masculin	m	masculine
mathématique	Math	mathematics
médecine	Méd, Med	medicine
météorologie	Mét, Met	meteorology
métallurgie	Métal, Metal	metallurgy
masculin et féminin	mf	masculine and feminine
militaire	Mil	military
mines	Min	mining
minéralogie	Minér, Miner	mineralogy
masculin pluriel	mpl	masculine plural
musique	Mus	music
mythologie	Myth	mythology
nom	n	noun
nord de l'Angleterre	N Angl	North of England
nautique	Naut	nautical, naval
négatif	nég, neg	negative
nord de l'Angleterre	N Engl	North of England
nom féminin	nf	feminine noun
nom masculin	nm	masculine noun
nom masculin et féminin	nmf	masculine and feminine noun
nom masculin, féminin	nm,f	masculine, feminine noun
non comptable	NonC	uncountable
nom pluriel	npl	plural noun
nom singulier	nsg	singular noun
nucléaire	Nucl	nuclear
numéral	num	numerical
objet	obj	object
œnologie	Œnol	oenology
opposé	opp	opposite
optique	Opt	optics
informatique	Ordin	computing
ornithologie	Orn	ornithology
emploi réfléchi	o.s.	oneself
parlement	Parl	parliament
passif	pass	passive
péjoratif	péj, pej	pejorative
personnel	pers	personal
pharmacie	Pharm	pharmacy
philatélie	Philat	philately
philosophie	Philos	philosophy
phonétique	Phon	phonetics
photographie	Photo, Phot	photography
physique	Phys	physics
physiologie	Physiol	physiology
pluriel	pl	plural
politique	Pol	politics
possessif	poss	possessive
préfixe	préf, pref	prefix
préposition	prép, prep	preposition
prétérit	prét, pret	preterite
pronom	pron	pronoun
proverbe	Prov	proverb
participe présent	prp	present participle
psychiatrie, psychologie	Psych	psychology, psychiatry
temps du passé	pt	past tense
participe passé	ptp	past participle
quelque chose	qch	something
quelqu'un	qn	somebody, someone
marque déposée	®	registered trademark
radio	Rad	radio
chemin de fer	Rail	rail(ways)
religion	Rel	religion
relatif	rel	relative
quelqu'un	sb	somebody, someone
sciences	Sci	science
science-fiction	Sci Fi	science fiction
école	Scol	school
écossais, Écosse	Scot	Scottish, Scotland
sculpture	Sculp	sculpture
séparable	sep	separable
singulier	sg	singular
ski	Ski	skiing
sociologie	Sociol	sociology
terme de spécialiste	SPÉC, SPEC	specialist term
statistique	Stat	statistics
Bourse	St Ex	Stock Exchange
quelque chose	sth	something
subjonctif	subj	subjunctive
suffixe	suf	suffix
superlatif	superl	superlative
chirurgie	Surg	surgery
arpentage	Surv	surveying
technique	Tech	technical
télécommunication	Télec, Telec	telecommunications
industrie textile	Tex	textiles
théâtre	Théât, Theat	theatre
télévision	TV	television
typographie	Typo, Typ	typography
université	Univ	university
américain, États-Unis	US	American, United States
verbe	vb	verb
médecine vétérinaire	Vét, Vet	veterinary medicine
verbe intransitif	vi	intransitive verb
verbe pronominal	vpr	pronominal verb
verbe transitif	vt	transitive verb
verbe transitif et intransitif	vti	transitive and intransitive verb
verbe transitif indirect	vt indir	indirect transitive verb
zoologie	Zool	zoology
langage familier, voir page xxix	*	informal language, see page xxix
langage très familier, voir page xxix	**	very informal language, see page xxix
langage vulgaire, voir page xxix	***	offensive language, see page xxix
emploi vieilli, voir page xxix	†	old-fashioned term or expression, see page xxix
emploi archaïque, voir page xxix	††	archaic term or expression, see page xxix
renvoi à la Grammaire active, voir page xxxii	▼	cross reference to Language in Use, see page xxxii

DICTIONNAIRE
FRANÇAIS - ANGLAIS
ANGLAIS - FRANÇAIS

FRENCH - ENGLISH
ENGLISH - FRENCH
DICTIONARY

COLLINS ROBERT

Unabridged

FRENCH-ENGLISH
ENGLISH-FRENCH
DICTIONARY

by
Beryl T. Atkins
Alain Duval   Rosemary C. Milne

and
Pierre-Henri Cousin
Hélène M. A. Lewis   Lorna A. Sinclair
Renée O. Birks   Marie-Noëlle Lamy

FIFTH EDITION

HarperCollins*Publishers*

LE ROBERT
& COLLINS

Senior

DICTIONNAIRE
FRANÇAIS - ANGLAIS
ANGLAIS - FRANÇAIS

par
Beryl T. Atkins
Alain Duval   Rosemary C. Milne

et
Pierre-Henri Cousin
Hélène M. A. Lewis   Lorna A. Sinclair
Renée O. Birks   Marie-Noëlle Lamy

CINQUIÈME ÉDITION

DICTIONNAIRES LE ROBERT

© Copyright 1978, 1987 William Collins Sons & Co. Ltd. and
Dictionnaires Le Robert

© Copyright 1993, 1995, 1998 HarperCollins Publishers and Dictionnaires Le Robert

fifth edition / cinquième édition 1998

fourth edition reprinted / quatrième édition: réimpressions
1996
1997

Dictionnaires Le Robert
27, rue de la Glacière - 75013 Paris
ISBN 2 85036 528-9

HarperCollins Publishers

P.O. Box, Glasgow G4 ONB, Great Britain

1995 Markham Road, Scarborough, Canada, AM1B 5M8

ISBN 0-00-470526-2
with thumb index 0-00-470527-0

10 East 53rd Street, New York
New York 10022
ISBN 0-06-270816-3

First HarperCollins edition published 1993

Library of Congress Cataloging-in-Publication Data:

Collins-Robert French-English, English French dictionary : unabridged
/ by Beryl T. Atkins ... [et al.]. – 5th ed.
  p.   cm.
  Added title page title: Robert & Collins dictionnaire français-anglais,
anglais-français.
  ISBN 0-06-270816-3 (hc)
  1. French language–Dictionaries–English. 2. English language–
Dictionaries–French. I. Atkins, Beryl T. II. Title: Robert & Collins
dictionnaire français-anglais, anglais-français.
PC2640.C69 1998
443'.21–dc21   97-46140

98 99 00 01 02 MI 10 9 8 7 6 5 4 3 2 1

Typeset by Morton Word Processing Ltd, Scarborough
Printed in France by Maury-Imprimeur S. A. – Malesherbes

CINQUIÈME ÉDITION/FIFTH EDITION

Direction éditoriale: société
Dictionnaires Le Robert représentée par

Pierre Varrod

Publishing Director
HarperCollins

Lorna Sinclair Knight

Direction de l'ouvrage

Alain Duval

Project management

Michela Clari
with
Carol MacLeod

Chef de projet

Martyn Back

Responsable de la rédaction

Dominique Le Fur
avec
Brigitte Vienne

Senior Editors

Janet Gough
Sabine Citron

Rédaction/Editors

Jean-François Allain, Claire Bigot, Harry Campbell, Gearóid Cronin, Daphne Day,
Christèle Éon, Hélène Fabre, Phyllis Gautier, Bob Grossmith, Frances Illingworth,
Jacques Lesca, Christine Penman, Christian Salzedo, Donald Watt

Anglais américain/American English

Kathleen Micham, John Wright

Coordination éditoriale/Editorial management

Vivian Marr
with
Isobel Gordon
Silke Zimmermann

Secrétariat de rédaction et correction/Editorial staff

Elspeth Anderson, Cécile Aubinière-Robb, Anne-Marie Banks, Anne Convery,
Sylvie Fontaine, Sandra Harper, Angela Jack, Irene Lakhani, Anne Lindsay,
Caitlin McMahon, Maggie Seaton, Jill Williams

Informatique éditoriale/Data management

Ray Carrick
Kamal Loudiyi
Jane Creevy, Paul Hasset, André Gautier

Nous tenons à remercier/We would like to thank

Geoffrey Bremner, Jeremy Butterfield, Gonzague Raynaud, Keith Foley, Hélène Bernaert, Chantal Testa,
Duncan Marshal, Hazel Mills, Gerry McIntyre, Brigitte Orcel, Anne-Marie Lentaigne

TROISIÈME ET QUATRIÈME ÉDITIONS/
THIRD AND FOURTH EDITIONS

direction rédactionnelle/general editors

Alain Duval   Lorna Sinclair Knight

rédacteurs/editors

Diana Feri   Stephen Clarke   Dominique Le Fur
Laurence Hautekeur   Françoise Morcellet   Jill Campbell

chef de projet/editorial management

Vivian Marr

autres collaborateurs/other contributors

Christine Penman   Jean-Benoît Ormal-Grenon   Cécile Aubinière-Robb

administration, secrétariat et correction/editorial staff

Elspeth Anderson   Luc Audrain   Anne Baudrillard   Linda Chestnutt
Chantal Combes   Elizabeth Cunningham   Annick Dehais   Anne Dickinson
Susan Dunsmore   Sylvie Fontaine   Élisabeth Huault   Lesley Johnston
Irene Lakhani   Joyce Littlejohn   Dominique Lopin   Kamal Loudiyi
Fiona MacGregor   Carol MacLeod   Maimie McGadie   Janice McNeillie
Val McNulty   Hellen Ranson   Gonzague Raynaud   Diane Robinson
Megan Thomson   Lydia Vigné   Silke Zimmermann

DEUXIÈME ÉDITION/SECOND EDITION

dirigée par/by

Beryl T. Atkins

Alain Duval   Rosemary C. Milne   Hélène M. A. lewis

Lorna Sinclair   Renée Birks

autres collaborateurs/other contributors

Guy Jean Forgue (Américanismes/American language)

Charles Lynn Clark   Susan Lochrie   Geneviève Lebaut

Jöelle Sampy   Ann Goodman   Renée Gillot-Gautier   Florence Millar

administration, secrétariat et correction/administrative staff

William T. McLeod   Richard Thomas   Barbara Christie   Carol Purdon

Elspeth Anderson   Catherine E. Love   Anne Marie Banks

PREMIÈRE ÉDITION/FIRST EDITION

par/by

Beryl T. Atkins

Alain Duval   Rosemary C. Milne

et/and

Pierre-Henri Cousin

Hélène M. A. Lewis   Lorna A. Sinclair

Renée O. Birks   Marie-Noëlle Lamy

autres collaborateurs/other contributors

John Scullard   Edwin Carpenter   Margaret Curtin   Kenneth Gibson

Gerry Kilroy   Michael Janes   Anthony Linforth   Trevor Peach   Elise Thomson

avec/with
comité de lecture/readers' panel

Paul Robert

Martine Bercot   Gilberte Gagnon   Maryline Hira   Lucette Jourdan   Denis Keen

Jean Mambrino   Jacques Mengin   Robert Mengin   Marie Christine de Montoussé

Alain Rey   Josette Rey-Debove   Colette Thompson   Elaine Williamson

TABLE DES MATIÈRES

CONTENTS

Introduction   xii
Comment utiliser le dictionnaire   xvii
Prononciation
    Prononciation du français   xxxvi
    Prononciation de l'anglais   xxxviii

DICTIONNAIRE FRANÇAIS-ANGLAIS   1-987

Grammaire active de l'anglais
    et du français   1-61

DICTIONNAIRE ANGLAIS-FRANÇAIS   989-2081

Annexes
    Le verbe français   3
    Le verbe anglais   25
    Nombres, heures et dates   33
    Poids, mesures et
        températures   41

Introduction   xiv
Using the dictionary   xvii
Pronunciation
    Pronunciation of French   xxxvi
    Pronunciation of English   xxxviii

FRENCH-ENGLISH DICTIONARY   1-987

Language in use: a grammar
    of communication in French
    and English   1-61

ENGLISH-FRENCH DICTIONARY   989-2081

Appendices
    The French verb   3
    The English verb   25
    Numbers, time and dates   33
    Weights, measures
        and temperatures   41

Le ROBERT & COLLINS SENIOR est considéré comme un ouvrage de référence majeur, et la réputation de sérieux dont il jouit ne s'est pas démentie depuis la première édition, parue en 1978. Son approche révolutionnaire du traitement de la langue, l'étendue du vocabulaire couvert, la clarté et la fiabilité de son contenu en ont fait, tant dans les pays francophones que dans les pays anglophones, un dictionnaire dont la qualité est reconnue par tous.

La manière la plus évidente d'actualiser un dictionnaire bilingue est d'y ajouter les néologismes et les expressions qui sont venus enrichir la langue courante. Nous avons cependant voulu aller plus loin dans notre démarche. Ce nouveau dictionnaire, qui contient des milliers de mots et de sens nouveaux, est également le résultat d'une réflexion méthodologique approfondie, visant à en faire un dictionnaire pour le XXIᵉ siècle.

Poursuivant plus avant dans la voie tracée par les précédentes éditions, nous avons affiné le traitement des entrées en explorant plus en profondeur le sens, le contexte et l'usage des mots. Pour cela, nous avons eu recours à la fois aux méthodes lexicographiques traditionnelles et à de puissants outils informatiques d'analyse. Les recherches en linguistique compu-

tationnelle menées par COLLINS en partenariat avec l'université de Birmingham depuis les années 70 et l'informatisation des bases de données monolingues du ROBERT ont prouvé combien pouvait se montrer précieuse, pour l'élaboration des dictionnaires bilingues, l'exploration méthodique de vastes corpus électroniques. Ces corpus sont des ensembles de textes manipulables par ordinateur, qui montrent comment les mots fonctionnent dans leur environnement contextuel naturel, que ce soit dans la conversation de tous les jours, dans les journaux, dans des rapports officiels ou dans la littérature. Tout comme dans le domaine des sciences, où les chercheurs se servent de données objectives pour vérifier leurs hypothèses, les lexicographes utilisent ces vastes banques de données pour vérifier leurs intuitions linguistiques en les confrontant à des données quantifiables, et pour explorer des aspects de la langue qui auraient pu leur échapper. Grâce à cette démarche, nous sommes à même de vous présenter une analyse plus approfondie et plus pointue du vocabulaire du français et de l'anglais d'aujourd'hui. Vous trouverez ci-dessous un exemple montrant comment les articles de notre dictionnaire reflètent l'usage réel, tel qu'il est présenté dans la « Bank of English » et dans la « Banque de français moderne ».

```
            affirmant " la réalité incontournable du marché " a été repoussé de
        sont devenus une réalité " incontournable " à Djibouti, a-t-il
    juridique adapté à une réalité incontournable. La loi ainsi complétée a été
            des flux est une réalité incontournable. A leur immense
    en restant conscient des réalités incontournables du monde, qu'entre les écologistes et
mais passe à côté de deux réalités incontournables : il n'y a que des cas particuliers
pas moins subsister plusieurs réalités incontournables. La fin de la guerre froide n'a pas
        part, que c'était un fait " incontournable que le conseil issu du suffrage
        plus rien non plus du fait incontournable d'être homme, yang, mâle.Il y a
    trouvé un argument de marketing incontournable pour vendre les services de
        organisée alors que demeure, incontournable, le problème de la légitimité
            ce domaine.Le problème était incontournable. Avec la victoire d'une
    problèmes qui apparaissent maintenant incontournables et pourraient empoisonner une campagne
        le personnage du conteur reste incontournable. Loin de le considérer comme un
                des lunettes, ce personnage incontournable de l'histoire de documentaire
        la renaissance (PR), personnage incontournable. Ce manipulateur des coulisses
    sans doute un de ces personnages incontournable qui pourraient l'aider à
        plus que jamais, l'interlocuteur incontournable dans toute tentative de
                en font un interlocuteur incontournable dans le domaine de la
            demeure l'interlocuteur incontournable des maires des petites
            demeure un interlocuteur incontournable, invité à développer, en son
        Mieux les 47 s. 02 de l'incontournable Edwin Moses en 1983, le double
        la programmation n'oublie ni l'incontournable Luis Bunuel ni les générations
            subir les " analyses " de incontournable Manu Dibango, excellent
    on trouve, en bonne position, l'incontournable Jane Fonda. La créatrice des
        aux deux visages. Reste enfin l'incontournable Sergio Leone : Il était une
Un produit étonnant et désormais incontournable tant ses utilisations sont
```

incontournable [ɛ̃kɔ̃tuʀnabl] ADJ [*réalité, fait*] inescapable; [*date, délai*] imperative; [*argument, problème, artiste*] that can't be ignored; [*personnage, interlocuteur*] key (*épith*); [*œuvre d'art*] major (*épith*); **c'est un livre ~** the book is essential reading; **ce produit est désormais ~** this product has become indispensable; (*hum*) **trois personnalités étaient invitées, dont l'~ Éliane Hotin** three celebrities were invited, including the inevitable Éliane Hotin

Nous avons présenté cette vaste matière d'une façon aussi claire que possible afin de vous offrir un outil de travail aussi convivial que sophistiqué. Outre l'accroissement de la couverture lexicale, cette nouvelle édition du ROBERT & COLLINS SENIOR propose une présentation entièrement nouvelle, qui offre l'avantage de mettre instantanément en évidence à l'intérieur des articles complexes les différents sens du mot, les expressions idiomatiques et les locutions figées. Il est parfois difficile de se repérer dans des entrées telles que «for», «to», «à», ou «avoir». Aussi avons-nous entièrement modifié la présentation de ces articles longs, qui sont devenus plus clairs et plus accessibles. Des remarques sur l'usage ont également été ajoutées afin de permettre au lecteur d'éviter les pièges de traduction.

Pour communiquer efficacement dans une langue étrangère, il faut une connaissance approfondie non seulement de la langue, mais aussi de la culture du pays. Nous sommes donc allés plus loin que les dictionnaires bilingues traditionnels et nous avons intégré dans le texte des données culturelles, que nous présentons sous forme d'encadrés. Ces encadrés encyclopédiques traitent d'institutions, d'événements culturellement importants, de traditions et de coutumes des pays anglophones et francophones. Le supplément «Grammaire active», salué par la critique depuis sa première parution pour sa présentation thématique originale des concepts que l'usager sera amené à exprimer, vient compléter des outils de communication désormais indispensables.

Ces innovations méthodologiques qui se fondent sur les traditionnels points forts du dictionnaire constituent pour nous le plus grand pas en avant dans le domaine de la lexicographie bilingue depuis notre première édition de 1978. Nous sommes convaincus que le ROBERT & COLLINS SENIOR continuera à être le fidèle compagnon des élèves, des étudiants, des enseignants, des traducteurs, des spécialistes de la langue, et plus généralement de tous ceux qui partagent notre amour de l'anglais.

Nous tenons à remercier pour leur aide et pour leur coopération tous ceux qui nous ont aimablement autorisés à incorporer leurs textes dans la «Bank of English» et dans la «Banque de français moderne».

INTRODUCTION

Since it was first published in 1978, the COLLINS ROBERT FRENCH DICTIONARY has become one of the most highly-respected reference works of its kind. Its revolutionary treatment of language, the extent of its coverage and the clarity and accuracy of the information it gives have made it a recognized authority in English- and French-speaking countries alike.

When working on a new version of any dictionary, the most obvious means of updating the text is to add any new words and expressions that have recently come into the language. However, for this major new edition we decided we wanted to do much more than simply expand the word list in this way. So, in addition to gathering the thousands of new words and senses that have gone into this volume, we put a great deal of thought into how we could still further develop and enrich the text to bring it into the 21st century.

Building on the strengths of the previous edition, one aim was to refine existing entries by exploring meaning, context and usage in greater depth than ever

before. To achieve this, we used both traditional lexicographical methods and the most up-to-date electronic tools available. Pioneering research into computational linguistics, carried out by COLLINS in partnership with the University of Birmingham since the 1970s, together with LE ROBERT's monolingual databases, has demonstrated how dictionaries can benefit from the use of large electronic corpora. These are collections of texts held on computer which provide evidence of the way words are actually used in a huge variety of contexts, whether in ordinary conversation, in newspapers, in official reports, or in literature. Much as scientists analyse objective data to test their hypotheses, editors use these vast databanks to validate their own linguistic intuition using hard evidence, and to explore aspects of meaning or usage that might otherwise have been overlooked. In this way we have achieved a depth and accuracy of coverage that would have been impossible using traditional methods alone. Here is an example of how our dictionary entries reflect authentic usage as found in our corpora, the Bank of English and the Banque de français moderne.

```
                  one. All NATO members now broadly accept that the alliance will
            all the other members of the EU broadly accept that European integration
          of work at all hours. The paper broadly agrees - and is also more
  and Shiite Mujahedeen factions have broadly agreed that the UN plan is a
        as well as conservatives, would broadly agree with their view that Mr
     and Futures Commission (SFC) has broadly agreed: Jardines, which accounts
        trade union, and evolved into a broadly-based movement for democracy, it
            were beginning to win more broadly based popular support. The
       there are growing signs of more broadly-based popular unrest. The colours
      they argue, are now much more broadly based than before, and disarmament
 health spending per head with some broadly defined results. You might
  them by giving them to everyone in broadly defined groups. It follows that
       people sit up. Privatisation, broadly defined to cover all sorts of
     than the year before. Staff costs, broadly defined, make up two-thirds of the
 to over-rule the provinces for five, broadly defined reasons? This week
fifth of the freight traffic in this broadly defined market. It hopes that the
     than external expansion. He hinted broadly that some form of America's commercial
      the American side. He also hinted broadly that American firms that hesitated
       percent for the Conservatives. Broadly similar results are published in
     other Arab states, and to follow broadly similar lines: that there must be
 says Britain's target is in fact broadly similar to the Japanese aim, which
    to the Gulf, in the light of the broadly similar approach taken by the two
       The late edition carries a broadly similar report, but the newspaper
 during their bloody rule) smile so broadly as they sip champagne at its
    ecstatic on television. He smiled broadly, gave his trademark thumbs-up and
The diplomat's son nodded and smiled broadly. All of a sudden, captain and
   of famous parents? She smiles broadly and warns that we should never
 embarrassed, afraid to smile too broadly in case it causes resentment. Real
    Community summit had accepted broadly speaking the EC Commission's
 open to us and is probably safer. Broadly speaking, there is growing
 Beverley Hills, and Century City - broadly speaking, the green zone, where
   years. In China, rocks perform, broadly speaking, the ornamental role of
    Defence Minister Dmitri Yazov broadly supported the official line of
its first big meeting this weekend broadly supports the Mazowiecki
  together Solidarity members who broadly support the government of the
   correspondents say the plan is broadly supported by the Russian
```

broadly ['brɔːdlɪ] ADV [a] (= *generally*) [*agree, accept, define*] dans les grandes lignes, d'une manière générale ; [*welcome*] généralement ; [*support*] largement ; **this is ~ true** c'est vrai, grosso modo ; **~ similar** à peu près semblable ; **~-based** large ; **~ speaking** en gros, généralement parlant [b] [*hint*] fortement [c] **to smile ~** avoir un large sourire

One of our greatest challenges, given the sheer wealth of information to be presented, was to find ways to make such a sophisticated reference work as simple as possible to use. Besides its increased breadth and depth of coverage, this new edition of the COLLINS ROBERT FRENCH DICTIONARY has a completely new layout designed to make different senses, idioms and set structures easier to locate in complex entries. Finding one's way around entries like 'for', 'to', 'à' and 'avoir' can be a daunting task, and we have completely redesigned these longer entries to make them clearer and more helpful. Guidance on usage has also been provided to help the user avoid the pitfalls of translation.

Since communication requires an understanding of both language and culture, we have also gone further than the traditional bilingual dictionary by including carefully selected encyclopedic information, presented in special boxed entries integral to the text, and giving details about institutions, culturally significant events, traditions and customs in French- and English-speaking countries. Together with the critically-acclaimed 'Language In Use' supplement, our comprehensive guide to self-expression in everyday situations, this new volume offers all the information the user needs for successful communication.

By combining the tried-and-tested strengths of the dictionary with a new and innovative approach, we feel that we have taken the most significant step forward in bilingual lexicography since our first edition in 1978. We are confident that the COLLINS ROBERT FRENCH DICTIONARY will continue to be a valued companion for students, teachers, translators, linguists and anyone who shares our love of the French language.

We would like to acknowledge the help and cooperation of all those who have kindly given permission for their material to be incorporated in the Bank of English and the Banque de français ⸱erne.

COMMENT UTILISER
LE DICTIONNAIRE

HOW TO USE
THE DICTIONARY

Les principales caractéristiques de ce dictionnaire sont mentionnées dans les éclatés des pages xviii à xxiii. Pour une explication détaillée de chacune de ces caractéristiques et pour tirer le meilleur parti de votre dictionnaire, reportez-vous aux pages xxiv – xxxiii.

BIZUTAGE

New arrivals at certain "grandes écoles" and other educational institutions are called "bizuts" or "bizuths", and when they arrive at school in September, they are often subjected to an initiation ceremony known as **bizutage**. *This usually involves being subjected to light-hearted ordeals by one's new classmates, but can sometimes degenerate into humiliating and cruel pranks. For this reason, the traditon has become more controversial in recent years, and many schools have outlawed it.*

note culturelle	
cultural information	

synonyme	
synonym	

blouse [bluz] NF (= *tablier*) overall; (= *chemisier*) blouse, smock; [*médecin*] (white) coat; [*paysan*] smock; (*Billard*) pocket; **les ~s blanches** (= *médecins*) hospital doctors

domaine	
specialist field	

blouser[1] [bluze] ▶conjug 1◀ VI [*robe, chemisier*] to be loose-fitting (*and gathered at the waist*)

numéros d'homographes	
homograph numbers	

sujet du verbe	
subject of verb	

blouser[2]: [bluze] ▶conjug 1◀ **1** VT to con•, trick, pull a fast one on•; **se faire ~** to be had ou conned• **2** **se blouser**† VPR (= *se tromper*) to make a mistake ou a blunder

blouser[3] [bluze] VT (*Billard*) to pot, pocket

blouson [bluzɔ̃] NM blouson (jacket); **~ de cuir** leather jacket; **~ d'aviateur** flying jacket; **~ noir**† ≈ hell's angel, ≈ teddy-boy (*Brit*)

bluff• [blœf] NM bluff; **c'est du ~ ou un coup de ~!** he's (*ou they're etc*) just bluffing ou just trying it on!• (*Brit*)

bluffer• [blœfe] ▶conjug 1◀ **1** VI to bluff, try it on• (*Brit*); (*Cartes*) to bluff **2** VT **a** (= *tromper*) to fool, put on•, have on (*Brit*); (*Cartes*) to bluff **b** (= *impressionner*) to impress; **j'ai été bluffé** I was really impressed; **elle m'a totalement bluffé** she really took my breath away, she really bowled me over

lettres signalant différents sens	
letters for different senses	

BN [been] NF (ABRÉV = **Bibliothèque nationale**) → **bibliothèque**

abréviations	
abbreviations	

BO [beo] NF (ABRÉV = **bande originale**) → **bande**[1]

renvoi	
cross-reference	

boa [bɔa] NM (*Habillement, Zool*) boa; **~ constricteur** boa constrictor

Boadicée [bɔadise] NF Boadicea

nom propre	
proper name	

bobard• [bɔbaʀ] NM (= *mensonge*) lie, fib•; (= *histoire*) tall story, yarn

bobèche [bɔbɛʃ] NF candle-ring

bobet, -ette [bɔbɛ, ɛt] ADJ (*Helv* = *sot*) stupid, foolish

helvétisme	
Swiss French	

bobinage [bɔbinaʒ] NM (*gén = action*) winding; (*Élec*) coil(s)

bobine [bɔbin] NF **a** [*fil*] reel, bobbin; [*métier à tisser*] bobbin, spool; [*machine à écrire, à coudre*] spool; (*Photo*) spool, reel; (*Élec*) coil; **~ d'induction** induction coil; **~ (d'allumage)** coil; **~ de pellicule** roll of film **b** (• = *visage*) face, mug•; **il a fait une drôle de ~!** what a face he made!; **tu en fais une drôle de ~!** you look a bit put out!•

bobineau [bɔbino] NM = **bobinot**

bobiner [bɔbine] ▶conjug 1◀ VT to wind

bobinette†† [bɔbinɛt] NF (wooden) latch

†† archaïque	
†† archaic	

bobo [bobo] NM (*langage enfantin*) (= *plaie*) sore; (= *coupure*) cut; **avoir ~** to be hurt, have a pain; **avoir ~ à la gorge** to have a sore throat; **ça (te) fait ~?** does it hurt?, is it sore?; **il n'y a pas eu de ~** there was no harm done

bobonne††• [bɔbɔn] NF (**sa**) **~** his old woman•, his missus• (*Brit*), his old lady• (*US*); (*hum*) **oui ~** yes love• ou dearie•

† vieilli	
† old-fashioned	

The main features of the dictionary are highlighted in the text extracts on pages xviii-xxiii. For a detailed explanation of each of these features and information on how to get the most out of your dictionary, see pages xxiv – xxxiii.

proper name	
nom propre	

Balkan ['bɔ:lkən] ADJ, N **the ~s** les Balkans *mpl*; **the ~ States** les États *mpl* balkaniques; **the ~ Peninsula** la péninsule Balkanique

parts of speech	
catégories grammaticales	

ball[1] [bɔ:l] [1] N [a] (*gen*, *Cricket, Golf, Hockey, Tennis*) balle *f*; (*inflated: Ftbl etc*) ballon *m*; (*Billiards*) bille *f*, boule *f*; (*Croquet*) boule *f*; **as round as a ~** rond comme une boule *or* bille; (*US fig*) **behind the eight ~*** dans le pétrin*; **cat curled up in a ~** chat *m* couché en rond *or* pelotonné (en boule); **tennis/golf** *etc* **~** balle *f* de tennis/de golf *etc*; **croquet ~** boule *f* de croquet; (*Met*) **~ of fire** ◊ **~ lightning** éclair *m* en boule

specialist field	
domaine	

[b] (*fig phrases*) (*US*) **that's the way the ~ bounces!*** c'est la vie!; **to keep a lot of ~s in the air** faire plein de choses à la fois; **take the ~ and run with it!** vas-y fonce!*, saisis ta chance!; **to keep the ~ rolling** (= *maintain conversation*) alimenter la conversation; (= *maintain activity*) maintenir le mouvement; (= *maintain interest*) soutenir l'intérêt; **to start** *or* **set the ~ rolling*** lancer une affaire (*or* la conversation *etc*); **he's got the ~ at his feet** c'est à lui de saisir cette chance; **the ~ is with you** *or* **in your court** (c'est) à vous de jouer; (*US*) **to have something on the ~*** en avoir là-dedans* *or* dans le ciboulot*; **to be on the ~*** (= *competent*) être à la hauteur (de la situation *or* des circonstances); (= *alert*) ouvrir l'œil et le bon*; **he's a real ~ of fire*** il est débordant d'activité; (*US*) **the whole ~ of wax** absolument tout → **eyeball, play, tennis**

different meanings of phrase	
différents sens d'une expression	

cross-references	
renvois	

[c] [*of rifle etc*] balle *f*; (*lit, fig*) **~ and chain** boulet *m* → **cannonball**

[d] [*of wool, string*] pelote *f*, peloton *m*; **to wind sth into a ~** mettre qch en pelote

noun complement of noun	
compléments de nom	

[e] (*Culin*) [*of meat, fish*] boulette *f*; [*of potato*] croquette *f*

[f] (*Tech*) bille *f* (de roulement)

[g] (*Anat*) **~ of the foot** (partie *f* antérieure de la) plante *f* du pied; **~ of the thumb** (partie *f* charnue du) pouce *m* → **eyeball**

[2] **balls**⁛ NPL (*Anat*) couilles⁛ *fpl*; (*Brit* = *nonsense*) conneries⁛ *fpl*, couillonnades⁛ *fpl*; (*Brit* = *courage*) **to have ~s**⁛ avoir des couilles⁛; (*esp US*) **~s!**⁛ quelles conneries!⁛; (*fig*) **to break sb's ~s** casser les couilles⁛ à qn

vulgar⁛	
vulgaire⁛	

[3] VT [*+ wool etc*] mettre en pelote, pelotonner

object of verb	
objet direct	

[4] VI s'agglomérer

[5] COMP ▶ **ball-and-socket joint** N (joint *m* à) rotule *f* ▶ **ball bearings** NPL roulement *m* à billes ▶ **ball boy** N (*Tennis*) ramasseur *m* de balles ▶ **ball cartridge** N cartouche *f* à balle ▶ **ball control** N (*NonC: Ftbl, Basketball etc*) contrôle *m* du ballon ▶ **ball game** N jeu *m* de balle (*or* ballon); (*US*) match *m* de baseball; (*fig*) **it's a whole new ~ game*** ◊ **it's not the same ~ game*** c'est une toute autre histoire ▶ **ball girl** N (*Tennis*) ramasseuse *f* de balles ▶ **ball gown** N robe *f* de bal ▶ **ballpoint (pen)** N stylo *m* (à) bille, (pointe *f*) Bic® *m* ▶ **ball-shaped** ADJ sphérique ▶ **balls-up**⁛, **ball-up**⁛ (*US*) N bordel⁛ *m*; **he made a ~s-up of the job** il a foutu le bordel⁛ *or* salopé le boulot⁛; (*Brit*) **the meeting was a ~s-up** la réunion a été bordélique⁛

compounds marked by ▶	
composés signalés par ▶	

trademark	
marque déposée	

▶ **ball up** [1] VI (*Ski etc*) botter [2] VT SEP⁛ = **balls up**

▶ **balls up**⁛ [1] VT SEP⁛ foutre la merde⁛ *or* le bordel⁛ dans; **to be/get ballsed up**⁛ être/se trouver dans la merde jusqu'au cou⁛ [2] **~s-up**⁛ N → **ball**[1]

homograph number	
numéro d'homographe	

ball[2] [bɔ:l] N (= *dance*) bal *m*; **to give a ~** donner un bal; (*lit, fig*) **to open the ~** ouvrir le bal; **to have a ~*** s'amuser comme des fous, se marrer* → **fancy**

synonym	
synonyme	

ballad ['bæləd] N (*Mus*) romance *f*; (*Literat*) ballade *f*

ballast ['bæləst] [1] N (*NonC*) [a] (*Aviat, Naut*) lest *m*; **ship in ~** vaisseau *m* en lest; **to sail in**

câble [kabl] **1** NM **a** (= *filin*) cable; ~ **métallique** wire cable **b** (*TV*) cable; **la télévision par ~** ◊ **le ~** cable (television), cablevision; **transmettre par ~** to broadcast on cable, cablecast (*US*) **c** († = *dépêche*) cable **2** COMP ▶ **câble d'accélérateur** accelerator cable ▶ **câble d'amarrage** mooring line ▶ **câble coaxial** coaxial cable ▶ **câble de démarreur** *ou* **de démarrage** (*Aut*) jump lead (*Brit*), jumper cable (*US*) ▶ **câble électrique** (electric) cable ▶ **câble de frein** brake cable ▶ **câble de halage** towrope, towline ▶ **câble hertzien** radio link (*by hertzian waves*) ▶ **câble de remorquage** = **câble de halage** ▶ **câble de transmission** transmission cable

câblé, e [kable] (*ptp de* **câbler**) ADJ **a** (*TV*) [*chaîne, réseau*] cable (*épith*); **la ville est ~e** the town has cable television **b** (*Ordin*) wired **c** (* = *à la mode*) [*personne*] trendy*, hip*; **il est ~ informatique/jazz** he's really into computers/jazz

caddie [kadi] NM **a** (*Golf*) caddie; **être le ~ de qn** to caddie for sb, be sb's caddie **b** ® (= *chariot*) (supermarket *ou* shopping) trolley (*Brit*), caddy (*US*), (grocery) cart (*US*)

cadeau (*pl* **cadeaux**) [kado] NM **a** (= *présent*) present, gift (**de qn** from sb); **faire un ~ à qn** to give sb a present *ou* gift; **~ de mariage/de Noël** wedding/Christmas present; **~ publicitaire** free gift, freebie*, giveaway* (*US*) **b** (*loc*) **faire ~ de qch à qn** (*offrir*) to make sb a present of sth, give sb sth as a present; (*laisser*) to let sb keep sth, give sb sth; **il a décidé d'en faire ~ (à quelqu'un)** he decided to give it away (to somebody); **je vous fais ~ des détails** I'll spare you the details; **ils ne font pas de ~x** [*examinateurs, police*] they don't let you off lightly; **ils ne nous ont pas fait de ~** [*équipe adverse*] they really gave us a run for our money; **garde la monnaie, je t'en fais ~** you can keep the change; **en ~** [*offrir, recevoir*] as a present; **les petits ~x entretiennent l'amitié** there's nothing like a little present between friends; **c'était un ~ empoisonné** it was more of a curse than a blessing, it was a poisoned chalice; **c'est pas un ~!** *it's (*ou* he's etc*) a real pain!*

cadenas [kadna] NM padlock; **fermer au ~** to padlock

cadenasser [kadnase] ▶conjug 1◀ **1** VT to padlock **2** **se cadenasser** VPR to lock o.s. in

cadencé, e [kadãse] (*ptp de* **cadencer**) ADJ **a** (= *rythmé*) rhythmic(al) → **pas¹** **b** (*Ordin*) **processeur ~ à 130 MHz** 130 MHz processor that runs at 130 MHz, 130 MHz processor

cadencer [kadãse] ▶conjug 3◀ VT [+ *débit, phrases, allure, marche*] to put rhythm into, give rhythm to

cadet, -ette [kade, ɛt] **1** ADJ (*de deux*) younger; (*de plusieurs*) youngest **2** NM **a** [*famille*] **le ~** the youngest child *ou* boy *ou* one; **le ~ des garçons** the youngest boy *ou* son; **mon (frère) ~** my younger brother; **le ~ de mes frères** my youngest brother; **le père avait un faible pour son ~** the father had a soft spot for his youngest boy **b** (*relation d'âges*) **il est mon ~** he's younger than me; **il est mon ~ de 2 ans** he's 2 years younger than me, he's 2 years my junior; **c'est le ~ de mes soucis** that's the least of my worries **c** (*Tennis, Ping-Pong, Ftbl etc*) *15-17 year-old player*; (*Athlétisme*) *15-17 year-old athlete*; (*Hist*) cadet (*gentleman who entered the army to acquire military skill and eventually a commission*)

Annotations (margin labels):

composés signalés par ▶ / compounds marked by ▶

participe passé adjectival / past participle used as adjective

marque déposée / trademark

anglais britannique et américain / British and American English

préposition souvent utilisée / preposition often used

exemples / examples

verbes souvent utilisés avec une expression / verbs often used with a phrase

• familier / • informal

verbe pronominal / pronominal verb

renvoi au tableau de conjugaison / reference to verb tables

renvoi / cross-reference

objets directs / objects of verb

catégories grammaticales / parts of speech

explication (pas d'équivalent anglais) / explanation (no English equivalent)

kiss [kɪs] **1** N baiser [m]; **to give sb a ~** donner un baiser à qn, embrasser qn; **give me a ~** embrasse-moi; *(to child)* fais-moi une bise•; *(esp Brit Med)* **~ of life** bouche-à-bouche *m*; *(in letter)* **"love and ~es"** « bons baisers », « grosses bises »•; *(fig)* **to give the ~ of death to ...** porter le coup fatal à ... → **blow**[1]

2 VT **a** embrasser, donner un baiser à; **to ~ sb's cheek** embrasser qn sur la joue; **to ~ sb's hand** baiser la main de qn; *(Diplomacy etc)* **to ~ hands** être admis au baisemain (du roi *or* de la reine); **they ~ed each other** ils se sont embrassés; **to ~ sb good night/goodbye** embrasser qn en lui souhaitant bonne nuit/en lui disant au revoir, souhaiter bonne nuit/dire au revoir à qn en l'embrassant; *(to hurt child)* **I'll ~ it better** un petit bisou• et ça ira mieux; *(esp US)* **to ~ ass**•• faire de la lèche•; *(esp US)* **to ~ sb's ass**•• lécher le cul à qn••; *(esp US)* **~ my ass!**•• va chier!•• → **goodbye**

b *(= touch lightly: also liter)* frôler; **the ball ~ed the top of the crossbar** le ballon a frôlé la barre transversale

3 VI s'embrasser; **to ~ and make up** faire la paix; **to ~ and tell** raconter ses secrets d'alcôve

4 COMP ► **kiss-and-tell**• ADJ [story, memoirs] divulguant des secrets d'alcôve *(avec une personnalité en vue)* ► **kiss curl** N *(Brit)* accroche-cœur *m* ► **kiss-off**•• N *(US)* **to give sb the ~-off** [+ employee] virer• qn; [+ girlfriend etc] plaquer• qn

► **kiss away** VT SEP **she ~ed away the child's tears** elle a séché les larmes de l'enfant en l'embrassant

► **kiss back** VT SEP [+ person] rendre un baiser à

kissagram ['kɪsəˌɡræm] N baiser télégraphié

KISSAGRAM

Un kissagram est un « baiser télégraphié » adressé à une personne pour lui faire une surprise, par exemple à l'occasion de son anniversaire. Le message est remis par un porteur costumé, qui lit un petit texte et embrasse le destinataire devant tout le monde.

kisser• ['kɪsə^r] N gueule• *f*

kit [kɪt] **1** N **a** *(NonC)* *(= equipment, gear)* *(for camping, skiing, climbing, photography etc)* matériel *m*, équipement *m*; *(Mil)* fourniment *m*, fourbi• *m*; *(= tools)* outils *mpl*; **fishing** *etc* **~** matériel *m* or attirail *m* de pêche *etc*; *(US)* **the whole ~ and caboodle**• tout le bataclan•, tout le fourbi•

b *(NonC•)* *(= belongings)* affaires *fpl*; *(= clothes)* fringues• *fpl*; *(for sports)* affaires *fpl*; *(= luggage)* bagages *mpl*; **get your ~ off!**•• à poil!•; **have you got your gym/football ~?** tu as tes affaires de gym/de football?

c *(= set of items)* trousse *f*; **puncture-repair ~** trousse *f* de réparations; **first-aid ~** trousse *f* d'urgence *or* de premiers secours → **survival**

d *(= parts for assembly)* kit *m*; **sold in ~ form** vendu en kit; **he built it from a ~** il l'a assemblé à partir d'un kit; **model aeroplane ~** maquette *f* d'avion (à assembler)

2 COMP ► **kit car** N voiture *f* en kit ► **kit inspection** N *(Mil)* revue *f* de détail

► **kit out, kit up** VT SEP *(Brit)* **a** *(Mil)* équiper **(with de)** **b** **to ~ sb out with sth** équiper qn de qch; **he arrived ~ted out in oilskins** il est arrivé équipé d'un ciré; **he had ~ted himself out in a bright blue suit** il avait mis un costume bleu vif

kitbag ['kɪtbæg] N *(esp Brit)* sac *m* de voyage, de sportif, de soldat, de marin etc)

Ordre des mots

Le principe général est l'ordre alphabétique. Les variantes orthographiques qui ne se suivent pas immédiatement dans l'ordre alphabétique figurent à leur place dans la nomenclature avec un renvoi à la forme qui est traitée. Pour l'ordre d'apparition des composés, voir **Les composés**.

clef ... NF = **clé**
caldron... N = **cauldron**

Les variantes orthographiques américaines sont traitées de la même manière.

honor ... (US) = **honour**

Les noms propres, ainsi que les sigles et acronymes, figurent à leur place dans l'ordre alphabétique général.

Les homographes sont suivis d'un chiffre qui permet de les distinguer, ex.: **raie**[1], **raie**[2]; **blow**[1], **blow**[2], **blow**[3].

Articles longs

Les articles qui sont particulièrement longs, soit parce qu'ils traitent de mots-outils (**à**, **faire**, **to**, **do** etc.), soit parce qu'ils couvrent beaucoup d'expressions lexicales (**affaire**, **heure**, **head**, **time** etc.), bénéficient d'un traitement spécifique dans notre dictionnaire. Les articles comprenant plus d'une catégorie grammaticale s'ouvrent par un «menu» qui présente leur structure. Des notes à l'intérieur même des articles expliquent certains points de grammaire et d'usage importants que les exemples seuls ne peuvent parfaitement illustrer. Le mot MAIS (ou BUT) attire l'attention de l'usager sur des exceptions aux règles énoncées. Chaque catégorie sémantique est clairement signalée par un indicateur mis en relief et les structures importantes sont présentées de manière à être très facilement repérables. Dans certaines séquences d'exemples très longues, les collocateurs les plus fréquents sont mis en valeur. Enfin, l'usager est régulièrement renvoyé à des articles moins denses pour y trouver plus aisément certaines expressions.

Notes culturelles

Des informations concernant des événements culturellement importants, des traditions et coutumes ou des institutions, qui ne pouvaient être données dans le corps même des articles sous forme de traductions ou de simples gloses, sont présentées dans des encadrés placés juste en-dessous de l'entrée.

Les composés

Certains articles comportent une section COMP (composés). En anglais, y figurent des groupes de mots avec trait d'union tels que **body-surf** (sous **body**) et **point-to-point** (sous **point**) ainsi que des groupes de mots sans trait d'union tels que **hazardous waste** (sous

Word order

Alphabetical order is followed throughout. If two variant spellings are not alphabetically adjacent each is treated as a separate headword and there is a cross-reference to the form treated in depth. For the alphabetical order of compounds, see **Compounds**.

American variations in spelling are treated in the same fashion.

Proper names, as well as abbreviations and acronyms, will be found in their alphabetical place in the word list.

Superior numbers are used to separate words of like spelling, **raie**[1], **raie**[2]; **blow**[1], **blow**[2], **blow**[3].

Complex entries

Entries that are very long because they cover function words (**to**, **do**, **à**, **faire** etc) or words that are used in a large number of set structures (**time**, **head**, **affaire**, **heure** etc) are given special treatment in this dictionary. Complex entries with more than one part of speech begin with a special "menu" that shows how they are structured. Special notes inside the entry either explain important points of grammar and usage that cannot be properly demonstrated by examples alone, or refer you to another part of the dictionary. The word BUT (or MAIS) introduces exceptions to any general point that has been made. The beginning of each semantic category is clearly signposted with indicators in boxes, and set structures have been given special prominence to make them easy to locate. Finally, in entries where there are long sequences of examples containing set collocates, these collocates are highlighted to make them stand out clearly.

Cultural notes

Extra information on culturally significant events, institutions, traditions and customs that cannot be given in an ordinary translation or gloss is given in the form of boxed notes following the relevant entry.

Compounds

In this dictionary, entries may include sections headed COMP (compounds). In these will be found English hyphenated words, such as **body-surf** (under **body**), and **point-to-point** (under **point**), and unhyphenated combinations of two or more elements, such as

hazardous), air traffic control (sous **air**) et **ear, nose and throat specialist** (sous **ear**).

Chaque composé est précédé d'un triangle noir et donné dans l'ordre alphabétique. Les catégories grammaticales sont mentionnées et, lorsqu'il y en a plusieurs, sont séparées par un losange noir :

▶ **back-heel** (*Ftbl*) N talonnade *f* ◆ VT **to back-heel the ball** faire une talonnade

Les mots soudés tels que **blackbird** et **partygoer** apparaissent comme des entrées normales à leur place dans l'ordre alphabétique.

L'orthographe anglaise est assez variable dans ce domaine et il existe souvent plusieurs variantes : **backhander/back-hander, paintbrush/paint brush/paint-brush** etc. Si la forme en un seul mot est la plus fréquente, le composé est présenté comme entrée à part entière. Ainsi **paintbrush** n'apparaît pas sous **paint**. Lors de sa recherche, l'utilisateur doit donc garder à l'esprit qu'un mot de ce type peut se trouver soit dans un groupe de composés, soit dans l'ordre alphabétique général.

En français, les composés sans trait d'union comme **gaz naturel, modèle déposé** ou **pont d'envol** apparaissent sous le premier mot, dans la catégorie COMP. La présence de prépositions n'influe pas sur l'ordre alphabétique : ainsi, **Casque bleu** précède **casque à pointe**. Les catégories grammaticales sont indiquées lorsqu'il y a un risque d'erreur ou que le composé traité appartient à plusieurs catégories grammaticales. Les composés à trait d'union comme **camion-citerne, arrière-pensée** ou **lave-glace** sont traités comme des entrées à part entière et donnés à leur place dans l'ordre alphabétique général. Lorsque les deux orthographes, avec et sans trait d'union, sont possibles, elles sont toutes deux signalées à l'utilisateur.

Locutions et exemples

Les formules figées et les expressions idiomatiques figurent généralement sous le premier terme qui reste inchangé, quelles que soient les modifications que l'on apporte à l'expression en question. Ainsi, **casser les pieds de qn** et **casser sa pipe** se trouvent sous **casser**. Lorsque le premier élément d'une expression peut varier, celle-ci est traitée sous le second élément. Ainsi, **savoir quelque chose sur le bout du doigt** est placé sous **bout** parce que l'on peut dire également **connaître quelque chose sur le bout du doigt**. Lorsque ce principe est abandonné, un renvoi prévient l'utilisateur.

Un certain nombre de mots sont très fréquents et servent à former un grand nombre de locutions verbales, par exemple :

faire honneur à, faire du ski, faire la tête *etc*
to make sense of something, to make an appointment, to make a mistake *etc*

Les articles où sont traités ces mots sont particulièrement longs et, pour faciliter leur lisibilité, beaucoup d'expressions ont été renvoyées sous d'autres entrées : **faire la tête** sous **tête**, **to make sense of something** sous **sense**.

hazardous waste (under **hazardous**), air traffic control (under **air**), ear, nose and throat specialist (under **ear**).

Each compound is preceded by a black triangle, and the order is alphabetical. Parts of speech are shown, and when there is more than one, this is signalled by a black lozenge:

Single words such as **blackbird** and **partygoer**, which are made up of two elements, but are not hyphenated, appear as headwords in the main alphabetical list.

English spelling is variable in this area, and there are possible alternatives: **backhander/back-hander, paintbrush/paint brush/paint-brush** etc. If the single word form is the most common, this will be treated as a headword; **paintbrush** therefore does not appear in the entry **paint**. When looking for a word of this type, users should bear in mind that it may be found either in a compound section, or as a headword.

On the French side, only unhyphenated combinations, such as **gaz naturel, modèle déposé** and **pont d'envol** appear in compound sections. Alphabetical order is not affected by linking prepositions, thus **Casque bleu** precedes **casque à pointe**. The part of speech is given where it could be ambiguous or where there is more than one. Hyphenated words, such as **camion-citerne, arrière-pensée** and **lave-glace** are treated as headwords. If a word can appear both with or without a hyphen, both spellings are given.

Set phrases and idioms

Set phrases and idioms are generally placed under the first invariable element: **to break the back of a task** and **to break sb's heart** are both included under **break**. When the first element of a phrase can be varied, as in the case of **to give** or **lend somebody a hand**, the phrase will be found at the second element (**hand**). When the "first element" principle has not been followed a cross-reference shows the user where to look. At **break**, cross-references to **record** and **ice** indicate that **to break a record** and **to break the ice** are treated at these entries.

Certain very common French and English verbs form the basis of a very large number of phrases.

The entries for these verbs are very long, and phrases are therefore treated under the second element so that the user will find them more easily in a shorter entry; **faire la tête** is thus under **tête**, and **to make sense of something** under **sense**.

Cette méthode a été appliquée pour les verbes français suivants : **avoir, être, faire, donner, mettre, passer, porter, prendre, remettre, reprendre, tenir, tirer** et pour les verbes anglais : **be, become, come, do, get, give, go, have, lay, make, put, set, take.**

This approach has been followed with the following verbs:
French: **avoir, être, faire, donner, mettre, passer, porter, prendre, remettre, reprendre, tenir, tirer.**
English: **be, become, come, do, get, give, go, have, lay, make, put, set, take.**

Répétition du mot dans l'article

Repetition of the headword within the entry

Par souci d'économie de place, le mot est remplacé par le signe ~ lorsqu'il est répété dans le corps de l'article sans subir de modification orthographique.

To save space, where the headword occurs in its full form within the entry it is replaced by ~.

> **age** ... she stayed for ~s
> **carry** ... to ~ authority ... *but* he carried his audience with him
> **abus** ... faire ~ de

Les formes conjuguées des verbes français sont reprises en toutes lettres (ex. : **porter...il porte...ils porteront**), ainsi que les composés dans les deux langues et que les verbes anglais à particule.

Inflected forms of French verbs are shown in full (eg **porter...il porte...ils porteront**), as are compounds in both languages, and phrasal verbs in English.

Pluriel

Plurals

Les formes plurielles qui présentent des difficultés sont données dans la langue de départ.

Irregular plural forms of English words are given in the English-French side, those of French words and compounds in the French-English side.

En français, les pluriels autres que ceux qui se forment par le simple ajout du -s sont indiqués, ex. : **cheval** (*pl* **-aux**); ceux des composés avec trait d'union sont également donnés.

In French, all plurals which do not consist of *headword* + s are shown, eg **cheval** (*pl* **-aux**). The plural form of hyphenated compounds is also shown.

En anglais, les pluriels formés régulièrement ne sont pas donnés.

In English a knowledge of the basic rules is assumed.

1 La plupart des noms prennent *-s* au pluriel : **bed-s, site-s.**

1 Most English nouns take *-s* in the plural: **bed-s, site-s.**

2 Les noms se terminant par *-s, -x, -z, -sh* et *-ch* [tʃ] prennent *-es* au pluriel : **boss-es, box-es, dish-es, patch-es.**

2 Nouns that end in *-s, -x, -z, -sh* and some in *-ch* [tʃ] take *-es* in the plural: **boss-es, box-es, dish-es, patch-es.**

3 Les noms se terminant par *-y* non précédé d'une voyelle changent au pluriel le *-y* en *-ies* : **lady-ladies, berry-berries** (mais **tray-s, key-s**).

3 Nouns that end in *-y* not preceded by a vowel change the *-y* to *-ies* in the plural: **lady-ladies, berry-berries** (but **tray-s, key-s**).

Quand le pluriel d'un mot est très différent du singulier, il figure à sa place dans la nomenclature générale avec un renvoi ; il est répété sous le singulier.

Plural forms of the headword which differ substantially from the singular form are listed in their alphabetical place in the word list with a cross-reference, and repeated under the singular form.

> **baux** ... *pl de* **bail**
> **bail** (*pl* **baux**) ...
> **children** ... NPL *of* **child**
> **child** (*pl* **children**) ... N

Dans la partie anglais-français, les mots français invariables au pluriel sont suivis de l'indication (*inv*).

French invariable plurals are marked (*inv*) on the English-French side.

Genre

Genders

Les formes féminines des mots français qui ne suivent pas directement le masculin dans l'ordre alphabétique

Feminine forms in French which are separated alphabetically from the masculine form in the word list sont données à leur place normale dans la nomenclature, avec un renvoi au masculin ; elles sont répétées sous celui-ci.

are shown as separate headwords, with a cross-reference to the masculine form.

belle ... → **beau**

Un mot féminin exigeant une traduction différente du masculin fait l'objet soit d'un article séparé soit d'une catégorie bien individualisée dans le cas d'articles complexes.

A feminine headword requiring a different translation from its masculine form is given either a separate entry or a separate category in the case of more complex entries.

blanchisseur ... NM ... launderer
blanchisseuse ... NF laundress
coiffeur ... NM *[dames]* hairdresser; *[hommes]* hairdresser, barber
coiffeuse ... NF *(= personne)* hairdresser; *(= meuble)* ...
baladeur, -euse ... ☐ ADJ ... ☐ NM ... ☐ **baladeuse** NF

Dans la partie anglais-français, le féminin des adjectifs français se construisant régulièrement n'est pas indiqué. Sont considérées comme régulières les formes suivantes :

In the English-French side the feminine forms of French adjectives are given only where these are not regular. The following are considered regular adjective inflections:

-, e ◇ -ef, -ève ◇ -eil, -eille ◇ -er, -ère ◇ -et, -ette ◇ -eur, -euse ◇ -eux, -euse ◇
-ien, -ienne ◇ -ier, -ière ◇ -if, -ive ◇ -il, -ille ◇ -on, -onne ◇ -ot, -otte

Par contre quand un nom anglais peut recevoir une traduction au masculin ou au féminin, selon le sexe, la forme du féminin est toujours mentionnée.

When the translation of an English noun could be either masculine or feminine, according to sex, the feminine form of the French noun translation is always given.

▶ **car-worker** N *(Ind)* ouvrier *m*, -ière *f* de l'industrie automobile
▶ **computer scientist** N informaticien(ne) *m(f)*

Indications d'emploi

Les indications guidant le lecteur prennent les formes suivantes :

Indicating material

General indicating material takes the following forms :

Entre crochets [ ]

☐ Les noms sujets précisant le sens d'une entrée verbe.

In square brackets [ ]

☐ Within verb entries, typical noun subjects of the headword.

décroître ... VI *[nombre, population, intensité, pouvoir]* to decrease, diminish, decline; *[eaux, fièvre]* to subside, go down; *[popularité]* to decline, drop
fade ... VI *[colour]* passer, perdre son éclat ; *[material]* passer, se décolorer ; *[light]* baisser, diminuer ; *[flower]* se faner, se flétrir

☐ Les noms compléments d'une entrée nom.

☐ Within noun entries, typical noun complements of the headword.

défigurement ... NF *[vérité]* distortion; *[texte, tableau]* mutilation; *[visage]* disfigurement
branch ... NF *[of tree, candelabra]* bras *m*, ... *[of mountain chain]* ramification *f* ; ... *[of subject, science etc]* branche *f*

[vérité] doit donc se lire « de la vérité ».

In such instances, *[vérité]* should be read as 'de la vérité'.

☐ Les noms que peut qualifier une entrée adjectif.

☐ Typical noun complements of adjectives.

élancé, e ... ADJ *[clocher, colonne, taille, personne]* slender
distinct ... ADJ ... *[increase, progress]* sensible

☐ Les verbes ou adjectifs modifiés par une entrée adverbe.

☐ Typical verb or adjective complements of adverbs.

bourgeoisement ... ADV [penser, réagir] conventionally; [vivre] comfortably
briskly ... ADV ... [move] vivement ; [walk] d'un bon pas ; [speak] brusquement ;
  [act] sans tarder

Entre crochets avec le signe +

Les compléments d'objet d'une entrée verbe.

In square brackets with +

Typical objects of verbs.

défaire ... VT ... [+ couture, tricot] to undo, unpick (Brit); [+ écheveau] to undo,
  unravel, unwind; [+ corde, nœud, ruban] to undo, untie; ... [+ valise] to unpack
impair ... VT ... [+ abilities, faculties] détériorer, diminuer ; [+ negotiations, relations]
  porter atteinte à ; [+ health] abîmer, détériorer ; [+ sight, hearing] abîmer, affaiblir

Entre parenthèses avec le signe =

Les synonymes

In parentheses with =

Synonyms

décent, e ... ADJ (= bienséant) decent, proper; (= discret, digne) proper;
  (= acceptable) [logement, salaire], decent
centenary ... N (= anniversary) centenaire m; (= century) siècle m

Entre parenthèses ( )

1 Les autres précisions et explications susceptibles de guider l'usager.

In parentheses ( )

1 Other information and hints which guide the user.

contender ... N ... (in contest, competition, race) concurrent(e) m(f); (in election,
  for a job) candidat m
décaper ... VT (gén) to clean, cleanse; (à l'abrasif) to scour;...(à la brosse) to scrub
employment ... N ... (= a job) emploi m, travail m; (modest) place f;
  (important) situation f

2 Les indications d'ordre grammatical permettant au lecteur étranger d'utiliser le mot correctement. Elles sont données après la traduction.

2 Syntactical information to allow the non-native speaker to use the word correctly. This is given after the translation.

différer ... VI ... to differ, be different (**de** from, **en**, **par** in)
dissimuler ... VT ... to conceal, hide (**à qn** from sb)
speak ... VI ... parler (to **à**, of, about **de**)
commit ... VT ... to ~ o.s. s'engager (**to sth** à qch, **to doing** à faire)

Autres indications d'emploi

NonC signifie « non comptable ». Il est utilisé pour indiquer qu'un nom ne s'emploie pas normalement au pluriel et ne se construit pas, en règle générale, avec l'article indéfini ou un numéral. NonC a pour but d'avertir de lecteur étranger dans les cas où celui-ci risquerait d'employer le mot de manière incorrecte ; mais notre propos n'est nullement de donner une liste exhaustive de ces mots en anglais. NonC est parfois utilisé comme indication dans la langue de départ, lorsque c'est le seul moyen de distinguer emplois « non comptables » et « comptables ».

Other indicators

NonC stands for 'uncountable' and serves to mark nouns which are not normally used in the plural or with the indefinite article or with numerals. NonC occurs only as a warning device in cases where a non-native speaker might otherwise use the word wrongly. There has been no attempt to give an exhaustive account of 'uncountability' in English. NonC has also been used as an indicator to distinguish meanings in the source language.

folâtrerie ... NF (NonC= caractère) playfulness
clignement ... NM ... blinking (NonC)
Callanetics® ... N (NonC) gymnastique douce (caractérisée par la répétition fréquente
  de légers exercices musculaires)
implement ... N ... ~s équipement m (NonC), matériel m (NonC)

SPÉC, SPEC signifie « terme de spécialiste ».

SPEC, SPÉC stands for 'technical term.'

tympan ... NM (Anat) eardrum, tympanum (SPÉC)

Cela veut dire que le mot anglais d'usage courant est « eardrum » et que « tympanum » ne se rencontre que dans le vocabulaire des spécialistes.

This indicates that the common English word is 'eardrum' and that 'tympanum' is restricted to the vocabulary of specialists.

≈ introduit une équivalence culturelle, lorsque ce que représente le terme de la langue de départ n'existe pas ou n'a pas d'équivalent exact dans la langue d'arrivée, et n'est donc pas à proprement parler traduisible.

≈ is used when the source language headword or phrase has no equivalent in the target language and is therefore untranslatable. In such cases the nearest cultural equivalent is given.

> **bêtise** ... NF ... **~ de Cambrai** ≈ mint humbug (*Brit*), ≈ piece of hard mint candy (*US*)
> **the National Health Service** N ≈ la Sécurité sociale

Une glose explicative peut être donnée lorsqu'il n'existe pas d'équivalent culturel assez proche dans la langue d'arrivée.

An explanatory gloss (in italics) is given in cases where there is no cultural equivalent in the target language.

> **Yorkshire pudding** N *pâte à crêpe cuite qui accompagne un rôti de bœuf*

On a eu recours aux petites capitales pour indiquer, dans certaines expressions anglaises, l'accent d'insistance qui rend, ou requiert, une nuance particulière du français.

Small capitals are used to indicate the spoken stress in certain English expressions.

> **mais enfin ! je viens de te le dire !** but I've just TOLD you!

Domaines

Les indications de domaine figurent dans les cas suivants :

1 Pour indiquer les différents sens d'un mot et introduire les traductions appropriées.

> **cuirasse** ... NF ... (*Hist*) [*chevalier*] breastplate; (*Naut*) armour(-plate *ou* plating) (*Brit*), armor(-plate *ou* plating) (*US*); (*Zool*) cuirass
> **grade** ... N ... (*Mil = rank*) rang *m*; ... (*Climbing*) degré *m* (de difficulté)

2 Quand la langue de départ n'est pas ambiguë, mais que la traduction peut l'être.

> **comprimé** ... NM (*Pharm*) tablet
> **parabola** ... N parabole *f* (*Math*)

La liste des indications de domaine apparaissant sous forme abrégée figure sur les pages de garde.

Niveaux de langue

Une quinzaine d'indications de registre accompagnent les mots et expressions qui présentent un écart par rapport à la langue courante. Ces indications sont données aussi bien dans la langue de départ que dans la langue d'arrivée et constituent avant tout un avertissement au lecteur utilisant la langue étrangère. Les paragraphes suivants précisent le sens des principaux niveaux de langue, dont la liste complète figure sous forme abrégée sur les pages de garde.

frm indique le style administratif, les formules officielles, la langue soignée.

Field labels

Labels indicating subject fields occur in the following cases:

1 To differentiate various meanings of the headword.

2 When the meaning in the source language is clear but may be ambiguous in the target language.

A full list of the abbreviated field labels is given on the inside covers of the dictionary.

Style labels

A dozen or so indicators of register are used to mark non-neutral words and expressions. These indicators are given for both source and target language and serve mainly as a warning to the reader using the foreign language. The following paragraphs explain the meaning of the most common style labels, of which a complete list is given, with explanations, on the inside covers of the dictionary.

frm denotes formal language such as that used on official forms, in pronouncements and other formal communications.

> **agréer** ... (*frm*) 1 VT (= *accepter*) [+ *demande, excuses*] to accept
> **heretofore** ... N (*frm*) (= *up to a specified point*) jusque-là

* marque la majeure partie des expressions familières employées dans la langue de tous les jours. Ce signe conseille au lecteur d'être prudent.

* indicates that the expression, while not forming part of standard language, is used by all educated speakers in a relaxed situation but would not be used in a formal essay or letter, or on an occasion when the speaker wishes to impress.

> **écraseur, -euse*** ... NM, F roadhog*
> **discuter le coup*** to have a chat
> **kidology*** ... N (*Brit*) bluff *m*
> **he laughed himself silly*** il a ri comme un bossu* *or* comme une baleine*

‡ marque les expressions très familières qui sont à employer avec la plus grande prudence par le lecteur étranger, qui devra posséder une grande maîtrise de la langue et savoir dans quel contexte elles peuvent être utilisées.

‡ indicates that the expression is used by some but not all educated speakers in a very relaxed situation. Such words should be handled with care by non-native speakers, unless they are very fluent in the language and sure of their company.

> **doucement les basses !‡** take it easy!*, go easy!*
> **kisser‡** ... N gueule‡ *f*

*‡ marque le petit nombre d'expressions courantes que le lecteur étranger doit pouvoir reconnaître, mais dont l'emploi risque d'être ressenti comme fortement indécent ou injurieux.

*‡ means 'Danger'. Such words are liable to offend in any situation, and therefore are to be avoided by the non-native speaker.

> **baiser** ... VT ... [b] *‡ to screw*‡, fuck*‡
> **shit*‡** ... N ... merde*‡ *f*

† marque les termes ou expressions démodés, qui ont quitté l'usage courant mais que l'étranger peut encore rencontrer au cours de ses lectures.

† denotes old-fashioned terms which are no longer in wide current use but which the foreign user will certainly find in reading.

> **indéfrisable†** ... NF perm, permanent (*US*)
> **botheration†** ... EXCL flûte !*, la barbe !*

†† marque les termes ou expressions archaïques, que le lecteur ne rencontrera en principe que dans les œuvres classiques.

†† denotes obsolete words which the user will normally find only in classical literature.

> **gageure** ... NF ... [b] †† (= *pari*) wager
> **burthen††** ... = **burden**

On évitera de confondre ces signes avec l'indication *Hist*, qui ne marque pas le niveau de langue du mot lui-même mais souligne que l'objet désigné ne se rencontre que dans un contexte historiquement daté.

The use of † and †† should not be confused with the label *Hist*. *Hist* does not apply to the expression itself but denotes the historical context of the object so named.

> **ordalie** ... NF (*Hist*) ordeal

littér, liter marquent les expressions de style poétique ou littéraire.

liter, littér denote an expression which belongs to literary or poetic language.

> **ostentatoire** ... ADJ (*littér*) ostentatious
> **beseech** ... VT (*liter*) [a] (= *ask for*) ... [b] (= *entreat*)

Le lecteur veillera à ne pas confondre ces indications avec *lit* d'une part (sens propre, emploi littéral) et *Littérat, Literat* de l'autre (domaine de la littérature).

The user should not confuse these style labels with the field labels *Literat, Littérat* which indicate that the expression belongs to the field of literature. Similarly the user should note that the abbreviation *lit* indicates the literal meaning, as opposed to the figurative (*fig*) meaning of a word.

L'indication *arg* (argot) désigne les termes appartenant au vocabulaire de groupes restreints (tels que les écoliers, les militaires) et l'indication du domaine approprié lui est adjointe dans la langue de départ.

For the purpose of this dictionary the indicator *arg* (argot) marks specific areas of vocabulary restricted to clearly defined groups of speakers (eg school-children, soldiers etc) and for this reason a field label is added to the label *arg* marking the source language expression.

camer (se) ... (*arg Drogue*) to be on drugs

Les indications de niveau de langue peuvent soit s'attacher à un mot ou à une expression isolés, soit marquer une catégorie entière ou même un article complet. Lorsqu'un mot est suivi d'astérisques, les locutions et exemples de l'article ne prendront à leur tour l'astérisque que si elles appartiennent à un niveau de langue différent. Tous les composés stylistiquement marqués prennent l'astérisque même s'ils sont du même niveau de langue que l'entrée.

The labels and symbols above are used to mark either an individual word or phrase, or a whole category, or even a complete entry. Where a headword is marked with asterisks any phrases in the entry will only have asterisks if they are of a different register from the headword. All compounds are marked even if their register matches that of the headword.

Ponctuation

Une virgule sépare les traductions considérées comme équivalentes ou pratiquement équivalentes.

Punctuation

A comma is used to separate translations which have the same or very similar meanings.

légitime ... 1 ADJ a (= *légal*) [*droits, gouvernement*] legitimate, lawful
I haven't seen him for ages il y a un siècle que je ne le vois plus, il y a une éternité que je ne l'ai vu

Un point-virgule sépare les traductions qui ne sont pas interchangeables. Le point-virgule est accompagné d'une indication qui précise la différence de sens.

A semi-colon separates translations which are not interchangeable. Indicators are given to differentiate between non-interchangeable translations.

mettre en danger [+ *personne*] to put in danger; [+ *vie, espèce*] to endanger; [+ *chances, réputation, carrière*] to jeopardize
melting ... 1 ADJ [*snow*] fondant ; (*fig*) [*voice, look*] attendri ; [*words*] attendrissant

Les traductions offrant plusieurs variantes interchangeables à partir d'un tronc commun sont séparées par *ou* ou par *or*.

In the translation of phrases, an alternative translation for part of the phrase is preceded by either *or* or *ou*.

je serai ravi de vous retrouver I'll be delighted to see *ou* meet you again
she is an eager student of English elle étudie l'anglais avec enthousiasme *or* ardeur

Le trait oblique / permet de regrouper des expressions de sens différent ayant un élément en commun, lorsque cette structure est reflétée dans la langue d'arrivée.

An oblique / indicates alternatives in the source language which are reflected exactly in the target language.

I'd give my eyeteeth* for a car like that/to go to China qu'est-ce que je ne donnerais pas pour avoir une voiture comme ça/pour aller en Chine
voiture haut/bas de gamme car at the top/lower end of the range, an upmarket/down-market car

Les parenthèses figurant à l'intérieur des expressions ou de leur traduction indiquent que les mots qu'elles contiennent sont facultatifs.

Parentheses within illustrative phrases or their translations indicate that the material so contained is optional.

bas les pattes ! ... (keep your) hands off!*, (keep your) paws off!⁎
(that's) too bad! (*indignant*) c'est un peu fort !

Ces parenthèses peuvent figurer en corrélation.

Such parentheses may be given for phrases in both source and target language.

our (highly) esteemed colleague notre (très) estimé collègue *or* confrère

Si une traduction est valable pour deux expressions synonymiques, ces expressions sont séparées par un losange (◇).

Phrases which can have the same translation are separated by a lozenge (◇).

tout à coup ◇ **tout d'un coup** all of a sudden, suddenly, all at once
to go back and forth ◇ **to go back and forward** [*person*] faire des allées et venues

Renvois

Ils renvoient le lecteur à l'article dans lequel est traitée une certaine expression, où figure un certain composé (voir **Locutions et exemples** ci-dessus).

> **nail** ... N ... → **bed**
> **bed of nails** N *(lit)* lit *m* de clous ...

Ils attirent également l'attention de l'usager sur certains mots-clés qui ont été traités en profondeur ; pour les numéraux, **six, sixième** et **soixante** ; pour les jours de la semaine, **samedi** ; pour les mois de l'année, **septembre**. Dans la nomenclature anglaise, ce seront les mots **six, sixth, sixty, Saturday, September**.

> **Friday** ... *for other phrases see* **Saturday**
> **vendredi** ... *pour autres locutions voir* **samedi**

Renvois en bas de page

Si l'un des mots que vous cherchez est accompagné d'un triangle (▼) dans la marge, vous trouverez ce mot répété en bas de page et suivi d'un ou de plusieurs numéros qui vous renvoient à la rubrique correspondante de la section **Grammaire active**. Par exemple :

permettre ...28.1, 30, 36.1, 37.4

vous renvoie aux rubriques *La suggestion* (chapitre 28, § 1), *Propositions* (chapitre 30), *La permission* (chapitre 36, § 1) et *L'obligation* (chapitre 37, § 4).

Verbes

Les tables de conjugaison des verbes français et anglais sont données en annexe à la fin de l'ouvrage. Dans la nomenclature française, chaque verbe est suivi d'un numéro à l'intérieur d'un carré qui renvoie le lecteur à ces tables. Dans la nomenclature anglaise, le prétérit et le participe passé des verbes forts anglais sont donnés après le verbe dans le corps de l'article. Une liste des principaux verbes forts figure également en annexe.

Dans la partie français-anglais, les emplois véritablement pronominaux des verbes sont traités dans une catégorie à part.

> **baisser** ... ☐3☐ **se baisser** VPR *(pour ramasser qch)* to bend down, stoop; *(pour éviter)* to duck

Les emplois pronominaux à valeur réciproque, réfléchie ou passive ne figurent que lorsque la traduction l'exige. En pareil cas, ils peuvent être simplement donnés dans la catégorie appropriée du verbe transitif, par exemple.

> **grandir** ... VT ... *(= faire paraître grand)* ... **ces chaussures te grandissent** those shoes make you (look) taller; **il se grandit en se mettant sur la pointe des pieds** he made himself taller by standing on tiptoe

Si la traduction d'un participe passé ne peut se déduire directement du verbe, ou si le participe a pris une

Cross-references

These are used to refer the user to the headword under which a certain compound or idiom has been treated (see **Set phrases and idioms** above).

They are also used to draw the user's attention to the full treatment of such words as numerals, days of the week and months of the year under certain key words. The key words which have been treated in depth are: French: **six, sixième, soixante, samedi, septembre.** English: **six, sixth, sixty, Saturday, September.**

References at the foot of the page

If a word you are looking up has a triangle (▼) next to it in the margin, you will find the word repeated at the foot of the page, together with a number or numbers referring you to relevant topics in **Language in Use**. For example:

refuse ...12, 8.3, 9.3

refers you to topics on *Disagreement* (chapter 12), *Intentions and Desires* (chapter 8, § 3) and *Permission* (Chapter 9, § 3).

Verbes

Tables of French and English verbs are included in the supplements at the end of the book. At each verb headword on the French-English side of the dictionary, a number inside a box refers the user to these tables. On the English–French side, the preterite and past participle of English strong verbs are given at the main verb entry.

In the French-English part of the dictionary verbs which are true pronominals are treated in a separate grammatical category.

Pronominal uses which indicate a reciprocal, reflexive or passive sense are shown only if the translation requires it. In such cases they may be given within the transitive category of the verb as an illustrative phrase.

If the translation of a past participle cannot be reached directly from the verb entry or if the past participle has valeur adjective, il est traité comme mot à part entière et figure à sa place alphabétique dans la nomenclature.

adjectival value then the past participle is treated as a headword.

étendu, e ... (*ptp de* **étendre**) ⬒1 ADJ ⬚a (= *vaste*) ... ⬚b (= *allongé*) ...
broken ... ⬒1 VB *ptp de* **break** ⬒2 ADJ ⬚a (= *cracked, smashed*) ...
⬚b (*Med* = *fractured*) ... ⬚c (= *not working*) ... ⬚d (*fig* = *ruined*) ...

PRONONCIATION

PRONUNCIATION

PRONUNCIATION OF FRENCH

Transcription

The symbols used to record the pronunciation of French are those of the International Phonetic Association. The variety of French transcribed is that shown in *Le Nouveau Petit Robert*, i.e. standard Parisian speech. Within this variety of French, variant pronunciations can be observed. In particular, there is a marked tendency among speakers today to make no appreciable distinction between: [a] and [ɑ], **patte** [pat] and **pâte** [pɑt] both tending towards the pronunciation [pat]; [ɛ̃] and [œ̃], **brin** [bʁɛ̃] and **brun** [bʁœ̃] both tending towards the pronunciation [bʁɛ̃]. The distinction between these sounds is maintained in the transcription.

Headwords

Each headword has its pronunciation transcribed between square brackets. In the case of words having a variant pronunciation (e.g. **tandis** [tɑ̃di], [tɑ̃dis]), the one pronunciation given is that regarded by the editorial team as preferable, often on grounds of frequency.

Morphological variations

Morphological variations of headwords are shown phonetically where necessary, without repetition of the root (e.g. **journal**, *pl*-**aux** [ʒuʁnal, o]).

Compound words

Compound words derived from headwords and shown within an entry are given without phonetic transcription (e.g. **casque** [kask], but **Casque bleu, casque de chantier**). The pronunciation of compounds is usually predictable, being that of the citation form of each element, associated with the final syllable stress characteristic of the language (see following paragraph).

Syllable stress

In normal, unemphatic speech, the final syllable of a word, or the final syllable of a sense group, carries a moderate degree of stress. The syllable stressed is given extra prominence by greater length and intensity. The exception to this rule is a final syllable containing a mute *e*, which is never stressed. In view of this simple rule, it has not been considered necessary to indicate the position of a stressed syllable of a word by a stress mark in the phonetic transcription.

Closing of [ɛ]

Under the influence of stressed [y], [i], or [e] vowels, an [ɛ] in an open syllable tends towards a closer [e] sound, even in careful speech. In such cases, the change has been indicated: **aimant** [ɛmɑ̃], but **aimer** [eme]; **bête** [bɛt], but **bêtise** [betiz].

Mute *e* [ə]

Within isolated words, a mute *e* [ə] preceded by a single pronounced consonant is regularly dropped (e.g. **follement** [fɔlmɑ̃]; **samedi** [samdi]).

Opening of [e]

As the result of the dropping of an [ə] within a word, an [e] occurring in a closed syllable tends towards [ɛ], as the transcription shows (e.g. **événement** [evɛnmɑ̃]; **élevage** [ɛlvaʒ]).

Aspirate *h*

Initial *h* in the spelling of a French word does not imply strong expulsion of breath, except in the case of certain interjections. Initial *h* is called 'aspirate' when it is incompatible with liaison (**des haricots** [de'aʁiko]) or with elision (**le haricot** [lə'aʁiko]). Aspirate *h* is shown in transcriptions by an apostrophe placed at the beginning of the word (e.g. **hibou** ['ibu]).

Consonants and assimilation

Within a word and in normal speech, a voiceless consonant may be voiced when followed by a voiced consonant (e.g. **exemple** [ɛgzɑ̃pl]), and a voiced consonant may be devoiced when followed by a voiceless consonant (e.g. **absolument** [apsɔlymɑ̃]). When this phenomenon is regular in a word, it is shown in transcription (e.g. **abside** [apsid]). In speech, its frequency varies from speaker to speaker. Thus, while the citation form of **tasse** is [tɑs], the group **une tasse de thé** may be heard pronounced [yntɑsdəte] or [yntɑzdəte].

Sentence stress

Unlike the stress pattern of English associated with meaning, sentence stress in French is associated with rhythm. The stress falls on the final syllable of the sense groups of which the sentence is formed (see **Syllable stress**). In the following example: *quand il m'a vu, il a traversé la rue en courant pour me dire un mot*, composed of three sense groups, the syllables **vu**, **-rant** and **mot** carry the stress, being slightly lengthened.

Intonation

French intonation is less mobile than English and is closely associated with sentence stress. The most marked rises and falls occur normally on the final syllable of sense groups. Thus, in the sentence given above, the syllables **vu** and **-rant** are spoken with a slight rise (indicating continuity), while the syllable **mot** is accompanied by a fall in the voice (indicating finality). In the case of a question, the final syllable will normally also be spoken with rising voice.

PHONETIC TRANSCRIPTION OF FRENCH

Phonetic alphabet used

Vowels

[i]	_il_, v_ie_, l_y_re
[e]	bl_é_, jou_er_
[ɛ]	l_ai_t, jou_et_, m_e_rci
[a]	pl_a_t, p_a_tte
[ɑ]	b_a_s, p_â_te
[ɔ]	m_o_rt, d_o_nner
[o]	m_o_t, d_ô_me, _eau_, g_au_che
[u]	gen_ou_, r_ou_e
[y]	r_u_e, vêt_u_
[ø]	p_eu_, d_eux_
[œ]	p_eu_r, m_eu_ble
[ə]	l_e_, pr_e_mier
[ɛ̃]	mat_in_, pl_ein_
[ã]	s_ans_, v_ent_
[ɔ̃]	b_on_, _om_bre
[œ̃]	l_un_di, br_un_

Semi-consonants

[j]	_y_eux, pa_ille_, p_i_ed
[w]	_ou_i, n_ou_er
[ɥ]	h_u_ile, l_u_i

Consonants

[p]	_p_ère, sou_p_e
[t]	_t_erre, vi_t_e
[k]	_c_ou, _qu_i, sa_c_, _k_épi
[b]	_b_on, ro_b_e
[d]	_d_ans, ai_d_e
[g]	_g_are, ba_gue_
[f]	_f_eu, neu_f_, _ph_oto
[s]	_s_ale, _c_elui, _ç_a, de_ss_ous, ta_ss_e, na_t_ion
[ʃ]	_ch_at, ta_che_
[v]	_v_ous, rê_v_e
[z]	_z_éro, mai_s_on, ro_s_e
[ʒ]	_j_e, _g_ilet, _g_eôle
[l]	_l_ent, so_l_
[ʀ]	_r_ue, veni_r_
[m]	_m_ain, fe_mm_e
[n]	_n_ous, to_nn_e, a_n_imal
[ɲ]	a_gn_eau, vi_gn_e
[h]	_h_op! (exclamative)
[']	_h_aricot (no liaison)
[ŋ]	words borrowed from English: campi_ng_
[x]	words borrowed from Spanish or Arabic: _j_ota

PRONONCIATION DE L'ANGLAIS

La notation adoptée est celle de l'Association phonétique internationale. L'ouvrage de base qui nous a servi constamment d'outil de référence est *l'English Pronouncing Dictionary* de Daniel Jones, qui, mis à jour par le Professeur A. C. Gimson, continue de faire autorité en France et partout où l'on apprend l'anglais britannique.

La transcription correspond à la *received pronunciation (RP)*, variété de l'anglais britannique la plus généralement étudiée dans le monde aujourd'hui. Elle correspond également, à quelques exceptions près, à celle de la 14ᵉ édition de *l'English Pronouncing Dictionary (EPD)* (Cambridge University Press). Ce système de transcription présente l'avantage d'utiliser des signes qui indiquent clairement la distinction à la fois quantitative et qualitative qui existe entre les voyelles tendues et relâchées (par exemple : 14ᵉ édition : [iː], [ɪ], [ɜː], [ə]).

Pour des raisons d'économie de place, une seule prononciation est donnée pour chaque mot, à l'exclusion des variantes courantes. La prononciation ainsi transcrite est celle la plus fréquemment entendue selon l'*EPD*, ou, dans le cas de néologismes et de mots nouveaux, selon les membres de l'équipe Collins-Le Robert.

Il a été jugé inutile de compliquer la tâche de l'utilisateur en indiquant au moyen de symboles appropriés la prononciation de mots sortant du cadre du vocabulaire britannique. Ainsi, **aluminium, aluminum** sont transcrits : [ˈæljʊˈmɪnɪəm], [əˈluːmɪnəm], bien que la seconde forme, exclusivement américaine, ne s'entend normalement qu'avec un accent américain. Il s'agit, dans de tels cas, d'une approximation qui ne met pas en cause la compréhension du mot employé.

Les formes réduites

Certains mots monosyllabiques, en nombre limité, ayant une fonction plus structurale que lexicale, sont sujets, surtout à l'intérieur d'un énoncé, à une réduction vocalique plus ou moins importante. Le mot **and**, isolé, se prononce [ænd] ; mais, dans la chaîne parlée, il se prononcera, à moins d'être accentué, [ənd, ən, n] selon le débit du locuteur et selon le contexte. Les mots qui sont le plus souvent touchés par cette réduction vocalique sont les suivants : *a, an, and, as, at, but, for, from, of, some, than, that, the, them, to, us, am, is, are, was, were, must, will, would, shall, should, have, has, had, do, does, can, could.*

L'accent tonique

Tout mot anglais, isolé, de deux syllabes ou plus, porte un accent tonique. Cet accent est noté au moyen du signe (ˈ) placé devant la syllabe intéressée ; par exemple : **composer** [kəmˈpəʊzə]. Le Français doit veiller à bien placer l'accent tonique sous peine de poser de sérieux problèmes de compréhension à ses interlocuteurs. Le tableau suivant indique un certain nombre de suffixes qui permettent de prévoir la place de l'accent tonique sur de nombreux mots. Ce tableau est donné à titre indicatif et ne cherche pas à être exhaustif.

Tableau des suffixes déterminant la position de l'accent tonique

SUFFIXE	EXEMPLE	EXCEPTIONS	REMARQUES
Accent sur syllabe finale			
-ee	refuˈgee	ˈcoffee, ˈtoffee, comˈmittee, ˈpedigree	
-eer	engiˈneer		
-ese	Japaˈnese		
-esque	pictuˈresque		
-ette	quarˈtette	ˈetiquette, ˈomelette	
-ate	creˈate		verbes de 2 syllabes
-fy	deˈfy		verbes de 2 syllabes
-ise, -ize	adˈvise		verbes de 2 syllabes
Accent sur pénultième			
-ial	comˈmercial		
-ian	lˈtalian		
-ic, -ics	ecoˈnomics	ˈArabic, aˈrithmetic, ˈCatholic, ˈheretic, ˈlunatic, ˈpolitics	les suffixes -ical, -ically *ne modifient pas la place de l'accent tonique, et n'admettent pas d'exceptions ; exemple :* poˈlitical, poˈlitically, arithˈmetical

SUFFIXE	EXEMPLE	EXCEPTIONS	REMARQUES
-ion	infor'mation	'dandelion ('television)	
-ish	di'minish	im'poverish	verbes en -ish
-itis	appendi'citis		
-osis	diag'nosis	(meta'morphosis)	

Accent sur antépénultième

-ety	so'ciety		
-ity	sin'cerity		
-itive	com'petitive		
-itude	'attitude		
-grapher	pho'tographer		
-graphy	pho'tography		
-logy	bi'ology		
-ate	ap'preciate		
-fy	'pacify		
-ise, -ize	'advertise	'characterize, 'regularize, 'liberalize, 'nationalize	pour les verbes de 2 syllabes, voir p.xxxviii

NB *Les mots placés entre parenthèses ont aussi une accentuation conforme au modèle.*

L'accent secondaire

Dans un mot, toute syllabe accentuée en plus de celle qui porte l'accent tonique porte un accent secondaire, c'est-à-dire un accent ayant moins d'intensité que l'accent tonique. L'accent secondaire est noté au moyen du signe (ˌ) devant la syllabe intéressée, par exemple: **composition** [ˌkɒmpəˈzɪʃən] (accent secondaire sur [ˌkɒm], accent tonique sur [ˈzɪʃ]).

Les composés

La prononciation des mots ou groupes de mots rassemblés dans la catégorie COMP d'un article n'est pas indiquée, car elle correspond à celle du mot-souche suivie de celle du mot ou des mots formant le reste du composé, mais avec une restriction importante: pour des raisons pratiques, on considérera que la grande majorité des composés à deux éléments ne sont accentués que sur le premier élément, cette accentuation s'accompagnant d'une chute de la voix. Exemple: **'left-wing, 'food prices.**

L'accent de phrase

À la différence du français dont l'accent de phrase (syllabe allongée) tombe normalement sur la dernière syllabe des groupes de souffle, l'anglais met en relief la syllabe accentuée de chaque mot apportant un nouvel élément d'information. Dans la pratique cela veut dire que les mots lexicaux reçoivent un accent de phrase, tandis que les mots grammaticaux n'en reçoivent pas (voir **Les formes réduites**). Il est logique, dans un tel système, que même les mots lexicaux ne soient pas accentués s'ils n'apportent pas de nouveaux éléments d'information; c'est le cas, notamment, de mots ou de concepts répétés dans une même séquence; ils sont accentués une première fois, mais ils perdent leur accent par la suite. De même, lorsqu'une idée est répétée dans une même séquence, les mots qui l'expriment ne sont plus mis en relief lors de sa réapparition. Par contre, les éléments contrastifs de la phrase anglaise sont toujours fortement accentués. Exemple: *John recently bought himself a car, and Peter's got a new one too.*
Accents sur: **John, recently, bought, car, Peter, too.**
Accents contrastifs sur: **John** (facultatif) et **Peter**. Absence d'accent sur: **'s got a new one**, qui n'apporte aucun nouvel élément d'information et pourrait être supprimé (**and Peter, too**).

L'intonation

L'intonation en anglais, beaucoup plus qu'en français, révèle le sentiment du locuteur vis-à-vis des propos qu'il tient. Dans les deux langues, l'intonation est liée à l'accent de phrase. L'intonation française, tout comme l'accent de phrase, se manifeste sur la dernière syllabe des groupes de souffle: légère montée de la voix à l'intérieur de la phrase, avec une chute ou une montée sur la syllabe finale, selon qu'il s'agit d'une déclarative ou d'une interrogative. En anglais, l'intonation est liée au sens, et se manifeste sur toutes les syllabes accentuées de la phrase (voir **L'accent de phrase**). La phrase anglaise type présente une intonation commençant relativement haut, et descendant progressivement vers le grave sur les syllabes accentuées. Sur la dernière syllabe accentuée de la phrase, la voix marque soit une chute, soit une montée, plus importante qu'en français, selon le type de phrase: une chute, s'il s'agit d'une indication de finalité (déclaratives, impératives etc); une montée s'il s'agit d'une invitation au dialogue (interrogatives, requêtes polies etc). Plus le discours est animé et plus l'écart entre l'aigu et le grave se creuse. Des mots ayant un sens affectif intense tendent à faire monter la voix beaucoup plus haut que ne l'exigent les habitudes du discours français.

TRANSCRIPTION PHONÉTIQUE DE L'ANGLAIS

Alphabet phonétique et valeur des signes

Voyelles et diphtongues

[i:] b*ea*d, s*ee*
[ɑ:] b*ar*d, c*al*m
[ɔ:] b*or*n, c*or*k
[u:] b*oo*n, f*oo*l
[ɜ:] b*u*m, f*er*n, w*or*k
[ɪ] s*i*t, p*i*ty
[e] s*e*t, l*e*ss
[æ] s*a*t, *a*pple
[ʌ] f*u*n, c*o*me
[ɒ] f*o*nd, w*a*sh
[ʊ] f*u*ll, s*oo*t
[ə] compos*er*, *a*bove
[eɪ] b*ay*, f*a*te
[aɪ] b*uy*, l*ie*
[ɔɪ] b*oy*, v*oi*ce
[əu] n*o*, ag*o*
[au] n*ow*, pl*ough*
[ɪə] t*ier*, b*eer*
[ɛə] t*are*, f*air*
[ʊə] t*our*

Consonnes

[p] *p*at, *p*o*p*e
[b] *b*at, *b*a*b*y
[t] *t*ab, s*t*rut
[d] *d*ab, men*d*e*d*
[k] *c*ot, *k*iss, *ch*ord
[g] *g*ot, a*gog*

[f] *f*ine, ra*ff*le
[v] *v*ine, ri*v*er
[s] pot*s*, *s*it, ri*c*e
[z] pod*s*, bu*zz*
[θ] *th*in, ma*th*s
[ð] *th*is, o*th*er
[ʃ] *sh*ip, *s*ugar
[ʒ] mea*s*ure
[tʃ] *ch*ance
[dʒ] *j*ust, e*dg*e
[l] *l*ittle, p*l*ace
[r] *r*an, sti*rr*ing
[m] ra*m*, *m*u*mm*y
[n] ra*n*, *n*ut
[ŋ] ra*ng*, ba*nk*
[h] *h*at, re*h*eat
[j] *y*et, mill*i*on
[w] *w*et, be*w*ail
[x] lo*ch*

Divers

Un caractère en italique
représente un son qui peut ne pas
être prononcé
[ʳ] représente un [r] entendu s'il
forme une liaison avec la voyelle
du mot suivant
['] accent tonique
[ˌ] accent secondaire

DICTIONNAIRE
FRANÇAIS-ANGLAIS

FRENCH-ENGLISH
DICTIONARY

A

A¹, a¹ [a] NM (= *lettre*) A, a; **de A à Z** from A to Z; **feuille A3/A4** sheet of A3/A4 paper; **c'est du format A4** it's A4 (paper); **prouver** *ou* **démontrer qch par A + B** to prove sth conclusively

A² (ABRÉV = **ampère**) amp

A³ [a] NF (ABRÉV = **autoroute**) ≈ M (*Brit*); **l'A10** the A10 motorway (*Brit*) *ou* highway (*US*)

A⁴ (ABRÉV = **apprenti conducteur**) P plate (*on car of newly qualified driver*)

a² (ABRÉV = **are**) a

à [a]

> Contraction **à + le = au**; **à + les = aux**.
> Lorsque *à* se trouve dans des locutions du type obéir à qn, apprendre à qn, lent à s'habiller, l'admission au club, *reportez-vous à l'autre mot.*

PRÉPOSITION

a | déplacement, direction | (= *vers*) to; (= *dans*) into; **aller** *ou* **se rendre à Lille/au Canada/aux Açores** to go to Lille/Canada/the Azores; **aller au marché/au théâtre** to go to the market/the theatre; **entrez au salon** come into the lounge; **au lit les enfants!** off to bed children!, time for bed children!

> *Notez qu'avec certains édifices l'anglais n'utilisera pas l'article si l'accent est mis sur leur fonction plutôt que sur leur localisation.*

aller à l'hôpital (*gén*) to go to the hospital; [*malade*] to go to hospital; **aller à l'église** (*gén*) to go to the church; [*pratiquant*] to go to church

b | position, localisation | in; **habiter à Paris/au Canada/à Bali** to live in Paris/in Canada/in Bali; **on s'est arrêté à Toulouse** we stopped in Toulouse; **je suis à la cuisine** I'm in the kitchen; **il faisait chaud à l'église/au théâtre** it was hot in church/in the theatre

> *Lorsque* à *est suivi d'un nom de petite île ou d'île dont la traduction comprend les mots* **island** *ou* **isle**, *il se traduit le plus souvent par* **on**.

vivre à Paros/l'île de Wight to live on Paros/the Isle of Wight

> *Lorsque* à *est suivi du nom d'un lieu où l'on exerce une activité, il se traduit par* **at**.

être à l'école/au bureau to be at school/the office

c | étape de voyage, adresse | at; **l'avion a atterri à Luton** the plane landed at Luton; **le train ne s'est pas arrêté à Montélimar** the train didn't stop at Montélimar; **j'habite au (numéro) 26 (de la rue Pasteur)** I live at number 26 (rue Pasteur); MAIS **habiter au 4ème étage** to live on the 4th floor

d | suivi d'une activité | **quand elle est à son tricot/à sa peinture*** when she's doing her knitting/painting; **allez Paul, à la vaisselle!** come on Paul, get cracking* with that washing-up!; **le livre est à la reliure** the book is (away) being bound; MAIS **au travail tout le monde!** come on everybody, let's get to work!; **elle est au tennis** (*gén*) she's playing tennis; (*à son cours*) she's at her tennis lesson

e | provenance | from; **je l'ai eu à la bibliothèque** I got it from the library; **prendre de l'eau au puits/à la rivière** to get water from the well/the river

f | distance, durée | **Paris est à 400 km de Londres** Paris is 400 km from London; **c'est à 3 km/5 minutes (d'ici)** it's 3 km/5 minutes away (from here); **c'est à 4 heures de route** it's a 4-hour drive

g | avec notion de temps | (*moment précis, fête, moment de l'année*) at; (*époque*) in; **à 6 heures** at 6 (o'clock); **je vous verrai aux vacances/à Noël** I'll see you in the holidays/at Christmas; **la poésie au 19e siècle** poetry in the 19th century

> *Lorsque* à *signifie* lors de, *l'anglais emploie souvent une proposition temporelle introduite par* **when**.

je n'étais pas là à leur arrivée I wasn't there when they arrived; **à sa naissance, il ne pesait que 3 kg** he only weighed 3 kilos when he was born; **vous serez payé à l'achèvement des travaux** you'll be paid when the work is finished

(*dans des exclamations*) **à lundi/la semaine prochaine!** see you on Monday/next week!

> *Avec la nuance de sens* à l'occasion de, à *se traduit par* **at**.

on se reverra à sa réception we'll see each other again at his party

h | appartenance, possession | **c'est à moi/à eux** it's mine/theirs, it belongs to me/to them; **ce livre est à Luc** this book belongs to Luc *ou* is Luc's; **à qui est ce stylo?** whose pen is this?; **c'est une amie à lui/à eux** she is a friend of his/theirs; **ils n'ont pas de maison à eux** they haven't got a house of their own; **la voiture à Paul*** Paul's car; **on avait la plage à nous (tous seuls)** we had the beach to ourselves; **à moi le Canada/Paris!** Canada/Paris here I come!; **à nous la belle vie!** it's the good life for us from now on!; **je suis à toi pour toujours** I'm yours forever; **je suis à vous dans deux minutes** I'll be with you in a couple of minutes

i | responsabilité | **c'était à toi d'y aller** it was up to you to go; **ce n'est pas à moi de le dire/de décider** it's not for me to say/to decide, it's not up to me to say/to decide

j | dans une dédicace | for, to; (*dans les souhaits*) to; **à mon fils, pour ses 20 ans** to *ou* for my son, on his 20th birthday; (*dans un toast*) **à Julie!** to Julie!; **à ta nouvelle maison!** to your new house!; MAIS **à tes 30 ans!** happy 30th birthday!; **à mon épouse regrettée** in memory of my dear wife

k | dans un ordre de passage | **à toi!** (*dans un jeu*) your turn (to play)!; (*aux échecs, aux dames*) your move!; (*en lançant une balle*) to you!; **c'est à qui (le tour)?** (*dans un jeu*) whose turn is it?; (*dans une file d'attente*) who's next?; (*TV, Rad*) **à vous les studios/Paris** over to you in the studio/in Paris

l | suivi d'un chiffre pour rapport, évaluation | **nous y sommes allés à cinq** five of us went; **ils**

l'ont soulevé à (eux) deux the two of them lifted it up together; **ils ont fait le travail à trois/à eux tous** they did the work between the three of them/between them; **ils couchent à trois dans la même chambre** they sleep three to a room; **à trois, nous irons plus vite** it'll be quicker if three of us do it; **nous n'entrerons jamais à six dans sa voiture** the six of us will never get into his car; **on peut rentrer à six dans la voiture** the car can hold six people; **gagner (par) 2 à 1** to win (by) 2 goals to 1; **il mène (par) 3 jeux à 2** he's leading (by) 3 games to 2

m | = par, chaque | **faire du 90 à l'heure** to do 90 km *ou* per hour; **c'est à 15 F le kilo** it's 15 francs a kilo; **être payé à la semaine/au mois** to be paid weekly/monthly, be paid by the week/the month

n | approximation | **il leur faut 4 à 5 heures/kilos** they need 4 to 5 hours/kilos; **on a fait 8 à 9 kilomètres** we did 8 or 9 kilometres

o | description |

> *Lorsque* à *est utilisé dans une description, il est rendu soit par* **with** *soit par une locution adjectivale.*

robe à manches dress with sleeves; **robe à manches courtes** short-sleeved dress; **enfant aux yeux bleus/aux cheveux longs** blue-eyed/long-haired child, child with blue eyes/long hair; **la dame au chapeau vert** the lady in *ou* with the green hat; **l'homme à la pipe** the man smoking a pipe, the man with the pipe; (*titre de tableau*) Man with Pipe

p | = au moyen de, avec | with; (*suivi du nom d'un instrument de musique*) on; **couper qch au couteau** to cut sth with a knife; **faire la cuisine à l'huile/au beurre** to cook with oil/butter; **canard aux petits pois/aux pruneaux** duck with peas/prunes; **il l'a joué au piano/violon** he played it on the piano/violin; MAIS **sardines à l'huile** sardines in oil; **regarder qch à la jumelle** to look at sth through binoculars; **le générateur marche au gazole** the generator runs on diesel; **j'y suis allé à pied** I went on foot

q | = d'après, au vu de | according to, from; (*avec valeur consécutive*) to; **à ce qu'il prétend** according to what he says; **à ce que j'ai compris** from what I understood; **à sa consternation** to his dismay; **à ma grande surprise** to my great surprise, much to my surprise; MAIS **à son expression, je dirais qu'il est content** judging from his expression I'd say he is pleased; **c'est aux résultats qu'on le jugera** he will be judged on his results

r | notion d'imminence | **le temps est à la pluie/neige** it looks like rain/snow, there's rain/snow on the way

s

♦ **à la ...** (= *à la manière de*) **cuisiné à la japonaise** cooked Japanese-style; **le socialisme à la française** French-style socialism; **une histoire à la Tolstoï** a story in the style of Tolstoy *ou* à la Tolstoy; **vivre à l'américaine** to live like an American

◆ **à** + infinitif

> à + infinitif se traduit le plus souvent par une proposition infinitive.

je n'ai rien à lire/faire I have nothing to read/do; **j'ai quelque chose à te montrer** I've got something to show you; **il a été le premier à le dire, mais ils sont plusieurs à le penser** he was the first one to say it, but there are quite a few people who think the same; **ils sont deux à l'avoir fait** two of them did it; **elle est toujours à le taquiner** she keeps teasing him, she's forever teasing him

(avec idée de nécessité, de devoir) **c'est à faire aujourd'hui** it has to be done ou it must be done today; **ce sont des choses à prévoir** these things have to be ou need to be thought about; **il est à ménager** he should be ou needs to be handled carefully; **le poisson est à manger tout de suite** the fish needs to be ou must be eaten at once; **tout est à refaire** it's all got to be done again; **ces journaux sont à jeter** these papers can be thrown out

> Lorsque à + infinitif a une valeur temporelle ou causale, il se traduit généralement par un gérondif ou une proposition temporelle.

à le voir si maigre, j'ai eu pitié when I saw how thin he was I felt sorry for him; **à le fréquenter, on se rend compte que ...** when you've been with him for a while, you realize that ...; **il nous fait peur à conduire si vite** he frightens us driving so fast; MAIS **à l'entendre/le voir, on dirait qu'il est ivre** to hear him/look at him you'd think he was drunk, he sounds/looks drunk; **vous le buterez à le punir ainsi** you'll antagonize him if you punish him like that

(valeur consécutive) **c'est à vous rendre fou** it's enough to drive you crazy; **c'est à se demander si** it makes you wonder if; **c'est à croire qu'ils nous prennent pour des idiots** you'd think that they took us for complete idiots

(indiquant la fonction) for, designed for; **c'est une machine à polir les pierres** it's a machine (designed) for polishing stones

Å (ABRÉV = **angström**) Å

Aaron [aʀɔ̃] NM Aaron

AB (ABRÉV = **assez bien**) quite good, ≈ C+

abaissable [abesabl] ADJ [siège] reclining (épith)

abaissant, e [abesɑ̃, ɑ̃t] ADJ degrading

abaisse [abes] NF rolled-out pastry; **faites une ~ de 3 cm** roll out the pastry to a thickness of 3 cm

abaisse-langue [abeslɑ̃g] NM INV tongue depressor, spatula (Brit)

abaissement [abesmɑ̃] NM a (= action) [levier] (en tirant) pulling down; (en poussant) pushing down; [température, valeur, taux] lowering, bringing down; **l'~ de l'âge de la retraite/des barrières douanières** lowering the retirement age/customs barriers b (= fait de s'abaisser) [température, valeur, taux] fall, drop (de in); [terrain] downward slope; **l'~ de la moralité** the decline in moral standards c (= conduite obséquieuse) subservience, self-abasement; (= conduite choquante) degradation d † (= humiliation) humiliation; (= déchéance) debasing; (Rel) humbling

abaisser [abese] ▸ conjug 1 ◂ 1 VT a [+ levier] (= tirer) to pull down; (= pousser) to push down; [+ store] to pull down; [+ siège] to put down; **cette vitre s'abaisse-t-elle ?** does this window go down?; (course automobile) **~ le drapeau** to lower the flag
b [+ température, valeur, taux] to lower, reduce, bring down; [+ niveau, mur] to lower; **~ le coût de la main d'œuvre** to bring down ou reduce labour costs; **~ l'âge de la retraite** to bring down ou lower the retirement age
c (Math) [+ chiffre] to bring down, carry; [+

perpendiculaire] to drop
d (= rabaisser) [personne] to humiliate; [vice] to debase; (Rel) to humble; **~ la puissance des nobles** to reduce the power of the nobles
e (Culin) [+ pâte] to roll out
2 **s'abaisser** VPR a (= diminuer) [température, valeur, taux] to fall, drop, go down; [terrain] to slope down; (Théât) [rideau] to fall (sur on)
b (= s'humilier) to humble o.s.; **je ne m'abaisserai pas à présenter des excuses** I won't stoop so low as to apologize

abaisseur [abesœʀ] ADJ M, NM (muscle) ~ depressor

abalone [abalɔn] NM abalone

abandon [abɑ̃dɔ̃] NM a (= délaissement) [personne, lieu] desertion, abandonment; **~ de poste** desertion of one's post; (Jur) **~ du domicile conjugal** desertion
b (= renonciation) [idée, privilège, fonction, recherches] giving up; [droit] giving up, relinquishment; [course, championnat] withdrawal (de from); (Sport) **après l'~ de notre équipe** after our team was forced to retire ou withdraw; **gagner par ~** to win by default; **faire ~ de ses biens à qn** to make over one's property to sb; **faire ~ de ses droits sur** to relinquish ou renounce one's right(s) to; **~ de soi-même** self-abnegation
c (= manque de soin) neglected state; **l'(état d')~ où se trouvait la ferme** the neglected state (that) the farm was in; **jardin à l'~** neglected garden, garden run wild ou in a state of neglect; **laisser qch à l'~** to neglect sth
d (= confiance) lack of constraint; **parler avec ~** to talk freely ou without constraint; **dans ses moments d'~** in his moments of abandon, in his more expansive moments
e (= nonchalance) **étendu sur le sofa avec ~** sprawled out on the sofa; **l'~ de son attitude/ses manières** his relaxed ou easy-going attitude/manners
f (Ordin) abort

abandonné, e [abɑ̃dɔne] (ptp de **abandonner**) ADJ a [attitude, position] relaxed; (avec volupté) abandoned b [jardin] neglected; [route, usine] disused; **vieille maison ~e** deserted old house c (= délaissé) [conjoint] abandoned; **enfants ~s à eux-mêmes** children left to their own devices; **tout colis ~ sera détruit** any luggage left unattended will be destroyed

abandonner [abɑ̃dɔne] ▸ conjug 1 ◂ 1 VT a (= délaisser) [+ lieu] to desert, abandon; [+ personne] (gén) to leave, abandon; (intentionnellement) to desert, abandon; [+ voiture, animal] to abandon; **il a été abandonné à la naissance** he was abandoned at birth; **son courage l'abandonna** his courage failed ou deserted him; **ses forces l'abandonnèrent** his strength failed him; **l'ennemi a abandonné ses positions** the enemy abandoned their positions; (Mil) **~ son poste** to desert one's post; **~ le terrain** (Mil) to take flight; (fig) to give up; (Jur) **~ le domicile conjugal** to desert ou abandon the family home; **il a été abandonné des médecins†** the doctors have given up on him
b (= renoncer à) [+ fonction] to give up, relinquish; [+ études, projet, recherches] to give up, abandon; [+ matière d'examen] to drop, give up; [+ technique] to abandon, give up; [+ hypothèse] to abandon, drop; [+ droit, privilèges] to give up, relinquish; [+ course] to withdraw ou retire from, abandon; **~ tout espoir (de faire qch)** to give up ou abandon all hope (of doing sth); **le joueur a dû ~** the player had to retire ou withdraw; **~ le pouvoir** to give up power; (lit, fig) **~ la lutte** ou **la partie** to give up the fight ou the struggle; (Jur) **~ les poursuites** to drop the charges; **j'abandonne !** I give up!
c (Ordin) to abort
d **~ à** (gén) to give ou leave to; **elle lui abandonna sa main** she let him take her hand;

~ à qn le soin de faire qch to leave it up to sb to do sth; **~ qn à son (triste) sort** to leave ou abandon (littér) sb to their fate; **~ qch au pillage/à la destruction** to leave sth to be pillaged/to be destroyed; **le verger a été abandonné aux herbes folles** the orchard has become overrun with weeds; **abandonnez votre corps aux délices d'un bain chaud** luxuriate in a hot bath
2 **s'abandonner** VPR a (= se relâcher) to let o.s. go; (= se confier) to open up; **elle s'abandonna dans mes bras** she sank into my arms
b **s'~ à** (= se laisser aller à) [+ passion, joie, débauche] to give o.s. up to; [+ paresse, désespoir] to give way to; **s'~ à la rêverie** to indulge in ou give o.s. up to daydreaming; **s'~ au bien-être** to luxuriate in a sense of wellbeing; **il s'abandonna au sommeil** he let himself drift off to sleep
c † (= se donner sexuellement) to give o.s. (à to)

abaque [abak] NM (= boulier) abacus; (= graphique) graph; (Archit) abacus

abasourdi, e [abazuʀdi] ADJ stunned, dumbfounded, stupefied

abasourdir [abazuʀdiʀ] ▸ conjug 2 ◂ VT a (= étonner) to stun, dumbfound b (= étourdir) [bruit] to stun, daze

abasourdissement [abazuʀdismɑ̃] NM bewilderment, stupefaction

abâtardir [abatɑʀdiʀ] ▸ conjug 2 ◂ 1 VT [+ race, vertu] to cause to degenerate; [+ qualité] to debase 2 **s'abâtardir** VPR [race, vertu] to degenerate; [qualité] to become debased; **langue abâtardie** bastardized ou debased language

abâtardissement [abatɑʀdismɑ̃] NM [race, vertu] degeneration; [qualité] debasement; [langue, style] bastardization, debasement

abat-jour [abaʒuʀ] NM INV [lampe] lampshade; (Archit) splay

abats [aba] NMPL [volaille] giblets; [bœuf, porc] offal

abat-son (pl abat-sons) [abasɔ̃] NM louvre (Brit) ou louver (US) (boards)

abattage [abataʒ] NM a [animal] slaughter, slaughtering; [arbre] felling, cutting (down); (Min) extracting b (Comm) (vente à l')~ selling in bulk at knock-down prices c * (= entrain) **avoir de l'~** to be dynamic, have plenty of go*; (= force) **il a de l'~** he's a strapping fellow d [prostituée] **faire de l'~** to get through dozens of punters* (Brit) a day (ou night), turn dozens of tricks‡ (US) a day (ou night)

abattant [abatɑ̃] NM [table] flap, leaf; [siège de W-C] lid

abattement [abatmɑ̃] NM a (= dépression) dejection, despondency; **être dans un extrême ~** to be in very low spirits b (= fatigue) exhaustion c (Fin) (= rabais) reduction; (fiscal) (tax) allowance; **~ forfaitaire** standard deduction ou allowance

abattis [abati] 1 NMPL [volaille] giblets; (* = bras et jambes) limbs → **numéroter** 2 NM (Can = terrain déboisé) brushwood; **faire un ~** to clear fell (Brit) ou clear cut (US) land

abattoir [abatwaʀ] NM slaughterhouse, abattoir; **envoyer des hommes à l'~*** to send men to the slaughter

abattre [abatʀ] ▸ conjug 41 ◂ 1 VT a (= faire tomber) [+ maison, mur] to pull ou knock down; [+ arbre] to cut down, fell; [+ roche, minerai] to break away, hew; [+ quilles] to knock down; [+ avion] to bring ou shoot down; (fig) [+ adversaire, rival] to bring down; **le vent a abattu la cheminée** the wind blew the chimney down; **la pluie abattait la poussière** the rain settled the dust
b (= tuer) [+ personne, oiseau] to shoot down; [+ fauve] to shoot, kill; [+ animal domestique] to destroy, put down; [+ animal de boucherie] to slaughter; (fig) **c'est l'homme à ~** he's the

one you've (ou we've etc) got to get rid of [c] (= ébranler) [fièvre] to weaken, drain (of energy); [mauvaise nouvelle, échec] to demoralize, shatter*; [efforts] to tire out, wear out; **la maladie l'a abattu** the illness left him very weak, the illness drained him of energy; **être abattu par la fatigue/la chaleur** ou to be overcome by tiredness/the heat; **se laisser ~ par des échecs** to be demoralized by failures; **ne te laisse pas ~** keep your spirits up, don't let things get you down
[d] (= affaiblir) [+ courage] to weaken; [+ fierté] to humble
[e] [+ carte] to lay down; (lit, fig) **~ son jeu ou ses cartes** to lay ou put one's cards on the table, show one's hand
[f] **~ du travail** to get through a lot of work
[2] **s'abattre** VPR [a] (= tomber) [personne] to fall (down), collapse; [cheminée] to fall ou crash down; **le mât s'est abattu** the mast came ou went crashing down
[b] **s'~ sur** [pluie] to beat down on; [ennemi] to swoop down on, fall on; [oiseau de proie] to swoop down on; [moineaux] to sweep down on(to); [coups, injures] to rain on

abattu, e [abaty] (ptp de **abattre**) ADJ (= fatigué) worn out, exhausted; (= faible) [malade] very weak, feeble; (= déprimé) downcast, demoralized → **bride**

abat-vent (pl **abat-vent(s)**) [abavã] NM [cheminée] chimney cowl; [fenêtre, ouverture] louvre (Brit) ou louver (US) (boards)

abbatial, e (mpl **-iaux**) [abasjal, jo] [1] ADJ abbey (épith) [2] **abbatiale** NF abbey-church

abbaye [abei] NF abbey

abbé [abe] NM [abbaye] abbot; (= prêtre) priest; **~ mitré** mitred abbot → **monsieur**

abbesse [abɛs] NF abbess

abc [abese] NM (= livre) ABC ou alphabet book; (= rudiments) ABC, fundamentals, rudiments; **c'est l'~ du métier** it's the most elementary ou the first requirement of the job

abcès [apsɛ] NM (Méd) abscess; [gencive] gumboil, abscess; (dans un conflit) **vider ou crever l'~** to clear the air; **il faut crever l'~ au sein du parti** it's time to sort out the party's problems once and for all; (fig) **~ de fixation** focal point for grievances

Abdias [abdjas] NM Obadiah

abdication [abdikasjɔ̃] NF (lit, fig) abdication; **l'~ des parents devant leurs enfants** parents' abdication of authority over their children

abdiquer [abdike] ▸conjug 1◂ [1] VI [roi] to abdicate; **la justice abdique devant le terrorisme** justice gives way in the face of ou before terrorism; **dans ces conditions j'abdique*** in that case I give up [2] VT **~ la couronne** to abdicate the throne; **~ ses croyances/son autorité** to give up ou renounce one's beliefs/one's authority

abdomen [abdɔmɛn] NM abdomen

abdominal, e (mpl **-aux**) [abdɔminal, o] [1] ADJ abdominal [2] **abdominaux** NMPL abdominals, stomach muscles; **faire des abdominaux** to do ou work one's abdominals

abdos* [abdo] NMPL (ABRÉV = **abdominaux**) abs*

abducteur [abdyktœʀ] ADJ M, NM (**muscle**) **~** abductor (muscle)

abduction [abdyksjɔ̃] NF (Anat) abduction

abécédaire [abesedɛʀ] NM alphabet primer

abeille [abɛj] NF bee; **~ maçonne** mason bee → **nid**, **reine**

Abel [abɛl] NM Abel

aber [abɛʀ] NM (Géog) aber

aberrant, e [abeʀã, ãt] ADJ [a] (= insensé) [conduite] aberrant; [histoire] absurd, nonsensical; **il est ~ qu'il parte** it's absurd that he should go, it makes no sense at all for him to go [b] (Bio) aberrant, deviant; (Ling) irregular

aberration [abeʀasjɔ̃] NF (gén) (mental) aberration; (Astron, Phys) aberration; **dans un moment ou instant d'~** in a moment of aberration; **par quelle ~ a-t-il accepté?** whatever possessed him to accept?; **~ chromosomique** chromosomal abnormality

abêtir VT, **s'abêtir** VPR [abetiʀ] ▸conjug 2◂ to turn into a moron* ou half-wit

abêtissant, e [abetisã, ãt] ADJ [travail] stupefying

abêtissement [abetismã] NM (= état) mindlessness; (= action) **l'~ des masses par la télévision** the stupefying effect of television on the masses

abhorrer [abɔʀe] ▸conjug 1◂ VT (littér) to abhor, loathe

Abidjan [abidʒã] N Abidjan

abîme [abim] NM [a] (= gouffre) abyss, gulf, chasm; (fig) **l'~ qui nous sépare** the gulf ou chasm between us [b] (loc) **au bord de l'~** [pays, banquier] on the brink ou verge of ruin; [personne] on the brink ou verge of despair; **être au fond de l'~** [personne] to be in the depths of despair ou at one's lowest ebb; [pays] to have reached rock-bottom; (littér) **les ~s de l'enfer/de la nuit/du temps** the depths of hell/night/time; **être plongé dans un ~ de perplexité** to be utterly ou deeply perplexed; **c'est un ~ de bêtise** he's abysmally ou incredibly stupid

abîmé, e [abime] (ptp de **abîmer**) ADJ (= détérioré) damaged, spoiled; **il était plutôt ~* après le match** he was a bit battered and bruised after the match

abîmer [abime] ▸conjug 1◂ [1] VT [a] (= endommager) to damage, spoil; **la pluie a complètement abîmé mon chapeau** the rain has ruined my hat [b] (‡ = frapper) **~ qn** to beat sb up; **je vais t'~ le portrait** I'll smash your face in* [2] **s'abîmer** VPR [a] [objet] to get damaged; [fruits] to go bad, spoil; **s'~ les yeux** to ruin ou strain one's eyes, spoil one's eyesight [b] (littér) [navire] to sink, founder; [personne] **s'~ dans** [+ réflexion] to be lost ou sunk in; [+ douleur] to lose o.s. in

abject, e [abʒɛkt] ADJ despicable, contemptible, abject; **être ~ envers qn** to treat sb in a despicable manner, behave despicably towards sb

abjectement [abʒɛktəmã] ADV abjectly

abjection [abʒɛksjɔ̃] NF abjection, abjectness

abjuration [abʒyʀasjɔ̃] NF abjuration, recantation (**de** of); **faire ~ de** to abjure

abjurer [abʒyʀe] ▸conjug 1◂ VT to abjure, recant

Abkhazie [abkazi] NF Abkhazia

ablatif [ablatif] NM ablative; **à l'~** in the ablative; **~ absolu** ablative absolute

ablation [ablasjɔ̃] NF (Méd) removal, ablation (SPÉC); (Géol) ablation

ablette [ablɛt] NF bleak

ablutions [ablysjɔ̃] NFPL (gén) ablutions; **faire ses ~** to perform one's ablutions

abnégation [abnegasjɔ̃] NF (self-)abnegation, self-denial; **avec ~** selflessly

aboiement [abwamã] NM [a] [chien] bark; **~s** barking (NonC) [b] (péj) (= cri) shout, bark; (= critiques, exhortations) **~s** rantings

abois [abwa] NMPL baying; **aux ~** [animal] at bay; [personne] in desperate straits; (financièrement) hard-pressed

abolir [abɔliʀ] ▸conjug 2◂ VT [+ coutume, loi] to abolish, do away with

abolition [abɔlisjɔ̃] NF abolition; **l'~ de l'esclavage** the Abolition of Slavery

abolitionnisme [abɔlisjɔnism] NM abolitionism

abolitionniste [abɔlisjɔnist] ADJ, NMF abolitionist

abominable [abɔminabl] ADJ abominable, appalling; (sens affaibli) awful, terrible; **l'~ homme des neiges** the abominable snowman

abominablement [abɔminabləmã] ADV [se conduire, s'habiller] abominably; **~ cher** terribly ou dreadfully expensive; **~ laid** horribly ou dreadfully ugly

abomination [abɔminasjɔ̃] NF [a] (= horreur, crime) abomination [b] (loc) **avoir qn/qch en ~** to loathe ou abominate sb/sth; **c'est une ~!** it's abominable! ou appalling!; **l'~ de la désolation** the abomination of desolation; **dire des ~s** to say abominable ou appalling things

abominer [abɔmine] ▸conjug 1◂ VT (littér = exécrer) to loathe, abominate

abondamment [abɔ̃damã] ADV (gén) abundantly, plentifully; [écrire] prolifically; [commenter] extensively; [manger, boire] copiously; [pleuvoir] heavily; [rincer] thoroughly; **prouver ~ qch** to provide ample proof ou evidence of sth

abondance [abɔ̃dãs] NF [a] (= profusion) abundance; **des fruits en ~** plenty of ou an abundance of fruit, fruit in abundance ou in plenty; **larmes qui coulent en ~** tears falling in profusion ou profusely; **il y a (une) ~ de** [+ nourriture, gibier] there is plenty of; [+ détails, dossiers] there are plenty of; **année d'~** year of plenty ■ (PROV) **~ de biens ne nuit pas** an abundance of goods does no harm → **corne** [b] (= richesses) affluence; **vivre dans l'~** to live in affluence; **~ d'idées** wealth of ideas [c] **parler d'~** (= improviser) to improvise, extemporize; (= parler beaucoup) to speak at length

abondant, e [abɔ̃dã, ãt] ADJ [documentation, bibliographie] extensive; [récolte] fine (épith), abundant; [réserves] plentiful; [végétation] lush, luxuriant; [chevelure] thick; [pluies] heavy; [larmes] profuse, copious; (Méd) [règles] heavy; **une ~e production littéraire** an extensive ou prolific literary output; **recevoir un courrier ~** to receive a great deal of mail ou a large quantity of mail; **il y a une ~e littérature sur ce sujet** a great deal has been written on the subject; **cela requiert une main-d'œuvre ~e** it requires a plentiful ou an abundant supply of labour; **il me fit d'~es recommandations** he gave me copious advice; **illustré d'~es photographies** illustrated with numerous photographs, lavishly illustrated with photographs; **les pêches sont ~es sur le marché** peaches are in plentiful ou generous supply; **il lui faut une nourriture ~e** he must have plenty to eat ou plenty of food

abonder [abɔ̃de] ▸conjug 1◂ VI [a] (= être nombreux) [exemples, projets, témoignages] to abound; **les erreurs abondent dans ce devoir** this essay is full of ou riddled with mistakes; **les légumes abondent cette année** there are plenty of vegetables this year, vegetables are plentiful ou in plentiful supply this year; **les rumeurs abondent sur le sujet** there are lots of rumours flying around about this [b] **~ en** (= être plein de) to be full of, abound with ou in; **les forêts abondent en gibier** the forests are teeming with ou abound with game; **son œuvre abonde en images** his work is rich in ou is full of imagery; **le marché abonde en nouveautés** the market is full of new products [c] (= être d'accord) **je ne peux qu'~ en ce sens** I fully agree ou I agree wholeheartedly (with that); **il a abondé dans notre sens** he was in complete ou full agreement with us

▼ **abonné, e** [abɔne] (ptp de **abonner**) [1] ADJ [a] (= inscrit) **être ~ à un journal** to subscribe to a paper; **être ~ au téléphone** to have a phone; **être ~ au gaz** to have gas, be a gas consumer; **être ~ au câble** to have cable (television); **être ~ à une messagerie électronique** to have ou to be on E-mail; **être ~ à Internet** to be on the Internet

▶ GRAMMAIRE ACTIVE: abonné 27.5

b * (= *habitué*) **il y est ~!** he makes (quite) a habit of it!; **il est ~ à la première/dernière place** he always comes first/last; **il semblait ~ au succès/à l'échec** he seemed to be on a winning/losing streak; **nos entreprises publiques sont ~es aux déficits** our state-owned companies have quite a talent for losing money

2 NM,F (*Presse, Téléc, TV*) subscriber; [*messagerie électronique, radiotéléphone*] user; (*Élec, Gaz*) consumer; (*Rail, Sport, Théât*) season-ticket holder; (*Téléc*) **il n'y a plus d'~ au numéro que vous avez demandé** the number you have dialled has been disconnected; **se mettre** *ou* **s'inscrire aux ~s absents** (*Téléc*) to put one's phone on to the answering service; (*fig*) **une fois encore, la commission est aux ~s absents** once again, there is no response from the commission

abonnement [abɔnmɑ̃] NM (*Presse*) subscription; (*Rail, Sport, Théât*) season ticket; **magazine vendu uniquement par** *ou* **sur ~** magazine available only on *ou* by subscription; **prendre** *ou* **souscrire un ~ à un journal** to subscribe to *ou* take out a subscription to a paper; **service (des) ~s** [*journal, magazine*] subscriptions sales office; **spectacle hors ~s** show not included on a season ticket; **l'~ pour 10 séances d'UV coûte 250 F** a course of 10 sunbed sessions costs 250 francs; **~ jeunes/familles** (*pour club, musée*) special (membership) rates for young people/families; (**coût de l'**)**~** (*Téléc*) rental; (*Gaz, Élec*) standing charge; **tarif ~** [*journal, magazine*] special subscription rate → **carte**

abonner [abɔne] ▸conjug 1◂ **1** VT **~ qn (à qch)** (*Presse*) to take out a subscription (to sth) for sb; (*Sport, Théât*) to buy sb a season ticket (for sth) **2** **s'abonner** VPR (*Presse*) to subscribe, take out a subscription (à to); (*Rail, Sport, Théât*) to buy a season ticket (à for); **s'~ au câble** to subscribe to cable (television); **s'~ à Internet** to get connected to *ou* get onto the Internet

▼ **abord** [abɔʀ] **1** NM **a** (= *manière d'accueillir*) manner; **être d'un ~ rude/rébarbatif** to have a rough/an off-putting manner; **être d'un ~ facile/difficile** to be approachable/not very approachable **b** (= *accès*) access, approach; **lieu d'un ~ difficile** place with difficult means of access, place that is difficult to get to; **lecture d'un ~ difficile** reading matter which is difficult to get into *ou* difficult to get to grips with **c** (*loc*) **dès l'~** from the outset, from the very beginning; **au premier ~** at first sight, initially → **prime, tout**

2 **abords** NMPL (= *environs*: *gén*) surroundings; [*ville, village*] outskirts, surroundings; **aux ~s de** [*lieu*] in the area around *ou* surrounding; [*âge*] around, about; [*date*] around; **dans ce quartier et aux ~s** in this neighbourhood and the surrounding area; **aux ~s de la soixantaine, il prit sa retraite** he retired when he was about sixty

3 **d'abord** LOC ADV (= *en premier lieu*) first; (= *au commencement*) at first; (= *essentiellement*) primarily; (*introduisant une restriction*) for a start, for one thing; **allons d'~ chez le boucher** let's go to the butcher's first; **il fut (tout) d'~ poli, puis il devint grossier** he was polite at first *ou* initially, and then became rude; **cette ville est d'~ un centre touristique** this town is primarily *ou* first and foremost a tourist centre; **d'~, il n'a même pas 18 ans** for a start *ou* in the first place, he's not even 18

abordable [abɔʀdabl] ADJ [*prix*] reasonable; [*marchandise, menu*] affordable, reasonably priced; [*personne*] approachable; [*lieu*] accessible; [*auteur, texte*] accessible; **livre peu ~** rather inaccessible book

abordage [abɔʀdaʒ] NM **a** (= *assaut*) attacking; **à l'~!** up lads and at 'em!, away boarding—

ers!; **ils sont allés à l'~** they boarded the ship → **sabre** **b** (= *accident*) collision

▼ **aborder** [abɔʀde] ▸conjug 1◂ **1** VT **a** (= *arriver à*) [+ *rivage, tournant, montée*] to reach; **les coureurs abordent la ligne droite** the runners are entering the home straight; **il aborde la vieillesse avec inquiétude** he's worried about getting old; **nous abordons une période difficile** we're about to enter a difficult phase **b** (= *approcher*) [+ *personne*] to approach, go *ou* come up to; **il m'a abordé avec un sourire** he came up to me *ou* approached me with a smile **c** [+ *sujet*] to broach; [+ *activité*] to take up, tackle; [+ *problème*] to tackle; **il n'a abordé le roman que vers la quarantaine** he didn't take up writing novels until he was nearly forty; **j'aborde maintenant le second point** I'll now move on to the second point **d** (*Naut*) (= *attaquer*) to board; (= *heurter*) to collide with **2** VI (*Naut*) to land, touch *ou* reach land; **ils ont abordé à Carnac** they landed at Carnac

aborigène [abɔʀiʒɛn] **1** ADJ (*gén*) aboriginal; (*relatif aux peuplades australiennes*) Aboriginal **2** NMF aborigine; **~ d'Australie** (Australian) Aborigine

abortif, -ive [abɔʀtif, iv] (*Méd*) **1** ADJ abortive **2** NM abortifacient (*SPÉC*)

abouchement [abuʃmɑ̃] NM (*Tech*) joining up end to end; (*Méd*) anastomosis

aboucher [abuʃe] ▸conjug 1◂ **1** VT (*Tech*) to join up (end to end); (*Méd*) to join up, anastomose (*SPÉC*); (*fig*) **~ qn avec** to put sb in contact *ou* in touch with **2** **s'aboucher** VPR **s'~ avec qn** to get in touch with sb, make contact with sb

Abou Dhabi [abudabi] N Abu Dhabi

aboulier [abule] ▸conjug 1◂ **1** VT (= *donner*) to hand over; **aboule!** hand it over!*, give it here!* **2** **s'abouler** VPR (= *venir*) to come; **aboule-toi!** come (over) here!

aboulie [abuli] NF ab(o)ulia

aboulique [abulik] **1** ADJ ab(o)ulic (*SPÉC*) **2** NMF (*Méd*) person suffering from ab(o)ulia; (*fig*) **son mari est un ~** her husband is utterly apathetic *ou* (totally) lacking in willpower

Abou Simbel [abusimbɛl] N Abu Simbel

about [abu] NM (*Tech*) butt

aboutement [abutmɑ̃] NM (= *action*) joining (end to end); (= *état*) join

abouter [abute] ▸conjug 1◂ VT to join (up) (end to end)

abouti, e [abuti] ADJ [*projet*] successfully completed; [*œuvre*] accomplished

▼ **aboutir** [abutiʀ] ▸conjug 2◂ VI **a** (= *réussir*) [*démarche, personne*] to succeed; **ses efforts/tentatives n'ont pas abouti** his efforts/attempts have come to nothing *ou* have failed; **faire ~ des négociations/un projet** to bring negotiations/a project to a successful conclusion **b** (= *arriver à, déboucher sur*) **~ à** *ou* **dans** to end (up) in *ou* at; **la route aboutit à un cul-de-sac** the road ends in a cul-de-sac; **une telle philosophie aboutit au désespoir** such a philosophy results in *ou* leads to despair; **~ en prison** to end up in prison; **les négociations n'ont abouti à rien** the negotiations have come to nothing, nothing has come of the negotiations; **en additionnant le tout, j'aboutis à 12 F** adding it all up I get 12 francs; **il n'aboutira jamais à rien dans la vie** he'll never get anywhere in life

aboutissants [abutisɑ̃] NMPL → **tenant**

aboutissement [abutismɑ̃] NM (= *résultat*) [*efforts, opération*] outcome, result; (= *succès*) [*plan*] success

aboyer [abwaje] ▸conjug 8◂ VI to bark; (*péj* = *crier*) to shout, yell; **~ après** *ou* **contre qn** to bark *ou* yell at sb → **chien**

aboyeur† [abwajœʀ] NM (*Théât*) barker†; (*dans une réception*) usher (*who announces guests at a reception*)

abracadabra [abʀakadabʀa] EXCL abracadabra

abracadabrant, e [abʀakadabʀɑ̃, ɑ̃t] ADJ fantastic, preposterous; **histoire ~e** cock-and-bull story

Abraham [abʀaam] NM Abraham

abraser [abʀaze] ▸conjug 1◂ VT to abrade

abrasif, -ive [abʀazif, iv] ADJ, NM abrasive

abrasion [abʀazjɔ̃] NF (*gén, Géog*) abrasion

abréaction [abʀeaksjɔ̃] NF abreaction

abrégé [abʀeʒe] NM [*livre, discours*] summary, synopsis; [*texte*] summary, précis; (= *manuel, guide*) short guide; **faire un ~ de** to summarize, précis; **~ d'histoire** concise guide to history; **en ~** (= *en miniature*) in miniature; (= *en bref*) in brief, in a nutshell; **répéter qch en ~** to repeat sth in a few words; **mot/phrase en ~** word/sentence in a shortened *ou* an abbreviated form; **voilà, en ~, de quoi il s'agissait** briefly *ou* to cut (*Brit*) *ou* make (*US*) a long story short, this is what it was all about

abrégement [abʀeʒmɑ̃] NM [*durée*] cutting short, shortening; [*texte*] abridgement

abréger [abʀeʒe] ▸conjug 3 et 6◂ VT [+ *vie*] to shorten; [+ *durée, visite*] to cut short, shorten; [+ *conversation, vacances*] to cut short; [+ *texte*] to shorten, abridge; [+ *mot*] to abbreviate, shorten; **~ les souffrances de qn** to put an end to sb's suffering; **pour ~ les longues soirées d'hiver** to while away the long winter evenings, to make the long winter evenings pass more quickly; **version abrégée** [*livre*] abridged version; **forme abrégée** shortened *ou* abbreviated form; **docteur s'abrège souvent en Dr** doctor is often shortened *ou* abbreviated to Dr; **abrège!** * come *ou* get to the point!

abreuver [abʀœve] ▸conjug 1◂ **1** VT **a** [+ *animal*] to water **b** (= *saturer*) **~ qn de** to overwhelm *ou* shower sb with; **~ qn d'injures** to heap *ou* shower insults on sb; **le public est abreuvé de films d'horreur** (*inondé*) the public is swamped with horror films; (*saturé*) the public has had its fill of *ou* has had enough of horror films **c** (= *imbiber*) (*gén*) to soak, drench (**de** with); (*Tech*) to prime; **terre abreuvée d'eau** sodden *ou* waterlogged ground **2** **s'abreuver** VPR [*animal*] to drink; * [*personne*] to quench one's thirst; (*péj*) **s'~ de télévision** to be addicted to television, be a television addict

abreuvoir [abʀœvwaʀ] NM (= *mare*) watering place; (= *récipient*) drinking trough

abréviation [abʀevjasjɔ̃] NF abbreviation

abri [abʀi] NM **a** (= *refuge, cabane*) shelter; **~ à vélos** bicycle shed; (*Mil*) **~ souterrain/antiatomique** air-raid/(atomic) fallout shelter; (*hum*) **tous aux ~s!** take cover!, run for cover!; **construire un ~ pour sa voiture** to build a car-port **b** (= *protection*) refuge (**contre** from), protection (**contre** against); **~ fiscal** tax shelter **c** (*loc*) **à l'~** : **être/mettre à l'~** (*des intempéries*) to be/put under cover; (*du vol, de la curiosité*) to be/put in a safe place; **être à l'~ de** (= *protégé de*) [+ *pluie, vent, soleil*] to be sheltered from; [+ *danger, soupçons*] to be safe *ou* shielded from; (= *protégé par*) [+ *mur, feuillage*] to be sheltered *ou* shielded by; **à l'~ des regards** hidden from view; **personne n'est à l'~ d'une erreur** we all make mistakes; **elle est à l'~ du besoin** she is free from financial worries; **la solution retenue n'est pas à l'~ de la critique** the solution opted for is open to criticism *ou* is not above criticism; **leur entreprise s'est développée à l'~ de toute concurrence** their company has grown because it has been shielded *ou* protected from competition; **mettre qch à l'~ de** [+ *intempéries*] to shelter sth from; [+ *regards*] to hide sth from; **mettre qch à l'~ d'un mur** to put sth in the shelter of a—

wall; (*sur étiquette*) **conserver à l'~ de la lumière/de l'humidité** store *ou* keep in a dark/dry place; **se mettre à l'~** to shelter, take cover; **se mettre à l'~ de** [+ *pluie, vent, soleil*] to take shelter from; [+ *soupçons*] to place o.s. above; **se mettre à l'~ du mur/du feuillage** to take cover *ou* shelter by the wall/under the trees → **indiscret**

Abribus® [abʀibys] NM bus shelter

abricot [abʀiko] 1 NM (*Bot*) apricot → **pêche¹** 2 ADJ INV apricot(-coloured)

abricoté, e [abʀikɔte] ADJ [*gâteau*] apricot (*épith*) → **pêche¹**

abricotier [abʀikɔtje] NM apricot tree

abriter [abʀite] ▸conjug 1◂ 1 VT a (= *protéger*) (*de la pluie, du vent*) to shelter (**de** from); (*du soleil*) to shelter, shade (**de** from); (*de radiations*) to screen (**de** from); **abritant ses yeux de sa main** shading his eyes with his hand; **le côté abrité** (*de la pluie*) the sheltered side; (*du soleil*) the shady side; **maison abritée** house in a sheltered spot

b (= *héberger*) [+ *réfugié*] to shelter, give shelter to; [+ *criminel*] to harbour (*Brit*), harbor (*US*); **ce bâtiment abrite 100 personnes/nos bureaux** the building accommodates 100 people/houses our offices; **le musée abrite de superbes collections** the museum houses some very fine collections; **la réserve abritait des espèces végétales uniques** the nature reserve provided a habitat for some unique plant species; **le parti abrite différents courants** different political tendencies are represented in the party; **l'écurie n'abrite plus que trois chevaux** only three horses are now kept in the stables

2 **s'abriter** VPR to (take) shelter (**de** from), take cover (**de** from); **s'~ derrière la tradition/un alibi** to hide behind tradition/an alibi; **s'~ derrière son chef/le règlement** to hide behind one's boss/the rules; **s'~ des regards indiscrets** to avoid prying eyes

abrogatif, -ive [abʀɔgatif, iv] ADJ rescissory, abrogative

abrogation [abʀɔgasjɔ̃] NF repeal, abrogation

abrogeable [abʀɔʒabl] ADJ repealable

abroger [abʀɔʒe] ▸conjug 3◂ VT to repeal, abrogate

abrupt, e [abʀypt] 1 ADJ a (= *escarpé*) [*pente*] abrupt, steep; [*falaise*] sheer b [*personne, ton*] abrupt, brusque; [*manières*] abrupt; **de façon ~e** abruptly 2 NM steep slope

abruptement [abʀyptəmɑ̃] ADV [*descendre*] steeply, abruptly; [*annoncer*] abruptly

abruti, e [abʀyti] (*ptp de* **abrutir**) 1 ADJ a (= *hébété*) stunned, dazed (**de** with); **~ par l'alcool** befuddled *ou* stupefied with drink b (* = *bête*) idiotic*, moronic* 2 NM,F* idiot*, moron*

abrutir [abʀytiʀ] ▸conjug 2◂ VT a (= *fatiguer*) to exhaust; **la chaleur m'abrutit** the heat makes me dopey* *ou* knocks me out; **~ qn de travail** to work sb silly *ou* stupid; **ces discussions m'ont abruti** these discussions have left me quite dazed; **s'~ à travailler** to work o.s. silly; **leur professeur les abrutit de travail** their teacher drives them stupid with work; **tu vas t'~ à force de lire** you'll overtax *ou* exhaust yourself reading so much b (= *abêtir*) **~ qn** to deaden sb's mind; **l'alcool l'avait abruti** he was stupefied with drink; **s'~ à regarder la télévision** to become mindless through watching (too much) television

abrutissant, e [abʀytisɑ̃, ɑ̃t] ADJ [*travail*] mind-destroying; **ce bruit est ~** this noise drives you mad *ou* wears you down

abrutissement [abʀytismɑ̃] NM (= *fatigue extrême*) (mental) exhaustion; (= *abêtissement*) mindless state; **l'~ des masses par la télévision** the stupefying effect of television on the masses

ABS [abeɛs] NM (ABRÉV = **Antiblockiersystem**) ABS

abscisse [apsis] NF abscissa; **en ~** on the abscissa

abscons, e [apskɔ̃, ɔ̃s] ADJ abstruse, recondite

absence [apsɑ̃s] NF a (*gén, Jur*) [*personne*] absence; **son ~ à la réunion** his absence from the meeting; (*Admin, Scol*) **3 ~s successives** 3 absences in succession; **cet élève/employé accumule les ~s** this pupil/employee is persistently absent → **briller** b (= *manque*) absence, lack (**de** of); **~ de goût** lack of taste; **l'~ de rideaux** the fact that there are (*ou* were) no curtains, the absence of curtains; **il constata l'~ de sa valise** he noticed that his suitcase was missing c (= *défaillance*) **~ (de mémoire)** mental blank; **il a des ~s** at times his mind goes blank d **en l'~ de** in the absence of; **en l'~ de sa mère, c'est Anne qui fait la cuisine** Anne's doing the cooking while her mother's away *ou* in her mother's absence; **en l'~ de preuves** in the absence of proof

absent, e [apsɑ̃, ɑ̃t] 1 ADJ a [*personne*] (*gén*) away (**de** from); (*pour maladie*) absent (**de** from), off*; **être ~ de son travail** to be absent from work, be off work*; **il est ~ de Paris/de son bureau en ce moment** he's out of *ou* away from Paris/his office at the moment; **conférence internationale dont la France était ~e** international conference from which France was absent b [*sentiment*] lacking, absent; [*objet*] missing; **discours d'où toute émotion était ~e** speech in which there was no trace of emotion; **il constata que sa valise était ~e** he noticed that his suitcase was missing c (= *distrait*) [*air*] vacant d [*Jur*] missing

2 NM,F (*Scol*) absentee; (*littér* = *mort, en voyage*) absent one (*littér*); (= *disparu*) missing person; **le ministre/le champion a été le grand ~ de la réunion** the minister/the champion was the most notable absentee at the meeting ▪ (*PROV*) **les ~s ont toujours tort** it's always the people who aren't there that get the blame

absentéisme [apsɑ̃teism] NM (*Agr, Écon, Ind, Scol*) absenteeism; (= *école buissonnière*) truancy

absentéiste [apsɑ̃teist] NMF (*Agr*) absentee; (*gén*) **c'est un ~** ◊ **il est du genre ~** he is always *ou* regularly absent; **propriétaire ~** absentee landlord; **élève ~** truant

absenter (s') [apsɑ̃te] ▸conjug 1◂ VPR (*gén*) to go out, leave; (*Mil*) to go absent; **s'~ de** [+ *pièce*] to go out of, leave; [+ *ville*] to leave; **s'~ quelques instants** to go out for a few moments; **je m'étais absenté de Paris** I was away from *ou* out of Paris; **elle s'absente souvent de son travail** she is frequently off work* *ou* away from work; **élève qui s'absente trop souvent** pupil who is too often absent *ou* away (from school) *ou* off school

abside [apsid] NF apse

absidial, e (*mpl* -iaux) [apsidjal, jo] ADJ apsidal

absidiole [apsidjɔl] NF apsidiole

absinthe [apsɛ̃t] NF (= *liqueur*) absinth(e); (= *plante*) wormwood, absinth(e)

absolu, e [apsɔly] 1 ADJ a (= *total*) absolute; **en cas d'~e nécessité** if absolutely necessary; **être dans l'impossibilité ~e de faire qch** to find it absolutely impossible to do sth; **c'est une règle ~e** it's a hard-and-fast rule, it's an unbreakable rule; **j'ai la preuve ~e de sa trahison** I have absolute *ou* positive proof of his betrayal → **alcool** b (= *entier*) [*ton*] peremptory; [*jugement, caractère*] rigid, uncompromising c (*opposé à relatif*) [*valeur, température*] absolute; **considérer qch de manière ~e** to consider sth absolutely *ou* in absolute terms d (*Hist, Pol*) [*majorité, roi, pouvoir*] absolute

e (*Ling*) [*construction*] absolute; **verbe employé de manière ~e** verb used absolutely *ou* in the absolute; **génitif/ablatif ~** genitive/ablative absolute → **superlatif**

2 NM **l'~** the absolute; **juger dans l'~** to judge out of context *ou* in the absolute

absolument [apsɔlymɑ̃] ADV a (= *entièrement*) absolutely; **avoir ~ tort** to be quite *ou* absolutely *ou* entirely wrong; **s'opposer ~ à qch** to be entirely *ou* absolutely opposed to sth, be completely *ou* dead* against sth; **~ pas!** certainly not!; **~ rien** absolutely nothing, nothing whatever b (= *à tout prix*) absolutely, positively; **vous devez ~** you absolutely *ou* positively *ou* simply must; **il veut ~ revenir** he (absolutely) insists upon returning c (= *oui*) absolutely; **vous êtes sûr? — ~!** are you sure? — definitely! *ou* absolutely! d (*Ling*) absolutely

absolution [apsɔlysjɔ̃] NF a (*Rel*) absolution (**de** from); **donner l'~ à qn** to give sb absolution b (*Jur*) dismissal (*of case, when defendant is considered to have no case to answer*)

absolutisme [apsɔlytism] NM absolutism

absolutiste [apsɔlytist] 1 ADJ absolutistic 2 NMF absolutist

absolutoire [apsɔlytwaʀ] ADJ (*Rel, Jur*) absolutory

absorbable [apsɔʀbabl] ADJ absorbable

absorbant, e [apsɔʀbɑ̃, ɑ̃t] 1 ADJ [*matière*] absorbent; [*tâche*] absorbing, engrossing; (*Bot, Zool*) [*fonction, racines*] absorptive; **société ~e** surviving company 2 NM absorbent

absorber [apsɔʀbe] ▸conjug 1◂ 1 VT a (= *avaler*) [+ *médicament*] to take; [+ *aliment, boisson*] to swallow; [+ *parti*] to absorb; [+ *firme*] to take over, absorb b (= *résorber*) (*gén*) to absorb; [+ *liquide*] to absorb, soak up; [+ *tache*] to remove, lift; [+ *dette*] to absorb; [+ *bruit*] to absorb; **crème vite absorbée par la peau** cream that is absorbed rapidly by the skin; **le noir absorbe la lumière** black absorbs light; **cet achat a absorbé presque toutes mes économies** I used up *ou* spent nearly all my savings when I bought that; **ces dépenses absorbent 39% du budget** this expenditure accounts for 39% of the budget c (= *accaparer*) [+ *attention, temps*] to occupy, take up; **mon travail m'absorbe beaucoup** ◊ **je suis très absorbé par mon travail** my work takes up *ou* claims a lot of my time; **absorbé par son travail/dans sa lecture, il ne m'entendit pas** he was engrossed in *ou* absorbed in his work/in his book and he didn't hear me; **cette pensée absorbait mon esprit** ◊ **j'avais l'esprit absorbé par cette pensée** my mind was completely taken up with this thought

2 **s'absorber** VPR (= *se plonger*) **s'~ dans une lecture/une tâche** to become absorbed *ou* engrossed in a book/a task

absorbeur [apsɔʀbœʀ] NM (*Tech*) absorber; **volant à ~ d'énergie** energy-absorbing steering wheel; **~ d'odeur(s)** air freshener; **~ d'humidité** dehumidifier

absorption [apsɔʀpsjɔ̃] NF a [*médicament*] taking; [*aliment*] swallowing; **l'~ d'alcool est fortement déconseillée** you are strongly advised not to drink alcohol b [*parti*] absorption; [*firme*] takeover, absorption c (= *résorption*: *gén*) absorption; [*tache*] removal; **les qualités d'~ des bruits du matériau** the ability of this material to absorb sound; **l'~ des rayons ultraviolets par l'ozone** the absorption of ultra-violet rays by the ozone layer

absoudre [apsudʀ] ▸conjug 51◂ VT (*Rel, littér*) to absolve (**de** from); (*Jur*) to dismiss → **absolution**

absoute [apsut] NF [*office des morts*] absolution; [*jeudi saint*] general absolution

abstenir (s') [apstəniʀ] ▸conjug 22◂ VPR a **s'~ de qch** to refrain *ou* abstain from sth;

s'~ de faire to refrain from doing; **s'~ de vin** to abstain from wine; **s'~ de boire du vin** to refrain from drinking wine; **s'~ de tout commentaire** ◊ **s'~ de faire des commentaires** to refrain from comment *ou* commenting; **dans ces conditions je préfère m'~** in that case I'd rather not → **doute** b (*Pol*) to abstain (**de voter** from voting)

abstention [apstɑ̃sjɔ̃] NF (*dans un vote*) abstention; (= *non-intervention*) non-participation

abstentionnisme [apstɑ̃sjɔnism] NM abstaining, non-voting

abstentionniste [apstɑ̃sjɔnist] NMF non-voter, abstainer

abstinence [apstinɑ̃s] NF abstinence; (*Rel*) **faire ~** to refrain from eating meat

abstinent, e [apstinɑ̃, ɑ̃t] ADJ abstemious, abstinent

abstract [abstrakt] NM abstract

abstraction [apstraksjɔ̃] NF (= *fait d'abstraire*) abstraction; (= *idée abstraite*) abstraction, abstract idea; **faire ~ de** to set *ou* leave aside, disregard; **en faisant ~ ou ~ faite des difficultés** setting aside *ou* leaving aside *ou* disregarding the difficulties

abstraire [apstrɛr] ▸conjug 50◂ 1 VT (= *isoler*) to abstract (**de** from), isolate (**de** from); (= *conceptualiser*) to abstract 2 **s'abstraire** VPR to cut o.s. off (**de** from)

abstrait, e [apstrɛ, ɛt] 1 ADJ abstract 2 NM a (= *artiste*) abstract painter; (= *genre*) **l'~** abstract art b (*Philos*) **l'~** the abstract; **dans l'~** in the abstract

abstraitement [apstrɛtmɑ̃] ADV abstractly, in the abstract

abstrus, e [apstry, yz] ADJ abstruse, recondite

absurde [apsyrd] 1 ADJ (*Philos*) absurd; (= *illogique*) absurd, preposterous; (= *ridicule*) absurd, ridiculous, ludicrous; **ne sois pas ~!** don't be ridiculous! *ou* absurd! 2 NM **l'~** the absurd; **l'~ de la situation** the absurdity of the situation; **raisonnement** *ou* **démonstration par l'~** reductio ad absurdum

absurdement [apsyrdəmɑ̃] ADV absurdly

absurdité [apsyrdite] NF a (*Philos*) absurdity; (= *illogisme*) absurdity, preposterousness; (= *ridicule*) absurdity, ridiculousness, ludicrousness b (= *parole, acte*) absurdity; **dire une ~** to say something absurd *ou* ridiculous; **dire des ~s** to talk nonsense

Abû Dhabî [abudabi] N = **Abou Dhabî**

Abuja [abuʒa] N Abuja

abus [aby] 1 NM a (= *excès*) [*médicaments, alcool*] abuse; [*force, autorité*] abuse, misuse; **faire ~ de** [+ *sa force, son pouvoir*] to abuse; **faire ~ de cigarettes** to smoke excessively; **l'~ (qu'il fait) d'aspirine** (his) excessive use *ou* (his) overuse of aspirin; **~ de boisson** excessive drinking, drinking to excess; **nous avons fait des** *ou* **quelques ~ hier soir** we overdid it *ou* things *ou* we overindulged last night; **il y a de l'~** !* that's going a bit too far!*, that's a bit much! b (= *injustice*) abuse, social injustice 2 COMP ▸ **abus d'autorité** abuse *ou* misuse of authority ▸ **abus de biens sociaux** misuse of company property ▸ **abus de confiance** (*Jur*) breach of trust; (*escroquerie*) confidence trick ▸ **abus de langage** misuse of language ▸ **abus de pouvoir** abuse *ou* misuse of power

abuser [abyze] ▸conjug 1◂ 1 VT INDIR a (= *exploiter*) [+ *situation, crédulité*] to exploit, take advantage of; [+ *autorité, puissance*] to abuse, misuse; [+ *hospitalité, amabilité, confiance*] to abuse; [+ *ami*] to take advantage of; **~ de sa force** to misuse one's strength; **je ne veux pas ~ de votre temps** I don't want to take up *ou* waste your time; **je ne voudrais pas ~ (de votre gentillesse)** I don't want to impose (upon your kindness); **~ d'une femme** (*gén*) to abuse a woman (sex-

ually); (*euph*) to take advantage of a woman; **alors là, tu abuses !** now you're going too far! *ou* overstepping the mark!; **je suis compréhensif, mais il ne faudrait pas ~** I'm an understanding sort of person but don't try taking advantage *ou* don't push me too far; **elle abuse de la situation** she's taking advantage* b (= *user avec excès*) **~ de l'alcool** to drink excessively *ou* to excess; **~ de ses forces** to over-exert o.s., overtax one's strength; **il ne faut pas ~ des médicaments/des citations** you shouldn't take too many medicines/use too many quotes; **il ne faut pas ~ des bonnes choses** you can have too much of a good thing, enough is as good as a feast (*PROV*); **il use et (il) abuse de métaphores** he's too fond *ou* overfond of metaphors 2 VT [*escroc*] to deceive; [*ressemblance*] to mislead; **se laisser ~ par de belles paroles** to be taken in *ou* misled by fine words 3 **s'abuser** VPR (*frm*) (= *se tromper*) to be mistaken; (= *se faire des illusions*) to delude o.s.; **si je ne m'abuse** if I'm not mistaken

abusif, -ive [abyzif, iv] ADJ [*pratique*] improper; [*mère, père*] over-possessive; [*prix*] exorbitant, excessive; [*punition*] excessive; **usage ~ de son autorité** improper use *ou* misuse of one's authority; **usage ~ d'un mot** misuse *ou* improper use *ou* wrong use of a word; **c'est peut-être ~ de dire cela** it's perhaps putting it a bit strongly to say that

Abû Simbel [abusimbɛl] N = **Abou Simbel**

abusivement [abyzivmɑ̃] ADV (*Ling* = *improprement*) wrongly, improperly; (= *excessivement*) excessively, to excess; **il s'est servi ~ de lui** he took advantage of him

abyme [abim] NM (*Littérat*) **mise en ~** mise en abyme

abyssal, e (*mpl -aux*) [abisal, o] ADJ (*Géog*) abyssal; (*fig*) unfathomable

abysse [abis] NM (*Géog*) abyssal zone

abyssin, e [abisɛ̃, in] ADJ = **abyssinien**

Abyssinie [abisini] NF Abyssinia

abyssinien, -ienne [abisinjɛ̃, jɛn] 1 ADJ Abyssinian 2 **Abyssinien(ne)** NM,F Abyssinian

AC [ase] N (*ABRÉV* = **appellation contrôlée**) appellation contrôlée (*label guaranteeing district of origin of a wine*)

acabit [akabi] NM (*péj*) **être du même ~** to be cast in the same mould; **ils sont tous du même ~** they're all the same *ou* all much of a muchness; **fréquenter des gens de cet ~** to mix with people of that type *ou* like that

acacia [akasja] NM (*gén* = *faux acacia*) locust tree, false acacia; (*Bot* = *mimosacée*) acacia

académicien, -ienne [akademisjɛ̃, jɛn] NM,F (*gén*) academician; [*Académie française*] member of the Académie française, Academician; (*Antiq*) academic

académie [akademi] NF a (= *société savante*) learned society; (*Antiq*) academy; **l'Académie royale de** the Royal Academy of; **l'Académie des sciences** the Academy of Science; **l'Académie de médecine** the Academy of Medicine; **l'Académie de chirurgie** the College of Surgeons; **l'Académie (française)** the Académie française, the French Academy b (= *école*) academy; **~ de dessin/danse** art/dancing school, academy of art/dancing; **~ de cinéma** film school; **~ militaire** military academy; **~ de billard** billiard hall (*where lessons are given*) c (*Scol, Univ* = *région*) regional education authority d (*Art* = *nu*) nude; (* = *anatomie*) anatomy (*hum*)

démies other than the one in which they originally lived.

Another significant feature of the **académies** is that their school holidays begin on different dates, partly to avoid congestion on popular holiday routes.

académique [akademik] ADJ (*péj, littér, Art*) academic; (*de l'Académie française*) of the Académie Française, of the French Academy; (*Scol*) of the regional education authority; (*Belg, Can, Helv*) **année ~** academic year → **inspection, palme**

académisme [akademism] NM (*péj*) academicism

Acadie [akadi] NF (*Hist*) Acadia; (*Géog*) **l'~** the Maritime Provinces

acadien, -ienne [akadjɛ̃, jɛn] 1 ADJ Acadian 2 NM (*Ling*) Acadian 3 **Acadien(ne)** NM,F Acadian

acajou [akaʒu] 1 NM (*à bois rouge*) mahogany; (= *anacardier*) cashew 2 ADJ INV mahogany (*épith*)

acalorique [akalɔrik] ADJ calorie-free

acanthe [akɑ̃t] NF (*Bot*) acanthus; (*Archit*) **(feuille d')~** acanthus

a cap(p)ella [akapela] LOC ADJ, LOC ADV a capella; **chanter ~** to sing a capella

acariâtre [akarjatr] ADJ [*caractère*] sour, cantankerous; [*personne*] cantankerous; **d'humeur ~** sour-tempered

acaricide [akarisid] 1 ADJ acaricidal 2 NM acaricide

acarien [akarjɛ̃] NM acarid, acaridan

accablant, e [akablɑ̃, ɑ̃t] ADJ [*chaleur*] oppressive; [*témoignage*] overwhelming, damning; [*responsabilité*] overwhelming; [*douleur*] excruciating; [*travail*] exhausting

accablement [akabləmɑ̃] NM (= *abattement*) despondency, dejection; (= *oppression*) exhaustion

accabler [akable] ▸conjug 1◂ VT a [*chaleur, fatigue*] to overwhelm, overcome; (*littér*) [*fardeau*] to weigh down; **accablé de chagrin** prostrate *ou* overwhelmed with grief; **les troupes, accablées sous le nombre** the troops, overwhelmed *ou* overpowered by numbers b [*témoignage*] to condemn, damn; **sa déposition m'accable** his evidence is overwhelmingly against me c (= *faire subir*) **~ qn d'injures** to heap abuse on sb; **~ qn de reproches/critiques** to heap reproaches/criticism on sb;

il **m'accabla de son mépris** he poured scorn on me; **~ qn d'impôts** to overburden sb with taxes; **~ qn de travail** to overburden sb with work, pile work on sb; **~ qn de questions** to bombard sb with questions; *(iro)* **il nous accablait de conseils** he overwhelmed us with advice

accalmie [akalmi] NF *(gén)* lull; *[vent, tempête]* lull **(de** in); *[fièvre]* respite **(dans** in), remission **(dans** of); *[affaires, transactions]* slack period; *[combat]* lull, break; *[crise politique ou morale]* period of calm, lull **(de** in); **profiter d'une ~ pour sortir** to take advantage of a calm spell to go out; **nous n'avons pas eu un seul moment d'~ pendant la journée** we didn't have a single quiet moment during the whole day

accaparant, e [akaparã, ãt] ADJ *[métier, enfant]* demanding

accaparement [akaparmã] NM *[pouvoir, production]* monopolizing; *[marché]* cornering, capturing

accaparer [akapaʀe] ▸conjug 1◂ VT [a] (= monopoliser) *[+ production, pouvoir, conversation, attention, hôte]* to monopolize; *[+ marché, vente]* to corner, capture; **les enfants l'ont tout de suite accaparée** the children claimed all her attention straight away; **ces élèves brillants qui accaparent les prix** those bright pupils who carry off all the prizes; **il accapare la salle de bains pendant des heures** he hogs* the bathroom for hours [b] (= absorber) *[travail]* to take up the time and energy of; **il est complètement accaparé par sa profession** his job takes up all his time and energy; **les enfants l'accaparent** the children take up all her time (and energy)

accapareur, -euse [akapaʀœʀ, øz] [1] ADJ monopolistic [2] NM,F *(péj)* monopolizer, grabber*

accastillage [akastijaʒ] NM *(Naut)* outfitting of the superstructures

accédant, e [aksedã, ãt] NM,F ~ **(à la propriété)** first-time property owner *ou* homeowner

▼**accéder** [aksede] ▸conjug 6◂ ◆ **accéder à** VT INDIR [a] (= atteindre) *[+ lieu, sommet]* to reach, get to; *[+ honneur, responsabilité]* to attain; *[+ grade]* to rise to; *[+ responsabilité]* to accede to; **~ directement à** to have direct access to; **on accède au château par le jardin** you can get to the castle through the garden, access to the castle is through the garden; **~ au trône** to accede to the throne; **~ à la propriété** to become a property owner *ou* homeowner, buy property for the first time [b] *(Ordin)* to access [c] (frm = exaucer) *[+ requête, prière]* to grant, accede to (frm); *[+ vœux]* to meet, comply with; *[+ demande]* to accommodate, comply with

accélérateur, -trice [akseleʀatœʀ, tʀis] [1] ADJ accelerating [2] NM *(Aut, Photo, Phys)* accelerator; **~ de particules** particle accelerator; **donner un coup d'~** *(lit)* to accelerate, step on it*; (= se dépêcher) to step on it*, get a move on*; **donner un coup d'~ à l'économie** to give the economy a boost; **donner un coup d'~ aux réformes** to speed up the reforms

accélération [akseleʀasjɔ̃] NF *(Aut, Tech)* acceleration; *[travail]* speeding up; *[pouls]* quickening; **l'~ de l'histoire** the speeding-up of the historical process

accéléré [akseleʀe] NM *(Ciné)* speeded-up motion; **film en ~** speeded-up film; *(Vidéo)* **faire défiler un film en ~** to fast-forward a film

accélérer [akseleʀe] ▸conjug 6◂ [1] VT *[+ rythme]* to speed up, accelerate; *[+ processus, travail]* to speed up; **~ le pas** to quicken one's pace *ou* step; **il faut ~ la baisse des taux d'intérêt** interest rates must be lowered more quickly; **~ le mouvement** to get things moving, hurry *ou* speed things up → **cours, formation, vitesse** [2] VI *(Aut, fig)* to accelerate, speed up; **accélère !*** hurry up!, get a move

on!* [3] **s'accélérer** VPR *[rythme]* to speed up, accelerate; *[pouls]* to quicken; *[événements]* to gather pace

accéléromètre [akseleʀɔmetʀ] NM accelerometer

accent [aksã] [1] NM [a] (= prononciation) accent; **avoir l'~ paysan/du Midi** to have a country/southern (French) accent; **parler sans ~** to speak without an accent [b] *(Orthographe)* accent; **e ~ grave/aigu** e grave/acute; **~ circonflexe** circumflex (accent) [c] *(Phon)* accent, stress; *(fig)* stress; **mettre l'~ sur** *(lit)* to stress, put the stress *ou* accent on; *(fig)* to stress, emphasize; **l'~ est mis sur la production** (the) emphasis *ou* accent is (placed *ou* put) on production [d] (= inflexion) tone (of voice); **~ suppliant/plaintif** beseeching/plaintive tone; **~ de sincérité/de détresse** note of sincerity/of distress; **récit qui a l'~ de la sincérité** story which has a ring of sincerity; **avec des ~s de rage** in accents of rage; **les ~s de cette musique** the strains of this music; **les ~s de l'espoir/de l'amour** the accents of hope/love; **les ~s déchirants de ce poète** the heartrending accents of this poet

[2] COMP ▸ **accent de hauteur** pitch ▸ **accent d'intensité** tonic *ou* main stress ▸ **accent de mot** word stress ▸ **accent nasillard** nasal twang ▸ **accent de phrase** sentence stress ▸ **accent tonique** = accent d'intensité ▸ **accent traînant** drawl

accenteur [aksãtœʀ] NM ~ **mouchet** dunnock, hedge sparrow

accentuation [aksãtɥasjɔ̃] NF *[lettre]* accentuation; *[syllabe]* stressing, accentuation; *(Phon)* **les règles de l'~** the rules of stress; **faire des fautes d'~** to get the stress wrong [b] *[silhouette, contraste]* emphasizing, accentuation; *[effort, poussée]* intensification, marked increase **(de** in); **une ~ de la récession** a deepening of the recession

accentué, e [aksãtɥe] (ptp de **accentuer**) ADJ (= marqué) marked, pronounced; (= croissant) increased

accentuel, -elle [aksãtɥel] ADJ *[syllabe]* stressed, accented; **système ~ d'une langue** stress *ou* accentual system of a language

accentuer [aksãtɥe] ▸conjug 1◂ [1] VT [a] *[+ lettre]* to accent; *[+ syllabe]* to stress, accent; **syllabe (non) accentuée** (un)stressed *ou* (un)accented syllable [b] *[+ silhouette, contraste]* to emphasize, accentuate; *[+ goût]* to bring out; *[+ effort, poussée]* to increase, intensify [2] **s'accentuer** VPR *[tendance, hausse, contraste, traits]* to become more marked *ou* pronounced; **l'inflation s'accentue** inflation is becoming more pronounced *ou* acute; **le froid s'accentue** it's becoming colder

acceptabilité [akseptabilite] NF *(Ling)* acceptability

▼**acceptable** [akseptabl] ADJ [a] (= passable) *[résultats, travail]* satisfactory, fair; **ce café/vin est ~** this coffee/wine is reasonable *ou* quite decent* *ou* quite acceptable [b] (= recevable) *[condition]* acceptable [c] *(Ling)* acceptable

acceptation [akseptasjɔ̃] NF *(gén)* acceptance; ~ **bancaire** bank acceptance

▼**accepter** [aksepte] ▸conjug 1◂ VT [a] (= gén, Comm) to accept; *[+ proposition, condition]* to agree to, accept; *[+ pari]* to take on, accept; **acceptez-vous les chèques?** do you take cheques?; **acceptez-vous Jean Leblanc pour époux?** do you take Jean Leblanc to be your husband?; **elle accepte tout de sa fille** she puts up with *ou* takes anything from her daughter; *(littér, hum)* **j'en accepte l'augure** I'd like to believe it; **~ le combat** *ou* **le défi** to take up *ou* accept the challenge; **elle a été bien acceptée dans le club** she's been well received at the club; **il n'accepte pas que la vie soit une routine** he won't accept that life should be a routine; **~ la compétence des tri-**

bunaux californiens to defer to California jurisdiction [b] (= être d'accord) to agree **(de faire** to do); **je n'accepterai pas que tu partes** I won't let you leave; **je n'accepte pas de partir** I refuse to leave, I will not leave

acception [aksepsjɔ̃] NF *(Ling)* meaning, sense, acceptation; **dans toute l'~ du mot** *ou* **terme** in every sense *ou* in the full meaning of the word, using the word in its fullest sense; **sans ~ de** without distinction of

accès [akse] NM [a] (= possibilité d'approche) access *(NonC)*; **une grande porte interdisait l'~ du jardin** a big gate prevented access to the garden; **« ~ interdit à toute personne étrangère aux travaux »** "no entry *ou* no admittance to unauthorized persons"; **d'~ facile** *[lieu, port]* (easily) accessible; *[personne]* approachable; *[traité, manuel]* easily understood; *[style]* accessible; **d'~ difficile** *[lieu]* hard to get to, not very accessible; *[personne]* not very approachable; *[traité, manuel]* not easily understood [b] (= voie) **les ~ de la ville** the approaches to *ou* means of access to the town; **les ~ de l'immeuble** the entrances to the building; **« ~ aux quais »** "to the trains" [c] *(loc)* **avoir ~ à qch** to have access to sth; **avoir ~ auprès de qn** to have access to sb; **donner ~ à** *[+ lieu]* to give access to; *(en montant)* to lead up to; *[+ carrière]* to open the door *ou* way to [d] (= crise) *[colère, folie]* fit; *[fièvre]* attack, bout; *[enthousiasme]* burst; **~ de toux** fit *ou* bout of coughing; **être pris d'un ~ de mélancolie/de tristesse** to be overcome by melancholy/sadness; **par ~** in fits [e] *(Ordin)* access; **port/temps/point d'~** access port/time/point; **~ protégé** restricted access; **~ aux données** access to data

accessibilité [aksesibilite] NF accessibility **(à** to)

accessible [aksesibl] ADJ *[lieu]* accessible **(à** to), get-at-able*; *[personne]* approachable; *[but]* attainable; *(Ordin)* accessible **(par** by); **parc ~ au public** gardens open to the public; **elle n'est ~ qu'à ses amies** only her friends are able *ou* allowed to see her; **ces études sont ~s à tous** *(sans distinction)* the course is open to everyone; *(financièrement)* the course is within everyone's pocket; *(intellectuellement)* the course is within the reach of everyone; **être ~ à la pitié** to be capable of pity

accession [aksesjɔ̃] NF ~ **à** *[+ pouvoir, fonction]* accession to; *[+ indépendance]* attainment of; *[+ rang]* rise to; *(frm)* *[+ requête, désir]* granting of, compliance with; **pour faciliter l'~ à la propriété** to facilitate home ownership

accessit [aksesit] NM *(Scol)* ≈ certificate of merit

accessoire [akseswaʀ] [1] ADJ *[idée]* of secondary importance; *[clause]* secondary; **l'un des avantages ~s de ce projet** one of the added *ou* incidental advantages of this plan; **c'est d'un intérêt tout ~** this is only of minor *ou* incidental interest; **frais ~s** *(gén)* incidental expenses; *(Fin, Comm)* ancillary costs; *(Jur)* **dommages-intérêts ~s** incidental damages [2] NM [a] *(Théât)* prop; *(Aut, Habillement)* accessory; **~s de toilette** toilet requisites → **magasin** [b] *(Philos)* **l'~** the unessential; **distinguer l'essentiel de l'~** to distinguish essentials from non-essentials

accessoirement [akseswaʀmã] ADV (= secondairement) secondarily, incidentally; (= si besoin est) if need be, if necessary

accessoiriser [akseswaʀize] ▸conjug 1◂ VT *[+ tailleur, costume]* to accessorize

accessoiriste [akseswaʀist] [1] NM prop(s) man [2] NF prop(s) woman

accident [aksidã] [1] NM [a] *(gén)* accident; *(Aut, Rail)* accident, crash; *(Aviat)* crash; *(Admin)* **il n'y a pas eu d'~ de personnes** there were no casualties, no one was injured; **il y a a**

eu plusieurs ~s mortels sur la route there have been several road deaths *ou* several fatalities on the roads; **avoir un** ~ to have an accident, meet with an accident

b (= *mésaventure*) **les ~s de sa carrière** the setbacks in his career; **les ~s de la vie** life's ups and downs, life's trials; **les ~s qui ont entravé la réalisation du projet** the setbacks *ou* hitches which held up the project; **c'est un simple ~, il ne l'a pas fait exprès** it was just an accident, he didn't do it on purpose

c (*Méd*) illness, trouble; **elle a eu un petit ~ de santé** she's had a little trouble with her health; **~ cardiaque** heart attack; **~ secondaire** minor complication

d (*Philos*) accident

e (*littér* = *hasard*) (pure) accident; (= *fait mineur*) minor event; **par ~** by chance, by accident; **si par ~ tu ...** if by chance you ..., if you happen to ...

f (*Mus*) accidental

2 COMP ► **accident d'avion** air *ou* plane crash ► **accident de la circulation** road accident ► **accidents domestiques** accidents in the home ► **accident de montagne** mountaineering *ou* climbing accident ► **accident de parcours** hiccup (*fig*) ► **accident de la route** = **accident de la circulation** ► **accident de terrain** accident (*SPÉC*), undulation; **les ~s de terrain** the unevenness of the ground ► **accident du travail** accident at work, industrial accident ► **accident de voiture** car accident *ou* crash

accidenté, e [aksidɑ̃te] (*ptp de* **accidenter**) **1** ADJ **a** [*région*] undulating, hilly; [*terrain*] uneven; [*vie, carrière*] chequered (*Brit*), checkered (*US*), eventful **b** [*véhicule*] damaged; [*avion*] crippled **2** NM,F casualty, injured person; **~ de la route** road accident victim; **~ du travail** victim of an accident at work *ou* of an industrial accident

accidentel, -elle [aksidɑ̃tɛl] ADJ (= *fortuit*) [*événement*] accidental, fortuitous; (= *par accident*) [*mort*] accidental → **signe**

accidentellement [aksidɑ̃tɛlmɑ̃] ADV **a** (= *par hasard*) accidentally, by accident *ou* chance; **il était là ~** he just happened to be there **b** [*mourir*] in an accident

accidenter [aksidɑ̃te] ▶conjug 1◀ VT [+ *personne*] to injure, hurt; [+ *véhicule*] to damage

accise [aksiz] NF (*Belg, Can*) excise; **droits d'~** excise duties

acclamation [aklamasjɔ̃] NF **élire qn par ~** to elect sb by acclamation; **~s** cheers, cheering; **il est sorti sous les ~s du public** he left to great cheering from the audience

acclamer [aklame] ▶conjug 1◀ VT to cheer, acclaim; **on l'acclama roi** they acclaimed him king

acclimatable [aklimatabl] ADJ acclimatizable, acclimatable (*US*)

acclimatation [aklimatasjɔ̃] NF acclimatization, acclimation (*US*) → **jardin**

acclimatement [aklimatmɑ̃] NM acclimatization, acclimation (*US*)

acclimater [aklimate] ▶conjug 1◀ **1** VT (*Bot, Zool*) to acclimatize, acclimate (*US*); [+ *idée, usage*] to introduce **2** **s'acclimater** VPR [*personne, animal, plante*] to become acclimatized, adapt (o.s. *ou* itself) (**à** to); [*usage, idée*] to become established *ou* accepted

accointances [akwɛ̃tɑ̃s] NFPL (*péj*) contacts, links; **avoir des ~** to have contacts (**avec** with, **dans** in, among)

accolade [akɔlad] NF **a** (= *embrassade*) embrace (on formal occasion); (*Hist* = *coup d'épée*) accolade; **donner/recevoir l'~** to embrace/be embraced (*Typo*) brace; **mots (mis) en ~** words bracketed together **c** (*Archit, Mus*) accolade

accoler [akɔle] ▶conjug 1◀ VT (*gén*) to place side by side; (*Typo*) to bracket together; **~ une chose à une autre** to place one thing beside *ou* next to another; **il avait accolé à son nom celui de sa mère** he had joined *ou* added his mother's maiden name to his surname

accommodant, e [akɔmɔdɑ̃, ɑ̃t] ADJ accommodating

accommodation [akɔmɔdasjɔ̃] NF (*Opt*) accommodation; (= *adaptation*) adaptation

accommodement [akɔmɔdmɑ̃] NM **a** (*littér* = *arrangement*) compromise, accommodation (*littér*); (*hum*) **trouver des ~s avec le ciel/avec sa conscience** to come to an arrangement with the powers above/with one's conscience **b** (*Culin*) preparation

accommoder [akɔmɔde] ▶conjug 1◀ **1** VT **a** (*Culin*) [+ *plat*] to prepare (**à** in, with); **~ les restes** to use up the left-overs **b** (= *concilier*) **~ le travail avec le plaisir** to combine business with pleasure; **~ ses principes aux circonstances** to adapt *ou* alter one's principles to suit the circumstances **c** †† (= *arranger*) [+ *affaire*] to arrange; [+ *querelle*] to put right; (= *réconcilier*) [+ *ennemis*] to reconcile, bring together; (= *malmener*) to treat harshly; (= *installer confortablement*) **~ qn** to make sb comfortable **2** VI (*Opt*) to focus (**sur** on) **3** **s'accommoder** VPR **a** † (= *s'adapter à*) **s'~ à** to adapt to **b** (= *supporter*) **s'~ de** [+ *personne*] to put up with; **il lui a bien fallu s'en ~** he just had to put up with it *ou* accept it; **je m'accommode de peu** I'm content *ou* I can make do with little; **elle s'accommode de tout** she'll put up with anything; **il s'accommode mal de la vérité** he's uncomfortable *ou* doesn't feel at home with the truth **c** (= *s'arranger avec*) **s'~ avec** † [+ *personne*] to come to an agreement *ou* arrangement with (**sur** about); **son allure s'accommode mal avec sa vie d'ascète** his appearance is hard to reconcile with his ascetic lifestyle **d** (*Culin*) **le riz peut s'~ de plusieurs façons** rice can be served in several ways

accompagnateur, -trice [akɔ̃paɲatœr, tris] NM,F (*Mus*) accompanist; (= *guide*) guide; (*Scol*) accompanying adult; [*voyage organisé*] courier

accompagnement [akɔ̃paɲmɑ̃] NM **a** (*Mus*) accompaniment; **sans ~** unaccompanied; **musique d'~** accompanying music **b** (*Culin*) accompaniment; (**servi**) **en ~ de** served with **c** (= *escorte*) escort; (*fig*) accompaniment; **l'~ d'un malade** giving (psychological) support to a terminally-ill patient; (*Pol*) **mesures/plan d'~** [*loi, réforme*] accompanying measures/programme; **livret d'~** [*vidéo*] accompanying booklet

accompagner [akɔ̃paɲe] ▶conjug 1◀ **1** VT **a** (= *escorter*) to accompany, go with, come with; [+ *malade*] to give (psychological) support to; **~ un enfant à l'école** to take a child to school; **~ qn chez lui/à la gare** to go home/to the station with sb, see sb home/to the station; **il s'était fait ~ de sa mère** he had got his mother to go with him *ou* to accompany him; **être accompagné de** *ou* **par qn** to be with sb, be accompanied by sb; **est-ce que vous êtes accompagné?** is there anybody with you?; **tous nos vœux vous accompagnent** all our good wishes go with you; **mes pensées t'accompagnent** my thoughts are with you; **~ qn de ses huées** to boo sb; **~ qn du regard** to follow sb with one's eyes **b** (= *assortir*) to accompany, go (together) with; **il accompagna ce mot d'une mimique expressive** he gestured expressively as he said the word; **une lettre accompagnait les fleurs** a letter came with the flowers; **crise de nerfs accompagnée de sanglots** hysteria accompanied by sobbing; **l'agitation qui accompagna**

son arrivée the stir *ou* fuss that accompanied his arrival **c** (*Mus*) to accompany (**à** on) **d** (*Culin*) **du chou accompagnait le rôti** the roast was served with cabbage; **le beaujolais est ce qui accompagne le mieux cette viande** a Beaujolais goes best with this meat, Beaujolais is the best wine to serve with this meat **2** **s'accompagner** VPR **a** **s'~ de** (= *s'assortir de*) to be accompanied by; **leurs discours doivent s'~ de mesures concrètes** their speeches must be backed up with concrete measures, they need to follow their speeches up with concrete measures; **la guerre s'accompagne toujours de privations** war is always accompanied by hardship; **le poisson s'accompagne d'un vin blanc sec** fish is served with a dry white wine **b** (*Mus*) **s'~ à** to accompany o.s. on; **il s'accompagna (lui-même) à la guitare** he accompanied himself on the guitar

accompli, e [akɔ̃pli] (*ptp de* **accomplir**) ADJ **a** (= *parfait, expérimenté*) accomplished; (*Ling*) accomplished **b** (= *révolu*) **avoir 60 ans ~s** to be over 60, have turned 60 → **fait**

accomplir [akɔ̃plir] ▶conjug 2◀ **1** VT **a** [+ *devoir, promesse*] to fulfil, carry out; [+ *mauvaise action*] to commit; [+ *tâche, mission*] to carry out, accomplish; [+ *exploit*] to achieve; [+ *rite*] to perform; **~ des merveilles** to work wonders, perform miracles; **les progrès accomplis dans ce domaine** advances (made) in this field; **il a enfin pu ~ ce qu'il avait décidé de faire** at last he managed to achieve *ou* accomplish what he had decided to do; **la satisfaction du devoir accompli** the satisfaction of having done one's duty **b** [+ *apprentissage, service militaire*] (= *faire*) to do; (= *terminer*) to complete **2** **s'accomplir** VPR **a** (= *se réaliser*) [*souhait*] to come true; **la volonté de Dieu s'est accomplie** God's will was done **b** (= *s'épanouir*) **elle s'accomplit dans son travail** she finds her work very fulfilling

accomplissement [akɔ̃plismɑ̃] NM **a** [*devoir, promesse*] fulfilment; [*mauvaise action*] committing; [*tâche, mission*] accomplishment; [*exploit*] achievement **b** (= *fin*) [*apprentissage, service militaire*] completion

▼**accord** [akɔr] **1** NM **a** (= *entente*) agreement; (= *concorde*) harmony; **l'~ fut général sur ce point** there was general agreement on this point; **nous avons son ~ de principe** he has agreed in principle; **le bon ~ régna pendant 10 ans** harmony reigned for 10 years → **commun**

b (= *traité*) agreement; **passer un ~ avec qn** to make an agreement with sb; **~ à l'amiable** informal *ou* amicable agreement; **~ de modération** restraint of trade clause; **~ bilatéral** bilateral agreement; **Accord général sur les tarifs douaniers et le commerce** General Agreement on Tariffs and Trade; **les ~s d'Helsinki/de Camp David** etc the Helsinki/Camp David etc agreement; **Accord de libre-échange nord-américain** North American Free Trade Agreement; (*Jur*) **~ complémentaire** additional agreement; **~s de crédit** credit arrangements; **~ salarial** wage settlement; **~ de sûreté** security agreement

c (= *permission*) consent, agreement **d** (= *harmonie*) [*couleurs*] harmony **e** (*Gram*) [*adjectif, participe*] agreement; (*Ling*) concord; **~ en genre/nombre** agreement in gender/number **f** (*Mus*) (= *notes*) chord, concord; (= *réglage*) tuning; **~ parfait** triad; **~ de tierce** third; **~ de quarte** fourth **g** (*loc*) **en ~ avec le paysage** in harmony *ou* in keeping with the landscape; **en ~ avec vos instructions** in accordance *ou* in line with your instructions; **en ~ avec le directeur** in agreement with the director

---

► GRAMMAIRE ACTIVE: **accord** 38.1, 38.2, 39.1, 53.6

2 **d'accord** LOC ADJ, LOC ADV **être d'~** to agree, be in agreement; **être d'~ avec qn** to agree with sb; **nous sommes d'~ pour dire que ...** we agree that ...; **se mettre** ou **tomber d'~ avec qn** to agree ou come to an agreement with sb; **être d'~ pour faire** to agree to do; **il est d'~ pour nous aider** he's willing to help us; **je ne suis pas d'~ pour le laisser en liberté** I don't agree that he should be left at large; **je ne suis pas d'~ avec toi** I disagree ou don't agree with you; **essayer de mettre deux personnes d'~** to try to get two people to come to ou to reach an agreement, try to get two people to see eye to eye; **je les ai mis d'~ en leur donnant tort à tous les deux** I ended their disagreement by pointing out that they were both wrong; **c'est d'~ ◊ nous sommes d'~** (we're) agreed, all right; **c'est d'~ pour demain** it's agreed for tomorrow, OK for tomorrow*; **d'~!** OK!*, (all) right!; **alors là, (je ne suis) pas d'~!*** I don't agree!, no way!*

accordable [akɔʀdabl] ADJ (*Mus*) tunable; [*faveur*] which can be granted

accordage [akɔʀdaʒ] NM tuning

accord-cadre (*pl* **accords-cadres**) [akɔʀkɑdʀ] NM outline ou framework agreement

accordement [akɔʀdmɑ̃] NM = **accordage**

accordéon [akɔʀdeɔ̃] NM accordion; **~ à clavier** piano-accordion; **en ~*** [*voiture*] crumpled up; [*pantalon, chaussette*] wrinkled (up); **on a eu une circulation en ~** the traffic was moving in fits and starts; **l'entreprise a procédé à un coup d'~ sur son capital** the company has gone from increasing to dramatically reducing its capital

accordéoniste [akɔʀdeɔnist] NMF accordionist

▼ **accorder** [akɔʀde] ▸ conjug 1 ◂ 1 VT a (= *donner*) [+ *faveur, permission*] to grant; [+ *allocation, pension*] to give, award (**à** to); **on lui a accordé un congé exceptionnel** he's been given ou granted special leave; **elle accorde à ses enfants tout ce qu'ils demandent** she lets her children have ou she gives her children anything they ask for; **pouvez-vous m'~ quelques minutes?** can you spare me a few minutes? → **main**
b (= *admettre*) **~ à qn que ...** to admit (to sb) that ...; **vous m'accorderez que j'avais raison** you'll admit ou concede I was right; **je vous l'accorde, j'avais tort** I admit ou accept ou concede that I was wrong, I was wrong, I'll grant you that
c (= *attribuer*) **~ de l'importance à qch** to attach importance to sth; **~ de la valeur à qch** to attach value to sth, value sth
d (*Mus*) [+ *instrument*] to tune; **ils devraient ~ leurs violons*** (*sur un récit, un témoignage*) they ought to get their story straight*
e (*Gram*) **(faire) ~ un verbe/un adjectif** to make a verb/an adjective agree (**avec** with)
f (= *mettre en harmonie*) [+ *personnes*] to bring together; **~ ses actions avec ses opinions** to act in accordance with one's opinions; **~ la couleur du tapis avec celle des rideaux** to match the colour of the carpet with (that of) the curtains

2 **s'accorder** VPR a (= *être d'accord*) to agree, be agreed; (= *se mettre d'accord*) to agree; **ils s'accordent pour** ou **à dire que le film est mauvais** they agree that it's not a very good film; **ils se sont accordés pour le faire élire** they agreed to get him elected
b (= *s'entendre*) [*personnes*] to get on together; **(bien/mal) s'~ avec qn** to get on (well/ badly) with sb
c (= *être en harmonie*) [*couleurs*] to match, go together; [*opinions*] to agree; [*sentiments, caractères*] to be in harmony; **s'~ avec** [*opinion*] to agree with; [*sentiments*] to be in harmony ou in keeping with; [*couleur*] to match, go with; **il faut que nos actions s'accordent avec nos opinions** we must act in accordance with our opinions
d (*Ling*) to agree (**avec** with); **s'~ en nombre/ genre** to agree in number/gender
e (= *se donner*) **il ne s'accorde jamais de répit** he never gives himself a rest, he never lets up*; **je m'accorde 2 jours pour finir** I'm giving myself 2 days to finish

accordeur [akɔʀdœʀ] NM (*Mus*) tuner

accordoir [akɔʀdwaʀ] NM tuning hammer ou wrench

accorte [akɔʀt] ADJ F (*hum*) winsome, comely

accostage [akɔstaʒ] NM (*Naut*) coming along- side; [*personne*] accosting

accoster [akɔste] ▸ conjug 1 ◂ 1 VT a (*gén, péj*) [+ *personne*] to accost b (*Naut*) [+ *quai, navire*] to come ou draw alongside; (*emploi absolu*) to berth

accotement [akɔtmɑ̃] NM (*Aut*) shoulder, verge (*Brit*), berm (*US*); (*Rail*) shoulder; **~ non stabilisé ◊ ~ meuble** soft shoulder ou verge (*Brit*); **~ stabilisé** hard shoulder

accoter [akɔte] ▸ conjug 1 ◂ 1 VT to lean, rest (**contre** against, **sur** on) 2 **s'accoter** VPR **s'~ à** ou **contre** to lean against

accotoir [akɔtwaʀ] NM [*bras*] armrest; [*tête*] headrest

accouchée [akuʃe] NF (new) mother

accouchement [akuʃmɑ̃] NM (= *naissance*) (child)birth, delivery; (= *travail*) labour (*Brit*), labor (*US*); **~ provoqué** induced labour; **~ à terme** delivery at full term, full-term delivery; **~ avant terme** early delivery, delivery before full term; **~ naturel** natural childbirth; **~ pré- maturé** premature birth; **~ sans douleur** pain- less childbirth; **pendant l'~** during the deliv- ery

accoucher [akuʃe] ▸ conjug 1 ◂ 1 VT **~ qn** to deliver sb's baby, deliver sb 2 VI a (= *être en travail*) to be in labour (*Brit*) ou labor (*US*); (= *donner naissance*) to have a baby, give birth; **où avez-vous accouché?** where did you have your baby?; **elle ~ en octobre** her baby is due in October; **~ avant terme** to have one's baby prematurely ou early ou before it is due; **~ d'un garçon** to give birth to a boy, have a (baby) boy b (*hum*) **~ de** [+ *roman*] to pro- duce (*with difficulty*); **accouche!*** spit it out!*, out with it!* → **montagne**

accoucheur, -euse [akuʃœʀ, øz] 1 NM,F (*médecin*) ~ obstetrician 2 **accoucheuse** NF (= *sage-femme*) midwife

accouder (s') [akude] ▸ conjug 1 ◂ VPR to lean (on one's elbows); **s'~ sur** ou **à** to lean (one's elbows) on, rest one's elbows on; **accoudé à la fenêtre** leaning on one's elbows at the win- dow

accoudoir [akudwaʀ] NM armrest

accouplement [akuplœmɑ̃] NM a [*roues*] coupling (up); [*wagons*] coupling (up), hitch- ing (up); [*générateurs*] connecting (up); [*tuyaux*] joining (up), connecting (up); [*moteurs*] coupling, connecting (up); (*fig*) [*mots, images*] linking b (= *copulation*) mat- ing, coupling

accoupler [akuple] ▸ conjug 1 ◂ 1 VT a (*en- semble*) [+ *animaux de trait*] to yoke; [+ *roues*] to couple (up); [+ *wagons*] to couple (up), hitch (up); [+ *générateurs*] to connect (up); [+ *tuyaux*] to join (up), connect (up); [+ *moteurs*] to couple, connect (up); [+ *mots, images*] to link; **ils sont bizarrement accouplés*** they make a strange couple, they're an odd pair b **~ une remorque/un cheval à** to hitch a trailer/horse (up) to; **~ un moteur/un tuyau à** to connect an engine/a pipe to c (= *faire copuler*) to mate (**à, avec, et** with) 2 **s'accoupler** VPR to mate, couple

accourir [akuʀiʀ] ▸ conjug 11 ◂ VI (*lit*) to rush up, run up (**à, vers** to); (*fig*) to hurry, hasten, rush (**à, vers** to); **à mon appel il accourut immédiatement** he came as soon as I called;

ils **sont accourus (pour) le féliciter** they rushed up ou hurried to congratulate him

accoutrement [akutʀəmɑ̃] NM (*péj*) getup*, rig-out* (*Brit*)

accoutrer [akutʀe] ▸ conjug 1 ◂ (*péj*) 1 VT (= *habiller*) to get up*, rig out* (*Brit*) (**de** in) 2 **s'accoutrer** VPR to get o.s. up*, rig o.s. out* (*Brit*) (**de** in); **il était bizarrement accou- tré** he was wearing the strangest getup*

accoutumance [akutymɑ̃s] NF (= *habitude*) habituation (**à** to); (= *besoin*) addiction (**à** to)

accoutumé, e [akutyme] (*ptp de* **accoutumer**) ADJ usual; **comme à l'~e** as usual; **plus/moins/ mieux qu'à l'~e** more/less/better than usual

accoutumer [akutyme] ▸ conjug 1 ◂ 1 VT **~ qn à qch/à faire qch** to accustom sb ou get sb used to sth/to doing sth; **on l'a accoutumé à** ou **il a été accoutumé à se lever tôt** he has been used ou accustomed to getting up early 2 **s'accoutumer** VPR **s'~ à qch/à faire qch** to get used ou accustomed to sth/to doing sth; **il s'est lentement accoutumé** he gradually got used ou accustomed to it

Accra [akʀa] N Accra

accréditation [akʀeditasjɔ̃] NF accreditation; **badge** ou **carte d'~** official pass; **accorder** ou **donner une ~** to accredit

accréditer [akʀedite] ▸ conjug 1 ◂ 1 VT [+ *ru- meur*] to substantiate, give substance to; [+ *idée, thèse*] to substantiate, back up; [+ *per- sonne*] to accredit (**auprès de** to); **banque ac- créditée** accredited bank 2 **s'accréditer** VPR [*rumeur*] to gain ground

accréditif, -ive [akʀeditif, iv] 1 ADJ accreditive; **carte accréditive** credit card 2 NM (*Fin*) letter of credit; (*Presse*) press card

accrétion [akʀesjɔ̃] NF (*Géol*) accretion; (*Astron*) **disque d'~** accretion disk

accro* [akʀo] ABRÉV = **accroché** 1 ADJ a (*Drogue*) **être ~** to have a habit (*arg*), be hooked*; **être ~ à l'héroïne** to be hooked on heroin* b (= *fanatique*) **être ~** to be hooked* 2 NMF addict; **les ~s du deltaplane** hang- gliding addicts

accroc [akʀo] NM a (= *déchirure*) tear; **faire un ~ à** to make a tear in, tear b [*réputation*] blot (**à** on); [*règle*] breach, infringement (**à** of); **fai- re un ~ à** [+ *règle*] to bend; [+ *réputation*] to tar- nish c (= *anicroche*) hitch, snag; **sans ~(s)** [*se dérouler*] without a hitch, smoothly; **quinze ans d'une passion sans ~(s)** fifteen years of unbroken passion

accrochage [akʀoʃaʒ] NM a (*Aut* = *collision*) collision, bump*, fender-bender* (*US*); (*Mil* = *combat*) skirmish; (*Boxe*) clinch b (= *dispute*) brush; (*plus sérieux*) clash c [*tableau*] hang- ing; [*wagons*] coupling, hitching (up) (**à** to)

accroche [akʀoʃ] NF (*Publicité*) lead-in, catch- er, catch line ou phrase; (*Presse*) **~ de une** splash headline

accroché, e* [akʀoʃe] (*ptp de* **accrocher**) ADJ a (= *amoureux*) **être ~** to be hooked* b (*Drogue*) **être ~** to have a habit (*arg*), be hooked*; **~ à l'héroïne** hooked on heroin*

accroche-cœur (*pl* **accroche-cœurs**) [akʀoʃ- kœʀ] NM kiss curl

accrocher [akʀoʃe] ▸ conjug 1 ◂ 1 VT a (= *suspendre*) [+ *chapeau, tableau*] to hang (up) (**à** on); (= *attacher*) [+ *wagons*] to couple, hitch together; **~ un wagon à** to hitch ou couple a carriage (up) to; **~ un ver à l'hameçon** to fasten ou put a worm on the hook; **maison accro- chée à la montagne** house perched on the mountainside → **cœur**
b (*accidentellement*) [+ *jupe, collant*] to catch (**à** on); [+ *aile de voiture*] to catch (**à** on), bump (**à** against); [+ *voiture*] to bump into; [+ *piéton*] to hit; [+ *pile de livres, meuble*] to catch (on); **rester accroché aux barbelés** to be caught on the barbed wire
c (= *attirer*) [+ *attention, lumière*] to catch; **~ le regard** to catch the eye; **la vitrine doit ~ le**

client the window display should attract customers
d (* = *saisir*) [+ *occasion*] to get; [+ *personne*] to get hold of; [+ *mots, fragments de conversation*] to catch
e (*Boxe*) to clinch
2 VI **a** [*fermeture éclair*] to stick, jam; [*pourparlers*] to come up against a hitch *ou* snag; **cette traduction accroche par endroits** this translation is a bit rough in places; **cette planche accroche quand on l'essuie** the cloth catches on this board when you wipe it
b * (= *plaire*) [*disque, slogan*] to catch on; **ça accroche entre eux** they hit it off (together)*
c (* = *s'intéresser*) **elle n'accroche pas en physique** she can't get into physics*; **l'art abstrait, j'ai du mal à ~** abstract art does nothing for me*
3 **s'accrocher** VPR **a** (= *se cramponner*) to hang on; **s'~ à** [+ *branche, pouvoir*] to cling to, hang on to; [+ *espoir, personne*] to cling to; **accroche-toi bien!** hold on tight!
b (* = *être tenace*) [*malade*] to cling on, hang on; [*étudiant*] to stick at it; [*importun*] to cling; **pour enlever la tache, tiens, accroche-toi!** you'll have a hell of a job getting the stain out!*
c (= *entrer en collision*) [*voitures*] to bump into each other, clip each other; (*Boxe*) to go *ou* get into a clinch; (*Mil*) to skirmish
d (= *se disputer*) to have a brush; (*plus sérieux*) to have a clash (**avec** with); **ils s'accrochent tout le temps** they're always at loggerheads *ou* always quarrelling
e **se l'~*** (= *en faire son deuil*): **tu peux te l'~** you can kiss it goodbye*, you've got a hope* (*Brit*) (*iro*)

accrocheur, -euse [akʀɔʃœʀ, øz] ADJ **a** [*concurrent*] tenacious; [*vendeur*] persistent, aggressive **b** [*affiche, titre*] eye-catching; [*méthode*] calculated to appeal; [*musique, slogan*] catchy; [*prix*] very attractive; [*film*] which (really) pulls the crowds *ou* pulls them in*

accroire [akʀwaʀ] VT (*frm ou hum*) **faire** *ou* **laisser ~ qch à qn** to delude sb into believing sth; **et tu veux me faire ~ que ...** and you expect me to believe that ...; **il veut nous en faire ~** he's trying to deceive us *ou* take us in; **il ne s'en est pas laissé ~** he wouldn't be taken in

accroissement [akʀwasmɑ̃] NM (*gén*) increase (**de** in); [*nombre, production*] growth (**de** in), increase (**de** in); **~ démographique nul** zero population growth

accroître [akʀwatʀ] ▶conjug 55◀ **1** VT [+ *somme, plaisir, confusion*] to increase, add to; [+ *réputation*] to enhance, add to; [+ *gloire*] to increase, heighten; [+ *production*] to increase (**de** by); **~ son avance sur qn** to increase one's lead over sb **2** **s'accroître** VPR to increase, grow; **sa part s'est accrue de celle de son frère** his share was increased by that of his brother

accroupi, e [akʀupi] (*ptp de* **s'accroupir**) ADJ squatting *ou* crouching (down); **en position ~e** in a squatting *ou* crouching position

accroupir (s') [akʀupiʀ] ▶conjug 2◀ VPR to squat *ou* crouch (down)

accroupissement [akʀupismɑ̃] NM squatting, crouching

accu* [aky] NM (*Aut etc*) (ABRÉV = **accumulateur**) battery

accueil [akœj] NM **a** (*gén* = *réception*) welcome, reception; [*sinistrés, film, idée*] reception; **rien n'a été prévu pour l'~ des touristes** no provision has been made to accommodate tourists, no tourist facilities have been provided; **quel ~ a-t-on fait à ses idées?** what sort of reception did his ideas get?, how were his ideas received?; **faire bon ~ à** [+ *idée, proposition*] to welcome; **faire bon ~ à qn** to welcome sb, make sb welcome; **faire mauvais ~ à** [+ *idée, suggestion*] to receive badly; **faire mauvais ~ à qn** to make sb feel unwelcome,

give sb a bad reception; **faire bon/mauvais ~ à un film** to give a film a good/bad reception; **le projet a reçu** *ou* **trouvé un ~ favorable** the plan was favourably *ou* well received; **d'~** [*centre, organisation*] reception (*épith*); [*paroles, cérémonie*] welcoming, of welcome → **famille, hôtesse, pays, structure, terre**
b (= *bureau*) reception; **adressez-vous à l'~** ask at reception

accueillant, e [akœjɑ̃, ɑ̃t] ADJ welcoming, friendly

accueillir [akœjiʀ] ▶conjug 12◀ VT **a** (= *aller chercher*) to meet, collect; (= *recevoir*) to welcome, greet; (= *donner l'hospitalité à*) to welcome, take in; (= *héberger*) to accommodate; **j'ai été l'~ à la gare** I went to meet *ou* collect him *ou* pick him up at the station; **il m'a bien accueilli** he made me very welcome, he gave me a warm welcome; **il m'a mal accueilli** he made me feel very unwelcome; **il m'a accueilli sous son toit/dans sa famille** he welcomed me into his house/his family; **cet hôtel peut ~ 80 touristes** this hotel can accommodate 80 tourists; **ils se sont fait ~ par des coups de feu/des huées** they were greeted with shots/boos *ou* catcalls
b [+ *idée, demande, film, nouvelle*] to receive; **être bien/mal accueilli** to be well/badly received; **il accueillit ma suggestion avec un sourire** he greeted *ou* received my suggestion with a smile

acculer [akyle] ▶conjug 1◀ VT **~ qn à** [+ *mur*] to drive sb back against; [+ *ruine, désespoir*] to drive sb to the brink of; [+ *choix, aveu*] to force sb into; **acculé à la mer** driven back to the edge of the sea; **~ qn contre** to drive sb back to *ou* against; **~ qn dans** [+ *impasse, pièce*] to corner sb in; (*lit, fig*) **nous sommes acculés, nous devons céder** we're cornered, we must give in

acculturation [akyltyʀasjɔ̃] NF acculturation (*frm*)

acculturer [akyltyʀe] ▶conjug 1◀ VT [+ *groupe*] to help adapt *ou* adjust to a new culture, acculturate (*frm*)

accumulateur [akymylatœʀ] NM accumulator, (storage) battery; (*Ordin*) accumulator; **~ de chaleur** storage heater

accumulation [akymylasjɔ̃] NF [*documents, richesses, preuves, marchandises*] accumulation; [*irrégularités, erreurs*] series; **une ~ de stocks** a build-up in stock; (*Élec*) **radiateur à ~ (nocturne)** (night-)storage heater

accumuler [akymyle] ▶conjug 1◀ VT [+ *documents, richesses, preuves, erreurs*] to accumulate, amass; [+ *marchandises*] to accumulate, stockpile; [+ *énergie*] to store; (*Fin*) **les intérêts accumulés pendant un an** the interest accrued over a year; **il accumule les gaffes** he makes one blunder after another; **le retard accumulé depuis un an** the delay that has built up over the past year **2** **s'accumuler** VPR [*objets, problèmes, travail*] to accumulate, pile up; **les dossiers s'accumulent sur mon bureau** I've got files piling up on my desk

accusateur, -trice [akyzatœʀ, tʀis] **1** ADJ [*doigt, regard*] accusing; [*documents, preuves*] accusatory, incriminating **2** NM,F accuser; (*Hist*) **~ public** public prosecutor (*during the French Revolution*)

accusatif, -ive [akyzatif, iv] **1** NM accusative case; **à l'~** in the accusative **2** ADJ accusative

accusation [akyzasjɔ̃] NF **a** (*gén*) accusation; (*Jur*) charge, indictment; **porter** *ou* **lancer une ~ contre** to make *ou* level an accusation against; **il a lancé des ~s de corruption/de fraude contre eux** he accused them of bribery/of fraud, he levelled accusations of bribery/of fraud against them; **mettre en ~†** to indict; **mise en ~†** indictment; **c'est une terrible ~ contre notre société** it's a terrible indictment of our society; (*Jur*) **abandonner**

l'~ to drop the charge → **acte, chambre, chef**
b (= *ministère public*) **l'~** the prosecution

accusatoire [akyzatwaʀ] ADJ (*Jur*) accusatory

accusé, e [akyze] (*ptp de* **accuser**) **1** ADJ (= *marqué*) marked, pronounced **2** NM,F accused; (*procès*) defendant; **~, levez-vous!** the defendant will rise → **banc 3** COMP
▶ **accusé de réception** acknowledgement of receipt

▼**accuser** [akyze] ▶conjug 1◀ **1** VT **a** [+ *personne*] (*gén*) to accuse (**de** of); (*Jur*) **~ de** to accuse of, charge with, indict for; **~ qn d'ingratitude** to accuse sb of ingratitude; **~ qn d'avoir volé de l'argent** to accuse sb of stealing *ou* having stolen money; **tout l'accuse** everything points to his guilt *ou* his being guilty
b (= *rendre responsable*) [+ *pratique, malchance, personne*] to blame (**de** for); **accusant son mari de ne pas s'être réveillé à temps** blaming her husband for not waking up in time; **accusant le médecin d'incompétence pour avoir causé la mort de l'enfant** blaming the doctor's incompetence for having caused the child's death, blaming the child's death on the doctor's incompetence
c (= *souligner*) [+ *effet, contraste*] to emphasize, accentuate, bring out; **cette robe accuse sa maigreur** this dress makes her look even thinner
d (= *montrer*) to show; **la balance accusait 80 kg** the scales registered *ou* read 80 kg; **~ la quarantaine** to look forty; (*lit, fig*) **~ le coup** to stagger under the blow, show that the blow has struck home; **elle accuse la fatigue de ces derniers mois** she's showing the strain of these last few months; **la Bourse accuse une baisse de 3 points/un léger mieux** the stock exchange is showing a 3-point fall/a slight improvement; **~ réception de** to acknowledge receipt of
2 **s'accuser** VPR **a** **s'~ de qch/d'avoir fait qch** (= *se déclarer coupable*) to admit to sth/to having done sth; (= *se rendre responsable*) to blame o.s. for sth/for having done sth; (*Rel*) **mon père, je m'accuse (d'avoir péché)** bless me, Father, for I have sinned; **en protestant, il s'accuse** by objecting, he is admitting his guilt
b (= *s'accentuer*) [*tendance*] to become more marked *ou* pronounced

ace [ɛs] NM (*Tennis*) ace; **faire un ~** to serve an ace

acerbe [asɛʀb] ADJ caustic, acid; **d'une manière ~** caustically, acidly

acéré, e [aseʀe] ADJ [*griffe, pointe*] sharp; [*lame*] sharp, keen; [*raillerie, réplique*] scathing, biting, cutting; **critique à la plume ~e** critic with a scathing pen

acétate [asetat] NM acetate

acétique [asetik] ADJ acetic

acétone [asetɔn] NF acetone

acétylène [asetilɛn] NM acetylene → **lampe**

acétylsalicylique [asetilsalisilik] ADJ **acide ~** acetylsalicylic acid

achalandé, e [aʃalɑ̃de] ◆**bien achalandé** LOC ADJ (= *bien fourni*) well-stocked; († = *très fréquenté*) well-patronized

achards [aʃaʀ] NMPL spicy relish made with finely chopped fruit and vegetables

acharné, e [aʃaʀne] (*ptp de* **s'acharner**) ADJ [*combat, concurrence, adversaire*] fierce, bitter; [*discussion*] heated; [*volonté*] dogged; [*campagne*] fierce; [*travail, efforts*] relentless, unremitting, strenuous; [*poursuivant, poursuite*] relentless; [*travailleur*] relentless, determined; [*défenseur, partisan*] staunch, fervent; [*joueur*] hardened; **~ contre** dead (set) against; **~ à faire** set *ou* bent *ou* intent on doing, determined to do; **c'est l'un des plus ~s à combattre la pauvreté** he is one of the most active campaigners in the fight against poverty; **~ à leur perte** intent on bringing about their downfall; **quelques ~s restaient encore** a dedicated few stayed on

acharnement [aʃaʀnəmɑ̃] NM [*combattant, résistant*] fierceness, fury; [*poursuivant*] relentlessness; [*travailleur*] determination, unremitting effort; **son ~ au travail** the determination with which he tackles his work; **avec ~** [*poursuivre*] relentlessly; [*travailler*] relentlessly, furiously; [*combattre*] bitterly, fiercely; [*résister*] fiercely; [*défendre*] staunchly; **se battant avec ~** fighting tooth and nail; **cet ~ contre les fumeurs m'agace** it gets on my nerves the way smokers are being hounded like this; **~ thérapeutique** prolongation of life by medical means (*when a patient would otherwise die*)

acharner (s') [aʃaʀne] ▶ conjug 1 ◀ VPR a (= *tourmenter*) **s'~ sur** [+ *victime, proie*] to go at fiercely and unrelentingly; **s'~ contre qn** [*malchance*] to dog sb; [*adversaire*] to set o.s. against sb, have got one's knife into sb; **elle s'acharne après cet enfant** she's always hounding that child b (= *s'obstiner sur*) **~ sur** [+ *calculs, texte*] to work away furiously at; **je m'acharne à le leur faire comprendre** I'm desperately trying to get them to understand it; **il s'acharne inutilement** he's wasting his efforts

achat [aʃa] 1 NM a (*action*) purchase, purchasing, buying; **faire l'~ de qch** to purchase ou buy sth; **faire un ~ groupé** to buy several items at once; **c'est cher à l'~ mais c'est de bonne qualité** it's expensive (to buy) but it's good quality; **la livre vaut 11 F à l'~** the buying rate for sterling is 11 francs; **ces titres ont fait l'objet d'~s massifs** these securities have been bought up in great numbers → **central, offre, ordre, pouvoir** *etc* b (= *chose achetée*) purchase; **faire un ~** to make a purchase; **il a fait un ~ judicieux** he made a wise buy ou purchase; **faire des ~s** to shop, go shopping; **il est allé faire quelques ~s** he has gone out to buy a few things ou to do some shopping; **faire ses ~s (de Noël)** to do one's (Christmas) shopping; **montre-moi tes ~s** show me what you've bought; **je ferai mes derniers ~s à l'aéroport** I'll buy the last few things I need at the airport

2 COMP ▶ **achat d'espace** (*Publicité*) space buying ▶ **achat d'impulsion** (= *action*) impulse buying; (= *chose*) impulse buy ou purchase

acheminement [aʃ(ə)minmɑ̃] NM [*courrier, colis*] delivery (**vers** to); [*troupes*] transporting; (*Comm*) **~ de marchandises** carriage of goods; **l'~ des secours aux civils** getting help to civilians

acheminer [aʃ(ə)mine] ▶ conjug 1 ◀ 1 VT [+ *courrier, colis*] to forward, dispatch (**vers** to); [+ *troupes*] to transport (**vers** to); [+ *train*] to route (**sur, vers** to); **~ un train supplémentaire sur Dijon** to put on an extra train to Dijon; **le pont aérien qui acheminera l'aide humanitaire dans la région** the airlift that will bring humanitarian aid to the region 2 **s'acheminer** VPR **s'~ vers** [+ *endroit*] to make one's way towards, head for; [+ *conclusion, solution*] to move towards; [+ *guerre, destruction, ruine*] to head for

acheter [aʃ(ə)te] ▶ conjug 5 ◀ VT a (*Comm*) to buy, purchase; **~ qch à qn** (*à un vendeur*) to buy ou purchase sth from sb; (*pour qn*) to buy sth for sb, buy sb sth; **~ en grosses quantités** to buy in bulk, bulk-buy (*Brit*); **j'achète mon fromage au détail** I buy my cheese loose; (*Bourse*) **~ à la hausse/à la baisse** to buy for a rise/for a fall; **ça s'achète dans les quincailleries** you can buy it ou it can be bought in hardware stores, it's on sale in hardware stores; **je me suis acheté une montre** I bought myself a watch; **(s')~ une conduite** to turn over a new leaf, mend one's ways → **comptant, crédit** b (*en corrompant*) [+ *vote,*

appui] to buy; [+ *électeur, juge*] to bribe, buy; **se laisser ~** to let o.s. be bribed ou bought; **on peut ~ n'importe qui** every man has his price, everyone has their price

acheteur, -euse [aʃ(ə)tœʀ, øz] NM,F buyer, purchaser; (*Jur*) vendee; (*Comm: professionnel*) buyer; **il est ~** he wants to buy it; **il n'a pas encore trouvé d'~ pour sa voiture** he hasn't yet found anyone to buy his car ou a buyer for his car; **article qui ne trouve pas d'~** item which does not sell ou which finds no takers; **la foule des ~s** the crowd of shoppers

achevé, e [aʃ(ə)ve] (*ptp de* **achever**) 1 ADJ [*canaille*] downright, out-and-out, thorough; [*artiste*] accomplished; [*art, grâce*] perfect; **d'un ridicule ~** perfectly ridiculous; **tableau d'un mauvais goût ~** picture in thoroughly bad taste 2 NM ▶ **d'imprimer** colophon

achèvement [aʃevmɑ̃] NM [*travaux*] completion; (*littér = perfection*) culmination → **voie**

achever [aʃ(ə)ve] ▶ conjug 5 ◀ 1 VT a (= *terminer*) [+ *discours, repas*] to finish, end; [+ *livre*] to finish, reach the end of; (= *parachever*) [+ *tâche, tableau*] to complete, finish; **~ ses jours à la campagne** to end one's days in the country; (*littér*) **le soleil achève sa course** the sun completes its course; **~ (de parler)** to finish (speaking); **il partit sans ~ (sa phrase)** he left in mid sentence ou without finishing his sentence; **~ de se raser/de se préparer** to finish shaving/getting ready; **le pays achevait de se reconstruire** the country was just finishing rebuilding itself b (= *porter à son comble*) **cette remarque acheva de l'exaspérer** the remark really brought his irritation to a head; **cette révélation acheva de nous plonger dans la confusion** this revelation was all we needed to confuse us completely c (= *tuer*) [+ *blessé*] to finish off; [+ *cheval*] to destroy; (= *fatiguer, décourager*) to finish (off); (* = *vaincre*) to finish off; **cette mauvaise nouvelle va ~ son père** this bad news will finish his father off; **cette longue promenade m'a achevé!** that long walk finished me (off)!

2 **s'achever** VPR (= *se terminer*) to end (**par, sur** with); (*littér*) [*jour, vie*] to come to an end, draw to a close; (*TV*) **ainsi s'achèvent nos émissions de la journée** that brings to an end our programmes for today

Achgabat [aʃgabat] N Ashkhabad

achigan [aʃigɑ̃] NM (*Can*) (black) bass; **~ à grande bouche** large-mouth bass; **~ à petite bouche** small-mouth bass; **~ de roche** rock bass

Achille [aʃil] NM Achilles → **talon**

achillée [akile] NF achillea

achoppement [aʃɔpmɑ̃] NM **pierre** ou **point d'~** stumbling block

achopper [aʃɔpe] ▶ conjug 1 ◀ VT INDIR **~ sur** [+ *difficulté*] to come up against; (*littér*) [+ *pierre*] to stumble against ou over; **les pourparlers ont achoppé** the talks came up against a stumbling block

achromatique [akʀomatik] ADJ achromatic

acide [asid] 1 ADJ (*lit, fig*) acid, sharp, tart; (*Chim*) acid → **pluie** 2 NM acid; (*arg Drogue*) acid; **~ aminé** amino-acid; **~ gras saturé/insaturé** saturated/unsaturated fatty acid

acidifiant, e [asidifjɑ̃, jɑ̃t] 1 ADJ acidifying 2 NM acidifier

acidificateur [asidifikatœʀ] NM acidifying agent, acidifier

acidification [asidifikasjɔ̃] NF acidification

acidifier VT, **s'acidifier** VPR [asidifje] ▶ conjug 7 ◀ to acidify

acidité [asidite] NF (*lit, fig*) acidity, sharpness, tartness; (*Chim*) acidity

acidose [asidoz] NF acidosis

acidulé, e [asidyle] ADJ [*goût*] slightly acid; [*voix*] shrill → **bonbon**

acier [asje] NM steel; **~ inoxydable/trempé** stainless/tempered steel; **~ rapide** high-speed steel; **d'~** [*poutre, colonne*] steel (*épith*), of steel; [*regard*] steely; **muscles d'~** muscles of steel → **gris, moral, nerf**

aciérie [asjeʀi] NF steelworks

aciériste [asjeʀist] NM steelmaker

acmé [akme] NF (*littér = apogée*) acme, summit; (*Méd*) crisis

acné [akne] NF acne; **avoir de l'~** to have acne, suffer from acne; **~ juvénile** teenage acne

acnéique [akneik] 1 ADJ prone to acne (*attrib*) 2 NMF acne sufferer

acolyte [akɔlit] NM (*péj = associé*) confederate, associate; (*Rel*) acolyte, server

acompte [akɔ̃t] NM (= *arrhes*) deposit; (*sur somme due*) down payment; (= *versement régulier*) instalment; (*sur salaire*) advance; (*à un entrepreneur*) progress payment; (*sur somme due*) **recevoir un ~** to receive something on account, receive a down payment; **ce weekend à la mer, c'était un petit ~ sur nos vacances** that weekend at the seaside was like a little foretaste of our holidays → **provisionnel**

aconier [akɔnje] NM lighterman

aconit [akɔnit] NM aconite, aconitum

a contrario [akɔ̃tʀaʀjo] ADV, ADJ a contrario

acoquiner (s') [akɔkine] ▶ conjug 1 ◀ VPR (*péj*) to get together, team up (**avec** with)

Açores [asɔʀ] NFPL **les ~** the Azores

à-côté (*pl* **à-côtés**) [akote] NM [*problème*] side issue; [*situation*] side aspect; (= *gain, dépense secondaire*) extra; **avec ce boulot, il se fait des petits ~s** with this job, he makes a bit extra ou on the side*

à-coup (*pl* **à-coups**) [aku] NM [*moteur*] cough; [*machine*] jolt, jerk; [*économie, organisation*] jolt; **travailler par ~s** to work by ou in fits and starts; **avancer par ~s** to move forward in ou by fits and starts, jerk ou jolt forward ou along; **sans ~s** smoothly; **le moteur eut quelques ~s** the engine coughed (and spluttered)

acousticien, -ienne [akustisjɛ̃, jɛn] NM,F acoustician

acoustique [akustik] 1 ADJ acoustic; (*Phon*) **trait distinctif ~** acoustic feature → **cornet** 2 NF (= *science*) acoustics *sg*; (= *sonorité*) acoustics; **il y a une mauvaise ~** the acoustics are bad

acquéreur [akeʀœʀ] NM buyer, purchaser; **j'ai trouvé/je n'ai pas trouvé ~ pour mon appartement** I have/I haven't found a purchaser ou buyer for my apartment, I've found someone/I haven't found anyone to buy my apartment; **cet objet n'a pas encore trouvé ~** the object has not yet found a purchaser ou buyer ou taker; **se porter ~ (de qch)** to announce one's intention to buy ou purchase (sth); **se rendre ~ de qch** to purchase ou buy sth

acquérir [akeʀiʀ] ▶ conjug 21 ◀ VT a [+ *propriété, meuble*] to acquire; (*en achetant*) to purchase, buy; (*Bourse*) [+ *titre*] to acquire, purchase, buy; [+ *société*] to acquire; **~ qch par succession** to come into sth, inherit sth → **bien** b (= *obtenir*) [+ *faveur, célébrité*] to win, gain; [+ *habileté, autorité, nationalité, habitude*] to acquire; [+ *importance, valeur, statut*] to acquire, gain; **~ la certitude de qch** to become certain of sth; **~ la preuve de qch** to gain ou obtain (the) proof of sth; **leur entreprise a acquis une dimension européenne** their company has acquired ou taken on a European dimension; **l'expérience s'acquiert avec le temps** experience is something you acquire with time; **il s'est acquis une solide réputation** he has built up a solid reputation c **il s'est acquis l'estime/l'appui de ses chefs** he won ou gained his superiors' esteem/support

acquêt [akɛ] NM acquest → **communauté**

acquiescement [akjɛsmɑ̃] NM [a] (= *approbation*) approval, agreement; **il leva la main en signe d'~** he raised his hand in approval *ou* agreement [b] (= *consentement*) acquiescence, assent; **donner son ~ à qch** to give one's assent to sth

acquiescer [akjese] ▸conjug 3◂ VI [a] (= *approuver*) to approve, agree; **il acquiesça d'un signe de tête** he nodded in agreement, he nodded his approval [b] (= *consentir*) to acquiesce, assent; **~ à une demande** to acquiesce to *ou* in a request, assent to a request

acquis, e [aki, iz] (*ptp de* **acquérir**) [1] ADJ [a] [*fortune, qualité, droit*] acquired; (*Bio*) **caractères ~** acquired characteristics → **vitesse** [b] [*fait*] established, accepted; **tenir qch pour ~** (*comme allant de soi*) to take sth for granted; (*comme décidé*) to take sth as settled *ou* agreed; **il est maintenant ~ que ...** it has now been established that ..., it is now accepted that ... [c] **être ~ à qn: ce droit nous est ~** we have now established this right as ours; **ses faveurs nous sont ~es** we can count on *ou* be sure of his favour; **être ~ à un projet/qn** to be in complete support of *ou* completely behind a plan/sb; **cette région est ~e à la gauche** this region is a left-wing stronghold *ou* is solidly left-wing [2] NM [a] (= *avantage*) asset; **sa connaissance de l'anglais est un ~ précieux** his knowledge of English is a valuable asset; **~ sociaux** social benefits; **~ territoriaux** territorial aquisitions [b] † (= *expérience, savoir*) experience; **avoir de l'~** to have experience; **un élève qui vit sur ses ~** a pupil who is content to get by on what he already knows

acquisition [akizisjɔ̃] NF [a] (= *action, processus*) acquisition, acquiring; **faire l'~ de qch** to acquire sth; (*par achat*) to purchase sth; **l'~ du langage** language acquisition; **l'~ de la nationalité française** the acquisition of French nationality; (*Ordin*) **l'~ de données** data acquisition [b] (= *objet*) acquisition; (*par achat*) purchase; **nouvelle ~** [*bibliothèque*] accession

acquit [aki] NM [a] (*Comm* = *décharge*) receipt; **« pour ~ »** "received" [b] **par ~ de conscience** to set one's mind at rest, be quite sure [c] **~ à-caution** bond note

acquittement [akitmɑ̃] NM [a] [*accusé*] acquittal; **verdict d'~** verdict of not guilty [b] [*facture*] payment, settlement; [*droit, impôt*] payment; [*dette*] discharge, settlement

acquitter [akite] ▸conjug 1◂ [1] VT [a] [+ *accusé*] to acquit [b] [+ *droit, impôt*] to pay; [+ *dette*] to pay (off), settle, discharge; [+ *facture*] (*gén*) to pay, settle; (*Comm*) to receipt [c] **~ qn de** [+ *dette, obligation*] to release sb from [2] **s'acquitter** VPR **s'~ de** [+ *dette*] to pay (off), settle; [+ *dette morale, devoir*] to discharge; [+ *promesse*] to fulfil, carry out; [+ *obligation*] to fulfil, discharge; [+ *fonction, tâche*] to fulfil, carry out; **comment m'~ (envers vous)?** how can I ever repay you? (**de** for)

acre [akʀ] [1] NF (*Hist*) ≈ acre [2] NM (*Can*) acre (4,046.86 m²)

âcre [akʀ] ADJ [*odeur, saveur*] acrid, pungent; (*littér*) acrid

âcreté [akʀəte] NF [*odeur, saveur*] acridness, acridity, pungency; (*littér*) acridness, acridity

acrimonie [akʀimɔni] NF acrimony, acrimoniousness

acrimonieux, -ieuse [akʀimɔnjø, jøz] ADJ acrimonious

acrobate [akʀɔbat] NMF (*lit, fig*) acrobat

acrobatie [akʀɔbasi] NF (= *tour*) acrobatic feat; (= *art*) acrobatics *sg*; **~ aérienne** aerobatics; **faire des ~s** to perform acrobatics; **il a fallu se livrer à des ~s comptables/budgétaires** we had to juggle the accounts/the budget; **à force**

d'~s financières, il a sauvé son entreprise he managed to save his company with some financial sleight of hand *ou* thanks to some financial gymnastics; **mon emploi du temps tient de l'~*** I have to tie myself in knots* to cope with my timetable

acrobatique [akʀɔbatik] ADJ (*lit, fig*) acrobatic

acronyme [akʀɔnim] NM acronym

Acropole [akʀɔpɔl] NF **l'~** the Acropolis

acrostiche [akʀɔstiʃ] NM acrostic

acrylique [akʀilik] ADJ, NM acrylic → **peinture**

actant [aktɑ̃] NM (*Ling*) agent

acte [akt] [1] NM [a] (= *action*) action, act; **~ instinctif/réflexe** instinctive/reflex action; **moins de paroles, des ~s** let's have less talk and more action; **plusieurs ~s de terrorisme ont été commis** several acts of terrorism have been committed; **~ de bravoure/de lâcheté/de cruauté** act of bravery/cowardice/cruelty, brave/cowardly/cruel act; **ce crime est un ~ de folie/l'~ d'un fou** this crime is an act of madness/the work of a madman; (*Psych*) **passer à l'~** to act out one's desires *ou* fantasies; **après avoir menacé en paroles il passa aux ~** having uttered verbal threats he proceeded to carry them out *ou* to put them into action; (*Philos*) **en ~** in actuality [b] (*Jur*) [*notaire*] deed; [*état civil*] certificate; (*Jur*) **dont ~** duly noted *ou* acknowledged [c] (*Théât, fig*) act; **pièce en un ~** one-act play; **le dernier ~ du conflit se joua en Orient** the final act of the struggle was played out in the East [d] [*congrès*] **~s** proceedings [e] (*loc*) **demander ~ que/de qch** to ask for formal acknowledgement that/of sth; **prendre ~ de qch** to note sth; **prendre ~ que ...** to record formally that ...; **nous prenons ~ de votre promesse** we have noted *ou* taken note of your promise; **donner ~ que** to acknowledge formally that; **donner ~ de qch** to acknowledge sth formally; **faire ~ de citoyen** to act *ou* behave as a citizen; **faire ~ d'autorité** to make a show of authority; **faire ~ de candidature** to apply, submit an application; **faire ~ de présence** to put in a token appearance; **il a au moins fait ~ de bonne volonté** he has at least shown *ou* made a gesture of goodwill *ou* willingness

[2] COMP ► **acte d'accusation** bill of indictment, charge (*Brit*) ► **acte d'amnistie** amnesty ► **les Actes des Apôtres** the Acts of the Apostles ► **acte d'association** partnership agreement *ou* deed, articles of partnership ► **acte authentique** = **acte notarié** ► **acte de banditisme** criminal act ► **acte de baptême** baptismal certificate ► **acte de charité** act of charity ► **acte de commerce** commercial act *ou* deed ► **acte constitutif** [*société*] charter ► **acte de contrition** act of contrition ► **acte de décès** death certificate ► **acte d'espérance** act of hope ► **acte de l'état civil** *birth, marriage or death certificate* ► **acte de foi** act of faith ► **acte gratuit** gratuitous act, free act ► **acte de guerre** act of war ► **acte judiciaire** judicial document; **signifier** *ou* **notifier un ~ judiciaire** to serve legal papers (à on) ► **acte manqué** (*Psych*) subconsciously deliberate mistake ► **acte de mariage** marriage certificate ► **acte médical** medical treatment (*NonC*) ► **acte de naissance** birth certificate ► **acte notarié** notarial deed, deed executed by notary ► **acte de notoriété** affidavit ► **acte officiel** (*Jur*) instrument ► **acte sexuel** sex act ► **acte de succession** attestation of inheritance ► **l'Acte unique (européen)** the Single European Act ► **acte de vente** bill of sale → **seing**

acteur [aktœʀ] NM (*Théât, Ciné*) actor; (*fig*) player; **~ de cinéma** film *ou* movie (*US*) actor; **~ de théâtre** stage *ou* theatre actor; **tous les ~s**

du film sont excellents the entire cast in this film are *ou* is excellent; **les principaux ~s économiques** the key economic players; **les ~s de la politique mondiale** the actors *ou* players on the world political stage; **les ~s sociaux** the main organized forces in society; (*fig*) **les trois ~s de ce drame** the three people involved in *ou* the three protagonists in the tragedy → **actrice**

actif, -ive [aktif, iv] [1] ADJ [*personne, participation*] active; [*poison, médicament*] active, potent; (*au travail*) [*population*] working; (*Bourse*) [*marché*] buoyant; (*Phys*) [*substance*] activated, active; (*Élec*) [*circuit, élément*] active; (*Ling*) active; **les principes ~s du médicament** the active principles of the drug; **prendre une part active à qch** to take an active part in sth; **dans la vie active** in his (*ou* one's *etc*) working life; **entrer dans la vie active** to begin one's working life → **armée²**, **charbon**, **corruption** *etc* [2] NM [a] (*Ling*) active (voice); **à l'~** in the active voice [b] (*Fin*) assets; [*succession*] credits; **~ circulant** current *ou* floating assets; **~ réalisable et disponible** current assets; **porter une somme à l'~** to put a sum on the assets side; **sa gentillesse est à mettre à son ~** his kindness is a point in his favour, on the credit *ou* plus* side there is his kindness (to consider); **il a plusieurs crimes à son ~** he has several crimes to his name; **il a plusieurs records à son ~** he has several records to his credit *ou* name [c] (= *qui travaille*) working person; **les ~s** people who work, the working population [3] **active** NF (*Mil*) **l'active** the regular army; **officier d'active** regular officer

actinide [aktinid] NM actinide, actinon

actinium [aktinjɔm] NM actinium

action¹ [aksjɔ̃] [1] NF [a] (= *acte*) action, act; **~ audacieuse** act of daring, bold deed *ou* action; **faire une bonne ~** to do a good deed; **j'ai fait ma bonne ~ de la journée** I've done my good deed for the day; **commettre une mauvaise ~** to do something (very) wrong, behave badly; **~ d'éclat** dazzling *ou* brilliant feat *ou* deed; (*Rel*) **~ de grâce(s)** thanksgiving [b] (= *activité*) action; **passer à l'~** (*gén, fig*) to take action; (*Mil*) to go into battle *ou* action; **le moment est venu de passer à l'~** the time has come for action; **être en ~** [*forces*] to be at work; **entrer en ~** [*troupes, canon*] to go into action; [*usine*] to go into operation; [*mécanisme*] to start; **mettre en ~** [+ *mécanisme*] to set going; [+ *plan*] to put into action; **le dispositif de sécurité se mit en ~** the security device went off *ou* was set off → **champ, feu¹, homme** [c] (= *effet*) [*machine*] action; [*éléments naturels, médicament*] effect; **ce médicament est sans ~** this medicine is ineffective *ou* has no effect; **la pierre s'est fendue sous l'~ du gel** the frost caused the stone to crack; **la transformation s'opère sous l'~ des bactéries** the transformation is caused by the action of bacteria [d] (= *initiative*) action; **engager une ~ commune** to take concerted action; **recourir à l'~ directe** to resort to *ou* have recourse to direct action; **~ revendicative** [*ouvriers*] industrial action (*NonC*); [*étudiants*] protest (*NonC*) → **journée** [e] (= *politique, mesures*) policies; **l'~ gouvernementale** the government's policies; **l'~ économique et sociale** economic and social policy; **l'~ humanitaire** humanitarian aid; **pour financer notre ~ en faveur des réfugiés** in order to finance our aid programme for refugees; **le développement de l'~ culturelle à l'étranger** the development of cultural initiatives abroad; **son ~ à la tête du ministère a été critiquée** he was criticized for what he did as head of the ministry → **programme** [f] [*pièce, film*] (= *mouvement, péripéties*) action; (= *intrigue*) plot; **~!** action!; **l'~ se passe en Grèce** the action takes place in Greece; **film**

d~ action film; **roman (plein) d'~** action-packed novel

[g] (Jur) action (at law), lawsuit; **~ juridique/ civile** legal/civil action; **~ en diffamation** libel action → **intenter**

[h] (Sport) **il a été blessé au cours de cette ~** he was injured during that bit of play; **il y a eu deux ~s dangereuses devant nos buts** there were two dangerous attacking moves right in front of our goal; **il y a eu de belles ~s au cours de ce match** there was some fine play during the match; **revoyons l'~** let's have an action replay

[i] (Helv Comm = vente promotionnelle) special offer; **robes en ~** dresses on special offer

action² [aksjɔ̃] NF (Fin) share; **~s** shares, stock(s); **~ cotée** listed ou quoted share; **~ gratuite/ordinaire/nominative/au porteur** free/ ordinary/registered/bearer share; **~ préférentielle** ou **à dividende prioritaire** preference share (Brit), preferred share (US); **~ de chasse** hunting rights; (fig) **ses ~s sont en hausse/ baisse** his stock is rising/falling → **société**

actionnaire [aksjɔnɛʀ] NMF shareholder

actionnariat [aksjɔnaʀja] NM (= détention d'actions) shareholding; (= personnes) shareholders

actionnement [aksjɔnmɑ̃] NM activating, activation

actionner [aksjɔne] ▸ conjug 1 ◂ VT [a] [+ levier, manette] to operate; [+ mécanisme] to activate; [+ machine] to drive, work; **moteur actionné par la vapeur** steam-powered ou -driven engine; **~ la sonnette** to ring the bell [b] (Jur) to sue, bring an action against; **~ qn en dommages et intérêts** to sue sb for damages

activateur, -trice [aktivatœʀ, tʀis] [1] ADJ activating (épith) [2] NM activator

activation [aktivasjɔ̃] NF (Chim, Phys) activation; (Bio) initiation of development

activé, e [aktive] (ptp de **activer**) ADJ (Sci) activated → **charbon**

activement [aktivmɑ̃] ADV actively; **participer ~ à qch** to take an active part ou be actively involved in sth; **le suspect est ~ recherché par la police** a major police search for the suspect is under way

activer [aktive] ▸ conjug 1 ◂ VT [a] (= accélérer) [+ processus, travaux] to speed up; (= aviver) [+ feu] to stoke [b] (Chim) to activate [c] (= actionner) [+ dispositif] to set going; (Ordin) to activate [2] VI (* = se dépêcher) to get a move on*, get moving* [3] **s'activer** VPR (= s'affairer) to bustle about; **s'~ à faire** to be busy doing; **active-toi !*** get a move on!*

activisme [aktivism] NM activism

activiste [aktivist] ADJ, NMF activist

activité [aktivite] NF [a] (= fonctionnement) activity; **l'~ économique** economic activity; (Comm) **cesser ses ~s** to cease trading ou operations; **la concurrence nous a forcé à cesser nos ~s** our competitors have put us out of business; **être en ~** [volcan] to be active; [entreprise] to be trading, be in business; [centrale nucléaire, usine] to function, be in operation; **être en pleine ~** [usine] to be operating at full strength, be in full operation; [personne] to be very busy; (hum) to be hard at it*; **pratiquer une ~ physique régulière** to take regular exercise, exercise regularly; **elle déborde d'~** [personne] she's incredibly active → **rapport, secteur** etc [b] (= occupation rémunérée, passe-temps) activity; **le club propose de multiples ~s culturelles** the club provides a wide range of cultural activities [c] (= emploi) job; **~ professionnelle** occupation; **avoir une ~ salariée** to be in paid ou gainful (frm) employment; **le passage de l'~ à la retraite** the transition from working life to retirement; (Mil) the transfer from the active to the retired list; **en ~** [salarié] working, in

active employment; **le nombre des médecins en ~** the number of practising doctors; **cesser son ~** [salarié] to stop working; [médecin] to stop practising

[d] (= domaine d'intervention) [entreprise] (line of) business; **notre ~ principale est l'informatique** our main line of business is computing; **ils ont étendu leurs ~s à la distribution** they have branched out into distribution

[e] (= animation) [rue, ville] bustle; **les rues sont pleines d'~** the streets are bustling with activity ou are very busy

actrice [aktʀis] NF (Théât, Ciné, fig) actress; **~ de cinéma** film ou movie (US) actress; **~ de théâtre** stage ou theatre actress

actuaire [aktɥɛʀ] NMF actuary

actualisation [aktɥalizasjɔ̃] NF [a] (= mise à jour) [ouvrage, règlement] updating; **ils réclament l'~ du salaire minimum** they are calling for a review of the minimum wage [b] (Fin) [coûts] updated forecast; [somme due] discounting [c] (Ling, Philos) actualization

actualiser [aktɥalize] ▸ conjug 1 ◂ VT [a] (= mettre à jour) [+ ouvrage, règlement] to update, bring up to date; [+ salaires] to review [b] (Fin) [+ coûts] to give an updated forecast of; [+ somme due] to discount; **cash-flow actualisé** discounted cash flow [c] (Ling, Philos) to actualize

actualité [aktɥalite] NF [a] [livre, sujet] topicality; **livre d'~** topical book [b] (= événements) **l'~** current events; **l'~ sportive** the sports news [c] (Ciné, Presse) **les ~s** the news; **il est passé aux ~s*** he was on the news; **~s télévisées/ régionales** television/local ou regional news [d] (Philos) actuality

actuariel, -elle [aktɥaʀjɛl] ADJ actuarial; **taux** ou **rendement ~ brut** gross annual interest yield ou return

actuel, -elle [aktɥɛl] ADJ [a] (= présent) present, current; **à l'heure ~le** at the present time; **à l'époque ~le** nowadays, in this day and age; **le monde ~** the world today, the present-day world; **l'~ Premier ministre** the current Prime Minister [b] (= d'actualité) [livre, problème] topical [c] (Philos, Rel) actual

actuellement [aktɥɛlmɑ̃] ADV at the moment, at present

acuité [akɥite] NF [son] shrillness; [douleur, problème, crise] acuteness; [sens] sharpness, acuteness; **~ visuelle** visual acuity

acuponcteur, acupuncteur [akypɔ̃ktœʀ] NM acupuncturist

acuponcture, acupuncture [akypɔ̃ktyʀ] NF acupuncture

acyclique [asiklik] ADJ (gén) non-cyclical; (Chim) acyclic

a/d (ABRÉV = **à dater, à la date de**) as from

ADAC [adak] NM (ABRÉV = **avion à décollage et atterrissage courts**) STOL

adage¹ [adaʒ] NM (= maxime) adage, saying

adage² [adaʒ] NM (Danse) adagio

adagio [ada(d)ʒjo] NM adagio

Adam [adɑ̃] NM Adam; (hum) **en costume** ou **tenue d'~** in one's birthday suit → **pomme**

adamantin, e [adamɑ̃tɛ̃, in] ADJ (littér) adamantine

adaptabilité [adaptabilite] NF adaptability

adaptable [adaptabl] ADJ adaptable

adaptateur, -trice [adaptatœʀ, tʀis] [1] NM,F (Ciné, Théât) adapter [2] NM (Tech) adapter

adaptatif, -ive [adaptatif, iv] ADJ adaptive; **système d'optique adaptative** adaptive optics system

adaptation [adaptasjɔ̃] NF [a] (gén) adaptation (à to); **faire un effort d'~** to try to adapt; **capacité** ou **faculté d'~** adaptability; **il lui a fallu un certain temps d'~** it took him some time to adapt (pour to) [b] (Ciné, Théât) adaptation; (Mus) arrangement; **~ cinéma-**

tographique/télévisée film ou screen/television adaptation

adapter [adapte] ▸ conjug 1 ◂ [1] VT [a] (= appliquer) **~ une prise/un mécanisme à** to fit a plug/a mechanism to; **~ la musique aux paroles** to fit the music to the words; **le traitement semble bien adapté (à la maladie)** the treatment seems to be appropriate (to the illness); **ces mesures sont-elles bien adaptées à la situation ?** are these measures really suited to the situation? [b] (= modifier) [+ conduite, méthode, organisation] to adapt (à to); [+ roman, pièce] to adapt (pour for) [2] **s'adapter** VPR [a] (= s'habituer) to adapt (o.s.) (à to) [b] (= s'appliquer) [objet, prise] **s'~ à** ou **sur qch** to fit sth

ADAV [adav] NM (ABRÉV = **avion à décollage et atterrissage verticaux**) VTOL

addenda [adɛ̃da] NM INV addenda

Addis Abeba [adisabeba] N Addis Ababa

additif, -ive [aditif, iv] [1] ADJ (Math) additive [2] NM (= note, clause) additional clause, rider; (= substance) additive; **~ budgétaire** supplemental budget; **~ alimentaire** food additive

addition [adisjɔ̃] NF [a] (Math) (gén) addition; (= problème) addition, sum; **faire une ~** to do a sum; **par ~ de** by adding, by the addition of [b] (= facture) bill, check (US); **payer** ou **régler l'~** (lit) to pay ou settle the bill; (fig) to pick up the tab; (fig) **l'~ va être lourde** the cost will be high

additionnel, -elle [adisjɔnɛl] ADJ additional → **centime**

additionner [adisjɔne] ▸ conjug 1 ◂ [1] VT (lit, fig) to add up; **~ qch à** to add sth to; **~ le vin de sucre** to add sugar to the wine, mix sugar with the wine; (sur étiquette) **additionné d'alcool** with alcohol added [2] **s'additionner** VPR to add up

additionneur [adisjɔnœʀ] NM adder (machine)

additivé, e [aditive] ADJ [carburant] high-octane (épith)

adducteur [adyktœʀ] ADJ M, NM (canal) **~** feeder (canal); (muscle) **~** adductor

adduction [adyksjɔ̃] NF (Anat) adduction; (Tech) **~ d'eau** water conveyance; **travaux d'~ d'eau** laying on water

Adélaïde [adelaid] NF Adelaïde

ADEME [adɛm] NF (ABRÉV = **Agence de l'environnement et de la maîtrise de l'énergie**) → **agence**

Aden [adɛn] N Aden

adénine [adenin] NF adenine

adénome [adenom] NM adenoma

adénosine [adenozin] NF adenosine

adénovirus [adenoviʀys] NM adenovirus

adepte [adɛpt] NMF (doctrine, mouvement) follower; (activité) enthusiast; **faire des ~s** to gain followers; **les ~s du deltaplane** hang-gliding enthusiasts

adéquat, e [adekwa(t), at] ADJ (gén) appropriate, suitable, fitting; (Gram) adequate; **utiliser le vocabulaire ~** to use the appropriate vocabulary; **ces installations ne sont pas ~es** these facilities are not suitable

adéquation [adekwasjɔ̃] NF appropriateness; [grammaire] adequacy

adhérence [adeʀɑ̃s] NF (gén) adhesion (à to); [pneus, semelles] grip (à on), adhesion (à to); [voiture] **~ (à la route)** roadholding

adhérent, e [adeʀɑ̃, ɑ̃t] [1] ADJ [pays] member (épith); **les pays ~s** the member nations; **les personnes non ~es à l'association** non-members of the association [2] NM,F member; **carte d'~** membership card

adhérer [adeʀe] ▸ conjug 6 ◂ ♦ **adhérer à** VT INDIR [a] (= coller) to stick to, adhere to; **~ à la route** [pneu] to grip the road; [voiture] to hold the road; **ça adhère bien** it sticks ou adheres well, it holds the road well [b] (= se rallier à)

[+ *plan, projet*] to subscribe to; [+ *traité*] to adhere to; [+ *point de vue*] to support, subscribe to; [+ *idéal, philosophie*] to adhere to [c] (= *devenir membre de*) to join; (= *être membre de*) to be a member of, belong to

adhésif, -ive [adezif, iv] [1] ADJ adhesive, sticky; **pansement ~** sticking plaster (*Brit*), Band-Aid® (*US*); **papier ~** sticky(-backed) paper [2] NM adhesive

adhésion [adezjɔ̃] NF [a] (= *accord*) support (**à** for), adherence (**à** to); **leur ~ au traité** their adherence to the treaty [b] (= *inscription*) joining; (= *fait d'être membre*) membership (**à** of); **son ~ au club** his joining the club; **ils ont demandé leur ~ à l'UE** they've applied to join the EU, they've applied for EU membership; **bulletin/campagne d'~** membership form/drive; **il y a 3 nouvelles ~s cette semaine** 3 new members joined this week, there have been 3 new memberships this week

ad hoc [adɔk] ADJ INV [a] (= *approprié*) [*formation, méthode, solution*] appropriate; **c'est l'homme ~** he's just the man we need; **j'ai trouvé le lieu ~ pour la réception** I've found the ideal *ou* the perfect place for the reception [b] [*organisme, mission*] ad hoc; **commission ~** ad hoc committee

adieu (*pl* **adieux**) [adjø] [1] NM [a] (= *salut*) goodbye, farewell (*littér*); **dire ~ à** to say goodbye to; **d'~** [*repas, visite*] farewell (*épith*); **baiser d'~** parting *ou* farewell kiss; **tu peux dire ~ à ta sieste !** you can forget about your nap!; **tu peux dire ~ à ton argent !** you can kiss your money goodbye!* [b] (= *séparation*) **~x** farewells; **faire ses ~x (à qn)** to say one's farewells (to sb); **il a fait ses ~x à la scène/au journalisme** he bade farewell to the stage/to journalism [2] EXCL (= *au revoir*) goodbye, farewell (*littér*); (*dial* = *bonjour*) hello, hi*; **~ la tranquillité/les vacances** goodbye to (our) peace and quiet/our holidays

à-Dieu-va(t) [adjøva(t)] EXCL it's all in God's hands!

adipeux, -euse [adipø, øz] ADJ (*Anat*) adipose; [*visage*] fleshy

adiposité [adipozite] NF adiposity

adjacent, e [adʒasɑ̃, ɑ̃t] ADJ adjacent, adjoining; **~ à** adjacent to, adjoining → **angle**

adjectif, -ive [adʒɛktif, iv] [1] ADJ adjectival, adjective (*épith*) [2] NM adjective; **~ substantivé/qualificatif** nominalized/qualifying adjective; **~ attribut/épithète** predicative/attributive adjective; **~ verbal** verbal adjective

adjectival, e (*mpl* **-aux**) [adʒɛktival, o] ADJ adjectival; **locution ~e** adjectival phrase

adjectivé, e [adʒɛktive] ADJ used as an adjective

adjectivement [adʒɛktivmɑ̃] ADV adjectivally, as an adjective

adjoindre [adʒwɛ̃dʀ] ▸ *conjug 49* ◂ VT [a] (= *associer*) **~ un collaborateur à qn** to appoint sb as an assistant to sb; **~ qn à une équipe** to give sb a place in a team; **s'~ un collaborateur** to take on *ou* appoint an assistant [b] (= *ajouter*) **~ une pièce/un dispositif à qch** to attach *ou* affix a part/device to sth; **~ un chapitre à un ouvrage** to add a chapter to a book; (*à la fin*) to append a chapter to a book; **à ces difficultés est venu s'~ un nouveau problème** in addition to all these difficulties there was now a new problem

adjoint, e [adʒwɛ̃, wɛ̃t] (*ptp de* **adjoindre**) [1] ADJ assistant; **commissaire/directeur ~** assistant commissioner/manager [2] NM,F deputy, assistant; **~ au maire** deputy mayor; **~ d'enseignement** non-certificated teacher (*with tenure*) [3] NM (*Ling*) adjunct

adjonction [adʒɔ̃ksjɔ̃] NF [a] (= *action*) [*collaborateur, produit, bâtiment*] addition (**à** to); [*article, chapitre*] addition; (*à la fin*) appending (**à** to); [*dispositif*] attaching, affixing

(**à** to); **l'~ de deux secrétaires à l'équipe** the addition of two secretaries to the team, the appointment of two extra *ou* additional secretaries to the team; **produits sans ~ de colorant/sel** products with no added colouring/salt [b] (= *chose ajoutée*) addition

adjudant [adʒydɑ̃] NM (*gén*) warrant officer; (*Aviat US*) senior master sergeant; **~ chef** warrant officer 1st class (*Brit*), chief warrant officer (*US*)

adjudicataire [adʒydikatɛʀ] NMF (*aux enchères*) purchaser; (= *soumissionnaire*) successful bidder

adjudicateur, -trice [adʒydikatœʀ, tʀis] NM,F [*enchères*] seller; [*contrat*] awarder

adjudication [adʒydikasjɔ̃] NF [a] (= *vente aux enchères*) sale by auction; (= *marché administratif*) invitation to tender, putting up for tender; (= *contrat*) contract; **par (voie d')~** by auction, by tender; **mettre en vente par ~** to put up for sale by auction; **offrir par ~** to put up for tender; **~ forcée** compulsory sale [b] (= *attribution*) [*contrat*] awarding (**à** to); [*meuble, tableau*] auctioning (**à** to)

adjuger [adʒyʒe] ▸ *conjug 3* ◂ [1] VT [a] (*aux enchères*) to knock down, auction (**à** to); **une fois, deux fois, trois fois, adjugé(, vendu) !** going, going, gone!; **le document a été adjugé pour 3 000 F** the document went for *ou* was sold for 3,000 francs [b] (= *attribuer*) [+ *contrat, avantage, récompense*] to award; (* = *donner*) [+ *place, objet*] to give [2] **s'adjuger** VPR (= *obtenir*) [+ *contrat, récompense*] to win; (*Sport*) [+ *place, titre*] to win; (= *s'approprier*) to take for o.s.; **il s'est adjugé la meilleure place** he has taken the best seat for himself, he has given himself the best seat; **ils se sont adjugé 24% du marché** they have taken over *ou* cornered 24% of the market; **leur parti s'est adjugé 60% des sièges** their party have won *ou* carried off 60% of the seats

adjuration [adʒyʀasjɔ̃] NF entreaty, plea

adjurer [adʒyʀe] ▸ *conjug 1* ◂ VT **~ qn de faire** to implore *ou* beg sb to do

adjuvant [adʒyvɑ̃] NM (= *médicament*) adjuvant; (= *additif*) additive; (= *stimulant*) stimulant; (*Ling*) adjunct

ad lib(itum) [adlib(itɔm)] ADV ad lib

admettre [admɛtʀ] ▸ *conjug 56* ◂ VT [a] (= *laisser entrer*) [+ *visiteur, démarcheur*] to admit, let in; **la salle ne pouvait ~ que 50 personnes** the room could only accommodate *ou* seat 50 people; **les chiens ne sont pas admis dans le magasin** dogs are not allowed in the shop; (*sur écriteau*) no dogs (allowed); **il fut admis dans une grande pièce** he was ushered *ou* shown *ou* admitted into a large room; (*Tech*) **l'air/le liquide est admis dans le cylindre** the air/the liquid is allowed to pass into the cylinder

[b] (= *recevoir*) [+ *hôte*] to receive; [+ *nouveau membre*] to admit; (*à l'hôpital*) to admit; **~ qn à sa table** to receive sb at one's table; **il a été admis chez le ministre** he was received by the minister, he was admitted to see the minister; **se faire ~ dans un club** to gain admittance to *ou* be admitted to a club

[c] (*Scol, Univ*) (*à un examen*) to pass; (*dans une classe*) to admit, accept; **ils ont admis 30 candidats** they passed 30 of the candidates; **il a été admis au concours** he passed *ou* got through the exam; **il a été admis dans un bon rang au concours** he came out well in *ou* got a good place in the exam; **il a/il n'a pas été admis en classe supérieure** he will move up into *ou* he will be admitted to/he didn't get into *ou* won't be admitted to the next class; **lire la liste des admis au concours** to read the list of successful candidates in the exam

[d] (= *convenir de*) [+ *défaite, erreur*] to admit, acknowledge; **il n'admet jamais ses torts** he never accepts *ou* admits he's in the wrong; **je suis prêt à ~ que vous aviez raison** I'm ready

to accept *ou* admit *ou* concede that you were right; **il est admis que** c'est chose admise **que** it's an accepted *ou* acknowledged fact that, it's generally admitted that; **admettons !** (*pour concéder*) if you say so!; **admettons qu'il ne l'ait pas fait exprès** let's say he didn't do it on purpose

[e] (= *accepter*) [+ *excuses, raisons, thèse*] to accept; (*Jur*) [+ *pourvoi*] to accept

[f] (= *supposer*) to suppose, assume; **en admettant que** supposing *ou* assuming that; **admettons qu'elle soit venue** let's suppose *ou* assume that she came

[g] (= *tolérer*) [+ *ton, attitude, indiscipline*] to allow, accept; **je n'admets pas qu'il se conduise ainsi** I won't allow *ou* permit him to behave like that, I won't stand for *ou* accept such behaviour (from him); (*Admin*) **~ qn à siéger** to admit sb (*as a new member*); (*Admin*) **admis à faire valoir ses droits à la retraite** entitled to retire

[h] (= *laisser place à*) to admit of; **ton qui n'admet pas de réplique** tone (of voice) which brooks no reply; **règle qui n'admet aucune exception** rule which allows of *ou* admits of no exception; **règle qui admet plusieurs exceptions** rule which allows for several exceptions

administrateur, -trice [administʀatœʀ, tʀis] NM,F (*gén*) administrator; [*banque, entreprise*] director; [*fondation*] trustee; **~ de biens** property manager; **~ judiciaire** receiver; **~ civil** high-ranking civil servant acting as aide to a minister

administratif, -ive [administʀatif, iv] ADJ administrative

administration [administʀasjɔ̃] NF [a] (= *gestion*) [*affaires, entreprise*] management, running; [*fondation*] administration; [*pays*] running, government; [*commune*] running; **je laisse l'~ de mes affaires à mon notaire** I leave my lawyer to deal with my affairs, I leave my affairs in the hands of my lawyer; **~ légale** guardianship; [*société*] **être placé sous ~ judiciaire** to go into receivership; **la ville a été mise sous ~ de l'ONU** the town has been placed under UN administration → **conseil** [b] [*médicament, sacrement*] administering, administration

[c] (= *service public*) (sector of the) public services; **l'Administration** ≈ the Civil Service; **l'~ locale** local government; **être** *ou* **travailler dans l'~** to work in the public services; **l'~ des Douanes** the Customs Service; **l'~ des Eaux et Forêts** ≈ the Forestry Commission (*Brit*), ≈ the Forestry Service (*US*); **l'~ fiscale** ◊ **l'~ des Impôts** the tax department, ≈ the Inland Revenue (*Brit*), ≈ the Internal Revenue (*US*); (*Police*) **l'~ centrale** police headquarters; **l'~ pénitentiaire** the prison authorities

[d] (= *gouvernement*) administration; **l'~ Carter** the Carter administration

administrativement [administʀativmɑ̃] ADV administratively; **interné ~** formally committed (to a psychiatric hospital), sectioned (*Brit*)

administré, e [administʀe] NM,F [*maire*] citizen; **informer ses ~s** to notify *ou* inform one's town (*ou* city)

administrer [administʀe] ▸ *conjug 1* ◂ VT [a] (= *gérer*) [+ *affaires, entreprise*] to manage, run; [+ *fondation*] to administer; [+ *pays*] to run, govern; [+ *commune*] to run [b] (= *dispenser*) [+ *justice, remède, sacrement*] to administer; [+ *coup, gifle*] to deal, administer; (*Jur*) [+ *preuve*] to produce

admirable [admiʀabl] ADJ admirable, wonderful; **être ~ de courage** to show admirable *ou* wonderful courage; **portrait ~ de vérité** portrait showing a wonderful likeness

admirablement [admiʀabləmɑ̃] ADV admirably, wonderfully

admirateur, -trice [admiʀatœʀ, tʀis] NM,F admirer

admiratif, -ive [admiratif, iv] ADJ admiring; **d'un air ~** admiringly

admiration [admirasjɔ̃] NF admiration; **faire l'~ de qn** ◊ **remplir qn d'~** to fill sb with admiration; **tomber/être en ~ devant qch/qn** to be filled with/lost in admiration for sth/sb

admirativement [admirativmɑ̃] ADV admiringly, in admiration

▼ **admirer** [admire] ▶ conjug 1 ◀ VT to admire; (iro) to marvel at

admissibilité [admisibilite] NF [postulant] eligibility (à for); (Scol, Univ) eligibility to sit the oral part of an exam

admissible [admisibl] [1] ADJ [a] [procédé] admissible, acceptable; [excuse] acceptable; **ce comportement n'est pas ~** this behaviour is quite inadmissible ou unacceptable [b] [postulant] eligible (à for); (Scol, Univ) eligible to sit the oral part of an exam [2] NMF eligible candidate

admission [admisjɔ̃] NF [a] (dans un lieu, club) admission, admittance, entry (à to); (Univ) **il a appris son ~ au concours** he found out that he had passed the exam; **son ~ (au club) a été obtenue non sans mal** he had some difficulty in gaining admission ou entry (to the club); **faire une demande d'~ à un club** to apply to join ou make an application to join a club, apply for membership of a club; (Douane) **~ temporaire d'un véhicule** temporary importation of a vehicle; **le nombre des ~s au concours** the number of successful candidates in the exam [b] (Tech = introduction) intake; (Aut) induction → **soupape**

admonestation [admɔnɛstasjɔ̃] NF (littér) admonition, admonishment

admonester [admɔnɛste] ▶ conjug 1 ◀ VT (gén, Jur) to admonish

admonition [admɔnisjɔ̃] NF (littér, Jur) admonition, admonishment

ADN [ɑdeɛn] NM (ABRÉV = **acide désoxyribonucléique**) DNA

adnominal, e (mpl -aux) [adnɔminal, o] ADJ (Ling) adnominal

ado* [ado] NMF (ABRÉV = **adolescent, e**) teenager, teen* (US)

adobe [adɔb] NM adobe

adolescence [adɔlesɑ̃s] NF adolescence; **ses années d'~** his adolescent ou teenage years

adolescent, e [adɔlesɑ̃, ɑ̃t] [1] ADJ (littér) adolescent (épith) [2] NM,F adolescent, teenager; (Méd, Psych) adolescent

Adonis [adɔnis] NM (Myth, fig) Adonis

adonner (s') [adɔne] ▶ conjug 1 ◀ **s'adonner à** VPR [+ art] to devote o.s. to; [+ études] to give o.s. over to, devote o.s. to; [+ sport, passe-temps] to devote o.s. to, go in for; [+ pratiques] to indulge in; **il s'adonnait à la boisson/au jeu** he was a confirmed drinker/gambler; **venez vous ~ aux joies du ski** come and experience the joys of skiing

adoptable [adɔptabl] ADJ [enfant] eligible for adoption; [mesure] that can be adopted

adoptant, e [adɔptɑ̃, ɑ̃t] NM,F person wishing to adopt

adopter [adɔpte] ▶ conjug 1 ◀ VT [a] (Jur) [+ enfant] to adopt [b] (= accueillir, accepter) [+ personne, animal] to adopt; **elle a su se faire ~ par ses nouveaux collègues** she's managed to gain acceptance with her new colleagues [c] [+ attitude, religion, nom, mesure] to adopt; [+ cause] to take up, adopt; **« l'essayer c'est l'~ ! »** "try it - you'll love it!" [d] [+ loi] to pass; [+ motion] to pass, adopt; **cette proposition a été adoptée à l'unanimité** the proposal was carried unanimously

adoptif, -ive [adɔptif, iv] ADJ enfant ~ (gén) adoptive child; (dans une famille d'accueil) ≈ foster child; **parent ~** (gén) adoptive parent; (= nourricier) ≈ foster parent

adoption [adɔpsjɔ̃] NF [a] [enfant] adoption; **~ plénière** adoption; **~ simple** ≈ fostering; **pays d'~** country of adoption; **un Londonien d'~** a Londoner by adoption [b] [attitude, religion, nom, mesure, cause] adoption [c] [loi] passing; [motion] passing, adoption

adorable [adɔrabl] ADJ [personne] adorable, delightful; [robe, village] lovely, delightful

adorablement [adɔrabləmɑ̃] ADV delightfully, adorably

adorateur, -trice [adɔratœr, tris] NM,F (Rel, fig) worshipper

adoration [adɔrasjɔ̃] NF adoration, worship; **être en ~ devant** to dote on, worship, idolize

▼ **adorer** [adɔre] ▶ conjug 1 ◀ VT [+ personne, dieu] to adore, worship; [+ chose] to adore → **brûler**

adosser [adose] ▶ conjug 1 ◀ [1] VT **~ à** ou **contre qch** [+ meuble] to stand against sth; [+ échelle] to stand ou lean against sth; [+ bâtiment] to build against ou onto sth; **~ un crédit à une hypothèque/un contrat d'assurance-vie** to secure a loan with a mortgage/a life-insurance policy [2] **s'adosser** VPR **s'~ à** ou **contre qch** [personne] to lean back against sth; [bâtiment] to be built against ou onto sth, back onto sth; **il était adossé au pilier** he was leaning back against the pillar; **le village est adossé à la montagne** the village is built right up against the mountain

adoubement [adubmɑ̃] NM (Hist) dubbing

adouber [adube] ▶ conjug 1 ◀ VT (Hist) to dub; (Dames, Échecs) to adjust

adoucir [adusir] ▶ conjug 2 ◀ [1] VT [a] [+ saveur, acidité] to make milder ou smoother; (avec sucre) to sweeten; [+ rudesse, voix, peau] to soften; [+ couleur, contraste] to soften, tone down; [+ caractère, personne] to mellow; [+ chagrin] to soothe, allay, ease; [+ conditions pénibles, épreuve, solitude] to ease; [+ dureté, remarque] to mitigate, soften; **cette coiffure lui adoucit le visage** that hairstyle softens her features; **pour ~ ses vieux jours** to comfort him in his old age; **le vent du sud a adouci la température** the south wind has made the weather milder; **~ la condamnation de qn** to reduce sb's sentence → **musique** [b] (Tech) [+ eau, métal] to soften [2] **s'adoucir** VPR [voix, couleur, peau] to soften; [caractère, personne] to mellow; **la température s'est adoucie** the weather has got milder

adoucissant, e [adusisɑ̃, ɑ̃t] [1] ADJ [crème, lotion] for smoother skin; [sirop] soothing [2] NM fabric softener, fabric conditioner

adoucissement [adusismɑ̃] NM [a] [saveur, acidité] (avec sucre) sweetening; [rudesse, voix, peau] softening; [couleur, contraste] softening, toning-down; [caractère, personne] mellowing; [chagrin] soothing, allaying, easing; [conditions pénibles, épreuve] easing; [dureté, remarque] softening; **on espère un ~ de la température** we are hoping for milder weather; **apporter des ~s aux conditions de vie des prisonniers** to make the living conditions of the prisoners easier ou less harsh [b] (Tech) [eau, métal] softening

adoucisseur [adusisœr] NM **~ (d'eau)** water softener

ad patres* [adpatrɛs] ADV (hum) **expédier** ou **envoyer qn ~** to send sb to kingdom come*

adrénaline [adrenalin] NF adrenaline

adressage [adresaʒ] NM [courrier] mailing; (Ordin) addressing; **mode d'~** addressing mode

▼ **adresse¹** [adrɛs] NF [a] (= domicile) address; **partir sans laisser d'~** to leave without giving a forwarding address; **je connais quelques bonnes ~s de restaurants** I know some good restaurants to go to; **c'est une/la bonne ~ pour les chaussures** it's a good place/the place to go for shoes → **carnet, tromper** [b] (frm = message) address [c] (Ordin, Ling) address; **(mot) ~** [dictionnaire] headword; **~ électronique** e-mail

address [d] **à l'~ de** (= à l'intention de) for the benefit of

adresse² [adrɛs] NF (= habileté) deftness, dexterity, skill; (= subtilité, finesse) shrewdness, skill, cleverness; (= tact) adroitness; **jeu/exercice d'~** game/exercise of skill; **il eut l'~ de ne rien révéler** he was adroit enough ou shrewd enough not to say anything → **tour**

▼ **adresser** [adrese] ▶ conjug 1 ◀ [1] VT [a] **~ une lettre/un colis à** (= envoyer) to send a letter/parcel to; (= écrire l'adresse) to address a letter/parcel to; **la lettre m'était personnellement adressée** the letter was addressed to me personally; **mon médecin m'a adressé à un spécialiste** my doctor sent ou referred me to a specialist [b] **~ une remarque/une requête à** to address a remark/a request to; **~ une accusation/un reproche à** to level an accusation/a reproach at ou against; **~ une allusion/un coup à** to aim a remark/a blow at; **~ un compliment/ses respects à** to pay a compliment/one's respects to; **~ une prière à** to address a prayer to; (à Dieu) to offer (up) a prayer to; **~ un regard furieux à qn** to direct an angry look at sb; **il m'adressa un signe de tête/un geste de la main** he nodded/waved at me; **~ un sourire à qn** to give sb a smile, smile at sb; **~ la parole à qn** to speak to sb; **il m'adressa une critique acerbe** he criticized me harshly; (sur lettre) **je vous adresse mes meilleurs vœux** please accept my best wishes [c] (Ordin) to address [2] **s'adresser** VPR [a] (= parler à) **s'~ à qn** [personne] to speak to sb, address sb; [remarque] to be aimed at sb; **il s'adresse à un public féminin** [discours, magazine] it is intended for ou aimed at a female audience; [auteur] he writes for ou is addressing a female readership; **ce livre s'adresse à notre générosité** this book appeals to our generosity; **et cela s'adresse aussi à vous !** and that goes for you too! [b] (= aller trouver) **s'~ à** [+ personne] to go and see; (Admin) [+ personne, bureau] to apply to; **adressez-vous au concierge** go and see (ou ask, tell etc) the concierge; **adressez-vous au secrétariat** enquire at the office, go and ask at the office; (hum) **il vaut mieux s'~ à Dieu qu'à ses saints** it's best to go straight to the top

adret [adrɛ] NM (Géog) south-facing slope

Adriatique [adrijatik] ADJ F, NF (mer) **~** Adriatic (Sea)

adroit, e [adrwa, wat] ADJ (= habile) skilful, deft; (= subtil) clever, shrewd; (= plein de tact) adroit; **~ de ses mains** clever with one's hands; **c'était très ~ de sa part** it was very clever ou shrewd of him

adroitement [adrwatmɑ̃] ADV (= habilement) skilfully, deftly; (= subtilement) cleverly, shrewdly; (= avec tact) adroitly

adsorber [atsɔrbe] ▶ conjug 1 ◀ VT to adsorb

adsorption [atsɔrpsjɔ̃] NF adsorption

adulateur, -trice [adylatœr, tris] NM,F (littér) (= admirateur) adulator; (= flatteur) sycophant

adulation [adylasjɔ̃] NF (littér) (= admiration) adulation; (= flatterie) sycophancy

aduler [adyle] ▶ conjug 1 ◀ VT (littér) (= admirer) to adulate; (= flatter) to flatter

adulte [adylt] [1] ADJ [personne] adult (épith); [animal, plante] fully-grown, mature; (= mûr) [attitude, comportement] adult, mature → **âge** [2] NMF adult, grown-up

adultère [adyltɛr] [1] ADJ [relations, désir] adulterous; **femme ~** adulteress; **homme ~** adulterer [2] NM (acte) adultery → **constat**

adultérin, e [adylterɛ̃, in] ADJ (Jur) [enfant] born of adultery

ad valorem [advalɔrɛm] LOC ADJ ad valorem

advenir [advənir] ▶ conjug 22 ◀ [1] VB IMPERS [a] (= survenir) **~ que ...** to happen that ..., come to pass that ... (littér); **~ à** to happen to,

---

befall (littér); **qu'est-il advenu au prisonnier?** what has happened to the prisoner?; **il m'advient de faire** I sometimes happen to do; **advienne que pourra** come what may; **quoi qu'il advienne** whatever happens ou may happen **b** (= devenir, résulter de) **~ de** to become of; **qu'est-il advenu du prisonnier/du projet?** what has become of the prisoner/the project?; **on ne sait pas ce qu'il en adviendra** nobody knows what will come of it ou how it will turn out **2** VI (= arriver) to happen

adventice [advãtis] ADJ (Bot) self-propagating; (Philos, littér = accessoire) adventitious

adventif, -ive [advãtif, iv] ADJ (Bot) [bourgeon, racine] adventitious

adventiste [advãtist] ADJ, NMF Adventist

adverbe [advɛʁb] NM adverb

adverbial, e (mpl -iaux) [advɛʁbjal, jo] ADJ adverbial

adverbialement [advɛʁbjalmã] ADV adverbially

adversaire [advɛʁsɛʁ] NMF (gén) opponent, adversary; (Mil) adversary, enemy; [théorie, traité] opponent (de of); **il ne faut pas sous-estimer l'~** (gén) you shouldn't underestimate your opponent ou your adversary; (Mil) you shouldn't underestimate the enemy

adversatif, -ive [advɛʁsatif, iv] ADJ, NM adversative

adverse [advɛʁs] ADJ [partie, forces, bloc] opposing; (littér) **la fortune ~** adverse fortune; (Jur) **la partie ~** the other side

adversité [advɛʁsite] NF adversity

ad vitam æternam* [advitametɛʁnam] LOC ADV till kingdom come

AE [ɑə] **1** NM (ABRÉV = **adjoint d'enseignement**) → **adjoint 2** NFPL (ABRÉV = **affaires étrangères**) → **affaire**

aède [aɛd] NM (Greek) bard

AELE [aaɛlə] NF (ABRÉV = **Association euro-péenne de libre-échange**) EFTA

aérage [aeʁaʒ] NM ventilation

aérateur [aeʁatœʁ] NM ventilator

aération [aeʁasjɔ̃] NF [pièce, literie] airing; [terre, racine] aeration; (= circulation d'air) ventilation → **conduit**

aéré, e [aeʁe] (ptp de **aérer**) ADJ [pièce] airy, well-ventilated; [page] well spaced out → **centre**

aérer [aeʁe] ▸conjug 6◂ **1** VT [+ pièce, literie] to air; [+ terre, racine] to aerate; (= alléger) [+ exposé, présentation] to lighten **2** **s'aérer** VPR [personne] to get some fresh air

aérien, -ienne [aeʁjɛ̃, jɛn] **1** ADJ **a** (Aviat) [espace, droit] air (épith); [navigation, photographie] aerial (épith); [attaque] aerial (épith); air (épith); **base aérienne** air base → **compagnie, ligne, métro b** (= léger) [silhouette] sylphlike; [démarche] light; [musique, poésie] ethereal **c** (Bot) [racine] aerial; (Téléc) [circuit, câble] overhead (épith); (Géog) [courant, mouvement] air (épith) **2** NM (Radio = antenne) aerial

aérium [aeʁjɔm] NM sanatorium, sanitarium (US)

aérobic [aeʁɔbik] NF aerobics sg

aérobie [aeʁɔbi] ADJ aerobic

aérobiologie [aeʁɔbjɔlɔʒi] NF aerobiology

aéro-club (pl aéro-clubs) [aeʁɔklœb] NM flying club

aérodrome [aeʁɔdʁom] NM airfield, aerodrome (Brit), airdrome (US)

aérodynamique [aeʁodinamik] **1** ADJ [expérience] aerodynamics (épith); [ligne, véhicule] streamlined, aerodynamic; **soufflerie ~** wind tunnel **2** NF aerodynamics sg

aérodynamisme [aeʁodinamism] NM aerodynamic shape

aérofrein [aeʁofʁɛ̃] NM air brake

aérogare [aeʁogaʁ] NF (air) terminal

aéroglisseur [aeʁoglisœʁ] NM hovercraft

aérogramme [aeʁogʁam] NM airmail letter

aérographe [aeʁogʁaf] NM airbrush

aérolit(h)e [aeʁɔlit] NM aerolite, aerolith

aéromobile [aeʁomɔbil] ADJ airborne

aéromodélisme [aeʁomɔdelism] NM model aircraft making

aéronaute [aeʁonot] NMF aeronaut

aéronautique [aeʁonotik] **1** ADJ [équipement, ingénieur] aeronautical; **construction/constructeur** ~ aircraft construction/constructor; **l'industrie** ~ the aviation ou aeronautics industry; **entreprise** ou **société** ~ aviation company, aeronautics firm **2** NF aeronautics sg

aéronaval, e (pl **aéronavals**) [aeʁonaval] **1** ADJ **forces ~es** air and sea forces, naval aviation forces; **groupe** ~ naval aviation unit; **base ~e** naval airbase **2** **aéronavale** NF **l'aéronavale** ≈ the Fleet Air Arm (Brit), ≈ Naval Aviation (US)

aéronef [aeʁonɛf] NM (Admin) aircraft

aérophagie [aeʁofaʒi] NF **il a** ou **fait de l'~** he suffers from abdominal wind

aéroplane† [aeʁoplan] NM aeroplane (Brit), airplane (US)

aéroport [aeʁopɔʁ] NM airport

aéroporté, e [aeʁopɔʁte] ADJ [opération, division, troupes] airborne; [matériel] airlifted, brought ou ferried by air (attrib); [missile] air-launched

aéroportuaire [aeʁopɔʁtɥeʁ] ADJ [installations, autorités] airport (épith)

aéropostal, e (mpl -aux) [aeʁopɔstal, o] **1** ADJ (air) airmail (épith) **2** **Aéropostale** NF **l'Aéropostale** (Hist) the (French) airmail service

aérosol [aeʁosɔl] NM aerosol; **bombe ~** spray ou aerosol can; **déodorant/peinture en ~** spray deodorant/paint

aérospatial, e (mpl -iaux) [aeʁospasjal, jo] **1** ADJ aerospace (épith) **2** **aérospatiale** NF aerospace science

aérostat [aeʁosta] NM aerostat

aérostatique [aeʁostatik] **1** ADJ aerostatic **2** NF aerostatics sg

aérotrain® [aeʁotʁɛ̃] NM hovertrain

AF [ɑɛf] NF (ABRÉV = **allocations familiales**) → **allocation**

AFAT [afat] NF (ABRÉV = **auxiliaire féminin de l'armée de terre**) member of the women's army

affabilité [afabilite] NF affability

affable [afabl] ADJ affable

affablement [afabləmã] ADV affably

affabulateur, -trice [afabylatœʁ, tʁis] NM,F inveterate liar, storyteller

affabulation [afabylasjɔ̃] NF **a** (= mensonges) **c'est de l'~** ◊ **ce sont des ~s** it's all made up, it's pure fabrication **b** [roman] (construction of) plot

affabuler [afabyle] ▸conjug 1◂ VI to invent ou make up stories

affacturage [afaktyʁaʒ] NM (Jur) factoring

affactureur [afaktyʁœʁ] NM (Jur) factor

affadir [afadiʁ] ▸conjug 2◂ **1** VT [+ aliment] to make tasteless ou insipid; [+ couleur] to make dull; [+ style] to make dull ou uninteresting **2** **s'affadir** VPR [couleur] to become dull; [style] to become dull, pall; [aliment] to lose its flavour (Brit) ou flavor (US), become tasteless ou insipid

affadissement [afadismã] NM [aliment] loss of flavour (Brit) ou flavor (US) (de in, from); [saveur, style] weakening (de of); [couleurs, sensations] dulling (de of)

affaiblir [afebliʁ] ▸conjug 2◂ **1** VT (gén) to weaken **2** **s'affaiblir** VPR [personne, autorité, résolution] to weaken, grow ou become weaker; [facultés] to deteriorate; [vue] to grow dim ou weaker; [son] to fade (away), grow fainter; [intérêt] to wane; [vent] to abate, die down; [monnaie] to weaken; **le sens de ce mot s'est affaibli** the word has lost much of its meaning; **utiliser un mot dans son sens affaibli** to use the weaker meaning of a word

affaiblissement [afeblismã] NM [personne, autorité, résolution] weakening; [facultés] deterioration; [bruit] fading (away); [monnaie] weakening; [intérêt] waning; **l'~ de notre pays au plan international** our country's waning influence on the international scene; **on note un ~ progressif des syndicats** the power of the unions is gradually weakening; **l'~ des valeurs morales** the sharp decline in ou deterioration of moral values

affaire [afɛʁ]

| **1** NOM FÉMININ | **3** COMPOSÉS |
| **2** NOM FÉMININ PL | |

1 NOM FÉMININ

a = problème, question matter, business; **j'ai une ~ urgente à régler** I've got (some) urgent business to deal with, I've got an urgent matter to settle; **ce n'est pas une petite** ou **une mince ~** it's no small matter; **ce n'est pas une petite ~ de le faire obéir** getting him to obey is no easy matter ou no mean task; **l'amour, c'est la grande ~ de sa vie** love is the most important thing in his life; **j'en fais une ~ de principe** it's a matter of principle (for me); **c'est une ~ de goût/de mode** it's a matter of taste/fashion; **le sport ne devrait pas être une ~ d'argent** sport shouldn't be about money; **c'est une ~ d'hommes** it's men's business; **c'est l'~ d'un spécialiste** it's a job for a specialist; **c'est mon ~, pas la tienne** it's my business ou affair, not yours; **ce n'est pas ton ~** it's none of your business; **comment je fais? — c'est ton ~!** what do I do? — that's YOUR problem!; **j'en fais mon ~** I'll deal with it, leave it to me; **il en a fait une ~ personnelle** he took it personally; **avec les ordinateurs, il est à son ~** when it comes to computers, he knows what he's about* ou he knows his stuff*; **dans les soirées, il est à son ~** he's in his element at parties; **il en a fait toute une ~** he made a dreadful fuss about it, he made a great song and dance about it; (aller à Glasgow,) **c'est toute une ~** it's quite a business (getting to Glasgow); **c'est une autre ~** that's quite another matter ou a different kettle of fish; **c'est l'~ de quelques minutes/quelques clous** it's a matter of a few minutes/a few nails, it'll only take a few minutes/a few nails; **le temps/l'âge ne fait rien à l'~** time/age has got nothing to do with it; **en voilà une ~!** what a (complicated) business!; **ce n'est pas une ~!** it's no big deal!, it's nothing to get worked up about!*; **quelle ~!** what a carry-on!*; **la belle ~!** big deal!, so what?; **tirer** ou **sortir qn de l'~** to help sb out, get sb out of a tight spot*; **ce médecin m'a tiré d'~** this doctor pulled me through; **il est tiré** ou **sorti d'~** (après une maladie) he's pulled through; (après des ennuis) he's got over it; **il est assez grand pour se tirer d'~ tout seul** he's big enough to manage on his own ou to sort it out by himself

b = ce qui convient **j'ai ton ~** I've got (just) what you want; **cet employé fera/ne fait pas l'~** this employee will do nicely/won't do (for the job); **ça fait mon ~** that's (just) what I want ou need; **cela fera bien l'~ de quelqu'un** that will (certainly) come in handy ou do nicely for somebody; **faire son ~ à qn** (= le malmener) to give sb a beating*; (= le tuer) to do sb in* → **connaître**

c = ensemble de faits connus du public affair; (= scandale) scandal; (= crise) crisis; **l'~ Dreyfus** the Dreyfus affair; **l'~ des otages** the hostage crisis; **l'~ du sang contaminé** the contaminated blood scandal ou affair; **la population est révoltée par les ~s** the country is up in arms over the scandals; **une grave ~ de corruption/**

d'espionnage a serious corruption/spy scandal; **c'est une sale ~** it's a nasty business → **suivre**

[d] [Jur, Police] case; **l'~ Dufeu** the Dufeu case; **être sur une ~** to be on a case; **une ~ de vol** a case of theft; **son ~ est claire** it's an open and shut case → **entendu**

[e] **= transaction** deal; (= *achat avantageux*) bargain; **une (bonne) ~** a good deal, a (good) bargain; **une mauvaise ~** a bad deal *ou* bargain; **faire ~ avec qn** to conclude *ou* clinch a deal with sb; **il est sur une grosse ~ avec la Russie** he's onto a big (business) deal with Russia; **l'~ est faite ! *ou* conclue !** that's the deal settled!; **l'~ est dans le sac*** it's in the bag*

[f] **= entreprise** business, concern; **il a monté/ il dirige une ~ d'import-export** he set up/he runs an import-export business; **c'est une ~ qui marche/en or** it's a going concern/a gold mine

[g]
♦ **avoir affaire à** [+ *cas, problème*] to be faced with, have to deal with; [+ *personne*] (= *s'occuper de*) to be dealing with; (= *être reçu ou examiné par*) to be dealt with by; **nous avons ~ à un dangereux criminel** we are dealing with a dangerous criminal; (*menace*) **tu auras ~ à moi/lui** you'll be hearing from me/him

[2] **affaires** NOM FÉMININ PL

[a] **= intérêts publics et privés** affairs; **les ~s culturelles/de la municipalité/publiques** cultural/municipal/public affairs; **les Affaires étrangères** Foreign Affairs; (*au Canada*) **Affaires extérieures** External Affairs (*Can*); (*Pol*) **être aux ~s** to be in office; **se mêler des ~s des autres** to interfere in other people's business; **occupe-toi *ou* mêle-toi de tes ~s !** mind your own business!

[b] **= activités commerciales** business *sg*; **être dans les ~s** to be in business; **parler (d')~** to talk *ou* discuss business; **ils font beaucoup d'~s ensemble** they do a lot of business together; **les ~s reprennent** business is picking up; **il est dur en ~s** he's a tough businessman; **être en ~s avec qn** to be doing business with sb; **il est venu pour ~s** he came on business; **les ~s sont les ~s** business is business → **carré, droit**

♦ **d'affaire(s)** [*repas, voyage, relations*] business (*épith*); **les milieux d'~s sont optimistes** the business community is optimistic → **chiffre**

[c] **= occupations**
♦ **toutes affaires cessantes** immediately, forthwith (*fml*)

[d] **= objets personnels** things, belongings; (= *habits*) clothes, things; **mes ~s de tennis** my tennis kit *ou* things; **range tes ~s !** put your things away!

[3] COMPOSÉS
▶ **affaire de cœur** love affair ▶ **affaire d'État** (*Pol*) affair of state; **il en a fait une ~ d'État*** he made a great song and dance about it *ou* a great issue of it ▶ **affaire d'honneur** matter *ou* affair of honour ▶ **affaire de famille** (= *entreprise*) family business *ou* concern; (= *problème*) family problem *ou* matter ▶ **affaire de mœurs** (*gén*) sex scandal; (*Jur*) sex case

affairé, e [afere] (*ptp de* **s'affairer**) ADJ busy
affairement [aferəmã] NM bustling activity
affairer (s') [afere] ▶conjug 1◀ VPR to busy o.s., bustle about; **s'~ auprès *ou* autour de qn** to fuss around sb; **s'~ à faire qch** to busy o.s. doing sth, bustle about doing sth
affairisme [aferism] NM (political) racketeering
affairiste [aferist] NM (*péj*) huckster, wheeler-dealer*; **sous ce régime il n'y a pas de place pour l'~** there is no place under this government for political racketeering *ou* for those who want to use politics to line their own pockets

affaissement [afesmã] NM [*route, sol*] subsidence, sinking; [*corps, muscles, poutre*] sagging; [*forces*] ebbing; [*volonté*] weakening; **~ de terrain** subsidence (*NonC*)
affaisser [afese] ▶conjug 1◀ [1] VT [+ *route, sol*] to cause to subside [2] **s'affaisser** VPR (= *fléchir*) [*route, sol*] to subside, sink; [*corps, poutre*] to sag; [*plancher*] to cave in, give way; [*forces*] to ebb; [*volonté*] to weaken; **le sol était affaissé par endroits** the ground had subsided *ou* sunk in places [b] (= *s'écrouler*) [*personne*] to collapse; **il s'était affaissé sur le sol** he had collapsed *ou* crumpled in a heap on the ground; **il était affaissé dans un fauteuil/sur le sol** he was slumped in an armchair/on the ground
affaler [afale] ▶conjug 1◀ [1] VT [+ *voile*] to lower, haul down [2] **s'affaler** VPR [a] (= *tomber*) to collapse, fall; (= *se laisser tomber*) to collapse, flop, slump; **affalé dans un fauteuil** slumped *ou* slouched in an armchair; **au lieu de rester là affalé à ne rien faire, viens m'aider** don't just sit there doing nothing, come and give me a hand [b] (*Naut*) **s'~ le long d'un cordage** to slide down a rope
affamé, e [afame] (*ptp de* **affamer**) ADJ starving, famished, ravenous; **~ de gloire** hungry *ou* greedy for fame → **ventre**
affamer [afame] ▶conjug 1◀ VT [+ *personne, ville*] to starve
affameur, -euse [afamœr, øz] NM,F (*péj*) tight-fisted employer (*who pays starvation wages*)
affect [afɛkt] NM affect
affectation [afɛktasjɔ̃] NF [a] [*immeuble, somme*] allocation, allotment (**à** to, for); **l'~ du signe + à un nombre** the addition of the plus sign to a number, the modification of a number by the plus sign [b] (= *nomination*) (*à un poste*) appointment; (*à une région, un pays*) posting; **rejoindre son ~** to take up one's appointment, to take up one's posting [c] (= *manque de naturel*) affectation, affectedness; **avec ~** affectedly [d] (= *simulation*) affectation, show; **avec une ~ de** with an affectation *ou* show of
affecté, e [afɛkte] (*ptp de* **affecter**) ADJ (= *feint*) affected, feigned, assumed; (= *maniéré*) affected
affecter [afɛkte] ▶conjug 1◀ VT [a] (= *feindre*) to affect, feign; **~ de faire qch** to pretend to do sth; **~ un grand chagrin** to affect *ou* feign great sorrow, put on a show of great sorrow; (*littér*) **~ un langage poétique** to affect *ou* favour a poetic style of language; **il affecta de ne pas s'y intéresser** he pretended not to be interested in it
[b] (= *destiner*) to allocate, allot (**à** to, for); **~ des crédits à la recherche** to earmark funds for research, allocate *ou* allot funds to *ou* for research
[c] (= *nommer*) (*à une fonction, un bureau*) to appoint; (*à une région, un pays*) to post (**à** to)
[d] (= *émouvoir*) to affect, move; (= *concerner*) to affect; **il a été très affecté par leur mort** he was deeply affected by their deaths
[e] (*Math*) to modify; **nombre affecté du coefficient 2/du signe plus** number modified by *ou* bearing the coefficient 2/a plus sign
[f] (*Méd*) to affect; **les oreillons affectent surtout les jeunes enfants** mumps mostly affects young children
[g] (= *prendre*) **ce muscle affecte la forme d'un triangle** this muscle is triangle-shaped *ou* is in the form of a triangle
affectif, -ive [afɛktif, iv] ADJ (*gén*) [*vie, terme, nuance*] emotional; (*Psych*) affective
affection [afɛksjɔ̃] NF [a] (= *tendresse*) affection, fondness; **avoir de l'~ pour qn** to feel affection for sb, be fond of sb; **prendre qn en ~** ◊ **se prendre d'~ pour qn** to become fond of *ou* attached to sb [b] (*Méd*) ailment, affection [c] (*Psych*) affection

affectionné, e [afɛksjɔne] (*ptp de* **affectionner**) ADJ (*frm*) **votre fils ~** your loving *ou* devoted son; **votre ~** yours affectionately
affectionner [afɛksjɔne] ▶conjug 1◀ VT [+ *chose*] to have a liking for, be fond of; [+ *personne*] to be fond of
affectivité [afɛktivite] NF affectivity
affectueusement [afɛktɥøzmã] ADV affectionately, fondly; **~ vôtre** yours affectionately
affectueux, -euse [afɛktɥø, øz] ADJ [*personne*] affectionate; [*pensée, regard*] affectionate, fond
afférent, e [aferã, ãt] ADJ [a] (*Admin*) **~ à** [*fonction*] pertaining to, relating to; **questions ~es** related questions; (*Jur*) **part ~e à** portion accruing to [b] (*Méd*) afferent
affermage [afɛrmaʒ] NM (*par le propriétaire*) leasing; (*par le fermier*) renting; **contrat d'~** lease
affermer [afɛrme] ▶conjug 1◀ VT [*propriétaire*] to lease; [*fermier*] to rent
affermir [afɛrmir] ▶conjug 2◀ [1] VT [+ *pouvoir, position*] to consolidate, strengthen; [+ *principes*] to strengthen; [+ *contrôle*] to tighten up; [+ *tendance*] to reinforce; [+ *autorité*] to reinforce, strengthen; [+ *muscles*] to tone up; **~ sa prise** (*Sport*) to tighten one's grip; **cela l'a affermi dans sa résolution** that strengthened his resolve; **d'autres preuves ont affermi ma certitude** new evidence convinced me even more [2] **s'affermir** VPR [*pouvoir*] to consolidate itself, be reinforced; [*détermination, principe*] to be strengthened; [*autorité, tendance*] to be reinforced; [*monnaie*] to strengthen; [*muscles*] to become firmer, firm up; **la reprise économique devrait s'~** the economic recovery should consolidate itself
affermissement [afɛrmismã] NM [*pouvoir, position*] consolidation, strengthening; [*tendance*] reinforcement; [*monnaie*] strengthening
affété, e [afete] ADJ (*littér*) precious, affected, mannered
afféterie [afetri] NF (*littér*) preciosity, affectation (*NonC*)
affichage [afiʃaʒ] NM [a] [*affiche, résultats*] putting *ou* sticking up, posting; (*Théât*) billing; **l'~** billsticking, billposting; **« ~ interdit »** "stick no bills", "post no bills"; **interdit à l'~** [*magazine*] not for public display; **campagne d'~** poster campaign → **panneau, tableau** [b] (*Ordin*) display; **montre à ~ numérique** digital watch
affiche [afiʃ] NF [a] (*officielle*) public notice; (*Admin*) bill; (*électorale*) poster; **la vente a été annoncée par voie d'~** the sale was advertised on public noticeboards [b] (*Théât*) (play)bill; **mettre à l'~** to bill; **quitter l'~** to come off, close; **tenir longtemps l'~** to have a long run; **ce spectacle est resté à l'~ plus d'un an** the show ran for over a year; **il y a une belle ~ pour cette pièce** this play has an excellent cast → **tête**
afficher [afiʃe] ▶conjug 1◀ [1] VT [a] [+ *résultats*] to put *ou* stick up, post; (*Théât*) to bill; (*Ordin*) to display; **« défense d'~ »** "stick no bills", "post no bills"; **~ complet** to be sold out [b] (+ *émotion, mépris*) to exhibit, display; [+ *qualité, vice*] to flaunt, parade, display; **~ ses opinions politiques** to make no secret of one's political views [2] **s'afficher** VPR (= *apparaître*) to be displayed; **un menu s'affiche à l'écran** a menu is displayed on the screen; **l'hypocrisie qui s'affiche sur tous les visages** the hypocrisy which is plain to see on everybody's face [b] (= *se montrer*) to flaunt o.s.; **s'~ avec son amant** to carry on openly in public with one's lover
affichette [afiʃɛt] NF (*officielle*) small public notice; (*Admin, Théât*) small bill *ou* poster; (*publicitaire, électorale*) small poster

afficheur, -euse [afiʃœʀ, øz] [1] NM,F bill-sticker, billposter [2] NM (*Tech*) display

affichiste [afiʃist] NMF poster designer *ou* artist

affidé, e [afide] NM,F (*péj*) accomplice, henchman

affilage [afilaʒ] NM [*couteau, outil*] sharpening, whetting; [*rasoir*] sharpening, honing

affilé, e[1] [afile] (*ptp de* **affiler**) ADJ [*outil, couteau*] sharp; [*intelligence*] keen → **langue**

affilée[2] [afile] ◆ **d'affilée** LOC ADV in a row; **8 heures d'~** 8 hours at a stretch *ou* solid; **boire plusieurs verres d'~** to drink several glasses in a row *ou* in succession

affiler [afile] ▶conjug 1◀ VT [+ *couteau, outil*] to sharpen, whet; [+ *rasoir*] to sharpen, hone

affiliation [afiljasjɔ̃] NF affiliation

affilié, e [afilje] (*ptp de* **affilier**) NM,F affiliated member

affilier [afilje] ▶conjug 7◀ [1] VT to affiliate (**à** to) [2] **s'affilier** VPR to become affiliated, affiliate o.s. (*ou* itself) (**à** to)

affiloir [afilwaʀ] NM (= *outil*) sharpener; (= *pierre*) whetstone; (*pour couteau*) steel

affinage [afinaʒ] NM [*métal*] refining; [*verre*] fining; [*fromage*] maturing

affinement [afinmã] NM [*analyse*] refinement, honing; [*concept*] refinement; [*goût, manières, style*] refinement

affiner [afine] ▶conjug 1◀ [1] VT [a] [+ *métal*] to refine; [+ *verre*] to fine; [+ *fromage*] to complete the maturing (process) of; **fromage affiné en cave** cheese matured in a cellar [b] [+ *analyse, image, style, stratégie*] to hone, refine; [+ *concept*] to refine; [+ *esprit, mœurs*] to refine; [+ *sens*] to make keener, sharpen [c] [+ *taille, hanches*] to slim (down); [+ *chevilles*] to make slender; **ce maquillage vous affinera le visage** this make-up will make your face look thinner [2] **s'affiner** VPR [a] [*analyse, concept*] to become (more) refined; [*style*] to become (more) refined *ou* polished; [*odorat, goût*] to become sharper *ou* keener [b] [*personne*] to slim (down); [*taille*] to become slimmer; [*chevilles*] to become (more) slender; [*visage*] to get thinner; [*grain de la peau*] to become finer

affineur, -euse [afinœʀ, øz] NM,F [*métal*] refiner; [*verre*] finer

affinité [afinite] NF (*entre personnes*) affinity; (*entre œuvres*) similarity; **avoir des ~ avec qn** to have a natural affinity with sb; (*petite annonce*) **«plus si ~s»** "possibly more"

affirmatif, -ive [afiʀmatif, iv] [1] ADJ [*réponse, proposition*] affirmative; [*personne, ton*] assertive, affirmative; (*Ling*) affirmative, positive; **il a été ~ à ce sujet** he was quite positive on that score *ou* about that; (*Mil, hum*) **~!** affirmative! → **signe** [2] NM (*Ling*) affirmative, positive; **à l'~** in the affirmative, in the positive [3] **affirmative** NF affirmative; **répondre par l'affirmative** to answer yes *ou* in the affirmative; **dans l'affirmative** in the event of the answer being yes *ou* of an affirmative reply (*frm*); **nous espérons que vous viendrez: dans l'affirmative, faites-le-nous savoir** we hope you'll come and if you can (come) please let us know

affirmation [afiʀmasjɔ̃] NF [a] (= *allégation*) assertion [b] (*Ling*) assertion [c] (= *manifestation*) [*talent, autorité*] assertion, affirmation

affirmativement [afiʀmativmã] ADV in the affirmative, affirmatively

▼**affirmer** [afiʀme] ▶conjug 1◀ VT [a] (= *soutenir*) to maintain, assert; **tu affirmes toujours tout sans savoir** you are always positive about everything without really knowing; **il affirme l'avoir vu s'enfuir** he maintains *ou* claims that he saw him run off; **il affirme que c'est de votre faute** he contends *ou* maintains that it is your fault; **pouvez-vous l'~ ?** can you swear to

it?, can you be positive about it?; **on ne peut rien ~ encore** we can't say anything positive *ou* for sure yet; **c'est lui, affirma-t-elle** it's him, she said; **~ qch sur l'honneur** to maintain *ou* affirm sth on one's word of honour; **~ sur l'honneur que ...** to give one's word of honour that ...
[b] (= *manifester*) [+ *originalité, autorité, position*] to assert; **talent/personnalité qui s'affirme** talent/personality which is asserting itself; **il s'affirme comme l'un de nos meilleurs romanciers** he is establishing himself as one of our best novelists
[c] (*frm* = *proclamer*) to affirm, assert; **le président a affirmé sa volonté de régler cette affaire** the president affirmed *ou* asserted his wish to settle the matter

affixe [afiks] NM (*Ling*) affix

affleurement [aflœʀmã] NM (*Géol*) outcrop; (*fig*) emergence; (*Tech*) flushing

affleurer [aflœʀe] ▶conjug 1◀ [1] VI [*rocs, récifs*] to show on the surface; [*filon, couche*] to show on the surface, outcrop (SPÉC); [*sentiment, sensualité*] to come *ou* rise to the surface; **quelques récifs affleuraient (à la surface de l'eau)** a few reefs showed on the surface (of the water) [2] VT (*Tech*) to make flush, flush

afflictif, -ive [afliktif, iv] ADJ (*Jur*) corporal

affliction [afliksjɔ̃] NF (*littér*) affliction; **être dans l'~** to be in a state of affliction

affligé, e [afliʒe] (*ptp de* **affliger**) ADJ **être ~ de** [*maladie*] to be afflicted with; **il était ~ d'une femme acariâtre** he was afflicted *ou* cursed with a cantankerous wife; (*littér*) **les ~s** the afflicted

affligeant, e [afliʒã, ãt] ADJ distressing; (*iro*) pathetic

affliger [afliʒe] ▶conjug 3◀ VT (= *attrister*) to distress, grieve; (*littér* = *accabler*) to smite (*littér*) (**de** with); **s'~ de qch** to be distressed *ou* grieved about sth; (*hum*) **la nature l'avait affligé d'un nez crochu** nature had afflicted *ou* cursed him with a hooked nose

affluence [aflyãs] NF [*gens*] crowds, throng (*littér*); **les heures d'~** [*trains, circulation*] the rush hour; [*magasin*] the peak shopping period, the busy period

affluent [aflyã] NM tributary, affluent (SPÉC)

affluer [aflye] ▶conjug 1◀ VI [*fluide, sang*] to rush, flow (**à, vers** to); [*foule*] to flock; **les dons affluaient de partout** donations came flooding in from all over; **l'argent afflue dans les caisses de la banque** money is flowing *ou* flooding into the coffers of the bank

afflux [afly] NM [*fluide*] inrush, inflow; [*argent, foule*] inrush, influx, flood; (*Élec*) flow; **~ de capitaux** capital inflow; **~ de main-d'œuvre** labour influx

affolant, e [afɔlã, ãt] ADJ (= *effrayant*) frightening; (*littér* = *troublant*) [*situation, nouvelle*] distressing, disturbing; **c'est ~!** it's alarming!; **à une vitesse ~e** at an alarming rate

affolé, e [afɔle] (*ptp de* **affoler**) ADJ [a] (= *effrayé*) panic- *ou* terror-stricken; **je suis ~ de voir ça** I'm appalled *ou* horrified at that; **air ~** look of panic [b] [*boussole*] wildly fluctuating

affolement [afɔlmã] NM [a] (= *effroi*) panic; (*littér* = *trouble*) turmoil; **pas d'~!** don't panic! [b] [*boussole*] wild fluctuations

affoler [afɔle] ▶conjug 1◀ [1] VT (= *effrayer*) to throw into a panic, terrify; (*littér* = *troubler*) to drive wild, throw into a turmoil [2] **s'affoler** VPR [*personne*] to lose one's head; [*gouvernement, Bourse*] to panic, lose one's nerve; **ne nous affolons pas*** let's not panic *ou* get in a panic*, let's keep our heads

affouillement [afujmã] NM undermining

affouiller [afuje] ▶conjug 1◀ VT to undermine

affranchi, e [afʀãʃi] (*ptp de* **affranchir**) NM,F (= *esclave*) emancipated *ou* freed slave; (= *libertin*) emancipated man (*ou* woman)

affranchir [afʀãʃiʀ] ▶conjug 2◀ [1] VT [a] (*avec des timbres*) to put a stamp *ou* stamps on, stamp; (*à la machine*) to frank; **lettre affranchie/non affranchie** stamped/unstamped letter, franked/unfranked letter; **j'ai reçu une lettre insuffisamment affranchie** I received a letter with insufficient postage on it; **machine à ~** franking machine [b] [+ *esclave*] to enfranchise, emancipate; [+ *peuple, pays*] to free; (*fig*) [+ *esprit, personne*] to free, emancipate; **~ qn de** [+ *contrainte, influence*] to free sb from [c] (*arg Crime* = *mettre au courant*) **~ qn** to give sb the low-down*, put sb in the picture* [d] (*Cartes*) to clear [2] **s'affranchir** VPR **~ de** [+ *domination, convenances*] to free o.s. from

affranchissement [afʀãʃismã] NM [a] (*avec des timbres*) stamping; (*à la machine*) franking; (= *prix payé*) postage [b] [*esclave*] emancipation, enfranchisement, freeing; [*peuple, pays*] freeing; (*fig*) [*esprit, personne*] freeing, emancipation

affres [afʀ] NFPL (*littér*) **les ~ de** the pangs *ou* the torments of; **être dans les ~ de la mort** to be in the throes of death

affrètement [afʀɛtmã] NM chartering

affréter [afʀete] ▶conjug 6◀ VT to charter

affréteur [afʀetœʀ] NM (*Aviat, Naut*) charterer; (*Aut*) hirer

affreusement [afʀøzmã] ADV [*souffrir, blesser*] horribly; [*difficile, vulgaire*] terribly; **~ laid** hideously ugly; **ce plat est ~ mauvais** this food is terrible *ou* awful; **on est ~ mal assis** these seats are terribly uncomfortable; **~ en retard** dreadfully late

affreux, -euse [afʀø, øz] [1] ADJ (= *très laid*) hideous, ghastly; (= *effroyable, abominable*) dreadful, awful, horrible; **quel temps ~!** what dreadful *ou* awful weather!; **j'ai un mal de tête ~** I've got a splitting *ou* a dreadful *ou* an awful headache → **jojo** [2] NM (*arg Mil*) (white) mercenary

affriander [afʀijãde] ▶conjug 1◀ VT (*littér*) to attract, allure, entice

affriolant, e [afʀijɔlã, ãt] ADJ [*perspective, programme*] appealing, exciting; [*femme*] alluring; [*vêtement*] alluring

affrioler [afʀijɔle] ▶conjug 1◀ VT to tempt

affriquée [afʀike] [1] ADJ F affricative [2] NF affricate

affront [afʀɔ̃] NM (*frm* = *insulte*) affront; **faire (un) ~ à qn** to affront sb

affrontement [afʀɔ̃tmã] NM (*Mil, Pol*) confrontation

affronter [afʀɔ̃te] ▶conjug 1◀ [1] VT [+ *adversaire, danger*] to confront, face; **~ la mort** to face *ou* brave death; **~ le mauvais temps** to brave the bad weather [2] **s'affronter** VPR [*adversaires*] to confront each other; **ces deux théories s'affrontent** these two theories clash *ou* are in direct opposition

affublement [afyblmã] NM (*péj*) attire

affubler [afyble] ▶conjug 1◀ VT **~ qn de** [+ *vêtement*] to deck *ou* rig* (*Brit*) sb out in; **~ qn d'un sobriquet** to attach a nickname to sb; **il s'affubla d'un vieux manteau** he donned an old coat; **affublé d'un vieux chapeau** wearing an old hat

affût [afy] NM [a] **~ (de canon)** (gun) carriage [b] (*Chasse*) hide (*Brit*), blind (*US*); **chasser à l'~** to hunt game from a hide (*Brit*) *ou* blind (*US*); **être à l'~** to be lying in wait; **se mettre à l'~** to lie in wait; (*fig*) **être à l'~ de qch** to be on the look-out for sth

affûtage [afytaʒ] NM sharpening, grinding

affûter [afyte] ▶conjug 1◀ VT [+ *lame*] to sharpen, grind; [+ *arguments, stratégie*] to hone

affûteur [afytœʀ] NM (= *personne*) grinder

affûteuse [afytøz] NF (= *machine*) grinder, sharpener

afghan, e [afgã, an] [1] ADJ Afghan → **lévrier**

▶ GRAMMAIRE ACTIVE: **affirmer** 53.3, 53.5

[2] NM (*Ling*) Afghan [3] **Afghan(e)** NM,F Afghan

Afghanistan [afganistã] NM Afghanistan

aficionado [afisjɔnado] NM aficionado

▼ **afin** [afɛ̃] PRÉP ~ **de** to, in order to, so as to; ~ **que nous le sachions** so that *ou* in order that we should know

AFNOR [afnɔʀ] NF (ABRÉV = **Association française de normalisation**) *French Industrial Standards Authority*, ≈ BSI (*Brit*), ≈ ANSI (*US*)

afocal, e (*mpl* -**aux**) [afɔkal, o] ADJ afocal

a fortiori [afɔʀsjɔʀi] LOC ADV all the more, a fortiori (*frm*)

AFP [aɛfpe] NF (ABRÉV = **Agence France-Presse**) French Press Agency

AFPA [afpa] NF (ABRÉV = **Association pour la formation professionnelle des adultes**) *adult professional education association*

africain, e [afʀikɛ̃, ɛn] [1] ADJ African [2] **Africain(e)** NM,F African

africanisation [afʀikanizasjɔ̃] NF Africanization

africanisme [afʀikanism] NM Africanism

africaniste [afʀikanist] NMF Africanist

afrikaans [afʀikãs] NM, ADJ INV Afrikaans

afrikander [afʀikãdeʀ], **afrikaner** [afʀikaneʀ] ADJ, NMF Afrikaner

Afrique [afʀik] NF Africa; **l'~ australe/du Nord** Southern/North Africa; **l'~ du Sud** South Africa; **l'~ noire** black Africa

afro* [afʀo] ADJ INV Afro; **coiffure ~** Afro (hairstyle *ou* hairdo*)

afro- [afʀo] PRÉF Afro-

afro-américain, e [afʀoameʀikɛ̃, ɛn] [1] ADJ Afro-American, African-American [2] **Afro-Américain(e)** NM,F Afro-American, African-American

afro-asiatique (*pl* **afro-asiatiques**) [afʀoazjatik] [1] ADJ Afro-Asian [2] **Afro-Asiatique** NMF Afro-Asian

afro-brésilien, -ienne [afʀobʀeziljɛ̃, jɛn] [1] ADJ Afro-Brazilian [2] **Afro-Brésilien(ne)** NM,F Afro-Brazilian

AG* [aʒe] NF (ABRÉV = **assemblée générale**) (*Écon*) AGM; [*étudiants*] EGM

agaçant, e [agasã, ãt] ADJ irritating, aggravating, annoying

agacement [agasmã] NM irritation, annoyance

agacer [agase] ▶ conjug 3 ◀ VT [a] ~ **qn** (= *énerver*) to get on sb's nerves, irritate *ou* aggravate* sb; (= *taquiner*) to pester *ou* tease sb; ~ **les dents de qn** to set sb's teeth on edge; ~ **les nerfs de qn** to get on sb's nerves; **ça m'agace !** it's getting on my nerves!; **agacé par le bruit** irritated *ou* annoyed by the noise; **agacé de l'entendre** irritated by what he said [b] (*littér* = *aguicher*) to excite, lead on

agaceries [agasʀi] NFPL coquetries, provocative gestures

Agamemnon [agamɛmnɔ̃] NM Agamemnon

agapes [agap] NFPL (*hum*) banquet, feast

agar-agar (*pl* **agars-agars**) [agaʀagaʀ] NM agar(-agar)

agate [agat] NF agate

agave [agav] NM agave

AGE [aʒeø] NF (ABRÉV = **assemblée générale extraordinaire**) EGM

âge [ɑʒ] [1] NM [a] (*gén*) age; **quel ~ avez-vous ?** how old are you?, what age are you?; **à l'~ de 8 ans** at the age of 8; **j'ai votre ~** I'm your age, I'm the same age as you; **ils sont du même ~** they're the same age; (*hum*) **il est d'un ~ canonique** he's a venerable age; **elle est d'un ~ avancé** she's getting on in years, she's quite elderly; **d'~ moyen** ◊ **entre deux ~s** middle-aged; **il ne paraît** *ou* **fait pas son ~** he doesn't look his age; **elle porte bien son ~** she looks good for her age; **il fait plus vieux que**

son ~ he looks older than he is; **sans ~** ◊ **qui n'a pas d'~** ageless; **on a l'~ de ses artères** you're as old as you feel; **il a vieilli avant l'~** he's got *ou* he's old before his time; **il a pris de l'~** he's aged; **amusez-vous, c'est de votre ~** enjoy yourself, you should (do) at your age; **à son ~** at his age; **j'ai passé l'~ de le faire** I'm too old for that; **avec l'~ il se calmera** he'll settle down as he gets older; **des gens de tout ~** people of all ages; **être en ~ de se marier** to be of marriageable age, be old enough to get married; **porto de 15 ans d'~** 15-year-old port; **le premier ~** the first three months → **bas¹, moyen, quatrième, troisième** [b] (= *ère*) age; **l'~ de (la) pierre/du bronze/du fer** the Stone/Bronze/Iron Age; (*hum*) **ça existait déjà à l'~ des cavernes !** that dates back to the Stone Age!

[2] COMP ▶ **l'âge adulte** (*gén*) adulthood; (*pour un homme*) manhood; (*pour une femme*) womanhood; **à l'~ adulte** in adulthood ▶ **l'âge bête** : **c'est l'~ bête** it's an awkward *ou* difficult age ▶ **l'âge critique** the change of life ▶ **l'âge d'homme** manhood ▶ **l'âge ingrat** = **l'âge bête** ▶ **l'âge légal** the legal age; **avoir l'~ légal** to be legally old enough ▶ **âge mental** mental age ▶ **l'âge mûr** maturity ▶ **l'âge d'or** the golden age ▶ **l'âge de la pierre polie** the neolithic age ▶ **l'âge de la pierre taillée** the palaeolithic age ▶ **l'âge de raison** the age of reason ▶ **l'âge de la retraite** retiring age ▶ **l'âge tendre** the tender years ▶ **l'âge viril** = **l'âge d'homme**

âgé, e [ɑʒe] ADJ **être ~** to be old, be elderly; **être ~ de 9 ans** to be 9 years old, be 9 years of age; **enfant ~ de 4 ans** 4-year-old child; **dame ~e** elderly lady; **les personnes ~es** the elderly

agence [aʒãs] [1] NF (= *succursale*) branch (office); (= *bureaux*) offices; (= *organisme*) agency, bureau, office

[2] COMP ▶ **agence commerciale** sales office *ou* agency ▶ **Agence pour l'énergie nucléaire** Atomic Energy Authority ▶ **Agence de l'environnement et de la maîtrise de l'énergie** *French energy conservation agency*, ≈ Energy Efficiency Office (*Brit*) ▶ **agence immobilière** estate agency (*Brit*), estate agent's (office) (*Brit*), real estate agency (*US*) ▶ **agence d'intérim** temping agency ▶ **Agence internationale de l'énergie atomique** International Atomic Energy Agency ▶ **agence matrimoniale** marriage bureau ▶ **Agence nationale pour l'emploi** *French national employment office*, ≈ job centre (*Brit*) ▶ **agence de placement** employment agency *ou* bureau ▶ **agence de presse** news *ou* press agency, news service (*US*) ▶ **agence de publicité** advertising *ou* publicity agency ▶ **agence de renseignements** information bureau *ou* office ▶ **Agence spatiale européenne** European Space Agency ▶ **agence de tourisme** tourist agency ▶ **agence de voyages** travel agency

agencé, e [aʒãse] (*ptp de* **agencer**) ADJ **bien ~** (*gén*) well-organized; [*phrase*] well-constructed; [*local*] (*en meubles*) well-equipped; (*en espace*) well-arranged, well laid-out; **mal ~** [*local*] (*en meubles*) poorly-equipped; (*en espace*) badly laid-out

agencement [aʒãsmã] NM [*éléments*] organization; [*phrase, roman*] construction; [*couleurs*] harmonization; [*local*] (= *disposition*) arrangement, layout; (= *équipement*) equipment; **~s modernes** modern fittings *ou* equipment

agencer [aʒãse] ▶ conjug 3 ◀ VT [+ *éléments*] to put together, organize, order; [+ *couleurs*] to harmonize; [+ *phrase, roman*] to put together, construct; [+ *local*] (= *disposer*) to lay out, arrange; (= *équiper*) to equip

agenda [aʒɛ̃da] NM [a] (= *carnet*) diary (*Brit*), datebook (*US*), calendar (*US*); ~ **de bureau**

desk diary (*Brit*) *ou* calendar (*US*); ~ **électronique** electronic organizer *ou* diary (*Brit*) [b] (= *activités*) schedule; ~ **très chargé** very busy schedule

agenouillement [aʒ(ə)nujmã] NM (*littér*) kneeling

agenouiller (s') [aʒ(ə)nuje] ▶ conjug 1 ◀ VPR to kneel (down); **être agenouillé** to be kneeling; **s'~ devant l'autorité** to bow before authority

agenouilloir [aʒ(ə)nujwaʀ] NM (= *escabeau*) hassock, kneeling stool; (= *planche*) kneeling plank

agent [aʒã] [1] NM [a] (*Police*) ~ **(de police)** policeman, (police) constable (*Brit*); ~ **de la circulation** ≈ policeman on traffic duty, ≈ traffic policeman; **pardon monsieur l'~** excuse me, officer *ou* constable (*Brit*); **elle est ~ (de police)** she's a policewoman

[b] (*Comm, Pol* = *représentant*) agent; (*Admin*) officer, official; **arrêter un ~ ennemi** to arrest an enemy agent; ~ **exclusif** sole agent; ~ **en franchise** franchised dealer

[c] (*Chim, Gram, Sci*) agent; ~ **de sapidité** (flavour) enhancer → **complément**

[2] COMP ▶ **agent administratif** administrative officer ▶ **agent artistique** (artistic) agent ▶ **agent d'assurances** insurance agent ▶ **agent de change†** stockbroker ▶ **agent commercial** (sales) representative ▶ **agent comptable** accountant ▶ **agent consulaire** consular official *ou* officer ▶ **agent double** double agent ▶ **agent électoral** campaign organizer *ou* aide ▶ **agent d'entretien** cleaning operative, maintenance person ▶ **agent de l'État** public sector employee ▶ **agent du fisc** tax official *ou* officer ▶ **agent de la force publique** member of the police force ▶ **agent du gouvernement** government official ▶ **agent immobilier** estate agent (*Brit*), real estate agent (*US*) ▶ **agent de liaison** (*Mil*) liaison officer ▶ **agent littéraire** literary agent ▶ **agent de maîtrise** supervisor ▶ **agent maritime** shipping agent ▶ **agent provocateur** agent provocateur ▶ **agent public** = **agent de l'État** ▶ **agent de publicité** advertising agent ▶ **agent de renseignements** intelligence agent ▶ **agent secret** secret agent ▶ **agent de surface** = **agent d'entretien** ▶ **agent technique** technician ▶ **agent de transmission** (*Mil*) despatch rider, messenger ▶ **agent voyer** ≈ borough surveyor

agentif [aʒãtif] NM (*Ling*) agentive

ageratum [aʒeʀatɔm] NM ageratum

aggiornamento [a(d)dʒɔʀnamɛnto] NM (*Rel*) aggiornamento; (*fig*) [*stratégie, politique*] adjustment, change

agglo* [aglo] NM ABRÉV = **aggloméré**

agglomérat [aglɔmeʀa] NM (*Géol*) agglomerate; [*personnes*] mixture; [*objets*] cluster

agglomération [aglɔmeʀasjɔ̃] NF [a] (= *ville*) (*Admin*) town; (*Aut*) built-up area; **l'~ parisienne** Paris and its suburbs, the urban area of Paris [b] [*nations, idées*] conglomeration; [*matériaux*] conglomeration, agglomeration

aggloméré, e [aglɔmeʀe] NM (= *bois*) chipboard, Masonite® (*US*); (= *pierre*) conglomerate; (= *charbon*) briquette

agglomérer [aglɔmeʀe] ▶ conjug 6 ◀ [1] VT (= *amonceler*) to pile up; [+ *bois, pierre*] to compress [2] **s'agglomérer** VPR to agglomerate; (= *s'amonceler*) to pile up; (= *se rassembler*) to conglomerate, gather; (*Admin*) **population agglomérée** dense population

agglutinant, e [aglytinã, ãt] [1] ADJ (*gén*) agglutinating; (*Ling*) agglutinative [2] NM agglutinant

agglutination [aglytinasjɔ̃] NF (*Bio, Ling*) agglutination

▶ GRAMMAIRE ACTIVE: **afin** 35.2

agglutiner [aglytine] ▶conjug 1◀ VT to stick together; (*Bio*) to agglutinate; **les passants s'agglutinaient devant la vitrine** passers-by gathered in front of the window

agglutinogène [aglytinɔʒɛn] NM agglutinogen

aggravant, e [agʀavɑ̃, ɑ̃t] ADJ [*facteur*] aggravating → **circonstance**

aggravation [agʀavasjɔ̃] NF [*mal, situation*] worsening, aggravation; [*impôt, chômage*] increase

aggraver [agʀave] ▶conjug 1◀ 1 VT (= *faire empirer*) to make worse, aggravate, worsen; (= *renforcer*) to increase; **tu aggraves ton cas** you're making things worse for yourself; **il a aggravé la marque** *ou* **le score à la 35ème minute** he increased their lead in the 35th minute 2 **s'aggraver** VPR (= *empirer*) to get worse, worsen; (= *se renforcer*) to increase; **le chômage s'est fortement aggravé** unemployment has increased sharply, there has been a sharp increase in unemployment

agile [aʒil] ADJ agile, nimble; **~ de ses mains** nimble with one's fingers; **d'un geste ~** with an agile *ou* a nimble *ou* quick gesture; **~ comme un singe** as nimble as a goat

agilement [aʒilmɑ̃] ADV nimbly, agilely

agilité [aʒilite] NF agility, nimbleness

agio [aʒjo] NM a (= *différence de cours*) Exchange premium b (= *frais*) **~s** (bank) charges

agiotage [aʒjɔtaʒ] NM speculation

agioter [aʒjɔte] ▶conjug 1◀ VI to speculate

agioteur, -euse [aʒjɔtœʀ, øz] NM,F speculator

▼**agir** [aʒiʀ] ▶conjug 2◀ 1 VI a (*gén*) to act; (= *se comporter*) to behave, act; **il faut ~ tout de suite** we must act *ou* do something at once, we must take action at once; **il a agi de son plein gré** *ou* **en toute liberté** he acted quite willingly/freely; **il agit comme un enfant** he acts *ou* behaves like a child; **il a bien/mal agi envers sa mère** he behaved well/badly towards his mother; **il a sagement agi** he did the right thing, he acted wisely; **le syndicat a décidé d'~** the union has decided to take action *ou* to act; **~ en ami** to behave *ou* act like a friend; **~ au nom de qn** to act on behalf of sb → **façon, manière**
b (= *exercer une influence*) **~ sur qch** to act on sth; **~ sur qn** to bring pressure to bear on sb; (*Bourse*) **~ sur le marché** to influence the market; **~ auprès de qn** to use one's influence with sb
c (*loc*) **faire ~ la loi** to put *ou* set the law in motion; **il a fait ~ son syndicat/ses amis** he got his union/friends to act *ou* take action; **je ne sais pas ce qui le fait ~ ainsi** I don't know what prompts him to *ou* makes him act like that
d (= *opérer*) [*médicament*] to act, work; [*influence*] to have an effect (**sur** on); **le remède agit lentement** the medicine is slow to take effect, the medicine acts *ou* works slowly; **laisser ~ la nature** to let nature take its course; **la lumière agit sur les plantes** light acts on *ou* has an effect on plants
2 **s'agir** VB IMPERS a (= *il est question de*) **il s'agit de ...** it is a matter *ou* question of ...; **dans ce film il s'agit de 3 bandits** this film is about 3 gangsters; **décide-toi, il s'agit de ton avenir** make up your mind, it's your future that's at stake; **les livres dont il s'agit** the books in question; **quand il s'agit de manger, il est toujours là** when it comes to food, he's never far away; **quand il s'agit de travailler, il n'est jamais là** when there's any work to be done, he's never there *ou* around; **on a trouvé des colonnes: il s'agirait/il s'agit d'un temple grec** some columns have been found: it would appear to be/it is a Greek temple; **de quoi s'agit-il?** what is it?, what's it (all) about?; **voilà ce dont il s'agit** that's what it's

(all) about: **il ne s'agit pas d'argent** it's not a question of money; **il ne s'agit pas de ça!** that's not it! *ou* the point!; (*iro*) **il s'agit bien de ça!** that's hardly the problem!; **il s'agissait bien de son frère** it was (about) his brother after all
b (= *il est nécessaire de faire*) **il s'agit de faire vite** we must act quickly, the thing (to do) is to act quickly; **il s'agit pour lui de réussir** what he has to do is succeed; **maintenant, il ne s'agit pas de plaisanter** this is no time for jokes; **avec ça, il ne s'agit pas de plaisanter** that's no joking matter; **maintenant il s'agit de garder notre avance** now it's a matter *ou* question of maintaining our lead, now what we have to do is maintain our lead; **il s'agit** *ou* **s'agirait de s'entendre: tu viens ou tu ne viens pas?** let's get one thing clear *ou* straight — are you coming or aren't you?; **il s'agit de savoir ce qu'il va faire** it's a question of knowing what he's going to do, what we have to establish is what he's going to do
c (*loc*) **s'agissant de qn/qch** as regards sb/sth; **s'agissant de sommes aussi importantes, il faut être prudent** when such large amounts are involved, one must be careful

AGIRC [aʒiʀk] NF (ABRÉV = **Association générale des institutions de retraite des cadres**) *confederation of executive pension funds*

âgisme [aʒism] NM ageism

agissant, e [aʒisɑ̃, ɑ̃t] ADJ (= *actif*) active; (= *efficace*) efficacious, effective; **minorité ~e** active *ou* influential minority

agissements [aʒismɑ̃] NMPL (*péj*) schemes, intrigues; **surveiller les ~ de qn** to keep an eye on what sb is up to*

agitateur, -trice [aʒitatœʀ, tʀis] 1 NM,F (*Pol*) agitator 2 NM (*Chim*) stirring rod

agitation [aʒitasjɔ̃] NF a [*personne*] (*ayant la bougeotte*) restlessness, fidgetiness; [*affairé*] bustle; (*troublé*) agitation b [*mer*] roughness, choppiness; [*air*] turbulence; [*lieu, rue*] hustle and bustle c (*Pol*) unrest, agitation

agité, e [aʒite] (*ptp de* **agiter**) 1 ADJ a [*personne*] (= *ayant la bougeotte*) restless, fidgety; [*affairé*] bustling (*épith*); (= *troublé*) agitated b [*mer*] rough, choppy; [*Naut*] moderate; [*vie*] hectic; [*époque*] troubled; [*nuit*] restless; **mer peu ~e** slight sea *ou* swell; **avoir le sommeil ~** to toss about in one's sleep 2 NM,F (*Psych*) manic person; **c'est un ~** he's manic

agiter [aʒite] ▶conjug 1◀ 1 VT a (= *secouer*) [+ *bras, mouchoir*] to wave; [+ *ailes*] to flap, flutter; [+ *queue*] to wag; [+ *bouteille, liquide*] to shake; [+ *menace*] to brandish; **~ avant l'emploi** shake (well) before use; **~ l'air de ses bras** to wave one's arms about; **le vent agite doucement les branches** the wind stirs *ou* sways the branches (gently); **le vent agite violemment les branches** the wind shakes the branches; **les feuilles, agitées par le vent** leaves, fluttering in the wind; **bateau agité par les vagues** boat tossed about *ou* rocked by the waves; **~ le spectre** *ou* **l'épouvantail de qch** to raise the spectre of sth
b (= *inquiéter*) to trouble, perturb, agitate
c (= *débattre*) [+ *question, problème*] to discuss, debate
2 **s'agiter** VPR a [*employé, serveur*] to bustle about; [*malade*] to move about *ou* toss restlessly; [*enfant, élève*] to fidget; [*foule, mer*] to stir; **s'~ dans son sommeil** to toss and turn in one's sleep; **les pensées qui s'agitent dans ma tête** the thoughts dancing about in my head; **le peuple s'agite** the masses are getting restless; **s'~ sur sa chaise** to wriggle about on one's chair
b (* = *se dépêcher*) to get a move on*

agit-prop [aʒitpʀɔp] NF INV agitprop

agneau (*pl* **agneaux**) [aɲo] NM lamb; (= *fourrure*) lambskin; **son mari est un véritable ~**

her husband is as meek as a lamb; (*iro*) **mes ~x** my dears (*iro*); **l'Agneau de Dieu** the Lamb of God; **Agneau pascal** Paschal Lamb; (*Rel*) **l'~ sans tache** the lamb without stain; **l'~ du sacrifice** the sacrificial lamb → **doux, innocent**

agnelage [aɲ(ə)laʒ] NM (= *mise bas*) lambing; (= *époque*) lambing season

agneler [aɲ(ə)le] ▶conjug 5◀ VI to lamb

agnelet [aɲ(ə)lɛ] NM small lamb, lambkin†

agneline [aɲ(ə)lin] NF lamb's wool

agnelle [aɲɛl] NF (female) lamb

agnosticisme [agnɔstisism] NM agnosticism

agnostique [agnɔstik] ADJ, NMF agnostic

agonie [agɔni] NF (*Méd*) death pangs; **entrer en ~** to begin to suffer the agony *ou* pangs of death, begin one's mortal agony (*frm*); **être à l'~** to be at death's door, be dying; **longue ~** slow death; **son ~ fut longue** he died a slow death; **l'~ d'un régime** the death throes of a régime

agonir [agɔniʀ] ▶conjug 2◀ VT to revile; **~ qn d'injures** to hurl insults *ou* abuse at sb, heap insults *ou* abuse on sb

agonisant, e [agɔnizɑ̃, ɑ̃t] ADJ (*littér ou fig*) dying; **la prière des ~s** prayers for the dying, last rites

agoniser [agɔnize] ▶conjug 1◀ VI (*littér ou fig*) to be dying; **un blessé agonisait dans un fossé** a wounded man lay dying in a ditch

agora [agɔʀa] NF (*Antiq*) agora; (= *espace piétonnier*) concourse

agoraphobe [agɔʀafɔb] ADJ, NMF agoraphobic

agoraphobie [agɔʀafɔbi] NF agoraphobia

agouti [aguti] NM (*Zool*) agouti

agrafage [agʀafaʒ] NM [*vêtement*] hooking (up), fastening (up); [*papiers*] stapling; (*Méd*) putting in of clips

agrafe [agʀaf] NF [*vêtement*] hook (and eye) fastener; [*papiers*] staple; (*Méd*) clip

agrafer [agʀafe] ▶conjug 1◀ VT a [+ *vêtement*] to hook (up), fasten (up); [+ *papiers*] to staple b (‡ = *arrêter*) to bust‡, nab‡

agrafeuse [agʀaføz] NF stapler

agraire [agʀɛʀ] ADJ [*politique, loi*] agrarian; [*mesure, surface*] land (*épith*) → **réforme**

agrammatical, e (*mpl* **-aux**) [agʀamatikal, o] ADJ agrammatical

agrandir [agʀɑ̃diʀ] ▶conjug 2◀ 1 VT a (= *rendre plus grand*) [+ *passage*] to widen; [+ *trou*] to make bigger, enlarge; [+ *usine, domaine*] to enlarge, extend; [+ *écart*] to increase; [+ *photographie*] to enlarge, blow up*; (*à la loupe*) to magnify; (*en photocopiant*) to enlarge; **ce miroir agrandit la pièce** this mirror makes the room look bigger *ou* larger; (**faire**) **~ sa maison** to extend one's house
b (= *développer*) to extend, expand; **pour ~ le cercle de ses activités** to widen *ou* extend *ou* expand the scope of one's activities
c (= *ennoblir*) [+ *âme*] to uplift, elevate, ennoble
2 **s'agrandir** VPR [*ville, famille*] to grow, expand; [*écart*] to widen, grow, get bigger; [*passage*] to get wider; [*trou*] to get bigger; **il nous a fallu nous ~** we had to expand, we had to find a bigger place; **ses yeux s'agrandirent sous le coup de la surprise** his eyes widened *ou* grew wide with surprise

agrandissement [agʀɑ̃dismɑ̃] NM [*local*] extension; [*puissance, ville*] expansion; (*Photo*) (= *action*) enlargement; (= *photo*) enlargement, blow-up*

agrandisseur [agʀɑ̃disœʀ] NM enlarger

agraphie [agʀafi] NF agraphia

agrarien, -ienne [agʀaʀjɛ̃, jɛn] ADJ, NM (*Hist, Pol*) agrarian

agréable [agʀeabl] ADJ pleasant, agreeable; **~ à voir** nice to see; **~ à l'œil** pleasing to the eye; **~ à vivre** [*personne*] easy *ou* pleasant to live

▶ GRAMMAIRE ACTIVE: **agir** 53.2

with; [lieu] pleasant to live in; **il est toujours ~ de ...** it is always pleasant ou nice ou agreeable to ...; **ce que j'ai à dire n'est pas ~** what I have to say isn't a (very) pleasant; **si ça peut lui être ~** if that will please him; **il me serait ~ de ...** it would be a pleasure for me to ..., I should be pleased to ...; **être ~ de sa personne**† to be pleasant-looking ou personable; **l'~ de la chose** the pleasant ou nice thing about it → **joindre**

agréablement [agreabləmã] ADV pleasantly, agreeably; **nous avons ~ passé la soirée** we spent a pleasant ou a nice evening, we spent the evening pleasantly; **~ surpris** pleasantly surprised

agréé, e [agree] (ptp de **agréer**) ① ADJ [bureau, infirmière, nourrice] registered; **fournisseur ~** authorized ou registered dealer → **comptable** ② (†: Jur) counsel, attorney (US) (appearing for parties before a commercial court)

agréer [agree] ▸ conjug 1 ◂ (frm) ① VT (= accepter) [+ demande, excuses] to accept; (+ fournisseur, matériel] to approve; (formule épistolaire) **veuillez ~, Monsieur** ou **je vous prie d'~, Monsieur, l'expression de mes sentiments distingués** ou **les meilleurs** ou **l'assurance de ma considération distinguée** yours sincerely, sincerely yours (US); (plus impersonnel) yours faithfully ② **agréer à** VT INDIR [+ personne] to please, suit; **si cela vous agrée** if it suits ou pleases you, if you are agreeable

agrég* [agreg] NF ABRÉV = **agrégation**

agrégat [agrega] NM (Constr, Écon, Géol) aggregate; (péj) [idées] mishmash

agrégatif, -ive [agregatif, iv] NM,F candidate for the agrégation

agrégation [agregasjɔ̃] NF ⓐ (Univ) high-level competitive examination for recruiting teachers in France ⓑ [particules] aggregation

---

┌─── AGRÉGATION ───┐

The **agrégation** or "agrég", as it is known informally, is the highest qualification available for teachers at secondary level. Many university lecturers are also "agrégés". Candidates take a series of written papers in which they are expected to demonstrate in-depth knowledge of a single chosen field (mathematics, philosophy, English, etc). The candidates who obtain the best results in the written papers then go on to take the oral examination. → CAPES

---

agrégé, e [agreʒe] (ptp de **agréger**) NM,F qualified teacher (holder of the agrégation) → **professeur**

agréger [agreʒe] ▸ conjug 3 et 6 ◂ VT [+ particules] to aggregate; **~ qn à un groupe** to incorporate sb into a group; **s'~ à un groupe** to incorporate o.s. into a group

agrément [agremã] NM ⓐ (littér = charme) [personne, conversation] charm; [visage] attractiveness, charm; [lieu, climat] pleasantness, agreeableness, amenity (littér); **sa compagnie est pleine d'~** he is very pleasant company; **ville/maison sans ~** unattractive town/house, town/house with no agreeable ou attractive features; **les ~s de la vie** the pleasures of life, the pleasant things in life; **faire un voyage d'~** to go on ou make a pleasure trip → **art, jardin, plante¹** ⓑ (frm = consentement) consent, approval; (Jur) assent; **donner son ~ à qch** to give one's consent ou assent to sth ⓒ (Mus) (**note d'**)~ grace note

agrémenter [agremãte] ▸ conjug 1 ◂ VT **~ qch de** (= décorer) to embellish ou adorn sth with; (= relever) to accompany sth with; **agrémenté de broderies** trimmed ou embellished with embroidery; **conférence agrémentée de projections** lecture accompanied by slides; **~ un récit d'anecdotes** to pepper ou enliven a story with anecdotes; (iro) **dispute agrémentée de coups** argument enlivened with blows

agrès [agrɛ] NMPL (Aviat, Naut) tackle; (Sport) apparatus sg; **exercices aux ~** exercises on the apparatus, apparatus work

agresser [agrese] ▸ conjug 1 ◂ VT to attack; **il s'est senti agressé** (physiquement) he felt they (ou you etc) were being aggressive towards him; (psychologiquement) he felt they (ou you etc) were hostile towards him; **il l'a agressée verbalement et physiquement** he subjected her to verbal and physical abuse; **agressé par la vie moderne** feeling the strains ou stresses of modern life

agresseur [agresœʀ] NM attacker, assailant, aggressor; (**pays**) ~ aggressor

agressif, -ive [agresif, iv] ADJ (gén) aggressive (**envers** towards, with); **d'un ton ~** aggressively; **campagne publicitaire agressive** aggressive advertising campaign

agression [agresjɔ̃] NF (contre une personne) attack; (contre un pays) aggression; (dans la rue) mugging; (Psych) aggression; **~ nocturne** attack ou assault at night; **être victime d'une ~** to be mugged; **les ~s de la vie moderne** the stresses ou strains of modern living ou life

agressivement [agresivmã] ADV aggressively

agressivité [agresivite] NF aggression, aggressiveness

agreste [agrɛst] ADJ (littér) rustic

agricole [agrikɔl] ADJ [accord, machine, ressources, enseignement] agricultural; [produits, travaux] farm (épith), agricultural; [population] farming (épith), agricultural; **syndicat ~** farmers' union; **lycée ~** ≈ secondary school (Brit) ou high school (US) which trains farmers; **le monde ~** the agricultural ou farming world → **comice, exploitation**

agriculteur, -trice [agrikyltœʀ, tʀis] NM,F farmer

agriculture [agrikyltyʀ] NF agriculture, farming

agripper [agripe] ▸ conjug 1 ◂ ① VT (= se retenir à) to grab ou clutch (hold of), grasp; (= arracher) to snatch, grab ② **s'agripper** VPR **s'~ à qch** to cling on to sth, clutch ou grip sth; **ne t'agrippe pas à moi** don't cling on to ou hang on to me

agroalimentaire [agroalimãtɛʀ] ① ADJ [industrie] food-processing; **produits ~s** processed foodstuffs ② NM **l'~** the food-processing industry

agrochimie [agroʃimi] NF agrochemistry

agrochimique [agroʃimik] ADJ agrochemical

agro-industrie [agroɛ̃dystʀi] (pl **agro-industries**) NF agribusiness

agro-industriel, -elle [agroɛ̃dystʀijɛl] ADJ agro-industrial

agronome [agrɔnɔm] NMF agronomist; **ingénieur ~** agricultural engineer

agronomie [agrɔnɔmi] NF agronomy, agronomics sg

agronomique [agrɔnɔmik] ADJ agronomic(al)

agrume [agrym] NM citrus fruit

aguerrir [agerir] ▸ conjug 2 ◂ VT to harden; **~ qn contre qch** to harden sb to ou against sth, inure sb to sth; **des troupes aguerries** (au combat) seasoned troops; (à l'effort) trained troops; **s'~** to become hardened; **s'~ contre** to become hardened to ou against, inure o.s. to

aguets [agɛ] **◂ aux aguets** LOC ADV on the look-out, on the watch

aguichant, e [agiʃã, ãt] ADJ enticing, tantalizing

aguiche [agiʃ] NF teaser

aguicher [agiʃe] ▸ conjug 1 ◂ VT to entice, lead on, tantalize

aguicheur, -euse [agiʃœʀ, øz] ① ADJ enticing, tantalizing ② NM (= enjôleur) seducer ③ **aguicheuse** NF (= allumeuse) teaser, vamp

ah [ʼɑ] ① EXCL ⓐ (réponse, réaction exclamative) ah!, oh!, ooh!; (question) **~ ? ◊ bon ? ◊ oui ?**

really?, is that so?; (résignation) **~ bon** oh ou ah well; (insistance) **~ oui** oh yes, yes indeed; (insistance) **~ non** oh no, certainly ou definitely not; **~ bien (ça) alors !** (surprise) well, well!, just fancy! (Brit); (indignation) well really!; **~ bien oui** well of course ⓑ (intensif) ah!, oh!; **~ ! j'allais oublier** oh! ou ah! I nearly forgot; **~, ~ ! je t'y prends** aha! ou oho! I've caught you at it; **~, qu'il est lent !** oh, he's so slow! ② NM **pousser un ~ de soulagement** to sigh with relief, give a sigh of relief; **des ~s d'allégresse** oohs and ahs of joy

ahan†† [aɑ̃] NM **à grand ~** with much striving

ahaner [aane] ▸ conjug 1 ◂ VI ⓐ (†† ou littér) (= peiner) to labour (Brit), labor (US), make great efforts; (= respirer) to breathe heavily; **ahanant sous le fardeau** labouring under the burden

ahuri, e [ayri] ① ADJ (ptp de **ahurir**) (= stupéfait) stunned, flabbergasted; (= hébété, stupide) stupefied; **avoir l'air ~** to look stunned ou stupefied; **ne prends pas cet air ~** don't look so flabbergasted ② NM,F (péj) blockhead*, nitwit*

ahurir [ayriʀ] ▸ conjug 2 ◂ VT to dumbfound, astound, stun

ahurissant, e [ayrisã, ãt] ADJ stupefying, astounding; (sens affaibli) staggering

ahurissement [ayrismã] NM stupefaction

aï [ai] NM (Zool) ai

aiche [ɛʃ] NF = **èche**

aide¹ [ɛd] ① NF ⓐ (= assistance) help, assistance; **apporter son ~ à qn** to help ou assist sb; **son ~ nous a été précieuse** he was a great help to us, his help was invaluable to us; **appeler/crier à l'~** to call/shout for help; **venir en ~ à qn** to help sb, come to sb's assistance ou aid; **à l'~ !** help!; **sans l'~ de personne** without any help (from anyone), completely unassisted ou unaided ⓑ **à l'~ de** with the help ou aid of; **ouvrir qch à l'~ d'un couteau** to open sth with a knife ⓒ (en équipement, en argent etc) aid; **l'~ humanitaire/alimentaire** humanitarian/food aid ou relief; **~ de l'État** government ou state aid ⓓ (Équitation) **~s** aids ⓔ (Ordin) help; **~ en ligne (contextuelle)** (context-sensitive) help ② COMP ▸ **aide au développement** development aid ▸ **aide à l'embauche** employment incentive ▸ **aide judiciaire** legal aid ▸ **aide médicale (gratuite)** (free) medical aid ▸ **aide personnalisée au logement** ≈ housing benefit (Brit) ou subsidy (US) ▸ **aide au retour** repatriation grant (for immigrants returning to their country of origin) ▸ **aide sociale** social security (Brit), welfare (US)

aide² [ɛd] ① NMF (= personne) assistant; **~-chimiste/-chirurgien** assistant chemist/surgeon; **~-maçon** builder's mate (Brit) ou labourer ② COMP ▸ **aide de camp** aide-de-camp ▸ **aide de cuisine** kitchen hand ▸ **aide électricien** electrician's mate (Brit) ou helper (US) ▸ **aide familiale** (= personne) mother's help (Brit) ou helper (US), home help ▸ **aide jardinier** gardener's helper ou mate (Brit), under-gardener (Brit) ▸ **aide de laboratoire** laboratory assistant ▸ **aide maternelle** = aide familiale

aide-comptable (pl **aides-comptables**) [ɛdkɔ̃tabl] NMF accountant's assistant

aide-mémoire [ɛdmemwaʀ] NM INV (gén) aide-mémoire; (Scol) crib

aide-ménagère (pl **aides-ménagères**) [ɛdmenaʒɛʀ] NF home help (Brit), home helper (US)

aider [ede] ▸ conjug 1 ◂ ① VT to help; **~ qn (à faire qch)** to help sb (to do sth); **~ qn à monter/à descendre/à traverser** to help sb up/down/across ou over; **il a aidé à sortir de la voiture** he helped him out of the car; **il m'a**

aidé de ses conseils he gave me some helpful advice; **~ qn financièrement** to help sb (out) *ou* assist sb financially, give sb financial help; **il m'aide beaucoup** he helps me a lot, he's a great help to me; **je me suis fait ~ par** *ou* **de mon frère** I got my brother to help *ou* assist me *ou* to give me a hand; **elle ne se déplace qu'aidée de sa canne** she can only get about with (the aid *ou* help of) her walking stick; (*hum*) **il n'est pas aidé !*** nature hasn't been kind to him!

② VI to help; **elle est venue pour ~** she came to help (out) *ou* to give *ou* lend a hand; **~ à la cuisine** to help (out) in *ou* give a hand in the kitchen; **le débat aiderait à la compréhension du problème** discussion would contribute towards an understanding of the problem, discussion would help us to understand the problem; **ça aide à passer le temps** it helps (to) pass the time; **l'alcool aidant, il se mit à parler** helped on by the alcohol *ou* with the help of alcohol, he began to speak → **dieu**

③ **s'aider** VPR ⓐ **s'~ de** to use, make use of; **atteindre le placard en s'aidant d'un escabeau** to reach the cupboard by using a stool *ou* with the aid of a stool; **en s'aidant de ses bras** using his arms to help him

ⓑ (*loc*) **entre voisins il faut s'~** neighbours should help each other (out) ▪ (*PROV*) **aide-toi, le ciel t'-a** God helps those who help themselves (*PROV*)

aide-soignant, e (*mpl* **aides-soignants**) [ɛdswaɲɑ̃, ɑ̃t] NM,F nursing auxiliary (*Brit*), nurse's aide (*US*)

aïe [aj] EXCL (*douleur*) ouch!, ow!; **aïe ~ ~!, ça se présente mal** dear oh dear, things don't look too good!

AIEA [aiea] NF (ABRÉV = **Agence internationale de l'énergie atomique**) IAEA

aïeul [ajœl] NM (*littér*) grandfather; **les ~s** the grandparents

aïeule [ajœl] NF (*littér*) grandmother

aïeux [ajø] NMPL (*littér*) forefathers, forebears, ancestors; **mes ~!** (*, † ou hum*) my godfathers!* †, by jingo!* †

aigle [ɛgl] ① NM (= *oiseau, lutrin*) eagle; **~ royal** golden eagle; **~ d'Amérique** American eagle; **~ de mer** (= *oiseau*) sea eagle; (= *poisson*) eagle ray; **il a un regard d'~** he has eyes like a hawk, he's eagle-eyed; **ce n'est pas un ~*** he's no genius ② NF (= *oiseau, insigne*) eagle

aiglefin [ɛgləfɛ̃] NM haddock

aiglon, -onne [ɛglɔ̃, ɔn] NM,F eaglet; (*Hist*) **l'Aiglon** Napoleon II

aigre [ɛgʀ] ① ADJ ⓐ [*fruit*] sour, sharp; [*vin*] vinegary, sour; [*goût, odeur, lait*] sour; (*fig*) **tourner à l'~** to turn sour → **crème** ⓑ [*son, voix*] sharp, shrill; ⓒ [*froid*] bitter; [*vent*] keen, cutting (*épith*); ⓓ [*propos, critique*] cutting (*épith*), harsh

aigre-doux, aigre-douce (*mpl* **aigres-doux**, *fpl* **aigres-douces**) [ɛgʀədu, dus] ADJ [*sauce*] sweet and sour; [*fruit*] bitter-sweet; [*propos*] bitter-sweet

aigrefin [ɛgʀəfɛ̃] NM swindler, crook

aigrelet, -ette [ɛgʀəlɛ, ɛt] ADJ [*petit-lait, pomme*] sourish; [*vin*] vinegarish; [*voix, son*] shrill

aigrement [ɛgʀəmɑ̃] ADV [*répondre, dire*] sourly

aigrette [ɛgʀɛt] NF (= *plume*) feather; (= *oiseau*) egret; (= *bijou*) aigret(te); (*Bot*) pappus

aigreur [ɛgʀœʀ] ① NF ⓐ (= *acidité*) [*petit-lait*] sourness; [*vin*] sourness, acidity; [*pomme*] sourness, sharpness ⓑ (= *acrimonie*) sharpness, harshness ② **aigreurs** NFPL **avoir des ~s (d'estomac)** to have heartburn

aigri, e [ɛgʀi] (*ptp de* **aigrir**) ADJ embittered, bitter

aigrir [ɛgʀiʀ] ▸ conjug 2 ◂ ① VT [+ *personne*] to embitter; [+ *caractère*] to sour ② **s'aigrir** VPR

[*aliment*] to turn sour; [*caractère*] to sour; **il s'est aigri** he has become embittered

aigu, -uë [egy] ① ADJ ⓐ [*son, voix*] high-pitched, shrill; [*note*] high-pitched, high ⓑ [*crise, problème*] acute; [*douleur*] acute, sharp; [*intelligence*] keen, acute ⓒ (= *pointu*) sharp, pointed → **accent, angle** ② NM (*Mus: sur bouton de réglage*) treble; **les ~s** the high notes; **passer du grave à l'~** to go from low to high pitch

aigue-marine (*pl* **aigues-marines**) [ɛgmaʀin] NF aquamarine

aiguière [ɛgjɛʀ] NF ewer

aiguillage [egɥijaʒ] NM (*Rail*) (= *action*) shunting (*Brit*), switching (*US*); (= *instrument*) points (*Brit*), switch (*US*); **le déraillement est dû à une erreur d'~** the derailment was due to faulty shunting (*Brit*) *ou* switching (*US*); (*fig*) **il y a eu une erreur d'~** (*gén*) it (*ou* he *etc*) was sent to the wrong place; (*orientation scolaire*) he was (*ou* they were *etc*) pointed *ou* steered in the wrong direction → **cabine, poste**

aiguille [egɥij] ① NF ⓐ (*Bot, Couture, Méd*) needle; **~ à coudre/à tricoter/à repriser** sewing/knitting/darning needle; **~ hypodermique** hypodermic needle; **travail à l'~** needlework → **chercher, fil, tirer** ⓑ [*compteur, boussole, gramophone*] needle; [*horloge*] hand; [*balance*] pointer, needle; [*cadran solaire*] pointer, index; [*clocher*] spire; (*Rail*) point (*Brit*), switch (*US*); (*Géog*) (= *pointe*) needle; (= *cime*) peak; **en forme d'~** needle-shaped; **la petite/grande ~** [*horloge*] the hour/minute hand, the little/big hand ② COMP ▸ **aiguille de glace** icicle ▸ **aiguille de pin** pine needle

aiguillée [egɥije] NF length of thread (*for use with needle at any one time*)

aiguiller [egɥije] ▸ conjug 1 ◂ VT ⓐ (= *orienter*) to direct; **~ un enfant vers le technique** to direct *ou* orientate *ou* steer a child towards technical studies; (*Scol*) **on l'a mal aiguillé** he was steered in the wrong direction; **~ la conversation sur un autre sujet** to steer the conversation onto another subject; **~ la police sur une mauvaise piste** to put the police onto the wrong track ⓑ (*Rail*) to shunt (*Brit*), switch (*US*)

aiguillette [egɥijɛt] NF [*pourpoint*] aglet; (*Culin, Mil*) aiguillette

aiguilleur [egɥijœʀ] NM (*Rail*) pointsman (*Brit*), switchman (*US*); (*Aviat*) **~ du ciel** air-traffic controller

aiguillon [egɥijɔ̃] NM [*insecte*] sting; [*bouvier*] goad; (*Bot*) thorn; (*fig*) spur, stimulus

aiguillonner [egɥijɔne] ▸ conjug 1 ◂ VT [+ *bœuf*] to goad; (*fig*) to spur *ou* goad on

aiguisage [egiza ʒ] NM [*couteau, outil*] sharpening

aiguiser [egize] ▸ conjug 1 ◂ VT ⓐ [+ *couteau, outil*] to sharpen ⓑ [+ *appétit*] to whet, stimulate; [+ *sens*] to excite, stimulate; [+ *esprit*] to sharpen; [+ *style*] to polish

aiguiseur, -euse [egizœʀ, øz] NM,F sharpener, grinder

aiguisoir [egizwaʀ] NM sharpener, sharpening tool

aïkido [aikido] NM aikido

ail (*pl* **ails, aulx**) [aj, o] NM garlic → **gousse, saucisson, tête**

ailante [ɛlɑ̃t] NM tree of heaven, ailanthus (*SPÉC*)

aile [ɛl] ① NF ⓐ [*oiseau, château*] wing; [*moulin*] sail; [*hélice, ventilateur*] blade, vane; [*nez*] wing; [*voiture*] wing (*Brit*), fender (*US*); [*pont*] abutment

ⓑ (*Sport*) wing; **il joue à l'~ gauche** he plays left wing

ⓒ (*Mil, Pol*) wing; **l'~ dure du parti** the hardline wing of the party, the hardliners in the party; (*Mil*) **~ marchante** wheeling flank

ⓓ (*loc*) **l'oiseau disparut d'un coup d'~** the bird disappeared with a flap of its wings; **d'un coup d'~ nous avons gagné Orly** we reached Orly in no time (at all); (*fig*) **avoir des ~s** to have wings; **l'espoir lui donnait des ~s** hope lent *ou* gave him wings; **prendre sous son ~ (protectrice)** to take under one's wing; **sous l'~ maternelle** under one's mother's *ou* the maternal wing; **avoir un coup dans l'~*** (= *être ivre*) to have had one too many*; (= *être en mauvaise posture*) to be in a very bad way* → **peur, plomb, tire-d'aile(s)** *etc*

② COMP ▸ **aile de corbeau** (= *couleur*) inky black, jet-black ▸ **aile delta** (*Aviat*) delta wing; (= *deltaplane*) hang-glider; **faire de l'~ delta** to go hang-gliding ▸ **aile libre** (*Sport*) hang-gliding; (= *appareil*) hang-glider

ailé, e [ele] ADJ (*lit, littér*) winged

aileron [ɛlʀɔ̃] NM [*poisson*] fin; [*oiseau*] pinion; [*avion*] aileron; (*Aut: de stabilisation*) aerofoil; (*Archit*) console

ailette [ɛlɛt] NF [*missile, radiateur*] fin; [*turbine, ventilateur*] blade; (*Aut*) **~ de refroidissement** cooling fan

ailier [elje] NM (*gén*) winger; (*Rugby*) flanker, wing-forward

aillade [ajad] NF (= *sauce*) garlic dressing *ou* sauce; (= *croûton*) garlic crouton

ailler [aje] ▸ conjug 1 ◂ VT to flavour with garlic

▼ **ailleurs** [ajœʀ] ADV ⓐ (= *autre part*) somewhere else, elsewhere; **nulle part ~** nowhere else; **partout ~** everywhere else; **il est ◊ l'esprit ~** his thoughts are *ou* his mind is elsewhere, he's miles away; **ils viennent d'~** they come from somewhere else; **nous sommes passés (par) ~** we went another way; **je l'ai su par ~** I heard of it from another source ⓑ **par ~** (= *autrement*) otherwise, in other respects; (= *en outre*) moreover, furthermore; **d'~ be-sides, moreover; d'~ il faut avouer que ...** anyway *ou* besides we have to admit that ...; **ce vin, d'~ très bon, n'est pas ...** this wine, which I may add is very good *ou* which is very good by the way, is not ...; **lui non plus d'~** neither does (*ou* is, has *etc*) he, for that matter

ailloli [ajɔli] NM aïoli, garlic mayonnaise

aimable [ɛmabl] ADJ ⓐ (= *gentil*) [*parole*] kind, nice; [*personne*] kind, nice, amiable (*frm*); **c'est un homme ~** he's a (very) nice man; **tu es bien ~ de m'avoir attendu** it was very nice *ou* kind of you to wait for me; **c'est très ~ à vous** *ou* **de votre part** it's most kind of you; (*frm*) **soyez assez ~ pour ...** would you be so kind *ou* good as to ...; **~ comme une porte de prison** like a bear with a sore head ⓑ († = *agréable*) [*endroit, moment*] pleasant ⓒ († = *digne d'amour*) lovable, amiable†

aimablement [ɛmabləmɑ̃] ADV [*agir*] kindly, nicely; [*répondre, recevoir*] amiably, nicely; [*re-fuser*] politely; **il m'a offert ~ à boire** he kindly offered me a drink

aimant¹ [ɛmɑ̃] NM magnet; **~ (naturel)** magnetite (*NonC*), lodestone

aimant², e [ɛmɑ̃, ɑ̃t] ADJ loving, affectionate

aimantation [ɛmɑ̃tasjɔ̃] NF magnetization

aimanté, e [ɛmɑ̃te] (*ptp de* **aimanter**) ADJ [*aiguille, champ*] magnetic

aimanter [ɛmɑ̃te] ▸ conjug 1 ◂ VT to magnetize

▼ **aimer** [eme] ▸ conjug 1 ◂ ① VT ⓐ (*d'amour*) to love; (*d'amitié, attachement, goût*) to like, be fond of; **~ beaucoup** [+ *personne*] to like very much *ou* a lot, be very fond of; [+ *animaux, choses*] to like very much *ou* a lot, be very fond of, love; **~ bien** to like, be fond of; **il l'aime d'amour** he really loves her; **il l'aime à la folie** he adores her, he's crazy about her*; **j'aime une bonne tasse de café après déjeuner** I like *ou* enjoy *ou* love a nice cup of coffee after lunch; **les hortensias aiment l'ombre** hydrangeas like shade; **tous ces trucs-là, tu aimes, toi ?*** do you go in for all that kind of stuff?*; **un enfant mal aimé** a child who doesn't get enough love; **il est mal aimé du public** the public don't like him; **je n'aime pas beaucoup cet acteur** I don't care for *ou* I don't like that actor very much, I'm not very keen on (Brit) that actor; **elle n'aime pas le tennis** she doesn't like tennis *ou* care for tennis, she's not keen on (Brit) tennis; **les enfants aiment qu'on s'occupe d'eux** children like *ou* love attention; **elle n'aime pas qu'il sorte le soir** she doesn't like him going out *ou* him to go out at night; **~ faire ◊ ~ à faire** (littér) to like doing *ou* to do; (frm *ou* hum) **j'aime à penser** *ou* **à croire que ...** I like to think that ...; (hum) **qui m'aime me suive!** anyone who wants to come with me is welcome! ■ (PROV) **qui m'aime aime mon chien** love me love my dog ■ (PROV) **qui aime bien châtie bien** spare the rod and spoil the child (PROV)

b (avec assez, autant, mieux) **j'aime autant vous dire que je n'irai pas!** I may as well tell you that I won't go!; **il aime** *ou* **aimerait autant ne pas sortir aujourd'hui** he'd just as soon not go out today, he'd be just as happy not going out today; **j'aimerais autant que ce soit elle qui m'écrive** I'd rather it was she who wrote to me; **j'aime autant qu'elle ne soit pas venue** I'm just as happy *ou* it's (probably) just as well she didn't come; **j'aime autant ça!** (ton menaçant) I'm pleased to hear it!, that sounds more like it!*; (soulagement) what a relief!; **on lui apporte des fleurs, elle aimerait mieux des livres** they bring her flowers but she'd rather *ou* sooner have *ou* she'd prefer books; **il aurait mieux aimé se reposer que d'aller au cinéma** he'd rather have rested *ou* he'd have preferred to rest than go to the cinema; **j'aime mieux te dire qu'il va m'entendre!*** I'm going to give him a piece of my mind, I can tell you!; **elle aime assez** *ou* **bien bavarder avec les voisins** she quite *ou* rather likes chatting with the neighbours

c (au conditionnel = vouloir) **aimeriez-vous une tasse de thé?** would you like a cup of tea?, would you care for a cup of tea?; **elle aimerait bien aller se promener** she'd like to go for a walk; **j'aimerais vraiment venir** I'd really like to come, I'd love to come; **je n'aimerais pas être dehors par ce temps** I wouldn't want *ou* like to be out in this (sort of) weather; **j'aimerais assez/je n'aimerais pas ce genre de manteau** I'd rather *ou* quite like/wouldn't like a coat like that

2 s'aimer VPR **a** (= s'apprécier) **ils s'aiment** they're in love, they love each other; **aimez-vous les uns les autres** love one another; **ces deux-là ne s'aiment guère** there's no love lost between those two; **elle a réussi à se faire ~ par lui** she managed to win his love *ou* heart; **essayer de se faire ~ de qn** to try to win sb's affection; **je ne m'aime pas avec ce chapeau** I don't like myself in this hat

b (= faire l'amour) to make love

aine [ɛn] NF (Anat) groin

aîné, e [ene] **1** ADJ (= plus âgé) elder, older; (= le plus âgé) eldest, oldest **2** NM **a** (famille) **l'~ (des garçons)** the eldest boy; **mon (frère) ~ (plus âgé)** my older *ou* elder brother; (le plus âgé) my oldest *ou* eldest brother; **mon ~** my oldest *ou* eldest boy *ou* son **b** (relation d'âges) **il est mon ~** he's older than me; **il est mon ~ de 2 ans** he's 2 years older than me, he's 2 years my senior; (littér) **respectez vos ~s** respect your elders **3 aînée** NF **a** (famille) **l'~e (des filles)** the oldest *ou* eldest girl *ou* daughter; **ma sœur ~e ◊ mon ~e** (plus âgée) my older *ou* elder sister; (la plus âgée) my oldest *ou* eldest sister **b** (relation d'âge) **elle est mon ~e** she's older than me; **elle est mon ~e de 2 ans** she's 2 years older than me, 2 years my senior

aînesse [ɛnɛs] NF → **droit³**

▼ **ainsi** [ɛ̃si] ADV **a** (= de cette façon) in this way *ou* manner; **je préfère agir ~** I prefer to do it this way; **il faut procéder ~** you have to pro-

---

ceed as follows *ou* thus *ou* in this manner, this is how to proceed; **c'est ~ que ça s'est passé** that's the way *ou* how it happened; **pourquoi me traites-tu ~?** why do you treat me like this? *ou* in this way?; **~ finit son grand amour** thus ended his great love; **il n'en est pas ~ pour tout le monde** it's not so *ou* the case for everyone; **s'il en est ~** *ou* **puisque c'est ~, je m'en vais** if *ou* since that's the way it is, I'm leaving, if *ou* since that's how it is, I'm leaving; **s'il en était ~** if this were the case; **il en sera ~ et pas autrement** that's the way it's going to be and that's that

b (littér = en conséquence) thus; (= donc) so; **ils ont perdu le procès, ~ ils sont ruinés** they lost the case and so they are ruined; **~ tu vas partir!** so, you're going to leave!

c (littér = de même) so, in the same way; **comme le berger mène ses moutons, ~ le pasteur guide ses ouailles** as the shepherd leads his sheep, so the minister guides his flock

d **~ que** (just) as; (littér) **~ qu'il vous plaira** (just) as it pleases you; **~ que nous avons dit hier** just as we said yesterday; **la jalousie, ~ qu'un poison subtil, s'insinuait en lui** like a subtle poison, jealousy was slowly taking hold of him; **sa beauté ~ que sa candeur me frappèrent** I was struck by her beauty as well as her innocence

e (loc) **pour ~ dire** so to speak, as it were; **ils sont pour ~ dire ruinés** they are ruined, so to speak *ou* as it were, you might say they are ruined; **~ soit-il** (gén) so be it; (Rel) amen; **et ~ de suite** and so on (and so forth); **~ va le monde** that's the way of the world

aïoli [ajɔli] NM = **ailloli**

air¹ [ɛr] **1** NM **a** (= gaz) air; (= brise) (light) breeze; (= courant d'air) draught (Brit), draft (US); **l'~ de la campagne/de la mer** the country/sea air; **l'~ de la ville ne lui convient pas** town air *ou* the air of the town doesn't suit him; **on manque d'~ ici** there's no air in here, it's stuffy in here; **donnez-nous un peu d'~** give us some (fresh) air; **sortir à l'~ libre** to go out into the open air; **mettre la literie à l'~** to put the bedclothes (out) to air *ou* out for an airing, air the bedclothes; **se promener les fesses à l'~** to walk around bare-bottomed; **sortir prendre l'~** to go out for some *ou* a breath of (fresh) air; (Naut) **il y a des ~s** there's a wind (up); **il y a un peu d'~ aujourd'hui** there's a light *ou* slight breeze today; **on sent de l'~ qui vient de la porte** you can feel a draught (Brit) *ou* draft (US) from the door → **bol, chambre, courant** etc

b **plein ~** open air; (Scol) **les enfants ont plein ~ le mercredi** the children have games *ou* sport on Wednesdays; **en plein ~** [piscine] outdoor (épith), open-air (épith); [spectacle, cirque] open-air (épith); [jouer] outdoors; [s'asseoir] outdoors, (out) in the open (air); **de plein ~** [activité, jeux] outdoor (épith)

c (= espace) air; **s'élever dans l'~** *ou* **dans les ~s** to rise (up) into the skies *ou* the air; **regarder en l'~** to look up; **avoir le nez en l'~** to gaze vacantly into space; **jeter qch en l'~** to throw sth (up) into the air; **transports par ~** air transport, transport by air; **l'avion a pris l'~** the plane has taken off; **de l'~** [hôtesse, ministère] air (épith) → **armée², école, mal**

d (= atmosphère, ambiance) atmosphere; **il est allé prendre l'~ du bureau** he has gone to see how things look *ou* what things look like at the office; **tout le monde se dispute, l'~ de la maison est irrespirable** everyone's quarrelling and the atmosphere in the house is unbearable; **il a besoin de l'~ de la ville** he needs the atmosphere of the town

e **ces idées étaient dans l'~ à cette époque** those ideas were in the air at that time; **il y a de la bagarre/de l'orage dans l'~** there's a fight/storm brewing; **la grippe est dans l'~** there's a lot of flu about; **vivre** *ou* **se nourrir de**

---

l'~ du temps to live on air *ou* on nothing at all; **c'est dans l'~ du temps** it's part of the current climate

f **en l'~** [paroles, promesses] idle, empty; [dire] rashly; **ce ne sont encore que des projets en l'~** the plans are still very much (up) in the air; (désordre) **tout était en l'~ dans la pièce** the room was in a total mess; **flanquer*** *ou* **ficher*** *ou* **foutre** **tout en l'~** (= jeter) to chuck* *ou* sling* (Brit) it all away *ou* out; (= abandonner) to chuck it all in* *ou* up* (Brit); **ce contretemps a fichu en l'~ mon week-end*** this hitch has completely messed up my weekend*; **en courant, il a flanqué le vase en l'~*** he knocked the vase over as he ran past; **se ficher*** *ou* **se foutre** **en l'~** (accidentellement) to smash o.s. up*; (= se suicider) to do o.s. in → **parler**

2 COMP ► **air comprimé** compressed air ► **air conditionné** (système) air conditioning; (atmosphère) conditioned air; **le bureau a l'~ conditionné** the office has air conditioning *ou* is air-conditioned ► **air liquide** liquid air

air² [ɛr] NM **a** (= apparence, manière) air; **d'un ~ décidé** in a resolute manner; **sous son ~ calme c'est un homme énergique** beneath his calm appearance he is a forceful man; **un garçon à l'~ éveillé** a lively-looking boy; **ils ont un ~ de famille** there's a family likeness between them; **ça lui donne l'~ d'un clochard** it makes him look like a tramp; **avoir grand ~** to look very impressive → **faux²**

b (= expression) look, air; **d'un ~ perplexe** with a look *ou* an air of perplexity, with a perplexed air *ou* look; **je lui trouve un drôle d'~** I think he looks funny *ou* very odd; **prendre un ~ éploré** to put on *ou* adopt a tearful expression; **elle a pris son petit ~ futé pour me dire** she told me in her sly little way, she put on that sly look she has *ou* hers of hers to tell me; **prendre un ~ entendu** to put on a knowing air; **prendre un ~ pincé** to put on a prim expression

c (loc) **elle a l'~ d'une enfant** she looks like a child; **ça m'a l'~ d'un mensonge** it looks to me *ou* sounds to me like a lie; **ça m'a l'~ d'être assez facile** it strikes me as being fairly easy, it looks fairly easy to me; **elle a l'~ intelligent(e)** she looks *ou* seems intelligent; **il a l'~ stupide — et il a l'~ et la chanson*** he looks idiotic — he doesn't just look it either!*; **il a eu l'~ de ne pas comprendre** he looked as if *ou* as though he didn't understand, he didn't seem to understand; (faire semblant) he pretended not to understand; **elle n'avait pas l'~ de vouloir travailler** she didn't look as if *ou* as though she wanted to work; **il est très ambitieux sans en avoir l'~** he might not look it but he's very ambitious, he's very ambitious although he might not look it *ou* doesn't really look it; **ça (m')a tout l'~ d'être une fausse alerte** it looks (to me) as if it's a false alarm; **il a l'~ de vouloir neiger** it looks like snow; **de quoi j'ai l'~ maintenant!*** ◊ **j'ai l'~ fin maintenant!*** I look like a real idiot *ou* a right fool now*; **il n'a l'~ de rien, mais il sait ce qu'il fait** you wouldn't think it to look at him but he knows what he's doing; **cette plante n'a l'~ de rien, pourtant elle donne de très jolies fleurs** this plant doesn't look much but it has very pretty flowers; **sans avoir l'~ de rien, filons discrètement** let's just behave naturally and slip away unnoticed; **ça m'a tout de même coûté 5 000 F, de l'~ de rien** even so, it still cost me 5,000 francs; **avec un ~ de ne pas y toucher ◊ sans avoir l'~ d'y toucher** looking as if butter wouldn't melt in his (*ou* her) mouth; **il a dit ça avec son ~ de ne pas y toucher** he said it with the most innocent expression on his face

air³ [ɛr] NM [opéra] aria; (= mélodie) tune, air; **~ d'une chanson** the tune of a song; **~ d'opéra** operatic aria; **~ de danse** dance tune; (lit,

➤ GRAMMAIRE ACTIVE: **ainsi** 53.5

fig) ~ **connu** familiar tune; **chanter des slogans sur l'~ des lampions** to chant slogans

airain [ɛRɛ̃] NM *(littér)* bronze

air-air [ɛRɛR] ADJ INV *(Mil)* air-to-air

airbag® [ɛRbag] NM *(Aut)* air bag

Airbus® [ɛRbys] NM Airbus®

aire [ɛR] NF *(= zone)* area, zone; *(Math)* area; *[aigle]* eyrie; **~ d'atterrissage** landing strip; *(pour hélicoptère)* landing pad; *(Agr)* **~ de battage** threshing floor; *(Géol)* **~s continentales** continental shields; **~ d'embarquement** boarding area; **~ de jeux** (adventure) playground; **~ de lancement** launching site; **~ linguistique** linguistic region; *(sur autoroute)* **~ de repos** rest area *(on motorway etc)*; **~ de service** service station, motorway services *(Brit)*, service plaza *(US)*; **~ de stationnement** *(Aut)* parking area; *(Aviat)* apron; *(Naut)* **~ de vent** rhumb; **suivant l'~ de vent** following the rhumb-line route, taking a rhumb-line course

airelle [ɛRɛl] NF *(= myrtille)* blueberry, bilberry, whortleberry; **~ des marais** cranberry

air-sol [ɛRsɔl] ADJ INV *(Mil)* air-to-ground

air-terre [ɛRtɛR] ADJ INV *(Mil)* air-to-ground

aisance [ɛzɑ̃s] NF [a] *(= facilité)* ease; **s'exprimer avec une rare ou parfaite ~** to express o.s. with great ease; **il patinait avec une rare ou parfaite ~** he skated with the greatest of ease ou with great ease; **il y a beaucoup d'~ dans son style** he has an easy ou a flowing style ou a very fluent style [b] *(= richesse)* affluence; **vivre dans l'~** to be comfortably off ou well-off, live comfortably [c] *(Couture)* **redonner de l'~ sous les bras** to give more freedom of movement under the arms → **pli** [d] → **cabinet, fosse, lieu¹**

aise [ɛz] [1] NF a *(littér)* joy, pleasure, satisfaction; **j'ai tant d'~ à vous voir** I'm so pleased to see you; **sourire d'~** to smile with pleasure; **tous ces compliments la comblaient d'~** she was overjoyed at all these compliments [b] *(loc)* **être à l'~ ou être à son ~** *(dans une situation)* to be ou feel at ease; *(dans un vêtement, fauteuil)* to be ou feel comfortable; *(= être riche)* to be comfortably off ou comfortable; **être mal à l'~ ou ◊ être mal à son ~** *(dans une situation)* to be ou feel ill at ease; *(dans un vêtement, fauteuil)* to be ou feel uncomfortable; **mettez-vous à l'~ ou à votre ~** make yourself comfortable, make yourself at home; **leur hôtesse les mit tout de suite à l'~** their hostess immediately put them at (their) ease ou made them feel immediately at home; **faire qch à l'~*** to do sth easily; **tu comptes faire ça en deux heures? — à l'~!** do you think you can do that in 2 hours? — easily! ou no problem!*; **en prendre à son ~ avec qch** to make free with sth, do exactly as one likes with sth; **vous en prenez à votre ~!** you're taking things nice and easy!; **tu en parles à ton ~!** it's easy (enough) ou it's all right for you to talk!; **à votre ~!** please yourself!, just as you like!; **on tient à quatre à l'~ dans cette voiture** this car holds four (quite) comfortably, four can get in this car (quite) comfortably

[2] **aises** NFPL **aimer ses ~s** to like ou be fond of one's (creature) comforts; *(iro)* **tu prends tes ~s!** make yourself at home, why don't you! *(iro)*

[3] ADJ *(littér)* **bien ~** delighted, most pleased *(de* to); **j'ai terminé — j'en suis fort ~** I've finished — I'm so glad ou I am most pleased

aisé, e [eze] ADJ [a] *(= facile)* easy *(à faire* to do) [b] *(= dégagé)* [démarche] easy, graceful; [style] flowing, fluent [c] *(= riche)* well-to-do, comfortably off *(attrib)*, well-off

aisément [ezemɑ̃] ADV *(= sans peine)* easily; *(= sans réserves)* readily; *(= dans la richesse)* comfortably

aisselle [ɛsɛl] NF *(Anat)* armpit, axilla *(SPÉC)*; *(Bot)* axil

AIT [aite] NF (ABRÉV = **Association internationale du tourisme**) → **association**

Aix-la-Chapelle [ɛkslaʃapɛl] N Aachen

Ajax [aʒaks] NM Ajax

ajonc [aʒɔ̃] NM gorse bush; **des ~s** gorse *(NonC)*, furze *(NonC)*

ajour [aʒuR] NM *(gén pl)* [broderie, sculpture] openwork *(NonC)*

ajouré, e [aʒuRe] *(ptp de* **ajourer**) ADJ [mouchoir] openwork *(épith)*, hemstitched; [bijou, sculpture] which has an openwork design

ajourer [aʒuRe] ▶conjug 1◀ VT [+ sculpture] to ornament with openwork; [+ mouchoir] to hemstitch

ajournement [aʒuRnəmɑ̃] NM [assemblée] adjournment; [réunion, élection, décision, rendez-vous] postponement; [candidat] referral; [conscrit] deferment

ajourner [aʒuRne] ▶conjug 1◀ VT [+ assemblée] to adjourn; [+ réunion, élection, décision, rendez-vous] to postpone, put off; [+ candidat] to refer; [+ conscrit] to defer; **réunion ajournée d'une semaine/au lundi suivant** meeting adjourned ou delayed for a week/until the following Monday

▼ **ajout** [aʒu] NM *[texte]* addition

▼ **ajouter** [aʒute] ▶conjug 1◀ [1] VT [a] *(= mettre, faire ou dire en plus)* to add; **ajoute un peu de sel** put a bit more salt in, add a bit of salt; **je dois ~ que ...** I should add that ...; **sans ~ un mot** without (saying ou adding) another word; **ajoutez à cela qu'il pleuvait** on top of that ou in addition to that ou what's more, it was raining; **ajoutez à cela sa maladresse naturelle** add to that his natural clumsiness [b] **~ foi aux dires de qn** to lend ou give credence to sb's statements, believe sb's statements

[2] **ajouter à** VT INDIR *(littér)* to add to, increase; **ton arrivée ajoute à mon bonheur** I am even happier now you are here, your arrival adds to my happiness

[3] **s'ajouter** VPR **s'~ à** to add to; **ces malheurs venant s'~ à leur pauvreté** these misfortunes adding further to their poverty; **ceci, venant s'~ à ses difficultés** this coming on top of ou to add further to his difficulties; **à ces dépenses viennent s'~ les impôts** on top of ou in addition to these expenses there are taxes

ajustage [aʒystaʒ] NM *(Tech)* fitting

ajusté, e [aʒyste] *(ptp de* **ajuster**) ADJ [vêtement] tailored; **robe étroitement ~e** tight-fitting dress

ajustement [aʒystəmɑ̃] NM [statistique, prix] adjustment; *(Tech)* fit; **~ monétaire** currency adjustment ou realignment; **le projet est finalisé, à quelques ~s près** the project is completed, give or take a few finishing touches

ajuster [aʒyste] ▶conjug 1◀ [1] VT [a] *(= régler)* [+ ceinture, prix, politique] to adjust; [+ vêtement] to alter; **il leur est difficile d'~ leurs vues** it's difficult for them to reconcile their views [b] *(= adapter)* [+ tuyau] to fit *(à* into); **~ l'offre à la demande** to adjust ou adapt supply to demand, match supply to ou and demand [c] *(= viser)* **~ qn** to aim at sb, take aim at sb; **son tir ou son coup** to adjust one's aim → **tir** [d] † [+ coiffure] to tidy, arrange; [+ tenue] to arrange; [+ cravate] to straighten [2] **s'ajuster** VPR [a] *(Tech)* to fit (together) [b] († *= se rhabiller)* to adjust ou tidy one's dress†

ajusteur [aʒystœR] NM metal worker

Alabama [alabama] NM Alabama

alacrité [alakRite] NF *(littér)* alacrity

Aladin [aladɛ̃] NM Aladdin

alaise [alɛz] NF undersheet, drawsheet

alambic [alɑ̃bik] NM *(Chim)* still

alambiqué, e [alɑ̃bike] ADJ *(péj)* [style, discours] convoluted, involved; [personne, esprit] oversubtle

alangui, e [alɑ̃gi] *(ptp de* **alanguir**) ADJ [attitude, geste] languid; [rythme, style] languid, lifeless

alanguir [alɑ̃giR] ▶conjug 2◀ [1] VT [a] [fièvre] to make feeble ou languid, enfeeble; [chaleur] to make listless ou languid; [plaisirs, vie paresseuse] to make indolent ou languid; **être tout alangui par la chaleur** to feel listless ou languid with the heat [b] [+ récit] to make nerveless ou lifeless [2] **s'alanguir** VPR to grow languid ou weak, languish

alanguissement [alɑ̃gismɑ̃] NM languidness, languor

alarmant, e [alaRmɑ̃, ɑ̃t] ADJ alarming

alarme [alaRm] NF [a] *(= signal de danger)* alarm; **donner ou sonner l'~** to give ou sound ou raise the alarm, give the alert; **(système d')~** alarm system → **pistolet, signal, sirène, sonnette** [b] *(= inquiétude)* alarm; **jeter l'~** to cause alarm; **à la première ~** at the first sign of danger

alarmer [alaRme] ▶conjug 1◀ [1] VT to alarm [2] **s'alarmer** VPR to become alarmed *(de, pour* about, at); **il n'a aucune raison de s'~** he has ou there is no cause for alarm

alarmisme [alaRmism] NM alarmism

alarmiste [alaRmist] ADJ, NMF alarmist

Alaska [alaska] NM Alaska; **la route de l'~** the Alaska Highway; **la chaîne de l'~** the Alaska Range

albacore [albakɔR] NM *(Zool)* albacore

albanais, e [albanɛ, ɛz] [1] ADJ Albanian [2] NM *(Ling)* Albanian [3] **Albanais(e)** NM,F Albanian

Albanie [albani] NF Albania

albâtre [albatR] NM alabaster; **d'~ ◊ en ~** alabaster *(épith)*

albatros [albatRos] NM *(= oiseau)* albatross; *(Golf)* albatross *(Brit)*, double eagle *(US)*

Alberta [albɛRta] NM Alberta

albigeois, e [albiʒwa, waz] [1] ADJ [a] *(Géog)* of ou from Albi [b] *(Hist)* Albigensian [2] **Albigeois(e)** NM,F inhabitant ou native of Albi [3] NMPL *(Hist)* **les Albigeois** the Albigenses, the Albigensians → **croisade**

albinisme [albinism] NM albinism

albinos [albinos] NMF, ADJ INV albino

Albion [albjɔ̃] NF **(la perfide) ~** (perfidious) Albion

album [albɔm] NM [a] *(= livre)* album; **~ (de) photos/de timbres** photo/stamp album; **~ à colorier ou de coloriages** colouring *(Brit)* ou coloring *(US)* book; **~ de presse** scrapbook; **~ de bandes dessinées** cartoon book [b] *(= disque)* album; **~ de 2 CD** double CD

albumen [albymɛn] NM albumen

albumine [albymin] NF albumin

albumineux, -euse [albyminø, øz] ADJ albuminous

albuminurie [albyminyRi] NF albuminuria

albuminurique [albyminyRik] ADJ albuminuric

alcade [alkad] NM alcalde

alcaïque [alkaik] ADJ Alcaic; **vers ~s** Alcaics

alcali [alkali] NM alkali; **~ volatil** ammonia

alcalin, e [alkalɛ̃, in] ADJ alkaline

alcalinité [alkalinite] NF alkalinity

alcaloïde [alkalɔid] NM alkaloid

alcalose [alkaloz] NF alkalosis

Alceste [alsɛst] NM Alcestis

alchémille [alkemij] NF lady's mantle

alchimie [alʃimi] NF *(lit, fig)* alchemy

alchimique [alʃimik] ADJ alchemical, of alchemy

alchimiste [alʃimist] NMF alchemist

alcool [alkɔl] NM [a] *(Chim)* alcohol; **~ absolu éthylique** pure ethyl alcohol; **~ à brûler** methylated spirit(s), meths *(Brit)*; **~ camphré** camphorated alcohol; **~ rectifié** rectified spirit; **~ à 90°** surgical spirit; **lampe à ~** spirit lamp

b (= *boisson*) alcohol (*NonC*); **l'~ au volant** drinking and driving, drink-driving (*Brit*), drunk-driving (*US*); **boire de l'~** (*gén*) to drink alcohol; (*eau-de-vie*) to drink spirits (*Brit*) *ou* (hard) liquor (*US*); **il ne tient pas l'~** he can't take his drink; **il ne prend jamais d'~** he never drinks *ou* touches alcohol; **le cognac est un ~** cognac is a brandy *ou* spirit (*Brit*); **vous prendrez bien un petit ~** you won't say no to a little brandy; **~ de prune/poire** plum/pear brandy; **~ de menthe** medicinal mint spirit; **~ blanc** colourless spirit; **~ de grain** grain alcohol; **bière/boisson sans ~** non-alcoholic *ou* alcohol-free beer/drink

alcoolémie [alkɔlemi] NF **taux d'~** alcohol level (in the blood)

alcoolier [alkɔlje] NM distiller

alcoolique [alkɔlik] ADJ, NMF alcoholic; **les Alcooliques anonymes** Alcoholics Anonymous

alcooliser [alkɔlize] ▶ conjug 1 ◀ VT to alcoholize; **boissons alcoolisées/non alcoolisées** alcoholic/soft drinks; **très peu alcoolisé** very low in alcohol; **déodorant alcoolisé** alcohol-based deodorant

alcoolisme [alkɔlism] NM alcoholism; **~ aigu/chronique/mondain** acute/chronic/social alcoholism

alcoolo [alkɔlo] **1** ADJ alcoholic **2** NMF alcoholic, lush*

alcoomètre [alkɔmetʀ] NM alcoholometer

alcootest® [alkɔtest] NM (= *objet*) Breathalyser® (*Brit*), Breathalyzer® (*US*); (= *épreuve*) breath-test; **faire subir un ~ à qn** to give sb a breath test, breath-test sb, breathalyse (*Brit*) *ou* breathalyze (*US*) sb

alcôve [alkov] NF alcove, recess (*in a bedroom*); (*fig*) **d'~** bedroom (*épith*), intimate → **secret**

alcyon [alsjɔ̃] NM (*Myth*) Halcyon

al dente [aldɛnte] LOC ADV, LOC ADJ al dente

ALE [ael] NF (ABRÉV = **Association de libre-échange**) FTA

aléa [alea] NM unknown quantity; **en comptant avec tous les ~s** taking all the unknown factors into account; **les ~s de l'existence** the vagaries of life; **les ~s de l'examen** the uncertainties of the exam; **après bien des ~s** after many ups and downs

aléatoire [aleatwaʀ] ADJ **a** (= *risqué*) [*gains, succès*] uncertain; [*marché*] chancy, risky, uncertain **b** (*Math*) [*grandeur*] random; (*Ordin*) [*nombre, accès*] random; (*Mus*) aleatoric, aleatory → **contrat**

aléatoirement [aleatwaʀmɑ̃] ADV randomly

alémanique [alemanik] ADJ, NM (*Ling*) Alemannic → **suisse**

ALENA [alena] NM (ABRÉV = **Accord de libre-échange nord-américain**) NAFTA

alène, alêne [alɛn] NF awl

alentour [alɑ̃tuʀ] ADV around; **tout ~** *ou* **à l'entour**†† all around; **~ de qch** around sth; **les villages d'~** the neighbouring *ou* surrounding villages

alentours [alɑ̃tuʀ] NMPL **a** (= *environs*) [*ville*] surroundings, neighbourhood (*Brit*), neighborhood (*US*); **les ~ sont très pittoresques** the surroundings *ou* environs are very picturesque; **dans les ~** in the vicinity *ou* neighbourhood; **aux ~ de Dijon** in the Dijon area; **il gagne aux ~ de 10 000 F** he earns (something) in the region of 10,000 francs, he earns around *ou* about 10,000 francs; **aux ~ de 8 heures** some time around 8 (o'clock), round about 8 (o'clock) (*Brit*) **b** (*Art*) [*tapisserie*] border

Aléoutiennes [aleusjɛn] ADJ FPL, NFPL **les (îles) ~** the Aleutian Islands, the Aleutians

Alep [alɛp] N Aleppo

alerte [alɛʀt] **1** ADJ [*personne, geste*] agile, nimble; [*esprit*] alert, agile, nimble; [*vieillard*] spry, agile; [*style*] brisk, lively **2** NF **a** (= *si-*

gnal de danger, durée du danger) alert, alarm; **donner l'~** to give the alert *ou* alarm; **donner l'~ à qn** to alert sb; **~ aérienne** air raid warning; **~ à la bombe** bomb scare; **en cas d'~** if there is an alert; **système d'~** alarm system; **les nuits d'~** nights on alert → **cote, état, faux**

b (= *avertissement*) warning sign; (= *inquiétude*) alarm; **à la première ~** at the first warning sign; **l'~ a été chaude** *ou* **vive** there was intense *ou* considerable alarm; **~ cardiaque** heart flutter **3** EXCL watch out!

alerter [alɛʀte] ▶ conjug 1 ◀ VT (= *donner l'alarme à*) to alert; (= *informer*) to inform, notify; (= *prévenir*) to warn; **~ l'opinion publique** to alert public opinion; **les pouvoirs publics ont été alertés** the authorities have been informed *ou* notified, it has been brought to the attention of the authorities

alésage [alezaʒ] NM (= *action*) reaming; (= *diamètre*) bore

alèse [alez] NF = **alaise**

aléser [aleze] ▶ conjug 6 ◀ VT to ream

alevin [alvɛ̃] NM alevin, young fish (*bred artificially*)

alevinage [alvinaʒ] NM (= *action*) stocking with alevins *ou* young fish; (= *pisciculture*) fish farming

aleviner [alvine] ▶ conjug 1 ◀ **1** VT (= *empoissonner*) to stock with alevins *ou* young fish **2** VI (= *pondre*) to spawn

Alexandre [alɛksɑ̃dʀ] NM Alexander; **~ le Grand** Alexander the Great

Alexandrie [alɛksɑ̃dʀi] N Alexandria

alexandrin, e [alɛksɑ̃dʀɛ̃, in] **1** ADJ [*art, poésie*] (*Hist*) Alexandrian; [*prosodie*] alexandrine **2** NM alexandrine

alezan, e [alzɑ̃, an] ADJ, NM,F (= *cheval*) chestnut; **~ clair** sorrel

alfa [alfa] NM (= *herbe*) Esparto (grass); (= *papier*) Esparto paper

algarade [algaʀad] NF (*littér*) (= *gronderie*) angry outburst; (= *dispute*) quarrel

algèbre [alʒɛbʀ] NF (*Math*) algebra; **par l'~** algebraically; **c'est de l'~ pour moi*** it's (all) Greek to me*

algébrique [alʒebʀik] ADJ algebraic

algébriquement [alʒebʀikmɑ̃] ADV algebraically

algébriste [alʒebʀist] NMF algebraist

Alger [alʒe] N Algiers

Algérie [alʒeʀi] NF Algeria

algérien, -ienne [alʒeʀjɛ̃, jɛn] **1** ADJ Algerian **2 Algérien(ne)** NM,F Algerian

algérois, e [alʒeʀwa, waz] **1** ADJ of *ou* from Algiers **2 Algérois(e)** NM,F inhabitant *ou* native of Algiers **3** NM (= *région*) **l'Algérois** the Algiers region

algie [alʒi] NF algia

ALGOL [algɔl] NM ALGOL

algonkin, e ou **algonquin, e** [algɔ̃kɛ̃, in] **1** ADJ Algonqui(a)n **2** NM (*Ling*) Algonqui(a)n **3 Algonkin(e)** NM,F Algonqui(a)n

algorithme [algɔʀitm] NM algorithm

algorithmique [algɔʀitmik] **1** ADJ algorithmic **2** NF study of algorithms

algothérapie [algoteʀapi] NF algotherapy, seaweed baths

algue [alg] NF (*de mer*) seaweed (*NonC*); (*d'eau douce*) alga; **~s** (*de mer*) seaweed; (*d'eau douce*) algae; (*Culin*) **~s séchées** dried seaweed; **~s brunes/vertes/marines** brown/green/marine algae; **bain d'~s** seaweed bath

Alhambra [alɑ̃bʀa] NM **l'~** the Alhambra

alias [aljas] ADV alias, also known as, a.k.a.

Ali Baba [alibaba] NM Ali Baba; **« ~ et les quarante voleurs »** "Ali Baba and the Forty Thieves" → **caverne**

alibi [alibi] NM alibi

Alice [alis] NF Alice; **« ~ au pays des merveilles »** "Alice in Wonderland"

aliénabilité [aljenabilite] NF alienability

aliénable [aljenabl] ADJ alienable

aliénant, e [aljenɑ̃, ɑ̃t] ADJ alienating

aliénataire [aljenatɛʀ] NMF alienee

aliénateur, -trice [aljenatœʀ, tʀis] NM,F (*Jur*) alienator

aliénation [aljenasjɔ̃] NF (*gén*) alienation; (*Méd*) **~ (mentale)** (mental) derangement, insanity

aliéné, e [aljene] NM,F insane person, lunatic (*péj*) → **asile**

aliéner [aljene] ▶ conjug 6 ◀ VT **a** (*Jur* = *céder*) to alienate; [+ *droits*] to give up; (*Jur*) **~ un bien** to dispose of property; **~ sa liberté entre les mains de qn** to relinquish one's freedom to sb; **un traité qui aliène leur liberté** a treaty which alienates their freedom **b** (= *rendre hostile*) [+ *partisans, opinion publique*] to alienate (**à qn** from sb); **s'~ ses partisans/l'opinion publique** to alienate one's supporters/public opinion; **s'~ un ami** to alienate *ou* estrange a friend; **s'~ l'affection de qn** to alienate sb's affections, estrange sb **c** (*Philos, Sociol*) **~ qn** to alienate sb

aliéniste† [aljenist] NMF psychiatrist

Aliénor [aljenɔʀ] NF Eleanor; **~ d'Aquitaine** Eleanor of Aquitaine

alignement [aliɲ(ə)mɑ̃] NM **a** (= *action*) aligning, lining up, bringing into alignment; (= *rangée*) alignment, line; **les ~s de Carnac** the Carnac menhirs *ou* alignments (*SPÉC*) **b** (*Mil*) **être à l'~** to be in line; **se mettre à l'~** to fall into line, line up; **sortir de l'~** to step out of line (*lit*); **à droite/gauche, ~ !** right/left, dress! **c** (*rue*) building line; **maison frappée d'~** house affected by a road widening scheme **d** (*Pol, Fin*) alignment; **~ monétaire** monetary alignment *ou* adjustment

aligner [aliɲe] ▶ conjug 1 ◀ **1** VT **a** [+ *objets*] to align, line up, bring into alignment (**sur** with); [+ *chiffres*] to string together, string up a line of; [+ *arguments*] to reel off; (*Mil*) to form into lines, draw up in lines; **il alignait des allumettes sur la table** he was lining up *ou* making lines of matches on the table; **il n'arrivait pas à ~ deux mots de suite** he couldn't string a sentence *ou* two words together; **les enfants étaient alignés le long de la route** the children were lined up along the roadside; (= *payer*) **pour acheter cette voiture, il va falloir les ~*** that car will set you back a bit*

b [+ *rue*] to modify the (statutory) building line of

c (*Fin, Pol*) to bring into alignment (**sur** with); **~ sa conduite sur** to bring one's behaviour into line with, modify one's behaviour to conform with

d (*⁂ = punir*) **~ qn** to do sb*; **il s'est fait ~** he got done* (**pour** for)

2 s'aligner VPR [*soldats*] to fall into line, line up; **s'~ sur** [+ *politique*] to conform to the line of; [+ *pays, parti*] to align o.s. with; **tu peux toujours t'~!*** just try and match that!, beat that!*

aligoté [aligɔte] ADJ M, NM aligoté

aliment [alimɑ̃] NM **a** (= *nourriture*) food; **bien mâcher les ~s** to chew one's food well; **le pain est un ~** bread is (a) food *ou* a type of food; **comment conserver vos ~s** how to keep food fresh; **~ riche/complet/liquide** rich/whole/liquid food; **~s pour chiens/chats** dog/cat food; **~s pour bétail** cattle feed **b** (*Jur*) maintenance

alimentaire [alimɑ̃tɛʀ] ADJ **a** [*aide, hygiène*] food (*épith*); [*besoins*] dietary (*épith*); [*habitudes*] eating (*épith*), dietary (*épith*); **notre comportement ~** our eating patterns **b** (*péj*) [*activité*] done to earn a living *ou* some cash; **c'est de la littérature/peinture ~** these kinds of books/paintings are just potboilers; **pour lui ce n'est qu'un travail ~** to him it's just a job that pays the rent

alimentation [alimɑ̃tasjɔ̃] NF a (= *action*) [*personne, chaudière*] feeding; [*moteur, circuit*] supplying, feeding; **l'~ en eau des grandes villes** supplying water to *ou* the supply of water to large towns; **d'~** [*pompe, ligne*] feed (*épith*) → **tuyau** b (= *régime*) diet; **~ de base** staple diet; **~ équilibrée/mal équilibrée** balanced/unbalanced diet; **~ lactée** milky food(s), milk diet; **bon** *ou* **ticket d'~** food voucher c (*Comm*) food trade; **il travaille dans l'~** he works in the food industry; **magasin d'~** food shop, grocery store (*US*); **rayon ~** food *ou* grocery section

alimenter [alimɑ̃te] ▶conjug 1◀ 1 VT a [+ *personne, animal*] to feed b [+ *chaudière*] to feed [+ *moteur, circuit*] to supply, feed; [+ *caisse, compte bancaire, fonds*] to put money into; [+ *marché*] to supply (**en** with); **le tuyau alimente le moteur en essence** the pipe supplies the engine with petrol (*Brit*) *ou* gasoline (*US*) *ou* feeds *ou* supplies petrol (*Brit*) *ou* gasoline (*US*) to the engine; **~ une ville en gaz/électricité** to supply a town with gas/electricity c [+ *conversation*] [*personne*] to keep going, sustain; [+ *curiosité*] to feed; [+ *inflation, polémique, rumeurs, soupçons*] to fuel; **cela a alimenté la conversation** it gave us (*ou* them etc) something to talk about; **ces faits vont ~ notre réflexion** these facts will provide food for thought 2 **s'alimenter** VPR [*personne*] to eat; **s'~ seul** to feed o.s.; **le malade recommence à s'~** the patient is starting to eat again *ou* to take food again

alinéa [alinea] NM (= *passage*) paragraph; (= *ligne*) indented line (*at the beginning of a paragraph*); **nouvel ~** new line

alisier [alizje] NM sorb, service tree

alitement [alitmɑ̃] NM confinement to (one's) bed

aliter [alite] ▶conjug 1◀ 1 VT to confine to (one's) bed; **rester alité** to remain confined to (one's) bed, remain bedridden; **infirme alité** bedridden invalid 2 **s'aliter** VPR to take to one's bed

alizé [alize] ADJ M, NM **(vent) ~** trade wind

alkékenge [alkekɑ̃ʒ] NM Chinese lantern, winter *ou* ground cherry

Allah [ala] NM Allah

allaitante [alɛtɑ̃t] ADJ F **femme ~** nursing mother; **vache ~** brood cow

allaitement [alɛtmɑ̃] NM [*bébé*] feeding; [*animal*] suckling; **~ maternel** breast-feeding; **~ mixte** mixed feeding; **~ au biberon** bottle-feeding; **pendant l'~** while breast-feeding

allaiter [alɛte] ▶conjug 1◀ VT [*femme*] to (breast-)feed; [*animal*] to suckle; **~ au biberon** to bottle-feed; **elle allaite encore** she's still breast-feeding (the baby)

allant, e [alɑ̃, ɑ̃t] 1 ADJ (*littér* = *alerte*) [*personne*] sprightly, active; [*musique*] lively 2 NM (= *dynamisme*) drive, energy; **avoir de l'~** to have plenty of drive *ou* energy; **avec ~** energetically

alléchant, e [aleʃɑ̃, ɑ̃t] ADJ [*odeur*] mouth-watering, tempting; [*proposition*] enticing, tempting, alluring; [*prix*] attractive

allécher [aleʃe] ▶conjug 6◀ VT [*odeur*] to make one's mouth water, tempt; [*proposition*] to entice, tempt, lure; **alléché par l'odeur** tempted by the smell; **alléché par des promesses fallacieuses** lured by false promises

allée [ale] NF a [*forêt*] lane, path; [*ville*] avenue; [*jardin*] path; [*parc*] path, walk; (*plus large*) avenue; (*menant à une maison*) drive, driveway; [*cinéma, autobus*] aisle; **~ cavalière** bridle path; **les ~s du pouvoir** the corridors of power b **~s et venues** comings and goings; **que signifient ces ~s et venues dans le couloir?** why all this to-ing and fro-ing in the corridor?; **ceci l'oblige à de constantes ~s et venues (entre Paris et la province)** this means

---

he has to keep shuttling back and forth (between Paris and the provinces); **j'ai perdu mon temps en ~s et venues** I've wasted my time going back and forth *ou* to-ing and fro-ing; **le malade l'obligeait à de constantes ~s et venues** the patient kept him constantly on the run *ou* running about (for him)

allégation [a(l)legasjɔ̃] NF (= *affirmation*) allegation; (= *citation*) citation

allégé, e [aleʒe] (*ptp de* **alléger**) ADJ low-fat; **(produits) ~s** low-fat products

allégeance [aleʒɑ̃s] NF allegiance; **faire ~ à qn** to swear allegiance to sb

allégement, allègement [aleʒmɑ̃] NM a [*fardeau, véhicule*] lightening b [*personnel*] reduction (**de** in) c [*coûts, impôts, charges sociales*] reduction (**de** in); **~ fiscal** tax relief; **notre objectif demeure l'~ de nos dettes** our aim remains to reduce our debts d [*contrôles*] easing; [*formalités*] simplification e [*douleur*] alleviation

alléger [aleʒe] ▶conjug 6 et 3◀ VT a (*en poids*) [+ *fardeau*] to lighten; [+ *véhicule*] to make lighter; [+ *skis*] to unweight; (*hum*) **~ qn de son portefeuille*** to relieve sb of their wallet b (*en nombre*) [+ *personnel*] to streamline, reduce; (*Scol*) **~ les effectifs** to reduce numbers in the classroom; **pour ~ notre dispositif militaire** to reduce our military presence c (*Fin*) [+ *coûts, impôts, charges sociales, dette*] to reduce d (= *simplifier*) [+ *contrôles*] to ease; [+ *formalités*] to simplify; **~ les programmes scolaires** to cut the number of subjects on the school syllabus e (= *rendre moins pénible*) [+ *douleur*] to alleviate, relieve, soothe; [+ *conditions de détention*] to ease

allégorie [a(l)legɔri] NF allegory

allégorique [a(l)legɔrik] ADJ allegorical

allégoriquement [a(l)legɔrikmɑ̃] ADV allegorically

allègre [a(l)lɛgr] ADJ [*personne, humeur*] gay, cheerful, light-hearted; [*démarche*] lively, jaunty; [*musique*] lively, merry; **il descendait la rue d'un pas ~** he was walking gaily *ou* cheerfully down the street

allégrement, allègrement [a(l)legrəmɑ̃] ADV a (= *gaiement*) gaily, cheerfully b (*hum*) **le coût de l'opération dépasse ~ les 50 millions** the cost of the operation is well over 50 million; **le virus voyage ~ d'un ordinateur à l'autre** the virus merrily travels from one computer to another

allégresse [a(l)legrɛs] NF elation; **ce fut l'~ générale** there was general rejoicing *ou* jubilation

alléguer [a(l)lege] ▶conjug 6◀ VT a [+ *fait*] to put forward (as proof *ou* as an excuse *ou* as a pretext); [+ *excuse, prétexte, raison, preuve*] to put forward; **il allégua comme prétexte que ...** he put forward as a pretext that ...; **ils refusèrent de m'écouter, alléguant (comme raison) que ...** they refused to listen to me, arguing that ... *ou* alleging that ... b (*littér* = *citer*) to cite, quote

allèle [alɛl] NM allele

alléluia [a(l)leluja] NM, EXCL (*Rel*) alleluia, hallelujah

Allemagne [almaɲ] NF Germany; **l'~ fédérale** the Federal German Republic; **~ de l'Ouest/de l'Est** West/East Germany → **république**

allemand, e [almɑ̃, ɑ̃d] 1 ADJ German → **république** 2 NM (*Ling*) German → **bas, haut** 3 **Allemand(e)** NM,F German 4 **allemande** NF (*Mus*) allemande

---

aller [ale]

▶conjug 9◀
1 VERBE INTRANSITIF	4 VERBE PRONOMINAL
2 VERBE IMPERSONNEL	5 LOC EXCLAMATIVES
3 VERBE AUXILIAIRE	6 NOM MASCULIN

1 VERBE INTRANSITIF
a (= *se déplacer, partir*) to go; **où vas-tu**

---

where are you going?; MAIS **il t'attend, va!** he's waiting for you, go on!

▸ *aller se traduit régulièrement par un verbe spécifique en anglais.*

j'allais par les rues désertes I walked *ou* wandered through the empty streets; **il allait trop vite quand il a eu son accident** he was driving *ou* going too fast when he had his accident; **en ville, on va plus vite à pied qu'en voiture** in town it is quicker to walk than to go by car; **~ à Paris en voiture/en avion** to drive/fly to Paris; **il y est allé à** *ou* **en vélo** he cycled there, he went there on his bike; **j'irai à pied** I'll walk, I'll go on foot

♦ **aller et venir** (*entre deux endroits*) to come and go; (*dans une pièce*) to pace up and down; **tu sais, la chance, ça va ça vient** luck comes and goes, you know, you win some, you lose some; **avec lui l'argent, ça va, ça vient** when it comes to money, it's easy come, easy go with him

♦ **aller + préposition** (= *se rendre à ou vers etc*) **~ à** to go to; **~ à Caen/à la campagne** to go to Caen/to the country; **~ au lit/à l'église/à l'école** to go to bed/to church/to school; **~ en Allemagne** to go to Germany; **~ chez le boucher/chez un ami** to go to the butcher's/to a friend's (place); **je vais sur** *ou* **vers Lille** (*en direction de*) I'm going towards Lille; (*but du voyage*) I'm heading for Lille; MAIS **~ aux renseignements/aux nouvelles** to go and inquire/and find out the news

---

Notez l'utilisation du perfect et du pluperfect **have/had been**; **have/had gone** implique que le sujet n'est pas encore revenu.

je ne suis jamais allé à New York/en Corse I've never been to New York/Corsica; **étiez-vous déjà allés en Sicile?** had you been to Sicily before?; **il n'est pas là?** — **non il est allé voir sa mère/au tennis** he's not there? — no, he's gone to see his mother/to play tennis

---

b euph (*aux toilettes*) to go to the toilet; **tu es allé ce matin?** have you been (to the toilet) this morning?; **ça fait ~*** it makes you go*

c dans le temps, une évolution **on va à la catastrophe/la ruine** we're heading for disaster/ruin; **~ sur ses 30 ans** to be getting on for (*Brit*) *ou* going on (*US*) 30; **on va vers une guerre civile** we're heading for civil war; **où allons-nous?** what are things coming to?; **j'irai (jusqu')à la Commission européenne s'il le faut** I'll take it to the European Commission if necessary

d (= *mener, s'étendre*) to go (à to); **cette route doit ~ quelque part** this road must go somewhere; **ses champs vont jusqu'à la forêt** his fields go *ou* stretch as far as the forest

e (= *durer*) **l'abonnement va jusqu'en juin** the subscription lasts *ou* runs till June; **le contrat allait jusqu'en mai** the contract ran until May; **la période qui va du 22 mai au 15 juillet** from 22nd May to 15th July

f (= *se porter*) **comment allez-vous?** how are you?; **comment va ton frère?** — **il va bien/mal** (*physiquement*) how's your brother? — he's fine/he's not very well; (*moralement*) how's your brother? — he's fine/not too happy; **cela fait des années qu'il va mal** he hasn't been well for years; **(comment) ça va?** — **ça va** how's things?* *ou* how are you doing? — fine *ou* not so bad*; **ça va mieux maintenant** I'm feeling better now; **ça va?** — **faudra bien que ça aille*** how's things* *ou* how are you doing? — fine *ou* not so bad; **ça va?** — **on fait ~*** you all right?* — so-so*; **non mais ça va pas (la tête)!*** you're crazy!*, you must be crazy!*; **non mais ça va, te gêne pas!*** don't mind me!

g (= *se passer, fonctionner*) **(comment) ça va au bureau?** — **ça va** how's it going at the office? — fine *ou* not so bad*; **ça va comme ça?** — **faudra bien que ça aille*** is it all right like that? — it'll have to be*; **comment vont les affaires?** — **elles vont bien/mal** how's business? — fine/not too good; **ça va mal en Asie/à la maison** things aren't going too well *ou* things aren't looking so good in Asia/at home; **ça va mal ~ si tu continues** there's going to be trouble if you carry on like that; **notre économie va mieux** the economy is doing better *ou* is looking up; **ça va mieux pour lui maintenant** things are going better for him now; **ça ne va pas mieux!** il veut une voiture pour son anniversaire! whatever next! he wants a car for his birthday!; **ça ne va pas sans difficulté** it's no easy job; **ça va tout seul** (= *c'est facile*) it's a cinch*, it's a doddle* (*Brit*); **ça ne va pas tout seul** it's not exactly easy

- **plus ça va** : **plus ça va, plus l'inquiétude grandit** people are getting more and more worried; **plus ça va, plus je me dis que j'ai eu tort** the more I think about it, the more I realize how wrong I was; **plus ça va, plus nous produisons des déchets** we just keep producing more and more waste; **plus ça va, moins ça va** things are going from bad to worse

h = **convenir** ~ **(bien)** avec to go (well) with; **~ bien ensemble** [*couleurs, styles*] to go well together; **ils vont bien ensemble** [*personnes*] they make a nice couple; **ce tableau va bien/mal sur ce mur** the picture looks right/doesn't look right on that wall; **ici, cette couleur n'ira pas** that colour just won't work *ou* go here; **la clé ne va pas dans la serrure** the key won't go in *ou* doesn't fit the lock; **les ciseaux ne vont pas pour couper du carton** scissors won't do *ou* are no good for cutting cardboard; **votre plan ne va pas** your plan won't work

- **aller à qn** (*forme, mesure*) to fit sb; (*style, genre*) to suit sb; **cette robe te va très bien** (*couleur, style*) that dress really suits you; (*taille*) that dress fits you perfectly; **vos projets me vont parfaitement** your plans suit me fine; **rendez-vous demain 4 heures? — ça me va*** tomorrow at 4? — OK, fine*; **ce climat ne leur va pas** the climate here doesn't suit them *ou* agree with them; **ça lui va mal** *ou* **bien** (*hum*) **de critiquer les autres** he's got a nerve* criticizing other people, he's a fine one* to criticize

i
- **aller à** (= *être attribué à*) [*prix, récompense, part d'héritage*] to go to; **le maison ira à la cadette** the house will go to the youngest daughter; (= *servir à*) **l'argent ira à la restauration du clocher** the money will go towards restoring the bell tower; **où sont allés les 2 000 F?** (= *qu'a-t-on acheté avec*) what did the 2,000 francs go on?; (*où l'argent est-il passé*) where did that 2,000 francs go?

j
- **aller en** + *participe présent*

Lorsque **aller** *sert à exprimer la progression, il est souvent rendu par un comparatif.*

~ en empirant to get worse and worse; **le bruit va croissant** the noise is getting louder and louder; **notre rythme de travail ira en s'accélérant** we'll have to work more and more quickly; *MAIS* **~ en augmentant** to keep increasing

- **y aller** : **on y va?** (*avant un départ*) shall we go?; (*avant d'agir*) shall we start?; **allons-y (Alonzo*)!** let's go!; **allez-y, c'est votre tour** go on, it's your turn; **allez-y, vous ne risquez rien** go ahead *ou* go on, you've nothing to lose; **comme vous y allez!** ◊ **vous y allez un peu fort!** that's going a bit far!; **non mais vas-y, insulte-moi!*** go on, insult me, why don't you!; **vas-y doucement** *ou* **mollo:** gently does it; (*Math*) **27 divisé par 7, il y a 3 (et il reste 6)** 27 divided by 7 goes 3 (remainder 6)

- **y aller de** (= *contribuer*) **chacun y est allé de son commentaire** everyone had their say, everyone put in their two cents* (*US*); **il y est allé de sa petite chanson*** he gave us a little song; **il y est allé de sa petite larme*** he had a little cry

2 VERBE IMPERSONNEL
- **il y va/allait de** (= *ce qui est/était en jeu*) **il y va de votre vie/de votre santé** your life/your health is at stake *ou* depends on it; **il y allait de notre honneur!** our honour was at stake!

- **il en va de** (= *c'est la même chose pour*) **il en va de même pour tous les autres** the same applies to *ou* goes for all the others; **il en va de l'édition comme des autres secteurs** it's the same in publishing as in other sectors, the same goes for publishing as for other sectors

- **ça y va/y allait*** (*valeur intensive*) **ça y va le whisky chez eux!** they certainly get through a lot of whisky!; **ça y va les billets de 500 F avec lui!** he certainly gets through those 500 franc notes!; **ça y allait les insultes!** you should have heard the abuse!

3 VERBE AUXILIAIRE
- **aller** + *infinitif*

Notez l'utilisation de and *et de* to *entre les deux verbes en anglais;* to *exprime généralement une idée d'intention alors que* and *met l'accent sur l'accomplissement de l'action.*

il est allé se renseigner (*gén*) he went to get some information; (*a obtenu les informations*) he went and got some information; **~ voir qn à l'hôpital** to go and visit sb in hospital; **va te laver les mains** go and wash your hands

Lorsque **aller** *exprime le futur immédiat, il est parfois traduit par le futur simple; la forme* be going to *s'utilise plutôt lorsque le locuteur met quelqu'un en garde ou exprime une intention.*

tu vas être en retard you're going to be late, you'll be late; **il va descendre dans une minute** he'll be (coming) down in a minute; **ça va prendre un quart d'heure** that'll take *ou* it's going to take a quarter of an hour; **je vais lui dire** I'm going to tell him; **je vais le faire tout de suite** I'll do it right away; **ils allaient commencer** they were going to start, they were about to start; *MAIS* **je vais te dire une chose** let me tell you something

(*valeur intensive*) **ne va pas te faire du souci inutilement** don't go and get *ou* don't go getting all worried for no reason; **allez donc voir si c'est vrai!** who knows if it's true!; **n'allez pas vous imaginer que …** don't you go imagining that …; **pourvu qu'il n'aille pas penser que …** as long as he doesn't get the idea that …; **va** *ou* **allez savoir*!** who knows?; **va lui expliquer ça, toi!** you try explaining that to him!; **va me dire pourquoi j'ai fait ça/il s'est mis en colère?** I have no idea why I did that/why he got angry

4 **s'en aller** VERBE PRONOMINAL

a = **partir** to go (away); (= *déménager*) to move, leave; **bon, je m'en vais** right, I'm off *ou* I'm going; **elle s'en va en vacances demain** she goes *ou* is going away on holiday tomorrow; **ils s'en vont à Paris** they are going *ou* off to Paris; **il s'en est allé** *ou* **s'est en allé*** sans rien dire he went away *ou* off *ou* he left without saying anything; **va-t'en!** ◊ **allez-vous-en!** go away!; **va-t-en de là!** get out of here!; **ils s'en vont du quartier** they are leaving the area, they are moving away from the area

Notez que lorsque **aller** *est suivi d'un adverbe de manière, l'anglais utilise un verbe spécifique; reportez-vous à l'adverbe.*

s'en ~ subrepticement to steal *ou* sneak away; **elle s'est en allée sur la pointe des pieds** she tiptoed away

b **euph** (= *mourir*) to go; **il s'en va** he's going *ou* fading; **quand je m'en irai** when I'm gone; *MAIS* **il s'en est allé paisiblement** he passed away peacefully

c = **quitter un emploi** to leave; (= *prendre sa retraite*) to retire, leave

d = **disparaître** [*tache*] (*gén*) to come off; (*sur tissu*) to come out; [*temps, années*] to pass, go by; **ça s'en ira au lavage** [*boue*] it'll wash off, it'll come off in the wash; [*tache*] it'll wash out; **tout son argent s'en va en CDs** all his money goes on CDs, he spends all his money on CDs

e |valeur intensive| **je m'en vais leur montrer de quoi je suis capable** I'll show them what I'm made of!; **va-t'en voir si c'est vrai!*** who knows if it's true!

5 LOC EXCLAMATIVES
- **allons!** ◊ **allez!** ◊ **va!** (*pour stimuler*) **allons!** ◊ **allez!** go on!, come on!; (*Sport*) **allez (la) France!** come on France!; **allez, allez** *ou* **allons, allons, circulez** come on now, move along; (*impatience*) **allons, cesse de m'ennuyer!** will you just stop bothering me!; (*pour encourager, réconforter*) **allons, allons, il ne faut pas pleurer** come on now *ou* come, come, you mustn't cry; **tu t'en remettras, va** don't worry, you'll get over it; **ce n'est pas grave, allez!** come on, it's not so bad *ou* serious!; **allez, au revoir!** 'bye then!*

- **allons bon!** (*agacement*) **allons bon! qu'est-ce qui t'est encore arrivé?** NOW what's happened?; (*ennui*) **il est tombé — allons bon!** he's fallen over — oh dear!; **allons bon, j'ai oublié mon sac!** oh dear, I've left my bag behind!

- **allons donc!** (*incrédulité*) come on!, come off it!*; **notre planète est menacée — allons donc!** the planet is in danger — oh come on!; **lui paresseux? allons donc! c'est lui qui fait tout** lazy, him? you've got to be kidding*, he's the one who does all the work; **lui m'aider? allons donc!** help me, him? that'll be the day!*

- **va donc!:** (*insulte*) **va donc, eh crétin!** you stupid idiot!*

- **ça va!*** (= *assez*) that's enough!; (= *d'accord*) OK, OK*; **tes remarques désobligeantes, ça va comme ça!** I've had just about enough of your nasty comments!; **alors, tu viens? — ça va(, ça va)** j'arrive! are you coming then? — OK, OK, I'm coming!; **ça va bien!** ça fait dix fois que je te le dis — ça va, je vais le faire! I've told you ten times — look, I'll do it, OK?

- **va pour …*:** **va pour une nouvelle voiture!** all right we'll GET a new car!; (*dans un marchandage*) **va pour 30 F!** OK, 30 francs then!; **j'aimerais ~ à Tokyo — alors va pour Tokyo!** I'd like to go to Tokyo — Tokyo it is then!

6 NOM MASCULIN
a = **trajet** outward journey; **l'~ s'est bien passé** the (outward) journey *ou* the journey there went off well; **j'irai vous voir à l'~** I'll come and see you on the way there; **je ne fais que l'~ et retour** *ou* **l'~-retour** I'm just going there and back; **j'ai fait plusieurs ~s et retours entre chez moi et la pharmacie** I made several trips to the chemist's; **le dossier a fait plusieurs ~s et retours entre nos services** the file has been shuttled between departments → **match**

b = **billet** single (ticket) (*Brit*), one-way ticket (*US*); **trois ~s (simples) pour Tours** three singles (*Brit*) *ou* one-way tickets (*US*) to Tours; **~-retour** *ou* **et retour** return (ticket) (*Brit*), round-trip ticket (*US*); **l'~-retour Paris-New York coûte 3 500 F** Paris-New York is 3,500 francs return (*Brit*) *ou* round-trip (*US*); **donner un ~-retour à qn*** (= *le gifler*) to give sb a box round the ears

---

allergène [alɛrʒɛn] **1** ADJ allergenic **2** NM allergen

allergénique [alɛrʒenik] ADJ allergenic

allergie [alɛrʒi] NF allergy; (*lit, fig*) **faire une ~** to be allergic (**à** to); **~ respiratoire/cutanée** respiratory/skin allergy

allergique [alɛrʒik] ADJ (*lit, fig*) allergic (**à** to)

allergisant, e [alɛrʒizɑ̃, ɑ̃t] **1** ADJ [*substance*] allergenic **2** NM allergen

allergologie [alɛrɡɔlɔʒi] NF study of allergies

allergologiste [alɛrɡɔlɔʒist], **allergologue** [alɛrɡɔlɔɡ] NMF allergist

alliacé, e [aljase] ADJ alliaceous

alliage [aljaʒ] NM alloy; (péj) **un ~ disparate de doctrines** a hotchpotch of doctrines; **roues en ~ léger** alloy wheels

alliance [aljɑ̃s] **1** NF **a** (Pol) alliance; (= entente) union; (Bible) covenant; **faire** ou **conclure une ~ avec un pays** to enter into an alliance with a country; **faire ~ avec qn** to ally oneself with sb → **saint, triple b** (frm = mariage) union, marriage; **neveu/oncle par ~** nephew/uncle by marriage; **entrer par ~ dans une famille** to marry into a family, become united by marriage with a family **c** (= bague) (wedding) ring **d** (= mélange) combination **2** COMP ► **alliance de mots** (Littérat) bold juxtaposition (of words), oxymoron

allié, e [alje] (ptp de **allier**) **1** ADJ [pays, forces] allied; **famille ~e** family ou relations by marriage **2** NM,F (= pays) ally; (= ami, soutien) ally; (= parent) relative by marriage; (Pol) **les Alliés** the Allies

allier [alje] ► conjug 7 ◄ **1** VT [+ efforts] to combine, unite; [+ couleurs] to match; (Pol) to ally; (Tech) to alloy; **elle allie l'élégance à la simplicité** she combines elegance with simplicity; **ils sont alliés à une puissante famille** they are related by marriage to a powerful family **2** **s'allier** VPR [efforts] to combine, unite; [couleurs] to match; [familles] to become united by marriage, become allied (à to, with); (Pol) to become allies ou allied; (Tech) to alloy; **la France s'allia à l'Angleterre** France became allied to ou with England ou allied itself to ou with England

alligator [aligatɔʀ] NM alligator

allitération [a(l)liteʀasjɔ̃] NF alliteration

allô [alo] EXCL (Téléc) hello!, hullo! (Brit)

allocataire [alɔkatɛʀ] NMF recipient

allocation [alɔkasjɔ̃] **1** NF **a** [argent] allocation; [indemnité] granting; (Fin) [actions] allotment; [temps] allotment, allocation **b** (= somme) allowance; **toucher les ~s** to draw ou get family allowance **2** COMP ► **allocation (de) chômage** unemployment benefit (NonC) (Brit), unemployment insurance (NonC) (US) ► **allocations familiales** (= argent) state allowance paid to families with dependent children; ≈ family allowance (Brit), ≈ child benefit (Brit), ≈ welfare (US); ≈ bureau) ≈ family allowance department (Brit), ≈ child benefit office (Brit), ≈ welfare center (US) ► **allocation (de) logement** rent allowance ou subsidy ► **allocation de maternité** maternity allowance ou benefit ► **allocation parentale (d'éducation)** allowance paid to a parent who has stopped work to bring up a young child ► **allocation de parent isolé** allowance for one-parent families

allocs [alɔk] NFPL (ABRÉV = **allocations familiales**) → **allocation**

allocutaire [a(l)lɔkytɛʀ] NMF addressee

allocution [a(l)lɔkysjɔ̃] NF (short) speech; **~ télévisée** (short) televised speech

allogène [alɔʒɛn] ADJ [population] non-native; (fig) [éléments] foreign

allonge [alɔ̃ʒ] NF (Tech) extension; [table] leaf; [boucherie] hook; (Boxe) reach; **avoir une bonne ~** to have a long reach

allongé, e [alɔ̃ʒe] (ptp de **allonger**) ADJ **a** (= étendu) **être ~** to be stretched out, be lying (sur on); **rester ~** to stay lying down; **~ sur le dos** lying on one's back, supine (frm) **b** (= long) long; (= étiré) elongated; (= oblong) oblong; **faire une mine ~e** to pull ou make a long face

allongement [alɔ̃ʒmɑ̃] NM **a** (Métal) elongation; (Ling) lengthening; (Aviat) aspect ratio **b** [distance, vêtement] lengthening; [route, voie ferrée] lengthening, extension **c** [durée] extension; **avec l'~ des jours** with the days getting ou growing longer; **contribuer à l'~ de**

la durée de vie ou **de l'espérance de vie** to contribute to greater ou higher ou increased life expectancy; **pour éviter l'~ des listes d'attente** to prevent waiting lists (from) getting any longer

allonger [alɔ̃ʒe] ► conjug 3 ◄ **1** VT **a** (= rendre plus long) [+ vêtement] to lengthen, make longer (de by); (en défaisant l'ourlet) to let down; [+ délai, durée] to extend; **~ le pas** to quicken one's pace; **cette coiffure lui allonge le visage** that hair style makes her face look longer **b** (= étendre) [+ bras, jambe] to stretch (out); [+ malade] to lay ou stretch out; **~ le cou (pour apercevoir qch)** to crane ou stretch one's neck (to see sth); **la jambe allongée sur une chaise** with one leg up on ou stretched out on a chair **c** [+ somme] to fork out*; [+ coup] to deal, land; **~ qn** to knock sb flat; **il va falloir les ~** we'll (ou you'll etc) have to cough up* **d** [+ sauce] to thin (down); (fig) **~ la sauce*** to spin it out **2** VI [jours] to get ou grow longer, lengthen **3** **s'allonger** VPR **a** (= devenir ou paraître plus long) [ombres, jours] to get ou grow longer, lengthen; [enfant] to grow taller; [discours, visite] to drag on; [durée] to get longer; [file, liste d'attente] to get longer, grow; **son visage s'allongea à ces mots** at these words he pulled ou made a long face ou his face fell; **la route s'allongeait devant eux** the road stretched away before them **b** (= s'étendre) to lie down, stretch (o.s.) out; (pour dormir) to lie down; **s'~ dans l'herbe** to lie down ou stretch (o.s.) out on the grass

allopathe [alɔpat] **1** ADJ allopathic **2** NMF allopath, allopathist

allopathie [alɔpati] NF allopathy

allopathique [alɔpatik] ADJ allopathic

allophone [alɔfɔn] NM allophone

allotropie [alɔtʀɔpi] NF allotropy

allotropique [alɔtʀɔpik] ADJ allotropic

allouer [alwe] ► conjug 1 ◄ VT [+ argent] to allocate; [+ indemnité] to grant; (Fin) [+ actions] to allot; [+ temps] to allot, allow, allocate; **pendant le temps alloué** during the allotted time, during the time allowed ou allocated

allumage [alymaʒ] NM **a** (= action) [feu] lighting, kindling; [poêle] lighting; [électricité] putting ou switching ou turning on; [gaz] lighting, putting ou turning on **b** (Aut) ignition; **avance à l'~** ignition ou spark advance; **régler l'~** to adjust the timing → **auto-allumage**

allumé, e [alyme] ADJ (= fou) crazy*, nuts*; (= ivre) smashed*, pissed* (Brit), trashed* (US)

allume-cigare (pl **allume-cigares**) [alymsigaʀ] NM cigar lighter

allume-feu (pl **allume-feu(x)**) [alymfø] NM firelighter

allume-gaz [alymgɑz] NM INV gas lighter (for cooker)

allumer [alyme] ► conjug 1 ◄ **1** VT **a** [+ feu] to light, kindle; [+ bougie, poêle] to light; [+ cigare, pipe] to light (up); [+ incendie] to start, light; **il alluma sa cigarette à celle de son voisin** he lit (up) his cigarette from his neighbour's, he got a light from his neighbour's cigarette; **le feu était allumé** the fire was lit, the fire was going; **laisse le poêle allumé** leave the stove on ou lit **b** [+ électricité, lampe, radio] to put ou switch ou turn on; [+ gaz] to light, put ou turn on; **laisse la lumière allumée** leave the light on; **allume dans la cuisine** put ou switch ou turn the light(s) on in the kitchen; **le bouton n'allume pas** ◊ **ça n'allume pas** the light doesn't come on ou work; **où est-ce qu'on allume ?** where is the switch? **c** (= éclairer) **~ une pièce** to put ou switch ou turn the light(s) on in a room; **sa fenêtre était allumée** there was a light (on) at his

window; **laisse le salon allumé** leave the light(s) on in the sitting-room, leave the sitting-room light(s) on **d** [+ colère, envie, haine] to arouse, stir up, kindle; [+ amour] to kindle **e** (* = aguicher) to turn on, tease **f** (‡ = tuer) to burn‡ **2** **s'allumer** VPR [incendie] to blaze, flare up; [lumière] to come ou go on; [radiateur] to switch (itself) on; [sentiment] to be aroused; **ça s'allume comment ?** how do you switch it on? **le désir s'alluma dans ses yeux** his eyes lit up with desire; **ses yeux s'allumèrent** his eyes lit up; **ce bois s'allume bien** this wood is easy to light ou burns easily; **sa fenêtre s'alluma** a light came ou went on at his window

allumette [alymɛt] NF **a** (pour allumer) match; [morceau de bois] match(stick); **~ de sûreté** ou **suédoise** safety match; **~ tison** fuse; **il a les jambes comme des ~s** he's got legs like matchsticks **b** (Culin) flaky pastry finger; **~ au fromage** cheese straw (Brit) ou stick (US) → **pomme**

allumeur [alymœʀ] NM (Aut) distributor; (Tech) igniter; (Hist) **~ de réverbères** lamplighter

allumeuse [alymøz] NF (péj) teaser, tease, vamp

allure [alyʀ] NF **a** (= vitesse) [véhicule] speed; [piéton] pace; **rouler** ou **aller à vive** ou **grande/faible** ou **petite ~** to drive ou go at high ou great/low ou slow speed; **à toute ~** [rouler] at top ou full speed, at full tilt; [réciter, dîner] as fast as one can; **à cette ~, nous n'aurons jamais fini à temps** at this rate we'll never be finished in time **b** (= démarche) walk, gait (littér); (= prestance) bearing; (= attitude) air, look; (* = aspect) [objet, individu] look, appearance; **avoir de l'~** ◊ **ne pas manquer d'~** to have style, have a certain elegance; **avoir fière** ou **grande** ou **belle/piètre ~** to cut a fine/a shabby figure; **avoir une drôle d'~/bonne ~** to look odd ou funny/fine; **d'~ sportive** sporty-looking; **d'~ louche/bizarre** fishy-/odd-looking; **les choses prennent une drôle d'~** things are taking a funny ou an odd turn; **la ville prend des ~s de fête foraine** the town is beginning to look like ou resemble a funfair **c** (= comportement) **~s** ways; **choquer par sa liberté d'~s** to shock people with ou by one's free ou unconventional behaviour; **il a des ~s de voyou** he behaves ou carries on* like a hooligan **d** (Équitation) gait; (Naut) trim

allusif, -ive [a(l)lyzif, iv] ADJ allusive

allusion [a(l)lyzjɔ̃] NF (= référence) allusion (à to); (avec sous-entendu) hint (à at); **~ malveillante** innuendo; **faire ~ à** to allude ou refer to, hint at, make allusions to; **par ~** allusively

alluvial, e (mpl **-iaux**) [a(l)lyvjal, jo] ADJ alluvial

alluvionnement [a(l)lyvjɔnmɑ̃] NM alluviation

alluvions [a(l)lyvjɔ̃] NFPL alluvial deposits, alluvium sg

Almaty [almati] N Almaty

almanach [almana] NM almanac

almée [alme] NF Egyptian dancing girl, almah

aloès [alɔɛs] NM aloe

aloi [alwa] NM **de bon ~** [plaisanterie, gaieté] honest, respectable; [individu] worthy, of sterling ou genuine worth; [produit] good quality; **de mauvais ~** [plaisanterie, gaieté] unsavoury, unwholesome; [individu] dubious; [produit] of doubtful quality

alopécie [alɔpesi] NF alopecia

alors [alɔʀ] ADV **a** (= à cette époque) then, in those days, at that time; **il était ~ étudiant** he was a student then ou at that time ou in those days; **les femmes d'~ portaient la crinoline** the women d'~ of those days ou at ou of that time wore crinolines; **le ministre d'~ M. Dupont** the then minister Mr Dupont, the minister at that time, Mr Dupont → **jusque** |b| (= *en conséquence*) then, in that case, so; **vous ne voulez pas de mon aide ? ~ je vous laisse** you don't want my help? I'll leave you to it then; **il ne connaissait pas l'affaire, ~ on l'a mis au courant** he wasn't familiar with the matter so they put him in the picture; **~ qu'est-ce qu'on va faire ?** what are we going to do then?, so what are we going to do? |c| **~ que** (*simultanéité*) while, when; (*opposition*) whereas; **~ même que** (= *même si*) even if, even though; (= *au moment où*) while, just when; **on a sonné ~ que j'étais dans mon bain** the bell rang while *ou* when I was in the bath; **elle est sortie ~ que le médecin le lui avait interdit** she went out although *ou* even though the doctor had told her not to; **il est parti travailler à Paris ~ que son frère est resté au village** he went to work in Paris whereas *ou* while his brother stayed behind in the village; **~ même qu'il me supplierait** even if he begged me, even if *ou* though he were to beg me |d| *** ~ tu viens (oui ou non) ?** well (then), are you coming (or not)?, are you coming then (or not)?; **~ ça, ça m'étonne** now that really does surprise me; **~ là je ne peux pas vous répondre** well that I really can't tell you; **~ là je vous arrête** well I must stop you there; **et (puis) ~ ?** and then what (happened)?; **il pleut — et ~ ?** it's raining — so (what)?; **alors ~ ! ◊ ~ quoi !** come on! → **non**

alose [aloz] NF shad

alouette [alwɛt] NF lark; **~ (des champs)** skylark; **attendre que les ~s vous tombent toutes rôties dans la bouche** to wait for things to fall into one's lap → **miroir**

alourdir [aluʀdiʀ] ▶conjug 2◀ |1| VT |a| [+ *véhicule*] to weigh *ou* load down, make heavy; [+ *phrase*] to make heavy *ou* cumbersome; [+ *démarche, traits*] to make heavy; [+ *esprit*] to dull; [+ *atmosphère, climat*] to make more tense; **il avait la tête alourdie par le sommeil** his head was heavy with sleep; **vêtements alourdis par la pluie** heavy, rain-soaked clothes; **les odeurs d'essence alourdissaient l'air** petrol fumes hung heavy on the air, the air was heavy with petrol fumes |b| (= *augmenter*) [+ *dette, facture, comptes*] to increase |2| **s'alourdir** VPR [*personne, paupières*] to become *ou* grow heavy; **sa taille/elle s'est alourdie** her waist/she has thickened out; **le bilan s'est encore alourdi** the death toll has risen again

alourdissement [aluʀdismã] NM |a| [*véhicule, objet*] increased weight, heaviness; [*phrase, style, pas*] heaviness; [*esprit*] dullness, dulling; [*taille*] thickening; **pour éviter l'~ de la procédure** to prevent the procedure from becoming more lengthy and cumbersome |b| [*dette, facture*] increase (**de** in)

aloyau [alwajo] NM sirloin

alpaga [alpaga] NM (*Tex, Zool*) alpaca

alpage [alpaʒ] NM (= *pré*) high mountain pasture; (= *époque*) season spent by sheep etc in mountain pasture

alpaguer* [alpage] ▶conjug 1◀ VT (*gén*) to collar*; (*Police*) to collar*, nab* (*Brit*); **se faire ~** to get collared*

alpe [alp] |1| NF (= *pré*) alpine pasture |2| **Alpes** NFPL **les Alpes** the Alps

alpestre [alpɛstʀ] ADJ alpine

alpha [alfa] NM alpha; (*Rel, fig*) **l'~ et l'oméga** the alpha and omega; (*Phys*) **particule ~** alpha particle

alphabet [alfabɛ] NM (= *système*) alphabet; (= *livre*) alphabet *ou* ABC book; **~ morse** Morse code

alphabétique [alfabetik] ADJ alphabetical; **par ordre ~** in alphabetical order

alphabétiquement [alfabetikmã] ADV alphabetically

alphabétisation [alfabetizasjɔ̃] NF elimination of illiteracy (**de** in); **l'~ d'une population** teaching a population to read and write; **campagne d'~** literacy campaign; **taux d'~** literacy rate

alphabétisé, e [alfabetize] (*ptp de* **alphabétiser**) ADJ literate; **population faiblement ~e** population with a low level of literacy

alphabétiser [alfabetize] ▶conjug 1◀ VT [+ *pays*] to eliminate illiteracy in; [+ *population*] to teach how to read and write

alphanumérique [alfanymeʀik] ADJ alphanumeric

alphapage® [alfapaʒ] NM radiopager (*which displays messages*); **envoyer qch par ~** to send sth via a radiopager

alpin, e [alpɛ̃, in] ADJ alpine → **chasseur, ski**

alpinisme [alpinism] NM mountaineering, mountain climbing

alpiniste [alpinist] NMF mountaineer, climber

alsacien, -ienne [alzasjɛ̃, jɛn] |1| ADJ Alsatian |2| NM (*Ling*) Alsatian |3| **Alsacien(ne)** NM,F Alsatian

altérabilité [alteʀabilite] NF alterability

altérable [alteʀabl] ADJ alterable; **~ à l'air** liable to oxidization

altération [alteʀasjɔ̃] NF |a| (= *falsification*) [*fait, texte, vérité*] distortion, falsification; [*monnaie*] falsification; [*vin, aliment, qualité*] adulteration |b| (= *détérioration*) [*vin, aliment, qualité, matière*] deterioration; **l'~ de sa santé** the change for the worse in *ou* the deterioration of *ou* in his health; **l'~ de son visage/de sa voix** his distorted features/broken voice; **l'~ de leurs relations** the deterioration of their relationship |c| (= *modification*) change, modification |d| (*Mus*) accidental; (*Géol*) weathering

altercation [alteʀkasjɔ̃] NF altercation

alter ego [alteʀego] NM INV alter ego; **il est mon ~** he is my alter ego

altérer [alteʀe] ▶conjug 6◀ |1| VT |a| (= *assoiffer*) to make thirsty; (*littér*) **altéré d'honneurs** thirsty *ou* thirsting for honours; **fauve altéré de sang** wild animal thirsting for blood; **il était altéré** his throat was parched |b| (= *falsifier*) [+ *texte, faits, vérité*] to distort, falsify; [+ *monnaie*] to falsify; (*Comm*) [+ *vin, aliments, qualité*] to adulterate |c| (= *abîmer*) [+ *vin, aliments, qualité*] to spoil; [+ *matière*] to alter, debase; [+ *sentiments*] to alter, spoil; [+ *couleur*] to alter; [+ *visage, voix*] to distort; [+ *santé, relations*] to impair, affect; **d'une voix altérée** in a broken voice; **la chaleur a altéré la viande** the heat made the meat go bad *ou* go off (*Brit*) |d| (= *modifier*) to alter, change, modify; **ceci n'a pas altéré mon amour pour elle** this has not altered my love for her |2| **s'altérer** VPR [*vin*] to become spoiled; [*viande*] to go bad, go off (*Brit*), spoil (*US*); [*matière, couleur*] to undergo a change; [*visage*] to change, become distorted; [*sentiments*] to alter, be spoilt; [*relations*] to deteriorate; **sa santé s'altère de plus en plus** his health is deteriorating further *ou* is getting progressively worse; **sa voix s'altéra sous le coup de la douleur** grief made his voice break, grief distorted his voice

altérité [alteʀite] NF otherness

alternance [alteʀnɑ̃s] NF |a| (*gén*) alternation; (*Pol*) changeover of political power between parties |b| **en ~ faire qch en ~** (= *se relayer*) to take it in turns to do sth; **les deux pièces sont jouées en ~** the two plays are performed alternately; **cette émission reprendra en ~ avec d'autres programmes** this broadcast will alternate with other programmes → **formation**

alternant, e [alteʀnɑ̃, ɑ̃t] ADJ alternating

alternateur [alteʀnatœʀ] NM alternator

alternatif, -ive¹ [alteʀnatif, iv] ADJ (= *périodique*) alternate; (*Philos*) alternative; (*Élec*) alternating; (*médecine*) alternative

alternative² [alteʀnativ] NF (= *dilemme*) alternative; (* = *possibilité*) alternative, option; (*Philos*) alternative; **être dans une ~** to have to choose between two alternatives

alternativement [alteʀnativmã] ADV alternately, in turn

alterne [alteʀn] ADJ (*Bot, Math*) alternate

alterné, e [alteʀne] (*ptp de* **alterner**) ADJ [*rimes*] alternate; (*Math*) [*série*] alternate; **circulation ~e** (*pour travaux*) contraflow (system); (*pour pollution*) selective ban on vehicle use (based on registration numbers) during periods of heavy pollution; **la prise ~e de deux médicaments** taking two medicines in alternation → **stationnement**

alterner [alteʀne] ▶conjug 1◀ |1| VT [+ *choses*] to alternate; [+ *cultures*] to rotate, alternate |2| VI to alternate (**avec** with); **ils alternèrent à la présidence** they took (it in) turns to be chairman

altesse [altɛs] NF (= *prince*) prince; (= *princesse*) princess; (= *titre*) **votre Altesse** your Highness; **Son Altesse sérénissime/royale** His *ou* Her Serene/Royal Highness

altier, -ière [altje, jɛʀ] ADJ [*caractère*] haughty; (*littér*) **cimes altières** lofty peaks (*littér*)

altimètre [altimɛtʀ] NM altimeter

altimétrie [altimetʀi] NF altimetry

altiport [altipɔʀ] NM altiport (*SPÉC*), mountain airfield

altiste [altist] NMF viola player, violist

altitude [altityd] NF |a| (*par rapport à la mer*) altitude, height above sea level; (*par rapport au sol*) height; (*fig*) **~s** heights; **être à 500 mètres d'~** to be at a height *ou* an altitude of 500 metres, be 500 metres above sea level; **en ~** at high altitude, high up; **les régions de basse ~** low-lying areas |b| (*Aviat*) **perdre de l'~** to lose altitude *ou* height; **prendre de l'~** to gain altitude; **voler à basse/haute ~** to fly at low/high altitude

alto [alto] |1| NM (= *instrument*) viola |2| NF contralto |3| ADJ **saxo(phone)/flûte ~** alto sax(ophone)/flute

altruisme [altʀyism] NM altruism

altruiste [altʀyist] |1| ADJ altruistic |2| NMF altruist

altuglas® [altyglas] NM thick form of Perspex®

alu [aly] NM ABRÉV = **aluminium**

aluminate [alyminat] NM aluminate

alumine [alymin] NF alumina

aluminium [alyminjɔm] NM aluminium (*Brit*), aluminum (*US*)

alun [alœ̃] NM alum

alunir [alyniʀ] ▶conjug 2◀ VI to land on the moon

alunissage [alynisaʒ] NM (moon) landing

alvéolaire [alveɔlɛʀ] ADJ alveolar

alvéole [alveɔl] NM ou M [*ruche*] alveolus, cell; (*Géol*) cavity; **~ dentaire** tooth socket, alveolus (*SPÉC*); **~s dentaires** alveolar ridge, teeth ridge, alveoli (*SPÉC*); **~ pulmonaire** air cell, alveolus (*SPÉC*)

alvéolé, e [alveɔle] ADJ honeycombed, alveolate (*SPÉC*)

Alzheimer [alzajmœʀ] NM **maladie d'~** Alzheimer's disease; **il a un ~*** he has got Alzheimer's (disease)

AM [aɛm] (ABRÉV = **assurance maladie**) → **assurance**

amabilité [amabilite] NF kindness; **ayez l'~ de** (would you) be so kind *ou* good as to; **plein d'~ envers moi** extremely kind to me; **faire des ~s à qn** to show politeness *ou* courtesy to sb

amadou [amadu] NM touchwood, tinder

amadouer [amadwe] ▶conjug 1 ◀ VT (= *enjôler*) to coax, cajole; (= *adoucir*) to mollify, soothe; **~ qn pour qu'il fasse qch** to wheedle *ou* cajole sb into doing sth

amaigrir [amegʀiʀ] ▶conjug 2 ◀ ⓵ VT ⓐ (= *rendre plus maigre*) to make thin *ou* thinner; **joues amaigries par l'âge** cheeks wasted with age; **je l'ai trouvé très amaigri** I found him much thinner, I thought he looked much thinner; **10 années de prison l'ont beaucoup amaigri** 10 years in prison have left him very much thinner ⓑ (*Tech*) to thin down, reduce ⓶ **s'amaigrir** VPR to get *ou* become thin *ou* thinner

amaigrissant, e [amegʀisɑ̃, ɑ̃t] ADJ [*produit, régime*] slimming (*Brit*), reducing (*US*)

amaigrissement [amegʀismɑ̃] NM ⓐ (*pathologique*) [*corps*] loss of weight; [*visage, membres*] thinness ⓑ (*volontaire*) slimming; **un ~ de 3 kg** a loss (in weight) of 3 kg → **cure¹**

amalgamation [amalgamasjɔ̃] NF (*Métal*) amalgamation

amalgame [amalgam] NM (*péj* = *mélange*) (strange) mixture *ou* blend; (*Métal, Dentisterie*) amalgam; **un ~ d'idées** a hotchpotch of ideas; **faire l'~ entre deux idées** to confuse two ideas; **il ne faut pas faire l'~ entre parti de droite et parti fasciste** you shouldn't lump the right-wing and fascist parties together

amalgamer [amalgame] ▶conjug 1 ◀ ⓵ VT (*Métal*) to amalgamate; (= *mélanger*) to combine (**à, avec** with); (= *confondre*) [+ *idées, réalités*] to confuse ⓶ **s'amalgamer** VPR (*Métal*) to be amalgamated; (= *s'unir*) to combine

amande [amɑ̃d] NF ⓐ (= *fruit*) almond; **~s amères/douces** bitter/sweet almonds; **~s pilées** ground almonds; **en ~** almond-shaped, almond (*épith*) → **pâte** ⓑ (= *noyau*) kernel ⓒ (*mollusque*) queen scallop

amandier [amɑ̃dje] NM almond (tree)

amandine [amɑ̃din] NF (= *gâteau*) almond tart

amanite [amanit] NF Amanita; **~ phalloïde** death cap; **~ tue-mouches** fly agaric

amant [amɑ̃] NM lover; **~ de passage** casual lover; **les deux ~s** the two lovers; **prendre un ~** to take a lover

amante†† [amɑ̃t] NF (= *fiancée*) betrothed†, mistress†

amarante [amaʀɑ̃t] ⓵ NF amaranth ⓶ ADJ INV amaranthine

amariner [amaʀine] ▶conjug 1 ◀ VT ⓐ [+ *navire ennemi*] to take over and man ⓑ [+ *matelot*] to accustom to life at sea; **elle n'est pas** *ou* **ne s'est pas encore amarinée** she hasn't got used to being at sea yet, she hasn't found her sea legs yet

amarrage [amaʀaʒ] NM (*Naut*) mooring; **être à l'~** to be moored

amarre [amaʀ] NF (*Naut* = *cordage*) rope *ou* line *ou* cable (for mooring); **les ~s** the moorings → **larguer, rompre**

amarrer [amaʀe] ▶conjug 1 ◀ VT [+ *navire*] to moor, make fast; [+ *cordage*] to make fast, belay; (*hum*) [+ *paquet, valise*] to tie down; **la navette s'est amarrée à la station orbitale** the shuttle has docked with the space station

amaryllis [amaʀilis] NF amaryllis

amas [amɑ] NM ⓐ (*lit* = *tas*) heap, pile, mass; [*souvenirs, idées*] mass; **tout un ~ de qch** a whole heap *ou* pile of sth ⓑ (*Astron*) star cluster ⓒ (*Min*) mass

amasser [amase] ▶conjug 1 ◀ ⓵ VT ⓐ (= *amonceler*) [+ *choses*] to pile *ou* store up, amass, accumulate; [+ *fortune*] to amass, accumulate; **il ne pense qu'à ~ (de l'argent)** all he thinks of is amassing *ou* accumulating wealth ⓑ (= *rassembler*) [+ *preuves, données*] to amass, gather (together) → **pierre** ⓶ **s'amasser** VPR [*choses, preuves*] to pile up, accumulate; [*foule*] to gather, mass; **les preuves s'amassent contre**

lui the evidence is building up *ou* piling up against him

amateur [amatœʀ] NM ⓐ (= *non-professionnel*) amateur; **équipe ~** amateur team; **talent d'~** amateur talent; **peintre/musicien/photographe ~** amateur painter/musician/photographer; **faire de la peinture en ~** to do a bit of painting (as a hobby) ⓑ (= *connaisseur*) **~ de** lover of; **~ d'art/de musique** art/music lover; **être ~ de films/de concerts** to be an avid *ou* a keen (*Brit*) film-/concert-goer, be keen on (*Brit*) films/concerts; **elle est très ~ de framboises** she is very fond of *ou* she loves raspberries; **le jazz, je ne suis pas ~** I'm not really a jazz fan, I'm not all that keen on jazz (*Brit*) ⓒ* (= *acheteur*) taker; (= *volontaire*) volunteer; **il reste des carottes, il y a des ~s?** *ou* **avis aux ~s!** there are some carrots left, are there any takers? → **trouver** ⓓ (*péj*) dilettante, mere amateur; **travail d'~** amateurish work; **faire qch en ~** to do sth amateurishly

amateurisme [amatœʀism] NM (*Sport*) amateurism; (*péj*) amateurism, amateurishness; **c'est de l'~!** it's so amateurish!

amazone [amazon] NF ⓐ (= *écuyère*) horsewoman; **tenue d'~** woman's riding habit; **monter en ~** to ride sidesaddle ⓑ (= *jupe*) long riding skirt ⓒ (* = *prostituée*) prostitute (*who picks up her clients in a car*) ⓓ **Amazone** (*Géog, Myth*) Amazon

Amazonie [amazɔni] NF Amazonia

amazonien, -ienne [amazɔnjɛ̃, jɛn] ADJ Amazonian

ambages [ɑ̃baʒ] ◆**sans ambages** LOC ADV without beating about the bush, in plain language

ambassade [ɑ̃basad] NF ⓐ (= *institution, bâtiment*) embassy; (= *charge*) ambassadorship, embassy; (= *personnel*) embassy staff *pl ou* officials, embassy; **l'~ de France** the French Embassy ⓑ (= *mission*) mission; **être envoyé en ~ auprès de qn** to be sent on a mission to sb

ambassadeur [ɑ̃basadœʀ] NM (*Pol, fig*) ambassador; **~ extraordinaire** ambassador extraordinary (**auprès de** to); **l'~ de la pensée française** the representative *ou* ambassador of French thought

ambassadrice [ɑ̃basadʀis] NF (= *diplomate*) ambassador, ambassadress (**auprès de** to); (= *épouse*) ambassador's wife, ambassadress; (*fig*) representative, ambassador, ambassadress

ambiance [ɑ̃bjɑ̃s] NF ⓐ (= *atmosphère*) atmosphere; (= *environnement*) surroundings; [*famille, équipe*] atmosphere; **l'~ de la salle** the atmosphere in the house, the mood of the audience; **il vit dans une ~ calme** he lives in calm *ou* peaceful surroundings; **il y a de l'~ ici!** there's a great atmosphere here!*; **il va y avoir de l'~ quand tu vas lui dire ça!*** things are going to get ugly* when you tell him that!; **mettre de l'~** to liven things up*; **mettre qn dans l'~** to put sb in the mood → **éclairage, musique**

ambiant, e [ɑ̃bjɑ̃, ɑ̃t] ADJ [*air*] surrounding, ambient; [*température*] ambient; [*idéologie, scepticisme*] prevailing, pervading

ambidextre [ɑ̃bidɛkstʀ] ADJ ambidextrous

ambigu, -uë [ɑ̃bigy] ADJ ambiguous

ambiguïté [ɑ̃biguite] NF ⓐ (*caractère*) ambiguousness, ambiguity; **une réponse sans ~** an unequivocal *ou* unambiguous reply; **parler/répondre sans ~** to speak/reply unambiguously *ou* without ambiguity ⓑ (*Ling*) ambiguity ⓒ (*terme*) ambiguity

ambitieusement [ɑ̃bisjøzmɑ̃] ADV ambitiously

ambitieux, -ieuse [ɑ̃bisjø, jøz] ⓵ ADJ ambitious; (*littér*) **~ de plaire** anxious to please, desirous to please (*littér*) ⓶ NM,F ambitious person

▼**ambition** [ɑ̃bisjɔ̃] NF ambition; **il met toute son ~ à faire** his only *ou* sole ambition is to do; **elle a l'~ de réussir** her ambition is to succeed; **il a de grandes ~s** he has great *ou* big ambitions

ambitionner [ɑ̃bisjɔne] ▶conjug 1 ◀ VT to seek *ou* strive after; **il ambitionne d'escalader l'Everest** it's his ambition to *ou* his ambition is to climb Everest

ambivalence [ɑ̃bivalɑ̃s] NF ambivalence

ambivalent, e [ɑ̃bivalɑ̃, ɑ̃t] ADJ ambivalent

amble [ɑ̃bl] NM [*cheval*] amble; **aller l'~** to amble

ambler [ɑ̃ble] ▶conjug 1 ◀ VI [*cheval*] to amble

amblyope [ɑ̃bljɔp] ⓵ ADJ **il est ~** he has a lazy eye, he is amblyopic (*SPÉC*) ⓶ NMF person with a lazy eye *ou* amblyopia (*SPÉC*)

amblyopie [ɑ̃bljɔpi] NF lazy eye, amblyopia (*SPÉC*)

ambre [ɑ̃bʀ] NM **~ (jaune)** amber; **~ gris** ambergris; **couleur d'~** amber(-coloured)

ambré, e [ɑ̃bʀe] ADJ [*couleur*] amber; [*parfum*] amber-based

ambroisie [ɑ̃bʀwazi] NF (*Myth*) ambrosia; (*Bot*) ambrosia, ragweed; (*fig*) **c'est de l'~!** this is food fit for the gods!

ambrosiaque [ɑ̃bʀozjak] ADJ ambrosial

ambulance [ɑ̃bylɑ̃s] NF ambulance; (*fig*) **on ne tire pas sur une ~** you don't kick somebody when they're down

ambulancier, -ière [ɑ̃bylɑ̃sje, jɛʀ] NM,F (*conducteur*) ambulance driver; (= *infirmier*) ambulance man (*ou* woman)

ambulant, e [ɑ̃bylɑ̃, ɑ̃t] ADJ [*comédien, musicien*] itinerant, strolling; [*cirque, théâtre*] travelling; **c'est un squelette/dictionnaire ~*** he's a walking skeleton/dictionary → **marchand, vendeur** *etc*

ambulatoire [ɑ̃bylatwaʀ] ADJ (*Méd*) outpatient (*épith*), ambulatory; **médecine ~** outpatient care

AME [aema] NM (ABRÉV = **accord monétaire européen**) EMA

âme [ɑm] NF ⓐ (*gén, Philos, Rel*) soul; **(que) Dieu ait son ~** (may) God rest his soul; **sur mon ~††** upon my soul† → **recommander, rendre** ⓑ (= *centre de qualités intellectuelles et morales*) heart, soul, mind; **avoir** *ou* **être une ~ généreuse** to have great generosity of spirit; **avoir** *ou* **être une ~ basse** *ou* **vile** to have an evil heart *ou* mind, be evil-hearted *ou* evilminded; **avoir** *ou* **être une ~ sensible** to be a sensitive soul, be very sensitive; (*frm*) **ce film n'est pas pour les ~s sensibles** this film is not for the squeamish *ou* the faint-hearted; **grandeur** *ou* **noblesse d'~** high- *ou* noble-mindedness; **en mon ~ et conscience** in all conscience *ou* honesty; (*littér*) **de toute mon ~** with all my soul; **il y a mis toute son ~** he put his heart and soul into it ⓒ (= *centre psychique et émotif*) soul; **faire qch avec ~** to do sth with feeling; **ému jusqu'au fond de l'~** profoundly moved; **c'est un corps sans ~** he has no soul; **il est musicien dans l'~** he's a musician through and through; **il a la technique mais son jeu est sans ~** his technique is good but he plays without feeling *ou* his playing is soulless ⓓ (= *personne*) soul; (*frm*) **un village de 600 ~s** a village of 600 souls; **on ne voyait ~ qui vive** you couldn't see a (living) soul, there wasn't a (living) soul to be seen; **bonne ~*** kind soul; **est-ce qu'il n'y aura pas une bonne ~ pour m'aider?** won't some kind soul give me a hand?; (*iro*) **il y a toujours de bonnes ~s pour critiquer** there's always some kind soul ready to criticize (*iro*); (*gén péj*) **~ charitable** well-meaning soul (*iro*); **il est là/il erre comme une ~ en peine** he looks like/he is wandering about like a lost soul; **être l'~ damnée de qn** to be sb's henchman *ou* tool; **il a trouvé l'~**

sœur he has found a soul mate
[e] (= *principe qui anime*) soul, spirit; **l'~ d'un peuple** the soul *ou* spirit of a nation; **l'~ d'un complot** the moving spirit in a plot; **être l'~ d'un parti** to be the soul *ou* leading light of a party; **elle a une ~ de sœur de charité** she is the very soul *ou* spirit of charity; **elle a une ~ de chef** she has the soul of a leader
[f] (*Tech*) [*canon*] bore; [*aimant*] core; [*violon*] soundpost → **charge, état, fendre** *etc*

améliorable [ameljɔʀabl] ADJ improvable

amélioration [ameljɔʀasjɔ̃] NF [a] (= *fait de s'améliorer*) improvement; **l'~ de son état de santé** the improvement in his health, the change for the better in his health; **on assiste à une ~ des conditions de travail** working conditions are improving; **une ~ de la conjoncture** an economic upturn, an improvement in the state of the economy [b] (= *travaux*) improvement; **faire des ~s dans** ◊ **apporter des ~s à** to make *ou* carry out improvements in *ou* to

améliorer [ameljɔʀe] ▸ conjug 1 ◂ [1] VT to improve; **~ sa situation** to improve one's situation; **pour ~ l'ordinaire** (*argent*) to top up one's basic income; (*repas*) to make things a bit more interesting [2] **s'améliorer** VPR to improve; **tu ne t'améliores pas avec l'âge!** you're not getting any better with age!, you don't improve with age, do you?

amen [amɛn] NM INV (*Rel*) amen; **dire ~ à qch/à tout** to say amen to sth/everything, agree religiously to sth/everything

aménageable [amenaʒabl] ADJ [*horaire*] flexible; [*grenier*] suitable for conversion (**en** into)

aménagement [amenaʒmɑ̃] NM [a] (= *agencement*) [*local*] fitting-out; [*parc*] laying-out; **l'~ d'une chambre en bureau** converting a bedroom into an office; **l'~ du territoire** national and regional development; ≈ town and country planning (*Brit*); **~ régional/urbain** regional/urban development; **plan d'~** development plan [b] (= *équipements*) **~s** facilities; **les nouveaux ~s de l'hôpital** the new hospital facilities [c] (= *ajustement*) adjustment; **~ du temps de travail** (*réforme*) reform of working hours; (*gestion*) flexible time management; **demander des ~s financiers/d'horaire** to request certain financial adjustments/adjustments to one's timetable; (*Jur*) **~ de peine** reduced sentencing [d] (= *création*) [*route*] making, building; [*gradins, placard*] putting in

aménager [amenaʒe] ▸ conjug 3 ◂ VT [a] (= *équiper*) [+ *local*] to fit out; [+ *parc*] to lay out; [+ *territoire*] to develop; [+ *horaire*] (*gén*) to plan, work out; (= *modifier*) to adjust; **horaire aménagé** (*travail*) flexible working hours; (*Scol*) flexible timetable; **~ une chambre en bureau** to convert a bedroom into a study; **s'~ des plages de repos** to take a rest from time to time [b] (= *créer*) [+ *route*] to make, build; [+ *gradins, placard*] to put in; **~ un bureau dans une chambre** to fix up a study in a bedroom

aménageur, -euse [amenaʒœʀ, øz] NM,F specialist in national and regional development, ≈ town and country planner (*Brit*), ≈ city planner (*US*)

amendable [amɑ̃dabl] ADJ (*Pol*) amendable; (*Agr*) which can be enriched

amende [amɑ̃d] NF fine; **mettre à l'~** to penalize; **il a eu 500 F d'~** he got a 500-franc fine, he was fined 500 francs; **« défense d'entrer sous peine d'~ »** "trespassers will be prosecuted *ou* fined"; **faire ~ honorable** to make amends

amendement [amɑ̃dmɑ̃] NM (*Pol*) amendment; (*Agr*) (= *opération*) enrichment; (= *substance*) enriching agent

amender [amɑ̃de] ▸ conjug 1 ◂ [1] VT (*Pol*) to amend; (*Agr*) to enrich; [+ *conduite*] to improve, amend [2] **s'amender** VPR to mend one's ways

amène [amɛn] ADJ (*littér* = *aimable*) [*propos, visage*] affable; [*personne, caractère*] amiable, affable; **des propos peu ~s** unkind words

amener [am(ə)ne] ▸ conjug 5 ◂ [1] VT [a] (= *faire venir*) [+ *personne, objet*] to bring (along); (= *acheminer*) [+ *cargaison*] to bring, convey; **on nous amène les enfants tous les matins** they bring the children to us every morning, the children are brought to us every morning; **amène-la à la maison** bring her round (*Brit*) *ou* around (*US*) (to the house), bring her home; **le sable est amené à Paris par péniche** sand is brought *ou* conveyed to Paris by barge; **qu'est-ce qui vous amène ici?** what brings you here?; **vous nous avez amené le beau temps!** you've brought the nice weather with you! → **mandat**
[b] (= *provoquer*) to bring about, cause; **~ la disette** to bring about *ou* cause a shortage; **~ le typhus** to cause typhus
[c] (= *inciter*) **~ qn à faire qch** (*circonstances*) to induce *ou* lead *ou* bring sb to do sth; (*personne*) to bring sb round to doing sth, get sb to do sth; (*par un discours persuasif*) to talk sb into doing sth; **la crise pourrait ~ le gouvernement à agir** the crisis might induce *ou* lead the government to take action; **elle a été finalement amenée à renoncer à son voyage** she was finally induced *ou* driven to give up her trip; **je suis amené à croire que ...** I am led to believe *ou* think that ...; **c'est ce qui m'a amené à cette conclusion** that is what led *ou* brought me to that conclusion
[d] (= *diriger*) to bring; **~ qn à ses propres idées/à une autre opinion** to bring sb round (*Brit*) *ou* around (*US*) to one's own ideas/to another way of thinking; **~ la conversation sur un sujet** to bring the conversation round (*Brit*) *ou* around (*US*) to a subject, lead the conversation on to a subject; **système amené à un haut degré de complexité** system brought to a high degree of complexity
[e] [+ *transition, conclusion, dénouement*] to present, introduce; **exemple bien amené** well-introduced example
[f] (*Pêche*) [+ *poisson*] to draw in; (*Naut*) [+ *voile, pavillon*] to strike; (*Mil*) **~ les couleurs** to strike colours
[g] (*Dés*) [+ *paire, brelan*] to throw
[2] **s'amener*** VPR (= *venir*) to come along; **amène-toi ici!** get over here!*; **tu t'amènes?** are you going to get a move on?*, come on!*; **il s'est amené avec toute sa bande** he came along *ou* turned up *ou* showed up* with the whole gang

aménité [amenite] NF (= *amabilité*) [*propos*] affability; [*personne, caractère*] amiability, affability; **sans ~** unkindly; (*iro*) **se dire des ~s** to exchange uncomplimentary remarks

aménorrhée [amenɔʀe] NF amenorrhoea

amenuisement [amənɥizmɑ̃] NM [*valeur, avance, espoir*] dwindling; [*chances*] lessening; [*ressources*] diminishing, dwindling

amenuiser [amənɥize] ▸ conjug 1 ◂ [1] **s'amenuiser** VPR [*valeur, avance, espoir*] to dwindle; [*chances*] to grow slimmer, lessen; [*risque*] to diminish, become less (and less) likely; [*différences*] to diminish, become less important *ou* evident; [*provisions, ressources*] to run low, diminish, dwindle; [*temps*] to run out [2] VT [+ *objet*] to thin down; (*fig*) to reduce

amer¹ [amɛʀ] NM (*Naut*) seamark

amer², -ère [amɛʀ] ADJ (*lit, fig*) bitter; **~ comme chicotin*** as bitter as anything; **avoir la bouche amère** to have a bitter taste in one's mouth

amérasien, -ienne [ameʀazjɛ̃, jɛn] [1] ADJ Amerasian [2] **Amérasien(ne)** NM,F Amerasian

amèrement [amɛʀmɑ̃] ADV bitterly

américain, e [ameʀikɛ̃, ɛn] [1] ADJ American → **œil** [2] NM (*Ling*) American (English) [3] **Américain(e)** NM,F American [4] **améri-**

caine NF (*automobile*) American car; **à l'~e** (*gén*) in the American style; (*Culin*) à l'Américaine; **course à l'~e** (bicycle) relay race

américanisation [ameʀikanizasjɔ̃] NF americanization

américaniser [ameʀikanize] ▸ conjug 1 ◂ [1] VT to americanize [2] **s'américaniser** VPR to become americanized

américanisme [ameʀikanism] NM americanism

américaniste [ameʀikanist] NMF Americanist, American specialist

américium [ameʀisjɔm] NM americium

amérindien, -ienne [ameʀɛ̃djɛ̃, jɛn] [1] ADJ Amerindian, American Indian [2] **Amérindien(ne)** NM,F Amerindian, American Indian

Amérique [ameʀik] NF America; **~ centrale/latine/du Nord/du Sud** Central/Latin/North/South America

Amerloque* [ameʀlɔk] NMF, **Amerlo(t)** [ameʀlo] NM Yankee*, Yank*

amerrir [ameʀiʀ] ▸ conjug 2 ◂ VI (*Aviat*) to land (on the sea), make a sea-landing; (*Espace*) to splash down

amerrissage [ameʀisaʒ] NM (*Aviat*) (sea) landing; (*Espace*) splashdown

amertume [amɛʀtym] NF (*lit, fig*) bitterness; **plein d'~** full of bitterness, very bitter

améthyste [ametist] NF, ADJ INV amethyst

ameublement [amœblamɑ̃] NM (= *meubles*) furniture; (*action*) furnishing; **articles d'~** furnishings; **commerce d'~** furniture trade

ameublir [amœbliʀ] ▸ conjug 2 ◂ VT (*Agr*) to loosen, break down

ameuter [amøte] ▸ conjug 1 ◂ [1] VT [a] (= *attrouper*) [+ *curieux, passants*] to draw a crowd of; [+ *voisins*] to bring out; (= *soulever*) [+ *foule*] to rouse, stir up, incite (**contre** against); **ses cris ameutèrent les passants** his shouts drew a crowd of passers-by; **elle a ameuté l'opinion internationale contre les pollueurs** she mobilized international opinion against the polluters; **tais-toi, tu vas ~ toute la rue!*** be quiet, you'll have the whole street out!; **tu n'as pas besoin d'~ tout le quartier!*** you don't have to tell the whole neighbourhood!, you don't have to shout it from the rooftops! [b] [+ *chiens*] to form into a pack [2] **s'ameuter** VPR (= *s'attrouper*) [*passants*] to gather, mass together; [*voisins*] to come out; (= *se soulever*) to band together, gather into a mob; **des passants s'ameutèrent** an angry crowd gathered

ami, e [ami] [1] NM,F [a] (= *personne proche*) friend; **un vieil ~ de la famille** *ou* **de la maison** an old friend of the family, an old family friend; **~ d'enfance** childhood friend; **~ intime** (very) close *ou* intimate friend, bosom friend; **il m'a présenté son ~e** he introduced his girlfriend to me; **elle est sortie avec ses ~es** she's out with her (girl)friends; **c'était signé « un ~ qui vous veut du bien »** it was signed "a well-wisher *ou* a friend"; **se faire un ~ de qn** to make *ou* become friends with sb; **faire ~~ avec qn*** to be buddy-buddy with sb*; **nous sommes entre ~s** (*deux personnes*) we're friends; (*plus de deux*) we're all friends; **je vous dis ça en ~** I'm telling you this as a friend; **nous sommes des ~s de vingt ans** we've been friends for twenty years; **~s des bêtes/de la nature** animal/nature lovers; **société** *ou* **club des ~s de Balzac** Balzac club *ou* society; **un célibataire/professeur de mes ~s** a bachelor/teacher friend of mine; **être sans ~s** to be friendless, have no friends; **parents et ~s** friends and relations *ou* relatives; **~ des arts** patron of the arts; **le meilleur ~ de l'homme** man's best friend; **nos ~s à quatre pattes** our four-legged friends
[b] (*euph* = *amant*) boyfriend; (= *maîtresse*) girlfriend; **l'~e de l'assassin** the murderer's

lady-friend → **bon¹, petit**
[c] (interpellation) **mes chers ~s** gentlemen; (auditoire mixte) ladies and gentlemen; **mon cher ~** my dear fellow ou chap (Brit); **ça, mon (petit) ~** now look here; **ben mon ~!** si j'avais su gosh!* ou blimey!* (Brit) ou crikey!* (Brit) if I had known that; (entre époux) **oui mon ~!** yes my dear!

[2] ADJ [visage, pays] friendly; [regard] kindly, friendly; **tendre à qn une main ~** to lend ou give sb a friendly ou helping hand; **être très ~ avec qn** to be very friendly ou great friends ou very good friends with sb; **nous sommes très ~s** we're very close ou good friends; **être ~ de l'ordre** to be a lover of order

amiable [amjabl] ADJ (Jur) amicable; **~ compositeur** conciliator; **à l'~** [divorce, solution] amicable; **vente à l'~** private sale, sale by private agreement; **partage à l'~** private ou amicable partition; **accord** ou **règlement à l'~** amicable agreement, out-of-court settlement; **régler une affaire à l'~** to settle a difference out of court

amiante [amjɑ̃t] NM asbestos; **plaque/fil d'~** asbestos sheet ou plate/thread

amibe [amib] NF amoeba

amibiase [amibjɑz] NF amoebiasis

amibien, -ienne [amibjɛ̃, jɛn] [1] ADJ [maladie] amoebic [2] **amibiens** NMPL Amoebae

amical, e (mpl -aux) [amikal, o] [1] ADJ [personne, relations] friendly; **match ~** ◊ **rencontre ~e** friendly (match); **peu ~** unfriendly [2] **amicale** NF association, club (of people having the same interest); **~e des anciens élèves** old boys' association (Brit), alumni association (US)

amicalement [amikalmã] ADV in a friendly way; **il m'a salué ~** he gave me a friendly wave; (formule épistolaire) **(bien) ~** kind regards, best wishes, yours (ever)

amidon [amidɔ̃] NM starch

amidonner [amidɔne] ▸ conjug 1 ◂ VT to starch

amincir [amɛ̃siʀ] ▸ conjug 2 ◂ [1] VT to thin (down); **cette robe l'amincit** this dress makes her look slim(mer) ou thin(ner); **visage aminci par la tension** face drawn with tension ou hollow with anxiety [2] **s'amincir** VPR [couche de glace, épaisseur de tissu] to get thinner

amincissant, e [amɛ̃sisɑ̃, ɑ̃t] ADJ [crème, régime] slimming (Brit), reducing (US)

amincissement [amɛ̃sismɑ̃] NM thinning (down); **l'~ de la couche de glace a causé l'accident** the ice had got thinner and that was what caused the accident

amine [amin] NF amine

aminé, e [amine] ADJ → **acide**

amiral, e (mpl -aux) [amiʀal, o] [1] ADJ **vaisseau** ou **bateau ~** flagship [2] NM admiral [3] **amirale** NF admiral's wife

amirauté [amiʀote] NF (gén) admiralty; (= fonction) admiralty, admiralship

▼**amitié** [amitje] NF [a] (= sentiment) friendship; **prendre qn en ~** ◊ **se prendre d'~ pour qn** to befriend sb; **se lier d'~ avec qn** to make friends with sb; (littér) **nouer une ~ avec qn** to strike up a friendship with sb; **avoir de l'~ pour qn** to be fond of sb, have a liking for sb; **faites-moi l'~ de venir** do me the kindness ou favour of coming; **l'~ franco-britannique** Anglo-French ou Franco-British friendship; (euph) **~ particulière** homosexual relationship [b] (formule épistolaire) **~s** all the very best, very best wishes ou regards; **~s, Paul** kind regards, Paul, yours, Paul; **elle vous fait** ou **transmet toutes ses ~s** she sends her best wishes ou regards [c] († = civilités) **faire mille ~s à qn** to give sb a warm and friendly welcome

Amman [aman] N Amman

ammoniac, -aque [amɔnjak] [1] ADJ ammoniac; **sel ~** sal ammoniac [2] NM (= gaz) ammonia [3] **ammoniaque** NF ammonia (water)

ammoniacal, e (mpl -aux) [amɔnjakal, o] ADJ ammoniacal

ammoniaqué, e [amɔnjake] ADJ ammoniated

ammonite [amɔnit] NF (Zool) ammonite

ammonium [amɔnjɔm] NM ammonium

amnésie [amnezi] NF amnesia; **~ collective** collective amnesia

amnésique [amnezik] [1] ADJ amnesic [2] NMF amnesiac, amnesic

amniocentèse [amnjosɛ̃tez] NF amniocentesis

amnios [amnjos] NM amnion

amnioscopie [amnjɔskɔpi] NF fetoscopy

amniotique [amnjɔtik] ADJ amniotic; **cavité/liquide ~** amniotic cavity/liquid

amnistiable [amnistjabl] ADJ who may be amnestied

amnistie [amnisti] NF amnesty; **loi d'~** law of amnesty; **bénéficier d'une ~ générale/partielle/totale** to be granted a general/partial/complete amnesty

---
AMNISTIE

The word **amnistie** has a particular meaning at the time of presidential elections in France, as it refers to the traditional waiving of penalties for minor offences (especially parking fines) by the new president as a gesture of goodwill when he comes to power. The tradition is now institutionalized, and in practice Parliament votes on which offences the **amnistie** should cover. The "amnistie présidentielle" is becoming increasingly controversial, and some people feel that it should be abandoned altogether.

---

amnistié, e [amnistje] (ptp de **amnistier**) [1] ADJ [personne, fait] amnestied [2] NM,F amnestied prisoner

amnistier [amnistje] ▸ conjug 7 ◂ VT [+ personne] to grant an amnesty to, amnesty; [+ délit] to grant an amnesty for

amocher: [amɔʃe] ▸ conjug 1 ◂ VT [+ objet, personne] to mess up*, make a mess of*; [+ véhicule] to bash up*; **tu l'as drôlement amoché** you've made a terrible mess of him*, you've messed him up with something terrible*; **se faire ~ dans un accident/une bagarre** to get messed up* in an accident/a fight; **elle/la voiture était drôlement amochée** she/the car was a terrible mess*; **il s'est drôlement amoché en tombant** he gave himself a terrible bash (Brit) ou he smashed himself up pretty well* (US) when he fell

amoindrir [amwɛ̃dʀiʀ] ▸ conjug 2 ◂ VT [+ autorité] to lessen, weaken, diminish; [+ forces] to weaken; [+ fortune, quantité] to diminish, reduce; [+ personne] (physiquement) to make weaker, weaken; (moralement, mentalement) to diminish; **~ qn (aux yeux des autres)** to diminish ou belittle sb (in the eyes of others) [2] **s'amoindrir** VPR [autorité, facultés] to grow weaker, weaken, diminish; [forces] to weaken, grow weaker; [quantité, fortune] to diminish

amoindrissement [amwɛ̃dʀismɑ̃] NM [autorité] lessening, weakening; [forces] weakening; [fortune, quantité] reduction; [personne] (physique) weakening; (moral, mental) diminishing

amollir [amɔliʀ] ▸ conjug 2 ◂ [1] VT [+ chose] to soften, make soft; [+ personne] (moralement) to soften; (physiquement) to weaken, make weak; [+ volonté, forces, résolution] to weaken; **cette chaleur vous amollit** this heat makes you feel (quite) limp ou weak [2] **s'amollir** VPR [chose] to go soft; [courage, énergie] to weaken; [jambes] to go weak; [personne] (= perdre cou-

rage) to grow soft, weaken; (= s'attendrir) to soften, relent

amollissant, e [amɔlisɑ̃, ɑ̃t] ADJ [climat, plaisirs] enervating

amollissement [amɔlismɑ̃] NM [chose] softening; [personne] (moral) softening; (physique) weakening; [volonté, forces, résolution] weakening; **l'~ général est dû à ...** the general weakening of purpose is due to ...

amonceler [amɔ̃s(ə)le] ▸ conjug 4 ◂ [1] VT [+ choses] to pile ou heap up; [+ richesses] to amass, accumulate; [+ documents, preuves] to pile up, accumulate, amass [2] **s'amonceler** VPR [choses] to pile ou heap up; [courrier, demandes] to pile up, accumulate; [nuages] to bank up; [neige] to drift into banks; [difficultés] to pile up; **les preuves s'amoncellent contre lui** the evidence is building up ou piling up against him

amoncellement [amɔ̃sɛlmɑ̃] NM [a] (= tas) [objets] pile, heap, mass; [problèmes] series; **~ de nuages** cloudbank [b] (= accumulation) devant l'~ des demandes faced with a growing number of requests; **~ de preuves** accumulation of evidence

amont [amɔ̃] [1] ADJ INV [ski, skieur] uphill (épith) [2] NM [a] [cours d'eau] upstream water; [pente] uphill slope; **les rapides/l'écluse d'~** the upstream rapids/lock; **l'~ était coupé de rapides** the river upstream was a succession of rapids [b] **en ~** (rivière) upstream, upriver; (pente) uphill; (dans l'industrie pétrolière) upstream; **les contrôles en ~** the checks carried out beforehand; **en ~ de** [+ rivière] upstream ou upriver from; [+ pente] uphill from, above; (fig) before; **en ~ de cette opération** prior to this operation; **intervenir en ~ d'une tâche** to intervene before a task is carried out

amoral, e (mpl -aux) [amɔʀal, o] ADJ amoral

amoralisme [amɔʀalism] NM amorality

amoralité [amɔʀalite] NF amorality

amorçage [amɔʀsaʒ] NM [a] (= action) [hameçon, ligne] baiting; [emplacement] ground baiting [b] [dynamo] energizing; [siphon, obus, pompe] priming [c] (= dispositif) priming cap, primer

amorce [amɔʀs] NF [a] (Pêche) [hameçon] bait; [emplacement] ground bait [b] (= explosif) [cartouche] cap, primer, priming; [obus] percussion cap; [mine] priming; [pistolet d'enfant] cap [c] (= début) [route] initial section; [trou] start; [pellicule, film] trailer; [conversations, négociations] starting up, beginning; [idée, projet] beginning, germ; **l'~ d'une réforme/d'un changement** the beginnings of a reform/change [d] (Ordin) [programme] ▸ bootstrap

amorcer [amɔʀse] ▸ conjug 3 ◂ VT [a] [+ hameçon, ligne] to bait; **il amorce au ver de vase** [+ ligne] he baits his line with worms; [+ emplacement] he uses worms as ground bait [b] [+ dynamo] to energize; [+ siphon, obus, pompe] to prime [c] [+ route, tunnel] to start ou begin building, make a start on; [+ travaux] to begin, make a start on; [+ trou] to begin ou start to bore; **la construction est amorcée depuis deux mois** work has been in progress ou been under way for two months [d] [+ réformes, évolution] to initiate, begin; [+ virage] to begin; **il amorça un geste pour prendre la tasse** he made as if to take the cup; [fusée] **~ la rentrée dans l'atmosphère** to initiate re-entry into the earth's atmosphere; **une descente s'amorce après le virage** after the bend the road starts to go down [e] (Pol = entamer) [+ dialogue] to start (up); [+ négociations] to start, begin; **une détente est amorcée** ou **s'amorce** there are signs of (the beginnings of) a détente

amorphe [amɔʀf] ADJ [a] (= apathique) [personne] passive, lifeless, spiritless; [esprit,

caractère, attitude] passive; [*marché*] dull
[b] (*Minér*) amorphous

amorti, e [amɔʀti] (*ptp de* **amortir**) 1 NM (*Tennis*) drop shot; (*Ftbl*) **faire un ~** to trap the ball; **faire un ~ de la poitrine** to chest the ball down 2 **amortie** NF (*Tennis*) drop shot

amortir [amɔʀtiʀ] ▸ conjug 2 ◂ VT [a] (= *diminuer*) [+ *choc*] to absorb, cushion; [+ *coup, chute*] to cushion, soften; [+ *bruit*] to deaden, muffle; [+ *passions, douleur*] to deaden, dull [b] (*Fin*) [+ *dette*] to pay off, amortize (SPÉC); [+ *titre*] to redeem; [+ *matériel*] to write off the cost of, depreciate (SPÉC); (*gén*) **il utilise beaucoup sa voiture pour l'~** he uses his car a lot to make it pay *ou* to recoup the cost to himself; **maintenant, notre équipement est amorti** we have now written off the (capital) cost of the equipment [c] (*Archit*) to put an amortizement *ou* amortization on

amortissable [amɔʀtisabl] ADJ (*Fin*) redeemable

amortissement [amɔʀtismã] NM [a] (*Fin*) [*dette*] paying off; [*titre*] redemption; (= *provision comptable*) reserve *ou* provision for depreciation; **l'~ de ce matériel se fait en trois ans** it takes three years to recoup *ou* to write off the cost of this equipment; **~s admis par le fisc** capital allowances [b] (= *diminution*) [*choc*] absorption [c] (*Archit*) amortizement, amortization

amortisseur [amɔʀtisœʀ] NM shock absorber

amour [amuʀ] 1 NM [a] (= *sentiment*) love; **parler de ~** to speak of love; **se nourrir** *ou* **vivre d'~ et d'eau fraîche*** to live on love alone; **j'ai rencontré le grand ~** I have met the love of my life; **vivre un grand ~** to be passionately *ou* deeply in love; **entre eux, ce n'est pas le grand ~** there's no love lost between them; **~ platonique** platonic love; **lettre/mariage/roman d'~** love letter/match/story; **fou d'~** madly *ou* wildly in love; **~ fou** wild love *ou* passion, mad love; **ce n'est plus de l'~, c'est de la rage*** it's not love, it's raving madness!* → **filer, saison**
[b] (= *acte*) love-making (NonC); **pendant l'~, elle murmurait des mots tendres** while they were making love *ou* during their love-making, she murmured tender words; **l'~ libre** free love; **l'~ physique** physical love; **faire l'~** to make love (**avec** to, with)
[c] (= *personne*) love; (= *aventure*) love affair; **premier ~** (= *personne*) first love; (= *aventure*) first love (affair); **ses ~s de jeunesse** (= *aventures*) the love affairs *ou* loves of his youth; (= *personnes*) the loves *ou* lovers of his youth; **c'est un ~ de jeunesse** she's one of his old loves *ou* flames*; **des ~s de rencontre** casual love affairs; (*hum*) **à tes ~s!*** (*quand on trinque*) here's to you!; (*quand on éternue*) bless you!; (*hum*) **comment vont tes ~s?*** how's your love life?*
[d] (= *terme d'affection*) **mon ~** my love, my sweet; **cet enfant est un ~** that child's a real darling; **passe-moi l'eau, tu seras un ~** be a darling *ou* dear and pass me the water, pass me the water, there's a darling *ou* a dear (*Brit*); **un ~ de bébé/de petite robe** a lovely *ou* sweet little baby/dress
[e] (*Art*) cupid; (*Myth*) (**le dieu**) **Amour** Eros, Cupid
[f] (*Bot*) **~ en cage** Chinese lantern, winter *ou* ground cherry
[g] (*loc*) **pour l'~ de Dieu** for God's sake, for the love of God; **pour l'~ de votre mère** for your mother's sake; **faire qch pour l'~ de l'art*** to do sth for the love of it; **avoir l'~ du travail bien fait** to love to see a job well done; **faire qch avec ~** to do sth with loving care
2 **amours** NFPL (*littér*) (= *personnes*) loves; (= *aventures*) love affairs → **ancillaire**

amouracher (s') [amuʀaʃe] ▸ conjug 1 ◂ VPR (*péj*) ♦ **s'amouracher de** to become infatuated with

amourette [amuʀɛt] NF (= *relation*) passing fancy, passing love affair

amoureusement [amuʀøzmã] ADV lovingly, amorously

amoureux, -euse [amuʀø, øz] 1 ADJ [a] (= *épris*) [*personne*] in love (**de** with); **tomber ~** to fall in love (**de** with); **être ~ de la musique/la nature** to be a music-/nature-lover, be passionately fond of music/nature; (*hum*) **il est ~ de sa voiture** he's in love with his car (*hum*) [b] (= *d'amour*) [*aventures*] love (*épith*), amorous; **déboires ~** disappointments in love; **vie amoureuse** love life [c] (= *ardent*) [*tempérament, personne*] amorous; [*regard*] tender; loving; (= *voluptueux*) amorous 2 NM,F (*gén*) lover; († = *soupirant*) love, sweetheart; **un ~ de la nature** a nature-lover, a lover of nature; **~ transi** bashful lover; **partir en vacances en ~** to go off on a romantic holiday

amour-propre (*pl* **amours-propres**) [amuʀpʀɔpʀ] NM self-esteem, pride

amovibilité [amɔvibilite] NF (*Jur*) removability

amovible [amɔvibl] ADJ [*doublure, housse, panneau*] removable, detachable; (*Jur*) removable

ampélopsis [ãpelɔpsis] NM ampelopsis

ampérage [ãpeʀaʒ] NM amperage

ampère [ãpeʀ] NM ampere, amp

ampèremètre [ãpeʀmɛtʀ] NM ammeter

amphétamine [ãfetamin] NF amphetamine; **être sous ~s** to be on amphetamines

amphi [ãfi] NM (*arg Univ*) ABRÉV = **amphithéâtre**

amphibie [ãfibi] 1 ADJ amphibious, amphibian 2 NM amphibian

amphibiens [ãfibjɛ̃] NMPL amphibia, amphibians

amphigouri [ãfiguʀi] NM amphigory

amphigourique [ãfiguʀik] ADJ amphigoric

amphithéâtre [ãfiteatʀ] NM (*Archit*) amphitheatre (*Brit*), amphitheater (*US*); (*Univ*) lecture hall *ou* theatre (*Brit*) *ou* theater (*US*); (*Théât*) (upper) gallery; (*Géol*) **~ morainique** morainic cirque *ou* amphitheatre

amphitryon [ãfitʀijɔ̃] NM (*hum ou littér* = *hôte*) host

amphore [ãfɔʀ] NF amphora

ample [ãpl] ADJ [*manteau*] roomy; [*jupe, manche*] full; [*geste*] wide, sweeping; [*voix*] sonorous; [*style*] rich, grand; [*projet*] vast; [*sujet*] wide-ranging, extensive; **faire ~(s) provision(s) de qch** to get into an ample *ou* a plentiful supply of sth; **donner ~ matériel à discussion** to give plenty to discuss; **pour plus ~ informé je tenais à vous dire ...** for your further information I should tell you ...; **veuillez m'envoyer de plus ~ renseignements sur ...** please send me further details of ... *ou* further information about ... → **jusque**

amplement [ãpləmã] ADV [*expliquer, mériter*] fully, amply; **gagner ~ sa vie** to earn a very good living; **ça suffit ~ ◊ c'est ~ suffisant** that's more than enough, that's ample; **les récents événements ont ~ démontré que ...** recent events have been ample proof that ...; **son attitude justifie ~ ma décision** his attitude is ample justification for my decision, his attitude fully *ou* amply justifies my decision

ampleur [ãplœʀ] NF [a] [*vêtement*] fullness; [*voix*] sonorousness; [*geste*] liberalness; [*style, récit*] opulence; **donner de l'~ à une robe** to give fullness to a dress [b] (= *importance*) [*crise, problème, dégâts*] scale, extent; [*déficit*] size, extent; [*sujet, projet*] scope; [*vues*] range; **vu l'~ des dégâts ...** in view of the extent of the scale of the damage ...; **l'~ des moyens mis en œuvre** the sheer size *ou* the massive scale of the measures implemented; **sans grande ~** of limited scope, small-scale (*épith*); **de grande/faible ~** large-/small-scale (*épith*); **des inondations d'une ~ sans précédent** flooding on an

unprecedented scale; **ces manifestations prennent de l'~** the demonstrations are increasing in scale

ampli* [ãpli] NM (ABRÉV = **amplificateur**) amp*; **~-tuner** tuner amplifier

ampliation [ãpliasjɔ̃] NF (= *duplicata*) certified copy; (= *développement*) amplification; **~ des offres de preuves** amplification of previous evidence

amplificateur [ãplifikatœʀ] NM (*Phys, Radio*) amplifier; (*Photo*) enlarger (*permitting only fixed enlarging*)

amplification [ãplifikasjɔ̃] NF [a] (= *développement*) [*tendance, mouvement, échanges, coopération*] development; (= *augmentation*) increase; **une ~ de l'agitation sociale** an increase in social unrest [b] (= *exagération*) [*incident*] exaggeration [c] (*Photo*) enlarging; (*Opt*) magnifying

amplifier [ãplifje] ▸ conjug 7 ◂ 1 VT [a] [+ *tendance*] to accentuate; [+ *mouvement, échanges, coopération*] to cause to develop [b] (= *exagérer*) [+ *incident*] to magnify, exaggerate [c] (*Tech*) [+ *son, courant*] to amplify; [+ *image*] (*Photo*) to enlarge; (*Opt*) to magnify 2 **s'amplifier** VPR (= *se développer*) [*mouvement, tendance, échange, pensée*] to develop; (= *s'aggraver*) to get worse; **les affrontements s'amplifient** the clashes are getting worse

amplitude [ãplityd] NF [a] (*Astron, Phys*) amplitude [b] [*températures*] range [c] (= *importance*) **l'~ de la catastrophe** the magnitude of the catastrophe

ampoule [ãpul] NF [a] (*Élec*) bulb; **~ à vis/à baïonnette** screw-fitting/bayonet bulb [b] (*Pharm*) phial, vial; (*pour seringue*) ampoule, ampule; **~ autocassable** phial (*with a snap-off top*) [c] (*Méd*) (*à la main, au pied*) blister, ampulla (SPÉC); (*Anat*) **~ rectale** rectal ampulla

ampoulé, e [ãpule] ADJ [*style*] turgid, pompous, bombastic

amputation [ãpytasjɔ̃] NF [*membre*] amputation; [*texte, roman, fortune*] drastic cut *ou* reduction (**de** in); [*budget*] drastic cutback *ou* reduction (**de** in)

amputé, e [ãpyte] (*ptp de* **amputer**) 1 ADJ [*membre*] amputated; [*personne*] who has had a limb amputated 2 NM,F amputee; **c'est un ~ he has lost an arm (*ou* a leg), he has had an arm (*ou* a leg) off*** (*Brit*); **c'est un ~ des deux jambes** he's lost both his legs

amputer [ãpyte] ▸ conjug 1 ◂ VT [a] [+ *membre*] to amputate; **il a été amputé** he had an amputation; **il a été amputé d'une jambe** he had his leg amputated [b] [+ *texte, fortune*] to cut *ou* reduce drastically; [+ *budget*] to cut back *ou* reduce drastically (**de** by); **~ un pays d'une partie de son territoire** to sever a country of a part of its territory

Amsterdam [amstɛʀdam] N Amsterdam

amuïr (s') [amɥiʀ] ▸ conjug 2 ◂ VPR (*Phon*) to become mute, be dropped (*in pronunciation*)

amuïssement [amɥismã] NM (*Phon*) dropping of a phoneme in pronunciation

amulette [amylɛt] NF amulet

amure [amyʀ] NF (*Naut*) tack; **aller bâbord/tribord ~s** to go on the port/starboard tack

amurer [amyʀe] ▸ conjug 1 ◂ VT [+ *voile*] to haul aboard the tack of, tack

amusant, e [amyzã, ãt] ADJ (= *distrayant*) [*jeu*] amusing, entertaining; (= *drôle*) [*film, remarque, convive*] amusing, funny; [*jeu*] **c'est (très) ~** it's (great) fun; **c'était ~ à voir** it was amusing *ou* funny to see; **l'~ de l'histoire c'est que ...** the funny *ou* amusing thing about it all is that ...

amuse-bouche (*pl* **amuse-bouche(s)**) [amyzbuʃ] NM appetizer, snack

amuse-gueule (*pl* **amuse-gueule(s)**) [amyz-gœl] NM appetizer, snack

amusement [amyzmɑ̃] NM a (= *divertissement*) amusement (*NonC*); **pour l'~ des enfants** for the children's amusement *ou* entertainment, to amuse *ou* entertain the children b (= *jeu*) game; (= *activité*) diversion, pastime c (= *hilarité*) amusement (*NonC*)

amuser [amyze] ▸conjug 1◂ 1 VT a (= *divertir*) to amuse, entertain; (*involontairement*) to amuse b (= *faire rire*) [*histoire drôle*] to amuse; **ces remarques ne m'amusent pas du tout** I don't find those remarks in the least bit funny *ou* amusing, I'm not in the least amused by such remarks; **tu m'amuses avec tes grandes théories** you make me laugh with your great theories; **faire le pitre pour ~ la galerie** to clown around and play to the crowd, clown around to amuse the crowd c (= *plaire*) **ça ne m'amuse pas de devoir aller leur rendre visite** I don't enjoy having to go and visit them; **si vous croyez que ces réunions m'amusent** if you think I enjoy these meetings d (= *détourner l'attention de*) [+ *ennemi, caissier*] to distract (the attention of), divert the attention of; **pendant que tu l'amuses, je prends l'argent** while you keep him busy *ou* distract his attention, I'll take the money e (= *tromper*) to delude, beguile

2 **s'amuser** VPR a (= *jouer*) [*enfants*] to play; **s'~ avec** [+ *jouet, personne, chien*] to play with; [+ *stylo, ficelle*] to play *ou* fiddle with; **s'~ à un jeu** to play a game; **ils se sont amusés tout l'après-midi à faire des châteaux de sable** they had fun *ou* they played all afternoon building sandcastles; **ils se sont amusés à arroser les passants** they were messing around* spraying passers-by with water; **pour s'~ ils allumèrent un grand feu de joie** they lit a big bonfire for fun *ou* a lark*; **ne t'amuse pas à recommencer, sinon!** don't you do *ou* start that again, or else!
b (= *se divertir*) to have fun *ou* a good time, enjoy o.s.; (= *rire*) to have a good laugh; **s'~ à faire qch** to have fun doing sth, enjoy o.s. doing sth; **nous nous sommes bien amusés** we had great fun *ou* a great time*; **qu'est-ce qu'on s'amuse!** this is great fun!; **j'aime autant te dire qu'on ne s'est pas amusés** it wasn't much fun, I can tell you; **on ne va pas s'~ à cette réunion** we're not going to have much fun *ou* enjoy it much at this meeting; **on ne faisait rien de mal, c'était juste pour s'~** we weren't doing any harm, it was just for fun *ou* for a laugh
c (= *batifoler*) to mess about* *ou* around*; **on n'a pas le temps de s'~** there's no time to mess around*
d (*littér = se jouer de*) **s'~ de qn** to make a fool of sb

amusette [amyzɛt] NF diversion; **elle n'a été pour lui qu'une ~** she was mere sport to him, she was just a passing fancy for him; **au lieu de perdre ton temps à des ~s tu ferais mieux de travailler** instead of frittering your time away on idle pleasures you should do some work

amuseur, -euse [amyzœr, øz] NM,F entertainer; (*péj*) **ce n'est qu'un ~** he's just a clown

amygdale [amidal] NF tonsil; **se faire opérer des ~s** to have one's tonsils removed *ou* out

amygdalite [amidalit] NF tonsillitis

amylacé, e [amilase] ADJ starchy

amylase [amilaz] NF amylase

amyle [amil] NM amyl; **nitrite d'~** amyl nitrite

amylique [amilik] ADJ **alcool ~** amyl alcohol

AN [aɛn] NF (ABRÉV = **Assemblée nationale**) → **assemblée**

an [ɑ̃] NM a (= *durée*) year; **après 5 ~s de prison** after 5 years in prison; **dans 3 ~s** in 3 years, in 3 years' time (*Brit*); **une amitié de 20 ~s** a friendship of 20 years' standing
b (= *âge*) year; **un enfant de six ~s** a six-year-old child, a six-year-old; **porto de 10 ~s d'âge** 10-year-old port; **il a 22 ~s** he's 22 (years old); **il n'a pas encore 10 ~s** he's not yet 10
c (= *point dans le temps*) year; **4 fois par ~** 4 times a year; **il reçoit tant par ~** he gets so much a year *ou* per annum; **le jour ou le premier de l'~ ◊ le nouvel ~** New Year's Day; **bon ~ mal ~** taking one year with another, on average; **en l'~ 300 de Rome** in the Roman year 300; **en l'~ de notre ère/avant Jésus-Christ 300** in (the year) 300 AD/BC; (*frm ou hum*) **en l'~ de grâce ...** in the year of grace ...; (*Hist*) **l'~ II de la république** the second year of the French Republic; **je m'en moque ou je m'en soucie comme de l'~ quarante** I couldn't care less (about it), I don't give a damn* (about it)
d (*littér*) **les ~s l'ont courbé** he is bent with age; **l'outrage des ~s** the ravages of time; **courbé sous le poids des ~s** bent under the weight of years *ou* age

ana (*pl* **ana(s)**) [ana] NM ana

anabaptisme [anabatism] NM anabaptism

anabaptiste [anabatist] ADJ, NMF anabaptist

anabolisant, e [anabɔlizɑ̃, ɑ̃t] 1 ADJ anabolic 2 NM anabolic steroid

anabolisme [anabɔlism] NM anabolism

anacarde [anakard] NM cashew (nut)

anacardier [anakardje] NM cashew (tree)

anachorète [anakɔrɛt] NM anchorite

anachronique [anakrɔnik] ADJ anachronistic, anachronous

anachronisme [anakrɔnism] NM anachronism

anacoluthe [anakɔlyt] NF anacoluthon

anaconda [anakɔ̃da] NM anaconda

Anacréon [anakreɔ̃] NM Anacreon

anacréontique [anakreɔ̃tik] ADJ anacreontic

anaérobie [anaerɔbi] ADJ anaerobic

anaglyphe [anaglif] NM anaglyph

anagrammatique [anagramatik] ADJ anagrammatical

anagramme [anagram] NF anagram

anal, e (*mpl* **-aux**) [anal, o] ADJ anal

analeptique [analɛptik] ADJ analeptic

analgésie [analʒezi] NF analgesia

analgésique [analʒezik] ADJ, NM analgesic

anallergique [analɛrʒik] ADJ hypoallergenic

analogie [analɔʒi] NF analogy; **par ~ avec** by analogy with

analogique [analɔʒik] ADJ analogical

analogiquement [analɔʒikmɑ̃] ADV analogically

analogue [analɔg] 1 ADJ analogous, similar (à to) 2 NM analogue

analphabète [analfabɛt] ADJ, NMF illiterate

analphabétisme [analfabetism] NM illiteracy

analysable [analizabl] ADJ analysable, analyzable (*US*)

analysant, e [analizɑ̃, ɑ̃t] NM,F analysand

analyse [analiz] 1 NF a (= *examen*) analysis; **faire l'~ de** to analyze; **ça ne résiste pas à l'~** it doesn't stand up to analysis; **avoir l'esprit d'~** to have an analytic(al) mind; **en dernière ~** in the final *ou* last analysis
b (*Méd*) test; **~ de sang/d'urine** blood/urine test; **(se) faire faire des ~s** to have some tests (done) → **laboratoire**
c (*Psych*) analysis, psychoanalysis; **il est en ~ ◊ il fait une ~** he's undergoing *ou* having analysis
d (*Math*) (= *discipline*) calculus; (= *exercice*) analysis

2 COMP ▸ **analyse combinatoire** combinatorial analysis ▸ **analyse en constituants immédiats** constituent analysis ▸ **analyse factorielle** factor *ou* factorial analysis ▸ **analyse financière** financial analysis ▸ **analyse fonctionnelle** functional job analysis ▸ **analyse grammaticale** parsing; **faire l'~ grammaticale de** to parse ▸ **analyse logique** sentence analysis (*Brit*), diagramming (*US*) ▸ **analyse de marché** market analysis *ou* survey ▸ **analyse sectorielle** cross-section analysis ▸ **analyse spectrale** spectrum analysis ▸ **analyse de système** systems analysis ▸ **analyse transactionnelle** transactional analysis ▸ **analyse du travail** job analysis

analysé, e [analize] NM,F (*Psych*) person who has undergone analysis

analyser [analize] ▸conjug 1◂ VT (*gén*) to analyze; (*Psych*) to (psycho)analyze; (*Méd*) [+ *sang, urine*] to test; (*analyse grammaticale*) to parse

analyseur [analizœr] NM (*Phys*) analyser; (*Ordin*) **~ syntaxique** parser

analyste [analist] NMF (*gén, Math*) analyst; (= *psychanalyste*) analyst, psychoanalyst; **~-programmeur** programme analyst; **~ financier/de marché** financial/market analyst; **~ de systèmes** systems analyst

analytique [analitik] 1 ADJ analytic(al) 2 NF analytics *sg*

analytiquement [analitikmɑ̃] ADV analytically

anamorphose [anamɔrfoz] NF anamorphosis

ananas [anana(s)] NM (= *fruit, plante*) pineapple

anapeste [anapɛst] NM anapaest

anaphore [anafɔr] NF anaphora

anaphorique [anafɔrik] ADJ anaphoric

anaphylactique [anafilaktik] ADJ anaphylactic; **choc ~** anaphylactic shock

anar* [anar] NMF ABRÉV = **anarchiste**

anarchie [anarʃi] NF (*Pol, fig*) anarchy

anarchique [anarʃik] ADJ anarchic(al); **de façon *ou* manière ~** anarchically

anarchiquement [anarʃikmɑ̃] ADV anarchically

anarchisant, e [anarʃizɑ̃, ɑ̃t] ADJ anarchistic

anarchisme [anarʃism] NM anarchism

anarchiste [anarʃist] 1 ADJ anarchistic 2 NMF anarchist

anarchosyndicalisme [anarkosɛ̃dikalism] NM anarcho-syndicalism

anarchosyndicaliste [anarkosɛ̃dikalist] NMF anarcho-syndicalist

anastigmat [anastigma(t)] ADJ M, NM (*objectif*) **~** anastigmat, anastigmatic lens

anastigmatique [anastigmatik] ADJ anastigmatic

anastrophe [anastrɔf] NF anastrophe

anathématiser [anatematize] ▸conjug 1◂ VT (*lit, fig*) to anathematize

anathème [anatɛm] NM (= *excommunication, excommunié*) anathema; (*Rel*) **prononcer un ~ contre qn ◊ frapper qn d'~** to excommunicate sb, anathematize sb; (*fig*) **jeter l'~ sur** to curse, anathematize (*frm*)

Anatolie [anatɔli] NF Anatolia

anatomie [anatɔmi] NF a (= *science*) anatomy b (= *corps*) anatomy; (*hum*) **dans ce film, elle montre beaucoup de son ~** she shows a lot of bare flesh in this film c (†† = *dissection*) (*Méd*) anatomy; (*fig*) analysis; (*fig*) **faire l'~ de** to dissect (*fig*), analyse; **pièce d'~** anatomical subject

anatomique [anatɔmik] ADJ (*gén*) anatomic(al); [*fauteuil, oreiller*] contour (*épith*) → **cire, planche**

anatomiquement [anatɔmikmɑ̃] ADV anatomically

anatomiste [anatɔmist] NMF anatomist

ANC [aɛnse] NM (ABRÉV = **African National Congress**) ANC

ancestral, e (*mpl* **-aux**) [ɑ̃sɛstʀal, o] ADJ ancestral

ancêtre [ɑ̃sɛtʀ] NMF a (= *aïeul*) ancestor; (* = *vieillard*) old man (*ou* woman); **nos ~s les Gaulois** our ancestors *ou* forefathers the Gauls b (= *précurseur*) [*personne, objet*] ancestor, forerunner, precursor; **c'est l'~ de la littérature moderne** he's the father of modern literature

anche [ɑ̃ʃ] NF (*Mus*) reed

anchoïade [ɑ̃ʃɔjad] NF anchovy sauce

anchois [ɑ̃ʃwa] NM anchovy

ancien, -ienne [ɑ̃sjɛ̃, jɛn] 1 ADJ a (= *vieux*: *gén*) old; [*coutume, château, loi*] ancient; [*objet d'art*] antique; **dans l'~ temps** in the olden days, in times gone by; **il est plus ~ que moi dans la maison** he has been with *ou* in the firm longer than me; **une ancienne amitié** an old *ou* long-standing friendship; **~s francs** old francs; **cela lui a coûté 10 millions ~s** it cost him 10 million old francs → **testament** b (*avant nom* = *précédent*) former; **son ancienne femme** his ex-wife, his former *ou* previous wife; **c'est mon ~ quartier/ancienne école** it's my old neighbourhood/school, that's where I used to live/go to school c (= *antique*) [*langue, civilisation, histoire*] ancient; **dans les temps ~s** in ancient times; **la Grèce/l'Égypte ancienne** ancient Greece/Egypt 2 NM (= *mobilier ancien*) **l'~** antiques 3 NM,F a (= *personne âgée*) elder, old man (*ou* woman); (*hum*) **et le respect pour les ~s ?** have some respect for your elders!; **les ~s du village** the village elders b (= *personne expérimentée*) senior *ou* experienced person; (*Mil*) old soldier; **c'est un ~ dans la maison** he has been with *ou* in the firm a long time c (*Hist*) **les ~s** the Ancients; (*Littérat*) **les ~s et les modernes** the Ancients and the Moderns d (*Scol*) **~ (élève)** former pupil, old boy (*Brit*), alumnus (*US*); **ancienne (élève)** former pupil, old girl (*Brit*), alumna (*US*) 4 **à l'ancienne** LOC ADJ, LOC ADV [*meuble*] old-style, traditional (-style); [*confiture*] made in the traditional way; **faire qch à l'ancienne** to do sth in the traditional way; **cuisiner à l'~ne** to use traditional cooking methods 5 COMP ► **ancien combattant** war veteran, ex-serviceman ► **l'Ancien Régime** the Ancien Régime

anciennement [ɑ̃sjɛnmɑ̃] ADV (= *autrefois*) formerly

ancienneté [ɑ̃sjɛnte] NF a (= *durée de service*) length of service; (= *privilèges obtenus*) seniority; **il a 10 ans d'~ dans la maison** he has been with *ou* in the firm (for) 10 years; **à l'~** by seniority b [*maison*] age; [*objet d'art*] age, antiquity; [*amitié, relation*] length; **compte tenu de l'~ de cette pratique/loi** considering how long this practice/law has been in existence

ancillaire [ɑ̃silɛʀ] ADJ **devoirs ~s** duties as a servant; (*hum*) **relations/amours ~s** relations/ amorous adventures with the servants

ancolie [ɑ̃kɔli] NF columbine

ancrage [ɑ̃kʀaʒ] NM a (*Naut*) anchorage b (= *attache*) [*poteau, câble*] anchoring; [*mur*] cramping c (= *incrustation*) **l'~ de nos valeurs dans la culture** the way our values are rooted in culture; **le vote confirme l'~ à gauche de la région** the polls confirm that the region is a left-wing stronghold; **pour faciliter l'~ d'entreprises dans la région** to help companies gain a foothold in the region; **point d'~** (*Aut*) anchorage point; (*fig*) [*politique*] foundation stone; **la monnaie d'~ du SME** the anchor currency of the EMS

ancre [ɑ̃kʀ] NF a (*Naut*) **~ (de marine)** anchor; **~ de miséricorde** *ou* **de salut** sheet anchor; **être à l'~** to be *ou* lie *ou* ride at anchor; **jeter l'~** to cast *ou* drop anchor → **lever** b (*Constr*) cramp(-iron), anchor; (*Horlogerie*) anchor escapement, recoil escapement

ancrer [ɑ̃kʀe] ▶conjug 1◀ 1 VT a (*Naut*) to anchor b (*Tech*) [+ *poteau, câble*] to anchor; [+ *mur*] to cramp c (= *incruster*) **~ qch dans la tête de qn** to fix sth firmly in sb's mind; **il a cette idée ancrée dans la tête** he's got this idea firmly fixed in his mind; (*Pol*) **la région reste profondément ancrée à gauche** the region is still firmly left-wing *ou* remains a left-wing stronghold 2 **s'ancrer** VPR a (*Naut*) to anchor, cast *ou* drop anchor b (= *s'incruster*) **quand une idée s'ancre dans l'esprit des gens** when an idea takes root *ou* becomes fixed in people's minds; **il s'est ancré dans la tête que ...** he got it into *ou* fixed in his head that ...; **le groupe cherche à s'~ économiquement dans la région** the group is trying to gain an economic foothold in the region

andain [ɑ̃dɛ̃] NM swath

andalou, -ouse [ɑ̃dalu, uz] 1 ADJ Andalusian 2 **Andalou(se)** NM,F Andalusian

Andalousie [ɑ̃daluzi] NF Andalusia, Andalucia

andante [ɑ̃dɑ̃t] ADV, NM andante

Andes [ɑ̃d] NFPL **les ~** the Andes

andin, e [ɑ̃dɛ̃, in] 1 ADJ Andean 2 **Andin(e)** NM,F Andean

andorran, e [ɑ̃dɔʀɑ̃, an] 1 ADJ Andorran 2 **Andorran(e)** NM,F Andorran

Andorre [ɑ̃dɔʀ] NF Andorra; **~-la-Vieille** Andorra la Vella

andouille [ɑ̃duj] NF a (*Culin*) andouille, *sausage made of chitterlings, eaten cold* b (: = *imbécile*) dummy*, twit* (*Brit*), prat: (*Brit*); **faire l'~** to act the fool; **espèce d'~ !** ◊ **triple ~ !** you dummy!*, you (stupid) prat!: (*Brit*)

andouiller [ɑ̃duje] NM tine, (branch of) antler

andouillette [ɑ̃dujɛt] NF andouillette, *small sausage made of chitterlings, eaten hot*

androcéphale [ɑ̃dʀosefal] ADJ with a human head

androgène [ɑ̃dʀoʒɛn] 1 ADJ [*hormone*] androgen; [*effet*] androgenic 2 NM androgen

androgyne [ɑ̃dʀoʒin] 1 ADJ androgynous 2 NM androgyne

androgynie [ɑ̃dʀoʒini] NF androgyny

androïde [ɑ̃dʀɔid] NM android

andrologie [ɑ̃dʀɔlɔʒi] NF andrology

andrologue [ɑ̃dʀɔlɔg] NMF andrologist

Andromaque [ɑ̃dʀɔmak] NF Andromache

Andromède [ɑ̃dʀɔmɛd] NF Andromeda

andropause [ɑ̃dʀopoz] NF male menopause

androstérone [ɑ̃dʀosteʀɔn] NF androsterone

âne [ɑn] NM a (*Zool*) donkey, ass; **être comme l'~ de Buridan** to be unable to decide between two alternatives; (*hum*) **il y a plus d'un ~ (à la foire) qui s'appelle Martin** a lot of people are called that, that's a very common name → **dos** b (: = *personne*) ass*, fool; **faire l'~ pour avoir du son** to act *ou* play dumb to find out what one wants to know; **~ bâté†** stupid ass* → **bonnet, pont**

┌─────────────────────┐
I'ÂNE DE BURIDAN
└─────────────────────┘
The origin of this expression is a philosophical text, supposedly written by Buridan in the 14th century, about an ass that starves to death because he cannot choose between two identical heaps of oats. The term has come to refer to any person who finds it impossible to make up their mind.

anéantir [aneɑ̃tiʀ] ▶conjug 2◀ 1 VT a (= *détruire*) [+ *ville, armée, peuple*] to annihilate, wipe out; [+ *efforts*] to wreck, ruin, destroy; [+ *espoirs*] to dash, ruin, destroy; [+ *sentiment*] to destroy b (= *déprimer, gén pass*) [*chaleur*] to overwhelm, overcome; [*fatigue*] to exhaust, wear out; [*chagrin*] to crush; **la nouvelle l'a anéanti** the news completely broke him 2 **s'anéantir** VPR [*espoir*] to be dashed

anéantissement [aneɑ̃tismɑ̃] NM a (= *destruction*) [*ville, armée, peuple*] annihilation, wiping out; [*efforts, sentiment*] destruction; **c'est l'~ de tous mes espoirs** that's the end of *ou* that has dashed all my hopes; **ce régime vise à l'~ de l'individu** this régime aims at the complete suppression *ou* annihilation of the individual b (= *fatigue*) exhaustion; (= *abattement*) dejection

anecdote [anɛkdɔt] NF (*gén*) anecdote; **l'~** (= *détails*) trivial detail *ou* details; **pour l'~** as a matter of interest; (*péj*) **cet historien ne s'élève pas au-dessus de l'~** this historian doesn't rise above the anecdotal

anecdotique [anɛkdɔtik] ADJ [*histoire, description*] anecdotal; (*péj*) [*peinture*] exclusively concerned with detail (*attrib*); (*péj*) **le caractère ~ de cet incident** the trivial nature of the incident; **ce sujet n'a qu'un intérêt ~** this subject is only of passing interest

anémiant, e [anemjɑ̃, ɑ̃t] ADJ (*Méd*) causing anaemia (*Brit*) *ou* anemia (*US*); (*fig*) debilitating

anémie [anemi] NF (*Méd*) anaemia (*Brit*), anemia (*US*); (*fig*) [*économie*] weakness; **~ pernicieuse** pernicious anaemia; **~ falciforme** sickle cell anaemia

anémié, e [anemje] (*ptp de* **anémier**) ADJ (*Méd*) anaemic (*Brit*), anemic (*US*); (*fig*) weakened, enfeebled

anémier [anemje] ▶conjug 7◀ 1 VT (*Méd*) to make anaemic (*Brit*) *ou* anemic (*US*); (*fig*) to weaken 2 **s'anémier** VPR (*Méd*) to become anaemic (*Brit*) *ou* anemic (*US*)

anémique [anemik] ADJ (*Méd, fig*) anaemic (*Brit*), anemic (*US*)

anémomètre [anemɔmɛtʀ] NM (*pour un fluide*) anemometer; (*pour le vent*) anemometer, wind gauge

anémone [anemɔn] NF anemone; **~ sylvie** wood anemone; **~ de mer** sea anemone

ânerie [ɑnʀi] NF a (*caractère*) stupidity; **il est d'une ~ !** he's a real ass!* b (= *parole*) stupid *ou* idiotic remark; (*action*) stupid mistake, blunder; **arrête de dire des ~s !** stop talking nonsense! *ou* rubbish (*Brit*)!; **faire une ~** to make a blunder, do something silly

anéroïde [aneʀɔid] ADJ → **baromètre**

ânesse [ɑnɛs] NF she-ass, jenny

anesthésiant, e [anɛstezjɑ̃, ɑ̃t] ADJ, NM anaesthetic (*Brit*), anesthetic (*US*); **~ local** local anaesthetic

anesthésie [anɛstezi] NF (= *état d'insensibilité, technique*) anaesthesia (*Brit*), anesthesia (*US*); (= *opération*) anaesthetic (*Brit*), anesthetic (*US*); **sous ~** under anaesthetic *ou* anaesthesia; **~ générale/locale** general/local anaesthetic; **je vais vous faire une ~** I'm going to give you an anaesthetic

anesthésier [anɛstezje] ▶conjug 7◀ VT (*Méd*) [+ *organe*] to anaesthetize (*Brit*), anesthetize (*US*); [+ *personne*] to give an anaesthetic (*Brit*) *ou* anesthetic (*US*) to, anaesthetize (*Brit*), anesthetize (*US*); (*fig*) to deaden, benumb, anaesthetize (*Brit*), anesthetize (*US*); (*fig*) **j'étais comme anesthésié** I felt completely numb

anesthésique [anɛstezik] 1 ADJ [*substance*] anaesthetic (*Brit*), anesthetic (*US*) 2 NM anaesthetic (*Brit*), anesthetic (*US*)

anesthésiste [anɛstezist] NMF anaesthetist (*Brit*), anesthesiologist (*US*)

aneth [anɛt] NM dill

anévrisme [anevʀism] NM aneurism → **rupture**

anfractuosité [ɑ̃fʀaktɥozite] NF [*falaise, mur, sol*] crevice

ange [ãʒ] **1** NM **a** (Rel) angel; **bon/mauvais ~** good/bad angel; **être le bon ~ de qn** to be sb's good ou guardian angel; **être le mauvais ~ de qn** to be an evil influence on sb **b** (= personne) angel; **oui mon ~** yes, darling; **va me chercher mes lunettes tu seras un ~** be an angel ou a darling and get me my glasses; **il est sage comme un ~** he's an absolute angel, he's as good as gold; **il est beau comme un ~** he's absolutely gorgeous; **avoir une patience d'~** to have the patience of a saint; **c'est un ~ de douceur/de bonté** he's sweetness/kindness itself **c** (Zool) angel fish **d** (loc) **un ~ passa** there was an awkward pause ou silence; **être aux ~s** to be in seventh heaven → **discuter**
2 COMP ► **ange déchu** (Rel) fallen angel ► **l'ange exterminateur** (Rel) the exterminating angel ► **ange gardien** (Rel, fig) guardian angel; (= garde du corps) bodyguard → **cheveu, faiseur**

angélique¹ [ãʒelik] ADJ (Rel, fig) angelic(al)
angélique² [ãʒelik] NF (Bot, Culin) angelica
angéliquement [ãʒelikmã] ADV angelically, like an angel
angélisme [ãʒelism] NM (Rel) angelism; **l'~ du gouvernement** the government's naïve optimism
angelot [ãʒ(ə)lo] NM (Art) cherub
angélus [ãʒelys] NM angelus
angine [ãʒin] NF (= amygdalite) tonsillitis; (= pharyngite) pharyngitis; **avoir une ~** to have a sore throat; **~ de poitrine** angina (pectoris); **couenneuse ◊ ~ diphtérique** diphtheria
angineux, -euse [ãʒinø, øz] ADJ anginal
angiome [ãʒjom] NM angioma
angioplastie [ãʒjoplasti] NF angioplasty
angiosperme [ãʒjospɛrm] **1** ADJ angiospermous **2** **les angiospermes** NFPL angiosperms, the Angiospermae (SPÉC)
anglais, e [ãglɛ, ɛz] **1** ADJ English → **assiette, broderie, crème** etc **2** NM **a** **Anglais** Englishman; **les Anglais** (en général) English people, the English; (abusivement = Britanniques) British people, the British; (= hommes) Englishmen; (euph) **les Anglais ont débarqué*** I've got the curse*, I've got my period **b** (Ling) English; → **canadien/britannique/américain** Canadian/British/American English; **parler ~** to speak English **3** **anglaise** NF **a** **Anglaise** Englishwoman **b** (Coiffure) **~es** ringlets **c** (Écriture) ≈ modern English handwriting **4** **à l'anglaise** LOC ADJ, LOC ADV [légumes] boiled; [parc, jardin] landscaped; **cuit à l'~e** boiled → **filer**

▼ **angle** [ãgl] **1** NM **a** [meuble, rue] corner; **à l'~ de ces deux rues** at ou on the corner of these two streets; **le magasin qui fait l'~** the shop on the corner; **la maison est en ~** the house stands directly ou is right on the corner; **meuble d'~** corner unit **b** (Math) angle; **~ saillant/rentrant** salient/re-entrant angle; **~ aigu/obtus** acute/obtuse angle; **~s alternes externes/internes** exterior/interior alternate angles **c** (= aspect) angle, point of view; **vu sous cet ~** seen from ou looked at from that angle ou point of view **d** [caractère, personne] rough edge → **arrondir**
2 COMP ► **angles adjacents** adjacent angles ► **angle de braquage** lock ► **angle de chasse** (Aut) castor angle ► **angle de couverture** (Photo) lens field ► **angle dièdre** dihedral angle ► **angle droit** right angle; **faire un ~ droit** to be at right angles (avec to) ► **angle facial** facial angle ► **angle d'incidence** angle of incidence ► **angle d'inclinaison** angle of inclination ► **angle inscrit (à un cercle)** inscribed angle (of a circle) ► **angle de marche = angle de route** ► **angle mort** dead angle, blind spot

► **angle optique** optic angle ► **angle de réfraction** angle of refraction ► **angle de route** (Mil) bearing, direction of march ► **angle de tir** firing angle ► **angle visuel** visual angle

Angleterre [ãglətɛr] NF England; (abusivement = Grande Bretagne) (Great) Britain
anglican, e [ãglikã, an] ADJ, NM,F Anglican
anglicanisme [ãglikanism] NM Anglicanism
angliche* [ãgliʃ] (hum ou péj) **1** ADJ English, British **2** NMF Brit*, Britisher*; **les ~s** the Brits*
angliciser [ãglisize] ▸ conjug 1 ◂ **1** VT to anglicize **2** **s'angliciser** VPR to become anglicized
anglicisme [ãglisism] NM anglicism
angliciste [ãglisist] NMF (= étudiant) student of English (language and civilization); (= spécialiste) anglicist, English specialist
anglo- [ãglo] PRÉF (dans les mots composés à trait d'union, le préfixe reste invariable) anglo-; **~irlandais** Anglo-Irish
anglo-américain, e (pl **anglo-américains**) [ãgloamerikɛ̃] **1** ADJ Anglo-American **2** NM (Ling) American English **3** **Anglo-Américain(e)** NM,F Anglo-American
anglo-arabe (pl **anglo-arabes**) [ãgloarab] ADJ, NM (= cheval) Anglo-Arab
anglo-canadien, -ienne (mpl **anglo-canadiens**) [ãglokanadjɛ̃, jɛn] **1** ADJ Anglo-Canadian **2** NM (Ling) Canadian English **3** **Anglo-Canadien(ne)** NM,F English Canadian
anglomane [ãgloman] NMF anglomaniac
anglomanie [ãglomani] NF anglomania
anglo-normand, e (mpl **anglo-normands**) [ãglonɔrmã, ãd] **1** ADJ Anglo-Norman → **île 2** NM **a** (Ling) Anglo-Norman, Norman French **b** (= cheval) Anglo-Norman (horse)
anglophile [ãglofil] ADJ, NMF anglophile
anglophilie [ãglofili] NF anglophilia
anglophobe [ãglofɔb] **1** ADJ anglophobic **2** NMF anglophobe
anglophobie [ãglofɔbi] NF anglophobia
anglophone [ãglofɔn] **1** ADJ [personne] English-speaking, Anglophone; [littérature] English-language (épith), in English (attrib) **2** NMF English speaker, Anglophone
anglo-saxon, -onne (mpl **anglo-saxons**) [ãglosaksɔ̃, ɔn] **1** ADJ Anglo-Saxon; **les pays ~s** Anglo-Saxon countries **2** NM (Ling) Anglo-Saxon **3** **Anglo-Saxon(ne)** NM,F Anglo-Saxon
angoissant, e [ãgwasã, ãt] ADJ [situation, silence] harrowing, agonizing; **nous avons vécu des jours ~s** we went through ou suffered days of anguish ou agony
angoisse [ãgwas] NF **a** (NonC) (gén, Psych) anguish, distress; **crises d'~** anxiety attacks; (Philos) **l'~ métaphysique** angst; **une étrange ~ le saisit** a strange feeling of anguish gripped him; **l'~ de la mort** the anguish of death; **il vivait dans l'~** he lived in anguish; **il vivait dans l'~ d'un accident** he lived in dread of ou he dreaded an accident; **vivre des jours d'~** to go through ou suffer days of anguish ou agony; **c'est l'~*** it's nerve-racking; **quelle ~, ces factures à payer !*** these bills are a terrible worry! **b** (= peur) dread (NonC), fear; (= sensation d'étouffement) **avoir des ~s** to feel one is suffocating
angoissé, e [ãgwase] (ptp de **angoisser**) **1** ADJ [geste, visage, voix] anguished; [question, silence] agonized; [personne] anxious, distressed; **être ~** (= inquiet) to be distressed ou in anguish; (= oppressé) to feel suffocated **2** NM,F anxious person
angoisser [ãgwase] ▸ conjug 1 ◂ **1** VT **a** (= inquiéter) to distress, cause anguish ou distress to; (= oppresser) to choke **2** VI (* = être angoissé) to be worried sick*
Angola [ãgɔla] NM Angola

angolais, e [ãgɔlɛ, ɛz] **1** ADJ Angolan **2** **Angolais(e)** NM,F Angolan
angor [ãgɔr] NM angina; **crise d'~** attack of angina
angora [ãgɔra] ADJ, NM angora
angstrœm, angström [aŋstrœm] NM angstrom (unit)
anguille [ãgij] NF (Culin, Zool) eel; **~ de mer** conger eel; **il m'a filé entre les doigts comme une ~** he slipped right through my fingers, he wriggled out of my clutches; **il y a ~ sous roche** there's something in the wind
angulaire [ãgylɛr] ADJ angular → **pierre**
anguleux, -euse [ãgylø, øz] ADJ [menton, visage] angular; [coude] bony
anharmonique [anarmɔnik] ADJ anharmonic
anhydre [anidr] ADJ anhydrous
anhydride [anidrid] NM anhydride
anicroche* [anikrɔʃ] NF hitch, snag; **sans ~s** [se passer] smoothly, without a hitch
ânier, -ière [ãnje, jɛr] NM,F donkey-driver
aniline [anilin] NF aniline
animal, e (mpl **-aux**) [animal, o] **1** ADJ **a** [espèce, règne, graisse, vie] animal (épith); **protéine (d'origine) ~e** animal protein **b** [force, réaction] animal (épith); [sensualité] raw, animal (épith) → **esprit 2** NM **a** (Zool) animal; **~ familier** ou **de compagnie** pet; **~ de laboratoire** laboratory animal; **animaux de boucherie** animals for slaughter **b** (* ou péj) (= personne brutale) animal; (= personne stupide) silly devil*; **où est parti cet ~ ?** where did that devil* go?
animalcule [animalkyl] NM animalcule
animalerie [animalri] NF [laboratoire] animal house; (= magasin) pet shop
animalier, -ière [animalje, jɛr] **1** ADJ [peintre, sculpteur] animal (épith), wildlife (épith); [film, photographie] wildlife (épith); **cinéaste ~** maker of wildlife films → **parc 2** NM **a** (Art) painter (ou sculptor) of animals, animal painter (ou sculptor) **b** [laboratoire] animal keeper
animalité [animalite] NF animality
animateur, -trice [animatœr, tris] NM,F **a** (= personne dynamique) **c'est un ~ né** he's a born organizer; **l'~ de cette entreprise** the driving force behind ou the prime mover in this undertaking; **ce poste requiert des qualités d'~ d'équipe** this post requires leadership qualities **b** (= professionnel) [spectacle, émission de jeux] host, compere (Brit), emcee (US); [émission culturelle] presenter; [music-hall] compere (Brit), emcee (US); [discothèque] disc jockey, DJ; [club] leader, sponsor (US); [camp de vacances] activity leader, camp counselor (US); **~ (de) radio** radio presenter **c** (Ciné = technicien) animator
animation [animasjɔ̃] NF **a** (= vie) [quartier, regard, personne] life, liveliness; [discussion] animation, liveliness; (= affairement) [rue, quartier, bureau] (hustle and) bustle; **son arrivée provoqua une grande ~** his arrival caused a great deal of excitement ou a great commotion; **parler avec ~** to talk animatedly; **mettre de l'~** to liven things up; **mettre de l'~ dans une soirée** to liven up a party **b** (= activités) activities; **chargé de l'~ culturelle/sportive** in charge of cultural/sports activities → **centre c** [équipe, groupe de travail] leading; **les cadres ont un rôle d'~** a manager's role is to lead **d** (Ciné) animation; (Mét) **comme on le voit sur l'~ satellite** as we can see from the satellite picture → **cinéma, film**
animé, e [anime] (ptp de **animer**) ADJ **a** [rue, quartier] (= affairé) busy; (= plein de vie) lively; [regard, visage] lively; [discussion] animated, lively, spirited; (Comm) [enchères, marché] brisk **b** (Ling, Philos) animate
animer [anime] ▸ conjug 1 ◂ **1** VT **a** (= mener) [+ spectacle, émission de jeux] to host, compere

(*Brit*), emcee (*US*); [+ *émission culturelle*] to present; [+ *discussion*] to lead; [+ *réunion*] to run, lead

b (= *dynamiser, motiver*) [+ *parti*] to be the driving force in; [+ *équipe*] to lead

c (= *donner de la vie à*) [+ *ville, soirée, conversation*] to liven up; [+ *visage*] to animate, light up; [+ *peinture, statue*] to bring to life; (*Philos*) [+ *nature, matière*] to animate; **l'enthousiasme qui animait son regard** the enthusiasm which shone in his eyes; **les meilleurs joueurs seront présents, ce qui va ► le tournoi** the top players will be there, which will make for an exciting tournament

d (= *stimuler*) [*haine, désir*] to drive (on); [*foi*] to sustain; [*espoir*] to nourish, sustain; **animé par** *ou* **de** [+ *volonté*] driven (on) by; [+ *désir*] prompted by; **animé des meilleures intentions** motivated by the best intentions; (*Bourse*) **~ le marché** to stimulate the market; **le patriotisme qui animait les soldats** the sense of patriotism that spurred the soldiers on

e (= *mouvoir*: *surtout au passif*) to drive; **l'objet est animé d'un mouvement de rotation/de translation** the object rotates/is translated; **le balancier était animé d'un mouvement régulier** the pendulum was moving in a steady rhythm *ou* swinging steadily

2 s'animer VPR [*personne, rue*] to come to life, liven up; [*statue*] to come to life; [*conversation*] to become animated, liven up; [*foule, objet inanimé*] to come to life; [*match*] to liven up; [*yeux, traits*] to light up; **les machines semblaient s'~ d'une vie propre** the machines seemed to have a life of their own

animisme [animism] NM animism

animiste [animist] **1** ADJ [*théorie*] animist(ic); [*société, population*] animist **2** NMF animist

animosité [animozite] NF (= *hostilité*) animosity (**contre** towards, against)

anion [anjɔ̃] NM anion

anis [ani(s)] NM (= *plante*) anise; (*Culin*) aniseed; (= *bonbon*) aniseed ball; **~ étoilé** star anise; **à l'~** aniseed (*épith*)

aniser [anize] ▸ conjug 1 ◂ VT to flavour with aniseed; **goût anisé** taste of aniseed

anisette [anizet] NF anisette

Ankara [ɑ̃kaʁa] N Ankara

ankylose [ɑ̃kiloz] NF ankylosis

ankyloser [ɑ̃kiloze] ▸ conjug 1 ◂ **1** VT to stiffen, ankylose (*SPÉC*); **être tout ankylosé** to be stiff all over; **mon bras ankylosé** my stiff arm; **cette routine qui nous ankylose** this mind-numbing routine **2 s'ankyloser** VPR [*membre*] to stiffen up, ankylose (*SPÉC*); [*institution*] to be stagnating; [*esprit*] to become stultified *ou* dulled

annales [anal] NFPL annals; **ça restera dans les ~*** that'll go down in history (*hum*); **un cas unique dans les ~ du crime** a case that is unique in the history of crime

annamite† [anamit] **1** ADJ Annamese, Annamite **2 Annamite** NMF Annamese, Annamite

Annapurna [anapuʁna] NM (*Géog*) Annapurna

Anne [an] NF Ann, Anne; **~ d'Autriche** Anne of Austria; **~ Boleyn** Anne Boleyn; **~ de Bretagne** Anne of Brittany

anneau (*pl* **anneaux**) [ano] **1** NM **a** (= *cercle, bague*) ring; (= *partie d'une bague*) hoop; (= *boucle d'oreille*) hoop (earring); [*chaîne*] link; [*préservatif*] rim; **~ de rideau** curtain ring **b** (*Algèbre*) ring; (*Géom*) ring, annulus **c** [*colonne*] annulet; [*champignon*] annulus; [*ver*] segment, metamere (*SPÉC*); [*serpent*] coil **d** (*Sport*) **les ~x** the rings; **exercices aux ~x** ring exercises **2** COMP ► **anneaux colorés** (*Opt*) Newton's rings ► **anneau de croissance** [*arbre*] annual *ou* growth ring ► **anneau épiscopal** bishop's ring ► **anneau nuptial** wedding ring ► **anneau**

oculaire (*Opt*) eye ring ► **anneaux olympiques** Olympic rings ► **anneaux de Saturne** Saturn's rings ► **anneau sphérique** (*Géom*) (spherical) annulus *ou* ring ► **anneau de vitesse** (*Sport*) race track

▼ **année** [ane] **1** NF **a** (= *durée*) year; **il y a bien des ~s qu'il est parti** he's been gone for many years, it's many years since he left; **la récolte d'une ~** a *ou* one year's harvest; **tout au long de l'~** the whole year (round), throughout the year; **payé à l'~** paid annually; (*Fin*) **en ~ pleine** in a full year; **les bénéfices en ~ pleine** the full-year profits; **~ de base** base year **b** (= *âge, Scol, Univ*) year; **il est dans sa vingtième ~** he is in his twentieth year; **l'~ universitaire** the academic year; (*Scol, Univ*) **de première/deuxième ~** first-/second-year (*épith*) **c** (= *point dans le temps*) year; **les ~s de guerre** the war years; **~ de naissance** year of birth; **les ~s 60** the sixties, the 60s; (*littér*) **en l'~ 700 de notre ère/avant Jésus-Christ** in (the year) 700 A.D./B.C. → **bon¹, souhaiter**

2 COMP ► **année bissextile** leap year ► **année budgétaire** financial year ► **année calendaire, année civile** calendar year ► **année de référence** (*Fin, Jur*) base year; **l'~ de référence 1984** (*Stat*) the 1984 benchmark ► **les années folles** the Roaring Twenties ► **année sainte** Holy Year

année-lumière (*pl* **années-lumière**) [anelymjɛʁ] NF light year; (*lit, fig*) **à des années-lumière de** light years away from; **c'est à des années-lumière de mes préoccupations** it's the last thing on my mind; **ma sœur et moi sommes à des années-lumière** there's a world of difference between my sister and me

annelé, e [an(ə)le] ADJ ringed; (*Bot, Zool*) annulate; (*Archit*) annulated

▼ **annexe** [anɛks] **1** ADJ **a** (= *secondaire*) [*activités, produits, services*] ancillary; [*tâches*] subsidiary; [*considérations*] secondary; [*budget, revenu*] supplementary; **avantages ~s** fringe benefits; **frais ~s** incidental expenses; **effets ~s** side effects; **il fait des travaux ~s** (*pour compléter son salaire*) he does other jobs on the side **b** (= *attaché*) [*document*] annexed, appended; **les bâtiments ~s** the annexes **2** NF **a** [*document*] (= *pièces complémentaires*) appendix; (= *pièces additives*) annex(e); [*contrat*] (*gén*) rider; (= *liste*) schedule (**de, à** to); **en ~ in** the appendix **b** (*Constr*) annex(e) **c** (= *embarcation*) tender, dinghy

annexer [anɛkse] ▸ conjug 1 ◂ **1** VT [+ *territoire*] to annex; [+ *document*] to append, annex (**à** to) **2 s'annexer** VPR (= *s'attribuer*) [+ *bureau, personne*] to commandeer (*hum*)

annexion [anɛksjɔ̃] NF (*Pol*) annexation

annexionnisme [anɛksjɔnism] NM annexationism

annexionniste [anɛksjɔnist] ADJ, NMF annexationist

Annibal [anibal] NM Hannibal

annihilation [aniilasjɔ̃] NF **a** [*efforts, espoirs, résistance*] destruction; [*peuple*] annihilation **b** (*Phys*) annihilation

annihiler [aniile] ▸ conjug 1 ◂ VT [+ *efforts*] to wreck, ruin, destroy; [+ *espoirs*] to dash, destroy, wreck; [+ *résistance*] to wipe out, destroy, annihilate; [+ *personne, esprit*] to crush; [+ *peuple*] to annihilate, wipe out

▼ **anniversaire** [anivɛʁsɛʁ] **1** ADJ [*date*] anniversary (*épith*); **la date** *ou* **le jour ~ de la victoire** the anniversary of the victory **2** NM [*naissance*] birthday; [*événement, mariage, mort*] anniversary; **bon ou joyeux ~ !** happy birthday!; **c'est l'~ de leur mariage** it's their wedding anniversary; **cadeau/carte d'~** birthday present/card

▼ **annonce** [anɔ̃s] NF **a** [*accord, décision, résultat*] announcement; **l'~ officielle des fiançailles** the official announcement of the engagement; **faire une ~** to make an announcement;

à l'~ de cet événement when the event was announced; **il cherche l'effet d'~** he wants to make an impact; **« ~ personnelle »** "personal message"; **~ judiciaire** *ou* **légale** legal notice **b** (*Cartes*) declaration; (*Bridge*) (*gén*) bid; (*finale*) declaration **c** (= *publicité*) (newspaper) advertisement; (*pour emploi*) job advertisement; **petites ~s ◊ ~s classées** classified advertisements *ou* ads*, classifieds, small ads* (*Brit*); **mettre** *ou* **passer une ~ (dans un journal)** to put *ou* place an advertisement in a paper; **journal d'~s** free sheet; (*dans un journal*) **page des petites ~s** classifieds page, small-ads page (*Brit*)

▼ **annoncer** [anɔ̃se] ▸ conjug 3 ◂ **1** VT **a** (= *informer de*) [+ *fait, décision, nouvelle*] to announce (**à** to); **~ à qn que ...** to tell sb that ..., announce to sb that ...; **on m'a annoncé par lettre que ...** I was informed *ou* advised by letter that ...; **je lui ai annoncé la nouvelle** (*gén*) I told her the news, I announced the news to her; (*mauvaise nouvelle*) I broke the news to her; **on annonce l'ouverture d'un nouveau magasin** they're advertising the opening of a new shop; **on annonce la sortie prochaine de ce film** the forthcoming release of this film has been announced; **les journaux ont annoncé leur mariage** their marriage has been announced in the papers; **on annonce un grave incendie** a serious fire is reported to have broken out

b (= *prédire*) [+ *pluie, détérioration*] to forecast; **on annonce un ralentissement économique dans les mois à venir** a slowdown in the economy is forecast *ou* predicted for the coming months; **la défaite annoncée du parti** the predicted defeat of the party

c (= *signaler*) [*présage*] to foreshadow, foretell; [*signe avant-coureur*] to herald; [*sonnerie, pas*] to announce, herald; **les nuages qui annoncent une tempête** clouds that herald a storm; **ça n'annonce rien de bon** it bodes ill; **ce radoucissement annonce la pluie/le printemps** this warmer weather is a sign that rain/spring is on the way; **la cloche qui annonce la fin des cours** the bell announcing *ou* signalling the end of classes

d (= *introduire*) [+ *personne*] to announce; **il entra sans se faire ~** he went in without being announced *ou* without announcing himself; **qui dois-je ~ ?** what name shall I say?, whom shall I announce?

e (*Cartes*) to declare; (*Bridge*) (*gén*) to bid; (= *demander un contrat*) to declare; **~ la couleur** (*lit*) to declare trumps; (*fig*) to lay one's cards on the table

2 s'annoncer VPR **a** (= *se présenter*) [*situation*] **comment est-ce que ça s'annonce ?** how is it shaping up? *ou* looking?; **le temps s'annonce orageux** the weather looks stormy; **l'année s'annonce excellente** it promises to be an excellent year; **ça s'annonce bien** that looks promising; **le projet s'annonce bien/mal** the project has got off to a good/bad start **b** (= *arriver*) [*événement, crise*] to approach; **la révolution qui s'annonçait** the signs of the coming revolution; **l'hiver s'annonçait** winter was on the way

c [*personne*] (= *donner son nom*) to announce o.s.; **annoncez-vous au concierge en arrivant** make yourself known *ou* say who you are to the concierge when you arrive; **il s'annonçait toujours en frappant 3 fois** he always announced himself by knocking 3 times; **tu viens ici quand tu veux, tu n'as pas besoin de t'~** you can come here whenever you like, you don't have to let me know in advance

annonceur, -euse [anɔ̃sœʁ, øz] **1** NM,F (*Radio, TV*) announcer **2** NM (= *publicité*) advertiser

annonciateur, -trice [anɔ̃sjatœʁ, tʁis] **1** ADJ **signe ~** [*maladie, crise*] warning sign; [*catastrophe*] portent; [*amélioration, reprise économique*] indication, sign; **~ de** [+

événement favorable] heralding; [+ *événement défavorable*] heralding, forewarning; **vent ~ de pluie** wind that heralds rain [2] NM,F herald, harbinger (*littér*)

Annonciation [anɔ̃sjasjɔ̃] NF **l'~** (= *événement*) the Annunciation; (= *fête*) Annunciation Day, Lady Day

annotateur, -trice [anɔtatœʀ, tʀis] NM,F annotator

annotation [anɔtasjɔ̃] NF annotation

annoter [anɔte] ▸ conjug 1 ◂ VT to annotate

▼ **annuaire** [anɥɛʀ] NM [*organisme*] yearbook, annual; [*téléphone*] (telephone) directory, phone book; **~ électronique** electronic directory; **je ne suis pas dans l'~** I'm ex-directory, I'm not in the phone book

annualisation [anɥalizasjɔ̃] NF [*comptes*] annualization; **l'~ du temps de travail** the calculation of working hours on a yearly basis

annualiser [anɥalize] ▸ conjug 1 ◂ VT (*gén*) to make annual; [+ *comptes*] to annualize; **taux annualisé** annualized rate; **travail à temps partiel annualisé** part-time work where the hours worked are calculated on a yearly basis

annualité [anɥalite] NF (*gén*) yearly recurrence; **l'~ du budget/de l'impôt** yearly budgeting/taxation

annuel, -elle [anɥɛl] ADJ annual, yearly → **plante[1]**

annuellement [anɥɛlmɑ̃] ADV annually, once a year, yearly

annuité [anɥite] NF (*gén*) annual instalment (*Brit*) *ou* installment (*US*), annual payment; [*dette*] annual repayment; [*pension*] **avoir toutes ses ~s** to have (made) all one's years' contributions

annulable [anɥlabl] ADJ annullable, liable to annulment (*attrib*)

annulaire [anɥlɛʀ] [1] ADJ annular, ring-shaped [2] NM ring finger, third finger

annulation [anɥlasjɔ̃] NF [*contrat*] invalidation, nullification; [*jugement, décision*] quashing; [*engagement, réservation, commande*] cancellation; [*élection, acte, examen*] nullification; [*mariage*] annulment; **ils demandent l'~ de leur dette** they are asking for their debt to be cancelled

▼ **annuler** [anɥle] ▸ conjug 1 ◂ [1] VT [+ *contrat*] to invalidate, void, nullify; [+ *jugement, décision*] to quash; [+ *engagement*] to cancel, call off; [+ *élection, acte, examen*] to nullify, declare void; [+ *mariage*] to annul; [+ *réservation*] to cancel; [+ *commande*] to cancel, withdraw; [+ *dette*] to cancel; **le fax annule les distances** fax machines make distance irrelevant [2] **s'annuler** VPR [*poussées, efforts*] to cancel each other out

anoblir [anɔbliʀ] ▸ conjug 2 ◂ VT to ennoble, confer a title of nobility on

anoblissement [anɔblismɑ̃] NM ennoblement

anode [anɔd] NF anode

anodin, e [anɔdɛ̃, in] ADJ [*personne*] insignificant; [*détail*] trivial, trifling, insignificant; [*propos, remarque*] innocuous, harmless; **ce n'est pas un acte ~** it's not a trivial matter; **dire qch de façon ~e** to say sth blandly; **s'il a dit cela, ce n'est pas ~** if he said that, he meant something by it

anodique [anɔdik] ADJ anodic

anodiser [anɔdize] ▸ conjug 1 ◂ VT to anodize

anomal, e (*mpl* **-aux**) [anɔmal, o] ADJ (*Gram*) anomalous

anomalie [anɔmali] NF (*gén, Astron, Gram*) anomaly; (*Bio*) abnormality; (*Tech*) (technical) fault; **~ chromosomique/génétique** chromosomal/genetic abnormality *ou* defect

anomie [anɔmi] NF anomie

ânon [anɔ̃] NM (= *petit de l'âne*) ass's foal; (= *petit âne*) little ass *ou* donkey

anone [anɔn] NF annona

ânonnement [anɔnmɑ̃] NM (*inexpressif*) drone; (*hésitant*) faltering *ou* mumbling (speech)

ânonner [anɔne] ▸ conjug 1 ◂ VTI (*de manière inexpressive*) to drone on; (*en hésitant*) to mumble away; **~ sa leçon** to mumble one's way through one's lesson

anonymat [anɔnima] NM anonymity; **sous (le) couvert de l'~** ◊ **sous couvert d'~** anonymously; **garder** *ou* **conserver l'~** to remain anonymous, preserve one's anonymity; **dans un total ~** in total anonymity; **respecter l'~ de qn** to respect sb's desire for anonymity *ou* desire to remain anonymous

anonyme [anɔnim] ADJ (= *sans nom*) [*auteur, interlocuteur, appel, lettre*] anonymous; [*main, voix*] unknown; (= *impersonnel*) [*décor, meubles*] impersonal → **alcoolique, société**

anonymement [anɔnimmɑ̃] ADV anonymously

anophèle [anɔfɛl] NM anopheles

anorak [anɔrak] NM anorak

anorexie [anɔrɛksi] NF anorexia; **~ mentale** anorexia nervosa

anorexigène [anɔrɛksiʒɛn] [1] ADJ [*substance, effet*] appetite-suppressing; **médicament ~** appetite suppressant (drug) [2] NM appetite suppressant

anorexique [anɔrɛksik] ADJ, NMF anorexic

anormal, e (*mpl* **-aux**) [anɔrmal, o] [1] ADJ [a] (*Sci, Méd*) abnormal; (= *insolite*) [*situation*] unusual; [*comportement*] abnormal, unusual; **si vous voyez quelque chose d'~, signalez-le** if you notice anything unusual *ou* irregular, report it [b] (= *injuste*) unfair; **il est ~ que ...** it isn't right *ou* it's unfair that ... [2] NM,F (*Méd*) abnormal person

anormalement [anɔrmalmɑ̃] ADV [*se développer*] abnormally; [*se conduire, agir*] unusually, abnormally; [*chaud, grand*] unusually, abnormally

anormalité [anɔrmalite] NF abnormality

anoxie [anɔksi] NF anoxia

anoxique [anɔksik] ADJ anoxic

ANPE [aɛnpe] NF (ABRÉV = **Agence nationale pour l'emploi**) → **agence**

anse [ɑ̃s] NF [*panier, tasse*] handle; (*Géog*) cove; (*Anat*) loop, flexura (*SPÉC*); (*Archit*) **~ (de panier)** basket-handle arch; (*hum*) **faire danser** *ou* **valser l'~ du panier** to make a bit out of the shopping money*

antagonique [ɑ̃tagɔnik] ADJ antagonistic

antagonisme [ɑ̃tagɔnism] NM antagonism

antagoniste [ɑ̃tagɔnist] [1] ADJ [*forces, propositions*] antagonistic; (*Anat*) [*muscles*] antagonist [2] NMF antagonist

antalgique [ɑ̃talʒik] ADJ, NM analgesic

antan [ɑ̃tɑ̃] NM (*littér*) **d'~** of yesteryear, of long ago; **ma jeunesse d'~** my long-lost youth; **ma force d'~** my strength of former days; **mes plaisirs d'~** my erstwhile pleasures

Antananarivo [ɑ̃tananarivo] N Antananarivo

Antarctide [ɑ̃tarktid] NF **l'~** Antarctica

antarctique [ɑ̃tarktik] [1] ADJ [*région*] Antarctic; **l'océan Antarctique** the Antarctic Ocean [2] **Antarctique** NM **l'Antarctique** (= *océan*) the Antarctic; (= *continent*) Antarctica

antécédence [ɑ̃tesedɑ̃s] NF antecedence

antécédent, e [ɑ̃tesedɑ̃, ɑ̃t] [1] NM [a] (*Gram, Math, Philos*) antecedent [b] (*Méd*: *surtout pl*) medical *ou* case history; **elle a des ~s d'hypertension artérielle** she has a past *ou* previous history of high blood pressure; **avez-vous des ~s familiaux de maladies cardiaques?** is there any history of heart disease in your family? [2] **antécédents** NMPL [*personne*] past *ou* previous history; [*affaire*] past *ou* previous history, antecedents; **avoir de bons/mauvais ~s** to have a good/bad previous history; **~s judiciaires** criminal record; **ses ~s politiques** his political background

antéchrist [ɑ̃tekrist] NM Antichrist

antécime [ɑ̃tesim] NF [*montagne*] foresummit, subsidiary summit

antédiluvien, -ienne [ɑ̃tedilyvjɛ̃, jɛn] ADJ (*lit, fig*) antediluvian

anténatal, e (*mpl* **s**) [ɑ̃tenatal] ADJ (*Méd*) [*diagnostic, examen, dépistage*] antenatal (*épith*), prenatal (*épith*)

antenne [ɑ̃tɛn] NF [a] (*Zool*) antenna, feeler; (*fig*) **avoir des ~s** to have a sixth sense; **avoir des ~s dans un ministère** to have contacts in a ministry [b] (= *dispositif*) (*Radio*) aerial, antenna; (*TV*) aerial; [*radar*] antenna; **~ parabolique** *ou* **satellite** satellite dish, dish aerial, dish antenna (*US*) [c] (*Radio, TV*) **je donne l'~ à Paris** (we'll go) over to Paris now; **garder/quitter l'~** to stay on/go off the air; **nous devons bientôt rendre l'~** we have to go back to the studio soon; **je rends l'~ au studio** and now back to the studio; **temps d'~** airtime; **vous avez droit à 2 heures d'~** you are entitled to 2 hours' broadcasting time *ou* airtime *ou* to 2 hours on the air; **leur parti est interdit d'~** their party is banned from radio and television, there is a broadcasting ban on their party; **hors ~, le ministre a déclaré que ...** off the air, the minister declared that ...; **être à l'~** to be on the air; **passer à l'~** to go *ou* be on the air; **sur notre ~** on our station; **le concert sera diffusé sur l'~ de France-Musique** the concert will be broadcast on France-Musique [d] (*Naut* = *vergue*) lateen yard [e] (= *succursale*) branch; (*Mil* = *poste avancé*) outpost; **~ médicale** medical unit

antépénultième [ɑ̃tepenyltjɛm] [1] ADJ antepenultimate [2] NF antepenultimate syllable, antepenult

antéposer [ɑ̃tepoze] ▸ conjug 1 ◂ VT to place *ou* put in front of the word; **sujet antéposé** subject placed *ou* put in front of the verb

antéposition [ɑ̃tepozisjɔ̃] NF (*Ling*) anteposition

antérieur, e [ɑ̃terjœr] ADJ [a] (*dans le temps*) [*époque, situation*] previous, earlier; **c'est ~ à la guerre** it was prior to the war; **cette décision était ~e à son départ** that decision was taken prior to his departure; **dans une vie ~e** in a former life [b] (*dans l'espace*) [*partie*] front (*épith*); **membre ~** forelimb; **patte ~e** [*cheval, vache*] forefoot; [*chien, chat*] forepaw [c] (*Ling*) [*voyelle*] front (*épith*) → **futur, passé**

antérieurement [ɑ̃terjœrmɑ̃] ADV earlier; **~ à** prior *ou* previous to

antériorité [ɑ̃terjɔrite] NF [*événement, phénomène*] precedence; (*Gram*) anteriority

anthologie [ɑ̃tɔlɔʒi] NF anthology → **morceau**

anthozoaires [ɑ̃tozɔɛr] NMPL **les ~** the Anthozoa

anthracite [ɑ̃trasit] [1] NM anthracite [2] ADJ INV dark grey (*Brit*) *ou* gray (*US*), charcoal grey (*Brit*) *ou* gray (*US*)

anthrax [ɑ̃traks] NM (= *tumeur*) carbuncle

anthropique [ɑ̃trɔpik] ADJ anthropic

anthropocentrique [ɑ̃trɔposɑ̃trik] ADJ anthropocentric

anthropocentrisme [ɑ̃trɔposɑ̃trism] NM anthropocentrism

anthropoïde [ɑ̃trɔpɔid] [1] ADJ anthropoid [2] NM anthropoid (ape)

anthropologie [ɑ̃trɔpɔlɔʒi] NF anthropology

anthropologique [ɑ̃trɔpɔlɔʒik] ADJ anthropological

anthropologiste [ɑ̃trɔpɔlɔʒist], **anthropologue** [ɑ̃trɔpɔlɔg] NMF anthropologist

anthropométrie [ɑ̃trɔpɔmetri] NF anthropometry

anthropométrique [ɑ̃tʀɔpɔmetʀik] ADJ anthropometric(al); **fiche ~** mugshot

anthropomorphe [ɑ̃tʀɔpɔmɔʀf] ADJ anthropomorphous

anthropomorphique [ɑ̃tʀɔpɔmɔʀfik] ADJ anthropomorphic

anthropomorphisme [ɑ̃tʀɔpɔmɔʀfism] NM anthropomorphism

anthropomorphiste [ɑ̃tʀɔpɔmɔʀfist] [1] ADJ anthropomorphist, anthropomorphic [2] NMF anthropomorphist

anthroponymie [ɑ̃tʀɔpɔnimi] NF (Ling) anthroponomy

anthropophage [ɑ̃tʀɔpɔfaʒ] [1] ADJ cannibalistic, cannibal (épith), anthropophagous (SPÉC) [2] NMF cannibal, anthropophagite (SPÉC)

anthropophagie [ɑ̃tʀɔpɔfaʒi] NF cannibalism, anthropophagy (SPÉC)

anthropopithèque [ɑ̃tʀɔpɔpitɛk] NM anthropopithecus

anthume [ɑ̃tym] ADJ [œuvre] published during the author's lifetime

anti [ɑ̃ti] [1] PRÉF anti(-) (dans les composés à traits d'union, le préfixe reste invariable) anti-; ~ **impérialisme** anti-imperialism; **l'~-art/-théâtre** anti-art/-theatre; **flash ~-yeux rouges** flash with red-eye reduction feature; **loi ~-casseur(s)** law against looting; **bombe ~-crevaison** (instant) puncture sealant [2] NM (hum) **le parti des ~s** those who are anti ou against, the anti crowd*

anti-acnéique [ɑ̃tiakneik] ADJ [traitement, préparation] anti-acne (épith)

antiacridien, -ienne [ɑ̃tiakʀidjɛ̃, jɛn] ADJ locust control (épith); **la lutte antiacridienne** the fight to control locusts

antiadhésif, -ive [ɑ̃tiadezif, iv] ADJ [poêle, revêtement] non-stick (épith)

antiaérien, -ienne [ɑ̃tiaeʀjɛ̃, jɛn] ADJ [batterie, canon, missile] anti-aircraft; [abri] air-raid (épith)

anti-âge [ɑ̃tiaʒ] ADJ INV anti-ageing

antialcoolique [ɑ̃tialkɔlik] ADJ **campagne ~** campaign against alcohol; **ligue ~** temperance league

antiallergique [ɑ̃tialɛʀʒik] [1] ADJ anti-allergic [2] NM anti-allergic drug

antiatomique [ɑ̃tiatɔmik] ADJ anti-radiation; **abri ~** fallout shelter

anti-aveuglant, e [ɑ̃tiavœɡlɑ̃, ɑ̃t] ADJ (Aut) anti-dazzle

anti-avortement [ɑ̃tiavɔʀtəmɑ̃] ADJ INV anti-abortion, pro-life

antibalistique [ɑ̃tibalistik] ADJ [missile] anti-ballistic

antibiothérapie [ɑ̃tibjoteʀapi] NF antibiotic therapy

antibiotique [ɑ̃tibjɔtik] ADJ, NM antibiotic; **être/mettre sous ~s** to be/put on antibiotics

antiblocage [ɑ̃tiblɔkaʒ] ADJ INV **système ~ des roues** antilock braking system, ABS

antibois [ɑ̃tibwa] NM chair-rail

antibrouillard [ɑ̃tibʀujaʀ] ADJ, NM (Aut) **(phare) ~** fog lamp (Brit), fog light (US)

antibruit [ɑ̃tibʀɥi] ADJ INV **mur ~** (= qui empêche le bruit) soundproof wall; (= qui diminue le bruit) noise-reducing wall; **campagne ~** campaign against noise pollution

antibuée [ɑ̃tibɥe] ADJ INV **dispositif ~** demister; **bombe/liquide ~** anti-mist spray/liquid

anticalcaire [ɑ̃tikalkɛʀ] [1] ADJ **poudre ~** water softener [2] NM water softener

anticancéreux, -euse [ɑ̃tikɑ̃seʀø, øz] ADJ cancer (épith); **centre ~** (= laboratoire) cancer research centre; (= hôpital) cancer hospital; **médicament ~** anti-cancer drug

anticellulite [ɑ̃tiselylit] ADJ INV anti-cellulite (épith)

anticerne [ɑ̃tisɛʀn] NM concealer (to cover shadows under the eyes)

antichambre [ɑ̃tiʃɑ̃bʀ] NF antechamber, anteroom; **faire ~†** to wait humbly ou patiently (for an audience with sb)

antichar [ɑ̃tiʃaʀ] ADJ anti-tank

antichoc [ɑ̃tiʃɔk] ADJ [montre] shockproof

antichute [ɑ̃tiʃyt] ADJ INV **lotion ~** hair restorer

anticipation [ɑ̃tisipasjɔ̃] NF [a] (gén, Sport, Fin) anticipation; **par ~** [rembourser] in advance; **paiement par ~** payment in advance ou anticipation, advance payment; **était-ce une réponse par ~?** was he anticipating the question by giving that reply? [b] (Écon) **~s** expectations; **~s inflationnistes** inflationary expectations [c] (futuriste) **littérature d'~** science fiction; **roman/film d'~** science-fiction ou futuristic novel/film [d] (Ordin) look-ahead [e] (Mus) anticipation

anticipé, e [ɑ̃tisipe] (ptp de **anticiper**) ADJ [élections, retour] early (épith); **remboursement ~** repayment before due date; **élections ~es** early elections; **retraite ~e** early retirement; **avec mes remerciements ~s** thanking you in advance ou in anticipation

anticiper [ɑ̃tisipe] ▶conjug 1 ◀ [1] VI (= prévoir, calculer) to anticipate; (en imaginant) to look ou think ahead, anticipate what will happen; (en racontant) to jump ahead; **n'anticipons pas!** let's not look ou think too far ahead, let's not anticipate; **mais j'anticipe!** but I'm getting ahead of myself! [2] **anticiper sur** VT INDIR [+ récit, rapport] to anticipate; **~ sur l'avenir** to anticipate the future; **sans vouloir ~ sur ce que je dirai tout à l'heure** without wishing to go into what I shall say later; (Sport) **il anticipe bien (sur les balles)** he's got good anticipation [3] VT (Comm) [+ paiement] to pay before due, anticipate; (Sport) to anticipate; [+ avenir, événement, reprise économique] to anticipate

anticlérical, e (mpl **-aux**) [ɑ̃tikleʀikal, o] [1] ADJ anticlerical [2] NM,F anticleric(al)

anticléricalisme [ɑ̃tikleʀikalism] NM anticlericalism

anticlinal, e (mpl **-aux**) [ɑ̃tiklinal, o] ADJ, NM anticlinal

anticoagulant, e [ɑ̃tikɔagylɑ̃, ɑ̃t] ADJ, NM anticoagulant

anticolonialisme [ɑ̃tikɔlɔnjalism] NM anticolonialism

anticolonialiste [ɑ̃tikɔlɔnjalist] ADJ, NMF anticolonialist

anticommunisme [ɑ̃tikɔmynism] NM anticommunism

anticommuniste [ɑ̃tikɔmynist] ADJ, NMF anticommunist

anticonceptionnel, -elle [ɑ̃tikɔ̃sɛpsjɔnɛl] ADJ contraceptive; **moyens ~s** contraceptive methods, methods of birth control

anticonformisme [ɑ̃tikɔ̃fɔʀmism] NM nonconformism

anticonformiste [ɑ̃tikɔ̃fɔʀmist] ADJ, NMF nonconformist

anticonstitutionnel, -elle [ɑ̃tikɔ̃stitysjɔnɛl] ADJ unconstitutional

anticonstitutionnellement [ɑ̃tikɔ̃stitysjɔnɛlmɑ̃] ADV unconstitutionally

anticorps [ɑ̃tikɔʀ] NM antibody

anticyclone [ɑ̃tisiklon] NM anticyclone

anticyclonique [ɑ̃tisiklonik] ADJ anticyclonic

antidater [ɑ̃tidate] ▶conjug 1 ◀ VT to backdate, predate, antedate

antidéflagration [ɑ̃tideflagʀasjɔ̃] ADJ INV **porte ~** blast-proof door

antidémarrage [ɑ̃tidemaʀaʒ] ADJ INV (Aut) **dispositif ~** (engine) immobiliser

antidémocratique [ɑ̃tidemɔkʀatik] ADJ (= opposé à la démocratie) antidemocratic; (= peu démocratique) undemocratic

antidépresseur [ɑ̃tidepʀɛsœʀ] ADJ M, NM antidepressant

antidérapant, e [ɑ̃tideʀapɑ̃, ɑ̃t] ADJ (Aut) non-skid; (Ski) non-slip

antidétonant, e [ɑ̃tidetɔnɑ̃, ɑ̃t] ADJ, NM anti-knock

antidiphtérique [ɑ̃tidifteʀik] ADJ [sérum] diphtheria (épith)

antidiurétique [ɑ̃tidjyʀetik] ADJ, NM antidiuretic

antidopage [ɑ̃tidɔpaʒ] ADJ [loi, contrôle] doping (épith), anti-doping (épith); **subir un contrôle ~** to be dope-tested

antidote [ɑ̃tidɔt] NM (lit, fig) antidote (**contre, de** for, against)

antidouleur [ɑ̃tidulœʀ] [1] ADJ INV [médicament, traitement] painkilling (épith); **centre ~** pain control unit [2] NM painkiller

antidrogue [ɑ̃tidʀɔg] ADJ INV [lutte] against drug abuse; [campagne] anti-drug(s); **brigade ~** drug squad

antidumping [ɑ̃tidœmpiŋ] ADJ INV anti-dumping

antiéconomique [ɑ̃tiekɔnɔmik] ADJ uneconomical

antieffraction [ɑ̃tiefʀaksjɔ̃] ADJ [vitres] burglar-proof

antiémétique [ɑ̃tiemetik] ADJ, NM antiemetic

anti-émeute(s) [ɑ̃tiemøt] ADJ INV [police, brigade, unité] riot (épith)

antienne [ɑ̃tjɛn] NF (Rel) antiphony; (fig littér) chant, refrain

antiépileptique [ɑ̃tiepilɛptik] [1] ADJ antiepileptic [2] NM antiepileptic drug

antiesclavagisme [ɑ̃tiesklavaʒism] NM opposition to slavery; (Hist US) abolitionism

antiesclavagiste [ɑ̃tiesklavaʒist] [1] ADJ anti-slavery, opposed to slavery (attrib); (Hist US) abolitionist [2] NMF opponent of slavery; (Hist US) abolitionist

anti-européen, -enne [ɑ̃tiøʀɔpeɛ̃, ɛn] [1] ADJ anti-European [2] NM,F anti-European; **les ~s du parti** the anti-European wing of the party

antifasciste [ɑ̃tifaʃist] ADJ, NMF antifascist

antifongique [ɑ̃tifɔ̃ʒik] ADJ, NM antifungal

anti-g [ɑ̃tiʒe] ADJ INV **combinaison ~** G-suit

antigang [ɑ̃tigɑ̃g] ADJ INV, NM **la brigade ~ ◊ l'~** the (police) commando squad

antigel [ɑ̃tiʒɛl] ADJ INV, NM antifreeze

antigène [ɑ̃tiʒɛn] NM antigen

antigivrant, e [ɑ̃tiʒivʀɑ̃, ɑ̃t] [1] ADJ anti-icing (épith) [2] NM anti-icer

Antigone [ɑ̃tigɔn] NF Antigone

antigouvernemental, e (mpl **-aux**) [ɑ̃tiguvɛʀnəmɑ̃tal, o] ADJ antigovernment(al)

antigravitationnel, -elle [ɑ̃tigʀavitasjɔnɛl] ADJ antigravity (épith)

antigrippe [ɑ̃tigʀip] ADJ INV **vaccin ~** flu vaccine

Antigua-et-Barbuda [ɑ̃tigwaebaʀbyda] NPL Antigua and Barbuda

antiguais, e [ɑ̃tigwɛ, ɛz] [1] ADJ Antiguan [2] **Antiguais(e)** NM,F Antiguan

antihausse [ɑ̃tios] ADJ INV [mesures] aimed at curbing price rises, anti-inflation (épith)

antihéros [ɑ̃tieʀo] NM anti-hero

antihistaminique [ɑ̃tiistaminik] ADJ, NM antihistamine

antihygiénique [ɑ̃tiiʒjenik] ADJ unhygienic

anti-inflammatoire [ɑ̃tiɛ̃flamatwaʀ] ADJ, NM anti-inflammatory

anti-inflationniste [ɑ̃tiɛ̃flasjɔnist] ADJ [mesure] anti-inflationary, counter-inflationary

antijeu [ɑ̃tiʒø] NM **faire de l'~** to be unsporting *ou* unsportsmanlike

antillais, e [ɑ̃tijɛ, ɛz] [1] ADJ West Indian [2] **Antillais(e)** NM,F West Indian

Antilles [ɑ̃tij] NFPL **les ~** the West Indies; **les Grandes/Petites ~** the Greater/Lesser Antilles; **les ~ françaises** the French West Indies; **la mer des ~** the Caribbean Sea

antilope [ɑ̃tilɔp] NF antelope

antimatière [ɑ̃timatjɛʀ] NF antimatter

antimilitarisme [ɑ̃timilitaʀism] NM antimilitarism

antimilitariste [ɑ̃timilitaʀist] ADJ, NMF antimilitarist

antimissile [ɑ̃timisil] ADJ antimissile

antimite [ɑ̃timit] [1] ADJ (anti-)moth (*épith*) [2] NM mothproofing agent, moth repellent; (= *boules de naphtaline*) mothballs

antimoine [ɑ̃timwan] NM antimony

antimonarchique [ɑ̃timɔnaʀʃik] ADJ antimonarchist, antimonarchic(al)

antimonarchiste [ɑ̃timɔnaʀʃist] NMF antimonarchist

antimycosique [ɑ̃timikozik] ADJ, NM antimycotic

antinational, e (*mpl* **-aux**) [ɑ̃tinasjɔnal, o] ADJ antinational

antinazi, e [ɑ̃tinazi] ADJ, NM,F anti-Nazi

antinomie [ɑ̃tinɔmi] NF antinomy

antinomique [ɑ̃tinɔmik] ADJ antinomic(al)

antinucléaire [ɑ̃tinykleɛʀ] ADJ anti-nuclear; **les (militants) ~s** anti-nuclear campaigners, the anti-nuclear lobby

Antioche [ɑ̃tjɔʃ] N Antioch

Antiope [ɑ̃tjɔp] NF (ABRÉV = **acquisition numérique et télévisualisation d'images organisées en pages d'écriture**) ≈ Videotex®, ≈ Teletext® (*Brit*), ≈ Ceefax® (*Brit*)

antioxydant, e [ɑ̃tiɔksidɑ̃, ɑ̃t] ADJ, NM antioxidant

antipaludéen, -enne [ɑ̃tipalydeɛ̃, ɛn] [1] ADJ anti-malarial [2] NM anti-malarial drug

antipaludique [ɑ̃tipalydik] [1] ADJ [*vaccin*] anti-malarial; **la lutte ~** the fight against malaria [2] NM anti-malarial drug

antipape [ɑ̃tipap] NM antipope

antiparasite [ɑ̃tipaʀazit] ADJ anti-interference (*épith*); **dispositif ~** suppressor

antiparasiter [ɑ̃tipaʀazite] ▶conjug 1◀ VT to fit a suppressor to

antiparlementaire [ɑ̃tipaʀləmɑ̃tɛʀ] ADJ antiparliamentary

antiparlementarisme [ɑ̃tipaʀləmɑ̃taʀism] NM antiparliamentarianism

antiparticule [ɑ̃tipaʀtikyl] NF (*Phys*) antiparticle; (*Tech*) **filtre ~s** dust filter

antipasti [ɑ̃tipasti] NMPL (*Culin*) antipasti

antipathie [ɑ̃tipati] NF antipathy; **l'~ entre ces deux communautés** the hostility *ou* antipathy between the two communities; **avoir de l'~ pour qn** to dislike sb

antipathique [ɑ̃tipatik] ADJ [*personne*] disagreeable, unpleasant; [*endroit*] unpleasant; **il m'est ~** I don't like him, I find him most disagreeable

antipatriotique [ɑ̃tipatʀijɔtik] ADJ antipatriotic; (= *peu patriote*) unpatriotic

antipatriotisme [ɑ̃tipatʀijɔtism] NM antipatriotism

antipelliculaire [ɑ̃tipelikylɛʀ] ADJ anti-dandruff (*épith*)

antipersonnel [ɑ̃tipɛʀsɔnɛl] ADJ INV antipersonnel

antiphrase [ɑ̃tifʀaz] NF antiphrasis; **par ~** ironically

antipode [ɑ̃tipɔd] NM (*Géog*) **les ~s** the antipodes; (*Géog*) **être aux ~s** to be on the other side of the world; **votre théorie est aux ~s de**

la mienne our theories are poles apart, your theory and mine are at opposite extremes

antipoétique [ɑ̃tipɔetik] ADJ unpoetic

antipoison [ɑ̃tipwazɔ̃] ADJ INV **centre ~** treatment centre for poisoning cases

antipoliomyélitique [ɑ̃tipɔljɔmjelitik] ADJ **vaccin ~** polio vaccine

antipollution [ɑ̃tipɔlysjɔ̃] ADJ INV antipollution (*épith*)

antiprotéase [ɑ̃tipʀɔteaz] ADJ, NF (*Méd*) (**molécule**) ~ protease inhibitor

antiprotectionniste [ɑ̃tipʀɔtɛksjɔnist] [1] ADJ free-trade (*épith*) [2] NMF free trader

antiprurigineux, -euse [ɑ̃tipʀyʀiʒinø, øz] ADJ, NM antipruritic

antipsychiatrie [ɑ̃tipsikjatʀi] NF antipsychiatry

antipyrétique [ɑ̃tipiʀetik] ADJ antipyretic

antipyrine [ɑ̃tipiʀin] NF antipyrine

antiquaille [ɑ̃tikaj] NF (*péj*) piece of old junk

antiquaire [ɑ̃tikɛʀ] NMF antique dealer

antique [ɑ̃tik] [1] ADJ a (= *de l'Antiquité*) [*vase, objet*] antique, ancient; [*style*] ancient; **objets d'art ~s** antiquities b (*littér* = *très ancien*) [*coutume, objet*] ancient; (*péj*) [*véhicule, chapeau*] antiquated, ancient; **l'art ~** (*de l'Antiquité*) classical art *ou* style

antiquité [ɑ̃tikite] NF a (= *période*) **l'Antiquité** antiquity; **l'Antiquité grecque/romaine** Greek/Roman antiquity; **dès la plus haute Antiquité** since earliest antiquity, from very ancient times b (= *ancienneté*) antiquity, (great) age; **de toute ~** from the beginning of time, from time immemorial c (= *objet de l'Antiquité*) piece of classical art; (= *objet ancien*) antique; **~s** (= *œuvres de l'Antiquité*) antiquities; (= *meubles anciens*) antiques; **marchand/magasin d'~s** antique dealer/shop

antirabique [ɑ̃tiʀabik] ADJ **vaccin ~** rabies vaccine

antirachitique [ɑ̃tiʀaʃitik] ADJ antirachitic

antiracisme [ɑ̃tiʀasism] NM antiracism

antiraciste [ɑ̃tiʀasist] ADJ, NMF antiracist, antiracialist (*Brit*)

antiradar [ɑ̃tiʀadaʀ] [1] ADJ [*missile*] anti-radar (*épith*) [2] NM anti-radar missile

antireflet [ɑ̃tiʀəflɛ] ADJ INV [*surface*] non-reflecting; (*Photo*) bloomed

antireligieux, -ieuse [ɑ̃tiʀ(ə)liʒjø, jøz] ADJ antireligious

antirépublicain, e [ɑ̃tiʀepyblikɛ̃, ɛn] ADJ antirepublican

antirétroviral, e (*mpl* **-aux**) [ɑ̃tiʀetʀoviʀal, o] [1] ADJ antiretroviral [2] NM antiretroviral drug

antirévolutionnaire [ɑ̃tiʀevɔlysjɔnɛʀ] ADJ antirevolutionary

antirides [ɑ̃tiʀid] ADJ anti-wrinkle (*épith*)

antiroman [ɑ̃tiʀɔmɑ̃] NM **l'~** the antinovel, the anti-roman

antirouille [ɑ̃tiʀuj] [1] ADJ INV anti-rust (*épith*) [2] NM INV rust inhibitor, anti-rust (paint *ou* primer)

antiroulis [ɑ̃tiʀuli] ADJ anti-roll (*épith*)

antiscorbutique [ɑ̃tiskɔʀbytik] ADJ antiscorbutic

antisèche [ɑ̃tisɛʃ] NF (*arg Scol*) crib, cheat sheet* (*US*)

antiségrégationniste [ɑ̃tisegʀegasjɔnist] ADJ antisegregationist

antisémite [ɑ̃tisemit] [1] ADJ anti-Semitic [2] NMF anti-Semite

antisémitisme [ɑ̃tisemitism] NM anti-Semitism

antisepsie [ɑ̃tisɛpsi] NF antisepsis

antiseptique [ɑ̃tisɛptik] ADJ, NM antiseptic

antisida [ɑ̃tisida] ADJ INV [*campagne, vaccin*] against AIDS, AIDS (*épith*); [*traitement*] for AIDS, AIDS (*épith*)

antisismique [ɑ̃tisismik] ADJ earthquake-proof (*épith*)

antisocial, e (*mpl* **-iaux**) [ɑ̃tisɔsjal, jo] ADJ (*Pol*) antisocial

anti-sous-marin, e [ɑ̃tisumaʀɛ̃, in] ADJ anti-submarine

antispasmodique [ɑ̃tispasmɔdik] ADJ, NM antispasmodic

antisportif, -ive [ɑ̃tispɔʀtif, iv] ADJ (*opposé au sport*) anti-sport; (*peu élégant*) unsporting, unsportsmanlike

antistatique [ɑ̃tistatik] ADJ, NM antistatic

antistrophe [ɑ̃tistʀɔf] NF antistrophe

antisubversif, -ive [ɑ̃tisybvɛʀsif, iv] ADJ counter-subversive

antitabac [ɑ̃titaba] ADJ INV **campagne ~** anti-smoking campaign; **loi ~** *law prohibiting smoking in public places*

antitache(s) [ɑ̃titaʃ] ADJ [*traitement*] stain-repellent

antiterroriste [ɑ̃titeʀɔʀist] ADJ antiterrorist

antitétanique [ɑ̃titetanik] ADJ [*sérum*] (anti-)tetanus (*épith*)

antithèse [ɑ̃titɛz] NF (*gén*) antithesis; (*fig* = *le contraire*) **c'est l'~ de** it is the opposite of

antithétique [ɑ̃titetik] ADJ antithetic(al)

antitout* [ɑ̃titu] [1] ADJ INV [*personne*] systematically opposed to everything [2] NMF INV person who is systematically opposed to everything

antitoxine [ɑ̃titɔksin] NF antitoxin

antitoxique [ɑ̃titɔksik] ADJ antitoxic

antitrust [ɑ̃titʀœst] ADJ INV [*loi, mesures*] anti-monopoly (*Brit*), anti-trust (*US*)

antituberculeux, -euse [ɑ̃titybɛʀkylø, øz] ADJ [*sérum*] tuberculosis (*épith*)

antitumoral, e (*pl* **-aux**) [ɑ̃titymɔʀal, o] ADJ (*Méd*) [*substance, action*] anti-tumour (*épith*) (*Brit*), anti-tumor (*épith*) (*US*)

antitussif, -ive [ɑ̃titysif] [1] ADJ [*comprimé*] cough (*épith*), antitussive (*SPÉC*) [2] NM cough mixture, antitussive (*SPÉC*)

antivariolique [ɑ̃tivaʀjɔlik] ADJ **vaccin ~** smallpox vaccine

antivénéneux, -euse [ɑ̃tivenenø, øz] ADJ antidotal

antivenimeux, -euse [ɑ̃tivənimø, øz] ADJ **sérum ~, substance antivenimeuse** antivenin, antivenene

antiviral, e (*mpl* **-aux**) [ɑ̃tiviʀal, o] ADJ, NM antiviral

antivirus [ɑ̃tiviʀys] NM (*Méd*) antiviral drug; (*Ordin*) antivirus

antivol [ɑ̃tivɔl] NM, ADJ INV (**dispositif**) **~** anti-theft device; [*cycle*] lock; (*sur volant de voiture*) (steering) lock; **mettre un ~ sur son vélo** to put a lock on *ou* to lock one's bike

antonomase [ɑ̃tɔnɔmaz] NF antonomasia

antonyme [ɑ̃tɔnim] NM antonym

antonymie [ɑ̃tɔnimi] NF antonymy

antre [ɑ̃tʀ] NM (*littér* = *caverne*) cave; [*animal*] den, lair; (*fig*) den; (*Anat*) antrum

anurie [anyʀi] NF anuria

anus [anys] NM anus; **~ artificiel** colostomy

Anvers [ɑ̃vɛʀ] N Antwerp

anxiété [ɑ̃ksjete] NF (= *inquiétude, Méd*) anxiety; **avec ~** anxiously; **être dans l'~** to be very anxious *ou* worried

anxieusement [ɑ̃ksjøzmɑ̃] ADV anxiously

anxieux, -ieuse [ɑ̃ksjø, jøz] [1] ADJ [*personne, regard*] anxious, worried; [*attente*] anxious; (*Méd*) **crises anxieuses** anxiety attacks; **~ de** anxious to [2] NM,F worrier

anxiogène [ɑ̃ksjɔʒɛn] ADJ [*situation, effet*] stressful, anxiety-provoking (*SPÉC*)

anxiolytique [ɑ̃ksjɔlitik] [1] ADJ tranquillizing [2] NM tranquillizer

AOC [aose] NF (ABRÉV = **appellation d'origine contrôlée**) **fromage/vin ~** AOC cheese/wine (*with a guarantee of origin*)

> **AOC**
>
> AOC *is the highest French wine classification. It indicates that the wine meets strict requirements concerning the vineyard of origin, the type of vine grown, the method of production, and the volume of alcohol present.* → VDQS

aoriste [aɔʀist] NM aorist

aorte [aɔʀt] NF aorta

aortique [aɔʀtik] ADJ aortic

août [u(t)] NM August; *pour locutions voir* **septembre** *et* **quinze**

aoûtat [auta] NM harvest tick *ou* mite (*Brit*), chigger (*US*)

aoûtien, -ienne* [ausjɛ̃, jɛn] NM,F August holiday-maker (*Brit*) *ou* vacationer (*US*)

AP [ape] NF (ABRÉV = **Assistance publique**) → **assistance**

ap. (ABRÉV = **après**) after; **en 300 ~ J.-C.** in 300 AD

apache [apaʃ] 1 ADJ a (= *indien*) Apache b († = *canaille*) **il a une allure ~** he has a tough *ou* vicious look (about him) 2 **Apache** NMF Apache; **les Apaches** the Apaches 3 NM († = *voyou*) ruffian, tough

apaisant, e [apɛzɑ̃, ɑ̃t] ADJ a (= *qui soulage*) [*musique, silence, crème*] soothing b (= *pacificateur*) [*discours*] conciliatory

apaisement [apɛzmɑ̃] NM a [*passion, désir, soif, faim*] appeasement; **après l'~ de la tempête** once the storm had died down b (= *soulagement*) relief; (= *assurance*) reassurance; **cela lui procura un certain ~** this brought him some relief; **donner des ~s à qn** to reassure sb c (*Pol*) appeasement; **une politique d'~** a policy of appeasement

apaiser [apeze] ▸conjug 1◂ 1 VT a [+ *personne, foule*] to calm (down), pacify, placate; [+ *animal*] to calm down b [+ *faim*] to appease; [+ *soif*] to slake, appease; [+ *conscience*] to salve, soothe; [+ *scrupules*] to allay; [+ *douleur*] to soothe; **pour ~ les esprits** to calm people down 2 **s'apaiser** VPR a [*personne, malade, animal*] to calm *ou* quieten down b [*vacarme, excitation, tempête*] to die down, subside; [*vagues, douleur*] to die down; [*passion, désir*] to cool; [*soif, faim*] to be assuaged *ou* appeased; [*scrupules*] to be allayed; **sa colère s'est un peu apaisée** he's calmed down a bit

apanage [apanaʒ] NM (= *privilège*) privilege; **être l'~ de qn/qch** to be the privilege *ou* prerogative of sb/sth; **avoir l'~ de qch** to have the sole *ou* exclusive right to sth, possess sth exclusively; **il croit avoir l'~ du bon sens** he thinks he's the only one with any common sense

aparté [aparte] NM (= *entretien*) private conversation (*in a group*); (*Théât, gén* = *remarque*) aside; **en ~** in an aside

apartheid [apaʀtɛd] NM apartheid; **politique d'~** apartheid policy

apathie [apati] NF apathy

apathique [apatik] ADJ apathetic

apathiquement [apatikmɑ̃] ADV apathetically

apatride [apatʀid] 1 ADJ stateless 2 NMF stateless person

APE [apea] NF (ABRÉV = **Assemblée parlementaire européenne**) EP

APEC [apɛk] NF (ABRÉV = **Association pour l'emploi des cadres**) executive employment agency

Apennin(s) [apenɛ̃] NM(PL) **l'Apennin** ◊ **les Apennins** the Apennines

aperception [apɛʀsɛpsjɔ̃] NF apperception

apercevoir [apɛʀsəvwaʀ] ▸conjug 28◂ 1 VT a (= *voir*) to see; (*brièvement*) to catch sight of, catch a glimpse of; (= *remarquer*) to notice; **on apercevait au loin un clocher** a church tower could be seen in the distance b (= *se rendre compte de*) [+ *danger, contradictions*] to see, perceive; [+ *difficultés*] to see, foresee; **si on fait cela, j'aperçois des problèmes** if we do that, I (can) see problems ahead *ou* I (can) foresee problems 2 **s'apercevoir** VPR [*personnes*] to see *ou* notice each other; **elle s'aperçut dans le miroir** she caught a glimpse *ou* caught sight of herself in the mirror; **s'~ de** [+ *erreur, omission*] to notice; [+ *présence, méfiance*] to notice, become aware of; [+ *dessein, manège*] to notice, see through, become aware of; **s'~ que ...** to notice *ou* realize that ...; **sans s'en ~** without realizing, inadvertently; **ça s'aperçoit à peine** it's hardly noticeable, you can hardly see it

aperçu [apɛʀsy] NM a (= *idée générale*) general survey; **~ sommaire** brief survey; **cela vous donnera un bon ~ de ce que vous allez visiter** that will give you a good idea *ou* a general idea of what you are about to visit b (= *point de vue personnel*) insight (**sur** into) c (*Ordin*) **~ avant impression** print preview

apéritif, -ive [apeʀitif, iv] 1 ADJ (*littér*) [*boisson*] that stimulates the appetite; **ils firent une promenade apéritive** they went for a walk to get up an appetite 2 NM aperitif, drink (*taken before lunch or dinner*); **prendre l'~** to have an aperitif; **venez prendre l'~** come for drinks; **ils sont arrivés à l'~** they came when we were having drinks

apéro* [apeʀo] NM ABRÉV = **apéritif**

aperture [apɛʀtyʀ] NF (*Ling*) aperture

apesanteur [apəzɑ̃tœʀ] NF weightlessness; **être en (état d')~** to be weightless

à-peu-près [apøpʀɛ] NM INV vague approximation; **il est resté dans l'~** he was very vague → **près**

apeuré, e [apœʀe] ADJ frightened, scared

apex [apɛks] NM (*Astron, Bot, Sci*) apex; (*Ling*) [*langue*] apex, tip; (= *accent latin*) macron

aphasie [afazi] NF aphasia

aphasique [afazik] ADJ, NMF aphasic

aphérèse [afeʀɛz] NF aphaeresis

aphone [afɔn] ADJ voiceless, aphonic (*SPÉC*); **je suis presque ~ d'avoir trop crié** I've nearly lost my voice *ou* I'm hoarse from shouting so much

aphonie [afɔni] NF aphonia

aphorisme [afɔʀism] NM aphorism

aphrodisiaque [afʀɔdizjak] ADJ, NM aphrodisiac

Aphrodite [afʀɔdit] NF Aphrodite

aphte [aft] NM ulcer, aphtha (*SPÉC*); **~ buccal** mouth ulcer

aphteux, -euse [aftø, øz] ADJ aphthous → **fièvre**

api [api] → **pomme**

Apia [apja] N Apia

à-pic [apik] NM cliff

apical, e (*mpl* -aux) [apikal, o] 1 ADJ apical; **r ~ trillé** r 2 **apicale** NF apical consonant

apico-alvéolaire [apikoalveɔlɛʀ] ADJ, NF apico-alveolar

apico-dental, e (*mpl* -aux) [apikodɑ̃tal, o] 1 ADJ apico-dental 2 **apico-dentale** NF apico-dental

apicole [apikɔl] ADJ beekeeping (*épith*), apiarian (*SPÉC*), apicultural (*SPÉC*)

apiculteur, -trice [apikyltœʀ, tʀis] NM,F beekeeper, apiarist (*SPÉC*), apiculturist (*SPÉC*)

apiculture [apikyltyʀ] NF beekeeping, apiculture (*SPÉC*)

apitoiement [apitwamɑ̃] NM (= *pitié*) pity, compassion

apitoyer [apitwaje] ▸conjug 8◂ 1 VT to move to pity; **~ qn sur le sort de qn** to make sb feel sorry for sb; **regard/sourire apitoyé** pitying look/smile 2 **s'apitoyer** VPR **s'~ sur qn** *ou* **le sort de qn** to feel pity for sb, feel sorry for sb; **s'~ sur son propre sort** to feel sorry for o.s.

ap. J.-C. (ABRÉV = **après Jésus-Christ**) AD

APL [apeɛl] NF (ABRÉV = **aide personnalisée au logement**) → **aide**

aplanir [aplaniʀ] ▸conjug 2◂ 1 VT [+ *terrain, surface*] to level; [+ *difficultés*] to smooth away *ou* out, iron out; [+ *obstacles*] to smooth away 2 **s'aplanir** VPR [*terrain*] to become level; **les difficultés se sont aplanies** the difficulties smoothed themselves out

aplanissement [aplanismɑ̃] NM [*terrain*] levelling; [*difficultés*] smoothing away, ironing out; [*obstacles*] smoothing away

aplat [apla] NM (= *teinte*) flat tint; (= *surface*) flat, solid (plate)

aplati, e [aplati] (*ptp de* aplatir) ADJ [*forme, objet, nez*] flat; **c'est ~ sur le dessus/à son extrémité** it's flat on top/at one end

aplatir [aplatiʀ] ▸conjug 2◂ 1 VT [+ *objet*] to flatten; [+ *couture*] to press flat; [+ *cheveux*] to smooth down, flatten; [+ *pli*] to smooth (out); [+ *surface*] to flatten (out); **~ qch à coups de marteau** to hammer sth flat; **~ qn*** to flatten sb*; (*Rugby*) **~ (le ballon** *ou* **un essai)** to score a try, touch down 2 **s'aplatir** VPR a [*personne*] **s'~ contre un mur** to flatten o.s. against a wall; **s'~ par terre** (= *s'étendre*) to lie flat on the ground; (* = *tomber*) to fall flat on one's face; (*fig* = *s'humilier*) **s'~ devant qn** to crawl to sb, grovel before sb b [*choses*] (= *devenir plus plat*) to become flatter; (= *être écrasé*) to be flattened *ou* squashed; **s'écraser*) s'~ contre*** to smash against

aplatissement [aplatismɑ̃] NM (*gén*) flattening; (*fig* = *humiliation*) grovelling; **l'~ de la terre aux pôles** the flattening-out *ou* -off of the earth at the poles

aplomb [aplɔ̃] NM a (= *assurance*) composure, (self-)assurance; (*péj* = *insolence*) nerve*, cheek* (*Brit*); **garder son ~** to keep one's composure, remain composed; **perdre son ~** to lose one's composure, get flustered; **tu ne manques pas d'~!** you've got a nerve* *ou* a cheek* (*Brit*)! b (= *équilibre*) balance, equilibrium; (= *verticalité*) perpendicularity; **perdre l'~** *ou* **son ~** [*personne*] to lose one's balance; **à l'~ du mur** at the base of the wall c (*Équitation*) **~s** stand d **d'~** [*corps*] steady, balanced; [*bâtiment, mur*] plumb; **se tenir d'~ (sur ses jambes)** to be steady on one's feet; **être d'~** [*objet*] to be balanced *ou* level; [*mur*] to be plumb; **ne pas être d'~** [*mur*] to be out of *ou* off plumb; **mettre** *ou* **poser qch d'~** to straighten sth (up); **le vase n'est pas (posé) d'~** the vase isn't level; **tu n'as pas l'air d'~*** you look under the weather, you look off-colour* (*Brit*); **remettre d'~** [+ *bateau*] to right; [+ *entreprise*] to put back on its feet; **ça va te remettre d'~*** that'll put you right *ou* on your feet again; **se remettre d'~** (*après une maladie*) to pick up, get back on one's feet again; **le soleil tombait d'~** the sun was beating down

apnée [apne] NF apnoea (*Brit*), apnea (*US*); **être en ~** to be holding one's breath; **plonger en ~** to dive without any breathing apparatus

apocalypse [apɔkalips] NF (*Rel*) apocalypse; (= *livre*) **l'Apocalypse** (the Book of) Revelation, the Apocalypse; **atmosphère d'~** doom-laden *ou* end-of-the-world atmosphere; **paysage/vision d'~** apocalyptic landscape/vision

apocalyptique [apɔkaliptik] ADJ (*Rel*) apocalyptic; (*fig*) [*paysage, vision*] apocalyptic

apocope [apɔkɔp] NF apocope

apocryphe [apɔkʀif] **1** ADJ apocryphal, of doubtful authenticity; (*Rel*) Apocryphal **2** NM apocryphal book; **les ~s** the Apocrypha

apode [apɔd] **1** ADJ apodal, apodous **2** NM apodal *ou* apodous amphibian; **les ~s** apodal *ou* apodous amphibians, the Apoda (*SPÉC*)

apodictique [apɔdiktik] ADJ apodictic

apogée [apɔʒe] NM (*Astron*) apogee; [*carrière*] peak, height; [*art, mouvement*] peak, zenith; **être à son ~** [*carrière*] to peak, reach its peak *ou* height; [*art, mouvement*] to reach its peak; **artiste à son ~** artist at his (*ou* her) peak; **à l'~ de sa gloire/carrière** at the height of his (*ou* her) fame/career

apolitique [apɔlitik] ADJ (= *indifférent*) apolitical, unpolitical; (= *indépendant*) non-political

apolitisme [apɔlitism] NM (= *indifférence*) apolitical *ou* unpolitical attitude; (= *indépendance*) non-political stand; [*organisme*] non-political character

apollon [apɔlɔ̃] NM **a** (*Myth*) **Apollon** Apollo **b** (= *homme*) Apollo, Greek god **c** (= *papillon*) apollo

apologétique [apɔlɔʒetik] **1** ADJ (*Philos, Rel*) apologetic **2** NF apologetics *sg*

apologie [apɔlɔʒi] NF **a** (= *défense*) apology, apologia; **faire l'~** (*gén*) to try and justify; (*Jur*) to vindicate **b** (= *éloge*) praise; **faire l'~ de** to praise, speak (very) highly of

apologiste [apɔlɔʒist] NMF apologist

apologue [apɔlɔg] NM apologue

apophyse [apɔfiz] NF apophysis

apoplectique [apɔplektik] ADJ apoplectic

apoplexie [apɔpleksi] NF apoplexy; **attaque d'~** stroke, apoplectic fit

apoptose [apɔptoz] NF apoptosis

aporie [apɔʀi] NF aporia

apostasie [apɔstazi] NF apostasy

apostasier [apɔstazje] ▶ conjug 7 ◀ VI to apostatize, renounce the faith

apostat, e [apɔsta, at] ADJ, NM,F apostate, renegade

a posteriori [apɔsteʀjɔʀi] LOC ADV, LOC ADJ (*Philos*) a posteriori; (*gén*) after the event; **il est facile, ~, de dire que ...** it is easy enough, after the event *ou* with hindsight, to say that ...

apostille [apɔstij] NF apostil

apostiller [apɔstije] ▶ conjug 1 ◀ VT to add an apostil to

apostolat [apɔstɔla] NM (*Bible*) apostolate, discipleship; (= *prosélytisme*) proselytism, preaching, evangelism; (*fig*) **ce métier est un ~** this job requires total devotion *ou* has to be a vocation

apostolique [apɔstɔlik] ADJ apostolic → **nonce**

apostrophe[1] [apɔstʀɔf] NF (*Rhétorique*) apostrophe; (= *interpellation*) rude remark (*shouted at sb*); **mot mis en ~** word used in apostrophe; **lancer des ~s à qn** to shout rude remarks at sb

apostrophe[2] [apɔstʀɔf] NF (*Gram*) apostrophe

apostropher [apɔstʀɔfe] ▶ conjug 1 ◀ **1** VT (= *interpeller*) to shout at, address sharply **2** **s'apostropher** VPR to shout at each other; **les deux automobilistes s'apostrophèrent violemment** the two motorists hurled abuse at each other

apothème [apɔtɛm] NM apothem

apothéose [apɔteoz] NF **a** (= *consécration*) apotheosis; **cette nomination est pour lui une ~** this appointment is a supreme honour for him; **les tragédies de Racine sont l'~ de l'art classique** Racine's tragedies are the apotheosis *ou* pinnacle of classical art; (*iro*) **ça a été l'~!** that was the last straw! **b** (*gén, Théât* = *bouquet*) grand finale; **finir dans une ~** to end in a blaze of glory **c** (*Antiq* = *déification*) apotheosis

apothicaire†† [apɔtikɛʀ] NM apothecary†; **des comptes d'~** complicated calculations

apôtre [apotʀ] NM (*Rel*) apostle; (= *porte-parole*) advocate, apostle; **faire le bon ~** to play the saint, have a holier-than-thou attitude; **se faire l'~ de** to make o.s. the advocate *ou* apostle of

Appalaches [apalaʃ] NMPL **les (monts) ~** the Appalachian Mountains, the Appalachians

appalachien, -ienne [apalaʃjɛ̃, jɛn] ADJ Appalachian

apparaître [apaʀɛtʀ] ▶ conjug 57 ◀ **1** VI **a** (= *se montrer*) [*jour, personne, fantôme*] to appear (à to); [*difficulté, vérité*] to appear, come to light; [*signes, obstacles*] to appear; [*fièvre, boutons*] to break out; **la vérité lui apparut soudain** the truth suddenly dawned on him; **la silhouette qui apparaît/les problèmes qui apparaissent à l'horizon** the figure/the problems looming on the horizon **b** (= *sembler*) to seem, appear (à to); **ces remarques m'apparaissent fort judicieuses** these comments seem *ou* sound very wise to me; **je dois t'~ comme un monstre** I must seem like a monster to you **2** VB IMPERS **il apparaît que ...** it appears *ou* turns out that ...

apparat [apaʀa] NM **a** (= *pompe*) pomp; **d'~** [*dîner, habit, discours*] ceremonial; **en grand ~** (*pompe*) with great pomp and ceremony; (*habits*) in full regalia; **sans ~** [*réception*] unpretentious **b** (*Littérat*) **~ critique** critical apparatus, apparatus criticus

apparatchik [apaʀatʃik] NM apparatchik

▶ **appareil** [apaʀɛj] **1** NM **a** (= *machine, instrument*) (*gén*) piece of apparatus, device; (*électrique, ménager*) appliance; (*Radio, TV* = *poste*) set; (*Photo*) camera **b** (= *téléphone*) (tele)phone; **qui est à l'~?** who's speaking?; **Paul à l'~** Paul speaking **c** (*Aviat*) (aero)plane (*Brit*), (air)plane (*US*), aircraft *inv*, craft *inv* (*US*) **d** (*Méd*) appliance; (*pour fracture*) splint; (*auditif*) hearing aid; (= *contention dentaire*) brace; (* = *dentier*) dentures, plate **e** (*Anat*) apparatus, system; **~ digestif/respiratoire/urogénital** digestive/respiratory/urogenital apparatus *ou* system; **~ phonatoire** vocal apparatus *ou* organs **f** (= *structures*) apparatus, machinery; **l'~ policier/du parti** the police/the party apparatus *ou* machinery; **l'~ législatif** *ou* **des lois** the legal apparatus *ou* machinery; **l'~ industriel/militaire/productif** the industrial/military/production apparatus **g** (*littér*) (= *dehors fastueux*) air of pomp; (= *cérémonie fastueuse*) ceremony; **l'~ magnifique de la royauté** the opulent trappings of royalty → **simple** **h** (*Archit* = *agencement*) **i** (*Gym*) **~s** apparatus *sg*; **exercices aux ~s** exercises on the apparatus, apparatus work **j** (*Culin : = préparation*) mixture **2** COMP ► **appareil critique** (*Littérat*) critical apparatus, apparatus criticus ► **appareil électroménager** household *ou* domestic appliance ► **appareil de levage** lifting appliance, hoist ► **appareil de mesure** measuring device ► **appareil orthopédique** orthopaedic (*Brit*) *ou* orthopedic (*US*) appliance ► **appareil photo, appareil photographique** camera ► **appareil à sous**† (= *distributeur*) vending machine; (= *jeu*) slot machine, fruit machine (*Brit*)

appareillage [apaʀejaʒ] NM **a** (*Naut*) (= *départ*) casting off, getting under way; (= *manœuvres*) preparations for casting off *ou* getting under way **b** (= *équipement*) equipment; **~ électrique** electrical equipment **c** [*handicapé*] fitting with a prosthesis; [*sourd*] fitting with a hearing aid **d** (*Archit* = *agencement*) bonding; (= *taille*) dressing

appareiller [apaʀeje] ▶ conjug 1 ◀ **1** VI (*Naut*) to cast off, get under way **2** VT **a** (*Naut*) [+

navire] to rig, fit out **b** (*Archit*) (= *agencer*) to bond; (= *tailler*) to dress **c** [+ *handicapé*] to fit with a prosthesis *ou* an artificial limb (*ou* hand *ou* arm etc); [+ *sourd*] to fit with a hearing aid **d** (= *coupler*) to pair; (= *assortir*) to match up; (= *accoupler*) to mate (**avec** with)

apparemment [apaʀamɑ̃] ADV (= *de toute évidence*) apparently; (= *en surface*) seemingly; **théories ~ contradictoires** seemingly contradictory theories; **remarques ~ insignifiantes** seemingly trivial remarks; **il va mieux ? — ~** is he any better? — apparently

apparence [apaʀɑ̃s] NF **a** (= *aspect*) [*maison, personne*] appearance, aspect; **~ physique** physical appearance; **bâtiment de belle ~** fine-looking building; **il a une ~ négligée** he looks shabby; **homme d'~** *ou* **à l'~ sévère** severe-looking man; **quelques fermes d'~ prospère** some farms that appeared prosperous, some prosperous-looking farms **b** (= *déguisement*) appearance; **sous cette ~ souriante** beneath that smiling exterior; **sous l'~ de la générosité** under the guise of generosity; **ce n'est qu'une (fausse) ~** it's a mere façade **c** **les ~s** appearances; **les ~s sont contre lui** appearances are against him; **il ne faut pas se fier aux ~s** don't be taken in *ou* fooled by appearances, you shouldn't go by appearances; **tu te fies trop aux ~s** you rely too much on appearances; **sauver les ~s** to keep up appearances; **comme ça, les ~s sont sauves** that way, nobody loses face **d** (= *semblant, vestige*) semblance; **une ~ de liberté** a semblance of freedom **e** (*Philos*) appearance **f** (*loc*) **malgré l'~** *ou* **les ~s** in spite of appearances; **contre toute ~** against all expectations; **selon toute ~, il s'agit d'un suicide** it would appear *ou* seem that it was suicide, there is every indication that it was suicide; **en ~, leurs critiques semblent justifiées** on the face of it, their criticism seems justified; **une remarque en ~ pertinente** an apparently *ou* a seemingly relevant remark; **les gens sont rassurés, au moins en ~** people are reassured, at least they seem to be *ou* at least on the face of it; **ce problème n'est facile qu'en ~** this problem only appears to be easy; **ce n'est qu'en ~ qu'il est heureux** it's only on the surface *ou* outwardly that he's happy

apparent, e [apaʀɑ̃, ɑ̃t] ADJ **a** (= *visible*) [*appréhension, gêne*] obvious, noticeable; [*ruse*] obvious; **de façon ~e** visibly, conspicuously; **sans raison/cause ~e** without apparent *ou* obvious reason/cause; **plafond avec poutres ~es** ceiling with exposed beams; **coutures ~es** topstitched seams **b** (= *superficiel*) [*solidité, causes*] apparent (*épith*); **ces contradictions ne sont qu'~es** these are only outward *ou* surface discrepancies **c** (= *trompeur*) [*bonhomie, naïveté*] seeming, apparent; **sous son ~e gentillesse** beneath his kind-hearted façade

apparenté, e [apaʀɑ̃te] (*ptp de* **apparenter**) ADJ (= *de la même famille*) related; (= *semblable*) similar (**à** to); (*Pol*) **~ (au parti) socialiste** in alliance with the Socialists; **les libéraux et ~s** the Liberals and their electoral allies

apparentement [apaʀɑ̃tmɑ̃] NM (*Pol*) grouping of electoral lists (*in proportional representation system*)

apparenter (s') [apaʀɑ̃te] ▶ conjug 1 ◀ VPR ♦ **s'apparenter à** (*Pol*) to ally o.s. with (*in elections*); (*par mariage*) to marry into; (= *ressembler à*) to be similar to, have certain similarities to

appariement [apaʀimɑ̃] NM (*littér*) (= *assortiment*) matching; (= *assemblage*) pairing; (= *accouplement*) mating

apparier [apaʀje] ▶ conjug 7 ◀ VT (*littér*) (= *assortir*) to match; (= *coupler*) to pair; (= *accoupler*) to mate

appariteur [apaʀitœʀ] NM (*Univ*) ≈ porter (*Brit*), ≈ campus policeman (*US*); (*hum*) **~ musclé** strong-arm attendant (*hired at times of student unrest*)

apparition [apaʀisjɔ̃] NF **a** (= *manifestation*) [*étoile, symptôme, signe*] appearance; [*personne*] appearance, arrival; [*boutons, fièvre*] outbreak; **faire son ~** [*personne*] to make one's appearance, appear; [*symptômes*] to appear; [*fièvre*] to break out; **il n'a fait qu'une (courte** ou **brève) ~** (*à une réunion*) he only put in ou made a brief appearance; (*dans un film*) he only made a brief appearance, he made a cameo appearance; (*au générique*) **par ordre d'~ à l'écran** in order of appearance **b** (= *vision*) apparition; (= *fantôme*) apparition, spectre (*Brit*), specter (*US*); **avoir des ~s** to see ou have visions

apparoir [apaʀwaʀ] VB IMPERS (*frm* ou *hum*) **il appert (de ces résultats) que ...** it appears (from these results) that ...

appartement [apaʀtəmɑ̃] NM **a** [*maison, immeuble*] flat (*Brit*), apartment (*surtout US*); [*hôtel*] suite; **vivre dans un** ou **en ~** to live in a flat (*Brit*) ou apartment (*surtout US*) → **chien, plante b ~s** [*château*] apartments; **elle s'est retirée dans ses ~s** [*reine*] she retired to her apartments; (*hum*) she retired to her room ou chamber **c** (*＊: Can* = *pièce*) room

appartenance [apaʀtənɑ̃s] NF (*à une race, une famille, un ensemble*) membership (**à** of); (*à un parti*) adherence (**à** to), membership (**à** of); **leur sentiment d'~ à cette nation** their sense of belonging to the nation

appartenir [apaʀtəniʀ] ▸conjug 22◂ **1** **appartenir à** VT INDIR **a** (= *être la possession de*) to belong to; **ceci m'appartient** this is mine, this belongs to me; **la maison m'appartient en propre** I'm the sole owner of the house; **pour des raisons qui m'appartiennent** for reasons of my own ou which concern me (alone); **le choix ne m'appartient pas** it isn't for me to choose; **un médecin ne s'appartient pas** a doctor's time ou life is not his own **b** (= *faire partie de*) [+ *famille, race, parti*] to belong to, be a member of **2** VB IMPERS **il appartient/n'appartient pas au comité de décider si ...** it is for ou up to/not for ou not up to the committee to decide if ..., it is/is not the committee's responsibility to decide if ...

appas [apa] NMPL (*littér*) charms

appât [apa] NM (*Pêche*) bait; (*fig*) lure, bait; **mettre un ~ à l'hameçon** to bait one's hook; **l'~ du gain/d'une récompense** the lure of gain/a reward → **mordre**

appâter [apate] ▸conjug 1◂ VT [+ *poissons, gibier, personne*] to lure, entice; [+ *piège, hameçon*] to bait

appauvrir [apovʀiʀ] ▸conjug 2◂ **1** VT [+ *personne, sol, langue*] to impoverish; [+ *sang*] to make thin, weaken **2** **s'appauvrir** VPR [*personne, sol, pays*] to grow poorer, become (more) impoverished; [*langue*] to become impoverished; [*sang*] to become thin ou weak; [*race*] to degenerate

appauvrissement [apovʀismɑ̃] NM [*personne, sol, langue, pays*] impoverishment; [*sang*] thinning; [*race*] degeneration; **l'~ de la couche d'ozone** the depletion of the ozone layer; **l'~ culturel et intellectuel** cultural and intellectual decline

appeau (*pl* **appeaux**) [apo] NM (= *instrument*) bird call; (= *oiseau, fig*) decoy; **servir d'~ à qn** to act as a decoy for sb

appel [apɛl] **1** NM **a** (= *cri*) call; **accourir à l'~ de qn** to come running in answer to sb's call; **~ à l'aide** ou **au secours** call for help; **elle a entendu des ~s** ou **des cris d'~** she heard someone calling out, she heard cries; **à son ~, elle se retourna** she turned round when he called; (*Hist*) **l'Appel du 18 juin** *General de Gaulle's radio appeal to the French people to resist the Nazi occupation* **b** (= *sollicitation*) call; (*dans aéroport*) **dernier ~**

pour le vol AF 850 last call for flight AF 850; **~ à l'insurrection/aux armes/aux urnes** call to insurrection/to arms/to vote; **lancer un ~ au calme** to appeal ou call for calm, issue an appeal for calm; **à l'~ des syndicats ...** in response to the appeal of the trade unions ...; **manifestation à l'~ d'une organisation** demonstration called by an organization; **il me fit un ~ du regard** he gave me a meaningful glance; **c'était un ~ du pied** it was an indirect ou a veiled appeal; **il a fait un ~ du pied au chef de l'autre parti** he made covert advances to the leader of the other party; **faire un ~ de phares** to flash one's headlights ou one's high beams (*US*); **offre/prix d'~** introductory offer/price; **article** ou **produit d'~** loss leader **c** **faire ~ à** (= *invoquer*) to appeal to; (= *avoir recours à*) to call on, resort to; (*fig* = *nécessiter*) to require; **faire ~ au bon sens/à la générosité de qn** to appeal to sb's common sense/ generosity; **faire ~ à ses souvenirs** to call up one's memories; **il a dû faire ~ à tout son courage** he had to summon up ou muster all his courage; **faire ~ à l'armée** to call out the army; **on a dû faire ~ aux pompiers** they had to call the firemen; **ils ont fait ~ au président pour que ...** they appealed to ou called on the president to ...; **ce problème fait ~ à des connaissances qu'il n'a pas** this problem calls for ou requires knowledge he hasn't got **d** (= *voix*) call; **l'~ du devoir/de la religion** the call of duty/of religion; **l'~ de la raison/de sa conscience** the voice of reason/of one's conscience; **l'~ du large** the call of the sea **e** (= *vérification de présence*) (*Scol*) register, registration; (*Mil*) roll call; **faire l'~** (*Scol*) to call the register (*Brit*), take attendance (*US*); (*Mil*) to call the roll; **faire l'~ nominal des candidats** to call out the candidates' names; **absent/présent à l'~** (*Scol*) absent/present (for the register ou at registration); (*Mil*) absent/present at roll call; (*Jur*) **l'~ des causes** the reading of the roll of cases (*to be heard*) → **cahier, manquer, numéro f** (*Jur* = *recours*) appeal (**contre** against, from); **faire ~ d'un jugement** to appeal against a judgment; **faire ~** to appeal, lodge an appeal; **juger en ~/sans ~** to judge on appeal/ without appeal; (*fig*) **sans ~** [*décision*] final; [*décider*] irrevocably → **cour g** (*Mil* = *mobilisation*) call-up; **~ de la classe 1995** 1995 call-up, call-up of the class of 1995 → **devancer h** (*Téléc*) **~ (téléphonique)** (telephone ou phone) call; **un poste avec signal d'~** a phone with call waiting function → **numéro i** (*Cartes*) signal (**à** for); **faire un ~ à pique** to signal for a spade **j** (*Athlétisme* = *élan*) take-off; **pied d'~** take-off foot **k** (*Ordin*) call

2 COMP ▸ **appel d'air** in-draught (*Brit*), in-draft (*US*), intake of air; **ça fait ~ d'air** there's a draught (*Brit*) ou draft (*US*) ▸ **appel en couverture** (*Bourse*) request for cover ▸ **appel de fonds** call for capital; **faire un ~ de fonds** to call up capital ▸ **appel à maxima** *appeal by prosecution against the harshness of a sentence* ▸ **appel à minima** *appeal by prosecution against the leniency of a sentence* ▸ **appel de note** (*Typo*) footnote reference, reference mark ▸ **appel d'offres** (*Comm*) invitation to tender ou bid (*US*) ▸ **appel au peuple** appeal ou call to the people

appelant, e [ap(ə)lɑ̃, ɑ̃t] (*Jur*) **1** ADJ **partie ~e** appellant **2** NM,F appellant

appelé [ap(ə)le] NM (*Mil*) conscript, draftee (*US*), selectee (*US*); (*Rel, fig*) **le nom de qn** to call out sb's name; **il y a beaucoup d'~s et peu d'élus** many are called but few are chosen

▾ **appeler** [ap(ə)le] ▸conjug 4◂ **1** VT **a** (= *interpeller*) to call; **~ qn** to call out sb's name; **~ qn à l'aide** ou **au secours** to call to sb for help; **~ qn (d'un**

geste) de la main to beckon (to) sb **b** (*Téléc*) [+ *personne*] phone (up), call (up), to ring (up) (*Brit*); [+ *numéro*] to dial, call, phone **c** (= *faire venir*) (*gén*) to call, summon; [+ *médecin, taxi, police*] to call, send for; [+ *pompiers*] to call out; [+ *ascenseur*] to call; **~ les fidèles à la prière** to summon ou call the faithful to prayer; (*Mil*) **~ une classe (sous les drapeaux)** to call up a class (of recruits); (*frm* ou *hum*) **Dieu/la République vous appelle** God/the Republic is calling you; (*hum*) **le devoir m'appelle** duty calls; **le patron l'a fait ~** the boss sent for him; **il a été appelé auprès de sa mère malade** he was called ou summoned to his sick mother's side; **~ la colère du ciel sur qn** to call down the wrath of heaven upon sb; **j'appelle la bénédiction de Dieu sur vous** may God bless you **d** (*Jur*) **~ une cause** to call (out) a case; **en attendant que notre cause soit appelée** waiting for our case to come up ou be called; **~ qn en justice** ou **à comparaître** to summon sb before the court **e** (= *nommer*) to call; **~ qn par son prénom** to call ou address sb by their first name; **~ qn Monsieur/Madame** to call sb Sir/Madam; **~ les choses par leur nom** to call things by their rightful name; **~ un chat un chat** to call a spade a spade; **voilà ce que j'appelle écrire !** now that's what I call writing!; **il va se faire ~ Arthur !＊** he's going to get a dressing down* ou a rollicking* (*Brit*) **f** (= *désigner*) **~ qn à** [+ *poste*] to appoint ou assign sb to; **être appelé à de hautes/ nouvelles fonctions** to be assigned important/new duties; **sa nouvelle fonction l'appelle à jouer un rôle important** his new duties will require him to play an important role; **être appelé à un brillant avenir** to be destined for a brilliant future; **la méthode est appelée à se généraliser** the method looks likely ou set to become widely used **g** (= *réclamer*) [*situation, conduite*] to call for, demand; **j'appelle votre attention sur ce problème** I call your attention to this problem; **les affaires l'appellent à Lyon** he has to go to Lyons on business **h** (= *entraîner*) **une lâcheté en appelle une autre** one act of cowardice leads to ou begets (*frm*) another; **ceci appelle une réflexion** ou **une remarque** this calls for comment **i** (*Cartes*) [+ *carte*] to call for **j** (*Ordin*) [+ *fichier*] to call (up)

2 VI **a** (= *crier*) **~ à l'aide** ou **au secours** to call for help; **elle appelait, personne ne venait** she called (out) but nobody came **b** **en ~ à** to appeal to; **en ~ de** to appeal against; **j'en appelle à votre bon sens** I appeal to your common sense

3 **s'appeler** VPR **a** (= *être nommé*) to be called; **il s'appelle Paul** his name is Paul, he's called Paul; **comment s'appelle cet oiseau ?** what's the name of this bird?, what's this bird called?; **comment ça s'appelle en français ?** what's that (called) in French?, what do you call that in French?; **voilà ce qui s'appelle une gaffe/être à l'heure !** now that's what's called a blunder/being on time!; **je te prête ce livre, mais il s'appelle Reviens !＊** I'll lend you this book but I want it back! **b** [*personnes*] to call to each other; **on s'appelle ce soir (au téléphone)** you ring me or I'll ring you this evening; **nous nous appelons par nos prénoms** we're on first-name terms, we call each other by our first names

appellatif [apelatif] ADJ M, NM (*Ling*) **(nom) ~** appellative

appellation [apelasjɔ̃] NF designation, appellation; (*littér* = *mot*) term, name; **~ d'origine** label of origin; **(d'origine) contrôlée** appellation (d'origine) contrôlée, *label guaranteeing the origin of wine and cheese*; **vin d'~** appellation contrôlée wine, wine carrying a guarantee of origin

appendice [apɛ̃dis] NM [*livre*] appendix; (*Anat*) (*gén*) appendage, appendix; [*intestin*] **l'~** the appendix; (*hum*) **~ nasal** proboscis (*hum*)

appendicectomie [apɛ̃disɛktɔmi] NF appendectomy

appendicite [apɛ̃disit] NF appendicitis; **faire de l'~ chronique** to have a grumbling appendix; **avoir une crise d'~** to have appendicitis; **se faire opérer de l'~** to have one's appendix removed

appendiculaire [apɛ̃dikylɛʀ] 1 ADJ appendicular 2 **appendiculaires** NMPL **les ~s** appendicularians, the Appendicularia (*SPÉC*)

appentis [apɑ̃ti] NM (= *bâtiment*) lean-to; (= *auvent*) penthouse (roof), sloping roof

appert [apɛʀ] → **apparoir**

appertisé, e [apɛʀtize] ADJ [*denrée*] sterilized (in a hermetic container)

appesantir [apəzɑ̃tiʀ] ▸ conjug 2 ◂ 1 VT [+ *tête, paupières*] to weigh down; [+ *objet*] to make heavier; [+ *gestes, pas*] to slow (down); [+ *esprit*] to dull; (*littér*) **~ son bras** *ou* **autorité sur** to strengthen one's authority over 2 **s'appesantir** VPR [*tête*] to grow heavier; [*gestes, pas*] to become slower; [*esprit*] to grow duller; [*autorité*] to grow stronger; **s'~ sur un sujet/des détails** to dwell at length on a subject/on details; **inutile de s'~** no need to dwell on that

appesantissement [apəzɑ̃tismɑ̃] NM [*démarche*] heaviness; [*esprit*] dullness; [*autorité*] strengthening

appétence [apetɑ̃s] NF appetence; **avoir de l'~ pour** to have a partiality for, be partial to

appétissant, e [apetisɑ̃, ɑ̃t] ADJ [*nourriture*] appetizing, mouth-watering; [*personne*] delectable; **peu ~** unappetizing

appétit [apeti] NM **a** (*pour la nourriture*) appetite; **avoir de l'~** *ou* **avoir bon ~** *ou* **avoir un solide ~** to have a good *ou* hearty appetite; **bon ~ !** (*hôte*) bon appétit!; (*serveur*) enjoy your meal!, enjoy! (*US*); **perdre l'~** to lose one's appetite; **il n'a pas d'~** he's got no appetite; **ouvrir l'~ de qn ◊ donner de l'~ à qn ◊ mettre qn en ~** to give sb an appetite; (*fig*) **ce premier essai m'a mis en ~** this first attempt has given me a taste for it *ou* has whetted my appetite; **avoir un ~ d'oiseau/d'ogre** to eat like a bird/horse; **manger avec ~** *ou* **de bon ~** to eat heartily *ou* with appetite; **manger sans ~** to eat without appetite; **l'~ vient en mangeant** (*lit*) appetite comes with eating; (*fig*) you get a taste for it **b** (= *désir*) appetite (**de** for); **~ sexuel** sexual appetite

applaudimètre [aplodimɛtʀ] NM applause meter, clapometer* (*Brit*); **elle a gagné à l'~** she got the loudest *ou* warmest applause

applaudir [aplodiʀ] ▸ conjug 2 ◂ 1 VT to applaud, clap; (= *approuver*) to applaud, commend; **applaudissons notre sympathique gagnant** let's give the winner a big hand 2 VI to applaud, clap; **~ à tout rompre** to bring the house down 3 **applaudir à** VT INDIR (*littér* = *approuver*) [+ *initiative*] to applaud, commend; **~ des deux mains à qch** to approve heartily of sth, commend sth warmly 4 **s'applaudir** VPR (= *se réjouir*) **je m'applaudis de n'y être pas allé !** I'm congratulating myself *ou* patting myself on the back for not having gone!

applaudissement [aplodismɑ̃] NM **a** (= *acclamations*) **~s** applause (*NonC*), clapping (*NonC*); **des ~s nourris éclatèrent** loud applause *ou* clapping broke out; **sortir sous les ~s** to go off to great applause; **un tonnerre d'~s** thunderous applause **b** (*littér = approbation*) approbation, commendation (**à** of)

applicabilité [aplikabilite] NF applicability

applicable [aplikabl] ADJ applicable; [*loi*] **être ~ à** to apply to, be applicable to; **ce règlement**

est difficilement ~ this rule is difficult to apply

applicateur [aplikatœʀ] 1 ADJ M applicator (*épith*) 2 NM (= *dispositif*) applicator

application [aplikasjɔ̃] NF **a** (= *pose*) [*enduit, peinture, pommade*] application; **renouveler l'~ tous les jours** apply every day
b (= *mise en pratique: gén*) application; [*peine*] enforcement; [*règlement, décision*] implementation; [*loi*] enforcement, application; [*remède*] administration; [*recette*] use; **mettre en ~** [+ *décision*] to put into practice, implement; [+ *loi*] to enforce, apply; [+ *théorie*] to put into practice, apply; **mise en ~** [*décision*] implementation; [*loi*] enforcement, application; [*théorie*] application; **mesures prises en ~ de la loi** measures taken to enforce *ou* apply the law; **entrer en ~** to come into force; **champ d'~** area of application
c **~s** [*théorie, méthode*] applications; **les ~s de cette théorie** the (possible) applications of the theory
d (= *attention*) application; **~ à qch** application to sth; **travailler avec ~** to work diligently, apply o.s.; **son ~ à faire qch** the zeal with which he does sth
e (*Couture*) appliqué (work); **~ de dentelles** appliqué lace; **~ de velours** velvet appliqué
f (*Math*) mapping
g (*Ordin*) application (program)

applique [aplik] NF (= *lampe*) wall light *ou* lamp; (*Couture*) appliqué

appliqué, e [aplike] (*ptp de appliquer*) ADJ **a** [*personne*] industrious, assiduous; [*écriture*] careful; **bien ~** [*baiser*] firm; [*coup*] well-aimed **b** [*linguistique, mathématiques*] applied

appliquer [aplike] ▸ conjug 1 ◂ 1 VT **a** (= *poser*) [+ *peinture, revêtement, cataplasme*] to apply (**sur** to); **~ une échelle sur** *ou* **contre un mur** to put *ou* lean a ladder against a wall; **~ son oreille sur** *ou* **à une porte** to put one's ear to a door
b (= *mettre en pratique: gén*) to apply; [+ *peine*] to enforce; [+ *règlement, décision*] to implement, put into practice; [+ *loi*] to enforce, apply; [+ *remède*] to administer; [+ *recette*] to use; **~ un traitement à une maladie** to apply a treatment to an illness
c (= *consacrer*) **~ son esprit à l'étude** to apply one's mind to study; **~ tous ses soins à faire qch** to put all one's efforts into doing sth
d (= *donner*) [+ *gifle, châtiment*] to give; [+ *qualificatif*] to use; **~ un baiser/sobriquet à qn** to give sb a kiss/nickname; **je lui ai appliqué ma main sur la figure** I struck *ou* slapped him across the face, I struck *ou* slapped his face
2 **s'appliquer** VPR **a** (= *coïncider*) **s'~ sur** to fit over; **le calque s'applique exactement sur son modèle** the tracing fits exactly over its model
b (= *correspondre*) **s'~ à** to apply to; **cette remarque ne s'applique pas à vous** this remark doesn't apply to you
c (= *s'acharner*) **s'~ à faire qch** to make every effort to do sth; **s'~ à l'étude de** to apply o.s. to the study of; **élève qui s'applique** pupil who applies himself

appog(g)iature [apɔ(d)ʒjatyʀ] NF appoggiatura

appoint [apwɛ̃] NM **a** (= *monnaie*) **l'~** the right *ou* exact money *ou* change; **faire l'~** to give the right *ou* exact money *ou* change; (*sur pancarte*) **« prière de faire l'~ »** "exact change only please" **b** (= *complément*) (extra) contribution, (extra) help; **salaire d'~** secondary *ou* extra income; **travail d'~** second job; **radiateur d'~** back-up *ou* extra heater

appointements [apwɛ̃tmɑ̃] NMPL salary

appointer [apwɛ̃te] ▸ conjug 1 ◂ VT to pay a salary to; **être appointé à l'année/au mois** to be paid yearly/monthly

appontage [apɔ̃taʒ] NM landing (*on an aircraft carrier*)

appontement [apɔ̃tmɑ̃] NM landing stage, wharf

apponter [apɔ̃te] ▸ conjug 1 ◂ VI to land (*on an aircraft carrier*)

apport [apɔʀ] NM **a** (= *approvisionnement*) [*capitaux*] contribution, supply; [*chaleur, air frais, eau potable*] supply; **l'~ de devises par le tourisme** the currency that tourism brings in; **leur ~ financier** their financial contribution; (*Fin*) **~ personnel** personal capital contribution, ≈ deposit (*when buying a house*); **l'~ d'alluvions d'une rivière** the alluvia brought *ou* carried down by a river; **l'~ de** *ou* **en vitamines d'un aliment** the vitamins provided by *ou* the vitamin content of a food; **~ calorique** [*aliment*] calorie content; **l'~ calorique quotidien** the daily calorie intake **b** (= *contribution*) contribution; **l'~ de notre civilisation à l'humanité** our civilization's contribution to humanity **c** (*Jur*) **~s** property; **~s en communauté** goods contributed by man and wife to the joint estate; (*Fin*) **~s en société** capital invested

apporter [apɔʀte] ▸ conjug 1 ◂ VT **a** [+ *objet*] to bring; **apporte-le-moi** bring it to me; **apporte-le-lui** take it to him; **apporte-le en montant** bring it up with you; **apporte-le en venant** bring it with you (when you come), bring it along; **qui a apporté toute cette boue ?** who brought in all this mud?; **le vent d'ouest nous apporte toutes les fumées d'usine** the west wind blows *ou* carries all the factory fumes our way; **vent qui apporte la pluie** wind that brings rain
b [+ *satisfaction, repos, soulagement*] to bring, give; [+ *ennuis, argent, nouvelles*] to bring; [+ *preuve, solution*] to supply, provide; **~ sa contribution à qch** to make one's contribution to sth; **~ des modifications à qch** [*ingénieur*] to make *ou* introduce changes in sth; [*progrès*] to bring about changes in sth; **~ du soin à qch/à faire qch** to exercise care in sth/in doing sth; **~ de l'attention à qch/à faire qch** to bring one's attention to bear on sth/on doing sth; **elle y a apporté toute son énergie** she put all her energy into it; **son livre n'apporte rien de nouveau** his book contributes *ou* says nothing new; **leur enseignement m'a beaucoup apporté** I got a lot out of their teaching; **s'~ beaucoup** (*couple*) to get a lot out of being together

apposer [apoze] ▸ conjug 1 ◂ VT (*frm*) [+ *sceau, timbre, plaque*] to affix; [+ *signature*] to append (*frm*); (*Jur*) [+ *clause*] to insert; (*Jur*) **~ les scellés** to affix the seals (*to prevent unlawful entry*); **~ une mention sur un produit** to display consumer information on a product

apposition [apozisjɔ̃] NF **a** (*Gram*) apposition; **en ~** in apposition **b** [*sceau, timbre, plaque, scellés*] affixing; [*signature*] appending (*frm*); (*Jur*) [*clause*] insertion

appréciable [apresjabl] ADJ **a** (= *évaluable*) appreciable, noticeable **b** (= *assez important*) appreciable; **un nombre ~ de gens** a good many *ou* a good few people, an appreciable number of people **c** (= *agréable*) [*qualité, situation*] nice, pleasant; **c'est ~ de pouvoir se lever tard** it's nice to be able to get up late

appréciateur, -trice [apresjatœʀ, tʀis] NM,F judge, appreciator

appréciatif, -ive [apresjatif, iv] ADJ (= *estimatif*) appraising, evaluative; (= *admiratif*) appreciative → **état**

appréciation [apresjasjɔ̃] NF **a** (= *évaluation*) [*distance, importance*] estimation, assessment; (= *expertise*) [*objet*] valuation; (*Assurances*) **~ des risques** estimation of risks, risk assessment **b** (= *jugement*) **soumettre qch à l'~ de qn** to ask for sb's assessment of sth; **je laisse cela à votre ~** I leave it to you to judge for yourself; **commettre une erreur d'~** to be mistaken in one's assessment; **les ~s du professeur sur un élève** the teacher's assessment of a pupil; (*sur livret*) **« ~ du professeur »** "teacher's comments *ou* remarks" c (= *augmentation*) [*monnaie*] appreciation

▼ **apprécier** [apʀesje] ▸conjug 7◂ 1 VT a (= *évaluer*) [+ *distance, importance*] to estimate, assess; (= *expertiser*) [+ *objet*] to value, assess the value of
b (= *discerner*) [+ *nuance*] to perceive, appreciate
c (= *aimer*) [+ *qualité, repas*] to appreciate; ~ qn (= *le trouver sympathique*) to like sb; (= *l'estimer*) to appreciate sb; un mets très apprécié a much appreciated dish, a highly-rated dish; son discours n'a pas été apprécié par la droite his speech was not appreciated by the right wing; je n'apprécie guère votre attitude I don't like your attitude; il n'a pas apprécié ! he didn't appreciate that!, he didn't much care for that!
2 **s'apprécier** VPR a (= *s'estimer*) to like each other; ils s'apprécient beaucoup they really like each other
b (*Fin*) to rise, appreciate; le franc s'est nettement apprécié par rapport au mark the franc has risen *ou* appreciated sharply against the mark

appréhender [apʀeɑ̃de] ▸conjug 1◂ VT a (= *arrêter*) to apprehend b (= *redouter*) to dread; ~ de (faire) qch to dread (doing) sth; ~ que ... to fear that ... c (= *comprendre*) [+ *situation*] to apprehend, grasp

appréhensif, -ive [apʀeɑ̃sif, iv] ADJ apprehensive, fearful (de of)

appréhension [apʀeɑ̃sjɔ̃] NF a (= *crainte*) apprehension, anxiety; envisager qch avec ~ to be apprehensive *ou* anxious about sth, dread sth; avoir de l'~ to be apprehensive; son ~ de l'examen/de l'avenir his apprehension about the exam/the future b (= *compréhension*) [*situation, réalité*] apprehension

apprenant, e [apʀənɑ̃, ɑ̃t] NM,F learner

apprendre [apʀɑ̃dʀ] ▸conjug 58◂ VT a [+ *leçon, métier*] to learn; ~ que/à lire/à nager to learn that/(how) to read/(how) to swim; ~ à se servir de qch to learn (how) to use sth; ~ à connaître qn to get to know sb; il apprend vite he's a quick learner, he learns quickly; l'espagnol s'apprend vite *ou* facilement Spanish is easy to learn → cœur
b [+ *nouvelle*] to hear, learn; [+ *événement, fait*] to hear of, learn of; [+ *secret*] to be told (de qn by sb); j'ai appris hier que ... I heard *ou* learnt *ou* it came to my knowledge (*frm*) yesterday that ...; j'ai appris son arrivée par des amis/par la radio I heard of *ou* learnt of his arrival through friends/on the radio; apprenez que je ne me laisserai pas faire ! be warned that *ou* let me make it quite clear that I won't be trifled with!
c (= *annoncer*) ~ qch à qn to tell sb (of) sth; il m'a appris la nouvelle he told me the news; il m'apprend à l'instant sa démission/qu'il va partir he has just told me of his resignation/ that he's going to leave; vous ne m'apprenez rien ! you haven't told me anything new! *ou* anything I don't know already!, that's no news to me!
d (= *enseigner*) ~ qch à qn to teach sb sth, teach sth to sb; ~ à qn à faire to teach sb (how) to do; il a appris à son chien à obéir/ qu'il doit obéir he taught his dog to obey/ that he must obey; je vais lui ~ à vivre I'll teach him a thing or two, I'll straighten *ou* sort (*Brit*) him out; ça lui apprendra (à vivre) ! that'll teach him (a lesson)!; on n'apprend pas à un vieux singe à faire des grimaces don't teach your grandmother to suck eggs

apprenti, e [apʀɑ̃ti] NM,F [*métier*] apprentice; (= *débutant*) novice, beginner; ~ conducteur learner driver (*Brit*), student driver (*US*); ~ mécanicien apprentice *ou* trainee mechanic, mechanic's apprentice; (*péj*) ~ philosophe novice philosopher; ~ sorcier sorcerer's apprentice;

jouer à l'~ sorcier *ou* aux ~s sorciers to play God

apprentissage [apʀɑ̃tisaʒ] NM (= *formation*) apprenticeship; (= *de l'anglais/de la lecture/ de l'amour* learning English/(how) to read/ about love; l'~ de la patience learning to be patient, learning patience; mettre qn en ~ to apprentice sb (chez to); être en ~ to be apprenticed *ou* an apprentice (chez to); faire son ~ to serve one's apprenticeship, do one's training (chez with); faire son ~ de mécanicien to serve one's apprenticeship as a mechanic; école *ou* centre d'~ training school; faire l'~ de [+ *douleur, vie active*] to have one's first experience of, be initiated into; le pays fait le difficile ~ de la démocratie the country is taking its first difficult steps in democracy
→ contrat, taxe

apprêt [apʀɛ] NM a (= *opération*) [*cuir, tissu*] dressing; [*papier*] finishing; (*Peinture*) sizing, priming b (= *substance*) [*cuir, tissu*] dressing; (= *peinture*) size, primer; couche d'~ coat of primer c (= *affectation*) sans ~ unaffected; elle est d'une beauté sans ~ she has a kind of natural beauty

apprêtage [apʀɛtaʒ] NM [*cuir, tissu*] dressing; [*papier*] finishing; [*peinture*] sizing, priming

apprêté, e [apʀɛte] (*ptp de* **apprêter**) ADJ (= *affecté*) [*manière, style*] affected

apprêter [apʀɛte] ▸conjug 1◂ 1 VT a [+ *nourriture*] to prepare, get ready; (= *habiller*) ~ un enfant/une mariée to get a child/bride ready, dress a child/bride b (*Tech*) [+ *peau, papier, tissu*] to dress, finish; (*Peinture*) to size, prime 2 **s'apprêter** VPR a s'~ à qch/à faire qch (= *se préparer*) to get ready for sth/to do sth, prepare (o.s.) for sth/to do sth; nous nous apprêtions à partir we were getting ready *ou* preparing to leave; je m'apprêtais à le dire I was just about to say so b (= *faire sa toilette*) to dress o.s., prepare o.s.

apprivoisable [apʀivwazabl] ADJ tameable; difficilement ~ difficult to tame

apprivoisé, e [apʀivwaze] (*ptp de* **apprivoiser**) ADJ tame, tamed

apprivoisement [apʀivwazmɑ̃] NM (= *action*) taming; (= *état*) tameness

apprivoiser [apʀivwaze] ▸conjug 1◂ 1 VT [+ *animal, personne difficile*] to tame; [+ *personne timide*] to bring out of his (*ou* her) shell; je commence tout juste à ~ l'ordinateur I'm just beginning to get to grips with the computer 2 **s'apprivoiser** VPR [*animal*] to become tame; [*personne difficile*] to become easier to get on with; [*personne timide*] to come out of one's shell

approbateur, -trice [apʀɔbatœʀ, tʀis] 1 ADJ approving; signe de tête ~ nod of approval, approving nod 2 NM,F (*littér*) approver

approbatif, -ive [apʀɔbatif, iv] ADJ = approbateur, -trice

▼ **approbation** [apʀɔbasjɔ̃] NF (= *jugement favorable*) approval, approbation; (= *acceptation*) approval; donner son ~ à un projet to give one's approval to a project; ce livre a rencontré l'~ du grand public this book has been well received by the public; conduite/ travail digne d'~ commendable behaviour/ work; (*Fin*) ~ des comptes approval of the accounts

approchable [apʀɔʃabl] ADJ [*chose*] accessible; [*personne*] approachable; le ministre est difficilement ~ the minister is rather inaccessible *ou* is not very accessible

approchant, e [apʀɔʃɑ̃, ɑ̃t] ADJ [*style, genre*] similar (de to); [*résultat*] close (de to); quelque chose d'~ something like that, something similar; rien d'~ nothing like that

approche [apʀɔʃ] NF a (= *arrivée*) [*personne, véhicule, événement*] approach; à mon ~ il sourit he smiled as I drew near *ou* approached; à

l'~ de l'hiver at the approach of winter, as winter drew near *ou* approached; (*dans une gare*) « (train) à l'~ » "train now approaching"; s'enfuir à l'~ du danger to flee at the first sign of danger; à l'~ *ou* aux ~s de la cinquantaine, il ... as he neared *ou* approached fifty, he ..., as fifty drew nearer, he ... → lunette, travail
b (= *abord*) être d'~ difficile/aisée [*personne*] to be unapproachable/approachable; [*lieu*] to be inaccessible/(easily) accessible, be difficult/ easy of access; [*musique, auteur*] to be difficult/easy to understand; manœuvres *ou* travaux d'~ (*Mil*) approaches, saps; (*fig*) manoeuvres, manoeuvrings
c (= *parages*) les ~s de la ville the area (immediately) surrounding the town; les ~s du port/de l'île sont dangereuses the waters around the port/island are dangerous; aux ~s de la ville elle pensa ... as she neared *ou* approached the town she thought ...
d (= *façon d'envisager*) approach; l'~ de ce problème the approach to this problem; ce n'est qu'une ~ sommaire de la question this is only a brief introduction to *ou* a cursory glance at the question
e (*Typo*) (= *espace*) spacing; (= *faute*) spacing error; (= *signe*) close-up mark
f (*Aviat*) nous sommes en ~ finale we are on our final approach
g (*Golf*) approach; coup d'~ approach shot

approché, e [apʀɔʃe] (*ptp de* **approcher**) ADJ [*résultat, idée*] approximate

approcher [apʀɔʃe] ▸conjug 1◂ 1 VT a [+ *objet*] to put near, move near; ~ une table d'une fenêtre to move a table near to a window; approche ta chaise draw *ou* bring up your chair, bring your chair nearer *ou* closer; il approcha les deux chaises l'une de l'autre he moved the two chairs closer together; il approcha le verre de ses lèvres he lifted *ou* raised the glass to his lips; elle approcha son visage du sien she moved her face near to his
b [+ *personne*] (= *aller*) to go near, approach; (= *venir*) to come near, approach; ne l'approchez pas ! don't go near him!, keep away from him!
c (= *côtoyer*) be in contact with; (= *entrer en contact avec*) to approach
2 VI [*date, saison*] to approach, draw near; [*personne, orage*] to approach, come nearer; [*nuit, jour*] to approach, draw on; le jour approche où ...; he was near when ...; approchez, approchez ! come closer!; approche que je t'examine come here and let me look at you
3 **approcher de** VT INDIR [+ *lieu*] to approach, get closer to; nous approchons du but we're getting there; ~ de la perfection [*appareil*] to come close to perfection; [*personne*] to near perfection; il approche de la cinquantaine he's getting on for (*Brit*) *ou* going on (*US*) *ou* approaching fifty; devoir qui approche de la moyenne exercise that is just below average; l'aiguille du compteur approchait du 80 the needle on the speedometer was approaching *ou* nearing 80
4 **s'approcher** VPR (= *venir*) to come near, approach; (= *aller*) to go near, approach; il s'est approché pour me parler he came up to speak to me; l'enfant s'approcha de moi the child came up to me; ne t'approche pas de moi don't come near me; s'~ du micro (*venir*) to come up to the mike; (*se rapprocher*) to get closer *ou* nearer to the mike; approche-toi ! come here!; approchez-vous du feu go and sit (*ou* stand) near the fire; s'~ de la réalité to come near to reality

approfondi, e [apʀɔfɔ̃di] (*ptp de* **approfondir**) ADJ [*connaissances, étude*] thorough, detailed; [*débat*] in-depth

approfondir [apʀɔfɔ̃diʀ] ▸conjug 2◂ VT a [+ *canal, puits*] to deepen, make deeper

---

➤ GRAMMAIRE ACTIVE: **apprécier** 34.2, 34.3　　**approbation** 40.2

b [+ *question, étude*] to go (deeper) into; [+ *connaissances*] to deepen, increase; **il vaut mieux ne pas ~ le sujet** it's better not to go into the matter too closely; **sans ~** superficially

approfondissement [apʀɔfɔ̃dismɑ̃] NM [*canal, puits*] deepening (*NonC*); [*connaissances*] deepening (*NonC*), increasing (*NonC*); **l'~ de cette étude serait souhaitable** it would be a good idea to take this study further

appropriation [apʀɔpʀijasjɔ̃] NF **a** (*Jur*) appropriation **b** (= *adaptation*) suitability, appropriateness (**à** to)

approprié, e [apʀɔpʀije] (*ptp de* **approprier**) ADJ [*réponse, méthode, remède*] appropriate, suitable; [*place*] proper, right, appropriate; **il faut des remèdes ~s au mal** we need remedies that are suited *ou* appropriate to the evil; **fournir une réponse ~e à une question** to provide an apt *ou* a suitable *ou* an appropriate reply to a question

approprier [apʀɔpʀije] ▸ conjug 7 ◂ **1** VT (= *adapter*) to suit, fit, adapt (**à** to); **~ son style à l'auditoire** to suit one's style to one's audience, adapt one's style to (suit) one's audience **2** **s'approprier** VPR **a** (= *s'adjuger*) [+ *bien*] to appropriate; [+ *pouvoir, droit, propriété, découverte*] to take over, appropriate **b** (= *s'adapter à*) **s'~ à** to be appropriate to, fit, suit

▼ **approuver** [apʀuve] ▸ conjug 1 ◂ VT (= *être d'accord avec*) [+ *attitude*] to approve of; **il a démissionné et je l'approuve** he resigned, and I agree with him *ou* approve (of his doing so); **on a besoin de se sentir approuvé** one needs to feel the approval of others; **je n'approuve pas qu'il parte maintenant** I don't approve of his leaving now **b** (= *avaliser*) [+ *comptes, médicament, procès-verbal, nomination*] to approve; [+ *projet de loi*] to approve, pass; [+ *contrat*] to ratify → **lu**

approvisionnement [apʀɔvizjɔnmɑ̃] NM (= *action*) supplying (**en, de** of); (= *réserves*) **~s** supplies, provisions, stock; **l'~ en légumes de la ville** supplying the town with vegetables, (the) supplying (of) vegetables to the town; **il avait tout un ~ de cigarettes** he was well stocked with cigarettes, he had a large stock of cigarettes; (*Écon*) **~s sauvages** panic buying

approvisionner [apʀɔvizjɔne] ▸ conjug 1 ◂ **1** VT [+ *magasin, commerçant*] to supply (**en, de** with); [+ *compte bancaire*] to pay *ou* put money into; [+ *fusil*] to load; **ils sont bien approvisionnés en fruits** they are well supplied *ou* stocked with fruit **2** **s'approvisionner** VPR to stock up (**en** with), lay in supplies (**en** of); **s'~ en bois** to stock up with wood, get supplies of wood; **je m'approvisionne au supermarché** I shop at the supermarket

approvisionneur, -euse [apʀɔvizjɔnœʀ, øz] NM,F supplier

approximatif, -ive [apʀɔksimatif, iv] ADJ [*calcul, évaluation, traduction*] rough; [*nombre, prix*] approximate; [*termes*] vague; **parler un français ~** to speak broken French

approximation [apʀɔksimasjɔ̃] NF (*gén*) approximation, (rough) estimate; (*Math*) approximation; **par ~s successives** by trial and error

approximativement [apʀɔksimativmɑ̃] ADV [*calculer, évaluer*] roughly; [*compter*] approximately

appt (ABRÉV = **appartement**) apt

appui [apɥi] **1** NM **a** (*lit, fig*) support; (*Alpinisme*) press hold; **prendre ~ sur** [*personne*] to lean on; (*du pied*) to stand on; [*objet*] to rest on; **son pied trouva un ~** he found a foothold; **avoir besoin d'~** to need (some) support; **trouver un ~ auprès de lui** I turned to him for support; **avoir l'~ de qn** to have sb's support *ou* backing; **il a des ~s au ministère** he has connections in the ministry

b (*Mus*) [*voix*] placing; (*Poésie*) **consonne d'~** supporting consonant; **voyelle d'~** support vowel

c **à l'~** in support of this, to back this up; **avec preuves à l'~** with evidence to prove it; **il m'a expliqué comment faire avec démonstration à l'~** he told me how to do it and backed this up with a demonstration; **à l'~ de son témoignage** in support of his evidence, to back up his evidence

2 COMP ▸ **appui aérien** air support ▸ **appui de fenêtre** window ledge ▸ **appui financier** financial support *ou* backing ▸ **appui logistique** logistic backup *ou* support ▸ **appui tactique** tactical support

appuie-bras [apɥibʀa] NM INV armrest

appuie-main (*pl* **appuie-main(s)**) [apɥimɛ̃] NM maulstick

appuie-tête (*pl* **appuie-tête(s)**) [apɥitɛt] NM [*voiture, fauteuil de dentiste*] headrest, head restraint; [*fauteuil*] antimacassar

appuyé, e [apɥije] (*ptp de* **appuyer**) ADJ (= *insistant*) [*regard*] fixed, intent; [*geste*] emphatic; (= *excessif*) [*politesse*] overdone; **il a rendu un hommage ~ à son collègue** he paid a glowing tribute to his colleague

▼ **appuyer** [apɥije] ▸ conjug 8 ◂ **1** VT **a** (= *poser*) [+ *objet, coudes, front*] to lean (**contre** against, **sur** on); **~ une échelle contre un mur** to lean *ou* rest a ladder against a wall, prop a ladder up against a wall; **~ sa main sur l'épaule de qn** to rest one's hand on sb's shoulder

b (= *presser*) to press; **il dut ~ son genou sur la valise pour la fermer** he had to press *ou* push the suitcase down with his knee to close it; **appuie ton doigt sur le pansement** put *ou* press your finger on the dressing **c** (= *étayer*) **~ un mur par qch** to support *ou* prop up a wall with sth

d (= *soutenir*) [+ *personne, candidature, politique*] to support, back (up); **il a appuyé sa thèse de documents convaincants** he backed up *ou* supported his thesis with convincing documents; **~ la demande de qn** to support sb's request

e (*Mil*) [+ *attaque*] to back up; **l'offensive sera appuyée par l'aviation** the offensive will be backed up from the air *ou* given air support

2 VI **a** (= *presser sur*) **~ sur** [+ *bouton*] to press, push; [+ *frein*] to apply, put one's foot on; [+ *pédales*] to press down on; [+ *levier*] to press (down); [+ *gâchette*] to press, pull, squeeze; (*Aut*) **~ sur le champignon*** to step on the gas*, put one's foot down (*Brit*)

b (= *reposer sur*) **~ sur** to rest on; **la voûte appuie sur des colonnes** the vault rests on columns *ou* is supported by columns

c (= *insister sur*) **~ sur** [+ *mot, argument, syllabe*] to stress, emphasize; (*Mus*) [+ *note*] to accentuate, accent; **n'appuyez pas trop** don't press the point; **~ sur la chanterelle** to harp on

d (= *se diriger*) **~ sur la droite** *ou* **à droite** to bear (to the) right

3 **s'appuyer** VPR **a** (= *s'accoter*) **s'~ sur/contre** to lean on/against; **appuie-toi à mon bras** lean on my arm

b (*fig* = *compter*) **s'~ sur** [+ *personne, autorité*] to lean on; (*Pol*) **s'~ sur un parti** to rely on the support of a party; **s'~ sur l'amitié de qn** to rely *ou* depend on sb's friendship; **s'~ sur des découvertes récentes pour démontrer ...** to use recent discoveries to demonstrate ...; **sur quoi vous appuyez-vous pour avancer cela?** what evidence do you have to support what you're saying?

c (‡ = *subir*) [+ *importun, discours ennuyeux*] to put up with*; [+ *corvée*] to take on; **qui va s'~ le ménage?** who'll get landed* with the

housework?; **chaque fois c'est nous qui nous appuyons toutes les corvées** it's always us who get stuck* *ou* landed* with all the chores; **il s'est appuyé le voyage de nuit** he ended up having to travel at night

âpre [ɑpʀ] ADJ **a** [*goût, vin*] pungent, acrid; [*hiver, vent, temps*] bitter, harsh; [*son, voix, ton*] harsh **b** [*vie*] harsh; [*combat, discussion*] bitter; [*détermination, résolution*] grim; [*concurrence, critique*] fierce; **après d'~s marchandages** after some intense haggling **c** **~ au gain** grasping, greedy

âprement [ɑpʀəmɑ̃] ADV [*lutter*] bitterly, grimly; [*critiquer*] fiercely

▼ **après** [apʀɛ]

| **1** PRÉPOSITION | **2** ADVERBE |

1 PRÉPOSITION

a temps after; **il est entré ~ elle** he came in after her; **venez ~ 8 heures** come after 8; **~ beaucoup d'hésitations il a accepté** after much hesitation he accepted; **~ tout ce que j'ai fait pour lui** after everything I've done for him; **tu l'injuries, et ~ ça tu t'étonnes qu'il se vexe** you insult him and then you're surprised that he takes offence; **jour ~ jour** day after day, day in day out; **page ~ page** page after page, page upon page

♦ **après + infinitif**: **~ avoir lu ta lettre, je ...** after I read *ou* after reading *ou* having read your letter, I ...; **elle s'est décidée ~ avoir longtemps hésité** she made up her mind after much hesitation; **~ être rentré chez lui, il ...** after he got home, he ...; **~ manger** when you've (*ou* I've *etc*) eaten; **ce sont des propos d'~ boire** it's the drink talking

♦ **après coup** after the event, afterwards, later; **il n'a compris/réagi qu'~ coup** he didn't understand/react until afterwards

♦ **après que** + *indicatif* after; **~ que je l'ai quittée** after I left her; **venez me voir ~ que vous lui aurez parlé** come and see me after *ou* when you've spoken to him

♦ **après quoi**: **elle l'a grondé, ~ quoi il a été sage** she told him off and after that he behaved himself

♦ **et (puis) après?** (*pour savoir la suite*) and then what?; (*pour marquer l'indifférence*) so what?*, what of it?

b ordre d'importance, hiérarchie | **sa famille passe ~ ses malades** his family comes after *ou* second to his patients; **~ le capitaine vient le lieutenant** after captain comes lieutenant; **~ vous, je vous en prie** after you

♦ **après tout** after all; **~ tout, ce n'est qu'un enfant** after all he is only a child; **et pourquoi pas, ~ tout?** after all, why not?

c espace (= *plus loin que*) after, past; (= *derrière*) behind, after; **~ le pont, la route rétrécit** the road narrows after the bridge; **sa maison est (juste) ~ la mairie** his house is (just) past *ou* after *ou* beyond the town hall; **j'étais ~ elle dans la queue** I was behind *ou* after her in the queue; **le chien court ~ sa balle** the dog's running after his ball; **elle traîne toujours ~ elle 2 petits chiens** she's always got 2 little dogs in tow

d en s'accrochant | **grimper ~ un poteau** to climb (up) a pole; **sa jupe s'accrochait ~ les ronces** her skirt kept catching on the brambles

e ‡: agressivité | at; **le chien aboyait ~ eux** the dog was barking at them; **il est furieux ~ eux** he's mad* at them; **~ qui en a-t-il?** who has he got it in for?*; **elle est toujours ~ lui** (*surveillance*) she's always breathing down his neck*; (*harcèlement*) she's always (going) on at him* (*Brit*) *ou* nagging (at) him, she keeps on at him all the time*

f
♦ **d'après**
(= *en suivant (un modèle, un auteur)*) **portrait peint d'~ nature** portrait painted from life;

dessin d'~ **Ingres** drawing after Ingres, drawing in the style *ou* manner of Ingres; **scénario d'~ un roman de Balzac** screenplay adapted from a novel by Balzac

(= *selon*) d'~ **lui/elle** according to him/her, in his/her opinion; **d'~ moi** in my opinion; **(à en juger) d'~ son regard/ce qu'il a dit** from the look he gave/what he said; **ne jugez pas d'~ les apparences** don't go *ou* judge by appearances; **ne jugez pas d'~ ce qu'il dit** don't go by what he says; **d'~ la météo/les sondages** according to the weather forecast/the polls; **d'~ ma montre** by my watch

2 ADVERBE

a dans le temps (= *ensuite*) afterwards, next; (= *plus tard*) later; **venez me voir ~** come and see me afterwards; **aussitôt ~** immediately *ou* straight after(wards); **longtemps ~** long *ou* a long time after(wards); **qu'allons-nous faire ~ ?** what are we going to do next? *ou* afterwards?; **~, c'est ton tour** it's your turn next; **deux jours/semaines ~** two days/weeks later; **les réformes, ce sera pour ~** reforms will come later; **~ tu iras dire que ...** next you'll be saying that ...; **il est resté deux jours, et ~ il est parti** he stayed two days and afterwards *ou* and then he left

b dans l'espace **tu vois la poste ? sa maison est juste ~** do you see the post office? his house is just a bit further on; **ce crochet là-bas, ton manteau est pendu ~** your coat's (hanging) on that peg over there

c dans un ordre **qu'est-ce qui vient ~ ?** what comes next?, what's to follow?; **il pense surtout à ses malades, sa famille passe ~** he thinks of his patients first, his family comes second; **~, nous avons des articles moins chers** otherwise we have cheaper things

d

♦ **d'après** (= *suivant*) (*dans le temps*) **la semaine/le mois d'~** the following *ou* next week/month, the week/month after; **le train d'~ est plus rapide** the next train is faster; (*dans l'espace*) **tu vois le cinéma ? c'est la rue d'~** do you see the cinema? it's the next street along (from there)

après-demain [apRɛd(ə)mɛ̃] ADV the day after tomorrow

après-dîner† (*pl* **après-dîners**) [apRedine] NM evening; **conversations d'~** after-dinner conversations

après-guerre (*pl* **après-guerres**) [apRɛgɛR] NM post-war years; **d'~** post-war (*épith*)

après-midi [apRemidi] NM *ou* F INV afternoon; **dans l'~** in the afternoon

après-rasage (*pl* **après-rasages**) [apReRazaʒ] **1** ADJ INV [*lotion, mousse*] aftershave (*épith*) **2** NM aftershave

après-shampo(o)ing (*pl* **après-shampo(o)ings**) [apReʃɑ̃pwɛ̃] NM (hair) conditioner

après-ski (*pl* **après-ski(s)**) [apReski] NM **a** (= *chaussure*) snow boot **b** (= *loisirs*) **l'~** après-ski; **tenue d'~** après-ski outfit

après-soleil [apResɔlɛj] **1** ADJ INV after-sun (*épith*) **2** NM INV after-sun cream (*ou* lotion)

après-vente [apRevɑ̃t] ADJ INV **(service) ~** after-sales service

âpreté [apRate] NF **a** [*goût, vin*] pungency; [*hiver, vent, temps*] bitterness, harshness; [*son, voix, ton*] harshness **b** [*vie*] harshness; [*discussion*] bitterness; [*détermination, résolution*] grimness; [*concurrence, critique*] fierceness

a priori [apRijɔRi] **1** LOC ADV (*Philos*) a priori; (*gén*) [*intéressant, surprenant*] at first sight; **refuser qch ~** to refuse sth out of hand; **~, la date ne devrait pas changer** in principle, the date shouldn't change; **tu es libre samedi ? — ~ oui** are you free on Saturday? — I should be **2** LOC ADJ (*Philos*) a priori **3** NM INV (*Philos*) apriorism; (*gén*) prejudice; **avoir des ~** to be

biased *ou* prejudiced (**envers** towards, **contre** against); **j'ai abordé le problème sans ~** I approached the problem with an open mind

apriorisme [apRiɔRism] NM apriorism

aprioriste [apRijɔRist] **1** ADJ aprioristic, apriorist (*épith*) **2** NMF a priori reasoner, apriorist

à-propos [apRopo] NM (= *présence d'esprit*) presence of mind; [*remarque, acte*] aptness; **avec beaucoup d'~ le gouvernement a annoncé ...** with consummate timing the government has announced ...; **répondre avec ~** to make an apt *ou* a suitable reply; **avoir beaucoup d'~** (*dans ses réponses*) to have the knack of saying the right thing; (*dans ses actes*) to have the knack of doing the right thing; **son manque d'~ lui nuit** his inability to say *ou* do the right thing does him a lot of harm; **avoir l'esprit d'~** to be quick off the mark

apte [apt] ADJ **a** **~ à qch** capable of sth; **~ à faire** capable of doing, able to do; **~ à exercer une profession** (*intellectuellement*) (suitably) qualified for a job; (*physiquement*) capable of doing a job; **je ne suis pas ~ à juger** I'm not able *ou* not in a position to judge; (*Mil*) **~ (au service)** fit for service **b** (*Jur*) **~ à** fit to *ou* for

aptère [aptɛR] ADJ (*Bot, Zool*) apterous; (*Art*) [*temple*] apteral; **la Victoire ~** the apteral Victory

aptéryx [apteRiks] NM (= *oiseau*) kiwi

aptitude [aptityd] NF **a** (= *faculté*) aptitude, ability; (= *don*) gift, talent; **test d'~** aptitude test; **son ~ à étudier** *ou* **à** *ou* **pour l'étude** his aptitude for study *ou* studying, his ability to study; **avoir de grandes ~s** to be very gifted *ou* talented **b** (*Jur*) fitness (**à** to)

apurement [apyRmɑ̃] NM [*comptes*] auditing; [*dette*] discharging, wiping off

apurer [apyRe] ▸ conjug 1 ◂ VT [+ *comptes*] to audit; [+ *dette*] to discharge, wipe off

aquacole [akwakɔl] ADJ **élevage ~** (= *activité*) aquaculture, fish farming; (= *entreprise*) fish farm

aquaculteur, -trice [akwakyltœR, tRis] NM,F (*gén*) aquiculturalist; [*poissons*] fish farmer

aquaculture [akwakyltyR] NF (*gén*) aquiculture, aquaculture; [*poissons*] fish farming

aquafortiste [akwafɔRtist] NMF aquafortist

aquagym [akwaʒim] NF aqua-aerobics *sg*

aquaplanage [akwaplanaʒ] NM aquaplaning

aquaplane [akwaplan] NM aquaplane

aquaplaning [akwaplaniŋ] NM = **aquaplanage**

aquarelle [akwaRɛl] NF (= *technique*) watercolours (*Brit*), watercolors (*US*); (= *tableau*) watercolour (*Brit*), watercolor (*US*); **faire de l'~** to paint in watercolours

aquarellé, e [akwaRele] ADJ [*dessin*] done in watercolour(s) (*Brit*) *ou* watercolor(s) (*US*)

aquarelliste [akwaRelist] NMF watercolourist (*Brit*), watercolorist (*US*)

aquariophile [akwaRjɔfil] NMF tropical fish enthusiast, aquarist

aquariophilie [akwaRjɔfili] NF keeping tropical fish

aquarium [akwaRjɔm] NM aquarium, fish tank; **~ d'eau de mer** marine aquarium

aquatique [akwatik] ADJ [*plante*] aquatic, water (*épith*); **animal ~** aquatic animal; **oiseau ~** aquatic bird, waterbird; **parc ~** aqua park; **paysage ~** (*sous l'eau*) underwater landscape; (*marécageux*) watery landscape

aquavit [akwavit] NM aquavit

aqueduc [ak(ə)dyk] NM (*Tech, Anat*) aqueduct

aqueux, -euse [akø, øz] ADJ aqueous → **humeur**

à quia [akɥija] LOC ADV (*littér*) **mettre qn ~** to nonplus sb; **être ~** to be at a loss for a reply

aquifère [akɥifɛR] **1** ADJ **nappe ~** aquifer, water-bearing layer *ou* stratum **2** NM aquifer

aquilin, e [akilɛ̃, in] ADJ aquiline

aquilon [akilɔ̃] NM (*littér*) north wind

A.R. a (ABRÉV = **Altesse royale**) → **altesse b** (ABRÉV = **aller (et) retour**) → **aller**

AR [aɛR] NM (ABRÉV = **accusé** *ou* **avis de réception**) → **accusé, avis**

ara [aRa] NM macaw

arabe [aRab] **1** ADJ [*désert*] Arabian; [*nation, peuple*] Arab; [*art, langue, littérature*] Arabic, Arab; **(cheval) ~** Arab (horse) → **république, téléphone 2** NM (*Ling*) Arabic; **l'~ littéral** written Arabic **3** **Arabe** NM Arab; **un jeune Arabe** an Arab boy **4** **Arabe** NF Arab woman (*ou* girl)

arabesque [aRabɛsk] NF arabesque; **~ de style** stylistic ornament, ornament of style

arabica [aRabika] NM arabica

Arabie [aRabi] NF Arabia; **~ Saoudite** Saudi Arabia; **le désert d'~** the Arabian desert

arabique [aRabik] ADJ Arabian → **gomme**

arabisant, e [aRabizɑ̃, ɑ̃t] NM,F Arabist, Arabic scholar

arabisation [aRabizasjɔ̃] NF arabization

arabiser [aRabize] ▸ conjug 1 ◂ VT to arabize

arabisme [aRabism] NM Arabism

arable [aRabl] ADJ arable

arabo-islamique (*pl* **arabo-islamiques**) [aRaboislamik] ADJ Arab-Islamic

arabophone [aRabɔfɔn] **1** ADJ Arabic-speaking (*épith*) **2** NMF Arabic speaker

arachide [aRaʃid] NF (= *plante*) groundnut (plant); (= *graine*) peanut, groundnut, monkey nut (*Brit*)

arachnéen, -enne [aRaknéɛ̃, ɛn] ADJ (*littér* = *léger*) gossamer (*épith*), of gossamer; (*Zool*) arachnidan

arachnide [aRaknid] NM arachnid; **les ~s** the Arachnida (*SPÉC*)

arachnoïde [aRaknɔid] NF arachnoid (membrane)

arachnoïdien, -ienne [aRaknɔidjɛ̃, jɛn] ADJ arachnoid

arack [aRak] NM arrack

araignée [aReɲe] NF **a** (= *animal*) spider; **~ d'eau** water strider *ou* skater, pond-skater; **~ de mer** spider crab; **il a une ~ au plafond*** he's got a screw loose*, he's got bats in the belfry* (*Brit*) ■ (*PROV*) **~ du matin, chagrin, ~ du soir, espoir** seeing a spider in the morning brings bad luck, seeing a spider in the evening brings good luck → **toile b** (= *crochet*) grapnel **c** (*Boucherie*) cut of beef used to make steaks **d** (*Pêche*) square net

araire [aRɛR] NM swing plough (*Brit*) *ou* plow (*US*)

arak [aRak] NM = **arack**

araméen, -enne [aRameɛ̃, ɛn] **1** ADJ Aram(a)ean, Aramaic **2** NM (*Ling*) Aramaic, Aram(a)ean **3** **Araméen(ne)** NM,F Aram(a)ean

Ararat [aRaRa(t)] N **le mont ~** Mount Ararat

arasement [aRazmɑ̃] NM **a** (= *mise à niveau*) [*mur*] levelling; [*bois*] (*en rabotant*) planing(-down); (*en sciant*) sawing **b** (*Géol*) [*relief*] erosion

araser [aRaze] ▸ conjug 1 ◂ VT **a** (= *mettre de niveau*) to level; (*en rabotant*) to plane (down); (*en sciant*) to saw; (= *diminuer*) to reduce **b** (*Géol*) [+ *relief*] to erode

aratoire [aRatwaR] ADJ ploughing (*Brit*), plowing (*US*); **travaux ~s** ploughing; **instrument ~** ploughing implement

araucaria [aRokaRja] NM monkey puzzle (tree), araucaria

arbalète [aRbalɛt] NF crossbow

arbalétrier [aRbaletRije] NM **a** (= *personne*) crossbowman **b** (= *poutre*) rafter

arbitrage [aRbitRaʒ] NM **a** (*Comm, Pol* = *action*) arbitration; (*Bourse*) arbitrage; (= *sen-*

tence) arbitrament; ~ **obligatoire** compulsory arbitration; **recourir à l'~** to go to arbitration b (*Boxe, Ftbl, Rugby*) refereeing; (*Cricket, Hockey, Tennis*) umpiring; **erreur d'~** refereeing *ou* referee's error, umpiring *ou* umpire's error

arbitragiste [aʀbitʀaʒist] NMF (*Bourse*) arbitrager, arbitrageur

arbitraire [aʀbitʀɛʀ] 1 ADJ (= *despotique, contingent*) arbitrary 2 NM **le règne de l'~** the reign of the arbitrary; **l'~ du signe linguistique/d'une décision** the arbitrary nature *ou* the arbitrariness of the linguistic sign/of a decision

arbitrairement [aʀbitʀɛʀmɑ̃] ADV arbitrarily

arbitral, e (*mpl* **-aux**) [aʀbitʀal, o] ADJ a (*Jur*) arbitral b (*Boxe, Ftbl, Rugby*) referee's (*épith*); (*Cricket, Hockey, Tennis*) umpire's (*épith*); **décision ~e** referee's *ou* umpire's decision *ou* ruling

arbitre [aʀbitʀ] NM a (*Boxe, Ftbl, Rugby*) referee, ref*; (*Cricket, Hockey, Tennis*) umpire; **faire l'~** to (be the) referee *ou* umpire; (*Tennis*) **~ de chaise** umpire → **libre** b (= *conciliateur*) arbiter; (*Jur*) arbitrator; **servir d'~ dans un conflit social** to act as an arbiter *ou* arbitrate in an industrial dispute; (*fig*) **~ du bon goût** arbiter of (good) taste

arbitrer [aʀbitʀe] ▶ conjug 1 ◀ VT a [+ *conflit*] to arbitrate; [+ *personnes*] to arbitrate between; (*Fin*) to carry out an arbitrage operation on b (*Boxe, Ftbl, Rugby*) to referee, ref*; (*Cricket, Hockey, Tennis*) to umpire

arboré, e [aʀboʀe] ADJ [*région*] wooded; [*jardin*] planted with trees

arborer [aʀboʀe] ▶ conjug 1 ◀ VT [+ *vêtement*] to sport; [+ *sourire*] to wear; [+ *air*] to display; [+ *décoration*] to sport, display; [+ *drapeau*] to bear, display; **le journal arbore un gros titre** the paper is carrying a big headline; **~ l'étendard de la révolte** to bear the standard of revolt

arborescence [aʀboʀesɑ̃s] NF (*Agr*) arborescence; (*Ling, Math*) tree (diagram); (*Ordin*) tree (structure)

arborescent, e [aʀboʀesɑ̃, ɑ̃t] ADJ [*plante*] arborescent; **fougère ~e** tree fern; **réseau ~** tree network; (*Ordin*) **menu ~** menu tree, tree-structured menu

arboretum [aʀboʀetɔm] NM arboretum

arboricole [aʀboʀikɔl] ADJ [*technique*] arboricultural; [*animal*] arboreal

arboriculteur, -trice [aʀboʀikyltœʀ, tʀis] NM,F tree grower, arboriculturist (*SPÉC*)

arboriculture [aʀboʀikyltyʀ] NF tree cultivation, arboriculture (*SPÉC*)

arborisé, e [aʀboʀize] ADJ arborized

arbouse [aʀbuz] NF arbutus berry

arbousier [aʀbuzje] NM arbutus, strawberry tree

arbre [aʀbʀ] 1 NM a (*Bot, Ling*) tree; **~ fruitier/d'agrément** *ou* **d'ornement** fruit/ornamental tree; **faire l'~ fourchu/droit** to do a handstand (with one's legs apart/together); (*fig*) **les ~s vous cachent la forêt** you can't see the wood (*Brit*) *ou* forest (*US*) for the trees; **c'est abattre** *ou* **couper l'~ pour avoir le fruit** that's sacrificing long-term gains for short-term profits; **faire grimper** *ou* **faire monter qn à l'~** to have sb on*, pull sb's leg* ■ (*PROV*) **entre l'~ et l'écorce il ne faut pas mettre le doigt** do not meddle in other people's affairs b (*Tech*) shaft 2 COMP ▶ **arbre à cames** camshaft; **avec ~ à cames en tête** with overhead camshaft ▶ **arbre d'entraînement** drive shaft ▶ **arbre généalogique** family tree; **faire son ~ généalogique** to draw up one's family tree ▶ **arbre d'hélice** propeller shaft ▶ **arbre de Judée** Judas tree ▶ **arbre de mai** May tree ▶ **arbre-manivelle** NM (*pl* **arbres-manivelles**) crankshaft ▶ **arbre mo-**

teur driving shaft ▶ **arbre de Noël** (= *sapin*) Christmas tree; (= *fête d'entreprise*) Christmas party ▶ **arbre à pain** breadfruit tree ▶ **arbre de transmission** propeller shaft ▶ **arbre de vie** (*Anat*) arbor vitae, tree of life; (*Bible*) tree of life

arbrisseau (*pl* **arbrisseaux**) [aʀbʀiso] NM shrub

arbuste [aʀbyst] NM small shrub, bush

arbustif, -ive [aʀbystif, iv] ADJ [*végétation*] shrubby; **culture arbustive** cultivation of shrubs *ou* bushes

ARC [aʀk] NM (ABRÉV = **AIDS-related complex**) ARC

arc [aʀk] 1 NM (= *arme*) bow; (*Géom*) arc; (*Anat, Archit*) arch; **l'~ de ses sourcils** the arch *ou* curve of her eyebrows; **la côte formait un ~** the coastline formed an arc → **corde, lampe, soudure, tir** 2 COMP ▶ **arc brisé** Gothic arch ▶ **arc de cercle** (*Géom*) arc of a circle; (*gén*) **ça forme un ~ de cercle** it forms an arc; **en ~ de cercle** in an arc ▶ **arc électrique** electric arc ▶ **arc outrepassé** Moorish arch ▶ **arc en plein cintre** Roman arch ▶ **arc réflexe** reflex arc ▶ **arc de triomphe** triumphal arch; **l'Arc de Triomphe** the Arc de Triomphe ▶ **arc voltaïque** = arc électrique

arcade [aʀkad] NF (*Archit*) arch, archway; **~s** arcade, arches; **les ~s d'un cloître/d'un pont** the arches *ou* arcade of a cloister/of a bridge; **se promener sous les ~s** to walk through the arcade *ou* underneath the arches; ▶ **dentaire** dental arch; **~ sourcilière** (*gén*) arch of the eyebrows; (*Boxe*) **il a été touché à l'~ sourcilière** he got a cut above the eye → **jeu**

Arcadie [aʀkadi] NF Arcadia

arcane [aʀkan] NM a (*fig : gén pl = mystère*) mystery b (*Alchimie*) arcanum

arcature [aʀkatyʀ] NF arcature

arc-boutant (*pl* **arcs-boutants**) [aʀkbutɑ̃] NM flying buttress

arc-bouter [aʀkbute] ▶ conjug 1 ◀ 1 VT (*Archit*) to buttress 2 **s'arc-bouter** VPR to lean, press (**à, contre** (up) against, **sur** on); **arc-bouté contre le mur, il essayait de pousser la table** pressing (up) *ou* bracing himself against the wall, he tried to push the table

arceau (*pl* **arceaux**) [aʀso] NM (*Archit*) arch; (*Croquet*) hoop; (*Méd*) cradle; (*Aut*) **~ (de sécurité)** roll bar

arc-en-ciel (*pl* **arcs-en-ciel**) [aʀkɑ̃sjɛl] NM rainbow

archaïque [aʀkaik] ADJ archaic

archaïsant, e [aʀkaizɑ̃, ɑ̃t] 1 ADJ archaistic 2 NM,F archaist

archaïsme [aʀkaism] NM archaism

archange [aʀkɑ̃ʒ] NM archangel; **l'~ (Saint) Michel/Gabriel** the Archangel Michael/Gabriel

arche [aʀʃ] NF a (*Archit*) arch b (*Rel*) ark; **l'~ de Noé** Noah's Ark; **l'~ d'alliance** the Ark of the Covenant

archéologie [aʀkeɔlɔʒi] NF archaeology (*Brit*), archeology (*US*)

archéologique [aʀkeɔlɔʒik] ADJ archaeological (*Brit*), archeological (*US*)

archéologue [aʀkeɔlɔg] NMF archaeologist (*Brit*), archeologist (*US*)

archer [aʀʃe] NM archer, bowman

archet [aʀʃɛ] NM (*Mus, gén*) bow; **donner des coups d'~** to bow; **coup d'~** bow-stroke

archétypal, e (*mpl* **-aux**) [aʀketipal, o] ADJ archetypal

archétype [aʀketip] 1 NM (*gén*) archetype; (*Bio*) prototype 2 ADJ (*gén*) archetypal; (*Bio*) prototypal, prototypic

archétypique [aʀketipik] ADJ archetypical

archevêché [aʀʃəveʃe] NM (= *territoire*) archdiocese, archbishopric; (= *charge*) archbishopric; (= *palais*) archbishop's palace

archevêque [aʀʃəvɛk] NM archbishop

archi... [aʀʃi] PRÉF a (* = *extrêmement*) tremendously, enormously; **~bondé** ◊ **~comble** ◊ **~plein** chock-a-block*, jampacked; **~connu** extremely *ou* very well-known; **~difficile** tremendously difficult; **~millionnaire** millionaire several times over b (*dans un titre*) arch... → **archidiacre, archiduc** *etc*

archidiaconat [aʀʃidjakɔna] NM (= *dignité*) archdeaconry

archidiaconé [aʀʃidjakɔne] NM (= *territoire*) archdeaconry

archidiacre [aʀʃidjakʀ] NM archdeacon

archidiocèse [aʀʃidjɔsez] NM archdiocese

archiduc [aʀʃidyk] NM archduke

archiduchesse [aʀʃidyʃes] NF archduchess

archiépiscopal, e (*mpl* **-aux**) [aʀʃiepiskɔpal, o] ADJ archiepiscopal

archiépiscopat [aʀʃiepiskɔpa] NM archbishopric (*office*), archiepiscopate

archimandrite [aʀʃimɑ̃dʀit] NM archimandrite

Archimède [aʀʃimed] NM Archimedes → **vis**

archimédien, -ienne [aʀʃimedjɛ̃, jɛn] ADJ Archimedean

archipel [aʀʃipɛl] NM archipelago; **l'~ malais** the Malay Archipelago; **l'~ des Kouriles** the Kuril Islands

archiphonème [aʀʃifɔnɛm] NM archiphoneme

archiprêtre [aʀʃipʀɛtʀ] NM archpriest

architecte [aʀʃitɛkt] NMF (*lit, fig*) architect; **~ d'intérieur** interior designer; **~ naval** naval architect; (*Ordin*) **~ de réseaux** network architect

architectonique [aʀʃitɛktɔnik] 1 ADJ architectonic 2 NF architectonics *sg*

architectural, e (*mpl* **-aux**) [aʀʃitɛktyʀal, o] ADJ architectural

architecturalement [aʀʃitɛktyʀalmɑ̃] ADV architecturally

architecture [aʀʃitɛktyʀ] NF (*lit, Ordin*) architecture; (*fig*) structure; **~ civile/militaire/religieuse** civil/military/religious architecture; **merveille d'~** marvellous piece of architecture

architecturé, e [aʀʃitɛktyʀe] ▶ conjug 1 ◀ ADJ **bien ~** [*œuvre musicale, roman*] well-structured; **des phrases savamment ~es** carefully crafted sentences

architrave [aʀʃitʀav] NF architrave

archivage [aʀʃivaʒ] NM (*gén*) filing; (*Ordin*) filing, archival storage; **~ électronique** electronic filing *ou* storage

archiver [aʀʃive] ▶ conjug 1 ◀ VT to archive, file

archives [aʀʃiv] NFPL archives, records; **les Archives nationales** the National Archives, ≈ the Public Records Office (*Brit*); **ça restera dans les ~!** that will go down in history!; **je vais chercher dans mes ~** I'll look through my files *ou* records

archiviste [aʀʃivist] NMF archivist

archivolte [aʀʃivɔlt] NF archivolt

arçon [aʀsɔ̃] NM (*Équitation*) tree → **cheval, pistolet, vider**

arc-rampant (*pl* **arcs-rampants**) [aʀkʀɑ̃pɑ̃] NM rampant arch

arctique [aʀktik] 1 ADJ [*région*] Arctic; **l'océan (glacial) Arctique** the Arctic ocean 2 **Arctique** NM **l'Arctique** the Arctic

ardemment [aʀdamɑ̃] ADV ardently, fervently

Ardenne [aʀdɛn] NF (= *région de France, Belgique et Luxembourg*) **l'~** the Ardennes

Ardennes [aʀdɛn] NFPL (= *département français*) **les ~** the Ardennes; **la bataille des ~** the Battle of the Bulge

ardent, e [aʀdɑ̃, ɑ̃t] ADJ a (= *brûlant : gén*) burning; [*tison*] glowing; [*feu*] blazing; [*yeux*] fiery (**de** with); [*couleur*] flaming, fiery;

[*chaleur, soleil*] scorching, blazing; [*fièvre, soif*] raging → **buisson, chapelle, charbon** [b] (= *vif*) [*foi*] burning, fervent, passionate; [*colère*] burning, raging; [*passion, désir*] burning, ardent; [*piété, haine, prière*] fervent, ardent; [*lutte*] ardent, passionate; [*discours*] impassioned, inflamed [c] (= *bouillant*) [*amant*] ardent, hot-blooded; [*jeunesse, caractère*] fiery, passionate; [*joueur*] keen; [*partisan*] ardent, keen; [*cheval*] mettlesome, fiery; **être ~ au travail/au combat** to be a zealous worker/an ardent fighter

ardeur [aʀdœʀ] NF (*gén*) ardour (*Brit*), ardor (*US*); [*partisan, joueur*] zeal; [*caractère*] fieriness; [*foi, prière*] fervour (*Brit*), fervor (*US*); (*littér*) **les ~s de l'amour** the ardour of love; (*littér ou hum*) **modérez vos ~s!** control yourself!; **défendre une cause avec ~** to defend a cause ardently *ou* fervently; **son ~ au travail** *ou* **à travailler** his zeal *ou* enthusiasm for work; **l'~ du soleil** the heat of the sun; (*littér*) **les ~s de l'été** the heat of summer

ardillon [aʀdijɔ̃] NM [*boucle*] tongue

ardoise [aʀdwaz] [1] NF (= *matière*) slate; (* = *dette*) unpaid bill; **toit d'~s** slate roof; **couvrir un toit d'~(s)** to slate a roof; (*fig*) **avoir une ~ de 300 F chez l'épicier** to owe 300 francs at the grocer's [2] ADJ INV (*couleur*) slate-grey (*Brit*) *ou* -gray (*US*)

ardoisé, e [aʀdwaze] ADJ slate-grey (*Brit*) *ou* -gray (*US*)

ardoisier, -ière [aʀdwazje, jɛʀ] [1] ADJ [*gisement*] slaty; [*industrie*] slate (*épith*) [2] NM (= *ouvrier*) slate-quarry worker; (= *propriétaire*) slate-quarry owner [3] **ardoisière** NF slate quarry

ardu, e [aʀdy] ADJ [*travail*] arduous, laborious; [*problème*] difficult; [*pente*] steep

are [aʀ] NM are, one hundred square metres

areligieux, -ieuse [aʀ(ə)liʒjø, jøz] ADJ areligious

aréna [aʀena] NF (*Can Sport*) arena, (skating) rink

arène [aʀɛn] NF [a] (= *piste*) arena; **l'~ politique** the political arena; (*fig*) **descendre dans l'~** to enter the arena [b] **~s** (*Archit*) amphitheatre (*Brit*), amphitheater (*US*); [*courses de taureaux*] bullring; **les ~s de Nîmes** the amphitheatre of Nîmes [c] (*Géol*) sand, arenite (*SPÉC*); (*Géol*) **~ granitique** granitic sand

arénicole [aʀenikɔl] NF sandworm

aréole [aʀeɔl] NF areola

aréomètre [aʀeɔmɛtʀ] NM hydrometer

aréométrie [aʀeɔmetʀi] NF hydrometry

aréopage [aʀeɔpaʒ] NM (*fig, hum*) learned assembly; (*Antiq*) **l'Aréopage** the Areopagus

arête [aʀɛt] NF [a] (*Zool*) (fish)bone; **~ centrale** backbone, spine; **c'est plein d'~s** it's full of bones, it's very bony; **enlever les ~s d'un poisson** to bone a fish; **sans ~s** boneless [b] (= *bord*) [*cube, pierre, ski*] edge; [*toit*] ridge; [*voûte*] groin; [*montagne*] ridge, crest; [*nez*] bridge [c] (*Bot*) [*seigle, orge*] beard; **~s** beard

areu [aʀø] EXCL (*langage de bébé*) **areu ~** goo-goo; **faire areu ~** to gurgle

argent [aʀʒɑ̃] [1] NM [a] (= *métal*) silver; **en ~ ◊ d'~** silver → **noce, parole** [b] (= *couleur*) silver; **cheveux/reflets (d') ~** silvery hair/glints [c] (*Fin*) money (*NonC*); **il a de l'~** he's got money, he's well off; **il l'a fait pour (de) l'~** he did it for money; **il se fait un ~ fou*** he makes pots* *ou* loads* of money; **c'est un homme/une femme d'~** he/she loves money; **politique de l'~ cher** tight *ou* dear (*Brit*) money policy → **couleur, manger, puissance** [d] (*loc*) **l'~ de la drogue** drug(s) money; **j'en ai/j'en veux pour mon ~** I've got/I want (to get) my money's worth; **on en a pour son ~** it's good value (for money), it's worth every penny; **on n'en a jamais que pour son ~** you get what you pay for; **faire ~ de tout** to turn

everything into cash, make money out of anything; **jeter l'~ par les fenêtres** to throw money away *ou* down the drain; **avoir de l'~ plein les poches*** to have plenty of money, be rolling in money* ■ (*PROV*) **l'~ n'a pas d'odeur** money has no smell ■ (*PROV*) **l'~ ne fait pas le bonheur** money can't buy happiness ■ (*PROV*) **l'~ va à l'~** money attracts money ■ (*PROV*) **point** *ou* **pas d'~, point** *ou* **pas de Suisse** nothing for nothing [e] (*Hér*) argent

[2] COMP ► **argent comptant**: **payer ~ comptant** to pay cash; **prendre qch/les paroles de qn pour ~ comptant** to take sth/what sb says at (its) face value ► **argent de poche** pocket money; **ils lui donnent 100 F par semaine d'~ de poche** they give him 100 francs a week pocket money ► **argent liquide** ready money, (ready) cash ► **argent sale** dirty money

argenté, e [aʀʒɑ̃te] ADJ (*ptp de* **argenter**) [*couleur, cheveux*] silver, silvery; [*couverts*] **en métal ~** silver-plated; **je ne suis pas très ~ en ce moment*** I'm pretty broke at the moment*, I'm not too well-off just now → **renard**

argenter [aʀʒɑ̃te] ▶ conjug 1 ◀ VT [+ *miroir*] to silver; [+ *couverts*] to silver(-plate); (*fig littér*) to give a silvery sheen to, silver (*littér*)

argenterie [aʀʒɑ̃tʀi] NF silver, silverware; (*de métal argenté*) silver plate; **faire l'~** to polish *ou* clean the silver

argenteur [aʀʒɑ̃tœʀ] NM silverer

argentier [aʀʒɑ̃tje] NM [a] (*Hist*) Superintendent of Finance; (*hum*) **le grand ~** the Minister of Finance [b] (= *meuble*) silver cabinet

argentifère [aʀʒɑ̃tifɛʀ] ADJ silver-bearing, argentiferous (*SPÉC*)

argentin[1], e [aʀʒɑ̃tɛ̃, in] ADJ [*son, voix*] silvery

argentin[2], e [aʀʒɑ̃tɛ̃, in] [1] ADJ Argentinian (*Brit*), Argentinean (*US*), Argentine (*épith*) [2] **Argentin(e)** NM,F Argentinian (*Brit*), Argentinean (*US*), Argentine

Argentine [aʀʒɑ̃tin] NF **l'~** Argentina, the Argentine

argenture [aʀʒɑ̃tyʀ] NF [*miroir*] silvering; [*couverts*] silver-plating, silvering

argile [aʀʒil] NF clay; **~ à silex** clay-with-flints → **colosse**

argileux, -euse [aʀʒilø, øz] ADJ clayey

argon [aʀgɔ̃] NM argon

argonaute [aʀgonot] NM (*Myth*) Argonaut; (*Zool*) argonaut, paper nautilus

Argos [aʀgɔs] N Argos

argot [aʀgo] NM slang; **~ de métier** trade slang; **parler ~** to use slang; **mot d'~** slang word

argotique [aʀgotik] ADJ (= *de l'argot*) slang; (= *très familier*) slangy

argotisme [aʀgotism] NM slang term

argousin †† [aʀguzɛ̃] NM (*péj ou hum*) rozzer † (*péj*), bluebottle † (*péj*)

arguer [aʀgɥe] ▶ conjug 1 ◀ (*littér*) [1] VT [a] (= *déduire*) to deduce; **il ne peut rien ~ de ces faits** he can draw no conclusion from these facts [b] (= *prétexter*) **~ que ...** to put forward the reason that ...; **il argua qu'il n'avait rien entendu** he protested that he had heard nothing [2] **arguer de** VT INDIR **il refusa, arguant de leur manque de ressources** he refused, putting forward their lack of resources as an excuse *ou* as a reason

▼ **argument** [aʀgymɑ̃] NM (*gén*) argument; **tirer ~ de qch** to use sth as an argument *ou* excuse; **~ frappant** strong *ou* convincing argument; (*hum* = *coup*) blow; **~ massue** sledgehammer argument; **~ publicitaire** advertising claim; **~ de vente** selling proposition *ou* point

argumentaire [aʀgymɑ̃tɛʀ] NM (*gén*) argument; (*Comm*) sales leaflet *ou* blurb

argumentation [aʀgymɑ̃tasjɔ̃] NF argumentation

argumenter [aʀgymɑ̃te] ▶ conjug 1 ◀ VI to argue (**sur** about); **~ de qch** to use sth as an argument; **discours bien argumenté** well-argued speech

argus [aʀgys] NM [a] **l'~ (de l'automobile)** guide to secondhand car prices, ≈ Glass's directory (*Brit*), ≈ the Blue Book (*US*); **~ de la photo** guide to secondhand photographic equipment prices → **coter** [b] (= *oiseau*) argus pheasant

argutie [aʀgysi] NF (*littér: gén péj*) quibble; **~s** pettifoggery, quibbles, quibbling

aria [aʀja] NF (*Mus*) aria

Ariane [aʀjan] NF Ariadne → **fil**

arianisme [aʀjanism] NM Arianism

aride [aʀid] ADJ (= *sec*) [*vent, climat*] dry; (= *stérile*) [*sol*] arid; [*sujet, matière*] dry; **tâche ~** thankless task; **cœur ~** heart of stone

aridité [aʀidite] NF (= *sécheresse*) [*vent, climat*] dryness; (= *stérilité*) [*sol*] aridity; [*sujet, matière*] dryness; [*tâche*] thanklessness; **l'~ de son cœur** his stony-heartedness

arien, -ienne [aʀjɛ̃, jɛn] ADJ, NM,F Arian

ariette [aʀjɛt] NF arietta, ariette

Arioste [aʀjɔst] NM **l'~** Ariosto

aristo* [aʀisto] NMF (*péj*) (ABRÉV = **aristocrate**) aristocrat, nob† (*Brit*), toff* † (*Brit*)

aristocrate [aʀistɔkʀat] NMF aristocrat

aristocratie [aʀistɔkʀasi] NF aristocracy

aristocratique [aʀistɔkʀatik] ADJ aristocratic

aristocratiquement [aʀistɔkʀatikmɑ̃] ADV aristocratically

Aristophane [aʀistɔfan] NM Aristophanes

Aristote [aʀistɔt] NM Aristotle

aristotélicien, -ienne [aʀistɔtelisjɛ̃, jɛn] ADJ, NM,F Aristotelian

aristotélisme [aʀistɔtelism] NM Aristotelianism

arithméticien, -ienne [aʀitmetisjɛ̃, jɛn] NM,F arithmetician

arithmétique [aʀitmetik] [1] NF (= *science*) arithmetic; (= *livre*) arithmetic book [2] ADJ arithmetical

arithmétiquement [aʀitmetikmɑ̃] ADV arithmetically

Arizona [aʀizona] NM **l'~** Arizona

Arkansas [aʀkɑ̃sas] NM **l'~** Arkansas

arlequin [aʀləkɛ̃] NM (*Théât*) Harlequin; **bas (d')~** harlequin stockings → **habit**

arlequinade [aʀləkinad] NF (*fig*) buffoonery; (*Théât*) harlequinade

arlésien, -ienne [aʀlezjɛ̃, jɛn] [1] ADJ of *ou* from Arles [2] **Arlésien(ne)** NM,F inhabitant *ou* native of Arles [3] **arlésienne** NF **jouer l'arlésienne** *ou* **les arlésiennes** [*personne*] to keep well out of sight, never show up; **le dialogue, cette arlésienne de la vie politique** dialogue, that elusive phenomenon in politics

---

L'ARLÉSIENNE

The origin of the expression "jouer l'arlésienne" is Georges Bizet's opera of the same name, adapted from a book by Alphonse Daudet, in which the main character never actually appears. It has come to refer to any person or thing which, although much talked about, never materializes.

---

armada [aʀmada] NF (*péj*) **une ~ de** [*personnes*] a whole army *ou* mob of; [*voitures*] a fleet of; **l'Invincible Armada** the Spanish Armada

armagnac [aʀmaɲak] NM armagnac

armateur [aʀmatœʀ] NM (= *propriétaire*) shipowner; (= *exploitant*) ship's manager; **~ affréteur** owner-charterer

armature [aʀmatyʀ] NF [a] (*gén* = *carcasse*) [*tente, montage, édifice*] frame; (*Constr*) framework, armature (*SPÉC*); (*fig* = *infrastructure*) framework; **~ de corset** corset bones *ou*

► GRAMMAIRE ACTIVE: **argument** 53.2, 53.3

stays; **soutien-gorge à/sans ~** underwired/ unwired bra **b** (*Mus*) key signature **c** (*Phys*) [*condensateur*] electrode; [*aimant*] armature

arme [aRm] **1** NF **a** (= *instrument*) (*gén*) weapon; (= *fusil, revolver*) gun; **~s** weapons, arms; **fabrique d'~s** arms factory; **l'~ du crime** the murder weapon; **soldats en ~s** (*avec des armes*) armed soldiers; (*prêts à se battre*) soldiers under arms; **un peuple en ~s** a nation in arms; **ils sont entrés en ~s dans la ville** they came into the town under arms; **des policiers sans ~(s)** unarmed police → **bretelle, maniement, port²** **b** (= *élément d'une armée*) arm; **les trois ~s** the three services *ou* arms; **l'~ de l'infanterie** the infantry; **dans quelle ~ sert-il?** which service is he in?, which branch (of the army) does he serve in? **c** (*Mil*) **la carrière** *ou* **le métier des ~s** soldiering; (*littér*) **le succès de nos ~s** the success of our armies; **aux ~s!** to arms!; **compagnon** *ou* **frère d'~s** comrade-in-arms; **appeler un régiment sous les ~s** to call up a regiment → **homme, place, prise** **d** (= *moyen d'action*) weapon; **~ à double tranchant** double-edged weapon *ou* sword; **il est sans ~** he's defenceless (*Brit*) *ou* defenseless (*US*) (**contre** against); **donner** *ou* **fournir des ~s à qn** to give sb weapons (**contre** against); **tu leur donnes des ~s contre toi-même** you're giving them a stick to beat you with **e** (*Escrime*) **les ~s** fencing; **faire des ~s** to fence → **maître, passe¹, salle** **f** (*Hér*) **~s** arms, coat of arms; **aux ~s de** bearing the arms of → **héraut** **g** (*loc*) **porter les ~s** to be a soldier; **prendre les ~s** (= *se soulever*) to rise up in arms; (*pour défendre son pays*) to take up arms; **avoir l'~ au bras** to have one's weapon in (one's) hand; **~ à la bretelle!** ≈ slope arms!; **~ sur l'épaule!** shoulder arms!; **~ au pied!** attention! (*with rifle on ground*); **rester** *ou* **demeurer l'~ au pied** (*fig*) to hold fire; **portez ~!** shoulder arms!; **présentez ~!** present arms!; **reposez ~!** order arms!; **déposer** *ou* **mettre bas les ~s** to lay down (one's) arms; **rendre les ~s** to lay down one's arms, surrender; **faire ses premières ~s** to start out, begin one's career (**dans** in); **il a fait ses (premières) ~s en Afrique** he started his military career in Africa, he first saw service in Africa; **partir avec ~s et bagages** to pack up and go; **passer l'~ à gauche*** to kick the bucket*; **à ~s égales** on equal terms; **passer qn par les ~s** to shoot sb by firing squad; **prendre le pouvoir/régler un différend par les ~s** to take power/settle a dispute by force; **mourir les ~s à la main** to die fighting; **ils ont défendu la ville les ~s à la main** they took up arms to defend the town → **appel, fait¹, gens¹, pris, suspension**

2 COMP ► **l'arme absolue** the ultimate weapon ► **arme atomique** atomic weapon ► **arme biologique** biological weapon ► **arme blanche** knife; **se battre à l'~ blanche** to fight with knives ► **arme de chasse** hunting weapon ► **arme chimique** chemical weapon ► **arme d'épaule** rifle ► **arme à feu** firearm ► **arme de guerre** weapon of war ► **arme de jet** projectile ► **arme légère** light weapon ► **arme lourde** heavy weapon ► **arme nucléaire** nuclear weapon; **avoir l'~ nucléaire** to have nuclear weapons ► **arme de poing** handgun ► **arme de service** [*policier*] service revolver *ou* gun

armé, e¹ [aRme] (*ptp de* **armer**) **1** ADJ [*personne, forces, conflit*] armed; **~ jusqu'aux dents** *ou* **de pied en cap** armed to the teeth; **attention, il est ~!** careful, he's armed!; **~ de** armed with; **être bien ~ pour passer un examen** to be well-equipped to take an examination; **bien ~ contre le froid** well-equipped against the cold; **canne ~e d'un bout ferré** stick fitted with a steel tip, stick tipped with

steel → **béton, ciment, force, vol 2** NM (= *position*) cock

armée² [aRme] **1** NF **a** (*Mil*) army; **~ de mercenaires** mercenary army; **l'~ d'occupation/de libération** the occupying/ liberating army *ou* forces; (*Hist*) **la Grande Armée** the Grande Armée, *army of Napoleon*; **être à l'~** to be doing one's military service; **être dans l'~** to be in the army **b** (*péj*) army; **une ~ de domestiques/rats** an army of servants/rats; **regardez-moi cette ~ d'incapables!** just look at this hopeless bunch* *ou* crew* → **corps, zone**

2 COMP ► **armée active** regular army ► **l'armée de l'air** the Air Force ► **armée de conscription** conscript army ► **armée de métier** professional army ► **l'armée des Ombres** (*Hist*) *the French Resistance* ► **armée permanente** standing army ► **armée régulière** regular army ► **l'Armée républicaine irlandaise** the Irish Republican Army ► **armée de réserve** reserve ► **l'Armée rouge** the Red Army ► **l'Armée du Salut** the Salvation Army ► **l'armée de terre** the Army

armement [aRməmã] NM **a** (= *action*) [*pays, armée*] armament; [*personne*] arming; [*fusil*] cocking; [*appareil-photo*] winding-on **b** (= *armes*) [*soldat*] arms, weapons; [*pays, troupe, avion*] arms, armament(s); **usine d'~** arms factory; **la limitation des ~s** arms limitation; **les dépenses d'~s de la France** France's expenditure on arms *ou* weapons → **course c** (*Naut* = *équipement*) fitting-out, equipping

Arménie [aRmeni] NF Armenia → **papier**

arménien, -ienne [aRmenjẽ, jɛn] **1** ADJ Armenian **2** (*Ling*) Armenian **3** **Arménien(ne)** NM,F Armenian

armer [aRme] ▸conjug 1◂ **1** VT **a** (*lit*) to arm (**de** with, **contre** against); **~ qn contre les difficultés de la vie** to equip sb to deal with life's difficulties, arm sb against life's difficulties **b** (*Hist*) **~ qn chevalier** to dub sb knight **c** [+ *navire*] to fit out, equip **d** [+ *fusil*] to cock; [+ *appareil-photo*] to wind on **e** (= *renforcer*) [+ *béton, poutre*] to reinforce (**de** with); **~ un bâton d'une pointe d'acier** to fit a stick with a steel tip, fit a steel tip on(to) a stick **2 s'armer** VPR (= *s'équiper*) to arm o.s. (**de** with, **contre** against); **s'~ de courage** to summon up one's courage, steel o.s.; **il faut s'~ de patience** you have to be patient

armistice [aRmistis] NM armistice; (= *fête*) **l'Armistice** Armistice Day

armoire [aRmwaR] **1** NF (*gén*) (tall) cupboard, closet (*US*); (= *penderie*) wardrobe **2** COMP ► **armoire frigorifique** cold room *ou* store ► **armoire à glace** (*lit*) wardrobe with a mirror; (*, fig* = *costaud*) great hulking brute* ► **armoire à linge** linen cupboard (*Brit*) *ou* closet (*US*) ► **armoire normande** large wardrobe ► **armoire à pharmacie** medicine chest *ou* cabinet ► **armoire de toilette** bathroom cabinet (with a mirror)

armoiries [aRmwaRi] NFPL coat of arms, armorial bearings

armoise [aRmwaz] NF artemisia

armorial, e (*mpl* -**iaux**) [aRmɔRjal, jo] ADJ, NM armorial

armoricain, e [aRmɔRikẽ, ɛn] ADJ Armorican → **homard**

armorier [aRmɔRje] ▸conjug 7◂ VT to emblazon

armure [aRmyR] NF **a** (*Mil*) armour (*NonC*) (*Brit*), armor (*NonC*) (*US*); **une ~** a suit of armour; **chevalier en ~** knight in armour **b** (*Tex*) weave **c** [*câble*] (metal) sheath **d** (*Mus*) key signature **e** (*Phys*) armature

armurerie [aRmyRRi] NF (= *fabrique*) arms factory; (= *magasin*) [*armes à feu*] gunsmith's; [*armes blanches*] armourer's (*Brit*), armorer's (*US*); (= *profession*) arms manufacture

armurier [aRmyRje] NM (= *fabricant, marchand*) [*armes à feu*] gunsmith; [*armes blanches*] armourer (*Brit*), armorer (*US*); (*Mil*) armourer (*Brit*), armorer (*US*)

ARN [aɛRɛn] NM (ABRÉV = **acide ribonucléique**) RNA; ► **messager/de transfert** messenger/ transfer RNA

arnaque* [aRnak] NF con (trick)*; **il a monté plusieurs ~s immobilières** he organized several property frauds; **ce régime amaigrissant, c'est une belle ~** this diet is a real con*; **c'est (de) l'~** (= *c'est trop cher*) it's a rip-off*, it's daylight robbery

arnaquer* [aRnake] ▸conjug 1◂ VT **a** (= *escroquer*) to swindle, do* (*Brit*), diddle* (*Brit*); **je me suis fait ~ de 200 F** I was cheated *ou* done* (*Brit*) *ou* diddled* (*Brit*) out of 200 francs **b** (= *arrêter*) to nab*; **se faire ~** to get nabbed*

arnaqueur, -euse* [aRnakœR, øz] NM,F swindler, cheat, con artist*

arnica [aRnika] NF arnica

aromate [aRɔmat] NM (= *herbe*) herb; (= *épice*) spice; **~s** seasoning (*NonC*); **ajoutez quelques ~s** add (some) seasoning *ou* a few herbs (*ou* spices)

aromathérapie [aRɔmateRapi] NF aromatherapy

aromatique [aRɔmatik] ADJ (*gén, Chim*) aromatic

aromatiser [aRɔmatize] ▸conjug 1◂ VT to flavour (*Brit*), flavor (*US*); **aromatisé à la vanille** vanilla-flavoured

arôme, arome [aRom] NM [*plat*] aroma; [*café, vin*] aroma, fragrance; [*fleur*] fragrance; (= *goût*) flavour (*Brit*), flavor (*US*); (*ajouté à un aliment*) flavouring (*Brit*), flavoring (*US*); **crème ~ chocolat** chocolate-flavoured cream dessert

aronde †† [aRɔd] NF swallow → **queue**

arpège [aRpɛʒ] NM arpeggio; **faire des ~s** to play arpeggios

arpéger [aRpeʒe] ▸conjug 6 et 3◂ VT [+ *passage*] to play in arpeggios; [+ *accord*] to play as an arpeggio, spread

arpent [aRpã] NM (*Hist*) arpent (*about an acre*); (*fig*) **il a quelques ~s de terre** he's got a few acres

arpentage [aRpãtaʒ] NM (= *technique*) (land) surveying; (= *mesure*) measuring, surveying

arpenter [aRpãte] ▸conjug 1◂ VT [+ *pièce, couloir*] to pace (up and down); (*Tech*) [+ *terrain*] to measure, survey

arpenteur [aRpãtœR] NM (land) surveyor → **chaîne**

arpète*, arpette* [aRpɛt] NMF apprentice

arpion* [aRpjɔ] NM hoof*, foot

arqué, e [aRke] (*ptp de* **arquer**) ADJ [*objet, sourcils*] arched, curved; **avoir le dos ~** to be hunchbacked; **le dos ~ sous l'effort** his back bowed under the strain; **il a les jambes ~es** he's bandy-legged *ou* bow-legged; **nez ~** hooknose, hooked nose

arquebuse [aRkəbyz] NF (h)arquebus

arquebusier [aRkəbyzje] NM (= *soldat*) (h)arquebusier

arquer [aRke] ▸conjug 1◂ **1** VT [+ *objet, tige*] to curve; [+ *dos*] to arch **2** VI [*objet*] to bend, curve; [*poutre*] to sag; **il ne peut plus ~*** he can't walk any more **3** **s'arquer** VPR to curve

arrachage [aRaʃaʒ] NM [*légume*] lifting; [*plante, arbre*] uprooting; [*dent*] extracting, pulling (*US*); [*sac*] snatching; **l'~ des mauvaises herbes** weeding

arraché [aRaʃe] NM (*Sport*) snatch; **il soulève 130 kg à l'~** he can do a snatch using 130 kg; **obtenir la victoire à l'~** to snatch victory; **ils ont eu le contrat à l'~** they just managed to snatch the contract

arrache-clou (pl **arrache-clous**) [aʀaʃklu] NM nail wrench

arrachement [aʀaʃmã] NM ⓐ (= *chagrin*) wrench; **ce fut un véritable ~ pour elle de partir** it was a real wrench for her to leave ⓑ (= *déchirement*) tearing

arrache-pied [aʀaʃpje] ◆ **d'arrache-pied** LOC ADV relentlessly

arracher [aʀaʃe] ▸conjug 1◂ ① VT ⓐ (= *déraciner*) [+ *légume*] to lift; [+ *souche, plante*] to pull up, uproot; [+ *mauvaises herbes*] to pull up; [+ *cheveux*] to tear *ou* pull out; [+ *dent*] to take out, extract, pull (*US*); [+ *poil, clou*] to pull out; **j'ai passé la matinée à ~ des mauvaises herbes** I've been weeding all morning; **je vais me faire ~ une dent** I'm going to have a tooth *ou* extracted *ou* pulled (*US*) ⓑ (= *enlever*) [+ *chemise, membre*] to tear off; [+ *affiche*] to tear down; [+ *feuille, page*] to tear out (**de** of); **je vais lui ~ les yeux** I'll scratch his eyes out; **cette séparation lui a arraché le cœur** he was heartbroken by this separation; **ce spectacle lui arracha le cœur** the sight of it broke his heart, it was a heartrending sight for him; **ça arrache (la gorge)**⁑ [*plat*] it'll blow your head off*; [*boisson*] it's really rough! ⓒ (= *prendre*) **~ à qn** [+ *portefeuille, arme*] to snatch *ou* grab from sb; [+ *argent*] to get out of sb; **~ des larmes/un cri à qn** to make sb cry/cry out; **ils ont arraché la victoire à la dernière minute** they snatched victory at the last minute; **il lui arracha son sac à main** he snatched *ou* grabbed her handbag from her; **je lui ai arraché cette promesse/ces aveux/la vérité** I dragged this promise/this confession/the truth out of him ⓓ (= *soustraire*) **~ qn à** [+ *famille, pays*] to tear *ou* drag sb away from; [+ *passion, vice, soucis*] to rescue sb from; [+ *sommeil, rêve*] to drag *ou* snatch sb out of *ou* from; [+ *sort, mort*] to snatch sb from; [+ *habitudes, méditation*] to force sb out of; **~ qn des mains d'un ennemi** to snatch sb from the hands of an enemy; **la mort nous l'a arraché** death has snatched *ou* torn him from us; **il m'a arraché du lit à 6 heures** he got *ou* dragged me out of bed at 6 o'clock

② **s'arracher** VPR ⓐ (= *se déchirer*) **tu t'es arraché les vêtements sur le grillage** you've torn your clothes on the fence; **s'~ les cheveux** (*lit*) to tear *ou* pull out one's hair; (*fig*) to tear one's hair out; (*fig*) **s'~ les yeux** to scratch each other's eyes out ⓑ **s'~ qn/qch** to fight over sb/sth; **on s'arrache leur dernier CD** everybody is desperate to get hold of their latest CD; **les cinéastes se l'arrachent** film directors are falling over themselves *ou* are fighting to get him to act in their films ⓒ **s'~ de** *ou* **à** [+ *pays, famille*] to tear o.s. away from; [+ *habitude, méditation, passion*] to force o.s. out of; [+ *lit*] to drag o.s. from, force o.s. out of; **on s'arrache ?**⁑ let's split!⁑

arracheur [aʀaʃœʀ] NM → **mentir**

arracheuse [aʀaʃøz] NF (*Agr*) lifter, grubber

arraisonnement [aʀɛzɔnmã] NM (*Naut*) inspection

arraisonner [aʀɛzɔne] ▸conjug 1◂ VT (*Naut*) to inspect

arrangeant, e [aʀãʒã, ãt] ADJ accommodating, obliging

arrangement [aʀãʒmã] NM ⓐ (= *action*) [*fleurs, coiffure, voyage*] arranging ⓑ (= *agencement*) [*mobilier, maison*] layout, arrangement; [*fiches*] order, arrangement; [*mots*] order; **l'~ de sa coiffure** the way her hair is done *ou* arranged; **l'~ de sa toilette** the way she is dressed ⓒ (= *accord*) agreement, settlement, arrangement; **arriver** *ou* **parvenir à un ~** to come to an agreement *ou* a settlement *ou* an arrangement; **sauf ~ contraire** unless other arrangements are made; (*Jur*) **~ de famille** family settlement (*in financial matters*) ⓓ (*Mus*) ar-

rangement; **~ pour guitare** arrangement for guitar ⓔ (*Math*) arrangement ⓕ (= *préparatifs*) **~s** arrangements

arranger [aʀãʒe] ▸conjug 3◂ ① VT ⓐ (= *disposer*: *gén*) to arrange; [+ *coiffure*] to tidy up; **~ sa cravate/sa jupe** to straighten (up) one's tie/skirt, set one's tie/skirt straight ⓑ (= *organiser*) [+ *voyage, réunion*] to arrange, organize; [+ *rencontre, entrevue*] to arrange, fix (up); **~ sa vie/ses affaires** to organize one's life/one's affairs; **il a tout arrangé pour ce soir** he has seen to *ou* he has arranged everything for tonight; **ce combat de catch était arrangé à l'avance** this wrestling match was fixed (in advance) *ou* was a put-up job* ⓒ (= *régler*) [+ *différend*] to settle; **il a essayé d'~ les choses** *ou* **le coup*** he tried to sort *ou* straighten the matter out; **tout est arrangé** everything is settled *ou* sorted out; **et ce qui n'arrange rien, il est en retard !** and he's late, which doesn't help matters!; **ce contretemps n'arrange pas nos affaires** this setback doesn't help matters ⓓ (= *contenter*) to suit, be convenient for; **ça ne m'arrange pas tellement** it doesn't really suit me; **cela m'arrange bien** that suits me nicely *ou* fine; **à 6 heures si ça vous arrange** at 6 o'clock if that suits you *ou* if that's convenient (for you); **tu le crois parce que ça t'arrange** you believe him because it suits you (to do so) ⓔ (= *réparer*) [+ *voiture, montre*] to fix, put right; [+ *robe*] (= *recoudre*) to fix, mend; (= *modifier*) to alter; **il faudrait ~ votre texte, il est confus** you'd better sort out your text, it looks awfully confused ⓕ (* = *malmener*) to work over*, sort out⁑ (*Brit*); **il s'est drôlement fait ~** he got a real working over*, they really sorted him out⁑ (*Brit*); **te voilà bien arrangé !** what a state *ou* mess you've got yourself in!*; **il s'est fait ~ le portrait** he got his face bashed in* *ou* smashed in* ⓖ (*Littérat, Mus*) to arrange

② **s'arranger** VPR ⓐ (= *se mettre d'accord*) to come to an agreement *ou* a settlement *ou* an arrangement; **arrangez-vous avec le patron** you'll have to sort it out with the boss; **s'~ à l'amiable** to come to a friendly *ou* an amicable agreement ⓑ (= *s'améliorer*) [*querelle*] to be settled; [*situation*] to work out, sort itself out (*Brit*); [*santé*] to get better; **le temps n'a pas l'air de s'~** it doesn't look as though the weather is improving *ou* getting any better; **tout va s'~** everything will work out (all right) *ou* sort itself out (*Brit*); **les choses s'arrangèrent d'elles-mêmes** things worked *ou* sorted (*Brit*) themselves out; **ça ne s'arrange pas*, il est plus têtu que jamais** he's not getting any better, he's more stubborn than ever; **il ne fait rien pour s'~** he doesn't do himself any favours; **alors, ça s'arrange entre eux ?** are things getting (any) better between them? ⓒ (= *se débrouiller*) to manage; **arrangez-vous comme vous voudrez mais je les veux demain** I don't know how you do it but I want them for tomorrow; **tu t'arranges toujours pour avoir des taches !** you always manage to dirty your clothes!; **il va s'~ pour finir le travail avant demain** he'll see to it that *ou* he'll make sure (that) he finishes the job before tomorrow; **il s'est arrangé pour avoir des places gratuites** he has managed to get some free seats; **arrangez-vous pour venir me chercher à la gare** arrange it so that you can come and meet me at the station; **c'est ton problème, arrange-toi !** it's your problem, you deal with it! ⓓ **s'~ de** to make do with, put up with; **il s'est arrangé du fauteuil pour dormir** he made do with the armchair to sleep in; **il faudra bien s'en ~** we'll just have to put up with it ⓔ (= *se classer*) to be arranged; **ses arguments s'arrangent logiquement** his arguments are

logically arranged ⓕ (= *se rajuster*) to tidy o.s. up; **elle s'arrange les cheveux** she's fixing her hair ⓖ (* = *se faire mal*) **tu t'es bien arrangé !** you've got yourself in a fine state!, you do look a mess!*

arrangeur, -euse [aʀãʒœʀ, øz] NM,F (*Mus*) arranger

arrérages [aʀeʀaʒ] NMPL arrears

arrestation [aʀɛstasjɔ̃] ① NF arrest; **procéder à l'~ de qn** to arrest sb; **être/mettre en état d'~** to be/place *ou* put under arrest; **se mettre en état d'~** to give o.s. up to the police; **ils ont procédé à une douzaine d'~s** they made a dozen arrests ② COMP ▸ **arrestation préventive** ≈ arrest ▸ **arrestation provisoire** taking into preventive custody

arrêt [aʀɛ] ① NM ⓐ [*machine, véhicule*] stopping; [*développement, croissance*] stopping, checking, arrest; [*hémorragie*] stopping, arrest; **attendez l'~ complet (du train/de l'avion)** wait until the train/aircraft has come to a complete stop *ou* standstill; **cinq minutes d'~** [*trajet*] a 5-minute stop; [*cours*] a 5-minute break; [*sur véhicule*] **« ~s fréquents »** "frequent stops"; **véhicule à l'~** stationary vehicle; [*véhicule, conducteur*] **être à l'~** to be stationary; **faire un ~** [*train*] to stop, make a stop; [*gardien de but*] to make a save; **le train fit un ~ brusque** the train came to a sudden stop *ou* standstill; **nous avons fait plusieurs ~s** we made several stops *ou* halts; **marquer un ~ avant de continuer à parler** to pause *ou* make a pause before speaking again; **~ buffet*** snack break, pit stop* (*US*); **~ pipi*** loo stop* (*Brit*), bathroom break (*US*); **donner un coup d'~ à** to check, put a brake on ⓑ (= *lieu*) stop; **~ d'autobus** bus stop; **~ fixe/facultatif** compulsory/request stop ⓒ (*Mil*) **~s** arrest; **~s simples/de rigueur** open/close arrest; **~s de forteresse** confinement (*in military prison*); **mettre qn aux ~s** to put sb under arrest → **maison, mandat** ⓓ (*Jur* = *décision*) judgment, decision, ruling; **faire ~ sur les appointements de qn** to issue a writ of attachment (*on debtor's salary*); (*littér*) **les ~s du destin** the decrees of destiny (*littér*) ⓔ (*Couture*) **faire un ~** to fasten off the thread → **point²** ⓕ (*Tech*) [*machine*] stop mechanism; [*serrure*] ward; [*fusil*] safety catch; **appuyez sur l'~** press the stop button; (*Audiov*) **~ sur image** (= *dispositif*) freeze frame; **faire un ~ sur image** to freeze on a frame ⓖ (*Ski*) stop; (*Boxe*) stoppage; **il a perdu/gagné par ~ de l'arbitre** he won/lost on a stoppage ⓗ (*Chasse*) **rester** *ou* **tomber en ~** (*lit*) to point; (*fig*) to stop short; **être en ~** (*lit*) to be pointing (**devant** at); (*fig*) to stand transfixed (**devant** before) → **chien** ② **sans arrêt** LOC ADV (= *sans interruption*) [*travailler, pleuvoir*] without stopping, non-stop; (= *très fréquemment*) [*se produire, se détraquer*] continually, constantly; **ce train est sans ~ jusqu'à Lyon** this train is non-stop to Lyon ③ COMP ▸ **arrêt du cœur** cardiac arrest, heart failure ▸ **l'arrêt des hostilités** the cessation of hostilities ▸ **arrêt de jeu** (*Sport*) stoppage; **jouer les ~s de jeu** to play injury time ▸ **arrêt (de) maladie** sick leave; **être en ~ (de) maladie** to be on sick leave; **se mettre en ~ (de) maladie** to go sick ▸ **arrêt de mort** death warrant; **il avait signé son ~ de mort** (*fig*) he had signed his own death warrant ▸ **arrêt de travail** (= *grève*) stoppage (of work); (= *congé de maladie*) sick leave; (= *certificat*) doctor's *ou* medical certificate ▸ **arrêt de volée** (*Rugby*) **faire un ~ de volée** to make a mark

arrêté, e [aʀete] (*ptp de* **arrêter**) ① ADJ [*décision, volonté*] firm, immutable; [*idée, opinion*] fixed, firm; **c'est une chose ~e** the matter *ou* it is settled **2** NM (= *décision administrative*) order, decree (*frm*); **~ ministériel** departmental *ou* ministerial order; **~ municipal** ≈ by(e)-law; **~ préfectoral** order of the prefect; **~ de compte** (*fermeture*) settlement of account; (*relevé*) statement of account (*to date*)

arrêter [aRete] ▶conjug 1◀ **1** VT **a** (= *immobiliser*) [+ *personne, machine, montre*] to stop; [+ *cheval*] to stop, pull up; [+ *moteur*] to switch off, stop; **arrêtez-moi près de la poste** drop me off by the post office; **il m'a arrêté dans le couloir pour me parler** he stopped me in the corridor to speak to me; (*dans la conversation*) **ici, je vous arrête!** I must stop *ou* interrupt you there!

b (= *entraver*) [+ *développement, croissance*] to stop, check, arrest; [+ *foule, ennemi*] to stop, halt; [+ *hémorragie*] to stop, arrest; **le trafic ferroviaire est arrêté à cause de la grève** trains have been brought to a standstill *ou* a halt because of the strike; **rien n'arrête la marche de l'histoire** nothing can stop *ou* check *ou* halt the march of history; (*hum*) **on n'arrête pas le progrès!** the wonders of modern science! (*hum*); **nous avons été arrêtés par un embouteillage** we were held up *ou* stopped by a traffic jam; **seul le prix l'arrête** it's only the price that stops him; **rien ne l'arrête** there's nothing to stop him; **arrête les frais!*** drop it!*; **bon, on arrête les frais*** OK, let's stop this before it gets any worse

c (= *abandonner*) [+ *études, compétition, sport*] to give up; [+ *représentations*] to cancel; **~ la fabrication d'un produit** to discontinue (the manufacture of) a product; **on a dû ~ les travaux à cause de la neige** we had to stop work *ou* call a halt to the work because of the snow

d (= *faire prisonnier*) to arrest; **il s'est fait ~ hier** he got himself arrested yesterday; **je vous arrête!** you're under arrest!

e (*Fin*) [+ *compte*] (= *fermer*) to settle; (= *relever*) to make up; **les comptes sont arrêtés chaque fin de mois** statements (of account) are made up at the end of every month

f (*Couture*) [+ *point*] to fasten off

g (= *fixer*) [+ *jour, lieu*] to appoint, decide on; [+ *plan*] to decide on; [+ *derniers détails*] to finalize; **~ son attention/ses regards sur** to fix one's attention/gaze on; **~ un marché** to make a deal; **il a arrêté son choix** he's made his choice; **ma décision est arrêtée** my mind is made up; (*Admin*) **~ que ...** to rule that ...

h (*Méd*) **~ qn** to give sb sick leave; **elle est arrêtée depuis 3 semaines** she's been on sick leave for 3 weeks

2 VI to stop; **~ de fumer** to give up *ou* stop *ou* quit* smoking; **il n'arrête pas** he just never stops, he's always on the go; **il n'arrête pas de critiquer tout le monde** he never stops criticizing people, he's always criticizing people; **arrête de parler!** stop talking!; **arrête!** stop it!, stop that!; **ça n'arrête pas!*** it never stops!

3 **s'arrêter** VPR **a** (= *s'immobiliser*) [*personne, machine, montre*] to stop; [*train, voiture*] (*gén*) to stop; (*en se garant*) to pull up; **nous nous sommes arrêtés sur le bas-côté** we pulled up *ou* stopped by the roadside; **s'~ court** *ou* **net** [*personne*] to stop dead *ou* short; [*cheval*] to pull up; [*bruit*] to stop suddenly; **le train ne s'arrête pas à toutes les gares** the train doesn't stop *ou* call at every station; **nous nous sommes arrêtés 10 jours à Lyon** we stayed *ou* stopped* 10 days in Lyons

b (= *s'interrompre*) to stop, break off; **la route s'arrête ici** the road ends *ou* stops here; **s'~ pour se reposer/pour manger** to break off *ou* stop for a rest/to eat; **arrête-toi un peu, tu vas t'épuiser** stop for a while *ou* take a break or you'll wear yourself out; **les ouvriers se sont arrêtés à 17 heures** (*grève*) the workmen stopped work *ou* downed tools (*Brit*) at 5 o'clock; (*heure de fermeture*) the workmen finished (work) *ou* stopped work at 5 o'clock;

sans s'~ without stopping, without a break; **ce serait dommage de s'~ en si bon chemin** it would be a shame to stop *ou* give up while things are going so well

c (= *cesser*) [*développement, croissance*] to stop, come to a halt, come to a standstill; [*hémorragie*] to stop; **le travail s'est arrêté dans l'usine en grève** work has stopped in the striking factory, the striking factory is at a standstill; **s'~ de manger/marcher** to stop eating/walking; **s'~ de fumer/boire** to give up *ou* stop *ou* quit* smoking/drinking; **l'affaire ne s'arrêtera pas là!** you (*ou* they *etc*) haven't heard the last of this!

d **s'~ sur** [*choix, regard*] to fall on; **il ne faut pas s'~ aux apparences** you should always look beyond appearances; **s'~ à des détails** to waste time worrying about details; **s'~ à un projet** to settle on *ou* fix on a plan; **arrêtons-nous un instant sur ce tableau** let us turn our attention to this picture for a moment

arrhes [aR] NFPL deposit; **verser des ~** to pay *ou* leave a deposit

arriération [aRjeRasjɔ̃] NF **a** (*Psych*) retardation; **~ affective** emotional retardation **b** **~ économique** [*pays*] economic backwardness; **certains villages sont en voie d'~** some villages are slipping into economic decline

arriéré, e [aRjeRe] **1** ADJ **a** (*Comm*) [*paiement*] overdue, in arrears (*attrib*); [*dette*] outstanding **b** (*Psych*) [*enfant, personne*] backward, retarded; (*Scol*) educationally subnormal; [*région, pays*] backward, behind the times (*attrib*); [*croyances, méthodes, personne*] out-of-date, behind the times (*attrib*) **2** NM (= *choses à faire, travail*) backlog; (= *paiement*) arrears; **il voulait régler l'~ de sa dette** he wanted to settle the arrears on his debt

arrière [aRjeR] **1** NM **a** [*voiture*] back; [*bateau*] stern; [*train*] rear; (*Naut*) à aft, at the stern; (*Naut*) **à l'~ de** at the stern of, abaft; **se balancer d'avant en ~** to rock backwards and forwards; **avec le moteur à l'~** with the engine at the back, with a rear-mounted engine; (*en temps de guerre*) **l'~ (du pays)** the home front, the civilian zone; **l'~ tient bon** morale on the home front *ou* behind the lines is high

b (*Sport* = *joueur*) (*gén*) fullback; (*Volley*) back-line player; **~ gauche/droit** (*Ftbl*) left/right back; (*Basket*) left/right guard; (*Ftbl*) **~ central** centre back; **~ volant** sweeper

c (*Mil*) **les ~s** the rear; **attaquer les ~s de l'ennemi** to attack the enemy in the rear; **assurer** *ou* **protéger ses ~s** (*lit*) to protect the rear; (*fig*) to leave o.s. a way out

d **en ~** (= *derrière*) behind; (= *vers l'arrière*) backwards; **être/rester en ~** to be/lag *ou* drop behind; **regarder en ~** (*lit*) to look back *ou* behind; (*fig*) to look back; **faire un pas en ~** to step back(wards), take a step back; **aller/marcher en ~** to go/walk backwards; **se pencher en ~** to lean back(wards); (*Naut*) **en toute!** full astern!; **100 ans en ~** 100 years ago *ou* back; **il faut remonter loin en ~ pour trouver une telle sécheresse** we have to go a long way back (in time) to find a similar drought; **revenir en ~** [*marcheur*] to go back, retrace one's steps; [*orateur*] to go back over what has been said; [*civilisation*] to regress; (*avec magnétophone*) to rewind; (*dans ses pensées*) to look back; **renverser la tête en ~** to tilt one's head back(wards); **le chapeau en ~** his hat tilted back(wards); **être peigné** *ou* **avoir les cheveux en ~** to have *ou* wear one's hair brushed *ou* combed back(wards)

e (*lit, fig*) **en ~ de** behind; **rester** *ou* **se tenir en ~ de qch** to stay behind sth; **il est très en ~ des autres élèves** he's a long way behind the other pupils

2 ADJ INV **roue/feu ~** rear wheel/light; **siège ~** [*voiture*] back seat; [*moto*] pillion → **machine, marche¹, vent**

3 EXCL **en ~!** vous gênez stand *ou* get back!

you're in the way; **~, misérable!**† behind me, wretch!†

arrière-ban (*pl* **arrière-bans**) [aRjɛRbɑ̃] NM → **ban**

arrière-bouche (*pl* **arrière-bouches**) [aRjɛRbuʃ] NF back of the mouth

arrière-boutique (*pl* **arrière-boutiques**) [aRjɛRbutik] NF back shop

arrière-chœur (*pl* **arrière-chœurs**) [aRjɛRkœR] NM retrochoir

arrière-cour (*pl* **arrière-cours**) [aRjɛRkuR] NF backyard

arrière-cuisine (*pl* **arrière-cuisines**) [aRjɛRkɥizin] NF scullery

arrière-fond (*pl* **arrière-fonds**) [aRjɛRfɔ̃] NM **a** [*tableau, scène*] background; **en ~** in the background **b** (*littér*) **dans l'~ obscur de son âme** in the dark recesses of his soul

arrière-garde (*pl* **arrière-gardes**) [aRjɛRgaRd] NF rearguard; (*lit, fig*) **livrer un combat** *ou* **une bataille d'~** to fight a rearguard action *ou* battle

arrière-gorge (*pl* **arrière-gorges**) [aRjɛRgɔRʒ] NF back of the throat

arrière-goût (*pl* **arrière-goûts**) [aRjɛRgu] NM (*lit, fig*) aftertaste; **ses propos ont un ~ de racisme** his comments smack of racism

arrière-grand-mère (*pl* **arrière-grands-mères**) [aRjɛRgRɑ̃mɛR] NF great-grandmother

arrière-grand-oncle (*pl* **arrière-grands-oncles**) [aRjɛRgRɑ̃tɔ̃kl] NM great-great-uncle

arrière-grand-père (*pl* **arrière-grands-pères**) [aRjɛRgRɑ̃pɛR] NM great-grandfather

arrière-grands-parents [aRjɛRgRɑ̃paRɑ̃] NMPL great-grandparents

arrière-grand-tante (*pl* **arrière-grands-tantes**) [aRjɛRgRɑ̃tɑ̃t] NF great-great-aunt

arrière-pays [aRjɛRpei] NM INV hinterland; **dans l'~ niçois** in the countryside just inland from Nice

arrière-pensée (*pl* **arrière-pensées**) [aRjɛRpɑ̃se] NF (= *motif inavoué*) ulterior motive; (= *réserves, doute*) reservation; **je l'ai dit/fait sans ~** I had no ulterior motive when I said/did it; **cette mesure n'est pas dénuée d'~s politiques** there's a political agenda behind this measure

arrière-petit-cousin (*pl* **arrière-petits-cousins**) [aRjɛRpətikuzɛ̃] NM cousin three times removed

arrière-petite-cousine (*pl* **arrière-petites-cousines**) [aRjɛRpətitkuzin] NF cousin three times removed

arrière-petite-fille (*pl* **arrière-petites-filles**) [aRjɛRpətitfij] NF great-granddaughter

arrière-petite-nièce (*pl* **arrière-petites-nièces**) [aRjɛRpətitnjɛs] NF great-great-niece

arrière-petit-fils (*pl* **arrière-petits-fils**) [aRjɛRpətifis] NM great-grandson

arrière-petit-neveu (*pl* **arrière-petits-neveux**) [aRjɛRpətin(ə)vø] NM great-grandnephew, great-great-nephew

arrière-petits-enfants [aRjɛRpətizɑ̃fɑ̃] NMPL great-grandchildren

arrière-plan (*pl* **arrière-plans**) [aRjɛRplɑ̃] NM background; **à l'~** in the background; **ces préoccupations ont été reléguées à l'~** these concerns were put on the back burner *ou* relegated to the background

arrière-port (*pl* **arrière-ports**) [aRjɛRpɔR] NM inner harbour

arriérer [aRjeRe] ▶conjug 6◀ (*Fin*) **1** VT [+ *paiement*] to defer **2** **s'arriérer** VPR to fall into arrears, fall behind with one's *ou* the payments

arrière-saison (*pl* **arrière-saisons**) [aRjɛRsezɔ̃] NF end of autumn, late autumn, late fall (*US*); **un soleil d'~** late-autumn *ou* late-fall (*US*) sunshine

arrière-salle (*pl* **arrière-salles**) [aRjɛRsal] NF back room; [*café, restaurant*] inner room

arrière-train (*pl* **arrière-trains**) [aRjɛRtRɛ̃] NM [*animal*] hindquarters; (*hum*) [*personne*] behind*, hindquarters

arrimage [aRimaʒ] NM (*Naut*) stowage, stowing

arrimer [aRime] ▸conjug 1◂ VT (*Naut*) [+ *cargaison*] to stow; (*gén*) [+ *colis*] to lash down, secure

arrimeur [aRimœR] NM stevedore

arrivage [aRivaʒ] NM [*marchandises*] consignment, delivery, load; (*fig hum*) [*touristes*] fresh load (*hum*) ou influx

arrivant, e [aRivɑ̃, ɑ̃t] NM,F newcomer; **nouvel ~** newcomer, new arrival; **combien d'~s y avait-il hier?** how many new arrivals were there yesterday?, how many newcomers ou people arrived yesterday?; **les premiers ~s de la saison** the first arrivals of the season

arrivée [aRive] NF a [*personne, train, courrier*] arrival; [*printemps, neige, hirondelles*] arrival, coming; [*course, coureur*] finish; **l'~ de ce produit sur le marché** the appearance of this product on the market; **c'est l'~ des abricots sur les marchés** apricots are beginning to arrive in ou are coming into the shops; **j'attends l'~ du courrier** I'm waiting for the post ou mail to come ou arrive; (*dans une gare, un aéroport*) **«~s»** "arrivals"; **contactez-nous à votre ~ à l'aéroport** contact us (up)on your arrival at the airport; **à son ~ chez lui** when he arrive ou got (ou arrives ou gets) home, on arriving home, on his arrival home; **à l'~** [*course*] at the finish; (* = *au bout du compte*) at the end of the day; **j'irai l'attendre à l'~ (du train)** I'll go and get him at the station, I'll go and meet him off the train (*Brit*); **à leur ~ au pouvoir** when they came (ou come) to power → **gare¹, juge, ligne¹**
b (*Tech*) **~ d'air/d'eau/de gaz** (= *robinet*) air/water/gas inlet; (= *processus*) inflow of air/water/gas

arriver [aRive] ▸conjug 1◂ 1 VI a (*au terme d'un voyage*) [*train, personne*] to arrive; **~ à** [+ *ville*] to arrive at, get to, reach; **~ de** [+ *ville, pays*] to arrive from; **~ en France** to arrive in ou reach France; **~ chez des amis** to arrive at friends'; **~ chez soi** to arrive ou get home; **nous sommes arrivés** we've arrived, we're there; **le train doit ~ à 6 heures** the train is due (to arrive) ou scheduled to arrive ou is due in at 6 o'clock; **il est arrivé par le train/en voiture** he arrived by train/by car ou in a car; **réveille-toi, on arrive!** wake up, we're almost there!; **cette lettre m'est arrivée hier** this letter reached me yesterday; **~ le premier** (*à une course*) to come in first; (*à une soirée, une réception*) to be the first to arrive, arrive first; **les premiers arrivés** the first to arrive, the first arrivals → **destination, mars, port**
b (= *approcher*) [*saison, nuit, personne, véhicule*] to come; **~ à grands pas/en courant** to stride up/run up; **j'arrive!** (I'm) coming!, just coming!; **le train arrive en gare** the train is pulling ou coming into the station; **la voici qui arrive** here she comes (now); **allez, arrive*, je suis pressé!** hurry up ou come on, I'm in a hurry!; **ton tour arrivera bientôt** it'll soon be your turn; **on va commencer à manger, ça va peut-être faire ~ ton père** we'll start eating, perhaps that will make your father come; **pour faire ~ l'eau jusqu'à la maison ...** to lay the water on for (*Brit*) ou to bring the water (up) to the house ...; **l'air/l'eau arrive par ce trou** the air/water comes in through this hole; **pour qu'arrive plus vite le moment où il la reverrait** to bring the moment closer when he would see her again → **chien**
c (= *atteindre*) **~ à** [+ *niveau, lieu*] to reach, get to, arrive at; [+ *personne, âge*] to reach, get to; [+ *poste, rang*] to attain, reach; [+ *résultat, but, conclusion*] to reach, arrive at; **la nouvelle est**

arrivée jusqu'à nous the news has reached us ou got to us; **le bruit arrivait jusqu'à nous** the noise reached us; **je n'ai pas pu ~ jusqu'au chef** I wasn't able to get as far as the boss; **comment arrive-t-on chez eux?** how do you get to their house?; **le lierre arrive jusqu'au 1er étage** the ivy goes up to ou goes up as far as the 1st floor; **l'eau lui arrivait (jusqu')aux genoux** the water came up to his knees, he was knee-deep in water; **et le problème des salaires? — j'y arrive** and what about the wages problem? — I'm just coming to that; (*fig*) **il ne t'arrive pas à la cheville** he can't hold a candle to you, he's not a patch on you (*Brit*); **~ au pouvoir** to come to power
d (= *réussir*) **~ à** (+ *infinitif*) to manage to do sth, succeed in doing sth; **pour ~ à lui faire comprendre qu'il a tort** to get him to understand he's wrong; **il n'arrive pas à le comprendre** he just doesn't understand it; **je n'arrive pas à comprendre son attitude** I just don't ou can't understand ou I fail to understand his attitude; **je n'arrive pas à faire ce devoir** I can't do this exercise; **tu y arrives?** how are you getting on?; **je n'y arrive pas** I can't do ou manage it; **~ à ses fins** to get one's way, achieve one's ends; **il n'arrivera jamais à rien** he'll never get anywhere, he'll never achieve anything; **on n'arrivera jamais à rien avec lui** we'll never get anywhere with him
e (= *atteindre une réussite sociale*) to succeed (in life), get on (in life); **il veut ~** he wants to get on ou succeed (in life); **il se croit arrivé** he thinks he's made it* ou he's arrived
f (= *se produire*) to happen; **c'est arrivé hier** it happened ou occurred yesterday; **ce genre d'accident n'arrive qu'à lui!** that sort of accident only (ever) happens to him!; **ce sont des choses qui arrivent** these things (will) happen; **cela peut ~ à n'importe qui** it could ou can happen to anyone; **tu n'oublies jamais? — ça m'arrive** don't you ever forget? — yes, sometimes; **cela ne m'arrivera plus!** I won't let it happen again!; **tu ne sais pas ce qui m'arrive!** you'll never guess what happened (to me)!; **il croit que c'est arrivé*** he thinks he's made it*; **ça devait lui ~** he had it coming to him*; **tu vas nous faire ~ des ennuis*** you'll get us into trouble
g **en ~ à** (= *finir par*) to come to; **on n'en est pas encore arrivé là!** (*résultat négatif*) we've not come to ou reached that (stage) yet!; (*résultat positif*) we've not got that far yet!; **on en arrive à se demander si ...** it makes you wonder whether ...; **il faudra bien en ~ là!** it'll have to come to that (eventually); **c'est triste d'en ~ là** it's sad to be reduced to that

2 VB IMPERS a (= *survenir*) **il est arrivé un télégramme** a telegram has come ou arrived; **il est arrivé un accident** there's been an accident; **il lui est arrivé un accident** he's had an accident, he has met with an accident; **il (lui) est arrivé un malheur** something dreadful has happened (to him); **il lui arrivera des ennuis** he'll get (himself) into trouble; **il m'arrive toujours des aventures incroyables** incredible things are always happening to me; **quoi qu'il arrive** whatever happens; **comme il arrive souvent** as is often the case
b **il arrive que** ou **de**: **il m'arrive d'oublier ◊ il arrive que j'oublie** I sometimes forget; **il peut ~ qu'elle se trompe ◊ il peut lui ~ de se tromper** she does occasionally make a mistake, it occasionally happens that she makes a mistake; **il peut ~ qu'elle se trompe mais ce n'est pas une raison pour la critiquer** she may make mistakes but that's no reason to criticize her; **il pourrait ~ qu'ils soient sortis** it could be that they've gone out, they might have gone out; **s'il lui arrive ou arrivait de faire une erreur, prévenez-moi** if he should happen ou if he happens to make a mistake, let me know; **il m'est arrivé plusieurs fois de le voir/faire** I have seen him/done it several times; **il**

ne lui arrive pas souvent de mentir it isn't often that he lies, he doesn't often lie

arrivisme [aRivism] NM (*péj*) (ruthless) ambition, pushiness; (*social*) social climbing

arriviste [aRivist] NMF (*péj*) go-getter*, careerist; (*social*) social climber

arroche [aRɔʃ] NF orache, orach (*US*)

arrogance [aRɔgɑ̃s] NF arrogance

arrogant, e [aRɔgɑ̃, ɑ̃t] ADJ arrogant

arroger (s') [aRɔʒe] ▸conjug 3◂ VPR [+ *pouvoirs, privilèges*] to assume (without right); [+ *titre*] to claim (falsely), claim (without right), assume; **s'~ le droit de ...** to assume the right to ..., take it upon o.s. to ...

arrondi, e [aRɔ̃di] (*ptp de* **arrondir**) 1 ADJ [*objet, forme, relief*] round, rounded; [*visage*] round; [*voyelle*] rounded 2 NM (*gén = contour*) roundness; (*Aviat*) flare-out, flared landing; (*Couture*) hemline (*of skirt*)

arrondir [aRɔ̃diR] ▸conjug 2◂ 1 VT a [+ *objet, contour*] to round, make round; [+ *rebord, angle*] to round off; [+ *phrases*] to polish, round out; [+ *gestes*] to make smoother; [+ *caractère*] to make more agreeable, smooth the rough edges off; [+ *voyelle*] to round, make rounded; [+ *jupe*] to level; [+ *visage, taille, ventre*] to fill out, round out; (*fig*) **~ les angles** to smooth things over b (= *accroître*) [+ *fortune*] to swell; [+ *domaine*] to increase, enlarge; **~ ses fins de mois** to supplement one's income c (= *simplifier*) [+ *somme, nombre*] to round off; **~ au franc inférieur/supérieur** to round down/up to the nearest franc 2 **s'arrondir** VPR [*relief*] to become round(ed); [*taille, joues, ventre, personne*] to fill out; [*fortune*] to swell

arrondissement [aRɔ̃dismɑ̃] NM a (*Admin*) district b [*voyelle*] rounding; [*fortune*] swelling; [*taille, ventre*] rounding, filling out

---

ARRONDISSEMENT

The French metropolitan and overseas "départements" are divided into over 300 smaller administrative areas known as **arrondissements,** *which in turn are divided into "cantons" and "communes". There are usually three or four* **arrondissements** *in a "département". The main town in an* **arrondissement** *(the "chef-lieu d'arrondissement") is the home of the "sous-préfecture". The "sous-préfet d'arrondissement" reports to the "préfet" and deals with local administration, development and public order.*

    Marseilles, Lyons and Paris are divided into city districts known as **arrondissements,** *each with its own local council (the "conseil d'arrondissement") and mayor. The number of the* **arrondissement** *appears in addresses at the end of the post code.*

→ COMMUNE ; CONSEIL ; DÉPARTEMENT

---

arrosage [aRozaʒ] NM [*pelouse*] watering; [*voie publique*] spraying; **cette plante nécessite des ~s fréquents** this plant needs frequent watering → **lance, tuyau**

arroser [aRoze] ▸conjug 1◂ VT a [*personne*] [+ *plante, terre*] (*gén*) to water; (*avec un tuyau*) to water, hose; (*légèrement*) to sprinkle; [+ *champ*] to spray; [+ *rôti*] to baste; **~ qch d'essence** to pour petrol (*Brit*) ou gasoline (*US*) over sth; (*Culin*) **arrosez d'huile d'olive** drizzle with olive oil
b [*pluie*] [+ *terre*] to water; [+ *personne*] (*légèrement*) to make wet; (*fortement*) to drench, soak; **c'est la ville la plus arrosée de France** it is the wettest city ou the city with the highest rainfall in France; **se faire ~*** to get drenched ou soaked
c (*Géog*) [*fleuve*] to water
d (*Mil*) (*avec fusil, balles*) to spray (*de* with); (*avec canon*) to bombard (*de* with)
e * [+ *événement, succès*] to drink to; [+ *repas*] to wash down (with wine)*; [+ *café*] to lace (with a spirit); **après un repas bien arrosé** after a meal washed down with plenty of wine, af-

ter a pretty boozy* meal; **... le tout arrosé de champagne** ... all washed down with champagne; **tu as gagné, ça s'arrose!** you've won — that calls for a drink! *ou* we must drink to that!

[f] (*TV, Radio*) [+ *territoire*] to cover

[g] (* = *soudoyer*) [+ *personne*] to grease *ou* oil the palm of

[h] (*littér*) [*sang*] to soak; **~ une photographie de ses larmes** to let one's tears fall upon a photograph; **terre arrosée de sang** blood-soaked earth

arroseur [arozœr] NM [a] [*jardin*] waterer; [*rue*] water cartman; **c'est l'~ arrosé** it's a case of the biter (being) bit [b] (= *tourniquet*) sprinkler

arroseuse [arozøz] NF [*rue*] water cart

arrosoir [arozwar] NM watering can

arrt ABRÉV = **arrondissement**

arsenal (*pl* **-aux**) [arsənal, o] NM (*Mil*) arsenal; [*mesures, lois*] arsenal; (* = *attirail*) gear* (*NonC*), paraphernalia (*NonC*); **l'~ du pêcheur/du photographe** the fisherman's/photographer's gear *ou* paraphernalia; **tout un ~ de vieux outils** a huge collection *ou* assortment of old tools; (*Naut*) **~ (de la marine ou maritime)** naval dockyard

arsenic [arsənik] NM arsenic; **empoisonnement à l'~** arsenic poisoning

arsenical, e (*mpl* **-aux**) [arsənikal, o] ADJ [*substance*] arsenical

arsénieux [arsenjø] ADJ M arsenic (*épith*); **oxyde** *ou* **anhydride ~** arsenic trioxide, arsenic

arsouille† [arsuj] NM *ou* F (= *voyou*) ruffian; **il a un air ~** (= *voyou*) he looks like a ruffian; (= *malin*) he looks crafty

art [ar] [1] NM [a] (= *esthétique*) art; **l'~ espagnol/populaire** Spanish/popular art; **l'~ pour l'~** art for art's sake; **livre/critique d'~** art book/critic; **c'est du grand ~!** (*activité*) it's poetry in motion!; (*travail excellent*) it's an excellent piece of work!; (*iro: tableau exécrable*) call that art?!; **le septième ~** cinema; **le huitième ~** television; **le neuvième ~** comic strips, strip cartoons (*Brit*), comics (*US*) → **amateur** [b] (= *technique*) art; **~ culinaire/militaire/oratoire** the art of cooking/of warfare/of public speaking; **l'~ de la conversation** the art of conversation; **il est passé maître dans l'~ de** he's a past master in the art of; **un homme/les gens de l'~** a man/the people in the profession; **demandons à un homme de l'~!** let's ask a professional! → **règle** [c] (= *adresse*) [*artisan*] skill, artistry; [*poète*] skill, art, artistry; **faire qch avec un ~ consommé** to do sth with consummate skill; **c'est tout un ~** it's quite an art; **il a l'~ et la manière** he's got the know-how *ou* he knows what he's doing and he does it in style [d] **l'~ de faire qch** the art of doing sth, a talent *ou* flair for doing sth, the knack of doing sth*; **il a l'~ de me mettre en colère** he has a talent *ou* a knack* for making me angry; **ce style a l'~ de me plaire** this style appeals to me; (*hum*) **ça a l'~ de m'endormir** it sends me to sleep every time; **réapprendre l'~ de marcher** to re-learn the art of walking

[2] COMP ▸ **arts d'agrément** accomplishments ▸ **arts appliqués** = arts décoratifs ▸ **art déco** art deco ▸ **arts décoratifs** decorative arts ▸ **l'art dramatique** dramatic art, drama ▸ **les arts du feu** ceramics *sg* ▸ **arts graphiques** graphic arts ▸ **les arts libéraux** the liberal arts ▸ **arts martiaux** martial arts ▸ **arts ménagers** home economics, homecraft (*NonC*), domestic science; **les Arts ménagers** (*salon*) ≈ the Ideal Home Exhibition ▸ **les Arts et Métiers** higher education institute for industrial art and design ▸ **l'art nègre** African art ▸ **art nouveau** Art Nouveau ▸ **les arts plastiques** the visual arts, the fine arts ▸ **art poétique** (= *technique*) poetic art; (= *doctrine*) ars

poetica, poetics *sg* ▸ **les arts de la rue** street performance ▸ **les arts de la scène** *ou* **du spectacle** the performing arts ▸ **les arts de la table** the art of entertaining (*preparing and presenting food*) ▸ **art de vivre** way of life

art. (ABRÉV = **article**) art

Arte [arte] N (*TV*) Franco-German cultural television channel

artefact [artefakt] NM artefact

Artémis [artemis] NF Artemis

artère [arter] NF (*Anat*) artery; (*Aut*) **(grande) ~** (*en ville*) main road, thoroughfare; (*entre villes*) main (trunk) road

artériel, -ielle [arterjɛl] ADJ (*Anat*) arterial → **tension**

artériographie [arterjografi] NF arteriography

artériole [arterjɔl] NF arteriole

artériosclérose [arterjoskleroz] NF arteriosclerosis

artérite [arterit] NF arteritis

artésien, -ienne [artezjɛ̃, jɛn] ADJ Artois (*épith*), of *ou* from Artois → **puits**

arthrite [artrit] NF arthritis; **avoir de l'~** to have arthritis

arthritique [artritik] ADJ, NMF arthritic

arthritisme [artritism] NM arthritism

arthropode [artropɔd] NM arthropod

arthrose [artroz] NF (degenerative) osteoarthritis

arthrosique [artrozik] [1] ADJ osteoarthritic [2] NMF osteoarthritis sufferer

Arthur [artyr] NM Arthur; **le roi ~** King Arthur → **appeler**

arthurien, -ienne [artyrjɛ̃, jɛn] ADJ [*cycle, mythe*] Arthurian

artichaut [artiʃo] NM artichoke → **cœur, fond**

article [artikl] [1] NM [a] (*Comm*) item, article; **baisse sur tous nos ~s** all (our) stock *ou* all items reduced, reduction on all items; **~ d'importation** imported product; **nous ne faisons plus cet ~** we don't stock that item *ou* product any more; **faire l'~** (*pour vendre qch*) to give the sales pitch; (*fig*) to sing sth's *ou* sb's praises [b] (*Presse*) [*journal*] article; [*dictionnaire*] entry [c] (= *chapitre*) point; [*loi, traité*] article; **les 2 derniers ~s de cette lettre** the last 2 points in this letter; **sur cet ~** on this point; **sur l'~ de** in the matter of, in matters of [d] (*Gram*) article; **~ contracté/défini/élidé/indéfini/partitif** contracted/definite/elided/indefinite/partitive article [e] (*Ordin*) record, item [f] **à l'~ de la mort** at death's door, at the point of death

[2] COMP ▸ **articles de bureau** office accessories ▸ **articles de consommation courante** convenience goods ▸ **article de foi** (*lit, fig*) article of faith ▸ **article de fond** (*Presse*) feature article ▸ **articles de luxe** luxury goods ▸ **articles de mode** fashion accessories ▸ **articles de Paris†** fancy goods ▸ **articles de sport** (*vêtements*) sportswear; (*objets*) sports equipment ▸ **articles de toilette** toiletries, toilet requisites *ou* articles ▸ **articles de voyage** travel goods *ou* requisites

articulaire [artikylɛr] ADJ articular → **rhumatisme**

articulation [artikylasjɔ̃] NF [a] (*Anat*) joint; (*Tech*) articulation; **~s des doigts** knuckles, finger joints; **~ du genou/de la hanche/de l'épaule** knee/hip/shoulder joint; **~ en selle** saddle joint [b] [*discours, raisonnement*] linking sentence; **la bonne ~ des parties de son discours** the sound structuring of his speech [c] (*Ling*) articulation; **point d'~** point of articulation [d] (*Jur*) enumeration, setting forth

articulatoire [artikylatwar] ADJ articulatory

articulé, e [artikyle] (*ptp de* **articuler**) [1] ADJ [*langage*] articulate; [*membre*] jointed, articulated; [*objet*] jointed; [*poupée*] with movable joints (*épith*), poseable; **autobus ~** articulated bus [2] NM **~ dentaire** bite

articuler [artikyle] ▸ conjug 1 ◂ VT [a] [+ *mot*] (= *prononcer clairement*) to articulate, pronounce clearly; (= *dire*) to pronounce, utter; **il articule bien/mal ses phrases** he articulates *ou* speaks/doesn't articulate *ou* speak clearly; **il articule mal** he doesn't articulate (his words) *ou* speak clearly; **articule!** speak clearly!

[b] (= *joindre*) [+ *mécanismes, os*] to articulate, joint; [+ *idées*] to link (up *ou* together); **élément/os qui s'articule sur un autre** element/bone that is articulated with *ou* is jointed to another; **~ un discours sur deux thèmes principaux** to structure a speech around *ou* on two main themes; **toute sa défense s'articule autour de cet élément** his entire defence hinges *ou* turns on this factor; **les parties de son discours s'articulent bien** the different sections of his speech are well linked *ou* hang together well; **une grande salle autour de laquelle s'articulent une multitude de locaux** a large room surrounded by a multitude of offices

[c] (*Jur*) [+ *faits, griefs*] to enumerate, set out

artifice [artifis] NM (clever *ou* ingenious) device, trick; (*péj*) trick; **~ de calcul** (clever) trick of arithmetic; **~ comptable** accounting device; **~ de style** stylistic device; **user d'~s pour paraître belle** to resort to tricks *ou* artifice to make oneself look beautiful; **l'~ est une nécessité de l'art** art cannot exist without (some) artifice; **sans ~(s)** [*présentation*] simple; [*s'exprimer*] straightforwardly, unpretentiously → **feu¹**

artificiel, -ielle [artifisjɛl] ADJ [a] (= *fabriqué*) artificial; [*fibre*] man-made; [*colorant*] artificial, synthetic; [*dent*] false; [*île*] artificial, man-made → **insémination, intelligence** etc [b] (*péj*) [*raisonnement, style*] artificial, contrived; [*vie, besoins*] artificial; [*gaieté*] forced, artificial

artificiellement [artifisjɛlmã] ADV artificially; **fabriqué ~** man-made, synthetically made

artificier [artifisje] NM (= *fabricant*) firework(s) manufacturer *ou* maker; (= *pyrotechnicien*) pyrotechnician; (*pour désamorçage*) bomb disposal expert

artificieux, -ieuse [artifisjø, jøz] ADJ (*littér*) guileful, deceitful

artillerie [artijri] NF artillery, ordnance; **~ de campagne** field artillery; **~ de marine** naval guns; (*lit, fig*) **grosse ~** (= ◊ **~ lourde** heavy artillery); **pièce d'~** piece of artillery, gun; **tir d'~** artillery fire

artilleur [artijœr] NM artilleryman, gunner

artimon [artimɔ̃] NM (= *voile*) mizzen; (= *mât*) mizzen(mast) → **mât**

artisan [artizã] NM [a] (= *patron*) (self-employed) craftsman, artisan; **les petits ~s** small craftsmen *ou* artisans; **il a été ~ avant de travailler pour moi** he ran his own business *ou* he was self-employed before coming to work for me; **~ boulanger** baker; (*sur vitrine*) **~ boucher** quality butcher [b] (= *auteur, cause*) [*accord, politique, victoire*] architect; **~ de la paix** peacemaker; **il est l'~ de sa propre ruine** he has brought about *ou* he is the author of his own ruin

artisanal, e (*mpl* **-aux**) [artizanal, o] ADJ [*production*] (= *limitée*) small-scale (*épith*), on a small scale (*attrib*); (= *traditionnelle*) traditional; **entreprise ~e** small company; **foire ~e** arts and crafts fair, craft fair; **pêche ~e** local *ou* small-scale fishing; **la production ~e de ce médicament** the production of this medicine on a small scale; **il exerce une activité ~e** he's a self-employed craftsman; **la fabrication se fait de manière très ~e** (*traditionnellement*) the style of production is very traditional; (*à pe-*

tite échelle) the style of production is very much that of a cottage industry; **bombe de fabrication ~e** home-made bomb; **produits artisanaux** crafts, handicrafts

artisanalement [aʀtizanalmɑ̃] ADV **fabriqué ~** [*pain, fromage*] made using traditional methods; [*objet*] hand-crafted

artisanat [aʀtizana] NM (= *métier*) craft industry; **l'~ local** (= *industrie*) local crafts *ou* handicrafts; **l'~ d'art** arts and crafts

artiste [aʀtist] **1** NMF [a] (*gén*) artist; (= *interprète*) performer; [*music-hall, cirque*] artiste, entertainer; **~ dramatique/de cinéma** stage/ film actor *ou* actress; **~ invité** guest artist; **~ peintre** artist, painter → **entrée, travail** [b] (*péj* = *bohème*) bohemian **2** ADJ [*personne, style*] artistic; (*péj*) **il est du genre ~** he's the artistic *ou* bohemian type

artiste-interprète (*pl* **artistes-interprètes**) [aʀtistɛ̃tɛʀpʀɛt] NMF [*musique*] composer and performer; [*chanson, pièce*] writer and performer

artistement [aʀtistəmɑ̃] ADV artistically

artistique [aʀtistik] ADJ artistic

artistiquement [aʀtistikmɑ̃] ADV artistically

arum [aʀɔm] NM arum lily

aryen, -yenne [aʀjɛ̃, jɛn] **1** ADJ Aryan **2** **Aryen(ne)** NM,F Aryan

arythmie [aʀitmi] NF arrhythmia

AS [aɛs] **1** NFPL (ABRÉV = **assurances sociales**) → **assurance** **2** NF (ABRÉV = **association sportive**) → **association**

as [as] NM [a] (= *carte, dé*) ace; (*Hippisme, au loto*) **l'~** number one [b] (* = *champion*) ace*; **un ~ de la route/du ciel** a crack driver/pilot; **l'~ de l'école** the school's star pupil [c] (*Tennis*) ace; **réussir** *ou* **servir un ~** to serve an ace [d] (*loc*) **être ficelé** *ou* **fagoté comme l'~ de pique*** to be dressed any old how*; **être (plein) aux ~:** to be loaded*, be rolling in it*; (*au restaurant*) **les apéritifs sont passés à l'~*** we got away without paying for the drinks, we got the drinks for free*; **mes vacances sont passées à l'~*** my holidays went by the board (*Brit*), my vacation went down the drain (*US*); **il n'y avait pas assez de place, mon texte est passé à l'~** there wasn't enough room so my article was ditched*

ASA [aza] NM INV (ABRÉV = **American Standards Association**) (*Photo*) ASA

asbeste [asbɛst] NM asbestos

asbestose [asbɛstoz] NF asbestosis

ascendance [asɑ̃dɑ̃s] NF [a] (*généalogique*) ancestry; **son ~ paternelle** his paternal ancestry; **être d'~ bourgeoise** to be of middle-class descent [b] (*Astron*) rising, ascent; (*Mét*) **~ thermique** thermal

ascendant, e [asɑ̃dɑ̃, ɑ̃t] **1** ADJ [*astre*] rising, ascending; [*mouvement, direction*] upward; [*courant*] rising; [*progression*] ascending; [*trait*] rising; (*Généalogie*) [*ligne*] ancestral; **mouvement ~ du piston** upstroke of the piston **2** NM [a] (= *influence*) (powerful) influence, ascendancy (*sur* over); **subir l'~ de qn** to be under sb's influence [b] (*Admin*) **~s** ascendants [c] (*Astron*) rising star; (*Astrol*) ascendant

ascenseur [asɑ̃sœʀ] NM lift (*Brit*), elevator (*US*); (*Ordin*) scroll bar → **renvoyer**

ascension [asɑ̃sjɔ̃] NF [a] [*ballon*] ascent, rising; [*fusée*] ascent; [*homme politique*] rise; (*sociale*) rise; (*Rel*) **l'Ascension** the Ascension; (= *jour férié*) Ascension (Day); **l'île de l'Ascension** Ascension Island; (*Astron*) **~ droite** right ascension; **~ professionnelle** professional advancement [b] [*montagne*] ascent; **faire l'~ d'une montagne** to climb a mountain, make the ascent of a mountain; **la première ~ de l'Everest** the first ascent of Everest; **c'est une ~ difficile** it's a difficult climb; **faire des ~s** to go (mountain) climbing

ascensionnel, -elle [asɑ̃sjɔnɛl] ADJ [*mouvement*] upward; [*force*] upward, elevatory; **vitesse ~le** climbing speed → **parachute**

ascensionniste [asɑ̃sjɔnist] NMF ascensionist

ascèse [asɛz] NF asceticism

ascète [asɛt] NMF ascetic

ascétique [asetik] ADJ ascetic

ascétisme [asetism] NM ascéticism

ASCII [aski] NM (ABRÉV = **American Standard Code for Information Interchange**) ASCII; **code ~** ASCII code

ascorbique [askɔʀbik] ADJ [*acide*] ascorbic

ASE [aɛsə] NF (ABRÉV = **Agence spatiale européenne**) ESA

asémantique [asemɑ̃tik] ADJ asemantic

asepsie [asɛpsi] NF asepsis

aseptique [asɛptik] ADJ aseptic

aseptisation [asɛptizasjɔ̃] NF [*pièce*] fumigation; [*pansement, ustensile*] sterilization; [*plaie*] disinfection

aseptisé, e [asɛptize] (*ptp de* **aseptiser**) ADJ (*Méd*) sterilized; [*univers, images*] sanitized; [*document, discours*] impersonal; [*relation entre personnes*] sterile; [*film, roman*] anodyne, bland

aseptiser [asɛptize] ▸ conjug 1 ◂ VT [+ *pièce*] to fumigate; [+ *pansement, ustensile*] to sterilize; [+ *plaie*] to disinfect

asexué, e [asɛksɥe] ADJ (*Bio*) asexual; [*personne*] sexless, asexual

ashkénaze [aʃkenaz] ADJ, NMF Ashkenazi

ashram [aʃʀam] NM ashram

asiate [azjat] NMF (*injurieux*) Asian

asiatique [azjatik] **1** ADJ Asian; **la grippe ~** Asian flu; **le Sud-Est ~** South-East Asia; **la communauté ~ de Paris** the far eastern community in Paris **2** **Asiatique** NMF Asian

Asie [azi] NF Asia; **~ Mineure** Asia Minor; **~ centrale** Central Asia; **~ du Sud-Est** Southeast Asia

asile [azil] NM [a] (= *institution*) **~ (de vieillards)**† old people's home, retirement home; **~ psychiatrique** mental home; **~ (d'aliénés)**† (lunatic) asylum†; **~ de nuit** night shelter, hostel [b] (= *refuge*) refuge; (*dans une église*) sanctuary; **demander ~ à qn** to ask sb for refuge; **demander l'~ politique** to seek political asylum; **il a trouvé ~ chez un ami** he found refuge at the home of a friend; **droit d'~** (*Rel*) right of sanctuary; (*politique*) right of asylum; **sans ~** homeless

Asmara [asmara] N Asmara

asocial, e (*mpl* **-iaux**) [asɔsjal, jo] **1** ADJ [*comportement*] antisocial **2** NM,F social misfit, socially maladjusted person

asparagus [asparagys] NM (= *plante d'ornement*) asparagus fern

aspartam(e) [aspaʀtam] NM aspartame

▼ **aspect** [aspɛ] NM [a] (= *allure*) [*personne, objet, paysage*] appearance, look; **homme d'~ sinistre** sinister-looking man, man of sinister appearance; **l'intérieur de cette grotte a l'~ d'une église** the inside of the cave resembles *ou* looks like a church; **les nuages prenaient l'~ de montagnes** the clouds took on the appearance of mountains; **ce château a un ~ mystérieux** the castle has an air of mystery (about it) [b] (= *angle*) [*question*] aspect, side; **vu sous cet ~** seen from that angle; **j'ai examiné le problème sous tous ses ~s** I considered all aspects *ou* sides of the problem [c] (*Astrol, Ling*) aspect [d] (*littér* = *vue*) sight; **à l'~ de** at the sight of

asperge [aspɛʀʒ] NF [a] (*Bot*) asparagus → **pointe** [b] (* = *personne*) **(grande) ~** beanpole*, string bean* (*US*)

asperger [aspɛʀʒe] ▸ conjug 3 ◂ VT [+ *surface*] to spray; (*légèrement*) to sprinkle; (*Rel*) to sprinkle; [+ *personne*] to splash (*de* with); **s'~ le visage** to splash one's face with water; **le bus**

nous a aspergés au passage* the bus splashed us *ou* sprayed water over us as it went past; **se faire ~*** (*par une voiture*) to get splashed; (*par un arroseur*) to get wet

aspérité [aspeʀite] NF [a] (= *partie saillante*) bump; **les ~s de la table** the bumps on the table, the rough patches on the surface of the table; **sans ~s** [*chemin, surface*] smooth [b] (*littér*) [*caractère, remarques, voix*] harshness; **sans ~s** [*caractère*] mild; [*remarques*] uncontroversial; [*voix*] smooth; **gommer les ~s de qch** to smooth the rough edges off sth

aspersion [aspɛʀsjɔ̃] NF spraying, sprinkling; (*Rel*) sprinkling of holy water, aspersion

asphalte [asfalt] NM asphalt

asphalter [asfalte] ▸ conjug 1 ◂ VT to asphalt

asphérique [asfeʀik] ADJ (*Photo*) [*lentille*] aspherical

asphodèle [asfɔdɛl] NM asphodel

asphyxiant, e [asfiksjɑ̃, jɑ̃t] ADJ [*fumée*] suffocating, asphyxiating; [*atmosphère*] stifling, suffocating → **gaz**

asphyxie [asfiksi] NF (*gén*) suffocation, asphyxiation; (*Méd*) asphyxia, [*plante*] asphyxiation; (*fig*) [*personne*] suffocation; [*industrie*] stifling

asphyxier [asfiksje] ▸ conjug 7 ◂ **1** VT (*lit*) to suffocate, asphyxiate; (*fig*) [+ *industrie, esprit*] to stifle; **mourir asphyxié** to die of suffocation *ou* asphyxiation **2** **s'asphyxier** VPR (*accident*) to suffocate, asphyxiate, be asphyxiated; (*suicide*) to suffocate o.s.; (*fig*) to suffocate; **il s'est asphyxié au gaz** he gassed himself

aspic [aspik] NM (*Zool*) asp; (*Bot*) aspic; (*Culin*) **~ de volaille/de foie gras** chicken/foie gras in aspic

aspirant, e [aspiʀɑ̃, ɑ̃t] **1** ADJ suction (*épith*), vacuum (*épith*) → **pompe¹** **2** NM,F (= *candidat*) candidate (*à* for) **3** NM (*Mil*) officer cadet; (*Naut*) midshipman, middie* (*US*)

aspirateur, -trice [aspiʀatœʀ, tʀis] **1** ADJ aspiratory **2** NM (*domestique*) vacuum (cleaner), Hoover® (*Brit*); (*Constr, Méd*) aspirator; **passer les tapis à l'~** to vacuum *ou* hoover the carpets, run the vacuum cleaner *ou* Hoover over the carpets; **passer l'~** to vacuum, hoover; **passer** *ou* **donner un coup d'~ dans la voiture** to give the car a quick going-over with the vacuum cleaner *ou* Hoover; **~(-)balai** upright vacuum cleaner *ou* Hoover®; **~(-)bidon** (*vertical*) cylinder vacuum cleaner *ou* Hoover®; **~(-)traîneau** (*horizontal*) cylinder vacuum cleaner *ou* Hoover®

aspiration [aspiʀasjɔ̃] NF [a] (*en inspirant*) inhaling (*NonC*), inhalation, breathing in (*NonC*); (*Ling*) aspiration; **de longues ~s** long deep breaths [b] [*liquide*] (*avec une paille*) sucking (up); (*gén, Tech : avec une pompe*) sucking up, drawing up, suction; (= *technique d'avortement*) vacuum extraction [c] (= *ambition*) aspiration (*vers, à* for, after); (= *souhait*) desire, longing (*vers, à* for)

aspiré, e [aspiʀe] (*ptp de* **aspirer**) **1** ADJ (*Ling*) aspirated; **h ~** aspirate h **2** **aspirée** NF aspirate

aspirer [aspiʀe] ▸ conjug 1 ◂ **1** VT [a] [+ *air, odeur*] to inhale, breathe in; [+ *liquide*] (*avec une paille*) to suck (up); (*Tech : avec une pompe*) to suck *ou* draw up; **~ et refouler** to pump in and out [b] (*Ling*) to aspirate **2** **aspirer à** VT INDIR [+ *honneur, titre*] to aspire to; [+ *genre de vie, tranquillité*] to desire, long for; **aspirant à quitter cette vie surexcitée** longing to leave this hectic life; **~ à la main de qn**† to be sb's suitor†, aspire to sb's hand†

aspirine [aspiʀin] NF aspirin; **(comprimé** *ou* **cachet d')~** aspirin; **prenez 2 ~s** take 2 aspirins → **blanc**

aspiro-batteur (*pl* **aspiro-batteurs**) [aspiʀobatœʀ] NM vacuum cleaner, Hoover® (*Brit*) (*which beats as it sweeps*)

▶ GRAMMAIRE ACTIVE: **aspect** 53.1, 53.2

assagir [asaʒiʀ] ▸ conjug 2 ◂ VT **a** (= calmer) [+ personne] to quieten (Brit) ou quiet (US) down, settle down; [+ passion] to subdue, temper, quieten (Brit), quiet (US); **elle n'arrivait pas à ~ ses cheveux rebelles** she couldn't do anything with her hair **b** (littér = rendre plus sage) to make wiser **2** **s'assagir** VPR [personne] to quieten (Brit) ou quiet (US) down, settle down; [style, passions] to become subdued

assagissement [asaʒismɑ̃] NM [personne] quietening (Brit) ou quieting (US) down, settling down; [passions] subduing

assaillant, e [asajɑ̃, ɑ̃t] NM,F assailant, attacker

assaillir [asajiʀ] ▸ conjug 13 ◂ VT (lit) to assail, attack; (fig) to assail (de with); **assailli de questions** assailed ou bombarded with questions

assainir [aseniʀ] ▸ conjug 2 ◂ VT [+ quartier, logement] to clean up, improve the living conditions in; [+ marécage] to drain; [+ air, eau] to purify, decontaminate; [+ finances, marché] to stabilize; [+ monnaie] to rehabilitate, re-establish; **la situation s'est assainie** the situation has become healthier; (fig) **~ l'atmosphère** to clear the air

assainissement [asenismɑ̃] NM [quartier, logement] cleaning up; [marécage] draining; [air, eau] purification, decontamination; [finances, marché] stabilization; **~ monétaire** rehabilitation ou re-establishment of a currency; **~ budgétaire** stabilization of the budget; **des travaux d'~** drainage work

assaisonnement [asɛzɔnmɑ̃] NM (= méthode) [salade] dressing, seasoning; [plat] seasoning; (= ingrédient) seasoning

assaisonner [asɛzɔne] ▸ conjug 1 ◂ VT **a** (Culin) (avec sel, poivre, épices) to season (de, avec with), add seasoning to; (avec huile, citron) to dress (de, avec with); (fig) [+ discours] to spice (up); **j'ai trop assaisonné la salade** I've put too much dressing on the salad **b** (‡, †) [+ personne] (verbalement) to tell off*; (financièrement) to clobber‡, sting‡

assassin, e [asasɛ̃, in] **1** ADJ [œillade] provocative; **lancer un regard ~ à qn** to look daggers at sb **2** NM (gén) murderer; (Pol) assassin; **l'~ court toujours** the killer ou murderer is still at large; **à l'~!** murder!

assassinat [asasina] NM murder; (Pol) assassination

assassiner [asasine] ▸ conjug 1 ◂ VT to murder; (Pol) to assassinate; **mes créanciers m'assassinent!** my creditors are bleeding me white!*

assaut [aso] NM (Mil) assault, attack (de on); (Boxe, Escrime) bout; (Alpinisme) assault; (fig) [temps] onslaught; **donner l'~ à ◊ monter à l'~ de** to storm, attack, launch an attack on; **ils donnent l'~** they're attacking; **à l'~!** charge!; **résister aux ~s de l'ennemi** to resist the enemy's attacks ou onslaughts; **partir à l'~ de** (lit) to attack; (fig) [de petites firmes qui sont parties à l'~ d'un marché international] small firms who have set out to take the international market by storm ou to capture the international market; **prendre d'~** (lit) to take by storm, assault; (fig) **prendre une place d'~** to grab a seat; **les libraires étaient prises d'~** people flocked to the bookshops; **ils faisaient ~ de politesse** they were falling over each other to be polite → char

assèchement [asɛʃmɑ̃] NM **a** (Tech) [terrain] draining; [réservoir] draining, emptying **b** (= processus naturel) [terrain] drying (out); [réservoir] drying (up) **c** (Fin) [marché, crédits] drying up

assécher [aseʃe] ▸ conjug 6 ◂ **1** VT **a** [+ terrain] (Tech) to drain; [vent, évaporation] to dry (out); [+ réservoir] (Tech) to drain, empty; [vent, évaporation] to dry (up) **b** (Fin) [+ mar-

ché, crédits] to dry up **2** **s'assécher** VPR [cours d'eau, réservoir] to dry up

ASSEDIC [asedik] NFPL (ABRÉV = **Association pour l'emploi dans l'industrie et le commerce**) organization managing unemployment insurance payments

assemblage [asɑ̃blaʒ] NM **a** (= action) [éléments, parties] assembling, putting together; (Menuiserie) assembling, jointing; [meuble, maquette, machine] assembling, assembly; (Ordin) assembly; (Typo) [feuilles] gathering; (Couture) [pièces] sewing together; [robe, pull-over] sewing together ou up, making up; **~ de pièces par soudure/collage** soldering/glueing together of parts **b** (Menuiserie = jointure) joint; **~ à vis/par rivets/à onglet** screwed/rivet(ed)/mitre joint **c** (= structure) **une charpente est un ~ de poutres** the framework of a roof is an assembly of beams; **toit fait d'~s métalliques** roof made of metal structures **d** (= réunion) [couleurs, choses, personnes] collection **e** (Art = tableau) assemblage

assemblé [asɑ̃ble] NM (Danse) assemblé

assemblée [asɑ̃ble] NF (gén = réunion, foule) gathering; (= réunion convoquée) meeting; (Pol) assembly; (Rel) **l'~ des fidèles** the congregation; **~ mensuelle/extraordinaire/plénière** monthly/extraordinary/plenary meeting; **~ générale** (Écon) annual general meeting (Brit), general meeting (US); [étudiants] (extraordinary) general meeting; **~ générale extraordinaire** extraordinary general meeting; **réunis en ~** gathered ou assembled for a meeting; **à la grande joie de l'~** to the great joy of the assembled company ou of those present; **l'Assemblée (nationale)** the French National Assembly; **l'Assemblée parlementaire européenne** the European Parliament; (Pol) **~ délibérante** deliberating assembly

---

ASSEMBLÉE NATIONALE

The term **Assemblée nationale** has been used to refer to the lower house of the French parliament since 1946, though the old term "la Chambre des députés" is sometimes still used. Its members are elected in the "élections législatives" for a five-year term. It has similar legislative powers to the House of Commons in Britain and the House of Representatives in the United States. Sittings of the **Assemblée nationale** are public, and take place in a semicircular amphitheatre ("l'Hémicycle") in the Palais Bourbon. → DÉPUTÉ ; ÉLECTIONS

---

assembler [asɑ̃ble] ▸ conjug 1 ◂ **1** VT **a** (= réunir) [+ données, matériaux] to gather (together), collect (together); (Pol) [+ comité] to convene, assemble; † [+ personnes] to assemble, gather (together); (Typo) [+ feuilles] to gather; (Danse) **~ les pieds** to take up third position **b** (= joindre) [+ idées, meuble, machine, puzzle] to assemble, put together; [+ pull, robe] to sew together ou up, make up; (Menuiserie) to assemble, joint; [+ couleurs, sons] to put together; **~ par soudure/collage** to solder/glue together **2** **s'assembler** VPR [foule] to gather, collect; [participants, conseil, groupe] to assemble, gather; (fig) [nuages] to gather → ressembler

assembleur, -euse [asɑ̃blœʀ, øz] **1** NM,F (= ouvrier) (gén) assembler, fitter; (Typo) gatherer **2** NM (Ordin) assembler **3** **assembleuse** NF (Typo = machine) gathering machine

assener, asséner [asene] ▸ conjug 5 ◂ VT [+ coup] to strike; [+ argument] to thrust forward; [+ propagande] to deal out; [+ réplique] to thrust ou fling back; **~ un coup à qn** to deal sb a blow

▼ **assentiment** [asɑ̃timɑ̃] NM (= consentement) assent, consent; (= approbation) approval; **sans mon ~** without my consent; **donner son ~ à** to give one's assent ou consent to

asseoir [aswaʀ] ▸ conjug 26 ◂ **1** VT **a** **~ qn** (personne debout) to sit sb down; (personne couchée) to sit sb up; **~ qn sur une chaise/dans un fauteuil** to sit ou seat sb on a chair/in an armchair; **~ un enfant sur ses genoux** to sit a child on one's knee; (fig) **~ un prince sur le trône** to put ou set a prince on the throne **b** **faire ~ qn** to ask sb to sit down; **faire ~ ses invités** to ask one's guests to sit down ou to take a seat; **je leur ai parlé après les avoir fait ~** I talked to them after asking them to sit down; **fais-la ~, elle est fatiguée** get her to sit down, she's tired **c** **être assis** to be sitting (down) ou seated; **reste assis!** (= ne bouge pas) sit still!; (= ne te lève pas) don't get up!; **nous sommes restés assis pendant des heures** we sat ou remained seated for hours; **nous étions très bien/mal assis** (sur des chaises) we had very comfortable/uncomfortable seats; (par terre) we were very comfortably/uncomfortably seated; **assis en tailleur** sitting cross-legged; **assis à califourchon sur** sitting astride, straddling → entre **d** (frm = affermir) [+ réputation] to establish, assure; [+ autorité, théorie] to establish; **une maison sur du granit** to build a house on granite; **~ les fondations sur** to lay ou build the foundations on; **~ sa réputation sur qch** to build one's reputation on sth; **~ une théorie sur des faits** to base a theory on facts; **~ son jugement sur des témoignages dignes de foi** to base one's judgment on reliable evidence **e** (* = stupéfier) to stagger, stun; **son inconscience m'assoit** his foolishness staggers me, I'm stunned by his foolishness; **j'en suis ou reste assis de voir que ...** I'm staggered ou stunned ou flabbergasted* to see that ... **f** (Fin) **~ un impôt** to base a tax, fix a tax (sur on) **2** **s'asseoir** VPR [personne debout] to sit (o.s.) down; [personne couchée] to sit up; **asseyez-vous donc** do sit down, do have ou take a seat; **asseyez-vous par terre** sit (down) on the floor; **il n'y a rien pour s'~** there's nothing to sit on; **le règlement, je m'assieds dessus!** you know what you can do with the rules!‡; **s'~ à califourchon (sur qch)** to sit (down) astride (sth); **s'~ en tailleur** to sit (down) cross-legged

assermenté, e [asɛʀmɑ̃te] ADJ [témoin, expert] on oath (attrib)

assertif, -ive [asɛʀtif, iv] ADJ [phrase] declarative

assertion [asɛʀsjɔ̃] NF assertion

asservi, e [asɛʀvi] (ptp de asservir) ADJ [peuple] enslaved; [presse] subservient; **moteur ~** servomotor

asservir [asɛʀviʀ] ▸ conjug 2 ◂ VT (= assujettir) [+ personne] to enslave; [+ pays] to reduce to slavery, subjugate; (littér = maîtriser) [+ passions, nature] to overcome, master; (Tech) **être asservi** to have servo-control; **être asservi à** to be a slave to

asservissant, e [asɛʀvisɑ̃, ɑ̃t] ADJ [règles] oppressive; **avoir un travail ~** to have a very demanding job

asservissement [asɛʀvismɑ̃] NM (= action) enslavement; (lit, fig = état) slavery, subservience (à to); (Élec) servo-control (NonC) (à by)

assesseur [asesœʀ] NM assessor

▼ **assez** [ase] ADV **a** (= suffisamment) (avec vb) enough; (devant adj, adv) enough, sufficiently; **bien ~** quite enough, plenty; **tu as (bien) ~ mangé** you've had ou eaten (quite) enough, you've had (quite) enough to eat; **c'est bien ~ grand** it's quite big enough; **plus qu'~** more than enough; **je n'ai pas ~ travaillé** I haven't done enough work, I haven't worked enough; **il ne vérifie pas ~ souvent** he doesn't check often enough; **tu travailles depuis ~ longtemps** you've been working (for) long enough; **ça a ~ duré!** this has gone on long enough!; **combien voulez-vous? est-ce que**

50F c'est ~ ? — **c'est bien ~** how much do you want? is 50 francs enough? *ou* will 50 francs do? — that will be plenty *ou* ample *ou* that will be quite enough; **il a juste ~** he has just enough → **peu**

[b] **~ de** (*quantité, nombre*) enough; **avez-vous acheté ~ de pain/d'oranges ?** have you bought enough *ou* sufficient bread/enough oranges?; **il n'y a pas ~ de viande** there's not enough meat; **ils sont ~ de deux pour ce travail** the two of them are enough *ou* will do* for this job; **j'en ai ~ de 3** 3 will be enough for me *ou* will do (for) me*; **n'apportez pas de verres, il y en a ~** don't bring any glasses, there are enough *ou* we have enough

[c] (*avec pour*) enough; **as-tu trouvé une boîte ~ grande pour tout mettre ?** have you found a big enough box *ou* a box big enough to put it all in?; **le village est ~ près pour qu'elle puisse y aller à pied** the village is near enough for her to walk there; **je n'ai pas ~ d'argent pour m'offrir cette voiture** I can't afford (to buy myself) this car, I haven't got enough money to buy myself this car; **il est ~ idiot pour refuser !** he's stupid enough to refuse!; **il n'est pas ~ sot pour le croire** he's not so stupid as to believe it

[d] (*intensif*) rather, quite, fairly, pretty*; **la situation est ~ inquiétante** the situation is rather *ou* somewhat *ou* pretty* worrying; **ce serait ~ agréable d'avoir un jour de congé** it would be rather *ou* quite nice to have a day off; **il était ~ tard quand ils sont partis** it was quite *ou* fairly *ou* pretty* late when they left; **j'ai oublié son adresse, est-ce ~ bête !** how stupid (of me), I've forgotten his address!; **je l'ai ~ vu !** I've seen (more than) enough of him!; **elle était déjà ~ malade il y a 2 ans** she was already quite ill 2 years ago; **je suis ~ de ton avis** I'm inclined to agree with you

[e] (*loc*) **en voilà ~ !** ◊ **c'est ~ !** ◊ **c'en est ~ !** I've had enough!, enough is enough!; **~ !** that will do!, that's (quite) enough!; **~ parlé *ou* de discours, des actes !** that's enough talk, let's have some action!; **j'en ai (plus qu')~ de toi et de tes jérémiades*** I've had (more than) enough of *ou* I'm (absolutely) sick (and tired)* of you and your moaning

assidu, e [asidy] ADJ [a] (= *régulier*) [*présence, client, lecteur*] regular; **élève/employé ~** pupil/employee with a good attendance record [b] (= *appliqué*) [*soins, effort*] constant, unremitting; [*travail*] diligent; [*relations*] sustained; [*personne*] diligent, assiduous [c] (= *empressé*) [*personne*] attentive (**auprès de** to); **faire une cour ~e à qn** to be assiduous in one's attentions to sb, woo sb assiduously

assiduité [asidɥite] NF ~ (= *ponctualité*) regularity; (= *empressement*) attentiveness, assiduity (**à** to); **son ~ aux cours** his regular attendance at classes; **fréquenter un bistrot avec ~** to be a regular at a bar; (*frm ou hum*) **poursuivre une femme de ses ~s** to woo a woman assiduously

assidûment [asidymɑ̃] ADV [*fréquenter*] faithfully, assiduously; [*travailler, s'entraîner*] assiduously

assiégé, e [asjeʒe] (*ptp de* **assiéger**) [1] ADJ [*garnison, ville*] besieged, under siege (*attrib*) [2] NM,F **les ~s** the besieged

assiégeant, e [asjeʒã, ãt] [1] NM,F besieger [2] ADJ **les troupes ~es** the besieging troops

assiéger [asjeʒe] ▶ conjug 3 *et* 6 ◀ VT (*Mil*) [+ *ville*] to besiege, lay siege to; [+ *armée*] to besiege; (*fig*) (= *entourer*) [+ *guichet, porte, personne*] to mob, besiege; (= *harceler*) to beset; **assiégé par l'eau/les flammes** hemmed in by water/flames; **à Noël les magasins étaient assiégés** the shops were taken by storm *ou* mobbed at Christmas; **ces pensées/tentations qui m'assiègent** these thoughts/temptations that beset *ou* assail me

assiette [asjɛt] [1] NF [a] (= *vaisselle*) plate; (= *contenu*) plate(ful)

[b] (= *équilibre*) [*cavalier*] seat; [*navire*] trim; [*colonne*] seating; (*Équitation*) **perdre son ~** to lose one's seat, be unseated; (*Équitation*) **avoir une bonne ~** to have a good seat, sit one's horse well; **il n'est pas dans son ~ aujourd'hui*** he's not feeling (quite) himself today, he's (feeling) a bit off-colour (*Brit*) today [c] [*hypothèque*] property or estate on which a mortgage is secured; **~ fiscale** *ou* **de l'impôt/de la TVA** tax/VAT base; **l'~ des cotisations sociales** the basis on which social security contributions are assessed

[2] COMP ► **assiette anglaise** *ou* **de charcuterie** assorted cold meats ► **assiette composée** mixed salad (*of cold meats and vegetables*) ► **assiette creuse** soup dish *ou* plate ► **assiette à dessert** dessert plate ► **assiette nordique** *ou* **scandinave** plate of assorted smoked fish ► **assiette à pain** side plate ► **assiette plate** (dinner) plate ► **assiette à potage** *ou* **à soupe** = **assiette creuse** ► **assiette scandinave** = **assiette nordique** ► **assiette à soupe** = **assiette creuse**

assiettée [asjete] NF (*gén*) plate(ful); [*soupe*] plate(ful), dish

assignable [asiɲabl] ADJ (= *attribuable*) [*cause, origine*] ascribable, attributable (**à** to)

assignat [asiɲa] NM (*Hist*) banknote used during the French Revolution

assignation [asiɲasjɔ̃] NF (*Jur*) [*parts*] assignation, allocation; **~ (en justice)** writ; **~ (à comparaître)** [*prévenu*] summons; [*témoin*] subpoena; **~ à résidence** house arrest

assigner [asiɲe] ▶ conjug 1 ◀ VT [a] (= *attribuer*) [+ *part, place, rôle*] to assign, allocate, allot; [+ *valeur, importance*] to attach, ascribe; [+ *cause, origine*] to ascribe, attribute (**à** to) [b] (= *affecter*) [+ *somme, crédit*] to allot, allocate (**à** to), earmark (**à** for) [c] (= *fixer*) [+ *limite, terme*] to set, fix (**à** to); **~ un objectif à qn** to set sb a goal [d] (*Jur*) (**à comparaître**) [+ *prévenu*] to summons; [+ *témoin*] to subpoena, summons; **~ qn (en justice)** to issue a writ against sb, serve a writ on sb, serve sb with a writ; **~ qn à résidence** to put sb under house arrest

assimilable [asimilabl] ADJ [a] [*connaissances*] which can be assimilated *ou* absorbed; [*nourriture*] assimilable; [*immigrant*] who can be assimilated [b] **~ à** (= *comparable à*) comparable to

assimilation [asimilasjɔ̃] NF [a] [*aliments, immigrants, connaissances*] assimilation; **~ chlorophyllienne** photosynthesis; **~ culturelle** cultural assimilation [b] (= *comparaison*) **l'~ de ce bandit à un héros/à Napoléon est un scandale** it's a scandal making this criminal out to be a hero/to liken *ou* compare this criminal to Napoleon; **l'~ des techniciens aux ingénieurs** the classification of technicians as engineers, the inclusion of technicians in the same category as engineers

assimilé, e [asimile] (*ptp de* **assimiler**) [1] ADJ (= *semblable*) comparable, similar; **ce procédé et les méthodes ~es** this process and other comparable *ou* similar methods; **farines et produits ~s** flour and related products [2] NM (*Mil*) non-combatant ranking with the combatants; **les cadres et ~s** management and employees of similar status; **les fonctionnaires et ~s** civil servants and those in a similar category

assimiler [asimile] ▶ conjug 1 ◀ [1] VT [a] [+ *connaissances*] to assimilate, take in; [+ *aliments, immigrants*] to assimilate; **un élève qui assimile bien** a pupil who assimilates things easily *ou* takes things in easily; **ses idées sont du Nietzsche mal assimilé** his ideas are just a few ill-digested notions (taken) from Nietzsche

[b] **~ qn/qch à** (= *comparer à*) to liken *ou* compare sb/sth to; (= *classer comme*) to put sb/sth into the same category as; **ils demandent à**

être assimilés à des fonctionnaires they are asking to be put in the same category as civil servants

[2] **s'assimiler** VPR [a] [*aliments, immigrants*] to assimilate, be assimilated; [*connaissances*] to be assimilated

[b] **s'~ à** (= *se comparer à*) [*personne*] to liken o.s. *ou* compare o.s. to; **cet acte s'assimile à un règlement de compte(s)** this act can be seen *ou* considered as a settling of (old) scores

assis, e¹ [asi, iz] (*ptp de* **asseoir**) ADJ [a] [*personne*] sitting (down), seated; **position** *ou* **station ~e** sitting position; **la position** *ou* **station ~e lui est douloureuse** he finds it painful to sit; **demeurer** *ou* **rester ~** to remain seated; **restez ~** (please) don't get up; **~ !** (*à un chien*) sit!; (*à une personne*) sit down! → **magistrature, place, position;** → **asseoir** [b] (= *assuré*) [*fortune*] secure; [*personne*] stable; [*autorité*] (well-)established; **maintenant que son fils a une situation bien ~e** now that his son is well-established

Assise [asiz] N Assisi; **Saint François d'~** Saint Francis of Assisi

assise² [asiz] NF (*Constr*) course; (*Bio, Géol*) stratum; [*raisonnement*] basis, foundation; **leur ~ politique** their political base

assises [asiz] NFPL (*Jur*) assizes; [*association, parti politique*] conference; **~ nationales** national conference; **tenir ses ~** to hold its conference; **procès d'~** trial → **cour**

assistanat [asistana] NM [a] (*Scol*) assistantship [b] (*Sociol*) (= *soutien*) (state) support; (*péj*) mollycoddling (*péj*), nannying (*péj, Brit*); (= *aide financière*) (state) aid; (*péj*) handouts (*péj*), charity (*péj*)

assistance [asistɑ̃s] [1] NF [a] (= *assemblée*) [*conférence*] audience; [*débat*] audience, house; [*meeting*] house; [*cérémonie*] gathering, audience; [*messe*] congregation

[b] (= *aide*) assistance; **donner/prêter ~ à qn** to give/lend sb assistance; **~ aux anciens détenus** prisoner after-care [c] (= *présence*) attendance (**à** at)

[2] COMP ► **assistance éducative** educational support (*for children with special needs*) ► **assistance judiciaire** legal aid ► **assistance médicale (gratuite)** (free) medical care ► **Assistance publique: les services de l'Assistance publique** ≈ the health and social security services; **être à l'Assistance publique** to be in (state *ou* public) care; **enfant de l'Assistance (publique)** child in care (*Brit*) *ou* in state custody (*US*); **les hôpitaux de l'Assistance publique** state- *ou* publicly-owned hospitals ► **assistance respiratoire** artificial respiration ► **assistance sociale** (= *aide*) social aid; (= *métier*) social work ► **assistance technique** technical aid

assistant, e [asistã, ãt] NM,F [a] (*gén, Scol*) assistant; (*Univ*) ≈ assistant lecturer (*Brit*), ≈ teaching assistant (*US*); **~e de direction** management secretary; **~ (de langue)** language assistant; **~e maternelle** child minder (*Brit*), child caregiver (*US*); **~e sociale** (*gén*) social worker; (*Scol*) school counsellor, school social worker; **le directeur et son ~e** the manager and his personal assistant *ou* his PA → **maître** [b] [*assemblée*] **les ~s** those present

assisté, e [asiste] (*ptp de* **assister**) [1] ADJ [a] (*Jur, Méd, Sociol*) supported by *ou* cared for by the state; [*financièrement*] receiving (state) aid; **enfant ~** child in care (*Brit*) *ou* state custody (*US*) [b] (*Tech*) [*freins*] servo-assisted; **~ par ordinateur** computer-aided, computer-assisted → **direction, procréation, publication, traduction** [2] NM,F **les ~s** (*recevant une aide financière*) people receiving (state) aid; (*péj*) people receiving handouts (*péj*), welfare scroungers (*péj*); **il a une mentalité d'~** he can't do anything for himself

assister [asiste] ▸conjug 1◂ **1** **assister à** VT INDIR (= être présent à) [+ cérémonie, conférence, messe] to be (present) at, attend; [+ match, spectacle] to be at; [+ dispute] to witness; **il a assisté à l'accouchement de sa femme** he was there when his wife gave birth, he was at the birth of his child; (TV) **vous pourrez ~ en direct à cet événement** you'll be able to see the event live (on television); **on assiste à une montée du chômage** unemployment is on the rise ou on the increase, we are witnessing a rise ou an increase in unemployment; **nous assistons actuellement en Europe à des changements fondamentaux** there are fundamental changes taking place in Europe, Europe is witnessing fundamental changes; **depuis le début de l'année, on assiste à une reprise de l'économie** the economy has picked up since the beginning of the year, there has been an upturn in the economy since the beginning of the year; **il a assisté à l'effondrement de son parti** he saw the collapse of his party

2 VT (= aider) to assist; (financièrement) to give aid to; (frm) **~ qn dans ses derniers moments** to succour (frm) ou comfort sb in their last hour; **~ les pauvres†** to minister to the poor (frm)

associatif, -ive [asɔsjatif, iv] ADJ **a** (Sociol) [réseau] of associations; **le mouvement ~** associations; **des représentants du milieu ~** representatives of associations; **la vie associative** community life; **il a de nombreuses activités associatives** he's involved in several associations **b** (Math) associative

association [asɔsjasjɔ̃] NF **a** (gén = société) association, society; (Comm, Écon) partnership; (Jur) **~ de malfaiteurs** criminal conspiracy; **~ de consommateurs** consumer association; **~ sportive** sports association; **~ loi (de) 1901** (non-profit-making) association; **Association internationale du tourisme** International Tourism Association; **Association européenne de libre-échange** European Free Trade Association **b** [idées, images] association; [couleurs, intérêts] combination **c** (= participation) association, partnership; **l'~ de ces deux écrivains a été fructueuse** the two writers have had a very fruitful partnership; **son ~ à nos travaux dépendra de ...** whether or not he joins us in our work will depend on ...; **travailler en ~** to work in partnership (avec with)

associationnisme [asɔsjasjɔnism] NM (Philos) associationism

associationniste [asɔsjasjɔnist] ADJ, NMF associationist

associativité [asɔsjativite] NF (Math) associativity

associé, e [asɔsje] (ptp de **associer**) **1** ADJ (Univ) [assistant, professeur] visiting; **membre ~** associate member **2** NM,F (gén) associate; (Comm, Fin) partner, associate; **~ principal** senior partner

associer [asɔsje] ▸conjug 7◂ **1** VT **a** **~ qn à** (= faire participer à) [+ profits] to give sb a share of; [+ affaire] to make sb a partner in; **~ qn à son triomphe** to let sb share in one's triumph **b** **~ qch à** (= rendre solidaire de) to associate ou link sth with; (= allier à) to combine sth with; **il associe la paresse à la malhonnêteté** he combines laziness with dishonesty **c** (= grouper) [+ idées, images, mots] to associate; [+ couleurs, intérêts] to combine (à with) **2** **s'associer** VPR **a** (= s'unir) [firmes] to join together, form an association; [personnes] (gén) to join forces, join together; (Comm) to form a partnership; **s'~ à ou avec** [firme] to join with, form an association with; [personne] (gén) to join (forces) with; (Comm) to go into partnership with; [bandits] to fall in with; **on va lui faire un cadeau, tu t'associes à nous ?** we're going to get him a present, do you want to come in with us?

b (= participer à) **s'~ à** [+ projet] to join in; [+ douleur] to share in; **je m'associe aux compliments que l'on vous fait** I would like to join with those who have complimented you **c** (= s'allier) [couleurs, qualités] to be combined (à with); **ces couleurs s'associent à merveille** these colours go together beautifully **d** (= s'adjoindre) **s'~ qn** to take sb on as a partner

assoiffé, e [aswafe] ADJ (lit) thirsty; (fig) **~ de** thirsting for ou after (littér); (littér ou hum) **monstre ~ de sang** bloodthirsty monster

assoiffer [aswafe] ▸conjug 1◂ VT [temps, course] to make thirsty

assolement [asɔlmɑ̃] NM (systematic) rotation (of crops)

assoler [asɔle] ▸conjug 1◂ VT [+ champ] to rotate crops on

assombri, e [asɔ̃bri] (ptp de **assombrir**) ADJ [ciel] dark, sombre (Brit), somber (US); [visage, regard] gloomy, sombre (Brit), somber (US)

assombrir [asɔ̃briR] ▸conjug 2◂ **1** VT **a** (= obscurcir: gén) to darken; [+ pièce] to make dark ou gloomy; [+ couleur] to make dark ou sombre (Brit) ou somber (US) **b** (= attrister) [+ personne] to fill with gloom; [+ assistance] to cast a gloom over; [+ visage, avenir, voyage] to cast a shadow over **2** **s'assombrir** VPR **a** [ciel, pièce] to darken, grow dark; [couleur] to grow sombre (Brit) ou somber (US), darken **b** [personne, caractère] to become gloomy ou morose; [visage, regard] to cloud over; **la situation politique s'est assombrie** the political situation has become gloomier

assombrissement [asɔ̃brismɑ̃] NM [ciel, pièce] darkening; **l'~ des perspectives économiques** the increasingly gloomy economic prospects

assommant, e* [asɔmɑ̃, ɑ̃t] ADJ (= ennuyeux) deadly* boring ou dull; **il est ~** he's a deadly* bore, he's deadly* dull ou boring

assommer [asɔme] ▸conjug 1◂ VT (lit) (= tuer) to batter to death; (= étourdir) [+ animal] to knock out, stun; [+ personne] to knock out, knock senseless; (fig = moralement) to crush; (* fig = ennuyer) to bore stiff*, bore to tears* ou to death*; **être assommé par le bruit/la chaleur** to be overwhelmed by the noise/overcome by the heat; **si je lui mets la main dessus je l'assomme*** if I can lay my hands on him I'll beat his brains out*

assommoir† [asɔmwaR] NM (= massue) club; (= café) café, grogshop† (Brit); (prix) **c'est le coup d'~!** it's extortionate!

Assomption [asɔ̃psjɔ̃] NF (Rel) **(la fête de) l'~** (the feast of) the Assumption; (= jour férié) Assumption Day

assonance [asɔnɑ̃s] NF assonance

assonant, e [asɔnɑ̃, ɑ̃t] ADJ assonant, assonantal

assorti, e [asɔrti] (ptp de **assortir**) ADJ **a** (= en harmonie) **des époux bien/mal ~s** a well/badly-matched ou -suited couple, a good/bad match; **être ~ à** [+ couleur] to match; **chemise avec cravate ~e** shirt with matching tie **b** [bonbons] assorted; **« hors-d'œuvre/fromages ~s »** "assortment of hors d'œuvres/cheeses"; (= achalandé) **magasin bien/mal ~** well/poorly-stocked shop **c** **être ~ de** [+ conditions, conseils] to be accompanied with

assortiment [asɔrtimɑ̃] NM **a** (= gamme) [bonbons, fromages, fruits, hors-d'œuvre] assortment; [livres] collection; [vaisselle] set; **je vous fais un ~ ?** shall I give you an assortment?; **il y avait tout un ~ d'outils** there was a whole set ou collection of tools **b** (= harmonie) [couleurs, formes] arrangement, ensemble **c** (Comm = lot, stock) stock, selection

assortir [asɔrtiR] ▸conjug 2◂ **1** VT **a** (= accorder) [+ couleurs, motifs] to match (à to, avec with); **elle assortit la couleur de son écharpe à** celle de ses yeux she chose the colour of her scarf to match her eyes; **elle avait su ~ ses invités** she had mixed ou matched her guests cleverly **b** (= accompagner de) **~ qch de** [+ conseils, commentaires] to accompany sth with **c** (Comm = approvisionner) [+ commerçant] to supply; [+ magasin] to stock (**de** with) **2** **s'assortir** VPR **a** [couleurs, motifs] to match, go (well) together; [caractères] to go together, be well matched; **le papier s'assortit aux rideaux** the wallpaper matches ou goes (well) with the curtains **b** (= s'accompagner de) **ce livre s'assortit de notes** this book has accompanying notes ou has notes with it

assoupi, e [asupi] (ptp de **assoupir**) ADJ [personne] dozing; [sens, intérêt, douleur] dulled; [haine] lulled

assoupir [asupiR] ▸conjug 2◂ **1** VT [+ personne] to make drowsy; [+ sens, intérêt, douleur] to dull; [+ passion] to lull **2** **s'assoupir** VPR [personne] to doze off; [intérêt] to be dulled

assoupissement [asupismɑ̃] NM **a** (= sommeil) doze; (= somnolence) drowsiness **b** (= action) [sens] numbing; [facultés, intérêt] dulling; [douleur] deadening

assouplir [asupliR] ▸conjug 2◂ **1** VT [+ cuir] to soften, make supple; [+ membres, corps] to make supple; [+ règlements, mesures] to relax; [+ principes] to make more flexible, relax; **~ le caractère de qn** to make sb more manageable; **~ les horaires** to produce a more flexible timetable **2** **s'assouplir** VPR [cuir] to soften, become supple; [membres, corps] to become supple; [règlements, mesures] to relax; [principes] to become more flexible, relax; **il faut que je m'assouplisse** I must loosen up; **son caractère s'est assoupli** he has become more manageable

assouplissant, e [asuplisɑ̃, ɑ̃t] **1** ADJ [produit, formule] softening **2** NM **~ (textile)** (fabric) softener

assouplissement [asuplismɑ̃] NM [cuir] softening; [membres, corps] suppling up; [règlements, mesures, principes] relaxing; **faire des exercices d'~** to limber up, do (some) limbering up exercises; (Écon) **mesures d'~ du crédit** easing of credit restrictions; **mesures d'~ des formalités administratives** measures to relax administrative regulations; **l'~ de la politique monétaire** the relaxing of monetary policy

assouplisseur [asuplisœR] NM (fabric) softener

assourdir [asuRdiR] ▸conjug 2◂ **1** VT **a** (= rendre sourd) [+ personne] to deafen **b** (= amortir) [+ bruit] to deaden, muffle **2** **s'assourdir** VPR (Ling) to become voiceless, become unvoiced

assourdissant, e [asuRdisɑ̃, ɑ̃t] ADJ deafening

assourdissement [asuRdismɑ̃] NM **a** [personne] (= état) (temporary) deafness; (= action) deafening **b** [bruit] deadening, muffling **c** (Ling) devoicing

assouvir [asuviR] ▸conjug 2◂ VT [+ faim] to satisfy, assuage (frm); [+ passion] to assuage (frm)

assouvissement [asuvismɑ̃] NM [faim] satisfaction, satisfying; [passion] assuaging (frm)

ASSU [asy] NF (ABRÉV = **Association du sport scolaire et universitaire**) university and school sports association

assujetti, e [asyʒeti] (ptp de **assujettir**) ADJ [peuple] subject, subjugated; **~ à** [norme, loi] subject to; [taxe] liable ou subject to; (Admin) **les personnes ~es à l'impôt** persons liable to ou for tax

assujettir [asyʒetiR] ▸conjug 2◂ **1** VT (= contraindre) [+ peuple] to subjugate, bring into subjection; (= fixer) [+ planches, tableau] to secure, make fast; **~ qn à une règle** to subject sb to a rule **2** **s'assujettir** VPR (à une règle) to submit (à to)

assujettissant, e [asyʒetisɑ̃, ɑ̃t] ADJ [*travail*] demanding, exacting

assujettissement [asyʒetismɑ̃] NM (= *contrainte*) constraint; (= *dépendance*) subjection; **~ à l'impôt** tax liability

assumer [asyme] ▶conjug 1◀ **1** VT **a** (= *prendre*: *gén*) to assume; [+ *responsabilité, tâche, rôle*] to take on, assume; [+ *commandement*] to take over; [+ *poste*] to take up; **~ la responsabilité de faire qch** to take it upon oneself to do sth; **~ les frais de qch** to meet the cost *ou* expense of sth; **tu as voulu te marier, alors assume!** you wanted to get married, so you'll just have to take *ou* accept the consequences. **b** (= *remplir*) [+ *poste*] to hold; [+ *rôle*] to fulfil; **après avoir assumé ce poste pendant 2 ans** having held the post for 2 years **c** (= *accepter*) [+ *conséquence, situation, douleur*] (*Philos*) [+ *condition*] to accept **2** **s'assumer** VPR to come to terms with o.s.

assurable [asyRabl] ADJ insurable

assurage [asyRaʒ] NM (*Alpinisme*) belay

assurance [asyRɑ̃s] **1** NF **a** (= *confiance en soi*) self-confidence, (self-)assurance; **avoir de l'~** to be self-confident *ou* (self-)assured; **prendre de l'~** to gain (self-)confidence *ou* (self-)assurance; **parler avec ~** to speak confidently *ou* with assurance *ou* with confidence **b** (= *garantie*) assurance, undertaking (*Brit*); **donner à qn l'~ formelle que ...** to give sb a formal assurance *ou* undertaking that ...; **il veut avoir l'~ que tout se passera bien** he wants to be sure that everything goes well; (*formule épistolaire*) **veuillez agréer l'~ de ma considération distinguée** *ou* **de mes sentiments dévoués** yours faithfully *ou* sincerely, sincerely yours (*US*) **c** (= *contrat*) insurance (policy); **contrat d'~** insurance policy; **compagnie** *ou* **société/groupe d'~s** insurance company/group; **produits d'~** insurance products; **contracter** *ou* **prendre une ~ contre qch** to take out insurance *ou* an insurance policy against sth; **il est dans les ~s** he's in insurance, he's in the insurance business → **police², prime¹** **d** (*Alpinisme*) belay

2 COMP ▶ **assurance automobile** car *ou* motor (*Brit*) *ou* automobile (*US*) insurance ▶ **assurance bagages** luggage insurance ▶ **assurance chômage** unemployment insurance; **le régime d'~ chômage** the state unemployment insurance scheme; **caisse d'~ chômage** (= *fonds*) unemployment insurance fund; (= *bureau*) unemployment insurance office ▶ **assurance décès** whole-life insurance ▶ **assurance incendie** fire insurance ▶ **assurance invalidité-vieillesse** disablement insurance ▶ **assurance maladie** health insurance; **régime d'~ maladie** health insurance scheme ▶ **assurance maritime** marine insurance ▶ **assurance multirisques** comprehensive insurance ▶ **assurance personnelle** personal insurance ▶ **assurance responsabilité-civile** = **assurance au tiers** ▶ **assurances sociales** ≈ social security, ≈ welfare (*US*); **il est (inscrit) aux ~s sociales** he's on the state health scheme (*Brit*) *ou* plan (*US*), he pays National Insurance (*Brit*) ▶ **assurance au tiers** third-party insurance ▶ **assurance tous risques** (*Aut*) comprehensive insurance ▶ **assurance vie** life assurance *ou* insurance (*Brit*); **contrat d'~ vie** life assurance *ou* insurance (*Brit*) policy ▶ **assurance vieillesse** pension scheme; **le régime d'~ vieillesse** the state pension scheme; **caisse d'~ vieillesse** (*fonds*) retirement fund; (*bureau*) pensions office ▶ **assurance contre le vol** insurance against theft ▶ **assurance voyage** travel insurance

assurance-crédit (*pl* **assurances-crédits**) [asyRɑ̃skRedi] NF credit insurance

assuré, e [asyRe] (*ptp de* **assurer**) **1** ADJ **a** [*réussite, échec*] certain, sure; [*situation, fortune*] assured; **son avenir est ~ maintenant** his future is certain *ou* assured now; **entreprise ~e du succès** undertaking which is sure *ou* assured of success **b** [*air, démarche*] assured, (self-)confident; [*voix*] assured, steady; [*main, pas*] steady; **mal ~** [*voix, pas*] uncertain, unsteady; **il est mal ~ sur ses jambes** he's unsteady on his legs **c** (*loc*) **tenir pour ~ que ...** to be confident that ..., take it as certain that ...; **tenez pour ~ que ...** rest assured that ...; **il se dit ~ de cela** he says he is confident of that **2** NM,F (*Assurances*) (*assurance-vie*) assured *ou* insured person; (*autres assurances*) insured person, policyholder; **l'~** the assured, the policyholder; **~ social** person paying social security contributions

assurément [asyRemɑ̃] ADV (*frm*) most certainly, assuredly; **~, ceci présente des difficultés** this does indeed present difficulties; **(oui)** ~ yes indeed, (yes) most certainly; **~ il viendra** he will most certainly come

▼**assurer** [asyRe] ▶conjug 1◀ **1** VT **a** (= *certifier*) **~ à qn que ...** to assure sb that ...; **~ que ...** to affirm *ou* contend *ou* assert that ...; **cela vaut la peine, je vous assure** it's worth it, I assure you; (*ton exaspéré*) **je t'assure!** really! **b** (= *confirmer*) **~ qn de** [+ *amitié, bonne foi*] to assure sb of; **sa participation nous est assurée** we have been assured of his participation *ou* that he'll take part **c** (*par contrat*) to insure (**contre** against); **~ qn sur la vie** to give sb (a) life assurance *ou* insurance (*Brit*), assure sb's life; **faire ~ qch** to insure sth, have *ou* get sth insured; **être assuré** to be insured **d** (= *exécuter, fournir*) [+ *fonctionnement, permanence*] to maintain; [+ *travaux*] to carry out, undertake; [+ *surveillance*] to ensure, provide, maintain; [+ *service*] to operate, provide; [+ *financement*] to provide; **~ la surveillance des locaux** to guard the premises; **l'avion qui assure la liaison entre Genève et Aberdeen** the plane that operates between Geneva and Aberdeen; **l'armée a dû ~ le ravitaillement des sinistrés** the army had to provide supplies for the victims; (*Jur*) **~ sa propre défense** to conduct one's own defence; **~ la direction d'un service** to head up a department, be in charge of a department; **~ le remplacement de pièces défectueuses** to replace faulty parts; **~ le suivi d'une commande** to follow up an order **e** (= *garantir*) [+ *bonheur, protection, stabilité*] to ensure; [+ *succès, paix*] to ensure, secure; [+ *avenir, fortune*] to secure; [+ *revenu*] to provide; **~ à ses enfants la meilleure éducation possible** to provide one's children with the best possible education; **cela devrait leur ~ une vie aisée** that should ensure that they lead a comfortable life; **ce but leur a assuré la victoire** this goal ensured their victory; **~ ses arrières** to ensure *ou* make sure one has something to fall back on; **cela m'assure un toit pour quelques jours** that means I'll have somewhere to stay for a few days **f** (= *affermir*) [+ *pas, prise, échelle*] to steady; (= *fixer*) [+ *échelle, volet*] to secure; (*Alpinisme*) to belay; **il assura ses lunettes sur son nez** he fixed his glasses firmly on his nose **g** (= *protéger*) [+ *frontières*] to protect (**contre** against)

2 VI (* = *être à la hauteur*) to be very good; **ne pas ~** to be useless* *ou* no good*; **je n'assure pas du tout en allemand** I'm absolutely useless* *ou* no good at German

3 **s'assurer** VPR **a** (= *vérifier*) **s'~ que/de qch** to make sure that/of sth, ascertain that/sth; **assure-toi qu'on n'a rien volé** make sure *ou* check that nothing has been stolen; **assure-toi si les volets sont fermés** make sure the shutters are closed; **je vais m'en ~** I'll make sure, I'll check **b** (= *contracter une assurance*) to insure o.s.

(**contre** against); (= *se prémunir*) **s'~ contre** [+ *attaque, éventualité*] to insure (o.s.) against; **s'~ sur la vie** to insure one's life, take out (a) life assurance *ou* insurance (*Brit*) **c** (= *se procurer*) [+ *aide, victoire*] to secure, ensure; **il s'est assuré un revenu** he made sure of an income for himself, he ensured *ou* secured himself an income; **s'~ l'accès de** to secure access to; **s'~ le contrôle de** [+ *banque, ville*] to take control of **d** (= *s'affermir*) to steady o.s. (**sur** on); (*Alpinisme*) to belay o.s.; **s'~ sur sa selle** to steady o.s. in one's saddle **e** (*frm* = *arrêter*) **s'~ de la personne de qn** to apprehend sb

assureur [asyRœR] NM (= *agent*) insurance agent; (= *société*) insurance company; (*Jur* = *partie*) insurers; [*entreprise*] underwriters; **~-conseil** insurance consultant

Assyrie [asiRi] NF Assyria

assyrien, -ienne [asiRjɛ̃, jɛn] **1** ADJ Assyrian **2** **Assyrien(ne)** NM,F Assyrian

aster [astɛR] NM aster

astérie [asteRi] NF starfish

astérisque [asteRisk] NM asterisk; **marqué d'un ~** asterisked

astéroïde [asteRɔid] NM asteroid

asthénie [asteni] NF asthenia

asthénique [astenik] ADJ, NMF asthenic

asthmatique [asmatik] ADJ, NMF asthmatic

asthme [asm] NM asthma

asticot [astiko] NM (*gén*) maggot; (*pour la pêche*) maggot, gentle

asticoter* [astikɔte] ▶conjug 1◀ VT to needle, get at* (*Brit*); **cesse donc d'~ ta sœur!** stop needling *ou* getting at* (*Brit*) *ou* plaguing (*Brit*) your sister!

astigmate [astigmat] **1** ADJ astigmatic **2** NMF astigmat(ic)

astigmatisme [astigmatism] NM astigmatism

astiquer [astike] ▶conjug 1◀ VT [+ *arme, meuble, parquet*] to polish; [+ *bottes, métal*] to polish, shine

astragale [astRagal] NM (*Anat*) talus, astragalus; (*Bot*) astragalus; (*Archit*) astragal

astrakan [astRakɑ̃] NM astrakhan

astral, e (*mpl* **-aux**) [astRal, o] ADJ astral

astre [astR] NM star; (*littér*) **l'~ du jour/de la nuit** the day/night star (*littér*)

astreignant, e [astRɛɲɑ̃, ɑ̃t] ADJ [*travail*] exacting, demanding

astreindre [astRɛ̃dR] ▶conjug 49◀ **1** VT **~ qn à faire** to compel *ou* oblige *ou* force sb to do; **~ qn à un travail pénible/une discipline sévère** to force a trying task/a strict code of discipline (up)on sb **2** **s'astreindre** VPR **s'~ à faire** to force *ou* compel o.s. to do; **elle s'astreignait à un régime sévère** she forced herself to keep to a strict diet; **astreignez-vous à une vérification rigoureuse** make yourself carry out a thorough check

astreinte [astRɛ̃t] NF (*littér* = *obligation*) constraint, obligation; (*Jur*) penalty (*imposed on daily basis for non-completion of contract*); **être d'~** [*médecin, technicien*] to be on call

astringence [astRɛ̃ʒɑ̃s] NF astringency

astringent, e [astRɛ̃ʒɑ̃, ɑ̃t] ADJ, NM astringent

astrolabe [astRɔlab] NM astrolabe

astrologie [astRɔlɔʒi] NF astrology

astrologique [astRɔlɔʒik] ADJ astrological

astrologue [astRɔlɔg] NMF astrologer

astronaute [astRɔnot] NMF astronaut

astronautique [astRɔnotik] NF astronautics *sg*

astronef† [astRɔnɛf] NM spaceship, spacecraft

astronome [astRɔnɔm] NMF astronomer

astronomie [astRɔnɔmi] NF astronomy

astronomique [astRɔnɔmik] ADJ (*lit, fig*) astronomical, astronomic

▶ GRAMMAIRE ACTIVE: **assurer** 42.1

astronomiquement [astʀɔnɔmikmɑ̃] ADV astronomically

astrophysicien, -ienne [astʀofizisjɛ̃, jɛn] NM,F astrophysicist

astrophysique [astʀofizik] [1] ADJ astrophysical [2] NF astrophysics *sg*

astuce [astys] NF [a] (= *caractère*) shrewdness, astuteness; **il a beaucoup d'~** he is very shrewd *ou* astute [b] (= *truc*) (clever) way, trick; **l'~ c'est d'utiliser de l'eau au lieu de pétrole** the trick *ou* the clever bit (*Brit*) here is to use water instead of oil; **les ~s du métier** the tricks of the trade; **c'est ça l'~!** that's the trick! *ou* the clever bit (*Brit*) [c]* (= *jeu de mots*) pun; (= *plaisanterie*) wisecrack*; **faire des ~s** to make wisecracks*; **~ vaseuse** lousy* pun

astucieusement [astysjøzmɑ̃] ADV shrewdly, cleverly, astutely

astucieux, -ieuse [astysjø, jøz] ADJ [*personne, réponse, raisonnement*] shrewd, astute; [*visage*] shrewd; [*moyen, solution*] shrewd, clever

Asturies [astyʀi] NFPL **les ~** the Asturias

Asuncion [asunsjɔ̃] N Asuncion

asymétrie [asimetʀi] NF asymmetry

asymétrique [asimetʀik] ADJ asymmetric(al)

asymptomatique [asɛ̃ptɔmatik] ADJ [*infection, personne*] asymptomatic; **porteur ~** asymptomatic carrier

asymptote [asɛ̃ptɔt] [1] ADJ asymptotic [2] NF asymptote

asymptotique [asɛ̃ptɔtik] ADJ asymptotic

asynchrone [asɛ̃kʀon] ADJ asynchronous

asyndète [asɛ̃dɛt] NF asyndeton

asyntaxique [asɛ̃taksik] ADJ asyntactic(al)

ataraxie [ataʀaksi] NF ataraxia, ataraxy

atavique [atavik] ADJ atavistic

atavisme [atavism] NM atavism; **c'est de l'~!** it's heredity coming out!

ataxie [ataksi] NF ataxia

ataxique [ataksik] [1] ADJ ataxic [2] NMF ataxia sufferer ·

atchoum [atʃum] EXCL atishoo

atèle [atɛl] NM spider monkey

atelier [atəlje] NM [a] (= *local*) [*artisan*] shop; [*artiste*] studio; [*couturières*] workroom; [*haute couture*] atelier; **~ de fabrication** workshop [b] (= *groupe*) (*Art*) studio; (*Scol*) workgroup; (*dans un colloque*) discussion group, workshop; (*Scol*) **les enfants travaillent en ~s** the children work in small groups; (*TV*) **~ de production** production unit [c] (*Ind*) [*usine*] shop, workshop; **~ protégé** sheltered workshop [d] [*franc-maçonnerie*] lodge → **chef**[1]

atemporel, -elle [atɑ̃pɔʀɛl] ADJ [*vérité*] timeless

atermoiement [atɛʀmwamɑ̃] NM prevarication, procrastination (*NonC*)

atermoyer [atɛʀmwaje] ▶conjug 8◀ VI (= *tergiverser*) to procrastinate, temporize

athée [ate] [1] ADJ atheistic [2] NMF atheist

athéisme [ateism] NM atheism

Athéna [atena] NF Athena, (Pallas) Athene

athénée [atene] NM (*Belg* = *lycée*) ≈ secondary school, ≈ high school (*US*)

Athènes [atɛn] N Athens

athénien, -ienne [atenjɛ̃, jɛn] [1] ADJ Athenian [2] **Athénien(ne)** NM,F Athenian; (*hum*) **c'est là que les Athéniens s'atteignirent** that's when all hell broke loose*

athérome [ateʀom] NM atheroma

athérosclérose [ateʀoskleʀoz] NF atherosclerosis

athlète [atlɛt] NMF athlete; **corps d'~** athletic body; (*hum*) **regarde l'~!** ◊ **quel ~!** just look at muscleman! (*hum*)

athlétique [atletik] ADJ athletic

athlétisme [atletism] NM athletics (*NonC*); **~ sur piste** track athletics

Atlantide [atlɑ̃tid] NF **l'~** Atlantis

atlantique [atlɑ̃tik] [1] ADJ Atlantic; (*Can*) **les Provinces ~s** the Atlantic Provinces [2] **Atlantique** NM **l'Atlantique** the Atlantic (Ocean)

atlantisme [atlɑ̃tism] NM Atlanticism

atlantiste [atlɑ̃tist] [1] ADJ [*politique*] Atlanticist, which promotes the Atlantic Alliance [2] NMF Atlanticist

atlas [atlas] NM [a] (= *livre, Anat*) atlas [b] **Atlas** (*Myth*) Atlas; (*Géog*) **l'Atlas** the Atlas Mountains

atmosphère [atmosfɛʀ] NF [a] (*Géog*) atmosphere; **haute/basse ~** upper/lower atmosphere; **essai nucléaire en ~** nuclear test in the atmosphere [b] (= *environnement*) atmosphere; **j'ai besoin de changer d'~** I need a change of air *ou* scenery; **en ~ normale/contrôlée/stérile** in a normal/controlled/sterile atmosphere *ou* environment [c] (= *ambiance*) atmosphere; **~ de fête** festive atmosphere [d] († : *Phys* = *unité de pression*) atmosphere

atmosphérique [atmosfeʀik] ADJ atmospheric → **courant, perturbation**

atoca [atɔka] NM (*Can* = *fruit*) cranberry

atoll [atɔl] NM atoll

atome [atom] NM atom; **~-gramme** gram atom; **il n'a pas un ~ de bon sens** he hasn't a grain *ou* an ounce of common sense; **avoir des ~s crochus avec qn** to have a lot in common with sb, hit it off with sb*

atomique [atɔmik] ADJ (*Chim, Phys*) atomic; (*Mil, Pol*) atomic, nuclear → **bombe**

atomisation [atɔmizasjɔ̃] NF atomization

atomisé, e [atɔmize] (*ptp de* **atomiser**) [1] ADJ [*savoir, marché*] fragmented; [*mouvement politique*] fragmented, splintered; (*fig*) **parti politique ~** atomized *ou* fragmented political party [2] NM,F victim of an atomic bomb explosion; **les ~s d'Hiroshima** the victims of the Hiroshima atom bomb

atomiser [atɔmize] ▶conjug 1◀ VT (*Phys*) to atomize; (*Mil*) to destroy with atomic *ou* nuclear weapons; [+ *marché*] to fragment; [+ *société*] to atomize, fragment; [+ *parti*] to break up

atomiseur [atɔmizœʀ] NM (*gén*) spray; [*parfum*] atomizer

atomiste [atɔmist] ADJ, NMF (**savant**) **~** atomic scientist

atomistique [atɔmistik] ADJ, NF (**théorie**) **~** atomic theory

atonal, e (*mpl* **atonals**) [atɔnal] ADJ atonal

atonalité [atɔnalite] NF atonality

atone [atɔn] ADJ [a] (= *sans vitalité*) [*être*] lifeless; (= *sans expression*) [*regard*] expressionless; (*Méd*) atonic [b] (*Ling*) unstressed, unaccented, atonic

atonie [atɔni] NF (*Ling, Méd*) atony; (= *manque de vitalité*) lifelessness

atours [atuʀ] NMPL († *ou hum*) attire, finery; **dans ses plus beaux ~** in her loveliest attire † (*hum*), in all her finery (*hum*)

atout [atu] NM [a] (*Cartes*) trump; **jouer ~** to play a trump; (*en commençant*) to lead (with) a trump; **on jouait ~ cœur** hearts were trumps; **~ maître** master trump; **roi/reine d'~** king/queen of trumps; **3 sans ~** 3 no trumps [b] (*fig*) (= *avantage*) asset; (= *carte maîtresse*) trump card; **l'avoir dans l'équipe est un ~** he's an asset to our team; **avoir tous les ~s (dans son jeu)** to hold all the cards *ou* aces; **avoir plus d'un ~ dans sa manche** to have more than one ace up one's sleeve

atoxique [atɔksik] ADJ non-poisonous

ATP [atepe] NF (*ABRÉV* = **Association des tennismen professionnels**) ATP

atrabilaire [atʀabilɛʀ] ADJ († *ou hum*) bilious, atrabilious (*frm*)

âtre [ɑtʀ] NM (*littér*) hearth

Atrée [atʀe] NM Atreus

Atrides [atʀid] NMPL **les ~** the Atridae

atrium [atʀijɔm] NM (*Archit, Anat*) atrium

atroce [atʀos] ADJ [a] [*crime*] atrocious, heinous; [*douleur*] excruciating; [*spectacle*] atrocious, horrifying; [*mort, sort, vengeance*] dreadful, terrible [b] [*goût, odeur, temps*] atrocious, foul; [*livre, acteur*] atrocious, dreadful; [*laideur, bêtise*] dreadful

atrocement [atʀosmɑ̃] ADV [a] [*souffrir*] atrociously, horribly; [*défigurer*] horribly; **il s'est vengé ~** he wreaked a terrible *ou* dreadful revenge; **elle avait ~ peur** she was terror-stricken [b] [*laid*] atrociously, dreadfully; [*bête*] dreadfully; [*mauvais, ennuyeux*] excruciatingly, dreadfully; **loucher ~** to have a dreadful squint

atrocité [atʀosite] NF [a] (= *qualité*) [*crime, action*] atrocity, atrociousness; [*spectacle*] ghastliness [b] (= *acte*) atrocity, outrage; **dire des ~s sur qn** to say wicked *ou* atrocious things about sb; **cette nouvelle tour est une ~** that new tower is an atrocity *ou* a real eyesore

atrophie [atʀofi] NF (*Méd*) atrophy; (*fig*) degeneration, atrophy

atrophié, e [atʀofje] (*ptp de* **atrophier**) ADJ (*lit, fig*) atrophied

atrophier [atʀofje] ▶conjug 7◀ [1] VT (*Méd*) to atrophy; (*fig*) to atrophy, cause the degeneration of [2] **s'atrophier** VPR [*membres, muscle*] to waste away, atrophy; (*fig*) to atrophy, degenerate

atropine [atʀopin] NF atropine, atropin

attabler (s') [atable] ▶conjug 1◀ VPR (*pour manger*) to sit down at (the) table; **s'~ autour d'une bonne bouteille** to sit (down) at the table for a drink; **s'~ à la terrasse d'un café** to sit at a table outside a café; **il vint s'~ avec eux** he came to sit at their table; **les clients attablés** the seated customers

attachant, e [ataʃɑ̃, ɑ̃t] ADJ [*film, roman*] captivating; [*enfant*] endearing

attache [ataʃ] NF [a] (*en ficelle*) (piece of) string; (*en métal*) clip, fastener; (= *courroie*) strap [b] (*Anat*) **~s** [*épaules*] shoulder joints; [*bassin*] hip joints; (= *poignets et chevilles*) wrists and ankles [c] (*fig*) (= *lien*) tie; (= *famille*) **~s** ties, connections; **avoir des ~s dans une région** to have family ties *ou* connections in a region [d] (*Bot*) tendril [e] (*loc*) **être à l'~** [*animal*] to be tied up; [*bateau*] to be moored; **point d'~** [*bateau*] mooring (post); (*fig*) base → **port**[1]

attaché, e [ataʃe] (*ptp de* **attacher**) [1] ADJ [a] **~ à** [+ *personne, animal, lieu, idée*] attached to; [+ *habitude*] tied to; **~ à la vie** attached to life; **pays très ~ à son indépendance** country that sets great store by its independence [b] **~ à** (= *affecté à*) **être ~ au service de qn** to be in sb's personal service; **les avantages ~s à ce poste** the benefits attached to *ou* that go with the position; **son nom restera ~ à cette découverte** his name will always be linked *ou* connected with this discovery [2] NM attaché; **~ d'ambassade/de presse/militaire** embassy/press/military attaché; **~ d'administration** administrative assistant; **~ commercial/culturel** commercial/cultural attaché; (*Banque*) **~ de clientèle** account manager

attaché-case (*pl* **attachés-cases**) [ataʃekɛz] NM attaché case

attachement [ataʃmɑ̃] NM [a] (*à une personne, à un animal*) affection (**à** for), attachment (**à** to); (*à un lieu, à une idée, à la vie*) attachment (**à** to); (*à une politique, à une cause*) commitment (**à** to); **vouer un ~ viscéral à** to be strongly *ou* deeply attached to; **leur ~ à lutter contre le chômage** their commitment to fighting unemployment [b] (*Constr*) daily statement (*of work done and expenses incurred*)

attacher [ataʃe] ▶conjug 1◀ [1] VT [a] [+ *animal, plante, paquet*] to tie up; [+ *prisonnier*] to tie

up, bind; (*avec une chaîne*) to chain up; [+ *volets*] to fasten, secure; (*plusieurs choses ensemble*) to tie together, bind together; **~ une étiquette à une valise** to tie a label on(to) a case; **il attacha sa victime sur une chaise** he tied his victim to a chair; **~ les mains d'un prisonnier** to tie a prisoner's hands together, bind a prisoner's hands (together); **la ficelle qui attachait le paquet** the string that was tied round the parcel; **est-ce bien attaché ?** is it well *ou* securely tied (up)?; **il ne les attache pas avec des saucisses*** he's a bit tight-fisted
b [+ *ceinture*] to do up, fasten; [+ *robe*] (*à boutons*) to do up, button up, fasten; (*à fermeture éclair*) to do up, zip up; [+ *lacets, chaussures*] to do up, tie up; [+ *fermeture, bouton*] to do up; (*Aviat*) **veuillez ~ votre ceinture** (please) fasten your seatbelts; (*hum*) **attachez vos ceintures !*** hold on to your hats!*
c [+ *papiers*] (= *épingler*) to pin together, attach; (= *agrafer*) to staple together, attach; **~ à** (= *épingler*) to pin to; (= *agrafer*) to staple onto
d (*fig* = *lier à*) **il a attaché son nom à cette découverte** he has linked *ou* put his name to this discovery; **des souvenirs l'attachent à ce village** (*qu'il a quitté*) he still feels attached to the village because of his memories; (*qu'il habite*) his memories keep him here in this village; **il a su s'~ ses étudiants** he has won the loyalty of his students; **plus rien ne l'attachait à la vie** nothing held her to life any more
e (= *attribuer*) to attach; **~ de la valeur** *ou* **du prix à qch** to attach great value to sth, set great store by sth
f (*frm* = *adjoindre*) **~ des gardes à qn** to give sb a personal guard; **~ qn à son service** to engage sb, take sb into one's service
g (= *fixer*) **~ son regard** *ou* **ses yeux sur** to fix one's eyes upon
2 VI (*Culin*) to stick; **le riz a attaché** the rice has stuck; **poêle qui n'attache pas** non-stick frying pan
3 s'attacher VPR **a** (*gén*) to do up, fasten (up) (**avec, par** with); [*robe*] (*à boutons*) to button up, do up; (*à fermeture éclair*) to zip up, do up; [*fermeture, bouton*] to do up; **ça s'attache derrière** it does up at the back, it fastens (up) at the back; **s'~ à** [+ *corde*] to attach o.s. to; [+ *siège*] to fasten o.s. to
b (= *se prendre d'affection pour*) **s'~ à** to become attached to; **cet enfant s'attache vite** this child soon becomes attached to people
c (= *accompagner*) **s'~ aux pas de qn** to follow sb closely, dog sb's footsteps; **les souvenirs qui s'attachent à cette maison** the memories attached to *ou* associated with that house
d (= *prendre à cœur*) **s'~ à faire qch** to endeavour (*Brit, frm*) *ou* endeavor (*US, frm*) *ou* attempt to do sth

attaquable [atakabl] ADJ (*Mil*) open to attack; [*testament*] contestable

attaquant, e [atakɑ̃, ɑ̃t] NM,F (*Mil, Sport*) attacker; (*Fin*) raider; **l'avantage est à l'~** the advantage is on the attacking side

attaque [atak] **1** NF **a** (*Mil, Police*) attack (**contre** on); **lancer** *ou* **mener une ~ contre** to launch *ou* make an attack on; **aller** *ou* **monter à l'~** to go into the attack; **à l'~ !** attack!; **passer à l'~** to move into the attack; **~ d'artillerie/nucléaire** artillery/nuclear attack; **~ à la bombe** bomb attack, bombing
b (= *agression*) [*banque, train*] raid; [*personne*] attack (**de** on)
c (*Sport*) attack; [*coureur*] spurt; (*Alpinisme*) start; (*Escrime*) attack; **il a lancé une ~ à 15 km de l'arrivée** he put on a spurt 15 km from the finishing line; **jeu/coup d'~** attacking game/ shot; **repartir à l'~** to go back on the attack
d (= *critique*) attack (**contre** on); **ce n'était pas une ~ personnelle** it wasn't a personal attack, it was nothing personal; **elle a été l'objet de violentes ~s dans la presse** she

came in for severe criticism from the press
e (*Méd*) attack (**de** of); **avoir une ~** (*cardiaque*) to have a heart attack; (*hémorragie cérébrale*) to have a stroke; (*d'épilepsie*) to have a seizure *ou* fit
f (*Mus*) attack
g (*Cartes*) lead
d **d'~*** on *ou* in (top) form; **il n'est pas d'~ ce matin** he's not on form this morning; **se sentir** *ou* **être assez d'~ pour faire** to feel up to doing
2 COMP ► **attaque aérienne** air raid *ou* attack ► **attaque d'apoplexie** apoplectic attack *ou* fit ► **attaque cardiaque** heart attack ► **attaque à main armée** hold-up, armed robbery; **commettre une ~ à main armée contre une banque** to hold up a bank ► **attaque de nerfs**† fit of hysteria

attaquer [atake] ▸conjug 1◂ **1** VT **a** (= *assaillir*) [+ *pays*] to attack, launch an attack (up)on; [+ *personne*] to attack, assault, set upon; **l'armée prussienne attaqua** the Prussian army attacked *ou* went into the attack; **~ de front/par derrière** to attack from the front/ from behind *ou* from the rear; **~ (qn) par surprise** to make a surprise attack (on sb); (*à un chien*) **allez, Rex attaque !** kill, Rex, kill!; **on a été attaqués par les moustiques** we were attacked by mosquitoes
b (= *critiquer*) [+ *abus, réputation, personne*] to attack
c (= *endommager*) [*rouille, infection*] to attack; [+ *humidité*] to damage; **la pollution attaque notre environnement** pollution is having a damaging effect on *ou* is damaging our environment; **l'acide attaque le fer** acid attacks *ou* eats into iron
d (= *aborder*) [+ *difficulté, obstacle*] to tackle; [+ *chapitre*] to make a start on; [+ *discours*] to launch into; [+ *travail*] to set about, get down to; (*Alpinisme*) to start; **il attaqua les hors-d'œuvre*** he got going on* *ou* tucked into* (*Brit*) the hors d'œuvres
e (*Mus*) [+ *morceau*] to strike up, launch into; [+ *note*] to attack
f (*Jur*) [+ *jugement, testament*] to contest; [+ *mesure*] to challenge; **~ qn en justice** to take sb to court, sue sb
g (*Cartes*) **~ trèfle/de la reine** to lead a club/ the queen
2 VI **a** (*Sport*) to attack; [*coureur*] to put on a spurt
3 s'attaquer VPR **s'~ à** [+ *personne, abus, mal*] to attack; [+ *problème*] to tackle, attack, take on; **s'~ à plus fort que soi** to take on more than one's match

attardé, e [ataʀde] **1** ADJ **a**† [*enfant*] retarded **b** (= *en retard*) [*promeneur*] late, belated (*littér*) **c** (= *démodé*) [*personne, goût*] old-fashioned, behind the times (*attrib*) **2** NM,F **a** ~ **(mental)**† (mentally) retarded child **b** (*Sport*) **les ~s** the stragglers

attarder [ataʀde] ▸conjug 1◂ **1** VT to make late **2 s'attarder** VPR **a** (= *se mettre en retard*) to linger (behind); **s'~ chez des amis** to stay on at friends'; **s'~ à boire** to linger over drinks *ou* a drink; **il s'est attardé au bureau pour finir un rapport** he's stayed late *ou* on at the office to finish a report; **s'~ au café** to linger at a café; **s'~ pour cueillir des fleurs** to stay behind to pick flowers; **elle s'est attardée en route** she dawdled *ou* lingered *ou* tarried (*littér*) on the way; **ne nous attardons pas ici** let's not stay any longer **b** (*fig*) **s'~ sur une description** to linger over a description; **s'~ à des détails** to dwell on details

atteindre [atɛ̃dʀ] ▸conjug 49◂ **1** VT **a** (= *parvenir à*) [+ *lieu, limite*] to reach; [+ *objet haut placé*] to reach, get at; [+ *objectif*] to reach, arrive at, attain; [+ *prix, valeur*] to reach; **~ son but** [*personne*] to reach one's goal, achieve one's aim; [*mesure*] to be effective; [*missile*] to hit its target, reach its objective; **il n'atteint**

pas mon épaule he doesn't come up to *ou* reach my shoulder; **la Seine a atteint la cote d'alerte** the Seine has risen to *ou* reached danger level; **il a atteint (l'âge de) 90 ans** he's reached his 90th birthday; **cette tour atteint 30 mètres** the tower is 30 metres high; **les peupliers peuvent ~ une très grande hauteur** poplars can grow to *ou* reach a very great height; **la corruption y atteint des proportions incroyables** corruption there has reached incredible proportions → **bave**
b (= *contacter*) [+ *personne*] to get in touch with, contact, reach
c (= *toucher*) [*pierre, balle, tireur*] to hit (**à** in); [*événement, maladie, reproches*] to affect; **il a atteint la cible** he hit the target; **il a eu l'œil atteint par un éclat d'obus** he was hit in the eye by a bit of shrapnel; **la maladie a atteint ses facultés mentales** the illness has affected *ou* impaired his mental faculties; **les reproches ne l'atteignent pas** criticism doesn't affect him, he is unaffected by criticism; **le malheur qui vient de l'~** the misfortune which has just struck him; **il a été atteint dans son amour-propre** his pride has been hurt *ou* wounded
2 atteindre à VT INDIR (*littér* = *parvenir à*) [+ *but*] to reach, achieve; **~ à la perfection** to attain (to) *ou* achieve perfection

atteint, e¹ [atɛ̃, ɛ̃t] ADJ **a** (= *malade*) **être ~ de** [+ *maladie*] to be suffering from; **il a été ~ de surdité** he became *ou* went deaf; **le poumon est gravement/légèrement ~** the lung is badly/slightly affected; **il est gravement/ légèrement ~** he is seriously/only slightly ill; **les malades les plus ~s** the worst cases, the worst affected **b** (* = *fou*) touched*, cracked*
c (*Admin*) **être ~ par la limite d'âge** to have to retire (*because one has reached the official retirement age*)

atteinte² [atɛ̃t] NF **a** (= *préjudice*) attack (**à** on); **~ à l'ordre public** breach of the peace; **~ à la sûreté de l'État** offence against national security; **~ à la vie privée** invasion of privacy; **porter ~ à** to strike a blow at, undermine; **porter ~ à la réputation de qn/d'une entreprise** to damage sb's/a company's reputation; **hors d'~** (*lit*) out of reach; (*fig*) beyond reach; **hors d'~ de** [+ *projectile*] out of range *ou* reach of **b** (*Méd* = *crise*) attack (**de** of); **les premières ~s du mal** the first effects of the illness

attelage [at(ə)laʒ] NM **a** [*cheval*] harnessing, hitching up; [*bœuf*] yoking, hitching up; [*charrette, remorque*] hitching up; (*Rail*) [*wagons*] coupling **b** (= *harnachement, chaînes*) [*chevaux*] harness; [*bœuf*] yoke; [*remorque*] coupling, attachment; (*Rail*) coupling **c** (= *équipage*) [*chevaux*] team; [*bœufs*] team; [*deux bœufs*] yoke

atteler [at(ə)le] ▸conjug 4◂ **1** VT [+ *cheval*] to harness, hitch up; [+ *bœuf*] to yoke, hitch up; [+ *charrette, remorque*] to hitch up; (*Rail*) [+ *wagons*] (*à un convoi*) to couple on; (*l'un à l'autre*) to couple; **le cocher était en train d'~** the coachman was getting the horses harnessed; (*fig*) **~ qn à un travail** to put sb on a job; **il est attelé à ce travail depuis ce matin** he has been working away at this job since this morning **2 s'atteler** VPR **s'~ à** [+ *travail, tâche, problème*] to get down to

attelle [atɛl] NF [*cheval*] hame; (*Méd*) splint

attenant, e [at(ə)nɑ̃, ɑ̃t] ADJ (= *contigu*) adjoining; **jardin ~ à la maison** garden adjoining the house; **la maison ~e à la mienne** (*ou* **la sienne** *etc*) the house next door

attendre [atɑ̃dʀ] ▸conjug 41◂ **1** VT **a** [*personne*] [+ *personne, événement*] to wait for, await (*littér*); **maintenant, nous attendons qu'il vienne/de savoir** we are now waiting for him to come/waiting to find out; **attendez qu'il vienne/de savoir pour partir** wait until he comes/you know before you leave, wait for him to come/wait and find out before you leave; **attends la fin du film** wait until the film is over *ou* until the end of the film; **aller ~ un train/qn au train** to (go and) meet a train/sb off the train; **il est venu m'~ à la gare** he came to meet me *ou* he met me at the station; **j'attends le** *ou* **mon train** I'm waiting for the *ou* my train; **~ le moment favorable** to bide one's time, wait for the right moment; **j'attends le week-end avec impatience** I'm looking forward to the weekend, I can't wait for the weekend; **~ qn comme le Messie** to wait eagerly for sb; **nous n'attendons plus que lui pour commencer** we're just waiting for him to arrive, then we can start; **qu'est-ce qu'on attend pour partir ?** what are we waiting for? let's go!; **il faut ~ un autre jour/ moment pour lui parler** we'll have to wait till another day/time to speak to him; **on ne t'attendait plus** we had given up on you; **êtes-vous attendu ?** are you expected?, is anyone expecting you?; **il attend son heure** he's biding his time; **je n'attends qu'une chose, c'est qu'elle s'en aille** I (just) can't wait for her to go; **il n'attendait que ça !** ◊ **c'est tout ce qu'il attendait !** that's just what he was waiting for!; **l'argent qu'il me doit, je l'attends toujours** he still hasn't given me the money he owes me, I'm still waiting for the money he owes me; **en attendant** (= *pendant ce temps*) meanwhile, in the meantime; (= *en dépit de cela*) all the same, be that as it may; **en attendant, j'ai le temps de finir mon travail** meanwhile *ou* in the meantime I've time to finish my work; **en attendant l'heure de partir, il jouait aux cartes** he played cards until it was time to go *ou* while he was waiting to go; **on ne peut rien faire en attendant de recevoir sa lettre** we can't do anything until we get his letter; **en attendant qu'il revienne, je vais vite faire une course** while I'm waiting for him to come back I'm going to pop down* to the shop; **en attendant, c'est moi qui fais tout !** all the same, it's me that does everything! → **dégel**

[b] [*voiture*] to be waiting for; [*maison*] to be ready for; [*mauvaise surprise*] to be in store for, await, wait for; [*gloire*] to be in store for, await; **il ne sait pas encore le sort qui l'attend !** he doesn't know yet what's in store for him! *ou* awaiting him!; **je sais ce qui m'attend si je lui dis ça !** I know what'll happen to me if I tell him that!; **une brillante carrière l'attend** he has a brilliant career in store (for him) *ou* ahead of him; **le dîner vous attend** dinner's ready (when you are)

[c] (*sans complément d'objet*) [*personne, chose*] to wait; [*chose*] (= *se conserver*) to keep; **j'ai attendu 2 heures** I waited (for) 2 hours; (*iro*) **j'ai failli ~ !** you took your time!; **attendez un instant** wait a moment, hang on a minute*; **attends, je vais t'expliquer** wait, let me explain; **attendez voir*** let me *ou* let's see *ou* think*; **attendez un peu** let's see, wait a second; (*menace*) just (you) wait!; (*Téléc*) **vous attendez ou vous voulez rappeler plus tard ?** will you hold on or do you want to call back later?; (*iro*) **tu peux toujours ~ !** ◊ **tu peux ~ longtemps !** you'll be lucky!, you've got a hope! (*Brit*), you haven't a prayer! (*US*); **le train n'attendra pas** the train won't wait; **ce travail attendra/peut ~** this work will/can wait; **ces fruits ne peuvent pas ~ (demain)** this fruit won't keep (until tomorrow); **un soufflé n'attend pas** a soufflé has to be eaten straight away; **sans (plus) ~** (= *immédiatement*) straight away; **faites-le sans ~** do it straight away *ou* without delay; **il faut agir sans plus ~** we must act without further delay *ou* straight away

[d] **faire ~ qn** to keep sb waiting; **se faire ~** to keep people waiting, be a long time coming; **le conférencier se fait ~** the speaker is late; **il aime se faire ~** he likes to keep you *ou* people waiting; **excusez-moi de m'être fait ~** sorry to have kept you (waiting); **la paix se fait ~** peace is a long time coming; **leur riposte ne**

se fit pas ~ they didn't take long to retaliate

[e] (= *escompter, prévoir*) [+ *personne, chose*] to expect; **~ qch de qn/qch** to expect sth from sb/sth; **il n'attendait pas un tel accueil** he wasn't expecting such a welcome; **on attendait beaucoup de ces pourparlers** they had great hopes *ou* they expected great things of the talks; **elle est arrivée alors qu'on ne l'attendait plus** she came when she was no longer expected *ou* when they'd given up on her; **j'attendais mieux de cet élève** I expected better of this pupil, I expected this pupil to do better; **je n'en attendais pas moins de vous** I expected no *ou* nothing less of you

[f] **~ un enfant** *ou* **un bébé** ◊ **~ famille** (*Belg*) to be expecting a baby, be expecting; **ils attendent la naissance pour le 10 mai** the baby is due on 10th May

[2] **attendre après*** VT INDIR [+ *chose*] to be in a hurry for, be anxious for; [+ *personne*] to be waiting for; **l'argent que je t'ai prêté, je n'attends pas après** I'm not desperate for the money I lent you; **je n'attends pas après lui/ son aide !** I can get along without him/his help!

[3] **s'attendre** VPR [a] [*personnes*] to wait for each other

[b] **s'~ à qch** (= *escompter, prévoir*) to expect sth (**de, de la part de** from); **il ne s'attendait pas à gagner** he wasn't expecting to win; **est-ce que tu t'attends vraiment à ce qu'il écrive ?** do you really expect him to write?; **on ne s'attendait pas à ça de sa part** we didn't expect that of him; **avec lui on peut s'~ à tout** you never know what to expect with him; **tu t'attendais à quoi ?** what did you expect?; **Lionel ! si je m'attendais (à te voir ici) !*** Lionel, fancy meeting you here!; **elle s'y attendait** she expected as much; **il fallait** *ou* **on pouvait s'y ~** it was to be expected; **comme il fallait s'y ~ ...** as one would expect ..., predictably enough ...

attendri, e [atɑ̃dʀi] (*ptp de* attendrir) ADJ [*air, regard*] melting (*épith*), tender

attendrir [atɑ̃dʀiʀ] ▶ conjug 2 ◀ [1] VT [+ *viande*] to tenderize; (*fig*) [+ *personne*] to move (**to** pity); [+ *cœur*] to soften, melt; **il se laissa ~ par ses prières** her pleadings made him relent *ou* yield [2] **s'attendrir** VPR to be moved *ou* touched (**sur** by); **s'~ sur (le sort de) qn** to feel (sorry *ou* pity *ou* sympathy) for sb; **s'~ sur soi-même** to feel sorry for o.s.

attendrissant, e [atɑ̃dʀisɑ̃, ɑ̃t] ADJ moving, touching

attendrissement [atɑ̃dʀismɑ̃] NM (*tendre*) emotion, tender feelings; (*apitoyé*) pity; **ce fut l'~ général** everybody got emotional; **pas d'~ !** let's not be emotional!

attendrisseur [atɑ̃dʀisœʀ] NM (*Boucherie*) tenderizer; **viande passée à l'~** tenderized meat

attendu, e [atɑ̃dy] (*ptp de* attendre) [1] ADJ [*personne, événement, jour*] long-awaited; (= *prévu*) expected [2] PRÉP (= *étant donné*) given, considering; **~ que** seeing that, since, given *ou* considering that; (*Jur*) whereas [3] NMPL (*Jur*) **~s du jugement** grounds for the decision

attentat [atɑ̃ta] NM (*gén : contre une personne*) murder attempt; (*Pol*) assassination attempt; (*contre un bâtiment*) attack (**contre** on); **~ à la bombe** bomb attack, (*terrorist*) bombing; **~ à la voiture piégée** car-bombing; **un ~ a été perpétré contre M. Dupont** an attempt has been made on the life of Mr Dupont, there has been an assassination attempt on Mr Dupont; **~ aux droits/à la liberté** violation of rights/of liberty; **~ contre la sûreté de l'État** conspiracy against the security of the state; **~ aux mœurs** offence against public decency; **~ à la pudeur** indecent assault

attentatoire [atɑ̃tatwaʀ] ADJ prejudicial (**à** to), detrimental (**à** to)

attente [atɑ̃t] NF [a] (= *expectative*) wait, waiting (*NonC*); **cette ~ fut très pénible** the wait was unbearable; **l'~ est ce qu'il y a de plus pénible** it's the waiting which is hardest to bear; **l'~ se prolongeait** the wait was growing longer and longer

[b] (= *espoir*) expectation; **répondre à l'~** *ou* **aux ~s de qn** to come *ou* live up to sb's expectations; **contre toute ~** contrary to (all) expectation(s)

[c] **délai** *ou* **temps d'~** waiting time; **il y a 10 minutes d'~** there's a 10-minute wait; **position d'~** wait-and-see attitude; **solution d'~** temporary solution → **salle**

[d] **demande en ~** request pending; **le projet est en ~** the project is on hold; **laisser un dossier en ~** to leave a file pending; (*Téléc*) **mettre qn en ~** to put sb on hold; (*sur répondeur*) **pour écouter les messages en ~, appuyez ...** to listen to messages, press ...; **malade en ~ de greffe** patient waiting for a transplant; **détenu en ~ de jugement** prisoner awaiting trial

[e] **vivre dans l'~ d'une nouvelle** to spend one's time waiting for (a piece of) news; **dans l'~ de vos nouvelles** looking forward to hearing from you

attenter [atɑ̃te] ▶ conjug 1 ◀ VT [a] **~ à la vie de qn** to make an attempt on sb's life; **~ à ses jours** to attempt suicide; **~ à la sûreté de l'État** to conspire against the security of the state [b] (*fig = violer*) **~ à** [+ *liberté, droits*] to violate

attentif, -ive [atɑ̃tif, iv] ADJ [a] (= *vigilant*) [*personne, air*] attentive; **regarder qn d'un œil ~** to look at sb attentively; **écouter d'une oreille attentive** to listen attentively; **être ~ à tout ce qui se passe** to pay attention to everything that's going on; **sois donc ~ !** pay attention! [b] (= *scrupuleux*) [*examen*] careful, close, searching; [*travail*] careful; [*soin*] scrupulous; **~ à son travail** careful *ou* painstaking in one's work; **~ à ses devoirs** heedful *ou* mindful of one's duties; **~ à ne blesser personne** careful not to hurt anyone [c] (= *prévenant*) [*soins*] thoughtful; [*prévenance*] watchful; **~ à plaire** anxious to please; **~ à ce que tout se passe bien** keeping a close watch to see that all goes well

▼ **attention** [atɑ̃sjɔ̃] NF [a] (= *concentration*) attention; (= *soin*) care; **avec ~** [*écouter*] carefully, attentively; [*examiner*] carefully, closely; **attirer/détourner l'~ de qn** to attract/divert *ou* distract sb's attention; **fixer son ~ sur** to focus one's attention on; **faire un effort d'~** to make an effort to concentrate; **demander un effort d'~** to require careful attention; **je demande toute votre ~** can I have your full attention?; **ce cas/projet mérite toute notre ~** this case/ project deserves our undivided attention; **« à l'~ de M. Dupont »** "for the attention of Mr Dupont"; **votre candidature a retenu notre ~** we considered your application carefully → **signaler**

[b] **faire** *ou* **prêter ~ à** (= *remarquer*) to pay attention *ou* heed to; **faire bien** *ou* **très ~** to pay careful attention; **as-tu fait ~ à ce qu'il a dit ?** did you pay attention to *ou* listen carefully to what he said?; **il n'a même pas fait ~ à moi/à ce changement** he didn't (even) take any notice of me/the change; **tu vas faire ~ quand il entrera et tu verras** look carefully *ou* have a good look when he comes in and you'll see what I mean; **ne faites pas ~ à lui** pay no attention to him, take no notice of him, never mind him

[c] **faire ~** (= *prendre garde*) to be careful, take care; (**fais**) **~ à ta ligne** you'd better watch your waistline; **fais ~ à ne pas trop manger** mind *ou* be careful you don't eat too much; **fais ~ (à ce) que la porte soit fermée** make sure *ou* mind the door's shut; **fais bien ~ à toi** (= *prends soin de toi*) take good care of yourself; (= *sois vigilant*) be careful

[d] (*loc*) **~ ! tu vas tomber** watch out! *ou* mind

➤ GRAMMAIRE ACTIVE: **attention** 29.2, 29.3, 53.6

(out)! (*Brit*) *ou* careful! you're going to fall!; **« ~ chien méchant »** "beware of the dog"; **« ~ travaux »** "caution, work in progress"; **« ~ à la marche »** "be careful of the step", "mind the step" (*Brit*); **~! je n'ai pas dit cela** careful! I didn't say that; **~ au départ!** the train is now leaving!; **«~, peinture fraîche »** "(caution) wet paint"; (*sur colis*) **« ~, fragile »** "fragile, handle with care"; **~ les yeux!** watch out!*
e (= *prévenance*) attention, thoughtfulness (*NonC*); **être plein d'~s pour qn** to be very attentive towards sb; **ses ~s me touchaient** I was touched by his attentions *ou* thoughtfulness; **quelle charmante ~!** how very thoughtful!, what a lovely thought!

attentionné, e [atɑ̃sjɔne] ADJ (= *prévenant*) thoughtful, considerate (**pour, auprès de** towards)

attentisme [atɑ̃tism] NM wait-and-see policy, waiting-game

attentiste [atɑ̃tist] **1** NMF partisan of a wait-and-see policy **2** ADJ [*politique*] wait-and-see (*épith*)

attentivement [atɑ̃tivmɑ̃] ADV [*lire, écouter*] attentively, carefully; [*examiner*] carefully, closely

atténuantes [atenɥɑ̃t] ADJ FPL → **circonstance**

atténuation [atenɥasjɔ̃] NF **a** (= *fait d'atténuer*) [*douleur*] alleviation, easing; [*faute*] mitigation; [*responsabilité*] lightening; [*coup, effet*] softening; (*Jur*) [*punition, peine*] mitigation; (*Méd*) **d'un virus** attenuation of a virus; **cette crème permet l'~ des rides** this cream smooths out wrinkles **b** (= *fait de s'atténuer*) [*douleur*] dying down, easing; [*sensation, bruit*] dying down; [*violence, crise*] subsiding, abatement; [*couleur*] softening **c** (= *adoucissement*) [*lumière*] subduing, dimming; [*couleur, son*] softening, toning down

atténuer [atenɥe] ▶conjug 1◀ **1** VT **a** [+ *douleur*] to alleviate, ease; [+ *rancœur*] to mollify, appease; [+ *propos, reproches*] to tone down; [+ *rides*] to smooth out **b** [+ *faute*] to mitigate; [+ *responsabilité*] to lighten; [+ *punition*] to mitigate; [+ *coup, effets*] to soften; [+ *faits*] to water down; (*Fin*) [+ *pertes*] to cushion; [+ *risques*] to limit **c** [+ *lumière*] to subdue, dim; [+ *couleur, son*] to soften, tone down **2** **s'atténuer** VPR **a** [*douleur*] to ease, die down; [*sensation*] to die down; [*violence, crise*] to subside, abate **b** [*bruit*] to die down; [*couleur*] to soften; **leurs cris s'atténuèrent** their cries grew quieter *ou* died down

atterrant, e [aterɑ̃, ɑ̃t] ADJ appalling

atterrer [atere] ▶conjug 1◀ VT to dismay, appal (*Brit*), appall (*US*); **il était atterré par cette nouvelle** he was aghast *ou* shattered (*Brit*) at the news; **sa bêtise m'atterre** his stupidity appals me, I am appalled by *ou* aghast at his stupidity; **air atterré** look of utter dismay

atterrir [aterir] ▶conjug 2◀ VI (*Aviat*) to land, touch down; (*Naut*) to land; **~ sur le ventre** [*personne*] to land flat on one's face; [*avion*] to make a belly landing; **~ en prison/dans un village perdu*** to land up* (*Brit*) *ou* land* (*US*) in prison/in a village in the middle of nowhere; **le travail a finalement atterri sur mon bureau*** the work finally landed on my desk; **atterris!*** come back down to earth!

atterrissage [aterisaʒ] NM (*Aviat, Naut*) landing; **à l'~** at the moment of landing, at touchdown; **~ en catastrophe/sur le ventre/sans visibilité** crash/belly/blind landing; **~ forcé** emergency *ou* forced landing; (*Aviat, Écon*) **~ en douceur** soft landing → **piste, terrain, train**

attestation [atɛstasjɔ̃] NF **a** [*fait*] attestation **b** (= *document*) certificate; [*diplôme*] certificate of accreditation *ou* of attestation; **~ médicale** doctor's certificate; **~ sur l'honneur** affidavit; **~ de nationalité française/domiciliation** proof of French citizenship/residence; **~ de conformité** safety certificate

attester [atɛste] ▶conjug 1◀ VT **a** (= *certifier*) [+ *fait*] to testify to, vouch for; **~ que ...** to testify that ..., vouch for the fact that ..., attest that ...; [*témoin*] to testify that ...; **ce fait est attesté par tous les témoins** this fact is borne out *ou* is attested by all the witnesses; **comme en attestent les procès-verbaux** as the statements attest; **~ (de) l'innocence de qn** to prove sb's innocence; **certains documents attestent de l'ancienneté de ce vase** certain documents prove that this vase is an antique **b** (= *démontrer*) [*chose, preuve*] to attest to, testify to; **comme en attestent les sondages** as the polls show; **cette attitude atteste son intelligence** *ou* **atteste qu'il est intelligent** this attitude testifies to his intelligence; **les fissures attestent de la violence de cette collision** the cracks attest to the force of the collision; (*Ling*) **forme attestée** attested form; **mot non attesté dans** *ou* **par les dictionnaires** word not attested by dictionaries **c** (*littér* = *prendre à témoin*) **j'atteste les dieux que ...** I call the gods to witness that ...

attiédir† [atjedir] ▶conjug 2◀ **1** VT (*littér*) [+ *eau*] to make lukewarm; [+ *climat*] to make more temperate, temper; [+ *désir, ardeur*] to temper, cool **2** **s'attiédir** VPR [*eau*] (*plus chaud*) to get warmer; (*plus frais*) to get cooler; [*climat*] to become more temperate; (*littér*) [*désir, ardeur*] to cool down, wane

attifer* [atife] ▶conjug 1◀ **1** VT (= *habiller*) to get up* (**de** in); **regardez comme elle est attifée!** look at her get-up!*; **attifée d'une robe à volants** dolled up* in a flounced dress **2** **s'attifer** VPR to get o.s. up* (**de** in)

attiger* [atiʒe] ▶conjug 3◀ VI to go a bit far*, overstep the mark

Attila [atila] NM Attila

attique¹ [atik] **1** ADJ (*Antiq*) Attic; **finesse/sel ~** Attic wit/salt **2** **Attique** NF **l'Attique** Attica

attique² [atik] NM (*Constr*) attic (storey (*Brit*) *ou* story (*US*))

attirail* [atiraj] NM gear*, paraphernalia; **~ de pêche** fishing tackle; **~ de bricoleur/cambrioleur** handyman's/burglar's tools *ou* tool kit

attirance [atirɑ̃s] NF attraction (**pour, envers** for); **éprouver de l'~ pour qch/qn** to be *ou* feel drawn towards sth/sb, be attracted to sth/sb; **l'~ du vide** the lure of the abyss

attirant, e [atirɑ̃, ɑ̃t] ADJ attractive, appealing; **femme très ~e** alluring *ou* very attractive woman

▼**attirer** [atire] ▶conjug 1◀ VT **a** (*gén, Phys*) to attract; (= *appâtant*) to lure, entice; **il m'attira dans un coin** he drew me into a corner; **~ qn dans un piège/par des promesses** to lure *ou* entice sb into a trap/with promises; **ce spectacle va ~ la foule** this show will really draw *ou* attract the crowds *ou* will be a real crowd-puller; **~ l'attention de qn sur qch** to draw sb's attention to sth; **il essaya d'~ son attention** he tried to attract *ou* catch his attention **b** (= *plaire à*) [*pays, projet*] to appeal to; [*personne*] to attract, appeal to; **être attiré par une doctrine/qn** to be attracted *ou* drawn to a doctrine/sb; **affiche/robe qui attire les regards** eye-catching poster/dress; **il est très attiré par elle** he finds her very attractive, he's very drawn to her **c** (= *causer*) [+ *ennuis*] to cause, bring; **tu vas t'~ des ennuis** you're going to cause trouble for yourself *ou* bring trouble upon yourself; **ses discours lui ont attiré des sympathies** his speeches won *ou* gained *ou* earned him sympathy; **s'~ des critiques/la colère de qn** to incur criticism/sb's anger, bring criticism on/sb's anger down on o.s.; **s'~ des ennemis** to make enemies for o.s.; **je me suis attiré sa gratitude** I won *ou* earned his gratitude

attiser [atize] ▶conjug 1◀ VT [+ *feu*] (*avec tisonnier*) to poke (up), stir up; (*en éventant*) to fan; [+ *curiosité, haine*] to stir, arouse; [+ *convoitise*] to arouse; [+ *désir*] to stir, kindle; [+ *querelle*] to stir up; **j'ai soufflé pour ~ la flamme** I blew on the fire to make it burn

attitré, e [atitre] ADJ **a** (= *habituel*) [*marchand, place*] regular, usual; (= *agréé*) [*marchand*] accredited, appointed, registered; [*journaliste*] accredited; **fournisseur ~ d'un chef d'État** purveyors by appointment to a head of state

▼**attitude** [atityd] NF (= *maintien*) bearing; (= *comportement*) attitude; (= *point de vue*) standpoint, attitude; (= *affectation*) façade; **prendre des ~s gracieuses** to adopt graceful poses; **avoir une ~ décidée** to have a determined air; **prendre une ~ ferme** to adopt a firm standpoint *ou* attitude; **le socialisme chez lui n'est qu'une ~** his socialism is only a façade

attouchement [atuʃmɑ̃] NM touch, touching (*NonC*); (*Méd*) palpation; **se livrer à des ~s sur qn** (*gén*) to fondle *ou* stroke sb; (*Jur*) to interfere with sb

attracteur [atraktœr] NM (*Sci*) attractor

attractif, -ive [atraktif, iv] ADJ (*Phys*) [*phénomène*] attractive; (= *attrayant*) [*offre, prix, taux*] attractive

attraction [atraksjɔ̃] NF **a** (*gén* = *attirance, Ling, Phys*) attraction; **~ universelle** gravitation; **~ moléculaire** molecular attraction **b** (= *centre d'intérêt*) attraction; (= *partie d'un spectacle*) attraction; (= *numéro d'un artiste*) number; **l'~ vedette** the star attraction; (*boîte de nuit*) **quand passent les ~s?** when is the cabaret *ou* floorshow on?; (*cirque*) **ils ont renouvelé leurs ~s** they have changed their programme (of attractions *ou* entertainments), they have taken on some new acts → **parc**

attractivité [atraktivite] NF [*région*] attractiveness, appeal; [*programme, émission*] appeal

attrait [atrɛ] NM **a** (= *séduction*) [*paysage, doctrine, plaisirs*] appeal, attraction; [*danger, aventure*] appeal; **ses romans ont pour moi beaucoup d'~** I find his novels very appealing, his novels appeal to me very much; **éprouver un ~** *ou* **de l'~ pour qch** to be attracted to sth, find sth attractive *ou* appealing **b** (= *charmes*) **~s** attractions

attrapade* [atrapad] NF row*, telling off*

attrape [atrap] NF (= *farce*) trick → **farce¹**

attrape-couillon‡   (*pl* **attrape-couillons**) [atrapkuʒ̃] NM con*, con game*

attrape-mouche   (*pl* **attrape-mouches**) [atrapmuʃ] NM (= *plante, piège*) flytrap; (= *oiseau*) flycatcher; (= *papier collant*) flypaper

attrape-nigaud*   (*pl* **attrape-nigauds**) [atrapnigo] NM con*, con game*

attraper [atrape] ▶conjug 1◀ **1** VT **a** [+ *ballon*] to catch; [+ *journal, crayon*] to pick up **b** * [+ *train*] to catch, get, hop* (*US*); [+ *contravention, gifle*] to get **c** [+ *personne, voleur, animal*] to catch; **toi, si je t'attrape!** if I catch you!; **que je t'y attrape!** don't let me catch you doing that!, if I catch you doing that! **d** [+ *maladie*] to catch, get; **tu vas ~ froid** *ou* **du mal** you'll catch cold; **j'ai attrapé un rhume/son rhume** I've caught a cold/a cold from him *ou* his cold; **j'ai attrapé mal à la gorge** I've got a sore throat; **tu vas ~ la mort** you'll catch your death (of cold); **il a attrapé un coup de soleil** he got sunburnt; **la grippe s'attrape facilement** flu is very catching **e** (= *intercepter*) [+ *mots*] to pick up **f** (= *acquérir*) [+ *style, accent*] to pick up; **il faut ~ le coup** *ou* **le tour de main** you have to get *ou* learn the knack **g** (* = *gronder*) to tell off*; **se faire ~ (par qn)** to be told off (by sb)*, get a telling off from sb)*; **mes parents vont m'~** I'm really going to get it* from my parents, my parents are going to give me a real telling off*; **ils se sont**

▶ GRAMMAIRE ACTIVE: **attirer** 53.6   **attitude** 33.1

attrapés pendant une heure they went at each other for a whole hour*

[h] (= *tromper*) to take in; **se laisser ~** to be had* *ou* taken in; **tu as été bien attrapé** (*trompé*) you were had all right*; (*surpris*) you were caught out there all right

attrape-touristes [atʀapuʀist] NM INV tourist trap

attrape-tout [atʀaptu] ADJ INV [*parti politique*] catch-all (*épith*)

attrayant, e [atʀɛjɑ̃, ɑ̃t] ADJ [*spectacle, taux*] attractive; [*idée*] appealing, attractive; [*projet*] appealing; **c'est une lecture ~e** it makes *ou* it's pleasant reading; **peu ~** [*travail*] unappealing; [*paysage*] unattractive; [*proposition*] unattractive, unappealing

attribuable [atʀibɥabl] ADJ attributable (**à** to)

▼ **attribuer** [atʀibɥe] ▶conjug 1◀ VT [a] (= *allouer*) [+ *prix*] to award; [+ *avantages, privilèges*] to grant, accord; [+ *place, rôle*] to allocate, assign; [+ *biens, part*] to allocate (**à** to); (*Téléc*) **le numéro que vous avez demandé n'est plus attribué** the number you have dialled is no longer available; **s'~ le meilleur rôle/la meilleure part** to give o.s. the best role/the biggest share, claim the best role/the biggest share for o.s.

[b] (= *imputer*) [+ *faute*] to attribute, impute; [+ *pensée, intention*] to attribute, ascribe (**à** to); **à quoi attribuez-vous cet échec/accident?** what do you put this failure/accident down to?, what do you attribute *ou* ascribe this failure/accident to?

[c] (= *accorder*) [+ *invention, mérite*] to attribute (**à** to); **on lui attribue l'invention de l'imprimerie** the invention of printing has been attributed to him, he has been credited with the invention of printing; **la critique n'attribue que peu d'intérêt à son livre** the critics find little of interest in his book *ou* consider his book of little interest; **~ de l'importance à qch** to attach importance to sth; **s'~ tout le mérite** to claim all the merit for o.s.

attribut [atʀiby] NM (= *caractéristique, symbole*) attribute; (*Gram*) complement; **adjectif ~** predicative adjective; **nom ~** noun complement

attributaire [atʀibytɛʀ] NMF [*prestations*] beneficiary; [*actions*] allotee; [*prix*] prizewinner

attributif, -ive [atʀibytif, iv] ADJ [a] (*Jur*) **acte ~** act of assignment [b] (*Ling*) **fonction attributive** complement function; **syntagme ~** complement; **verbe ~** link verb, copula

attribution [atʀibysjɔ̃] NF [a] [*prix*] awarding; [*avantages*] granting; [*place, rôle, part*] allocation; [*œuvre, invention*] attribution [b] (= *prérogatives, pouvoirs*) **~s** remit, attributions; **cela n'entre pas dans mes ~s** that's not part of my remit

attristant, e [atʀistɑ̃, ɑ̃t] ADJ [*nouvelle, spectacle*] saddening

attrister [atʀiste] ▶conjug 1◀ [1] VT to sadden; **cette nouvelle nous a profondément attristés** we were greatly saddened by *ou* grieved at the news [2] **s'attrister** VPR to be saddened (**de** by), become sad (**de qch** at sth, **de voir que** at seeing that)

attroupement [atʀupmɑ̃] NM [*foule*] gathering; (= *groupe*) crowd, mob (*péj*)

attrouper (s') [atʀupe] ▶conjug 1◀ VPR to gather (together), flock together, form a crowd

atypique [atipik] ADJ atypical

au [o] → **à**

aubade [obad] NF dawn serenade; **donner une ~ à qn** to serenade sb at dawn

aubaine [obɛn] NF godsend; (*financière*) windfall; **profiter de l'~** to make the most of one's good fortune *ou* of the opportunity; **quelle (bonne) ~!** what a godsend! *ou* stroke of luck!

aube¹ [ob] NF [a] (= *lever du jour*) dawn, daybreak, first light; **à l'~** at dawn *ou* daybreak *ou*

first light; **avant l'~** before dawn *ou* daybreak [b] (= *début*) dawn, beginning; **à l'~ de** at the dawn of

aube² [ob] NF (*Rel*) alb

aube³ [ob] NF (*Tech*) [*bateau*] paddle, blade; [*moulin*] vane; [*ventilateur*] blade, vane; **roue à ~s** paddle wheel

aubépine [obepin] NF hawthorn; **fleurs d'~** may (blossom), hawthorn blossom

auberge [obɛʀʒ] NF inn; **il prend la maison pour une ~!** he treats this place like a hotel!; **~ de (la) jeunesse** youth hostel; **c'est l'~ espagnole** (*repas*) everyone's bringing some food along, it's potluck (*US*); (*situation chaotique*) it's a madhouse* → **sortir**

aubergine [obɛʀʒin] [1] NF [a] (= *légume*) aubergine (*Brit*), eggplant (*US*); **caviar d'~** ≈ aubergine (*Brit*) *ou* eggplant (*US*) dip [b] (†,* = *contractuelle*) traffic warden (*Brit*), meter maid* (*US*) [2] ADJ INV aubergine(-coloured)

aubergiste [obɛʀʒist] NMF [*hôtel*] hotelkeeper; [*auberge*] innkeeper, landlord; [*auberge de jeunesse*] **père** *ou* **mère ~** (youth-hostel) warden

aubette [obɛt] NF (*Belg*) bus shelter

aubier [obje] NM sapwood

auburn [obœʀn] ADJ INV auburn

aucun, e [okœ̃, yn] [1] ADJ [a] (*négatif*) no, not any; **~ historien n'en a parlé** no historian spoke of it; **il n'a ~e preuve** he has no proof, he doesn't have any proof; **sans faire ~ bruit** without making a noise *ou* any noise; **ils ne prennent ~ soin de leurs vêtements** they don't take care of their clothes (at all); **ils n'ont eu ~ mal à trouver le chemin** they had no trouble finding the way, they found the way without any trouble

[b] (*interrogatif, positif*) any; **il lit plus qu'~ autre enfant** he reads more than any other child; **croyez-vous qu'~ auditeur aurait osé le contredire?** do you think that any listener would have dared to contradict him?

[2] PRON [a] (*négatif*) none; **il n'aime ~ de ces films** he doesn't like any of these films; **~ de ses enfants ne lui ressemble** none of his children are like him; **je ne pense pas qu'~ d'entre nous puisse y aller** I don't think any of us can go; **combien de réponses avez-vous eues? — ~e** how many answers did you get? — not one *ou* none

[b] (*interrogatif, positif*) any, any one; **il aime ses chiens plus qu'~ de ses enfants** he is fonder of his dogs than of any (one) of his children; **pensez-vous qu'~ ait compris?** do you think anyone *ou* anybody understood?

[c] (*littér*) **d'~s** some; **d'~s aiment raconter que ...** there are some who like to say that ...

aucunement [okynmɑ̃] ADV in no way, not in the least, not in the slightest; **il n'est ~ à blâmer** he's not in the least to blame, he's in no way *ou* not in any way to blame; **accepterez-vous? — ~** are you going to accept? — certainly not

audace [odas] NF [a] (= *témérité*) daring, boldness, audacity; (*Art* = *originalité*) daring; (= *effronterie*) audacity, effrontery; **avoir l'~ de** to have the audacity to, dare to [b] (= *geste osé*) daring gesture; (= *innovation*) daring idea *ou* touch; **elle lui en voulait de ses ~s** she held his boldness *ou* his bold behaviour against him; **une ~ de génie** a daring touch of genius; **~s de style** daring innovations of style; **les ~s de la mode** the daring inventions *ou* creations of high fashion

audacieusement [odasjøzmɑ̃] ADV boldly; **robe ~ décolletée** daringly low-cut dress

audacieux, -ieuse [odasjø, jøz] ADJ [*soldat, action, architecture*] daring, bold; [*artiste, projet*] daring; **un geste ~** a bold gesture; **les plus ~** the boldest among them → **fortune**

au-delà [od(ə)la] [1] LOC ADV → **delà** [2] NM **l'~** the beyond

au-dessous, au-dessus → **dessous, dessus**

au-devant [od(ə)vɑ̃] [1] **au-devant de** LOC PRÉP ahead of; **aller ~ de qn** to go and meet sb; **aller ~ des désirs de qn** to anticipate sb's wishes [2] LOC ADV ahead

audibilité [odibilite] NF audibility

audible [odibl] ADJ audible

audience [odjɑ̃s] NF [a] (*frm* = *entretien*) interview, audience; **donner ~ à qn** to grant sb an audience

[b] (*Jur* = *séance*) hearing; **l'~ reprendra à 14 heures** the court will reconvene at 2 o'clock

[c] (= *attention*) interest; **ce projet eut beaucoup d'~** the project aroused much interest; **cet écrivain a trouvé ~ auprès des étudiants** this author has had a favourable reception from students *ou* is popular with students; **ce parti bénéficie de la plus large ~** this party has the largest following

[d] (= *spectateurs, auditeurs*) audience; (*Radio, TV*) **faire de l'~** to attract a large audience; **gagner des points d'~** to go up in the ratings; **taux d'~** (*TV*) viewing figures; (*Radio*) listening figures; **part d'~** audience share; **9,4 points d'~** 9.4 points in the ratings, 9.4 rating points (*US*); **cette série a battu tous les records d'~** the series has broken all viewing *ou* listening records; **heure de grande ~** (*TV*) peak viewing time; (*Radio*) peak listening time

audimat® [odimat] NM INV (= *appareil*) audience research device; (= *taux d'écoute*) ratings; **avoir un bon ~** ◊ **faire de l'~** to have good ratings

audimètre [odimɛtʀ] NM audience research device

audio [odjo] ADJ INV [*fréquence, matériel, cassette*] audio

audioconférence [odjokɔ̃feʀɑ̃s] NF audio-conference

audio-électronique (*pl* **audio-électroniques**) [odjoelɛktʀɔnik] ADJ audiotronic

audiofréquence [odjofʀekɑ̃s] NF audio frequency

audiogramme [odjogʀam] NM audiogram

audioguide [odjogid] NM tape guide

audiomètre [odjomɛtʀ] NM audiometer

audiométrie [odjometʀi] NF audiometry

audionumérique [odjonymeʀik] ADJ digital

audio-oral, e (*mpl* **audio-oraux**) [odjoɔʀal, o] ADJ [*exercices, méthode*] audio (*épith*)

audiophone [odjofɔn] NM hearing aid

audioprothésiste [odjopʀɔtezist] NMF hearing aid specialist

audiotexte [odjotɛkst] NM audiotext

audiotypie [odjotipi] NF audiotyping

audiotypiste [odjotipist] NMF audiotypist

audiovisuel, -elle [odjovizɥɛl] [1] ADJ audiovisual [2] NM **l'~** (= *équipement*) audiovisual aids; (= *méthodes*) audiovisual techniques *ou* methods; (= *radio et télévision*) radio and television

audit [odit] NM [a] (= *contrôle*) audit; **faire l'~ de** to audit [b] (= *personne*) auditor

auditer [odite] ▶conjug 1◀ VT to audit

auditeur, -trice [oditœʀ, tʀis] NM,F (*gén, Radio*) listener; (*Ling*) hearer; (*Fin*) auditor; **le conférencier avait charmé ses ~s** the lecturer had captivated his audience; (*Univ*) **~ libre** *person who registers to sit in on lectures*, auditor (*US*); **~ à la Cour des comptes** junior official (*at the Cour des Comptes*)

auditif, -ive [oditif, iv] ADJ auditory; **troubles ~s** hearing problems *ou* difficulties; **aide** *ou* **prothèse auditive** hearing aid

audition [odisjɔ̃] NF [a] (*Mus, Théât* = *essai*) audition; (= *récital*) recital; (= *concert d'élèves*) concert (**de** by); **passer une ~** to audition, have an audition [b] (*Jur*) hearing; **après une heure d'~ par le juge** after a one-hour hearing before the judge; **procéder à l'~ d'un témoin** to hear a witness c (= *écoute*) listening (**de** to); **salle conçue pour l'~ de la musique** room designed for listening to music d (= *ouïe*) hearing

auditionner [oditsjɔne] ▸conjug 1◂ 1 VT to audition, give an audition to 2 VI to be auditioned, audition

auditoire [oditwaʀ] 1 NM audience 2 ADJ (*Ling*) auditory

auditorium [oditɔʀjɔm] NM auditorium

auge [oʒ] NF (*Agr, Constr*) trough; (*Géog*) **vallée en ~ ◇~ ◇~ glaciaire** U-shaped valley, trough; (*hum*) **passe ton ~!*** give us your plate!*

Augias [oʒjas] NM Augeas → **écurie**

augmentatif, -ive [ɔgmãtatif, iv] ADJ (*Gram*) augmentative

augmentation [ɔgmãtasjɔ̃] NF (= *accroissement*) (*gén*) increase; [*prix, population, production*] increase, rise (**de** in); (= *de capital*) increase in capital; **~ de salaire** pay rise (*Brit*), (pay) raise (*US*); **réclamer une ~ (de salaire)** (*collectivement*) to make a wage claim; (*individuellement*) to put in for a pay rise (*Brit*) ou raise (*US*); **l'~ des salaires par la direction** the management's raising of salaries; **l'~ des prix par les commerçants** the raising ou putting up of prices by shopkeepers

augmenter [ɔgmãte] ▸conjug 1◂ 1 VT a [+ *salaire, prix, impôts*] to increase, raise, put up; [+ *nombre*] to increase, raise, augment; [+ *production, quantité, dose*] to increase, step up, raise; [+ *durée*] to increase; [+ *difficulté, inquiétude*] to add to, increase; [+ *intérêt*] to heighten; **~ les prix de 10 %** to increase ou raise ou put up prices by 10%; **il augmente ses revenus en faisant des heures supplémentaires** he augments ou supplements his income by working overtime; **sa collection s'est augmentée d'un nouveau tableau** he has extended ou enlarged his collection with a new painting, he has added a new painting to his collection; (*Tricot*) **~ (de 5 mailles)** to increase (5 stitches); (*Mus*) **tierce augmentée** augmented third; **ceci ne fit qu'~ sa colère** this only added to his anger → **édition**

b **~ qn (de 500 F)** to increase sb's salary (by 500 francs), give sb a (500-franc) rise (*Brit*) ou raise (*US*); **il n'a pas été augmenté depuis 2 ans** he has not had ou has not been given a rise (*Brit*) ou raise (*US*) ou a salary increase for 2 years

2 VI (= *grandir*) [*salaire, prix, impôts*] to increase, rise, go up; [*marchandises*] to go up; [*poids, quantité*] to increase; [*population, production*] to grow, increase, rise; [*douleur*] to grow ou get worse, increase; [*difficulté, inquiétude*] to grow, increase; **~ de poids/volume** to increase in weight/volume → **vie**

augure [ogyʀ] NM a (= *devin*) (*Hist*) augur; (*hum*) soothsayer, oracle; **consulter les ~s** to consult the oracle b (= *présage*) omen; (*Hist*) augury; **être de bon ~** to be of good omen, augur well; **résultat de bon ~** promising ou encouraging result; **être de mauvais ~** to be ominous ou of ill omen, augur ill; **cela me paraît de bon/mauvais ~** that's a good/bad sign, that augurs well/badly ou ill → **accepter, oiseau**

augurer [ogyʀe] ▸conjug 1◂ VT **que faut-il ~ de son silence?** what must we gather ou understand from his silence?; **je n'augure rien de bon de cela** I don't foresee ou see any good coming from ou out of it; **cela augure bien/mal de la suite** that augurs well/ill (for what is to follow)

Auguste [ogyst] NM Augustus; (*Antiq*) **le siècle d'~** the Augustan age

auguste [ogyst] 1 ADJ [*personnage, assemblée*] august; [*geste*] noble, majestic 2 NM **l'~ ≈** Coco the clown

augustin, e [ogystɛ̃, in] NM,F (*Rel*) Augustinian

augustinien, -ienne [ogystinjɛ̃, jɛn] ADJ Augustinian

aujourd'hui [oʒuʀdɥi] ADV a (= *ce jour-ci*) today; **~ en huit** a week from today, a week today (*Brit*), today week (*Brit*); **il y a ~ 10 jours que ...** it's 10 days ago today that ...; **c'est tout pour ~** that's all ou that's it for today; **à dater** ou **à partir d'~** (as) from today, from today onwards; **je le ferai ~** I'll do it this very day; (*hum*) **alors cette bière, c'est pour ~ ou pour demain?** any chance of getting that beer sometime today?; **ça ne date pas d'~** [*objet*] it's not exactly new; [*situation, attitude*] it's nothing new → **jour** b (= *de nos jours*) today, nowadays, these days; **les jeunes d'~** young people nowadays, (the) young people of today

aulne [o(l)n] NM alder

aulx [o] NMPL → **ail**

aumône [omon] NF (= *don*) charity (*NonC*), alms; (= *action de donner*) almsgiving; **vivre d'~(s)** to live on charity; **demander l'~** (*lit*) to ask ou beg for charity ou alms; (*fig*) to beg (for money *etc*); **faire l'~** to give alms (**à** to); **cinquante francs! c'est une ~** fifty francs, that's a beggarly sum!; **je ne vous demande pas l'~** I'm not asking for charity; **faire** ou **accorder l'~ d'un sourire à qn** to favour sb with a smile

aumônerie [omonʀi] NF chaplaincy

aumônier [omonje] NM chaplain

aumônière [omonjɛʀ] NF (*Hist, Rel*) purse

aune¹ [on] NM = **aulne**

aune² [on] NF ≈ ell; **il fit un nez long d'une ~** ou **son visage s'allongea d'une ~** he pulled a long face ou a face as long as a fiddle (*Brit*)

auparavant [opaʀavã] ADV (= *d'abord*) before(hand), first; (= *avant*) before(hand), previously

auprès [opʀɛ] 1 ADV (*littér*) nearby 2 **auprès de** LOC PRÉP a (= *à côté de*) next to, close to, by; (= *au chevet de, aux côtés de*) with; **rester ~ d'un malade** to stay with an invalid; **s'asseoir ~ de la fenêtre/de qn** to sit down by ou close to the window/by ou next to ou close to sb

b (= *comparé à*) compared with, in comparison with, next to; **notre revenu est élevé ~ du leur** our income is high compared with ou in comparison with ou next to theirs

c (= *s'adressant à*) **faire une demande ~ des autorités** to apply to the authorities, lodge a request with the authorities; **faire une démarche ~ du ministre** to approach the minister, apply to the minister; **ambassadeur ~ du Vatican** ambassador to the Vatican

d (= *dans l'opinion de*) in the opinion of; **il passe pour un incompétent ~ de ses collègues** his colleagues regard him as incompetent, he is incompetent in the opinion of his colleagues

auquel [okɛl] → **lequel**

aura [ɔʀa] NF aura

auréole [ɔʀeɔl] NF a (*Art, Astron*) halo, aureole; **~ de cheveux blonds** halo of blond hair; **entouré de l'~ du succès** flushed with success; **paré de l'~ du martyre** wearing a martyr's crown ou the crown of martyrdom; **parer qn d'une ~** to glorify sb b (= *tache*) ring

auréoler [ɔʀeɔle] ▸conjug 1◂ 1 VT (*gén ptp*) (= *glorifier*) to glorify; (*Art*) to encircle with a halo; **tête auréolée de cheveux blancs** head with a halo of white hair; **auréolé de gloire** wreathed in ou crowned with glory; **être auréolé de prestige** to have an aura of prestige 2 **s'auréoler** VPR **s'~ de** to take on an aura of

auréomycine [ɔʀeɔmisin] NF aureomycin (*Brit*), Aureomycin® (*US*)

auriculaire [ɔʀikylɛʀ] 1 NM little finger 2 ADJ auricular → **témoin**

auriculothérapie [ɔʀikylɔteʀapi] NF aural acupuncture

aurifère [ɔʀifɛʀ] ADJ gold-bearing

aurification [ɔʀifikasjɔ̃] NF (*dent*) filling with gold

aurifier [ɔʀifje] ▸conjug 7◂ VT (+ *dent*) to fill with gold

aurige [ɔʀiʒ] NM charioteer; (*Art*) **l'Aurige de Delphes** the Charioteer of Delphi

Aurigny [ɔʀiɲi] NF Alderney

aurochs [ɔʀɔk] NM aurochs

aurore [ɔʀɔʀ] NF a (= *lever du jour*) dawn, daybreak, first light; **à l'~** at dawn ou first light ou daybreak; **avant l'~** before dawn ou daybreak; **se lever/partir aux ~s** to get up/leave at the crack of dawn; **~ australe** aurora australis; **~ boréale** northern lights, aurora borealis; **~ polaire** polar lights b (*littér = début*) dawn, beginning; **à l'~ de** at the dawn of

auscultation [ɔskyltasjɔ̃] NF auscultation

ausculter [ɔskylte] ▸conjug 1◂ VT to sound (the chest of), auscultate (*SPÉC*)

auspices [ɔspis] NMPL a (*Antiq*) auspices b **sous de bons/mauvais ~** under favourable/unfavourable auspices; **sous les ~ de qn** under the patronage ou auspices of sb; **la réunion a commencé sous les meilleurs ~** the meeting got off to a most auspicious start

▾ **aussi** [osi] 1 ADV a (= *également*) too, also; **je suis fatigué et eux ~** I'm tired and so are they ou and they are too; **il travaille bien et moi ~** he works well and so do I; **il parle ~ l'anglais** he also speaks English, he speaks English as well ou too; **lui ~ parle l'anglais** he speaks English too ou as well, he too speaks English; **il parle l'italien et ~ l'anglais** he speaks Italian and English too ou as well, he speaks Italian and also English; **il a la grippe — lui ~?** he's got the flu — him too?* ou him as well?; **c'est ~ mon avis** I think so too ou as well, that's my view too ou as well; **faites bon voyage — vous ~** have a good journey — you too ou (the) same to you; **il ne suffit pas d'être doué, il faut ~ travailler** it's not enough to be talented, you also have to work; **toi ~, tu as peur?** so you are afraid too? ou as well?

b (*comparaison*) **~ grand** *etc* **que** as tall *etc* as; **il est ~ bête que méchant** ou **qu'il est méchant** he's as stupid as he is ill-natured; **viens ~ souvent que tu voudras** come as often as you like; **s'il pleut ~ peu que l'an dernier** if it rains as little as last year; **il devint ~ riche qu'il l'avait rêvé** he became as rich as he had dreamt he would; **pas ~ riche qu'on le dit** not as rich as he is said to be; **la piqûre m'a fait tout ~ mal que la blessure** the injection hurt me just as much as the injury (did); **~ vite que possible** as quickly as possible; **d'~ loin qu'il nous vit il lui fit signe** far away though he was he shouted as soon as he saw us

c (= *si, tellement*) so; **je ne te savais pas ~ bête** I didn't think you were so ou that* stupid; **comment peut-on laisser passer une ~ bonne occasion?** how can one let slip such a good opportunity? ou so good an opportunity?; **je ne savais pas que cela se faisait ~ facilement (que ça)** I didn't know that could be done as easily (as that) ou so easily ou that easily*; **~ léger qu'il fût** light though he was; **~ idiot que ça puisse paraître** silly though ou as it may seem

d (= *tout autant*) **bien** just as well, just as easily; **tu peux ~ bien dire non** you can just as easily ou well say no; (*littér*) **puisqu'~ bien tout est fini** since everything is finished; **ça peut ~ bien représenter une montagne qu'un animal** it could just as well ou easily represent a mountain as an animal; **~ sec*** straight away, there and then

► GRAMMAIRE ACTIVE: **aussi** 32.3, 53.5

2 CONJ (= *en conséquence*) therefore, consequently; **je suis faible, ~ ai-je besoin d'aide** I'm weak, therefore *ou* consequently I need help; **tu n'as pas compris, ~ c'est ta faute : tu n'écoutais pas** you haven't understood, well, it's your own fault — you weren't listening

aussitôt [osito] ADV straight away, immediately; **~ arrivé/descendu il s'attabla** as soon as he arrived/came down he sat down at table; **~ le train arrêté, elle descendit** as soon as *ou* immediately (*Brit*) the train stopped she got out; **~ dit, ~ fait** no sooner said than done; **~ après son retour** straight *ou* directly *ou* immediately after his return; **il est parti ~ après** he left straight *ou* directly *ou* immediately after; **~ que** as soon as; **~ que je le vis** as soon as *ou* the moment I saw him

austère [ostɛʀ] ADJ [*personne, vie, style, monument*] austere; [*livre, lecture*] dry; **coupe ~ d'un manteau** severe cut of a coat

austérité [osteʀite] NF [*personne, vie, style, monument*] austerity; [*livre, lecture*] dryness; (*Rel*) **~s** austerities; (*Pol*) **mesures/politique d'~** austerity measures/policy

austral, e (*mpl* **australs**) [ostʀal] ADJ southern, austral (*SPÉC*); **pôle ~** South Pole → **aurore**

Australasie [ostʀalazi] NF Australasia; **d'~** [*produit, habitant*] Australasian

Australie [ostʀali] NF **l'~** (the Commonwealth of) Australia; **~-Méridionale/-Occidentale** South/Western Australia

australien, -ienne [ostʀaljɛ̃, jɛn] **1** ADJ Australian **2** **Australien(ne)** NM,F Australian

australopithèque [ostʀalopitɛk] NM Australopithecus

autan [otɑ̃] NM (**vent d')autan** (strong and hot) southerly wind

autant [otɑ̃] **1** ADV **a** **~ de** (*quantité*) as much (**que** as); (*nombre*) as many (**que** as); **il y a (tout) ~ de place ici (que là-bas)** there's (just) as much room here (as over there); **il n'y a pas ~ de neige que l'année dernière** there isn't as much *ou* there's not so much snow as last year; **nous avons ~ de voitures qu'eux** we have as many cars as they have; **nous sommes ~ qu'eux** we are as many as they are *ou* as them, there are as many of us as of them; **il nous prêtera ~ de livres qu'il pourra** he'll lend us as many books as he can; **ils sont ~ à plaindre l'un que l'autre** you have to feel just as sorry for both of them; **ils ont ~ de mérite l'un que l'autre** they have equal merit; **ils ont ~ de talent l'un que l'autre** they are both equally talented; **j'en voudrais encore ~** I'd like as much again; **tous ces enfants sont ~ de petits menteurs** all these children are so many little liars; **tous ~ que vous êtes** every single one of you, the whole lot of you (*Brit*)

b (*intensité*) as much (**que** as); **il travaille toujours ~** he works as hard as ever, he's still working as hard; **pourquoi travaille-t-il ~ ?** why does he work so much? *ou* so hard?; **rien ne lui plaît ~ que de regarder les autres travailler** there is nothing he likes so much as *ou* likes better than watching others work; **intelligent, il l'est ~ que vous** he's just as intelligent as you are; **il peut crier ~ qu'il veut** he can scream as much as he likes; **cet avertissement vaut pour vous ~ que pour lui** this warning applies to you as much as to him; **courageux ~ que compétent** courageous as well as competent, as courageous as he is competent; **~ prévenir la police** it would be as well to tell the police → **aimer**

c (= *tant*) (*quantité*) so much, such; (*nombre*) so many, such a lot of; **elle ne pensait pas qu'il aurait ~ de succès/qu'il mangerait ~** she never thought that he would have so much *ou* such success *ou* be so successful/that he would eat so much *ou* such a lot; **vous invitez toujours ~ de gens ?** do you always invite so many people? *ou* such a lot of people?; **j'ai ra-** **rement vu ~ de monde** I've seldom seen such a crowd *ou* so many people

d (*avec en* = *à la même chose*) the same; **je ne peux pas en dire ~** I can't say the same (for myself); **je peux en faire ~** I can do as much *ou* the same

e (*loc*) **~ il est généreux, ~ elle est avare** he is as generous as she is miserly; **~ il aime les chiens, ~ il déteste les chats** he likes dogs as much as he hates cats; **~ que possible** as much *ou* as far as possible; **il voudrait, ~ que possible, éviter les grandes routes** he would like to avoid the major roads as much *ou* as far as possible ■ (*PROV*) **~ d'hommes, ~ d'avis** every man to his own opinion; **« Autant en emporte le vent »** "Gone with the Wind"; (*pour*) **~ que je** (*ou* **qu'il etc**) **sache** as far as I know (*ou* he *etc* knows), to the best of my (*ou* his *etc*) knowledge; **c'est ~ de gagné** *ou* **de pris** that's something at least; **c'est ~ de fait** that's that done at least; **~ dire qu'il ne sait rien/qu'il est fou** you *ou* one might as well say that he doesn't know anything/that he's mad; **~ pour moi !** my mistake!; **pour ~** for all that; **vous l'avez aidé mais il ne vous remerciera pas pour ~** you helped him but you won't get any thanks from him for all that; **il a gagné, cela ne signifie pas pour ~ qu'il est le meilleur** he won, but that doesn't mean that he's the best; **il ne le fera qu'~ qu'il saura que vous êtes d'accord** he'll only do it in so far as he knows you agree

2 **d'autant** LOC ADV **ce sera augmenté d'~** it will be increased accordingly *ou* in proportion; **d'~ que ◊ d'~ plus que** all the more so since *ou* because *ou* as; **c'est d'~ plus dangereux qu'il n'y a pas de parapet** it's all the more dangerous since *ou* because there is no parapet; **écrivez-lui, d'~ (plus) que je ne suis pas sûr qu'il vienne demain** you'd better write to him especially as *ou* since I'm not sure if he's coming tomorrow; **d'~ plus !** all the more reason!; **cela se gardera d'~ mieux (que ...)** it will keep even better *ou* all the better (since ...); **nous le voyons d'~ moins qu'il habite très loin maintenant** we see him even less now *ou* we see even less of him now that he lives a long way away

autarcie [otaʀsi] NF autarchy, autarky

autarcique [otaʀsik] ADJ autarchic, autarkic

autel [otɛl] NM **a** (*Rel*) altar; **~ portatif** portable altar; **conduire qn à l'~** (= *l'épouser*) to lead sb to the altar; **conduire** *ou* **mener sa fille à l'~** to take one's daughter down the aisle → **trône** **b** (*littér*) altar; **dresser un ~** *ou* **des ~s à qn** to worship sb, put sb on a pedestal; **sacrifier qch sur l'~ de** to sacrifice sth on the altar of

auteur [otœʀ] NM **a** [*texte, roman*] author, writer; [*opéra*] composer; [*procédé*] originator, author; [*crime, coup d'état*] perpetrator; **l'~ de l'invention** the inventor; **il en est l'~** (*invention*) he invented it; (*texte*) he wrote it, he's the author; **l'~ de ce canular** the hoaxer; **l'~ de l'accident** the person who caused the accident; **l'~ de ce tableau** the painter, the artist who painted the picture; **qui est l'~ de cette affiche ?** who designed this poster?; (*dans un musée*) **« ~ inconnu »** "anonymous", "artist unknown"; **il fut l'~ de sa propre ruine** he was the author of his own ruin; **Prévert est l'~ des paroles, Kosma de la musique** Prévert wrote the words *ou* lyrics and Kosma composed the music; († *ou hum*) **l'~ de mes jours** my noble progenitor† (*hum*); **~-compositeur (-interprète)** singer-songwriter; **film/cinéma d'~** arthouse film *ou* movie (*US*) /films *ou* movies (*US*) → **droit³**
b (= *écrivain*) author; **lire tout un ~** to read all of an author's works; (*femme*) **c'est un ~ connu** she is a well-known author *ou* authoress → **femme**

authenticité [otãtisite] NF [*œuvre d'art, récit, document, signature*] authenticity

authentification [otãtifikasjɔ̃] NF authentication

authentifier [otãtifje] ▶conjug 7◀ VT to authenticate

authentique [otãtik] ADJ [*œuvre d'art, récit*] authentic, genuine; [*signature, document*] authentic; [*sentiment*] genuine; **c'est vrai ? — ~ !** really? — really!; **un ~ Van Gogh** a genuine Van Gogh → **acte**

authentiquement [otãtikmã] ADV genuinely, authentically; [*rapporter*] faithfully

autisme [otism] NM autism

autiste [otist] ADJ, NMF autistic

autistique [otistik] ADJ autistic

auto [oto] **1** NF (= *voiture*) car, automobile (*US*); **~s tamponneuses** bumper cars, dodgems (*Brit*) → **salon, train** **2** ADJ INV **assurance ~** car *ou* motor (*Brit*) *ou* automobile (*US*) insurance; **frais ~** running costs (of a car)

auto... [oto] PRÉF **a** (= *fait sur soi*) self-; (*Alpinisme*) **~-assurance** self-belay, self-belaying system; **~discipline** self-discipline; **tendances ~destructrices** self-destructive tendencies **b** (= *qui se fait tout seul*) **~(-)contrôle** automatic control; **~(-)régulation** self-regulating system; **~(-)adhésif** self-adhesive **c** (*se rapportant à l'automobile*) **train ~s-couchettes** car sleeper train

autoallumage [otoalymaʒ] NM pre-ignition

autoberge [otobɛʀʒ] NF riverside *ou* embankment expressway

autobiographie [otobjɔgʀafi] NF autobiography

autobiographique [otobjɔgʀafik] ADJ autobiographic(al)

autobronzant, e [otobʀɔ̃zɑ̃, ɑ̃t] ADJ self-tanning (*épith*), instant tanning (*épith*)

autobus [otobys] NM bus; (*Hist*) **~ à impériale** double decker (bus); (*Can*) **~ scolaire** school bus

autocar [otokaʀ] NM coach (*Brit*), bus (*US*); (*de campagne*) country bus

autocaravane [otokaʀavan] NF motor caravan (*Brit*), motorhome (*US*), camper (*US*)

autocariste [otokaʀist] NM coach *ou* bus operator

autocassable [otokasabl] ADJ [*ampoule*] with a snap-off top

autocélébration [otoselebʀasjɔ̃] NF (*péj*) self-congratulation; **l'heure est à l'~ chez les élus** the newly-elected representatives are in a self-congratulatory mood *ou* are busy patting themselves on the back

autocensure [otosɑ̃syʀ] NF self-censorship

autocensurer (s') [otosɑ̃syʀe] ▶conjug 1◀ VPR to practise self-censorship, censor o.s.

autocéphale [otosefal] ADJ (*Rel*) autocephalous

autochenille [otoʃ(ə)nij] NF half-track

autochrome [otokʀom] **1** ADJ [*film, plaque*] autochrome **2** NF (= *plaque*) autochrome (*early colour photograph*)

autochtone [otɔktɔn] **1** ADJ native, autochthonous (*SPÉC*); (*Géol*) autochthonous **2** NMF native, autochthon (*SPÉC*)

autoclave [otoklav] ADJ, NM (*Méd, Tech*) (**appareil** *ou* **marmite**) ~ autoclave

autocollant, e [otokɔlɑ̃, ɑ̃t] **1** ADJ [*étiquette*] self-adhesive, self-sticking; [*papier*] self-adhesive; [*enveloppe*] self-seal, self-adhesive **2** NM sticker

autocopiant, e [otokɔpjɑ̃, ɑ̃t] ADJ [*papier*] self-copy

autocorrection [otokɔʀɛksjɔ̃] NF autocorrection

autocrate [otokʀat] NM autocrat

autocratie [otokʀasi] NF autocracy

autocratique [otokʀatik] ADJ autocratic

autocratiquement [otokʀatikmɑ̃] ADV autocratically

autocritique [otokʀitik] NF self-criticism; **faire son ~** to criticize o.s.

autocuiseur [otokɥizœʀ] NM pressure cooker

autodafé [otodafe] NM auto-da-fé

autodéfense [otodefɑ̃s] NF self-defence; **groupe d'~** vigilante group *ou* committee

autodérision [otodeʀizjɔ̃] NF self-mockery, self-derision; **pratiquer l'~** to mock o.s.

autodestructeur, -trice [otodɛstʀyktœʀ, tʀis] ADJ self-destructive

autodestruction [otodɛstʀyksjɔ̃] NF self-destruction

autodétermination [otodetɛʀminasjɔ̃] NF self-determination

autodétruire (s') [otodetʀɥiʀ] ▸ conjug 38 ◂ VPR [*bande*] to self-destruct; [*entreprise, pays, civilisation*] to destroy itself; [*personne*] to destroy o.s.

autodidacte [otodidakt] ① ADJ self-taught ② NMF self-taught person, autodidact (*frm*)

autodrome [otodʀom] NM motor-racing track, autodrome

auto-école (*pl* **auto-écoles**) [otoekɔl] NF driving school; **moniteur d'~** driving instructor

autoérotique [otoeʀɔtik] ADJ auto-erotic

autoérotisme [otoeʀɔtism] NM auto-eroticism, auto-erotism

autofécondation [otofekɔ̃dasjɔ̃] NF self-fertilization

autofinancement [otofinɑ̃smɑ̃] NM self-financing

autofinancer (s') [otofinɑ̃se] ▸ conjug 1 ◂ VPR [*entreprise*] to be *ou* become self-financing; **programme de recherches autofinancé** self-supporting *ou* self-financed research programme

autofocus [otofɔkys] ADJ, NM autofocus

autogène [otoʒɛn] ADJ → **soudure**

autogérer (s') [otoʒeʀe] ▸ conjug 1 ◂ VPR to be self-managing; **organisme autogéré** self-managed *ou* -run body

autogestion [otoʒɛstjɔ̃] NF (*gén*) self-management; (*avec les ouvriers*) joint worker-management control

autogestionnaire [otoʒɛstjɔnɛʀ] ADJ self-managing (*épith*)

autogire [otoʒiʀ] NM autogiro, autogyro

autographe [otɔgʀaf] ADJ, NM autograph

autogreffe [otogʀɛf] NF autograft

autoguidage [otogidaʒ] NM self-steering, self-guiding; (*Mil*) **système d'~** homing system

autoguidé, e [otogide] ADJ self-guided

auto-immune [otoi(m)myn] ADJ F autoimmune

auto-immunisation [otoimynizasjɔ̃] NF auto-immunization

auto-induction [otoɛ̃dyksjɔ̃] NF (*Phys*) self-induction

auto-intoxication [otoɛ̃tɔksikasjɔ̃] NF auto-intoxication

autolimitation [otolimitasjɔ̃] NF [*importations*] voluntary restraint; **accords d'~** voluntary restraint agreements

autolubrifiant, e [otolybʀifjɑ̃, jɑ̃t] ADJ self-lubricating

autolyse [otoliz] NF autolysis

automate [otomat] NM ⓐ (= *robot, personne*) automaton; **marcher comme un ~** to walk like a robot ⓑ [*tickets de transport*] (automatic) ticket machine

automaticité [otomatisite] NF automaticity

automation [otomasjɔ̃] NF automation

▼ **automatique** [otomatik] ① ADJ automatic → **distributeur** ② NM (*Téléc*) ≈ subscriber trunk

dialling (*Brit*), ≈ STD (*Brit*), ≈ direct distance dialing (*US*); (= *revolver*) automatic

automatiquement [otomatikmɑ̃] ADV automatically

automatisation [otomatizasjɔ̃] NF automation

automatiser [otomatize] ▸ conjug 1 ◂ VT to automate

automatisme [otomatism] NM automatism; [*machine*] automatic functioning, automatism; **s'entraîner pour acquérir des ~s** to practice in order to develop automatic reflexes

automédication [otomedikasjɔ̃] NF self-medication; **faire de l'~** to medicate o.s.

automédon [otomedɔ̃] NM († *ou hum*) coachman

automitrailleuse [otomitʀajøz] NF armoured (*Brit*) *ou* armored (*US*) car

automnal, e (*mpl* **-aux**) [ɔtɔnal, o] ADJ autumnal

automne [ɔtɔn] NM autumn, fall (*US*); **en ~** in (the) autumn, in the fall; (*fig*) **il est à l'~ de ses jours** he's in the autumn *ou* fall (*US*) of his life

automobile [ɔtɔmɔbil] ① ADJ [*véhicule*] self-propelled, motor (*épith*), automotive; [*course, sport*] motor (*épith*); [*assurance, industrie*] motor (*épith*), car (*épith*), automobile (*épith*) (*US*) → **canot** ② NF (= *voiture*) motor car (*Brit*), automobile (*US*); **l'~** (= *industrie*) the car *ou* motor *ou* automobile (*US*) industry; (*Sport*, = *conduite*) driving, motoring (*Brit*); **termes d'~** motoring terms; **être passionné d'~** to be a car fanatic; **aimer les courses d'~s** to like motor (*Brit*) *ou* car (*US*) racing

automobilisme [ɔtɔmɔbilism] NM driving, motoring (*Brit*)

automobiliste [ɔtɔmɔbilist] NMF driver, motorist (*Brit*)

automoteur, -trice [ɔtɔmɔtœʀ, tʀis] ① ADJ self-propelled, motorized, motor (*épith*), automotive ② **automotrice** NF electric railcar

automutilation [otomytilasjɔ̃] NF self-mutilation

automutiler (s') [otomytile] ▸ conjug 1 ◂ VPR [*personne, animal*] to mutilate o.s.

autoneige [otonɛʒ] NF (*Can*) snowmobile (*US, Can*), snowcat

autonettoyant, e [otonetwajɑ̃, ɑ̃t] ADJ self-cleaning (*épith*)

autonome [ɔtɔnɔm] ADJ ⓐ [*territoire*] autonomous, self-governing; **groupuscule ~** group of political extremists → **port** ⓑ [*personne*] self-sufficient; (*Philos*) [*volonté*] autonomous; (*Ordin*) off-line → **scaphandre**

autonomie [ɔtɔnɔmi] NF ⓐ (*Admin, Fin, Philos, Pol*) autonomy; **certains Corses/Bretons veulent l'~** some Corsicans/Bretons want home rule *ou* autonomy *ou* self-government ⓑ (*Aut, Aviat*) range; **cette voiture a une ~ de 100 kilomètres** the car has a range of 100 kilometres; **ce baladeur a une ~ de 3 heures** this personal stereo has a 3-hour charge

autonomiste [ɔtɔnɔmist] ADJ, NMF (*Pol*) separatist

autonyme [otonim] ADJ autonymous

autoparodie [otopaʀɔdi] NF self-parody

autopont [otopɔ̃] NM flyover (*Brit*), overpass (*US*)

autoportrait [otopɔʀtʀɛ] NM self-portrait

autoproclamé, e [otopʀɔklame] (*ptp de* **s'autoproclamer**) ADJ (*péj*) self-proclaimed

autoproclamer (s') [otopʀɔklame] ▸ conjug 1 ◂ VPR (*péj*) [*personne*] to proclaim o.s.; **il s'est autoproclamé expert** he has set himself up as an expert, he has proclaimed himself (to be) an expert

autopropulsé, e [otopʀɔpylse] ADJ self-propelled

autopropulsion [otopʀɔpylsjɔ̃] NF self-propulsion

autopsie [ɔtɔpsi] NF autopsy, post-mortem (examination); (*fig*) post-mortem; **faire** *ou* **pratiquer une ~** to carry out an autopsy *ou* a post-mortem (examination) (**sur** on)

autopsier [ɔtɔpsje] ▸ conjug 7 ◂ VT [+ *corps*] to carry out an autopsy *ou* a post-mortem (examination) on

autopunition [otopynisjɔ̃] NF self-punishment

autoradio [otoʀadjo] NM car radio

autoradiographie [otoʀadjɔgʀafi] NF auto-radiograph

autorail [otoʀaj] NM railcar

autorégulateur, -trice [otoʀegylatœʀ, tʀis] ADJ self-regulating

autorégulation [otoʀegylasjɔ̃] NF self-regulation

autorisation [ɔtɔʀizasjɔ̃] NF (= *permission*) permission, authorization (*Admin*) (**de qch** for sth, **de faire** to do); (= *permis*) permit; **nous avions l'~ du professeur** we had the teacher's permission; **avoir l'~ de faire qch** to have permission *ou* be allowed to do sth; (*Admin*) to be authorized to do sth; **le projet doit recevoir l'~ du comité** the project must be authorized *ou* passed by the committee; **~ d'absence** leave of absence; (*Ordin*) **~ d'accès** access permission; **~ de crédit** credit line, line of credit; **~ de mise sur le marché** permit to market a product; **~ de vol** flight clearance; **~ parentale** parental consent

autorisé, e [ɔtɔʀize] (*ptp de* **autoriser**) ADJ [*agent, version*] authorized; [*opinion*] authoritative; **dans les milieux ~s** in official circles; **nous apprenons de source ~e que ...** we have learnt from official sources that ...

▼ **autoriser** [ɔtɔʀize] ▸ conjug 1 ◂ ① VT ⓐ **~ qn à faire** (= *donner la permission de*) to give *ou* grant sb permission to do, authorize sb to do (*Admin*); (= *habiliter à*) [*personne, décret*] to give sb authority to do, authorize sb to do; **il nous a autorisés à sortir** he has given *ou* granted us permission to go out, we have his permission to go out; **sa faute ne t'autorise pas à le condamner** the fact that he made a mistake doesn't give you the right to pass judgment on him; **tout nous autorise à croire que ...** everything leads us to believe that ...; **se croire autorisé à dire que ...** to feel one is entitled *ou* think one has the right to say that ...

ⓑ (= *permettre*) [*personne*] [+ *manifestation, sortie*] to authorize, give permission for; [+ *projet*] to pass, authorize; **le sel ne m'est pas autorisé** I'm not allowed to eat salt; **« stationnement autorisé sauf le mardi »** "car parking every day except Tuesdays"

ⓒ (= *rendre possible*) [*chose*] to admit of, allow (of); **l'imprécision de cette loi autorise les abus** the imprecisions in this law admit of *ou* allow (of) abuses; **expression autorisée par l'usage** expression sanctioned *ou* made acceptable by use

ⓓ (*littér* = *justifier*) to justify

② **s'autoriser** VPR ⓐ (= *invoquer*) **s'~ de qch pour faire** to use sth as an excuse to do; **je m'autorise de notre amitié pour ...** in view of our friendship I permit myself to ...

ⓑ (= *se permettre*) on **s'autorise à penser que ...** one is justified in thinking that ...; **s'~ un cigare de temps en temps** to allow o.s. a cigar from time to time

autoritaire [ɔtɔʀitɛʀ] ADJ, NMF authoritarian

autoritairement [ɔtɔʀitɛʀmɑ̃] ADV in an authoritarian way

autoritarisme [ɔtɔʀitaʀism] NM authoritarianism

autorité [ɔtɔʀite] NF ⓐ (= *pouvoir*) authority (**sur** over); **l'~ que lui confère son expérience/âge** the authority conferred upon him by experience/age; **avoir de l'~ sur qn** to have

➤ GRAMMAIRE ACTIVE: **automatique** 27.3   **autoriser** 36.2

authority over sb; **être sous l'~ de qn** to be under sb's authority; **avoir ~ pour faire** to have authority to do; **air d'~** authoritative air, air of authority; **il n'a aucune ~ sur ses élèves** he has no control over his pupils

b (= *expert, ouvrage*) authority; **l'une des grandes ~s en la matière** one of the great authorities on the subject

c (*Admin*) **l'~ ◊ les ~s** the authorities; **l'~ militaire/législative** the military/legislative authorities; **les ~s civiles et religieuses/locales** the civil and religious/local authorities; **agent** *ou* **représentant de l'~** representative of authority; **adressez-vous à l'~** *ou* **aux ~s compétente(s)** apply to the proper authorities

d (*Jur*) **l'~ de la loi** the authority *ou* power of the law; **l'~ de la chose jugée** res judicata; **être déchu de l'~ parentale** to lose one's parental rights; **vendu par ~ de justice** sold by order of the court

e (*loc*) **d'~** (= *de façon impérative*) on one's own authority; (= *sans réflexion*) out of hand, straight off, unhesitatingly; **de sa propre ~** on one's own authority; [*livre, expert*] **faire ~** to be accepted as an authority, be authoritative

autoroute [otoʀut] NF motorway (*Brit*), highway (*US*), freeway (*US*); **~ de dégagement** *toll-free stretch of motorway leading out of a big city*; **~ urbaine** urban *ou* inner-city motorway (*Brit*), throughway (*US*), expressway (*US*); **~ à péage** toll motorway (*Brit*), turnpike (*US*); **l'~ du soleil** *the A6 motorway to the south of France*; **~s électroniques/de l'information** electronic/information highways

autoroutier, -ière [otoʀutje, jɛʀ] ADJ motorway (*épith*) (*Brit*), freeway (*épith*) (*US*), highway (*épith*) (*US*)

autosatisfaction [otosatisfaksjɔ̃] NF self-satisfaction

auto-stop [otostɔp] NM hitch-hiking, hitching*; **pour rentrer, il a fait de l'~** (*long voyage*) he hitched *ou* hitch-hiked home; (*courte distance*) he thumbed *ou* hitched* a lift home; **il a fait le tour du monde en ~** he hitch-hiked around the world, he hitched* his way round the world; **j'ai pris quelqu'un en ~** I picked up a *ou* gave a lift to a hitch-hiker *ou* hitcher*; **il nous a pris en ~** he picked us up, he gave us a lift

auto-stoppeur, -euse (*mpl* auto-stoppeurs) [otostɔpœʀ, øz] NM,F hitch-hiker, hitcher*; **prendre un ~** to pick up a hitch-hiker *ou* hitcher*

autostrade† [otostʀad] NF motorway (*Brit*), freeway (*US*), highway (*US*)

autosubsistance [otosybzistɑ̃s] NF self-sufficiency; **agriculture d'~** subsistence farming

autosuffisance [otosyfizɑ̃s] NF self-sufficiency

autosuffisant, e [otosyfizɑ̃, ɑ̃t] ADJ self-sufficient

autosuggestion [otosygʒɛstjɔ̃] NF autosuggestion

autotracté, e [ototʀakte] ADJ self-propelled

autotransfusion [ototʀɑ̃sfyzjɔ̃] NF autologous transfusion

autour¹ [otuʀ] **1** ADV around; **tout ~** all around; **maison avec un jardin ~** house surrounded by a garden, house with a garden around *ou* round (*Brit*) it **2 autour de** LOC PRÉP (*lieu*) around, round (*Brit*); (*temps, somme*) about, around, round about (*Brit*); **il regarda de lui** he looked around (him) *ou* about (him); **discussion ~ d'un projet** discussion on *ou* about a project; **d'un bon café** over a nice cup of coffee → **tourner**

autour² [otuʀ] NM (*Orn*) goshawk

autovaccin [otovaksɛ̃] NM autogenous vaccine, autovaccine

▼ **autre** [otʀ] **1** ADJ INDÉF **a** (= *différent*) other, different; **je préfère l'~ robe/les ~s chaussures** I prefer the other dress/the other shoes; **revenez une ~ fois/un ~ jour** come back another *ou* some other time/another *ou* some other day; **il n'y a pas d'~ moyen d'entrer** there's no other way *ou* there isn't any other way of getting in; **c'est une ~ question/un ~ problème** that's another *ou* a different question/problem; **la réalité est tout ~** the reality is quite *ou* altogether different; **je fais ça d'une ~ façon** I do it a different way *ou* another way *ou* differently; **ils ont un (tout) ~ mode de vie/point de vue** they have a (completely) different way of life/point of view; **vous ne le reconnaîtrez pas, c'est un (tout) ~ homme** you won't know him, he's completely different *ou* he's a changed man; **après ce bain je me sens un ~ homme** I feel (like) a new man after that swim; **en d'~s lieux** elsewhere ■ (*PROV*) **~s temps ~s mœurs** customs change with the times, autres temps autres mœurs → **côté, part**

b **~ chose**: **c'est (tout) ~ chose** that's a different *ou* another matter (altogether); **parlons d'~ chose** let's talk about something else *ou* different; **c'est ça et pas ~ chose** it's that or nothing; **ce n'est pas ~ chose que de la jalousie** that's just jealousy, that's nothing but jealousy; **ah ~ chose! j'ai oublié de vous dire que ...** oh, one more thing! I forgot to tell you that ...; **une chose est de rédiger un rapport, ~ chose est d'écrire un livre** it's one thing to draw up a report, but quite another thing *ou* but another thing altogether to write a book; (*admiratif*) **c'est quand même ~ chose!** it's really something else!, it's in a different league!; **voilà ~ chose!** (*incident*) that's all I (*ou* we) need!; (*impertinence*) what a nerve*! *ou* cheek!, the cheek of it!

c (= *supplémentaire*) other; **elle a 2 ~s enfants** she has 2 other *ou* 2 more children; **donnez-moi un ~ livre/une ~ tasse de thé** give me another book/cup of tea; **donne-lui une ~ chance** give him another *ou* one more chance; **il y a beaucoup d'~s solutions** there are many other *ou* many more solutions; **bien** *ou* **beaucoup d'~s choses encore** many *ou* plenty more besides; **c'est un ~ Versailles** it's another Versailles; **c'est un ~ moi-même** he's my alter ego; **des couteaux, des verres et ~s objets indispensables** knives, glasses and other necessary items; **il m'a dit ça sans ~ précision** he didn't go into any more detail than that; **~ chose, Madame?** anything else, madam?

d (*de deux: marque une opposition*) other; **de l'~ côté de la rue** on the other *ou* opposite side of the street; **dans l'~ sens** in the other *ou* opposite direction; **mets ton ~ manteau** put your other coat on; **ses premiers films étaient d'une ~ qualité** his first films were of an altogether different quality *ou* in a different league → **monde**

e (*dans le temps*) **l'~ jour ◊ l'~ fois** the other day; **l'~ lundi*** (= *lundi dernier*) last Monday; (*dans un passé récent*) one Monday recently; **l'~ semaine** the other week; **tu me le diras une ~ fois** tell me another time

f (*avec pron pers*) **faut pas nous raconter des histoires, à nous ~s!** * there's no point telling fibs to US!; **nous ~s, on est prudents*** WE are *ou* WE'RE cautious; **taisez-vous, vous ~s*** be quiet, you people *ou* the rest of you *ou* you lot*** (*Brit*); **et vous ~s qu'en pensez-vous?** what do you people *ou* you lot* (*Brit*) think?; **nous ~s Français, nous aimons la bonne cuisine** we French like good food

2 PRON INDÉF **a** (= *qui est différent*) another (one); **il en aime une ~** he's in love with another woman, he loves another; **d'~s** others; **aucun ~ ◊ nul ~** no one else, nobody else; **les deux ~s** the other two, two others; **prendre qn pour un ~/une chose**

---

pour une ~ to take *ou* mistake sb for sb else/sth for sth else; **envoyez-moi bien ce livre, je n'en veux pas d'~** make sure you send me that book, I don't want any other; **un ~ que moi/lui aurait refusé** anyone else (but me/him) would have refused; **elle n'est pas plus bête qu'une ~** she's no more stupid than anyone else; **X, Y, Z, et ~s** X, Y, Z and others *ou* etc; **il en a vu d'~s!** he's seen worse!; **il n'en fait jamais d'~s!** that's just typical of him!, that's just what he always does!; **et l'~ (là)*, il vient avec nous?** what about him, is he coming with us?; **et l'~ qui n'arrête pas de klaxonner!*** and then there's that idiot who keeps blowing his horn!; **vous en êtes un ~!†*** you're a fool!; **à d'~s!*** (that's) a likely story!, go tell it to the marines!* → **entre, rien**

b (= *qui vient en plus*) **donnez-m'en un ~** give me another (one) *ou* one more; **qui/quoi d'~?** who/what else?; **quelqu'un/quelque chose d'~** somebody *ou* someone/something else; **rien/personne d'~** nothing/nobody *ou* no one else; **deux enfants, c'est assez, je n'en veux pas d'~/d'~s** two children are enough, I don't want another (one)/any more

c (*marque une opposition*) **l'~** the other (one); **les ~s** (= *choses*) the others, the other ones; (= *personnes*) the others; **les ~s ne veulent pas venir** the others don't want to come; **il se moque de l'opinion des ~s** he doesn't care what other people think; **avec toi, c'est toujours les ~s qui ont tort** you always think that other people are in the wrong *ou* that it's the other person who's in the wrong → **côté, ni**

d (*dans le temps*) **d'une minute/semaine à l'~** (= *bientôt*) any minute/week (now); **d'un instant à l'~** (= *n'importe quand*) any time; (= *soudain*) from one moment to the next; (= *bientôt*) very soon

3 NM (*Philos*) **l'~** the other

autrefois [otʀəfwa] ADV in the past, once, formerly; **d'~** of the past, of old, past (*épith*); **~ ils s'éclairaient à la bougie** in the past *ou* in bygone days they used candles for lighting; **~ je préférais le vin** (in the past) I used to prefer wine

autrement [otʀəmɑ̃] ADV **a** (= *différemment*) differently; **il faut s'y prendre (tout) ~** we'll have to go about it in (quite) another way *ou* (quite) differently; **avec ce climat il ne peut en être ~** with the climate the way it is, it can't be any other way *ou* how else could it be!; **cela ne peut s'être passé ~** it can't have happened any other way; **agir ~ que d'habitude** to act differently from usual; **comment aller à Londres ~ que par le train?** how can we get to London other than by train?; **~ appelé** otherwise known as; **tu pourrais me parler ~!** don't you talk to me like that!

b (*avec faire*) **il n'y a pas moyen de faire ~ ◊ on ne peut pas faire ~** it's impossible to do otherwise *ou* to do anything else; **il n'a pas pu faire ~ que de me voir** he couldn't help seeing me *ou* help but see me

c (= *sinon*) otherwise; (*idée de menace*) otherwise, or else; **travaille bien, ~ tu auras de mes nouvelles!** work hard, otherwise *ou* or else you'll be hearing a few things from me!

d (* = *à part cela*) otherwise, apart *ou* aside from that; **la viande était bonne, ~ le repas était quelconque** the meat was good but apart from that *ou* but otherwise the meal was pretty nondescript

e (* *comparatif*) far (more); **il est ~ intelligent** he is far more intelligent, he is more intelligent by far; **c'est ~ meilleur** it's far better, it's better by far (**que** than)

f **pas ~** (* = *pas spécialement*) not particularly *ou* especially; **cela ne m'a pas ~ surpris** that didn't particularly surprise me

g **~ dit** (= *en d'autres mots*) in other words

Autriche [otʀiʃ] NF Austria

autrichien, -ienne [otʀiʃjɛ̃, jɛn] **1** ADJ Austrian **2 Autrichien(ne)** NM,F Austrian

autruche [otʀyʃ] NF ostrich; (fig) **faire l'~** to bury one's head in the sand → **estomac**, **politique**

autrui [otʀɥi] PRON (littér) others; **respecter le bien d'~** to respect other people's property ou the property of others; **ne fais pas à ~ ce que tu ne voudrais pas qu'on te fît** do unto others as you would have them do unto you, do as you would be done by

auvent [ovã] NM [maison] canopy; [tente] awning, canopy

auvergnat, e [ovɛʀɲa, at] **1** ADJ of ou from (the) Auvergne **2** NM (Ling) Auvergne dialect **3** **Auvergnat(e)** NM,F inhabitant ou native of (the) Auvergne

aux [o] → **à**

auxiliaire [ɔksiljɛʀ] **1** ADJ (Ling, Mil, gén) auxiliary (épith); [cause, raison] secondary, subsidiary; **bureau** ~ sub-office; (Ordin) **mémoire** ~ additional ou extra memory; (Ordin) **programme** ~ auxiliary routine → **maître 2** NMF (= assistant) assistant, helper; ~ **de justice** representative of the law; ~ **médical** medical auxiliary **3** NM (Gram, Mil) auxiliary

auxiliairement [ɔksiljɛʀmã] ADV (Ling) as an auxiliary; (fig = secondairement) secondarily, less importantly

auxiliariat [ɔksiljaʀja] NM (Scol) **pendant mon ~** during my time as a supply (Brit) ou substitute (US) teacher

AV [ave] (ABRÉV = **avis de virement**) → **avis**

av.[1] ABRÉV = **avenue**

av.[2] (ABRÉV = **avant**) before; **en 300 ~ J.-C.** in 300 BC

avachi, e [avaʃi] (ptp de **avachir**) ADJ **a** [cuir, feutre] limp; [chaussure, vêtement] misshapen, out of shape; **pantalon** ~ baggy trousers **b** [personne] (= fatigué) drained; (péj = indolent) sloppy; ~ **sur son bureau** slumped over his desk; ~ **sur la plage** lounging ou stretched out lazily on the beach

avachir [avaʃiʀ] ▸ conjug 2 ◂ **1** VT **a** [+ cuir, feutre] to make limp; [+ chaussure, vêtement] to make shapeless, put out of shape **b** [+ personne] (physiquement) to drain; (péj: moralement) to make sloppy **2** **s'avachir** VPR **a** [cuir] to become limp; [vêtement] to go out of shape, become shapeless **b** [personne] (physiquement) to become flabby; (péj: moralement) to become sloppy

avachissement [avaʃismã] NM **a** [vêtement, cuir] loss of shape **b** [personne] (physique) flabbiness; (péj: moral) sloppiness

aval[1] [aval] NM [cours d'eau] downstream water; [pente] downhill slope; **l'~ était coupé de rapides** the river downstream was a succession of rapids; **les rapides/l'écluse d'~** the downstream rapids/lock; **skieur/ski** ~ downhill skier/ski; **en** ~ (cours d'eau) downstream, down-river; (pente) downhill; (dans une hiérarchie) lower down; **en ~ de** [+ cours d'eau] downstream ou down-river from; [+ pente] downhill from; (Écon) **les opérations en ~ de la production** the operations coming after ou following production

aval[2] (pl **avals**) [aval] NM (= soutien) backing, support; (Comm, Jur) guarantee (**de** for); **donner son ~ à qn** to give sb one's support, back sb; **donner son ~ à une traite** to guarantee ou endorse a draft

avalanche [avalãʃ] NF (Géog) avalanche; [coups] hail, shower; [compliments] flood, torrent; [réclamations, prospectus] avalanche; ~ **poudreuse/de fond** dry/wet avalanche; **cône d'~** avalanche cone → **couloir**

avalancheux, -euse [avalãʃø, øz] .ADJ [zone, pente] avalanche-prone

avaler [avale] ▸ conjug 1 ◂ VT **a** [+ nourriture] to swallow (down); [+ boisson] to swallow (down), drink (down); [+ roman] to devour; (Alpinisme) [+ corde] to take in; ~ **la fumée** [fumeur] to inhale (the smoke); ~ **qch d'un**

trait ou **d'un seul coup** to swallow sth in one gulp, down sth in one gulp; ~ **son café à petites gorgées** to sip one's coffee; ~ **sa salive** to swallow; (fig) **j'ai eu du mal à ~ ma salive** I gulped; **il a avalé de travers** it went down the wrong way; **il n'a rien avalé depuis 2 jours** he hasn't eaten a thing ou had a thing to eat for 2 days; **la machine a avalé ma carte de crédit** the machine ate ou swallowed my credit card **b** (* = accepter) to swallow; [+ mensonge, histoire] to swallow; [+ affront] to swallow, take; [+ mauvaise nouvelle] to accept; **on lui ferait ~ n'importe quoi** he would swallow anything; (fig) **il a eu du mal à ~ la pilule** it was a hard ou bitter pill for him to swallow; **c'est dur ou difficile à ~** it's hard ou difficult to swallow; ~ **des couleuvres** (affront) to swallow an affront; (mensonge) to swallow a lie, be taken in; ~ **ses mots** to mumble; ~ **les kilomètres** to eat up the miles; [cheval] ~ **l'obstacle** to take the jump in its stride **c** (loc) **on dirait qu'il a avalé son parapluie** ou **sa canne** he's so (stiff and) starchy; (hum) **son bulletin de naissance** to kick the bucket*, snuff it*; **j'avalerais la mer et les poissons !** I could drink gallons (and gallons)!; [ambitieux] **il veut tout ~** he thinks he can take anything on

avaleur, -euse [avalœʀ, øz] NM,F ~ **de sabres** sword swallower

avaliser [avalize] ▸ conjug 1 ◂ VT [+ plan, entreprise] to back, support; (Comm, Jur) to endorse, guarantee

à-valoir [avalwaʀ] NM INV advance (**sur** on); **j'ai un ~ de 90 F dans ce grand magasin** I've 90 francs' credit at this store

avance [avãs] NF **a** (= marche, progression) advance; **accélérer/ralentir son ~** to speed up/ slow down one's advance **b** (sur un concurrent) lead; **avoir/prendre de l'~ sur qn** to have/take the lead over sb; **10 minutes/3 kilomètres d'~** a 10-minute/3-kilometre lead; **avoir une longueur d'~** to be a length ahead; (Scol) **il a un an d'~** he's a year ahead; **leur ~ dans le domaine scientifique** their lead in the field of science; **perdre son ~** to lose one's ou the lead; **cet élève est tombé malade et a perdu son ~** this pupil fell ill and lost the lead he had (on the rest of the class); (iro) **je t'accompagnerai — la belle ~!** I'll go with you — that'll really help! (iro) **c** (sur un horaire) **avoir/prendre de l'~** to be/ get ahead of schedule; (dans son travail) to be/get ahead ou in with one's work; **le train a dix minutes d'~** the train is 10 minutes early; **le train a pris de l'~/dix minutes d'~** the train has got ahead/has got 10 minutes ahead of schedule; **arriver avec cinq minutes d'~** [train] to arrive 5 minutes early ou 5 minutes ahead of time; [personne] to arrive 5 minutes early; **avec cinq minutes d'~ sur les autres** 5 minutes earlier than the others; **le train a perdu son ~** the train has lost the time it had gained; **ma montre a dix minutes d'~** my watch is 10 minutes fast; **ma montre prend de l'~/beaucoup d'~** my watch is gaining ou gains/gains a lot; (Aut) ~ **à l'allumage** ignition advance **d** (Comm, Fin = acompte) advance; ~ **de fonds** advance; **faire une ~ de 100 F à qn** to advance sb 100 francs, make sb an advance of 100 francs; ~ **(sur salaire)** advance (on one's salary); ~ **sur marché/sur recettes** advance on contract/against takings **e** ~**s** (= ouvertures) overtures; (galantes) advances; **faire des ~s à qn** to make overtures ou advances to sb **f** **en** ~ (sur l'heure fixée) early; (sur l'horaire) ahead of schedule; **être en ~ sur qn** to be ahead of sb; **être en ~ d'une heure** (sur l'heure fixée) to be an hour early; (sur l'horaire) to be an hour ahead of schedule; **dépêche-toi, tu n'es pas en ~!** hurry up, you haven't got much time! ou you're running out of time!; **tous ces problèmes ne m'ont pas mis en ~** all

these problems haven't helped; **les crocus sont en ~ cette année** the crocuses are early this year; **leur fils est très en ~ dans ses études/sur les autres enfants** their son is well ahead in his studies/ahead of the other children; **il est en ~ pour son âge** he's advanced for his age, he's ahead of his age group; **leur pays est en ~ dans le domaine scientifique** their country leads ou is ahead in the field of science; **il était très en ~ sur son temps** ou **son époque** he was well ahead of ou in advance of his time; **nous sommes en ~ sur le programme** we're ahead of schedule **g** (loc) **à l'~ ◊ d'~ ◊ par ~** in advance; **réserver une place un mois à l'~** to book a seat one month ahead ou in advance; **prévenir qn deux heures à l'~** to give sb 2 hours' notice, notify ou warn sb 2 hours beforehand ou in advance; **payable à l'~** ou **d'~** payable in advance; **en vous remerciant à l'~** ou **d'~** thanking you in advance ou in anticipation; **merci d'~** thanks (in advance); **d'~ je peux vous dire que ...** I can tell you in advance ou right now that ...; **d'~ il pouvait deviner** already ou even then he could guess; **je m'en réjouis d'~** I'm already looking forward to it; **ça a été arrangé d'~** it was prearranged, it was arranged beforehand ou in advance

avancé, e[1] [avãse] (ptp de **avancer**) ADJ **a** [élève, civilisation, technique] advanced; **la saison/journée était ~e** it was late in the season/day; **la nuit était ~e** it was well into the night; **il est très ~ dans son travail** he's well ahead with his work; **il est rentré à une heure ~e de la nuit** he got home late at night; **elle a travaillé jusqu'à une heure ~e de la nuit** she worked late into the night; **son roman est déjà assez ~** he's already quite a long way on ou quite far ahead with his novel; **je suis peu/très ~ dans mon roman** I haven't got very far into/I'm well into my novel; **les pays les moins ~s** the least developed countries; **cet enfant n'est vraiment pas ~ pour son âge** this child is not at all advanced for his age; **être d'un âge ~** to be getting on ou be advanced in years; **dans un état ~ de ...** in an advanced state of ...; **sa maladie est à un stade très ~** his illness is at a very advanced stage; **après toutes ses démarches, il n'en est pas plus ~** after all the steps he has taken, he's no further on than he was before; (iro) **nous voilà bien ~s!** a long way that's got us! (iro), a (fat) lot of good that's done us!* (iro) **b** (= d'avant-garde) [opinion, idée] progressive, advanced **c** (= qui se gâte) [fruit, fromage] overripe; **ce poisson est ~** this fish is bad ou is going off (Brit) **d** (Mil) [poste] advanced **e** (Sport) [match] early

avancée[2] [avãse] NF overhang

avancement [avãsmã] NM **a** (= promotion) promotion; **avoir** ou **prendre de l'~** to be promoted, get promotion; ~ **à l'ancienneté** promotion according to length of service; **possibilités d'~** prospects ou chances of promotion **b** (= progrès) [travaux] progress; [sciences, techniques] advancement **c** (= mouvement) forward movement **d** (Jur) ~ **d'hoirie** advancement

avancer [avãse] ▸ conjug 3 ◂ **1** VT **a** [+ objet] to move ou bring forward; [+ tête] to move forward; [+ main] to hold out, put out (vers to); [+ pion] to move forward; ~ **le cou** to crane one's neck; ~ **un siège à qn** to draw up ou bring forward a seat for sb; **le blessé avança les lèvres pour boire** the injured man put his lips forward to drink; († ou hum) **la voiture de Madame est avancée** your carriage awaits, Madam † (hum); ~ **(les aiguilles d') une pendule** to put (the hands of) a clock forward ou on (Brit) **b** [+ opinion, hypothèse] to put forward, advance; **ce qu'il avance paraît vraisemblable**

what he is putting forward *ou* suggesting seems quite plausible

c [+ *date, départ*] to bring forward; **il a dû ~ son retour** he had to bring forward the date of his return

d (= *faire progresser*) [+ *travail*] to speed up; **est-ce que cela vous avancera si je vous aide ?** will it speed things up (for you) *ou* will you get on more quickly if I lend you a hand?; **ça n'avance pas nos affaires** that doesn't improve matters for us; **cela t'avancera à quoi de courir ?** what good will it do you to run?; **cela ne t'avancera à rien de crier*** shouting won't get you anywhere, you won't get anywhere by shouting

e [+ *argent*] to advance; (= *prêter*) to lend

2 VI **a** (= *progresser*) to advance, move forward; [*bateau*] to make headway; **l'armée avance sur Paris** the army is advancing on Paris; **il avança d'un pas** he took *ou* moved a step forward; **il avança d'un mètre** he moved one metre forward, he came one metre nearer; **mais avance donc !** move on *ou* forward *ou* up, will you!; **il essayait de faire ~ son âne** he tried to get his donkey to move (on) *ou* to make his donkey move (on); **ça n'avançait pas sur la route** the traffic was almost at a standstill *ou* was crawling along

b (*fig*) to make progress; **la nuit avance** night is wearing on; **faire ~** [+ *travail*] to speed up; [+ *élève*] to bring on, help to make progress; [+ *science, recherche*] to further; **~ vite/lentement dans son travail** to make good/slow progress in one's work; **~ péniblement dans son travail** to plod on slowly with *ou* make halting progress in one's work; **~ en âge** to be getting on (in years); **~ en grade** to be promoted, get promotion; **et les travaux, ça avance ?*** how's the work coming on?*; **son livre n'avance guère** he's not making much headway *ou* progress with his book; **tout cela n'avance à rien** that doesn't get us any further *ou* anywhere; **je travaille mais il me semble que je n'avance pas** I'm working but I don't seem to be getting anywhere

c [*montre, horloge*] to gain; **~ de dix minutes par jour** to gain 10 minutes a day; **ma montre avance ◊ j'avance** my watch is fast; **ma montre avance ou j'avance de dix minutes** my watch is *ou* I'm 10 minutes fast

d [*cap, promontoire*] to project, jut out (**dans** into); [*lèvre, menton*] to protrude; **un balcon qui avance (de 3 mètres) sur la rue** a balcony that juts out *ou* projects (3 metres) over the street

3 **s'avancer** VPR **a** (= *aller en avant*) to move forward; (= *progresser*) to advance; **il s'avança vers nous** he came towards us; **la procession s'avançait lentement** the procession advanced slowly *ou* moved slowly forward; **il s'est avancé dans son travail** he made some progress with his work; **je profite de cette heure libre pour m'~** I'm making the most of this free hour to get ahead with my work

b (= *s'engager*) to commit o.s., stick one's neck out*; **je ne peux pas m'~ sans connaître la question** I don't know enough about it to venture *ou* hazard an opinion, I can't commit myself without knowing more about it; **je ne crois pas trop m'~ en disant que ...** I don't think I'm going too far if I say that ...

avanie [avani] NF snub; **subir une ~** to be snubbed; **faire ou infliger des ~s à qn** to snub sb

▼**avant** [avɑ̃]

1 PRÉPOSITION	**3** NOM MASCULIN
2 ADVERBE	**4** ADJECTIF INVARIABLE

1 PRÉPOSITION

a dans le temps before; **il est parti ~ nous/la fin** he left before us/the end; **~ son accident il était très gai** he was very cheerful before his accident; **peu ~ mon mariage** shortly *ou* a short

time before I got married; **il n'est pas arrivé ~ 9 heures** he didn't arrive until 9

◆ **avant de** + *infinitif* before; **à prendre ~ (de) manger** to be taken before food *ou* meals; **dînez donc ~ de partir** do have a meal before you go; **consultez-moi ~ de prendre une décision** consult me before making your decision *ou* before you decide

◆ **avant que** + *subjonctif* before; **je veux lire sa lettre ~ qu'elle (ne) l'envoie** I want to read her letter before she sends it (off); **n'envoyez pas cette lettre ~ que je (ne) l'aie lue** don't send this letter before *ou* until I have read it

b précédant une durée for; **il n'arrivera pas ~ une demi-heure** he won't be here for another half hour yet *ou* for half an hour yet; **ça ne pourra pas débuter ~ plusieurs jours** it can't start for another few days (yet) *ou* for a few days yet; **~ peu** shortly; **on ne le reverra pas ~ longtemps** we won't see him again for a while *ou* for some time

c = au plus tard by; **il me le faut ~ demain** I must have it by tomorrow

d = en moins de within; **ça doit être terminé ~ une semaine/un mois** it has to be finished within a week/a month

e dans l'espace before; **sa maison est (juste) ~ la poste** his house is just before the post office; **j'étais ~ lui dans la queue** I was in front of him *ou* before him in the queue (*Brit*) *ou* in the line (*US*); **on s'est arrêté juste ~ Paris** we stopped just outside *ou* before Paris; **la poste est juste ~ d'arriver à la gare** the post office is just before you come to the station

f indiquant une priorité before; (*dans une liste, un classement*) ahead of; **il met sa santé ~ sa carrière** he puts his health before *ou* above his career, he values his health above his career; **le capitaine est ~ le lieutenant** captain comes before *ou* is above lieutenant; **en classe, elle est ~ sa sœur** she is ahead of her sister at school

◆ **avant tout ◊ avant toute chose** (= *ce qui est le plus important*) above all; (= *tout d'abord, en premier*) first and foremost; **~ tout, il faut éviter la guerre** above all (things) war must be avoided; **il faut ~ tout vérifier l'état du toit** first and foremost we must see what state the roof is in

2 ADVERBE

a = auparavant before, beforehand, first; **venez me parler ~** come and talk to me first *ou* beforehand; **le voyage sera long, mangez ~** it's going to be a long journey so have something to eat beforehand *ou* before you go *ou* first

◆ **d'avant** (= *précédent*) before, previous; **la semaine/le mois d'~** the week/the month before, the previous week/month; **les gens d'~ étaient plus aimables** the previous people were nicer, the people who were there before were nicer; **le train d'~ était plein** the earlier *ou* previous train was full

b = autrefois (*suivi de l'imparfait*) **~, je mangeais plus de viande** I used to eat more meat; **~, je n'aimais pas la physique** I didn't use *ou* used to like physics, I never used to like physics; **~, c'était très beau ici** it used to be very beautiful here

c précédé d'une durée before(hand), previously, earlier; **quelques semaines/mois ~** a few *ou* some weeks/months before(hand) *ou* previously *ou* earlier; **bien ou longtemps ~** long before (that); **peu (de temps) ~** not long before (that), shortly before that *ou* beforehand

d dans l'espace before; **tu vois la boulangerie ? le fleuriste est juste ~** you see the baker's? the florist's is just this side of it; **n'avancez pas plus ~, c'est dangereux** don't go any further (forward), it's dangerous; **il s'était engagé trop ~ dans le bois** he had gone too far *ou* too deep into the wood

◆ **en avant** [+ *mouvement*] forward; [+ *position*]

in front, ahead (**de** of); **en ~, marche !** forward march!; (*Naut*) **en ~ toute !** full steam ahead!; **la voiture fit un bond en ~** the car lurched forward; **être en ~** (*d'un groupe de personnes*) to be (out) in front; **marcher en ~ de la procession** to walk in front of the procession; **les enfants sont partis en ~** the children have gone on ahead; **partez en ~, on vous rejoindra** you go on (ahead), we'll catch up with you; (*fig*) **regarder en ~** to look ahead

(*fig*) **mettre qch en ~** to put sth forward, advance sth; **mettre qn en ~** (*pour se couvrir*) to use sb as a front, hide behind sb; (*pour aider qn*) to push sb forward *ou* to the front; **il aime se mettre en ~** he likes to push himself forward, he likes to be in the forefront

e progression **ils sont assez ~ dans leurs recherches** they have come a long way in their research; **n'hésitez pas à aller plus ~** don't hesitate to go further *ou* on; **il s'est engagé trop ~** he has got *ou* become too involved, he has committed himself too deeply; **fort ~ dans la nuit** far *ou* well into the night

3 NOM MASCULIN

a = partie antérieure [*avion, voiture, train*] front; [*navire*] bow(s)

◆ **à l'avant** : **voyager à l'~ du train** to travel in the front of the train; **dans cette voiture on est mieux à l'~** it's more comfortable in the front of this car

◆ **aller de l'avant** to forge ahead

b Sport = joueur (*gén*) forward; (*Volley*) frontline player; **la ligne des ~s** the forward line

c Mil l'~ the front

4 ADJECTIF INVARIABLE
= antérieur [*roue, siège*] front; **la partie ~** the front part → traction

▼**avantage** [avɑ̃taʒ] NM **a** (= *intérêt*) advantage; **cette solution a l'~ de ne léser personne** this solution has the advantage of not hurting anyone; **il a ~ à y aller** it will be to his advantage to go, it will be worth his while to go; **j'ai ~ à acheter en gros** it's worth my while *ou* it's worth it for me to buy in bulk; **tu aurais ~ à te tenir tranquille*** you'd do better to keep quiet, you'd do well to keep quiet; **il aurait grand ~ à** it would be very much to his advantage to, he would be well advised to; **tirer ~ de la situation ◊ tourner une situation à son ~** to take advantage of the situation, turn the situation to one's advantage

b (= *supériorité*) advantage; **avoir un ~ sur qn** to have an advantage over sb; **j'ai sur vous l'~ de l'expérience** I have the advantage of experience over you; **ils ont l'~ du nombre** they have the advantage of numbers (**sur** over)

c (*Fin* = *gain*) benefit; **~s accessoires** additional benefits; **~s en nature** fringe benefits, benefits in kind; **~ pécuniaire** financial benefit; **~s sociaux** welfare benefits; **~ fiscal** tax break

d (*Mil, Sport, fig*) advantage; (*Tennis*) advantage, vantage (*Brit*); **avoir l'~** to have the advantage (**sur** over), have the upper hand, be one up* (**sur** on); (*Tennis*) **service/dehors** advantage in/out, van(tage) in/out (*Brit*), ad in/out* (*US*)

e (*frm* = *plaisir*) pleasure; **j'ai (l'honneur et) l'~ de vous présenter M. Leblanc** it is my (honour and) privilege to introduce Mr Leblanc; **que me vaut l'~ de votre visite ?** to what do I owe the pleasure *ou* honour of your visit? (*frm*)

f (*loc*) **être à son ~** (*sur une photo*) to look one's best; (*dans une conversation*) to be at one's best; **elle est à son ~ avec cette coiffure** that hair style really flatters her; **il s'est montré à son ~** he was seen in a favourable light *ou* to advantage; **c'est (tout) à ton ~** it's (entirely) to your advantage; **changer à son ~** to change for the better

➤ GRAMMAIRE ACTIVE: **avant** 53.1   **avantage** 28.1, 53.4

avantager

avantager [avɑ̃taʒe] ▸conjug 3◂ VT a (= *donner un avantage à*) to favour (*Brit*), favor (*US*), give an advantage to; **elle a été avantagée par la nature** she's blessed with natural beauty; **il a été avantagé par rapport à ses frères** he has been given an advantage over his brothers; (*dans la vie*) **être avantagé dès le départ** to have a head start (**par rapport à** on) b (= *mettre en valeur*) to flatter; **ce chapeau l'avantage** that hat's very flattering on her, she looks good in that hat

avantageusement [avɑ̃taʒøzmɑ̃] ADV [*vendre*] at a good price; [*décrire*] favourably (*Brit*), favorably (*US*), flatteringly; **la situation se présente** ~ the situation looks favourable

avantageux, -euse [avɑ̃taʒø, øz] ADJ a (= *profitable*) [*affaire*] worthwhile, profitable; [*prix*] attractive; **ce serait plus ~ de ...** it would be more profitable *ou* worthwhile to ...; **en grands paquets, c'est plus ~** large packets are better value *ou* more economical b (= *présomptueux*) [*air, personne*] conceited; **il a une idée assez avantageuse de lui-même** he has a very high opinion of himself, he thinks a lot of himself c (= *flatteur*) [*portrait, chapeau*] flattering; **prendre des poses avantageuses** to show o.s. off to one's best advantage

avant-bras [avɑ̃bʀɑ] NM INV forearm

avant-centre (*pl* **avants-centres**) [avɑ̃sɑ̃tʀ] NM centre-forward (*Brit*), center-forward (*US*); **il est** *ou* **joue** ~ he plays centre-forward

avant-coureur (*pl* **avant-coureurs**) [avɑ̃kuʀœʀ] ADJ M precursory, premonitory; **signe** ~ forerunner, harbinger (*littér*)

avant-dernier, -ière (*mpl* **avant-derniers**) [avɑ̃dɛʀnje, jɛʀ] ADJ, NM,F next to last, last but one (*Brit*) *sg seulement*, penultimate

avant-garde (*pl* **avant-gardes**) [avɑ̃gaʀd] NF (*Mil*) vanguard; (*Art, Pol*) avant-garde; **art/poésie/idées d'~** avant-garde art/poetry/ideas; **être à l'~ de** to be in the vanguard of

avant-gardisme [avɑ̃gaʀdism] NM avant-gardism

avant-gardiste (*pl* **avant-gardistes**) [avɑ̃gaʀdist] ADJ, NMF avant-gardist

avant-goût (*pl* **avant-goûts**) [avɑ̃gu] NM foretaste

avant-guerre (*pl* **avant-guerres**) [avɑ̃gɛʀ] 1 NM *ou* F pre-war years; **d'~** pre-war (*épith*) 2 ADV before the war

avant-hier [avɑ̃tjɛʀ] ADV the day before yesterday

avant-main (*pl* **avant-mains**) [avɑ̃mɛ̃] NF forequarters

avant-midi [avɑ̃midi] NM *ou* NF INV (*Belg, Can*) morning

avant-mont (*pl* **avant-monts**) [avɑ̃mɔ̃] NM foothills

avant-port (*pl* **avant-ports**) [avɑ̃pɔʀ] NM outer harbour

avant-poste (*pl* **avant-postes**) [avɑ̃pɔst] NM outpost; **aux ~s du combat pour la liberté** in the vanguard of the struggle for freedom; **aux ~s des technologies nouvelles** on the cutting edge of new technology

avant-première (*pl* **avant-premières**) [avɑ̃pʀəmjɛʀ] NF preview; **j'ai vu le film en** ~ I saw a preview of the film; **ce film sera projeté en** ~ **au Rex** the film will be previewing at the Rex

avant-projet (*pl* **avant-projets**) [avɑ̃pʀɔʒe] NM pilot study

avant-propos [avɑ̃pʀɔpo] NM INV foreword

avant-scène (*pl* **avant-scènes**) [avɑ̃sɛn] NF (*Théât*) (= *partie de la scène*) apron, proscenium; (= *loge*) box (*at the front of the house*)

avant-toit (*pl* **avant-toits**) [avɑ̃twa] NM eaves

avant-train (*pl* **avant-trains**) [avɑ̃tʀɛ̃] NM [*animal*] foreparts, forequarters; [*véhicule*] front axle assembly *ou* unit

avant-veille (*pl* **avant-veilles**) [avɑ̃vɛj] NF **l'~** two days before *ou* previously; **c'était l'~ de Noël** it was the day before Christmas Eve *ou* two days before Christmas

avare [avaʀ] 1 ADJ a [*personne*] miserly; ~ **de paroles/compliments** sparing of *ou* with words/compliments; **elle n'est pas ~ de discours/de promesses** she's full of talk/promises; **il n'est pas ~ de confidences** he's quite happy to confide in people b (*littér = peu abondant*) [*terre*] meagre (*Brit*), meager (*US*); [*lumière*] dim, weak 2 NMF miser

avarice [avaʀis] NF miserliness

avaricieux, -ieuse [avaʀisjø, jøz] (*littér*) 1 ADJ miserly, niggardly, stingy 2 NM miser, niggard, skinflint

avarie [avaʀi] NF [*navire, véhicule*] damage (*NonC*); (*Tech*) [*cargaison, chargement*] damage (*NonC*) (in transit), average (*SPÉC*)

avarié, e [avaʀje] (*ptp de* **avarier**) ADJ [*aliment*] rotting; [*navire*] damaged; **cette viande est ~e** this meat has gone bad *ou* off (*Brit*)

avarier [avaʀje] ▸conjug 7◂ 1 VT to spoil, damage 2 **s'avarier** VPR [*fruits, viande*] to go bad, rot

avatar [avataʀ] NM (*Rel*) avatar; (*fig*) metamorphosis; (= *péripéties*) **~s*** misadventures

à vau-l'eau [avolo] ADV → **vau-l'eau**

Ave [ave] NM INV ~ **(Maria)** Hail Mary, Ave Maria

avec [avɛk] 1 PRÉP a (*accompagnement, accord*) with; **elle est sortie ~ les enfants** she's gone out with the children; **son mariage ~ Marc a duré 8 ans** her marriage to Marc lasted (for) 8 years; **ils ont les syndicats ~ eux** they've got the unions on their side *ou* behind them; **je pense ~ cet auteur que ...** I agree with this writer that ...; **elle est ~ Robert** (= *elle le fréquente*) she's going out with Robert; (= *ils vivent ensemble*) she's living with Robert; **séparer/distinguer qch d'~ qch d'autre** to separate/distinguish sth from sth else; **divorcer d'~ qn** to divorce sb; **se séparer d'~ qn** to leave sb, part from sb; **elle s'est séparée d'~ X** she has separated from X b (*comportement = envers*) to, towards, with; **comment se comportent-ils ~ vous ?** how do they behave towards *ou* with you?; **il est très doux/gentil ~ moi** he's very gentle with/kind to me c (*moyen, manière*) with; (*ingrédient*) with, from, out of; **vous prenez votre thé ~ du lait ?** do you have *ou* take your tea with milk?, do you have *ou* take milk in your tea?; **boire ~ une paille** to drink through a straw; **maison ~ jardin** house with a garden; **faire qch ~ (grande) facilité** to do sth with (great) ease *ou* (very) easily; **(il) faudra bien faire ~** he (*ou* we etc) will have to make do; **parler ~ colère/bonté/lenteur** to speak angrily *ou* with anger/kindly/slowly; **chambre ~ salle de bain** room with a bathroom *ou* its own bathroom; **couteau ~ (un) manche en bois** knife with a wooden handle, wooden-handled knife; **gâteau fait ~ du beurre** cake made with butter; **ragoût fait ~ des restes** stew made out of *ou* from (the) left-overs; **c'est fait (entièrement) ~ du plomb** it's made (entirely) of lead; **voyageant ~ un passeport qui ...** travelling on a passport which ... d (*cause, simultanéité, contraste*) with; **on oublie tout ~ le temps** one forgets everything in time *ou* in the course of time *ou* with (the passing of) time; ~ **les élections, on ne parle plus que politique** with the elections (on) no one talks anything but politics; ~ **l'inflation et le prix de l'essence, les voitures se vendent mal** what with inflation and the price of petrol, cars aren't selling very well; **il est difficile de marcher ~ ce vent** it's difficult to walk in *ou* with this wind; ~ **un peu de travail, il aurait gagné le prix** with a little work *ou* if (only) he had done a little work he would have won

the prize; ~ **toute ma bonne volonté, je ne suis pas parvenu à l'aider** with the best will in the world *ou* for all my goodwill I couldn't help him; **se lever ~ le jour** to get up *ou* rise with the sun *ou* dawn, get up at daybreak; **ils sont partis ~ la pluie** they left in the rain e (*opposition*) with; **rivaliser/combattre ~ qn** to vie/fight with sb; **elle s'est fâchée ~ tous leurs amis** she has fallen out with all their friends f (*cela* ◊ *~ ça* ◊ *~ et ça, madame ?* (*dans un magasin*) anything else?; **il conduit mal et ~ ça il conduit trop vite** he drives badly and what's more *ou* on top of that he drives too fast; ~ **cela que tu ne le savais pas !** what do you mean you didn't know!, as if you didn't know!; (*iro*) **et ~ ça qu'il est complaisant !** and it's not as if he were helpful either!, and he's not exactly *ou* even helpful either!; ~ **tout ça j'ai oublié le pain** in the midst of all this I forgot about the bread 2 ADV* **tiens mes gants, je ne peux pas conduire ~** hold my gloves, I can't drive with them on; **rends-moi mon stylo, tu allais partir ~ !** give me back my pen, you were going to walk off with it!

aveline [av(ə)lin] NF (= *noix*) filbert

avelinier [av(ə)linje] NM (= *arbre*) filbert

aven [avɛn] NM sinkhole, pothole, swallow hole (*Brit*)

avenant, e [av(ə)nɑ̃, ɑ̃t] 1 ADJ [*personne, sourire*] pleasant, welcoming; [*manières*] pleasant, pleasing; [*maison*] attractive 2 NM a **à l'~** in keeping (**de** with); **la maison était luxueuse, et le mobilier était à l'~** the house was luxurious, and the furniture was equally so *ou* was in keeping with it; **la table coûtait 8 000 F, et tout était à l'~** the table cost 8,000 francs and everything else was just as expensive b [*police d'assurance*] endorsement; [*contrat*] amendment (**à** to); **faire un ~ à** [+ *police d'assurance*] to endorse; [+ *contrat*] to amend

avènement [avɛnmɑ̃] NM [*roi*] accession (**à** to); [*régime, politique, idée*] advent; [*Messie*] Advent, Coming

avenir¹ [av(ə)niʀ] NM a (= *futur*) future; (= *postérité*) future generations; **avoir des projets d'~** to have plans for the future, have future plans; **dans un proche ~** in the near future; **elle m'a prédit mon ~** she told my fortune; **l'~ le dira** only time will tell ∎ (*PROV*) **l'~ appartient à ceux qui se lèvent tôt** the early bird catches the worm (*PROV*) b (= *bien-être*) future (well-being); **assurer l'~ de ses enfants** to secure one's children's future c (= *carrière*) future, prospects; **il a de l'~** he has a good future *ou* good prospects; **artiste/entreprise pleine d'~** up-and-coming artist/company; **son ~ est derrière lui** his future is behind him, he's got no future; **métier d'~** job with a future *ou* with prospects; **il n'y a aucun ~ dans ce métier** there's no future *ou* there are no prospects in this job, this is a dead-end job; **projet sans ~** project without prospects of success *ou* without a future d **à l'~** (= *dorénavant*) from now on, in future

avenir² [av(ə)niʀ] NM (*Jur*) writ of summons (*from one counsel to another*)

Avent [avɑ̃] NM **l'~** Advent

aventure [avɑ̃tyʀ] NF a (= *péripétie, incident*) adventure; (= *entreprise*) venture; (= *liaison amoureuse*) affair; **fâcheuse ~** unfortunate experience; ~ **effrayante** terrifying experience; **film/roman d'~s** adventure film/story; ~ **amoureuse** *ou* **sentimentale** love affair; **avoir une ~ (galante) avec qn** to have an affair with sb b **l'~** adventure; **esprit d'~** spirit of adventure; **sortir la nuit dans ce quartier, c'est l'~** going out at night in this area is a risky business!; **j'ai du travail pour 6 mois, après c'est l'~** I've got work for 6 months, but after that, who knows? **c** **dire la bonne ~** to tell fortunes; **dire la bonne ~ à qn** to tell sb's fortune → **diseur** **d** (loc) **marcher à l'~** to walk aimlessly; (littér) **si, d'~ ou par ~** if by any chance

aventuré, e [avãtyʀe] (ptp de **aventurer**) ADJ [entreprise] risky, chancy; [hypothèse] risky, venturesome

aventurer [avãtyʀe] ▸conjug 1◂ **1** VT [+ somme, réputation, vie] to risk, put at stake, chance; [+ remarque, opinion] to venture **2** **s'aventurer** VPR to venture (**dans** into, **sur** onto); **s'~ à faire qch** to venture to do sth; (fig) **s'~ sur un terrain glissant** to tread on dangerous ground, skate on thin ice

aventureux, -euse [avãtyʀø, øz] ADJ [personne, esprit] adventurous, enterprising, venturesome; [imagination] bold; [projet, entreprise] risky, rash, chancy; [vie] adventurous

aventurier [avãtyʀje] NM adventurer

aventurière [avãtyʀjɛʀ] NF adventuress

aventurisme [avãtyʀism] NM (Pol) adventurism

aventuriste [avãtyʀist] ADJ (Pol) adventurist

avenu, e[1] [av(ə)ny] ADJ → **nul**

avenue[2] [av(ə)ny] NF [ville] (= boulevard) avenue; [parc] (= allée) drive, avenue; (littér) **les ~s du pouvoir** the roads to power

avéré, e [aveʀe] (ptp de **s'avérer**) ADJ [fait] established, known; [terroriste, criminel] known; **il est ~ que ...** it is a known ou recognized fact that ...

avérer (s') [aveʀe] ▸conjug 6◂ VPR **il s'avère que ...** it turns out that ...; **ce remède s'avéra inefficace** this remedy proved (to be) ou turned out to be ineffective; **il s'est avéré un employé consciencieux** he proved (to be) ou turned out to be a conscientious employee

avers [avɛʀ] NM obverse (of coin, medal)

averse [avɛʀs] NF (= pluie) shower (of rain); [insultes, pierres] shower; **forte ~** heavy shower, downpour; **~ orageuse** thundery shower; **être pris par ou recevoir une ~** to be caught in a shower; (fig) **il n'est pas né ou tombé de la dernière ~** he wasn't born yesterday

▼**aversion** [avɛʀsjɔ̃] NF aversion (**pour** to), loathing (**pour** for); **avoir en ~** ◊ **avoir de l'~ pour** to have an aversion to, loathe; **prendre en ~** to take a (strong) dislike to

averti, e [avɛʀti] (ptp de **avertir**) ADJ [public] informed; [connaisseur, expert] well-informed; **c'est un film réservé à des spectateurs ~s** this film is only suitable for an informed audience; **~ de** [+ problèmes etc] aware of; **être très ~ des travaux cinématographiques contemporains** to be very well up on ou well informed about the contemporary film scene → **homme**

avertir [avɛʀtiʀ] ▸conjug 2◂ VT (= prévenir) to tell, inform (**de qch** of sth); (= mettre en garde) to warn (**de qch** of sth); **avertissez-le de ne pas recommencer** tell ou warn him not to do it again; **tenez-vous pour averti** be warned, don't say you haven't been warned; **avertissez-moi dès que possible** let me know as soon as possible

avertissement [avɛʀtismã] NM (= avis) warning (**à** to); (= présage) warning, warning sign; (= réprimande) (Sport) caution; (Scol) warning; **recevoir un ~** to receive a warning; **les syndicats ont adressé un sévère ~ au gouvernement** the unions have issued a stern warning to the government; (= préface) **(au lecteur)** foreword; **~ sans frais** (Jur) notice of assessment; (fig) clear warning (**à** to)

avertisseur, -euse [avɛʀtisœʀ, øz] **1** ADJ warning **2** NM (Aut) horn, hooter (Brit); **~ (d'incendie)** (fire) alarm

aveu (pl **aveux**) [avø] NM **a** [crime] confession; [amour] confession, avowal (littér); [fait, faiblesse] admission; **c'est l'~ d'un échec de la**

part **du gouvernement** it's an admission of defeat on the part of the government; **un ~ d'impuissance** an admission of helplessness ou powerlessness; **faire l'~ d'un crime** to confess to a crime; **faire des ~x complets** to make a full confession; **passer aux ~x** to make a confession; **revenir sur ses ~x** to retract one's confession; **je dois vous faire un ~, je ne les aime pas non plus** I have a confession to make, I don't like them either **b** (frm : selon) **de l'~ de qn** according to sb; **de l'~ même du témoin** on the witness's own testimony **c** (frm) **sans ~** [homme, politicien] disreputable **d** (littér = assentiment) consent; **sans l'~ de qn** without sb's authorization ou consent

aveuglant, e [avœglã, ãt] ADJ [lumière] blinding, dazzling; [vérité] glaring (épith)

aveugle [avœgl] **1** ADJ [personne] blind; [passion, dévouement, obéissance] blind; [attentat, violence] indiscriminate, random; [terrorisme] indiscriminate; [fenêtre, façade, mur, couloir] blind; (Anat) **point ~** blind spot; **devenir ~** to go blind; **~ d'un œil** blind in one eye; **je ne suis pas ~ !** I'm not blind!; **son amour le rend ~** he's blinded by love; **l'amour est ~** love is blind; **avoir une confiance ~ en qn** to trust sb blindly, have blind faith in sb; **être ~ aux défauts de qn** to be blind to sb's faults; **l'instrument ~ du destin** the blind ou unwitting instrument of fate → **naissance** **2** NM blind man; **les ~s** the blind; **faire qch en ~** to do sth blindly; **c'est un ~-né** he was born blind, he has been blind from birth → **double, royaume** **3** NF blind woman

aveuglement [avœgləmã] NM (littér = égarement) blindness

aveuglément [avœglemã] ADV blindly

aveugler [avœgle] ▸conjug 1◂ **1** VT **a** (lit, fig) (= rendre aveugle) to blind; (= éblouir) to dazzle, blind **b** [+ fenêtre] to block ou brick up; [+ voie d'eau] to stop up **2** **s'aveugler** VPR **s'~ sur qn/qch** to be blind to ou shut one's eyes to sb's defects/sth

aveuglette [avœglɛt] **▸à l'aveuglette** LOC ADV **avancer à l'~** to grope (one's way) along, feel one's way along; **descendre à l'~** to grope one's way down; **prendre des décisions à l'~** to take decisions in the dark ou blindly

aveulir [avøliʀ] ▸conjug 2◂ (littér) **1** VT to enfeeble, enervate **2** **s'aveulir** VPR to weaken

aveulissement [avølismã] NM (littér) enfeeblement, enervation

aviaire [avjɛʀ] ADJ avian

aviateur [avjatœʀ] NM airman, aviator

aviation [avjasjɔ̃] **1** NF **a** (Mil) (= corps d'armée) air force; (= avions) aircraft, air force **b** **l'~** (= sport, métier de pilote) flying; (= secteur commercial) aviation; (= moyen de transport) air travel; **coupe/meeting d'~** flying cup/meeting; **usine d'~** aircraft factory; **compagnie d'~** airline company → **champ**; **terrain** **2** COMP ▸ **aviation de chasse** fighter force ▸ **aviation navale** fleet air arm (Brit), naval air force (US)

aviatrice [avjatʀis] NF airwoman, aviator, aviatrix

avicole [avikɔl] ADJ poultry (épith); **établissement ~** poultry farm

aviculteur, -trice [avikyltœʀ, tʀis] NM,F poultry farmer

aviculture [avikyltyʀ] NF poultry farming

avide [avid] ADJ (= cupide) [personne] greedy, grasping; [regard, yeux] greedy; (= passionné) [lecteur] avid; **~ de** [plaisir, sensation] eager ou avid for; [+ argent, nourriture] greedy for; [+ pouvoir, honneurs, succès, connaissances] hungry for; **~ de faire qch** eager to do sth; **~ de sang ou de carnage** bloodthirsty

avidement [avidmã] ADV [écouter] eagerly; [lire] avidly; [regarder] intently, eagerly; [compter, manger] greedily

avidité [avidite] NF (= passion) eagerness; (= cupidité, voracité) greed; **lire avec ~** to read avidly; **manger avec ~** to eat greedily

avifaune [avifon] NF avifauna

AVIGNON

Created by the actor-director Jean Vilar in 1947, the Festival d'Avignon *is one of the most important events in the French cultural calendar. The town is taken over by theatregoers in late July and early August, and many of its historic buildings are transformed into performance spaces. The most prestigious shows of the festival take place in the courtyard of the "Palais des Papes", the old Papal palace in the town centre.*

Note that when translating the phrase "in Avignon" the preposition "en" can be used instead of the usual "à", especially in formal speech or writing (for example, "ce spectacle a été créé en Avignon").

avilir [aviliʀ] ▸conjug 2◂ **1** VT [+ personne] to degrade, debase, demean; [+ monnaie] to debase; [+ marchandise] to cause to depreciate **2** **s'avilir** VPR [personne] to degrade o.s., debase o.s., demean o.s.; [monnaie, marchandise] to depreciate

avilissant, e [avilisã, ãt] ADJ [spectacle] degrading, shameful, shaming (épith); [conduite, situation, travail] degrading, demeaning

avilissement [avilismã] NM [personne] degradation, debasement; [monnaie] debasement; [marchandise] depreciation

aviné, e [avine] ADJ (littér) [personne] inebriated, intoxicated; [voix] drunken; **il a l'haleine ~e** his breath smells of alcohol

avion [avjɔ̃] **1** NM (= appareil) plane, aircraft pl inv, aeroplane (Brit), airplane (US); (Sport) **l'~** flying; **défense/batterie contre ~s** anti-aircraft defence/battery; **ils sont venus en ~** they came by air ou by plane, they flew (here); (sur lettre) **par ~** by air(mail) **2** COMP ▸ **avion de bombardement** bomber ▸ **avion de chasse** fighter (plane), interceptor ▸ **avion commercial** commercial aircraft ▸ **avion à décollage et atterrissage courts** short takeoff and landing aircraft, STOL aircraft ▸ **avion à décollage et atterrissage verticaux** vertical takeoff and landing aircraft, VTOL aircraft ▸ **avion furtif** stealth bomber ou plane ▸ **avion de ligne** airliner ▸ **avion en papier** paper aeroplane ▸ **avion postal** mail plane ▸ **avion à réaction** jet (plane) ▸ **avion de reconnaissance** reconnaissance aircraft ou plane ▸ **avion renifleur** sniffer plane ▸ **avion sanitaire** air ambulance ▸ **avion de tourisme** private aircraft ou plane ▸ **avion de transport** transport aircraft

avion-cargo (pl **avions-cargos**) [avjɔ̃kaʀgo] NM (air) freighter, cargo aircraft

avion-cible (pl **avions-cibles**) [avjɔ̃sibl] NM target aircraft

avion-citerne (pl **avions-citernes**) [avjɔ̃sitɛʀn] NM air tanker

avion-école (pl **avions-écoles**) [avjɔ̃ekɔl] NM training plane

avionique [avjɔnik] NF avionics sg

avionneur [avjɔnœʀ] NM aircraft manufacturer

avion-radar (pl **avions-radars**) [avjɔ̃ʀadaʀ] NM radar plane

avion-suicide (pl **avions-suicide**) [avjɔ̃sɥisid] NM suicide plane

avion-taxi (pl **avions-taxis**) [avjɔ̃taksi] NM taxi-plane

aviron [aviʀɔ̃] NM **a** (= rame) oar; (= sport) rowing; **faire de l'~** to row **b** (Can) paddle

avironner [aviʀɔne] ▸conjug 1◂ VT (Can) to paddle

▼**avis** [avi] **1** NM **a** (= *opinion*) opinion; **donner son ~** to give one's opinion *ou* views (**sur** on, about); **les ~ sont partagés** opinion is divided; **être du même ~ que qn** ◊ **être de l'~ de qn** to be of the same opinion as sb, share sb's view; **on ne te demande pas ton ~!** who asked you?; **je ne suis pas de votre ~** I don't agree (with you); **à mon ~ c'est ...** in my opinion *ou* to my mind it is ...; **si tu veux mon ~, il est ...** if you ask me *ou* if you want my opinion, he's ...; **c'est bien mon ~** I quite agree; (*iro*) **à mon humble ~** in my humble opinion; **de l'~ de tous, il ne sera pas élu** the unanimous view *ou* the general opinion is that he won't be elected → **changer, deux**
b (= *conseil*) advice (*NonC*); **un ~ amical** a friendly piece of advice, a piece of friendly advice; **suivre l'~ ou les ~ de qn** to take *ou* follow sb's advice; **sur l'~ de qn** on sb's advice
c (= *notification*) notice; (*Fin*) advice; **lettre d'~** letter of advice; **~ de crédit/de débit** credit/debit advice; **~ d'appel d'offres** invitation to tender *ou* to bid; **jusqu'à nouvel ~** until further notice; **sauf ~ contraire** unless otherwise informed, unless one hears to the contrary; (*sur étiquette*) unless otherwise indicated; (*Naut*) **~ de coup de vent** gale warning; **~ de tempête** storm warning; **~ aux amateurs !*** any takers?*; **donner ~ de/que ...**† to give notice of/that ... → **préalable**
d (*Admin* = *recommandation*) opinion; **les membres ont émis un ~** the members put forward an opinion; **on a pris l'~ du conseil** they took the opinion of the council; (*Admin*) **~ favorable/défavorable** accepted/rejected
e (*loc*) **il était d'~ de partir** *ou* **qu'on parte immédiatement** he thought *ou* he was of the opinion that we should leave at once; († *ou hum*) **m'est ~ que ...** methinks† (*hum*) ...
2 COMP ▶ **avis de décès** death notice ▶ **avis d'expédition** (*Comm*) advice of dispatch ▶ **avis d'imposition** tax notice ▶ **avis au lecteur** foreword ▶ **avis de mise en recouvrement** (*Fin*) notice of assessment ▶ **avis de mobilisation** mobilization notice ▶ **avis au public** public notice; (= *entête*) notice to the public ▶ **avis de réception** acknowledgement of receipt ▶ **avis de recherche** (= *affiche*) [*criminel*] wanted poster; [*disparu*] missing person poster; **lancer un ~ de recherche** (*pour criminel*) to issue a description of a wanted person; (*pour disparu*) to issue a description of a missing person ▶ **avis de virement** advice of bank transfer

avisé, e [avize] (*ptp de* **aviser**) ADJ sensible, wise; **être bien/mal ~ de faire** to be well-/ill-advised to do

aviser [avize] ▶ conjug 1 ◀ **1** VT **a** (*frm* = *avertir*) to advise, inform (**de** of), notify (**de** of, about); **il ne m'en a pas avisé** he didn't notify me of *ou* about it **b** (*littér* = *apercevoir*) to catch sight of, notice **2** VI **cela fait, nous aviserons** once that's done, we'll see where we stand; **sur place, nous aviserons** we'll see once we're there; **~ à qch** to see to sth **3** **s'aviser** VPR **a** (= *remarquer*) **s'~ de qch** to realize *ou* become aware of sth suddenly; **il s'avisa que ...** he suddenly realized that ... **b** (= *s'aventurer à*) **s'~ de faire qch** to dare (to) do sth, take it into one's head to do sth; **et ne t'avise pas d'aller lui dire** and don't you dare go and tell him

aviso [avizo] NM advice-boat

avitaminose [avitaminoz] NF vitamin deficiency, avitaminosis (*SPÉC*)

aviver [avive] ▶ conjug 1 ◀ **1** VT **a** [+ *douleur physique, appétit*] to sharpen; [+ *regrets, chagrin*] to deepen; [+ *intérêt, désir*] to kindle, arouse; [+ *colère*] to stir up; [+ *souvenirs*] to stir up, revive; [+ *querelle*] to stir up, add fuel to; [+ *passion*] to arouse, excite, stir up; [+ *regard*] to brighten; [+ *couleur*] brighten (up); [+ *feu*]

to revive, stir up; **l'air frais leur avait avivé le teint** the fresh air had given them some colour *ou* had put some colour into their cheeks **b** (*Méd*) [+ *plaie*] to open up; (*Tech*) [+ *bronze*] to burnish; [+ *poutre*] to square off **2** **s'aviver** VPR [+ *douleur*] to sharpen; [*regrets*] to deepen; [*regard*] to brighten

av. J.-C. (ABRÉV = *avant Jésus-Christ*) BC

avocaillon [avɔkajɔ̃] NM (*péj*) pettifogger, small-town lawyer

avocasserie [avɔkasʀi] NF (*péj*) pettifoggery, chicanery

avocassier, -ière [avɔkasje, jɛʀ] ADJ (*péj*) pettifogging

avocat¹, e [avɔka, at] **1** NM,F **a** (*Jur*) lawyer, attorney(-at-law) (*US*), advocate (*Écos*); (*d'assises*) ≈ barrister (*Brit*); **consulter son ~** to consult one's lawyer; **l'accusé et son ~** the accused and his counsel **b** (*fig* = *défenseur*) advocate, champion; **se faire l'~ d'une cause** to advocate *ou* champion *ou* plead a cause; **faistoi mon ~ auprès de lui** plead with him on my behalf **2** COMP ▶ **avocat d'affaires** business lawyer ▶ **avocat de la défense** counsel for the defence *ou* defendant, defending counsel (*Brit*), defense counsel (*US*) ▶ **l'avocat du diable** (*Rel, fig*) the devil's advocate; (*fig*) **se faire l'~ du diable** to be *ou* play devil's advocate ▶ **avocat d'entreprise** company *ou* corporate lawyer ▶ **avocat général** counsel for the prosecution, prosecuting attorney (*US*), assistant procurator fiscal (*Écos*) ▶ **l'avocat de la partie civile** the counsel for the plaintiff ▶ **avocat plaidant** court lawyer (*Brit*), trial lawyer (*US*) ▶ **avocat sans cause** briefless barrister (*Brit*) *ou* attorney (*US*)

avocat² [avɔka] NM (= *fruit*) avocado (pear)

avocatier [avɔkatje] NM avocado (tree), avocado pear tree

avocette [avɔsɛt] NF avocet

avoine [avwan] NF oats → **farine, flocon, fou**

---

avoir [avwaʀ]

▶ conjug 34 ◀

1 VERBE TRANSITIF	4 NOM MASCULIN
2 VERBE AUXILIAIRE	5 NOM MASCULIN PL
3 VERBE IMPERSONNEL	

1 VERBE TRANSITIF

Lorsque **avoir** *fait partie d'une expression figée comme* **avoir raison, avoir peur, avoir faim,** *reportez-vous au nom.*

a possession

Lorsque **avoir** *signifie* **posséder, disposer de,** *il se traduit généralement par* **have** *ou plus familièrement par* **have got,** *mais uniquement au présent ; cette dernière forme est moins courante en anglais américain.*

j'ai la réponse/trois frères I have *ou* I've got the answer/three brothers; **il n'a pas d'argent** he has *ou* he's got no money, he hasn't got any money, he doesn't have any money; **il n'avait pas d'argent** he had no money *ou* didn't have any money; **on ne peut pas tout ~** you can't have everything; **as-tu son adresse ?** have you got his address?, do you have his address?

b localisation

Lorsque **avoir** *est utilisé pour localiser un bâtiment, un objet etc, il peut se traduire par* **have (got)** *mais l'anglais préférera souvent une tournure avec* **be.**

vous avez la gare tout près the station is nearby; **vous avez un parc au bout de la rue** you've got *ou* there's a park down the road; **vous tournez à droite et vous aurez la poste juste en face de vous** you turn right and you'll see the post office just opposite *ou* and the post office is just opposite; **tu as les verres sur la dernière étagère** the glasses are on the top shelf, you'll find the glasses on the top shelf

c

La tournure familière dans laquelle **avoir** *est suivi d'un adjectif possessif en corrélation avec un participe passé ou une relative n'est pas traduite ou est rendue par* **have** *et un possessif.*

j'ai eu mon appareil photo volé I had my camera stolen; **ils ont leur fille qui part au Québec** they've got their daughter going to Quebec; **j'ai mes rhumatismes qui me font souffrir** my rheumatism's playing me up*

d = obtenir [+ *produit, renseignement, train*] to get; **nous avons très bien la BBC** we (can) get the BBC very clearly; **pouvez-vous nous ~ ce livre ?** can you get this book for us?, can you get us this book?; **essayez de m'~ Paris** (au téléphone) could you put me through to Paris *ou* get me Paris?; **je n'ai pas pu ~ Luc** (au téléphone) I couldn't get through to Luc, I didn't manage to get Luc on the phone; **je n'arrive pas à ~ Paris** I can't get through to Paris

e = porter [+ *vêtements*] to wear, have on; **il avait un pantalon beige** he was wearing beige trousers; **qu'est-ce qu'il avait sur lui ?** what was he wearing?, what did he have on?; **elle a toujours des gants/un foulard** she always wears gloves/a scarf; MAIS **la femme qui a le chapeau/le corsage bleu** the woman with *ou* in the blue hat/blouse

f caractérisation

Lorsque **avoir** *introduit une caractéristique physique ou morale, il est rendu soit par* **have** *soit par* **be** + *adjectif.*

il a les yeux bleus he has (got) blue eyes; **son regard a quelque chose de méchant** ◊ **il a quelque chose de méchant dans le regard** he's got a nasty look in his eye; **il a du courage/de l'ambition/du toupet** he has (got) courage/ambition/cheek, he is courageous/ambitious/cheeky; MAIS **il avait les mains qui tremblaient** his hands were shaking

g avec forme, dimension to be; **~ 3 mètres de haut/4 mètres de long** to be 3 metres high/4 metres long; **cette chaise a une jolie ligne** this chair is a nice shape; **je veux une chaise qui ait cette forme** I want a chair (that's) this shape; MAIS **je voudrais un pull qui ait cette couleur** I'd like a jumper (in) this colour

h avec un âge to be; **il a dix ans** he is ten (years old); **j'ai l'impression d'~ 20 ans** I feel as if I were 20; **il a dans les cinquante ans** he's about *ou* around 50; **il a dans les** *ou* **environ 45 ans** he's in his mid-forties; **elle a entre 50 et 60 ans** she's between 50 and 60, she's in her fifties; MAIS **elle venait d'~ 38 ans** she had just turned 38

Lorsque **avoir** *l'on a une proposition relative, l'anglais peut employer une tournure adjectivale.*

les étudiants qui ont 18 ans 18-year-old students, students who are 18 (years old); **des enfants qui ont entre 10 et 15 ans** children (who are) between 10 and 15, 10-to-15 year olds; **des bâtiments qui ont plus de 250 ans** buildings (that are) more than 250 years old

i = souffrir de [+ *rhume, maladie*] to have; **il a la rougeole** he's got measles; **il a eu la rougeole à 10 ans** he had measles when he was 10; MAIS **il ne veut pas dire ce qu'il a** he won't say what's wrong (with him)

j = éprouver **~ le sentiment/l'impression que** to have the feeling/the impression that; **qu'est-ce que tu as ?** what's the matter (with you)?, what's wrong (with you)?; **il a sûrement quelque chose** I'm sure there's something the matter with him *ou* something wrong with him; **qu'est-ce que tu as ? — j'ai que je suis exténué** what's the matter? — I'll tell you what the matter is, I'm worn out; **il a qu'il est jaloux** he's jealous, that's what's wrong *ou* the matter with him; **qu'est-ce qu'il a à pleurer ?** what's he crying for?

k = faire

Lorsque **avoir** *signifie* **exprimer** *ou* **faire,** *il se traduit généralement par un verbe spécifique en anglais ; cherchez sous le substantif.*

▶ GRAMMAIRE ACTIVE: **avis** 28.1, 29.1, 29.2, 33.1, 33.2, 38.1, 40.1, 53.5

il eut un geste d'énervement he made an irritated gesture; **elle eut un sourire malin** she gave a knowing smile, she smiled knowingly; **il eut une grimace de douleur** he winced; **elle a eu un regard haineux** she gave us a spiteful look; **ils ont eu des remarques malheureuses** they made *ou* passed (*Brit*) some unfortunate remarks

$\boxed{\text{l}}$ **= recevoir** ~ **des amis à dîner** to have friends to dinner; **j'ai eu mon frère à déjeuner** I had my brother round for lunch; **il aime ~ des amis** he likes to have friends over *ou* round (*Brit*), he likes to entertain friends

$\boxed{\text{m}}$ **suivi d'une activité** to have; **ils ont des soirées deux ou trois fois par semaine** they have parties two or three times a week; **je n'ai rien ce soir** I've nothing on this evening, I'm not doing anything this evening; **j'ai français à 10 heures** I've got French at 10

$\boxed{\text{n}}$ **= toucher, attraper, vaincre** to get; **je l'ai eu !** (*cible*) got it!; **ils ont fini par ~ le coupable** they got the culprit in the end; **dans la fusillade, ils ont eu le chef de la bande** in the shoot-out they got the gang leader; **on les aura !** we'll have *ou* get them!*; **je t'aurai !** I'll get you!*; **elle m'a eu au sentiment** she took advantage of my better nature

$\boxed{\text{o}}$ *** = duper** [*escroc*] to have*, take in*, con*; [*plaisantin*] to take in*; **ils m'ont eu** *ou* **j'ai été eu** I've been had*; **je t'ai bien eu !** got you there!*; **se faire ~** (*par escroc*) to be had*, be taken in*; (*par un plaisantin*) to be taken in*; **je me suis fait ~ de 30 F** I was conned out of 30 francs*; **il s'est laissé ~** he let himself be taken in*

$\boxed{\text{p}}$
♦ **en avoir** (= *être courageux*) to have guts* *ou* balls**

$\boxed{\text{q}}$
♦ **avoir à** + *infinitif* (= *devoir*) **j'ai à travailler** I've got some work to do; **il a un bouton à recoudre** he's got a button that needs sewing on

♦ **n'avoir qu'à** : **tu n'as qu'à me téléphoner demain** just give me a ring tomorrow; **tu n'as qu'à appuyer sur le bouton, et ça se met en marche** (you) just press the knob, and it starts working; **c'est simple, vous n'avez qu'à lui écrire** it's simple, all you have to do is write to him; **tu n'avais qu'à ne pas y aller** you shouldn't have gone (in the first place); **s'il n'est pas content, il n'a qu'à partir** if he doesn't like it, he can always leave

$\boxed{\text{2}}$ VERBE AUXILIAIRE

En tant qu'auxiliaire, avoir se traduit par have sauf dans certains emplois du passé qui sont rendus par des prétérits.

j'ai déjà couru 10 km I've already run 10 km; **il a été renvoyé deux fois** he has been dismissed twice; **quand il eut** *ou* **a eu parlé** when he had spoken; **il n'est pas bien, il a dû trop manger** he is not well, he must have eaten too much; **nous aurons terminé demain** we'll have finished tomorrow; **si je l'avais vu** if I had seen him; **j'étais pressé, j'ai couru** I was in a hurry so I ran; **il a fini hier** he finished yesterday

$\boxed{\text{3}}$ **il y a** VERBE IMPERSONNEL

$\boxed{\text{a}}$ **réalité, existence** (*suivi d'un nom singulier*) there is; (*suivi d'un nom pluriel*) there are; **il y a un chien à la porte** there's a dog at the door; **il n'y avait que moi** there was only me, I was the only one; **il y a eu trois blessés** three people were injured, there were three injured; **il y a voiture et voiture !** there are cars and cars!

♦ **il y en a** (*avec antécédent au singulier*) there is some; (*avec antécédent au pluriel*) there are some; **j'achète du pain ? — non, il y en a (encore)** shall I buy some bread? — no, there's some left; **quand y en a pour deux, y en a pour trois*** (*nourriture*) there's plenty for everyone; (*place*) there's plenty of room for everyone; **il y en a pour dire** *ou* **qui disent ...** there are some *ou* those who say ..., some say ...; **quand il n'y en a plus, il y en a encore !*** there's plenty more where that came from!*; [*MAIS*] **il y en a qui feraient mieux de se taire !** some people

would do better to keep quiet!; **il y en a, je vous jure !*** some people, honestly!*, really, some people!*

♦ **il n'y en a que pour** : **il n'y en a que pour mon petit frère, à la maison** my little brother gets all the attention at home; **il n'y en a eu que pour lui pendant l'émission** the whole programme revolved around him

♦ **qu'y a-t-il ?** ◊ **qu'est-ce qu'il y a ?** (= *que se passe-t-il*) what is it?, what's the matter?, what's up?*; (= *qu'est-ce qui ne va pas*) what's wrong?, what's the matter?, what's up?*

♦ **il y a que** : **il y a que nous sommes mécontents !** we're annoyed, that's what!*

♦ **il n'y a (pas) que** : **il n'y a pas que toi** you're not the only one!; **il n'y a que lui pour faire cela !** only HE would do that!, trust him to do that!; **il n'y a pas que nous à le dire** we're not the only ones who say *ou* to say that

♦ **(il n')y a pas*** : **il n'y a pas, (il) faut que je parte** it's no good, I've got to go; **y a pas, il faut qu'il désobéisse** he just won't do as he's told; **il n'y a pas à dire, il est très intelligent** there's no denying he's very intelligent

♦ **il n'y a qu'à** + *infinitif* ◊ **y a qu'à** + *infinitif** : **il n'y a qu'à les laisser partir** just let them go; **il y a qu'à protester** we'll just have to protest, why don't we protest; **y a qu'à lui dire*** why don't we just tell him; **y avait qu'à le prendre, alors !*** why didn't you take it then!

$\boxed{\text{b}}$ **= il se passe** **il y a eu des émeutes dans la capitale** there have been riots in the capital; **il y a eu un accident/une inondation** there has been an accident/flooding; **qu'est-ce qu'il y a eu ?** what's happened?; **il y a eu quelque chose de grave** something serious has happened

♦ **il y avait une fois ...** once upon a time, there was ...

$\boxed{\text{c}}$ **avec une durée**

Dans le cas d'une action non révolue, for s'emploie avec le present perfect lorsque le verbe français est au présent, et avec le pluperfect lorsque le verbe français est à l'imparfait.

il y a 10 ans que je le connais I've known him (for) 10 years; **il y avait longtemps qu'elle désirait ce livre** she had wanted *ou* been wanting this book for a long time

Dans le cas d'une action révolue, on emploie ago et le prétérit.

il y a 10 ans, nous étions à Paris 10 years ago we were in Paris; **il est né il y a tout juste un an** he was born just one year ago; **il y a 10 jours/10 minutes que nous sommes rentrés** ◊ **nous sommes rentrés il y a 10 jours/10 minutes** we got back 10 days/10 minutes ago, we have been back 10 days/10 minutes; **il n'y a pas un quart d'heure qu'il est parti** he left not a quarter of an hour ago; [*MAIS*] **il y aura 10 ans demain que je ne l'ai vu** it will be 10 years tomorrow since I last saw him

$\boxed{\text{d}}$ **suivi d'une distance** **il y a 10 km d'ici à Paris** it is 10 km from here to Paris; **combien y a-t-il d'ici à Lille ?** how far is it from here to Lille?

$\boxed{\text{4}}$ NOM MASCULIN

$\boxed{\text{a}}$ **= bien** assets; **il a investi tout son ~ dans l'entreprise** he invested all his assets in the firm; **son ~ était bien peu de chose** what he had wasn't much

$\boxed{\text{b}}$ Comm (= *actif*) credit (side); (= *billet de crédit*) credit note; (*Fin*) ~ **fiscal** tax credit; **vous pouvez me faire un ~ ?** can you give me a credit note?

$\boxed{\text{5}}$ **avoirs** NMPL holdings, assets; ~**s à l'étranger** foreign assets *ou* holdings; ~**s en caisse** *ou* **en numéraire** cash holdings; ~**s financiers** financial resources

avoirdupoids [avwaʀdypwa] NM avoirdupois

avoisinant, e [avwazinɑ̃, ɑ̃t] ADJ [*région, pays*] neighbouring (*Brit*), neighboring (*US*); [*rue, ferme*] nearby, neighbouring (*Brit*), neighbor-

ing (*US*); **dans les rues ~es** in the nearby streets, in the streets close by *ou* nearby

avoisiner [avwazine] ▶conjug 1◀ VT [+ *lieu*] (= *être proche de*) to be near *ou* close to; (= *être contigu à*) to border on; [*prix, température, taux*] to be close to; (*fig*) **son indifférence avoisine le mépris** his indifference borders *ou* verges on contempt

avortement [avɔʀtəmɑ̃] NM (*Méd*) abortion; (*fig*) ~ **de** failure of; **campagne contre l'~** anti-abortion campaign; ~ **thérapeutique** termination (of pregnancy) (*for medical reasons*)

avorter [avɔʀte] ▶conjug 1◀ $\boxed{\text{1}}$ VI $\boxed{\text{a}}$ (*Méd*) to have an abortion, abort; **faire ~ qn** [*personne*] to give sb an abortion, abort sb; [*remède*] to make sb abort; **se faire ~** to have an abortion $\boxed{\text{b}}$ (*fig*) to fail, come to nothing; **faire ~ un projet** to frustrate *ou* wreck a plan; **projet avorté** abortive plan $\boxed{\text{2}}$ VT (*Méd*) to abort, perform an abortion on

avorteur, -euse [avɔʀtœʀ, øz] NM,F abortionist

avorton [avɔʀtɔ̃] NM (*péj = personne*) little runt (*péj*); (= *arbre, plante*) puny *ou* stunted specimen; (= *animal*) puny specimen

avouable [avwabl] ADJ blameless; **procédés peu ~s** fairly disreputable methods, methods which don't bear mentioning

avoué, e [avwe] (*ptp de avouer*) $\boxed{\text{1}}$ ADJ [*ennemi, revenu, but*] avowed $\boxed{\text{2}}$ NM ≈ solicitor (*Brit*), ≈ attorney-at-law (*US*)

avouer [avwe] ▶conjug 1◀ $\boxed{\text{1}}$ VT [+ *amour*] to confess, avow (*littér*); [+ *crime*] to confess (to), own up to; [+ *fait*] to acknowledge, admit; [+ *faiblesse, vice*] to admit to, confess to; ~ **avoir menti** to admit *ou* confess that one has lied, admit *ou* own up to lying; ~ **que ...** to admit *ou* confess that ...; **elle est douée, je l'avoue** she is gifted, I (must) admit → **faute** $\boxed{\text{2}}$ VI $\boxed{\text{a}}$ (= *se confesser*) [*coupable*] to confess, own up $\boxed{\text{b}}$ (= *admettre*) to admit, confess; **tu avoueras, c'est un peu fort !** you must admit *ou* confess, it is a bit much! $\boxed{\text{3}}$ **s'avouer** VPR **s'~ coupable** to admit *ou* confess one's guilt; **s'~ vaincu** to admit *ou* acknowledge defeat; **s'~ déçu** to admit to being disappointed

avril [avʀil] NM April ∎ (*PROV*) **en ~ ne te découvre pas d'un fil** ne'er cast a clout till May is out (*PROV*) → **poisson, premier**; *pour autres locutions voir* **septembre**

avunculaire [avɔ̃kylɛʀ] ADJ avuncular

AWACS [awaks] NM (ABRÉV = **Airborne Warning And Control System**) AWACS; **(avion) ~** AWACS (plane); **avion-radar ~** AWACS early-warning (radar) plane

axe [aks] NM $\boxed{\text{a}}$ (*Tech*) axle; (*Anat, Astron, Bot, Math*) axis $\boxed{\text{b}}$ (= *route*) trunk road (*Brit*), main highway (*US*); **les grands ~s (routiers)** the main roads, the major trunk roads (*Brit*), the main highways (*US*); **les vols réguliers sur l'~ Paris-Marseille** the regular flights on the Paris-Marseilles route; **(à Paris) ~ rouge** no stopping zone, clearway (*Brit*) $\boxed{\text{c}}$ (*fig*) [*débat, théorie, politique*] main line $\boxed{\text{d}}$ (*Hist, Pol*) **l'Axe** the Axis; **l'~ Paris-Bonn dans la construction européenne** the Paris-Bonn axis in the construction of Europe ∎ **dans l'~ de** (= *dans le prolongement*) **cette rue est dans l'~ de l'église** this street is directly in line with the church; **mets-toi bien dans l'~ (de la cible)** line up on the target, get directly in line with the target

axel [aksɛl] NM axel

axer [akse] ▶conjug 1◀ VT ~ **qch sur/autour de** to centre (*Brit*) *ou* center (*US*) sth on/around; **il est très axé sur la politique** he's very interested in politics; **leur rapport est axé sur l'environnement** their report focuses on the environment

axial, e (*mpl* -**iaux**) [aksjal, jo] ADJ axial; **éclairage ~** central overhead lighting

axillaire [aksilɛʀ] ADJ axillary

axiomatique [aksjɔmatik] ① ADJ axiomatic ② NF axiomatics *sg*

axiome [aksjom] NM axiom

axis [aksis] NM axis (vertebra)

axone [akson] NM axon(e)

ayant cause (*pl* **ayants cause**) [ɛjɑ̃koz] NM (*Jur*) legal successor, successor in title; **les ayants cause du défunt** the beneficiaries of the deceased

ayant droit (*pl* **ayants droit**) [ɛjɑ̃dRwa] NM ⓐ (*Jur*) = **ayant cause** ⓑ [*prestation, pension*] eligible party; **~ à** party entitled to *ou* eligible for

ayatollah [ajatɔla] NM ayatollah; (*fig*) **les ~s de la morale** moral zealots

azalée [azale] NF azalea

Azerbaïdjan [azɛRbaidʒɑ̃] NM Azerbaijan

azerbaïdjanais, e [azɛRbaidʒanɛ, ɛz] ① ADJ Azerbaijani ② NM (*Ling*) Azerbaijani ③ **Azerbaïdjanais(e)** NM,F Azerbaijani

azéri, e [azeRi] ① ADJ Azeri, Azerbaijani ② NM (*Ling*) Azerbaijani ③ **Azéri(e)** NM,F Azeri, Azerbaijani

AZERTY [azɛRti] ADJ INV **clavier ~** AZERTY keyboard

azimut [azimyt] NM ⓐ (*Astron*) azimuth ⓑ (*, fig*) **tous ~s** (= *dans toutes les directions*) everywhere, all over the place; [*offensive, campagne*] all-out (*épith*); [*négociation*] wide-ranging (*épith*); [*réformes*] wholesale; **la banque a connu une expansion tous ~s** the bank has undergone a dramatic expansion; **il attaque tous ~s** he lashes out in all directions; **elle téléphonait tous ~s** she phoned around everywhere; **chercher qn dans tous les ~s** to look everywhere *ou* all over the place for sb, search high and low for sb

azimutal, e (*mpl* **-aux**) [azimytal, o] ADJ azimuthal

azimuté, e* [azimyte] ADJ crazy*, nuts*, mad

Azincourt [azɛ̃kuR] N Agincourt

azote [azɔt] NM nitrogen

azoté, e [azɔte] ADJ [*substance, base*] nitrogenous → **engrais**

AZT [azɛdte] NM (ABRÉV = **azidothymidine**) AZT

aztèque [astɛk] ① ADJ Aztec ② **Aztèque** NMF Aztec

azur [azyR] NM (*littér*) (= *couleur*) azure, sky blue; (= *ciel*) skies, sky; (*Hér*) azure → **côte**

azuré, e [azyRe] (*ptp de* **azurer**) ADJ azure

azuréen, -enne [azyReɛ̃, ɛn] ADJ ⓐ (= *de la côte d'Azur*) of the French Riviera ⓑ (*littér*) [*yeux, bleu, ciel*] azure

azurer [azyRe] ▶ conjug 1 ◀ VT [+ *linge*] to blue; (*littér*) to azure, tinge with blue

azyme [azim] ① ADJ unleavened → **pain** ② NM unleavened bread; **fête des Azymes** Passover

B

B, b [be] NM (= *lettre*) B, b

b (ABRÉV = **bien**) (*Scol*) g, good

B. A. [bea] NF (ABRÉV = **bonne action**) good deed; **faire sa ~ (quotidienne)** to do one's good deed for the day

B.A.-BA [beaba] NM SG **le ~** the ABC (**de** of); **il n'en est qu'au ~** he's just starting off, he's just a beginner

baba¹* [baba] NM (*Culin*) baba; **~ au rhum** rum baba

baba² [baba] ① NM **il l'a eu dans le ~:** it was one in the eye for him* ② ADJ **j'en suis resté ~*** I was flabbergasted *ou* dumbfounded, I was gobsmacked* (*Brit*)

baba³* [baba], **baba cool*** (*pl* **babas cool** [babakul]) NMF ≈ hippy

Babel [babɛl] N Babel → **tour¹**

babeurre [babœʀ] NM buttermilk

babil [babil] NM [*littér*] [*bébé*] babble; [*enfant*] prattle; [*adulte*] chatter; [*oiseau*] twittering; [*ruisseau*] babbling

babillage [babijaʒ] NM [*enfant*] prattle; [*adulte*] chatter

babillard, e [babijaʀ, aʀd] ① ADJ (*littér*) [*adulte*] chattering; [*bébé*] babbling; [*oiseau*] twittering; [*ruisseau*] babbling, chattering ② NM,F (*personne*) chatterbox ③ NM (*Can*) notice *ou* bulletin board; **~ électronique** electronic bulletin board ④ **babillarde*** NF (= *lettre*) letter, note

babiller [babije] ▸ conjug 1 ◂ VI [*personne*] to chatter; [*bébé*] to babble; [*enfant*] to prattle; [*oiseau*] to twitter; [*ruisseau*] to babble, chatter

babines [babin] NFPL [*animal*] chops; * [*personne*] chops*, lips → **lécher**

babiole [babjɔl] NF (= *bibelot*) trinket, knick-knack; (= *vétille*) trifle, triviality; (= *cadeau*) **offrir une ~** to give a small token *ou* a little something

bâbord [babɔʀ] NM port (side); **par ou à ~** on the port side, to port; **par ~ arrière** aft on the port side

babouche [babuʃ] NF babouche, Turkish *ou* oriental slipper

babouin [babwɛ̃] NM baboon

baboune* [babun] NF (*Can*) lip; **faire la ~** (*de déception, de dédain*) to pout; (*de dégoût*) to grimace; **elle m'a fait la ~ toute la journée** she was sulky *ou* huffy* with me all day

baby [babi] ① ADJ INV **taille ~** baby size ② NM (= *whisky*) shot of scotch

baby-blues [babibluz] NM INV baby blues*, postnatal depression; **avoir le ~** to have the baby blues*, be suffering from postnatal depression

baby-boom (*pl* **baby-booms**) [babibum] NM baby boom; **les enfants du ~** the baby-boomers

baby-foot (*pl* **baby-foots**) [babifut] NM INV (= *jeu*) table football; (= *appareil*) football table

Babylone [babilɔn] N Babylon

babylonien, -ienne [babilɔnjɛ̃, jɛn] ① ADJ

Babylonian ② **Babylonien(ne)** NM,F Babylonian

baby-sitter (*pl* **baby-sitters**) [babisitœʀ] NMF baby-sitter

baby-sitting (*pl* **baby-sittings**) [babisitiŋ] NM baby-sitting; **faire du ~** to baby-sit, do baby-sitting

bac¹ [bak] NM ⓐ (= *bateau*) (*gén*) ferry, ferryboat; (*pour voitures*) car-ferry; **~ aérien** air ferry ⓑ (= *récipient*) tub; (*Ind*) tank, vat; (*Peinture, Photo*) tray; [*évier*] sink; [*courrier, imprimante*] tray; **~ à douche** shower tray; **~ (à fleurs)** planter, tub; **~ à glace** ice-tray; **~ à laver** washtub, (deep) sink; **~ à légumes** vegetable compartment *ou* tray; **~ à réserve d'eau** self-watering planter; **~ à sable** sandpit; **évier (à) deux ~s** double sink unit; **glace vendue en ~s de deux litres** ice-cream sold in two-litre tubs

bac²* [bak] NM ABRÉV = **baccalauréat** ⓐ (*en France*) **formation ~ + 3** ≈ 3 years' higher education → **baccalauréat** ⓑ (*au Canada* = *licence*) ≈ BA

baccalauréat [bakalɔʀea] NM ⓐ (*en France*) baccalauréat, school leaving certificate, ≈ A-levels (*Brit*), ≈ high school diploma (*US*) ⓑ (*au Canada* = *licence*) ≈ BA; **~ en droit** law degree, LLB (*Brit*)

> ┌─ **BACCALAURÉAT** ──────────────
>
> The "bac", as it is popularly known, is the school leaving examination all French schoolchildren take in their final year at the "lycée". Before beginning their **baccalauréat** studies, pupils choose a specialization known as a "série", represented by an initial letter: a "bac" with a scientific bias is known as a "bac S" (for "scientifique") while an arts-oriented "bac" is referred to as a "bac L" (for "littéraire"), for example. When the word "bac" is followed by a plus sign and a number, this refers to the number of years of formal study completed since obtaining the baccalauréat qualification: "bac" + 3 refers to the "licence" or equivalent, "bac" + 4 to the "maîtrise", etc. These abbreviations are often used in job advertisements to indicate the level of qualification required.

---

baccara [bakaʀa] NM (*Casino*) baccara(t)

baccarat [bakaʀa] NM (**cristal de**) **~** Baccarat crystal

bacchanale [bakanal] NF ⓐ (= *danse*) bacchanalian *ou* drunken dance; († = *orgie*) orgy, drunken revel ⓑ (*Antiq*) **~s** Bacchanalia

bacchante [bakɑ̃t] ① NF (*Antiq*) bacchante ② **bacchantes*** NFPL moustache, whiskers (*hum*)

Bacchus [bakys] NM Bacchus

Bach [bak] NM Bach

bâchage [baʃaʒ] NM covering

bâche [baʃ] NF ⓐ (= *toile*) canvas cover *ou* sheet; [*camion*] tarpaulin, tarp (*US*); [*piscine*] (plastic *ou* canvas) cover; **~ goudronnée** tarpaulin, tarp (*US*) ⓑ (*Tech*) (= *réservoir*) tank,

---

cistern; (= *carter*) housing; (= *serre*) forcing frame

bachelier, -ière [baʃəlje, jɛʀ] NM,F *person who has passed the baccalauréat*

bâcher [baʃe] ▸ conjug 1 ◂ VT to cover with a canvas sheet, put a canvas sheet over; **camion bâché** covered truck *ou* lorry (*Brit*)

bachique [baʃik] ADJ (*Antiq, fig*) Bacchic; **fêtes ~s** bacchanalian revels; **chanson ~** drinking song

bachot¹†* [baʃo] NM = **baccalauréat**; → **boîte**

bachot² [baʃo] NM (small) boat, skiff

bachotage [baʃɔtaʒ] NM (*Scol*) cramming, swotting (*Brit*); **faire du ~** to cram *ou* swot (*Brit*) (for an exam)

bachoter [baʃɔte] ▸ conjug 1 ◂ VI (*Scol*) to cram *ou* swot (*Brit*) (for an exam)

bacillaire [basilɛʀ] ADJ [*maladie*] bacillary; [*malade*] tubercular

bacille [basil] NM (*gén*) germ, bacillus (*SPÉC*); **le ~ virgule** the comma bacillus; **le ~ de Koch/de Hansen** Koch's/Hansen('s) bacillus

bacillose [basiloz] NF (*gén*) bacillus infection; (= *tuberculose*) tuberculosis

backgammon [bakgamɔn] NM backgammon

bâclage [baklaʒ] NM botching

bâcler [bakle] ▸ conjug 1 ◂ VT [+ *travail, devoir*] to botch (up); [+ *cérémonie*] to skip through, hurry over; **~ sa toilette** to have a quick wash; **la fin du film est bâclée** the ending of the film is a bit of a mess; **c'est du travail bâclé** it's slapdash work

bacon [bekɔn] NM (= *lard*) bacon; (= *jambon fumé*) smoked loin of pork; **œufs au ~** bacon and eggs

bactéricide [bakteʀisid] ① ADJ bactericidal ② NM bactericide

bactérie [bakteʀi] NF bacterium; **~s** bacteria; **on a découvert une nouvelle ~** a new strain of bacteria *ou* a new bacterium has been discovered

bactérien, -ienne [bakteʀjɛ̃, jɛn] ADJ [*contamination, pollution*] bacterial

bactériologie [bakteʀjɔlɔʒi] NF bacteriology

bactériologique [bakteʀjɔlɔʒik] ADJ [*arme, examen*] bacteriological

bactériologiste [bakteʀjɔlɔʒist] NMF bacteriologist

bactériophage [bakteʀjɔfaʒ] NM bacteriophage

badaboum* [badabum] EXCL crash, bang, wallop!; **et ~! voilà bébé par terre** whoops! baby falls down!

badaud, e [bado, od] ① NM,F (*qui regarde*) curious *ou* gaping (*péj*) onlooker; (*qui se promène*) stroller ② ADJ **les Parisiens sont très ~s** Parisians love to stop and stare *ou* are full of idle curiosity

badauder† [badode] ▸ conjug 1 ◂ VI (= *se promener*) to stroll (**dans** about); (= *regarder*) to gawk, gawp

badauderie† [badodʀi] NF (idle) curiosity

baderne [badɛʀn] NF (péj) **(vieille)** ~ old fogey*

badge [badʒ] NM (gén) badge, button (US); (d'identité) name badge ou tag; (pour visiteur) visitor's badge, (visitor's) pass; (= carte électronique) swipe card

badgé, e [badʒe] ADJ [personne] wearing a badge

badiane [badjan] NF star anis, badian

badigeon [badiʒɔ̃] NM [mur intérieur] distemper; [mur extérieur] (lait de chaux) whitewash; (coloré) coloured distemper, colourwash (Brit); **un coup de** ~ a coat of distemper ou whitewash

badigeonnage [badiʒɔnaʒ] NM [a] [mur intérieur] distempering; [mur extérieur] (au lait de chaux) whitewashing; (coloré) colourwashing [b] [plaie] painting

badigeonner [badiʒɔne] ▸ conjug 1 ◂ VT [a] [+ mur intérieur] to distemper; [+ mur extérieur] to whitewash (Brit); (en couleur) to colourwash (Brit) [b] (= barbouiller) [+ visage, surface] to smear, daub, cover (**de** with); **se** ~ **de crème** to smear o.s. with cream [c] [+ plaie] to paint (**à, avec** with); **se** ~ **la gorge** to paint one's throat (**à** with); ~ **une plaie de qch** to swab a wound with sth [d] (Culin) to brush (**de** with)

badin[1], e[1]† [badɛ̃, in] ADJ [personne] jocular; [humeur] light-hearted, playful; [propos] bantering, playful; **sur un** ou **d'un ton** ~ playfully, in a bantering ou jesting tone

badin[2] [badɛ̃] NM (Aviat) airspeed indicator

badinage [badinaʒ] NM (= propos légers) banter (NonC); **sur un ton de** ~ in a bantering ou jesting tone, playfully

badine[2] [badin] NF switch, rod

badiner [badine] ▸ conjug 1 ◂ VI [a] († = plaisanter) to (exchange) banter, jest†; **pour** ~ for a jest†, in jest [b] (en négation) **c'est quelqu'un qui ne badine pas** he doesn't stand for any nonsense; **il ne badine pas sur la discipline** he's a stickler for discipline, he has strict ideas about discipline; **il ne faut pas** ~ **avec ce genre de maladie** this sort of illness is not to be treated lightly; **et je ne badine pas** ! and I'm not joking!

badinerie† [badinʀi] NF jest†

badminton [badminton] NM badminton

bâdrant, e* [bɑdʀɑ̃, ɑ̃t] ADJ (Can) bothersome; **t'es vraiment** ~ **avec tes questions** you're being a real nuisance ou a real pain in the neck* with your questions

bâdrer* [bɑdʀe] ▸ conjug 1 ◂ VT (Can) to bother; **tu commences à me** ~ **avec tes questions** you're beginning to get on my nerves with your questions

BAFA [bafa] NM (ABRÉV = **brevet d'aptitude à la fonction d'animateur**) → **brevet**

baffe* [baf] NF slap, clout* (Brit); **donner une paire de** ~**s à qn** to slap sb across the face; **recevoir une** ~ to get slapped, get a clip on ou round the ear* (Brit)

Baffin [bafin] NM **mer** ou **baie de** ~ Baffin Bay; **terre de** ~ Baffin Island

baffle [bafl] NM [a] (= panneau) baffle (board ou plate); (= enceinte) speaker

bafouer [bafwe] ▸ conjug 1 ◂ VT [+ autorité] to flout, scorn; [+ droit, valeurs] to scorn, scoff at; **mari bafoué†** cuckold†

bafouillage [bafujaʒ] NM (= bredouillage) spluttering, stammering; (= propos incohérents) gibberish (NonC), babble (NonC)

bafouille* [bafuj] NF (= lettre) letter, note

bafouiller [bafuje] ▸ conjug 1 ◂ [1] VI (= bredouiller) to splutter, stammer; (= divaguer) to talk gibberish, babble [2] VT to splutter (out), stammer (out); **qu'est-ce qu'il bafouille ?** what's he babbling ou jabbering on about?*

bafouilleur, -euse* [bafujœʀ, øz] NM,F splutterer, stammerer

bâfrer* [bafʀe] ▸ conjug 1 ◂ [1] VI to guzzle*, stuff one's face* [2] VT to guzzle (down)*, gobble (down), wolf (down)*

bâfreur, -euse* [bafʀœʀ, øz] NM,F guzzler*, greedy guts* (Brit)

bagage [bagaʒ] NM [a] (= valises) ~**s** luggage (NonC), baggage (NonC); **faire/défaire ses** ~**s** to pack/unpack (one's luggage ou bags), do one's packing/unpacking; **envoyer qch en** ~**s accompagnés** to send sth as registered luggage; (dans un aéroport) **« (livraison des)** ~**s »** "baggage claim ou reclaim (Brit)" [b] (= valise) bag, piece of luggage; (Mil) kit; ~ **à main** piece of hand luggage, carry-on bag; **il avait pour tout** ~ **une serviette** his only luggage was a briefcase [c] (= connaissances) stock of knowledge; (= diplômes) qualifications; **son** ~ **intellectuel/littéraire** his stock ou store of general/literary knowledge; **ce métier exige un bon** ~ **technique** you need a good technical background for this profession

bagagerie [bagaʒʀi] NF luggage shop

bagagiste [bagaʒist] NM (= manutentionnaire) baggage ou luggage handler; (= porteur) porter

bagarre* [bagaʀ] NF [a] **la** ~ fighting; **il cherche/veut la** ~ he's looking for/wants a fight; **il va y avoir de la** ~ **pour la première place** there's going to be a tough fight for first place; **dès qu'ils sont ensemble, c'est la** ~ as soon as they're together, they're at each other's throats [b] (= rixe) fight, scuffle; (entre ivrognes) brawl; (fig : entre deux orateurs) set-to, barney* (Brit); **de** ~ **générale** free-for-all; **de violentes** ~**s ont éclaté** violent scuffles broke out

bagarrer* [bagaʀe] ▸ conjug 1 ◂ [1] VI (en paroles) to argue, wrangle; (physiquement) to fight; **ça bagarrait dur à l'Assemblée** things got very rowdy ou heated in Parliament [2] **se bagarrer** VPR (= se battre) to fight, scuffle, scrap*; (= se disputer) to have a set-to; **on s'est bagarré dur dans les rues** there was violent fighting in the streets

bagarreur, -euse* [bagaʀœʀ, øz] [1] ADJ [caractère] aggressive, fighting (épith); **il est** ~ (= batailleur) he's always getting into fights; (= ambitieux) he's a fighter [2] NM,F (= ambitieux) fighter; (Sport) battler

bagasse [bagas] NF bagasse

bagatelle [bagatɛl] NF [a] (= objet) small thing, trinket; († = bibelot) knick-knack, trinket [b] (= somme) trifling ou paltry sum, trifle; (iro) **ça m'a coûté la** ~ **de 3 000 F** it cost me the trifling sum of 3,000 francs (iro) ou a mere 3,000 francs (iro) [c] (= vétille) trifle; **perdre son temps à des** ~**s** to fritter away one's time, waste time on trifles [d] († ou hum) **être porté sur la** ~ [homme] to be a bit of a philanderer, be fond of the women; [femme] to be fond of the men [e] ~**s** !† fiddlesticks!†

Bagdad [bagdad] N Baghdad

bagnard [baɲaʀ] NM convict; (fig) **une vie de** ~ a slave's existence

bagne [baɲ] NM (Hist) (= prison) penal colony; (= peine) penal servitude, hard labour; **être condamné au** ~ to be sentenced to hard labour; (fig) **quel** ~ !* ◊ **c'est le** ~ !* it's sheer slavery!

bagnole* [baɲɔl] NF car; **vieille** ~ jalopy*, old banger* (Brit); **il aime faire de la** ~ he likes driving; **ça, c'est de la** ~ ! now that's what I call a car!

bagou(t)* [bagu] NM volubility, glibness (péj); **avoir du** ~ to have the gift of the gab, have a glib tongue (péj); **quel bagout il a !** he'd talk the hind leg(s) off a donkey!*

bagouse* [baguz] NF (= bijou) ring

baguage [bagaʒ] NM [oiseau, arbre] ringing

bague [bag] NF [a] (= bijou) ring; [cigare] band; [oiseau] ring; [boîte de bière] ring-pull, pull-tab; ~ **de fiançailles** engagement ring; (hum) **il a la** ~ **au doigt** he's married ou hitched* (hum) [b] (Tech) collar; ~ **allonge** extension tube; ~ **d'assemblage** bushing; (Photo) ~ **intermédiaire/de réglage** adapter/setting ring; ~ **de serrage** jubilee clip

bagué, e [bage] (ptp de **baguer**) ADJ [oiseau] ringed, banded (US); [main, doigt] beringed; [homard] with its pincers tied together; **cigare** ~ **(d'or)** cigar with a (gold) band

baguenaude* [bagnod] NF **être en** ~ to be gallivanting about

baguenauder VI, **se baguenauder*** VPR [bagnode] ▸ conjug 1 ◂ (= faire un tour) to go for a stroll; (= traîner) to trail around, mooch about* (Brit)

baguer [bage] ▸ conjug 1 ◂ VT [a] [+ oiseau, arbre] to ring; (Tech) to collar [b] (Couture) to baste, tack

baguette [bagɛt] NF [1] [a] (= bâton) stick, switch; (pour manger) ~**s** chopsticks; ~ **de chef d'orchestre** (conductor's) baton; **sous la** ~ **de Luc Petit** under the baton of Luc Petit, conducted by Luc Petit, with Luc Petit conducting; **mener** ou **faire marcher qn à la** ~ to rule sb with a rod of iron ou an iron hand [b] (= pain) baguette, French stick [c] (Constr) beading, strip of wood; (= cache-fils) (plastic ou wood) casing [d] (= motif sur chaussette, bas) clock [2] COMP ▸ **baguette de coudrier** hazel stick ou switch ▸ **baguette de fée** magic wand ▸ **baguette de fusil** ramrod ▸ **baguette magique** magic wand; **résoudre qch d'un coup de** ~ **magique** to solve sth by waving a magic wand ▸ **baguette de protection latérale** (Aut) side trim ▸ **baguette de sourcier** divining rod ▸ **baguette de tambour** (lit) drumstick; **cheveux raides comme des** ~**s de tambour** dead straight ou really straight hair ▸ **baguette viennoise** stick of Vienna bread

bah [ba] EXCL (indifférence) pooh!; (doute) well!, really!

Bahamas [baamas] NFPL **les (îles)** ~ the Bahamas

bahamien, -ienne [baamjɛ̃, ɛn] [1] ADJ Bahamian [2] **Bahamien(ne)** NM,F Bahamian

Bahreïn [baʀɛn] NM Bahrain; **à** ~ in Bahrain

bahreïni, e [baʀe(i)ni] [1] ADJ Bahraini, Bahreini [2] **Bahreïni(e)** NM,F Bahraini, Bahreini

bahut [bay] NM [a] (= coffre) chest; (= buffet) sideboard [b] (arg Scol) school [c]* (= camion) lorry (Brit), truck (surtout US); (= voiture) car; (= taxi) cab

bai, e[1] [bɛ] ADJ [cheval] bay

baie[2] [bɛ] NF [a] (Géog) bay; **la** ~ **d'Hudson** Hudson Bay; **la** ~ **de Somme** the Baie de Somme; **la** ~ **des Anges** the Baie des Anges (in Nice); **la Grande Baie australienne** the Great Australian Bight; **la** ~ **James** James Bay; **la** ~ **des Cochons** the Bay of Pigs [b] (Archit) opening; (= fenêtre) ~ **vitrée** (gén) plate glass window; (panoramique) picture window

baie[3] [bɛ] NF (Bot) berry; (Culin) ~**s rouges** red berries; ~**s roses** pink peppercorns

baignade [bɛɲad] NF (= action) swimming; (= lieu) swimming place; **« ~ interdite »** "no swimming", "swimming prohibited"; **c'est l'heure de la** ~ it's time for a swim

baigner [beɲe] ▸ conjug 1 ◂ [1] VT [a] [+ bébé, chien] to bath (Brit), bathe (US); [+ pieds, visage, yeux] to bathe; **visage baigné de larmes/sueur** face bathed in tears/sweat [b] [mer, rivière] to wash, bathe; [lumière] to bathe; **baigné de soleil** bathed in sunlight [2] VI [a] (= tremper dans) [linge] to soak, lie soaking (dans in); (= tremper dans l'alcool) [fruits] to steep, soak (dans in); **la viande baignait dans la graisse** the meat was swimming in grease; **la victime baignait dans son sang** the victim was lying in a pool of blood; **la ville baigne dans la brume** the town is shrouded ou wrapped in mist; **tout baigne (dans**

l'huile)* everything's everything's looking great*; **ça baigne!*** great!*, couldn't be better!*

[b] (fig) **il baigne dans la joie** his joy knows no bounds, he is bursting with joy; **~ dans le mystère** [affaire] to be shrouded ou wrapped in mystery; [personne] to be completely mystified ou baffled; **~ dans la culture** to be immersed in culture ou surrounded by culture

[3] se baigner VPR (dans la mer, une piscine) to go swimming, have a swim; (dans une baignoire) to have a bath

baigneur, -euse [bɛɲœʀ, øz] **[1]** NM,F swimmer, bather (Brit) **[2]** NM (= jouet) baby doll

baignoire [bɛɲwaʀ] NF **[a]** [salle de bains] bath(tub), tub (US); **~ sabot** ≈ hip-bath; **~ à remous** whirlpool ou spa bath **[b]** (Théât) ground floor box, baignoire **[c]** [sous-marin] conning tower

Baïkal [bajkal] NM **le (lac) ~** Lake Baikal

bail (pl **baux**) [baj, bo] **[1]** NM lease; **prendre à ~** to lease, take out a lease on; **donner à ~** to lease (out); **faire/passer un ~** to draw up/enter into a lease; (fig) **ça fait un ~ que je ne l'ai pas vu!*** it's ages since I (last) saw him!, I haven't seen him for ages! **[2]** COMP **► bail commercial** commercial lease **► bail à ferme** farming lease **► bail à loyer** (house-) letting lease (Brit), rental lease (US)

baille [baj] NF **[a]** (Naut = baquet) (wooden) bucket **[b]** (* = eau) **la ~** (gén) the water; (= mer) the drink*; **tomber à la ~** to fall into the water ou the drink*; **à la ~!** (= tous dans l'eau!) everybody in!

bâillement [bajmɑ̃] NM **[a]** [personne] yawn **[b]** [col] gaping ou loose fit

bailler [baje] **►** conjug 1 **◄** VT (†† ou hum) to give; **vous me la baillez belle! ou bonne!** that's a tall tale!

bâiller [baje] **►** conjug 1 **◄** VI **[a]** [personne] to yawn; **~ de sommeil ou de fatigue/d'ennui** to yawn with tiredness/with ou from boredom; **~ à s'en décrocher la mâchoire ou comme une carpe** to yawn one's head off **[b]** (= être trop large) [col] to gape; [chaussure] to be too loose **[c]** (= être entrouvert) [couture, boutonnage] to gape; [porte] to be ajar ou half-open; (= être décousu) [chaussure] to be split open, gape

bailleur, bailleresse [bajœʀ, bajʀɛs] NM,F [local] lessor; **~ de fonds** backer, sponsor; **~ de licence** licensor, licenser

bailli [baji] NM bailiff

bailliage [bajaʒ] NM bailiwick

bâillon [bajɔ̃] NM (lit, fig) gag; **mettre un ~ à qn** to gag sb

bâillonner [bajɔne] **►** conjug 1 **◄** VT [+ personne] to gag; [+ presse, opposition, opinion] to gag, muzzle

bain [bɛ̃] **[1]** NM **[a]** (dans une baignoire) bath; (dans une piscine, la mer) swim; **~ d'algues/de boue** seaweed/mud bath; **~ de sang** blood bath; **ce séjour à la campagne fut pour elle un ~ de fraîcheur ou de jouvence** that stay in the country put new life into her ou revitalized her; **prendre un ~** (dans une baignoire) to have a bath; (dans la mer, une piscine) to have a swim, take a dip **[b]** (= liquide) bath(water); (Chim, Photo) bath; **~ (de teinture)** dye bath; (Photo) **~ de fixateur/de révélateur** fixing/developing bath **[c]** (= récipient, baignoire) bath(tub), tub (US); [teinturier] vat **[d]** (= piscine) **petit/grand ~** shallow/deep end; (= lieu) **~s** baths **[e]** (* : loc) **nous sommes tous dans le même ~** we're all in the same boat; **tu seras vite dans le ~** you'll soon pick it up ou get the hang of it* ou find your feet (Brit); **mettre qn dans le ~** (= informer) to put sb in the picture; (= compromettre) to incriminate sb, implicate sb; **en avouant, il nous a tous mis dans le ~** by owning up, he's involved us all (in it) ou

mixed us all up in it; **se (re)mettre dans le ~** to get (back) into the swing of things

[2] COMP **► bain de bouche** (= liquide) mouthwash, oral rinse; **faire des ~s de bouche** to use a mouthwash ou an oral rinse **► bain de foule** walkabout; **prendre un ~ de foule** to mingle with the crowd, go on a walkabout **► bain linguistique** ou **de langue** : **il n'y a rien de tel que le ~ linguistique ou de langue pour apprendre l'anglais** there's nothing like total immersion as a way of learning English **► bains de mer** sea bathing (Brit) ou swimming **► bain moussant** bubble ou foam bath **► bain d'œil** ou **oculaire** (= soin) eye bath; (= liquide) eyewash **► bain de pieds** foot-bath **► bains publics** (public) baths **► bain à remous** whirlpool ou spa bath **► bains romains** Roman baths **► bain de siège** sitz bath; **prendre un ~ de siège** to have a sitz bath **► bain de soleil** (= corsage) sun top, halter; **robe ~ de soleil** sun dress; **prendre un ~ de soleil** to sunbathe; **les ~s de soleil lui sont déconseillés** he has been advised against sunbathing **► bain turc** Turkish bath **► bain de vapeur** steam bath

bain-marie (pl **bains-marie**) [bɛ̃maʀi] NM (hot water in) double boiler, bain-marie; **faire chauffer au ~** [+ sauce] to heat in a bain-marie ou a double boiler; [+ boîte de conserve] to immerse in boiling water

bains-douches [bɛ̃duʃ] NMPL **~ municipaux** public baths (with showers)

baïonnette [bajɔnɛt] NF (Élec, Mil) bayonet; **charger ~ au canon** to charge with fixed bayonets → **ampoule, douille**

baisable** [bɛzabl] ADJ fuckable**; **elle est tout à fait ~** I'd like to give her one*

baise** [bɛz] NF screwing**; **il ne pense qu'à la ~** all he ever thinks about is sex; **une bonne ~** a good screw** ou fuck**

baise-en-ville* [bɛzɑ̃vil] NM INV overnight bag

baisemain [bɛzmɛ̃] NM **il lui fit le ~** he kissed her hand; **le ~ ne se pratique plus** it is no longer the custom to kiss a woman's hand

baisement [bɛzmɑ̃] NM kissing; **~ de main** kissing of hands

baiser [beze] **[1]** NM kiss; **gros ~** (great) big kiss, smacking kiss*; **un ~ rapide (sur la joue)** a quick peck (on the cheek); **~ d'adieu** parting kiss; (en fin de lettre) **bons ~s** (with) love, much love; **~ de paix** kiss of peace; **~ de Judas** (Bible) kiss of Judas; (= trahison) Judas kiss; **donner ou faire/envoyer un ~ à qn** to give/blow a kiss to sb **[2]** ► conjug 1 **◄** VT **[a]** (frm) [+ main, visage, sol] to kiss **[b]**** to screw**, lay**, fuck**; (péj) **c'est une mal(-)baisée** she could do with a good lay** (= tromper, vaincre) to have*, screw**; **il a été baisé** ◊ **il s'est fait ~** he was really had*, he really got screwed** **[d]** (** = comprendre) **ses histoires, on y baise rien** you can't understand a fucking** ou bloody** (Brit) thing of what he says **[3]** VI** to screw**, fuck**; **il/elle baise bien** he's/she's a good fuck**

baiseur, -euse* [bɛzœʀ, øz] NM,F **c'est un sacré ~** (actif) he's always at it*; (doué) he's a really good screw**, he's really good in bed

baisse [bɛs] NF [température, prix, niveau, pouvoir d'achat] fall, drop (**de** in); [baromètre, pression] fall; (Bourse) fall; [popularité] decline, drop (**de** in); **~ de l'activité économique** downturn ou downswing in the economy; **« ~ sur les légumes »** (par surproduction) "vegetables down in price"; (en réclame) "special offer on vegetables"; **sans ~ de salaire** without salary cuts, without lowering salaries; **être à la ~** (Bourse) to be falling; **jouer à la ~** (Bourse) to play for a fall, go a bear; **réviser ou revoir les chiffres à la ~** to revise figures downwards; **être en ~** [prix, chômage, actions] to be going down, be dropping; [niveau] to be dropping;

[demande] to be slackening; [natalité] to be falling; [popularité] to be declining ou on the wane; **les affaires sont en ~** there's a slump in business, business is on a downturn; **son moral est en ~** his morale is getting lower and lower; **la production est en ~ de 8% par rapport à l'année dernière** production is 8% down on last year

baisser [bese] ► conjug 1 **◄** **[1]** VT **[a]** [+ objet] to lower; [+ store] to lower, pull down; [+ vitre] to lower, let down; (à la manivelle) to wind down; [+ col] to turn down; [+ rideau] to lower, ring down; **baisse la branche pour que je puisse l'attraper** pull the branch down so (that) I can reach it; **~ pavillon** (Naut) to lower ou strike the flag; (fig) to show the white flag, give in; (Théât) **une fois le rideau baissé** once the curtain was down **[b]** [+ main, bras] to lower; **~ la tête** to lower ou bend one's head; (de chagrin, honte) to hang ou bow one's head; [plantes] to wilt, droop; **baisse la tête, il y a une poutre** watch ou mind your head, there's a beam in the way; **~ les yeux** to look down, lower one's eyes; **elle entra, les yeux baissés** she came in with downcast eyes; **faire ~ les yeux à qn** to outstare sb, stare sb out ou out of countenance (frm); **~ le nez*** (de honte) to hang one's head; **~ le nez dans son livre*** to bury one's nose in one's book; **~ le nez dans son assiette*** to bend over one's plate; (fig) **~ les bras** to give up, throw in the towel* ou sponge* **[c]** [+ chauffage, éclairage, radio, son] to turn down; [+ voix] to lower; (Culin) **~ le feu** turn down ou lower the heat → **ton²** **[d]** [+ prix] to lower, bring down, reduce; **faire ~ la tension/le chômage** to reduce tension/unemployment **[e]** [+ mur] to lower

[2] VI **[a]** [température, prix] to fall, drop, go down; [baromètre] to fall; [pression] (Bourse) to drop, fall; [marée] to go out, ebb; [eaux] to subside, go down; [réserves, provisions] to run ou get low; [popularité] to decline; [soleil] to go down, sink → **estime** **[b]** [vue, mémoire, forces, santé] to fail, dwindle; [talent] to decline, wane; **le jour baisse** the light is failing ou dwindling; **il a beaucoup baissé ces derniers temps** he has really gone downhill recently

[3] se baisser VPR (pour ramasser) to bend down, stoop; (pour éviter) to duck; **il n'y a qu'à se ~ (pour les ramasser)** (lit) they're lying thick on the ground; (fig) they're there for the taking

baissier, -ière [besje, jɛʀ] (Bourse) **[1]** ADJ [marché, tendance] bear (épith), bearish (épith) **[2]** NM bear

bajoues [baʒu] NFPL [animal] cheeks, pouches; [personne] jowls, heavy cheeks

bakchich [bakʃiʃ] NM baksheesh

bakélite® [bakelit] NF Bakelite®

bakongo [bakɔ̃go] **[1]** ADJ Bakongo **[2]** **Bakongo** NMF Bakongo; **les Bakongos** the Bakongo (people)

Bakou [baku] N Baku

bal (pl **bals**) [bal] **[1]** NM (= réunion) dance; (habillé) ball; (= lieu) dance hall; **aller au ~** to go dancing; **ouvrir le ~** to lead ou open the dancing; (fig) **mener ou conduire le ~** to call the tune ou the shots*, say what goes* **[2]** COMP **► bal champêtre** open-air dance **► bal costumé** fancy dress ball (Brit), costume ball (US) **► bal des débutantes** ou **des débs*** coming-out ball **► bal masqué** masked ball **► bal musette** popular dance (to the accordion) **► bal populaire** ou **public** ≈ local dance ou hop* † **► bal du 14 juillet** Bastille Day dance (free and open to all) → *LE QUATORZE JUILLET*

balade* [balad] NF (à pied) walk, stroll; (en voiture) drive, run, ride; (à vélo) ride, run; (en *bateau*) ride, trip; **être en ~** to be out for a walk (*ou* a drive *etc*); **faire une ~ ◊ aller en ~** to go for a walk (*ou* a drive *etc*); **j'ai fait une ~ à ski** I went skiing *ou* for a ski

balader* [balade] ▸ conjug 1 ◂ 1 VT a (= *traîner*) [+ *chose*] to trail around, carry about; [+ *personne*] to trail around
b (= *promener*) [+ *personne*] to take for a walk; [+ *animal*] to walk, take for a walk; (*en voiture*) to take for a drive *ou* a ride
c (*Tennis*) **elle s'est fait ~ pendant le premier set** her opponent had her running all over the place in the first set; (*Rugby, Ftbl*) **ils nous ont baladés pendant la première mi-temps** they walked us all over us* in the first half
2 **se balader** VPR a (*à pied*) to go for a walk *ou* a stroll; (*en voiture*) to go for a drive *ou* ride *ou* run; (*à vélo*) to go for a ride *ou* run; (*en bateau*) to go for a ride; (= *traîner*) to traipse round; **pendant qu'ils se baladaient** while they were out for a walk (*ou* drive *etc*); **aller se ~ en Afrique** to go touring round Africa; **la lettre s'est baladée de bureau en bureau** the letter was sent *ou* shuttled around from one office to another
b (= *être en désordre*) **des câbles se baladent partout** there are cables trailing all over the place; **mes cassettes se sont baladées dans la valise** my tapes got knocked around my suitcase
c (* = *être très à l'aise*) **il s'est baladé en chimie** he sailed through his chemistry exam, his chemistry exam was a piece of cake* for him

baladeur, -euse [baladœʀ, øz] 1 ADJ wandering, roving; **avoir la main baladeuse** *ou* **les mains baladeuses** to have wandering *ou* groping* hands; **un micro ~ circulait dans le public** a microphone circulated round the audience
2 NM (= *magnétophone*) Walkman®, personal stereo 3 **baladeuse** NF (= *lampe*) inspection lamp

baladin† [baladɛ̃] NM wandering entertainer *ou* actor, strolling player†

balafon [balafɔ̃] NM balafon, African xylophone

balafre [balafʀ] NF (= *blessure au visage*) gash; (*intentionnelle*) slash; (= *cicatrice*) scar

balafrer [balafʀe] ▸ conjug 1 ◂ VT a (= *blesser au visage*) to gash; (*intentionnellement*) to slash, scar; **il s'est balafré** he gashed his face; **une cicatrice lui balafrait la joue** he had a scar running down his cheek b (= *enlaidir*) [+ *ville, paysage*] to scar; [+ *vitrine, bâtiment*] to deface; **de grandes lézardes balafrent les édifices** the buildings are scarred *ou* disfigured by huge cracks

balai [balɛ] 1 NM a (*gén*) broom, brush; [*bruyère, genêt*] broom; (*Élec*) brush; [*essuie-glace*] blade; **passer le ~** to sweep the floor, give the floor a sweep; **donner un coup de ~** (*lit*) to give the floor a (quick) sweep, sweep the floor; (*fig*) to make a clean sweep; **il y a eu un coup de ~ dans la société** they've made a clean sweep in the company, there have been across-the-board redundancies in the company; **du ~*** beat it!*, clear off!* b (* = *an*) **il a 80 ~s** he's 80 (years old) c (*Mus*) (wire) brush 2 COMP ▸ **balai de crin** horsehair brush ▸ **balai éponge** squeezy (*Brit*) *ou* sponge (*US*) mop ▸ **balai mécanique** carpet sweeper

balai-brosse (*pl* **balais-brosses**) [balɛbʀɔs] NM (long-handled) scrubbing brush

balaise‡ [balɛz] ADJ = **balèze**

balalaïka [balalaika] NF balalaika

balance¹ [balɑ̃s] 1 NF a (*gén*) scales; (*à deux plateaux*) pair of scales; (*à bascule*) weighing machine; (*pour salle de bains*) (bathroom) scales; (*pour cuisine*) (kitchen) scales; (*Chim, Phys*) balance; **monter sur la ~** to get on the scales
b (*loc*) **tenir la ~ égale entre deux rivaux** to hold the scales even between two rivals; **être en ~** [*proposition, sort*] to hang in the balance; [*candidat*] to be under consideration; **mettre dans la** *ou* **en ~ le pour et le contre** to weigh up the pros and cons; **mettre tout son poids dans la ~** to use one's power to tip the scales; **si on met dans la ~ son ancienneté** if you take his seniority into account
c (*Écon, Élec, Pol*) balance; **~ de l'actif et du passif** balance of assets and liabilities
d (*Astron*) **la Balance** Libra, the Balance; **être (de la) Balance** to be (a) Libra *ou* a Libran
e (*Pêche*) drop-net
2 COMP ▸ **balance automatique** electronic scales ▸ **balance commerciale** *ou* **du commerce** balance of trade ▸ **balance des comptes** balance of payments ▸ **balance électronique** electronic scales ▸ **balance des forces** balance of power ▸ **balance de ménage** kitchen scales ▸ **balance des paiements** = **balance des comptes** ▸ **balance des pouvoirs** balance of power ▸ **balance de précision** precision balance ▸ **balance (de) Roberval** (Roberval's) balance ▸ **balance romaine** steelyard

balance² [balɑ̃s] NF (*arg Crime*) stool pigeon*, grass‡ (*Brit*), fink‡ (*US*)

balancé, e [balɑ̃se] (*ptp de* **balancer**) ADJ **phrase bien/harmonieusement ~e** well-turned/nicely balanced phrase; **elle est bien ~e*** she's well put together*, she's got a good chassis* (*US*)

balancelle [balɑ̃sɛl] NF couch hammock (*Brit*), glider (*US*)

balancement [balɑ̃smɑ̃] NM a (= *mouvement*) [*corps*] sway(ing); [*bras*] swing(ing); [*bateau*] rocking, motion; [*hanches, branches*] swaying b (*Littérat, Mus*) balance

balancer [balɑ̃se] ▸ conjug 3 ◂ 1 VT a [+ *chose, bras, jambe*] to swing; [+ *bateau, bébé*] to rock; (*sur une balançoire*) to swing, push; **veux-tu que je te balance?** do you want me to push you? *ou* give you a push?; **le vent balançait les branches** the wind rocked the branches *ou* set the branches swaying
b (* = *lancer*) to fling, chuck*; **balance-moi mon crayon** throw *ou* chuck* me over my pencil (*Brit*), toss me my pencil; **~ qch à la tête de qn** to fling *ou* chuck* sth at sb's head
c (* = *dire*) [+ *méchanceté, insanités*] to hurl; **il m'a balancé ça en pleine figure** he just came out with it* straight to my face; **qu'est-ce qu'il leur a balancé!** he really let them have it!*
d (* = *se débarrasser de*) [+ *vieux meubles*] to chuck out* *ou* away*, toss out; **balance ça à la poubelle** chuck it* in the bin (*Brit*) *ou* the trash (*US*); **j'ai envie de tout ~** (*travail*) I feel like throwing *ou* chucking* it all in; **~ qn** (= *renvoyer*) to give sb the boot‡ *ou* the push‡ (*Brit*), chuck sb out*; **il s'est fait ~ de son club** he got kicked out* *ou* chucked out* of his club
e (= *équilibrer*) [+ *compte, phrases, paquets*] to balance; **~ le pour et le contre**† to weigh (up) the pros and cons; **tout bien balancé** (*frm*) all things considered
f (*arg Crime* = *dénoncer*) to finger‡, grass on‡
2 VI a († = *hésiter*) to waver, hesitate, dither; (*frm*) **entre les deux mon cœur balance** I'm torn between the two
b (= *osciller*) [*objet*] to swing
c (* = *être rythmé*) **ça balance!** it's rocking! *ou* swinging!
3 **se balancer** VPR a (= *osciller*) [*bras, jambes*] to swing; [*bateau*] to rock; [*branches*] to sway; [*personne*] (*sur une balançoire*) to swing, have a swing; (*sur une bascule*) to seesaw, play on a seesaw; **se ~ sur ses jambes** to sway about, sway from side to side; **ne te balance pas sur ta chaise!** don't tip back on your chair!; **se ~ sur ses ancres** to ride at an-

chor
b (* = *se jeter*) to throw o.s.; **il s'est balancé du 10ᵉ étage** he threw himself from the 10th floor
c **s'en ~*** (= *s'en ficher*) **je m'en balance** I don't give a damn* *ou* darn* (*US*) (about it), I couldn't care less (about it)

balancier [balɑ̃sje] NM [*pendule*] pendulum; [*montre*] balance wheel; [*équilibriste*] (balancing) pole; [*bateau*] outrigger

balançoire [balɑ̃swaʀ] NF (*suspendue*) swing; (*sur pivot*) seesaw, teeter-totter (*US*); **faire de la ~** to have a go on a (*ou* the) swing

balane [balan] NF acorn barnacle *ou* shell

balayage [balɛjaʒ] NM (= *nettoyage*) sweeping; (*Élec, Radio*) scanning; [*essuie-glace*] wipe; [*cheveux*] highlighting; **se faire faire un ~** to have highlights (put in one's hair), have one's hair highlighted

balayer [balɛje] ▸ conjug 8 ◂ VT a (= *ramasser*) [+ *poussière, feuilles mortes*] to sweep up, brush up b (= *nettoyer*) [+ *pièce*] to sweep (out); [+ *trottoir*] to sweep; [+ *pare-brise*] to wipe; **le vent balayait la plaine** the wind swept across *ou* scoured the plain; (*fig*) **ils feraient mieux de ~ devant leur porte** they should clean up their own back yard c (= *chasser*) [+ *feuilles mortes*] to sweep away; [+ *soucis, obstacles*] to brush aside, sweep away; [+ *objections*] to brush aside; **l'armée balayait tout sur son passage** the army swept aside all that lay in its path; **le gouvernement a été balayé** the government was swept out of office d (= *parcourir*) [*phares*] to sweep (across); [*vague, regard*] to sweep over; (*Élec, Radio*) [*radar*] to scan; [*tir*] to sweep (across)

balayette [balɛjɛt] NF small (hand)brush

balayeur, -euse [balɛjœʀ, øz] 1 NM,F roadsweeper (*Brit*), streetsweeper (*US*) 2 **balayeuse** NF (= *machine*) roadsweeping (*Brit*) *ou* streetsweeping (*US*) machine, roadsweeper (*Brit*), streetsweeper (*US*)

balayures [balɛjyʀ] NFPL sweepings

balbutiant, e [balbysjɑ̃, ɑ̃t] ADJ [*voix*] stammering; [*discours*] hesitant; [*science*] in its infancy (*attrib*); **une démocratie ~e** a fledgling democracy

balbutiement [balbysimɑ̃] NM (= *paroles confuses*) stammering, mumbling; [*bébé*] babbling; **les premiers ~s de l'enfant** the child's first faltering attempts at speech; (= *débuts*) **~s** beginnings; **cette science en est à ses premiers ~s** this science is still in its infancy

balbutier [balbysje] ▸ conjug 7 ◂ 1 VI [*bègue, personne ivre*] to stammer; [*bébé*] to babble 2 VT to stammer (out), falter out

balbuzard [balbyzaʀ] NM **~ (pêcheur)** osprey

balcon [balkɔ̃] NM (*Constr*) balcony; (*Théât*) **(premier) ~** dress *ou* lower circle, mezzanine (*US*); **deuxième ~** upper circle, balcony (*Brit*); **loge/fauteuil de ~** box/seat in the dress circle → **monde**

balconnet [balkɔnɛ] NM **(soutien-gorge à) ~** half-cup bra

baldaquin [baldakɛ̃] NM (= *dais*) baldaquin, canopy; [*lit*] tester, canopy → **lit**

Bâle [bɑl] N Basle, Basel

Baléares [baleaʀ] NFPL **les (îles) ~** the Balearic Islands, the Balearics; **en vacances aux ~** ≈ on holiday in Majorca (*ou* Minorca *ou* Ibiza)

baleine [balɛn] NF a (= *animal*) whale; **~ blanche/bleue/franche** white/blue/right whale; **~ à bosse** humpback whale; **rire** *ou* **se marrer comme une ~*** to laugh like a drain* b (= *fanon*) (piece of) whalebone, baleen; **soutien-gorge à/sans ~s** underwired/unwired bra; **~ de corset** (corset-)stay; **~ de parapluie** umbrella rib

baleiné, e [balene] ADJ [*col*] stiffened; [*corset*] boned; [*soutien-gorge*] (*gén*) boned; (*sous les bonnets*) underwired

baleineau (*pl* **baleineaux**) [balɛno] NM whale calf

baleinier, -ière [balenje, jɛʀ] ① ADJ whaling ② NM (= *pêcheur, bateau*) whaler ③ **baleinière** NF whaler, whale *ou* whaling boat

balèze [balɛz] ① ADJ (= *musclé*) brawny, strapping (*épith*); (= *excellent*) terrific*, great* (**en** at) ② NMF strapping fellow (*ou* woman etc)

Bali [bali] N Bali

balinais, e [baline, ɛz] ① ADJ Balinese ② **Balinais(e)** NM,F Balinese

balisage [balizaʒ] NM ⓐ (= *balises*) (*Naut*) beacons, buoys; (*Aviat*) beacons, runway lights; (*Aut*) (road) signs; (*Ski*) markers ⓑ (= *pose de balises*) (*Naut*) marking with buoys; [*chemin de randonnée, piste de ski*] marking out ⓒ (*Ordin*) [*texte*] tagging, marking up

balise¹ [baliz] NF ⓐ (*Naut*) beacon, (marker) buoy; (*Aviat*) beacon, runway light; (*Aut*) (road) marker; (*Ski*) marker; **~ radio** radio beacon; **~ de détresse** distress beacon ⓑ (*Ordin*) tag

balise² [baliz] NF (= *fruit*) canna fruit

baliser [balize] ▶conjug 1◀ ① VT ⓐ (*Naut*) to mark out with beacons *ou* buoys; (*Aviat*) to mark out with beacons *ou* buoys; [+ *sentier, piste de ski*] to mark out; **sentier balisé** way-marked footpath ⓑ (*fig*) **~ son avenir** to map out one's future; **~ le terrain** to prepare the ground; **~ le chemin** to pave the way; **nos chercheurs avancent sur un terrain déjà bien balisé** our researchers are exploring well-charted territory; (*Écon*) **un marché bien balisé** a well-defined market ⓒ (*Ordin*) [+ *texte*] to tag, mark up ② VI (* = *avoir peur*) to have the jitters*; **il balise pour son examen** he's freaking out* *ou* he's really worked up about his exam

baliseur [balizœʀ] NM (= *personne*) ≈ (Trinity House) buoy-keeper; (= *bateau*) ≈ Trinity House boat

balistique [balistik] ① ADJ ballistic; **expertise ~** ballistic test ② NF ballistics *sg*

baliveau (*pl* **baliveaux**) [balivo] NM (= *arbre*) sapling; (*Constr*) scaffold(ing) pole

baliverne [balivɛʀn] NF (= *propos*) fatuous remark; **dire des ~s** to talk nonsense *ou* twaddle; **s'amuser à des ~s** to fool around; **~(s)!**† balderdash!†, fiddlesticks!†

balkanique [balkanik] ADJ Balkan; **les États ~s** the Balkan States

balkanisation [balkanizasjɔ̃] NF (*Pol*) Balkanization; (*fig*) balkanization

balkaniser [balkanize] ▶conjug 1◀ VT (*Pol*) to Balkanize; (*fig*) to balkanize

Balkans [balkɑ̃] NMPL **les ~** the Balkans

ballade [balad] NF (= *poème court, Mus*) ballade; (= *poème long*) ballad

ballant, e [balɑ̃, ɑ̃t] ① ADJ **les bras ~s** with arms dangling, with swinging arms; **ne reste pas là, les bras ~s*** don't just stand there looking helpless; **les jambes ~es** with legs dangling ② NM (= *mou*) [*câble*] slack, play; [*chargement*] sway, roll; **avoir du ~** [*câble*] to be slack; [*chargement*] to be slack *ou* loose; **donner du ~ à une corde** to give some slack *ou* play to a rope

ballast [balast] NM (*Rail*) ballast, roadbed (*US*); (*Naut*) ballast tank

balle¹ [bal] NF ⓐ (= *projectile*) bullet; **~ dum-dum/explosive/traçante** dum-dum/explosive/tracer bullet; **~ en caoutchouc/de plastique** rubber/plastic bullet; **~ à blanc** blank; **~ perdue** stray bullet; **tirer à ~s réelles** to use live bullets; **finir avec douze ~s dans la peau*** to end up in front of a firing squad; **prendre une ~ dans la peau*** to get shot *ou* plugged*; **tué par ~s** shot dead ⓑ (*Sport*) ball; **~ de ping-pong/de golf** table tennis/golf ball; **jouer à la ~** to play (with a)

ball; **à toi la ~!** catch!; (*fig*) **la ~ est dans leur camp** the ball is in their court → **saisir** ⓒ (*Sport – coup*) shot, ball; **c'est une belle ~** that's a nice ball *ou* a good shot; (*Tennis, Ping-Pong*) **faire des** *ou* **quelques ~s** to knock the ball around a bit, have a knock-up (*Brit*); (*Tennis*) **~ de jeu/match/set** game/match/set point; **~ de service** service ball; **deuxième ~** second serve *ou* service; **c'est une ~ de 3 jeux à 2** it's game point at 2 games all ⓓ (* = *franc*) franc

balle² [bal] NF (*Agr, Bot*) husk, chaff

balle³ [bal] NF [*coton, laine*] bale

balle⁴* [bal] NF chubby face; **il a une bonne ~** he's got a jolly face

baller [bale] ▶conjug 1◀ VI [*bras, jambes*] to dangle, hang loosely; [*tête*] to hang; [*chargement*] to be slack *ou* loose

ballerine [bal(ə)ʀin] NF (= *danseuse*) ballerina, ballet dancer; (= *chaussure*) ballet shoe

ballet [balɛ] NM ⓐ (= *spectacle*) ballet; (= *musique*) ballet music; (= *compagnie*) **les Ballets russes** the Russian Ballet; **~ aquatique** water ballet; (*fig*) **~s roses/bleus** sexual orgies organized by paedophiles and involving young girls/boys ⓑ **~ diplomatique** flurry of diplomatic activity

ballon¹ [balɔ̃] ① NM ⓐ (*gén*) ball; **~ de football** football (*Brit*), soccer ball (*US*); **~ de rugby** rugby ball; **~ de basket** basketball; **~ de volley** volleyball; **jouer au ~** to play (with a) ball; **le ~ rond** (= *football*) soccer; **le ~ ovale** (= *rugby*) rugby, rugger* (*Brit*) ⓑ (= *jouet*) **~** (**en ou de baudruche**) balloon ⓒ (*Aviat*) balloon; **monter en ~** to go up in a balloon; **voyager en ~** to travel by balloon ⓓ (= *verre*) round wineglass; (*à cognac*) balloon *ou* brandy glass; **un ~ de rouge*** a glass of red wine ⓔ (* = *Alcootest*) **souffler dans le ~** to take a breath test *ou* Breathalyzer test®; **soufflez dans le ~, s'il vous plaît** blow in(to) the bag, please ⓕ (*Chim*) balloon ⓖ (*fig*) **avoir le ~*** (= *être enceinte*) to have a bun in the oven*, be up the spout* (*Brit*) ② COMP ▶ **ballon de barrage** barrage balloon ▶ **ballon captif** captive balloon ▶ **ballon dirigeable** airship ▶ **ballon d'eau chaude** hot-water tank ▶ **ballon d'essai** (*Mét*) pilot balloon; (= *test*) experiment (*to test reaction*), trial balloon (*US*); (*fig*) **lancer un ~ d'essai** to put out feelers, fly a kite (*Brit*), send out a trial balloon (*US*) ▶ **ballon d'oxygène** (*lit*) oxygen bottle; (*fig*) lifesaver; **cet argent a apporté un ~ d'oxygène à l'entreprise** the money has given the company a much-needed shot in the arm

ballon² [balɔ̃] NM (*Géog*) rounded mountain in the Vosges

ballonné, e [balɔne] (*ptp de* **ballonner**) ADJ [*ventre*] bloated, distended; **je suis** *ou* **je me sens ~** ◊ **j'ai le ventre ~** I feel bloated

ballonnement [balɔnmɑ̃] NM feeling of distension, flatulence; (*Vét*) bloat

ballonner [balɔne] ▶conjug 1◀ VT [+ *ventre*] to distend, to blow out; (*Vét*) [+ *animal*] to cause bloat in

ballonnet [balɔnɛ] NM (*gén, Aviat, Mét*) (small) balloon; (*Chir*) balloon

ballon-panier [balɔ̃panje] NM INV (*Can*) basketball

ballon-sonde (*pl* **ballons-sondes**) [balɔ̃sɔ̃d] NM meteorological *ou* weather *ou* pilot balloon

ballon-volant [balɔ̃vɔlɑ̃] NM INV (*Can*) volleyball

ballot [balo] ① NM ⓐ (= *paquet*) bundle, package ⓑ (* = *nigaud*) nitwit*, dumdum* ② ADJ silly; **tu es/c'est ~ de l'avoir oublié** you're/it's a bit silly *ou* daft (*Brit*) to have forgotten it

baliotin [balɔtɛ̃] NM **~ de chocolats** (small punnet-shaped) box of chocolates

ballottage [balɔtaʒ] NM (*Pol*) **il y a ~** there will have to be a second ballot, people will have to vote again; **M. Dupont est en ~** Mr Dupont has to stand again at (*Brit*) *ou* run again on (*US*) the second ballot; **être en ~ favorable** to stand a very good chance of winning at the second ballot

ballottement [balɔtmɑ̃] NM [*objet*] banging about, rolling around; [*tête, membres*] lolling; [*train*] jolting; [*poitrine*] bouncing; [*bateau*] tossing, bobbing; [*personne*] shaking

ballotter [balɔte] ▶conjug 1◀ ① VI [*objet*] to roll around, bang about; [*tête, membres*] to loll; [*poitrine*] to bounce; [*bateau*] to toss, bob about; [*train*] to jolt along ② VT (*gén pass*) ⓐ (= *secouer*) [+ *personne*] to shake about, jolt; [+ *bateau*] to toss (about); **on est ballotté dans ce train** you get shaken about *ou* thrown about in this train ⓑ (= *tirailler*) **ballotté par des choix difficiles** torn between difficult choices ⓒ (= *déplacer sans ménagement*) to shunt (around); **cet enfant a été ballotté entre plusieurs écoles** this child has been shifted around *ou* shunted around from school to school

ballottine [balɔtin] NF ≈ meat loaf (*made with poultry*)

ball-trap (*pl* **ball-traps**) [baltʀap] NM (= *lieu*) shooting ground; (= *sport*) clay-pigeon shooting, trap-shooting; (*avec 2 cibles*) skeet-shooting; (= *machine*) trap

balluchon [balyʃɔ̃] NM† bundle (of clothes), belongings; **faire son ~*** to pack up one's bags

balnéaire [balneɛʀ] ADJ swimming, bathing (*Brit*) → **station**

balnéothérapie [balneoteʀapi] NF balneotherapy

balourd, e [baluʀ, uʀd] ① ADJ (= *maladroit*) clumsy, oafish ② NM,F (= *lourdaud*) dolt, oaf ③ NM (*Tech*) unbalance

balourdise [baluʀdiz] NF ⓐ (= *maladresse*) clumsiness, oafishness; (= *manque de finesse*) oafishness, doltishness ⓑ (= *gaffe*) blunder, boob* (*Brit*)

balsa [balza] NM balsa (wood)

balsamier [balzamje] NM balsam tree

balsamine [balzamin] NF balsam

balsamique [balzamik] ADJ balsamic

balte [balt] ADJ [*pays, peuple*] Baltic; **les pays ~s** the Baltic States

balthazar [baltazaʀ] NM ⓐ († = *banquet*) feast, banquet ⓑ (= *bouteille*) balthazar ⓒ **Balthazar** Belshazzar

baltique [baltik] ① ADJ [*mer, région*] Baltic ② **Baltique** NF **la Baltique** the Baltic (Sea)

baluchon [balyʃɔ̃] NM = **balluchon**

balustrade [balystʀad] NF (*Archit*) balustrade; (= *garde-fou*) railing, handrail

balustre [balystʀ] NM ⓐ (*Archit*) baluster; [*siège*] spoke ⓑ (**compas à**) **~** bow(-spring) compass

balzacien, -ienne [balzasjɛ̃, jɛn] ADJ (= *qui appartient à Balzac*) of Balzac; (= *qui rappelle Balzac*) typical of Balzac

balzan, e [balzɑ̃, an] ① ADJ [*cheval*] with white stockings ② **balzane** NF (= *tache*) white stocking

Bamako [bamako] N Bamako

bambara [bɑ̃baʀa] ① ADJ Bambara ② NM (*Ling*) Bambara ③ **Bambara** NMF Bambara; **les Bambaras** the Bambara (people)

bambin [bɑ̃bɛ̃] NM small child, little kid*

bambochard, e [bɑ̃bɔʃaʀ, aʀd] ADJ, NM,F = **bambocheur, -euse**

bambocher† [bɑ̃bɔʃe] ▶conjug 1◀ VI (= *faire la noce*) to live it up*, have a wild time

bambocheur, -euse† [bɑ̃bɔʃœʀ, øz] ① ADJ

[*tempérament*] revelling **2** NM,F (= *noceur*) reveller

bambou [bãbu] NM **a** (= *plante*) bamboo; (= *canne*) bamboo (walking) stick → **pousse** **b** coup de ~* (= *insolation*) attraper un coup de ~† to get a touch of sunstroke*; **avoir le coup de ~** (= *être fatigué*) to be bushed* *ou* shattered* (*Brit*); (= *prix exorbitant*) **dans ce restaurant, c'est le coup de ~** they really fleece* you in that restaurant

bamboula* [bãbula] NF **faire la ~** to live it up*, have a wild time

bambouseraie [bãbuzʀɛ] NF bamboo plantation

ban [bã] NM **a** [*mariage*] ~s banns **b** [*applaudissements*] round of applause; [*tambour*] drum roll; [*clairon*] bugle call, fanfare; **faire un ~** to applaud *ou* cheer; **un ~ pour Marc Durand!** (*applaudissements*) (let's have) a big hand for* *ou* a round of applause for Marc Durand!; (*acclamations*) ≈ three cheers for Marc Durand! **c** (*Hist*) proclamation **d** (*loc*) (*Hist*) **être/mettre au ~ de l'Empire** to be banished/banish from the Empire; **être/mettre au ~ de la société** to be outlawed/outlaw from society; (*Hist*) **le ~ et l'arrière-~** the barons and vassals; **le ~ et l'arrière-~ de sa famille/de ses amis** all of *ou* every last one of his relatives/his friends

banal[1], e[1] (*mpl* **banals**) [banal] ADJ **a** (= *sans originalité*) [*roman, conversation, idée*] banal, trite; [*vie*] humdrum, banal; [*personne*] run-of-the-mill, ordinary; **un personnage peu ~** an unusual character; **ça, ce n'est pas ~!** that's rather out of the ordinary!; **haïr le ~** to hate what is banal *ou* what is trite **b** (= *courant*) [*nom*] commonplace; [*incident*] everyday (*épith*), commonplace; **il n'y a rien là que de très ~** there is nothing at all unusual *ou* out of the ordinary about that; **une grippe ~e** a common-or-garden case of flu; **quoi de plus ~ qu'un mariage?** what could be more mundane *ou* ordinary than a wedding? **c** (*Ordin*) general-purpose; **mémoire ~e** general-purpose storage

banal[2], e[2] (*mpl* **-aux**) [banal, o] ADJ (*Hist*) **four/moulin ~** communal *ou* village oven/mill

banalement [banalmã] ADV [*commencer, arriver*] in the most ordinary way

banalisation [banalizasjɔ̃] NF **a** **la ~ de la violence** the way in which violence has become a feature of everyday life; **la ~ des greffes** the fact that organ transplants are now quite commonplace *ou* widely practised **b** [*campus*] opening to the police

banaliser [banalize] ▸ *conjug 1* ◂ **1** VT **a** (+ *pratique*) (= *rendre courant*) to make commonplace; (= *minimiser*) to trivialize; **ce qui banalise la violence quotidienne** what makes life humdrum *ou* robs life of its excitement; **~ la violence** to make violence seem ordinary *ou* part of everyday life **b** (+ *campus*) to open to the police; (*Police*) **voiture banalisée** unmarked police car **c** (*Rail*) (+ *locomotive*) to man with several crews; (+ *voie*) to make two-way **2** **se banaliser** VPR [*pratiques*] to become commonplace; [*violence*] to become part of everyday life

banalité [banalite] NF **a** (= *caractère*) [*roman, conversation, idée*] banality, triteness; [*vie*] banality; [*personne*] ordinariness; [*incident*] triviality; **d'une ~ affligeante** appallingly trite **b** (= *propos*) truism, platitude, trite remark; **on a échangé des ~s** we made small talk, we talked about this and that

banane [banan] NF **a** (= *fruit*) banana; **~ plantain** plantain **b** (*Aut*) overrider **c** (*Coiffure*) quiff (*Brit*), pompadour (*US*) → **chignon** **d** (*arg Mil*) medal, decoration, gong* (*Brit*) **e** (*arg Aviat*) twin-rotor helicopter, chopper; **f** (= *sac*) hip bag, waist-bag (*Brit*), bum-bag* (*Brit*), fanny pack* (*US*) **g** (*Élec*)

(fiche-)banane banana plug **h** (* = *idiot*) ~! you silly twit!*, you dork!* (*US*)

bananeraie [bananʀɛ] NF banana plantation

bananier, -ière [bananje, jɛʀ] **1** ADJ banana (*épith*) **2** NM (= *arbre*) banana tree; (= *bateau*) banana boat

banc [bã] **1** NM **a** (= *siège*) seat, bench; ~ **public** park bench; ~ (**d'école**) (school) bench; **nous nous sommes connus sur les ~s de l'école** we've known each other since we were at school together; (*Pol*) **les ~s de l'opposition** the opposition benches **b** (*Géol*) (= *couche*) layer, bed; [*coraux*] reef; ~ **de vase** mudbank; ~ **de brouillard** (*gén*) fog patch; (*en mer*) fog bank; ~ **de brume** bank of mist; ~ **de glace** ice floe; **les ~s de Terre-Neuve** the Grand Banks of Newfoundland **c** [*poissons*] school, shoal (*Brit*) (**de** of) **d** (*Tech* = *établi*) (work) bench **2** COMP ▸ **banc des accusés** dock, bar; **être au ~ des accusés** to be in the dock ▸ **banc des avocats** bar ▸ **banc d'église** pew ▸ **banc d'essai** (*Tech*) test bed; (*fig*) testing ground, test bed; **mettre qch au ~ d'essai** to test sth out ▸ **banc d'huîtres** (= *huîtrière*) oyster bed; (*de restaurant*) oyster display ▸ **banc des ministres** ≈ government front bench ▸ **banc de musculation** weight *ou* exercise bench ▸ **banc de nage** thwart ▸ **banc de neige** (*Can*) snowdrift, snowbank ▸ **banc de sable** sandbank, sandbar ▸ **banc des témoins** (*Jur*) witness box (*Brit*), witness stand (*US*) ▸ **banc de touche** (substitutes') bench

bancable [bãkabl] ADJ bankable

bancaire [bãkɛʀ] ADJ [*système*] banking; **chèque ~** (bank) cheque (*Brit*) *ou* check (*US*)

bancal, e (*mpl* **bancals**) [bãkal] ADJ **a** [*personne*] (= *boiteux*) lame; (= *aux jambes arquées*) bandy-legged **b** [*table, chaise*] wobbly, rickety **c** [*idée, raisonnement*] shaky, unsound

bancarisé, e [bãkaʀize] ADJ (*Fin*) [*population, pays*] with banking facilities; **pays peu/fortement ~** country with few/extensive banking facilities

banco [bãko] NM (*Jeux*) banco; **faire ~** to go banco; (*fig*) ~ **!** you're on*!

banc-titre (*pl* **bancs-titres**) [bãtitʀ] NM (*Audiov*) caption stand

bandage [bãdaʒ] NM **a** (= *objet*) [*blessé*] bandage; [*roue*] (*en métal*) band, hoop; (*en caoutchouc*) tyre (*Brit*), tire (*US*); ~ **herniaire** surgical appliance, truss **b** (= *action*) [*blessé*] bandaging; [*ressort*] stretching; [*arc*] bending

bandana [bãdana] NM banda(n)na

bandant, e: [bãdã, ãt] ADJ [*film, livre*] sexy*; **elle est vachement ~e** she's a real turn-on*; **ce n'est pas très ~** it's not exactly thrilling

bande[1] [bãd] **1** NF **a** (= *ruban*) (*en tissu, métal*) band, strip; (*en papier*) strip; (*de sable*) strip, tongue; (*Ciné*) film; (*magnétophone*) tape; (*Presse*) wrapper; (*Méd*) bandage; ~ (**de mitrailleuse**) (ammunition) belt; ~ **de terre** strip *ou* tongue of land; **la ~ de Gaza** the Gaza strip **b** (= *dessin, motif*) stripe; [*chaussée*] line; [*assiette*] band; (*Hér*) bend **c** (*Billard*) cushion; **jouer la ~** to play (the ball) off the cushion; **faire/obtenir qch par la ~** to do/get sth by devious means *ou* in a roundabout way; **apprendre qch par la ~** to hear of sth indirectly *ou* through the grapevine* **d** (*Naut*) list; **donner de la ~** to list **e** (*Élec, Phys, Radio*) band; ~ (**de fréquence**) waveband, frequency band; **sur la ~ AM/FM** on AM/FM **2** COMP ▸ **bande d'absorption** (*Phys*) absorption band ▸ **bande amorce** [*pellicule, cassette*] leader ▸ **bande d'arrêt d'urgence** hard shoulder, berm (*US*) ▸ **bande chromosomique** chromosome band ▸ **bande des-**

sinée comic strip, strip cartoon (*Brit*); (= *livre*) comic book ▸ **bande d'émission** emission band ▸ **bande d'essai** (*Photo*) test strip ▸ **bande étalon** (*Photo*) reference strip, test gauge ▸ **bande gaufrée** (*Photo*) apron ▸ **bande magnétique** magnetic tape ▸ **bande de manœuvre** (*Ordin*) scratch tape ▸ **bande molletière** puttee ▸ **bande originale** (original) soundtrack ▸ **bande passante** pass band ▸ **bande perforée** punched *ou* perforated *ou* paper tape ▸ **bande protectrice** (*Photo*) duplex paper ▸ **bande de roulement** (*pneu*) tread ▸ **bandes rugueuses** rumble strips ▸ **bande sonore** (*Ciné*) soundtrack; (*Aut*) rumble strip ▸ **bande Velpeau®** crêpe bandage (*Brit*), Ace® bandage (*US*) ▸ **bande vidéo** videotape

┌─────────────────────────────┐
│ **BANDE DESSINÉE** │
└─────────────────────────────┘

The **bande dessinée** *or* **BD** *enjoys a huge following in France and Belgium amongst adults as well as children. The strip cartoon is accorded both literary and artistic status, and is known as "le huitième art". An international strip cartoon festival takes place in the French town of Angoulême at the end of January each year.*

bande[2] [bãd] NF **a** (= *groupe*) band, group; **une ~ d'amis** a group of friends; **ils sont partis en ~** they set off in a group, they all went off together **b** (= *gang*) [*pirates*] band; [*voleurs*] gang, band; ~ **armée** armed gang *ou* band; **il ne fait pas partie de leur ~** he's not in their crowd *ou* gang; (*Pol*) **la ~ des Quatre** the Gang of Four; **faire ~ à part** to go off on one's own **c** (*•: péj*) ~ **de** bunch of*, pack of*; ~ **d'imbéciles!** pack of idiots!*, bunch of fools!*; **c'est une ~ de paresseux** they're a lazy bunch* *ou* crowd* *ou* lot (*Brit*) **d** [*oiseaux*] flock; [*loups, chiens*] pack; [*lions, singes*] troop

bandé, e [bãde] (*ptp de* **bander**) ADJ (*Hér*) bendy

bande-annonce (*pl* **bandes-annonces**) [bãdanɔ̃s] NF (*Ciné*) trailer

bandeau (*pl* **bandeaux**) [bãdo] NM **a** (= *ruban*) headband, bandeau; (= *pansement*) head bandage; (*pour les yeux*) blindfold; **mettre un ~ à qn** to blindfold sb; **avoir un ~ sur l'œil** to wear an eye patch; **avoir un ~ sur les yeux** to be blind **b** (*Coiffure*) **porter les cheveux en ~x** to wear one's hair parted down the middle and looped back at the sides **c** (*Archit*) string course **d** [*livre*] publicity strip

bandelette [bãdlɛt] NF strip of cloth, (narrow) bandage; [*momie*] wrapping, bandage

bander [bãde] ▸ *conjug 1* ◂ **1** VT **a** (= *entourer*) (+ *genou, plaie*) to bandage; ~ **les yeux à qn** to blindfold sb; **les yeux bandés** blindfold(ed) **b** (= *tendre*) (+ *corde*) to strain, tauten; (+ *arc*) to bend; (+ *ressort*) to stretch, tauten; (+ *muscles*) to tense **2** VI: to have a hard-on:

banderille [bãdʀij] NF banderilla

banderole [bãdʀɔl] NF (= *drapeau*) banderole; ~ **publicitaire** advertising streamer

bande-son (*pl* **bandes-son**) [bãdsɔ̃] NF (*Ciné*) soundtrack

bandit [bãdi] NM (= *brigand*) bandit; (= *voleur*) thief; (= *assassin*) murderer; (= *escroc*) crook, shark*; (* = *enfant*) rascal; ~ **armé** gunman, armed gangster; ~ **de grand chemin** highwayman; ~ **manchot†** one-armed bandit

banditisme [bãditism] NM crime (*NonC*); **le grand ~** organized crime; (*fig*) **900 F pour cette réparation, c'est du ~!** 900 francs for this repair job — it's daylight robbery!

bandonéon [bãdoneɔ̃] NM bandoneon

bandoulière [bãduljɛʀ] NF (*gén*) shoulder strap; (*Mil*) bandoleer, bandolier; **en ~** slung across the shoulder

bang [bɑ̃g] **1** NM INV [*avion supersonique*] supersonic bang, sonic boom **2** EXCL bang!, crash!

Bangkok [bɑ̃kɔk] N Bangkok

bangladais, e [bɑ̃ɡlade, ɛz] **1** ADJ Bangladeshi **2 Bangladais(e)** NM,F Bangladeshi

Bangladesh [bɑ̃ɡladeʃ] NM Bangladesh

Bangui [bɑ̃ɡi] N Bangui

banian [banjɑ̃] ADJ banyan, banian; **figuier ~** banyan tree

banjo [bɑ̃(d)ʒo] NM banjo

Banjul [bɑ̃ʒul] N Banjul

banlieue [bɑ̃ljø] NF suburbs, outskirts; **proche/moyenne/grande ~** inner *ou* near/intermediate/outer suburbs; **Paris et sa ~** Greater Paris; **la grande ~ de Paris** the outer suburbs of Paris, the commuter belt of Paris; **la ~ rouge** the Communist-controlled suburbs of Paris; **une ~ ouvrière** a working-class suburb; **habiter en ~** to live in the suburbs; **de ~** [*maison, ligne de chemin de fer*] suburban (*épith*); [*train*] commuter (*épith*)

> ┌─ **BANLIEUE** ─┐
>
> The connotations of suburbia in France are quite different from those that prevail in many English-speaking countries. For historical, economic and social reasons, many suburbs of large French towns have become severely depressed in recent years; the word **banlieue** thus tends to conjure up images of violence and urban decay, and has similar connotations to the English term "inner city". Young people in many such suburbs have developed a strong cultural identity that includes rap music and "verlan". → VERLAN

banlieusard, e [bɑ̃ljøzaʀ, aʀd] NM,F (suburban) commuter, suburbanite (*hum*)

banne [ban] NF **a** (= *toile*) canopy **b** (= *panier*) wicker basket

bannette [banɛt] NF **a** (*Naut* = *couchette*) bunk **b** (= *corbeille*) small wicker basket

banni, e [bani] (*ptp de* **bannir**) NM,F exile

bannière [banjɛʀ] NF **a** (= *drapeau*) banner; **la ~ étoilée** the Star-Spangled Banner; **se battre** *ou* **se ranger sous la ~ de qn** to fight on sb's side *ou* under sb's banner **b** (* = *pan de chemise*) **se promener en ~** to be walking round with one's shirt-tail hanging out

bannir [baniʀ] ▸ conjug 2 ◂ VT [+ *citoyen*] to banish; [+ *pensée*] to banish, dismiss; [+ *mot, sujet, aliment*] to banish, exclude (**de** from); [+ *usage*] to prohibit, put a ban on

bannissement [banismɑ̃] NM banishment

banque [bɑ̃k] **1** NF **a** (= *établissement*) bank; **il a 3 millions en ~** he's got 3 million in the bank; **mettre des chèques en ~** to bank cheques; **la grande ~ appuie sa candidature** the big banks are backing his candidature; **la Banque de France/d'Angleterre** the Bank of France/of England **b** (= *activité, métier*) ~ banking **c** (*Jeux*) bank; **tenir la ~** to be (the) banker **d** (*Méd*) **~ des yeux/du sang/du sperme/d'organes** eye/blood/sperm/organ bank

2 COMP ▸ **banque d'affaires** merchant bank ▸ **banque alimentaire** food bank ▸ **banque centrale** central bank ▸ **Banque centrale européenne** European Central Bank ▸ **banque de dépôt** deposit bank ▸ **banque directe** (= *activité*) direct banking ▸ **banque de données** data bank ▸ **banque d'émission** bank of issue ▸ **banque d'escompte** discount bank ▸ **Banque européenne d'investissement** European Investment Bank ▸ **Banque européenne pour la reconstruction et le développement** European Bank for Reconstruction and Development ▸ **banque d'images** picture library ▸ **Banque internationale pour la reconstruction et le développement** International Bank for Reconstruction and Development ▸ **Banque mondiale** World Bank ▸ **Banque des règlements internationaux** Bank for International Settlements

banquer* [bɑ̃ke] ▸ conjug 1 ◂ VI to cough up*, stump up* (*Brit*)

banqueroute [bɑ̃kʀut] NF (*Fin*) (fraudulent) bankruptcy; (*Pol*) bankruptcy; (*littér*) failure; **faire ~** to go bankrupt

banqueroutier, -ière [bɑ̃kʀutje, jɛʀ] NM,F (fraudulent) bankrupt

banquet [bɑ̃kɛ] NM dinner; (*d'apparat*) banquet

banqueter [bɑ̃k(ə)te] ▸ conjug 4 ◂ VI (*lit*) to banquet; (= *festoyer*) to feast

banquette [bɑ̃kɛt] NF **a** [*train*] seat; [*auto*] (bench) seat; [*restaurant*] (wall) seat; [*piano*] (duet) stool; [*Théât*] **jouer devant les ~s** to play to an empty house; (*dans un bal*) **faire ~** to be a wallflower **b** (*Archit*) window seat **c** (*Mil*) **~ de tir** banquette, fire-step **d** (= *talus*) berm(e); (= *chemin*) path

banquier [bɑ̃kje] NM (*Fin, Jeux*) banker

banquise [bɑ̃kiz] NF ice field; (*flottante*) ice floe

bantou, e [bɑ̃tu] **1** ADJ Bantu **2** NM (*Ling*) Bantu **3 Bantou(e)** NM,F Bantu

bantoustan [bɑ̃tustɑ̃] NM Bantustan

banyuls [banjuls, banjyls] NM Banyuls (*sweet fortified wine drunk as an apéritif*)

banzaï* [bɑ̃(d)zaj] EXCL bingo!

baobab [baɔbab] NM baobab

baoulé, e [baule] **1** ADJ Baoule **2 Baoulé(e)** NM,F Baoule; **les Baoulés** the Baoule people

baptême [batɛm] **1** NM **a** (= *sacrement*) baptism; (= *cérémonie*) christening, baptism; **donner le ~ à** to baptize, christen; **recevoir le ~** to be baptized *ou* christened **b** [*cloche*] blessing, dedication; [*navire*] naming, christening **2** COMP ▸ **baptême de l'air** first flight ▸ **baptême du feu** baptism of fire ▸ **baptême de la ligne** (*Naut*) (first) crossing of the line ▸ **baptême du sang** (*littér*) baptism of blood

baptiser [batize] ▸ conjug 1 ◂ VT **a** (*Rel*) to baptize, christen; **faire ~ un enfant** to have a child baptized *ou* christened **b** [+ *cloche*] to bless, dedicate; [+ *navire*] to name, christen **c** (= *appeler*) to call, christen, name; **on le baptisa Paul** he was christened Paul; **on baptisa la rue du nom du maire** the street was named after the mayor **d** (* = *surnommer*) to christen, dub; (*hum*) **la pièce qu'il baptisait pompeusement salon** the room which he pompously dubbed the drawing room **e*** [+ *vin, lait*] to water down

baptismal, e [batismal, o] ADJ (*mpl* **-aux**) baptismal

baptisme [batism] NM baptism

baptiste [batist] ADJ, NMF Baptist

baptistère [batistɛʀ] NM baptistry

baquet [bakɛ] NM tub → **siège¹**

bar¹ [baʀ] NM (= *établissement, comptoir*) bar; **~ américain** cocktail bar; **~ à vin(s)/à huîtres** wine/oyster bar; **~ à bière(s)** bar specializing in a wide variety of beers

bar² [baʀ] NM (= *poisson*) bass

bar³ [baʀ] NM (*Phys*) bar

Barabbas [barabas] NM Barabbas

barachois [baʀaʃwa] NM (*Can*) lagoon

baragouin* [baʀaɡwɛ̃] NM gibberish, double Dutch

baragouinage* [baʀaɡwinaʒ] NM (= *façon de parler*) gibbering; (= *propos*) gibberish, double Dutch

baragouiner* [baʀaɡwine] ▸ conjug 1 ◂ **1** VI to gibber, talk gibberish *ou* double Dutch **2** VT [+ *langue*] to speak badly; [+ *discours, paroles*] to jabber out, gabble; **il baragouine un peu l'espagnol** he can speak a bit of Spanish; (*péj*) **qu'est-ce qu'il baragouine ?** what's he jabbering on about?*

baragouineur, -euse* [baʀaɡwinœʀ, øz] NM,F jabberer

baraka* [baraka] NF luck; **avoir la ~** to be lucky

baraque [baʀak] NF **a** (= *cabane*) shed, hut; (= *boutique*) stand, stall; **~ foraine** fairground stall **b** * (= *maison*) place*, shack*; (= *appartement*) place*; (*péj* = *entreprise*) dump*, hole*; **une belle ~** a smart place*; **quand je suis rentré à la ~** when I got back to my place*; **quelle (sale) ~ !** what a lousy dump!*, what a hole!* → **casser** **c** (** = *homme*) burly *ou* beefy* guy

baraqué, e* [baʀake] ADJ hefty, well-built

baraquement [baʀakmɑ̃] NM **~(s)** group of huts; (*Mil*) camp

baratin* [baʀatɛ̃] NM (= *boniment*) sweet talk*, smooth talk*; (= *verbiage*) chatter, hot air*; (*Comm*) patter*, sales talk, sales pitch; **assez de ~ !** cut the cackle!* *ou* the chat!* (*Brit*); (*gén*) **faire son** *ou* **du ~ à qn** to sweet-talk sb*, chat sb up* (*Brit*), feed sb some lines* (*US*); (*Comm*) **faire son** *ou* **le ~ à un client** to give a customer the sales talk *ou* pitch* *ou* patter*; **avoir du ~** to have all the patter*, be a smooth talker

baratiner* [baʀatine] ▸ conjug 1 ◂ VT **~ qn** (= *amadouer*) to sweet-talk sb*, chat sb up* (*Brit*); (= *draguer*) to chat sb up* (*Brit*), feed sb some lines* (*US*); **~ le client** to give a customer the sales talk *ou* pitch* *ou* patter* **2** VI (= *bavarder*) to chatter, natter* (*Brit*)

baratineur, -euse* [baʀatinœʀ, øz] **1** NM,F (= *beau parleur, menteur*) smooth talker; (= *bavard*) gasbag*, windbag* **2** NM (= *dragueur*) smooth talker

baratte [baʀat] NF [*beurre*] churn

baratter [baʀate] ▸ conjug 1 ◂ VT to churn

barbacane [baʀbakan] NF (= *bastion*) barbican; (= *meurtrière*) loophole; (= *drain*) weeper

Barbade [baʀbad] NF **la ~** Barbados

barbadien, -ienne [baʀbadjɛ̃, ɛn] **1** ADJ Barbadian **2 Barbadien(ne)** NM,F Barbadian

barbant, e* [baʀbɑ̃, ɑ̃t] ADJ boring, deadly dull; **qu'il est/que c'est ~ !** what a bore he/it is!

barbaque* [baʀbak] NF (*péj*) meat

barbare [baʀbaʀ] **1** ADJ [*invasion, peuple*] barbarian, barbaric; (*péj*) [*mœurs, musique, crime*] barbaric, barbarous **2** NM (*Hist, fig*) barbarian

barbarement [baʀbaʀmɑ̃] ADV barbarously, barbarically

barbaresque [baʀbaʀɛsk] ADJ (*Hist = d'Afrique du Nord*) Barbary Coast (*épith*); **les États ~s** the Barbary Coast

Barbarie [baʀbaʀi] NF (*Hist*) **la ~** the Barbary Coast

barbarie [baʀbaʀi] NF (= *manque de civilisation*) barbarism; (= *cruauté*) barbarity, barbarousness

barbarisme [baʀbaʀism] NM (*Gram*) barbarism

barbe¹ [baʀb] **1** NF **a** [*personne*] beard; **une ~ de 3 mois** 3 months' (growth of) beard; **il a une ~ de 3 jours** he's got 3 days' stubble on his chin; **sans ~** [*adulte*] clean-shaven, beardless; [*adolescent*] (= *imberbe*) beardless; **il a de la ~ (au menton)** [*adulte*] he needs a shave; [*adolescent*] he already has a few hairs on his chin; **avoir une ◊ porter la** *ou* **une ~** to have a beard; **faire la ~ à qn** to trim sb's beard; (*hum*) **il n'a pas encore de ~ au menton et il croit tout savoir** he's still in short pants *ou* he's still wet behind the ears* and he thinks he knows it all **b** [*chèvre, singe, oiseau*] beard **c** [*plume*] barb; [*poisson*] barbel; [*orge*] beard

(*NonC*); **~s** whiskers
[d] (= *aspérités*) **~s** [*papier*] ragged edge; [*métal*] jagged edge
[e] (*loc*) **à la ~ de qn** under sb's nose; **dérober qch à la ~ de qn** to take* sth from under sb's nose; **vieille ~*** old stick-in-the-mud*, old fogey*; **marmonner dans sa ~** to mumble *ou* mutter into one's beard; **rire dans sa ~** to laugh up one's sleeve; **la ~!*** damn (it)!*, blast!* (*Brit*); **il faut que j'y retourne, quelle ~!*** I've got to go back — what a drag!*; **oh toi, la ~!*** oh shut up, you!*
[2] COMP ► **barbe de capucin** wild chicory ► **barbe à papa** candy-floss (*Brit*), cotton candy (*US*)

barbe² [barb] NM (*Zool*) (**cheval**) **~** barb

barbeau (*pl* **barbeaux**) [barbo] NM (*Zool*) barbel; (*Bot*) cornflower; (‡ = *souteneur*) pimp, ponce

Barbe-Bleue [barbəblø] NM Bluebeard

barbecue [barbəkju] NM (= *repas, cuisine*) barbecue; (= *matériel*) barbecue set; **faire un ~** to have a barbecue; **faire cuire qch au ~** to barbecue sth

barbelé, e [barbəle] ADJ, NM (**fil de fer**) **~** barbed wire (*NonC*); **les ~s** the barbed wire fence *ou* fencing; **s'égratigner après les ~s** to get scratched on the barbed wire; (*fig*) **derrière les ~s** [*prisonnier*] in a prison camp

barber* [barbe] ►conjug 1◄ [1] VT to bore stiff*, bore to tears* [2] **se barber** VPR to be bored stiff*, be bored to tears* (**à faire** doing)

Barberousse [barbəRus] NM Barbarossa

barbet¹ [barbε] NM (**rouget**) **~** red mullet, goatfish (*US*)

barbet² [barbε] NM (**chien**) **~** water spaniel

barbiche [barbiʃ] NF goatee (beard)

barbichette* [barbiʃεt] NF (small) goatee (beard)

barbichu, e [barbiʃy] [1] ADJ [*personne*] with a goatee (beard) [2] NM man with a goatee (beard)

barbier [barbje] NM†† barber; (*Can*) (men's) hairdresser

barbillon [barbijɔ̃] NM [a] [*plume, hameçon*] barb; [*poisson*] barbel; **~s** [*bœuf, cheval*] barbs [b] (*Zool = petit barbeau*) (small) barbel

barbiturique [barbityRik] [1] ADJ barbituric [2] NM barbiturate

barbon [barbɔ̃] NM (†† *ou péj*) (**vieux**) **~** greybeard, old fogey*

barbotage [barbɔtaʒ] NM [a] (* = *vol*) filching*, pinching* (*Brit*) [b] (*dans l'eau*) paddling (*en éclaboussant*) splashing about; [*canard*] dabbling [c] (*dans la boue*) paddling *ou* squelching (*Brit*) around [d] [*gaz*] bubbling

barboter [barbɔte] ►conjug 1◄ [1] VT (* = *voler*) to pinch* (*Brit*), whip* (**à** from, off); **elle lui a barboté son briquet** she's filched* his lighter [2] VI [a] (*dans l'eau*) to paddle; (*en éclaboussant*) to splash about; [*canard*] to dabble; (*dans la boue*) to paddle *ou* squelch (*Brit*) around [b] [*gaz*] to bubble

barboteur, -euse¹ [barbɔtœR, øz] [1] ADJ **il est (du genre) ~*** ◊ **c'est un ~** he's a bit light-fingered (*Brit*) *ou* sticky-fingered (*US*) [2] NM (*Chim*) bubble chamber

barboteuse² [barbɔtøz] NF (= *vêtement*) rompers

barbouillage [barbujaʒ] NM [a] (= *peinture*) daub; (= *écriture*) scribble, scrawl; **feuille couverte de ~** sheet of paper covered with scrawls *ou* scribblings [b] (= *action de peindre*) daubing; (= *action d'écrire*) scribbling, scrawling

barbouille* [barbuj] NF (*péj*) painting; (*hum*) **il fait de la ~** he does a bit of painting

barbouiller [barbuje] ►conjug 1◄ [1] VT [a] (= *couvrir, salir*) to smear, daub (**de** with), cover (**de** with, in); **il a le visage tout barbouillé de chocolat** he's got chocolate (smeared) all

over his face, he's got his face all covered in chocolate
[b] (*péj = peindre*) [+ *mur*] to daub *ou* slap paint on; **il barbouille (des toiles) de temps en temps** he does a bit of painting from time to time
[c] (*péj = écrire, dessiner*) to scribble (**sur** on); **~ une feuille de dessins** to scribble *ou* scrawl drawings on a piece of paper; **~ du papier** to cover a piece of paper with scrawls, scrawl all over a piece of paper; **~ un slogan sur un mur** to daub a slogan on a wall
[d] **~ l'estomac** to upset the stomach; **être barbouillé** ◊ **avoir l'estomac barbouillé** to feel queasy *ou* sick
[2] **se barbouiller** VPR **se ~ qch** to smear o.s. with sth; **il s'est barbouillé de confiture** he's smeared jam all over his face

barbouilleur, -euse [barbujœR, øz] NM,F (*péj*) (= *artiste*) dauber; (= *peintre en bâtiment*) bad *ou* slapdash painter; **~ de papier** hack (writer)

barbouillis [barbuji] NM (= *écriture*) scribble, scrawl; (= *peinture*) daub

barbouze* [barbuz] NM *ou* NF [a] (= *barbe*) beard [b] (= *policier*) secret (government) police agent; (= *garde du corps*) bodyguard

barbu, e [barby] [1] ADJ [*personne*] bearded; (*Bio*) barbate [2] NM bearded man, man with a beard; (*hum ou péj = islamiste*) Islamic fundamentalist [3] **barbue** NF (*Zool*) brill

barcarolle [barkaRɔl] NF barcarolle

barcasse [barkas] NF boat

Barcelone [barsəlɔn] N Barcelona

barda* [barda] NM gear*; (*Mil*) kit; **il a tout un ~ dans la voiture** he's got a whole load* of stuff in the car

bardage [bardaʒ] NM (*Constr*) weatherboarding, cladding (*Brit*), siding (*US*)

bardane [bardan] NF burdock

barde¹ [bard] NM (= *poète*) bard

barde² [bard] NF (*Culin, Mil*) bard

bardeau¹ (*pl* **bardeaux**) [bardo] NM [*toit*] shingle

bardeau² (*pl* **bardeaux**) [bardo] NM = **bardot**

barder [barde] ►conjug 1◄ [1] VT [a] (*Culin*) to bard [b] (*Mil*) [+ *cheval*] to bard; **bardé de fer** [*cheval*] barded; [*soldat*] armour-clad; [*porte*] with iron bars; **poitrine bardée de décorations** chest bedecked with medals; **bardé de diplômes** with a whole string *ou* array of qualifications [c] (*fig*) **être bardé** to be immune (**contre** to) [2] VB IMPERS* **ça va ~** things are going to get hot, all hell is going to break loose; **ça a bardé!** (*dans une réunion*) the sparks really flew!; (*dans les rues*) things got pretty hot!

bardot [bardo] NM hinny

barème [barεm] NM (= *table de référence*) table, list; (= *tarif*) (*Comm*) scale of charges, price list; (*Rail*) fare schedule; **~ de l'impôt** tax scale; (*Scol*) **~ de correction** marking (*Brit*) *ou* grading (*US*) scheme; **hors ~** off the (salary) scale (*attrib*)

barge¹ [barʒ] NF (= *bateau*) barge; (= *meule*) (rectangular) haystack

barge²* [barʒ] ADJ = **barjo(t)**

barguigner [barɡiɲe] ►conjug 1◄ VI (*littér ou hum*) **sans ~** without shilly-shallying

baril [baRi(l)] NM [*pétrole*] barrel; [*vin*] barrel, cask; [*poudre*] keg, cask; [*harengs*] barrel; [*lessive*] drum

barillet [baRijε] NM [a] (*Tech*) [*serrure, revolver*] cylinder; [*pendule*] barrel; **serrure à ~** cylinder *ou* Yale® lock [b] (= *petit baril*) small barrel *ou* cask

bariolage [baRjɔlaʒ] NM (= *résultat*) riot *ou* medley of colours; (= *action*) daubing

bariolé, e [baRjɔle] (*ptp de* **barioler**) ADJ [*vêtement*] many-coloured, rainbow-coloured,

gaudy (*péj*); [*groupe*] colourfully dressed, gaily coloured

barioler [baRjɔle] ►conjug 1◄ VT to splash *ou* daub bright colours on, streak with bright colours

barjo(t)* [baRʒo] ADJ nuts*, crazy*, barmy* (*Brit*); **bande de barjots!** bunch of nutcases*!

barmaid [barmεd] NF barmaid

barman [barman] (*pl* **barmans** *ou* **barmen** [barmεn]) NM barman, bartender (*surtout US*)

bar-mitsva [barmitsva] NF INV Bar Mitzvah

barnache [barnaʃ], **barnacle** [barnakl] NF = **bernache**

baromètre [barɔmεtR] NM (*lit, fig*) barometer; **le ~ baisse** the glass *ou* barometer is falling; **le ~ est au beau fixe/à la pluie** the barometer is set (at) fair/is pointing to rain; (*fig*) **le ~ est au beau (fixe)*** things are looking good*; **~ enregistreur/anéroïde** recording/aneroid barometer

barométrique [barɔmetRik] ADJ barometric(al)

baron¹ [barɔ̃] NM [a] (= *titre*) baron → **Monsieur** [b] (*fig = magnat*) baron, lord; **les ~s de la presse** the press barons *ou* lords

baron² [barɔ̃] NM **~ d'agneau** baron of lamb

baronnage [barɔnaʒ] NM (= *titre*) barony; (= *corps des barons*) baronage

baronne [barɔn] NF baroness

baronnet [barɔnε] NM baronet

baronnie [barɔni] NF barony

baroque [barɔk] [1] ADJ [*idée*] weird, strange, wild; (*Archit, Art, Mus*) baroque; **perle ~** baroque pearl [2] NM baroque

barotraumatisme [barotRomatism] NM barotrauma

baroud [baRud] NM (*arg Mil*) fighting; **~ d'honneur** last-ditch struggle, gallant last stand

baroudeur [baRudœR] NM (*arg Mil*) firebrand, fighter; **c'est un ~** he knocks about* *ou* travels around a lot

barouf* [baRuf(lə)] NM (= *vacarme*) row*, din*, racket*; **faire du ~** to create a racket*, make a row*; (= *protester*) to kick up a fuss* *ou* stink*

barque [bark] NF small boat, small craft; **~ à moteur** (small) motorboat; **~ de pêche** small fishing boat; **il mène bien sa ~** he's doing alright for himself, he manages his affairs very well; (*fig*) **charger la ~** (= *exagérer*) to overdo it

barquette [barkεt] NF [a] (= *tarte*) pastry boat, small tart [b] (= *récipient*) container; (*pour fruits*) punnet, carton

barracuda [baRakyda] NM barracuda

barrage [baRaʒ] NM [a] [*rivière, lac*] dam, barrage; (*à fleur d'eau*) **~ de retenue** flood barrier; **~ flottant** floating boom *ou* barrier [b] (= *barrière*) barrier; (*d'artillerie, de questions*) barrage; **~ de police** (police) roadblock; (= *cordon d'agents*) police cordon; (= *chevaux de frise*) (police) barricade; **établir un ~ (routier)** [*manifestants*] to set up a roadblock; **faire ~ à** to hinder, stand in the way of; **il y a eu un ~ de la direction** the management has put up a barrier; (*Sport*) **match de ~** relegation match [c] (*Cartes*) pre-emptive bid, pre-empt

barre [bar] [1] NF [a] (*gén = tige, morceau*) bar; (*de fer*) rod, bar; (*de bois*) piece, rod; (*d'or*) bar; (*Ftbl, Rugby*) **~ (transversale)** crossbar; (*sur une voiture*) **~s de fixation** *ou* **de toit** roof bars; **~ de savon**† cake *ou* bar of soap; **c'est le coup de ~ dans ce restaurant*** you pay through the nose* in that restaurant*; (*fatigue*) **j'ai un coup de ~*** I feel drained *ou* shattered*
[b] (*Danse*) barre; **exercices à la ~** exercises at the barre, barre exercises
[c] (*Naut*) helm; [*petit bateau*] tiller; (*lit, fig*) **être à la** *ou* **tenir la ~** to be at the helm; (*lit, fig*) **prendre la ~** to take the helm; **redresser la ~** (*lit*) to right the helm; (*fig*) to get things back on an even keel

[d] (*Jur*) ~ **du tribunal** bar; ~ **(des témoins)** witness box (*Brit*), witness stand (*US*); **être appelé à la** ~ to be called as a witness; **comparaître à la** ~ to appear as a witness

[e] (*Géog*) (= *houle*) (*gén*) race; (*à l'estuaire*) bore; (= *banc de sable*) (sand) bar; (= *crête de montagne*) ridge

[f] (= *trait*) line, dash, stroke; (*du t, f*) stroke; **faire des ~s** to draw lines (on a page); **mets une ~ à ton t** cross your t; (*Math*) ~ **de fraction/d'addition** fraction/addition line; (*Typo*) ~ **oblique** slash, oblique (stroke), solidus (*SPÉC*)

[g] (= *niveau*) mark; **franchir la ~ des 10%** to pass the 10% mark; (*Scol*) **placer la ~ à 10** to set the pass mark *ou* the passing grade (*US*) at 10; **mettre** *ou* **placer la ~ plus haut** to raise the stakes; **vous placez la ~ trop haut** you set your standards too high

[h] († = *jeu*) **~s** ≈ prisoners' base; (*frm*) **avoir ~(s) sur qn** (*avantage*) to have an advantage over sb; (*pouvoir*) to have power over *ou* a hold on sb

[i] (*Zool*) [*cheval*] bar

[j] († = *douleur*) pain; **j'ai une ~ sur la poitrine** my chest feels tight

[k] (*Hér*) bar

[2] COMP ► **barre d'accouplement** tie-rod ► **barre antiroulis** anti-roll bar ► **barre d'appui** (window) rail ► **barres asymétriques** asymmetric bars ► **barre de céréales** muesli (*Brit*) *ou* granola (*US*) bar ► **barre chocolatée** chocolate bar, bar of chocolate, candy bar (*US*) ► **barre à disques** (*Sport*) barbell ► **barre d'espacement** space bar ► **barre fixe** horizontal *ou* chinning bar ► **barre de mesure** (*Mus*) bar line ► **barre à mine** crowbar ► **barre omnibus** (*Élec*) busbar ► **barre de remorquage** (*Aut*) tow bar ► **barre de reprise** (*Mus*) repeat mark(s) *ou* sign ► **barres parallèles** parallel bars ► **barre de torsion** torsion bar

barré, e [baʀe] (*ptp de* **barrer**) [1] ADJ [a] (*Hér*) [*écu*] barred [b] [*dent*] impacted [c] (* = *engagé, parti*) **il/c'est mal** ~ he's/it's off to a bad start; **il est mal ~ pour avoir son examen** his chances of passing the exam are pretty slim; (*iro*) **on est bien ~ avec un chef comme lui!** we won't get very far with a boss like him! [2] NM (*Mus*) barré

barreau (*pl* **barreaux**) [baʀo] NM [a] [*échelle*] rung; [*cage, fenêtre*] bar; **être derrière les ~x** [*prisonnier*] to be behind bars; ~ **de chaise** (*lit*) (chair) rung *ou* crossbar; (* = *cigare*) fat cigar [b] (*Jur*) bar; **entrer** *ou* **être admis** *ou* **reçu au** ~ to be called to the bar

barrement [baʀmɑ̃] NM [*chèque*] crossing

barrer [baʀe] ►conjug 1◄ [1] VT [a] (= *obstruer*) [+ *porte*] to bar; [+ *fenêtre*] to bar up; [+ *chemin, route*] (*par accident*) to block; (*pour travaux, par la police*) to close (off), seal *ou* shut off; (*par barricades*) to barricade; ~ **le passage** *ou* **la route à qn** (*lit*) to stand in sb's way, block *ou* bar sb's way; (*fig*) to stand in sb's way; **il est barré par son supérieur** his boss is standing in his way; **des rochers nous barraient la route** rocks blocked *ou* barred our way; **« rue barrée »** "road closed" [b] (= *rayer*) [+ *mot, phrase*] to cross out, score out; [+ *surface, feuille*] to cross; [+ *chèque*] to cross; **chèque barré** crossed cheque (*Brit*), check for deposit only (*US*); **chèque non barré** open *ou* uncrossed cheque (*Brit*); **barre ton t** cross your t; **les rides qui barraient son front** the wrinkles which lined his forehead [c] (*Naut*) to steer; (*Sport*) **quatre/deux barré** coxed four/pair

[2] VI (*Naut*) to steer, take the helm

[3] **se barrer** VPR [*personne*] to clear off*; [*fixations*] to come out; **barre-toi!** clear off!*, beat it!*, scram!‡; **le tuyau se barre** the pipe is falling off; **il s'est barré de chez lui** he walked out on his family*

barrette [baʀɛt] NF [a] (*pour cheveux*) (hair) slide (*Brit*), barrette (*US*); (= *bijou*) brooch; (= *médaille*) bar [b] (*Ordin*) ~ **(de mémoire)** memory module [c] (*arg Drogue*) ~ **(de cannabis)** (one gram) bar of cannabis [d] (*Rel*) biretta; **recevoir la** ~ to receive the red hat

barreur, -euse [baʀœʀ, øz] NM,F (*gén*) (*homme*) helmsman; (*femme*) helmswoman; (*Aviron*) cox(swain); **quatre avec/sans** ~ coxed/coxless four

barricade [baʀikad] NF barricade → **côté**

barricader [baʀikade] ►conjug 1◄ [1] VT [+ *porte, fenêtre, rue*] to barricade [2] **se barricader** VPR **se** ~ **dans/derrière** to barricade o.s. in/behind; **se** ~ **chez soi** to lock *ou* shut o.s. in

barrière [baʀjɛʀ] [1] NF (= *clôture*) fence; (= *porte*) gate; (*lit, fig* = *obstacle*) barrier; (*Hist* = *octroi*) tollgate; **dresser une** ~ to put up a barrier (**entre** between); **franchir la** ~ **de la langue** to break through the language barrier [2] COMP ► **barrière de corail** coral reef; **la Grande Barrière (de corail)** the Great Barrier Reef ► **barrière de dégel** *roadsign warning of dangerous road conditions during a thaw* ► **barrière douanière** trade *ou* tariff barrier ► **barrière naturelle** natural barrier ► **barrière (de passage à niveau)** level (*Brit*) *ou* grade (*US*) crossing gate ► **barrière de sécurité** (*dans les rues*) crowd barrier; (*pour un bébé*) safety gate

barrique [baʀik] NF barrel, cask → **plein**

barrir [baʀiʀ] ►conjug 2◄ VI [*éléphant*] to trumpet

barrissement [baʀismɑ̃] NM trumpeting

bartavelle [baʀtavɛl] NF rock partridge

barycentre [baʀisɑ̃tʀ] NM barycentre (*Brit*), barycenter (*US*)

baryton [baʀitɔ̃] ADJ, NM baritone; **~-basse** base-baritone

baryum [baʀjɔm] NM barium

bas[1], basse[1] [ba, bas]

[1] ADJECTIF	[3] NOM MASCULIN
[2] ADVERBE	[4] COMPOSÉS

[1] ADJECTIF

[a] **= de faible hauteur** [*siège, porte, colline, nuages*] low; [*ciel*] low, overcast; [*maison*] low-roofed; [*terrain*] low(-lying); **le soleil est ~ sur l'horizon** the sun is low on the horizon; **les basses branches** *ou* **les branches basses d'un arbre** the lower *ou* bottom branches of a tree; **les branches de cet arbre sont basses** the branches of this tree hang low; **il a le front ~** he has a low brow *ou* forehead; ~ **sur pattes** [*animal*] short-legged; * [*personne*] short-legged, stumpy-legged; * [*meuble*] with short legs → **main, oreille, plafond, table** etc

[b] **= peu élevé** [*prix, chiffre, température, niveau, rendement*] low; (*Élec*) [*fréquence*] low; **les ~ salaires** low salaries; **la Seine est très basse en ce moment** the Seine is very low at the moment; **c'est (la) marée basse** ◊ **c'est la basse mer** the tide is low *ou* out, it's low tide; **à marée basse** at low tide *ou* water; **un enfant en ~ âge** a young *ou* small child

[c] **= peu audible** [*son*] low → **messe, voix**

[d] **= grave** [*note*] low; [*voix*] deep, low

[e] **= humble** [*naissance*] low, lowly; **personnes de basse condition** people from humble backgrounds; **basses besognes** menial tasks; (*péj*) dirty work; **les ~ quartiers de la ville** the seedy *ou* poor parts of the town; (*Boucherie*) **les ~ morceaux** the cheap cuts

[f] **= mesquin** [*jalousie, vengeance*] base, petty; [*action*] base, mean; **c'était ~ de sa part** it was a mean *ou* despicable thing for him to do; **c'est encore un exemple de basses manœuvres politiciennes** this is yet another example of base political manoeuvring; **elle n'a pas agi pour de**

basses raisons (commerciales) she didn't act out of base (commercial) motives → **coup**

[g] Ling **le** ~ **latin** low Latin; **le** ~ **allemand** Low German, plattdeutsch (*SPÉC*)

[h] Géog **la Basse Seine** the Lower Seine; **le Bas Languedoc** Lower Languedoc; **les Bas Bretons** the inhabitants of Lower Brittany; (*Hist Can*) **le Bas Canada** Lower Canada

[2] ADVERBE

[a] **dans l'espace** [*voler, viser*] low; **mets tes livres/le tableau plus** ~ put your books/the picture lower down; **ma maison est plus** ~ **dans la rue** my house is further down the street; **comme l'auteur le dit plus** ~ as the author says further on; **voir plus** ~ see below; **mettre** *ou* **traiter qn plus** ~ **que terre** to treat sb like dirt

[b] **dans une hiérarchie** **il est assez** ~ **dans la hiérarchie** he's quite low down in the hierarchy; **être au plus** ~ [*prix*] to be at their lowest, have reached rock bottom; [*cote de popularité, inflation*] to be at its lowest; **le dollar n'a jamais été aussi** ~ the dollar has reached a new *ou* an all-time low

[c] **= mal en point, en mauvaise posture** **le malade est bien** ~ the patient is very low; **être au plus** ~ [*personne*] to be very low, be at a very low ebb; [*secteur économique*] to be at a very low ebb; **la Bourse est au plus** ~ **depuis 1988** the stock exchange is at its lowest since 1988; **son image est au plus** ~ **dans l'opinion** his public image is at an all-time low

[d] **= doucement** [*parler*] softly, in a low voice; **dire qch/parler tout** ~ to say sth/speak in a whisper *ou* in a very low voice; **mets la télé tout** ~ put the TV on very low; **mettez la radio/le chauffage plus** ~ turn the radio/heating down

[e] Mus **= dans les graves** [*chanter*] low

[f] **locutions figées**

♦ **à bas** : **à** ~ **le fascisme/les tyrans!** down with fascism/tyrants!

♦ **bas les** + *nom*: ~ **les masques!** drop the pretence!; ~ **les pattes!** (*à un chien*) down!; (*: à une personne*) (keep your) hands off!*, (keep your) paws off!‡

♦ **mettre bas** (*Vét*) to give birth, drop (*SPÉC*); **mettre** ~ **les armes** (*Mil*) to lay down one's arms; (*fig*) to throw in the sponge; **mettre** ~ **les masques** to stop pretending, drop one's mask; **mise** ~ (*Vét*) birth, dropping → **chapeau, jeter**

[3] NOM MASCULIN

[*page, escalier, colline*] foot, bottom; [*visage*] lower part; [*mur*] foot; [*jupe, pantalon*] bottom; **le** ~ **du ventre** the lower abdomen; **une maison du** ~ **de la rue Blanche** a house at the bottom (end) of rue Blanche; **il a une malformation du** ~ **de la colonne vertébrale** he has a malformation of the lower spine; **faire les** ~ **d'un pantalon** to hem a pair of trousers

♦ **au bas** ◊ **dans le bas** at the bottom; **la colonne est évasée dans le** ~ the pillar widens out at the bottom

♦ **au bas de** ◊ **dans le bas de** [*page, escalier, colline, côte*] at the bottom *ou* foot of; [*armoire, immeuble, écran*] at the bottom of; [*vêtement*] (*gén*) at the bottom of; (*tout autour*) round the bottom of; **au** ~ **de l'échelle sociale** at the bottom of the social ladder; **dans le** ~ **du corps** in the lower part of the body; **j'ai mal au** *ou* **dans le** ~ **du dos** my lower back is aching, I've got a pain in my lower back; **dans le** ~ **de la ville** at the lower end of the town; **l'équipe se retrouve au** *ou* **dans le** ~ **du classement** the team is at the bottom of the league

♦ **de bas en haut** [*s'ouvrir*] from the bottom up(wards); [*compter, lire*] from the bottom up; **il la contempla de** ~ **en haut** he looked her up and down

♦ **d'en bas** : **les dents/la mâchoire d'en** ~ the lower teeth/jaw; **les chambres d'en** ~ the downstairs rooms; **le supermarché d'en** ~ **vend du pain** the supermarket below sells bread;

ceux d'en ~ (= *voisins*) the people (who live) below; (= *personnes humbles*) the lower orders; **le bruit vient d'en ~** the noise is coming from downstairs *ou* from down below; **vu d'en ~,** cela ressemble à ... seen from below, it looks like ...

♦ **du bas** [*dents, mâchoire*] lower; **l'étagère/le tiroir du ~** the bottom shelf/drawer; **les appartements du ~** the downstairs flats (*Brit*) *ou* apartments (*US*), the flats (*Brit*) *ou* apartments (*US*) downstairs *ou* down below

♦ **en bas** (*dans une maison*) downstairs; **il habite en ~** he lives downstairs *ou* down below; **les voleurs sont passés par en ~** the thieves got in downstairs; **je ne peux pas rester la tête en ~ trop longtemps** I can't stay upside down for too long; **il se tenait à la branche, la tête en ~** he was hanging upside down from the branch; **le tableau est posé la tête en ~*** the picture is upside down

♦ **en bas de** (*dans l'espace*) **en ~ de la côte/de l'escalier** at the bottom *ou* foot of the hill/of the stairs; **il m'attend en ~ de l'immeuble** he's waiting for me outside the building; **signez en ~ de cette page** sign at the bottom of this page; **ils sont au ~ du classement** they're at the bottom of the league; (*Can*) **en ~ de 100 dollars** under 100 dollars

4 COMPOSÉS
  ▸ **bas de casse** (*Typo*) NM lower case

bas² [ba] NM stocking; (*de footballeur*) sock; (*de bandit masqué*) stocking mask; **~ de contention** *ou* **à varices*** support stockings *ou* hose; **~ fins** sheer stockings; **~ (de) nylon** nylon stockings, nylons; **~ sans couture** seamless stockings; **~ résille** fishnet stockings; **~ de soie** silk stockings; **~ de laine** (*lit*) woollen stockings; (*fig*) savings, nest egg (*fig*)

basal, e (*mpl* **-aux**) [bazal, o] ADJ basal

basalte [bazalt] NM basalt

basaltique [bazaltik] ADJ basalt(ic)

basane [bazan] NF (= *peau*) basan, bazan; [*pantalon de cavalier*] leather padding

basané, e [bazane] **1** ADJ [*teint, visage*] [*vacancier*] (sun-)tanned, sunburnt (*Brit*); [*marin*] tanned, weather-beaten; (= *foncé*) swarthy; **individu au teint ~** dark-skinned individual **2** NM,F (*injurieux*) ≈ darky (*injurieux*)

bas-côté (*pl* **bas-côtés**) [bakote] NM **a** [*route*] verge, shoulder (*US*) **b** [*église*] (side) aisle **c** (*Can* = *appentis*) lean-to (shed), penthouse

basculant, e [baskylã, ãt] ADJ [*siège*] tip-up (*épith*) ▸ **benne**

bascule [baskyl] NF **a** (= *balance*) [*marchandises*] weighing machine; [*personne*] **~ (automatique)** scales **b** (= *balançoire*) seesaw, teeter-totter (*US*); **cheval/fauteuil à ~** rocking horse/chair; **mouvement de ~** (*lit*) rocking motion; (*fig*) turnaround; **le mouvement de ~ de l'électorat** the swing in the mood of the electorate; **pratiquer une politique de ~** to run with the hare and hunt with the hounds **c** (= *mécanisme*) bascule; (*Ordin*) **~ (bistable)** flip-flop; (*Élec*) **interrupteur à ~** toggle switch **d** (*Lutte*) lift-over

basculer [baskyle] ▸ conjug 1 ◂ **1** VI **a** [*personne*] to topple *ou* fall over, overbalance; [*objet*] to fall *ou* tip over; [*benne, planche, wagon*] to tip up; [*tas*] to topple (over); **il bascula dans le vide** he toppled over the edge **b** (= *changer*) [*match, débat*] to take a sudden turn; **ma vie a basculé** my life was turned upside down; (*Pol*) **~ dans l'opposition** to swing *ou* go over to the opposition; **~ dans le chaos** to be plunged into chaos **c** (*Ordin*) to toggle; (*Élec*) to switch (**sur** to) **2** VT **a** (*plus gén*) **faire ~** [+ *benne*] to tip up; [+ *contenu*] to tip out; [+ *personne*] to knock off balance, topple over **b** [+ *appel téléphonique*] to divert (to another telephone)

basculeur [baskylœR] NM **a** (*Élec*) rocker switch **b** [*benne*] tipper

base [baz] **1** NF **a** [*bâtiment, colonne, triangle*] base; [*montagne*] base, foot; [*gâteau, maquillage*] base; (*Anat, Chim, Math, Ordin*) base; (*Ling* : = *racine*) root; **calculer en ~ 2/10** to calculate in base 2/10; **~ (de vernis à ongles)** (nail varnish) base coat
b (= *lieu, Mil*) base; **~ navale/aérienne** naval/air base; **rentrer à sa** *ou* **la ~** to return to base
c (*Pol*) **la ~** the rank and file, the grass roots; **militant de ~** grassroots activist
d (= *fondement*) basis; **~s** basis *sg*, foundations; **~s d'un traité/d'un accord** basis of a treaty/of an agreement; **raisonnement fondé sur des ~s solides** solidly-based argument; **il a des ~s solides en anglais** he has a good grounding in English *ou* a sound basic knowledge of English; **jeter/saper les ~s de ...** to lay/undermine the foundations of ...
e (*loc*) **produit à ~ de soude** soda-based product; **cocktail à ~ de gin** gin-based cocktail; **à la ~** (= *fondamentalement*) basically, fundamentally; **être à la ~ de** to be at the root of; **de ~** (*gén*) basic; [*employé*] low-ranking; [*vocabulaire*] basic, core; **les métiers de ~ d'une entreprise** a company's core activities; **forme de ~** base form; **sur la ~ de ces renseignements** on the basis of this information; **ces départs s'effectuent sur la ~ du volontariat** the redundancies will take place on a voluntary basis → **camp, taux**

2 COMP ▸ **base de départ** (*fig*) starting point (*fig*) ▸ **base de données** database (*fig*) ▸ **base d'imposition** taxable amount ▸ **base de lancement** launching site ▸ **base de loisirs** sports and recreation park ▸ **base d'opérations** base of operations, operations base ▸ **base de ravitaillement** supply base ▸ **base de temps** (*Ordin*) clock

base(-)ball (*pl* **base(-)balls**) [bɛzbol] NM baseball

Bas-Empire [bazãpiR] NM **le ~** the late Roman Empire

baser [baze] ▸ conjug 1 ◂ **1** VT [+ *théorie*] to base (**sur** on); (*gén, Mil*) **être basé à** to be based at *ou* in; **économie basée sur le pétrole** oil-based economy **2** **se baser** VPR **se ~ sur** to base one's judgement on; **sur quoi vous basez-vous?** what is the basis of your argument?

bas-fond (*pl* **bas-fonds**) [bafɔ̃] NM **a** (*Naut*) (= *haut-fond*) shallow, shoal; (= *dépression*) depression **b** (*péj*) **les ~s de la société** the lowest depths *ou* the dregs of society; **les ~s de la ville** the seediest *ou* slummiest parts of the town

BASIC [bazik] NM BASIC

basilic [bazilik] NM (*Bot*) basil; (*Zool*) basilisk

basilique [bazilik] NF (*Rel*) basilica

basique [bazik] **1** ADJ (*gén, Chim*) basic **2** NM (= *vêtement*) basic item

basket [baskɛt] NM basketball; **~s** (*gén*) sneakers, trainers (*Brit*), ≈ tennis shoes (*US*); (*pour joueur*) basketball boots (*Brit*), high-tops (*US*); **être à l'aise dans ses ~s*** to be at ease with o.s. → **lâcher**

basket-ball (*pl* **basket-balls**) [baskɛtbol] NM basketball

basketteur, -euse [baskɛtœR, øz] NM,F basketball player

basmati [basmati] ADJ **riz ~** basmati rice

basquaise [baskɛz] **1** ADJ F (*Culin*) **poulet ~** basquaise chicken **2 Basquaise** NF Basque (woman)

basque¹ [bask] **1** ADJ Basque; **le Pays ~** the Basque Country **2** NM (*Ling*) Basque **3 Basque** NMF Basque

basque² [bask] NF [*habit*] skirt(s); [*robe*] basque → **pendu**

bas-relief (*pl* **bas-reliefs**) [baRəljɛf] NM bas-relief, low relief; **en ~** bas-relief (*épith*), low-relief (*épith*), in bas *ou* low relief

basse² [bas] NF **a** (= *chanteur*) bass; (= *voix*) bass (voice); (= *contrebasse*) (double) bass; (= *guitare*) bass; **flûte/trombone ~** bass flute/trombone; **~ de viole** bass viol, viola da gamba → **doucement b** (= *partie*) **~ chiffrée** figured bass; **~ continue** (basso) continuo, thorough bass; **~ contrainte** *ou* **obstinée** ground bass

basse-cour (*pl* **basses-cours**) [baskuR] NF (= *lieu*) farmyard; (= *animaux*) farmyard animals; (*péj*) **c'est une vraie ~ ce bureau!** this office is like a henhouse!

basse-fosse (*pl* **basses-fosses**) [basfos] NF (*littér*) dungeon

bassement [basmã] ADV basely, meanly, despicably

bassesse [bases] NF **a** (= *servilité*) servility; (= *mesquinerie*) meanness, baseness, lowness **b** (= *acte servile*) servile act; (= *acte mesquin*) low *ou* mean *ou* base *ou* despicable act; **il ferait des ~s pour avoir de l'avancement** he'd stoop to anything to get promoted

basset [basɛ] NM (*Zool*) basset (hound)

basse-taille (*pl* **basses-tailles**) [bastaj] NF (*Mus*) bass baritone

bassin [basɛ̃] NM **a** (= *pièce d'eau*) ornamental lake; (*plus petit*) pond; [*piscine*] pool; [*fontaine*] basin; **petit/grand ~** [*piscine*] small/main pool; **~ de décantation** settling basin *ou* tank **b** (= *cuvette*) bowl; (*Méd*) bedpan **c** (*Géog, Géol*) basin; **~ houiller/minier** coal/mineral field *ou* basin; **~ hydrographique** catchment basin *ou* area; **le Bassin parisien** the Paris Basin; **~ de retenue (d'un barrage)** (dam) reservoir **d** (*Écon*) area; **~ d'emploi(s)** labour market area **e** (*Anat*) pelvis **f** (*Naut*) dock; **~ de radoub/de marée** dry *ou* graving/tidal dock

bassine [basin] NF **a** (= *cuvette*) bowl, basin; **~ à confiture** preserving pan **b** (= *contenu*) bowl(ful)

bassiner [basine] ▸ conjug 1 ◂ VT **a** [+ *plaie*] to bathe; (*Agr*) to sprinkle *ou* spray (water on) **b** [+ *lit*] to warm (with a warming pan) **c** (* = *ennuyer*) to bore; **elle nous bassine** she's a pain in the neck*

bassinet [basinɛ] NM (*Anat*) renal pelvis → **cracher**

bassinoire [basinwaR] NF (*Hist*) warming pan

bassiste [basist] NMF (= *contrebassiste*) double bass player; (= *guitariste*) bass guitarist

basson [basɔ̃] NM (= *instrument*) bassoon; (= *musicien*) bassoonist

bassoniste [basɔnist] NMF bassoonist

basta* [basta] EXCL that's enough!

baste†† [bast] EXCL (= *indifférence*) never mind!, who cares?; (= *dédain*) pooh!

bastide [bastid] NF **a** (= *maison*) (country) house (*in Provence*) **b** (*Hist* = *village*) walled town (*in S.W. France*)

bastille [bastij] NF fortress, castle; (*Hist*) **la Bastille** the Bastille

bastingage [bastɛ̃gaʒ] NM (*Naut*) (ship's) rail; (*Hist*) bulwark

bastion [bastjɔ̃] NM (= *fortification*) bastion; (*fig*) bastion, stronghold

baston* [bastɔ̃] NM *ou* F fight, punch-up* (*Brit*); **il va y avoir du ~** things are going to get nasty

bastonnade†† [bastɔnad] NF drubbing, beating

bastonner (se)* [bastɔne] ▸ conjug 1 ◂ VPR to fight

bastos [bastos] NF (*arg Crime* = *balle*) slug*

bastringue* [bastRɛ̃g] NM **a** (= *objets*) junk*, clobber* (*Brit*); **et tout le ~** the whole caboodle* (*Brit*) *ou* kit and caboodle* (*US*) **b** (= *bruit*) racket*, din* **c** (= *bal*) (local) dance hall; (= *orchestre*) band

Basutoland [basytɔlãd] NM Basutoland

bas-ventre (pl **bas-ventres**) [bavɑ̃tʀ] NM (= région génitale) groin (area); (= abdomen) lower abdomen; **il a reçu un coup de genou dans le ~** he was kneed in the groin

BAT [beate] NM (ABRÉV = **bon à tirer**) → **bon 1**

bat. ABRÉV = **bâtiment**

bât [ba] NM [âne, mule] packsaddle; (fig) **c'est là où le ~ blesse** there's the rub

bataclan* [bataklɑ̃] NM junk*, clobber* (Brit); **et tout le ~** the whole caboodle* (Brit) ou kit and caboodle* (US)

bataille [batɑj] 1 NF a (Mil) battle; (= rixe) fight; (= querelle) fight, struggle; (= controverse) fight, dispute; **~ de rue** street fight ou battle; **~ juridique** legal battle; **la vie est une dure ~** life is a hard fight ou struggle; (fig) **il arrive toujours après la ~** he always turns up when it's too late b (Cartes) beggar-my-neighbour c (loc) **en ~** (Mil, Naut) in battle order ou formation; **il a les cheveux en ~** his hair's a mess; **le chapeau en ~** with his hat on askew; **être garé en ~** to be parked at an angle (to the kerb) 2 COMP ► **bataille aérienne** air battle ► **bataille aéronavale** sea and air battle ► **bataille de boules de neige** snowball fight ► **bataille électorale** electoral battle ► **bataille navale** (Mil) naval battle; (= jeu) battleships; **faire une ~ navale** to play battleships ► **bataille rangée** pitched battle

batailler [batɑje] ▸ conjug 1 ◂ VI (= lutter) to fight, battle; **~ ferme** to fight hard

batailleur, -euse [batɑjœʀ, øz] 1 ADJ pugnacious, aggressive; **il est ~** he loves a fight 2 NM,F (= arriviste) fighter

bataillon [batɑjɔ̃] NM (Mil) battalion; (fig) crowd, herd

bâtard, e [bɑtaʀ, aʀd] 1 ADJ [enfant]† illegitimate, bastard† (péj); (fig) [œuvre, solution] hybrid (épith); **chien ~** mongrel 2 NM,F (péj) (= personne) illegitimate child, bastard† (péj); (= chien) mongrel 3 NM (Boulangerie) (short) loaf of bread 4 **bâtarde** NF (écriture) ~ slanting round-hand

bâtardise [bɑtaʀdiz] NF bastardy† (péj), illegitimacy

batave [batav] 1 ADJ (Hist) Batavian; (hum) Dutch; **la République ~** the Batavian Republic 2 **Batave** NMF (Hist) Batavian; (hum) Dutch person

batavia [batavja] NF Webb lettuce

bateau (pl **bateaux**) [bato] 1 NM a (gén) boat; (grand) ship; **~ à moteur/à rames/à voiles** motor/rowing/sailing boat; **prendre le ~** (= embarquer) to embark, take the boat (à at); (= voyager) to go by boat, sail; **faire du ~** (à voiles) to go sailing; (à rames, à moteur) to go boating; (fig) **mener qn en ~** to take sb for a ride*, lead sb up the garden path* b [trottoir] dip (in front of a driveway entrance); **il s'est garé devant le ~** he parked in front of the driveway entrance c (Couture) **encolure** ou **décolleté ~** boat neck d (* = mystification) hoax, joke; **monter un ~ (à qn)** to play a practical joke (on sb) 2 ADJ INV (* = banal) hackneyed; **c'est (un sujet) ~** it's the same old theme* ou the favourite topic (that crops up every time) 3 COMP ► **bateau amiral** flagship ► **bateau de commerce** merchant ship ou vessel ► **bateau de guerre** warship, battleship ► **bateau de pêche** fishing boat ► **bateau de plaisance** yacht ► **bateau pneumatique** inflatable boat ► **bateau de sauvetage** lifeboat ► **bateau à vapeur** steamer, steamship

bateau-citerne (pl **bateaux-citernes**) [batositɛʀn] NM tanker

bateau-école (pl **bateaux-écoles**) [batoekɔl] NM training ship

bateau-feu (pl **bateaux-feux**) [batofø] NM lightship

bateau-lavoir (pl **bateaux-lavoirs**) [batolavwaʀ] NM wash-shed (on river); (péj ou hum) **capitaine** ou **amiral de ~** freshwater sailor

bateau-mouche (pl **bateaux-mouches**) [batomuʃ] NM river boat (for sightseeing, especially in Paris)

bateau-phare (pl **bateaux-phares**) [batofaʀ] NM lightship

bateau-pilote (pl **bateaux-pilotes**) [batopilɔt] NM pilot boat

bateau-pompe (pl **bateaux-pompes**) [batopɔ̃p] NM fireboat

bateleur, -euse [batlœʀ, øz] NM,F† tumbler; (péj) buffoon

batelier [batəlje] NM (gén) boatman, waterman; [bac] ferryman

batelière [batəljɛʀ] NF (gén) boatwoman; [bac] ferrywoman

batellerie [batɛlʀi] NF a (= transport) inland water transport ou navigation, canal transport b (= bateaux) river and canal craft

bâter [bate] ▸ conjug 1 ◂ VT to put a packsaddle on → **âne**

bat-flanc [baflɑ̃] NM INV [lit] boards

bath†* [bat] ADJ INV [personne, chose] super*, great*, smashing* (surtout Brit)

bathymètre [batimɛtʀ] NM bathometer, bathymeter

bathymétrie [batimetʀi] NF bathometry, bathymetry

bathymétrique [batimetʀik] ADJ bathymetric

bathyscaphe [batiskaf] NM bathyscaphe

bathysphère [batisfɛʀ] NF bathysphere

bâti, e [bati] (ptp de **bâtir**) 1 ADJ a **être bien/mal ~** [personne] to be well-built/of clumsy build; [dissertation] to be well/badly constructed b **terrain ~/non ~** developed/undeveloped site 2 NM a (Couture) tacking (NonC); **point de ~** tacking stitch b (Constr) [porte] frame; [machine] stand, support, frame

batifolage [batifɔlaʒ] NM a (= folâtrerie) frolicking ou larking (Brit) about b (= flirt) dallying, flirting c (= perte de temps) messing ou larking (Brit) about

batifoler* [batifɔle] ▸ conjug 1 ◂ VI a (= folâtrer) to frolic ou lark (Brit) about b (= flirter) to dally, flirt (avec with) c (péj = perdre son temps) to mess ou lark (Brit) about

batik [batik] NM batik

bâtiment [batimɑ̃] NM a (= édifice) building; **~s d'habitation** living quarters; **~s d'exploitation** farm buildings ou sheds b (= industrie) **le ~** the building industry ou trade; **être dans le ~** to be in the building trade, be a builder c (Naut) ship, vessel; **~ de guerre** warship

bâtir [batiʀ] ▸ conjug 2 ◂ VT a (Constr) to build; (se) **faire ~ une maison** to have a house built; **se ~ une maison** to build o.s. a house; **la maison s'est bâtie en 3 jours** the house was built ou put up in 3 days; (lit, fig) **sur le roc/sable** to build on rock/sand; **terrain/pierre à ~** building land/stone b (fig) [+ hypothèse] to build up; [+ phrase] to construct, build; [+ fortune] to amass, build up; [+ réputation] to build (up), make (sur on); [+ plan] to draw up c (Couture) to tack, baste; **fil/coton à ~** tacking ou basting thread/cotton

bâtisse [batis] NF a (= maison) building; (péj) great pile ou edifice b (Tech) masonry

bâtisseur, -euse [batisœʀ, øz] NM,F builder; **~ d'empire** empire builder

batiste [batist] NF batiste, cambric, lawn

bâton [batɔ̃] 1 NM a (= morceau de bois) stick; (= canne) stick, staff (littér); (Rel = insigne) staff; (= trique) club, cudgel; (à deux mains) staff; [agent de police] baton b [craie, encens, réglisse] stick; **~ de rouge (à lèvres)** lipstick c (= trait) vertical line ou stroke; (Scol) **faire des ~s** to draw vertical lines (when learning to write); (Typo) **caractères ~(s)** sans-serif characters d (* = million de centimes) ten thousand francs e (loc) **il m'a mis des ~s dans les roues** he put a spoke in my wheel, he put a spanner (Brit) ou wrench (US) in the works (for me); **parler à ~s rompus** to talk about this and that; **conversation à ~s rompus** desultory conversation; (hum) **il est mon ~ de vieillesse** he is the prop ou staff of my old age (hum) 2 COMP ► **bâton de berger** shepherd's crook ► **bâton blanc†** [agent de police] policeman's baton ► **bâton de chaise** chair rung ► **bâton de maréchal** (lit) marshal's baton; (fig) **ce poste, c'est son ~ de maréchal** that's the highest post he'll ever hold ► **bâton de pèlerin** (Rel) pilgrim's staff; **prendre son ~ de pèlerin** to set out on a mission ► **bâton de ski** ski stick ou pole

bâtonner†† [batɔne] ▸ conjug 1 ◂ VT to beat with a stick, cudgel

bâtonnet [batɔnɛ] NM short stick ou rod; (Anat) rod; (pour nettoyer les oreilles) cotton bud; **~ glacé** ice pop; **~s de poisson pané** fish fingers (Brit), fish sticks (US)

bâtonnier [batɔnje] NM ≈ president of the Bar

batracien [batʀasjɛ̃] NM batrachian

battage [bataʒ] NM a [tapis, or] beating; [céréales] threshing b (* = publicité) hype*; **~ médiatique** media hype; **faire du ~ autour de qch/qn** to give sth/sb a plug*, hype sth/sb*

battant, e [batɑ̃, ɑ̃t] 1 ADJ → **battre, pluie, tambour** 2 NM a [cloche] clapper, tongue; [volet] shutter, flap; **~ (de porte)** (left-hand ou right-hand) door (of a double door); **~ (de fenêtre)** (left-hand ou right-hand) window; **porte à double ~** ou **à deux ~s** double door(s) 3 NM,F (= personne) fighter (fig), go-getter*

batte [bat] NF (à beurre) dasher; [blanchisseuse] washboard; (Sport) bat

battement [batmɑ̃] NM a (= claquement) [porte, volet] banging (NonC); [pluie] beating (NonC), (pitter-)patter (NonC); [tambour] beating (NonC), rattle (NonC); [voile, toile] flapping (NonC) b (= mouvement) [ailes] flapping (NonC), flutter (NonC), beating (NonC); [cils] fluttering (NonC); [rames] plash (NonC), splash (NonC); **~ de paupières** blinking (NonC); **~s de jambes** leg movements c (Méd) [cœur] beat, beating (NonC); [pouls] beat, throbbing (NonC), beating (NonC); (irrégulier) fluttering (NonC); [tempes] throbbing (NonC); **avoir/donner des ~s de cœur** to get ou have/give palpitations d (= intervalle) **deux minutes de ~** (= pause) a two-minute break; (= attente) two minutes' wait; (= temps libre) two minutes to spare; **j'ai une heure de ~ de 10 à 11** I'm free for an hour ou I've got an hour to spare between 10 and 11 e (Radio) beat; (Phon) flap

batterie [batʀi] NF a (Mil) battery; **~ de missiles/antichars/côtière** missile/anti-tank/coastal battery; **mettre des canons en ~** to unlimber guns; (fig) **les journalistes attendaient, caméras en ~** the journalists were waiting with their cameras at the ready; (fig) **changer/dresser ses ~s** to change/lay ou make one's plans; (fig) **dévoiler ses ~s** to unmask one's guns b (Mus = percussion) percussion (instruments); (Jazz = instruments) drum kit; **Luc Cohen à la ~** Luc Cohen on drums ou percussion c (Aut, Élec) battery → **recharger** d (= groupe) [tests, radars, mesures] battery; **~ de projecteurs** bank of spotlights e **~ de cuisine** (Culin) pots and pans, kitchen utensils; (* = décorations) gongs*, ironmongery* (Agr) = battery; **élevage en ~** battery farming ou rearing; **poulets de ~** battery chickens g (Danse) batterie

batteur [batœʀ] NM [a] (Culin) whisk, beater [b] (Mus) drummer, percussionist [c] (= métier) (Agr) thresher; (Métal) beater; (Cricket) batsman; (Base-ball) batter

batteuse [batøz] NF [a] (Agr) threshing machine [b] (Métal) beater

battle-dress [batœldʀɛs] NM INV battle-dress

battoir [batwaʀ] NM [a] [laveuse] beetle, battledore; (à tapis) (carpet) beater [b] (= grandes mains) ~s* (great) mitts* ou paws*

battre [batʀ] ▸conjug 41◂ [1] VT [a] [+ personne] to beat, strike, hit; **elle ne bat jamais ses enfants** she never hits ou smacks her children; **~ qn comme plâtre*** to beat the living daylights out of sb*, thrash ou beat sb soundly; **~ qn à mort** to batter ou beat sb to death; **regard de chien battu** hangdog ou cowering look; **femmes battues** battered women [b] (= vaincre) [+ adversaire, équipe] to beat, defeat; **se faire ~** to be beaten ou defeated; **il ne se tient pas pour battu** he doesn't consider himself beaten ou defeated; (Sport) **~ qn (par) 6 à 3** to beat sb 6-3; **~ qn à plate(s) couture(s)** to thrash sb, beat sb hands down → **record** [c] (= frapper) [+ tapis, linge, fer, or] to beat; [+ blé] to thresh ▪ (PROV) **~ le fer pendant qu'il est chaud** to strike while the iron is hot (PROV); **il battit l'air/l'eau des bras** his arms thrashed the air/water; **~ le fer à froid** to cold hammer iron; **son manteau lui bat les talons** his coat is flapping round his ankles; **~ le briquet†** to strike a light [d] (= agiter) [+ beurre] to churn; [+ blanc d'œuf] to beat (up), whip, whisk; [+ crème] to whip; [+ cartes] to shuffle → **neige** [e] (= parcourir) [+ région] to scour, comb; **~ le pays** to scour the countryside; (Chasse) **~ les buissons** to beat the bushes (for game); **hors des sentiers battus** off the beaten track; (fig) **~ la campagne** to let one's mind wander; **~ le pavé** to wander aimlessly about ou around [f] (= heurter) [pluie] to beat ou lash against; [mer] to beat ou dash against; (Mil) [+ positions, ennemis] to batter; **littoral battu par les tempêtes** storm-lashed coast [g] (Mus) **~ la mesure** to beat time; **~ le tambour** (lit) to beat the drum; (fig) to shout from the rooftops; **~ le rappel** to call to arms; (fig) **~ le rappel de ses souvenirs** to summon up one's old memories; **~ le rappel de ses amis** to rally one's friends; **~ la retraite** to sound the retreat [h] (loc) **~ la breloque†** [appareil] to be erratic; **son cœur bat la breloque** his heart is none too good, he has a bad ou dicky* (Brit) heart; **son cœur battait la chamade** his heart was pounding ou beating wildly; **~ en brèche une théorie** to demolish a theory; **~ froid à qn** to cold-shoulder sb, give sb the cold shoulder; **~ son plein** [saison touristique] to be at its height; [fête] to be going full swing; **~ la semelle** to stamp one's feet (to keep warm); **~ pavillon britannique** to fly the British flag, sail under the British flag; **~ monnaie** to strike ou mint coins; **~ sa coulpe** to beat one's breast (fig)

[2] VI [cœur, pouls] to beat; [montre, métronome] to tick; [pluie] to beat, lash (contre against); [porte, volets] to bang, rattle; [voile, drapeau] to flap; [tambour] to beat; (fig, hum) **son cœur bat pour lui** he's her heart-throb; **son cœur battait d'émotion** his heart was beating wildly ou pounding with emotion; **le cœur battant** with beating ou pounding heart → **retraite**

[3] **battre de** VT INDIR **~ des mains** to clap one's hands; (fig) to dance for joy, exult; **~ du tambour** to beat the drum; **l'oiseau bat des ailes** the bird is beating ou flapping its wings; (fig) **~ de l'aile** to be in a bad way

[4] **se battre** VPR [a] (dans une guerre, un combat) to fight (avec with, contre against); (= disputer) to fall out; (fig) to fight, battle, struggle (contre against); **se ~ comme des**

chiffonniers to fight like cat and dog; **se ~ au couteau/à la baïonnette** to fight with knives/bayonets; **nos troupes se sont bien battues** our troops fought well ou put up a good fight; **se ~ en duel** to fight a duel; **se ~ contre des moulins à vent** to tilt at windmills; **il faut se ~ pour arriver à obtenir quelque chose** you have to fight to get what you want; **se ~ avec un problème** to struggle ou battle with a problem [b] (fig) **se ~ les flancs** to rack one's brains; **je m'en bats l'œil**‡ I don't care a fig* ou a damn‡

battu, e¹ [baty] (ptp de **battre**) ADJ → **battre**, **jeté, œil, pas¹, terre**

battue² [baty] NF (Chasse) battue, beat; (pour retrouver qn) search

batture [batyʀ] NF (Can) sand bar, strand

bau (pl **baux**) [bo] NM (Naut) beam

baud [bo] NM (Ordin) baud

baudelairien, -ienne [bodlɛʀjɛ̃, jɛn] ADJ of Baudelaire, Baudelairean

baudet [bodɛ] NM [a] (Zool) donkey, ass [b] (Menuiserie) trestle, sawhorse

baudrier [bodʀije] NM [épée] baldric; [drapeau] shoulder-belt; (Alpinisme) harness; (pour matériel) gear sling → **Orion**

baudroie [bodʀwa] NF angler (fish)

baudruche [bodʀyʃ] NF (= caoutchouc) rubber; (péj) (= personne) wimp*, spineless character; (= théorie) empty theory, humbug*; **ça s'est dégonflé comme une ~** it came to nothing ou vanished into thin air → **ballon¹**

bauge [boʒ] NF [sanglier, porc] wallow

baume [bom] NM (lit) balm, balsam; (fig) balm; **~ après-rasage/pour les lèvres** aftershave/lip balm; **ça lui a mis du ~ au cœur** (consolé) it was a great comfort to him; (rassuré) it heartened him

Baumé [bome] N **~ degré**

baux [bo] pl de **bail, bau**

bauxite [boksit] NF bauxite

bavard, e [bavaʀ, aʀd] [1] ADJ [personne] talkative; [discours, récit] long-winded, wordy; **il est ~ comme une pie** he's a real chatterbox [2] NM,F chatterbox, prattler; (péj) gossip, blabbermouth*

bavardage [bavaʀdaʒ] NM (= papotage) chatting, talking; (= jacasserie) chattering, prattling; (= commérage) gossiping; **j'entendais leur ~(s)** I could hear them talking ou chattering

bavarder [bavaʀde] ▸conjug 1◂ VI [a] (= papoter) to chat, talk; (= jacasser) to chatter, prattle; (= commérer) to gossip; **arrêtez de ~ !** stop that chattering! [b] (= divulguer un secret) to blab*, give the game away, talk

bavarois, e [bavaʀwa, waz] [1] ADJ Bavarian [2] NM,F [a] (= personne) **Bavarois(e)** Bavarian [b] (Culin) bavarois; **~(e) aux fraises** strawberry bavarois

bavasser* [bavase] ▸conjug 1◂ VI (= bavarder) to blather (on)*, natter* (Brit)

bave [bav] NF [a] [personne] dribble; [animal] slaver, slobber; [chien enragé] foam, froth; [escargot] slime; [crapaud] spittle; (fig) venom, malicious words ▪ (PROV) **la ~ du crapaud n'atteint pas la blanche colombe !** sticks and stones might break my bones but names will never hurt me (PROV)

baver [bave] ▸conjug 1◂ [1] VI [a] [personne] to dribble; (beaucoup) to slobber, drool; [animal] to slaver, slobber; [chien enragé] to foam ou froth at the mouth; [stylo] to leak; [pinceau] to drip; [liquide] to run [b] (*: loc) **en ~ d'admiration** to gasp in admiration; **en ~ d'envie** to be green with envy; **en ~** (= souffrir) to have a rough ou hard time of it*; **il m'en a fait ~** he really gave me a rough ou hard time*; **elle n'a pas fini d'en ~ avec son fils** she hasn't seen the last of her troubles with her son yet [c] (littér) **~ sur la réputation de qn** to besmear

ou besmirch sb's reputation [2] VT **il en a bavé des ronds de chapeau**‡ his eyes nearly popped out of his head*

bavette [bavɛt] NF [a] [tablier, enfant] bib; (Aut = garde-boue) mudguard, mud flap [b] (= viande) undercut → **tailler**

baveux, -euse [bavø, øz] ADJ [bouche] dribbling, slobbery; [enfant] dribbling; **omelette baveuse** runny omelette; (Typo) **lettre baveuse** blurred ou smeared letter

Bavière [bavjɛʀ] NF Bavaria

bavoir [bavwaʀ] NM bib

bavolet [bavɔlɛ] NM [manteau] (gun) flap

bavure [bavyʀ] NF (= tache) smudge, smear; (Tech) burr; (= erreur) blunder; **~ policière** police blunder; **sans ~(s)** [travail] flawless, faultless

bayadère [bajadɛʀ] [1] NF bayadère [2] ADJ [tissu] colourfully striped

bayer [baje] ▸conjug 1◂ VI **~ aux corneilles** to stand gaping, stand and gape

bayou [baju] NM bayou

bazar [bazaʀ] NM [a] (= magasin) general store; (oriental) bazaar [b] (* = effets personnels) junk* (NonC), gear‡ (NonC), things* [c] (* = désordre) clutter, jumble, shambles (NonC); **quel ~ !** what a shambles!*; **il a mis le ~ dans mes photos** he jumbled all my photos up; **et tout le ~** and all the rest, and what have you*, the whole caboodle*, the whole kit and caboodle* (US)

bazarder* [bazaʀde] ▸conjug 1◂ VT (= jeter) to get rid of, chuck out*, ditch*; (= vendre) to get rid of, sell off, flog‡ (Brit)

bazooka [bazuka] NM bazooka

BCBG [besebeʒe] ADJ (ABRÉV = **bon chic bon genre**) → **bon**

BCBG

The adjective "bon chic bon genre" or **BCBG** refers to a particular stereotype of the French upper middle class. To be **BCBG** is to be quite well-off (though not necessarily wealthy), to be conservative in both outlook and dress, and to attach importance to social standing and outward signs of respectability.

BCE [beseə] NF (ABRÉV = **Banque centrale européenne**) ECB

BCG [beseʒe] NM (ABRÉV = **bacille Bilié Calmette et Guérin**) BCG

BD [bede] NF [a] (ABRÉV = **bande dessinée**) **la BD** comic strips, strip cartoons (Brit), comics (US); **une BD** (dans un journal) a comic strip, a strip cartoon (Brit); (= livre) a comic book; **auteur de BD** comic strip writer, strip cartoonist (Brit); **l'histoire romaine en BD** a comic-strip book of Roman history [b] (ABRÉV = **base de données**) DB

bd ABRÉV = **boulevard**

bê [bɛ] EXCL baa!

beagle [bigl] NM beagle

béance [beãs] NF (Méd) **~ du col** ou **cervico-isthmique** incompetence of the cervix

béant, e [beã, ãt] ADJ [blessure] gaping, open; [bouche] gaping, wide open; [yeux] wide open; [gouffre] gaping, yawning

béarnais, e [beaʀnɛ, ɛz] [1] ADJ [personne] from the Béarn; (sauce) **~e** Béarnaise sauce [2] **Béarnais(e)** NM,F inhabitant ou native of the Béarn

béat, e [bea, at] ADJ [a] (hum) (= heureux) [personne] blissfully happy; (= content de soi) smug [b] (= niais) [sourire, air] beatific, blissful; **optimisme ~** blind optimism; **admiration ~e** blind ou dumb admiration; **être ~ d'admiration** to be struck dumb with admiration; **regarder qn d'un air ~** to look at sb in open-eyed wonder

béatement [beatmɑ̃] ADV [*sourire*] beatifically; **il contemplait ~ son assiette** he was looking at his plate with an expression of blissful contentment; **on s'endormit ~ jusqu'à l'heure du dîner** we slept blissfully until dinner time

béatification [beatifikasjɔ̃] NF beatification

béatifier [beatifje] ▶ conjug 7 ◀ VT to beatify

béatitude [beatityd] NF (*Rel*) beatitude; (= *bonheur*) bliss; **les Béatitudes** the Beatitudes

beatnik [bitnik] NMF beatnik; **la génération ~** the beat generation

Béatrice [beatris] NF Beatrice

beau, belle [bo, bɛl]

Devant nom masculin commençant par voyelle ou h muet = **bel**; masculin pluriel = **beaux**.
  1 ADJECTIF   3 NOM FÉMININ
  2 NOM MASCULIN

1 ADJECTIF

a = qui plaît au regard, à l'oreille [*objet, paysage, jambes*] beautiful, lovely; [*femme*] beautiful, good-looking; [*homme*] handsome, good-looking; **il m'a fait un très ~ cadeau** he gave me a really nice *ou* a lovely present; **il a une belle tête** he's got a nice face; **les ~x quartiers** the smart *ou* posh* districts; (*hum*) **~ Serge était là** the gorgeous Serge was there; **il est ~ comme le jour** *ou* **comme un dieu** he's like a Greek god; (*hum*) **tu es ~ comme un camion tout neuf!*** don't you look smart!; **il est ~ garçon** he's good-looking; **se faire ~** to get dressed up *ou* spruced up; **se faire belle** (= *s'habiller, se maquiller*) to do o.s. up; **avec lui, c'est sois belle et tais-toi** he expects you to just sit there and look pretty; (*littér*) **porter ~** to look dapper; **mettre ses ~x habits** to put on one's best clothes

b = qui plaît à l'esprit, digne d'admiration [*discours, match*] fine; [*film, poème, roman*] beautiful, fine; [*nom*] beautiful; **il a fait du ~ travail** he did a really good job; **il y a quelques ~x moments dans cette pièce** there are some fine moments in the play; **elle a fait une belle carrière** she had a successful career; **c'est une belle mort** it's a good way to go; **une belle âme** a fine *ou* noble nature; **un ~ geste** a noble act, a fine gesture; **ce n'est pas ~ de mentir** it isn't nice to tell lies; **il ferait ~ voir que ...** it would be a fine thing if ...; **il ferait ~ voir qu'il mente!** he'd better not be lying! → **joueur** *etc*

c = agréable [*voyage*] lovely; [*journée*] beautiful, fine; **par une belle soirée d'été** on a beautiful *ou* fine summer's evening; **il fait ~** the weather's fine *ou* nice; **il fait très ~** the weather's beautiful; **la mer était belle** (*sans vagues*) the sea was calm; **c'est le bel âge** those are the best years of your life; **c'est le plus ~ jour de ma vie!** this is the best day of my life!; **c'est trop ~ pour être vrai** it's too good to be true; **ce serait trop ~!** that would be too much to hope for! → **jeu, rôle** *etc*

d intensif [*revenu, profit*] handsome; [*résultat, occasion*] excellent, fine; [*brûlure, peur*] nasty; **ça fait une belle somme!** that's a tidy* sum (of money)!; **il en reste un ~ morceau** there's still a good bit (of it) left; **le film a remporté un ~ succès** the film was a big *ou* great success; **ça a fait un ~ scandale** it caused quite a scandal, it caused a big scandal; **95 ans, c'est un bel âge** 95 is a good age *ou* a fine old age; **il est arrivé un ~ matin/jour** he turned up one fine morning/day; **il a attrapé une belle bronchite** he's got a nasty attack *ou* a bad bout of bronchitis; **c'est un ~ menteur** he's a terrible *ou* the most awful liar; **c'est un ~ salaud*** he's a real bastard**

e locutions figées

♦ **avoir beau** + *infinitif* : **on a ~ faire/dire, ils n'apprennent rien** whatever you do/say ou no matter what you do/say, they don't learn anything; **on a ~ protester, personne n'écoute** however much *ou* no matter how much you

protest, no one listens; **il a eu ~ essayer, il ...** however much *ou* whatever he tried, he ...; **try as he might, he ...; on a ~ dire, il n'est pas bête** say what you like, he is not stupid

♦ **l'avoir belle de** + *infinitif* * : **il l'avait belle de s'échapper/de lui dire ce qu'il pensait** it would have been easy for him to escape/to say what he thought

♦ **bel et bien** well and truly; **il s'est bel et bien trompé** he got it well and truly wrong; **cet homme a bel et bien existé** the man really did exist; **il est bel et bien mort** he's well and truly dead, he's dead all right*; **ils sont bel et bien entrés par la fenêtre** they got in through the window, there's no doubt about that, they got in through the window all right*

♦ **de plus belle** even more; **crier de plus belle** to shout even louder; **rire de plus belle** to laugh even louder *ou* harder; **reprendre de plus belle** [*combat, polémique, violence*] to start up again with renewed vigour; **continuer de plus belle** [*discrimination, répression*] to be worse than ever

♦ **tout beau(, tout beau)!**† steady on!, easy does it! → **bailler, échapper**

2 NOM MASCULIN

a esthétiquement le ~ the beautiful; **le culte du ~** the cult of beauty; **elle n'aime que le ~** she only likes what is beautiful; **elle n'achète que du ~** she only buys the best quality

b loc c'est du ~! (*iro*) lovely! (*iro*); (*reproche*) that was a fine thing to do! (*iro*); (*consternation*) this is a fine business! *ou* a fine mess!; **être au ~** [*temps*] to be fine, be set fair; **être au ~ (fixe)** [*baromètre*] to be set fair; [*relations*] to be as good as ever; **nos rapports ne sont pas au ~ fixe** things are a bit strained between us; **son moral n'est pas au ~ fixe** he's in low spirits; **la situation n'est pas au ~ fixe** things aren't looking too good; **faire le ~** [*chien*] to sit up and beg; (*péj*) [*personne*] to curry favour (devant with); **le plus ~ de l'histoire, c'est que ...** the best part is that ...

3 belle NOM FÉMININ

a = femme beautiful woman; (= *compagne*) **sa belle** his lady friend; **ma belle!*** sweetie!*, sweetheart!; (*Littérat*) **« la Belle au bois dormant »** "Sleeping Beauty"; (*Littérat*) **« la Belle et la Bête »** "Beauty and the Beast"

b Jeux, Sport decider, deciding match; **on fait la belle ?** shall we play a decider?

c * : iro = action, parole en faire de belles to get up to mischief; **il en a fait de belles quand il était jeune** he was a bit wild when he was young; **en apprendre/dire de belles sur qn** to hear/say things about sb (*euph*); **j'en ai entendu de belles sur son compte** I've heard some stories about him

d prisonnier se faire la belle* to break out of jail, go over the wall*

beaucoup [boku] ADV **a** (*modifiant verbe*) a lot, (very) much, a great deal; **il mange ~** he eats a lot; **elle lit ~** she reads a great deal *ou* a lot; **elle ne lit pas ~** she doesn't read much *ou* a great deal *ou* a lot; **la pièce ne m'a pas ~ plu** I didn't like the play very much; **il s'intéresse ~ à la peinture** he's very interested in painting, he takes a lot *ou* a great deal of interest in painting; **il y a ~ à faire/voir** there's a lot to do/see; **il a ~ voyagé/lu** he has travelled/read a lot *ou* extensively *ou* a great deal

b (*modifiant adv*) much, far, a good deal, a lot; **~ plus rapide** much *ou* a good deal *ou* a lot quicker; **elle travaille ~ trop** she works far too much; **elle travaille ~ trop lentement** she works much *ou* far too slowly; **se sentir ~ mieux** to feel much *ou* miles* better; **~ plus d'eau** much *ou* a lot *ou* far more water; **~ moins de gens** many *ou* a lot *ou* far fewer people; **il est susceptible, il l'est même ~** he's touchy, in fact he's very touchy indeed

c (*employé seul = personnes*) many; **ils sont ~**

à croire que ... ◊ ~ croient que ... many *ou* a lot of people think that ...; **~ d'entre eux** a lot *ou* many of them

d ~ de (*quantité*) a great deal of, a lot of, much; (*nombre*) many, a lot of, a good many; **~ de monde** a lot of people, a great *ou* good many people; **avec ~ de soin/plaisir** with great care/pleasure; **il ne reste pas ~ de pain** there isn't a lot of *ou* isn't (very) much bread left; **j'ai ~ (de choses) à faire** I have a lot (of things) to do; **pour ce qui est de l'argent/du lait, il en reste ~/il n'en reste pas ~** as for money/milk, there is a lot left/there isn't a lot *ou* much left; **vous attendiez des touristes, y en a-t-il eu ~ ? — oui (il y en a eu) ~** you were expecting tourists and were there many *ou* a lot (of them)? — yes there were (a good many *ou* a lot of them); **j'en connais ~ qui pensent que ...** I know a great many (people) *ou* a lot of people who think that ...; **il a ~ d'influence** he has a great deal *ou* a lot of influence, he is very influential; **il a eu ~ de chance** he's been very lucky

e de ~ by far, by a long way; **elle est de ~ la meilleure élève** she's by far *ou* she's far and away the best pupil, she's the best pupil by far; **il l'a battu de ~** he beat him by miles* *ou* by a long way; **il est de ~ ton aîné** he's very much *ou* a great deal older than you; **il est de ~ supérieur** he is greatly *ou* far superior; **il préférerait de ~ s'en aller** he'd much rather leave; **il s'en faut de ~ qu'il soit au niveau** he is far from being up to standard, he's nowhere near up to standard

f (*loc*) **c'est déjà ~ de l'avoir fait** *ou* **qu'il l'ait fait** it was quite something *ou* quite an achievement to have done it at all; **à ~ près** far from it; **c'est ~ dire** that's an exaggeration *ou* an overstatement, that's saying a lot; **être pour ~ dans une décision/une nomination** to be largely responsible for a decision/an appointment, have a big hand in making a decision/an appointment; **il y est pour ~** he's largely responsible for it, he had a lot to do with it

beauf: [bof] NM **a** (= *beau-frère*) brother-in-law **b** (*péj*) narrow-minded Frenchman with conservative attitudes and tastes

BEAUF

The word **beauf** is an abbreviation of "beau-frère" (brother-in-law). It is a pejorative and humorous term used to refer to stereotypical ordinary Frenchmen who are perceived as being somewhat vulgar, narrow-minded and chauvinistic.

beau-fils (*pl* **beaux-fils**) [bofis] NM (= *gendre*) son-in-law; (*d'un remariage*) stepson

beaufort [bofɔr] NM **a** (= *fromage*) type of gruyère cheese **b Beaufort** → **échelle**

beau-frère (*pl* **beaux-frères**) [bofrɛr] NM brother-in-law

beaujolais [boʒɔlɛ] NM **a** (= *région*) **le Beaujolais** the Beaujolais region **b** (= *vin*) beaujolais, Beaujolais; **le ~ nouveau** (the) beaujolais *ou* Beaujolais nouveau, (the) new beaujolais *ou* Beaujolais

beau-papa* (*pl* **beaux-papas**) [bopapa] NM father-in-law, dad-in-law* (*Brit*)

beau-père (*pl* **beaux-pères**) [bopɛr] NM (= *père dua conjoint*) father-in-law; (= *nouveau mari de la mère*) stepfather

beaupré [bopre] NM bowsprit

beauté [bote] NF **a** (*gén*) beauty; [*femme*] beauty, loveliness; [*homme*] handsomeness; **de toute ~** very beautiful, magnificent; **c'est ça la ~ de la chose** that's the beauty of it; **se (re)faire une ~** to powder one's nose, do one's face*; **vous êtes en ~ ce soir** you look radiant this evening; **finir** *ou* **terminer qch en ~** to complete sth brilliantly, finish sth with a flourish; **finir en ~** to end with a flourish, finish brilliantly; **faire qch pour la ~ du geste** to do sth for the sake of it; **la ~ du diable** youthful beauty *ou* bloom → **concours, produit, reine, soin** b (= *belle femme*) beauty c **~s** beauties; **les ~s de Rome** the beauties of Rome

beaux [bo] ADJ MPL → **beau**

beaux-arts [bozaʀ] NMPL **les ~** fine arts; (= *école*) (à l'École des) Beaux-Arts (*the French national college of art and architecture*); (*en province*) the college of art

beaux-parents [bopaʀɑ̃] NMPL [*homme*] wife's parents, in-laws*; [*femme*] husband's parents, in-laws*

bébé [bebe] NM (= *enfant, animal*) baby; (= *poupée*) dolly*; **avoir** *ou* **faire un ~** to have a baby; **faire le ~** to behave *ou* act like a baby; **il est resté très ~** he's stayed very babyish; **~ éléphant/girafe** baby elephant/giraffe; **~-bulle** bubble baby (*baby who has to live in a sterile environment because of an immune deficiency*); **~-éprouvette** test-tube baby; **elle attend un ~** she's expecting a baby; **jeter le ~ avec l'eau du bain** to throw out the baby with the bathwater; **on lui a repassé** *ou* **refilé le ~*** he was left holding the baby

bebelle [bəbɛl], **bébelle** [bebɛl] NF (*Can = bibelot*) knick-knack; **range tes bébelles** tidy away your things

bébête* [bebɛt] 1 ADJ silly 2 NF bug; **une petite ~** a creepy crawly*, a bug

be-bop (*pl* be-bops) [bibɔp] NM (be)bop

bec [bɛk] 1 NM a (*Orn*) beak, bill; **oiseau qui se fait le ~** bird that sharpens its beak (**contre** on); (**nez en**) **~ d'aigle** aquiline *ou* hook nose; **coup de ~** (*lit*) peck; (*fig*) dig, cutting remark b (= *pointe*) [*plume*] nib; [*carafe, casserole*] lip; [*théière*] spout; [*flûte, trompette*] mouthpiece; (*Géog*) bill, headland; (*sur vêtement*) pucker; **ça fait un ~ dans le dos** it puckers in the back c (* = *bouche*) mouth; **ouvre ton ~!** open your mouth!, mouth open!*; **ferme ton ~!** just shut up!*; **il n'a pas ouvert le ~** he never opened his mouth, he didn't say a word; **la pipe au ~** with his pipe stuck* in his mouth; **clore** *ou* **clouer le ~ à qn** to reduce sb to silence, shut sb up* → **prise²** d (*loc*) **tomber sur un ~*** (*obstacle temporaire*) to hit a snag; (*impasse*) to be stymied*; (*échec*) to come unstuck*; **être** *ou* **rester le ~ dans l'eau*** to be left in the lurch, be left high and dry; **défendre qch ~ et ongles** to fight tooth and nail for sth e (*: Can, Belg, Helv = baiser*) kiss, peck 2 COMP ► **bec Auer** Welsbach burner ► **bec Bunsen** Bunsen burner ► **bec fin*** gourmet ► **bec de gaz** lamppost, gaslamp ► **bec verseur** pourer

bécane* [bekan] NF (= *vélo*) bike*; (= *machine*) machine

bécarre [bekaʀ] NM (*Mus*) natural; **sol ~** G natural

bécasse [bekas] NF (*Zool*) woodcock; (* = *sotte*) (silly) goose*

bécasseau (*pl* bécasseaux) [bekaso] NM sandpiper; (= *petit de la bécasse*) young woodcock

bécassine [bekasin] NF (*Zool*) snipe; (* = *sotte*) (silly) goose*

bec-croisé (*pl* becs-croisés) [bɛkkʀwaze] NM crossbill

bec-de-cane (*pl* becs-de-cane) [bɛkdəkan] NM (= *poignée*) doorhandle; (= *serrure*) catch

bec-de-lièvre (*pl* becs-de-lièvre) [bɛkdəljɛvʀ] NM harelip

bec-de-perroquet (*pl* becs-de-perroquet) [bɛkdəpɛʀɔkɛ] NM (*Méd*) osteophyte

bêchage [beʃaʒ] NM digging, turning over

béchamel [beʃamɛl] NF (**sauce**) **~** béchamel (sauce), white sauce

bêche [bɛʃ] NF spade

bêcher [beʃe] ▶conjug 1◀ 1 VT (*Agr*) to dig, turn over 2 VI (* = *crâner*) to be stuck-up *ou* toffee-nosed*

bêcheur, -euse* [beʃœʀ, øz] 1 ADJ stuck-up*, toffee-nosed* (*Brit*) 2 NM,F stuck-up* *ou* toffee-nosed* (*Brit*) person

bécot* [beko] NM kiss, peck; **gros ~** smacker*

bécoter* [bekɔte] ▶conjug 1◀ 1 VT to kiss 2 **se bécoter** VPR to smooch

becquée [beke] NF beakful; **donner la ~ à** to feed

becquerel [bɛkʀɛl] NM becquerel

becquet [bekɛ] NM (*Alpinisme*) (rocky) spike; (= *adhésif*) (removable) self-stick note, Post-it (note)®; (*Aut*) **(arrière)** spoiler

becquetance: [bɛktɑ̃s] NF grub:, chow: (*US*)

becqueter [bekte] ▶conjug 4◀ VT (*Orn*) to peck (at); (: = *manger*) to eat; **qu'y a-t-il à ~ ce soir?** what's for dinner tonight?

bectance: [bɛktɑ̃s] NF = **becquetance**

becter: [bɛkte] ▶conjug 4◀ VT = **becqueter**

bedaine* [bədɛn] NF paunch, potbelly:

bédé* [bede] NF = **BD** a

bedeau (*pl* bedeaux) [bədo] NM verger, beadle†

bédéphile [bedefil] NMF comic strip *ou* strip cartoon fan*

bedon* [bədɔ̃] NM paunch, potbelly:

bedonnant, e* [bədɔnɑ̃, ɑ̃t] ADJ potbellied:, paunchy, portly

bedonner* [bədɔne] ▶conjug 1◀ VI to get a paunch, get potbellied:

bédouin, -ouine [bedwɛ̃, win] 1 ADJ Bedouin 2 **Bédouin(e)** NM,F Bedouin

BEE [beøø] NM (ABRÉV = **Bureau européen de l'environnement**) → **bureau**

bée [be] ADJ F **être** *ou* **rester bouche ~** (*lit*) to stand open-mouthed *ou* gaping (**de** with); (*d'admiration*) to be lost in wonder; (*de surprise*) to be flabbergasted (**devant** at); **il en est resté bouche ~** his jaw dropped, he was flabbergasted*

béer [bee] ▶conjug 1◀ VI (*littér*) a [*ouverture, bouche*] to be (wide) open b [*personne*] **~ d'admiration/d'étonnement** to gape *ou* stand gaping in admiration/amazement

beffroi [befʀwa] NM belfry

bégaiement [begɛmɑ̃] NM (*lit*) stammering, stuttering; (*fig = débuts*) **~s** faltering *ou* hesitant beginnings

bégayant, e [begɛjɑ̃, ɑ̃t] ADJ stammering, stuttering

bégayement [begɛmɑ̃] NM = **bégaiement**

bégayer [begeje] ▶conjug 8◀ 1 VI to stammer, stutter, have a stammer 2 VT to stammer (out), falter (out)

bégonia [begɔnja] NM begonia

bègue [bɛg] 1 NMF stammerer, stutterer 2 ADJ **être ~** to stammer, have a stammer

bégueule [begœl] 1 NF prude 2 ADJ prudish

bégueulerie† [begœlʀi] NF prudishness, prudery

béguin [begɛ̃] NM a (* *toquade*) **avoir le ~ pour qn** to have a crush on sb*, be sweet on sb*; **elle a eu le ~ pour cette petite ferme** she took quite a fancy to that little farmhouse b (= *bonnet*) bonnet

béguinage [beginaʒ] NM (*Rel*) Beguine convent

béguine [begin] NF (*Rel*) Beguine

bégum [begɔm] NF begum

behaviorisme [bievjɔʀism] NM behaviourism

behavioriste [bievjɔʀist] ADJ, NMF behaviourist

Behring [beʀiŋ] N = **Béring**

BEI [beøi] NF (ABRÉV = **Banque européenne d'investissement**) EIB

beige [bɛʒ] ADJ, NM beige

beigeasse [bɛʒas], **beigeâtre** [bɛʒɑtʀ] ADJ (*péj*) dirty beige (*péj*), oatmeal (*épith*)

beigne¹: [bɛɲ] NF slap, clout* (*Brit*); **donner une ~ à qn** to slap sb, clout sb* (*Brit*), give sb a clout* (*Brit*)

beigne² [bɛɲ] NM (*Can*) doughnut

beignet [beɲɛ] NM [*fruits, légumes*] fritter; (= *pâte frite*) doughnut; **~ aux pommes** apple doughnut *ou* fritter

Beijing [bɛidʒiŋ] N Beijing

béké [beke] NMF (*terme des Antilles françaises*) white Creole (*in the French West Indies*)

bel [bɛl] ADJ → **beau**

bêlement [bɛlmɑ̃] NM (*Zool, fig*) bleat(ing)

bêler [bele] ▶conjug 1◀ VI (*Zool, fig*) to bleat

belette [bəlɛt] NF weasel

belge [bɛlʒ] 1 ADJ Belgian; **histoires ~s** *jokes told against Belgians by the French* 2 **Belge** NMF Belgian

belgicisme [bɛlʒisism] NM Belgian-French word (*ou phrase*)

Belgique [bɛlʒik] NF Belgium

Belgrade [bɛlgʀad] N Belgrade

bélier [belje] NM (*Zool*) ram; (*Tech*) ram, pile driver; (*Mil*) (battering) ram; **coup de ~** waterhammer; **~ hydraulique** hydraulic ram; (*Astron*) **le Bélier** Aries, the Ram; **être (du) Bélier** to be (an) Aries *ou* an Arian → **voiture**

**bélître†† ** [belitʀ] NM rascal, knave†

Belize [beliz] NM Belize

belizien, -ienne [belizjɛ̃, jɛn] 1 ADJ Belizean 2 **Belizien(ne)** NM,F Belizean

belladone [beladɔn] NF (*Bot*) deadly nightshade, belladonna; (*Méd*) belladonna

bellâtre [belɑtʀ] NM buck, swell*

belle [bɛl] ADJ, NF → **beau**

belle-de-jour (*pl* belles-de-jour) [bɛldəʒuʀ] NF a (*Bot*) convolvulus, morning glory b (*euph* = *prostituée*) prostitute, lady of the night (*euph*)

belle-de-nuit (*pl* belles-de-nuit) [bɛldənɥi] NF a (*Bot*) marvel of Peru b (*euph* = *prostituée*) prostitute, lady of the night (*euph*)

belle-doche: (*pl* belles-doches) [bɛldɔʃ] NF (*péj*) mother-in-law

belle-famille (*pl* belles-familles) [bɛlfamij] NF [*homme*] wife's family, in-laws*; [*femme*] husband's family, in-laws*

belle-fille (*pl* belles-filles) [bɛlfij] NF (= *bru*) daughter-in-law; (*d'un remariage*) stepdaughter

belle-maman* (*pl* belles-mamans) [bɛlmamɑ̃] NF mother-in-law, mum-in-law* (*Brit*)

bellement [bɛlmɑ̃] ADV (= *bel et bien*) well and truly; († = *avec art*) nicely, gently

belle-mère (*pl* belles-mères) [bɛlmɛʀ] NF = *mère du conjoint*) mother-in-law; (= *nouvelle épouse du père*) stepmother

belles-lettres [bɛllɛtʀ] NFPL **les ~** great literature, belles-lettres

belle-sœur (*pl* belles-sœurs) [bɛlsœʀ] NF sister-in-law

bellicisme [belisism] NM bellicosity, warmongering

belliciste [belisist] 1 ADJ warmongering, bellicose 2 NMF warmonger

belligérance [beliʒeʀɑ̃s] NF belligerence, belligerency

belligérant, e [beliʒeʀɑ̃, ɑ̃t] ADJ, NM,F belligerent

belliqueux, -euse [belikø, øz] ADJ [*humeur, personne*] quarrelsome, aggressive; [*politique, peuple*] warlike, bellicose, hawkish; **multiplier les déclarations belliqueuses** to do a lot of sabre-rattling

bellot, -otte†* [belo, ɔt] ADJ [*enfant*] pretty, bonny (*Brit*)

Belmopan [bɛlmɔpan] N Belmopan

belon [bəlɔ̃] NF *ou* M Belon oyster

belote [bəlɔt] NF (= *jeu*) belote; (= *partie*) game of belote

bélouga, béluga [beluga] NM beluga

belvédère [belvedɛʀ] NM (= *terrasse*) panoramic viewpoint, belvedere; (= *édifice*) belvedere

bémol [bemɔl] NM (*Mus*) flat; **en si ~** in B flat; (*fig*) **mettre un ~*** to tone it *ou* things down a bit*

ben* [bɛ̃] ADV well, er*; **~ oui/non** well, yes/no; **~ quoi ?** so (what)?; **eh ~** well, er*

bénard* [benaʀ] NM trousers, pants (*US*)

bénédicité [benedisite] NM grace, blessing; **dire le ~** to say grace *ou* the blessing

bénédictin, e [benediktɛ̃, in] ADJ, NM,F Benedictine → **travail¹**

bénédiction [benediksjɔ̃] NF [a] (*Rel* = *consécration*) benediction, blessing; [*église*] consecration; [*drapeau, bateau*] blessing; **donner la ~ à** to bless; **~ nuptiale** marriage ceremony; (*partie de la cérémonie*) marriage blessing [b] (= *assentiment, faveur*) blessing; **donner sa ~ à** to give one's blessing to [c] (* = *aubaine*) **~ (du ciel)** blessing, godsend

bénef* [benɛf] NM (ABRÉV = **bénéfice**) profit

bénéfice [benefis] [1] NM [a] (*Comm*) profit; **réaliser de gros ~s** to make a big profit *ou* big profits; **faire du ~** to make *ou* turn a profit; (*Fin*) **prise de ~(s)** profit-taking [b] (= *avantage*) advantage, benefit; **c'est tout ~** it's to your (*ou our etc*) advantage; (*Jur*) **il a obtenu un divorce à son ~** he obtained a divorce in his favour; **il perd tout le ~ de sa bonne conduite** he loses all the benefits he has gained from his good behaviour; **concert donné au ~ des aveugles** concert given to raise funds for *ou* in aid of the blind; **conclure une affaire à son ~** to complete a deal to one's advantage; **pourquoi nier, quel ~ peux-tu en tirer ?** what's the point of (your) denying it?, what good is there in (your) denying it?; **le ~ du doute** the benefit of the doubt; (*Jur*) **au ~ de l'âge** by virtue of age [c] (*Rel*) benefice, living [2] COMP ▸ **bénéfice d'exploitation** operating profit ▸ **bénéfice d'inventaire : sous ~ d'inventaire** (*Fin*) without liability to debts beyond assets descended; (*fig*) **je n'accepte leur théorie que sous ~ d'inventaire** it's only with certain reservations that I accept their theory ▸ **bénéfice net par action** (*Fin*) price earning ratio ▸ **bénéfices non distribués** (*Fin*) (accumulated) retained earnings

bénéficiaire [benefisjɛʀ] [1] ADJ [*opération*] profit-making, profitable; **solde ~** credit balance → **marge** [2] NMF (*gén*) beneficiary; [*testament*] beneficiary; [*chèque*] payee; **être le ~ de qch** to benefit by sth

bénéficier [benefisje] ▸ conjug 7 ◂ VT INDIR [a] **~ de** (= *jouir de*) [+ *avantage*] to have, enjoy; (= *obtenir*) [+ *remise*] to get, have; (= *tirer profit de*) [+ *situation, mesure*] to benefit by *ou* from, gain by; **~ d'un préjugé favorable** to be favourably considered; **~ d'un non-lieu** to be (unconditionally) discharged; **~ de circonstances atténuantes** to be granted mitigating circumstances; **faire ~ qn de certains avantages** to enable sb to enjoy certain advantages; **faire ~ qn d'une remise** to give *ou* allow sb a discount [b] **~ à** (= *profiter à*) to benefit; **ces mesures doivent ~ aux plus démunis** these measures should benefit the poorest elements of society

bénéfique [benefik] ADJ [*effet, aspect*] beneficial; (*Astrol*) **l'influence ~ de Vénus** the benign *ou* favourable influence of Venus

Bénélux [benelyks] NM **le ~** Benelux, the Benelux countries

benêt [bənɛ] [1] NM simpleton; **grand ~** big

ninny*, stupid lump*; faire le ~ to act stupid *ou* daft* (*Brit*) [2] ADJ M simple(-minded), silly

bénévolat [benevɔla] NM voluntary help

bénévole [benevɔl] [1] ADJ [*aide*] voluntary; [*travail*] voluntary, unpaid; **à titre ~** on a voluntary basis [2] NMF volunteer, voluntary helper *ou* worker

bénévolement [benevɔlmã] ADV [*travailler*] voluntarily, for nothing

Bengale [bɛ̃gal] NM Bengal → **feu¹**

bengali [bɛ̃gali] [1] ADJ Bengali, Bengalese [2] NM (*Ling*) Bengali; (= *oiseau*) waxbill [3] **Bengali** NMF Bengali, Bengalese

bénigne [benin] ADJ F → **bénin**

bénignité [beniɲite] NF [*maladie*] mildness; (*littér*) [*personne*] benignancy, kindness

Bénin [benɛ̃] NM Benin; **République populaire du ~** People's Republic of Benin

bénin, -igne [benɛ̃, iɲ] ADJ [a] [*accident*] slight, minor; [*punition*] mild; [*maladie, remède*] mild, harmless; [*tumeur*] benign [b] (*littér*) [*humeur, critique*] benign, kindly

béninois, e [beninwa,waz] [1] ADJ Beninese [2] **Béninois(e)** NM,F Beninese

béni-oui-oui* [beniwiwi] NM INV (*péj*) yes man* (*péj*)

bénir [beniʀ] ▸ conjug 2 ◂ VT [a] (*Rel*) [+ *fidèle, objet*] to bless; [+ *mariage*] to bless, solemnize → **dieu** [b] (= *remercier*) to be eternally grateful to, thank God for; **soyez béni !** bless you!; (*iro*) **ah, toi, je te bénis !** oh curse you! *ou* damn you!; **~ le ciel de qch** to thank God for sth; **béni soit le jour où ...** thank God for the day (when) ...; **je bénis cette coïncidence** (I) thank God for this coincidence

bénit, e [beni, it] ADJ [*pain, cierge*] consecrated; [*eau*] holy

bénitier [benitje] NM (*Rel*) stoup, font → **diable, grenouille**

benjamin, e [bɛ̃ʒamɛ̃, in] NM,F [*famille*] youngest child; (*Sport*) ≈ junior (12-13 years old)

benjoin [bɛ̃ʒwɛ̃] NM benzoin

benne [bɛn] NF [a] (*Min*) skip (*Brit*), truck, tub [b] [*camion*] (*basculante*) tipper; (*amovible*) skip; [*grue*] scoop, bucket; [*téléphérique*] (*cable-*)car; **~ à ordures** dustcart (*Brit*), garbage truck (*US*); **camion à ~ basculante** dump truck, tipper lorry (*Brit*)

benoît, e [bənwa, wat] ADJ (*littér*) bland, ingratiating

benoîtement [bənwatmã] ADV (*littér*) blandly, ingratiatingly

benzène [bɛ̃zɛn] NM benzene

benzine [bɛ̃zin] NF benzine

benzol [bɛ̃zɔl] NM benzol

Béotie [beɔsi] NF Boeotia

béotien, -ienne [beɔsjɛ̃, jɛn] [1] ADJ Boeotian [2] NM,F (*péj*) philistine [3] **Béotien(ne)** NM,F Boeotian

BEP [beøpe] NM (ABRÉV = **brevet d'études professionnelles**) → **brevet**

BEPC [beøpese] NM (ABRÉV = **brevet d'études du premier cycle**) → **brevet**

béquée [beke] NF = **becquée**

béquet [bekɛ] NM = **becquet**

béqueter [bɛkte] VT = **becqueter**

béquille [bekij] NF [a] [*infirme*] (*fig*) crutch; **marcher avec des ~s** to walk *ou* be on crutches [b] [*motocyclette, mitrailleuse*] stand; (*Aviat*) tail skid; (*Naut*) shore, prop; **mettre une ~ sous qch** to prop *ou* shore sth up [c] [*serrure*] handle

béquiller [bekije] ▸ conjug 1 ◂ [1] VT (*Naut*) to shore up [2] VI* to walk with *ou* on crutches

ber [bɛʀ] NM (*Can* = *berceau*) cradle

berbère [bɛʀbɛʀ] [1] ADJ Berber [2] NM (*Ling*) Berber [3] **Berbère** NMF Berber

bercail [bɛʀkaj] NM (*Rel, fig*) fold; (*hum*) **rentrer au ~** to return to the fold

berçante* [bɛʀsãt] NF (*Can*) (**chaise**) **~** rocking chair

berce¹ [bɛʀs] NF (*Bot*) hogweed

berce² [bɛʀs] NF (*Belg* = *berceau*) cradle, crib

berceau (*pl* **berceaux**) [bɛʀso] NM [a] (= *lit*) cradle, crib; (= *lieu d'origine*) birthplace; [*civilisation*] cradle; **dès le ~** from birth, from the cradle; **il les prend au ~ !*** he snatches them straight from the cradle!, he's a baby *ou* cradle snatcher! [b] (*Archit*) barrel vault; (= *charmille*) bower, arbour; (*Naut*) cradle → **voûte**

bercelonnette [bɛʀsəlɔnɛt] NF rocking cradle, cradle on rockers

bercement [bɛʀsəmã] NM rocking (movement)

bercer [bɛʀse] ▸ conjug 3 ◂ [1] VT [a] [+ *bébé*] to rock; (*dans ses bras*) to rock, cradle; [+ *navire*] to rock; **les chansons qui ont bercé notre enfance** the songs that we grew up with; **je me suis laissé ~ par sa voix** his voice lulled me; (*hum*) **il a été bercé trop près du mur*** he's a bit soft in the head* [b] (= *apaiser*) [+ *douleur*] to lull, soothe; (= *tromper*) **~ de** to delude with [2] **se bercer** VPR **se ~ de** to delude o.s. with; **se ~ d'illusions** to harbour illusions, delude o.s.

berceur, -euse [bɛʀsœʀ, øz] [1] ADJ [*rythme*] lulling, soothing [2] **berceuse** NF [a] (= *chanson*) lullaby, cradlesong; (*Mus*) berceuse [b] (= *fauteuil*) rocking chair

BERD [bɛʀd] NF (ABRÉV = **Banque européenne pour la reconstruction et le développement**) EBRD

béret [beʀɛ] NM beret; **~ basque** Basque beret; (*Mil*) **les ~s bleus/verts** the Blue/Green Berets

Bérézina [beʀezina] NF (*Géog*) **la ~** the Berezina river; (*fig*) **c'est la ~ !** it's a complete disaster!

bergamasque [bɛʀgamask] NF bergamask

bergamote [bɛʀgamɔt] NF bergamot orange

bergamotier [bɛʀgamɔtje] NM bergamot

berge [bɛʀʒ] NF [a] [*rivière*] bank; **route** *ou* **voie sur ~** riverside *ou* embankment expressway [b] (* = *année*) **il a 50 ~s** he's 50 (years old)

berger [bɛʀʒe] NM (*lit, Rel*) shepherd; (**chien de**) **~** sheepdog; **~ allemand** German shepherd, alsatian (*Brit*); **~ des Pyrénées** Pyrenean mountain dog → **étoile, réponse**

bergère [bɛʀʒɛʀ] NF [a] (= *personne*) shepherdess [b] (= *fauteuil*) wing chair

bergerie [bɛʀʒəʀi] NF [a] (= *abri*) sheepfold → **loup** [b] (*Littérat* = *pièce, poème*) pastoral [c] (*Comm* = *comptoir*) counter

bergeronnette [bɛʀʒəʀɔnɛt] NF wagtail; **~ flavéole/des ruisseaux** yellow/grey wagtail

béribéri [beʀibeʀi] NM beriberi

Béring [beʀiŋ] N **le détroit de ~** the Bering Strait; **mer de ~** Bering Sea

berk* [bɛʀk] EXCL yuk!‡

berkélium [bɛʀkeljɔm] NM berkelium

berlander* [bɛʀlãde] ▸ conjug 1 ◂ VI (*Can*) to prevaricate, equivocate

Berlin [bɛʀlɛ̃] N Berlin; (*Hist*) **~-Est/-Ouest** East/West Berlin

berline [bɛʀlin] NF [a] (*Aut*) saloon (car) (*Brit*), sedan (*US*); (†† : *à chevaux*) berlin [b] (*Min*) truck

berlingot [bɛʀlɛ̃go] NM [a] (= *bonbon*) ≈ boiled sweet (*Brit*), ≈ piece of hard candy (*US*) [b] (= *emballage*) (pyramid-shaped) carton; (*pour shampooing*) sachet

berlinois, e [bɛʀlinwa, waz] [1] ADJ of *ou* from Berlin [2] **Berlinois(e)** NM,F Berliner

berlot [bɛʀlo] NM (*Can*) sleigh

berlue [bɛʀly] NF **j'ai la ~** I must be seeing things

berme [bɛʀm] NF [*canal*] path; [*fossé*] verge

bermuda [bɛʀmyda] NM bermuda shorts, bermudas

Bermudes [bɛʀmyd] NFPL Bermuda → **triangle**

bermudien, -ienne [bɛʀmydjɛ̃, jɛn] [1] ADJ Bermudan, Bermudian [2] **Bermudien(ne)** NM,F Bermudan, Bermudian

bernache [bɛʀnaʃ] NF (= crustacé) barnacle; (= oie) ~ **(nonnette)** barnacle goose; ~ **cravant** brent goose

bernacle [bɛʀnakl] NF barnacle goose

bernardin, e [bɛʀnaʀdɛ̃, in] NM,F Bernardine, Cistercian

bernard-l'(h)ermite [bɛʀnaʀlɛʀmit] NM INV hermit crab

Berne [bɛʀn] N Bern

berne [bɛʀn] NF **en ~ ≈** at half-mast; **mettre en ~ ≈** to half-mast; **avoir le moral en ~** to feel dispirited

berner [bɛʀne] ▶conjug 1 ◀ VT (= tromper) to fool, hoax; (Hist) [+ personne] to toss in a blanket; **il s'est laissé ~ par leurs promesses** he was taken in by their promises

bernicle [bɛʀnikl] NF = **bernique¹**

Bernin [bɛʀnɛ̃] NM **le ~** Bernini

bernique¹ [bɛʀnik] NF (Zool) limpet

bernique²* [bɛʀnik] EXCL (= rien à faire) nothing doing!*, not a chance! ou hope!

béryl [beʀil] NM beryl

béryllium [beʀiljɔm] NM beryllium

berzingue* [bɛʀzɛ̃g] ADV **à tout(e) ~** flat out*

besace [bəzas] NF beggar's bag ou pouch

bésef* [bezef] ADV **il n'y en a pas ~** (quantité) there's not much (of it) ou a lot (of it); (nombre) there aren't many (of them) ou a lot (of them)

besicles [bezikl] NFPL (Hist) spectacles; (hum) glasses, specs*

bésigue [bezig] NM bezique

besogne [bəzɔɲ] NF (= travail) work (NonC), job; **se mettre à la ~** to set to work; **c'est de la belle ~** (lit) this is nice work; (iro) this is a nice mess; **une sale ~** a nasty job; **les basses ~s** the dirty work; **ce serait aller vite en ~ (que de croire que ...)** it would be jumping the gun ou it would be a bit premature (to think that ...)

besogner [bəzɔɲe] ▶conjug 1 ◀ VI to toil (away), drudge

besogneux, -euse [bəzɔɲø, øz] ADJ († = miséreux) needy, poor; (= travailleur) industrious, hard-working

besoin [bəzwɛ̃] NM [a] (= exigence) need (de for); ~**s (d'argent)** financial needs; ~**s essentiels** basic needs; **nos ~s en énergie** our energy needs ou requirements; **subvenir ou pourvoir aux ~s de qn** to provide for sb's needs; **éprouver le ~ de faire qch** to feel the need to do sth; **mentir est devenu un ~ chez lui** lying has become compulsive ou a need with him

[b] (= pauvreté) **le ~** need, want; **être dans le ~** to be in need ou want; **cela les met à l'abri du ~** that will keep the wolf from their door; **une famille dans le ~** a needy family; **pour ceux qui sont dans le ~** for the needy, for those in straitened circumstances; **c'est dans le ~ qu'on reconnaît ses vrais amis** in times of trouble you find out who your true friends are, a friend in need is a friend indeed (PROV)

[c] (euph) ~**s naturels** nature's needs; **faire ses ~s** [personne] to relieve o.s. (Brit); [animal domestique] to do its business; **satisfaire un ~ pressant** to answer an urgent call of nature

[d] (avec avoir) **avoir ~ de qn** to need sb; **avoir ~ de qch** to need sth, be in need of sth, want sth; **avoir ~ de faire qch** to need to do sth; **il n'a pas ~ de venir** he doesn't need ou have to come, there's no need for him to come; **il a ~ que vous l'aidiez** he needs your help ou you to help him; **pas ~ de dire qu'il ne m'a pas cru** it goes without saying ou needless to say he didn't believe me; **je n'ai pas ~ de vous rappeler que ...** there's no need (for me) to remind you that ...; **ce tapis a ~ d'être nettoyé** this

carpet needs ou wants (Brit) cleaning; **il a grand ~ d'aide** he needs help badly, he's badly in need of help; (iro) **il avait bien ~ de ça !** that's just what he needed! (iro); **est-ce que tu avais ~ d'y aller ?*** did you really have to go?, what did you want to go for anyway!

[e] (avec être : littér) **si ~ est ◊ s'il en est ~** if need(s) be, if necessary; **il n'est pas ~ de mentionner que ...** there is no need to mention that ...

[f] (loc) **au ~** if necessary, if need(s) be; **si le ~ s'en fait sentir ◊ en cas de ~** if the need arises, in case of necessity; **pour les ~s de la cause** for the purpose in hand

Bessarabie [besaʀabi] NF Bessarabia

bestiaire [bɛstjɛʀ] NM [a] (= livre) bestiary [b] (= gladiateur) gladiator

bestial, e (mpl -iaux) [bɛstjal, jo] ADJ [meurtre, violence] brutal; [personne, plaisir] bestial; **sa force ~e** his brute strength

bestialement [bɛstjalmɑ̃] ADV bestially, brutishly

bestialité [bɛstjalite] NF (= sauvagerie) bestiality, brutishness; (= perversion) bestiality

bestiaux [bɛstjo] NMPL (gén) livestock; (= bovins) cattle; **ils ont été parqués comme des ~ dans des camps** they were herded ou corralled into camps

bestiole [bɛstjɔl] NF (gén) creature; (= insecte) insect, bug*; (rampant) creepy crawly*

best of* [bɛstɔf] NM INV **un ~ des Beatles** a compilation of the greatest hits of the Beatles; **un ~ de leurs émissions** a selection of highlights of their programmes

best-seller (pl **best-sellers**) [bɛstselœʀ] NM best seller

bêta¹, -asse* [bɛta, as] [1] ADJ silly, stupid [2] NM,F goose*, silly billy*; **gros ~ !** big ninny!*, silly goose!*

bêta² [bɛta] NM (Ling, Phys, Méd) beta

bêtabloquant [bɛtablɔkɑ̃] NM beta-blocker

bêtacarotène [bɛtakaʀɔtɛn] NM betacarotene

bétail [betaj] NM (gén) livestock; (= bovins, fig) cattle; **gros ~** cattle; **petit ~** small livestock; **le ~ humain qu'on entasse dans les camps** the people who are crammed like cattle into the camps

bétaillère [betajɛʀ] NF livestock truck

bêta-test (pl **bêta-tests**) [bɛtatɛst] NM (Ordin) beta-test

bêta-version (pl **bêta-versions**) [bɛtavɛʀsjɔ̃] NM (Ordin) beta version

bête [bɛt] [1] NF [a] (= animal) animal; (= insecte) insect, creature; ~ **(sauvage)** (wild) beast; **nos amies les ~s** our four-legged friends; **aller soigner les ~s** to go and see to the animals; **gladiateur livré aux ~s** gladiator flung to the beasts; **pauvre petite ~** poor little thing* ou creature; **ce chien est une belle ~** this dog is a fine animal ou beast; (hum) **c'est une belle ~ !*** (= homme) what a hunk!; **tu as une petite ~ sur ta manche** there's an insect ou a creepy crawly* on your sleeve; **ces sales ~s ont mangé mes carottes** those wretched creatures have been eating my carrots

[b] (= personne) (bestial) beast; († : stupide) fool; **c'est une méchante ~** he is a wicked creature; **quelle sale ~ !** (enfant) what a wretched pest!; (adulte) what a horrible creature!, what a beast!; **faire la ~** to act stupid ou daft*, play the fool; (hum) **c'est une brave ou une bonne ~ !** he is a good-natured sort ou soul; (terme d'affection) **grande ou grosse ~ !*** you big silly!*; (admiratif) **en maths, c'est la ~ !*** he's a wizard ou he's an ace* at maths!

[c] (* : loc) **travailler comme une ~** to work like a dog; **malade comme une ~** sick as a dog; **on s'est éclatés comme des ~s** we had a whale of a time*

[2] ADJ [a] (= stupide) [personne, idée, sourire] stupid, silly, foolish, idiotic; **ce qu'il peut être**

~**!** what a fool he is!; **il est plus ~ que méchant** he may be stupid but he's not malicious, he's stupid rather than really nasty; **il est loin d'être ~ ◊ il a oublié d'être ~** he's far from ou anything but stupid, he's no fool; **et moi, ~ et discipliné, j'ai obéi** and I did exactly what I was told, without asking myself any questions; **être ~ comme ses pieds*** ou **à manger du foin*** to be too stupid for words, be as thick as a brick*; **lui, pas si ~, est parti à temps** knowing better ou being no fool, he left in time; **ce film est ~ à pleurer** this film is too stupid for words; **c'est ~, on n'a pas ce qu'il faut pour faire des crêpes** it's a shame ou it's too bad we haven't got what we need for making pancakes; **que je suis ~ !** how silly ou stupid of me!, what a fool I am!; **ce n'est pas ~** that's not a bad idea

[b] (* = très simple) **c'est tout ~** it's quite ou dead* simple; ~ **comme chou** simplicity itself, as easy as pie* ou as winking*

[3] COMP ► **bête à bon dieu** ladybird, ladybug (US) ► **bête à concours** swot* (Brit), grind* (US) ► **bête à cornes** horned animal; (hum) snail ► **bête curieuse** (iro) queer ou strange animal:; **ils nous ont regardés comme des ~s curieuses** they looked at us as if we had just landed from Mars ou as if we had two heads ► **bête fauve** big cat; (fig) wild animal ou beast ► **bête féroce** wild animal ou beast ► **bête noire : c'est ma ~ noire** (chose) that's my pet hate ou my bête noire ou my pet peeve* (US); (personne) I just can't stand him ► **bête de race** pedigree animal ► **bête sauvage = bête féroce** ► **bête de scène** great performer ► **bête de sexe:** sex machine* ► **bête de somme** beast of burden ► **bête de trait** draught animal

bétel [betɛl] NM betel

bêtement [bɛtmɑ̃] ADV stupidly, foolishly, idiotically; **tout ~** quite simply

Bethléem [betleɛm] N Bethlehem

Bethsabée [betsabe] NF Bathsheba

bêtifiant, e [betifjɑ̃, jɑ̃t] ADJ [livre, film, ton] inane, asinine

bêtifier [betifje] ▶conjug 7 ◀ VI to prattle stupidly, talk twaddle; **en parlant aux enfants, elle bêtifie toujours** she always tends to talk down to children

bêtise [betiz] NF [a] (NonC = stupidité) stupidity, foolishness, folly; **être d'une ~ crasse** to be incredibly stupid; **j'ai eu la ~ d'accepter** I was foolish enough to accept; **c'était de la ~ d'accepter** it was folly to accept [b] (= action stupide) silly ou stupid thing; (= erreur) blunder; **ne dis pas de ~s** don't talk nonsense ou rubbish (Brit); **ne faites pas de ~s, les enfants** don't get into ou up to mischief, children; **faire une ~** (= action stupide, tentative de suicide) to do something stupid ou silly; (= erreur) to make a blunder, boob* [c] (= bagatelle) trifle, triviality; **dépenser son argent en ~s** to spend ou squander one's money on rubbish (Brit) ou garbage; **ils se disputent sans arrêt pour des ~s** they're forever arguing over trifles [d] (= bonbon) ~ **de Cambrai ≈** mint humbug (Brit), ≈ piece of hard mint candy (US) [e] (Can) ~**s*** insults, rude remarks

bêtisier [betizje] NM (= livre) collection of howlers; (Radio, TV) collection of out-takes

béton [betɔ̃] NM concrete; ~ **armé** reinforced concrete; ~ **cellulaire** air-entrained concrete; **en ~** (lit) concrete (épith); **(en) ~*** [alibi, argument, contrat] cast-iron; [garantie, certitude] cast-iron, ironclad; [organisation] ultra-efficient; (en justice) **un dossier en ~** a watertight case; (Ftbl) **faire ou jouer le ~** to play defensively; **laisse ~ !*** forget it!*

bétonnage [betɔnaʒ] NM (Constr) concreting; **pour éviter le ~ du littoral** to prevent the coast from becoming a sprawl of concrete [b] (Ftbl) defensive play

bétonner [betɔne] ▶ conjug 1◀ [1] VT [a] (Constr) to concrete; **surface bétonnée** concrete surface; (péj) **ils bétonnent nos côtes** our coastline is becoming very built-up ou is being turned into a concrete jungle [2] VI (Ftbl) to play defensively

bétonneur [betɔnœʀ] NM (péj) (building) developer

bétonneuse [betɔnøz], **bétonnière** [betɔnjɛʀ] NF cement mixer

bette [bɛt] NF ~**s** (Swiss) chard; **une ~** a piece of chard

betterave [bɛtʀav] NF ~ **fourragère** mangel-wurzel, beet; ~ **(rouge)** beetroot (Brit), beet (US); ~ **sucrière** sugar beet

betteravier, -ière [bɛtʀavje, jɛʀ] [1] ADJ [culture, exploitation] (sugar) beet (épith) [2] NM beet grower

beuglant [bøglɑ̃] NM honky-tonk*

beuglante [bøglɑ̃t] NF (= cri) yell, holler*; (= chanson) song; **pousser une ~** to yell, give a yell ou holler*

beuglement [bøgləmɑ̃] NM [a] [vache] lowing (NonC), mooing (NonC); [taureau] bellowing (NonC) [b] [personne] bawling (NonC), bellowing (NonC), hollering* (NonC); **pousser des ~s** to bawl, bellow [c] [radio, télévision] blaring (NonC)

beugler [bøgle] ▶ conjug 1◀ [1] VI [a] [vache] to low, moo; [taureau] to bellow [b]* [personne] to bawl, bellow, holler* [c] [radio, TV] to blare; **faire ~ sa télé** to have one's TV on (at) full blast* [2] VT (péj) [+ chanson] to bellow out, belt out*

beur [bœʀ] [1] NMF second-generation North African living in France [2] ADJ [culture, musique] of second-generation North Africans living in France

---
BEUR

Beur is the term used to refer to a person born in France of North African immigrant parents. It is not a racist term and is often used by the media, anti-racist groups and second-generation North Africans themselves. The word itself originally came from the "verlan" rendering of the word "arabe". → VERLAN
---

beurk [bœʀk] EXCL = **berk**

beurre [bœʀ] [1] NM [a] (laitier) butter; ~ **salé/demi-sel** salted/slightly salted butter; ~ **doux** unsalted butter; **au ~** [plat] (cooked) in butter; [pâtisserie] made with butter; **faire la cuisine au ~** to cook with butter; ~ **fondu** melted butter → **inventer, motte, œil** [b] (Culin) paste; ~ **d'anchois/d'écrevisses** anchovy/shrimp paste; (= substance végétale) ~ **de cacao/de cacahuètes** cocoa/peanut butter [c] (*: loc) **le couteau entre dans cette viande comme dans du ~** this meat is like butter to cut; **c'est entré comme dans du ~** it went like a (hot) knife through butter; **cette viande, c'est du ~!** this is very tender meat; **ça va mettre du ~ dans les épinards** that'll be some handy extra money for you (ou him etc), that'll help you (ou him etc) make ends meet; **faire son ~** to make a packet* ou a pile*; **il n'y en a pas plus que de ~ en broche** there is (ou are) none at all; **on ne peut pas avoir le ~ et l'argent du ~** you can't have your cake and eat it → **compter** [2] COMP ▶ **beurre d'escargot = beurre persillé** ▶ **beurre laitier** dairy butter ▶ **beurre noir** (Culin) brown (butter) sauce ▶ **beurre persillé** garlic and parsley butter

beurré, e [bœʀe] (ptp de **beurrer**) [1] ADJ (*: = ivre) plastered* [2] NM butter-pear, beurré [3] **beurrée†** NF (Can) slice of bread and peanut butter

beurre-frais [bœʀfʀɛ] ADJ INV (= couleur) buttercup yellow

beurrer [bœʀe] ▶ conjug 1◀ [1] VT to butter; **tartine beurrée** slice of bread and butter [2] **se beurrer:** VPR to get plastered‡

beurrier, -ière [bœʀje, jɛʀ] [1] ADJ [industrie, production] butter (épith); **région beurrière** butter-producing region [2] NM butter dish

beuverie [bøvʀi] NF drinking bout ou session, binge*

bévue [bevy] NF blunder; **commettre une ~** to make a blunder

bey [bɛ] NM bey

Beyrouth [beʀut] N Beirut

bézef‡ [bezɛf] ADV = **bésef**

Bhoutan, Bhutân [butɑ̃] NM Bhutan

bhoutanais, e [butanɛ, ɛz] [1] ADJ Bhutanese [2] **Bhoutanais(e)** NM,F Bhutanese

bi¹ [bi] ADJ, NMF (ABRÉV = **bisexuel, -elle**) bi*

bi² [bi] NM (Can = baiser) kiss; **fais-moi un ~** kiss me, give me a kiss

bi... [bi] PRÉF bi...; **~dimensionnel** two-dimensional

biacide [biasid] ADJ, NM diacid

Biafra [bjafʀa] NM Biafra

biafrais, e [bjafʀɛ, ɛz] [1] ADJ Biafran [2] **Biafrais(e)** NM,F Biafran

biais, e [bjɛ, jɛz] [1] ADJ [arc] skew [2] NM [a] (= moyen) way, means; (= détour, artifice) expedient, dodge*; **chercher un ~ pour obtenir qch** to find some means of getting sth ou some expedient for getting sth; **il a trouvé le ~ (pour se faire exempter)** he found a dodge* ou he managed to find a way (to get himself exempted); **par quel ~ a-t-il réussi à s'introduire dans le pays?** by what roundabout means did he manage to get into the country?; **par le ~ de** (= par l'intermédiaire de) through; (= au moyen de) by means of; **réserver par le ~ d'une agence** to book through an agency; **communiquer par le ~ du fax** to communicate by ou via fax [b] (= aspect) angle, way; **c'est par ce ~ qu'il faut aborder le problème** the problem should be approached from this angle ou in this way [c] (Tex) (= sens) bias; (= bande) bias binding; **coupé** ou **taillé dans le ~** cut on the bias ou the cross; **jupe en ~** skirt cut on the bias [d] (= ligne oblique) slant [e] (Sociol) bias [f] (loc) **en ~** ◊ **de ~** (poser) slantwise, at an angle; [aborder un sujet] indirectly, in a roundabout way; **une allée traverse le jardin en ~** a path cuts diagonally across the garden; **regarder qn de ~** to give sb a sidelong glance

biaisé, e [bjeze] (ptp de **biaiser**) ADJ [a] (Stat) [échantillon, données] biased; (= faussé) [vision] distorted; **une perception ~e de la réalité** a distorted ou skewed view of reality; **depuis cet incident, les relations entre les deux pays sont un peu ~es** since this incident the two countries have had a somewhat skewed relationship; **leurs questions sont toujours ~es** their questions always have a certain slant to them [b] (= avec un parti pris) [reportage, conclusion, raisonnement, analyse] biased; **la composition du jury était ~e** the jury was made up of an unrepresentative sample of people

biaiser [bjeze] ▶ conjug 1◀ [1] VI [a] (= louvoyer) to sidestep the issue, prevaricate [b] (= obliquer) to change direction [2] VT (Stat) [+ résultat] to bias

biathlon [biatlɔ̃] NM biathlon

bibelot [biblo] NM (sans valeur) trinket, knick-knack; (de valeur) bibelot, curio

biberon [bibʀɔ̃] NM feeding bottle, baby's bottle; **élevé au ~** bottle-fed; **l'heure du ~** (baby's) feeding time; **élever** ou **nourrir au ~** to bottle-feed; **il est à 6 ~s (par jour)** he's on 6 feeds (a day)

biberonner [bibʀɔne] ▶ conjug 1◀ VI to tipple*, booze*

bibi¹ [bibi] NM woman's hat

bibi² [bibi] PRON me, yours truly (hum)

bibine [bibin] NF (weak) beer, dishwater (hum); **une infâme ~** a foul ou loathsome brew

bibi(t)te [bibit] NF (Can) insect, bug*

bible [bibl] NF (= livre, fig) bible; **la Bible** the Bible

bibli [bibli] NF ABRÉV = **bibliothèque**

bibliobus [biblijobys] NM mobile library, bookmobile (US)

bibliographe [biblijɔgʀaf] NMF bibliographer

bibliographie [biblijɔgʀafi] NF bibliography

bibliographique [biblijɔgʀafik] ADJ bibliographic(al)

bibliomane [biblijɔman] NMF booklover

bibliomanie [biblijɔmani] NF bibliomania

bibliophile [biblijɔfil] NMF bibliophile (frm), booklover

bibliophilie [biblijɔfili] NF bibliophilism (frm), love of books

bibliothécaire [biblijɔtekɛʀ] NMF librarian

bibliothéconomie [biblijɔtekɔnɔmi] NF library science

bibliothèque [biblijɔtɛk] NF (= édifice, pièce) library; (= meuble) bookcase; (= collection) library, collection (of books); ~ **de gare** station bookstall (Brit) ou newsstand (US); ~ **municipale/universitaire** public/university library; ~ **de prêt** lending library

---
BIBLIOTHÈQUE NATIONALE

The "BN", as it is popularly known, was founded in 1537 by Francis I. Situated in the rue de Richelieu in Paris, it is a copyright deposit library holding important historic collections of printed and manuscript material. The building has become too small to house the collections adequately, and most of its material is being transferred to a vast new library complex in the south-east of the city.
---

biblique [biblik] ADJ biblical

bibliquement [biblikmɑ̃] ADV biblically; (hum ou frm) **connaître ~ qn** to know sb in the biblical sense (hum), have carnal knowledge of sb (frm)

bic® [bik] NM **(pointe) ~** ≈ Biro®, ≈ ballpoint pen, ≈ Bic® (pen) (US)

bicaméral, e (mpl **-aux**) [bikameʀal, o] ADJ bicameral, two-chamber (épith)

bicaméralisme [bikameʀalism], **bicamérisme** [bikameʀism] NM bicameral ou two-chamber system

bicarbonate [bikaʀbɔnat] NM bicarbonate; ~ **de soude** bicarbonate of soda, sodium bicarbonate, baking soda

bicarré, e [bikaʀe] ADJ (Math) biquadratic

bicentenaire [bisɑ̃t(ə)nɛʀ] NM bicentenary, bicentennial

bicéphale [bisefal] ADJ two-headed, bicephalous (SPÉC)

biceps [bisɛps] NM biceps; **avoir des** ou **du ~*** to have a strong ou good pair of arms

biche [biʃ] NF hind, doe; **un regard** ou **des yeux de ~** doe-like eyes; (terme d'affection) **ma ~** darling, pet*

bicher [biʃe] ▶ conjug 1◀ VI [a] [personne] to be pleased with o.s. [b] (= aller) **ça biche?** how's things?*, things O.K. with you?*

bichette [biʃɛt] NF (terme d'affection) **(ma) ~** darling, pet*

Bichkek [biʃkɛk] N Pishpek

bichlorure [biklɔʀyʀ] NM bichloride

bichon, -onne [biʃɔ̃, ɔn] NM,F (= chien) bichon frise; **mon ~** pet*, love*

bichonner [biʃɔne] ▶ conjug 1◀ [1] VT [+ personne] to pamper, cosset; **il bichonne sa moto/la pelouse** he lavishes care on his motorbike/the lawn [2] **se bichonner** VPR to dress up, spruce o.s. up; (péj) **elle est en train de se ~ dans sa chambre** she's getting dolled up* in her room

bichromate [bikʀɔmat] NM bichromate

bichromie [bikʀɔmi] NF two-colour process

biclou* [biklu] NM (= bicyclette) bike

bicolore [bikɔlɔʀ] ADJ bicolour(ed) (Brit), bicolor(ed) (US), two-colour(ed) (Brit), two-color(ed) (US), two-tone; (Cartes) two-suited

biconcave [bikɔ̃kav] ADJ biconcave

biconvexe [bikɔ̃vɛks] ADJ biconvex

bicoque [bikɔk] NF (péj) dump*; (* : hum) **ils ont une petite ~ au bord de la mer** they've got a little place by the sea

bicorne [bikɔʀn] 1 NM cocked hat 2 ADJ two-horned

bicot⁜ [biko] NM (injurieux) (North African) Arab

bicross [bikʀɔs] NM (= vélo) ≈ mountain bike; (= sport) ≈ mountain biking

biculturel, -elle [bikyltyʀɛl] ADJ bicultural

bicycle [bisikl] NM (Hist, à grande et petite roues) penny farthing (bicycle) (Brit), ordinary (US); (Can) bicycle

bicyclette [bisiklɛt] NF a (= véhicule) bicycle, bike*; **aller à la ville à** ou **en ~** to go to town by bicycle, cycle to town; **faire de la ~** to go cycling, cycle; **sais-tu faire de la ~?** can you cycle?, can you ride a bike?* b (Sport) cycling

bidasse* [bidas] NM (= conscrit) soldier, squaddy (arg Mil, Brit)

bide [bid] NM a (⁜ = ventre) belly*; **avoir du ~** to have a potbelly b (* = échec) (gén) flop*, fiasco; **il a essayé de la draguer, mais ça a été le ~** he tried to pick her up but failed miserably; (Théât, Ciné) **être** ou **faire un ~** to be a flop* ou a washout ou a bomb* (US)

bidet [bidɛ] NM a (= cuvette) bidet b (= cheval) (old) nag

bidirectionnel, -elle [bidiʀɛksjɔnɛl] ADJ bidirectional

bidoche⁜ [bidɔʃ] NF meat

bidon [bidɔ̃] 1 NM a (gén) can, tin; (à huile, à essence) can; (à peinture) tin; [cycliste, soldat] water bottle, flask; **~ à lait** milk-churn; **huile en ~** oil in a can b (⁜ = ventre) belly* c (⁜ = bluff) **c'est du ~** that's a load of hot air ou bull⁜ ou codswallop⁜ (Brit); **ce n'est pas du ~** I'm (ou he's etc) not kidding!* 2 ADJ INV (⁜ = simulé) [attentat, attaque] mock (épith); [déclaration, prétexte] phoney*, phony* (US); [élection] rigged; [maladie, émotion] sham (épith); **société ~** ghost company; **il est ~** he's phoney* ou phony* (US)

bidonnage* [bidɔnaʒ] NM [reportage, CV] faking; **cette interview, c'était du ~** that interview was faked ou was a put-up* job

bidonnant, e⁜ [bidɔnɑ̃, ɑ̃t] ADJ hilarious; **c'était ~** it was a scream*, it was sidesplittingly funny*

bidonner [bidɔne] ▶ conjug 1 ◀ 1 **se bidonner** VPR to split one's sides (laughing)*, be doubled up (with laughter), crease up* 2 VT (* = truquer) [+ reportage, CV] to fake

bidonville [bidɔ̃vil] NM shanty town

bidouillage* [bidujaʒ] NM **c'est du ~** it's just been cobbled together

bidouiller* [biduje] ▶ conjug 1 ◀ VT a (gén = réparer) to (have a) tinker with; (Ordin) [+ programme] to hack up; **j'ai réussi à le ~** I've managed to fix it for the time being b (péj = truquer) [+ compteur] to fiddle with, fix; [+ élection] to rig

bidouilleur, -euse* [bidujœʀ, øz] NM,F **c'est un ~** (= habile) he's quite good with his hands; (péj) he's a bit of a botcher*

bidous* [bidu] NMPL (Can) money, dough⁜

bidule* [bidyl] NM (= machin) contraption, thingumajig*, thingummy* (Brit), whatsit*

(Brit); (= personne) what's-his-name* (ou what's-her-name*), whatsit* (Brit); **eh ~!** hey (you) what's-your-name!*

bief [bjɛf] NM a [canal] reach b [moulin] **~ d'amont** headrace; **~ d'aval** tail race ou water

bielle [bjɛl] NF [locomotive] connecting rod; [voiture] track rod

biellette [bjɛlɛt] NF (Aut) stub axle

biélorusse [bjelɔʀys] 1 ADJ Byelorussian 2 **Biélorusse** NMF Byelorussian

Biélorussie [bjelɔʀysi] NF Byelorussia

---

bien [bjɛ̃]

1 ADVERBE	3 NOM MASCULIN
2 ADJECTIF INVARIABLE	4 COMPOSÉS

1 ADVERBE

a = **de façon satisfaisante** [jouer, dormir, travailler] well; [conseiller, choisir] well, wisely; [fonctionner] properly, well; **aller** ou **se porter ~** ◊ **être ~ portant** to be well, be in good health; **comment vas-tu?** — **~/très ~ merci** how are you? — fine/very well, thanks; **nous avons ~ travaillé aujourd'hui** we've done some good work today; **il a ~ réussi** he's done well (for himself); **cette porte ne ferme pas ~** this door doesn't shut properly; **la télé ne marche pas ~** the TV isn't working properly ou right; **il s'habille ~** he dresses well ou smartly; **il parle ~ l'anglais** he speaks good English, he speaks English well; **elle est ~ coiffée aujourd'hui** her hair looks nice today; **on est ~ nourri dans cet hôtel** the food's good in that hotel; **il a ~ pris ce que je lui ai dit** he took what I said in good part ou quite well; **il s'y est ~ pris (pour le faire)** he went about it the right way; **si je me rappelle ~** if I remember right(ly) ou correctly; **ni ~ ni mal** so-so*; (auteur) **il n'écrit ni ~ ni mal** he's so-so as an author

b = **selon les convenances, la morale, la raison** [se conduire, agir] well, decently; **il pensait ~ faire** he thought he was doing the right thing; **vous avez ~ fait** you did the right thing, you did right; **il a ~ fait de partir** he was quite right ou he did right to go; **faire ~ les choses** to do things properly ou in style; **vous faites ~ de me le dire!** you did well to tell me!, it's a good thing you've told me!; **vous feriez ~ de partir tôt** you'd do well ou you'd be well advised to leave early; **ça commence à ~ faire!** this has gone on quite long enough!, this is getting beyond a joke!; **~ lui en a pris** it was just as well he did it

c = **sans difficulté** [supporter] well; [se rappeler] well, clearly; **on comprend très ~ pourquoi** you can certainly understand ou see why; **il peut très ~ le faire** he's perfectly capable of doing it

d **exprimant le degré** (= très) very, really; (= beaucoup) very much, thoroughly; (= trop) rather; **~ mieux** much better; **~ souvent** quite often; **nous sommes ~ contents de vous voir** we're very ou awfully glad to see you; **~ plus heureux/ex** far ou much happier/more expensive; **c'est un ~ beau pays** it's a really ou truly beautiful country; **nous avons ~ ri** we had a good laugh; **les enfants se sont ~ amusés** the children thoroughly enjoyed themselves ou had great fun; **vos œufs sont ~ frais?** are your eggs really fresh?; **question ~ délicate** highly sensitive question; **~ trop bête** far too stupid; **elle est ~ jeune (pour se marier)** she is very ou rather young (to be getting married); **c'est ~ moderne pour mes goûts** it's rather too modern for my taste; **il me paraît ~ sûr de lui** he seems to be rather ou pretty* sure of himself to me

e **effectivement** indeed, definitely; (interrog = réellement) really; **nous savons ~ où il se cache** we know perfectly well ou quite well where he's hiding; **j'avais ~ dit que je ne viendrais pas** I (certainly) did say that I wouldn't come; **je trouve ~ que c'est un peu cher mais**

tant pis I do think it's rather expensive ou I agree it's rather expensive but never mind; **c'est ~ une erreur** it's definitely ou certainly a mistake; **était-ce ~ une erreur?** was it really ou in fact a mistake?; **c'est ~ à ton frère que je pensais** it was indeed your brother I was thinking of; **ce n'est pas lui mais ~ son frère qui est docteur** it's his brother not him who is a doctor; **dis-lui ~ que** be sure to ou and tell him that ...; make sure you tell him that ...; **je vous avais ~ averti** I gave you ample warning, I did warn you; **c'est ~ mon manteau?** that is my coat, isn't it?

f **dans une exclamative** (= vraiment, justement) **il s'agit ~ de ça!** as if that's the point!; **voilà ~ les femmes!** that's women for you!; **c'est ~ ça, on t'invite et tu te décommandes!** that's you all over ou that's just like you! — we invite you over and then you say you can't come!

g **avec valeur intensive** **ferme ~ la porte** shut the door properly, make sure you shut the door; **tourne ~ ton volant à droite** turn your wheel hard to the right; **écoute-moi ~** listen to me carefully; **regardez ~ ce qu'il va faire** watch what he does carefully; **mets-toi ~ en face** stand right ou straight opposite; **percez un trou ~ au milieu** drill a hole right in the centre; **tiens-toi ~ droit** stand quite straight; **il est mort et ~ mort** he's dead and gone; **c'est ~ compris?** is that quite clear ou understood?; **c'est ~ promis?** is that a firm promise?; **il arrivera ~ à se débrouiller** he'll manage to cope all right; **j'espère ~!** I should hope so (too)!; **où peut-il ~ être?** where on earth can he be?; (dans une lettre) **~ à vous** yours

h = **malgré tout** **il fallait ~ que ça se fasse** it just had to be done; **il faut ~ le supporter** you've just got to put up with it; **il pourrait ~ venir nous voir de temps en temps!** he could at least come and see us now and then!

i = **volontiers** (précédé d'un verbe au conditionnel) **je mangerais ~ un morceau** I could do with a bite to eat, I wouldn't mind something to eat; **je l'aiderais ~, mais ...** I wish I could help him, but ...; **j'irais ~, mais ...** I'd love to go but ...; **je voudrais ~ t'y voir!** I'd like ou love to see you try!, I'd sure like* (US) to see you try!; **je te verrais ~ en jaune** I think you'd look good in yellow

j = **au moins** at least; **il y a ~ 3 jours que je ne l'ai vu** I haven't seen him for at least 3 days; **cela vaut ~ ce prix là** it's worth at least that

k **locutions figées**

♦ **bien du, de la** a great deal of; **elle a eu ~ du mal** ou **de la peine à le trouver** she had a good ou great deal of difficulty in ou no end of trouble* in finding it; **ça fait ~ du monde** that's an awful lot of people; **ils ont eu ~ de la chance** they were really very lucky

♦ **bien des** a good many; **je connais ~ des gens qui auraient protesté** I know a good many ou quite a few people who would have protested

♦ **bien que** although, though; **~ que je ne puisse pas venir** although ou though I can't come

♦ **bien sûr** of course; **~ sûr qu'il viendra!** of course he'll come!

♦ **pour bien faire** : **pour ~ faire il faudrait partir maintenant** the best thing would be to leave now; **pour ~ faire, il aurait fallu terminer hier** it would have been better if we had finished yesterday

2 ADJECTIF INVARIABLE

a = **satisfaisant** [film, tableau, livre] good; [personne] **elle est très ~ comme secrétaire** she's a very good ou competent secretary; **donnez-lui quelque chose de ~** give him something really good; **ce serait ~ s'il venait** it would be good if he were to come; **~!** (approbation) good!, fine!; (pour changer de sujet) O.K.!, all right!; (exaspération) **bien ~!** ◊ **c'est ~!** all right! all right!, O.K.! O.K.!

b Scol, sur copie good; **assez ~** quite good; **très ~** very good

c = en bonne forme well, in good form ou health; **je ne suis pas ~** I don't feel very well; **tu n'es pas ~?** are you feeling OK?; **il n'était pas très ~ ce matin** he was out of sorts ou off colour* (Brit) this morning

d = beau [personne] good-looking, nice-looking; [chose] nice; **elle était très ~ quand elle était jeune** she was very attractive ou good-looking when she was young; **il est ~ de sa personne** he's a good-looking man ou a fine figure of a man; **ils ont une maison tout ce qu'il y a de ~*** they've got a really lovely ou nice house; **ce bouquet fait ~ sur la cheminée** those flowers look nice on the mantelpiece

e = à l'aise il est **~ partout** he is ou feels at home anywhere; **on est ~ à l'ombre** it's pleasant ou nice in the shade; **on est ~ ici** it's nice here, we like it here; **je suis ~ dans ce fauteuil** I'm very comfortable in this chair; **elle se trouve ~ dans son nouveau poste** she's very happy in her new job; **laisse-le, il est ~ où il est!** leave him alone — he's quite all right where he is ou he's fine where he is; (iro) **vous voilà ~!** now you've done it!, you're in a fine mess now!

f = acceptable (socialement) nice; (moralement) right; **c'est pas ~ de dire ça** it's not nice to say that; **ce n'est pas ~ de faire ça** it's not nice ou right to do that; **c'est ~ ce qu'il a fait là** it was very good ou decent ou nice of him to do that; **c'est ~ à vous de les aider** it's good ou nice of you to help them; **c'est un type ~*** he's a nice guy* ou bloke* (Brit); **c'est une femme ~** she's a very nice woman; **des gens ~** very nice ou decent people

g = en bons termes être **~ avec qn** to be on good terms ou get on well with sb; **ils sont ~ ensemble** they're on the best of terms; **se mettre ~ avec qn** to get on the good ou right side of sb, get into sb's good books*

3 NOM MASCULIN

a NonC = ce qui est avantageux, agréable good; **le ~ public** the public good; **c'est pour ton ~!** it's for your own good!; **pour le (plus grand) ~ de l'humanité** for the (greater) good of humanity; **faire du ~ à qn/qch** to do sb/sth good; **ça ne va pas faire de ~ à sa réputation** that's not going to do his reputation any good; **ses paroles m'ont fait du ~** what he said did me good; **ça fait du ~ de se confier** it's good to talk; **je me suis cogné la tête, ça ne fait pas de ou du ~!** I bumped my head and it really hurt ou it didn't half* (Brit) hurt; **ça fait du ~ par où ça passe*!** that hits the spot!; **dire du ~ de qn** to speak well of sb; **on a dit le plus grand ~ de ce livre/de cet acteur** this book/this actor has been highly praised, people have spoken very highly ou favourably of this book/this actor; **on dit beaucoup de ~ de ce restaurant** this restaurant has got a very good name, people speak very highly of this restaurant; **vouloir du ~ à qn** to wish sb well; (iro) **un ami qui vous veut du ~** a well-wisher (iro); (iro) **grand ~ vous fasse!** much good may it do you!; **vous y êtes le ~ venu to it!**; (littér) **être du dernier ~ avec qn** to be on the closest possible terms ou on intimate terms with sb

♦ **en bien je trouve qu'il a changé en ~** I find he has changed for the better ou he has improved; **parler en ~ de qn** to speak favourably ou well of sb

b = avantage finalement cet échec temporaire **a été un ~** in the end this setback was a good thing; **son départ a été un ~ pour l'entreprise** it was a good thing for the firm that he left

c = ce qui a une valeur morale **le ~** good; **savoir discerner le ~ du mal** to be able to tell good from evil ou right from wrong; **faire le ~** to do good; **rendre le ~ pour le mal** to return good for evil

d = possession possession, property (NonC); (= argent) fortune; (= terre) estate; **~s** goods; **cet ordinateur est son ~ le plus cher** this computer is his most treasured possession; **la tranquillité est le seul ~ qu'il désire** peace of mind is all he asks for; **il considère tout comme son ~** he regards everything as being his property ou his own; **il a dépensé tout son ~** he has gone through his entire fortune; **avoir du ~ (au soleil)** to have property; **laisser tous ses ~s à qn** to leave all one's (worldly) goods ou possessions to sb; **il est très attaché aux ~s de ce monde** he lays great store by worldly goods ou possessions ■ (PROV) **~ mal acquis ne profite jamais** ill-gotten gains seldom prosper (PROV), ill gotten ill spent

4 COMPOSÉS

▶ **biens de consommation** consumer goods ▶ **biens durables** consumer durables ▶ **biens d'équipement** capital equipment ou goods; (Ind) plant ▶ **biens d'équipement ménager** household goods ▶ **bien de famille** family estate ▶ **biens immeubles, biens immobiliers, biens fonciers** real estate, property (Brit), landed property ▶ **biens immédiatement disponibles** off-the-shelf goods ▶ **biens intermédiaires** (Admin) intermediate goods ▶ **bien marchand** commodity ▶ **biens meubles, biens mobiliers** personal property ou estate, movables ▶ **biens privés** private property ▶ **biens publics** public property

bien-aimé, e (mpl **bien-aimés**) [bjɛ̃neme] ADJ, NM,F beloved

bien-être [bjɛ̃nɛtʀ] NM INV (physique, psychologique) well-being; (matériel) comfort, material well-being

bienfaisance [bjɛ̃fəzɑ̃s] NF charity; **association ou œuvre de ~** charitable organization, charity; **l'argent sera donné à des œuvres de ~** the money will be given to charity

bienfaisant, e [bjɛ̃fəzɑ̃, ɑ̃t] ADJ **a** [effets] salutary, beneficial; [pluie] life-giving; **eaux aux vertus ~es** health-giving waters; (Astrol) **l'influence ~e de Vénus** the favourable ou benign influence of Venus **b** † [personne] beneficent (fml), kindly

bienfait [bjɛ̃fe] NM (= faveur) kindness, kind deed; (surtout pl = avantage) benefit; **c'est un ~ du ciel!** it's a godsend! ou a blessing! ■ (PROV) **un ~ n'est jamais perdu** a good turn ou deed never goes amiss; **les ~s du progrès** the benefits of progress; **les ~s d'un traitement** the beneficial effects of a course of treatment; **il commence à ressentir les ~s de son séjour à la campagne** he is beginning to feel the benefit of his stay in the country

bienfaiteur [bjɛ̃fɛtœʀ] NM benefactor
bienfaitrice [bjɛ̃fɛtʀis] NF benefactress

bien-fondé (pl **bien-fondés**) [bjɛ̃fɔ̃de] NM [opinion, assertion] validity; (Jur) [plainte] cogency

bien-fonds (pl **biens-fonds**) [bjɛ̃fɔ̃] NM real estate, landed property

bienheureux, -euse [bjɛ̃nœʀø, øz] ADJ **a** (Rel) blessed, blest (littér); **les ~** the blessed, the blest **b** (littér) happy; **~ ceux qui ...** lucky are those who ...

biennal, e (mpl **-aux**) [bjenal, o] **1** ADJ biennial **2** **biennale** NF biennial event

bien-pensant, e (mpl **bien-pensants**) [bjɛ̃pɑ̃sɑ̃, ɑ̃t] **1** ADJ (Rel) God-fearing; (péj = conformiste) right-thinking **2** NM,F **les ~s** (Rel) God-fearing people; (péj = conformistes) right-thinking people

bienséance [bjɛ̃seɑ̃s] NF propriety, decorum; **les ~s** the proprieties

bienséant, e [bjɛ̃seɑ̃, ɑ̃t] ADJ [action, conduite] proper, seemly, becoming; **il n'est pas ~ de bâiller** it is unbecoming ou unseemly to yawn

bientôt [bjɛ̃to] ADV soon; **à ~!** see you soon!, bye for now!*; **c'est ~ dit** it's easier said than done, it's easy to say; **on est ~ arrivé** we'll soon be there, we'll be there shortly; **on ne pourra ~ plus circuler dans Paris** before long it will be impossible to drive in Paris; **c'est pour ~?** is it due soon?, any chance of its being ready soon?; (naissance) is the baby expected ou due soon?; **il est ~ minuit** it's nearly midnight; **il aura ~ 30 ans** he'll soon be 30; **il eut ~ fait de finir son travail†** he finished his work in no time, he lost no time in finishing his work

bienveillance [bjɛ̃vɛjɑ̃s] NF benevolence, kindness (envers to); **avec ~** [dire, regarder] benevolently, kindly; [parler] kindly; **examiner un cas avec ~** to give favourable consideration to a case; (Admin) **je sollicite de votre haute ~ ...** I beg (leave) to request ...

bienveillant, e [bjɛ̃vɛjɑ̃, ɑ̃t] ADJ benevolent, kindly

bienvenu, e [bjɛ̃v(ə)ny] **1** ADJ **remarque ~e** apposite ou well-chosen remark **2** NM,F **vous êtes le ~, soyez le ~** you're very welcome, pleased to see you*; **une tasse de café serait la ~e** a cup of coffee would be (most) welcome **3** **bienvenue** NF **souhaiter la ~ à qn** to welcome sb; **~e à vous!** welcome (to you)!, you are most welcome!; **allocution de ~e** welcoming speech; **~e à Paris/en Italie!** welcome to Paris/to Italy!; **~e parmi nous!** welcome (to the department ou company ou neighbourhood etc)!; (Can = je vous en prie) **~e!** you're welcome!

bière¹ [bjɛʀ] NF beer; **garçon, deux ~s!** waiter, two beers!; **~ blanche** type of Belgian beer brewed from wheat; **~ blonde** ≈ lager, ≈ light ale (Brit), ≈ light beer (US); **~ brune** ≈ brown ale, ≈ dark beer (US) → **petit, pression**

bière² [bjɛʀ] NF coffin, casket (US); **mettre qn en ~** to put ou place sb in their coffin; **la mise en ~ a eu lieu ce matin** the body was placed in the coffin this morning

biface [bifas] NM (Archéol) flint, biface
biffage [bifaʒ] NM crossing out
biffer [bife] ▶ conjug 1 ◀ VT to cross out, strike out; **~ à l'encre/au crayon** to cross out in ink/pencil out
biffeton [biftɔ̃] NM (bank)note, bill (US)
biffin [bifɛ̃] NM (arg Mil) foot soldier, infantryman; (†* = chiffonnier) rag-and-bone man
biffure [bifyʀ] NF crossing out
bifide [bifid] ADJ bifid
bifidus [bifidys] NM bifidus; **yaourt au ~** yogurt containing bifidus, bio yogurt
bifocal, e (mpl **-aux**) [bifɔkal, o] ADJ bifocal; **lunettes ~es** bifocals
bifteck [biftɛk] NM steak; **~ de cheval** horsemeat steak; **deux ~s** two steaks, two pieces of steak → **défendre, gagner, haché**
bifurcation [bifyʀkasjɔ̃] NF [route] fork, junction; (Rail) fork; [artère, tige] branching; (fig = changement) change
bifurquer [bifyʀke] ▶ conjug 1 ◀ VI **a** [route, voie ferrée] to fork, branch off **b** [véhicule] to turn off (vers, sur for, towards); (fig) [personne] to branch off (vers into); **~ sur la droite** to turn ou bear right
bigame [bigam] **1** ADJ bigamous **2** NMF bigamist
bigamie [bigami] NF bigamy
bigarade [bigaʀad] NF Seville ou bitter orange
bigarré, e [bigaʀe] (ptp de **bigarrer**) ADJ **a** (= bariolé) [vêtement] many-coloured, rainbow-coloured; [groupe] colourfully dressed, gaily coloured **b** (fig) [foule] motley (épith); [société, peuple] heterogeneous, mixed
bigarreau (pl **bigarreaux**) [bigaʀo] NM bigarreau, bigaroon (cherry); **yaourt aux ~x** cherry yogurt
bigarrer [bigaʀe] ▶ conjug 1 ◀ VT to colour in many hues

bigarrure [bigaʀyʀ] NF coloured pattern; **la ~ ou les ~s d'un tissu** the medley of colours in a piece of cloth, the gaily-coloured pattern of a piece of cloth

Big Bang, **big(-)bang** [bigbɑ̃g] NM INV (*Astron*) big bang; (*fig* = *réorganisation*) shake-up

bigle† [bigl] ADJ → **bigleux, -euse b**

bigler†‡ [bigle] ▸conjug 1◂ ① VT [+ *personne*] to look at ② VI (= *loucher*) to squint, have a squint; **arrête de ~ sur ou dans mon jeu** stop peeping at my cards*, take your beady eyes off my cards*

bigleux, -euse* [biglø, øz] ADJ ⓐ (= *myope*) short-sighted; **quel ~ tu fais!** you need glasses! ⓑ (= *qui louche*) squint(-eyed), cross-eyed

bigophone* [bigɔfɔn] NM phone, blower‡ (*Brit*), horn* (*US*); **passer un coup de ~ à qn** to get on the blower‡ (*Brit*) ou horn* (*US*) to sb, give sb a buzz* ou ring

bigophoner* [bigɔfɔne] ▸conjug 1◂ VI to be on the blower‡ (*Brit*) ou horn* (*US*); **~ à qn** to give sb a buzz* ou a ring

bigorneau (*pl* **bigorneaux**) [bigɔʀno] NM winkle

bigorner†‡ [bigɔʀne] ▸conjug 1◂ ① VT [+ *voiture*] to smash up ② **se bigorner** VPR (= *se battre*) to come to blows, scrap* (**avec** with)

bigot, e [bigo, ɔt] (*péj*) ① ADJ sanctimonious, holier-than-thou ② NM,F sanctimonious ou holier-than-thou person

bigoterie [bigɔtʀi] NF (*péj*) sanctimoniousness

bigouden, -ène [bigudɛ̃, ɛn] ① ADJ of ou from the Pont-l'Abbé region (*in Brittany*) ② **Bigouden(ène)** NM,F native ou inhabitant of the Pont-l'Abbé region ③ **bigoudène** NF (= *coiffe*) *woman's headdress worn in the Pont-l'Abbé region*

bigoudi [bigudi] NM (hair-)curler, roller; **elle était en ~s** her hair was in curlers ou rollers

bigre* [bigʀ] EXCL (*hum*) gosh!*, holy smoke!*

bigrement* [bigʀəmɑ̃] ADV [*bon, chaud, cher*] darned*, jolly* (*Brit*); [*changer, ressembler*] a heck of a lot*; **on a ~ bien mangé** we had a jolly good meal* (*Brit*), we had one dandy meal* (*US*)

biguine [bigin] NF beguine

Bihar [biaʀ] NM **le ~** Bihar

bihebdomadaire [biɛbdɔmadɛʀ] ADJ twice-weekly

bijection [biʒɛksjɔ̃] NF bijection

bijou (*pl* **bijoux**) [biʒu] NM jewel; (= *chef-d'œuvre*) gem; **les ~x d'une femme** a woman's jewels ou jewellery; **un ~ de précision** a marvel of precision; **~x (de) fantaisie** costume jewellery; **mon ~** (*terme d'affection*) my love, pet; **~x de famille** (*lit*) family jewels; (‡ *hum*) wedding tackle‡ (*Brit*), family jewels‡ (*US*)

bijouterie [biʒutʀi] NF (= *boutique*) jeweller's (shop); (= *commerce*) jewellery business ou trade; (= *art*) jewellery-making; (= *bijoux*) jewellery

bijoutier, -ière [biʒutje, jɛʀ] NM,F jeweller

bikini® [bikini] NM bikini

bilabial, e (*mpl* **-iaux**) [bilabjal, jo] ① ADJ bilabial ② **bilabiale** NF bilabial

bilame [bilam] NM (*Phys*) bimetallic strip

bilan [bilɑ̃] NM ⓐ (*Fin*) balance sheet, statement of accounts; **dresser ou établir son ~** to draw up the balance sheet; **~ de liquidation** statement of affairs (*in a bankruptcy petition*) ⓑ (= *évaluation*) appraisal, assessment; (= *résultats*) results; (= *conséquences*) consequences; **le ~ du gouvernement** the government's track record; **quel a été le ~ de ces négociations?** what was the upshot ou the end result of the negotiations?; **faire le ~ d'une situation** to take stock of ou assess a situation; **quand on arrive à 50 ans on fait le ~** when you

reach 50 you take stock (of your life) ⓒ [*catastrophe*] (= *nombre de morts*) (death) toll; **d'après un premier ~ ou un ~ provisoire** according to the first reports coming in; **«émeute dans la capitale, ~: 3 morts»** "riots in the capital: 3 dead"; **~ provisoire: 300 blessés** so far, 300 people are known to have been injured ⓓ (*Méd*) **~ de santé** (medical) checkup; **se faire faire un ~ de santé** to go for ou have a checkup; (*fig*) **faire le ~ de santé de l'économie** to assess the current state of the economy

bilatéral, e (*mpl* **-aux**) [bilateʀal, o] ADJ bilateral; **stationnement ~** parking on both sides (of the road)

bilatéralement [bilateʀalmɑ̃] ADV bilaterally

bilboquet [bilbɔkɛ] NM ≈ cup-and-ball game

bile [bil] NF (*Anat, fig* = *amertume*) bile; (*fig*) **se faire de la ~ (pour)** to get worried (about), worry o.s. sick (about)* → **échauffer**

biler (se)* [bile] ▸conjug 1◂ VPR (*gén nég*) to worry o.s. sick* (**pour** about); **ne vous bilez pas!** don't get all worked up!* ou het up!*, don't get yourself all worried!; **il ne se bile pas** he's not one to worry, he doesn't let things bother him

bileux, -euse* [bilø, øz] ADJ easily upset ou worried; **il n'est pas ~!◊ce n'est pas un ~!** he's not one to worry, he doesn't let things bother him; **quel ~ tu fais!** what a fretter* ou worrier you are!

bilharziose [bilaʀzjoz] NF bilharziasis, schistosomasis

biliaire [biljɛʀ] ADJ biliary → **calcul, vésicule**

bilieux, -euse [biljø, øz] ADJ [*teint*] bilious, yellowish; [*personne, tempérament*] irritable, testy

bilingue [bilɛ̃g] ADJ bilingual

bilinguisme [bilɛ̃gɥism] NM bilingualism

billard [bijaʀ] ① NM ⓐ (= *jeu*) billiards sg; (= *table*) billiard table; (= *salle*) billiard room; **faire un ~ ou une partie de ~** to play (a game of) billiards ⓑ (* : *loc*) **passer sur le ~** to go under the surgeon's knife, have an operation; **c'est du ~** it's quite ou dead easy*, it's a piece of cake* ou a cinch; **cette route est un vrai ~** this road is incredibly smooth ou as smooth as a billiard table ② COMP ▸ **billard américain** pool ▸ **billard électrique** pinball machine ▸ **billard français** French billiards ▸ **billard japonais** (= *partie*) (game of) pinball; (= *table*) pinball machine ▸ **billard russe** bar billiards

bille [bij] NM ⓐ (= *boule*) [*enfant*] marble; [*billard*] (billiard) ball; **jouer aux ~s** to play marbles, have a game of marbles; **déodorant à ~** roll-on deodorant; (*fig*) **il a attaqué ou foncé ~ en tête*** he didn't beat about the bush*; (*fig*) **reprendre ou récupérer ou retirer ses ~s*** to pull out; (*fig*) **il a su placer ses ~s*** he made all the right moves; **toucher sa ~ au tennis/en histoire*** to know a thing or two about tennis/history → **roulement, stylo** ⓑ (* = *visage*) **de bois** billet, block of wood ⓒ (* = *visage*) mug‡, face; **il a fait une drôle de ~!** you should have seen his face!; **~ de clown** funny face; **il a une bonne ~** he's got a jolly face ⓓ (* = *yeux*) **~s** round eyes

billet [bijɛ] ① NM ⓐ (= *ticket*) ticket; **~ de quai/train/loterie** platform/train/lottery ticket; **~ collectif** group ticket → **aller** ⓑ (= *argent*) note, bill (*US*); **~ de 100 francs** 100-franc note; **ça coûte 500 ~s*** it costs 5,000 francs → **faux²** ⓒ († = *lettre*) note, short letter; (*Presse*) **~ d'humeur** column ⓓ (*loc*) **je te fiche ou flanque mon ~ qu'il ne viendra pas!*** I bet my bottom dollar* ou I bet you anything he won't come! ② COMP ▸ **billet de banque** banknote, ▸ **billet de commerce** promissory note,

bill of exchange ▸ **billet doux** billet doux (*hum*), love letter ▸ **billet de faveur** complimentary ticket ▸ **billet de logement** (*Mil*) billet ▸ **billet à ordre** promissory note, bill of exchange ▸ **billet de parterre** prendre ou ramasser un ~ de parterre to fall flat on one's face, come a cropper* (*Brit*) ▸ **billet au porteur** bearer order ▸ **billet de retard** (*Scol*) late slip, tardy slip (*US*); (*Admin*) note from public transport authorities attesting late running of train etc ▸ **billet de trésorerie** commercial paper ▸ **le billet vert** (*Écon*) the dollar

billetterie [bijetʀi] NF [*argent*] cash dispenser, cash point, ATM, automatic teller machine; [*tickets*] (automatic) ticket machine

billevesées [bijvəze] NFPL (*littér* = *sornettes*) nonsense (*NonC*)

billion [biljɔ̃] NM million million, trillion (*surtout US*)

billot [bijo] NM [*boucher, bourreau, cordonnier*] block; (*Can*) log (of wood); (*fig*) **j'en mettrais ma tête sur le ~** I'd stake my life on it

bilobé, e [bilɔbe] ADJ bilobate, bilobed

bimbeloterie [bɛ̃blɔtʀi] NF (= *objets*) knick-knacks, fancy goods (*Brit*); (= *commerce*) knick-knack ou fancy goods (*Brit*) business

bimensuel, -elle [bimɑ̃sɥɛl] ① ADJ twice monthly, bimonthly, fortnightly (*Brit*), semimonthly (*US*) ② NM (= *revue*) fortnightly review (*Brit*), semimonthly (*US*)

bimensuellement [bimɑ̃sɥɛlmɑ̃] ADV twice a month, fortnightly (*Brit*), semimonthly (*US*)

bimestriel, -elle [bimɛstʀijɛl] ADJ bimonthly

bimétallique [bimetalik] ADJ bimetallic

bimétallisme [bimetalism] NM bimetallism

bimoteur [bimɔtœʀ] ① ADJ twin-engined ② NM twin-engined plane

binage [binaʒ] NM hoeing, harrowing

binaire [binɛʀ] ① ADJ binary ② NM (*Ordin*) binary code; **codé en ~** binary coded

binational, e (*mpl* **-aux**) [binasjɔnal, o] ① ADJ [*personne*] having dual nationality ② NM,F person with dual nationality

biner [bine] ▸conjug 1◂ VT to hoe, harrow

binette [binɛt] NF ⓐ (*Agr*) hoe ⓑ (* = *visage*) face, mug‡

bing [biŋ] EXCL smack!, thwack!

bingo [biŋgo] NM (*Can*) (= *jeu*) ≈ bingo (*using letters as well as numbers*); (= *partie*) ≈ game of bingo; **~!** bingo!

biniou [binju] NM (*Mus*) (Breton) bagpipes; (* = *téléphone*) **donner un coup de ~ à qn** to give sb a buzz* ou a ring

binoclard, e* [binɔklaʀ, aʀd] ADJ, NM,F **il est ou c'est un ~** he wears specs*, he's a four-eyes*

binocle [binɔkl] NM pince-nez

binoculaire [binɔkylɛʀ] ADJ binocular

binôme [binom] ① NM (*Math, Bio*) binomial; (= *deux personnes*) two-person team; **travailler en ~** to work in pairs ② NMF (= *une personne*) partner; **mon/ma ~** my partner

bio* [bjo] ① NF ⓐ (ABRÉV = **biographie**) bio* ⓑ ABRÉV = **biologie** ② ADJ (ABRÉV = **biologique**) [*agriculture, engrais, nourriture*] organic; **produits ~(s)** (= *aliments*) organic food; (= *non-polluants*) eco-friendly products

biocarburant [bjokaʀbyʀɑ̃] NM biofuel

biochimie [bjoʃimi] NF biochemistry

biochimique [bjoʃimik] ADJ biochemical

biochimiste [bjoʃimist] NMF biochemist

biodégradabilité [bjodegʀadabilite] NF biodegradability

biodégradable [bjodegʀadabl] ADJ biodegradable

biodégradation [bjodegʀadasjɔ̃] NF biodegradation

biodiversité [bjodivɛʀsite] NF biodiversity

bioénergétique [bjoenɛRʒetik] [1] ADJ bioenergetic [2] NF bioenergetics *sg*

bioénergie [bjoenɛRʒi] NF bioenergy

bioéthique [bjoetik] NF bioethics *sg*

biographe [bjɔgʀaf] NMF biographer

biographie [bjɔgʀafi] NF biography; ~ romancée biographical novel

biographique [bjɔgʀafik] ADJ biographical

bio-industrie (*pl* **bio-industries**) [bjoɛ̃dystʀi] NF bioindustry

biologie [bjɔlɔʒi] NF biology; ~ **animale/végétale** animal/plant biology; ~ **cellulaire/médicale/moléculaire** cellular/medical/molecular biology

biologique [bjɔlɔʒik] ADJ (*gén*) biological; [*produits, aliments*] natural, organic; [*parent*] biological; **agriculture** ~ organic farming

biologiquement [bjɔlɔʒikmɑ̃] ADV biologically; **produit** ~ **cultivé** organically grown product

biologiste [bjɔlɔʒist] NMF biologist

biomasse [bjɔmas] NF biomass

biomatériau (*pl* **biomatériaux**) [bjɔmateʀjo] NM biomaterial

bionique [bjɔnik] [1] NF bionics *sg* [2] ADJ bionic

biophysicien, -ienne [bjofizisjɛ̃, jɛn] NM,F biophysicist

biophysique [bjofizik] NF biophysics *sg*

biopsie [bjɔpsi] NF biopsy

biorythme [bjɔʀitm] NM biorhythm

biosphère [bjɔsfɛʀ] NF biosphere

biosynthèse [bjɔsɛ̃tɛz] NF biosynthesis

biotechnique [bjɔteknik], **biotechnologie** [bjɔteknɔlɔʒi] NF biotechnology

biotope [bjɔtɔp] NM biotope

bioxyde [bijɔksid] NM dioxide

▼ **bip** [bip] NM [a] (= *son*) (*court*) b(l)eep; (*continu*) b(l)eeping; **faire** ~ to b(l)eep; **parlez après le** ~ **sonore** speak after the tone *ou* beep [b] (= *appareil*) bleep(er), beeper

bipale [bipal] ADJ twin-bladed

biparti, e [bipaʀti], **bipartite** [bipaʀtit] ADJ (*Bot*) bipartite; (*Pol*) two-party, bipartite, bipartisan

bipartisme [bipaʀtism] NM (*Pol*) bipartisanship

bipasse [bipas] NM = **by-pass**

bip-bip (*pl* **bips-bips**) [bipbip] NM = **bip** b

bipède [bipɛd] ADJ, NM biped

biper¹ [bipe] ▶ conjug 1 ◀ VT to page

biper² [bipœʀ] NM (*Téléc*) beeper, bleeper

biphasé, e [bifaze] ADJ diphase, two-phase

biplace [biplas] ADJ, NM two-seater

biplan [biplɑ̃] [1] ADJ **avion** ~ biplane [2] NM biplane

bipolaire [bipɔlɛʀ] ADJ bipolar

bipolarisation [bipɔlaʀizasjɔ̃] NF (*Pol*) polarization (**entre** of, between); **la** ~ **Est-Ouest de l'Europe** the way Europe is polarized between East and West

bipolarité [bipɔlaʀite] NF bipolarity

bique [bik] NF nanny-goat; (*péj*) **vieille** ~* old hag, old bag*; **grande** ~* beanpole

biquet, -ette [bikɛ, ɛt] NM,F (*Zool*) kid; (*terme d'affection*) **mon** ~ love

biquotidien, -ienne [bikɔtidjɛ̃, jɛn] ADJ twice-daily

birbe [biʀb] NM (*péj*) **vieux** ~ old fuddy-duddy*, old fogey*

BIRD [biʀd] NF (ABRÉV = **Banque internationale pour la reconstruction et le développement**) IBRD

biréacteur [biʀeaktœʀ] NM twin-engined jet

biréfringence [biʀefʀɛ̃ʒɑ̃s] NF birefringence

biréfringent, e [biʀefʀɛ̃ʒɑ̃, ɑ̃t] ADJ birefringent

birème [biʀɛm] NF (*Antiq*) bireme

birman, e [biʀmɑ̃, an] [1] ADJ Burmese [2] NM (*Ling*) Burmese [3] **Birman(e)** NM,F Burmese

Birmanie [biʀmani] NF Burma

biroute [biʀut] NF [a] (**:** = *pénis*) dick**:**, cock**:**, prick**:** [b] (*arg Mil* = *manche à air*) wind sock

bis¹ [bis] [1] ADV (*Mus*: *sur partition*) repeat, twice; (*Théât*) ~ **!** encore!; (*numéro*) **12** ~ 12a; ~ **repetita** it's the same story (all over) again → **itinéraire** [2] NM (*Théât*) encore

bis², e¹ [bi, biz] ADJ greyish-brown, brownish-grey → **pain**

bisaïeul [bizajœl] NM great-grandfather

bisaïeule [bizajœl] NF great-grandmother

bisannuel, -elle [bizanɥɛl] ADJ biennial

bisbille* [bisbij] NF squabble, tiff; **être en** ~ **avec qn** to be at loggerheads with sb

bisbrouille [bizbʀuj] NF (*Belg* = *fâcherie*) tiff; **ils sont en** ~ they've had a tiff *ou* falling-out

biscornu, e [biskɔʀny] ADJ [*forme*] irregular, crooked; [*maison*] crooked, oddly shaped; [*idée, esprit*] quirky, peculiar; [*raisonnement*] tortuous, quirky; **un chapeau** ~ a shapeless hat

biscoteaux* [biskɔto] NMPL biceps; **avoir des** ~ to have a good pair of biceps

biscotte [biskɔt] NF rusk (*Brit*), melba toast (*US*)

biscuit [biskɥi] [1] NM [a] (*Culin*) (= *pâte*) sponge cake; (= *gâteau sec*) biscuit (*Brit*), cookie (*US*); ~ **salé** cracker, cheese biscuit (*Brit*); (*fig*) **ne t'embarque pas** *ou* **ne pars pas sans** ~**s** mind you're fully prepared [b] (= *céramique*) biscuit, bisque [2] COMP ▶ **biscuit (à) apéritif** cracker, cocktail snack ▶ **biscuit pour chien** dog biscuit ▶ **biscuit à la cuiller** sponge finger (*Brit*), lady finger (*US*) ▶ **biscuit de Savoie** sponge cake

biscuiterie [biskɥitʀi] NF (= *usine*) biscuit (*Brit*) *ou* cookie (*US*) factory; (= *commerce*) biscuit (*Brit*) *ou* cookie (*US*) trade

bise² [biz] NF (= *vent*) North wind

bise³ [biz] NF (= *baiser*) kiss; **faire une** *ou* **la** ~ **à qn** to kiss sb, give sb a kiss; **faire une grosse** ~ **à qn** to give sb a big kiss; **il lui a fait une petite** ~ he gave her a quick peck* *ou* kiss; (*sur lettre*) **grosses** ~**s** lots of love (**de** from), much love (**de** from)

biseau (*pl* **biseaux**) [bizo] NM [a] (= *bord*) (*gén*) bevel, bevelled edge; (*à 45°*) chamfer, chamfered edge; **en** ~ (*gén*) bevelled, with a bevelled edge; (*à 45°*) chamfered, with a chamfered edge; **tailler en** ~ (*gén*) to bevel; (*à 45°*) to chamfer [b] (= *outil*) bevel

biseautage [bizota ʒ] NM (*gén*) bevelling; (*à 45°*) chamfering

biseauter [bizote] ▶ conjug 1 ◀ VT (*Tech*) (*gén*) to bevel; (*à 45 degrés*) to chamfer; [+ *cartes*] to mark

bisexualité [bisɛksɥalite] NF bisexuality, bisexualism

bisexué, e [bisɛksɥe] ADJ bisexual

bisexuel, -elle [bisɛksɥɛl] [1] ADJ bisexual [2] NM,F bisexual

bismuth [bismyt] NM bismuth

bison [bizɔ̃] NM (*d'Amérique*) (American) bison, buffalo (*US*); (*d'Europe*) European bison, wisent; **Bison futé** *traffic monitoring service that informs drivers about congestion on French roads and suggests alternative routes*

bisou* [bizu] NM kiss; **faire un** ~ **à qn** to give sb a kiss; **faire un petit** ~ **à qn** to give sb a peck* *ou* kiss; (*sur lettre*) **gros** ~**s** lots of love (**de** from)

bisque [bisk] NF (*Culin*) bisk, bisque; ~ **de homard** lobster soup, bisque of lobster

bisquer* [biske] ▶ conjug 1 ◀ VI to be riled* *ou* nettled; **faire** ~ **qn** to rile* *ou* nettle sb

Bissau [bisao] N Bissau

bissecteur, -trice [bisɛktœʀ, tʀis] [1] ADJ bisecting [2] **bissectrice** NF bisector, bisecting line

bissection [bisɛksjɔ̃] NF bissection

bisser [bise] ▶ conjug 1 ◀ VT (= *faire rejouer*) [+ *acteur, chanson*] to encore; (= *rejouer*) [+ *morceau*] to play again, sing again

bissextile [bisɛkstil] ADJ F → **année**

bisexué, e [bisɛksɥe] ADJ = **bisexué, e**

bisexuel, -elle [bisɛksɥɛl] ADJ, NM,F = **bisexuel, elle**

bistable [bistabl] ADJ (*Élec*) bistable

bistouri [bistuʀi] NM bistoury (SPÉC), surgical knife; **enlever qch au** ~ to remove sth surgically; (*fig*) **donner un coup de** ~ to take drastic action *ou* measures

bistre [bistʀ] [1] ADJ [*couleur*] blackish-brown, bistre; [*objet*] bistre-coloured, blackish-brown; [*peau, teint*] swarthy [2] NM bistre

bistré, e [bistʀe] (*ptp de* **bistrer**) ADJ [*teint*] tanned, swarthy

bistrer [bistʀe] ▶ conjug 1 ◀ VT [+ *objet*] to colour with bistre; [+ *peau*] to tan

bistro(t) [bistʀo] NM [a] (*= café*) ≈ pub, ≈ bar (*US*), ≈ café; **faire les bistros** to go on a bar-crawl [b] (*† = cafetier*) ≈ café owner

bistrotier, -ière [bistʀɔtje, jɛʀ] NM,F ≈ publican (*Brit*), bar manager (*US*)

BIT [beite] NM (ABRÉV = **Bureau international du travail**) ILO

bit [bit] NM (*Ordin*) bit

bite:** [bit] NF = **bitte** b

biter, bitter:** [bite] ▶ conjug 1 ◀ VT **j'y bitte rien** I can't understand a fucking thing**:**

bithérapie [biteʀapi] NF double therapy

bitoniau* [bitɔnjo] NM whatsit*

bitos* [bitos] NM hat, headgear* (NonC)

bitte [bit] NF [a] [*navire*] bitt; [*quai*] ~ (**d'amarrage**) mooring post, bollard [b] (**:** = *pénis*) prick**:**, cock**:**, dick**:**

biture:** [bityʀ] NF = **biture**

bitumage [bitymaʒ] NM asphalting

bitume [bitym] NM (*Chim, Min*) bitumen; (= *revêtement*) asphalt, Tarmac®, blacktop (*US*); (*fig* = *route*) road; **arpenter le** ~ to walk the streets

bitumé, e [bityme] (*ptp de* **bitumer**) ADJ [*route*] asphalted, asphalt (*épith*), tarmac (*épith*); [*carton*] bitumized

bitum(in)er [bitym(in)e] ▶ conjug 1 ◀ VT [+ *route*] to asphalt, tarmac

bitum(in)eux, -euse [bitym(in)ø, øz] ADJ bituminous

biture:** [bityʀ] NF **prendre une** ~ to get drunk *ou* plastered*; **il tient une de ces** ~**s** he's plastered*; **il tient une de ces** ~**s** he's blind drunk*

biturer (se):** [bityʀe] ▶ conjug 1 ◀ VPR to get drunk *ou* plastered*

biunivoque [biynivɔk] ADJ (*fig*) one-to-one; (*Math*) → **correspondance**

bivalent, e [bivalɑ̃, ɑ̃t] ADJ (*Chim*) bivalent; [*professeur*] teaching two subjects

bivalve [bivalv] ADJ, NM bivalve

bivouac [bivwak] NM bivouac, bivvy**:**

bivouaquer [bivwake] ▶ conjug 1 ◀ VI to bivouac

bizarre [bizaʀ] [1] ADJ [*personne, conduite*] strange, odd, peculiar; [*idée, raisonnement, temps*] odd, strange, funny*; [*vêtement*] strange *ou* funny-(looking); **tiens, c'est** ~ that's odd *ou* funny* [2] NM **le** ~ the bizarre; **le** ~ **dans tout cela** ... what's strange *ou* peculiar about all that ...

bizarrement [bizaʀmɑ̃] ADV strangely, oddly

bizarrerie [bizaʀʀi] NF [*personne*] odd *ou* strange *ou* peculiar ways; [*idée*] strangeness, oddness; [*situation, humeur*] strange *ou* odd nature; ~**s** [*langue, règlement*] peculiarities, oddities, quirks; **ce sont les ~s du système** these are the quirks *ou* the vagaries of the system

bizarroïde* [bizaʀɔid] ADJ weird

bizness* [biznɛs] NM = **business**

bizut [bizy] NM (*arg Scol*) freshman, first-year student, fresher (*Brit*)

bizutage [bizytaʒ] NM (*arg Scol*) ragging (*Brit*), hazing (*US*) (of new student etc)

┌─────────────┐
│ **BIZUTAGE** │
└─────────────┘

*New arrivals at certain "grandes écoles" and other educational institutions are called "bizuts" or "bi-zuths", and when they arrive at school in September, they are often subjected to an initia-tion ceremony known as **bizutage**. This usually involves being subjected to light-hearted ordeals by one's new classmates, but can sometimes de-generate into humiliating and cruel pranks. For this reason, the tradition has become more controversial in recent years, and many schools have outlawed it.*

bizuter [bizyte] ▶ conjug 1 ◀ VT (*arg Scol*) to rag (*Brit*), haze (*US*) (*new student etc*)

bizuth [bizy] NM = **bizut**

BK [beka] NM (ABRÉV = **bacille de Koch**) Koch's bacillus

blabla(bla)* [blabla(bla)] NM twaddle*, clap-trap*; **il y a beaucoup de ~ dans sa disserta-tion** there's a lot of waffle* (*Brit*) in his paper

blablater* [blablate] ▶ conjug 1 ◀ VI to blabber on*, waffle on* (*Brit*)

black* [blak] ① ADJ [*personne, culture, musique*] black ② NMF black person; **les ~s** black peo-ple, blacks

blackboulage [blakbulaʒ] NM blackballing

blackbouler [blakbule] ▶ conjug 1 ◀ VT (*à une élection*) to blackball; (*: *à un examen*) to fail

black-jack (*pl* **black-jacks**) [blak(d)ʒak] NM blackjack

black-out [blakaut] NM (*Élec, Mil, fig*) black-out; (*fig*) **faire le ~ sur qch** to impose a (news) blackout on sth

blafard, e [blafaʀ, aʀd] ADJ [*teint*] pale, pallid, wan; [*couleur, lumière, soleil*] pale; **l'aube ~e** the pale light of dawn

blague [blag] NF ① ① (= *histoire, plaisanterie*) joke; (= *farce*) practical joke, trick; **faire une ~ à qn** to play a trick *ou* a joke on sb; **sans ~?** really?, you're kidding!‡; **sans ~ ◊ ~ à part** se-riously, joking apart, kidding aside* (*US*); **non mais sans ~, tu me prends pour qui ?** no really *ou* come on, what do you take me for?; **il prend tout à la ~** he can never take anything seriously; **ne me raconte pas de ~s!** you're having (*Brit*) *ou* putting (*US*) me on!*, pull the other one!* (*Brit*); **c'est de la ~ tout ça !** it's all talk, it's all bull‡ ⓑ (* = *erreur*) silly thing, blunder, stupid mistake; **faire une ~** to make a blunder *ou* a stupid mistake; **faire des ~s** to do silly *ou* stupid things; **attention, pas de ~s !** be careful!, no messing about!* ⓒ ~ (**à tabac**) (tobacco) pouch

blaguer* [blage] ▶ conjug 1 ◀ ① VI to be joking *ou* kidding* (**sur** about); **j'ai dit cela pour ~** I said it for a joke *ou* lark* (*Brit*); **on ne blague pas avec ça** you shouldn't joke about that, that's not something to joke about ② VT to tease, make fun of, kid*, take the mickey out of‡ (*Brit*)

blagueur, -euse [blagœʀ, øz] ① ADJ [*sourire, air*] ironical, teasing; [*ton, manière*] jokey*; **il est (très)~** he's (really) good fun ② NM,F (*gén*) joker; (= *farceur*) practical joker

blair‡ [blɛʀ] NM nose, beak‡, hooter‡ (*Brit*)

blaireau (*pl* **blaireaux**) [blɛʀo] NM ① (*Zool*) badger ⓑ (*pour barbe*) shaving brush ⓒ (‡: *péj*) nerd* (*péj*)

blairer‡ [blɛʀe] ▶ conjug 1 ◀ VT **je ne peux pas le ~** I can't stand *ou* bear him

blâmable [blɑmabl] ADJ blameful

blâme [blɑm] NM ⓐ (= *désapprobation*) blame; (= *réprimande*) reprimand, rebuke; **encourir le ~ de qn** [*personne, action*] to incur sb's con-demnation *ou* censure; **rejeter le ~ sur qn** to blame sb, put the blame on sb ⓑ (*Admin, Sport* = *punition*) reprimand; **donner un ~ à qn** to reprimand sb; **recevoir un ~** to be repri-manded, incur a reprimand

blâmer [blɑme] ▶ conjug 1 ◀ VT (= *désavouer*) to blame; (= *réprimander*) to reprimand, rebuke; **je ne te blâme pas de** *ou* **pour l'avoir fait** I don't blame you for having done it

blanc, blanche [blɑ̃, blɑ̃ʃ] ① ADJ ⓐ (= *sans couleur*) white; (= *pâle*) white, pale; **~ de colère/de peur** white with anger/fear; **~ comme neige** (as) white as snow, snow-white; **~ comme un cachet d'aspirine** white as a sheet; **il devint ~ comme un linge** he went *ou* turned as white as a sheet → **arme, bois, bon-net** ⓑ [*page, bulletin de vote*] blank; [*papier non quadrillé*] unlined, plain; (*Scol*) **il a rendu co-pie blanche** *ou* **sa feuille blanche** he handed in a blank paper; **prenez une feuille blanche** take a clean *ou* blank piece of paper; **voter ~** to return a blank vote → **carte, examen** ⓒ (= *innocent*) pure, innocent; **~ comme nei-ge** *ou* **comme la blanche hermine** as pure as the driven snow ⓓ [*domination, justice, pouvoir*] white; **la race blanche** the white *ou* Caucasian race; **de race blanche** white, Caucasian; **l'Afrique blanche** white Africa ⓔ (*Sci*) [*bruit*] white ⓕ (*Fin*) **ça a été une opération blanche** we (*ou* they *etc*) broke even, we (*ou* they *etc*) didn't lose or gain by it; **cette privatisation sera une opération blanche pour l'État** the government will neither gain nor lose from this privatiza-tion ⓖ (*Tennis*) **jeu ~** love game ② NM ⓐ (= *couleur*) white; **peindre qch en ~** to paint sth white; **le ~ de sa robe tranchait sur sa peau brune** her white dress *ou* the white of her dress contrasted sharply with her dark skin → **but** ⓑ (= *linge*) **laver séparément le ~ et la couleur** to wash whites and coloureds separately; **vente de ~** white sale, sale of household lin-en; **magasin de ~** linen shop; **la quinzaine du ~** (annual) sale of household linen, (annual) white sale ⓒ (*Cosmétique*) white (face-)powder ⓓ (= *espace non écrit*) blank, space; [*bande magnétique*] blank; [*domino*] blank; **il y a eu un ~ (dans la conversation)** there was a break *ou* a lull in the conversation; (*dû à la gêne*) there was an embarrassed silence; **laisser un ~** to leave a blank *ou* space; **il faut laisser le nom en ~** the name must be left blank *ou* must not be filled in → **chèque, signer** ⓔ (= *vin*) white wine ⓕ (*Culin*) ~ (**d'œuf**) (egg) white; **~ (de poulet)** white (meat), breast of chicken; **elle n'aime pas le ~** she doesn't like the white (meat) *ou* the breast ⓖ **le ~ (de l'œil)** the white (of the eye) → **regarder, rougir** ⓗ (= *personne*) **un Blanc** a White, a white man; (*Ethnol*) **les Blancs** white people ⓘ (*loc*) **à ~** [*charger*] with blanks; **tirer à ~** to fire blanks; **balle à ~** blank; **cartouche à ~** blank (cartridge) → **chauffer, saigner** ③ **blanche** NF ⓐ (= *femme*) **une Blanche** a white woman ⓑ (*Mus*) minim (*Brit*), half-note (*US*) ⓒ (*Billard*) white (ball) ⓓ (*arg Drogue*) horse (*arg*), smack (*arg*) ④ COMP ▶ **blanc de baleine** spermaceti ▶ **blanc de blanc(s)** blanc de blanc(s)

▶ **blanc cassé** off-white ▶ **blanc de céru-se** white lead ▶ **blanc de chaux** whitewash ▶ **blanc d'Espagne** whiting, whitening ▶ **blanc de zinc** zinc oxide

blanc-bec (*pl* **blancs-becs**) [blɑ̃bɛk] NM greenhorn*, tenderfoot*

blanc-bleu‡ [blɑ̃blø] ADJ INV **il n'est pas ~ dans cette affaire** he's not entirely blameless *ou* innocent in this affair

blanc-cassis (*pl* **blancs-cassis**) [blɑ̃kasi(s)] NM kir (*apéritif made with white wine and blackcur-rant liqueur*)

blanchâtre [blɑ̃ʃɑtʀ] ADJ whitish, off-white

blanche [blɑ̃ʃ] ADJ, NF → **blanc**

Blanche-Neige [blɑ̃ʃnɛʒ] NF Snow White; **~ et les Sept Nains** Snow White and the Seven Dwarfs

blancheur [blɑ̃ʃœʀ] NF whiteness

blanchiment [blɑ̃ʃimɑ̃] NM (= *décoloration*) bleaching; (= *badigeonnage*) whitewashing; [*argent*] laundering

blanchir [blɑ̃ʃiʀ] ▶ conjug 2 ◀ ① VT ⓐ (*gén*) to whiten, lighten; [+ *mur*] to whitewash; [+ *cheveux*] to turn grey *ou* white; [+ *toile*] to bleach; **le soleil blanchit l'horizon** the sun is lighting up the horizon; **la neige blanchit les collines** the snow is turning the hills white; **~ à la chaux** to whitewash ⓑ (= *nettoyer*) [+ *linge*] (*fig*) [+ *argent*] to laun-der; **il est logé, nourri et blanchi** he gets bed and board and his laundry is done for him ⓒ (= *disculper*) [+ *personne*] to exonerate, ab-solve, clear; [+ *réputation*] to clear; **il en est sorti blanchi** he cleared his name ⓓ (*Culin, Agr*) (**faire**) **~** to blanch ⓔ (*Typo*) [+ *page*] to white out, blank ② VI [*personne, cheveux*] to turn *ou* go grey *ou* white; [*couleur, horizon*] to become lighter; **son teint a blanchi** he is looking *ou* has got paler, he has lost colour; **~ de peur** to blanch *ou* blench *ou* go white with fear; (*littér*) **blan-chi sous le harnais** *ou* **harnois** worn down by hard work ③ **se blanchir** VPR to exonerate o.s. (**de** from), clear one's name

blanchissage [blɑ̃ʃisaʒ] NM [*linge*] launder-ing; [*sucre*] refining; **donner du linge au ~** to send linen to the laundry; **note de ~** laundry bill

blanchissant, e [blɑ̃ʃisɑ̃, ɑ̃t] ADJ [*agent, produit*] whitening

blanchissement [blɑ̃ʃismɑ̃] NM whitening; **ce shampooing retarde le ~ des cheveux** this shampoo stops your hair (from) going grey *ou* white

blanchisserie [blɑ̃ʃisʀi] NF laundry

blanchisseur [blɑ̃ʃisœʀ] NM (*lit*) launderer; (*fig hum*) [*argent sale*] money launderer

blanchisseuse [blɑ̃ʃisøz] NF laundress

blanc-manger (*pl* **blancs-mangers**) [blɑ̃mɑ̃ʒe] NM (*Culin*) blancmange

blanc-seing (*pl* **blancs-seings**) [blɑ̃sɛ̃] NM (*lit*) signature to a blank document; (*fig*) **donner un ~ à qn** to give sb a blank cheque

blanquette [blɑ̃kɛt] NF ⓐ (*Culin*) **~ de veau/ d'agneau** blanquette of veal/of lamb, veal/ lamb in white sauce ⓑ (= *vin*) sparkling white wine

blasé‡ [blɑʒ] NM = **blaze**

blasé, e [blaze] (*ptp de blaser*) ① ADJ blasé ② NM,F blasé individual; **faire le ~** to affect indifference

blaser [blaze] ▶ conjug 1 ◀ ① VT to make blasé *ou* indifferent; **être blasé de** to be bored with *ou* tired of ② **se blaser** VPR to become bored (**de** with), become tired (**de** of), become blasé (**de** about)

blason [blazɔ̃] NM ⓐ (= *armoiries*) coat of arms, blazon → **redorer** ⓑ (= *science*) herald-ry ⓒ (*Littérat* = *poème*) blazon

blasonner [blazɔne] ▸conjug 1◂ VT (= orner d'armoiries) to blazon, emblazon

blasphémateur, -trice [blasfematœʀ, tʀis] [1] ADJ [personne] blaspheming, blasphemous [2] NM,F blasphemer

blasphématoire [blasfematwaʀ] ADJ [parole] blasphemous

blasphème [blasfɛm] NM blasphemy

blasphémer [blasfeme] ▸conjug 6◂ VTI to blaspheme

blatérer [blateʀe] ▸conjug 6◂ VI [chameau] to bray

blatte [blat] NF cockroach

blaze: [blaz] NM (= nez) beak:, hooter: (Brit); (= nom) name

blazer [blazœʀ] NM blazer

blé [ble] NM [a] (= céréale) wheat, corn (Brit); le ~ en herbe (Agr) wheat on the blade; ~ dur hard wheat, durum wheat; ~ noir buckwheat; (Can) ~ d'Inde* maize, (Indian) corn (US, Can); les ~s the corn (Brit), the wheat → blond, fauché [b] (: = argent) dough:, lolly: (Brit)

bled [blɛd] NM [a]* village; (péj) hole*, godforsaken place*; c'est un ~ perdu ou paumé it's a godforsaken place* ou hole* (in the middle of nowhere) [b] (en Afrique du Nord) le ~ the interior (of North Africa); (fig) habiter dans le ~* to live in the middle of nowhere ou at the back of beyond

blême [blɛm] ADJ [teint] pallid, deathly pale; [lumière] pale, wan; ~ de rage/de colère livid ou white with rage/anger

blêmir [blemiʀ] ▸conjug 2◂ VI [personne] to turn ou go pale, pale; [lumière] to grow pale; ~ de colère to go livid ou white with anger

blêmissement [blemismɑ̃] NM [teint, lumière] paling

blende [blɛd] NF blende

blennie [bleni] NF (Zool) blenny

blennorragie [blenɔʀaʒi] NF gonorrhoea

blèsement [blɛzmɑ̃] NM lisping

bléser [bleze] ▸conjug 6◂ VI to lisp

blessant, e [blesɑ̃, ɑ̃t] ADJ (= offensant) cutting, biting, hurtful

blessé, e [blese] (ptp de blesser) [1] ADJ (= meurtri) hurt, injured; (dans une agression) wounded; (= offensé) hurt, upset; être ~ à la tête/au bras to have a head/an arm injury ou wound; il était ~ dans son amour-propre his pride was hurt [2] NM wounded ou injured man, casualty; (Mil) wounded soldier, casualty; les ~s (dans un accident) the injured; (Mil) the wounded; l'accident a fait 10 ~s 10 people were injured ou hurt in the accident; grand ~ seriously injured person [3] blessée NF wounded ou injured woman, casualty [4] COMP ▸ blessé grave seriously ou severely injured ou wounded person ▸ blessé de guerre person who was wounded in the war; les ~s de guerre the war wounded ▸ blessé léger slightly injured person; l'attentat a fait 30 ~s légers 30 people were slightly injured ou suffered minor ou slight injuries in the bomb attack ▸ blessés de la route road casualties, people ou persons injured in road accidents

blesser [blese] ▸conjug 1◂ [1] VT [a] (= meurtrir, dans un accident) to hurt, injure; (Mil, dans une agression) to wound; [ceinture, chaussure] to hurt; il a été blessé d'un coup de couteau he received a knife wound, he was stabbed (with a knife); être blessé dans un accident de voiture to be injured in a car accident; ses chaussures lui blessent le talon his shoes are making his heels sore → bât [b] (= agresser) sons qui blessent l'oreille sounds which offend the ear ou grate on the ear; couleurs qui blessent la vue colours

which offend ou shock the eye [c] (= offenser) to hurt (the feelings of), upset, wound; ~ qn au vif to cut sb to the quick; il s'est senti blessé dans son orgueil ou son amour-propre his pride was hurt; des paroles qui blessent cutting words, wounding ou cutting remarks [d] (littér = porter préjudice à) [+ règles, convenances] to offend against; [+ intérêts] to go against, harm; cela blesse son sens de la justice that offends his sense of justice [2] se blesser VPR [a] (= se faire mal) to hurt o.s.; il s'est blessé en tombant he fell and injured himself; il s'est blessé (à) la jambe he injured ou hurt his leg [b] (= se vexer) to take offence; il se blesse pour un rien he's easily hurt ou offended, he's quick to take offence

blessure [blesyʀ] NF (accidentelle) injury; (intentionnelle, morale) wound; quelle ~ d'amour-propre pour lui! what a blow to his pride ou self-esteem! → coup

blet, blette¹ [blɛ, blɛt] ADJ [fruit] overripe

blette² [blɛt] NF = bette

blettir [bletiʀ] ▸conjug 2◂ VI to become overripe

blettissement [bletismɑ̃] NM overripeness

bleu, e [blø] [1] ADJ [a] [couleur] blue; ~ de froid blue with cold; être ~ de colère to be livid ou purple with rage; il avait le menton ~ he had a five-o'clock shadow → enfant, fleur, maladie, peur [b] (= meurtri) bruised; (= marbré) avoir les jambes toutes ~es to have mottled legs (due to bad circulation) [c] [steak] very rare, underdone [2] NM [a] (= couleur) blue; (fig) il n'y a vu que du ~* he didn't notice a thing, he didn't catch on*; regarde le ~ de ce ciel look how blue the sky is; le ~ des mers du Sud the blue of the South Seas; le grand ~ the blue depths of the sea [b] ~ (de lessive) (dolly) blue; passer le linge au ~ to blue the laundry [c] (= marque sur la peau) bruise; être couvert de ~s to be covered in bruises, be black and blue*; se faire un ~ au genou/bras to bruise one's knee/arm; avoir des ~s à l'âme to be emotionally bruised [d] (= vêtement) ~(s) (de travail) overalls; ~ (de chauffe) overalls, boiler suit (Brit) [e] (arg Mil = recrue) rookie (arg), new ou raw recruit; (gén = débutant) beginner, greenhorn*; tu me prends pour un ~? do you take me for a novice? [f] (= fromage) blue(-veined) cheese [g] (Culin) truite au ~ trout au bleu [h] (Can) les Bleus the Conservatives [3] COMP ▸ bleu acier steel blue ▸ bleu ardoise slaty ou slate blue ▸ bleu canard peacock blue ▸ bleu ciel sky blue ▸ bleu de cobalt cobalt blue ▸ bleu glacier ice blue ▸ bleu horizon sky blue ▸ bleu indigo indigo blue ▸ bleu lavande lavender blue ▸ bleu marine navy blue ▸ bleu de méthylène (Méd) methylene blue ▸ bleu noir blue-black ▸ bleu nuit midnight blue ▸ bleu outremer ultramarine ▸ bleu pervenche periwinkle blue ▸ bleu pétrole petrol blue ▸ bleu de Prusse Prussian blue ▸ bleu roi royal blue ▸ bleu turquoise turquoise blue ▸ bleu vert blue-green

bleuâtre [bløatʀ] ADJ bluish

bleuet [bløɛ] NM cornflower; (Can) blueberry

bleuetière [bløɛtjɛʀ], **bleuetterie** [bløɛtʀi] NF (Can) blueberry grove

bleuir [bløiʀ] ▸conjug 2◂ VTI to turn blue

bleuissement [bløismɑ̃] NM turning blue

bleusaille [bløzaj] NF (arg Mil = recrue) rookie (arg), new ou raw recruit; (collectivement) la ~ the rookies (arg)

bleuté, e [bløte] ADJ [reflet] bluish; [verre] blue-tinted

blindage [blɛ̃daʒ] NM [a] (= action) [porte] reinforcing; (Mil) fitting of armour plating; (Élec) screening; (Constr) timbering, shoring up [b] (= résultat) [porte] reinforcement; (Mil) armour plating; (Élec) screening; (Constr) shoring up, timbering

blinde [blɛ̃d] ◆ à tout(e) blinde* LOC ADV [rouler] flat out*; [partir] like a shot*; il est arrivé à toute ~ (en voiture) he drove up at top ou breakneck speed; (à pied) he arrived like a shot*

blindé, e [blɛ̃de] (ptp de blinder) [1] ADJ [a] (Mil) [division] armoured; [engin, train] armoured, armour-plated; [abri] bombproof; [porte] reinforced [b] (* = endurci) immune, hardened (contre to); il a essayé de me faire peur mais je suis ~ he tried to frighten me but I'm immune to his threats [c] (: = ivre) plastered:, sloshed: [2] NM (Mil) tank; ~ léger de campagne combat car; ~ de transport de troupes armoured personnel carrier; les ~s the armour

blinder [blɛ̃de] ▸conjug 1◂ [1] VT [a] [+ porte] to reinforce [b] (Mil) to armour, put armour plating on [c] (Élec) to screen [d] (Constr) to shore up, timber [e] (* = endurcir) to harden, make immune (contre to) [f] (: = soûler) ~ qn to get sb plastered* ou sloshed* [2] se blinder VPR (* = s'endurcir) to harden o.s., become immune (contre to) [b] (: = se soûler) to get plastered* ou sloshed*

blinis [blinis] NM blini; des ~ blinis

blister [blistɛʀ] NM blister pack; mettre sous ~ to blisterpack

blizzard [blizaʀ] NM blizzard

bloc [blɔk] [1] NM [a] [pierre, marbre, bois] block; fait d'un seul ~ made in one piece; ça forme un seul ~ it forms a single block; ça s'est détaché d'un seul ~ it came off all in one piece; (Géol) ~ erratique erratic block [b] (Papeterie) pad; ~ de bureau office notepad, desk pad; ~ de papier à lettres writing pad [c] (= système d'éléments) unit; (Ordin) block; ces éléments forment (un) ~ these elements make up a unit; (Ordin) ~ de mémoire storage ou memory block [d] (= groupe, union) group; (Pol) bloc; ~ économique/monétaire/régional economic/ monetary/regional bloc; (Pol) le ~ communiste/capitaliste the communist/ capitalist bloc; (Pol) pays divisé en deux ~s adverses country split into two opposing blocks ou factions [e] (Bourse) [actions] block; achat/vente en ~ block purchase/sale → 1h [f] (Méd) ~ (opératoire) (operating) theatre suite; il est au ~ he's in (the) theatre, he's in the operating room (US) [g] (: = prison) mettre qn au ~ to clap sb in clink: ou in the nick: (Brit); j'ai eu 10 jours de ~ I got 10 days in clink: ou in the nick: (Brit) [h] (loc) faire ~ to join forces, unite (avec with, contre against); serrer ou visser qch à ~ to screw sth up as tight as possible ou as far as it will go; fermer un robinet à ~ to turn a tap right off ou off hard; en ~ [acheter, vendre] as a whole; [refuser, nier] out of hand, outright; ils ont condamné en ~ l'attitude des USA they were united ou unanimous in their condemnation of the US attitude; se retourner tout d'un ~ to swivel round → freiner, gonflé [2] COMP ▸ bloc à appartements (Can) block of flats (Brit), apartment building ou house (US) ▸ bloc de culasse breech-block ▸ bloc de départ (Sport) starting-block ▸ bloc optique (Aut) headlamp assembly ▸ bloc sonore (Ciné) sound unit

blocage [blɔkaʒ] NM [a] [prix, salaires] freeze, freezing; [compte bancaire] freezing [b] (Constr) rubble [c] (Psych) block; avoir ou faire un ~ to have a mental block [d] [*frein, roues*] locking; [*écrou*] overtightening; (*Ordin*) ~ **de mémoire** memory block

bloc-cuisine (*pl* **blocs-cuisines**) [blɔkkɥizin] NM compact kitchen unit (*incorporating a sink, fridge and hob*)

bloc-cylindres (*pl* **blocs-cylindres**) [blɔksilɛ̃dr] NM (*Aut*) cylinder block

bloc-diagramme (*pl* **blocs-diagrammes**) [blɔkdjagram] NM (*Géog*) block diagram

bloc-évier (*pl* **blocs-éviers**) [blɔkevje] NM sink unit

blockhaus [blɔkos] NM (*Mil*) blockhouse, pillbox

bloc-moteur (*pl* **blocs-moteurs**) [blɔkmɔtœr] NM (*Aut*) engine block

bloc-notes (*pl* **blocs-notes**) [blɔknɔt] NM (= *cahier*) desk pad, scratch pad; (*avec pince*) clipboard

bloc-système (*pl* **blocs-systèmes**) [blɔksistɛm] NM (*Rail*) block system

blocus [blɔkys] NM blockade; (*Hist*) **le ~ continental** the Continental System; **~ économique** economic blockade; **lever/forcer le ~** to raise/run the blockade; **faire le ~ de** to blockade

blond, blonde [blɔ̃, blɔ̃d] [1] ADJ [*cheveux*] fair, blond(e); [*personne*] fair, fair-haired, blond(e); [*blé, sable*] golden; **~ cendré** ash-blond; **~ roux** sandy, light auburn; **~ vénitien** strawberry blonde, titian (*littér*) **tabac** ≈ mild *ou* light *ou* Virginia tobacco; **bière** ≈ lager; **il est ~ comme les blés** his hair is golden blond(e), he has golden blond(e) hair [2] NM (= *couleur*) blond, light gold; (= *homme*) fair-haired man [3] **blonde** NF (= *femme*) blonde; (**: Can = compagne*) girlfriend, sweetheart; **~e incendiaire** blonde bombshell (*hum*); **~e oxygénée/platinée** *ou* **platine** peroxide/platinum blonde; **une vraie ~e** a natural blonde; **c'est une fausse ~e** she's not a real blonde, she's a peroxide blonde *ou* a bottle blonde* (*péj*) [b] (= *bière*) lager, ≈ light ale (*Brit*) [c] (= *cigarette*) Virginia cigarette

blondasse [blɔ̃das] ADJ (*péj*) dull blond(e)

blondeur [blɔ̃dœr] NF (*littér*) [*cheveux*] fairness; [*blés*] gold

blondin [blɔ̃dɛ̃] NM fair-haired child *ou* young man; (†† = *élégant*) dandy

blondine [blɔ̃din] NF fair-haired child *ou* young girl

blondinet [blɔ̃dinɛ] NM fair-haired boy

blondinette [blɔ̃dinɛt] NF fair-haired girl

blondir [blɔ̃dir] ▶ conjug 2 ◀ [1] VI [*cheveux*] to go fairer; (*littér*) [*blés*] to turn golden; [*oignons*] to become transparent; **faire ~ des oignons** to fry onions lightly (until they are transparent) [2] VT [+ *cheveux, poils*] to bleach

bloquer [blɔke] ▶ conjug 1 ◀ [1] VT [a] (= *immobiliser accidentellement*) [+ *freins, machine, porte*] to jam; [+ *écrou*] to overtighten; [+ *roue*] to lock; **le mécanisme est bloqué** the mechanism is jammed *ou* stuck; **être bloqué par les glaces** to be stuck in the ice, be icebound; **être bloqué par un accident/la foule** to be held up by an accident/the crowd; **je suis bloqué chez moi** I'm stuck at home; **je suis bloqué** (*physiquement*) I can't move, I'm stuck; **j'ai les reins bloqués** my back has seized up [b] (= *immobiliser volontairement*) [+ *objet en mouvement*] to stop; [+ *roue*] (*avec une cale*) to put a block under; (*avec une pierre*) to wedge; [+ *écrou*] to tighten; [+ *porte*] (*avec une cale*) to wedge; **j'ai bloqué la porte avec une chaise** (*ouverte*) I propped the door open with a chair; (*fermée*) I propped a chair against the door to keep it shut; **~ qn contre un mur** to pin sb against a wall; **bloque la roue pendant que je la regonfle** hold the wheel still while I pump it up [c] (= *obstruer*) to block (up); (*Mil*) to block-

ade; **route bloquée par la glace/la neige** icebound/snowbound road; **un camion bloque la route** a truck is blocking the road, the road is blocked by a truck; **des travaux bloquent la route** there are road works in *ou* blocking the way; **les enfants bloquent le passage** the children are standing in *ou* blocking the way, the children are stopping me (*ou* us *etc*) getting past; **des manifestants bloquent la circulation** demonstrators are holding up the traffic [d] [+ *processus*] to bring to a standstill; **les négociations sont bloquées** the talks are deadlocked *ou* are at a standstill; **la situation est complètement bloquée** the situation is at a complete standstill; **ça bloque au niveau de la direction** management are holding things up [e] (= *grouper*) to lump together, put *ou* group together; (*Scol*) **les cours sont bloqués sur six semaines** the classes are spread over six weeks [f] (*Sport*) [+ *ballon*] to block; (*Billard*) [+ *bille*] to jam, wedge [g] [+ *marchandises*] to stop, hold up; [+ *crédit, salaires*] to freeze; [+ *compte en banque*] to stop, freeze [h] (*psychologiquement*) **ça me bloque d'être devant un auditoire** I freeze (up) if I have to speak in public; **quand on le critique, ça le bloque** whenever people criticize him he tenses up *ou* gets all tensed up; **il est bloqué** (*dans sa réflexion*) he has a mental block (about things) [i] (** = réserver*) [+ *jour*] to reserve, put aside [j] (**: Belg*) [+ *examen*] to cram for, swot for* (*Brit*)

[2] **se bloquer** VPR [*porte*] to jam, get stuck, stick; [*machine*] to jam; [*roue*] to lock; [*frein*] to jam, lock on; [*clé*] to get stuck; [*genou*] to lock; (*Psych*) to have a mental block; **devant un auditoire, il se bloque** in front of an audience he just freezes (up)

bloqueur [blɔkœr] NM (*Belg*) swot* (*Brit*)

blottir (se) [blɔtir] ▶ conjug 2 ◀ VPR to curl up, huddle up; **se blottir contre qn** to snuggle up to sb; **se blottir dans les bras de qn** to snuggle up in sb's arms; **blottis les uns contre les autres** curled up *ou* huddled up (close) against one another; **blotti parmi les arbres** nestling *ou* huddling among the trees

blousant, e [bluzɑ̃, ɑ̃t] ADJ [*robe, chemisier*] loose-fitting (*and gathered at the waist*)

blouse [bluz] NF (= *tablier*) overall; (= *chemisier*) blouse, smock; [*médecin*] (white) coat; [*paysan*] smock; (*Billard*) pocket; **les ~s blanches** (= *médecins*) hospital doctors

blouser¹ [bluze] ▶ conjug 1 ◀ VI [*robe, chemisier*] to be loose-fitting (*and gathered at the waist*)

blouser²* [bluze] ▶ conjug 1 ◀ [1] VT to con*, trick, pull a fast one on*; **se faire ~** to be had* *ou* conned* [2] **se blouser**† VPR (= *se tromper*) to make a mistake *ou* a blunder

blouser³ [bluze] VT (*Billard*) to pot, pocket

blouson [bluzɔ̃] NM blouson (jacket); **~ de cuir** leather jacket; **~ d'aviateur** flying jacket; **~ noir**† (*hum*) hell's angel, ≈ teddy-boy (*Brit*)

blue-jean (*pl* **blue-jeans**) [bludʒin] NM (pair of) jeans

blues [bluz] NM INV [a] (= *chanson*) blues song; **aimer le ~** to like the blues; **écouter du ~** to listen to the blues *ou* to blues music [b] (** = mélancolie*) **le ~ the blues*; avoir le ~** *ou* **◊ avoir un coup de ~** to have the blues*, feel blue*

bluette† [blyɛt] NF [a] (= *étincelle*) spark, sparkle [b] (= *livre*) witty little piece (of writing); (= *film*) sentimental film

bluff* [blœf] NM bluff; **c'est du ~** *ou* **un coup de ~!** he's (*ou* they're *etc*) just bluffing *ou* just trying it on!* (*Brit*)

bluffer* [blœf] ▶ conjug 1 ◀ [1] VI to bluff, try it on* (*Brit*); (*Cartes*) to bluff [2] VT [a] (= *tromper*) to fool, put on*, have on (*Brit*); (*Cartes*) to bluff [b] (= *impressionner*) to im-

press; **j'ai été bluffé** I was really impressed; **elle m'a totalement bluffé** she really took my breath away, she really bowled me over

bluffeur, -euse* [blœfœr, øz] NM,F bluffer

blush [blœʃ] NM blusher

blutage [blytaʒ] NM [*farine*] bo(u)lting

bluter [blyte] ▶ conjug 1 ◀ VT [+ *farine*] to bo(u)lt

BN [been] NF (ABRÉV = **Bibliothèque nationale**) → **bibliothèque**

BO [beo] NF (ABRÉV = **bande originale**) → **bande¹**

boa [bɔa] NM (*Habillement, Zool*) boa; **~ constricteur** boa constrictor

Boadicée [bɔadise] NF Boadicea

boat people [botpipœl] NMPL boat people

bob¹ [bɔb] NM (*Sport*) bob(sleigh)

bob² [bɔb] NM (= *chapeau*) cotton sunhat

bobard* [bɔbar] NM (= *mensonge*) lie, fib*; (= *histoire*) tall story, yarn

bobèche [bɔbɛʃ] NF candle-ring

bobet, -ette [bɔbɛ, ɛt] ADJ (*Helv = sot*) stupid, foolish

bobinage [bɔbinaʒ] NM (*gén = action*) winding; (*Élec*) coil(s)

bobine [bɔbin] NF [a] [*fil*] reel, bobbin; [*métier à tisser*] bobbin, spool; [*machine à écrire, à coudre*] spool; (*Photo*) spool, reel; (*Élec*) coil; **~ d'induction** induction coil; **~ (d'allumage)** coil; **~ de pellicule** roll of film [b] (* = *visage*) face, mug*; **il a fait une drôle de ~!** what a face he made!; **tu en fais une drôle de ~!** you look a bit put out!*

bobineau [bɔbino] NM = **bobinot**

bobiner [bɔbine] ▶ conjug 1 ◀ VT to wind

bobinette†† [bɔbinɛt] NF (wooden) latch

bobineur, -euse [bɔbinœr, øz] [1] NM,F [*personne*] winder [2] NM (= *appareil*) coiler [3] **bobineuse** NF winding machine

bobinoir [bɔbinwar] NM winding machine

bobinot [bɔbino] NM (*Tex*) reel, bobbin

bobo [bobo] NM (*langage enfantin*) (= *plaie*) sore; (= *coupure*) cut; **avoir ~** to be hurt, have a pain; **avoir ~ à la gorge** to have a sore throat; **ça (te) fait ~?** does it hurt?, is it sore?; **il n'y a pas eu de ~** there was no harm done

bobonne†* [bɔbɔn] NF (*sa*) ~ his old woman*, his missus* (*Brit*), his old lady* (*US*); (*hum*) **oui** ~ yes love* *ou* dearie*

bobsleigh [bɔbslɛg] NM bobsleigh

bocage [bɔkaʒ] NM [a] (*Géog*) bocage (*farmland criss-crossed by hedges and trees*) [b] (*littér = bois*) grove, copse

bocager, -ère [bɔkaʒe, ɛr] ADJ (*littér = boisé*) wooded; (*Géog*) **paysage ~** bocage landscape

bocal (*pl* **-aux**) [bɔkal, o] NM jar; **~ à poissons rouges** goldfish bowl; **mettre en bocaux** [+ *fruits, légumes*] to preserve, bottle

Boccace [bɔkas] NM Boccaccio

boche** [bɔʃ] (*péj*) [1] ADJ Boche [2] **Boche** NM Jerry, Kraut*

Bochimans [bɔʃimɑ̃] NMPL Bushmen

bock [bɔk] NM (= *verre*) beer glass; (= *bière*) glass of beer

body [bɔdi] NM (*gén*) body(suit); (*Sport*) leotard

Boers [bur] NMPL **les ~** the Boers; **la guerre des ~** the Boer war

bœuf (*pl* **bœufs**) [bœf, bø] [1] NM [a] (= *bête*) ox; (*de boucherie*) bullock, steer (*US*); (= *viande*) beef; **~s de boucherie** beef cattle; **~ mode** stewed beef with carrots; **~ en daube** bœuf en daube, beef stew; **il a un ~ sur la langue** he has been paid to keep his mouth shut*; **on n'est pas des ~s!** we're not galley slaves!* → **charrue, fort, qui** [b] (*arg Mus*) jam session; **faire un ~** to jam [2] ADJ INV **effet/succès ~*** tremendous* *ou* fantastic* effect/success

bof [bɔf] EXCL **il est beau! — ~** he's good-looking! — do you really think so? *ou* d'you reckon?*; **qu'en penses-tu ?** — ~ what do you think of it? — not a lot; **ça t'a plu ?** — ~ did you like it? — not really; **~, si tu y tiens vraiment** oh, alright, if you really want to; **la ~ génération ◊ la génération ~** the couldn't-care-less generation

bogee, bogey [bɔgi] NM (*Golf*) bogy, bogey, bogie

bogomile [bɔgɔmil] ADJ, NM Bogomil

Bogota [bɔgɔta] N Bogota

bogue¹ [bɔg] NF (*Bot*) husk

bogue² [bɔg] NM (*Ordin*) bug

boguet [bɔgɛ] NM a (*: Helv = cyclomoteur*) moped b = **boghei**

Bohême [bɔɛm] NF Bohemia

bohème [bɔɛm] 1 ADJ bohemian 2 NMF bohemian; **mener une vie de ~** to lead a bohemian life 3 NF (= *milieu*) **la ~** Bohemia 4 NM (= *verre*) Bohemian glass; **un vase en ~** a Bohemian glass vase

bohémien, -ienne [bɔemjɛ̃, jɛn] 1 ADJ Bohemian 2 NM (*Ling*) Bohemian 3 NM,F (= *gitan*) gipsy; (= *de Bohême*) **Bohémien(ne)** Bohemian

boire [bwaʀ] ◢ conjug 53 ◀ 1 VT a (= *ingurgiter*) to drink; **offrir/donner à ~ à qn** to get sb/give sb something to drink *ou* a drink; **~ à la santé/au succès de qn** to drink sb's health/to sb's success; **on a bu une bouteille à nous deux** we drank a (whole) bottle between the two of us; **~ jusqu'à plus soif** to drink one's fill, drink until one's thirst is quenched; **il boit l'argent du ménage** he drinks away the housekeeping money, he spends all the housekeeping money on drink; (*fig*) **~ une** *ou* **la tasse*** (*en nageant*) to swallow *ou* get a mouthful of water; **ce vin se boit bien** *ou* **se laisse ~** this wine goes down nicely*, this wine is very drinkable; **donner à ~ à un enfant** to give a child something to drink; **faire ~ un malade** to help a sick person to drink; **faire ~ un cheval** to water a horse → **coup, vin**

b (*gén emploi absolu = boire trop*) to drink; **il s'est mis à ~** he has taken to drink, he has started drinking; **il a bu, c'est évident** he has obviously been drinking; **~ comme un trou*** *ou* **comme une éponge*** to drink like a fish; **il boit sec** he's a heavy drinker

c (= *absorber*) to soak up, absorb; **ce papier boit l'encre** the ink soaks into this paper; **ce buvard boit bien l'encre** this blotter soaks up the ink well; **la plante a déjà tout bu** the plant has already soaked up all the water; **cette plante boit beaucoup*** this is a very thirsty plant*

d (*loc*) **~ les paroles de qn** to drink in sb's words, lap up what sb says*; **~ le calice jusqu'à la lie** to drain one's cup to the (last) dregs *ou* last drop; **il y a à ~ et à manger là-dedans** (*dans une boisson*) there are bits floating about in it; (*fig*) (= *qualités et défauts*) it's got its good points and its bad; (= *vérités et mensonges*) you have to pick and choose what to believe ■ (*PROV*) **qui a bu boira** a leopard never changes its spots (*PROV*), once a thief always a thief (*PROV*) → **lait**

2 NM **le ~ et le manger** food and drink; (*fig*) **il en perd le ~ et le manger** he's losing sleep over it (*ou* her etc), he can't eat or sleep because of it (*ou* her etc)

bois [bwa] 1 NM a (= *forêt, matériau*) wood; **c'est en ~** it's made of wood; **chaise de** *ou* **en ~** wooden chair; **ramasser du petit ~** to collect sticks *ou* kindling; (*fig*) **son visage était de ~** his face was impassive, he was poker-faced; (*fig*) **je ne suis pas de ~** I'm only human, I'm only flesh and blood → **chèque**

b (= *objet en bois*) (*gravure*) woodcut; (*manche*) shaft, handle

c (*Zool*) antler

d (*Mus*) woodwind instrument; **les ~** the woodwind (instruments *ou* section)

e (*Golf*) wood

f (*loc*: *Tennis*) **faire un ~** to hit the ball off the wood; **je ne suis pas du ~ dont on fait les flûtes** I'm not going to let myself be pushed around, I'm not just anyone's fool; **touchons du ~ !*** touch wood!* (*Brit*), knock on wood!* (*US*); **il va voir de quel ~ je me chauffe !** I'll show him (what I'm made of)!, just let me get my hands on him!; **il fait feu** *ou* **flèche de tout ~** he'll use any means available to him

2 COMP ► **bois blanc** deal; **table en ~ blanc** deal table ► **bois à brûler** firewood ► **bois de charpente** timber, lumber (*US*) ► **bois de chauffage** *ou* **de chauffe** firewood ► **bois de construction** timber, lumber (*US*) ► **bois debout** (*Can*) standing timber ► **bois d'ébène** (*Hist péj = esclaves*) black gold ► **bois exotique** tropical hardwood ► **les bois de justice** the guillotine ► **bois de lit** bedstead ► **bois de menuiserie** timber, lumber (*US*) ► **bois mort** deadwood ► **bois d'œuvre** timber, lumber (*US*) ► **bois rond** (*Can*) unhewn timber ► **bois de rose** rosewood ► **bois tropical** = **bois exotique** ► **bois vert** green wood; (*Menuiserie*) unseasoned *ou* green timber

boisage [bwazaʒ] NM (= *action*) timbering; (= *matière*) timber work

bois-brûlé, e† [*mpl* **bois-brûlés**] [bwabʀyle] NM,F (*Can*) half-breed Indian, bois-brûlé (*Can*)

boisé, e [bwaze] (*ptp de boiser*) ADJ [*région, parc*] wooded; [*vin*] woody, boisé; **région très/peu ~e** densely *ou* thickly/sparsely wooded area

boisement [bwazmã] NM afforestation

boiser [bwaze] ◢ conjug 1 ◀ VT [+ *région*] to afforest, plant with trees; [+ *galerie*] to timber

boiserie [bwazʀi] NF **~(s)** panelling, wainscot(t)ing, wood trim (*US*)

boisseau (*pl* **boisseaux**) [bwaso] NM a (= *mesure*)†† (*Can*) bushel (36,36 litres); **c'est un vrai ~ de puces !*** he's a menace!* *ou* a pest!*; **garder** *ou* **mettre sous le ~** [+ *projet*] to keep secret; [+ *problème embarrassant*] to brush *ou* sweep under the carpet b (= *tuyau*) flue

boisson [bwasɔ̃] NF drink; (*: Can*) hard liquor, spirits; **ils apportent la ~** they're bringing the drinks; (*littér*) **être pris de ~** to be drunk, be under the influence (*hum*); **il est porté sur la ~** he likes his drink, he's a bit of a boozer*; **~ alcoolisée** alcoholic drink *ou* beverage (*frm*); **~ non alcoolisée** soft drink; **~ fraîche/chaude** cold/hot drink

boîte [bwat] 1 NF a (= *récipient*) (*en carton, bois*) box; (*en métal*) box, tin; (*conserves*) tin (*Brit*), can; **mettre des haricots en ~** to can beans; **des tomates en ~** tinned (*Brit*) *ou* canned (*US*) tomatoes; **il a mangé toute la ~ de caramels** he ate the whole box of toffees; (*fig*) **mettre qn en ~*** to pull sb's leg*, take the mickey out of sb* (*Brit*); **la mise en ~* du gouvernement par les journaux satiriques** the ridiculing of the government by the satirical press; **il ne supporte pas la mise en ~*** he can't stand having his leg pulled, he can't stand being made a joke of; (*Ciné*) **c'est dans la ~*** it's in the can*

b (*: = cabaret*) nightclub; **aller** *ou* **sortir en ~** to go (out) to a nightclub, go (night-)clubbing*

c * (= *lieu de travail, firme*) company; (= *école*) school; **quelle (sale) ~ !** what a dump!*, what a crummy hole!*; **je veux changer de ~** (= *entreprise*) I want to work for another company; (= *école*) I want to change schools; **j'en ai marre de cette ~ !** I'm fed up with this place!; **il s'est fait renvoyer de la ~** (= *entreprise*) he got fired*; (= *école*) he got thrown out *ou* expelled; **elle travaille pour une ~ de pub*** she works for an advertising company

2 COMP ► **boîte d'allumettes** box of matches ► **boîte à archives** box file

► **boîte à bachot** (*péj*) crammer('s), cramming school ► **boîte à bijoux** jewellery (*Brit*) *ou* jewelry (*US*) box ► **boîte de camembert** camembert box; **ferme ta ~ à camembert !*** shut up!*, shut your face* ► **boîte de conserve** tin (*Brit*) *ou* can (*US*) of food ► **boîte de couleurs** box of paints, paintbox ► **boîte à couture** = **boîte à ouvrage** ► **boîte crânienne** (*Anat*) cranium, brainpan* ► **boîte d'essieu** axle box ► **boîte expressive** (*Orgue*) swell (box) ► **boîte à gants** (*Aut*) glove compartment ► **boîte à idées** suggestion box ► **boîte à images** télévision ► **boîte à** *ou* **aux lettres** (*publique*) post box, mailbox (*US*); (*privée*) letterbox (*Brit*), mailbox (*US*); **mettre une lettre à la ~** to post (*Brit*) *ou* mail a letter; **je leur sers de ~ à lettres** I'm their go-between ► **boîte à lettres électronique** electronic mailbox ► **boîte à malice** bag of tricks ► **boîte à musique** musical box ► **boîte noire** (*Aviat*) black box ► **boîte de nuit** nightclub; **faire les ~s de nuit** to go (night)clubbing* ► **boîte à ordures** dustbin (*Brit*), garbage *ou* trash can (*US*) ► **boîte à outils** (*Tech*) toolbox; (*Ordin*) toolkit ► **boîte à ouvrage** sewing box, workbox ► **boîte de Pandore** Pandora's box ► **boîte de Pétri** Petri dish ► **boîte postale 150** P.O. Box 150 ► **boîte à rythmes** beatbox ► **boîte à thé** tea caddy ► **boîte de vitesses** gearbox ► **boîte vocale** (*Téléc*) voice mail (*NonC*)

boitement [bwatmã] NM limping

boiter [bwate] ◢ conjug 1 ◀ VI [*personne*] to limp, walk with a limp; [*meuble*] to wobble; [*raisonnement*] to be unsound *ou* shaky; **~ bas** to limp badly; **~ de la jambe gauche** to limp with one's left leg

boiteux, -euse [bwatø, øz] 1 ADJ [*personne*] lame, who limps (*attrib*); [*meuble*] wobbly, rickety; [*paix, projet, compromis*] shaky; [*union*] ill-assorted; [*raisonnement*] unsound, shaky; [*explication*] lame, weak; [*vers*] lame; [*phrase*] (*incorrecte*) grammatically wrong; (*mal équilibrée*) cumbersome, clumsy; **c'était un mariage ~** it was a shaky marriage 2 NM,F lame person, gimp*

boîtier [bwatje] NM (*gén*) case; (*pour appareil photo*) body; (*Aut*) **~ de différentiel** differential housing; **~ électrique** electric torch (*Brit*), flashlight (*US*); **~ de montre** watchcase

boitillement [bwatijmã] NM slight limp

boitiller [bwatije] ◢ conjug 1 ◀ VI to limp slightly, have a slight limp

boit-sans-soif* [bwasɑ̃swaf] NMF INV drunkard, lush*, piss artist* (*Brit*)

bol [bɔl] NM a (= *récipient*) bowl; (= *contenu*) bowl, bowlful; (*fig*) **prendre un (bon) ~ d'air** to get a breath of fresh air; **cheveux coupés au ~** pudding-basin haircut (*Brit*), bowl cut (*US*) b (*Pharm*) bolus; **~ alimentaire** bolus c (*: loc*) **avoir du ~** to be lucky *ou* jammy* (*Brit*); **ne pas avoir de ~** to be unlucky; **pas de ~, il est déjà parti** no luck, he's already left d (*: Can*) = **bolle**

bolchevik, bolchevique [bɔlʃevik] ADJ, NMF Bolshevik, Bolshevist

bolchevisme [bɔlʃevism] NM Bolshevism

bolcheviste [bɔlʃevist] ADJ, NMF = **bolchevik**

bolduc [bɔldyk] NM curling ribbon, gift-wrap ribbon, bolduc (*SPÉC*)

bolée [bɔle] NF bowl(ful)

boléro [bɔleʀo] NM (*Habillement, Mus*) bolero

bolet [bɔlɛ] NM boletus

bolide [bɔlid] NM (*Astron*) meteor, bolide (*SPÉC*); (= *voiture*) (high-powered) racing car; **comme un ~** [*arriver, passer*] at top speed; **il fonce comme un ~ ◊ c'est un vrai ~** he really whizzes along

Bolivie [bɔlivi] NF Bolivia

bolivien, -ienne [bɔlivjɛ̃, jɛn] ①ADJ Bolivian ② **Bolivien(ne)** NM,F Bolivian

bollard [bɔlaʀ] NM (*Naut*) bollard

bolle* [bɔl] NF (*Can*) head, bonce* (*Brit*); **j'ai mal à la ~** I've got a headache

bolognais, e [bɔlɔɲɛ, ɛz] ①ADJ Bolognese; (*Culin*) bolognese ② **Bolognais(e)** NM,F Bolognese

bombance†* [bɔ̃bɑ̃s] NF feast, beanfeast* (*Brit*); **faire ~** to revel, have a beanfeast* (*Brit*)

bombarde [bɔ̃baʀd] NF (*Mil, Mus*) bombard

bombardement [bɔ̃baʀdəmɑ̃] NM ⓐ (= *pilonnage*) bombardment; (*avec bombes*) bombing; (*avec obus*) shelling; **~ aérien** air raid, aerial bombing (*NonC*) ⓑ (*avec des cailloux, des tomates*) pelting ⓒ (*Phys*) bombardment; **~ atomique** atomic bombardment

bombarder [bɔ̃baʀde] ▸conjug 1◂ VT ⓐ (*Mil*) to bombard; (*avec bombes*) to bomb; (*avec obus*) to shell ⓑ **~ de** (+ *cailloux, tomates*) to pelt with; (+ *questions, critiques, appels*) to bombard with ⓒ (*Phys*) to bombard ⓓ (* = *catapulter*) **on l'a bombardé directeur** he was thrust into *ou* pitchforked into the position of manager

bombardier [bɔ̃baʀdje] NM (= *avion*) bomber; (= *aviateur*) bombardier; **~ d'eau** fire-fighting aircraft, tanker plane (*US*)

Bombay [bɔ̃bɛ] N Bombay

bombe [bɔ̃b] ① NF ⓐ (*Mil*) bomb; **attentat à la ~** bombing, bomb attack; (*fig*) **comme une ~** unexpectedly, out of the blue; **la nouvelle a éclaté comme une ~** *ou* **a fait l'effet d'une ~** the news came as a bombshell *ou* was a bolt from the blue ⓑ (= *atomiseur*) spray; (*gén*) **en ~** in an aerosol (*attrib*); **peinture/chantilly en ~** aerosol paint/cream; **déodorant/insecticide en ~** deodorant/insect spray ⓒ (*Équitation*) riding cap *ou* hat ⓓ (*loc*) **faire la ~*** to have a wild time ② COMP ▸ **bombe aérosol** aerosol can *ou* spray ▸ **bombe anti-crevaison** instant puncture sealant ▸ **bombe antigel** (*Aut*) de-icing spray ▸ **bombe atomique** atom(ic) bomb; **la ~ atomique** the Bomb ▸ **bombe à billes** = **bombe à fragmentation** ▸ **bombe au cobalt** (*Méd*) cobalt therapy unit, telecobalt machine ▸ **bombe déodorante** deodorant spray ▸ **bombe à eau** water bomb ▸ **bombe à fragmentation** cluster bomb ▸ **bombe glacée** (*Culin*) bombe glacée, ice-cream pudding (*Brit*) ▸ **bombe H** H-bomb ▸ **bombe à hydrogène** hydrogen bomb ▸ **bombe incendiaire** incendiary *ou* fire bomb ▸ **bombe insecticide** insect spray, fly spray ▸ **bombe lacrymogène** teargas grenade ▸ **bombe de laque** hair spray ▸ **bombe logique** (*Ordin*) logic bomb ▸ **bombe au napalm** napalm bomb ▸ **bombe à neutrons** neutron bomb ▸ **bombe de peinture** paint spray, can of aerosol paint ▸ **bombe à retardement** time bomb ▸ **bombe sexuelle*** sex bomb* ▸ **bombe volcanique** (*Géol*) volcanic bomb

bombé, e [bɔ̃be] (*ptp de* **bomber**) ADJ [*forme*] rounded, convex; [*cuiller*] rounded; [*poitrine*] thrown out; [*front*] domed; [*mur*] bulging; [*dos*] humped, hunched; [*route*] cambered; **verre ~** balloon-shaped glass

bombement [bɔ̃bmɑ̃] NM [*forme*] convexity; [*route*] camber; [*front*] bulge

bomber¹ [bɔ̃be] ▸conjug 1◂ ① VT ⓐ **~ le torse** *ou* **la poitrine** (*lit*) to stick out *ou* throw out one's chest; (*fig*) to puff out one's chest, swagger about ⓑ (*Peinture*) to spray(-paint) ② VI ⓐ [*route*] to camber; [*mur*] to bulge; (*Menuiserie*) to warp ⓑ (* = *rouler vite*) to belt along*

bomber² [bɔ̃bœʀ] NM (= *blouson*) bomber jacket

bombonne [bɔ̃bɔn] NF = **bonbonne**

bombyx [bɔ̃biks] NM bombyx

bôme [bom] NF (*Naut*) boom

▼**bon¹, bonne¹** [bɔ̃, bɔn]

① ADJECTIF	④ NOM MASCULIN
② ADVERBE	⑤ NOM FÉMININ
③ EXCLAMATION	⑥ COMPOSÉS

① ADJECTIF

ⓐ = **de qualité** (*gén*) good; [*fauteuil, lit*] good, comfortable; **il a de bonnes jambes** he has a good *ou* strong pair of legs; **une bonne paire de chaussures** a good (strong) pair of shoes; **il a fait du ~ travail** he's done a good job; **marchandises/outils de bonne qualité** good quality goods/tools

ⓑ = **adéquat, compétent, sûr** [*docteur, élève, employé*] good; [*instrument, système, remède*] good, reliable; [*conseil*] good, sound; [*excuse, raison*] good, valid; [*placement, monnaie, entreprise*] sound; **être ~ en anglais** to be good at English; **pour le ~ fonctionnement du moteur** for the motor to work efficiently *ou* properly; **tout lui est ~ pour me discréditer** he'll stop at nothing to discredit me; (*Mil*) **~ pour le service** fit for service

ⓒ = **agréable** [*odeur, vacances, repas*] good, pleasant, nice; [*surprise*] pleasant, nice; **un ~ petit vin** a nice (little) wine; **un ~ vin** a good wine; **une bonne tasse de thé** a nice (hot) cup of tea; **un ~ bain chaud** a nice hot bath; **elle aime les bonnes choses** she likes good food and drink; **nous avons passé une bonne soirée** we had a pleasant *ou* nice evening; **c'était vraiment ~** (*à manger, à boire*) it was *ou* tasted really good *ou* nice; **l'eau est bonne** (*à la mer, à la piscine*) the water's warm *ou* nice; (*iro*) **elle est bien bonne celle-là** ! that's a good one!

ⓓ = **moralement ou socialement irréprochable** [*lectures, fréquentations, pensées, famille*] good; **les bonnes gens** good *ou* honest people; **il est ~ père et ~ fils** he's a good father and a good son; **d'un ~ milieu social** from a good social background

ⓔ = **charitable** [*personne*] good, kind (-hearted); [*action*] good, kind; [*parole*] kind, comforting; **une bonne dame m'a fait entrer** some good woman let me in; **être ~ pour les animaux** to be kind to animals; **vous êtes bien ou trop ~** you are really too kind, it's really too kind *ou* good of you; **il est ~ comme du ~ pain** he has a heart of gold; **elle est bonne fille** she's a nice *ou* good-hearted girl, she's a good sort*; (*iro*) **vous êtes ~ vous** (*avec vos idées impossibles*)!* you're a great help (with your wild ideas)!; (*iro*) **vas-y demain — tu es ~ toi !*** je n'ai pas que ça à faire! go tomorrow — you've got a nerve!* I've got things to do!

ⓕ = **valable, utilisable** [*billet, passeport, timbre*] valid; **médicament/yaourt ~ jusqu'au 5 mai** medicine/yoghurt to be consumed *ou* used before 5th May; **est-ce que la soupe va être encore bonne avec cette chaleur ?** will the soup have kept *ou* will the soup still be all right in this heat?; **ce joint de caoutchouc n'est plus ~** this rubber washer is no longer any good; **est-ce que ce pneu/ce vernis est encore ~ ?** is this tyre/varnish still fit to be used? *ou* still usable?; (*Tennis*) **la balle est/n'est pas bonne** the ball was in/was out

ⓖ = **favorable** [*opinion, rapport*] good, favourable; (*Scol*) [*bulletin, note*] good; **le diagnostic du médecin n'est pas très ~** the doctor's diagnosis isn't very good

ⓗ = **recommandé** [*alimentation*] good; **ce n'est pas un ~ champignon** it's not an edible mushroom; **cette eau est-elle bonne (à boire)?** is this water fit *ou* all right to drink?; **est-ce bien ~ de fumer tant ?** is it a good thing *ou* is it wise to smoke so much?; **ce serait une bonne chose s'il restait là-bas** it would be a good thing if he stayed

there; **il serait ~ que vous les préveniez** it would be a good idea *ou* thing to let them know; **il est ~ de louer tôt** it's as well *ou* it's advisable to book early; **croire** *ou* **juger** *ou* **trouver ~ de faire qch** to think *ou* see fit to do sth; **il semblerait ~ de ...** it would seem sensible *ou* a good idea to ...; **trouvez-vous ~ qu'il y aille ?** do you think it's a good thing for him to go?; **quand/comme vous le jugerez ~** when/as you see fit; **quand/comme ~ vous semble** when/as you think best; **allez-y si ~ vous semble** go ahead if you think it best; **~ pour la santé/pour le mal de tête** good for your health/for headaches; **c'est ~ pour ce que tu as !** it'll do you good!; **la baisse des taux, c'est ~ pour l'économie** the reduction in interest rates is good for the economy; **la télévision, c'est ~ pour ceux qui n'ont rien à faire** television is all right *ou* fine for people who have nothing to do; **cette solution, c'est ~ pour toi, mais pas pour moi** that solution's OK for you but not for me

ⓘ * = **attrapé, condamné** **je suis ~ !** I've had it!*; **le voilà ~ pour une contravention** he's in for a fine now*; **le voilà ~ pour recommencer** now he'll have to start all over again

ⓙ **sur imprimé** **~ pour pouvoir** procuration given by; (*Comm : sur coupon*) **~ pour un lot de 6 bouteilles** this voucher *ou* coupon may be exchanged for a pack of 6 bottles; **~ pour une réduction de 2 F** 2 francs off next purchase

ⓚ = **utile** **c'est ~ à savoir** that's useful to know, that's worth knowing; **c'est toujours ~ à prendre** there's no reason to turn it down, it's better than nothing; **tout n'est pas ~ à dire** some things are better left unsaid; **puis-je vous être ~ à quelque chose ?** can I be of any use *ou* help to you?, can I do anything for you?; **ce drap est (tout juste) ~ à faire des torchons** this sheet is (just) about good enough for *ou* is only fit for dusters (*Brit*) *ou* dustcloths (*US*); **c'est (tout juste) ~ à nous créer des ennuis** it will only create problems for us, all it will do is create problems for us; **c'est ~ à jeter** it's fit for the dustbin, it might as well be thrown out

ⓛ = **correct** [*solution, méthode, réponse, calcul*] right, correct; **au ~ moment** at the right *ou* proper time; **sur le ~ côté de la route** on the right *ou* proper side of the road; **le ~ côté du couteau** the cutting *ou* sharp edge of the knife; **le ~ usage** correct usage (of language); (*en positionnant qch*) **c'est ~ ?*** is this O.K.?, how's that? ■ (*PROV*) **les ~s comptes font les ~s amis** bad debts make bad friends

ⓜ **intensif de quantité** good; **un ~ kilomètre** a good kilometre; **une bonne livre/semaine/heure** a good pound/week/hour; **il a reçu une bonne fessée** he got a good spanking; **la voiture en a pris un ~ coup*** the car got pretty smashed up*; **ça fait un ~ bout de chemin !** that's quite a distance *ou* a good way!; **il est tombé une bonne averse/couche de neige** there has been a heavy shower/fall of snow; **après un ~ moment** after quite some time *ou* a good while; **laissez une bonne marge** leave a good *ou* wide margin; **il faudrait une bonne gelée pour tuer la vermine** what's needed is a hard frost to kill off the vermin; **ça aurait besoin d'une bonne couche de peinture/d'un ~ coup de balai** it needs *ou* would need a good coat of paint/a good sweep-out; **ça fait un ~ poids à traîner** that's quite a *ou* some load to drag round!; **une bonne moitié** at least half

ⓝ **en apostrophe** **mon ~ monsieur** my good man; **ma bonne dame** my good woman; **mon ~ ami** my dear *ou* good friend

ⓞ **dans des souhaits** **bonne (et heureuse) année !** happy New Year!; **bonne chance !** good luck!, all the best!; **~ courage !** good luck!; **~ dimanche !** have a nice Sunday!; **bonne fin de semaine !** enjoy the rest of the week!, have a good weekend!; **~ match !** (*à un spectateur*) enjoy the game!; (à un joueur) have a good game!; **bonne promenade**! have a nice walk!; (Scol) **bonne rentrée**! I hope the new term starts well!; ~ **retour**! safe journey back!, safe return!; **bonne route**! safe journey!; **bonne santé**! (I) hope you keep well!; **bonnes vacances**! have a good holiday! (Brit) ou vacation! (US); ~ **voyage**! safe journey!, have a good journey!; **au revoir et bonne continuation** goodbye and I hope all goes well (for you) ou and all the best! → **anniversaire, appétit, souhaiter** etc

[p] = **amical** [ambiance] good, pleasant, nice; [regard, sourire] warm, pleasant; **relations de ~ voisinage** good neighbourly relations; **un ~ (gros) rire** a hearty ou cheery laugh; **c'est un ~ camarade** he's a good friend

[2] ADVERBE

◆ **faire bon** : **il fait ~ ici** it's nice ou pleasant here; **il fait ~ au soleil** it's nice and warm in the sun; **il fait ~ vivre à la campagne** it's a nice life in the country; **une ville où il fait ~ vivre** a town that's really nice to live in; **il ne ferait pas ~ le contredire** we (ou you etc) would be ill-advised to contradict him

◆ **pour de bon** (= définitivement) for good; (= vraiment) really; **si tu continues, je vais me fâcher pour de ~** if you keep that up, I'm really going to get angry

[3] EXCLAMATION

= **d'accord** all right!, OK!*; (énervement) (all) right!, OK!*; ~ ! **ça suffit maintenant**! (all) right! ou OK! that's enough!; **bon**! ~ ! all right! all right!; ~ ! **je le ferai moi-même** (all) right then I'll do it myself

[4] NOM MASCULIN

[a] = **personne** good ou upright person; **les ~s et les méchants** good people and bad people; (dans un western) the goodies and the baddies (Brit), the good guys and the bad guys

[b] = **morceau, partie** **mange le ~ et laisse le mauvais** eat the good part and leave the bad part; **avoir du ~** [solution, principe] to have its advantages ou its good points; **il y a du ~ dans ce qu'il dit** there is some merit ou there are some good points in what he says; **il y a du ~ et du mauvais** it has its good and its bad points; **il y a du ~ et du moins ~** parts of it are good and parts of it are not so good, some bits are better than others

[5] **bonne** NOM FÉMININ

[a] = **histoire** **en voilà une bonne**! that's a good one!; (iro) **tu en as de bonnes, toi**!* you're kidding!*, you must be joking!*

[b]

◆ **avoir qn à la bonne*** to like sb, be in* ou in solid* (US) with sb; **il m'a à la bonne** I'm in his good books*

[6] COMPOSÉS

► **bonne amie** († ou hum) girlfriend, sweetheart ► **bon chic bon genre** [personne] chic but conservative, Sloaney* (Brit), preppy* (US); [bar, soirée] chic but conservative, Sloaney* (Brit); **le style ~ chic ~ genre des villes bourgeoises** the conservative chic of middle-class towns ► **bon enfant** LOC ADJ [personne, sourire] good-natured [atmosphère] friendly ► **bonne femme** (péj = femme) woman; (péj = épouse) **sa bonne femme** his old woman*, his missus*; **pauvre petite bonne femme** (= enfant) poor little thing ► **une bonne pâte** an easy-going fellow, a good sort ► **bon à rien, bonne à rien** ADJ **cet enfant n'est à rien** this child is no good ou use at anything; **cet appareil n'est ~ à rien** this instrument is useless ou isn't much good ou use for anything ◆ NM,F good-for-nothing, ne'er-do-well ► **bon Samaritain** (Bible, fig) good Samaritan ► **bonne sœur*** nun, fast; (fig) [syndicaliste] staunch, dyed-in-the-wool ► **bon à tirer** ADJ passed for press ◆ NM final corrected proof; **donner le ~ à tirer** to pass for press ► **bon vivant** NM bon viveur ou vivant; **c'est un ~ vi-**

vant he's a bon viveur ou vivant, he likes the good things in life

bon² [bɔ̃] [1] NM (= formulaire) slip, form; (= coupon d'échange) coupon, voucher; (Fin = titre) bond [2] COMP ► **bon de caisse** cash voucher ► **bon de commande** order form ► **bon d'épargne** savings certificate ► **bon d'essence** petrol (Brit) ou gas (US) coupon ► **bon de garantie** guarantee (slip) ► **bon de livraison** delivery slip ► **bon de réduction** reduction coupon ou voucher ► **bon du Trésor** (Government) Treasury bill ► **bon à vue** demand note

Bonaparte [bɔnapaʀt] NM Bonaparte

bonapartisme [bɔnapaʀtism] NM Bonapartism

bonapartiste [bɔnapaʀtist] ADJ, NMF Bonapartist

bonasse [bɔnas] ADJ (gén) easy-going; (péj) meek; **accepter qch d'un air ~** (gén) to accept sth good-naturedly; (péj) to accept sth meekly

bonbec* [bɔ̃bɛk] NM (= bonbon) sweetie* (Brit), candy (US)

bonbon [bɔ̃bɔ̃] [1] NM sweet (Brit), sweetie* (Brit), piece of candy (US); **j'en ai ras le ~*** I'm fed up to the back teeth* → **casser** [2] COMP ► **bonbon acidulé** acid drop ► **bonbon anglais** fruit drop ► **un bonbon au chocolat** a chocolate ► **bonbon fourré** sweet (Brit) ou piece of candy (US) with soft centre ► **bonbon à la menthe** mint, humbug (Brit) ► **bonbon au miel** honey drop

bonbonne [bɔ̃bɔn] NF (recouverte d'osier) demijohn; (à usage industriel) carboy

bonbonnière [bɔ̃bɔnjɛʀ] NF (= boîte) sweet (Brit) ou candy (US) box, bonbonnière; (fig = appartement) bijou flat (Brit), exquisite apartment (US), bijou residence (hum)

bond [bɔ̃] NM [a] [personne, animal] (gén) leap, bound, jump; (de la position accroupie) spring; [balle] bounce; **faire des ~s** (= sauter) to leap ou spring up ou into the air; (= gambader) to leap ou jump about; **faire un ~ d'indignation** to leap ou jump up indignantly; **faire un ~ de surprise** to start with surprise; **franchir qch d'un ~** to clear sth with one jump ou bound; **se lever d'un ~** to leap ou jump ou spring up; **d'un ~ il fut près d'elle** in a single leap ou bound he was at her side; **il ne fit qu'un ~ jusqu'à l'hôpital** he rushed ou dashed off to the hospital; **j'ai pris ou saisi l'occasion au ~** I jumped at ou I seized the opportunity; **saisir une remarque au ~** to pounce ou jump on a remark → **saisir, faux²**

[b] (= progression) **les prix ont fait un ~** prices have shot up ou soared; **la science a fait un grand ~ en avant** science has taken a great leap forward; **l'économie nationale a fait un ~ (en avant)** the country's economy has leapt forward ou taken a leap forward; **progresser par ~s** to progress by leaps and bounds; (Mil) to advance by successive dashes

bonde [bɔ̃d] NF [a] (= bouchon) [tonneau] bung, stopper; [étang] plug; [évier, baignoire] plug; [b] (= trou) [tonneau] bunghole; [évier, baignoire] plughole

bondé, e [bɔ̃de] ADJ packed, jam-packed*

bondieusard, e* [bɔ̃djøzaʀ, aʀd] (péj) [1] ADJ sanctimonious, churchy* [2] NM,F sanctimonious ou churchy* person, Holy Joe* (péj) (Brit)

bondieuserie [bɔ̃djøzʀi] NF (péj) (= piété) religiosity, devoutness; (= bibelot) religious trinket ou bric-à-brac (NonC)

bondir [bɔ̃diʀ] ▸ conjug 2 ◂ VI [a] (= sauter) [homme, animal] to jump ou leap ou spring up; [balle] to bounce (up); ~ **de joie** to jump ou leap for joy; ~ **de colère** to fume with anger; **il bondit d'indignation** he leapt up indignantly; (fig) **cela me fait ~*** it makes my blood

boil*, it makes me hopping mad* (Brit) [b] (= gambader) to jump ou leap about (= sursauter) to start; ~ **de surprise/de frayeur** to start with surprise/fright [d] (= se précipiter) ~ **vers** ou **jusqu'à** to dash ou rush to; ~ **sur sa proie** to pounce on one's prey

bondissant, e [bɔ̃disɑ̃, ɑ̃t] ADJ leaping, jumping

bondissement [bɔ̃dismɑ̃] NM [animal] leaping (NonC)

bongo [bɔ̃go] NM (Mus) bongo (drum)

▼ **bonheur** [bɔnœʀ] [1] NM [a] (= félicité) happiness; (= joie) joy; **trouver le ~** to find true happiness; **le ~ de vivre/d'aimer** the joy of living/of loving; **avoir le ~ de voir son enfant réussir** to have the joy of seeing one's child succeed; **faire le ~ de qn** to make sb happy, bring happiness to sb; **si ce ruban peut faire ton ~, prends-le** if this ribbon is what you're looking for ou can be any use to you, take it; **alors, tu as trouvé ton ~?** so, did you find what you wanted ou what you were looking for?; **des vacances**! **quel ~**! holidays! what bliss! ou what a delight!; **quel ~ de vous revoir**! what a pleasure it is to see you again!

[b] (= chance) (good) luck, good fortune; **il ne connaît pas son ~**! he doesn't know ou realize (just) how lucky he is!, he doesn't know ou realize his luck!*; **avoir le ~ de faire** to be lucky enough ou have the good fortune to do; **il eut le rare ~ de gagner 3 fois** he had the unusual good fortune of winning ou to win 3 times; **porter ~** to bring sb luck; **ça porte ~ de ...** it's lucky to ...; **par ~** fortunately, luckily; **par un ~ inespéré** by an unhoped-for stroke of luck ou good fortune

[c] (loc: littér) **avec ~** felicitously; **mêler avec ~ le tragique et le comique** to blend the tragic and the comic skilfully; **au petit ~ (la chance)*** [répondre] off the top of one's head*; [faire] haphazardly, any old how*; **il n'y a pas de véritable sélection, c'est au petit ~ la chance** there's no real selection (process), it's just pot luck ou the luck of the draw ■ (PROV) **le ~ des uns fait le malheur des autres** one man's meat is another man's poison (PROV)

bonheur-du-jour (pl **bonheurs-du-jour**) [bɔnœʀdyʒuʀ] NM escritoire, writing desk

bonhomie [bɔnɔmi] NF affability, bonhomie

bonhomme [bɔnɔm] [1] NM (pl **bonshommes**) [a]* (= homme) guy*, chap* (Brit), fellow*, bloke* (Brit); (= mari) old man*; **dessiner des bonshommes** to draw little men; **un petit ~ de 4 ans** a little chap* ou lad* ou fellow* of 4; **dis-moi, mon ~** tell me, sonny* ou little fellow*; **c'était un grand ~** he was a great man*; **aller ou suivre son petit ~ de chemin** to carry on ou go on in one's own sweet way [b] (*: Can = père) old man*, father [2] ADJ (pl **bonhommes**) [air, regard] good-natured [3] COMP ► **bonhomme de neige** snowman ► **bonhomme de pain d'épice** gingerbread man

boni † [bɔni] NM (= bénéfice) profit; **100 F de ~** a 100-franc profit

boniche* [bɔniʃ] NF (péj) maid, skivvy* (Brit); **je ne suis pas ta ~** I'm not your skivvy (Brit) ou slave; **faire la ~ pour qn** to be sb's slave, to skivvy for sb* (Brit)

bonification¹ [bɔnifikasjɔ̃] NF [a] (= amélioration) [terre, vins] improvement [b] (Sport) (= points) bonus (points); (= avantage) advantage, start

bonification² [bɔnifikasjɔ̃] NF (Fin = remise) discount, rebate; **~s d'intérêt** interest rate subsidies, preferential interest rates

bonifier¹ [bɔnifje] VT, **se bonifier** VPR ▸ conjug 7 ◂ to improve

bonifier² [bɔnifje] ▸ conjug 7 ◂ VT (Fin) to give as a bonus; **prêt ou crédit (à taux) bonifié** government subsidized ou low-interest loan

► GRAMMAIRE ACTIVE: **bonheur** 50.3

boniment [bɔnimɑ̃] NM (= *baratin*) sales talk (*NonC*), patter* (*NonC*); (* = *mensonge*) tall story, humbug (*NonC*); **faire le** ou **du ~ à qn** to give sb the sales talk ou patter*; **faire du ~ à une femme** to try and pick up a woman*, chat a woman up* (*Brit*); **raconter des ~s** to spin yarns ou tall stories

bonimenter [bɔnimɑ̃te] ▶ conjug 1 ◀ VI to give the sales talk ou patter*

bonimenteur, -euse [bɔnimɑ̃tœʀ, øz] NM,F smooth talker; [*foire*] barker

bonite [bɔnit] NF bonito

▼ **bonjour** [bɔ̃ʒuʀ] NM **a** (*gén*) hello; (*matin*) (good) morning; (*après-midi*) (good) afternoon; (*Can* = *au revoir*) good day (*frm*), good morning, good afternoon; **~ chez vous !** hello to everybody at home!; **avec lui, c'est ~ bonsoir** I only ever say hello to him; **donnez-lui le ~ de ma part** give him my regards, remember me to him; **dire ~ à qn** to say hello to sb; **est-ce que je peux passer te dire un petit ~ ?** can I drop in (to say hello)? **b** (*: loc*) **le bus aux heures de pointe, ~ (les dégâts) !*** taking the bus in the rush hour is absolute hell!*; **tu aurais vu sa moto après l'accident ! ~ (les dégâts) !*** you should've seen his bike after the accident! what a mess!; **si son père l'apprend, ~ (les dégâts) !** if his father finds out about it, sparks will fly ou all hell will be let loose!*; **si tu l'invites, ~ l'ambiance !** if you invite him, it'll ruin the atmosphere!; **pour l'ouvrir, ~ !** there's no way to get it open

Bonn [bɔn] N Bonn

bonne² [bɔn] NF maid, domestic; **~ d'enfants** nanny, child's nurse (*US*); **~ à tout faire** maid of all work, skivvy (*Brit*); (*hum*) general dogsbody ou factotum; **je ne suis pas ta ~** I'm not your skivvy ou slave → **bon¹**

bonne-maman (*pl* **bonnes-mamans**) [bɔnmamɑ̃] NF granny, grandma

bonnement [bɔnmɑ̃] ♦ **tout bonnement** LOC ADV just, (quite) simply; **dire tout ~ que ...** to say quite simply that ...

bonnet [bɔnɛ] **1** NM **a** (= *coiffure*) bonnet, hat; [*bébé*] bonnet **b** [*soutien-gorge*] cup **c** (*Zool*) reticulum **d** (*loc*) **prendre qch sous son ~** to make sth one's concern ou responsibility, take it upon o.s. to do sth; **c'est blanc et blanc ~** it amounts to the same thing; **jeter son ~ par-dessus les moulins** to kick over the traces, have one's fling → **gros**, **tête 2** COMP ▶ **bonnet d'âne** dunce's cap ▶ **bonnet de bain** bathing cap ▶ **bonnet de nuit** (*Habillement*) nightcap; (*: fig*) wet blanket*, killjoy, spoilsport ▶ **bonnet phrygien** Phrygian cap ▶ **bonnet à poils** bearskin ▶ **bonnet de police** forage cap, garrison ou overseas cap (*US*) → MARIANNE

bonneteau [bɔnto] NM three card trick ou monte (*US*)

bonneterie [bɔnɛtʀi] NF (= *objets*) hosiery; (= *magasin*) hosier's shop, hosiery; (= *commerce*) hosiery trade

bonnetier, -ière [bɔntje, jɛʀ] NM,F hosier

bonnette [bɔnɛt] NF (*Photo*) supplementary lens; (*Naut*) studding sail, stuns'l; (*Mil*) [*fortification*] bonnet

bonniche [bɔniʃ] NF = **boniche**

bon-papa (*pl* **bons-papas**) [bɔ̃papa] NM grandad*, grandpa

bonsaï [bɔ̃zaj] NM bonsai

bonsoir [bɔ̃swaʀ] NM **a** (*en arrivant*) hello, good evening; (*en partant*) good evening, good night; (*en se couchant*) good night; **souhaiter le ~ à qn** to say good night to sb, wish sb goodnight **b** (*: loc*) **~ !** (= *rien à faire*) nothing doing!*, not a chance!*, not on your life!*; **pour s'en débarrasser ~ !** it's going to be sheer ou absolute hell* getting rid of it

bonté [bɔ̃te] NF **a** (= *caractère*) kindness, goodness; **ayez la ~ de faire** would you be so kind ou good as to do?; **faire qch par pure ~**

---

d'âme to do sth out of the goodness of one's heart; **avec ~** kindly; **~ divine ! ou du ciel !** good heavens!* **b** (= *acte*) (act of) kindness; **merci de toutes vos ~s** thank you for all your kindness ou for all the kindness you've shown me; **avoir des ~s pour qn** to be very kind to sb

bonus [bɔnys] NM (*Assurances*) no-claims bonus

bonze [bɔ̃z] NM (*Rel*) bonze; (* = *personnage important*) bigwig*; **vieux ~:** old fossil:

bonzerie [bɔ̃zʀi] NF Buddhist monastery

bonzesse [bɔ̃zɛs] NF bonze

boogie-woogie (*pl* **boogie-woogies**) [bugiwugi] NM boogie-woogie

book [buk] NM = **press book**

bookmaker [bukmekœʀ] NM bookmaker

booléen, -enne [buleɛ̃, ɛn] ADJ (*Math, Ordin*) boolean

boom [bum] NM (= *expansion*) boom; **être en plein ~** [*secteur*] to be booming; (* = *en plein travail*) to be really busy

boomerang [bumʀɑ̃g] NM (*lit, fig*) boomerang; (*fig*) **faire ~, avoir un effet ~** to backfire

booster [bustœʀ] NM [*fusée*] booster, launching vehicle; [*autoradio*] booster

boots [buts] NMPL boots

boqueteau (*pl* **boqueteaux**) [bɔkto] NM copse

borax [bɔʀaks] NM borax

borborygme [bɔʀbɔʀigm] NM rumble, rumbling noise (in one's stomach), borborygmus (*SPÉC*)

bord [bɔʀ] NM **a** [*route*] side, edge; [*rivière*] side, bank; [*lac*] edge, side, shore; [*cratère*] edge, rim, lip; [*forêt, table*] edge; [*précipice*] edge, brink; [*verre, tasse*] brim, rim; [*assiette*] edge, rim; [*plaie*] edge; **le ~ des paupières** the rim of the eye; **le ~ de la mer** the seashore; **~ du trottoir** edge of the pavement, kerb (*Brit*), curb (*US*); **une maison au ~ du lac** a house by the lake ou at the lakeside, a lakeside house; **se promener au ~ de la rivière** to go for a walk along the riverside ou the river bank ou by the river; **passer ses vacances au ~ de la mer** to spend one's holidays at the seaside ou by the sea, go to the seaside for one's holidays; **pique-niquer au ~ ou sur le ~ de la route** to (have a) picnic at ou by the roadside; **au ~ de l'eau** at the water's edge; **se promener au ~ de l'eau** to go for a walk by the lake (ou river ou sea); **en été les ~s du lac sont envahis de touristes** in summer the shores of the lake are overrun by tourists; **il a regagné le ~ à la nage** (*dans la mer*) he swam ashore ou to the shore; (*dans une rivière*) he swam to the bank; **verre rempli jusqu'au ~ ou à ras ~** glass full ou filled to the brim
b [*vêtement, mouchoir*] edge, border; [*chapeau*] brim; **chapeau à large(s) ~(s)** wide- ou broad-brimmed hat; **le ~ ourlé d'un mouchoir** the rolled hem of a handkerchief; **~ à ~** [*coudre, coller*] edge to edge; **veste ~ à ~** edge-to-edge jacket
c (*Naut*) side; **les hommes du ~** the crew; (*Naut*) **jeter par-dessus ~** to throw overboard; (*Aviat, Naut*) **à ~** on board, aboard; **monter à ~** to go on board ou aboard; **prendre qn à son ~** to take sb aboard ou on board; **monter à ~ d'un navire** to board a ship, go on board ou aboard ship; **la marchandise a été expédiée à ~ du SS Wallisdown** the goods were shipped on SS Wallisdown; **M. Morand, à ~ d'une voiture bleue** Mr Morand, driving ou in a blue car; **journal ou livre de ~** log(book), ship's log
d (*Naut* = *bordée*) tack; **tirer des ~s** to tack, make tacks; **tirer un ~** to tack, make a tack
e (*: Can*) side; **de mon ~** on my side; **prendre le ~** to make off
f (*loc*) **être au ~ de la ruine/du désespoir** to be on the verge ou brink of ruin/despair; **au ~ de la tombe** on the brink of death; **au ~ des**

---

larmes on the verge of tears; **nous sommes du même ~** we are on the same side, we are of the same opinion; (*socialement*) we are all of a kind; **à pleins ~s** abundantly, freely; **il est un peu fantaisiste/sadique sur les ~s*** he's a bit of an eccentric/a sadist

bordage [bɔʀdaʒ] **1** NM (*Couture*) edging, trimming **2** **bordages** NMPL **a** (*Naut*) (*en bois*) planks, planking; (*en fer*) plates, plating **b** (*Can*) inshore ice

bordé [bɔʀde] **1** NM **a** (*Couture*) braid, trimming **b** (*Naut*) (*en bois*) planking; (*en fer*) plating

bordeaux [bɔʀdo] **1** NM (= *vin*) Bordeaux (wine); **~ rouge** red Bordeaux, claret (*Brit*) **2** ADJ INV maroon, burgundy

bordée [bɔʀde] NF **a** (= *salve*) broadside; (*fig*) **~ d'injures** torrent ou volley of abuse **b** (*Naut* = *quart*) watch **c** (= *parcours*) tack; **tirer des ~s** to tack, make tacks; (*fig*) **tirer une ~** to go on a spree* ou binge* **d** (*: Can*) **une ~ de neige** a heavy snowfall

bordel: [bɔʀdɛl] NM (= *hôtel*) brothel, whorehouse*; (= *chaos*) mess, shambles *sg*; **quel ~ !** what a bloody‡ (*Brit*) ou goddamned‡ (*US*) shambles!; **si tout le monde a accès aux dossiers, ça va être le ~** if everyone has access to the files it'll be bloody‡ (*Brit*) ou goddamned‡ (*US*) chaos; **mettre ou foutre: le ~** to create havoc, cause bloody‡ (*Brit*) ou goddamned‡ (*US*) chaos; **mettre ou foutre: le ~ dans qch** to screw: ou bugger‡ (*Brit*) sth up; **~ ! hell!*, bloody hell!: (*Brit*), shit!:*:; **arrête de gueuler, ~ (de merde) !** stop shouting for Christ's sake!:* ou for fuck's sake!:*; **... et tout le ~ ...** and God knows what else*

bordelais, e [bɔʀdəlɛ, ɛz] **1** ADJ of ou from Bordeaux, Bordeaux (*épith*) **2** **Bordelais(e)** NM,F inhabitant ou native of Bordeaux **3** NM (= *région*) **le Bordelais** the Bordeaux region **4** **bordelaise** NF (*Culin*) **entrecôte (à la) ~e** Bordelaise entrecôte steak

bordélique: [bɔʀdelik] ADJ chaotic, shambolic* (*Brit*)

border [bɔʀde] ▶ conjug 1 ◀ VT **a** (*Couture*) (= *entourer*) to edge, trim (**de** with); (= *ourler*) to hem, put a hem on **b** (= *longer*) [*arbres, immeubles, maisons*] to line; [*sentier*] to run alongside; **allée bordée de fleurs** path edged ou bordered with flowers; **rue bordée de maisons** road lined with houses; **rue bordée d'arbres** tree-lined road **c** [+ *personne, couverture*] to tuck in; **~ un lit** to tuck the blankets in **d** (*Naut*) (*en bois*) to plank; (*en fer*) to plate **e** (*Naut*) [+ *voile*] to haul on, pull on; [+ *avirons*] to ship

bordereau (*pl* **bordereaux**) [bɔʀdəʀo] **1** NM (= *formulaire*) note, slip; (= *relevé*) statement, summary; (= *facture*) invoice **2** COMP ▶ **bordereau d'achat** purchase note ▶ **bordereau d'envoi** dispatch note ▶ **bordereau de livraison** delivery slip ou note ▶ **bordereau de versement** pay(ing)-in slip

bordure [bɔʀdyʀ] NF (= *bord*) edge; (= *cadre*) surround, frame; [*gazon, fleurs*] border; [*arbres*] line; (*Couture*) border, edging, edge; [*voile*] foot; **~ de trottoir** kerb (*Brit*), curb (*US*), kerbstones (*Brit*), curbstones (*US*); **en ~ de** (= *le long de*) running along, alongside, along the edge of; (= *à côté de*) next to, by; (= *près de*) near (to); **en ~ de route** [*maison, champ*] by the roadside (*attrib*); [*restaurant, arbre*] roadside (*épith*); **papier à ~ noire** black-edged paper, paper with a black edge

bore [bɔʀ] NM boron

boréal, e (*mpl* **-aux**) [bɔʀeal, o] ADJ boreal → **aurore**

borgne [bɔʀɲ] ADJ **a** [*personne*] one-eyed, blind in one eye; **fenêtre ~** obstructed window **b** (*fig* = *louche*) [*hôtel, rue*] shady

borique [bɔʀik] ADJ boric

➤ GRAMMAIRE ACTIVE: **bonjour** 48.2

bornage [bɔʀnaʒ] NM [terrain] boundary marking, demarcation

borne [bɔʀn] NF **a** (kilométrique) kilometre-marker, ≈ milestone; [terrain] boundary stone ou marker; (autour d'un monument) bollard (Brit), post; **~ d'incendie** fire hydrant; **ne reste pas là planté comme une ~ !*** don't just stand there like a statue! **b** (fig) **~s** limit(s), bounds; **il n'y a pas de ~s à la bêtise humaine** human folly knows no bounds; **franchir** ou **dépasser les ~s** to go too far; **sans ~s** limitless, unlimited, boundless; **il lui vouait une admiration sans ~(s)** his admiration for her knew no bounds; **mettre des ~s à** to limit **c** (* = kilomètre) kilometre **d** (Élec) terminal **e** (Téléc) **~ téléphonique** ou **d'appel** (pour taxi) taxi rank (Brit) ou stand (US) telephone; (pour secours) emergency telephone; **~ de paiement** pay point **f** (Ordin) **~ interactive/Minitel** interactive/Minitel terminal **g** (Math) bound; **~ inférieure/supérieure** lower/upper bound

borné, e [bɔʀne] (ptp de **borner**) ADJ **a** [personne] narrow-minded, short-sighted; [esprit, vie] narrow; [intelligence] limited **b** (Math) bounded

borne-fontaine (pl **bornes-fontaines**) [bɔʀn(ə)fɔ̃tɛn] NF **a** [eau potable] public drinking fountain **b** (Can = bouche d'incendie) fire hydrant

Bornéo [bɔʀneo] N Borneo

borner [bɔʀne] ▶ conjug 1 ◀ **1** VT **a** [+ ambitions, besoins, enquête] to limit, restrict (**à faire** to doing, **à qch** to sth) **b** [+ terrain] to mark out ou off, mark the boundary of; **arbres qui bornent un champ** trees which border a field; **immeubles qui bornent la vue** buildings which limit ou restrict one's view **2 se borner** VPR (= se contenter de) **se ~ à faire** to content o.s. with doing, be content to do; **se ~ à qch** to content o.s. with sth; (= se limiter à) **se ~ à faire/à qch** [personne] to restrict ou confine o.s. to doing/to sth; [visite, exposé] to be limited ou restricted to doing/to sth; **je me borne à vous faire remarquer que …** I would just ou merely like to point out to you that …; **il s'est borné à resserrer les vis** he just ou merely tightened up the screws

bort(s)ch [bɔʀtʃ] NM bors(c)h

bosco [bɔsko] NM (Naut) quartermaster

bosniaque [bɔsnjak] **1** ADJ Bosnian **2 Bosniaque** NMF Bosnian

Bosnie [bɔsni] NF Bosnia

Bosnie-Herzégovine [bɔsniɛʀzegɔvin] NF Bosnia-Herzegovina

bosnien, -ienne [bɔsnjɛ̃, jɛn] ADJ, NM,F = **bosniaque**

boson [bozɔ̃] NM boson

Bosphore [bɔsfɔʀ] NM **le ~** the Bosphorus; **le détroit du ~** the Bosphorus Strait(s)

bosquet [bɔskɛ] NM copse, grove

bossage [bɔsaʒ] NM (Archit) boss; **~s** bosses, bossage

bossa-nova (pl **bossas-novas**) [bɔsanɔva] NF bossa nova

bosse [bɔs] NF **a** [chameau, bossu] hump; (en se cognant) bump, lump; (= éminence) bump; (Ski) mogul, bump; **se faire une ~ au front** to get a bump on one's forehead; **route pleine de ~s** bumpy road; **ski sur ~s** mogul skiing → **rouler b** (Naut) **~ d'amarrage** pointer **c** (* : loc) **avoir la ~ des maths** to have a good head for maths, be good at maths; **avoir la ~ du commerce** to be a born businessman (ou businesswoman)

bosselage [bɔslaʒ] NM embossment

bosseler [bɔsle] ▶ conjug 4 ◀ VT (= déformer) to dent; (= marteler) to emboss; **tout bosselé** [+ théière] battered, badly dented; [+ front] bruised, covered in bumps (attrib); [+ sol] bumpy

bossellement [bɔsɛlmɑ̃] NM embossing

bosselure [bɔslyʀ] NF (= défaut) dent; (= relief) embossment

bosser* [bɔse] ▶ conjug 1 ◀ **1** VI (= travailler) to work (**dans** in); (= travailler dur) (intellectuellement) to work hard, slog away* (Brit); (physiquement) to slave away, work one's guts out* **2** VT [+ examen] to slog away for* (Brit), swot for (Brit); **~ son anglais** to slog away at ou swot for* one's English

bosseur, -euse* [bɔsœʀ, øz] **1** ADJ hard-working **2** NM,F slogger* (Brit), hard worker

bossoir [bɔswaʀ] NM [bateau] davit; [ancre] cathead

bossu, e [bɔsy] **1** ADJ [personne] hunchbacked; **dos ~** hunch(ed) back; **redresse-toi, tu es tout ~** sit up, you're getting round-shouldered **2** NM,F hunchback → **rire**

boston [bɔstɔ̃] NM (= danse, jeu) boston

bot, bote [bo, bɔt] ADJ **main ~e** club-hand; **pied ~** club-foot

botanique [bɔtanik] **1** ADJ botanical **2** NF botany

botaniste [bɔtanist] NMF botanist

Botnie [bɔtni] NF **le golfe de ~** the Gulf of Bothnia

botrytis [bɔtʀitis] NM (Agr) botrytis

Botswana [bɔtswana] NM Botswana

botswanais, e [bɔtswanɛ, ɛz] **1** ADJ of ou from Botswana **2 Botswanais(e)** NM,F inhabitant ou native of Botswana

botte¹ [bɔt] NF (high) boot; **~ de caoutchouc** wellington (boot) (Brit), gumboot (Brit), rubber boot (US); **~ de cheval** ou **de cavalier** riding boot; **~ d'égoutier** waders; **les ~s de sept lieues** the seven-league boots; **la ~ (de l'Italie)** the boot (of Italy); **être à la ~ de qn** to be under sb's heel ou thumb, be sb's puppet; **avoir qn à sa ~** to have sb under one's heel ou thumb; **cirer** ou **lécher les ~s de qn*** to lick sb's boots; **être sous la ~ de l'ennemi** to be under the enemy's heel

botte² [bɔt] NF [fleurs, légumes] bunch; [foin] (en gerbe) bundle, sheaf; (au carré) bale

botte³ [bɔt] NF (Escrime) thrust; **porter une ~ à** (lit) to make a thrust at; (fig) to hit out at; (fig) **~ secrète** secret weapon

botter [bɔte] ▶ conjug 1 ◀ **1** VT **a** (= mettre des bottes à) to put boots on; (= vendre des bottes à) to sell boots to; **se ~** to put one's boots on; **botté de cuir** with leather boots on, wearing leather boots **b** **~ les fesses** ou **le derrière de qn*** to kick ou boot* sb in the behind*, give sb a kick up the backside* ou in the pants* **c** (* = plaire) **ça me botte*** I fancy* (Brit) ou like ou dig* that; **ce film m'a botté** I really liked that film **d** (Ftbl) to kick; **~ la balle en touche** to kick the ball into touch **2** VI (Ftbl) to kick the ball; (Ski) to ball up

botteur [bɔtœʀ] NM (Rugby) kicker

bottier [bɔtje] NM [bottes] bootmaker; [chaussures] shoemaker

bottillon [bɔtijɔ̃] NM ankle boot; [bébé] bootee

bottin ® [bɔtɛ̃] NM telephone directory, phonebook; **Bottin mondain** ≈ Who's Who

bottine [bɔtin] NF (ankle) boot; **~ à boutons** button-boot

botulique [bɔtylik] ADJ **bacille ~** botulinus

botulisme [bɔtylism] NM botulism

boubou [bubu] NM boubou, bubu

bouc [buk] NM (Zool) (billy) goat; (= barbe) goatee (beard); **sentir ou puer le ~** to stink*, pong* (Brit); (fig) **~ émissaire** scapegoat, fall guy

boucan* [bukɑ̃] NM din*, racket*; **faire du ~** (= bruit) to kick up* a din* ou a racket*; (= protestation) to kick up* a fuss

boucane* [bukan] NF (Can) smoke

boucaner [bukane] ▶ conjug 1 ◀ VT [+ viande] to smoke, cure; [+ peau] to tan

boucanier [bukanje] NM (= pirate) buccaneer

bouchage [buʃaʒ] NM **a** [bouteille] corking **b** [trou, fente] filling up ou in; [fuite] plugging, stopping **c** [fenêtre, porte] blocking (up) **d** [lavabo] blocking (up), choking up

bouche [buʃ] **1** NF **a** (Anat) mouth; [volcan, fleuve, four] mouth; [canon] muzzle; **embrasser à pleine ~** to kiss full on the lips ou mouth; **parler la ~ pleine** to talk with one's mouth full; **avoir la ~ amère** to have a bitter taste in one's mouth; **j'ai la ~ sèche** my mouth feels ou is dry; **j'ai la ~ pâteuse** my tongue feels thick ou coated; **il a 5 ~s à nourrir** he has 5 mouths to feed; (dans une population) **les ~s inutiles** the non-active ou unproductive population; **provisions de ~** provisions; **dépenses de ~** food bills; **vin court/long en ~** wine with no finish/a long ou lingering finish → **garder**

b (= organe de la communication) mouth; **fermer la ~ à qn** to shut sb up; **garder la ~ close** to keep one's mouth shut; **il n'a pas ouvert la ~ de la soirée** he didn't open his mouth ou he didn't say a word all evening; **dans sa ~, ce mot surprend** when he says ou uses it, that word sounds odd; **il a toujours l'injure à la ~** he's always ready with an insult; **il n'a que ce mot-là à la ~** that's all he ever talks about; **de ~ à oreille** by word of mouth, confidentially; **~ cousue !*** don't breathe a word!, mum's the word!*; **son nom est dans toutes les ~s** his name is a household word ou is on everyone's lips; **aller ou passer de ~ en ~** to be rumoured about; **il en a plein la ~** he can talk of nothing else; **nos sentiments s'expriment par sa ~** our feelings are expressed through his words

c (loc) **s'embrasser à ~ que veux-tu** to kiss eagerly; **faire la fine ou petite ~** to turn one's nose up; **avoir la ~ en cœur** to simper; **et pour la bonne ~, le dernier roman de Legrand** and last but by no means least, Legrand's latest novel; **nous avons gardé ou réservé pour la bonne ~ un enregistrement inédit de Bechet** we have saved the best till last ou and last but not least — a previously unreleased Bechet recording → **bée**

2 COMP ▶ **bouche d'aération** air vent ou inlet ▶ **bouche de chaleur** hot-air vent ou inlet ▶ **bouche d'égout** manhole ▶ **bouche à feu** (Hist) piece (of ordnance), gun ▶ **bouche d'incendie** fire hydrant ▶ **bouche de métro** metro entrance

bouché, e¹ [buʃe] (ptp de **boucher¹**) ADJ **a** [temps, ciel] cloudy, overcast **b** (= obstrué) [passage] blocked; **j'ai les oreilles ~es** my ears are blocked (up); **j'ai le nez ~** my nose is blocked (up) ou stuffed up **c** (* = stupide) [personne] stupid, thick*; **~ à l'émeri** dead from the neck up*, as thick as a brick* (Brit) **d** (= sans avenir) **le secteur de la publicité est ~** there are absolutely no openings in the advertising industry; **il n'a devant lui qu'un horizon ~** his prospects don't look very bright

bouche-à-bouche [buʃabuʃ] NM INV kiss of life (Brit), mouth-to-mouth resuscitation (Brit) ou respiration (US); **faire du ~ à qn** to give sb the kiss of life, give sb mouth-to-mouth resuscitation (Brit) ou respiration (US)

bouchée² [buʃe] NF **a** (= quantité) mouthful; **pour une ~ de pain** for a song, for next to nothing; **mettre les ~s doubles** to put on a spurt, work twice as hard; **ne faire qu'une ~ d'un plat** to gobble up ou polish off a dish in next to no time; **ne faire qu'une ~ d'un adversaire** to make short work of an opponent **b** (Culin) **~ (au chocolat)** chocolate; **~ à la reine** vol-au-vent filled with chopped sweetbreads in a rich sauce

boucher¹ [buʃe] ▶ conjug 1 ◀ **1** VT **a** (= fermer) [+ bouteille] to cork, put the ou a cork in **b** (= *colmater*) [+ *trou, fente*] to fill up *ou* in; [+ *fuite*] to plug, stop; **ça** (*ou* **elle** *etc*) **lui en a bouché un coin** he was staggered* *ou* flabbergasted* *ou* gobsmacked* (*Brit*) **c** (= *condamner*) [+ *fenêtre, porte*] to block (up) **d** (= *engorger*) [+ *lavabo*] to block (up), choke (up); **sécrétions qui bouchent les pores** secretions which block up *ou* clog up the pores; **j'ai les oreilles bouchées** my ears are blocked (up); **j'ai le nez bouché** my nose is blocked (up) *ou* stuffed up *ou* bunged up*; **~ le passage** to be *ou* stand in the way; **~ le passage à qn** to be *ou* stand in sb's way, block sb's way; **~ la vue** to block the view; **on l'a employé pour ~ les trous** we used him as a stopgap **2 se boucher** VPR [*évier*] to get blocked *ou* choked *ou* clogged up; [*temps*] to get cloudy, become overcast; **se ~ le nez** to hold one's nose; **se ~ les oreilles** to put one's fingers in one's ears *ou* one's hands over one's ears; (= *refuser d'entendre*) to turn a deaf ear; **se ~ les yeux** to put one's hands over one's eyes, hide one's eyes; (= *refuser de voir*) to turn a blind eye

boucher² [buʃe] NM (*lit, fig*) butcher

bouchère [buʃɛʀ] NF (woman) butcher; (= *épouse*) butcher's wife

boucherie [buʃʀi] NF (= *magasin*) butcher's (shop); (= *métier*) butchery (trade); (*fig*) slaughter; **animaux de ~** animals for slaughter; **~ chevaline** *ou* **hippophagique** horse(meat) butcher's; **~ charcuterie** butcher's (shop) with delicatessen

bouche-trou (*pl* **bouche-trous**) [buʃtʀu] NM (= *personne*) fill-in, stopgap, stand-in; (= *chose*) stopgap, pinch-hitter* (*NonC*)

bouchon [buʃɔ̃] NM **a** (*en liège*) cork; (*en verre*) stopper; (*en plastique*) stopper, top; (*en chiffon, papier*) plug, bung (*Brit*); [*bidon, réservoir*] cap; [*tube*] top; [*évier*] plug; (*Photo*) **~ d'objectif** lens cap; **~ antivol** locking petrol (*Brit*) *ou* gas (*US*) cap; **~ de vidange** drain plug; **vin qui sent le ~** corked *ou* corky wine; **~ de cérumen** earwax *ou* cerumen plug → **pousser** **b** (*Pêche*) float **c** (*pour un cheval*) wisp; **~ de paille** wisp [*Aut* = *embouteillage*] holdup, traffic jam; **un ~ de 12 km** a 12-km tailback

bouchonnage [buʃɔnaʒ] NM [*cheval*] rubbing-down, wisping-down (*Brit*)

bouchonné, e [buʃɔne] ADJ [*vin*] corked, corky

bouchonner [buʃɔne] ▸ conjug 1 ◂ **1** VT [+ *cheval*] to rub down, wisp down (*Brit*) **2** VI (*Aut*) **ça bouchonne en ville** there's heavy congestion in town

bouchot [buʃo] NM mussel bed

bouclage [bukla ʒ] NM (* = *mise sous clés*) locking up *ou* away, imprisonment; [*encerclement*] surrounding, sealing off; (*Presse*) [*journal*] closing, putting to bed

boucle [bukl] NF [*ceinture, soulier*] buckle; [*cheveux*] curl, lock; [*ruban, voie ferrée, rivière*] loop; (*Sport*) lap; (*Aviat*) loop; (*Ordin*) loop; **fais une ~ à ton j** put a loop on your j; **fais une ~ à ton lacet** tie your shoelace in a bow; **Boucles d'or** Goldilocks; **~ d'oreille** earring; **~ d'oreille à vis** (*ou* **à crochets**) pierced earring, earring for pierced ear; **~ d'oreille à clip** *ou* **à pince** clip-on (earring)

bouclé, e [bukle] (*ptp de* **boucler**) ADJ [*cheveux, fourrure*] curly; [*personne*] curly-haired; **il avait la tête ~e** his hair was curly *ou* all curls

boucler [bukle] ▸ conjug 1 ◂ **1** VT **a** (= *fermer*) [+ *ceinture*] to buckle, fasten (up); * [+ *porte*] to lock; **~ sa valise** (*lit*) to fasten one's suitcase; (*fig*) to pack one's bags; **tu vas la ~ !** will you shut your trap!*, will you belt up!* (*Brit*) **b** (= *terminer*) [+ *affaire*] to finish off, settle; [+ *circuit*] to complete, go round; [+ *budget*] to balance; [+ *article*] to finish; **il faut ~** (*Presse*)

we've got to put the paper to bed; (*Jur*) **le dossier est bouclé** all the background work on the case has been completed; **arriver à ~ ses fins de mois** to manage to stay in the black *ou* to make ends meet at the end of the month; **~ la boucle** (*Aviat*) to loop the loop; **on est revenu par l'Espagne pour ~ la boucle** we came back through Spain to make (it) a round trip; **la boucle est bouclée** we've (*ou* they've) come full circle; **dans le cycle de production la boucle est bouclée** the cycle of production is now completed **c** (* = *enfermer*) to lock up, put under lock and key; **ils ont bouclé le coupable** they've locked up the criminal *ou* put the criminal under lock and key; **être bouclé chez soi** to be cooped up *ou* stuck* at home **d** (*Mil, Police* = *encercler*) to seal off, cordon off **2** VI **a** [*cheveux*] to curl, be curly; **elle commence à ~** her hair is getting curly **b** (*Ordin*) to get stuck in a loop

bouclette [buklɛt] NF small curl

bouclier [buklije] NM (*Mil, fig*) shield; (*Police*) riot shield; **faire un ~ de son corps à qn** to shield sb with one's body; (*Espace*) **~ thermique** heat shield; **~ atomique** *ou* **nucléaire** nuclear defences; **~ humain** human shield

Bouddha [buda] NM Buddha; (= *statuette*) **bouddha** Buddha

bouddhique [budik] ADJ Buddhist

bouddhisme [budism] NM Buddhism; **~ zen** zen Buddhism

bouddhiste [budist] ADJ, NMF Buddhist; **~ zen** zen Buddhist

bouder [bude] ▸ conjug 1 ◂ **1** VI to sulk **2** VT [+ *personne*] to refuse to talk to *ou* have anything to do with; [+ *produit*] to be reluctant to buy; [+ *conférence, exposition*] to stay away from; **~ la nourriture** to have no appetite; **~ son plaisir** to deny o.s. a good thing; **ils ont boudé mon gâteau** they hardly touched my cake; **le public a boudé sa pièce** hardly anybody went to see his play; **les électeurs ont boudé ce scrutin** many voters stayed away from the polls; **cet événement a été boudé par les médias** the event received hardly any media coverage; **le soleil va ~ le nord du pays** the north of the country won't see much of the sun; **ils se boudent** they're not on speaking terms, they're not speaking

bouderie [budʀi] NF (= *état*) sulkiness (*NonC*); (= *action*) sulk

boudeur, -euse [budœʀ, øz] **1** ADJ sulky, sullen **2 boudeuse** NF (= *siège*) dos-à-dos

boudin [budɛ̃] NM **a** (*Culin*) **~ (noir)** ≈ black pudding (*Brit*), ≈ blood sausage (*US*); **~ blanc** ≈ white pudding (*Brit*) *ou* sausage (*US*); **~ antillais** small, spicy black pudding; **faire du ~*** (= *bouder*) to sulk → **eau** **b** (*gonflable*) ring, tube **c** (* = *doigt*) podgy *ou* fat finger **d** (* = *fille*) fat lump (of a girl) (*péj*), fatty* (*péj*)

boudiné, e [budine] (*ptp de* **boudiner**) ADJ **a** [*doigt*] podgy **b** (= *serré*) **dans** squeezed into, bursting out of; **~ dans un corset** strapped into *ou* bulging out of a tight-fitting corset; **je me sens ~e dans cette robe** I feel like I can't breathe in this dress

boudiner [budine] ▸ conjug 1 ◂ VT **a** (*Tex*) to rove; [+ *fil métallique*] to coil **b** (* = *serrer*) **sa robe la boudine** her dress is much too tight for her

boudoir [budwaʀ] NM (= *salon*) boudoir; (= *biscuit*) sponge (*Brit*) *ou* lady (*US*) finger

boue [bu] NF (*gén*) mud; [*mer, canal*] sludge; (= *dépôt*) sediment; **~s thermales** heated mud; **~s d'épuration** sewage sludge (*NonC*), silt; (*Méd*) **~s activées** activated sludge (*NonC*); (*fig*) **traîner qn dans la ~** to drag sb's name through the mud; (*fig*) **couvrir qn de ~** to throw *ou* sling mud at sb

bouée [bwe] NF (*de signalisation*) buoy; (*d'enfant*) rubber ring; **~ de corps-mort** mooring buoy; **~ de sauvetage** (*lit*) lifebelt; (*fig*) lifeline; **~ sonore** radio buoy

boueux, -euse [bwø, øz] **1** ADJ muddy; (*Typo*) blurred, smudged **2** NM (* = *éboueur*) dustman (*Brit*), bin man* (*Brit*), garbage man (*US*)

bouffant, e [bufɑ̃, ɑ̃t] **1** ADJ [*manche*] puff(ed) (*épith*), full; [*cheveux*] bouffant; [*pantalon*] baggy **2** NM [*jupe, manche*] fullness; [*cheveux*] fullness, volume; [*pantalon*] bagginess

bouffarde* [bufaʀd] NF pipe

bouffe¹ [buf] ADJ → **opéra**

bouffe²* [buf] NF food, grub*, nosh* (*Brit*); **il ne pense qu'à la ~** he only ever thinks of his stomach, all he ever thinks about is food; **faire la ~** to do the cooking, get the grub ready*; **ils font de la bonne ~ dans ce resto** they do good food in that restaurant; **on se téléphone et on se fait une ~** I'll give you a ring and we'll meet up for a bite* (to eat)

bouffée [bufe] NF [*parfum*] whiff; [*pipe, cigarette*] puff, draw, drag*; [*colère*] outburst; [*orgueil*] fit; **~ d'air** *ou* **de vent** puff *ou* breath *ou* gust of wind; (*lit, fig*) **une ~ d'air pur** a breath of fresh air; **~ de chaleur** (*Méd*) hot flush (*Brit*) *ou* flash (*US*); (*gén*) gust *ou* blast of hot air; **~ délirante** (*Psych*) delirious episode; **par ~s** in gusts → **oxygène**

bouffer¹ [bufe] ▸ conjug 1 ◂ VI [*cheveux*] to be full, have volume; **faire ~ une jupe/une manche** to make a skirt fuller/a sleeve puff out; **faire ~ ses cheveux** to add volume *ou* fullness to one's hair

bouffer²* [bufe] ▸ conjug 1 ◂ VT **a** (*gén*) to eat; (= *engloutir*) to gobble up*, wolf down; **cette voiture bouffe de l'essence** this car really drinks petrol (*Brit*) *ou* guzzles gas (*US*); **se ~ le nez** (*constamment*) to be always at each other's throat(s); (*ponctuellement*) to have a go at one another*, scratch each other's eyes out*; **~ du curé** to be violently anticlerical; **je l'aurais bouffé !** I could have murdered him!; **j'ai cru qu'elle allait le ~** I thought she was going to eat him alive **b** (*emploi absolu*) to eat; **on bouffe mal ici** the food *ou* grub* (*Brit*) here isn't up to much; **on a bien bouffé ici** the food was great* here **c** (* = *accaparer*) **il ne faut pas se laisser ~ par ses enfants/son travail** you shouldn't let your children/work eat up *ou* take up all your time (and energy); **ça me bouffe tout mon temps** it eats up *ou* takes up all my time

bouffetance* [buftɑ̃s] NF = **bouffe***

bouffeur, -euse* [bufœʀ, øz] NM,F (greedy) pig*, greedy guts* (*Brit*)

bouffi, e [bufi] (*ptp de* **bouffir**) ADJ [*visage*] puffed up, bloated; [*yeux*] swollen, puffy; (*fig*) swollen, puffed up (**de** with); (*hareng*) **~** bloater; (*hum*) **tu l'as dit ~ !** you said it!

bouffir [bufiʀ] ▸ conjug 2 ◂ **1** VT to puff up **2** VI to become bloated, puff up

bouffissure [bufisyʀ] NF puffiness (*NonC*), bloatedness (*NonC*), puffy swelling

bouffon, -onne [bufɔ̃, ɔn] **1** ADJ farcical, comical **2** NM (= *pitre*) buffoon, clown; (*Hist*) jester; **le ~ du roi** the court jester

bouffonnerie [bufɔnʀi] NF **a** [*personne*] clownishness; [*situation*] drollery **b** **~s** (= *comportement*) antics, buffoonery; (= *paroles*) jesting; **faire des ~s** to clown around, play the fool

bougainvillée [bugɛ̃vile] NF, **bougainvillier** [bugɛ̃vilje] NM bougainvillea

bouge [buʒ] NM (= *taudis*) hovel, dump*; (= *bar louche*) low dive*

bougé [buʒe] NM (*Photo*) (*dû au photographe*) camera shake; (*dû au sujet*) blur

bougeoir [buʒwaʀ] NM (bas) candle-holder; (haut) candlestick

bougeotte* [buʒɔt] NF **avoir la ~** (= voyager) to be always on the move; (= remuer) to fidget, have the fidgets*, have ants in one's pants*

bouger [buʒe] ▶ conjug 3 ◀ 1 VI a (= remuer) to move; (= se révolter) to be restless; **ne bouge pas** keep still, don't move ou budge; **il n'a pas bougé (de chez lui)** he stayed in ou at home; **la terre a bougé** (tremblement de terre) the ground shook; **un métier où l'on bouge** an active job, a job where you are always on the move; (fig) **quand la police l'a arrêté, personne n'a bougé** when the police arrested him no-one lifted a finger (to help)

b (= changer) to change; **les prix n'ont pas bougé** prices have stayed put* ou the same; **ça ne bouge pas beaucoup dans ce service** nothing much ever changes in this department; **ce tissu ne bouge pas** (gén) this material wears ou will wear well; (en dimensions) this material neither shrinks nor goes out of shape; **les couleurs ne bougeront pas** the colours won't fade; **ses idées n'ont pas bougé** his ideas haven't altered, he hasn't changed his ideas

c (* = être actif) [personne] to get out and about; **secteur qui bouge** fast-moving sector; **c'est une ville qui bouge** it's a very lively town, there's a lot happening in this town

2 VT* [+ objet] to move, shift*; **il n'a pas bougé le petit doigt** he didn't lift a finger (to help)

3 se bouger* VPR to move; **bouge-toi de là !** shift over!*, shift out of the way!*, scoot over!* (US); **je m'ennuie — alors bouge-toi un peu !** I'm bored — then get up off your backside*! (Brit) ou butt*! (US); **si tu veux le contrat, il faut que tu te bouges** if you want the contract, you'd better get moving or get a move on*; **elle ne s'est pas beaucoup bougée pour m'aider** she didn't go out of her way to help me

bougie [buʒi] NF a (= chandelle) candle; (Aut) spark(ing) plug, plug; **ampoule de 40 ~s†** 40 candle-power bulb b (†* = visage) face, dial*; **faire une drôle de ~** to make ou pull (Brit) a face

bougna(t)†* [buɲa] NM (= charbonnier) coalman; (= marchand de charbon) coal merchant (who also runs a small café)

bougnoul(e)*‡ [buɲul] NMF (injurieux) (= Noir) nigger*‡ (injurieux); (= Arabe) Arab

bougon, -onne [bugɔ̃, ɔn] 1 ADJ grumpy, grouchy 2 NM,F grumbler, grouch*

bougonnement [bugɔnmɑ̃] NM grumbling, grouching*

bougonner [bugɔne] ▶ conjug 1 ◀ VI to grouch* (à o.s.), grumble

bougre* [bugʀ] 1 NM (= type) guy*, fellow*, chap* (Brit); (= enfant) (little) rascal; **bon ~** good sort* ou chap*; **pauvre ~** poor devil* ou blighter*; **ce ~ d'homme** that confounded man; **~ d'idiot !** ou **d'animal !** stupid ou confounded idiot!*, silly blighter!* (Brit); **ce n'est pas un mauvais ~** he's not a bad guy*; **il le savait, le ~ !** the so-and-so knew it! 2 EXCL good Lord!*, strewth!* (Brit), I'll be darned!* (US)

bougrement* [bugʀəmɑ̃] ADV (hum) damn*, damned‡

bougresse‡ [bugʀɛs] NF woman; (péj) hussy, bitch*‡

bouiboui*, boui-boui (pl **bouis-bouis**) [bwibwi] NM (gén) unpretentious (little) restaurant; (péj) greasy spoon*

bouif†* [bwif] NM cobbler

bouillabaisse [bujabɛs] NF bouillabaisse, fish soup

bouillant, e [bujɑ̃, ɑ̃t] ADJ (= brûlant) [boisson] boiling (hot), scalding; (qui bout) [eau, huile] boiling; [tempérament] fiery; [personne] (= emporté) fiery-natured, hotheaded; (= fiévreux) boiling (hot)*; **~ de colère** seething ou boiling with anger

bouillasse* [bujas] NF (= gadoue) muck

bouille* [buj] NF (= visage) face, mug* (péj); **avoir une bonne ~** to have a cheerful friendly face

bouilleur [bujœʀ] NM (= distillateur) distiller; **~ de cru** home distiller; **~ de cru clandestin** moonshiner

bouilli, e¹ [buji] (ptp de **bouillir**) 1 ADJ boiled 2 NM boiled meat; **~ de bœuf** beef stew

bouillie² [buji] NF [bébé] baby's cereal; [vieillard] gruel, porridge; **réduire en ~** [légumes, fruits] to reduce to a pulp; [+ adversaire] to beat to a pulp; **~ bordelaise** Bordeaux mixture; (fig) **c'est de la ~ pour les chats** it's gibberish*; **il a été réduit en ~** [adversaire] he was beaten to a pulp; **sa voiture a été réduite en ~** his car was smashed to pieces

bouillir [bujiʀ] ▶ conjug 15 ◀ 1 VI a (lit) to boil, be boiling; **commencer à ~** to reach boiling point, be nearly boiling; **l'eau bout** the water is boiling; **l'eau ne bout plus** the water has stopped boiling, the water has gone ou is off the boil (Brit); **faire ~ de l'eau** to boil water, bring water to the boil; **faire ~ du linge/des poireaux** to boil clothes/leeks; **faire ~ un biberon** to sterilize a (baby's) bottle by boiling; **~ à gros bouillons** to boil fast; (fig) **avoir de quoi faire ~ la marmite** to have enough to keep the pot boiling; **c'est elle qui fait ~ la marmite** she's the breadwinner, she's the one who brings home the bacon

b (fig) to boil; **à voir ça, je bous !** seeing that makes my blood boil!; **faire ~ qn** to make sb's blood boil; **~ d'impatience** to seethe with impatience; **~ de rage/de haine** to seethe ou boil with anger/hatred

2 VT [+ eau, linge] to boil

bouilloire [bujwaʀ] NF kettle; **~ électrique** (gén) electric kettle; (haute) jug kettle

bouillon [bujɔ̃] 1 NM a (= soupe) stock, bouillon; **~ de légumes/poulet** vegetable/chicken stock; **prendre** ou **boire un ~*** (en nageant) to swallow ou get a mouthful; (Fin) to take a tumble*, come a cropper* (Brit) b (= bouillonnement) bubble (in boiling liquid); **au premier ~** as soon as it starts to boil; **couler à gros ~s** to gush out, come gushing out c (arg Presse) **~s** unsold copies d (Couture) puff; **rideau à ~s** Austrian blind 2 COMP ▶ **bouillon cube** stock ou bouillon cube ▶ **bouillon de culture** culture fluid ▶ **bouillon gras** meat stock ▶ **bouillon maigre** clear stock ▶ **bouillon d'onze heures*** poisoned drink, lethal potion

bouillonnant, e [bujɔnɑ̃, ɑ̃t] ADJ [liquide chaud] bubbling; [torrent] foaming, frothing; **bain ~** whirlpool bath

bouillonné [bujɔne] NM (Couture) ruffle

bouillonnement [bujɔnmɑ̃] NM [liquide chaud] bubbling; [torrent] foaming, frothing; **~ d'idées** ferment of ideas

bouillonner [bujɔne] ▶ conjug 1 ◀ VI [liquide chaud] to bubble; [torrent] to foam, froth; [idées] to bubble up; **~ de colère** to seethe ou boil with anger; **il bouillonne d'idées** his mind is teeming with ideas, he's bubbling with ideas

bouillotte [bujɔt] NF hot-water bottle

boulange* [bulɑ̃ʒ] NF bakery trade; **être dans la ~** to be a baker (by trade)

boulanger [bulɑ̃ʒe] NM baker

boulangère [bulɑ̃ʒɛʀ] NF (woman) baker; (= épouse) baker's wife → **pomme**

boulangerie [bulɑ̃ʒʀi] NF (= magasin) baker's (shop), bakery; (= commerce) bakery trade; **~-pâtisserie** bread and pastry shop

boulangisme [bulɑ̃ʒism] NM right-wing movement led by General Boulanger, who staged an abortive coup d'État in 1889

boulangiste [bulɑ̃ʒist] ADJ, NMF Boulangist → **boulangisme**

boule [bul] 1 NF a (Billard, Croquet) ball; (Boules) bowl; (Géol) tor; **jouer aux ~s** to play bowls; (Casino) **jouer à la ~** to play (at) boule; **roulé en ~** [animal] curled up in a ball; [paquet] rolled up in a ball; **petite ~ de poil** (= animal) little ball of fluff; (fig) **être en ~*** to be in a temper, be hopping mad* (Brit); **se mettre en ~** [hérisson] to roll up into a ball; * [personne] to fly off the handle*; **ça me met en ~*** it drives me mad ou really gets my goat*

b (* = grosseur) lump; (fig) **avoir une ~ dans la gorge** to have a lump in one's throat; **j'ai les ~s*** (= anxieux) I've got butterflies* (in my stomach); (= furieux) I'm really ou hopping mad* (Brit); **ça fout les ~s‡** (= ça angoisse) it's really scary*, it gives you the creeps*; (= ça énerve) it's damn annoying*

c (* = tête) head, nut*; **perdre la ~** to go bonkers* ou nuts*, go off one's rocker*; **coup de ~‡** headbutt; **avoir la ~ à zéro** to have a shaven head

2 COMP ▶ **boule de billard** billiard ball; (fig) **avoir une ~ de billard** to be as bald as a coot* ou an egg* ▶ **boule de cristal** crystal ball; (fig) **je ne lis pas dans les ~s de cristal !** I haven't got a crystal ball!, I'm not a clairvoyant! ▶ **boule de feu** fireball ▶ **boule de gomme** (Pharm) throat pastille; (= bonbon) fruit pastille ou gum, gumdrop ▶ **boules de gui** mistletoe berries ▶ **boule de loto** lotto ou lottery ball; **yeux en ~s de loto** big round eyes ▶ **boule de neige** snowball; (fig) **faire ~ de neige** to snowball ▶ **boule puante** stink bomb ▶ **boule de pain** round loaf ▶ **boule Quiès®** (wax) earplug, (wax) ear stopper

---

| BOULES |

This popular French game takes several forms, including "pétanque", which originated in the South of France, and "boule lyonnaise" from Lyons. The idea of the game is to throw steel balls towards a small wooden ball called the "cochonnet", if necessary knocking one's opponent's **boules** out of the way in the process. The winner is the player who finishes closest to the "cochonnet".

---

bouleau (pl **bouleaux**) [bulo] NM (silver) birch

boule-de-neige (pl **boules-de-neige**) [buldəneʒ] NF (= fleur) guelder-rose; (= arbre) snowball tree

bouledogue [buldɔg] NM bulldog

bouler [bule] ▶ conjug 1 ◀ VI to roll along; **elle a boulé dans l'escalier** she fell head over heels down the stairs; **envoyer ~ qn*** to send sb packing*, send sb away with a flea in their ear*

boulet [bulɛ] NM a [forçat] ball and chain; (de canon) cannonball; (fig) **traîner un ~** to have a millstone around ou round (Brit) one's neck; **c'est un (véritable) ~ pour ses parents** he's a millstone around ou round (Brit) his parents' neck; **arriver comme un ~ de canon** to come bursting in ou crashing in; **tirer à ~s rouges sur qn** to lay into sb tooth and nail b [charbon] (coal) nut c (Vét) fetlock

boulette [bulɛt] NF a [papier] pellet; (Culin) meat croquette, meatball; **~ empoisonnée** lump of poisoned meat b (* = bévue) blunder, bloomer*; **faire une ~** to make a blunder ou bloomer*, drop a brick* ou clanger* (Brit)

boulevard [bulvaʀ] NM boulevard; **les ~s extérieurs** the outer boulevards of Paris; **les grands ~s** the grand boulevards; **pièce** ou **comédie de ~** light comedy → **périphérique, théâtre**

boulevardier, -ière [bulvaʀdje, jɛʀ] **1** ADJ **le comique ~** light comedy (*typical of the théâtre de Boulevard*) **2** NM,F *writer of light comedy for the theatre*

bouleversement [bulvɛʀsəmɑ̃] NM [*habitudes, vie politique*] disruption; **le ~ de son visage** the utter distress on his face, his distraught face; **ce fut un vrai ~** it was a real upheaval

bouleverser [bulvɛʀse] ▸ conjug 1 ◂ VT **a** (= *émouvoir*) to move deeply; (= *causer un choc à*) to shatter; **bouleversé par l'angoisse/la peur** distraught with anxiety/fear; **la nouvelle les a bouleversés** they were deeply distressed *ou* upset by the news, they were shattered by the news **b** (= *modifier*) [+ *plan, habitude*] to disrupt, change completely *ou* drastically **c** (= *déranger*) to turn upside down

boulgour [bulguʀ] NM (*Culin*) bulg(h)ur (*wheat*)

boulier [bulje] NM (= *abaque*) abacus; (*Billard*) scoring board

boulimie [bulimi] NF bulimia, binge-eating syndrome (*US*); **il fait de la ~** he's a compulsive eater; **être saisi d'une ~ de lecture/de cinéma** to be seized by a compulsive desire to read/to go the cinema

boulimique [bulimik] **1** ADJ bulimic **2** NMF bulimiac, compulsive eater

boulingrin [bulɛ̃gʀɛ̃] NM lawn

bouliste [bulist] NMF bowls player

Boulle [bul] NM INV **style/commode ~** boul(l)e *ou* buhl style/chest of drawers

boulocher [bulɔʃe] ▸ conjug 1 ◂ VI [*pull, tissu*] to pill

boulodrome [bulɔdʀom] NM bowling pitch

boulon [bulɔ̃] NM bolt; (*avec son écrou*) nut and bolt; (*fig*) **(res)serrer les ~s** to tighten a few screws

boulonnage [bulɔnaʒ] NM (= *assemblage*) bolting (on); (= *serrage*) bolting (down)

boulonnais, e [bulɔnɛ, ɛz] **1** ADJ of *ou* from Boulogne **2 Boulonnais(e)** NM,F inhabitant *ou* native of Boulogne **3** NM (= *cheval*) type of draught horse bred in the Boulogne region

boulonner [bulɔne] ▸ conjug 1 ◂ **1** VT (= *serrer*) to bolt (down); (= *assembler*) to bolt (on) **2** VI* to work; **~ (dur)** to slog* *ou* slave* away

boulot¹, -otte [bulo, ɔt] ADJ (= *trapu*) plump, tubby*

boulot² [bulo] NM **a** (= *travail*) work (*NonC*); **on a du ~** (*gén*) we've got work to do; (= *tâche difficile*) we've got our work cut out for us; **j'ai un ~ fou en ce moment** I'm up to my eyes in work *ou* I'm snowed under with work at the moment*; **ce n'est pas du ~!** that's not work!, (do you) call that work!; **elle a 4 enfants à élever, quel ~!** she has 4 children to bring up, that's quite a job! *ou* that's a lot of work!; **il est ~ ~** with him it's just work, work, work*; **faire le ~** to do the work; **ça/elle a fait du bon ~** it's/she's done a good job; **se mettre au ~** to get down *ou* knuckle* down to work; **allez, au ~!** let's get cracking!*, let's get this show on the road!; **allez, faut retourner au ~!** come on, back to the grind!*; **je suis au ~ depuis 7 h du matin** I've been at work since 7 o'clock this morning; **il a repeint la cuisine, t'aurais vu le ~!** he repainted the kitchen and it was an absolute disaster! → **métro, sale b** (= *emploi*) job, work (*NonC*); **il a trouvé du ~ ou un ~** he's found work *ou* a job; **petit ~** casual job; **j'ai fait des petits ~s** I did odd jobs *ou* casual work; **être sans ~** to be out of work *ou* unemployed; **gardien de musée, c'est le bon ~** a job as a museum attendant is a cushy number* **c** (= *lieu de travail*) work (*NonC*), place of work; **aller au ~** to go to work; **je sors du ~ à**

18 h I finish work *ou* I knock off* (*work*) at 6 o'clock

boulotter [bulɔte] ▸ conjug 1 ◂ **1** VI to eat; **on a bien boulotté** we had a good meal; **qu'est-ce qu'elle boulotte !** you should see what she can put away! **2** VT to eat, gobble up

boum [bum] **1** EXCL (*chute*) bang!, wallop!; (*explosion*) boom!, bang!; (*langage enfantin*) **faire ~** to go bang*; **~ par terre !** whoops a daisy! **2** NM (= *explosion*) bang; **on entendit un grand ~** there was an enormous bang; (*loc*) **être en plein ~** to be in full swing, be going full blast* **3** NF (* = *fête*) party

boumer⁎ [bume] ▸ conjug 1 ◂ VI **ça boume** everything's going fine *ou* dandy* (*US*); **ça boume ?** how's things?* *ou* tricks?*

boumerang [bumʀɑ̃g] NM = **boomerang**

bounioul⁎ [bunjul] NM = **bougnoul(e)**

bouquet¹ [bukɛ] NM **a** [*fleurs*] bunch (of flowers); (*soigneusement composé, grand*) bouquet; (*petit*) posy; (* : *Can* = *plante d'ornement*) (house) plant; **~ d'arbres** clump of trees; **faire un ~** to make up a bouquet; **le ~ de la mariée** the bride's bouquet; **~ de persil/thym** bunch of parsley/thyme; (*Culin*) **~ garni** bouquet garni (*bunch of mixed herbs*) **b** [*feu d'artifice*] finishing *ou* crowning piece (*in a firework display*); (*fig*) **c'est le ~!** that takes the cake!* *ou* the biscuit!* (*Brit*) **c** [*vin*] bouquet, nose; **vin qui a du ~** wine which has a good bouquet *ou* nose **d** (*Jur*) [*viager*] initial payment **e** (*TV*) multi-channel package

bouquet² [bukɛ] NM (= *crevette*) prawn

bouquetière [buk(ə)tjɛʀ] NF flower seller, flower girl

bouquetin [buk(ə)tɛ̃] NM ibex

bouquin⁎ [bukɛ̃] NM book

bouquiner⁎ [bukine] ▸ conjug 1 ◂ VTI to read; **il passe son temps à ~** he always has his nose in a book

bouquiniste [bukinist] NMF secondhand bookseller (*esp along the Seine in Paris*)

bourbe [buʀb] NF mire, mud

bourbeux, -euse [buʀbø, øz] ADJ miry, muddy

bourbier [buʀbje] NM (*quag*)mire; (*fig*) (= *situation*) mess; (= *entreprise*) unsavoury *ou* nasty business, quagmire

bourbon [buʀbɔ̃] NM (= *whisky*) bourbon

bourbonien, -ienne [buʀbɔnjɛ̃, jɛn] ADJ Bourbon (*épith*); **nez ~** long aquiline nose

bourdaine [buʀdɛn] NF alder buckthorn

bourde⁎ [buʀd] NF (= *gaffe*) blunder, boob*; (= *faute*) slip, mistake; **faire une ~** (= *gaffe*) to boob* (*Brit*), blunder, drop a clanger* (*Brit*); (= *faute*) to make a (silly) mistake, goof up* (*US*)

bourdon¹ [buʀdɔ̃] NM **a** (*Zool*) bumblebee; **avoir le ~⁎** to have the blues* **b** (*Mus* = *cloche*) great bell; [*cornemuse*] bourdon, drone; [*orgue*] bourdon → **faux²**

bourdon² [buʀdɔ̃] NM (*Typo*) omission, out

bourdon³ [buʀdɔ̃] NM (= *bâton*) pilgrim's staff

bourdonnant, e [buʀdɔnɑ̃, ɑ̃t] ADJ [*insecte*] buzzing, humming, droning; [*ville*] buzzing with activity; **il avait la tête ~e ou les oreilles ~es** his ears were buzzing *ou* ringing

bourdonnement [buʀdɔnmɑ̃] NM [*insecte*] buzz(ing) (*NonC*); [*abeille*] buzz(ing) (*NonC*), drone (*NonC*); [*voix*] buzz (*NonC*), hum (*NonC*); [*moteur*] hum(ming) (*NonC*), drone (*NonC*); [*avion*] drone (*NonC*); **j'ai un ~ dans les oreilles ou des ~s d'oreilles** my ears are buzzing *ou* ringing

bourdonner [buʀdɔne] ▸ conjug 1 ◂ VI [*insecte*] to buzz; [*abeille*] to buzz, drone; [*moteur*] to hum, drone; **ça bourdonne dans mes oreilles** my ears are buzzing *ou* ringing

bourg [buʀ] NM (*gén*) market town; (*petit*) village; **au ~ ◊ dans le ~** in town, in the village

bourgade [buʀgad] NF village, (small) town

bourge⁎ [buʀʒ] ADJ, NMF (ABRÉV = **bourgeois**) (*péj*) bourgeois (*péj*)

bourgeois, e [buʀʒwa, waz] **1** ADJ **a** (*Sociol*) middle-class **b** (*gén péj* = *conventionnel*) [*culture, préjugé, goûts*] bourgeois, middle-class; **avoir l'esprit ~** to have a conventional outlook; **mener une petite vie ~e** to lead a comfortable middle-class existence **c** (= *cossu*) [*quartier*] middle-class; [*appartement*] plush **2** NM,F **a** (*Sociol*) middle-class person; **grand ~** upper middle-class person; (*péj*) **les ~** the wealthy (classes) → **épater b** (*Hist*) (= *citoyen*) burgher; (= *riche roturier*) bourgeois **3** NM (*Can*) head of household, master **4** **bourgeoise⁎** NF (*hum* = *épouse*) **la ou ma ~e** the wife*, the missus*

bourgeoisement [buʀʒwazmɑ̃] ADV [*penser, réagir*] conventionally; [*vivre*] comfortably

bourgeoisie [buʀʒwazi] NF **a** (*Sociol*) middle class(es), bourgeoisie; **petite/moyenne ~** lower middle/middle class; **grande ~** upper middle class **b** (*Hist* = *citoyenneté*) bourgeoisie, burgesses

bourgeon [buʀʒɔ̃] NM (*Bot*) bud; († = *bouton*) pimple, spot (*Brit*); **~ gustatif** (*Anat*) taste bud

bourgeonnement [buʀʒɔnmɑ̃] NM (*Bot*) budding; (*Méd*) granulation (*SPÉC*)

bourgeonner [buʀʒɔne] ▸ conjug 1 ◂ VI (*Bot*) to (come into) bud; (*Méd*) [*plaie*] to granulate (*SPÉC*); (*fig*) **son visage bourgeonne** he's getting pimples *ou* spots (*Brit*)

bourgmestre [buʀgmɛstʀ] NM burgomaster

bourgogne [buʀgɔɲ] **1** NM (= *vin*) burgundy **2** **Bourgogne** NF (= *région*) **la Bourgogne** Burgundy

bourguignon, -onne [buʀgiɲɔ̃, ɔn] **1** ADJ Burgundian; (*Culin*) **un (bœuf) ~** bœuf bourguignon, beef stewed in red wine **2** **Bourguignon(ne)** NM,F Burgundian

bourlinguer [buʀlɛ̃ge] ▸ conjug 1 ◂ VI **a** (= *naviguer*) to sail; (* = *voyager*) to travel around a lot*, knock about a lot*; **il a bourlingué dans tout l'hémisphère sud** he has travelled all over the southern hemisphere **b** (*Naut* = *avancer péniblement*) to labour

bourlingueur, -euse⁎ [buʀlɛ̃gœʀ, øz] NM,F **c'est un ~** he knocks about a lot*, he travels around a lot*

bourrache [buʀaʃ] NF borage

bourrade [buʀad] NF (*du poing*) thump; (*du coude*) dig, prod

bourrage [buʀaʒ] NM [*coussin*] stuffing; [*poêle, pipe*] filling; [*fusil*] wadding; [*imprimante, photocopieur*] paper jam; **il y a un ~ (de papier)** the paper has got stuck *ou* jammed in the machine; **~ de crâne** (= *propagande*) brainwashing; (= *récits exagérés*) eyewash*, hot air*; (*Scol*) cramming

bourrasque [buʀask] NF gust of wind, squall; **~ de neige** flurry of snow; **le vent souffle en ~s** the wind is blowing in gusts

bourrasser⁎ [buʀase] ▸ conjug 1 ◂ VT (*Can*) to browbeat, bully

bourratif, -ive [buʀatif, iv] ADJ (*gén*) filling; (*péj*) stodgy

bourre¹ [buʀ] NF [*coussin*] stuffing; (*en poils*) hair; (*en laine, coton*) wadding, flock; [*bourgeon*] down; [*fusil*] wad; **de première ~⁎** great*, brilliant* (*Brit*); **à la ~⁎** (= *en retard*) late; (= *pressé*) pushed for time*; **être à la ~ dans son travail⁎** to be behind with one's work

bourre² †⁎ [buʀ] NM (= *policier*) cop*; **les ~s** the fuzz*, the cops*

bourré, e¹ [buʀe] (*ptp de* **bourrer**) ADJ **a** (= *plein à craquer*) [*salle, compartiment*] packed, jam-packed*, crammed (**de** with); [*sac*] crammed, stuffed (**de** with); **portefeuille ~ de billets** wallet stuffed with notes; **devoir ~ de fautes** exercise riddled with mistakes; **il est ~ de tics** he's always twitching; **il est ~ de complexes** he's got loads of hang-ups*, he's really hung-up*; **il est /le film est ~ d'idées** he's/the film is bursting with ideas; **c'est ~ de vitamines** it's packed with vitamins b (♯ = *ivre*) sloshed♯, plastered♯

bourreau (*pl* **bourreaux**) [buʀo] 1 NM a (= *tortionnaire*) torturer b (*Hist*) [*guillotine*] executioner, headsman; [*pendaison*] executioner, hangman 2 COMP ► **bourreau des cœurs** ladykiller ► **bourreau d'enfants** child-batterer, baby-batterer ► **bourreau de travail** glutton for work*, workaholic*

bourrée² [buʀe] NF (*Mus*) bourrée

bourrelé, e [buʀ(ə)le] ADJ (*littér*) **~ de remords** stricken with *ou* racked by remorse; **~ de soupçons** racked by suspicion

bourrelet [buʀlɛ] NM a (*gén*) roll; [*porte, fenêtre*] draught excluder (*Brit*), weather strip (*US*) b (**de chair**) fold *ou* roll of flesh; **~ (de graisse)** (*gén*) roll of fat; (*à la taille*) spare tyre*

bourrelier [buʀəlje] NM saddler

bourrellerie [buʀɛlʀi] NF saddlery

bourrer [buʀe] ▸ conjug 1 ◂ 1 VT a (= *remplir*) [+ *coussin*] to stuff; [+ *pipe, poêle*] to fill; [+ *valise*] to stuff *ou* cram full; **~ une dissertation de citations** to cram an essay with quotations; **~ un sac de papiers** to stuff *ou* cram papers into a bag; (*Pol*) **les urnes** to rig the ballot b **~ qn de nourriture** to stuff sb with food; **ne te bourre pas de gâteaux** don't stuff* yourself *ou* fill yourself up* with cakes; **les frites, ça bourre** chips really fill you up! c (*loc*) **~ le crâne à qn*** (= *endoctriner*) to stuff* sb's head full of ideas, brainwash sb; (= *en faire accroire*) to feed sb a lot of eyewash*; (*Scol*) to cram sb; **~ qn de coups** to beat sb up; **se faire ~ la gueule**♯♯ to get one's head bashed in♯; **se ~ la gueule**♯♯ (= *se battre*) to beat one another up♯; (= *se soûler*) to get sloshed♯ *ou* plastered♯ *ou* pissed♯♯ (*Brit*) 2 VI a (♯ = *se dépêcher*) (*en voiture, en moto*) to go flat out*, tear along*; (*au travail*) to go *ou* work flat out* b [*papier*] to jam

bourriche [buʀiʃ] NF [*huîtres*] hamper, basket; (*Pêche*) keep-net

bourrichon* [buʀiʃɔ̃] NM **se monter le ~** to get a notion in one's head; **monter le ~ à qn** to put ideas into sb's head (**contre** against)

bourricot [buʀiko] NM (small) donkey

bourrin* [buʀɛ̃] NM horse, nag*

bourrique [buʀik] NF a (*Zool*) (= *âne*) donkey, ass; (= *ânesse*) she-ass b* (= *imbécile*) ass, blockhead*; (= *têtu*) pigheaded* person; **faire tourner qn en ~** to drive sb to distraction *ou* up the wall* → **soûl, têtu**

bourriquet [buʀikɛ] NM = **bourricot**

bourru, e [buʀy] ADJ [*personne, air*] surly; [*voix*] gruff

bourrure [buʀyʀ] NF (*Can*) stuffing (*in saddle etc*)

bourse [buʀs] 1 NF a (= *porte-monnaie*) purse; **la ~ ou la vie !** your money or your life!, stand and deliver!; **sans ~ délier** without spending a penny; **avoir la ~ dégarnie** to be hard-up*; **avoir la ~ bien garnie** (*ponctuellement*) to be flush*; (*en permanence*) to have well-lined pockets, have a well-lined purse; **ils font ~ commune** they share expenses; **il nous a ouvert sa ~** he lent us some money; **c'est trop cher pour ma ~** I can't afford it, it's more than I can afford → **cordon, portée²** b (= *marché boursier*) **la Bourse** the Stock Exchange; **la Bourse de Paris** the Bourse, the Paris Stock Exchange; **la Bourse de Londres/de New York** the London/New York Stock Exchange; **la Bourse monte/descend** the market is going up/down; **valoir tant en Bourse** to be worth so much on the Stock Exchange *ou* Market; **jouer à la Bourse** to speculate *ou* gamble on the Stock Exchange *ou* Market → **coter** c [*objets d'occasion*] sale; **~ aux livres** second-hand book sale

d **~ (d'études)** (*Scol*) school maintenance allowance (*NonC*); (*Univ*) grant; (*obtenue par concours*) scholarship, bursary

e (*Anat*) **~ séreuse** bursa; **~s** scrotum

2 COMP ► **Bourse du** *ou* **de commerce** produce exchange, commodity market ► **Bourse de l'emploi** ≈ job centre ► **Bourse des marchandises** = **Bourse du commerce** ► **Bourse du travail** *trades union centre*, ≈ trades council (*Brit*) ► **Bourse des valeurs** Stock Market, Stock *ou* Securities Exchange

boursicotage [buʀsikɔtaʒ] NM dabbling on the stock exchange

boursicoter [buʀsikɔte] ▸ conjug 1 ◂ VI to dabble on the stock exchange

boursicoteur, -euse [buʀsikɔtœʀ, øz], **boursicotier, -ière** [buʀsikɔtje, jɛʀ] NM,F small-time speculator, small investor

boursier, -ière [buʀsje, jɛʀ] 1 ADJ a (*Scol, Univ*) **étudiant ~** grant holder; (*par concours*) scholarship holder b (*Bourse*) stock-market (*épith*), stock-exchange (*épith*); **marché ~** stock market; **indice ~** stock market index; **valeurs boursières** stocks and shares 2 NM,F a (= *étudiant*) grant holder; (*par concours*) scholarship holder b (= *agent de change*) stockbroker; (= *opérateur*) stock exchange operator

boursouflage [buʀsuflaʒ] NM [*visage*] swelling, puffing-up; [*style*] turgidity

boursouflé, e [buʀsufle] (*ptp de* **boursoufler**) ADJ [*visage*] puffy, swollen, bloated; [*main*] swollen; [*surface peinte*] blistered; (*fig*) [*style, discours*] bombastic, turgid

boursouflement [buʀsufləmɑ̃] NM = **boursouflage**

boursoufler [buʀsufle] ▸ conjug 1 ◂ 1 VT to puff up, bloat 2 **se boursoufler** VPR [*peinture*] to blister; [*visage, main*] to swell (up)

boursouflure [buʀsuflyʀ] NF [*visage*] puffiness; [*style*] turgidity, pomposity; (= *cloque*) blister; (= *enflure*) swelling

bouscaud, e [busko, od] ADJ (*Can*) thickset

bouscueil [buskœj] NM (*Can*) break-up of ice (in rivers and lakes)

bousculade [buskylad] NF (= *remous*) hustle, jostle, crush; (= *hâte*) rush, scramble; **dans la ~** in the rush *ou* crush; **pas de ~ !** don't push!; **ça a été la ~ ce week-end** it was a real rush *ou* scramble this weekend

bousculer [buskyle] ▸ conjug 1 ◂ 1 VT a [+ *personne*] (= *pousser*) to jostle, shove; (= *heurter*) to bump into *ou* against, knock into *ou* against; (= *presser*) to rush, hurry (up); (*Mil*) to drive from the field; (*fig*) **je n'aime pas qu'on me bouscule** I don't like to be pressured *ou* rushed; (*fig*) **être (très) bousculé** to be rushed off one's feet
b [+ *objet*] (= *heurter*) to knock *ou* bump into; (= *faire tomber*) to knock over; (= *déranger*) to knock about
c [+ *idées*] to shake up, liven up; [+ *traditions*] to shake up; [+ *habitudes*] to upset; [+ *emploi du temps*] to upset, disrupt
2 **se bousculer** VPR (= *se heurter*) to jostle each other; (* = *se dépêcher*) to get a move on*; **les souvenirs/idées se bousculaient dans sa tête** his head was buzzing with memories/ideas; **on se bouscule pour aller voir ce film** there's a mad rush on* to see the film; **ça se bouscule au portillon*** (= *bégayer*) he can't get his words out fast enough; (= *s'enthousiasmer*) **les gens ne se bousculent pas (au portillon)*** people aren't exactly queuing up* (*Brit*) *ou* lining up (*US*)

bouse [buz] NF (cow *ou* cattle) dung (*NonC*), cow pat

bouseux♯ [buzø] NM (*péj*) bumpkin, yokel

bousier [buzje] NM dung-beetle

bousillage* [buzijaʒ] NM a [*travail*] botch-

ing, bungling b [*appareil, moteur*] wrecking, busting up♯; [*voiture, avion*] smashing up*

bousiller* [buzije] ▸ conjug 1 ◂ VT a (= *bâcler*) [+ *travail*] to botch, bungle, louse up* b (= *détériorer*) [+ *appareil, moteur*] to bust up♯, wreck; [+ *voiture, avion*] to smash up*, total* (*US*); **ça a bousillé sa vie/carrière** it wrecked his life/career; **se ~ la santé** to ruin one's health; **on est en train de ~ les forêts** we're decimating the forests c (= *tuer*) [+ *personne*] to bump off♯, do in♯; **se faire ~** to get done in♯ *ou* bumped off♯

bousilleur, -euse* [buzijœʀ, øz] NM,F bungler, botcher

boussole [busɔl] NF compass; (*fig*) **perdre la ~*** to go off one's head, lose one's marbles*

boustifaille♯ [bustifaj] NF grub♯, nosh♯ (*Brit*)

bout [bu]

1 NOM MASCULIN	2 COMPOSÉS

1 NOM MASCULIN

a = **extrémité, fin** [*ficelle, planche, rue, table*] end; [*nez, langue, oreille*] tip; [*canne*] end, tip; **~ du doigt** fingertip; **~ du sein** nipple; **à ~ rond/carré** round-/square-ended; **cigarette à ~ liège** cork-tipped cigarette; **à l'autre ~ du couloir** at the other *ou* far end of the corridor; **commençons par un ~ et nous verrons** let's get started *ou* make a start and then we'll see; **cette vieille voiture s'en va par tous les ~s*** this old car is falling apart; **on ne sait pas par quel ~ le prendre** you just don't know how to tackle *ou* handle him; **prendre qch par le bon ~** to approach *ou* handle sth the right way; (*fig*) **tenir le bon ~*** (= *être sur la bonne voie*) to be on the right track; (= *avoir fait le plus gros du travail*) to be getting near the end of one's work, be past the worst (*hum*); **on n'en voit pas le ~** there doesn't seem to be any end to it → **monde, nez, tunnel**

b = **morceau** [*ficelle, pain, papier*] piece, bit; **un ~ de terrain** a patch *ou* plot of land; **un ~ de pelouse/de ciel bleu** a patch of lawn/of blue sky; **un petit ~ d'homme*** a (mere) scrap of a man; **un petit ~ de femme** a slip of a woman; **un (petit) ~ de chou*** *ou* **de zan*** a little kid* *ou* nipper* (*Brit*); **bonjour, ~ de chou** hello, poppet* (*Brit*) *ou* my little love; **on a fait un ~ de chemin ensemble** (*lit*) we walked part of the way together; (*fig*) (*en couple*) we were together for a while; **jusqu'à Paris, cela fait un (bon) ~ de chemin** *ou* **un ~*** it's some distance *ou* quite a long way to Paris; **il m'a fait un ~ de conduite** he went part of the way with me; **il est resté un bon ~ de temps** he stayed a while *ou* quite some time; **avoir un ~ de rôle dans une pièce** to have a small *ou* bit part *ou* walk-on part in a play; **mettre les ~s**♯ to hop it♯ (*Brit*), skedaddle*, scarper♯ (*Brit*) → **connaître**

c Naut = **cordage** [but] (length of) rope

d **expressions figées**

◆ **à bout** : **être à ~** (= *fatigué*) to be exhausted, be all in♯; (= *en colère*) to have had enough, be at the end of one's patience; **ma patience est à ~** I'm at the end of my patience; **pousser qn à ~** to push sb to the limit (of his patience)

◆ **à bout de** : **à ~ de bras** [*tenir, porter*] (*lit*) at arm's length; (*fig*) **nous avons porté le club à ~ de bras pendant 2 ans** we struggled to keep the club going for 2 years; **être à ~ d'arguments** to have run out of arguments; **être à ~ de force(s)** to have no strength left; **à ~ de forces, il s'écroula** worn out *ou* exhausted, he collapsed; **être à ~ de nerfs** to be at the end of one's tether, be just about at breaking point; **à ~ de souffle** (*lit*) breathless, out of breath (*attrib*); (*fig*) [*machine, gouvernement*] on its last legs*; **le moteur est à ~ de souffle** the engine is about to give up the ghost; **venir à ~ de** [+ *travail*] to get through, get to the end of; [+ *adversaire*] to get the better of, overcome;

[+ *repas, gâteau*] to get through; **je n'en vien-drai jamais à ~** I'll never manage it, I'll never get through it → **course**

♦ **à bout portant ◊ à bout touchant**† LOC ADV [*tirer, tuer*] point-blank, at point-blank range

♦ **à tout bout de champ** all the time; **il m'interrompait à tout ~ de champ** he interrupted me at every opportunity, he kept on interrupting me; **elle se regarde dans la glace à tout ~ de champ** she's forever looking at herself in the mirror

♦ **au bout de**
(*dans l'espace*) **au ~ de la rue** at the end of the street; **au ~ du jardin** at the bottom *ou* end of the garden; **la poste est tout au ~ du village** the post office is at the far end of the village
(*dans le temps*) after; **au ~ d'un mois** after a month, a month later; **au ~ d'un moment** after a while; **il est parti au ~ de trois minutes** he left after three minutes
[e] [fig] **au ~ du compte** in the last analysis, all things considered; **il n'est pas au ~ de ses pei-nes** he's not out of the wood (*Brit*) *ou* woods (*US*) yet, his troubles still aren't over; **être au ~ du rouleau*** (= *n'avoir plus rien à dire*) to have run out of ideas; (= *être sans ressources*) to be running short (of money); (= *être épuisé*) to be exhausted; (= *être près de la mort*) to have come to the end of the road

♦ **bout à bout** end to end; **mettre des planches/tuyaux ~ à ~** to lay planks/pipes end to end; **il a reconstitué l'histoire en mettant ~ à ~ tous les indices** he reconstructed what had happened by piecing all the clues *ou* evidence together

♦ **de bout en bout** : **lire un livre de ~ en ~** to read a book from cover to cover *ou* right through *ou* from start to finish; **parcourir une rue de ~ en ~** to go from one end of a street to the other

♦ **du bout de** : **manger du ~ des dents** to pick *ou* nibble at one's food; **du ~ des doigts** [*effleurer, pianoter*] with one's fingertips; (*fig*) **le public a applaudi du ~ des doigts** the audience clapped half-heartedly; **du ~ des lèvres** [*accepter, approuver*] reluctantly, half-heartedly; **il écarta les feuilles mortes du ~ du pied** he pushed aside the dead leaves with his toe

♦ **d'un bout à l'autre** from one end to the other; **il a traversé le pays/continent d'un ~ à l'autre** he travelled the length and breadth of the country/continent; **je l'ai lu d'un ~ à l'autre sans m'arrêter** I read it right through *ou* from cover to cover without stopping; **ce film est passionnant d'un ~ à l'autre** the film is compelling from start to finish *ou* right through; **d'un ~ à l'autre de la ville** from one end of the town to the other; **d'un ~ à l'autre de ses œu-vres** throughout *ou* all through his works; **d'un ~ de l'année à l'autre** all year round; **d'un ~ à l'autre du voyage** from the beginning of the journey to the end, throughout *ou* right through the journey

♦ **en bout de** at the end *ou* bottom of; **assis en ~ de table** sitting at the end *ou* bottom *ou* foot of the table → **chaîne, course**

♦ **jusqu'au bout** : **nous sommes restés jusqu'au ~** we stayed right to the end; **ce travail lui dé-plaît mais il ira jusqu'au ~** he doesn't like this job but he'll see it through; **ils ont combattu jusqu'au ~** they fought to the bitter end; **re-belle jusqu'au ~** rebellious to the end *ou* the last

♦ **jusqu'au bout de** (*fig*) **il faut aller jusqu'au ~ de ce qu'on entreprend** if you take something on you must see it through (to the end); **aller jusqu'au ~ de ses idées** to follow (one's ideas) through; (*fig*) **il est aristocrate/russe jusqu'au ~ des ongles** he's an aristocrat/he's Russian through and through; **elle est professionnelle jusqu'au ~ des ongles** she's a professional to her fingertips

♦ **sur le bout de** (*fig*) **j'ai son nom sur le ~ de la langue** his name is on the tip of my tongue; **il sait sa leçon sur le ~ du doigt** *ou* **des doigts** he knows his lesson backwards *ou* off pat* (*Brit*); **elle connaît la question sur le ~ des doigts** she knows the subject inside out

[2] COMPOSÉS
► **bout de l'an** (*Rel*) memorial service (*held on the first anniversary of a person's death*)
► **bout d'essai** (*Ciné*) screen test, test film; **tourner un ~ d'essai** to do a screen test
► **bout filtre** filter tip; **cigarettes (à) ~ filtre** filter tip cigarettes, tipped cigarettes

boutade [butad] NF [a] (= *trait d'esprit*) witti-cism, sally (*littér*); (= *plaisanterie*) joke; **il a ré-pondu par une ~** he made a witty reply; **il s'en est sorti par une ~** he joked his way out of it; **elle l'a dit par ~** she said it in jest; **ce n'est pas une ~** it's not a joke, I'm not joking [b] († = *caprice*) whim; **par ~** as the whim takes him (*ou her etc*), by fits and starts

bout-dehors (*pl* **bouts-dehors**) [budɔR] NM (*Naut*) boom

boute-en-train [butɑ̃trɛ̃] NM INV live wire*; **c'était le ~ de la soirée** he was the life and soul of the party; **on ne peut pas dire que c'est un ~** he's not exactly the life and soul of the party

boutefeu [butfø] NM (*Hist*) linstock; († = *personne*) firebrand

bouteille [butɛj] NF [a] (= *récipient*) bottle; (= *contenu*) bottle(ful); **boire à la ~** to drink (straight) from the bottle; **~ d'air comprimé/ de butane/de gaz** cylinder of compressed air/ of butane gas/of gas; **~ de Leyde** Leyden jar; **~ d'un litre/de 2 litres** litre/2-litre bottle; **~ de vin** (= *récipient*) wine bottle; (= *contenu*) bottle of wine; **bière en ~** bottled beer; **mettre du vin en ~s** to bottle wine; **mise en ~** bottling; **vin qui a 10 ans de ~** wine that has been in (the) bottle for 10 years; **boire une (bonne) ~** to drink *ou* have a bottle of (good) wine; (*hum*) **aimer la ~** to be fond of the bottle, like one's tipple* [b] (*loc*) **prendre de la ~*** to be getting on in years, be getting long in the tooth* (*hum*); **il a de la ~*** (*dans son métier*) he's been around a long time; **c'est la ~ à l'encre** the whole business is about as clear as mud, you can't make head nor tail of it

bouter [bute] ▸ conjug 1 ◂ VT† to drive, push (**hors de** out of)

bouteur [butœR] NM bulldozer; **~ biais** angledozer

boutique [butik] NF [a] (= *magasin*) shop, sto-re (*surtout US*); [*grand couturier*] boutique; **~ en plein vent** open-air stall; **robe/tailleur ~** de-signer dress/suit **~ fermer, parler** [b] (* = *lieu de travail*) place*, hole*; **quelle sale ~ !** what a crummy* place!, what a dump!*

boutiquier, -ière [butikje, jɛR] NM,F shop-keeper (*Brit*), storekeeper (*US*)

boutoir [butwaR] NM [*sanglier*] snout; **coup de ~** (*Mil, Sport, gén*) thrust; [*vent, vagues*] batter-ing (*NonC*)

bouton [butɔ̃] [1] NM [a] (*Couture*) button [b] (= *mécanisme: Élec*) switch; [*porte, radio*] knob; [*sonnette*] (push-)button [c] (*Bot*) bud; **en ~** in bud; **~ de rose** rosebud [d] (*Méd*) pim-ple, spot (*Brit*), zit* (*surtout US*); **~ d'acné** pim-ple, spot (*Brit*) (*caused by acne*); **avoir des ~s** to have pimples *ou* spots (*Brit*), have a pimply face; (* : *fig*) **ça me donne des ~s** it makes my skin crawl [2] COMP ► **bouton de chemise** shirt button ► **bouton de col** collar stud ► **bouton de culotte** trouser *ou* pant (*US*) button ► **bouton de fièvre** cold sore, fever blister *ou* sore ► **bouton de guêtre** gaiter button; (*fig*) **il ne manque pas un ~ de guêtre** everything is in apple-pie order ► **bouton de manchette** cufflink

bouton-d'or (*pl* **boutons-d'or**) [butɔdɔR] NM (= *fleur*) buttercup; (= *couleur*) buttercup yel-low

boutonnage [butɔnaʒ] NM buttoning(-up); **avec ~ à droite/à gauche** right/left buttoning (*épith*), which buttons on the right/left; **manteau à double ~** double-buttoning coat

boutonner [butɔne] ▸ conjug 1 ◂ [1] VT [a] [+ *vêtement*] to button *ou* fasten (up) [b] (*Escrime*) to button [2] **se boutonner** VPR [*vêtement*] to button (up); [*personne*] to button (up) one's coat (*ou* trousers *etc*)

boutonneux, -euse [butɔnø, øz] ADJ pimply, spotty (*Brit*)

boutonnière [butɔnjɛR] NF (*Couture*) button-hole; (= *bouquet*) buttonhole (*Brit*), boutonni-ere (*US*); **avoir une fleur à la ~** to wear a flower in one's buttonhole, wear a buttonhole (*Brit*) *ou* boutonniere (*US*); **porter une décoration à la ~** to wear a decoration on one's lapel; (*Chir*) **faire une ~ (à qn)** to make a small incision (in sb's abdomen)

bouton-poussoir (*pl* **boutons-poussoirs**) [butɔpuswaR] NM push button

bouton-pression (*pl* **boutons-pression**) [butɔpResjɔ̃] NM snap fastener, press stud (*Brit*)

boutre [butR] NM dhow

bout-rimé (*pl* **bouts-rimés**) [buRime] NM (*Littérat*) (= *poème*) poem in set rhymes; **bouts-rimés** (= *fins de vers*) rhyme endings, bouts rimés

bouturage [butyRaʒ] NM taking (of) cuttings, propagation (by cuttings)

bouture [butyR] NF cutting; **faire des ~s** to take cuttings

bouturer [butyRe] ▸ conjug 1 ◂ [1] VT to take a cutting from, propagate (by cuttings) [2] VI to put out suckers

bouvet [buvɛ] NM (*Menuiserie*) rabbet plane

bouvier [buvje] NM (= *personne*) herdsman, cattleman, herder (*US*); (= *chien*) sheep dog

bouvillon [buvijɔ̃] NM bullock, steer (*US*)

bouvreuil [buvRœj] NM bullfinch

bouzouki [buzuki] NM bouzouki

bovarysme [bɔvaRism] NM bovarism, bovarysm

bovidé [bɔvide] [1] ADJ M bovid [2] NM bovid; **~s** bovids, bovidae (*SPÉC*)

bovin, e [bɔvɛ̃, in] [1] ADJ (*lit, fig*) bovine [2] NM bovine; **~s** cattle, Bovini (*SPÉC*)

bowling [buliŋ] NM (= *jeu*) (tenpin) bowling; (= *salle*) bowling alley

box [bɔks] NM [*hôpital, dortoir*] cubicle; [*écurie*] loose box; [*porcherie*] stall, pen; (= *garage*) lock-up (garage); (*Jur*) **~ des accusés** dock; (*lit, fig*) **dans le ~ des accusés** in the dock

box(-calf) [bɔks(kalf)] NM box calf; **sac en ~** calfskin bag

boxe [bɔks] NF boxing; **match de ~** boxing match; **~ anglaise** boxing; **~ française** ≈ kick boxing; **~ thaï** Thai boxing; **faire de la ~** to box

boxer¹ [bɔkse] ▸ conjug 1 ◂ [1] VI to box, be a boxer; **~ contre** to box against, fight [2] VT (*Sport*) to box against, fight; (* = *frapper*) to thump*, punch

boxer² [bɔksɛR] NM boxer (dog)

boxer-short (*pl* **boxer-shorts**) [bɔksœRʃɔRt] NM boxer shorts, boxers

boxeur [bɔksœR] NM boxer

box-office (*pl* **box-offices**) [bɔksɔfis] NM box office; **film en tête du ~** box-office success *ou* hit

boxon: [bɔksɔ̃] NM [a] (= *maison close*) brothel, whorehouse* † [b] (= *désordre*) **c'est le ~ !** it's a shambles!

boy [bɔj] NM (= *serviteur*) (native) servant boy, (house)boy; (*Music-hall*) ≈ male dancer

boyard [bɔjaR] NM (*Hist*) boyar(d)

boyau (pl **boyaux**) [bwajo] NM [a] (= intestins) **~x** [animal] guts, entrails; * [personne] insides*, guts*; **elle a le ~ de la rigolade*** she's always giggling*; **il a toujours un ~ de vide*** he's always hungry → **tripe** [b] (= corde) **~ (de chat)** (cat)gut [c] (= passage) (narrow) passageway; (= tuyau) narrow pipe; (Mil) communication trench, sap; (Min) (narrow) gallery [d] [bicyclette] (racing) tyre, tubeless tyre [e] (pour saucisse) casing

boycott [bɔjkɔt], **boycottage** [bɔjkɔtaʒ] NM boycotting (NonC), boycott

boycotter [bɔjkɔte] ▸ conjug 1 ◂ VT to boycott

boy-scout† (pl **boy(s)-scouts**) [bɔjskut] NM (boy) scout; **avoir une mentalité de ~*** to have a (rather) naïve ou ingenuous outlook

BP [bepe] (ABRÉV = **boîte postale**) P.O. Box

BPF (ABRÉV = **bon pour francs**) amount payable on a cheque

brabançon, -onne [brabɑ̃sɔ̃, ɔn] [1] ADJ of ou from Brabant [2] **Brabançon(ne)** NM,F inhabitant ou native of Brabant [3] NM **(cheval) ~** type of draught horse bred in the Brabant region [4] **Brabançonne** NF **la Brabançonne** the Belgian national anthem

brabant [brabɑ̃] NM [a] (Agr) **double ~** swivel plough (Brit) ou plow (US) [b] (Géog) **le Brabant** Brabant

bracelet [braslɛ] [1] NM [a] [poignet] bracelet; [bras] bangle; [cheville] ankle bracelet, bangle; [montre] strap, bracelet; [nouveau-né] identity bracelet, name tag [b] (= élastique) rubber band (→ menottes) **~s** handcuffs; **on lui a passé les ~s** they handcuffed him [2] COMP ▸ **bracelet de force** (leather) wristband

bracelet-montre (pl **bracelets-montres**) [braslɛmɔ̃tr] NM wristwatch

brachial, e (mpl **-iaux**) [brakjal, jo] ADJ brachial

brachiopode [brakjɔpɔd] NM brachiopod

brachycéphale [brakisefal] [1] ADJ brachycephalic [2] NMF brachycephalic person

brachycéphalie [brakisefali] NF brachycephaly

braconnage [brakɔnaʒ] NM poaching

braconner [brakɔne] ▸ conjug 1 ◂ VI to poach

braconnier, -ière [brakɔnje, jɛr] NM,F poacher

bradage [bradaʒ] NM selling off

brader [brade] ▸ conjug 1 ◂ VT [a] (= vendre à prix réduit) to sell cut-price (Brit) ou cut-rate (US); (= vendre en solde) to have a clearance sale of; (lit, fig = se débarrasser de) to sell off; **à ce prix-là, c'est bradé** at that price, it's a giveaway

braderie [bradri] NF (= magasin) discount centre; (= marché) market (held once or twice a year, where goods are sold at reduced prices); (péj) **la grande ~ des entreprises publiques** the massive ou wholesale sell-off of state-owned companies

bradeur, -euse [bradœr, øz] NM,F discounter

bradycardie [bradikardi] NF abnormally low rate of heartbeat, bradycardia (SPÉC)

braguette [bragɛt] NF [pantalon] fly, flies; (Hist) codpiece

brahmane [braman] NM Brahmin, Brahman

brahmanique [bramanik] ADJ Brahminical

brahmanisme [bramanism] NM Brahminism, Brahmanism

Brahmapoutre [bramaputr], **Brahmaputra** [bramaputra] NM Brahmaputra

brahmine [bramin] NF Brahmani, Brahmanee

brai [brɛ] NM pitch, tar

braies [brɛ] NFPL (Hist) breeches (worn by Gauls)

braillard, e* [brajar, ard] [1] ADJ [a] (= criard) bawling (épith), yelling (épith); **des haut-parleurs ~s** blaring loudspeakers; **des mouettes ~es** screeching gulls [b] (= pleurard) [enfant] bawling (épith), howling (épith), squalling (épith) [2] NM,F bawler

braille [braj] NM Braille

braillement* [brajmɑ̃] NM [a] (= cris) bawling (NonC), yelling (NonC) [b] (= pleurs) bawling (NonC), howling (NonC), squalling (NonC); **les ~s de l'enfant** the bawling of the child

brailler* [braje] ▸ conjug 1 ◂ [1] VI (= crier) to bawl, yell; (= pleurer) to bawl, howl; **il faisait ~ sa radio** his radio was blaring, he had his radio blaring ou on full blast [2] VT [+ chanson, slogan] to bawl out

brailleur, -euse [brajœr, øz] ADJ, NM,F = **braillard**

braiment [bremɑ̃] NM bray(ing)

brain-trust (pl **brain-trusts**) [brɛntrœst] NM brain trust, brains trust

braire [brɛr] ▸ conjug 50 ◂ VI (lit, fig) to bray; **faire ~ qn*** to get on sb's nerves ou wick* (Brit)

braise [brɛz] NF [a] [feu] **la ~ ◊ les ~s** the (glowing) embers; (= charbon de bois) live charcoal; (fig) **être sur la ~** to be on tenterhooks; **yeux de ~** fiery eyes, eyes like coals [b] (‡ = argent) cash*, dough‡, bread‡

braiser [breze] ▸ conjug 1 ◂ VT to braise; **bœuf/chou braisé** braised beef/cabbage

bramement [bramɑ̃] NM [a] [cerf] bell, troat [b] (= hurlement) wailing

bramer [brame] ▸ conjug 1 ◂ VI [a] [cerf] to bell, troat [b]* (= brailler) to bawl; (= se lamenter) to wail

bran [brɑ̃] NM bran; **~ de scie** sawdust

brancard [brɑ̃kar] NM [a] (= bras) [charrette] shaft; [civière] shaft, pole → **ruer** [b] (= civière) stretcher

brancarder [brɑ̃karde] ▸ conjug 1 ◂ VT [+ personne] to carry on a stretcher

brancardier, -ière [brɑ̃kardje, jɛr] NM,F stretcher-bearer

branchage [brɑ̃ʃaʒ] NM branches, boughs; **~s** fallen ou lopped-off branches, lops

branche [brɑ̃ʃ] NF [a] (Bot) branch, bough; **~ mère** main branch; **sauter de ~ en ~** to leap from branch to branch; **céleri en ~s** (sticks of) celery; (fig) **n'essaie pas de te raccrocher** ou **de te rattraper aux ~s*** don't try to make up for what you've said → **vieux** [b] (= ramification) [nerfs, veines] branch, ramification; [rivière, canalisation, bois de cerf] branch; [lunettes] side-piece; [compas] leg; [ciseaux] blade; [fer à cheval] half; [famille] branch; **la ~ aînée** ou **eldest branch** of the family; **la ~ maternelle** the maternal branch of the family, the mother's side of the family; **avoir de la ~*** to be of good stock [c] (= secteur) branch; **les ~s de la science moderne** the different branches of modern science; **notre fils s'orientera vers une ~ technique** our son will specialize in technical subjects; **la ~ politique/militaire de cette organisation** the political/military wing ou arm of the organization

branchement [brɑ̃ʃmɑ̃] NM [a] (= fils connectés) connection; **vérifiez les ~s** check the connections [b] (= action) [appareil à gaz, tuyau] connecting (up); [eau, gaz, électricité, réseau] linking up [c] (Rail) branch line [d] (Ordin) branch

brancher [brɑ̃ʃe] ▸ conjug 1 ◂ [1] VT [a] [+ appareil électrique] (à une prise) to plug in; **~ qch sur qch** to plug sth into sth, connect sth up with sth [b] [+ appareil à gaz, tuyau, eau, gaz, électricité] to connect (up); **être branché sur un réseau** to be linked ou connected to a network [c] (= allumer) [+ télévision] to turn on [d] (* = mettre en relation) **~ qn avec qn** to put sb in contact with sb [e] (= orienter) **~ qn sur un sujet** to start sb off on a subject; **quand on l'a branché** ou **quand il est branché là-dessus il est intarissable** when he's launched on that ou when somebody gets him started on that he can go on forever [f] (* = intéresser) **ce qui me branche** what grabs me* ou gives me a buzz*; **ça ne me branche pas** [idée] it doesn't grab me*; [musique, activité] it doesn't do anything for me; **ça te brancherait d'aller au ciné ?** (do you) fancy going to see a film?*; **il ne me branche pas trop son frère** I'm not too gone* on ou too keen on his brother

[2] **se brancher** VPR [a] (= se connecter) **où est-ce que ça se branche ?** where does that plug in?; **où est-ce que je peux me ~ ?** where can I plug it in?; **se ~ sur un réseau/Internet** to get onto ou connect to a network/the Internet [b] (* = entrer en relation) **se ~ avec qn** to get in contact with sb

branchette [brɑ̃ʃɛt] NF small branch, twig

branchial, e (mpl **-iaux**) [brɑ̃ʃjal, jo] ADJ branchial

branchies [brɑ̃ʃi] NFPL (Zool) gills, branchiae (SPÉC)

branchiopode [brɑ̃ʃjɔpɔd] NM branchiopod

branchu, e [brɑ̃ʃy] ADJ branchy

brandade [brɑ̃dad] NF **~ (de morue)** brandade (dish made with cod)

brande [brɑ̃d] NF (= lande) heath(land); (= plantes) heath, heather, brush

brandebourg [brɑ̃dbur] [1] NM (Habillement) frog; **à ~(s)** frogged [2] **Brandebourg** N Brandenburg; **la porte de Brandebourg** the Brandenburg Gate

brandebourgeois, e [brɑ̃dburʒwa, waz] [1] ADJ Brandenburg (épith); (Mus) **« les concertos ~ »** "the Brandenburg Concertos" [2] **Brandebourgeois(e)** NM,F inhabitant ou native of Brandenburg

brandir [brɑ̃dir] ▸ conjug 2 ◂ VT [+ arme] to brandish; [+ document] to brandish, flourish

brandon [brɑ̃dɔ̃] NM firebrand (lit); **~ de discorde** bone of contention

brandy [brɑ̃di] NM brandy

branlant, e [brɑ̃lɑ̃, ɑ̃t] ADJ [dent] loose; [mur] shaky; [escalier, meuble] rickety, shaky; [pas] unsteady, tottering, shaky; (fig) [régime] tottering, shaky; [raison] shaky

branle [brɑ̃l] NM [cloche] swing; **mettre en ~** [+ cloche] to swing, set swinging; (fig) [+ forces] to set in motion, set off; **donner le ~ à** to set in motion, set rolling; **se mettre en ~** to get going ou moving

branle-bas [brɑ̃lba] NM INV bustle, commotion; **dans le ~ du départ** in the confusion ou bustle of departure; **être en ~** to be in a state of commotion; **mettre qch en ~** to turn sth upside down, cause commotion in sth; (Naut) **~ de combat** (= manœuvre) preparations for action; (= ordre) "action stations!"; **sonner le ~ de combat** to sound action stations; **mettre en ~ de combat** to clear the decks (for action)

branlée [brɑ̃le] NF [a] (‡ = coups) hammering*; **recevoir une ~** to get hammered*, get a hammering* [b] (‡ = masturbation) [homme] hand job‡, wank‡‡ (Brit)

branlement [brɑ̃lmɑ̃] NM [tête] wagging, shaking

branler [brɑ̃le] ▸ conjug 1 ◂ [1] VT [a] **~ la tête** ou **(hum) du chef** to shake ou wag one's head [b] (‡‡ = faire) **qu'est-ce qu'ils branlent ?** what the hell are they up to?‡; **il n'en branle pas une** he does fuck all‡‡ ou bugger all‡‡ (Brit); **j'en ai rien à ~** I don't give a fuck‡‡ [2] VI [échafaudage] to be shaky ou unsteady; [meuble] to be shaky ou rickety; [dent] to be loose; **ça branle dans le manche** things are a bit shaky [3] **se branler**** VPR [homme] to jerk off**, have a wank** (Brit); [femme] to masturbate; (fig) **je m'en branle** I don't give a (flying) fuck**

branlette** [brɑ̃lɛt] NF **la ~** wanking** (Brit), jerking off**; **se faire une ~**** to (have a) wank** (Brit), jerk (o.s.) off**

branleur, -euse** [brɑ̃lœr, øz] NM,F (= paresseux) lazy swine ou bugger** (Brit)

branleux, -euse** [brɑ̃lø, øz] ADJ (Can) shilly-shallying*

branque* [brɑ̃k], **branquignol*** [brɑ̃kiɲɔl] [1] ADJ crazy*, barmy* (Brit) [2] NM crackpot*, nutter* (Brit)

braquage [brakaʒ] NM (Aut) (steering) lock; (arg Crime) stickup (arg) → **angle, rayon**

braque [brak] [1] ADJ* crazy*, barmy* (Brit) [2] NM (Zool) pointer

braquemart [brakmar] NM [a] (Hist = épée) brackmard ††, (double-bladed) sword [b] (** = pénis) dick**, cock**

braquer [brake] ▸ conjug 1 ◂ [1] VT [a] (= diriger) **une arme sur** to point ou aim a weapon at; **~ un télescope/un projecteur sur** to train a telescope/a spotlight on; **~ son regard/attention sur** to turn one's gaze/attention towards, fix one's gaze/attention on; **tous les regards étaient braqués sur eux** all eyes were upon them; **les (feux des) projecteurs sont braqués sur la famille royale** the royal family are in the spotlight [b] (Aut) [+ roue] to swing [c] ‡ (= attaquer) [+ banque, personne] to hold up; (= menacer) [+ personne] to pull one's gun on, to hold up [d] (= buter) **~ qn** to put sb's back up*, make sb dig in his heels; **~ qn contre qch** to turn sb against sth; **il est braqué** he won't budge, he's dug his heels in [2] VI (Aut) to turn the (steering) wheel; [voiture] **bien/mal** to have a good/bad lock; **à fond** to put on the full lock; **braquez vers la gauche/la droite** turn hard left/right, left hand/right hand hard down [3] **se braquer** VPR to dig one's heels in; **se ~ contre qch** to set one's face against sth

braquet [brakɛ] NM [bicyclette] gear ratio; **changer de ~** (lit) to change gear; (*: fig) to get into gear; **mettre le petit ~** to change into lower gear; **mettre le grand ~** (lit) to change into higher gear; (*: fig) to get a move-on*, shift into high gear* (US)

braqueur‡ [brakœr] NM (= gangster) hold-up man*

bras [brɑ] [1] NM [a] (Anat) arm; **une serviette sous le ~** with a briefcase under one's arm; **un panier au ~** with a basket on one's arm; **donner le ~ à qn** to give sb one's arm; **prendre le ~ de qn** to take sb's arm; **être au ~ de qn** to be on sb's arm; **se donner le ~** to link arms; **~ dessus, ~ dessous** arm in arm; **on a dû transporter tout cela à ~** we had to carry all that; **les ~ en croix** with one's arms spread; (lit) **les ~ croisés** with one's arms folded; (fig) **rester les ~ croisés** to sit idly by; **tendre** ou **allonger le ~ vers qch** to reach out for sth, stretch out one's hand ou arm for sth; **tomber dans les ~ de qn** to fall into sb's arms; **il est mort dans mes ~** he died in my arms; **(viens) dans mes ~ mon fils !** come and let me kiss ou hug you, my son! → **arme, force, plein** etc [b] (= travailleur) hand, worker; **manquer de ~** to be short-handed, be short of manpower ou labour [c] (= pouvoir) **le ~ de la justice** the arm of the law; (Rel) **le ~ séculier** the secular arm; **le ~ armé du parti** the military wing ou arm of the party [d] [manivelle, outil, pompe] handle; [fauteuil] arm(rest); [grue] jib; [sémaphore, ancre, électrophone, moulin, essuie-glace] arm; [croix] limb;

[aviron, brancard] shaft; (Naut) [vergue] brace [e] [fleuve] branch [f] [cheval] shoulder; [mollusque] tentacle [g] (Ordin) **d'accès** ou **de lecture-écriture** access ou positioning arm [h] (loc) **en ~ de chemise** in (one's) shirt sleeves; **saisir qn à ~-le-corps** to seize sb round the waist, seize sb bodily; (fig) **avoir le ~ long** to have a long arm; (lit, fig) **à ~ ouverts** ◊ **les ~ ouverts** with open arms; **les ~ tendus** with outstretched arms; **tomber sur qn à ~ raccourcis*** to set (up)on sb, pitch into sb*; **lever les ~ au ciel** to throw up one's arms; **les ~ m'en tombent** I'm flabbergasted* ou stunned; **avoir** ou **se retrouver avec qch/qn sur les ~*** to have sth/sb on one's hands, be stuck* ou landed* with sth/sb; **il a une nombreuse famille sur les ~*** he's got a large family to look after; **avoir une sale histoire sur les ~*** to have a nasty business on one's hands; **partir avec qch sous le ~** to make off with sth; (hum) **(être) dans les ~ de Morphée** (to be) in the arms of Morpheus; **faire un ~ d'honneur à qn** ≈ put two fingers up at sb*, ≈ give sb the V-sign (Brit) ou the finger** (US) → **bout, couper, gros** etc [2] COMP ▸ **bras droit** (fig) right-hand man ▸ **bras de fer** (Sport) Indian wrestling (NonC), arm-wrestling (NonC); **faire une partie de ~ de fer avec qn** to arm-wrestle with sb; (fig) **la partie de ~ de fer entre patronat et syndicats** the trial of strength between the bosses and the unions ▸ **bras de levier** lever arm; **faire ~ de levier** to act as a lever ▸ **bras de mer** arm ou stretch of the sea, sound ▸ **bras mort** (gén) backwater; (= lac) oxbow lake, cutoff

brasage [brazaʒ] NM brazing

braser [braze] ▸ conjug 1 ◂ VT to braze

brasero [brazero] NM brazier

brasier [brazje] NM (= incendie) (blazing) inferno, furnace; (fig = foyer de guerre) inferno; **son cœur/esprit était un ~** his heart/mind was on fire ou ablaze

Brasilia [brazilja] N Brasilia

brasiller [brazije] ▸ conjug 1 ◂ VI [mer] to glimmer; [bougie] to glow red

brassage [brasaʒ] NM [a] [bière] brewing [b] (= mélange) mixing; **~ des peuples** intermixing of ethnic groups; (Aut) **~ des gaz** mixing [c] (Naut) bracing

brassard [brasar] NM armband; **~ de deuil** black armband

brasse [bras] NF [a] (= sport) breast-stroke; (= mouvement) stroke; **~ coulée** breast-stroke; **~ papillon** butterfly(-stroke); **nager la ~** to swim breast-stroke; **faire quelques ~s** to do a few strokes [b] †† (= mesure) ≈ 6 feet; (Naut) fathom

brassée [brase] NF armful; (‡: Can) [machine à laver] load; **par ~s** in armfuls

brasser [brase] ▸ conjug 1 ◂ VT [a] (= remuer) to stir (up); (= mélanger) to mix; [+ pâte] to knead; [+ salade] to toss; [+ cartes] to shuffle; [+ argent] to handle a lot of; **~ des affaires** to be in big business; (fig) **~ du vent** to blow hot air* [b] [+ bière] to brew [c] (Naut) to brace

brasserie [brasri] NF [a] (= café) ≈ pub, ≈ bar (US), ≈ brasserie [b] (= fabrique de bière) brewery; (= industrie) brewing industry

brasseur, -euse [brasœr, øz] NM,F [a] [bière] brewer [b] (Comm) **~ d'affaires** big businessman [c] (Sport) breast-stroke swimmer

brassière [brasjɛr] NF [a] [bébé] (baby's) vest (Brit) ou undershirt (US); **~ (de sauvetage)** life jacket [b] (= soutien-gorge) cropped bra; (Can) bra

brasure [brazyr] NF (= procédé) brazing; (= résultat) brazed joint, braze; (= métal) brazing metal

Bratislava [bratislava] N Bratislava

bravache [bravaʃ] [1] NM braggart, blusterer; **faire le ~** to swagger about [2] ADJ swaggering, blustering

bravade [bravad] NF act of bravado; **par ~** out of bravado

brave [brav] [1] ADJ [a] (= courageux) [personne, action] brave, courageous, gallant (littér); **faire le ~** to act brave, put on a bold front [b] (avant n) (= bon) good, nice, fine; (= honnête) decent, honest; **c'est une ~ fille** she's a nice girl; **c'est un ~ garçon** he's a good ou nice fellow ou lad (Brit); **ce sont de ~s gens** they're good ou decent people ou souls; **il est bien ~** he's not a bad chap* (Brit) ou guy* (US), he's a nice enough fellow; **mon ~ (homme)** my good man ou fellow; **ma ~ dame** my good woman [2] NM (gén) brave man; (= Indien) brave; **~ entre les ~s**† bravest of the brave†

bravement [bravmɑ̃] ADV (= courageusement) bravely, courageously, gallantly (littér); (= résolument) boldly

braver [brave] ▸ conjug 1 ◂ VT (= défier) [+ personne] to stand up to; [+ autorité, tabou] to defy; [+ règle] to defy; [+ danger, mort] to brave; **~ l'opinion** to fly in the face of (public) opinion; **~ les océans** to brave the seas

▾ **bravo** [bravo] [1] EXCL (= félicitations) well done!, bravo!; (= approbation) hear! hear!; (iro) well done! [2] NM cheer; **un grand ~ pour ...!** a big cheer for ...!, let's hear it for ...!

bravoure [bravur] NF bravery, braveness, gallantry (littér) → **morceau**

Brazzaville [brazavil] N Brazzaville

break [brɛk] NM [a] (Aut) estate (car) (Brit), station wagon (US) [b] (= pause) break; **(se) donner un ~** to take a break [c] (Boxe, Tennis) break; **balle de ~** break point; **faire le ~** to break

brebis [brəbi] NF (Zool) ewe; (Rel) **les ~** the flock; **~ égarée** stray ou lost sheep; **~ galeuse** black sheep ■ (PROV) **à ~ tondue Dieu mesure le vent** the Lord tempers the wind to the shorn lamb (PROV)

brèche [brɛʃ] NF [mur] breach, opening, gap; (Mil) breach; [lame] notch, nick; (Mil) **faire** ou **ouvrir une ~ dans le front ennemi** to make a breach in ou to breach the enemy line; (fig) **s'engouffrer dans la ~** to leap ou step into the breach; **faire une ~ à sa fortune** to make a hole in one's fortune; (fig) **il est toujours sur la ~** he's always beavering away* → **battre**

bréchet [breʃɛ] NM wishbone

brechtien, -ienne [breʃtjɛ̃, jɛn] ADJ Brechtian

bredouillage [brədujaʒ] NM mumbling

bredouille [brəduj] ADJ (gén) empty-handed; (Chasse, Pêche) **rentrer ~** to go ou come home empty-handed ou with an empty bag

bredouillement [brədujmɑ̃] NM = **bredouillage**

bredouiller [brəduje] ▸ conjug 1 ◂ [1] VI (= bégayer) to stammer; (= marmonner) to mumble [2] VT (= bégayer) to stammer (out); (= marmonner) to mumble

▾ **bref, brève** [brɛf, ɛv] [1] ADJ [rencontre, discours, lettre] brief, short; [voyelle, syllabe] short; **d'un ton ~** sharply, curtly; **soyez ~ et précis** be brief and to the point; **à ~ délai** shortly [2] ADV (enfin) ~ (= pour résumer) to make ou cut (Brit) a long story short, in short, in brief; (= passons) let's not waste any more time; (= donc) anyway; **en ~** in short, in brief [3] NM (Rel) (papal) brief [4] **brève** NF (= syllabe) short syllable; (= voyelle) short vowel; (Journalisme) news sg in brief; **brèves de comptoir** bar-room philosophising (NonC)

brelan [brəlɑ̃] NM (Cartes) three of a kind; **~ d'as** three aces

breloque [brələk] NF (bracelet) charm → **battre**

brème [brɛm] NF [a] (Zool) bream [b] (arg Cartes) card

▸ GRAMMAIRE ACTIVE: **bravo** 40.1, 50.6 **bref** 53.4

brésil [bʀezil] NM [a] (= *bois*) brazil (wood) [b] **Brésil** Brazil

brésilien, -ienne [bʀeziljɛ̃, jɛn] [1] ADJ Brazilian [2] NM (*Ling*) Brazilian Portuguese [3] **Brésilien(ne)** NM,F Brazilian

Bretagne [bʀətaɲ] NF Brittany

bretèche [bʀətɛʃ] NF gatehouse, bartizan

bretelle [bʀətɛl] NF [a] [*sac*] (shoulder) strap; [*lingerie*] strap; [*fusil*] sling; [*pantalon*] **~s** braces (*Brit*), suspenders (*US*); **porter l'arme** *ou* **le fusil à la ~** to carry one's weapon slung over one's shoulder → **remonter** [b] (*Rail*) crossover; (*Aut*) slip road (*Brit*), entrance (*ou* exit) ramp, on (*ou* off) ramp (*US*); **~ de raccordement** access road; **~ de contournement** bypass

breton, -onne [bʀətɔ̃, ɔn] [1] ADJ Breton [2] NM (*Ling*) Breton [3] **Breton(ne)** NM,F Breton

bretonnant, e [bʀətɔnɑ̃, ɑ̃t] ADJ (*Ling*) Breton-speaking; (*attaché aux traditions*) preserving Breton culture

bretteur [bʀetœʀ] NM†† swashbuckler; (= *duelliste*) duellist

bretzel [bʀɛtzɛl] NM pretzel

breuvage [bʀœvaʒ] NM drink, beverage; (*magique*) potion

brève [bʀɛv] ADJ, NF → **bref**

brevet [bʀəvɛ] [1] NM [a] (= *diplôme*) diploma, certificate; (*Hist* = *note royale*) royal warrant; (*Scol*) exam taken at the age of 16, ≈ GCSE (*Brit*); (*Scol*) **avoir son ~** ≈ to have (passed) one's GCSEs (*Brit*) [b] (*Naut*) certificate, ticket; **~ de capitaine** master's certificate *ou* ticket; (*Mil*) **~ de commandant** major's brevet [c] (*Jur*) **~ (d'invention)** letters patent, patent; **~ en cours d'homologation** patent pending [d] (*fig* = *garantie*) guarantee; **donner à qn un ~ d'honnêteté** to testify to *ou* guarantee sb's honesty; **on peut lui décerner un ~ de persévérance** he deserves a medal for perseverance [2] COMP ► **brevet d'apprentissage** ≈ certificate of apprenticeship ► **brevet d'aptitude à la fonction d'animateur** *certificate for activity leaders in a holiday camp* ► **brevet des collèges, brevet d'études du premier cycle**† *exam taken at the age of 16,* ≈ GCSE (*Brit*) ► **brevet d'études professionnelles** *technical school certificate* ► **brevet de pilote** *pilot's licence* ► **brevet de secourisme** *first aid certificate* ► **brevet de technicien** *vocational training certificate taken at age 16* ► **brevet de technicien supérieur** *vocational training certificate taken after the age of 18*

brevetable [bʀəv(ə)tabl] ADJ patentable

breveté, e [bʀəv(ə)te] (*ptp de* **breveter**) [1] ADJ [a] [*invention*] patented; **~ sans garantie du gouvernement** patented (*without official government approval*) [b] (= *diplômé*) [*technicien*] qualified, certificated; (*Mil*) [*officier*] commissioned [2] NM,F (*Admin, Jur*) patentee

breveter [bʀəv(ə)te] ▶ conjug 4 ◀ VT [+ *invention*] to patent; **faire ~ qch** to take out a patent for sth

bréviaire [bʀevjɛʀ] NM (*Rel*) breviary; (*fig*) bible

BRI [beɛʀi] NF (ABRÉV = **Banque des règlements internationaux**) BIS

briard, e [bʀijaʀ, aʀd] [1] ADJ of *ou* from Brie [2] **Briard(e)** NM,F inhabitant *ou* native of Brie [3] NM (= *chien*) Briard (sheepdog)

bribe [bʀib] NF (= *fragment*) bit, scrap; **~s de conversation** snatches of conversation; **~s de nourriture** scraps of food; **les ~s de sa fortune** the remnants of his fortune; **par ~s** in snatches, piecemeal

bric-à-brac [bʀikabʀak] NM INV [a] (= *objets*) bric-a-brac, odds and ends; (*fig*) bric-a-brac, trimmings [b] (= *magasin*) junk shop

bric et de broc [bʀikedbʀɔk] **♦de bric et de broc** LOC ADV (= *de manière disparate*) any old way*, any old how*; **meublé de ~** furnished with bits and pieces *ou* with odds and ends

brick [bʀik] NM [a] (*Naut*) brig [b] (*Culin*) ≈ fritter (*with a filling*); **~ à l'œuf/au thon** egg/tuna fritter

bricolage [bʀikɔlaʒ] NM [a] (= *passe-temps*) do-it-yourself, D.I.Y.* (*Brit*); (= *travaux*) odd jobs; **j'ai du ~ à faire** I've got a few (odd) jobs to do; **rayon ~** do-it-yourself department [b] (= *réparation*) makeshift repair *ou* job; (*péj*) **c'est du ~!** it's a rush job!*

bricole [bʀikɔl] NF [a]* (= *babiole*) trifle; (= *cadeau*) something small, token; (= *menu travail*) easy job, small matter; **il ne reste que des ~s** there are only a few bits and pieces *ou* a few odds and ends; **il ne me reste que quelques ~s à faire** I only have a few odd things left to do; **ça coûte 10 F et des ~s** it costs 10 francs *ou* so; **il va lui arriver des ~s*** he's going to run into trouble [b] [*cheval*] breast harness [c] (*Can* = *bretelles*) **~s*** braces (*Brit*), suspenders (*US*)

bricoler [bʀikɔle] ▶ conjug 1 ◀ [1] VI (*menus travaux*) to do odd jobs, potter about (*Brit*), putter around (*US*); (*réparations*) to do odd repairs, do odd jobs; (*passe-temps*) to tinker about *ou* around; **elle aime ~** she likes D.I.Y.; **j'aime bien ~ dans la maison** I like doing odd jobs around the house [2] VT (= *réparer*) to fix (up), mend; (= *mal réparer*) to tinker *ou* mess (about) with; (= *fabriquer*) to cobble up *ou* together, knock up* (*Brit*)

bricoleur [bʀikɔlœʀ] NM handyman, do-it-yourselfer*, D.I.Y. man* (*Brit*); **il est ~** he's good with his hands, he's very handy*; **je ne suis pas très ~** I'm not much of a handyman

bricoleuse [bʀikɔløz] NF handywoman, do-it-yourselfer*, D.I.Y. woman* (*Brit*)

bride [bʀid] NF [a] (*Équitation*) bridle; **tenir un cheval en ~** to curb a horse; **tenir ses passions/une personne en ~** to keep one's passions/a person in check, keep a tight rein on one's passions/a person; **jeter** *ou* **laisser** *ou* **mettre la ~ sur le cou** *ou* **col à un cheval** to give a horse the reins, give a horse his head; **laisser la ~ sur le cou à qn** to give *ou* leave sb a free hand; **les jeunes ont maintenant la ~ sur le cou** young people can just do as they like nowadays; **tu lui laisses trop la ~ sur le cou** you don't keep a tight enough rein on him; **tenir la ~ haute à un cheval** to rein in a horse; (*fig*) **tenir la ~ à qn** to keep a tight rein on sb; **aller à ~ abattue** *ou* **à toute ~** to ride flat out*, ride hell for leather*; **tourner ~** (*lit*) to turn back; (*fig*) to do an about-turn → **lâcher** [b] [*bonnet*] string; (*en cuir*) strap [c] (*Couture*) [*boutonnière*] bar; [*bouton*] loop; [*dentelle*] string [d] (*Tech*) [*bielle*] strap; [*tuyau*] flange [e] (*Méd*) adhesion

bridé, e [bʀide] (*ptp de* **brider**) ADJ **avoir les yeux ~s** to have slanting *ou* slit eyes

brider [bʀide] ▶ conjug 1 ◀ VT [a] [+ *cheval*] to bridle; [+ *moteur*] to restrain; [+ *impulsion*] to curb, restrain; [*croissance, consommation, investissement, liberté*] to curb; [+ *création, imagination*] to curb, keep in check; [+ *personne*] to keep in check; **~ sa colère** to restrain one's anger; **logiciel bridé** restricted-access software, crippleware*; **il est bridé dans son costume** ◊ **son costume le bride** his suit is too tight for him [b] (*Culin*) to truss [c] [+ *boutonnière*] to bind; [+ *tuyau*] to clamp, flange; (*Naut*) to lash together

bridge¹ [bʀidʒ] NM (*Cartes*) bridge; **~ contrat** contract bridge; **~ aux enchères** auction bridge; **faire un ~** to play *ou* have a game of bridge

bridge² [bʀidʒ] NM (= *prothèse*) bridge

bridger [bʀidʒe] ▶ conjug 3 ◀ VI to play bridge

bridgeur, -euse [bʀidʒœʀ, øz] NM,F bridge player

bridon [bʀidɔ̃] NM snaffle

brie [bʀi] NM Brie (cheese)

briefer [bʀife] ▶ conjug 1 ◀ VT to brief

briefing [bʀifiŋ] NM briefing; **faire un ~ à l'intention de l'équipe de vente** to brief the sales force

brièvement [bʀijɛvmɑ̃] ADV briefly, concisely

brièveté [bʀijɛvte] NF brevity, briefness

brigade [bʀigad] [1] NF (*Mil*) brigade; (*Police*) squad; (*gén* = *équipe*) gang, team [2] COMP ► **brigade anti-émeute** riot police (*NonC*) *ou* squad ► **brigade antigang** anti-terrorist squad ► **brigade canine** dog-handling unit (*in the police*) ► **brigade criminelle** Crime *ou* Murder Squad ► **brigade financière** Fraud Squad ► **brigade de gendarmerie** (*corps*) gendarmerie squad; (*bâtiment*) gendarmerie ► **Brigades internationales** International Brigades ► **brigade des mineurs** juvenile liaison police, juvenile bureau ► **brigade des mœurs, brigade mondaine**† Vice Squad ► **brigade de recherche dans l'intérêt des familles** ≈ missing persons bureau ► **brigade de répression et d'intervention** = brigade anti-gang ► **les Brigades rouges** the Red Brigades ► **brigade de sapeurs-pompiers** fire brigade ► **brigade des stupéfiants** *ou* **des stups*** drug(s) squad ► **brigade volante** flying squad

brigadier [bʀigadje] NM (*Police*) ≈ sergeant; (*Mil*) [*artillerie*] bombardier; [*blindés, cavalerie, train*] corporal; **~-chef** ≈ lance sergeant

brigand [bʀigɑ̃] NM († = *bandit*) brigand, bandit; (*péj* = *filou*) twister, sharpie* (*US*), crook; (*hum* = *enfant*) rascal, imp

brigandage [bʀigɑ̃daʒ] NM (armed) robbery, banditry†, brigandage; **commettre des actes de ~** to engage in robbery with violence; (*fig*) **c'est du ~!** it's daylight robbery!

brigantin [bʀigɑ̃tɛ̃] NM (*Naut*) brig

brigantine [bʀigɑ̃tin] NF (*Naut*) spanker

brigue [bʀig] NF (*littér*) intrigue; **obtenir qch par ~** to get sth by intrigue

briguer [bʀige] ▶ conjug 1 ◀ VT [+ *poste*] to covet, aspire to, bid for; [+ *honneur, faveur*] to aspire after, crave; [+ *amitié*] to court, solicit; [+ *suffrages*] to solicit, canvass (for); **il brigue la succession du président** he has his eye on the presidency; **il brigue un second mandat de président** he is seeking a second term of office as president

brillamment [bʀijamɑ̃] ADV brilliantly; **réussir ~ un examen** to pass an exam with flying colours; **il a ~ remporté les élections** he won the election hands down

brillance [bʀijɑ̃s] NF (*Astron*) brilliance; (= *éclat*) sheen; [*cheveux*] sheen, lustre; [*peau*] shininess; [*tissu*] sheen

brillant, e [bʀijɑ̃, ɑ̃t] [1] ADJ [a] (= *luisant*) shiny; (= *étincelant*) sparkling, bright; [*chaussures*] well-polished, shiny; [*cheveux*] glossy; [*couleur*] bright, brilliant; **elle avait les yeux ~s de fièvre/d'impatience** her eyes were bright with fever/impatience; **il avait les yeux ~s de convoitise/colère** his eyes glittered with envy/anger → **peinture, sou** [b] (= *remarquable*) brilliant, outstanding; [*situation*] excellent; [*carrière*] brilliant; [*succès*] brilliant, dazzling, outstanding; [*avenir*] brilliant, bright; [*conversation*] brilliant, sparkling; **avoir une intelligence ~e** to be outstandingly intelligent, be brilliant; **c'est un ~ orateur** he is a brilliant speaker; **elle a été ~e à l'examen** she did brilliantly in her exam; **sa santé n'est pas ~e** his health isn't too good; **ce n'est pas ~** [*travail*] it's not too good, it's not up to much (*Brit*); [*situation*] it's far from satisfactory

2 NM **a** (= *éclat*) (*étincelant*) sparkle, brightness; (*luisant*) shine; [*cheveux*] glossiness; [*couleur*] brightness, brilliance; [*étoffe*] sheen; (*par usure*) shine; **le ~ de son esprit/style** the brilliance of his mind/style; **donner du ~ à un cuir** to polish up a piece of leather **b** (= *diamant*) brilliant; **taillé/monté en ~** cut/mounted as a brilliant **c** (= *cosmétique*) **~ à lèvres** lip gloss

brillantine [bʀijɑ̃tin] NF brilliantine

briller [bʀije] ▸conjug 1◂ VI **a** (*gén*) [*lumière, soleil*] to shine; [*diamant, eau*] to sparkle, glitter; [*étoile*] to twinkle, shine (brightly); [*métal*] to glint, shine; [*feu, braises*] to glow (brightly); [*flammes*] to blaze; [*éclair*] to flash; [*chaussures*] to shine; [*surface polie, humide*] to shine, glisten, **frotte fort, il faut que ça brille** rub hard, it's got to have a good shine on it; **faire ~ les meubles/l'argenterie** to polish the furniture/the silver; **faire ~ ses chaussures** to shine *ou* polish one's shoes; **tout brille dans sa salle de bains** everything is spick and span in his bathroom; **faire ~ les avantages de qch à qn** to paint a glowing picture of sth to sb → **tout** **b** [*yeux*] to shine, sparkle; [*nez, peau*] to be shiny; [*larmes*] to glisten; **ses yeux brillaient de joie** his eyes sparkled with joy; **ses yeux brillaient de convoitise** his eyes glinted greedily **c** [*personne*] to shine, stand out; **~ en société** to be a success in society; **~ à un examen** to do brilliantly in an exam, come through an exam with flying colours; **~ par son talent/éloquence** to be outstandingly talented/eloquent; **il ne brille pas par le courage/la modestie** courage/modesty is not his strong point *ou* his forte; **~ par son absence** to be conspicuous by one's absence; **le désir de ~** the longing to stand out (from the crowd), the desire to be the centre of attention

brimade [bʀimad] NF (= *vexation*) vexation; (*Mil, Scol: d'initiation*) ragging (*NonC*) (*Brit*), hazing (*NonC*) (*US*); **faire subir des ~s à qn** to harry sb, harass sb; (*Mil, Scol*) to rag sb (*Brit*), haze sb (*US*)

brimbalement* [bʀɛ̃balmɑ̃] NM = **bringuebalement**

brimbaler* [bʀɛ̃bale] ▸conjug 1◂ VI, VT = **bringuebaler**

brimborion [bʀɛ̃bɔʀjɔ̃] NM (= *colifichet*) bauble, trinket

brimer [bʀime] ▸conjug 1◂ VT (= *soumettre à des vexations*) to aggravate, bully; (*Mil, Scol*) [+ *nouveaux*] to rag (*Brit*), haze (*US*); **il se sent brimé** he feels he's being got at* (*Brit*) *ou* gotten at* (*US*), he feels he's being done down* (*Brit*); **je suis brimé*** I'm being got* (*Brit*) *ou* gotten at* (*US*), I'm being done down* (*Brit*)

brin [bʀɛ̃] NM **a** [*blé, herbe*] blade; [*bruyère, mimosa, muguet*] sprig; [*osier*] twig; [*paille*] wisp; (*fig*) **un beau ~ de fille** a fine-looking girl **b** [*chanvre, lin*] yarn, fibre; [*corde, fil, laine*] strand **c** (= *un peu*) **un ~ de** a touch *ou* grain *ou* bit of; **il n'a pas un ~ de bon sens** he hasn't got an ounce *ou* a grain of common sense; **avec un ~ de nostalgie** with a touch *ou* hint of nostalgia; **il y a en lui un ~ de folie/méchanceté** there's a touch of madness/malice in him; **faire un ~ de causette** to have a bit of a chat*, have a little chat; **faire un ~ de cour à une femme** to flirt a little with a woman; **faire un ~ de toilette** to have a quick wash; **il n'y a pas un ~ de vent** there isn't a breath of wind; **s'amuser un ~** to have a bit of fun; **un ~ plus grand/haut** a bit *ou* a little *ou* a fraction *ou* a shade bigger/higher; **je suis un ~ embêté*** I'm a trifle *ou* a shade worried **d** (*Radio*) [*antenne*] wire

brindille [bʀɛ̃dij] NF twig

bringue¹* [bʀɛ̃g] NF **grande ~** beanpole*

bringue²* [bʀɛ̃g] NF **faire la ~** to have a wild time; **~ à tout casser** rave-up* (*Brit*), hot party (*US*)

bringuebalement* [bʀɛ̃g(ə)balmɑ̃] **brinquebalement*** [bʀɛ̃kbalmɑ̃] NM (= *mouvement*) shaking (about); (= *bruit*) rattle

bringuebaler* [bʀɛ̃g(ə)bale] **brinquebaler*** [bʀɛ̃kbale] ▸conjug 1◂ VI **[***tête***]** to shake about, joggle; [*voiture*] to shake *ou* jolt about, joggle; (*avec bruit*) to rattle; **une vieille auto toute bringuebalante** a ramshackle *ou* broken-down old car; **il y a à quelque chose qui bringuebale dans ce paquet** something is rattling in this packet **2** VT to cart (about)

brio [bʀijo] NM (= *virtuosité*) brilliance; (*Mus*) brio; **avec ~** (*Mus*) with con brio; **réussir un examen) with flying colours; **faire qch avec ~** to do sth brilliantly, carry sth off with great panache

brioche [bʀijɔʃ] NF brioche; **jambon en ~** ham in a pastry case; (*fig*) **prendre de la ~*** to develop a paunch, get a bit of a tummy*

brioché, e [bʀijɔʃe] ADJ (baked) like a brioche → **pain**

brique [bʀik] **1** NF **a** (*Constr*) brick; [*savon*] bar, cake; [*tourbe*] block, slab; [*lait*] carton; **mur de** *ou* **en ~(s)** brick wall; **~ pleine/creuse** solid/hollow brick; (*fig*) **bouffer des ~s‡** to have nothing to eat **b** (* = *dix mille francs*) **une ~** ten thousand francs **c** (*Naut*) **~ à pont** holystone **2** ADJ INV brick red

briquer [bʀike] ▸conjug 1◂ VT* to polish up; (*Naut*) to holystone, scrub down

briquet¹ [bʀikɛ] NM (cigarette) lighter; **~-tempête** windproof lighter → **battre**

briquet² [bʀikɛ] NM (*Zool*) beagle

briquetage [bʀik(ə)taʒ] NM (= *mur*) brickwork; (= *enduit*) imitation brickwork

briqueter [bʀik(ə)te] ▸conjug 4◂ VT **a** (= *bâtir*) to brick, build with bricks **b** (= *peindre*) to face with imitation brickwork

briqueterie [bʀik(ə)tʀi] NF brickyard, brickfield

briqueteur [bʀik(ə)tœʀ] NM bricklayer

briquetier [bʀik(ə)tje] NM (= *ouvrier*) brickyard worker, brickmaker; (= *entrepreneur*) brick merchant

briquette [bʀikɛt] NF briquette; **c'est de la ~*** it's not up to much (*Brit*)

bris [bʀi] NM breaking; (*Jur*) **~ de clôture** trespass, breaking-in; (*Aut*) **~ de glaces** broken windows; (*Jur*) **~ de scellés** breaking of seals

brisant, e [bʀizɑ̃, ɑ̃t] **1** ADJ high-explosive (*épith*); **obus ~** high-explosive shell **2** NM **a** (= *vague*) breaker **b** (= *écueil*) shoal, reef **c** (= *brise-lames*) groyne, breakwater

briscard [bʀiskaʀ] NM (*Hist Mil*) veteran, old soldier; **c'est un vieux ~*** de la politique he's a veteran of *ou* an old hand in politics

brise [bʀiz] NF breeze; **~ de mer/terre** sea/land breeze

brisé, e [bʀize] (*ptp de* **briser**) ADJ **~ (de fatigue)** worn out, exhausted; **~ (de chagrin)** overcome by sorrow, brokenhearted → **arc, ligne¹, pâte**

brise-bise [bʀizbiz] NM INV half-curtain

brisées [bʀize] NFPL **marcher sur les ~ de qn** to poach *ou* intrude on sb's preserve *ou* territory; **suivre les ~ de qn** to follow in sb's footsteps

brise-fer [bʀizfɛʀ] NMF INV **cet enfant est un vrai ~!** that child is a real little vandal!

brise-glace (*pl* **brise-glaces**) [bʀizglas] NM (= *navire*) icebreaker; [*pont*] icebreaker, ice apron

brise-jet (*pl* **brise-jets**) [bʀizʒe] NM tap swirl (*Brit*), anti-splash faucet nozzle (*US*)

brise-lame(s) (*pl* **brise-lames**) [bʀizlam] NM breakwater, mole

brise-motte(s) (*pl* **brise-mottes**) [bʀizmɔt] NM harrow

briser [bʀize] ▸conjug 1◂ **1** VT **a** (= *casser*) [+ *objet*] to break, smash; [+ *mottes de terre*] to break up; [+ *chaîne, fers*] to break; **~ qch en mille morceaux** to smash sth to smithereens, break sth into little pieces *ou* bits, shatter sth (into little pieces); (*lit, fig*) **~ la glace** to break the ice **b** (= *saper, détruire*) [+ *carrière, vie*] to ruin, wreck; [+ *personne*] (= *épuiser*) to tire out, exhaust; [+ *abattre la volonté de*] to break, crush; [+ *espérance*] to smash, shatter, crush; [+ *cœur, courage*] to break; [+ *traité, accord*] to break; [+ *amitié*] to break up, bring to an end; **~ l'élan de qn** to kill sb's enthusiasm; **d'une voix brisée par l'émotion** in a voice choked with emotion; **ces épreuves l'ont brisé** these trials and tribulations have left him a broken man; **il en a eu le cœur brisé** it broke his heart, he was heartbroken about it; **chagrin qui brise le cœur** heartbreaking grief *ou* sorrow; **tu me les brises!‡** you're really pissing me off**, you're really getting on my tits!** (*Brit*) **c** (= *avoir raison de*) [+ *volonté*] to break, crush; [+ *rebelle*] to crush, subdue; [+ *opposition, résistance*] to crush, break down; [+ *grève*] to break (up); [+ *révolte*] to crush, quell; **il était décidé à ~ les menées de ces conspirateurs** he was determined to put a stop to *ou* to put paid to (*Brit*) the schemings of these conspirators **d** (= *mettre fin à*) [+ *silence, rythme*] to break; (*frm*) [+ *entretien*] to break off **2** VI (*littér*) **a** (= *rompre*) **~ avec qn** to break with sb; **brisons là!†** enough said! **b** (= *déferler*) [*vagues*] to break **3** **se briser** VPR **a** [*vitre, verre*] to break, shatter, smash; [*bâton, canne*] to break, snap **b** [*vagues*] to break (**contre** against) **c** [*résistance*] to break down, snap; [*assaut*] to break up (**sur** on, **contre** against); [*espoir*] to be dashed; **nos efforts se sont brisés sur cette difficulté** our efforts were frustrated *ou* thwarted by this difficulty **d** [*cœur*] to break, be broken; [*voix*] to falter, break

brise-soleil [bʀizsɔlej] NM INV (slatted) canopy *ou* awning

brise-tout [bʀiztu] NMF INV (= *maladroit*) butterfingers*; **cet enfant est un vrai ~!** that child is a real little vandal!

briseur, -euse [bʀizœʀ, øz] NM,F breaker, wrecker; **~ de grève** strikebreaker

brise-vent (*pl* **brise-vent(s)**) [bʀizvɑ̃] NM windbreak

brisquard [bʀiskaʀ] NM = **briscard**

bristol [bʀistɔl] NM (= *papier*) Bristol board; (= *carte de visite*) visiting card

brisure [bʀizyʀ] NF (= *cassure*) break, crack; [*charnière*] joint, break; (*Hér*) mark of cadency, brisure; (*Culin*) **~s de riz** rice which has not been sorted and is of inconsistent quality

britannique [bʀitanik] **1** ADJ British **2** **Britannique** NMF British person, Britisher (*US*), Briton; **c'est un Britannique** he's British *ou* a Britisher (*US*); **les Britanniques** the British, British people

brittonique [bʀitɔnik] ADJ, NM Brythonic, Brittonic

broc [bʀo] NM pitcher, ewer

brocante [bʀɔkɑ̃t] NF (= *commerce*) secondhand trade, secondhand market; (= *objets*) secondhand goods; **il est dans la ~** he deals in secondhand goods; **acheter qch à la ~** to buy sth at the flea market

brocanter [bʀɔkɑ̃te] ▸conjug 1◂ VI to deal in secondhand goods

brocanteur, -euse [bʀɔkɑ̃tœʀ, øz] NM,F secondhand goods dealer

brocard¹ [bʀɔkaʀ] NM (*Zool*) brocket

brocard² [bʀɔkaʀ] NM († = *moquerie*) gibe, taunt

brocarder [bʀɔkaʀde] ▶conjug 1◀ VT† to gibe at, taunt

brocart [bʀɔkaʀ] NM brocade

brochage [bʀɔʃaʒ] NM [a] (*Imprim*) binding (*with paper*); [b] (*Tex*) brocading [c] (*Tech*) broaching

broche [bʀɔʃ] NF [a] (= *bijou*) brooch [b] (*Culin*) spit; (*Tex*) spindle; (*Tech*) drift, pin, broach; (*Élec*) pin; (*Méd*) pin; (*Alpinisme*) **~ (à glace)** ice piton; (*Culin*) **faire cuire à la ~** to spit-roast; **poulet/agneau à la ~** spit-roasted chicken/lamb

broché, e [bʀɔʃe] (*ptp de* **brocher**) [1] NM (*Tex*) (= *procédé*) brocading; (= *tissu*) brocade [2] ADJ **livre ~** paperback; **édition ~e** paperback edition, book with paperback cover

brocher [bʀɔʃe] ▶conjug 1◀ VT [a] (*Imprim*) to bind (*with paper*), put a paperback cover on [b] (*Tex*) to brocade; **tissu broché d'or** gold brocade [c] (*Tech*) to broach

brochet [bʀɔʃɛ] NM (*Zool*) pike

brochette [bʀɔʃɛt] NF (*Culin*) (= *ustensile*) skewer; (= *plat*) kebab, brochette; **rognons en ~** kidney kebab; **~ de décorations** row of medals; **~ de personnalités/de criminels** bunch of VIPs/criminals

brocheur, -euse [bʀɔʃœʀ, øz] [1] NM,F (= *personne*) (*Imprim*) book binder; (*Tex*) brocade weaver [2] NM (*Tex* = *machine*) brocade loom [3] **brocheuse** NF (*Imprim* = *machine*) binder, binding machine

brochure [bʀɔʃyʀ] NF [a] (= *magazine*) brochure, booklet, pamphlet; **~ touristique** tourist brochure [b] [*livre*] (*paper*) binding [c] (*Tex*) brocaded pattern *ou* figures

brocoli [bʀɔkɔli] NM broccoli

brodequin [bʀɔd(ə)kɛ̃] NM (*laced*) boot; (*Hist Théât*) buskin, sock; (*Hist* = *supplice*) **les ~s** the boot

broder [bʀɔde] ▶conjug 1◀ [1] VT [+ *tissu*] to embroider (**de** with); [+ *récit*] to embroider [2] VI (= *exagérer*) to embroider, embellish; (= *trop développer*) to elaborate; **~ sur un sujet** to elaborate on a subject

broderie [bʀɔdʀi] NF (= *art*) embroidery; (= *objet*) piece of embroidery, embroidery (*NonC*); (= *industrie*) embroidery trade; **faire de la ~** to embroider, do embroidery; **~ anglaise** broderie anglaise

brodeur [bʀɔdœʀ] NM embroiderer

brodeuse [bʀɔdøz] NF (= *ouvrière*) embroideress; (= *machine*) embroidery machine

broiement [bʀwamɑ̃] NM = **broyage**

bromate [bʀɔmat] NM bromate

brome [bʀɔm] NM (*Chim*) bromine

bromique [bʀɔmik] ADJ bromic

bromure [bʀɔmyʀ] NM [a] (*Chim*) bromide; **~ d'argent/de potassium** silver/potassium bromide [b] (= *papier*) bromide paper; (= *épreuve*) bromide (proof)

bronca [bʀɔ̃ka] NF (*dans une arène*) cheering; (= *huées de mécontentement*) booing

bronche [bʀɔ̃ʃ] NF bronchus (*SPÉC*); **les ~s** the bronchial tubes; **il est faible des ~s** he has a weak chest

broncher [bʀɔ̃ʃe] ▶conjug 1◀ VI [*cheval*] to stumble; **personne n'osait ~*** no one dared move a muscle *ou* say a word; **le premier qui bronche ...!*** the first person to budge ...!* *ou* make a move ...!; **sans ~** (= *sans peur*) without turning a hair, without flinching; (* = *sans protester*) uncomplainingly, meekly; (* = *sans se tromper*) faultlessly, without faltering

bronchiole [bʀɔ̃ʃjɔl] NF (*Anat*) bronchiole

bronchique [bʀɔ̃ʃik] ADJ bronchial

bronchite [bʀɔ̃ʃit] NF bronchitis (*NonC*); **avoir une bonne ~** to have (got) a bad bout *ou* attack of bronchitis

bronchiteux, -euse [bʀɔ̃ʃitø, øz] [1] ADJ [*personne*] suffering from bronchitis, bronchitic (*SPÉC*) [2] NM,F person suffering from bronchitis, bronchitic (*SPÉC*)

bronchitique [bʀɔ̃ʃitik] ADJ bronchitic (*SPÉC*); **il est ~** he suffers from bronchitis

bronchopneumonie [bʀɔ̃kɔpnœmɔni] NF bronchopneumonia (*NonC*)

brontosaure [bʀɔ̃tozɔʀ] NM brontosaurus

bronzage [bʀɔ̃zaʒ] NM [a] [*peau*] (sun) tan; **~ intégral** allover tan; **séance de ~ artificiel** tanning session [b] [*métal*] bronzing

bronzant, e [bʀɔ̃zɑ̃, ɑ̃t] ADJ [*lait, lotion*] tanning (*épith*), suntan (*épith*)

bronze [bʀɔ̃z] NM (= *métal, objet*) bronze

bronzé, e [bʀɔ̃ze] (*ptp de* **bronzer**) ADJ (sun)tanned, sunburnt (*Brit*)

bronzer [bʀɔ̃ze] ▶conjug 1◀ [1] VT [+ *peau*] to tan; [+ *métal*] to bronze [2] VI [*peau, personne*] to get a tan; **les gens qui (se) bronzent** *ou* **se font ~ sur la plage** people who sunbathe on the beach; **je bronze vite** I tan easily

bronzette* [bʀɔ̃zɛt] NF **faire de la ~** to do a bit of sunbathing

bronzeur [bʀɔ̃zœʀ] NM (= *fondeur*) bronze-smelter; (= *fabricant*) bronze-smith

broquette [bʀɔkɛt] NF (= *clou*) tack

brossage [bʀɔsaʒ] NM brushing

brosse [bʀɔs] [1] NF [a] (= *ustensile*) brush; [*peintre*] (paint)brush; **donne un coup de ~ à ta veste** give your jacket a brush; **passer le tapis à la ~** to give the carpet a brush, brush the carpet; **passer le carrelage à la ~** to give the (stone) floor a scrub; **passer la ~ à reluire à qn** to suck up to sb*; **il sait manier la ~ à reluire** he really knows how to suck up to people* *ou* butter people up [b] (*Coiffure*) crew cut; **avoir les cheveux en ~** to have a crew cut (*Can*) **prendre une ~:** to get drunk *ou* smashed: [2] COMP ▶ **brosse à chaussures** shoebrush ▶ **brosse à cheveux** hairbrush ▶ **brosse en chiendent** scrubbing brush ▶ **brosse à dents** toothbrush ▶ **brosse à habits** clothesbrush ▶ **brosse métallique** wire brush ▶ **brosse à ongles** nailbrush

brosser [bʀɔse] ▶conjug 1◀ [1] VT [a] (= *nettoyer*) to brush; [+ *cheval*] to brush down; [+ *plancher, carrelage*] to scrub; **viens ici que je te brosse** come here and let me give you a brush; **~ des miettes sur une table** to brush crumbs off a table [b] (*Art, fig* = *peindre*) to paint; **~ un vaste tableau de la situation** to paint a broad picture of the situation [c] (*Sport*) [+ *balle*] to put spin on [d] (*: *Belg*) [+ *cours*] to skip [2] **se brosser** VPR [a] (= *frotter*) to brush one's clothes, give one's clothes a brush; **se ~ les dents** to brush *ou* clean one's teeth; **se ~ les cheveux** to brush one's hair [b] (*: *loc*) **se ~ le ventre** to go without food; **tu peux (toujours) te ~!** you'll have to do without!, nothing doing!:, you can whistle for it!:

brosserie [bʀɔsʀi] NF (= *usine*) brush factory; (= *commerce*) brush trade

brossier, -ière [bʀɔsje, jɛʀ] NM,F (= *ouvrier*) brush maker; (= *commerçant*) brush dealer

brou [bʀu] NM (= *écorce*) husk, shuck (*US*); **~ de noix** (*Menuiserie*) walnut stain; (= *liqueur*) walnut liqueur

broue: [bʀu] NF (*Can*) [*bière*] froth; [*mer*] foam

brouet [bʀuɛ] NM (†† = *potage*) gruel; (*péj ou hum*) brew

brouette [bʀuɛt] NF wheelbarrow

brouettée [bʀuete] NF (wheel)barrowful

brouetter [bʀuete] ▶conjug 1◀ VT to (carry in a) wheelbarrow

brouhaha [bʀuaa] NM (= *tintamarre*) hubbub

brouillage [bʀujaʒ] NM (*Radio*) (*intentionnel*) jamming; (*accidentel*) interference; (*TV*) scrambling; (*fig*) [*points de repère*] blurring; **~ des pistes** confusion

brouillard [bʀujaʀ] NM [a] (*dense*) fog; (*léger*) mist; (*mêlé de fumée*) smog; **~ de chaleur** heat haze; **~ givrant** freezing fog; **~ à couper au couteau** thick *ou* dense fog, peasouper*; **il fait** *ou* **il y a du ~** it's foggy; (*fig*) **être dans le ~** to be in the dark → **foncer¹** [b] (*Comm*) daybook

brouillasser [bʀujase] ▶conjug 1◀ VI to drizzle

brouille [bʀuj] NF disagreement, breach, quarrel; **~ légère** tiff; **être en ~ avec qn** to have fallen out with sb, be on bad terms with sb

brouillé, e [bʀuje] (*ptp de* **brouiller**) ADJ [a] (= *fâché*) **être ~ avec qn** to have fallen out with sb, be on bad terms with sb; **être ~ avec les dates/l'orthographe*** to be hopeless *ou* useless* at dates/spelling [b] **avoir le teint ~** to have a muddy complexion → **œuf**

brouiller [bʀuje] ▶conjug 1◀ [1] VT [a] (= *troubler*) [+ *contour, vue, yeux*] to blur; [+ *papiers, idées*] to mix up, muddle up; [+ *combinaison de coffre*] to scramble; [+ *message*] (*lit*) to scramble; (*fig*) to confuse; [+ *frontières, repères*] to blur; **la buée brouille les verres de mes lunettes** my glasses are misting up; **la pluie a brouillé l'adresse** the rain has smudged *ou* blurred the address; **~ les pistes** *ou* **cartes** to confuse *ou* cloud the issue; **cette déclaration a brouillé l'image du président** the statement has tarnished the president's image [b] (= *fâcher*) to set at odds, put on bad terms; **cet incident l'a brouillé avec sa famille** the incident set him at odds with *ou* put him on bad terms with his family; **elle m'a brouillé avec l'informatique** she really put me off computers [c] (*Radio*) [+ *émission*] (*volontairement*) to jam; (*par accident*) to cause interference to; (*TV*) to scramble [2] **se brouiller** VPR [a] (= *se troubler*) [*vue*] to become blurred; [*souvenirs, idées*] to get mixed up *ou* muddled up, become confused; **tout se brouilla dans sa tête** everything became confused *ou* muddled in his mind [b] (= *se fâcher*) **se ~ avec qn** to fall out *ou* quarrel with sb; **depuis qu'ils se sont brouillés** since they fell out (with each other) [c] (*Mét*) [*ciel*] to cloud over; **le temps se brouille** it's going *ou* turning cloudy, the weather is breaking

brouillerie [bʀujʀi] NF = **brouille**

brouilleur [bʀujœʀ] NM jammer

brouillon, -onne [bʀujɔ̃, ɔn] [1] ADJ (= *qui manque de soin*) untidy; (= *qui manque d'organisation*) unmethodical, unsystematic, muddle-headed; **élève ~** careless pupil; **avoir l'esprit ~** to be muddle-headed [2] NM,F (= *personne*) muddler, muddlehead [3] NM [*lettre, devoir*] rough copy; (= *ébauche*) (rough) draft; [*calculs, notes*] rough work; (*papier*) **~** rough paper; **prendre qch au ~** to make a rough copy of sth → **cahier**

broum [bʀum] EXCL brum

broussaille [bʀusaj] NF **~s** undergrowth, brushwood, scrub; **avoir les cheveux en ~** to have tousled hair; **sourcils en ~** bushy eyebrows

broussailleux, -euse [bʀusajø, øz] ADJ [*terrain, sous-bois*] bushy, scrubby; [*ronces*] brambly; [*jardin*] overgrown; [*sourcils, barbe*] bushy; [*cheveux*] bushy, tousled

broussard* [bʀusaʀ] NM bushman

brousse [bʀus] NF **la ~** the bush; (*fig*) **c'est en pleine ~*** it's at the back of beyond*, it's in the middle of nowhere

broutage [bʀutaʒ] NM = **broutement**

broutard [bʀutaʀ] NM grass-fed calf

broutement [bʀutmɑ̃] NM [a] [*mouton*] grazing; [*lapin*] nibbling; [*vache, cerf*] browsing [b] [*rabot*] chattering

brouter [bʀute] ▸conjug 1◂ ① VT ⓐ [+ *herbe*] to graze on, browse on ⓑ* [+ *sexe féminin*] to go down on*⁑; **il nous les broute!** he's a fucking pain in the neck! ② VI ⓐ [*mouton, vache, cerf*] to graze, browse ⓑ (*Tech*) [*rabot*] to chatter ⓒ [*freins*] to grab; [*embrayage, voiture*] to judder

broutille [bʀutij] NF (= *bagatelle*) trifle; **c'est de la ~*** (*de mauvaise qualité*) it's just junk, it's cheap rubbish (*Brit*); (*sans importance*) it's not worth mentioning, it's nothing of any consequence; **perdre son temps à des ~s** to lose one's time over trifles *ou* trivial matters

brownie [bʀɔni] NM (*Culin*) brownie

brownien, -ienne [bʀɔnjɛ̃, jɛn] ADJ [*mouvement, particules*] Brownian; (*fig*) **agité de mouvements ~s** rushing about in all directions

broyage [bʀwajaʒ] NM ⓐ [*pierre, sucre, os*] grinding, crushing; [*poivre, blé, couleurs*] grinding ⓑ [*chanvre, lin*] braking

broyer [bʀwaje] ▸conjug 8◂ VT ⓐ (= *concasser*) [+ *pierre, sucre, os*] to grind (to a powder), crush; [+ *poivre, blé, couleurs*] to grind ⓑ (= *mastiquer*) [+ *aliments*] to grind, break up; **~ du noir** to mope, brood ⓒ [+ *chanvre, lin*] to brake; [+ *doigt, main*] to crush; **il a été broyé par une machine** he was crushed to death in a machine

broyeur, -euse [bʀwajœʀ, øz] ① ADJ crushing, grinding ② NM (= *ouvrier*) grinder, crusher; (= *machine*) grinder, crusher; [*chanvre, lin*] brake; **~ (de cailloux)** pebble grinder

brrr [bʀʀ] EXCL brr!

bru [bʀy] NF daughter-in-law

bruant [bʀyɑ̃] NM bunting (*bird*); **~ jaune** yellowhammer; **des roseaux** reed bunting

brucelles [bʀysɛl] NFPL tweezers

brucellose [bʀyseloz] NF brucellosis

brugnon [bʀyɲɔ̃] NM nectarine

brugnonier [bʀyɲɔnje] NM nectarine tree

bruine [bʀyin] NF (fine) drizzle, Scotch mist

bruiner [bʀyine] ▸conjug 1◂ VI to drizzle

bruineux, -euse [bʀyinø, øz] ADJ drizzly

bruire [bʀyiʀ] ▸conjug 2◂ VI [*feuilles, tissu, vent*] to rustle; [*ruisseau*] to murmur; [*insecte*] to buzz, hum; **le marché financier s'est mis à ~ des rumeurs les plus bizarres** the money market has started buzzing with the strangest rumours

bruissement [bʀyismɑ̃] NM [*feuilles, tissu, vent*] rustle, rustling; [*ruisseau*] murmur; [*insecte*] buzz(ing), humming

bruit [bʀyi] NM ⓐ (*gén*) sound, noise; (*désagréable*) noise; **j'ai entendu un ~** I heard a noise; **un ~ de vaisselle** the clatter of dishes; **un ~ *ou* des ~s de moteur/voix** the sound of an engine/of voices; **un ~ *ou* des ~s de marteau** (the sound of) hammering; **un ~ de verre brisé** the tinkle *ou* sound of broken glass; **un ~ de pas** (the sound of) footsteps; **le ~ d'un plongeon** a splash; **le ~ de la pluie contre les vitres** the sound *ou* patter of the rain against the windows; **le ~ des radios** the noise *ou* blare of radios; **les ~s de la rue** street noises; **le ~ de fond** background noise; **le ~ familier des camions** the familiar rumble of the lorries; **~ sourd** thud; **~ strident** screech, shriek; **on n'entend aucun ~ d'ici** you can't hear a sound from here; **passer dans un ~ de tonnerre** to thunder past ⓑ (*opposé à silence*) **le ~** noise; **j'ai entendu du ~** I heard a noise; **il y a trop de ~** there's too much noise, it's too noisy; **je ne peux pas travailler dans le ~** I can't work in a noisy environment; **le ~ est insupportable ici** the noise is unbearable here; **sans ~** noiselessly, without a sound, silently; **faire du ~** [*objet, machine*] to make a *ou* some noise; **les enfants font du ~, c'est normal** it's natural for children to be noisy; **arrêtez de faire du ~** stop

being so noisy; **cette machine fait un ~ infernal** this machine makes a dreadful noise *ou* racket* ⓒ (= *perturbation*) **beaucoup de ~ pour rien** much ado about nothing, a lot of fuss about nothing; **faire grand ~** [*affaire, déclaration, film, nouvelle*] to cause quite a stir; **faire grand ~ *ou* beaucoup de ~ autour de qch** to make a great fuss *ou* to-do about sth; **cette nouvelle a été annoncée à grand ~** the news was announced amid much publicity *ou* fanfare; **il fait plus de ~ que de mal** his bark is worse than his bite ⓓ (= *nouvelle*) rumour; **le ~ de son départ ...** the rumour of his departure ...; **le ~ court qu'il doit partir** there's a rumour going about that he is to leave; **c'est un ~ qui court** it's a rumour that's going around; **c'est un ~ qui court** it's a rumour that's going around; **se faire l'écho d'un ~** to repeat a rumour; **répandre de faux ~s (sur)** to spread false rumours *ou* tales (about); **les ~s de couloir à l'Assemblée nationale** parliamentary rumours; **~s de guerre** rumours of war; **~ de bottes** sabre-rattling; **il n'est ~ †† dans la ville que de son arrivée** his arrival is the talk of the town, his arrival has set the town agog ⓔ (*Téléc*) noise; (*Méd*) **~ de souffle** murmur; (*Méd*) **~ de galop** galop rhythm

bruitage [bʀyitaʒ] NM sound effects

bruiter [bʀyite] ▸conjug 1◂ VT to add the sound effects to

bruiteur, -euse [bʀyitœʀ, øz] NM,F sound-effects engineer

brûlage [bʀylaʒ] NM [*cheveux*] singeing; [*café*] roasting; [*herbes*] burning; **faire un ~ à qn** to singe sb's hair

brûlant, e [bʀylɑ̃, ɑ̃t] ADJ ⓐ (= *chaud*) [*objet*] burning (hot), red-hot; [*plat*] burning (hot), red-hot; [*liquide*] boiling (hot), scalding; [*soleil*] scorching, blazing; [*air*] burning; **il a le front ~ (de fièvre)** his forehead is burning (with fever) ⓑ (= *passionné*) [*regard, pages*] fiery, impassioned ⓒ (= *controversé*) [*sujet*] highly topical; **être sur un terrain ~** to touch on a hotly debated issue; **c'est d'une actualité ~e** it's the burning question *ou* issue of the hour

brûlé, e [bʀyle] (*ptp de brûler*) ① ADJ **il est ~*** (*gén*) he's had* *ou* blown* it; [*espion*] his cover is blown* ② NM,F ⓐ [*crème, terre, tête*] ② NM,F (= *personne*) burnt person; **grand ~** victim of third-degree burns, badly burnt person ③ NM **ça sent le ~** (*lit*) there's a smell of burning; (*fig*) there's trouble brewing; **cela a un goût de ~** it tastes burnt *ou* has a burnt taste

brûle-gueule (*pl* **brûle-gueules**) [bʀylgœl] NM short (clay) pipe

brûle-parfum (*pl* **brûle-parfums**) [bʀylpaʀfœ̃] NM perfume burner

brûle-pourpoint [bʀylpuʀpwɛ̃] **▸à brûle-pourpoint** LOC ADV ⓐ (= *brusquement*) point-blank ⓑ († = *à bout portant*) at point-blank range

brûler [bʀyle] ▸conjug 1◂ ① VT ⓐ (= *détruire*) [+ *objet, ordures, corps*] to burn; [+ *maison, village*] to burn down; **être brûlé vif** (*accident*) to be burnt alive *ou* burnt to death; (*supplice*) to be burnt at the stake; (*fig*) **il a brûlé ses dernières cartouches** he's shot his bolt; (*fig*) **~ ses vaisseaux** to burn one's bridges *ou* one's boats (*Brit*); **~ le pavé†** to ride *ou* run hell for leather*; (*Théât*) **~ les planches** to give a spirited performance; **~ ce que l'on a adoré** to burn one's old idols ⓑ (= *endommager*) [*flamme*] to burn; [*eau bouillante*] to scald; [*fer à repasser*] to singe, scorch; [*soleil*] [+ *herbe*] to scorch; [+ *peau*] to burn; [*gel*] [+ *bourgeon*] to nip, damage; [*acide*] [+ *peau*] to burn, sear; [+ *métal*] to burn, attack, corrode; **il a la peau brûlée par le soleil** his skin is sunburnt; **le soleil nous brûle** the sun is scorching *ou* burning ⓒ (= *traiter*) [+ *café*] to roast; [+ *pointes de cheveux*] to singe; (*Méd*) to cauterize

ⓓ (= *consommer*) [+ *électricité, charbon*] to burn, use; [+ *cierge, encens, calories*] to burn; **ils ont brûlé tout leur bois** they've burnt up *ou* used up all their wood; **~ la chandelle par les deux bouts** to burn the candle at both ends; (*hum*) **j'irai ~ un cierge pour toi** I'll go and light a candle for you, I'll cross my fingers for you ⓔ (= *ignorer*) (*Aut*) **~ un stop** to ignore a stop sign; **~ un feu rouge** to go through a red light, run a red light (*US*); (*Rail*) **~ un signal/une station** to go through *ou* past a signal/a station (without stopping); **~ une étape** to cut out a stop; (*fig*) **~ les étapes** (= *réussir rapidement*) to shoot ahead; (= *trop se précipiter*) to cut corners, take short cuts; **~ la politesse à qn** to leave sb abruptly (without saying goodbye) ⓕ (= *donner une sensation de brûlure*) to burn; **le radiateur me brûlait le dos** the radiator was burning *ou* scorching my back; **j'ai les yeux qui me brûlent ◊ les yeux me brûlent** my eyes are smarting *ou* stinging; **j'ai la figure qui (me) brûle** my face is burning; **la gorge lui brûle** he's got a burning sensation in his throat; **l'argent lui brûle les doigts** money burns a hole in his pocket; **cette question me brûlait les lèvres** I was dying to ask that question

② VI ⓐ [*charbon, feu*] to burn; [*maison, forêt*] to be on fire; (*Culin*) to burn; **ce bois brûle très vite** this wood burns (up) very quickly; **j'ai laissé ~ le rôti** I burnt the roast; **on a laissé ~ l'électricité *ou* l'électricité a brûlé toute la journée** the lights have been left on *ou* have been burning away all day → **torchon** ⓑ (= *être très chaud*) to be burning (hot) *ou* scalding; **son front brûle de fièvre** his forehead is burning; **ne touche pas, ça brûle** don't touch that, you'll burn yourself *ou* you'll get burnt; (*jeu, devinette*) **tu brûles!** you're getting hot! ⓒ (*fig*) **~ de faire qch** to be burning *ou* be dying to do sth; **~ d'impatience** to seethe with impatience; († *ou hum*) **~ (d'amour) pour qn** to be infatuated *ou* madly in love with sb; **~ d'envie *ou* du désir de faire qch** to be dying *ou* longing to do sth

③ **se brûler** VPR ⓐ (*gén*) to burn o.s.; (= *s'ébouillanter*) to scald o.s.; **je me suis brûlé la langue** I burnt my tongue; **se ~ les doigts** (*lit*) to burn one's fingers; (*fig*) to get one's fingers burnt; **le papillon s'est brûlé les ailes à la flamme** the moth burnt *ou* singed its wings in the flame; **se ~ la cervelle** to blow one's brains out ⓑ (*: Can*) to exhaust o.s., wear o.s. out

brûlerie [bʀylʀi] NF [*café*] (= *usine*) coffee-roasting plant; (= *magasin*) coffee-roasting shop; [*alcool*] (brandy) distillery

brûleur [bʀylœʀ] NM (= *dispositif*) burner

brûlis [bʀyli] NM (= *technique*) slash-and-burn technique; (= *terrain*) field (*where vegetation has been slashed and burnt*); **culture sur ~** slash-and-burn agriculture *ou* farming

brûloir [bʀylwaʀ] NM (= *machine*) coffee roaster

brûlot [bʀylo] NM ⓐ (*Hist Naut*) fire ship; (= *personne*) firebrand; (*fig*) **lancer un ~ contre** to launch a scathing *ou* blistering attack on ⓑ (*Can*) midge, gnat

brûlure [bʀylyʀ] NF (= *lésion*) burn; (= *sensation*) burning sensation; (= *d'eau bouillante*) scald; **~ de cigarette** cigarette burn; **~ du premier degré** first-degree burn; **~s d'estomac** heartburn (*NonC*)

brumaire [bʀymɛʀ] NM Brumaire (*second month of French Republican calendar*)

brume [bʀym] NF (= *brouillard*) (*léger*) mist; (*de chaleur*) haze; (*dense*) fog; (*Naut*) fog; **être dans les ~s du sommeil/de l'alcool** to be half asleep/in a drunken stupor → **banc, corne**

brumeux, -euse [bʀymø, øz] ADJ ⓐ [*temps*] misty, foggy; [*ciel*] hazy ⓑ [*poésie, philosophie,* raisonnement] obscure, hazy; [idée, souvenir] vague, hazy

brumisateur® [bʀymizatœʀ] NM spray, atomiser

brun, brune [bʀœ̃, bʀyn] **1** ADJ [yeux, couleur] brown; [cheveux] brown, dark; [peau] dusky, swarthy, dark; (= bronzé) tanned, brown; [tabac] dark; [bière] brown; **il est ~** (cheveux) he's dark-haired; (bronzé) he's tanned; **il est ~ (de peau)** he's dark-skinned; **~ roux** (dark) auburn **2** NM (= couleur) brown; (= homme) dark-haired man **3** **brune** NF **a** (= bière) brown ale, stout **b** (= cigarette) cigarette made of dark tobacco **c** (= femme) brunette **d** (littér) **à la ~e** at twilight, at dusk

brunante [bʀynɑ̃t] NF (Can) **à la ~** at twilight, at dusk

brunâtre [bʀynɑtʀ] ADJ brownish

brunch [bʀœ(t)ʃ] NM brunch

Brunei [bʀynei] NM Brunei

brunéien, -ienne [bʀynejɛ̃, jɛn] **1** ADJ of ou from Brunei **2** **Brunéien(ne)** NM,F inhabitant ou native of Brunei

brunette [bʀynɛt] NF brunette

brunir [bʀyniʀ] ▶conjug 2◀ **1** VI [personne, peau] to get a tan, get sunburnt (Brit); [cheveux] to go darker; [caramel] to brown **2** VT **a** [+ peau] to tan; [+ cheveux] to darken **b** [+ métal] to burnish, polish

brunissage [bʀynisaʒ] NM (Tech) burnishing; (Culin) browning

brunissement [bʀynismɑ̃] NM [peau] tanning

brunissoir [bʀyniswaʀ] NM burnisher

brunissure [bʀynisyʀ] NF [métal] burnish; (Agr) potato rot; [vigne] brown rust

brunoise [bʀynwaz] NF (Culin) diced vegetable; **fine ~ de carottes** finely diced carrots; **taillez la courgette en ~** dice the courgette

brushing [bʀœʃiŋ] NM blow-dry; **faire un ~ à qn** to blow-dry sb's hair

brusque [bʀysk] ADJ **a** (= rude, sec) [personne, manières] brusque, abrupt, blunt; [geste] brusque, abrupt, rough; [ton] curt, abrupt, blunt; **être ~ avec qn** to be curt ou abrupt with sb **b** (= soudain) [départ, changement] abrupt, sudden; [virage] sharp; [envie] sudden; **la ~ aggravation de la crise économique** the sudden worsening of the economic crisis

brusquement [bʀyskəmɑ̃] ADV **a** (= sèchement) brusquely, abruptly, bluntly **b** (= subitement) suddenly

brusquer [bʀyske] ▶conjug 1◀ VT **a** (= précipiter) to rush, hasten; **attaque brusquée** surprise attack; **il ne faut rien ~** we mustn't rush things **b** [+ personne] to rush, chivvy*

brusquerie [bʀyskəʀi] NF brusqueness, abruptness

brut, e[1] [bʀyt] **1** ADJ **a** [diamant] uncut, rough; [pétrole] crude; [minerai] crude, raw; [sucre] unrefined; [soie, métal] raw; [toile] unbleached; [laine] untreated; [idée] crude, raw; [art] primitive; [donnée] raw; **les faits ~s** hard facts; **à l'état ~** [diamant] in the rough; [matière] untreated, unprocessed; **informations à l'état ~** raw data; **~ de béton ou de décoffrage** [pilier, mur] raw concrete; (fig) rough and ready; **~ de fonderie** [pièce] unpolished; (fig) rough and ready; **force ~e** brute force ou physical violence **b** [champagne] brut, dry; [cidre] dry **c** (Comm, Fin) [bénéfice, poids, salaire] gross; **il touche 25 000 F ~s par mois** he earns 25,000 francs gross per month; **ils ont fait un bénéfice ~ de 5 millions** they made a gross profit of ou they grossed 5 million; **ça fait 100 F/100 kg ~ ◊ ça fait ~ 100 F/100 kg** that makes 100 francs/100 kg gross → **marge, produit, résultat** **2** NM **a** (= pétrole) crude (oil); **lourd/léger** heavy/light crude **b** (= champagne) brut ou dry champagne; (=

cidre) dry cider **c** (= salaire) gross salary

brutal, e (mpl **-aux**) [bʀytal, o] ADJ **a** (= violent) [personne, caractère] rough, brutal, violent; [instinct] savage; [jeu] rough; **être ~ avec qn** to be rough with sb; **force ~e** brute force **b** (= abrupt, cru) [langage, franchise] blunt; [vérité] plain, unvarnished; [réalité] stark; **il a été très ~ dans sa réponse** he gave a very blunt answer **c** (= soudain) [mort, changement] [choc, coup] brutal

brutalement [bʀytalmɑ̃] ADV **a** (= violemment) [pousser, saisir, attaquer] brutally **b** (= sèchement) [dire, répondre, déclarer] bluntly **c** (= subitement) [chuter, mourir, changer] suddenly

brutaliser [bʀytalize] ▶conjug 1◀ VT [+ personne] (gén) to ill-treat; (physiquement) to knock about*, manhandle; [+ enfant] (à l'école) to bully; [+ machine] to treat roughly; **femme brutalisée par son mari** battered wife

brutalité [bʀytalite] NF **a** (= violence) roughness; (plus cruelle) brutality; (Sport) rough play (NonC); **avec ~** brutally; **il l'a dit fermement mais sans ~** he was firm about it without being brutal **b** (= acte) brutality; **~s policières** police brutality **c** (= soudaineté) suddenness, abruptness

brute[2] [bʀyt] NF (= homme brutal) brute, animal; (= homme grossier) boor, lout; (littér = animal) brute, beast; **taper sur qch comme une ~*** to bash* away at sth (savagely); **frapper qn comme une ~** to lay into ou at sb brutishly; **travailler comme une ~*** to work like a dog; **~ épaisse*** brutish lout; **c'est une sale ~!*** he's a real brute!*; **tu es une grosse ~!*** you're a big bully!

Brutus [bʀytys] NM Brutus

Bruxelles [bʀysɛl] N Brussels → **chou**[1]

bruxellois, e [bʀykselwa, waz] **1** ADJ of ou from Brussels **2** **Bruxellois(e)** NM,F inhabitant ou native of Brussels

bruyamment [bʀɥijamɑ̃] ADV [rire, parler] noisily, loudly; [protester] loudly

bruyant, e [bʀɥijɑ̃, ɑ̃t] ADJ [personne, réunion] noisy, boisterous; [rire] noisy; [rire] loud; [succès] resounding (épith); **ils ont accueilli la nouvelle avec une joie ~e** they greeted the news with whoops* ou with loud cries of joy

bruyère [bʀɥijɛʀ] NF (= plante) heather; (= terrain) heath(land); **pipe en (racine de) ~** briar pipe → **coq**[1], **terre**

bryophytes [bʀijɔfit] NFPL bryophytes

BT [bete] NM (ABRÉV = **brevet de technicien**) → **brevet**

BTP [betepe] NMPL (ABRÉV = **bâtiments et travaux publics**) public buildings and works sector

BTS [beteɛs] NM (ABRÉV = **brevet de technicien supérieur**) → **brevet**

BU [bey] NF (ABRÉV = **bibliothèque universitaire**) → **bibliothèque**

bu, e [by] ptp de **boire**

buanderette [bɥɑ̃dʀɛt] NF (Can) launderette (Brit), Laundromat® (US)

buanderie [bɥɑ̃dʀi] NF wash house, laundry; (Can = blanchisserie) laundry

Buba* [buba] NF (ABRÉV = **Bundesbank**) **la ~** the Bundesbank

bubale [bybal] NM bubal

bubon [bybɔ̃] NM bubo

bubonique [bybɔnik] ADJ bubonic → **peste**

Bucarest [bykaʀɛst] N Bucharest

buccal, e (mpl **-aux**) [bykal, o] ADJ oral → **cavité, voie**

buccin [byksɛ̃] NM whelk

buccodentaire [bykodɑ̃tɛʀ] ADJ [hygiène] oral

bûche [byʃ] NF **a** [bois] log; (Culin) **~ de Noël** Yule log; **~ glacée** ice-cream Yule log **b** (* = lourdaud) blockhead*, clot* (Brit), clod* (US); **lump***; **rester (là) comme une ~** to sit there

like a (great) lump* **c** (* = chute) fall, spill; **ramasser une ~** to come a cropper* (Brit), take a (headlong) spill (US)

bûcher[1] [byʃe] NM **a** (= remise) woodshed **b** (funéraire) (funeral) pyre; (= supplice) stake; **être condamné au ~** to be condemned to (be burnt at) the stake

bûcher[2]* [byʃe] ▶conjug 1◀ **1** VT [étudiant] to bone up on*, swot up* (Brit) **2** VI to swot* (Brit), grind away*

bûcher[3] [byʃe] ▶conjug 1◀ (Can) **1** VT [+ arbres] to fell, cut down, chop down **2** VI to fell trees

bûcheron, -onne [byʃʀɔ̃, ɔn] NM,F woodcutter, lumberjack

bûchette [byʃɛt] NF (dry) twig, stick (of wood); (pour compter) rod, stick

bûcheur, -euse* [byʃœʀ, øz] **1** ADJ hardworking **2** NM,F slogger*, swot* (Brit), grind* (US)

bucolique [bykɔlik] **1** ADJ bucolic, pastoral **2** NF bucolic, pastoral (poem)

Budapest [bydapɛst] N Budapest

budget [bydʒɛ] NM budget; **~ annexe** supplementary budget; **~ d'exploitation** working ou operating ou trading budget; **~ de fonctionnement** operating budget; **~ d'investissement** capital budget; **~ prévisionnel** provisional budget; **~ publicitaire** [annonceur] advertising budget; [agence de publicité] advertising account; **le client au ~ modeste** the customer on a tight budget ou with a low income; **vacances pour petits ~s ou ~s modestes** low-cost ou -budget holidays; **film à gros ~** big-budget film → **boucler**

budgétaire [bydʒetɛʀ] ADJ [dépenses, crise, politique] budget (épith); [déficit] budgetary; **débat ~** budget debate, debate on the budget

budgéter [bydʒete] ▶conjug 1◀ VT = **budgétiser**

budgétisation [bydʒetizasjɔ̃] NF inclusion in the budget

budgétiser [bydʒetize] ▶conjug 1◀ VT to include in the budget, budget for

budgétivore [bydʒetivɔʀ] ADJ high-spending (épith)

buée [bɥe] NF [haleine] condensation, steam; [eau chaude] steam; (sur vitre) mist, steam, condensation; (sur miroir) mist; **couvert de ~** misted up, steamed up; **faire de la ~** to make steam

Buenos Aires [bwenɔzɛʀ] N Buenos Aires

buffet [byfɛ] NM **a** (= meuble) sideboard; **~ de cuisine** kitchen dresser (Brit), kitchen cabinet (US) → **danser** **b** (réception) (= table) buffet; (= repas) buffet (meal); **~ campagnard** ≈ cold table; **~ froid** cold buffet; **~ (de gare)** station buffet, refreshment room ou bar; **~ roulant** refreshment trolley (Brit) ou cart (US) **c** (* = ventre) stomach, belly*; **il n'a rien dans le ~** (à jeun) he hasn't had anything to eat; (peureux) he has no guts* **d** **~ (d'orgue)** (organ) case

buffle [byfl] NM buffalo

bug [bœg] NM (Ordin) bug

buggy [bygi] NM (Aut) buggy

bugle[1] [bygl] NM (Mus) bugle

bugle[2] [bygl] NF (Bot) bugle

bugne [byɲ] NF (Culin) piece of fried batter coated with sugar, a Lyon speciality

building [bildiŋ] NM tower block

buire [bɥiʀ] NF ewer

buis [bɥi] NM (= arbre) box(wood) (NonC), box tree; (= bois) box(wood)

buisson [bɥisɔ̃] NM (Bot) bush; (Culin) **~ de langoustines** buisson of langoustines; (Bible) **~ ardent** burning bush

buissonnant, e [bɥisɔnɑ̃, ɑ̃t] ADJ [plante] bush-like; [favoris] bushy, luxuriant

buissonneux, -euse [bɥisɔnø, øz] ADJ [ter-

rain] bushy, full of bushes; [*végétation*] scrubby
buissonnière [bɥisɔnjɛʀ] ADJ F → **école**
Bujumbura [buʒumbuʀa] N Bujumbura
bulbe [bylb] NM (*Bot*) bulb, corm; (*Archit*)
onion-shaped dome; (*Anat*) **~ pileux** hair
bulb; **~ rachidien** medulla (oblongata)
bulbeux, -euse [bylbø, øz] ADJ (*Bot*) bulbous;
[*forme*] bulbous, onion-shaped
bulgare [bylgaʀ] **1** ADJ Bulgarian **2** NM
(*Ling*) Bulgarian **3 Bulgare** NMF Bulgarian,
Bulgar
Bulgarie [bylgaʀi] NF Bulgaria
bulldog [buldɔg] NM = **bouledogue**
bulldozer [buldozɛʀ] NM bulldozer; (*fig*) **c'est
un vrai ~** he steamrollers (his way) through
everything
bulle¹ [byl] NF **a** [*air, boisson, savon, verre*]
bubble; (*Méd = cloque*) blister, bulla (SPÉC);
faire des ~s [*liquide*] to bubble; [*personne*] to
blow bubbles; **~ d'air** air bubble; (*Tech*) airlock
→ **coincer, chambre, chier b** (= *enceinte stérile*) bubble **c** (= *espace protégé*) cocoon; **la ~
familiale** the family cocoon; (*Écon*) **~
financière/spéculative** financial/speculative
bubble **d** [*bande dessinée*] balloon
e [*emballage*] **film à ~s** ◊ **emballage-~**
bubble-wrap; **enveloppe à ~s** padded envelope **f** (*Rel*) bull **g** (*arg Scol = zéro*)
nought, zero
bulle² [byl] NM **(papier) ~** Manilla paper
bullé, e [byle] ADJ bubble (*épith*); **verre ~** bubble glass
buller* [byle] ▶conjug 1◀ VI (= *paresser*) to laze
around
bulletin [byltɛ̃] **1** NM **a** (= *reportage, communiqué*) bulletin, report; (= *magazine*) bulletin;
(= *formulaire*) form; (= *certificat*) certificate; (=
billet) ticket; (*Scol*) report
b (*Pol*) ballot paper; **voter à ~ secret** to vote
by secret ballot
2 COMP ▶ **bulletin de bagage** luggage
ticket, baggage check (*surtout US*) ▶ **bulletin
blanc** (*Pol*) blank vote ▶ **bulletin de
commande** order form ▶ **bulletin de
consigne** left-luggage (*Brit*) ou checkroom
(*US*) ticket ▶ **bulletin des cours** (*Bourse*) official list, stock-exchange list ▶ **bulletin
d'information** news bulletin ▶ **bulletin
météorologique** weather forecast ou report
▶ **bulletin de naissance** birth certificate
▶ **bulletin de notes** = **bulletin scolaire**
▶ **bulletin nul** (*Pol*) spoiled ou spoilt (*Brit*)
ballot paper ▶ **bulletin de paie** = **bulletin
de salaire** ▶ **bulletin de participation**
(*dans un concours*) entry form ▶ **bulletin de
salaire** pay-slip, wage slip, salary advice (*Brit*)
▶ **bulletin de santé** medical bulletin
▶ **bulletin scolaire** (school) report (*Brit*), report (card) (*US*) ▶ **bulletin trimestriel** end-
of-term report ▶ **bulletin de vote** (*Pol*) ballot paper
bulletin-réponse (*pl* **bulletins-réponses**)
[byltɛ̃ʀepɔ̃s] NM (*dans un concours*) entry form,
reply slip
bull-terrier (*pl* **bull-terriers**) [bultɛʀje] NM
bull terrier
bulot [bylo] NM whelk
bungalow [bœ̃galo] NM (*en Inde*) bungalow;
[*motel*] chalet
bunker¹ [bœnkœʀ] NM (*Golf*) bunker, sand
trap (*US*)
bunker² [bunkœʀ, bankɛʀ] NM bunker
Bunsen [bœnsɛn] N → **bec**
buraliste [byʀalist] NMF [*bureau de tabac*] tobacconist (*Brit*), tobacco dealer (*US*), smoke
shop (*US*) (*selling stamps and newspapers*);
[*poste*] clerk
bure [byʀ] NF (= *étoffe*) frieze, homespun; (=
vêtement) [*moine*] frock, cowl; **porter la ~** to be
a monk

bureau (*pl* **bureaux**) [byʀo] **1** NM **a** (=
meuble) desk
b (= *cabinet de travail*) study
c (= *lieu de travail, pièce, édifice*) office; **le ~ du
directeur** the manager's office; **pendant les
heures de ~** during office hours; **nos ~x seront fermés** our premises ou the office will be
closed; **il travaille dans les ~x*** he has a desk
ou an office job; (*hum*) **le ~ des pleurs est
fermé** moaning (about it) will get you nowhere; **emploi de ~** desk ou office job;
équipement/mobilier de ~ office equipment/
furniture ou **chef¹, deuxième**
d (= *section*) department; (*Mil*) branch, department
e (= *comité*) committee; (*exécutif*) board; **
aller à une réunion du ~** to go to a committee
meeting; **élire le ~** [*syndicats*] to elect the officers (of the committee)
2 COMP ▶ **bureau d'accueil** reception
▶ **bureau d'aide sociale** welfare office
▶ **bureau de bienfaisance** welfare office
▶ **bureau de change** bureau de change
(*Brit*), foreign exchange office (*US*) ▶ **bureau
des contributions** tax office ▶ **bureau à
cylindre** roll-top desk ▶ **bureau de
douane** customs house ▶ **bureau d'études**
[*entreprise*] research department; (= *cabinet*)
research consultancy ▶ **Bureau européen
de l'environnement** European Environment Office ▶ **bureau exécutif** executive
committee ▶ **Bureau international du travail** International Labour Office ▶ **bureau
de location** booking ou box office
▶ **bureau ministre** pedestal desk ▶ **bureau
des objets trouvés** lost and found (office),
lost property office (*Brit*) ▶ **bureau de placement** employment agency ▶ **bureau politique** [*parti*] party executives; [*parti
communiste*] politburo ▶ **bureau de poste**
post office ▶ **bureau de renseignements**
information service ▶ **bureau de tabac** tobacconist's (shop) (*Brit*), tobacco ou smoke
shop (*US*) (*selling stamps and newspapers*)
▶ **bureau de tri** sorting office ▶ **Bureau
de vérification de la publicité** *independent
body which regulates the advertising industry*, ≈
Advertising Standards Authority (*Brit*)
▶ **bureau de vote** polling station
bureaucrate [byʀokʀat] NMF bureaucrat
bureaucratie [byʀokʀasi] NF (*péj*) (*gén*) bureaucracy; (= *employés*) officials, officialdom
(*NonC*); **toute cette ~ m'agace** all this red
tape gets on my nerves
bureaucratique [byʀokʀatik] ADJ bureaucratic
bureaucratisation [byʀokʀatizasjɔ̃] NF bu-
reaucratization
bureaucratiser [byʀokʀatize] ▶conjug 1◀ VT
to bureaucratize
bureautique [byʀotik] NF office automation;
application ~ office automation application
burette [byʀɛt] NF **a** (*Chim*) burette; (*Culin,
Rel*) cruet; [*mécanicien*] oilcan **b** (**:** =
testicules) **~s** balls**
burgrave [byʀgʀav] NM (*Hist*) burgrave
burin [byʀɛ̃] NM (*Art*) (= *outil*) burin, graver; (=
gravure) engraving, print; (*Tech*) (cold) chisel
buriné, e [byʀine] (*ptp de* **buriner**) ADJ [*visage*]
(deeply) lined, craggy
buriner [byʀine] ▶conjug 1◀ VT (*Art*) to engrave; (*Tech*) to chisel, chip
Burkina(-Faso) [byʀkina(faso)] NM Burkina-
Faso
burkinabé [byʀkinabe] **1** ADJ of ou from
Burkina-Faso **2 Burkinabé** NMF inhabitant
ou native of Burkina-Faso
burlat [byʀla] NF *type of cherry*
burlesque [byʀlɛsk] ADJ (*Théât*) burlesque; (=
comique) comical, funny; (= *ridicule*) ludicrous,
ridiculous; **le ~** the burlesque

burnes:: [byʀn] NFPL (= *testicules*) balls::; **tu
me casses les ~!** you're getting on my wick!*
(*Brit*), you're really pissing me off!**
burnous [byʀnu(s)] NM [*Arabe*] burnous(e);
[*bébé*] baby's cape → **suer**
burundais, e [buʀundɛ, ɛz] **1** ADJ Burundian
2 Burundais(e) NM,F Burundian
Burundi [buʀundi] NM Burundi
bus [bys] NM (*Aut, Ordin*) bus
busard [byzaʀ] NM (*Orn*) harrier; **~ Saint-
Martin** hen harrier
buse¹ [byz] NF (*Orn*) buzzard; (* = *imbécile*)
dolt*
buse² [byz] NF (= *tuyau*) (*gén*) pipe; (*Tech*)
duct; **~ d'aération** ventilation duct; **~ de
carburateur** carburettor choke tube; **~ de haut
fourneau** blast nozzle; **~ d'injection** injector
(nozzle)
bush [buʃ] NM (*Géog*) bush
business* [biznɛs] NM **a** (= *affaires*) business;
qu'est-ce que c'est que ce ~? what's all this
mess about?* **b** (= *truc, machin*) thingumajig*, thingummy* (*Brit*)
busqué, e [byske] ADJ **avoir le nez ~** to have a
hooked ou a hook nose
buste [byst] NM (= *torse*) chest; (= *seins*)
bust; (= *sculpture*) bust; **photographier qn en
~** to take a head-and-shoulder photograph
of sb
bustier [bystje] NM (= *sous-vêtement*) long-line
(strapless) bra; (= *corsage*) off-the-shoulder
top → **robe**
▼**but** [by(t)] NM **a** (= *objectif*) aim, goal, objective; **il n'a aucun ~ dans la vie** he has no aim
in life; **il a pour ~ ou il s'est donné pour ~ de
faire** his aim is to do, he is aiming to do; **aller
droit au ~** to come ou go straight to the
point; **nous touchons au ~** the end ou our
goal is in sight; **être encore loin du ~** to have
a long way to go; **prenons comme ~ (de promenade) le château** let's go ou walk as far as
the castle; **leur ~ de promenade favori** their favourite walk; **aller ou errer sans ~** to wander
aimlessly about ou around; **à ~ lucratif** profit-
making, profit-seeking; **à ~ non lucratif** ◊ **sans
~ lucratif** non-profit-making (*Brit*), non-profit
(*US*), not-for-profit (*US*)
b (= *intention*) aim, purpose, object; (= *raison*) reason; (*Gram*) purpose; **dans le ~ de faire**
with the intention ou aim of doing, in order
to do; **je lui écris dans le ~ de ...** my aim in
writing to him is to ...; **je fais ceci dans le seul
~ de ...** my sole aim in doing this is to ...;
c'est dans ce ~ que nous partons it's with this
aim in view that we're leaving; **faire qch dans
un ~ déterminé** to do sth for a definite reason
ou aim, do sth with one aim ou object in
view; **c'était le ~ de l'opération** that was the
object ou point of the operation; **qui va à
l'encontre du ~ recherché** self-defeating;
(*Gram*) **complément de ~** purpose clause
c (*Sport, Ftbl etc*) goal; (*Tir*) target, mark; (*Pétanque = cochonnet*) jack; **gagner/perdre (par) 3
~s à 2** to win/lose by 3 goals to 2; **marquer** ou
rentrer* un ~ to score a goal
d (*loc*) **de ~ en blanc** suddenly, point-blank,
just like that*; **il me demanda de ~ en blanc si
...** he asked me point-blank ou straight out
if ...
butane [bytan] NM **(gaz) ~** (*Camping, Ind*) butane; (*à usage domestique*) calor gas®
butanier [bytanje] NM butane tanker
buté, e¹ [byte] (*ptp de* **buter**) ADJ [*personne, air*]
stubborn, obstinate, mulish
butée² [byte] NF **a** (*Archit*) abutment
b (*Tech*) stop; [*piscine*] end wall; (*Ski*) toe-
piece
buter [byte] ▶conjug 1◀ VI **a** (= *achopper*)
to stumble, trip; **~ contre qch** (= *trébucher*) to
stumble over sth, catch one's foot on sth; (=
cogner) to bump ou bang into ou against sth;
(= *s'appuyer*) to be supported by sth, rest

▶ GRAMMAIRE ACTIVE: **but** 35.2

against sth; **~ contre une difficulté** to come up against a difficulty, hit a snag*; **nous butons sur ce problème depuis le début** this problem has been a stumbling block right from the start; **~ sur un mot** to stumble over *ou* trip over a word b (*Ftbl*) to score a goal 2 VT a [+ *personne*] to antagonize; **cela l'a buté** it made him dig his heels in b (= *renforcer*) [+ *mur, colonne*] to prop up c (*‡ = tuer*) to bump off‡, do in‡ 3 **se buter** VPR a (= *s'entêter*) to dig one's heels in, get obstinate *ou* mulish b (= *se heurter*) **se ~ à une personne** to bump into a person; **se ~ à une difficulté** to come up against a difficulty, hit a snag*

buteur [bytœʀ] NM (*Ftbl*) striker

butin [bytɛ̃] NM [*armée*] spoils, booty, plunder; [*voleur*] loot; (*fig*) booty; **~ de guerre** spoils of war

butiner [bytine] ▸ conjug 1 ◂ 1 VI [*abeilles*] to gather pollen (and nectar) 2 VT [*abeilles*] [+ *fleurs*] to gather pollen (and nectar) from; [+ *nectar, pollen*] to gather; (*fig*) to gather, glean, pick up

butineur, -euse [bytinœʀ, øz] 1 ADJ pollen-gathering (*épith*) 2 **butineuse** NF pollen-gathering bee

butoir [bytwaʀ] NM (*Rail*) buffer; (*Tech*) stop; **~ de porte** doorstop, door stopper → **date**

butor [bytɔʀ] NM a (*‡: péj = malotru*) boor b (*Orn*) bittern

buttage [bytaʒ] NM earthing-up

butte [byt] NF a (= *tertre*) mound, hillock; **~ de tir** butt; **~-témoin** outlier b **être en ~ à** [+ *difficultés*] to be exposed to

butter [byte] ▸ conjug 1 ◂ VT a (*Agr*) [+ *plante*] to earth up; [+ *terre*] to ridge b (*‡ = tuer*) to bump off‡, do in‡

buvable [byvabl] ADJ drinkable, fit to drink; (*Méd*) **ampoule ~** phial to be taken orally; **c'est ~ !*** it's not too bad!; **ce type n'est pas ~*** the guy's unbearable *ou* insufferable

buvard [byvaʀ] NM (= *papier*) blotting paper (*NonC*); (= *sous-main*) blotter

buvette [byvɛt] NF a (= *café*) refreshment room; (*en plein air*) refreshment stall b [*ville d'eaux*] pump room

buveur, -euse [byvœʀ, øz] NM,F a (= *ivrogne*) drinker b (= *consommateur*) drinker; [*café*] customer; **~ de bière** beer drinker; **c'est une grande buveuse de café** she drinks a lot of coffee

BVP [bevepe] NM (ABRÉV = **Bureau de vérification de la publicité**) ≈ ASA (*Brit*)

by-pass [bajpas] NM (*Élec, Tech*) by-pass; (*Méd*) by-pass operation

byssus [bisys] NM byssus

Byzance [bizɑ̃s] N Byzantium; (*fig*) **c'est ~ !*** what luxury!

byzantin, e [bizɑ̃tɛ̃, in] ADJ (*Hist*) Byzantine; (*péj*) [*débat*] protracted and trivial; **des querelles ~es** protracted wrangling

byzantinisme [bizɑ̃tinism] NM logic-chopping, (love of) hair-splitting

byzantiniste [bizɑ̃tinist], **byzantinologue** [bizɑ̃tinɔlɔg] NMF Byzantinist, specialist in Byzantine art

BZH (ABRÉV = **Breizh**) Britanny

C

C¹, c¹ [se] NM (= *lettre*) C, c; (*Ordin*) **(langage) C** C (language); **c cédille** c cedilla

C² (ABRÉV = **Celsius, centigrade**) C

c² ABRÉV = **centime**

c', ç' [s] ABRÉV = **ce²**

CA [sea] NM **a** (ABRÉV = **chiffre d'affaires**) → **chiffre b** (ABRÉV = **conseil d'administration**) → **conseil**

ça¹ [sa] PRON DÉM **a** (*gén*) that, it; (* : *pour désigner*) (*près*) this; (*plus loin*) that; **je veux ça, non pas ça, ça là-bas** I want that one, not this one, that one over there; **qu'est-ce que ça veut dire?** what does that *ou* this mean?; **ça m'agace de l'entendre se plaindre** it gets on my nerves hearing him complain; **faire des études, ça ne le tentait guère** studying didn't really appeal to him **b** (*péj : désignant qn*) he, she, they; **et ça va à l'église!** and to think he (*ou* she *etc*) goes to church!

c (*insistance*) **il ne veut pas venir — pourquoi ça?** he won't come — why not? *ou* why's that? *ou* why won't he?; **j'ai vu Pierre Borel — qui ça?/quand ça?/où ça?** I saw Pierre Borel — who?/when was that?/where was that?

d (*loc*) **tu crois ça!** that's what YOU think!; **ça ne fait rien** it doesn't matter; **on dit ça!** that's what (they *ou* you *etc*) say!; **voyez-vous ça!** how do you like that!, did you ever hear of such a thing!; **(ah) ça non!** most certainly not!; **(ah) ça oui!** absolutely!, (yes) definitely!; (*iro*) **c'est ça, continue!** that's right, just you carry on!* (*iro*); **ça par exemple!** (*indignation*) well!, well really!; (*iro*) **ça alors!** (*surprise*) well I never!; **ça alors!** (my) goodness!*; **me faire ça à moi!** fancy doing that to me (of all people)!; **on dirait un Picasso/du champagne — il y a de ça*** it looks like a Picasso/tastes like champagne — yes, (I suppose) it does a bit; **tu pars à cause du salaire? — il y a de ça*** are you leaving because of the salary? — it is partly that; **j'ai 5 jours de congé, c'est déjà *ou* toujours ça (de pris)** I've got 5 days off, that's something at least → **faire, pas²**

ça² [sa] NM (*Psych = inconscient*) id

çà [sa] ADV **a** **çà et là** here and there **b** (†† = *ici*) hither† (*aussi hum*)

cabale [kabal] NF **a** (= *complot*) cabal, conspiracy; **monter une ~ contre qn** to mount a conspiracy against sb **b** (*Hist*) cab(b)ala, kab(b)ala

cabaliste [kabalist] NMF cab(b)alist

cabalistique [kabalistik] ADJ **a** (= *mystérieux*) [*signe*] cabalistic, arcane; (*Hist*) cabalistic

caban [kabã] NM (= *veste longue*) car coat, three-quarter (length) coat; [*marin*] reefer *ou* pea jacket

cabane [kaban] **1** NF **a** (*en bois*) hut, cabin; (*en terre*) hut; (*pour rangements, animaux*) shed **b** (* : *péj = bicoque*) shack **c** (* = *prison*) **en ~** in (the) clink*, in the nick*; (*Brit*) **3 ans de ~** 3 years in (the) clink* *ou* in the nick* (*Brit*) *ou* inside* **2** COMP ► **cabane à lapins** (*lit*) rabbit hutch; (*fig*) rabbit hutch, box ► **cabane à outils** toolshed ► **cabane de rondins**

log cabin ► **cabane à sucre** (* : *Can*) sap house (*Can*)

cabanon [kabanõ] NM **a** (*en Provence* = *maisonnette*) [*campagne*] (country) cottage; [*littoral*] cabin, chalet **b** (= *remise*) shed, hut **c** (= *cellule*) [*aliénés*] padded cell

cabaret [kabaʀɛ] NM (= *boîte de nuit*) night club, cabaret; († = *café*) tavern, inn → **danseur**

cabaretier, -ière† [kabaʀ(ə)tje, jɛʀ] NM,F innkeeper

cabas [kaba] NM (= *sac*) shopping bag

cabestan [kabestã] NM capstan → **virer**

cabillaud [kabijo] NM (fresh) cod *pl inv*

▼ **cabine** [kabin] **1** NF [*navire, véhicule spatial*] cabin; [*avion*] cockpit; [*train, grue*] cab; [*piscine*] cubicle; [*laboratoire de langues*] booth; (*Can*) motel room, cabin (*US, Can*); (*Scol*) **entraînement en ~s** language lab training *ou* practice **2** COMP ► **cabine d'aiguillage** signal box ► **cabine (d'ascenseur)** lift (cage) (*Brit*), (elevator) car (*US*) ► **cabine de bain** (*gén*) beach *ou* bathing hut; (*sur roulettes*) bathing machine ► **cabine de douche** shower cubicle *ou* stall (*US*) ► **cabine d'essayage** fitting room ► **cabine de pilotage** (*gén*) cockpit; (*dans avion de ligne*) flight deck ► **cabine de plage** beach *ou* bathing hut ► **cabine de projection** projection room ► **cabine de téléphérique** cablecar ► **cabine téléphonique** telephone booth *ou* kiosk, pay-phone, call *ou* (tele)phone box (*Brit*)

cabinet [kabinɛ] **1** NM **a** (= *local professionnel*) [*dentiste*] surgery (*Brit*), office (*US*); [*médecin*] consulting-room, surgery (*Brit*), office (*US*); [*notaire, huissier*] office; [*avocat, juge*] chambers; [*agent immobilier*] agency **b** (= *clientèle*) [*avocat, médecin*] practice **c** (*Pol*) [*gouvernement*] cabinet; (= *collaborateurs*) staff; **le ~ du ministre** the minister's (personal *ou* private) staff → **chef¹** **d** [*exposition*] exhibition room **e** (= *meuble*) cabinet **f** † (= *bureau*) study; (= *réduit*) closet† **2** **cabinets** NMPL (= *toilettes*) toilet, lavatory, loo* (*Brit*), bathroom (*US*); **aller aux ~s** to go to the toilet (*Brit*) *ou* the bathroom (*US*); **il est aux ~s** he's in the toilet *ou* loo* (*Brit*) *ou* bathroom (*US*); **~s extérieurs** outdoor lavatory, outhouse (*US*) **3** COMP ► **cabinet d'affaires** business consultancy ► **cabinet d'aisances**† water closet†, lavatory ► **cabinet d'architectes** firm of architects ► **cabinet d'assurances** insurance firm *ou* agency ► **cabinet d'avocats** law firm ► **cabinet-conseil, cabinet de consultants** consulting firm ► **cabinet de consultation** consulting-room, surgery (*Brit*), doctor's office (*US*) ► **cabinet dentaire** dental surgery (*Brit*), dentist's office (*US*) ► **cabinet d'études** consultancy ► **cabinet d'experts comptables** *ou* **d'expertise**

comptable chartered accountant's (*Brit*), certified public accountant's (*US*) ► **cabinet juridique** law consultancy ► **cabinet de lecture**† reading room ► **cabinet médical** (*sur une plaque*) medical practice, surgery (*Brit*); (= *bureau*) surgery (*Brit*), doctor's office (*US*) ► **cabinet particulier** private dining room ► **cabinet de recrutement** recruitment agency *ou* consultancy ► **cabinet de toilette** bathroom ► **cabinet de travail** study

câblage [kɑblaʒ] NM **a** [*dépêche, message*] cabling **b** (*Tech*) [*torons*] twisting together **c** (*Élec = fils*) wiring **d** (*TV*) [*quartier, rue*] cabling

câble [kɑbl] **1** NM **a** (= *filin*) cable; **~ métallique** wire cable **b** (*TV*) cable; **la télévision par ~** ◊ **le ~** cable (television), cablevision; **transmettre par ~** to broadcast on cable, cablecast (*US*) **c** († = *dépêche*) cable **2** COMP ► **câble d'accélérateur** accelerator cable ► **câble d'amarrage** mooring line ► **câble coaxial** coaxial cable ► **câble de démarreur** *ou* **de démarrage** (*Aut*) jump lead (*Brit*), jumper cable (*US*) ► **câble électrique** (electric) cable ► **câble de frein** brake cable ► **câble de halage** towrope, towline ► **câble hertzien** radio link (by hertzian waves) ► **câble de remorquage** = **câble de halage** ► **câble de transmission** transmission cable

câblé, e [kɑble] (*ptp de* **câbler**) ADJ **a** (*TV*) [*chaîne, réseau*] cable (*épith*); **la ville est ~e** the town has cable television **b** (*Ordin*) wired **c** (* = *à la mode*) [*personne*] trendy*, hip*; **il est ~ informatique/jazz** he's really into computers/jazz

câbler [kɑble] ► conjug 1 ◄ VT **a** [+ *dépêche, message*] to cable **b** (*Tech*) [+ *torons*] to twist together (into a cable) **c** (*TV*) [+ *quartier, rue*] to install cable television in, cable

câblerie [kɑbləʀi] NF cable-manufacturing plant

câblier [kɑblije] NM (= *navire*) cable ship

câblo-distributeur (*pl* **câblo-distributeurs**) [kɑblodistʀibytœʀ] NM cable company

câblo-distribution (*pl* **câblo-distributions**) [kɑblodistʀibysjõ] NF cable television, cablevision

câblo-opérateur (*pl* **câblo-opérateurs**) [kɑbloopeʀatœʀ] NM cable (television) operator

cabochard, e* [kabɔʃaʀ, aʀd] ADJ (= *têtu*) pigheaded*, mulish; **c'est un ~** he's pigheaded*

caboche [kabɔʃ] NF **a** (* = *tête*) noddle*, head; **mets-toi ça dans la ~** get that into your head *ou* noddle* *ou* thick skull*; **quand il a quelque chose dans la ~** when he's got something into his head **b** (= *clou*) hobnail

cabochon [kabɔʃõ] NM (= *bouchon*) stopper; (= *brillant*) cabochon; (= *clou*) stud

cabossé, e [kabɔse] (*ptp de* **cabosser**) ADJ [*chapeau, instrument, voiture*] battered; **une cassero-**

► GRAMMAIRE ACTIVE: **cabine** 27.2

le toute ~e a battered *ou* badly dented saucepan

cabosser [kabɔse] ▶conjug 1◀ VT (= *bosseler*) to dent

cabot [kabo] **1** NM **a** (*péj* = *chien*) dog, mutt* **b** (*arg Mil* = *caporal*) ≈ corporal, ≈ corp (*arg, Brit*) **2** ADJ, NM = **cabotin**

cabotage [kabɔtaʒ] NM (*Naut*) coastal navigation; **petit/grand ~** inshore/seagoing navigation

caboter [kabɔte] ▶conjug 1◀ VI (*Naut*) to coast, ply (along the coast); **~ le long des côtes d'Afrique** to ply along the African coast

caboteur [kabɔtœʀ] NM (= *bateau*) tramp, coaster

cabotin, e [kabɔtɛ̃, in] (*péj*) **1** ADJ theatrical; **il est très ~** he likes to show off *ou* hold the centre of the stage **2** NM,F (*gén*) show-off; (*acteur*) ham (actor)*

cabotinage [kabɔtinaʒ] NM [*personne, enfant*] showing off; [*acteur*] ham* *ou* third-rate acting

cabotiner [kabɔtine] ▶conjug 1◀ VI [*acteur*] to ham it up*

caboulot† [kabulo] NM (= *bistro*) sleazy* *ou* seedy* dive* (*péj*) *ou* pub

cabrer [kabʀe] ▶conjug 1◀ **1** VT [+ *cheval*] to rear (up); [+ *avion*] to nose up; **faire ~ son cheval** to make one's horse rear (up); **~ qn** to put sb's back up; **~ qn contre qn** to turn *ou* set sb against sb **2 se cabrer** VPR [*cheval*] to rear (up); [*avion*] to nose up; [*personne, orgueil*] to revolt, rebel; **se ~ contre qn** to turn *ou* rebel against sb; **se ~ devant** to jib at

cabri [kabʀi] NM (*Zool*) kid

cabriole [kabʀijɔl] NF (= *bond*) [*enfant, chevreau*] caper; (= *culbute*) [*clown, gymnaste*] somersault; (*Danse*) cabriole; (*Équitation*) capriole, spring; (*péj*) **les ~s de certains politiciens** the antics of some politicians; **faire des ~s** [*chevreau, enfant*] to caper *ou* cavort (about); [*cheval*] to cavort

cabrioler [kabʀijɔle] ▶conjug 1◀ VI (= *gambader*) to caper *ou* cavort (about)

cabriolet [kabʀijɔlɛ] NM (*Hist*) cabriolet; (= *voiture décapotable*) convertible

cabus [kaby] NM → **chou¹**

CAC [kak] NF (ABRÉV = **compagnie des agents de change**) *institute of stockbrokers*; **l'indice ~ 40** the CAC(-40) index

caca [kaka] NM **a** (*langage enfantin*) poo* (*langage enfantin*) (*Brit*), poop* (*US*); **faire ~** to do a big job* (*langage enfantin*) *ou* a poo* (*langage enfantin*) (*Brit*) *ou* a number two* (*langage enfantin*) (*US*); **il a marché dans du ~ de chien** he stepped in some dog dirt; **son travail, c'est (du) ~** his work is absolute garbage; **on est dans le ~** we're in a (bit of a) mess*; **c'est ~ boudin** it's yucky* *ou* yukky* **b** (= *couleur*) **~ d'oie** greenish-yellow

cacah(o)uète, cacahouette [kakawɛt] NF (*gén*) peanut; (*Agr*) groundnut → **beurre, pesant**

cacao [kakao] NM (= *poudre*) cocoa (powder); (= *boisson*) cocoa; (*Bot*) cocoa bean

cacaoté, e [kakaɔte] ADJ [*farine*] cocoa- *ou* chocolate-flavoured

cacaotier [kakaɔtje], **cacaoyer** [kakaɔje] NM cacao (tree)

cacarder [kakaʀde] ▶conjug 1◀ VI [*oie*] to gaggle, honk

cacatoès [kakatɔɛs] NM cockatoo

cacatois [kakatwa] NM (= *voile*) royal; **mât de ~ royal** royal mast; **grand/petit ~** main/fore royal

cachalot [kaʃalo] NM sperm whale

cache¹ [kaʃ] NM (*Ciné, Photo*) mask; (*gén*) card (*for covering one eye, masking out a section of text*); (*Ordin*) cache

cache² [kaʃ] NF (= *cachette*) hiding place; (*pour butin*) cache; **~ d'armes** arms cache

caché, e [kaʃe] (*ptp de* **cacher**) ADJ [*trésor, charmes, vertus*] hidden; [*asile*] secluded, hidden; [*sentiments*] inner(most), secret; [*sens*] hidden, secret; **je n'ai rien de ~ pour eux** I have no secrets from them; **vie ~e** (*secrète*) secret *ou* hidden life; (*retirée*) secluded life

cache-cache [kaʃkaʃ] NM INV (*lit, fig*) hide-and-seek; **jouer à ~** to play hide-and-seek; **faire une partie de ~** to play hide-and-seek (**avec** with)

cache-cœur (*pl* **cache-cœurs**) [kaʃkœʀ] NM crossover top (*ou* sweater *etc*)

cache-col (*pl* **cache-col(s)**) [kaʃkɔl] NM scarf, muffler

Cachemire [kaʃmiʀ] NM Kashmir

cachemire [kaʃmiʀ] NM (= *laine*) cashmere; **motif** *ou* **impression** *ou* **dessin ~** paisley pattern; **écharpe en ~** cashmere scarf; **écharpe (à motif) ~** paisley(-pattern) scarf

cachemirien, -ienne [kaʃmiʀjɛ̃, ɛn] **1** ADJ Kashmiri **2 Cachemirien(ne)** NM,F Kashmiri

cache-misère* [kaʃmizɛʀ] NM INV (= *vêtement*) wrap or coat worn to hide old or dirty clothes; **le rideau servait de ~** the curtain was there to hide unsightly things

cache-nez [kaʃne] NM INV scarf, muffler

cache-plaque (*pl* **cache-plaque(s)**) [kaʃplak] NM hob cover

cache-pot (*pl* **cache-pot(s)**) [kaʃpo] NM flowerpot holder

cache-prise (*pl* **cache-prise(s)**) [kaʃpʀiz] NM socket cover

cacher [kaʃe] ▶conjug 1◀ **1** VT **a** (= *dissimuler volontairement*) [+ *objet*] to hide, conceal; [+ *malfaiteur*] to hide; **le chien est allé ~ son os** the dog's gone to bury its bone; **~ ses cartes** *ou* **son jeu** (*lit*) to keep one's cards *ou* hand up; (*fig*) to keep *ou* play one's cards close to one's chest

b (= *masquer*) [+ *accident de terrain, trait de caractère*] to hide, conceal; **les arbres nous cachent le fleuve** we can't see the river because of the trees; **tu me caches la lumière** you're in my light; **son silence cache quelque chose** he's hiding something by not saying anything; **qu'est-ce que ça cache?** I wonder what's going on?; **les mauvaises herbes cachent les fleurs** you can't see the flowers for the weeds → **arbre**

c (= *garder secret*) [+ *fait, sentiment*] to hide, conceal (**à qn** from sb); **~ son âge** to keep one's age a secret; **on ne peut plus lui ~ la nouvelle** you can't keep *ou* hide the news from him (*ou* her) any longer; **pour ne rien vous ~** to be perfectly honest (with you); **il ne m'a pas caché qu'il désire partir** he's been quite open with me about wanting to leave; **il n'a pas caché que cela lui déplaisait** he made no secret of the fact that he didn't like it

2 se cacher VPR **a** (= *se dissimuler*) [*personne, soleil*] to hide; **va te ~!** get out of my sight!, be gone!† (*aussi hum*); **se ~ de qn** to hide from sb; **il se cache pour fumer** he goes and hides to (have a) smoke; **il se cache d'elle pour boire** he drinks behind her back; **je ne m'en cache pas** I'm quite open about it, I make no secret of it, I don't hide *ou* conceal it

b (= *être caché*) [*personne*] to be hiding; [*malfaiteur, évadé*] to be in hiding; [*chose*] to be hidden; **il se cache de peur d'être puni** he's keeping out of sight *ou* he's hiding in case he gets punished

c (= *être masqué*) [*accident de terrain, trait de caractère*] to be concealed; **la maison se cache derrière le rideau d'arbres** the house is concealed *ou* hidden behind the line of trees

d **faire qch sans se ~** *ou* **s'en ~** to do sth openly, do sth without hiding *ou* concealing the fact; **il l'a fait sans se ~ de nous** he did it without hiding *ou* concealing it from us

cache-radiateur (*pl* **cache-radiateur(s)**) [kaʃʀadjatœʀ] NM radiator cover

cachère [kaʃɛʀ] ADJ INV = **kascher**

cache-sexe (*pl* **cache-sexe(s)**) [kaʃsɛks] NM G-string

cache-sommier (*pl* **cache-sommiers**) [kaʃsɔmje] NM valance

cachet [kaʃɛ] NM **a** (= *comprimé*) tablet; **un ~ d'aspirine** an aspirin (tablet) → **blanc b** (= *timbre*) stamp; (= *sceau*) seal; **~ (de la poste)** postmark; **sa lettre porte le ~ de Paris** his letter is postmarked Paris *ou* has a Paris postmark; **à envoyer le 15 septembre au plus tard, le ~ de la poste faisant foi** to be postmarked 15th September at the latest; **le ~ de l'originalité/du génie** the stamp of originality/genius → **lettre c** (= *style, caractère*) style, character; **cette petite église avait du ~** there was something very characterful about that little church, that little church had (great) character; **c'est le toit qui donne son ~ à** *ou* **fait le ~ de la maison** it's the roof that gives character to the house **d** (= *rétribution*) fee → **courir**

cachetage [kaʃtaʒ] NM sealing

cache-tampon [kaʃtɑ̃pɔ̃] NM INV hunt the thimble

cacheter [kaʃte] ▶conjug 4◀ VT to seal; **envoyer qch sous pli cacheté** to send sth in a sealed envelope; **vin cacheté** wine in a sealed bottle → **cire**

cachette [kaʃɛt] NF (*gén*) hiding-place; [*fugitif*] hideout; **en ~** [*agir, fumer*] on the sly, secretly; [*économiser, voir qn*] secretly; **il boit en ~** he's a secret drinker, he drinks secretly; **en ~ de qn** (*action répréhensible*) behind sb's back; (*action non répréhensible*) unknown to sb

cachexie† [kaʃɛksi] NF cachexia, cachexy

cachot [kaʃo] NM **a** (= *cellule*) dungeon; (= *punition*) solitary confinement

cachotterie [kaʃɔtʀi] NF (= *secret*) mystery; **c'est une nouvelle ~ de sa part** it's another of his (little) mysteries; **faire des ~s** to be secretive, act secretively; **faire des ~s à qn** to keep secrets *ou* things from sb

cachottier, -ière [kaʃɔtje, jɛʀ] ADJ secretive; **cet enfant est (un) ~** he's a secretive child

cachou [kaʃu] NM (= *bonbon*) cachou

cacique [kasik] NM (= *Indien*) cacique; **les ~s du parti** the party bosses; (*arg Scol*) **c'était le ~** he came first, he got first place

cacochyme† [kakɔʃim] ADJ († *ou hum*) **vieillard ~** doddery old man

cacophonie [kakɔfɔni] NF cacophony; (*péj*) **quelle ~!** what a racket!*

cacophonique [kakɔfɔnik] ADJ cacophonous

cactée [kakte], **cactacée** [kaktase] NF cactus; **les ~s** *ou* **cactacées** cacti, Cactaceae (*SPÉC*)

cactus [kaktys] NM INV cactus

c.-à-d. (ABRÉV = **c'est-à-dire**) i.e.

cadastral, e (*mpl* **-aux**) [kadastʀal, o] ADJ cadastral; **plan ~** cadastral map

cadastre [kadastʀ] NM (= *registre*) cadastre (*Brit*), cadaster (*US*); (= *service*) cadastral survey

cadastrer [kadastʀe] ▶conjug 1◀ VT to survey and register (*in the cadastre*)

cadavéreux, -euse [kadaveʀø, øz] ADJ [*teint*] deathly pale; [*pâleur*] deathly; **les blessés au teint ~** the deathly-looking *ou* deathly pale injured

cadavérique [kadaveʀik] ADJ [*teint*] deathly pale; [*pâleur*] deathly; [*visage*] cadaverous → **rigidité**

cadavre [kadavʀ] NM **a** (*humain*) body, corpse; (*animal*) carcass, body; **~ ambulant** walking *ou* living corpse; **il y a un ~ entre eux** they've got someone's blood on their hands; **il y a un ~ dans le placard** there's a skeleton in the cupboard (*Brit*) *ou* closet (*US*) **b** (* =

bouteille vide, de vin etc) empty (bottle), dead soldier*, dead man* (*Brit*)

caddie [kadi] NM a (*Golf*) caddie; **être le ~ de qn** to caddie for sb, be sb's caddie b ® (= *chariot*) (supermarket *ou* shopping) trolley (*Brit*), caddy (*US*), (grocery) cart (*US*)

cade [kad] NM (*Bot*) cade; **huile de ~** oil of cade

cadeau (*pl* **cadeaux**) [kado] NM a (= *présent*) present, gift (**de qn** from sb); **faire un ~ à qn** to give sb a present *ou* gift; **~ de mariage/de Noël** wedding/Christmas present; **~ publicitaire** free gift, freebie*, giveaway* (*US*) b (*loc*) **faire ~ de qch à qn** (*offrir*) to make sb a present of sth, give sb sth as a present; (*laisser*) to let sb keep sth, give sb sth; **il a décidé d'en faire ~ (à quelqu'un)** he decided to give it away (to somebody); **je vous fais ~ des détails** I'll spare you the details; **ils ne font pas de ~x** [*examinateurs, police*] they don't let you off lightly; **ils ne nous ont pas fait de ~** [*équipe adverse*] they really gave us a run for our money; **garde la monnaie, je t'en fais ~** you can keep the change; **en ~** [*offrir, recevoir*] as a present; **les petits ~x entretiennent l'amitié** there's nothing like a little present between friends; **c'était un ~ empoisonné** it was more of a curse than a blessing, it was a poisoned chalice; **c'est pas un ~!*** it's (*ou* he's *etc*) a real pain!*

cadenas [kadna] NM padlock; **fermer au ~** to padlock

cadenasser [kadnase] ▶conjug 1◀ 1 VT to padlock 2 **se cadenasser** VPR to lock o.s. in

cadence [kadɑ̃s] NF a (= *rythme*) [*vers, chant, danse*] rhythm; **marquer la ~** to beat out the rhythm b (= *vitesse, taux*) rate, pace; **~ de tir/de production** rate of fire/of production; **à la ~ 10 par jour** at the rate of 10 a day; **à une bonne ~** at a good pace *ou* rate; **ils nous font travailler à une ~ infernale** we have to work at a furious pace; **forcer la ~** to force the pace c (*Mus*) [*succession d'accords*] cadence; [*concerto*] cadenza d (*loc*) **en ~** (= *régulièrement*) rhythmically; (= *ensemble, en mesure*) in time

cadencé, e [kadɑ̃se] (*ptp de* **cadencer**) ADJ a (= *rythmé*) rhythmic(al) → **pas¹** b (*Ordin*) **processeur ~ à 130 MHz** processor that runs at 130 MHz, 130 MHz processor

cadencer [kadɑ̃se] ▶conjug 3◀ VT [+ *débit, phrases, allure, marche*] to put rhythm into, give rhythm to

cadet, -ette [kadɛ, ɛt] 1 ADJ (*de deux*) younger; (*de plusieurs*) youngest 2 NM a [*famille*] **le ~** the youngest child *ou* boy *ou* one; **le ~ des garçons** the youngest boy *ou* one; **mon (frère) ~** my younger brother; **le ~ de mes frères** my youngest brother; **le père avait un faible pour son ~** the father had a soft spot for his youngest boy b (*relation d'âges*) **il est mon ~** he's younger than me; **il est mon ~ de 2 ans** he's 2 years younger than me, he's 2 years my junior; **c'est le ~ de mes soucis** that's the least of my worries c (*Tennis, Ping-Pong, Ftbl etc*) 15-17 year-old player; (*Athlétisme*) 15-17 year-old athlete; (*Hist*) cadet (*gentleman who entered the army to acquire military skill and eventually a commission*) 3 **cadette** NF a [*famille*] **la cadette** the youngest child *ou* girl *ou* one; **la cadette des filles** the youngest girl *ou* daughter; **ma (sœur) cadette** my younger sister b (*relation d'âge*) **elle est ma cadette** she's younger than me c (*Tennis, Ping-Pong, Ftbl etc*) 15-17 year-old player; (*Athlétisme*) 15-17 year-old athlete

cadmium [kadmjɔm] NM cadmium; **jaune de ~** cadmium yellow

cador [kadɔʀ] NM (= *chien*) dog, mutt*, pooch* (*US*); (*péj = personne importante*) heavy-

weight*; (*péj*) **c'est pas un ~** he's no bright spark*

cadrage [kadʀaʒ] NM a (*Photo, Ciné*) (= *action*) framing; (= *résultat*) composition b [*budget, projet*] guidelines; **lettre de ~ (budgétaire) du Premier ministre** budget guidelines (*sent by the Prime Minister to ministers and the managers of state-controlled companies*)

cadran [kadʀɑ̃] 1 NM [*téléphone, boussole, compteur*] dial; [*montre, horloge*] dial, face; [*baromètre*] face → **tour²** 2 COMP ▶ **cadran solaire** sundial

cadrat [kadʀa] NM (*Typo*) quad

cadratin [kadʀatɛ̃] NM (*Typo*) em quad

cadre [kadʀ] NM a [*tableau, porte, bicyclette*] frame; **il roulait à bicyclette avec son copain sur le ~** he was riding his bicycle with his friend on the crossbar b (= *tableau*) picture c (= *caisse*) **~ (d'emballage** *ou* **de déménagement)** crate, packing case; **~-conteneur** container d (*sur formulaire*) space, box; **ne rien écrire dans ce ~** do not write in this space, leave this space blank e (= *décor*) setting; (= *entourage*) surroundings; **vivre dans un ~ luxueux/austère** to live in luxurious/austere surroundings; **maison située dans un ~ de verdure** house in a leafy setting; **quel ~ magnifique!** what a magnificent setting!; **~ de vie** (living) environment f (= *limites*) scope; **rester/être dans le ~ de** to remain/be *ou* fall within the scope of; **cette décision sort du ~ de notre accord** this decision is outside *ou* beyond the scope of our agreement; **il est sorti du ~ de ses fonctions** he went beyond the scope of *ou* overstepped the limits of his responsibilities; **respecter le ~ de la légalité** to remain within (the bounds of) the law; **sortir du ~ étroit de la vie quotidienne** to get out of the straitjacket *ou* the narrow confines of everyday life g (= *contexte*) context, framework; **dans le ~ de** [*réformes, recherches, festival*] within the context *ou* framework of h (= *structure*) structure, framework; **le ~ juridique/institutionnel** the legal/institutional framework → **loi-cadre** i (= *chef, responsable*) executive, manager; (*Mil*) officer; **les ~s** management, the managerial staff; **elle est passée ~** she has been upgraded to a managerial position *ou* to the rank of manager, she's been made an executive; **~ subalterne** junior executive *ou* manager; **~ supérieur** *ou* **de direction** senior executive *ou* manager; **~ moyen** middle executive *ou* manager; **les ~s moyens** middle management, middle-grade managers (*US*); (*hum*) **jeune ~ dynamique** upwardly mobile young executive j (*Admin = liste du personnel*) **entrer dans/figurer sur les ~s (d'une compagnie)** to be (placed) on/be on the books (of a company); **être rayé des ~s** (= *licencié*) to be dismissed; (= *libéré*) to be discharged; **hors ~** detached, seconded (*Brit*) k [*radio*] frame antenna l (*Photo*) **~ de développement** processing rack; **viseur à ~ lumineux** collimator viewfinder

cadrer [kadʀe] ▶conjug 1◀ 1 VI (= *coincider*) to tally (**avec** with), conform (**avec** to, with) 2 VT a (*Ciné, Photo*) to centre (*Brit*), center (*US*) b (= *définir*) [+ *projet*] to define the parameters of

cadreur [kadʀœʀ] NM (*Ciné*) cameraman

caduc, caduque [kadyk] ADJ a (*Bot*) **à feuilles caduques** deciduous b (*Jur*) (= *nul*) null and void; (= *périmé*) lapsed; **devenir ~** [*legs*] to become null and void; [*loi*] to lapse; **rendre ~** to render null and void, invalidate

c (= *périmé*) [*théorie*] outmoded, obsolete d (*Ling*) **e ~** mute e

caducée [kadyse] NM caduceus

caducifolié, e [kadysifɔlje] ADJ (*Bot*) deciduous

cæcum [sekɔm] NM caecum

cæsium [sezjɔm] NM caesium

CAF¹ [kaf] (ABRÉV = **coût, assurance, fret**) CIF

CAF² [kaf] NF (ABRÉV = **caisse d'allocations familiales**) → **caisse**

cafard¹ [kafaʀ] NM a (= *insecte*) cockroach b (* = *mélancolie*) **un coup de ~** a fit of depression *ou* of the blues*; **avoir le ~** to be feeling down* *ou* low*, be down in the dumps*; **ça lui donne le ~** it depresses him, it gets him down*

cafard², e [kafaʀ, aʀd] NM,F (*péj*) a (* = *rapporteur*) sneak, telltale, tattletale (*US*) b († = *hypocrite*) hypocrite

cafardage* [kafaʀdaʒ] NM (= *rapportage*) sneaking, taletelling, tattling (*US*)

cafarder* [kafaʀde] ▶conjug 1◀ 1 VT (= *dénoncer*) to tell tales on, sneak on* (*Brit*), tattle on (*US*) 2 VI a (= *rapporter*) to tell tales, sneak* (*Brit*), tattle (*US*) b (= *être déprimé*) to be feeling down* *ou* low*, be down in the dumps*

cafardeur, -euse¹ [kafaʀdœʀ, øz] NM,F (*péj*) sneak, telltale, tattletale (*US*)

cafardeux, -euse² [kafaʀdø, øz] ADJ a (= *déprimé*) [*personne*] feeling down *ou* low* (*attrib*), down in the dumps* (*attrib*); [*tempérament*] gloomy, melancholy b (= *déprimant*) depressing

caf'conc'* [kafkɔ̃s] NM ABRÉV = **café-concert**

café [kafe] 1 NM a (= *plante, boisson, produit*) coffee → **cuiller, service** b (= *moment du repas*) coffee; **au ~, on parlait politique** we talked politics over coffee; **il est arrivé au ~** he came in when we were having coffee c (= *lieu*) café, ≈ pub; **le ~ du coin** the local café, ≈ the local* (*Brit*); **ce ne sont que des propos de ~ du Commerce** (*gén*) it's just barroom philosophizing; (*politique*) it's just barroom politics 2 COMP ▶ **café complet** ≈ continental breakfast ▶ **café crème** coffee with hot, frothy milk ▶ **café décaféiné** decaffeinated coffee ▶ **café express** espresso coffee ▶ **café filtre** filter(ed) coffee ▶ **café en grains** coffee beans ▶ **café instantané** instant coffee ▶ **café au lait** coffee with milk, white coffee (*Brit*); **robe ~ au lait** coffee-coloured dress ▶ **café liégeois** coffee ice cream (*with whipped cream*) ▶ **café lyophilisé** (freeze-dried) instant coffee ▶ **café noir** *ou* **nature** black coffee ▶ **café en poudre** instant coffee ▶ **café soluble** instant coffee

café-bar (*pl* **cafés-bars**) [kafebaʀ] NM café bar

café-concert (*pl* **cafés-concerts**) [kafekɔ̃sɛʀ] NM *café where singers entertain customers*

caféier [kafeje] NM coffee tree

caféière [kafejɛʀ] NF coffee plantation

caféine [kafein] NF caffeine

café-restaurant (*pl* **cafés-restaurants**) [kaferɛstɔʀɑ̃] NM café restaurant

cafet'*, cafét'* [kafet] NF ABRÉV = **cafétéria**

café-tabac (*pl* **cafés-tabacs**) [kafetaba] NM café (*where cigarettes may be purchased*)

cafetan [kaftɑ̃] NM caftan

cafeter* [kafte] VTI = **cafter**

cafétéria [kafeterja] NF cafeteria

cafeteur, -euse* [kaftœʀ, øz] NM,F = **cafteur, -euse**

café-théâtre (*pl* **cafés-théâtres**) [kafeteatʀ] NM (= *genre*) light entertainment performed in small theatres; (= *endroit*) small theatre (*Brit*) *ou* theater (*US*); **il a fait trois ans de ~** ≈ he did three years as a stand-up comedian

cafetier, -ière [kaftje, jɛʀ] **1** NM,F café-owner **2 cafetière** NF **a** (= *pot*) coffeepot; (= *machine*) coffee-maker; **cafetière électrique** electric coffee-maker; **cafetière à l'italienne** espresso maker; **cafetière à piston** cafetiere **b** (⁑ = *tête*) head, nut*, noodle*

cafouillage* [kafujaʒ] NM muddle, shambles *sg*

cafouiller* [kafuje] ▸conjug 1◂ VI [*organisation, administration*] to be in a shambles *ou* mess; [*discussion*] to turn into a shambles, fall apart; [*candidat*] to flounder, get into a muddle; [*moteur, appareil*] to work in fits and starts; [*télévision*] to be on the blink*; **dans cette affaire le gouvernement cafouille** the government's in a real shambles over this business; **en seconde mi-temps, leur équipe a cafouillé** their team fell apart in the second half

cafouilleur, -euse* [kafujœʀ, øz] **1** ADJ [*organisation, discussion*] chaotic, shambolic* (*Brit*); **il est ~** he always gets (things) into a muddle **2** NM,F muddler, bungler

cafouillis [kafuji] NM = **cafouillage**

cafter* [kafte] ▸conjug 1◂ **1** VT (= *dénoncer*) to tell tales on*, sneak on* (*US*) **2** VI to tell tales, sneak* (*Brit*), tattle (*US*)

cafteur, -euse* [kaftœʀ, øz] NM,F sneak, tell-tale, tattletale (*US*)

cage [kaʒ] **1** NF **a** [*animaux*] cage; **mettre en ~** (*lit*) to put in a cage; (*fig*) [+ *voleur*] to lock up; **dans ce bureau, je me sens comme un animal en ~** I feel cooped up in this office **b** [*roulement à billes, pendule*] casing; [*maison*] shell **c** (⁑: *Sport* = *but*) goal **2** COMP ► **cage d'ascenseur** lift (*Brit*) *ou* elevator (*US*) shaft ► **cage d'escalier** (stair)well ► **cage d'extraction** (*Min*) cage ► **cage de Faraday** Faraday cage ► **cage à oiseaux** birdcage ► **cage à lapins** (*lit*) (rabbit) hutch; (*fig*) rabbit hutch, box ► **cage à poules** (*lit*) hen-coop; (*pour enfants*) jungle-gym, climbing frame; (*péj = immeuble*) rabbit hutch, box ► **cage thoracique** ribcage

cageot [kaʒo] NM **a** [*légumes, fruits*] crate **b** (⁑ = *femme laide*) dog⁑

cagette [kaʒɛt] NF [*légumes, fruits*] crate

cagibi [kaʒibi] NM (= *débarras*) boxroom (*Brit*), storage room (*US*), glory hole* (*Brit*); (= *remise*) shed

cagna [kaɲa] NM (*arg Mil* = *abri*) dugout

cagne [kaɲ] NF → **khâgne**

cagneux¹, -euse [kaɲø, øz] ADJ [*cheval, personne*] knock-kneed; [*jambes*] crooked; **genoux ~** knock knees

cagneux², -euse [kaɲø, øz] NM,F → **khâgneux, -euse**

cagnotte [kaɲɔt] NF (= *caisse commune*) kitty; [*jeu*] pool, kitty; (⁑ = *économies*) nest egg

cagot, e [kago, ɔt] (†† *ou péj*) **1** ADJ [*allure, air*] sanctimonious **2** NM,F sanctimonious hypocrite

cagoule [kagul] NF [*moine*] cowl; [*pénitent*] hood, cowl; [*bandit*] hood, mask; (= *passe-montagne*) balaclava

cagoulé, e [kagule] ADJ [*bandit*] hooded, masked, wearing a balaclava

cahier [kaje] **1** NM **a** (*Scol*) notebook, exercise book **b** (= *revue*) journal; (= *partie détachable*) pull-out supplement **c** (*Typo*) signature, gathering **2** COMP ► **cahier d'appel** (*Scol*) register (*Brit*), attendance sheet (*US*) ► **cahier de brouillon** roughbook (*Brit*), notebook (for rough drafts) (*US*) ► **cahier des charges** (*production*) specifications, requirements (*US*); (*contrat*) terms of reference, terms and conditions ► **cahier de cours** notebook, exercise book ► **cahier de devoirs** homework book ► **cahier de doléances** (*Hist*) register of grievances ► **cahier d'exercices** exercise

book ► **cahier à spirale** spiral notebook ► **cahier de textes** homework notebook *ou* diary ► **cahier de travaux pratiques** lab book

cahin-caha* [kaɛ̃kaa] ADV **aller ~** [*troupe, marcheur*] to hobble along; [*affaires*] to struggle along; **la vie continue ~** life trundles on; (*santé*) **alors ça va ? — ~** how are you? — (I'm) so-so

cahors [kaɔʀ] NM (= *vin*) cahors (*red wine made in the south west of France*)

cahot [kao] NM (= *secousse*) jolt, bump; (*fig*) **~s** ups and downs

cahotant, e [kaɔtɑ̃, ɑ̃t] ADJ [*route*] bumpy, rough; [*véhicule*] jolting

cahotement [kaɔtmɑ̃] NM bumping, jolting

cahoter [kaɔte] ▸conjug 1◂ **1** VT [+ *véhicule*] to jolt; [+ *voyageurs*] to jolt *ou* bump about; [*vicissitudes*] to buffet about; **une famille cahotée par la guerre** a family buffeted *ou* tossed about by the war **2** VI [*véhicule*] to trundle along; **le petit train cahotait le long du canal** the little train trundled along by the canal

cahoteux, -euse [kaɔtø, øz] ADJ [*route*] bumpy, rough

cahute [kayt] NF (= *cabane*) shack, hut; (*péj*) shack

caïd [kaid] NM **a*** (= *meneur*) [*pègre*] boss, big chief*; [*classe, bureau*] big shot*; (= *as, crack*) ace*; **le ~ de l'équipe** the star of the team, the team's top man; **il est ~ en mécanique, c'est un ~** he's an ace* at mechanics; **jouer les ~s** *ou* **au ~** to swagger about **b** (*en Afrique du Nord* = *fonctionnaire*) kaid

caillasse [kajas] NF loose stones; **pente couverte de ~** scree-covered slope, slope covered with loose stones; (*péj*) **ce n'est que de la ~** it's just like gravel, it's just loose stones

caille [kaj] NF (= *oiseau*) quail; **chaud comme une ~** warm as toast; **rond comme une ~** plump as a partridge; (*affectueusement*) **oui ma ~*** yes poppet* (*Brit*) *ou* honey* (*US*)

caillé [kaje] NM curds

caillebotis [kajbɔti] NM (= *treillis*) grating; (= *plancher*) duckboards

caillement [kajmɑ̃] NM [*lait*] curdling; [*sang*] coagulating, clotting

cailler [kaje] ▸conjug 1◂ **1** VI **a** [+ *lait*] to curdle; **faire ~ du lait** to curdle milk **b** (⁑ = *avoir froid*) to be freezing; **ça caille dehors** it's freezing outside, it's brass monkey weather⁑; **ça caille ici !** it's freezing in here! **2** **se cailler** VPR **a** [*lait*] to curdle; [*sang*] to coagulate, clot → **lait b** (⁑ = *avoir froid*) to be freezing; **on se (les) caille !** ◊ **on se caille les miches** *ou* **les meules** it's freezing cold!, it's bloody freezing!⁑⁂ (*Brit*)

caillette [kajɛt] NF (*Zool*) rennet stomach, abomasum (*SPÉC*)

caillot [kajo] NM (blood) clot

caillou (*pl* **cailloux**) [kaju] NM **a** (*gén*) stone; (= *petit galet*) pebble; (= *grosse pierre*) boulder; (⁑ = *diamant*) stone; **des tas de ~x d'empierrement** heaps of road metal; (= *mauvaise terre*) **c'est du ~** it's nothing but stones; **il a un ~ à la place du cœur** he has a heart of stone **b** (= *îlot*) rock; **le Caillou*** New Caledonia **c** (*arg Drogue*) rock **d** (⁑ = *tête*) head, nut*; **il n'a pas un poil** *ou* **cheveu sur le ~*** he's as bald as a coot *ou* an egg

cailloutage [kajutaʒ] NM (= *action*) metalling; (= *cailloux*) (road) metal, ballast

caillouter [kajute] ▸conjug 1◂ VT (= *empierrer*) to metal

caillouteux, -euse [kajutø, øz] ADJ [*route, terrain*] stony; [*plage*] pebbly, shingly

cailloutis [kajuti] NM (*gén*) gravel; [*route*] (road) metal, ballast

caïman [kaimɑ̃] NM cayman, caiman

Caïmans [kaimɑ̃] NFPL **les (îles) ~** the Cayman Islands

Caïn [kaɛ̃] NM Cain

Caire [kɛʀ] NM **le ~** Cairo

cairn [kɛʀn] NM **a** (*Alpinisme*) cairn **b** (= *chien*) cairn (terrier)

caisse [kɛs] **1** NF **a** (*pour emballage*) box; [*fruits, légumes*] crate; [*bouteilles*] case; [*plantes*] tub; (= *litière de chat*) litter tray; **mettre des arbres en ~** to plant trees in tubs **b** (*Tech* = *boîte, carcasse*) [*horloge*] casing; [*orgue*] case; [*véhicule*] bodywork; [*tambour*] cylinder **c** (*Fin*) (= *tiroir*) till; (= *machine*) cash register, till; (*portable*) cashbox; (= *somme d'argent*) **petite ~** petty cash, float* (*US*); **avoir de l'argent en ~** to have ready cash; **ils n'ont plus un sou en ~** they haven't got a penny *ou* a cent (*US*) left in the bank; **faire la ~** to count up the money in the till, do the till; **être à la ~** (*temporairement*) to be at *ou* on the cashdesk; (= *être caissier*) to be the cashier; **tenir la ~** to be the cashier; (*hum*) to hold the purse strings; **les ~s de l'État** the state coffers; **se servir** *ou* **piquer* dans la ~** to have one's fingers *ou* hand in the till; **partir avec la ~** to make off with the contents of the till *ou* the takings → **bon², livre¹** **d** (= *guichet*) [*boutique*] cashdesk; [*banque*] cashier's desk; [*supermarché*] check-out; **passer à la ~** (*lit*) to go to the cashdesk *ou* cashier; (= *être payé*) to collect one's money; (= *être licencié*) to get paid off; **on l'a prié de passer à la ~** he was asked to collect his last wages and go **e** (= *établissement, bureau*) office; (= *organisme*) fund; **~ d'entraide** mutual aid fund **f** (*Mus* = *tambour*) drum → **gros** **g** (⁑ = *poitrine*) chest; **il s'en va** *ou* **part de la ~** his lungs are giving out **h** (* = *voiture*) motor* (*Brit*), auto* (*US*); **vieille ~** old heap*, old banger* (*US*), jalopy (*US*) **2** COMP ► **caisse d'allocations familiales** family allowance office (*Brit*), ≈ welfare center (*US*) ► **caisse claire** (*Mus*) side *ou* snare drum ► **caisse comptable** = **caisse enregistreuse** ► **caisse des dépôts et consignations** deposit and consignment office ► **caisse à eau** (*Naut, Rail*) water tank ► **caisse d'emballage** packing case ► **caisse enregistreuse** cash register ► **caisse d'épargne** savings bank ► **Caisse nationale d'assurance maladie** national state health insurance office ► **caisse noire** secret funds ► **caisse à outils** toolbox ► **caisse de prévoyance** contingency *ou* reserve fund ► **caisse de résonance** resonance chamber ► **caisse de retraite** superannuation *ou* pension fund ► **caisse à savon** (*lit*) soapbox; (*péj = meuble*) old box ► **caisse de secours** relief *ou* emergency fund ► **caisse primaire d'assurance maladie** state health insurance office, ≈ Department of Health office (*Brit*), ≈ Medicaid office (*US*) ► **caisse de sécurité sociale** Social Security office ► **caisse de solidarité** (*Scol*) school fund ► **caisse du tympan** middle ear, tympanic cavity (*SPÉC*)

caissette [kɛsɛt] NF (small) box

caissier, -ière [kesje, jɛʀ] NM,F [*banque*] cashier; [*magasin*] cashier, assistant at the cashdesk; [*supermarché*] check-out assistant (*Brit*) *ou* clerk (*US*), checker (*US*); [*cinéma*] cashier, box-office assistant

caisson [kesɔ̃] NM **a** (= *caisse*) box, case; [*bouteilles*] crate; (= *coffrage*) casing; (*Mil* = *chariot*) caisson **b** (*Tech : immergé*) caisson; **hyperbare** hyperbaric chamber; **le mal** *ou* **la maladie des ~s** caisson disease, decompression sickness, the bends* **c** [*plafond*] caisson, coffer → **plafond, sauter**

cajoler [kaʒɔle] ▸conjug 1◂ VT (= *câliner*) cuddle, make a fuss of; († = *amadouer*) to wheedle, coax, cajole; **~ qn pour qu'il donne qch** *ou* **pour obtenir qch** to try to wheedle sth out of sb

cajolerie [kaʒɔlʀi] NF [a] (= *caresses*) ~s cud-dling; **faire des ~s à qn** to make a fuss of sb, give sb a cuddle [b] († = *flatterie*) flattery, ca-joling (NonC), cajolery; **arracher une pro-messe à qn à force de ~s** to coax *ou* cajole a promise out of sb

cajoleur, -euse [kaʒɔlœʀ, øz] [1] ADJ (= *câlin*) [*mère*] loving, affectionate; (= *flatteur*) [*voix, personne*] wheedling, coaxing [2] NM,F (= *flatteur*) wheedler, coaxer

cajou [kaʒu] NM **(noix de) ~** cashew nut

cajun [kaʒœ] [1] ADJ INV Cajun [2] NM (*Ling*) Cajun [3] **Cajun** NMF Cajun

cake [kɛk] NM fruit cake

cal [kal] NM (*Bot, Méd*) callus

cal. (ABRÉV = **calorie**) cal

calabrais, e [kalabʀɛ, ɛz] [1] ADJ Calabrian [2] **Calabrais(e)** NM,F Calabrian

Calabre [kalabʀ] NF Calabria

calage [kalaʒ] NM [a] (*avec une cale, un coin*) [*meuble, fenêtre, porte*] wedging; [*roue*] chock-ing, wedging; (*avec une vis, une goupille*) [*poulie*] keying; [*cheville, objet pivotant*] wedg-ing, locking [b] [*moteur*] stalling; **après deux ~s successifs** having stalled twice

calamar [kalamaʀ] NM = **calmar**

calamine [kalamin] NF [a] (*Minér*) calamine [b] (*Aut = résidu*) carbon deposits

calaminer (se) [kalamine] ▸conjug 1◂ VPR [*cylindre etc*] to be caked with soot, coke up (*Brit*), get coked up (*Brit*)

calamistré, e [kalamistʀe] ADJ [*cheveux*] waved and brilliantined

calamité [kalamite] NF (= *malheur*) calamity; (*: hum*) disaster; **ce type est une ~*** that guy is a (walking) disaster*

calamiteux, -euse [kalamitø, øz] ADJ calami-tous

calancher* [kalɑ̃ʃe] ▸conjug 1◂ VI to croak*, kick the bucket*, snuff it* (*Brit*)

calandre [kalɑ̃dʀ] NF [*automobile*] radiator grill; (= *machine*) calender

calanque [kalɑ̃k] NF (= *crique*) rocky inlet (*in the Mediterranean*)

calao [kalao] NM hornbill

calcaire [kalkɛʀ] [1] ADJ [a] (= *qui contient de la chaux*) [*sol, terrain*] chalky, calcareous (SPÉC); [*eau*] hard [b] (*Géol*) [*roche, plateau, relief*] limestone (*épith*) [c] (*Méd*) [*dégénérescence*] calcareous; (*Chim*) [*sels*] calcium (*épith*) [2] NM (*Géol*) limestone; [*bouilloire*] fur (*Brit*), sedi-ment (*US*); **faire un coup de ~*** (*déprimé*) to have a touch of the blues*; (*en colère*) to fly off the handle

calcanéum [kalkaneɔm] NM calcaneum

calcédoine [kalsedwan] NF chalcedony

calcémie [kalsemi] NF plasma calcium level

calcif* [kalsif] NM = **calecif**

calcification [kalsifikasjɔ̃] NF (*Méd*) calcifica-tion

calcifié, e [kalsifje] (*ptp de* **calcifier**) ADJ calci-fied

calcifier [kalsifje] ▸conjug 7◂ VI, **se calcifier** VPR to calcify

calcination [kalsinasjɔ̃] NF calcination

calciné, e [kalsine] (*ptp de* **calciner**) ADJ [*débris, os*] charred, burned to ashes (*attrib*); [*rôti*] charred, burned to a cinder (*attrib*)

calciner [kalsine] ▸conjug 1◂ [1] VT (*Tech = brûler*) [+ *pierre, bois, métal*] to calcine (SPÉC); [+ *rôti*] to burn to a cinder; (*littér*) **la plaine calcinée par le soleil** the sun-scorched *ou* sun-baked plain [2] **se calciner** VPR [*rôti*] to burn to a cinder; [*débris*] to burn to ashes

calcique [kalsik] ADJ calcic; **déficit ~** calcium deficiency

calcite [kalsit] NF calcite

calcium [kalsjɔm] NM calcium

calcul [kalkyl] [1] NM [a] (= *opération*) calcula-tion; (= *exercice scolaire*) sum; (*Admin*) **~ des re-traites** pension calculation; **~ de l'impôt** (*sur le revenu*) tax assessment; **se tromper dans ses ~s ◊ faire une erreur de ~** to miscalculate, make a miscalculation, make a mistake in one's calculations; **si on fait le ~** when you add it all up → **règle** [b] (= *discipline*) **le ~** arithmetic; **fort en ~** good at arithmetic *ou* sums; **le ~ différentiel/intégral/des prédicats** differential/integral/predicate calculus [c] (= *estimation*) **~s** reckoning(s), calcula-tions; **d'après mes ~s** by my reckoning, ac-cording to my calculations [d] (= *plan*) calculation (NonC); (= *arrière-pensée*) ulterior motive; **~s intéressés** self-interested motives; **par ~** with an ulterior motive, out of (calculated) self-interest; **faire un bon ~** to calculate correctly *ou* right; **faire un mauvais ~** to miscalculate, make a miscal-culation [e] (*Méd*) stone, calculus (SPÉC) [2] COMP ▸ **calcul algébrique** calculus ▸ **calcul biliaire** gallstone ▸ **calcul mental** (= *discipline*) mental arithmetic; (= *opération*) mental calculation ▸ **calcul des probabili-tés** probability theory; **un simple ~ des pro-babilités vous indiquera que ...** calculating the probability will show you that ... ▸ **calcul rénal** kidney stone, renal calculus (SPÉC)

calculable [kalkylabl] ADJ calculable, which can be calculated *ou* worked out

calculateur, -trice [kalkylatœʀ, tʀis] [1] ADJ (= *intéressé*) calculating [2] NM (= *machine*) computer; **~ numérique/analogique** digital/analog computer [3] **calculatrice** NF (= *ma-chine*) calculator; **calculatrice de poche** pocket *ou* hand-held calculator [4] NM,F (= *personne*) calculator

calculer [kalkyle] ▸conjug 1◂ [1] VT [a] [+ *prix, quantité, surface*] to work out, calculate; **il calcule vite** he calculates quickly, he's quick at figures *ou* at calculating; **il calcula mentale-ment la distance** he worked out *ou* calculated the distance in his head → **machine, règle** [b] (= *évaluer*) [+ *chances, conséquences*] to cal-culate, work out, weigh up; (*Sport*) **~ son élan** to judge one's run-up; **~ que ...** to work out *ou* calculate that ...; **tout bien calculé** every-thing *ou* all things considered → **risque** [c] (= *préméditer*) [+ *geste, effets*] to plan, calcu-late; [+ *plan, action*] to plan; **elle calcule conti-nuellement** she's always calculating; **~ son coup** to plan one's move (carefully); **ils avaient calculé leur coup** they had it all fig-ured out*; **avec une gentillesse calculée** with calculated kindness [2] VI (= *économiser*) to budget carefully, count the pennies; (*péj*) **ces gens qui calculent** peo-ple who are always counting their pennies *ou* who work out every penny

calculette [kalkylɛt] NF pocket *ou* hand-held calculator

caldoche [kaldɔʃ] [1] ADJ white New Caledo-nian (*épith*) [2] **Caldoche** NMF white New Caledonian

cale¹ [kal] NF [a] (= *soute*) hold → **fond** [b] (= *chantier, plan incliné*) slipway; **~ de chargement** slipway; **~ sèche** *ou* **de radoub** dry *ou* graving dock

cale² [kal] NF (= *coin*) [*meuble, caisse*] wedge; (*Golf*) wedge; [*roue*] chock, wedge; **mettre une voiture sur ~s** to put a car on blocks

calé, e* [kale] (*ptp de* **caler**) ADJ [a] (= *savant*) [*personne*] bright; **être ~ en chimie** to be a wiz-ard* at chemistry; **c'est drôlement ~ ce qu'il a fait** what he did was terribly clever [b] (= *ardu*) [*problème*] tough

calebasse [kalbas] NF (= *récipient*) calabash, gourd

calèche [kalɛʃ] NF barouche

calecif* [kalsif] NM pants (*Brit*), shorts (*US*)

caleçon [kalsɔ̃] NM [a] [*homme*] boxer shorts, shorts (*US*); **3 ~s** 3 pairs of boxer shorts *ou* shorts (*US*); **~ de bain** swimming *ou* bathing trunks; **~(s) long(s)** long johns* [b] [*femme*] leggings

Calédonie [kaledɔni] NF Caledonia

calédonien, -ienne [kaledɔnjɛ̃, jɛn] [1] ADJ Caledonian [2] **Calédonien(ne)** NM,F Cal-edonian

calembour [kalɑ̃buʀ] NM pun, play on words (NonC)

calembredaine [kalɑ̃bʀədɛn] NF (= *plai-santerie*) silly joke; (= *balivernes*) **~s** balderdash (NonC), nonsense (NonC)

calendaire [kalɑ̃dɛʀ] ADJ calendar (*épith*)

calendes [kalɑ̃d] NFPL (*Antiq*) calends → renvoyer

calendos* [kalɑ̃dos] NM Camembert (cheese)

calendrier [kalɑ̃dʀije] NM (= *jours et mois*) cal-endar; (= *programme*) schedule; **~ d'amortisse-ment** repayment schedule; **~ à effeuiller/perpétuel** tear-off/everlasting calendar; **le ~ républicain** the French Revolutionary Calen-dar; **~ des examens** exam timetable; (*Ftbl*) **~ des rencontres** fixture(s) timetable *ou* list; **~ de travail** work schedule *ou* programme; **~ scolaire** school schedule

cale-pied [kalpje] NM INV [*vélo*] toe clip

calepin [kalpɛ̃] NM notebook

caler [kale] ▸conjug 1◂ [1] VT [a] (*avec une cale, un coin*) [+ *meuble*] to put a wedge under, wedge; [+ *fenêtre, porte*] (*pour la maintenir ouverte*) to wedge open; (*pour la maintenir fermer*) to wedge shut; [+ *roue*] to chock, wedge [b] (*avec une vis, une goupille*) [+ *poulie*] to key; [+ *cheville, objet pivotant*] to wedge, lock [c] (*avec des coussins etc*) [+ *malade*] to prop up; **~ sa tête sur l'oreiller** to prop *ou* rest one's head on the pillow; **des coussins lui calaient la tête ◊ il avait la tête (bien) calée par des coussins** his head was propped up on *ou* sup-ported by cushions [d] (= *appuyer*) [+ *pile de livres, de linge*] to prop up; **~ qch dans un coin/contre qch** to prop sth up in a corner/against sth [e] [+ *moteur, véhicule*] to stall [f] (*Naut*) [+ *mât*] to house [g] (* = *bourrer*) **ça cale (l'estomac)** it fills you up; **non merci, je suis calé** no thanks, I'm full up* *ou* I've eaten more than my fill [2] VI [a] [*véhicule, moteur, conducteur*] to stall [b] * (= *être bloqué*) to be stuck; (= *abandonner*) to give up; **~ sur un exercice difficile** to be stuck on a difficult exercise; **il a calé avant le dessert** he gave up before the dessert; **il a calé sur le dessert** he couldn't finish his dessert [c] (*Naut*) **~ trop** to have too great a draught; **~ 8 mètres** to draw 8 metres of water [3] **se caler** VPR **se ~ dans un fauteuil** to plant o.s. firmly *ou* settle o.s. comfortably in an armchair; **se ~ les joues*** to stuff o.s., have a good feed* (*Brit*)

caleter [kalte] VI, **se caleter** VPR [kalte] ▸conjug 1◂ = **calter**

calfatage [kalfataʒ] NM (*Naut*) ca(u)lking

calfater [kalfate] ▸conjug 1◂ VT (*Naut*) to ca(u)lk

calfeutrage [kalføtʀaʒ], **calfeutrement** [kalføtʀəmɑ̃] NM [*pièce, porte*] draughtproofing (*Brit*), draftproofing (*US*); [*fissure*] filling, stop-ping up

calfeutrer [kalføtʀe] ▸conjug 1◂ [1] VT [+ *pièce, porte*] to (make) draughtproof (*Brit*) *ou* draftproof (*US*); [+ *fissure*] to fill, stop up; **calfeutré** [*pièce, porte*] draughtproof (*Brit*) (*épith*), draftproof (*US*) (*épith*); **~ une fenêtre avec un bourrelet** to put (a) weather-strip round a window [2] **se calfeutrer** VPR (=

s'enfermer) to shut o.s. up *ou* away; (*pour être au chaud*) to get cosy

calibrage [kalibraʒ] NM [*œufs, fruits, charbon*] grading; [*conduit, cylindre, fusil*] calibration; [*pièce travaillée*] gauging; (*Imprim*) [*texte*] cast-off

calibre [kalibr] NM [a] (= *diamètre*) [*fusil, canon*] calibre (*Brit*), caliber (*US*), bore; [*tuyau*] bore, diameter; [*obus, balle*] calibre (*Brit*), caliber (*US*); [*cylindre, instrument de musique*] bore; [*câble*] diameter; [*œufs, fruits*] grade; [*boule*] size; **de gros ~** [*pistolet*] large-bore (*épith*); [*obus*] large-calibre (*épith*); **pistolet de ~ 7,35** 7.35 mm (*calibre*) pistol [b] (*arg Crime* = *pistolet*) rod (*arg*), gat (*arg*) [c] (= *instrument*) (*pour mesurer*) gauge; (*pour reproduire*) template [d] (= *envergure*) calibre (*Brit*), caliber (*US*); **son frère est d'un autre ~** his brother is of another calibre altogether; **c'est rare un égoïsme de ce ~** you don't often see selfishness on such a scale

calibrer [kalibre] ▶conjug 1◀ VT [a] (= *mesurer*) [+ *œufs, fruits, charbon*] to grade; [+ *conduit, cylindre, fusil*] to calibrate; (*Imprim*) [*texte*] to cast off [b] (= *finir*) [+ *pièce travaillée*] to gauge

calice [kalis] NM (*Rel*) chalice; (*Bot, Physiol*) calyx → **boire**

calicot [kaliko] NM (= *tissu*) calico; (= *banderole*) banner

califat [kalifa] NM caliphate

calife [kalif] NM caliph; **il veut être ~ à la place du ~** he likes to play God

Californie [kalifɔrni] NF California

californien, -ienne [kalifɔrnjɛ̃, jɛn] [1] ADJ Californian [2] **Californien(ne)** NM,F Californian

californium [kalifɔrnjɔm] NM californium

califourchon [kalifurʃɔ] ♦**à califourchon** LOC ADV astride; **s'asseoir à ~ sur qch** to straddle sth, sit astride sth; **être à ~ sur qch** to be astride sth; (*Équitation*) **monter à ~** to ride astride

câlin, e [kɑlɛ̃, in] [1] ADJ (= *qui aime les caresses*) [*enfant, chat*] cuddly, cuddlesome; (= *qui câline*) [*mère, ton, regard*] tender, loving [2] NM cuddle; **faire un (petit) ~** *ou* **des ~s à qn** to make a fuss of sb, give sb a cuddle

câliner [kɑline] ▶conjug 1◀ VT to cuddle, make a fuss of

câlinerie [kɑlinri] NF (= *tendresse*) tenderness; (= *caresses*) **~s** caresses; **faire des ~s à qn** to cuddle sb, make a fuss of sb

calisson [kalisɔ] NM calisson (*lozenge-shaped sweet made of ground almonds*)

calleux, -euse [kalø, øz] ADJ [*peau*] horny, callous

calligramme [kaligram] NM (= *poème*) calligramme

calligraphe [ka(l)ligraf] NMF calligrapher, calligraphist

calligraphie [ka(l)ligrafi] NF (= *technique*) calligraphy, art of handwriting; **c'est de la ~** it's lovely handwriting, the handwriting is beautiful

calligraphier [ka(l)ligrafje] ▶conjug 7◀ VT [+ *titre, phrase*] to write artistically, calligraph (*SPÉC*)

calligraphique [ka(l)ligrafik] ADJ calligraphic

callipyge [ka(l)lipiʒ] ADJ (*hum*) callipygian, big-bottomed; **la Vénus ~** Callipygian Venus

callosité [kalozite] NF callosity

calmant, e [kalmã, ãt] [1] ADJ [a] (*Pharm*) (= *tranquillisant*) tranquillizing (*épith*); (*contre la douleur*) painkilling (*épith*) [b] (= *apaisant*) [*paroles*] soothing [2] NM (= *tranquillisant*) tranquilizer, sedative; (= *antidouleur*) painkiller

calmar [kalmar] NM squid

calme [kalm] [1] ADJ [a] (*gén*) quiet, calm; (= *paisible*) peaceful; (*Naut*) [*mer*] calm; [*nuit, air*] still; [*chambre*] quiet; (*Fin*) [*marché, affaires*]

quiet; **malgré leurs provocations il restait très ~** he remained quite calm *ou* cool *ou* unruffled in spite of their taunts; **le malade a eu une nuit ~** the patient has had a quiet *ou* peaceful night [2] NM [a] (= *sang-froid*) coolness, composure; **garder son ~** to keep cool *ou* calm, keep one's composure *ou* one's cool*; **perdre son ~** to lose one's composure *ou* one's cool*; **avec un ~ incroyable** with incredible composure; **recouvrant son ~** recovering *ou* regaining his composure [b] (= *tranquillité*) (*gén*) peace (and quiet), calm; [*nuit*] stillness; [*endroit*] peacefulness; **il me faut du ~ pour travailler** I need peace and quiet to work; **du ~ !** (= *restez tranquille*) keep quiet!; (= *pas de panique*) keep calm! *ou* cool!; **le malade doit rester au ~** the patient needs quiet; **ramener le ~** (= *arranger les choses*) to calm things down; (= *rétablir l'ordre*) to restore calm; **le ~ avant la tempête** the calm *ou* lull before the storm [c] (*Naut*) (**zones des**) **~s équatoriaux** doldrums (*lit*); **~ plat** dead *ou* flat calm; **c'est le ~ plat dans les affaires** business is dead quiet *ou* practically at a standstill; **depuis que je lui ai envoyé cette lettre c'est le ~ plat** I haven't heard a thing since I sent him that letter

calmement [kalməmã] ADV (*agir*) calmly; **la journée s'est passée ~** the day passed quietly

calmer [kalme] ▶conjug 1◀ [1] VT [a] (= *apaiser*) [+ *personne*] to calm (down), pacify; [+ *querelle, discussion*] to quieten down (*Brit*), quiet down (*US*); [+ *révolte*] to subdue; (*littér*) [+ *tempête, flots*] to calm; **~ les esprits** to calm people down, pacify people; **attends un peu, je vais te ~ !*** just you wait, I'll (soon) quieten (*Brit*) *ou* quiet (*US*) you down!; (*lit, fig*) **~ le jeu** to calm things down [b] (= *réduire*) [+ *douleur, inquiétude*] to soothe, ease; [+ *nerfs, agitation, crainte, colère*] to calm, soothe; [+ *fièvre*] to bring down; [+ *impatience*] to curb; [+ *faim*] to appease; [+ *soif*] to quench; [+ *ardeur*] to cool, subdue [2] **se calmer** VPR [a] [*personne*] (= *s'apaiser*) to calm down, cool down; (= *faire moins de bruit*) to quieten down (*Brit*), quiet down (*US*); (= *se tranquilliser*) to calm down; [*discussion, querelle*] to quieten down (*Brit*), quiet down (*US*); [*tempête*] die down; [*mer*] to become calm; **on se calme !*** (= *taisez-vous*) be quiet!; (= *pas de panique*) calm down! [b] (= *diminuer*) [*douleur*] to ease, subside; [*faim, soif, inquiétude*] to ease; [*crainte, impatience, fièvre*] to subside; [*colère, ardeur*] to cool, subside

calomel [kalɔmɛl] NM calomel

calomniateur, -trice [kalɔmnjatœr, tris] [1] ADJ (= *diffamateur*) slanderous; (*par écrit*) libellous [2] NM,F (= *diffamateur*) slanderer; (*par écrit*) libeller

calomnie [kalɔmni] NF slander (*NonC*), calumny; (*écrite*) libel; (*sens affaibli*) maligning (*NonC*); **cette ~ l'avait profondément blessé** he'd been deeply hurt by this slander *ou* calumny; **écrire des ~s** to write libellous things; **dire une ~/des ~s** to say something slanderous/slanderous things

calomnier [kalɔmnje] ▶conjug 7◀ VT (= *diffamer*) to slander; (*par écrit*) to libel; (*sens affaibli = vilipender*) to malign

calomnieux, -ieuse [kalɔmnjø, jøz] ADJ [*propos*] slanderous; (*par écrit*) libellous; (*Jur*) **dénonciation calomnieuse** false accusation

caloporteur [kalɔpɔrtœr] ADJ, NM = **caloriporteur**

calorie [kalɔri] NF calorie; **aliment riche/pauvre en ~s** food with a high/low calorie content, high-/low-calorie food; **menu basses ~s** low-calorie meal; **ça donne des ~s*** it warms you up; **tu aurais besoin de ~s !*** you need building up!

calorifère [kalɔrifɛr] [1] ADJ heat-giving [2] NM† stove

calorifique [kalɔrifik] ADJ calorific

calorifuge [kalɔrifyʒ] [1] ADJ (heat-)insulating, heat-retaining [2] NM insulating material

calorifugeage [kalɔrifyʒaʒ] NM lagging, insulation

calorifuger [kalɔrifyʒe] ▶conjug 3◀ VT to lag, insulate (against loss of heat)

calorimètre [kalɔrimɛtr] NM calorimeter

calorimétrie [kalɔrimetri] NF calorimetry

calorimétrique [kalɔrimetrik] ADJ calorimetric(al)

caloriporteur [kalɔripɔrtœr] ADJ, NM (**fluide**) **~ coolant**

calorique [kalɔrik] ADJ (*diététique*) calorie (*épith*); (*chaleur*) calorific; **ration ~** calorie requirements; **valeur ~** calorific value

calot [kalo] NM [a] (*Mil* = *coiffure*) forage cap, overseas cap (*US*) [b] (= *bille*) (large) marble, alley

calotin, e [kalɔtɛ̃, in] (*péj*) [1] ADJ sanctimonious, churchy* [2] NM,F sanctimonious churchgoer, Holy Joe*

calotte [kalɔt] [1] NF [a] (= *bonnet*) skullcap [b] (*péj*) **la ~** (= *le clergé*) the priests, the cloth; (= *le parti dévot*) the church party [c] (= *partie supérieure*) [*chapeau*] crown; [*voûte*] calotte [d] (* = *gifle*) slap; **il m'a donné une ~** he gave me a slap in the face [2] COMP ► **la calotte des cieux** the dome *ou* vault of heaven ► **calotte crânienne** top of the skull ► **calotte glaciaire** icecap ► **calotte sphérique** segment of a sphere

calotter* [kalɔte] ▶conjug 1◀ VT (= *gifler*) to slap

calquage [kalkaʒ] NM tracing

calque [kalk] NM [a] (= *dessin*) tracing; **prendre un ~ d'un plan** to trace a plan [b] (= *papier transparent*) tracing paper [c] (= *reproduction*) [*œuvre d'art*] exact copy; [*événement*] carbon copy; [*personne*] spitting image [d] (*Ling*) calque, loan translation

calquer [kalke] ▶conjug 1◀ VT (= *copier*) [+ *plan, dessin*] to trace; (*fig*) to copy exactly; (*Ling*) **calqué de l'anglais** translated literally from English; **~ son comportement sur celui de son voisin** to model one's behaviour on that of one's neighbour, copy one's neighbour's behaviour exactly

calter* VI, **se calter*** VPR [kalte] ▶conjug 1◀ (= *décamper*) to make o.s. scarce*, scarper* (*Brit*), buzz off* (*Brit*)

calumet [kalymɛ] NM peace pipe; **fumer le ~ de la paix** (*lit*) to smoke the pipe of peace; (*fig*) to bury the hatchet

calva* [kalva] NM ABRÉV = **calvados**

calvados [kalvados] NM [a] (= *eau-de-vie*) calvados [b] **Calvados** (= *département*) **le Calvados** Calvados

calvaire [kalvɛr] NM [a] (= *croix*) (*au bord de la route*) roadside cross *ou* crucifix, calvary; (= *peinture*) Calvary, road *ou* way to the Cross [b] (= *épreuve*) suffering, martyrdom; **le ~ du Christ** Christ's martyrdom *ou* suffering on the cross; **sa vie fut un long ~** his life was one long martyrdom *ou* agony *ou* tale of suffering; **un enfant comme ça, c'est un ~ pour la mère** a child like that must be a real burden to his mother [c] (*Rel*) **Le Calvaire** Calvary

Calvin [kalvɛ̃] NM Calvin

calvinisme [kalvinism] NM Calvinism

calviniste [kalvinist] [1] ADJ Calvinist, Calvinistic [2] NMF Calvinist

calvitie [kalvisi] NF baldness (*NonC*); **~ précoce** premature baldness (*NonC*)

calypso [kalipso] NM calypso

camaïeu [kamajø] NM (= *peinture*) monochrome; **en ~** [*paysage, motif*] monochrome (*épith*); **en ~ bleu** in blue monochrome; **un ~ de roses** various shades of pink

camail [kamaj] NM (*Rel*) cappa magna

camarade [kamaʀad] [1] NMF friend; (*Pol*) **le ~ Durand** comrade Durand; **elle voyait en lui un bon ~** she saw him as a good friend [2] COMP ► **camarade d'atelier** workmate (*Brit*), shop buddy* (*US*) ► **camarade de classe** classmate ► **camarade d'étude** fellow student ► **camarade de jeu** playmate ► **camarade de promotion** fellow student (*from a grande école*) ► **camarade de régiment** friend from one's army days

camaraderie [kamaʀadʀi] NF (*entre deux personnes*) good companionship, good fellowship; (*dans un groupe*) camaraderie

camard, e [kamaʀ, aʀd] [1] ADJ [*nez*] pug (*épith*); [*personne*] pug-nosed [2] **Camarde** NF (*littér*) **la Camarde** the (Grim) Reaper

camarguais, e [kamaʀgɛ, ɛz] [1] ADJ of *ou* from the Camargue; (*bottes*) **~es** suede cowboy boots [2] **Camarguais(e)** NM,F inhabitant *ou* native of the Camargue

Camargue [kamaʀg] NF **la ~** the Camargue

cambiste [kãbist] NM foreign exchange broker *ou* dealer; [*devises des touristes*] money-changer

Cambodge [kãbɔdʒ] NM Cambodia

cambodgien, -ienne [kãbɔdʒjɛ̃, jɛn] [1] ADJ Cambodian [2] **Cambodgien(ne)** NM,F Cambodian

cambouis [kãbwi] NM dirty oil *ou* grease

cambré, e [kãbʀe] (*ptp de* **cambrer**) ADJ être **~** ◊ **avoir les reins ~s** to have an arched back; **avoir le pied très ~** to have very high insteps *ou* arches

cambrer [kãbʀe] ▸ conjug 1 ◂ [1] VT [a] [+ *pied*] to arch; **~ la taille** *ou* **le dos** *ou* **les reins** to throw back one's shoulders, arch one's back [b] (*Tech*) [+ *pièce de bois*] to bend; [+ *métal*] to curve; [+ *tige, semelle*] to arch [2] **se cambrer** VPR (= *se redresser*) to throw back one's shoulders, arch one's back

cambrien, -ienne [kãbʀijɛ̃, ijɛn] ADJ, NM Cambrian

cambriolage [kãbʀijɔlaʒ] NM (= *activité, méthode*) burglary, housebreaking, breaking and entering (*Jur*); (= *coup*) break-in, burglary

cambrioler [kãbʀijɔle] ▸ conjug 1 ◂ VT to break into, burgle, burglarize (*US*)

cambrioleur, -euse [kãbʀijɔlœʀ, øz] NM,F burglar, housebreaker

cambrousse [kãbʀus] NF (= *campagne*) country; **en pleine ~** out in the sticks*, in the back of beyond; (*péj*) **frais arrivé de sa ~** fresh from the backwoods *ou* the sticks*

cambrure [kãbʀyʀ] NF [a] (= *courbe, forme*) [*poutre, taille, reins*] curve; [*semelle, pied*] arch; [*route*] camber; **sa ~ de militaire** his military bearing [b] (= *partie*) ► **du pied** instep; **~ des reins** small *ou* hollow of the back; **pieds qui ont une forte ~** feet with high insteps; **reins qui ont une forte ~** back which is very arched

cambuse [kãbyz] NF [a]* (= *pièce*) pad*; (= *maison*) shack*, place; (= *taudis*) hovel [b] (*Naut*) storeroom

came¹ [kam] NF (*Tech*) cam → **arbre**

came² [kam] NF (*arg Drogue*) (*gén*) dope*; (= *héroïne*) junk*; (= *cocaïne*) snow*; (*= marchandise*) stuff*; (*péj = pacotille*) junk*, trash*

camé, e¹* [kame] (*ptp de* **se camer**) [1] ADJ high*, spaced out*; **complètement ~** completely spaced out*, high as a kite* [2] NM,F druggy*; (*à l'héroïne*) junkie*

camée² [kame] NM cameo

caméléon [kamele ̃ɔ̃] NM (*Zool*) chameleon; (*fig*) chameleon; (*péj*) turncoat

camélia [kamelja] NM camellia

camélidé [kamelide] NM member of the cam-

---

el family; **les ~s** members of the camel family, the Camelidae (*SPÉC*)

camelot [kamlo] NM street pedlar *ou* vendor; (*Hist*) **les Camelots du roi** militant royalist group in 1930s

camelote* [kamlɔt] NF [a] (= *pacotille*) **c'est de la ~** it's junk* *ou* rubbish* (*Brit*) *ou* schlock‡ (*US*) [b] (= *marchandise*) stuff*; **il vend de la belle ~** he sells nice stuff*

camembert [kamãbɛʀ] NM (= *fromage*) Camembert (cheese); (* = *graphique*) pie chart

camer (se) [kame] VPR (*arg Drogue*) to be on drugs

caméra [kameʀa] NF (*Ciné, TV*) camera; [*amateur*] cine-camera, movie camera (*US*); **~ sonore** sound camera; **~ vidéo** video camera, camcorder; **devant les ~s de (la) télévision** in front of the television cameras, on TV; **être derrière la ~** [*réalisateur*] to be behind the camera; **la ~ invisible** *ou* **cachée** (= *émission*) candid camera

cameraman [kameʀaman] (*pl* **cameramen** [kameʀamɛn]) NM cameraman

cámériste [kameʀist] NF (= *femme de chambre*) chambermaid; (*Hist*) lady-in-waiting

Cameroun [kamʀun] NM Cameroon; (*Hist*) Cameroons; **République unie du ~** United Republic of Cameroon

camerounais, e [kamʀunɛ, ɛz] [1] ADJ Cameroonian [2] **Camerounais(e)** NM,F Cameroonian

caméscope [kameskɔp] NM camcorder, video camera

camion [kamjɔ̃] [1] NM [a] (= *poids lourd*) lorry (*Brit*), truck (*surtout US*); (*dont l'arrière fait corps avec la cabine*) van (*Brit*), truck (*surtout US*) [b] (= *chariot*) wag(g)on, dray [c] [*peintre*] (= *seau*) (paint-)pail [2] COMP ► **camion (à) benne** tipper (truck) ► **camion de déménagement** removal (*Brit*) *ou* moving (*US*) van ► **camion militaire** army lorry (*Brit*) *ou* truck ► **camion (à) remorque** lorry (*Brit*) *ou* truck (*US*) with a trailer, tractor-trailer (*US*) ► **camion (à) semi-remorque** articulated lorry (*Brit*), trailer truck (*US*)

camion-citerne (*pl* **camions-citernes**) [kamjɔ̃sitɛʀn] NM tanker (lorry) (*Brit*), tank truck (*US*)

camion-grue (*pl* **camions-grues**) [kamjɔ̃gʀy] NM crane-truck

camionnage [kamjɔnaʒ] NM haulage (*Brit*), trucking (*US*)

camionnette [kamjɔnɛt] NF (small) van; (*ouverte*) pick-up (truck); **~ de livraison** delivery van

camionneur [kamjɔnœʀ] NM (= *chauffeur*) lorry (*Brit*) *ou* truck (*US*) driver, trucker (*US*); (= *entrepreneur*) haulage contractor (*Brit*), road haulier (*Brit*), trucking contractor (*US*); **pull (à) col ~** sweater with a zip-up collar

camisard [kamizaʀ] NM Camisard (*French Protestant insurgent after the revocation of the Edict of Nantes*)

camisole [kamizɔl] [1] NF†† (= *blouse*) camisole†; (= *chemise de nuit*) nightshirt [2] COMP ► **camisole chimique** suppressants ► **camisole de force** straitjacket

camomille [kamɔmij] NF (*Bot*) camomile; (= *tisane*) camomile tea

Camorra [kamɔʀa] NF **la ~** the Camorra

camouflage [kamuflaʒ] NM [a] (*Mil*) (= *action*) camouflaging; (= *résultat*) camouflage [b] [*argent*] concealing, hiding; [*erreur*] camouflaging, covering-up; **le ~ d'un crime en accident** disguising a crime as an accident

camoufler [kamufle] ▸ conjug 1 ◂ [1] VT (*Mil*) to camouflage; (= *cacher*) [+ *argent*] to conceal, hide; [+ *erreur, embarras*] to conceal, cover up; (= *déguiser*) [+ *défaite, intentions*] to disguise; **~ un crime en accident** to disguise a crime as an

---

accident, make a crime look like an accident [2] **se camoufler** VPR to camouflage o.s.

camouflet [kamuflɛ] NM (*littér*) snub; **infliger un ~ à qn** to snub sb

camp [kã] [1] NM [a] (*Alpinisme, Mil, Sport* = *emplacement*) camp; **~ de prisonniers/de réfugiés** prison/refugee camp; **rentrer au ~** to come *ou* go back to camp; **le Camp du drap d'or** the Field of the Cloth of Gold → **aide, feu¹** [b] (= *séjour*) **faire un ~ d'une semaine** to go camping for a week, go for a week's camping holiday (*Brit*) *ou* vacation (*US*); **le ~ vous fait découvrir beaucoup de choses** you discover lots of things when you go camping [c] (= *parti, faction*) (*Jeux, Sport*) side; (*Pol*) camp; **changer de ~** [*joueur*] to change sides; [*soldat*] to go over to the other side; **à cette nouvelle la consternation/l'espoir changea de ~** on hearing this, it was the other side which began to feel dismay/hopeful; **dans le ~ opposé/victorieux** in the opposite/winning camp; **passer dans le ~ adverse** to go over to the opposite *ou* enemy camp → **balle¹** [2] COMP ► **camp de base** base camp ► **camp de camping** campsite, camping site ► **camp de concentration** concentration camp ► **camp d'entraînement** training camp ► **camp d'extermination** extermination camp ► **camp fortifié** fortified camp ► **camp de la mort** death camp ► **camp de nudistes** nudist camp ► **camp retranché** = **camp fortifié** ► **camp de toile** campsite, camping site ► **camp de travail** labour (*Brit*) *ou* labor (*US*) camp ► **camp de vacances** ≈ children's holiday camp (*Brit*), ≈ summer camp (*US*) ► **camp volant** camping tour *ou* trip; (*Mil*) temporary camp; **vivre** *ou* **être en ~ volant†** to live out of a suitcase

campagnard, e [kãpaɲaʀ, aʀd] [1] ADJ [*vie, manières*] country (*épith*); (*péj*) rustic → **gentilhomme** [2] NM countryman, country fellow; (*péj*) rustic (*péj*), hick (*péj*); **~s** countryfolk, country people; (*péj*) rustics (*péj*) [3] **campagnarde** NF countrywoman

campagne [kãpaɲ] NF [a] (= *habitat*) country; (= *paysage*) countryside; (*Agr* = *champs ouverts*) open country; **la ville et la ~** town and country; **la ~ anglaise** the English countryside; **dans la ~ environnante** in the surrounding countryside; **en pleine ~** right in the middle of the country(side); **à la ~** in the country; **auberge/chemin de ~** country inn/lane; **les travaux de la ~** farm *ou* agricultural work → **battre, maison** etc [b] (*Mil*) campaign; **faire ~** to fight (a campaign); **les troupes en ~** the troops on campaign *ou* in the field; **entrer en ~** to embark on a campaign; **la ~ d'Italie/de Russie** the Italian/Russian campaign; **artillerie/canon de ~** field artillery/gun [c] (*Pol, Presse*) campaign (**pour** for, **contre** against); **~ électorale** election campaign; **~ d'affichage** poster campaign; **~ publicitaire** *ou* **de publicité** advertising *ou* publicity campaign; **~ de vente** sales campaign *ou* drive; **~ de fouilles** series of excavations; **faire ~ pour un candidat** to campaign *ou* canvass for *ou* on behalf of a candidate; **partir en ~** to launch a campaign (**contre** against); **mener une ~ pour/contre** to campaign for/against, lead a campaign for/against; **tout le monde se mit en ~ pour lui trouver une maison** everybody set to work *ou* got busy to find him a house [d] (= *récolte*) harvest; **~ sucrière** sugar cane (*ou* sugar beet) harvest; **~ de pêche** fishing season

campagnol [kãpaɲɔl] NM vole

campanaire [kãpanɛʀ] ADJ **l'art ~** campanology; **inscription ~** inscription on a bell

campanile [kãpanil] NM [*église*] campanile; (= *clocheton*) bell-tower

campanule [kãpanyl] NF bellflower, campanula

campement [kɑ̃pmɑ̃] NM (= camp) camp, encampment; **matériel de ~** camping equipment; **chercher un ~ pour la nuit** to look for somewhere to set up camp *ou* for a camping place for the night; **établir son ~ sur les bords d'un fleuve** to set up (one's) camp on the bank of a river; **~ de nomades/d'Indiens** camp *ou* encampment of nomads/of Indians; (*Mil*) **revenir à son ~** to return to camp

camper [kɑ̃pe] ▸conjug 1◂ **1** VI to camp; (*hum*) **on campait à l'hôtel/dans le salon** we were camping out at *ou* in a hotel/in the lounge → **position** **2** VT **a** [+ *troupes*] to camp out; **campés pour 2 semaines près du village** camped (out) for 2 weeks by the village **b** (= *esquisser*) [+ *caractère, personnage*] to portray; [+ *récit*] to construct; [+ *portrait*] to fashion, shape; **personnage bien campé** vividly sketched *ou* portrayed character **c** (= *poser*) **~ sa casquette sur l'oreille** to pull *ou* clap one's cap on firmly over one ear; **se ~ des lunettes sur le nez** to plant* a pair of glasses on one's nose **3** **se camper** VPR **se ~ devant qn** to plant o.s. in front of sb*; **se ~ sur ses jambes** to stand firm

campeur, -euse [kɑ̃pœʀ, øz] NM,F camper

camphre [kɑ̃fʀ] NM camphor

camphré, e [kɑ̃fʀe] ADJ camphorated → **alcool**

camphrier [kɑ̃fʀije] NM camphor tree

camping [kɑ̃piŋ] NM **a** (= *activité*) **le ~** camping; **faire du ~** to go camping → **sauvage** **b** (= *lieu*) campsite, camping site

camping-car (*pl* camping-cars) [kɑ̃piŋkaʀ] NM camper, Dormobile® (*Brit*), motorhome (*US*), RV (*US*)

camping-gaz® [kɑ̃piŋgaz] NM INV camp(ing) stove

campo(s)†* [kɑ̃po] NM **demain on a campos** tomorrow is a day off, we've got tomorrow off *ou* free; **on a eu** *ou* **on nous a donné campos à 4 heures** we were free *ou* told to go at 4 o'clock

campus [kɑ̃pys] NM campus

camus, e [kamy, yz] ADJ [*nez*] pug (*épith*); [*personne*] pug-nosed

Canaan [kanaɑ̃] NM Canaan

Canada [kanada] NM Canada

canada [kanada] NF *apple of the pippin variety*

Canadair® [kanadɛʀ] NM fire-fighting aircraft, tanker plane (*US*)

canadianisme [kanadjanism] NM Canadianism

canadien, -ienne [kanadjɛ̃, jɛn] **1** ADJ Canadian **2** **Canadien(ne)** NM,F Canadian; **Canadien(ne) français(e)** French Canadian **3** **canadienne** NF (= *veste*) fur-lined jacket; (= *canoë*) (Canadian) canoe; (= *tente*) (ridge) tent

canaille [kanaj] **1** ADJ [*manières*] cheap, coarse; **sous ses airs ~s, il est sérieux** he might look a bit rough and ready, but he is reliable **2** NF (*péj* = *salaud*) bastard*****; (= *escroc*) crook, shyster (*US*), chiseler (*US*); (*hum* = *enfant*) rascal, rogue, (little) devil; (*péj* = *populace*) **la ~**† the rabble (*péj*), the riffraff (*péj*)

canaillerie [kanajʀi] NF **a** [*allure, ton*] vulgarity, coarseness **b** (= *malhonnêteté*) [*procédés, personne*] crookedness **c** (= *action malhonnête*) dirty *ou* low trick

canal (*pl* -aux) [kanal, o] **1** NM **a** (*artificiel*) canal; (= *détroit*) channel; (= *tuyau, fossé*) conduit, (*Anat*) canal, duct; (*TV, Ordin*) channel; **le ~ de Panama/Suez** the Panama/Suez Canal; **le ~ de Mozambique** the Mozambique Channel; **~ lacrymal** tear *ou* lacrimal (*SPÉC*) duct; **Canal Plus** ◊ **Canal +** *French pay TV channel* **b** (= *intermédiaire*) **par le ~ d'un collègue** through *ou* via a colleague; **par le ~ de la presse** through the medium of the press; (*littér*) **par un ~ amical** through a friend

▸ GRAMMAIRE ACTIVE: **candidature** 46.1

2 COMP ▶ **canal d'amenée** feeder canal ▶ **canal biliaire** biliary canal, bile duct ▶ **canal déférent** vas deferens ▶ **canal de dérivation** diversion canal ▶ **canal de distribution** distribution channel ▶ **canal de fuite** tail-race ▶ **canal d'irrigation** irrigation canal ▶ **canal maritime** ship canal ▶ **canal médullaire** medullary cavity *ou* canal ▶ **canal de navigation** ship canal

canalisation [kanalizasjɔ̃] NF **a** (= *tuyau*) (main) pipe; **~s** (= *réseau*) pipes, piping, pipework; (*Élec*) cables **b** (= *aménagement*) [*cours d'eau*] canalization **c** [*demandes, foule*] channelling, funnelling

canaliser [kanalize] ▸conjug 1◂ VT **a** [+ *foule, demandes, énergie*] to channel, funnel **b** [+ *fleuve*] to canalize; [+ *région*] to provide with a network of canals

cananéen, -enne [kananeɛ̃, ɛn] **1** ADJ Canaanite **2** NM (*Ling*) Canaanite **3** **Cananéen(ne)** NM,F Canaanite

canapé [kanape] NM **a** (= *meuble*) sofa, settee, couch; **~ transformable** *ou* **convertible** sofa bed, bed settee (*Brit*) **b** (*Culin*) open sandwich; (*pour apéritif*) canapé; **crevettes sur ~** shrimp canapé, canapé of shrimps

canaque [kanak] **1** ADJ Kanak **2** **Canaque** NMF Kanak

canard [kanaʀ] **1** NM **a** (= *oiseau, Culin*) duck; (*mâle*) drake → **froid, mare, vilain b*** (= *journal*) rag*; (= *fausse nouvelle*) false report, rumour, canard (*frm*) **c** (*Mus* = *couac*) false note; **faire un ~** to hit a false note **d** (*terme d'affection*) **mon (petit) ~** pet, poppet* (*Brit*) **e** (* = *sucre*) sugar lump dipped in brandy or coffee **2** COMP ▶ **canard de Barbarie** Muscovy *ou* musk duck ▶ **canard boiteux*** lame duck ▶ **canard laqué** Peking duck ▶ **canard mandarin** mandarin duck ▶ **canard à l'orange** duck in orange sauce ▶ **canard sauvage** wild duck ▶ **canard siffleur** wigeon ▶ **canard souchet** shoveler

canardeau (*pl* canardeaux) [kanaʀdo] NM duckling

canarder* [kanaʀde] ▸conjug 1◂ **1** VT (*au fusil*) to snipe at, take potshots at; (*avec pierres*) to pelt (*avec* with); **ça canardait de tous les côtés** there were bullets flying all over the place **2** VI (*Mus*) to hit a false note

canardière [kanaʀdjɛʀ] NF (= *mare*) duck-pond; (= *fusil*) punt gun

canari [kanaʀi] NM, ADJ INV canary; **(jaune) ~** canary yellow

Canaries [kanaʀi] NFPL **les (îles) ~** the Canary Islands, the Canaries

canasson [kanasɔ̃] NM (*péj* = *cheval*) nag (*péj*)

canasta [kanasta] NF canasta

Canberra [kɑ̃beʀa] N Canberra

cancan [kɑ̃kɑ̃] NM **a** (= *racontar*) piece of gossip; **~s** gossip, tittle-tattle; **faire courir des ~s (sur qn)** to spread gossip *ou* stories (about sb), tittle-tattle (about sb) **b** (= *danse*) cancan

cancaner [kɑ̃kane] ▸conjug 1◂ VI **a** (= *bavarder*) to gossip; (= *médire*) to spread scandal *ou* gossip, tittle-tattle **b** [*canard*] to quack

cancanier, -ière [kɑ̃kanje, jɛʀ] **1** ADJ gossipy, scandalmongering (*épith*), tittle-tattling (*épith*) **2** NM,F gossip, scandalmonger, tittle-tattle

cancer [kɑ̃sɛʀ] NM **a** (*Méd, fig*) cancer; **avoir un ~ du sein/du poumon** to have breast/lung cancer, have cancer of the breast/lung; **~ du sang** leukaemia (*Brit*), leukemia (*US*) **b** (*Astron*) **le Cancer** Cancer; **il est (du signe) du Cancer** he's (a) Cancer → **tropique**

cancéreux, -euse [kɑ̃seʀø, øz] **1** ADJ [*tumeur*] cancerous; [*personne*] with cancer **2** NM,F person with cancer; (*à l'hôpital*) cancer patient

cancériforme [kɑ̃seʀifɔʀm] ADJ cancer-like

cancérigène [kɑ̃seʀiʒɛn] ADJ carcinogenic, cancer-producing

cancérisation [kɑ̃seʀizasjɔ̃] NF **on peut craindre la ~ de l'organe** there is a risk of the organ becoming cancerous

cancériser (se) [kɑ̃seʀize] ▸conjug 1◂ VPR to become cancerous; **cellules cancérisées** cancerous cells

cancérogène [kɑ̃seʀoʒɛn] ADJ = **cancérigène**

cancérogenèse [kɑ̃seʀoʒənez] NF carcinogenesis

cancérologie [kɑ̃seʀɔlɔʒi] NF (= *recherche*) cancer research; (= *traitement*) cancer treatment; **il est hospitalisé en ~** he's in the (*ou* a) cancer ward

cancérologique [kɑ̃seʀɔlɔʒik] ADJ [*médecine, recherche*] cancer (*épith*)

cancérologue [kɑ̃seʀɔlɔg] NMF cancer specialist

cancre [kɑ̃kʀ] NM (*péj* = *élève*) dunce

cancrelat [kɑ̃kʀəla] NM cockroach

candélabre [kɑ̃delabʀ] NM (= *chandelier*) candelabra, candelabrum

candeur [kɑ̃dœʀ] NF ingenuousness, naïvety

candi [kɑ̃di] ADJ M → **sucre**

candida [kɑ̃dida] NM INV candida (albicans)

candidat, e [kɑ̃dida, at] NM,F (*à un concours, une élection*) candidate (**à** at); (*à un poste*) applicant, candidate (**à** for); **~ sortant** present *ou* outgoing incumbent; **les ~s à l'examen** the examination candidates, the examinees; **les ~s à l'embauche** job applicants; **être ~ à la députation** to run *ou* stand (*Brit*) for the post of deputy; **se porter ~ à un poste** to apply for a job, put o.s. forward for a job; (*Pol*) **être ~ à la présidence** to run *ou* stand (*Brit*) for president, run for the presidency; **les ~s à la retraite** candidates for retirement; **je ne suis pas ~** (*fig*) I'm not interested

▼ **candidature** [kɑ̃didatyʀ] NF (*Pol*) candidacy, candidature; (*à un poste*) application (**à** for); **~ officielle** (*à un poste*) formal application; (*Pol*) official candidacy *ou* candidature; **~ spontanée** (*à un poste*) (*action*) unsolicited application; (*lettre*) unsolicited letter of application; **poser sa ~ à un poste** to apply for a job, submit one's application for a job; **poser sa ~ à une élection** to stand in an election (*Brit*), put o.s. forward as a candidate in an election, run for election (*US*)

candide [kɑ̃did] ADJ ingenuous, naïve

candidement [kɑ̃didmɑ̃] ADV ingenuously, naïvely

candidose [kɑ̃didoz] NF thrush, candidiasis (*SPÉC*)

candir [kɑ̃diʀ] ▸conjug 2◂ VTI **(faire) ~** to candy

candomblé [kɑ̃dɔbl] NM candomblé

cane [kan] NF (female) duck

caner* [kane] ▸conjug 1◂ VI **a** (= *mourir*) to kick the bucket‡, snuff it‡; (= *flancher*) to chicken out*, funk it‡ (*Brit*), wimp out* (*US*) **(devant** in the face of)

caneton [kantɔ̃] NM duckling

canette¹ [kanɛt] NF (= *animal*) duckling

canette² [kanɛt] NF [*machine à coudre*] spool; **~ (de bière)** (= *bouteille*) small bottle of beer; (= *boîte*) can of beer

canevas [kanva] NM **a** [*livre, discours*] framework, basic structure **b** (*Couture*) (= *toile*) canvas; (= *ouvrage*) tapestry (work) **c** (*Cartographie*) network

caniche [kaniʃ] NM poodle; **~ nain** toy poodle

caniculaire [kanikylɛʀ] ADJ [*chaleur, jour*] scorching; **une journée ~** a scorcher*, a scorching (hot) day

canicule [kanikyl] NF (= *forte chaleur*) scorching heat; (= *vague de chaleur*) heatwave; (*spécialement juillet-août*) **la ~** the midsummer heat, the dog days; **aujourd'hui c'est la ~** it's a scorcher today*

canidé [kanide] NM canine; **les ~s** canines, the dog family, the Canidae (*SPÉC*)

canif [kanif] NM penknife, pocket knife; **donner un coup de ~ dans le contrat (de mariage)*** to have a bit on the side*

canin, e [kanɛ̃, in] **1** ADJ [*espèce*] canine; [*exposition*] dog (*épith*) **2 canine** NF (= *dent*) canine (tooth); (*supérieure*) eyetooth; [*chien, vampire*] fang

caninette [kaninɛt] NF pooper-scooper motor bike* (*motor bike used to clean streets of dog mess*)

canisses [kanis] NFPL (type of) wattle fence

caniveau (*pl* **caniveaux**) [kanivo] NM gutter (*in roadway etc*)

canna [kana] NM (= *fleur*) canna

cannabis [kanabis] NM cannabis

cannage [kanaʒ] NM (= *partie cannée*) canework; (= *opération*) caning

canne [kan] **1** NF **a** (= *bâton*) (walking) stick, cane; [*souffleur de verre*] blowpipe **b** (* = *jambe*) leg; **il ne tient pas sur ses ~s** he's not very steady on his pins*; **il a des ~s de serin*** he has spindly little legs → **sucre 2** COMP ▶ **canne anglaise** crutch ▶ **canne blanche** [*aveugle*] white stick ▶ **canne à pêche** fishing rod ▶ **canne à sucre** sugar cane

canné, e [kane] (*ptp de* **canner**) ADJ [*siège*] cane (*épith*)

canneberge [kanbɛʀʒ] NF cranberry

canne-épée (*pl* **cannes-épées**) [kanepe] NF swordstick

cannelé, e [kanle] (*ptp de* **canneler**) ADJ [*colonne*] fluted

canneler [kanle] ▶ conjug 4 ◀ VT to flute

cannelier [kanəlje] NM cinnamon tree

cannelle [kanɛl] NF (*Culin*) cinnamon; (= *robinet*) tap, spigot

cannelure [kan(ə)lyʀ] NF [*meuble, colonne*] flute; [*plante*] striation; **~s** [*colonne*] fluting; [*neige*] corrugation; **~s glaciaires** striae, striations

canner [kane] ▶ conjug 1 ◀ VT [+ *chaise*] to cane

cannette [kanɛt] NF = **canette²**

canneur, -euse [kanœʀ, øz] NM,F cane worker, caner

cannibale [kanibal] **1** ADJ [*tribu, animal*] cannibal (*épith*), cannibalistic **2** NMF cannibal

cannibalisation [kanibalizasjɔ̃] NF [*machine*] cannibalization; (*Comm*) **pour éviter la ~ de leurs produits** to prevent their products losing their market share *ou* the cannibalization (*US*) of their products

cannibaliser [kanibalize] ▶ conjug 1 ◀ VT [+ *machine*] to cannibalize; (*Comm*) [+ *produit*] to eat into the market share of, cannibalize (*US*); **ce produit a été cannibalisé par ...** this product has lost (some of its) market share to ...

cannibalisme [kanibalism] NM cannibalism

cannisses [kanis] NFPL = **canisses**

canoë [kanɔe] NM (= *bateau*) canoe; (= *sport*) canoeing

canoéisme [kanɔeism] NM canoeing

canoéiste [kanɔeist] NMF canoeist

canoë-kayak [kanɔekajak] NM INV **faire du ~** to go canoeing; **descendre une rivière en ~** to go down a river in a canoe, canoe down a river

canon¹ [kanɔ̃] **1** NM **a** (= *arme*) gun, cannon; (*Hist*) cannon; **~ de 75/125** 75/125-mm gun; **coup de ~** (*moderne*) artillery shot; (*Hist*) cannon shot; **des coups de ~** (*moderne*) artillery fire; (*Hist*) cannon fire; (*Tennis*) **service ~*** cannonball (serve); (*Ftbl*) **tir ~*** bullet-like shot → **chair**
b (= *tube*) [*revolver*] barrel; **fusil à ~ scié** sawn-off (*Brit*) *ou* sawed-off (*US*) shotgun; **à deux ~s** double-barrelled → **baïonnette**
c (*Tech*) [*clé, seringue*] barrel; [*arrosoir*] spout
d (*Vét*) [*bœuf, cheval*] cannonbone
e (*Hist Habillement*) canion
f (* = *verre*) glass (of wine)
2 COMP ▶ **canon à eau** water cannon ▶ **canon antiaérien** anti-aircraft *ou* A.A. gun ▶ **canon antichar** anti-tank gun ▶ **canon antigrêle** anti-hail gun ▶ **canon à électrons** electron gun ▶ **canon lisse** smooth *ou* unrifled bore ▶ **canon de marine** naval gun ▶ **canon à neige** snow cannon ▶ **canon à particule** particle beam weapon ▶ **canon rayé** rifled bore

canon² [kanɔ̃] NM **a** (= *modèle*) model, perfect example; (= *normes*) **~s** canons; **les ~s de la beauté** the canons of beauty; **elle/il est ~*** ◊ **c'est un ~*** *ou* **une fille/un mec ~*** she/he's gorgeous, she's/he's a bit of alright* (*Brit*)
b (*Rel*) canon → **droit³**

canon³ [kanɔ̃] NM (*Mus*) canon; **~ à 2 voix** canon for 2 voices; **chanter en ~** to sing in a round *ou* in canon

cañon [kaɲɔ̃] NM canyon, cañon

canonicat [kanɔnika] NM canonicate, canonry

canonique [kanɔnik] ADJ canonical; **forme ~** (*Ling*) base form → **âge**

canonisation [kanɔnizasjɔ̃] NF canonization

canoniser [kanɔnize] ▶ conjug 1 ◀ VT to canonize

canonnade [kanɔnad] NF cannonade; **le bruit d'une ~** the noise of a cannonade *ou* of (heavy) gunfire

canonner [kanɔne] ▶ conjug 1 ◀ VT to bombard, shell

canonnier [kanɔnje] NM gunner

canonnière [kanɔnjɛʀ] NF gunboat

canope [kanɔp] NM **(vase) ~** Canopic jar (*ou* urn *ou* vase)

canopée [kanɔpe] NF (forest) canopy

canot [kano] NM (= *barque*) (small *ou* open) boat, dinghy; (*Can*) Canadian canoe; **~ automobile** motorboat; **~ pneumatique** rubber *ou* inflatable dinghy; **~ de sauvetage** lifeboat

canotage [kanɔtaʒ] NM boating, rowing, canoeing (*Can*); **faire du ~** to go boating *ou* rowing; (*Can*) to go canoeing

canoter [kanɔte] ▶ conjug 1 ◀ VI to go boating *ou* rowing; (*Can*) to go canoeing

canoteur, -euse [kanɔtœʀ, øz] NM,F rower

canotier [kanɔtje] NM (= *personne, chapeau*) boater

cantal [kɑ̃tal] NM **a** (= *fromage*) Cantal (cheese) **b** (= *région*) **le Cantal** the Cantal

cantaloup [kɑ̃talu] NM cantaloup(e), muskmelon

cantate [kɑ̃tat] NF cantata

cantatrice [kɑ̃tatʀis] NF [*opéra*] (opera) singer, prima donna; [*chants classiques*] (professional) singer

cantharide [kɑ̃taʀid] NF **a** (*Zool*) cantharid **b** (= *poudre*) cantharis, cantharides, Spanish fly

cantilène [kɑ̃tilɛn] NF song, cantilena

cantine [kɑ̃tin] NF **a** (= *réfectoire*) [*entreprise*] canteen; [*école*] cafeteria, dining hall (*Brit*), lunch room (*US*); **manger à la ~** (*gén*) to eat in the canteen; (*Scol*) to have school meals; **ticket de ~** meal voucher *ou* ticket **b** (= *malle*) tin trunk

cantinière [kɑ̃tinjɛʀ] NF (*Hist Mil*) canteen woman

cantique [kɑ̃tik] NM (= *chant*) hymn; (*Bible*) canticle; **le Cantique des ~s** the Song of Songs, the Song of Solomon

canton [kɑ̃tɔ̃] NM **a** (*Pol*) (*en France*) canton, ≈ district; (*en Suisse*) canton **b** (= *section*) [*voie ferrée, route*] section **c** († = *région*) district; (*Can*) township

⸻ **CANTON** ⸻

The **cantons** *are electoral areas into which France's "arrondissements" are divided for administration purposes. Each* **canton** *usually includes several "communes", and corresponds to the constituency of a "conseiller général" who is elected in the "élections cantonales". The main town in the* **canton** *has a "gendarmerie", a local tax office and sometimes a "tribunal d'instance".*

Of the self-governing **cantons** *that make up the Swiss Confederation, six are French-speaking: Jura, Vaud, Neuchâtel, Genève, Valais (also German-speaking) and Fribourg (also German-speaking).* → ARRONDISSEMENT; COMMUNE; ÉLECTIONS

cantonade [kɑ̃tɔnad] **♦ à la cantonade** LOC ADV **parler à la ~** (*gén*) to speak to the company at large; (*Théât*) to speak (in an aside) to the audience; **c'est à qui ? dit-elle à la ~** whose is this? she asked the assembled company

cantonais, e [kɑ̃tɔnɛ, ɛz] **1** ADJ Cantonese **2** NM (*Ling*) Cantonese **3 Cantonais(e)** NM,F Cantonese

cantonal, e (*mpl* **-aux**) [kɑ̃tɔnal, o] ADJ (*en France*) cantonal, ≈ district (*épith*); (*en Suisse*) cantonal; **sur le plan ~** (*en France*) at (the) local level; (*en Suisse*) at the level of the cantons; **les (élections) ~es** cantonal elections → ÉLECTIONS

cantonnement [kɑ̃tɔnmɑ̃] NM **a** (*Mil*) (= *action*) stationing; (*chez l'habitant*) billeting, quartering; (= *lieu*) quarters, billet; (= *camp*) camp; **établir un ~** to set up (a) camp; **troupes en ~** billeted troops; **prendre ses ~s** to take up one's quarters **b** (*Rail*) block system **c** (*Admin*) [*forêt*] range

cantonner [kɑ̃tɔne] ▶ conjug 1 ◀ **1** VT **a** (*Mil*) (= *établir*) to station; (*chez l'habitant*) to quarter, billet (**chez, dans** on) **b** (= *reléguer*) to confine; **~ qn dans un travail** to confine sb to a job; **~ qn à** *ou* **dans un rôle** to limit *ou* restrict sb to a role **2** VI (*Mil*) to be stationed (**à, dans** at); (*chez l'habitant*) to be quartered *ou* billetted **3 se cantonner** VPR **se ~ à** *ou* **dans** to confine o.s. to

cantonnier [kɑ̃tɔnje] NM (= *ouvrier*) roadmender, roadman

cantonnière [kɑ̃tɔnjɛʀ] NF (= *tenture*) pelmet

canular [kanylaʀ] NM hoax; **monter un ~** to think up *ou* plan a hoax; **faire un ~ à qn** to hoax sb, play a hoax on sb

canule [kanyl] NF cannula

canuler* [kanyle] ▶ conjug 1 ◀ VT (= *ennuyer*) to bore; (= *agacer*) to pester

Canut [kanyt] NM Canute, Knut

canut, -use [kany, yz] NM,F silk worker (*in Lyons*)

canyon [kanjɔ̃, kanjɔn] NM canyon, cañon; **le Grand Canyon** the Grand Canyon

canyoning [kanjɔniŋ] NM (*Sport*) canyoning; **faire du ~** to go canyoning

CAO [seao] NF (ABRÉV = **conception assistée par ordinateur**) CAD

caoua* [kawa] NM = **kawa**

caoutchouc [kautʃu] NM **a** (= *matière*) rubber; **en ~** rubber (*épith*); **~ mousse**® foam *ou* sponge rubber; **balle en ~ mousse** rubber *ou* sponge ball; **~ synthétique** synthetic rubber → **botte¹** **b** (= *élastique*) rubber *ou* elastic band **c** († = *imperméable*) waterproof; (= *chaussures*) **~s** overshoes, galoshes **d** (= *plante verte*) rubber plant

caoutchouter [kautʃute] ▶ conjug 1 ◀ VT to rubberize, coat with rubber

caoutchouteux, -euse [kautʃutø, øz] ADJ rubbery

CAP [seape] NM (ABRÉV = **certificat d'aptitude professionnelle**) vocational training certificate, ≈ City and Guilds examination (Brit); **il a un ~ de menuisier/soudeur** he's a qualified joiner/welder, ≈ he's got a City and Guilds in joinery/welding (Brit)

cap¹ [kap] NM [a] (Géog) cape; (= promontoire) point, headland; **le ~ Canaveral** Cape Canaveral; **le ~ Horn** Cape Horn; **le ~ de Bonne Espérance** the Cape of Good Hope; (Naut) **passer** ou **doubler un ~** to round a cape; [malade] **il a passé le ~** he's over the worst, he's turned the corner; **il a passé le ~ de l'examen** he's got over the hurdle of the exam; **dépasser** ou **franchir** ou **passer le ~ des 40 ans** to turn 40; **dépasser** ou **franchir le ~ des 50 millions** to pass the 50-million mark [b] (= direction) course; (lit, fig) **changer de ~** to change course; **mettre le ~ au vent** to head into the wind; **mettre le ~ au large** to stand out to sea; **mettre le ~ sur** to head for; **~ magnétique** magnetic course ou heading → **pied** [c] (= ville) **Le Cap** Cape Town; **la province du Cap** the Cape Province

cap²* [kap] ADJ (ABRÉV = **capable**) (langage enfantin) **t'es pas ~ de le faire!** you couldn't do it if you tried!

▼ **capable** [kapabl] ADJ [a] (= compétent) able, capable [b] (= apte à) **~ de faire** capable of doing; **te sens-tu ~ de tout manger?** do you feel you can eat it all?, do you feel up to eating it all?; **tu n'en es pas ~** you're not up to it, you're not capable; **viens te battre si tu en es ~** come and fight if you've got it in you ou if you dare; **cette conférence est ~ d'intéresser beaucoup de gens** this lecture is likely to interest a lot of people [c] (= qui fait preuve de) **~ de** [+ dévouement, courage, incartade] capable of; **il est ~ du pire comme du meilleur** he's capable of (doing) the worst as well as the best; **il est ~ de tout** he'll stop at nothing, he's capable of anything [d] * **il est ~ de l'avoir perdu/de réussir** he's quite likely to have lost it/to succeed, he's quite capable of having lost it/of succeeding; **il est bien ~ d'en réchapper** he may well get over it [e] (Jur) competent

capacité [kapasite] [1] NF [a] (= contenance, potentiel) capacity; [accumulateur] capacitance, capacity; **la ~ d'accueil d'une ville** the total amount of tourist accommodation in a town; **de grande ~** [avion, stade] with a large seating capacity; **~ de mémoire/de stockage** (Ordin) memory/disk capacity [b] (= aptitude) ability (à to); **~s intellectuelles** intellectual abilities ou capacities; **en-dehors de mes ~s** beyond my capabilities ou capacities; **sa ~ d'analyse/d'analyser les faits** his capacity for analysis/for analysing facts; **il a une grande ~ d'adaptation** he's very adaptable [c] (Jur) capacity; **avoir ~ pour qch** to be (legally) entitled to sth [2] COMP ▶ **capacité civile** civil capacity ▶ **capacité contributive** ability to pay tax ▶ **capacité en droit** basic legal qualification ▶ **capacité électrostatique** capacitance ▶ **capacité légale** legal capacity ▶ **capacité thoracique** (Méd) vital capacity

caparaçon [kaparasɔ̃] NM (Hist) caparison

caparaçonner [kaparasɔne] ▶conjug 1◀ VT (Hist) [+ cheval] to caparison; (hum) **caparaçonné de cuir** all clad in leather

cape [kap] NF (Habillement) (courte) cape; (longue) cloak; **roman** (ou **film**) **de ~ et d'épée** swashbuckler → **rire**

capeline [kaplin] NF wide-brimmed hat

CAPES [kapes] NM (ABRÉV = **certificat d'aptitu-**
de au professorat de l'enseignement secondaire) → **certificat**

━━━ **CAPES** ━━━

The **CAPES** *is a competitive examination for the recruitment of French secondary school teachers. It is taken after the "licence". Successful candidates become fully-qualified teachers ("professeurs certifiés").* → AGRÉGATION ; CONCOURS

capésien, -ienne* [kapesjɛ̃, jɛn] NM,F holder of the CAPES, ≈ qualified graduate teacher

CAPET [kapet] NM (ABRÉV = **certificat d'aptitude au professorat de l'enseignement technique**) → **certificat**

capétien, -ienne [kapesjɛ̃, jɛn] [1] ADJ Capetian [2] **Capétien(ne)** NM,F Capetian

capharnaüm* [kafarnaɔm] [1] NM (= bric-à-brac, désordre) shambles*; **quel ~!** what a shambles!* [2] **Capharnaüm** N Capernaum

cap-hornier (pl **cap-horniers**) [kapɔrnje] NM Cape Horner

capillaire [kapilɛr] [1] ADJ (Anat, Bot, Phys) capillary; [soins, lotion] hair (épith) → **vaisseau** [2] NM (Anat) capillary; (Bot = fougère) maidenhair fern

capillarité [kapilarite] NF capillarity; **par ~** by capillary action

capilliculteur, -trice [kapilikyltœr, tris] NM,F specialist in hair care

capilotade [kapilɔtad] ♦**en capilotade** LOC ADJ [fruits, nez] in a pulp; [objet cassable] in smithereens; **j'ai les reins en ~** my back's killing me*

capitaine [kapitɛn] [1] NM [a] (armée de terre) captain; (armée de l'air) flight lieutenant (Brit), captain (US); [grand bateau] captain, master; [bateau de pêche] captain, skipper; (Sport) captain, skipper*; (littér = chef militaire) (military) leader → **instructeur** [b] (Zool) threadfin [2] COMP ▶ **capitaine de corvette** lieutenant commander ▶ **capitaine de frégate** commander ▶ **capitaine de gendarmerie** captain of the gendarmerie ▶ **capitaine d'industrie** captain of industry ▶ **capitaine au long cours** master mariner ▶ **capitaine de la marine marchande** captain in the merchant navy (Brit) ou in the marine (US) ▶ **capitaine des pompiers** fire chief, firemaster (Brit), fire marshal (US) ▶ **capitaine de port** harbour (Brit) ou harbor (US) master ▶ **capitaine de vaisseau** captain

capitainerie [kapitɛnri] NF harbour (Brit) ou harbor (US) master's office

capital, e (mpl **-aux**) [kapital, o] [1] ADJ [a] (= principal) [erreur, question] major (épith); [rôle] cardinal, major (épith); **d'une importance ~e** of major ou capital importance; **c'est l'œuvre ~e de Gide** it is Gide's major work; **son erreur ~e** his major ou chief mistake → **péché, sept** [b] (= essentiel) essential; **il est ~ d'y aller ou que nous y allions** it is of the utmost importance ou it is absolutely essential that we go [c] (Jur) capital → **peine** [2] NM (Fin = avoirs) capital; **50 millions de francs de ~** a 50-million-franc capital, a capital of 50 million francs; **au ~ de** with a capital of → **augmentation** [b] (= placements) **capitaux** money, capital; **la circulation/fuite des capitaux** the circulation/flight of capital [c] (= possédants) **le ~** capital; **le ~ et le travail** capital and labour; **le grand ~** big investors [d] (= fonds, richesse) stock, fund; **le ~ de connaissances acquis à l'école** the stock ou fund of knowledge acquired at school; **la connaissance d'une langue constitue un ~ appréciable** knowing a language is a significant ou major asset; **le ~ artistique de la région** the artistic wealth ou resources of the region; **accroître son ~(-)santé** to build up one's health;
elle a su se bâtir un ~(-)confiance she managed to gain ou win everybody's trust [3] **capitale** NF [a] (Typo) (lettre) **~e** capital (letter); **en grandes/petites ~e** in large/small capitals; **en ~es d'imprimerie** in block letters ou block capitals [b] (= métropole) capital (city); **le dimanche, les Parisiens quittent la ~e** on Sundays Parisians leave the capital; **~e régionale** regional capital; **la ~e du vin** the wine capital [4] COMP ▶ **capital circulant** working capital, circulating capital ▶ **capital constant** constant capital ▶ **capital décès** death benefit ▶ **capital d'exploitation** working capital ▶ **capitaux fébriles** hot money ▶ **capital fixe** fixed (capital) assets ▶ **capitaux flottants** floating capital ou assets ▶ **capital initial** ou **de lancement** seed ou start-up money ▶ **capital social** authorized capital, share capital ▶ **capitaux spéculatifs** = capitaux fébriles ▶ **capital variable** variable capital

capitalisable [kapitalizabl] ADJ capitalizable

capitalisation [kapitalizasjɔ̃] NF capitalization; **~ boursière** market capitalization ou valuation

capitaliser [kapitalize] ▶conjug 1◀ [1] VT [a] (= amasser) [+ somme] to amass; [+ expériences, connaissances] to build up, accumulate; **l'intérêt capitalisé pendant un an** an interest accrued ou accumulated in a year [b] (Fin = ajouter au capital) [+ intérêts] to capitalize [c] (= calculer le capital de) [+ rente] to capitalize [2] VI [a] (= amasser de l'argent) to save, put money by [b] **~ sur** [+ événement, situation] to capitalize on

capitalisme [kapitalism] NM capitalism

capitaliste [kapitalist] ADJ, NMF capitalist

capitalistique [kapitalistik] ADJ capital (épith); **intensité ~** capital intensity; **industrie ~** capital-intensive industry

capital-risque [kapitalrisk] NM venture capital

capitation [kapitasjɔ̃] NF (Hist) poll tax, capitation

capiteux, -euse [kapitø, øz] ADJ [vin, parfum] heady; [femme, beauté] intoxicating, alluring

Capitole [kapitɔl] NM **le ~** the Capitol

capitolin, e [kapitɔlɛ̃, in] ADJ Capitoline; **le (mont) Capitolin** the Capitoline (Hill)

capiton [kapitɔ̃] NM (= bourre) padding; [cellulite] node of fat (SPÉC); **les ~s** orange-peel skin

capitonnage [kapitɔnaʒ] NM padding

capitonner [kapitɔne] ▶conjug 1◀ VT [+ siège, porte] to pad (de with); (fig) **capitonné de** lined with; **nid capitonné de plumes** nest lined with feathers

capitulaire [kapitylɛr] ADJ (Rel) capitular; **salle ~** chapter house

capitulard, e [kapitylar, ard] ADJ, NM,F defeatist

capitulation [kapitylasjɔ̃] NF (Mil, fig) capitulation, surrender; (= traité) capitulation (treaty); **~ sans conditions** unconditional surrender

capituler [kapityle] ▶conjug 1◀ VI (Mil = se rendre) to capitulate, surrender; (fig = céder) to surrender, give in, capitulate

capon, -onne†† [kapɔ̃, ɔn] [1] ADJ cowardly [2] NM,F coward

caporal (pl **-aux**) [kapɔral, o] NM [a] (Mil) lance corporal (Brit), private first class (US); **~ d'ordinaire** mess corporal; **~-chef** corporal [b] (= tabac) caporal

caporalisme [kapɔralism] NM [personne, régime] petty officiousness

capot [kapo] [1] NM [a] (véhicule, moteur) bonnet (Brit), hood (US) [b] (Naut) (= bâche de protection) cover; (= trou d'homme) companion hatch [2] ADJ INV (Cartes) **être ~** to have lost all the tricks; **il nous a mis ~** he took all the tricks

capotage [kapɔtaʒ] NM [*véhicule*] overturning; [*projet*] failure; [*négociations*] breakdown

capote [kapɔt] NF **a** [*voiture*] top, hood (*Brit*) **b** (*gén Mil = manteau*) greatcoat **c** ~ (**anglaise**)**:** French letter*, rubber**:**, safe**:** (*US*) **d** († = *chapeau*) bonnet

capoter [kapɔte] ▸ conjug 1 ◂ VI [*véhicule*] to overturn; [*négociations*] to founder; **faire** ~ [+ *véhicule*] to overturn; [+ *négociations, projet*] to ruin, scupper* (*Brit*), put paid to (*Brit*)

cappuccino [kaputʃino] NM cappuccino

câpre [kɑpʀ] NF (*Culin*) caper

Capri [kapʀi] NF Capri

caprice [kapʀis] NM **a** (= *lubie*) whim, caprice; (= *toquade amoureuse*) (passing) fancy; **agir par** ~ to act out of capriciousness; **ne lui cède pas, c'est seulement un** ~ don't give in to him, it's only a whim; **faire un** ~ to throw a tantrum; **cet enfant fait des** ~**s** the child's being awkward *ou* temperamental; **cet arbre est un vrai** ~ **de la nature** that tree is a real freak of nature; **une récolte exceptionnelle due à quelque** ~ **de la nature** an exceptional crop due to some quirk *ou* trick of nature **b** (= *variations*) ~**s** [*nuages, vent, marché*] vagaries, caprices; **les** ~**s de la mode** the vagaries *ou* whims of fashion; **les** ~**s du sort** *ou* **du hasard** the quirks of fate **c** (*Mus*) capriccio, caprice

capricieusement [kapʀisjøzmɑ̃] ADV capriciously, whimsically

capricieux, -ieuse [kapʀisjø, jøz] ADJ **a** (= *fantasque*) (*gén*) capricious, whimsical; [*appareil*] temperamental; (*littér*) [*brise*] capricious; [*chemin*] winding **b** (= *coléreux*) wayward; **cet enfant est (un)** ~ the child's awkward *ou* temperamental, the child throws tantrums

capricorne [kapʀikɔʀn] NM **a** (*Astron*) **le Capricorne** Capricorn; **il est (du signe) du Capricorne** he's (a) Capricorn → **tropique** **b** (*Zool*) capricorn beetle

câprier [kɑpʀije] NM caper bush *ou* shrub

caprin, e [kapʀɛ̃, in] **1** ADJ (*Zool*) [*espèce*] goat (*épith*), caprine (*SPÉC*) **2** NM **les** ~**s** members of the goat family, the Caprinae (*SPÉC*)

capriné [kapʀine] NM = **caprin**

capsulage [kapsylaʒ] NM [*bouteille de vin*] capsuling; [*bouteille de bière, d'eau*] capping

capsule [kapsyl] NF **a** (*Anat, Bot, Pharm*) capsule **b** [*bouteille*] cap; (*couvrant le goulot*) capsule **c** [*arme à feu*] (percussion) cap, primer; [*pistolet d'enfant*] cap → **pistolet** **d** ~ **spatiale** space capsule

capsuler [kapsyle] ▸ conjug 1 ◂ VT [+ *bouteille de bière, eau*] to put a cap on; [+ *bouteille de vin*] to put a capsule on

captage [kaptaʒ] NM [*cours d'eau*] harnessing; [*message, émission*] picking up

captateur, -trice [kaptatœʀ, tʀis] NM,F (*Jur*) ~ **d'héritage** *ou* **de succession** legacy hunter

captation [kaptasjɔ̃] NF **a** [*marché, pouvoir*] capturing; [*clientèle*] poaching; (*Jur*) ~ **d'héritage** captation (*SPÉC*) *ou* improper solicitation of a legacy **b** [*cours d'eau, source*] harnessing; (*Bio*) [*substance*] uptake

capter [kapte] ▸ conjug 1 ◂ VT **a** [+ *énergie, cours d'eau*] to harness; [+ *courant*] to tap; [+ *lumière*] to catch; [+ *atmosphère*] to capture **b** [+ *suffrages, attention*] to win, capture; [+ *confiance, bienveillance*] to win, gain; **cette entreprise a capté 12 % du marché** this firm has captured 12% of the market **c** (*Téléc*) [+ *message, émission, chaîne*] to pick up

capteur [kaptœʀ] NM sensor; ~ **solaire** solar panel

captieux, -ieuse [kapsjø, jøz] ADJ specious

captif, -ive [kaptif, iv] **1** ADJ [*personne, marché, clientèle*] captive; [*nappe d'eau*] confined → **ballon¹** **2** NM,F captive, prisoner

captivant, e [kaptivɑ̃, ɑ̃t] ADJ [*film, lecture*] gripping, enthralling; [*personne*] fascinating, captivating

captiver [kaptive] ▸ conjug 1 ◂ VT [+ *personne*] to fascinate, enthrall, captivate; [+ *attention, esprit*] to captivate

captivité [kaptivite] NF captivity; **en** ~ in captivity; **pendant sa** ~ while he was in captivity

capture [kaptyʀ] NF **a** (= *action*) [*malfaiteur, animal*] catching, capture; [*objet*] catching; [*navire*] capture **b** (= *animal, objet*) catch; (= *personne*) captured person **c** (*Phys, Géog*) capture; ~ **électronique** electron capture

capturer [kaptyʀe] ▸ conjug 1 ◂ VT [+ *malfaiteur, animal*] to catch, capture; [+ *objet*] to catch; [+ *navire*] to capture

capuche [kapyʃ] NF hood

capuchette [kapyʃɛt] NF rainhood

capuchon [kapyʃɔ̃] NM **a** (*Couture*) hood; (*Rel*) cowl; (= *pèlerine*) hooded raincoat **b** [*stylo*] top, cap **c** [*cheminée*] cowl

capucin [kapysɛ̃] NM (*Rel*) Capuchin; (*Zool*) capuchin → **barbe¹**

capucine [kapysin] NF (*Bot*) nasturtium; (*Rel*) Capuchin nun

cap(-)verdien, -ienne [kapvɛʀdjɛ̃, jɛn] **1** ADJ Cape Verdean **2** **Cap(-)verdien(ne)** NM,F Cape Verdean

Cap-Vert [kapvɛʀ] NM **le** ~ Cape Verde; **les îles du** ~ the Cape Verde Islands

caque [kak] NF herring barrel ■ (*PROV*) **la** ~ **sent toujours le hareng** what's bred in the bone will (come) out in the flesh (*PROV*)

caquelon [kaklɔ̃] NM earthenware *ou* cast-iron fondue-dish

caquet* [kakɛ] NM [*personne*] gossip, prattle, blether* (*Brit*); [*poule*] cackle, cackling; **rabattre** *ou* **rabaisser le** ~ **de** *ou* **à qn*** to bring *ou* pull sb down a peg or two

caquetage [kaktaʒ], **caquètement** [kaketmɑ̃] NM [*poule*] cackle, cackling; [*personne*] prattle, prattling

caqueter [kakte] ▸ conjug 4 ◂ VI [*personne*] to prattle; [*poule*] to cackle

car¹ [kaʀ] NM coach (*Brit*), bus (*US*); ~ **de police** police van; ~ (**de ramassage**) **scolaire** school bus

car² [kaʀ] CONJ because, for

carabin [kaʀabɛ̃] NM (*arg Méd*) medical student

carabine [kaʀabin] NF rifle, gun, carbine (*SPÉC*); [*stand de tir*] rifle; ~ **à air comprimé** air rifle *ou* gun

carabiné, e* [kaʀabine] ADJ [*fièvre, vent, orage*] raging, violent; [*cocktail, facture, punition*] stiff; [*amende*] heavy, stiff; [*rhume*] stinking*, shocking; [*migraine*] splitting, blinding; **mal de dents** ~ raging toothache

carabinier [kaʀabinje] NM (*en Espagne*) carabinero, customs officer; (*en Italie*) carabiniere, police officer; (*Hist Mil*) carabineer; **les** ~**s siciliens** the Sicilian carabinieri

carabosse [kaʀabɔs] NF → **fée**

Caracas [kaʀakas] N Caracas

caraco [kaʀako] NM († = *chemisier*) (woman's) loose blouse; (= *sous-vêtement*) camisole

caracoler [kaʀakɔle] ▸ conjug 1 ◂ VI [*cheval*] (= *évoluer*) to prance; (= *gambader*) to gambol *ou* caper about; (*Dressage*) to caracole; ~ **sur un cheval** to ride proud; [*concurrent*] ~ **en tête** to be well ahead of the others; **il caracole en tête des sondages** he's riding high in the polls

caractère [kaʀaktɛʀ] NM **a** (= *tempérament*) character, nature; **être d'un** *ou* **avoir un** ~ **ouvert** to have an outgoing nature; **être d'un** *ou* **avoir un** ~ **fermé** to be withdrawn; **être d'un** *ou* **avoir un** ~ **froid/passionné** to be a cold/passionate person; **avoir bon/mauvais** ~ to be good-/bad-tempered, be good-/ill-natured; **il est très jeune de** ~ [*adolescent*] he's

very immature; [*adulte*] he has a very youthful outlook; **son** ~ **a changé** his character has changed, he has changed; **les chats ont un** ~ **sournois** cats have a sly nature; **il a** *ou* **c'est un heureux** ~ he has a happy nature; **ce n'est pas dans son** ~ **de faire** ◊ **il n'a pas un** ~ **à faire** it is not in his nature to do; **le** ~ **méditerranéen/latin** the Mediterranean/Latin character; **il a un sale** ~* ◊ **il a un** ~ **de cochon*** he's a difficult *ou* an awkward so-and-so*; **il a un** ~ **en or** he's very good-natured, he has a delightful nature **b** (= *nature, aspect*) nature; **sa présence confère à la réception un** ~ **officiel** his being here gives an official character *ou* flavour to the reception; **la situation n'a aucun** ~ **de gravité** the situation shows no sign *ou* evidence of being serious; **mission à** ~ **humanitaire** humanitarian mission, mission of a humanitarian nature **c** (= *fermeté*) character; **il a du** ~ he has *ou* he's got character; **il n'a pas de** ~ he's got no backbone, he's spineless; **style sans** ~ characterless style **d** (= *cachet, individualité*) character; **la maison/cette vieille rue a du** ~ the house/this old street has got character **e** (*littér = personne*) character; **ces** ~**s ne sont pas faciles à vivre** these characters *ou* people are not easy to live with → **comique** **f** (= *caractéristique*) characteristic; ~ **héréditaire/acquis** hereditary/acquired characteristic **g** (*Écriture, Typo*) character; ~ **gras/maigre** heavy-/light-faced letter; (*Typo*) ~**s gras** bold type (*NonC*); **en gros/petits** ~**s** in large/small characters; **en** ~**s d'imprimerie** in block capitals; **les** ~**s de ce livre** the print in this book **h** (*Ordin*) character; ~ **de commande** control character; ~ **générique** *ou* **de remplacement** wildcard

caractériel, -elle [kaʀakteʀjɛl] **1** ADJ **a** [*personne*] (*Psych*) emotionally disturbed, maladjusted; (= *lunatique*) **il est un peu** ~ he has mood swings **b** **traits** ~**s** traits of character; **troubles** ~**s** emotional disturbance *ou* problems **2** NM,F (= *adulte*) emotionally disturbed person; (= *enfant*) problem *ou* maladjusted child

caractérisation [kaʀakteʀizasjɔ̃] NF characterization

caractérisé, e [kaʀakteʀize] (*ptp de* **caractériser**) ADJ [*erreur*] blatant; **une rubéole** ~**e** a clear *ou* straightforward case of German measles; **c'est de l'insubordination** ~**e** it's sheer *ou* downright insubordination

caractériser [kaʀakteʀize] ▸ conjug 1 ◂ VT to characterize; **avec l'enthousiasme qui le caractérise** with his characteristic enthusiasm; **ça se caractérise par** it is characterized *ou* distinguished by; **ce qui caractérise ce paysage** the main *ou* characteristic features of this landscape

▾ **caractéristique** [kaʀakteʀistik] **1** ADJ characteristic (**de** of) **2** NF characteristic, (typical) feature; (*Admin*) ~**s signalétiques** particulars, personal details; ~**s techniques** design features

caractérologie [kaʀakteʀɔlɔʒi] NF characterology

carafe [kaʀaf] NF **a** (= *récipient*) decanter; [*eau, vin ordinaire*] carafe; **une demi-**~ **de vin** half a carafe of wine; **tomber en** ~* to break down; **rester en** ~* to be left stranded, be left high and dry; **laisser qn en** ~* to leave sb high and dry **b** (* = *tête*) head, nut*

carafon [kaʀafɔ̃] NM **a** (= *récipient*) small decanter; [*eau, vin ordinaire*] small carafe **b** (* = *tête*) head, nut*

caraïbe [kaʀaib] **1** ADJ Caribbean; **les îles Caraïbes** the Caribbean islands; **les Indiens** ~**s** the Carib Indians **2** **Caraïbe** NMF (= *personne*) Carib **3** **Caraïbe(s)** NF(PL) **la Caraï-**

➤ GRAMMAIRE ACTIVE: **caractéristique** 53.1, 53.6

be ◊ **les Caraïbes** the Caribbean (islands); **la mer des Caraïbes** the Caribbean (Sea)

carambolage [kaʀɑ̃bɔlaʒ] NM [autos] multiple crash, pile-up; (Billard) cannon (Brit), carom (US)

carambole [kaʀɑ̃bɔl] NF [a] (Billard) red (ball) [b] (= fruit) star fruit, carambola

caramboler [kaʀɑ̃bɔle] ▸conjug 1◂ [1] VT to collide with, run into; **5 voitures se sont carambolées** there was a 5-car pile-up, 5 cars ran into each other ou collided [2] VI (Billard) to cannon (Brit), get ou make a cannon (Brit) ou carom (US)

carambouillage [kaʀɑ̃bujaʒ] NM, **carambouille** [kaʀɑ̃buj] NF (Jur) reselling of unlawfully owned goods

caramel [kaʀamɛl] [1] NM (= sucre fondu) caramel; (= bonbon) (mou) caramel, fudge, chewy toffee; (dur) toffee [2] ADJ INV caramel(-coloured)

caramélisation [kaʀamelizasjɔ̃] NF caramelization

caramélisé, e [kaʀamelize] (ptp de **caraméliser**) ADJ [aliment] (= enrobé de caramel) coated with caramel, caramel-coated; [moule, plat] caramel-lined; (= très cuit, au goût de caramel) caramelized

caraméliser [kaʀamelize] ▸conjug 1◂ [1] VT [+ sucre] to caramelize; [+ moule, pâtisserie] to coat with caramel; [+ boisson, aliment] to flavour (Brit) ou flavor (US) with caramel [2] VI, **se caraméliser** VPR [sucre] to caramelize

carapace [kaʀapas] NF [crabe, tortue] shell, carapace; **~ de boue** crust of mud; **sommet recouvert d'une ~ de glace** summit encased in a sheath of ice; **il est difficile de percer sa ~ d'égoïsme** it's difficult to penetrate the armour of his egoism ou his thickskinned self-centredness

carapater (se)* [kaʀapate] ▸conjug 1◂ VPR to skedaddle*, run off, hop it* (Brit)

carat [kaʀa] NM (Bijouterie) carat; **de l'or 18 ~s** ◊ **du 18 ~s** 18-carat gold; **il faut partir à midi, dernier ~*** we have to leave by midday ou noon at the latest

Caravage [kaʀavaʒ] NM **le ~** Caravaggio

caravane [kaʀavan] NF (= convoi) caravan; (= véhicule) caravan, trailer (US); **une ~ de voitures** a procession ou stream of cars; **une ~ de touristes** a stream of tourists; **la ~ du Tour de France** the whole retinue of the Tour de France; **la ~ publicitaire** the publicity caravan → **chien**

caravanier, -ière [kaʀavanje, jɛʀ] [1] ADJ [itinéraire, chemin] caravan (épith); **tourisme ~** caravanning (Brit), RV ou camper vacationing (US) [2] NM [a] (= conducteur de caravane) caravaneer [b] (= vacancier) caravanner (Brit), person vacationing in an RV ou a camper (US)

caravaning [kaʀavaniŋ] NM **faire du ~** to go caravanning (Brit), go on vacation in an RV ou a camper (US); **camp de ~** caravan site, trailer camp (US) ou court (US) ou park (US)

caravansérail [kaʀavɑ̃seʀaj] NM (lit, fig) caravanserail

caravelle [kaʀavɛl] NF (Hist Naut) caravel

carbochimie [kaʀbɔʃimi] NF organic chemistry

carbonade [kaʀbɔnad] NF (= viande) char-grilled meat; **~ flamande** beef stew

carbonate [kaʀbɔnat] NM carbonate; **~ de soude** sodium carbonate, washing soda

carbone [kaʀbɔn] NM (= matière, feuille) carbon; **le ~ 14** carbon-14; **(papier) ~** carbon (paper) → **datation**

carboné, e [kaʀbɔne] ADJ carbonaceous

carbonifère [kaʀbɔnifɛʀ] [1] ADJ (Minér) carboniferous; (Géol) Carboniferous [2] NM Carboniferous

carbonique [kaʀbɔnik] ADJ carbonic → **gaz, neige** etc

carbonisation [kaʀbɔnizasjɔ̃] NF carbonization

carbonisé, e [kaʀbɔnize] (ptp de **carboniser**) ADJ [arbre, restes] charred; **il est mort ~** he was burned to death

carboniser [kaʀbɔnize] ▸conjug 1◂ VT [+ bois, substance] to carbonize; [+ forêt, maison] to burn to the ground, reduce to ashes; [+ rôti] to burn to a cinder

carbonnade [kaʀbɔnad] NF = **carbonade**

carburant [kaʀbyʀɑ̃] [1] ADJ M **mélange ~** mixture of petrol (Brit) ou gasoline (US) and air (in internal combustion engine) [2] NM fuel; **les ~s** fuel oils

carburateur [kaʀbyʀatœʀ] NM carburettor (Brit), carburetor (US)

carburation [kaʀbyʀasjɔ̃] NF [essence] carburation; [fer] carburization

carbure [kaʀbyʀ] NM carbide → **lampe**

carburé, e [kaʀbyʀe] (ptp de **carburer**) ADJ [air, mélange] carburetted; [métal] carburized

carburer [kaʀbyʀe] ▸conjug 1◂ [1] VI [a] [moteur] **ça carbure bien/mal** it is well/badly tuned [b]*‡ [personne] **il carbure au vin rouge** he drinks red wine as if it was water; **elle carbure aux amphétamines/au café** she lives on amphetamines/on coffee; **ça carbure sec ici!** (boisson) they're really knocking it back in here!; (travail) they're working flat out!* [2] VT [+ air] to carburet; [+ métal] to carburize

carburol [kaʀbyʀɔl] NM gasohol

carcajou [kaʀkaʒu] NM wolverine

carcan [kaʀkɑ̃] NM (Hist) iron collar; (= contrainte) yoke, shackles; **ce col est un vrai ~** this collar is like a vice; **le ~ de la tradition** the straitjacket of tradition, the fetters of tradition

carcasse [kaʀkas] NF [a] [animal] carcass; [maison] shell; **je vais réchauffer ma ~ au soleil*** I'm going to toast myself in the sun*; **j'ai du mal à traîner ma vieille ~*** I'm finding it difficult to drag my old bones around*; **des ~s de voitures calcinées** burnt-out cars [b] (= armature) [abat-jour] frame; [bateau] skeleton; [immeuble] shell, skeleton; **pneu à ~ radiale/diagonale** radial/cross-ply tyre

carcéral, e [kaʀseʀal, o] ADJ prison (épith); **régime ~** prison regime; **l'univers ~** prison life

carcinogène [kaʀsinɔʒɛn] ADJ carcinogenic

carcinogenèse [kaʀsinɔʒənɛz] NF carcinogenesis

carcinome [kaʀsinom] NM carcinoma

cardage [kaʀdaʒ] NM carding

cardamine [kaʀdamin] NF cuckooflower, lady's-smock

cardamome [kaʀdamɔm] NF cardamom

cardan [kaʀdɑ̃] NM universal joint → **joint**

carde [kaʀd] NF (Tex) card

carder [kaʀde] ▸conjug 1◂ VT to card; **laine cardée** carded wool

cardeur, -euse [kaʀdœʀ, øz] [1] NM,F carder [2] **cardeuse** NF (= machine) carding machine, carder

cardiaque [kaʀdjak] [1] ADJ (Anat) cardiac, heart (épith); **malade ~** heart case ou patient; **être ~** to suffer from ou have a heart condition; **chirurgie ~** heart surgery → **crise** [2] NMF heart case ou patient

Cardiff [kaʀdif] N Cardiff

cardigan [kaʀdigɑ̃] NM cardigan

cardinal, e (mpl **-aux**) [kaʀdinal, o] [1] ADJ [nombre] cardinal; (littér = capital) cardinal → **point**¹ [2] NM [a] (Rel) cardinal; **~-archevêque** Cardinal Archbishop [b] (= nombre) cardinal number [c] (Orn) cardinal (bird)

cardinalat [kaʀdinala] NM cardinalate, cardinalship

cardinalice [kaʀdinalis] ADJ of a cardinal; **conférer à qn la dignité ~** to make sb a cardinal, raise sb to the purple → **pourpre**

cardiogramme [kaʀdjɔgʀam] NM cardiogram

cardiographe [kaʀdjɔgʀaf] NM cardiograph

cardiographie [kaʀdjɔgʀafi] NF cardiography

cardiologie [kaʀdjɔlɔʒi] NF cardiology

cardiologique [kaʀdjɔlɔʒik] ADJ cardiological

cardiologue [kaʀdjɔlɔg] NMF cardiologist, heart specialist

cardio-pulmonaire (pl **cardio-pulmonaires**) [kaʀdjopylmɔnɛʀ] ADJ cardiopulmonary

cardiotonique [kaʀdjɔtɔnik] NM heart tonic

cardiovasculaire [kaʀdjovaskylɛʀ] ADJ cardiovascular

cardite [kaʀdit] NF carditis

cardon [kaʀdɔ̃] NM cardoon

carême [kaʀɛm] NM (= jeûne) fast; (Rel = période) **le Carême** Lent; **sermon de ~** Lent sermon; **faire ~** to observe ou keep Lent, fast during Lent; **rompre le ~** to break the Lent fast; **le ~ qu'il s'est imposé** the fast he has undertaken; **face** ou **figure** ou **mine de ~*** long face (fig)

carême-prenant †† (pl **carêmes-prenants**) [kaʀɛmpʀənɑ̃] NM (= période) Shrovetide ††; (= personne) Shrovetide reveller ††

carénage [kaʀenaʒ] NM [a] (Naut) (= action) careening; (= lieu) careenage [b] [véhicule] (= action) streamlining; (= partie) fairing

carence [kaʀɑ̃s] NF [a] (Méd) deficiency; **~ alimentaire** nutritional deficiency; **~ vitaminique** ou **en vitamines** vitamin deficiency; **maladie de ou par ~** deficiency disease [b] (= manque) shortage; **une grave ~ en personnel qualifié** a serious shortage of qualified staff; **~ affective** emotional deprivation [c] (= incompétence) [gouvernement] shortcomings, incompetence; [parents] inadequacy [d] (= défauts) **les ~s de** [+ système, organisation] the inadequacies ou shortcomings of [e] (Jur) insolvency

carencé, e [kaʀɑ̃se] ADJ [personne] nutritionally deficient, suffering from nutritional deficiency; [régime] deficient (**en** in); **régime ~ en fer** diet deficient in iron, iron-deficient diet; **gravement ~ en vitamine F** seriously deficient in vitamin F

carène [kaʀɛn] NF [a] (Naut) (lower part of the) hull; **mettre en ~** to careen [b] (Bot) carina, keel

caréner [kaʀene] ▸conjug 6◂ VT [a] (Naut) to careen [b] (Tech) [+ véhicule] to streamline

caressant, e [kaʀesɑ̃, ɑ̃t] ADJ [enfant, animal] affectionate; [regard, voix] caressing, tender; [brise] caressing

caresse [kaʀɛs] NF [a] (= câlinerie) caress; (à un animal) stroke; **faire des ~s à** [+ personne] to caress; [+ animal] to stroke, pet; (littér) **la ~ de la brise/des vagues** the caress of the breeze/of the waves [b] (†† = flatterie) cajolery (NonC), flattery (NonC); **endormir la méfiance de qn par des ~s** to use cajolery to allay ou quieten sb's suspicions

caresser [kaʀese] ▸conjug 1◂ VT [a] [+ personne] to caress; [+ animal] to stroke, pet; [+ objet] to stroke; **il lui caressait les jambes/les seins** he was stroking ou caressing her legs/caressing ou fondling her breasts; **il ressait les touches du piano** he stroked ou caressed the keys of the piano; **~ qn du regard** to gaze fondly at sb; **~ qn dans le sens du poil** to stay on the right side of sb; **il vaut mieux le ~ dans le sens du poil** you'd better not rub him up the wrong way; (hum) **je vais lui ~ les côtes*** ou **l'échine*** I'm going to give him such a hiding [b] [+ espoir] to entertain, toy with; **~ le projet de faire qch** to toy with the idea of doing sth [c] († = flatter) to flatter, fawn on

car-ferry (pl **car-ferrys** ou **car-ferries**) [kaʀfeʀi] NM (car) ferry

cargaison [kaʀgɛzɔ̃] NF a (Aviat, Naut) cargo, freight; **une ~ de bananes** a cargo of bananas b * load, stock; **des ~s de** [+ lettres, demandes] heaps ou piles of; **des ~s de touristes** busloads (ou shiploads ou planeloads) of tourists

cargo [kaʀgo] NM cargo boat, freighter; **~ mixte** cargo and passenger vessel

cargue [kaʀg] NF (Naut) brail

carguer [kaʀge] ▸conjug 1◂ VT [+ voiles] to brail, furl

cari [kaʀi] NM = **curry**

cariatide [kaʀjatid] NF caryatid

caribou [kaʀibu] NM caribou

caricatural, e (mpl -aux) [kaʀikatyʀal, o] ADJ (= ridicule) [aspect, traits] ridiculous, grotesque; (= exagéré) [description, interprétation] caricatured

caricature [kaʀikatyʀ] NF a (= dessin, description) caricature; (politique) (satirical) cartoon; **faire la ~ de** to make a caricature of, caricature; **une ~ de procès** a mere mockery of a trial; **une ~ de la vérité** a caricature ou gross distortion of the truth; **c'est une ~ de l'Anglais en vacances** he is a caricature of the Englishman on holiday b (* = personne laide) fright*

caricaturer [kaʀikatyʀe] ▸conjug 1◂ VT to caricature

caricaturiste [kaʀikatyʀist] NMF caricaturist; (à intention politique) (satirical) cartoonist

carie [kaʀi] NF a (Méd) [dents, os] caries (NonC); **la ~ dentaire** tooth decay, (dental) caries; **j'ai une ~** I need a filling, I've got a cavity b (Bot) [arbre] blight; [blé] smut, bunt

carié, e [kaʀje] (ptp de **carier**) ADJ [dent] decayed, bad

carier [kaʀje] ▸conjug 7◂ 1 VT to decay, cause to decay; **dent cariée** bad ou decayed tooth 2 **se carier** VPR to decay

carillon [kaʀijɔ̃] NM a [église] (= cloches) (peal ou set of) bells; (= air) chimes; **on entendait le ~ de St Pierre/des ~s joyeux** we could hear the chimes of St Pierre/hear joyful chimes b [horloge] (= système de sonnerie) chime; (= air) chimes; **une horloge à ~** un ~ a chiming clock c [sonnette d'entrée] (door) chime

carillonner [kaʀijɔne] ▸conjug 1◂ 1 VI a [cloches] to ring, chime; (à toute volée) to peal out b (à la porte) to ring very loudly; **ça ne sert à rien de ~, il n'y a personne** no use ringing away on the doorbell like that — there's no one in 2 VT [+ fête] to announce with a peal of bells; [+ heure] to chime, ring; (fig) [+ nouvelle] to broadcast

carillonneur [kaʀijɔnœʀ] NM bell ringer

cariste [kaʀist] NM fork-lift truck operator

caritatif, -ive [kaʀitatif, iv] ADJ charitable; **association** ou **organisation caritative** charity, charitable organization

carlin [kaʀlɛ̃] NM pug(dog)

carlingue [kaʀlɛ̃g] NF (Aviat) cabin; (Naut) keelson

carliste [kaʀlist] ADJ, NMF Carlist

carmagnole [kaʀmaɲɔl] NF (= chanson, danse) carmagnole; (Hist = veste) short jacket (worn during the French revolution)

carme [kaʀm] NM Carmelite, White Friar

carmel [kaʀmɛl] NM (= monastère) [carmes] Carmelite monastery; [carmélites] Carmelite convent; **le Carmel** (= ordre) the Carmelite order

carmélite [kaʀmelit] NF Carmelite nun

carmin [kaʀmɛ̃] 1 NM (= colorant) cochineal; (= couleur) carmine, crimson 2 ADJ INV carmine, crimson

carminé, e [kaʀmine] ADJ carmine, crimson

carnage [kaʀnaʒ] NM (lit, fig) carnage, slaughter; **quel ~!** what a massacre!; **faire un ~** (lit) to cause absolute carnage; (fig) **je vais faire un ~!** I'm going to murder someone!

carnassier, -ière [kaʀnasje, jɛʀ] 1 ADJ [animal] carnivorous, flesh-eating; [dent] carnassial 2 NM carnivore; **~s** carnivores, Carnivora (SPÉC) 3 **carnassière** NF (= dent) carnassial; (= gibecière) gamebag

carnation [kaʀnasjɔ̃] NF (= teint) complexion; (Peinture) flesh tint

carnaval (pl **carnavals**) [kaʀnaval] NM (= fête) carnival; (= période) carnival (time); (= mannequin) **(Sa Majesté) Carnaval** King Carnival; **de ~** [tenue, ambiance] carnival (épith)

carnavalesque [kaʀnavalɛsk] ADJ (= grotesque) carnivalesque

carne * [kaʀn] NF (péj = viande) tough ou leathery meat; († = cheval) nag*, hack; **quelle ~!** (homme) what a swine!‡ ou bastard!*‡; (femme) what a bitch!*‡

carné, e [kaʀne] ADJ a [alimentation] meat (épith) b [littér] [fleur, ton] flesh-coloured

carnet [kaʀnɛ] 1 NM (= calepin) notebook; (= liasse) book 2 COMP ▸ **carnet d'adresses** address book; **avoir un ~ d'adresses bien rempli** to have a lot of (good) contacts ▸ **carnet de bal** dance card ▸ **carnet de billets** book of tickets ▸ **carnet de bord** (Naut, Aviat) log(book) ▸ **carnet de chèques** chequebook (Brit), checkbook (US) ▸ **carnet de commandes** order book; **nos ~s de commandes sont pleins** we have a full order book ▸ **carnet à croquis** ou **dessins** sketchbook ▸ **carnet de maternité** medical record of pregnancy ▸ **carnet mondain** (Presse) society column ▸ **carnet de notes** (= calepin) notebook; (Scol) report card, school report (Brit); **avoir un bon ~ de notes** to have a good report ▸ **carnet de route** travel diary ▸ **carnet rose** (Presse) births column ▸ **carnet de santé** health record ▸ **carnet à souches** counterfoil book ▸ **carnet de timbres** book of stamps ▸ **carnet de vol** (Aviat) log(book)

carnier [kaʀnje] NM gamebag

carnivore [kaʀnivɔʀ] 1 ADJ [animal] carnivorous, flesh-eating; [insecte, plante] carnivorous; (hum) [personne] **il est très ~** he's a big meat-eater, he loves his meat 2 NM carnivore; **~s carnivores**, Carnivora (SPÉC)

Caroline [kaʀɔlin] NF **~ du Nord** North Carolina; **~ du Sud** South Carolina

carolingien, -ienne [kaʀɔlɛ̃ʒjɛ̃, jɛn] 1 ADJ Carolingian 2 **Carolingien(ne)** NM,F Carolingian

caroncule [kaʀɔ̃kyl] NF (Zool) caruncle, wattle

carotène [kaʀɔtɛn] NM carotene, carotin

carotide [kaʀɔtid] ADJ, NF carotid

carottage [kaʀɔtaʒ] NM a (* = vol) swiping*‡, pinching* b (Tech) core boring

carotte [kaʀɔt] 1 NF a (Bot, Culin) carrot; **les ~s sont cuites!** * they've (ou we've etc) had it!*, it's all up* (Brit) ou over! → **poil** b (* = promesse) carrot; **manier la ~ et le bâton** to use the carrot and stick approach c (Tech) core d [tabac] plug; (= enseigne) tobacconist's (Brit) ou tobacco shop (US) sign 2 ADJ INV [cheveux] red, carroty*; [couleur] carroty; **objet (couleur) ~** carrot-coloured object; **rouge ~** carrot red

carotter [kaʀɔte] ▸conjug 1◂ 1 VT a (* = voler) to swipe‡, pinch*; **~ qch à qn** to pinch* ou nick‡ sth from sb; **il m'a carotté (de) 5 F ◊ je me suis fait ~ (de) 5 F** he did* ou diddled* me out of 5 francs b (Tech) to bore 2 VI **il essaie toujours de ~** he's always trying to fiddle a bit for himself; **elle carotte sur l'argent des commissions** she fiddles the housekeeping money

carotteur, -euse * [kaʀɔtœʀ, øz], **carottier, -ière** * [kaʀɔtje, jɛʀ] NM,F diddler*

caroube [kaʀub] NF (= fruit) carob

caroubier [kaʀubje] NM carob (tree)

carpaccio [kaʀpatʃ(j)o] NM carpaccio

Carpates [kaʀpat] NFPL **les ~** the Carpathians

carpe[1] [kaʀp] NF (Zool) carp → **muet**, **saut**

carpe[2] [kaʀp] NM (Anat) carpus

carpeau (pl **carpeaux**) [kaʀpo] NM young carp

carpette [kaʀpɛt] NF (= tapis) rug; (péj = personne servile) servile person, doormat (fig); **s'aplatir comme une ~ devant qn** to fawn on sb

carpien, -ienne [kaʀpjɛ̃, jɛn] ADJ carpal

carquois [kaʀkwa] NM quiver

carrare [kaʀaʀ] NM (= marbre) Carrara (marble)

carre [kaʀ] NF [ski] edge; **prendre des ~s** to dig in the edges of one's skis

Carré [kaʀe] N (Vét) **maladie de ~** canine distemper

carré, e [kaʀe] 1 ADJ a [table, jardin, menton] square; **aux épaules ~es** square-shouldered → **partie**[3] b (Math) square; **mètre/kilomètre ~** square metre/kilometre; **il n'y avait pas un centimètre ~ de place** there wasn't an inch of room, there wasn't (enough) room to swing a cat (Brit) → **racine** c (= franc) [personne] forthright, straightforward; [réponse] straight, straightforward; **être ~ en affaires** to be aboveboard ou straightforward in one's (business) dealings 2 NM a (gén) square; (= foulard) scarf; **découper qch en petits ~s** to cut sth up into little squares; **~ de soie** silk scarf; **~ de terre** patch ou plot (of land); **un ~ de choux/de salades** a cabbage/lettuce patch; **avoir les cheveux coupés au ~** ◊ **avoir une coupe au ~** to wear ou have one's hair in a bob; **~ blanc**† (TV) sign indicating that a film is unsuitable for children or sensitive viewers; **~ de service** (Tennis) service court b (Mil = disposition) square → **former** c (Naut = mess, salon) wardroom; **le ~ des officiers** the (officers') wardroom d (Math) square; **le ~ de 4** 4 squared, the square of 4; **3 au ~** 3 squared; **élever** ou **mettre** ou **porter un nombre au ~** to square a number e (Cartes) **un ~ d'as** four aces f (Culin) **~ de l'Est** soft, mild, fermented cheese; (Boucherie) **~ d'agneau** loin of lamb g (= groupe) **le dernier ~** the last handful h (arg Scol) student repeating the preparation for the grandes écoles 3 **carrée** NF a (‡ = chambre) bedroom b (Hist Mus) breve

carreau (pl **carreaux**) [kaʀo] NM a (par terre) (floor) tile; (au mur) (wall) tile; **~ de plâtre** plaster block b (= carrelage, sol) tiled floor; **le ~ des Halles** the market at les Halles c (= vitre) (window) pane; (* = lunettes) **~x** glasses, specs*; **faire les ~x** to clean the windows; **remplacer un ~** to replace a pane; **regarder au ~** to look out of the window; **des vandales ont cassé les ~x** vandals have smashed the windows d (sur un tissu) check; (sur du papier) square; **à ~x** [papier] [mouchoir] check (épith), checked; **veste à grands/petits ~x** jacket with a large/small check; (Scol) **laisser 3 ~x de marge** leave 3 squares margin, leave a margin of 3 squares; (Tech) **mettre un plan au ~** to square a plan e (Cartes) diamond; **jouer ~** to play diamonds; **le dix de ~** the ten of diamonds f (Pétanque) **faire un ~** to hit the bowl nearest the jack and stay on its spot g [mine] bank h (Hist = flèche) bolt i (*: loc) (bagarre) **laisser qn sur le ~** to lay ou knock sb out*; **il est resté sur le ~** (bagarre) he was laid ou knocked out*; (examen) he didn't make the grade; (chômage) he's out of a job;

se tenir à ~ to keep one's nose clean*, watch one's step

carrefour [kaʀfuʀ] NM [a] [*routes*] crossroads *sg*; **le ~ de l'Europe/de la drogue** the crossroads of Europe/of drug trafficking; **une science au ~ de plusieurs disciplines** a science at the junction *ou* meeting point of several different disciplines; **se trouver à un ~ (de sa vie/carrière)** to be at a crossroads (in one's life/career) [b] (= *rencontre, forum*) forum, symposium; **~ des métiers** careers convention; (*fig*) **~ d'idées** forum for ideas

carrelage [kaʀlaʒ] NM (= *action*) tiling; (= *carreaux*) tiles, tiling (*NonC*); **poser un ~** to lay a tiled floor; **laver le ~** to wash the floor

carreler [kaʀle] ▸conjug 4◂ VT [+ *mur, sol*] to tile; [+ *papier*] to draw squares on

carrelet [kaʀlɛ] NM [a] (= *poisson*) plaice [b] (= *filet*) square fishing net [c] (*Tech*) [*bourrelier*] half-moon needle; [*dessinateur*] square ruler

carreleur, -euse [kaʀlœʀ, øz] NM,F tiler

carrément [kaʀemɑ̃] ADV [a] (= *franchement*) bluntly, straight out; **je lui ai dit ~ ce que je pensais** I told him straight out what I thought [b] (= *sans hésiter*) straight; **il a ~ écrit au proviseur** he wrote straight to the headmaster; **vas-y** go right ahead; **j'ai pris ~ à travers champs** I struck straight across the fields [c] (*intensif*) **il est ~ timbré*** he's definitely cracked*; **cela nous fait gagner ~ 10 km/2 heures** it saves us 10 whole km *ou* a full 10 km/a whole 2 hours *ou* 2 full hours

carrer [kaʀe] ▸conjug 1◂ [1] VT (*Math, Tech*) to square [2] **se carrer** VPR **se ~ dans un fauteuil** to settle (o.s.) comfortably *ou* ensconce o.s. in an armchair; **bien carré dans son fauteuil** comfortably settled *ou* ensconced in his armchair

carrier [kaʀje] NM (= *ouvrier*) quarryman, quarrier; (= *propriétaire*) quarry owner; **maître ~** quarry master

carrière¹ [kaʀjɛʀ] NF [*sable*] (sand)pit; [*roches etc*] quarry

carrière² [kaʀjɛʀ] NF [a] (= *profession*) career; **en début/fin de ~** at the beginning/end of one's career; (*Pol*) **la ~** the diplomatic service; **embrasser la ~ des armes†** to embark on a career of arms†; **faire ~ dans l'enseignement** to make one's career in teaching; **il est entré dans l'industrie et y a fait (rapidement) ~** he went into industry and (quickly) made a career for himself; **officier/militaire de ~** career officer/soldier [b] (*littér* = *cours*) course; **le jour achève sa ~** the day is drawing to a close *ou* has run its course; **donner (libre) ~ à** to give free rein to

carriérisme [kaʀjeʀism] NM (*péj*) careerism

carriériste [kaʀjeʀist] NMF (*péj*) careerist

carriole [kaʀjɔl] NF [a] (= *charrette*) cart [b] (*Can*) sleigh, ca(r)riole (*US, Can*), carryall (*US, Can*)

carrossable [kaʀɔsabl] ADJ [*route etc*] suitable for (motor) vehicles

carrosse [kaʀɔs] NM (horse-drawn) coach; **~ d'apparat** state coach → **cinquième, rouler**

carrosser [kaʀɔse] ▸conjug 1◂ VT (*Aut*) (= *mettre une carrosserie à*) to fit a body to; (= *dessiner la carrosserie de*) to design a body for *ou* the body of; **voiture bien carrossée** car with a well-designed body; [*personne*] **elle est bien carrossée*** she's got curves in all the right places

carrosserie [kaʀɔsʀi] NF (*Aut*) (= *coque*) body(work), coachwork; (= *métier*) coach-building (*Brit*), car-body making (*US*); **atelier de ~** body shop

carrossier [kaʀɔsje] NM (= *constructeur*) coachbuilder (*Brit*), car-body maker (*US*); (= *dessinateur*) car designer; **ma voiture est chez le ~** my car is in the body shop

carrousel [kaʀuzɛl] NM [a] (*Équitation*) carousel; (*fig* = *succession rapide*) merry-go-round; **le ~ des voitures officielles** the to-ing and fro-ing of official cars; **un ~ d'avions dans le ciel** planes weaving patterns *ou* circling in the sky [b] [*diapositives*] Carousel® [c] (*Belg* = *manège*) merry-go-round, roundabout (*Brit*), carousel (*US*)

carrure [kaʀyʀ] NF [a] (= *largeur d'épaules*) [*personne*] build; [*vêtement*] breadth across the shoulders; **manteau un peu trop étroit de ~** coat which is a little tight across the shoulders; **une ~ d'athlète** an athlete's build; **homme de belle/forte ~** well-built/burly man [b] [*mâchoire*] squareness; [*bâtiment*] square shape [c] (= *envergure*) calibre (*Brit*), caliber (*US*), stature

carry [kaʀi] NM = **curry**

cartable [kaʀtabl] NM (*à poignée*) (school)bag; (*à bretelles*) satchel

carte [kaʀt] [1] NF [a] (*gén*) card; **~ (postale)** (post)card; **~ de visite** (*lit*) visiting card, calling card (*US*); (*fig* = *expérience*) CV; **ce poste au Japon, c'est une très bonne ~ de visite** having worked in Japan looks good on a CV; **~ de visite professionnelle** business card

[b] (*Jeux*) **(à jouer)** (playing) card; **battre** *ou* **brasser** *ou* **mêler les ~s** to shuffle the cards; **donner les ~s** to deal (the cards); **faire** *ou* **tirer les ~s à qn** to read sb's cards; **avoir toutes les ~s en main** (*lit*) to have all the cards; (*fig*) to hold all the cards; **jouer la ~ du charme** to turn on the charm; **jouer la ~ de l'Europe** to turn towards Europe; **jouer la ~ de la privatisation/la transparence** to opt for privatisation/openness; **pendant sa campagne il a joué la ~ nationaliste** he played the nationalist card during his campaign; **~ maîtresse** (*lit*) master (card); (*fig*) trump card; (*lit*) **~ forcée** forced card; (*fig*) **c'est la ~ forcée !** we have no choice!, it's Hobson's choice!; (*lit, fig*) **jouer ~s sur table** to put *ou* lay one's cards on the table → **brouiller, château**

[c] (*Géog*) map; (*Astron, Mét, Naut*) chart; **~ du relief/géologique** relief/geological map; **~ routière** roadmap; **~ du ciel** sky chart; **~ de la lune** chart *ou* map of the moon; **~ météorologique** *ou* **du temps** weather chart → **rayer**

[d] (*au restaurant*) menu; **on prend le menu ou la ~ ?** shall we have the set menu or shall we eat à la carte?; **une très bonne/très petite ~** a very good/very small menu *ou* choice of dishes

[e] (*Fin*) credit card; **payer par ~** to pay by credit card

[f] (*Ordin*) board

[g] **à la ~** [*repas*] à la carte; [*retraite, plan d'investissement, voyage*] tailor-made; **manger à la ~** to eat à la carte; **programme à la ~** (*Scol*) free-choice curriculum, curriculum allowing pupils a choice of subjects; **télévision à la ~** pay-per-view television *ou* TV; **avoir un horaire à la ~** to have flexible working hours; **faire du tourisme à la ~** to go on a tailor-made *ou* an à la carte holiday

[h] **en ~ :** [*fille ou femme ou prostituée en ~*] registered prostitute

[2] COMP ► **carte d'abonnement** (*train*) season ticket, pass; (*Théât*) season ticket ► **carte d'alimentation** = **carte de rationnement** ► **carte d'anniversaire** birthday card ► **carte d'assuré social** ≈ National Insurance card (*Brit*), ≈ social security card (*US*) ► **carte bancaire** banker's card ► **carte blanche:** **avoir ~ blanche** to have carte blanche *ou* a free hand; **donner ~ blanche à qn** to give sb carte blanche *ou* a free hand ► **Carte Bleue®** debit card ► **carte de chemin de fer** railway (*Brit*) *ou* train (*US*) season ticket ► **carte de correspondance** (plain) postcard ► **carte de crédit** credit card ► **carte d'électeur** voting card, voter registration card (*US*) ► **carte d'état-major** Ordnance Survey map (*Brit*), Geological Sur-

vey map (*US*) ► **carte d'étudiant** student card ► **carte d'extension de mémoire** memory expansion board ► **carte de famille nombreuse** card issued to members of large families, allowing reduced fares etc ► **carte de fidélité** (regular customer's) discount card ► **carte graphique** graphics board ► **carte grise** ≈ (car) registration book (*Brit*) *ou* papers (*US*), ≈ logbook (*Brit*) ► **carte d'identité** identity *ou* I.D. card ► **carte d'identité scolaire** pupil's identity card, student I.D. (card) ► **carte d'interface** interface board ► **carte d'invalidité** disability card ► **carte d'invitation** invitation card ► **carte jeune** young persons' discount card ► **carte journalière** (*Ski*) day-pass, day-ticket ► **carte de lecteur** library card, reader's ticket (*Brit*), library ticket (*Brit*) ► **carte magnétique** magnetic (strip) card; **cabine téléphonique à ~ (magnétique)** cardphone ► **carte mécanographique** = **carte perforée** ► **carte à mémoire** smart card, intelligent card; (*pour téléphone*) phone card ► **carte mère** motherboard ► **carte de Noël** Christmas card ► **carte orange** monthly (*ou* weekly *ou* yearly) season ticket (*for all types of transport in Paris*) ► **carte de paiement** credit card ► **carte perforée** punch card ► **carte de presse** press card ► **carte privative** charge *ou* store card ► **carte à puce** smart card, intelligent card ► **carte de rationnement** ration card ► **carte de résident** residence permit ► **carte scolaire** list of schools (*showing forecasts for regional requirements*) ► **carte de Sécurité sociale** = **carte d'assuré social** ► **carte de séjour** residence permit ► **carte syndicale** union card ► **carte téléphonique** *ou* **de téléphone** phonecard ► **carte de travail** work permit ► **carte vermeil** ≈ senior citizen's rail pass ► **carte verte** (*Aut*) green card (*Brit*), certificate of insurance (*US*) ► **carte des vins** wine list ► **carte de vœux** greetings card (*Brit*), greeting card (*US*)

─────────
CARTES
─────────

French people over the age of eighteen are normally required to carry a "carte d'identité" that provides proof of identity in France and can also be used instead of a passport for travel to some countries. They also have a "carte d'électeur" (voting card) and a "carte d'assuré social" bearing their social security number. Foreign nationals residing in France for more than three months must have a "carte de séjour", which is issued by their local "préfecture", and a "carte de travail" if they are employed. All car owners must have a "carte grise", which provides proof of ownership and must be shown along with one's driving licence if one is stopped by the police.

cartel [kaʀtɛl] NM [a] (*Pol*) cartel, coalition; (*Écon*) cartel, combine [b] (= *pendule*) wall clock [c] (*Hist* = *défi*) cartel

carte-lettre (*pl* **cartes-lettres**) [kaʀtəlɛtʀ] NF letter-card

cartellisation [kaʀtelizasjɔ̃] NF (*Écon*) formation of combines

carter [kaʀtɛʀ] NM [*bicyclette*] chain guard; (*Aut*) [*huile*] sump, oilpan (*US*); [*boîte de vitesses*] (gearbox) casing; [*différentiel*] cage; [*moteur*] crankcase

carte-réponse (*pl* **cartes-réponses**) [kaʀt(ə)-ʀepɔ̃s] NF (*gén*) reply card; [*concours*] entry form

carterie [kaʀt(ə)ʀi] NF postcard shop

cartésianisme [kaʀtezjanism] NM Cartesianism

cartésien, -ienne [kaʀtezjɛ̃, jɛn] ADJ, NM,F Cartesian

Carthage [kaʀtaʒ] N Carthage

carthaginois, e [kaʀtaʒinwa, waz] **1** ADJ Carthaginian **2 Carthaginois(e)** NM,F Carthaginian

cartilage [kaʀtilaʒ] NM (Anat) cartilage; [viande] gristle

cartilagineux, -euse [kaʀtilaʒinø, øz] ADJ (Anat) cartilaginous; [viande] gristly

cartographe [kaʀtɔgʀaf] NMF cartographer

cartographie [kaʀtɔgʀafi] NF cartography, map-making; **~ génique** ou **génétique** gene ou genetic mapping

cartographier [kaʀtɔgʀafje] ▸ conjug 1 ◂ VT [+ pays, planète] to map, draw a map of; [+ génome humain] to map

cartographique [kaʀtɔgʀafik] ADJ cartographic(al)

cartomancie [kaʀtɔmɑ̃si] NF fortune-telling (with cards), cartomancy

cartomancien, -ienne [kaʀtɔmɑ̃sjɛ̃, jɛn] NM,F fortune-teller (who uses cards)

carton [kaʀtɔ̃] **1** NM **a** (= matière) cardboard; **écrit/collé sur un ~** written/pasted on (a piece of) cardboard; **masque de** ou **en ~** cardboard mask **b** (= boîte) (cardboard) box, carton (US); (= contenu) boxful; († = cartable) (school)bag; (à bretelles) satchel; **~ de lait** (boîte) carton of milk; (plusieurs boîtes) pack of milk; **~-repas** pre-packaged meal; (fig) **c'est quelque part dans mes ~s** it's somewhere in my files; **le projet a dormi** ou **est resté dans les ~s plusieurs années** the project was shelved ou mothballed for several years **c** (= cible) target; **faire un ~** (à la fête) to have a go on the rifle range; (* : sur l'ennemi) to take a potshot (sur at); **faire un bon ~** to get a good score; **j'ai fait un ~ en anglais*** I did really well in English, I got really good grades in English (US); **elle fait un ~ au hit-parade*** she's riding high ou she's a huge success in the charts; (fig) **~ plein pour*** ... full marks for ... (Brit), A+ for ... (US) **d** (Peinture) sketch; (Géog) inset map; [tapisserie, mosaïque] cartoon **e** (= carte) card; **~ d'invitation** invitation card → **taper f** (* = accident) smash-up* **2** COMP ▸ **carton à chapeau** hatbox ▸ **carton à chaussures** shoebox ▸ **carton à dessin** portfolio ▸ **carton gris** newsboard ▸ **carton jaune** (Ftbl) yellow card; **il a reçu un ~ jaune** he got a yellow card, he was booked ▸ **carton ondulé** corrugated cardboard ▸ **carton pâte** pasteboard; **de ~ pâte** [décor] (fig) [personnages] cardboard (épith) ▸ **carton rouge** (Ftbl) red card; **il a reçu un ~ rouge** he got the red card, he was sent off

cartonnage [kaʀtɔnaʒ] NM **a** (= industrie) cardboard industry **b** (= emballage) cardboard (packing) **c** (Reliure) (= action) boarding; (= couverture) **~ pleine toile** cloth binding; **~ souple** limp binding

cartonner [kaʀtɔne] ▸ conjug 1 ◂ **1** VT **a** (= relier) to bind in boards; **livre cartonné** hardback (book) **b** (* = heurter) to smash into* **2** VI* **a** (= réussir) to do brilliantly* (en in) **b** (en voiture) to have a smash(-up)*; **ça cartonne souvent à ce carrefour** there are quite a few crashes at this crossroads

cartonnerie [kaʀtɔnʀi] NF (= industrie) cardboard industry; (= usine) cardboard factory

cartonnier, -ière [kaʀtɔnje, jɛʀ] **1** NM,F (= artiste) tapestry ou mosaic designer **2** NM (= meuble) filing cabinet

cartophile [kaʀtɔfil] NMF postcard collector

cartouche[1] [kaʀtuʃ] NF (gén, Mil, Ordin) cartridge; [cigarettes] carton → **brûler**

cartouche[2] [kaʀtuʃ] NM (Archéol, Archit) cartouche

cartoucherie [kaʀtuʃʀi] NF (= fabrique) cartridge factory; (= dépôt) cartridge depot

cartouchière [kaʀtuʃjɛʀ] NF (= ceinture) cartridge belt; (= sac) cartridge pouch

caryatide [kaʀjatid] NF = **cariatide**

caryotype [kaʀjotip] NM karyotype

▼ **cas** [ka] **1** NM **a** (= situation) case; (= événement) occurrence; **~ tragique/spécial** tragic/special case; **~ urgent** urgent case, emergency; **comme c'est son ~** as is the case with him; **un ~ très rare** a very rare occurrence; **exposez-lui votre ~** state your case; (à un médecin) describe your symptoms; **il s'est mis dans un mauvais ~** he's got himself into a tricky situation ou position; **dans le premier ~** in the first case ou instance **b** (Jur) case; **~ d'homicide/de divorce** murder/divorce case; **l'adultère est un ~ de divorce** adultery is grounds for divorce; **soumettre un ~ au juge** to submit a case to the judge; (hum) **c'est un ~ pendable** he deserves to be shot (hum) **c** (Méd, Sociol) case; **il y a plusieurs ~ de choléra dans le pays** there are several cases of cholera in the country; **~ social** person with social problems, social misfit; (fig) **c'est vraiment un ~!** he's (ou she's) a real case!* **d** (Ling) case **e** (loc) **faire (grand) ~ de/peu de ~ de** to attach great/little importance to, set great/little store by; **il ne fait jamais aucun ~ de nos observations** he never pays any attention to ou takes any notice of our comments; **c'est le ~ ou jamais** it's now or never; **c'est le ~ ou jamais de réclamer** if ever there was a case for complaint this is it; **c'est (bien) le ~ de le dire!** you said it!; **au ~ ou dans le ~ ou pour le ~ où il pleuvrait** in case it rains, in case it should rain; **je prends un parapluie au ~ où** ou **en ~*** I'm taking an umbrella (just) in case; **dans** ou **en ce ~ téléphonez-nous** in that case give us a ring; **dans le ~ présent** in this particular case; **le ~ échéant ◊ en ~ de besoin** if the need arises, if need be; **en ~ d'absence** in case of ou in the event of absence; **en ~ d'urgence** in an emergency; **en aucun ~ vous ne devez vous arrêter** on no account ou under no circumstances are you to stop; **en tout ~ ou en tout cas ou dans tous les ~** anyway, in any case, at any rate; **mettre qn dans le ~ d'avoir à faire qch** to put sb in the situation ou position of having to do sth; **il accepte ou il refuse selon les ~** he accepts or refuses according to the circumstances **2** COMP ▸ **cas de conscience** moral dilemma; **il a un ~ de conscience** he's in a moral dilemma ▸ **cas d'école** textbook case, classic example ▸ **cas d'espèce** individual case ▸ **cas de figure** scenario; **dans ce ~ de figure** in this case ▸ **cas de force majeure** case of absolute necessity ▸ **cas de légitime défense** case of legitimate self-defence; **c'était un ~ de légitime défense** he acted in self-defence ▸ **cas limite** borderline case

casanier, -ière [kazanje, jɛʀ] **1** ADJ [personne, habitudes, vie] stay-at-home* (épith) **2** NM,F stay-at-home, homebody (US)

casaque [kazak] NF [jockey] blouse; † [femme] overblouse; (Hist) [mousquetaire] tabard; **tourner ~** (= fuir) to turn tail, flee; (= changer de camp) to change sides; (= changer d'opinion) to do a U-turn

casbah [kazba] NF (en Afrique) kasbah; (* = maison) house, place*; **rentrer à la ~** to go home

cascade [kaskad] NF **a** [eau] waterfall, cascade (littér); [mots, chiffres] stream; [événements] spate; [réformes, révélations] series; [erreurs] string, series; [rires] peal; **des démissions en ~** a spate of resignations **b** (= acrobatie) stunt; **dans ce film, c'est lui qui fait les ~s** he does the stunts in this film

cascader [kaskade] ▸ conjug 1 ◂ VI (littér) to cascade

cascadeur [kaskadœʀ] NM [film] stuntman; [cirque] acrobat

cascadeuse [kaskadøz] NF [film] stuntwoman; [cirque] acrobat

case [kaz] NF **a** (sur papier) square, space; (sur formulaire) box; [échiquier] square; (Jeux) **la ~ départ** the start; (fig) **nous voilà revenus à la ~ départ ◊ retour à la ~ départ** (we're) back to square one **b** (pupitre) compartment, shelf; [courrier] pigeonhole (Brit), mail box (US); [boîte, tiroir] compartment; **~ postale** post-office box; (Ordin) **~ de réception** card stacker; **il a une ~ vide*** ou **en moins*** ◊ **il lui manque une ~*** he has a screw loose* **c** (= hutte) hut; **« la Case de l'oncle Tom »** "Uncle Tom's Cabin"

caséeux, -euse [kazeø, øz] ADJ caseous

caséine [kazein] NF casein

casemate [kazmat] NF blockhouse, pillbox

caser* [kaze] ▸ conjug 1 ◂ **1** VT **a** (= placer) [+ objets] to shove*, stuff; (= loger) [+ amis] to put up **b** (= marier) [+ fille] to find a husband for; (= pourvoir d'une situation) to find a job for; **ses enfants sont casés maintenant** (emploi) his children have got jobs now ou are fixed up now; (mariage) his children are (married and) off his hands now **2** se caser VPR (= vivre ensemble) to settle down; (= trouver un emploi) to find a (steady) job; (= se loger) to find a place to live; (célibataire) **il va avoir du mal à se ~** he's going to have a job finding someone to settle down with

caserne [kazɛʀn] NF (Mil, fig) barracks; **~ de pompiers** fire station, fire ou station house (US); **cet immeuble est une vraie ~** this building looks like a barracks

casernement [kazɛʀnəmɑ̃] NM (Mil) (= action) quartering in barracks; (= bâtiments) barrack buildings

caserner [kazɛʀne] ▸ conjug 1 ◂ VT (Mil) to barrack, quarter in barracks

cash* [kaʃ] **1** ADV (= comptant) **payer ~** to pay cash down; **il m'a donné 40 000 F ~** he gave me 40,000 francs cash down ou on the nail* (Brit) ou on the barrel* (US) **2** NM cash (NonC)

casher [kaʃɛʀ] ADJ INV kosher

cash-flow (pl cash-flows) [kaʃflo] NM cash flow

cashmere [kaʃmiʀ] NM = **cachemire**

casier [kazje] **1** NM **a** (= compartiment) compartment; (= tiroir) drawer; (fermant à clé) locker; [courrier] pigeonhole (Brit), mail box (US); **~ de consigne automatique** luggage locker **b** (= meuble) set of compartments ou pigeonholes (Brit) ou (mail)boxes (US); (à tiroirs) filing cabinet **c** (Pêche) (lobster etc) pot; **poser des ~s** to put out lobster pots **2** COMP ▸ **casier à bouteilles** bottle rack ▸ **casier fiscal** tax record ▸ **casier à homards** lobster pot ▸ **casier judiciaire** police ou criminal record; **avoir un ~ judiciaire vierge/chargé** to have a clean (police) record/ a long record ▸ **casier à musique** music cabinet

casino [kazino] NM casino

casoar [kazɔaʀ] NM (Orn) cassowary; (= plumet) plume

Caspienne [kaspjɛn] NF **la (mer) ~** the Caspian Sea

casque [kask] **1** NM **a** (qui protège) [soldat, alpiniste] helmet; [motocycliste] crash helmet; [ouvrier] hard hat; **« le port du ~ est obligatoire »** "this is a hard hat area", "hard hats must be worn at all times"; **j'ai le ~ depuis ce matin*** I've had a headache ou a bit of a head* (Brit) since this morning **b** (pour sécher les cheveux) (hair-)drier **c** (à écouteurs : gén) headphones, headset, earphones; [hi-fi] headphones **d** (Zool) casque **e** (Bot) helmet, galea **2** COMP ▸ **Casque bleu** blue helmet ou beret; **les Casques bleus** the U.N. peacekeeping force, the blue helmets *ou* berets ► **casque de chantier** hard hat ► **casque colonial** pith helmet, topee ► **casque intégral** full-face helmet ► **casque à pointe** spiked helmet

casqué, e [kaske] ADJ [*motocycliste, soldat*] wearing a helmet, helmeted

casquer* [kaske] ► conjug 1 ◀ VTI (= *payer*) to cough up*, fork out*

casquette [kasket] NF cap; **~ d'officier** officer's (peaked) cap; (*fig*) **avoir plusieurs/une double ~** to wear several hats/two hats; **il en a sous la ~*** he's really brainy*

cassable [kasabl] ADJ breakable

Cassandre [kasɑ̃dR] NF (*Myth*) Cassandra; **les ~ de l'écologie** the ecological prophets of doom; **jouer les ~** to spread doom and gloom

cassant, e [kasɑ̃, ɑ̃t] ADJ a (*glace, substance*) brittle; [*métal*] short; [*bois*] easily broken *ou* snapped b [*ton*] curt, abrupt, brusque; [*attitude, manières*] brusque, abrupt c (* = *difficile*) **ce n'est pas ~** it's not exactly back-breaking *ou* tiring work

cassate [kasat] NF cassata

cassation [kasasjɔ̃] NF a (*Jur*) cassation → **cour, pourvoir** b (*Mil*) reduction to the ranks

casse [kɑs] 1 NF a (= *action*) breaking, breakage; (= *objets cassés*) damage, breakages; **il y a eu beaucoup de ~ pendant le déménagement** a lot of things were broken *ou* there were a lot of breakages during the move; **payer la ~** to pay for the damage *ou* breakages; (*fig*) **il va y avoir de la ~*** there's going to be (some) rough stuff*; **pas de ~ !** (*lit*) don't break anything!; (* : *fig*) no rough stuff!* b (* = *endroit*) scrap yard; **mettre à la ~** to scrap; **vendre à la ~** to sell for scrap; **bon pour la ~** fit for scrap, ready for the scrap heap; **envoyer une voiture à la ~** to send a car to the breakers c (*Typo*) case; (= *caractère*) **bas de ~** lower-case letter d (*Bot*) cassia 2 NM (*arg Crime* = *cambriolage*) break-in; **faire un ~ dans une bijouterie** to break into a jeweller's shop, do a break-in at a jeweller's shop

cassé, e [kɑse] (*ptp de casser*) ADJ a [*voix*] broken, cracked; [*vieillard*] bent → **blanc, col** b (* = *éreinté*) done in*, (dead-)beat*, knackered‡ (*Brit*)

casse-cou* [kasku] 1 ADJ INV [*personne*] reckless; [*opération, entreprise*] risky, dangerous 2 NMF INV (= *personne*) daredevil, reckless person; (*en affaires*) reckless person; **crier ~ à qn** to warn sb

casse-couilles‡ [kaskuj] 1 ADJ INV **t'es ~ avec tes questions !** you're being a real pain in the arse‡ (*Brit*) *ou* ass‡ (*US*) with all your questions! 2 NMF INV pain in the arse‡ (*Brit*) *ou* ass‡ (*US*) *ou* butt‡ (*US*)

casse-croûte [kaskRut] NM INV (= *repas*) snack, lunch (*US*); (= *sandwich*) sandwich; (*Can* = *restaurant*) snack bar; **manger/emporter un petit ~** to have/take along a bite to eat* *ou* a snack

casse-cul‡ [kasky] ADJ INV damn *ou* bloody (*Brit*) annoying‡; **il est ~** he's a pain in the arse‡ (*Brit*) *ou* ass‡ (*US*) *ou* butt‡ (*US*)

casse-dalle: (*pl* **casse-dalle(s)**) [kasdal] NM (= *repas*) snack, lunch (*US*); (= *sandwich*) sandwich

casse-graine* [kasgRen] NM INV (= *repas*) snack, lunch (*US*)

casse-gueule‡ [kasgœl] 1 ADJ INV [*sentier*] dangerous, treacherous; [*opération, entreprise*] risky, dangerous 2 NM INV (= *opération, entreprise*) risky *ou* dangerous business; (= *endroit*) dangerous *ou* nasty spot

casse-noisette(s) (*pl* **casse-noisettes**) [kasnwazet] NM (pair of) nutcrackers (*Brit*), nutcracker (*US*); (*Mus*) « **Casse-Noisette** » "The Nutcracker"

---

casse-noix [kasnwa] NM INV = **casse-noisette(s)**

casse-pattes* [kaspat] NM INV a (= *escalier, côte*) **c'est un vrai ~** it's a real slog* b † (* = *alcool*) rotgut*

casse-pieds* [kaspje] 1 ADJ INV **ce qu'elle est ~ !** (= *importune*) she's a pain in the neck!*; (= *ennuyeuse*) what a bore *ou* drag* she is!; **corriger des copies, c'est ~** it's a real drag* having to correct exam papers 2 NMF INV (= *importun*) nuisance, pain in the neck*; (= *personne ennuyeuse*) bore

casse-pipe* [kaspip] NM INV **aller au ~** (= *aller à la guerre*) to go to the front; (= *se faire tuer*) to go to be slaughtered; **vouloir faire de la morale en politique, c'est aller au ~** if you try to preach morality in politics you're courting disaster

casser [kase]

┌─────────────────────────────────────┐
│ ► conjug 1 ◀ │
│ 1 VERBE TRANSITIF   3 VERBE PRONOMINAL │
│ 2 VERBE INTRANSITIF │
└─────────────────────────────────────┘

1 VERBE TRANSITIF

a = **briser** [+ *objet*] to break; [+ *noix*] to crack; [+ *latte, branche*] to snap, break; **~ une dent/un bras à qn** to break sb's tooth/arm; **~ qch en deux/en morceaux** to break sth in two/into pieces; **~ un morceau de chocolat** to break off *ou* snap off a piece of chocolate; **~ un carreau** (*volontairement*) to smash a pane; (*accidentellement*) to break a pane; **il s'est mis à tout ~ autour de lui** he started smashing *ou* breaking everything in sight; **je casse tout *ou* beaucoup en ce moment** I break everything I touch at the moment ■ (*PROV*) **qui casse les verres les paye** you pay for your mistakes

b = **endommager** [+ *appareil*] to break, bust*; [+ *volonté, moral*] to break; [+ *vin*] to spoil the flavour of; **cette maladie lui a cassé la voix** this illness has ruined his voice; **je veux ~ l'image qu'on a de moi** I want to change the image people have of me

c = **interrompre** [+ *rythme, grève*] to break; **si l'on s'arrête, ça va ~ notre moyenne horaire** if we stop, we're going to fall behind on our hourly average

d = **dégrader** [+ *militaire*] to reduce to the ranks; [+ *fonctionnaire*] to demote; (*fig = nuire à*) **~ qn** to cause sb's downfall

e ‡ = **molester** **~ du facho/flic** to go fascist-/cop-bashing‡

f Admin, Jur = **annuler** [+ *jugement*] to quash; [+ *arrêt*] to nullify, annul; **faire ~ un jugement pour vice de forme** to have a sentence quashed on a technicality

g Comm **~ les prix** to slash prices

h loc **à tout ~*** (= *extraordinaire*) [*film, repas*] stupendous, fantastic; [+ *succès*] runaway (*épith*); (= *tout au plus*) **tu en auras pour 100 F à tout ~** that'll cost you 100 francs at the outside *ou* at the most; (*Aviat*) **~ du bois** to smash up one's plane; (*fig*) **~ la baraque*** (= *avoir du succès*) to bring the house down; **~ la baraque à qn*** (= *tout gâcher*) to mess *ou* foul* everything up (for sb); **~ la croûte* *ou* la graine*** to have a bite to eat* *ou* something to eat; **~ la figure* *ou* la gueule:** à qn to smash sb's face in‡, knock sb's block off‡; **~ le morceau:** (= *avouer*) to spill the beans, come clean; (= *trahir*) to give the game away*, blow the gaff* (*Brit*); **~ les pieds à qn*** (= *fatiguer*) to bore sb stiff; (= *irriter*) to get on sb's nerves; **il nous les casse‡** he's a pain (in the neck)!*; **tu me casses les bonbons‡** you're a pain in the neck!*, you're getting on my nerves *ou* wick (*Brit*)!*; **~ sa pipe*** to kick the bucket‡, snuff it* (*Brit*); **ça/il ne casse pas des briques*** ◊ **ça/il ne casse rien*** ◊ **ça/il ne casse pas trois pattes à un canard*** it's/he's nothing to write home about*; **~ du sucre sur le dos de qn** to gossip *ou* talk about sb behind his back; **il nous casse**

---

la tête *ou* les oreilles avec sa trompette* he makes a terrible racket with that trumpet of his; **il nous casse la tête avec ses histoires*** he bores us stiff with his stories → **omelette, rein**

2 VERBE INTRANSITIF

a = **se briser** [*objet*] to break; [*baguette, corde, plaque*] to break, snap; **ça casse facilement** it breaks easily; **ça casse comme du verre** it's very brittle; **le pantalon doit ~ sur la chaussure** the trouser (leg) should rest on the shoe

b * = **endommager sa voiture, son bateau** [*personne*] (*Aut*) to break down; **dans le Paris-Dakar, il a cassé au kilomètre 152** he broke down at kilometre 152 in the Paris-Dakar race; (*Naut* = **démâter**) **elle a cassé juste avant l'arrivée** her mast broke just before the end of the race

c = **rompre** [*couple*] to break *ou* split up; **il était avec une actrice, mais il a cassé** he was going out with an actress but he broke up with her

3 VERBE PRONOMINAL

a = **se briser** [*objet*] to break; **la tasse s'est cassée en tombant** the cup broke when it fell; **l'anse s'est cassée** the handle came off *ou* broke (off); **se ~ net** to break *ou* snap clean off; (*en deux morceaux*) to snap in two

b = **briser *ou* endommager une partie de son corps** [*personne*] **se ~ la jambe/une jambe/une dent** to break one's leg/a leg/a tooth; **tu vas te ~ le cou!** you'll break your neck!; (*fig*) **se ~ la figure* *ou* la gueule:** (= *tomber*) to fall flat on one's face, come a cropper* (*Brit*); (*d'une certaine hauteur*) to crash down; (= *faire faillite*) to go bankrupt, come a cropper* (*Brit*); **se ~ la figure contre qch** to crash into sth; (*fig*) **se ~ le nez** (= *trouver porte close*) to find no one in; (= *échouer*) to fail, come a cropper* (*Brit*); (*fig*) **se ~ les dents** to fall flat on one's face, come a cropper* (*Brit*)

c * = **se fatiguer** **il ne s'est rien cassé** *ou* **il ne s'est pas cassé pour écrire cet article** he didn't strain himself writing this article; (*fig*) **il ne s'est pas cassé la tête* *ou* la nénette:** *ou* **le tronc:** *ou* **le cul:*** he didn't put himself out! *ou* overexert himself! *ou* bust a gut:*; (*fig*) **cela fait deux jours que je me casse la tête sur ce problème** I've been racking my brains over this problem for two days

d * = **partir** to split*; **casse-toi !** get lost!:

casserole [kasRɔl] NF a (= *ustensile*) saucepan; (= *contenu*) saucepan(ful); **du veau à la *ou* en ~** braised veal b (*péj*) **c'est une vraie ~*** (*piano*) it's a tinny piano; (*voiture*) it's a tinny car; **chanter comme une ~*** to be a lousy singer*; **faire un bruit de ~** to clank c (*arg Ciné*) projector; (* = *scandale*) scandal; **traîner une ~ *ou* des ~s** to be haunted by a scandal e (*loc*) **passer à la ~:** (*sexuellement*) to get screwed:* *ou* laid:*; (= *être tué*) to be bumped off‡

casse-tête (*pl* **casse-tête(s)**) [kastet] NM (*Hist* = *massue*) club; **~ (chinois)** (= *problème difficile*) headache (*fig*); (= *jeu*) puzzle, brain-teaser

cassette [kaset] NF a (= *coffret*) casket; (= *trésor*) [*roi*] privy purse; (*hum*) **il a pris l'argent sur sa ~ personnelle** he paid out of his own pocket b [*magnétophone, magnétoscope, ordinateur*] cassette; **~ vidéo** video (cassette); **~ audio** audio cassette → **magnétophone**

casseur [kasœr] NM a (= *ferrailleur*) scrap dealer *ou* merchant b (= *manifestant*) rioter, rioting demonstrator c (: = *cambrioleur*) burglar d (* = *bravache*) tough guy*; **jouer les ~s*** to play tough* e **~ de pierres** stone breaker

Cassiopée [kasjɔpe] NF Cassiopeia

cassis [kasis] NM a (= *fruit*) blackcurrant; (= *arbuste*) blackcurrant bush; (= *liqueur*) blackcurrant liqueur, cassis [b] (‡ = *tête*) head, nut*, block* [c] [*route*] bump, ridge

cassolette [kasɔlɛt] NF (= *ustensile*) earthenware dish; (= *mets*) cassolette

cassonade [kasɔnad] NF brown sugar

cassoulet [kasulɛ] NM cassoulet (*meat and bean casserole, a specialty of SW France*)

cassure [kɑsyʀ] NF [a] (*lit, fig*) break; [*col*] fold; **à la ~ du pantalon** where the trousers rest on the shoe [b] (*Géol*) (*gén*) break; (= *fissure*) crack; (= *faille*) fault

castagne‡ [kastaɲ] NF [a] (= *action*) fighting; **il aime la ~** he loves a good fight *ou* punch-up* (*Brit*) [b] (= *rixe*) fight, punch-up* (*Brit*)

castagner (se)‡ [kastaɲe] ▶conjug 1◀ VPR to fight, have a punch-up* (*Brit*)

castagnettes [kastaɲɛt] NFPL castanets; **il avait les dents/les genoux qui jouaient des ~*** he could feel his teeth chattering/his knees knocking

caste [kast] NF (*lit, péj*) caste → **esprit**

castel [kastɛl] NM mansion, small castle

castillan, e [kastijɑ̃, an] [1] ADJ Castilian [2] NM (*Ling*) Castilian [3] **Castillan(e)** NM,F Castilian

Castille [kastij] NF Castile

castor [kastɔʀ] NM (= *animal, fourrure*) beaver

castrat [kastʀa] NM (= *chanteur*) castrato

castrateur, -trice [kastʀatœʀ, tʀis] ADJ (*Psych*) castrating

castration [kastʀasjɔ̃] NF [*homme, animal mâle*] castration; [*animal femelle*] spaying; [*cheval*] gelding; **complexe de ~** castration complex

castrer [kastʀe] ▶conjug 1◀ VT (*gén*) [+ *homme, animal mâle*] to castrate; [+ *animal femelle*] to spay; [+ *cheval*] to geld

castrisme [kastʀism] NM Castroism

castriste [kastʀist] [1] ADJ Castro (*épith*), Castroist [2] NMF supporter *ou* follower of Castro

casuel, -elle [kazɥɛl] [1] ADJ [a] (*Ling*) désinences **~les** case endings; **système ~** case system [b] (*littér*) fortuitous [2] NM† (= *gain variable*) commission money; [*curé*] casual offerings

casuiste [kazɥist] NM (*Rel, péj*) casuist

casuistique [kazɥistik] NF (*Rel, péj*) casuistry

casus belli [kazysbelli] NM INV casus belli

catabolisme [katabɔlism] NM catabolism, katabolism

catachrèse [katakʀɛz] NF catachresis

cataclysme [kataklism] NM cataclysm

cataclysmique [kataklismik] ADJ cataclysmic, cataclysmal

catacombes [katakɔ̃b] NFPL catacombs

catadioptre [katadjɔptʀ] NM (*sur voiture*) reflector; (*sur chaussée*) cat's eye, Catseye® (*Brit*)

catafalque [katafalk] NM catafalque

catalan, e [katalɑ̃, an] [1] ADJ Catalan, Catalonian [2] NM (*Ling*) Catalan [3] **Catalan(e)** NM,F Catalan

catalepsie [katalɛpsi] NF catalepsy; **tomber en ~** to have a cataleptic fit

cataleptique [katalɛptik] ADJ, NMF cataleptic

catalogage [katalɔgaʒ] NM [*articles, objets*] cataloguing, cataloging (*US*); [*personne*] categorizing, labelling, pigeonholing (*péj*)

Catalogne [katalɔɲ] NF Catalonia

catalogne [katalɔɲ] NF (*Can*) cloth made from woven strips of fabric

catalogue [katalɔg] NM (*gén*) catalogue, catalog (*US*); (*Ordin*) directory; **prix ~** list price; **faire le ~ de** to catalogue, catalog (*US*); **acheter qch sur ~** to buy sth from a catalogue

cataloguer [katalɔge] ▶conjug 1◀ VT to catalogue, catalog (*US*), pigeonhole; * [+ *personne*] to categorize, label (**comme** as)

catalpa [katalpa] NM catalpa

catalyse [kataliz] NF catalysis

catalyser [katalize] ▶conjug 1◀ VT (*Chim, fig*) to catalyse

catalyseur [katalizœʀ] NM (*Chim, fig*) catalyst

catalytique [katalitik] ADJ catalytic → **pot**

catamaran [katamaʀɑ̃] NM (= *voilier*) catamaran; [*hydravion*] floats

cataphote® [katafɔt] NM = **catadioptre**

cataplasme [kataplasm] NM (*Méd*) poultice, cataplasm; **~ sinapisé** mustard poultice *ou* plaster; **c'est un véritable ~ sur l'estomac** it lies like a lead weight on the stomach

catapultage [katapyltaʒ] NM (*lit, fig*) catapulting; (*Aviat*) catapult launch

catapulte [katapylt] NF (*Aviat, Hist*) catapult

catapulter [katapylte] ▶conjug 1◀ VT (*lit*) to catapult; **il a été catapulté à ce poste** he was pitchforked *ou* catapulted into this job

cataracte [kataʀakt] NF [a] (= *chute d'eau*) cataract; **des ~s de pluie** torrents of rain [b] (*Méd*) cataract; **il a été opéré de la ~** he's had a cataract operation, he's been operated on for (a) cataract

catarrhal, e (*mpl* **-aux**) [kataʀal, o] ADJ catarrhal

catarrhe [kataʀ] NM catarrh

catarrheux, -euse [kataʀø, øz] ADJ [*voix*] catarrhal, thick; **vieillard ~** wheezing old man

catastase [katastaz] NF (*Phon*) on-glide

catastrophe [katastʀɔf] NF disaster, catastrophe; **~ écologique** ecological disaster; **~ aérienne** air crash *ou* disaster; **~ naturelle** (*gén*) natural disaster; (*Assurances*) act of God; **~ ! le prof est arrivé !** panic stations! the teacher's here!; **~ ! je l'ai perdu !** Hell's bells!* I've lost it!; **atterrir en ~** to make a forced *ou* an emergency landing; **partir en ~** to leave in a terrible *ou* mad rush; **c'est la ~ cette voiture/ces chaussures !*** this car is/these shoes are a disaster!; **film ~** disaster movie *ou* film; (*fig*) **scénario ~** nightmare scenario

catastrophé, e* [katastʀɔfe] ADJ [*personne, air*] stunned; **être ~** to be stunned

catastropher* [katastʀɔfe] ▶conjug 1◀ VT to shatter*, stun

catastrophique [katastʀɔfik] ADJ disastrous, catastrophic

catastrophisme [katastʀɔfism] NM [a] (*Géol*) catastrophism [b] (= *pessimisme*) gloom-mongering; **faire du ~** to spread doom and gloom

catastrophiste [katastʀɔfist] [1] ADJ [*vision*] gloomy, (utterly) pessimistic [2] NMF [a] (*Géol*) catastrophist [b] (= *pessimiste*) gloom-monger, (utter) pessimist

catch [katʃ] NM (all-in) wrestling; **il fait du ~** he's a wrestler

catcher [katʃe] ▶conjug 1◀ VI to wrestle

catcheur, -euse [katʃœʀ, øz] NM,F wrestler

catéchèse [kateʃɛz] NF catechetics *sg*, catechesis

catéchisation [kateʃizasjɔ̃] NF catechization

catéchiser [kateʃize] ▶conjug 1◀ VT (*Rel*) to catechize; (= *endoctriner*) to indoctrinate, catechize; (= *sermonner*) to lecture

catéchisme [kateʃism] NM (= *enseignement, livre, fig*) catechism; **aller au ~** to go to catechism (class), ≈ go to Sunday school, ≈ go to CCD* (*US*)

catéchiste [kateʃist] NMF catechist → **dame**

catéchumène [katekymɛn] NMF (*Rel*) catechumen; (*fig*) novice

catégorie [kategɔʀi] NF (*gén, Philos*) category; (*Boxe, Hôtellerie*) class; (*Admin*) [*personnel*] grade; (*Boucherie*) **morceaux de première/deuxième ~** prime/second cuts; **hors ~** exceptional, outstanding; **ranger par ~** to categorize; **il est de la ~ de ceux qui ...** he comes in *ou* he belongs to the category of those who

...; **~ socioprofessionnelle** socio-professional group

catégoriel, -elle [kategɔʀjɛl] ADJ [a] (*Pol, Syndicats*) **revendications ~les** sectional claims [b] (*Gram*) **indice ~** category index

catégorique [kategɔʀik] ADJ [a] [*ton, personne*] categorical, adamant; [*démenti, refus*] flat (*épith*), categorical; **ne sois pas si ~ !** don't make such categorical statements!; **il nous a opposé un refus** *ou* **un non ~** he refused our request point-blank *ou* categorically [b] (*Philos*) categorical

catégoriquement [kategɔʀikmɑ̃] ADV [*refuser*] point-blank, categorically; [*rejeter, condamner, démentir, nier*] categorically

catégorisation [kategɔʀizasjɔ̃] NF categorization

catégoriser [kategɔʀize] ▶conjug 1◀ VT to categorize

caténaire [katenɛʀ] ADJ, NF (*Rail*) catenary

catgut [katgyt] NM (*Méd*) catgut

cathare [kataʀ] ADJ, NM,F Cathar

catharisme [kataʀism] NM Catharism

catharsis [kataʀsis] NF (*Littérat, Psych*) catharsis

cathartique [kataʀtik] ADJ cathartic

Cathay [kate] NM Cathay

cathédrale [katedʀal] NF cathedral → **verre**

Catherine [katʀin] NF Catherine, Katherine; **~ la Grande** Catherine the Great → **coiffer**

catherinette [katʀinɛt] NF *girl of 25 still unmarried by the Feast of St Catherine*

┌─── **CATHERINETTE** ───┐

*The tradition of the **catherinettes** has its origins in the dressmaking trade, where seamstresses still not married on their twenty-fifth birthday would go to a ball called "le bal des catherinettes" on Saint Catherine's Day (25th November) wearing a hat they made specially for the occasion. To wear such a hat was known as "coiffer sainte Catherine", and the expression, though a little old-fashioned, survives as a way of referring to a 25-year-old-woman who is still single.*

cathéter [katetɛʀ] NM catheter

cathétérisme [kateteʀism] NM catheterization

catho* [kato] ADJ, NMF ABRÉV = **catholique**

cathode [katɔd] NF cathode

cathodique [katɔdik] ADJ (*Phys*) cathodic → **écran, rayon, tube**

catholicisme [katɔlisism] NM (Roman) Catholicism

catholicité [katɔlisite] NF [a] (= *fidèles*) **la ~** the (Roman) Catholic Church [b] (= *orthodoxie*) catholicity

catholique [katɔlik] [1] ADJ [a] (*Rel*) [*foi, dogme*] (Roman) Catholic [b]* **pas (très) ~** a bit fishy*, not very kosher* (*US*) [2] NMF (Roman) Catholic

catimini [katimini] ◆ **en catimini** LOC ADV on the sly *ou* quiet; **sortir en ~** to steal *ou* sneak out; **il me l'a dit en ~** he whispered it in my ear

catin† [katɛ̃] NF (= *prostituée*) trollop†, harlot†

cation [katjɔ̃] NM cation

catogan [katɔgɑ̃] NM bow (*tying hair on the neck*)

Caton [katɔ̃] NM Cato

cattleya [katleja] NM cattleya

Catulle [katyl] NM Catullus

Caucase [kokaz] NM **le ~** the Caucasus

caucasien, -ienne [kokazjɛ̃, jɛn] [1] ADJ Caucasian [2] **Caucasien(ne)** NM,F Caucasian

cauchemar [koʃmaʀ] NM nightmare; **faire des ~s** to have nightmares; **c'est mon ~** it's a nightmare; **vision de ~** nightmarish sight

cauchemarder [koʃmaʀde] ▸conjug 1◂ VI to have nightmares; **faire ~ qn** to give sb nightmares

cauchemardesque [koʃmaʀdɛsk] ADJ nightmarish

cauchemardeux, -euse [koʃmaʀdø, øz] ADJ a = **cauchemardesque** b **sommeil ~** sleep disturbed by nightmares

caudal, e (mpl -aux) [kodal, o] ADJ caudal

caudillo [kaodijo] NM caudillo; (péj) **ses manières de ~** his dictatorial style

cauri [koʀi] NM cowrie ou cowry (shell)

causal, e (mpl -aux) [kozal, o] ADJ causal

causalité [kozalite] NF causality

causant, e* [kozɑ̃, ɑ̃t] ADJ talkative, chatty; **il n'est pas très ~** he doesn't say very much, he's not very forthcoming ou talkative

causatif, -ive [kozatif, iv] ADJ (Gram) [conjonction] causal; [construction, verbe] causative

cause [koz] NF a (= motif, raison) cause; **quelle est la ~ de l'accident?** what caused the accident?, what was the cause of the accident?; **on ne connaît pas la ~ de son absence** the reason for ou the cause of his absence is not known; **être (la) ~ de qch** to be the cause of sth; **la chaleur en est la ~** it is caused by the heat; **la ~ en demeure inconnue** the cause remains unknown, the reason for it remains unknown; **les ~s qui l'ont poussé à agir** the reasons that caused him to act ■ (PROV) **à petite ~ grands effets** great oaks from little acorns grow (PROV) → **relation** b (Jur) lawsuit, case; (à plaider) brief; **~ civile** civil action; **~ criminelle** criminal proceedings; **la ~ est entendue** (lit) both sides have put their case; (fig) there's no doubt about it; **~ célèbre** cause célèbre, famous trial ou case; **plaider sa ~** to plead one's case; **avocat sans ~(s)** briefless barrister → **ayant cause, connaissance** c (= ensemble d'intérêts) cause; **grande/noble ~** great/noble cause; **pour la bonne ~** for a good cause; **il ment, mais c'est pour la bonne ~** he's lying but it's for a good reason; **~ perdue** lost cause; **faire ~ commune avec qn** to make common cause with sb, side ou take sides with sb → **fait¹** d (Philos) cause; **~ première/seconde/finale** primary/secondary/final cause e (loc) **à ~ de** (= en raison de) because of, owing to; (= par égard pour) because of, for the sake of; **à ~ de cet incident technique** because of ou owing to this technical failure; **à ~ de son âge** on account of ou because of his age; **il est venu à ~ de vous** he came for your sake ou because of you; (iro) **ce n'est pas à ~ de lui que j'y suis arrivé!** it's no thanks to him I managed to do it!; **être en ~** [personne] to be involved ou concerned; [intérêts] to be at stake, be involved; **son honnêteté n'est pas en ~** there is no question about his honesty, his honesty is not in question; **mettre en ~** [+ innocence, nécessité, capacité] to (call into) question; [+ personne] implication; **mise en ~** [personne] implication; **remettre en ~** [+ principe, tradition] to question, challenge; **sa démission remet tout en ~** his resignation means we're back to square one; **remise en ~** calling into question; **mettre qn hors de ~** to clear ou exonerate sb; **fermé pour ~ d'inventaire/de maladie** closed for stocktaking (Brit) ou inventory (US)/on account of illness; **et pour ~!** and for (a very) good reason!; **non sans ~!** not without (good) cause ou reason!

causer¹ [koze] ▸conjug 1◂ VT (= provoquer) to cause; (= entraîner) to bring about; **~ des ennuis à qn** to get sb into trouble, bring sb trouble; **~ de la peine à qn** to hurt sb; **l'explosion a causé la mort de dix personnes** ten people died in the explosion; **cette erreur a causé sa perte** this mistake brought about his downfall

causer² [koze] ▸conjug 1◂ 1 VI a (= s'entretenir) to chat, talk; (* = discourir) to speak, talk; **~ de qch** to talk about sth; (propos futiles) to chat about sth; **on n'a même pas compris de quoi ça causait*** we didn't even understand what it was all about; **~ à qn*** to talk ou speak to sb; **assez causé!** that's enough talk!; (iro) **cause toujours, tu m'intéresses!** oh, come off it!* b (= jaser) to talk, gossip (sur qn about sb); **on cause dans le village/le bureau** people are talking in the village/the office c (‡ = avouer) to talk; **pour le faire ~** to loosen his tongue, to make him talk 2 VT to talk; **~ politique/travail** to talk politics/shop; **elles causaient chiffons** they were talking ou chatting about clothes

causerie [kozʀi] NF (= discours) talk; (= conversation) chat

causette [kozɛt] NF chat, natter* (Brit); **faire la ~ ◊ faire un brin de ~** to have a chat ou natter* (Brit) (**avec** with)

causeur, -euse [kozœʀ, øz] 1 ADJ talkative, chatty 2 NM,F talker, conversationalist 3 **causeuse** NF (= siège) causeuse, love seat

causse [kos] NM causse (limestone plateau (in south-central France))

causticité [kostisite] NF (lit, fig) causticity

caustique¹ [kostik] 1 ADJ (lit, fig) caustic; **surface ~** caustic (surface) 2 NM (Chim) caustic

caustique² [kostik] NF (Opt) caustic

cautèle [kotɛl] NF (littér) cunning, guile

cauteleux, -euse [kotlø, øz] ADJ (littér) cunning

cautère [kotɛʀ] NM cautery; **c'est un ~ sur une jambe de bois** it's of absolutely no use, it won't do any good at all

cautérisation [koteʀizasjɔ̃] NF cauterization

cautériser [koteʀize] ▸conjug 1◂ VT to cauterize

caution [kosjɔ̃] NF a (= somme d'argent) (Fin) guarantee, security; (Jur) bail (bond); (pour appartement, véhicule loué) deposit; **~ bancaire** bank guarantee; **~ de soumission** bid bond; **~ solidaire** joint and several guarantee; **il vous faut une ~ parentale** your parents have to stand guarantor ou surety for you; **verser une ~ de 1 000 F** to put ou lay down a security ou a guarantee of 1,000 francs; **libérer sous ~** to release ou free on bail; **libération ou mise en liberté sous ~** release on bail; **payer la ~ de qn** to bail sb out, stand (Brit) ou go (US) bail for sb, put up bail for sb (US) b (= appui) backing, support; **apporter ou donner sa ~ à qn/qch** to lend one's support to sb/sth c (= personne) guarantor; **se porter ~ pour qn ◊ servir de ~ à qn** to stand surety ou security (Brit) for sb → **sujet**

cautionnement [kosjɔnmɑ̃] NM (= somme) guarantee, security; (= contrat) security ou surety bond; (= soutien) support, backing; **~ électoral** deposit (required of candidates in an election)

cautionner [kosjɔne] ▸conjug 1◂ VT a (= répondre ou moralement) to answer for, guarantee; (financièrement) to guarantee, stand surety ou guarantor for b (= soutenir) [+ politique, gouvernement] to support, give one's support ou backing to

cavaillon [kavajɔ̃] NM cavaillon melon

cavalcade [kavalkad] NF a (= course tumultueuse) stampede; (* = troupe désordonnée) stampede, stream b [cavaliers] cavalcade c (= défilé, procession) cavalcade, procession

cavalcader [kavalkade] ▸conjug 1◂ VI (= courir) to stream, swarm, stampede; († = chevaucher) to cavalcade, ride in a cavalcade

cavale [kaval] NF a (littér = jument) mare b (arg Prison = évasion) **être en ~** to be on the run; **après une ~ de trois jours** after having been on the run for three days

cavaler [kavale] ▸conjug 1◂ 1 VI a* (= courir) to run; (= se hâter) to be on the go*; **j'ai dû ~ dans tout New York pour le trouver** I had to rush all around New York to find it b (‡ = draguer) [homme] to chase anything in a skirt*; [femme] to chase anything in trousers*; **~ après qn** to run ou chase after sb 2 VT (‡ = énerver) to piss off*‡, tee off* (US); **il commence à nous ~** we're beginning to get pissed off*‡ ou cheesed off* (Brit) with him 3 **se cavaler*** VPR (= se sauver) [personne] to clear off*, leg it*, skedaddle*; [animal] to run off

cavalerie [kavalʀi] NF (Mil) cavalry; [cirque] horses; (Mil) **~ légère** light cavalry ou horse; (Mil) **grosse ~ ◊ ~ lourde** heavy ou armoured cavalry; **c'est de la grosse ~** (humour) it's rather heavyhanded; (nourriture) it's really stodgy

cavaleur‡ [kavalœʀ] NM wolf, womanizer; **il est ~** he chases anything in a skirt*

cavaleuse‡ [kavaløz] NF hot piece‡; **elle est ~** she chases anything in trousers*

cavalier, -ière [kavalje, ɛʀ] 1 ADJ a (= impertinent) [attitude, parole] cavalier, offhand, casual; **c'est un peu ~ de sa part (de faire cela)** it's a bit cavalier of him (to do that) b **allée ou piste cavalière** bridle path 2 NM,F a (Équitation) rider; **les (quatre) ~s de l'Apocalypse** the (Four) Horsemen of the Apocalypse; **faire ~ seul** to go it alone b [danseur] partner; **changez de ~!** change partners! 3 NM a (Mil) trooper, cavalryman; **une troupe de 20 ~s** a troop of 20 horses b (Échecs) knight c (= accompagnateur) escort d (= clou) staple; [balance] rider; [dossier] tab; (Ordin) [carte-mère] jumper e (Hist Brit) cavalier f († = gentilhomme) gentleman

cavalièrement [kavaljɛʀmɑ̃] ADV casually, in a cavalier fashion, off-handedly

cavatine [kavatin] NF cavatina

cave¹ [kav] NF a (= pièce) cellar; (voûtée) vault; (= cabaret) cellar nightclub; **chercher ou fouiller de la ~ au grenier** to search the house from top to bottom b (Œnol) cellar; **avoir une bonne ~** to have ou keep a fine cellar; **~ à vin** (= armoire) refrigerated wine cabinet c (= coffret à liqueurs) liqueur cabinet; (= coffret à cigares) cigar box d (Can) [maison] basement

cave² [kav] ADJ (= creux) [yeux, joues] hollow, sunken → **veine**

cave³‡ [kav] NM a (arg Crime) straight (arg), someone who does not belong to the underworld b (= imbécile) sucker‡; **il est ~** he's a sucker‡

cave⁴ [kav] NM (Poker) bet

caveau (pl **caveaux**) [kavo] NM a (= cave) (small) cellar b (= sépulture) vault, tomb; **~ de famille** family vault c (= cabaret) cellar club

caverne [kavɛʀn] NF a (= grotte) cave, cavern; **c'est la ~ d'Ali Baba!** it's an Aladdin's cave! → **homme** b (Anat) cavity

caverneux, -euse [kavɛʀnø, øz] ADJ a [voix] hollow, cavernous b (Anat, Méd) [respiration] cavernous; [poumon] with cavitations, with a cavernous lesion → **corps** c (littér) [montagne, tronc] cavernous

cavernicole [kavɛʀnikɔl] ADJ (Zool) cave-dwelling (épith)

caviar [kavjaʀ] NM a (Culin) caviar(e); **~ rouge** salmon roe; **~ d'aubergines** aubergine (Brit) ou eggplant (US) dip, aubergine with fromage frais and olive oil; **la gauche ~** champagne socialists b (Presse) **passer au ~** to blue-pencil, censor

caviarder [kavjaʀde] ▸conjug 1◂ VT (Presse) to blue-pencil, censor

caviste [kavist] NM cellarman

cavité [kavite] NF cavity; **~ articulaire** socket (of bone); **~ pulpaire** (tooth) pulp cavity; **~ buccale** oral cavity

Cayenne [kajɛn] N Cayenne → **poivre**

cayeu (*pl* **cayeux**) [kajø] NM = **caïeu**

CB (ABRÉV = **Cartes bancaires**) → **carte**

C.B. [sibi] NF (ABRÉV = **Citizens' Band**) la ~ CB radio

C.C. [sese] NM ⓐ (ABRÉV = **compte courant**) C/A ⓑ (ABRÉV = **corps consulaire**) → **corps**

CCI [sesei] NF (ABRÉV = **Chambre de commerce et d'industrie**) → **chambre**

CCP [sesepe] NM ⓐ (ABRÉV = **centre de chèques postaux**) → **centre** ⓑ (ABRÉV = **compte chèque postal**) → **compte**

CD¹ [sede] NM (ABRÉV = **compact disc**) CD; **CD audio/vidéo** audio/video CD

CD² [sede] (ABRÉV = **corps diplomatique**) CD

CDD [sedede] NM (ABRÉV = **contrat à durée déterminée**) → **contrat**

CDDP [sededepe] NM (ABRÉV = **centre départemental de documentation pédagogique**) → **centre**

CDI¹ [sedei] NM ⓐ (ABRÉV = **centre de documentation et d'information**) → **centre** ⓑ (ABRÉV = **centre des impôts**) → **centre** ⓒ (ABRÉV = **contrat à durée indéterminée**) → **contrat**

CD-I, CD² [sedei] NM (ABRÉV = **compact disc interactif**) CDI; **film sur ~** CDI film

CD-ROM [sederɔm] NM INV (ABRÉV = **compact disc read only memory**) CD-ROM

CDS [sedeɛs] NM (ABRÉV = **Centre des démocrates sociaux**) *French political party*

CDV [sedeve] NM (ABRÉV = **compact disc video**) CDV

CD-vidéo [sedevideo] NM INV (ABRÉV = **compact disc vidéo**) CD-video

CE [seə] ① NM ⓐ (ABRÉV = **comité d'entreprise**) → **comité** ⓑ (ABRÉV = **Conseil de l'Europe**) → **conseil** ⓒ (ABRÉV = **cours élémentaire**) → **cours** ② NF (ABRÉV = **Communauté européenne**) EC

ce¹ [sə]

> *Devant voyelle ou* **h** *muet au masculin* = **cet**, *féminin* = **cette**, *pluriel* = **ces**.

ADJECTIF DÉMONSTRATIF

ⓐ

> *Lorsque* **ce** *est employé pour désigner quelqu'un ou quelque chose qui est proche, on le traduit par* **this** *; lorsqu'il désigne quelqu'un ou quelque chose qui est éloigné, on le traduit généralement par* **that** *;* **ces** *se traduit respectivement par* **these** *et* **those**.

ce chapeau (*tout proche, que je pourrais toucher*) this hat; (*plus loin ou ailleurs*) that hat; **si seulement ce mal de tête s'en allait** if only this headache would go away; **que faisais-tu avec ce type ?*** what were you doing with that guy?*; **que fais-tu avec ce vélo dans ta chambre ?** what are you doing with that bike in your room?; **je ne monterai jamais dans cette voiture !** I'm never getting into that car!

ⓑ

> *Lorsque* **ce** *se réfère à quelqu'un ou quelque chose dont le locuteur vient de parler ou qu'il a présent à l'esprit, on le traduit souvent par* **this** *; si* **ce** *se réfère à quelqu'un ou quelque chose mentionné par un autre locuteur, on le traduit plutôt par* **that** *;* **ces** *se traduit respectivement par* **these** *et* **those**.

j'aime beaucoup ce concerto (*dont je viens de parler*) I'm very fond of this concerto; (*dont tu viens de parler*) I'm very fond of that concerto; **ces questions ne m'intéressent pas** (*celles que je viens de mentionner*) these questions are of no interest to me

> *Notez que là où le français pourrait employer l'article défini à la place de* **ce**, *l'anglais utilise régulièrement comme substitut* **this** *ou* **that**.

ce petit idiot a perdu son ticket the ou that little twerp* has gone and lost his ticket; **il a quitté cette entreprise en 1983** he left the com-

pany in 1983; **je leur ai dit qu'il fallait le vendre mais cette idée ne leur a pas plu** I told them they should sell it but they didn't like the ou that idea

> *Notez l'emploi de* **that** *ou d'un possessif lorsqu'il y a reprise par un pronom.*

alors, cet examen, il l'a eu ?* so, did he pass that ou his exam?; **alors, cette bière, elle arrive ?*** where's that ou my beer got to?*; **et ce rhume/cette jambe, comment ça va ?*** how's that ou your cold/leg? → **ci**, **là**

ⓒ

> *Lorsque* **ce** *est employé pour un événement ou un moment dans le présent ou dans un avenir proche, on le traduit par* **this** *; lorsqu'il désigne un événement ou un moment passé ou dans un avenir éloigné, on le traduit généralement par* **these** *et* **those**.

on a bien travaillé ce matin we've worked well this morning; **venez cet après-midi** come this afternoon; **le 8 de ce mois(-ci)** the 8th of this month; **le 8 de ce mois(-là)** the 8th of that month; **il m'a semblé fatigué ces derniers jours** he's been looking tired these past few days; **ces années furent les plus heureuses de ma vie** those ou these were the happiest years of my life; *MAIS* **cette nuit** (*qui vient*) tonight; (*passée*) last night

ⓓ

> *Lorsque* **ce** *a une valeur intensive, il peut se traduire par un adjectif.*

comment peut-il raconter ces mensonges ! how can he tell such lies!; **cette générosité me semble suspecte** (all) this generosity strikes me as suspicious; **aurait-il vraiment ce courage ?** would he really have that much courage?; **cette idée !** what an idea!; **l'idée !**; *MAIS* **ah, cette Maud !** that Maud!; **ce Paul Durat est un drôle de personnage !** that Paul Durat is quite a character!

ⓔ formules de politesse, *aussi hum* **si ces dames veulent bien me suivre** if you ladies will be so kind as to follow me; **ces messieurs sont en réunion** the gentlemen are in a meeting

ⓕ
◆ *avec* **qui**, **que** : **cette amie chez qui elle habite est docteur** the friend she lives with is a doctor; **elle n'est pas de ces femmes qui ...** she's not one of those ou these women who ...; **il a cette manie qu'ont les enseignants de ...** he has this ou that habit teachers have of ...

ce² [sə]

> *Devant* **en** *et les formes du verbe* **être** *commençant par une voyelle* = **c'**; *devant* **a** = **ç'**. *Pour les locutions figées telles que* **c'est**, **ce sont**, **c'est lui qui**, **c'est que** *etc, reportez-vous à* **être**.

PRONOM DÉMONSTRATIF

ⓐ
◆ **ce** + *pronom relatif* ◊ **ce que/qui** what; (*reprenant une proposition*) which; **ce qui est important c'est ...** what really matters is ...; **elle fait ce qu'on lui dit** she does what she is told ou as she is told; **il ne sait pas ce que sont devenus ses amis** he doesn't know what has become of his friends; **ce qui est dommage, c'est que nous n'ayons pas de jardin** we haven't got a garden, which is a pity; **il faut être diplômé, ce qu'il n'est pas** you have to have qualifications, which he hasn't; **ce à quoi il pense** what he's thinking about; **il a été reçu à son examen, ce à quoi il s'attendait fort peu** he passed his exam, which he wasn't really expecting

> *Notez la place de la préposition en anglais.*

voilà exactement ce dont j'ai peur that's just what I'm afraid of; **c'est ce pour quoi ils luttent** that's what they're fighting for; **ce sur quoi il comptait, c'était ...** what he was counting on was ...; *MAIS* **ce qu'entendant/que voyant, je ...** on hearing/seeing which (*frm*) I ...

> *Notez que* **all** *n'est jamais suivi de* **what** *et que* **that** *peut être omis.*

tout ce que je sais all (that) I know; **voilà tout ce que j'ai pu savoir** that's all I managed to find out

ⓑ
◆ *préposition* + **ce que** + *indicatif* : **à ce qu'on dit/que j'ai appris** from what they say/what I've heard; **il est resté insensible à ce que je lui ai dit** he remained unmoved by what I said; **je ne crois pas à ce qu'il raconte** I don't believe what he says

◆ *préposition* + **ce que** + *subjonctif* : **on ne s'attendait pas à ce qu'il parle** ou **parlât** (*frm*) they were not expecting him ou he was not expected to speak; **il se plaint de ce qu'on ne l'ait pas prévenu** he is complaining that no one warned him; **déçue de ce qu'il ait oublié** disappointed that he had forgotten

ⓒ
◆ **ce que** (*valeur intensive*) **ce que ce train est lent !** this train is so slow!; **ce que les gens sont bêtes !** people are so stupid!, how stupid people are!; **ce qu'on peut s'amuser !** isn't this fun!; **ce qu'il parle bien !** he's a wonderful speaker!, isn't he a wonderful speaker!; **ce qu'elle joue bien !** doesn't she play well!, what a good player she is!; **ce que c'est que le destin !** that's fate for you!; **ce qu'il m'agace !** he's so annoying!; **ce qu'il ne faut pas entendre tout de même !** the things you hear sometimes!, the things people say!; **ce qu'il ne faut pas faire pour la satisfaire !** the things you have to do to keep her happy!

◆ **ce disant** so saying, saying this

◆ **ce faisant** in so doing, in doing so; **il a démissionné et, ce faisant, il a pris un gros risque** he resigned, and by ou in doing so, he took a big risk

◆ **et ce** (*frm*) **j'y suis arrivé, et ce grâce à toi** I managed it, and it was all thanks to you; **elle a tout jeté, et ce sans me le dire** she threw everything away without asking me; **il a refusé, et ce malgré notre insistance** he refused despite our urging

◆ **pour ce faire** to do this, to this end; **il veut développer son entreprise, et pour ce faire il doit emprunter** he wants to develop his company, and to do this ou to this end he will have to borrow money; **on utilise pour ce faire une pince minuscule** to do this you use a tiny pair of pliers

CEA [seaa] ① NM (ABRÉV = **compte d'épargne en actions**) → **compte** ② NF (ABRÉV = **Commissariat à l'énergie atomique**) ≈ AEA (*Brit*), ≈ AEC (*US*)

céans †† [seã] ADV here, in this house → **maître**

CECA [seka] NF (ABRÉV = **Communauté européenne du charbon et de l'acier**) ECSC

ceci [səsi] PRON DÉM this; **ce cas a ~ de surprenant que ...** this case is surprising in that ...; the surprising thing about this case is that ...; **à ~ près que ...** except that ..., with the ou this exception that ...; **~ compense cela** one thing makes up for another

cécité [sesite] NF blindness; **~ des neiges** snow-blindness; **~ verbale** word blindness; **être frappé de ~** to be struck blind, go blind

cédant, e [sedã, ãt] (*Jur*) ① ADJ assigning ② NM,F assignor

céder [sede] ▸ conjug 6 ◂ ① VT ⓐ (= *donner*) [+ part, place, tour] to give up; **~ qch à qn** to let sb have sth, give sth up to sb; **je m'en vais, je vous cède ma place** ou **je cède la place** I'm going so you can have my place ou I'll let you have my place; **~ le pouvoir à qn** to hand over ou yield power to sb; **et maintenant je cède l'antenne à notre correspondant à Paris** and now (I'll hand you) over to our Paris correspondent; (*Jur*) **~ ses biens** to make over ou transfer one's property → **parole**

b (= *vendre*) [+ *commerce*] to sell, dispose of; **~ qch à qn** to let sb have sth, sell sth to sb; **le fermier m'a cédé un litre de lait** the farmer let me have a litre of milk; **~ à bail** to lease; **« bail à ~ »** "lease for sale"; (*petite annonce*) **« cède maison avec jardin »** "house with garden for sale"; **il a bien voulu ~ un bout de terrain** he agreed to part with a plot of land

c (*loc*) **~ le pas à qn** to give way to sb; **son courage ne le cède en rien à son intelligence** he's as brave as he is intelligent; **il ne le cède à personne en égoïsme** he's as selfish as they come; **il ne lui cède en rien** he is every bit his equal → **terrain**

2 VI **a** (= *capituler*) to give in; **~ par faiblesse/lassitude** to give in out of weakness/tiredness; **aucun ne veut ~** no one wants to give in ou give way; **sa mère lui cède en tout** his mother always gives in to him **b** **~ à** (= *succomber à*) [+ *force, tentation*] to give way to, yield to; (= *consentir*) [+ *caprice, prière*] to give in to; **~ à qn** (*à ses raisons, ses avances*) to give in ou yield to sb; **il cède facilement à la colère** he loses his temper easily **c** (= *se rompre*) [*digue, chaise, branche*] to give way; (= *fléchir*) [+ *fièvre, colère*] to subside; **la glace a cédé sous le poids** the ice gave (way) under the weight

cédétiste [sedetist] **1** ADJ CFDT (*épith*) **2** NMF member of the CFDT

Cedex [sedɛks] NM (ABRÉV = **courrier d'entreprise à distribution exceptionnelle**) express postal service (*for bulk users*)

cédille [sedij] NF cedilla

cédrat [sedʀa] NM (= *fruit*) citron; (= *arbre*) citron (tree)

cédratier [sedʀatje] NM citron (tree)

cèdre [sɛdʀ] NM (= *arbre*) cedar (tree); (*Can* = *thuya*) cedar, arbor vitae; (= *bois*) cedar (wood)

cédrière [sedʀijɛʀ] NF (*Can*) cedar grove

CEE [seəə] NF (ABRÉV = **Communauté économique européenne**) EEC

CEEA [seəəa] NF (ABRÉV = **Communauté européenne de l'énergie atomique**) EAEC

CEGEP, Cegep [seʒɛp] NM (ABRÉV = **Collège d'enseignement général et professionnel**) (*Can*) → **collège**

cégétiste [seʒetist] **1** ADJ CGT (*épith*) **2** NMF member of the CGT

CEI [seai] NF (ABRÉV = **Communauté des États indépendants**) CIS

ceindre [sɛ̃dʀ] ▶ conjug 52 ◀ VT (*littér*) **a** (= *entourer*) **~ sa tête d'un bandeau** to put a band round one's head; **la tête ceinte d'un diadème** wearing a diadem; **~ une ville de murailles** to encircle a town with walls; (*Bible*) **se ~ les reins** to gird one's loins **b** (= *mettre*) [+ *armure, insigne d'autorité*] to don, put on; **~ son épée** to buckle ou gird on one's sword; **~ l'écharpe municipale** ≈ to put on ou don the mayoral chain; **~ la couronne** to assume the crown

ceinture [sɛ̃tyʀ] **1** NF **a** [*manteau, pantalon*] belt; [*pyjama, robe de chambre*] cord; (= *écharpe*) sash; (= *gaine*) girdle; **se serrer la ~** to tighten one's belt (*fig*); **elle a tout, et nous, ~ !** she's got everything and we've got zilch*! ou sweet FA*! (*Brit*) ou nix*! (*US*); **faire ~** to have to go without; **personne ne lui arrive à la ~** no one can hold a candle to him*, no one can touch him* **b** (*Couture* = *taille*) [*pantalon, jupe*] waistband **c** (*Aut, Aviat*) seat belt; **attacher ou mettre sa ~** (*Aut*) to put on one's seat belt; (*Aviat*) to fasten one's seat belt **d** (*Anat*) waist; **nu jusqu'à la ~** stripped to the waist; **l'eau lui arrivait (jusqu')à la ~** the water came up to his waist, he was waist-deep in ou up to his waist in water **e** (*Arts martiaux* = *niveau*) belt; **(prise de) ~** waistlock; **~ noire/blanche** black/white belt;

elle est ~ bleue she's a blue belt; (*Boxe, fig*) **coup au-dessous de la ~** blow below the belt **f** [*fortifications, murailles*] ring; [*arbres, montagnes*] belt **g** (= *métro, bus*) circle line; **petite/grande ~** inner/outer circle

2 COMP ▶ **ceinture de chasteté** chastity belt ▶ **ceinture de flanelle** flannel binder ▶ **ceinture fléchée** (*Can*) arrow sash ▶ **ceinture de grossesse** maternity girdle ou support ▶ **ceinture herniaire** truss ▶ **ceinture médicale** → **ceinture orthopédique** ▶ **ceinture de natation** swimmer's float belt ▶ **ceinture orthopédique** surgical corset ▶ **ceinture pelvienne** pelvic girdle ▶ **ceinture rouge** working-class suburbs around Paris which have traditionally voted Communist ▶ **ceinture de sauvetage** lifebelt (*Brit*), life preserver (*US*) ▶ **ceinture scapulaire** pectoral girdle ▶ **ceinture de sécurité** seat belt; **~ de sécurité à enrouleur** inertia reel seat ou safety belt ▶ **ceinture verte** green belt

ceinturer [sɛ̃tyʀe] ▶ conjug 1 ◀ VT [+ *personne*] (*gén*) to grasp ou seize round the waist; (*Sport*) to tackle (round the waist); [+ *ville*] to surround, encircle

ceinturon [sɛ̃tyʀɔ̃] NM (*gén*) (wide) belt; [*uniforme*] belt

CEL [seɛl] NM (ABRÉV = **compte d'épargne logement**) → **compte**

cela [s(ə)la] PRON DÉM **a** (*gén, en opposition à ceci*) that; (*en sujet apparent*) it; **qu'est-ce que ~ veut dire ?** what does that ou this mean?; **on ne s'attendait pas à ~** that was (quite) unexpected, we weren't expecting that; **~ n'est pas très facile** that's not very easy; **~ m'agace de l'entendre se plaindre** it annoys me to hear him complain; **~ vaut la peine qu'il essaie** it's worth his trying; **~ me donne du souci** it gives me a lot of worry; **faire des études, ~ ne le tentait guère** studying did not really appeal to him

b (*forme d'insistance*) **il ne veut pas venir — pourquoi ~ ?** he won't come — why not? ou why won't he?; **comment ~ ?** what do you mean?; **j'ai vu Marie — qui ~ ?/quand ~ ?/où ~ ?** I've seen Marie — who (do you mean)?/when was that?/where was that?

c (*dans le temps*) **il y a deux jours de ~** ◊ **il y a de ~ deux jours** two days ago; **~ fait dix jours/longtemps qu'il est parti** it is ten days/a long time since he left, he has been gone ten days/a long time, he left ten days/a long time ago

d (*loc*) **voyez-vous ~ !** did you ever hear of such a thing!; **~ ne fait rien** it ou that doesn't matter; **et en dehors de ou à part ~ ?** apart from that?; **à ~ près que ...** except that ..., with the exception that ...; **avec eux, il y a ~ de bien qu'ils ...** there's one thing to their credit and that's that they ..., I'll say this for them, they ...

céladon [seladɔ̃] NM, ADJ INV (*vert*) **~** celadon

Célèbes [selɛb] NFPL Celebes, Sulawesi

célébrant [selebʀɑ̃] (*Rel*) **1** ADJ M officiating **2** NM celebrant

célébration [selebʀasjɔ̃] NF celebration

célèbre [selebʀ] ADJ famous (**pour, par** for); **cette ville est ~ pour son festival** this town is famous for its festival; **cet escroc, tristement ~ par ses vols** this crook, notorious for his robberies ou whose robberies have won him notoriety; **se rendre ~ par** to achieve celebrity for ou on account of

▼ **célébrer** [selebʀe] ▶ conjug 6 ◀ VT **a** [+ *anniversaire, fête*] to celebrate; [+ *cérémonie*] to hold; [+ *mariage*] to celebrate, solemnize; **~ la messe** to celebrate mass **b** (= *glorifier*) [+ *exploit*] to celebrate, extol; **~ les louanges de qn** to sing sb's praises

célébrité [selebʀite] NF (= *renommée*) fame,

celebrity; (= *personne*) celebrity; **parvenir à la ~** to rise to fame

celer [səle] ▶ conjug 5 ◀ VT († ou *littér*) to conceal (**à qn** from sb)

céleri [selʀi] NM **~ (en branches)** celery; **~(-rave)** celeriac; **~ rémoulade** celeriac in remoulade (dressing) → **pied**

célérité [seleʀite] NF promptness, speed, swiftness; **avec ~** promptly, swiftly

célesta [selɛsta] NM celeste, celesta

céleste [selɛst] ADJ **a** (= *du ciel, divin*) celestial, heavenly; **colère/puissance ~** celestial anger/power, anger/power of heaven; **le Céleste Empire** the Celestial Empire **b** (*fig* = *merveilleux*) heavenly

célibat [seliba] NM [*homme*] single life, bachelorhood; [*femme*] single life; (*par abstinence*) (period of) celibacy; [*prêtre*] celibacy; **vivre dans le ~** [*prêtre*] to be celibate

célibataire [selibatɛʀ] **1** ADJ (*gén*) single, unmarried; [*prêtre*] celibate; (*Admin*) single; **mère ~** unmarried ou single mother; **père ~** single father **2** NM (= *homme*) single man, bachelor; (*Admin*) single man; **la vie de ~** the life of a single man, the bachelor's life, (the) single life; **club pour ~s** singles club **3** NF (= *femme*) single woman, unmarried woman; (*Admin*) single woman; **la vie de ~** (the) single life, the life of a single woman

célioscopie [seljɔskɔpi] NF = **cœlioscopie**

celle [sɛl] PRON DÉM → **celui**

cellier [selje] NM storeroom (*for wine and food*)

cellophane® [selɔfan] NF Cellophane®; **sous ~** [*aliment*] Cellophane-wrapped, wrapped in Cellophane

cellulaire [selylɛʀ] ADJ **a** (*Bio*) cellular; (*Tech*) **béton ~** air-entrained concrete → **téléphone b** (= *pénitentiaire*) **régime ~** confinement; **voiture ou fourgon ~** prison van

cellule [selyl] NF (*Bio, Bot, Jur, Mil, Photo, Pol*) cell; (*Constr* = *module*) unit; [*avion*] airframe; (*Mil*) **6 jours de ~** 6 days in the cells; **~ familiale** family unit; **~ de réflexion** think tank; **réunir une ~ de crise** to convene an emergency committee; **~ photo-électrique** electric eye, photoelectric cell; **~ photovoltaïque** photovoltaic cell; **~ de lecture** cartridge

cellulite [selylit] NF (= *graisse*) cellulite; (= *inflammation*) cellulitis; **avoir de la ~** to have cellulite

celluloïd [selylɔid] NM celluloid

cellulose [selyloz] NF cellulose; **~ végétale** dietary fibre

cellulosique [selylozik] ADJ cellulose (*épith*)

Celsius [selsjys] N **degré ~** degree Celsius

celte [sɛlt] **1** ADJ Celtic **2** **Celte** NMF Celt

celtique [seltik] ADJ, NM Celtic

celtitude [seltityd] NF Celtic identity

celui [səlɥi], **celle** [sɛl] (*mpl* **ceux** [sø]) (*fpl* **celles** [sɛl]) PRON DÉM **a** (*fonction démonstrative*) **~-ci** ◊ **celle-ci** this one; **ceux-ci** ◊ **celles-ci** these (ones); **~-là** ◊ **celle-là** that one; **ceux-là** ◊ **celles-là** those (ones); **vous avez le choix, celle-ci est plus élégante, mais celle-là est plus confortable** you can choose, this one's more elegant, but that one's more comfortable; **une autre citation, plus littéraire celle-là** another quotation, this time a more literary one ou this one more literary

b (*référence à un antécédent*) **j'ai rendu visite à mon frère et à mon oncle, ~-ci était malade** I visited my brother and my uncle and the latter was ill; **elle écrivit à son frère : ~-ci ne répondit pas** she wrote to her brother, who did not answer ou but he did not answer; **ceux-là, ils auront de mes nouvelles !** as for them ou that lot* (*Brit*), I'll give them a piece of my mind; **il a vraiment de la chance, ~-là !** that guy* certainly has a lot of luck!; **elle est forte ou bien bonne, celle-là !** that's a bit much! ou steep!* ou stiff!*

c (+ *de*) ~ **de** : **je n'aime pas cette pièce, celle de Labiche est meilleure** I don't like this play, Labiche's is better; **c'est ~ des 3 frères que je connais le mieux** of the 3 brothers he's the one I know (the) best, he's the one I know (the) best of the 3 brothers; **il n'a qu'un désir, ~ de devenir ministre** he only wants one thing — (that's) to become a minister; **s'il cherche un local, ~ d'en-dessous est libre** if he's looking for a place, the one below is free; **ce livre est pour ~ d'entre vous que la peinture intéresse** this book is for whichever one of you is interested in painting; **pour ceux d'entre vous qui …** for those of *ou* among you who …

d (*avec qui, que, dont*) **ses romans sont ceux qui se vendent le mieux** his novels are the ones *ou* those that sell best; **c'est celle que l'on accuse** she is the one who is being accused; **donnez-lui le ballon jaune, c'est ~ qu'il préfère** give him the yellow ball — it's *ou* that's the one he likes best; **~ dont je t'ai parlé** the one I told you about; **il a fait ~ qui ne voyait pas** he acted as if he didn't see

e (**: avec adj, participe*) **cette marque est celle recommandée par les fabricants de machines à laver** this brand is the one recommended by washing machine manufacturers, this is the brand recommended by washing machine manufacturers; **~ proche de la fontaine** the one near the fountain; **tous ceux ayant le même âge** all those of the same age

cément [semã] NM (*Métal*) cement; (*dents*) cementum, cement

cénacle [senakl] NM (*frm = cercle*) (literary) coterie *ou* set; (*Rel*) cenacle; **pénétrer dans le ~ des décideurs** to penetrate the inner sanctums of the decision-makers

cendre [sãdʀ] NF **a** (= *substance*) ash, ashes; (*charbon*) ~**(s)** ash, ashes, cinders; **~ de bois** wood ash; **~s volcaniques** volcanic ash; **des ~s** *ou* **de la ~ (de cigarette)** (cigarette) ash; **réduire en ~s** to reduce to ashes; **cuire qch sous la ~** to cook sth in the (the) embers; **couleur de ~** ashen, ash-coloured; (*littér*) **goût de ~** bitter taste → **couver b** (*mort*) **~s** ashes; **le jour ou le mercredi des Cendres** ◊ **les Cendres** Ash Wednesday → **renaître**

cendré, e [sãdʀe] **1** ADJ (= *couleur*) ashen; **gris/blond ~** ash grey/blond; **chèvre ~** *goat's cheese coated in wood ash* **2 cendrée** NF (*Sport = piste*) cinder track; (*Chasse*) **de la ~e** dust shot

cendreux, -euse [sãdʀø, øz] ADJ (*terrain, substance*) ashy; (*couleur*) ash (*épith*), ashy; (*teint*) ashen

cendrier [sãdʀije] NM (*fumeur*) ashtray; (*poêle*) ash pan; (*locomotive*) **~ de foyer** ash box

Cendrillon [sãdʀijɔ̃] NF Cinderella

cène [sɛn] NF **a** (*Peinture, Bible*) **la Cène** the Last Supper **b** (= *communion protestante*) (Holy) Communion, Lord's Supper, Lord's Table

cénesthésie [senɛstezi] NF coen(a)esthesia

cénesthésique [senɛstezik] ADJ cenesthesic, cenesthetic

cénobite [senɔbit] NM cenobite

cénotaphe [senɔtaf] NM cenotaph

cénozoïque [senɔzɔik] **1** ADJ Cenozoic **2** NM **le ~** the Cenozoic

cens [sãs] NM (*Hist*) **a** (= *quotité imposable*) taxable quota *ou* rating (*as an electoral qualification*) **b** (= *redevance féodale*) rent (*paid by tenant of a piece of land to feudal superior*) **c** (= *recensement*) census; **~ électoral** ≈ poll tax

▼ **censé, e** [sãse] ADJ **être ~ faire qch** to be supposed to do sth; **je suis ~ travailler** I'm supposed to be *ou* I should be working; **nul n'est ~ ignorer la loi** ignorance of the law is no excuse

censément [sãsemã] ADV (= *en principe*) sup-

posedly; (= *pratiquement*) virtually; (= *pour ainsi dire*) to all intents and purposes

censeur [sãsœʀ] NM **a** (*Ciné, Presse*) censor **b** (*fig = critique*) critic **c** (†: *Scol*) ≈ deputy *ou* assistant head (*Brit*), ≈ assistant *ou* vice-principal (*US*) **d** (*Hist*) censor

censitaire [sãsitɛʀ] (*Hist*) **1** ADJ **suffrage** *ou* **système ~** voting system based on the poll tax **2** NM **(électeur) ~** eligible voter (*through payment of the poll tax*)

censurable [sãsyʀabl] ADJ censurable

censure [sãsyʀ] NF **a** (*Ciné, Presse*) (= *examen*) censorship; (= *censeurs*) (board of) censors; (*Psych*) censor **b** (†= *critique*) censure; (*Jur, Pol = réprimande*) reprimand; **la ~s de l'Église** the censure of the Church → **motion**

censurer [sãsyʀe] ▶ conjug 1 ◀ VT **a** (+ *spectacle, journal*) to censor; (+ *souvenirs*) to censor; (+ *sentiments*) to suppress **b** (*Jur, Pol, Rel = critiquer*) to censure

cent[1] [sã] **1** ADJ **a** (*cardinal: gén*) a hundred; (*100 exactement*) one hundred, a hundred; (*multiplié par un nombre*) **quatre ~s** four hundred; **quatre ~ un/treize** four hundred and one/thirteen; **~/deux ~s chaises** a hundred/two hundred chairs; **courir un ~ mètres** to run a one-hundred-metre race *ou* sprint *ou* dash (*US*); **piquer un ~ mètres*** (*pour rattraper qn*) to sprint; (*pour s'enfuir*) to leg it*

b (*ordinal: inv*) **en l'an treize ~** in the year thirteen hundred

c (*beaucoup de*) **il a eu ~ occasions de le faire** he has had hundreds of opportunities to do it; **je te l'ai dit ~ fois** I've told you a hundred times, if I've told you once I've told you a hundred times; **il a ~ fois raison** he's absolutely right; **~ fois mieux/pire** a hundred times better/worse; **je préférerais ~ fois faire votre travail** I'd far rather do your job, I'd rather do your job any day*; **c'est ~ fois trop grand** it's far too big → **mot**

d (*loc*) **il est aux ~ coups** he's frantic, he doesn't know which way to turn; **faire les ~ pas** to pace up and down; (*Sport*) **(course de) quatre ~s mètres haies** 400 metres hurdles; **tu ne vas pas attendre ~ sept ans*** you can't wait for ever; (*Hist*) **la guerre de Cent Ans** the Hundred Years' War; (*Hist*) **les Cent-Jours** the Hundred Days; **s'ennuyer** *ou* **s'emmerder* à ~ sous (de) l'heure*** to be bored to tears*, be bored out of one's mind*; **il vit à ~ à l'heure*** he leads a very hectic life → **donner, quatre**

2 NM **a** (= *nombre*) a hundred; **il y a ~ contre un à parier que …** it's a hundred to one that … → **gagner**

b **pour ~** per cent; **argent placé à cinq pour ~** money invested at five per cent; (*fig*) **je suis ~ pour ~ sûr** I'm a hundred per cent certain; **j'en suis à quatre-vingt-dix pour ~ sûr** I'm ninety per cent certain of it

c (*Comm*) **un ~** *ou* one hundred; **un ~ de billes/d'œufs** a *ou* one hundred marbles/eggs; **c'est 12 F le ~** they're 12 francs a hundred; *pour autres locutions voir* **six**

cent[2] [sɛnt, (*Can*) sɛn] NM (*aux USA, au Canada = monnaie*) cent

centaine [sãtɛn] NF **a** (= *environ cent*) **une ~ de** about a hundred, a hundred or so; **la ~ de spectateurs qui …** the hundred *ou* so spectators who …; **plusieurs ~s (de)** several hundred; **des ~s de personnes** hundreds of people; **ils vinrent par ~s** they came in their hundreds **b** (= *cent unités*) hundred; **10 F la ~** 10 francs a hundred; **atteindre la ~** (*collection*) to reach the (one) hundred mark; (*Math*) **la colonne des ~s** the hundreds column

centaure [sãtɔʀ] NM (*Myth*) centaur

centaurée [sãtɔʀe] NF centaury

centenaire [sãt(ə)nɛʀ] **1** ADJ hundred-year-old (*épith*); **cet arbre est ~** this tree is a hundred years old, this is a hundred-year-old tree; **cette maison est plusieurs fois ~** this house is several hundred years old **2** NMF (=

personne) centenarian **3** NM (= *anniversaire*) centenary

centenier [sãtənje] NM (*Hist*) centurion

centésimal, e (*mpl* **-aux**) [sãtezimal, o] ADJ centesimal

centiare [sãtjaʀ] NM centiare

centième [sãtjɛm] **1** ADJ, NMF hundredth; **je n'ai pas retenu le ~ de ce qu'il a dit** I can hardly remember a single word of what he said; *pour autres locutions voir* **sixième 2** NF (*Théât*) hundredth performance

centigrade [sãtigʀad] ADJ centigrade

centigramme [sãtigʀam] NM centigramme (*Brit*), centigram (*US*)

centile [sãtil] NM (per)centile

centilitre [sãtilitʀ] NM centilitre (*Brit*), centiliter (*US*)

centime [sãtim] NM centime; (*fig*) **je n'ai pas un ~** I haven't got a penny *ou* a cent (*US*); **~ additionnel** ≈ additional tax

centimètre [sãtimɛtʀ] NM **a** (= *mesure*) centimetre (*Brit*), centimeter (*US*); (= *ruban*) tape measure, measuring tape

centrafricain, e [sãtʀafʀikɛ̃, ɛn] **1** ADJ of *ou* from the Central African Republic; **la République ~e** the Central African Republic **2 Centrafricain(e)** NM,F Central African

centrage [sãtʀaʒ] NM centring (*Brit*), centering (*US*)

central, e (*mpl* **-aux**) [sãtʀal, o] **1** ADJ **a** (= *du centre*) (*quartier*) central; (*partie, point*) central, centre (*Brit*) (*épith*), center (*US*) (*épith*); **mon bureau occupe une position très ~e** my office is very central; **Amérique/Asie ~e** Central America/Asia → **chauffage, unité b** (= *le plus important*) (*problème, idée*) central; (*bureau*) central, head (*épith*), main (*épith*) **c** (*Jur*) (*pouvoir, administration*) central **d** (*voyelle*) centre (*épith*) (*Brit*), center (*épith*) (*US*)

2 NM **a** (*Téléc*) **~ (téléphonique)** (telephone) exchange **b** (*Tennis = court*) centre (*Brit*) *ou* center (*US*) court

3 centrale NF **a** (*Phys, Élec*) **~e électrique** power station *ou* plant (*US*); **~e thermique au charbon/au fioul** coal-fired/oil-fired power station *ou* plant (*US*); **~e nucléaire** nuclear power station *ou* plant (*US*) **b** (= *groupement*) **~e syndicale** *ou* **ouvrière** group of affiliated trade unions **c** (*Comm*) **~e d'achat(s)** central buying office **d** (= *prison*) prison, ≈ county jail (*US*), ≈ (state) penitentiary (*US*) **e Centrale** (*Univ*) → **école**

centralien, -ienne [sãtʀaljɛ̃, jɛn] NM,F student (*ou* former student) of the École centrale

centralisateur, -trice [sãtʀalizatœʀ, tʀis] ADJ centralizing (*épith*)

centralisation [sãtʀalizasjɔ̃] NF centralization

centraliser [sãtʀalize] ▶ conjug 1 ◀ VT to centralize; **économie centralisée** centralized economy

centralisme [sãtʀalism] NM centralism

centraliste [sãtʀalist] **1** ADJ centralist(ic) **2** NMF centralist

centre [sãtʀ] **1** NM **a** (*gén*) centre (*Brit*), center (*US*); **le ~ (de la France)** central France; **il habite en plein ~ (de la ville)** he lives right in the centre (of town); **il se croit le ~ du monde** he thinks the universe *ou* the world revolves around him; **au ~ du débat** at the centre of the debate; **mot ~** key word; **idée ~** central idea

b (= *lieu d'activités, bâtiment, services*) centre (*Brit*), center (*US*); **les grands ~s urbains/ industriels/universitaires** the great urban/ industrial/academic centres

c (*Pol*) centre (*Brit*), center (*US*); **~ gauche/ droit** centre left/right; **député du ~** deputy of the centre

d (*Ftbl*) († = *joueur*) centre (*Brit*), center (*US*); (= *passe*) centre (*Brit*) *ou* center (*US*) pass

2 COMP ► **centre d'accueil** reception centre ► **centre aéré** (school's) outdoor centre ► **centre anti-douleur** pain clinic ► **centre d'animation** youth centre ► **centre d'attraction** centre of attraction ► **centre de chèques postaux** *postal banking organization*, ≈ National Girobank (*Brit*) ► **centre commercial** shopping centre *ou* arcade, shopping mall (*US*) ► **centre de contrôle** (*Espace*) mission control ► **centre culturel** arts centre ► **centre départemental de documentation pédagogique** *local teachers' resource centre* ► **centre de dépression** (*Mét*) depression, low pressure area ► **centre de détention préventive** remand centre *ou* prison ► **centre de documentation** resource centre, reference library ► **centre de documentation et d'information** school library ► **centre d'éducation surveillée** reformatory, reform school ► **centre d'études** research centre ► **centre de formation professionnelle** professional training centre ► **centre de gravité** (*Phys*) centre of gravity ► **centre de haute pression** (*Mét*) high pressure area ► **centre d'hébergement** reception centre ► **centre hospitalier** hospital ► **centre hospitalier régional** regional hospital ► **centre hospitalier spécialisé** psychiatric hospital ► **centre hospitalier universitaire** teaching *ou* university hospital ► **centre des impôts** tax collection office (*Brit*), Internal Revenue Service office (*US*) ► **centre d'influence** centre of influence ► **centre d'information et de documentation de la jeunesse** careers advisory centre ► **centre d'information et d'orientation** careers advisory centre ► **centre d'intérêt** centre of interest ► **centre médical** medical *ou* health centre ► **Centre national de cinématographie** *French national film institute*, ≈ British Film Institute (*Brit*), ≈ Academy of Motion Picture Arts and Sciences (*US*) ► **Centre national de documentation pédagogique** *national teachers' resource centre* ► **Centre national d'enseignement à distance** *national centre for distance learning*, ≈ Open University (*Brit*) ► **Centre national de la recherche scientifique** ≈ Science and Engineering Research Council (*Brit*), ≈ National Science Foundation (*US*) ► **centres nerveux** (*Physiol*, *fig*) nerve centres ► **Centre régional de documentation pédagogique** *regional teachers' resource centre* ► **Centre régional des œuvres universitaires et scolaires** *students' welfare office* ► **centre de rétention (administrative)** detention centre (*for illegal immigrants*) ► **centre de tri** (*Poste*) sorting office ► **centres vitaux** (*Physiol*) vital organs, vitals; [*entreprise*] vital organs → **serveur**

centré, e [sɑ̃tʀe] (*ptp de* **centrer**) ADJ ~ **sur** [*débat, texte, politique*] centered on, focused on; **le reportage est trop ~ sur la politique** the report focuses *ou* concentrates too much on politics

centrer [sɑ̃tʀe] ▶conjug 1◀ VT **a** (*gén, Sport, Tech*) to centre (*Brit*), center (*US*); **le sujet est mal/bien centré** the subject is off-centre (*Brit*) *ou* off-center (*US*)/right in the centre (*Brit*) *ou* center (*US*); (*Sport*) **il n'a pas pu ~** he was unable to centre the ball **b** (= *orienter*) ~ **une pièce/une discussion sur** to focus a play/a discussion (up)on

centre-ville (*pl* **centres-villes**) [sɑ̃tʀəvil] NM town *ou* city centre (*Brit*) *ou* center (*US*), downtown (*US*); **au** *ou* **en ~** in the town *ou* city centre, downtown (*US*)

centrifugation [sɑ̃tʀifygasjɔ̃] NF centrifugation

centrifuge [sɑ̃tʀify3] ADJ centrifugal

centrifuger [sɑ̃tʀify3e] ▶conjug 3◀ VT to centrifuge

centrifugeur [sɑ̃tʀify3œR] NM, **centrifugeuse** [sɑ̃tʀify3øz] NF (*Tech*) centrifuge; (*Culin*) juice extractor

centripète [sɑ̃tʀipɛt] ADJ centripetal

centrisme [sɑ̃tʀism] NM (*Pol*) centrism, centrist policies

centriste [sɑ̃tʀist] ADJ, NMF centrist

centuple [sɑ̃typl] **1** ADJ a hundred times as large (**de** as); **mille est un nombre ~ de dix** a thousand is a hundred times ten **2** NM **le ~ de 10** a hundred times 10; **au ~** a hundredfold; **on lui a donné le ~ de ce qu'il mérite** he was given a hundred times more than he deserves

centupler [sɑ̃typle] ▶conjug 1◀ VTI to increase a hundred times *ou* a hundredfold; **~ un nombre** to multiply a number by a hundred

centurie [sɑ̃tyʀi] NF (*Hist Mil*) century

centurion [sɑ̃tyʀjɔ̃] NM centurion

CEP [seap] NM (ABRÉV = **certificat d'études primaires**) → **certificat**

cep [sep] NM **a** ~ (**de vigne**) (vine) stock **b** [*charrue*] stock

cépage [sepa3] NM (type of) vine

cèpe [sep] NM (*Culin*) cep; (*Bot*) (edible) boletus

▼ **cependant** [s(ə)pɑ̃dɑ̃] CONJ **a** (= *pourtant*) nevertheless, however, yet; **ce travail est dangereux, nous allons ~ essayer de le faire** it's a dangerous job — we shall try to do it nevertheless *ou* but we'll try to do it all the same; **c'est incroyable et ~ c'est vrai** it's incredible and yet it's true **b** (*littér*) (= *pendant ce temps*) meanwhile, in the meantime; (= *tandis que*) **~ que** while

céphalée [sefale] NF cephalalgia (*SPÉC*), headache

céphalique [sefalik] ADJ cephalic

céphalopode [sefalɔpɔd] NM cephalopod; **~s** cephalopods, Cephalopoda (*SPÉC*)

céphalo-rachidien, -ienne [sefalɔʀaʃidjɛ̃, jɛn] ADJ cephalo-rachidian (*SPÉC*), cerebrospinal

céramide [seramid] NM (*Cosmétique*) ceramide

céramique [seramik] **1** ADJ ceramic **2** NF (= *matière, objet*) ceramic; (= *art*) **la ~** ceramics, pottery; **vase en ~** ceramic *ou* pottery vase; **~ dentaire** dental ceramics

céramiste [seramist] NMF ceramist

cerbère [sɛʀbɛʀ] NM **a** (*péj*) fierce doorkeeper *ou* doorman; (*hum* = *concierge*) janitor **b** **Cerbère** (*Myth*) Cerberus

cerceau (*pl* **cerceaux**) [sɛʀso] NM [*enfant, tonneau, crinoline*] hoop; [*capote, tonnelle*] half-hoop; **jouer au ~** to play with a hoop, bowl a hoop; **avoir les jambes en ~** to be bandy-legged *ou* bow-legged, have bandy *ou* bow legs

cerclage [sɛʀkla3] NM (= *action*) hooping; **~ du col de l'utérus** cervical cerclage

cercle [sɛʀkl] **1** NM **a** (= *forme, figure*) circle, ring; (*Géog, Géom*) circle; **l'avion décrivait des ~s** the plane was circling (overhead); **itinéraire décrivant un ~** circular route; **entourer d'un ~ le chiffre correct** to circle *ou* ring *ou* put a circle *ou* a ring round the correct number; **faire ~ (autour de qn/qch)** to gather round (sb/sth) in a circle *ou* ring, form a circle *ou* ring (round sb/sth); **~s imprimés sur la table par les** (*fonds de*) **verres** rings left on the table by the glasses; **un ~ de badauds/de chaises** a circle *ou* ring of onlookers/chairs → **arc, quadrature**
b (= *étendue*) [*activités*] scope, circle, range; **étendre le ~ de ses relations/de ses amis** to widen the circle of one's acquaintances/one's circle of friends
c (= *groupe*) circle; **le ~ de famille** the family

circle; **un ~ d'amis** a circle of friends; **~ de qualité** quality circle
d (= *club*) society, club; **~ littéraire** literary circle *ou* society; **aller dîner au ~** to go and dine at the club
e (= *cerceau*) hoop, band; **~ de tonneau** barrel hoop *ou* band; **~ de roue** tyre (*Brit*) *ou* tire (*US*) (made of metal)
f (= *instrument*) protractor
2 COMP ► **cercle horaire** horary circle ► **cercle polaire** polar circle; **~ polaire arctique** Arctic Circle; **~ polaire antarctique** Antarctic Circle ► **cercle vertueux** virtuous circle ► **cercle vicieux** vicious circle

cercler [sɛʀkle] ▶conjug 1◀ VT (*gén*) to ring; [+ *tonneau*] to hoop; [+ *roue*] to tyre (*Brit*), tire (*US*) (**de** with); **lunettes cerclées d'écaille** horn-rimmed spectacles

cercueil [sɛʀkœj] NM coffin, casket (*US*)

céréale [sereal] NF (*Bot*) cereal; (*pour petit-déjeuner*) **~s** (breakfast) cereal

céréaliculture [serealikyltyʀ] NF cereal growing

céréalier, -ière [serealje, jɛʀ] **1** ADJ cereal (*épith*) **2** NM (= *producteur*) cereal grower; (**navire**) ~ grain carrier *ou* ship

cérébelleux, -euse [serebelø, øz] ADJ cerebellar

cérébral, e (*mpl* **-aux**) [serebral, o] ADJ (*Méd*) [*hémisphère, cortex*] cerebral; (= *intellectuel*) [*travail*] mental; **c'est un ~** he's quite cerebral

cérébro-spinal, e (*mpl* **-aux**) [serebrospinal, o] ADJ cerebrospinal

cérémonial (*pl* **cérémonials**) [seremɔnjal] NM ceremonial

cérémonie [seremɔni] NF ceremony; **sans ~** [*manger*] informally; [*proposer*] without ceremony, unceremoniously; [*réception*] informal; **avec ~** ceremoniously; **faire des ~s** to stand on ceremony; **ne fais pas tant de ~s** there's no need to stand on ceremony; **tenue** *ou* **habit de ~** formal dress (*NonC*), ceremonial dress (*NonC*); (*Mil*) **tenue de ~** dress uniform → **maître**

cérémoniel, -ielle [seremɔnjɛl] ADJ ceremonial

cérémonieusement [seremɔnjøzmɑ̃] ADV ceremoniously, formally

cérémonieux, -ieuse [seremɔnjø, jøz] ADJ [*ton, accueil*] ceremonious, formal; [*personne*] formal; **il est très ~** he has a very formal manner

cerf [sɛʀ] NM stag, hart (*littér*)

cerfeuil [sɛʀfœj] NM chervil

cerf-volant (*pl* **cerfs-volants**) [sɛʀvɔlɑ̃] NM **a** (= *jouet*) kite; **jouer au ~** to fly a kite **b** (*Zool*) stag beetle

cerisaie [s(ə)ʀizɛ] NF cherry orchard

cerise [s(ə)ʀiz] **1** NF cherry; (*fig*) **la ~ sur le gâteau** the icing on the cake **2** ADJ INV cherry(-red), cerise → **rouge**

cerisier [s(ə)ʀizje] NM (= *arbre*) cherry (tree); (= *bois*) cherry (wood)

cérium [serjɔm] NM cerium

CERN [sɛʀn] NM (ABRÉV = **Conseil européen pour la recherche nucléaire**) CERN

cerne [sɛʀn] NM [*yeux, lune*] ring; (= *tache*) ring, mark; [*arbre*] annual ring; **les ~s de** *ou* **sous les yeux** the (dark) rings *ou* shadows under his eyes

cerné, e [sɛʀne] ADJ **avoir les yeux ~s** to have (dark) rings *ou* shadows under one's eyes; **ses yeux ~s trahissaient sa fatigue** the (dark) rings *ou* shadows under his eyes showed how tired he was

cerneau (*pl* **cerneaux**) [sɛʀno] NM unripe walnut; (*Culin*) **~x (de noix)** shelled walnuts

cerner [sɛʀne] ▶conjug 1◀ VT **a** (= *entourer*) to encircle, surround; (*Peinture*) [+ *visage, silhouette*] to outline (**de** with, in); **ils étaient**

cernés de toute(s) part(s) they were surrounded on all sides, they were completely surrounded **b** (= *comprendre*) [+ *problème*] to delimit, define, zero in on; [+ *personne*] to work out, figure out **c** [+ *noix*] to shell (*while unripe*); [+ *arbre*] to ring

▼ **certain, e** [sɛʀtɛ̃, ɛn] **1** ADJ **a** (*après nom = incontestable*) [*fait, succès, événement*] certain; [*indice*] sure; [*preuve*] positive, sure; [*cause*] undoubted, sure; **c'est la raison ~e de son départ** it's undoubtedly the reason he's going; **ils vont à une mort ~e** they're heading for certain death; **il a fait des progrès ~s** he has made definite progress; **la victoire est ~e** victory is assured *ou* certain; **c'est une chose ~e** it's absolutely certain; **c'est ~** there's no doubt about it; **c'est un crétin ! — c'est ~ !** he's a moron!* — that's for sure!*; **il est maintenant ~ qu'elle ne reviendra plus** it's now (quite) certain that she won't come back, she's sure *ou* certain not to come back now; **je le tiens pour ~ !** I'm certain *ou* sure of it!, I know it for a fact!; **il est ~ que ce film ne convient guère à des enfants** this film is definitely unsuitable for children
b (= *convaincu, sûr*) [*personne*] sure, certain, convinced; **es-tu ~ de rentrer ce soir ?** are you sure *ou* certain you'll be back this evening? *ou* of being back this evening?; **il est ~ de leur honnêteté** he's convinced of their honesty, he's certain *ou* sure they are honest; **on n'est jamais ~ du lendemain** you can never be sure what tomorrow will bring; **elle est ~e qu'ils viendront** she's sure *ou* certain *ou* convinced they'll come → **sûr**
c (*Comm = déterminé*) [*date, prix*] definite
2 ADJ INDÉF (*avant nom*) **a** (= *plus ou moins défini*) **un ~** a certain, some; **elle a un ~ charme** there's something quite attractive about her, she has a certain charm; **dans une ~e mesure** to a certain extent, to some extent; **il y a un ~ village où** there is a certain *ou* some village where; **dans un ~ sens, je le comprends** in a way *ou* in a certain sense I can see his point; **jusqu'à un ~ point** up to a (certain) point; **il a manifesté un ~ intérêt** he showed a certain (amount of) *ou* some interest; **un ~ nombre d'éléments font penser que ...** a (certain) number of things lead one to think that ...
b (*parfois péj = personne*) **un ~** a (certain); **un ~ M. Leblanc vous a demandé** a Mr Leblanc asked for you; **un ~ ministre disait même que ...** a certain minister even said that ...
c (*intensif*) some; **c'est à une ~e distance d'ici** it's quite a *ou* some distance from here; **cela demande une ~e patience/un ~ courage** it takes a fair amount of patience/some *ou* a fair amount of courage; **au bout d'un ~ temps** after a while *ou* some time; **il a un ~ âge** he's getting on (in years); **une personne d'un ~ âge** an elderly person; (*hum*) **il est d'un âge ~** he's past his prime
d (*pl = quelques*) **~s** some, certain; **dans ~s cas** in some *ou* certain cases; **~es personnes ne l'aiment pas** some people don't like him; **~es fois ◊ à ~s moments** at (certain) times; **sans ~es notions de base** without some *ou* certain (of the) basic notions
3 **certains** PRON INDÉF PL (= *personnes*) some (people); (= *choses*) some; **dans ~s de ces cas** in certain *ou* some of these cases; **parmi ses récits ~s sont amusants** some of his stories are amusing; **pour ~s** some (people) say that ...; **~s d'entre vous** some of you; **il y en a ~s qui ...** there are some (people) *ou* there are those who ...
4 NM (*Fin*) fixed *ou* direct rate of exchange

certainement [sɛʀtɛnmɑ̃] ADV (= *très probablement*) most probably, most likely; (= *sans conteste*) certainly; (= *bien sûr*) certainly, of course; **il va ~ venir ce soir** he'll most probably *ou* most likely come tonight; **il est ~ le plus intelligent** he's certainly *ou* without doubt the most intelligent; **il y a ~ un moyen**

de s'en tirer there must be some way out; **puis-je emprunter votre stylo ? — ~** can I borrow your pen? — certainly *ou* of course

certes [sɛʀt] ADV **a** (*de concession*) (= *sans doute*) certainly, admittedly; (= *bien sûr*) of course, certainly; **il est ~ le plus fort, mais ...** he is admittedly *ou* certainly the strongest, but ...; **~ je n'irai pas jusqu'à le renvoyer mais ...** of course I wouldn't *ou* I certainly wouldn't go so far as dismissing him but ... **b** (*d'affirmation*) indeed, most certainly; **l'avez-vous apprécié ? — ~** did you like it? — I did indeed *ou* I most certainly did

certif* [sɛʀtif] NM (ABRÉV = **certificat d'études (primaires)**) → **certificat**

certificat [sɛʀtifika] **1** NM (= *attestation*) certificate, attestation; (= *diplôme*) certificate, diploma; (= *recommandation*) [*domestique*] testimonial; (*fig*) guarantee
2 COMP ▶ **certificat d'aptitude professionnelle** vocational training certificate, ≈ City and Guilds examination (*Brit*) ▶ **certificat d'aptitude au professorat de l'enseignement du second degré** secondary school teacher's diploma ▶ **certificat d'aptitude au professorat de l'enseignement technique** technical teaching diploma ▶ **certificat de bonne vie et mœurs** character reference ▶ **certificat de concubinage** document certifying that an unmarried couple are living together as husband and wife ▶ **certificat de décès** death certificate ▶ **certificat de dépôt** (*Fin*) certificate of deposit ▶ **certificat d'études primaires** certificate formerly obtained by pupils at the end of primary school ▶ **certificat d'hébergement** proof of residence (*required by foreign nationals who apply to come and live in France*) ▶ **certificat d'investissement** non-voting preference share (*Brit*) *ou* preferred share (*US*) ▶ **certificat de licence**† (*Univ*) part of first degree ▶ **certificat de mariage** marriage certificate ▶ **certificat médical** medical *ou* doctor's certificate ▶ **certificat de navigabilité** (*Naut*) certificate of seaworthiness; (*Aviat*) certificate of airworthiness ▶ **certificat d'origine** (*Comm*) certificate of origin ▶ **certificat prénuptial** prenuptial medical certificate ▶ **certificat de résidence** (*Admin*) certificate of residence *ou* domicile ▶ **certificat de scolarité** attestation of attendance at school *ou* university ▶ **certificat de travail** attestation of employment

certificateur [sɛʀtifikatœʀ] **1** ADJ [*personne*] who acts as a guarantor *ou* as surety; **organisme ~** certification body **2** NM (*Jur*) guarantor, certifier; **~ de caution** countersurety, countersecurity

certification [sɛʀtifikasjɔ̃] NF **a** (*Jur = assurance*) attestation, witnessing; **~ de signature** attestation of signature **b** [*entreprise, produit*] certification; **~ ISO 9000** ISO 9000 certification

certifié, e [sɛʀtifje] (*ptp de* **certifier**) NM,F (qualified) secondary school (*Brit*) *ou* high-school (*US*) teacher, *holder of the CAPES*

certifier [sɛʀtifje] ▶ conjug 7 ◀ VT **a** (= *assurer*) **~ qch à qn** to assure sb of sth, guarantee sb sth *ou* sth to sb; **je te certifie qu'ils vont créer affaire à moi !** I can assure you *ou* I'm telling you* they'll have me to reckon with! **b** (*Jur = authentifier*) [+ *document*] to certify, guarantee; [+ *signature*] to attest, witness; [+ *caution*] to counter-secure; **copie certifiée conforme à l'original** certified copy of the original

▼ **certitude** [sɛʀtityd] NF certainty; **c'est une ~ absolue** it's absolutely certain *ou* an absolute certainty; **avoir la ~ de qch/de faire** to be certain *ou* (quite) sure *ou* confident of sth/of doing; **j'ai la ~ d'être le plus fort** I am certain of being *ou* that I am the strongest

céruléen, -enne [seʀyleɛ̃, ɛn] ADJ (*littér*) cerulean

cérumen [seʀymɛn] NM (ear) wax, cerumen (*SPÉC*)

cérumineux, -euse [seʀyminø, øz] ADJ ceruminous

céruse [seʀyz] NF ceruse → **blanc**

cérusé, e [seʀyze] ADJ [*bois, meuble*] white-leaded

Cervantes [sɛʀvɑ̃tɛs] NM Cervantes

cerveau (*pl* cerveaux) [sɛʀvo] **1** NM **a** (*Anat*) brain; (*fig = intelligence*) brain(s), mind; **le ~ humain** the human brain; **avoir le ~ dérangé** *ou* (*hum*) **fêlé** to be deranged *ou* (a bit) touched* *ou* cracked*; **fais travailler ton ~** use your brain → **rhume, transport** **b** (= *personne intelligente*) brain, mind; **c'est un grand ~** he has a great brain *ou* mind; **la fuite** *ou* **l'exode des ~x** the brain drain **c** (= *organisateur*) brains; **c'était le ~ de l'affaire** he was the brains behind the job, he masterminded the job; **le ~ de la bande** the brains of the gang **2** COMP ▶ **cerveau antérieur** forebrain ▶ **cerveau électronique** electronic brain ▶ **cerveau moyen** midbrain ▶ **cerveau postérieur** hindbrain

cervelas [sɛʀvəla] NM saveloy

cervelet [sɛʀvəlɛ] NM cerebellum

cervelle [sɛʀvɛl] NF (*Anat*) brain; (*Culin*) brains; (*Culin*) **~ d'agneau** lamb's brains; (*Culin*) **~ de canut** *fromage blanc with chopped chives (Lyons speciality)*; **se brûler** *ou* **se faire sauter la ~** to blow one's brains out; **quand il a quelque chose dans la ~** when he gets something into his head; **sans ~** brainless; **il n'a rien dans la ~*** he's completely brainless, he's as thick as two short planks* (*Brit*); **avoir une ~ d'oiseau** *ou* **de moineau** to be feather-brained *ou* bird-brained; **toutes ces ~s folles** all these scatter-brains → **creuser, trotter**

cervical, e (*mpl* -**aux**) [sɛʀvikal, o] ADJ cervical

cervidé [sɛʀvide] NM cervid (*SPÉC*); **~s** Cervidae (*SPÉC*)

Cervin [sɛʀvɛ̃] NM **le ~** the Matterhorn

cervoise [sɛʀvwaz] NF barley beer

CES [seəɛs] NM **a** (ABRÉV = **collège d'enseignement secondaire**) → **collège** **b** (ABRÉV = **contrat emploi-solidarité**) → **contrat**

ces [se] PRON DÉM → **ce**

César [sezaʀ] NM **a** (*Hist*) Caesar ■ (*PROV*) **il faut rendre à ~ ce qui appartient à ~** render unto Caesar the things which are Caesar's (*PROV*) **b** (*Ciné*) French film award, ≈ Oscar, ≈ BAFTA award (*Brit*)

Césarée [sezaʀe] NF Caesarea

césarien, -ienne [sezaʀjɛ̃, jɛn] **1** ADJ (*Hist*) Caesarean **2** **césarienne** NF (*Méd*) Caesarean (section); **elle a eu** *ou* **on lui a fait une césarienne** she had a Caesarean (birth *ou* delivery)

césarisé, e [sezaʀize] ADJ **a** (*Ciné*) [*comédien*] who has won a César; [*film*] that has won a César **b** **les femmes ~es** women who have had Caesareans *ou* Caesarean births *ou* deliveries

césariser [sezaʀize] ▶ conjug 1 ◀ VT (*Méd*) to perform a Caesarean (section) on

césium [sezjɔm] NM = **cæsium**

cessant, e [sesɑ̃, ɑ̃t] ADJ → **affaire**

cessation [sesasjɔ̃] NF (*frm*) [*activité, pourparlers*] cessation; [*hostilités*] cessation, suspension; [*paiements*] suspension; **être en ~ de paiements** to be insolvent, be unable to meet one's financial obligations

cesse [sɛs] NF **a** **sans ~** (= *tout le temps*) continually, constantly, incessantly; (= *sans interruption*) continuously, incessantly; **elle est sans ~ après lui** she's continually *ou* constantly nagging (at) him, she's forever nagging (at) him; **la pluie tombe sans ~ depuis hier** it has been raining continuously *ou* non-stop

▶ GRAMMAIRE ACTIVE: certain 42.1, 43.1, 53.6   certitude 42.1

since yesterday b (frm) **il n'a de ~ que ...** he will not rest until ...; **il n'a eu de ~ qu'elle ne lui cède** he gave her no peace ou rest until she gave in to him

cesser [sese] ▸ conjug 1 ◂ 1 VT a [+ bavardage, bruit, activité] to stop; [+ relations] to (bring to an) end, break off; **nous avons cessé la fabrication de cet article** we have stopped making this item, this line has been discontinued; **~ ses fonctions** to leave office; **~ ses paiements** to stop ou discontinue payment; **~ le combat** to stop ou cease fighting; **~ le travail** to stop work ou working

b **~ de faire qch** to stop doing sth; **il a cessé de fumer** he's given up ou stopped ou quit* smoking; **il a cessé de venir il y a un an** he stopped coming a year ago; **il n'a pas cessé de pleuvoir de toute la journée** it hasn't stopped raining all day, the rain hasn't let up all day; **la compagnie a cessé d'exister en 1943** the company ceased to exist ou ceased trading in 1943; **quand cesseras-tu ou tu vas bientôt ~ de faire le clown ?** when are you going to stop ou quit* ou leave off* acting the fool?; **son effet n'a pas cessé de se faire sentir** its effects are still being felt

c (frm : répétition fastidieuse) **ne ~ de : il ne cesse de m'importuner** he's constantly ou forever bothering me; **il ne cesse de dire que ...** he's constantly ou continually saying that ...

2 VI a [bavardage, bruit, activités, combat] to stop, cease; [relations, fonctions] to come to an end; [douleur] to stop; [fièvre] to pass, die down; **le vent a cessé** the wind has stopped (blowing); **tout travail a cessé** all work has stopped ou come to a halt ou a standstill

b **faire ~** [+ bruit] to put a stop to, stop; [+ scandale] to put an end ou a stop to; (Jur) **pour faire ~ les poursuites** in order to have the proceedings dropped

cessez-le-feu [sesel(ə)fø] NM INV ceasefire

cessible [sesibl] ADJ (Jur) transferable, assignable

cession [sesjɔ̃] NF [bail, biens, droit] transfer; **faire ~ de** to transfer, assign; **~-bail** lease-back

cessionnaire [sesjɔnɛʀ] NMF [bien, droit] transferee, assignee

c'est-à-dire [sɛtadiʀ] CONJ a (= à savoir) that is (to say), i.e; **un lexicographe, ~ quelqu'un qui fait un dictionnaire** a lexicographer, that is (to say), someone who compiles a dictionary b **~ que** (= en conséquence) **l'usine a fermé, ~ que son frère est maintenant en chômage** the factory has shut down, which means that his brother is unemployed now; (manière d'excuse) **viendras-tu dimanche ? — ~ que j'ai du travail** will you come on Sunday? — well actually ou well the thing is I've got some work to do; (rectification) **je suis fatigué — ~ que tu as trop bu hier** I'm tired — you mean ou what you mean is you had too much to drink yesterday

césure [sezyʀ] NF caesura

CET [seate] NM (ABRÉV = **collège d'enseignement technique**) → **collège**

cet [sɛt] ADJ DÉM → **ce**

cétacé [setase] NM cetacean

ceux [sø] PRON DÉM → **celui**

Ceylan [selɑ̃] NM Ceylon

cf [seɛf] (ABRÉV = **confer**) cf

CFA [seɛfa] (ABRÉV = **Communauté financière africaine**) → **franc²**

CFAO [seɛfao] NF (ABRÉV = **conception et fabrication assistées par ordinateur**) CADCAM

CFC [seɛfse] NMPL (ABRÉV = **chlorofluorocarbures**) CFCs

CFDT [seɛfdete] NF (ABRÉV = **Confédération française démocratique du travail**) French trade union

CFP [seɛfpe] NM (ABRÉV = **centre de formation professionnelle**) → **centre**

CFTC [seɛftese] NF (ABRÉV = **Confédération française des travailleurs chrétiens**) French trade union

cg (ABRÉV = **centigramme**) cg

CGC [segese] NF (ABRÉV = **Confédération générale des cadres**) French management union

CGT [seʒete] NF (ABRÉV = **Confédération générale du travail**) French trade union

ch (ABRÉV = **cheval-vapeur**) HP, h.p.

chablis [ʃabli] NM a (= vin) Chablis (dry white Burgundy wine) b (= bois) windfall

chacal (pl chacals) [ʃakal] NM (Zool) jackal; (* : péj) vulture

cha-cha(-cha) [tʃatʃa(tʃa)] NM INV cha-cha(-cha)

chacun, e [ʃakœ̃, yn] PRON INDÉF a (d'un ensemble bien défini) each (one); **~ d'entre eux** each (one) of them, every one of them; **~ des deux** each ou both of them, each of the two; **ils me donnèrent ~ 10 F/leur chapeau** they each (of them) gave me 10 francs/their hat, each (one) of them gave me 10 francs/their hat; **il leur donna (à) ~ 10 F ◊ il leur donna 10 F (à) ~** he gave them 10 francs each, he gave them each 10 francs, he gave each (one) of them 10 francs; **il remit les livres ~ à sa ou leur place** he put each of the books back in its place; **nous sommes entrés ~ à notre tour** we each went in in turn

b (d'un ensemble indéfini) everyone, everybody; **comme ~ le sait** as everyone ou everybody knows; **~ son tour !** wait your turn!, everyone's got to have a turn!; **~ son goût ou ses goûts** each to his own; **~ ses idées** everyone has a right to their (own) opinion, each to his own; **~ pour soi (et Dieu pour tous !)** every man for himself (and God for us all!); **~ voit midi à sa porte** people always act in their own interests ■ (PROV) **(à) ~ son métier(, les vaches seront bien gardées)** each man to his own trade → **tout**

chafouin, e [ʃafwɛ̃, in] ADJ [visage, mine] sly

chagrin¹, e [ʃagʀɛ̃, in] 1 ADJ a (littér) (= triste) [air, humeur, personne] despondent, woeful, dejected; (= bougon) [personne] ill-humoured (Brit) ou -humored (US), morose; **les esprits ~s disent que ...** disgruntled people say that ... 2 NM a (= affliction) grief, sorrow; (à un enfant) **alors, on a un gros ~ !** well, we do look sorry for ourselves! ou unhappy!; **avoir un ~ d'amour** to have an unhappy love affair, be disappointed in love; **plonger qn dans un profond ~** to plunge sb deep in grief; **faire du ~ à qn** to cause sb grief ou distress ou sorrow, grieve ou distress sb; **avoir du ~** to be grieved ou distressed → **noyer²** b (†† = mélancolie) ill-humour (Brit) ou -humor (US)

chagrin² [ʃagʀɛ̃] NM (= cuir) shagreen → **peau**

chagrinant, e [ʃagʀinɑ̃, ɑ̃t] ADJ distressing

chagriner [ʃagʀine] ▸ conjug 1 ◂ VT a (= désoler) to grieve, distress, upset; (= tracasser) to worry, bother

chah [ʃa] NM = **shah**

chahut [ʃay] NM (= tapage) uproar; **faire du ~** to make ou create an uproar

chahuter [ʃayte] ▸ conjug 1 ◂ 1 VI (Scol) (= faire du bruit) to make ou create an uproar; (= faire les fous) to mess around, lark around* (avec with) 2 VT a [+ professeur] to play up, rag, bait; † [+ fille] to tease; [+ ministre] to heckle; **un professeur chahuté** a teacher who can't control his pupils; **il se fait ~ par ses élèves** his pupils create mayhem in his class b (* = cahoter) [+ objet] to knock about c (Bourse) [+ valeur, monnaie] to put under pressure

chahuteur, -euse [ʃaytœʀ, øz] 1 ADJ rowdy, unruly 2 NM,F rowdy

chai [ʃɛ] NM wine and spirit store(house)

chaînage [ʃɛnaʒ] NM a (Ordin) chaining b (Constr) clamp; **poutre de ~** (wall) tie

chaîne [ʃɛn] 1 NF a (de métal, ornementale) chain; **~ de bicyclette/de montre** bicycle/watch chain; **attacher un chien à une ~** to chain up a dog, put a dog on a chain; (Aut) **~s** (snow) chains

b (= esclavage) **~s** chains, bonds, fetters, shackles; **briser ses ~s** to cast off one's chains ou bonds ou shackles

c (= suite : gén), (Anat, Chim, Méd) chain; [montagnes] chain, range; **la ~ des Alpes** the Alpine range; **faire la ~ ◊ former une ~ (humaine)** to form a (human) chain; **en ~** [catastrophes, faillites] a series of → **réaction**

d (Ind) (= de fabrication) production line; **produire qch à la ~** to mass-produce sth, make sth on an assembly line ou a production line; **travailler à la ~** to work on an assembly line ou a production line; **il produit des romans à la ~** he churns out one novel after another; (fig) **en bout de ~** at the end of the chain → **travail¹**

e (TV) channel; **~ culturelle/musicale** cultural/music channel; **sur la première/deuxième ~** on the first/second channel

f (Radio) music system; **~ hi-fi/stéréo** hi-fi/stereo system; **~ compacte** mini-system, music centre (Brit)

g (Comm) [journaux] string; [magasins] chain, string

h (Tex) warp

i (= lettre) chain letter

2 COMP ► **chaîne alimentaire** food chain ► **chaîne d'arpenteur** (surveyor's) chain, chain measure ► **chaîne câblée** cable channel ► **chaîne de caractères** (Ordin) character string ► **chaîne du froid** cold chain; **respecter la ~ du froid** to make sure the recommended low temperature is maintained ► **chaîne de montage** assembly line ► **la chaîne parlée** (Ling) connected speech ► **chaîne payante** ou **à péage** (TV) pay TV channel ► **chaîne privée** (TV) private channel ► **chaîne publique** (TV) publicly-owned channel, public service channel (US) ► **chaîne sans fin** endless chain ► **chaîne de solidarité** support network ► **chaîne de sûreté** (gén) safety chain; [porte] door ou safety chain

chaîner [ʃɛne] ▸ conjug 1 ◂ VT (Ordin) to chain; (Constr) to clamp

chaînette [ʃɛnɛt] NF (small) chain; (Math) **courbe** ou **arc en ~** catenary curve → **point²**

chaînon [ʃɛnɔ̃] NM (lit, fig) [chaîne] link; [filet] loop; (Géog) secondary range (of mountains); **le ~ manquant** the missing link; (Ordin) **~ de données** data link

chair [ʃɛʀ] 1 NF a [homme, animal, fruit] flesh; **entrer dans les ~s** to penetrate the flesh; **en ~ et en os** in the flesh, as large as life (hum); **ce n'est qu'un être de ~ et de sang** he's only flesh and blood, he's only human; **être ni ~ ni poisson** (indécis) to be indecisive; (indéfinissable) to be neither fish nor fowl; **l'ogre aime la ~ fraîche** the ogre likes a diet of warm young flesh; (hum) **il aime la ~ fraîche** (des jeunes femmes) he likes firm young flesh ou bodies; **avoir/donner la ~ de poule** (froid) to have/give goosepimples ou gooseflesh; (chose effrayante) **ça vous donne** ou **on en a la ~ de poule** it makes your flesh creep, it gives you gooseflesh; **~ à canon** cannon fodder; **~ (à saucisse)** sausage meat; **je vais en faire de la ~ à pâté** ou **à saucisse*** I'm going to make mincemeat of him; **bien en ~** well-padded (hum), plump

b (littér, Rel : opposé à l'esprit) flesh; **souffrir dans/mortifier sa ~** to suffer in/mortify the flesh; **fils/parents selon la ~** natural son/parents; **sa propre ~ ◊ la ~ de sa ~** his own flesh and blood; **la ~ est faible** the flesh is weak → **péché**

c (Peinture) **~s** flesh tones ou tints

2 ADJ INV (couleur) **~** flesh-coloured (Brit) ou -colored (US)

chaire [ʃɛʀ] NF [a] (= estrade) [prédicateur] pulpit; [professeur] rostrum; **monter en ~** to go up into *ou* ascend the pulpit [b] (= poste) (Scol) post; (Univ) chair; **créer une ~ de français** to create a chair of French [c] **la ~ pontificale** the papal throne

chaise [ʃɛz] [1] NF chair; **faire la ~** (pour porter un blessé) to link arms to make a seat *ou* chair; **être assis** *ou* **avoir le cul: entre deux ~s** to be caught between two stools, be on the horns of a dilemma → **politique** [2] COMP ► **chaise de bébé** highchair ► **chaise berçante** *ou* **berceuse** (Can) rocking chair ► **chaise de cuisine** kitchen chair ► **chaise électrique** electric chair ► **chaise haute** highchair ► **chaise de jardin** garden chair ► **chaise longue** (= siège pliant) deckchair; (= canapé) chaise longue; **faire de la ~ longue** to lie back *ou* relax in a deckchair; (= se reposer) to put one's feet up ► **chaises musicales** (= jeu, fig) musical chairs ► **chaise percée** commode ► **chaise (à porteurs)** sedan(-chair) ► **chaise de poste** poste chaise ► **chaise roulante** wheelchair, bathchair† (Brit)

chaisier, -ière [ʃɛzje, jɛʀ] NM,F [a] (= loueur) chair attendant [b] (= fabricant) chair maker

chaland¹ [ʃalɑ̃] NM (Naut) barge

chaland², e† [ʃalɑ̃, ɑ̃d] NM,F (= client) customer

chalandise [ʃalɑ̃diz] NF **zone de ~** customer catchment area

chalazion [ʃalazjɔ̃] NM (Méd) sty(e), chalazion (SPÉC)

chalcographie [kalkɔgʀafi] NF (= gravure) chalcography; (= salle) chalcography room

Chaldée [kalde] NF Chaldea

chaldéen, -enne [kaldeɛ̃, ɛn] [1] ADJ Chaldean, Chaldee [2] NM (Ling) Chaldean [3] **Chaldéen(ne)** NM,F Chaldean, Chaldee

châle [ʃal] NM shawl → **col**

chalet [ʃalɛ] NM chalet; (Can) summer cottage; **~ de nécessité**†† public convenience

chaleur [ʃalœʀ] NF [a] (gén, Phys) heat; (modérée, agréable) warmth; **quelle ~!** it's hot!, it's boiling!*; **il fait une ~ accablante** the heat's oppressive, it's oppressively hot; **il faisait une ~ lourde** the air was sultry, it was very close; **les grandes ~s (de l'été)** the hot (summer) days *ou* weather; (sur étiquette) « **craint la ~ »** "keep in a cool place"; **~ massique** *ou* **spécifique/latente** specific/latent heat; **~ animale** body heat [b] [discussion, passion] heat; [accueil, voix, couleur] warmth; [convictions] fervour (Brit), fervor (US); **manquer de ~ humaine** to lack the human touch; **chercher un peu de ~ humaine** to look for a bit of company; **prêcher avec ~** to preach with fire *ou* fervour; **défendre une cause/un ami avec ~** to put up a passionate defence of a cause/a friend [c] (Zool) **la période des ~s** the heat; **en ~** on (Brit) *ou* in (US) heat [d] (= malaise) flush; **éprouver des ~s** to have hot flushes (Brit) *ou* flashes (US) → **bouffée**

chaleureusement [ʃalœʀøzmɑ̃] ADV warmly

chaleureux, -euse [ʃalœʀø, øz] ADJ [accueil, applaudissements, remerciements] warm; [félicitations] hearty, warm; **il parla de lui en termes ~** he spoke of him most warmly

châlit [ʃali] NM bedstead

challenge [ʃalɑ̃ʒ] NM (= épreuve) contest, tournament (in which a trophy is at stake); (= trophée) trophy; (= gageure, défi) challenge

challenger [ʃalɑ̃ʒɛʀ], **challengeur** [ʃalɑ̃ʒœʀ] NM challenger

chaloir [ʃalwaʀ] VI → **chaut**

chaloupe [ʃalup] NF launch; (*: Can) rowing boat (Brit), rowboat (US, Can); **~ de sauvetage** lifeboat

chaloupé, e [ʃalupe] ADJ [danse] swaying; [démarche] rolling

chalumeau (pl **chalumeaux**) [ʃalymo] NM [a] (Tech) blowtorch, blowlamp (Brit); **~ oxyacétylénique** oxyacetylene torch; **ils ont découpé le coffre-fort au ~** they used a blowtorch to cut through the safe [b] (Mus) pipe [c] († = paille) (drinking) straw [d] (Can) spout (fixed on the sugar maple tree for collecting maple sap)

chalut [ʃaly] NM trawl (net); **pêcher au ~** to trawl

chalutage [ʃalytaʒ] NM trawling

chalutier [ʃalytje] NM (= bateau) trawler; (= pêcheur) trawlerman

chamade [ʃamad] NF → **battre**

chamaille [ʃamaj] NF squabble, (petty) quarrel

chamailler (se) [ʃamaje] ▸conjug 1◂ VPR to squabble, bicker

chamaillerie [ʃamajʀi] NF squabble, (petty) quarrel; **~s** squabbling (NonC), bickering (NonC)

chamailleur, -euse [ʃamajœʀ, øz] [1] ADJ quarrelsome [2] NM,F quarrelsome person

chaman [ʃaman] NM shaman

chamanisme [ʃamanism] NM shamanism

chamarré, e [ʃamaʀe] (ptp de **chamarrer**) ADJ [étoffe, rideaux] richly coloured (Brit) *ou* colored (US) *ou* brocaded; **~ d'or/de pourpre** bedecked with gold/purple

chamarrer [ʃamaʀe] ▸conjug 1◂ VT (littér = orner) to bedeck, adorn

chamarrure [ʃamaʀyʀ] NF (gén pl) [étoffe] vivid *ou* loud (péj) combination of colours; [habit, uniforme] rich trimming

chambard* [ʃɑ̃baʀ] NM (= vacarme) racket*, rumpus*, row* (Brit); (= protestation) rumpus*, row* (Brit); (= bagarre) scuffle, brawl; (= désordre) shambles sg, mess; (= bouleversement) upheaval; **faire du ~** (= protester) to kick up a rumpus* *ou* a row* (Brit); **ça va faire du ~!** it's bound to cause a rumpus* *ou* row!* (Brit)

chambardement* [ʃɑ̃baʀdəmɑ̃] NM (= bouleversement) upheaval; (= nettoyage) clear-out

chambarder* [ʃɑ̃baʀde] ▸conjug 1◂ VT (= bouleverser) [+ objets, pièce] to turn upside down; [+ projets, habitudes] to turn upside down, upset; (= se débarrasser de) to chuck out*, throw out, get rid of

chambellan [ʃɑ̃belɑ̃] NM chamberlain

chamboulement* [ʃɑ̃bulmɑ̃] NM (= désordre) chaos, confusion; (= bouleversement) upheaval

chambouler* [ʃɑ̃bule] ▸conjug 1◂ VT (= bouleverser) [+ objets, pièce] to turn upside down; **cela a chamboulé nos projets** that messed up* our plans *ou* threw our plans right out*; **il a tout chamboulé dans la maison** he has turned the (whole) house upside down

chamboule-tout [ʃɑ̃bultu] NM INV (= jeu) fairground game in which balls are thrown to knock down a pyramid of tins, ≈ coconut shy (Brit)

chambranle [ʃɑ̃bʀɑ̃l] NM [porte] (door) frame, casing; [fenêtre] (window) frame, casing; [cheminée] mantelpiece; **il s'appuya au ~** he leant against the doorpost

chambre [ʃɑ̃bʀ] [1] NF [a] (pour dormir) bedroom; (†† = pièce) chamber†, room; **~ à un lit/à deux lits** single-/twin-bedded room; **~ double** *ou* **pour deux personnes** double room; **~ individuelle** single room; (Méd) **~ seule** private room; **va dans ta ~!** go to your (bed)room!; **faire ~ à part** to sleep apart *ou* in separate rooms → **femme, robe, valet** [b] (Pol) House, Chamber; **à la Chambre** in the House; **système à deux ~s** two-house *ou* -chamber system; **Chambre haute/basse** Upper/Lower House *ou* Chamber; **ce n'est plus qu'une simple ~ d'enregistrement** it simp-

ly rubber-stamps the government's decisions [c] (Jur = section judiciaire) division; (Admin = assemblée, groupement) chamber [d] (Tech) [fusil, mine, canon] chamber [e] **en ~: travailler en ~** to work at home, do outwork; **couturière en ~** dressmaker working at home; (péj) **stratège/alpiniste en ~** armchair strategist/mountaineer → **musique, orchestre** [2] COMP ► **chambre d'accusation** court of criminal appeal ► **chambre à air** (inner) tube; **sans ~ à air** tubeless ► **chambre d'amis** spare *ou* guest room ► **chambre de bonne** (lit) maid's room; (sous les toits) garret ► **chambre à bulles** bubble chamber ► **chambre des cartes** (Naut) charthouse ► **chambre claire** (Opt) camera lucida ► **chambre de combustion** combustion chamber ► **chambre de commerce (et d'industrie)** Chamber of Commerce (and Industry) ► **la Chambre des communes** the House of Commons ► **chambre de compensation** clearing house ► **chambre correctionnelle** ≈ magistrates' *ou* district court ► **chambre à coucher** (= pièce) bedroom; (= mobilier) bedroom furniture ► **chambre criminelle** court of criminal appeal (in the Cour de Cassation) ► **la Chambre des députés** the Chamber of Deputies ► **chambre d'enfant** child's (bed)room, nursery ► **chambre d'étudiant** student room ► **chambre d'explosion** = chambre de combustion ► **chambre forte** strongroom ► **chambre frigorifique, chambre froide** cold room ► **chambre à gaz** gas chamber ► **chambre d'hôte** ≈ bed and breakfast ► **chambre d'hôtel** hotel room ► **la Chambre des lords** the House of Lords ► **chambre des machines** engine room ► **chambre des métiers** guild chamber, chamber of trade ► **chambre meublée** furnished room, bed-sitter (Brit) ► **chambre noire** (Photo) darkroom ► **les chambres de l'œil** the aqueous chambers of the eye ► **la Chambre des représentants** the House of Representatives ► **chambre des requêtes** (preliminary) civil appeal court ► **chambre sourde** anechoic chamber ► **chambre de sûreté** [prison] lockup ► **chambre syndicale** employers' federation

chambrée [ʃɑ̃bʀe] NF (= pièce, occupants) room; [soldats] barrack-room; **camarades** *ou* **compagnons de ~** army buddies (quartered in the same barrack room)

chambrer [ʃɑ̃bʀe] ▸conjug 1◂ VT [a] [+ vin] to bring to room temperature, chambré; [+ personne] (= prendre à l'écart) to corner, collar*; (= tenir enfermé) to keep in, confine, keep cloistered; **les organisateurs ont chambré l'invité d'honneur** the organisers kept the V.I.P. guest out of circulation *ou* to themselves [b] (* = taquiner) to tease; (canular) **tu me chambres?** are you having me on?*, are you pulling my leg?*

chambrette [ʃɑ̃bʀɛt] NF small bedroom

chambrière [ʃɑ̃bʀijɛʀ] NF (= béquille de charrette) cart-prop; († = servante) chambermaid

chambriste [ʃɑ̃bʀist] NMF chamber-music player

chameau (pl **chameaux**) [ʃamo] NM [a] (Zool) camel → **poil** [b] (*: péj) (= enfant) little beast*; (= femme) cow:; (= homme) swine*; **elle devient ~ avec l'âge** the older she gets the nastier she is; **quel vieux ~!** (= femme) old bag!:; (= homme) nasty old man!

chamelier [ʃaməlje] NM camel driver

chamelle [ʃamɛl] NF female camel

chamelon [ʃam(ə)lɔ̃] NM young camel

chamois [ʃamwa] [1] NM (Zool) chamois; (Ski) skiing badge (marking degree of proficiency) → **peau** [2] ADJ INV fawn, buff(-coloured) (Brit) *ou* -colored (US))

chamoisine [ʃamwazin] NF shammy leather

champ¹ [ʃɑ̃] **1** NM **a** (*Agr*) field; **~ de blé** wheatfield, field of corn (*Brit*) *ou* wheat; **~ d'avoine/de trèfle** field of oats/clover; **travailler aux ~s** to work in the fields; **on s'est retrouvé en plein(s) ~(s)** we found ourselves in the middle of *ou* surrounded by fields **b** (= *campagne*) **~s** country(side); **la vie aux ~s** life in the country, country life; **fleurs des ~s** wild flowers → **clé**, **travers²** **c** (*fig* = *domaine*) field, area; **élargir le ~ de ses recherches/de ses investigations** to broaden the scope of one's research/one's investigations **d** (*Élec, Ling, Ordin, Phys*) field **e** (*Ciné, Photo*) **dans le ~** in (the) shot *ou* the picture; **être dans le ~** to be in shot; **sortir du ~** to go out of shot; **pas assez de ~** not enough depth of focus; **hors ~** off-camera (*attrib*) → **profondeur** **f** (*Hér*) [*écu, médaille*] field **g** (*loc*) **avoir du ~** to have elbowroom *ou* room to move; **laisser du ~ à qn** to leave sb room to manoeuvre; **laisser le ~ libre à qn** to leave sb a clear field; **vous avez le ~ libre** you're free to do as you please; **prendre du ~** (*lit*) to step back, draw back; (*fig*) to stand back; (*Mil*) **sonner aux ~s** to sound the general salute

2 COMP ► **champ d'action** *ou* **d'activité** sphere of activity ► **champ d'aviation** airfield ► **champ de bataille** battlefield ► **champ clos** combat area; (*fig*) **en ~ clos** behind closed doors ► **champ de courses** racecourse ► **champ électrique** electric field ► **les Champs Élysées** (*Myth*) the Elysian Fields; (*à Paris*) the Champs Élysées ► **champ de foire** fairground ► **champ d'honneur** field of honour; **mourir** *ou* **tomber au ~ d'honneur** to be killed in action ► **champ magnétique** magnetic field ► **champ de manœuvre** parade ground ► **champ de Mars** ≈ military esplanade ► **champ de mines** minefield ► **champ de neige** snowfield ► **champ opératoire** operative field ► **champ optique** optical field ► **champ ouvert** (*Agr*) open field ► **champ sémantique** semantic field ► **champ de tir** (= *terrain*) rifle *ou* shooting range, practice ground; (= *angle de vue*) field of fire ► **champ visuel** *ou* **de vision** field of vision *ou* view, visual field

champ² [ʃɑp] NM (ABRÉV = **champagne**) bubbly*, champers* (*Brit*)

champagne [ʃɑpaɲ] **1** ADJ INV champagne **2** NM champagne; **elle a réussi ses examens, ~ !** she passed her exams, let's get out the champagne to celebrate!; **~ rosé** pink champagne **3** **Champagne** NF **la Champagne** Champagne, the Champagne region → **fine²**

champagnisation [ʃɑpaɲizasjɔ̃] NF champagnization

champagniser [ʃɑpaɲize] ▶conjug 1◀ VT to champagnize

champenois, e [ʃɑpənwa, waz] **1** ADJ of *ou* from Champagne; **vin méthode ~e** champagne-type *ou* sparkling wine **2** **Champenois(e)** NM,F inhabitant *ou* native of Champagne

champêtre [ʃɑpɛtʁ] ADJ (*gén*) rural; [*vie*] country (*épith*), rural; [*odeur, route*] country (*épith*); [*bal, fête*] village (*épith*); **fleurs ~s** wild flowers; **dans un décor ~** in a rural *ou* pastoral setting → **garde²**

champignon [ʃɑpiɲɔ̃] NM **a** (*gén*) mushroom; (*terme générique*) fungus; (*vénéneux*) toadstool, poisonous mushroom *ou* fungus; (*Méd*) fungus; **aller aux ~s** to go mushroom-picking, go collecting mushrooms; **~ comestible** (edible) mushroom, edible fungus; **certains ~s sont comestibles** some fungi are edible; **~ de Paris** *ou* **de couche** cultivated mushroom; **~ hallucinogène** hallucinogenic

mushroom, magic mushroom*; **ces nouvelles industries ont proliféré comme des ~s** these new industries have sprung up *ou* sprouted like mushrooms *ou* have mushroomed → **pousser, ville** **b** (*Phys Nucl*) **~ (atomique)** mushroom cloud **c** (*: Aut*) accelerator → **appuyer**

champignonnière [ʃɑpiɲɔnjɛʁ] NF mushroom bed

champion, -ionne [ʃɑpjɔ̃, jɔn] **1** ADJ* A1, first-rate; **c'est ~ !** that's great!* *ou* first-rate! **2** NM,F (*Sport,* = *défenseur*) champion; **~ du monde de boxe** world boxing champion; **se faire le ~ d'une cause** to champion a cause; (*hum*) **c'est le ~ de la gaffe** there's no one to beat him for tactlessness

championnat [ʃɑpjɔna] NM championship; **~ du monde/d'Europe** world/European championship

chançard, e* [ʃɑsaʁ, aʁd] **1** ADJ lucky **2** NM,F lucky devil*, lucky dog*

▼**chance** [ʃɑs] NF **a** (= *bonne fortune*) (good) luck; **tu as de la ~ d'y aller** you're lucky *ou* fortunate to be going; **il a la ~ d'y aller** he's lucky *ou* fortunate enough to be going, he has the good luck *ou* good fortune to be going; **avec un peu de ~** with a bit of luck; **quelle ~ !** what a bit *ou* stroke of (good) luck!, how lucky!; **c'est une ~ que ...** it's lucky *ou* fortunate that ..., it's a bit of *ou* a stroke of luck that ...; **coup de ~** stroke of luck; **il était là, une ~ !** *ou* **un coup de ~ !** he was there, luckily; **jour de ~ !** lucky day!; **ce n'est pas mon jour de ~ !** it's not my day!; **la ~ a voulu qu'il y eût un médecin** by a stroke of luck *ou* luckily there was a doctor; **par ~** luckily, fortunately; **pas de ~ !** hard *ou* bad *ou* tough* luck!, hard lines!* (*Brit*); (*iro*) **c'est bien ma ~** (that's) just my luck! → **porter** **b** (= *hasard, fortune*) luck, chance; **courir** *ou* **tenter sa ~** to try one's luck; **la ~ a tourné** his (*ou* her *etc*) luck has changed; **la ~ lui sourit** fortune smiles on him; **mettre toutes les ~s de son côté** to take no chances; **sa mauvaise ~ le poursuit** he is dogged by bad luck *ou* ill-luck → **bon¹** **c** (= *possibilité de succès*) chance; **donner sa ~** *ou* **ses ~s à qn** to give sb his chance; **quelles sont ses ~s (de réussir** *ou* **de succès)?** what are his chances *ou* what chance has he got (of success *ou* of succeeding)?; **elle a ses** *ou* **des ~s (de gagner)** she's stands a good chance (of winning); **il/son tir n'a laissé aucune ~ au gardien de but** he/his shot didn't give the goalkeeper a chance; **les ~s d'un accord ...** the chances of a settlement ...; **il n'a aucune ~** he hasn't got *ou* doesn't stand a (dog's) chance; **il y a une ~ sur cent (pour) que ...** there's one chance in a hundred *ou* a one-in-a-hundred chance that ...; **elle a une ~ sur deux de s'en sortir** she's got a fifty-fifty chance of pulling through; **il y a peu de ~s (pour) qu'il la voie** there's little chance (that) he'll see her, there's little chance of his seeing her, the chances of his seeing her are slim; **il y a toutes les ~s que ...** there's every chance that ..., the chances *ou* odds are that ...; **il y a de grandes** *ou* **fortes ~s pour qu'il vienne** there's a strong *ou* good chance he'll come, he's very likely to come; **il y a des ~s*** it's very likely, I wouldn't be surprised; **ils ont des ~s égales** they have equal chances *ou* an equal chance

chancelant, e [ʃɑs(ə)lɑ̃, ɑ̃t] ADJ [*démarche*] unsteady, faltering, tottering; [*objet*] wobbly, unsteady; [*mémoire*] failing, shaky; [*santé*] frail (*épith*), failing; [*conviction, courage, résolution*] wavering, faltering, shaky; [*autorité*] faltering, flagging; [*régime*] tottering

chanceler [ʃɑs(ə)le] ▶conjug 4◀ VI [*personne*] to totter, stagger; [*ivrogne*] to reel; [*objet*] to wobble, totter; [*autorité*] to falter, flag; [*régime*] to totter; [*conviction, résolution, courage*] to waver, falter; [*mémoire*] to fail; **sa santé chancelle** he's in failing health, his health is failing; **il**

s'avança en chancelant he tottered *ou* staggered *ou* reeled forward; **une société qui chancelle sur ses bases** a society which is tottering upon its foundations

chancelier [ʃɑsəlje] NM (*en Allemagne, Autriche*) chancellor; [*ambassade*] secretary; (*Hist*) chancellor; **le ~ de l'Échiquier** the Chancellor of the Exchequer; **grand ~ de la Légion d'honneur** high-ranking officer in the French Legion of Honour → **recteur**

chancelière [ʃɑsəljɛʁ] NF footwarmer

chancellerie [ʃɑsɛlʁi] NF [*ambassade, consulat*] chancellery, chancery; (*Hist*) chancellery

chanceux, -euse [ʃɑsø, øz] ADJ lucky, fortunate; (†† = *hasardeux*) hazardous

chancre [ʃɑkʁ] NM (*Bot, Méd, fig*) canker; **~ syphilitique** chancre; **~ mou** chancroid, soft chancre; **manger** *ou* **bouffer comme un ~** to make a pig of oneself*, pig out*, pig oneself* (*Brit*)

chancrelle [ʃɑkʁɛl] NF chancroid

chandail [ʃɑdaj] NM (thick) sweater, (thick) jumper (*Brit*)

Chandeleur [ʃɑdlœʁ] NF **la ~** Candlemas

chandelier [ʃɑdəlje] NM (*à une branche*) candlestick, candleholder; (*à plusieurs branches*) candelabra

chandelle [ʃɑdɛl] NF **a** (= *bougie*) (tallow) candle; **un dîner aux ~s** a dinner by candlelight, a candlelit dinner; **~ romaine** roman candle **b** (*Aviat*) chandelle; (*Rugby*) up-and-under; (*Tennis*) lob; (*Gym*) shoulder stand; (*: = morve*) trickle of snot* **c** (*loc*) (*hum*) **tenir la ~** to play gooseberry (*Brit*), be a third wheel (*US*); **je ne tenais pas la ~ !** I wasn't there at the time!; (*Aviat*) **monter en ~** to climb vertically; (*Golf*) **lancer en ~** to loft; **voir trente-six ~s** to see stars → **brûler, économie, jeu**

chanfrein [ʃɑfʁɛ̃] NM **a** (*Tech*) bevelled edge; (*à 45 degrés*) chamfer **b** [*cheval*] nose

change [ʃɑʒ] NM **a** (*Fin*) [*devises*] exchange; (*Banque*) **faire le ~** to exchange money; **opération de ~** (= foreign) exchange transaction → **agent, bureau** *etc* **b** (*Fin = taux d'échange*) exchange rate; **le ~ est avantageux** the exchange rate is favourable; **la cote des ~s** the (list of) exchange rates; **au cours actuel du ~** at the current rate of exchange **c** (*Can = petite monnaie*) change **d** **~ (complet)** (disposable) nappy (*Brit*) *ou* diaper (*US*) **e** (*loc*) **gagner/perdre au ~** (*Fin*) to gain/lose money on the exchange; (*fig*) to gain/lose on the exchange *ou* deal; **donner le ~** to allay suspicion; **donner le ~ à qn** to put sb off the scent *ou* off the track

changeable [ʃɑʒabl] ADJ (= *transformable*) changeable, alterable

changeant, e [ʃɑʒɑ̃, ɑ̃t] ADJ [*personne, fortune, humeur*] changeable, fickle, changing (*épith*); [*couleur, paysage*] changing (*épith*); [*temps*] changeable, unsettled; **son humeur est ~e** he's a man of many moods *ou* of uneven temper

changement [ʃɑʒmɑ̃] NM **a** (= *remplacement*) changing; **le ~ de la roue nous a coûté 100 F** the wheel change cost us 100 francs; **le ~ de la roue nous a pris une heure** it took us an hour to change the wheel **b** (= *fait de se transformer*) change (**de** in); **le ~ soudain de la température/la direction du vent** the sudden change in temperature/wind direction **c** (= *transformation*) change, alteration; **il n'aime pas le(s) ~(s)** he doesn't like change(s); **elle a trouvé de grands ~s dans le village** she found the village greatly changed *ou* altered; **il y a eu du ~** (= *situation*) things have changed; **il y a eu du ~ dans cette pièce** there have been a few changes (made) in this room; **la situation reste sans ~** there has been no change in the situation, the situation remains unchanged *ou* unaltered; **~ en bien** *ou* **en mieux** change for the better d ~ **de** change of; ~ **d'adresse/d'air/de mi-nistère** change of address/air/government; ~ **de programme** [*projet*] change of plan *ou* in the plan(s); [*spectacle*] change of programme *ou* in the programme; ~ **de direction** (*sens*) change of course *ou* direction; (*dirigeants*) change of management; (*sur un écriteau*) under new management; **il y a eu un ~ de propriétaire** it has changed hands, it has come under new ownership; (*Mus*) ~ **de ton** change of key; ~ **de décor** (*paysage*) change of scenery; (*Théât*) scene-change; (*Théât*) ~ **à vue** transformation (scene)

e (*Admin = mutation*) transfer; **demander son ~** to apply for a transfer

f (*Aut*) ~ **de vitesse** (= *dispositif*) gears, gear change (*Brit*), gear stick *ou* lever (*Brit*); (= *action*) change of gears, gear change (*Brit*), gearshift (*US*); [*bicyclette*] gear(s)

g (*Transport*) change; **il y a deux ~s pour aller de Paris à Lamballe** you have to change twice *ou* make two changes to get from Paris to Lamballe

changer [ʃɑ̃ʒe] ▶ conjug 3 ◀ 1 VT a (= *modifier*) [+ *projets, personne*] to change; **on ne le changera pas** nothing will change him *ou* make him change, you'll never change him; **ce chapeau la change** that hat makes her look different; **ça change tout!** that makes all the difference!, that changes everything!; **une promenade lui changera les idées** a walk will take his mind off things; **il n'a pas changé une virgule au rapport** he hasn't changed *ou* altered a single comma in the report; **il ne veut rien ~ à ses habitudes** he doesn't want to change *ou* alter his habits in any way; **je ne vois pas ce que ça change** I don't see what difference that makes; **ça ne change rien (à l'affaire)** it doesn't make the slightest difference, it doesn't alter things one bit; **ça ne change rien au fait que ...** it doesn't change *ou* alter the fact that ...; **vous n'y changerez rien!** there's nothing you can do (about it)!

b (= *remplacer, échanger*) to change; (*Théât*) [+ *décor*] to change, shift; (*Fin*) [+ *argent, billet*] to change; (*Can*) [+ *chèque*] to cash; ~ **100 F contre des livres** to change 100 francs into pounds, exchange 100 francs for pounds; ~ **les draps/une ampoule** to change the sheets/a bulb; **il a changé sa voiture** he changed his car; **ce manteau était trop petit, j'ai dû le ~** that coat was too small — I had to change *ou* exchange it; **je changerais bien ma place pour la sienne** I'd like to change *ou* swap* places with him; **il a changé sa montre contre celle de son ami** he exchanged his watch for his friend's, he changed *ou* swapped* watches with his friend

c (= *déplacer*) ~ **qn de poste** to move sb to a different job; ~ **qn/qch de place** to move sb/sth (to a different place), shift sb/sth; **ils ont changé tous les meubles de place** they've changed *ou* moved all the furniture around → **fusil**

d (= *transformer*) ~ **qch/qn en** to change *ou* turn sth/sb into; **la citrouille fut changée en carrosse** the pumpkin was changed *ou* turned into a carriage

e (= *mettre d'autres vêtements à*) ~ **un enfant/malade** to change a child/patient; ~ **un bébé** to change a baby's nappy (*Brit*) *ou* diaper (*US*)

f (= *procurer un changement à*) **des voisins silencieux, ça nous change** it makes a change for us to have quiet neighbours, having quiet neighbours makes a change for us; **ça m'a changé agréablement de ne plus entendre de bruit** it was a pleasant *ou* nice change for me not to hear any noise; **ils vont en Italie, ça les changera de l'Angleterre!** they're going to Italy — it will be *ou* make a change for them after England!

2 **changer de** VT INDIR a (= *remplacer*) to change; (= *modifier*) to change, alter; ~ **d'adresse/de nom/de voiture** to change one's address/name/car; ~ **de domicile** to move (house); ~ **d'appartement** to move (into a new flat (*Brit*) *ou* apartment (*surtout US*)); ~ **de vêtements** to change (one's clothes); **elle a changé de coiffure** she's changed her hairstyle, she's got a new hairstyle; ~ **de sexe** to have a sex change; ~ **de peau** (*Zool*) to shed its skin; (*fig*) to become a different person; ~ **d'avis** *ou* **d'idée/de ton** to change one's mind/tune; **il change d'avis comme de chemise*** he's always changing his mind; **elle a changé de couleur quand elle m'a vu** (= *elle a blêmi*) she went pale *ou* she blanched when she saw me; (= *elle a rougi*) she coloured visibly when she saw me; **la rivière a changé de cours** the river has altered *ou* shifted its course; **elle a changé de visage** her face has changed *ou* altered; (*d'émotion*) her expression changed *ou* altered; **change de disque!‡** put another record on!‡, don't keep (harping) on *ou* don't go on about it!*

b (= *passer dans une autre situation*) to change; ~ **de train/compartiment/pays** to change trains/compartments/countries; (*Aut*) ~ **de vitesse** to change gear; **changeons de crémerie‡** *ou* **d'auberge‡** let's take our business *ou* custom (*Brit*) elsewhere; **pour mieux voir, change de place** move to another seat if you want a better view; ~ **de position** to alter *ou* shift *ou* change one's position; **j'ai besoin de ~ d'air** I need a change of air; **pour ~ d'air** for a change of air, to get a change of air; ~ **de côté** (*gén*) to go over *ou* across to the other side, change sides; (*dans la rue*) to cross over (to the other side); ~ **de propriétaire** *ou* **de mains** to change hands; **changeons de sujet** let's change the subject; **il a changé de chemin pour m'éviter** he went a different way to avoid me → **camp, cap**

c (= *échanger*) to exchange, change, swap* (**avec qn** with sb); ~ **de place avec qn** to change *ou* exchange *ou* swap* places with sb; **j'aime bien ton sac, tu changes avec moi?*** I like your bag — will you swap* (with me)? *ou* will you exchange *ou* do a swap* (with me)?

3 VI a (= *se transformer*) to change, alter; ~ **en bien** *ou* **en mieux/en mal** *ou* **en pire** to change for the better/the worse; **il n'a pas du tout changé** he hasn't changed *ou* altered at all *ou* a bit; **il a changé du tout au tout** he's transformed; **les temps ont bien changé!** *ou* **sont bien changés!** (how) times have changed!; **le vent a changé** the wind has changed (direction)

b (*Transport*) to change; **j'ai dû ~ à Rome** I had to change at Rome

c (*loc iro*) **pour ~!** that makes a change!; **et pour (pas*) ~, c'est nous qui faisons le travail** and as per usual* *ou* and just for a change (*iro*) we'll be doing the work

d (= *procurer un changement*) **ça change des films à l'eau de rose** it makes a change from sentimental films

4 **se changer** VPR a (= *mettre d'autres vêtements*) to change (one's clothes); **va te ~ avant de sortir** go and change (your clothes) before you go out

b (= *se transformer*) **se ~ en** to change *ou* turn into

changeur, -euse [ʃɑ̃ʒœʀ, øz] 1 NM,F (= *personne*) moneychanger 2 NM (= *machine*) ~ **(de disques)** record changer; ~ **de monnaie** change machine

chanoine [ʃanwan] NM (*Rel*) canon (*person*) → **gras**

chanoinesse [ʃanwanɛs] NF (*Rel*) canoness

chanson [ʃɑ̃sɔ̃] 1 NF song; ~ **d'amour/à boire/de marche/populaire** love/drinking/marching/popular song; ~ **enfantine/d'étudiant** children's/student song; (*fig*) **c'est toujours la même ~** it's always the same old story; **l'air ne fait pas la ~** do not judge by appearances, appearances are deceptive; **~s que tout cela!†††** fiddle-de-dee!†, poppycock!†;

ça, c'est une autre ~ that's quite a different matter *ou* quite another story → **connaître**

2 COMP ► **chanson folklorique** folksong ► **chanson de geste** chanson de geste ► **chanson de marins** (sea) shanty ► **chanson de Noël** (Christmas) carol ► **« la Chanson de Roland »** "the Chanson de Roland", "the Song of Roland" ► **chanson de toile** chanson de toile, weaving song

┌─ **CHANSON FRANÇAISE** ─┐

The term **la chanson française** *refers to a very diverse popular musical genre. Traditional French "chansons" gained international renown in the forties thanks to stars like Edith Piaf and Charles Trenet, and in the fifties and sixties thanks to Yves Montand, Charles Aznavour and Juliette Gréco.* **La chanson française** *has always been characterized by the quality of its lyrics, exemplified by the work of singer-poets like Jacques Brel, Georges Brassens, Léo Ferré and Barbara.*

chansonnette [ʃɑ̃sɔnɛt] NF ditty, light-hearted song

chansonnier [ʃɑ̃sɔnje] NM (= *artiste*) chansonnier, cabaret singer (*specializing in political satire*); (= *livre*) song-book

chant¹ [ʃɑ̃] NM a (= *sons*) [*personne*] singing; [*oiseau*] singing, warbling; (= *mélodie habituelle*) [*insecte*] chirp(ing); [*coq*] crow(ing); [*mer, vent, instrument*] sound, song; (*littér*) **entendre des ~s mélodieux** to hear melodious singing; **au ~ du coq** at cockcrow; **le ~ du cygne d'un artiste** an artist's swan song; **écouter le ~ des sirènes** to let o.s. be led astray

b (= *chanson*) song; ~ **patriotique/populaire** patriotic/popular song; ~ **de Noël** (Christmas) carol; ~ **religieux** *ou* **sacré** *ou* **d'Église** hymn; ~ **de guerre** battle song

c (= *action de chanter, art*) singing; **nous allons continuer par le ~ d'un cantique** we shall continue by singing a hymn; **cours/professeur de ~** singing lessons/teacher; **apprendre le ~** to learn to sing; **j'aime le ~ choral** I like choral *ou* choir singing; ~ **grégorien** Gregorian chant; ~ **à une/à plusieurs voix** song for one voice/several voices

d (= *mélodie*) melody

e (*Poésie*) (= *genre*) ode; (= *division*) canto; ~ **funèbre** funeral lament; ~ **nuptial** nuptial song *ou* poem; **épopée en douze ~s** epic in twelve cantos; (*fig*) **le ~ désespéré de ce poète** the despairing song of this poet

chant² [ʃɑ̃] NM (= *côté*) edge; **de** *ou* **sur ~** on edge, edgewise

chantage [ʃɑ̃taʒ] NM blackmail; **se livrer à un** *ou* **exercer un ~ sur qn** to blackmail sb; **faire du ~** to use blackmail; ~ **affectif** emotional blackmail; **il (nous) a fait le ~ au suicide** he threatened suicide to blackmail us, he blackmailed us with suicide *ou* by threatening suicide

chantant, e [ʃɑ̃tɑ̃, ɑ̃t] ADJ a (= *mélodieux*) [*accent, voix*] singsong, lilting b (= *qui se chante aisément*) [*air*] tuneful, catchy

chanter [ʃɑ̃te] ▶ conjug 1 ◀ 1 VT a [+ *chanson, opéra, messe*] to sing; **l'oiseau chante ses trilles** the bird sings *ou* warbles its song; **chante-nous quelque chose!** sing us a song!, sing something for us!

b (= *célébrer*) to sing of, sing; ~ **les exploits de qn** to sing (of) sb's exploits; ~ **l'amour** to sing of love; ~ **les louanges de qn** to sing sb's praises → **victoire**

c (* = *raconter*) **qu'est-ce qu'il nous chante là?** what's this he's telling us?, what's he (going) on about now?*; **j'ai eu beau le ~ sur tous les tons** no matter how many times I've said it

2 VI a [*personne*] to sing; (* : *de douleur*) to howl; [*oiseau*] to sing, warble; [*coq*] to crow;

[*poule*] to cackle; [*insecte*] to chirp; [*ruisseau*] to babble; [*bouilloire*] to sing; [*eau qui bout*] to hiss, sing; ~ **juste/faux** to sing in tune/out of tune *ou* flat; ~ **pour endormir un enfant** to sing a child to sleep; **chantez donc plus fort!** sing up! (*Brit*) *ou* out! (*US*); **c'est comme si on chantait*** it's like talking to a brick wall, it's a waste of breath; **il chante en parlant** he's got a lilting *ou* singsong voice

b (*par chantage*) **faire ~ qn** to blackmail sb **c** (* = *plaire*) **vas-y si le programme te chante** (you) go if the programme appeals to you *ou* if you fancy (*Brit*) the programme; **cela ne me chante guère de sortir ce soir** I don't really feel like *ou* fancy (*Brit*) going out tonight; **il vient quand** *ou* **si** *ou* **comme ça lui chante** he comes when *ou* if *ou* as the fancy takes him

chanterelle [ʃɑ̃tʀɛl] NF **a** chanterelle **b** (*Mus*) E-string → **appuyer** **c** (= *oiseau*) decoy (bird)

chanteur, -euse [ʃɑ̃tœʀ, øz] NM,F singer; ~ **de charme** crooner; ~ **de(s) rues** street singer, busker (*Brit*) → **maître, oiseau**

chantier [ʃɑ̃tje] **1** NM **a** (*Constr*) building site; [*plombier, peintre*] job; (*Can*) [*bûcherons*] lumber camp (*US*, *Can*), shanty (*Can*); **le matin il est au ~** he's on (the) site in the mornings; **j'ai laissé mes pinceaux sur le ~** I left my brushes at the job; «**~ interdit au public**» "no entry *ou* admittance (to the public)"; (*sur une route*) «**fin de ~**» "road clear", "end of roadworks"

b (= *entrepôt*) depot, yard **c** (*: *fig* = *désordre*) shambles*; **quel ~ dans ta chambre!** what a shambles* *ou* mess in your room!

d **mettre en ~** *ou* **sur le ~** [+ *projet*] to get started *ou* going; **il a deux livres en ~** *ou* **sur le ~** he has two books on the go, he's working on two books; **à la maison nous sommes en ~ depuis deux mois** we've had work *ou* alterations going on in the house for two months now

2 COMP ► **chantier de construction** building site ► **chantier de démolition** demolition site ► **chantier d'exploitation** (*Min*) opencast working ► **chantier d'exploitation forestière** tree-felling *ou* lumbering (*US*, *Can*) site ► **chantier naval** shipyard ► **chantier de réarmement** refit yard

chantilly [ʃɑ̃tiji] NF (**crème**) ~ ≈ whipped cream

chantonnement [ʃɑ̃tɔnmɑ̃] NM (soft) singing, humming, crooning

chantonner [ʃɑ̃tɔne] ▸ conjug 1 ◂ **1** VI [*personne*] to sing to oneself; [*eau qui bout*] to hiss, sing; ~ **pour endormir un bébé** to sing a baby to sleep **2** VT to sing, hum; ~ **une berceuse à un bébé** to sing a lullaby to a baby

chantoung [ʃɑ̃tuŋ] NM Shantung (silk)

chantourner [ʃɑ̃tuʀne] ▸ conjug 1 ◂ VT to jigsaw → **scie**

chantre [ʃɑ̃tʀ] NM (*Rel*) cantor; (*fig littér* = *poète*) bard, minstrel; (= *laudateur*) exalter, eulogist; (*Rel*) **premier ~** precentor; (*fig*) **le grand ~ de** the high priest of

chanvre [ʃɑ̃vʀ] NM hemp; **de ~** hemp (*épith*), hempen (*épith*); ~ **du Bengale** jute; ~ **indien** Indian hemp; ~ **de Manille** Manila hemp, abaca → **cravate**

chanvrier, -ière [ʃɑ̃vʀije, ijɛʀ] **1** ADJ hemp (*épith*) **2** NM,F (= *cultivateur*) hemp grower; (= *ouvrier*) hemp dresser

chaos [kao] NM (*lit*, *fig*) chaos; **dans le ~** in (a state of) chaos

chaotique [kaɔtik] ADJ chaotic

chap. (ABRÉV = **chapitre**) chap

chapardage* [ʃapaʀdaʒ] NM petty theft, pilfering (*NonC*)

chaparder* [ʃapaʀde] ▸ conjug 1 ◂ VTI to pinch, pilfer (**à** from)

chapardeur, -euse* [ʃapaʀdœʀ, øz] **1** ADJ light-fingered **2** NM,F pilferer, petty thief

chape [ʃap] NF **a** (*Rel*) cope **b** (*Tech*) [*pneu*] tread; [*bielle*] strap; [*poulie*] shell; [*voûte*] coating; (*sur béton*) screed; ~ **de béton** (concrete) screed; **une ~ de plomb s'est abattue sur le pays** a wall of silence has surrounded the country **c** (*Hér*) chape

chapeau (*pl* **chapeaux**) [ʃapo] **1** NM **a** (= *coiffure*) hat; **saluer qn ~ bas** (*lit*) to doff one's hat to sb; (*fig*) to take one's hat off to sb; **saluer qn d'un coup de ~** to raise one's hat to sb; **ça mérite un coup de ~** it's quite an achievement; **coup de ~ à Paul pour sa nouvelle chanson** hats off to Paul for his new song; **tirer son ~ à qn*** to take one's hat off to sb; **il a réussi? eh bien ~!** he managed it? hats off to him! *ou* well, you've got to hand it to him!; **~, mon vieux!*** well done *ou* jolly good (*Brit*), old man!*; **il a dû manger son ~ en public** he had to eat his words in public → **porter, travailler**

b (*Tech*) [*palier*] cap; (*Aut*) ~ **de roue** hub cap; **démarrer sur les ~x de roues*** [*véhicule, personne*] to shoot off at top speed, take off like a shot; [*affaire, soirée*] to get off to a good start; **prendre un virage sur les ~x de roues** to screech round a corner

c (*Presse*) [*article*] introductory paragraph **d** (*Bot*) [*champignon*] cap; (*Culin*) [*vol-au-vent*] lid, top

2 COMP ► **chapeau de brousse** safari hat ► **chapeau chinois** (*Mus*) crescent, jingling Johnny; (*Zool*) limpet ► **chapeau cloche** cloche hat ► **chapeau de gendarme** (*en papier*) (folded) paper hat ► **chapeau haut-de-forme** top hat ► **chapeau melon** bowler (hat) (*Brit*), derby (*US*) ► **chapeau mou** trilby (hat) (*Brit*), fedora (*US*) ► **chapeau de paille** straw hat ► **chapeau de plage** *ou* **de soleil** sun hat ► **chapeau tyrolien** Tyrolean hat

chapeauté, e [ʃapote] (*ptp de* **chapeauter**) ADJ with a hat on, wearing a hat

chapeauter [ʃapote] ▸ conjug 1 ◂ VT (= *superviser*) to head (up), oversee

chapelain [ʃaplɛ̃] NM chaplain

chapelet [ʃaplɛ] NM **a** (= *objet*) rosary, beads; (= *prières*) rosary; **réciter** *ou* **dire son ~** to say the rosary, tell *ou* say one's beads†; **le ~ à cinq heures** the rosary is at five o'clock; (*fig*) **dévider** *ou* **défiler son ~*** to recite one's grievances **b** (*fig* = *succession*) ~ **de** [*oignons, injures, îles*] string of; ~ **de bombes** stick of bombs

chapelier, -ière [ʃapəlje, jɛʀ] **1** ADJ hat (*épith*) **2** NM,F hatter

chapelle [ʃapɛl] NF **a** (*Rel* = *lieu*) chapel; (*Mus* = *chœur*) chapel; ~ **absidiale/latérale** absidial/side chapel; ~ **de la Sainte Vierge** Lady Chapel; ~ **ardente** (= *église*) chapel of rest; **l'école a été transformé en ~ ardente** the school was turned into a temporary morgue → **maître b** (= *coterie*) coterie, clique

chapellerie [ʃapɛlʀi] NF (= *magasin*) hat shop, hatter('s); (= *commerce*) hat trade, hat industry

chapelure [ʃaplyʀ] NF (dried) breadcrumbs

chaperon [ʃapʀɔ̃] NM **a** (= *personne*) chaperon **b** (*Constr*) [*mur*] coping **c** († = *capuchon*) hood → **petit 5**

chaperonner [ʃapʀɔne] ▸ conjug 1 ◂ VT **a** [+ *personne*] to chaperon **b** (*Constr*) [+ *mur*] to cope

chapiteau (*pl* **chapiteaux**) [ʃapito] NM **a** [*colonne*] capital; [*niche*] canopy **b** [*cirque*] big top, marquee; **sous le ~** under the big top; **sous le plus grand ~ du monde** in the biggest circus in the world **c** [*alambic*] head

chapitre [ʃapitʀ] NM **a** [*livre, traité*] chapter; [*budget, statuts*] section, item; **inscrire un nouveau ~ au budget** to make out a new budget

head; (*fig*) **un nouveau ~ de sa vie** a new chapter of *ou* in his life **b** (*fig* = *sujet*) subject, matter; **il est imbattable sur ce ~** he's unbeatable on that subject *ou* score; **il est très strict sur le ~ de la discipline** he's very strict in matters of discipline *ou* about discipline; **au ~ des faits divers** under the heading of news in brief **c** (*Rel* = *assemblée*) chapter → **salle, voix**

chapitrer [ʃapitʀe] ▸ conjug 1 ◂ VT **a** (= *réprimander*) to admonish, reprimand; (= *faire la morale à*) to lecture (**sur** on, about); **dûment chapitré par sa mère** duly coached by his mother **b** [+ *texte*] to divide into chapters; [+ *budget*] to divide into headings, itemize

chapka [ʃapka] NF Russian fur hat

chapon [ʃapɔ̃] NM capon

chaptalisation [ʃaptalizasjɔ̃] NF (*vin*) chaptalization

chaptaliser [ʃaptalize] ▸ conjug 1 ◂ VT [+ *vin*] to chaptalize

chaque [ʃak] ADJ **a** (*ensemble défini*) each, every; ~ **élève (de la classe)** each *ou* every pupil (in the class); **ils coûtent 10 F ~*** they're 10 francs each *ou* apiece **b** (*ensemble indéfini*) every; ~ **homme naît libre** every man is born free; **il m'interrompt à ~ instant** he interrupts me every other second, he keeps interrupting me; ~ **10 minutes, il éternuait*** he sneezed every 10 minutes; ~ **chose à sa place/en son temps** everything in its place/in its own time → **à**

char¹ [ʃaʀ] **1** NM **a** (*Mil*) tank; **régiment de ~s** tank regiment **b** [*carnaval*] (carnival) float; **le défilé des ~s fleuris** the procession of flower-decked floats **c** († = *charrette*) wagon, cart **d** (*: *Can*) car, automobile (*US*) **e** (*Antiq*) chariot; (*littér*) ~ **de l'Aurore** the chariot of the dawn; **le ~ de l'État** the ship of state **f** (*loc*) **arrête ton ~*** (*raconter des histoires*) shut up!*, belt up!‡ (*Brit*); (*se vanter*) stop showing off! **2** COMP ► **char d'assaut** tank ► **char à banc** horse-drawn wagon with seats ► **char à bœufs** oxcart ► **char de combat** = char d'assaut ► **char funèbre** hearse ► **char à voile** sand yacht, land yacht; **faire du ~ à voile** to go sand-yachting

char²* [ʃaʀ] NM (= *bluff*) **c'est du ~ tout ça!** he's (*ou* they're *etc*) just bluffing, he's (*ou* they're *etc*) just trying it on* (*Brit*); **sans ~!** no kidding!*

charabia* [ʃaʀabja] NM gibberish, gobbledygook*

charade [ʃaʀad] NF (*parlée*) riddle, word puzzle; (*mimée*) charade

charançon [ʃaʀɑ̃sɔ̃] NM weevil

charançonné, e [ʃaʀɑ̃sɔne] ADJ weevilly, weevilled

charbon [ʃaʀbɔ̃] **1** NM **a** (= *combustible*) coal (*NonC*); (= *escarbille*) speck of coal dust, piece of grit; **être sur les ~s ardents** to be like a cat on hot bricks *ou* on a hot tin roof (*US*); **aller au ~*** (*travail*) to go to work; (*tâche ingrate, risquée*) to stick one's neck out; (*se démener*) **il faut aller au ~** we've got to get out there and do what's got to be done **b** (= *maladie*) [*blé*] smut, black rust; [*bête, homme*] anthrax **c** (*Art*) (= *instrument*) piece of charcoal; (= *dessin*) charcoal drawing **d** (*Pharm*) charcoal; **pastilles au ~** charcoal tablets **e** (*Élec*) [*arc électrique*] carbon **2** COMP ► **charbon actif** *ou* **activé** active *ou* activated carbon ► **charbon animal** animal black ► **charbon de bois** charcoal; **cuit au ~ de bois** char-grilled, charcoal-grilled, barbecued ► **charbon de terre** †† coal

charbonnage [ʃaʀbɔnaʒ] NM (*gén pl* = *houillère*) colliery, coalmine; **les Charbonnages (de France)** the French Coal Board

charbonner [ʃaʀbɔne] ▸ conjug 1 ◂ **1** VT [+ *inscription*] to scrawl in charcoal; ~ **un mur de dessins** to scrawl (charcoal) drawings on a wall; **avoir les yeux charbonnés** to have eyes heavily rimmed with eyeliner; **se ~ le visage** to blacken *ou* black one's face [2] VI [*lampe, poêle, rôti*] to char, go black; (*Naut*) to take on coal

charbonneux, -euse [ʃaʀbɔnø, øz] ADJ [a] [*apparence, texture*] coal-like; (*littér = noirci, souillé*) sooty [b] (*Méd*) **tumeur charbonneuse** anthracoid *ou* anthrasic tumour; **mouche charbonneuse** anthrax-carrying fly

charbonnier, -ière [ʃaʀbɔnje, jeʀ] [1] ADJ coal (*épith*); **navire ~** collier, coaler → **mésange** [2] NM (= *personne*) coalman; (†† = *fabriquant de charbon de bois*) charcoal burner ∎ (*PROV*) **est maître dans sa maison** *ou* **chez soi** a man is master in his own home, an Englishman's home is his castle (*Brit*), a man's home is his castle (*US*) → **foi** [3] **charbonnière** NF (= *four*) charcoal kiln *ou* oven

charcutage [ʃaʀkytaʒ] NM (*péj*) **~ électoral** gerrymandering

charcuter* [ʃaʀkyte] ▸ conjug 1 ◂ [1] VT [+ *personne*] (*dans une rixe*) to hack about*; (= *opérer*) to butcher*; [+ *rôti, volaille*] to mangle, hack to bits; [+ *texte*] to hack; **il va se faire ~** he's going to go under the (surgeon's) knife [2] **se charcuter** VPR to cut o.s. to ribbons; (*bagarre*) **ils se sont charcutés** they cut each other to ribbons, they hacked each other to bits

charcuterie [ʃaʀkytʀi] NF (= *magasin*) pork butcher's shop and delicatessen; (= *produits*) cooked pork meats; (= *commerce*) pork meat trade; (*de traiteur*) delicatessen trade

┌─ **CHARCUTERIE** ─┐

This is a generic term referring to a wide variety of products made with pork, such as pâté, "rillettes", ham and sausages. The terms **charcuterie** *or* "**boucherie-charcuterie**" *also refer to the shop where these products are sold. The "charcutier-traiteur" sells ready-prepared dishes to take away as well as* **charcuterie**.

charcutier, -ière [ʃaʀkytje, jeʀ] NM,F pork butcher; (= *traiteur*) delicatessen dealer; (* : *péj* = *chirurgien*) butcher* (*fig*)

chardon [ʃaʀdɔ̃] NM (*Bot*) thistle; [*grille, mur*] **~s** spikes

chardonnay [ʃaʀdɔne] NM (= *vin*) Chardonnay

chardonneret [ʃaʀdɔnʀɛ] NM goldfinch

charentais, e [ʃaʀɑ̃tɛ, ɛz] [1] ADJ of *ou* from Charente [2] **Charentais(e)** NM,F inhabitant *ou* native of Charente [3] **charentaise** NF carpet slipper

charge [ʃaʀʒ] [1] NF [a] (= *fardeau lit*) load, burden; (*fig*) burden; [*véhicule*] load; [*navire*] freight, cargo; (*Archit* = *poussée*) load; **~ maximale** [*camion*] maximum load; **fléchir** *ou* **plier sous la ~** to bend under the load *ou* burden; **~ de travail** workload; **c'est une grosse ~ de travail** it's an awful lot of work; **l'éducation des enfants est une lourde ~ pour eux** educating the children is a heavy burden for them; **leur mère infirme est une ~ pour eux** their invalid mother is a burden to *ou* on them [b] (= *rôle, fonction*) responsibility; (*Admin*) office; (*Jur*) practice; **~ publique/élective** public/elective office; **avoir une ~ d'avocat** to have a lawyer's practice; **les hautes ~s qu'il occupe** the high office that he holds; **les devoirs de la ~** the duties of (the) office; **on lui a confié la ~ de (faire) l'enquête** he was given the responsibility of (carrying out) the inquiry; **il a la ~ de faire ◊ la pour ~ de faire** the onus is upon him to do, he is responsible for doing → **femme** [c] (*envers qn*) **avoir la ~ de qn** to be responsible for sb, have charge of sb; **les enfants dont j'ai la ~** the children (who are) in my care; **avoir ~ d'âmes** [*prêtre*] to be responsible for people's spiritual welfare, have the cure

of souls; [*personne*] to be responsible for people's welfare [d] (= *obligations financières*) **~s** [*commerçant*] expenses, costs, outgoings; [*locataire*] maintenance *ou* service charges; **~s familiales** family expenses *ou* outgoings; **la ~ fiscale** the tax burden; **~s fiscales** taxes, taxation; **dans ce commerce, nous avons de lourdes ~s** we have heavy expenses *ou* costs *ou* our overheads are high in this trade; **les ~s de l'État** government expenditure → **cahier** [e] (*Jur*) charge; **les ~s qui pèsent contre lui** the charges against him → **témoin** [f] (*Mil* = *attaque*) charge; (*Sport*) **~ irrégulière** illegal tackle → **pas¹, revenir, sonner** [g] (*Tech*) [*fusil*] loading, charging; [*explosifs*] charge; (*Élec*) (= *action*) charging; (= *quantité*) charge [h] (= *caricature*) caricature → **portrait** [i] (*Naut* = *chargement*) loading [j] **il a sa mère à (sa) ~** he has a dependent mother, he has his mother to support; **enfants à ~** dependent children; **personnes à ~** dependents; **à ~ pour lui de payer** on condition that he meets the costs [k] **être à la ~ de qn** [*frais, réparations*] to be chargeable to sb, be payable by sb; [*personne*] to be dependent upon sb, be a charge on sb, be supported by sb; **les frais sont à la ~ de l'entreprise** the costs will be borne by the firm, the firm will pay the expenses; **j'accepte ton aide à ~ de revanche** I'll let you help me but on condition that you let me return the favour sometime [l] **en ~** (*Élec*) **conducteur en ~** live conductor; **mettre une batterie en ~** to charge a battery, put a battery on charge (*Brit*); **la batterie est en ~** the battery is being charged *ou* is on charge (*Brit*); **prendre en ~** [+ *frais, remboursement*] to take care of; [+ *passager*] to take on; **prendre un enfant en ~** (= *gén*) to take charge of a child; [*Assistance publique*] to take a child into care (*Brit*), take a child into court custody (*US*); **l'adolescent doit se prendre en ~** the adolescent must take responsibility for himself; **prise en ~** (*par un taxi*) (= *action*) picking up; (= *prix*) minimum (standard) fare; (*par la Sécurité sociale*) undertaking to reimburse medical expenses [m] **être en ~ de** to deal with, be in charge of, handle [2] COMP ▸ **charge affective** (*Psych*) emotive power ▸ **charge creuse** (*Mil*) hollow-charge ▸ **charge émotionnelle** = **charge affective** ▸ **charges de famille** dependents ▸ **charges locatives** maintenance *ou* service charges ▸ **charges patronales** employers' contributions ▸ **charges sociales** social security contributions ▸ **charge utile** live load ▸ **charge à vide** weight (when) empty, empty weight

chargé, e [ʃaʀʒe] (*ptp de* **charger**) [1] ADJ [a] (*lit*) [*personne, véhicule*] loaded, laden (**de** with); **~ comme un mulet*** *ou* **un baudet*** loaded *ou* laden (down) like a mule [b] (= *responsable de*) **être ~ de** [+ *travail, enfants*] to be in charge of [c] (*fig* = *rempli de*) **~ d'honneurs** laden with honours; (*littér*) **~ d'ans** *ou* **d'années** weighed down by (the) years; **mot ~ de sens** word full of *ou* pregnant with meaning; **regard ~ de menaces** menacing *ou* baleful look; **nuage ~ de neige** snow-laden cloud, cloud laden *ou* heavy with snow; **air ~ de parfums** air heavy with scent *ou* fragrance (*littér*) [d] (= *occupé*) [*emploi du temps*] full, heavy; **notre programme est très ~** we have a very busy schedule *ou* a very full programme [e] (*fig* = *lourd*) [*conscience*] troubled; [*ciel*] overcast, heavy; [*style*] overelaborate, intricate; **c'est un homme qui a un passé ~** he is a man with a past → **hérédité** [f] (*Méd*) [*estomac*] overloaded; [*langue*] coated, furred; **il a l'haleine ~e** his breath smells

[g] (*Tech*) [*arme, appareil*] loaded [h] ‡ (= *ivre*) plastered‡ (*attrib*), sloshed‡ (*attrib*); (= *drogué*) stoned‡ (*attrib*), spaced (out)‡ (*attrib*) [2] COMP ▸ **chargé d'affaires** NM chargé d'affaires ▸ **chargé de cours** NM junior lecturer *ou* fellow ▸ **chargé de famille : être ~ de famille** to have family responsibilities ▸ **chargé de mission** (*gén*) project leader; (*Pol*) (official) representative ▸ **chargé de recherches** researcher

chargement [ʃaʀʒəmɑ̃] NM [a] (= *action*) [*camion, bagages*] loading [b] (= *marchandises*) load; [*navire*] freight, cargo; **le ~ a basculé** the load toppled over [c] (*Comm*) (= *remise*) registering; (= *paquet*) registered parcel [d] [*arme, caméra, logiciel*] loading; [*chaudière*] stoking

charger [ʃaʀʒe] ▸ conjug 3 ◂ [1] VT [a] [+ *animal, personne, véhicule, étagère*] to load; **~ qn de paquets** to load sb up *ou* weigh sb down with parcels; **je vais ~ la voiture** I'll go and load the car (up); **on a trop chargé cette voiture** this car has been overloaded; **table chargée de mets appétissants** table laden *ou* loaded with mouth-watering dishes; **~ le peuple d'impôts** to burden the people with *ou* weigh the people down with taxes; **~ sa mémoire (de faits)/ un texte de citations** to overload one's memory (with facts)/a text with quotations; **plat qui charge l'estomac** dish that lies heavy on the stomach [b] (= *placer, prendre*) [+ *objet, bagages*] to load (**dans** into); **il a chargé le sac/le cageot sur son épaule** he loaded the sack/the crate onto his shoulder, he heaved the sack over/the crate onto his shoulder; [*taxi*] **~ un client** to pick up a passenger *ou* a fare [c] [+ *fusil, caméra, logiciel*] to load; [+ *batterie*] to charge; [+ *chaudière*] to stoke, fire; (*Couture*) [+ *bobine, canette*] to load *ou* fill with thread [d] (= *donner une responsabilité*) **~ qn de qch** to put sb in charge of sth; **~ qn de faire qch** to give sb the responsibility *ou* job of doing sth, ask sb to do sth; **être chargé de faire qch** to be put in charge of doing sth, be made responsible for doing sth; **il m'a chargé d'un petit travail** he gave me a little job to do; **on l'a chargé d'une mission importante** he was given an important job to do; **on l'a chargé de la surveillance des enfants** *ou* **de surveiller les enfants** he was put in charge of the children, he was given the job of looking after the children; **il m'a chargé de mettre une lettre à la poste** he asked me to post a letter; **on m'a chargé d'appliquer le règlement** I've been instructed to apply the rule; **il m'a chargé de m'occuper de la correspondance** he gave me the responsibility *ou* job of seeing to the correspondence; **il m'a chargé de ses amitiés pour vous** *ou* **de vous transmettre ses amitiés** he asked me to give you his regards [e] (= *accuser*) [+ *personne*] to bring all possible evidence against; **~ qn de** [+ *crime*] to charge sb with [f] (= *attaquer*) (*Mil*) to charge (at); (*Sport*) to charge, tackle; **chargez!** charge!; **il a chargé dans le tas*** he charged into them [g] (= *caricaturer*) [+ *portrait*] to make a caricature of; [+ *description*] to overdo, exaggerate; (*Théât*) [+ *rôle*] to overact, ham it up*; **il a tendance à ~** he has a tendency to overdo it *ou* to exaggerate [2] **se charger** VPR [a] **se ~ de** [+ *tâche*] to see to, take care *ou* charge of, take on; [+ *enfant, prisonnier*] to attend to, take care of; (*iro*) [+ *ennemi*] to see to, attend to; **se ~ de faire qch** to undertake to do sth, take it upon o.s. to do sth; **il s'est chargé des enfants** he is seeing to *ou* taking care *ou* charge of the children; **d'accord je m'en charge** O.K., I'll see to it *ou* I'll take care of it; **je me charge de le faire venir** I'll make sure *ou* I'll see to it that he comes, I'll make it my business to see that he comes

b **:** (= *se soûler*) to get plastered**:**; (= *se droguer*) to get stoned**:**

chargeur [ʃaʀʒœʀ] NM **a** (= *personne*) (*gén, Mil*) loader; (*Naut*) (= *négociant*) shipper; (= *affréteur*) charterer **b** (= *dispositif*) [*arme à feu*] magazine, cartridge clip; (*Photo*) cartridge; **il vida son ~ sur les gendarmes** he emptied his gun *ou* magazine into the police officers; **~ de batterie** (battery) charger

charia [ʃaʀja] NF sharia, sheria

chariot [ʃaʀjo] NM (= *charrette*) wagon, waggon (*Brit*); (*plus petit*) truck, cart; (= *table, panier à roulettes*) trolley (*Brit*), cart (*US*); (= *appareil de manutention*) truck, float (*Brit*); [*machine à écrire, machine-outil*] carriage; [*hôpital*] trolley; **~ (à bagages)** (baggage *ou* luggage trolley (*Brit*) *ou* cart (*US*); (*Ciné*) **~ (de caméra)** dolly; **~ (à fourche)** fork-lift truck; (*Astron*) **le Petit/Grand Chariot** the Little/Great Bear

charismatique [kaʀismatik] ADJ charismatic

charisme [kaʀism] NM charisma

charitable [ʃaʀitabl] ADJ **a** (= *qui fait preuve de charité*) charitable (**envers** towards); **organisation ~** charitable organization, charity **b** (= *gentil*) kind (**envers** to, towards); **ce n'est pas très ~ de votre part** that's rather uncharitable *ou* unkind of you; (*iro*) **merci de tes conseils ~s** thanks for your kind advice (*iro*) → **âme**

charitablement [ʃaʀitabləmɑ̃] ADV (= *avec charité*) charitably; (= *gentiment*) kindly; (*iro*) **je vous avertis ~ que la prochaine fois ...** let me give you a friendly warning that next time ...

charité [ʃaʀite] NF **a** (= *bonté, amour*) charity; (= *gentillesse*) kindness; (*Rel*) charity, love; **il a eu la ~ de faire** he was kind enough to do; **faites-moi la ~ de ...** ◊ **ayez la ~ de ...** be so kind as to ...; **ce serait une ~ à lui faire que de ...** it would be doing him a kindness *ou* a good turn to ... → **dame, sœur** **b** (= *aumône*) charity; **demander la ~** (*lit*) to ask *ou* beg for charity; (*fig*) to come begging; **faire la ~ à** to give to charity; **faire la ~ à** [+ *mendiants*] to give (something) to; **je ne veux pas qu'on me fasse la ~** I don't want charity; **la ~, ma bonne dame !** could you spare me some change?; **vivre de la ~ publique** to live on (public) charity; **vivre des ~s de ses voisins** to live on the charity of one's neighbours ∎ (*PROV*) **~ bien ordonnée commence par soi-même** charity begins at home (*PROV*); **fête de ~** charity fête → **vente**

charivari [ʃaʀivaʀi] NM hullabaloo

charlatan [ʃaʀlatɑ̃] NM (*péj*) (= *médecin*) quack, charlatan; (= *pharmacien, vendeur*) crook, mountebank (*littér*); (= *plombier, maçon*) cowboy*; (= *politicien*) charlatan, phoney*

charlatanerie [ʃaʀlatanʀi] NF = **charlatanisme**

charlatanesque [ʃaʀlatanesk] ADJ (= *de guérisseur*) [*remède, méthodes*] quack (*épith*); (= *de démagogue, d'escroc*) [*méthodes*] phoney*, bogus

charlatanisme [ʃaʀlatanism] NM [*guérisseur*] quackery, charlatanism; [*politicien*] charlatanism, trickery

Charlemagne [ʃaʀləmaɲ] NM Charlemagne

Charles [ʃaʀl] NM Charles; **~ le Téméraire** Charles the Bold; **~Quint** Charles the Fifth (of Spain); **~ Martel** Charles Martel

charleston [ʃaʀlɛstɔn] NM (= *danse*) charleston

charlot [ʃaʀlo] NM **a** (*Ciné*) **Charlot** (= *personnage*) Charlie Chaplin; (= *film*) Charlie Chaplin film **b** (*péj*) (= *peu sérieux*) phoney*; (= *paresseux*) shirker, skiver*

charlotte [ʃaʀlɔt] NF (= *gâteau*) charlotte; (= *coiffure*) mobcap

charmant, e [ʃaʀmɑ̃, ɑ̃t] ADJ **a** (= *aimable*) [*hôte, jeune fille, employé*] charming; [*enfant*]

sweet, delightful; [*sourire, manières*] charming, engaging; **il s'est montré ~** he was charming; **c'est un collaborateur ~** he is a charming *ou* delightful man to work with → **prince** **b** (= *agréable*) [*séjour, soirée*] delightful, lovely; (*iro*) **eh bien c'est ~** charming! (*iro*); (*iro*) **~e soirée !** great evening! (*iro*) **c** (= *ravissant*) [*robe, village, jeune fille, sourire*] lovely, charming

charme¹ [ʃaʀm] NM (*Bot*) hornbeam

charme² [ʃaʀm] **1** NM **a** (= *attrait*) [*personne, musique, paysage*] charm; **elle a beaucoup de ~** she has great charm; **ça lui donne un certain ~** that gives him a certain charm *ou* appeal; **cette vieille maison a son ~** this old house has its charm; **c'est ce qui en fait (tout) le ~** that's where its attraction lies, that's what is so delightful about it; **ça ne manque pas de ~** it's not without (a certain) charm; **ça a peut-être du ~ pour vous, mais ...** it may appeal to you but ...; (*hum*) **je suis assez peu sensible aux ~s d'une promenade sous la pluie** a walk in the rain holds few attractions for me; **hôtel de ~** attractive privately-run hotel; **opération** *ou* **offensive de ~** charm offensive; **magazine de ~** (*euph*) girlie magazine*; **émission/photos de ~** soft porn programme/photographs **b** (= *envoûtement*) spell; **subir** *ou* **être sous le ~ de qn** to be under sb's spell; **exercer un ~ sur qn** to have sb under one's spell; **il est tombé sous son ~** he has fallen under her spell; **tenir qn sous le ~ (de)** to captivate sb (with), hold sb spellbound (with); **le ~ est rompu** the spell is broken → **chanteur** **c** (*loc*) **faire du ~** to turn *ou* switch on the charm; **faire du ~ à qn** to try to charm sb, use one's charm on sb; **aller** *ou* **se porter comme un ~** to be *ou* feel as fit as a fiddle

2 charmes NMPL (*hum* = *attraits d'une femme*) charms (*hum*); **il doit avoir des ~s cachés** he must have hidden talents → **commerce**

charmé, e [ʃaʀme] (*ptp de* **charmer**) ADJ **être ~ de faire qch** to be delighted to do sth

charmer [ʃaʀme] ▶ conjug 1 ◀ VT [+ *public*] to charm, enchant; [+ *serpents*] to charm; (†, *littér*) [+ *peine, douleur*] to charm away; **elle a des manières qui charment** she has charming *ou* delightful ways; **spectacle qui charme l'oreille et le regard** performance that charms *ou* enchants both the ear and the eye

charmeur, -euse [ʃaʀmœʀ, øz] **1** ADJ [*sourire, manières*] winning, engaging **2** NM,F (= *séducteur*) charmer; **~ de serpent** snake charmer

charmille [ʃaʀmij] NF arbour (*Brit*), arbor (*US*); (= *allée d'arbres*) tree-covered walk

charnel, -elle [ʃaʀnel] ADJ (*frm*) [*passions, instincts*] carnal; [*désirs*] carnal, fleshly; **l'acte ~** ◊ **l'union ~le** the carnal act (*frm*); **enveloppe ~le** mortal coil; **liens ~s** blood ties

charnellement [ʃaʀnelmɑ̃] ADV (*frm, littér*) [*convoiter*] sexually; **connaître ~** to have carnal knowledge of (*littér*); **pécher ~** to commit the sin of the flesh (*littér*)

charnier [ʃaʀnje] NM [*victimes*] mass grave; (†† = *ossuaire*) charnel house

charnière [ʃaʀnjeʀ] NF **a** [*porte, fenêtre, coquille*] hinge; [*timbre de collection*] (stamp) hinge → **nom** **b** (= *transition*) turning point; **époque/rôle ~** pivotal period/role; **moment ~** turning point (**de** in); **parti ~** party that occupies the middle ground; **roman ~** novel marking a turning point *ou* a transition; **à la ~ de deux époques** at the cusp of two eras; **la ville est située à la ~ de l'Occident et l'Orient** it's a city where East meets West **c** (*Mil*) pivot

charnu, e [ʃaʀny] ADJ [*lèvres*] fleshy, thick; [*fruit, bras*] plump, fleshy; **les parties ~es du corps** the fleshy parts of the body; (*hum*) **sur la partie ~e de son individu** on the fleshy part of his person (*hum*)

charognard [ʃaʀɔɲaʀ] NM (*lit*) carrion eater; (*fig*) vulture

charogne [ʃaʀɔɲ] NF (= *cadavre*) carrion (*NonC*), decaying carcass; (**:** = *salaud*) (*femme*) bitch**:**; (*homme*) bastard**:**, sod**:** (*Brit*)

charolais, e [ʃaʀɔle, ez] **1** ADJ of *ou* from Charolais **2 Charolais** NM (= *région*) **le Charolais** Charolais **3** NM,F (= *bétail*) Charolais

charpente [ʃaʀpɑ̃t] NF **a** [*bâtiment*] frame(work), skeleton; [*toit*] (roof) structure; **~ en bois/métallique** timber/steel frame(work) → **bois** **b** [*feuille*] skeleton; [*roman*] structure, framework; **le squelette est la ~ du corps** the skeleton is the framework of the body **c** (= *carrure*) build, frame; **quelle solide ~ !** he's well-built!; **~ fragile/épaisse** fragile/stocky build

charpenté, e [ʃaʀpɑ̃te] ADJ **bien/solidement ~** [*personne*] well/solidly built; [*texte*] well/solidly structured *ou* constructed

charpentier [ʃaʀpɑ̃tje] NM (*Constr*) carpenter; **~ de marine** shipwright

charpie [ʃaʀpi] NF **a** (*Hist* = *pansement*) shredded linen (*used to dress wounds*) **b** (*loc*) **c'est de la ~** [*viande*] it's been cooked to shreds; [*vêtements*] they're (all) in shreds *ou* ribbons, they're falling to pieces; **mettre** *ou* **réduire en ~** [+ *papier, vêtements*] (= *déchirer*) to tear to shreds; [+ *viande*] (= *hacher menu*) to mince; **je vais le mettre en ~** I'll tear him to shreds!, I'll make mincemeat of him!; **il s'est fait mettre en ~ par le train** he was mangled by the train

charre: [ʃaʀ] NM = **char²**

charretée [ʃaʀte] NF (*lit*) cartload (**de** of); (* = *grande quantité de*) **une ~ de*** ◊ **des ~s de*** loads* *ou* stacks* of

charretier, -ière [ʃaʀtje, jeʀ] NM,F carter; (*péj*) **de ~** [*langage, manières*] coarse → **chemin, jurer**

charrette [ʃaʀet] NF **a** (*lit*) cart; **~ à bras** handcart, barrow; **~ anglaise** dogcart; **~ des condamnés** tumbril; (*fig* = *licenciement*) **il a fait partie de la dernière ~** he went in the last round of redundancies (*Brit*) *ou* lay-offs **b** (= *travail urgent*) spate of work; **faire une ~*** to work flat out*; **être (en pleine) ~*** to be working against the clock

charriage [ʃaʀjaʒ] NM **a** (= *transport*) carriage, cartage **b** (*Géol* = *déplacement*) overthrusting → **nappe**

charrier [ʃaʀje] ▶ conjug 7 ◀ **1** VT **a** (= *transporter*) (*avec brouette*) to cart (along), trundle along, wheel (along); (*sur le dos*) to hump (*Brit*) *ou* lug along, heave (along), cart (along); [*camion*] to carry, cart; **on a passé des heures à ~ du charbon** we spent hours heaving *ou* carting coal **b** (= *entraîner*) [*fleuve*] to carry (along), wash along, sweep (along); [*coulée, avalanche*] to carry (along), sweep (along); (*littér*) **le ciel** *ou* **le vent charriait de lourds nuages** the wind sent heavy clouds scudding across the sky; (*péj*) **l'idéologie qu'il charrie** the ideology he propounds; **les obscénités charriées par ses romans** the obscenities with which his novels are littered **c** * **~ qn** (= *taquiner qn*) to tease sb, take the mickey out of sb* (*Brit*); (= *raconter des histoires à qn*) to kid sb*, have sb on* (*Brit*), put sb on* (*US*) **2** VI**:** (= *abuser*) to go too far, overstep the mark; (= *plaisanter*) to be kidding*, be joking*; **tu charries, elle n'est pas si vieille !** come on* *ou* come off it* (*Brit*) — she's not that old!; **faut pas** *ou* **faudrait pas ~ !** that's a bit much! *ou* rich!* (*Brit*)

charrieur, -euse: [ʃaʀjœʀ, øz] NM,F **c'est un ~** (= *il abuse*) he's always going too far *ou* overstepping the mark; (= *il plaisante*) he's always having (*Brit*) *ou* putting (*US*) people on*; **il est un peu ~** he's a bit of a joker*

charroi †† [ʃaʀwa] NM (= *transport*) cartage

charron [ʃaʀɔ̃] NM cartwright, wheelwright

charroyer [ʃaRwaje] ▸conjug 8◂ VT (littér) (par charrette) to cart; (laborieusement) to cart (along), heave (along)

charrue [ʃaRy] NF plough (Brit), plow (US); (fig) **mettre la ~ devant ou avant les bœufs** to put the cart before the horse

charte [ʃaRt] NF (Hist, Pol = convention) charter; (Hist = titre, contrat) title, deed; **accorder une ~ à** to grant a charter to, charter; **la Charte des Nations Unies** the United Nations Charter; **l'École (nationale) des ~s ◊ les Chartes** the École des Chartes (French national school of archival studies and palaeography)

charter [ʃaRtɛR] 1 NM (= vol) charter flight; (= avion) charter(ed) plane 2 ADJ INV [vol, billet, prix] charter (épith); **avion ~** charter(ed) plane

chartisme [ʃaRtism] NM (Pol Brit) Chartism

chartiste [ʃaRtist] 1 ADJ (Pol Brit) Chartist 2 NMF (= élève) student of the École des Chartes; (Pol Brit) Chartist; (= analyste) chartist

chartreuse [ʃaRtRøz] NF (= liqueur) chartreuse; (= couvent) Charterhouse, Carthusian monastery; (= religieuse) Carthusian nun

chartreux [ʃaRtRø] NM (= religieux) Carthusian monk; (= chat) Chartreux

Charybde [kaRibd] NM Charybdis; **tomber de ~ en Scylla** to jump out of the frying pan into the fire

chas [ʃa] NM eye (of needle)

chasse¹ [ʃas] 1 NF a (gén) hunting; (au fusil) shooting, hunting; **aller à la ~** (gén) to go hunting; (avec fusil) to go shooting ou hunting; **aller à la ~ aux papillons** to go catching butterflies; **~ au faisan** pheasant shooting; **~ au lapin** rabbit shooting, rabbiting; **~ au renard/au chamois/au gros gibier** fox/ chamois/big game hunting; **air/habits de ~** hunting tune/clothes → **chien, cor', fusil** etc b (= période) (gén) hunting season; (au fusil) hunting season, shooting season; **la ~ est ouverte/fermée** it's the open/close season (Brit), it's open/closed season (US) c (= gibier) game; **manger/partager la ~** to eat/share the game; **faire (une) bonne ~** to get a good bag; **bonne ~!** (lit) have a good day's shooting!; (fig) happy hunting! d (= domaine) shoot, hunting ground; **louer une ~** to rent a shoot, rent land to shoot ou hunt on; **une ~ giboyeuse** a well-stocked shoot e (= chasseurs) **la ~** the hunt f (Aviat) **la ~** the fighters → **avion, pilote** g (= poursuite) chase; **une ~ effrénée dans les rues** a frantic chase through the streets h (loc) **faire la ~ à** [+ souris, moustiques] to hunt down, chase; [+ abus, erreurs] to hunt down, track down; **faire la ~ aux appartements/occasions** to go flat- (Brit) ou apartment- (US)/bargain-hunting; **faire la ~ au mari** to be searching ou looking for a husband, be in search of a husband; **prendre en ~ ◊ donner la ~ à** [+ fuyard, voiture] to give chase to, chase after; [+ avion, navire, ennemi] to give chase to; (Aviat, Mil, Naut) **donner la ~** to give chase; **se mettre en ~ pour trouver qch** to go hunting for sth; **être en ~** [chienne] to be on (Brit) ou in (US, Ir) heat; [chien] to be on the trail ▪ (PROV) **qui va à la ~ perd sa place** he who leaves his place loses it

2 COMP ▸ **chasse à l'affût** hunting (from a hide (Brit) ou blind (US)) ▸ **chasse au chevreuil** deer hunting, deer-stalking ▸ **chasse à courre** (= sport) hunting with hounds; (= partie de chasse) hunt ▸ **chasse au furet** ferreting ▸ **chasse gardée** (lit) private hunting (ground), private shoot; (fig) exclusive preserve ou domain; **elle est mignonne — attention, c'est ~ gardée!** she's cute — hands off! she's already spoken for ou taken*; (panneau) « **~ gardée** » "private, poachers will be prosecuted" ▸ **chasse à l'homme** manhunt ▸ **chasse aux sorcières** witch hunt;

faire la ~ aux sorcières to conduct a witch hunt ▸ **chasse sous-marine** harpooning, harpoon fishing ▸ **chasse au trésor** treasure hunt

chasse² [ʃas] NF a **~ (d'eau ou des cabinets)** (toilet) flush; **actionner ou tirer la ~** to flush the toilet; (avec chaîne) to pull the chain b (Typo) body (width), set (width)

chassé [ʃase] NM (= danse) chassé

châsse [ʃas] NF (= reliquaire) reliquary, shrine; (‡ = œil) eye, peeper*; (= monture) [bague, bijou] setting; [lancette] handle

chasse-clou (pl **chasse-clous**) [ʃasklu] NM nail punch

chassé-croisé (pl **chassés-croisés**) [ʃasekRwaze] NM a (Danse) chassé-croisé, set to partners b (fig) **avec tous ces chassés-croisés nous ne nous sommes pas vus depuis six mois** with all these to-ings and fro-ings we haven't seen each other for six months; **une période de chassés-croisés sur les routes** a period of heavy two-way traffic; **les ferries vont et viennent en un ~ régulier** the ferries ply to and fro continuously

chasselas [ʃasla] NM chasselas grape

chasse-mouche (pl **chasse-mouches**) [ʃasmuʃ] NM flyswatter, fly whisk (Brit)

chasse-neige (pl **chasse-neige(s)**) [ʃasnɛʒ] NM a (= instrument) snowplough (Brit), snowplow (US); (= position du skieur) snowplough (Brit), snowplow (US), wedge; **~ à soufflerie** snow-blower; **descendre une pente en ~** to snowplough (Brit) ou snowplow (US) down a slope

chasse-pierres [ʃaspjɛR] NM INV cowcatcher

chassepot [ʃaspo] NM (Hist) chassepot (rifle)

chasser [ʃase] ▸conjug 1◂ 1 VT a (gén) to hunt; (au fusil) to shoot, hunt; **~ à l'affût/au filet** to hunt from a hide (Brit) ou blind (US) with a net; **~ le faisan/le cerf** to go pheasant-shooting/deer hunting; **il chasse le lion en Afrique** he is shooting lions ou lion-shooting in Africa; (fig: être dans la lignée) **il chasse de race** it runs in the family, he is carrying on the family tradition → **chien** b (= faire partir) [+ importun, animal, ennemi] to drive ou chase out ou away; [+ domestique, fils indigne] to turn out; [+ immigrant] to drive out, expel; [+ touristes, clients] to drive away, chase away; **chassant de la main les insectes** brushing away ou driving off (the) insects with his hand; **il a chassé les gamins du jardin** he chased ou drove the kids out of the garden; **mon père m'a chassé de la maison** my father has turned ou thrown me out of the house; **le brouillard nous a chassés de la plage** we were driven off the beach by the fog; **ces touristes, ils vont finir par nous ~ de chez nous** these tourists will end up driving us away from our own homes; **il a été chassé de son pays par le nazisme** he was forced to flee his country because of the Nazis, Nazism drove him from his country ▪ (PROV) **chassez le naturel, il revient au galop** what's bred in the bone comes out in the flesh (PROV) → **faim** c (= dissiper) [+ odeur] to dispel, drive away; [+ idée] to dismiss, chase away; [+ souci, doute] to dispel, drive away, chase away; [+ brouillard] to dispel; **essayant de ~ ces images obsédantes** trying to chase away ou dismiss these haunting images; **il faut ~ cette idée de ta tête** you must get that idea out of your head ou dismiss that idea from your mind d (= pousser) [+ troupeau, nuages, pluie] to drive; (Tech) [+ clou] to drive in e (= éjecter) [+ douille, eau d'un tuyau] to drive out → **clou**

2 VI a (= aller à la chasse) (gén) to go hunting; (au fusil) to go shooting ou hunting; (fig) **~ sur les terres de qn** to poach on sb's territory

b (= déraper) [véhicule, roues] to skid; [ancre] to drag; **~ sur ses ancres** to drag its anchors

chasseresse [ʃasRɛs] NF (littér) huntress (littér) → **Diane**

chasseur [ʃasœR] 1 NM a (gén) hunter; (à courre) hunter, huntsman; (Anthropologie) **~-cueilleur** hunter-gatherer; **~ de baleines** whaler; **~ de phoques** sealer; **~ de papillons** butterfly catcher; **c'est un très bon ~** (gén) he's a very good hunter; (au fusil) he's an excellent shot; **c'est un grand ~ de renards** he's a great one for foxhunting, he's a great foxhunter b (Mil) (= soldat) chasseur; (= avion) fighter; (= régiment) **le 3e ~** the 3rd (regiment of) chasseurs c (= garçon d'hôtel) page (boy), messenger (boy), bellboy (US) d (Culin) **poulet/lapin ~** chicken/rabbit chasseur (chicken/rabbit cooked with mushrooms and white wine)

2 COMP ▸ **chasseur alpin** mountain infantryman; **les ~s alpins** the mountain infantry, the alpine chasseurs ▸ **chasseur d'autographes** autograph hunter ▸ **chasseur à cheval** (Hist Mil) cavalryman; **les ~s à cheval** the cavalry ▸ **chasseur d'images** roving amateur photographer ▸ **chasseur de mines** minesweeper ▸ **chasseur à pied** (Hist Mil) infantryman; **les ~s à pied** the infantry ▸ **chasseur de primes** bounty hunter ▸ **chasseur à réaction** jet fighter ▸ **chasseur de sous-marins** submarine chaser ▸ **chasseur de têtes** (lit, fig) headhunter

chasseur-bombardier (pl **chasseurs-bombardiers**) [ʃasœRbɔ̃baRdje] NM (Aviat Mil) fighter-bomber

chasseuse [ʃasøz] NF huntswoman, hunter, huntress (littér)

chassie [ʃasi] NF [yeux] sticky matter (in eye), sleep*

chassieux, -ieuse [ʃasjø, jøz] ADJ [yeux] sticky, gummy; [personne, animal] gummy- ou sticky-eyed; **avoir les yeux ~** to have sleep* in one's eyes

châssis [ʃasi] NM a [véhicule] chassis; [machine] sub- ou under-frame b (= encadrement) [fenêtre] frame; [toile, tableau] stretcher; (Typo) chase; (Photo) (printing) frame; **~ mobile/dormant** opening/fixed frame c (‡ = corps féminin) body, figure, chassis‡ (US); **elle a un beau ~!** she's got a hell of a figure!‡ d (Agr) cold frame

chaste [ʃast] ADJ chaste; (hum) [oreilles] delicate; **de ~s jeunes filles** chaste young girls; **mener une vie ~** to lead a celibate life, live the life of a nun (ou a monk)

chastement [ʃastəmɑ̃] ADV chastely

chasteté [ʃastəte] NF chastity → **ceinture**

chasuble [ʃazybl] NF chasuble → **robe**

chat [ʃa] 1 NM a (= animal) (gén) cat; (mâle) tomcat; **~ persan/siamois** Persian/Siamese cat; **petit ~** kitten; (terme d'affection) **mon petit ~** (à un enfant) pet*, poppet* (Brit); (à une femme) sweetie* b (= jeu) tag, tig (Brit); **jouer à ~** to play tag ou tig (Brit), have a game of tag ou tig (Brit); **(c'est toi le) ~!** you're it! c (loc) **il n'y avait pas un ~ dehors** there wasn't a soul outside; **avoir un ~ dans la gorge** to have a frog in one's throat; **il a acheté cette voiture ~ en poche** he bought a pig in a poke when he got that car, he hardly even looked at the car before buying it; **jouer au ~ et à la souris** to play cat and mouse; **j'ai d'autres ~s à fouetter** I've other fish to fry; **il n'y a pas de quoi fouetter un ~** it's nothing to make a fuss about ▪ (PROV) **~ échaudé craint l'eau froide** once bitten, twice shy (PROV) ▪ (PROV) **quand le ~ n'est pas là les souris dansent** when the cat's away the mice will play (_PROV_) ■ (_PROV_) **à bon ~ bon rat** tit for tat → **appeler, chien** _etc_

[2] COMP ► **le Chat botté** Puss in Boots ► **chat de gouttière** ordinary cat, alley cat ► **chat à neuf queues** cat-o'-nine-tails ► **chat perché** (= _jeu_) "off-ground" tag _ou_ tig (_Brit_) ► **chat sauvage** wildcat

châtaigne [ʃatɛɲ] NF [a] (= _fruit_) (sweet) chestnut; **~ d'eau** water chestnut [b] (‡ = _coup de poing_) punch, clout* (_Brit_) **flanquer une ~ à qn** to punch _ou_ clout* (_Brit_) sb, give sb a clout* (_Brit_) [c] (* = _décharge électrique_) (electric) shock

châtaigneraie [ʃatɛɲʀɛ] NF chestnut grove

châtaignier [ʃatɛɲe] NM (= _arbre_) (sweet) chestnut tree; (= _bois_) chestnut

châtain [ʃatɛ̃] [1] NM chestnut brown [2] ADJ M [_cheveux_] chestnut (brown); [_personne_] brown-haired; **elle est ~ clair/roux** she has light brown hair/auburn hair

château (_pl_ **châteaux**) [ʃato] [1] NM [a] (= _forteresse_) castle; (= _résidence royale_) palace, castle; (= _gentilhommière_) mansion, stately home; (_en France_) château; (= _vignoble_) château; **les ~x de la Loire** the châteaux of the Loire; **le ~ de Versailles** the Palace of Versailles; (_fig_) **bâtir** _ou_ **faire des ~x en Espagne** to build castles in the air _ou_ in Spain; **il est un peu ~ branlant** he's not very steady on his legs, he's a bit wobbly on his pins* (_Brit_) → **vie** [b] (*: _Culin_) chateaubriand [2] COMP ► **château d'arrière** (_Naut_) aftercastle ► **château d'avant** (_Naut_) fo'c'sle ► **château de cartes** (_Cartes, fig_) house of cards ► **château d'eau** water tower ► **château fort** stronghold, fortified castle ► **château de sable** sand castle

chateaubriand, châteaubriant [ʃatobʀijɑ̃] NM (_Culin_) chateaubriand, chateaubriant

Château-la-Pompe [ʃatolapɔ̃p] NM INV (_hum_) Adam's ale (_hum_)

châtelain [ʃat(ə)lɛ̃] NM [a] (_Hist_ = _seigneur_) (feudal) lord; **le ~** the lord of the manor [b] (= _propriétaire_) (_d'ancienne date_) squire; (_nouveau riche_) owner of a manor

châtelaine [ʃat(ə)lɛn] NF [a] (= _propriétaire_) owner of a manor [b] (= _épouse_) lady (of the manor), chatelaine [c] (= _ceinture_) chatelaine, châtelaine

chat-huant (_pl_ **chats-huants**) [ʃayɑ̃] NM screech owl, barn owl

châtié, e [ʃatje] (_ptp de_ **châtier**) ADJ [_style_] polished, refined; [_langage_] refined

châtier [ʃatje] ► conjug 7 ◄ VT [a] (_littér_ = _punir_) [+ _coupable_] to chastise (_littér_), castigate (_littér_), punish; [+ _faute_] to punish; (_Rel_) [+ _corps_] to chasten, mortify; **~ l'insolence de qn** to chastise _ou_ punish sb for his insolence → **qui** [b] (= _soigner_) [+ _style_] to polish, refine; [+ _langage_] to refine

chatière [ʃatjɛʀ] NF (= _porte_) cat-flap; (= _trou d'aération_) (air-)vent, ventilation hole; (= _piège_) cat-trap

châtiment [ʃatimɑ̃] NM (_littér_) chastisement (_littér_), castigation (_littér_), punishment; **~ corporel** corporal punishment

chatoiement [ʃatwamɑ̃] NM [_vitraux_] glistening; [_reflet, étoffe_] shimmer(ing); [_bijoux, plumage_] glistening, shimmer(ing); [_couleurs, style_] sparkle

chaton¹ [ʃatɔ̃] NM [a] (_Zool_) kitten [b] (_Bot_) catkin; **~s de poussière** balls of fluff

chaton² [ʃatɔ̃] NM (= _monture_) bezel, setting; (= _pierre_) stone

chatouille* [ʃatuj] NF tickle; **faire des ~s à qn** to tickle sb; **craindre les ~s** _ou_ **la ~** to be ticklish

chatouillement [ʃatujmɑ̃] NM (_gén_) tickling (_NonC_); (_dans le nez, la gorge_) tickle; **des ~s la faisaient se trémousser** a tickling sensation made her fidget

chatouiller [ʃatuje] ► conjug 1 ◄ VT [a] (_lit_) to tickle; **arrête, ça chatouille !** don't, that tickles! _ou_ you're tickling! [b] [+ _amour-propre, curiosité_] to tickle, titillate; [+ _palais, odorat_] to titillate [c] († _ou hum_) **~ les côtes à qn** to tan sb's hide

chatouilleux, -euse [ʃatujø, øz] ADJ [a] (_lit_) ticklish [b] (= _susceptible_) [_personne, caractère_] touchy, (over)sensitive; **être ~ sur l'honneur/l'étiquette** to be touchy _ou_ sensitive on points of honour/etiquette

chatouillis* [ʃatuji] NM light _ou_ gentle tickling; **faire des ~ à qn** to tickle sb lightly _ou_ gently

chatoyant, e [ʃatwajɑ̃, ɑ̃t] ADJ [_vitraux_] glistening; [_reflet, étoffe_] shimmering; [_bijoux, plumage_] glistening, shimmering; [_couleurs, style_] sparkling; **l'éclat ~ des pierreries** the way the gems sparkle in the light

chatoyer [ʃatwaje] ► conjug 8 ◄ VI [_vitraux_] to glisten; [_reflet, étoffe_] to shimmer; [_bijoux, plumage_] to glisten, shimmer; [_couleurs, style_] to sparkle

châtré* [ʃatʀe] NM (_lit, fig_) eunuch; **voix de ~** squeaky little voice

châtrer [ʃatʀe] ► conjug 1 ◄ VT [+ _taureau, cheval_] to castrate, geld; [+ _chat_] to neuter, castrate, fix (_US_); [+ _homme_] to castrate, emasculate; (_littér_) [+ _texte_] to mutilate, bowdlerize

chatte [ʃat] NF (_Zool_) (female) cat; (‡‡ = _vagin_) pussy‡‡; **elle est très ~** she's very kittenish; (_terme d'affection_) **ma (petite) ~** (my) pet*, sweetie(-pie)*

chattemite [ʃatmit] NF **faire la ~** to be a bit of a coaxer

chatterie [ʃatʀi] [1] NF (= _friandise_) titbit, dainty morsel; **aimer les ~s** to love a little delicacy _ou_ a dainty morsel [2] **chatteries** NFPL† (= _caresses_) playful attentions _ou_ caresses; (= _minauderies_) kittenish ways; **faire des ~ à qn** to make a fuss of sb

chatterton [ʃatɛʀtɔn] NM (adhesive) insulating tape

chat-tigre (_pl_ **chats-tigres**) [ʃatigʀ] NM tiger cat

chaud, chaude [ʃo, ʃod] [1] ADJ [a] [_température_] warm; (_très chaud_) hot; **les climats ~s** warm climates; (_très chaud_) hot climates; **l'eau du lac n'est pas assez ~e pour se baigner** the lake isn't warm enough for bathing; **bois ton thé pendant qu'il est ~** drink your tea while it's hot; **repas ~** hot meal; **tous les plats étaient servis très ~s** all the dishes were served up piping hot; **cela sort tout ~ du four** it's (piping) hot from the oven; **il a des nouvelles toutes ~es** he's got some news hot from the press _ou_ some hot news; (_fig_) **sa place est encore ~e et il y en a déjà qui se pressent pour le remplacer** he's only just left and some people can't wait to step into his shoes → **battre, main** _etc_ [b] [_couverture, vêtement_] warm [c] (= _vif, passionné_) [_félicitations_] warm, hearty; (_littér_) [_amitié_] warm; [_partisan_] keen, ardent; [_admirateur_] warm, ardent; [_recommandation_] wholehearted, enthusiastic; [_discussion_] heated; **la bataille a été ~e** it was a fierce battle, the battle was fast and furious; **être ~ (pour faire/pour qch)*** to be enthusiastic (about doing/about sth), be keen (on doing/on sth) (_Brit_); **il n'est pas très ~ pour conduire de nuit*** he doesn't much like driving at night, he is not very _ou_ too keen (_Brit_) on driving at night [d] (= _difficile_) **les endroits ~s de la ville** the city's trouble spots; **les points ~s du globe** the world's hot spots _ou_ flashpoints; **la rentrée sera ~e** there's going to be a lot of social unrest in the autumn; **l'alerte a été ~e** it was a near _ou_ close thing [e] [_voix, couleur_] warm [f] (* = _sensuel_) [_personne, tempérament_] hot, randy‡ (_Brit_); **quartier ~** red-light district [g] (_Phys Nucl_) [_produits, zone_] hot

[2] NM [a] (= _chaleur_) **le ~** (the) heat; **elle souffre autant du ~ que du froid** she suffers as much from the heat as from the cold [b] **restez donc au ~** stay in the warm; **garder** _ou_ **tenir qch au ~** to keep sth warm _ou_ hot; **garder un enfant enrhumé au ~** to keep a child with a cold (indoors) in the warmth [c] **à ~** (_Tech_) [_travailler_] under heat; **reportage à ~** on-the-spot report; **il a été opéré à ~** he had an emergency operation → **souder**

[3] ADV **avoir ~** to be warm, feel warm; (_très chaud_) to be hot, feel hot; **avez-vous assez ~ ?** are you warm enough?; **on a trop ~ ici** it's too hot in here; **j'ai eu ~ !*** (= _de la chance_) I had a lucky _ou_ narrow escape, it was a close shave; **il fait ~** it's hot _ou_ warm; **il fera ~ le jour où il voudra bien travailler*** that'll be the day when he decides to work; **ça ne me fait ni ~ ni froid** I couldn't care less, it makes no difference to me; **ça fait ~ au cœur** it's heart-warming; **manger ~** to have a hot meal, eat something hot; **boire ~** to have _ou_ take hot drinks; **il a fallu tellement attendre qu'on n'a pas pu manger ~** we had to wait so long the food had gone cold; **« servir ~ »** "serve hot"; **~ devant !** mind your back (_ou_ backs)!; **une robe qui tient ~** a warm dress; **tenir trop ~ à qn** to make sb too hot; [_course_] **ça m'a donné ~** it made me really hot → **souffler**

[4] **chaude** NF († = _flambée_) blaze

[5] COMP ► **chaud et froid** (_Méd_) chill ► **chaud lapin:** horny _ou_ randy (_Brit_) devil:

chaudement [ʃodmɑ̃] ADV [_s'habiller_] warmly; [_féliciter, recommander_] warmly, heartily; [_argumenter_] heatedly, hotly; **~ disputé** hotly disputed; (_hum_) **comment ça va ? — ~ !** how are you? — (I'm) hot!

chaude-pisse: (_pl_ **chaudes-pisses**) [ʃodpis] NF clap:‡

chaud-froid (_pl_ **chauds-froids**) [ʃofʀwa] NM (_Culin_) chaudfroid

chaudière [ʃodjɛʀ] NF [_locomotive, chauffage central_] boiler; **~ à gaz** gas-fired boiler

chaudron [ʃodʀɔ̃] NM cauldron

chaudronnerie [ʃodʀɔnʀi] NF [a] (= _métier_) boilermaking, boilerwork; (= _industrie_) boilermaking industry [b] (= _boutique_) coppersmith's workshop; (= _usine_) boilerworks [c] (= _produits_) **grosse ~** industrial boilers; **petite ~** pots and pans

chaudronnier, -ière [ʃodʀɔnje, jɛʀ] NM,F (= _artisan_) coppersmith; (= _ouvrier_) boilermaker

chauffage [ʃofaʒ] NM (= _action_) heating; (= _appareils_) heating (system); **il y a le ~ ?** is there any heating?, is it heated?; **avoir un bon ~** to have a good heating system; **~ au charbon/au gaz/à l'électricité** solid fuel/gas/electric heating; **~ central** central heating; **~ par le sol** underfloor heating; **~ urbain** urban _ou_ district heating system; **mets le ~** (_maison_) put the heating on; (_voiture_) put the heater on → **bois**

chauffagiste [ʃofaʒist] NM heating engineer _ou_ specialist

chauffant, e [ʃofɑ̃, ɑ̃t] ADJ [_surface, élément_] heating (_épith_) → **couverture, plaque**

chauffard [ʃofaʀ] NM (_péj_) reckless driver; (_qui s'enfuit_) hit-and-run driver; **(espèce de) ~ !** roadhog!*; **c'est un vrai ~** he's a real menace _ou_ maniac on the roads; **tué par un ~** killed by a reckless driver; **on n'a pas retrouvé le ~ responsable de l'accident** the driver responsible for the accident has not yet been found

chauffe [ʃof] NF (= _lieu_) fire-chamber; (= _processus_) stoking; **surface de ~** heating-surface, fire surface; (_Naut_) **chambre de ~** stokehold; **tour de ~** [_voiture de course_] warm-up lap; [_candidat, sportif_] practice run → **bleu**

chauffe-assiette(s) (_pl_ **chauffe-assiettes**) [ʃofasjet] NM plate-warmer

chauffe-bain (_pl_ **chauffe-bains**) [ʃofbɛ̃] NM water-heater

chauffe-biberon (*pl* **chauffe-biberons**) [ʃof-bibrɔ̃] NM bottle-warmer

chauffe-eau [ʃofo] NM INV (*gén*) water-heater; (*électrique*) immersion heater

chauffe-pieds [ʃofpje] NM INV foot-warmer

chauffe-plat (*pl* **chauffe-plats**) [ʃofpla] NM dish-warmer, chafing dish

chauffer [ʃofe] ▸conjug 1◂ **1** VT **a** (**faire**) **~** [+ *soupe*] to warm up, heat up; [+ *assiette*] to warm; [+ *eau du bain*] to heat (up); [+ *eau du thé*] to boil, heat up; **~ qch au four** to heat sth up in the oven, put sth in the oven to heat up; **mets l'eau à ~** (*gén*) put the water on; (*dans une bouilloire*) put the water on to boil, put the kettle on; (*hum: quand on casse qch*) **faites ~ la colle!** get the glue out!; **je vais te ~ les oreilles!** I'll box your ears!, you'll get a clip round the ear!* (*Brit*)

b [+ *appartement*] to heat; **on va ~ un peu la pièce** we'll heat (up) the room a bit **c** [*soleil*] to warm, make warm; [*soleil brûlant*] to heat, make hot **d** (*Tech*) [+ *métal, verre, liquide*] to heat; [+ *chaudière, locomotive*] to stoke (up), fire; (*lit, fig*) **~ qch à blanc** to make sth white-hot; **~ qn à blanc** to galvanize sb into action **e** (* = *préparer*) [+ *candidat*] to cram; [+ *commando*] to train up; [+ *salle, public*] to warm up **f** [+ *muscle*] to warm up **g** († = *voler*) to pinch*, swipe*

2 VI **a** (= *être sur le feu*) [*aliment, eau du bain*] to be heating up, be warming up; [*assiette*] to be warming (up); [*eau du thé*] to be heating up **b** (= *devenir chaud*) [*moteur, télévision*] to warm up; [*four*] to heat up; [*chaudière, locomotive*] to get up steam **c** (= *devenir trop chaud*) [*freins, appareil, moteur*] to overheat **d** (= *donner de la chaleur*) **le soleil chauffe** the sun's really hot; **le poêle chauffe bien** the stove gives out a lot of heat; **ils chauffent au charbon** they use coal for heating, their house is heated by coal; **le mazout chauffe bien** oil gives out a lot of heat **e** (*: loc*) **ça chauffe** (*il y a de la bagarre*) things are getting heated; (*il y a de l'ambiance*) things are livening up; **ça va ~!** sparks will fly!; **le but/l'essai chauffe** there must be a goal/try now!, they're on the brink of a goal/try!; (*cache-tampon*) **tu chauffes!** you're getting warm(er)!

3 se chauffer VPR **a** (*près du feu*) to warm o.s.; (* : *en faisant des exercices*) to warm up; **se ~ au soleil** to warm o.s. in the sun **b** (= *avoir comme chauffage*) **se ~ au bois/charbon** to burn wood/coal, use wood/coal for heating; **se ~ à l'électricité** to have electric heating, use electricity for heating → **bois**

chaufferette [ʃofʀɛt] NF (= *chauffe-pieds*) foot-warmer; (= *réchaud*) plate warmer

chaufferie [ʃofʀi] NF [*maison, usine*] boiler room; [*navire*] stokehold

chauffeur [ʃofœʀ] **1** NM **a** (= *conducteur*) (*gén*) driver; (*privé*) chauffeur; **~ d'autobus** bus driver; **voiture avec/sans ~** chauffeur-driven/self-drive car **b** [*chaudière*] fireman, stoker **2** COMP ▸ **chauffeur de camion** lorry (*Brit*) *ou* truck (*US*) driver ▸ **chauffeur du dimanche** (*hum*) Sunday driver ▸ **chauffeur de maître** chauffeur ▸ **chauffeur de taxi** taxi driver, cab driver

chauffeuse [ʃoføz] NF low armless chair, unit chair

chaulage [ʃolaʒ] NM [*sol, arbre, raisins*] liming; [*mur*] whitewashing

chauler [ʃole] ▸conjug 1◂ VT [+ *sol, arbre, raisins*] to lime; [+ *mur*] to whitewash

chaume [ʃom] NM **a** (= *reste des tiges*) stubble; (*littér* = *champs*) **les ~s** the stubble fields **b** (= *toiture*) thatch; **couvrir de ~** to thatch → **toit**

chaumer [ʃome] ▸conjug 1◂ **1** VT to clear stubble from **2** VI to clear the stubble

chaumière [ʃomjɛʀ] NF (*littér ou hum*) (little) cottage; (*à toit de chaume*) thatched cottage; **on en parlera encore longtemps dans les ~s** people will talk about it for a long time to come; **ça fait pleurer dans les ~s** [*feuilleton, film*] it's a real tear-jerker*

chaumine [ʃomin] NF† small (thatched) cottage

chaussant, e [ʃosɑ̃, ɑ̃t] ADJ (= *confortable*) well-fitting, snug-fitting; **articles ~s** footwear (*NonC*); **ces souliers sont très ~s** these shoes are a very good fit *ou* fit very well

chausse [ʃos] **1** NF (*Tech*) linen funnel **2 chausses** NFPL (*Hist*) hose

chaussée [ʃose] NF **a** (= *route, rue*) road, roadway; **traverser la ~** to cross the road; **ne reste pas sur la ~** don't stay in *ou* on the road *ou* on the roadway; **l'entretien de la ~** road maintenance; **~ pavée** (= *rue*) cobbled street; (= *route*) cobbled *ou* flagged road; **~ bombée** cambered road; **"~ glissante"** "slippery road"; **"~ déformée"** "uneven road surface" → **pont b** (= *chemin surélevé*) causeway; (= *digue*) embankment; **la ~ des Géants** the Giants' Causeway

chausse-pied (*pl* **chausse-pieds**) [ʃospje] NM shoehorn

chausser [ʃose] ▸conjug 1◂ **1** VT **a** (= *mettre des chaussures à*) [+ *personne*] to put shoes on; (= *acheter des chaussures à*) to buy shoes for; **chausse les enfants pour sortir** put the children's shoes on *ou* help the children on with their shoes and we'll go out; **chaussé de bottes/sandales** wearing boots/sandals, with boots/sandals on → **cordonnier**

b (= *mettre*) [+ *chaussures, lunettes, skis*] to put on; (*Équitation*) **~ les étriers** to put one's feet into the stirrups **c** (= *fournir en chaussures*) **ce marchand nous chausse depuis 10 ans** this shoemaker has been supplying us with shoes for 10 years **d** (= *convenir à*) to fit; **ces chaussures vous chaussent bien** those shoes fit you well *ou* are a good fit **e** (*Agr*) [+ *arbre*] to earth up **f** (*Aut*) [+ *voiture*] to fit tyres (*Brit*) *ou* tires (*US*) on; **voiture bien chaussée** car with good tyres (*Brit*) *ou* tires (*US*)

2 VI **a** **~ du 40** to take size 40 in shoes, take a (size) 40 shoe; **ces chaussures chaussent grand** *ou* **large** these shoes are wide-fitting; **chaussures qui chaussent bien le pied** well-fitting shoes

3 se chausser VPR (= *mettre ses chaussures*) to put one's shoes on; (= *acheter des chaussures*) **se (faire) ~ chez ...** to buy *ou* get one's shoes at ...; **se (faire) ~ sur mesure** to have one's shoes made to measure

chausse-trap(p)e (*pl* **chausse-trap(p)es**) [ʃostʀap] NF (*lit, fig*) trap; **tomber dans/éviter une chausse-trappe** to fall into/avoid a trap

chaussette [ʃosɛt] NF sock; **j'étais en ~s** I was in my socks; **~s russes** foot-bindings; **~s tombantes** slouch socks; **elle m'a laissé tomber comme une vieille ~*** she ditched* *ou* jilted me

chausseur [ʃosœʀ] NM (= *fabricant*) shoemaker; (= *fournisseur*) footwear specialist

chausson [ʃosɔ̃] NM **a** (= *pantoufle*) slipper; [*bébé*] bootee; [*danseur*] ballet shoe *ou* pump; **~ à pointe** blocked shoe; **~s d'escalade** climbing shoes → **point² b** (*Culin*) turnover; **~ aux pommes** apple turnover

chaussure [ʃosyʀ] **1** NF **a** (= *soulier*) shoe; **la ~ est une partie importante de l'habillement** footwear is *ou* shoes are an important part of one's dress; **rayon ~s** shoe *ou* footwear department; **trouver ~ à son pied** to find a suitable match **b** **la ~** (= *industrie*) the shoe industry; (= *commerce*) the shoe trade *ou* business

2 COMP ▸ **chaussures basses** flat shoes ▸ **chaussures cloutées** *ou* **à clous** hobnailed boots ▸ **chaussures montantes** ankle boots ▸ **chaussures de ski** ski boots ▸ **chaussures de sport** sports shoes ▸ **chaussures à talon haut** high-heeled shoes, (high) heels* ▸ **chaussures de ville** smart shoes

chaut [ʃo] VI († *ou hum*) **peu me ~** it matters little to me, it is of no import *ou* matter to me

chauve [ʃov] ADJ [*personne*] bald(-headed); [*crâne*] bald; (*littér*) [*colline, sommet*] bare; **~ comme un œuf*** *ou* **une bille*** *ou* **mon genou*** as bald as a coot

chauve-souris (*pl* **chauves-souris**) [ʃovsuʀi] NF (*Zool*) bat

chauvin, e [ʃovɛ̃, in] **1** ADJ (= *nationaliste*) chauvinistic; (*en temps de guerre*) jingoistic; (*en sport, dans ses goûts*) biased, prejudiced **2** NM,F (= *nationaliste*) chauvinist; (*en temps de guerre*) jingoist

chauvinisme [ʃovinism] NM (= *nationalisme*) chauvinism; (*en temps de guerre*) jingoism; (*en sport, dans ses goûts*) bias, prejudice

chaux [ʃo] NF **~ lime; ~ éteinte** slaked lime; **~ vive** quicklime; **blanchi** *ou* **passé à la ~** whitewashed; **bâti à ~ et à sable** (*littér*) [*maison*] as solid as a rock; [*personne*] as strong as an ox

chavirage [ʃaviʀaʒ] NM [*bateau*] capsizing, keeling over, overturning

chavirement [ʃaviʀmɑ̃] NM upheaval (**de** in)

chavirer [ʃaviʀe] ▸conjug 1◂ **1** VI **a** [*bateau*] to capsize, keel over, overturn; [*gouvernement*] to founder; **faire ~ un bateau** to keel a boat over, capsize *ou* overturn a boat **b** [*pile d'objets*] to keel over; [*charrette*] to overturn, tip over; [*yeux*] to roll; [*paysage, chambre*] to reel, spin; [*esprit*] to reel; **mon cœur a chaviré** (*de dégoût*) my stomach heaved; (*d'émotion*) my heart leapt **2** VT **a** (= *renverser*) [+ *bateau*] [*vagues*] to capsize, overturn; (*en cale sèche*) to keel over; [+ *meubles*] to overturn **b** (= *bouleverser*) [+ *personne*] **j'en étais tout chaviré*** (*ému*) I was quite overcome; (*affligé*) I was quite shaken; **musique qui chavire l'âme** music that tugs at the heartstrings

chéchia [ʃeʃja] NF tarboosh, fez

check-list (*pl* **check-lists**) [(t)ʃɛklist] NF check list

check-point (*pl* **check-points**) [(t)ʃɛkpojnt] NM checkpoint

check-up [(t)ʃekœp] NM INV check-up

chef¹ [ʃɛf] **1** NM,F **a** (= *patron, dirigeant*) head, boss*; [*tribu*] chief(tain), headman; **~ indien** Indian chief; **il a l'estime de ses ~s** he is highly thought of by his superiors *ou* bosses; **la ~*** the boss*; **grand ~*** big chief *ou* boss*; (*péj*) **faire le** *ou* **jouer au petit ~** to throw one's weight around

b [*expédition, révolte, syndicat*] leader; **~ spirituel** spiritual leader; **avoir une âme** *ou* **un tempérament de ~** to be a born leader **c** (* = *champion*) **tu es un ~** you're the greatest*, you're the tops*; **elle se débrouille comme un ~** she is doing a first-class job **d** (*Mil: au sergent*) **oui, ~!** yes, Sarge! **e** (*Culin*) chef; **spécialité du ~** chef's speciality; **pâté du ~** chef's special pâté; **~ de cuisine** head chef; **grand ~** master chef **f** (*Hér*) chief **g** **commandant en ~** commander-in-chief; **général en ~** general-in-chief; **ingénieur en ~** chief engineer; **le général commandait en ~ les troupes alliées** the general was the commander-in-chief of the allied troops

2 ADJ INV **gardien/médecin ~** chief warden/consultant

3 COMP ▸ **chef d'antenne** branch manager ▸ **chef d'atelier** (shop) foreman ▸ **chef de bande** gang leader ▸ **chef de bataillon** major (in the infantry) ▸ **chef de bureau**

head clerk ► **chef de cabinet** principal private secretary (de to) ► **chef de chantier** (works (*Brit*) *ou* site) foreman ► **chef des chœurs** choirmaster ► **chef de classe** ≈ class monitor *ou* prefect (*Brit*) *ou* president (*US*) ► **chef de clinique** ≈ senior registrar ► **chef comptable** chief accountant ► **chef de dépôt** shed *ou* yard master ► **chef d'école** (*Art, Littérat*) leader of a school ► **chef d'entreprise** company director ► **chef d'équipe** foreman ► **chef d'escadron** major (in the cavalry) ► **chef d'État** head of state; **le ~ de l'État** the Head of State ► **chef d'état-major** chief of staff; **~s d'état-major** Joint Chiefs of Staff ► **chef de famille** head of the family *ou* household; (*Admin*) householder ► **chef de file** (*gén, Art*) leader; (*Pol*) party leader; (*Naut*) leading ship; (*Banque*) lead bank ► **chef de gare** station master ► **chef de gouvernement** head of government ► **chef mécanicien** chief mechanic; (*Rail*) head driver (*Brit*), chief engineer (*US*) ► **chef de musique** bandmaster ► **chef de nage** stroke (oar) ► **chef d'orchestre** (*gén*) conductor, director (*US*); (*jazz etc*) (band) leader ► **chef de patrouille** patrol leader ► **chef de pièce** (*Mil*) captain of a gun ► **chef de produit** product manager, brand manager ► **chef de projet** project manager ► **chef de rayon** department(al) supervisor, departmental manager ► **chef de service** section *ou* departmental head; (*Méd*) ≈ consultant ► **chef de train** guard (*Brit*), conductor (*US*)

chef² [ʃɛf] NM ⓐ (†† *ou hum* = *tête*) head ⓑ (*Jur* = *charge*) **~ d'accusation** charge, count (of indictment) ⓒ (*loc*) (*Jur*) **posséder qch de son ~** to own sth in one's own right; (*frm*) **de son propre ~** on his own initiative, off his own bat; (*littér*) **au premier ~** greatly, exceedingly; **cela m'intéresse au premier ~** it's of the greatest *ou* utmost interest to me; (*littér*) **de ce ~** accordingly, hence

chef-d'œuvre (*pl* **chefs-d'œuvre**) [ʃɛdœvʀ] NM masterpiece, chef-d'œuvre; (*fig*) **c'est un ~ d'hypocrisie/d'ironie** it is the ultimate hypocrisy/irony

chefferie [ʃɛfʀi] NM (*Anthropologie*) chieftainship; (*Méd*) consultancy

chef-lieu (*pl* **chefs-lieux**) [ʃɛfljø] NM ≈ county town

cheftaine [ʃɛftɛn] NF [*louveteaux*] cubmistress (*Brit*), den mother (*US*); [*jeunes éclaireuses*] Brown Owl (*Brit*), troop leader (*US*); [*éclaireuses*] (guide) captain, guider

cheik [ʃɛk] NM sheik

chelem [ʃlɛm] NM (*Cartes*) slam; **petit/grand ~** small/grand slam; (*Sport*) **faire le grand ~** to do the grand slam

chemin [ʃ(ə)mɛ̃] ① NM ⓐ (*gén*) path; (= *route*) lane; (= *piste*) track → **croisée², voleur** ⓑ (= *parcours, trajet, direction*) way (**de, pour** to); **demander/trouver le** *ou* **son ~** to ask/find the *ou* one's way; **montrer le ~ à qn** to show sb the way; **il y a bien une heure de ~** it takes a good hour to get there; **quel ~ a-t-elle pris ?** which way did she go?; **de bon matin, ils prirent le ~ de la côte** they set out *ou* off for the coast early in the morning; **le ~ le plus court entre deux points** the shortest distance between two points; **ils ont fait tout le ~ à pied/en bicyclette** they walked/cycled all the way *ou* the whole way; **on a fait du ~ depuis une heure** we've come quite a way in an hour; **se mettre en ~** to set out *ou* off; **poursuivre son ~** to carry on *ou* continue on one's way; (*littér*) **passez votre ~** go your way (*littér*), be on your way; **~ faisant** ◊ **en ~** on the way; **pour venir, nous avons pris le ~ des écoliers** we came the long way round; (*fig*) **aller son ~** to go one's own sweet way; **être toujours sur les ~s** to be always on the road ■ (*PROV*) **tous les ~s mènent à Rome** all roads

lead to Rome (*PROV*) → **rebrousser** ⓒ (*fig*) path, way, road; **le ~ de l'honneur/de la gloire** the path *ou* way of honour/to glory; **le ~ de la ruine** the road to ruin; **nos ~s se sont croisés** our paths crossed → **droit²** ⓓ (*loc*) **il a encore du ~ à faire** he's still got a long way to go; **faire son ~ dans la vie** to make one's way in life; **il a fait du ~ !** (*arriviste, jeune cadre*) he has come up in the world; (*savant, chercheur*) he has come a long way; **cette idée a fait son ~** this idea has gained ground; (*concession*) **faire la moitié du ~** to meet sb half-way; **se mettre dans** *ou* **sur le ~ de qn** to stand *ou* get in sb's way, stand in sb's path; **il est toujours sur mon ~** (*présent*) he turns up wherever I go; (*comme obstacle*) he always stands in my way; **montrer le ~** to lead the way; **il n'y arrivera pas par ce ~** he won't achieve anything this way, he won't get far if he goes about it this way; **être sur le bon ~** to be on the right track; **ne t'arrête pas en si bon ~ !** don't stop now when you're doing so well *ou* after such a good start; **trouver des difficultés sur son ~** to meet with difficulties; **cela n'en prend pas le ~** it doesn't look very likely; **est-ce qu'il va réussir ? — il n'en prend pas le ~** will he succeed? — not if he goes about it like that; (*Rel*) **le ~ de Damas** the road to Damascus; **trouver son ~ de Damas** to see the light

② COMP ► **chemin d'accès** (*Ordin*) access path ► **chemin charretier** cart track ► **chemin creux** sunken lane ► **chemin critique** (*Ordin*) critical path ► **le chemin de croix (du Christ)** the Way of the Cross; (*dans une église*) the Stations of the Cross ► **chemin de fer** railway (*Brit*), railroad (*US*); (= *moyen de transport*) rail; **par ~ de fer** by rail; **employé des ~s de fer** railway (*Brit*) *ou* railroad (*US*) worker ► **chemin de halage** towpath ► **chemin de ronde** parapet *ou* rampart walk ► **chemin de table** table runner ► **chemin de terre** dirt track ► **chemin de traverse** path across *ou* through the fields ► **chemin vicinal** country road *ou* lane, minor road

chemineau (*pl* **chemineaux**) [ʃ(ə)mino] NM (†† = *vagabond*) vagabond

cheminée [ʃ(ə)mine] ① NF ⓐ (*extérieure*) [*maison, usine*] chimney (stack); [*paquebot, locomotive*] funnel, smokestack ⓑ (*intérieure*) fireplace; (= *foyer*) fireplace, hearth; (= *encadrement*) mantelpiece, chimney piece; **un feu crépitait dans la ~** a fire was crackling in the hearth *ou* fireplace *ou* grate → **feu¹** ⓒ [*volcan*] vent; (*Alpinisme*) chimney; [*lampe*] chimney ② COMP ► **cheminée d'aération** ventilation shaft ► **cheminée des fées** earth pillar ► **cheminée prussienne** (closed) stove ► **cheminée d'usine** factory chimney

cheminement [ʃ(ə)minmɑ̃] NM (= *progression*) [*caravane, marcheurs*] progress, advance; [*troupes*] advance (under cover); [*sentier, itinéraire, eau*] course, way; [*idées, pensée*] development, progression; **il est difficile de suivre son ~ intellectuel** it is difficult to follow his reasoning *ou* line of thought

cheminer [ʃ(ə)mine] ▶ conjug 1 ◀ VI (*littér*) ⓐ (= *marcher*) to walk (along); (*Mil* = *avancer à couvert*) to advance (under cover); **~ péniblement** to trudge (wearily) along; **après avoir longtemps cheminé** having plodded along for ages; **nous cheminions vers la ville** we wended (*littér*) our way towards the town ⓑ [*sentier*] to make its way (**dans** along); [*eau*] to make its way, follow its course (**dans** along); [*idées*] to follow their course; **l'idée cheminait lentement dans sa tête** the idea was slowly taking root in his mind, he was slowly coming round to the idea; **sa pensée cheminait de façon tortueuse** his thoughts followed a tortuous course; **les eaux de la Durance cheminent entre les falaises** the waters of the

Durance flow between cliffs *ou* make their way between cliffs

cheminot [ʃ(ə)mino] NM railwayman (*Brit*), railroad man (*US*)

chemisage [ʃ(ə)mizaʒ] NM (*intérieur*) lining; (*extérieur*) jacketing

chemise [ʃ(ə)miz] ① NF ⓐ (*Habillement*) [*homme*] shirt; †† [*femme*] chemise†, shift†; [*bébé*] vest (*Brit*), undershirt (*US*); **~ de soirée/de sport** dress/sports shirt; **être en manches** *ou* **bras de ~** to be in one's shirt sleeves; **col/manchette de ~** shirt collar/cuff; **je m'en moque comme de ma première ~*** I couldn't care less*, I don't care a hoot* *ou* two hoots* ⓑ (= *dossier*) folder; (*Tech*) (= *revêtement intérieur*) lining; (= *revêtement extérieur*) jacket; (*Aut*) **~ de cylindre** cylinder liner ② COMP ► **chemise (américaine)** (woman's) vest (*Brit*) *ou* undershirt (*US*) ► **chemises brunes** (*Hist*) Brown Shirts ► **chemise d'homme** man's shirt ► **chemise de maçonnerie** facing ► **chemises noires** (*Hist*) Blackshirts ► **chemise de nuit** [*femme*] nightdress, nightie*; [*homme*] nightshirt ► **chemises rouges** (*Hist*) Redshirts

chemiser [ʃ(ə)mize] ▶ conjug 1 ◀ VT [+ *intérieur*] to line; [+ *extérieur*] to jacket

chemiserie [ʃ(ə)mizʀi] NF (= *magasin*) (men's) shirt shop; (= *rayon*) shirt department; (= *commerce*) shirt(-making) trade *ou* business

chemisette [ʃ(ə)mizɛt] NF [*homme*] short-sleeved shirt; [*femme*] short-sleeved blouse

chemisier, -ière [ʃ(ə)mizje, jɛʀ] ① NM,F (= *marchand*) (gentlemen's) shirtmaker; (= *fabricant*) shirtmaker ② NM (= *vêtement*) blouse → **col, robe**

chênaie [ʃɛnɛ] NF oak grove

chenal (*pl* **-aux**) [ʃənal, o] ① NM (= *canal*) channel, fairway; (= *rigole*) channel; [*moulin*] millrace; [*forge, usine*] flume ② COMP ► **chenal de coulée** (*Ind*) gate, runner ► **chenal pro-glaciaire** glaciated valley

chenapan [ʃ(ə)napɑ̃] NM (*hum* = *garnement*) scallywag (*hum*), rascal (*hum*); (*péj* = *vaurien*) scoundrel, rogue

chêne [ʃɛn] ① NM (= *arbre*) oak (tree); (= *bois*) oak ② COMP ► **chêne pubescent** pubescent oak ► **chêne rouvre** *ou* **sessile** durmast *ou* sessile oaktree ► **chêne vert** holm oak, ilex

chéneau (*pl* **chéneaux**) [ʃeno] NM [*toit*] gutter

chêne-liège (*pl* **chênes-lièges**) [ʃɛnljɛʒ] NM cork oak

chenet [ʃ(ə)nɛ] NM firedog, andiron

chènevis [ʃɛnvi] NM hempseed

chenil [ʃ(ə)nil] NM kennels (*Brit*), kennel (*US*); **mettre son chien dans un ~** to put one's dog in kennels

chenille [ʃ(ə)nij] ① NF ⓐ (*Aut, Zool*) caterpillar; **véhicule à ~s** tracked vehicle ⓑ (*Tex*) chenille ② COMP ► **chenille du mûrier** silkworm ► **chenille processionnaire** processionary caterpillar

chenillé, e [ʃ(ə)nije] ADJ [*véhicule*] with caterpillar tracks, tracked

chenillette [ʃ(ə)nijɛt] NF (= *véhicule*) tracked vehicle

chenu, e [ʃəny] ADJ (*littér*) [*vieillard, tête*] hoary; [*arbre*] leafless with age

cheptel [ʃɛptɛl] ① NM (= *bétail*) livestock; (*Jur*) livestock (leased); **~ ovin d'une région** sheep population of an area ② COMP ► **cheptel mort** farm implements ► **cheptel vif** livestock

chèque [ʃɛk] ① NM ⓐ (*Banque*) cheque (*Brit*), check (*US*); **faire/toucher un ~** to write *ou* make out/cash a cheque; **~ de 100 F** cheque for 100 francs → **barrer** ⓑ (= *bon*) voucher; **~-déjeuner**® *ou* **-repas** *ou* **-restaurant**® luncheon voucher (*Brit*), meal ticket (*US*); **~-cadeau** gift token; **~-essence**

petrol (*Brit*) *ou* gasoline (*US*) coupon *ou* voucher

② COMP ▶ **chèque bancaire** cheque ▶ **chèque de banque** banker's *ou* cashier's cheque ▶ **chèque en blanc** (*lit, fig*) blank cheque ▶ **chèque en bois*** dud cheque* (*Brit*), rubber cheque* ▶ **chèque certifié** certified cheque ▶ **chèque de dépannage** loose cheque (*supplied by bank when customer does not have his own chequebook*) ▶ **chèque emploi service** *automatic welfare deduction system for pay cheques for domestic help* ▶ **chèque à ordre** cheque to order, order cheque ▶ **chèque au porteur** bearer cheque ▶ **chèque postal** *cheque drawn on a post office account*; **les ~s postaux** (= *service*) the banking departments of the post office ▶ **chèque sans provision** bad cheque ▶ **chèque de voyage** traveller's cheque

chéquier [ʃekje] NM chequebook (*Brit*), checkbook (*US*)

cher, chère¹ [ʃɛʀ] ① ADJ ⓐ (*gén après nom* = *aimé*) [*personne, souvenir, vœu*] dear (**à** to); **ceux qui** *ou* **les êtres qui nous sont ~s** our nearest and dearest, our loved ones; **des souvenirs ~s** fond memories; **des souvenirs ~s à mon cœur** memories dear to my heart; **c'est mon vœu le plus ~** it's my fondest *ou* dearest wish; **mon désir le plus ~** *ou* **mon plus ~ désir est de ...** my greatest *ou* most cherished desire is to ...; **l'honneur est le bien le plus ~** honour is one's most precious possession, one's honour is to be treasured above all else; **selon une formule chère au président** as a favourite saying of the president goes, to quote a favourite expression of the president
ⓑ (*avant nom*) dear; **(mes) ~s auditeurs** dear listeners; (*Rel*) **mes bien ~s frères** my dear(est) brethren; **Monsieur et ~ collègue** dear colleague; **ce ~ (vieux) Louis !*** that old Louis!*; (*hum*) **le ~ homme n'y entendait pas malice** the dear man didn't mean any harm to it; **il était content de retrouver ses ~s livres** he was glad to be back with his beloved books; **elle a retrouvé ses chères habitudes** she slipped back into the old habits she holds so dear; (*sur lettre*) **~s tous** dear all
ⓒ (*après nom* = *coûteux*) expensive, dear (*Brit*); **un petit restaurant pas ~** an inexpensive *ou* a reasonably priced little restaurant; **c'est vraiment pas ~ !** it's really cheap!; **la vie est chère à Paris** the cost of living is high in Paris, Paris is an expensive place to live; **c'est moins ~ qu'en face** it's cheaper than *ou* less expensive than in the shop opposite; **cet épicier est trop ~** this grocer is too expensive *ou* too dear (*Brit*) *ou* charges too much; **c'est trop ~ pour ce que c'est** it's overpriced → **vie**

② NM,F (*frm ou hum*) **mon ~** ◊ **ma chère** my dear; **oui, très ~** yes, dearest; **son ~ et tendre** her other *ou* better half (*hum*)

③ ADV [*valoir, coûter, payer*] a lot (of money), a great deal (of money); **article qui vaut** *ou* **coûte ~** expensive item, item that costs a lot *ou* a great deal; **as-tu payé ~ ton costume?** did you pay much *ou* a lot for your suit?, was your suit (very) expensive?; **il se fait payer ~** ◊ **il prend** ~ he charges a lot, he's expensive; **il vend ~** his prices are high, he charges high prices; **ça s'est vendu ~** it went for *ou* fetched a high price *ou* a lot (of money); **je ne l'ai pas acheté ~** ◊ **je l'ai eu pour pas ~** I didn't pay much for it, I got it cheap*; **je donnerais ~ pour savoir ce qu'il fait*** I'd give anything to know what he's doing; **je ne donne pas ~ de sa vie/de sa réussite** I wouldn't like to bet on his chances of survival/succeeding, I wouldn't rate his chances of survival/ succeeding very highly; **il ne vaut pas ~** he's a good-for-nothing; **tu ne vaux pas plus ~ que lui** you're no better than he is *ou* than him, you're just as bad as he is; **son imprudence lui a coûté ~** his rashness cost him dear (*Brit*) *ou*

a great deal (*US*); **il a payé ~ son imprudence** he paid dearly *ou* heavily for his rashness

chercher [ʃɛʀʃe] ▶ conjug 1 ◀ ① VT ⓐ (= *essayer de trouver*) [+ *personne, chose égarée, emploi*] to look for, search for, try to find; [+ *solution, moyen*] to look for, seek, try to find; [+ *ombre, lumière, tranquillité*] to seek; [+ *citation, heure de train*] to look up; [+ *nom, terme*] to try to remember; [+ *raison, excuse*] to cast about for, try to find, look for; **~ un mot dans un dictionnaire** to look up a word in a dictionary; **~ qn du regard** *ou* **des yeux** to look *ou* glance around for sb; **~ qch à tâtons** to grope *ou* fumble for sth; **attends, je cherche** wait a minute, I'm trying to think; **il n'a pas bien cherché** he didn't look very hard; **~ partout qch/qn** to search *ou* hunt everywhere for sth/ sb; **~ sa voie** to look for *ou* seek a path in life; **il cherchait ses mots** he was struggling to find the right words; (*à un chien*) **cherche ! cherche !** fetch!; **ce n'est pas la peine de ~ bien loin, c'est lui qui l'a fait** you don't have to look too far, he's the one who did it
ⓑ (= *viser à*) [+ *gloire, succès*] to seek (after); (= *rechercher*) [+ *alliance, faveur*] to seek; **il ne cherche que son intérêt** he's only out for himself
ⓒ (= *provoquer*) [+ *danger, mort*] to court; **~ la difficulté** to look for difficulties; **~ la bagarre** to be looking *ou* spoiling for a fight; **tu l'auras cherché !** you've been asking for it!; **il l'a bien cherché** he asked for it, he had it coming to him; **si on me cherche, on me trouve*** if anyone asks for it they'll get it*; **tu me cherches?*** are you looking for trouble?; **~ le contact avec l'ennemi** to try to engage the enemy in combat
ⓓ (= *prendre, acheter*) **aller ~ qch/qn** to go for sth/sb, go and get *ou* fetch (*Brit*) sth/sb; **il est venu ~ Paul** he called *ou* came for Paul, he came to get *ou* to fetch (*Brit*) Paul; **il est allé me ~ de la monnaie** he's gone to get me some change; **va me ~ mon sac** go and get *ou* fetch (*Brit*) my bag; **qu'est-ce que tu vas ~?** **je n'ai rien dit !** what do you mean? I didn't say a thing!; **où est-ce qu'il va ~ toutes ces idées idiotes !** where does he get all those stupid ideas from!; **monter/descendre ~ qch** to go up/down for sth *ou* to get sth; **aller ~ qch dans un tiroir** to go and get sth out of a drawer; **il est allé/venu le ~ à la gare** he went/came to meet *ou* collect him at the station; **aller ~ les enfants à l'école** to go to get *ou* collect *ou* fetch (*Brit*) the children from school; **envoyer ~ le médecin** to send for the doctor; **envoyer qn ~ le médecin** to send sb to get the doctor; **ça va ~ dans les 300 F** it'll come to around 300 francs; **ça va ~ dans les 5 ans de prison** it will mean something like 5 years in prison; (*amende*) **ça peut aller ~ loin** it could mean a heavy fine
ⓔ **~ à faire** to try to do, attempt to do; **~ à comprendre** to try to understand; **faut pas ~ à comprendre*** don't even try and understand; **~ à faire plaisir à qn** to try *ou* endeavour to please sb; **~ à obtenir qch** to try to get *ou* obtain sth; **~ à savoir qch** to try *ou* attempt to find out sth
ⓕ (*loc*) **~ midi à quatorze heures** to complicate the issue; **~ la petite bête** to split hairs; **~ une aiguille dans une botte** *ou* **meule de foin** to look for a needle in a haystack; **~ des poux dans la tête de qn*** to try to make trouble for sb; **~ querelle à qn** to try to pick a quarrel with sb; **cherchez la femme !** chercher la femme! → **crosse, fortune, histoire, noise, salut**

② **se chercher** VPR (= *chercher sa voie*) to search for an identity; **il se cherche encore** he hasn't found himself yet

chercheur, -euse [ʃɛʀʃœʀ, øz] ① ADJ [*esprit*] inquiring → **tête** ② NM [*télescope*] finder; [*détecteur à galène*] cat's whisker; **~ de fuites** gas-leak detector ③ NM,F (= *scientifique*) re-

searcher, research worker; **~ de** (*gén*) seeker of; **~ d'aventure(s)** adventure seeker, seeker after adventure; **~ d'or** gold digger; **~ de trésors** treasure hunter

chère² [ʃɛʀ] NF (†† *ou hum*) food, fare, cheer†; **faire bonne ~** to eat well, have a good meal; **aimer la bonne ~** to love one's food

chèrement [ʃɛʀmɑ̃] ADV ⓐ (= *durement*) dearly; **~ acquis** *ou* **payé** [*avantage, victoire*] dearly bought *ou* won; **vendre ~ sa vie** to sell one's life dearly ⓑ (= *avec affection*) [*aimer*] dearly ⓒ († = *au prix fort*) [*vendre*] at a high price, dearly†

chéri, e [ʃeʀi] (*ptp de chérir*) ① ADJ (= *bien-aimé*) beloved, darling, dear(est); **quand il a revu son fils ~** when he saw his beloved son again; **c'est l'enfant ~ du parti** he's the darling of the party; **maman ~e** mother dear, mother darling; (*sur tombe*) **« à notre père ~ »** "to our dearly beloved father" ② NM,F ⓐ (*terme d'affection*) darling; **mon ~** (my) darling; (*hum*) **bonjour mes ~s** hullo darlings (*hum*) ⓑ (*péj = préféré*) **c'est le ~ à sa maman*** he's mummy's (*Brit*) *ou* mommy's (*US*) little darling *ou* blue-eyed boy; **c'est la ~e de ses parents** she's the apple of her parents' eye, her parents dote on her

chérif [ʃeʀif] NM sherif

chérir [ʃeʀiʀ] ▶ conjug 2 ◀ VT (*littér*) [+ *personne*] to cherish, love dearly; [+ *liberté, idée*] to cherish, hold dear; [+ *souvenir*] to cherish, treasure

Cherokee [ʃeʀoki] NMF Cherokee

chérot* [ʃeʀo] ADJ M (= *coûteux*) pricey* (*Brit*), expensive

cherry [ʃeʀi], **cherry brandy** [ʃeʀibʀɑ̃di] NM cherry brandy

cherté [ʃɛʀte] NF [*article*] high price, dearness (*Brit*); [*époque, région*] high prices (**de** in); **la ~ de la vie** the high cost of living, the cost of things*

chérubin [ʃeʀybɛ̃] NM (*lit, fig*) cherub; **~s** (*Art*) cherubs; (*Rel*) cherubim

chétif, -ive [ʃetif, iv] ADJ ⓐ (= *malingre*) [*personne*] puny, sickly; [*plante*] scrawny, stunted; **enfant à l'aspect ~** weedy-looking *ou* puny-looking child ⓑ (= *minable*) [*récolte*] meagre (*Brit*), meager (*US*), poor; [*existence*] meagre (*Brit*), meager (*US*), mean; [*repas*] skimpy, scanty; [*raisonnement*] paltry, feeble

chétivement [ʃetivmɑ̃] ADV [*pousser*] punily

chevaine [ʃ(ə)vɛn] NM = **chevesne**

cheval [ʃ(ə)val] (*pl* **-aux**) [ʃ(ə)val, o] ① NM ⓐ (= *animal*) horse; (= *viande*) horsemeat; **carrosse à deux/à six chevaux** coach and pair/and six; **faire du ~** to go horse-riding; **tu sais faire du ~?** can you ride (a horse)?; (*péj*) **c'est un grand ~, cette fille** she's a strapping lass; **au travail, c'est un vrai ~** he works like a Trojan; **ce n'est pas le mauvais ~** he's not a bad sort *ou* soul; **tu as mangé** *ou* **bouffé* du ~ !** you're full of beans!*; **c'est changer un ~ borgne pour un aveugle** it's jumping out of the frying pan into the fire; **ça ne se trouve pas sous le pas** *ou* **le sabot d'un ~** it doesn't grow on trees; **on ne change pas de ~ au milieu du gué** you don't change horses in midstream → **miser, monter¹, petit 5**
ⓑ (*Aut*) horsepower (*NonC*); **elle fait combien de chevaux?** how many cc's is it?, what horsepower is it?; **c'est une 6 chevaux** it's a 6 horsepower car
ⓒ (*arg Drogue*) horse, (big) H
ⓓ (*loc*) **à ~** on horseback; **se tenir bien à ~** to have a good seat, sit well on horseback; **être à ~ sur une chaise** to be (sitting) astride a chair, be straddling a chair; **village à ~ sur deux départements** village straddling two departments; **à ~ sur deux mois** overlapping two (different) months, running from one month into the next; **être à ~ sur deux cultures** [*ville, pays*] to be at the crossroads of two cultures; [*personne*] to have roots in two cultures;

[œuvre] to be rooted in ou to span two cultures; **être (très) à ~ sur le règlement/les principes** to be a (real) stickler for the rules/ for principles; **monter sur ses grands chevaux** to get on one's high horse; **de ~*** [remède] drastic; [fièvre] raging

② COMP ► **cheval d'arçons** pommel horse ► **cheval d'attelage** plough (Brit) ou plow (US) horse ► **cheval à bascule** rocking horse ► **cheval de bataille** (Mil) battle horse, charger; (fig) **il a ressorti son ~ de bataille** he's back on his hobby-horse ou his favourite theme again; **l'opposition en a fait son ~ de bataille** the opposition have made it their key issue ou main concern ► **cheval de bois** wooden horse; **monter ou aller sur les chevaux de bois** to go on the merry-go-round ou roundabout (Brit); († ou hum) **manger avec les chevaux de bois** to miss a meal, go dinnerless ► **cheval de chasse** hunter ► **cheval de cirque** circus horse ► **cheval de course** racehorse ► **cheval de fiacre** carriage horse ► **cheval fiscal** horsepower (for tax purposes) ► **chevaux de frise** chevaux-de-frise ► **cheval de labour** carthorse, plough (Brit) ou plow (US) horse ► **cheval de manège** school horse ► **cheval marin** ou **de mer** sea horse ► **cheval de poste** ou **de relais** post horse ► **(vieux) cheval de retour** recidivist, old lag* (Brit) ► **cheval de saut** vaulting horse ► **cheval de selle** saddle horse ► **cheval de trait** draught horse (Brit), draft horse (US) ► **le cheval de Troie** (lit, fig) the Trojan horse, the Wooden Horse of Troy

chevalement [ʃ(ə)valmã] NM [mur] shoring; [galerie] (pit)head frame

chevaler [ʃ(ə)vale] ▶ conjug 1 ◀ VT [+ mur] to shore up

chevaleresque [ʃ(ə)valʀɛsk] ADJ [caractère, conduite] chivalrous, gentlemanly; **règles ~s** rules of chivalry; **l'honneur ~** the honour of a knight, knightly honour

chevalerie [ʃ(ə)valʀi] NF (Hist = institution) chivalry; (= dignité, chevaliers) knighthood → **roman¹**

chevalet [ʃ(ə)valɛ] NM a (peintre) easel; (Menuiserie) trestle, sawhorse (Brit), sawbuck (US); [violon] bridge; (à feuilles mobiles) flip chart b (Hist = torture) **le ~ rack**

chevalier [ʃ(ə)valje] ① NM a (Hist) knight; **faire qn ~** to knight sb, dub sb knight; **« je te fais ~ »** "I dub you knight" b (= membre) [ordre français] chevalier; [ordre britannique] knight; ► **de la Légion d'honneur** Knight of the Legion of Honour c (= oiseau) sandpiper ② COMP ► **chevalier aboyeur** (Orn) greenshank ► **chevalier blanc** (Fin) white knight ► **chevalier errant** knight-errant ► **chevalier gambette** (Orn) redshank ► **chevalier gris** (Fin) grey knight ► **chevalier d'industrie** crook, swindler ► **chevalier noir** (Fin) black knight ► **chevalier servant** (attentive) escort ► **chevalier de la Table ronde** Knight of the Round Table ► **chevaliers teutoniques** Teutonic Knights ► **le chevalier à la Triste Figure** the Knight of the Sorrowful Countenance

chevalière [ʃ(ə)valjɛʀ] NF signet ring

chevalin, e [ʃ(ə)valɛ̃, in] ADJ [race] of horses, equine; [visage, œil] horsy → **boucherie**

cheval-vapeur (pl **chevaux-vapeur**) [ʃ(ə)valvapœʀ] NM horsepower

chevauchée [ʃ(ə)voʃe] NF (= course) ride; (= cavaliers, cavalcade) cavalcade

chevauchement [ʃ(ə)voʃmã] NM (gén) overlapping; (Géol) thrust fault

chevaucher [ʃ(ə)voʃe] ▶ conjug 1 ◀ ① VT a [+ cheval, âne] to be astride; [+ chaise] to sit astride, straddle; **de grosses lunettes lui chevauchaient le nez** a large pair of glasses sat on his nose; **le pont chevauche l'abîme** the

bridge spans the abyss b [+ tuiles] to overlap, lap over ② **se chevaucher** VPR [dents, tuiles, lettres] to overlap (each other); (Géol) [couches] to overthrust, override ③ VI a († ou littér = aller à cheval) to ride (on horseback) b = **se chevaucher**

chevau-léger (pl **chevau-légers**) [ʃ(ə)voleʒe] NM (Hist = soldat) member of the Household Cavalry; (= troupe) **~s** Household Cavalry

chevêche [ʃ(ə)vɛʃ] NF little owl

chevelu, e [ʃəv(ə)ly] ADJ [personne] (gén) with a good crop of ou a long mane of hair; (péj) long-haired; [tête] hairy; [épi] tufted; [racine] bearded → **cuir**

chevelure [ʃəv(ə)lyʀ] NF a (= cheveux) hair (NonC); **une ~ malade/terne** unhealthy/dull hair; **elle avait une ~ abondante/une flamboyante ~ rousse** she had thick hair ou a thick head of hair/a shock of flaming red hair; **sa ~ était magnifique** her hair was magnificent b [comète] tail

chevesne [ʃ(ə)vɛn] NM chub

chevet [ʃ(ə)vɛ] NM a (lit) bed(head); **au ~ de qn** at sb's bedside → **lampe, livre¹, table** b (Archit) [église] chevet

cheveu (pl **cheveux**) [ʃ(ə)vø] ① NM a (gén pl) hair; (= chevelure) **~x** hair (NonC); (collectif) **il a le ~ rare** he's balding, his hair is thinning; **une femme aux ~x blonds/frisés** a fair-haired/curly-haired woman, a woman with fair/curly hair; **avoir les ~x en désordre** ou **en bataille** ou **hirsutes** to have untidy ou disheveled hair; **(les) ~x au vent** hair streaming in the wind; **elle s'est trouvé 2 ~x blancs** she has found 2 white hairs; **en ~x†** hatless, bareheaded; **il n'a pas un ~ sur la tête** ou **le caillou*** he hasn't a (single) hair on his head → **coupe², brosse, épingle, filet** b (loc) **leur survie n'a tenu qu'à un ~ ◊ il s'en est fallu d'un ~ qu'ils ne se tuent** they escaped death by a whisker; **son accord n'a tenu qu'à un ~** it was touch and go whether he would agree; **il s'en faut d'un ~ qu'il ne change d'avis** it's touch and go whether he'll change his mind; **si vous osez toucher à un ~ de cet enfant** if you dare touch ou if you so much as touch a hair of this child's head; **avoir mal aux ~x*** to have a hangover; **avoir un ~ (sur la langue)*** to have a lisp; **se faire des ~x (blancs)*** to worry o.s. sick*; **arriver comme un ~ sur la soupe*** [personne] to turn up at the most awkward moment; [remarque] to be completely irrelevant; **tiré par les ~x** [histoire] far-fetched; **il y a un ~*** there's a hitch* ou snag*; **il va y trouver un ~*** he's not going to like it one bit; **se prendre aux ~x** to come to blows → **arracher, couper**

② COMP ► **cheveux d'ange** (= vermicelle) angel hair pasta; (= décoration) Christmas floss ► **cheveux de Vénus** maidenhair (fern)

chevillard [ʃ(ə)vijaʀ] NM wholesale butcher

cheville [ʃ(ə)vij] NF a (Anat) ankle; **l'eau lui venait** ou **arrivait à la ~** ou **aux ~s** he was ankle-deep in water, the water came up to his ankles; (fig) **aucun ne lui arrive à la ~** he's head and shoulders above the others, there's no one to touch him; (péj) **avoir les ~s qui enflent*** to be full of oneself, have a swollen ou swelled head* (US); (péj) **t'as pas les ~s qui enflent?*** you're very full of yourself, aren't you?; (péj) **ça va les ~s?*** bighead!* b (= fiche) (pour joindre) dowel, peg, pin; (pour vis) plug; (Mus) [instrument à cordes] peg; (Boucherie = crochet) hook; **vendre de la viande à la ~** to sell meat wholesale; **~ ouvrière** (Aut) kingpin; (fig) kingpin, mainspring c (Littérat) [poème] cheville; (péj = remplissage) padding (NonC) d (loc) **être en ~ avec qn pour faire qch** to be in cahoots* with sb to do sth, collude with sb in doing sth

cheviller [ʃ(ə)vije] ▶ conjug 1 ◀ VT (Menuiserie) to peg; **avoir l'âme chevillée au corps** to have

nine lives; **avoir l'espoir chevillé au cœur** ou **au corps** to refuse to give up hope, have a never-say-die attitude; **avoir la méchanceté chevillée au corps** to be nasty through and through, be downright nasty ou malicious

chèvre [ʃɛvʀ] ① NF a (Zool) (gén) goat; (femelle) nanny-goat; **devenir ~*** to go crazy; **je deviens ~ moi avec tous ces formulaires/enfants!*** all these forms/these children are driving me up the wall!*; **rendre** ou **faire devenir qn ~*** to drive sb up the wall* → **fromage** b (Tech) (= treuil) hoist, gin; (= chevalet) sawhorse, sawbuck (US), trestle ② NM (= fromage) goat('s) cheese, goat's-milk cheese

chevreau (pl **chevreaux**) [ʃəvʀo] NM (= animal, peau) kid; **bondir comme un ~** to gambol like a lamb

chèvrefeuille [ʃɛvʀəfœj] NM honeysuckle

chevrette [ʃəvʀɛt] NF a (= jeune chèvre) kid, young she-goat b (= chevreuil femelle) roe, doe; (= fourrure) goatskin c (= trépied) (metal) tripod

chevreuil [ʃəvʀœj] NM (Zool) roe deer; (= mâle) roebuck; (Can = cerf de Virginie) deer; (Culin) venison

chevrier [ʃəvʀije] NM (= berger) goatherd; (= haricot) (type of) kidney bean

chevrière [ʃəvʀijɛʀ] NF goatherd

chevron [ʃəvʀõ] NM (= poutre) rafter; (= galon) stripe, chevron; (= motif) chevron, V(-shape); **~s** (petits) herringbone (pattern); (grands) chevron pattern; **à ~s** (petits) herringbone; (grands) chevron-patterned

chevronné, e [ʃəvʀɔne] ADJ [alpiniste] experienced, seasoned; [soldat] seasoned; [conducteur] experienced; **un parlementaire ~** a seasoned parliamentarian

chevrotant, e [ʃəvʀɔtã, ãt] ADJ [voix] quavering, shaking; [vieillard] with a quavering voice

chevrotement [ʃəvʀɔtmã] NM [voix] quavering, shaking; [vieillard] quavering (voice)

chevroter [ʃəvʀɔte] ▶ conjug 1 ◀ VI [personne] to quaver; [voix] to quaver, shake

chevrotine [ʃəvʀɔtin] NF buckshot (NonC)

chewing-gum (pl **chewing-gums**) [ʃwingɔm] NM chewing gum (NonC); **un ~** a piece of chewing-gum

Cheyenne [ʃejɛn] NMF Cheyenne; **les ~s** the Cheyenne

chez [ʃe] PRÉP a (à la maison) **~ soi** at home; **être/rester ~ soi** to be/stay at home, be/stay in; **est-ce qu'elle sera ~ elle aujourd'hui ?** will she be at home ou in today?; **venez ~ moi** come to my place; **nous rentrons ~ nous** we are going home; **j'ai des nouvelles de ~ moi** I have news from home; **faites comme ~ vous** make yourself at home; **on n'est plus ~ soi avec tous ces touristes !** it doesn't feel like home any more with all these tourists around!; **nous l'avons trouvée ~ elle** we found her at home b **~ qn** (maison) at sb's house ou place; (appartement) at sb's place ou flat (Brit) ou apartment (US); (famille) in sb's family ou home; **~ moi nous sommes 6** there are 6 of us in my ou our family; **près de/devant/de ~ qn** near/in front of/from sb's place ou house; **de/près de ~ nous** from/near (our) home ou our place ou our house; **~ Robert/le voisin** at Robert's (house)/the neighbour's (house); **moi/son frère, c'est tout petit** my/his brother's place is tiny; **je vais ~ lui/Robert** I'm going to his place/to Robert's (place); **il séjourne ~ moi** he is staying at my place ou with me; **la personne ~ qui je suis allé** the person to whose house I went; **passons par ~ eux/mon frère** let's drop in on them/my brother, let's drop by their place/my brother's place; (sur une adresse) **~ M. Lebrun** c/o Mr Lebrun; (enseigne de café) **~ Rosalie** Rosalie's, chez Rosalie; **~ nous** (pays) in our country, at home, back home*; (région) at home, back home*; (maison) in our house, at home; ~ **nous au Canada/en Bretagne** (là-bas) back (home) in Canada/Brittany; (ici) here in Canada/Brittany; **c'est une coutume/paysanne (bien) de ~ nous** it/she is one of our typical local customs/country girls; ~ **eux/vous, il n'y a pas de parlement** in their/your country there's no parliament; **il a été élevé ~ les Jésuites** he was brought up in a Jesuit school ou by the Jesuits

☐c (avec nom de métier) ~ **l'épicier/le coiffeur** at the grocer's/the hairdresser's; **je vais ~ le boucher** I'm going to the butcher's; **il va ~ le dentiste/le médecin** he's going to the dentist('s)/the doctor('s)

☐d (avec groupe humain ou animal) among; ~ **les Français/les Romains** among the French/the Romans; ~ **les fourmis/le singe** in ants/monkeys; **on trouve cet instinct ~ les animaux** you find this instinct in animals; ~ **les politiciens** among politicians; (Sport) ~ **les hommes/les femmes** in the men's/women's

☐e (avec personne, œuvre) ~ **Balzac/Picasso on trouve de tout** in Balzac/Picasso you find a bit of everything; **c'est rare ~ un enfant de cet âge** it's rare in a child of that age; ~ **lui, c'est une habitude** it's a habit with him; ~ **lui c'est le foie qui ne va pas** it's his liver that gives him trouble

chez-soi [ʃeswa] NM INV home (of one's own); **avoir un ~** to have a home of one's own ou a home to call one's own

chiadé, e: [ʃjade] (ptp de **chiader**) ADJ (= difficile) [problème] tough*, stiff*; (= approfondi) [exposé] thorough; (= perfectionné) [appareil] clever, nifty*

chiader: [ʃjade] ▸ conjug 1 ◂ ① VT [+ leçon] to swot up* (Brit), cram; [+ examen] to cram for*, swot for* (Brit); [+ exposé] to work on, swot up* for (Brit); **il a chiadé sa lettre** he worked on his letter till it was perfect ② VI (= travailler) to swot* (Brit), slog away* (Brit), grind away* (US)

chialer* [ʃjale] ▸ conjug 1 ◂ VI (= pleurer) to blubber*

chialeur, -euse* [ʃjalœʀ, øz] NM,F crybaby*

chiant, chiante: [ʃjɑ̃, ʃjɑ̃t] ADJ [personne, problème] damn: ou bloody: (Brit) annoying; **ce roman est ~** this novel's damn: ou bloody: (Brit) boring; **c'est ~** it's a damn: ou bloody: (Brit) nuisance, it's damn: ou bloody: (Brit) annoying; ~ **comme la pluie** ou **un lundi** as boring as hell:; **tu es ~ avec tes questions!** you're a pain in the arse:: (Brit) ou ass:: (US) with all your questions!

chiard: [ʃjaʀ] NM brat

chiasme [kjasm] NM (Littérat) chiasmus

chiasse: [ʃjas] ① NF ☐a (= colique) **avoir/attraper la ~** (lit) to have/get the runs* ou the trots*; (peur) to have/get the willies*, be/get scared witless ou shitless::; **ça lui donne la ~** (lit) it gives him the runs*; (peur) it scares him witless ou shitless:: ☐b (= poisse) **c'est la ~ ◊ quelle ~** what a damn: ou bloody: (Brit) pain ② COMP ▸ **chiasse de mouche** fly speck

chiatique: [ʃjatik] ADJ [personne, problème] damn: ou bloody: (Brit) annoying

chic [ʃik] ① NM ☐a (= élégance) [toilette, chapeau] stylishness; [personne] style; **avoir du ~** [toilette, chapeau] to have style, be stylish; [personne] to have (great) style; **être habillé avec ~** to be stylishly dressed → **bon¹** ☐b (loc) **avoir le ~ pour faire qch** to have the knack of doing sth; **de ~** [peindre, dessiner] without a model, from memory; **traduire/écrire qch de ~** to translate/write sth off the cuff ② ADJ INV ☐a (= élégant) [chapeau, toilette, personne] stylish, smart ☐b (= de la bonne société) [dîner] smart, posh*; **deux messieurs ~** two smart(-looking) gentle-

men; **les gens ~** the smart set, posh* people ☐c (* = gentil, généreux) decent*, nice; **c'est une ~ fille** she's a nice girl; **c'est un ~ type** he's a decent sort ou a nice guy* ou a nice bloke* (Brit); **elle a été très ~ avec moi** she's been very nice ou decent to me; **c'est très ~ de sa part** that's very decent ou nice of him

③ EXCL ~ (alors)!* great!*

chicane [ʃikan] NF ☐a (= zigzag) [barrage routier] ins and outs, twists and turns; [circuit automobile] chicane; [gymkhana] in and out, zigzag; **des camions stationnés en ~ gênaient la circulation** lorries parked at intervals on both sides of the street held up the traffic ☐b (†: Jur = objection) quibble; (= querelle) squabble, petty quarrel; **aimer la ~ ◊ avoir l'esprit de ~** (disputes) to enjoy picking quarrels with people, enjoy bickering; (procès) to enjoy bickering over points of procedure; **chercher ~ à qn ◊ faire des ~s à qn** to pick petty quarrels with sb; **gens de ~** pettifoggers

chicaner [ʃikane] ▸ conjug 1 ◂ ① VT ☐a († ou littér) (= mesurer) ~ **qch à qn** to quibble with sb about ou over sth; (= contester) **nul ne lui chicane son courage** no one disputes his courage ou calls his courage into question ☐b († ou littér = chercher querelle à) ~ **qn (sur** ou **au sujet de qch)** to quibble ou squabble with sb (over sth); **ils se chicanent continuellement** they're constantly bickering ② VI ☐a (= ergoter) ~ **sur** to quibble about ☐b (†: Jur) to pettifog †

chicanerie† [ʃikanʀi] NF (= disputes) wrangling, petty quarrelling (NonC); (= tendance à ergoter) (constant) quibbling; **toutes ces ~s** all this quibbling

chicaneur, -euse [ʃikanœʀ, øz] ① ADJ argumentative, pettifogging ② NM,F quibbler

chicanier, -ière [ʃikanje, jɛʀ] ① ADJ quibbling ② NM,F quibbler

chicano [ʃikano] ① ADJ Chicano (souvent injurieux) ② **Chicano** NMF Chicano (souvent injurieux)

chiche¹ [ʃiʃ] ADJ → **pois**

chiche² [ʃiʃ] ADJ ☐a (= mesquin) [personne] niggardly, mean; [rétribution] niggardly, paltry, mean; [repas] scanty, meagre (Brit), meager (US); **comme cadeau, c'est un peu ~** it's a rather mean ou paltry gift; **être ~ de paroles/compliments** to be sparing with one's words/compliments ☐b (* = capable) **être ~ de faire qch** to be able to do sth ou capable of doing sth; **tu n'es pas ~ (de le faire)** you couldn't (do that); ~ **que je le fais!** I bet you I do it!, (I) bet you I will!:; ~? — ~! are you on?* ou are you game?* — you're on!*

chiche-kebab (pl **chiche(s)-kebab(s)**) [ʃiʃkebab] NM shish kebab

chichement [ʃiʃmɑ̃] ADV (récompenser, nourrir) meanly, meagrely (Brit), meagerly (US); [vivre, se nourrir] (= pauvrement) poorly; (= mesquinement) meanly

chichi* [ʃiʃi] NM ☐a ~(s) (= embarras) fuss (NonC), carry-on* (NonC); (= manières) fuss (NonC); **faire des ~(s)** (= embarras) to fuss, make a fuss; (manières) to make a fuss; **ce sont des gens à ~(s)** they're the sort of people who make a fuss; **on vous invite sans ~(s)** we're inviting you informally; **ce sera sans ~** it'll be quite informal ☐b (= beignet) ≈ doughnut

chichiteux, -euse [ʃiʃitø, øz] ADJ (péj) (= faiseur d'embarras) troublesome; (= maniéré) fussy

chicon [ʃikɔ̃] NM (= romaine) cos (lettuce) (Brit), romaine (US); (Belg = endive) chicory (NonC) (Brit), endive (US)

chicorée [ʃikɔʀe] NF (= salade) endive (Brit), chicory (US); (à café) chicory; ~ **frisée** curly endive (Brit), escarole (US)

chicos* [ʃikos] ADJ [personne] stylish, smart; [quartier, appartement] posh*; **c'est ~ chez toi!** your place is very plush!*

chicot [ʃiko] NM [dent, arbre] stump

chicotin [ʃikɔtɛ̃] NM → **amer²**

chié, e¹: [ʃje] ADJ ☐a (= bien) damn: ou bloody: (Brit) good; **elle est ~e, sa moto** his motorbike's something else!* ou wicked!:; ☐b (= difficile) tough*, stiff*; **il est ~, ce problème** it's a hell of a problem; ☐c (= qui exagère) **t'es (pas) ~ d'arriver toujours en retard!** it's a bit much you always turning up late!; **avoir menti comme ça, c'est ~** what a nerve* to have lied like that

chiée²: [ʃje] NF **une ~ de ◊ des ~s de** a hell of a lot of:

chien [ʃjɛ̃] ① NM ☐a (= animal) dog; **petit ~** (jeune) puppy, pup; (de petite taille) small dog; **le ~ est le meilleur ami de l'homme** a man's best friend is his dog; **«(attention) ~ méchant»** "beware of the dog"; **faire le ~ fou** to fool about ☐b [fusil] hammer, cock ☐c (injure) **quel ~!** (you) swine!* ☐d (* = frange) ~**s** fringe (Brit), bangs (US) ☐e (Naut) **coup de ~** squall ☐f (loc) **coiffée à la ~** wearing a fringe (Brit), wearing bangs (US); **oh le beau ~~!** nice doggy!, good doggy!; (péj) **c'est le ~~ à sa mémère!** who's mummy's (Brit) ou mommy's (US) little boy then!; **en ~ de fusil** curled up; **quel ~ de temps!** ou **temps de ~!** what filthy ou foul weather!; **ce métier de ~** this rotten job*; **comme un ~** [mourir, traiter] like a dog; **elle a du ~*** she has a certain something*, she's very attractive; **c'est pas fait pour les ~s!** it's there to be used; **être** ou **vivre** ou **s'entendre comme ~ et chat** to fight like cat and dog, always be at one another's throats; **ils se sont regardés en ~s de faïence** they just stood ou sat glaring at each other; **arriver comme un ~ dans un jeu de quilles** to turn up when least needed ou wanted; **recevoir qn comme un ~ dans un jeu de quilles** to give sb a cold reception; **faire les** ou **tenir la rubrique des ~s écrasés*** to write nothing but fillers; **je ne suis pas ton ~!** I'm not your slave ou servant!; **je lui garde** ou **réserve un ~ de ma chienne*** I'll get even with him*; **entre ~ et loup** at dusk ■ (PROV) **un ~ regarde bien un évêque** a cat may look at a king (PROV) ■ (PROV) **les ~s aboient, la caravane passe** let the world say what it will ■ (PROV) **bon ~ chasse de race** like father like son (PROV)

② ADJ INV ☐a (= avare) mean, stingy* ☐b (= méchant) rotten*; **elle n'a pas été ~ avec toi** she was quite decent to you

③ COMP ▸ **chien d'appartement** house dog ▸ **chien d'arrêt** pointer ▸ **chien d'attaque** attack dog ▸ **chien d'avalanche** mountain rescue dog ▸ **chien d'aveugle** guide dog ▸ **chien de berger** sheepdog ▸ **chien de chasse** gun dog ▸ **chien couchant** setter; **faire le ~ couchant** to kowtow, toady (auprès de to) ▸ **chien courant** hound ▸ **chien de garde** guard dog, watchdog ▸ **chien de manchon** lapdog ▸ **chien de mer** dogfish ▸ **chien de meute** hound ▸ **chien policier** police dog, tracker dog ▸ **chien des Pyrénées** Pyrenean mountain dog, Great Pyrenees (US) ▸ **chien de race** pedigree dog ▸ **chien de salon** = **chien de manchon** ▸ **chien savant** (lit) performing dog; (fig) know-all ▸ **chien de traîneau** husky

chien-assis (pl **chiens-assis**) [ʃjɛ̃asi] NM ≈ dormer window (Brit), ≈ dormer (US)

chiendent [ʃjɛ̃dɑ̃] NM ☐a (Bot) couch grass, quitch (grass) → **brosse** ☐b (†* = l'ennui) **le ~** the trouble ou rub

chienlit [ʃjɑ̃li] NF ☐a (= pagaille) **c'est la ~** it's havoc ou chaos ☐b († = mascarade) fancy-dress (Brit) ou costume (US) parade

chien-loup (pl **chiens-loups**) [ʃjɛ̃lu] NM wolfhound

chienne [ʃjɛn] NF bitch; (= *injure*) ~! (you) bitch!**⁚**; **quelle ~ de vie!** it's a dog's life!

chier⁑ [ʃje] ▶conjug 7◀ VI **a** (= *déféquer*) to shit**⁑**, crap**⁑**; **~ un coup** to have a crap**⁑** ou shit**⁑** **b** (*loc*) **faire ~ qn** [*personne*] (= *ennuyer*) to bore the pants off sb**⁑**; (= *tracasser, harceler*) to bug sb**⁑**, piss sb off**⁑**, get up sb's nose**⁑** (*Brit*); **ça me fait ~** it pisses me off**⁑**, it's a pain in the arse**⁑** (*Brit*) ou ass**⁑** (*US*); **envoyer ~ qn** to tell sb to piss off**⁑** ou bugger off**⁑** (*Brit*); **je me suis fait ~ pendant trois heures à réparer la voiture** I sweated my guts out**⁑** for three hours repairing the car; **qu'est-ce qu'on se fait ~ à ses conférences!** what a fucking**⁑** ou bloody**⁑** (*Brit*) bore his lectures are!; **ça va ~ (des bulles)!** there'll be one hell of a row!**⁑**; **y a pas à ~, c'est lui le meilleur** say what you damn ou bloody (*Brit*) well like**⁑**, he's the best; **il faut quand même pas ~ dans la colle!** you've got a fucking nerve!**⁑**; **il est ~** (= *mauvais*) [*film, livre, service*] crappy**⁑**, crap**⁑** (*attrib*); [*personne, appareil*] fucking**⁑** ou bloody**⁑** (*Brit*) useless; (= *laid*) fucking**⁑** ou bloody**⁑** (*Brit*) hideous

chierie⁑ [ʃiʀi] NF (real) pain in the butt**⁑** ou arse**⁑** (*Brit*) ou ass**⁑** (*US*)

chiffe [ʃif] NF **a** (*sans volonté*) spineless individual, drip*; (*fatigué*) **je suis comme une ~ (molle)** I feel like a wet rag → **mou¹** **b** (= *chiffon*) rag

chiffon [ʃifɔ̃] **1** NM **a** (*usagé*) (piece of) rag; (*pour essuyer*) duster (*Brit*), dust cloth (*US*); **donner un coup de ~ à qch** ◊ **passer un coup de ~ sur qch** to give sth a wipe ou go over sth with a cloth; **vieux ~s** old rags; **votre devoir est un vrai ~** your homework is extremely messy ou a dreadful mess; **mettre ses vêtements en ~** to throw down one's clothes in a crumpled heap; **parler ~s⁎** to talk about clothes; (*fig*) **agiter le ~ ou un ~ rouge** to wave the ou a red rag **b** (*Papeterie*) **le ~** rag; **fait avec du ~** made from rags → **papier**

2 COMP ▶ **chiffon à chaussures** shoe cloth ou rag ▶ **chiffon à meubles** = **chiffon à poussière** ▶ **chiffon de papier**: **écrire qch sur un ~ de papier** to write sth (down) on a (crumpled) scrap of paper; **ce traité n'est qu'un ~ de papier** this treaty isn't worth the paper it's written on ou is just a useless scrap of paper ▶ **chiffon à poussière** duster (*Brit*), dust cloth (*US*)

chiffonnade [ʃifɔnad] NF chiffonnade

chiffonné, e [ʃifɔne] (*ptp de* **chiffonner**) ADJ **a** (= *fatigué*) [*visage*] worn-looking **b** (= *sympathique*) **un petit nez ~** a pert little nose; **un joli minois ~** a funny little face

chiffonner [ʃifɔne] ▶conjug 1◀ VT **a** (*lit*) [+ *papier*] to crumple; [+ *habits*] to crease, rumple, crumple; [+ *étoffe*] to crease, crumple; **ce tissu se chiffonne facilement** this material creases ou crumples easily ou is easily creased **b** (* = *contrarier*) **ça me chiffonne** it bothers ou worries me; **qu'est-ce qui te chiffonne?** what's bothering ou worrying you?

chiffonnier [ʃifɔnje] NM **a** (= *personne*) ragman, rag-and-bone man (*Brit*); **se battre** ou **se disputer comme des ~s** to fight like cat and dog; **c'est une bataille de ~s** it's no holds barred → EMMAÜS **b** (= *meuble*) chiffon(n)ier

chiffrable [ʃifʀabl] ADJ **ce n'est pas ~** it's impossible to put a figure on it

chiffrage [ʃifʀaʒ] NM **a** [*message*] (en)coding, ciphering; (*Ordin*) [*données, télégramme*] ciphering **b** [*dépenses, dommages*] assessing **c** [*pages*] numbering **d** [*effets personnels, linge*] marking (with one's ou sb's initials) **e** (*Mus*) [*accord*] figuring

chiffre [ʃifʀ] NM **a** (= *caractère*) figure, numeral, digit (*Math*); (= *nombre*) number; **donne-moi un ~ entre 1 et 8** give me a number between 1 and 8; **~ arabe/romain** Arab/

Roman numeral; **nombre** ou **numéro de 7 ~s** 7-figure ou 7-digit number; **inflation à deux/trois ~s** double-/triple-digit inflation, two-/three-figure inflation; **écrire un nombre en ~s** to write out a number in figures; **science des ~s** science of numbers; **aligner des ~s** to draw up columns of figures

b (= *résultat*) figure; (= *montant*) total; **15 blessés, c'est le ~ provisoire** there's a total of 15 wounded so far, at the last count there were 15 wounded; **je n'ai pas les ~s en tête** I can't recall the figures; **ça atteint des ~s astronomiques** it reaches an astronomical figure ou sum; **selon les ~s officiels** according to official figures; **les ~s du chômage** the unemployment ou jobless figures, the number of unemployed; **en ~s ronds** in round figures **c** (*Comm*) **~ (d'affaires)** turnover; **il fait un ~ (d'affaires) de 3 millions** he has a turnover of 3 million francs; **~ net/brut** net/gross figure ou turnover; **faire du ~⁎** to have a big turnover; **~s de vente** sales figures; **ils ont doublé leurs ~s de vente** they have doubled their sales → **impôt**

d (= *code*) [*message*] code, cipher; [*coffre-fort*] combination; **écrire une lettre en ~s** to write a letter in code ou cipher; **on a trouvé leur ~** their code has been broken; **le (service du) ~** the cipher office

e (= *initiales*) (set of) initials, monogram; **mouchoir brodé à son ~** handkerchief embroidered with one's initials ou monogram **f** (*Mus* = *indice*) figure

chiffré, e [ʃifʀe] (*ptp de* **chiffrer**) ADJ **a** (= *évalué*) [*analyse, argument*] backed up by figures; **données ~es** detailed facts and figures; **le rapport fixe des objectifs ~s** the report sets out targets in precise figures; **aucune précision ~e n'a été donnée** no figures were given **b** (= *codé*) **langage ~** code (language), cipher; **message ~** coded message, message in code ou cipher **c** (*Mus*) **basse ~e** thorough ou figured bass

chiffrement [ʃifʀəmɑ̃] NM [*texte*] (en)coding, ciphering

chiffrer [ʃifʀe] ▶conjug 1◀ **1** VT **a** (= *coder*) [+ *message*] to (en)code, cipher; (*Ordin*) [+ *données, télégramme*] to encode → **message** **b** (= *évaluer*) [+ *dépenses, dommages*] to put a figure to, assess (the amount of); **faire une proposition chiffrée** to propose a figure **c** (= *numéroter*) [+ *pages*] to number **d** (= *marquer*) [+ *effets personnels, linge*] to mark (with one's ou sb's initials) **e** (*Mus*) [+ *accord*] to figure **2** VI, **se chiffrer** VPR **(se) ~ à** to add up to, amount to, come to; **ça (se) chiffre à combien?** what ou how much does that add up to? ou amount to? ou come to?; **ça (se) chiffre par millions** it adds up to ou amounts to ou comes to millions; **ça commence à ~!** it's starting to mount up!; **ça finit par ~*** it all adds up

chiffreur, -euse [ʃifʀœʀ, øz] NM,F coder

chignole [ʃiɲɔl] NF (= *outil*) (à *main*) (hand) drill; (*électrique*) (electric) drill; (* = *voiture*) jalopy* (*hum*)

chignon [ʃiɲɔ̃] NM bun, chignon; **~ banane** French pleat; **se faire un ~** ◊ **relever ses cheveux en ~** to put one's hair into a bun → **crêper**

chihuahua [ʃiwawa] NM chihuahua

chiisme [ʃiism] NM Shiism

chiite [ʃiit] ADJ, NMF Shiite

Chili [ʃili] NM Chile

chilien, -ienne [ʃiljɛ̃, jɛn] **1** ADJ Chilean **2 Chilien(ne)** NM,F Chilean

chimère [ʃimɛʀ] NF **a** (= *illusion*) (wild) dream, pipe dream, chim(a)era (*frm*); **le bonheur est une ~** happiness is just a dream ou an illusion; **c'est une ~ que de croire ...** it's an illusion to think that ...; **tes grands projets, ~s (que tout cela)!** your grand plans are nothing but pipe dreams ou (idle) fancies; **un**

monde peuplé de vagues **~s** a world filled with vague imaginings; **poursuivre** ou **caresser des ~s** to chase rainbows **b** (*Myth*) **la Chimère** chim(a)era, Chim(a)era **c** (*Bio*) chim(a)era **d** (= *poisson*) chimaera

chimérique [ʃimeʀik] ADJ **a** (= *utopique*) [*esprit, projet, idée*] fanciful; [*rêve*] wild (*épith*), idle (*épith*); **c'est un esprit ~** he's a real dreamer **b** (= *imaginaire*) [*personnage*] imaginary, chimerical

chimie [ʃimi] NF chemistry; **~ organique/minérale** organic/inorganic chemistry; **cours/expérience de ~** chemistry class/experiment; **la merveilleuse ~ de l'amour** love's marvellous chemistry

chimiothérapie [ʃimjoteʀapi] NF chemotherapy

chimiothérapique [ʃimjoteʀapik] ADJ chemotherapeutic

chimique [ʃimik] ADJ chemical → **produit**

chimiquement [ʃimikmɑ̃] ADV chemically

chimiste [ʃimist] NMF chemist (*scientist*) → **ingénieur**

chimpanzé [ʃɛ̃pɑ̃ze] NM chimpanzee, chimp*

chinchilla [ʃɛ̃ʃila] NM (= *animal, fourrure*) chinchilla

Chine [ʃin] NF China; **~ populaire/nationaliste** Communist ou Red/nationalist China; **la République populaire de ~** the Chinese People's Republic, the People's Republic of China → **crêpe²**, **encre**

chine¹ [ʃin] NM **a** (= *papier*) rice paper **b** (= *vase*) china vase; (= *porcelaine*) china

chine²⁎ [ʃin] NF **a** (= *brocante*) **faire de la ~** to hunt (around) for antiques **b** (= *porte à porte*) **vente à la ~** door-to-door selling

chiné, e [ʃine] (*ptp de* **chiner**) ADJ (*Tex*) mottled, chiné (*SPÉC*)

chiner [ʃine] ▶conjug 1◀ **1** VT **a** (*Tex*) [+ *étoffe*] to dye the warp of **b** (* = *taquiner*) to kid, have on* (*Brit*), rag*; **tu ne vois pas qu'il te chine** don't you see he's kidding you ou having you on* (*Brit*); **je n'aime pas qu'on me chine** I don't like being ragged* **2** VI* to hunt (around) for antiques

Chinetoque⁑ [ʃintɔk] NMF (*injurieux* = *Chinois*) Chink** (*injurieux*)

chineur, -euse* [ʃinœʀ, øz] NM,F (= *brocanteur*) antique dealer; (= *amateur*) antique-hunter

chinois, e [ʃinwa, waz] **1** ADJ **a** (*de Chine*) Chinese → **ombre¹** **b** (*péj* = *pointilleux*) [*personne*] pernickety, fussy; [*règlement*] hair-splitting **2** NM **a** (*Ling*) Chinese; (*péj*) **c'est du ~*** it's all Greek to me*, it's double Dutch* (*Brit*) **b** **Chinois** Chinese, Chinese man; **les Chinois** the Chinese **c** (* : *péj* = *maniaque*) hair-splitter **d** (*Culin* = *passoire*) (small conical) strainer **3 Chinoise** NF Chinese, Chinese woman

chinoiser [ʃinwaze] ▶conjug 1◀ VI to split hairs; **~ sur** to quibble over

chinoiserie [ʃinwazʀi] NF **a** (= *subtilité excessive*) hair-splitting (*NonC*) **b** (= *complications*) **~s** unnecessary complications ou fuss; **les ~s de l'administration** red tape; **tout ça, ce sont des ~s** all this is unnecessarily complicated **c** (*Art*) (= *décoration*) chinoiserie; (= *objet*) Chinese ornament, Chinese curio

chintz [ʃints] NM (*Tex*) chintz

chiot [ʃjo] NM pup(py)

chiotte [ʃjɔt] NF ou M **a** (** = *W.-C.*) **~s** bog**⁑** (*Brit*), can**⁑** (*US*), john**⁑** (*US*); **aux ~s l'arbitre!** what a shitty referee!**⁑**; **quelle ~!** ◊ **c'est la ~!** what a pain in the arse**⁑** (*Brit*) ou ass**⁑** (*US*); **quel temps de ~!** what shitty weather!**⁑**; **c'est de la musique de ~** it's crap(py) music**⁑**; **avoir un goût de ~** [*personne*] to have crap taste**⁑** → **corvée** **b** (** = *voiture*) jalopy* (*hum*)

chiper⁎ [ʃipe] ▶conjug 1◀ VT (= *voler*) [+

portefeuille, idée] to pinch*, filch*; [+ *rhume*] to catch

chipeur, -euse* [ʃipœr, øz] **1** ADJ [*gamin*] thieving **2** NM,F thief

chipie* [ʃipi] NF vixen (*péj*); **petite ~ !** you little devil!*

chipolata [ʃipɔlata] NF chipolata

chipotage* [ʃipɔtaʒ] NM (= *marchandage, ergotage*) quibbling; (*pour manger*) picking *ou* nibbling at one's food)

chipoter* [ʃipɔte] ▸ conjug 1 ◂ **1** VI (= *manger*) to be a fussy eater; (= *ergoter*) to quibble (**sur** about, over); (= *marchander*) to quibble (**sur** over); **~ sur la nourriture** to nibble *ou* pick at one's food; **tu chipotes là !** now you're quibbling!; **vous n'allez pas ~ pour 2 F !** you're not going to quibble about 2 francs! **2 se chipoter** VPR to squabble (**sur** over)

chipoteur, -euse* [ʃipɔtœr, øz] **1** ADJ (= *marchandeur*) haggling; (= *ergoteur*) quibbling; (*en mangeant*) fussy **2** NM,F (= *marchandeur*) haggler; (= *ergoteur*) quibbler; (*en mangeant*) fussy eater

chips [ʃips] NFPL **(pommes) ~** (potato) crisps (*Brit*) *ou* chips (*US*)

chique [ʃik] NF (= *tabac*) quid, chew; (* = *enflure*) (facial) swelling, lump (on the cheek); (= *puce*) chigoe, chigger → **couper**

chiqué* [ʃike] NM **a** (= *bluff*) pretence (*NonC*), bluffing (*NonC*); **il a fait ça au ~** he bluffed it out; **il prétend que cela le laisse froid mais c'est du ~** he claims it leaves him cold but it's all put on* **b** (*factice*) sham (*NonC*); **ces combats de catch c'est du ~** these wrestling matches are all sham *ou* all put on* *ou* are faked; **combat sans ~** fight that's for real*; **~!, remboursez !** what a sham!, give us our money back! **c** (= *manières*) **faire du ~** to put on airs (and graces)

chiquement* [ʃikmɑ̃] ADV [*s'habiller*] smartly, stylishly; [*traiter, accueillir*] kindly, decently

chiquenaude [ʃiknod] NF (= *pichenette*) flick, flip; **il l'enleva d'une ~** he flicked *ou* flipped it off; **une ~ suffirait à renverser le gouvernement** it wouldn't take much to overturn the government

chiquer [ʃike] ▸ conjug 1 ◂ **1** VT [+ *tabac*] to chew → **tabac 2** VI to chew tobacco

chiqueur, -euse* [ʃikœr, øz] NM,F tobacco-chewer

chirographaire [kirɔgrafɛr] ADJ unsecured

chirographie [kirɔgrafi] NF = **chiromancie**

chiromancie [kirɔmɑ̃si] NF palmistry, chiromancy (*SPÉC*)

chiromancien, -ienne [kirɔmɑ̃sjɛ̃, jɛn] NM,F palmist, chiromancer (*SPÉC*)

chiropracteur [kirɔpraktœr] NM chiropractor

chiropracticien, -ienne [kirɔpraktisjɛ̃, jɛn] NM,F chiropractor

chiropractie [kirɔprakti], **chiropraxie** [kirɔpraksi] NF chiropractic

chirurgical, e (*mpl* **-aux**) [ʃiryrʒikal, o] ADJ (*lit, fig*) surgical; **acte ~** surgical procedure; (*Mil*) **frappe ~e** surgical strike

chirurgie [ʃiryrʒi] NF surgery (*science*); **~ esthétique/dentaire/réparatrice** cosmetic/dental/reconstructive surgery

chirurgien, -ienne [ʃiryrʒjɛ̃, jɛn] NM,F surgeon; **~-dentiste** dental surgeon; (*Mil*) **~ major** army surgeon

Chisinau [ʃizino] N Kishinev, Chisinau

chistera [(t)ʃistera] NF *ou* M wicker basket (*in game of pelota*)

chiure [ʃjyr] NF **~ de mouche** fly speck

chlamydia (*pl* **chlamydiae**) [klamidja] NF chlamydia

chlâsse* [ʃlas] ADJ → **schlass**

chleuh* [ʃlø] (*injurieux*) **1** ADJ Kraut** (*injurieux*) **2 Chleuh** NMF Kraut** (*injurieux*)

---

chlinguer [ʃlɛ̃ge] VI = **schlinguer**

chlorate [klɔrat] NM chlorate

chlore [klɔr] NM chlorine

chloré, e [klɔre] (*ptp de* **chlorer**) ADJ chlorinated

chlorer [klɔre] ▸ conjug 1 ◂ VT to chlorinate

chlorhydrique [klɔridrik] ADJ hydrochloric

chlorique [klɔrik] ADJ chloric

chlorofluorocarbone [klɔroflyɔrokarbɔn] NM chlorofluorocarbon

chlorofluorocarbure [klɔroflyɔrokarbyr] NM chlorofluorocarbon

chloroforme [klɔrɔfɔrm] NM chloroform

chloroformer [klɔrɔfɔrme] ▸ conjug 1 ◂ VT to chloroform

chlorophylle [klɔrɔfil] NF chlorophyll

chlorophyllien, -ienne [klɔrɔfiljɛ̃, jɛn] ADJ chlorophyllous

chlorose [klɔroz] NF (*Méd*) chlorosis, green-sickness (*NonC*); (*Bot*) chlorosis

chlorure [klɔryr] NM chloride; **~ de sodium** sodium chloride; **~ de chaux** chloride of lime

chlorurer [klɔryre] ▸ conjug 1 ◂ VT = **chlorer**

chnoque* [ʃnɔk] NM (*péj*) **quel vieux ~ !** what an old fart!*; **eh ! du ~ !** hey! you!

chnouf† [ʃnuf] NF (*arg Drogue*) dope*

choc [ʃɔk] **1** NM **a** (= *heurt*) [*objets*] impact, shock; [*vagues*] crash; **le ~ de billes d'acier qui se heurtent** the impact of steel balls as they collide; **cela se brise au moindre ~** it breaks at the slightest bump *ou* knock; **« résiste au(x) ~(s) »** "shock-resistant"; **la résistance au ~ d'un matériau** a material's resistance to shock; **la carrosserie se déforma sous le ~** the coachwork twisted with *ou* under the impact; **la corde se rompit sous le ~** the sudden wrench made the rope snap *ou* snapped the rope

b (= *collision*) [*véhicules*] crash, smash; [*personnes*] blow; (*plus léger*) bump; **le ~ entre les véhicules fut très violent** the vehicles crashed together with tremendous force; **~ meurtrier** fatal crash *ou* smash; **il tituba sous le ~** the blow *ou* bump threw him off balance

c (= *bruit*) (*violent*) crash, smash; (*sourd*) thud, thump; (*métallique*) clang, clash; (*cristallin*) clink, chink; [*gouttes, grêlons*] drumming (*NonC*); **le ~ sourd des obus** the thud of shellfire

d (= *affrontement*) [*troupes, émeutiers*] clash; [*intérêts, cultures, passions*] clash, collision; **il y a eu un ~ sanglant entre la police et les émeutiers** there has been a violent clash between police and rioters; **la petite armée ne put résister au ~** the little army could not stand up to the onslaught

e (= *émotion*) shock; **le ~ est rude** it comes as *ou* it's quite a shock; **il ne s'est pas remis du ~** he hasn't got over *ou* recovered from the shock; **ça m'a fait un drôle de ~ de le voir dans cet état** it gave me a nasty shock *ou* quite a turn* to see him in that state; **il est encore sous le ~** (*à l'annonce d'une nouvelle*) he's still in a state of shock; (*après un accident*) he's still in shock; **tenir le ~*** [*personne*] to cope; [*machine*] to hold out; **après la mort de sa femme il n'a pas tenu le ~** he couldn't cope after his wife's death → **état**

f de ~ [*troupe, unité*] shock; [*traitement, thérapeutique, tactique*] shock; [*évêque, patron*] high-powered

2 ADJ INV (= *à sensation*) **argument/discours/ formule(-)choc** shock argument/speech/ formula; **film/photo(-)choc** shock film/photo; **mesures(-)choc** shock measures; **« notre prix ~ : 99 F »** "our special price: 99 francs"

3 COMP ► **choc anesthésique** shock due to anaesthetics ► **choc culturel** culture shock ► **choc électrique** electric shock ► **choc nerveux** (nervous) shock ► **choc opératoire** post-operative shock ► **choc pétrolier** (*Écon*) oil crisis ► **choc psycholo-**

---

gique psychological shock ► **choc en retour** (*Elec*) return shock; (*fig*) backlash ► **choc septique** toxic shock; **faire un ~ septique** to suffer from toxic shock ► **choc thermique** thermal shock

chochotte* [ʃɔʃɔt] **1** NF (= *femme chichiteuse*) fusspot* (*Brit*), fussbudget (*US*); (= *homme : mauviette*) sissy*; (= *homme efféminé*) namby-pamby*; **arrête de faire la ou ta ~ !** stop making such a fuss (about nothing)!* **2** ADJ INV **elle est très ~** she fusses too much; **il est très ~** (*mauviette*) he's a real sissy*; (*efféminé*) he's a real namby-pamby*

chocolat [ʃɔkɔla] **1** NM **a** (= *substance, boisson, bonbon*) chocolate; **mousse/crème au ~** chocolate mousse/cream; **~ au lait/aux noisettes** milk/hazelnut chocolate → **barre, plaque b** (= *couleur*) chocolate (brown) **c être ~†*** to be thwarted *ou* foiled **2** ADJ INV chocolate(-brown) **3** COMP ► **chocolat amer** bitter chocolate; (*poudre*) cocoa powder ► **chocolat blanc** white chocolate ► **chocolat chaud** hot chocolate ► **chocolat à croquer** plain dark chocolate ► **chocolat à cuire** cooking chocolate ► **chocolat fondant** fondant chocolate ► **chocolat liégeois** chocolate sundae ► **chocolat de ménage** = **chocolat à cuire** ► **chocolat noir** dark chocolate ► **chocolat à pâtisser** = **chocolat à cuire** ► **chocolat en poudre** drinking chocolate

chocolaté, e [ʃɔkɔlate] ADJ (= *additionné de chocolat*) chocolate-flavoured (*Brit*) *ou* -flavored (*US*), chocolate (*épith*); (= *au goût de chocolat*) chocolate-flavoured (*Brit*) *ou* -flavored (*US*), chocolat(e)y*

chocolaterie [ʃɔkɔlatri] NF (= *fabrique*) chocolate factory; (= *magasin*) chocolate shop

chocolatier, -ière [ʃɔkɔlatje, jɛr] **1** ADJ chocolate (*épith*) **2** NM,F (= *fabricant*) chocolate maker; (= *commerçant*) chocolate seller

chocottes‡ [ʃɔkɔt] NFPL **avoir les ~** to have the jitters* *ou* the heebie-jeebies*; **ça m'a filé les ~** it gave me the jitters* *ou* the heebie-jeebies*

chœur [kœr] NM **a** (= *chanteurs : gén, Rel*) choir; [*opéra, oratorio*] chorus **b** (*Théât : récitants*) chorus **c** (*fig*) (= *concert*) **un ~ de récriminations** a chorus of recriminations; (= *groupe*) **le ~ des mécontents** the band of malcontents **d** (*Archit*) choir, chancel → **enfant e** (*Mus*) (= *composition*) chorus; (= *hymne*) chorale; (*Théât* = *texte*) chorus; **~ à 4 parties** (*opéra*) 4-part chorus; (*Rel*) 4-part chorale **f** (*loc*) **en ~** (*Mus*) in chorus; (*fig* = *ensemble*) [*chanter*] in chorus; [*répondre, crier*] in chorus *ou* unison; (*hum*) **on s'ennuyait en ~** we were all getting bored (together); **tous en ~ !** all together now!

choir [ʃwar] VI († *ou hum*) to fall; **faire ~** to cause to fall; **laisser ~ qch** to drop sth; (*fig*) **laisser ~ ses amis** to let one's friends down; **se laisser ~ dans un fauteuil** to drop into an armchair

choisi, e [ʃwazi] (*ptp de* **choisir**) ADJ **a** (= *sélectionné*) [*morceaux, passages*] selected **b** (= *raffiné*) [*langage, termes*] carefully chosen; [*clientèle, société*] select

choisir [ʃwazir] ▸ conjug 2 ◂ VT **a** (*gén*) to choose (**entre** between); **des deux solutions, j'ai choisi la première** I chose *ou* picked the first of the two solutions, I opted *ou* plumped* (*Brit*) for the first of the two solutions; **choisissez une carte/un chiffre** pick a card/a number; **il faut savoir ~ ses amis** you must know how to pick *ou* choose your friends; **dans les soldes, il faut savoir ~** in the sales, you've got to know what to choose *ou* how to be selective; **se ~ un mari** to choose a husband; **on l'a choisi parmi des douzaines de candidats** he was picked (out) *ou* selected *ou* chosen from among dozens of applicants; (*iro*) **tu as (bien) choisi ton moment !** you really choose your moments, don't you?; **tu as mal choisi ton moment si tu veux une augmentation !** you picked the wrong time to ask for a rise

b ~ **de faire qch** to choose to do sth; **à toi de ~ si et quand tu veux partir** it's up to you to choose if and when you want to leave

▼ **choix** [ʃwa] **1** NM **a** (= décision) choice; **je n'avais pas le ~ ou d'autre ~** I had no choice, I had no other option; **de ton ~** of your (own) choosing; **le ~ d'un cadeau est souvent difficile** choosing a gift is often difficult, it's often difficult to choose a gift; **avoir le ~** to have a ou the choice; **faire son ~** to take ou make one's choice, take one's pick; **mon ~ est fait** I've made my choice; **c'est un ~ à faire** it's a choice you have (ou he has etc) to make; **faire un ~ de société** to choose the kind of society one wants to live in; **~ de vie** life choice; (frm) **faire ~ de qch** to select sth; **laisser le ~ à qn** to leave sb (free) to choose (**de faire** to do); **donner le ~ à qn** to give sb the choice (**de faire** of doing); **arrêter** ou **fixer** ou **porter son ~ sur qch** to fix one's choice on sth, settle on sth → **embarras**

b (= variété) choice, selection, variety; **ce magasin offre un grand ~** this shop has a wide ou large selection (of goods); **il y a du ~** there is a choice; **il n'y a pas beaucoup de ~** there isn't a great deal of ou much choice, there isn't a great selection (to choose from)

c (= échantillonnage) ~ **de** selection of; **il avait apporté un ~ de livres** he had brought a selection of books

d (loc) **de ~** (= de qualité) choice (épith); **cible de ~** prime target; **morceau de ~** (viande) prime cut; **c'est un morceau de ~** [prestation, poème] it's first-rate; **de premier ~** [fruits] class ou grade one; [agneau, bœuf] prime (épith); **il n'achète que du premier ~** he only buys top-quality products; **de second ~** (gén) low-quality, low-grade; [fruits, viande] class ou grade two (Brit), market grade (US); **articles de second ~** seconds

2 **au choix** LOC ADV **vous pouvez prendre, au ~, fruits ou fromages** you have a choice between ou of fruit or cheese; **« dessert au ~ »** "choice of desserts"; (Admin) **avancement au ~** promotion on merit ou by selection; **au ~ du client** as the customer chooses, according to (the customer's) preference

choke* [(t)ʃɔk] NM (Helv: Aut) choke

choléra [kɔleʀa] NM cholera

cholérique [kɔleʀik] **1** ADJ (gén) choleroid; [patient] cholera (épith) **2** NMF cholera patient ou case

cholestérol [kɔlesteʀɔl] NM cholesterol

cholestérolémie [kɔlesteʀɔlemi] NF cholestorolaemia (Brit), cholestorolemia (US)

chômage [ʃomaʒ] **1** NM unemployment; **le ~ des cadres** executive unemployment, unemployment among executives; **le ~ des jeunes** youth unemployment; **le taux de ~** the unemployment ou jobless rate; **~ saisonnier/chronique** seasonal/chronic unemployment; **être au ~** to be unemployed ou out of work; **s'inscrire au ~** to apply for unemployment benefit (Brit) ou welfare (US), sign on the dole* (Brit); **mettre qn au ~** to lay sb off, make sb redundant (Brit); **beaucoup ont été mis au ~** there have been many layoffs ou redundancies (Brit); **toucher le ~*** to get unemployment benefit (Brit), be on the dole* (Brit), be on welfare (US) → **allocation, indemnité** **2** COMP ► **chômage de longue durée** long-term unemployment ► **chômage partiel** short-time working ► **chômage structurel** structural unemployment ► **chômage technique : mettre en ~ technique** to lay off (temporarily); **le nombre de travailleurs en ~ technique** the number of workers laid off, the number of layoffs

chômé, e [ʃome] (ptp de **chômer**) ADJ **jour ~** (férié) public holiday, ≈ bank holiday (Brit); (pour chômage technique) shutdown day; (de grève) strike day; **fête ~e** public holiday, ≈ bank holiday (Brit)

chômedu: [ʃomdy] NM (= inactivité) unemployment; (= indemnités) dole* (Brit), unemployment (US); **être au ~** to be on the dole* (Brit) ou on unemployment (US)

chômer [ʃome] ▶ conjug 1 ◀ **1** VI **a** (fig = être inactif) [capital, équipements] to be unemployed, be idle, lie idle; [esprit, imagination] to be idle, be inactive; **on n'a pas chômé** we didn't just sit around doing nothing **b** (= être sans travail) [travailleur] to be unemployed, be out of work ou out of a job; [usine] to be ou stand idle, be at a standstill; [industrie] to be at a standstill **c** (†† = être en congé) to be on holiday (Brit) ou vacation (US) **2** VT †† [+ jour férié] to keep

chômeur, -euse [ʃomœʀ, øz] NM,F (gén) unemployed person ou worker; (mis au chômage) redundant worker (Brit), laid-off worker (US); **les ~s (de longue durée)** the (long-term) unemployed; **le nombre des ~s** the number of unemployed ou of people out of work; **3 millions de ~s** 3 million unemployed ou people out of work

chope [ʃɔp] NF (= récipient) tankard, mug; (= contenu) pint

choper: [ʃɔpe] ▶ conjug 1 ◀ VT **a** (= voler) to pinch*, nick* (Brit) **b** (= attraper) [+ balle, personne, maladie] to catch; **se faire ~ par la police** to get nabbed* by the police **c** (Tennis) to chop; **balle chopée** chop

chopine [ʃɔpin] NF (* = bouteille) bottle (of wine); (†† = mesure) half-litre (Brit) ou -liter (US), ≈ pint; (Can = 0,568 l) pint; **on a été boire une ~*** we went for a drink

chopper [(t)ʃɔpœʀ] NM (= moto) chopper

choquant, e [ʃɔkɑ̃, ɑ̃t] ADJ (= qui heurte le goût) shocking, appalling; (= injuste) outrageous, scandalous; (= indécent) shocking, offensive

choquer [ʃɔke] ▶ conjug 1 ◀ **1** VT **a** (= scandaliser) to shock; (plus fort) to appal; (= blesser) to offend, shock; **ça m'a choqué de le voir dans cet état** I was shocked ou appalled to see him in that state; **ce roman risque de ~** some people may find this novel offensive ou shocking; **j'ai été vraiment choqué par son indifférence** I was really shocked ou appalled by his indifference; **ne vous choquez pas de ma question** don't be shocked at ou by my question; **il a été très choqué de ne pas être invité** he was most offended at not being invited; **cette scène m'a beaucoup choqué** I was deeply shocked by that scene **b** (= aller à l'encontre de) [+ délicatesse, pudeur, goût] to offend (against); [+ raison] to offend against, go against; [+ vue] to offend; [+ oreilles] [son, musique] to jar on, offend; [propos] to shock, offend; **cette question a choqué sa susceptibilité** the question offended his sensibilities **c** (= commotionner) [chute] to shake (up); [accident] to shake (up), shock; [deuil, maladie] to shake; (Méd) **être choqué** to be in shock; **il sortit du véhicule, durement choqué** he climbed out of the vehicle badly shaken ou shocked; **la mort de sa mère l'a beaucoup choqué** the death of his mother has shaken him badly **d** (= heurter: gén) to knock (against); [+ verres] to clink; **choquant son verre contre le mien** clinking his glass against mine **e** (Naut) [+ cordage, écoute] to slacken **2** **se choquer** VPR (= s'offusquer) to be shocked; **il se choque facilement** he's easily shocked

choral, e [ʃɔʀal] (mpl **chorals**) **1** ADJ choral **2** NM choral(e) **3** **chorale** NF choral society, choir

chorée [kɔʀe] NF (Méd) ~ **(de Huntington)** Huntington's chorea

chorégraphe [kɔʀeɡʀaf] NMF choreographer

chorégraphie [kɔʀeɡʀafi] NF choreography

chorégraphier [kɔʀeɡʀafje] ▶ conjug 7 ◀ VT (lit, fig) to choreograph

chorégraphique [kɔʀeɡʀafik] ADJ choreographic

choreute [kɔʀøt] NM chorist

choriste [kɔʀist] NMF [église] choir member, chorister; [opéra, théâtre antique] member of the chorus; **les ~s** the choir, the chorus

chorizo [ʃɔʀizo] NM chorizo

chorus [kɔʀys] NM **faire ~** to chorus ou voice one's agreement ou approval; **faire ~ avec qn** to voice one's agreement with sb; **ils ont fait ~ avec lui pour condamner ces mesures** they joined with him in voicing their condemnation of the measures

chose [ʃoz] **1** NF **a** (= truc) thing; **je viens de penser à une ~** I've just thought of something; **il a un tas de ~s à faire à Paris** he has a lot of things ou lots to do in Paris; **il n'y a pas une seule ~ de vraie là-dedans** there isn't a (single) word of truth in it; **critiquer est une ~, faire le travail en est une autre** criticizing is one thing, doing the work is another; **ce n'est pas ~ facile** ou **aisée de ...** it's not an easy thing to ...; **~ étrange** ou **curieuse, il a accepté** strangely ou curiously enough, he accepted, the strange ou curious thing is (that) he accepted; **c'est une ~ admise que ...** it's an accepted fact that ...

b (= événements, activités) **les ~s** things; **les ~s se sont passées ainsi** it (all) happened like this; **les ~s vont mal** things are going badly; **dans l'état actuel des ~s** ◊ **au point où en sont les ~s** as things ou matters stand (at present), the way things are at the moment; **ce sont des ~s qui arrivent** it's just one of those things, these things happen; **regarder les ~s en face** to face up to things; **prendre les ~s à cœur** to take things to heart; **mettons les ~s au point** let's get things clear ou straight; **en mettant les ~s au mieux/au pire** at best/worst; **parler de ~(s) et d'autre(s)** to talk about this and that; **elle a fait de grandes ~s** she has done great things → **force, ordre[1]**

c (= ce dont il s'agit) **la ~ est d'importance** it's no trivial matter, it's a matter of some importance; **la ~ dont j'ai peur, c'est que ...** what ou the thing I'm afraid of is that ...; **il va vous expliquer la ~** he'll tell you all about it ou what it's all about; **la ~ en question** the matter in hand; **la ~ dont je parle** the thing I'm talking about; **il a très bien pris la ~** he took it all very well; **c'est la ~ à ne pas faire** that's the one thing ou the very thing not to do

d (= réalités matérielles) **les ~s** things; **les ~s de ce monde** the things of this world; **quand ils reçoivent, ils font bien les ~s** when they have guests they really do things properly; **elle ne fait pas les ~s à demi** ou **à moitié** she doesn't do things by halves

e (= mot) thing; **j'ai plusieurs ~s à vous dire** I've got several things to tell you; **vous lui direz bien des ~s de ma part** give him my regards

f (= objet) thing; **ils vendent de jolies ~s** they sell some nice things

g (= personne, animal) thing; **pauvre ~ !** poor thing!; **c'est une petite ~ si fragile encore** he (ou she) is still such a delicate little thing; **être la ~ de qn** to be sb's plaything

h (Jur) **la ~ jugée** the res judicata, the final decision; (Pol) **la ~ publique** the state ou nation; († ou hum) **la ~ imprimée** the printed word

i (loc) **c'est ~ faite** it's done; **voilà une bonne ~ de faite** that's one thing out of the way; **c'est bien peu de ~** it's nothing really; **(très) peu de ~** nothing much, very little; **avant toute ~** above all (else); **toutes ~s égales** all (other) things being equal, all things considered; **de deux ~s l'une : soit ..., soit ...** there are two possibilities: either ..., or ... ■ (PROV) **~ promise, ~ due** promises are made to be kept → **porté**

2 NM* **a** (= truc, machin) thing, thingumajig*; **qu'est-ce que c'est que ce ~ ?** what's this thing here?, what's this thingumajig?* **b** (= personne) what's-his-name*, thingumajig*; **j'ai vu le petit ~** I saw young what's-his-name*; **Monsieur Chose** Mr what's-his-name*; **eh ! Chose** hey, you!

3 ADJ INV* **être/se sentir tout ~** (bizarre) to be/feel not quite oneself, feel a bit peculiar; (malade) to be/feel out of sorts ou under the weather; **ça l'a rendu tout ~ d'apprendre cette nouvelle** it made him go all funny when he heard the news

chosifier [ʃozifje] ▶ conjug 7 ◀ VT to reify

chou¹ (pl **choux**) [ʃu] **1** NM **a** (Bot) cabbage **b** (= ruban) rosette **c** (= gâteau) choux bun → **pâte** **d** (* = tête) **il n'a rien dans le ~** he's got nothing up top*; **elle a en dans le ~** she's really brainy* **e** (* loc) **être dans les ~x** [projet] to be up the spout* (Brit), be a write-off; (Sport) to be right out of the running; [candidat] to have had it; **faire ~ blanc** to draw a blank; **le gouvernement va faire ses ~x gras de la situation** the government will cash in on ou capitalize on the situation; **ils vont faire leurs ~x gras de ces vieux vêtements** they'll be only too glad to make use of these old clothes → **bout** **2** COMP ► **chou de Bruxelles** Brussels sprout ► **chou cabus** white cabbage ► **chou chou** chayote ► **chou à la crème** cream-puff ► **chou frisé** kale ► **chou palmiste** cabbage tree ► **chou rouge** red cabbage

chou², -te* (mpl **choux**) [ʃu, ʃut, ʃu] **1** NM,F (= amour) darling; **c'est un ~** he's a darling ou a dear; **oui ma choute** yes, darling ou honey (US) ou poppet* (Brit) **2** ADJ INV (= ravissant) delightful, cute* (surtout US); **ce qu'elle est ~ ou c'est d'un ~, cette robe !** what a lovely ou cute* little dress!; **ce qu'elle est ~ dans ce manteau !** doesn't she look just adorable in that coat!

chouan [ʃwɑ̃] NM 18th century French counter-revolutionary in the Vendée

Chouannerie [ʃwan(ə)ri] NF 18th century French counter-revolutionary movement in the Vendée

choucas [ʃuka] NM jackdaw

chouchou, -te [ʃuʃu, ut] **1** NM,F (* = favori) pet, darling, blue-eyed boy (ou girl); **le ~ du prof** the teacher's pet **2** NM (= élastique) scrunchy

chouchoutage* [ʃuʃutaʒ] NM (= favoritisme) pampering

chouchouter* [ʃuʃute] ▶ conjug 1 ◀ VT to pamper, coddle

choucroute [ʃukrut] NF **a** (Culin) sauerkraut; **~ garnie** sauerkraut with meat **b** (* = coiffure) beehive (hairstyle)

chouette¹* [ʃwɛt] **1** ADJ **a** (= beau) [objet, personne] great* **b** (= gentil) nice; (= sympathique) great*; **sois ~, prête-moi 100 F** be a dear ou an angel* and lend me 100 francs **2** EXCL **~ (alors) !** great!*

chouette² [ʃwɛt] NF (Zool) owl; **~ chevêche** little owl; **~ effraie** barn owl, screech owl; **~ hulotte** tawny owl; (péj) **quelle vieille ~ !** silly old bag!*

chou-fleur (pl **choux-fleurs**) [ʃuflœr] NM cauliflower; **oreilles en ~** cauliflower ears; **nez en ~** swollen nose

chouia* [ʃuja] NM [sucre, bonne volonté, impatience, place] smidgin; **c'est pas ~** that's not much; **un ~ trop grand/petit** (just) a shade too big/small; **il manque un ~ pour que tu puisses te garer** there's not quite enough room for you to park

chouiner* [ʃwine] ▶ conjug 1 ◀ VI (= pleurer) to whine

chou-navet (pl **choux-navets**) [ʃunavɛ] NM swede (Brit), rutabaga (US)

choupette [ʃupɛt] NF [cheveux] top-knot

chouquette [ʃukɛt] NF ball of choux pastry sprinkled with sugar

chou-rave (pl **choux-raves**) [ʃurav] NM kohlrabi

chouraver* [ʃurave], **chourer*** [ʃure] ▶ conjug 1 ◀ VT to pinch*, swipe*, nick* (Brit)

chow-chow (pl **chows-chows**) [ʃoʃo] NM chow (dog)

choyer [ʃwaje] ▶ conjug 8 ◀ VT (frm = dorloter) to cherish; (avec excès) to pamper; [+ idée] to cherish

CHR [seaʃɛr] NM (ABRÉV = **centre hospitalier régional**) → **centre**

chrême [krɛm] NM chrism, holy oil

chrétien, -ienne [kretjɛ̃, jɛn] ADJ, NM,F Christian

chrétien-démocrate, chrétienne-démocrate (mpl **chrétiens-démocrates**) [kretjɛ̃demɔkrat, kretjɛndemɔkrat] ADJ, NM,F Christian Democrat

chrétiennement [kretjɛnmɑ̃] ADV [agir] in a Christian way; [mourir] as a Christian; **être enseveli ~** to have a Christian burial

chrétienté [kretjɛ̃te] NF Christendom

christ [krist] NM **a** **le Christ** Christ **b** (Art) crucifix, Christ (on the cross); **peindre un ~** to paint a figure of Christ

christiania [kristjanja] NM (Ski) (parallel) christie, christiania

christianisation [kristjanizasjɔ̃] NF conversion to Christianity

christianiser [kristjanize] ▶ conjug 1 ◀ VT to convert to Christianity

christianisme [kristjanism] NM Christianity

christique [kristik] ADJ Christlike

Christmas [kristmas] N **île ~** Christmas Island

chromage [kromaʒ] NM chromium-plating

chromate [krɔmat] NM chromate

chromatique [krɔmatik] ADJ **a** (Mus, Peinture, Opt) chromatic **b** (Bio) chromosomal

chromatisme [krɔmatism] NM (Mus) chromaticism; (Opt) (= aberration) chromatum, chromatic aberration; (= coloration) colourings (Brit), colorings (US)

chromatographie [krɔmatɔgrafi] NF chromatography

chrome [krom] NM (Chim) chromium; (Peinture) **jaune/vert de ~** chrome yellow/green; (Aut) **faire les ~s*** to polish the chrome

chromé, e [krome] (ptp de **chromer**) ADJ [métal, objet] chrome (épith), chromium-plated

chromer [krome] ▶ conjug 1 ◀ VT to chromium-plate

chromo [kromo] NM chromo

chromosome [kromozom] NM chromosome; **~ X/Y** X/Y chromosome

chromosomique [kromozomik] ADJ [anomalie] chromosomal; [analyse] chromosome (épith), chromosomal

chromosphère [kromosfɛr] NF chromosphere

chronicité [krɔnisite] NF chronicity

chronique [krɔnik] **1** ADJ chronic **2** NF (Littérat) chronicle; (Presse) column, page; **~ financière** financial column ou page ou news; **~ locale** local news and gossip; (Bible) **le livre des Chroniques** the Book of Chronicles → **défrayer**

chroniquement [krɔnikmɑ̃] ADV chronically

chroniqueur, -euse [krɔnikœr, øz] NM,F (Littérat) chronicler; (Presse, gén) columnist; **~ parlementaire/sportif** parliamentary/sports editor

chrono* [krono] NM (ABRÉV = **chronomètre**) stopwatch; (Aut) **faire du 80 (km/h) ~** ou **au ~** to be timed ou clocked at 80; (temps chronométré) **faire un bon ~** to do a good time

chronobiologie [krɔnobjɔlɔʒi] NF chronobiology

chronologie [krɔnɔlɔʒi] NF chronology

chronologique [krɔnɔlɔʒik] ADJ chronological

chronologiquement [krɔnɔlɔʒikmɑ̃] ADV chronologically

chronométrage [krɔnometraʒ] NM (Sport) timing

chronomètre [krɔnometr] NM (= montre de précision) chronometer; (Sport) stopwatch; **~ de marine** marine ou box chronometer

chronométrer [krɔnometre] ▶ conjug 6 ◀ VT to time

chronométreur, -euse [krɔnometrœr, øz] NM,F (Sport) timekeeper

chronométrique [krɔnometrik] ADJ chronometric

chrysalide [krizalid] NF chrysalis; (fig) **sortir de sa ~** to blossom, come out of one's shell

chrysanthème [krizɑ̃tɛm] NM chrysanthemum

chrysolithe [krizɔlit] NF chrysolite, olivine

CHS [seaʃɛs] NM (ABRÉV = **centre hospitalier spécialisé**) → **centre**

chtimi, ch'timi [ʃtimi] **1** ADJ of ou from northern France **2** NM (Ling) dialect spoken in northern France **3** NMF native ou inhabitant of northern France

chtouille* [ʃtuj] NF (= blennorragie) clap**; (= syphilis) pox*

CHU [seaʃy] NM (ABRÉV = **centre hospitalier universitaire**) → **centre**

chu [ʃy] ptp de **choir**

chuchotement [ʃyʃɔtmɑ̃] NM [personne, vent, feuilles] whisper, whispering (NonC); [ruisseau] murmur

chuchoter [ʃyʃɔte] ▶ conjug 1 ◀ VTI [personne, vent, feuilles] to whisper; [ruisseau] to murmur; **~ qch à l'oreille de qn** to whisper sth in sb's ear

chuchoterie [ʃyʃɔtri] NF whisper; **~s** whisperings

chuchoteur, -euse [ʃyʃɔtœr, øz] **1** ADJ whispering **2** NM,F whisperer

chuchotis [ʃyʃɔti] NM = **chuchotement**

chuintant, e [ʃɥɛ̃tɑ̃, ɑ̃t] ADJ, NF (Ling) (consonne) **~e** palato-alveolar fricative, hushing sound

chuintement [ʃɥɛ̃tmɑ̃] NM (Ling) pronunciation of s sound as sh; (= bruit) soft ou gentle hiss

chuinter [ʃɥɛ̃te] ▶ conjug 1 ◀ VI **a** (Ling) to pronounce s as sh **b** [chouette] to hoot, screech **c** (= siffler) to hiss softly ou gently

chut [ʃyt] EXCL sh!, shush!

chute [ʃyt] NF **a** [pierre] fall; (Théât) [rideau] fall; **faire une ~** [personne] to (have a) fall; [chose] to fall; **faire une ~ de 3 mètres/mortelle** to fall 3 metres/to one's death; **faire une ~ de cheval/de vélo** to fall off ou come off a horse/bicycle; **faire une mauvaise ~** to have a bad fall; **loi de la ~ des corps** law of gravity; **~ libre** (en parachutisme) free fall; **être en ~ libre** [économie, ventes] to plummet, take a nose dive; **« attention, ~ de pierres »** "danger, falling rocks" → **point¹** **b** [cheveux] loss; [feuilles] fall(ing); **lotion contre la ~ des cheveux** hair restorer **c** (= ruine) [empire] fall, collapse; [commerce] collapse; [roi, ministre] (down)fall; (Mil) [ville] fall; [monnaie, cours] fall, drop (de in); [pièce, auteur] failure; (Rel) **la ~** the Fall; **il a entraîné le régime dans sa ~** he dragged the régime down with him (in his fall); **plus dure sera la ~** the harder they fall boxed{d} (*Géog*) fall; **~ d'eau** waterfall; **les ~s du Niagara/Zambèze** the Niagara/Victoria Falls; **barrage de basse/moyenne/haute ~** dam with a low/medium/high head; **de fortes ~s de pluie/neige** heavy falls of rain/snow, heavy rainfall/snowfalls

boxed{e} (= *baisse*) [*température, pression*] drop, fall (*de in*) → **tension**

boxed{f} (= *déchet*) [*papier, tissu*] offcut, scrap; [*bois*] offcut

boxed{g} (= *fin*) [*toit*] pitch, slope; [*vers*] cadence; [*histoire drôle*] punch line; **la ~ des reins** the small of the back; **~ du jour** nightfall

boxed{h} (*Cartes*) **faire 3 (plis) de ~** to be 3 (tricks) down

chuter [ʃyte] ▸conjug 1◂ VI boxed{a} (= *tomber*) [*personne*] to fall, fall flat on one's face, come a cropper* (*Brit*); [*prix, bourse*] to fall, drop; (*lit, fig*) **faire ~ qn** to bring sb down boxed{b} (= *échouer*) to fail, come a cropper* (*Brit*); (*Cartes*) **~ de deux (levées)** to go down two

chyle [ʃil] NM (*Physiol*) chyle

chyme [ʃim] NM (*Physiol*) chyme

Chypre [ʃipʀ] N Cyprus; **à ~** in Cyprus

chypriote [ʃipʀiɔt] boxed{1} ADJ Cypriot boxed{2} Chypriote NMF Cypriot

▼**ci** [si] ADV boxed{a} (*dans l'espace*) **celui-ci, celle-ci** this one; **ceux-ci** these (ones); **ce livre-ci** this book; **cette table-ci** this table; **cet enfant-ci** this child; **ces livres-/tables-ci** these books/tables boxed{b} (*dans le temps*) **à cette heure-ci** (= *à une heure déterminée*) at this time; (= *à une heure indue*) at this hour of the day, at this time of night; (= *à l'heure actuelle*) by now, at this moment; **ces jours-ci** (*avenir*) in the next few days; (*passé*) these past few days, in the last few days; (*présent*) these days; **ce dimanche-ci/cet après-midi-ci je ne suis pas libre** I'm not free this Sunday/this afternoon; **non, je pars cette nuit-ci** no, I'm leaving tonight boxed{c} **de ci de là** here and there → **comme, par-ci par-là**

CIA [seia] NF (ABRÉV = **Central Intelligence Agency**) CIA

ci-après [siapʀɛ] ADV (*gén*) below; (*Jur*) hereinafter

cibiche* [sibiʃ] NF (= *cigarette*) ciggy*, fag* (*Brit*)

cibiste [sibist] NMF CB user, CBer (*US*)

ciblage [siblaʒ] NM (*Comm*) targeting; **~ des prix** target pricing

cible [sibl] NF (*Mil, Écon*) target; **~ mouvante** moving target; (*lit, fig*) **être la ~ de** ◊ **servir de ~** to be a target for, be the target of; (*lit, fig*) **prendre qch pour ~** to take sth as one's target → **langue**

cibler [sible] ▸conjug 1◂ VT [+ *catégorie d'acheteurs*] to target; **produit mal ciblé** product not targeted at the right market; **campagne électorale bien ciblée** well-targeted election campaign

ciboire [sibwaʀ] NM (*Rel*) ciborium (*vessel*)

ciboule [sibul] NF (*Bot*) (larger) chive; (*Culin*) chives

ciboulette [sibulet] NF (*Bot*) (smaller) chive; (*Culin*) chives

ciboulot‡ [sibulo] NM (= *tête*) head, nut* ; (= *cerveau*) brain; **il s'est mis dans le ~ de ...** he got it into his head *ou* nut* to ...; **il n'a rien dans le ~** he's got nothing up top*

cicatrice [sikatʀis] NF (*lit, fig*) scar

cicatriciel, -ielle [sikatʀisjɛl] ADJ cicatricial (*SPÉC*), scar (*épith*) → **tissu**

cicatrisant, e [sikatʀizɑ̃, ɑ̃t] boxed{1} ADJ healing boxed{2} NM healing substance

cicatrisation [sikatʀizasjɔ̃] NF [*égratignure*] healing; [*plaie profonde*] closing up, healing

cicatriser [sikatʀize] ▸conjug 1◂ boxed{1} VT (*lit, fig*) to heal (over); **sa jambe est cicatrisée** his leg has healed boxed{2} VI [*plaie*] to heal (up), form a scar, cicatrize (*SPÉC*); [*personne*] to heal (up);

je cicatrise mal I don't heal very easily boxed{3} **se cicatriser** VPR to heal (up), form a scar, cicatrize (*SPÉC*)

Cicéron [siseʀɔ̃] NM Cicero

cicérone [siseʀɔn] NM (*hum*) guide, cicerone; **faire le ~** to act as a guide *ou* cicerone

ciclosporine [siklospoʀin] NF cyclosporin-A

ci-contre [sikɔ̃tʀ] ADV opposite

CICR [seiseɛʀ] NM (ABRÉV = **Comité international de la Croix-Rouge**) → **comité**

ci-dessous [sidəsu] ADV below

ci-dessus [sidəsy] ADV above

ci-devant [sidəvɑ̃] boxed{1} ADV (†† *ou hum*) formerly; **mes ~ collègues** my erstwhile *ou* former colleagues boxed{2} NMF (*Hist*) ci-devant (*aristocrat who lost his title in the French Revolution*)

CIDEX [sidɛks] NM (ABRÉV = **courrier individuel à distribution exceptionnelle**) *special post office sorting service for individual clients*

CIDJ [seideʒi] NM (ABRÉV = **centre d'information et de documentation de la jeunesse**) → **centre**

cidre [sidʀ] NM cider; **~ bouché** *fine bottled cider*; **~ doux** sweet cider

cidrerie [sidʀəʀi] NF (= *industrie*) cidermaking; (= *usine*) cider factory

Cie (ABRÉV = **compagnie**) Co

ciel [sjɛl] boxed{1} NM boxed{a} (*pl littér* **cieux**) (= *espace*) sky, heavens (*littér*); **les bras tendus vers le ~** with his arms stretched out heavenwards *ou* skywards; **les yeux tournés vers le ~** eyes turned heavenwards *ou* skywards, gazing heavenwards *ou* skywards; **haut dans le ~** *ou* **dans les cieux** (*littér*) high (up) in the sky, high in the heavens; **suspendu entre ~ et terre** [*personne, objet*] suspended in mid-air; [*village*] suspended between sky and earth; (*fig*) **tomber du ~** to be a godsend, be heaven-sent; **sous un ~ plus clément** ◊ **sous des cieux plus cléments** (*littér*) : (*climat*) beneath more clement skies *ou* a more clement sky; (*hum: endroit moins dangereux*) in healthier climes; **sous d'autres cieux** in other climes; **sous le ~ de Paris/de Provence** beneath the Parisian/Provençal sky; **le ~ ne va pas te tomber sur la tête !** the sky isn't going to fall (in)!, it's not the end of the world! → **remuer, septième, tomber**

boxed{b} (*pl* **ciels**) (*Peinture* = *paysage*) sky; **les ~s de Grèce** the skies of Greece; **les ~s de Turner** Turner's skies

boxed{c} (*pl* **cieux**) (*Rel*) heaven; **il est au ~** he is in heaven; **le royaume des cieux** the kingdom of heaven; **notre Père qui es aux cieux** our Father who *ou* which art in heaven

boxed{d} (= *providence*) heaven; **le ~ a écouté leurs prières** heaven heard their prayers; **(juste) ~ !** good heavens!; **le ~ m'est témoin que ...** heaven knows that ...; **le ~ soit loué !** thank heavens!; **c'est le ~ qui vous envoie !** you're heaven-sent!

boxed{e} **à ~ ouvert** [*égout*] open; [*piscine*] open-air; [*mine*] opencast (*Brit*), open cut (*US*)

boxed{2} COMP ▸ **ciel de carrière** quarry ceiling ▸ **ciel de lit** canopy, tester

cierge [sjɛʀʒ] NM (*Rel*) candle; (*Bot*) cereus → **brûler**

cieux [sjø] *nmpl de* **ciel**

cigale [sigal] NF cicada

cigare [sigaʀ] NM (*lit*) cigar; (* = *tête*) head, nut* ; (* = *bateau*) **~ (des mers)** powerboat

cigarette [sigaʀɛt] NF boxed{a} (*à fumer*) cigarette; **~ (à) bout filtre** filter tip, (filter-)tipped cigarette; **la ~ du condamné** the condemned man's last smoke *ou* cigarette; (= *biscuit*) **~ russe** rolled sweet biscuit often served with ice cream boxed{b} (* = *bateau*) Cigarette ®, cigarette boat

cigarettier [sigaʀetje] NM cigarette manufacturer *ou* maker

cigarillo [sigaʀijo] NM cigarillo

ci-gît [siʒi] ADV here lies

cigogne [sigɔɲ] NF (*Orn*) stork; (*Tech*) crank brace

ciguë [sigy] NF (*Bot*, = *poison*) hemlock; **grande ~** giant hemlock

ci-inclus, e [siɛ̃kly, yz] boxed{1} ADJ enclosed; **l'enveloppe ~e** the enclosed envelope boxed{2} ADV enclosed; **~ une enveloppe** envelope enclosed

ci-joint, e (*mpl* **ci-joints**) [siʒwɛ̃] boxed{1} ADJ enclosed; **les papiers ~s** the enclosed papers boxed{2} ADV enclosed; **vous trouverez ~ ...** you will find enclosed ..., please find enclosed ...

cil [sil] NM (*Anat*) eyelash; (*Bio*) **~s vibratiles** cilia

ciliaire [siljɛʀ] ADJ (*Anat*) ciliary

cilice [silis] NM hair shirt

cilié, e [silje] boxed{1} ADJ ciliate(d) boxed{2} **les ciliés** NMPL ciliates, the Ciliata (*SPÉC*)

cillement [sijmɑ̃] NM blinking

ciller [sije] ▸conjug 1◂ VI **~ (des yeux)** to blink (one's eyes); (*fig*) **il n'a pas cillé** he didn't bat an eyelid

cimaise [simɛz] NF (*Peinture*) picture rail, picture moulding (*Brit*) *ou* molding (*US*); (*Archit*) cyma → **honneur**

cime [sim] NF [*montagne*] summit; (= *pic*) peak; [*arbre*] top; (*fig*) [*gloire*] peak, height

ciment [simɑ̃] NM cement; **~ armé** reinforced concrete; **~ prompt** *ou* **(à prise) rapide** quick-setting cement; **~ colle** glue cement

cimenter [simɑ̃te] ▸conjug 1◂ VT boxed{a} (*Constr*) [+ *sol*] to cement, cover with concrete; [+ *bassin*] to cement, line with cement; [+ *piton, anneau, pierres*] to cement boxed{b} (*fig*) [+ *amitié, accord, paix*] to cement; **l'amour qui cimente leur union** the love which binds them together

cimenterie [simɑ̃tʀi] NF cement works

cimentier, -ière [simɑ̃tje, jɛʀ] boxed{1} ADJ cement (*épith*) boxed{2} NM cement manufacturer

cimeterre [simtɛʀ] NM scimitar

cimetière [simtjɛʀ] NM [*ville*] cemetery; [*église*] graveyard, churchyard; **~ des chiens** pet cemetery; **~ de voitures** scrapyard; **~ des éléphants** elephant's graveyard; **aller au ~** to visit the cemetery

cimier [simje] NM [*casque*] crest; [*arbre de Noël*] *decorative bauble for the top of the Christmas tree*

cinabre [sinabʀ] NM cinnabar

ciné [sine] NM* (ABRÉV = **cinéma**) (= *art, procédé*) cinema; (= *salle*) cinema, movie theater (*US*); **aller au ~** to go to the cinema *ou* the movies (*US*)

cinéaste [sineast] NMF (*gén*) film-maker, moviemaker (*US*); (= *réalisateur connu*) (film) director

ciné-club (*pl* **ciné-clubs**) [sineklœb] NM film society *ou* club

cinéma [sinema] boxed{1} NM boxed{a} (= *procédé, art, industrie*) cinema; (= *salle*) cinema, movie theater (*US*); **roman adapté pour le ~** novel adapted for the cinema *ou* the screen; **faire du ~** to be a film *ou* movie (*US*) actor (*ou* actress); **de ~** [*technicien, studio*] film (*épith*); [*projecteur, écran*] cinema (*épith*); **acteur/vedette de ~** film *ou* movie (*US*) actor/star; **être dans le ~** to be in the film *ou* movie (*US*) business *ou* in films *ou* movies (*US*); **le ~ français/italien** French/Italian cinema; **le ~ de Carné** Carné films; **aller au ~** to go to the cinema *ou* movies (*US*); **elle se fait du ~** she's deluding herself

boxed{b} (* = *simagrées*) **c'est du ~** it's all put on*, it's all an act; **arrête ton ~ !** give it a rest!; **faire tout un ~** to put on a great act*

boxed{c} (* = *complication*) fuss; **c'est toujours le même ~** it's always the same old to-do* *ou* business; **tu ne vas pas nous faire ton ~ !** you're not going to make a fuss *ou* a great scene *ou* a song and dance* about it!

boxed{2} COMP ▸ **cinéma d'animation** (= *technique*) animation; (= *films*) animated films ▸ **cinéma d'art et d'essai** avant-garde *ou* experimental films *ou* cinema; (= *salle*) art house ► **cinéma muet** silent films *ou* movies (*US*) ► **cinéma parlant** talking films *ou* pictures, talkies* ► **cinéma permanent** continuous performance ► **cinéma de plein air** open-air cinema ► **cinéma à salles multiples** multiplex cinema

Cinémascope® [sinemaskɔp] NM Cinemascope®

cinémathèque [sinematɛk] NF film archive *ou* library; (= *salle*) film theatre (*Brit*), movie theater (*US*)

cinématique [sinematik] NF kinematics *sg*

cinématographe [sinematɔgraf] NM cinematograph

cinématographie [sinematɔgrafi] NF film-making, movie-making (*US*), cinematography

cinématographier [sinematɔgrafje] ▶conjug 7◀ VT to film

cinématographique [sinematɔgrafik] ADJ film (*épith*), cinema (*épith*)

cinéma-vérité [sinemaverite] NM INV cinéma-vérité, ciné vérité

ciné-parc, **cinéparc** (*pl* ciné(-)parcs) [sinepark] NM (*Can*) drive-in (cinema)

cinéphile [sinefil] 1 ADJ [*public*] cinemagoing (*épith*) 2 NMF film *ou* cinema enthusiast, film buff*, movie buff* (*US*)

cinéraire [sinerɛr] 1 ADJ [*vase*] cinerary 2 NF (*Bot*) cineraria

Cinérama® [sinerama] NM Cinerama®

ciné-roman (*pl* ciné-romans) [sinerɔmɑ̃] NM film story

cinétique [sinetik] 1 ADJ kinetic 2 NF kinetics *sg*

cing(h)alais, e [sɛ̃galɛ, ɛz] 1 ADJ Sin(g)halese 2 NM (*Ling*) Sin(g)halese 3 **Cing(h)alais(e)** NM,F Sin(g)halese

cinglant, e [sɛ̃glɑ̃, ɑ̃t] ADJ [*vent*] biting, bitter; [*pluie*] lashing, driving; [*propos, ironie*] biting, scathing, cutting

cinglé, e* [sɛ̃gle] (*ptp de* cingler) 1 ADJ screwy*, cracked* 2 NM,F crackpot*, nut*

cingler [sɛ̃gle] ▶conjug 1◀ 1 VT [*personne*] to lash; [*vent, pluie, branche*] to sting, whip (against); [*pluie*] to lash (against); (*fig*) to lash, sting; **il cingla l'air de son fouet** he lashed the air with his whip 2 VI (*Naut*) **~ vers** to make for

cinoche* [sinɔʃ] NM (= *salle*) cinema, movie theater (*US*); **aller au ~** to go to the cinema *ou* movies (*US*)

cinoque‡ [sinɔk] ADJ = **sinoque**

cinq [sɛ̃k] ADJ INV, NM INV five; **dire les ~ lettres** *ou* **le mot de ~ lettres** to use a rude word *ou* a four-letter word; **je lui ai dit les ~ lettres** I told him where to go*; **en ~ sec*** in a flash, before you could say Jack Robinson*; (= *rendez-vous*) **à sept** afternoon tryst; *pour autres locutions voir* **six**; **recevoir**

cinq-dix-quinze†‡ [sɛ̃diskɛ̃z] NM (*Can*) cheap store, dime store (*US, Can*), five-and-ten (*US, Can*)

cinquantaine [sɛ̃kɑ̃tɛn] NF (= *âge, nombre*) about fifty

cinquante [sɛ̃kɑ̃t] ADJ INV, NM INV fifty; *pour locutions voir* **six**

cinquantenaire [sɛ̃kɑ̃tnɛr] 1 ADJ [*arbre, objet*] fifty-year-old (*épith*); **il est ~** it (*ou* he) is fifty years old 2 NM (= *anniversaire*) fiftieth anniversary, golden jubilee

cinquantième [sɛ̃kɑ̃tjɛm] ADJ, NMF fiftieth; *pour locutions voir* **sixième**

cinquantièmement [sɛ̃kɑ̃tjɛmmɑ̃] ADV in the fiftieth place

cinquième [sɛ̃kjɛm] 1 ADJ fifth; **la ~ semaine (de congés payés)** the fifth week of paid holiday (*Brit*) *ou* vacation (*US*); **je suis la ~ roue du carrosse*** I feel like a spare part* (*Brit*), I feel

like a fifth wheel (*US*); ~ **colonne** fifth column; *pour autres locutions voir* **sixième** 2 NMF fifth 3 NF a (*Scol*) ≈ second form *ou* year (*Brit*), ≈ seventh grade (*US*) b (*Aut*) fifth gear c (*TV*) **la Cinquième** French cultural TV channel broadcasting in the afternoon

cinquièmement [sɛ̃kjɛmmɑ̃] ADV in the fifth place

cintrage [sɛ̃traʒ] NM [*tôle, bois*] bending

cintre [sɛ̃tr] NM a (*Archit*) arch → **voûte** b (= *porte-manteau*) coathanger c (*Théât*) **les ~s** the flies

cintré, e [sɛ̃tre] (*ptp de* cintrer) ADJ [*porte, fenêtre*] arched; [*galerie*] vaulted, arched; [*veste*] fitted; (‡, *fig* = *fou*) nuts*, crackers*; **chemise ~e** close-fitting *ou* slim-fitting shirt

cintrer [sɛ̃tre] ▶conjug 1◀ VT (*Archit*) [+ *porte*] to arch, make into an arch; [+ *galerie*] to vault, give a vaulted *ou* arched roof to; (*Tech*) to bend, curve; (*Habillement*) to take in at the waist

CIO [seio] NM a (ABRÉV = **centre d'information et d'orientation**) → **centre** b (ABRÉV = **Comité international olympique**) IOC

cirage [siraʒ] NM a (= *produit*) (shoe) polish b (= *action*) [*chaussures*] polishing; [*parquets*] polishing, waxing c **être dans le ~*** (*après anesthésie*) to be a bit groggy* *ou* whoozy*; (= *être mal réveillé*) to be a bit whoozy*; (*arg Aviat*) to be flying blind; **quand il est sorti du ~*** when he came to *ou* round → **noir**

circa [sirka] ADV circa

circadien, -ienne [sirkadjɛ̃, jɛn] ADJ circadian

circoncire [sirkɔ̃sir] ▶conjug 37◀ VT to circumcize

circoncis [sirkɔ̃si] (*ptp de* circoncire) ADJ circumcized

circoncision [sirkɔ̃sizjɔ̃] NF circumcision

circonférence [sirkɔ̃ferɑ̃s] NF circumference

circonflexe [sirkɔ̃flɛks] ADJ **accent ~** circumflex

circonlocution [sirkɔ̃lɔkysjɔ̃] NF circumlocution; **employer des ~s pour annoncer qch** to announce sth in a roundabout way

circonscription [sirkɔ̃skripsjɔ̃] NF (*Admin, Mil*) district, area; ~ **(électorale)** [*député*] constituency (*Brit*), district (*US*)

circonscrire [sirkɔ̃skrir] ▶conjug 39◀ VT [+ *feu, épidémie*] to contain, confine; [+ *territoire*] to mark out; [+ *sujet*] to define, delimit; ~ **un cercle/carré à** to draw a circle/square round; **le débat s'est circonscrit à** *ou* **autour de cette seule question** the debate limited *ou* restricted itself to *ou* was centred round *ou* around that one question; **les recherches sont circonscrites au village** the search is being limited *ou* confined to the village

circonspect, e [sirkɔ̃spɛ(kt), ɛkt] ADJ [*personne*] circumspect, cautious; [*silence, remarque*] prudent, cautious

circonspection [sirkɔ̃spɛksjɔ̃] NF caution, circumspection

circonstance [sirkɔ̃stɑ̃s] NF a (= *occasion*) occasion; **en la ~** in this case, on this occasion; **en pareille ~** in such a case, in such circumstances; **il a profité de la ~ pour me rencontrer** he took advantage of the occasion to meet me → **concours** b (= *situation*) **~s** circumstances; **~s économiques** economic circumstances; **être à la hauteur des ~s** to be equal to the occasion; **en raison des ~s** ◊ **étant donné les ~s** in view of *ou* given the circumstances; **dans ces ~s** under *ou* in these circumstances; **dans les ~s présentes** *ou* **actuelles** in the present circumstances c [*crime, accident*] circumstance; (*Jur*) **~s atténuantes** mitigating *ou* extenuating circumstances; ~ **aggravante** aggravating circumstance, aggravation; **il y a une ~ troublante**

there's one disturbing circumstance *ou* point; **dans des ~s encore mal définies** in circumstances which are still unclear

d **de ~** [*parole, mine, conseil*] appropriate, apt; [*œuvre, poésie*] occasional (*épith*); [*habit*] appropriate, suitable

circonstancié, e [sirkɔ̃stɑ̃sje] ADJ [*rapport*] detailed

circonstanciel, -ielle [sirkɔ̃stɑ̃sjɛl] ADJ (*Gram*) adverbial; **complément ~ de lieu/temps** adverbial phrase of place/time

circonvenir [sirkɔ̃v(ə)nir] ▶conjug 22◀ VT (*frm*) [+ *personne*] to circumvent (*frm*), get round

circonvoisin, e [sirkɔ̃vwazɛ̃, in] ADJ (*littér*) surrounding, neighbouring (*Brit*), neighboring (*US*)

circonvolution [sirkɔ̃vɔlysjɔ̃] NF (*Anat*) convolution; [*rivière, itinéraire*] twist; **décrire des ~s** [*rivière, route*] to twist and turn; ~ **cérébrale** cerebral convolution

circuit [sirkɥi] 1 NM a (= *itinéraire touristique*) tour, (round) trip; ~ **d'autocar** bus trip, coach (*Brit*) tour *ou* trip; **il y a un très joli ~ (à faire) à travers bois** there's a very nice trip (you can do) through the woods; **faire le ~ (touristique) des volcans d'Auvergne** to tour *ou* go on a tour of the volcanoes in Auvergne b (= *parcours compliqué*) roundabout *ou* circuitous route; **il faut emprunter un ~ assez compliqué pour y arriver** you have to take a rather circuitous *ou* roundabout route to get there; **j'ai dû refaire tout le ~ en sens inverse** I had to go right back round the way I'd come *ou* make the whole journey back the way I'd come c (*Sport*) circuit; ~ **automobile** (motor-) racing circuit; **course sur ~** circuit racing; **sur le ~ international** on the international circuit d (*Élec*) circuit; **couper/rétablir le ~** to break/restore the circuit; **mettre qch en ~** to connect sth up; **mettre hors ~** [+ *appareil*] to disconnect; [+ *personne*] to push aside; **tous les ~s ont grillé** (*machine*) all the fuses have blown, there's been a burnout e (*Écon*) circulation f (= *enceinte*) [*ville*] circumference g (*Ciné*) circuit h (‡ : *loc*) **être dans le ~** to be around; **est-ce qu'il est toujours dans le ~?** is he still around?; **se remettre dans le ~** to get back into circulation; **mettre qch dans le ~** to put sth into circulation, feed sth into the system 2 COMP ► **circuit de distribution** (*Comm*) distribution network *ou* channels ► **circuit électrique** (*Élec*) electric(al) circuit; [*jouet*] (electric) track ► **circuit fermé** (*Élec, fig*) closed circuit; **vivre en ~ fermé** to live in a closed world; **ces publications circulent en ~ fermé** this literature has a limited *ou* restricted circulation ► **circuit hydraulique** (*Aut*) hydraulic circuit ► **circuit imprimé** printed circuit ► **circuit intégré** integrated circuit ► **circuit de refroidissement** cooling system

circulaire [sirkylɛr] ADJ, NF (*gén*) circular; ~ **d'application** decree specifying how a law should be enforced

circulairement [sirkylɛrmɑ̃] ADV in a circle

circulant, e [sirkylɑ̃, ɑ̃t] ADJ a (*Fin*) circulating; **actif ~** current assets; **capitaux ~s** circulating capital b (*Bio*) [*molécule*] circulating in the bloodstream; **sang ~** circulating blood

circularité [sirkylarite] NF circularity

circulation [sirkylasjɔ̃] NF [*air, sang, argent*] circulation; [*marchandises*] movement; [*nouvelle*] spread; [*trains*] running; (*Aut*) traffic; **la (du sang)** the circulation; (*Méd*) **avoir une bonne/mauvaise ~** to have good/bad circulation; **la libre ~ des travailleurs** the free movement of labour; (*Aut*) **pour rendre le ~ plus fluide** to improve traffic flow; **route à grande ~** major road, main highway (*US*); **mettre en**

~ [+ *argent*] to put into circulation; [+ *livre, produit, voiture*] to put on the market, bring out; [+ *fausse nouvelle*] to circulate, spread (about); **mise en ~** [*argent*] circulation; [*livre, produit, voiture*] marketing; **retirer de la ~** [+ *argent*] to take out of *ou* withdraw from circulation; [+ *médicament, produit, livre*] to take off the market, withdraw; (*euph*) [+ *personne*] to get rid of; **~ aérienne** air traffic; (*Anat*) **~ générale** systemic circulation; **~ monétaire** money *ou* currency circulation; (*Aut*) **« ~ interdite »** "no vehicular traffic"; (*fig*) **disparaître de la ~** to drop out of sight, disappear from the scene → **accident, agent**

circulatoire [siʀkylatwaʀ] ADJ circulation (*épith*), circulatory; **troubles ~s** circulatory disorders

circuler [siʀkyle] ▸conjug 1◂ VI a [*sang, air, marchandise, argent*] to circulate; [*rumeur*] to circulate, go around *ou* about; **l'information circule mal entre les services** communication between departments is poor; **il circule bien des bruits à son propos** there's a lot of gossip going around about him, there's a lot being said about him; **faire ~** [+ *air, sang, argent, document*] to circulate; [+ *marchandises*] to put into circulation; [+ *bruits*] to spread b [*voiture*] to go, move; [*train*] to go, run; [*passant*] to walk; [*foule*] to move (along); [*plat, bonbons, lettre*] to be passed *ou* handed round; **un bus sur trois circule** one bus in three is running; **~ à droite/à gauche** to drive on the right/on the left; **circulez!** move along!; **faire ~** [+ *voitures, piétons*] to move on; [+ *plat, pétition*] to hand *ou* pass round

circumnavigation [siʀkɔmnavigasjɔ̃] NF circumnavigation

circumpolaire [siʀkɔmpɔlɛʀ] ADJ circumpolar

cire [siʀ] 1 NF a (*gén*) wax; (*pour meubles, parquets*) polish; (*Méd*) [*oreille*] (ear)wax; **~ d'abeille** beeswax; **~ à cacheter/à épiler** sealing/depilatory wax; **s'épiler les jambes à la ~** to wax one's legs; **personnage en ~** waxwork dummy → **musée** b (*Zool*) cirrus 2 COMP ▸ **cire anatomique** wax anatomical model ▸ **cire perdue** cire perdue, lost wax

ciré [siʀe] NM (*Habillement*) oilskin

cirer [siʀe] ▸conjug 1◂ VT to polish; **j'en ai rien à ~:** I don't give a damn:; **~ les bottes** *ou* **pompes de qn*** to lick sb's boots*, suck up to sb: → **toile**

cireur, -euse [siʀœʀ, øz] 1 NM,F (= *personne*) [*chaussures*] shoe-shiner, bootblack†; [*planchers*] (floor) polisher; **~ de bottes** *ou* **pompes*** bootlicker* 2 **cireuse** NF (= *appareil*) floor polisher

cireux, -euse [siʀø, øz] ADJ [*matière*] waxy; [*teint*] waxen

ciron [siʀɔ̃] NM (*littér, Zool*) mite

cirque [siʀk] NM a (= *chapiteau*) big top; (= *spectacle*) circus b (*Antiq* = *arène*) circus, amphitheatre (*Brit*), amphitheater (*US*) → **jeu** c (*Géog*) cirque d (* = *embarras*) **quel ~ pour garer sa voiture ici!** it's such a performance* *ou* to-do* finding a place to park around here!; **quel ~ il a fait quand il a appris la nouvelle!** what a scene he made when he heard the news!; **arrête ton ~!** give it a rest!*; **c'est le ~ ici aujourd'hui** it's absolute chaos here today, the place is a real circus today (*US*)

cirrhose [siʀoz] NF cirrhosis; **~ du foie** cirrhosis of the liver

cirrocumulus [siʀokymylys] NM cirrocumulus

cirrostratus [siʀostratys] NM cirrostratus

cirrus [siʀys] NM cirrus

cisaille(s) [sizaj] NF(PL) [*pour métal*] shears; [*pour fil métallique*] wire cutters; [*jardinier*] (gardening) shears

cisaillement [sizajmɑ̃] NM a [*métal*] cut-ting; [*branches*] clipping, pruning b [*rivet, boulon*] shearing off

cisailler [sizaje] ▸conjug 1◂ 1 VT a (= *couper*) [+ *métal*] to cut; [+ *branches*] to clip, prune; (*fig*) [+ *carrière*] to cripple b (= *user*) [+ *rivet, boulon*] to shear off c (* = *tailler maladroitement*) [+ *tissu, planche, cheveux*] to hack at 2 **se cisailler** VPR (= *se couper*) to cut o.s.

cisalpin, e [sizalpɛ̃, in] ADJ cisalpine

ciseau (*pl* **ciseaux**) [sizo] NM a **(paire de) ~x** (*pour tissu, papier*) (pair of) scissors; (*pour métal, laine*) shears; (*pour fil métallique*) wire cutters; **~x de brodeuse** embroidery scissors; **~x de couturière** dressmaking shears *ou* scissors; **~x à ongles** nail scissors; **en un coup de ~x** with a snip of the scissors; **donner des coups de ~x dans un texte*** to make cuts in a text b (*Sculp, Tech*) chisel; **~ à froid** cold chisel c (*Sport = prise*) scissors (hold *ou* grip); (*Ski*) **montée en ~x** herringbone climb; (*Catch*) **~ de jambes** leg scissors; **faire des ~x** to do scissor kicks → **sauter**

ciselage [siz(ə)laʒ] NM chiselling

ciseler [siz(ə)le] ▸conjug 5◂ VT [+ *pierre*] to chisel, carve; [+ *métal*] to chase, chisel; [+ *persil*] to chop finely; [+ *style*] to polish; **les traits finement ciselés de son visage** his finely chiselled features

ciseleur, -euse [siz(ə)lœʀ, øz] NM, F [*bois, marbre*] carver; (*en orfèvrerie*) engraver

ciselure [siz(ə)lyʀ] NF a [*bois, marbre*] carving, chiselling; [*orfèvrerie*] engraving, chasing b (= *dessin*) [*bois*] carving; [*orfèvrerie*] engraved *ou* chased pattern *ou* design, engraving

Cisjordanie [sisʒɔʀdani] NF **la ~** the West Bank

cistercien, -ienne [sistɛʀsjɛ̃, jɛn] ADJ, NM,F Cistercian

citadelle [sitadɛl] NF (*lit, fig*) citadel

citadin, e [sitadɛ̃, in] 1 ADJ (*gén*) town (*épith*), urban; [*grande ville*] city (*épith*), urban 2 NM,F city dweller, urbanite (*US*)

citation [sitasjɔ̃] NF a [*auteur*] quotation; **« fin de ~ »** "unquote", "end of quotation" b (*Jur*) summons; **~ à comparaître** (*à accusé*) summons to appear; (*à témoin*) subpoena c (= *mention*) citation; (*Mil*) **~ à l'ordre du jour** *ou* **de l'armée** mention in dispatches

cité [site] 1 NF (*littér, Antiq* = *grande ville*) city; (= *petite ville*) town; (= *immeubles*) (housing) estate (*Brit*), project (*US*); **le problème des ~s** the problem of social unrest in deprived estates (*Brit*) *ou* projects (*US*); (*à Québec*) **~ parlementaire** Parliament buildings; **la ~ des Papes** Avignon; **la Cité du Vatican** Vatican City; **la ~ des Doges** Venice → **droit³** 2 COMP ▸ **cité ouvrière** ≈ (workers') housing estate (*Brit*) *ou* development (*US*) ▸ **cité de transit** ≈ halfway house *ou* hostel for homeless families ≈ (temporary) hostel ▸ **cité universitaire** ≈ (student) hall(s) of residence

cité-dortoir (*pl* **cités-dortoirs**) [sitedɔʀtwaʀ] NF dormitory (*Brit*) *ou* bedroom (*US*) town

cité-jardin (*pl* **cités-jardins**) [siteʒaʀdɛ̃] NF garden city

citer [site] ▸conjug 1◂ VT a (= *rapporter*) [+ *texte, exemples, faits*] to quote, cite; **il n'a pas pu ~ 3 pièces de Sartre** he couldn't name 3 plays by Sartre b (= **en exemple**) [+ *personne*] to hold up as an example (**pour** for); **~ un soldat (à l'ordre du jour** *ou* **de l'armée)** to mention a soldier in dispatches c (*Jur*) **~ (à comparaître)** [+ *accusé*] to summon to appear; [+ *témoin*] to subpoena

citerne [sitɛʀn] NF tank; (*à eau*) water tank

cithare [sitaʀ] NF zither; (*Antiq*) cithara

citoyen, -yenne [sitwajɛ̃, jɛn] 1 ADJ (= *faisant preuve de civisme*) [*entreprise*] socially aware; **une nation citoyenne** a nation where the notion of citizenship is central 2 NM,F citizen; **~/citoyenne d'honneur d'une ville** freeman/freewoman of a town; **~ du monde** citizen of the world 3 NM (* = *type*) guy*, bloke* (*Brit*); **drôle de ~** oddbod*, oddball* (*US*)

citoyenneté [sitwajɛnte] NF citizenship

citrin, e [sitʀɛ̃, in] 1 ADJ citrine-coloured 2 **citrine** NF (= *pierre*) citrine

citrique [sitʀik] ADJ citric

citron [sitʀɔ̃] 1 NM (= *fruit*) lemon; (:: = *tête*) head, nut*; **un** *ou* **du ~ pressé** a (fresh) lemon juice; **~ vert** lime → **thé** 2 ADJ INV lemon(-coloured (*Brit*) *ou* -colored (*US*)); **jaune ~** lemon-yellow

citronnade [sitʀɔnad] NF lemon squash (*Brit*), still lemonade (*Brit*), lemonade (*US*)

citronné, e [sitʀɔne] ADJ [*goût, odeur*] lemony; [*gâteau*] lemon(-flavoured (*Brit*) *ou* -flavored (*US*)); [*liquide*] with lemon juice added, lemon-flavoured (*Brit*) *ou* -flavored (*US*); [*eau de toilette*] lemon-scented

citronnelle [sitʀɔnɛl] NF (= *graminée*) lemon grass; (= *mélisse*) lemon balm; (= *verveine*) lemon verbena; (= *huile*) citronella (oil); (= *liqueur*) lemon liqueur

citronnier [sitʀɔnje] NM lemon tree

citrouille [sitʀuj] NF pumpkin; (:: = *tête*) head, nut*; **j'ai la tête comme une ~*** I feel like my head's going to explode

citrus [sitʀys] NM citrus

cive [siv] NF (*Bot*) chive; (*Culin*) chives

civet [sivɛ] NM stew; **lièvre en ~ ◇ ~ de lièvre** ≈ jugged hare

civette¹ [sivɛt] NF (*Zool*) civet (cat); (= *parfum*) civet

civette² [sivɛt] NF (*Bot*) chive; (*Culin*) chives

civière [sivjɛʀ] NF stretcher

civil, e [sivil] 1 ADJ a (= *entre citoyens*) [*guerre, mariage*] civil; (*Pol*) **personne de la société ~e** lay person **~ code, partie²** (= *non militaire*) civilian c (*littér = poli*) civil, courteous 2 NM a (= *non militaire*) civilian; **se mettre en ~** [*soldat*] to dress in civilian clothes, wear civvies*; [*policier*] to dress in plain clothes; **policier en ~** plain-clothes policeman, policeman in plain clothes; **soldat en ~** soldier in civvies* *ou* in mufti *ou* in civilian clothes; **dans le ~** in civilian life, in civvy street* (*Brit*) b (*Jur*) **poursuivre qn au ~** to take civil action against sb, sue sb in the (civil) courts

civilement [sivilmɑ̃] ADV a (*Jur*) **poursuivre qn ~** to take civil action against sb, sue sb in the (civil) courts; **être ~ responsable** to be legally responsible; **se marier ~** to have a civil wedding, ≈ get married in a registry office (*Brit*), ≈ be married by a judge (*US*) b (*littér = poliment*) civilly

civilisable [sivilizabl] ADJ civilizable

civilisateur, -trice [sivilizatœʀ, tʀis] 1 ADJ civilizing 2 NM,F civilizer

civilisation [sivilizasjɔ̃] NF civilization

civilisé, e [sivilize] (*ptp de* **civiliser**) ADJ civilized

civiliser [sivilize] ▸conjug 1◂ 1 VT to civilize 2 **se civiliser** VPR [*peuple*] to become civilized; * [*personne*] to become more civilized

civilité [sivilite] NF (= *politesse*) civility; (*frm* = *compliments*) **~s** civilities; **faire** *ou* **présenter ses ~s à** to pay one's compliments to

civique [sivik] ADJ civic; **avoir le sens ~** to be public-spirited → **éducation, instruction**

civisme [sivism] NM public-spiritedness; **cours de ~** civics *sg*

cl (ABRÉV = *centilitre*) cl

clabaudage [klabodaʒ] NM (*littér*) [*personne*] moaning, whingeing; [*chien*] yapping

clabauder [klabode] ▸conjug 1◂ VI (*littér*) [*personne*] to moan, whinge (**contre** about);

[*chien*] to yap; **~ contre qn** to make denigrating remarks about sb

clabauderie [klabodʀi] NF (*littér*) = **clabaudage**

clabaudeur, -euse [klabodœʀ, øz] (*littér*) [1] ADJ (= *médisant*) gossiping; (= *aboyant*) yapping [2] NM,F (= *cancanier*) gossip

clac [klak] EXCL [*porte*] slam!; [*élastique, stylo*] snap!; [*fouet*] crack!

clafoutis [klafuti] NM clafoutis (*type of tart made of fruit and batter*)

claie [klɛ] NF [*fruit, fromage*] rack; (= *crible*) riddle; (= *clôture*) hurdle

▼ **clair, e**[1] [klɛʀ] [1] ADJ [a] (= *lumineux*) [*pièce*] bright, light; [*ciel*] clear; [*couleur, flamme*] bright; **par temps ~** on a clear day, in clear weather
[b] (= *pâle*) [*teint, couleur*] light; [*tissu, robe*] light-coloured (*Brit*) ou -colored (*US*); **bleu/vert ~** light blue/green
[c] (= *limpide*) [*eau, son, conscience, voyelle*] clear; **d'une voix ~e** in a clear voice
[d] (= *peu consistant*) [*sauce, soupe*] thin; [*tissu*] thin; [*blés*] sparse
[e] (= *sans ambiguïté*) [*exposé, pensée, position*] clear; **cette affaire n'est pas ~e** there's something slightly suspicious about all this; **avoir un esprit ~** to be a clear thinker; **je serai ~ avec vous** I'll be frank with you; **c'est ~ et net** it's perfectly clear; **son message était ~ et net** his message was loud and clear; **je ne ferai jamais ça, c'est ~ et net!** I'll never do that, there's no question ou no two ways* about it!
[f] (= *évident*) clear, obvious, plain; **il est ~ qu'il se trompe** it is clear ou obvious that he's mistaken; **son affaire est ~e, il est coupable** it's quite clear ou obvious that he's guilty; **c'est ~ comme le jour** ou **comme de l'eau de roche** it's as clear as daylight, it's crystal-clear; **il passe le plus ~ de son temps à rêver** he spends most of his time daydreaming; **le plus ~ de son argent** the better part of his money
[2] ADV **il fait ~** it's light; **il ne fait guère ~ dans cette pièce** it's not very light in this room; **il fait aussi ~ ou on voit aussi ~ qu'en plein jour** it's as bright as daylight; **voir ~** (*lit*) to see well; **voir ~ dans un problème/une situation** to have a clear understanding of a problem/a situation, grasp a problem/situation clearly; **maintenant j'y vois plus ~** now I've got a better idea; **je vois ~ dans son jeu** I can see what his game is, I know exactly what he's up to*; **parlons ~** let's be frank
[3] **au clair** LOC ADV **tirer qch au ~** to clear sth up, clarify sth; **il faut tirer cette affaire au ~** we must get to the bottom of this business, we must sort this business out; **être au ~ sur qch** to be clear about ou on sth; **mettre ses idées au ~** to organize one's thoughts; **mettre les choses au ~** to make things clear; **mettre les choses au ~ avec qn** to get things straight with sb → **sabre**
[4] **en clair** LOC ADV (= *c'est-à-dire*) to put it plainly; (= *non codé*) [*message*] in clear; [*émission*] unscrambled
[5] NM [a] († = *partie usée*) **~s** worn parts, thin patches
[b] (*Art*) **~s** light (*NonC*), light areas; **les ~s et les ombres** the light and shade
[6] COMP ► **clair de lune** moonlight; **au ~ de lune** in the moonlight; **promenade au ~ de lune** stroll in the moonlight

claire[2] [klɛʀ] NF (= *parc*) oyster bed; **(huître de) ~** fattened oyster → **fine**[2]

clairement [klɛʀmɑ̃] ADV clearly

clairet, -ette [klɛʀɛ, ɛt] [1] ADJ [*soupe*] thin; [*voix*] high-pitched; **(vin) ~** light red wine
[2] **clairette** NF light sparkling wine

claire-voie (*pl* **claires-voies**) [klɛʀvwa] NF (= *clôture*) openwork fence; [*église*] clerestory; **à ~** openwork (*épith*)

clairière [klɛʀjɛʀ] NF clearing, glade

clair-obscur (*pl* **clairs-obscurs**) [klɛʀɔpskyʀ] NM (*Art*) chiaroscuro; (*gén*) twilight

clairon [klɛʀɔ̃] NM (= *instrument*) bugle; (= *joueur*) bugler; [*orgue*] clarion (stop)

claironnant, e [klɛʀɔnɑ̃, ɑ̃t] ADJ [*voix*] strident, resonant

claironner [klɛʀɔne] ▶ conjug 1 ◀ [1] VT [+ *succès, nouvelle*] to trumpet, shout from the rooftops [2] VI (= *parler fort*) to speak at the top of one's voice

clairsemé, e [klɛʀsəme] ADJ [*arbres, maisons, applaudissements, auditoire*] scattered; [*blés, gazon, cheveux*] thin, sparse; [*population*] sparse, scattered

clairvoyance [klɛʀvwajɑ̃s] NF [*personne*] clear-sightedness, perceptiveness; [*esprit*] perceptiveness

clairvoyant, e [klɛʀvwajɑ̃, ɑ̃t] [1] ADJ [a] (= *perspicace*) [*personne*] clear-sighted, perceptive; [*œil, esprit*] perceptive [b] († = *doué de vision*) sighted [2] NM,F († : *doué de vision*) sighted person; (= *médium*) clairvoyant

clam [klam] NM (*Zool*) clam

clamecer[ː] [klamse] ▶ conjug 3 ◀ VI (= *mourir*) to kick the bucket[ː], snuff it[ː] (*Brit*)

clamer [klame] ▶ conjug 1 ◀ VT to shout out, proclaim; **~ son innocence/son indignation** to proclaim one's innocence/one's indignation

clameur [klamœʀ] NF clamour; **les ~s de la foule** the clamour of the crowd; (*fig*) **les ~s des mécontents** the protests of the discontented

clamser[ː] [klamse] ▶ conjug 1 ◀ VI = **clamecer**

clan [klɑ̃] NM (*lit, fig*) clan; **esprit de ~** clannishness

clandé [klɑ̃de] NM (*arg Crime*) (= *maison close*) brothel, knocking-shop[ː] (*Brit*); (= *maison de jeu*) gambling joint

clandestin, e [klɑ̃dɛstɛ̃, in] [1] ADJ [*réunion*] secret, clandestine; [*revue, organisation, imprimerie*] underground (*épith*); [*mouvement*] underground (*épith*), clandestine; [*commerce*] clandestine, illicit; [*travailleur, travail, immigration, avortement*] illegal [2] NM (= *ouvrier*) illegal worker; **(passager) ~** stowaway

clandestinement [klɑ̃dɛstinmɑ̃] ADV (= *secrètement*) secretly; (= *illégalement*) illegally; **faire entrer qn ~ dans un pays** to smuggle sb into a country

clandestinité [klɑ̃dɛstinite] NF [a] [*activité*] secret nature; **dans la ~** (= *en secret*) [*travailler*] in secret, clandestinely; (= *en se cachant*) [*vivre*] underground; **entrer dans la ~** to go underground; **le journal interdit a continué de paraître dans la ~** the banned newspaper went on being published underground ou clandestinely [b] (*Hist* = *la Résistance*) **la ~** the Resistance

clanique [klanik] ADJ [*rivalité, société*] clan (*épith*); **guerre ~** clan warfare

clap [klap] NM (*Ciné*) clapperboard

clapet [klapɛ] NM [a] (*Tech*) valve; (*Élec*) rectifier; (*Aut*) **~ d'admission/d'échappement** induction/exhaust valve [b] (ː = *bouche*) **ferme ton ~** hold your tongue*, shut up*; **quel ~!** what a chatterbox!*

clapier [klapje] NM [a] (= *cabane à lapins*) hutch; (*péj* = *logement surpeuplé*) dump[ː], hole* [b] (= *éboulis*) scree

clapotement [klapɔtmɑ̃] NM lap(ping) (*NonC*)

clapoter [klapɔte] ▶ conjug 1 ◀ VI [*eau*] to lap

clapotis [klapɔti] NM lap(ping) (*NonC*)

clappement [klapmɑ̃] NM click(ing) (*NonC*)

clapper [klape] ▶ conjug 1 ◀ VI **~ de la langue** to click one's tongue

claquage [klakaʒ] NM (= *action*) pulling ou straining (of a muscle); (= *blessure*) pulled ou

strained muscle; **se faire un ~** to pull ou strain a muscle

claquant, e[ː] [klakɑ̃, ɑ̃t] ADJ (= *fatigant*) killing*, exhausting

claque[1] [klak] NF [a] (= *gifle*) slap; **donner ou flanquer* ou filer* une ~ à** to slap sb, give sb a slap ou clout* (*Brit*); (*fig humiliation*) **il a pris une ~ aux dernières élections** the last election was a slap in the face for him; (*fig = choc*) **elle a pris une ~ quand son mari est parti*** it was a real blow to her when her husband left; **mes économies ont pris une ~ pendant les vacances** the holidays made a hole in my savings → **tête** [b] (*loc*) **il en a sa ~*** (*excédé*) he's fed up to the back teeth* (*Brit*) ou to the teeth* (*US*); (*épuisé*) he's dead beat* ou all in* [c] (*Théât*) **faire la ~** to cheer [d] (*Can* = *protection*) galosh, overshoe

claque[2] [klak] ADJ, NM **(chapeau) ~** opera hat

claque[3]: [klak] NM brothel, whorehouse† *, knocking-shop[ː] (*Brit*)

claqué, e[ː] [klake] (*ptp de* **claquer**) ADJ (= *fatigué*) all in*, dead beat*, knackered* (*Brit*)

claquement [klakmɑ̃] NM [a] (= *bruit répété*) [*porte*] banging (*NonC*), slamming (*NonC*); [*fouet*] cracking (*NonC*); [*langue*] clicking (*NonC*); [*doigts*] snap(ping) (*NonC*); [*talons*] click(ing) (*NonC*); [*dents*] chattering (*NonC*); [*drapeau*] flapping (*NonC*) [b] (= *bruit isolé*) [*porte*] bang, slam; [*fouet*] crack; [*langue*] click; **la corde cassa avec un ~ sec** the rope broke with a sharp snap

claquemurer [klakmyʀe] ▶ conjug 1 ◀ [1] VT to coop up; **il reste claquemuré dans son bureau toute la journée** he stays cooped up ou shut up ou shut away in his office all day [2] **se claquemurer** VPR to shut o.s. away ou up

claquer [klake] ▶ conjug 1 ◀ [1] VI [a] [*porte, volet*] to bang; [*drapeau*] to flap; [*fouet*] to crack; [*coup de feu*] to ring out; **faire ~** [+ *porte*] to bang, slam; [+ *fouet*] to crack
[b] (= *produire un bruit*) **~ des doigts** ◊ **faire ses doigts** to click ou snap one's fingers; (*Mil*) **~ des talons** to click one's heels; (*fig*) **~ du bec**[ː] to be famished*; **il claquait des dents** his teeth were chattering; **faire ~ sa langue** to click one's tongue
[c] (= *casser*) [*ficelle*] to snap
[d] * [*télévision, moteur, lampe*] to conk out[ː], pack in*; (ː = *mourir*) to kick the bucket[ː], snuff it[ː] (*Brit*); **il a claqué d'une crise cardiaque** a heart attack finished him off; **~ dans les mains** ou **les doigts de qn** [*malade*] to die on sb; [*entreprise*] to go bust on sb*; **le sèche-cheveux m'a claqué entre les mains** ou **les doigts** the hair-drier packed in on me* ou died on me*
[2] VT [a] (= *gifler*) [+ *enfant*] to slap
[b] (= *refermer avec bruit*) [+ *livre*] to snap shut; **~ la porte** (*lit*) to slam the door; (*fig*) to storm out; **il a claqué la porte du gouvernement** he left the government in high dudgeon; **il m'a claqué la porte au nez** (*lit*) he slammed the door in my face; (*fig*) he refused to listen to me
[c] (* = *fatiguer*) [*travail*] to exhaust, tire out; **le voyage m'a claqué** I felt dead tired* ou knackered[ː] (*Brit*) after the journey; **~ son cheval** to wear out ou exhaust one's horse; **ne travaille pas tant, tu vas te ~** don't work so hard or you'll knock ou wear yourself out
[d] (* = *casser*) [+ *élastique, fermeture éclair*] to bust*
[e] (ː = *dépenser*) [+ *argent*] to blow*; **j'ai beaucoup claqué à Noël** I blew* a lot of cash at Christmas
[3] **se claquer** VPR (*Sport*) **se ~ un muscle** to pull ou strain a muscle

claquette [klakɛt] NF [a] (*Danse*) **~s** tap-dancing; **faire des ~s** to tap-dance → **danseur** [b] (= *claquoir*) clapper; (*Ciné*) clapperboard [c] (= *tong*) flip-flop, thong (*US*)

claquoir [klakwaʀ] NM clapper

► **GRAMMAIRE ACTIVE:** clair 42.1, 53.6

clarification [klaʀifikasjɔ̃] NF (lit, fig) clarification

clarifier [klaʀifje] ▶conjug 7◀ VT 1 VT (lit, fig) to clarify 2 **se clarifier** VPR [situation] to become clearer, be clarified

clarine [klaʀin] NF cowbell

clarinette [klaʀinɛt] NF clarinet

clarinettiste [klaʀinɛtist] NMF clarinettist

clarisse [klaʀis] NF (Poor) Clare

clarté [klaʀte] NF a (= lumière) light; **la ~ de la lune** the light of the moon, the moonlight; **à la ~ de la lampe** in the lamplight, in ou by the light of the lamp b (= luminosité) [flamme, pièce, jour, ciel] brightness; [eau, son, verre] clearness; [teint] (= pureté) clearness; (= pâleur) lightness; c (fig = netteté) [explication, pensée, attitude, conférencier] clarity; **~ d'esprit** clear thinking; **pour plus de ~** to be perfectly ou absolutely clear d (fig = précisions) **avoir des ~s sur une question** to have some (further ou bright) ideas on a subject; **cela projette quelques ~s sur la question** this throws some light on the subject

clash [klaʃ] NM clash

classable [klasabl] ADJ [document, plante] classifiable; **elle est difficilement ~** it's hard to know how to categorize her

classe [klas] 1 NF a (= catégorie sociale) class; (Démographie) **~s creuses** age groups depleted by war deaths or low natality; **les ~s moyennes** the middle classes; **les basses/hautes ~s (sociales)** the lower/upper (social) classes; **la ~ laborieuse ou ouvrière** the working class; **la ~ politique** the political community; **selon sa ~ sociale** according to one's social status ou social class; **société sans ~** classless society b (gén, Sci = espèce) class; (Admin = rang) grade; **toutes les ~s d'utilisateurs** every category of user; **il est vraiment à mettre dans une ~ à part** he's really in a class of his own ou a class apart; **hôtel de première ~** first-class hotel; **~ grammaticale ou de mots** grammatical category, part of speech; **~ d'âge** age group; **établissement de ~** high-class establishment; **de ~ internationale** world-class; **hors ~** exceptional c (Aviat, Rail) class; **compartiment/billet de 1ère/2ème ~** 1st/2nd class compartment/ticket; **voyager en 1ère ~** to travel 1st class; (Aviat) **~ affaires/club/touriste** business/club/economy class d (gén, Sport = valeur) class; **liqueur/artiste de grande ~** liqueur/artist of great distinction; **de ~ internationale** of international class; **elle a de la ~** she's got class; **ils n'ont pas la même ~** they're not in the same class; **robe qui a de la ~** stylish ou chic dress; **ils sont descendus au Ritz — la ~ quoi !*** they stayed at the Ritz — classy, eh?* e (Scol) (= ensemble d'élèves) class, form (Brit), grade (US); (= année d'études secondaires) year; **les grandes/petites ~s** the senior/junior classes; **il est en ~ de 6ème** ≈ he is in the 1st year (Brit) ou 5th grade (US); **monter de ~** to go up a class; **il est (le) premier/(le) dernier de la ~** he is top/bottom of the class; **~ enfantine** playschool; **partir en ~ verte ou de nature** ≈ to go to the country with the school; **partir en ~ de neige/de mer** ≈ to go skiing/to the seaside with the school → **préparatoire, redoubler** f (Scol) (= cours) class; (= l'école) **la ~** school; **la ~ d'histoire/de français** the history/French class; **~ de solfège/de danse** musical theory/dancing lesson; **aller en ~** ou **à la ~** to go to school; **pendant/après la ~** ou **les heures de ~** during/after school ou school hours; **la ~ se termine** ou **les élèves sortent de ~ à 16 heures** school finishes ou classes finish at 4 o'clock; **il est en ~** (en cours) [professeur] he is in class, he is teaching; [élève] he is in class; (à l'école) [élève] he is at school; **c'est M. Renan qui leur fait la ~**

(habituellement) Mr Renan is their (primary school) teacher, Mr Renan takes them at (primary) school; (en remplacement) Mr Renan is their replacement (primary school) teacher g (Scol = salle) classroom; (d'une classe particulière) form room (Brit), homeroom (US); **il est turbulent en ~** he's disruptive in class ou in the classroom; **les élèves viennent d'entrer en ~** the pupils have just gone into class h (Mil = rang) **militaire ou soldat de 1ère ~** (armée de terre) ≈ private (Brit), ≈ private first class (US); (armée de l'air) ≈ leading aircraftman (Brit), ≈ airman first class (US); **militaire ou soldat de 2ème ~** (terre) private (Brit), (air) aircraftman (Brit), airman basic (US); (= contingent) **la ~ de 1997** the class of '97; **ils sont de la même ~** they were called up at the same time; **faire ses ~s** (lit) to do one's recruit training; (fig) to learn the ropes*, serve one's apprenticeship (fig)

2 ADJ INV* [personne, vêtements, voiture] classy*; **ça fait ~** it adds a touch of class*

classé, e [klase] ADJ [bâtiment, monument] listed (Brit), with a preservation order on it; [vins] classified; [joueur] (= Tennis) ≈ ranked player; (Bridge) graded ou master player

classement [klasmɑ̃] NM a (= rangement) [papiers, documents] filing; [livres] classification; [fruits] grading; **~ alphabétique** alphabetical classification; **j'ai fait du ~ toute la journée** I've spent all day filing; **j'ai fait un peu de ~ dans mes factures** I've put my bills into some kind of order b (= classification) [fonctionnaire, élève] grading; [joueur] grading, ranking; [hôtel] grading, classification c (= rang) [élève] place (Brit) ou rank (US) (in class), position in class; [coureur] placing; **avoir un bon/mauvais ~** [élève] to get a high/low place in class (Brit), be ranked high/low in class (US); [coureur] to be well/poorly placed; **le ~ des coureurs à l'arrivée** the placing of the runners at the finishing line d (= liste) [élèves] class list (in order of merit); [coureurs] finishing list; [équipes] league table; **je vais vous lire le ~** I'm going to read you your (final) placings (Brit) (in class) ou rankings (US); (Cyclisme) **~ général** overall placings (Brit) ou rankings (US); **premier au ~ général/au ~ de l'étape** first overall/for the stage e (= clôture) [affaire, dossier] closing

classer [klase] ▶conjug 1◀ 1 VT a (= ranger) [+ papiers] to file; [+ livres] to classify; [+ documents] to file, to classify; **~ des livres par sujet** to classify books by ou according to subject (matter); **~ des factures par année/client** to file invoices according to the year/the customer's name b (Sci = classifier) [+ animaux, plantes] to classify c (= hiérarchiser) [+ employé, élève, joueur, copie] to grade; [+ hôtel] to grade, classify; **~ un édifice monument historique** to list a building (Brit), put a building on the historical register (US); **Jean Suchet, que l'on classe parmi les meilleurs violonistes** Jean Suchet, who ranks ou is rated among the top violinists d (= clore) [+ affaire, dossier] to close; **c'est une affaire classée maintenant** the matter is closed now e (péj = cataloguer) [+ personne] to categorize; **celui-là, je l'ai classé dès que je l'ai vu** I sized him up* as soon as I saw him

2 **se classer** VPR **se ~ premier/parmi les premiers** to come (Brit) ou come in (US) first/among the first; **ce livre se classe au nombre des grands chefs-d'œuvre littéraires** this book ranks among the great works of literature

classeur [klasœʀ] NM (= meuble) filing cabinet; (= dossier) (loose-leaf) file; (à tirette) binder; **~ à anneaux** ring binder; **~ à rideau** roll-top cabinet

classicisme [klasisism] NM (Art) classicism; (= conformisme) conventionality

classieux, -ieuse* [klasjø, jøz] ADJ classy*

classificateur, -trice [klasifikatœʀ, tʀis] 1 ADJ [procédé, méthode] classifying; (= méthodique) [esprit] methodical, orderly; **obsession classificatrice** mania for categorizing ou classifying things 2 NM,F classifier

classification [klasifikasjɔ̃] NF classification

classificatoire [klasifikatwaʀ] ADJ classificatory

classifier [klasifje] ▶conjug 7◀ VT to classify

classique [klasik] 1 ADJ a (Art) [auteur, genre, musique] classical; (Ling) [langue] classical b (= sobre) [coupe, vêtement, décoration] classic, classical c (= habituel) [argument, réponse, méthode, maladie] classic, standard; [conséquence] usual; [symptôme] classic, usual; [produit] ordinary, regular (US); **c'est ~** it's classic!; **c'est le coup ~ !*** it's the usual story; **c'est la question/la plaisanterie ~** it's the classic question/joke; **le cambriolage s'est déroulé suivant le plan ~** the burglary followed the standard ou recognized pattern; **grâce à une opération maintenant ~** thanks to an operation which is now quite usual ou standard d (Scol = littéraire) **faire des études ~s** to study classics, do classical studies; **il est en section ~** he's in the classics stream (Brit), he's in the classic program (US) → **lettre**

2 NM a (= auteur) (Antiq) classical author; (classicisme français) classic, classicist; (= grand écrivain) (auteur) **~** classic (author) b (= ouvrage) classic; **un ~ du cinéma** a cinema classic, a classic film; **c'est un ~ du genre** it's a classic of its kind; (hum) **je connais mes ~s !*** I know my classics! c (= genre) **le ~** (= musique) classical music; (= style) the classic ou classical style 3 NF (Sport) classic; (Cyclisme) one-day road race

classiquement [klasikmɑ̃] ADV classically

claudication [klodikasjɔ̃] NF (littér) limp

claudiquer [klodike] ▶conjug 1◀ VI (littér) to limp

clause [kloz] NF (Gram, Jur) clause; **~ de conscience** conscience clause; **~ dérogatoire ou échappatoire** escape clause; **~ de la nation la plus favorisée** most-favoured-nation trading status; **~ pénale** penalty clause; **~ de style** standard ou set clause; **~ résolutoire** resolutive clause → **sauvegarde**

claustral, e (mpl -aux) [klostʀal, o] ADJ monastic, cloistral, claustral

claustration [klostʀasjɔ̃] NF confinement

claustrer [klostʀe] ▶conjug 1◀ 1 VT (= enfermer) to confine 2 **se claustrer** VPR to shut o.s. up ou away; (fig) **se ~ dans** to wrap ou enclose o.s. in

claustrophobe [klostʀɔfɔb] ADJ, NMF claustrophobic

claustrophobie [klostʀɔfɔbi] NF claustrophobia

clausule [klozyl] NF clausula

clavecin [klav(ə)sɛ̃] NM harpsichord

claveciniste [klav(ə)sinist] NMF harpsichordist

clavette [klavɛt] NF (Tech) [boulon] key, cotter pin

clavicorde [klavikɔʀd] NM clavichord

clavicule [klavikyl] NF collarbone, clavicle (SPÉC)

clavier [klavje] NM (lit) keyboard; (fig = registre) range; **à un/deux ~(s)** [orgue, clavecin] single-/double-manual (épith); **~ AZERTY/QWERTY** AZERTY/QWERTY keyboard

claviste [klavist] NMF keyboard operator, keyboarder

clayette [klɛjɛt] NF (= étagère) wicker ou wire rack; (= cageot à fruits) tray; [réfrigérateur] shelf

clayon [klɛjɔ̃] NM (= étagère) rack; (= plateau) tray

clé [kle] **1** NF **a** [serrure, pendule, boîte de conserve] key; [poêle] damper; **la ~ de la porte d'entrée** the (front) door key; **la ~ est sur la porte** the key is in the door; **Avignon, ~ de la Provence** Avignon, the gateway to Provence; **les ~s du Paradis** the keys to the Kingdom; **les ~s de saint Pierre** St Peter's keys → **fermer, tour²** **b** (Tech) spanner (Brit), wrench (surtout US); **un jeu de ~s** a set of spanners ou wrenches **c** (Mus) [guitare, violon] peg; [clarinette] key; [gamme] clef; [accordeur] key; **~ de fa/de sol/d'ut** bass ou F/treble ou G/alto ou C clef; **il y a trois dièses à la ~** the key signature has 3 sharps; **avec une altération à la ~** with a change in the key signature **d** [mystère, réussite, code, rêve] key (**de** to); **la préface nous fournit quelques ~s** the preface offers a few clues **e** (Lutte) lock; **il lui a fait une ~ au bras** he got him in an armlock **f** (loc) **personnage à ~s** real-life character disguised under a fictitious name; **roman à ~s** roman à clef (novel in which actual persons appear as fictitious characters); **il y a une récompense à la ~** there's a reward at the end of it all ou at the end of the day; **je vais les mettre en retenue, avec un devoir à la ~** I'll keep them behind, and give them an exercise into the bargain; **mettre sous ~** to put under lock and key; **mettre la ~ sous la porte** ou le **paillasson** (= faire faillite) to shut up shop; (= s'enfuir) to clear out, do a bunk* (Brit); **prendre la ~ des champs** to run away ou off **g** **~s en main: acheter un appartement ~s en main** to buy an apartment ready for immediate occupation ou with immediate entry; **prix ~s en main** [voiture] price on the road, on-the-road price (Brit), sticker price (US); [appartement] price with immediate entry ou possession ou occupation; **solution/usine ~s en main** turnkey solution/factory

2 ADJ INV [industrie, mot, position, rôle] key (épith)

3 COMP ▸ **clé Allen** Allen wrench ou key (Brit) ▸ **clé anglaise** = **clé à molette** ▸ **clé à bougie** spark plug swivel ▸ **clé de contact** ignition key ▸ **clé à crémaillère** monkey wrench, shifting spanner ou wrench ▸ **clé crocodile** alligator spanner ou wrench ▸ **clé en croix** wheel brace ▸ **clé dynamométrique** torque wrench ▸ **clé à ergot** spanner wrench ▸ **clé à fourche** = **clé plate** ▸ **clé mixte** combination spanner ou wrench ▸ **clé à molette** monkey wrench, adjustable spanner ou wrench ▸ **clé à pipe** box ou socket spanner, socket wrench ▸ **clé plate** open-end spanner ou wrench ▸ **clé polygonale** ring spanner ou wrench ▸ **clé RIB** personal code (that appears on official slip giving bank account details) ▸ **clé en tube** hex key (wrench) ▸ **clé universelle** adjustable spanner ou wrench ▸ **clé de voûte** (Archit, fig) keystone

clean* [klin] ADJ INV **a** [homme] wholesome-looking, clean-cut; [femme] wholesome-looking; [vêtements] smart; [décor] stark **b** (arg Drogue) clean

clébard* [klebaʀ], **clebs*** [klɛps] NM (péj = chien) dog, hound (hum), mutt*

clef [kle] NF = **clé**

clématite [klematit] NF clematis

clémence [klemɑ̃s] NF (= douceur) [temps] mildness, clemency (frm); (= indulgence) [juge] clemency, leniency

clément, e [klemɑ̃, ɑ̃t] ADJ (= doux) [temps] mild, clement (frm); (= indulgent) [personne] lenient; **se montrer ~** to show clemency (**envers** towards) → **ciel**

clémentine [klemɑ̃tin] NF clementine

clenche [klɑ̃ʃ] NF latch

Cléopâtre [kleopatʀ] NF Cleopatra

cleptomane [klɛptɔman] NMF = **kleptomane**

cleptomanie [klɛptɔmani] NF = **kleptomanie**

clerc [klɛʀ] NM **a** [notaire] clerk → **pas¹** **b** (Rel) cleric **c** (†† = lettré) (learned) scholar; **être (grand) ~ en la matière** to be an expert on the subject; **on n'a pas besoin d'être grand ~ pour deviner ce qui s'est passé !** you don't need to be a genius to guess what happened!

clergé [klɛʀʒe] NM clergy; **le bas/haut ~** the lower/higher clergy

clérical, e (mpl **-aux**) [klerikal, o] **1** ADJ (Rel) clerical **2** NM,F clerical, supporter of the clergy

cléricalisme [klerikalism] NM clericalism

clic [klik] NM **a** (= bruit Ordin) click; **le menu s'ouvre d'un ~ de souris** the menu opens with a mouse click **b** (TV) **~s** sparkles, sparklies*

clic-clac [klikklak] **1** EXCL [appareil-photo] click!; [pas] clickety-clack!; [sabots] clip(pety)-clop! **2** NM INV **a** (= bruit) [sabots] clip(pety)-clop; [talons] click **b** (canapé ou convertible) **~** sofa bed (with reclining back)

cliché [kliʃe] NM (= lieu commun) cliché; (Photo) negative; (Typo) plate

client, cliente [klijɑ̃, klijɑ̃t] NM,F **a** [magasin, restaurant] customer; [coiffeur] client, customer; [avocat] client; [hôtel] guest, patron; [médecin] patient; [taxi] fare; **être ~ d'un magasin** to patronize a shop, be a regular customer at a shop; **le boucher me sert bien parce que je suis (une) ~** the butcher gives me good service because I'm a regular customer (of his) ou because I'm one of his regulars; (Écon) **la France est un gros ~ de l'Allemagne** France is a large trading customer of Germany; (fig) **je ne suis pas ~*** it's not my thing* ou my cup of tea* **b** (* : péj = individu) guy*, bloke* (Brit); **un drôle de ~** he's an odd customer ou bloke* (Brit); **pour le titre de champion du monde, Suard est un ~ sérieux** Suard is a hot contender for ou is making a strong bid for the world championship **c** (Ordin) client **d** (Antiq = protégé) client

clientèle [klijɑ̃tɛl] NF **a** (= ensemble des clients) [restaurant, hôtel, coiffeur] clientele; [magasin] customers, clientele; [avocat, médecin] practice; [taxi] fares; [parti politique] supporters; **le boucher a une nombreuse ~** the butcher has many customers; **le candidat a conservé sa ~ électorale au deuxième tour** the candidate held on to his voters in the second round **b** (= fait d'être client) custom, business; **accorder sa ~ à qn** to give sb one's custom ou business, patronize sb; **retirer sa ~ à qn** to withdraw one's custom from sb, take one's business away from sb **c** (Antiq = protégés) clients

clientélisme [klijɑ̃telism] NM (péj) vote-catching, clientelism; **c'est du ~** it's just a vote-catching gimmick

clientéliste [klijɑ̃telist] ADJ [système, tradition] based on patronage, clientelist; **il y a un risque de pressions ~s** there is a danger of pressure being exerted by influential voters

clignement [kliɲ(ə)mɑ̃] NM blinking (NonC); **cela l'obligeait à des ~s d'yeux continuels** it made him blink continually; **un ~ d'œil** a wink

cligner [kliɲe] ▸ conjug 1 ◂ VT, VT INDIR **~ les** ou **des yeux** (clignoter) to blink; (fermer à moitié) to screw up one's eyes; **~ de l'œil** to wink (**en direction de** at)

clignotant, e [kliɲɔtɑ̃, ɑ̃t] **1** ADJ [lumière] vacillant) flickering; (= intermittent, pour signal) flashing, winking **2** NM **a** (Aut) indicator; (fig = indice de danger) warning light (fig); (Aut) **mettre son ~** to indicate (Brit), put one's turn signal on (US); (fig) **tous les ~s sont allumés** all

the warning signs ou danger signals are flashing

clignotement [kliɲɔtmɑ̃] NM [yeux] blinking; [étoile, guirlande] twinkling; [phares] flashing; [lumière] (vacillante) flickering; (vue de loin) twinkling; (= signal) flashing; **les ~s de la lampe** the flickering of the lamplight

clignoter [kliɲɔte] ▸ conjug 1 ◂ VI [yeux] to blink; [étoile, guirlande] to twinkle; [phares] to flash; [lumière] (= vaciller) to flicker; (vue de loin) to twinkle; (= signal) to flash, wink; **~ des yeux** to blink

clim* [klim] NF ABRÉV = **climatisation**

climat [klima] NM (lit, fig) climate; (littér = contrée) clime (littér); **dans** ou **sous nos ~s** in our climate; **~ économique/politique** economic/political climate; **le ~ social est très mauvais en ce moment** the public mood is very bad at the moment; **pour améliorer le ~ social dans cette profession/cette usine** to improve relations between management and workers in this profession/this factory

climatique [klimatik] ADJ climatic → **station**

climatisation [klimatizasjɔ̃] NF air conditioning

climatiser [klimatize] ▸ conjug 1 ◂ VT [+ pièce, atmosphère] to air-condition; (Tech) [+ appareil] to adapt for use in severe conditions; **bureau climatisé** air-conditioned office

climatiseur [klimatizœʀ] NM air conditioner

climatologie [klimatɔlɔʒi] NF climatology

climatologique [klimatɔlɔʒik] ADJ climatological

clin [klɛ̃] NM ▸ **d'œil** (pl **clins d'œil** ou **d'yeux**) (lit) wink; (fig: dans un roman, un film) allusion, veiled reference; (fig) **c'est un ~ d'œil aux Marx Brothers** it's a nod in the direction of the Marx Brothers; **c'est un ~ d'œil au lecteur** it is a veiled message to the reader; **faire un ~ d'œil** (lit) to wink (**à** at); (fig) to make a veiled reference (**à** to); **en un ~ d'œil** in a flash, in the twinkling of an eye

clinfoc [klɛ̃fɔk] NM flying jib

clinicien, -ienne [klinisjɛ̃, jɛn] NM,F clinician

clinique [klinik] **1** ADJ clinical → **mort¹** **2** NF **a** (= établissement) nursing home, private hospital, private clinic; (= section d'hôpital) clinic; **~ d'accouchement** maternity hospital, maternity home (Brit) → **chef¹** **b** (= enseignement) clinic

cliniquement [klinikmɑ̃] ADV clinically

clinquant, e [klɛ̃kɑ̃, ɑ̃t] **1** ADJ [bijoux, décor, langage] flashy **2** NM **a** [lamelles brillantes] tinsel; (= faux bijoux) tawdry jewellery (Brit) ou jewelery (US); [opéra, style] flashiness

clip [klip] NM **a** (= broche) brooch **b** (= boucle d'oreille) clip-on **c** ~ (vidéo) (pop) video, (music) video clip; (promotionnel) (promo) video **d** (Chir) clamp

clipper [klipœʀ] NM (Naut) clipper

clique [klik] NF **a** (péj = bande) clique, set **b** (Mil = orchestre) drum and bugle band **c** **prendre ses ~s et ses claques (et s'en aller)*** to pack up and go, pack one's bags and leave

cliquer [klike] ▸ conjug 1 ◂ VI (Ordin) to click (**sur** on)

cliquet [klikɛ] NM pawl

cliqueter [klik(ə)te] ▸ conjug 4 ◂ VI [monnaie] to jingle, clink, chink; [dés] to rattle; [vaisselle] to clatter; [verres] to clink, chink; [chaînes] to clank; [ferraille] to jangle; [mécanisme] to go clickety-clack; [armes] to clash; [moteur] to pink, knock; **j'entends quelque chose qui cliquette** I can hear something clinking

cliquetis [klik(ə)ti], **cliquettement** [klikɛtmɑ̃] NM [clés] jingle (NonC), jingling (NonC); [vaisselle] clatter (NonC); [verres] clink (NonC), clinking (NonC); [chaînes] clank (NonC), clanking (NonC); [ferraille] jangle (NonC), jangling

(NonC); [mécanisme] clickety-clack (NonC); [armes] clash (NonC); [moteur] pinking ou knocking sound, pinking (NonC); [machine à écrire] rattle (NonC), clicking (NonC); **on entendait un ~ ou des ~ de vaisselle** we could hear the clatter of dishes; **des ~ se firent entendre** clinking noises could be heard

clisse [klis] NF **a** [fromage] wicker tray **b** [bouteille] wicker covering

clisser [klise] ▶conjug 1◀ VT [+ bouteille] to cover with wicker(work)

clitoridectomie [klitɔʀidɛktɔmi] NF clitoridectomy

clitoridien, -ienne [klitɔʀidjɛ̃, jɛn] ADJ clitoral

clitoris [klitɔʀis] NM clitoris

clivage [klivaʒ] NM **a** (Géol = fissure) cleavage **b** (Minér) (= action) cleaving; (= résultat) cleavage **c** [groupes] split, division; [idées] distinction, split (**de** in)

cliver VT, **se cliver** VPR [klive] ▶conjug 1◀ (Minér) to cleave

cloaque [klɔak] NM (Zool) cloaca; (= lieu de corruption) cesspool, cesspit; (= endroit sale) pigsty, dump*, tip* (Brit)

clochard, e [klɔʃaʀ, aʀd] NM,F down-and-out, tramp, bum* (US)

clochardisation [klɔʃaʀdizasjɔ̃] NF **les hommes sont plus touchés par la ~ que les femmes** men are more liable than women to become down-and-outs ou to end up living on the streets; **marginaux en voie de ~** drop-outs on the road to vagrancy

clochardiser [klɔʃaʀdize] ▶conjug 1◀ **1** VT [+ personne] to turn into a down-and-out ou a tramp ou a bum* (US); **les toxicomanes clochardisés** down-and-out drug addicts **2** **se clochardiser** VPR [personne] to become a down-and-out ou a tramp ou a bum* (US); **la ville se clochardise** there are more and more down-and-outs ou tramps ou bums* (US) in the town

cloche [klɔʃ] **1** NF **a** [église] bell; **en forme de ~** bell-shaped; **courbe en ~** bell curve; **il a été élevé sous ~** he had a very sheltered upbringing, he was wrapped in cotton wool as a child (Brit); **il ne faut pas mettre nos entreprises sous ~** we shouldn't cosset our companies → **son²** **b** (= couvercle) [plat] dishcover, lid; [plantes, légumes] cloche **c** * (= imbécile) idiot, clot* (Brit); (= clochard) down-and-out, tramp, bum* (US); **la ~** (= les clochards) down-and-outs, tramps, bums* (US); (= style de vie) the life of a tramp **d** (Chim) bell jar **2** ADJ **a** (= évasé) [jupe] bell-shaped → **chapeau** **b** * (= idiot) idiotic, silly; **qu'il est ~ ce type !** what an idiot ou a clot!* (Brit) **3** COMP ► **cloche à fromage** cheese cover ► **cloche à plongeur** ou **de plongée** diving bell

Clochemerle [klɔʃmɛʀl] NM (hum) **c'est un peu ~ ici** there's a touch of parish-pump politics about this place, a lot of petty small-town squabbling goes on here

┌─── **CLOCHEMERLE** ───┐
This term is an allusion to the title of a humorous novel, written in 1934 by Gabriel Chevallier, describing the pandemonium that erupts in a French village community following the decision to erect a public urinal next to the local church.

cloche-pied (à) [klɔʃpje] LOC ADV hopping; **arriver à cloche-pied** to come hopping along, hop in; **il est parti (en sautant) à cloche-pied** he hopped away ou off

clocher¹ [klɔʃe] NM **a** (Archit) (en pointe) steeple; (carré) church tower **b** (fig = village) village; **revoir son ~** to see one's home town again; **de ~** [mentalité] parochial, small-town (épith); [querelles] local, parochial → **esprit**

► GRAMMAIRE ACTIVE: **clore** 53.4

clocher*² [klɔʃe] ▶conjug 1◀ VI (= être défectueux) [raisonnement] to be cockeyed*; **qu'est-ce qui cloche ?** what's up (with you)?*; **pourvu que rien ne cloche** provided nothing goes wrong ou there are no hitches; **il y a quelque chose qui cloche (dans ce qu'il dit)** there's something which doesn't quite fit ou something not quite right (in what he says); **il y a quelque chose qui cloche dans le moteur** there's something wrong ou there's something up* with the engine

clocheton [klɔʃtɔ̃] NM (Archit) pinnacle

clochette [klɔʃɛt] NF (small) bell; (= partie de fleur) bell; **~s** (= campanules) bellflowers; **~s bleues** (= jacinthes des bois) bluebells

clodo* [klodo] NM tramp, bum* (US)

cloison [klwazɔ̃] NF **a** (Constr) partition (wall) **b** (Anat, Bot) septum, partition; **~ nasale** nasal septum **c** (Naut) bulkhead; **~ étanche** watertight compartment **d** (fig) barrier; **les ~s entre les différentes classes sociales** the barriers between the different social classes

cloisonné, e [klwazɔne] (ptp de **cloisonner**) **1** ADJ **être ~** [sciences, services administratifs] to be isolated ou cut off from one another; **nous vivons dans un monde ~** we live in a compartmentalized world **2** NM (Art) cloisonné

cloisonnement [klwazɔnmã] NM [société, système] compartmentalization; **le ~ des services** the fact that the departments work in isolation (from one another); **à cause du ~ culturel et social** because of cultural and social barriers

cloisonner [klwazɔne] ▶conjug 1◀ VT [+ pièce] to divide up, partition off; [+ tiroir] to divide up; [+ société] to divide, compartmentalize; [+ secteurs] to isolate

cloître [klwatʀ] NM cloister

cloîtrer [klwatʀe] ▶conjug 1◀ **1** VT (= enfermer) to shut away (**dans** in); (Rel) to cloister; **~ une jeune fille** (lit) to put a girl in a convent; (fig) to keep a girl shut away (from the rest of society); **religieuse cloîtrée** nun belonging to an enclosed order **2** **se cloîtrer** VPR (= s'enfermer) to shut o.s. up ou away, cloister o.s. (**dans** in); (Rel) to enter a convent ou monastery; **il est resté cloîtré dans sa chambre pendant 2 jours** he stayed shut up ou away in his room for 2 days; **ils vivent cloîtrés chez eux sans jamais voir personne** they cut themselves off from the world ou they lead cloistered lives and never see anyone

clonage [klonaʒ] NM (lit, fig) cloning

clone [klon] NM (lit, fig) clone

cloner [klone] ▶conjug 1◀ VT (lit, fig) to clone

clope* [klɔp] **1** NF (= cigarette) cig*, smoke*, fag* (Brit) **2** NM (= mégot) butt, dog end*

cloper* [klɔpe] ▶conjug 1◀ VI to smoke; **il était en train de ~** he was having a smoke, he was smoking

clopin-clopant [klɔpɛ̃klɔpã] ADV **a** (= en boitillant) **marcher ~** to hobble ou limp along; **il vint vers nous ~** he hobbled towards us; **sortir/entrer ~** to hobble out/in **b** (fig) **les affaires allaient ~** business was struggling along ou was just ticking over; **comment ça va ? — ~** how are things? — so-so*

clopiner [klɔpine] ▶conjug 1◀ VI (= boitiller) to hobble ou limp along; **~ vers** to hobble ou limp towards

clopinettes* [klɔpinɛt] NFPL **travailler pour/gagner des ~** to work for/earn peanuts*

cloporte* [klɔpɔʀt] NM (Zool) woodlouse; (péj) creep*

cloque [klɔk] NF [peau, peinture] blister; (Bot) leaf curl ou blister; **être en ~⁑** to be pregnant, be in the club⁑ (Brit); **il l'a mise en ~⁑** he knocked her up⁑, he put her in the club⁑ (Brit)

cloqué, e [klɔke] (ptp de **cloquer**) **1** ADJ [feuilles, peinture] blistered; **étoffe ~e** seersucker (NonC) **2** NM (Tex) seersucker

cloquer [klɔke] ▶conjug 1◀ VI [peau, peinture] to blister

▼ **clore** [klɔʀ] ▶conjug 45◀ VT **a** (= clôturer) [+ liste, débat] to close; [+ livre, discours, spectacle] to end, conclude; (Fin) [+ compte] to close; **la séance est close** the meeting is closed ou finished; **l'incident est clos** the matter is closed; **les inscriptions sont closes depuis hier** yesterday was the closing date for registration; **une description clôt le chapitre** the chapter closes ou ends ou concludes with a description; **le débat s'est clos sur cette remarque** the discussion ended ou closed with that remark **b** († ou littér = conclure) [+ accord, marché] to conclude **c** (littér = entourer) [+ terrain, ville] to enclose (**de** with) **d** (littér = fermer) [+ porte, volets] to close, shut; [+ lettre] to seal; [+ chemin, passage] to close off, seal off → **bec**

clos, close [klo, kloz] (ptp de **clore**) **1** ADJ [système, ensemble] closed; [espace] enclosed; **les yeux ~** ou **les paupières ~es, il ...** with his eyes closed ou shut, he ... → **huis, maison** **2** NM (= pré) (enclosed) field; (= vignoble) vineyard; **un ~ de pommiers** an apple orchard

clôture [klotyʀ] NF **a** (= enceinte) (en planches) fence, paling; (en fil de fer) (wire) fence; (d'arbustes) hedge; (en ciment) wall; **mur/grille de ~** outer ou surrounding wall/ railings → **bris** **b** (= fermeture) [débat, liste, compte] closing, closure; [bureaux, magasins] closing; [inscriptions] closing date (**de** for); (Ciné, Théât) **~ annuelle** annual closure; **il faut y aller avant la ~** (du festival) we must go before it ends ou is over; (d'une pièce) we must go before it closes ou ends; (du magasin) we must go before it closes ou shuts; **séance/date de ~** closing session/date; (Bourse) **cours de ~** closing price; **combien valait le dollar en ~ ?** what did the dollar close at?; **débat de ~** adjournment debate

clôturer [klotyʀe] ▶conjug 1◀ **1** VT **a** [+ jardin, champ] to enclose, fence **b** [+ débats, liste, compte] to close; [+ inscriptions] to close (the list of) **2** VI (Bourse) to close; **la séance a clôturé en baisse** prices were down at the close (of dealing), prices closed down; **le dollar a clôturé à 6 F** the dollar closed at 6 francs

clou [klu] **1** NM **a** (gén) nail; (décoratif) stud; **fixe-le avec un ~** nail it up (ou down ou on); **pendre son chapeau à un ~** to hang one's hat on a nail **b** [chaussée] stud; **traverser dans les ~s ◊ prendre les ~s (pour traverser)** to cross at the pedestrian ou zebra (Brit) crossing, cross at the crosswalk (US) **c** (Méd) boil **d** (= attraction principale) [spectacle] star attraction ou turn; **le ~ de la soirée** the highlight ou the star turn of the evening **e** (* = mont-de-piété) **mettre sa montre au ~** to pawn one's watch, put one's watch in hock* **f** (* = instrument) ancient machine ou implement; (vieux) (= voiture) old jalopy* ou banger* (Brit); (= vélo) rickety old bike, old boneshaker* (Brit) **g** (loc) **des ~s !⁑** no way!*, nothing doing!*; **il lui a tout expliqué mais des ~s !⁑** he explained everything to him but he was just wasting his breath!; **je l'ai fait pour des ~s*** I did it all for nothing, I was just wasting my time; **j'y suis allé pour des ~s*** it was a wild-goose chase ■ (PROV) **un ~ chasse l'autre** one man goes and another steps in ou another takes his place → **valoir** **2** COMP ► **clou à béton** masonry nail ► **clou de girofle** (Culin) clove ► **clou de tapissier** (upholstery) tack ► **clou à tête homme** veneer pin ► **clou à tête plate** flat-headed nail ► **clou sans tête** brad

clouer [klue] ▸conjug 1◂ VT [a] [+ planches, couvercle, caisse] to nail down; [+ tapis] to tack ou nail down; [+ tapisserie] to nail up; **il l'a cloué au sol d'un coup d'épée** he pinned him to the ground with a thrust of his sword [b] (= immobiliser) [+ ennemi] to pin down; **ça l'a cloué sur place** [étonnement, peur] it left him rooted to the spot; **~ qn au lit** to keep sb stuck in bed* ou confined to bed; **~ au sol** [personne] to pin down (to the ground); [+ avion] to ground; (Échecs) **~ une pièce** to pin a piece; **être** ou **rester cloué de stupeur** to be glued ou rooted to the spot with amazement → **bec**

cloué, e [klue] (ptp de **clouer**) ADJ [ceinture, porte] studded; [chaussures] hobnailed → **passage**

clouterie [klutʀi] NF nail factory

clovisse [klɔvis] NF clam

clown [klun] NM clown; **faire le ~** to clown (about), play the fool; **c'est un vrai ~** he's a real comic; **~ blanc** whiteface clown

clownerie [klunʀi] NF clowning (NonC), silly trick; **faire des ~** to clown (about), play the fool; **arrête tes ~s** stop your (silly) antics

clownesque [klunesk] ADJ [comportement] clownish; [situation] farcical

club [klœb] [1] NM [a] (= association) club; **le ~ des pays riches** the club of rich nations [b] (= crosse de golf) club [2] ADJ **sandwich ~** ham salad sandwich, ≈ club sandwich; **cravate ~** (diagonally) striped tie → **fauteuil** [3] COMP ▸ **club de gymnastique** gym ▸ **club d'investissement** investment club ▸ **club de jazz** jazz club ▸ **club privé** exclusive night club ▸ **club de rencontre(s)** singles club ▸ **club sportif** sports club ▸ **club du troisième âge** club for retired people, Darby and Joan club (Brit) ▸ **club de vacances** holiday (Brit) ou vacation (US) village

cluse [klyz] NF (Géog) transverse valley (in the Jura), cluse (SPÉC)

clystère [klister] NM (Hist Méd) clyster

Clytemnestre [klitɛmnɛstʀ] NF Clytemnestra

CM [seɛm] NM (ABRÉV = **cours moyen**) → **cours**

cm (ABRÉV = **centimètre**) cm; **cm²** cm², sq. cm; **cm³** cm³, cu. cm

CNAM [knam] [1] NM (ABRÉV = **Conservatoire national des arts et métiers**) → **conservatoire** [2] NF (ABRÉV = **Caisse nationale d'assurance maladie**) → **caisse**

CNC [seense] NM [a] (ABRÉV = **Centre national de cinématographie**) ≈ BFI (Brit), ≈ Academy of the Movie Picture (US) [b] (ABRÉV = **Comité national de la consommation**) ≈ National Consumer Council (Brit), ≈ CA (Brit), ≈ CPSC (US)

CNDP [seɛndepe] NM (ABRÉV = **Centre national de documentation pédagogique**) → **centre**

CNED [kned] NM (ABRÉV = **Centre national d'enseignement à distance**) → **centre**

CNIL [knil] NF (ABRÉV = **Commission nationale de l'informatique et des libertés**) → **commission**

CNIT [knit] NM (ABRÉV = **Centre national des industries et des techniques**) exhibition centre in Paris

CNPF [seɛnpeɛf] NM (ABRÉV = **Conseil national du patronat français**) national council of French employers, ≈ CBI (Brit)

CNRS [seɛneɛʀɛs] NM (ABRÉV = **Centre national de la recherche scientifique**) ≈ SERC (Brit), ≈ NSF (US)

coaccusé, e [kɔakyze] NM,F codefendant, co-accused

coacquéreur [kɔakeʀœʀ] NM joint purchaser

coadjuteur [kɔadʒytœʀ] NM coadjutor

coadjutrice [kɔadʒytʀis] NF coadjutress

coadministrateur, -trice [kɔadministʀatœʀ, tʀis] NM,F (Comm) co-director; (Jur) co-trustee

coagulant, e [kɔagylɑ̃, ɑ̃t] [1] ADJ coagulative [2] NM coagulant

coagulateur, -trice [kɔagylatœʀ, tʀis] ADJ coagulative

coagulation [kɔagylasjɔ̃] NF coagulation

coaguler VTI, **se coaguler** VPR [kɔagyle] ▸conjug 1◂ [sang] to coagulate (SPÉC), clot, congeal; [lait] to curdle

coalisé, e [kɔalize] (ptp de **coaliser**) [1] ADJ (= allié) [pays] allied; (= conjoint) [efforts] united [2] NMPL **les ~s** the members of the coalition

coaliser [kɔalize] ▸conjug 1◂ [1] VT to unite (in a coalition) [2] **se coaliser** VPR (= se liguer : gén) to unite; [pays] to form a coalition; **deux des commerçants se sont coalisés contre un troisième** two of the shopkeepers joined forces ou united against a third

coalition [kɔalisjɔ̃] NF coalition; **ministère de ~** coalition government

coaltar [kɔltaʀ] NM (lit) coal tar; **être dans le ~*** (après anesthésie) to be a bit groggy* ou whoozy*; (= être mal réveillé) to be a bit whoozy*, be half-asleep

coassement [kɔasmɑ̃] NM croaking (NonC)

coasser [kɔase] ▸conjug 1◂ VI to croak

coassocié, e [kɔasɔsje] NM,F copartner

coassurance [kɔasyʀɑ̃s] NF mutual assurance

coati [kɔati] NM coati

coauteur [kɔotœʀ] NM [a] (Littérat) co-author, joint author [b] (Jur) accomplice

coaxial, e [mpl **-aux**] [kɔaksjal, jo] ADJ coaxial

COB [kɔb] NF (ABRÉV = **Commission des opérations de Bourse**) French stock exchange regulatory body, ≈ SIB (Brit), ≈ SEC (US)

cobalt [kɔbalt] NM cobalt → **bombe**

cobaye [kɔbaj] NM (lit, fig) guinea-pig; **servir de ~ à** to act as ou be used as a guinea-pig for

cobelligérant, e [kobeliʒeʀɑ̃, ɑ̃t] [1] ADJ co-belligerent [2] NMPL **les ~s** the cobelligerent nations

Cobol [kɔbɔl] NM (Ordin) COBOL

cobra [kɔbʀa] NM cobra

coca [kɔka] [1] NM (ABRÉV = **Coca-Cola**)® Coke®; **un whisky ~** a whisky and Coke® [2] NF (= substance) coca extract [3] NM ou F (= plante) coca

cocagne [kɔkaɲ] NF → **mât, pays¹**

cocaïne [kɔkain] NF cocaine

cocaïnomane [kɔkainɔman] NMF cocaine addict

cocard* [kɔkaʀ] NM black eye, shiner*

cocarde [kɔkaʀd] NF (en tissu) rosette; (Hist : sur la coiffure) cockade; [avion] roundel; (sur voiture officielle) **~ (tricolore)** ≈ official sticker

cocardier, -ière [kɔkaʀdje, jɛʀ] [1] ADJ jingoistic, chauvinistic [2] NM,F jingoist, chauvinist

cocasse [kɔkas] ADJ comical, funny

cocasserie [kɔkasʀi] NF comicalness, funniness; **c'était d'une ~!** it was so funny! ou comical!

coccinelle [kɔksinɛl] NF (= insecte) ladybird, ladybug (US); (* = voiture) beetle (Brit), bug (US)

coccyx [kɔksis] NM coccyx

coche [kɔʃ] NM (= diligence) (stage)coach; (Hist) **~ d'eau** horse-drawn barge; (fig) **louper** ou **manquer** ou **rater le ~** to miss the boat* ou one's chance → **mouche**

cochenille [kɔʃnij] NF (gén) mealybug; (pour teinture) cochineal insect

cocher¹ [kɔʃe] ▸conjug 1◂ VT (au crayon) to check off, tick (off) (Brit); (d'une entaille) to notch

cocher² [kɔʃe] NM (gén) coachman, coach driver; [fiacre] cabman, cabby*

cochère [kɔʃɛʀ] ADJ F → **porte**

Cochinchine [kɔʃɛ̃ʃin] NF Cochin China

cochlée [kɔkle] NF cochlea

cochon, -onne [kɔʃɔ̃, ɔn] [1] ADJ [a] (‡ = obscène) [chanson, histoire] dirty, smutty; [personne] dirty-minded [b] (* = sale) **il est ~** (sur lui) he's filthy; (dans son travail) he's a messy worker; **c'est pas ~!** it's not at all bad! [2] NM [a] (= animal) pig, hog (US); (* = viande) pork (NonC); **~ d'Inde** guinea-pig; **~ de lait** (gén) piglet; (Culin) suck(l)ing-pig [b] (‡ : péj = personne) (sale, vieux) dirty pig‡; (= goujat) swine‡; **manger/écrire comme un ~** to be a messy eater/writer; **vieux ~** dirty old man; **petit ~!** you messy thing!; **ce ~ de voisin** that swine‡ of a neighbour; (terme amical) **eh bien, mon ~!** you old devil!* [c] (loc) **quel temps de ~!** what lousy ou filthy weather!*; (hum) **(et) ~ qui s'en dédit*** let's shake (hands) on it, cross my heart (and hope to die)*; **un ~ n'y retrouverait pas ses petits** it's like a pigsty in there, it's a real mess in there; (hum) **si les petits ~s ne te mangent pas** if the bogeyman doesn't get you; (hum) **elle ira loin si les petits ~s ne la mangent pas avant** she'll go far if nothing gets in her way; **tout homme a dans son cœur un ~ qui sommeille** there's a bit of the animal in every man → **confiture, copain** [3] **cochonne** NF (= personne) (sale) dirty pig‡; (vicieuse) dirty cow‡

cochoncetés* [kɔʃɔ̃ste] NFPL (= obscénités) filth (NonC), smut (NonC); (= plaisanteries) smutty ou dirty jokes; (saletés) **faire des ~** to make a mess; **arrête de dire des ~** stop talking dirty*

cochonnaille* [kɔʃɔnaj] NF (= charcuterie) pork products; **assiette de ~** selection of cold pork ou ham

cochonner* [kɔʃɔne] ▸conjug 1◂ VT (= mal faire) [+ travail] to botch (up), bungle; (= salir) [+ vêtements] to mess up*, make filthy

cochonnerie* [kɔʃɔnʀi] NF (= nourriture) disgusting ou foul food, pigswill* (NonC); (= marchandise) rubbish (NonC), trash (NonC); (= plaisanterie) smutty ou dirty joke; (= tour) dirty ou low trick; (= saleté) filth (NonC); **manger des ~s** to eat junk food; **faire une ~ à qn** to play a dirty trick on sb; **le chien a fait des ~s dans la cuisine** the dog has made a mess in the kitchen; **ne regarde pas ces ~s!** don't look at that filth!

cochonnet [kɔʃɔne] NM (Zool) piglet; (Boules) jack

cocker [kɔkɛʀ] NM cocker spaniel

cockpit [kɔkpit] NM cockpit

cocktail [kɔktɛl] NM (= réunion) cocktail party; (= boisson) cocktail; (fig) mixture, potpourri; **~ de fruits/crevettes** fruit/prawn cocktail; **~ Molotov** Molotov cocktail, petrol bomb; (fig) **~ explosif** explosive cocktail ou mixture

coco¹ [koko] NM [a] (langage enfantin = œuf) egg [b] (terme d'affection) pet, darling, poppet* (Brit); **oui, mon ~** yes, darling [c] (‡ : péj = type) guy*, bloke* (Brit), an odd guy* ou bloke* (Brit), an oddball* ou oddbod* (Brit); **toi mon ~, tu vas voir!** you've got it coming to you, buster ou mate!* [d] (* : péj = communiste) commie* [e] (= réglisse) liquorice powder; (= boisson) liquorice water [f] († = noix) coconut; **beurre de ~** coconut butter; **tapis en (fibre de) ~** coconut ou coir mat ou matting (NonC) → **lait, noix** [g] (= haricot) small white haricot bean

coco²† [koko] NF (arg Drogue = cocaïne) coke*, snow (arg)

cocon [kɔkɔ̃] NM (lit, fig) cocoon; **sortir du ~ familial** to leave the family nest

cocontractant, e [kokɔ̃tʀaktɑ̃, ɑ̃t] NM,F contracting partner

cocooning [kɔkuniŋ] NM staying at home, cocooning (US); **j'ai envie d'une petite soirée**

~ I feel like spending a nice cosy evening at home

cocorico [kɔkɔʀiko] **1** NM [*coq*] cock-a-doodle-do; (*fig*) cheer of victory; **pousser un ~** ◊ **faire ~** [*coq*] to crow; (*fig*) to crow (over one's victory); **ils ont fait ~ un peu trop tôt** their victory celebrations were premature, they started celebrating a bit too soon **2** EXCL [*coq*] cock-a-doodle-do!; **~! on a gagné!** hooray! we won!

cocoter* [kɔkɔte] ▶conjug 4◀ VI (= *sentir mauvais*) to stink, pong* (*Brit*)

cocoteraie [kɔkɔtʀɛ] NF (*naturelle*) coconut grove; (*cultivée*) coconut plantation

cocotier [kɔkɔtje] NM coconut palm *ou* tree → **secouer**

cocotte [kɔkɔt] **1** NF **a** (*langage enfantin* = *poule*) hen, cluck-cluck (*langage enfantin*) **b** (*: *péj* = *femme*) tart*; **ça sent** *ou* **pue la ~** it smells like a perfume factory **c** (*à un cheval*) **allez ~! hue ~!** gee up! **d** (*: *terme d'affection*) (**ma**) **~ pet, sweetie* e** (= *marmite*) casserole; **faire un poulet à la** *ou* **en ~** to casserole a chicken; **poulet/veau (à la) ~** chicken/veal casserole **2** COMP ▶ **Cocotte Minute**® pressure cooker ▶ **cocotte en papier** paper hen

cocotter* [kɔkɔte] ▶conjug 4◀ VI = **cocoter**

cocu, e* [kɔky] **1** ADJ deceived, cuckolded†; **elle l'a fait ~** she was unfaithful to him, she cuckolded him† **2** NM deceived husband, cuckold† → **veine 3 cocue** NF deceived wife

cocufier* [kɔkyfje] ▶conjug 7◀ VT to be unfaithful to, cuckold†

coda [kɔda] NF (*Mus*) coda

codage [kɔdaʒ] NM coding, encoding

code [kɔd] **1** NM **a** (*Jur*) code; **le ~ civil** the civil code, ≈ common law; **~ pénal** penal code; **le ~ maritime/de commerce** maritime/commercial law; **~ du travail** labour regulations *ou* laws; **~ de la route** highway code; (*Aut*) **il a eu le ~, mais pas la conduite** he passed on the highway code but not on the driving **b** (= *règles*) code; **~ de la politesse/de l'honneur** code of politeness/honour **c** (= *écriture, message*: *gén*) (*Sci*) code; **~ secret** secret code; **écrire qch en ~** to write sth in code **d** (*Aut*) **phares ~ ◊ ~s** dipped (head)lights (*Brit*), low beams (*US*); **mettre ses ~s** *ou* **ses phares en ~(s) ◊ se mettre en ~(s)** to dip one's (head)lights (*Brit*), put on the low beams (*US*); **rouler en ~(s)** to drive with dipped (head)lights (*Brit*) *ou* on low beams (*US*) **2** COMP ▶ **code d'accès** (*à un immeuble*) entry code; (*à une base de données*) access code ▶ **code ASCII** ASCII code ▶ **code à barres** bar code ▶ **code confidentiel** PIN number ▶ **code génétique** genetic code ▶ **code personnel** ▶ **code confidentiel** ▶ **code postal** postcode (*Brit*), zip code (*US*)

codé, e [kɔde] (*ptp de coder*) ADJ (*Ordin*) [*message*] coded; (*TV*) [*émission*] scrambled, coded; (*fig*) **le langage ~ de certains milieux** the secret language used by certain social groups; **c'est une société très ~e** it's a society where everything is very coded; **je n'aime pas les tailleurs, c'est trop ~** I don't like wearing suits, they're too bound up with a certain image

code-barre(s) (*pl* **codes-barres**) [kɔdbaʀ] NM bar code

codébiteur, -trice [kɔdebitœʀ, tʀis] NM,F joint debtor

codécision [kɔdesizjɔ̃] NF joint decision

codéine [kɔdein] NF codeine

codemandeur, -eresse [kɔd(ə)mɑ̃dœʀ, dʀɛs] NM,F joint plaintiff

coder [kɔde] ▶conjug 1◀ VT to code

codétenteur, -trice [kodetɑ̃tœʀ, tʀis] NM,F (*Jur, Sport*) joint holder

codétenu, e [kodet(ə)ny] NM,F prisoner, inmate; **avec ses ~s** with his fellow prisoners *ou* inmates

CODEVI [kodevi] NM (ABRÉV = **compte pour le développement industriel**) → **compte**

codex [kɔdɛks] NM (officially approved) pharmacopoeia

codicillaire [kɔdisileʀ] ADJ (*Jur*) codicillary

codicille [kɔdisil] NM (*Jur*) codicil

codification [kɔdifikasjɔ̃] NF codification

codifier [kɔdifje] ▶conjug 7◀ VT (*Jur, systématiser*) to codify

codirecteur, -trice [kodiʀɛktœʀ, tʀis] NM,F co-director, joint manager (*ou* manageress)

codirection [kodiʀɛksjɔ̃] NF [*entreprise*] joint management

coéditer [koedite] ▶conjug 1◀ VT to co-publish

coéditeur, -trice [koeditœʀ, tʀis] NM,F co-publisher

coédition [koedisjɔ̃] NF co-edition

coefficient [kɔefisjɑ̃] **1** NM (*Math, Phys*) coefficient; (*Scol*) **cette matière est affectée d'un ~ trois** marks (*Brit*) *ou* grades (*US*) in this subject are weighted by a factor of three **2** COMP ▶ **coefficient d'erreur** margin of error ▶ **coefficient de sécurité** safety margin ▶ **coefficient d'élasticité** modulus of elasticity ▶ **coefficient de dilatation** coefficient of expansion ▶ **coefficient d'occupation des sols** planning density ▶ **coefficient de marée** tidal range ▶ **coefficient de pénétration dans l'air** drag coefficient *ou* factor

cœlacanthe [selakɑ̃t] NM coelacanth

cœlialgie [seljalʒi] NF coeliac disease

cœlioscopie [seljɔskɔpi] NF laparoscopy

cœnesthésie [senestezi] NF = **cénesthésie**

coentreprise [koɑ̃tʀəpʀiz] NF (*Écon*) joint venture

coépouse [koepuz] NF co-wife

coéquipier, -ière [koekipje, jɛʀ] NM,F team mate

coercibilité [kɔɛʀsibilite] NF coercibility

coercible [kɔɛʀsibl] ADJ coercible

coercitif, -ive [kɔɛʀsitif, iv] ADJ coercive

coercition [kɔɛʀsisjɔ̃] NF coercion

cœur [kœʀ]

1 NOM MASCULIN   **2** COMPOSÉS

1 NOM MASCULIN
a Anat (= *organe*) heart; (= *poitrine*) heart, breast; **avoir le ~ malade** to have a weak heart *ou* a heart condition; (*lit ou hum*) **heureusement que j'ai le ~ solide** it's a good thing I haven't got a weak heart; **serrer qn contre** *ou* **sur son ~** to hold *ou* press sb to one's heart *ou* breast; (*Boucherie*) **~ de bœuf/de poulet** beef/chicken heart; **opération à ~ ouvert** open-heart surgery; **on l'a opéré à ~ ouvert** he had open-heart surgery → **battement, greffe**[1]

b = **estomac** il faut **avoir le ~ bien accroché pour être ambulancier** you need a strong stomach to be an ambulance man; **j'avais le ~ au bord des** *ou* **sur les lèvres** I thought I was going to be sick (any minute) → **mal, soulever**

c = **siège de l'amour** heart; **avoir un coup de ~ pour qch** to fall in love with sth; **nos coups de ~ parmi les livres du mois** our favourites among this month's new books; **donner son ~ à qn** to lose one's heart to sb, give sb one's heart; **je ne le porte pas dans mon ~** I am not exactly *ou* overly fond of him; (*forme d'adresse*) **mon ~** sweetheart; **c'est un homme selon mon ~** he's a man after my own heart; **c'est un film/un paysage selon mon ~** it's the kind of film/landscape I love; **avoir un** *ou* **le ~ sensible** to be sensitive *ou* tender-hearted → **joli**

d = **bonté, générosité** **avoir bon ~** to be kind-hearted *ou* good-hearted, have one's heart in the right place; **à votre bon ~** (m'sieurs-dames)! thank you kindly!; **homme/femme de ~** kind-hearted *ou* good-hearted man/woman; **avoir le ~ sur la main** to be open-handed; **manquer de ~** to be unfeeling *ou* heartless; **il a** *ou* **c'est un ~ d'or** he has a heart of gold; **elle a un ~ gros comme ça*** she's really big-hearted; **héros au grand ~** big-hearted hero; **il a une pierre** *ou* **un caillou à la place du ~** he has a heart of stone; **c'est un homme sans ~** ◊ **il n'a pas de ~** he's really heartless

e = **humeur** **avoir le ~ à faire qch** to feel like doing sth; **je n'ai pas le ~ à rire/à sortir** I don't feel like laughing/going out, I'm not in the mood for laughing/going out; **il n'a plus le ~ à rien** his heart isn't in anything any more; **si le ~ vous en dit** if you feel like it, if you're in the mood; **avoir le ~ joyeux** *ou* **gai** to feel happy; **d'un ~ léger** light-heartedly; **il est parti le ~ léger** he left in a light-hearted mood; **il avait le ~ lourd** his heart was heavy, he was heavy-hearted; **il est parti le ~ lourd** he left with a heavy heart; **avoir le ~ gros** *ou* **serré** to have a heavy heart; **mon ~ se serre à cette pensée** my heart sinks at the thought

♦ **de bon ~** [*manger, rire*] heartily; [*faire, accepter*] willingly, readily

f = **âme, pensées intimes** **c'est un ~ pur** he is a candid soul; **ouvrir son ~ à qn** to open one's heart to sb; **ça vient du ~!** it comes *ou* is straight from the heart!; **des paroles venues du ~** words from the heart, heartfelt words; **je veux en avoir le ~ net** I want to be clear in my own mind (about it); **ce geste/ce discours lui est allé (droit) au ~** he was (deeply) moved *ou* (very) touched by this gesture/these words, this gesture/these words went straight to his heart → **cri**

♦ **à cœur** : **avoir à ~ de faire qch** to be very keen to do sth; **prendre les choses à ~** to take things to heart; **ce voyage me tient à ~** I've set my heart on this trip; **cette cause me tient à ~** this cause is close to my heart; **c'est un sujet qui me tient vraiment à ~** it's an issue I feel very strongly about

♦ **à cœur ouvert** : **il m'a parlé à ~ ouvert** he opened his heart to me; **nous avons eu une conversation à ~ ouvert** we had a heart-to-heart (talk)

♦ **avoir qch sur le cœur** : **ce qu'il m'a dit, je l'ai sur le ~** *ou* **ça m'est resté sur le ~** what he said to me still rankles with me, I still feel sore about what he said to me; **je vais lui dire ce que j'ai sur le ~** (*gén*) I'm going to tell him what's on my mind; (*ce que je pense de lui*) I'm going to give him a piece of my mind

♦ **cœur à cœur** : **on s'est parlé ~ à ~** we had a heart-to-heart (talk)

♦ **de tout (son) cœur** [*remercier, souhaiter*] with all one's heart, from the bottom of one's heart; **être de tout ~ avec qn dans la joie/une épreuve** to share (in) sb's happiness/sorrow; **je suis de tout ~ avec vous** my thoughts are with you

g = **courage, ardeur** heart, courage; **comment peut-on avoir le ~ de refuser?** how can one have *ou* find the heart to refuse?; **le ~ lui manqua (pour ...)** his courage failed him (when it came to ...); **mettre tout son ~ dans qch/à faire qch** to put all one's heart into sth/into doing sth; **avoir du ~ au ventre*** to have guts*; **donner du ~ au ventre à qn*** to buck sb up*; **avoir du ~ à l'ouvrage** to put one's heart into one's work; **il travaille mais le ~ n'y est pas** he does the work but his heart isn't in it; **redonner du ~ à qn** to give sb new heart

♦ **à cœur joie** : **s'en donner à ~ joie** (= *s'amuser*) to have a tremendous time, have a whale of a time*; (= *critiquer*) to have a field day, go to town; **les pillards s'en sont donné à ~ joie** the looters really went to town

h = partie centrale [*chou*] heart; [*arbre, poutre*] heart, core; [*fruit, pile atomique*] core; [*problème, ville*] heart; (*Boucherie*) ~ de rumsteck/de filet prime cut of rump steak/of fillet

◆ à cœur: fromage fait à ~ fully ripe cheese; viande cuite à ~ medium-cooked meat; viande tendre à ~ very tender meat

◆ au cœur de [*région, ville, forêt*] in the heart of; au ~ de l'été at the height of summer; au ~ de l'hiver in the depths *ou* heart of winter

i = objet heart; en (forme de) ~ heart-shaped; volets percés de ~s shutters with heart-shaped holes → **bouche**

j Cartes heart; roi/as de ~ king/ace of hearts; avez-vous du ~? have you got any hearts? → **atout**

k

◆ par cœur [*réciter, apprendre*] by heart; connaître ~ [+ *poème, formule*] to know (off) by heart; [+ *endroit*] to know like the back of one's hand; il connaît Racine par ~ he knows (the works of) Racine inside out; je te connais par ~ I know you inside out, I know you like the back of my hand; tes arguments, je les connais par ~! I've heard all your arguments before!, I know your arguments by heart!; savoir par ~ [+ *leçon*] to know (off) by heart

2 COMPOSÉS

► cœur d'artichaut (*lit*) artichoke heart; (*fig*) c'est *ou* il a un ~ d'artichaut he falls in love with every girl he meets ► cœur de céleri celery heart ► cœur de palmier heart of palm

cœur-de-pigeon (*pl* cœurs-de-pigeon) [kœʀdəpiʒɔ̃] NM *variety of red cherry*

coexistence [kɔɛgzistɑ̃s] NF coexistence; ~ pacifique peaceful coexistence

coexister [kɔɛgziste] ▸ conjug 1 ◂ VI to coexist

coffrage [kɔfʀaʒ] NM (*pour protéger, cacher*) boxing (*NonC*); [*galerie, tranchée*] (= dispositif, action) coffering (*NonC*); [*béton*] (= dispositif) form, formwork (*NonC*), shuttering (*NonC*), (= action) framing

coffre [kɔfʀ] **1** NM **a** (= meuble) chest; ~ à linge/à outils linen/tool chest **b** (*Aut*) boot (*Brit*), trunk (*US*); ~ avant/arrière front/rear boot (*Brit*) *ou* trunk (*US*) **c** (= coffrage: *gén*) case; [*piano*] case; [*radio*] cabinet **d** [*banque, hôtel*] safe; (= compartiment) safe- *ou* safety-deposit box; (*Hist, fig* = cassette) coffer; les ~s de l'État the coffers of the state; (*Banque*) la salle des ~s the strongroom, the (bank) vault **e** (* = poitrine) le ~ the chest; il a du ~ he's got a lot of blow* *ou* puff* (*Brit*) **2** COMP ► coffre à jouets toybox ► coffre de nuit night safe ► coffre de voyage† trunk

coffre-fort (*pl* coffres-forts) [kɔfʀəfɔʀ] NM safe

coffrer [kɔfʀe] ▸ conjug 1 ◂ VT **a** (* = emprisonner) to throw *ou* put inside*; se faire ~ to get put inside* **b** (*Tech*) [+ béton] to place a frame *ou* form for; [+ tranchée, galerie] to coffer

coffret [kɔfʀɛ] NM (*gén*) casket; [*disques, livres*] (= contenant) box; (= contenu) boxed set; ~ à bijoux jewel box, jewellery case; ~-cadeau presentation box

cofinancement [kofinɑ̃smɑ̃] NM co-financing

cofinancer [kofinɑ̃se] ▸ conjug 3 ◂ VT to finance jointly, co-finance

cofondateur, -trice [kɔfɔ̃datœʀ, tʀis] NM,F cofounder

cogérant [kɔʒeʀɑ̃] NM joint manager

cogérante [kɔʒeʀɑ̃t] NF joint manageress

cogérer [kɔʒeʀe] ▸ conjug 6 ◂ VT to manage jointly

cogestion [kɔʒɛstjɔ̃] NF co-management, joint management

cogitation [kɔʒitasjɔ̃] NF (*hum*) cogitation

cogiter [kɔʒite] ▸ conjug 1 ◂ **1** VI (*hum = réfléchir*) to cogitate **2** VT qu'est-ce qu'il cogite? what's he thinking up?

cogito [kɔʒito] NM (*Philo*) cogito; le ~ cartésien Descartes's cogito

cognac [kɔɲak] **1** NM cognac, (French) brandy **2** ADJ INV brandy-coloured (*Brit*) *ou* -colored (*US*)

cognassier [kɔɲasje] NM quince (tree), japonica

cogne† [kɔɲ] NM (= policier) cop*; les ~s the cops*, the fuzz*

cognée [kɔɲe] NF felling axe *ou* ax (*US*) → **manche**

cognement [kɔɲmɑ̃] NM (= bruit, action) banging; (*Aut*) knocking

cogner [kɔɲe] ▸ conjug 1 ◂ **1** VT **a** (= heurter) to knock; fais attention à ne pas ~ les verres mind you don't knock the glasses against anything; quelqu'un m'a cogné en passant somebody knocked (into) me as they went by **b** (* = battre) to beat up **2** VI **a** [*personne*] ~ sur [+ clou, piquet] to hammer on; [+ mur] to bang *ou* knock on; (*fort*) to hammer on; ~ du poing sur la table to bang *ou* thump one's fist on the table; ~ à la porte/au plafond to knock at the door/on the ceiling; (*fort*) to bang *ou* rap at the door/on the ceiling **b** [*volet, battant, branche*] to bang; [*grêle*] to hammer, pound (contre against); ~ contre [*projectile*] to hit, strike; un caillou est venu ~ contre le pare-brise a stone hit the windscreen; il y a un volet qui cogne (contre le mur) there's a shutter banging (against the wall); le moteur cogne the engine's knocking **c** * [*boxeur, bagarreur*] to hit out; ça va ~ à la manif* there's going to be some rough stuff at the demo*; ce boxeur-là, il cogne dur that boxer's a hard hitter, that boxer packs a mean punch*; ~ sur qn to lay into sb* **d** * [*soleil*] to beat down; ça cogne!* it's scorching!* **e** (* = sentir mauvais) to stink to high heaven*, pong* (*Brit*) **3** se cogner VPR **a** se ~ contre un mur to bump into a wall; se ~ la tête/le genou contre un poteau to bang one's head/knee on a post; (*fig*) c'est à se ~ la tête contre les murs it's like banging your head against a brick wall **b** se ~ (dessus)* (= se battre) to lay into each other*

cogneur* [kɔɲœʀ] NM (= bagarreur, boxeur) bruiser*

cogniticien, -ienne [kɔɲitisjɛ̃, jɛn] NM,F cognitive scientist

cognitif, -ive [kɔɡnitif, iv] ADJ cognitive

cognition [kɔɡnisjɔ̃] NF cognition

cohabitant, e [kɔabitɑ̃, ɑ̃t] **1** ADJ couple ~ couple who are living together, cohabiting couple **2** NM,F cohabitee; (*euph* = concubin) live-in lover

cohabitation [kɔabitasjɔ̃] NF [*couple*] living together, cohabitation; [*plusieurs personnes*] living under the same roof; (*Pol*) cohabitation; la ~ avec mon mari était devenue impossible it had become impossible for me and my husband to carry on living together *ou* living under the same roof

---

COHABITATION

The situation which occurs when, as a result of a presidential or general election, the French people find themselves with a president who represents one political party and a government which represents another. A recent example of **cohabitation** *is the combination of a Socialist Prime Minister,*

Lionel Jospin, with a Gaullist President, Jacques Chirac.

---

cohabiter [kɔabite] ▸ conjug 1 ◂ VI [*couple*] to live together, cohabit; [*plusieurs personnes*] to live under the same roof; (*Pol*) to cohabit; ils cohabitent avec leurs parents they live with their parents

cohérence [kɔeʀɑ̃s] NF **a** (= logique) [*arguments, politique*] coherence; [*conduite*] consistency; le manque de ~ de sa politique the incoherence of his policy; la ~ d'ensemble du projet the overall coherence of the project **b** (= homogénéité) [*groupe*] cohesion; pour améliorer la ~ de cette gamme to make the range more comprehensive; la ~ de l'équipe laisse à désirer the team is not as well-knit as it could be **c** (*Phys*) coherence

cohérent, e [kɔeʀɑ̃, ɑ̃t] ADJ **a** (= logique) [*arguments*] coherent; [*politique*] coherent; [*conduite*] consistent; sois ~ (avec toi-même) be true to yourself **b** (= homogène) [*équipe*] well-knit; [*groupe*] cohesive; [*gamme de produits*] comprehensive, complete **c** (*Phys*) coherent

cohéritier [kɔeʀitje] NM joint heir, coheir

cohéritière [kɔeʀitjɛʀ] NF joint heiress, coheiress

cohésif, -ive [kɔezif, iv] ADJ cohesive

cohésion [kɔezjɔ̃] NF cohesion

cohorte [kɔɔʀt] NF (= groupe) troop; (*Hist Mil*) cohort

cohue [kɔy] NF (= foule) crowd; (= bousculade) crush; c'était la ~ à l'entrée du cinéma there was such a crush at the entrance to the cinema

coi, coite [kwa, kwat] ADJ se tenir ~ ◊ rester ~ to remain silent; en rester ~ to be rendered speechless

coiffage [kwafaʒ] NM hairdressing; produit de ~ hairstyling product

coiffant, e [kwafɑ̃, ɑ̃t] ADJ → gel, mousse¹

coiffe [kwaf] NF **a** [*costume régional, religieuse*] headdress **b** [*chapeau*] lining; (*Tech*) [*fusée*] cap; (*Anat*) [*nouveau-né*] caul

coiffé, e [kwafe] (*ptp de* **coiffer**) ADJ **a** [*peigné*] est-ce que tu es ~? have you done your hair?; comment était-elle ~e? what was her hair like?, how did she have her hair?; il est toujours bien/mal ~ his hair always looks nice/a mess; être ~ en brosse to have a crew-cut; être ~ en chien fou to have dishevelled hair; il était ~ en arrière he had his hair brushed *ou* combed back → naître **b** (= couvert) être ~ d'un béret to be wearing a beret; le clown entra ~ d'une casserole the clown came in with a saucepan on his head

coiffer [kwafe] ▸ conjug 1 ◂ **1** VT **a** (= peigner) ~ qn to do sb's hair; il coiffe bien he's a good hairdresser; cheveux difficiles à ~ unmanageable hair; (aller) se faire ~ to (go and) have one's hair done **b** (= couvrir la tête de) ~ (la tête d')un bébé d'un bonnet to put a bonnet on a baby's head; ce chapeau la coiffe bien that hat suits her *ou* looks good on her; le béret qui la coiffait the beret she had on *ou* was wearing **c** (= mettre) [+ chapeau] to put on; ~ la mitre/la tiare to be mitred/made Pope; ~ la couronne to be crowned (king *ou* queen); elle allait bientôt ~ sainte Catherine she would soon be 25 and still unmarried → CATHERINETTE **d** (= surmonter) des nuages coiffaient le sommet clouds covered the summit, the summit was topped with clouds; pic coiffé de neige snow-capped peak **e** (= diriger) [+ services] to head up, have overall responsibility for **f** (* = dépasser) ~ qn à l'arrivée *ou* au poteau to nose sb out*, pip sb at the post* (*Brit*); se

faire ~ to be nosed out*, be pipped at the post* (*Brit*)

2 **se coiffer** VPR **a** (= *se peigner*) to do one's hair; **elle se coiffe toujours mal** she never manages to do anything nice with her hair; (*hum*) **tu t'es coiffé avec un râteau ou un clou** you look like you've been dragged through a hedge backwards; **tu t'es coiffé avec un pétard** your hair's all sticking up **b** (= *mettre comme coiffure*) **se ~ d'une casquette** to put on a cap; **d'habitude, elle se coiffe d'un chapeau de paille** she usually wears a straw hat **c** (= *acheter ses chapeaux*) **se ~ chez Legrand** to buy one's hats from Legrand

coiffeur [kwafœʀ] NM [*dames*] hairdresser; [*hommes*] hairdresser, barber; **les grands ~s parisiens** top Paris hairstylists

coiffeuse [kwaføz] NF (= *personne*) hairdresser; (= *meuble*) dressing table

coiffure [kwafyʀ] NF (= *façon d'être peigné*) hairstyle, hairdo*; (= *chapeau*) hat, headgear* (*NonC*); (*métier*) **la ~** hairdressing → **salon**

coin [kwɛ̃] NM **a** (= *angle*) [*objet, chambre*] corner; **armoire/place de ~** corner cupboard/seat; (*Scol*) **va au ~!** go and stand in the corner!; (*Scol*) **envoyer ou mettre un enfant au ~** to send a child to stand in the corner, put a child in the corner; (*Rail*) **~(-)fenêtre/(-)couloir** window/aisle seat, seat by the window/on the aisle **b** [*rue*] corner; **le boucher du ~** the butcher's on the corner; **la blanchisserie fait le ~** the laundry is right on the corner; **à tous les ~s de rue** on every street corner **c** [*yeux, bouche*] corner; **sourire en ~** half smile; **regard en ~** sidelong glance; **regarder/surveiller qn du ~ de l'œil** to look at/watch sb out of the corner of one's eye **d** (= *espace restreint*) [*village, maison*] part; **un ~ de terre/ciel bleu** a patch of land/blue sky; **un ~ de plage** a spot on the beach; **le ~ du bricoleur** (*dans un magasin*) the DIY department (*Brit*), the home improvement department (*US*); (*dans un journal*) DIY tips (*Brit*), home improvement tips (*US*); **~-bureau/-repas** work/dining area; **rester dans son ~** to keep to oneself; **laisser qn dans son ~** to leave sb alone; **dans un ~ de ma mémoire** in the recesses of my mind ou memory; **dans quel ~ l'as-tu mis?** where did you put it?; **je l'ai mis dans un ~** I put it somewhere; **j'ai cherché dans tous les ~s (et recoins)** I looked in every nook and cranny → **petit** **e** (= *région*) area; **dans quel ~ habitez-vous?** whereabouts do you live?; **les gens du ~** the local people, the locals; **vous êtes du ~?** do you live locally? ou around here? **ou** are you from the area?; **je ne suis pas du ~** I'm not from around here, I'm a stranger here; **le supermarché du ~** the local supermarket; **un ~ perdu ou paumé*** a place miles from anywhere; **un ~ de Paris/de la France que je connais bien** an area of Paris/of France that I know well; **on a trouvé un petit ~ pas cher/tranquille pour le week-end** we found somewhere nice and cheap/nice and quiet for the weekend, we found a nice inexpensive/quiet little spot for the weekend; **de tous les ~s du monde** from every corner of the world; **de tous les ~s du pays** from all over the country **f** (= *objet triangulaire*) [*reliure, cartable, sous-main*] corner (piece); (*pour coincer, écarter*) wedge; (*pour graver*) die; (= *poinçon*) hallmark; (*Typo*) (= *de serrage*) quoin; **être frappé ou marqué au ~ du bon sens** to bear the stamp of commonsense **g** (*loc*) **je n'aimerais pas le rencontrer au ~ d'un bois** I wouldn't like to meet him on a dark night; **au ~ du feu** by the fireside; **causerie/rêverie au ~ du feu** fireside chat/daydream → **boucher¹, quatre**

coinçage [kwɛ̃saʒ] NM wedging

coincé, e* [kwɛ̃se] ADJ [*personne*] hung up*, uptight*; **il est très ~** he has a lot of hang-ups*, he's very uptight*

coincement [kwɛ̃smã] NM jamming (*NonC*)

coincer [kwɛ̃se] ▸conjug 3◂ **1** VT **a** (= *bloquer*) (*intentionnellement*) to wedge; (*accidentellement*) [+ *tiroir, fermeture éclair*] to jam; **le tiroir est coincé** the drawer is stuck ou jammed; **le vélo était coincé sous le camion** the bike was wedged under the lorry; **il se trouva coincé contre un mur par la foule** he was pinned against a wall by the crowd; **il m'a coincé entre deux portes pour me dire ...** he cornered me to tell me ...; **nous étions coincés dans le couloir/dans l'ascenseur** we were stuck ou jammed in the corridor/in the lift; (*fig*) **je suis coincé à la maison/au bureau** I'm stuck at home/at the office; **ils ont coincé l'armoire en voulant la faire passer par la porte** they got the wardrobe jammed ou stuck trying to get it through the door **b** (*: *fig* = *attraper*) [+ *voleur*] to nab*; [+ *faussaire, fraudeur*] to catch up with; **je me suis fait ~ ou ils m'ont coincé sur cette question** they got me on ou caught me out on that question, I was caught out on that question; **coincé entre son désir et la peur** caught between his desire and fear; **nous sommes coincés, nous ne pouvons rien faire** we're stuck ou cornered ou in a corner and can't do anything; **~ la bulle*** to bum around*

2 VI [*porte*] to stick; (*fig*) **ça coince au niveau de la direction*** there are problems at management level

3 **se coincer** VPR [*fermeture, tiroir*] to jam, stick, get jammed ou stuck; **se ~ le doigt dans une porte** to catch one's finger in a door; **se ~ un nerf*** to trap ou pinch a nerve; **se ~ une vertèbre*** to trap a nerve in one's spine

coinceur [kwɛ̃sœʀ] NM (*Alpinisme*) nut

coïncidence [kɔɛ̃sidãs] NF (*gén*, *Géom*) coincidence

coïncident, e [kɔɛ̃sidã, ãt] ADJ [*surfaces, faits*] coincident

coïncider [kɔɛ̃side] ▸conjug 1◂ VI [*surfaces, opinions, dates*] to coincide (**avec** with); [*témoignages*] to tally; **nous sommes arrivés à faire ~ nos dates de vacances** we've managed to get the dates of our holidays to coincide

coin-coin [kwɛ̃kwɛ̃] NM INV [*canard*] quack; **~!** quack! quack!

coïnculpé, e [kɔɛ̃kylpe] NM,F co-defendant, co-accused

coing [kwɛ̃] NM quince

coït [kɔit] NM coitus, coition; **~ interrompu** coitus interruptus

coite [kwat] ADJ F → **coi**

coke¹ [kɔk] NM (= *combustible*) coke

coke² [kok] NF (*arg Drogue* = *cocaïne*) coke*

cokéfaction [kɔkefaksjɔ̃] NF coking

cokéfier [kɔkefje] ▸conjug 7◂ VT to coke

cokerie [kɔkʀi] NF cokeworks, coking works

col [kɔl] **1** NM **a** [*chemise, manteau*] collar; **ça bâille du ~** it gapes at the neck; **pull à ~ rond** round-neck pullover → **faux²** **b** (*Géog*) pass; **le ~ du Simplon** the Simplon pass **c** (= *partie étroite*) [*carafe, vase*] neck; **~ du fémur/de la vessie** neck of the thighbone/of the bladder; **elle s'est cassé le ~ du fémur** she has broken her hip; **~ de l'utérus** neck of the womb, cervix **d** († ou *littér* = *cou*) neck; **un homme au ~ de taureau** a man with a bull neck, a bull-necked man

2 COMP ▸ **col blanc** (= *personne*) white-collar worker ▸ **col bleu** (= *ouvrier*) blue-collar worker; (= *marin*) bluejacket ▸ **col cassé** wing collar ▸ **col châle** shawl collar ▸ **col cheminée** high round neck, turtleneck (*Brit*) ▸ **col chemisier** shirt collar ▸ **col Claudine** Peter Pan collar ▸ **col dur** stiff collar ▸ **col Mao** Mao collar ▸ **col marin** sailor's collar ▸ **col mou** soft collar ▸ **col officier** mandarin collar ▸ **col polo** polo shirt collar ▸ **col ras du cou** round neck, turtleneck (*Brit*) ▸ **col roulé** roll neck (*Brit*), polo neck (*Brit*), turtleneck (*US*) ▸ **col (en) V** V-neck

cola [kɔla] NM (= *arbre*) cola ou kola (tree); **(noix de) ~** cola ou kola nut

colback* [kɔlbak] NM **attraper** ou **prendre qn par le ~** to grab sb by the collar

colbertisme [kɔlbɛʀtism] NM *economic policy based on a high degree of state control (an allusion to Colbert, chief minister under Louis XIV)*

colbertiste [kɔlbɛʀtist] ADJ [*pays, modèle*] with a policy of strong state intervention in the economy

colchique [kɔlʃik] NM autumn crocus, meadow saffron, colchicum (*SPÉC*)

col-de-cygne (*pl* **cols-de-cygne**) [kɔldəsiɲ] NM [*plomberie, mobilier*] swan neck

colégataire [kolegatɛʀ] NMF joint legatee

coléoptère [kɔleɔptɛʀ] NM beetle, coleopterous insect (*SPÉC*); **~s** Coleoptera (*SPÉC*)

colère [kɔlɛʀ] **1** NF **a** (= *irritation*) anger; **la ~ est mauvaise conseillère** anger is a bad counsellor; **être/se mettre en ~** to be/get angry ou cross; **mettre qn en ~** to make sb angry ou cross; **passer sa ~ sur qn** to work off ou take out one's anger on sb; **en ~ contre moi-même** angry ou cross with myself, mad at myself*; **dit-il avec ~** he said angrily **b** (= *accès d'irritation*) (fit of) rage; **il fait des ~s terribles** he has terrible fits of anger ou rage; **il est entré dans une ~ noire** he flew into a terrible rage; **faire** ou **piquer une ~** to throw a tantrum **c** (*littér*) wrath; **la ~ divine** divine wrath; **la ~ des flots/du vent** the rage ou wrath of the sea/of the wind **2** ADJ INV† (= *coléreux*) irascible; (= *en colère*) irate

coléreux, -euse [kɔleʀø, øz], **colérique** [kɔleʀik] ADJ [*caractère*] quick-tempered, irascible; [*enfant*] quick-tempered, easily angered; [*vieillard*] irascible

colibacille [kɔlibasil] NM colon bacillus

colibacillose [kɔlibasiloz] NF colibacillosis

colibri [kɔlibʀi] NM hummingbird

colifichet [kɔlififɛ] NM (= *bijou*) trinket, bauble; (= *babiole*) knickknack

colimaçon [kɔlimasɔ̃] NM† snail → **escalier**

colin [kɔlɛ̃] NM (= *merlu*) hake; (= *lieu noir*) coalfish, coley, saithe

colineau (*pl* **colineaux**) [kɔlino] NM = **colinot**

colin-maillard (*pl* **colin-maillards**) [kɔlɛ̃majaʀ] NM blind man's buff

colinot [kɔlino] NM (= *merlu*) small hake; (= *lieu noir*) small coalfish

colin-tampon* (*pl* **colin-tampons**) [kɔlɛ̃tɑ̃pɔ̃] NM **il s'en soucie ou s'en moque comme de ~** he doesn't give ou care a fig* about it

colique [kɔlik] **1** NF **a** (= *diarrhée*) diarrhoea; **avoir la ~** (*lit*) to have diarrhoea; (*fig* = *avoir peur*) to be scared stiff* **b** (*gén pl* = *douleur*) stomach pain, colic pain, colic (*NonC*); **être pris de violentes ~s** to have violent stomach pains; **~ hépatique/néphrétique** biliary/renal colic; **quelle ~!*** (*personne*) what a pain in the neck!*; (*chose*) what a drag!* **2** ADJ (*Anat*) colonic

colis [kɔli] NM parcel; **envoyer/recevoir un ~ postal** to send/receive a parcel through the post ou mail; **par ~ postal** by parcel post

Colisée [kɔlize] NM **le ~** the Coliseum ou Colosseum

colistier, -ière [kolistje, jɛʀ] NM,F (*Pol*) fellow candidate

colite [kɔlit] NF colitis

collabo* [kɔ(l)labo] NMF (ABRÉV = **collabora-**

teur, -trice (péj: Hist Pol) collaborator, collaborationist

collaborateur, -trice [kɔ(l)labɔratœr, tris] NM,F [collègue] colleague; [journal] contributor; [livre] collaborator; (Hist Pol) [ennemi] collaborator, collaborationist

collaboration [kɔ(l)labɔrasjɔ̃] NF (Pol, à un travail, un livre) collaboration (à on); (à un journal) contribution (à to); (Hist) **la ~** the Collaboration; **s'assurer la ~ de qn** to enlist the services of sb; **en ~ (étroite) avec** in (close) collaboration with

collaborationniste [kɔ(l)labɔrasjɔnist] ☐ ADJ [groupe, journal, politique] collaborationist (épith) ② NMF collaborator, collaborationist, quisling

collaborer [kɔ(l)labɔre] ▸ conjug 1 ◂ VI ⓐ **~ avec qn** to collaborate ou work with sb; **~ à** [+ travail, livre] to collaborate on; [+ journal] to contribute to ⓑ (Pol) to collaborate

collage [kɔlaʒ] NM ⓐ (à la colle forte) sticking, gluing; (à la colle blanche) pasting; [étiquettes] sticking; **~ de papiers peints** paperhanging; **~ d'affiches** billposting ⓑ (Art) collage ⓒ (= apprêt) [vin] fining; [papier] sizing ⓓ (†: péj = concubinage) affair; **c'est un ~** they're living together

collagène [kɔlaʒɛn] NM collagen

collant, e [kɔlɑ̃, ɑ̃t] ① ADJ (= ajusté) [vêtement] skintight, tight-fitting, clinging; (= poisseux) sticky; [importun] **être ~*** to cling, stick like a leech → **papier** ② NM ⓐ [maillot] [femme] body stocking; [danseur, acrobate] leotard ⓑ (= bas: gén) tights (Brit), pantyhose (US); [danseuse] tights ③ **collante** NF (arg Scol = convocation) notification; (= feuille de résultats) results slip

collapsus [kɔlapsys] NM [malade, organe] collapse

collatéral, e (mpl -aux) [kɔ(l)lateral, o] ADJ [parent, artère] collateral; **(nef) ~e** (side) aisle; **les collatéraux** (= parents) collaterals; (Archit) (side) aisles

collation [kɔlasjɔ̃] NF ⓐ (= repas) light meal; (= en-cas) snack ⓑ (= comparaison) [manuscrit] collation; (= vérification) [liste] checking; (Typo) collation ⓒ (frm) [titre, grade] conferment

collationnement [kɔlasjɔnmɑ̃] NM (= comparaison) [manuscrits] collation; (= vérification) [liste] checking; (Typo) checking

collationner [kɔlasjɔne] ▸ conjug 1 ◂ VT (= comparer) [+ manuscrits] to collate (**avec** with); (= vérifier) [+ liste] to check; (Typo) to collate

colle [kɔl] NF ⓐ (gén) glue; [papiers peints] wallpaper paste; (= apprêt) size; **~ (blanche ou d'écolier ou de pâte)** paste; **~ (forte)** (strong) glue, adhesive; **~ à bois** wood glue; **~ de poisson** fish glue; (fig) **ce riz, c'est de la vraie ~ (de pâte)** this rice is like paste ou is a gluey ou sticky mass → **chauffer, pot** ⓑ (* = question) teaser, poser* (Brit); **poser une ~ à qn** to set sb a poser*; **là, vous me posez une ~** you've stumped me there* ⓒ (arg Scol) (= examen blanc) mock oral exam; (= retenue) detention; **mettre une ~ à qn** to give sb a detention; **j'ai eu trois heures de ~** I got a three-hour detention, I was kept back for three hours ⓓ**:** **vivre** ou **être à la ~** to live together, be shacked up together*

collecte [kɔlɛkt] NF ⓐ (= quête) [vêtements, verre, sang] collection; [informations, données] collection, gathering; **~ de fonds** fund-raising event ⓑ (Rel = prière) collect

collecter [kɔlɛkte] ▸ conjug 1 ◂ VT (gén) to collect; [+ informations, données] to collect, gather

collecteur, -trice [kɔlɛktœr, tris] ① ADJ [canal] collecting; **égout ~** main sewer; **organisme ~** collection agency ② NM,F [personne] collector; **~ d'impôts** tax collector; **~ de fonds** fund-raiser ③ NM (Aut) manifold; (Élec) commutator; (Radio) **~ d'ondes** aerial; **~ d'égouts** ◊ **(grand) ~** main sewer

collectif, -ive [kɔlɛktif, iv] ① ADJ [travail, responsabilité, punition] collective; [sport] team (épith); [billet, réservation] group (épith); [hystérie, licenciements] mass (épith); [installations] public; (Ling) [terme, sens] collective; **faire une démarche collective auprès de qn** to approach sb collectively ou as a group; **immeuble ~** (large) block (of flats) (Brit), apartment building (US) → **convention, ferme²** ② NM (= mot) collective noun; (= groupe de travail) collective; **~ budgétaire** minibudget

collection [kɔlɛksjɔ̃] NF ⓐ [timbres, papillons] collection; (Comm) [échantillons] line; (hum = groupe) collection; **objet/timbre de ~** collector's item/stamp; **faire (la) ~ de** to collect; **voiture de ~** classic car; (de l'entre-deux-guerres) vintage car ⓑ (Mode) collection ⓒ (Édition = série) series, collection; **notre ~ « jeunes auteurs »** our "young authors" series ou collection; **il a toute la ~ des œuvres de Larbaud** he's got the complete collection ou set of Larbaud's works ⓓ (Méd) **~ de pus** gathering of pus

collectionner [kɔlɛksjɔne] ▸ conjug 1 ◂ VT (gén, hum) to collect

collectionneur, -euse [kɔlɛksjɔnœr, øz] NM,F collector

collectivement [kɔlɛktivmɑ̃] ADV (gén) collectively; [démissionner, protester] in a body, collectively

collectivisation [kɔlɛktivizasjɔ̃] NF collectivization

collectiviser [kɔlɛktivize] ▸ conjug 1 ◂ VT to collectivize

collectivisme [kɔlɛktivism] NM collectivism

collectiviste [kɔlɛktivist] ADJ, NMF collectivist

collectivité [kɔlɛktivite] NF ⓐ (= groupement) group; (= le public) **la ~** the community; **la ~ nationale** the nation (as a community); **la ~ des citoyens** the citizens as a whole ou as a body; **les ~s locales/publiques** the local/public authorities; **~s professionnelles** professional bodies ou organizations ⓑ (= vie en communauté) **la ~** community life ou living; **vivre en ~** to live in a community ⓒ (= possession commune) collective ownership

collège [kɔlɛʒ] NM ⓐ (= école) school; (privé) private school; **~ (d'enseignement secondaire)** secondary school (Brit), junior high school (US); **~ (d'enseignement) technique** technical school; **le Collège de France** prestigious state-run institution of higher education which does not grant diplomas; (Can) **Collège d'enseignement général et professionnel** general and vocational college (Can), ≈ sixth-form college (Brit), ≈ junior college (US) ⓑ (Pol, Rel = assemblée) college; **~ électoral** electoral college → **sacré¹**

┌─────────────┐
│ **COLLÈGE** │
└─────────────┘

The term **collège** refers to the type of state secondary school French children attend between the ages of 11 and 15 (ie after "école primaire" and before "lycée"). **Collège** covers the school years referred to as "sixième", "cinquième", "quatrième" and "troisième". At the end of "troisième", pupils take the examination known as the "brevet des collèges". → LYCÉE

┌──────────────────────┐
│ **COLLÈGE DE FRANCE** │
└──────────────────────┘

The **Collège de France** in Paris is an unusual higher education establishment in that it neither organizes examinations nor confers diplomas. Professors at this prestigious place of learning are appointed by the French President and give lectures that are open to all. **Collège de France** professors in recent times have included such major intellectual figures as Roland Barthes, Michel Foucault and Claude Lévi-Strauss.

collégial, e (mpl -iaux) [kɔleʒjal, jo] ① ADJ (Rel) collegiate; (Pol) collegial, collegiate; **décision ~e** group ou collective decision ② **collégiale** NF collegiate church

collégialement [kɔleʒjalmɑ̃] ADV collectively

collégialité [kɔleʒjalite] NF (Pol) collegial administration; (Rel) collegiality

collégien [kɔleʒjɛ̃] NM schoolboy; (fig = novice) **c'est un ~** he's an innocent, he's a bit green

collégienne [kɔleʒjɛn] NF schoolgirl

collègue [kɔ(l)lɛg] NMF colleague; **un ~ de travail/bureau** a colleague from work/the office → **Monsieur**

coller [kɔle] ▸ conjug 1 ◂ ① VT ⓐ (à la colle forte) to stick, glue; (à la colle blanche) to paste; [+ étiquette, timbre] to stick; [+ affiche] to stick (up) (à, sur on); [+ enveloppe] to stick down; [+ papier peint] to hang; [+ film] to splice; (Ordin) [+ texte, image] to paste; **~ deux morceaux (ensemble)** to stick ou glue ou paste two pieces together; **~ qch à** ou **sur qch** to stick sth on(to) sth; **les cheveux collés de sang** his hair stuck together ou matted with blood; **les yeux encore collés de sommeil** his eyes still half-shut with sleep

ⓑ (= appliquer) **~ son oreille à la porte/son nez contre la vitre** to press one's ear to ou against the door/one's nose against the window; **il colla l'armoire contre le mur** he stood the wardrobe right against the wall; **il se colla contre le mur pour les laisser passer** he pressed himself against the wall to let them pass; (Mil) **ils l'ont collé au mur** they stuck him up against the wall

ⓒ (* = mettre) to stick, shove*; **colle tes valises dans un coin** stick ou shove* ou dump* your bags in a corner; **il en colle des pages** he writes reams*; **dans ses devoirs il colle n'importe quoi** he puts ou sticks ou shoves* any old thing (down) in his homework; **il se colla devant moi** he plonked* ou planted himself in front of me; **ils se collent devant la télé dès qu'ils rentrent** they plonk themselves* in front of the TV as soon as they come in; **se ~ un chapeau sur la tête** to stick ou shove a hat on one's head*; **ils l'ont collé ministre** they've gone and made him a minister* → **poing**

ⓓ (* = donner) to give; **il m'a collé une contravention/une punition/une gifle** he gave me a fine/a punishment/a slap; **on m'a collé une fausse pièce** I've been palmed off with a false coin; **on lui a collé trois ans de prison** they've stuck him in prison ou sent him down* for three years, they've given him three years; **on lui a collé la responsabilité/la belle-mère** he's got (himself) stuck* ou lumbered* (Brit) with the responsibility/his mother-in-law

ⓔ (arg Scol) (= consigner) to put in detention, keep back; (= recaler) to fail, flunk* (US); **se faire ~** (en retenue) to be put in detention; (à l'examen) to be failed, be flunked* (US)

ⓕ (* = embarrasser par une question) to catch out

ⓖ (* = suivre) [+ personne] to cling to; **la voiture qui nous suit nous colle de trop près** the car behind is sitting right on our tail*; **il m'a collé (après) toute la journée** he clung to me all day

ⓗ (= apprêter) [+ vin] to fine; [+ papier] to size

② VI ⓐ (= être poisseux) to be sticky; (= adhérer) to stick (à to)

ⓑ (fig) **~ à** to cling to; **~ au peloton** to stick close to the pack; **robe qui colle au corps** tight-fitting ou clinging dress; **ils nous collent au derrière*** they're right on our tail*; **voiture qui colle à la route** car that grips the road; **un rôle qui lui colle à la peau** a part tailor-made for him, a part which fits him like a glove; **depuis, cette réputation lui colle à la peau** he's been stuck with this reputation ever since; **~ au sujet** to stick to the subject; **ce ro-**

man **colle à la réalité** this novel is very faithful to reality; **mot qui colle à une idée** word which fits an idea closely

c (* = *bien marcher*) **ça colle?** OK?*; **ça ne colle pas entre eux** they aren't hitting it off* *ou* getting on (*Brit*) *ou* getting along (together); **il y a quelque chose qui ne colle pas** there's something wrong *ou* not right here; **ça ne colle pas, je ne suis pas libre** that's no good *ou* that won't do, I'm not free; **son histoire ne colle pas** his story doesn't hold together *ou* doesn't gibe (*US*)

d (*jeux d'enfants*) **c'est à toi de ~** it's your turn to be it, you're it now

3 se coller VPR a (‡ = *subir*) [+ *tâche, personne*] to be *ou* get stuck* *ou* landed with* *ou* lumbered with* (*Brit*); **il va falloir se ~ la belle-mère pendant trois jours !** we'll have to put up with my mother-in-law for three days!

b (‡ = *se mettre à*) **se ~ à (faire) qch** to get stuck into (doing) sth*, get down to (doing) sth, set about (doing) sth

c (= *s'accrocher à*) **se ~ à qn** [*danseur*] to press o.s. against sb, cling to sb; [*importun*] to stick to sb like glue *ou* like a leech; **elle dansait collée à** *ou* **contre lui** she was dancing tightly pressed against him *ou* clinging tightly to him; **ces deux-là sont toujours collés ensemble**‡ those two *ou* that pair always go around together *ou* are never apart

d (‡† = *vivre ensemble*) **se ~ ensemble** to live together, shack up together‡

collerette [kɔlʀɛt] NF (= *col*) collaret; (*Hist* = *fraise*) ruff; [*champignon*] ring, annulus; [*tuyau*] flange

collet [kɔlɛ] NM (= *piège*) snare, noose; (= *petite cape*) short cape; [*dent*] neck; (*Boucherie, Bot*) neck; (*Tech*) collar, flange; **prendre** *ou* **saisir qn au ~** to seize sb by the collar; **mettre la main au ~ de qn** to get hold of sb, collar sb*; **elle est très ~ monté** she's very strait-laced *ou* stuffy

colleter [kɔlte] ▸ conjug 4 ◂ 1 VT [+ *adversaire*] to seize by the collar; **il s'est fait ~ par la police*** he was collared* by the police 2 **se colleter** VPR (= *se battre*) to have a tussle, tussle; **se ~ avec** to wrestle *ou* grapple *ou* tussle with

colleur, -euse [kɔlœʀ, øz] 1 NM,F a **~ d'affiches** billsticker, billposter b (*arg Scol*) *mock oral examiner* 2 **colleuse** NF (*Ciné*) splicer; (*Photo*) mounting press

colley [kɔlɛ] NM collie

collier [kɔlje] NM a [*femme*] necklace; [*chevalier, maire*] chain; [*chien, cheval, chat*] (= *courroie, pelage*) collar; (*Boucherie*) neck; **~ de perles** pearl necklace; **~ de fleurs** garland; **~ de chien** *ou* **ras du cou** (= *bijou*) choker; **~ anti-puces** flea collar; **reprendre le ~*** to get back into harness; **donner un coup de ~** to put one's back into it* → **franc¹** b (= *barbe*) **~ (de barbe)** beard (*along the line of the jaw*) c (*Tech*) **~ de serrage** clamp collar

collimateur [kɔlimatœʀ] NM (= *lunette*) collimator; (*fig, fig*) **avoir qn/qch dans son** *ou* **le ~** (*lit*) to have sb/sth in one's sights; (*fig*) to have one's eye on sb/sth

colline [kɔlin] NF hill

collision [kɔlizjɔ̃] NF [*véhicules, bateaux*] collision; (*Phys, Géog*) collision; (*fig*) [*intérêts, manifestants*] clash; **entrer en ~** to collide (**avec** with); (*Aut*) **~ en chaîne** pile-up

collisionneur [kɔlizjɔnœʀ] NM collider

collocation [kɔlɔkasjɔ̃] NF (*Jur*) classification of creditors in order of priority; (*Ling*) collocation

collodion [kɔlɔdjɔ̃] NM collodion

colloïdal, e (*mpl* **-aux**) [kɔlɔidal, o] ADJ colloidal; **solution ~e** colloidal solution *ou* suspension

colloïde [kɔlɔid] NM colloid

---

colloque [kɔ(l)lɔk] NM colloquium, symposium; (*hum*) confab*

collusion [kɔlyzjɔ̃] NF (= *complicité*) collusion (**avec** with, **entre** between)

collutoire [kɔlytwaʀ] NM oral medication (*NonC*); (*en bombe*) throat spray

collyre [kɔliʀ] NM eye lotion, collyrium (*SPÉC*)

colmatage [kɔlmataʒ] NM a [*fuite*] sealing(-off), plugging; [*fissure, trou*] filling-in, plugging, closing; [*déficit*] making good b (*Agr*) [*terrain*] warping

colmater [kɔlmate] ▸ conjug 1 ◂ VT a [+ *fuite*] to seal (off), plug; [+ *fissure, trou*] to fill in, plug; [+ *déficit*] to make good, make up; **la fissure s'est colmatée toute seule** the crack has filled itself in *ou* sealed itself; (*Mil*) **~ une brèche** to seal *ou* close a gap b (*Agr*) [+ *terrain*] to warp

colo* [kɔlo] NF (ABRÉV = **colonie de vacances**) → **colonie**

colocataire [kɔlɔkatɛʀ] NMF [*immeuble*] fellow tenant, co-tenant (*Admin*); [*appartement*] flatmate (*Brit*), roommate (*US*); [*maison*] housemate

Cologne [kɔlɔɲ] N Cologne → **eau**

Colomb [kɔlɔ̃] NM **Christophe ~** Christopher Columbus

colombage [kɔlɔ̃baʒ] NM half-timbering; **maison à ~(s)** half-timbered house

colombe [kɔlɔ̃b] NF (*Orn, fig Pol*) dove

Colombie [kɔlɔ̃bi] NF Colombia; **~ britannique** British Columbia

colombien, -ienne [kɔlɔ̃bjɛ̃, jɛn] 1 ADJ Colombian 2 **Colombien(ne)** NM,F Colombian

colombier [kɔlɔ̃bje] NM dovecote

colombin¹ [kɔlɔ̃bɛ̃] NM (**pigeon**) **~** stockdove

colombin² [kɔlɔ̃bɛ̃] NM [*argile*] clay coil; (‡ = *étron*) turd‡*

Colombine [kɔlɔ̃bin] NF (*Théât*) Columbine

Colombo [kɔlɔ̃bo] N Colombo

colombophile [kɔlɔ̃bɔfil] 1 ADJ **société ~** pigeon-fanciers' club 2 NMF pigeon fancier

colombophilie [kɔlɔ̃bɔfili] NF pigeon fancying

colon [kɔlɔ̃] NM a (= *pionnier*) settler, colonist b (*en vacances*) child (*at a children's holiday camp*) c (*arg Mil*) colonel; **eh bien, mon ~ !*** heck!*, blimey!* (*Brit*)

côlon [kolɔ̃] NM (*Anat*) colon

colonel [kɔlɔnɛl] NM [*armée de terre*] colonel; [*armée de l'air*] group captain (*Brit*), colonel (*US*)

colonelle [kɔlɔnɛl] NF a (= *officier*) [*armée de terre*] colonel; [*armée de l'air*] group captain (*Brit*), colonel (*US*) b († = *épouse*) [*armée de terre*] colonel's wife; [*armée de l'air*] group captain's wife (*Brit*), colonel's wife (*US*)

colonial, e (*mpl* **-iaux**) [kɔlɔnjal, jo] 1 ADJ colonial → **casque** 2 NM (= *soldat*) soldier of the colonial troops; (= *habitant*) colonial 3 **coloniale** NF **la ~e** (the French) Colonial Army

colonialisme [kɔlɔnjalism] NM colonialism; **~ culturel** cultural imperialism

colonialiste [kɔlɔnjalist] ADJ, NMF colonialist

colonie [kɔlɔni] NF (*Bio, Pol, Zool*) colony; (= *communauté ethnique*) community; **vivre aux ~s** to live in the colonies; **~ de vacances** ≈ (children's) holiday camp (*Brit*), ≈ summer camp (*US*); **~ pénitentiaire** penal settlement *ou* colony

---

COLONIE DE VACANCES

The **colonie de vacances** or "**colo**" is an important part of life for many French children. **Colonies de vacances** are residential centres in the countryside, in the mountains or at the seaside where

---

children, supervised by trained "moniteurs" and "monitrices", can participate in a range of open-air activities. The **colonie de vacances** helps break up the two-month summer holiday for parents and children alike.

---

colonisateur, -trice [kɔlɔnizatœʀ, tʀis] 1 ADJ colonizing (*épith*) 2 NM,F colonizer

colonisation [kɔlɔnizasjɔ̃] NF colonization

colonisé, e [kɔlɔnize] (*ptp de* **coloniser**) 1 ADJ colonized 2 NMPL **les ~s** colonized peoples, those who have been subjected to colonialization

coloniser [kɔlɔnize] ▸ conjug 1 ◂ VT to colonize

colonnade [kɔlɔnad] NF colonnade

colonne [kɔlɔn] 1 NF (*gén*) column; (*Archit*) column, pillar; **en ~ par deux** [*enfants*] in twos, in a crocodile* (*Brit*); [*soldats*] in twos; **mettez-vous en ~ par quatre** line up four abreast; (*Presse*) **titre sur cinq ~s à la une** headline splashed across the front page; [*nombre*] **~ des unités/dizaines** unit/tens column → **cinquième, titre, titrer** 2 COMP ► **colonne d'air** airstream ► **colonne barométrique** barometric column ► **colonne blindée** armoured column ► **colonne de direction** (*Aut*) steering column ► **les Colonnes d'Hercule** the Pillars of Hercules ► **colonne montante** rising main ► **colonne Morris** (pillar-shaped) billboard ► **colonne sèche** dry riser ► **colonne de secours** rescue party ► **colonne vertébrale** spine, spinal *ou* vertebral column (*SPÉC*)

colonnette [kɔlɔnɛt] NF small column

colopathie [kɔlɔpati] NF colitis, colonitis

colophane [kɔlɔfan] NF rosin

coloquinte [kɔlɔkɛ̃t] NF (*Bot*) colocynth (*SPÉC*), bitter apple; (‡† = *tête*) head, nut*, bonce‡ (*Brit*)

Colorado [kɔlɔʀado] NM Colorado

colorant, e [kɔlɔʀɑ̃, ɑ̃t] 1 ADJ colouring (*Brit*) *ou* coloring (*US*) → **shampooing** 2 NM (*gén*) colouring (*Brit*) *ou* coloring (*US*) agent, colorant; (*pour textiles*) dye; (*sur étiquette*) « **sans ~s artificiels** » "(contains) no artificial colouring"; **~s vitaux** vital stains

coloration [kɔlɔʀasjɔ̃] NF a (= *teinture*) [*substance*] colouring (*Brit*), coloring (*US*); [*tissu*] dyeing; [*bois*] staining; **~ naturelle** *ou* **artificielle** natural *ou* artificial colouring b (*pour les cheveux*) colour (*Brit*), color (*US*); **se faire faire une ~** to have one's hair coloured (*Brit*) *ou* colored (*US*) c (= *couleur, nuance*) shade, colour(ing) (*Brit*), color(ing) (*US*); [*peau*] colouring (*Brit*), coloring (*US*); (*fig*) [*voix, ton*] coloration; (*fig*) [*discours*] complexion; **~ politique** [*journal, mouvement*] political complexion; **à** *ou* **de ~ socialiste** of *ou* with a socialist bent

colorature [kɔlɔʀatyʀ] NF coloratura

coloré, e [kɔlɔʀe] (*ptp de* **colorer**) ADJ [*teint*] florid, ruddy; [*objet*] coloured (*Brit*), colored (*US*); [*foule*] colourful (*Brit*), colorful (*US*); [*style, récit*] vivid, colourful (*Brit*), colorful (*US*)

colorer [kɔlɔʀe] ▸ conjug 1 ◂ 1 VT a (= *teindre*) (= *substance*) to colour (*Brit*), color (*US*); [+ *tissu*] to dye; [+ *bois*] to stain; **~ qch en bleu** to colour (*ou* dye *ou* stain) sth blue; (*litt*) **le soleil colore les cimes neigeuses** the sun tinges the snowy peaks with colour; (*Culin*) **faire ~ la viande dans le beurre** brown the meat in butter b (*littér = enjoliver*) [+ *récit, sentiments*] to colour (*Brit*), color (*US*) (**de** with) 2 **se colorer** VPR a (= *prendre de la couleur*) [*fruit*] to turn red (*ou* yellow *ou* orange etc), colour (*Brit*), color (*US*); **le ciel se colore de rose** the sky takes on a rosy tinge *ou* hue; **son teint se colora** her face became flushed, her colour rose b (= *être empreint de*) **se ~ de** to be coloured (*Brit*) *ou* colored (*US*) *ou* tinged with

coloriage [kɔlɔRjaʒ] NM (= *action*) colouring (*NonC*) (*Brit*), coloring (*NonC*) (*US*); (= *dessin*) coloured (*Brit*) *ou* colored (*US*) drawing

colorier [kɔlɔRje] ▶ conjug 7 ◀ VT [+ *carte, dessin*] to colour (*Brit*) *ou* color (*US*) (in); **images à ~** pictures to colour (in)

coloris [kɔlɔRi] NM (*gén*) colour (*Brit*), color (*US*), shade; [*visage, peau*] colouring (*Brit*), coloring (*US*); (*Comm*) **carte de ~** shade card

colorisation [kɔlɔRizasjɔ̃] NF colourization (*Brit*), colorization (*US*)

coloriser [kɔlɔRize] ▶ conjug 1 ◀ VT to colourize (*Brit*), colorize (*US*)

coloriste [kɔlɔRist] ① NMF (= *peintre*) colourist (*Brit*), colorist (*US*); (= *enlumineur*) colourer (*Brit*), colorer (*US*) ② NF (= *coiffeuse*) hairdresser (*specializing in tinting and rinsing*)

coloscopie [kɔlɔskɔpi] NF colonoscopy

colossal, e (*mpl* **-aux**) [kɔlɔsal, o] ADJ colossal, huge

colossalement [kɔlɔsalmɑ̃] ADV colossally, hugely

colosse [kɔlɔs] NM (= *personne*) giant (*fig*); (= *institution, État*) colossus, giant; **le ~ de Rhodes** the Colossus of Rhodes; **~ aux pieds d'argile** idol with feet of clay

colostrum [kɔlɔstRɔm] NM colostrum

colportage [kɔlpɔRtaʒ] NM [*marchandises, ragots*] hawking, peddling → **littérature**

colporter [kɔlpɔRte] ▶ conjug 1 ◀ VT [+ *marchandises, ragots*] to hawk, peddle

colporteur, -euse [kɔlpɔRtœR, øz] NM,F (= *vendeur*) hawker, pedlar; **~ de rumeurs** *ou* **ragots*** gossipmonger

colt® [kɔlt] NM (= *revolver*) gun, Colt®

coltiner [kɔltine] ▶ conjug 1 ◀ ① VT [+ *fardeau*] to carry, lug* *ou* hump* (*Brit*) around ② **se coltiner** VPR [+ *colis*] to lug* *ou* hump* (*Brit*) around, carry; * [+ *travail, personne*] to be *ou* get stuck* *ou* landed* *ou* lumbered* (*Brit*) with; **il va falloir se ~ ta sœur** we'll have to put up with your sister

columbarium [kɔlɔ̃baRjɔm] NM (= *cimetière*) columbarium

colvert [kɔlvɛR] NM mallard

colza [kɔlza] NM rape, colza

coma [kɔma] NM coma; **être/entrer dans le ~** to be in/go into a coma; **dans un ~ dépassé** brain-dead; **~ diabétique** diabetic coma

comateux, -euse [kɔmatø, øz] ① ADJ comatose; **état ~** state of coma, comatose state ② NM,F patient in a coma, comatose patient

combat [kɔ̃ba] ① NM ⓐ (*Mil*) battle, fight; **le ~ ◊ les ~s** the fighting (*NonC*); **~ aérien** air battle, dogfight; **~ naval** naval action; **ils s'entraînent au ~ aérien/naval** they're training in aerial/naval combat; (*lit, fig*) **~ d'arrière-garde** rearguard action; **~ de** [*avion*] combat (*épith*); [*troupes*] combat (*épith*), fighting; [*zone*] combat (*épith*), battle (*épith*); **aller au ~** to go into battle, enter the fray (*littér*); **mort au ~** killed in action; **les ~s continuent** the fighting goes on; **mettre hors de** [+ *soldat*] to put out of action; [+ *adversaire politique*] to put out of the running; (*Sport*) to put out of the fight *ou* contest → **branle-bas, char, sport**

ⓑ (*fig*) fight (**contre** against, **pour** for); **des ~s continuels entre parents et enfants** endless fighting between parents and children; **le ~ contre la vie chère** the fight against the high cost of living; **la vie est un ~ de tous les jours** life is a daily struggle; **« étudiants, professeurs : même ~ ! »** "students and teachers fighting together", "students and teachers united"; **quel ~ pour le faire manger !** it's such a struggle getting him to eat!; **discours de ~** fighting speech

ⓒ (*Sport*) match, fight; **~ de boxe/de catch** boxing/wrestling match

ⓓ (*littér = concours*) **ce fut un ~ de**

générosité/d'esprit they vied with each other in generosity/wit

② COMP ▶ **combat de coqs** cockfight; **les ~s de coqs ont été interdits** cockfighting has been banned ▶ **combat de gladiateurs** gladiatorial combat *ou* contest ▶ **combat rapproché** close combat ▶ **combat de rues** street fighting (*NonC*), street battle ▶ **combat singulier** single combat

combatif, -ive [kɔ̃batif, iv] ADJ [*troupes*] ready to fight; [*personne*] with a fighting spirit; [*esprit, humeur*] fighting (*épith*)

combativité [kɔ̃bativite] NF [*troupe*] readiness to fight; [*personne*] fighting spirit

combattant, e [kɔ̃batɑ̃, ɑ̃t] ① ADJ [*troupe*] fighting (*épith*), combatant (*épith*) ② NM,F [*guerre*] combatant; [*bagarre*] brawler → **ancien** ③ NM (= *oiseau*) (*mâle*) ruff; (*femelle*) reeve; (= *poisson*) fighting fish

combattre [kɔ̃batR] ▶ conjug 41 ◀ ① VT [+ *incendie, adversaire*] to fight; [+ *théorie, politique, inflation, vice*] to combat, fight (against); [+ *maladie*] [*malade*] to fight against; [*médecin*] to fight, combat ② VI to fight (**contre** against, **pour** for)

combe [kɔ̃b] NF (*Géog*) coomb, comb(e)

combien [kɔ̃bjɛ̃] ① ADV ⓐ (= *quantité*) how much; how many; **~ de lait/de bouteilles veux-tu ?** how much milk/how many bottles do you want?; **~ y en a-t-il en moins ?** (*quantité*) how much less is there (of it)?; (*nombre*) how many fewer are there (of them)?; **tu en as pour ~ de temps ?** how long will you be?; **depuis ~ de temps travaillez-vous ici ?** how long have you been working here?; **~ de fois ?** (*nombre*) how many times?; (*fréquence*) how often?

ⓑ (= *d'entre eux*) how many (of them); **~ n'ouvrent jamais un livre !** just think of how many people there are who never open a book!; **~ sont-ils ?** how many (of them) are there?, how many are they?

ⓒ (*frm = à quel point*) **si tu savais ~/~ plus je travaille maintenant !** if you only knew how much/how much more I work now!; **tu vois ~ il est paresseux** you can see how lazy he is; **c'est étonnant de voir ~ il a changé** it's surprising to see how changed he is *ou* how (much) he has changed; **~ vous avez raison !** how right you are!

ⓓ (= *tellement*) **~ peu de gens/d'argent** how few people/little money; **~ plus/moins de gens** how many more/fewer people; **~ plus d'argent** how much more money; **c'est plus long à faire mais ~ meilleur !** it takes longer to do but it's so much better!; († *ou hum*) **il est bête, ô ~ !** he is stupid, (oh) so stupid!; **~ d'ennui je vous cause** what a lot of trouble I'm causing you

ⓔ (= *avec mesure*) **~ est-ce ? ◊ ~ ça coûte ? ◊ ça fait ~ ?*** how much is it?; **~ pèse ce colis ?** how much does this parcel weigh?, how heavy is this parcel?; **~ mesure-t-il ?** (*personne*) how tall is he?; (*colis*) how big is it?; (*en longueur*) how long is it?, what length is it?; **vous le voulez en ~ de large ?** what width do you want (it)?; **ça va augmenter de ~ ?** how much more will it go up? *ou* be?; **ça va faire une différence de ~ ?** what will the difference be?; **~ y a-t-il d'ici à la ville ?** how far is it from here to the town?; **ça fait ~ de haut ?** how high is it?, what height is it?; (*Sport*) **~ a-t-il fait ~ aux essais ?** what was his time in the trials?

② NM* (*rang*) **le ~ êtes-vous ?** where did you come?, where were you placed?; (*date*) **le ~ sommes-nous ?** what's the date?, what date is it?; (*fréquence*) [*trains, bus*] **il y en a tous les ~ ?** how often do they run?

combientième* [kɔ̃bjɛ̃tjɛm] ① ADJ **Lincoln était le ~ président ?** what number president was Lincoln?; **c'est la ~ fois que ça arrive !** how many times has that happened now!

② NMF ⓐ (= *rang*) **il est le ~ ?** where did he come?, where was he placed?; **ce coureur est arrivé le ~ ?** where did this runner come (in)? ⓑ (= *énumération*) **encore un attentat, c'est le ~ ?** another attack, how many does that make *ou* is that of?; **donne-moi le troisième — le ~ ?** give me the third one — which one did you say?

combinaison [kɔ̃binɛzɔ̃] NF ⓐ (= *action*) combining; [*éléments, sons, chiffres*] combination; **~ (ministérielle)** government; **~ (chimique)** (*entre plusieurs corps*) combination; (= *corps composé*) compound ⓑ [*coffre-fort, loto*] combination ⓒ (= *vêtement*) [*femme*] slip; [*aviateur*] flying suit; [*mécanicien*] boiler suit (*Brit*), (one-piece) overalls (*US*); (*Ski*) ski-suit; **~ de plongée (sous-marine)** (underwater) diving suit; **~ spatiale** space suit ⓓ (= *astuce*) device, trick; (= *manigance*) scheme; **des ~s louches** shady schemes *ou* scheming (*NonC*)

combinaison-short (*pl* **combinaisons-shorts**) [kɔ̃binɛzɔ̃ʃɔRt] NF culotte suit

combinard, e* [kɔ̃binaR, aRd] ADJ, NM,F (*péj*) **il est ~ ◊ c'est un ~** (*astuces*) he knows all the tricks; (*manigances*) he's a schemer

combinat [kɔ̃bina] NM (industrial) complex

combinatoire [kɔ̃binatwaR] ① ADJ (*Ling*) combinative; (*Math*) combinatorial, combinatory ② NF (= *analyse*) combinatorial analysis, combinatorics *sg*

combine* [kɔ̃bin] NF (= *astuce*) trick (**pour faire** to do); (*péj* = *manigance*) **la ~** scheming; **il est dans la ~** he knows (all) about it, he's in on it**; **entrer dans la ~** to play the game; **ça sent la ~** I smell a rat, it sounds a bit fishy*; **toutes leurs ~s** all their little schemes

combiné [kɔ̃bine] NM (*Chim*) compound; [*téléphone*] receiver, handset; **~ (gaine-soutien-gorge)** corselette; **~ (batteur-mixeur)** mixer and liquidizer *ou* blender; **~ (avion-hélicoptère)** convertible helicopter, convertiplane; (*Ski*) **~ alpin/nordique** alpine/nordic combination; (*Ski*) **il est 3ème au ~** he's 3rd overall

combiner [kɔ̃bine] ▶ conjug 1 ◀ ① VT ⓐ (= *grouper*) [+ *éléments, sons, chiffres*] to combine (**à, avec** with); **opération combinée** joint *ou* combined operation; **l'oxygène et l'hydrogène combinés** oxygen and hydrogen combined; **l'inquiétude et la fatigue combinées** a combination of anxiety and tiredness ⓑ (= *élaborer*) [+ *affaire, mauvais coup, plan*] to devise, work out, think up; [+ *horaire, emploi du temps*] to devise; **bien combiné** well devised ② **se combiner** VPR [*éléments*] to combine (**avec** with)

comble [kɔ̃bl] ① ADJ [*pièce, autobus*] packed (full), jam-packed* ► **mesure, salle** ② NM ⓐ (= *degré extrême*) height; **c'est le ~ du ridicule !** that's the height of absurdity!; **au ~ de la joie** overjoyed; **au ~ du désespoir** in the depths of despair; **être (porté) à son ~** [*joie, colère*] to be at its peak *ou* height; **ceci mit le ~ à sa fureur** this brought his anger to its climax *ou* a peak (*loc*) **c'est le ~ ! ◊ c'est un ~ !** that's the last straw!, that takes the biscuit!* (*Brit*) *ou* cake!* (*US*); **le ~, c'est qu'il est parti sans payer** and to cap it all* he left without paying; **pour ~ (de malheur) il ...** to cap *ou* crown (*Brit*) it all he ... ⓒ (= *charpente*) roof trussing (*SPÉC*), roof timbers; **les ~s** the attic, the loft; **loger (dans une chambre) sous les ~s** to live in a garret *ou* an attic; **faux ~ ◊ ~ perdu** inconvertible (part of the) attic → **fond**

combler [kɔ̃ble] ▶ conjug 1 ◀ VT ⓐ (= *boucher*) [+ *trou, fente*] to fill in; **ça comblera un trou dans nos finances** that'll fill a gap in our finances ⓑ (= *résorber*) [+ *déficit*] to make good, make up; [+ *lacune, vide*] to fill; **~ son retard** to make up lost time ⓒ (= *satisfaire*) [+ *désir, espoir*] to fulfil; [+ *besoin*] to fulfil, fill; [+ *personne*] to gratify; **parents comblés par la naissance d'un enfant** parents overjoyed at the birth of a child; **c'est une femme comblée** she has all that she could wish for [d] (= *couvrir*) **~ qn de** [+ *cadeaux, honneurs*] to shower sb with; **il mourut comblé d'honneurs** he died laden with honours; **vous me comblez d'aise** *ou* **de joie** you fill me with joy; **vraiment, vous nous comblez!** really, you're too good to us!

combo [kɔ̃bo] NM (*Mus*) combo

comburant, e [kɔ̃byrã, ãt] [1] ADJ combustive [2] NM oxidizer, oxidant

combustibilité [kɔ̃bystibilite] NF combustibility

combustible [kɔ̃bystibl] [1] ADJ combustible [2] NM fuel; **les ~s** fuels, kinds of fuel; **~ fossile/irradié/nucléaire** fossil/spent/nuclear fuel; **~ organique** biofuel, organic fuel

combustion [kɔ̃bystjɔ̃] NF combustion; **poêle à ~ lente** slow-burning stove

come-back [kɔmbak] NM INV comeback; **faire son ~** to make a comeback

COMECON [kɔmekɔn] NM (ABRÉV = **Council for Mutual Economic Assistance**) COMECON

comédie [kɔmedi] [1] NF [a] (*Théât*) comedy; **~ de mœurs/d'intrigue** comedy of manners/of intrigue; **~ de caractères** character comedy; **~ de situation** situation comedy; (*Théât, Ciné*) **~ dramatique** drama; **de ~** [*personnage, situation*] (*Théât*) comedy (*épith*); (*fig*) comical [b] (*fig* = *simulation*) playacting; **c'est de la ~** it's all an act, it's all a sham; **jouer la ~** to put on an act, put it on* [c] (* = *caprice, histoires*) palaver, fuss; **faire la ~** to make a fuss *ou* a scene; **allons, pas de ~** come on, no nonsense *ou* fuss; **c'est toujours la même ~** it's always the same palaver [2] COMP ▶ **comédie de boulevard** light comedy ▶ **la comédie humaine** the comédie humaine ▶ **comédie musicale** musical

Comédie-Française [kɔmedifrãsez] NF **la ~** the Comédie-Française (*the French National Theatre*)

comédien, -ienne [kɔmedjɛ̃, jɛn] [1] NM,F [a] (= *hypocrite*) sham; **quel ~ tu fais!** you're always putting it on!* [b] (= *pitre*) show-off [2] NM actor; (= *comique*) comedy actor, comedian [3] **comédienne** NF (= *actrice*) actress; (= *comique*) comedy actress, comedienne

comédogène [kɔmedɔʒɛn] ADJ comedogenic

comédon [kɔmedɔ̃] NM blackhead, comedo (*SPÉC*)

comestible [kɔmɛstibl] [1] ADJ edible [2] **comestibles** NMPL (fine) foods, delicatessen; **magasin de ~s** ≈ delicatessen

comète [kɔmɛt] NF (*Astron*) comet → **plan¹**

cométique [kɔmetik] NM (*Can*) Eskimo sled, komatik (*US, Can*)

comice [kɔmis] [1] NM **~(s) agricole(s)†** agricultural show *ou* meeting [2] NF Comice pear

comique [kɔmik] [1] ADJ (*Théât*) [*acteur, film, genre*] comic; (*fig*) [*incident, personnage*] comical [2] NM [a] [*tenue, aspect physique*] comic look *ou* appearance; **le ~ de la situation** the funny side of the situation; **d'un ~ irrésistible** hilariously *ou* irresistibly funny; **le ~ de la chose, c'est que ...** the funny *ou* amusing thing about it is that ... [b] (*Littérat*) **le ~** comedy; **~ de caractère/de situation** character/

situation comedy; **~ de répétition** comedy of repetition; **le ~ de boulevard** light comedy; **~ troupier** coarse comedy; **avoir le sens du ~** to have a sense of the comic [3] NM,F (= *artiste*) comic; (= *dramaturge*) comedy writer

comiquement [kɔmikmã] ADV comically

comité [kɔmite] [1] NM (*gén*) committee; (*permanent, élu*) board, committee; (= *consultatif/exécutif/restreint* advisory/executive/select committee; **~ de défense/soutien** protection/support committee; (*fig*) **se réunir en petit ~** (*gén*) to meet in a select group; (*petite réception*) to have a small get-together [2] COMP ▶ **comité central** central committee ▶ **comité directeur** *ou* **de direction** management committee ▶ **Comité économique et social** *French regional commission on economic and social affairs* ▶ **comité d'entreprise** workers' *ou* works council ▶ **Comité national d'éthique** *national research ethics committee in France* ▶ **comité des fêtes** ≈ recreation committee ▶ **comité de gestion** board of management ▶ **Comité international de la Croix-Rouge** International Committee of the Red Cross ▶ **Comité international olympique** International Olympic Committee ▶ **comité de lecture** reading panel *ou* committee ▶ **comité de liaison** liaison committee ▶ **comité monétaire (européen)** (European) monetary committee ▶ **Comité national de la consommation** ≈ National Consumer Council (*Brit*), ≈ Consumers' Association (*Brit*), ≈ Consumer Product Safety Council (*US*) ▶ **comité de pilotage** steering committee

commandant [kɔmɑ̃dɑ̃] [1] NM [*armée de terre*] major; [*armée de l'air*] squadron leader (*Brit*), major (*US*); (*Aviat, Naut*) captain; (*gén : dans toute fonction de commandement*) commander, commandant; **«oui mon ~»** "yes Sir" [2] COMP ▶ **commandant de bord** (*Aviat*) captain ▶ **commandant en chef** commander-in-chief ▶ **commandant en second** second in command

commandante [kɔmɑ̃dɑ̃t] NF major's (*ou* captain's etc) wife

▼ **commande** [kɔmɑ̃d] NF [a] (*Comm*) order; **passer (une) ~** to put in *ou* place an order (**de** for); **prendre la ~** to take the order; **on vous livrera vos ~s jeudi** your order will be delivered to you on Thursday; **payable à la ~** cash with order; **cet article est en ~** the item is on order; **fait sur ~** made to order; **agir sur ~** to act on orders; **je ne peux pas jouer ce rôle/m'amuser sur ~** I can't act the role/enjoy myself to order; **carnet/bulletin de ~s** order book/form; **les ~s publiques** state *ou* government orders [b] (*Littérat, Art*) commission; **passer une ~ à qn** to commission sb; **travailler sur ~** to work to commission; **ouvrage écrit/composé sur ~** commissioned work/composition; **film de ~** commissioned film [c] (*Aviat, Tech*) (= *action*) control (*NonC*), controlling (*NonC*); (= *dispositif*) **les ~s** the controls; **les organes** *ou* **leviers de ~** ◊ **les ~s** the controls; **~ à distance** remote control; **~ nu-**

mérique numerical *ou* digital control; **à ~ vocale** voice-activated; **à ~ par effleurement** touch-controlled; **câble de ~** control cable; **véhicule à double ~** dual control vehicle, vehicle with dual controls; **se mettre aux ~s** ◊ **prendre les ~s** (*lit*) to take control, take (over) the controls; (*fig*) to take control; (*lit, fig*) **passer les ~s à qn** to hand over control *ou* the controls to sb; **être aux ~s** ◊ **tenir les ~s** (*lit*) to be in control, be at the controls; (*fig*) to be in control → **poste, tableau** [d] (*loc*) **de ~** [*sourire*] forced, affected; [*optimisme*] fake; [*livre, film, tableau*] commissioned

commandement [kɔmɑ̃dmɑ̃] [a] (= *direction*) [*armée, navire*] command; **avoir/prendre le ~ de** to be in *ou* have/take command of; **sur un ton de ~** in a commanding tone; **avoir l'habitude du ~** to be used to being in command → **poste²** [b] (= *état-major*) command; **le ~ a décidé que ...** it has been decided at higher command that ... → **haut** [c] (*Rel*) commandment [d] (= *ordre*) command; (*Mil*) **à mon ~, marche!** on my command, march!; **avoir ~ de faire qch†** to have orders to do sth [e] (*Jur*) **~ d'huissier** court order to pay

▼ **commander** [kɔmɑ̃de] ▶ conjug 1 ◀ [1] VT [a] (= *ordonner*) [+ *obéissance, attaque*] to order, command; **~ à qn de faire qch** to order *ou* command sb to do sth; **il me commanda le silence** he ordered *ou* commanded me to keep quiet; **sans vous ~, pourriez-vous taper cette lettre?** if it's no trouble, could you type this letter?; **l'amitié ne se commande pas** you can't make friends to order; **l'amour ne se commande pas** you don't choose who you love; **je ne peux pas le sentir, ça ne se commande pas** I can't stand him — you can't help these things [b] (= *imposer*) [+ *respect, admiration*] to command [c] (= *requérir*) [*événements, circonstances*] to demand; **la prudence commande que ...** prudence demands that ... [d] (*Comm*) [+ *marchandise, repas*] to order; (*Art*) [+ *œuvre*] to commission; (*au café*) **avez-vous déjà commandé?** have you ordered?, has somebody taken your order?; **qu'as-tu commandé pour Noël?** what have you asked for for Christmas?; (*hum*) **nous avons commandé le soleil** we've ordered some sunshine (*hum*) [e] (= *diriger*) [+ *armée, navire, expédition, attaque*] to command; (*emploi absolu*) to be in command, be in charge; **~ le feu** to give the order to shoot *ou* to (open) fire; **c'est lui qui commande ici** he's in charge here; **je n'aime pas qu'on me commande** I don't like to be ordered about *ou* to be given orders; **à la maison, c'est elle qui commande** she's the boss at home, she's the one who gives the orders at home [f] (= *contrôler*) to control; **ce bouton commande la sirène** this switch controls the siren; **forteresse qui commande l'entrée du détroit** fortress which commands the entrance to the straits [2] **commander à** VT INDIR [+ *passions, instincts*] to have command *ou* control over; **il ne commande plus à sa jambe gauche** he no longer has any control over his left leg; **il ne sait pas se ~** he can't control himself [3] **se commander** VPR (= *communiquer*) [*pièces*] to connect, lead into one another

commanderie [kɔmɑ̃dri] NF (*Hist*) (= *bénéfice*) commandership; (= *maison*) commander's residence

commandeur [kɔmɑ̃dœr] NM commander (of an Order); (*Littérat*) **la statue du ~** the statue of the Commendatore

commanditaire [kɔmɑ̃ditɛr] NM (*Comm*) limited *ou* sleeping (*Brit*) *ou* silent (*US*) partner; [*exposition*] sponsor; **les ~s d'un meurtre** the people behind a murder

commandite [kɔmɑ̃dit] NF (*Comm* = *fonds*) share (*of limited partner*); **(société en) ~** limited partnership

commandité, e [kɔmɑ̃dite] NM,F active *ou* acting *ou* ordinary partner

commanditer [kɔmɑ̃dite] ▶conjug 1◀ VT (*Comm* = *financer*) to finance; [+ *exposition*] to sponsor; [+ *crime*] to be behind

commando [kɔmɑ̃do] NM commando (group); **les membres du ~** the commando members, the commandos

---

▼ **comme** [kɔm]

1 CONJONCTION	**3** ADVERBE
2 LOC ADVERBIALE	

1 CONJONCTION

a |temps| as; **elle entra (juste) ~ le rideau se levait** she came in (just) as the curtain was rising

b |cause| as, since; **~ il pleuvait, j'ai pris la voiture** as *ou* since it was raining I took the car; **~ il est lâche, il n'a pas osé parler** being a coward *ou* coward that he is, he didn't dare speak out

♦ **comme quoi**
(= *disant que*) to the effect that; **j'ai reçu une lettre ~ quoi j'étais licencié** I got a letter to the effect that *ou* telling me I was fired
(= *d'où il s'ensuit que*) which goes to show that; **~ quoi tout le monde peut se tromper** which (just) goes to show that anybody can make a mistake; **~ quoi!** it just goes to show!

c |comparaison| as, like (*devant n et pron*); (*avec idée de manière*) as, the way*; **elle a soigné son chien ~ elle aurait soigné un enfant** she nursed her dog as she would have done a child; **il pense ~ nous** he thinks as we do *ou* like us; **c'est un homme ~ lui qu'il nous faut** we need a man like him *ou* such as him; **un homme ~ lui, on n'en fait plus** they don't make men like that any more; **ce pantalon est pratique pour le travail ~ pour les loisirs** these trousers are practical for work as well as leisure; **il s'ennuie en ville ~ à la campagne** he gets bored both in town and in the country, he gets bored in town as he does in the country; **il écrit ~ il parle** he writes as *ou* the way he speaks; **c'est une excuse ~ une autre** it's as good an excuse as any; **c'est un client ~ un autre** he's just another customer; **c'est une façon ~ une autre de résoudre les problèmes** that's one way of solving problems; **il voudrait une moto ~ celle de son frère/la mienne*** he would like a motorbike like his brother's/ mine; **il voudrait une moto, ~ son frère** he would like a motorbike (just) like his brother; **le héros du film n'agit pas ~ dans la pièce** the hero in the film does not act as he does *ou* the way he does in the play; **si, ~ nous le pensons, il a oublié** if he has forgotten, as we think he has; **faites ~ vous voulez** do as you like; **choisissez ~ pour vous choose** as you would for yourself, choose as if it were for yourself; **~ pour faire** as if to do; **il fit un geste ~ pour la frapper** he made as if to hit her *ou* he was going to hit her; **il y a ~ un problème** there's a bit of a problem → **dire, hasard, juste, plaire, tout** *etc*

♦ **comme ça** ◊ **comme cela**
(= *ainsi*) like that; **il est ~ ça, tu ne le changeras pas** that's the way he is, you won't change him; **vous aimeriez une robe ~ ça?** would you like a dress like that?; **des choses ~ ça** things like that, that sort of thing; **il a pêché un saumon ~ ça!** he caught a salmon (that was) this big!
(** : admiratif*) great!*, fantastic!*, terrific!*; **on a vu un film ~ ça!** we saw a great* *ou* fantastic* *ou* terrific* film!

2 LOC ADVERBIALE

a |intensif| alors, **~ ça, vous nous quittez?** so you're leaving us just like that?; **le docteur m'a dit ~ ça*, prenez des calmants** the doctor just told me to take some tranquillizers

b = **de cette manière** **je l'ai enfermé, ~ ça il ne peut pas nous suivre** I locked him in — that way he can't follow us; **c'est ~ ça et pas autrement** *ou* **un point c'est tout** that's just the way it is, that's all there is to it; **c'est ~ ça que je m'y prendrais** that's how I'd do it; **puisque** *ou* **si c'est ~ ça, je m'en vais!** if that's how *ou* the way it is, I'm leaving!

♦ **comme ci comme ça** so-so*, fair to middling; **comment ça va? — ~ ci ~ ça** how are you? — so-so* *ou* fair to middling

♦ **comme il faut** († *ou hum* = *convenable*) **une dame très ~ il faut** a fine upstanding woman; (= *convenablement*) properly; **mange/tiens-toi ~ il faut** eat/sit up properly

♦ **comme les autres**
c'est un jour/métier ~ les autres it's just like any other day/job; **il n'est pas ~ les autres** he's not like everybody else, he's different; **un roman/ une grève pas ~ les autres** a different kind of novel/strike
faire ~ les autres to do as everybody does *ou* like everybody else

♦ **comme si** as if, as though; **il se conduit ~ si de rien n'était** he behaves as if *ou* as though nothing had happened; **~ si nous ne savions pas!** as if we didn't know!; **ce n'est pas ~ si on ne l'avait pas prévenu!** it's not as if *ou* as though he hadn't been warned!; **tu n'es pas gai mais tu peux faire ~ si*** you're not happy but you can pretend (to be)

♦ *adjectif* + **comme tout**: **elle est gentille ~ tout** she's so nice, she's as nice as can be; **c'est facile ~ tout** it's as easy as can be; **c'était amusant ~ tout** it was so *ou* terribly funny; **il est menteur ~ tout** he's such a liar, he's a terrible *ou* dreadful liar

♦ **comme tout le monde** like everybody else; **il a applaudi pour faire ~ tout le monde** he clapped to be like everybody else; **je veux vivre ~ tout le monde** I want to lead a normal life

d = **en tant que** as; **nous l'avons eu ~ président** we had him as (our) president; **~ étudiant, il est assez médiocre** as a student, he is rather poor

e = **tel que** like, such as; **les fleurs ~ la rose et l'iris sont fragiles** flowers such as *ou* like roses and irises are fragile; **bête ~ il est … stupid** as he is …; **elle n'a jamais vu de maison ~ la nôtre** she's never seen a house like ours *ou* such as ours

f
♦ **comme** + *adjectif ou participe présent* as though, as if; **il était ~ fasciné par ces oiseaux** it was as though *ou* as if he were fascinated by these birds, he was as though *ou* as if fascinated by these birds; **il était ~ fou** he was behaving like a madman; **il était ~ perdu dans cette foule** it was as though *ou* as if he were lost in this crowd; **~ se parlant à lui-même** as if *ou* as though talking to himself

3 ADVERBE
how; **~ ces enfants sont bruyants!** how noisy those children are!, those children are so noisy!; **~ il fait beau!** what a lovely day (it is)!, what lovely weather!; **tu sais ~ elle est** you know what she's like *ou* how she is; **écoute ~ elle chante bien** listen (to) how beautifully she sings; **~ vous y allez, vous!*** (now) hold on a minute!*, don't get carried away! → **voir**

---

commémoratif, -ive [kɔmemɔʁatif, iv] ADJ [*cérémonie, plaque*] commemorative (*épith*), memorial (*épith*); [*service*] memorial (*épith*); **monument ~** memorial

commémoration [kɔmemɔʁasjɔ̃] NF commemoration; **en ~ de** in commemoration of

commémorer [kɔmemɔʁe] ▶conjug 1◀ VT to commemorate

commençant, e [kɔmɑ̃sɑ̃, ɑ̃t] **1** ADJ beginning (*épith*) **2** NM,F (= *débutant*) beginner; **grand ~** absolute beginner

---

commencement [kɔmɑ̃smɑ̃] NM **a** (= *début*) beginning, commencement (*frm*); (= *départ*) start; **il y a eu un ~ d'incendie** a small fire broke out; (*Jur*) **~ d'exécution** initial steps in the commission of a crime; (*Jur*) **~ de preuve** prima facie evidence; **au/dès le ~** in/from the beginning, at/from the outset *ou* start; **du ~ à la fin** from beginning to end, from start to finish; **c'est le ~ de la fin** it's the beginning of the end; **il y a un ~ à tout** you've (always) got to start somewhere **b** **~s** [*science, métier*] (= *premiers temps*) beginnings; (= *rudiments*) basic knowledge; **les ~s ont été durs** the beginning was hard

▼ **commencer** [kɔmɑ̃se] ▶conjug 3◀ **1** VT **a** (= *entreprendre*) [+ *travail, opération, repas*] to begin, start, commence (*frm*); **ils ont commencé les travaux de l'autoroute** they've started *ou* begun work on the motorway; **j'ai commencé un nouveau chapitre** I've started *ou* begun (on) a new chapter; **je vais ~ le judo/le violon** I'm going to take up judo/the violin; **quelle façon de ~ l'année!** what a way to begin *ou* start the (new) year!
b (= *entamer*) [+ *bouteille, produit*] to open
c [*chose*] to begin; **mot/phrase qui commence un chapitre** word/sentence which begins a chapter, opening word/sentence of a chapter; **une heure de méditation commence la journée** the day begins *ou* starts with an hour of meditation

2 VI **a** (= *débuter*) to begin, start, commence (*frm*); **le concert va ~** the concert is about to begin *ou* start; **tu ne vas pas ~!*** ◊ **ne commence pas!*** don't start!*; (*lit ou iro*) **ça commence bien!** that's a good start!, we're off to a good start!; **ça commence mal!** that's a bad start!, that's not a very good start!; **pour ~** (*lit*) to begin *ou* start with; (*fig*) to begin *ou* start with, for a start; **elle commence demain chez Legrand** she starts (work) tomorrow at Legrand's; **c'est lui qui a commencé!** he started it!; **leurs jupes commencent à 80 F** they've got skirts from 80 francs upwards
b **~ à** (*ou* **de**) **faire** to begin *ou* start to do, begin *ou* start doing; **il commençait à neiger** it was beginning *ou* starting to snow; **il commençait à s'inquiéter/à s'impatienter** he was getting *ou* beginning to get nervous/impatient; **je commence à en avoir assez*** I've had just about enough (of it); **ça commence à bien faire*** it's getting a bit much*
c **~ par qch/par faire qch** to start *ou* begin with sth/by doing sth; **par quoi voulez-vous ~?** what would you like to begin *ou* start with?; **commençons par le commencement** let's begin at the beginning; **commence par faire tes devoirs, on verra après** do your homework for a start, and then we'll see; **ils m'ont tous déçu, à ~ par Jean** they all let me down, especially Jean; **il faut apporter du changement, à ~ par trouver de nouveaux locaux** we have to make some changes, and the first thing to do is to find new premises

commensal, e (*mpl* **-aux**) [kɔmɑ̃sal, o] NM,F (*littér* = *personne*) companion at table, table companion; (*Bio*) commensal

commensalisme [kɔmɑ̃salism] NM (*Bio*) commensalism

commensurable [kɔmɑ̃syʁabl] ADJ commensurable

comment [kɔmɑ̃] **1** ADV **a** (= *de quelle façon*) how; **~ a-t-il fait?** how did he do it?, how did he manage that?; **je ne sais pas ~ il a fait cela** I don't know how he did it; **~ s'appelle-t-il?** what's his name?, what's he called?; **~ appelles-tu cela?** what do you call that?; **~ allez-vous?** *ou* **vas-tu?** how are you?; **~ est-il, ce type?** what sort of guy* is he?, what's he like?; **~ va-t-il?** how is he?; **~ faire?** how shall we do it? *ou* go about it?; **~ se fait-il que …?** how is it that …?, how come …?*; **~ se peut-il que …?** how can it be that …?

▶ GRAMMAIRE ACTIVE: **comme** 44.1   **commencer** 53.1, 53.2

b (*excl*) ~? (I beg your) pardon?, pardon me?; (*US*) sorry?, what?*; ~ **cela**? what do you mean?; ~, **il est mort**? what? he's dead?; **tu as assez mangé**? — **et** ~! have you had enough to eat? — I (most) certainly have! *ou* I should say so! *ou* and how!*; **avez-vous bien travaillé**? — **et** ~! did you work well? — I should say so! *ou* not half!* (*Brit*) *ou* and how!*; ~ **donc**! by all means!, of course!; **Dieu sait** ~! goodness* *ou* God* knows how!

2 NM **le** ~ the how; **les** ~**(s)** the hows → **pourquoi**

commentaire [kɔmɑ̃tɛʀ] NM **a** (= *remarque*) comment; **faire des** ~**s sur qch** to comment on *ou* about sth; **quels ont été ses** ~**s sur ce qui s'est passé**? what did he say about what happened?; ~**s de presse** press comments; **je vous dispense de vos** ~**s** I can do without your comments *ou* remarks, I don't want (to hear) any comments *ou* remarks from you; **tu feras comme je te l'ordonne, et pas de** ~**s**! you will do as I say and no arguments!; **son attitude se passe de** ~**s** his attitude speaks for itself; **vous avez entendu ce qu'il a dit**! — **sans** ~! did you hear him! — no comment!; **sa conduite donne lieu à bien des** ~**s**! his behaviour has really set people talking!
b (= *exposé*) commentary (**de** on); (*Radio, TV*) commentary; (*Littérat* = *mémoires*) **les** «**Commentaires**» **de César** Caesar's "Commentaries"; **un bref** ~ **de la séance** some brief comments on the meeting
c (*Littérat* = *explication*) commentary; **faire le** ~ **d'un texte** to do *ou* give a commentary on a text; **édition avec** ~**(s)** annotated edition
d (*Ordin, Ling*) comment

commentateur, -trice [kɔmɑ̃tatœʀ, tʀis] NM,F (*gén, Radio, TV*) commentator

commenter [kɔmɑ̃te] ▸conjug 1◂ VT **a** [+ *poème*] to comment (on); [+ *conduite*] to make comments on, comment on; [+ *événement, actualité*] to comment on; (*Radio, TV*) [+ *match*] to commentate on; [+ *cérémonie officielle*] to provide the commentary for; **le match sera commenté par André Leduc** the commentary on the match will be given by André Leduc, André Leduc will be commentating on the match

commérage [kɔmeʀaʒ] NM piece of gossip; ~**s** gossip (*NonC*), gossiping (*NonC*)

commerçant, e [kɔmɛʀsɑ̃, ɑ̃t] **1** ADJ **a** [*nation*] trading (*épith*), commercial; [*quartier*] shopping (*épith*); [*ville, activité*] commercial; **rue très** ~**e** busy shopping street, street with many shops **b** (= *habile*) [*procédé*] commercially shrewd; **il est très** ~ he's got good business sense; **ce n'est pas très** ~ it's not a very good way to do business **2** NM shopkeeper, tradesman, merchant (*US*), storekeeper (*US*); ~ **en gros** wholesale dealer; **les** ~**s du quartier** (the) local tradesmen *ou* shopkeepers *ou* merchants **3** **commerçante** NF shopkeeper, storekeeper (*US*)

commerce [kɔmɛʀs] NM **a** **le** ~ (= *activité*) trade, commerce; (= *affaires*) business, trade; **le** ~ **n'y est pas encore très développé** commerce *ou* trade isn't very highly developed there yet; **depuis quelques mois le** ~ **ne marche pas très bien** business *ou* trade has been bad for a few months; **opération/maison/traité de** ~ commercial operation/firm/treaty; ~ **en** *ou* **de gros/détail** wholesale/retail trade; ~ **extérieur/international** foreign/international trade *ou* commerce; **faire du** ~ **(avec)** to trade (with); **être dans le** ~ to be in trade; **faire** ~ **de** ~ to trade in; **faire** ~ **de ses charmes/son nom** to trade on one's charms/name ~ **effet**
b (= *circuit commercial*) [*objet*] **dans le** ~ in the shops *ou* stores (*US*); **hors** ~ for restricted sale only (*attrib*); **exemplaires hors** ~ privately printed copies
c (= *commerçants*) **le** ~ shopkeepers, merchants (*US*); **le petit** ~ small shopkeepers *ou*

traders; **le grand** ~ large *ou* big retailers; **le monde du** ~ the commercial world, trading *ou* commercial circles
d (= *boutique*) business; **tenir** *ou* **avoir un** ~ **d'épicerie** to have a grocery business; **un gros/petit** ~ a big/small business → **proximité**
e († *ou littér*) (= *fréquentation*) (social) intercourse; (= *compagnie*) company; (= *rapport*) dealings; **être d'un** ~ **agréable** to be pleasant company; **avoir** ~ **avec qn** to have dealings with sb

commercer [kɔmɛʀse] ▸conjug 3◂ VI to trade (**avec** with)

commercial, e (*mpl* -**iaux**) [kɔmɛʀsjal, jo] **1** ADJ (*gén*) commercial; [*activité, société, port*] commercial, trading (*épith*); [*déficit, stratégie, guerre*] trade (*épith*); **accord** ~ trade *ou* trading agreement; **service** ~ [*entreprise*] sales department; **chaîne de télévision** ~**e** commercial television channel; **anglais** ~ business English; (*péj*) **sourire** ~ phoney professional smile **2** NM marketing man; **l'un de nos commerciaux** one of our marketing people **3** **commerciale** NF (= *véhicule*) estate car (*Brit*), station wagon (*US*)

commercialement [kɔmɛʀsjalmɑ̃] ADV commercially

commercialisable [kɔmɛʀsjalizabl] ADJ marketable, tradable

commercialisation [kɔmɛʀsjalizasjɔ̃] NF marketing

commercialiser [kɔmɛʀsjalize] ▸conjug 1◂ VT to market

commère [kɔmɛʀ] NF (*péj* = *bavarde*) gossip

commérer† [kɔmeʀe] ▸conjug 6◂ VI to gossip

commettant [kɔmetɑ̃] NM (*Jur, Fin*) principal

commettre [kɔmɛtʀ] ▸conjug 56◂ **1** VT **a** (= *perpétrer*) [+ *crime, injustice*] to commit; [+ *erreur*] to make; (*hum*) **il a commis 2 ou 3 romans** he's responsible for 2 or 3 novels (*hum*) → **faute** **b** (*littér* = *confier*) ~ **qch à qn** to commit sth to sb, entrust sth to sb **c** (*frm* = *nommer*) [+ *arbitre*] to appoint, nominate; ~ **qn à une charge** to appoint *ou* nominate sb to an office; **avocat commis d'office** lawyer *ou* barrister (*Brit*) appointed by the court **2** **se commettre** VPR (*péj, frm*) to endanger one's reputation, lower o.s.; **se** ~ **avec des gens peu recommandables** to associate with rather undesirable people

comminatoire [kɔminatwaʀ] ADJ [*ton, lettre*] threatening; (*Jur*) appointing a penalty for non-compliance

commis [kɔmi] NM (= *vendeur*) (shop *ou* store (*US*)) assistant; (= *employé de bureau*) office clerk; ~ **aux écritures** book-keeper; ~-**greffier** assistant to the clerk of the court; ~ **de cuisine/de salle** apprentice chef/waiter; (*Naut*) ~ **aux vivres** ship's steward; ~ **voyageur** commercial traveller, travelling salesman; **un grand** ~ **(de l'État)** a top-ranking *ou* senior civil servant

commisération [kɔmizeʀasjɔ̃] NF commiseration

commissaire [kɔmisɛʀ] **1** NM **a** ~ **(de police)** ≈ (police) superintendent (*Brit*), (police) captain (*US*); ~ **principal** ◊ **divisionnaire** ≈ chief superintendent (*Brit*), police chief (*US*); ~ **de police judiciaire** detective superintendent (*Brit*), (police) captain (*US*) **b** (= *responsable*) [*rencontre sportive, fête*] steward; [*exposition*] organizer; (*Aut*) ~ **de courses** marshal **c** (= *envoyé*) representative **d** [*commission*] commission member, commissioner **2** COMP ▸ **commissaire de l'Air** chief administrator (*in Air Force*) ▸ **commissaire du bord** purser ▸ **commissaire aux comptes** auditor ▸ **commissaire européen** European Commissioner ▸ **commissaire du gouvernement** government commissioner ▸ **Commissaire aux langues officielles** (*Can*) Commissioner of Official Languages

(*Can*) ▸ **commissaire de la Marine** chief administrator (*in the Navy*) ▸ **commissaire au Plan** planning commissioner ▸ **commissaire de la République** ≈ prefect

commissaire-priseur (*pl* **commissaires-priseurs**) [kɔmisɛʀpʀizœʀ] NM auctioneer

commissariat [kɔmisaʀja] NM **a** (= *poste*) ~ **(de police)** police station **b** (*Admin* = *fonction*) commissionership; ~ **du bord** pursership; ~ **aux comptes** auditorship **c** (= *commission*) commission; **Commissariat à l'énergie atomique** Atomic Energy Commission; **Commissariat général du Plan** State Planning Commission **d** (= *corps*) ▸ **de la Marine** ≈ Admiralty Board (*Brit*), ≈ Naval Command (*US*) **e** (= *service*) ~ **hôtelier** catering service (*for rail companies and airlines*)

commission [kɔmisjɔ̃] NF **1** **a** (= *comité restreint*) committee; (= *bureau nommé*) commission; (*Pol*) **la** ~ **du budget** the Budget committee; **les membres sont en** ~ the members are in committee; **travail en** ~ work in committee; (*Pol*) **renvoi d'un texte en** ~ committal of a bill
b (= *message*) message; **est-ce qu'on vous a fait la** ~? did you get *ou* were you given the message?
c (= *course*) errand; **faire des** ~**s** to run errands (**pour** for); **on l'a chargé d'une** ~ he was sent on an errand
d (= *emplettes*) ~**s** shopping; **faire les/des** ~**s** to do the/some shopping; **partir en** ~**s** to go shopping; **l'argent des** ~**s** the shopping money
e (*langage enfantin*) **faire la petite/grosse** ~ to do number one/two (*langage enfantin*)
f (= *pourcentage*) commission; **toucher 10 % de** ~ *ou* **une** ~ **de 10 %** to get 10% commission (**sur** on); **travailler à la** ~ to work on commission
g (*Comm, Jur* = *mandat*) commission; **avoir la** ~ **de faire** to be empowered *ou* commissioned to do; ~ **d'office** court appointment of a barrister (*Brit*) *ou* counselor (*US*)
2 COMP ▸ **commission d'arbitrage** arbitration committee ▸ **commission d'armistice** armistice council ▸ **Commission de développement économique régional** French commission for regional economic development ▸ **commission d'enquête** committee *ou* commission of inquiry ▸ **Commission européenne** European Commission ▸ **commission d'examen** board of examiners ▸ **la commission des finances** finance committee ▸ **commission interparlementaire** ≈ joint (parliamentary) committee ▸ **la commission des lois** the law commission ▸ **commission militaire** army exemption tribunal ▸ **Commission nationale de l'informatique et des libertés** French data protection watchdog ▸ **Commission des opérations de Bourse** French stock exchange regulatory body, ≈ Securities and Investment Board (*Brit*), ≈ Securities and Exchange Commission (*US*) ▸ **commission paritaire** joint commission (with equal representation of both sides) ▸ **commission parlementaire** parliamentary commission *ou* committee ▸ **commission permanente** standing committee, permanent commission ▸ **commission rogatoire** letters rogatory ▸ **commission temporaire** ad hoc committee

commissionnaire [kɔmisjɔnɛʀ] NM **a** (= *livreur*) delivery boy; (*adulte*) delivery man; (= *messager*) messenger boy; (*adulte*) messenger; (= *chasseur*) page (boy); (*adulte*) commissionaire **b** (= *intermédiaire*) agent, broker; ~ **en douane** customs agent *ou* broker; ~ **de transport** forwarding agent; ~ **de roulage** carrier, haulage contractor (*Brit*), haulier (*Brit*)

commissionner [kɔmisjɔne] ▸conjug 1◂ VT (*Comm, Jur* = *mandater*) to commission

commissure [kɔmisyʀ] NF [bouche] corner; (Anat, Bot) commissure

commode [kɔmɔd] 1 ADJ a (= pratique) [appartement, meuble] convenient; [outil] handy (pour for, pour faire for doing); [itinéraire] handy, convenient; **ce pinceau n'est pas très ~ pour les coins** this brush isn't very practical for doing corners b (= facile) easy; **ce n'est pas ~** it's not easy (à faire to do); **ce serait trop ~!** that would be too easy! c († = souple) [morale, caractère] easy-going; **~ à vivre** easy to get along with ou get on (Brit) with; **il n'est pas ~** (= sévère) he's so strict; (= difficile) he's really awkward ou difficult 2 NF (= meuble) chest of drawers

commodément [kɔmɔdemã] ADV [porter] conveniently; [s'asseoir] comfortably

commodité [kɔmɔdite] NF a (= confort) convenience; **pour plus de ~** for greater convenience; **les ~s de la vie moderne** the conveniences ou comforts of modern life b (†† = toilettes) **~s** toilet

commotion [kɔmosjɔ̃] NF (= secousse) shock; **~ cérébrale** concussion; **les grandes ~s sociales** the great social upheavals

commotionner [kɔmosjɔne] ▶conjug 1◀ VT [secousse, nouvelle] **~ qn** to give sb a shock, shake sb; **être fortement commotionné par qch** to be badly ou severely shocked ou shaken by sth

commuable [kɔmɥabl] ADJ [peine] commutable

commuer [kɔmɥe] ▶conjug 1◀ VT [+ peine] to commute (**en** to)

▼**commun, e**[1] [kɔmœ̃, yn] 1 ADJ a (= collectif, de tous) common; (= fait ensemble) [décision, effort, réunion] joint (épith); **pour le bien ~** for the common good; **dans l'intérêt ~** in the common interest; **ils ont une langue ~e qui est l'anglais** they have English as a common language; **d'un ~ accord** of a common accord, of one accord → **sens** b (= partagé) [élément] common; [pièce, cuisine] communal, shared; [dénominateur, facteur, angle] common (à to); **ces deux maisons ont un jardin ~** the two houses share the same garden; **le jardin est ~ aux deux maisons** the garden is shared by the two houses; **les parties ~es de l'immeuble** the communal parts of the building; **tout est ~ entre eux** they share everything; **un ami ~** a mutual friend; **la vie ~e** [couple] conjugal life, life together; [communauté] communal life → **point**[1] c (= comparable) [goût, intérêt, caractère] common (épith); **ils n'ont rien de ~** they have nothing in common; **ce métal n'a rien de ~ avec l'argent** this metal has nothing in common with ou is nothing like silver; **il n'y a pas de ~e mesure entre eux** there's no possible comparison between them → **nom** d **en ~** in common; **faire la cuisine/les achats en ~** to share (in) the cooking/the shopping; **vivre en ~** to live communally; **faire une démarche en ~** to take joint steps; **mettre ses ressources en ~** to share ou pool one's resources; **tout mettre en ~** to share everything; **ces plantes ont en ~ de pousser sur les hauteurs** these plants have in common the fact that they grow at high altitudes e (= ordinaire) [accident, erreur] common; [opinion] commonly held, widespread; [métal] common; **peu ~** out of the ordinary, uncommon; **d'une force peu ~e** unusually ou uncommonly strong; **il est ~ de voir ...** it is quite common ou quite a common thing to see ... → **lieu** f (péj = vulgaire) [manières, voix, personne] common 2 NM a (= le peuple) **le ~ des mortels** ordinary mortals, the common run of people; (†, péj) **le ~ ◊ les gens du ~** the common people ou herd; **hors du ~** [personne, destin] extraordinary

b (= bâtiments) **les ~s** the outbuildings, the outhouses

communal, e (mpl -aux) [kɔmynal, o] ADJ [dépenses] council (épith) (Brit), community (épith) (US); [fête, aménagements] local (épith); **l'école ~e ◊ la ~e*** (= bâtiment) the local (primary) school, the local grade ou elementary school (US); (= éducation) state education; **les (terrains) communaux** common land

communard, e [kɔmynaʀ, aʀd] 1 ADJ (Hist) of the Commune 2 NM,F (Hist) communard; (péj = communiste) red (péj), commie* (péj)

communautaire [kɔmynotɛʀ] ADJ community (épith); (Pol) [droit, politique] Community (épith)

communautariste [kɔmynotaʀist] ADJ [modèle, politique] that takes account of minorities

communauté [kɔmynote] NF a (= similitude) [intérêts, culture] community; **~ d'idées/de sentiments** shared ideas/feelings; **~ de langue** common ou shared language b (= groupe: gén), (Rel) community; **la ~ internationale/scientifique** the international/scientific community; **~ urbaine** urban community; **~ linguistique** speech community; **vivre en ~** to live in a commune; **mettre qch en ~** to pool sth c (Jur: entre époux) **biens qui appartiennent à la ~** joint estate (of husband and wife); **mariés sous le régime de la ~** married with a communal estate; **~ légale** communal estate; **~ réduite aux acquêts** communal estate comprising only property acquired after marriage d (Pol) **la Communauté économique européenne** the European Economic Community; **la Communauté européenne de l'énergie atomique** the European Atomic Energy Community; **les pays de la Communauté** the members of the Community; **la Communauté des États indépendants** the Commonwealth of Independent States; (Hist) **la Communauté européenne du charbon et de l'acier** the European Coal and Steel Community

commune[2] [kɔmyn] NF a (= ville) town; (= village) village; (= administration) town (ou village) council, municipality (Admin); (territoire) **sur toute l'étendue de la ~** throughout the entire district b (Hist) **la Commune** the Commune c (Pol) **la Chambre des ~s ◊ les Communes** the (House of) Commons

---
┌─ **COMMUNE** ─┐

The **commune** is the smallest administrative subdivision in France. There are 38,000 communes in all, 90% of them having less than 2,000 inhabitants. Several small villages may make up a single **commune**. Each **commune** is administered by a "maire", who is elected by the "conseil municipal". The inhabitants of the **commune** vote for the "conseil municipal" in the "élections municipales". → ARRONDISSEMENT ; CANTON ; DÉPARTEMENT ; ÉLECTIONS ; MAIRE
---

communément [kɔmynemã] ADV commonly

communiant, e [kɔmynjã, jãt] NM,F (Rel) communicant; (premier) **~** young boy making his first communion; **me voici en première ~e** this is me in my communion dress

communicable [kɔmynikabl] ADJ [expérience, sentiment] which can be communicated; [droit] transferable; [dossier] which may be made available; **ces renseignements ne sont pas ~s par téléphone** this information cannot be given over the telephone

communicant, e [kɔmynikã, ãt] 1 ADJ a [pièces] communicating (épith) → **vase**[1] b [entreprise] that communicates effectively 2 NM,F (= communicateur) communicator (dans un colloque) speaker (person giving a paper)

communicateur, -trice [kɔmynikatœʀ, tʀis] 1 ADJ (Tech) [fil, pièce] connecting (épith) 2 NM,F communicator

communicatif, -ive [kɔmynikatif, iv] ADJ [rire, ennui] infectious; [personne] communicative

▼**communication** [kɔmynikasjɔ̃] NF a (gén, Philo = relation) communication; **il a des problèmes de ~** he has trouble ou problems communicating; **être en ~ avec** [+ ami, société savante] to be in communication ou contact with; [+ esprit] to communicate ou be in communication with; **entrer en ~ avec** [+ esprit, extraterrestre] to communicate with; [+ personne] to get in touch ou contact with; **mettre qn en ~ avec qn** to put sb in touch ou in contact with sb b (= transmission) [fait, nouvelle] communication; [dossier] transmission; **avoir ~ d'un fait** to be informed of a fact; **demander ~ d'un dossier** to ask for a file; **donner ~ d'une pièce** to communicate a document (à qn to sb); (en entreprise) **~ interne** internal communications c (= message) message, communication; (à une conférence) paper; **j'ai une ~ importante à vous faire** I have an important announcement to make; [conférencier] **faire une ~** to read ou give a paper d (Téléc) **~ (téléphonique)** (telephone ou phone) call; **être en ~** to be on the (tele)phone (avec qn to sb); **entrer en ~ avec qn** to get through to sb (on the phone); **mettre qn en ~** to put sb through (avec to), connect sb (avec with); **~ interurbaine** inter-city call, trunk call (Brit); **~ à longue distance** long-distance call; **~ en PCV** reverse charge call (Brit), collect call (US); **~ avec préavis** personal call (Brit), person-to-person call (US); **vous avez la ~** you're through, I'm connecting you now; **je n'ai pas pu avoir la ~** I couldn't get through e (= moyen de liaison) communication; **les grands axes de ~** the major communication routes; **porte de ~** communicating door; **moyens de ~** means of communication; **toutes les ~s ont été coupées** all communications ou all lines of communication were cut off → **voie** f (= relations publiques) **la ~** public relations; **conseil(ler) en ~** media ou communications consultant; **action ou opération de ~** public relations exercise; **agence/groupe de ~** communications firm/group; **campagne de ~** publicity campaign ou drive; **un homme de ~** a communicator

communier [kɔmynje] ▶conjug 7◀ VI (Rel) to receive communion; **~ sous les deux espèces** to receive communion under both kinds; **~ dans** [+ sentiment] to be united in; **~ avec** [+ sentiment] to share

communion [kɔmynjɔ̃] NF (Rel, fig) communion; **faire sa (première) ~ ou sa ~ privée** to make one's first communion; **~ solennelle†** solemn communion; **être en ~ avec** [+ personne] to be in communion with; [+ sentiments] to be in sympathy with; **être en ~ d'esprit avec qn** to be of the same intellectual outlook as sb; **la ~ des saints** the communion of the saints

communiqué [kɔmynike] NM communiqué; **~ de presse** press release

communiquer [kɔmynike] ▶conjug 1◀ 1 VT a [+ nouvelle, renseignement, demande] to pass on, communicate, convey (à to); [+ dossier, document] (= donner) to give (à to); (= envoyer) to send, transmit (à to); **~ un fait à qn** to inform sb of a fact; **se ~ des renseignements** to pass on information to one another b [+ enthousiasme, peur] to communicate, pass on (à to); (Méd) [+ maladie] to pass on, give (à qn to sb) c [+ mouvement] to communicate, transmit, impart (à to); [+ lumière, chaleur] to transmit (à to)

▶ GRAMMAIRE ACTIVE: **commun** 32.5   **communication** 27.3, 27.6, 27.7

[2] VI [a] (= *correspondre*) to communicate (**avec** with); **~ avec qn par lettre/téléphone** to communicate with sb by letter/phone; **il communique bien** he's a good *ou* an effective communicator [b] [*pièces, salles*] to communicate (**avec** with); **pièces qui communiquent** connecting rooms, rooms which communicate with one another; **couloir qui fait ~ les chambres** corridor that links *ou* connects the rooms

[3] **se communiquer** VPR [*feu, maladie*] **se ~ à** to spread to

communisant, e [kɔmynizɑ̃, ɑ̃t] [1] ADJ communistic [2] NM,F communist sympathizer

communisme [kɔmynism] NM communism

communiste [kɔmynist] ADJ, NMF communist

COMMUNISTE

The Communist Party has played a far more influential role in French politics than in most other democracies. Evidence of the French Communist Party's importance can be seen in the "banlieues rouges" (Paris suburbs with communist mayors), in the party's annual festival (la "fête de l'Humanité" which continues to draw huge crowds, and in its newspaper, "L'Humanité", which still has a wide circulation.

commutable [kɔmytabl] ADJ = **commuable**

commutateur [kɔmytatœʀ] NM (*Élec*) (changeover) switch, commutator; (*Téléc*) commutation switch; (= *bouton*) (light) switch

commutatif, -ive [kɔmytatif, iv] ADJ (*Jur, Ling, Math*) commutative

commutation [kɔmytasjɔ̃] NF (*Jur, Math*) commutation; (*Ling*) substitution, commutation; (*Élec*) commutation, switching; **~ de peine** commutation of sentence *ou* penalty; (*Ordin*) **~ des messages** message switching

commutativité [kɔmytativite] NF [*élément*] commutative property, commutability; [*addition*] commutative nature

commuter [kɔmyte] ▶ conjug 1 ◀ VT (*Math*) [+ *éléments*] to commute; (*Ling*) [+ *termes*] to substitute, commute

Comores [kɔmɔʀ] NFPL **les (îles) ~** the Comoro Islands, the Comoros

comorien, -ienne [kɔmɔʀjɛ̃, jɛn] [1] ADJ of *ou* from the Comoros [2] **Comorien(ne)** NM,F inhabitant *ou* native of the Comoros

compacité [kɔ̃pasite] NF [*foule*] density; [*véhicule, appareil*] compactness

compact, e [kɔ̃pakt] [1] ADJ (= *dense*) [*foule, substance*] dense; [*brouillard*] dense, thick; [*quartier*] closely *ou* densely built-up; (= *faible encombrement*) [*véhicule, appareil, meuble*] compact; [*poudre*] pressed; **disque → ◊ Compact Disc®** compact disc → **chaîne** [2] NM [a] (= *chaîne hi-fi*) compact music system; (= *disque*) compact disc, CD; **réédition en ~** CD re-release [b] [*poudre*] powder compact [c] (*Photo*) compact camera [3] **compacte** NF (*Aut*) compact car

compactage [kɔ̃paktaʒ] NM [*sol, ordures*] compaction; (*Ordin*) compressing

compacter [kɔ̃pakte] ▶ conjug 1 ◀ VT (*gén*) to compact; [+ *données*] to compress

compagne [kɔ̃paɲ] NF (= *camarade, concubine, littér* = *épouse*) companion; (= *maîtresse*) (lady) friend; [*animal*] mate; **~ de classe** classmate; **~ de jeu** playmate

compagnie [kɔ̃paɲi] [1] NF [a] (= *présence, société*) company; **il n'a pour toute ~ que sa vieille maman** he has only his old mother for company; **ce n'est pas une ~ pour lui** he (*ou* she) is no company for him; **en ~ de** [+ *personne*] in the company of, in company with; [+ *chose*] alongside, along with; **il n'est heureux qu'en ~ de ses livres** he's only happy when (he's) surrounded by his books; **en**

bonne/mauvaise/joyeuse ~ in good/bad/cheerful company; **tenir ~ à qn** to keep sb company; **être d'une ~ agréable** *ou* **de bonne ~** to be pleasant *ou* good company; **voyager de ~** to travel together; **aller de ~ avec** to go hand in hand with **→ fausser** [b] (= *réunion*) gathering, party; **bonsoir la ~!** goodnight all! [c] (*Comm*) company; (= *groupe de savants, écrivains*) body; **~ d'assurances/théâtrale** insurance/theatrical company; **~ aérienne/maritime** airline/shipping company; **la banque X et ~** the X and company bank, the bank of X and company; **tout ça, c'est voleurs et ~*** they're all a bunch* of thieves [d] (*Mil*) company

[2] COMP ▶ **compagnie de discipline** punishment company (*made up of convicted soldiers*) ▶ **la Compagnie des Indes** (*Hist*) the East India Company ▶ **la Compagnie de Jésus** the Society of Jesus ▶ **compagnie de perdreaux** covey of partridges ▶ **compagnies républicaines de sécurité** state security police force in France

compagnon [kɔ̃paɲɔ̃] [1] NM [a] (= *camarade, concubin, littér* = *époux*) companion; (= *écuyer*) companion; **~ d'études** fellow student; **~ de travail** workmate; **~ d'exil/de misère/d'infortune** companion in exile/in suffering/in misfortune [b] (= *ouvrier*) journeyman; **il a deux ~s** he has two employees *ou* two people working for him [c] (= *franc-maçon*) companion [2] COMP ▶ **compagnon d'armes** companion- *ou* comrade-in-arms ▶ **compagnon de bord** shipmate ▶ **compagnon de jeu** playmate ▶ **Compagnon de la Libération** French Resistance fighter ▶ **compagnon de route** (*lit, Pol*) fellow traveller ▶ **compagnon de table** companion at table, table companion ▶ **compagnon de voyage** travelling companion, fellow traveller (*lit*) ▶ **compagnon du Tour de France, compagnon du voyage** journeyman (*touring France after his apprenticeship*)

compagnonnage [kɔ̃paɲɔnaʒ] NM (*Hist*) ≈ (trade) guilds

▼ **comparable** [kɔ̃paʀabl] ADJ [*grandeur, élément*] comparable (**à** to, **avec** with); **je n'avais jamais rien vu de ~** I'd never seen anything like it; **ce n'est pas ~** there's (just) no comparison

▼ **comparaison** [kɔ̃paʀɛzɔ̃] NF [a] (*gén*) comparison (**à** to, **avec** with); **mettre qch en ~ avec** to compare sth with; **faire une ~ entre X et Y** to compare X and Y, make a comparison between X and Y; **vous n'avez qu'à faire la ~** you only need to compare them; **et c'est mieux ? — aucune ~!** is it better? — (there's) no comparison!; **ça ne soutient pas la ~** that doesn't bear *ou* stand comparison [b] (*Gram*) comparison; **adjectif/adverbe de ~** comparative adjective/adverb [c] (*Littérat*) simile, comparison [d] (*loc*) **en ~ (de)** in comparison (with); **par ~ à** by comparison (**avec, à** with); **il est sans ~ le meilleur** he is far and away the best; **c'est sans ~ avec ...** it cannot be compared with ... ▪ (*PROV*) **~ n'est pas raison** comparisons are odious

comparaître [kɔ̃paʀɛtʀ] ▶ conjug 57 ◀ VI (*Jur*) appear in court; **~ devant un juge** to appear before a judge → **citation, citer**

comparant, e [kɔ̃paʀɑ̃, ɑ̃t] NM,F (*Jur*) party (*appearing in court*)

comparatif, -ive [kɔ̃paʀatif, iv] [1] ADJ [*publicité*] comparative; **essai ~** comparison test [2] NM comparative; (*Gram*) **au ~** in the comparative; **~ d'infériorité/de supériorité/d'égalité** comparative of lesser/greater/similar degree

comparatisme [kɔ̃paʀatism] NM comparative studies, comparat(iv)ism

comparatiste [kɔ̃paʀatist] ADJ, NMF comparatist

comparativement [kɔ̃paʀativmɑ̃] ADV comparatively, by comparison; **~ à** in comparison to *ou* with, compared to *ou* with

▼ **comparé, e** [kɔ̃paʀe] (*ptp de* **comparer**) ADJ [*étude, littérature*] comparative

▼ **comparer** [kɔ̃paʀe] ▶ conjug 1 ◀ VT [a] (= *confronter*) to compare (**à, avec** with); **~ deux choses (entre elles)** to compare two things; **vous n'avez qu'à ~** you've only to compare; **comparé à** compared to *ou* with [b] (= *identifier*) to compare, liken (**à** to); **Molière peut se ~** *ou* **être comparé à Shakespeare** Molière can be compared *ou* likened to Shakespeare; **c'est un bon écrivain mais il ne peut quand même pas se ~ à X** he's a good writer but he still can't compare with X; **il ose se ~ à Picasso** he dares to compare himself with Picasso; **ça ne se compare pas** there's no comparison, they can't be compared

comparse [kɔ̃paʀs] NMF (*Théât*) supernumerary, walk-on; (*péj*) associate, stooge*; **rôle de ~** (*Théât*) walk-on part; (*péj*) minor part; **nous n'avons là que les ~s, il nous faut le vrai chef** these are only the small fry, we want the real leader

compartiment [kɔ̃paʀtimɑ̃] NM (*gén, Rail*) compartment; [*damier*] square; (*Bourse*) section; **~ à glace** freezer compartment; **dans tous les ~s du jeu** in every area of the game

compartimentage [kɔ̃paʀtimɑ̃taʒ] NM, **compartimentation** [kɔ̃paʀtimɑ̃tasjɔ̃] NF [*armoire*] partitioning, compartmentation; [*administration, problème*] compartmentalization

compartimenter [kɔ̃paʀtimɑ̃te] ▶ conjug 1 ◀ VT [+ *armoire*] to partition, divide into compartments, put compartments in; [+ *problème, administration*] to compartmentalize

comparution [kɔ̃paʀysjɔ̃] NF (*Jur*) appearance in court

compas [kɔ̃pa] [1] NM (*Géom*) (pair of) compasses; (*Naut*) compass; **tracer qch au ~** to draw sth with (a pair of) compasses; **avoir le ~ dans l'œil** to have an accurate eye → **naviguer** [2] COMP ▶ **compas à balustre** bow compass ▶ **compas d'épaisseur** callipers (*Brit*), calipers (*US*) ▶ **compas à pointes sèches** dividers ▶ **compas quart de cercle** wing compass ▶ **compas de réduction** proportional dividers

compassé, e [kɔ̃pase] ADJ (= *guindé*) formal, stuffy, starchy

compassion [kɔ̃pasjɔ̃] NF compassion; **avec ~** compassionately

compatibilité [kɔ̃patibilite] NF (*gén, Méd, Ordin*) compatibility (**entre** between); (*Ordin*) **~ ascendante/descendante** upward/downward compatibility

compatible [kɔ̃patibl] [1] ADJ (*gén, Méd, Ordin*) compatible (**avec** with); **difficilement/parfaitement ~s** hardly/perfectly *ou* fully compatible [2] NM (*Ordin*) compatible (computer)

compatir [kɔ̃patiʀ] ▶ conjug 2 ◀ VI to sympathize; **~ à la douleur de qn** to share sb's grief

compatissant, e [kɔ̃patisɑ̃, ɑ̃t] ADJ compassionate, sympathetic

compatriote [kɔ̃patʀijɔt] [1] NM compatriot, fellow countryman [2] NF compatriot, fellow countrywoman

compensable [kɔ̃pɑ̃sabl] ADJ [a] [*perte*] that can be compensated for (**par** by) [b] [*chèque*] **~ à Paris** to be cleared in Paris

compensateur, -trice [kɔ̃pɑ̃satœʀ, tʀis] [1] ADJ [*indemnité, élément, mouvement*] compensatory, compensating (*épith*); **repos ~** time off in lieu [2] NM compensator; **(pendule) ~** compensation pendulum

compensation [kɔ̃pɑ̃sasjɔ̃] NF [a] (= *dédommagement*) compensation; **donner qch en ~ d'autre chose** to give sth in compensation for sth else, make up for sth with sth else; **en**

~ (des dégâts) ◊ à titre de ~ (pour les dégâts) in compensation *ou* by way of compensation (for the damage); **c'est une pietre ~ de le savoir** it's not much of (a) compensation to know that; **il y en a peu mais en ~ c'est bon** there's not much of it but on the other hand *ou* to make up for that it's good [b] (= équilibre) balance; (= neutralisation) balancing; (Phys) [forces] compensation; [maladie, infirmité] compensation; (Naut) [compas] correction; (Psych) compensation; [dette] set-off (Brit), offsetting; [chèques] clearing; (Math) **loi de ~** law of large numbers; (Jur) **~ des dépens** division *ou* sharing of the costs → **chambre**

compensatoire [kɔ̃pɑ̃satwaʀ] ADJ compensatory, compensating; (Fin) **droits ~s** countervailing duties → **montant**

compensé, e [kɔ̃pɑ̃se] (ptp de **compenser**) ADJ [gouvernail] balanced; [horloge] compensated; **chaussures à semelles ~es** platform shoes, shoes with platform soles

compenser [kɔ̃pɑ̃se] ▶conjug 1◀ VT [+ perte, dégâts] to compensate for, make up for; [+ infirmité] to compensate (for); (Naut) [+ compas] to correct; [+ dette] to set off, offset; **~ une peine par une joie** to make up for a painful experience with a happy one; **ses qualités et ses défauts se compensent** his qualities compensate for *ou* make up for his faults; **les gains et les pertes se compensent** the gains and losses cancel each other out; **pour ~** to compensate, to make up for it, as a compensation; (Jur) **~ les dépens** to divide *ou* share the costs, tax each party for its own costs; (Phys) **forces qui se compensent** compensating forces → **ceci**

compère [kɔ̃pɛʀ] NM [a] (gén = complice) accomplice; (aux enchères) puffer [b]† (= ami) crony*, comrade; (= personne, type) fellow

compère-loriot (pl **compères-loriots**) [kɔ̃pɛʀlɔʀjo] NM (Méd = orgelet) sty(e); (Orn) golden oriole

compète* [kɔ̃pɛt] NF = **compétition**

compétence [kɔ̃petɑ̃s] NF [a] (= expérience) competence (en matière de in); **faire qch avec ~** to do sth competently; **avoir des ~s** to be competent; **faire appel à la ~ ou aux ~s d'un spécialiste** to call (up)on the skills of a specialist; **savoir utiliser les ~s** to know how to put people's skills *ou* abilities to the best use [b] (= personne) specialist, expert [c] (= rayon d'activité) scope of activities, domain; (Jur) competence; (Jur) **~ territoriale** jurisdiction; **c'est de la ~ de ce tribunal** it's within the competence of this court; **ce n'est pas de ma ~ ◊ cela n'entre pas dans mes ~s** that's not (in) my sphere *ou* domain

compétent, e [kɔ̃petɑ̃, ɑ̃t] ADJ [a] (= capable) competent, capable; **~ en** competent in; **très ~ en législation du travail** very well-versed in *ou* conversant with labour legislation; **je ne suis pas ~ pour vous répondre** I'm not qualified to answer [b] (= concerné) [service] relevant, concerned (attrib); (Jur) competent; **adressez-vous à l'autorité ~e** apply to the authority concerned; [tribunal] **être ~ pour faire qch** to have the jurisdiction to do sth

compétiteur, -trice [kɔ̃petitœʀ, tʀis] NM,F competitor

compétitif, -ive [kɔ̃petitif, iv] ADJ competitive

compétition [kɔ̃petisjɔ̃] NF [a] (Sport = activité) **la ~** competitive sport; **faire de la ~** to go in for competitive sport; **la ~ automobile** motor racing; **abandonner la ~** to retire from competitive sport, stop going in for competitions; **sport de ~** competitive sport [b] (Sport = épreuve) event; **~ sportive** sporting event; **une ~ automobile** a motor-racing event; **film présenté hors ~** film presented out of competition [c] (gén, Scol, Sport = rivalité) competition (NonC); (Comm, Pol) rivalry, competition (NonC); **entrer en ~ avec** to compete with;

être en ~ to be competing, be in competition (avec with)

compétitivité [kɔ̃petitivite] NF competitiveness

compilateur, -trice [kɔ̃pilatœʀ, tʀis] [1] NM,F (souvent péj) compiler [2] NM (Ordin) compiler; **~ croisé** cross compiler

compilation [kɔ̃pilasjɔ̃] NF [a] (= action) compiling, compilation; [textes, chansons] compilation; (péj = plagiat) plagiarism; **une ~ des meilleures chansons de Brel** the best of Brel [b] (Ordin) [programme] compilation

compiler [kɔ̃pile] ▶conjug 1◀ VT [a] [+ documents, chansons, ouvrage] to compile [b] (Ordin) [+ programme] to compile

complainte [kɔ̃plɛ̃t] NF (Littérat, Mus) lament

complaire [kɔ̃plɛʀ] ▶conjug 54◀ [1] **complaire à** VT INDIR to (try to) please [2] **se complaire** VPR **se ~ dans qch/à faire qch** to take pleasure in sth/in doing sth, delight *ou* revel in sth/in doing sth

complaisamment [kɔ̃plɛzamɑ̃] ADV (avec obligeance) obligingly, kindly; (avec indulgence) indulgently; (avec fatuité) complacently, smugly

complaisance [kɔ̃plɛzɑ̃s] NF [a] (= obligeance) kindness (**envers** to, towards); (= esprit accommodant) accommodating attitude; (frm) **il a eu la ~ de m'accompagner** he was kind *ou* good enough to *ou* he was so kind as to accompany me; **par ~** out of kindness [b] (= indulgence coupable) indulgence, leniency; (= connivence malhonnête) connivance; (= servilité) servility, subservience; [conjoint trompé] tacit consent; **avoir des ~s pour qn** to treat sb indulgently; **sourire de ~** polite smile; **certificat ou attestation de ~** medical *ou* doctor's certificate (issued for non-genuine illness to oblige a patient); (Comm) **billet de ~** accommodation bill → **pavillon** [c] (= fatuité) self-satisfaction, complacency; **il parlait avec ~ de ses succès** he spoke smugly about his successes

complaisant, e [kɔ̃plɛzɑ̃, ɑ̃t] ADJ [a] (= obligeant) kind, obliging; (= arrangeant) accommodating [b] (= trop indulgent) indulgent, lenient; (= trop arrangeant) over-obliging; (= servile) servile, subservient; **c'est un mari ~** he turns a blind eye to his wife's goings-on; **prêter une oreille ~e à qn/qch** to listen to sb/sth readily, lend a willing ear to sb/sth [c] (= fat) self-satisfied, smug, complacent

complément [kɔ̃plemɑ̃] NM [a] (gén, Bio, Math, Ordin) complement; (= reste) rest, remainder; **~ d'information** further *ou* additional information (NonC) [b] (Gram) (gén) complement; (= complément d'objet) object; **~ circonstanciel de lieu/de temps** adverbial phrase of place/time; **~ (d'objet) direct/indirect** direct/indirect object; **~ d'agent** agent; **~ de nom** possessive phrase

complémentaire [kɔ̃plemɑ̃tɛʀ] [1] ADJ (gén, Math) complementary; (= additionnel) supplementary; **couleurs ~s** complementary colours; **pour tout renseignement ~** for any further *ou* additional information → **cours** [2] NM (Math) complement

complémentarité [kɔ̃plemɑ̃taʀite] NF complementarity, complementary nature

complet, -ète [kɔ̃plɛ, ɛt] [1] ADJ [a] (= exhaustif, entier: gén) complete, full; [rapport, analyse] comprehensive, full; **procéder à un examen ~ de qch** to make a full *ou* thorough examination of sth; **il reste encore trois tours/jours ~s** there are still three complete *ou* full laps/three full *ou* whole days to go; **pour vous donner une idée complète de la situation** to give you a complete idea of the situation; **les œuvres complètes de Voltaire** the complete works of Voltaire; **le dossier est-il ~?** is the file complete?; **une collection très complète** a very comprehensive *ou* full collection; **la lecture complète de ce livre prend**

deux heures it takes two hours to read this book right through *ou* from cover to cover → **aliment, pension, riz** [b] (= total) [échec, obscurité] complete, total, utter; [découragement] complete, total; **dans la misère la plus complète** in the most abject poverty; **l'aviron est un sport très ~** rowing exercises your whole body [c] (= consommé: après nom) [homme, acteur] complete; **c'est un athlète ~** he's an all-round athlete [d] (= plein) [autobus, train] full, full up (attrib); (écriteau) **« ~ »** [hôtel] "no vacancies"; [parking] "full"; [cinéma] "sold out"; [match] "ground full"; **le théâtre affiche ~ tous les soirs** the theatre has a full house every evening [e] * **c'est ~!** that's the end! *ou* the limit!, that's all we needed! [2] NM (= costume) **~(-veston)** suit [3] **au (grand) complet** LOC ADV **maintenant que nous sommes au ~** now that we are all here; **le groupe/bureau au grand ~** the whole *ou* entire group/office

complètement [kɔ̃plɛtmɑ̃] ADV [a] (= en entier) [démonter, nettoyer, repeindre] completely; [lire] right through, from cover to cover; [citer] in full; **~ nu** completely *ou* stark naked; **~ trempé/terminé** completely soaked/finished; **~ équipé** fully equipped; **écouter ~ un CD** to listen to a CD right through, listen to the whole of a CD [b] (= absolument) [+ fou] completely, absolutely; [+ faux] completely, absolutely, utterly; [+ découragé] completely, totally [c] (= à fond) [étudier, faire une enquête] fully, thoroughly

compléter [kɔ̃plete] ▶conjug 6◀ [1] VT [a] (= terminer, porter au total voulu) [+ somme, effectifs] to make up; [+ mobilier, collection, dossier] to complete; **pour ~ votre travail/l'ensemble ...** to complete your work/the whole ...; **il compléta ses études en suivant un cours de dactylographie** he completed *ou* rounded off *ou* finished off his studies by taking a course in typing; **et pour ~ le tableau, il arriva en retard!** and to crown *ou* top it all, he arrived late! [b] (= augmenter) [+ études, formation] to complement, supplement; [+ connaissances, documentation, collection] to supplement, add to; [+ mobilier, garde-robe] to add to; **sa collection se complète lentement** his collection is slowly building up [2] **se compléter** VPR [caractères, partenaires, fonctions] to complement one another

complétif, -ive [kɔ̃pletif, iv] [1] ADJ substantival [2] **complétive** NF (proposition) complétive noun *ou* substantival clause

complétude [kɔ̃pletyd] NF completeness

complexe [kɔ̃plɛks] [1] ADJ [intrigue, mécanisme] intricate, complex; [calcul, situation] complex, complicated; [nombre, quantité, phrase] complex; **sujet ~** compound subject [2] NM [a] (Psych) complex; **~ d'Œdipe/d'infériorité/de supériorité** Oedipus/inferiority/superiority complex; **faire des ~s ◊ être bourré de ~s*** to have loads of hang-ups*, be full of complexes; (hum) **il est vraiment sans ~** he's got a nerve*; **c'est une équipe de France sans ~ qui va jouer ce soir** the French team are in a very relaxed frame of mind for tonight's match [b] (Écon: industriel, universitaire, touristique) complex; **~ routier** road network; **~ hôtelier/sportif** hotel/sports complex [c] (Chim, Math) complex

complexer [kɔ̃plɛkse] ▶conjug 1◀ VT **ça le complexe terriblement** it gives him a terrible complex; **être très complexé** to be very hung-up* *ou* mixed up* (**par** about)

complexification [kɔ̃plɛksifikasjɔ̃] NF increasing complexity; **cela entraîne une ~ des rapports sociaux** this makes social relationships more and more complex *ou* increasingly complex

complexifier [kɔ̃plɛksifje] ▶conjug 7◀ **1** VT to make more complex, complicate **2** **se complexifier** VPR to become more complex *ou* complicated

complexion †† [kɔ̃plɛksjɔ̃] NF (= *constitution*) constitution; (= *teint*) complexion; (= *humeur*) disposition, temperament

complexité [kɔ̃plɛksite] NF [*intrigue, mécanisme*] intricacy, complexity; [*calcul, situation*] complexity

complication [kɔ̃plikasjɔ̃] NF (= *complexité*) complexity; (= *ennui*) complication; (*Méd*) **~s** complications; **faire des ~s** to make life difficult *ou* complicated

complice [kɔ̃plis] **1** ADJ **a** **être ~ de qch** to be (a) party to sth **b** [*regard, sourire*] knowing (*épith*), of complicity (*attrib*); [*attitude*] conniving; (*littér*) **la nuit ~ protégeait leur fuite** the friendly night conspired to shelter their flight (*littér*); [*amis*] **on est très ~s** we're very close, we understand each other completely **2** NMF **a** (= *criminel*) accomplice; **être (le) ~ de qn** to be sb's accomplice, be in collusion with sb; **être ~ d'un meurtre** to be an accessory *ou* an accomplice to murder; **~ par instigation/par assistance** accessory before/after the fact **b** (*dans un adultère*) (*Jur*) co-respondent; (= *amant*) lover; (= *maîtresse*) mistress **c** (= *compère*) [*farce, projet*] partner; (*hum*) **mon vieux ~** my old partner-in-crime (*hum*)

complicité [kɔ̃plisite] NF (*Jur, fig*) complicity; **agir en ~ avec** to act in complicity *ou* collusion with; **accusé de ~ de vol** accused of aiding and abetting a theft *ou* of being an accessory to theft; (= *bonne entente*) **la ~ qui existe entre eux** the rapport they have

complies [kɔ̃pli] NFPL compline

compliment [kɔ̃plimɑ̃] NM **a** (= *félicitations*) **~s** congratulations; **recevoir les ~s de qn** to receive sb's congratulations, be congratulated by sb; **faire des ~s à qn** to congratulate sb (**pour** on); (*lit ou iro*) (**je vous fais**) **mes ~s !** congratulations!, well done! **b** (= *louange*) compliment; **elle rougit sous le ~** she blushed at the compliment; **faire un ~ à qn** to pay sb a compliment; **faire des ~s à qn sur sa bonne mine** ◊ **faire ~ à qn de sa bonne mine** to compliment sb on how well they look; **il lui fait sans cesse des ~s** he's always paying her compliments; **avec les ~s de la direction** with the compliments of the management; **faites-lui mes ~s** give him my regards **d** (= *petit discours*) congratulatory speech

complimenter [kɔ̃plimɑ̃te] ▶conjug 1◀ VT (= *féliciter*) to congratulate (**pour, sur, de** on); (= *louanger*) to compliment (**pour, sur, de** on)

compliqué, e [kɔ̃plike] (*ptp de* **compliquer**) ADJ [*mécanisme*] complicated, intricate; [*affaire, explication, phrase*] complicated, involved; [*histoire, esprit*] tortuous; [*personne*] complicated; [*fracture*] compound (*épith*); **ne sois pas si ~ !** don't make life so difficult!; **puisque tu refuses, ce n'est pas ~, moi je pars** since you refuse, that makes it easy *ou* that simplifies things— I'm leaving; **il ne m'écoute jamais, c'est pas ~ !*** it's quite simple, he never listens to a word I say!; **cette histoire est d'un ~ !** what a complicated story!

compliquer [kɔ̃plike] ▶conjug 1◀ **1** VT to complicate; **il nous complique l'existence** *ou* **la vie** he makes life difficult *ou* complicated for us; **~ les choses** to complicate matters **2** **se compliquer** VPR **a** [*situation, problème*] to become *ou* get complicated; **ça se complique** things are getting more and more complicated **b** [*personne*] **se ~ l'existence** to make life difficult *ou* complicated for o.s.

complot [kɔ̃plo] NM plot; **~ contre la sûreté de l'État** plot to destabilize national security; **mettre qn dans le ~*** to let sb in on the plot

comploter [kɔ̃plɔte] ▶conjug 1◀ VTI to plot (**de** **faire** to do, **contre** against); **qu'est-ce que vous complotez ?*** what are you up to?

comploteur, -euse [kɔ̃plɔtœʀ, øz] NM,F plotter

componction [kɔ̃pɔ̃ksjɔ̃] NF (*péj*) (affected) gravity; (*Rel*) contrition; **avec ~** solemnly, with a great show of dignity

comportement [kɔ̃pɔʀtəmɑ̃] NM (*gén*) behaviour (*Brit*), behavior (*US*) (**envers, avec** towards); [*matériel, pneus, monnaie*] performance; **~ d'achat** buying patterns

comportemental, e (*mpl* **-aux**) [kɔ̃pɔʀtəmɑ̃tal, o] ADJ behavioural (*Brit*), behavioral (*US*)

comportementalisme [kɔ̃pɔʀtəmɑ̃talism] NM behaviourism (*Brit*), behaviorism (*US*)

comportementaliste [kɔ̃pɔʀtəmɑ̃talist] ADJ, NMF behaviourist (*Brit*), behaviorist (*US*)

comporter [kɔ̃pɔʀte] ▶conjug 1◀ **1** VT **a** (= *consister en*) to be composed of, be made up of, consist of, comprise; **ce roman comporte deux parties** this novel is made up of *ou* is composed of *ou* comprises two parts; **la maison comporte 5 pièces et une cuisine** the house comprises 5 rooms and a kitchen **b** (= *être muni de*) to have, include; **son livre comporte une préface** his book has *ou* includes a preface; **cette machine ne comporte aucun dispositif de sécurité** this machine has no safety mechanism; **cette règle comporte des exceptions** there are certain exceptions to this rule **c** (= *impliquer*) [+ *risques*] to entail, involve; **je dois accepter avec tout ce que cela comporte (de désavantages)** I must accept with all (the disadvantages) that it entails *ou* involves **2** **se comporter** VPR **a** (= *se conduire*) to behave; **se ~ en** *ou* **comme un enfant gâté** to behave like a spoilt child; **il s'est comporté d'une façon odieuse** he behaved horribly (**avec** towards) **b** (= *réagir*) [*personne*] to behave; [*machine, voiture*] to perform; **comment s'est-il comporté après l'accident ?** how did he behave after the accident?; **notre équipe s'est très bien comportée** our team played *ou* acquitted itself very well, our team put up a good performance; **comment le matériel s'est-il comporté en altitude ?** how did the equipment perform at high altitude?; **ces pneus se comportent très bien sur chaussée glissante** these tyres perform very well on slippery roads; (*Bourse*) **le franc se comporte bien aujourd'hui** the franc is performing *ou* doing well today

composant, e [kɔ̃pozɑ̃, ɑ̃t] **1** ADJ, NM component, constituent; **~s électroniques** electronic components **2** **composante** NF (*gén, Phys*) component; (*Pol*) **les diverses ~es du parti** the various elements in the party

composé, e [kɔ̃poze] (*ptp de* **composer**) **1** ADJ **a** (*Chim, Gram, Math, Mus*) compound (*épith*); (*Bot*) [*fleur*] composite (*épith*); [*feuille*] compound (*épith*); [*bouquet, salade*] mixed → **passé b** (*guindé*) [*maintien, attitude*] studied **2** NM (*Chim, Gram*) compound; (*fig*) combination, mixture **3** **composée** NF (*Bot*) composite; **~es** composites, Compositae (*SPÉC*)

composer [kɔ̃poze] ▶conjug 1◀ **1** VT **a** (= *confectionner*) [+ *plat, médicament*] to make (up); [+ *équipe sportive*] to select, put together; [+ *assemblée, équipe scientifique*] to form, set up **b** (= *élaborer*) [+ *poème, lettre*] to write, compose; [+ *musique*] to compose; [+ *tableau*] to paint; [+ *programme*] to work out, draw up **c** [+ *numéro de téléphone*] to dial; [+ *code*] to enter **d** (= *disposer*) [+ *bouquet*] to arrange, make up; [+ *vitrine*] to arrange, lay out **e** (= *constituer*) [+ *ensemble, produit, groupe*] to make up; [+ *assemblée*] to form, make up; **pièces qui composent une machine** parts which

(go to) make up a machine; **composé à 50% de papier recyclé** made of 50% recycled paper; **ces objets composent un ensemble harmonieux** these objects form *ou* make a harmonious group **f** (*Typo*) to set **g** (*frm* = *étudier artificiellement*) **~ son visage** to compose one's features; **~ ses gestes** to use affected gestures; **il s'était composé un personnage de dandy** he had established his image as that of a dandy; **se ~ un visage de circonstance** to assume a suitable expression **2** VI **a** (*Scol*) to do a test; **~ en anglais** to take *ou* sit (*surtout Brit*) an English test **b** (= *traiter*) to compromise; **~ avec** [+ *adversaire*] to come to terms with, compromise with **3** **se composer** VPR (= *consister en*) **se ~ de** ◊ **être composé de** to be composed of, be made up of, consist of, comprise; **la vitrine se compose** *ou* **est composée de robes** the window display is made up of *ou* composed of dresses; **notre équipe est composée à 70% de femmes** our team is 70% women, 70% of our team are women

composite [kɔ̃pozit] **1** ADJ **a** = *hétérogène*) [*éléments, mobilier, matériau, groupe*] composite; [*public*] mixed; [*foule*] motley (*épith*) **b** (*Archit*) composite **2** NM (*Archit*) composite order; (= *matériau*) composite

compositeur, -trice [kɔ̃pozitœʀ, tʀis] NM,F (*Mus*) composer; (*Typo*) typesetter, compositor → **amiable**

composition [kɔ̃pozisjɔ̃] NF **a** (= *confection*) [*plat, médicament*] making(-up); [*assemblée*] formation, setting-up; [*équipe sportive*] selection; [*équipe de chercheurs*] setting-up; [*bouquet, vitrine*] arranging; **les boissons qui entrent dans la ~ du cocktail** the drinks that go into the cocktail → **rôle** **b** (= *élaboration*) [*lettre, poème*] writing, composition; [*symphonie*] composition; [*tableau*] painting; **une œuvre de ma ~** a work of my own composition **c** (= *œuvre*) (*musicale, picturale*) composition; (*architecturale*) structure; **~ florale** flower arrangement **d** (= *structure*) [*plan, ensemble*] structure; **quelle est la ~ du passage ?** what is the structure of the passage?; **la répartition des masses dans le tableau forme une ~ harmonieuse** the distribution of the masses in the picture makes for a harmonious composition **e** (= *constituants*) [*mélange*] composition; [*équipe, assemblée*] composition, line-up; **quelle est la ~ du gâteau ?** what is the cake made of?, what ingredients go into the cake?; **la nouvelle ~ du Parlement européen** the new line-up in the European Parliament **f** (*Scol* = *examen*) test; **~ de français** (*en classe*) French test *ou* exam; (*à l'examen*) French paper; (= *rédaction*) **~ française** French essay *ou* composition **g** (*Typo*) typesetting, composition **h** (*loc*) **venir à ~** to come to terms; **amener qn à ~** to get sb to come to terms; **être de bonne ~** to be good-natured

compost [kɔ̃pɔst] NM compost

compostage [kɔ̃pɔstaʒ] NM **a** (*pour mettre une date*) (date) stamping; (= *poinçonnage*) punching **b** (*Agr*) composting

composter [kɔ̃pɔste] ▶conjug 1◀ VT **a** (= *dater*) to (date) stamp; (= *poinçonner*) to punch; **n'oubliez pas de ~ votre billet** don't forget to get your ticket punched **b** (*Agr*) to compost

composteur [kɔ̃pɔstœʀ] NM (= *timbre dateur*) date stamp; (= *poinçon*) ticket punching machine; (*Typo*) composing stick

compote [kɔ̃pɔt] NF stewed fruit, compote; **~ de pommes/de poires** stewed apples/pears, compote of apples/pears; **j'ai les jambes en ~*** (*de fatigue*) my legs are killing me* *ou* aching;

(par l'émotion, la maladie) my legs are like jelly *ou* cotton wool *(Brit)*; **il a le visage en ~*** his face is black and blue *ou* is a mass of bruises

compotier [kɔ̃pɔtje] NM fruit dish *ou* bowl

compréhensibilité [kɔ̃pReãsibilite] NF [*texte*] comprehensibility

compréhensible [kɔ̃pReãsibl] ADJ (= *clair*) comprehensible, easily understood; (= *concevable*) understandable

compréhensif, -ive [kɔ̃pReãsif, iv] ADJ **ⓐ** (= *tolérant*) understanding **ⓑ** (*Logique*) comprehensive

compréhension [kɔ̃pReãsjɔ̃] NF (= *indulgence*) understanding; (= *fait ou faculté de comprendre*) understanding, comprehension; (= *clarté*) understanding, intelligibility; (*Logique, Ling, Math, Scol*) comprehension; **~ orale/écrite** listening *ou* aural/reading comprehension; **exercice de ~** comprehension exercise

▼ **comprendre** [kɔ̃pRãdR] ▶conjug 58◀ VT **ⓐ** (= *être composé de*) to be composed of, be made up of, consist of, comprise; (= *être muni de, inclure*) to include; **ce manuel comprend 3 parties** this textbook is composed of *ou* is made up of *ou* comprises 3 parts; **cet appareil comprend en outre un flash** this camera also has *ou* comes with a flash; **le loyer ne comprend pas le chauffage** the rent doesn't include *ou* cover heating, the rent is not inclusive of heating; **je n'ai pas compris là-dedans les frais de déménagement** I haven't included the removal expenses

ⓑ [+ *problème, langue*] to understand; [+ *plaisanterie*] to understand, get*; [+ *personne*] (*ce qu'elle dit ou écrit*) to understand; **je ne le comprends pas/je ne comprends pas ce qu'il dit, il parle trop vite** I can't understand him/I can't make out *ou* understand what he says, he speaks too quickly; **vous m'avez mal compris** you've misunderstood me; **il comprend mal ce qu'on lui dit** he doesn't understand what he is told; **il ne comprend pas l'allemand** he doesn't understand German; **~ la vie/les choses** to understand life/things; **il ne comprend pas la plaisanterie** he can't take a joke; **il ne comprend rien à rien** he hasn't a clue about anything, he doesn't understand a thing (about anything); **c'est à n'y rien ~** it's completely baffling, it's beyond me; **se faire ~** to make o.s. understood; **il est difficile de bien se faire ~** it's difficult to get one's ideas across (**de qn** to sb); **j'espère que je me suis bien fait ~ ou que c'est compris** I hope I've made myself quite clear; **il comprend vite** he's quick, he catches on fast; **tu comprends, ce que je veux c'est ... you see,** what I want is ...; **il a bien su me faire ~ que je le gênais** he made it quite clear *ou* plain to me that I was annoying him; **dois-je ~ que ...?** am I to take it *ou* understand that ...?; **oui, enfin, je me comprends** well, I know what I mean

ⓒ (= *être compréhensif envers*) [+ *personne*] to understand; **j'espère qu'il comprendra** I hope he'll understand; **~ les jeunes/les enfants** to understand young people/children; **je le comprends, il en avait assez** I can understand him *ou* I know just how he felt — he'd had enough

ⓓ (= *concevoir*) [+ *attitude, point de vue*] to understand; **je comprends mal son attitude** I find it hard to understand his attitude; **c'est comme ça que je comprends les vacances** that's what I think of as a holiday; **c'est comme ça que je comprends le rôle de Hamlet** that's how I see *ou* understand the role of Hamlet; **ça se comprend, il voulait partir** it's quite understandable *ou* it's perfectly natural, he wanted to go; **nous comprenons vos difficultés mais nous ne pouvons rien faire** we understand *ou* appreciate your difficulties but there's nothing we can do

ⓔ (= *se rendre compte de*) to realize, understand (**pourquoi** why, **comment** how); **il n'a**

pas encore compris la gravité de son acte he hasn't yet understood *ou* grasped the seriousness of what he did; **j'ai compris ma douleur*** I realized what I'd let myself in for*; **il m'a fait ~ que je devais faire attention** he made me realize that I should be careful; **il a enfin compris qu'elle ne voulait pas revenir** he finally understood that she didn't want to come back

comprenette* [kɔ̃pRanɛt] NF **il est dur ou lent à la ~ ◊ il a la ~ difficile** he's slow on the uptake*, he's slow to catch on*

compresse [kɔ̃pRES] NF compress

compresser [kɔ̃pRese] ▶conjug 1◀ VT (*gén*) to squash; (*Tech*) to compress; (*Ordin, Téléc*) [+ *images, données, signaux*] to compress; [+ *coûts, dépenses*] to cut, reduce; **des vêtements compressés dans une valise** clothes squashed *ou* crammed into a suitcase

compresseur [kɔ̃pREsœR] NM compressor → **rouleau**

compressibilité [kɔ̃pResibilite] NF (*Phys*) compressibility; (*Fin*) **la ~ des dépenses** the extent to which expenses can be reduced *ou* cut

compressible [kɔ̃pResibl] ADJ (*Phys*) compressible; [*dépenses*] reducible; **ces dépenses ne sont pas ~s à l'infini** these costs cannot be reduced *ou* cut down indefinitely

compressif, -ive [kɔ̃pResif, iv] ADJ [*pansement*] compressive

compression [kɔ̃pResjɔ̃] NF **ⓐ** (= *action*) [*gaz, substance*] compression; [*dépenses, personnel*] reduction, cutback, cutting-down (**de** in); (*Ordin*) compression; **~ numérique** digital compression; **procéder à des ~s de crédits** to set up credit restrictions *ou* a credit squeeze; **~s budgétaires** cutbacks in spending, budget restrictions *ou* cuts; **~ des profits** squeeze on profits, reduction in profits; **~ des coûts** cost-cutting (*NonC*); **des mesures de ~ sont nécessaires** restrictions *ou* cutbacks are needed **ⓑ** (*Aut, Phys = pression*) compression; **pompe de ~** compression pump; **meurtri par ~** bruised by crushing; (*Méd*) **point de ~** pressure point

comprimé [kɔ̃pRime] NM (*Pharm*) tablet; **médicament en ~s** medicine in tablet form

comprimer [kɔ̃pRime] ▶conjug 1◀ VT **ⓐ** (= *presser*) [+ *air, gaz, artère*] to compress; [+ *substance à emballer*] to press *ou* pack tightly together; **sa ceinture lui comprimait l'estomac** his belt was pressing *ou* digging into his stomach; **ces chaussures me compriment les pieds** these shoes pinch my feet; **nous étions tous comprimés dans la voiture** we were all jammed together* *ou* packed tightly together in the car → **air** **ⓑ** (= *réduire*) [+ *dépenses, personnel*] to cut down *ou* back, reduce; (*Ordin*) to compress **ⓒ** (= *contenir*) [+ *larmes, colère, sentiments*] to hold back, hold in check

compris, e [kɔ̃pRi, iz] (*ptp de* **comprendre**) ADJ **ⓐ** (= *inclus*) **10 F emballage ~** 10 francs inclusive of *ou* including packaging, 10 francs packaging included; **10 F emballage non ~** 10 francs exclusive of *ou* excluding *ou* not including packaging; **service ~** service included; **service non ~** service not included, service extra; **tout ~** all inclusive, everything included; **c'est 100 F tout ~** it's 100 francs all inclusive *ou* all in*; **il va vendre ses terres, la ferme comprise/non comprise** he's selling his land including/excluding the farm **ⓑ** **700 F ~ l'électricité ou l'électricité y ~e** 700 francs including electricity *ou* electricity included; **y ~ moi** myself included, including me *ou* myself **ⓒ** (= *situé*) **être ~ entre** to be contained between *ou* by, be bounded by; **la zone ~e entre les falaises et la mer** the area (lying) between the cliffs and the sea, the area bounded by the cliffs and the sea; **tous les chapitres qui sont ~ entre les pages 12 et 145** all the chap-

ters (which are) contained *ou* included in pages 12 to 145

ⓓ (= *d'accord*) **(c'est) ~!** (it's) agreed!; **alors c'est ~, on se voit demain** so it's agreed then, we'll see each other tomorrow; **tu t'y mets tout de suite, ~!** start right away, understand? *ou* is that understood?

compromettant, e [kɔ̃pRɔmɛtã, ãt] ADJ compromising; **signer cette pétition, ce n'est pas très ~** you won't commit yourself to very much by signing this petition, there's no great commitment involved in signing this petition; (*péj*) **un homme ~** an undesirable associate

compromettre [kɔ̃pRɔmɛtR] ▶conjug 56◀ **①** VT [+ *personne, réputation*] to compromise; [+ *avenir, chances, santé*] to compromise, jeopardize **②** **se compromettre** VPR (= *s'avancer*) to commit o.s.; (= *se discréditer*) to compromise o.s.; **se ~ dans une affaire louche** to get mixed up *ou* involved in a shady deal

compromis, e [kɔ̃pRɔmi, iz] (*ptp de* **compromettre**) **①** ADJ **être ~** [*personne, réputation*] to be compromised; [*avenir, projet, chances*] to be jeopardized *ou* in jeopardy; **notre sortie/collaboration me semble bien ou très ~e** our trip/continuing collaboration looks very doubtful to me; **un ministre serait ~ dans cette affaire** a minister is alleged to be involved in the affair **②** NM compromise; **solution de ~** compromise solution; **~ de vente** (provisional) sales agreement; **trouver un ~ (entre)** to find *ou* reach a compromise (between)

compromission [kɔ̃pRɔmisjɔ̃] NF dishonest compromise; **c'est là une ~ avec votre conscience** now you're compromising with your conscience

comptabilisation [kɔ̃tabilizasjɔ̃] NF (*Fin*) posting

comptabiliser [kɔ̃tabilize] ▶conjug 1◀ VT (*Fin*) to post; (= *compter*) to count

comptabilité [kɔ̃tabilite] NF (= *science*) accountancy, accounting; (*d'une petite entreprise*) book-keeping; (= *comptes*) accounts, books; (= *bureau, service*) accounts office *ou* department; (= *profession*) accountancy, accounting; **il s'occupe de la ~ de notre entreprise** he does the accounting *ou* keeps the books for our firm; **~ analytique** cost accounting; **~ publique** public finance; **~ à partie simple/double** single-/double-entry book-keeping

comptable [kɔ̃tabl] **①** ADJ **ⓐ** (*Fin*) [+ *règles etc*] accounting, book-keeping; **il manque une pièce ~** one of the accounts is missing; (*Ling*) **nom ~** countable *ou* count noun **ⓑ** (= *responsable*) accountable (**de** for) **②** NMF accountant; **~ agréé** chartered accountant (*Brit*), certified accountant (*Brit*), certified public accountant (*US*); **~ du Trésor** local Treasury official; **chèque adressé au ~ du Trésor** cheque addressed to the Treasury → **chef¹**

comptage [kɔ̃taʒ] NM (= *action*) counting; **faire un ~ rapide** to do a quick count (**de** of)

comptant [kɔ̃tã] **①** ADV [*payer*] cash, in cash; [*acheter, vendre*] for cash; **verser 100 F ~** to pay 100 francs down, put down 100 francs **②** NM (= *argent*) cash; **au ~** [*payer*] cash; [*acheter, vendre*] for cash; **achat/vente au ~** cash purchase/sale → **argent**

---

compte [kɔ̃t]

① NOM MASCULIN	② COMPOSÉS

① NOM MASCULIN

ⓐ = **calcul** count; **faire le ~ des visiteurs/erreurs** to count (up) the visitors/mistakes, make a count of the visitors/mistakes; **faire le ~ des dépenses** to calculate *ou* work out the expenditure/one's wealth; (*fig*) **comment as-tu fait ton ~ pour arriver si tard?** how did you manage to arrive so late?; **l'as-tu**

compte-fils

inclus dans le ~ ? have you counted ou included him?; prendre qch en ~ to take sth into account; ils exigent la prise en ~ des préoccupations écologiques they're demanding that ecological considerations be taken into account

• **à ce compte(-là)** (= dans ce cas) in that case; (= à ce train-là) at this ou that rate

• **tout compte fait** ◊ **tous comptes faits** all things considered, when all's said and done

b = nombre exact (right) number; le ~ y est (paiement) that's the right amount; (inventaire) that's the right number, they're all there; ça ne fait pas le ~ (paiement) that's not enough ou the right amount; (inventaire) there's (still) something missing, they're not all there; j'ai ajouté 3 cuillerées/15 F pour faire le ~ I've added 3 spoonfuls/15 francs to make up the full amount; ça devrait faire (largement) le ~ that should be (more than) enough; avez-vous le bon ~ ou votre ~ de chaises ? have you got the right number of chairs? ou the number of chairs you want?; je n'arrive jamais au même ~ I never get the same figure ou number ou total twice; (Comm) pour faire bon ~ to make up the amount → loin, rond

c Comptab account; les ~s de la nation the national accounts; faire ses ~s to do one's accounts ou books; tenir les ~s du ménage to keep the household accounts; tenir les ~s d'une entreprise to keep the books ou accounts of a firm; publier à ~ d'auteur to publish at the author's expense; passer en ~ to place ou pass to account; nous sommes en ~ we have business to settle → apothicaire, ligne[1]

• **de compte à demi** : ils sont de ~ à demi dans cette affaire they're equal partners in this venture

• **être laissé pour compte** [question, aspect] to be neglected ou overlooked; [personne] to be left by the wayside → laissé-pour-compte

d Banque ~ (en banque ou bancaire) (bank) account; ~ rémunéré interest-bearing account; ~ non rémunéré non-interest-bearing account; avoir un ~ dans une banque/à la Banque de France to have an account with a bank/with the Banque de France; avoir de l'argent en ~ to have money in an account

e = dû donner ou régler son ~ à un employé (lit) to settle up with an employee; (fig = renvoyer) to give an employee his cards* (Brit) ou pink slip* (US); [employé] demander son ~ to hand in one's notice; (fig) il a son ~* (épuisé, mort) he's had it*, he's done for*; (ivre) he's had more than he can hold ou take; (fig) son ~ est bon his number's up*, he's had it* → régler

f = facture, addition (gén) account, invoice, bill; [hôtel, restaurant] bill (Brit), check (US); pourriez-vous me faire mon ~ ? would you make me out my bill?; mettez-le sur mon ~ ? (au restaurant, à l'hôtel) put it on my bill; (dans un magasin) charge it to ou put it on my account

g = avantage cela fait mon ~ that suits me; il y a trouvé son ~ he's got something out of it, he did well out of it; chacun y trouve son ~ there's something in it for everybody; si cette situation continue, c'est parce que le gouvernement y trouve son ~ if this situation continues, it's because it's to the government's advantage ou because it suits the government

• **à bon compte** [obtenir] (on the) cheap, for very little, for a song; s'en tirer à bon ~ to get off lightly

h = explications, justifications demander ou réclamer des ~s à qn to ask sb for an explanation; il me doit des ~s à propos de cette perte he owes me an explanation for this loss; rendre des ~s à qn to explain o.s. to sb; il va bien falloir qu'il me rende des ~s he's going to have to explain himself to me; je n'ai de ~s à rendre à personne I'm accountable to nobody, I

don't owe anybody any explanations; rendre ~ de qch à qn to give sb an account of sth; il doit rendre ~ de tous ses déplacements he has to account for all his movements; elle rendra ~ de la réunion à ses collègues she will brief her colleagues on the meeting

i

• **se rendre compte de qch** (= réaliser) to realize sth, be aware of sth; se rendre ~ que ... to realize that ..., be aware that ...; je me rends très bien ~ de la situation I am very well aware of the situation; est-ce que tu te rends vraiment ~ de ce que tu dis/fais ? do you realize ou do you really know what you are saying/doing?; tu ne te rends pas ~ du travail que ça représente you have no idea ou you just don't realize how much work that represents; rendez-vous ~ ! just imagine! ou think!; il a osé me dire ça, à moi, tu te rends ~ ! he dared say that to me — can you believe it!

• **tenir compte de qch/qn** to take sth/sb into account; il n'a pas tenu ~ de nos avertissements he didn't take any notice of our warnings, he disregarded ou ignored our warnings; tenir ~ à qn de son dévouement to take sb's devotion into account; on lui a tenu ~ de son passé they took his past into account ou consideration

• **compte tenu de** considering

k expressions figées

• **au compte de qn** ou **qch** : mettre qch au ~ de (= attribuer à) to put sth down to, attribute ou ascribe sth to; prendre qch à son ~ (responsabilité financière) to pay for sth; (responsabilité morale) to take responsibility for sth; je reprends cette maxime à mon ~ I shall make that saying my motto; il a repris la boutique à son ~ he's taken over the shop in his own name; être/s'établir ou se mettre ou s'installer à son ~ to be/set up in business for o.s., have/set up one's own business; travailler à son ~ to be self-employed

• **pour le compte de qn** (= au nom de) on behalf of; pour mon ~ (personnel) (= en ce qui me concerne) personally; (= pour mon propre usage) for my own use; (= mon profit) for my own benefit; chacun négocie pour son propre ~ everybody negotiates for himself; la banque agit pour son propre ~ the bank is acting on its own behalf

• **sur le compte de qn** ou **qch** (= à propos de) about; on m'en a raconté de belles sur son ~ ! I was told a few interesting stories about him! (= attribuer à) mettre qch sur le ~ de to put sth down to, attribute ou ascribe sth to

l

• **pour le compte** (Boxe) aller au tapis pour le ~ to be out for the count; (hum) tes sarcasmes l'ont envoyé au tapis pour le ~ your sarcastic remarks really knocked him for six*

2 COMPOSÉS

▸ **compte bloqué** escrow account ▸ **compte chèque postal** post office account, ≈ National Girobank account (Brit) ▸ **compte(-)chèques** = compte courant ▸ **compte courant** current ou checking (US) account ▸ **compte d'épargne en actions** stock market investment savings account ▸ **compte d'épargne logement** house purchase savings account giving the saver a reduced mortgage rate, ≈ building society account (Brit) ▸ **compte d'exploitation** trading ou operating ou working account ▸ **compte joint** joint account ▸ **compte numéroté** ou **à numéro** numbered account ▸ **compte pour le développement industriel** industrial development savings account ▸ **compte des profits et pertes** profit and loss account ▸ **compte à rebours** (Espace, fig) countdown ▸ **compte rendu** (= rapport) (gén) account, report; [livre, film] review; (sur travaux en cours) progress re-

port; ~ rendu d'audience court record; faire le ~ rendu d'un match/d'une réunion to give an account of ou a report on a match/meeting, give a rundown on a match/meeting ▸ **compte sur livret** deposit account

compte-fils [kɔ̃tfil] NM INV (Tech) linen tester
compte-gouttes [kɔ̃tgut] NM INV (= pipette) dropper; (fig) au ~ [distribuer, dépenser] sparingly, in dribs and drabs; [rembourser, entrer, sortir] in dribs and drabs

▼ **compter** [kɔ̃te]

▸ conjug 1 ◂
1 VERBE TRANSITIF **2** VERBE INTRANSITIF

1 VERBE TRANSITIF

a = calculer [+ choses, personnes, argent, jours] to count; combien en avez-vous compté ? how many did you count?, how many did you make it?; 40 cm ? j'avais compté 30 40 cm? I made it 30; il a 50 ans bien comptés he's a good 50 (years old); on peut ~ (sur les doigts de la main) ceux qui comprennent vraiment you can count on (the fingers of) one hand the number of people who really understand; on ne compte plus ses gaffes ◊ ses gaffes ne se comptent plus we've lost count of his blunders, he's made countless blunders; ~ les jours/les minutes to count the days/the minutes; ~ les points (lit) to count (up) the points; (fig) pendant qu'ils se disputaient moi je comptais les points I just sat back and watched while they argued; pendant qu'ils se battaient je comptais les coups I just sat back and watched while they fought; (Boxe) il a été compté 7 he took a count of 7 → mouton

b = escompter, prévoir to reckon, allow; combien as-tu compté qu'il nous fallait de chaises ? how many chairs did you reckon we'd need?; j'ai compté qu'il nous en fallait 10 I reckoned we'd need 10; combien de temps/d'argent comptez-vous pour finir les travaux ? how much time/money do you reckon it'll take to finish the work?, how much time/money are you allowing to finish the work?; il faut (bien) ~ 10 jours/100 F you must allow (a good) 10 days/100 francs, you must reckon on it taking (a good) 10 days/costing (a good) 100 francs; j'ai compté 90 cm pour le frigo, j'espère que ça suffira I've allowed 90 cm for the fridge, I hope that'll do

c = inclure to include; cela fait un mètre en comptant l'ourlet that makes one metre counting ou including the hem; t'es-tu compté ? did you count ou include yourself?; ne me comptez pas don't include me

• **sans compter** : nous étions dix, sans ~ l'instituteur there were ten of us, not counting the teacher; ils nous apportèrent leurs connaissances, sans ~ leur bonne volonté they gave us their knowledge, not to mention ou to say nothing of their helpfulness → **2b**

d = tenir compte de to take into account; ta bonne volonté te sera comptée your helpfulness will be taken into account

• **sans compter que** (= et de plus) not to mention that (= d'autant plus que) especially since ou as; il aurait dû venir, sans ~ qu'il n'avait rien à faire he ought to have come especially since ou as he had nothing to do

• **tout bien compté** (frm) all things considered, all in all

e = facturer to charge for; ~ qch à qn to charge sb for sth, charge sth to sb; ils n'ont pas compté le café they didn't charge for the coffee; combien vous ont-ils compté le café ? how much did they charge you for the coffee?; ils nous l'ont compté trop cher/10 F/au prix de gros they charged us too much/10 francs/the wholesale price (for it)

f = avoir to have; la ville compte quelques très beaux monuments the town has some very

> GRAMMAIRE ACTIVE: compter 35.2

beautiful monuments; **il compte 2 ans de règne/de service** he has been on the throne/in the firm for 2 years; **il ne compte pas d'enne-mis** he has no enemies; **cette famille compte trois musiciens** this family has *ou* boasts three musicians

$\boxed{g}$ **= classer, ranger** to consider; **on compte ce livre parmi les meilleurs de l'année** this book is considered (to be) *ou* ranks among the best of the year; **il le compte au nombre de ses amis** he considers him one of his friends, he numbers him among his friends

$\boxed{h}$ **= verser** to pay; **le caissier va vous ~ 600 F** the cashier will pay you 600 francs; **vous lui compterez 1000 F pour les heures supplémentai-res** you will pay him 1,000 francs' overtime

$\boxed{i}$ **= donner avec parcimonie** **il compte chaque sou qu'il nous donne** he counts every penny he gives us; **les permissions leur sont comptées** their leave is rationed; **il ne compte pas sa pei-ne** he spares no trouble; **ses jours sont comptés** his days are numbered; **le temps m'est compté** my time is precious

$\boxed{j}$ **= avoir l'intention de** to intend, plan; (= *s'attendre à*) to expect, reckon; **ils comptent partir demain** they intend *ou* plan to go to-morrow; **je compte recevoir la convocation de-main** I'm expecting to (receive) the summons tomorrow; **je ne compte pas qu'il vienne aujourd'hui** I'm not expecting *ou* I don't ex-pect him to come today

$\boxed{2}$ VERBE INTRANSITIF

$\boxed{a}$ **= calculer** to count; **il sait ~ (jusqu'à 10)** he can count (up to 10); **comment est-ce que tu as compté?** how did you work it out?; **~ sur ses doigts** to count on one's fingers; **~ de tête** to count in one's head; **tu as mal compté** you counted wrong, you miscounted

♦ **à compter de** (starting *ou* as) from; **cette loi prendra effet à ~ du 1ᵉʳ mai** this law will take effect (as) from May 1st

$\boxed{b}$ **= être économe** to economize; **avec la montée des prix, il faut ~ sans cesse** with the rise in prices you have to watch every penny (you spend); **dépenser sans ~** (= *être dépensier*) to spend extravagantly; (= *donner géné-reusement*) to give without counting the cost; **il s'est dépensé sans ~ pour cette cause** he spared no effort in supporting the cause, he gave himself body and soul to the cause

$\boxed{c}$ **= avoir de l'importance** to count, matter; **c'est le résultat qui compte** it's the result that counts *ou* matters; **c'est le geste qui compte** it's the thought that counts; **35 ans de maria-ge, ça compte!** 35 years of marriage, that's quite something!; **c'est un succès qui compte** it's an important success; **ce qui compte c'est de savoir dès maintenant** the main thing is to find out right away; **sa mère compte beaucoup pour lui** his mother is very important to him; **ça ne compte pas** that doesn't count

$\boxed{d}$ **= valoir** to count; **pour la retraite, les années de guerre comptent double** for the pur-poses of retirement, war service counts dou-ble; **après 60 ans les années comptent double** after 60 every year counts double

$\boxed{e}$ **= figurer** **~ parmi** to be *ou* rank among; **~ au nombre de** to be one of; **il compte pour deux** he's worth two men; **il compte pour quatre quand il s'agit de bagages/manger** he takes enough luggage/eats enough for four; **ça compte pour beaucoup dans sa réussite/dans sa décision** that has a lot to do with his success/his decision, that is a major factor in his success/his decision; **ça compte pour rien dans sa réussite/dans sa décision** that has noth-ing to do with his success/his decision; **ça compte pour du beurre*** that counts for noth-ing, that doesn't count

$\boxed{f}$

♦ **compter avec** (= *tenir compte de*) to reckon with, take account of, allow for; **il faut ~ avec l'opinion** you've got to reckon with *ou* take ac-count of public opinion; **il faut ~ avec le temps incertain** you have to allow for changeable weather; **un nouveau parti avec lequel il faut ~ a** new party to be reckoned with; **il faudra ~ avec lui** you'll have him to reckon with

♦ **compter sans** : on avait compté sans la grève we hadn't reckoned on there being a strike, we hadn't allowed for the strike

♦ **compter sur** (= *se fier à*) to count on, rely on; **~ sur la discrétion/la bonne volonté de qn** to count on *ou* rely on sb's discretion/goodwill; **nous comptons sur vous (pour) demain** we're expecting you (to come) tomorrow; **j'y compte bien!** I should hope so!; **n'y comptez pas trop ◊ ne comptez pas trop là-dessus** don't bank on it, don't count on it; **je compte sur vous** I'm counting *ou* relying on you; **vous pouvez ~ là-dessus** you can depend upon it; **ne comptez pas sur moi** (you can) count me out; **tu peux ~ sur lui pour le répéter partout!** you can bet (your life) he'll go and tell every-one!, you can count on him to go and tell everyone!; **compte (là-)dessus et bois de l'eau (fraîche)*** you've got a hope! (*Brit*), you haven't a prayer! (*US*), you'll be lucky!

compte-tours [kɔ̃tuʀ] NM INV (*Aut*) rev *ou* revolution counter, tachometer; (*Tech*) rev *ou* revolution counter

compteur [kɔ̃tœʀ] NM meter; **~ d'eau/électrique/à gaz** water/electricity/gas meter; **~ Geiger** Geiger counter; **~ (kilométrique)** mi-lometer (*Brit*), odometer (*US*); **~ (de vitesse)** speedometer; **remettre un ~ à zéro** to reset a meter at *ou* to zero; (*fig*) **remettre les ~s à zéro** to wipe the slate clean → **relever**

comptine [kɔ̃tin] NF (= *chanson*) nursery rhyme; (= *pour compter*) counting rhyme *ou* song

comptoir [kɔ̃twaʀ] NM $\boxed{a}$ [*magasin*] counter; [*bar*] bar $\boxed{b}$ (*colonial*) trading post $\boxed{c}$ (*Comm* = *cartel*) syndicate (*for marketing*) $\boxed{d}$ (*Fin* = *agence*) branch

compulsation [kɔ̃pylsasjɔ̃] NF consultation

compulser [kɔ̃pylse] ▶ conjug 1 ◀ VT to consult

compulsif, -ive [kɔ̃pylsif, iv] ADJ (*Psych*) com-pulsive

compulsion [kɔ̃pylsjɔ̃] NF (*Psych*) compulsion

comput [kɔ̃pyt] NM (*Rel*) *reckoning of the dates of movable feasts in the religious calendar*

computation [kɔ̃pytasjɔ̃] NF calculation, computation; **cela échappe aux ~s** this is im-possible to calculate

computationnel, -elle [kɔ̃pytasjɔnɛl] ADJ computational; **linguistique ~le** computa-tional linguistics

comte [kɔ̃t] NM count; (*britannique*) earl

comté [kɔ̃te] NM $\boxed{a}$ (*Hist*) earldom; (*Admin Brit, Can*) county $\boxed{b}$ (= *fromage*) comté (*kind of gru-yère cheese*)

comtesse [kɔ̃tɛs] NF countess

con, conne [kɔ̃, kɔn] $\boxed{1}$ ADJ (*f aussi inv* :* = stupide*) damned* *ou* bloody* (*Brit*) stupid*; **qu'il est ~!** what a stupid bastard*:* *ou* bloody* (*Brit*) fool (he is)!; **qu'elle est ~!** *ou* **conne!** silly bitch!*:*, silly cow!* (*Brit*); **il est ~ comme la lune** *ou* **comme un balai** he's a damn:* *ou* bloody* (*Brit*) fool *ou* idiot; **c'est pas ~ comme idée** it's not a bad idea $\boxed{2}$ NM,F (:* = *crétin*) damn fool*:*, bloody (*Brit*) idiot*:*, wally* (*Brit*), schmuck* (*US*); **sale ~ !*:*** bas-tard!*:*, bloody* (*Brit*) swine!; **bande de ~s** load of cretins:* *ou* bloody idiots:* (*Brit*); **faire le ~** to mess around*, muck about* (*Brit*), piss about*:*; **serrure/gouvernement à la ~** lousy:* *ou* crummy* lock/government; **comme un ~** like a damn fool* *ou* bloody idiot* (*Brit*) $\boxed{3}$ NM (*:* = *vagin*) cunt*:*

Conakry [kɔnakʀi] N Conakry

conard: [kɔnaʀ] NM = **connard**

conarde: [kɔnaʀd] NF = **connarde**

conasse: [kɔnas] NF = **connasse**

concassage [kɔ̃kasaʒ] NM crushing

concasser [kɔ̃kase] ▶ conjug 1 ◀ VT to crush; **poivre concassé** crushed peppercorns

concasseur [kɔ̃kasœʀ] $\boxed{1}$ ADJ M crushing $\boxed{2}$ NM crusher

concaténation [kɔ̃katenasjɔ̃] NF concatena-tion

concave [kɔ̃kav] ADJ concave

concavité [kɔ̃kavite] NF (*Opt*) concavity; (*gén* = *cavité*) hollow, cavity; **les ~s d'un rocher** the hollows *ou* cavities in a rock

concédant [kɔ̃sedɑ̃] NM (*Écon*) licensor

concéder [kɔ̃sede] ▶ conjug 6 ◀ VT [+ *privilège, droit, exploitation*] to grant; [+ *point*] to con-cede; [+ *but, corner*] to concede, give away; **je vous concède que …** I'll grant you that …

concélébrant [kɔ̃selebʀɑ̃] NM concelebrant

concélébrer [kɔ̃selebʀe] ▶ conjug 1 ◀ VT to concelebrate

concentration [kɔ̃sɑ̃tʀasjɔ̃] NF $\boxed{a}$ (*gén, Chim*) concentration; **les grandes ~s urbaines des Midlands** the great conurbations of the Mid-lands → **camp** $\boxed{b}$ (= *fusion*) **la ~ des entrepri-ses** the merging of businesses; **~ horizontale/verticale** horizontal/vertical integration $\boxed{c}$ **~ (d'esprit)** concentration

concentrationnaire [kɔ̃sɑ̃tʀasjɔnɛʀ] ADJ [*sys-tème*] concentration camp (*épith*)

concentré, e [kɔ̃sɑ̃tʀe] (*ptp de* **concentrer**) $\boxed{1}$ ADJ $\boxed{a}$ [*acide*] concentrated; [*lait*] con-densed $\boxed{b}$ [*candidat, athlète*] concentrating hard (*attrib*) $\boxed{2}$ NM (*chimique*) concentrated solution; (= *bouillon*) concentrate, extract; **~ de tomates** tomato purée

concentrer [kɔ̃sɑ̃tʀe] ▶ conjug 1 ◀ $\boxed{1}$ VT (*gén*) to concentrate; **~ son attention sur qch** to concentrate *ou* focus one's attention on sth $\boxed{2}$ **se concentrer** VPR [*foule, troupes*] to con-centrate; **le candidat se concentra avant de ré-pondre** the candidate gathered his thoughts *ou* thought hard before replying; **je me concentre!** I'm concentrating!; **se ~ sur un problème** to concentrate on a problem; **les regards se concentrèrent sur moi** everybody's gaze was fixed *ou* focused on me

concentrique [kɔ̃sɑ̃tʀik] ADJ [*cercle*] concen-tric

concept [kɔ̃sɛpt] NM concept

concepteur, -trice [kɔ̃sɛptœʀ, tʀis] NM,F (*Ind, Comm*) designer; **~ graphique** graphic de-signer; **~ de réseaux** network designer; **~(-rédacteur) publicitaire** advertising copywriter

conception [kɔ̃sɛpsjɔ̃] NF $\boxed{a}$ (*Bio*) conception → **immaculé** $\boxed{b}$ (= *action*) [*idée*] conception, conceiving; (*Ind, Comm*) design; **la ~ d'un tel plan est géniale** it is a brilliantly conceived plan; **voilà quelle est ma ~ de la chose** this is how I see it; **machine d'une ~ révolutionnaire** machine of revolutionary design; **~ assistée par ordinateur** computer-aided *ou* computer-assisted design $\boxed{c}$ (= *idée*) notion, idea; (= *réalisation*) creation

conceptualisation [kɔ̃sɛptɥalizasjɔ̃] NF con-ceptualization

conceptualiser [kɔ̃sɛptɥalize] ▶ conjug 1 ◀ VT to conceptualize

conceptuel, -elle [kɔ̃sɛptɥɛl] ADJ conceptual

concernant [kɔ̃sɛʀnɑ̃] PRÉP $\boxed{a}$ (= *se rapportant à*) concerning, relating to, regarding; **des me-sures ~ ce problème seront bientôt prises** steps will soon be taken concerning *ou* re-garding this problem $\boxed{b}$ (= *en ce qui concerne*) with regard to, as regards; **~ ce problème, des mesures seront bientôt prises** with regard to this problem *ou* as regards this problem *ou* as far as this problem is concerned, steps will soon be taken

▼ **concerner** [kɔ̃sɛʀne] ▶ conjug 1 ◀ VT to con-cern; **cela ne vous concerne pas** (= *ce n'est pas votre affaire*) it's no concern of yours; (= *on ne*

➤ GRAMMAIRE ACTIVE: **concerner** 33.2

parle pas de vous) it doesn't concern you; (= ça n'a pas d'incidence sur vous) it doesn't affect you; **en ce qui concerne cette question** with regard to this question, concerning this question, as far as this question is concerned; **en ce qui me concerne** as far as I'm concerned; (Admin) **pour affaire vous concernant** to discuss a matter which concerns you ou a matter concerning you; **je ne me sens pas concerné par sa remarque/son rapport** his remark/report doesn't apply to ou concern me

concert [kɔsɛʀ] NM [a] (Mus) concert; **~ spirituel** concert of sacred music; **~ de louanges/de lamentations/d'invectives** chorus of praise/lamentation(s)/invective; **on entendit un ~ d'avertisseurs** a chorus of horns started up → **salle** [b] (littér) (= harmonie) chorus; (= accord) entente, accord; **un ~ de voix** a chorus of voices; **le ~ des grandes puissances** the entente ou accord between the great powers [c] **de ~** [partir, décider] together; [rire] in unison; [agir] together, in concert, in unison; **ils ont agi de ~ pour éviter ...** they took concerted action to avoid ...; **de ~ avec** (= en accord avec) in cooperation ou conjunction with; (= ensemble) together with

concertant, e [kɔsɛʀtã, ãt] ADJ → **symphonie**

concertation [kɔsɛʀtasjɔ] NF (= échange de vues, dialogue) dialogue; (= rencontre) meeting; **sans ~ préalable** without preliminary consultation(s)

concerté, e [kɔsɛʀte] (ptp de **concerter**) ADJ concerted

concerter [kɔsɛʀte] ▶conjug 1◀ [1] VT (= organiser) [+ plan, entreprise, projet] to devise [2] **se concerter** VPR (= délibérer) to consult (each other), take counsel together

concertina [kɔsɛʀtina] NM concertina

concertino [kɔsɛʀtino] NM concertino

concertiste [kɔsɛʀtist] NMF concert artiste ou performer

concerto [kɔsɛʀto] NM concerto; **~ pour piano (et orchestre)** piano concerto, concerto for piano and orchestra; **~ grosso** concerto grosso

concessif, -ive [kɔsesif, iv] (Gram) [1] ADJ concessive [2] **concessive** NF concessive clause

concession [kɔsesjɔ] NF [a] (= faveur) concession (à to); **faire des ~s** to make concessions; **sans ~** [morale, reportage] uncompromising; [débat] ruthless [b] (= cession) [terrain, exploitation] concession; **faire la ~ d'un terrain** to grant a piece of land [c] (= exploitation, terrain, territoire) concession; [cimetière] burial plot; **~ minière** mining concession; **~ à perpétuité** burial plot held in perpetuity

concessionnaire [kɔsesjɔnɛʀ] [1] ADJ (Comm, Écon) [entreprise, service] concessionary; (travaux publics) **société** ~ contractor [2] NMF (= marchand agréé) agent, dealer, franchise holder; (= bénéficiaire d'une concession) concessionaire, concessionary; **~ automobile** car dealer; **disponible chez votre ~** available from your dealer

concevable [kɔs(ə)vabl] ADJ conceivable; **il est très ~ que ...** it's quite conceivable that ...

concevoir [kɔs(ə)vwaʀ] ▶conjug 28◀ VT [a] (= penser) to imagine; [+ fait, concept, idée] to conceive of; **je n'arrive pas à ~ que c'est fini** I can't conceive ou believe that it's finished; **il ne conçoit pas qu'on puisse souffrir de la faim** he cannot imagine ou conceive that people can suffer from starvation [b] (= élaborer, étudier) [+ voiture, maison, produit] to design; [+ solution, projet, moyen] to conceive, devise, think up; **bien/mal conçu** [projet, livre] well/badly thought out; [voiture, maison] well/badly designed [c] (= envisager) [+ question] to see, view; **voilà comment je conçois la chose** that's how I see

it ou view it ou look at it [d] (= comprendre) to understand; **je conçois sa déception** ou **qu'il soit déçu** I can understand his disappointment ou his being disappointed; **cela se conçoit facilement** it's quite understandable, it's easy to understand; **on concevrait mal qu'il puisse refuser** a refusal on his part would be difficult to understand; **ce qui se conçoit bien s'énonce clairement** what is clearly understood can be clearly expressed [e] (= rédiger) [+ lettre, réponse] to compose; **ainsi conçu ◊ conçu en ces termes** expressed ou couched in these terms [f] (= éprouver) to conceive; **je conçois des doutes quant à son intégrité** I have some doubts as to his integrity; **il en conçut une terrible jalousie** he conceived a terrible feeling of jealousy; **il conçut de l'amitié pour moi** he took a liking to me [g] (= engendrer) to conceive

conchyliculteur, -trice [kɔkilikyltœʀ, tʀis] NM,F shellfish farmer

conchyliculture [kɔkilikyltyʀ] NF shellfish farming

concierge [kɔsjɛʀʒ] NMF [immeuble] caretaker, manager (of an apartment building) (US); [hôtel] porter; (en France) concierge; (fig) **c'est un(e) vrai(e) ~** he (ou she) is a real gossip

---

◼ **CONCIERGE**

Many apartment buildings in French cities still have a "loge" near the entrance where the concierge lives with his or her family. The stereotypical image of the concierge is that of an amiable busybody with a tendency to spread gossip about tenants. Nowadays the term is considered slightly demeaning, and the words "gardien/gardienne d'immeuble" are often thought more acceptable.

---

conciergerie [kɔsjɛʀʒəʀi] NF [lycée, château] caretaker's lodge; (Can) apartment house; (Hist) **la Conciergerie** the Conciergerie

concile [kɔsil] NM (Rel) council; **~ œcuménique** ecumenical council; **le ~ de Trente** the Council of Trent

conciliable [kɔsiljabl] ADJ (= compatible) [opinions] reconcilable; **ce n'est pas ~ avec ...** it's not compatible with ...

conciliabule [kɔsiljabyl] NM [a] (= entretien) consultation, confab*; (iro) **tenir de grands ~s** to have great consultations ou confabs* [b] († = réunion) secret meeting

conciliaire [kɔsiljɛʀ] ADJ conciliar; **les pères ~s** the fathers of the council

conciliant, e [kɔsiljã, jãt] ADJ conciliatory, conciliating

conciliateur, -trice [kɔsiljatœʀ, tʀis] [1] ADJ conciliatory, conciliating [2] NM,F (= médiateur) conciliator

conciliation [kɔsiljasjɔ] NF (gén) conciliation, reconciliation; (entre époux) reconciliation; **esprit de ~** spirit of conciliation; **comité de ~** arbitration committee; **la ~ d'intérêts opposés** the reconciliation ou reconciling of conflicting interests; **tentative de ~** (gén, Pol) attempt at (re)conciliation; (entre époux) attempt at reconciliation → **procédure**

conciliatoire [kɔsiljatwaʀ] ADJ (Jur) conciliatory

concilier [kɔsilje] ▶conjug 7◀ [1] VT [a] (= rendre compatible) [+ exigences, opinions, sentiments] to reconcile (avec with) [b] (= attirer) to win, gain; **sa bonté lui a concilié les électeurs** his kindness won ou gained him the support of the voters ou won over the voters [c] (littér, Jur = réconcilier) [+ ennemis] to reconcile, conciliate [2] **se concilier** VPR (= s'attirer) to win, gain; **se ~ les bonnes grâces de qn** to win ou gain sb's favour

concis, e [kɔsi, iz] ADJ concise; **en termes ~** concisely

concision [kɔsizjɔ] NF concision, conciseness, succinctness

concitoyen, -yenne [kɔsitwajɛ, jɛn] NM,F fellow citizen

conclave [kɔklav] NM (Rel) conclave

concluant, e [kɔklyã, ãt] ADJ conclusive

▼ **conclure** [kɔklyʀ] ▶conjug 35◀ [1] VT [a] (= signer) [+ affaire, accord] to conclude; **~ un marché** to conclude ou clinch a deal; **marché conclu!** it's a deal! [b] (= terminer) [+ débat, discours, texte] to conclude, end; **et pour ~** and to conclude; **je vous demande de ~** will you please conclude; **il conclut par ces mots/en disant ...** he concluded with these words/by saying ...; **~ sa plaidoirie** to rest one's case [c] (= déduire) to conclude (qch de qch sth from sth); **j'en conclus que ...** I therefore conclude that ... [2] VI (Jur) [témoignage] **~ contre qn** to convict sb; [personne] **~ contre/en faveur de qn** to find against/in favour (Brit) ou favor (US) of sb [3] **conclure à** VT INDIR **ils ont conclu à son innocence** they concluded that he was innocent; **les juges ont conclu à l'acquittement** the judges decided on an acquittal

conclusif, -ive [kɔklyzif, iv] ADJ concluding (épith)

▼ **conclusion** [kɔklyzjɔ] [1] NF (gén) conclusion; [discours] close; **en ~** in conclusion; **~, il n'est pas venu*** the net result was that he didn't come; **~, on s'était trompé*** in other words, we had made a mistake [2] **conclusions** NFPL (Jur) [demandeur] pleadings, submissions; [avocat] summing-up; [jury] findings, conclusions; **déposer des ~s auprès d'un tribunal** to file submissions with a court

concocter* [kɔkɔkte] ▶conjug 1◀ VT [+ breuvage, discours, loi] to concoct

concoction* [kɔkɔksjɔ] NF concoction

concombre [kɔkɔbʀ] NM cucumber

concomitamment [kɔkɔmitamã] ADV concomitantly

concomitance [kɔkɔmitãs] NF concomitance

concomitant, e [kɔkɔmitã, ãt] ADJ concomitant

concordance [kɔkɔʀdãs] NF [a] (gén) agreement; **la ~ de deux témoignages** the agreement of two testimonies, the fact that two testimonies tally ou agree; **la ~ de deux résultats/situations** the similarity of ou between two results/situations; **mettre ses actes en ~ avec ses principes** to act in accordance with one's principles [b] (= index) (Bible) concordance; (Géol) conformability; (Gram) **des temps** sequence of tenses; (Phys) **~ de phases** synchronization of phases

concordant, e [kɔkɔʀdã, ãt] ADJ [faits] corroborating; (Géol) conformable; **deux témoignages ~s** two testimonies which agree ou which are in agreement ou which tally

concordat [kɔkɔʀda] NM (Rel) concordat; (Comm) composition; [faillite] winding-up arrangement

concorde [kɔkɔʀd] NF (littér = harmonie) concord

concorder [kɔkɔʀde] ▶conjug 1◀ VI [faits, dates, témoignages] to agree, tally; [idées] to coincide, match; [caractères] to match; **faire ~ des chiffres** to make figures agree ou tally; **ses actes concordent-ils avec ses idées ?** is his behaviour in accordance with his ideas?

concourant, e [kɔkuʀã, ãt] ADJ (= convergent) [droites] convergent; [efforts] concerted (épith), united

concourir [kɔkuʀiʀ] ▶conjug 11◀ [1] VI [a] [concurrent] to compete (pour for); **les films qui concourent au festival** the films competing (for a prize) at the festival [b] (Math = converger) to converge (vers towards, on) [2] **concourir à** VT INDIR **~ à qch/à faire qch** [personnes] to work towards sth/towards doing sth; [*circonstances*] to contribute to sth/to doing sth; **tout concourt à notre réussite** everything is working in our favour; **son intransigeance a concouru à son échec** his inflexibility contributed *ou* was a factor in his failure

concours [kɔ̃kuʀ] NM [a] (= *jeu, compétition*) competition; (= *examen*) competitive examination; ~ **agricole** agricultural show; ~ **hippique** (= *sport*) show-jumping; **un ~ hippique** (= *épreuve*) a horse show; **promotion par (voie de)** ~ promotion by (competitive) examination; ~ **de beauté** beauty contest; ~ **d'entrée (à)** (competitive) entrance examination (for); ~ **de recrutement** competitive entry examination; ~ **général** *competitive examination with prizes, open to secondary school children*; **être présenté hors** ~ to be shown outside the competition (*because of outstanding merit*); **être mis hors** ~ to be declared ineligible to compete, be disqualified; (*fig*) **il est hors** ~ he's in a class of his own [b] (= *participation*) aid, help; **prêter son** ~ **à qch** to lend one's support to sth; **avec le** ~ **de** (*participation*) with the participation of; (*aide*) with the support *ou* help *ou* assistance of; **il a fallu le** ~ **des pompiers** the firemen's help was needed [c] (= *rencontre*) ~ **de circonstances** combination of circumstances; **un grand** ~ **de peuple**† a large concourse† *ou* throng of people

┌─ **CONCOURS** ─┐

In France, the cultural significance of competitive examinations with a predetermined quota of successful candidates is considerable. Gruelling "classes préparatoires" after secondary school level are designed to prepare high-flying students for the "grandes écoles" entrance exams, and have tended to promote a competitive and elitist approach to learning in these schools. Other examples of the importance of **concours** *are the competitive recruitment procedures for public sector teaching posts ("CAPES" and "agrégation"), civil service appointments in ministries, and even jobs in the Post Office.*

concret, -ète [kɔ̃kʀɛ, ɛt] [1] ADJ [*situation, détail, objet*] concrete; **esprit** ~ practical mind; **il en a tiré des avantages** ~**s** it gave him certain real *ou* positive advantages → **musique** [2] NM **le** ~ **et l'abstrait** the concrete and the abstract; **ce que je veux, c'est du** ~ I want something concrete

concrètement [kɔ̃kʀetmã] ADV (*gén*) in concrete terms; (= *pratiquement*) in practical terms; **je me représente très** ~ **la situation** I can visualize the situation very clearly; ~**, à quoi ça va servir?** what practical use will it have?, in concrete terms, what use will it be?

concrétion [kɔ̃kʀesjɔ̃] NF (*Géol, Méd*) concretion

concrétisation [kɔ̃kʀetizasjɔ̃] NF [*promesse*] realization

concrétiser [kɔ̃kʀetize] ▸conjug 1◂ [1] VT to give concrete expression to [2] VI (*Sport* = *marquer*) to score [3] **se concrétiser** VPR [*espoir, projet*] to materialize; **ses promesses/menaces ne se sont pas concrétisées** his promises/threats didn't come to anything *ou* didn't materialize; **le projet commence à se** ~ the project is beginning to take shape

concubin, e [kɔ̃kybɛ̃, in] [1] NM,F (*Jur*) cohabitant, cohabitee, common-law husband (*ou* wife) [b] († *ou hum*) lover [2] **concubine** NF (*Hist*) concubine

concubinage [kɔ̃kybinaʒ] NM cohabitation; **ils vivent en** ~ they're living together *ou* as husband and wife; (*Jur*) ~ **notoire** common-law marriage

concupiscence [kɔ̃kypisãs] NF concupiscence

concupiscent, e [kɔ̃kypisã, ãt] ADJ concupiscent

concurremment [kɔ̃kyʀamã] ADV [a] (= *conjointement*) conjointly; **il agit** ~ **avec le président** he acts conjointly with *ou* in conjunction with the president [b] (= *en même temps*) concurrently

concurrence [kɔ̃kyʀãs] NF [a] (*gén, Comm* = *compétition*) competition; **prix défiant toute** ~ absolutely unbeatable price, rock-bottom price; ~ **déloyale** unfair trading *ou* competition; **faire** ~ **à qn** to be in competition with sb; **être en** ~ **avec qn** to be in competition with sb, compete with sb [b] (*limite*) **jusqu'à** ~ **de ...** up to ...

concurrencer [kɔ̃kyʀãse] ▸conjug 3◂ VT to compete with; **il nous concurrence dangereusement** he is a serious threat *ou* challenge to us; **leurs produits risquent de** ~ **les nôtres** their products could well pose a serious threat *ou* challenge to ours

concurrent, e [kɔ̃kyʀã, ãt] [1] ADJ [a] (= *rival*) rival, competing [b] († = *concourant*) [*forces, actions*] concurrent, cooperative [2] NM,F (*Comm, Sport*) competitor; (*Scol*) [*concours*] candidate

concurrentiel, -elle [kɔ̃kyʀãsjɛl] ADJ [*secteur, produit, prix*] competitive

concussion [kɔ̃kysjɔ̃] NF misappropriation of public funds

concussionnaire [kɔ̃kysjɔnɛʀ] [1] ADJ embezzling (*épith*) [2] NMF embezzler of public funds

condamnable [kɔ̃danabl] ADJ [*action, opinion*] reprehensible, blameworthy; **il n'est pas** ~ **d'avoir pensé à ses intérêts** he cannot be blamed for having thought of his own interests

condamnation [kɔ̃danasjɔ̃] NF [a] (*Jur*) [*coupable*] (= *action*) sentencing (**à** to, **pour** for); (= *peine*) sentence; **il a 3** ~**s à son actif** he already has 3 convictions; ~ **à mort** death sentence, sentence of death; ~ **à une amende** imposition of a fine; ~ **à 5 ans de prison** 5-year (prison) sentence; ~ **(aux travaux forcés) à perpétuité** life sentence (of hard labour); ~ **aux dépens** order to pay costs; ~ **pour meurtre** sentence for murder [b] [*livre, délit, conduite, idée*] condemnation [c] (= *faillite*) [*espoir, théorie, projet*] end; **c'est la** ~ **du petit commerce** it means the end of *ou* it spells the end for the small trader [d] (= *action*) locking; (= *système*) locking device; ~ **centralisée des portes** central-locking device

condamné, e [kɔ̃dane] (*ptp de* **condamner**) NM,F sentenced person, convict; (*à mort*) condemned person; **un** ~ **à mort s'est échappé** a man under sentence of death *ou* a condemned man has escaped; **les malades** ~**s** the terminally ill → **cigarette**

▼**condamner** [kɔ̃dane] ▸conjug 1◂ VT [a] [+ *coupable*] to sentence (**à** to, **pour** for); ~ **à mort** to sentence to death; ~ **qn à une amende** to fine sb, impose a fine on sb; ~ **qn à 5 ans de prison** to sentence sb to 5 years' imprisonment, pass a 5-year (prison) sentence on sb; **être condamné aux dépens** to be ordered to pay costs; ~ **qn par défaut/par contumace** to sentence sb by default/in his absence *ou* in absentia; ~ **pour meurtre** to sentence for murder; **Serge Despins, plusieurs fois condamné pour vol ...** Serge Despins, several times convicted of theft ... [b] (= *interdire*) [+ *délit, livre*] to condemn; **la loi condamne l'usage de stupéfiants** the law condemns the use of drugs; **ces délits sont sévèrement condamnés** these offences carry heavy sentences *ou* penalties [c] (= *blâmer*) [+ *action, idées, impropriété*] to condemn; **il ne faut pas le** ~ **d'avoir fait cela** you mustn't condemn *ou* blame him for doing that [d] (= *accuser*) to condemn; **sa rougeur le**

condamne the fact that he's blushing points to his guilt [e] [+ *malade*] to give up hope for; [+ *théorie, espoir*] to put an end to; **ce projet est maintenant condamné** this project is now doomed; **il était condamné depuis longtemps** there had been no hope for him *ou* he had been doomed for a long time; **il est condamné par les médecins** the doctors have given up hope (for him) [f] (= *obliger, vouer*) ~ **à** [+ *silence*] to condemn to; **je suis condamné** *ou* **ça me condamne à me lever tôt** I'm obliged to get up early; **condamné à sombrer dans l'oubli** doomed to sink into oblivion [g] [+ *porte, fenêtre*] (*gén*) to fill in, block up; (*avec briques*) to brick up; (*avec planches*) to board up; [+ *pièce*] to lock up; [+ *portière de voiture*] to lock; (*fig*) ~ **sa porte à qn** to bar one's door to sb

condé [kɔ̃de] NM (*arg Police* = *policier*) cop*; (= *accord*) deal (*which allows one to pursue illegal activities in exchange for information*)

condensable [kɔ̃dãsabl] ADJ condensable

condensateur [kɔ̃dãsatœʀ] NM (*Élec*) capacitor, condenser; (*Opt*) condenser

condensation [kɔ̃dãsasjɔ̃] NF condensation

condensé, e [kɔ̃dãse] (*ptp de* **condenser**) [1] ADJ [*gaz, vapeur, lait*] condensed; [*exposé, pensée*] condensed, compressed [2] NM (*gén*) summary; (*Presse*) digest

condenser [kɔ̃dãse] ▸conjug 1◂ [1] VT [+ *gaz, vapeur*] to condense; [+ *exposé, pensée*] to condense, compress [2] **se condenser** VPR [*vapeur*] to condense

condenseur [kɔ̃dãsœʀ] NM (*Opt, Phys*) condenser

condescendance [kɔ̃desãdãs] NF condescension; **avec** ~ condescendingly

condescendant, e [kɔ̃desãdã, ãt] ADJ condescending

condescendre [kɔ̃desãdʀ] ▸conjug 41◂ ✦**condescendre à** VT INDIR to condescend to; ~ **à faire qch** to condescend *ou* deign to do sth

condiment [kɔ̃dimã] NM condiment (*including pickles, spices, and any other seasoning*)

condisciple [kɔ̃disipl] NMF (*Scol*) schoolmate; (*Univ*) fellow student

condition [kɔ̃disjɔ̃] NF [a] (= *circonstances*) ~**s** conditions; ~**s atmosphériques/sociologiques** atmospheric/sociological conditions; ~**s de travail/vie** working/living conditions; **dans ces** ~**s, je refuse** under these conditions, I refuse; **dans les** ~**s actuelles** in *ou* under (the) present conditions; **améliorer la** ~ **des travailleurs émigrés** to improve the lot of foreign workers [b] (= *stipulation*) [*traité*] condition; (= *exigence*) [*acceptation*] condition, requirement; ~ **préalable** prerequisite; **la** ~ **nécessaire et suffisante pour que ...** the necessary and sufficient condition for ...; ~ **sine qua non** sine qua non, necessary condition; **l'honnêteté est la** ~ **du succès** honesty is the (prime) requirement for *ou* condition of success; **dicter/poser ses** ~**s** to state/lay down his conditions; **il ne remplit pas les** ~**s requises (pour le poste)** he doesn't fulfil the requirements (for the job); ~**s d'admission** terms *ou* conditions of admission *ou* entry (**dans** to); **sans** ~**(s)** [*capitulation*] unconditional; [*capituler*] unconditionally [c] (*Comm*) term; ~**s de vente/d'achat** terms of sale/of purchase; ~**s de paiement** terms (of payment); **obtenir des** ~**s intéressantes** to get favourable terms; **faire ses** ~**s** to make *ou* name his (one's) own terms; **acheter/envoyer à** *ou* **sous** ~ to buy/send on approval; **dans les** ~**s normales du commerce** in the ordinary course of business [d] (= *état*) condition; **en bonne** ~ [*aliments,* *envoi*] in good condition; **en bonne** *ou* **grande ~ (physique)** in good condition, fit; **en mauvaise ~ (physique)** out of condition, unfit; **mettre en ~** [+ *sportif*] to make *ou* get fit; [+ *candidat*] to prepare (mentally); [+ *spectateurs*] to condition; **la mise en ~ des téléspectateurs** the conditioning of television viewers; (*avant un examen*) **se mettre en ~** to prepare o.s. mentally

[e] (= *rang social*) station, condition; **vivre selon sa ~** to live according to one's station; **étudiant de ~ modeste** student from a modest home *ou* background; **personne de ~**†† person of quality; **la ~ ouvrière** the conditions of working-class life; **la ~ de prêtre** the priesthood; **la ~ d'artisan/d'intellectuel** the situation of the craftsman/intellectual

[f] (*loc*) **entrer/être en ~ chez qn**†† to enter sb's service/be in service with sb; **à une ~** on one condition; **je le ferai, à la seule ~ que toi aussi tu fasses un effort** I'll do it but only on one condition - you have to make an effort as well; **tu peux rester, à ~ d'être sage** *ou* **à ~ que tu sois sage** you can stay provided (that) *ou* so long as you're good; **sous ~** conditionally

conditionné, e [kɔ̃disjɔne] (*ptp de* **conditionner**) ADJ [a] (= *emballé*) packaged; (= *sous vide*) vacuum-packed [b] (= *influencé*) conditioned; **réflexe ~** conditioned response *ou* reflex [c] (= *climatisé*) → **air**

conditionnel, -elle [kɔ̃disjɔnɛl] ADJ, NM (*gén*) conditional; **réflexe ~** conditioned response *ou* reflex; (*Ling*) **au ~** in the conditional; **cette information est à mettre au ~** this information has still to be confirmed

conditionnellement [kɔ̃disjɔnɛlmɑ̃] ADV conditionally

conditionnement [kɔ̃disjɔnmɑ̃] NM (= *emballage*) packaging; [*air, personne, textile, blé*] conditioning

conditionner [kɔ̃disjɔne] ▸ conjug 1 ◂ VT (= *emballer*) to package; (= *influencer*) to condition; [+ *textiles, blé*] to condition; **ceci conditionne notre départ** our departure is dependent on *ou* is conditioned by this

conditionneur, -euse [kɔ̃disjɔnœʀ, øz] [1] NM,F (= *emballeur*) packer [2] NM [*denrées*] packaging machine; [*air*] air conditioner; (*pour cheveux*) conditioner

▾ **condoléances** [kɔ̃dɔleɑ̃s] NFPL condolences; **offrir** *ou* **faire ses ~ à qn** to offer sb one's sympathy *ou* condolences; **toutes mes ~** (please accept) all my condolences *ou* my deepest sympathy; **lettre de ~** letter of condolence

condom [kɔ̃dɔm] NM condom

condominium [kɔ̃dɔminjɔm] NM (= *souveraineté, logement*) condominium

condor [kɔ̃dɔʀ] NM condor

conductance [kɔ̃dyktɑ̃s] NF conductance

conducteur, -trice [kɔ̃dyktœʀ, tʀis] [1] ADJ (*Élec*) conductive, conducting → **fil** [2] NM,F (*Aut, Rail*) driver; [*machine*] operator; **~ d'engins** heavy plant driver; **~ d'hommes** leader; **~ de travaux** clerk of works [3] NM (*Élec*) conductor; (*TV*) continuity

conductibilité [kɔ̃dyktibilite] NF conductivity

conductible [kɔ̃dyktibl] ADJ conductive

conduction [kɔ̃dyksjɔ̃] NF (*Méd, Phys*) conduction

conductivité [kɔ̃dyktivite] NF conductivity

conduire [kɔ̃dɥiʀ] ▸ conjug 38 ◂ [1] VT [a] (= *emmener*) **~ qn quelque part** to take sb somewhere; (*en voiture*) to take *ou* drive sb somewhere; **~ un enfant à l'école/chez le médecin** to take a child to school/to the doctor; **~ la voiture au garage** to take the car to the garage; **~ les bêtes aux champs** to take *ou* drive the animals to the fields; **~ qn à la gare** (*en voiture*) to take *ou* drive sb to the station; (*à pied*) to walk *ou* see sb to the station; **il me**

---

conduisit à ma chambre he showed me *ou* took me to my room

[b] (= *guider*) to lead; **il conduisit les hommes à l'assaut** he led the men into the attack; **le guide nous conduisait** the guide was leading us; **il nous a conduits à travers Paris** he guided us through Paris

[c] (= *piloter*) [+ *véhicule*] to drive; [+ *embarcation*] to steer; [+ *avion*] to pilot; [+ *cheval*] [*cavalier*] to ride; [*cocher*] to drive; **~ un cheval par la bride** to lead a horse by the bridle

[d] (*Aut: emploi absolu*) to drive; **il conduit bien/mal** he is a good/bad driver, he drives well/badly → **permis**

[e] (= *mener*) **~ qn quelque part** [*véhicule*] to take sb somewhere; [*route, traces*] to lead *ou* take sb somewhere; [*études, événement*] to lead sb somewhere; **la sociologie ne conduit à rien** sociology doesn't lead to anything *ou* leads nowhere; **où cela va-t-il nous ~ ?** where will all this lead us?; **cela nous conduit à penser que ...** this leads us to believe that ...; **cet escalier conduit à la cave** this staircase leads (down) to the cellar; **où ce chemin conduit-il ?** where does this road lead *ou* go?; (*littér*) **~ ses pas vers** to bend one's steps towards; **ses dérèglements l'ont conduit en prison** his profligacy landed him in prison

[f] (= *diriger*) [+ *affaires*] to run, manage; [+ *travaux*] to supervise; [+ *pays*] to run, lead; [+ *négociations, enquête*] to lead, conduct; [+ *orchestre*] to conduct; [*premier violon*] to lead; **les fouilles sont conduites par P. Brunel** the excavation is being led *ou* directed by P. Brunel

[g] (= *transmettre*) [+ *chaleur, électricité*] to conduct; (= *transporter*) to carry; **un aqueduc conduit l'eau à la ville** an aqueduct carries water to the town

[2] **se conduire** VPR to behave; **il sait se ~ (en société)** he knows how to behave (in polite company); **ce ne sont pas des façons de se ~** that's no way to behave; **conduisez-vous comme il faut !** behave properly!; **il s'est mal conduit** he behaved badly

conduit [kɔ̃dɥi] [1] NM [a] (*Tech*) conduit, pipe; **~ de fumée** flue; **~ d'air** *ou* **de ventilation** ventilation shaft; **~ d'alimentation** supply pipe; **~ d'aération** air duct [b] (*Anat*) duct, canal, meatus (*SPÉC*) [2] COMP ▸ **conduit auditif** auditory canal ▸ **conduit urinaire** ureter, urinary canal

conduite [kɔ̃dɥit] [1] NF [a] (= *pilotage*) [*véhicule*] driving; [*embarcation*] steering; [*avion*] piloting; **la ~ d'un gros camion demande de l'habileté** driving a big truck takes a lot of skill; **~ accompagnée** driving as a learner accompanied by an experienced driver; **~ en état d'ivresse** drunk driving, driving while under the influence (of alcohol); **en Angleterre la ~ est à gauche** in England you drive on the left; **voiture avec ~ à gauche/à droite** left-hand-drive/right-hand-drive car; **faire un brin de ~ à qn*** to go *ou* walk part of the way with sb, walk along with sb for a bit*

[b] (= *direction*) [*affaires*] running, management; [*travaux*] supervision; [*pays*] running, leading; [*négociations, enquête*] leading, conducting; (*Littérat*) [*intrigue*] conducting; **sous la ~ de** [+ *homme politique, capitaine*] under the leadership of; [+ *guide*] accompanied by; [+ *instituteur*] under the supervision of; [+ *chef d'orchestre*] under the baton *ou* leadership of

[c] (= *comportement*) behaviour (*Brit*), behavior (*US*); (*Scol*) conduct; **avoir une ~ bizarre** to behave strangely; **quelle ~ adopter ?** what course of action shall we take?; **zéro ou no marks (*Brit*) for conduct; (*Prison*) **relâché** *ou* **libéré pour bonne ~** released for good behaviour → **acheter, écart, ligne**[1]

[d] (= *tuyau*) pipe; **~ d'eau/de gaz** water/gas main

---

[2] COMP ▸ **conduite d'échec** defeatist behaviour ▸ **conduite forcée** (*Hydro-Élec*) pressure pipeline ▸ **conduite intérieure** (*Aut*) saloon (car) (*Brit*), sedan (*US*) ▸ **conduite montante** rising main

condyle [kɔ̃dil] NM (*Anat*) condyle

cône [kon] NM (*gén, Sci*) cone; **en forme de ~** cone-shaped; **~ de déjection** alluvial cone; **~ d'ombre/de lumière** cone of shadow/light

confection [kɔ̃fɛksjɔ̃] NF [a] (= *exécution*) [*appareil, vêtement*] making; [*repas*] making, preparation, preparing; **un plat de ma ~** a dish that I made *ou* prepared myself [b] (*Habillement*) **la ~** the clothing industry; **être dans la ~** to be in the clothing business; **vêtement de ~** ready-made garment; **il achète tout en ~** he buys everything ready-to-wear *ou* off-the-peg (*Brit*) *ou* off-the-rack (*US*) → **magasin**

confectionner [kɔ̃fɛksjɔne] ▸ conjug 1 ◂ VT [+ *mets*] to prepare, make; [+ *appareil, vêtement*] to make

confectionneur, -euse [kɔ̃fɛksjɔnœʀ, øz] NM,F clothes manufacturer

confédéral, e (*mpl* **-aux**) [kɔ̃federal, o] ADJ confederal

confédération [kɔ̃federasjɔ̃] NF (*Pol*) confederation, confederacy; (= *syndicats*) confederation; **la Confédération helvétique** the Swiss Confederation

confédéré, e [kɔ̃federe] (*ptp de* **confédérer**) [1] ADJ [*nations*] confederate [2] NMPL (*Hist US*) **les Confédérés** the Confederates

confédérer [kɔ̃federe] ▸ conjug 6 ◂ VT to confederate

conférence [kɔ̃feʀɑ̃s] NF [a] (= *exposé*) (*gén*) lecture, talk; (*Univ*) lecture; **faire une ~ sur qch** to lecture on sth, give a lecture on sth → **salle, maître** [b] (= *réunion*) conference, meeting; **être en ~** to be in conference *ou* in a *ou* at a meeting; **~ au sommet** summit (meeting *ou* conference); **~ de presse** press conference [c] (= *poire*) conference pear

conférencier, -ière [kɔ̃feʀɑ̃sje, jɛʀ] NM,F speaker, lecturer

conférer [kɔ̃feʀe] ▸ conjug 6 ◂ [1] VT (= *décerner*) [+ *dignité*] to confer (**à** on); [+ *baptême, ordres sacrés*] to give; (*frm* = *donner*) [+ *prestige, autorité*] to impart (**à** to); **~ un certain sens/ aspect à qch** to endow sth with a certain meaning/look, give sth a certain meaning/ look; **ce titre lui confère un grand prestige** the title confers great prestige on him [2] VI (= *s'entretenir*) to confer (**sur** on, about)

confesse [kɔ̃fɛs] NF **être/aller à ~** to be at/go to confession

confesser [kɔ̃fese] ▸ conjug 1 ◂ [1] VT [a] (= *avouer*) [+ *péchés, erreur*] to confess; **~ que ...** to confess that ...; **~ sa foi** to confess one's faith [b] **~ qn** (*Rel*) to hear sb's confession, confess sb; (* = *faire parler qn*) to draw the truth out of sb, make sb talk; **l'abbé X confesse de 4 à 6** Father X hears confession from 4 to 6 [2] **se confesser** VPR (*Rel*) to go to confession; **se ~ à** [+ *prêtre*] to confess to, make confession to; [+ *ami*] to confess to; **se ~ de** [+ *péchés, méfait*] to confess

confesseur [kɔ̃fesœʀ] NM confessor

confession [kɔ̃fesjɔ̃] NF (= *aveu*) confession; (= *acte du prêtre*) hearing of confession; (= *religion*) denomination → **dieu**

confessionnal (*pl* **-aux**) [kɔ̃fesjɔnal, o] NM confessional

confessionnel, -elle [kɔ̃fesjɔnɛl] ADJ denominational; **école ~le** denominational *ou* sectarian school; **non ~** nondenominational, nonsectarian

confetti [kɔ̃feti] NM a piece of confetti; **des ~s** confetti (*NonC*); (*fig*) **tu peux en faire des ~s !*** [+ *contrat, chèque*] it's not worth the paper it's written on!

---

confiance [kɔ̃fjɑ̃s] NF (*en l'honnêteté de qn*) confidence, trust; (*en la valeur de qn, le succès de qch, la solidité d'un appareil*) confidence, faith (**en** in); **avoir ~ en** *ou* **dans ◊ faire ~ à** to have confidence *ou* faith in, trust; **quelqu'un en qui on peut avoir ~** someone you can rely on *ou* trust; **je l'aurai, tu peux me faire ~**! I'll get it — believe me!; **voter la ~** (*au gouvernement*) to pass a vote of confidence (in the government); **restaurer** *ou* **rétablir la ~** to restore peoples' *ou* public confidence; **il faut avoir ~** one must have confidence; **je n'ai pas ~ dans leur matériel** I have no faith *ou* confidence in their equipment; **il a toute ma ~** he has my complete trust *ou* confidence; **mettre qn en ~** to win sb's trust; **placer** *ou* **mettre sa ~ dans** to place *ou* put one's trust in; **avec ~** [*se confier*] trustingly; [*espérer*] confidently; **en (toute) ~ de ~** [*acheter*] with confidence; **de ~** [*personne, maison*] trustworthy, reliable; **c'est l'homme de ~ du ministre** he's the minister's right-hand man; **poste de ~** position of trust; **~ en soi** self-confidence; (*iro*) **la ~ rè-gne**! I can see you really trust me! → **abus, inspirer, question**

confiant, e [kɔ̃fjɑ̃, jɑ̃t] ADJ **a** (= *assuré, plein d'espoir*) confident; (*en soi-même*) (self-)confident **b** (= *sans défiance*) [*caractère, regard*] confiding

confidence [kɔ̃fidɑ̃s] NF (= *secret*) confidence, little (personal) secret; **je vais vous faire une ~** let me tell you a secret; **faire des ~s à qn** to confide in sb; **~ pour ~, je ne l'aime pas non plus** since we're speaking frankly, I don't like him either; **en ~** in confidence; **mettre qn dans la ~** to let sb into the secret; **sur le ton de la ~** in a confidential tone (of voice); **~s sur l'oreiller** pillow talk

confident [kɔ̃fidɑ̃] NM (= *personne*) confidant; (= *siège*) tête-à-tête, confidante

confidente [kɔ̃fidɑ̃t] NF confidante

confidentialité [kɔ̃fidɑ̃sjalite] NF confidentiality

confidentiel, -ielle [kɔ̃fidɑ̃sjɛl] ADJ (= *secret*) confidential; (*sur une enveloppe*) private (and confidential); (*pour public limité*) [*roman*] for a narrow readership; [*film*] for a limited audience

confidentiellement [kɔ̃fidɑ̃sjɛlmɑ̃] ADV confidentially

confier [kɔ̃fje] ▶ conjug 7 ◀ **1** VT **a** (= *dire en secret*) to confide (**à** to); **il me confie ses projets** he confides his plans to me, he tells me about his plans; **il me confie tous ses secrets** he shares all his secrets with me, he tells me all his secrets; **dans ce livre il confie ses joies et ses peines** in this book he tells of *ou* reveals his sorrows and his joys **b** (= *laisser aux soins de qn*) to entrust, confide (**à** to); **~ qn/qch aux soins de qn** to leave sb/sth in sb's care, entrust sb/sth to sb's care; **~ qn/qch à la garde de qn** to leave sb to look after sb/sth, entrust sb/sth to sb's safekeeping; **je vous confie le soin de le faire** I'll leave you to do it, I entrust you with the task of doing it **2** **se confier** VPR **a** (= *dire un secret*) **se ~ à qn** to confide in sb; **ils se confièrent l'un à l'autre leur chagrin** they confided their grief to each other **b** (*frm = se fier à*) **se ~ à** *ou* **en qn** to place o.s. in sb's hands

configuration [kɔ̃figyʀasjɔ̃] NF **a** (= *aspect général*) (general) shape, configuration; **la ~ des lieux** the layout of the premises; **suivant la ~ du terrain** following the lie of the land **b** (*Ordin*) configuration; **~ multipostes** multi-user system

configurer [kɔ̃figyʀe] ▶ conjug 1 ◀ VT (*Ordin*) to configure

confiné, e [kɔ̃fine] (*ptp de* **confiner**) ADJ **a** (= *enfermé*) **vivre ~ chez soi** to live shut away in

one's own home **b** (= *renfermé*) [*atmosphère*] enclosed; [*air*] stale

confinement [kɔ̃finmɑ̃] NM [*malade*] confining; [*déchets, site*] containment; (*Phys*) containment, confinement

confiner [kɔ̃fine] ▶ conjug 1 ◀ **1** VT (= *enfermer*) **~ qn à** *ou* **dans** to confine sb to *ou* in **2** **confiner à** VT INDIR (= *toucher à*) (*lit*) to border on, adjoin; (*fig*) to border *ou* verge on **3** **se confiner** VPR to confine o.s. (**à** to); **se ~ chez soi** to confine o.s. to the house, shut o.s. up at home

confins [kɔ̃fɛ̃] NMPL (= *frontières*) borders; (= *partie extrême*) fringes; **aux ~ de la Bretagne et de la Normandie/du rêve et de la réalité** on the borders of Brittany and Normandy/dream and reality; **aux ~ de la Bretagne/la science** at the outermost *ou* furthermost bounds of Brittany/science

confire [kɔ̃fiʀ] ▶ conjug 37 ◀ VT (*au sucre*) to preserve, candy; (*au vinaigre*) to pickle; (*dans de la graisse*) to preserve → **confit**

confirmand, e [kɔ̃fiʀmɑ̃, ɑ̃d] NM,F confirmand (*SPÉC*), confirmation candidate

▼ **confirmation** [kɔ̃fiʀmasjɔ̃] NF (*gén, Rel*) confirmation; **en ~ de** confirming, in confirmation of; **apporter ~ de** to confirm, provide confirmation of; **c'est la ~ de** it provides *ou* is confirmation of; **j'en attends ~** I'm waiting for confirmation

▼ **confirmer** [kɔ̃fiʀme] ▶ conjug 1 ◀ VT (*gén, Rel*) to confirm; **il m'a confirmé que ...** he confirmed that ...; (*dans une lettre*) **je souhaite ~ ma réservation du ...** I wish to confirm my reservation of ...; **cela l'a confirmé dans ses idées** it confirmed *ou* strengthened him in his ideas; **~ qn dans ses fonctions** to confirm sb's appointment; **la nouvelle se confirme** the news has been confirmed, there is some confirmation of the news → **exception**

confiscable [kɔ̃fiskabl] ADJ liable to confiscation *ou* seizure, confiscable

confiscation [kɔ̃fiskasjɔ̃] NF confiscation, seizure

confiserie [kɔ̃fizʀi] NF (= *magasin*) confectioner's (shop), sweetshop (*Brit*), candy store (*US*); (= *métier*) confectionery; (= *bonbons*) confectionery (*NonC*), sweets (*Brit*), candy (*NonC*) (*US*); **une ~** a sweet (*Brit*), a candy (*US*)

confiseur, -euse [kɔ̃fizœʀ, øz] NM,F confectioner

confisquer [kɔ̃fiske] ▶ conjug 1 ◀ VT (*gén, Jur*) to confiscate, seize

confit, e [kɔ̃fi, it] (*ptp de* **confire**) **1** ADJ [*fruit*] crystallized, candied; [*cornichon*] pickled; **gésiers ~s** gizzards preserved in fat; **la salade est ~e** the salad has gone soggy; (*fig*) **~ de** *ou* **en dévotion** steeped in piety **2** NM **~ d'oie/de canard** goose/duck confit

confiture [kɔ̃fityʀ] NF jam; **~ de prunes/d'abricots** plum/apricot jam; **~ d'oranges** (orange) marmalade; **~ de citrons** lemon marmalade; **faire des ~s** to make jam; **donner de la ~ aux cochons** to throw pearls before swine

confiturerie [kɔ̃fityʀʀi] NF jam factory

confiturier, -ière [kɔ̃fityʀje, jɛʀ] **1** NM,F jam *ou* preserves (*Brit*) maker **2** NM (= *pot*) jam jar

conflagration [kɔ̃flagʀasjɔ̃] NF (*frm = conflit*) cataclysm

conflictualité [kɔ̃fliktɥalite] NF conflict, conflictual situations

conflictuel, -elle [kɔ̃fliktɥɛl] ADJ [*pulsions, intérêts*] conflicting; **situation ~le** situation of conflict; **avoir des rapports ~s avec qn** to have a conflictual relationship with sb

conflit [kɔ̃fli] NM (*gén, Mil, Psych*) conflict; (*Ind* = *grève*) dispute; **pour éviter le ~** to avoid (a) conflict *ou* a clash; **entrer en ~ avec qn** to come into conflict with sb, clash with sb; **être en ~ avec qn** to be in conflict with sb; **~ d'intérêts** conflict *ou* clash of

interests; **le ~ des générations** the generation gap; **~ armé** armed conflict; **~ social ◊ ~ du travail** industrial dispute; **~s internes** infighting; (*Jur*) **~ de juridiction** jurisdictional dispute

confluence [kɔ̃flyɑ̃s] NF [*cours d'eau*] confluence, flowing together; (*fig*) mingling, merging

confluent [kɔ̃flyɑ̃] NM (*Géog*) confluence; (*fig*) **au ~ de deux cultures** at the bridge of two cultures, where two cultures meet; (*fig*) **au ~ du rêve et de la réalité** where dream meets reality

confluer [kɔ̃flye] ▶ conjug 1 ◀ VI [*cours d'eau*] to join, flow together; (*littér*) [*foule, troupes*] to converge (**vers** on); **~ avec** to flow into, join

confondant, e [kɔ̃fɔ̃dɑ̃, ɑ̃t] ADJ astounding

confondre [kɔ̃fɔ̃dʀ] ▶ conjug 41 ◀ **1** VT **a** (= *mêler*) [+ *choses, dates*] to mix up, confuse; **on confond toujours ces deux frères** people always mix up *ou* confuse the two brothers *ou* get the two brothers mixed up; **les deux sœurs se ressemblent au point qu'on les confond** the two sisters are so alike that you take *ou* mistake one for the other; **~ qch/qn avec qch/qn d'autre** to mistake sth/sb for sth/sb else; **elle a confondu sa valise avec la mienne** she mistook my suitcase for hers; **j'ai dû ~** I must have made a mistake, I must have been mistaken; **mes réserves ne sont pas de la lâcheté, il ne faudrait pas ~** my reservations aren't cowardice, let there be no mistake about that *ou* you shouldn't confuse the two
b (= *déconcerter*) to astound; **il me confondit par l'étendue de ses connaissances** he astounded me with the extent of his knowledge; **son insolence a de quoi vous ~** his insolence is astounding *ou* is enough to leave you speechless; **je suis confondu devant** *ou* **de tant d'amabilité** I'm overcome *ou* overwhelmed by such kindness; **être confondu de reconnaissance** to be overcome with gratitude
c (= *démasquer*) [+ *ennemi, menteur*] to confound
d (= *réunir, fusionner*) to join, meet; **deux rivières qui confondent leurs eaux** two rivers which flow together *ou* join; **toutes classes d'âge/dépenses confondues** all age groups/expenses taken into account; **les députés, toutes appartenances confondues** the deputies, irrespective of which party they belong to
2 **se confondre** VPR **a** (= *ne faire plus qu'un*) to merge; (= *se rejoindre*) to meet; (= *s'embrouiller*) to become confused; **les silhouettes se confondaient dans la brume** the silhouettes merged (together) in the mist; **les couleurs se confondent de loin** the colours merge in the distance; **tout se confondait dans sa mémoire** everything became confused in his memory; **nos intérêts se confondent** our interests are one and the same; **les deux fleuves se confondent à cet endroit** the two rivers flow together *ou* join here
b **se ~ en excuses** to apologize profusely; **il se confondit en remerciements** he thanked me (*ou* them *etc*) profusely *ou* effusively

conformation [kɔ̃fɔʀmasjɔ̃] NF conformation → **vice**

conforme [kɔ̃fɔʀm] ADJ **a** (= *semblable*) true (**à** to); **~ à l'original/au modèle** true to the original/pattern; **c'est ~ à l'échantillon** it matches the sample; **c'est peu ~ à ce que j'ai dit** it bears little resemblance to what I said; **ce n'est pas ~ à l'original** it does not match the original → **copie**
b (= *fidèle*) **être ~ à** [+ *norme, règle, commande*] to be in accordance with, comply with; [+ *loi*] to be in accordance *ou* conformity with; **l'exécution des travaux est ~ au plan prévu** the work is being carried out in accordance with the agreed plan; **être ~ aux normes**

de sécurité to conform to *ou* meet safety standards c (= *en harmonie avec*) **~ à** [+ *promesse*] in keeping with, consonant with (*frm*); **un niveau de vie ~ à nos moyens** a standard of living in keeping *ou* consonant with (*frm*) our means; **il a des vues ~s aux miennes** his views are in keeping with my own; **ces mesures sont ~s à notre politique** these measures are in line with our policy; **c'est ~ à ce que j'espérais** it is as I hoped

conformé, e [kɔ̃fɔʀme] (*ptp de conformer*) ADJ [*corps, enfant*] **bien/mal ~** well-/ill-formed; **bizarrement ~** strangely shaped *ou* formed

conformément [kɔ̃fɔʀmemɑ̃] ♦ **conformément à** LOC ADV a (= *en respectant*) [+ *loi*] in accordance *ou* conformity with; [+ *plan*] in accordance with, according to; **ce travail a été exécuté ~ au modèle/à l'original** this piece of work was done to conform to the pattern/original *ou* to match the pattern/original exactly b (= *suivant*) in accordance with; **~ à ce que j'avais promis/prédit** in accordance with what I had promised/predicted

conformer [kɔ̃fɔʀme] ▸conjug 1◂ 1 VT (= *calquer*) **~ qch à** to model sth on; **sa conduite à celle d'une autre personne** to model one's (own) conduct on somebody else's; **~ sa conduite à ses principes** to match one's conduct to one's principles 2 **se conformer** VPR **se ~ à** to conform to

conformisme [kɔ̃fɔʀmism] NM (*gén, Rel*) conformism

conformiste [kɔ̃fɔʀmist] ADJ, NMF (*gén, Rel*) conformist

conformité [kɔ̃fɔʀmite] NF a (= *identité*) similarity, correspondence (**à** to); **la ~ de deux choses** the similarity of *ou* between two things, the close correspondence of *ou* between two things b (= *fidélité*) faithfulness (**à** to); **~ à la règle/aux ordres reçus** compliance with the rules/orders received; **en ~ avec le plan prévu/avec les ordres reçus** in accordance *ou* conformity with the proposed plan/orders received; **en ~ avec le modèle** in accordance with the pattern; **certificat de ~** certificate of compliance c (= *harmonie*) conformity, agreement (**avec** with); **la ~ de nos vues sur la question** ◊ **notre ~ de vues sur la question** the convergence of our views on the question; **sa conduite est en ~ avec ses idées** his conduct is in keeping *ou* in conformity with his ideas

confort [kɔ̃fɔʀ] NM comfort; **villa tout ~** *ou* **avec (tout) le ~ moderne** villa with all modern conveniences *ou* mod cons (*Brit*); **il aime le ~** *ou* **son ~** he likes his creature comforts *ou* his comfort; **dès que ça dérange son ~ personnel il refuse de nous aider** as soon as it inconveniences him *ou* puts him out he refuses to help us; **pour notre ~ intellectuel** for our peace of mind; **~ psychologique** psychological well-being; **améliorer le ~ d'écoute** to improve the sound quality; **cette présentation apporte un grand ~ de lecture** this presentation makes for easy reading

confortable [kɔ̃fɔʀtabl] ADJ a (= *douillet*) [*appartement*] comfortable, cosy; [*vêtement, vie*] comfortable, comfy*; **peu ~** [*fauteuil*] rather uncomfortable; [*situation*] rather uncomfortable, awkward b (= *opulent*) [*fortune, retraite, situation, vie*] comfortable c (= *important*) [*majorité, marge*] comfortable; **il dispose d'une avance ~ sur ses rivaux** he has a comfortable lead over his rivals

confortablement [kɔ̃fɔʀtabləmɑ̃] ADV comfortably; **vivre ~** (*dans le confort*) to live in comfort; (*dans la richesse*) to live very comfortably, lead a comfortable existence

conforter [kɔ̃fɔʀte] ▸conjug 1◂ VT [+ *thèse*] to reinforce, back up; [+ *détermination*] to reinforce; **ceci me conforte dans mon analyse** this backs up *ou* reinforces my analysis

confraternel, -elle [kɔ̃fʀatɛʀnɛl] ADJ [*relations, amitié*] between colleagues

confrère [kɔ̃fʀɛʀ] NM [*profession*] colleague; [*association*] fellow member; (= *journal*) **selon notre ~ Le Monde** according to Le Monde

confrérie [kɔ̃fʀeʀi] NF brotherhood

confrontation [kɔ̃fʀɔ̃tasjɔ̃] NF a [*opinions, personnes*] confrontation; [*textes*] comparison, collation; **au cours de la ~ des témoins** when the witnesses were brought face to face b (= *conflit*) clash, confrontation

confronter [kɔ̃fʀɔ̃te] ▸conjug 1◂ VT (= *opposer*) [+ *opinions, personnes*] to confront; (= *comparer*) [+ *textes*] to compare, collate; **être confronté à** to be confronted with

confucianisme [kɔ̃fysjanism] NM Confucianism

confucianiste [kɔ̃fysjanist] 1 ADJ Confucian 2 NMF Confucian, Confucianist

Confucius [kɔ̃fysjys] NM Confucius

confus, e [kɔ̃fy, yz] ADJ a (= *peu clair*) [*bruit, texte, souvenir, mélange*] confused; [*esprit, personne, affaire*] confused, muddled b (= *honteux*) [*personne*] ashamed, embarrassed; **il était ~ d'avoir fait cela/de son erreur** he was embarrassed at having done that/about his mistake; **vous avez fait des folies, nous sommes ~!** you've been far too kind, we're quite overwhelmed!

confusément [kɔ̃fyzemɑ̃] ADV [*distinguer*] vaguely; [*comprendre, ressentir*] vaguely, in a confused way; [*parler*] unintelligibly, confusedly

confusion [kɔ̃fyzjɔ̃] NF a (= *honte*) embarrassment, confusion; **à ma grande ~** to my great embarrassment; **rouge de ~** red *ou* blushing with embarrassment b (= *erreur*) [*noms, personnes, dates*] mix-up, confusion (**de** in); **vous avez fait une ~** (*sur la personne*) you've made a mistake; (*sur des choses*) you've got things confused *ou* mixed up; **cela peut prêter à ~** this can lead to confusion c (= *désordre*) [*esprits, idées*] confusion; [*assemblée, pièce, papiers*] confusion, disorder (**de** in); **ses idées sont dans la plus grande ~** his ideas are extremely confused; **c'était dans une telle ~** it was in such confusion *ou* disorder; **mettre** *ou* **jeter la ~ dans les esprits/l'assemblée** to throw people/the audience into confusion *ou* disarray; **~ mentale** mental confusion d (*Jur*) **~ des dettes** confusion; **~ de part** *ou* **de paternité** doubt over paternity; **~ des peines** concurrency of sentences; **~ des pouvoirs** *non-separation of legislative, executive and judicial powers*

confusionnel, -elle [kɔ̃fyzjɔnɛl] ADJ (*Psych*) [*délire, état*] confusional

confusionnisme [kɔ̃fyzjɔnism] NM (*Psych*) *confused thinking of a child*; (*Pol*) *policy of spreading confusion in people's minds*

congé [kɔ̃ʒe] 1 NM a (= *vacances*) holiday (*Brit*), vacation (*US*); (= *arrêt momentané de travail*) leave (*NonC*); (*Mil* = *permission*) leave (*NonC*); **c'est son jour de ~** it's his day off; **avoir ~ le mercredi** to have Wednesdays off, be off on Wednesdays; **quel jour avez-vous ~?** which day do you have off?, which day are you off?; **j'ai pris deux semaines de ~ pour** *ou* **à Noël** I took two weeks off *ou* two weeks' leave at Christmas, I took two weeks' holiday (*Brit*) *ou* vacation (*US*) at Christmas; **il me reste trois jours de ~ à prendre** I've got three days' holiday (*Brit*) *ou* vacation (*US*) still to come; **~ sans solde** unpaid leave b **en ~** [*écolier*] on holiday (*Brit*) *ou* vacation (*US*); [*salarié*] on holiday (*Brit*) *ou* vacation (*US*), on leave; [*soldat*] on leave; (*fig*) **se mettre en ~ de son parti** to leave the party temporarily c (= *avis de départ*) notice; (= *renvoi*) notice

(to quit *ou* leave); **mon locataire m'a donné son ~** my tenant gave me notice that he was leaving; **donner (son) ~ à un locataire/employé** to give a tenant/an employee (his) notice; **donner ~ huit jours à l'avance** to give a week's notice; **il a demandé son ~** he has asked to leave d (= *adieu*) **prendre ~** to take one's leave (**de qn** of sb); **donner ~ à qn** (*en fin d'un entretien*) to dismiss sb e (*Admin* = *autorisation*) clearance certificate; [*transports d'alcool*] release (*of alcohol from bond*); **~ (de navigation)** clearance

2 COMP ► **congé annuel** annual holiday (*Brit*) *ou* vacation (*US*) *ou* leave ► **congé pour convenance personnelle** ≈ compassionate leave ► **congé de conversion** retraining period ► **congé (individuel) de formation** (personal) training leave ► **congé de longue durée** extended *ou* prolonged leave of absence ► **congé (de) maladie** sick leave; ► **de longue maladie** prolonged *ou* extended sick leave ► **congé (de) maternité** maternity leave ► **congé parental (d'éducation)** (unpaid) extended maternity *ou* paternity leave ► **les congés payés** (= *vacances*) (annual) paid holidays (*Brit*) *ou* vacation (*US*) *ou* leave; (*péj* = *vacanciers*) riff-raff (*péj*) on holiday (*Brit*) *ou* on vacation (*US*) ► **congés scolaires** school holidays (*Brit*) *ou* vacation (*US*) → **sabbatique**

congédier [kɔ̃ʒedje] ▸conjug 7◂ VT to dismiss

congelable [kɔ̃ʒlabl] ADJ suitable for freezing

congélateur [kɔ̃ʒelatœʀ] NM (= *meuble*) freezer, deep-freeze; (= *compartiment*) freezer compartment; **~ armoire** upright freezer; **~ bahut** chest freezer

congélation [kɔ̃ʒelasjɔ̃] NF [*eau, aliment, embryon*] freezing; [*huile*] congealing; **sac de ~** freezer bag → **point¹**

congeler [kɔ̃ʒ(ə)le] ▸conjug 5◂ 1 VT [+ *eau*] to freeze; [+ *aliments*] to (deep-)freeze; [+ *huile*] to congeal; **produits congelés** frozen foods 2 **se congeler** VPR to freeze

congénère [kɔ̃ʒenɛʀ] 1 ADJ congeneric 2 NMF (= *semblable*) fellow, fellow creature; **toi et tes ~s** you and your like *ou* kind

congénital, e (*mpl* -aux) [kɔ̃ʒenital, o] ADJ congenital; (*hum*) **elle est optimiste, c'est ~** she's a born optimist

congère [kɔ̃ʒɛʀ] NF snowdrift

congestif, -ive [kɔ̃ʒɛstif, iv] ADJ congestive

congestion [kɔ̃ʒɛstjɔ̃] NF congestion; **~ (cérébrale)** stroke; **~ (pulmonaire)** congestion of the lungs

congestionner [kɔ̃ʒɛstjɔne] ▸conjug 1◂ VT [+ *rue*] to congest; [+ *personne, visage*] to make flushed; **être congestionné** [*personne, visage*] to be flushed; [*rue*] to be congested

conglomérat [kɔ̃glɔmeʀa] NM (*Écon, Géol*) conglomerate; (*fig* = *amalgame*) conglomeration

conglomération [kɔ̃glɔmeʀasjɔ̃] NF conglomeration

conglomérer [kɔ̃glɔmeʀe] ▸conjug 6◂ VT to conglomerate

Congo [kɔ̃go] NM **le ~** (= *pays, fleuve*) the Congo; **au ~** in the Congo; **la République démocratique du ~** the Democratic Republic of Congo

congolais, e [kɔ̃gɔlɛ, ɛz] 1 ADJ Congolese 2 **Congolais(e)** NM,F Congolese 3 NM (= *gâteau*) coconut cake

congratulations [kɔ̃gʀatylasjɔ̃] NFPL († *ou hum*) congratulations

congratuler [kɔ̃gʀatyle] ▸conjug 1◂ VT († *ou hum*) to congratulate

congre [kɔ̃gʀ] NM conger (eel)

congrégation [kɔ̃gʀegasjɔ̃] NF (*Rel*) congregation; (*fig*) assembly

congrès [kɔ̃gʀɛ] NM (gén) congress; (Pol = conférence) conference; (Pol US) **le Congrès** Congress; **membre du Congrès** (gén) member of Congress; (homme) congressman; (femme) congresswoman

congressiste [kɔ̃gʀesist] NMF (gén) participant at a congress; (Pol) participant at a conference

congru, e [kɔ̃gʀy] ADJ [a] → **portion** [b] = **congruent**

congruence [kɔ̃gʀyɑ̃s] NF (Math) congruence

congruent, e [kɔ̃gʀyɑ̃, ɑ̃t] ADJ (Math) congruent

conifère [kɔnifɛʀ] NM conifer

conique [kɔnik] [1] ADJ conical; **de forme ~** cone-shaped, conical [2] NF conic (section)

conjectural, e (mpl -aux) [kɔ̃ʒɛktyʀal, o] ADJ conjectural

conjecture [kɔ̃ʒɛktyʀ] NF conjecture; **se perdre en ~s quant à qch** to lose o.s. in conjectures about sth; **nous en sommes réduits aux ~s** we can only conjecture ou guess (about this)

conjecturer [kɔ̃ʒɛktyʀe] ▶conjug 1◀ VT (frm) [+ causes, résultat] to conjecture, speculate about; **~ que ...** to conjecture ou surmise that ...

conjoint, e [kɔ̃ʒwɛ̃, wɛ̃t] [1] ADJ [démarche, action, débiteurs, legs] joint (épith); [problèmes] linked, related; **financement ~** joint financing; (Mus) **degrés ~s** conjunct degrees [2] NM,F (Admin = époux) spouse; **lui et sa ~e** he and his spouse; **le maire a félicité les ~s** the mayor congratulated the couple; **les (deux) ~s** the husband and wife; **les futurs ~s** the bride and groom to be

conjointement [kɔ̃ʒwɛ̃tmɑ̃] ADV jointly; **~ avec** together with; **la notice explicative vous sera expédiée ~ (avec l'appareil)** the explanatory leaflet will be enclosed (with the machine); (Jur) **~ et solidairement** jointly and severally

conjonctif, -ive [kɔ̃ʒɔ̃ktif, iv] [1] ADJ (Gram) conjunctive; (Anat) [tissu] connective [2] **conjonctive** NF (Anat) conjunctiva

conjonction [kɔ̃ʒɔ̃ksjɔ̃] NF [a] (Astron, Gram) conjunction; **~ de coordination/de subordination** coordinating/subordinating conjunction [b] (frm = union) union, conjunction

conjonctivite [kɔ̃ʒɔ̃ktivit] NF conjunctivitis

conjoncture [kɔ̃ʒɔ̃ktyʀ] NF (= circonstances) situation, circumstances; **dans la ~ (économique) actuelle** in the present (economic) situation ou circumstances; **crise de ~** economic crisis; **enquête de ~** study of the overall economic climate ou of the present state of the economy; **institut de ~** economic(s) research institute

conjoncturel, -elle [kɔ̃ʒɔ̃ktyʀɛl] ADJ [phénomène, reprise] linked to the present economic climate; [situation, tendance, prévisions] economic; **chômage ~** cyclical unemployment; **fluctuations ~les** current economic fluctuations

conjoncturiste [kɔ̃ʒɔ̃ktyʀist] NMF economic analyst

conjugable [kɔ̃ʒygabl] ADJ which can be conjugated

conjugaison [kɔ̃ʒygɛzɔ̃] NF (Bio, Gram) conjugation; (frm = union) union, uniting; **grâce à la ~ de nos efforts** thanks to our joint efforts

conjugal, e (mpl -aux) [kɔ̃ʒygal, o] ADJ [amour, union] conjugal; **devoir ~** conjugal duty; **vie ~e** married ou conjugal life → **domicile**

conjugalement [kɔ̃ʒygalmɑ̃] ADV **vivre ~** to live (together) as a (lawfully) married couple

conjugalité [kɔ̃ʒygalite] NF conjugality

conjugué, e [kɔ̃ʒyge] (ptp de **conjuguer**) [1] ADJ (Bot, Math) conjugate; [efforts, actions] joint, combined [2] **conjuguées** NFPL (Bot) conjugatae

conjuguer [kɔ̃ʒyge] ▶conjug 1◀ VT (Gram) to conjugate; (= combiner) to combine [2] **se conjuguer** VPR [efforts] to combine; **ce verbe se conjugue avec avoir** this verb is conjugated with avoir

conjuration [kɔ̃ʒyʀasjɔ̃] NF (= complot) conspiracy; (= rite) conjuration; **c'est une véritable ~ !** it's a conspiracy!, it's all a big plot!

conjuré, e [kɔ̃ʒyʀe] (ptp de **conjurer**) NM,F conspirator

conjurer [kɔ̃ʒyʀe] ▶conjug 1◀ [1] VT [a] (= éviter) [+ danger, échec] to avert [b] (littér = exorciser) [+ démons] to ward off, cast out; **essayer de ~ le sort** to try to ward off ill fortune [c] (= implorer) **~ qn de faire qch** to beseech ou entreat ou beg sb to do sth; **je vous en conjure** I beseech ou entreat ou beg you [d] (†† = conspirer) [+ mort, perte de qn] to plot; **~ contre qn** to plot ou conspire against sb [2] **se conjurer** VPR (= s'unir) [circonstances] to conspire; [conspirateurs] to plot, conspire (**contre** against); (frm ou hum) **vous vous êtes tous conjurés contre moi !** you're all in league against me!

connaissable [kɔnɛsabl] ADJ knowable

▼**connaissance** [kɔnɛsɑ̃s] NF [a] (= savoir) **la ~** knowledge; **la ~ intuitive/expérimentale** intuitive/experimental knowledge; **sa ~ de l'anglais** his knowledge of English; **il a une bonne ~ des affaires** he has a good ou sound knowledge of business matters; **une profonde ~ du cœur humain** a deep understanding of ou insight into the human heart; **la ~ de soi** self-knowledge [b] (= choses connues, science) **~s** knowledge; **faire étalage de ses ~s** to display one's knowledge ou learning; **approfondir/enrichir ses ~s** to deepen ou broaden/enhance one's knowledge; **avoir ou posséder des ~s en** to have some knowledge of; **c'est un garçon qui a des ~s** he's a knowledgeable fellow; **il a de bonnes/vagues ~s en anglais** he has a good command of/a smattering of English; **il a de vagues ~s en physique** he has a vague knowledge of ou a nodding acquaintance with physics [c] (= personne) acquaintance; **c'est une vieille/simple ~** he is an old/a mere acquaintance; **faire de nouvelles ~s** to make new acquaintances, meet new people [d] (= conscience, lucidité) consciousness; **être sans ~** to be unconscious; **perdre ~** to lose consciousness; **reprendre ~** to regain consciousness, come to ou round (Brit) [e] (loc) **à ma/sa/leur ~** to (the best of) my/his/their knowledge, as far as I know/he knows/they know; **pas à ma ~** not to my knowledge, not as far as I know; **venir à la ~ de qn** to come to sb's knowledge; **donner ~ de qch à qn** to inform ou notify sb of sth; **porter qch à la ~ de qn** to notify sb of sth, bring sth to sb's attention; **avoir ~ d'un fait** to be aware of a fact; **en (toute) ~ de cause** with full knowledge of the facts; **nous sommes parmi gens de ~** we are among familiar faces; **un visage de ~** a familiar face; **en pays de ~** (personnes) among familiar faces; (sujet) on familiar ground ou territory; **il avait amené quelqu'un de sa ~** he had brought along an acquaintance of his ou someone he knew; **faire ~ avec qn** ◊ **faire la ~ de qn** (rencontrer) to meet sb, make sb's acquaintance; (apprendre à connaître) to get to know sb; **(je suis) heureux de faire votre ~** (I am) pleased to meet you; **prendre ~ de** [+ lettre] to read; [+ faits] to become acquainted with, be informed of; **nous avons fait ~ à Paris** we met in Paris; **je leur ai fait faire ~** I introduced them (to each other)

connaissement [kɔnɛsmɑ̃] NM (Comm) bill of lading; **~ sans réserves** clean bill of lading

connaisseur, -euse [kɔnɛsœʀ, øz] [1] ADJ [coup d'œil, air] expert [2] NM,F connoisseur; **être ~ en vins** to be a connoisseur of wines; **il juge en ~** his opinion is that of a connoisseur

connaître [kɔnɛtʀ] ▶conjug 57◀ [1] VT [a] [+ date, nom, adresse] to know; [+ fait] to know, be acquainted with; [+ personne] (gén) to know, be acquainted with; (= rencontrer) to meet; **connaît-il la nouvelle ?** has he heard ou does he know the news?; **vous connaissez la dernière (nouvelle) ?** have you heard the latest (news)?; **connais-tu un bon restaurant ?** do you know of a good restaurant?; **~ qn de vue/nom/réputation** to know sb by sight/by name/by reputation; **chercher à ~ qn** to try to get to know sb; **apprendre à ~ qn** to get to know sb; **il l'a connu à l'université** he met ou knew him at university; **je l'ai connu enfant ou tout petit** I knew him when he was a child; (= je le vois encore) I have known him since he was a child; (hum) **si tu te conduis comme ça je ne te connais plus !** if you behave like that (I'll pretend) I'm not with you; **je ne lui connaissais pas ce chapeau/ces talents** I didn't know he had that hat/these talents; **je ne lui connais pas de défauts/d'ennemis** I'm not aware of his having any faults/enemies; **tu le connais mal** ◊ **c'est mal le ~** you're underestimating him/misjudging him [b] [+ langue, science] to know; [+ méthode, auteur, texte] to know, be acquainted with; **~ les oiseaux/les plantes** to know about birds/plants; **tu connais la mécanique/la musique ?** do you know anything ou much about engineering/music?; **~ un texte** to know a text, be familiar with a text; **il connaît son affaire** he knows what he's talking about; **elle connaît son métier** she (really) knows her job; **il en connaît un bout*** ou **un rayon*** he knows a thing or two about it*; **un poète qui connaît la vie/l'amour** a poet who knows what life/love is ou knows (about) life/love; **tu connais ce village ? — si je connais* ! j'y suis né !** do you know this village? — do I know it! I was born here!; **il ne connaît pas grand-chose à cette machine** he doesn't know (very) much about this machine; **il n'y connaît rien** he doesn't know anything ou a thing about it, he doesn't have a clue about it*; **je ne connais pas bien les coutumes du pays** I'm not really familiar with ou I'm not (very) well acquainted with ou I'm not very well up on* the customs of the country; **je connais la chanson** ou **la musique*** I've heard it all before; **il ne connaît pas sa force** he doesn't know ou realize his own strength; **il ne connaît pas son bonheur** ou **sa chance** he doesn't know how lucky he is; **il ne connaît que son devoir** duty first is his motto [c] (= éprouver) [+ faim, privations] to know, experience; [+ crise, événement] to experience; [+ humiliations] to experience, suffer, go through; **il ne connaît pas la pitié** he knows no pity; **ils ont connu des temps meilleurs** they have known ou seen better days; **nous connaissons de tristes heures** we are going through sad times; **le pays connaît une crise économique grave** the country is going through ou experiencing a serious economic crisis [d] (= avoir) [+ succès] to enjoy, have; [+ sort] to experience; **~ un échec** to fail; **sa patience ne connaît pas de bornes** his patience knows no bounds; **cette règle ne connaît qu'une exception** there is only one exception to this rule; **l'histoire de ce pays ne connaît qu'une tentative de coup d'État** in the history of this country there has only been one attempted coup [e] **faire ~** [+ idée, sentiment] to make known; [+ décision] to announce, make public; **faire ~ qn à qn** to introduce sb to sb; **cette pièce/ce traducteur l'a fait ~ en Angleterre** this play/translator brought him to the attention of the English public; **il m'a fait ~ les joies de la pêche** he introduced me to ou initiated me

▶ GRAMMAIRE ACTIVE: **connaissance** 46.2

in(to) the joys of fishing; **se faire ~** (*par le suc-cès*) to make a name for o.s., make one's name; (*aller voir qn*) to introduce o.s., make o.s. known

f (*loc*) **ça le/me connaît !*** he knows/I know all about it!; **je ne connais que lui/que ça !** do I know him/it!*, don't I know him/it!*; **une bonne tasse de café après le repas, je ne connais que ça** there's nothing like a good cup of coffee after a meal; **je ne le connais ni d'Ève ni d'Adam** I don't know him from Adam; **je te connais comme si je t'avais fait** I know you inside out

2 se connaître VPR **a** **se ~ (soi-même)** to know o.s.; **connais-toi toi-même** know thyself; (*fig*) **il ne se connaît plus** he's beside himself (*with joy or rage etc*)

b (= *se rencontrer*) to meet; **ils se sont connus en Grèce** they met *ou* became acquainted in Greece

c **s'y ~ en qch** to know (a lot) about sth, be well up on* *ou* well versed in sth; **il s'y connaît en voitures** he knows (all) about cars, he's an expert on cars; **c'est de l'or ou je ne m'y connais pas*** unless I'm very much mistaken, this is gold; **quand il s'agit d'embêter les autres, il s'y connaît !*** when it comes to annoying people he's an expert!*

3 connaître de VT INDIR (*Jur*) to take cognizance of

connard: [kɔnaʀ] NM damn fool:, wally:, bloody (*Brit*) idiot:, schmuck: (*US*)

connarde: [kɔnaʀd], **connasse:** [kɔnas] NF (silly) bitch:* *ou* cow: (*Brit*)

conne: [kɔn] NF → **con**

connecter [kɔnɛkte] ▶conjug 1◀ **1** VT (*Élec, Ordin*) to connect (**à** to, **avec** with) **2 se connecter** VPR (*Ordin*) (*à la prise*) to get connected, connect (**à** to); (*à un serveur*) to log on; **se ~ sur Internet** to log onto *ou* into the Internet

connecteur [kɔnɛktœʀ] NM (*Logique, Ling*) connective; (*Élec*) connector

Connecticut [kɔnɛktikœt] NM Connecticut

connectique [kɔnɛktik] NF (= *industrie*) connector industry; (= *connexions*) connections, wiring

connement: [kɔnmã] ADV bloody: (*Brit*) *ou* damn: stupidly; **j'ai dit ça un peu ~** it was a bit thick* *ou* stupid of me to say that

connerie: [kɔnʀi] NF **a** (*NonC*) damned *ou* bloody (*Brit*) stupidity:* **b** (= *remarque, acte*) damned *ou* bloody (*Brit*) stupid thing to say *ou* do:; (= *livre, film*) bullshit:* (*NonC*), bloody rubbish: (*Brit*) (*NonC*); **arrête de dire des ~s** stop talking bullshit:* *ou* such bloody rubbish: (*Brit*); **il a encore fait une ~** he's gone and done another damned stupid thing:; **c'est de la ~ !** that's (a load of) bullshit!:* *ou* cobblers!: (*Brit*)

connétable [kɔnetabl] NM (*Hist*) constable

connexe [kɔnɛks] ADJ (closely) related

connexion [kɔnɛksjɔ̃] NF (*gén*) link, connection; (*Élec*) connection (**entre** between, **avec** with); **le nombre d'heures de ~ sur le réseau** the number of hours people spend on the network; **temps de ~** connection time

connivence [kɔnivãs] NF connivance; **être/agir de ~ avec qn** to be/act in connivance with sb; **un sourire de ~** a smile of complicity; **ils sont de ~** they're in league with each other

connotatif, -ive [kɔ(n)nɔtatif, iv] ADJ (*Ling*) [*sens*] connotative

connotation [kɔ(n)nɔtasjɔ̃] NF connotation

connoter [kɔ(n)nɔte] ▶conjug 1◀ VT to connote, imply; (*Ling*) to connote

connu, e [kɔny] (*ptp de* **connaître**) ADJ (= *non ignoré*) [*terre, animal*] known; (= *célèbre*) [*idée, méthode, auteur, livre*] well-known (*épith*); **(bien) ~** well-known (*épith*); **très ~** very well

known, famous; **ces faits sont mal ~s** these facts are not well *ou* widely known; **il est ~ comme le loup blanc** everybody knows him; (*Stat*) **chiffres non encore ~s** figures not yet available → **ni**

conque [kɔk] NF (= *coquille*) conch; (*Anat*) concha

conquérant, e [kɔ̃keʀã, ãt] **1** ADJ [*pays, peuple*] conquering; [*ardeur*] masterful; [*air, regard*] swaggering **2** NM,F conqueror

conquérir [kɔ̃keʀiʀ] ▶conjug 21◀ VT [+ *pays, place forte, montagne*] to conquer; [+ *part de marché*] to capture; (*littér*) [+ *femme, cœur*] to conquer (*littér*), win; (*littér*) [+ *estime, respect*] to win, gain; [+ *supérieur, personnage influent, public*] to win over; **conquis à une doctrine** won over *ou* converted to a doctrine → **pays¹**

conquête [kɔ̃kɛt] NF conquest; **faire la ~ de** [+ *pays, montagne*] to conquer; [+ *femme*] to conquer (*littér*), win; [+ *supérieur, personnage influent*] to win over; **s'élancer** *ou* **partir à la ~ de** (*gén*) to set out to conquer; [+ *record*] to set out to break; (*hum*) **faire des ~s** to break a few hearts, make a few conquests

conquistador [kɔ̃kistadɔʀ] NM conquistador

consacré, e [kɔ̃sakʀe] (*ptp de* **consacrer**) ADJ **a** (= *béni*) [*hostie, église*] consecrated; [*lieu*] consecrated, hallowed **b** (= *habituel, accepté*) [*coutume*] established, accepted; [*itinéraire, visite*] traditional; [*écrivain*] established, recognized; **c'est l'expression ~e** it's the accepted way of saying it; **selon la formule ~e** as the expression goes **c** (= *destiné à*) **~ à** given over to; **talents ~s à faire le bien** talents given over to *ou* dedicated to doing good

consacrer [kɔ̃sakʀe] ▶conjug 1◀ VT **a** **~ à** (= *destiner, dédier à*) to devote to, dedicate to; (= *affecter à, utiliser pour*) to devote to, give (over) to; **~ son temps à faire qch** to devote one's time to doing sth; **~ sa vie à Dieu** to devote *ou* dedicate one's life to God; **il consacre toutes ses forces/tout son temps à son travail** he devotes all his energies/time to his work, he gives all his energies/time (over) to his work; **pouvez-vous me ~ un instant ?** can you spare me a moment?; **se ~ à une profession/à Dieu** to dedicate *ou* devote o.s. to a profession/God, give o.s. to a profession/God; **il a consacré plusieurs articles à ce sujet** he devoted several articles to this subject **b** (*Rel*) [+ *reliques, lieu*] to consecrate, hallow (*littér*); [+ *église, évêque, hostie*] to consecrate; **temple consacré à Apollon** temple dedicated to Apollo; (*littér*) **leur mort a consacré cette terre** their death has made this hallowed ground **c** (= *entériner*) [+ *coutume, droit*] to establish; [+ *abus*] to sanction; **expression consacrée par l'usage** expression sanctioned by use *ou* which has become accepted through use; **consacré par le temps** time-honoured (*épith*); **la fuite de l'ennemi consacre notre victoire** the enemy's flight makes our victory complete

consanguin, e [kɔ̃sãgɛ̃, in] **1** ADJ **frère ~** half-brother (*on the father's side*); **mariage ~** intermarriage, marriage between blood relations; **les mariages ~s sont à déconseiller** marriages between blood relations *ou* intermarrying should be discouraged **2** NM,F **les ~s** blood relations

consanguinité [kɔ̃sãg(ɥ)inite] NF (*du même père, d'ancêtre commun*) consanguinity; (= *union consanguine*) intermarrying

consciemment [kɔ̃sjamã] ADV consciously, knowingly

conscience [kɔ̃sjãs] NF **a** (= *faculté psychologique*) (*gén*) awareness, consciousness (**de** of); (*Philo, Psych*) consciousness; **~ de soi** self-awareness; **~ individuelle/collective/ nationale/de classe** individual/collective/

national/class consciousness; **~ politique/ écologique** ecological/political awareness; **avoir ~ que ...** to be aware *ou* conscious that ...; **avoir ~ de sa faiblesse/de l'importance de qch** to be aware *ou* conscious of one's own weakness/of the importance of sth; **avoir une ~ claire/aiguë de ses responsabilités** to be fully/keenly aware of one's responsibilities; **prendre ~ de qch** to become aware of sth, realize sth, awake to sth; **il prit soudain ~ d'avoir dit ce qu'il ne fallait pas** he was suddenly aware that *ou* he suddenly realized that he had said something he shouldn't have; **cela lui a donné** *ou* **fait prendre ~ de son importance** it made him aware of his importance, it made him realize how important he was; **prise de ~** awareness, realization; **il faut qu'il y ait une prise de ~ du problème** people must be made aware of the problem

b (= *éveil*) consciousness; **perdre/reprendre ~** to lose/regain consciousness

c (= *faculté morale*) conscience; **avoir la ~ tranquille/chargée** ◊ **avoir bonne/mauvaise ~** to have a clear/guilty conscience; **il n'a pas la ~ tranquille** he has a guilty *ou* an uneasy conscience, his conscience is troubling him; **j'ai ma ~ pour moi** I have a clear conscience; **avoir qch sur la ~** to have sth on one's conscience; **donner bonne ~ à qn** to ease sb's conscience; **donner mauvaise ~ à qn** to give sb a guilty *ou* bad conscience; **se donner bonne ~** to salve *ou* ease one's conscience; **agir selon sa ~** to act according to one's conscience *ou* as one's conscience dictates; **étouffer les ~s** to stifle consciences *ou* people's conscience; **en (toute) ~** in all conscience *ou* honesty; **sans ~** without conscience; **il a plusieurs morts/un mensonge sur la ~** he has several deaths/a lie on his conscience; **son déjeuner lui est resté sur la ~*** his lunch is lying heavy on his stomach → **acquit, objecteur**

d **~ (professionnelle)** conscientiousness; **faire un travail avec beaucoup de ~** to do a piece of work very conscientiously

consciencieusement [kɔ̃sjãsjøzmã] ADV conscientiously

consciencieux, -ieuse [kɔ̃sjãsjø, jøz] ADJ conscientious

conscient, e [kɔ̃sjã, ãt] **1** ADJ (= *non évanoui*) conscious; (= *lucide*) [*personne*] lucid; [*mouvement, décision*] conscious; **~ de/que** conscious *ou* aware of/that **2** NM (*Psych*) **le ~** the conscious

conscription [kɔ̃skʀipsjɔ̃] NF conscription, draft (*US*)

conscrit [kɔ̃skʀi] NM conscript, draftee (*US*)

consécration [kɔ̃sekʀasjɔ̃] NF **a** (*Rel*) [*personne*] consecration; [*temple*] consecration, dedication (**à** to) **b** [*coutume, droit, artiste*] establishment; [*abus*] sanctioning; **la ~ du temps** time's sanction; **cette exposition fut la ~ de son œuvre** this exhibition established his reputation as an artist; **ce traité fut la ~ de sa politique** this treaty was the apotheosis of his policy

consécutif, -ive [kɔ̃sekytif, iv] ADJ (= *successif*) consecutive; (= *résultant*) consequential; **pendant trois jours ~s** for three days running, for three consecutive days; **elle a eu trois succès ~s** she had three hits in a row; **sa blessure est consécutive à un accident** his injury is the result of an accident → **proposition**

consécution [kɔ̃sekysjɔ̃] NF consecution

consécutivement [kɔ̃sekytivmã] ADV consecutively; **elle eut ~ deux accidents** she had two consecutive accidents, she had two accidents in a row *ou* one after the other; **~ à** following

▼**conseil** [kɔ̃sɛj] **1** NM **a** (= *recommandation*) piece of advice, advice (*NonC*), counsel (*frm*); (= *simple suggestion*) hint; **donner des ~s à qn** to give sb some advice; **écouter/suivre le ~** *ou* **les ~s de qn** to listen to/follow sb's advice;

demander ~ à qn to ask *ou* seek sb's advice, ask sb for advice; **prendre ~ de qn** to take advice from sb; **je lui ai donné le ~ d'attendre** I advised him to wait; **un petit ~** a word *ou* a few words *ou* a bit of advice; **ne pars pas, c'est un ~ d'ami** don't go — that's (just) a friendly piece of advice; **écoutez mon ~** take my advice, listen to my advice; **un bon ~** a good *ou* sound piece of advice; **un bon ~: reposez-vous** a bit of advice: get some rest; **ne suivez pas les ~s de la colère** don't let yourself be guided by anger; **il est de bon ~** he gives good *ou* sound advice; (*frm*) **un homme de bon ~** a man of sound advice; (*Admin, Comm*) **~s à ...** advice to ...; **~s à la ménagère/ au débutant** hints *ou* tips for the housewife/ the beginner → **nuit**

[b] (= *activité professionnelle*) consultancy; **cabinet** *ou* **société de ~** consultancy *ou* consulting firm, firm of consultants; **activité de ~** consultancy

[c] (= *personne*) consultant, adviser (**en** in); **~ en brevets d'invention** patent engineer; **~ fiscal** tax consultant; **~ juridique** legal consultant *ou* adviser; **~ en communication** communications *ou* media consultant; **~ en propriété industrielle** patent lawyer *ou* attorney (*US*); **ingénieur(-)conseil** consulting engineer, engineering consultant; **avocat-/ esthéticienne-~** legal/beauty consultant

[d] (= *assemblée*) [*entreprise*] board; [*organisme politique ou professionnel*] council, committee; (= *séance*) meeting; **tenir ~** (= *se réunir*) to hold a meeting; (= *délibérer*) to deliberate

2 COMP [*société anonyme*] **conseil d'administration** board of directors; [*hôpital, école*] board of governors ► **conseil de classe** (*Scol*) staff meeting (*to discuss the progress of individual members of a class*) ► **conseil communal** (*Belg*) ≈ local council ► **Conseil constitutionnel** Constitutional Council ► **conseil de discipline** (*Scol, Univ*) disciplinary committee ► **conseil d'établissement** (*Scol*) ≈ governing board (*Brit*), board of education (*US*) ► **Conseil économique et social** Economic and Social Council ► **Conseil d'État** Council of State ► **Conseil de l'Europe** Council of Europe ► **Conseil européen** European Council ► **conseil exécutif** executive council ► **conseil de famille** board of guardians ► **conseil général** (French) departmental council, ≈ county council (*Brit*), ≈ county commission (*US*) ► **conseil de guerre** (= *réunion*) war council; (= *tribunal*) court-martial; **passer en ~ de guerre** to be court-martialled; **faire passer qn en ~ de guerre** to court-martial sb ► **Conseil des ministres** (= *personnes*) (*en Grande-Bretagne*) Cabinet; (*en France*) (French) Cabinet, council of ministers; (= *réunion*) Cabinet meeting ► **conseil municipal** town council ► **Conseil national du patronat français** French national employers' federation, ≈ Confederation of British Industry (*Brit*) ► **Conseil œcuménique des Églises** World Council of Churches ► **le conseil de l'Ordre** [*avocats*] lawyers' governing body, ≈ the Bar Council (*Brit*), the Bar (*US*); [*médecins*] doctors' governing body, ≈ British Medical Association (*Brit*) ► **conseil des prud'hommes** industrial arbitration court, ≈ industrial tribunal ► **conseil régional** regional council ► **conseil de révision** (*Mil*) recruiting board, draft board (*US*) ► **Conseil de sécurité** Security Council ► **Conseil supérieur de l'audiovisuel** French broadcasting regulatory body, ≈ Independent Broadcasting Authority (*Brit*), ≈ Federal Communications Commission (*US*) ► **Conseil supérieur de la magistrature** French magistrates' council (*which also hears appeals*) ► **conseil de surveillance** supervisory board ► **conseil d'UFR** (*Univ*) departmental (management) committee ► **conseil d'universi-**

té university management committee, ≈ governing body (*Brit*), ≈ Board of Trustees *ou* Regents (*US*)

CONSEIL

The Conseil constitutionnel *is made up of nine appointed members and the surviving former presidents of France. It ensures that the constitution is respected in matters of legislation and during elections.*

The Conseil d'État *examines bills before they are submitted to the* Conseil des ministres. *It is also the highest administrative court in the land, dealing with legal irregularities within public bodies and at government level.*

The Conseil régional, Conseil général, Conseil municipal *and* Conseil d'arrondissement *are elected local councils, respectively at the level of the "région", the "département", the "commune" and (in Paris, Lyons and Marseilles) the "arrondissement".* → ARRONDISSEMENT ; COMMUNE ; DÉPARTEMENT ; MAIRE ; RÉGION

▼ **conseiller**[1] [kɔ̃seje] ▶ conjug 1◀ VT [a] (= *recommander*) [+ *méthode, bonne adresse*] to recommend (**à qn** to sb); **prix conseillé** recommended price; **il conseille la prudence/le silence** he recommends *ou* counsels caution/ silence; **il m'a conseillé ce médecin** he advised me to go to this doctor, he recommended this doctor to me; **~ à qn de faire qch** to advise sb to do sth; **je vous conseille vivement de ...** I strongly advise you to ...; **la peur/ prudence lui conseilla de ...** fear/prudence prompted him to ...; **il est conseillé de s'inscrire à l'avance** it is advisable to enrol in advance; **il est conseillé aux parents de ...** parents are advised to ...

[b] (= *guider*) to advise, give advice to; **~ un étudiant dans ses lectures** to advise a student in his reading; **il a été bien/mal conseillé** he has been given good/bad advice, he has been well/badly advised

conseiller[2], **-ère** [kɔ̃seje, ɛʀ] 1 NM,F [a] (= *expert*) consultant, adviser (**en** in); (= *personne d'expérience*) counsellor, adviser; **~ diplomatique/économique/technique** diplomatic/economic/technical adviser; **~ financier** financial consultant *ou* adviser; **il est ~ auprès du président** he is an adviser to the president; (*fig*) **que ta conscience soit ta conseillère** may your conscience be your guide → **colère**

[b] (*Admin, Pol* = *fonctionnaire*) council member, councillor

2 COMP ► **conseiller d'État** senior member of the Council of State ► **conseiller général** (French) departmental councillor ► **conseiller en image** image consultant ► **conseiller matrimonial** marriage guidance counsellor ► **conseiller municipal** town councillor (*Brit*), city council man (*US*) ► **conseiller d'orientation** (*Scol*) careers adviser (*Brit*), (school) counselor (*US*), guidance counselor (*US*) ► **conseiller pédagogique** educational adviser ► **conseiller (principal) d'éducation** year head (*Brit*), dean (*US*) ► **conseiller régional** regional councillor ► **conseiller spécial** special adviser

conseilleur, -euse [kɔ̃sejœʀ, øz] NM,F (*péj*) dispenser of advice ∎ (*PROV*) **les ~s ne sont pas les payeurs** givers of advice don't pay the price

consensuel, -elle [kɔ̃sɑ̃sɥɛl] ADJ [*programme, gouvernement, solution*] consensus (*épith*); [*volonté, point de vue, société*] consensual; [*patron*] who seeks consensus; [*accord*] consensual; **dans un esprit ~** in a spirit of consensus

consensus [kɔ̃sɛsys] NM consensus (of opinion); **~ politique/social/national** political/ social/national consensus; **cette évolution fait l'objet d'un très large ~** there is a broad

consensus on this development; (*hum, péj*) **~ mou** loose consensus

consentant, e [kɔ̃sɑ̃tɑ̃, ɑ̃t] ADJ [*partenaire sexuel, otage, victime*] willing; (*Jur*) [*personnes, parties*] in agreement, agreeable; **(entre) adultes ~s** (between) consenting adults; **ce mariage ne peut avoir lieu que si les parents sont ~s** this marriage can only take place with the parents' consent *ou* if the parents consent to it

consentement [kɔ̃sɑ̃tmɑ̃] NM consent; **divorce par ~ mutuel** divorce by mutual consent; **donner son ~ à qch** to consent to sth, give one's consent to sth; (*littér*) **le ~ universel** universal *ou* common assent

▼ **consentir** [kɔ̃sɑ̃tiʀ] ▶ conjug 16◀ 1 VI (= *accepter*) to agree, consent (**à** to); **~ à faire qch** to agree to do(ing) sth; **je consens à ce qu'il vienne** I consent *ou* agree to his coming; **espérons qu'il va (y)** — let's hope he'll agree *ou* consent to it → **mot** 2 VT (= *accorder*) [+ *permission, délai, prêt*] to grant (**à** to)

conséquemment [kɔ̃sekamɑ̃] ADV (*littér* = *donc*) consequently; († *ou littér* = *avec cohérence*) consequentially; **~ à** as a result of

conséquence [kɔ̃sekɑ̃s] NF [a] (= *effet, résultat*) outcome (*NonC*), consequence; **cela pourrait avoir ou entraîner des ~s graves pour ...** this could have serious consequences for *ou* repercussions on ...; **cela a eu pour ~ de l'obliger à réfléchir** the result *ou* consequence of this was that he was forced to think again, he was forced to think again as a result; **accepter/subir les ~s de ses actions** to accept/suffer the consequences of one's actions; **c'est une erreur grosse ou lourde de ~s** this mistake will have serious consequences *ou* repercussions; **avoir d'heureuses ~s** to have a happy outcome

[b] (*Philo* = *suite logique*) consequence → **proposition, voie**

[c] (= *conclusion, déduction*) inference, conclusion (**de** to be drawn from); **tirer les ~s to** draw conclusions *ou* inferences (**de** from)

[d] (*loc*) **de ~** [*affaire, personne*] of (some) consequence *ou* importance; **en ~** (= *donc*) consequently; (= *comme il convient*) accordingly; **en ~ de** (= *par suite de*) in consequence of, as a result of; (= *selon*) according to; **sans ~** (= *sans suite fâcheuse*) without repercussions; (= *sans importance*) of no consequence *ou* importance; **cela ne tire ou ne porte ou ne prête pas à ~** (= *sans importance*) it's of no consequence; (= *sans suites fâcheuses*) it's unlikely there will be any repercussions

▼ **conséquent, e** [kɔ̃sekɑ̃, ɑ̃t] 1 ADJ [a] (= *logique*) logical, rational; (= *doué d'esprit de suite*) consistent; (*littér*) **à** consistent with, in keeping *ou* conformity with; **être ~ avec soi-même** to be consistent; **~ dans ses actions** consistent in one's actions [b] (* = *important*) sizeable [c] (*Géol*) [*rivière, percée*] consequent [d] (*Mus*) **partie ~e** answer 2 NM (*Ling, Logique, Math*) consequent; **par ~** consequently, therefore 3 **conséquente** NF (*Mus*) answer

conservateur, -trice [kɔ̃sɛʀvatœʀ, tʀis] 1 ADJ (*gén*) conservative; (*Pol Brit*) Conservative, Tory; (*Can*) **le parti ~** the Progressive-Conservative Party (*Can*) 2 NM,F [a] (= *gardien*) [*musée*] curator; [*bibliothèque*] librarian; **~ des eaux et forêts** ≈ forestry commissioner; **~ des hypothèques** ≈ land registrar [b] (*Pol*) conservative; (*Pol Brit*) Conservative, Tory; (*Can*) Conservative (*Can*) 3 NM (= *produit chimique*) preservative; (= *réfrigérateur*) freezer compartment

conservation [kɔ̃sɛʀvasjɔ̃] NF [a] (= *action*) [*aliments*] preserving; [*monuments*] preserving, preservation; [*archives*] keeping; [*accent, souplesse*] retention, retaining, keeping; [*habitudes*] keeping up; **date limite de ~** (*gén*) use-by date; [*aliments*] best-before date → **instinct,**

long [b] (= état) [aliments, monuments] preservation; **en bon état de ~** [fruits] well-preserved; [monument] well-preserved, in a good state of preservation [c] (Admin = charge) **~ des eaux et forêts** ≈ Forestry Commission; **~ des hypothèques** ≈ Land Registry

conservatisme [kɔ̃sɛʀvatism] NM conservatism

conservatoire [kɔ̃sɛʀvatwaʀ] [1] ADJ (Jur) protective → **saisie** [2] NM school, academy (of music, drama etc); **le Conservatoire (de musique et de déclamation)** the (Paris) Conservatoire; **le Conservatoire national des arts et métiers** national school of engineering and technology

conserve [kɔ̃sɛʀv] [1] NF **les ~s** (en boîtes) canned ou tinned (Brit) food(s); (en bocaux) preserves; **~s de viande/poisson** canned ou tinned (Brit) meat/fish; **l'industrie de la ~** the canning industry; **mettre en ~** to can; **se nourrir de ~s** to live out of cans ou tins (Brit); **faire des ~s de haricots** to bottle beans; (fig) **tu ne vas pas en faire des ~s!** you're not going to hoard it away for ever! → **boîte** [2] **de conserve** LOC ADV (= ensemble) [naviguer] in convoy; [agir] in concert

conserver [kɔ̃sɛʀve] ▶conjug 1◀ [1] VT [a] (= garder dans un endroit) [+ objets, papiers] to keep; **« ~ à l'abri de la lumière »** "keep ou store away from light"; **« à ~ au froid »** "keep refrigerated" [b] (= ne pas perdre) (gén) to keep, retain; [+ usage, habitude] to keep up; [+ espoir] to retain; [+ qualité, droits] to conserve, retain; (Sport) [+ titre] to retain, hold on to; **~ son calme** to keep ou remain calm, keep cool; **ça conserve tout son sens** it retains its full meaning; **~ la vie** to conserve life; **il a conservé toute sa tête** he still has his wits about him, he's still all there*; (Naut) **~ l'allure** to maintain speed; (Naut) **~ sa position** to hold one's position; (Mil) **~ ses positions** to hold its (ou their) positions [c] (= maintenir en bon état) [+ aliments, santé, monument] to preserve; **la vie au grand air, ça conserve!** the open-air life keeps you young; **bien conservé pour son âge** well-preserved for one's age [d] (Culin) to preserve, can; (dans du vinaigre) to pickle; (en bocal) to bottle [2] **se conserver** VPR [aliments] to keep

conserverie [kɔ̃sɛʀvʀi] NF (= usine) canning factory; (= industrie) canning industry

considérable [kɔ̃sideʀabl] ADJ [somme] considerable, sizeable; [foule] sizeable; [retard] considerable; [rôle, succès, changement, risque, dégâts, tort] considerable, significant; († ou littér) [personnage, situation] eminent, important; **saisi d'une émotion ~** considerably ou deeply moved

considérablement [kɔ̃sideʀabləmã] ADV considerably; **ceci nous a ~ retardés** this delayed us considerably; **ceci a ~ modifié la situation** this has changed things considerably

considérant [kɔ̃sideʀã] NM [loi, jugement] preamble

considération [kɔ̃sideʀasjɔ̃] NF [a] (= examen) [argument, problème] consideration; **ceci mérite ~** this is worth considering ou consideration ou looking into; **prendre qch en ~** to take sth into consideration ou account; **la prise en ~ de qch** taking sth into consideration ou account [b] (= motif, aspect) consideration, issue; **n'entrons pas dans ces ~s** let's not go into these considerations; **c'est une ~ dont nous n'avons pas à nous préoccuper** it's a question ou an issue we don't need to bother ourselves with; **~s d'ordre personnel** personal considerations [c] (= remarques, observations) **~s** reflections; **il se lança dans des ~s interminables sur la crise** he launched into lengthy reflections on the crisis

▶ GRAMMAIRE ACTIVE: considérer 53.1

[d] (= respect) esteem, respect; **jouir de la ~ de tous** to enjoy everyone's esteem ou respect; **par ~ pour** out of respect ou regard for → **agréer** [e] **en ~ de** (= en raison de) **en ~ de son âge** because of ou given his age; (= par rapport à) **en ~ de ce qui aurait pu se passer** considering what could have happened; **en ~ des services rendus** for services rendered [f] **sans ~ de** [+ dangers, conséquences, prix] heedless ou regardless of; **sans ~ de personne** without taking personalities into account ou consideration

▼**considérer** [kɔ̃sideʀe] ▶conjug 6◀ VT [a] (= envisager) [+ problème, situation] to consider, think about; **il faut ~ (les) avantages et (les) inconvénients** one must consider ou take into account the advantages and disadvantages; **considère bien ceci** think about this carefully; **il ne considère que son intérêt** he only thinks about ou considers his own interests; **tout bien considéré** all things considered, taking everything into consideration ou account; **c'est à ~** (pour en tenir compte) this has to be considered ou borne in mind ou taken into account; (à étudier) this has to be gone into ou examined [b] **~ comme** (= juger) to consider (to be); (= assimiler à) to look upon as, regard as, consider (to be); **je le considère comme mon fils** I look upon him as ou regard him as my son, I consider him to be my son; **je le considère comme intelligent** I consider him intelligent, I deem him to be intelligent (frm); **il se considère comme un personnage important** he sees himself as an important person, he considers himself (to be) an important person [c] (= juger) to consider, deem (frm); **je le considère intelligent** I consider him intelligent, I deem him to be intelligent (frm); **je considère qu'il a raison** I consider that he is right; **c'est très mal considéré (d'agir ainsi)** that's not an acceptable way to act, it's very bad form (to act like that) (Brit); **considérant que ...** (gén) considering that ...; (Jur) whereas ... [d] (frm = regarder) to consider, study [e] (= respecter: gén ptp) to respect, have a high regard for; **il est très considéré** he is highly regarded ou respected, he is held in high regard ou high esteem; **métier peu considéré** profession held in low esteem ou regard; **le besoin d'être considéré** the need to have people's respect ou esteem

consignataire [kɔ̃siɲatɛʀ] NM [biens, marchandises] consignee; [navire] consignee, forwarding agent; [somme] depositary

consignation [kɔ̃siɲasjɔ̃] NF (= dépôt d'argent) deposit; (= dépôt de marchandise) consignment; **la ~ d'un emballage** charging a deposit on a container; **marchandises en ~** goods on consignment → **caisse**

consigne [kɔ̃siɲ] NF [a] (= instructions) instructions; **donner/recevoir/observer la ~** to give/get ou be given/follow instructions; **c'est la ~** those are our instructions [b] (= punition) (Mil) confinement to barracks; (Scol†) detention [c] (pour les bagages) left-luggage (office) (Brit), checkroom (US); **~ automatique** (left-luggage) lockers [d] (Comm = somme remboursable) deposit; **il y a 2 F de ~ ou une ~ de 2 F sur la bouteille** there's a 2-franc deposit ou a deposit of 2 francs on the bottle, you get 2 francs back on the bottle

consigné, e [kɔ̃siɲe] (ptp de **consigner**) ADJ (Comm) [bouteille, emballage] returnable; **non ~** non-returnable

consigner [kɔ̃siɲe] ▶conjug 1◀ VT [a] [+ fait, pensée, incident] to record; **~ qch par écrit** to put sth down in writing ou on paper [b] (= interdire de sortir à) [+ troupe] to confine to barracks; [+ élève] to give detention to, keep in (after school); (= interdire l'accès de) [+ salle, établissement] to bar entrance to; **consigné à la** caserne confined to barracks; **établissement consigné aux militaires** establishment out of bounds to troops [c] (= mettre en dépôt) [+ somme, marchandise] to deposit; [+ navire] to consign; [+ bagages] to deposit ou put in the left-luggage (office) (Brit) ou checkroom (US) [d] (= facturer provisoirement) [+ emballage, bouteille] to put a deposit on; **les bouteilles sont consignées 2 F** there is a deposit of 2 francs on the bottles; **je vous le consigne** I'm giving it to you on a deposit

consistance [kɔ̃sistãs] NF [sauce, neige, terre] consistency; [caractère] strength; **~ sirupeuse/élastique** syrupy/elastic consistency; **manquer de ~** [sauce] to lack consistency; [idée, personnage, texte, film] to lack substance; [rumeur] to be unsupported by evidence; **donner de la ~ à** [+ pâte] to give body to; [+ rumeur] to give strength to; [+ idée, théorie] to give substance to; **prendre ~** [liquide] to thicken; [idée, projet, texte, personnage] to take shape; **sans ~** [caractère] spineless, colourless; [rumeur] ill-founded, groundless; [substance] lacking in consistency (attrib); **cette rumeur prend de la ~** this rumour is gaining ground

consistant, e [kɔ̃sistã, ãt] ADJ [repas] solid (épith), substantial; [nourriture] solid (épith); [mélange, peinture, sirop] thick; [argument] solid, sound

consister [kɔ̃siste] ▶conjug 1◀ VI [a] (= se composer de) **~ en** to consist of, be made up of; **le village consiste en 30 maisons et une église** the village consists of ou is made up of 30 houses and a church; **en quoi consiste votre travail ?** what does your work consist of? [b] (= résider dans) **~ dans** to consist in; **leur salut consistait dans l'arrivée immédiate de renforts** their salvation lay in the immediate arrival of reinforcements; **~ à faire** to consist in doing

consistoire [kɔ̃sistwaʀ] NM consistory

consistorial, e (mpl **-iaux**) [kɔ̃sistɔʀjal, jo] [1] ADJ consistorial, consistorian [2] NM consistorian

conso* [kɔ̃so] NF (ABRÉV = **consommation**) (= boisson) drink

consœur [kɔ̃sœʀ] NF (hum) (lady) colleague

consolable [kɔ̃sɔlabl] ADJ consolable

consolant, e [kɔ̃sɔlã, ãt] ADJ consoling, comforting

consolateur, -trice [kɔ̃sɔlatœʀ, tʀis] [1] ADJ consolatory [2] NM,F (littér) comforter

consolation [kɔ̃sɔlasjɔ̃] NF (= action) consoling, consolation; (= réconfort) consolation (NonC), comfort (NonC), solace (NonC) (littér); **nous prodiguant ses ~s** offering us comfort; **paroles de ~** words of consolation ou comfort; **elle est sa ~** she is his consolation ou comfort ou solace (littér); **il n'y a pas de dégâts, c'est une ~** there's no damage, that's one consolation; **lot ou prix de ~** consolation prize

console [kɔ̃sɔl] NF [a] (= table) console (table); (Archit) console [b] (Mus) [harpe] neck; [orgue] console; (Ordin, Tech: d'enregistrement) console; **~ de visualisation** visual display unit, VDU; **~ de mixage** mixing desk

consoler [kɔ̃sɔle] ▶conjug 1◀ [1] VT [+ personne] to console; [+ chagrin] to soothe; **ça me consolera de mes pertes** that will console me for my losses; **je ne peux pas le ~ de sa peine** I cannot console ou comfort him in his grief; **si ça peut te ~ ...** if it is of any consolation ou comfort to you ...; **le temps console** time heals [2] **se consoler** VPR to console o.s., find consolation; **se ~ d'une perte/de son échec** to be consoled for ou to get over a loss/one's failure; (hum) **il s'est vite consolé avec une autre** he soon consoled himself with another woman, he soon found comfort ou consolation with another woman; **il ne s'en consolera jamais** he'll never get over it

consolidation [kɔ̃sɔlidasjɔ̃] NF [a] (gén) [maison, table, mur] strengthening, reinforcement; (Méd) [fracture] setting [b] [accord, acquis, amitié, parti, fortune] consolidation; [monnaie] strengthening; **~ de l'unité européenne** strengthening of European unity [c] (Fin) funding; **~ de la dette** debt funding ou consolidation

consolidé, e [kɔ̃sɔlide] (ptp de **consolider**) [1] ADJ [a] (Fin) [bénéfice, bilan, chiffre d'affaires] consolidated; **dette ~e** (gén) consolidated debt; (comptabilité publique) funded debt; **rente ~e** consolidated government stock, consols [b] (Méd) **la fracture est ~e** the fracture has healed, the bone has set; **l'état du patient est ~** the patient's condition has stabilized ou is stable [2] **consolidés** NMPL (Fin) consols

consolider [kɔ̃sɔlide] ▸ conjug 1 ◂ [1] VT [a] [+ maison, table] to strengthen, reinforce; [+ mur] to reinforce; (Méd) [+ fracture] to set [b] [+ accord, amitié, parti, fortune] to consolidate; (Écon) [+ monnaie] to strengthen; **~ sa position** to consolidate one's position; **~ son avance** to extend one's lead [c] (Fin) [+ rente, emprunt] to guarantee; [+ dette] to fund, consolidate [2] **se consolider** VPR [régime, parti] to strengthen ou consolidate its position; [fracture] to set, knit; **la position de la gauche/droite s'est encore consolidée** the position of the left/right has been further consolidated ou strengthened

consommable [kɔ̃sɔmabl] [1] ADJ [solide] edible; [liquide] drinkable; **cette viande n'est ~ que bouillie** this meat can only be eaten boiled [2] NM (gén, Ordin) consumable

consommateur, -trice [kɔ̃sɔmatœʀ, tʀis] [1] NM,F (= acheteur) consumer; (= client d'un café) customer; **les plus grands** ou **gros ~s de thé** the biggest ou largest consumers of tea; **ce sont de gros ~s d'énergie/de médicaments** they consume a lot of energy/medicines; **c'est un grand ~ de romans** he reads a lot of novels; **défense/information des ~s** consumer protection/information [2] ADJ **industrie consommatrice d'énergie/de pétrole** energy-consuming/oil-consuming industry; **le premier pays ~ d'eau** the country with the highest water consumption

consommation [kɔ̃sɔmasjɔ̃] NF [a] [nourriture, gaz, matière première, essence] consumption; **faire une grande ~ de** to get through ou use a lot of; (Aut) **~ aux 100 km** (fuel) consumption per 100 km, ≈ miles per gallon, ≈ gas mileage (US); **ampoule basse ~** low-energy light bulb [b] (Écon) **la ~** consumption; **la ~ des ménages** household ou private consumption; **la ~ intérieure** domestic consumption; **~ ostentatoire** conspicuous consumption; **de ~** [biens, société] consumer (épith); **produits de ~** consumables, consumer goods; **article** ou **produit de ~ courante** ou **de grande ~** staple [c] (dans un café) (= boisson) drink; (= commande) order [d] (frm) [mariage] consummation; [ruine] confirmation; [crime] perpetration; (littér) **jusqu'à la ~ des siècles** until the end of time

consommé, e [kɔ̃sɔme] (ptp de **consommer**) [1] ADJ [habileté] consummate (épith); [écrivain, artiste] accomplished; **tableau qui témoigne d'un art ~** picture revealing consummate artistry [2] NM (Culin) consommé; **~ de poulet** chicken consommé, consommé of chicken

consommer [kɔ̃sɔme] ▸ conjug 1 ◂ VT [a] [+ nourriture] to eat, consume (frm); [+ boissons] to drink, consume (frm); **on consomme beaucoup de fruits chez nous** we eat a lot of fruit in our family; **la France est le pays où l'on consomme** ou **où il se consomme le plus de vin** France is the country where the most wine is consumed ou drunk; **il est interdit de ~ de l'alcool dans les bureaux** alcohol is not allowed ou may not be consumed in the office;

« à ~ de préférence avant le » "best before"; **« à ~ avec modération »** "to be drunk in moderation" [b] [+ combustible, matière première] to use, consume; **cette machine consomme beaucoup d'eau** this machine uses (up) a lot of water; **combien consommez-vous aux 100 km?** how much do you use per 100 km?, what's your petrol (Brit) ou gas (US) consumption?, ≈ how many miles per gallon do you get? (Brit), ≈ what's your gas mileage? (US); (Aut) **elle consomme beaucoup d'huile** it's heavy on oil, it uses a lot of oil [c] [frm = accomplir] [+ acte sexuel] to consummate; [+ crime] to perpetrate, commit; **le mariage n'a pas été consommé** the marriage has not been consummated; **cela a consommé sa ruine** this finally confirmed his downfall; **ce qui a consommé la rupture ...** what put the seal on the break-up ...; **la rupture est consommée** the break-up is complete

consomption [kɔ̃sɔpsjɔ̃] NF († ou littér = dépérissement) wasting; († = tuberculose) consumption†

consonance [kɔ̃sɔnɑ̃s] NF consonance (NonC); **nom aux ~s étrangères/douces** foreign-sounding/sweet-sounding name

consonant, e [kɔ̃sɔnɑ̃, ɑ̃t] ADJ consonant

consonantique [kɔ̃sɔnɑ̃tik] ADJ consonantal, consonant (épith); **groupe ~** consonant cluster

consonantisme [kɔ̃sɔnɑ̃tism] NM consonant system

consonne [kɔ̃sɔn] NF consonant; **~ d'appui** intrusive consonant; **~ de liaison** linking consonant

consort [kɔ̃sɔʀ] [1] ADJ → **prince** [2] NMPL (péj) **Pierre Renaud et ~s** (= acolytes) Pierre Renaud and company, Pierre Renaud and his bunch* (péj); (= pareils) Pierre Renaud and his like (péj)

consortial, e (mpl **-iaux**) [kɔ̃sɔʀsjal, jo] ADJ [prêt] syndicated

consortium [kɔ̃sɔʀsjɔm] NM consortium; **former un ~ (de prêt)** to syndicate a loan, form a loan consortium

conspirateur, -trice [kɔ̃spiʀatœʀ, tʀis] [1] ADJ conspiratorial [2] NM,F conspirer, conspirator, plotter

conspiration [kɔ̃spiʀasjɔ̃] NF conspiracy, plot; (Hist) **la Conspiration des poudres** the Gunpowder Plot

conspirer [kɔ̃spiʀe] ▸ conjug 1 ◂ [1] VI (= comploter) to conspire, plot (contre against) [2] **conspirer à** VT INDIR (= concourir à) **~ à faire qch** to conspire to do sth; **tout semblait ~ à notre succès** everything seemed to be conspiring to bring about our success [3] VT† [+ mort, ruine de qn] to conspire († ou littér), plot

conspuer [kɔ̃spɥe] ▸ conjug 1 ◂ VT to boo, shout down

constamment [kɔ̃stamɑ̃] ADV (= sans trêve) constantly, continuously; (= très souvent) constantly, continually

Constance [kɔ̃stɑ̃s] N (Géog) Constance; **le lac de ~** Lake Constance

constance [kɔ̃stɑ̃s] NF [a] (= permanence) consistency, constancy [b] (littér = persévérance, fidélité) constancy, steadfastness; **travailler avec ~** to work steadfastly; (iro) **vous avez de la ~!** you don't give up easily! [c] († = courage) fortitude, steadfastness

constant, e [kɔ̃stɑ̃, ɑ̃t] [1] ADJ [a] (= invariable) constant; (= continu) constant, continuous; (= très fréquent) constant, continual; **francs ~s** inflation-adjusted francs, constant francs [b] (littér = persévérant) [effort] steadfast; [travail] constant; **être ~ dans ses efforts** to be steadfast ou constant in one's efforts [2] **constante** NF (Math, Phys) constant; (fig = caractéristique) permanent feature; **une ~ de**

son caractère/sa politique an abiding feature of his character/policies

Constantin [kɔ̃stɑ̃tɛ̃] NM Constantine

Constantinople [kɔ̃stɑ̃tinɔpl] N Constantinople

constat [kɔ̃sta] NM [a] (= procès-verbal) **~ (d'huissier)** affidavit drawn up by a bailiff; **~ (d'accident)** (accident) report; **~ (à l')amiable** jointly-agreed statement for insurance purposes; **~ d'adultère** recording of adultery [b] (= constatation) **~ de décès** death certificate; **~ d'échec/d'impuissance** acknowledgement of failure/impotence; **je suis forcé de faire le triste ~ que ...** I regret to have to say that ...

▾**constatation** [kɔ̃statasjɔ̃] NF [a] (NonC) [fait] noting, noticing; [erreur] seeing, noticing; (frm) [effraction, état de fait, authenticité] recording; [décès] certifying [b] (= observation) observation; **~s** [enquête] findings; **c'est une simple ~ et non un reproche** it's just a statement of fact ou an observation, not a criticism; **faire une ~** to make an observation; (Police) **procéder aux ~s d'usage** to make a routine report

constater [kɔ̃state] ▸ conjug 1 ◂ VT [a] (= remarquer) [+ fait] to note, notice; [+ erreur] to see; **il constata la disparition de son carnet** he noticed ou saw that his notebook had disappeared; **je ne critique pas, je ne fais que ~** I'm not criticizing, I'm merely stating a fact; **je constate que vous n'êtes pas pressé de tenir vos promesses** I see ou notice that you aren't in a hurry to keep your promises; **vous pouvez ~ par vous-même les erreurs** you can see the mistakes for yourself [b] (frm = consigner) [+ effraction, état de fait, authenticité, dégâts] to record; [+ décès] to certify; **le médecin a constaté le décès** the doctor certified that death had taken place ou occurred

constellation [kɔ̃stelasjɔ̃] NF (Astron) constellation; (fig littér) **~ de** [+ lumières, poètes] constellation ou galaxy of

constellé, e [kɔ̃stele] (ptp de **consteller**) ADJ **~ (d'étoiles)** star-studded, star-spangled; **~ de** [+ astres, joyaux, lumières] spangled ou studded with; [+ taches] spotted ou dotted with

consteller [kɔ̃stele] ▸ conjug 1 ◂ VT **des lumières constellaient le ciel** the sky was studded with lights; **des taches constellaient le tapis** the carpet was spotted ou dotted with marks

consternant, e [kɔ̃stɛʀnɑ̃, ɑ̃t] ADJ dismaying, disquieting; **d'une bêtise ~e** incredibly stupid

consternation [kɔ̃stɛʀnasjɔ̃] NF consternation, dismay

consterner [kɔ̃stɛʀne] ▸ conjug 1 ◂ VT to dismay, fill with consternation ou dismay; **air consterné** air of consternation ou dismay

constipation [kɔ̃stipasjɔ̃] NF constipation

constipé, e [kɔ̃stipe] (ptp de **constiper**) ADJ (Méd) constipated; (péj = guindé) **avoir l'air** ou **être ~** to look stiff ou ill-at-ease

constiper [kɔ̃stipe] ▸ conjug 1 ◂ VT to constipate

constituant, e [kɔ̃stitɥɑ̃, ɑ̃t] [1] ADJ [a] [élément] constituent [b] (Pol) **assemblée ~e** constituent assembly; (Hist) **l'Assemblée ~e** the Constituent Assembly [2] NM [a] (Jur, Fin) settlor; (Gram) constituent; **~ immédiat** immediate constituent; **analyse en ~s immédiats** constituent analysis; **~ ultime** ultimate constituent [b] (Hist) **les ~s** the members of the Constituent Assembly [3] **constituante** NF [a] (au Québec) [université] branch [b] (Hist) **la Constituante** the Constituent Assembly

constitué, e [kɔ̃stitɥe] (ptp de **constituer**) ADJ [a] (Méd) **bien/mal ~** of sound/unsound constitution [b] (Pol) → **corps**

constituer [kɔ̃stitɥe] ▸ conjug 1 ◂ [1] VT [a] (= fonder) [+ comité, ministère, gouvernement, société anonyme] to set up, form; [+ bibliothèque] to build up; [+ collection] to build up, put together; [+ dossier] to make up, put together [b] (= composer) to make up, constitute, compose; **les pièces qui constituent cette collection** the pieces that (go to) make up *ou* that constitute this collection; **sa collection est surtout constituée de porcelaines** his collection is made up *ou* is composed *ou* consists mainly of pieces of porcelain [c] (= *être, représenter*) to constitute; **ceci constitue un délit/ne constitue pas un motif** that constitutes an offence/does not constitute a motive; **ceci constitue toute ma fortune** this constitutes *ou* represents my entire fortune; **ils constituent un groupe homogène** they make *ou* form a well-knit group [d] (*Jur* = *établir*) [+ *rente, pension, dot*] to settle (**à** on); **~ qn son héritier** to appoint sb one's heir

2 se constituer VPR [a] **se ~ prisonnier** to give o.s. up [b] (*Comm*) **se ~ en société** to form o.s. into a company [c] (= *amasser*) **se ~ un capital** to build (up) capital

constitutif, -ive [kɔstitytif, iv] ADJ constituent, component

constitution [kɔstitysjɔ̃] NF [a] (*NonC* = *création*) [*comité, ministère, gouvernement, société anonyme*] setting-up, forming; [*bibliothèque*] building-up; [*collection*] building-up, putting together; [*dossier*] making-up, putting together; (*Jur*) [*rente, pension, dot*] settlement, settling; [*avocat*] retaining; **~ de stocks** stockpiling [b] (= *éléments*) [*substance, ensemble, organisation*] make-up, composition; [*équipe, comité*] composition [c] (*Méd* = *santé*) constitution; **être de ~ délicate** to have a delicate constitution; **il a une robuste ~** he has a sturdy constitution [d] (*Pol*) constitution; **la Constitution française** the French constitution; **c'est contraire à la ~** it's unconstitutional, it's against the constitution

constitutionnaliser [kɔstitysjɔnalize] ▸conjug 1◂ VT to constitutionalize

constitutionnalité [kɔstitysjɔnalite] NF constitutionality

constitutionnel, -elle [kɔstitysjɔnɛl] ADJ constitutional → **droit³**

constitutionnellement [kɔstitysjɔnɛlmɑ̃] ADV constitutionally

constricteur [kɔstriktœr] ADJ M, NM (*Anat*) (**muscle**) **~** constrictor (muscle); **boa ~** boa constrictor

constrictif, -ive [kɔstriktif, iv] ADJ (*Phon*) constricted

constriction [kɔstriksjɔ̃] NF constriction

constrictor [kɔstriktɔr] ADJ M, NM (**boa**) **~** (boa) constrictor

constructeur, -trice [kɔstryktœr, tris] **1** ADJ (*Zool*) home-making (*épith*); (*fig*) [*imagination*] constructive **2** NM (= *fabricant*) manufacturer; (= *bâtisseur*) builder, constructor; **~ d'automobiles/d'ordinateurs** car/computer manufacturer; **~ de navires** shipbuilder

constructible [kɔstryktibl] ADJ **terrain ~** building land; **zone/terrain non ~** area/land *where no building is permitted*

constructif, -ive [kɔstryktif, iv] ADJ constructive

construction [kɔstryksjɔ̃] NF [a] (= *action*) [*machine, bâtiment, route, navire, chemin de fer*] building, construction; [*théorie, phrase, intrigue*] construction, building; **la ~ européenne** European construction; **la ~ de l'immeuble/du navire a pris deux ans** building the flats/ship *ou* the construction of the flats/ship took two years, it took two years to build the flats/ship; **la ~ automobile/navale/aéronautique européenne est menacée** European car/shipbuilding/aircraft industry is under threat; **ça va bien dans la ~** things are going well in the building trade (*Brit*) *ou* construction business; **entreprise de ~** construction company; **matériaux de ~** building ma-

terials; **de ~ récente** newly *ou* recently built; **de ~ française/anglaise** French/British built; **en (cours de) ~** under construction → **jeu** [b] (= *structure*) [*roman, thèse*] construction; [*phrase*] structure; **c'est une simple ~ de l'esprit** it's pure hypothesis [c] (= *édifice, bâtiment*) building, construction [d] (*Ling* = *expression, tournure*) construction, structure [e] (*Géom* = *figure*) figure, construction

constructivisme [kɔstryktivism] NM constructivism

constructiviste [kɔstryktivist] ADJ, NMF constructivist

construire [kɔstryir] ▸conjug 38◂ **1** VT [+ *machine, bâtiment, route, navire, chemin de fer*] to build, construct; [+ *figure géométrique*] to construct; [+ *théorie, phrase, intrigue*] to construct, put together; [+ *famille*] to start; **~ un couple** to build a relationship; **~ l'Europe** to build Europe; **ils font ~ à la campagne** they're having a house built in the countryside; **devoir bien construit** well-constructed essay **2 se construire** VPR **ça s'est beaucoup construit ici depuis la guerre** there's been a lot of building here since the war; **l'oiseau s'est construit un nid** the bird built itself a nest; **il s'est construit un personnage** he created a personality for himself; (*Ling*) **ça se construit avec le subjonctif** it takes the subjunctive, it takes a subjunctive construction

consubstantialité [kɔsypstɑ̃sjalite] NF consubstantiality

consubstantiation [kɔsypstɑ̃sjasjɔ̃] NF consubstantiation

consubstantiel, -elle [kɔsypstɑ̃sjɛl] ADJ consubstantial (**à, avec** with)

consul [kɔsyl] NM consul; **~ général** consul general; **~ de France** French Consul

consulaire [kɔsylɛr] ADJ consular

consulat [kɔsyla] NM [a] (= *bureaux*) consulate; (= *charge*) consulate, consulship [b] (*Hist*) **le Consulat** the Consulate

consultable [kɔsyltabl] ADJ (= *disponible*) [*ouvrage, livre*] available for consultation, which may be consulted; (= *utilisable*) **cette carte est trop grande pour être aisément ~** this map is too big to be used easily

consultant, e [kɔsyltɑ̃, ɑ̃t] **1** ADJ [*avocat*] consultant (*épith*); **médecin ~** consulting physician **2** NM,F (= *conseiller*) consultant; **~ en relations publiques** public relations consultant [b] (= *patient*) patient

consultatif, -ive [kɔsyltatif, iv] ADJ consultative, advisory; **à titre ~** in an advisory capacity

consultation [kɔsyltasjɔ̃] NF [a] (= *action*) consulting, consultation; **pour faciliter la ~ du dictionnaire/de l'horaire** to make the dictionary/timetable easier to consult; **après ~ de son agenda** having consulted his diary; **d'une ~ difficile** [*livre*] difficult to use *ou* consult; **~ électorale** (= *élection*) election; (= *référendum*) referendum; **faire une ~ électorale** to ask the electorate's opinion, go to the country (*Brit*) [b] (= *séance*: *chez le médecin, un expert*) consultation; (*Méd*) **aller à la ~** to go to the surgery (*Brit*) *ou* doctor's office (*US*); **donner une ~** to give a consultation; (*Méd*) **les heures de ~** consulting *ou* surgery (*Brit*) hours; **service (hospitalier) de ~ externe** outpatients' department [c] (= *échange de vues*) consultation; **être en ~ avec des spécialistes** to be in consultation with specialists [d] (*frm* = *avis donné*) professional advice (*NonC*)

consulter [kɔsylte] ▸conjug 1◂ **1** VT [+ *médecin, astrologue*] to consult; [+ *expert, avocat*] to consult, seek advice from; [+ *dictionnaire, documents*] to consult, refer to; [+ *base de données*] to consult; [+ *boussole, baromètre, horaire*] to look at, check; **la population a été consultée par référendum** the

people's opinion was canvassed in a referendum; (*littér*) **ne ~ que sa raison/son intérêt** to be guided only by one's reason/self-interest, look only to one's reason/self-interest **2** VI (*médecin*) (= *recevoir*) to hold surgery (*Brit*), be in (the office) (*US*); (= *conférer*) to hold a consultation **3** **se consulter** VPR (= *s'entretenir*) to confer, consult each other; **ils se consultèrent du regard** they looked questioningly at each other

consumer [kɔsyme] ▸conjug 1◂ **1** VT [a] (= *brûler*) to consume, burn; **l'incendie a tout consumé** the fire consumed *ou* wiped out everything; **des débris à demi consumés** charred debris; **une bûche se consumait dans l'âtre** a log was burning away in the hearth [b] (= *dévorer*) [*fièvre, mal*] to consume, devour; **consumé par l'ambition** consumed with *ou* devoured by ambition [c] (*littér* = *dépenser*) [+ *forces*] to expend; [+ *fortune*] to squander; **il consume sa vie en plaisirs frivoles** he fritters away his life in idle pleasures **2** **se consumer** VPR (*littér* = *dépérir*) to waste away; **se ~ de chagrin/de désespoir** to waste away with sorrow/despair; **il se consume à petit feu** he is slowly wasting away

consumérisme [kɔsymerism] NM consumerism

consumériste [kɔsymerist] ADJ, NMF consumerist

contact [kɔtakt] NM [a] (= *toucher*) touch, contact; **le ~ de deux surfaces** contact between two surfaces; (*Méd*) **ça s'attrape par (le) ~** it can be caught through contact; **le ~ de la soie est doux** silk is soft to the touch; **au point de ~ des deux lignes** at the point of contact *ou* the meeting point of the two lines → **lentille, verre** [b] (*Aut, Élec*) contact; (*Aut*) **mettre/couper le ~** to switch on/switch off the ignition; **~ électrique** electrical contact; **appuyer sur le ~** to press the contact button *ou* lever; **~!** (*Aviat*) contact!; (*auto-école*) switch on the ignition!; (*machine*) switch on!; **il y a un faux ~** there's a bad connection, there's a wire loose; **avoir un ou être en ~ radio avec qn** to be in radio contact with sb → **clé** [c] (= *rapport*) contact; **il a beaucoup de ~s (avec l'étranger)** he has got a lot of contacts *ou* connections (abroad); **notre ~ à Moscou** our contact in Moscow; **dès le premier ~, ils ...** from their first meeting, they ...; **en ~ étroit avec** in close touch *ou* contact with; **garder le ~ avec qn** to keep in touch *ou* contact with sb; **elle a besoin de ~ humain** she needs human contact; **j'ai un bon/mauvais ~ avec eux** my relations with them are good/bad, I have a good/bad relationship with them; (*dans une offre d'emploi*) **« bon ~ »** "ability to get on well with people"; **être de ~ facile/difficile** to be easy/not very easy to talk to; (*Mil*) **établir/rompre le ~** to make/break off contact (**avec** with) [d] (*loc*) **prendre ~ ◊ entrer en ~** (*Aviat, Mil, Radio*) to make contact (**avec** with); [+ *ami, clients*] to get in touch *ou* contact (**avec** with); **prise de ~** (= *première entrevue*) first meeting; (*Mil*) first contact; **perdre (le) ~** (*Aviat, Mil, Radio*) to lose contact (**avec** with); [+ *client, ami*] to lose touch *ou* contact (**avec** with); **rester/être en ~** (*Aviat, Mil, Radio*) to remain in/be in contact (**avec** with); [+ *client, ami*] to keep in/be in touch (**avec** with), remain in/be in contact (**avec** with); **se mettre en ~** to make contact with, contact; **entrer/être en ~** [*objets*] to come into/be in contact; [*fils électriques*] to make/be making contact; **mettre en ~** [+ *objets*] to bring into contact; [+ *relations d'affaires*] to put in touch; (*Aviat, Radio*) to put in contact [e] **au ~ de**: **au ~ de sa main** at the touch of his hand; **au ~ de ces jeunes gens il a acquis de l'assurance** through his contact *ou* association with these young people he has gained self-assurance; **métal qui s'oxyde au ~ de l'air/ de l'eau** metal that oxidizes on contact with air/water

▼ **contacter** [kɔ̃takte] ▸conjug 1◂ VT to contact, get in touch with

contagieux, -ieuse [kɔ̃taʒjø, jøz] ADJ [*maladie*] (*gén*) infectious, catching (*attrib*); (*par le contact*) contagious; [*personne*] infectious, contagious; [*enthousiasme, peur, rire*] infectious, contagious, catching (*attrib*); **l'isolement des ~** the isolation of contagious patients *ou* of patients with contagious diseases

contagion [kɔ̃taʒjɔ̃] NF (*Méd*) contagion, contagiousness; (*fig*) infectiousness; **être exposé à la ~** to be in danger of becoming infected; **pour éviter tout risque de ~** to avoid any risk of contagion

contagiosité [kɔ̃taʒjozite] NF contagiousness

container [kɔ̃tɛnɛʀ] NM = **conteneur**

contaminant, e [kɔ̃taminɑ̃, ɑ̃t] ADJ infectious (**pour** to)

contaminateur, -trice [kɔ̃taminatœʀ, tʀis] ① ADJ [*agent*] infectious; [*aiguille*] causing infection ② NM,F (*Méd*) contaminator

contamination [kɔ̃taminasjɔ̃] NF ⓐ (= *contagion*) [*personne*] infection, contamination; (= *pollution*) [*cours d'eau, zone*] contamination; **~ radioactive** radioactive contamination ⓑ (*littér : morale*) pollution ⓒ (*Ling*) contamination

contaminer [kɔ̃tamine] ▸conjug 1◂ VT ⓐ (= *infecter*) [+ *personne, animal*] to infect, contaminate; [+ *aliment, linge*] to contaminate; (= *polluer*) [+ *cours d'eau, zone*] to contaminate ⓑ (= *influencer*) to corrupt; **il s'est laissé ~ par le pessimisme ambiant** he gave in to the prevailing mood of pessimism

conte [kɔ̃t] NM (= *récit*) tale, story; († *ou littér = histoire mensongère*) (tall) story; (*lit, fig*) **~ de fée** fairy tale *ou* story; **~ de Noël** Christmas tale; **les ~s pour enfants** children's stories; **~s d'Andersen/de Grimm** Andersen's/Grimm's fairy tales

contemplateur, -trice [kɔ̃tɑ̃platœʀ, tʀis] NM,F contemplator

contemplatif, -ive [kɔ̃tɑ̃platif, iv] ① ADJ [*air, esprit*] contemplative, meditative; (*Rel*) [*ordre*] contemplative ② NM (*Rel*) contemplative

contemplation [kɔ̃tɑ̃plasjɔ̃] NF (= *action*) contemplation; **la ~** (*Philo*) contemplation, meditation; (*Rel*) contemplation; **rester en ~ devant qch** to stand gazing at sth

contempler [kɔ̃tɑ̃ple] ▸conjug 1◂ VT (= *regarder*) to contemplate, gaze at, gaze upon (*littér*); (= *envisager*) to contemplate, consider; **se ~ dans un miroir** to gaze at o.s. in a mirror

contemporain, e [kɔ̃tɑ̃pɔʀɛ̃, ɛn] ① ADJ ⓐ (= *de la même époque*) [*personne*] contemporary; [*événement*] contemporaneous, contemporary (**de** with) ⓑ (= *actuel*) [*problème*] contemporary, present-day (*épith*); [*art, mobilier*] contemporary ② NM contemporary (**de** of)

contemporanéité [kɔ̃tɑ̃pɔʀaneite] NF contemporaneousness

contempteur, -trice [kɔ̃tɑ̃ptœʀ, tʀis] NM,F (*littér*) denigrator

contenance [kɔ̃t(ə)nɑ̃s] NF ⓐ (= *capacité*) [*bouteille, réservoir*] capacity; [*navire*] (carrying) capacity; **avoir une ~ de 45 litres** to have a capacity of 45 litres, hold 45 litres ⓑ (= *attitude*) bearing, attitude; **~ humble/fière** humble/proud bearing; **~ gênée** embarrassed attitude; **il fumait pour se donner une ~** he was smoking to give an impression of composure *ou* to disguise his lack of composure; **faire bonne ~ (devant)** to put on a bold front (in the face of); **perdre ~** to lose one's composure

contenant [kɔ̃t(ə)nɑ̃] NM **le ~ (et le contenu)** the container (and the contents)

conteneur [kɔ̃t(ə)nœʀ] NM container

contenir [kɔ̃t(ə)niʀ] ▸conjug 22◂ ① VT ⓐ (= *avoir une capacité de*) [*récipient*] to hold, take; [*cinéma, avion, autocar*] to seat, hold ⓑ (= *renfermer*) [*récipient, livre, minerai*] to contain; **ce minerai contient beaucoup de fer** this ore contains a lot of iron *ou* has a lot of iron in it ⓒ (= *maîtriser*) [+ *surprise*] to contain; [+ *colère*] to contain, suppress; [+ *sanglots, larmes*] to contain, hold back; [+ *foule*] to contain, restrain, hold in check; [+ *inflation*] to control, curb; (*Mil*) **l'ennemi** to contain the enemy, hold the enemy in check ② **se contenir** VPR to contain o.s., control one's emotions

content, e [kɔ̃tɑ̃, ɑ̃t] ① ADJ ⓐ (= *heureux*) pleased, glad, happy; **avoir l'air ~** to look happy *ou* pleased; **je serais ~ que vous veniez** I'd be pleased *ou* glad *ou* happy if you came; **je suis ~ d'apprendre cela** I'm pleased to hear that; **il était très ~ de ce changement** he was very pleased *ou* glad about the change; **je suis très ~ ici** I'm very happy *ou* contented here; **voilà, c'est cassé, tu es ~ ?** there, it's broken, are you happy *ou* satisfied now? ⓑ **~ de** (= *satisfait de*) [+ *élève, voiture, situation*] pleased *ou* happy with; **être ~ de peu** to be content with little, be easily satisfied; **être ~ de soi** to be pleased with o.s. ⓒ **non ~ d'être/d'avoir fait ...** not content with being/with having done ... ② NM **avoir (tout) son ~ de qch** to have had one's fill of sth

contentement [kɔ̃tɑ̃tmɑ̃] NM (= *action de contenter*) satisfaction, satisfying; (= *état*) contentment, satisfaction; **éprouver un profond ~ à la vue de ...** to feel great contentment *ou* deep satisfaction at the sight of ...; **~ d'esprit** spiritual contentment; **~ de soi** self-satisfaction ■ (*PROV*) **~ passe richesse** happiness is worth more than riches

▼ **contenter** [kɔ̃tɑ̃te] ▸conjug 1◂ ① VT [+ *personne, besoin, envie, curiosité*] to satisfy; **facile à ~** easy to please, easily pleased *ou* satisfied; **cette explication l'a contenté** he was satisfied *ou* happy with this explanation, this explanation satisfied him; **il est difficile de ~ tout le monde** it's difficult to please everyone ② **se contenter** VPR **se ~ de qch/de faire qch** to content o.s. with sth/with doing sth; **se ~ de peu/de ce qu'on a** to make do *ou* be content with very little/with what one has; **il a dû se ~ d'un repas par jour/de manger les restes** he had to content himself *ou* make do with one meal a day/with eating the leftovers; **contentez-vous d'écouter/de regarder** just listen/watch; **il se contenta d'un sourire/ de sourire** he merely gave a smile/smiled

contentieux, -ieuse [kɔ̃tɑ̃sjø, jøz] ① ADJ (*Jur*) contentious ② NM (= *litige*) dispute, disagreement; (*Comm*) litigation; (= *service*) legal department; **~ administratif/commercial** administrative/commercial actions *ou* litigation

contention [kɔ̃tɑ̃sjɔ̃] NF (*Méd*) (= *procédé*) [*membre, dents*] support; (= *appareil*) brace; **de ~** [*collants, chaussettes*] support (*épith*)

contenu, e [kɔ̃t(ə)ny] (*ptp de* **contenir**) ① ADJ [*colère, sentiments*] restrained, suppressed ② NM [*récipient, dossier*] contents; [*loi, texte*] content; (*Ling*) content; **la table des matières indique le ~ du livre** the contents page shows what's in the book; **le ~ subversif de ce livre** the subversive content of this book

conter [kɔ̃te] ▸conjug 1◂ VT ⓐ (*littér*) [+ *histoire*] to recount, relate; (*hum*) **contez-nous vos malheurs** let's hear your problems, tell us all about your problems ⓑ (*loc*) **que me contez-vous là ?** what are you trying to tell me?; **il lui en a conté de belles !** he really spun him some yarns!* *ou* told him some incredible stories!; **elle ne s'en laisse pas ~** she's not easily taken in, she doesn't let herself be taken in (easily); **il ne faut pas lui en ~** don't bother trying those stories on him, it's no use trying it on with him* (*Brit*); († *ou hum*) **~**

fleurette à qn to whisper sweet nothings in sb's ear

contestable [kɔ̃tɛstabl] ADJ [*théorie, idée*] questionable, disputable; [*raisonnement*] questionable, doubtful

contestataire [kɔ̃tɛstatɛʀ] ① ADJ [*journal, étudiants, tendances*] anti-establishment ② NMF **c'est un ~** he's anti-establishment *ou* anti-authority; **les ~s ont été expulsés** the protesters were made to leave

contestateur, -trice [kɔ̃tɛstatœʀ, tʀis] ADJ contentious

contestation [kɔ̃tɛstasjɔ̃] NF ⓐ (*NonC = dénégation*) [*succession, droit, compétence, résultats*] contesting; [*légitimité, bien-fondé*] questioning, challenging; [*fait*] questioning, disputing, contesting; [*décision*] challenging, disputing, contesting ⓑ (= *objection*) dispute; **il y a matière à ~** there are grounds for contention *ou* dispute; **sans ~ possible** beyond dispute; **il n'y a aucune ~ possible** it's beyond dispute ⓒ (*gén, Pol = opposition*) **la ~** protest

conteste [kɔ̃tɛst] ◆ **sans conteste** LOC ADV unquestionably, indisputably

contester [kɔ̃tɛste] ▸conjug 1◂ ① VT (*Jur*) [+ *succession, droit, compétence*] to contest; [+ *légitimité, bien-fondé*] to question, challenge; [+ *fait*] to question, dispute, contest; [+ *décision*] to challenge, dispute, contest; **~ les résultats électoraux** to contest *ou* challenge the election results; **je ne conteste pas que vous ayez raison** I don't dispute that you're right; **je ne lui conteste pas ce droit** I don't question *ou* dispute *ou* contest his right; **ce roman/cet écrivain est très contesté** this novel/writer is very controversial ② VI (*gén*) to take issue (**sur** over); (*Pol*) to protest; **il ne conteste jamais** he never takes issue over anything; **il conteste toujours sur des points de détail** he's always taking issue over points of detail; **les jeunes ne pensent qu'à ~** all young people think about is protesting

conteur, -euse [kɔ̃tœʀ, øz] NM,F (= *écrivain*) storywriter; (= *narrateur*) storyteller

contexte [kɔ̃tɛkst] NM context; **pris hors ~** taken out of context

contextuel, -elle [kɔ̃tɛkstɥɛl] ADJ (*Ling*) contextual; (*Ordin*) [*aide en ligne*] context-sensitive

contexture [kɔ̃tɛkstyʀ] NF [*organisme*] texture; [*œuvre*] structure

contigu, -uë [kɔ̃tigy] ADJ [*maison, pièce, jardin*] adjoining, adjacent, contiguous (*frm*); [*domaines, sujets*] (closely) related; **être ~ à qch** to be adjacent *ou* next to sth

contiguïté [kɔ̃tigɥite] NF [*choses*] proximity, contiguity (*frm*); (*fig*) [*sujets*] relatedness; **la ~ de ces deux sujets** the fact that the two subjects are (closely) related

continence [kɔ̃tinɑ̃s] NF continence, continency

continent¹, e [kɔ̃tinɑ̃, ɑ̃t] ADJ continent

continent² [kɔ̃tinɑ̃] NM (*gén, Géog*) continent; (*par rapport à une île*) mainland

continental, -e (*mpl* -aux) [kɔ̃tinɑ̃tal, o] ① ADJ [*région, climat*] continental; (*opposé à côtier, insulaire*) mainland (*épith*); **petit déjeuner ~** continental breakfast ② NM,F (*gén*) mainlander; (= *Européen*) Continental

continentalité [kɔ̃tinɑ̃talite] NF continental character

contingence [kɔ̃tɛ̃ʒɑ̃s] NF ⓐ (*Philo*) contingency ⓑ **les ~s** contingencies; **il ne se soucie pas des ~s matérielles** he doesn't bother with the routine *ou* the chores of everyday life; **les ~s de la vie** the (little) chance happenings of life; **tenir compte des ~s** to take account of all contingencies *ou* eventualities

contingent, e [kɔ̃tɛ̃ʒɑ̃, ɑ̃t] ① ADJ contingent ② NM ⓐ (*Mil = groupe*) contingent; (*en France*) **le ~** the conscripts called up for national *service*, the draft (*US*) [b] (*Comm, Jur* = *quota*) quota [c] (= *part, contribution*) share

contingentement [kɔ̃tɛ̃ʒɑ̃tmɑ̃] NM **le ~ des exportations/importations** the fixing *ou* establishing of export/import quotas, the placing of quotas on exports/imports

contingenter [kɔ̃tɛ̃ʒɑ̃te] ▸conjug 1◂ VT [+ *importations, exportations*] to place *ou* fix a quota on; [+ *produits, matière première*] to distribute by a system of quotas

continu, e [kɔ̃tiny] [1] ADJ [*mouvement, série, bruit*] continuous; [*ligne, silence*] unbroken, continuous; [*effort*] continuous, unremitting; [*souffrance*] endless; (*Math*) continuous → **jet¹**, **journée** [2] NM (*Math, Philo, Phys*) continuum; (*Élec*) direct current; **utilisation en ~** continuous use; **faire qch en ~ pendant cinq heures** to do sth continuously *ou* non-stop for five hours, do sth for five hours non-stop; (*Ordin*) **papier (en) ~** continuous stationery [3] **continue** NF (*Phon*) continuant

continuateur, -trice [kɔ̃tinɥatœʀ, tʀis] NM,F (= *successeur*) successor; [*œuvre littéraire*] continuator; **les ~s de cette réforme** those who carried on (*ou* carry on *etc*) the reform

continuation [kɔ̃tinɥasjɔ̃] NF continuation; **nous comptons sur la ~ de cette entente** we count on the continuation of this agreement → **bon¹**

continuel, -elle [kɔ̃tinɥɛl] ADJ (= *continu*) continuous; (= *très fréquent*) continual, constant; **il lui fait des reproches ~s** he's always *ou* forever criticizing her

continuellement [kɔ̃tinɥɛlmɑ̃] ADV (= *sans interruption*) continuously; (= *très fréquemment*) continually, constantly; **elle se plaint ~** she's always *ou* she never stops complaining

continuer [kɔ̃tinɥe] ▸conjug 1◂ [1] VT [a] (= *poursuivre*) [+ *démarches, politique*] to continue (with), carry on with; [+ *tradition*] to continue, carry on; [+ *travaux, études*] to continue (with), carry on with, go on with; **~ son chemin** to continue on *ou* along one's way, go on one's way; **~ l'œuvre de son maître** to carry on *ou* continue the work of one's master; **Pompidou continua de Gaulle** Pompidou carried on *ou* continued where de Gaulle left off [b] (= *prolonger*) [+ *droite, route*] to continue [2] VI [a] [*bruit, spectacle, guerre*] to continue, go on; [*voyageur*] to go on, continue on one's way; **je continuerai par le saumon** I'll have the salmon to follow; **« mais » continua-t-il** "but", he went on *ou* continued; **dis-le, continue !** go on, say it!; **s'il continue, je vais ...** if he goes on *ou* keeps on *ou* continues, I'm going to ...; **si ça continue, je vais ...** if this keeps up *ou* continues, I'm going to ...; **la route (se) continue jusqu'à la gare** the road goes (on) *ou* continues as far as the station; **le chemin (se) continue par un sentier** the road turns into a path [b] **~ de** *ou* **à marcher/lire** to go on *ou* keep on *ou* continue walking/reading, continue to walk/read, walk/read on

continuité [kɔ̃tinɥite] NF [*politique, tradition*] continuation; [*action*] continuity; **la ~ de l'État** the continuity of the state; **assurer la ~ d'une politique** to ensure continuity in applying a policy, ensure the continuation of a policy → **solution**

continûment [kɔ̃tinymɑ̃] ADV continuously

continuum [kɔ̃tinɥɔm] NM continuum; **le ~ espace-temps** the space-time continuum

contondant, e [kɔ̃tɔ̃dɑ̃, ɑ̃t] ADJ [*instrument*] blunt; **arme ~e** blunt instrument

contorsion [kɔ̃tɔʀsjɔ̃] NF contortion

contorsionner (se) [kɔ̃tɔʀsjɔne] ▸conjug 1◂ VPR [*acrobate*] to contort o.s.; (*péj*) to contort o.s.; **il se contorsionnait pour essayer de se détacher** he was writhing about *ou* contorting himself in an attempt to get free

contorsionniste [kɔ̃tɔʀsjɔnist] NMF contortionist

contour [kɔ̃tuʀ] NM [a] [*objet*] outline; [*montagne, visage, corps*] outline, contour [b] **~s** [*route, rivière*] windings

contourné, e [kɔ̃tuʀne] (*ptp de* **contourner**) ADJ (*péj*) [*raisonnement, style*] tortuous; (*péj*) [*colonne, pied de table*] (over)elaborate

contournement [kɔ̃tuʀnəmɑ̃] NM [*obstacle*] bypassing; [*règle, difficulté*] circumventing, bypassing; **le ~ de la ville** driving round *ou* skirting (round) *ou* bypassing the town; **autoroute de ~** bypass

contourner [kɔ̃tuʀne] ▸conjug 1◂ VT [a] [+ *ville*] to skirt (round), bypass; [+ *montagne*] to skirt (round), walk (*ou* drive *etc*) round; [+ *mur, véhicule*] to walk (*ou* drive *etc*) round; [+ *règle, difficulté*] to circumvent, bypass, get round [b] (= *façonner*) [+ *arabesques*] to trace (out); [+ *vase*] to fashion [c] (= *déformer*) to twist, contort

contraceptif, -ive [kɔ̃tʀaseptif, iv] ADJ, NM contraceptive

contraception [kɔ̃tʀasepsjɔ̃] NF contraception; **moyens de ~** methods of contraception, contraceptive methods; **être sous ~ orale** to use oral contraception

contractant, e [kɔ̃tʀaktɑ̃, ɑ̃t] [1] ADJ (*Jur*) contracting [2] NM,F contracting party

contracté, e [kɔ̃tʀakte] (*ptp de* **contracter**) ADJ [a] (*Ling*) contracted [b] [*personne, muscle*] tense

contracter¹ [kɔ̃tʀakte] ▸conjug 1◂ [1] VT [a] (= *raidir*) [+ *muscle*] to tense, contract; (*fig*) [+ *personne*] to make tense; **la peur lui contracta la gorge** fear gripped his throat; **l'émotion lui contracta la gorge** his throat tightened with emotion; **les traits contractés par la souffrance** his features contorted with pain; **un sourire forcé contracta son visage** his face stiffened into a forced smile [b] (*Phys* = *réduire*) **~ un corps/fluide** to make a body/fluid contract [2] **se contracter** VPR [*muscle*] to tense (up), contract; [*gorge*] to tighten; [*traits, visage*] to tense (up); [*cœur*] to contract; (*fig*) [*personne*] to become tense; (*Phys*) [*corps*] to contract; [*mot, syllabe*] to be (able to be) contracted

contracter² [kɔ̃tʀakte] ▸conjug 1◂ VT [a] [+ *dette, obligation*] to contract, incur; [+ *alliance*] to contract, enter into; **~ une assurance** to take out an insurance policy; (*Admin*) **~ mariage avec** to contract (a) marriage with [b] [+ *maladie*] to contract; [+ *manie*] to acquire, contract

contractile [kɔ̃tʀaktil] ADJ contractile

contractilité [kɔ̃tʀaktilite] NF contractility

contraction [kɔ̃tʀaksjɔ̃] NF [a] (= *action*) [*corps, liquide*] contraction; [*muscle*] tensing, contraction [b] (= *état*) [*muscles, traits, visage*] tenseness [c] (= *spasme*) contraction; **elle a des ~s** [*femme enceinte*] she's having contractions [d] (*Scol*) **~ de texte** summary, précis

contractualisation [kɔ̃tʀaktɥalizasjɔ̃] NF [*accord, rapports*] formalization by contract; **une politique de ~ des universités** a policy of setting up contract-based links between universities and the state

contractualiser [kɔ̃tʀaktɥalize] ▸conjug 1◂ VT [a] [+ *personne*] to put on contract (*in a department of the public services*) [b] [+ *accord, rapports*] to formalize by contract; [+ *université*] to set up contract-based links with

contractuel, -elle [kɔ̃tʀaktɥɛl] [1] ADJ [*obligation*] contractual; [*emploi*] under contract (*attrib*); [*clause*] contract (*épith*), in the contract (*attrib*) [2] NM (**agent**) **~** (*gén*) contract worker (*in the public sector*); (*stationnement*) traffic warden (*Brit*), ≈ traffic policeman (*US*); (*sortie d'école*) ≈ lollipop man* (*Brit*), ≈ crossing guard (*US*) [3] **contractuelle** NF (*gén*) contract worker (*working for local authority*); (*stationnement*) ≈ traffic warden (*Brit*), ≈ meter maid* (*US*); (*sortie d'école*) ≈ lollipop lady* (*Brit*), ≈ crossing guard (*US*)

contractuellement [kɔ̃tʀaktɥɛlmɑ̃] ADV by contract, contractually

contracture [kɔ̃tʀaktyʀ] NF (*Archit*) contracture; (*Physiol*) spasm, (prolonged) contraction; **~ musculaire** cramp

contradicteur [kɔ̃tʀadiktœʀ] NM opponent, contradictor

contradiction [kɔ̃tʀadiksjɔ̃] NF [a] (*NonC* = *contestation*) **porter la ~ dans un débat** to introduce counter-arguments in a debate, add a dissenting voice to a debate; **je ne supporte pas la ~** I can't bear to be contradicted → **esprit** [b] (= *discordance*) contradiction, inconsistency; **texte plein de ~s** text full of contradictions *ou* inconsistencies; **le monde est plein de ~s** the world is full of contradictions; **dans les termes** contradiction in terms; **il y a ~ entre ...** there is a contradiction between ...; **être en ~ avec soi-même** to contradict o.s.; **il est en ~ avec ce qu'il a dit précédemment** he's contradicting what he said before; **leurs témoignages sont en ~** their testimonies contradict each other

contradictoire [kɔ̃tʀadiktwaʀ] ADJ [*idées, théories, récits*] contradictory, conflicting; **débat ~** debate; **réunion politique ~** political meeting with an open debate; **~ à** in contradiction to, in conflict with; (*Jur*) **arrêt/jugement ~** order/judgment given after due hearing of the parties

contradictoirement [kɔ̃tʀadiktwaʀmɑ̃] ADV (*Jur*) after due hearing of the parties

contraignant, e [kɔ̃tʀeɲɑ̃, ɑ̃t] ADJ [*horaire*] restricting, constraining; [*obligation, occupation*] restricting

contraindre [kɔ̃tʀɛ̃dʀ] ▸conjug 52◂ [1] VT **~ qn à faire qch** to force *ou* compel sb to do sth; **contraint à** *ou* **de démissionner** forced *ou* compelled to resign; **il/cela m'a contraint au silence/au repos** he/this forced *ou* compelled me to be silent/to rest; **~ par voie de justice** to constrain by law (*to pay debt*) [2] **se contraindre** VPR to restrain o.s.; **se ~ à être aimable** to force o.s. to be polite, make o.s. be polite

▼**contraint, e¹** [kɔ̃tʀɛ̃, ɛ̃t] (*ptp de* **contraindre**) ADJ [a] (= *gêné*) constrained, forced; **d'un air ~** with an air of constraint, constrainedly [b] **et forcé** under constraint *ou* duress

contrainte² [kɔ̃tʀɛ̃t] NF [a] (= *violence*) constraint; (*littér*) **vivre dans la ~** to live in bondage; **par ~** *ou* **sous la ~** under constraint *ou* duress; **empêcher qn d'agir par la ~** to prevent sb from acting by force, forcibly prevent sb from acting [b] (= *gêne*) constraint, restraint; (*Ling*) constraint; **sans ~** unrestrainedly, without restraint *ou* constraint [c] (*Jur*) **~ par corps** civil imprisonment [d] (*Phys*) stress

▼**contraire** [kɔ̃tʀɛʀ] [1] ADJ [a] (= *inverse*) [*sens, effet, mouvement*] opposite; (*Naut*) [*vent*] contrary, adverse; **dans le cas ~** otherwise → **avis** [b] (= *contradictoire*) [*opinions, propositions, intérêts*] conflicting [c] (= *nuisible*) [*forces, action*] contrary; [*destin*] adverse [d] **~ à** [+ *loi*] against; **c'est ~ à mes principes/intérêts** it is *ou* goes against my principles/interests; **~ à la santé** bad for the health, injurious *ou* prejudicial to the health (*frm*); **l'alcool m'est ~** alcohol doesn't agree with me; **le sort lui fut ~** fate was against him [2] NM [a] [*mot, concept*] opposite; **c'est le ~ de son frère** he's the opposite of his brother; **et pourtant c'est tout le ~** and yet it's just the reverse *ou* opposite; **il fait toujours le ~ de ce qu'on lui dit** he always does the opposite of what he's told; **je ne vous dis pas le ~** I'm not saying anything to the contrary, I'm not disputing *ou* denying it; **il dit/promet tout et son ~** he says/promises anything and everything

▸ GRAMMAIRE ACTIVE: **contraint** 37.1, 48.3 **contraire** 53.3

[b] **au ~** on the contrary; **je ne te reproche rien, (bien** *ou* **tout) au ~** I'm not criticising you at all, quite the reverse *ou* the opposite [c] **au ~ de** unlike; **au ~ des autres** unlike the others

contrairement [kɔ̃tRεRmɑ̃] ◆ **contrairement à** LOC ADV contrary to; (*dans une comparaison*) **~ aux autres ...** unlike the others ...

contralto [kɔ̃tRalto] NM contralto

contrapuntique [kɔ̃tRapɔ̃tik] ADJ (*Mus*) contrapuntal

contrariant, e [kɔ̃tRaRjɑ̃, jɑ̃t] ADJ [*personne*] perverse, contrary; [*incident*] tiresome, annoying, irksome

▼ **contrarier** [kɔ̃tRaRje] ▶ conjug 7 ◀ VT [a] (= *irriter*) to annoy; (= *ennuyer*) to bother; **il cherche à vous ~** he's trying to annoy you [b] (= *gêner*) [+ *projets*] to frustrate, thwart; [+ *amour*] to thwart; **~ la marche d'un bateau** to impede a ship's progress; **~ les mouvements de l'ennemi** to impede the enemy's movements; **forces qui se contrarient** forces which act against each other; **pour lui, la cuisine a été un don contrarié** his gift for cooking was never given a chance to develop [c] (= *contraster*) to alternate (for contrast) [d] [+ *gaucher*] to force to write with his (*ou* her) right hand

contrariété [kɔ̃tRaRjete] NF (= *irritation*) annoyance, vexation; **éprouver une ~** to feel annoyed *ou* vexed; **un geste de ~** a gesture of annoyance; **toutes ces ~s l'ont rendu furieux** all these annoyances *ou* vexations made him furious

contrastant, e [kɔ̃tRastɑ̃, ɑ̃t] ADJ [*couleurs, figures, effets*] contrasting (*épith*)

▼ **contraste** [kɔ̃tRast] NM (*gén, TV*) contrast; **par ~** by contrast; **faire ~ avec** to contrast with; **en ~ avec** in contrast to; **mettre en ~** to contrast

contrasté, e [kɔ̃tRaste] (*ptp de* **contraster**) ADJ [*composition, image, style*] full of contrasts; [*bilan, résultats*] uneven, mixed; **une photographie trop/pas assez ~e** a photograph with too much/not enough contrast; **couleurs très ~es** strongly contrasting colours; **les marchés ont connu des évolutions très ~es** the markets have developed in very different ways

contraster [kɔ̃tRaste] ▶ conjug 1 ◀ [1] VT [+ *éléments, caractères*] to contrast; [+ *photographie*] to give contrast to, put contrast into; **ce peintre contraste à peine son sujet** this painter hardly brings out his subject (at all) *ou* hardly makes his subject stand out [2] VI to contrast (**avec** with)

contrastif, -ive [kɔ̃tRastif, iv] ADJ (*Ling*) contrastive

contrat [kɔ̃tRa] [1] NM (= *convention, document*) contract, agreement; (*fig* = *accord, pacte*) agreement; **passer un ~ (avec qn)** to sign a contract (with sb); **être sous ~** to be under contract (**avec** to); **être employé sous ~** to be employed on contract; **établissement privé (placé) sous ~ (d'association)** ≈ grant-aided school; **réaliser** *ou* **remplir son ~** (*Bridge*) to make one's contract; (*fig, Pol*) to fulfil one's pledges; (*arg Crime*) **lancer un ~ contre qn** to take a contract out on sb → **bridge**
[2] COMP ► **contrat administratif** public service contract ► **contrat aléatoire** aleatory contract ► **contrat d'apprentissage** apprenticeship contract ► **contrat d'assurance** insurance contract ► **contrat collectif** collective agreement ► **contrat conclu dans les conditions normales du commerce** arm's length agreement ► **contrat à durée déterminée** fixed-term contract ► **contrat à durée indéterminée** permanent *ou* open-ended contract ► **contrat emploi-solidarité** government-sponsored work contract for the unemployed which includes professional training ► **contrat de garantie** guarantee, warranty ► **contrat**

de louage d'ouvrage contract for services ► **contrat de mariage** marriage contract ► **contrat de retour à l'emploi** *incentive scheme to encourage employers to hire the long-term unemployed* ► **contrat social** (*Hist, Pol*) social contract *ou* compact ► **contrat de travail** work contract ► **contrat de vente** sales contract ► **contrat verbal** verbal agreement

contravention [kɔ̃tRavɑ̃sjɔ̃] NF [a] (*Aut*) (*pour infraction au code*) fine; (*pour stationnement interdit*) (= *amende*) (parking) fine; (= *procès-verbal*) parking ticket; **dresser ~ (à qn)** (*stationnement interdit*) to issue a parking ticket (to sb); (*autres infractions*) to fine sb, book sb* (*Brit*) [b] (*Jur* = *infraction*) **~ à** contravention *ou* infraction of; **être en (état de) ~** to be contravening the law; **être en ~ à** to be in contravention of

▼ **contre** [kɔ̃tR] [1] PRÉP [a] (*contact, juxtaposition*) against; **se mettre ~ le mur** to stand against the wall; **s'appuyer ~ un arbre** to lean against a tree; **(la) face ~ terre** face downwards; **son bateau est amarré ~ le mien** his boat is moored alongside mine; **serrer qn ~ sa poitrine** *ou* **son cœur** to hug sb (to one), hug *ou* clasp sb to one's breast *ou* chest; **pousse la table ~ la fenêtre** push the table (up) against the window; **son garage est juste ~ notre maison** his garage is built onto our house; **elle se blottit ~ sa mère** she nestled *ou* cuddled up to her mother; **elle s'assit (tout) ~ lui** she sat down (right) next to *ou* beside him; **il s'est cogné la tête ~ le mur** he banged his head against *ou* on the wall; **joue ~ joue** cheek to cheek; **les voitures étaient pare-chocs ~ pare-chocs** the cars were bumper to bumper
[b] (*opposition, hostilité*) against; **se battre/voter ~ qn** to fight/vote against sb; **courir ~ la montre** to race against the clock; (*fig*) **lutter/travailler ~ la montre** to be up/work against the clock; **course** *ou* **épreuve ~ la montre** (*Sport*) race against the clock, time-trial; (*fig*) **le ~ la montre individuel/par équipe** individual/team time-trial; (*fig*) **ils sont engagés dans une course ~ la montre** they are in a race against time; (*Sport*) **Poitiers ~ Lyon** Poitiers versus Lyon; **être furieux/en colère ~ qn** to be furious/angry with sb; **jeter une pierre ~ la fenêtre** to throw a stone at the window; **agir ~ l'avis/les ordres de qn** to act against *ou* contrary to *ou* counter to sb's advice/orders; **aller/nager ~ le courant** to go/swim against the current; **acte ~ nature** unnatural act, act contrary to *ou* against nature; **je n'ai rien ~ (cela)** *ou* **là ~** (*frm*) I have nothing against it; **il a les ouvriers ~ lui** he's got the workers against him; **je suis (tout à fait) ~!** I'm (completely) against it! → **envers**[1], **gré, vent**
[c] (*défense, protection*) **s'abriter ~ le vent/la pluie** to take shelter from the wind/rain; **des comprimés ~ la grippe** flu tablets, tablets for flu; **sirop ~ la toux** cough mixture *ou* syrup; **s'assurer ~ les accidents/l'incendie** to insure (o.s.) against accidents/fire
[d] (*échange*) (in exchange) for; **échanger** *ou* **troquer qch ~** to exchange *ou* swap* sth for; **donner qch ~** to give sth (in exchange) for; **il a cédé ~ la promesse/l'assurance que ...** he agreed in return for the promise/assurance that ...
[e] (*proportion, rapport*) **il y a un étudiant qui s'intéresse ~ neuf qui bâillent** for every one interested student there are nine who are bored; **9 voix ~ 4** 9 votes to 4; **à 100 ~ 1** at 100 to 1
[f] (*loc* = *contrairement à*) **~ toute attente** *ou* **toute prévision** against all expectations, contrary to (all) expectation(s); **~ toute apparence** despite (all) appearances to the contrary; **par ~** on the other hand

[2] ADV **appuyez-vous ~** lean against *ou* on it; **laisse la porte ~*** push the door to
[3] NM [a] → **pour**
[b] (*fig* = *riposte*) counter, retort; (*Billard*) rebound; (*Sport*) (= *contre-attaque*) counterattack; (= *blocage*) block; (*Cartes*) double; (*Rugby*) **faire un ~** to charge down a kick; **l'art du ~** the art of repartee
[4] PRÉF (*le préfixe reste invariable dans les mots composés à trait d'union*) **~-** counter-, anti-

contre-accusation [kɔ̃tRakyzasjɔ̃] NF countercharge, counter-accusation

contre-alizé [kɔ̃tRalize] NM anti-trade (wind)

contre-allée [kɔ̃tRale] NF (*en ville*) service road (*Brit*), frontage road (*US*); (*dans un parc*) side path (*running parallel to the main drive*)

contre-amiral (*pl* **contre-amiraux**) [kɔ̃tRamiRal, o] NM rear admiral

contre-analyse [kɔ̃tRanaliz] NF second analysis, counter-analysis

contre-attaque [kɔ̃tRatak] NF counter-attack

contre-attaquer [kɔ̃tRatake] ▶ conjug 1 ◀ VI to counter-attack

contrebalancer [kɔ̃tRəbalɑ̃se] ▶ conjug 3 ◀ [1] VT [*poids*] to counterbalance; (*fig* = *égaler, compenser*) to offset [2] **se contrebalancer‡** VPR **je m'en contrebalance** I don't give a damn‡

contrebande [kɔ̃tRəbɑ̃d] NF (= *activité*) smuggling; (= *marchandises*) contraband, smuggled goods; **faire de la ~** to be involved in smuggling; **faire la ~ du tabac** to smuggle tobacco; **produits de ~** contraband (goods), smuggled goods

contrebandier, -ière [kɔ̃tRəbɑ̃dje, jεR] NM,F smuggler; **navire ~** smugglers' ship

contrebas [kɔ̃tRəba] ◆ **en contrebas** LOC ADV (down) below; **en ~ de** below

contrebasse [kɔ̃tRəbas] NF (= *instrument*) (double) bass; (= *musicien*) (double) bass player

contrebassiste [kɔ̃tRəbasist] NMF (double) bass player

contrebasson [kɔ̃tRəbasɔ̃] NM contrabassoon, double bassoon

contre-boutant [kɔ̃tRəbutɑ̃] NM (*en bois*) shore; (*en pierre*) buttress

contrebraquage [kɔ̃tRəbRakaʒ] NM (*en dérapage*) steering into the skid (*NonC*); **grâce à ce ~ instantané** because he immediately steered into the skid

contrebraquer [kɔ̃tRəbRake] ▶ conjug 1 ◀ VI (*en dérapant*) to steer into the skid; (*pour se garer*) to steer in the opposite direction

contrebutement [kɔ̃tRəbytmɑ̃] NM = **contre-boutant**

contrecarrer [kɔ̃tRəkaRe] ▶ conjug 1 ◀ VT [+ *projets*] to thwart, foil; † [+ *personne*] to thwart

contrechamp [kɔ̃tRəʃɑ̃] NM (*Ciné*) reverse shot

contrechant, contre-chant [kɔ̃tRəʃɑ̃] NM (*Mus*) descant, discant

contrechâssis [kɔ̃tRəʃasi] NM double (window) frame

contrechoc [kɔ̃tRəʃɔk] NM repercussions, after-effects; **~ pétrolier** impact of the oil slump

contreclef [kɔ̃tRəkle] NF stone adjoining the keystone

contrecœur[1] [kɔ̃tRəkœR] ◆ **à contrecœur** LOC ADV (be)grudgingly, reluctantly

contrecœur[2] [kɔ̃tRəkœR] NM [a] (= *fond de cheminée*) fire-back [b] (*Rail*) guardrail

contrecollé, e [kɔ̃tRəkɔle] ADJ [*cuir, laine*] foam-backed; **bois ~** plywood

contrecoup [kɔ̃tRəku] NM [a] (= *ricochet*) [*balle*] ricochet [b] (= *répercussion*) repercussions; **ce pays subit le ~ de la crise** this coun-

► GRAMMAIRE ACTIVE: **contrarier** 45.3   **contraste** 32.1   **contre** 39.2, 53.4

try is suffering from the (after-)effects of the crisis; **par ~** as an indirect consequence

contre-courant [kɔ̃tʀəkuʀɑ̃] NM [*cours d'eau*] counter-current; **à ~** (*lit*) upstream, against the current; (*fig*) against the current *ou* tide; **aller à ~ de la tendance générale** to go against the (general) trend

contre-culture [kɔ̃tʀəkyltyʀ] NF counterculture

contredanse [kɔ̃tʀədɑ̃s] NF [a]* (*gén*) fine; (*pour stationnement interdit*) (parking) ticket [b] (†† = *danse*) quadrille

contredire [kɔ̃tʀədiʀ] ▸conjug 37◂ [1] VT [*personne*] to contradict; [*faits*] to be at variance with, refute [2] **se contredire** VPR [*personne*] to contradict o.s.; [*témoins, témoignages*] to contradict each other

contredit [kɔ̃tʀədi] NM (*frm*) **sans ~** unquestionably, without question

contrée [kɔ̃tʀe] NF (*littér*) (= *pays*) land; (= *région*) region

contre-écrou (*pl* **contre-écrous**) [kɔ̃tʀekʀu] NM lock nut

contre-électromotrice [kɔ̃tʀelɛktʀɔmɔtʀis] ADJ F → **force**

contre-emploi [kɔ̃tʀɑ̃plwa] NM (*Théât*) **il joue** *ou* **est utilisé à ~** he's cast against type

contre-enquête [kɔ̃tʀɑ̃kɛt] NF counterinquiry

contre-épreuve [kɔ̃tʀepʀœv] NF (*Typo*) counter-proof; (= *vérification*) countercheck

contre-espionnage [kɔ̃tʀɛspjɔnaʒ] NM counter-espionage

contre-essai [kɔ̃tʀesɛ] NM control test, counter test

contre-étude [kɔ̃tʀetyd] NF control study

contre-exemple [kɔ̃tʀegzɑ̃pl] NM counterexample

contre-expert [kɔ̃tʀekspɛʀ] NM [*dommages*] second assessor; [*antiquité, bijou*] second valuer

contre-expertise [kɔ̃tʀekspɛʀtiz] NF [*dommages*] second assessment; [*antiquité, bijou*] second valuation

contrefaçon [kɔ̃tʀəfasɔ̃] NF [a] (*NonC = falsification*) [*argent, signature*] counterfeiting, forgery, forging; [*produits, édition*] counterfeiting; [*disques compacts*] pirating; **~ involontaire d'un brevet** innocent infringement of a patent; **poursuivre qn en ~** to take legal action against sb for counterfeiting *ou* forgery [b] (= *faux*) [*édition*] unauthorized *ou* pirated edition; [*produit*] imitation; [*disque compact*] pirate copy; [*billets, signature*] forgery, counterfeit; (*Comm*) **méfiez-vous des ~s** beware of imitations

contrefacteur [kɔ̃tʀəfaktœʀ] NM (*Jur*) forger, counterfeiter

contrefaire [kɔ̃tʀəfɛʀ] ▸conjug 60◂ VT [a] (*littér* = *imiter*) to imitate; († = *parodier*) to mimic, imitate [b] (= *déguiser*) [+ *voix, écriture*] to disguise [c] (= *falsifier*) [+ *argent, signature*] to counterfeit, forge; [+ *produits, édition*] to counterfeit; [+ *brevet*] to infringe [d] († = *feindre*) [+ *douleur, folie*] to feign [e] (= *déformer*) to distort

contrefait, e [kɔ̃tʀəfɛ, ɛt] (*ptp de* **contrefaire**) ADJ (= *difforme*) misshapen, deformed

contre-fenêtre [kɔ̃tʀəfənɛtʀ] NF inner window (*of a double window*)

contre-fer [kɔ̃tʀəfɛʀ] NM iron cap

contre-feu (*pl* **contre-feux**) [kɔ̃tʀəfø] NM (= *plaque*) fire-back; (= *feu*) backfire

contreficher (se)† [kɔ̃tʀəfiʃe] ▸conjug 1◂ VPR **je m'en contrefiche** I don't give a damn‡

contrefil, contre-fil [kɔ̃tʀəfil] NM (*Menuiserie*) **à ~** against the grain

contre-filet [kɔ̃tʀəfilɛ] NM (= *morceau*) sirloin; (= *tranche*) sirloin steak

contrefort [kɔ̃tʀəfɔʀ] NM [a] (*Archit*) [*voûte, terrasse*] buttress [b] [*chaussure*] stiffener [c] (*Géog*) [*arête*] spur; [*chaîne*] **~s** foothills

contrefoutre (se)‡ [kɔ̃tʀəfutʀ] VPR **je m'en contrefous** I don't give a damn‡

contre-fugue [kɔ̃tʀəfyg] NF counterfugue

contre-gouvernement [kɔ̃tʀəguvɛʀnəmɑ̃] NM shadow government, shadow cabinet (*surtout Brit*)

contre-haut [kɔ̃tʀəo] ◆**en contre-haut** LOC ADV above

contre-indication [kɔ̃tʀɛ̃dikasjɔ̃] NF (*Méd, Pharm*) contraindication

contre-indiquer [kɔ̃tʀɛ̃dike] ▸conjug 1◂ VT (*Méd*) to contraindicate; (*gén*) **c'est contre-indiqué** it is not recommended

contre-insurrection [kɔ̃tʀɛ̃syʀɛksjɔ̃] NF counterinsurgency

contre-interrogatoire [kɔ̃tʀɛ̃tɛʀɔgatwaʀ] NM cross-examination; **faire subir un ~ à qn** to cross-examine sb

contre-jour [kɔ̃tʀəʒuʀ] NM (= *éclairage*) backlighting (*NonC*), contre-jour (*NonC*); (*photographie*) backlit *ou* contre-jour shot; **à ~** [*se profiler, se détacher*] against the sunlight; [*photographier*] into the light; [*travailler, coudre*] with one's back to the light

contremaître [kɔ̃tʀəmɛtʀ] NM foreman

contremaîtresse [kɔ̃tʀəmɛtʀɛs] NF forewoman

contre-manifestant, e [kɔ̃tʀəmanifɛstɑ̃, ɑ̃t] NM,F counter demonstrator

contre-manifestation [kɔ̃tʀəmanifɛstasjɔ̃] NF counter demonstration

contre-manifester [kɔ̃tʀəmanifɛste] VI to hold a counter demonstration

contremarche [kɔ̃tʀəmaʀʃ] NF [a] (*Mil*) countermarch [b] [*marche d'escalier*] riser

contremarque [kɔ̃tʀəmaʀk] NF [a] (*Comm* = *marque*) countermark [b] (*Ciné, Théât* = *ticket*) ≈ voucher

contre-mesure [kɔ̃tʀəm(ə)zyʀ] NF [a] (= *action*) countermeasure [b] (*Mus*) **à ~** against the beat, offbeat

contre-offensive [kɔ̃tʀɔfɑ̃siv] NF counteroffensive

contre-offre [kɔ̃tʀɔfʀ] NF counterbid, counter offer

contre-OPA [kɔ̃tʀɔpea] NF INV counterbid, counter offer (*in a takeover battle*)

contre-ordre, contrordre [kɔ̃tʀɔʀdʀ] NM counter order, countermand; **ordres et ~s** orders and counter orders; **il y a ~** there has been a change of orders; **sauf ~** unless otherwise directed

contrepartie [kɔ̃tʀəpaʀti] NF [a] (*gén* = *compensation*) compensation; **en ~** (= *en échange, en retour*) in return; (= *en revanche*) to make up for it; (*Jur, Fin*) **moyennant ~ valable** ≈ for a good and valuable consideration; **obtenir de l'argent en ~** to get money in compensation; **prendre qch sans ~** to take sth without offering compensation [b] (*littér* = *contre-pied*) opposing view [c] (*Comm* = *registre*) duplicate register; (= *écritures*) counterpart entries

contrepente, contre-pente [kɔ̃tʀəpɑ̃t] NF opposite slope

contre-performance [kɔ̃tʀəpɛʀfɔʀmɑ̃s] NF (*Sport, Écon*) poor performance; **sa ~ aux élections** his poor performance *ou* showing in the elections

contrepet [kɔ̃tʀəpɛ] NM, **contrepèterie** [kɔ̃tʀəpɛtʀi] NF spoonerism

contre-pied [kɔ̃tʀəpje] NM [a] [*opinion, attitude*] (exact) opposite; **prendre le ~** (*d'une opinion*) to take the opposing *ou* opposite view; (*d'une action*) to take the opposite course; **il a pris le ~ de ce qu'on lui demandait** he did the exact opposite of what he was

asked [b] (*Sport*) **à ~** on the wrong foot; **prendre qn à ~** (*lit*) to wrong-foot sb; (*fig*) to wrong-foot sb, catch sb off-guard; (*Chasse*) **prendre le ~** to (run) heel; **les électeurs ont pris à ~ les instituts de sondage** the voters foiled the predictions of the pollsters

contreplaqué [kɔ̃tʀəplake] NM plywood

contre-plongée [kɔ̃tʀəplɔ̃ʒe] NF low-angle shot; **filmer en ~** to film from below

contrepoids [kɔ̃tʀəpwa] NM (*lit*) counterweight, counterbalance; [*acrobate*] balancing-pole; (*lit, fig*) **faire ~** to act as a counterbalance; **porter un panier à chaque main pour faire ~** to carry a basket in each hand to balance oneself; (*fig*) **servir de ~ à ◊ apporter un ~ à** to counterbalance

contre-poil [kɔ̃tʀəpwal] ◆**à contre-poil** LOC ADV (*lit, fig*) the wrong way

contrepoint [kɔ̃tʀəpwɛ̃] NM (*Mus*) counterpoint; (*lit, fig*) **en ~** in counterpoint; **thème joué en ~** theme played in counterpoint, contrapuntal theme; **en ~ de** as a counterpoint to

contrepoison [kɔ̃tʀəpwazɔ̃] NM antidote, counterpoison

contre-porte [kɔ̃tʀəpɔʀt] NF [*voiture*] inner door; **dans la ~ du réfrigérateur** in the inside of the fridge door

contre-pouvoir [kɔ̃tʀəpuvwaʀ] NM opposition force; **les syndicats doivent jouer leur rôle de ~** the unions should fulfil their role in challenging established authority

contre-productif, -ive [kɔ̃tʀəpʀɔdyktif, iv] ADJ [*attitude, effet, mesure*] counter-productive

contre-projet [kɔ̃tʀəpʀɔʒɛ] NM counterplan

contre-propagande [kɔ̃tʀəpʀɔpagɑ̃d] NF counter-propaganda

contre-proposition [kɔ̃tʀəpʀɔpozisjɔ̃] NF counterproposal

contre-publicité [kɔ̃tʀəpyblisite] NF adverse publicity; **ça leur fait de la ~** it's bad *ou* adverse publicity for them

contrer [kɔ̃tʀe] ▸conjug 1◂ [1] VT [a] [+ *personne, menées*] to counter; **se faire ~** to be countered (**par** by) [b] (*Cartes*) to double; (*Rugby*) **un coup de pied** to charge down a kick [2] VI (*Cartes*) to double

contre-rail (*pl* **contre-rails**) [kɔ̃tʀəʀaj] NM checkrail (*Brit*), guard-rail

Contre-Réforme [kɔ̃tʀəʀefɔʀm] NF (*Hist*) **la ~** the Counter-Reformation

contre-révolution [kɔ̃tʀəʀevɔlysjɔ̃] NF counter-revolution

contre-révolutionnaire [kɔ̃tʀəʀevɔlysjɔnɛʀ] ADJ, NMF counter-revolutionary

contrescarpe [kɔ̃tʀɛskaʀp] NF counterscarp

contreseing [kɔ̃tʀəsɛ̃] NM countersignature

contresens [kɔ̃tʀəsɑ̃s] NM (= *erreur*) misinterpretation; (*de traduction*) mistranslation; (= *absurdité*) nonsense (*NonC*), piece of nonsense; **à ~** (*Aut*) the wrong way; (*Couture*) against the grain; **à ~ de** against; **il a pris mes paroles à ~** he misinterpreted what I said; **faire un ~** (*en traduction*) to mistranslate a word (*ou* a phrase); (*sur les intentions de qn*) to misinterpret sb totally

contresigner [kɔ̃tʀəsiɲe] ▸conjug 1◂ VT to countersign

contretemps [kɔ̃tʀətɑ̃] NM [a] (= *complication, retard*) hitch, contretemps (*fml, aussi hum*) [b] (*Mus*) off-beat rhythm [c] **à ~** (*Mus*) off the beat; (*fig*) at an inopportune moment

contre-ténor [kɔ̃tʀətenɔʀ] NM countertenor

contre-terrorisme [kɔ̃tʀəteʀɔʀism] NM counterterrorism

contre-terroriste [kɔ̃tʀəteʀɔʀist] ADJ, NMF counterterrorist

contre-torpilleur [kɔ̃tʀətɔʀpijœʀ] NM destroyer

contre-ut [kɔ̃tʀyt] NM INV top *ou* high C

contre-valeur [kɔ̃tʀavalœʀ] NF (*Fin, Écon*) exchange value

contrevenant, e [kɔ̃tʀəv(ə)nã, ãt] (*Jur*) [1] ADJ offending [2] NM,F offender

contrevenir [kɔ̃tʀəv(ə)niʀ] ▸conjug 22◂
♦ **contrevenir à** VT INDIR (*Jur, littér*) [+ *loi, règlement*] to contravene

contrevent [kɔ̃tʀəvã] NM [a] (= *volet*) shutter [b] [*charpente*] brace, strut

contrevérité [kɔ̃tʀaveʀite] NF untruth, falsehood

contrevirage [kɔ̃tʀaviʀaʒ] NM (*Ski*) counterturn

contre-visite [kɔ̃tʀavizit] NF (*gén*) follow-up inspection; (*Méd*) second examination

contre-voie [kɔ̃tʀavwa] NF opposite track (of a railway line); **à ~** (= *en sens inverse*) on the wrong track; (= *du mauvais côté*) on the wrong side (of the train)

contribuable [kɔ̃tʀibɥabl] NMF taxpayer

contribuer [kɔ̃tʀibɥe] ▸conjug 1◂
♦ **contribuer à** VT INDIR [+ *résultat, effet*] to contribute to(wards); [+ *effort, dépense*] to contribute towards; **de nombreux facteurs ont contribué au déclin de .../à réduire le ...** numerous factors contributed to(wards) the decline in .../to(wards) the reduction in the ... *ou* to reducing the ...

contributeur, -trice [kɔ̃tʀibytœʀ, tʀis] [1] ADJ contributing; **les pays ~s de** *ou* **en troupes** the countries contributing troops [2] NM,F contributor; **~s de** *ou* **en troupes/de fonds** contributors of troops/funds; **~s de l'ONU** UN contributors

contributif, -ive [kɔ̃tʀibytif, iv] ADJ (*Jur*) [*part*] contributory

contribution [kɔ̃tʀibysjɔ̃] NF [a] (= *participation*) contribution; **mettre qn à ~** to call upon sb's services, make use of sb; **mettre qch à ~** to make use of sth; **apporter sa ~ à qch** to make one's contribution to sth [b] (= *impôts*) **~s** (*à la commune*) local taxes; (*à l'État*) taxes; **~s directes/indirectes** direct/indirect taxation; **~ sociale généralisée** supplementary social security contribution in aid of the underprivileged [c] (= *administration*) **~s** tax office, ≈ Inland Revenue (*Brit*), ≈ Internal Revenue Service (*US*); **travailler aux ~s** to work in the tax office, work for *ou* in the Inland Revenue (*Brit*) *ou* Internal Revenue (*US*)

contrister [kɔ̃tʀiste] ▸conjug 1◂ VT (*littér*) to grieve, sadden

contrit, e [kɔ̃tʀi, it] ADJ contrite

contrition [kɔ̃tʀisjɔ̃] NF contrition → **acte**

contrôlable [kɔ̃tʀolabl] ADJ [*opération*] that can be checked; [*affirmation*] that can be checked *ou* verified, verifiable; [*sentiment, inflation*] controllable; **un billet ~ à l'arrivée** a ticket that is inspected *ou* checked on arrival

contrôle [kɔ̃tʀol] NM [a] (= *vérification*) checking (*NonC*), check; **~ antidopage** doping control; (*Fin*) **~ des comptes** audit; **~ d'identité** identity check; **~ de police** police check; **~ de vitesse** speed check; **~ fiscal** tax inspection; **le ~ des passeports** passport control; **~ des passeports** passports please!; **le ~ des billets s'effectue à bord** tickets are checked *ou* inspected on board; (*Comm*) **~ de qualité** quality control; **~ sanitaire** health check; (*Élec*) **~ automatique de gain** automatic gain control → **visite**
[b] (= *surveillance*) [*opérations, agissements, gestion*] controlling, supervising, supervision; [*prix, loyers*] monitoring, controlling; **exercer un ~ sévère sur les agissements de qn** to maintain strict control over sb's actions; (*Jur*) **sous ~ judiciaire** ≈ on probation; **sous ~ médical** under medical supervision; (*Fin*) **~ des changes/des prix** exchange/price control; **~ des naissances** birth control; (*Aut*) **~ radar** radar speed trap; (*Aut*) **~ technique** MOT (test) (*Brit*), inspection (*US*)

[c] (= *maîtrise*) control; **~ de soi** self-control; **garder/perdre le ~ de son véhicule** to remain in/lose control of one's vehicle; **prendre le ~ d'une entreprise** to take control of *ou* take over a firm; **prise de ~** [*entreprise*] takeover; **sous ~ étranger** [*firme*] foreign-owned; [*territoire*] under foreign control; **sous ~ militaire** under military control; **avoir une région sous son ~** to be in control of a region, have a region under one's control
[d] (*Scol* = *épreuve*) (written) test; **le ~ continu** continuous assessment; **le ~ des connaissances** pupil *ou* student assessment; **avoir un ~ de chimie** to have a chemistry test
[e] (= *bureau*) (*gén*) office; (*Théât*) (advance) booking office; reservation office (*US*)
[f] (*Mil* = *registres*) **~s** rolls, lists; **rayé des ~s de l'armée** removed from the army lists
[g] (= *poinçon*) hallmark

contrôler [kɔ̃tʀole] ▸conjug 1◂ [1] VT [a] (= *vérifier*) [+ *billets, passeports*] to inspect, check; [+ *comptes*] to check, inspect; [+ *texte, traduction*] to check (*sur* against); [+ *régularité de qch*] to check; [+ *qualité*] to control, check; [+ *affirmations, alibi*] to check, verify; (*Scol*) [+ *connaissances*] to test; **~ le bon fonctionnement d'un appareil** to check that a machine is working properly
[b] (= *surveiller*) [+ *opérations, agissements, gestion*] to control, supervise; [+ *employés, travail*] to supervise; [+ *prix, loyers*] to monitor, control
[c] (= *maîtriser*) [+ *colère, réactions, nerfs, respiration*] to control; [+ *véhicule*] to control, be in control of; [+ *situation*] to be in control of; (*Mil*) [+ *zone, pays*] to be in control of; (*Écon*) [+ *secteur, firme*] to control; (*Aut, Sport*) [+ *ballon, skis, jeu*] to control; **les rebelles contrôlent l'aéroport** the rebels have taken control of the airport; **nous contrôlons cette société à 80%** we have an 80% (controlling) stake in this company
[d] (*Orfèvrerie*) to hallmark
[2] **se contrôler** VPR to control o.s.; **il ne se contrôlait plus** he was no longer in control of himself

contrôleur, -euse [kɔ̃tʀolœʀ, øz] NM,F [a] (*dans le train, le métro, le bus*) (ticket) inspector; (*sur le quai*) ticket collector; **~ aérien** ◊ **~ de la navigation aérienne** air-traffic controller [b] (*Fin*) [*comptabilité*] auditor; [*contributions*] inspector; **~ de gestion** financial controller, management *ou* cost accountant [c] (*Tech*) regulator; (*Ordin*) controller; **~ de ronde** time-clock

contrordre [kɔ̃tʀɔʀdʀ] NM = **contre-ordre**

controuvé, e [kɔ̃tʀuve] ADJ (*littér*) [*fait, nouvelle*] fabricated; [*histoire, anecdote*] fabricated, concocted

controverse [kɔ̃tʀɔvɛʀs] NF controversy; **prêter à ~** to be debatable

controversé, e [kɔ̃tʀɔvɛʀse] ADJ (*très*) **~** [*théorie, question*] much debated

contumace [kɔ̃tymas] [1] ADJ absconding [2] NF (*Jur*) contumacy (*refusal to appear in court*); **par ~** in absentia, in his (*ou* her *etc*) absence [3] NMF absconder

contumax [kɔ̃tymaks] NMF *person who fails to appear in court*

contus, e [kɔ̃ty, yz] ADJ (*Méd*) [*membre*] bruised, contused

contusion [kɔ̃tyzjɔ̃] NF bruise, contusion (*SPÉC*)

contusionner [kɔ̃tyzjɔne] ▸conjug 1◂ VT to bruise, contuse (*SPÉC*); **son corps était tout contusionné** his body was covered in bruises

conurbation [kɔnyʀbasjɔ̃] NF conurbation

▾ **convaincant, e** [kɔ̃vɛ̃kã, ãt] ADJ convincing

convaincre [kɔ̃vɛ̃kʀ] ▸conjug 42◂ VT [a] [+ *personne sceptique*] to convince (**de qch** of sth); [+ *personne hésitante*] to persuade (**de faire**

re qch to do sth); **je ne suis pas convaincu par son explication** I'm not convinced by his explanation; **je ne demande qu'à me laisser ~** I'm open to persuasion; **il m'a convaincu de renoncer à cette idée** he persuaded *ou* convinced me to give up the idea, he talked me into giving up the idea; **se laisser ~** to let o.s. be persuaded [b] (= *déclarer coupable*) **~ qn de meurtre/trahison** to prove sb guilty of *ou* convict sb of murder/treason

▾ **convaincu, e** [kɔ̃vɛ̃ky] (*ptp de* **convaincre**) ADJ convinced; **d'un ton ~** with conviction

convalescence [kɔ̃valesãs] NF convalescence; **être en ~** to be convalescing; **entrer en ~** to start one's convalescence; **période de ~** (period of) convalescence; **maison de ~** convalescent home

convalescent, e [kɔ̃valesã, ãt] ADJ, NM,F convalescent

convecteur [kɔ̃vɛktœʀ] NM convector (heater)

convection [kɔ̃vɛksjɔ̃] NF convection

convenable [kɔ̃vnabl] ADJ [a] (= *approprié*) [*parti*] fitting, suitable; [*moment, endroit*] fitting, suitable, appropriate [b] (= *décent*) [*manières*] acceptable, correct; [*vêtements*] decent, respectable; [*personne, famille*] respectable; **peu ~** [*manières*] improper, unseemly; [*vêtements*] unsuitable; **ne montre pas du doigt, ce n'est pas ~** don't point — it's not polite, it's bad manners to point [c] (= *acceptable*) [*devoir*] adequate, passable; [*salaire, logement*] decent, acceptable, adequate; **des conditions de vie à peine ~s** barely adequate living conditions

convenablement [kɔ̃vnabləmã] ADV [*placé, choisi*] suitably, appropriately; [*s'exprimer*] properly; [*payé, logé*] decently; **je vous demande de travailler ~** I'm asking you to do your work properly; **s'habiller ~** (*décemment*) to dress respectably *ou* properly; (*en fonction du temps*) to dress appropriately

convenance [kɔ̃vnãs] NF [a] (*frm* = *ce qui convient*) **trouver qch à sa ~** to find sth to one's liking, find sth suitable; **la chambre est-elle à votre ~?** is the room to your liking?; **le service est-il à votre ~?** is the service to your satisfaction?; **choisissez un jour à votre ~** choose a day to suit you *ou* to suit your convenience; **pour des raisons de ~(s) personnelle(s)** ◊ **pour ~s personnelles** for personal reasons → **mariage** [b] (= *étiquette*) **les ~s** propriety, the proprieties; **contraire aux ~s** contrary to the proprieties [c] (*littér* = *harmonie*) [*goûts, caractères*] affinity; († = *caractère adéquat*) [*terme, équipement*] appropriateness, suitability

▾ **convenir** [kɔ̃vniʀ] ▸conjug 22◂ [1] **convenir à** VT INDIR (= *être approprié à*) to suit, be suitable for; (= *être utile à*) to suit, be convenient for; (= *être agréable à*) to be agreeable to, suit; **ce chapeau ne convient pas à la circonstance** this hat is not suitable for the occasion *ou* does not suit the occasion; **le climat ne lui convient pas** the climate doesn't suit him *ou* doesn't agree with him; **oui, cette chambre me convient très bien** yes, this room suits me very well; **cette maison convient à une personne seule** this house is suitable for a person living on their own; **j'irai si cela me convient** I'll go if it is convenient (for me); (*ton péremptoire*) I'll go if it suits me; **si l'heure/la date vous convient** if the time/date is convenient for you *ou* suits you; **c'est tout à fait ce qui me convient** this is exactly what I need *ou* want; **j'espère que cela vous conviendra** I hope you will find this acceptable, I hope this will be acceptable to you
[2] **convenir de** VT INDIR [a] (= *avouer*) to admit (to), acknowledge; **il convint d'avoir été un peu brusque** he admitted (to) having been a little abrupt, he acknowledged (that) he'd been a bit abrupt; **tu as eu tort, conviens-en**

➤ GRAMMAIRE ACTIVE: convaincant 53.4   convaincu 33.2, 43.1, 53.6   convenir 36.1

you were wrong, admit it [b] (= *s'accorder sur*) to agree on; **~ d'une date/d'un lieu** to agree on a date/place; **une date a été convenue** a date has been agreed [3] VT **~ que ...** (= *avouer*) to admit that ..., acknowledge the fact that ...; (= *s'accorder sur*) to agree that ...; **il est convenu que nous nous réunissons demain** it is agreed that we should meet tomorrow [4] VB IMPERS **il convient de faire** (= *il vaut mieux*) it is advisable to do; (= *il est bienséant de*) it would be proper to do; **il convient d'être prudent** caution is advised, it is advisable to be cautious; **il convient qu'elle remercie ses hôtes de leur hospitalité** it is proper *ou* right for her to thank her host and hostess for their hospitality; (*frm*) **il convient de faire remarquer ...** we should point out ... [5] **se convenir** VPR [*personnes*] to be well-suited (to each other)

convent [kɔ̃vɑ̃] NM *general assembly of Freemasons*

convention [kɔ̃vɑ̃sjɔ̃] NF [a] (= *pacte*) (*gén*) agreement, covenant (*frm*); (*Pol*) convention; (*Ind*) **~ collective** collective agreement; **cela n'entre pas dans nos ~s** that doesn't enter into our agreement [b] (= *accord tacite*) (*gén*) understanding; (*Art, Littérat*) convention; **les ~s (sociales)** conventions, social conventions; (*Littérat, Théât*) **décor/personnage/langage de ~** conventional set/character/language; **mots/amabilité de ~** conventional words/kindness [c] (= *assemblée*) (*Pol US*) convention; (*Hist*) **la Convention** the Convention

conventionné, e [kɔ̃vɑ̃sjɔne] ADJ [*établissement, médecin*] *linked to the state health scheme*; ≈ National Health (*Brit*) (*épith*); [*prix*] government-regulated; [*prêt*] subsidized, low-interest (*épith*)

conventionnel, -elle [kɔ̃vɑ̃sjɔnɛl] [1] ADJ (*gén*) conventional; (*Jur*) [*acte, clause*] contractual [2] NM (*Hist*) **les ~s** the members of the Convention

conventionnellement [kɔ̃vɑ̃sjɔnɛlmɑ̃] ADV conventionally

conventionnement [kɔ̃vɑ̃sjɔnmɑ̃] NM *state health service contract*, ≈ National Health (*Brit*) contract

conventionner (se) [kɔ̃vɑ̃sjɔne] ▶conjug 1◀ VPR [*médecin*] *to register as a practitioner within the state health scheme*

conventuel, -elle [kɔ̃vɑ̃tɥɛl] ADJ [*vie, règle, monde, bâtiment*] [*moines*] monastic; [*nonnes*] convent (*épith*), conventual; [*simplicité, paix*] monastic

convenu, e [kɔ̃vny] (*ptp de* **convenir**) ADJ [a] (= *décidé*) [*heure, prix, mot*] agreed; **comme ~** as agreed [b] (*littér péj* = *conventionnel*) conventional

convergence [kɔ̃vɛʁʒɑ̃s] NF convergence; **point de ~** (*Sci, Math*) point of convergence; (*Pol*) point of agreement; **nous avons des points de ~** there are points on which we agree; **le point de ~ entre les deux théories** the meeting point between the two theories; **objectif/programme de ~** convergence target/programme → **critère**

convergent, e [kɔ̃vɛʁʒɑ̃, ɑ̃t] ADJ convergent

converger [kɔ̃vɛʁʒe] ▶conjug 3◀ VI [*lignes, rayons, routes*] to converge; **~ sur** [*regards*] to focus on; **nos pensées convergent sur le sujet** we think along the same lines on the subject

convers, e [kɔ̃vɛʁ, ɛʁs] ADJ (*Rel*) lay (*épith*)

conversation [kɔ̃vɛʁsasjɔ̃] NF [a] (= *entretien*) (*gén*) conversation; (*politique, diplomatique*) talk; **la ~** conversation; **~ téléphonique** (tele)phone conversation; **en (grande) ~ avec** (deep) in conversation with; **faire la ~ à** to make conversation with → **frais²** [b] (= *art de parler*) conversation; **avoir de la ~** to be a good conversationalist; **il n'a pas de ~** he's got no conversation; **elle a de la ~†** she's well-

stacked‡, she has big breasts [c] (= *langage familier*) **dans la ~ courante** in informal *ou* conversational *ou* everyday speech; **employer le style de la ~** to use a conversational style

conversationnel, -elle [kɔ̃vɛʁsasjɔnɛl] ADJ (*Ordin*) conversational

converser [kɔ̃vɛʁse] ▶conjug 1◀ VI to converse (**avec** with)

conversion [kɔ̃vɛʁsjɔ̃] NF [a] (*à une religion*) conversion (**à** to, **en** into); (*à une théorie*) winning over (**à** to), conversion (**à** to) [b] (*Écon* = *reconversion*) (*professionnelle*) retraining; (*industrielle*) conversion; **convention de ~** retraining scheme [c] [*chiffres, mesures, devises*] conversion; **taux de ~** conversion rate; **~ de dollars en francs** conversion of dollars into francs; **faire une ~ de fractions en ...** to convert fractions into ... [d] (= *demi-tour*) (*Mil*) wheel; (*Ski*) kick turn [e] (*Ordin*) conversion [f] (*Psych*) conversion

converti, e [kɔ̃vɛʁti] (*ptp de* **convertir**) [1] ADJ converted [2] NM,F convert → **prêcher**

convertibilité [kɔ̃vɛʁtibilite] NF (*Fin*) convertibility

convertible [kɔ̃vɛʁtibl] [1] ADJ convertible (**en** into) [2] NM (= *avion*) convertiplane; (= *canapé*) sofa bed, bed-settee (*Brit*)

convertir [kɔ̃vɛʁtiʁ] ▶conjug 2◀ VT [a] (= *rallier*) (*à une religion*) to convert (**à** to); (*à une théorie*) to win over, convert (**à** to) [b] (= *transformer*) to convert (**en** into); **~ une terre en blés** to convert a field over to wheat [2] **se convertir** VPR (= *devenir croyant*) to become a convert; (= *changer de religion*) to change religion; (*à une théorie*) to be converted (**à** to)

convertissage [kɔ̃vɛʁtisaʒ] NM (*Métal*) conversion

convertissement [kɔ̃vɛʁtismɑ̃] NM (*Fin*) conversion

convertisseur [kɔ̃vɛʁtisœʁ] NM (*Élec, Métal*) converter; **~ Bessemer** Bessemer converter; **~ d'images** image converter; (*Aut*) **~ de couple** torque converter; (*Ordin*) **~ numérique** digitizer; **~ numérique analogique** digital-analogue converter

convexe [kɔ̃vɛks] ADJ convex

convexion [kɔ̃vɛksjɔ̃] NF = **convection**

convexité [kɔ̃vɛksite] NF convexity

conviction [kɔ̃viksjɔ̃] NF [a] (= *certitude*) conviction, (firm) belief; **j'en ai la ~** I'm convinced of it; **parler avec ~** to speak with conviction; **faire qch avec/sans ~** to do sth with/without conviction; **manquer de ~** to lack conviction [b] (= *sérieux, enthousiasme*) conviction; [c] (= *opinions*) **~s** beliefs, convictions [d] → **pièce**

▼**convier** [kɔ̃vje] ▶conjug 7◀ VT (*frm*) **~ à** [+ *soirée, concert*] to invite to; **~ qn à faire qch** (*pousser*) to urge sb to do sth; (*inviter*) to invite sb to do sth; **la chaleur conviait à la baignade** the hot weather made it very tempting to swim

convive [kɔ̃viv] NMF guest (*at a meal*)

convivial, e (*mpl* **-iaux**) [kɔ̃vivjal, jo] ADJ (*gén*) [*ambiance, lieu*] convivial; (*Ordin*) user-friendly

convivialité [kɔ̃vivjalite] NF (= *rapports*) social interaction; (= *jovialité*) conviviality; (*Ordin*) user-friendliness

convocation [kɔ̃vɔkasjɔ̃] NF [a] (*NonC* [*assemblée*]) convening, convoking; [*membre de club*] inviting; [*témoin, prévenu, subordonné*] summoning; **la ~ des membres doit se faire longtemps à l'avance** members must be invited a long time in advance; **cette ~ chez le directeur l'intriguait** he was intrigued to know why the chairman had asked to see him; **la ~ des membres/candidats doit se faire par écrit** members/candidates must be given written notification to attend [b] (= *lettre, carte*) (written) notification to attend; (*Jur*) summons; **je**

n'ai pas encore reçu ma ~ I haven't had notification yet

convoi [kɔ̃vwa] NM [a] (= *cortège funèbre*) funeral procession [b] (= *train*) train; **~ de marchandises** goods train [c] [*véhicules, navires, prisonniers*] convoy [d] (*Aut*) **~ exceptionnel** ≈ wide (*ou* long *ou* dangerous) load

convoiement [kɔ̃vwamɑ̃] NM (= *escorte*) escorting; (*Mil, Naut*) escorting, convoying; (= *transport*) conveying

convoiter [kɔ̃vwate] ▶conjug 1◀ VT [+ *héritage, objet, poste*] to covet; [+ *personne*] to lust after; **poste très convoité** highly-coveted job

convoitise [kɔ̃vwatiz] NF (= *désir*) (*gén*) covetousness; (*pour une personne*) lust, desire; **la ~ des richesses** the lust for wealth; **la ~ de la chair** the lusts of the flesh; **l'objet de sa ~** the object of his desire; **regarder avec ~** [+ *objet*] to cast covetous looks at; [+ *personne*] to look *ou* gaze lustfully at; **regard brillant de ~** covetous (*ou* lustful) look; **l'objet des ~s de tous** the object of everyone's desire

convoler [kɔ̃vɔle] ▶conjug 1◀ VI († *ou hum*) **~ (en justes noces)** to be wed † (*aussi hum*)

convoquer [kɔ̃vɔke] ▶conjug 1◀ VT [+ *assemblée*] to convene, convoke; (= *convier*) to invite (**à** to); [+ *témoin, prévenu, subordonné*] to summon; **~ qn (pour une entrevue)** to call *ou* invite sb for an interview; **~ un candidat (à un examen)** to send a candidate written notification (of an exam); **il va falloir ~ les membres** we're going to have to call a meeting of the members *ou* call the members together; **as-tu été convoqué à la réunion ?** have you been invited to (attend) the meeting?; **le président a convoqué la presse pour annoncer...** the president called a press conference to announce...; **j'ai été convoqué à dix heures (pour mon oral)** I've been asked to attend at ten o'clock (for my oral); **le chef m'a convoqué** the boss sent for me *ou* asked to see me; **le chef m'a convoqué dans son bureau** the boss called *ou* summoned me to his office; **le juge m'a convoqué** I was summoned to appear before the judge, I was called before the judge

convoyage [kɔ̃vwajaʒ] NM = **convoiement**

convoyer [kɔ̃vwaje] ▶conjug 8◀ VT (= *escorter*) to escort; (*Mil, Naut*) to escort, convoy; (= *transporter*) to convey

convoyeur [kɔ̃vwajœʁ] NM (= *navire*) convoy, escort ship; (= *personne*) escort; (*Tech*) conveyor; **~ de fonds** security guard, Securicor® guard (*Brit*)

convulser [kɔ̃vylse] ▶conjug 1◀ VT [+ *visage*] to convulse, distort; [+ *corps*] to convulse; **la douleur lui convulsa le visage** his face was distorted *ou* convulsed with pain; **son visage se convulsait** his face was distorted

convulsif, -ive [kɔ̃vylsif, iv] ADJ convulsive

convulsion [kɔ̃vylsjɔ̃] NF (*gén, Méd, fig*) convulsion

convulsionnaire [kɔ̃vylsjɔnɛʁ] NMF convulsionary

convulsionner [kɔ̃vylsjɔne] ▶conjug 1◀ VT to convulse; **visage convulsionné** distorted *ou* convulsed face

convulsivement [kɔ̃vylsivmɑ̃] ADV convulsively

coobligé, e [kɔɔbliʒe] NM,F (*Jur*) joint obligor

cooccurrence [kɔɔkyʁɑ̃s] NF (*Ling*) co-occurrence

cool* [kul] ADJ cool*

coolie [kuli] NM coolie

coopé [kɔpe] NF [a] ABRÉV = **coopération** [b] (ABRÉV = **coopérative**) co-op

coopérant, e [kɔɔpeʁɑ̃, ɑ̃t] [1] ADJ cooperative [2] NM ≈ VSO volunteer, ≈ Peace Corps volunteer (*US*)

coopérateur, -trice [kɔ(ɔ)peʁatœʁ, tʁis] [1] ADJ cooperative [2] NM,F [a] (= *associé*) collaborator, cooperator ⓑ (= *membre d'une coopérative*) member of a cooperative, co-operator

coopératif, -ive [k(ɔ)ɔperatif, iv] **1** ADJ co-operative **2 coopérative** NF (= *organisme*) cooperative; (= *magasin*) co-op; **coopérative scolaire** school fund

coopération [kɔɔperasjɔ̃] NF ⓐ (*gén* = col-laboration) cooperation; **apporter sa ~ à une entreprise** to cooperate *ou* collaborate in an undertaking ⓑ (*Pol*) ≈ Voluntary Service Overseas *ou* VSO (*Brit*), ≈ Peace Corps (*US*) (usually as form of military service); **il a été envoyé en Afrique comme professeur au titre de la ~** ≈ he was sent to Africa as a VSO teacher (*Brit*), ≈ he was sent to Africa by the Peace Corps to be a teacher (*US*)

▸ COOPÉRATION

The French government, through the "Ministère de la coopération", provides aid to developing countries by setting up and supporting educa-tional and training schemes abroad. Most people who work abroad as part of coopération (known as "coopérants") do so as volunteers instead of doing military service. → SERVICE MILITAIRE

---

coopératisme [k(ɔ)ɔperatism] NM (*Écon*) co-operation

coopérer [kɔɔpere] ▸conjug 6◂ **1** VI to co-operate **2 coopérer à** VT INDIR to cooperate in

cooptation [kɔɔptasjɔ̃] NF coopting, coopta-tion

coopter [kɔɔpte] ▸conjug 1◂ VT to coopt

coordinateur, -trice [kɔɔʀdinatœʀ, tʀis] NM, F = **coordonnateur**

coordination [kɔɔʀdinasjɔ̃] NF (*gén, Ling*) co-ordination; **~ ouvrière/étudiante** workers'/students' committee → **conjonction**

coordonnant [kɔɔʀdɔnɑ̃] NM (*Ling*) co-ordinating conjunction

coordonnateur, -trice [kɔɔʀdɔnatœʀ, tʀis] **1** ADJ coordinating **2** NM,F coordinator

coordonné, e [kɔɔʀdɔne] (*ptp de* **coordonner**) **1** ADJ coordinated; (*Ling*) (*proposition*) **~e** coordinate clause; **papiers peints ~s** match-ing wallpapers **2 coordonnés** NMPL (*Habillement*) coordinates **3 coordonnées** NFPL (*Math*) coordinates; **donnez-moi vos ~es** can I have your name and address please?

coordonner [kɔɔʀdɔne] ▸conjug 1◂ VT to co-ordinate

copain* [kɔpɛ̃] NM (= *ami*) friend, mate* (sur-tout *Brit*), buddy* (surtout *US*); (= *amoureux*) **son ~** her boyfriend; **de bons ~s** good friends, great pals*; **~ de régiment** army pal* *ou* bud-dy*; **il est très ~ avec le patron** he's really in with the boss*, he's very pally* (*Brit*) with the boss; **avec eux, c'est ou on est ~ ~** we're very chummy* *ou* dead pally* (*Brit*) with them; **ils sont ~s comme cochons** they are great bud-dies*, they're as thick as thieves; (*péj*) **les meilleures postes sont toujours pour les petits ~s** they always give the best jobs to their cro-nies*, it's always jobs for the boys*

coparticipant, e [kɔpaʀtisipɑ̃, ɑ̃t] (*Jur*) **1** ADJ in copartnership *ou* joint account **2** NM,F copartner

coparticipation [kɔpaʀtisipasjɔ̃] NF (*Jur*) co-partnership; **~ aux bénéfices** profit-sharing

copeau (*pl* **copeaux**) [kɔpo] NM [*bois*] shaving; [*métal*] turning; **brûler des ~x** to burn wood shavings

Copenhague [kɔpənag] N Copenhagen

Copernic [kɔpɛʀnik] NM Copernicus

copernicien, -ienne [kɔpɛʀnisjɛ̃, jɛn] ADJ, NM,F Copernican; **révolution ~ne** Copernican revolution

copiage [kɔpjaʒ] NM (*gén*) copying; (*Scol*) copying, cribbing

copie [kɔpi] NF ⓐ (= *reproduction, exemplaire*) [*diplôme, film*] copy; [*tableau*] copy, reproduc-tion; [*sculpture, bijou*] copy, reproduction, rep-lica; (*Admin*) **~ certifiée conforme** certified copy; (*Admin*) **pour ~ conforme** certified accu-rate; (*Ciné, TV*) **~ étalon** master print; (*Ciné*) **~ d'exploitation** release print; (*Ciné*) **~ neuve** new copy; (*Ordin*) **~ papier** hard copy; **pren-dre ~ de qch** to make a copy of sth; **je vous ai mis en ~** I've copied it to you

ⓑ (= *action de copier*) copying

ⓒ (= *reproduction frauduleuse*) copy, imita-tion; **pâle ~** pale imitation

ⓓ (*Scol*) (= *feuille de papier*) sheet (of paper), paper; (= *devoir*) exercise; (= *composition, exa-men*) paper, script; **~ simple/double** single/double sheet (of paper); **~ d'examen** examina-tion script; **rendre** *ou* **remettre ~ blanche** to hand in a blank sheet of paper; **rendre** *ou* **re-mettre sa ~** (*lit*) to hand in one's paper; (*fig*) to turn in one's report; (*fig*) **revoir sa ~** to try and come up with something better → **mal**

ⓔ (*Typo*) copy

ⓕ (*Presse*) copy → **pisseur**

copier [kɔpje] ▸conjug 7◂ **1** VT ⓐ (= *reproduire légalement*) [+ *écrit, texte, acte*] to copy, make a copy of; (*Ordin*) to copy; [+ *ta-bleau, sculpture*] to copy, reproduce; **~ qch au propre** to make a fair copy of sth, copy sth out neatly; **~ une leçon trois fois** to copy out a lesson three times; **vous me la copierez !*** I won't forget that in a hurry!* ⓑ (= *reproduire frauduleusement*) [+ *tableau, sculpture, bijou, logiciel*] to copy, make a copy of; (*Scol* = *tricher*) to copy, crib; **~ le voisin** to copy *ou* crib from one's neighbour ⓒ (= *imiter*) [+ *style, démarche, auteur*] to copy **2** VI (*Scol* = *tricher*) to copy, crib (**sur** from)

copieur, -ieuse [kɔpjœʀ, jøz] **1** NM,F (*Scol*) copier, cribber **2** NM (= *machine*) copier

copieusement [kɔpjøzmɑ̃] ADV [*manger, boire*] copiously, heartily; **repas ~ arrosé** meal generously washed down with wine; **on s'est fait ~ arroser/engueuler*** we got well and truly soaked/told off*; **~ illustré/annoté** copiously illustrated/annotated

copieux, -ieuse [kɔpjø, jøz] ADJ [*repas*] copi-ous, hearty; [*portion*] generous; [*notes, exemples*] copious

copilote [kɔpilɔt] NMF (*Aviat*) co-pilot; (*Aut*) navigator

copin* [kɔpɛ̃] NM = **copain**

copinage* [kɔpinaʒ] NM (*péj*) pally* (*Brit*) *ou* buddy-buddy* (surtout *US*) relationship; **obte-nir qch par ~** to get sth through friendly con-tacts

copine* [kɔpin] NF (= *amie*) friend; (= *amoureuse*) girlfriend; **une ~ de ma mère** one of my mother's friends *ou* girlfriends; **~ de classe** school friend *ou* mate; **elle sont très ~s** they're great friends; **elle est très ~ avec le voisin** she's very friendly *ou* pally* (*Brit*) with the next-door neighbour

copiner* [kɔpine] ▸conjug 1◂ VI to be pally* (*Brit*) *ou* great buddies* (surtout *US*) (**avec** with)

copiste [kɔpist] NMF (*Hist, Littérat*) copyist, transcriber

coposséder [kɔpɔsede] ▸conjug 6◂ VT to own jointly

copossession [kɔpɔsesjɔ̃] NF co-ownership, joint ownership

copra(h) [kɔpʀa] NM copra

coprésidence [kɔpʀezidɑ̃s] NF co-presidency, co-chairmanship

coprésident [kɔpʀezidɑ̃] NM co-president, co-chairman

coprésidente [kɔpʀezidɑ̃t] NF co-president, co-chairwoman

coprin [kɔpʀɛ̃] NM ink cap, coprinus (SPÉC)

coproducteur, -trice [kɔpʀɔdyktœʀ, tʀis] NM,F coproducer

coproduction [kɔpʀɔdyksjɔ̃] NF (*Ciné, TV*) coproduction, joint production; **une ~ franco-italienne** a French-Italian copro-duction, a joint French-Italian production

coproduire [kɔpʀɔdɥiʀ] ▸conjug 38◂ VT to coproduce

coprophage [kɔpʀɔfaʒ] ADJ coprophagous

copropriétaire [kɔpʀɔpʀijetɛʀ] NMF co-owner, joint owner

copropriété [kɔpʀɔpʀijete] NF (= *statut*) co-ownership, joint ownership; (= *propriétaires*) co-owners; **immeuble en ~** block of flats (*Brit*) *ou* apartment building (*US*) in co-ownership, condominium (*US*)

copte [kɔpt] **1** ADJ Coptic **2** NM (*Ling*) Cop-tic **3 Copte** NMF Copt

copulatif, -ive [kɔpylatif, iv] ADJ (*Ling*) copu-lative

copulation [kɔpylasjɔ̃] NF copulation

copule [kɔpyl] NF (*Ling*) copulative verb, copula

copuler [kɔpyle] ▸conjug 1◂ VI to copulate

copyright [kɔpiʀajt] NM copyright

coq¹ [kɔk] **1** NM [*basse-cour*] cock, rooster; (= *girouette*) weather cock *ou* vane; (= *oiseau mâle*) **~ faisan/de perdrix** cock pheasant/partridge; **jeune ~** cockerel; (*Boxe*) **~ ◊ poids ~** bantam-weight; **être comme un ~ en pâte** to be in clover, live the life of Riley; **jambes** *ou* **mollets de ~** wiry legs; **sauter** *ou* **passer du ~ à l'âne** to jump from one subject to another → **chant¹, rouge 2** COMP ▸ **coq de bruyère** (*grand*) capercaillie; (*petit*) black grouse ▸ **coq de combat** fighting cock ▸ **le coq gaulois** the French cockerel (*emblem of the French fighting spirit*) ▸ **coq nain** bantam cock ▸ **coq de roche** cock-of-the-rock ▸ **coq de village** (*fig*) local ladykiller ▸ **coq au vin** (*Culin*) coq au vin

coq² [kɔk] NM (*Naut*) (ship's) cook

coq-à-l'âne [kɔkalan] NM INV abrupt change of subject; **faire un ~** to jump from one sub-ject to another

coquard‡**, coquart**‡ [kɔkaʀ] NM black eye, shiner‡

coque [kɔk] NF ⓐ [*bateau*] hull; [*avion*] fu-selage; [*auto*] shell, body ⓑ [*noix, amande*] shell; † [*œuf*] shell; (*Culin*) **œuf (à la) ~** (soft-) boiled egg; (*Naut*) **~ de noix** cockleshell ⓒ (= *mollusque*) cockle

coquelet [kɔkle] NM (*Culin*) cockerel

coquelicot [kɔkliko] NM poppy → **rouge**

coqueluche [kɔklyʃ] NF (*Méd*) whooping cough; **être la ~ de** to be the idol *ou* darling of

coquemar [kɔkmaʀ] NM cauldron, big kettle

coqueret [kɔkʀe] NM Chinese lantern, winter *ou* ground cherry

coquerico [kɔk(ə)ʀiko] NM, EXCL = **cocorico**

coquerie [kɔkʀi] NF (*Naut*) (*à bord*) (ship's) galley, caboose (*Brit*); (*à terre*) cookhouse

coquet, -ette [kɔkɛ, ɛt] **1** ADJ ⓐ (= *bien habillé*) smart, well turned-out; (= *soucieux de son apparence*) appearance-conscious, clothes-conscious; **homme trop ~** man who takes too much interest in *ou* who is too par-ticular about his appearance *ou* who is too clothes-conscious ⓑ († = *flirteur*) flirtatious ⓒ [*ville*] pretty, charming; [*logement*] charm-ing; [*robe*] smart, stylish ⓓ (*: *intensif*) [*somme d'argent, revenu*] tidy† (*épith*) **2 co-quette** NF **c'est une coquette** she's a co-quette *ou* a flirt, she's very coquettish *ou* flir-tatious; **faire sa coquette** to play hard to get*; (*fig*) **jouer les grandes coquettes** to flirt a lot, be very coquettish

coquetier [kɔk(ə)tje] NM egg cup; **gagner** *ou* **décrocher le ~** †* to hit the jackpot

coquettement [kɔkɛtmɑ̃] ADV [*sourire, re-garder*] coquettishly; [*s'habiller*] smartly, styl-ishly; [*meubler*] charmingly

coquetterie [kɔketri] NF [a] (= élégance) [personne] interest in one's appearance, consciousness of one's appearance; [toilette, coiffure] smartness, stylishness [b] (= galanterie) coquetry, flirtatiousness (NonC); (littér = amour propre) **il mettait sa ~ à marcher sans canne/parler sans notes** he prided himself on ou made a point of walking without a stick/talking without notes [c] (hum) **avoir une ~ dans l'œil*** to have a cast in one's eye

coquillage [kɔkijaʒ] NM (= mollusque) shellfish (NonC); (= coquille) shell

coquillard* [kɔkijar] NM → **tamponner**

coquille [kɔkij] [1] NF [a] [mollusque, œuf, noix] shell; (fig) **rentrer dans/sortir de sa ~** to go ou withdraw into/come out of one's shell [b] (= récipient) (shell-shaped) dish, scallop; (= mets) **~ de poisson/crabe** scallop of fish/crab, fish/crab served in scallop shells [c] (= décoration) scallop; [épée] coquille, shell [d] (Typo) misprint [e] (Sport = protection) box [f] (Méd = plâtre) spinal bed [2] COMP ► **coquille de beurre** shell of butter ► **coquille de noix*** (Naut) cockleshell ► **coquille d'œuf** (= couleur) eggshell (épith) ► **coquille Saint-Jacques** (= animal) scallop; (= carapace) scallop shell

coquillettes [kɔkijɛt] NFPL pasta shells

coquillier, -ière [kɔkije, jɛr] [1] ADJ conchiferous (SPÉC) [2] NM† shell collection

coquin, e [kɔkɛ̃, in] [1] ADJ [a] (= malicieux) [enfant, air] mischievous; **~ de sort!*** the devil!, the deuce!† * [b] (= polisson) [histoire, regard] naughty, suggestive [2] NM,F (= enfant) rascal, mischief; **tu es un petit ~!** you little monkey! ou rascal! [3] NM (†† = gredin) rascal, rogue [4] **coquine**†† NF (= débauchée) loose woman, strumpet†

coquinerie [kɔkinri] NF [a] (= caractère) [enfant] mischievousness; [gredin] roguery [b] (= action) [enfant] mischievous trick; [personne peu honnête] low-down trick

cor[1] [kɔr] NM (Mus) horn; **~ anglais** cor anglais (Brit), English horn (US); **~ de chasse** hunting horn; **~ d'harmonie** French horn; **~ à pistons** valve horn; **~ de basset** basset horn; **premier ~** principal horn; **chasser à ~ et à cri** to hunt with the hounds; **réclamer ou demander qch/qn à ~ et à cri** to clamour for sth/sb

cor[2] [kɔr] NM (Méd) **~ (au pied)** corn

cor[3] [kɔr] NM [cerf] tine; **un (cerf) 10 ~s** a 10-point stag, a 10-pointer

corail (pl **-aux**) [kɔraj, o] [1] NM coral; **la mer de Corail** the Coral Sea [2] ADJ INV [a] (= couleur) coral (pink) [b] **(train) Corail**® ≈ express (train), ≈ inter-city train (Brit) [c] (Zool) **serpent ~** coral snake

corallien, -ienne [kɔraljɛ̃, jɛn] ADJ coralline (littér), coral (épith)

corallin, e [kɔralɛ̃, in] ADJ (littér) [lèvre, coquille] coralline (littér), coral (red)

Coran [kɔrɑ̃] NM **le ~** the Koran

coranique [kɔranik] ADJ Koranic

corbeau (pl **corbeaux**) [kɔrbo] NM [a] (= oiseau = terme générique) crow; **(grand) ~** raven; **~ freux** rook [b] († péj = prêtre) black-coat† (péj), priest [c] (Archit) corbel [d] (* = diffamateur) writer of poison-pen letters

corbeille [kɔrbɛj] [1] NF [a] (= panier) basket; (pour courrier) tray; **~ arrivée/départ** in/out tray [b] (Théât) (dress) circle [c] (Archit) [chapiteau] bell, basket [d] († : Bourse) **la ~** the trading floor ou pit (in Paris Stock Exchange) [e] (= parterre) (round ou oval) flowerbed [2] COMP ► **corbeille d'argent** (Bot) sweet alyssum ► **corbeille à courrier** mail tray ► **corbeille de mariage** wedding presents; **sa femme a apporté une fortune dans la ~ de mariage** his wife brought him a fortune when she married him; **dans cette fusion, leur société apporte 10 millions de francs dans la ~ de mariage** their company brings (a dowry

of) 10 million francs to this merger ► **corbeille d'or** (Bot) golden alyssum ► **corbeille à ouvrage** workbasket ► **corbeille à pain** breadbasket ► **corbeille à papier(s)** wastepaper basket ou bin

corbillard [kɔrbijar] NM hearse

cordage [kɔrdaʒ] NM [a] (= corde, lien) rope; **~s** (gén) ropes, rigging; (Naut : de voilure) rigging [b] [raquette de tennis] stringing

corde [kɔrd] [1] NF [a] (gén = câble, cordage) rope; **attacher qn avec une ~ ou de la ~** to tie sb up with a (piece of) rope; **attacher ou lier qn à un arbre avec une ~** to rope sb to a tree, tie sb to a tree with a (piece of) rope; **en ~** ◊ **de ~** [tapis] whipcord (épith); **à semelle de ~** rope-soled; **grimper ou monter à la ~** to climb a rope, pull o.s. up a rope → **danseur, sauter** [b] (Mus) string; **instruments à ~s** stringed instruments; **les ~s** the strings; **orchestre/quatuor à ~s** string orchestra/quartet; **~ à vide** open string; **instrument à ~s pincées/frottées** plucked/bowed instrument; **à ~s croisées** [piano] overstrung [c] (Sport) [raquette, arc] string; (Boxe) **être envoyé dans les ~s** to be thrown against the ropes [d] [funambule] tightrope, high wire [e] (Courses) rails; **à la ~** (gén : sur piste) on the inside; (Courses) on the rails ou the inside; **prendre un virage à la ~** to hug a bend, take a bend on the inside; **prendre/tenir la ~** (gén : sur piste) to get on/be on the inside; (Courses) to get close to/be on the rails, get on/be on the inside; (fig) **c'est lui qui tient la ~** he's in with the best chance (of winning) [f] (= trame d'un tissu) thread → **user** [g] (Math) chord [h] († = mesure) cord [i] (loc) **mériter la ~†** to deserve to hang ou be hanged; **il s'est mis la ~ au cou** (= il s'est marié) he's tied the knot, he's got hitched*; **il a dû y aller la ~ au cou** (humble, soumis) he had to go cap in hand; **être ou marcher ou danser sur la ~ raide** to walk a tightrope; **politique de la ~ raide** brinkmanship; **parler de (la) ~ dans la maison du pendu** to bring up a sore point, make a tactless remark; **avoir plus d'une ~ ou plusieurs ~s à son arc** to have more than one string to one's bow; **c'est dans ses ~s** it's right up his street (Brit) ou alley (US); **est-ce que c'est dans ses ~s?** is he up to it?; **ce n'est pas dans mes ~s** it's not my line (of country); **tirer sur la ~** to push one's luck a bit*, go too far; **toucher ou faire vibrer la ~ sensible** to touch the right chord; **il pleut ou il tombe des ~s*** it's raining cats and dogs* ou bucketing (down)* (Brit) → **sac[1]**

[2] COMP ► **corde cervicale** cervical nerve ► **corde dorsale** spinal cord ► **corde à linge** clothes line, washing line ► **corde lisse** (climbing) rope ► **corde à nœuds** knotted climbing rope ► **corde à** ou **de piano** piano wire ► **corde de rappel** abseiling rope ► **corde à sauter** skipping rope, jump rope (US) ► **corde du tympan** chorda tympani ► **cordes vocales** vocal cords

cordeau (pl **cordeaux**) [kɔrdo] NM [a] (= corde) string, line; (= de jardinier) gardener's line; (fig) **fait** ou **tiré au ~** as straight as a die [b] (= mèche) fuse; **~ Bickford** Bickford fuse, safety fuse; **~ détonant** detonator fuse [c] (Pêche) ledger line

cordée [kɔrde] NF [a] [alpinistes] rope, roped party; **premier de ~** leader [b] [bois] cord

cordelette [kɔrdəlɛt] NF cord

Cordelier [kɔrdəlje] NM (= religieux) Cordelier

cordelière [kɔrdəljɛr] NF [a] (= corde) cord [b] (Archit) cable moulding (Brit) ou molding (US) [c] (= religieuse) **Cordelière** Franciscan nun

corder [kɔrde] ► conjug 1 ◄ VT [a] (Tech) [+ chanvre, tabac] to twist [b] (= lier) [+ malle] to tie up (with rope), rope up [c] (= mesurer) [+ bois] to cord [d] [+ raquette] to string

corderie [kɔrdəri] NF [a] (= industrie) rope-making industry; (= atelier) rope factory

cordial, e (mpl **-iaux**) [kɔrdjal, jo] [1] ADJ [accueil] hearty, warm, cordial; [sentiment, personne] warm; [manières] cordial; [antipathie, haine] cordial, hearty → **entente** [2] NM heart tonic, cordial

cordialement [kɔrdjalmɑ̃] ADV **se serrer la main ~** to shake hands warmly; **ils nous ont reçus très ~** they gave us a hearty ou very warm welcome; **vous êtes tous ~ invités** you are all cordially invited; **détester qn ~** to detest sb cordially ou heartily; (en fin de lettre) **~ (vôtre)** kind regards; **« bien ~ »** "kindest regards"

cordialité [kɔrdjalite] NF [accueil] warmth, cordiality; [sentiment, personne] warmth; [manières] cordiality; **tout s'est passé dans la plus parfaite ~** it all went off in the most cordial fashion

cordier [kɔrdje] NM [a] (= fabricant) rope-maker [b] (Mus) tailpiece

cordillère [kɔrdijɛr] NF mountain range, cordillera; **la ~ des Andes** the Andes cordillera; **la ~ australienne** the Great Dividing Range

cordite [kɔrdit] NF cordite

cordon [kɔrdɔ̃] [1] NM [a] [sonnette, rideau] cord; [tablier] tie; [sac, bourse] string; [chaussures] lace; **~ de sonnette** bell-pull; (fig) **tenir/délier/resserrer les ~s de la bourse** to hold/loosen/tighten the purse strings; **tenir les ~s du poêle** to be a pallbearer [b] [soldats] cordon [c] (Archit) string-course, cordon [d] (= décoration) sash; **~ du Saint-Esprit** ribbon of the order of the Holy Ghost; **~ de la Légion d'honneur** sash ou cordon of the Légion d'Honneur [2] COMP ► **cordon Bickford** Bickford fuse, safety fuse ► **cordon littoral** offshore bar ► **cordon médullaire** spinal cord ► **cordon ombilical** (lit, fig) umbilical cord; (fig) **couper** ou **rompre le ~ (ombilical)** to cut ou sever the umbilical cord ► **cordon sanitaire** (Méd, Pol) quarantine line, cordon sanitaire

cordon-bleu (pl **cordons-bleus**) [kɔrdɔ̃blø] NM (= cuisinier) cordon-bleu cook; (= décoration) cordon bleu

cordonner [kɔrdɔne] ► conjug 1 ◄ VT [+ soie, cheveux] to twist

cordonnerie [kɔrdɔnri] NF (= boutique) shoe-repair shop, cobbler's†; (= métier) shoe-repairing

cordonnet [kɔrdɔnɛ] NM (= petit cordon) braid (NonC), cord (NonC); (pour boutonnière) buttonhole twist

cordonnier, -ière [kɔrdɔnje, jɛr] NM,F (= réparateur) shoe-repairer, cobbler†; († = fabricant) shoemaker ■ (PROV) **les ~s sont toujours les plus mal chaussés** the shoemaker's children always go barefoot (PROV)

Cordoue [kɔrdu] N Cordoba

coréalisateur, -trice [kɔrealizatœr, tris] NM,F (Ciné, TV) codirector

Corée [kɔre] NF Korea; **~ du Sud/du Nord** South/North Korea

coréen, -enne [kɔreɛ̃, ɛn] [1] ADJ Korean [2] NM (Ling) Korean [3] **Coréen(ne)** NM,F Korean

coreligionnaire [kɔr(ə)liʒɔnɛr] NMF co-religionist

coresponsabilité [kɔrɛspɔ̃sabilite] NF joint responsibility

coresponsable [kɔrɛspɔ̃sabl] [1] ADJ [personne] co-responsible, jointly responsible (de for) [2] NMF person sharing responsibility (de for)

Corfou [kɔrfu] N Corfu

coriace [kɔrjas] ADJ (lit, fig) tough; **il est ~ en affaires** he's a hard-headed ou tough businessman

coriandre [kɔrjɑ̃dr] NF coriander

coricide [kɔrisid] NM corn remover

corindon [kɔrɛ̃dɔ̃] NM corundum

Corinthe [kɔrɛ̃t] N Corinth → **raisin**

corinthien, -ienne [kɔrɛ̃tjɛ̃, jɛn] ADJ Corinthian

Coriolan [kɔrjɔlɑ̃] NM Coriolanus

cormier [kɔrmje] NM (= arbre) service tree; (= bois) service wood

cormoran [kɔrmɔrɑ̃] NM cormorant; **~ huppé** shag

cornac [kɔrnak] NM [éléphant] mahout, elephant driver

cornaline [kɔrnalin] NF carnelian

cornaquer* [kɔrnake] ▶ conjug 1 ◀ VT to show around; **il m'a cornaqué à travers la ville** he showed me round the town

cornard: [kɔrnar] NM cuckold†

corne [kɔrn] **1** NF **a** [escargot, vache] horn; [cerf] antler; [narval] tusk; **~s** horns; **donner un coup de ~ à qn** to butt sb; **blesser qn d'un coup de ~** to gore sb; (fig) **avoir** ou **porter des ~s*** to be a cuckold†; **sa femme lui fait porter des ~s*** his wife is unfaithful to him; **faire les ~s à qn** to make a face at sb, make a jeering gesture at sb → **bête, taureau**
b (= substance) horn **c** (= instrument) horn; (Chasse) hunting horn; (Aut† = avertisseur) hooter, horn **d** (= coin) [page] dog-ear; **faire une ~ à la page d'un livre** to turn down the corner of the page in a book **e** (* = peau dure) **avoir de la ~** to have patches of hard skin, have calluses
2 COMP ▶ **corne d'abondance** horn of plenty, cornucopia ▶ **la corne de l'Afrique** the Horn of Africa ▶ **corne de brume** foghorn ▶ **corne à chaussures** shoehorn ▶ **cornes de gazelle** (Culin) sugar-covered shortbread crescents

cornée [kɔrne] NF cornea

cornéen, -enne [kɔrneɛ̃, ɛn] ADJ corneal → **lentille**

corneille [kɔrnɛj] NF crow; **~ mantelée** hooded crow; **~ noire** carrion crow → **bayer**

cornélien, -ienne [kɔrneljɛ̃, jɛn] ADJ (Littérat) Cornelian; (fig) [situation] where love and duty conflict; [héros] who puts duty before everything

cornemuse [kɔrnəmyz] NF bagpipes; **joueur de ~** piper, bagpiper

corner[1] [kɔrne] ▶ conjug 1 ◀ **1** VT **a** [+ livre, carte] to make ou get dog-eared; [+ page] to turn down the corner of **b** (†† : = claironner) [+ nouvelle] to blare out; **arrête de nous ~ (ça) aux oreilles*** stop shouting about it! **2** VI [chasseur] to sound a horn; † [automobiliste] to hoot (Brit) ou sound one's horn; [sirène] to sound

corner[2] [kɔrner] NM (Ftbl) corner (kick); **tirer un ~** to take a corner (kick); **sortir en ~** to go out of play for a corner (kick)

cornet [kɔrne] **1** NM **a** (= récipient) **~ (de papier)** paper cone; **~ de dragées/de frites** cornet ou paper cone of sweets/chips, ≈ bag of sweets/chips; **~ de glace** ice-cream cone ou cornet (Brit); **mettre sa main en ~ à cup one's hand to one's ear** (Belg = combiné téléphonique) handset, receiver **c** (Helv = sachet) (paper ou plastic) bag **d** (Mus) [orgue] cornet stop **2** COMP ▶ **cornet acoustique** ear trumpet ▶ **cornet à dés** dice cup ▶ **cornets du nez** turbinate bones ▶ **cornet (à pistons)** cornet ▶ **cornet de poste** ou **de postillon** posthorn

cornette [kɔrnɛt] NF [religieuse] cornet; (Naut = pavillon) burgee

cornettiste [kɔrnetist] NMF cornet player

corniaud [kɔrnjo] NM (= chien) mongrel; (* = imbécile) nitwit*, twit* (Brit)

corniche [kɔrniʃ] NF **a** (Archit = moulure) cornice; [piédestal] entablement **b** (Alpinisme) ledge; **(route en) ~** coast road, cliff road **c** [neige] cornice

cornichon [kɔrniʃɔ̃] NM (= concombre) gherkin; (en condiment) gherkin (Brit), pickle (US); (* = personne) nitwit*, nincompoop*; (arg Scol) pupil in the class preparing for Saint-Cyr

cornière [kɔrnjɛr] NF (= pièce métallique) corner iron; (= pièce d'écoulement) valley

cornique [kɔrnik] **1** ADJ Cornish **2** NM (Ling) Cornish

corniste [kɔrnist] NMF horn player

Cornouaille [kɔrnwaj] NF **la ~** Cornouaille (area of Brittany)

Cornouailles [kɔrnwaj] NF **les ~** Cornwall

cornouiller [kɔrnuje] NM dogwood

cornu, e [kɔrny] **1** ADJ [animal, démon] horned **2 cornue** NF (= récipient) retort; (Tech = four) retort

corollaire [kɔrɔlɛr] NM (Logique, Math) corollary; (gén = conséquence) consequence, corollary; **et ceci a pour ~ ...** and this has as a consequence ..., and the corollary of this is ...

corolle [kɔrɔl] NF corolla

coron [kɔrɔ̃] NM (= maison) mining cottage; (= quartier) mining village

coronaire [kɔrɔnɛr] ADJ (Anat) coronary

coronarien, -ienne [kɔrɔnarjɛ̃, jɛn] ADJ (Méd) coronary

corossol [kɔrɔsɔl] NM soursop

corporatif, -ive [kɔrpɔratif, iv] ADJ [mouvement, système] corporative; [esprit] corporate

corporation [kɔrpɔrasjɔ̃] NF [notaires, médecins] corporate body; (Hist) guild; **dans notre ~** in our profession

corporatisme [kɔrpɔratism] NM corporatism

corporatiste [kɔrpɔratist] ADJ corporatist

corporel, -elle [kɔrpɔrɛl] ADJ [châtiment] corporal; [sévices] physical; [intégrité] physical, bodily; [accident] involving physical injury; [besoin] bodily; **lait ~** body lotion ou milk; (Jur) **bien ~** corporeal property

corps [kɔr] **1** NM **a** (Anat) body; (= cadavre) corpse, (dead) body; **le ~ humain** the human body; **frissonner** ou **trembler de tout son ~** to tremble all over; **jusqu'au milieu du ~** up to the waist; **je n'ai rien dans le ~** I've had nothing to eat; **robe près du ~** close-fitting dress → **contrainte**[2], **diable**
b (Astron, Chim, Phys = objet, substance) body; **~ simples/composés** simple/compound bodies → **chute**
c (= partie essentielle) [bâtiment, lettre, article, ouvrage] (main) body; [meuble] main part, body; [pompe] barrel; (Typo) body
d [vêtement] bodice; [armure] cors(e)let
e (= consistance) [étoffe, papier, vin] body; **ce vin a du ~** this wine is full-bodied ou has (got) body
f (= groupe) body, corps; (Mil) corps; **~ de sapeurs-pompiers** fire brigade; **les grands ~ de l'État** the senior branches of the civil service → **esprit**
g (= recueil de textes) corpus, body; **~ de doctrines** body of doctrines
h (loc) **se donner ~ et âme à qch** to give o.s. body and soul to sth; **sombrer ~ et biens** [bateau] to go down with all hands; [entreprise] to sink without trace; **perdu ~ et biens** lost with all hands; **s'élancer** ou **se jeter à ~ perdu dans une entreprise/la mêlée** to throw o.s. wholeheartedly ou headlong into a venture/ into the fray; **donner ~ à qch** to give substance to sth; **faire ~** [idées] to form one body (avec with); [choses concrètes] to be joined (avec to); **prendre ~** to take shape; **s'ils veulent faire cela, il faudra qu'ils me passent sur le ~** if they want to do that, it'll be over my dead body; **pour avoir ce qu'il veut, il vous passerait sur le ~** he'd trample you underfoot

to get his own way; **faire qch à son ~ défendant** to do sth against one's will ou unwillingly; **mais qu'est-ce qu'il a dans le ~?** whatever's got into him?; **j'aimerais bien savoir ce qu'il a dans le ~** I'd like to know what makes him tick; **tenir au ~** [aliment] to be filling
2 COMP ▶ **corps d'armée** army corps ▶ **corps de ballet** corps de ballet ▶ **corps de bâtiment** main body (of a building) ▶ **corps caverneux** erectile tissue (of the penis) ▶ **corps céleste** celestial ou heavenly body ▶ **corps constitués** constitutional bodies (of the state) ▶ **corps consulaire** consular corps ▶ **corps à corps** clinch; **se battre (au) ~ à ~** to fight hand-to-hand ▶ **corps du délit** (Jur) corpus delicti ▶ **le Corps diplomatique** the Diplomatic Corps, the Foreign Service (US) ▶ **corps électoral** electorate ▶ **le corps enseignant** (gén) the teaching profession, teachers; [lycée, collège] the teaching staff ▶ **corps étranger** (Méd) foreign body ▶ **le corps européen** the Eurocorps ▶ **corps expéditionnaire** task force ▶ **corps franc** irregular force ▶ **corps de garde** (local) guardroom; (= troupe) guard; (péj) **plaisanteries de ~ de garde** barrack-room ou guardroom jokes ▶ **corps gras** greasy substance, glyceride (SPEC) ▶ **corps jaune** (Physiol) yellow body, corpus luteum (SPEC) ▶ **corps législatif** legislative body ▶ **corps de logis** main building, central building ▶ **le corps médical** the medical profession ▶ **corps de métier** trade association, guild ▶ **corps noir** (Phys) black body ▶ **corps politique** body politic ▶ **corps strié** (Anat) striate body ▶ **corps de troupe** unit (of troops) ▶ **corps vitré** (Anat) vitreous body

corps-mort (pl **corps-morts**) [kɔrmɔr] NM (Naut) mooring

corpulence [kɔrpylɑ̃s] NF stoutness, corpulence; **(être) de forte/moyenne ~** (to be) of stout/medium build

corpulent, e [kɔrpylɑ̃, ɑ̃t] ADJ stout, corpulent

corpus [kɔrpys] NM (gén, Jur, Ling) corpus

corpusculaire [kɔrpyskyler] ADJ (Anat, Phys) corpuscular

corpuscule [kɔrpyskyl] NM (Anat, Phys) corpuscle

correct, e [kɔrɛkt] ADJ **a** (= exact) [plan, copie] accurate; [phrase] correct, right; [emploi, fonctionnement] proper, correct; (en réponse) **~!** correct!, right! **b** (= convenable) [tenue] proper, correct **c** (= courtois) [conduite] correct; [personne] polite; **ce n'est pas très ~ de sa part** that's rather impolite of him **d** (= honnête) correct; **il est ~ en affaires** he's very correct in business matters **e** (= acceptable) [repas, hôtel, salaire] reasonable, decent → **politiquement**

correctement [kɔrɛktəmɑ̃] ADV [fonctionner] properly; [parler, écrire] properly, correctly; [évaluer] accurately; [se nourrir] properly; [rémunérer] decently, reasonably well; **vivre ~** to live reasonably well

correcteur, -trice [kɔrɛktœr, tris] **1** ADJ [dispositif] corrective → **verre** **2** NM,F [examen] examiner, marker (Brit), grader (US); (Typo) proofreader **3** NM (Tech = dispositif) corrector; **~ de tonalité** tone control; (Ordin) **~ d'orthographe** ou **orthographique** spellchecker; **~ liquide** correcting fluid

correctif, -ive [kɔrɛktif, iv] **1** ADJ [gymnastique, substance] corrective **2** NM (lit, fig) (= médicament) corrective (à to); (= mise au point) qualifying statement; **apporter un ~ à qch** (= corriger) to rectify ou correct an error in sth; (= ajouter une précision à) to qualify sth

correction [kɔrɛksjɔ̃] NF (NonC = action) [erreur, abus] correction, putting right; [manuscrit] correction, emendation; [mauvaise habitude] correction; (*Naut*) [*compas*] correction; [*trajectoire*] correction; [*examen*] (*gén*) correcting; (*en notant*) marking (*Brit*), grading (*US*); (*Ordin*) [*programme*] patching; [*mise au point*] debugging; [*Édition*] **~ d'épreuves** proofreading; **apporter une ~ aux propos de qn** to amend what sb has said; **la ~ des copies lui a pris toute la soirée** it took him all evening to correct *ou* mark the homework; **j'ai fait la ~ du devoir avec les élèves** I went through the pupils' essays with them; **après ~ des variations saisonnières** after seasonal adjustments → **maison**

[b] (= *surcharge, rature*) correction; (*Typo*) **~s d'auteur** author's corrections *ou* emendations [c] (= *châtiment*) (corporal) punishment, thrashing; **recevoir une bonne ~** to get a good hiding *ou* thrashing [d] (*NonC* = *exactitude*) [*plan, copie*] accuracy; [*phrase*] correctness; [*emploi, fonctionnement*] propriety, correctness [e] (= *bienséance*) [*tenue*] propriety, correctness; (= *honnêteté*) [*conduite, personne*] correctness; (= *courtoisie*) good manners; **il a fait preuve d'une parfaite ~** he behaved impeccably; **je l'ai fait par ~** it was the polite thing to do, it was only good manners

correctionnel, -elle [kɔʀɛksjɔnɛl] [1] ADJ **peine ~le** penalty (*imposed by courts*); **tribunal (de police) ~** ≈ magistrate's court (*dealing with criminal matters*) [2] **correctionnelle** NF ≈ magistrate's court; **passer en ~le** to go before the magistrate

Corrège [kɔʀɛʒ] N **le ~** Correggio

corrélat [kɔʀela] NM correlate

corrélatif, -ive [kɔʀelatif, iv] ADJ, NM correlative

corrélation [kɔʀelasjɔ̃] NF correlation; **être en ~ étroite avec** to be closely related to *ou* connected with, be in close correlation with; **mettre en ~** to correlate

corréler [kɔʀele] ▸conjug 6◂ VT to correlate

correspondance [kɔʀɛspɔ̃dɑ̃s] NF [a] (= *conformité*) correspondence, conformity; (*Archit* = *symétrie*) balance; **~ de goûts/d'idées entre deux personnes** conformity of two people's tastes/ideas; **être en parfaite ~ d'idées avec qn** to have ideas that correspond perfectly to sb's *ou* that are perfectly in tune with sb's [b] (*Math*) relation; **~ biunivoque** one-to-one mapping, bijection [c] (= *échange de lettres*) correspondence; **avoir** *ou* **entretenir une longue ~ avec qn** to engage in *ou* keep up a lengthy correspondence with sb; **être en ~ commerciale avec qn** to have a business correspondence with sb; **nous avons été en ~** we have corresponded, we have been in correspondence; **être en ~ téléphonique avec qn** to be in touch by telephone with sb; **cours par ~** correspondence course; **il a appris le latin par ~** he learned Latin through a *ou* by correspondence course [d] (= *ensemble de lettres*) mail, post (*surtout Brit*), correspondence; (*Littérat*) [*auteur*] correspondence; (*Presse*) letters to the Editor; **il reçoit une volumineuse ~** he receives large quantities of mail; **dépouiller/lire sa ~** to go through/read one's mail *ou* one's correspondence [e] (= *transports*) connection; **~ ferroviaire/ d'autobus** rail/bus connection; **attendre la ~** to wait for the connection; **l'autobus n'assure pas la ~ avec le train** the bus does not connect with the train

correspondancier, -ière [kɔʀɛspɔ̃dɑ̃sje, jɛʀ] NM,F correspondence clerk

correspondant, e [kɔʀɛspɔ̃dɑ̃, ɑ̃t] [1] ADJ (*gén : qui va avec, par paires*) corresponding; (*Géom*) [*angles*] corresponding; **ci-joint un chèque ~ à la facture** enclosed a cheque in the amount of *ou* in respect of (*Brit*) the invoice [2] NM,F [a] (*gén, Presse*) correspondent;

(*Scol*) penfriend; (*Banque*) correspondent bank; **~ de guerre/à l'étranger** war/foreign correspondent; **de notre ~ permanent à Londres** from our correspondent in London; (**membre**) **~** [*société savante*] corresponding member [b] (*Téléc*) **mon ~** (= *appelé*) the person I was calling; (= *appelant*) the caller; **le numéro de votre ~ a changé** the number you dialled has been changed; **nous recherchons votre ~** we are trying to connect you *ou* to put you through [c] (*Scol* = *responsable d'un interne*) guardian (*for child at boarding school*)

▾ **correspondre** [kɔʀɛspɔ̃dʀ] ▸conjug 41◂ [1] **correspondre à** VT INDIR [a] (= *s'accorder avec*) [+ *goûts*] to suit; [+ *capacités*] to fit; [+ *description*] to correspond to, fit; **sa version des faits ne correspond pas à la réalité** his version of the facts doesn't square *ou* tally with what happened in reality [b] (= *être l'équivalent de*) [+ *système, institutions, élément symétrique*] to correspond to; **le yard correspond au mètre** the yard corresponds to the metre [2] VI [a] (= *écrire*) to correspond (**avec** with) [b] (= *communiquer*) [*mers*] to be linked; [*chambres*] to communicate (**avec** with) [c] (*Transport*) **~ avec** to connect with [3] **se correspondre** VPR [*chambres*] to communicate (with one another); [*éléments d'une symétrie*] to correspond

corrida [kɔʀida] NF bullfight; (* : *fig* = *désordre*) to-do*, carry-on* (*Brit*); (*fig*) **ça va être la (vraie) ~ !*** all hell will break loose*

corridor [kɔʀidɔʀ] NM corridor, passage; (*Géog, Hist*) **le ~ polonais** the Polish Corridor

corrigé [kɔʀiʒe] NM (*Scol*) [*exercice*] correct version; [*traduction*] fair copy; **~s** (*en fin de manuel*) key to exercises; (*livre du professeur*) answer book; [*examens*] past papers

corriger [kɔʀiʒe] ▸conjug 3◂ [1] VT [a] (= *repérer les erreurs de*) [+ *manuscrit*] to correct, emend; (*Typo*) [+ *épreuves*] to correct, (proof)read; (*Scol*) [+ *examen, dictée*] to correct; (*en notant*) to mark (*Brit*), grade (*US*) [b] (= *rectifier*) [+ *erreur, défaut*] to correct, put right; [+ *théorie*] to put right; [+ *abus*] to remedy, put right; [+ *manières*] to improve; (*Naut*) [+ *compas*] to correct, adjust; [+ *trajectoire, vue, vision*] to correct; **~ ses actions** to mend one's ways; **j'ai corrigé mon jugement sur lui** I've changed my opinion of him; (*frm*) **~ l'injustice du sort** to mitigate the injustice of fate, soften the blows of unjust Fate (*littér*); (*fig*) **corrigé des variations saisonnières** seasonally adjusted → **tir** [c] (= *guérir*) **~ qn de** [+ *défaut*] to cure *ou* rid sb of; **tu ne le corrigeras pas à son âge** it's too late to make him change his ways now [d] (= *punir*) to thrash [2] **se corriger** VPR (= *devenir raisonnable*) to mend one's ways; **se ~ de** [+ *défaut*] to cure *ou* rid o.s. of

corrigible [kɔʀiʒibl] ADJ rectifiable, which can be put right

corroboration [kɔʀɔbɔʀasjɔ̃] NF corroboration

▾ **corroborer** [kɔʀɔbɔʀe] ▸conjug 1◂ VT to corroborate

corrodant, e [kɔʀɔdɑ̃, ɑ̃t] ADJ, NM corrosive

corroder [kɔʀɔde] ▸conjug 1◂ [1] VT [+ *métal*] to corrode, eat into; (*littér*) [+ *sentiments*] to erode [2] **se corroder** VPR [*métal*] to corrode

corrompre [kɔʀɔ̃pʀ] ▸conjug 4◂ [1] VT [a] (= *soudoyer*) [+ *témoin, fonctionnaire*] to bribe, corrupt [b] (*frm* = *pervertir*) [+ *mœurs, esprit, jeunesse*] to corrupt; [+ *langage*] to debase; **mots corrompus par l'usage** words corrupted *ou* debased by usage [c] [+ *air, eau, aliments*] to taint; (*Méd*) [+ *sang*] to contaminate [2] **se corrompre** VPR [*mœurs, jeunesse*] to become corrupt; [*goût*] to become debased; [*aliments*] to go off (*Brit*), go bad

corrompu, e [kɔʀɔ̃py] (*ptp de* **corrompre**) ADJ corrupt

corrosif, -ive [kɔʀozif, iv] [1] ADJ [*acide, substance*] corrosive; [*ironie, œuvre, écrivain*] caustic, scathing [2] NM corrosive

corrosion [kɔʀozjɔ̃] NF [*métaux*] corrosion; [*rochers*] erosion; [*volonté, bon sens*] erosion

corroyage [kɔʀwajaʒ] NM [*cuir*] currying; [*métal*] welding

corroyer [kɔʀwaje] ▸conjug 8◂ VT [+ *cuir*] to curry; [+ *métal*] to weld; [+ *bois*] to trim

corroyeur [kɔʀwajœʀ] NM currier

corrupteur, -trice [kɔʀyptœʀ, tʀis] [1] ADJ (*littér*) [*spectacle, journal*] corrupting [2] NM,F (= *qui soudoie*) briber; (*littér* = *qui déprave*) corrupter

corruptible [kɔʀyptibl] ADJ (*littér*) [*personne*] corruptible; † [*matière*] perishable

corruption [kɔʀypsjɔ̃] NF [a] (*gén*) corruption; (*en soudoyant*) bribery, corruption; **~ active** bribery; **~ passive** accepting bribes; **~ de fonctionnaire** bribery of a public official [b] (= *dépravation*) [*mœurs, esprit, jeunesse, texte*] corruption; [*langage*] debasement [c] (= *décomposition*) [*aliments*] decomposition; [*sang*] contamination

corsage [kɔʀsaʒ] NM (= *chemisier*) blouse; [*robe*] bodice

corsaire [kɔʀsɛʀ] NM [a] (*Hist* = *marin, navire*) privateer [b] (= *pirate*) pirate, corsair [c] (**pantalon**) **~** breeches

Corse [kɔʀs] NF Corsica

corse [kɔʀs] [1] ADJ Corsican [2] NM (*Ling*) Corsican [3] **Corse** NMF Corsican

corsé, e [kɔʀse] (*ptp de* **corser**) ADJ [a] [*vin*] full-bodied; [*café*] (= *parfumé*) full-flavoured (*Brit*) *ou* -flavored (*US*); (= *fort*) strong; [*mets, sauce*] spicy [b] (= *scabreux*) [*histoire*] spicy [c] (* *intensif*) [*addition*] high, steep* (*attrib*); [*exercice, problème*] tough

corselet [kɔʀsəlɛ] NM [a] (= *cuirasse*) cors(e)let; (= *vêtement*) corselet [b] (*Zool*) corselet

corser [kɔʀse] ▸conjug 1◂ VT [a] [+ *repas*] to make spicier, pep up*; [+ *vin*] to strengthen; [+ *boisson*] to spike; [+ *assaisonnement*] to pep up* [b] [+ *difficulté*] to intensify, aggravate; [+ *histoire, intrigue*] to liven up; **l'histoire** *ou* **l'affaire se corse** the plot thickens! (*hum*); **le premier exercice est facile mais après ça se corse** the first exercise is easy but then it gets much tougher; **les choses ont commencé à se ~ quand il a voulu discuter le prix** things started to get heated when he tried to haggle

corset [kɔʀsɛ] NM (= *sous-vêtement*) corset; (= *pièce de costume*) bodice; **~ orthopédique** *ou* **médical** surgical corset

corseter [kɔʀsəte] ▸conjug 5◂ VT (*lit*) to corset; (*fig* = *enserrer*) to constrain, constrict

corsetier, -ière [kɔʀsətje, jɛʀ] NM,F corsetmaker

corso [kɔʀso] NM **~ (fleuri)** procession of floral floats

cortège [kɔʀtɛʒ] NM [*fête*] procession; [*président*] cortège, retinue; **~ nuptial** bridal procession; **~ funèbre** funeral procession *ou* cortège; **~ de** [+ *manifestants, grévistes*] procession of; (*littér*) [+ *malheurs, fatalité*] trail of; [+ *visions, souvenirs*] succession of; **la faillite et son ~ de licenciements** bankruptcy and the accompanying lay-offs

cortex [kɔʀtɛks] NM cortex

cortical, e (*mpl* **-aux**) [kɔʀtikal, o] ADJ (*Anat, Bot*) cortical

corticoïde [kɔʀtikɔid] NM corticoid

corticostéroïde [kɔʀtikosteʀɔid] NM corticosteroid

corticosurrénale [kɔʀtikosyʀenal] [1] ADJ F adrenocortical [2] NF adrenal cortex

corticothérapie [kɔʀtikoteʀapi] NF corticosteroid *ou* corticoid therapy

---

▸ **GRAMMAIRE ACTIVE:** **correspondre** 32.4 **corroborer** 38.1

cortisone [kɔʀtizɔn] NF cortisone

corvéable [kɔʀveabl] ADJ (*Hist*) liable to the corvée → **taillable**

corvée [kɔʀve] NF **a** (*Mil*) (= *travail*) fatigue (duty); (= *soldats*) fatigue party; **être de ~** to be on fatigue (duty); **~ de chiottes***: latrine duty; **~ de vaisselle** (*Mil*) cookhouse fatigue; (*hum*) dishwashing duty; **~ de ravitaillement** supply duty; **~ de pommes de terre ou de patates*** spud-bashing (*arg Mil*) (*NonC*); **être de ~ de pommes de terre ou de patates*** to be on spud duty* **b** (= *tâche pénible*) chore, drudgery (*NonC*); **quelle ~!** what drudgery!, what a chore! **c** (*Hist*) corvée (*statute labour*) **d** (*Can*) voluntary work, bee* (*US, Can*)

corvette [kɔʀvet] NF corvette → **capitaine**

coryphée [kɔʀife] NM (*Théât*) coryphaeus

coryza [kɔʀiza] NM (*Méd*) coryza (*SPÉC*), head cold

COS [kɔs] NM (ABRÉV = **coefficient d'occupation des sols**) → **coefficient**

cosaque [kɔzak] NM cossack

cosécante [kosekɑ̃t] NF cosecant

cosignataire [kosiɲatɛʀ] ADJ, NMF cosignatory

cosigner [kosiɲe] ▶conjug 1◀ VT [+ *document*] [*une personne*] to be a joint signatory to (*frm*); [*deux personnes*] to be joint signatories to (*frm*), sign jointly; **un document cosigné par X et Y** a document signed jointly by X and Y

cosinus [kosinys] NM cosine

cosmétique [kɔsmetik] **1** ADJ, NM cosmetic **2** NF **la ~** the cosmetics industry

cosmétologie [kɔsmetɔlɔʒi] NF beauty care

cosmétologue [kɔsmetɔlɔg] NMF cosmetics expert

cosmique [kɔsmik] ADJ cosmic → **rayon**

cosmogonie [kɔsmɔgɔni] NF cosmogony

cosmogonique [kɔsmɔgɔnik] ADJ cosmogonic(al), cosmogonal

cosmographie [kɔsmɔgʀafi] NF cosmography

cosmographique [kɔsmɔgʀafik] ADJ cosmographic

cosmologie [kɔsmɔlɔʒi] NF cosmology

cosmologique [kɔsmɔlɔʒik] ADJ cosmological

cosmonaute [kɔsmɔnot] NMF cosmonaut

cosmopolite [kɔsmɔpɔlit] ADJ cosmopolitan

cosmopolitisme [kɔsmɔpɔlitism] NM cosmopolitanism

cosmos [kɔsmos] NM (= *univers*) cosmos; (*Aviat* = *espace*) (outer) space

cossard, e* [kɔsaʀ, aʀd] **1** ADJ lazy **2** NM,F lazybones

cosse [kɔs] NF **a** [*pois, haricots*] pod, hull **b** (*Élec*) terminal spade tag; (*Aut*) **~ de batterie** battery lead connection **c** (* = *flemme*) lazy mood; **avoir la ~** to feel as lazy as anything, be in a lazy mood

cossu, e [kɔsy] ADJ [*personne*] well-off, well-to-do; [*maison*] rich-looking, opulent(-looking)

costal, e (*mpl* **-aux**) [kɔstal, o] ADJ (*Anat*) costal

costar(d)* [kɔstaʀ] NM suit → **tailler**

Costa Rica [kɔstaʀika] NM Costa Rica

costaricien, -ienne [kɔstaʀisjɛ̃, jɛn] **1** ADJ Costarican **2** **Costaricien(ne)** NM,F Costarican

costaud, e* [kɔsto, od] **1** ADJ [*personne*] strong, sturdy; [*vin, tissu*] strong; **une voiture ~ ou ~e** a sturdy car **2** NM (= *homme*) strong ou sturdy ou strapping man **b** **c'est du ~** [*alcool, tissu*] it's strong stuff; [*maison*] it's strongly built **3** **costaude** NF strong ou sturdy ou strapping woman

costume [kɔstym] **1** NM **a** (*régional, traditionnel*) costume, dress; **~ national** na-

tional costume ou dress; (*hum*) **en ~ d'Adam/ d'Ève** in his/her birthday suit (*hum*) **b** (*Ciné, Théât*) costume **c** (= *complet*) suit; **~ deux/ trois pièces** two-/three-piece suit; **~ cravate** in a suit and tie **2** COMP ▶ **costume de bain** bathing suit ou costume (*Brit*) ▶ **costume de cérémonie** ceremonial dress (*NonC*) ▶ **costume de chasse** hunting gear (*NonC*) ▶ **costume marin** sailor suit

costumé, e [kɔstyme] (*ptp de* **costumer**) ADJ [*personne*] (*dans un bal*) in costume, in fancy dress (*Brit*); (*au théâtre*) in costume → **bal**

costumer [kɔstyme] ▶conjug 1◀ **1** VT **~ qn en monstre/en Zorro** to dress sb up as a monster/as Zorro **2** **se costumer** VPR (= *porter un déguisement*) to put on a costume ou fancy dress (*Brit*); [*acteur*] to get into costume; **se ~ en fée** to dress up as a fairy

costumier [kɔstymje] NM (= *fabricant, loueur*) costumier, costumer; (*Théât* = *employé*) wardrobe master

costumière [kɔstymjɛʀ] NF (*Théât*) wardrobe mistress

cosy [kozi] ADJ [*atmosphère, confort, appartement*] cosy, snug

cosy(-corner) (*pl* **cosys** ou **cosy-corners**) [kozi(kɔʀnɶʀ)] NM corner divan (*with shelves attached*)

cotangente [kotɑ̃ʒɑ̃t] NF cotangent

cotation [kɔtasjɔ̃] NF [*valeur boursière*] listing, quotation; [*timbre, voiture*] valuation; [*devoir scolaire*] marking (*Brit*), grading (*US*); **~ en Bourse/au second marché/à New York** listing ou quotation on the stock exchange/on the second market/in New York

cote [kɔt] **1** NF **a** (= *fixation du prix*) [*valeur boursière*] quotation; [*timbre, voiture d'occasion*] quoted value; (*Bourse* = *liste*) **~ officielle** official list; **consulter la ~** to look at the share prices; **inscrit à la ~** quoted (*Brit*) ou listed (*US*) on the stock exchange list **b** (= *évaluation*) [*devoir scolaire*] mark (*Brit*), grade (*US*); (*Courses*) [*cheval*] odds (**de** on); **la ~ de Banjo est de 3 contre 1** the odds on Banjo are 3 to 1 **c** (= *popularité*) rating, standing; **avoir une bonne ou grosse ~** to be (very) highly thought of, be highly rated (**auprès de** by); **avoir la ~*** to be very popular (**auprès de** with), be very well thought of ou highly rated (**auprès de** by); **elle a/n'a pas la ~*** **auprès du patron** she is/isn't in the boss's good books; **~ de popularité** ou **de confiance** popularity ou approval rating **d** (*sur une carte* = *altitude*) spot height; (*sur un croquis* = *dimension*) dimension; **il y a une ~ qui est effacée** one of the dimensions has been rubbed out; **l'ennemi a atteint la ~ 215** the enemy reached hill 215; **les explorateurs ont atteint la ~ 4.550/-190** the explorers reached the 4,550-metre mark above sea level/190-metre mark below ground **e** (= *marque de classement*: *gén*) classification mark, serial number ou mark; [*livre de bibliothèque*] class(ification) mark (*Brit*), call number (*US*) **f** (= *part*: *Fin*) **~ mobilière/foncière** property/land assessment **2** COMP ▶ **cote d'alerte** [*rivière*] danger mark ou level, flood level; [*chômage, épidémie*] atteindre la **~ d'alerte** to reach ou hit crisis point ▶ **cote d'amour**: **il jouit d'une ~ d'amour** his charm works in his favour ▶ **cote mal taillée** rough-and-ready settlement

coté, e [kɔte] (*ptp de* **coter**) ADJ **être très ~** to be highly thought of ou rated; **il est mal ~** he's not very highly thought of; **vin (très) ~** highly-rated wine

côte [kot] NF **a** (*Anat*) rib; **~s flottantes** floating ribs; **vraie/fausse ~** true/false rib; **on peut**

lui compter les **~s** ◊ **on lui voit les ~s** he's all skin and bone; (*fig*) **avoir les ~s en long** to feel stiff; (*fig*) **se tenir les ~s (de rire)** to split one's sides (with laughter); **~ à ~** side by side → **caresser**

b (*Boucherie*) [*bœuf*] rib; [*veau, agneau, mouton, porc*] chop; **~ première** loin chop → **faux²**

c (= *nervure*) [*chou, coupole*] rib; [*tissu*] rib, wale (*US*); **veste à ~s** ribbed jacket; **velours à larges ~s** wide rib ou wide wale (*US*) corduroy, elephant cord; (*Tricot*) **faire les poignets en ~s** to do the cuffs in rib(bing)

d (= *pente*) [*colline*] slope, hillside; (*Aut*) [*route*] hill; **il a dû s'arrêter dans la ~** he had to stop on the hill; **ne pas dépasser au sommet d'une ~** do not overtake when approaching the top of a hill ou on the brow of a hill (*Brit*); (*Aut*) **en ~** on a hill → **course, démarrage**

e (= *littoral*) coast; (= *ligne du littoral*) coastline; **les ~s de France** the French coast(s) ou coastline; **la Côte (d'Azur)** the (French) Riviera; **la ~ d'Émeraude** the northern coast of Brittany; **la Côte-d'Ivoire** the Ivory Coast; **~ rocheuse/découpée/basse** rocky/indented/low coastline; **sur la ~** ou **les ~s, il fait plus frais** it is cooler along ou on ou at the coast; **la route qui longe la ~** the coast road; (*Naut*) **aller à la ~** to run ashore

▼**côté** [kote] **1** NM **a** (= *partie du corps*) side; **être blessé au ~** to be wounded in the side; **l'épée au ~** with his sword by his side; **être couché sur le ~** to be lying on one's side; **à son ~** at his side, beside him; **aux ~s de** by the side of → **point¹**

b (= *face, partie latérale*) [*objet, route, feuille*] side; **de chaque ~** ou **des deux ~s de la cheminée** on each side ou on both sides of the fireplace; **il a sauté de l'autre ~ du mur/du ruisseau** he jumped over the wall/across the stream; **le bruit vient de l'autre ~ de la rivière/ de la pièce** the sound is coming from across ou from over the river ou from the other side of the river/from the other side of the room; **de l'autre ~ de la forêt il y a des prés** on the other side of the forest ou beyond the forest there are meadows; (*fig*) **de l'autre ~ de la barricade** ou **de la barrière** on the other side of the fence; (*Sport*) **le ~ fermé** ◊ **le petit ~** the inside; (*Sport*) **le ~ ouvert** ◊ **le grand ~** the outside; (*Tennis*) **changer de ~** to change ends; (*Naut*) **un navire sur le ~** a ship on her beamends

c (= *aspect*) side, point; **le ~ pratique/ théorique** the practical/theoretical side; **les bons et les mauvais ~s (de qn)** the good and bad sides ou points; (*de qch*) the pros and cons; **il a un ~ sympathique** there's a likeable side to him; **son attitude/ce film a un ~ pervers** there's something perverse about his attitude/this film; **prendre qch du bon/ mauvais ~** to take sth well/badly; **par certains ~s** in some respects ou ways; **de ce ~(-là)** in that respect; **d'un ~ ... d'un autre ~ ...** (*alternative*) on (the) one hand ... on the other hand ...; (*hésitation*) in one respect ou way ... in another respect ou way ...; (*du*) **santé tout va bien*** healthwise* ou as far as health is concerned everything is fine; **~ argent, tout va bien*** all's well on the money side, moneywise* everything is fine

d (= *parti, branche familiale*) side; **de mon ~** on my side (of the family); **se ranger** ou **se mettre du ~ du plus fort** to side with the strongest; **du ~ paternel** on his father's side

e (*précédé de* «*de*» = *direction*) way, direction, side; **de ce ~-ci/-là** this/that way; **de l'autre** ou **~ l'autre** the other way, in the other direction; **nous habitons du ~ de la poste** we live over by the post office; **le vent vient du ~ de la mer/du ~ opposé** the wind is blowing from the sea/from the opposite direction; **ils se di-**

▶ GRAMMAIRE ACTIVE: **côté** 32.3, 53.3, 53.5

rigeaient du ~ des prés/du ~ opposé they were heading towards the meadows/in the opposite direction; **nous pourrions regarder du ~ de la littérature médiévale** we could take a look at medieval literature; **venir de tous ~s** to come from all directions; **assiégé de tous ~s** besieged on ou from all sides; **chercher qn de tous ~s** to look for sb everywhere ou all over the place, search high and low for sb; **je l'ai entendu dire de divers ~s** I've heard it from several quarters ou sources; **de ~ et d'autre** here and there; **de mon ~, je ferai tout pour l'aider** for my part, I'll do everything I can to help him; **renseigne-toi de ton ~, je me renseignerai du mien** you find out what you can and I'll do the same; (fig) **voir de quel ~ vient le vent** to see which way the wind is blowing; ~ **du vent** windward side; ~ **sous le vent** leeward side; **ils ne sont pas partis du bon ~** they didn't go the right way ou in the right direction

[f] (Théât) ~ **cour** stage left, prompt side (Brit); ~ **jardin** stage right, opposite prompt side (Brit); **une chambre ~ rue** a bedroom overlooking the street

[2] **à côté** LOC ADV [a] (proximité) nearby; (pièce ou maison adjacente) next door; **la maison/les gens (d')à ~** the house/the people next door; **nos voisins d'à ~** our next-door neighbours; **l'hôtel est (tout) à ~** the hotel is (very) nearby ou close by

[b] (= en dehors du but) **ils ont mal visé, les bombes sont tombées à ~** their aim was bad and the bombs went astray ou fell wide; (fig) **je suis tombé à ~** (= se tromper) I got it all wrong

[c] (= en comparaison) in comparison; **elle a été très malade, ton rhume n'est rien à ~** she's been very ill, your cold is nothing in comparison

[3] **à côté de** LOC PRÉP [a] (= à proximité de) next to, beside; **on passe à ~ de beaucoup de choses en ne voyageant pas** you miss a lot by not travelling; **il est à ~ de la plaque** he hasn't got a clue*

[b] (= en dehors de) **à ~ de la cible** off target, wide of the target; **il a répondu à ~ de la question** (sans le faire exprès) his answer was off the point; (intentionnellement) he avoided the question

[c] (= en comparaison de) compared to, by comparison with, beside; **leur maison est grande à ~ de la nôtre** their house is big compared to ours; **il est paresseux, à ~ de ça il aime son travail** he's lazy, but on the other hand he does like his work

[4] **de côté** LOC ADV [a] (= de biais) [marcher, regarder, se tourner] sideways; **regard de ~** sidelong look; **porter son chapeau de ~** to wear one's hat (tilted) to ou on one side

[b] (= en réserve) [mettre, garder] aside; **mettre de l'argent de ~** to put money by ou aside

[c] (= à l'écart) **se jeter de ~** to leap aside ou to the ou to one side; **laisser qn/qch de ~** to leave sb/sth to one side ou out

coteau (pl coteaux) [kɔto] NM (= colline) hill; (= versant) slope, hillside → **flanc**

côtelé, e [kot(ə)le] ADJ ribbed → **velours**

côtelette [kotlɛt] NF (Culin) cutlet; **~s découvertes** middle neck chops; (* = côtes, flanc) **~s** ribs, side

coter [kɔte] ▸ conjug 1 ◂ [1] VT [a] [+ valeur boursière] to quote, list; [+ timbre-poste, voiture d'occasion] to quote the market price of; [+ cheval] to put odds on; (Scol) [+ devoir] to mark (Brit), grade (US); [+ film, roman] to rate; **coté en Bourse/au comptant** quoted ou listed on the stock exchange/on the spot market; **être coté à l'Argus** quoted ou listed (in the secondhand car book) [b] [+ carte] to put spot heights on; [+ croquis] to mark in the dimensions on [c] [+ pièce de dossier] to put a classification mark ou serial number ou serial mark

on; [+ livre de bibliothèque] to put a class(ification) mark (Brit) ou call number (US) ou shelf-mark ou pressmark (Brit) on [2] VI (Bourse) **valeur qui cote 500 F** share quoted ou listed at 500 francs

coterie [kɔtri] NF (gén péj) set; ~ **littéraire** literary coterie ou clique ou set

cothurne [kotyRn] NM buskin

côtier, -ière [kotje, jɛR] ADJ [pêche] inshore; [navigation, région, fleuve, ville] coastal (épith); **(bateau) ~** coaster

cotillon [kɔtijɔ̃] NM [a] (serpentins etc) **~s** party novelties (confetti, streamers, paper hats etc) [b] (†† = jupon) petticoat → **courir** [c] (= danse) cotillion, cotillon

cotisant, e [kɔtizɑ̃, ɑ̃t] NM,F [club, syndicat] subscriber, contributor (à to); [Sécurité sociale, pension] contributor (à to); **seuls les ~s y ont droit** only those who pay their subscriptions (ou dues ou contributions) qualify

cotisation [kɔtizasjɔ̃] NF (= quote-part) [club] subscription; [syndicat] subscription, dues; [Sécurité sociale, pension, mutuelle] contributions; **la ~ est obligatoire** there is a mandatory subscription charge

cotiser [kɔtize] ▸ conjug 1 ◂ [1] VI (dans un club) to subscribe, pay one's subscription; (à la Sécurité sociale) to pay one's contributions (à to); **tu as cotisé pour le cadeau ?** did you chip in* for the present? [2] **se cotiser** VPR to club together; **ils se sont cotisés pour lui faire un cadeau** they clubbed together to get him a present

côtoiement [kotwamɑ̃] NM (= contact) [danger, artistes] contact (**de** with)

coton [kɔtɔ̃] NM [a] (= plante, fil) cotton; ~ **à broder** embroidery thread; ~ **à repriser** darning thread ou cotton; ~ **hydrophile** cotton wool (Brit), absorbent cotton (US); **robe de ou en ~** cotton dress [b] (= tampon) (cotton-wool (Brit) ou cotton (US)) swab; **mets un ~ dans ton nez** put some ou a bit of cotton wool (Brit) ou cotton (US) in your nose [c] (loc) **avoir du ~ dans les oreilles*** to be deaf, have cloth ears* (Brit); **j'ai les bras/jambes en ~** my arms/legs feel like jelly ou cotton wool (Brit); **c'est ~*** it's tricky* → **élever, filer**

cotonnade [kɔtɔnad] NF cotton (fabric)

cotonneux, -euse [kɔtɔnø, øz] ADJ [a] [fruit, feuille] downy [b] [brouillard] wispy; [nuage] fluffy, fleecy, cotton-wool (Brit) (épith); [bruit] muffled

cotonnier, -ière [kɔtɔnje, jɛR] [1] ADJ cotton (épith) [2] NM (Bot) cotton plant

Coton-tige® (pl **Cotons-tiges**) [kɔtɔ̃tiʒ] NM cotton bud (Brit), Q-tip®

côtoyer [kotwaje] ▸ conjug 8 ◂ [1] VT [a] (= être à côté de) to be next to; (= fréquenter) to mix with, rub shoulders with; ~ **le danger** to flirt with danger [b] (= longer: en voiture, à pied etc) to drive (ou walk etc) along ou alongside; [rivière] to run ou flow alongside; [route] to skirt, run along ou alongside [c] (= frôler) [procédé, situation] to be bordering ou verging on; **cela côtoie la malhonnêteté** that is bordering ou verging on dishonesty; **il aime à ~ l'illégalité** he likes to do things that verge on illegality ou that come close to being illegal [2] **se côtoyer** VPR [individus] to mix, rub shoulders; [genres, extrêmes] to meet, come close

cotre [kɔtR] NM (Naut) cutter

cottage [kɔtedʒ] NM cottage

cotte [kɔt] NF [a] (Hist) ~ **de mailles** coat of mail; ~ **d'armes** (= tunique) coat of arms (surcoat) [b] (= salopette) overalls, (pair of) dungarees (Brit); (†† = jupe) petticoat

cotutelle [kotytɛl] NF joint guardianship

cotuteur, -trice [kotytœR, tRis] NM,F joint guardian

cotylédon [kɔtiledɔ̃] NM (Anat, Bot) cotyledon

cou [ku] NM (Anat, Couture) [bouteille] neck; **porter qch au ~ ou autour du ~** to wear sth round one's neck; **elle a un vrai ~ de girafe** she's got a neck like a giraffe; **jusqu'au ~** (lit) up to one's neck; **endetté jusqu'au ~** up to one's eyes in debt; **être impliqué jusqu'au ~ dans un scandale** to be heavily implicated in a scandal; **il est impliqué jusqu'au ~** he's in it up to his neck*; **sauter ou se jeter au ~ de qn** to throw one's arms around sb's neck, fall on sb's neck → **bride, casser, taureau** etc

couac [kwak] NM (Mus) [instrument] false note, goose note (Brit); [voix] false note; (fig) **il y a eu des ~s pendant les discussions avec les syndicats** there were moments of friction during the talks with the unions

couard, couarde [kwaR, kwaRd] (frm) [1] ADJ cowardly; **il est trop ~ pour cela** he's too cowardly ou too much of a coward for that [2] NM,F coward

couardise [kwaRdiz] NF (frm) cowardice

couchage [kuʃaʒ] NM (= matelas, draps) bedding (NonC); (= installation) **il faudra organiser le ~ en route** we'll have to organize our sleeping arrangements on the way; **matériel de ~** sleeping equipment, bedding; (= matelas) **pour ~ 90/135** for mattress size 90/135 cm → **sac¹**

couchant [kuʃɑ̃] [1] ADJ **soleil ~** setting sun; **au soleil ~** at sunset ou sundown (US) → **chien** [2] NM (= ouest) west; (= aspect du ciel, de l'ouest) sunset, sundown (US)

couche [kuʃ] [1] NF [a] (= épaisseur) [peinture] coat; [beurre, fard, bois, neige] layer; (Culin) layer; **ils avaient une ~ épaisse de crasse** they were covered in ou coated with dirt, they were covered in a thick layer of dirt; **en tenir ou avoir une ~*** to be really thick* ou dumb* [b] (Hort) hotbed → **champignon** [c] (= zone) layer, stratum; (= catégorie sociale) level, stratum; **la ~ d'ozone** ozone layer; **~s de l'atmosphère** layers ou strata of the atmosphere; (Bot) **~s ligneuses** woody ou ligneous layers; **dans toutes les ~s de la société** at all levels of society, in every social stratum [d] [bébé] nappy (Brit), diaper (US); **~-culotte** disposable nappy (Brit) ou diaper (US) [e] (littér = lit) bed; **une ~ de feuillage** a bed of leaves [2] **couches** NFPL (Méd = accouchement) confinement†; **mourir en ~s** to die in childbirth; **femme en ~s** woman in labour; **elle a eu des ~s pénibles** she had a difficult confinement† ou labour → **faux², relever, retour**

couché, e [kuʃe] (ptp de **coucher**) ADJ [a] (= étendu) lying (down); (au lit) in bed; **Rex, ~ !** lie down, Rex!; ~ **sur son guidon** bent over his handlebars [b] (= penché) [écriture] sloping, slanting [c] → **papier**

couche-dehors* [kuʃdəɔR] NM INV down-and-out, homeless person

coucher [kuʃe] ▸ conjug 1 ◂ [1] VT [a] (= mettre au lit) to put to bed; (= donner un lit à) to put up; **on peut vous ~** we can put you up, we can offer you a bed; **nous pouvons ~ 4 personnes** we can put up ou sleep 4 people → **nom**

[b] (= étendre) [+ blessé] to lay out; [+ échelle] to lay down; [+ bouteille] to lay on its side; **il y a un arbre couché en travers de la route** there's a tree lying across the road; **la rafale a couché le bateau** the gust of wind made the boat keel over ou keeled the boat over; **le vent a couché les blés** the wind has flattened the corn → **joue**

[c] (frm = inscrire) to inscribe; ~ **qn dans un testament** to name sb in a will; ~ **qn sur une liste** to inscribe ou include sb's name on a list; ~ **un article dans un contrat** to insert a clause into a contract

[d] (Hort) [+ branches] to layer

[2] VI [a] (= passer la nuit, séjourner) to sleep; **nous avons couché à l'hôtel/chez des amis** we spent the night at a hotel/with friends; **nous**

couchions à l'hôtel/chez des amis we were staying in a hotel/with friends; ~ sous la tente to sleep under canvas; il faudra qu'il couche par terre he'll have to sleep on the floor; on peut ~ à 5 dans le bateau the boat sleeps 5; ma voiture couche dehors* my car stays outside at night → étoile

[b] (* = se coucher) to go to bed; cela nous a fait ~ très tard that kept us up very late

[c] (* = avoir des rapports sexuels) ~ avec qn to sleep ou go to bed with sb; ils couchent ensemble they're sleeping together; avant le mariage, je ne couche pas I don't believe in (having) sex before marriage

3 **se coucher** VPR [a] (= aller au lit) to go to bed; se ~ comme les poules to go to bed early ou when the sun goes down; (fig) va te ~!* clear off!* → comme

[b] (= s'étendre) to lie down; il se coucha sur l'enfant pour le protéger he lay on top of the child to protect him; (Sport) se ~ sur les avirons/le guidon to bend over the oars/the handlebars; un poteau s'est couché au travers de la route there's a telegraph pole lying across the road; (péj) se ~ devant qn* to crawl to sb, grovel before sb

[c] [soleil, lune] to set, go down

[d] (Naut) [bateau] to keel over

[e] (Cartes = s'incliner) (gén) to throw in one's hand; (Poker) to fold

4 NM [a] (= moment) **surveiller le ~ des enfants** to see the children into bed; **le ~ était toujours à 9 heures** bedtime was always at 9 o'clock; (Hist) **le ~ du roi** the king's going-to-bed ceremony

[b] († = logement) accommodation; **le ~ et la nourriture** board and lodging

[c] (= tombée de la nuit) **(au) ~ du soleil** (at) sunset ou sundown (US); **le soleil à son ~** the setting sun

coucherie [kuʃʀi] NF (gén pl: péj) sleeping around (NonC)

couche-tard* [kuʃtaʀ] NMF INV night owl*

couche-tôt* [kuʃto] NMF INV **c'est un ~** he always goes to bed early

couchette [kuʃɛt] NF (Rail) couchette, berth; (Naut) [voyageur] couchette, berth; [marin] bunk

coucheur [kuʃœʀ] NM → mauvais

couci-couça* [kusikusa] ADV so-so*

coucou [kuku] **1** NM [a] (= oiseau) cuckoo; (= pendule) cuckoo clock; **maigre comme un ~*** as thin as a rake [b] (péj = avion) (old) crate* [c] (= fleur) cowslip [d] (* = bonjour) **faire un petit ~** to say hello (à to); **elle a fait un ~ à la caméra** she waved to the camera **2** EXCL (à cache-cache) peek-a-boo!; (= bonjour) cooey!, hello!; **~, c'est moi!** hi! ou hello!, it's me!

coude [kud] NM [a] (Anat = partie de la manche) elbow; **~s au corps** (lit) (with one's) elbows in; [courir] at the double; (fig) **se tenir ou serrer les ~s** to stick together; **coup de ~** nudge; **prendre un coup de ~ dans la figure** to get an elbow in the face; **écarter qn d'un coup de ~** to elbow sb out of the way; **d'un coup de ~ il attira son attention** he nudged him to attract his attention; **donner un coup de ~ à qn** (légèrement) to give sb a nudge, nudge sb; (plus brutalement) to elbow sb; **~ à ~** [travailler] shoulder to shoulder, side by side; [coureurs, candidats] **être au ~ à ~** to be neck and neck; **j'ai ou je garde votre dossier sous le ~** I am holding on to your file; **j'ai toujours ce dictionnaire sous le ~** I always keep this dictionary handy → **doigt**, **huile** etc [b] [rivière] bend, elbow; [route, tuyau, barre] bend

coudé, e [kude] (ptp de **couder**) ADJ [tuyau, barre] angled, bent at an angle, with a bend in it

coudée [kude] NF†† cubit†; (fig) **avoir ses ou les ~s franches** to have elbow room; (fig) **dépasser qn de cent ~s**† to stand head and shoulders above sb, be worth a hundred times more than sb

cou-de-pied (pl **cous-de-pied**) [kud(ə)pje] NM instep

couder [kude] ▸conjug 1◂ VT [+ tuyau, barre de fer] to put a bend in, bend (at an angle)

coudoyer [kudwaje] ▸conjug 8◂ VT [+ gens] to rub shoulders with, mix with, come into contact with; **dans cet article, la stupidité coudoie la mesquinerie** in this article, stupidity stands side by side with pettiness

coudre [kudʀ] ▸conjug 48◂ VT [+ pièces de tissu] to sew (together); [+ pièce, bouton] to sew on; [+ vêtement] to sew up, stitch up; (Reliure) [+ cahiers] to stitch; (Méd) [+ plaie] to sew up, stitch (up); **coudre un bouton/une pièce à une veste** to sew a button/patch on a jacket; **~ une semelle (à l'empeigne)** to stitch a sole (to the upper); **~ à la main/la machine** to sew by hand/by machine → **dé**, **machine**

coudrier [kudʀije] NM hazel tree

Coué [kwe] N **méthode ~** autosuggestion, Couéisme (SPÉC); **il faut pratiquer ou utiliser la méthode ~** you need to try self-persuasion

couenne [kwan] NF [a] [lard] rind [b] (‡ = peau) hide* [c] (Méd) [peau] membrane

couenneux, -euse [kwanø, øz] ADJ → **angine**

couette [kwɛt] NF [a] [cheveux] **~s** bunches [b] (= couverture) continental quilt, duvet, comforter (US); **se mettre sous la ~** to go to bed, turn in* [c] (Tech) bearing; (Naut) ways

couffin [kufɛ̃] NM [bébé] Moses basket; († = cabas) (straw) basket

coug(o)uar [kugwaʀ] NM cougar

couic [kwik] EXCL erk!, squeak!; **je n'y comprends que ~**†‡ I don't understand a blooming* (Brit) ou darn* (US) thing (= mourir) **faire ~*** to croak*, snuff it*

couille‡ [kuj] NF [a] (= testicule) ball‡; **~s** balls‡, bollocks‡ (Brit); (courage) **avoir des ~s** to have balls‡; **c'est une ~ molle** he has no balls‡; **se faire des ~s en or** to get filthy rich‡ [b] (= erreur, problème) balls-up‡ (Brit), cock-up‡ (Brit), ball-up‡ (US); **faire une ~** to screw up‡, fuck up‡; **je n'ai eu que des ~s cette semaine** it's been one cock-up‡ (Brit) ou balls-up‡ (Brit) ou ball-up‡ (US) after another this week

couillon‡ [kujɔ̃] **1** ADJ M damn‡ ou bloody‡ (Brit)‡ stupid **2** NM damn‡ ou bloody‡ (Brit) idiot ou cretin‡

couillonnade‡ [kujɔnad] NF bullshit‡ (NonC); **c'est de la ~** it's a load of bullshit‡

couillonner‡ [kujɔne] ▸conjug 1◂ VT to con*, do* (Brit); **on t'a couillonné ◊ tu t'es fait ~** you've been had* ou conned* ou done* (Brit)

couinement [kwinmɑ̃] NM [porc, freins] squealing (NonC), squeal; [souris etc] squeaking (NonC), squeak; [porte, ressort] creaking (NonC); (péj) [personne] whining (NonC), whine; **pousser un ~** [porc] to squeal; [souris etc] to squeak

couiner* [kwine] ▸conjug 1◂ VI [porc, freins] to squeal; [souris etc] to squeak; [porte, ressort] to creak; (péj) [personne] to whine

coulage [kulaʒ] NM [a] [cire, ciment] pouring; [statue, cloche] casting [b] (Écon) (= gaspillage) waste; (= vol) pilferage

coulant, e [kulɑ̃, ɑ̃t] **1** ADJ [a] [pâte] runny; [vin] smooth; [style] (free-)flowing, smooth → **nœud** [b] (* = indulgent) [personne] easy-going **2** NM [a] [ceinture] sliding loop [b] (Bot) runner

coule [kul] NF [a]‡ **être à la ~** to know the ropes, know the tricks of the trade [b] (= capuchon) cowl

coulé, e [kule] (ptp de **couler**) **1** ADJ [jeu de bataille navale] **(touché) ~!** she's gone under! → **brasse** **2** NM (Mus) slur; (Danse) glide; (Billard) follow **3** **coulée** NF [métal] casting;

~e de lave lava flow; ~e de boue mudslide; ~e de neige snowslide; [peinture] **il y a une ~e** the paint has run; **il y a des/trois ~es** the paint has run (in several places)/in three places; **~e verte** pedestrian zone (bordered with trees and grass)

coulemelle [kulmɛl] NF parasol mushroom

couler [kule] ▸conjug 1◂ **1** VI [a] [liquide] to run, flow; [sang, larmes] to flow; [fromage, bougie] to run; [rivière] to flow; **la sueur coulait sur son visage** he had sweat running down his face; (plus fort) he had sweat pouring down his face; **~ à flots** [vin, champagne] to be flowing freely; (fig) **le sang a coulé** blood has been shed

[b] **faire ~** [+ eau] to run; **faire ~ un bain** to run a bath, run water for a bath; (fig) **faire ~ le sang** to cause bloodshed; (fig) **ça a fait ~ beaucoup d'encre** it has caused a lot of ink to flow; **ça fera ~ de la salive** that'll set (the) tongues wagging

[c] [robinet] to run; (= fuir) to leak; [récipient, stylo] to leak; **ne laissez pas ~ les robinets** don't leave the taps (Brit) ou faucets (US) running ou on; **il a le nez qui coule** his nose is running, he has a runny nose

[d] [paroles] to flow; [roman, style] to flow (along); **~ de source** (= être clair) to be obvious; (= s'enchaîner) to follow naturally

[e] [vie, temps] to slip by, slip past

[f] [bateau, personne] to sink; [entreprise] to go under, fold; **~ à pic** to sink straight to the bottom

2 VT [a] [+ cire, ciment] to pour; [+ métal, statue, cloche] to cast; (Aut) **~ une bielle** to run a big end

[b] (= passer) **~ une existence paisible/des jours heureux** to enjoy a peaceful existence/happy days

[c] [+ bateau] to sink, send to the bottom; (= discréditer) [+ personne] to discredit; (* = faire échouer) [+ candidat] to bring down; [+ entrepreneur, firme] to wreck, ruin; **c'est son accent/l'épreuve de latin qui l'a coulé*** it was his accent/the Latin test that brought him down

[d] (= glisser) [+ regard, sourire] to steal; [+ pièce de monnaie] to slip

[e] (= filtrer) [+ liquide] to pour

3 **se couler** VPR [a] (= se glisser) **se ~ dans/à travers** to slip into/through; [personne] **se ~ dans un moule** to conform to a norm

[b] **se la ~ douce*** (= avoir la belle vie) to have it easy*, have an easy time (of it)*; (= paresser) to take it easy

couleur [kulœʀ] **1** NF [a] (= coloris) colour (Brit), color (US); (= nuance) shade, tint, hue (littér); **~s fondamentales/complémentaires** primary/complementary colours; **une robe de ~ bleue** a blue dress; **de ~ claire/sombre** light-/dark-coloured; **une belle ~ rouge** a beautiful shade of red, a beautiful red colour; **aux ~s délicates** delicately coloured, with delicate colours; **film/cartes en ~s** colour film/postcards; **vêtements noirs ou de ~** dark or colourful clothes; (= linge de couleur) **la ~ ◊ les ~s** coloureds; **je n'aime pas les ~s de la chambre** I don't like the colour scheme ou the colours in the bedroom; **les feuilles prenaient une ~ dorée** the leaves were turning golden-brown ou taking on a golden-brown colour; **se faire faire sa ou une ~** to have one's hair coloured → **goût**

[b] (= peinture) paint; **~s à l'eau** watercolours; **~s à l'huile** oil colours, oil paint; **boîte de ~s** paintbox, box of paints → **crayon**, **marchand**

[c] (= carnation) **~s** colour (Brit), color (US); **avoir des ~s** to have a good colour; **perdre ses/(re)prendre des ~s** to lose/get back one's colour; (bronzage) **tu as pris des ~s** you've caught the sun → **changer**, **haut**

[d] (= vigueur) colour (Brit), color (US); **ce récit a de la ~** this tale is very vivid ou colourful; **sans ~** colourless

couleuvre
208

e (= *caractère*) colour (*Brit*), color (*US*), flavour (*Brit*), flavor (*US*); **le poème prend soudain une ~ tragique** the poem suddenly takes on a tragic colour *ou* note

f (*Pol* = *étiquette*) colour (*Brit*), color (*US*); **~ politique** political persuasion

g (*Cartes*) suit → **annoncer**

h (*Sport*) [*club, écurie*] **~s** colours (*Brit*), colors (*US*); **les ~s** (*drapeau*) the colours (*Brit*) *ou* colors (*US*)

i **~ locale** local colour; **ces costumes font très ~ locale** these costumes give plenty of local colour

j (*loc*) **homme/femme de ~** coloured man/woman; **sous ~ de qch** under the guise of sth; **sous ~ de faire** while pretending to do; **montrer/présenter qch sous de fausses ~s** to show/present sth in a false light; **décrire** *ou* **peindre qch sous les plus sombres/vives ~s** to paint the darkest/rosiest picture of sth, paint sth in the darkest/rosiest colours; **l'avenir se présente sous les plus sombres ~s** the future looms very dark *ou* looks very gloomy; **elle n'a jamais vu la ~ de son argent*** she's never seen the colour of his money*; **il m'a promis un cadeau mais je n'en ai jamais vu la ~*** he promised me a present but I've yet to see it → **voir**

2 ADJ INV **yeux ~ d'azur** sky-blue eyes; **tissu cyclamen/mousse** cyclamen-coloured/moss-green material; **~ chair** flesh-coloured, flesh (*épith*); **~ paille** straw-coloured

couleuvre [kulœvʀ] NF **~ (à collier)** grass snake; **~ lisse** smooth snake; **~ vipérine** viperine snake → **avaler**

couleuvrine [kulœvʀin] NF (*Hist*) culverin

coulis [kuli] **1** ADJ M → **vent** **2** NM **a** (*Culin*) coulis; **~ de framboise/de cassis/de tomates** raspberry/blackcurrant/tomato coulis; **~ d'écrevisses** crayfish bisque **b** (*Tech*) (= *mortier*) grout; (= *métal*) molten metal (*filler*)

coulissant, e [kulisã, ãt] ADJ [*porte, panneau*] sliding (*épith*); **ceinture ~e** drawstring belt

coulisse [kulis] NF **a** (*Théât: gén pl*) wings; **en ~** ◊ **dans les ~s** (*Théât*) in the wings; (*fig*) behind the scenes; **les ~s de la politique** what goes on behind the political scenes; (*fig*) **rester dans la ~** to work behind the scenes **b** [*porte, tiroir*] runner; [*rideau*] top hem; [*robe*] casing; (= *panneau mobile*) sliding door; (*Tech* = *glissière*) slide; **porte à ~** sliding door; **regard en ~** sidelong glance *ou* look → **pied, trombone** **c** († : *Bourse*) unofficial Stock Market

coulisseau (*pl* **coulisseaux**) [kuliso] NM [*tiroir*] runner; (*Tech*) slide

coulisser [kulise] ▶conjug 1◀ **1** VT [+ *tiroir, porte*] to provide with runners; [+ *rideau*] to hem (the top of); **jupe coulissée** skirt with a drawstring waist **2** VI [*porte, rideau, tiroir*] to slide, run

coulissier† [kulisje] NM unofficial broker

couloir [kulwaʀ] NM [*bâtiment*] corridor, passage; [*wagon*] corridor; [*avion, train*] aisle; [*appareil de projection*] channel, track; (*Athlétisme, Natation*) lane; (*Géog*) gully, couloir (*SPÉC*); (*Tennis*) tramlines (*Brit*), alley (*surtout US*); (*Ski*) corridor; (*pour bus, taxi*) lane; **~ aérien** air (traffic) lane; **~ humanitaire** safe *ou* humanitarian corridor; **~ de navigation** shipping lane; (*Géog*) **~ d'avalanches** avalanche corridor; (*Pol etc*) **bruits de ~(s)** rumours; (*Pol etc*) **intrigues de ~(s)** backstage manoeuvring

coulommiers [kulɔmje] NM Coulommiers cheese (kind of soft cheese)

coulpe [kulp] NF (*littér ou hum*) **battre sa ~** to beat one's breast

coulure [kulyʀ] NF **a** [*fruit*] failure (due to washing off of pollen) **b** (= *trace*) [*métal*] run-

off; [*peinture*] **il y a des ~s** the paint has run (in several places)

coup [ku]

Lorsque **coup** *est suivi d'un complément de nom désignant une partie du corps ou un instrument* (coup de main/pied/balai/marteau/téléphone, coup d'œil *etc*), *cherchez à ce nom.*

NOM MASCULIN

a **= heurt, choc** knock, blow; (*affectif*) blow, shock; (*marquant l'agression*) blow; **il a pris un ~ sur la tête** (= *il s'est cogné*) he knocked *ou* banged his head, he got a blow on the head; (= *on l'a frappé*) he was hit on the head, he got a blow on the head; **la voiture a reçu un ~** the car has had a knock (*Brit*) *ou* bump; **donner des ~s dans la porte** to bang *ou* hammer at the door; **donner un ~ sec pour dégager qch** to give sth a sharp rap *ou* knock to release it; **ça a porté un ~ sévère à leur moral** it dealt a severe blow to their morale; **en prendre un** (bon *ou* sacré *ou* sérieux) **~*** [*carrosserie*] to have a (nasty) bash* (*Brit*) *ou* bang; [*personne, confiance, moral*] to take a (nasty) blow *ou* a (real) knock; **ça lui a fait** *ou* **fichu un ~*** it's given him a (bit of a) shock, it was a bit of a blow (for him); **~ dur** hard blow; **il m'a donné un ~** he hit me; **en venir aux ~s** to come to blows; **les ~s tombaient dru** *ou* **pleuvaient** the blows rained down *ou* fell thick and fast; (*Jur*) **~s et blessures** assault and battery, aggravated assault → **accuser, marquer**

b **Sport = geste** (*Cricket, Golf, Tennis*) stroke; (*Boxe*) blow, punch; (*Tir*) shot; (*Échecs*) move; (*aux dés*) throw; **il a fait 421 en deux ~s** he got 421 in two throws; (*Tennis*) **~ droit** drive; (*Tennis*) **~ droit croisé** cross-court drive; **renvoyer la balle en ~ droit** to do a forehand drive; **~ bas** (*Boxe*) blow *ou* punch below the belt; (*fig*) blow below the belt; **c'était un ~ bas** that was below the belt; **~ franc** (*Ftbl, Rugby*) free kick; (*Basket*) free-throw shot; **tous les ~s sont permis** no holds barred; **un ~ pour rien** (*lit*) a go for nothing, a free go; (*fig*) **c'était un ~ pour rien** it was all for nothing → **discuter, marquer**

c **= habileté** **avoir le ~** to have the knack; **attraper** *ou* **prendre le ~** to get the knack → **main**

d **effort** **en mettre un ~*** to pull out all the stops*; **il en met un sacré ~*** he's really going at it

e **= décharge, détonation** [*arme à feu*] shot; **à six ~s** six-shot (*épith*); **il jouait avec le fusil quand le ~ est parti** he was playing with the rifle when it went off; **faire ~ double** (*Chasse*) to do a right and left; (*fig*) to kill two birds with one stone → **feu¹, grâce, tirer**

f **= bruit de choc** knock; (*sec*) rap; **il y eut un ~ à la porte** there was a knock at the door; **sonner 3 ~s** to ring 3 times; **les douze ~s de midi** the twelve strokes of noon; **sur le ~ de minuit** at *ou* on the stroke of midnight; **sur le ~ des 10-11 heures** around 10 or 11 → **frapper**

g **= événement fortuit** **~ du sort** *ou* **du destin** blow dealt by fate; **~ de chance** *ou* **de veine*** ◊ **~ de pot*** *ou* **de bol*** stroke *ou* piece of luck; **~ de malchance** rotten luck → **sale**

h *** = action concertée, hasardeuse** [*cambrioleurs*] job*; *** = médiatique** media stunt; **il est sur un ~*** he's up to something; **elle voulait cette maison, mais ils étaient plusieurs sur le ~** she wanted that house but there were several people after it; **ça vaut** *ou* **ça vaut le ~*** it's worth (having) a go* *ou* a bash* (*Brit*); **réussir un beau ~** to pull it off; **il a manqué** *ou* **raté son ~** he blew it*, he didn't pull it off*; **c'est un ~ à se tuer!*/à se faire virer!*** you could get yourself killed doing that!/fired for doing that!; **c'est encore un ~ de 1 000 F*** that'll be another 1,000 francs to fork out* → **cent¹, quatre**

♦ **dans le coup** : **être dans le ~** (*impliqué*) to be in on it*; (*au courant*) to know all about it; (*expert*) to know what's what; (*à la page*) to be

with it*; **une grand-mère dans le ~** a with-it* *ou* hip* grandmother; **mettre qn dans le ~** to get sb involved, bring sb in; **pendant le match, il n'était pas dans le ~** he wasn't really with it* during the match

♦ **valoir le coup** : **ça vaut le ~** it's worth it; **c'est un film qui vaut le ~** the film is worth seeing; **cela valait le ~ d'essayer** it was worth trying *ou* a try; **ça ne vaut pas le ~ de partir pour 2 jours** it's not worth going just for 2 days

i ♦ **à coup(s) de** (= *au moyen de*) **la société boucle son budget à ~s de subventions** the firm manages to balance its budget by using *ou* through subsidies; **réussir à ~ de publicité** to succeed through repeated advertising *ou* through a massive publicity drive

j **= action contre qn** trick; **~ monté** setup; **c'est bien un ~ à lui** that's just like him *ou* typical of him; **tu ne vas pas nous faire le ~ d'être malade** you're not going to go and be ill on us*; **il nous fait le ~ chaque fois** he always does that; **un ~ en vache*** a dirty trick*; **faire un ~ en vache à qn*** to do the dirty on sb*, pull a dirty trick on sb*; **un ~ en traître** a stab in the back → **mauvais, panne, sale**

k *** = fois** time; **à chaque ~** ◊ **à tous (les) ~s** ◊ **à tout** every time; **à tous les ~s on gagne!** every one a winner!; **du même ~** at the same time; **pleurer/rire un bon ~** to have a good cry/laugh

♦ **au coup par coup** [*agir*] on an ad hoc basis; [*embaucher, acheter*] as and when the need arises

♦ **coup sur coup** in quick succession; **deux victoires ~ sur ~, c'est bon pour l'équipe!** two wins one after the other *ou* two successive wins, that's good for the team!

♦ **d'un seul coup** : **d'un seul ~, les lumières s'éteignirent** all at once *ou* all of a sudden the lights went out; **il a sauté 4 marches d'un seul ~** he leaped *ou* took 4 steps in one go *ou* at a time

♦ **du premier coup** ◊ **au premier coup** straight away, right away; **il a eu son permis de conduire du premier ~** he got his driving licence first time round *ou* first go*

l *** = quantité bue** **boire un ~** to have a drink *ou* something to drink; **aller boire un ~** (*gén*) to go and have something to drink; (*au café*) to go for a drink; **je te paie un ~ (à boire)** I'll buy you a drink; **vous boirez bien un ~ de rouge avec nous?** come and have a glass of red wine with us; **il a bu un ~ de trop** ◊ **il a un ~ dans le nez*** he's had one too many*, he's had one over the eight*

m **** = partenaire sexuel** **être un bon ~** to be a good screw** *ou* fuck**

n **expressions figées**

♦ **à coup sûr** (= *sûrement*) definitely

♦ **après coup** afterwards, after the event

♦ **du coup** as a result

♦ **pour le coup** : **c'est pour le ~ qu'il se fâcherait** then he'd really get angry; **là, pour le ~, il m'a étonné** he really surprised me there

♦ **sous le coup de** (= *sous l'effet de*) [+ *surprise, colère*] in the grip of; **sous le ~ d'une forte émotion** in a highly emotional state, in the grip of a powerful emotion

(*Admin*) **être sous le ~ d'une condamnation** to have a current conviction; **être sous le ~ d'une mesure d'expulsion** to be under an expulsion order; **il est sous le ~ d'un mandat d'arrêt** there is a warrant out for his arrest; **tomber sous le ~ de la loi** [*activité, acte*] to be a statutory offence

♦ **sur le coup** (= *instantanément*) outright; **mourir sur le ~** (= *assassinat*) to be killed outright; (*accident*) to die *ou* be killed instantly; **sur le ~ je n'ai pas compris** at the time I didn't understand

♦ **tout à coup** ◊ **tout d'un coup** all of a sudden, suddenly, all at once

coupable [kupabl] **1** ADJ **a** (= *fautif*) [*personne*] guilty (**de** of) → **non**, **plaider** **b** (= *blâmable*) [*désirs, amour*] guilty (*épith*); [*action, négligence*] culpable, reprehensible; [*faiblesse*] reprehensible **2** NMF culprit, guilty party (*hum*); **le grand ~ c'est le jeu** the real culprit is gambling, gambling is chiefly to blame

coupage [kupaʒ] NM [*vin*] (*avec un autre vin*) blending (*NonC*); (*avec de l'eau*) dilution (*NonC*), diluting (*NonC*); **ce sont des ~s ◊ ce sont des vins de ~** these are blended wines

coupant, e [kupɑ̃, ɑ̃t] ADJ [*lame, brin d'herbe*] sharp(-edged); [*ton, réponse*] sharp

coup-de-poing (*pl* **coups-de-poing**) [kud(ə)pwɛ̃] NM **a** (*Archéol*) biface, bifacial flint **b** (= *arme*) knuckle-duster(s), brass knuckles

coupe¹ [kup] NF **a** (*à dessert, à glace*) dish, bowl; (= *contenu*) dish(ful), bowl(ful); (*à boire*) goblet; **une ~ de champagne** a glass of champagne; **~ à fruits** (= *saladier*) fruit bowl; (*individuelle*) fruit dish, coupe; (*fig*) **la ~ est pleine** I've had enough, that's the limit → **boire**, **loin** **b** (*Sport* = *objet, épreuve*) cup; **~ d'Europe/du monde** European/World cup; **la ~ de France de football** the French football (*Brit*) ou soccer (*US*) cup

coupe² [kup] **1** NF **a** (*Couture*) (= *action*) cutting(-out); (= *pièce de tissu*) length; (= *façon d'être coupé*) cut; **robe de belle ~/de ~ sobre** beautifully/simply cut dress; **~ nette** ou **franche** clean cut
b (*Sylviculture*) (= *action*) cutting (down); (= *étendue de forêt*) felling area; (= *surface, tranche*) section
c [*herbe*] cutting; [*gâteau*] cutting up, slicing; [*rôti*] carving, cutting up; **fromage/beurre vendu à la ~** cheese/butter sold loose
d [*cheveux*] cutting; **~ (de cheveux)** (hair)cut; **~ au rasoir** razor-cut; **faites-moi une ~ toute simple** just do something simple
e (*pour examen au microscope*) section; **~ histologique** histological section
f (= *dessin, plan*) section; **le navire vu en ~** a (cross) section of the ship; **~ transversale** cross ou transversal section; **~ longitudinale** longitudinal section
g (*Littérat*) [*vers*] break, caesura
h (*Cartes*) cut, cutting (*NonC*); **jouer sous la ~ de qn** to lead (after sb has cut)
i (= *réduction*) cut; **faire des ~s dans qch** to make cuts in sth
j (*loc*) **être sous la ~ de qn** [*personne*] (= *être dominé*) to be under sb's thumb; (*hiérarchiquement*) to be under sb; [*entreprise, organisation*] to be under sb's control; **tomber sous la ~ de qn** to fall prey to sb, fall into sb's clutches

2 COMP ► **coupe claire** clear-cutting, clear-felling; (*fig*) **faire des ~s claires dans qch** to make drastic cuts in sth ► **coupe d'ensemencement** thinning (out) (*to allow space for sowing new trees*) ► **coupe réglée** periodic felling; (*fig*) **mettre en ~ réglée** to bleed systematically ► **coupe sombre** (slight) thinning (out); **faire des ~s sombres dans** to make drastic cuts in; **~s sombres dans le personnel** severe staff reductions ou cutbacks

coupé, e¹ [kupe] (*ptp de* **couper**) **1** ADJ **a** [*vêtement*] **bien/mal ~** well/badly cut **b** [*communications, routes*] cut off (*attrib*) **c** [*vin*] blended **d** (*Vét* = *castré*) neutered **2** NM (*Aut, Danse*) coupé

coupe-chou(x)* (*pl* **coupe-choux**) [kupʃu] NM (= *épée*) short sword; (= *rasoir*) open razor

coupe-cigare (*pl* **coupe-cigares**) [kupsigar] NM cigar cutter

coupe-circuit (*pl* **coupe-circuits**) [kupsirkɥi] NM cutout, circuit breaker

coupe-coupe [kupkup] NM INV machete

coupée² [kupe] NF (*Naut*) gangway (*opening, with ladder*) → **échelle**

coupe-faim (*pl* **coupe-faim(s)**) [kupfɛ̃] NM appetite suppressant; **le tabac a un effet ~** smoking takes away your appetite

coupe-feu (*pl* **coupe-feu(x)**) [kupfø] NM (= *espace*) firebreak; (= *chose*) fireguard; **porte ~** fire door

coupe-file (*pl* **coupe-files**) [kupfil] NM (= *carte de priorité*) pass

coupe-frites [kupfrit] NM INV chip-cutter ou -slicer (*Brit*), French-fry-cutter ou -slicer (*US*)

coupe-gorge (*pl* **coupe-gorge(s)**) [kupgɔrʒ] NM (= *quartier*) dangerous ou no-go area; (= *rue*) dangerous back-alley; **ce café/cette banlieue est un vrai ~!** you take your life in your hands when you go into that café/that area!

coupe-jarret (*pl* **coupe-jarrets**) [kupʒare] NM († *ou hum*) cutthroat

coupe-légume(s) (*pl* **coupe-légumes**) [kuplegym] NM vegetable-cutter

coupelle [kupɛl] NF **a** (= *petite coupe*) (small) dish **b** (*Chim*) cupel

coupe-œufs [kupø] NM INV egg-slicer

coupe-ongle(s) (*pl* **coupe-ongles**) [kupɔ̃gl] NM (= *pince*) nail clippers; (= *ciseaux*) nail scissors

coupe-papier [kuppapje] NM INV paper knife

▼ **couper** [kupe] ▶conjug 1◀ **1** VT **a** (= *sectionner*) to cut; [+ *bois*] to chop; [+ *arbre*] to cut down, fell; (= *séparer*) to cut off; (= *découper*) [+ *rôti*] to carve, cut up; (= *partager*) [+ *gâteau*] to cut, slice; (= *entailler*) [*vent*] to sting; **~ qch en (petits) morceaux** to cut sth up, cut sth into (little) pieces; **~ qch en tranches** to slice sth, cut sth into slices; (*lit*) **~ qch en deux** to cut sth in two ou in half; (*fig*) **le parti/l'électorat est coupé en deux** the party is/the voters are split down the middle; (*Mét*) **le pays sera coupé en deux** the country will be split in two; (*Ordin*) ~ **coller** to cut and paste; **~ la gorge à qn** to slit ou cut sb's throat; **~ la tête** ou **le cou à qn** to cut ou chop sb's head off; **~ (les pages d')un livre** to slit open ou cut the pages of a book; **livre non coupé** book with uncut pages; **coupez-lui une tranche de pain** cut him a slice of bread; **se faire ~ les cheveux** to get ou have one's hair cut, have a haircut → **six**, **tête**, **vif**
b (*Couture*) [+ *vêtement*] to cut out; [+ *étoffe*] to cut
c (= *retrancher*) [+ *passages inutiles*] to cut (out), take out, delete; (= *raccourcir*) [+ *émission*] to cut (down)
d (= *arrêter*) [+ *eau, gaz, courant*] to cut off; (*au compteur*) to turn off; [+ *communications, route, pont*] to cut off; [+ *relations diplomatiques*] to cut off, break off; (*Téléc*) to cut off; [+ *crédits*] to cut off; (*Ciné*) [+ *prise de vues*] to cut; (*Ciné*) **coupez!** cut!; (*Aut*) **~ le contact** ou **l'allumage** to switch off the ignition; **~ l'appétit à qn** (*un peu*) to take the edge off sb's appetite; (*complètement*) to spoil sb's appetite, take away sb's appetite; **~ la faim à qn** to take the edge off sb's hunger; **~ la fièvre à qn** to bring down sb's fever; (*fig*) **~ les ponts avec qn** to break off communications with sb; **~ la retraite à qn** to cut ou block off sb's line of retreat; **~ la route à qn** to cut sb off, cut in front of sb; **~ la route d'un véhicule** to cut a vehicle off; **la route était coupée par le bombardement** the road was completely cut off by the bombing; **~ le vent** to cut out the wind; **~ les vivres à qn** to cut off sb's means of subsistence
e (= *interrompre*) **~ qn** to interrupt sb; **~ la parole à qn** [*personne*] to cut sb short; [*émotion*] to leave ou render sb speechless; **~ le sifflet** ou **la chique* à qn** to shut sb up*, take the wind out of sb's sails; **ça te la coupe!*** that's shut you up!*
f (= *rompre la continuité de*) [+ *voyage*] to break; [+ *journée*] to break up; **nous nous arrêterons à Caen pour ~ le voyage** we'll stop at Caen to break the journey, we'll break the journey at Caen

g (= *isoler*) **~ qn de qch** to cut sb off from sth
h (= *traverser*) [*ligne*] to intersect, cut; [*route*] to cut across, cross; **le chemin de fer coupe la route en 2 endroits** the railway cuts across ou crosses the road at 2 points; **une cloison coupe la pièce** the room is divided by a partition
i (*Cartes*) [+ *jeu*] to cut; (= *prendre avec l'atout*) to trump
j (*Sport*) [+ *balle*] to slice, undercut
k [+ *vin*] (*à table*) to dilute, add water to; [+ *vin*] (*à la production*) to blend; **vin coupé d'eau** wine diluted with water
l (*Vét* = *castrer*) to neuter
m (*loc*) **~ les bras** ou **bras et jambes à qn** [*travail*] to wear sb out; [*nouvelle*] to knock sb for six* (*Brit*) ou for a loop* (*US*); **j'en ai les jambes coupées** I'm stunned; **coupons la poire en deux** let's meet halfway; **~ les cheveux en quatre** to split hairs, quibble; **~ la respiration à qn** (*lit*) to wind sb; (*fig*) to take sb's breath away → **couteau**, **effet**, **herbe**, **souffle** etc

2 **couper à** VT INDIR (= *échapper à*) [+ *corvée*] to get out of; **tu n'y couperas pas d'une amende** you won't get away without paying a fine, you won't get out of paying a fine; **tu n'y couperas pas** you won't get out of it → **court¹**

3 VI **a** (= *être tranchant*) [*couteau, verre*] to cut; [*vent*] to be biting; **ce couteau coupe bien** this knife cuts well ou has a good cutting edge
b (= *prendre un raccourci*) **~ à travers champs** to cut across country ou the fields; **~ au plus court** to go the quickest way; **~ par un sentier/la forêt** to cut along a path/through the forest
c (*Cartes*) (= *diviser le jeu*) to cut; (= *jouer atout*) to trump; **~ à trèfle/à carreau** etc to trump with a club/diamond etc

4 **se couper** VPR **a** (= *s'entailler la peau*) to cut o.s.
b (= *retrancher une partie de son corps*) **se ~ les cheveux/les ongles** to cut one's hair/nails
c (= *être usé*) [*tissu*] to come apart; [*cuir*] to crack
d (= *perdre contact*) **se ~ de** [+ *amis, famille, pays*] to cut o.s. off from, cut all ties with
e (= *se trahir*) to give o.s. away

couperet [kupre] NM [*boucher*] chopper, cleaver; [*guillotine*] blade, knife; **la décision est tombée comme un ~** the decision came as a bombshell ou was a bolt from the blue

couperose [kuproz] NF blotches (*on the face*), rosacea (*SPÉC*)

couperosé, e [kuproze] ADJ blotchy, affected by rosacea (*attrib*) (*SPÉC*)

coupeur, -euse [kupœr, øz] NM,F (*Couture*) cutter; **~ de tête** headhunter; **~ de cheveux en quatre** hairsplitter, quibbler

coupe-vent (*pl* **coupe-vent(s)**) [kupvɑ̃] NM (= *haie*) windbreak; (= *vêtement*) windcheater (*Brit*), windbreaker (*US*)

couplage [kuplaʒ] NM (*Élec, Tech*) coupling

couple [kupl] **1** NM **a** (= *époux, amoureux, danseurs*) couple; (= *patineurs, animaux*) pair; **~ Martin** the Martins; **ils ont des problèmes de ~ ◊ leur ~ a des problèmes** they have problems with their relationship; (*Patinage*) **l'épreuve en** ou **par ~s** the pairs (event) **b** (*Phys*) couple; **~ moteur** torque; **~ de torsion** torque **c** (*Naut*) (square) frame; (*Aviat*) frame; **s'amarrer à ~** to moor alongside another boat → **nage, nager** **2** NF ou M († = *deux*) **un** ou **une ~ de** a couple of **3** NF (*Chasse*) couple

couplé [kuple] NM (*pari*) ~ first and second place double (*on two horses in the same race*)

coupler [kuple] ▶conjug 1◀ VT **a** (*Chasse*) to couple (together), leash together **b** (*Tech*) to couple together ou up; (*Ordin*) to interface (**avec** with); (*Photo*) **télémètre couplé** coupled rangefinder; (Rail) **bielles couplées** coupling rods

couplet [kuplɛ] NM (= strophe) verse; (péj) tirade; (= chanson) **~s satiriques** satirical song; **y aller de son ~ sur qch** to give a little speech about sth

coupleur [kuplœʀ] NM (Élec) coupler; (Ordin) **~ acoustique** acoustic coupler

coupole [kupɔl] NF [a] (Archit) dome; **petite ~** cupola, small dome; **être reçu sous la Coupole** to become ou be made a member of the Académie française → ACADÉMIE [b] (Mil) [char d'assaut] revolving gun turret

coupon [kupɔ̃] NM [a] (Couture, Tex = reste) remnant; (= rouleau) roll [b] (Fin) **~ (de dividende)** coupon; **avec ~ attaché/détaché** cum-/ex-dividend) note, bill (US); **petites/grosses ~s** small/big notes, notes of small/large denomination [e] (= interruption) **~ (de courant)** power cut; **il y aura des ~s ce soir** (électricité) there'll be power cuts tonight; (gaz, eau) the gas (ou water) will be cut off tonight [f] (= arrêt, pause) break; **la ~ estivale** the summer break; **~ publicitaire** commercial break [g] (= division) divide (**entre** between); (Pol) **la ~ droite-gauche** the left-right divide

cour [kuʀ] [1] NF [a] [bâtiment] yard, courtyard; **être sur (la) ~** to look onto the (back)yard; **la ~ de la caserne** the barracks square; **~ de cloître** cloister garth; **~ d'école** schoolyard, playground; **~ de ferme** farmyard; **la ~ de la gare** the station forecourt; **~ d'honneur** main courtyard; **~ d'immeuble** courtyard of a block of flats (Brit) ou an apartment building (US); **~ intérieure** inner courtyard; **~ de récréation** playground; **la ~ des grands** (lit) the older children's playground; (fig) **jouer dans la ~ des grands** to play with the big boys* ou in the major league (US) → côté [b] (Jur) court; **Messieurs, la Cour!** ≈ all rise!, ≈ be upstanding in court! (Brit); **la Cour suprême** the Supreme Court → haut [c] [roi] court; [personnage puissant, célèbre] following; **vivre à la ~** to live at court; **faire sa ~ à** [+ roi] to pay court to; [+ supérieur, femme] to pay one's respects to; **être bien/mal en ~** to be in/out of favour (**auprès de qn** with sb); **homme/habit de ~** court gentleman/clothes; **gens de ~** courtiers, people at court; **c'est la ~ du roi Pétaud** it's absolute bedlam* [d] [femme] (= soupirants) following; (= essai de conquête) wooing (NonC), courting (NonC); **faire la ~ à une femme** to woo ou court a woman; **faire un brin de ~ à une femme*** to flirt with a woman

[2] COMP ► **cour d'appel** ≈ Court of Appeal, ≈ appellate court (US) ► **cour d'assises** ≈ Crown Court (Brit), ≈ court of assizes ► **cour de cassation** Court of Cassation, (final) Court of Appeal ► **cour des comptes** revenue court, ≈ Government Accounting Office (US) ► **Cour européenne des droits de l'homme** European Court of Human Rights ► **Cour européenne de justice** European Court of Justice ► **Cour internationale de justice** International Court of Justice ► **cour de justice** court of justice ► **cour martiale** court martial; **passer en ~ martiale** to be court-martialled ► **la Cour des Miracles** (Hist) area of Paris

famed for its disreputable population; (fig) **chez eux c'est une vraie ~ des miracles** their place is always full of shady characters; **ce quartier est une vraie ~ des miracles** this is a very unsavoury area ► **Cour de sûreté de l'État** state security court

courage [kuʀaʒ] NM [a] (= bravoure) courage, bravery, guts*; **avoir du ~** to be brave ou courageous, have guts*; **~ physique/moral** physical/moral courage; **se battre avec ~** to fight courageously ou with courage ou bravely; **s'il y va, il a du ~!** if he goes, it means he has guts!*; **je n'ai pas eu le ~ de lui refuser** I didn't have the heart to refuse [b] (= ardeur) will, spirit; **entreprendre une tâche/un travail avec ~** to undertake a task/job with a will; **je voudrais finir ce travail, mais je ne m'en sens pas** ou **je n'en ai pas le ~** I'd like to get this work finished, but I don't feel up to it; **je n'ai pas beaucoup de ~ ce soir** I don't feel up to much this evening; **il se lève tous les jours à 5 heures?** — **quel ~!/il a du ~!** he gets up at 5am every day? — what willpower!/he must have a lot of willpower!; **un petit verre pour vous donner du ~*** just a little drink to buck you up* [c] (loc) **~! nous y sommes presque!** cheer up! ou take heart! we're almost there!; **avoir le ~ de ses opinions** to have the courage of one's convictions; **prendre son ~ à deux mains** to take one's courage in both hands; **perdre ~** to lose heart, become discouraged; **reprendre ~** to take fresh heart

courageusement [kuʀaʒøzmɑ̃] ADV bravely, courageously; **entreprendre ~ une tâche** to tackle a task with a will

courageux, -euse [kuʀaʒø, øz] ADJ brave, courageous; **il n'est pas très ~ pour l'étude** he's lazy when it comes to studying, he hasn't got much will for studying; **je ne suis pas très ~ aujourd'hui** I don't feel up to very much today

couramment [kuʀamɑ̃] ADV [a] (= aisément) fluently; **parler le français ~** to speak French fluently ou fluent French [b] (= souvent) commonly; **ce mot s'emploie ~** this word is in current ou common usage; **ça se dit ~** it's a common ou an everyday expression; **cela arrive ~** it's a common occurrence; **cela se fait ~** it's quite a common thing to do, it's quite common practice

courant, e [kuʀɑ̃, ɑ̃t] [1] ADJ [a] (= normal, habituel) [dépenses] everyday, standard, ordinary; (Comm) [modèle, taille, marque] standard; **l'usage ~** everyday ou ordinary ou standard usage; **en utilisant les procédés ~s on gagne du temps** it saves time to use the normal ou ordinary ou standard procedures; **il nous suffit pour le travail ~** he'll do for the routine ou everyday business → **vie** [b] (= fréquent) common; **c'est un procédé ~** it's quite common practice ou quite a common procedure, it's quite commonplace; **ce genre d'incident est très ~ ici** this kind of incident is very common here, this kind of thing is a common occurrence here [c] (= en cours, actuel) [année, semaine] current, present; (Écon) [francs, prix] current; (Comm) **votre lettre du 5 ~** your letter of the 5th inst. ou instant ou of the 5th of this month → **expédier, monnaie** [d] (= qui court) → **chien, compte, eau**

[2] NM [a] [cours d'eau, mer, atmosphère] current; **~ (atmosphérique)** airstream, current; **~ d'air** draught (Brit), draft (US); **plein de ~s d'air** very draughty; (Mét) **~ d'air froid/chaud** cold/warm airstream; (fig) **c'est un vrai ~ d'air** one minute he's there, the next he's gone; **il y a trop de ~** the current's too strong; **suivre le ~** (lit) to go with the current; (fig) to go with the stream, follow the crowd; **remonter le ~** (lit) to go against the current; (fig) to get back on one's feet [b] (= déplacement) [population, échanges

commerciaux] movement; **~s de population** movements ou shifts of (the) population [c] (= mouvement: gén) movement; [opinion, pensée] trend, current; **les ~s de l'opinion** trends of public opinion; **un ~ de scepticisme/de sympathie** a wave of scepticism/sympathy; **le ~ romantique/surréaliste** the romantic/surrealist movement [d] (Élec) current, power; **~ continu/alternatif** direct/alternating current; **couper le ~** to cut off the power; **rétablir le ~** to put the power back on; **on s'est rencontré un soir et le ~ est tout de suite passé** we met one evening and hit it off straight away*; **le ~ ne passe pas entre nous** we don't get on; **entre ce chanteur et le public le ~ passe très bien** this singer really gets through to his audience ou has a really good rapport with his audience → **coupure, prise** [e] (= cours) **dans le ~ de la semaine/du mois** in the course of the week/month; **je dois le voir dans le ~ de la semaine** I'm to see him some time during the week; **dans le ~ de la conversation** in the course of the conversation; **le projet doit être fini ~ mai** the project is due to finish some time in May

[3] **au courant** LOC ADJ, LOC ADV **être au ~** (= savoir la nouvelle) to know (about it); (= bien connaître la question) to be well-informed; **tu m'as l'air très** ou **bien au ~ de ce qu'il fait !** you seem to know a lot about ou to be very well-informed about what he's doing!; **être au ~ de** [+ accident, projet] to know about; [+ nouvelles] to be well up on*, be up to date on; **mettre qn au ~ de** [+ faits, affaire] to tell sb about, put sb in the picture about*, fill sb in on*; [+ méthodes nouvelles] to bring sb up to date on; **il s'est vite mis au ~ dans son nouvel emploi** he soon got the hang of things* in his new job; **tenir qn au ~ de** [+ faits, affaire] to keep sb informed of ou posted about*; [+ méthodes] to keep sb up to date on; **si jamais ça recommence, tenez-moi au ~** if it happens again let me know; **s'abonner à une revue scientifique pour se tenir au ~** to subscribe to a science magazine to keep o.s. up to date

[4] **courante** NF [a] (* = diarrhée) **la ~e** the runs* [b] (Mus = danse, air) courante, courant

courbatu, e [kuʀbaty] ADJ stiff, stiff ou aching all over

courbature [kuʀbatyʀ] NF ache; **ce match de tennis m'a donné des ~s** I'm stiff ou aching all over after that game of tennis; **plein de ~s** stiff ou aching all over

courbaturé, e [kuʀbatyʀe] ADJ stiff ou aching all over

courbe [kuʀb] [1] ADJ curved [2] NF (gén, Géom) curve; **le fleuve fait une ~** the river curves; **~ de niveau** contour line; **~ de température** temperature curve

courber [kuʀbe] ▶conjug 1◀ [1] VT [a] (= plier) [+ branche, tige] to bend; **branches courbées sous le poids de la neige** branches bowed down with ou bent under the weight of the snow; **l'âge l'avait courbé** he was bowed ou bent with age [b] (= pencher) **~ la tête** to bow ou bend one's head; **courbant le front sur son livre** his head bent over a book; (fig) **~ la tête** ou **le front** ou **le dos** to submit (**devant** to) → **échine** [2] VI to bend; **~ sous le poids** to bend under the weight [3] **se courber** VPR [a] [arbre, branche, poutre] to bend, curve [b] [personne] (pour entrer, passer) to bend (down), stoop; (signe d'humiliation) to bow down; (signe de déférence) to bow (down); **il se courba pour le saluer** he greeted him with a bow; **se ~ en deux** to bend (o.s.) double [c] (littér = se soumettre) to bow down (**devant** before)

courbette [kuʀbɛt] NF [a] (= salut) low bow; (fig) **faire des ~s à** ou **devant qn** to kowtow to sb, bow and scrape to sb [b] [cheval] curvet

courbure [kuʀbyʀ] NF [ligne, surface] curvature; **~ rentrante/sortante/en S** inward/outward/S curve; **~ du nez/des reins** curve of the nose/the back

courette [kuʀɛt] NF (small) courtyard

coureur, -euse [kuʀœʀ, øz] **1** NM,F (Athlétisme) runner; (Cyclisme) cyclist, competitor; (Aut) driver, competitor; **~ de fond/de demi-fond** long-distance/middle-distance runner; **~ de 110 mètres haies** 110 metres hurdler **2** NM **a** (Zool) (oiseaux) **~s** running birds **b** (péj = amateur de) **c'est un ~ de cafés/de bals** he hangs round (Brit) ou around cafés/dances; **(de filles ou femmes ou jupons)** womanizer, skirt-chaser; **il est assez ~** he's a bit of a womanizer ou a skirt-chaser ou a wolf* **3** **coureuse** NF (péj = débauchée) manhunter; **elle est un peu coureuse** she's always chasing after men, she's a bit of a manhunter **4** COMP ▶ **coureur automobile** racing(-car) driver ▶ **coureur de ou des bois** (Hist Can) trapper, coureur de bois (US, Can) ▶ **coureur cycliste** racing cyclist ▶ **coureur de dot** (péj) fortune-hunter ▶ **coureur motocycliste** motorcycle ou motorbike racer

courge [kuʀʒ] NF **a** (= plante, fruit) gourd, squash (US, Can); (Culin) marrow (Brit), squash (US, Can) **b**‡ idiot, berk‡ (Brit)

courgette [kuʀʒɛt] NF courgette (Brit), zucchini (US)

courir [kuʀiʀ] ▶conjug 11◀ **1** VI **a** (gén, Athlétisme) to run; (Aut, Cyclisme) to race; (Courses) to run, race; **entrer/sortir en courant** to run in/out; **se mettre à ~** to break into a run, start to run, start running; **~ sur Ferrari** to race with Ferrari; **il courait à toutes jambes** ou **à perdre haleine** he ran as fast as his legs could carry him; **~ comme un dératé** ou **ventre à terre** to run flat out; **elle court comme un lapin** ou **lièvre** she runs ou can run like a hare ou the wind; **le voleur court encore** ou **toujours** the thief is still at large; **faire ~ un cheval** to race ou run a horse; **il ne fait plus ~** he doesn't race ou run horses any more; **un cheval trop vieux pour ~** a horse too old to race ou to be raced

b (= se précipiter) to rush; **~ chez le docteur/chercher le docteur** to rush ou run to the doctor's/for the doctor; **je cours l'appeler** I'll go ou run and call him straight away (Brit) ou right away; **ce spectacle fait ~ tout Paris** all Paris is rushing to see the show; **faire qch en courant** to do sth in a rush ou hurry; **elle m'a fait ~** she had me running all over the place; **elle est toujours en train de ~** she's always rushing about; **un petit mot en courant** just a (quick) note ou a few hurried lines; **~ partout pour trouver qch** to hunt everywhere for sth; **tu peux toujours ~!*** you can (go) whistle for it!*; **pour enlever les taches, tu peux toujours ~*** if you think you can get rid of those stains you've got another think coming*

c (avec à, après, sur) **~ à l'échec/à une déception** to be heading ou headed for failure/a disappointment; **~ à sa perte** ou **ruine** to be on the road to ruin; **~ à la catastrophe** to be rushing headlong into disaster; **~ après qch** to chase after sth; **~ après un ballon** to run after a ball; **l'autobus démarra et il courut après** the bus started and he ran after it; **gardez cet argent pour l'instant, il ne court pas après** keep this money for now as he's not in any hurry ou rush for it ou he's not desperate for it; **les épinards, je ne cours pas après** I'm not that keen on spinach; (lit, fig) **~ après qn** to run after sb; **~ après les femmes** to be a womanizer; **~ sur ses 60/70 ans** to be approaching ou pushing* ou getting on for 60/70; **~ sur le système** ou **le haricot à qn‡** to get on sb's nerves* ou wick* (Brit)

d [nuages] to speed, race, scud (littér); [ombres, reflets] to speed, race; [eau] to rush; [chemin] to run; **un frisson lui courut par tout**

le corps a shiver went ou ran through his body; **sa plume courait sur le papier** his pen was racing across the paper; **laisser ~ ses doigts sur un clavier** to tinkle away at a piano

e (= se répandre) **faire ~ une nouvelle** to spread a piece of news; **le bruit court que ...** rumour has it that ..., there is a rumour that ..., the rumour is that ...; **le bruit a récemment couru que ...** there has been a rumour going around that ...; **il court sur leur compte de curieuses histoires** there are some strange stories going around about them

f (= se passer) **l'année/le mois qui court** the current ou present year/month; **laisser ~*** to let things alone; **laisse ~!*** forget it!*, drop it!*

g (Naut) to sail

h (Fin) [intérêt] to accrue; [bail] to run

2 VT **a** (Sport) [+ épreuve] to compete in; **~ un 100 mètres** to run (in) ou compete in a 100 metres race; **~ le Grand Prix** to race in the Grand Prix

b (Chasse) **~ le cerf/le sanglier** to hunt stag/boar, go staghunting/boarhunting → **lièvre**

c (= rechercher) [+ honneurs] to seek avidly; (s'exposer à) **~ de grands dangers** to be in great danger; **~ les aventures** ou **l'aventure** to seek adventure; **~ un (gros) risque** to run a (high ou serious) risk; **~ sa chance** to try one's luck; **il court le risque d'être accusé** he runs the risk of being accused; **c'est un risque à ~** it's a risk we'll have to take ou run; (Théât) **~ le cachet** to chase after any sort of work

d (= parcourir) [+ mers, monde] to roam, rove; [+ campagne, bois] to roam ou rove (through); (= faire le tour de) [+ magasins, bureaux] to go round; **j'ai couru les agences toute la matinée** I've been going round the agencies all morning; **~ les rues** (lit) to wander ou roam the streets; (fig) to be run-of-the-mill, be nothing out of the ordinary; **le vrai courage ne court pas les rues** real courage is hard to find; **des gens comme lui, ça ne court pas les rues*** there aren't many like him

e (= fréquenter) **~ les théâtres/les bals** to do the rounds of (all) the theatres/dances; **~ les filles** to chase the girls; **~ la gueuse†** to go wenching†; **~ le guilledou†** ou **la prétentaine†** ou **le cotillon** to go gallivanting†, go wenching†

f (‡ = ennuyer) **~ qn** to bug sb‡, get up sb's nose‡ (Brit) ou on sb's wick* (Brit)

courlis [kuʀli] NM curlew

couronne [kuʀɔn] NF **a** [fleurs] wreath, circlet; **~ funéraire** ou **mortuaire** (funeral) wreath; **~ de fleurs d'oranger** orange-blossom headdress, circlet of orange-blossom; **~ de lauriers** laurel wreath, crown of laurels; **~ d'épines** crown of thorns; **en ~** in a ring → **fleur b** (= diadème) [roi, pape] crown; [noble] coronet **c** (= autorité royale) **la ~** the Crown; **la ~ d'Angleterre/de France** the crown of England/of France, the English/French crown; **aspirer/prétendre à la ~** to aspire to/lay claim to the throne ou the crown; **de la ~** [joyaux, colonie] crown (épith) **d** (= objet circulaire) crown; (= pain) ring-shaped loaf; [dent] crown; (Archit, Astron) corona; (Aut) **~ dentée** crown wheel; **la grande/petite ~** the outer/inner suburbs (of Paris) **e** (= monnaie) crown

couronnement [kuʀɔnmɑ̃] NM **a** [roi, empereur] coronation, crowning **b** [édifice, colonne] top, crown; [mur] coping; [toit] ridge **c** [carrière, œuvre, recherche] crowning achievement

couronner [kuʀɔne] ▶conjug 1◀ **1** VT **a** [+ souverain] to crown; **on le couronna roi** he was crowned king, they crowned him king → **tête**

b [+ ouvrage, auteur] to award a prize to; (Hist) [+ lauréat, vainqueur] to crown with a laurel wreath

c (littér = orner, ceindre) to crown; [diadème]

[+ front] to encircle; **couronné de fleurs** wreathed ou encircled with flowers; **remparts qui couronnent la colline** ramparts which crown the hill; **pic couronné de neige** snow-capped peak, peak crowned with snow

d (= parachever) to crown; **cela couronne son œuvre/sa carrière** that is the crowning achievement of his work/his career; (iro) **et pour ~ le tout** and to crown it all; **ses efforts ont été couronnés de succès** his efforts were crowned with success

e [+ dent] to crown

2 **se couronner** VPR **se ~ (le genou)** [cheval] to graze its knee; [personne] to graze one's knee

courre [kuʀ] VT → **chasse¹**

courrier [kuʀje] NM **a** (= lettres reçues) mail, post (Brit), letters; (= lettres à écrire) letters; **le ~ de 11 heures** the 11 o'clock post (Brit) ou mail; **avoir** ou **recevoir un ~ de ministre** to be inundated with mail ou letters, have a huge postbag* (Brit); (sur bac) **« ~ arrivée/départ »** "in/out"; (Ordin) **~ électronique** e-mail, electronic mail; **envoyer qch par ~ électronique** to e-mail sth, send sth by e-mail **~ retour b** † (= avion, bateau) mail; (Mil = estafette) courrier; (de diligence) post; **l'arrivée du ~ de Bogota** the arrival of the Bogota mail → **long-courrier c** (Presse) (= rubrique) column; (= nom de journal) ≈ Mail; **~ du cœur** problem page, agony column (Brit); **~ des lecteurs** letters to the Editor; **~ littéraire** literary column; **~ économique** financial page

courriériste [kuʀjeʀist] NMF columnist

courroie [kuʀwa] NF (= attache) strap; (Tech) belt; (Tech) **~ de transmission** driving belt; **je ne suis qu'une simple ~ de transmission** I'm just a cog in the machine ou in the wheel; (Aut) **~ de ventilateur** fan belt

courroucé, e [kuʀuse] (ptp de **courroucer**) ADJ (littér) wrathful, incensed

courroucer [kuʀuse] ▶conjug 3◀ (littér) **1** VT to anger, incense **2** **se courroucer** VPR to become incensed

courroux [kuʀu] NM (littér) ire (littér), wrath

cours [kuʀ] **1** NM **a** (= déroulement, Astron) course; [événements] course, run; (saisons) course, progression; [guerre, maladie] progress, course; [pensées, idées] course; **donner (libre) ~ à** [+ imagination] to give free rein to; [+ douleur] to give way to; [+ joie, sentiment] to give vent to, give free expression to; **il donna (libre) ~ à ses larmes** he let his tears flow freely → **suivre**

b [rivière] (= cheminement) course; (= écoulement) flow; **avoir un ~ rapide/régulier** to be fast-/smooth-flowing; **sur une partie de son ~** on ou along part of its course; **descendre le ~ de la Seine** to go down the Seine; **~ d'eau** (gén) watercourse; (= ruisseau) stream; (= rivière) river

c [valeurs, matières premières] price; [devises] rate; **avoir ~** [monnaie] to be legal tender; (fig) to be current, be in current use; **avoir ~ légal** to be legal tender; **ne plus avoir ~** [monnaie] to be no longer legal tender, be out of circulation; [expression] to be obsolete, be no longer in use ou no longer current; **ces plaisanteries n'ont plus ~ ici** jokes like that are no longer appreciated here; (Bourse) **~ d'ouverture** opening price; **~ de clôture** ◊ closing price, latest quotations; **~ des devises** ou **du change** foreign exchange rate; **au ~ (du jour)** at the price of the day; **au ~ du marché** at (the) market price; **le ~ des voitures d'occasion** the (selling) price of secondhand cars

d (= leçon) class; (Univ = conférence) lecture; (= série de leçons) course; (= manuel) coursebook, textbook; **~ de solfège/de danse** musical theory/dancing lesson; **~ de chimie** (= leçon) chemistry class ou lesson; (= conférence) chemistry lecture; (= enseignement) chemistry course; (= manuel) chemistry coursebook *ou* textbook; (= *notes*) ~ **de droit** law (course) notes; **faire** *ou* **donner un** ~ **sur** to give a class (*on* lecture *ou* course) on; **il donne des** ~ **en fac*** he lectures at (the) university; **qui vous fait** ~ **en anglais ?** who takes you for English?, who have you got for English?; **je ne ferai pas** ~ **demain** I won't be teaching tomorrow; **j'ai (un)** ~ **d'histoire à quatorze heures** I've got a history class at two o'clock; (*Univ*) ~ **accéléré** crash course (**de** in); ~ **du soir** (*pl*) evening classes; ~ **par correspondance** correspondence course; ~ **de vacances** summer school, holiday course (*Brit*); ~ **intensif** intensive course (**de, en** in); **donner/prendre des** ~ **particuliers** to give/have private lessons *ou* tuition (*Brit*); ~ **particuliers de piano** private piano lessons

[e] (*Scol* = *établissement*) school; ~ **privé** private school; ~ **de jeunes filles** girls' school *ou* college; ~ **de danse** dancing school

[f] (*Scol* = *enseignement primaire*) class; ~ **préparatoire/élémentaire/moyen** first/second or third/fourth or fifth year in primary school; (*Hist*) ~ **complémentaire** final year in elementary school

[g] (= *avenue*) walk

[2] **au cours de** LOC PRÉP in the course of, during

[3] **en cours** LOC ADJ [*année*] current (*épith*); [*affaires*] in hand, in progress; [*essais*] in progress, under way

[4] **en cours de** LOC PRÉP in the process of; **c'est en** ~ **de réparation/réfection** it's (in the process of) being repaired/rebuilt; **le projet est en** ~ **d'étude** the project is under consideration; (*lit, fig*) **en** ~ **de route** on the way; (*Jur*) **brevet en** ~ **d'agrément** patent pending

course [kuʀs] [1] NF [a] (= *action de courir*) running; (*littér*) **prendre sa** ~ to start running; **le cheval, atteint d'une balle en pleine** ~ the horse, hit by a bullet in mid gallop; **il le rattrapa à la** ~ he ran after him and caught up with him; **quelle** ~ **pour attraper le bus !** I had to run like mad* to catch the bus!; **la** ~ **folle de la voiture s'est terminée dans le ravin** the car careered out of control and ended up in the ravine; **c'est la** ~***** it's a race against the clock; **depuis que le bébé est né, c'est la** ~***** we've been run off our feet ever since the baby was born → **pas**[1]

[b] (= *discipline, Courses, Cyclisme, Naut*) racing; (*Athlétisme*) **la** ~ (**à pied**) running; **faire de la** ~ **pour s'entraîner** to go running to get fit; (*Aut, Cyclisme*) **tu fais de la** ~**?** do you race?; **la** ~ **de fond/demi-fond** long-distance/middle-distance running; **la** ~ **sur piste/route** track/road racing; **faire la** ~ **avec qn** to race with sb; **allez, on fait la** ~**!** let's have a race!, I'll race you! → **champ**[1], **écurie**

[c] (= *compétition*) race; ~ **de fond/sur piste** long-distance/track race; ~ **autour du monde** (**à la voile**) round-the-world (yacht) race; **les** ~**s** [*chevaux*] horse racing; **aller aux** ~**s** to go to the races; **parier aux** ~**s** to bet on the races; **les** ~**s de lévriers** greyhound racing; **être/ne plus être dans la** ~ [*candidat*] to be in the running/out of the running; **il n'est plus dans la** ~***** (*dépassé*) he's out of touch; **hors** ~ [*pilote, voiture*] out of the race; [*candidat*] out of the running; **il a été mis hors** ~ (*Sport*) he was disqualified; [*candidat*] he was put out of the running → **solitaire**

[d] (*pour l'obtention de qch*) race; **la** ~ **aux armements** the arms race; **la** ~ **à la présidence/à l'Élysée/au pouvoir** the race for the presidency/the Élysée/power; **la** ~ **à la productivité** the drive to be ultraproductive; **la** ~ **au diplôme** the rush to obtain as many diplomas as possible

[e] (= *voyage*) (*en autocar*) trip, journey (*Brit*); (*en taxi*) ride; **payer (le prix de) la** ~ to pay the fare; (*taxi*) **il n'a fait que 3** ~**s hier** he only picked up *ou* had 3 fares yesterday

[f] [*projectile*] flight; [*navire*] rapid course; [*nuages, ombres*] racing, swift passage; [*temps*] swift passage, swift passing (*NonC*); [*étoiles*] path

[g] (= *excursion*) (*à pied*) hike; (= *ascension*) climb

[h] (= *commission*) errand; (*dans un magasin*) ~**s** shopping (*NonC*); **faire une** ~ to (go and) get something from the shop(s) (*Brit*) *ou* store(s) (*US*); **faire les** ~**s** to do the shopping (*Brit*); **il est sorti faire des** ~**s** he has gone out to do *ou* get some shopping; **j'ai quelques** ~**s à faire** I've got some shopping to do; **les** ~**s sont sur la table** the shopping is on the table

[i] (*Tech*) [*pièce mobile*] movement; [*piston*] stroke; **à bout de** ~ (*Tech*) at full stroke; (*fig*) **en bout de** ~ (= *finalement*) at the end of the day, ultimately; **nous n'intervenons qu'en bout de** ~ we only intervene in the final stage of the process; **à** *ou* **en bout de** ~ [*institution, industrie, machine*] on its last legs*; [*personne*] on one's last legs* → **fin**[2]

[j] (*corsaire*) privateering; **faire la** ~ to privateer, go privateering

[2] COMP ▸ **course attelée** harness race ▸ **course automobile** motor race ▸ **course de chevaux** horse-race ▸ **course de côte** (*Sport Aut*) hill climb ▸ **course contre la montre** (*Sport*) race against the clock, time-trial; (*fig*) race against time *ou* the clock ▸ **course par étapes** stage race ▸ **course de haies** hurdling; **faire de la** ~ **de haies** to hurdle ▸ **course hippique** = **course de chevaux** ▸ **course d'obstacles** (*Sport*) obstacle race; (*Hippisme*) steeplechase; (*fig*) obstacle course *ou* race ▸ **course d'orientation** orienteering race ▸ **course de relais** relay race ▸ **course en sac** sack race ▸ **course de taureaux** bullfight ▸ **course au trésor** treasure hunt ▸ **course de trot** trotting race ▸ **course au trot attelé** harness race ▸ **course de vitesse** sprint

course-poursuite (*pl* **courses-poursuites**) [kuʀspuʀsɥit] NF (*Cyclisme*) pursuit; (*après un voleur*) chase

courser* [kuʀse] ▸ conjug 1 ◂ VT to chase *ou* hare* after

coursier[1] [kuʀsje] NM (*littér = cheval*) charger (*littér*), steed (*littér*)

coursier[2], **-ière** [kuʀsje, jɛʀ] NM,F (*gén*) messenger, courier; (*à moto*) dispatch rider; **on vous l'enverra par** ~ we'll send it to you by courier, we'll courier it over to you

coursive [kuʀsiv] NF (*Naut*) gangway (*connecting cabins*)

court[1], **e** [kuʀ, kuʀt] [1] ADJ [a] (*gén*) short; [*introduction, séjour*] short, brief; **de** ~**e durée** [*enthousiasme, ardeur*] short-lived; **il connaît un chemin plus** ~ he knows a quicker *ou* shorter way; **la journée m'a paru** ~**e** the day seemed to go very quickly *ou* to fly by; **avoir l'haleine** *ou* **la respiration** ~**e** *ou* **le souffle** ~ to be out of *ou* short of breath → **idée, manche**[1], **mémoire**[1]

[b] (= *insuffisant*) [*avance, majorité*] narrow, small; **il lui a donné 10 jours, c'est** ~ he's given him 10 days, which is (a bit) on the short side *ou* which isn't very long; **100 F pour le faire, c'est** ~ 100 francs for doing that — that's not very much *ou* that's a bit stingy*; **20 minutes, c'est bien** ~ 20 minutes is a bit tight

[c] (*loc*) **tirer à la** ~**e paille** to draw lots *ou* straws (*US*); **à sa** ~**e honte** to his humiliation; **d'une** ~**e tête** by a short head; **prendre au plus** ~ to go the shortest way; (*fig*) **aller au plus** ~ to cut corners

[2] ADV [a] [*coiffer, habiller*] short; **elle s'habille très** ~ she wears very short skirts (*ou* dresses); **les cheveux coupés** ~ with short hair

[b] (*loc*) **s'arrêter** ~ to stop short; **couper** ~ **à** [+ *débat, rumeur, critiques*] to put a stop to; **il faut faire** ~***** (= *être concis*) you (*ou* we) need to be brief; (= *être rapide*) you'd (*ou* we'd) better make it quick*; **prendre qn de** ~ to catch sb unawares *ou* on the hop* (*Brit*); **rester** *ou* **demeurer** ~ to be at a loss; **tourner** ~ [*projet, débat*] to come to a sudden end; **être à** ~ **d'argent/d'arguments** to be short of money/arguments; **être à** ~ **d'idées** to be short of ideas; **appelez-moi Bob tout** ~ just call me Bob; **ils veulent l'indépendance tout** ~ they want independence, nothing more and nothing less; **il n'est pas un peu hypocrite, il est hypocrite tout** ~ he's not just a bit of a hypocrite — he's a hypocrite full stop (*Brit*) *ou* he's a hypocrite, period (*US*) → **pendre**

court[2] [kuʀ] NM (*Sport*) (tennis) court; ~ **central** centre court

courtage [kuʀtaʒ] NM (= *métier*) brokerage; (= *commission*) commission; **vendre qch par** ~ to sell sth through *ou* by a broker; **maison** *ou* **société de** ~ brokerage company → **vente**

courtaud, **e** [kuʀto, od] ADJ [a] [*personne*] dumpy, squat [b] (**chien/cheval**) ~ docked and crop-eared dog/horse

court-bouillon (*pl* **courts-bouillons**) [kuʀbujɔ̃] NM (*Culin*) court-bouillon; **faire cuire qch au** ~ to cook sth in a court-bouillon

court-circuit (*pl* **courts-circuits**) [kuʀsiʀkɥi] NM (*Élec*) short(-circuit)

court-circuitage* (*pl* **court-circuitages**) [kuʀsiʀkɥitaʒ] NM [*personne, service*] bypassing

court-circuiter [kuʀsiʀkɥite] ▸ conjug 1 ◂ VT (*Élec*) to short(-circuit); [+ *personne*] to bypass, go over the head of; [+ *service*] to bypass

courtepointe [kuʀtəpwɛ̃t] NF counterpane

courtier, **-ière** [kuʀtje, jɛʀ] NM,F broker; ~ **d'assurances** *ou* **en assurances** insurance broker; ~ **en vins** wine broker; ~ **maritime** ship broker

courtilière [kuʀtiljɛʀ] NF mole cricket

courtine [kuʀtin] NF curtain

courtisan [kuʀtizɑ̃] NM (*Hist*) courtier; (*fig*) sycophant; **des manières de** ~ sycophantic ways

courtisane [kuʀtizan] NF (*Hist, littér*) courtesan

courtiser [kuʀtize] ▸ conjug 1 ◂ VT († *ou littér*) [+ *femme*] to woo, court, pay court to; (= *flatter*) to pay court to, fawn on (*péj*)

court-jus* (*pl* **courts-jus**) [kuʀʒy] NM short(-circuit)

court-métrage (*pl* **courts-métrages**) [kuʀmetʀaʒ] NM → **métrage**

courtois, **e** [kuʀtwa, waz] ADJ courteous; (*Littérat*) courtly

courtoisement [kuʀtwazmɑ̃] ADV courteously

courtoisie [kuʀtwazi] NF courtesy, courteousness; (*Jur*) ~ **internationale** comity of nations

court-vêtu, **e** (*mpl* **court-vêtus**) [kuʀvety] ADJ wearing a short skirt *ou* dress

couru, **e** [kuʀy] (*ptp de* **courir**) ADJ [a] [*restaurant, spectacle*] popular; **ce festival est moins** ~ **que l'autre** this festival is less popular *ou* draws less of a crowd than the other one [b] **c'est** ~ (**d'avance**)* it's a foregone conclusion, it's a sure thing*, it's a (dead) cert* (*Brit*)

couscous [kuskus] NM couscous

couscoussier [kuskusje] NM couscous-maker

cousette† [kuzet] NF (= *ouvrière*) dressmaker's apprentice; (= *nécessaire*) sewing kit

couseur, **-euse** [kuzœʀ, øz] [1] NM,F (= *personne*) stitcher [2] **couseuse** NF (= *machine*) (industrial) sewing machine

cousin[1], **e** [kuzɛ̃, in] NM,F cousin; ~ **germain** first cousin; ~**s issus de germains** second cousins; ~**s au 3e/4e degré** 3rd/4th cousins; **ils sont un peu** ~**s** they are related (in some way) *ou* are distant relations → **mode**[1], **petit, roi**

cousin[2] [kuzɛ̃] NM (*Zool*) cranefly, daddy longlegs (*Brit*)

cousinage † [kuzinaʒ] NM (*entre germains*) cousinhood, cousinship; (= *vague parenté*) relationship

cousiner † [kuzine] ▸ conjug 1 ◂ VI to be on familiar terms (**avec** with)

coussin [kusɛ̃] NM [*siège*] cushion; (*Tech*) [*collier de cheval*] padding; (*Belg* = *oreiller*) pillow; **~ d'air** air cushion

coussinet [kusinɛ] NM [a] [*siège, genoux*] (small) cushion; [*animal*] pad [b] (*Tech*) bearing; **~ de tête de bielle** [*arbre de transmission*] big end bearing; [*rail*] chair [c] (*Archit*) (volute) cushion

cousu, e [kuzy] (*ptp de* **coudre**) ADJ sewn, stitched; (*fig*) **être (tout) ~ d'or** to be extremely wealthy; (*fig*) **c'est ~ de fil blanc** it's a blatant lie; **~ main** (*lit*) handsewn, handstitched; (*fig*) **c'est du ~ main*** it's top quality stuff; **~ machine** machine-sewn → **bouche, motus**

coût [ku] NM (*lit, fig*) cost; **le ~ de la vie** cost of living; **~ d'acquisition** original cost; **~s de base** baseline costs; **~ du crédit** credit charges; **~ de distribution** distribution cost; **~ d'investissement** capital cost; **~ de production** production cost; **~ salarial** wage(s) bill; **~ d'utilisation** cost-in-use → **indice**

coûtant [kutã] ADJ M **prix ~** cost price; **vendre à prix ~** to sell at cost (price)

couteau (*pl* **couteaux**) [kuto] [1] NM [a] (*pour couper*) knife; [*balance*] knife edge; (= *coquillage*) razor-shell (*Brit*), razor clam (*US*); **~ à beurre/dessert/fromage/poisson/huîtres** butter/dessert/cheese/fish/oyster knife → **lame** [b] (*loc*) **vous me mettez le ~ sous ou sur la gorge** you're holding a gun to my head; **être à ~(x) tiré(s)** to be at daggers drawn (**avec** with); **remuer ou retourner le ~ dans la plaie** to twist the knife in the wound, rub it in*; (*fig*) **second ~** minor figure; **ce ne sont que des seconds ~x** they're only the small fry [2] COMP ► **couteau de chasse** hunting knife ► **couteau de cuisine** kitchen knife ► **couteau à découper** carving knife ► **couteau électrique** electric carving knife ► **couteau à éplucher, couteau à légumes** (potato) peeler ► **couteau à pain** breadknife ► **couteau à palette** *ou* **de peintre** (*Peinture*) palette knife ► **couteau de table** table knife → **cran**

couteau-scie (*pl* **couteaux-scies**) [kutosi] NM serrated knife

coutelas [kutlɑ] NM (= *couteau*) large (kitchen) knife; (= *épée*) cutlass

coutelier, -ière [kutəlje, jɛʀ] NM,F (= *fabricant, marchand*) cutler

coutellerie [kutɛlʀi] NF (= *industrie*) cutlery industry; (= *atelier*) cutlery works; (= *magasin*) cutlery shop, cutler's (shop); (= *produits*) cutlery

coûter [kute] ▸ conjug 1 ◂ VTI [a] (*lit*) to cost; **combien ça coûte?** how much is it?, how much does it cost?; **ça coûte cher?** is it expensive?, does it cost a lot?; **ça m'a coûté 10 F** it cost me 10 francs; **les vacances, ça coûte!*** holidays (*Brit*) *ou* vacations (*US*) are expensive *ou* cost a lot!; **ça coûte une fortune** *ou* **les yeux de la tête*** it costs a fortune *ou* the earth*; **ça coûte la peau des fesses*** it costs an arm and a leg*; **ça va lui ~ cher** (*lit*) it'll cost him a lot; [*erreur, impertinence*] he'll pay for that, it will cost him dear(ly); **ça coûtera ce que ça coûtera*** never mind the expense *ou* cost, hang the expense*; **tu pourrais le faire, pour ce que ça te coûte!** you could easily do it — it wouldn't make any difference to you *ou* it wouldn't put you to any trouble; **ça ne coûte rien d'essayer** it costs nothing to try

[b] (*fig*) **cette démarche me coûte** this is a painful step for me (to take); **il m'en coûte de refuser** it pains *ou* grieves me to have to refuse; **ça m'a coûté bien des mois de travail** it cost me many months' work; **ça lui a coûté la tête/la vie** it cost him his head/life; **je sais ce qu'il en coûte** I know what it costs → **premier** [c] **coûte que coûte** at all costs, no matter what; **il faut qu'il y arrive coûte que coûte** we must get there at all costs *ou* by hook or by crook

coûteux, -euse [kutø, øz] ADJ [*objet*] costly, expensive; [*erreur*] costly; [*expérience*] painful; **procédé ~ en temps/énergie** process costly in time/energy

coutil [kuti] NM [*vêtements*] drill, twill; [*matelas*] ticking

coutre [kutʀ] NM coulter (*Brit*), colter (*US*)

coutume [kutym] NF [a] (= *usage : gén, Jur*) custom; (*Jur* = *recueil*) customary [b] (*= habitude*) **avoir ~ de** to be in the habit of; **plus/moins que de ~** more/less than usual; **comme de ~** as usual; **selon sa ~** as is his custom *ou* wont → **fois**

coutumier, -ière [kutymje, jɛʀ] [1] ADJ (*gén*) customary, usual; [*loi*] customary; **droit ~** (= *concept*) customary law; (= *lois*) common law; (*gén péj*) **il est ~ du fait** that is what he usually does, that's his usual trick* [2] NM (*Jur*) customary

couture [kutyʀ] NF [a] (= *action, ouvrage*) sewing; (= *profession*) dressmaking; **faire de la ~** to sew; **veste/robe (haute) ~** designer jacket/dress → **haut, maison, point**² [b] (= *suite de points*) seam; **sans ~(s)** seamless; **faire une ~ à grands points** to tack *ou* baste a seam; **~ apparente** *ou* **sellier** topstitching, overstitching; **~ anglaise/plate** *ou* **rabattue** French/flat seam; **regarder qch/qn sous toutes les ~s** to examine sth/sb from every angle → **battre** [c] (= *cicatrice*) scar [d] (= *suture*) stitches

couturé, e [kutyʀe] ADJ [*visage*] scarred

couturier [kutyʀje] NM [a] (= *personne*) couturier, fashion designer; **grand ~** top designer [b] (*Anat*) **(muscle) ~** sartorial muscle, sartorius

couturière [kutyʀjɛʀ] NF [a] (= *personne*) dressmaker; (*en atelier*) dressmaker, seamstress† [b] (*Théât*) rehearsal preceding the full dress rehearsal, when alterations are made to the costumes

couvain [kuvɛ̃] NM (= *œufs*) brood; (= *rayon*) brood cells

couvaison [kuvɛzɔ̃] NF (= *période*) incubation; (= *action*) brooding, sitting

couvée [kuve] NF [*poussins*] brood, clutch; [*œufs*] clutch; [*enfants*] brood → **naître**

couvent [kuvã] NM [a] [*sœurs*] convent, nunnery†; [*moines*] monastery; **entrer au ~** to enter a convent [b] (= *internat*) convent (school)

couventine [kuvãtin] NF (= *religieuse*) conventual; (= *jeune fille élevée au couvent*) convent schoolgirl

couver [kuve] ▸ conjug 1 ◂ [1] VI [*feu, incendie*] to smoulder; [*haine, passion*] to smoulder, simmer; [*émeute*] to be brewing; [*complot*] to be hatching; **~ sous la cendre** (*lit*) to smoulder under the embers; [*passion*] to smoulder, simmer; [*émeute*] to be brewing [2] VT [a] [+ *œufs*] [*poule*] to sit on; [*appareil*] to hatch; **la poule était en train de ~** the hen was sitting on its eggs *ou* was brooding [b] [+ *enfant*] to be overcareful with, cocoon; [+ *maladie*] to be getting, be coming down with; [+ *vengeance*] to brew, plot; [+ *révolte*] to plot; **enfant couvé par sa mère** child cosseted by his mother, child brought up by an overcautious *ou* overprotective mother; **~ qn/qch des yeux** *ou* **du regard** (*tendresse*) to gaze lovingly *ou* devotedly at sb/sth; (*convoitise*) to look covetously *ou* longingly at sb/sth

couvercle [kuvɛʀkl] NM [*casserole, boîte, bocal*] lid; [*aérosol*] cap, top; (*qui se visse*) (screw-)cap, (screw-)top; (*Tech*) [*piston*] cover

couvert, e¹ [kuvɛʀ, ɛʀt] (*ptp de* **couvrir**) [1] ADJ [a] (= *habillé*) covered (up); **il est trop ~ pour la saison** he's dressed too warmly for the time of year; **il est resté ~ dans l'église** he kept his hat on inside the church [b] **~ de** [+ *boutons, taches*] covered in *ou* with; **pics ~s de neige** snow-covered *ou* snow-clad (*littér*) peaks; **~ de chaume** [*toit, maison*] thatched; **le rosier est ~ de fleurs** the rosebush is a mass of *ou* is covered in flowers [c] (= *voilé*) [*ciel*] overcast; **par temps ~** when the sky is overcast → **mot** [d] [*rue, cour*] covered; [*piscine, court de tennis*] indoor (*épith*), indoors (*attrib*) → **marché** [e] (= *protégé par un supérieur, une assurance*) covered [f] [*syllabe*] closed

[2] NM [a] (= *couteau, fourchette, cuillère, verre, assiette*) place setting; **une ménagère de 12 ~s** a canteen of 12 place settings; **~s** (= *couteaux, fourchettes, cuillères*) cutlery (*Brit*), flatware (*US*), silverware (*US*); **j'ai sorti les ~s en argent** I've brought out the silver *ou* the silver cutlery (*Brit*); **des ~s en plastique** plastic knives and forks

[b] (*à table*) **mettre le ~** to lay *ou* set the table; **mettre 4 ~s** to lay *ou* set 4 places, lay *ou* set the table for 4; **table de 4 ~s** table laid *ou* set for 4; **mets un ~ de plus** lay *ou* set another place; **il a toujours son ~ mis chez nous** there's always a place for him at our table; (*fig*) **remettre le ~*** (*gén*) to do it again; (*sexuellement*) to be at it again*; **le vivre** *ou* **gîte et le ~** board (*Brit*) *ou* food (*US*) and lodging, room *ou* bed (*Brit*) and board

[c] (*au restaurant = prix*) cover charge

[d] (= *abri*) (*littér*) **sous le ~ d'un chêne** under the shelter of an oak tree; **à ~ de la pluie** sheltered from the rain; (*Mil*) **être à ~** to be under cover; **se mettre à ~** (*Mil*) to get under *ou* take cover; (*fig*) to cover *ou* safeguard o.s.

[e] **sous (le) ~ de** (*prétexte*) under cover of; **ils l'ont fait sous le ~ de leurs supérieurs** they did it by hiding behind the authority of their superiors; **sous (le) ~ de la plaisanterie** under the guise of a joke; **Monsieur le Ministre sous ~ de Monsieur le Recteur** the Minister through the person of the Director of Education

couverte² [kuvɛʀt] NF (*Tech*) glaze

couverture [kuvɛʀtyʀ] NF [a] (= *literie*) blanket; **~ de laine/chauffante** wool *ou* woollen/electric blanket; **~ de voyage** travelling rug; (*fig*) **tirer la ~ à soi** (= *s'attribuer tout le succès*) to take (all) the credit; (= *monopoliser la parole*) to hog the stage [b] (= *toiture*) roofing; **~ de chaume** thatch, thatched roof; **~ en tuiles** tiles, tiled roof [c] [*cahier, livre*] cover; (= *jaquette*) dust cover; **en ~** on the cover; **première/quatrième de ~** (outside) front/back cover [d] (*Mil*) cover; (= *prétexte*) cover; **troupes de ~** covering troops; **~ aérienne** aerial cover [e] (*Fin*) cover, margin; **~ sociale** social security cover *ou* coverage; **~ médicale** medical *ou* health cover(age); **~ des risques** risk insurance coverage [f] (*Journalisme*) coverage; **assurer la ~ d'un événement** to provide coverage of an event; **~ médiatique** media coverage

couveuse [kuvøz] NF [a] (= *poule*) broody hen; **~ (artificielle)** incubator [b] [*bébé*] incubator; **être en ~** to be in an incubator

couvrant, e [kuvʀã, ãt] [1] ADJ [*peinture, fond de teint*] that covers well [2] **couvrante*** NF blanket, cover

couvre-chef (*pl* **couvre-chefs**) [kuvʀəʃɛf] NM (*hum*) hat, headgear (*NonC*) (*hum*)

couvre-feu (*pl* **couvre-feux**) [kuvʀəfø] NM curfew

couvre-lit (*pl* **couvre-lits**) [kuvʀəli] NM bedspread, coverlet

couvre-livre (*pl* **couvre-livres**) [kuvʀəlivʀ] NM book cover *ou* jacket

couvre-pied(s) (*pl* **couvre-pieds**) [kuvʀəpje] NM quilt

couvre-plat (*pl* **couvre-plats**) [kuvʀəpla] NM dish cover

couvre-théière (*pl* **couvre-théières**) [kuvʀə-tejeʀ] NM tea cosy

couvreur [kuvʀœʀ] NM roofer

couvrir [kuvʀiʀ] ▶ conjug 18 ◀ 1 VT a (*gén*) [+ *livre, sol, chargement*] to cover (**de, avec** with); [+ *récipient*] to cover (**de, avec** with), put the lid on; (*Jeux*) [+ *carte*] to cover; **~ un toit d'ardoises/de chaume/de tuiles** to slate/thatch/tile a roof; **des tableaux couvraient tout un mur** one whole wall was covered in pictures; **~ le feu** to bank up the fire

b (= *habiller*) to cover; **couvre bien les enfants** wrap *ou* cover the children up well; **un châle lui couvrait les épaules** she had a shawl around her shoulders

c (*fig*) **~ qch/qn de** to cover sth/sb with *ou* in; **couvert de bleus** bruised all over, covered in *ou* with bruises; **~ qn de cadeaux** to shower sb with gifts, shower gifts (up)on sb; **~ qn de caresses/baisers** to cover *ou* shower sb with caresses/kisses; **~ qn d'injures/d'éloges** to shower sb with insults/praise, heap insults/praise on sb; **cette aventure l'a couvert de ridicule** this affair has covered him with ridicule → **boue**

d (= *masquer*) [+ *son, voix*] to drown (out); [+ *énigme*] to conceal; **le bruit de la rue couvrait la voix du conférencier** the noise from the street drowned (out) the lecturer's voice; (*lit, fig*) **~ son jeu** to hold *ou* keep one's cards close to one's chest; **sa frugalité couvre une grande avarice** his frugality conceals great avarice; **~ qch du nom de charité** to pass sth off as charity

e (= *protéger*) to cover; **~ qn de son corps** to cover *ou* shield sb with one's body; (*Mil*) **~ sa retraite** to cover one's retreat; (*fig*) **~ qn** to cover up for *ou* shield sb; **~ une erreur** to cover up a mistake

f [+ *frais, dépenses*] to cover; [*assurance*] to cover; **pourriez-vous nous ~ de la somme de 1000 F** would you remit to us the sum of 1,000 francs; **~ l'enchère de qn** to make a higher bid than sb

g (= *parcourir*) [+ *kilomètres, distance*] to cover

h (*Zool*) [+ *jument*] to cover

i (*Journalisme*) [+ *événement*] to cover

2 **se couvrir** VPR a [*arbre*] **se ~ de fleurs/feuilles** to come into bloom/leaf; **les prés se couvrent de fleurs** the meadows are becoming a mass of flowers; [*personne*] **se ~ de taches** to cover o.s. in splashes, get covered in splashes; **se ~ de boutons** to become covered in *ou* with spots; **se ~ de gloire** to cover o.s. with glory; **se ~ de honte/ridicule** to bring shame/ridicule upon o.s., cover o.s. with shame/ridicule

b (= *s'habiller*) to cover up, wrap up; (= *mettre son chapeau*) to put on one's hat; **il fait froid, couvrez-vous bien** it's cold so wrap *ou* cover (yourself) up well

c [*ciel*] to become overcast, cloud over; **le temps se couvre** it's clouding over, the sky is *ou* it's becoming (very) overcast

d (*Boxe, Escrime*) to cover o.s.; (*fig*) **pour se ~** to cover *ou* shield himself

covalence [kɔvalãs] NF (*Chim*) covalency, covalence (*US*); **liaison de ~** covalent bond

covalent, e [kɔvalã, ãt] ADJ (*Chim*) covalent

cover-girl (*pl* **cover-girls**) [kɔvœʀgœʀl] NF cover girl

covoiturage [kɔvwatyʀaʒ] NM car sharing

cow-boy (*pl* **cow-boys**) [kɔbɔj] NM cowboy; **jouer aux ~s et aux Indiens** to play (at) cowboys and Indians

coxalgie [kɔksalʒi] NF coxalgia

coyote [kɔjɔt] NM coyote

CP [sepe] NM (ABRÉV = **cours préparatoire**) → **cours**

CPAM [sepeaɛm] NF (ABRÉV = **caisse primaire d'assurance maladie**) → **caisse**

CQFD [sekyɛfde]   (ABRÉV = **ce qu'il fallait démontrer**) QED

crabe [kʀab] NM a (*Zool*) crab; **marcher en ~** to walk crabwise *ou* crabways → **panier** b (= *véhicule*) caterpillar-tracked vehicle

crac [kʀak] EXCL [*bois, glace*] crack; [*étoffe*] rip

crachat [kʀaʃa] NM a (*gén*) spit (*NonC*), spittle (*NonC*); **il a reçu un ~ dans la figure** someone spat in his face b (**† = plaque, insigne*) decoration

craché, e* [kʀaʃe] (*ptp de* **cracher**) ADJ **c'est son père tout ~** he's the spitting image of his father; **c'est lui tout ~** that's just like him, that's him all over*

crachement [kʀaʃmã] NM a (= *expectoration*) spitting (*NonC*); **~ de sang** spitting of blood; **~s de sang** spasms of spitting blood *ou* of blood-spitting b (= *projection*) [*flammes, vapeur*] burst; [*étincelles*] shower (= *bruit*) [*radio, mitrailleuses*] crackling (*NonC*), crackle

cracher [kʀaʃe] ▶ conjug 1 ◀ 1 VI a (*avec la bouche*) to spit; **rincez-vous la bouche et crachez** rinse your mouth and spit it out; **~ sur qn** (*lit*) to spit at sb; (*fig*) to spit on sb; **il ne crache pas sur le caviar*** he doesn't turn his nose up at caviar; **il ne faut pas ~ sur cette offre*** this offer is not to be sneezed at; **il ne faut pas ~ dans la soupe*** don't bite the hand that feeds you; **c'est comme si je crachais en l'air*** I might as well be whistling in the wind; **~ au bassinet*** to cough up*

b [*stylo, plume*] to splutter, splotch; [*micro*] to crackle

2 VT a [*personne*] [+ *sang*] to spit; [+ *bouchée*] to spit out; [+ *injures*] to spit (out); ‡ [+ *argent*] to cough up*, stump up* (*Brit*); **~ ses poumons*** to cough up one's lungs* → **venin** b [*canon*] [+ *flammes*] to spit (out); [+ *projectiles*] to spit out; [*cheminée, volcan, dragon*] to belch (out); **le moteur crachait des étincelles** the engine was sending out showers of sparks; **le tuyau crachait une eau brunâtre** the pipe was spitting out dirty brown water

cracheur, -euse [kʀaʃœʀ, øz] NM,F **~ de feu** *ou* **de flammes** fire-eater

crachin [kʀaʃɛ̃] NM drizzle

crachiner [kʀaʃine] ▶ conjug 1 ◀ VI to drizzle

crachoir [kʀaʃwaʀ] NM spittoon, cuspidor (*US*); **tenir le ~*** to hold the floor; **j'ai tenu le ~ à ma vieille tante tout l'après-midi** I had to sit and listen to my old aunt spouting all afternoon*

crachotement [kʀaʃɔtmã] NM [*haut-parleur, téléphone, radio*] crackling (*NonC*), crackle; [*robinet*] spluttering (*NonC*)

crachoter [kʀaʃɔte] ▶ conjug 1 ◀ VI [*haut-parleur, téléphone, radio*] to crackle; [*robinet*] to splutter

crachouiller* [kʀaʃuje] ▶ conjug 1 ◀ VI [*personne*] to splutter

crack¹ [kʀak] NM a (= *poulain*) crack *ou* star horse b (* = *as*) ace; **un ~ en informatique** an ace *ou* a wizard* at computing; **c'est un ~ au saut en longueur** he's a first-class long jumper

crack² [kʀak] NM (*Drogue*) crack (cocaine)

cracking [kʀakiŋ] NM (*Chim*) cracking

Cracovie [kʀakɔvi] N Cracow

cracra* [kʀakʀa] ADJ INV, **crade*** [kʀad], **cradingue*** [kʀadɛ̃g], **crado*** [kʀado], **cradoque*** [kʀadɔk] ADJ [*personne, vêtement*] dirty, scuzzy‡; [*endroit, meuble*] dirty, grotty* (*Brit*)

craie [kʀɛ] NF (= *substance, bâtonnet*) chalk; **~ de tailleur** tailor's chalk, French chalk; **écrire qch à la ~ sur un mur** to chalk sth up on a wall

craignos‡ [kʀɛɲos] ADJ INV [*personne, quartier*] shady*, dodgy* (*Brit*); **il est vraiment ~ ce type** he's a really freaky guy*

craindre [kʀɛ̃dʀ] ▶ conjug 52 ◀ 1 VT a [*personne*] to fear, be afraid *ou* scared of; **je ne crains pas la mort/la douleur** I'm not afraid of dying/pain; **ne craignez rien** don't be afraid

---

ou frightened; **oui, je le crains !** yes, I'm afraid so!; **je crains le pire** I fear the worst; **il voulait se faire ~** he wanted to be feared

b **~ de faire qch** to be afraid of doing sth; **il craint de se faire mal** he's afraid of hurting himself; **je ne crains pas de dire que …** I am not afraid of saying that …; **je crains d'avoir bientôt à partir** I'm afraid I may have to leave soon; **craignant de manquer le train** afraid of missing *ou* afraid (that) he might miss the train

c **~ que …** to be afraid that …, fear that …; **je crains qu'il (n')attrape froid** I'm afraid (that) he might catch cold; **ne craignez-vous pas qu'il arrive ?** aren't you afraid he'll come? *ou* he might come?; **je crains qu'il (ne) se soit perdu** I'm afraid that he might *ou* may have got lost; **il est à ~ que …** it is to be feared that …; **je crains que vous ne vous trompiez** I fear you are mistaken

d **~ pour** [+ *vie, réputation, personne*] to fear for

e [*aliment, produit*] **~ le froid** to be easily damaged by (the) cold; **« craint l'humidité/la chaleur »** "keep *ou* store in a dry place/cool place", "do not expose to a damp atmosphere/to heat"; **vêtement qui ne craint rien** hard-wearing *ou* sturdy garment; **c'est un vieux tapis, ça ne craint rien** don't worry, it's an old carpet; **ces animaux craignent la chaleur** these animals can't stand the heat

2 VI‡ **il craint, ce type** that guy's really creepy*; **ça craint dans ce quartier** (*louche*) this is a really shady* *ou* dodgy (*Brit*)* area; (*dangereux*) this is a really dangerous area; **ça craint, leur émission** that programme's the pits‡; **s'il est élu, ça craint pour la démocratie** if he gets elected, it'll be a bad day for democracy

▼ **crainte** [kʀɛ̃t] NF a (= *peur*) fear; **la ~ de la maladie** *ou* **d'être malade l'arrête** fear of illness *ou* of being ill stops him; **soyez sans ~** ◊ **n'ayez ~** have no fear, never fear; **j'ai des ~s à son sujet** I'm worried about him; **sans ~** [*personne*] fearless; [*affronter, parler*] without fear, fearlessly; **avec ~** fearfully; **la ~ qu'on les entende** the fear that they might be overheard ■ (*PROV*) **la ~ est le commencement de la sagesse** only the fool knows no fear b (*loc*) **dans la ~ de** ◊ **par ~ de** for fear of; **de ~ d'une erreur** for fear of (there being) a mistake, lest there be a mistake (*frm*); **(par) ~ d'être suivi, il courut** he ran for fear of being followed *ou* fearing that he might be followed; **de ~ que … ou … que** for fear that …, fearing that …; **de ~ qu'on ne le suive, il courut** he ran for fear of being followed *ou* fearing that he might be followed

craintif, -ive [kʀɛ̃tif, iv] ADJ timid

craintivement [kʀɛ̃tivmã] ADV timidly

cramé, e* [kʀame] 1 ADJ burnt, burned (*US*) 2 NM **ça sent le ~** (*lit*) I (can) smell burning; (*fig*) there's trouble brewing; **ça a un goût de ~** it tastes burnt; **ne mange pas le ~** don't eat the burnt bit(s)

cramer* [kʀame] ▶ conjug 1 ◀ 1 VI [*maison*] to burn down, go up in flames; [*mobilier*] to go up in flames *ou* smoke; [*tissu, papier*] to burn 2 VT (*gén*) to burn; [+ *maison*] to burn down

cramoisi, e [kʀamwazi] ADJ crimson

crampe [kʀãp] NF cramp; **avoir une ~ au mollet** to have cramp (*Brit*) *ou* a cramp (*US*) in one's calf; **~ d'estomac** stomach cramp; (*hum*) **la ~ de l'écrivain** writer's cramp (*hum*)

crampon [kʀãpɔ̃] NM a (*Tech*) cramp (iron), clamp b [*chaussures de football*] stud; [*chaussures de course*] spike; [*fer à cheval*] calk; [*alpiniste*] **~ (à glace)** crampon c (*Bot*) tendril d (* = *personne*) leech; **elle est ~** she clings like a leech, you can't shake her off

cramponnage [kʀãpɔnaʒ] NM (*Alpinisme*) crampon technique, cramponning

cramponner [kʀɑ̃pɔne] ▸conjug 1◂ 1 VT a (*Tech*) to cramp (together), clamp (together) b (*: fig*) to cling to 2 **se cramponner** VPR (*pour ne pas tomber*) to hold on, hang on; (*dans son travail*) to stick at it*; **elle se cramponne** (= *ne vous lâche pas*) she clings like a leech, you can't shake her off; (= *ne veut pas mourir*) she's hanging on (to life); **se ~ à** [+ *branche, volant, bras*] to cling (on) to, clutch, hold on to; [+ *personne*] (*lit*) to cling (on) to; (*fig*) [+ *vie, espoir, personne*] to cling to

cran [kʀɑ̃] NM a (*pour accrocher, retenir*) [*pièce dentée, crémaillère*] notch; [*arme à feu*] catch; [*ceinture, courroie*] hole; **hausser un rayon de plusieurs ~s** to raise a shelf a few notches *ou* holes; **~ de sécurité** *ou* **de sûreté** safety catch; **(couteau) à ~ d'arrêt** flick-knife b (*servant de repère*: Couture), (*Typo*) nick; **~ de mire** bead c [*cheveux*] wave; **le coiffeur lui avait fait un ~** *ou* **des ~s** the hairdresser had put her hair in waves d (*: courage*) guts*; **elle a un drôle de ~** she's got a lot of guts* *ou* bottle* (*Brit*) e (*loc*) **monter/descendre d'un ~** (*dans la hiérarchie*) to move up/come down a rung *ou* peg; **elle est montée/descendue d'un ~ dans mon estime** she's gone up/down a notch *ou* peg in my estimation; **être à ~** to be very edgy; **ne le mets pas à ~** don't make me mad*

crâne¹ [kʀɑn] NM (*Anat*) skull, cranium (*SPÉC*); (*fig*) head; **avoir mal au ~*** to have a splitting headache; (*fig*) **avoir le ~ dur*** to be thick(skulled)* → **bourrage, bourrer, fracture**

crâne²† [kʀɑn] ADJ gallant

crânement† [kʀɑnmɑ̃] ADV gallantly

crâner* [kʀɑne] ▸conjug 1◂ VI to swank*, show off*, put on the dog* (*US*); **ce n'est pas la peine de ~** it's nothing to swank* *ou* show off* about

crânerie† [kʀɑnʀi] NF gallantry

crâneur, -euse* [kʀɑnœʀ, øz] NM,F swank*, show-off*; **faire le ~** to swank* *ou* show off*; **elle est un peu crâneuse** she's a bit of a show-off*

crânien, -ienne [kʀɑnjɛ̃, jɛn] ADJ cranial → **boîte**

craniologie [kʀɑnjɔlɔʒi] NF craniology

cranter [kʀɑ̃te] ▸conjug 1◂ VT (*Tech*) [+ *pignon, roue*] to put notches in; **~ ses cheveux** to put one's hair in waves; **tige crantée** notched stem

crapahuter [kʀapayte] ▸conjug 1◂ VI (*arg Mil*) to yomp; (= *faire une randonnée*) **on a crapahuté dans la montagne toute la journée** we trudged *ou* trekked through the mountains all day

crapaud [kʀapo] 1 NM a (*Zool*) toad → **bave, fauteuil, laid, piano** b (*: gamin*) brat* c [*diamant*] flaw 2 COMP ▸ **crapaud de mer** angler(-fish)

crapaud-buffle (*pl* **crapauds-buffles**) [kʀapobyfl] NM buffalo frog

crapaudine [kʀapodin] NF [*tuyau*] grating; [*gond*] gudgeon; (= *pierre*) toadstone

crapoter* [kʀapɔte] ▸conjug 1◂ VI [*fumeur*] **il crapote** he doesn't inhale

crapoteux, -euse* [kʀapɔtø, øz] ADJ [*lieu*] murky, gloomy; [*personne*] grimy-looking

crapule [kʀapyl] NF (= *escroc*) crook; (*††* = *racaille*) riffraff, scum*

crapulerie [kʀapylʀi] NF a (= *caractère*) villainy b (= *acte*) villainy

crapuleux, -euse [kʀapylø, øz] ADJ [*action*] villainous; [*vie*] dissolute → **crime**

craquage [kʀakaʒ] NM (*Chim*) cracking

craquant, e* [kʀakɑ̃, ɑ̃t] ADJ [*biscuit*] crunchy; (*: séduisant*) [*objet, personne*] gorgeous, lovely

craque*† [kʀak] NF whopper*, whopping lie*;

tu m'as raconté des ~s you've been trying to put one over on me

craquelé, e [kʀakle] (*ptp de* **craqueler**) ADJ [*terre, chemin*] covered with cracks; [*glace, peinture, cuir*] cracked; **des chaussures toutes ~es** cracked leather shoes

craqueler [kʀakle] ▸conjug 4◂ 1 VT [+ *vernis, faïence, terre*] [*usure, âge*] to crack; (*Tech*) [*artisan*] to crackle 2 **se craqueler** VPR [*vernis, faïence, terre*] to crack

craquellement [kʀakɛlmɑ̃] NM = **craquèlement**

craquelure [kʀaklyʀ] NF (*accidentelle*) crack; **~s** (*volontaires*) [*porcelaine, verre*] crackle (*NonC*); [*tableau*] craquelure (*NonC*) (*SPÉC*); **couvert de ~s** covered in cracks

craquement [kʀakmɑ̃] NM (= *bruit*) [*arbre, branche qui se rompt*] crack, snap; [*plancher, boiserie*] creak; [*feuilles sèches, neige*] crackle, crunch; [*chaussures*] squeak; **le ~ continuel des arbres/de la banquise** the constant creak of the trees/icefield

craquer [kʀake] ▸conjug 1◂ 1 VI a (= *produire un bruit*) [*parquet*] to creak, squeak; [*feuilles mortes, disque*] to crackle; [*neige*] to crunch; [*chaussures*] to squeak; [*biscuit*] to crunch; **faire ~ ses doigts** to crack one's fingers; **faire ~ une allumette** to strike a match b (= *céder*) [*bas*] to rip, go* (*Brit*); [*bois, couche de glace*] to crack; [*branche*] to crack, snap; **veste qui craque aux coutures** jacket which is coming apart at the seams → **plein** c (= *s'écrouler*) [*entreprise, gouvernement*] to be falling apart (at the seams), be on the verge of collapse; [*athlète*] to collapse; [*accusé, malade*] to break down, collapse; **ils ont craqué en deuxième mi-temps** they gave way in the second half; **je craque** (*: je n'en peux plus*) I've had enough; (= *je deviens fou*) I'm cracking up* → **nerf** d (*: être enthousiasmé*) **j'ai craqué** I couldn't resist it (*ou* them *ou* him *etc*); **il est à ~!** he's irresistible!

2 VT a [+ *pantalon*] to rip, split; **~ un bas*** to rip *ou* tear a stocking b **~ une allumette** to strike a match c [+ *produit pétrolier*] to crack

crash* [kʀaʃ] NM crash

crasher (se)* [kʀaʃe] ▸conjug 1◂ VPR [*voiture, train*] to crash; [*chauffeur, motard*] to crash, have a crash; [*avion*] (*accidentellement*) to crash; (*volontairement*) to crash-land; **il s'est crashé contre un arbre** he crashed into *ou* hit a tree; **se crasher en moto/voiture** to crash one's motorbike/car

crassane [kʀasan] NF → **passe-crassane**

crasse [kʀas] 1 NF a (= *saleté*) grime, filth b (*: sale tour*) dirty trick*; **faire une ~ à qn** to play a dirty trick on sb*, do the dirty on sb* c (*Tech*) (= *scorie*) dross, scum, slag; (= *résidus*) scale 2 ADJ [*ignorance, bêtise*] crass; [*paresse*] unashamed; **être d'une ignorance ~** to be abysmally ignorant *ou* pig ignorant*

crasseux, -euse [kʀasø, øz] ADJ grimy, filthy

crassier [kʀasje] NM slag heap

cratère [kʀatɛʀ] NM crater

cravache [kʀavaʃ] NF (*riding*) crop, quirt (*US*); (*fig*) **mener qn à la ~** to drive sb ruthlessly

cravacher [kʀavaʃe] ▸conjug 1◂ 1 VT [+ *cheval*] to use the crop on, whip, quirt (*US*); [+ *personne*] to strike with a riding crop; (= *rouer de coups*) to horsewhip 2 VI* (= *foncer*) to belt along*; (*pour finir un travail*) to work like mad*, pull out all the stops*

cravate [kʀavat] 1 NF a [*chemise*] tie; (*hum*) **~ de chanvre** hangman's rope; **~ de commandeur de la Légion d'honneur** ribbon of commander of the Legion of Honour → **épingle, jeter** b (*Lutte*) headlock c (*Naut*) sling

cravater [kʀavate] ▸conjug 1◂ VT a (*lit*) [+ *personne*] to put a tie on; **cravaté de neuf**

wearing a new tie; **se ~** to put one's *ou* a tie on b (= *prendre au collet*) (*gén*) to grab round the neck; (*Lutte*) to put in a headlock; (*: = arrêter*) to collar*; **se faire ~ par un journaliste** to be collared* *ou* buttonholed* by a journalist

crawl [kʀol] NM (= *nage*) crawl; **nager le ~** to do *ou* swim the crawl

crawler [kʀole] ▸conjug 1◂ VI to do *ou* swim the crawl; **dos crawlé** backstroke

crayeux, -euse [kʀɛjø, øz] ADJ [*terrain, substance*] chalky; [*teint*] chalk-white

crayon [kʀɛjɔ̃] 1 NM a (*pour écrire*) pencil; **écrire au ~** to write with a pencil; **écrivez cela au ~** write that in pencil; **notes au ~** pencilled notes; **avoir le ~ facile** to be good at drawing; **coup de ~** pencil stroke; **avoir un bon coup de ~** to be good at sketching b (= *bâtonnet*) pencil c (*Art*) (= *matière*) crayon; (= *dessin*) crayon (drawing); **colorier qch au ~** to crayon sth

2 COMP ▸ **crayon de couleur** crayon ▸ **crayon feutre** felt-tip pen ▸ **crayon gomme** pencil with rubber (*Brit*) *ou* eraser (*US*) ▸ **crayon gras** soft lead pencil ▸ **crayon hémostatique** styptic pencil ▸ **crayon khôl** eyeliner (pencil) ▸ **crayon à lèvres** lip pencil ▸ **crayon lithographique** litho pen ▸ **crayon au nitrate d'argent** silver-nitrate pencil, caustic pencil ▸ **crayon noir** *ou* **à papier** lead pencil ▸ **crayon optique** light pen ▸ **crayon à sourcils** eyebrow pencil ▸ **crayon pour les yeux** eyeliner (pencil)

crayonnage [kʀɛjɔnaʒ] NM (= *gribouillage*) scribble, doodle; (= *dessin*) (pencil) drawing, sketch

crayonner [kʀɛjɔne] ▸conjug 1◂ VT a [+ *notes*] to scribble, jot down (in pencil); [+ *dessin*] to sketch b (*péj* = *gribouiller*) [+ *traits*] to scribble; [+ *dessins*] to doodle

CRDP [seɛʀdepe] NM (*ABRÉV* = **Centre régional de documentation pédagogique**) → **centre**

CRDS [seɛʀdeɛs] NF (*ABRÉV* = **contribution au remboursement de la dette sociale**) → **remboursement**

créance [kʀeɑ̃s] NF a (*Fin, Jur*) (financial) claim, debt (*seen from the creditor's point of view*); (= *titre*) letter of credit; **~ hypothécaire** mortgage loan (*seen from the creditor's point of view*); **~s** accounts receivable; **~ irrécouvrable** bad debt → **lettre** b († *ou littér* = *crédit, foi*) credence (*frm*); **donner ~ à qch** (= *rendre croyable*) to lend credibility to sth; (= *ajouter foi à*) to give credence to sth (*frm*)

créancier, -ière [kʀeɑ̃sje, jɛʀ] NM,F creditor; **~-gagiste** lienor; **~ privilégié** preferential creditor

créateur, -trice [kʀeatœʀ, tʀis] 1 ADJ creative 2 NM,F (*gén, Rel*) creator; **~ de mode** fashion designer; **~ publicitaire** commercial artist; **le Créateur** the Creator

créatif, -ive [kʀeatif, iv] 1 ADJ creative, inventive 2 NM (*Publicité*) designer

créatine [kʀeatin] NF creatine, creatin

créatinine [kʀeatinin] NF creatinine

création [kʀeasjɔ̃] NF a (= *invention, conception*) [*vêtement, style, produit*] creation; (= *chose créée*) creation; **ses ~s les plus originales** his most original creations b (= *production, fondation*) [*empire, association*] creation, founding; [*firme*] creation, setting up; **la ~ d'emplois** job creation; **il y a eu 200 ~s d'emplois/de postes** 200 jobs/posts were created; **je travaille dans cette entreprise depuis sa ~** I've worked in this company since it was first set up; **il y a eu plusieurs ~s d'entreprises** several new companies have been created; (*Rel*) **la Création** (the) Creation; **depuis la ~ du monde** since the world began c (*Théât*) [*pièce*] first production d (*Phys*) **théorie de la ~ continue** steady-state theory

créationnisme [kreasjɔnism] NM creationism

créationniste [kreasjɔnist] **1** ADJ creationistic **2** NMF creationist

créativité [kreativite] NF creativeness, creativity; (Ling) creativity

créature [kreatyr] NF (gén, péj) creature

crécelle [kresɛl] NF rattle → **voix**

crécerelle [kres(ə)rɛl] NF kestrel

crèche [krɛʃ] NF **a** (Rel: de Noël) nativity scene, crib (Brit), crèche (US) **b** (= établissement) crèche, day nursery, day-care centre (Brit) ou center (US), child care center (US); **familiale** crèche in the home of a registered child minder; **~ parentale** crèche run by parents; **mettre son bébé à la ~** to put one's baby in a crèche

---

CRÈCHE DE NOËL

In France the Christmas crib usually contains figurines representing a miller, a woodcutter and other villagers in addition to the Holy Family and the traditional cow, donkey and shepherds. Figurines representing the Magi are added to the nativity scene at Epiphany.

---

crécher[*] [kreʃe] ▶ conjug 6 ◀ VI to hang out*; **je ne sais pas où ~ cette nuit** I don't know where I'm going to crash[*] ou kip down[*] (Brit) tonight

crédence [kredãs] NF **a** (= desserte) credence **b** (Rel) credence table, credenza

crédibiliser [kredibilize] ▶ conjug 1 ◀ VT [+ histoire] to back up, give credibility to; [+ candidature, situation financière] to support

crédibilité [kredibilite] NF credibility

▼**crédible** [kredibl] ADJ credible; **peu ~** [discours, témoin] unconvincing; **il n'est plus très ~** he doesn't have much credibility any more

crédirentier, -ière [kredirãtje, jɛr] NM,F recipient of an annuity

crédit [kredi] **1** NM **a** (= paiement différé) credit; **12 mois de ~** 12 months' credit; **faire ~ à qn** to give sb credit; **faites-moi ~, je vous paierai la semaine prochaine** let me have (it on) credit — I'll pay you next week; **« la maison ne fait pas (de) ~ »** "we are unable to give credit to our customers", "no credit is given here"; **« possibilités de ~ »** "credit (terms) available"; **acheter/vendre qch à ~** to buy/sell sth on credit; **ces gens qui achètent tout à ~** these people who buy everything on credit ou on time (US) → **carte**
b (= prêt) loan, credit; **établissement de ~** credit institution; **l'ouverture d'un ~** the granting of credit; **~ à taux préférentiel** preferential credit; **~ à taux fixe/révisable** fixed rate/adjustable rate loan; **accorder/obtenir un ~** to grant/obtain credit; **prendre un ~ sur dix ans** to take out a ten-year loan → **lettre**
c (dans une raison sociale) bank
d (= excédent d'un compte) credit; **porter une somme au ~ de qn** to credit sb ou sb's account with a sum, credit a sum to sb ou sb's account
e (Pol: gén pl = fonds) **~s** funds; **~s publics** public funds; **~s budgétaires** budget allocation; **~s extraordinaires** extraordinary funds; **débloquer un ~ de 35 millions de francs** to release 35 million francs of funding; **les ~s alloués à la défense** the funds allocated to defence, defence funding
f (Can Univ = unité de valeur) credit
g (= confiance) credit; (= réputation) reputation; **firme/client qui a du ~** creditworthy firm/client; **jouir d'un très grand ~** to enjoy an excellent reputation; **cette théorie connaît un grand ~** this theory is very widely accepted (**auprès de** by); **ça donne du ~ à ce qu'il affirme** that lends credibility to what he says; **faire ~ à l'avenir** to put one's trust in the future, have faith in the future; **bonne action à**

▶ GRAMMAIRE ACTIVE: **crédible** 53.6

mettre ou **porter au ~ de qn** good deed which is to sb's credit ou which counts in sb's favour; **perdre tout ~ auprès de qn** to lose all credit with sb, lose sb's confidence; **trouver ~ auprès de qn** [racontars] to find credence with sb (frm); [personne] to win sb's confidence; **il a utilisé son ~ auprès de lui pour ...** he used his influence with him to ...
2 COMP ▶ **crédit acheteur** buyer credit ▶ **crédit d'appoint** standby credit ▶ **crédit bancaire** bank credit ▶ **crédit en blanc** loan without security ▶ **crédit à la consommation** consumer credit ▶ **crédit documentaire** documentary (letter of) credit ▶ **crédits d'enseignement** (Admin Scol) government grant (to each school) ▶ **crédit à l'exportation** export credit ▶ **crédit fournisseur** supplier credit ▶ **crédit gratuit** (interest-)free credit ▶ **crédit hypothécaire** mortgage ▶ **crédit immobilier** ≈ mortgage ▶ **crédit d'impôt** tax credit ▶ **crédit municipal** state-owned pawnshop ou pawnbroker's

crédit-bail (pl **crédits-bails**) [kredibaj] NM (= système) leasing; (= contrat) lease, leasing agreement ou arrangement; **acquérir qch en ~** to buy sth under a leasing agreement ou arrangement

créditer [kredite] ▶ conjug 1 ◀ VT **a** (Fin) **~ qn/un compte de** [+ somme] to credit sb/an account with **b** (= complimenter) **~ qn de qch** to give sb credit for sth **c** (Sport) **être crédité de** [+ temps] to be credited with

créditeur, -trice [kreditœr, tris] **1** ADJ [banque, pays] creditor (épith); **compte/solde ~** credit account/balance; **leur compte est de nouveau ~** their account is in credit ou in the black[*] again **2** NM,F customer in credit

crédit-relais (pl **crédits-relais**) [kredir(ə)lɛ] NM bridging loan

credo [kredo] NM **a** (Rel) **le Credo** the (Apostle's) Creed **b** (= principes) credo, creed

crédule [kredyl] ADJ credulous, gullible

crédulité [kredylite] NF credulity, gullibility

créer [kree] ▶ conjug 1 ◀ **1** VT **a** (= inventer, concevoir) [+ vêtement, bijou] to create, design; [+ style, produit] to create; [+ mot] to coin, invent; **il a créé cette histoire de toutes pièces** he made up the story from beginning to end; **la joie de ~** the joy of making things ou creating something **b** (= produire, fonder) [+ empire, association] to create, found; [+ entreprise] to create, set up, form; [+ emplois] to create; **~ des ennuis/difficultés à qn** to create problems/difficulties for sb, cause sb problems/difficulties → **événement, fonction, précédent** etc **c** (Théât) [+ rôle] to create; [+ pièce] to produce (for the first time) **2** **se créer** VPR **se ~ une clientèle** to build up a clientèle; **se ~ des problèmes** to create ou make problems for o.s.

crémaillère [kremajɛr] NF **a** [cheminée] trammel → **pendre** **b** (Rail, Tech) rack; **chemin de fer à ~** rack railway, cog railway; **engrenage/direction à ~** rack-and-pinion gear/steering

crémant [kremã] ADJ M, NM cremant (sparkling wine)

crémation [kremasjɔ̃] NF cremation

crématoire [krematwar] **1** ADJ crematory → **four** **2** NM crematorium, crematory (furnace)

crématorium [krematɔrjɔm] NM crematorium

crème [krɛm] **1** NF **a** (Culin) (= produit laitier) cream; (= peau sur le lait) skin; (= entremets) cream dessert; (potage) **d'asperges/de champignons/tomates** cream of asparagus/of mushroom/of tomato (soup); (= liqueur) **~ de cassis** crème de cassis; **~ de marron** sweetened chestnut purée; **fraises à la ~** strawberries and cream; **gâteau à la ~** cream cake → **chou¹, fromage** etc

b (= produit pour la toilette, le nettoyage) cream; **~ de beauté** beauty cream; **~ pour le visage/de jour/de nuit** face/day/night cream; **~ pour les chaussures** shoe polish ou cream (Brit)
c (= les meilleurs) **la ~** the cream of the crop, the crème de la crème; **c'est la ~ des pères** he's the best of (all) fathers; **ses amis ce n'est pas la ~** his friends aren't exactly the cream of society ou la crème de la crème
2 ADJ INV cream(-coloured (Brit) ou -colored (US))
3 NM (= café au lait) coffee with milk ou cream, white coffee (Brit); **un grand/petit ~** a large/small cup of white coffee
4 COMP ▶ **crème aigre** sour cream ▶ **crème anglaise** thin custard made with eggs ▶ **crème antirides** anti-wrinkle cream ▶ **crème au beurre** butter cream ▶ **crème brûlée** crème brûlée ▶ **crème (au) caramel** crème caramel, caramel cream ou custard ▶ **crème démaquillante** cleansing cream, make-up removing cream ▶ **crème fleurette** ≈ single cream (Brit), ≈ light cream (US) ▶ **crème fond de teint** fluid foundation ou makeup ▶ **crème fouettée** (sweetened) whipped cream ▶ **crème fraîche** crème fraîche; **~ fraîche épaisse** ≈ double cream (Brit), ≈ heavy cream (US) ▶ **crème glacée** ice cream ▶ **crème grasse** dry-skin cream ▶ **crème de gruyère** ≈ cheese spread ▶ **crème hydratante** moisturizing cream, moisturizer ▶ **crème pâtissière** confectioner's custard ▶ **crème à raser** shaving cream ▶ **crème renversée** cream mould (Brit), cup custard (US)

crémerie [krɛmri] NF (= magasin) dairy; **changeons de ~***[*]* let's push off[*] somewhere else, let's take our custom (Brit) ou business (US) elsewhere! (hum)

crémeux, -euse [kremø, øz] ADJ creamy

crémier, -ière [kremje, jɛr] NM,F dairy owner

crémone [kremɔn] NF window catch

créneau (pl **créneaux**) [kreno] NM **a** [rempart] crenel, crenelle; (Mil) [tranchée] slit; **les ~x** (= forme) the crenelations; (= chemin de ronde) the battlements; (fig) **monter au ~ pour défendre sa politique** to leap to the defence of one's policies **b** (Aut) **faire un ~** to reverse into a parking space (between two cars) (Brit), parallel park (US); **j'ai raté mon ~** I've parked badly **c** (Comm) gap, niche; [emploi du temps] gap; (TV) **~ (horaire)** (time) slot; **~ publicitaire** advertising slot; **il y a un ~ pour les voitures économiques** there is a niche ou a ready market for fuel-efficient cars; [fusée] **~ de lancement** (launch) window

crénelage [kren(ə)laʒ] NM (Tech) milling

crénelé, e [kren(ə)le] (ptp de **créneler**) ADJ [mur, arête] crenellated; [feuille, bordure] scalloped, crenate (Bot)

créneler [kren(ə)le] ▶ conjug 4 ◀ VT **a** [+ muraille] to crenellate, crenel; [+ tranchée] to make a slit in **b** [+ roue] to notch; [+ pièce de monnaie] to mill

crénom [krenɔ̃] EXCL **~ de nom !**† confound it!, dash it all! (surtout Brit)

créole [kreɔl] **1** ADJ [accent, parler] creole → **riz** **2** (Ling) Creole **3** NMF Creole **4** NF (= boucle d'oreille) large hoop earring

créolité [kreɔlite] NF Creole identity

Créon [kreɔ̃] NM Creon

créosote [kreɔzɔt] NF creosote

crêpage [krɛpaʒ] NM **a** [cheveux] backcombing **b** **~ de chignon**[*] dust-up[*], free-for-all, set-to[*] (Brit) **c** (Tex) crimping

crêpe¹ [krɛp] NF (Culin) pancake (Brit), crêpe; **faire sauter une ~** to toss a pancake; **~ Suzette** crêpe suzette → **dentelle, pâte, retourner**

crêpe² [krɛp] NM **a** (Tex) crepe, crêpe, crape; **~ de Chine** crepe de Chine; **~ georgette** georgette (crepe); **~ de soie** silk crepe [b] (*noir: de deuil*) black mourning crepe; **voile de ~** mourning veil; **porter un ~** (*au bras*) to wear a black armband; (*autour du chapeau*) to wear a black hatband; (*aux cheveux, au revers*) to wear a black ribbon [c] (= *matière*) **semelles (de) ~** crepe soles

crêper [kʀepe] ▶conjug 1◀ [1] VT [a] [+ *cheveux*] to backcomb [b] (*Tex*) to crimp [2] **se crêper** VPR **se ~ les cheveux** to backcomb one's hair; (*fig*) **se ~ le chignon*** to tear each other's hair out, have a dust-up* *ou* a set-to* (*Brit*)

crêperie [kʀepʀi] NF crêperie, pancake house *ou* restaurant (*Brit*)

crépi, e [kʀepi] (*ptp de* **crépir**) ADJ, NM roughcast

crêpier, -ière [kʀepje, jɛʀ] [1] NM,F (= *personne*) pancake (*Brit*) *ou* crêpe seller [2] **crêpière** NF (= *plaque*) pancake (*Brit*) *ou* crêpe griddle; (= *poêle*) shallow frying pan (*for making pancakes*)

crépine [kʀepin] NF [a] [*tuyau*] strainer; [*passementerie*] fringe [b] (*Zool*) omentum, caul; (*Culin*) caul

crépinette [kʀepinɛt] NF flat sausage (*in caul*)

crépir [kʀepiʀ] ▶conjug 2◀ VT to roughcast

crépissage [kʀepisaʒ] NM roughcasting

crépitation [kʀepitɑsjɔ̃] NF [*feu, électricité*] crackling; (*Méd*) **~ osseuse** crepitus; **~ pulmonaire** crepitations

crépitement [kʀepitmɑ̃] NM [*feu, électricité*] crackling (*NonC*); [*chandelle, friture*] sputtering (*NonC*), spluttering (*NonC*); [*pluie*] pattering (*NonC*); [*mitrailleuse*] rattle (*NonC*); [*grésil*] rattle (*NonC*), patter (*NonC*); **sous le ~ des flashs** with flashguns going off all around

crépiter [kʀepite] ▶conjug 1◀ VI [*feu, électricité*] to crackle; [*chandelle, friture*] to sputter, splutter; [*pluie*] to patter; [*flashs*] to go off; [*mitrailleuse*] to rattle out; [*grésil*] to rattle, patter; **les applaudissements crépitèrent** there was a ripple of applause

crépon [kʀepɔ̃] NM ≈ seersucker → **papier**

crépu, e [kʀepy] ADJ [*cheveux*] frizzy; **elle est toute ~e** her hair's all frizzy

crépusculaire [kʀepyskylɛʀ] ADJ (*littér, Zool*) crepuscular; **lumière ~** twilight glow

crépuscule [kʀepyskyl] NM (*lit*) twilight, dusk; (*fig*) twilight; **au ~** at twilight; **au ~ de sa vie** in his twilight years

crescendo [kʀeʃɛndo] [1] ADV [a] (*Mus*) crescendo [b] **aller ~** [*vacarme, acclamations*] to rise in a crescendo, grow louder and louder, crescendo; [*colère, émotion*] to grow *ou* become ever greater [2] NM (*Mus*) crescendo; **le ~ de sa colère/de son émotion** the rising tide of his anger/emotion

cresson [kʀesɔ̃] NM **~ (de fontaine)** watercress; **~ des prés** cardamine, lady's-smock

cressonnette [kʀesɔnɛt] NF cardamine, lady's-smock

cressonnière [kʀesɔnjɛʀ] NF watercress bed

Crésus [kʀezys] NM Croesus → **riche**

crésyl, Crésyl® [kʀezil] NM *type of disinfectant containing cresol*

crétacé, e [kʀetase] [1] ADJ Cretaceous [2] NM **le ~** the Cretaceous period

crête [kʀɛt] NF [a] (*Zool*) [*coq*] comb; [*oiseau*] crest; [*batracien*] horn; **~ de coq** cockscomb [b] (= *arête*) [*mur*] top; [*toit*] ridge; [*montagne*] ridge, crest; [*vague*] crest; [*graphique*] peak; **la ~ du tibia** the edge *ou* crest (*SPÉC*) of the tibia, the shin; (*Géog*) **(ligne de) ~** watershed

Crète [kʀɛt] NF Crete

crétin, e [kʀetɛ̃, in] [1] ADJ (*péj*) cretinous*, idiotic, moronic* [2] NM,F (*péj*) moron*, cretin*

crétinerie* [kʀetinʀi] NF [a] (= *caractère*) idiocy, stupidity [b] (= *acte, parole*) idiotic *ou* stupid thing to do *ou* say

crétiniser [kʀetinize] ▶conjug 1◀ VT to turn into a moron* *ou* half-wit

crétinisme [kʀetinism] NM (*Méd*) cretinism; (*péj*) idiocy, stupidity

crétois, e [kʀetwa, waz] [1] ADJ Cretan [2] NM (*Ling*) Cretan [3] **Crétois(e)** NM,F Cretan

cretonne [kʀetɔn] NF cretonne

creusage [kʀøzaʒ], **creusement** [kʀøzmɑ̃] NM [*fondations*] digging; [*canal*] digging, cutting

creuser [kʀøze] ▶conjug 1◀ [1] VT [a] (= *évider*) [+ *bois, falaise*] to hollow (out); [+ *sol, roc*] to make *ou* dig a hole in, dig out; (*au marteau-piqueur*) to drill a hole in; **~ la neige de ses mains** to dig out the snow with one's hands [b] [+ *puits*] to sink, bore; [+ *fondations, mine*] to dig; [+ *canal*] to dig, cut; [+ *tranchée, fosse*] to dig (out); [+ *sillon*] to plough (*Brit*), plow (*US*); [+ *trou*] (*gén*) to dig, make; (*au marteau-piqueur*) to drill; **~ un tunnel sous une montagne** to bore *ou* drive a tunnel under a mountain; **~ un terrier** to burrow, make a burrow; **la taupe creuse des galeries** moles make *ou* dig tunnels in the soil; **~ sa propre tombe** to dig one's own grave; **ça a creusé un abîme** *ou* **un fossé entre eux** that has created *ou* thrown a great gulf between them

[c] (= *approfondir*) [+ *problème, sujet*] to go into (deeply *ou* thoroughly), look into (closely); **c'est une idée à ~** it's something to be gone into more deeply *ou* thoroughly, it's an idea worth pursuing; (*fig*) **si on creuse un peu** if you scratch the surface

[d] (*fig*) **la fatigue lui creusait les joues** he was so tired his face was gaunt; **visage creusé de rides** face furrowed with wrinkles; **~ les reins** to draw o.s. up, throw out one's chest; **la promenade, ça creuse (l'estomac)*** walking gives you a real appetite; (*lit, fig*) **~ l'écart** to establish a convincing lead (**par rapport à** over)

[2] VI [*personne*] to dig; [*lapin*] to burrow; **il a fallu ~ beaucoup** *ou* **profond** we had to dig deep (**dans** into)

[3] **se creuser** VPR [a] [*joues, visage*] to become gaunt *ou* hollow; **la mer se creuse** there's a swell coming on; (*lit, fig*) **l'écart se creuse entre eux** the gap between them is widening

[b] * [*personne*] **se ~ (la cervelle** *ou* **la tête)** to rack *ou* cudgel one's brains; **il ne s'est pas beaucoup creusé !** he didn't exactly put himself out *ou* overexert himself!; **ils ne se sont pas beaucoup creusés pour trouver un cadeau** they didn't look very hard to find a present

creuset [kʀøze] NM [a] (*Chim, Ind*) crucible; [*haut fourneau*] heart, crucible; **~ de verrerie** glassmaker's crucible [b] (= *lieu de brassage*) melting pot [c] (*littér* = *épreuve*) crucible (*littér*), trial

Creutzfeldt-Jakob [kʀɔjtsfɛldʒakɔb] N **maladie de ~** Creutzfeldt-Jakob disease, CJD

creux, creuse [kʀø, kʀøz] [1] ADJ [a] [*arbre, dent*] hollow; [*toux, voix*] hollow, deep; [*son*] hollow; [*estomac*] empty; **j'ai la tête** *ou* **la cervelle creuse** my mind's a blank → **nez, sonner, ventre**

[b] (= *concave*) [*surface*] concave, hollow; [*yeux*] deep-set, sunken; [*joue*] gaunt, hollow; [*visage*] gaunt; **aux yeux ~** hollow-eyed → **assiette, chemin**

[c] (= *vide de sens*) [*paroles*] empty, hollow; [*idées*] barren, futile; [*raisonnement*] weak, flimsy

[d] (= *sans activité*) **les jours ~** slack days; **les heures creuses** (*gén*) slack periods; (*métro, électricité, téléphone*) off-peak periods; **période creuse** (*gén*) slack period; (*Tourisme*) low season → **classe**

[2] NM [a] (= *cavité*) [*arbre*] hollow, hole; [*rocher, dent*] cavity, hole; **avoir un ~ (dans l'estomac)*** to feel *ou* be hungry *ou* peckish* (*Brit*)

[b] (= *dépression*) hollow; **être plein de ~ et de bosses** to be full of bumps and holes *ou* hollows; **le ~ de la main** the hollow of one's hand; **ça tient dans le ~ de la main** it's small enough to hold in your hand; **des écureuils qui mangent dans le ~ de la main** squirrels which eat out of your hand; **le ~ de l'aisselle** the armpit; **le ~ de l'estomac** the pit of the stomach; **le ~ de l'épaule** the hollow of one's shoulder; **au ~ des reins** in the small of one's back → **gravure**

[c] (= *activité réduite*) slack period

[d] (*Naut*) [*voile*] belly; [*vague*] trough; **il y avait des ~ de 10 mètres** there were 10-metre-high waves, the waves were 10 metres high; (*fig*) **être au** *ou* **dans le ~ de la vague** [*marché*] to have hit rock bottom; [*économie*] to be in the doldrums, be at its lowest ebb; [*entreprise*] to be in the doldrums; **il est au** *ou* **dans le ~ de la vague** his fortunes are at their lowest ebb

[e] (*Art*) **graver en ~** to do intaglio engraving

crevaison [kʀəvɛzɔ̃] NF (*Aut*) puncture (*Brit*), flat

crevant, e* [kʀəvɑ̃, ɑ̃t] ADJ (= *fatigant*) gruelling, killing* (*Brit*); (= *amusant*) priceless*

crevasse [kʀəvas] NF [*mur, rocher*] crack, fissure, crevice; [*sol*] crack, fissure; [*glacier*] crevasse; [*peau*] crack; **avoir des ~s aux mains** to have chapped hands

crevassé, e [kʀəvase] (*ptp de* **crevasser**) ADJ [*sol*] fissured; [*mains, peau*] chapped; **glacier très ~** glacier with a lot of crevasses

crevasser [kʀəvase] ▶conjug 1◀ [1] VT [+ *sol*] to cause cracks *ou* fissures in, crack; [+ *mains*] to chap [2] **se crevasser** VPR [*sol*] to crack, become cracked; [*mains*] to chap, become *ou* get chapped

crevé, e [kʀəve] (*ptp de* **crever**) [1] ADJ [a] [*pneu*] burst, punctured [b]* (= *mort*) dead; (= *fatigué*) dead beat*, bushed*, exhausted, knackered‡ (*Brit*) [2] (*Couture*) slash; **des manches à ~s** slashed sleeves

crève‡ [kʀɛv] NF (*bad*) cold; **j'ai la ~** I've got a bad cold; **elle a attrapé** *ou* **chopé* la ~** she's caught a bad cold

crève-cœur (*pl* **crève-cœurs**) [kʀɛvkœʀ] NM heartbreak

crève-la-faim* [kʀɛvlafɛ̃] NMF INV (*péj*) (= *miséreux*) miserable wretch; (= *clochard*) down-and-out

crever [kʀəve] ▶conjug 5◀ [1] VT [a] (= *percer*) [+ *pneu*] to burst, puncture; [+ *ballon*] to burst; **j'ai un pneu (de) crevé** I've got a puncture (*Brit*), I've got a flat tyre (*Brit*) *ou* tire (*US*), I've got a flat*; **~ les yeux à qn** (*intentionnellement*) to gouge (out) *ou* put out sb's eyes; (*accidentellement*) to blind sb (in both eyes); **ça crève les yeux** it's as plain as the nose on your face; (*fig*) **ça te crève les yeux !** it's staring you in the face!; **le prix a crevé le plafond** the price has gone through the roof; (*fig*) **~ le cœur à qn** to break sb's heart; **cet acteur crève l'écran** this actor has a tremendous screen presence

[b] (* = *exténuer*) **~ qn** [*personne*] to wear sb out, work sb to death*; [*tâche, marche*] to wear sb out, kill sb*; **~ un cheval** to ride *ou* work a horse into the ground *ou* to death

[c] ‡ **~ la faim** *ou* **la dalle** to be starving* *ou* famished*; **on la crève ici!** they starve us here!

[2] VI [a] (= *s'ouvrir*) [*fruit, sac, abcès*] to burst; **les nuages crevèrent** the clouds burst, the heavens opened; (*Culin*) **faire ~ du riz** to boil rice until the grains burst *ou* split

[b] (*péj* = *être plein de*) **~ de** [+ *santé*] to be bursting with; [+ *orgueil*] to be bursting *ou* puffed up with; [+ *jalousie*] to be full of, be bursting with; [+ *dépit*] to be full of; **~ d'envie de faire qch** to be dying to do sth* → **rire**

[c] ‡ (= *mourir*) [*animal, plante*] to die (off); [*personne*] to die, kick the bucket‡, snuff it‡ (*Brit*); **un chien crevé** a dead dog; **~ de faim/**

froid: to starve/freeze to death; (*fig*) **on crève de froid ici*** it's freezing (cold) in here; **on crève de chaud ici*** it's boiling in here*; **je crève de faim*** I'm starving* *ou* famished* *ou* ravenous; **je crève de soif*** I'm dying of thirst*, I'm parched*; **~ d'ennui*** to be bored to tears *ou* death*, be bored out of one's mind*; **tu veux nous faire ~!*** do you want to kill us or what!; **faire ~ qn de soif** to make sb die of thirst

d (*Aut*) [*pneu, automobiliste*] to have a flat tyre (*Brit*) *ou* tire (*US*), have a puncture (*Brit*); **faire 10 000 km sans ~** to drive 10,000 km without getting a flat* *ou* a puncture (*Brit*)

3 se crever VPR (‡ = *se fatiguer*) to kill o.s. (**à faire** doing); **se ~ (au travail)*** (*gén*) to work o.s. to death; [*ménagère*] to work one's fingers to the bone*; **se ~ le cul**‡ to slog one's guts out‡ (**à faire** doing); **je ne vais pas me ~ le cul à transporter toutes ces briques!***‡ I'm not going to bust a gut‡ *ou* to kill myself* carrying all those bricks around!

crevette [krəvɛt] NF **~ (rose)** prawn; **~ grise** shrimp → **filet**

crevettier [krəvetje] NM (= *filet*) shrimp net; (= *bateau*) shrimp boat

cri [kri] **1** NM **a** (= *éclat de voix*) [*personne*] cry, shout; (*très fort*) scream; (*ton aigu*) shriek, screech; (= *pleurs*) cry, scream; (*de douleur, de peur*) scream, cry, yell; **le ~ du nouveau-né** the cry of the newborn baby; **pousser des ~s de joie/triomphe** to cry out in joy/triumph; **~ de surprise** cry *ou* exclamation of surprise; **~ aigu** *ou* **perçant** piercing cry *ou* scream, shrill cry; [*animal*] squeal; **~ sourd** *ou* **étouffé** muffled cry *ou* shout; **pousser un ~ de colère** to shout angrily; **pousser un ~ de rage** to cry out in rage, give a cry of rage; **jeter** *ou* **pousser des ~s** to shout (out), cry out; **elle jeta un ~ de douleur** she cried out in pain, she gave a cry of pain; **pousser des ~s d'orfraie** to scream, shriek → **étouffer**

b (= *exclamation*) cry, shout; **~ d'alarme/ d'approbation** cry *ou* shout of alarm/ approval; **le ~ des marchands ambulants** the hawkers' cries; **marchant au ~ de « liberté »** marching to shouts *ou* cries of "freedom"; (*fig*) **le ~ des opprimés** the cries of the oppressed; (*fig*) **une tentative de suicide est souvent un ~ (de détresse)** a suicide attempt is often a cry for help; **ce poème est un véritable ~ d'amour** this poem is a cry of love; (*fig*) **le ~ de la conscience** the voice of conscience → **haut**

c (*terme générique*) noise; [*oiseau*] call; [*canard*] quack; [*cochon*] squeal; (*terme générique*) **le ~ d'un animal** the noise an animal makes

d (*littér* = *crissement*) squeal, screech

e (*loc*) **c'est le dernier ~** it's the (very) latest thing; **un ordinateur dernier ~** a state-of-the-art computer; **à grands ~s** vociferously

2 COMP ► **cri du cœur** heartfelt cry, cry from the heart, cri de cœur ► **cri de guerre** (*lit*) war cry; (*fig*) slogan, war cry ► **cri primal** primal scream

criaillement [krijajmɑ̃] NM **a** (*gén pl*) [*oie*] squawking (*NonC*); [*paon*] squawking (*NonC*), screeching (*NonC*); [*bébé*] bawling (*NonC*), squalling (*NonC*) **b** = **criailleries**

criailler [krijaje] ▶ conjug 1 ◀ VI **a** [*oie*] to squawk; [*paon*] to squawk, screech; [*bébé*] to bawl, squall **b** (= *rouspéter*) to grouse*, grumble; (= *houspiller*) **~ après qn** to nag (at) sb

criailleries [krijajri] NFPL **a** (= *rouspétance*) grousing* (*NonC*), grumbling (*NonC*); (= *houspillage*) nagging (*NonC*)

criailleur, -euse [krijajœr, øz] **1** ADJ grouchy* **2** NM,F (= *rouspéteur*) grouch*, grouser*

criant, e [krijɑ̃, ɑ̃t] ADJ [*erreur*] glaring (*épith*); [*injustice*] rank (*épith*), blatant, glaring (*épith*); [*preuve*] striking (*épith*), glaring (*épith*);

[*contraste, vérité*] striking (*épith*); **portrait ~ de vérité** amazingly true-to-life portrait

criard, e [krijar, ard] ADJ (*péj*) [*enfant*] yelling, squalling; [*oiseau*] squawking; [*son, voix*] piercing; [*couleurs, vêtement*] loud, garish

criblage [kriblaʒ] NM (= *tamisage*) [*graines*] sifting; [*sable*] riddling, sifting; [*minerai*] screening, jigging; (= *calibrage*) [*fruits*] grading; [*charbon*] riddling, screening

crible [kribl] NM (*à main*) riddle; (*Ind, Min*) screen, jig, jigger; **~ mécanique** screening machine; **passer au ~** (*lit*) to riddle, put through a riddle; [+ *idée, proposition*] to examine closely; [+ *déclaration, texte*] to go through with a fine-tooth comb

criblé, e [krible] (*ptp de* **cribler**) ♦ **criblé de** LOC ADJ [+ *balles, flèches, trous*] riddled with; [+ *taches*] covered in; **visage ~ de boutons** face covered in spots *ou* pimples, spotty face; **~ de dettes** crippled with debts, up to one's eyes in debt

cribler [krible] ▶ conjug 1 ◀ VT **a** (= *tamiser*) [+ *graines*] to sift; [+ *sable*] to riddle, sift; (= *trier*) [+ *minerai*] to screen, jig; (= *calibrer*) [+ *charbon*] to riddle, screen; [+ *fruits*] to grade **b** (= *percer*) **~ qch/qn de balles/flèches** to riddle sth/sb with bullets/arrows; (= *accabler*) **~ qn de questions** to bombard sb with questions; **~ qn d'injures** to heap insults on sb

cribleur, -euse [kriblœr, øz] **1** NM,F (= *ouvrier*) [*graines*] sifter; [*fruits*] grader; [*sable*] riddler, sifter; [*charbon*] riddler, screener; [*minerai*] screener, jigger **2** **cribleuse** NF (= *machine*) sifter, sifting machine

cric [krik] NM **~ (d'automobile)** (car) jack; **soulever qch au ~** to jack sth up; **~ hydraulique** hydraulic jack; **~ à vis** screw jack

cric-crac [krikkrak] EXCL, NM (*gén*) creak; (= *bruit de clé*) click

cricket [kriket] NM (*Sport*) cricket

cricoïde [krikɔid] **1** ADJ (*Anat*) cricoid **2** NM **le ~** the cricoid cartilage

cricri [krikri] NM, **cri-cri** [krikri] NM INV = *cri du grillon*) chirping; (* = *grillon*) cricket

criée [krije] NF **a** **(vente à la) ~** (sale by) auction; **vendre des poissons à la ~** to auction fish, sell fish by auction **b** (= *salle*) auction room, salesroom

crier [krije] ▶ conjug 7 ◀ **1** VI **a** [*personne*] to shout; (*très fort*) to scream; (*ton aigu*) to shriek, screech; (= *vagir*) to cry, scream; (*de douleur, peur*) to scream, cry out, yell (out); **~ de douleur** to give a scream *ou* cry *ou* yell of pain, scream *ou* cry *ou* yell out in pain; **« oh non ! » cria-t-il** "oh no!", he cried; **~ à tue-tête** *ou* **comme un sourd** *ou* **comme un putois** to shout one's head off; **tes parents vont ~** your parents are going to make a fuss; **tu ne peux pas parler sans ~?** do you have to shout?, can't you talk without shouting?

b [*oiseau*] to call; [*canard*] to quack; [*cochon*] to squeal; [*dindon*] to gobble; [*hibou, singe*] to call, screech, hoot; [*mouette*] to cry; [*oie*] to honk; [*perroquet*] to squawk; [*souris*] to squeak **c** (= *grincer*) [*porte, plancher, roue*] to creak, squeak; [*frein*] to squeal, screech; [*chaussure, étoffe*] to squeal; [*tissu, couleur*] to scream, shriek; **faire ~ la craie sur le tableau** to make the chalk squeak on the blackboard

d (*avec prép*) **~ contre** *ou* **après* qn** to nag (at) *ou* scold sb, go on at sb*; **~ contre qch** to shout about sth; **elle passe son temps à lui ~ après*** *ou* **dessus*** she's forever going on at him*, she's always shouting at him; **~ à la trahison/au scandale** to call it treason/a scandal, start bandying words like treason/ scandal about; **~ au miracle** to hail it as a miracle, call it a miracle; **~ à l'assassin** *ou* **au meurtre** to shout "murder"; **~ au loup/au voleur** to cry wolf/thief; **quand il a demandé une augmentation de 50% son patron a crié au fou**

when he asked for a 50% rise his boss called him a madman *ou* said he was crazy

2 VT **a** [+ *ordre, injures*] to shout (out), yell (out); (= *proclamer*) [+ *mépris, indignation*] to proclaim; [+ *innocence*] to protest; **~ qch sur (tous) les toits** to shout *ou* proclaim sth from the rooftops *ou* housetops; **elle cria qu'elle en avait assez** she shouted that she had had enough; (*plus fort*) she screamed (out) that she had had enough; **~ à qn de se taire** *ou* **qu'il se taise** to shout at sb to be quiet

b (*pour vendre*) **au coin de la rue, un gamin criait les éditions spéciales** at the street corner a kid was shouting out *ou* calling out the special editions

c (*pour avertir, implorer*) **sans ~ gare** without a warning; **~ grâce** (*lit*) to beg for mercy; (*fig*) to beg for mercy *ou* a respite; **quand j'ai parlé de me lancer seul dans l'entreprise, ils ont crié casse-cou** when I spoke of going it alone, they said I was crazy → **victoire**

crieur, -euse [krijœr, øz] NM,F **~ de journaux** newspaper seller; (*Hist*) **~ public** town crier

crime [krim] NM **a** (= *meurtre*) murder; **il s'agit bien d'un ~** it's definitely (a case of) murder; **retourner sur les lieux du ~** to go back to the scene of the crime; **la victime/ l'arme du ~** the murder victim/weapon; **~ de sang** murder; **~ crapuleux** foul crime; **~ passionnel** crime of passion, crime passionnel; **~ sexuel** sex murder *ou* crime; **le ~ parfait** the perfect crime; **cherchez à qui profite le ~** find someone with a motive

b (*Jur* = *délit grave*) crime, offence, ≈ felony (*US*); **~s et délits** crimes; **~ contre la sûreté de l'État** offence *ou* crime against the state; **~ de lèse-majesté** crime of lèse-majesté; **~ contre les mœurs** sexual offence, offence against public decency; **~ contre la paix** crime against peace; **~ contre un particulier** crime against a private individual; **~ contre nature** unnatural act, crime against nature; **~s de guerre** war crimes; **~ contre l'humanité** crime against humanity ■ (*PROV*) **le ~ ne paie pas** crime doesn't pay (*PROV*) → **syndicat**

c (*sens affaibli*) crime; **c'est un ~ de faire** it's criminal *ou* a crime to do; **il est parti avant l'heure ? ce n'est pas un ~ !** he left early? well, that's hardly a crime!

d († *ou littér* = *péché, faute*) sin, crime

Crimée [krime] NF **la ~** the Crimea, the Crimean peninsula; **la guerre de ~** the Crimean War

criminalisation [kriminalizasjɔ̃] NF criminalization

criminaliser [kriminalize] ▶ conjug 1 ◀ VT (*Jur*) to criminalize

criminaliste [kriminalist] NMF criminal lawyer

criminalité [kriminalite] NF (= *actes criminels*) criminality, crime; **la ~ juvénile** juvenile criminality; **la grande/petite ~** serious/petty crime; **la ~ organisée** organized crime

criminel, -elle [kriminɛl] **1** ADJ (*gén, Jur*) [*acte, personne, procès*] criminal; (*sens affaibli*) **ce serait ~ de laisser ces fruits se perdre** it would be criminal *ou* a crime to let this fruit go to waste → **incendie 2** NM,F (= *meurtrier*) murderer (*ou* murderess); (*Jur* = *auteur d'un délit grave*) criminal; **~ de guerre** war criminal; (*hum* = *coupable*) **voilà le ~** there's the culprit *ou* the guilty party **3** NM (*juridiction*) **avocat au ~** criminal lawyer; **poursuivre qn au ~** to take criminal proceedings against sb, prosecute sb in a criminal court **4 criminelle** NF **la ~le** (= *police*) the crime *ou* murder squad

criminellement [kriminɛlmɑ̃] ADV [*agir*] criminally; (*Jur*) **poursuivre qn ~** to take criminal proceedings against sb, prosecute sb in a criminal court

criminogène [kriminɔʒɛn] ADJ [*facteur*] encouraging criminality *ou* crime

criminologie [kriminɔlɔʒi] NF criminology

criminologiste [kʀiminɔlɔʒist], **criminologue** [kʀiminɔlɔg] NMF criminologist

crin [kʀɛ̃] NM a (= poil) [cheval] hair (NonC);
[matelas, balai] horse hair; **~ végétal** vegetable
(horse)hair → **gant** b **à tous ~s** ◊ **à tout ~**
[conservateur, républicain] diehard, dyed-in-
the-wool; **révolutionnaire à tout ~** out-and-
out revolutionary

crincrin* [kʀɛ̃kʀɛ̃] NM (péj) (= violon) squeaky
fiddle; (= son) squeaking, scraping

crinière [kʀinjɛʀ] NF a (Méd) [rhumatisme,
b* [personne] mane of hair, flowing mane;
elle avait une ~ rousse she had a mane of red
hair c [casque] plume

crinoline [kʀinɔlin] NF crinoline petticoat;
robe à ~ crinoline (dress)

crique [kʀik] NF creek, inlet

criquet [kʀikɛ] NM (Zool) locust; (gén =
sauterelle) grasshopper

crise [kʀiz] 1 NF a (Méd) [rhumatisme,
goutte] attack; [épilepsie, apoplexie] fit; **~ de
toux** fit ou bout of coughing
b (= accès) outburst, fit; **~ de
colère/rage/jalousie** fit of anger/rage/jealousy;
~ de rire laughing fit; **être pris d'une ~ de rire**
to be in fits (of laughter); **la ~ (de rire)!*** what
a scream!*; **j'ai été pris d'une ~ de rangement** I
got a sudden urge to tidy the place up; **travailler par ~s** to work in fits and starts; **je vais
au cinéma/je lis par ~s** I go through phases
when I go to the cinema/I read a lot
c (* = colère) rage, tantrum; **piquer** ou **faire
une** ou **sa ~** to throw a tantrum ou a fit*, fly
off the handle
d (= bouleversement, Pol, Écon) crisis; **en période de ~** in times of crisis ou of trouble; **pays/
économie en (état de) ~** country/economy in
(a state of) crisis; **la ~ de l'immobilier** the
property market crisis; **~ financière/politique**
financial/political crisis
e (= pénurie) shortage; **~ de main-d'œuvre**
shortage of manpower
2 COMP ► **crise d'appendicite** attack of
appendicitis ► **crise d'asthme** asthma attack, attack of asthma ► **crise cardiaque**
heart attack ► **crise de confiance** crisis of
confidence ► **crise de conscience** crisis of
conscience ► **crise économique** economic
crisis, slump ► **crise d'épilepsie** epileptic
fit ► **crise de foie** bilious attack, bad attack
of indigestion ► **crise d'identité** identity
crisis ► **crise de larmes** crying fit ► **crise
du logement** housing shortage ► **crise ministérielle** cabinet crisis ► **crise morale**
moral crisis ► **crise de nerfs** (Méd) fit of
hysterics; (caprice) tantrum ► **crise du pétrole** oil crisis ► **crise du pouvoir** leadership crisis ► **crise de la quarantaine** midlife crisis ► **crise religieuse** crisis of belief

crispant, e [kʀispɑ̃, ɑ̃t] ADJ (= énervant) irritating, aggravating*, annoying; **ce qu'il est ~ !***
he really gets on my nerves!*, he's a real pain
in the neck!*

crispation [kʀispasjɔ̃] NF a (= contraction)
[traits, visage] tensing; [muscles] contraction;
[cuir] shrivelling-up b (= spasme) twitch; **des
~s nerveuses** nervous twitches ou twitching;
une ~ douloureuse de la main a painful
twitching of the hand; (fig) **donner des ~s à
qn** to get on sb's nerves* c (= nervosité) state
of tension

crispé, e [kʀispe] (ptp de **crisper**) ADJ [sourire]
nervous, tense; [personne] tense, on edge
(attrib); [style] tense, awkward

crisper [kʀispe] ▸ conjug 1 ◂ 1 VT a (=
contracter) [+ muscles, membres] to tense, flex;
[+ poings] to clench; **la douleur crispait les visages** their faces were contorted with grief;
les mains crispées sur le volant clutching the
wheel b (= plisser) [+ cuir] to shrivel (up); **le
froid crispe la peau** the cold makes one's skin
feel taut ou tight c (* = agacer) **~ qn** to get
on sb's nerves* 2 **se crisper** VPR [visage] to

tense; [sourire] to become strained ou tense;
[poings] to clench; [personne] to get edgy* ou
tense; **ses mains se crispèrent sur le manche
de la pioche** his hands tightened on the pickaxe, he clutched the pickaxe

crispin [kʀispɛ̃] NM **gants à ~** gauntlets

criss [kʀis] NM kris, creese

crissement [kʀismɑ̃] NM [neige, gravier]
crunch(ing) (NonC); [pneus, freins] screech(-
ing) (NonC), squeal(ing) (NonC); [soie, taffetas]
rustling (NonC), rustle (NonC); [cuir] squeaking (NonC); [plume] scratching (NonC); **s'arrêter dans un ~ de pneus** to screech to a halt; **le
~ de la craie sur le tableau** the squeaking of
chalk on the blackboard

crisser [kʀise] ▸ conjug 1 ◂ VI [neige, gravier] to
crunch; [pneus, freins] to screech, squeal; [soie,
taffetas] to rustle; [cuir] to squeak; [plume] to
scratch; [craie] to squeak

cristal (pl **-aux**) [kʀistal, o] NM a (Chim, Min)
crystal; **~ (de roche)** rock crystal (NonC),
quartz (NonC); **~ (de plomb)** (lead) crystal; **~
de Baccarat** Baccarat crystal; **cristaux de givre**
(sur arbre) ice crystals; (sur vitre) ice patterns;
cristaux liquides liquid crystals; **écran à
cristaux liquides** liquid crystal screen; **de** ou
en ~ crystal (épith); (littér) **le ~ de sa voix** ◊ **sa
voix de ~** his crystal-clear voice; **~ de Bohême**
Bohemian crystal; **~ d'Islande** Iceland spar →
boule b (= objet) crystal(ware) (NonC), piece
of crystal(ware) ou fine glassware; **les cristaux
du lustre** the crystal droplets of the chandelier c (pour le nettoyage) **cristaux (de soude)**
washing soda

cristallerie [kʀistalʀi] NF (= fabrication) crystal
(glass-)making; (= fabrique) (crystal) glassworks; (= objets) crystal(ware), fine glassware

cristallier [kʀistalje] NM (Hist) (= chercheur)
crystal seeker; (= ouvrier) crystal engraver

cristallin, e [kʀistalɛ̃, in] 1 ADJ (Min) crystalline; [son, voix] crystal-clear; [eau] crystal(-
clear), crystalline 2 NM (Anat) crystalline
lens

cristallisation [kʀistalizasjɔ̃] NF (lit, fig) crystallization

cristallisé, e [kʀistalize] (ptp de **cristalliser**) ADJ
[minerai, sucre] crystallized

cristalliser VTI, **se cristalliser** VPR
[kʀistalize] ▸ conjug 1 ◂ (lit, fig) to crystallize

cristallisoir [kʀistalizwaʀ] NM crystallizing
dish

cristallographie [kʀistalɔgʀafi] NF crystallography

cristallomancie [kʀistalɔmɑ̃si] NF crystal-
gazing, crystallomancy

criste-marine (pl **cristes-marines**) [kʀist(ə)-
maʀin] NF (rock) samphire

critère [kʀitɛʀ] NM a (= référence) criterion;
son seul ~ est l'avis du parti his only criterion
is the opinion of the party; **le style n'est pas
le seul ~ pour juger de la valeur d'un roman**
style is not the only yardstick ou criterion by
which one can judge the value of a novel; **~s
de sélection** selection criteria
b (= stipulation) requirement; **il n'y a pas de ~
d'âge** there are no special requirements as far
as age is concerned; **~s de qualité** quality requirements; (Europe) **~s de convergence** convergence criteria; **~s d'attribution d'un prêt** requirements ou criteria for the granting of a
loan; **quels sont vos ~s de choix en littérature ?** what are the main factors you take into
account when choosing a book to read? →
convergence
c (= preuve) criterion; **ce n'est pas un ~
suffisant pour prouver l'authenticité du document** this is not a good enough criterion
on which to prove the document's authenticity; **la richesse n'est pas un ~ de succès**
wealth is not a criterion ou an indication of
success

critérium [kʀiteʀjɔm] NM a (Cyclisme) rally;
(Natation) gala b † = **critère**

criticisme [kʀitisism] NM (Philo) critical approach

critiquable [kʀitikabl] ADJ [attitude] reprehensible; [politique] open to criticism (attrib); **les
aspects les plus ~s de la procédure** the aspects of the procedure which are most open
to criticism

critique¹ [kʀitik] ADJ (= alarmant) [situation,
période] critical; (= décisif) [phase, situation,
période] crucial, critical; (Sci) [vitesse, masse,
point] critical; **dans les circonstances ~s, il
perd la tête** in critical situations ou in emergencies ou in a crisis he loses his head → **âge**

critique² [kʀitik] 1 ADJ a (= qui analyse)
[jugement, notes, édition] critical → **apparat, esprit**
b (= sévère) critical, censorious (frm); **d'un
œil ~** with a critical eye; **il s'est montré très ~
(au sujet de ...)** he was very critical of (...)
2 NF a (= blâme) criticism; **il ne supporte
pas la ~** ou **les ~s** he can't tolerate criticism;
malgré les nombreuses ~s despite the many
criticisms; **faire une ~ à (l'endroit de) qch/qn**
to criticize sth/sb; **une ~ que je lui ferais est
qu'il ...** one criticism I would make of him is
that he ... **la ~ est aisée** it's easy to criticize
b (= analyse) [texte, œuvre] appreciation, critique; [livre, spectacle] review; (= art de juger) **la
~** criticism; **la ~ littéraire/musicale** literary/
music criticism; **faire la ~ de** [+ livre, film] to
review, do a write-up on; [+ poème] to write
an appreciation ou a critique of
c (= personnes) **la ~** the critics; **la ~ a bien
accueilli sa pièce** his play was well received
by the critics
3 NMF (= commentateur) critic; **~ d'art/de cinéma** art/cinema ou film critic; **~ littéraire** literary critic

critiquer [kʀitike] ▸ conjug 1 ◂ VT a (= blâmer)
to criticize; **il critique tout/tout le monde** he
finds fault with ou criticizes everything/
everybody b (= juger) [+ livre, œuvre] to assess, make an appraisal of; (= examiner) to examine (critically)

croassement [kʀɔasmɑ̃] NM caw, cawing
(NonC)

croasser [kʀɔase] ▸ conjug 1 ◂ VI to caw

croate [kʀɔat] 1 ADJ Croatian 2 NM (Ling)
Croat, Croatian 3 **Croate** NMF Croat, Croatian

Croatie [kʀɔasi] NF Croatia

croato-musulman, e [kʀɔatomyzylmɑ̃, an]
ADJ Muslim-Croat (épith)

crobard* [kʀɔbaʀ] NM sketch

croc [kʀo] NM a (= dent) fang; **montrer les ~s**
[animal] to bare its teeth, show its teeth ou
fangs; * [personne] to show one's teeth; **avoir
les ~s!*** to be starving, be famished* b (= objet) hook; **~ de boucherie/de marinier** meat/
boat hook; **~ à fumier** muck rake

croc-en-jambe (pl **crocs-en-jambe**) [kʀɔk-
ɑ̃ʒɑ̃b] NM **faire un ~ à qn** (lit) to trip sb (up);
(fig) to trip sb up, pull a fast one on sb*; **un ~
me fit perdre l'équilibre** I was tripped up and
lost my balance

croche [kʀɔʃ] NF (Mus) quaver (Brit), eighth
(note) (US); **double ~** semiquaver (Brit), sixteenth (note) (US); **triple/quadruple ~**
demisemiquaver/hemidemisemiquaver (Brit),
thirty-second/sixty-fourth note (US)

croche-patte* (pl **croche-pattes**) [kʀɔʃpat]
NM = **croc-en-jambe**

croche-pied (pl **croche-pieds**) [kʀɔʃpje] NM =
croc-en-jambe

crochet [kʀɔʃɛ] NM a (= fer recourbé) (gén)
hook; [chiffonnier] spiked stick; [patte de
pantalon] fastener, clip, fastening; [cam-
brioleur, serrurier] picklock; (Rail) **~ d'attelage** coupling; **~ de boucherie** ou **de boucher**

meat hook; **~ à boutons** ou **bottines** button-hook; **vivre aux ~s de qn*** to live off sb, sponge off* **sb** [b] (= *aiguille*) crochet hook; (= *technique*) crochet; **couverture au ~** crocheted blanket; **faire du ~** to crochet; **faire qch au ~** to crochet sth [c] (*Boxe*) **~ du gauche/du droit** left/right hook [d] (= *détour*) [*véhicule*] sudden swerve; [*route*] sudden turn; [*voyage*] detour; **il a fait un ~ pour éviter l'obstacle** he swerved to avoid the obstacle; **faire un ~ par une ville** to make a detour through a town [e] (*Typo*) **~s** square brackets; **entre ~s** in square brackets [f] [*serpent*] fang [g] (*Archit*) crocket [h] (†: *Radio*) **~ radiophonique** talent show

crochetage [krɔʃtaʒ] NM [*serrure*] picking

crocheter [krɔʃte] ▶conjug 5◀ VT [a] [+ *serrure*] to pick; [+ *porte*] to pick the lock on [b] (= *faire tomber*) to trip (up) [c] (*Tricot*) to crochet

crocheteur [krɔʃtœr] NM (= *voleur*) picklock

crochu, e [krɔʃy] ADJ [*nez*] hooked; [*mains, doigts*] claw-like; **au nez ~** hook-nosed → **atome**

croco* [krɔko] NM (ABRÉV = **crocodile**) crocodile skin; **en ~** crocodile (*épith*)

crocodile [krɔkɔdil] NM (= *animal, peau*) crocodile; (*Rail*) contact ramp; **sac en ~** crocodile(-skin) handbag → **larme**

crocus [krɔkys] NM crocus

▼ **croire** [krwar]

▶conjug 44◀
[1] VERBE TRANSITIF [4] VERBE TRANSITIF
[2] VERBE INTRANSITIF   INDIR
[3] VERBE TRANSITIF [5] VERBE
   INDIR   PRONOMINAL
---

[1] VERBE TRANSITIF

[a] **= tenir pour vrai ou sincère** [+ *personne, fait, histoire*] to believe; **auriez-vous cru cela de lui?** would you have believed that of him?; **le croira qui voudra, mais ...** believe it or not (but) ...; **je veux bien le ~** I can quite ou well believe it; **je n'en crois rien** I don't believe a word of it; **croyez moi** believe me → **fer, parole**

♦ **je te** ou **vous crois!*** you bet!*, rather!

[b]

♦ **croire** + *infinitif* ou *que* (= *penser, estimer*) to believe, think; (= *déduire*) to believe, assume, think; **nous croyons qu'il a dit la vérité** we believe ou think that he told the truth; **je n'arrive pas à ~ qu'il a réussi** I (just) can't believe he has succeeded; **elle croyait avoir perdu son sac** she thought she had lost her bag; **il a bien cru manquer son train** he really thought he would miss his train; **il n'y avait pas de lumière, j'ai cru qu'ils étaient couchés** there was no light on so I thought ou assumed they had gone to bed; **il a cru bien faire** he meant well, he thought he was doing the right thing ou acting for the best; **je crois que oui** I think so; **je crois que non** I don't think so, I think not; **il n'est pas là? — je crois que si** isn't he in? — (yes) I think he is; **on ne croyait pas qu'il viendrait** we didn't think he'd come; **elle ne croit pas/elle ne peut pas ~ qu'il mente** she doesn't think/can't believe he is lying; **non, mais qu'est-ce que vous croyez?*** what do you imagine?; **je ne suis pas celle que vous croyez!** I'm not that sort of person! → **dire, rêver**

♦ **à croire que**: (c'est) **à ~ qu'il est amoureux** you'd ou anyone would think he was in love; (*frm*) **il est à ~ que** it is to be supposed ou presumed that

♦ **il faut croire que** it would seem ou appear that; **j'entends rien, faut ~ que je deviens sourde** I can't hear a thing, I must be going deaf; **faut pas ~!*** make no mistake (about it)

[c]

♦ **croire** + *adjectif* ou *adverbe* (= *juger, estimer*) to think, believe, consider; (= *supposer*) to think, believe; **croyez-vous cette réunion nécessaire?** do you think ou believe this meeting is necessary?, do you consider this meeting (to be)

▶ GRAMMAIRE ACTIVE: **croire** 33.2, 53.5

necessary?; **il n'a pas cru utile** ou **nécessaire de me prévenir** he didn't think it necessary to warn me; **on a cru préférable de refuser** we thought it preferable for us to refuse, we thought that it would be better for us to refuse; **on l'a cru mort** he was believed ou presumed (to be) dead; **on les croyait en France** they were believed ou thought to be in France; **je la croyais ailleurs/avec vous** I thought she was somewhere else/with you; **où vous croyez-vous?** where do you think you are?; **tu ne peux pas ~** ou **vous ne sauriez ~** (*frm*) **combien il nous manque** you cannot (begin) to imagine how much we miss him

[d]

♦ **on croirait** ◊ **on aurait cru**: **on croirait une hirondelle** it looks like a swallow; **on aurait cru (voir) un fantôme** he looked like a ghost; **on croirait (entendre) une clarinette** it sounds like ou it could be a clarinet (playing); **on croirait entendre son père** it could (almost) be his father talking, you'd think it was his father talking; **on croirait qu'elle ne comprend pas** she doesn't seem to understand, you might almost think she didn't understand

[e]

♦ **en croire qn** ou **qch** (= *s'en rapporter à*) **à l'en ~** to listen to ou hear him, if you (were to) go by what he says; **s'il faut en ~ les journaux** if we (are to) go by what the papers say, if we are to believe the papers, if the papers are anything to go by; **croyez-m'en** believe me; **vous pouvez m'en ~** ◊ **croyez-en mon expérience** (you can) take it from me, take it from one who knows; **si vous m'en croyez** if you want my opinion; **il n'en croyait pas ses oreilles/ses yeux** he couldn't believe his ears/his eyes

[2] VERBE INTRANSITIF

Rel **= avoir la foi** to believe, be a believer

[3] **croire à** VT INDIR [+ *innocence de qn, vie éternelle, Père Noël*] to believe in; [+ *justice, médecine*] to have faith ou confidence in, believe in; [+ *promesses*] to believe (in), have faith in; **il ne croit plus à rien** he no longer believes in anything; **ses histoires, je n'y crois plus** I don't believe his stories any more; **on a cru d'abord à un accident** at first they believed ou thought it was accident, at first they took it for an accident; **pour faire ~ à un suicide** to make people think it was suicide, to give the impression ou appearance of a suicide; **il ne croit pas à la guerre** (= *il pense qu'elle n'aura pas lieu*) he doesn't think ou believe there will be a war; (= *il pense qu'elle ne sert à rien*) he doesn't believe in war; **non, mais tu crois au Père Noël!** you really do live in cloud-cuckoo land! (*Brit*), you must believe in Santa Claus too!; **c'est à n'y pas ~!** it's beyond belief!, it's unbelievable!, it's hardly credible!; (*frm: formule épistolaire*) **veuillez ~ à mes sentiments dévoués** yours sincerely, I am, sir, your devoted servant (*frm*)

[4] **croire en** VT INDIR to believe in; **~ en Dieu** to believe in God; **~ en qn** to believe in sb, have faith ou confidence in sb

[5] **se croire** VERBE PRONOMINAL

[a] **= penser être tel ou dans telle situation** **se ~ fort/malin** to think one is strong/clever; **il se croit un génie** he thinks he's a genius; **elle se croit tout permis** she thinks she can do whatever she likes ou she can get away with anything; **on se croirait en vacances** I feel as if I'm on holiday; **on se croirait en Bretagne/été** it could almost be Brittany/summer; **le patron lui a dit qu'elle avait une espoir de promotion et elle s'y croit déjà*** the boss told her she had a chance of promotion and she acts as if she'd already got it

[b] **= être prétentieux** **qu'est-ce qu'il se croit, celui-là?** who does he think he is?*; (*péj*) **il s'y croit*** he thinks he's really something*

croisade [krwazad] NF (*Hist, fig*) crusade; **les Croisades** the (Holy) Crusades; **la ~ des Albigeois** the Albigensian Crusade; **partir en ~** (*lit*) to go on a crusade; (*fig*) to launch ou mount a crusade (**contre** against)

croisé[1], e[1] [krwaze] (*ptp de* **croiser**) [1] ADJ [*veste*] double-breasted; [*rimes, vers*] alternate; **race ~e** crossbreed; **tissu ~** twill → **bras, feu[1], mot** [2] NM (*Tex*) twill

croisé[2] [krwaze] NM (*Hist*) crusader

croisée[2] [krwaze] NF [a] (= *jonction*) **~ de chemins** crossroads, crossing; (*fig*) **à la ~ des chemins** at a crossroads; **~ d'ogives** ribbed vault; **~ du transept** transept crossing; **leur musique est à la ~ de plusieurs cultures** their music is a blend of several cultural influences [b] (*littér = fenêtre*) window, casement (*littér*)

croisement [krwazmɑ̃] NM [a] [*fils, brins*] crossing; **l'étroitesse de la route rendait impossible le ~** the narrowness of the road made it impossible for vehicles to pass (one another) → **feu[1]** [b] [*races, espèces*] crossing (*NonC*), crossbreeding (*NonC*), interbreeding (*NonC*) (**avec** with); **faire des ~s de race** to rear ou produce crossbreeds, cross(breed); **est-ce un ~?** ou **le produit d'un ~?** is it a cross(breed)? [c] (= *carrefour*) crossroads, junction; **au ~ de la route et de la voie ferrée** where the road crosses the railway

croiser [krwaze] ▶conjug 1◀ [1] VT [a] [+ *bras*] to fold, cross; [+ *jambes*] to cross; [+ *fils, lignes*] to cross; **elle croisa son châle sur sa poitrine** she folded her shawl across ou over her chest; **les jambes croisées** cross-legged; **~ les doigts** (*lit*) to cross one's fingers; (*fig*) to keep one's fingers crossed, cross one's fingers; (*fig*) **croisons les doigts!** fingers crossed!; **je croise les doigts pour qu'il fasse beau** I'm keeping my fingers crossed that the weather will be good; (*lit, fig*) **~ le fer** to cross swords (**avec** with); (*fig*) **se ~ les bras** to lounge around, sit around idly

[b] (= *couper*) [+ *route*] to cross, cut across; [+ *ligne*] to cross, cut across, intersect

[c] (= *passer à côté de*) [+ *véhicule, passant*] to pass; **notre train a croisé le rapide** our train passed the express going in the other direction; **son regard croisa le mien** his eyes met mine; **je l'ai croisé plusieurs fois dans des réunions** I've seen him several times at meetings; **j'ai croisé Jean dans la rue** I bumped into Jean in the street

[d] (= *accoupler*) [+ *espèces, races*] to cross(breed), interbreed (**avec** with); **l'âne peut se ~ avec le cheval** an ass can crossbred with a horse

[e] (*Sport*) [+ *tir, coup droit*] to angle; **passe croisée** diagonal pass

[2] VI [a] (*Habillement*) **cette veste croise bien** that jacket has got a nice ou good overlap; **cette saison les couturiers font ~ les vestes** this season fashion designers are making jackets double-breasted; **il avait tellement grossi qu'il ne pouvait plus (faire) ~ sa veste** he'd got so fat that he couldn't get his jacket to fasten

[b] (*Naut*) to cruise

[3] **se croiser** VPR [a] [*chemins, lignes*] to cross, cut (across) each other, intersect; **se ~ à angle droit** to cross at right angles; **nos regards** ou **nos yeux se croisèrent** our eyes met; **il a les yeux qui se croisent*** he's cross-eyed

[b] [*personnes, véhicules*] to pass each other; **ma lettre s'est croisée avec la tienne** ◊ **nos lettres se sont croisées** my letter crossed yours (in the post), our letters crossed (in the post); **nous nous sommes croisés hier** we bumped ou ran into each other yesterday; **nous nous sommes croisés plusieurs fois dans des réunions** we've seen each other several times at meetings

[c] (*Hist*) to take the cross, go on a crusade

croiseur [krwazœr] NM (= *bateau*) cruiser

croisière [kʀwazjɛʀ] NF cruise; **partir en ~ ◊ faire une ~** to go on a cruise; **être en ~** to be on a cruise; **ce voilier est idéal pour la ~** this boat is ideal for cruising; **allure** ou **régime** ou **rythme** ou **vitesse de ~** cruising speed

croisiériste [kʀwazjeʀist] NMF cruise passenger

croisillon [kʀwazijɔ̃] NM [croix, charpente] crosspiece, crossbar; [église] transept; **~s** [fenêtre] lattice work; [tarte] lattice → **fenêtre**

croissance [kʀwasɑ̃s] NF [enfant, ville, industrie] growth, development; [plante] growth; **~ économique** economic growth ou development; **~ interne/externe** [entreprise] internal/external growth; **~ zéro** zero (economic) growth; **arrêté dans sa ~** stunted; **maladie de ~** growth disease; **entreprise en pleine ~** expanding company

croissant[1] [kʀwasɑ̃] NM [a] (= forme) crescent; **~ de lune** crescent of the moon; **en ~** crescent-shaped [b] (Culin) croissant

croissant[2], **e** [kʀwasɑ̃, ɑ̃t] ADJ [nombre, tension] growing, increasing, rising; [chaleur] rising; [froid] increasing; [Math] [fonction] increasing; **aller ~** [peur, enthousiasme] to grow, increase; [bruit] to grow ou get louder; **le rythme ~ des accidents** the increasing number of accidents, the rising accident rate

croissanterie [kʀwasɑ̃tʀi] NF croissant shop

Croissant-Rouge [kʀwasɑ̃ʀuʒ] NM **le ~** the Red Crescent

croître [kʀwatʀ] ► conjug 55 ◄ VI [enfant, plante] to grow; [ville] to grow, increase in size; **~ en beauté/sagesse** to grow in beauty/ wisdom; **~ dans l'estime de qn** to rise ou grow in sb's esteem [b] [ambition, bruit, quantité] to grow, increase; **les jours croissent** the days are getting longer ou are lengthening; **~ en nombre/volume** to increase in number/size ou volume; **l'inquiétude sur son état de santé ne cessait de ~** there was increasing concern over the state of his health; **son enthousiasme ne cessa de ~** he grew more and more enthusiastic; **la chaleur ne faisait que ~** the heat got more and more intense, the temperature kept on rising [c] [rivière] to swell, rise; [lune] to wax; [vent] to rise [d] (loc) (Bible) **croissez et multipliez!** go forth and multiply!; (iro) **ça ne fait que ~ et embellir!** (things are getting) better and better!

croix [kʀwa] [1] NF [a] (gén, Hér, Rel) cross; **~ celtique/grecque/latine** Celtic/Greek/Latin cross; **~ de Malte/de Saint-André** Maltese/St Andrew's cross; **~ ancrée/fleuretée** cross moline/fleury ou flory; **~ fleuronnée** ou **tréflée** cross tréflée; **~ de Jérusalem** cross of Jerusalem; **~ potencée** potent cross; **mettre des bâtons en ~** in the form of a cross; **mettre les bâtons en ~** to lay sticks crosswise; **être disposé en ~** to form a cross ou be arranged crosswise; **chemins qui se coupent en ~** paths which cross at right angles (to one another); **mettre en ~ ◊ mettre à mort sur la ~** to crucify; **mise en ~** crucifixion; **mettre les bras en ~** to stretch one's arms out sideways; **pour le faire sortir, c'est la ~ et la bannière*** it's the devil's own job ou a devil of a job to get him to go out*; **~ de bois ~ de fer (, si je mens je vais en enfer)** cross my heart (and hope to die) → **chemin, signe** [b] (= décoration) cross; (Scol = récompense) prize, medal [c] (= marque) cross; **faire** ou **mettre une ~ devant un nom** to put a cross in front of ou by a name; **(appeler) les noms marqués d'une ~** (to call out) the names with a cross against (Brit) ou by (US) them; **ta prime, tu peux faire une ~ dessus*** you might just as well forget all about your bonus ou write your bonus off*; **si tu lui prêtes ton livre, tu peux faire une ~ dessus!*** if you lend him your book, you can say goodbye to it!* ou you can kiss it goodbye!*; (iro) **il faut faire une ~ à la cheminée** ou

sur le calendrier it's a red-letter day [d] (= souffrance, épreuve) cross, burden; **chacun a** ou **porte sa ~** we all have our cross to bear [2] COMP ► **croix de fer** (Gym) crucifix ► **croix gammée** swastika ► **Croix de guerre** (Mil) Military Cross ► **croix de Lorraine** cross of Lorraine ► **Croix-du-Sud** Southern Cross

Croix-Rouge [kʀwaʀuʒ] NF **la ~** the Red Cross

cromlech [kʀɔmlɛk] NM cromlech

cromorne [kʀɔmɔʀn] NF krumhorn

croquant[1]† [kʀɔkɑ̃] NM (péj) yokel, (country) bumpkin

croquant[2], **e** [kʀɔkɑ̃, ɑ̃t] [1] ADJ crisp, crunchy [2] NM [volaille] gristle; **le ~ de l'oreille** the cartilage in the ear

croque* [kʀɔk] NM ABRÉV = **croque-monsieur**

croque au sel [kʀɔkosɛl] ♦ **à la croque au sel** LOC ADV with salt (and nothing else), with a sprinkling of salt

croque-madame [kʀɔkmadam] NM INV toasted ham and cheese sandwich with a fried egg on top

croquembouche [kʀɔkɑ̃buʃ] NM pyramid of cream-filled choux pastry balls

croque-mitaine (pl **croque-mitaines**) [kʀɔkmitɛn] NM bog(e)y man, ogre; **ce maître est un vrai ~** this schoolmaster is a real ogre

croque-monsieur [kʀɔkməsjø] NM INV toasted ham and cheese sandwich

croque-mort* (pl **croque-morts**) [kʀɔkmɔʀ] NM undertaker's ou mortician's (US) assistant; **avoir un air de ~** to have a funereal look ou a face like an undertaker

croquenot* [kʀɔkno] NM (= chaussure) clodhopper*

croquer [kʀɔke] ► conjug 1 ◄ [1] VT [a] (= manger) [+ biscuits, noisettes, bonbons] to crunch; [+ fruit] to bite into; **à laisser fondre dans la bouche sans ~** to be sucked slowly and not chewed ou crunched; **~ le marmot**†* to hang around (waiting)*, kick ou cool one's heels*; **Adam croqua la pomme** Adam took a bite out of the apple; **je ne peux pas ~ avec mon dentier** I can't bite properly with my dentures → **chocolat** [b] (* = dépenser) to squander; **~ de l'argent** to squander money, go through money like water*; **~ un héritage** to squander ou blow* an inheritance [c] (= dessiner) to sketch; **être (joli) à ~** to be as pretty as a picture, look good enough to eat; **tu es à ~ avec ce chapeau** you look good enough to eat in that hat [d] (= camper) [+ personnage] to sketch, outline, give a thumbnail sketch of [e] (arg Crime) **il en croque** [indicateur] he's a (copper's) nark*; [policier] he gets paid off* [2] VI [a] [fruit] to be crunchy; [salade] to be crisp; **le sucre croque sous la dent** sugar is crunchy [b] (= mordre) to bite; **~ dans une pomme** to bite into an apple

croquet [kʀɔkɛ] NM (Sport) croquet

croquette [kʀɔkɛt] NF (Culin) croquette; **~s de chocolat** chocolate croquettes; **~s pour chiens/chats** dry dogfood/catfood

croqueuse [kʀɔkøz] NF **~ de diamants** gold digger, fortune-hunter

croquignolet, -ette* [kʀɔkiɲɔlɛ, ɛt] ADJ (= mignon) sweet, cute*, dinky*; (iro) **ça promet d'être ~** that sounds like great fun (iro)

croquis [kʀɔki] NM (= dessin) (rough) sketch; (= description) sketch; **faire un ~ de qch** to make a (rough) sketch of sth; **faire un ~ rapide de la situation** to give a rapid outline ou thumbnail sketch of the situation; **~ d'audience** court-room sketches

crosne [kʀon] NM Chinese artichoke

cross(-country) [kʀɔs(kuntʀi)] NM (= course) (à pied) cross-country race ou run; (Équitation) cross-country race; (= sport) (à pied) cross-country racing ou running; (Équitation) cross-country racing ou running; **faire du ~** (à pied) to do cross-country running

crosse [kʀɔs] NF [a] (= poignée) [fusil] butt; [revolver] grip; **frapper qn à coups de ~** to hit sb with the butt of one's rifle; **mettre** ou **lever la ~ en l'air** (= se rendre) to show the white flag, lay down one's arms; (= se mutiner) to mutiny, refuse to fight [b] (= bâton) (Rel) crook, crosier, crozier; (Sport) **~ de golf** golf club; **~ de hockey** hockey stick [c] (= partie recourbée) [violon] head, scroll; **~ de piston** cross-head; **~ de l'aorte** arch of the aorta, aortic arch; **~ de fougère** crosier (of fern) [d]: **chercher des ~s à qn** to pick a quarrel with sb; **s'il me cherche des ~s** if he's looking for a chance to make trouble ou to pick a quarrel with me [e] (Culin) **~ de bœuf** knuckle of beef

crotale [kʀɔtal] NM rattlesnake, rattler* (US)

crotte [kʀɔt] [1] NF [a] (= excrément) [brebis, lapin, souris] dropping; **~ de nez:** bog(e)y: (Brit), booger: (US); **son chien a déposé une ~ sur le palier** his dog has messed ou done its business on the landing; **c'est plein de ~(s) de chien** it's covered in dog mess; **c'est de la ~** it's a load of (old) rubbish*; **c'est pas de la ~** it's not cheap rubbish; **il ne se prend pas pour une ~** he thinks he's God's gift to mankind ou the bee's knees* (Brit); (terme d'affection) **ma (petite) ~** my little sausage* [b] (= bonbon) **~ de chocolat** chocolate [c] († = boue) mud [2] EXCL* oh heck!*, blast (it)!* (Brit); **je te dis ~!** get lost!*

crotté, e [kʀɔte] (ptp de **crotter**) ADJ [chaussure, vêtement] muddy, caked in ou covered in mud; **il était tout ~** he was all covered in mud ou all muddy

crotter [kʀɔte] ► conjug 1 ◄ [1] VT to muddy [2] VI [chien] to do its business, mess

crottin [kʀɔtɛ̃] NM [a] [cheval, âne] droppings, dung (NonC), manure (NonC) [b] (= fromage) small, round goat's milk cheese

crouillat:, [kʀuja], **crouille:** [kʀuj] NM (injurieux) North African

croulant, e [kʀulɑ̃, ɑ̃t] [1] ADJ [mur] crumbling, tumbledown (épith); [maison] ramshackle, tumbledown (épith), crumbling; [autorité, empire] crumbling, tottering [2] NM: old fogey*, crumbly (Brit)*

crouler [kʀule] ► conjug 1 ◄ VI [a] (= s'écrouler) [maison, mur] to collapse, tumble down, fall down; [masse de neige] to collapse; [terre] to give (way); [empire] to collapse; **la terre croula sous ses pas** the ground gave (way) beneath ou under his feet; **le tremblement de terre a fait ~ les maisons** the earthquake has brought the houses down; **la salle croulait sous les applaudissements** the auditorium resounded with applause; (fig) **~ sous le poids de qch** to collapse under the weight of sth; **ils croulent sous les dettes** they are crippled by debts [b] (= être délabré) **qui croule** [maison] ramshackle, tumbledown, crumbling; [mur] crumbling, tumbledown; [civilisation] crumbling

croup [kʀup] NM (Méd) croup; **faux ~** spasmodic croup

croupe [kʀup] NF [a] [cheval] croup, crupper, rump, hindquarters; **monter en ~** to ride pillion; **il monta en ~ et ils partirent** he got on behind and off they went; **il avait son ami en ~** he had his friend behind him (on the pillion) [b]* [personne] rump* [c] [colline] hilltop

croupetons [kʀuptɔ̃] ADV **se tenir** ou **être à ~** to be crouching, be squatting, be down on one's haunches; **se mettre à ~** to crouch ou squat down, go down on one's haunches

croupi, e [kʀupi] (ptp de **croupir**) ADJ [eau] stagnant

croupier, -ière[1] [kʀupje, jɛʀ] NM,F croupier

croupière[2] [kʀupje] NF (= harnais) crupper; **tailler des ~s à qn**† to put a spoke in sb's wheel

croupion [kʀupjɔ̃] NM (Orn) rump; (Culin) parson's nose, pope's nose (US); (‡ hum) [personne] rear (end)*, backside*; (péj) **parlement/parti** ~ rump parliament/party

croupir [kʀupiʀ] ▶conjug 2◀ VI [eau] to stagnate; **feuilles qui croupissent dans la mare** leaves rotting in the pond; ~ **dans son ignorance/dans le vice** to wallow ou remain sunk in one's own ignorance/in vice; **je n'ai pas envie de ~ dans ce bled*** I don't want to stay and rot in this dump*; ~ **en prison** to rot in prison

croupissant, e [kʀupisɑ̃, ɑ̃t] ADJ [eau] stagnant; **une vie ~e** a dreary existence

CROUS [kʀus] NM (ABRÉV = **centre régional des œuvres universitaires et scolaires**) → **centre**

croustade [kʀustad] NF croustade

croustillant, e [kʀustijɑ̃, ɑ̃t] ADJ [a] [pain, pâte] crusty; [croissant, galette, chips] crisp, crunchy [b] (= grivois) spicy

croustiller [kʀustije] ▶conjug 1◀ VI [pain, pâte] to be crusty; [croissant, galette, chips] to be crisp ou crunchy

croûte [kʀut] [1] NF [a] [pain, pâte] crust; [fromage] rind; [vol-au-vent] case; **jambon en ~** ham en croute; **morue en ~ de pommes de terre** cod baked in a potato crust → **pâté** [b] (* = nourriture) food, grub‡; **à la ~!**‡ (= venez manger) come and get it!*, grub's up!‡ (Brit), grub's on!‡ (US); (= allons manger) let's go and eat!* → **casser**, **gagner** [c] (= couche) layer; (sur plaie) scab; (sur pot de peinture) skin; **couvert d'une ~ de glace** crusted with ice, covered with a crust ou a layer of ice; **recouvert d'une ~ de boue** caked with mud; ~ **calcaire** ou **de tartre** layer of scale ou fur; **gratter des ~s de cire sur une table** to scrape candlewax off a table [d] (= apparence) ~ **de culture** veneer of culture; ~ **de bêtise** (thick) layer of stupidity [e] ~ **(de cuir)** undressed leather ou hide; **sac en** ~ hide bag [f] (péj = tableau) lousy painting [g] (péj = personne) old fossil

[2] COMP ▶ **croûte aux champignons** mushrooms on toast ▶ **croûte au fromage** cheese on toast, toasted cheese, ≈ Welsh rarebit ou rabbit ▶ **croûte de pain** crust of bread; ~**s de pain** (péj) old crusts; (quignons) hunks ou chunks of bread ▶ **la croûte terrestre** (Géol) the earth's crust

croûté, e [kʀute] ADJ (Ski) **neige** ~**e** crusted snow

croûter‡ [kʀute] ▶conjug 1◀ VI to have some grub‡, nosh‡ (Brit)

croûteux, -euse [kʀutø, øz] ADJ scabby, covered with scabs

croûton [kʀutɔ̃] NM [a] (= bout du pain) crust; (Culin) crouton [b] (péj = personne) **(vieux)** ~ fuddy-duddy*, old fossil*

croyable [kʀwajabl] ADJ **ce n'est pas ~!** it's unbelievable!, it's incredible!; **c'est à peine** ~ it's hard to believe

croyance [kʀwajɑ̃s] NF [a] (= foi) ~ **à** ou **en** belief in, faith in [b] (= religion, opinion) belief; ~**s religieuses** religious beliefs; **la ~ populaire** folk ou conventional wisdom

croyant, e [kʀwajɑ̃, ɑ̃t] [1] ADJ **être** ~ to be a believer; **ne pas être** ~ to be a non-believer [2] NM,F believer; **les** ~**s** people who believe in God

CRS [seeɛʀɛs] ABRÉV = **Compagnie républicaine de sécurité** [1] NM member of the state security police, ≈ member of the riot police; **les** ~ ≈ the riot police [2] NF company of the state security police, ≈ riot police

cru[1]**, e**[1] [kʀy] ADJ [a] (= non cuit) [aliments] raw, uncooked; **je ne vais pas te manger tout** ~ I won't eat you; **je l'aurais avalée** ou **mangée toute ~e*** (= j'étais furieux) I could have strangled ou murdered her*; (= elle était belle à croquer) she looked good enough to eat* → **lait** [b] (Tech = non apprêté) [soie] raw; [chanvre, toile] raw, untreated; [métal] crude, raw; **cuir** ~ untreated ou raw leather, rawhide [c] [lumière, couleur] harsh, garish [d] (= franc, réaliste) [mot] forthright, blunt; [description] raw, blunt; [réponse] straight, blunt, forthright; **je vous le dis tout** ~ I'll tell you straight out*, I'll give it to you straight* [e] (= choquant) [histoire, chanson, langage] crude, coarse; **parler** ~ to speak coarsely ou crudely [f] (loc) **à** ~ : **construire à** ~ to build without foundations; (Équitation) **monter à** ~ to ride bareback

cru[2] [kʀy] NM [a] (= vignoble) vineyard; **un vin d'un bon** ~ a good vintage [b] (= vin) wine; **un grand** ~ a great wine → **bouilleur** [c] (loc) **du** ~ local; **les gens du** ~ the locals; **de son (propre)** ~ of his own invention ou devising

cruauté [kʀyote] NF [a] [personne, destin] cruelty **(envers** to); [bête sauvage] ferocity [b] (= action) (act of) cruelty, cruel act

cruche [kʀyʃ] NF [a] (= récipient) jug (Brit), pitcher (US); (= contenu) jug(ful) (Brit), pitcher(ful) (US) ▪ (PROV) **tant va la** ~ **à l'eau qu'à la fin elle se casse** if you keep playing with fire you must expect to get burnt [b] (* = imbécile) ass*, twit* (Brit); **ce qu'il est** ~ ! he's such a ninny*

cruchon [kʀyʃɔ̃] NM (= récipient) small jug (Brit) ou pitcher (US); (= contenu) small jug(ful) (Brit) ou pitcher(ful) (US)

crucial, e (mpl -iaux) [kʀysjal, jo] ADJ crucial

crucifère [kʀysifɛʀ] ADJ cruciferous

crucifiement [kʀysifimɑ̃] NM crucifixion; (fig) **le ~ de la chair** the crucifying of the flesh

crucifier [kʀysifje] ▶conjug 7◀ VT (lit, fig) to crucify

crucifix [kʀysifi] NM crucifix

crucifixion [kʀysifiksjɔ̃] NF crucifixion

cruciforme [kʀysifɔʀm] ADJ cruciform; **tournevis** ~ Phillips screwdriver®; **vis** ~ Phillips screw®

cruciverbiste [kʀysivɛʀbist] NMF crossword-puzzle enthusiast

crudité [kʀydite] NF [a] [langage] crudeness, coarseness; [description] bluntness; [lumière, couleur] harshness, garishness [b] (= propos) ~**s** coarse remarks, coarseness (NonC); **dire des** ~**s** to make coarse remarks [c] (Culin) ~**s** raw vegetables; **salade de** ~**s** ≈ mixed salad, crudités

crue[2] [kʀy] NF (= montée des eaux) rise in the water level; (= inondation) flood; **en** ~ in spate; **les** ~**s du Nil** the Nile floods; **la fonte des neiges provoque des** ~**s subites** the spring thaw produces a sudden rise in river levels

cruel, -elle [kʀyɛl] ADJ [a] (= méchant) [personne, acte, paroles] cruel; [animal] ferocious [b] (= douloureux) [perte] cruel; [destin, sort, épreuve] cruel, harsh; [remords, froid, nécessité] cruel, bitter; [manque] desperate, severe

cruellement [kʀyɛlmɑ̃] ADV [a] (= méchamment) cruelly; **traiter qn** ~ to be cruel to sb, treat sb cruelly [b] (= douloureusement) [décevoir] bitterly; [souffrir] terribly; **manquer** ~ **de qch** to be desperately short of sth; **l'argent fait** ~ **défaut** the lack of money is sorely felt; ~ **éprouvé par ce deuil** sorely ou grievously distressed by this bereavement

crûment [kʀymɑ̃] ADV [dire, parler] (= nettement) bluntly, forthrightly; (= grossièrement) crudely, coarsely; **éclairer** ~ to cast a harsh ou garish light over

crustacé [kʀystase] NM (Zool) shellfish pl inv (crabs, lobsters and shrimps), crustacean (SPÉC); (Culin) ~**s** seafood, shellfish

cryobiologie [kʀijɔbjɔlɔʒi] NF cryobiology

cryochirurgie [kʀijɔʃiʀyʀʒi] NF cryosurgery

cryoconservation [kʀijokɔ̃sɛʀvasjɔ̃] NF cryogenic preservation

cryogénie [kʀijɔʒeni] NF cryogenics sg

cryogénique [kʀijɔʒenik] ADJ cryogenic; **moteur** ~ cryogenic (first-stage) engine; **fusée à propulsion** ~ cryogenically-powered rocket

cryologie [kʀijɔlɔʒi] NF cryogenics sg

cryptage [kʀiptaʒ] NM [message, émission, données] encryption

crypte [kʀipt] NF (Archit, Anat) crypt

crypter [kʀipte] ▶conjug 1◀ VT [+ message, émission, données] to encrypt; **chaîne/émission** ~**ée** encrypted channel/programme

cryptique [kʀiptik] ADJ [a] (= secret) cryptic [b] (Anat) cryptal

cryptocommuniste† [kʀiptokɔmynist] NMF crypto-communist

cryptogame [kʀiptɔgam] [1] ADJ cryptogamic [2] NM ou F cryptogam

cryptogramme [kʀiptɔgʀam] NM cryptogram

cryptographie [kʀiptɔgʀafi] NF cryptography, cryptology

cryptographique [kʀiptɔgʀafik] ADJ cryptographic

crypton [kʀiptɔ̃] NM = **krypton**

CSA [seɛsa] NM (ABRÉV = **Conseil supérieur de l'audiovisuel**) → **conseil**

CSCE [seɛssea] NF (ABRÉV = **Conférence sur la Sécurité et la Coopération en Europe**) CSCE

CSG [seɛsʒe] NF (ABRÉV = **contribution sociale généralisée**) → **contribution**

CSM [seɛsɛm] NM (ABRÉV = **Conseil supérieur de la magistrature**) → **conseil**

Cuba [kyba] N Cuba; **à** ~ in Cuba

cubage [kybaʒ] NM [a] (= action) cubage [b] (= volume) cubage, cubature, cubic content; ~ **d'air** air space

cubain, e [kybɛ̃, ɛn] [1] ADJ Cuban [2] **Cubain(e)** NM,F Cuban

cube [kyb] [1] NM (gén, Géom, Math) cube; [jeu] building block, (wooden) brick; (Math) **le** ~ **de 2 est 8** 2 cubed is 8, the cube of 2 is 8; **élever au** ~ to cube; (= moto) **gros** ~* big bike* [2] ADJ **centimètre/mètre** ~ cubic centimetre/metre → **cylindrée**

cuber [kybe] ▶conjug 1◀ [1] VT [+ nombre] to cube; [+ volume, solide] to cube, measure the volume of; [+ espace] to measure the cubic capacity of [2] VI [récipient] ~ **20 litres** to have a cubic capacity of 20 litres; (fig) **avec l'inflation leurs dépenses vont** ~* with inflation their expenses are going to mount up

cubique [kybik] [1] ADJ cubic; **racine** [2] NF (Math = courbe) cubic

cubisme [kybism] NM Cubism

cubiste [kybist] ADJ, NMF Cubist

cubitainer® [kybitɛnɛʀ] NM square plastic container (for holding liquids)

cubital, e (mpl -aux) [kybital, o] ADJ ulnar

cubitus [kybitys] NM ulna

cucu(l)* [kyky] ADJ ~ **(la praline)** [personne] silly; [film, livre] corny*

cucurbitacée [kykyʀbitase] NF cucurbitaceous plant, cucurbit; **les** ~**s** the Cucurbitaceae (SPÉC)

cueillette [kœjɛt] NF [a] [fleurs, fraises, mûres] picking, gathering; [pommes, poires etc] picking; (Ethnol) gathering; **la** ~ **du houblon/des pommes** hop-/apple-picking; **cette tribu pratique la** ~ the people of this tribe are gatherers [b] (= récolte) harvest, crop; **elle me montra sa** ~ she showed me what she'd picked; **quelle** ~**!** what a harvest! ou crop! [c] (Can) [données] collection

cueilleur, -euse [kœjœʀ, øz] NM,F [fruits] gatherer

cueillir [kœjiʀ] ▸conjug 12◂ VT a [+ *fleurs, fraises, mûres*] to pick; (*en quantité*) to gather; [+ *pommes, poires*] to pick b (*fig*) (= *attraper*) [+ *ballon*] to catch; [+ *baiser*] to snatch, steal; (* = *arrêter*) to nab*, catch; **~ les lauriers de la victoire** to win ou bring home the laurels (of victory); **le voleur s'est fait ~ par la police*** the thief was ou got nabbed by the police*; **il est venu nous ~ à la gare*** he came to collect ou get us ou pick us up at the station; **il m'a cueilli à froid** (= *pris au dépourvu*) he caught me off guard ou on the hop* (*Brit*)

cuesta [kwɛsta] NF cuesta

cui-cui [kɥikɥi] EXCL, NM tweet-tweet; **faire ~** to go tweet-tweet

cuiller, cuillère [kɥijɛʀ] 1 NF a (= *ustensile*) spoon; (= *contenu*) spoonful; **petite ~** (*à thé, à dessert*) teaspoon; **faire manger qn à la ~** to spoonfeed sb; **manger son dessert à la ou avec une ~** to use a spoon to eat one's dessert; (*Tennis*) **service à la ~** underarm serve; **servir à la ~** to serve underarm → **dos, ramasser** b (* = *main*) **serrer la ~ à qn** to shake sb's paw* c (*Pêche*) spoon, spoonbait; **~ tournante** spinner; **pêche à la ~** spoonbait fishing, fishing with a spoon(bait) d (*Tech*) [*grenade*] (safety) catch 2 COMP ▶ **cuiller de bois** (*gén, Rugby*) wooden spoon ▶ **cuiller à café** coffee spoon, ≈ teaspoon; **prenez une ~ à café de sirop** take a teaspoonful of cough mixture ▶ **cuiller à dessert** dessertspoon ▶ **cuiller à moka** (small) coffee spoon ▶ **cuiller à moutarde** mustard spoon ▶ **cuiller à pot** ladle; **en deux ou trois coups de ~ à pot*** in two shakes of a lamb's tail*, in a flash, in no time (at all) ▶ **cuiller à soupe** (= *ustensile*) soup spoon; (*pour mesurer*) tablespoon ▶ **cuiller de verrier** (glassblower's) ladle

cuillerée [kɥijʀe] NF spoonful; **~ à soupe** ≈ tablespoonful; **~ à café** ≈ teaspoonful

cuir [kɥiʀ] 1 NM a (= *peau apprêtée*) leather; (= *industrie, artisanat*) leathercraft, leatherwork; (* = *blouson*) leather jacket; **ceinture/semelles de ~** leather belt/soles; **objets ou articles en ~** leather articles ou goods; **le style ~** the leather look → **relier, tanner** b (*sur l'animal vivant, ou avant tannage*) hide; * [*personne*] hide*; **avoir le ~ dur** (= *être résistant*) to be as tough ou as hard as nails; (= *être insensible à la critique*) to be thick-skinned c (* = *faute de liaison*) incorrect liaison (*due to an intrusive z- or t-sound*) d (*Ftbl*) ball 2 COMP ▶ **cuir bouilli** cuir-bouilli ▶ **cuir brut** rawhide ▶ **cuir chevelu** (*Anat*) scalp ▶ **cuir de crocodile** crocodile skin ▶ **cuir en croûte** undressed leather ▶ **cuir à rasoir** (barber's ou razor) strop ▶ **cuir suédé** suede ▶ **cuir de vache** cowhide ▶ **cuir de veau** calfskin ▶ **cuir verni** patent leather ▶ **cuir vert** = cuir brut

cuirasse [kɥiʀas] NF (*Hist*) [*chevalier*] breastplate; (*Naut*) armour(-plate ou -plating (*Brit*), armor(-plate ou -plating) (*US*); (*Zool*) cuirass; (*fig*) armour (*Brit*), armor (*US*) → **défaut**

cuirassé, e [kɥiʀase] (*ptp de cuirasser*) 1 ADJ [*soldat*] breastplated; [*navire*] armour-plated (*Brit*), armor-plated (*US*), armoured (*Brit*), armored (*US*); (*fig*) **être ~ contre qch** to be hardened against sth, be proof against sth 2 NM battleship

cuirasser [kɥiʀase] ▸conjug 1◂ 1 VT [+ *chevalier*] to put a breastplate on; [+ *navire*] to armour-plate (*Brit*), armor-plate (*US*); (*fig* = *endurcir*) to harden (**contre** against) 2 **se cuirasser** VPR [*chevalier*] to put on a breastplate b (*fig* = *s'endurcir*) to harden o.s. (**contre** against); **se ~ contre la douleur/l'émotion** to harden o.s. against suffering/emotion

cuirassier [kɥiʀasje] NM (*Hist*) cuirassier; (*Mil* = *soldat*) (armoured (*Brit*) ou armored (*US*))

cavalryman; (= *régiment*) **le 3ème ~** the 3rd (armoured) cavalry

cuire [kɥiʀ] ▸conjug 38◂ 1 VT a (*faire*) **~** [+ *plat, dîner*] to cook; **~ à feu doux ou doucement** to cook gently ou slowly; **~ à petit feu** to simmer; **laisser ou faire ~ à feu doux ou à petit feu pendant 20 minutes** (allow to) simmer ou cook gently for 20 minutes; **~ à la broche** to cook on the spit, spit-roast; **~ au four** [+ *pain, gâteau, pommes*] to bake; [+ *viande*] to roast; [+ *pommes de terre*] to roast, bake; **~ qch à la vapeur/au gril/à la poêle/à l'eau/à la casserole** to steam/grill/fry/boil/stew sth; **~ au beurre/à l'huile** to cook in butter/in oil; **faites-le ~ dans son jus** cook ou stew it in its own juice; **faire bien/peu ~ qch** to cook sth thoroughly ou well/slightly ou lightly; **faire trop ~ qch** to overcook sth; **ne pas faire assez ~ qch** to undercook sth; **il l'a fait ~ à point** he cooked it to a turn → **carotte, cuit, dur, œuf** b **four qui cuit mal la viande** oven which cooks ou does meat badly ou unevenly c [+ *briques, porcelaine*] to fire d **à ~** [*chocolat*] cooking (*épith*); [*prunes, poires*] stewing (*épith*); **pommes à ~** cooking apples 2 VI a [*aliment*] to cook; **~ à gros bouillon(s)** to boil hard ou fast; **le dîner cuit à feu doux ou à petit feu** the dinner is cooking gently ou is simmering ou is on low; **~ dans son jus** to cook in its own juice, stew b [*personne*] **~ au soleil** to roast in the sun; **~ dans son jus*** (= *avoir très chaud*) to be boiling* ou roasting*; (= *se morfondre*) to stew in one's own juice; **on cuit ici!*** it's boiling (hot)* ou roasting* ou sweltering in here! c (= *brûler*) **les mains/yeux me cuisaient** my hands/eyes were smarting ou stinging; **mon dos me cuit** my back is burning d (*frm*) **il lui en a cuit** he suffered for it, he had good reason to regret it; **il vous en cuira** you'll rue the day (*frm*)

cuisant, e [kɥizɑ̃, ɑ̃t] ADJ a [*douleur*] smarting, sharp; [*blessure*] burning, stinging; [*froid*] bitter, biting b [*remarque*] caustic, stinging; [*échec, regret*] bitter

cuisine [kɥizin] 1 NF a (= *pièce*) kitchen; (= *mobilier*) kitchen furniture (*NonC*); (*Naut*) galley; **les ~s** the kitchens; (*dans un restaurant*) **la mère est à la caisse et le fils en ~** the mother works at the till and the son in the kitchen; **studio avec coin-~** studio flat with kitchen area ou kitchenette; **table/couteau de ~** kitchen table/knife → **batterie, intégré, latin, livre¹** b (= *art culinaire*) cookery, cooking; (= *préparation*) cooking; (= *nourriture apprêtée*) cooking, food; **~ allégée ou légère ou minceur** low-fat ou low-calorie foods; **la ~ chinoise/italienne** Chinese/Italian food; **faire la ~ au beurre/à l'huile** to cook with butter/oil; **je ne supporte pas la ~ au beurre/à l'huile** I can't stand things cooked in butter/oil; **apprendre la ~** to learn (how) to cook, learn cookery ou cooking; **la ~ prend du temps** cooking takes time; **une ~ épicée** hot ou spicy dishes ou food; **une ~ soignée** carefully prepared dishes ou food; **la bonne ~** good cooking ou food; **il est en train de faire la ~** he's busy cooking ou making the meal; **chez eux, c'est le mari qui fait la ~** the husband does the cooking ou the husband is the cook in their house; **savoir faire la ~** = ◊ **faire de la bonne ~** to be a good cook, be good at cooking → **nouveau** c (= *personnel*) [*maison privée*] kitchen staff; [*cantine*] kitchen ou catering staff d (*fig péj*) **~ électorale** electoral schemings ou jiggery-pokery* (*Brit*); **je n'aime pas beaucoup sa petite ~** I'm not very fond of his underhand tricks ou his little fiddles (*Brit*); **faire sa petite ~** to do one's own thing 2 COMP ▶ **cuisine américaine** open-plan kitchen ▶ **cuisine bourgeoise** (good) plain cooking ou fare ▶ **cuisine de cantine** can-

teen food ▶ **la cuisine française** French cooking ou cuisine ▶ **cuisine de restaurant** restaurant meals ou food ▶ **cuisine roulante** (*Mil*) field kitchen

cuisiner [kɥizine] ▸conjug 1◂ 1 VT a [+ *plat*] to cook b (*fig*) [+ *personne*] to grill*, give the third degree to* 2 VI to cook; **il cuisine bien** he's a good cook; **ne la dérange pas quand elle cuisine** don't bother her when she's cooking

cuisinier, -ière [kɥizinje, jɛʀ] 1 NM,F (= *personne*) cook 2 **cuisinière** NF (*à gaz, électrique*) stove, cooker (*Brit*); (*à bois*) (kitchen) range, wood-burning stove; **cuisinière à gaz** gas stove ou cooker (*Brit*); **cuisinière à charbon** solid-fuel stove; (*vieux modèle*) kitchen range (*Brit*), stove (*US*)

cuissage [kɥisaʒ] NM → **droit³**

cuissard [kɥisaʀ] NM [*armure*] cuisse; [*cycliste*] (cycling) shorts

cuissardes [kɥisaʀd] NFPL [*pêcheur*] waders; [*femme*] thigh boots

cuisse [kɥis] NF (*Anat*) thigh; (*Culin*) **~ de mouton** leg of mutton ou lamb; **~ de poulet** chicken leg; **~s de grenouilles** frogs' legs; (*fig*) **il se croit sorti de la ~ de Jupiter*** he thinks he's God's gift to mankind; **elle a la ~ légère*** she is generous with her favours (*euph*)

cuisseau (*pl* **cuisseaux**) [kɥiso] NM haunch (of veal)

cuisse-madame (*pl* **cuisses-madame**) [kɥismadam] NF (= *poire*) cuisse madame pear

cuisson [kɥisɔ̃] NF a [*aliments*] cooking; [*pain, gâteau*] baking; [*gigot*] roasting; **ceci demande une longue ~** this needs to be cooked (ou baked) for a long time; **temps de ~** cooking time; **~ à la vapeur/au four** steam/oven cooking; **la pâte gonfle à la ~** the dough rises as it bakes ou is baked; (*au restaurant*) **quelle ~ ?** how would you like it cooked? b [*briques, céramique*] firing c (= *sensation de brûlure*) stinging ou smarting sensation

cuissot [kɥiso] NM haunch (of venison ou wild boar)

cuistance‡ [kɥistɑ̃s] NF (= *préparation*) cooking, preparing the grub‡; (= *nourriture*) grub‡, nosh‡ (*Brit*)

cuistot* [kɥisto] NM cook

cuistre† [kɥistʀ] NM prig, priggish pedant

cuistrerie† [kɥistʀəʀi] NF priggish pedantry

cuit, e¹ [kɥi, kɥit] (*ptp de cuire*) ADJ a [*aliment, plat*] cooked; [*viande*] done (*attrib*); [*pomme*] baked; **bien ~** well done; **je voudrais une baguette bien ~e** I'd like a nice crisp baguette; **trop ~** overdone; **pas assez ~** underdone; **~ à point** (= *peu saignant*) medium-cooked; (*parfaitement*) done to a turn b (* = *perdu*) **il est ~** (= *il va se faire prendre*) he's done for*, his goose is cooked*; (= *il va perdre*) it's all up (*Brit*) ou over for him, he's had it*; **c'est ~ (pour ce soir)** we've had it (for tonight)* c (* = *ivre*) plastered‡, sloshed‡ d (*loc*) **c'est du tout ~*** it's ou it'll be a cinch* ou a walkover*; **il attend toujours que ça lui arrive ou tombe tout ~ (dans le bec)*** he expects everything to be handed to him on a plate

cuite² [kɥit] NF a‡ **prendre une ~** to get plastered‡ ou sloshed‡; **il a pris une sacrée ~** he got really plastered‡ ou roaring drunk* b (*Tech* = *cuisson*) firing

cuiter (se) [kɥite] ▸conjug 1◂ VPR to get plastered‡ ou sloshed‡

cuivre [kɥivʀ] NM a **~ (rouge)** copper; **~ jaune** brass; **~ blanc** white copper; **objets ou articles en ~** copperware; **casseroles à fond (de) ~** copper-bottomed pans → **gravure** b (*Art*) copperplate c (= *ustensiles*) **~s** (*de cuivre*) copper; (*de cuivre et laiton*) brasses; **faire (briller) les ~s** to do the brass ou the brasses d (*Mus*) brass instrument; **les ~s** the brass (section); **orchestre de ~s** brass band

cuivré, e [kɥivʀe] (*ptp de* **cuivrer**) ADJ [*reflets*] coppery; [*peau, teint*] bronzed; [*voix*] resonant, sonorous; **cheveux aux reflets ~s** hair with copper glints *ou* lights in it

cuivrer [kɥivʀe] ▶conjug 1◀ VT (*Tech*) to copper(plate), cover with copper; [+ *peau, teint*] to bronze

cuivreux, -euse [kɥivʀø, øz] ADJ (*Chim*) cuprous; **oxyde ~** cuprous oxide, cuprite

cul [ky] **1** NM **a** ** (*Anat*) backside*, bum* (*Brit*), arse** (*Brit*), ass** (*US*); **~ nu** bare-bottomed; **il est tombé le ~ dans l'eau** he fell arse first in the water** (*Brit*), he fell on his ass in the water** (*US*); **un coup de pied au ~** a kick *ou* boot up the arse** (*Brit*), a kick in the ass** (*US*); **gros ~*** (*camion*) heavy truck *ou* lorry (*Brit*), rig; (*tabac*) ≈ shag → **faux¹, feu¹, trou** *etc*
b (*Hist Habillement*) (**faux**) **~** bustle
c (*fig = fond, arrière*) [*bouteille*] bottom; **faire un cendrier d'un ~ de bouteille** to make an ashtray with *ou* from the bottom of a bottle; **pousser une voiture au ~*** to give a car a shove
d (** = *amour physique*) **le ~** sex; **film de ~** porn movie*, skinflick*; **revue** *ou* **magazine de ~** (*gén*) porn mag*; (*montrant des femmes*) girlie mag*; **une histoire de ~** (= *plaisanterie*) a dirty joke; **il nous a raconté ses histoires de ~** he told us all about his sexual exploits
e (*loc*) **faire ~ sec** to down one's drink in one go*; **allez, ~ sec!** right, bottoms up!*; **renverser ~ par-dessus tête** to turn head over heels; **on l'a dans le ~*** that's really screwed us (up)**; **être sur le ~*** (= *être fatigué*) to be dead-beat* *ou* knackered* (*Brit*); **montrer son ~*** to bare all, strip naked; **en tomber** *ou* **rester sur le ~*** to be taken aback, be flabbergasted; **être comme ~ et chemise*** to be as thick as thieves (**avec** with); **tu peux te le mettre** *ou* **foutre au ~!*** go and fuck yourself!* *ou* stuff yourself!* (*Brit*); **mon ~!*** my arse!* (*Brit*), my ass!* (*US*); **avoir le ~ bordé de nouilles*** ◊ **avoir du ~*** to be a lucky *ou* jammy (*Brit*) bastard*; **parle à mon ~, ma tête est malade*** you don't give a fuck* about what I'm saying, do you?
2 ADJ (* = *stupide*) silly; **qu'il est ~, ce type!** that guy's a real twerp* *ou* wally* (*Brit*)!

culasse [kylas] NF **a** [*moteur*] cylinder head → **joint b** [*canon, fusil*] breech; **~ (mobile)** breechblock → **bloc**

cul-bénit* (*pl* **culs-bénits**) [kybeni] NM (*péj*) religious nut*

cul-blanc (*pl* **culs-blancs**) [kyblã] NM wheat-ear

culbute [kylbyt] NF **a** (= *cabriole*) somersault; (= *chute*) tumble, fall; **faire une ~** (= *cabriole*) to (turn a) somersault; (*chute*) to (take a) tumble, fall (head over heels) **b** (* *fig* = *faillite*) [*ministère*] collapse, fall; [*banque*] collapse; **faire la ~** (= *être ruiné*) [*banque*] to collapse; [*entreprise*] to go bust*; [*spéculateur*] to take a tumble, come a cropper* (*Brit*); (= *doubler ses gains*) to double one's money

culbuter [kylbyte] ▶conjug 1◀ **1** VI [*personne*] to (take a) tumble, fall (head over heels); [*chose*] to topple (over), fall (over); [*voiture*] to somersault, turn a somersault, overturn; **il a culbuté dans l'étang** he tumbled *ou* fell into the pond **2** VT [+ *chaise*] to upset, knock over; [+ *personne*] to knock over; [+ *ennemi*] to overwhelm; [+ *ministère*] to bring down, topple; ‡ [+ *femme*] to lay‡, screw**

culbuteur [kylbytœʀ] NM **a** [*moteur*] rocker arm **b** [*benne*] tipper ‡ (= *jouet*) tumbler

culbuto [kylbyto] NM wobbly toy, Weeble®

cul-de-basse-fosse (*pl* **culs-de-basse-fosse**), **cul de basse-fosse** [kyd(ə)basfos] NM dungeon

cul-de-four (*pl* **culs-de-four**) [kyd(ə)fuʀ] NM (*Archit*) cul-de-four

cul-de-jatte (*pl* **culs-de-jatte**) [kyd(ə)ʒat] NM legless cripple

cul-de-lampe (*pl* **culs-de-lampe**) [kyd(ə)lãp] NM (*Archit*) cul-de-lampe; (*Typo*) tailpiece

cul-de-poule [kyd(ə)pul] ◆**en cul-de-poule** LOC ADJ **avoir la bouche en ~** to purse one's lips

cul-de-sac (*pl* **culs-de-sac**) [kyd(ə)sak] NM (= *rue*) cul-de-sac, dead end; (*fig*) blind alley

culer [kyle] ▶conjug 1◀ VI (*Naut*) [*bateau*] to go astern; [*vent*] to veer astern; **brasser à ~** to brace aback

culinaire [kylineʀ] ADJ culinary; **l'art ~** cookery

culminant, e [kylminã, ãt] ADJ → **point¹**

culminer [kylmine] ▶conjug 1◀ VI **a** [*sommet, massif*] to tower (**au-dessus de** above); **~ à** to reach its highest point at; **le Mont-Blanc culmine à 4 807 mètres** Mont Blanc reaches 4,807 metres at its highest point **b** [*colère, manifestation*] to come to a head; [*salaire, bénéfice, récession*] to reach, reach a peak (**à** at); **la crise culmina avec l'abdication du roi** the crisis culminated in the king's abdication **c** (*Astron*) to reach its highest point

culot [kylo] NM **a** (* = *effronterie*) nerve*, cheek* (*Brit*); **il a du ~** he's got a nerve* *ou* cheek* (*Brit*); **tu ne manques pas de ~!** you've got a nerve!* *ou* a cheek!* (*Brit*); **il y est allé au ~** he bluffed his way through it **b** [*ampoule*] cap; [*cartouche*] cap, base; [*bougie*] body; [*obus, bombe*] base **c** (= *dépôt*) [*pipe*] dottle; [*creuset*] residue; (*Géog*) **~ volcanique** volcanic cone

culottage [kylɔtaʒ] NM [*pipe*] seasoning

culotte [kylɔt] **1** NF **a** (= *slip*) [*femme*] pants (*Brit*), knickers (*Brit*), panties (*US*); [*homme*] underpants; **petite ~** [*femme*] panties (*US*); **trois ~s** three pairs of underpants
b (= *pantalon*) trousers, pants (*US*); (*Hist*) breeches; (= *short*) shorts
c (*Boucherie*) rump
d (*loc*) **baisser (sa) ~** (*lit*) to pull *ou* take one's knickers (*Brit*) *ou* panties (*US*) down; (‡ *fig*) to back down; **c'est elle qui porte la ~** she wears the trousers *ou* pants (*US*); **prendre une ~*** (*au jeu*) to lose one's shirt, lose heavily; **faire dans sa ~** (*uriner*) to wet oneself *ou* one's pants; (*déféquer*) to dirty one's pants; (*fig*) **trembler** *ou* **faire dans sa ~‡** ◊ **mouiller sa ~‡** to wet oneself‡, pee one's pants‡; **il n'a rien dans la ~** (*impuissant*) he can't get it up‡; (*lâche*) he has no balls** *ou* no guts‡
2 COMP ▶ **culotte de bain†** (swimming *ou* bathing) trunks ▶ **culotte(s) bouffante(s)** jodhpurs ▶ **culotte(s) de cheval** (*lit*) riding breeches; (*fig*) **avoir une ~ de cheval** to have jodhpur thighs *ou* saddlebags ▶ **culotte(s) courte(s)** short trousers *ou* pants (*US*); (*fig*) **j'étais encore en ~(s) courte(s)** I was still in short trousers *ou* short pants (*US*) ▶ **culotte de golf** plus fours, knicker-bockers ▶ **culotte(s) longue(s)** long trousers *ou* pants (*US*) ▶ **culotte de peau** (*péj Mil*) **une (vieille) ~ de peau** a colonel Blimp

culotté, e [kylɔte] (*ptp de* **culotter**) ADJ **a** (* = *effronté*) cheeky* (*Brit*), sassy* (*US*) **b** [*pipe*] seasoned; [*cuir*] mellowed

culotter [kylɔte] ▶conjug 1◀ **1** VT **a** [+ *pipe, théière*] to season **b** [+ *enfant*] to put trousers on **2 se culotter** VPR **a** [*pipe*] to season **b** [*enfant*] to put one's trousers on

culottier, -ière† [kylɔtje, jɛʀ] NM,F trouser maker, breeches maker†

culpabilisant, e [kylpabilizã, ãt] ADJ [*discours, idée*] that induces feelings of guilt; **c'est un peu ~ de laisser les enfants seuls** you feel a bit guilty about leaving the children on their own

culpabilisation [kylpabilizasjɔ̃] NF (= *action*) making guilty; (= *état*) guilt

culpabiliser [kylpabilize] ▶conjug 1◀ **1** VT **~ qn** to make sb feel guilty **2** VI, **se culpabiliser** VPR to feel guilty, blame o.s.

culpabilité [kylpabilite] NF (*gén*) guilt; (*Jur*) guilt, culpability → **sentiment**

cul-rouge (*pl* **culs-rouges**) [kyʀuʒ] NM great spotted woodpecker

culte [kylt] **1** NM **a** (= *vénération*) worship; **le ~ de Dieu** the worship of God; **le ~ du feu/du soleil** fire-/sun-worship; **avoir le ~ de** [+ *justice, tradition*] to make a cult *ou* religion of; [+ *argent*] to worship; **avoir un ~ pour qn** to (hero-)worship sb; **vouer** *ou* **rendre un ~ à qn/la mémoire de qn** to worship sb/sb's memory; **~ de la personnalité** personality cult; **son ~ du secret** his cult of secrecy **b** (= *pratiques*) form of worship; (= *religion*) religion; **le ~ catholique** the Catholic form of worship; **les objets du ~** liturgical objects; **lieu de ~** place of worship → **denier, liberté, ministre c** (= *office protestant*) (church) service; **assister au ~** to attend a (church) service **2** ADJ [*film, livre*] cult (*épith*)

cul-terreux* (*pl* **culs-terreux**) [kyteʀø] NM (*péj*) yokel, country bumpkin, hick* (*US*)

cultivable [kyltivabl] ADJ [*terrain*] suitable for cultivation, cultivable

cultivar [kyltivar] NM (*Hort*) cultivar

cultivateur, -trice [kyltivatœʀ, tʀis] **1** ADJ [*peuple*] agricultural, farming (*épith*) **2** NM,F farmer **3** NM (= *machine*) cultivator

cultivé, e [kyltive] (*ptp de* **cultiver**) ADJ (= *instruit*) cultured, cultivated

cultiver [kyltive] ▶conjug 1◀ **1** VT **a** [+ *champ*] to cultivate; **~ la terre** to cultivate the soil, farm the land; **terrains cultivés** cultivated land, land under cultivation **b** [+ *céréales, légumes, vigne*] to grow, cultivate; [+ *moules, huîtres*] to breed, farm **c** [+ *goût, don, image*] to cultivate; **~ son esprit** to improve *ou* cultivate one's mind **d** (= *pratiquer*) [+ *art, sciences, genre*] to cultivate; **~ l'esprit de famille** to have a strong sense of family; **il cultive la grossièreté/le paradoxe** he goes out of his way to do the unexpected **e** (= *fréquenter*) [+ *personne, amitié*] to cultivate; **c'est une relation à ~** it's a connection which should be cultivated **2 se cultiver** VPR to improve *ou* cultivate one's mind

cultuel, -elle [kyltɥɛl] ADJ **édifices ~s** places of worship; **association ~le** religious organization

culture [kyltyʀ] NF **a** [*champ*] cultivation; [*légumes*] growing, cultivating, cultivation; [*moules, huîtres*] breeding, farming; **méthodes de ~** farming methods, methods of cultivation; **~ mécanique** mechanized farming; **intensive/extensive** intensive/extensive farming; **pays de moyenne/grande ~** country with a medium-scale/large-scale farming industry; **~ maraîchère** market gardening; **~ fruitière** fruit farming; **mettre en ~** [+ *terrain*] to bring under cultivation; **j'ai deux cents hectares en ~** I have two hundred hectares of farmland *ou* of land under cultivation
b **~s** (= *terres cultivées*) land under cultivation, arable land
c (= *espèce cultivée*) crop; **~ de rapport** ◊ **~ commerciale** cash crop; **~ vivrière** food crop
d **la ~** culture; **homme de ~** man of culture, cultured man; **il manque de ~** he's not very cultured; **la ~ occidentale** western culture; **~ scientifique** scientific knowledge *ou* education; **~ générale** general knowledge; **~ classique** classical culture *ou* education; **~ de masse** mass culture; **~ d'entreprise** corporate culture, house style
e (*Bio*) culture; **~ microbienne/de tissus** microbe/tissue culture; **mettre des tissus en ~** to put tissue in a culture medium → **bouillon**
f **~ physique** physical culture *ou* training, PT; **faire de la ~ physique** to do physical training

culturel, -elle [kyltyʀɛl] ADJ cultural

culturellement [kyltyʀɛlmɑ̃] ADV culturally

culturisme [kyltyʀism] NM body-building

culturiste [kyltyʀist] NMF body-builder

cumin [kymɛ̃] NM (= faux anis) cumin; (= carvi) caraway; (= graines) cumin; (de carvi) caraway seeds

cumul [kymyl] NM a [fonctions] plurality; [salaires] concurrent drawing; **pour limiter le ~ des mandats** in order to limit the number of mandates that may be held at the same time ou concurrently b (Jur) [droits] accumulation; **avec ~ de peines** sentences to run consecutively; **~ d'infractions** combination of of-fences

cumulable [kymylabl] ADJ [fonctions] which may be held concurrently ou simultaneously; [traitements] which may be drawn concurrently ou simultaneously; **les réductions sur ces articles ne sont pas ~s** not more than one discount can be applied to each item

cumulard, e [kymylaʀ, aʀd] NM,F (péj) person drawing several salaries at the same time

cumulatif, -ive [kymylatif, iv] ADJ cumulative

cumulativement [kymylativmɑ̃] ADV [exercer des fonctions] simultaneously, concurrently; [purger des peines] consecutively

cumuler [kymyle] ▶conjug 1◀ 1 VT a [+ fonctions] to hold concurrently ou simultaneously; [+ salaires] to draw concurrently ou simultaneously; **~ deux traitements** to draw two separate salaries; **~ les fonctions de directeur et de comptable** to act simultaneously as manager and accountant, hold concurrently the positions of manager and accountant; **~ plusieurs handicaps** to suffer from a combination of handicaps b (Jur) [+ droits] to accumulate; (Fin) **calcul des intérêts cumulés** calculation of the interests accrued 2 **se cumuler** VPR [effets, handicaps, facteurs] to accumulate; **cette augmentation se cumulera avec celle de la TVA** this rise will come along on top of the increase in VAT

cumulonimbus [kymylɔnɛ̃bys] NM cumulo-nimbus

cumulus [kymylys] NM a (Mét) cumulus; **~ de beau temps/d'orage** (pl) fine-weather/storm clouds b (= chauffe-eau) water heater

cunéiforme [kyneifɔʀm] ADJ a [écriture, caractère] wedge-shaped, cuneiform (SPÉC) b (Anat) **les (os) ~s** the cuneiform bones (of the tarsus)

cunnilingus [kynilɛ̃gys] NM cunnilingus, cun-nilinctus

cupide [kypid] ADJ [air] greedy; [personne] grasping, greedy, moneygrubbing

cupidement [kypidmɑ̃] ADV greedily

cupidité [kypidite] NF greed, greediness, cu-pidity (littér)

Cupidon [kypidɔ̃] NM Cupid

cuprifère [kypʀifɛʀ] ADJ copper-bearing, cu-priferous (SPÉC)

cupule [kypyl] NF (Bot) cupule; [gland] (acorn) cup

curabilité [kyʀabilite] NF curability

curable [kyʀabl] ADJ curable

curaçao [kyʀaso] NM curaçao

curage [kyʀaʒ] NM [fossé, égout] clearing- ou cleaning-out; [puits] cleaning-out

curaillon* [kyʀajɔ̃] NM (péj) priest

curare [kyʀaʀ] NM curare

curatelle [kyʀatɛl] NF (Jur) [mineur, aliéné] guardianship; [succession] trusteeship

curateur, -trice [kyʀatœʀ, tʀis] NM,F (Jur) [mineur, aliéné] guardian; [succession] trustee

curatif, -ive [kyʀatif, iv] ADJ curative

curcuma [kyʀkyma] NM turmeric

cure[1] [kyʀ] NF a (= traitement) course of treat-ment; **~ (thermale)** ≈ course of treatment ou a cure at a spa; **faire une ~ (thermale) à Vichy** to

take the waters at Vichy; **suivre une ~ d'amai-grissement** to go on a slimming course (Brit), have reducing treatment (US); **faire une ~ de sommeil** to have sleep therapy; **~ de thalasso-thérapie** course of seawater therapy; **la ~ (psy-chanalytique)** the talking cure → **désintoxica-tion** b (= consommation) [aliments] diet; **j'ai fait une ~ de lecture/théâtre** I've done noth-ing but read/but go to the theatre; **faire une ~ de fruits** to eat a lot of fruit, go on a fruit diet c (littér, hum) **n'avoir ~ de qch** to care little about sth, pay no attention to sth; **il n'en a ~** he's not worried about that, he pays no at-tention to that; **je n'ai ~ de ces formalités** I've no time for these formalities, I can't be doing with these formalities (Brit)

cure[2] [kyʀ] NF (Rel) (= fonction) cure; (= paroisse) cure, ≈ living (Brit); (= maison) pres-bytery, ≈ vicarage

curé [kyʀe] NM parish priest; **~ de campagne** country priest; **se faire ~*** to go in for the priesthood; (péj) **les ~s** clerics, priests; **élevé chez les ~s** brought up by priests ou clerics → **bouffer[2], Monsieur**

cure-dent (pl **cure-dents**) [kyʀdɑ̃] NM tooth-pick

curée [kyʀe] NF a (Chasse) quarry; **donner la ~ aux chiens** to give the quarry to the hounds b (fig = ruée) scramble (for the spoils); **se ruer ou aller à la ~** to scramble for the spoils; (attaque violente) **les journalistes ont donné le signal de la ~** the press had everybody baying for his (ou their etc) blood

cure-ongle (pl **cure-ongles**) [kyʀɔgl] NM nail-cleaner

cure-oreille (pl **cure-oreilles**) [kyʀɔʀɛj] NM (= coton-tige) cotton bud (Brit), Q-tip® (US)

cure-pipe (pl **cure-pipes**) [kyʀpip] NM pipe cleaner

curer [kyʀe] ▶conjug 1◀ VT a [+ fossé, égout] to clear ou clean out; [+ puits] to clean out; [+ pipe] to clean out, scrape out b **se ~ les dents/le nez** to pick one's teeth/nose; **se ~ les ongles/oreilles** to clean one's nails/ears

curetage [kyʀtaʒ] NM curetting, curettage

cureter [kyʀte] ▶conjug 5◀ VT to curette

cureton* [kyʀtɔ̃] NM (péj) priestling

curette [kyʀɛt] NF (Tech) scraper; (Méd) cu-rette

curie[1] [kyʀi] NF (Hist romaine) curia; (Rel) Curia

curie[2] [kyʀi] NM (Phys) curie

curieusement [kyʀjøzmɑ̃] ADV (= avec curiosité) curiously; (= étrangement) strangely, curiously, oddly; **~, ils n'ont pas protesté** strangely ou oddly enough, they didn't pro-test

curieux, -ieuse [kyʀjø, jøz] 1 ADJ a (= intéressé) interested, curious; **esprit ~** inquir-ing mind; **~ de tout** curious about every-thing; **~ de mathématiques** interested in ou keen on (Brit) mathematics; **~ d'apprendre** in-terested in learning, keen to learn (Brit); **je se-rais ~ de voir/savoir** I'd be interested ou curi-ous to see/know b (= indiscret) curious, inquisitive, nos(e)y*; **jeter un regard ~ sur qch** to glance inquisi-tively ou curiously at sth c (= bizarre) strange, curious, odd; **ce qui est ~, c'est que ...** the odd ou strange ou curious thing is that ... → **bête, chose** 2 NM (= étrangeté) **le ~/le plus ~ de la chose** the funny ou strange thing/the funniest ou strangest thing about it 3 NM,F a (= indiscret) inquisitive person, nos(e)y parker*, busybody*; **petite curieuse !** little nos(e)y parker!*, nos(e)y little thing!* b (gén mpl = badaud) (inquisitive) onlooker, bystander; **éloigner les ~** to move the by-standers along; **venir en ~** to come just for a look ou to have a look

curiosité [kyʀjozite] NF a (= intérêt) curios-ity; **cette ~ de tout** this curiosity about every-thing; **ayant eu la ~ d'essayer** having been cu-rious enough to try; **il n'a pas eu la ~ de véri-fier** he didn't even bother to check b (= in-discrétion) curiosity, inquisitiveness, nosi-ness*; **~ malsaine** unhealthy curiosity; **par (pure) ~** out of (sheer) curiosity; **avec ~** curi-ously ▪ (PROV) **la ~ est un vilain défaut** curios-ity killed the cat (PROV) c (= site, monument) curious ou unusual sight ou feature; (= bibelot) curio; **les ~s de la ville** the (interesting ou un-usual) sights of the town; **magasin de ~s** curio ou curiosity shop; **ce timbre est une ~ pour les amateurs** this stamp has curiosity value for collectors d (= caractéristique) oddity; **c'est une des ~s de son esprit** it's one of the quirks ou oddities of his mind

curiste [kyʀist] NMF person taking the waters (at a spa)

curium [kyʀjɔm] NM curium

curling [kœʀliŋ] NM curling

curriculum (vitæ) [kyʀikylɔm(vite)] NM INV curriculum vitae, résumé (US)

curry [kyʀi] NM curry; **poulet au ~ ◊ ~ de pou-let** curried chicken, chicken curry

curseur [kyʀsœʀ] NM [règle] slide, cursor; [fermeture éclair] slider; [ordinateur] cursor

cursif, -ive [kyʀsif, iv] ADJ a (= lié) [écriture, lettre] cursive; **écrire en cursive** to write in cur-sive script b (= rapide) [lecture, style] cursory

cursus [kyʀsys] NM (Univ) ≈ degree course; [carrière] career path

curule [kyʀyl] ADJ **chaise ~** curule chair

curviligne [kyʀvilin] ADJ curvilinear

cutané, e [kytane] ADJ skin (épith), cutaneous (SPÉC); **affection ~e** skin trouble

cuti* [kyti] NF (ABRÉV = **cuti-réaction**) → **virer**

cuticule [kytikyl] NF (Bot, Zool) cuticle

cuti-réaction [kytiʀeaksjɔ̃] NF skin test; **faire une ~** to take a skin test

cutter [kœtœʀ] NM (petit) craft knife; (gros) Stanley knife®

cuvage [kyvaʒ] NM, **cuvaison** [kyvezɔ̃] NF [raisins] fermentation (in a vat)

cuve [kyv] NF [fermentation, teinture] vat; [bras-serie] mash tun; [mazout] tank; [eau] cistern, tank; [blanchissage] laundry vat; (Photo) **~ de développement** developing tank

cuvée [kyve] NF (= contenu) vatful; (= cru, année) vintage; [étudiants, films] crop; **la ~ 1937** the 1937 vintage; (= examen) **une ex-cellente ~** an excellent crop of graduates → **tête**

cuver [kyve] ▶conjug 1◀ 1 VT **~ (son vin)*** to sleep it off*; **~ sa colère** to sleep (ou work ou walk) off one's anger 2 VI [vin, raisins] to fer-ment

cuvette [kyvɛt] NF a (= récipient) basin, bowl; (pour la toilette) washbowl; (Photo) dish; **~ de plastique** plastic bowl b [lavabo] washbasin, basin; [évier] basin; [W.C.] pan c (Géog) ba-sin d [baromètre] cistern, cup e [montre] cap

▼**CV** [seve] NM a (ABRÉV = **curriculum vitæ**) CV b (ABRÉV = **cheval-vapeur**) hp

cyanose [sjanoz] NF cyanosis

cyanosé, e [sjanoze] ADJ cyanotic (SPÉC); **avoir le visage ~** to be blue in the face

cyanure [sjanyʀ] NM cyanid(e)

cyber(-) [sibɛʀ] PRÉF cyber(-); **cyberculture** cyberculture

cybercafé, cyber-café (pl **cyber-cafés**) [sibɛʀkafe] NM cybercafé

cyberespace [sibɛʀɛspas] NM cyberspace

cybermonde [sibɛʀmɔ̃d] NM cyberspace

cybernaute [sibɛʀnot] NMF cybersurfer, cybernaut

cybernéticien, -ienne [sibɛʀnetisjɛ̃, jɛn] NM,F cyberneticist

cybernétique [sibɛʀnetik] NF cybernetics *sg*

cyberpunk* [sibɛʀpœk] ADJ, NMF, NM cyberpunk

cyclable [siklabl] ADJ **piste ~** cycle track *ou* path (*Brit*)

cyclamen [siklamɛn] NM cyclamen

cycle¹ [sikl] NM [a] (*Astron, Bio, Élec*) cycle; **~ du carbone/de l'azote** carbon/nitrogen cycle; **~ menstruel** *ou* **ovarien** menstrual *ou* ovarian cycle; **le ~ infernal de la violence** the vicious circle of violence
[b] (*Écon*) cycle; **~ de vie d'un produit** product life cycle
[c] (*Littérat*) cycle; **le ~ arthurien** the Arthurian cycle; **~ de chansons** song cycle
[d] (*Scol*) **~ (d'études)** academic cycle; **~ élémentaire** ≈ first five years of primary school (*Brit*), ≈ grades one through five (*US*); **~ d'orientation** ≈ middle school (*transition classes*); **~ long** *studies leading to the baccalauréat*; **~ court** *studies leading to vocational training instead of the baccalauréat*; **premier/ deuxième ~** middle/upper school
[e] (*Univ*) **~ court** two-year vocational course (*taken after the baccalauréat*); **~ long** higher education course; **premier ~** ≈ first and second year; **deuxième** *ou* **second ~** ≈ Final Honours; **troisième ~** ≈ postgraduate studies; **diplôme de troisième ~** ≈ postgraduate degree, ≈ Ph.D.; **étudiant de troisième ~** ≈ postgraduate *ou* Ph.D. student
[f] (= *cours*) course; **~ de conférences** course of lectures; **~ de formation** training course

---

┌─ **CYCLE** ─────────────────────────┐

In France, primary and secondary education is split into four broad age-group divisions known as **cycles** *(similar to "key stages" in Britain). Le "cycle élémentaire" corresponds to primary school, "le cycle d'observation" covers the first two years of "collège" (referred to as "sixième" and "cinquième"), and "le premier cycle" the final two years of "collège" ("quatrième" and "troisième"). "Second cycle" corresponds to the three years spent at the "lycée" (referred to as "seconde", "première" and "terminale").*

Higher education in France has three **cycles***: "premier cycle" (up to "DEUG" level), "deuxième cycle" (up to "licence" and "maîtrise"), and "troisième cycle" ("doctorat", "DEA" and "DESS").* →
COLLÈGE ; LYCÉE

└─────────────────────────────────────┘

cycle² [sikl] NM (= *bicyclette*) cycle; **magasin de ~s** cycle shop; **marchand de ~s** bicycle seller; **tarif: ~s 50 F, automobiles 245 F** charge: cycles and motorcycles 50 francs, cars 245 francs

cyclique [siklik] ADJ cyclic(al)

cyclisme [siklism] NM cycling

cycliste [siklist] [1] ADJ **course/champion ~** cycle race/champion; **coureur ~** racing cyclist [2] NMF cyclist [3] NM (= *short*) cycling shorts

cyclocross, cyclo-cross [siklokʀɔs] NM INV (*Sport*) cyclo-cross; (= *épreuve*) cyclo-cross race

cycloïdal, e (*mpl* **-aux**) [sikloidal, o] ADJ cycloid(al)

cycloïde [sikloid] NF cycloid

cyclomoteur [siklomɔtœʀ] NM moped, motorized bike *ou* bicycle

cyclomotoriste [siklomɔtɔʀist] NMF moped rider

cyclonal, e (*mpl* **-aux**) [siklonal, o] ADJ cyclonic

cyclone [siklon] NM (= *typhon*) cyclone; (= *basse pression*) zone of low pressure; (= *vent violent*) hurricane; (*fig*) whirlwind; **entrer comme un ~** to sweep *ou* come in like a whirlwind → **œil**

cyclonique [siklonik] ADJ = **cyclonal**

cyclope [siklɔp] NM [a] (*Myth*) **Cyclope** Cyclops [b] (*Zool*) cyclops

cyclopéen, -enne [siklopeɛ̃, ɛn] ADJ (*Myth*) Cyclopean

cyclopousse [siklopus] NM INV (bicycle-powered) rickshaw

cyclosporine [siklospɔʀin] NF = **ciclosporine**

cyclothymie [siklotimi] NF manic-depression, cyclothymia (*SPÉC*)

cyclothymique [siklotimik] ADJ, NMF manic-depressive, cyclo-thymic (*SPÉC*)

cyclotourisme [siklotuʀism] NM bicycle touring; (*vacances*) **faire du ~** to go on a cycling holiday

cyclotron [siklotʀɔ̃] NM cyclotron

cygne [siɲ] NM swan; **jeune ~** cygnet; **~ mâle** male swan, cob → **chant¹**

cylindre [silɛ̃dʀ] NM [a] (*Géom*) cylinder; **~ droit/oblique** right (circular)/oblique (circular) cylinder; **~ de révolution** cylindrical solid of revolution [b] (= *rouleau*) roller; (*rouleau-compresseur*) wheel, roller; **~ d'impression** printing cylinder → **bureau, presse** [c] [moteur] cylinder; **moteur à 4 ~s en ligne** straight-4 engine; **moteur à 6 ~s en V** V6 engine; **moteur à 2 ~s opposés** flat-2 engine; **une 6 ~s** a 6-cylinder (car)

cylindrée [silɛ̃dʀe] NF capacity; **une ~ de 1 600 cm³** a capacity of 1,600 ccs; **une (voiture de) grosse/petite ~** a big-/small-engined car; (*arg Sport*) **grosse ~** (= *personne*) top athlete; (= *équipe*) big-league team

cylindrer [silɛ̃dʀe] ▶conjug 1◀ VT (= *rouler*) [+ *métal*] to roll; [+ *papier*] to roll (up); (= *aplatir*) [+ *linge*] to press; [+ *route*] to roll

cylindrique [silɛ̃dʀik] ADJ cylindrical

cymbale [sɛ̃bal] NF cymbal

cymbalier [sɛ̃balje] NM, **cymbaliste** [sɛ̃balist] NMF cymbalist, cymbale(e)r

cymbalum [sɛ̃balɔm] NM dulcimer, cymbalo

cynégétique [sineʒetik] [1] ADJ cynegetic [2] NF cynegetics *sg*

cynique [sinik] [1] ADJ cynical; (*Philo*) Cynic [2] NM cynic; (*Philo*) Cynic

cyniquement [sinikmɑ̃] ADV cynically

cynisme [sinism] NM cynicism; (*Philo*) Cynicism

cynocéphale [sinosefal] NM dog-faced baboon, cynocephalus (*SPÉC*)

cynodrome [sinodʀom] NM greyhound track

cynor(r)hodon [sinɔʀɔdɔ̃] NM rosehip

cyphose [sifoz] NF kyphosis

cyprès [sipʀɛ] NM cypress

cypriote [sipʀijɔt] ADJ, NMF = **chypriote**

cyrillique [siʀilik] ADJ Cyrillic

cystite [sistit] NF cystitis (*NonC*)

Cythère [siter] NF Cythera

cytise [sitiz] NM laburnum

cytogénéticien, -ienne [sitoʒenetisjɛ̃, jɛn] NM,F cytogenetics specialist

cytogénétique [sitoʒenetik] NF cytogenetics *sg*

cytologie [sitɔlɔʒi] NF cytology

cytologique [sitɔlɔʒik] ADJ cytological

cytomégalovirus [sitomegaloviʀys] NM cytomegalovirus, CMV

cytoplasme [sitɔplasm] NM cytoplasm

czar [tsaʀ] NM = **tsar**

czarewitch [tsaʀevitʃ] NM = **tsarévitch**

czariste [tsaʀist] ADJ = **tsariste**

D

D, d [de] NM (= *lettre*) D, d → **système**

d' [d] → **de¹, de²**

da [da] INTERJ → **oui**

DAB [dab] NM (ABRÉV = **distributeur automatique de billets**) ATM

dab †‡ [dab] NM (= *père*) old man*, father

d'abord [dabɔʀ] LOC ADV → **abord**

Dacca [daka] N Dacca

d'accord [dakɔʀ] LOC ADV, LOC ADJ → **accord**

Dacron® [dakʀɔ̃] NM Terylene® (*Brit*), Dacron® (*US*)

dactyle [daktil] NM [a] (*Poésie*) dactyl [b] (*Bot*) cocksfoot

dactylique [daktilik] ADJ dactylic

dactylo [daktilo] NF ABRÉV = **dactylographe, dactylographie**

dactylographe † [daktilɔgʀaf] NF typist

dactylographie [daktilɔgʀafi] NF typing, typewriting; **elle apprend la ~** she's learning to type

dactylographier [daktilɔgʀafje] ▸conjug 7◂ VT to type (out)

dactylographique [daktilɔgʀafik] ADJ typing (*épith*)

dactyloscopie [daktilɔskɔpi] NF fingerprinting

dada¹ [dada] NM [a] (*langage enfantin = cheval*) horsey (*langage enfantin*), gee-gee (*Brit, langage enfantin*); **viens faire à ~** come and ride the horsey *ou* the gee-gee; **jeu de ~s** ≈ ludo (*Brit*), ≈ Parcheesi (*US*) [b] (= *marotte*) hobby-horse (*fig*); **enfourcher son ~** to get on one's hobby-horse, launch o.s. on one's pet subject

dada² [dada] ADJ (*Art, Littérat*) Dada, dada

dadais [dadɛ] NM (**grand**) **~** awkward lump (of a youth) (*péj*); **espèce de grand ~!** you great lump!

dadaïsme [dadaism] NM Dadaism, Dada

dadaïste [dadaist] [1] ADJ Dadaist [2] NMF Dadaist

DAF [daf] NM (ABRÉV = **directeur administratif et financier**) → **directeur**

dague [dag] NF [a] (= *arme*) dagger [b] [*cerf*] spike

daguerréotype [dagereɔtip] NM daguerreotype

daguet [dagɛ] NM young stag, brocket

dahlia [dalja] NM dahlia

dahoméen, -enne [daɔmeɛ̃, ɛn] [1] ADJ Dahomean [2] **Dahoméen(ne)** NM,F Dahomean

Dahomey [daɔmɛ] NM Dahomey

dahu [day] NM *imaginary animal which gullible people are lured into chasing*

daigner [deɲe] ▸conjug 1◂ VT to deign, condescend; **il n'a même pas daigné nous regarder** he didn't even deign to look at us; (*frm*) **daignez nous excuser** be so good as to excuse us

daim [dɛ̃] NM (*gén*) (fallow) deer; (*mâle*) buck; (= *peau*) buckskin, doeskin; (= *cuir suédé*) suede; **chaussures en ~** suede shoes

---

daine [dɛn] NF (fallow) doe

dais [dɛ] NM canopy

Dakar [dakaʀ] N Dakar

dakin, Dakin [dakɛ̃] NM **solution** *ou* eau de Dakin Dakin's solution

Dakota [dakɔta] NM Dakota; **~ du Nord/du Sud** North/South Dakota

dalaï-lama (*pl* **dalaï-lamas**) [dalailama] NM Dalaï Lama

Dalila [dalila] NF Delilah

dallage [dalaʒ] NM (*NonC = action*) paving, flagging; (= *surface, revêtement*) paving, pavement

dalle [dal] NF [a] (= *pavement*) [*trottoir*] paving stone, flag(stone); (*Constr*) slab; **~ flottante/de béton** floating/concrete slab; **la ~ de couverture du parking** the concrete slab roof of the car park; **~ funéraire** tombstone; **~ de moquette** carpet tile [b] [*paroi de rocher*] slab [c]* **que ~** nothing at all, damn all‡ (*Brit*); **j'y pige ou entrave que ~** I don't get it*, I don't understand a bloody‡ (*Brit*) thing; **je n'y vois que ~** I can't see a damn‡ *ou* bloody‡ (*Brit*) thing [d] (* = *gosier*) **avoir la ~ en pente** to be a bit of a boozer‡; (= *avoir faim*) **avoir ou crever la ~** to be starving* *ou* famished* → **rincer**

daller [dale] ▸conjug 1◂ VT to pave, lay paving stones *ou* flagstones on; **cour dallée de marbre** courtyard paved with marble, marble courtyard

dalleur [dalœʀ] NM flag layer, paviour

Dalmatie [dalmasi] NF Dalmatia

dalmatien, -ienne [dalmasjɛ̃, jɛn] NM,F (= *chien*) dalmatian

daltonien, -ienne [daltɔnjɛ̃, jɛn] [1] ADJ colour-blind (*Brit*), color-blind (*US*) [2] NM,F colour-blind (*Brit*) *ou* color-blind (*US*) person

daltonisme [daltɔnism] NM colour blindness (*Brit*), color-blindness (*US*), daltonism (*SPÉC*)

dam [dɑ̃] NM **au (grand) ~ de qn** to sb's great displeasure

Damas [damas] N Damascus → **chemin**

damas [dama(s)] NM (= *tissu*) damask; (= *acier*) Damascus steel, damask; (= *prune*) damson

damasquinage [damaskinaʒ] NM damascening

damasquiner [damaskine] ▸conjug 1◂ VT to damascene

damassé, e [damase] (*ptp de* **damasser**) ADJ, NM damask

dame [dam] [1] NF [a] (= *femme*) lady; (* = *épouse*) wife; **il y a une ~ qui vous attend** there is a lady waiting for you; **votre ~ m'a dit que*** ... your wife told me that ...; **alors ma petite ~!** now then, dear!; **vous savez, ma bonne ~!** you know, my dear!; (*Jur*) **la ~ Dubois** Mrs Dubois; **coiffeur pour ~s** ladies' hairdresser; **de ~** [*sac, manteau*] lady's; **la Dame de fer** Iron Lady; (*hum*) **une vieille ~ indigne** an eccentric old lady; (*Sport*) **la finale ~s** the women's final → **vertu**
[b] (*de haute naissance*) lady; **une grande ~** (= *noble*) a highborn *ou* great lady; (= *artiste*) a

---

great lady (**de** of); **la grande ~ du roman policier** the grande dame *ou* the doyenne of crime fiction; **jouer les grandes ~s** to play the fine lady; **les belles ~s des quartiers chic** the fashionable *ou* fine ladies from the posh districts; **la première ~ de France** France's first lady; (*hum*) **la ~ de ses pensées** his lady-love (*hum*); **la Vieille Dame du Quai Conti** the French Academy
[c] (*Cartes, Échecs*) queen; (*Dames*) crown; (*Jacquet*) piece, man; **le jeu de ~s** ◊ **les ~s** draughts *sg* (*Brit*), checkers *sg* (*US*); **jouer aux ~s** to play draughts (*Brit*) *ou* checkers (*US*); **aller à ~** (*Dames*) to make a crown; (*Échecs*) to make a queen; **la ~ de pique** the queen of spades
[d] (*Tech = hie*) beetle, rammer; (*Naut*) rowlock

[2] EXCL **~ oui/non!** † why yes!/no!, indeed yes/no!

[3] COMP ▸ **dame blanche** (= *chouette*) barn owl ▸ **dame catéchiste** catechism mistress, ≈ Sunday school teacher ▸ **dame de charité** benefactress ▸ **dame de compagnie** (lady's) companion ▸ **dame d'honneur** lady-in-waiting ▸ **Dame Nature** Mother Nature ▸ **dame patronnesse** († *ou péj*) Lady Bountiful ▸ **dame pipi*** lady toilet attendant

dame-jeanne (*pl* **dames-jeannes**) [damʒan] NF demijohn

damer [dame] ▸conjug 1◂ VT [a] [+ *terre, neige, piste de ski*] to pack (down) [b] [+ *pion*] (*Dames*) to crown; (*Échecs*) to queen; (*fig*) **~ le pion à qn** to get the better of sb, checkmate sb

dameuse [damøz] NF (*Ski*) snow-grooming machine

damier [damje] NM (*Dames*) draughtboard (*Brit*), checkerboard (*US*); (= *dessin*) check (pattern); **en** *ou* **à ~** [*motif*] checkered, chequered (*Brit*); **tissu/foulard à ~** checked *ou* check fabric/scarf; **ville/rues en ~** town/streets in a grid pattern; **les champs formaient un ~** the fields were laid out like a draughtboard (*Brit*) *ou* a checkerboard (*US*)

damnable [danabl] ADJ (*Rel*) damnable; [*passion, idée*] despicable, abominable

damnation [danasjɔ̃] NF damnation; **~!** † damnation!, tarnation!† (*US*) → **enfer**

damné, e [dane] (*ptp de* **damner**) [1] ADJ (*, avant le n = maudit*) cursed*, confounded* † → **âme** [2] NM,F damned person; **les ~s** the damned → **souffrir**

damner [dane] ▸conjug 1◂ [1] VT to damn; **faire ~ qn*** to drive sb mad*; (*hum*) **c'est bon à faire ~ un saint*** it's so good it's wicked*; (*hum*) **elle est belle à faire ~ un saint*** she's so lovely she would tempt a saint (in heaven)* [2] **se damner** VPR to damn o.s.; **se ~ pour qn** to risk damnation for sb

Damoclès [damɔkles] NM Damocles → **épée**

damoiseau (*pl* **damoiseaux**) [damwazo] NM (*Hist*) page, squire; († *hum*) young beau †

damoiselle [damwazɛl] NF (*Hist*) damsel†

dan [dan] NM (*Arts martiaux*) dan; **il est deuxième ~** he's a second dan

danaïde [danaid] NF (*Zool*) monarch butterfly

Danaïdes [danaid] NFPL → **tonneau**

dancing [dãsiŋ] NM dance hall

dandinement [dãdinmã] NM [*canard, personne*] waddle

dandiner (se) [dãdine] ▶ conjug 1 ◀ VPR [*canard, personne*] to waddle; **avancer** *ou* **marcher en se dandinant** to waddle along

dandy [dãdi] NM dandy

dandysme [dãdism] NM dandyism

Danemark [danmark] NM Denmark

danger [dãʒe] NM [a] (= *risque*) danger; **un grave ~ nous menace** we are in serious *ou* grave danger; **courir un ~** to run a risk; **en cas de ~** in case of emergency; **être en ~** to be in danger; **ses jours sont en ~** his life is in danger; **mettre en ~** [+ *personne*] to put in danger; [+ *vie, espèce*] to endanger; [+ *chances, réputation, carrière*] to jeopardize; **adolescents en ~** moral teenagers in danger of being corrupted *ou* led astray; **en ~ de** in danger of; **il est en ~ de mort** he is in danger *ou* peril of his life; **ce pays est en grand ~ de perdre son indépendance** this country is in grave danger of losing its independence; **il est hors de ~** he is out of danger, he is safe; **sans ~** [*opération, expérience*] safe; [*utiliser, agir*] safely; **ça ne présente aucun ~** ◊ **c'est sans ~** it doesn't present any danger (**pour** to), it's quite safe (**pour** for); **il y aurait (du) ~ à faire cela** it would be dangerous to do that; **cet automobiliste est un ~ public** that driver is a public menace; **les ~s de la route** road hazards; **attention ~!** look out!; **« ~ de mort »** "danger of death"

[b] **(il n'y a) pas de ~!** no fear!*; **pas de ~ qu'il vienne!** there's no danger that he'll come

dangereusement [dãʒrøzmã] ADV dangerously

dangereux, -euse [dãʒrø, øz] ADJ [*route, ennemi, doctrine, animal*] dangerous (**pour** to); [*entreprise*] dangerous, hazardous, risky; **~ à manipuler** dangerous to handle; **zone dangereuse** danger zone; **il joue un jeu ~** he's playing a dangerous game; **« abus ~ »** "to be taken in moderation"

dangerosité [dãʒrozite] NF dangerousness

danois, e [danwa, waz] [1] ADJ Danish [2] NM [a] (*Ling*) Danish [b] (= *chien*) **(grand) ~** Great Dane [3] **Danois(e)** NM,F Dane

---

dans [dã]
PRÉPOSITION

[a] *sans changement de lieu* in; (= *à l'intérieur de*) in, inside; **il habite ~ Londres même/l'Est/le Jura** he lives in London itself/the East/the Jura; **le ministère est ~ la rue de Grenelle** the ministry is in the rue de Grenelle; **courir ~ l'herbe/les champs** to run around in *ou* run through the grass/fields; **il a plu ~ toute la France** there has been rain throughout France; **elle erra ~ la ville/les rues/la campagne** she wandered through *ou* round *ou* about the town/the streets/the countryside; **ne marche pas ~ l'eau** don't walk in *ou* through the water; **vous êtes ~ la bonne direction** you are going the right way *ou* in the right direction; **ils ont voyagé ~ le même train/avion** they travelled on the same train/plane; **cherche** *ou* **regarde ~ la boîte** look inside *ou* in the box; **~ le fond/le bas/le haut de l'armoire** at *ou* in the back/the bottom/the top of the wardrobe; **il reconnut le voleur ~ la foule/l'assistance** he recognized the thief in *ou* among the crowd/among the spectators; **qu'est-ce qui a bien pu se passer ~ sa tête?** what can he have been thinking of?; **il avait ~ l'esprit** *ou* **l'idée que ...** he had a feeling that ...; **elle avait ~ l'idée** *ou* **la tête de ... ** she had a mind to ...; **il y a de la tristesse ~ son regard/sourire** there's a certain sadness in his eyes/smile → **fouiller, recevoir, tomber** etc

[b] *changement de lieu* into, to; **s'enfoncer/pénétrer ~ la forêt** to plunge deep into/go into *ou* enter the forest; **ils sont partis ~ la montagne** they have gone off into the mountains; **mettre qch ~ un tiroir** to put sth in *ou* into a drawer; **verser du vin ~ un verre** to pour wine into a glass; **jeter l'eau sale ~ l'évier** to pour the dirty water down the sink

[c] **= dans des limites de** within; **~ le périmètre/un rayon très restreint** within the perimeter/a very restricted radius; **ce n'est pas ~ ses projets** he's not planning to do *ou* on doing that

[d] *indiquant l'action de prélever* out of, from; **prendre qch ~ un tiroir** to take sth out of *ou* from a drawer; **boire du café ~ une tasse/un verre** to drink coffee out of *ou* from a cup/glass; **la chèvre lui mangeait ~ la main** the goat was eating out of his hand; **le chien a mangé ~ mon assiette** the dog ate off my plate; **bifteck ~ le filet** fillet steak; **il l'a appris/copié ~ un livre** he learnt/copied it from *ou* out of a book

[e] **= pendant** in; **~ ma jeunesse/mon jeune temps** in my youth/my younger days; **~ les siècles passés** in previous centuries; **~ les mois à venir** in the months to come; **~ le cours ou le courant de l'année** in the course of the year; **il est ~ sa 6e année** he's in his 6th year → **temps**[1], **vie**

[f] *période ou délai dans l'avenir* in; (= *dans les limites de*) within, inside, in (the course of); **il part ~ deux jours/une semaine** he leaves in two days *ou* two days' time/a week *ou* a week's time; **~ combien de temps serez-vous prêt?** how long will it be before you are ready?; **il sera là ~ une minute** *ou* **un instant** he'll be here in a minute; **cela pourrait se faire ~ le mois/la semaine** it could be done within the month/week *ou* inside a month/week; **il mourut ~ l'heure qui suivit** he died within the hour; **je l'attends ~ la matinée/la nuit** I'm expecting him some time this morning/some time tonight, I'm expecting him some time in the course of the morning/night

[g] *état, condition, manière* in; **être ~ les affaires/l'industrie/le textile** to be in business/industry/textiles; **vivre ~ la misère/la peur** to live in poverty/fear; **vivre ~ l'oisiveté** to live a life of idleness; **~ le brouillard/l'obscurité** in fog/darkness, in the fog/the dark; **il n'est pas ~ le complot/le secret** he's not in on* the plot/the secret; **je l'aime beaucoup ~ cette robe/ce rôle** I really like her in that dress/that part; **et ~ tout cela, qu'est-ce que vous devenez?** and with all this going on, how are things with you?; **il est difficile de travailler ~ ce bruit/ces conditions** it's difficult to work with this noise/in these conditions; **le camion passa ~ un bruit de ferraille** the truck rattled past; **elles sortirent ~ un frou-frou de soie** they left in a rustle of silk; **faire les choses ~ les règles** to work within the rules

[h] *situation, cause* in, with; **~ son effroi, elle poussa un cri** she cried out in fright; **~ sa hâte il oublia son chapeau** in his haste he forgot his hat; **~ ces conditions** *ou* **ce cas-là, je refuse** in that case *ou* if that's the way it is* I refuse; **elle partit tôt, ~ l'espoir de trouver une place** she left early in the hope of getting *ou* hoping to get a seat; **il l'a fait ~ ce but** he did it with this aim in view

[i] *destination* mettre son espoir **~ qn/qch** to pin one's hopes on sb/sth; **avoir confiance ~ l'honnêteté de qn/le dollar** to have confidence in sb's honesty/the dollar

[j]

◆ **dans les** + *nombre* (= *environ*) (*prix*) (round) about, (something) in the region of; (*temps, grandeur*) (round) about, something like, some; **cela vaut/coûte ~ les 50 F** it's worth/it costs in the region of 50 francs *ou* (round)

about 50 francs; **il faut compter ~ les 3 ou 4 mois** we'll have to allow something like 3 or 4 months *ou* some 3 or 4 months; **il vous faut ~ les 3 mètres de tissu** you'll need something like 3 metres of fabric *ou* about *ou* some 3 metres of fabric; **cette pièce fait ~ les 8 m²** this room is about *ou* some 8 m²; **il a ~ les 30 ans** he's about 30, he's 30 or so

---

dansant, e [dãsã, ãt] ADJ [*mouvement, lueur*] dancing; [*musique*] lively; **thé ~** tea dance; **soirée ~e** dance

danse [dãs] NF [a] (= *valse, tango etc*) dance; **la ~** (= *art*) dance; (= *action*) dancing; **la ~ folklorique** folk *ou* country dancing; **~ classique** ballet; **~ contemporaine** contemporary dance; **~ de salon** ballroom dance; **la ~ du ventre** belly dancing; **faire la ~ du ventre** to belly-dance, do a belly dance; **~ de guerre** war dance; **~ macabre** danse macabre, dance of death; **ouvrir la ~** to open the dancing; **avoir la ~ de Saint-Guy** (*Méd*) to have St Vitus's dance; (*fig*) to have the fidgets; **~ de** [*professeur, leçon*] dancing; [*musique*] dance; **entrer dans la ~** (*lit*) to join in the dance *ou* dancing; (*fig*) **s'il entre dans la ~ ...** if he decides to get involved *ou* to join in ... [b] **~ mener, piste** [b]‡ (= *volée*) belting‡, (good) hiding; **filer** *ou* **flanquer une ~ à qn** to belt sb‡, give sb a (good) hiding

danser [dãse] ▶ conjug 1 ◀ [1] VI (*gén*) to dance; [*ombre, flamme*] to flicker, dance; [*flotteur, bateau*] to bob (up and down), dance; **elle danse bien** she's a good dancer; **faire ~ qn** to (have a) dance with sb; **après dîner il nous a fait ~** after dinner he got us dancing; **voulez-vous (avec moi)?** ◊ **vous dansez?** shall we dance?, would you like to dance?; **~ de joie** to dance for joy; (*fig*) **à l'époque, on dansait devant le buffet*** those were lean times; **les lignes dansaient devant mes yeux** the lines were dancing before my eyes; **personne ne savait sur quel pied ~** nobody knew what to do [2] VT to dance; **~ le tango** to dance the tango; **~ un rock** to jive; **elle danse « le Lac des cygnes »** she's dancing "Swan Lake"

danseur, -euse [dãsœr, øz] [1] NM,F (*gén*) dancer; (= *partenaire*) partner; **~ classique** *ou* **de ballet** ballet dancer; (*Opéra*) **~ étoile** principal dancer; **danseuse étoile** prima ballerina; **~ de corde** tightrope walker; **~ de claquettes** tap dancer; **~ mondain** professional ballroom dancing host [2] NF **danseuse de cabaret** cabaret dancer; **pédaler en danseuse** to pedal standing up; **entretenir une danseuse** (*maîtresse*) to keep a mistress; **l'État ne peut pas se permettre d'entretenir des danseuses** the state cannot afford to support unprofitable ventures; **les voiliers de course, c'est sa danseuse** he spends all his money on racing yachts

dantesque [dãtesk] ADJ Dantesque, Dantean

Danube [danyb] NM Danube

DAO [deao] NM (ABRÉV = **dessin assisté par ordinateur**) CAD

daphnie [dafni] NF daphnia

dard [dar] NM [*animal*] sting; (*Mil*†) javelin, spear

Dardanelles [dardanɛl] NFPL **les ~** the Dardanelles

darder [darde] ▶ conjug 1 ◀ VT [a] (= *lancer*) [+ *flèche*] to shoot; **le soleil dardait ses rayons sur la maison** the sun was beating down on the house; **il darda un regard haineux sur son rival** he shot a look full of hate at his rival [b] (= *dresser*) [+ *piquants, épines*] to point; **le clocher dardait sa flèche vers le ciel** the church spire thrust upwards into the sky

dare-dare* [dardar] LOC ADV double-quick*; **accourir ~** to come running up double-quick* *ou* at the double

darne [darn] NF [*poisson*] steak

dartre [dartr] NF dry patch, scurf (*NonC*)

darwinien, -ienne [daʀwinjɛ̃, jɛn] ADJ Darwinian

darwinisme [daʀwinism] NM Darwinism

darwiniste [daʀwinist] ADJ, NMF Darwinist

DAT [deate] NM (ABRÉV = **Digital Audio Tape**) DAT

datable [databl] ADJ dat(e)able; **manuscrit facilement ~** manuscript which can easily be dated

DATAR [dataʀ] NF (ABRÉV = **Délégation à l'aménagement du territoire et à l'action régionale**) → **délégation**

datation [datasjɔ̃] NF [*contrat, manuscrit*] dating; **~ au carbone 14** carbon dating

datcha [datʃa] NF dacha

date [dat] NF date; **~ de naissance/mariage/ paiement** date of birth/marriage/payment; **~ d'exigibilité** due *ou* maturity date; **~ de péremption/clôture** expiry/closing date; **~ butoir** *ou* **limite** deadline; **~ limite de consommation/de vente** use-by/sell-by date; **~ limite de fraîcheur** *ou* **de conservation** best-before date; **~ de valeur** [*chèque*] processing date; **pourriez-vous faire ce virement avec ~ de valeur le 15 juin?** could you process this payment on 15th June?; **note ce rendez-vous à la ~ du 12 mai** note down this appointment for May 12th; **à quelle ~ cela s'est-il produit?** on what date did that occur?; **à cette ~ il ne le savait pas encore** at that time he did not yet know about it; **à cette ~-là il était déjà mort** by that time *ou* by then he was already dead; **la ~ à laquelle je vous ai vu** the day I saw you; **le comité se réunit à ~ fixe** the committee meets on a fixed *ou* set date; **lettre en ~ du 23 mai** letter dated May 23rd; **j'ai pris ~ avec lui pour le 18 mai** I have set *ou* fixed a date with him for May 18th; **cet événement fait ~ dans l'histoire** this event stands out in *ou* marks a milestone in history; **sans ~** undated; **le premier en ~** the first *ou* earliest; **le dernier en ~** the latest *ou* most recent; **de longue** *ou* **vieille ~** [*amitié*] long-standing; [*ami*] long-standing, long-time; **je le connais de longue ~** I've known him for a (very) long time; **nous sommes des amis de longue ~** we go back a long way; **de fraîche ~** [*ami*] recent; **arrivé de fraîche ~ à Paris** newly arrived in Paris

dater [date] ▶ conjug 1 ◀ **1** VT [+ *lettre, événement*] to date; **lettre datée du 6/de Paris** letter dated the 6th/from Paris; **non daté** undated **2** VI **a ~ de** (= *remonter à*) to date back to, date from; **ça ne date pas d'hier** *ou* **d'aujourd'hui** [*maladie*] it has been going a long time; [*amitié, situation*] it goes back a long way; [*objet*] it's far from new; **à ~ de demain** as from tomorrow, from tomorrow onwards; **de quand date votre dernière rencontre?** when did you last meet? **b** (= *être important*) **cet événement a daté dans sa vie** this event marked a milestone in his life **c** (= *être démodé*) to be dated; **ça commence à ~** it's beginning to date; **le film est un peu daté** the film is a little dated

dateur [datœʀ] NM [*montre*] date indicator; **(timbre** *ou* **tampon) ~** date stamp

datif, -ive [datif, iv] ADJ, NM dative; **au ~** in the dative

dation [dasjɔ̃] NF (*Jur*) payment in kind; [*œuvres d'art*] donation

datte [dat] NF (*Bot, Culin*) date

dattier [datje] NM date palm

datura [datyʀa] NM datura

daube [dob] NF (= *viande*) stew, casserole; **faire une ~** *ou* **de la viande en ~** to make a stew *ou* casserole; **bœuf en ~** casserole of beef, beef stew

dauber [dobe] ▶ conjug 1 ◀ VI (*littér*) **~ sur qn/ qch** to jeer (at) sb/sth; **il serait facile de ~ sur nos erreurs** it would be easy to sneer *ou* scoff at our mistakes

dauphin [dofɛ̃] NM **a** (*Zool*) dolphin **b** (*Hist*) **le Dauphin** the Dauphin **c** (= *successeur*) heir apparent

Dauphine [dofin] NF Dauphine, Dauphiness

dauphinois, e [dofinwa, waz] **1** ADJ of *ou* from the Dauphiné → **gratin 2 Dauphinois(e)** NM,F inhabitant *ou* native of the Dauphiné

daurade [doʀad] NF gilthead bream, sea bream; **~ rose** red sea bream

davantage [davɑ̃taʒ] ADV **a** (= *plus*) [*gagner, acheter*] more; (*négatif*) any more; (*interrogatif*) (any) more; **bien/encore/même ~** much/still/even more; **je n'en sais pas ~** I don't know any more about it, I know no more *ou* nothing further about it; **il s'approcha ~** he drew closer *ou* nearer **b** (= *plus longtemps*) longer; (*négatif, interrogatif*) any longer; **sans s'attarder/rester ~** without lingering/staying any longer **c** (= *de plus en plus*) more and more; **les prix augmentent chaque jour ~** prices go up more and more every day **d ~ de** (some) more; (*négatif*) any more; **vouloir ~ de pain/temps** to want (some) more bread/time; **veux-tu ~ de viande?** do you want (any *ou* some) more meat?; **il n'en a pas voulu ~** he didn't want any more (of it) **e ~ que** (= *plus*) more than; (= *plus longtemps*) longer than; **tu te crois malin mais il l'est ~ (que toi)** you think you're sharp but he is more so than you *ou* but he is sharper (than you)

David [david] NM David

davier [davje] NM (*Chir*) forceps; (*Menuiserie*) cramp

db (ABRÉV = **décibel**) dB, db

DCA [desea] NF (ABRÉV = **défense contre avions**) anti-aircraft defence

DDASS [das] NF (ABRÉV = **Direction départementale de l'action sanitaire et sociale**) local department of social services; **un enfant de la ~** (*orphelin*) a state orphan; (*retiré de la garde de ses parents*) a child who has been taken into care (*Brit*), a child in court custody (*US*)

DDT [dedete] NM (ABRÉV = **dichloro-diphényl-trichloréthane**) DDT

---

de¹ [də]

> *Devant une voyelle ou un h muet* = d'; *contraction* de + le = du; de + les = des.
> *Lorsque* de *fait partie d'une locution du type* décider de faire, content de qch, *c'est l'occasion de,* se nourrir de, s'aider de, de plus en plus *etc,* reportez-vous à l'autre mot.

PRÉPOSITION

a déplacement, provenance   from; **être/ provenir/s'échapper de** to be/come/escape from; **sauter du toit** to jump off *ou* from the roof; **de sa fenêtre elle voit la mer** she can see the sea from her window; **il arrive du Japon** he has just arrived from Japan; **il y a une lettre de Paul** there's a letter from Paul; **nous recevons des amis du Canada** we have friends from Canada staying (with us); **ce sont des gens de la campagne/la ville** they are people from the country/town; **on apprend de Londres que ...** we hear *ou* it is announced from London that ...; **des pommes de notre jardin** apples from our garden; **le train/l'avion de Londres** the train/plane from London, the London train/ plane; MAIS **je l'ai vu en sortant de la maison** I saw him as I was coming out of the house

b localisation   in; **les magasins de Londres/ Paris** the shops in London/Paris, the London/Paris shops; **les gens de ma rue** the people in my street; MAIS **les voisins du 2e (étage)** the neighbours on the 2nd floor

c destination   for, to; **le train/l'avion de Bruxelles** the Brussels train/plane, the train/ plane for *ou* to Brussels; **la route de Tours** the Tours road, the road for Tours

---

d appartenance

Lorsque de *sert à exprimer l'appartenance, il peut se traduire par* of; *on préférera toutefois souvent le génitif lorsque le possesseur est une personne ou un pays, plus rarement une chose.*

la maison de David/de notre ami David's/our friend's house; **le mari de la reine d'Angleterre** the Queen of England's husband; **la patte du chien** the dog's paw; **le roi de France** the King of France; **l'attitude du Canada** Canada's attitude, the attitude of Canada; **un ami de mon père** a friend of my father's; **c'est le médecin de mes cousins** he's my cousins' doctor; **un ami de la famille** a friend of the family, a family friend; MAIS **un programmeur d'IBM** *ou* **de chez IBM** a programmer with IBM; **ses collègues de** *ou* **du bureau** his colleagues at work

Après un pluriel régulier ou un pluriel irrégulier se terminant par un s, *l'apostrophe s'utilise toujours seule; après un pluriel irrégulier ne se terminant pas par un* s, 's *est obligatoire.*

la maison de nos amis our friends' house; **la loge des actrices** the actresses' dressing-room; **les amis de nos enfants** our children's friends

Après un nom commun se terminant par ss, 's *est obligatoire.*

la loge de l'actrice the actress's dressing-room

Après un nom propre se terminant par s *ou* ss, *l'apostrophe peut être utilisée seule dans un registre plus soutenu.*

la vie de Jésus Jesus's life, Jesus' life; **la maison de Wells/Burgess** Wells's/Burgess's house, Wells'/Burgess' house

Dans le cas où le possesseur est un inanimé, l'anglais juxtapose parfois les noms.

le pied de la table the leg of the table, the table leg; **le bouton de la porte** the door knob

e caractérisation

Lorsque de *est utilisé pour la caractérisation, il peut être traduit par* of, *mais l'anglais utilise souvent des tournures adjectivales.*

(*caractérisation par le contenu*) **une bouteille de vin/lait** a bottle of wine/milk; **une tasse de thé** a cup of tea; **une pincée/cuillerée de sel** a pinch/spoonful of salt; **une poignée de gens** a handful of people; **une collection de timbres** a stamp collection; **une boîte de bonbons** a box of sweets

(*caractérisation par la matière*) **vase de cristal** crystal vase; **robe de soie** silk dress

(*caractérisation par la qualité*) **un homme de goût/d'une grande bonté** a man of taste/great kindness; **quelque chose de beau/cher** something lovely/expensive; **rien de neuf/ d'intéressant** nothing new/interesting *ou* of interest

(*caractérisation par la fonction*) **il est professeur d'anglais** he's an English teacher *ou* a teacher of English

(*caractérisation par le temps*) **les romanciers du 20e siècle** 20th-century novelists, novelists of the 20th century; **les journaux d'hier/du dimanche** yesterday's/the Sunday papers

♦ **de + participe passé:** **il y a deux verres de cassés** there are two broken glasses *ou* glasses broken; **il y a cinq enfants de disparus** five children are missing

f valeur intensive   **et elle de se moquer de nos efforts!** and she made fun of our efforts!; **et lui d'ajouter: « jamais! »** "never!" he added

La valeur intensive de de + *article ou démonstratif est souvent rendue par un adjectif ou un adverbe en anglais.*

il est d'une bêtise! he's so stupid!, he's incredibly stupid!; **il a un de ces appétits!** he's got an incredible appetite; **j'ai de ces douleurs!** I've got this terrible pain!; **elle a de ces initiatives!** some of the things she gets up to!; **tu as de ces idées!** you have the strangest ideas sometimes!

g

Lorsque **de** *introduit un nom en apposition, il est rarement traduit.*

le jour de Noël Christmas Day; le prénom de Paul est très courant the name Paul is very common; le mot de « liberté » the word "freedom"; cette saleté de temps nous gâche nos vacances this rotten weather is spoiling our holiday; MAIS ton idiot de fils that stupid son of yours; la ville de Paris the city of Paris; le mois de juin (the month of) June

h

♦ **de** + *nombre* (= *parmi*) of; de six qu'ils étaient (au départ), ils ne sont plus que deux of the original six there are only two left

Lorsque **de** *est suivi d'une mesure, d'un poids, d'un âge, d'une durée, d'un montant etc, il est souvent rendu en anglais par une simple apposition.*

une pièce de 6 m² a room 6 metres square; une plage de plusieurs kilomètres a beach several kilometres long; un rôti de 2 kg a 2-kilo joint; une table de 2 mètres de large a table 2 metres wide *ou* in width; un enfant de 5 ans a 5-year-old (child); un bébé de 6 mois a 6-month(-old) baby, a baby of 6 months; une attente de 2 heures a 2-hour wait; un voyage de trois jours a three-day journey; une promenade de 3 km/3 heures a 3-km/3-hour walk; un bébé de quelques mois a baby just a few months old; il y aura une attente de quelques heures there will be a few hours' wait, you will have to wait a few hours; un chèque de 100 F a cheque for 100 francs; elle est plus grande que lui de 5 cm she is 5 cm taller than he is, she is taller than him by 5 cm

i agent animé by; un film de Fellini a Fellini film, a film by Fellini; un concerto de Brahms a concerto by Brahms, a Brahms concerto; le message a été compris de tous the message was understood by everybody; c'est de qui? who is it by?; MAIS le poème n'est pas de moi I didn't write the poem; c'est bien de lui de sortir sans manteau it's just like him *ou* it's typical of him to go out without a coat

j agent inanimé

Lorsque **de** *introduit un agent inanimé, la traduction dépend étroitement du verbe; reportez-vous à celui-ci.*

couvert de boue/d'un drap covered in mud/with a sheet; rempli de fumée filled with smoke

k = avec, manière, cause

Lorsque **de** *signifie avec, au moyen de, à l'aide de, ou exprime la manière ou la cause, la traduction dépend étroitement du contexte; reportez-vous au verbe ou au nom.*

il l'attrapa de la main gauche he caught it with his left hand; de rien/d'un bout de bois, il peut faire des merveilles he can make wonderful things out of nothing/a bit of wood; il les encourageait de la voix he cheered them on; marcher d'un pas lent/d'un bon pas to walk slowly/briskly; parler d'une voix émue/ferme to speak emotionally/firmly *ou* in an emotional/a firm voice; regarder qn d'un air tendre to look at sb tenderly, give sb a tender look; rougir de dépit/de honte to blush with vexation/with *ou* for shame; de colère, il la gifla he slapped her in anger; être fatigué du voyage/de répéter to be tired from the journey/of repeating; elle rit de le voir si maladroit she laughed to see him *ou* on seeing him so clumsy; contrarié de ce qu'il se montre si peu coopératif annoyed at his being so uncooperative

l = par, chaque il gagne 90 F de l'heure he earns 90 francs an hour *ou* per hour; ça coûte 80 F du mètre it costs 80 francs a metre

m = durant de jour/nuit by day/night, during the day/the night; 3 heures du matin/de

l'après-midi 3 (o'clock) in the morning/afternoon, 3 am/pm

Notez l'emploi de **all** *dans les phrases suivantes.*

il n'a rien fait de la semaine/l'année he hasn't done a thing all week/year; de (toute) ma vie je n'ai entendu pareilles sottises I've never heard such nonsense in all my life; je ne l'avais pas vu de la semaine/de la soirée I hadn't seen him all week/all evening

n valeur emphatique t'en as une, de moto?* have you got a motorbike?; moi j'en ai vu deux, de lions!* I saw two lions, I did!; c'en est un, d'imbécile* he's a real idiot

♦ **de ... à** from ... to

(*dans l'espace*) de chez moi à la gare, il y a 5 km it's 5 km from my house to the station

(*dans le temps*) je serai là de 6 à 8 I'll be there from 6 to 8; du 2 au 7 mai (*écrit*) from 2nd to 7th May; (*parlé*) from the 2nd to the 7th of May; le magasin est ouvert du mardi au samedi the shop is open from Tuesday to Saturday; MAIS d'une minute/d'un jour à l'autre (= *très rapidement*) from one minute/day to the next; (= *incessamment, n'importe quand*) any minute/day now

(*avec un âge, une durée, une estimation*) les enfants de 9 à 12 ans children from 9 to 12, children between (the ages of) 9 and 12; ça peut coûter de 100 à 150 F it can cost from 100 to 150 francs *ou* between 100 and 150 francs

(*pour exprimer l'exhaustivité*) ils ont tout pris, des petites cuillères à l'armoire they took everything, from the teaspoons to the wardrobe → ici, là

♦ **de ... en** from ... to

(*dans l'espace*) il va de village en village/de porte en porte he goes from village to village/from door to door

(*dans le temps*) de mois en mois/jour en jour from month to month/day to day; MAIS le nombre diminue d'année en année the number is decreasing year on year *ou* every year; de minute en minute, l'espoir s'amenuisait hope faded as the minutes went by

(*dans une succession, une évolution*) il va d'échec en échec he goes from one failure to the next; nous allions de surprise en surprise we had one surprise after another

---

de² [də]

Devant une voyelle ou un **h** *muet* = **d'**; *contraction* **de** + **le** = **du**; **de** + **les** = **des**.
1 ARTICLE PARTITIF | **2** ARTICLE INDÉFINI PL

1 ARTICLE PARTITIF

a dans une affirmation

de *se traduit généralement par* **some**, *mais celui-ci peut être omis.*

au déjeuner, nous avons eu du poulet we had (some) chicken for lunch; j'ai du travail à faire I've got (some) work to do; il but de l'eau au robinet he drank some water from the tap; j'ai acheté des pommes/de la viande I bought some apples/some meat; j'ai acheté des fruits, des légumes et du vin I bought (some) fruit, (some) vegetables and (some) wine; j'ai acheté de la laine I bought some wool; il a joué du Chopin/des valses de Chopin he played (some) Chopin/some Chopin waltzes; cela demande du courage/de la patience it takes (some) courage/patience; c'est du chantage/vol! that's blackmail/robbery!

de *ne se traduit pas lorsque l'on ne veut pas ou ne peut pas préciser la quantité.*

boire du vin/de la bière/de l'eau to drink wine/beer/water; ils vendent des pommes/de la viande they sell apples/meat; on peut acheter de la laine chez Dupont you can buy wool at Dupont's; il mange des biscuits toute la journée he eats biscuits all day; les ânes mangent du foin donkeys eat hay; MAIS il y avait de

l'agressivité dans ses paroles there was something aggressive about what he said

Dans certaines expressions, **de** *se traduit par l'article* **a, an.**

faire du bruit to make a noise; avoir de l'humour to have a sense of humour

b dans une interrogation, une hypothèse

de *se traduit généralement par* **any**; **some** *est utilisé si l'on s'attend à une réponse positive.*

avez-vous du pain/des œufs à me passer? do you have any bread/eggs you could let me have?, I wonder if you could let me have some bread/eggs?; voulez-vous du pain/des œufs? would you like some bread/eggs?; vous ne voulez vraiment pas de vin? are you sure you don't want some *ou* any wine?; si on prenait de la bière/du vin? what about some beer/wine?; s'il y avait du pain, j'en mangerais if there was some *ou* any bread, I'd eat it

Lorsqu'il s'agit d'une alternative, **de** *ne se traduit généralement pas.*

voulez-vous du thé ou du café? would you like tea or coffee?

c dans une négation

de *se traduit généralement par* **any** *ou* **no.**

je n'ai pas acheté de pommes/de laine I didn't buy (any) apples/wool; il n'y a pas de pain there's no bread, there isn't any bread

d dans une comparaison il y a du poète chez cet homme he has something of the poet about him; il y a du puritain chez lui he has something of the puritan about him, there's something puritanical about him; il y a du Fellini chez lui his work is somewhat reminiscent of Fellini

2 ARTICLE INDÉFINI PL

a dans une affirmation

des, de *peuvent se traduire par* **some** *mais ce dernier est souvent omis.*

des enfants ont cassé les carreaux some children have broken the window panes; il y a des vers dans le fromage there are (some) maggots in the cheese; j'ai des voisins charmants *ou* de charmants voisins I've got (some) lovely neighbours; il y a des gens qui attendent there are (some) people waiting; il y a des gens qui disent que ... some people say that ...; elle a des taches de rousseur she's got freckles; elle a de petites taches de rousseur sur les joues she's got (some) little freckles on her cheeks

Lorsque le nom suivant **de** *appartient à un ensemble d'éléments fixes,* **some** *ne peut être employé.*

elle a de jolies mains/de jolis doigts she's got lovely hands/lovely fingers; il a de beaux enfants he's got beautiful kids; il portait des lunettes he was wearing glasses

Dans les oppositions, **de** *ne se traduit pas.*

elle élève des chats mais pas de chiens she breeds cats but not dogs

b dans une interrogation

des, de *se traduisent par* **any**; **some** *est utilisé lorsque l'on s'attend à une réponse positive.*

as-tu rencontré des randonneurs? did you meet any hikers?; tu veux vraiment des livres pour ton anniversaire? do you really want (some) books for your birthday?

c dans une négation

de *se traduit par* **any** *ou* **no.**

je n'ai pas de voisins I haven't got any neighbours, I have no neighbours; il n'a pas eu de client ce matin he hasn't had any customers this morning; je n'ai jamais vu de loups ici I have never seen (any) wolves here; MAIS je n'ai jamais vu de loups (de ma vie) I've never seen a wolf (in my life)

d valeur intensive elle est restée des mois et des mois sans nouvelles she was without news for months and months, she went for months and months without news; **j'ai attendu des heures** I waited (for) hours; **nous n'avons pas fait des kilomètres** we didn't exactly walk miles; **ils en ont cueilli des kilos (et des kilos)** they picked kilos (and kilos); **il y en a des qui exagèrent*** some people do exaggerate

dé [de] NM [a] **dé (à coudre)** thimble; (= *petit verre*) tiny glass; (*fig*) **ça tient dans un dé à coudre** it will fit into a thimble [b] (*Jeux*) die, dice *pl*; **dés (à jouer)** dice; **jouer aux dés** to play dice; **les dés sont jetés** the die is cast; (*Culin*) **couper des carottes en dés** to dice carrots; **sur un coup de dés** (*lit, fig*) on a throw of the dice; **jouer son avenir sur un coup de dés** to risk one's future on a throw of the dice, (take) a gamble with one's future

DEA [deǝa] NM (ABRÉV = **diplôme d'études approfondies**) → **diplôme**

deal [dil] NM [a] (*Drogue*) drug dealing [b]* (= *transaction*) deal; **passer un ~** to do *ou* strike a deal (**avec** with)

dealer[1] [dile] ▶conjug 1◀ VI (*Drogue*) to push drugs*

dealer[2] [dilœʀ] NM (*Drogue*) (drug) dealer*

déambulateur [deɑ̃bylatœʀ] NM walking frame, walker, zimmer (aid)®

déambulatoire [deɑ̃bylatwaʀ] NM ambulatory

déambuler [deɑ̃byle] ▶conjug 1◀ VI (*gén*) to wander; [*promeneur*] to stroll; **j'aime ~ dans les rues de Paris** I like to stroll through the streets of Paris

déb* [deb] NF (ABRÉV = **débutante**) deb*

débâcle [debɑkl] NF [*armée*] debacle, rout; [*régime*] collapse; [*glaces*] breaking up, debacle (*SPÉC*); **c'est une vraie ~!** it's a complete disaster!; **la ~ de la livre (face au dollar)** the collapse of the pound (against the dollar)

déballage [debalaʒ] NM [a] (= *action*) [*objets*] unpacking [b] [*marchandises*] display (of loose goods) [c]* (= *paroles, confession*) outpouring

déballer [debale] ▶conjug 1◀ VT [+ *objets*] to unpack; [+ *marchandises*] to display, lay out; * [+ *histoires, souvenirs*] to let out; * [+ *sentiments*] to pour out, give vent to; (* *péj*) [+ *connaissances*] to air (*péj*); **elle lui a tout déballé** she poured out her heart to him

déballonner (se)* [debalɔne] ▶conjug 1◀ VPR to chicken out*

débander [debɑ̃de] ▶conjug 1◀ [1] VT [a] (*Méd*) to unbandage, take the bandages off; **~ les yeux de qn** to remove a blindfold from sb's eyes [b] [+ *arc, ressort*] to relax, slacken (off) [2] VI (‡: *sexuellement*) to lose one's hard-on*‡; (*fig*) **travailler 10 heures sans ~‡** to work 10 hours without letting up* [3] **se débander** VPR [*armée, manifestants*] to scatter, break up; [*arc, ressort*] to relax, slacken

débaptiser [debatize] ▶conjug 1◀ VT to change the name of, rename

débarbouillage [debaʀbujaʒ] NM [*visage*] quick wash, cat-lick* (*Brit*)

débarbouiller [debaʀbuje] ▶conjug 1◀ [1] VT [+ *visage*] to give a quick wash *ou* cat-lick* (*Brit*) to [2] **se débarbouiller** VPR to give one's face a quick wash *ou* a cat-lick* (*Brit*)

débarbouillette [debaʀbujet] NF (*Can*) face cloth, flannel (*Brit*), wash cloth (*US*)

débarcadère [debaʀkadɛʀ] NM landing stage

débardage [debaʀdaʒ] NM (*Naut*) unloading, unlading; (*Sylviculture*) skidding

débarder [debaʀde] ▶conjug 1◀ VT (*Naut*) to unload, unlade; (*Sylviculture*) to skid

débardeur [debaʀdœʀ] NM (*Naut*) docker, stevedore; (*Sylviculture*) skidder; (= *vêtement*) (= T-shirt) singlet, sleeveless T-shirt; (*pardessus une chemise*) tank top, slipover (*Brit*)

débarqué, e [debaʀke] (*ptp de* **débarquer**) NM,F (*lit*) disembarked passenger; (*fig*) **un nouveau ~ dans le service** a new arrival in the department; **un jeune auteur fraîchement ~ de sa province** a young writer just up *ou* newly arrived from the provinces

débarquement [debaʀkǝmɑ̃] NM [*marchandises*] unloading, landing; [*passagers*] disembarkation, landing; [*troupes*] landing; **navire ou péniche de ~** landing craft *inv*; (*Hist*: *en Normandie*) **le ~** the Normandy landings

débarquer [debaʀke] ▶conjug 1◀ [1] VT [a] [+ *marchandises*] to unload, land; [+ *passagers*] to disembark, land; [+ *troupes*] to land [b]* (= *congédier*) to fire, sack* (*Brit*), kick out*; **se faire ~** to get the push* *ou* sack* (*Brit*), get kicked out* [2] VI [a] (*Aviat, Naut*) [*passagers*] to disembark (**de** from); [*troupes*] to land [b]* (= *arriver subitement*) to turn up; **il a débarqué chez moi hier soir** he turned up at my place last night; **j'ai débarqué à Paris quand j'avais 20 ans** I arrived in Paris when I was 20 [c]* (= *ne pas être au courant*) **tu débarques!** where have you been?*; **je n'en sais rien, je débarque** I don't know, that's the first I've heard of it

débarras [debaʀɑ] NM [a] (= *pièce*) junk room, boxroom (*Brit*); (= *placard, soupente*) junk cupboard, junk closet (*US*) [b]* **bon ~!** good riddance!; **il est parti, quel ~!** thank goodness he's gone!

débarrasser [debaʀase] ▶conjug 1◀ [1] VT [a] [+ *local*] to clear (de of); **~ (la table)** to clear the table; **débarrasse le plancher!*** beat it!*, hop it!* (*Brit*) [b] **~ qn de** [+ *fardeau, manteau, chapeau*] to relieve sb of; [+ *habitude*] to break *ou* rid sb of; [+ *ennemi, mal*] to rid sb of; [+ *liens*] to release sb from; **écris ces lettres tout de suite, tu en seras débarrassé** write those letters now to get them out of the way; **je peux vous ~?** can I take your coat (*ou* jacket *etc*)? [2] **se débarrasser** VPR **se ~ de** [+ *objet, personne*] to get rid of, rid o.s. of; [+ *sentiment*] to rid o.s. of, get rid of, shake off; [+ *mauvaise habitude*] to rid o.s. of; (= *ôter*) [+ *vêtement*] to take off, remove; **débarrassez-vous!** [+ *objets*] put your things down; [+ *manteau*] take your coat off

débat [deba] NM (= *discussion*) discussion, debate; (= *polémique*) debate; **~ intérieur** inner struggle; **dîner-~** dinner debate; (*TV*) **émission-~** televised *ou* television debate; (*Jur, Pol = séance*) **~s** proceedings, debates; (*Jur*) **~s à huis clos** hearing in camera; (*Parl*) **~ de clôture** ≈ adjournment debate; **~ d'idées** ideological debate; **un grand ~ de société sur l'éthique médicale** a major public debate *ou* controversy about medical ethics

débâter [debɑte] ▶conjug 1◀ VT [+ *bête de somme*] to unsaddle

débâtir [debɑtiʀ] ▶conjug 2◀ VT (*Couture*) to take out *ou* remove the tacking *ou* basting

débatteur [debatœʀ] NM debater

débattre [debatʀ] ▶conjug 41◀ [1] VT [+ *problème, question*] to discuss, debate; [+ *prix, clauses d'un traité*] to discuss; **le prix reste à ~** the price has still to be discussed; (*petite annonce*) **à vendre 1 000 F à ~** for sale: 1,000 francs or nearest offer [2] **débattre de** *ou* **sur** VT INDIR [+ *question*] to discuss, debate [3] **se débattre** VPR (*contre un adversaire*) to struggle (**contre** with); (*contre le courant*) to struggle (**contre** against); (*contre les difficultés*) to struggle (**contre** against, **avec** with), wrestle (**contre** with); **se ~ comme un beau diable** *ou* **comme un forcené** to struggle like the very devil *ou* like one possessed

débauchage [deboʃaʒ] NM (= *licenciement*) laying off, dismissal; [*salarié d'une autre entreprise*] hiring away, poaching; **il y a eu**

plusieurs ~s (*licenciements*) there were several layoffs, several people were laid off; (*d'autres entreprises*) several people were hired away *ou* poached

débauche [deboʃ] NF [a] (= *vice*) debauchery; **mener une vie de ~** ◊ **vivre dans la ~** to lead a debauched life *ou* a life of debauchery; **scène de ~** scene of debauchery; (*Jur*) **incitation de mineurs à la ~** corruption of minors → **lieu[1]** [b] (= *abondance*) **~ de** profusion *ou* abundance *ou* wealth of; **~ de couleurs** riot of colour

débauché, e† [deboʃe] [1] ADJ [*personne, vie*] debauched [2] NM,F debauched individual; **c'est un ~** he leads a debauched life *ou* a life of debauchery

débaucher [deboʃe] ▶conjug 1◀ [1] VT [a] **~ un salarié d'une autre entreprise**: (*gén*) to hire away, poach (**de** from); [*chasseur de tête*] to head-hunt; **il s'est fait ~ par un chasseur de tête** he was head-hunted [b] (= *licencier*) to lay off, make redundant (*Brit*); **on débauche dans ce secteur** a lot of people are being laid off *ou* made redundant in this sector; **les usines qui débauchent** factories that are laying off workers [c] († = *détourner*) (*du droit chemin*) to debauch, corrupt; (*: *d'une occupation*) to entice away, tempt away; (= *inciter à la grève*) to incite to strike [2] VI (= *sortir du travail*) to stop work for the day, knock off*

débecter‡ [debɛkte] ▶conjug 1◀ VT (= *dégoûter*) to disgust; **ça me débecte** it makes me sick, it makes me want to throw up* *ou* to puke‡

débile [debil] [1] ADJ [a] (= *faible*) [*enfant*] sickly, weak; [*corps, membre*] weak, feeble; [*esprit*] feeble; [*santé*] frail, poor [b]* (= *stupide*) [*personne*] moronic*; [*film, discours, raisonnement*] pathetic*, stupid [2] NMF (*Méd*) **~ mental** (mentally) retarded person; **~ léger/ moyen/profond** mildly/moderately/severely (mentally) retarded *ou* handicapped person; (*péj*) **quel ~, celui-là!** what a moron!*

débilitant, e [debilitɑ̃, ɑ̃t] ADJ (= *anémiant*) [*climat, régime*] debilitating, enervating; (= *déprimant*) [*atmosphère*] demoralizing; (* = *abêtissant*) [*travail*] mind-numbing; [*musique, spectacle*] mindless

débilité [debilite] NF († = *faiblesse*) debility; (*péj*) [*propos, attitude*] stupidity; **~ mentale** mental retardation *ou* deficiency; **enfant atteint d'une ~ légère** mildly (mentally) retarded *ou* handicapped child

débiliter [debilite] ▶conjug 1◀ VT (= *affaiblir*) [*climat, régime*] to debilitate, enervate; (= *déprimer*) [*endroit, propos*] to demoralize

débinage* [debinaʒ] NM knocking*, running down

débine†* [debin] NF **être dans la ~** to be hard up, be on one's uppers* (*Brit*); **tomber dans la ~** to fall on hard times

débiner* [debine] ▶conjug 1◀ [1] VT (= *dénigrer*) [+ *personne*] to knock*, run down [2] **se débiner** VPR (= *se sauver*) to clear off*

débineur, -euse* [debinœʀ, øz] NM,F backbiter*

débirentier, -ière [debiʀɑ̃tje, jɛʀ] NM,F (*Jur*) payer of an annuity

débit [debi] [1] NM [a] (*Fin*) debit; [*relevé de compte*] debit side; **mettre ou porter 100 F au ~ de qn** to debit sb *ou* sb's account with 100 francs, charge 100 francs to sb's account; **pouvez-vous me faire le ou mon ~?** can I pay for it please? [b] (*Comm = vente*) turnover (of goods), sales; **cet article a un bon/faible ~** this item sells well/poorly; **n'achète pas ton fromage dans cette boutique, il n'y a pas assez de ~** don't buy your cheese in this shop, there isn't a quick enough turnover [c] [*fleuve*] (rate of) flow; [*gaz, électricité*] output; [*pompe*] flow, outflow; [*tuyau*] discharge; [*machine*] output; [*moyen de transport*] passenger flow; (*Ordin*) [*données*] output; **il n'y a pas assez de ~ au robinet** there is not enough pressure in the tap; (*Méd*) **~ cardiaque** cardiac output; **~ sanguin** blood flow (from the heart) [d] (= *élocution*) delivery; **~ rapide/monotone** rapid/monotonous delivery; **elle a un sacré ~*** she's a real chatterbox, she's a great talker* [e] (*Menuiserie*) cutting up, sawing up

[2] COMP ► **débit de boissons** (= *petit bar ou café*) bar; (*Admin, terme générique*) drinking establishment ► **débit de tabac** tobacconist's (shop) (*Brit*), tobacco *ou* smoke shop (*US*)

débitable [debitabl] ADJ [*bois*] which can be sawn *ou* cut up

débitant, e [debitɑ̃, ɑ̃t] NM,F **~ (de boissons)** ≈ off-license manager (*Brit*), ≈ liquor store manager (*US*); **~ (de tabac)** tobacconist (*Brit*), tobacco dealer (*US*)

débiter [debite] ▸conjug 1◂ VT [a] (*Fin*) [+ *personne, compte*] to debit; **j'ai été débité de 300 F** 300 francs has been debited from my account [b] (*Comm*) [+ *marchandises*] to retail, sell [c] [*usine, machine*] to produce; (*Ordin*) to output; **ce fleuve/tuyau débite 3 m³/s** the flow of this river/through this pipe is 3 cu m per second [d] (*péj = dire*) [+ *sottises, banalités*] to utter, mouth; [+ *insultes*] to pour forth; [+ *sermon*] to spout, spiel off* (*US*); [+ *injures*] to churn out; **il me débita tout cela sans s'arrêter** he poured all that out to me without stopping [e] (= *découper*) [+ *bois*] to cut up, saw up (**en** into); [+ *viande*] to cut up

débiteur, -trice [debitœʀ, tʀis] [1] ADJ (*Fin*) [*compte, solde*] debit (*épith*); **mon compte est ~ (de 500 F)** my account has a debit balance of 500 francs) *ou* is (500 francs) in the red*; **l'organisme ~** the organisation that owes the money; **toute personne débitrice paiera des agios** account holders with a debit balance must pay charges [2] NM,F (*Fin, fig*) debtor; (*Jur*) **~-gagiste** lienee; (*lit, fig*) **être le ~ de qn** to be indebted to sb, be in sb's debt

déblai [deblɛ] [1] NM (= *nettoyage*) clearing; (*Tech* = *terrassement*) earth-moving, excavation [2] **déblais** NMPL (= *gravats*) rubble, debris *sg*; (= *terre*) (excavated) earth

déblaiement [deblɛmɑ̃] NM [*chemin, espace*] clearing

déblatérer* [deblatere] ▸conjug 6◂ VI (= *parler longuement et violemment*) to rant and rave (**contre** about); (= *médire*) **~ contre** *ou* **sur** to go *ou* rant on about*

déblayage [deblɛjaʒ] NM [a] = **déblaiement** [b] (*fig*) **le ~ d'une question** (doing) the spadework on a question

déblayer [deblɛje] ▸conjug 8◂ VT [a] (= *retirer*) [+ *décombres*] to clear away, remove; [+ *neige*] to clear away; (= *dégager*) [+ *route, porte, espace*] to clear; [+ *pièce*] to clear up, tidy up; (*Tech*) [+ *terrain*] to level off [b] [+ *travail*] to prepare, do the spadework on; **~ le terrain** (*avant des négociations, une réflexion*) to clear the ground *ou* the way; (= *déguerpir*) **déblaye (le terrain)!*** get lost!*, shove off!*, push off!* (*Brit*)

déblocage [deblɔkaʒ] NM [a] (*Écon*) [*crédits, fonds, aide, marchandises*] releasing; [*prix, salaires, loyers*] unfreezing; (*Fin*) [*compte*] freeing [b] (*Tech*) [*machine*] unjamming; [*écrou, frein*] releasing; [*route*] unblocking; **ceci a permis le ~ de la situation/des négociations** this has broken the deadlock in the situation/the negotiations

débloquer [deblɔke] ▸conjug 1◂ [1] VT [a] (*Écon*) [+ *crédits, fonds, aide, marchandises*] to release; [+ *prix, salaires, loyers*] to unfreeze; (*Fin*) [+ *compte*] to free [b] (*Tech*) [+ *machine*] to unjam; [+ *écrou, freins*] to release; [+ *route*] to unblock; [+ *négociations, situation*] to break the deadlock in **~ qn** (= *le rendre moins timide*) to bring sb out of their shell; (* = *désinhiber*) to rid sb of their complexes *ou* inhibitions

[2] VI* (= *dire des bêtises*) to talk nonsense *ou* rot* (*Brit*); (= *être fou*) to be off one's rocker* [3] **se débloquer** VPR [*personne*] to loosen up; **la situation commence à se ~** things are starting to get moving again

débobiner [debɔbine] ▸conjug 1◂ VT (*Couture*) to unwind, wind off; (*Élec*) to unwind, uncoil

déboguer [debɔge] ▸conjug 1◂ VT (*Ordin*) to debug

débogueur [debɔgœʀ] NM (*Ordin*) debugger

déboires [debwaʀ] NMPL (= *déceptions*) disappointments; (= *échecs*) setbacks; (= *ennuis*) trials, difficulties

déboisage [debwazaʒ], **déboisement** [debwazmɑ̃] NM [*montagne, région*] deforestation; [*forêt*] clearing

déboiser [debwaze] ▸conjug 1◂ VT [+ *montagne, région*] to deforest; [+ *forêt*] to clear of trees

déboîtement [debwatmɑ̃] NM [a] (*Méd*) dislocation [b] (*Aut*) (*du trottoir*) pulling out; (*d'une file*) changing lanes, pulling out

déboîter [debwate] ▸conjug 1◂ [1] VT [+ *épaule, cheville, mâchoire*] to dislocate; [+ *porte*] to take off its hinges; [+ *tuyaux*] to disconnect; [+ *objet*] to dislodge, knock out of place; **se ~ l'épaule** to dislocate one's shoulder [2] VI (*Aut*) (*du trottoir*) to pull out; (*d'une file*) to change lanes, pull out; (*Mil*) to break rank

débonder [debɔ̃de] ▸conjug 1◂ [1] VT [+ *tonneau*] to remove the bung *ou* stopper from; [+ *baignoire*] to pull the plug out of [2] **se débonder** VPR [*personne*] to open one's heart, pour out one's feelings

débonnaire [debɔnɛʀ] ADJ (= *bon enfant*) easy-going, good-natured; († = *trop bon, faible*) soft, weak; **air ~** kindly appearance

débordant, e [debɔʀdɑ̃, ɑ̃t] ADJ [a] [*activité*] exuberant; [*enthousiasme, joie*] overflowing, unbounded; [*imagination*] overactive; **elle était ~e de vie** she was bursting with vitality [b] (*Mil*) **mouvement ~** outflanking manœuvre

débordé, e [debɔʀde] ADJ **~ (de travail)** snowed under with work, up to one's eyes in work; **les hôpitaux sont ~s** the hospitals are unable to cope

débordement [debɔʀdəmɑ̃] [1] NM [a] [*rivière, liquide*] overflowing (*NonC*); [*liquide en ébullition*] boiling over (*NonC*); (*Ordin*) memory overflow; (*Mil, Sport*) outflanking (*NonC*); (*dans une manifestation*) **afin d'éviter les ~s** to prevent things from getting out of hand; **le ~ du parti par la base** the outflanking of the party by the rank and file [b] [*joie, violence*] outburst; [*énergie*] burst; [*paroles, injures*] torrent, rush; [*activité*] explosion; **~ de vie** bubbling vitality [2] **débordements** NMPL (= *excès*) excesses

déborder [debɔʀde] ▸conjug 1◂ [1] VI [a] [*récipient, liquide*] to overflow; [*fleuve, rivière*] to burst its banks, overflow; [*liquide bouillant*] to boil over; **les pluies ont fait ~ le réservoir** the rains caused the reservoir to overflow; **faire ~ le lait** to let the milk boil over; **tasse/boîte pleine à ~** cup/box full to the brim *ou* to overflowing (**de** with); **l'eau a débordé du vase/de la casserole** the water has overflowed out of the vase/has boiled over; **les vêtements débordaient de la valise** the clothes were spilling out of the suitcase; **la foule débordait sur la chaussée** the crowd was overflowing onto the roadway; (*fig*) **cela a fait ~ le vase ◊ c'est la goutte qui a fait ~ le vase** that was the last straw, that was the straw that broke the camel's back; **son cœur débordait, il fallait qu'il parle** his heart was (full to) overflowing and he just had to speak [b] (*en coloriant, en mettant du rouge à lèvres*) to go over the edge [c] (*fig*) **~ de santé** to be bursting with health; **~ de joie** to be brimming over *ou* bubbling *ou*

bursting with joy; **~ d'activité** [*lieu*] to be bustling *ou* buzzing with activity; [*personne*] to be bursting with vitality; **~ de vie** to be bursting with vitality; **~ d'imagination** to be full of imagination; **son cœur débordait de reconnaissance** his heart was overflowing *ou* bursting with gratitude; **il débordait de tendresse pour elle** his heart was overflowing with tenderness for her

[2] VT [a] (= *dépasser*) [+ *enceinte, limites*] to extend beyond; (*Mil, Pol, Sport*) [+ *ennemi*] to outflank; **leur maison déborde les autres** their house juts out from the others; **la nappe doit ~ la table** the tablecloth should hang over the edge of the table; **le conférencier/cette remarque déborde le cadre du sujet** the lecturer/that remark goes beyond the bounds of the subject; **il a débordé (le temps imparti)** he has run over (the allotted time); (*Mil, Pol, Sport*) **se laisser ~ sur la droite** to allow o.s. to be outflanked on the right; **le service d'ordre s'est laissé ~** the stewards were unable to cope [b] [+ *couvertures*] to untuck; **~ qn** to untuck sb *ou* sb's bed [c] (*Couture*) [+ *vêtement*] to remove the border from

[3] **se déborder** VPR **il s'est débordé en dormant** he *ou* his bed came untucked in his sleep

débosseler [debɔs(ə)le] ▸conjug 4◂ VT [+ *carrosserie*] to beat *ou* hammer (back) into shape; [+ *chapeau*] (*à coups de poing*) to beat back into shape

débotté [debɔte] ◆**au débotté** LOC ADV (*littér*) **je ne peux pas répondre au ~** I can't answer off the cuff; **prendre qn au ~** to catch sb unawares, take sb by surprise; **il m'a reçu au ~** he received me straight away

débotter [debɔte] ▸conjug 1◂ [1] VT **~ qn** to take off sb's boots [2] **se débotter** VPR to take one's boots off

débouchage [debuʃaʒ] NM [*bouteille*] uncorking, opening; [*tuyau*] unblocking

débouché [debuʃe] NM [a] (*gén pl*) (*Comm* = *marché, créneau*) outlet; (= *carrière*) opening, prospect [b] (= *sortie, ouverture*) opening; **au ~ de la vallée (dans la plaine)** where the valley opens out (into the plain); **au ~ de la rue** at the end of the street; **la Suisse n'a aucun ~ sur la mer** Switzerland has no outlet to the sea

déboucher [debuʃe] ▸conjug 1◂ [1] VT [a] [+ *lavabo, tuyau*] to unblock [b] [+ *bouteille de vin*] to uncork, open; [+ *carafe, flacon*] to unstopper, take the stopper out of; [+ *tube*] to uncap, take the cap *ou* top off

[2] VI to emerge, come out; **~ de** [*personne, voiture*] to emerge from, come out of; **~ sur** *ou* **dans** [*rue*] to run into, open onto *ou* into; [*personne, voiture*] to come out onto *ou* into, emerge onto *ou* into; **sur quoi ces études débouchent-elles ?** what does this course lead on to?; **les négociations ont débouché sur une impasse** the talks have reached an impasse *ou* a dead end; **~ sur des mesures concrètes** to result in *ou* lead to concrete measures; **ne ~ sur rien** to lead nowhere; **les discussions n'ont pas débouché** the discussions led nowhere

[3] **se déboucher** VPR [*bouteille*] to come uncorked; [*tuyau*] to unblock, come unblocked

déboucheur [debuʃœʀ] NM caustic cleaner, Liquid Plumber® (*US*)

débouchoir [debuʃwaʀ] NM [*lavabo*] plunger, plumber's helper (*US*)

déboucler [debukle] ▸conjug 1◂ VT [+ *ceinture*] to unbuckle, undo; **je suis toute débouclée** my hair has all gone straight, the curl has come out of my hair

déboulé [debule] NM (*Danse*) déboulé; (*Courses*) charge; (*Chasse*) **tirer un lapin au ~** to shoot a rabbit as it breaks cover

débouler [debule] ▶ conjug 1 ◀ ⓵ VI ⓐ (*Chasse*) [*lapin*] to bolt ⓑ* (= *surgir*) **attention, les voitures déboulent à toute vitesse ici** watch out, the cars come out of nowhere around here; **le vélo déboula d'une rue adjacente** the bike shot out of a side street; **~ chez qn** to turn up at sb's home ⓒ (= *dégringoler*) to tumble down ⓶ VT* (= *dévaler*) to charge down; **~ l'escalier** to come charging down the stairs*

déboulonnage [debulɔnaʒ], **déboulonnement** [debulɔnmɑ̃] NM ⓐ (= *dévissage*) removal of bolts (**de** from); [*statue*] dismantling, taking down ⓑ* [*personne*] (= *action de discréditer*) discrediting, debunking; (= *renvoi*) ousting

déboulonner [debulɔne] ▶ conjug 1 ◀ VT ⓐ (= *dévisser*) to remove the bolts from, take the bolts out of; **~ la statue de qn** (*lit*) to dismantle *ou* take down sb's statue; (*fig*) to knock sb off their pedestal ⓑ* [+ *personne*] (= *discréditer*) to discredit, debunk; (= *renvoyer*) to oust

débourber [deburbe] ▶ conjug 1 ◀ VT [+ *fossé*] to clear of mud, clean out; [+ *canal*] to dredge; [+ *véhicule*] to pull out of the mud; (*Œnol*) **~ du vin** to decant wine

débourrage [debuʁaʒ] NM [*cheval*] breaking in

débourrer [debuʁe] ▶ conjug 1 ◀ ⓵ VT ⓐ [+ *cheval*] to break in ⓑ [+ *cuir*] to deburr ⓒ [+ *pipe*] to empty ⓶ VI [*bourgeon*] to open out

débours [debuʁ] NM (= *dépense*) outlay; **pour rentrer dans ses ~** to recover one's outlay; **sans ~ d'argent** without any financial outlay

déboursement [debuʁsəmɑ̃] NM laying out, disbursement (*frm*)

débourser [debuʁse] ▶ conjug 1 ◀ VT to pay out, lay out, disburse (*frm*); **sans ~ un sou** without paying *ou* laying out a penny

déboussoler* [debusɔle] ▶ conjug 1 ◀ VT to disorientate; **il est complètement déboussolé** he is completely lost *ou* disorientated

debout [d(ə)bu] ADV, ADJ INV ⓐ [*personne*] (= *en position verticale*) standing (up); (= *levé*) up; **être** *ou* **se tenir ~** to stand; **être ~** (= *levé*) to be up; (= *guéri*) to be up (and about); **se mettre ~** to stand up, get up; **il préfère être** *ou* **rester ~** he prefers to stand *ou* remain standing; **hier, nous sommes restés ~ jusqu'à minuit** yesterday we stayed up till midnight; **il l'aida à se (re)mettre ~** he helped her (back) up, he helped him (back) to his feet; **leur fils se tient ~ maintenant** their son can stand (up) now; **le plafond est si bas qu'on ne peut pas se tenir ~** the ceiling is so low that it's impossible to stand upright; **il est très fatigué, il tient à peine ~** he's so tired he can hardly stand; **je ne tiens plus ~** I'm fit *ou* ready to drop*; **elle est ~ toute la journée** she's on her feet all day; **ces gens ~ nous empêchent de voir** we can't see because of the people standing in front of us; **~ ! get up!, on your feet!; ~ là-dedans !*** get up, you guys *ou* you lot!* (*Brit*); (*fig*) **il veut mourir ~** he wants to die on his feet *ou* with his boots on → **dormir, magistrature, place** ⓑ [*bouteille, meuble*] (*position habituelle*) standing up(right); (*position inhabituelle*) standing (up) on end; **mettre qch ~** to stand sth up(right), stand sth (up) on end; **les tables, ~ le long du mur** the tables, standing (up) on end along the wall; **mets les bouteilles ~** stand the bottles up(right); **tenir ~** [*objet*] to stay upright; **je n'arrive pas à faire tenir le livre ~** I can't keep the book upright, I can't make the book stand *ou* stay up ⓒ [*édifice, mur*] standing (*attrib*); (*fig*) **ces institutions sont** *ou* **tiennent encore ~** these institutions are still going; **cette théorie tient ~** this theory holds up *ou* holds water; **ça ne tient pas ~ ce que tu dis** what you say doesn't stand up; **son histoire ne tient pas ~** his story doesn't make sense *ou* doesn't hold together

débouté [debute] NM (*Jur*) ≈ nonsuit

déboutement [debutmɑ̃] NM (*Jur*) ≈ nonsuiting

débouter [debute] ▶ conjug 1 ◀ VT (*Jur*) ≈ to nonsuit; **~ qn de sa plainte** ≈ to nonsuit a plaintiff; **être débouté de sa demande** to be ruled out of court, see one's case dismissed by the court, ≈ be nonsuited

déboutonner [debutɔne] ▶ conjug 1 ◀ ⓵ VT to unbutton, undo ⓶ **se déboutonner** VPR ⓐ [*personne*] to unbutton *ou* undo one's jacket (*ou* coat etc); [*vêtement*] to come unbuttoned *ou* undone ⓑ* (= *se confier*) to open up*

débraillé, e [debʁaje] (*ptp de* **débrailler**) ⓵ ADJ [*tenue, personne*] untidy, slovenly-looking; [*manières*] slovenly; [*style*] sloppy, slipshod ⓶ NM [*tenue, manières*] slovenliness; [*style*] sloppiness; **être en ~** to be slovenly dressed

débrailler (se)* [debʁaje] ▶ conjug 1 ◀ VPR [*personne*] to loosen one's clothing

débranchement [debʁɑ̃ʃmɑ̃] NM (*gén*) disconnecting; [*appareil électrique*] unplugging, disconnecting; (*Rail*) [*wagons*] splitting up

débrancher [debʁɑ̃ʃe] ▶ conjug 1 ◀ ⓵ VT [+ *appareil électrique*] to unplug, disconnect; [+ *prise*] to disconnect, pull out; [+ *téléphone, perfusion*] to disconnect; (*Rail*) [+ *wagons*] to split up; (*Méd*) **ils l'ont débranché*** they switched him off* ⓶ VI* (= *ne plus prêter attention*) to switch off*; (= *arrêter de parler, de s'agiter*) **débranche un peu, tu veux ?** why don't you give it a break?*

débrayage [debʁɛjaʒ] NM ⓐ [*objet*] [*voiture*] clutch; [*appareil-photo*] release button ⓑ (= *action*) [*moteur*] disengagement of the clutch, declutching (*Brit*); [*appareil-photo*] releasing; (*Aut*) **faire un double ~** to double-declutch ⓒ (= *grève*) stoppage

débrayer [debʁɛje] ▶ conjug 8 ◀ ⓵ VI ⓐ (*Aut*) to disengage the clutch, declutch (*Brit*); (*Tech*) to operate the release mechanism ⓑ (= *faire grève*) to stop work, come out on strike; **le personnel a débrayé à 4 heures** the staff stopped work at 4 o'clock ⓶ VT (*Tech*) to release

débridé, e [debʁide] (*ptp de* **débrider**) ADJ unbridled, unrestrained

débridement [debʁidmɑ̃] NM [*instincts*] unbridling, unleashing; [*plaie*] lancing, incising

débrider [debʁide] ▶ conjug 1 ◀ VT [+ *cheval*] to unbridle; [+ *volaille*] to untruss; [+ *plaie*] to lance, incise; **travailler sans ~** to work nonstop

débris [debʁi] NM ⓐ (*pl = morceaux*) fragments, pieces; (= *décombres*) debris *sg*; (= *détritus*) rubbish (*NonC*); **des ~ de métal** scraps of metal ⓑ (*pl: littér = restes*) [*mort*] remains; [*plat, repas*] left-overs, scraps; [*armée, fortune*] remains, remnants; [*État*] ruins; [*édifice*] ruins, remains ⓒ (= *éclat, fragment*) fragment ⓓ (*péj = personne*) **(vieux) ~** old wreck, old dodderer

débronzer [debʁɔ̃ze] ▶ conjug 1 ◀ VI to lose one's tan

débrouillage [debʁujaʒ] NM [*fils*] disentangling, untangling; [*énigme*] unravelling

débrouillard, e [debʁujaʁ, aʁd] ⓵ ADJ (= *ingénieux*) resourceful; (= *malin*) smart ⓶ NM,F **c'est un ~** he's resourceful *ou* smart

débrouillardise [debʁujaʁdiz], **débrouille*** [debʁuj] NF (= *ingéniosité*) resourcefulness; (= *astuce*) smartness

débrouillement [debʁujmɑ̃] NM = **débrouillage**

débrouiller [debʁuje] ▶ conjug 1 ◀ ⓵ VT ⓐ [+ *fils*] to disentangle, untangle; [+ *affaire*] to sort out; [+ *problème*] to sort out, untangle; [+ *énigme*] to unravel ⓑ (* = *éduquer*) **~ qn** (*gén*) to teach sb how to look after himself (*ou* herself); (*à l'école*) to teach sb the basics; **~ qn en anglais/en informatique** to teach sb the basics *ou* give sb a grounding in English/computing ⓶ **se débrouiller** VPR to manage; **débrouillez-vous** you'll have to manage on your own *ou* sort things out yourself; **il m'a laissé me ~ tout seul** he left me to cope alone *ou* on my own; **il a fallu qu'il se débrouille tout seul dans la vie** he had to cope on his own, he had to fend for himself; **il s'est débrouillé pour obtenir la permission d'y aller** he somehow managed to get permission to go, he wangled* permission to go; **c'est toi qui as fait l'erreur, maintenant débrouille-toi pour la réparer** you made the mistake so now you can sort it out yourself; **il faudra bien nous en ~** we'll have to sort it out; **pour les boissons, je me débrouillerai avec mon frère*** I'll look after *ou* I'll organize the drinks with my brother; **elle se débrouille en allemand*** she can get by in German; **il se débrouille bien en anglais*** he gets by fairly well in English; **elle se débrouille bien*** (= *elle gagne bien sa vie*) she does well for herself

débroussaillage [debʁusajaʒ], **débroussaillement** [debʁusajmɑ̃] NM [*terrain*] clearing (**de** of); [*problème*] spadework (**de** on)

débroussailler [debʁusaje] ▶ conjug 1 ◀ VT [+ *terrain*] to clear (of brushwood); [+ *problème*] to do the spadework on

débroussailleuse [debʁusajøz] NF edge trimmer, strimmer ® (*Brit*), weedeater ® (*US*)

débucher [debyʃe] ▶ conjug 1 ◀ ⓵ VI [*animal*] to break cover ⓶ VT to force to break cover

débudgétisation [debydʒetizasjɔ̃] NF debudgeting

débudgétiser [debydʒetize] ▶ conjug 1 ◀ VT to debudget

débusquer [debyske] ▶ conjug 1 ◀ VT [+ *lièvre, cerf*] to drive out (from cover); [+ *oiseau*] to flush out, drive out (from cover); [+ *personne*] to drive out, flush out

début [deby] ⓵ NM ⓐ [*semaine, livre, action*] beginning, start; [*discours*] beginning, opening; **le chômage augmente, et ce n'est qu'un ~** unemployment is getting worse, and it's only the beginning; **ce n'est pas mal pour un ~** it's not bad for a first attempt; **j'ai un ~ de grippe** I've got the beginnings *ou* first signs of the flu; **l'incident a déclenché un ~ de panique** the incident caused some initial panic; **trouver un ~ de solution** to find the beginnings of a solution; **il y a** *ou* **il faut un ~ à tout** there's a first time for everything ⓑ (*loc*) **au ~** at first, in *ou* at the beginning; **au ~ du mois prochain** early next month, at the beginning of next month; **au tout ~ du siècle** right at the beginning of the century, at the very beginning of the century; **~ mai** at the beginning of May, in early May; **dès le ~** from the outset *ou* the start *ou* the (very) beginning; (*hum*) **du ~ à la fin** from beginning to end, from start to finish; **en ~ de soirée** early on in the evening; **salaire de ~** starting salary; **les scènes du ~ sont très belles** the opening scenes are very beautiful ⓶ **débuts** NMPL **ses ~s furent médiocres** he made an indifferent start; **à mes ~s (dans ce métier)** when I started (in this job); **ce projet n'en est qu'à ses ~s** the project is still in its early stages; **faire ses ~s dans le monde** to make one's début in society; **faire ses ~s sur la scène** to make one's début *ou* one's first appearance on the stage

débutant, e [debytɑ̃, ɑ̃t] ⓵ ADJ novice (*épith*) ⓶ NM,F (*gén*) beginner, novice; (*Théât*) debutant actor; **cours pour ~s** beginners' course; **grand/faux ~ en anglais** absolute/false beginner in English ⓷ **débutante** NF (*Théât*) debutant actress; (*dans la haute société*) debutante

débuter [debyte] ▸conjug 1◂ 1 VI a [*personne*] to start (out); **~ bien/mal** to make a good/bad start, start well/badly; **il a débuté (dans la vie) comme livreur** he started (life) as a delivery boy; **elle a débuté dans mon film** she made her début *ou* her first appearance in my film; **il débute (dans le métier), soyez indulgent** he is just starting (in the business) so don't be too hard on him; **l'orateur a débuté par des excuses** the speaker started (off) *ou* began *ou* opened by apologizing; **~ dans le monde** to make one's début in society; **pour ~** to start (off) with b [*livre, concert, manifestation*] to start, begin, open (**par, sur** with) 2 VT [+ *semaine, réunion, discours*] to start, begin, open (**par, sur** with); **il a bien débuté l'année** he has begun *ou* started the year well

deçà [dəsa] ADV a **en ~ de** (= *de ce côté-ci de*) (on) this side of; (= *en dessous de*) [+ *limite, prévisions*] below; **en ~ du fleuve/de la montagne** this side of the river/of the mountain; **tu vois la rivière, sa maison se trouve en ~** you see the river — his house is this side of it; **en ~ d'une certaine intensité, on ne peut plus rien entendre** below a certain intensity, one can no longer hear anything; **ce qu'il dit est très** *ou* **bien en ~ de la vérité** what he says is well short of the truth; **en ~ de ses moyens** within his means b †† **~, delà** here and there

déca* [deka] NM (ABRÉV = **décaféiné**) decaf*

déca- [deka] PRÉF deca-

décabosser [dekabɔse] ▸conjug 1◂ VT [+ *chapeau*] (*à coups de poing*) to beat back into shape; [+ *carrosserie*] to beat *ou* hammer (back) into shape

décachetage [dekaʃtaʒ] NM unsealing, opening

décacheter [dekaʃ(ə)te] ▸conjug 4◂ VT [+ *lettre*] to unseal, open

décade [dekad] NF (= *dix jours*) period of ten days; (= *décennie*) decade

décadenasser [dekadnase] ▸conjug 1◂ VT [+ *porte*] to unpadlock, remove the padlock from

décadence [dekadɑ̃s] NF (= *processus*) decline, decadence; (= *état*) decadence; **la ~ de l'empire romain** the decline of the Roman empire; **tomber en ~** to fall into decline → **grandeur**

décadent, e [dekadɑ̃, ɑ̃t] 1 ADJ (*gén*) decadent, declining; (*Art*) decadent 2 NM,F decadent

décaèdre [dekaɛdʀ] 1 ADJ decahedral 2 NM decahedron

décaféiné, e [dekafeine] (*ptp de* **décaféiner**) 1 ADJ decaffeinated, caffeine-free 2 NM decaffeinated coffee

décaféiner [dekafeine] ▸conjug 1◂ VT to decaffeinate

décagonal, e (*mpl* **-aux**) [dekagɔnal, o] ADJ decagonal

décagone [dekagon] NM decagon

décagramme [dekagʀam] NM decagram(me)

décaissement [dekɛsmɑ̃] NM payment, disbursement

décaisser [dekese] ▸conjug 1◂ VT [+ *argent*] to pay out; [+ *objet*] to uncrate, unpack

décalage [dekalaʒ] NM a (= *écart*) gap, interval; (*entre deux concepts*) gap, discrepancy; (*entre deux actions successives*) interval, time-lag (**entre** between); **le ~ entre le rêve et la réalité** the gap between dream and reality; **il y a un ~ entre le coup de feu et le bruit de la détonation** there is an interval *ou* a time-lag between firing and the sound of the shot; **le ~ horaire entre l'est et l'ouest des USA** the time difference between the east and the west of the USA; (*en avion*) (**fatigue due au**) **~ horaire** jet lag; **mal supporter le ~ horaire** to suffer from jet lag; (*fig*) **ses créations sont en ~ avec son**

époque/par rapport aux tendances actuelles his designs are out of step with the times/with contemporary trends b (= *déplacement*) move forward *ou* back; **il y a eu un ~ d'horaire/de date pour cette réunion** (*avance*) the time/date of this meeting has been brought forward; (*retard*) the time/date of this meeting has been put back c (*dans l'espace*) (= *avancée*) jutting out; (= *retrait*) standing back; (= *déplacement*) [*meuble, objet*] shifting forward *ou* back

décalaminage [dekalaminaʒ] NM decarbonization, decoking (*Brit*)

décalaminer [dekalamine] ▸conjug 1◂ VT to decarbonize, decoke (*Brit*)

décalcification [dekalsifikasjɔ̃] NF decalcification

décalcifier VT, **se décalcifier** VPR [dekalsifje] ▸conjug 7◂ to decalcify

décalcomanie [dekalkɔmani] NF transfer, decal; **faire des ~s** to do transfers

décaler [dekale] ▸conjug 1◂ 1 VT a [+ *horaire, départ, repas*] (= *avancer*) to bring *ou* move forward; (= *retarder*) to put back; **décalé d'une heure** (= *avancé*) brought *ou* moved forward an hour; (= *retardé*) put back an hour b [+ *pupitre, meuble*] (= *avancer*) to move *ou* shift forward; (= *reculer*) to move *ou* shift back; **décale le tableau (de 20 cm) vers la droite** move the picture (20 cm) to the right; **une série d'immeubles décalés par rapport aux autres** a row of buildings out of line with *ou* jutting out from the others; (*fig*) **il est complètement décalé par rapport à la réalité** he's completely out of touch with reality c (= *déséquilibrer*) [+ *meuble, objet*] **le buffet est décalé** the sideboard isn't straight 2 **se décaler** VPR [*rythme*] to go out of sync*; **décalez-vous d'un rang** move forward (*ou* back) a row; **décalez-vous d'une place** move up a seat

décalitre [dekalitʀ] NM decalitre (*Brit*), decaliter (*US*)

décalogue [dekalɔg] NM Decalogue

décalotter [dekalɔte] ▸conjug 1◂ VT (*gén*) to take the top off; (*Méd*) **~ le pénis** to pull back the foreskin

décalquer [dekalke] ▸conjug 1◂ VT (= *reproduire*) (*avec papier transparent*) to trace; (*par pression, à chaud*) to transfer; (*fig* = *imiter*) to copy

décamètre [dekamɛtʀ] NM decametre (*Brit*), decameter (*US*)

décamper* [dekɑ̃pe] ▸conjug 1◂ VI (= *déguerpir*) to clear out* *ou* off*; **décampez d'ici!** clear off!*, scram!*; **faire ~ qn** to chase sb out (**de** from)

décan [dekɑ̃] NM (*Astrol*) decan

décanal, e (*mpl* **-aux**) [dekanal, o] ADJ decanal

décanat [dekana] NM (= *dignité, durée*) deanship

décaniller* [dekanije] ▸conjug 1◂ VI (= *partir*) to clear out* *ou* off*, decamp*; **il nous a fait ~** he sent us packing* (**de** from)

décantation [dekɑ̃tasjɔ̃] NF [*liquide, vin*] settling (and decanting); **bassin de ~** settling *ou* sedimentation tank

décanter [dekɑ̃te] ▸conjug 1◂ 1 VT [+ *liquide, vin*] to settle, allow to settle (and decant); **il faut laisser ~ ce liquide pendant une nuit** this liquid must be allowed to settle overnight; (*fig*) **~ ses idées** to allow the dust to settle around one's ideas 2 **se décanter** VPR [*liquide, vin*] to settle; (*fig*) [*idées*] to become clear; **il faut laisser les choses se ~, après on verra** we'll have to let things clarify themselves *ou* we'll have to allow the dust to settle and then we'll see; **attendre que la situation se décante** to wait until the situation becomes clearer

---

décanteur [dekɑ̃tœʀ] NM [*station d'épuration*] settling *ou* sedimentation tank

décapage [dekapaʒ] NM (*gén*) cleaning, cleansing; (*à l'abrasif*) scouring; (*à l'acide*) pickling; (*à la brosse*) scrubbing; (*au papier de verre*) sanding; (*à la sableuse*) sandblasting; (*au chalumeau*) burning off; [*peinture*] stripping

décapant [dekapɑ̃] 1 ADJ [*produit*] abrasive, caustic; [*humour, critique*] scathing, caustic 2 NM (= *acide*) pickle, acid solution; (= *abrasif*) scouring agent, abrasive; (*pour peinture, vernis*) paint stripper

décaper [dekape] ▸conjug 1◂ VT (*gén*) to clean, cleanse; (*à l'abrasif*) to scour; (*à l'acide*) to pickle; (*à la brosse*) to scrub; (*au papier de verre*) to sand; (*à la sableuse*) to sandblast; (*au chalumeau*) to burn off; (= *enlever la peinture*) to strip; **décapez d'abord la surface pour enlever la rouille** first scrub the surface to remove the rust; * **un savon qui décape la peau** an abrasive soap; * **un humour qui décape** scathing *ou* caustic humour; * **ça décape!** it's strong stuff!

décapitation [dekapitasjɔ̃] NF [*personne*] beheading

décapiter [dekapite] ▸conjug 1◂ VT [+ *personne*] to behead; (*accidentellement*) to decapitate; [+ *arbre*] to top, cut the top off; **la police a décapité un réseau terroriste** the police have arrested the ringleaders of a terrorist network; **à la suite de l'attentat le parti s'est trouvé décapité** the party was left leaderless *ou* without a leader as a result of the attack

décapode [dekapɔd] NM decapod; **les ~s** the Decapoda

décapotable [dekapɔtabl] ADJ, NF (**voiture**) **~** convertible

décapoter [dekapɔte] ▸conjug 1◂ VT **~ une voiture** to put down the top *ou* roof (*Brit*) of a car

décapsuler [dekapsyle] ▸conjug 1◂ VT a [+ *bouteille*] to take the cap *ou* top off b (*Méd*) [+ *rein*] to decapsulate

décapsuleur [dekapsylœʀ] NM bottle-opener

décarcasser (se)* [dekaʀkase] ▸conjug 1◂ VPR to go to a lot of trouble (**pour faire** to do); **si tu veux des tickets, il faut que tu te décarcasses** if you want to get tickets, you'd better get a move on*

décarreler [dekaʀle] ▸conjug 4◂ VT to remove the tiles from

décarrer* [dekaʀe] ▸conjug 1◂ VI to split*, make tracks*, hit the road*

décasyllabe [dekasi(l)lab] 1 ADJ decasyllabic 2 NM decasyllable

décasyllabique [dekasi(l)labik] ADJ decasyllabic

décathlon [dekatlɔ̃] NM decathlon

décathlonien [dekatlɔnjɛ̃] NM decathlete

décati, e [dekati] ADJ (*péj*) [*vieillard*] decrepit; [*visage*] aged; [*beauté*] faded; [*immeuble, façade*] shabby-looking

décatir [dekatiʀ] ▸conjug 2◂ 1 VT [+ *étoffe*] to remove the gloss from 2 **se décatir** VPR [*personne*] to become decrepit

décavé, e [dekave] ADJ a (= *ruiné*) [*joueur*] ruined, cleaned out* (*attrib*); * [*banquier*] ruined b * (= *hâve*) [*visage*] haggard, drawn

▾ **décéder** [desede] ▸conjug 6◂ VI (*frm*) to die; **M. Leblanc, décédé le 14 mai** Mr Leblanc, who died on May 14th; **il est décédé depuis 20 ans** he died 20 years ago, he's been dead 20 years; **les biens des personnes décédées** the property of deceased persons *ou* of those who have died

décelable [des(ə)labl] ADJ detectable, discernible

déceler [des(ə)le] ▸conjug 5◂ VT a (= *repérer*) to detect; **on a décelé des traces de poison** traces of poison have been detected; **on peut**

~ dans ce poème l'influence germanique the Germanic influence can be discerned *ou* detected in this poem **b** (= *indiquer*) to indicate, reveal

décélération [deselerasjɔ̃] NF [*véhicule*] deceleration; **la ~ de la croissance économique** the slowdown in *ou* deceleration of economic growth

décélérer [deselere] ▸ conjug 1 ◂ VI [*véhicule*] to decelerate; [*investissements, rythme*] to slow down

décembre [desɑ̃bʀ] NM December; *pour locutions voir* **septembre**

décemment [desamɑ̃] ADV [*vivre, se nourrir*] decently, properly; [*se conduire*] decently; **je ne peux ~ pas accepter** it wouldn't be right for me *ou* proper of me to accept

décence [desɑ̃s] NF (= *bienséance*) decency, propriety; (= *réserve*) (sense of) decency; **il aurait pu avoir la ~ de ...** he could *ou* might have had the decency to ...

décennal, e (*mpl* **-aux**) [desenal, o] ADJ decennial

décennie [deseni] NF decade

décent, e [desɑ̃, ɑ̃t] ADJ (= *bienséant*) decent, proper; (= *discret, digne*) proper; (= *acceptable*) [*logement, salaire*] decent; [*prix*] reasonable, fair; **je vais mettre une robe pour être un peu plus ~e** I'm going to put on a dress to look a bit more decent; **il eût été plus ~ de refuser** it would have been more proper to refuse

décentrage [desɑ̃tʀaʒ] NM (*gén*) decentring (*Brit*), decentering (*US*); (*Opt*) decentration

décentralisateur, -trice [desɑ̃tʀalizatœʀ, tʀis] **1** ADJ decentralizing (*épith*), decentralization (*épith*) **2** NM,F advocate of decentralization

décentralisation [desɑ̃tʀalizasjɔ̃] NF decentralization

décentraliser [desɑ̃tʀalize] ▸ conjug 1 ◂ **1** VT [+ *administration, décisions*] to decentralize **2** se **décentraliser** VPR [*usine*] to be decentralized

décentration [desɑ̃tʀasjɔ̃] NF, **décentrement** [desɑ̃tʀəmɑ̃] NM (*Opt*) decentration; (= *action*) decentring (*Brit*), decentering (*US*), throwing off centre

décentrer [desɑ̃tʀe] ▸ conjug 1 ◂ **1** VT to decentre (*Brit*), decenter (*US*), throw off centre **2** se **décentrer** VPR to move off centre

déception [desɛpsjɔ̃] NF disappointment, let-down; **~ sentimentale** unhappy love affair; **j'ai eu la ~ de voir que ...** I was disappointed to see that ...

décérébration [deseʀebʀasjɔ̃] NF (*Physiol*) decerebration

décérébrer [deseʀebʀe] ▸ conjug 6 ◂ VT (*lit*) to decerebrate; (*fig*) to make moronic

décernement [desɛʀnəmɑ̃] NM awarding

décerner [desɛʀne] ▸ conjug 1 ◂ VT **a** [+ *prix, récompense*] to give, award; [+ *titre*] to award **b** (*Jur*) [+ *mandat d'arrêt, de dépôt*] to issue

décervelage [desɛʀvəlaʒ] NM (= *abrutissement*) making moronic; (= *lavage de cerveau*) brainwashing; **l'entreprise de ~ menée par la télévision** the way television turns people into morons

décerveler [desɛʀvəle] ▸ conjug 4 ◂ VT (= *abrutir*) to make moronic; (= *laver le cerveau de*) to brainwash; **machine à ~** (*allusion littéraire*) debraining machine; (*péj*) propaganda machine

▾ décès [desɛ] NM death, decease (*frm*); **« fermé pour cause de ~ »** "closed owing to bereavement" → **acte**

décevant, e [des(ə)vɑ̃, ɑ̃t] ADJ disappointing

décevoir [des(ə)vwaʀ] ▸ conjug 28 ◂ VT **~ qn** to disappoint sb, let sb down; **je ne veux pas ~ vos espoirs** I don't want to dash your hopes

déchaîné, e [deʃene] (*ptp de* **déchaîner**) ADJ [*flots, éléments*] raging; [*passion*] unbridled;

raging; [*personne*] wild; [*foule*] raging, wild; [*opinion publique*] furious; **il est ~ contre moi** he is furious with me

déchaînement [deʃenmɑ̃] NM **a** [*fureur, passions, haine*] outburst, explosion; **l'événement a provoqué un ~ de violence** the incident triggered an outburst of violence **b** (= *colère, violence*) (raging) fury; **un tel ~ contre son fils** such an outburst of fury at his son; **les ~s des médias/du public contre la réforme** angry outbursts from the media/the public against the reform

déchaîner [deʃene] ▸ conjug 1 ◂ **1** VT **a** [+ *tempête, violence, passions, colère*] to unleash; [+ *enthousiasme*] to arouse; [+ *opinion publique*] to rouse; **~ l'hilarité générale** to cause great *ou* much hilarity; **~ les huées/les cris/les rires** to raise a storm of booing/shouting/laughter; **les critiques** to unleash a barrage of criticism **b** [+ *chien*] to unchain, let loose **2** se **déchaîner** VPR [*fureur, passions*] to explode; [*personne*] to fly into a rage; [*foule*] to go wild; **il s'est déchaîné contre elle** he blew up at her *ou* let fly at her; **la presse se déchaîna contre lui/cette décision** the press railed against him/the decision; **la tempête se déchaînait** the storm was raging furiously

déchant [deʃɑ̃] NM (*Mus*) descant

déchanter [deʃɑ̃te] ▸ conjug 1 ◂ VI to become disillusioned *ou* disenchanted; **il commence à ~** he is becoming (somewhat) disillusioned *ou* disenchanted

décharge [deʃaʀʒ] NF **a** (*Élec*) **~ (électrique)** electrical discharge; **il a pris une ~ (électrique) dans les doigts** he got an electric shock in his fingers; (*Physiol*) **~ d'adrénaline** rush of adrenalin; (*Psych*) **~ émotionnelle** emotional release **b** (= *salve*) volley of shots, salvo; **on entendit le bruit de plusieurs ~s** a volley of shots was heard; **il a reçu une ~ de chevrotines dans le dos** he was hit in the back by a volley of buckshot **c** (*Jur*) discharge; (*Comm* = *reçu*) receipt; (*Hôpital*) (= *action*) discharge; (= *document*) discharge form; (*Scol*) **~ (de service)** reduction in teaching load; **je vais signer la ~ pour ce colis** I'll sign the receipt for this parcel; (*fig*) **il faut dire à sa ~ que ...** it must be said in his defence that ... → **témoin d** (= *dépôt*) **~ (publique** *ou* **municipale)** rubbish tip *ou* dump (*Brit*), garbage dump (*US*); **la mise en ~ des déchets toxiques** the dumping of toxic waste → **sauvage e** (*Typo*) offset sheet **f** (*Archit*) **voûte/arc de ~** relieving *ou* discharging vault/arch

déchargement [deʃaʀʒəmɑ̃] NM [*cargaison, véhicule, arme*] unloading; **commencer le ~ d'un véhicule** to start unloading a vehicle

décharger [deʃaʀʒe] ▸ conjug 3 ◂ **1** VT **a** [+ *véhicule, animal*] to unload; [+ *bagages, marchandises*] to unload (**de** from); **je vais vous ~: donnez-moi vos sacs/votre manteau** let me take your bags/your coat off you **b** (= *soulager*) [+ *conscience, cœur*] to unburden, disburden (**auprès de** to); **~ sa colère** *ou* **bile** (*littér*) to vent one's anger *ou* spleen (**sur qn** (up)on sb) **c** (*Jur*) **~ un accusé** to discharge an accused person **d** **~ qn de** [+ *dette*] to release sb from; [+ *impôt*] to exempt sb from; [+ *responsabilité, fonction, tâche*] to relieve sb of *ou* from; **le juge a demandé à être déchargé du dossier** the judge asked to be taken off the case **e** [+ *arme*] (= *enlever le chargeur*) to unload; (= *tirer*) to discharge, fire; **il déchargea son revolver sur la foule** he emptied his revolver into the crowd **f** (*Élec*) to discharge **g** (*Tech*) [+ *bassin*] to drain off the excess

from; [+ *support, étai*] to take the load *ou* weight off **2** VI **a** [*tissu*] to lose its colour **b** ‡ (= *éjaculer*) to come‡, shoot one's load‡ **3** se **décharger** VPR **a** (*Élec*) [*pile, batterie*] to run down, go flat **b** se **~ de** [+ *responsabilité, problème*] to offload, pass off (**sur qn** onto sb); **il s'est déchargé sur moi du soin de prévenir sa mère** he offloaded the job of telling his mother onto me **c** (= *être expulsé*) **l'excès de vapeur d'eau se décharge dans l'atmosphère** excess steam is released into the atmosphere

décharné, e [deʃaʀne] (*ptp de* **décharner**) ADJ [*corps, membre*] all skin and bone (*attrib*), emaciated; [*doigts*] bony, fleshless; [*visage*] fleshless, emaciated; [*squelette*] fleshless; (*fig*) [*paysage*] bare; [*style*] bald

décharner [deʃaʀne] ▸ conjug 1 ◂ VT (= *amaigrir*) to emaciate; **cette maladie l'a complètement décharné** this illness has left him completely emaciated

déchaussé, e [deʃose] (*ptp de* **déchausser**) ADJ [*personne*] barefoot(ed); [*pied*] bare; [*carmélite*] discalced (*frm*); [*dent, pavé*] loose; [*mur*] exposed

déchaussement [deʃosmɑ̃] NM [*dent*] loosening

déchausser [deʃose] ▸ conjug 1 ◂ **1** VT [+ *arbre*] to expose the roots of; [+ *mur*] to lay bare the foundations of; **~ un enfant** to take a child's shoes off; **~ ses skis** to take one's skis off **2** VI (*Ski*) to lose one's skis **3** se **déchausser** VPR [*personne*] to take one's shoes off; [*skieur*] to take one's skis off; [*dents*] to come *ou* work loose

dèche‡ [deʃ] NF **on est dans la ~** ◇ **c'est la ~** we're flat broke*

déchéance [deʃeɑ̃s] NF **a** (*morale*) decay, decline; (*physique*) degeneration; (*intellectuelle*) intellectual decline *ou* degeneration; (*Rel*) fall; (*civilisation*) decline, decay **b** (*Pol*) [*souverain*] deposition, dethronement; (*Jur*) **~ de l'autorité parentale** loss of parental rights **c** (*Fin*) **remboursement par ~ du terme** repayment by acceleration

déchet [deʃɛ] **1** NM **a** (= *reste*) [*viande, tissu, métal*] scrap **b** (*gén, Comm* = *perte*) waste, loss; **il y a du ~** (*dans une marchandise*) there is some waste *ou* wastage; (*dans un examen*) there are (some) failures, there is some wastage (of students) (*Brit*); (*viande*) there's a lot of waste; **~ de route** loss in transit **c** (*péj*) (= *raté*) failure, wash-out*, dead loss*; (= *épave*) wreck, dead-beat*; **les ~s de l'humanité** the dregs *ou* scum of the earth **2** **déchets** NMPL (= *restes, résidus*) [*viande, métal, tissu*] scraps; (= *épluchures*) peelings; (= *ordures*) waste (*NonC*), refuse (*NonC*), rubbish (*NonC*) (*Brit*); (*Physiol*) waste (*NonC*); **~s domestiques/industriels** household/industrial waste *ou* wastes (*US*); **~s nucléaires/radioactifs/toxiques** nuclear/radioactive/toxic waste

déchetterie® [deʃɛtʀi] NF waste collection centre *ou* site

déchiffonner [deʃifɔne] ▸ conjug 1 ◂ VT to smooth out, uncrease; **sa robe s'est déchiffonnée toute seule** the creases have come out of her dress (on their own)

déchiffrable [deʃifʀabl] ADJ [*message, écriture*] decipherable; [*code*] decodable, decipherable

déchiffrage [deʃifʀaʒ], **déchiffrement** [deʃifʀəmɑ̃] NM [*message, hiéroglyphe*] deciphering; [*code*] decoding; [*code-barres*] scanning; [*écriture*] deciphering; (*Mus*) sight-reading

déchiffrer [deʃifʀe] ▸ conjug 1 ◂ VT [+ *message, hiéroglyphe*] to decipher; [+ *code*] to decode; [+ *code-barres*] to scan; [+ *écriture*] to make out, decipher; (*Mus*) to sight-read; [+ *énigme*] to unravel, fathom; [+ *avenir*] to read; [+ *sentiment*] to read, make out

déchiffreur, -euse [deʃifʀœʀ, øz] NM,F [*code*] decoder; [*inscriptions, message*] decipherer

déchiqueté, e [deʃikte] ADJ (*ptp de* **déchiqueter**) [*montagne, relief, côte*] jagged, ragged; [*feuille*] jagged(-edged); [*corps*] mutilated

déchiqueter [deʃikte] ▶conjug 4◀ VT [+ *papier, tissu*] to tear to pieces *ou* shreds; [+ *viande, victime*] to pull *ou* tear to pieces; **elle a été déchiquetée par le train/l'explosion** she was mangled by the train/blown to pieces by the explosion; **déchiqueté par un lion** mauled *ou* savaged by a lion

déchiqueteur [deʃiktœʀ] NM, **déchiqueteuse** [deʃik(ə)tøz] NF (= *machine*) shredder

déchiqueture [deʃik(ə)tyʀ] NF [*tissu*] slash; [*feuille*] notch; **~s** [*côte, montagne*] jagged *ou* ragged outline

déchirant, e [deʃiʀɑ̃, ɑ̃t] ADJ [*drame*] heartbreaking, heartrending; [*cri, spectacle*] heartrending, harrowing; [*douleur*] agonizing, searing; [*adieux*] heartbreaking

déchirement [deʃiʀmɑ̃] NM a [*tissu*] tearing, ripping; [*muscle, tendon*] tearing b (= *peine*) wrench, heartbreak; **pour lui, l'exil fut un véritable ~** exile was a heartrending experience for him c **~s** (= *divisions*) rifts, splits

déchirer [deʃiʀe] ▶conjug 1◀ 1 VT a (= *mettre en morceaux*) [+ *papier, lettre*] to tear up, tear to pieces; (= *faire un accroc à*) [+ *vêtement*] to tear, rip; (= *arracher*) [+ *page*] to tear out (**de** from); (= *ouvrir*) [+ *sac, enveloppe*] to tear open; [+ *bande de protection*] to tear off; (= *mutiler*) [+ *corps*] to tear to pieces; **~ un papier/tissu en deux** to tear a piece of paper/cloth in two *ou* in half

b (*fig*) **leurs cris déchirèrent l'air/le silence** their cries rent the air/pierced the silence; **ce bruit me déchire les oreilles** that noise is ear-splitting; **la toux lui déchirait la poitrine** his chest was racked by a terrible cough; **un spectacle qui déchire (le cœur)** a heartrending *ou* harrowing sight; **elle est déchirée par le remords/la douleur** she is torn by remorse/racked by pain; **les dissensions continuent à ~ le pays** the country continues to be torn (apart) by dissension, dissension is still tearing the country apart; **~ qn à belles dents** to tear *ou* pull sb to pieces

2 **se déchirer** VPR a [*vêtement*] to tear, rip; [*sac*] to burst; **attention, tu vas te ~*** be careful, you'll tear your clothes; **se ~ un muscle** to tear a muscle; **se ~ les mains** to graze *ou* skin one's hands; **le brouillard s'est déchiré** the fog has broken up; **son cœur se déchira** his heart broke; **le pays se déchira en deux camps** the country was split into two camps

b [*personnes*] **ils ne cessent de se ~** they are constantly tearing each other apart

déchirure [deʃiʀyʀ] NF [*tissu*] tear, rip, rent; [*ciel*] break *ou* gap in the clouds; **~ musculaire** torn muscle; **se faire une ~ musculaire** to tear a muscle; **le chômage fait planer la menace d'une ~ sociale** unemployment threatens to rip society *ou* the social fabric apart

déchoir [deʃwaʀ] ▶conjug 25◀ (*frm*) 1 VI a [*personne*] to lower o.s., demean o.s.; **ce serait ~ que d'accepter** you would be lowering *ou* demeaning yourself if you accepted; **~ de son rang** to fall from rank b [*réputation, influence*] to decline, wane 2 VT **~ qn de sa nationalité/son titre** to strip *ou* deprive sb of their nationality/title; **être déchu de ses droits** to be deprived of one's rights

déchristianisation [dekʀistjanizasjɔ̃] NF dechristianization

déchristianiser [dekʀistjanize] ▶conjug 1◀ 1 VT to dechristianize 2 **se déchristianiser** VPR to become dechristianized

déchu, e [deʃy] ADJ (*ptp de* **déchoir**) [*roi*] de-

---

posed, dethroned; [*président, champion*] deposed; (*Rel*) [*ange, humanité*] fallen

déci [desi] NM (*Helv*) ≈ glass of wine (*containing one decilitre*)

décibel [desibɛl] NM decibel

décidé, e [deside] (*ptp de* **décider**) ADJ a (= *résolu, volontaire*) [*air, ton*] determined, decided; [*personne*] determined; (= *net, marqué*) [*goût*] decided, definite; **maintenant je suis ~** now I have made up my mind; **il est bien ~ à agir** he is determined to act; **il est ~ à tout** he is prepared to do anything; **il était ~ à ce que ça change** he was determined that this should change; **j'y suis tout à fait ~** I am quite determined (to do it); **les mesures sont ~es en comité** the measures are decided in committee b (= *fixé*) [*question*] settled, decided; **bon, c'est ~** right, that's settled *ou* decided (then); **c'est une chose ~e** the matter is settled

décidément [desidemɑ̃] ADV (= *en fait*) certainly, undoubtedly, indeed; **oui, c'est ~ une question de chance** yes, it is certainly *ou* undoubtedly *ou* indeed a matter of luck; (*intensif*) **~, je perds toujours mes affaires !** I'm ALWAYS losing my things!; **~, tu m'ennuies aujourd'hui** you're really annoying me today, you ARE annoying me today; **~, il est fou** he's really crazy, there's no doubt about it — he's crazy

▼ **décider** [deside] ▶conjug 1◀ 1 VT a [*personne*] (= *déterminer, établir*) **~ qch** to decide on sth; **~ que** to decide that; **~ de faire qch** to decide to do sth; **comment ~ qui a raison ?** how is one to decide who is right?; **elle décida qu'elle devait démissionner** she decided *ou* came to the decision that she must resign; **ils ont décidé la grève/de faire grève/de ne pas faire grève** they decided on a strike/to go on strike/against a strike *ou* not to go on strike; **c'est à lui de ~** it's up to him to decide; **c'est souvent lui qui décide pour les autres** he often decides for the others

b (= *persuader*) [*personne*] to persuade; [*conseil, événement*] to decide, convince; **~ qn à faire qch** to persuade *ou* induce sb to do sth; **c'est moi qui l'ai décidé à ce voyage** I'm the one who persuaded *ou* induced him to go on this trip; **la bonne publicité décide les clients éventuels** good advertising wins over potential customers

c [*chose*] (= *provoquer*) to cause, bring about; **ces scandales ont finalement décidé son renvoi** these scandals finally brought about *ou* caused his dismissal

2 **décider de** VT INDIR (= *être l'arbitre de*) to decide; (= *déterminer*) to decide, determine; **~ de l'importance/de l'urgence de qch** to decide on the *ou* as to the importance/urgency of sth, decide how important/urgent sth is; **les résultats de son examen décideront de sa carrière** the results of his exam will decide *ou* determine his career; **le sort en a décidé autrement** fate has decided *ou* ordained *ou* decreed otherwise; **ainsi en a décidé le gouvernement** this was the decision the government reached

3 **se décider** VPR a [*personne*] to come to *ou* make a decision, make up one's mind; **se ~ à qch** to decide on sth; **se ~ à faire qch** to make up one's mind to do sth, make the decision to do sth; **je ne peux pas me ~ à lui mentir** I cannot bring myself to lie to him; **se ~ pour qch** to decide on sth *ou* in favour of sth; **allez, décide-toi !** come on, make up your mind!

b [*problème, affaire*] to be decided *ou* settled *ou* resolved; **la question se décide aujourd'hui** the question is being decided *ou* settled *ou* resolved today; **leur départ s'est décidé très vite** they very quickly decided to leave

c * **est-ce qu'il va se ~ à faire beau ?** do you think it'll turn out fine after all?; **ça ne veut pas se ~** it won't make up its mind*; **la voitu-**

---

re ne se décide pas à partir the car just won't start

décideur, -euse [desidœʀ, øz] NM,F decision-maker; **avoir un rôle de ~** to have a decision-making role

décidu, e [desidy] ADJ [*forêt*] deciduous

décigramme [desigʀam] NM decigram(me)

décilitre [desilitʀ] NM decilitre (*Brit*), deciliter (*US*)

décimal, e [mpl -aux] [desimal, o] 1 ADJ decimal 2 **décimale** NF decimal place; **nombre à quatre ~es** number given to four decimal places; **jusqu'à la deuxième/troisième ~e** to two/three decimal places

décimalisation [desimalizasjɔ̃] NF decimalization

décimation [desimasjɔ̃] NF decimation

décimer [desime] ▶conjug 1◀ VT to decimate

décimètre [desimɛtʀ] NM decimetre (*Brit*), decimeter (*US*)

décisif, -ive [desizif, iv] ADJ [*argument, combat*] decisive, conclusive; [*intervention, influence*] decisive; [*preuve*] conclusive; [*moment, rôle*] decisive, critical; [*ton*] decisive, authoritative; **tournant** ≈ watershed; **le facteur ~** the deciding factor; **porter un coup ~ au terrorisme** to deal terrorism a decisive blow → **jeu**

décision [desizjɔ̃] NF a (= *choix*) decision; **prendre une ~** to take *ou* make a decision; **prendre la ~ de faire qch** to take *ou* make the decision to do sth; **il n'a pas encore pris sa ~** he hasn't yet made his decision; **le processus de prise de ~ dans l'entreprise** the decision-making process in the company; **parvenir à une ~** to come to *ou* reach a decision; **la ~ t'appartient** it's your decision, it's for you to decide; **soumettre qch à la ~ de qn** to ask sb to make a decision about sth → **pouvoir²**

b (= *verdict*) decision; **~ administrative/gouvernementale** administrative/government decision; **par ~ judiciaire** *ou* **de justice** by court order; **nommé à un poste de ~** appointed to a decision-making job; **organe de ~** decision-making body; **faire la ~** (*Sport*) to win the match; **leurs trois voix ont fait la ~** their three votes swung the result

c (= *qualité*) decision, decisiveness; **montrer de la ~** to be decisive; **avoir l'esprit de ~** to be decisive

décisionnaire [desizjɔnɛʀ] 1 ADJ [*organisme, pouvoir*] decision-making (*épith*) 2 NMF decision-maker

décisionnel, -elle [desizjɔnɛl] ADJ [*rôle, responsabilité*] decision-making (*épith*)

déclamateur, -trice [deklamatœʀ, tʀis] (*péj*) 1 ADJ ranting, declamatory 2 NM,F ranter, declaimer

déclamation [deklamasjɔ̃] NF (= *art*) declamation (*NonC*); (*péj*) ranting (*NonC*), spouting (*NonC*); **toutes leurs belles ~s** all their ranting

déclamatoire [deklamatwaʀ] ADJ a (*péj*) [*ton*] ranting, bombastic, declamatory; [*style*] bombastic, turgid b [*rythme*] declamatory

déclamer [deklame] ▶conjug 1◀ 1 VT to declaim; (*péj*) to spout 2 VI (*péj*) to rant; (*littér*) **~ contre** to inveigh *ou* rail against

déclarable [deklaʀabl] ADJ [*marchandise*] declarable, dutiable; [*revenus*] declarable

déclarant, e [deklaʀɑ̃, ɑ̃t] NM,F (*Jur*) informant

déclaratif, -ive [deklaʀatif, iv] ADJ (*Jur*) declaratory; (*Ling, Ordin*) declarative

déclaration [deklaʀasjɔ̃] NF a (= *manifeste, proclamation, Ordin*) declaration; (= *discours, commentaire*) statement; (= *aveu*) admission; (= *révélation*) revelation; **dans une ~ télévisée** in a televised statement; **le ministre n'a fait aucune ~** the minister did not make a statement; **je n'ai aucune ~ à faire** I have no comment to make; **selon sa propre ~, il était ivre** by his own admission he was drunk; **Déclara-**

tion (universelle) des droits de l'homme (Universal) Declaration of Human Rights; (*Hist US*) **Déclaration d'indépendance** Declaration of Independence; **~ d'intention** declaration of intent; **~ de principe** statement *ou* declaration of principle [b] (*amoureuse*) **~ (d'amour)** declaration of love; **faire une** *ou* **sa ~ à qn** to make a declaration of love to sb, declare one's love to sb [c] (*Admin, Jur*) [*naissance, décès*] registration, notification; [*vol, perte, changement de domicile*] notification; **envoyer une ~ de changement de domicile** to send notification of change of address; **faire une ~ d'accident** (*à l'assurance*) to file an accident claim; (*à la police*) to report an accident; **~ en douane** customs declaration; **~ de faillite** declaration of bankruptcy; **~ de guerre** declaration of war; **~ d'impôts** *ou* **de revenus** tax declaration; (*formulaire*) tax return (form); **faire sa ~ d'impôts** to fill in one's tax return (form); **~ d'utilité publique** public notice → IMPÔTS

---

déclaratoire [deklaRatwaR] ADJ (*Jur*) declaratory

déclaré, e [deklaRe] (*ptp de* **déclarer**) ADJ [*opinion*] professed; [*athée, révolutionnaire*] declared, self-confessed; [*ennemi*] sworn, avowed; [*intention*] avowed, declared; [*travailleur*] registered, declared; **revenus non ~s** undeclared income

déclarer [deklaRe] ▶conjug 1◀ [1] VT [a] (= *annoncer*) to announce, state, declare; (= *proclamer*) to declare; (= *avouer*) to admit, confess to; **«c'est un moment historique », déclara le ministre** "it's an historic moment", the minister declared; **~ son amour (à qn)** to declare one's love to sb, make a declaration of love (to sb); **~ la guerre à une nation/à la pollution** to declare war on a nation/on pollution; **le président déclara la séance levée** the chairman declared the meeting closed; **~ qn coupable/innocent** to find sb guilty/innocent
[b] **~ que ...** to declare *ou* say that ...; **je vous déclare que je n'y crois pas** I tell you I don't believe it; **ils ont déclaré que nous avions menti** they claimed that we had lied
[c] (*Admin*) [+ *marchandises, revenus, employés*] to declare; [+ *naissance, décès*] to register, notify; **le père doit aller ~ l'enfant à la mairie** the father has to go and register the child at the town hall; **~ qn en faillite** to declare sb bankrupt; (*Douane*) **avez-vous quelque chose à ~ ?** do you have anything to declare?; **~ qch au-dessus/au-dessous de sa valeur** to overvalue/undervalue sth; **rien à ~** nothing to declare

[2] **se déclarer** VPR [a] (= *se prononcer*) to declare *ou* state one's opinion; **se ~ en faveur de qch** to declare o.s. *ou* profess o.s. in favour of sth; **se ~ pour/contre qch** to come out in favour of/against sth; **il s'est déclaré l'auteur de ces poèmes/crimes** he stated that he had written the poems/committed the crimes; **se ~ satisfait** to declare o.s. satisfied; **il s'est déclaré prêt à signer ce document** he said he was ready *ou* declared himself ready to sign the document; (*Jur*) **se ~ incompétent** to decline a jurisdiction

[b] (= *apparaître*) [*incendie, épidémie*] to break out
[c] [*amoureux*] to make a declaration of one's love, declare *ou* avow (*littér*) one's love

déclassé, e [deklase] (*ptp de* **déclasser**) ADJ [a] [*coureur*] relegated (*in the placing*); [*hôtel, restaurant, vin*] downgraded; (*Bourse*) **valeurs ~es** displaced stocks *ou* securities [b] [*fiche, livre*] out of order (*attrib*)

déclassement [deklasmã] NM [a] (*social, dans une hiérarchie*) fall *ou* drop in status [b] (*Sport*) [*coureur*] relegation (*in the placing*); (*Rail*) [*voyageur*] change of class; (*Admin*) [*hôtel*] downgrading; [*monument*] delisting; (*Bourse*) [*valeur*] displacement [c] [*fiches, livres*] **pour éviter le ~** to stop things getting out of order

déclasser [deklase] ▶conjug 1◀ VT [a] (*socialement, dans une hiérarchie*) to lower in status; **il estimait qu'on l'avait déclassé en le mettant dans l'équipe B** he felt that he had suffered a drop in status *ou* that he had been downgraded by being put in the B team; **il se déclassait par de telles fréquentations** he was lowering himself socially *ou* demeaning himself by keeping such company [b] (= *rétrograder*) (*Sport*) [+ *coureur*] to relegate (*in the placing*); (*Rail*) [+ *voyageur*] to put in second class; (*Admin*) [+ *hôtel*] to downgrade; [+ *monument*] to delist; (*Bourse*) [+ *valeur*] to displace [c] (= *déranger*) [+ *fiches, livres*] to get out of order, put back in the wrong order

déclenchement [deklãʃmã] NM [a] (= *actionnement*) [*ressort, mécanisme*] release; [*sonnerie, alarme*] setting off, activating [b] (= *provocation*) [*insurrection*] launching, starting; [*catastrophe, guerre, crise, grève, processus, polémique*] triggering *ou* sparking off; [*accouchement*] inducement; **le rôle du psychisme dans le ~ de certaines maladies** the role of psychological factors in triggering certain illnesses [c] (*Mil*) [*tir*] opening; [*attaque*] launching

déclencher [deklãʃe] ▶conjug 1◀ [1] VT [a] (= *actionner*) [+ *ressort, mécanisme*] to release; [+ *sonnerie, alarme*] to set off, activate; **ce bouton déclenche l'ouverture/la fermeture de la porte** this button opens/closes the door; (*Photo*) **faire la mise au point avant de ~** to focus before releasing the shutter
[b] (= *provoquer*) [+ *insurrection*] to launch, start; [+ *catastrophe, guerre, crise, processus, polémique*] to trigger *ou* spark off; [+ *accouchement*] to induce; **c'est ce mot qui a tout déclenché** this is the word which triggered everything off; **~ une grève** [*meneur*] to launch *ou* start a strike; [*incident*] to trigger *ou* spark off a strike; **ça m'a déclenché une sciatique** it gave me sciatica; **quand je me penche ça me déclenche une douleur dans le dos** when I bend down my back hurts *ou* I get backache
[c] (*Mil*) [+ *tir*] to open; [+ *attaque*] to launch; **~ l'offensive** to launch the offensive

[2] **se déclencher** VPR [*ressort, mécanisme*] to release itself; [*sonnerie, alarme*] to go off; [*attaque, grève*] to start, begin; [*catastrophe, crise, réaction nerveuse*] to be triggered off

déclencheur [deklãʃœR] NM (*Tech*) release mechanism; (*Photo*) shutter release; **~ souple** cable release; **~ automatique** *ou* **à retardement** self-timer; **cet incident a servi de ~ à la crise** this incident sparked off *ou* triggered (off) the crisis

déclic [deklik] NM (= *bruit*) click; (= *mécanisme*) trigger mechanism; (*mentalement*) **ça a été le ~** it triggered something off in my (*ou* his *etc*) mind

déclin [deklɛ̃] NM [a] (*gén*) decline; [*malade, santé, vue*] deterioration; [*talent, forces, beauté, sentiment*] waning, fading; **~ de la production/de l'activité économique** decline in production/in economic activity; **le ~ du parti** the party's decline, the decline of the party; **le ~ du jour** the close of day; (*littér*) **au ~ de la vie** in the twilight years (*littér*); **~ démographique** population decline [b] (*loc*) **être à son ~** [*soleil*] to be setting; [*lune*] to be on the wane, be waning; **être sur le** *ou* **son ~** [*malade*] to be going downhill; [*acteur, homme politique*] to be on the decline *ou* on the wane; **être en ~** [*talent, prestige*] to be on the decline *ou* on the wane; [*forces, intelligence, civilisation, art*] to be in decline *ou* on the wane; [*marché, secteur*] to be in decline; **marché/industrie en ~** declining market/industry

déclinable [deklinabl] ADJ [a] (*Gram*) declinable [b] (= *adaptable*) **ce produit est facilement ~** it's easy to develop a whole range from this product; **coupe de cheveux ~ en trois longueurs** hairstyle that can be adapted to three different lengths of hair

déclinaison [deklinɛzɔ̃] NF (*Ling*) declension; (*Astron, Phys*) declination

déclinant, e [deklinã, ãt] ADJ [*pouvoir*] declining; [*santé*] declining, deteriorating; [*vue*] failing; [*prestige, popularité, forces*] waning, declining; [*beauté, sentiment*] fading

déclinatoire [deklinatwaR] NM [a] (= *boussole*) surveyor's compass [b] (*Jur*) **~ (de compétence)** (*gén*) challenge to jurisdiction; (*fait par le tribunal*) declining *ou* denial of jurisdiction

décliner [dekline] ▶conjug 1◀ [1] VT [a] (*frm* = *refuser*) [+ *offre, invitation, honneur*] to decline, turn down, refuse; **la direction décline toute responsabilité en cas de perte ou de vol** the management accepts no responsibility *ou* refuses to accept responsibility for loss or theft of articles; (*Jur*) **~ la compétence de qn/la compétence d'une juridiction** to refuse to recognize sb's competence/the competence of a court
[b] (*Ling*) to decline; **ce mot ne se décline pas** this word does not decline
[c] (*frm* = *réciter*) **~ son identité** to give one's personal particulars; **déclinez vos nom, prénoms, titres et qualités** state your name, forenames, qualifications and status
[d] (*Comm*) [+ *produit*] to offer in a variety of forms; **un rouge à lèvres décliné en cinq nuances** a lipstick available in *ou* that comes in five shades

[2] VI [a] (= *s'affaiblir*) to decline; [*malade, santé, vue*] to deteriorate, go downhill; [*talent, forces, beauté, sentiment*] to wane, fade; [*prestige, popularité*] to wane, fall off; [*production, ventes*] to fall, be on the decline; [*marché, secteur*] to be on the decline; **le revenu par habitant décline** per capita income is falling
[b] [*jour*] to draw to a close; [*soleil*] to be setting, go down; [*lune*] to wane, be on the wane; (*Tech*) [*aiguille aimantée*] to deviate

[3] **se décliner** VPR (*Comm*) [*produit*] to come in a variety of forms; **ce yaourt se décline en trois saveurs** this yoghurt is available in *ou* comes in three flavours

déclive [dekliv] ADJ [*terrain*] inclined

déclivité [deklivite] NF slope, incline, declivity (*frm*)

décloisonnement [deklwazɔnmã] NM decompartmentalization

décloisonner [deklwazɔne] ▶conjug 1◀ VT to decompartmentalize

déclouer [deklue] ▶conjug 1◀ VT [+ *caisse*] to open; [+ *planche*] to remove

déco [deko] [1] ADJ INV (ABRÉV = **décoratif**) → **art** [2] NF* (ABRÉV = **décoration**) **j'ai refait la ~ de ma chambre** I've redecorated my bedroom

décocher [dekɔʃe] ▶conjug 1◀ VT [a] [+ *flèche*] to shoot, fire; [+ *coup de pied*] to give, deliver; [+ *coup de poing*] to throw; [+ *ruade*] to let fly [b] [+ *œillade, regard*] to shoot, flash, dart; [+ *sourire*] to flash; [+ *remarque*] to fire, let fly

décoction [dekɔksjɔ̃] NF decoction

décodage [dekɔdaʒ] NM [*code*] decoding, cracking; (*TV, Ordin, Ling*) decoding; [*message*] deciphering; **système de ~ numérique** digital decoding system

décoder [dekɔde] ▸ conjug 1 ◂ VT [+ *code*] to decode, break; (*TV, Ordin, Ling*) to decode; [+ *message*] to decipher; (= *comprendre*) [+ *poème, comportement*] to understand

décodeur [dekɔdœʀ] NM [*code*] (*TV, Ordin, Ling*) decoder; [*message*] decipherer

décoffrage [dekɔfʀaʒ] NM (*Constr*) removal of the formwork → **brut**

décoffrer [dekɔfʀe] ▸ conjug 1 ◂ VT (*Constr*) to remove the formwork from

décoiffer [dekwafe] ▸ conjug 1 ◂ VT **a** (= *ébouriffer*) **~ qn** to mess up sb's hair; **il s'est/le vent l'a décoiffé** he/the wind has disarranged *ou* messed up his hair; **je suis toute décoiffée** my hair is in a mess *ou* is (all) messed up; (*fig*) **ça décoiffe!*** it really takes your breath away! **b** (= *ôter le chapeau*) **~ qn** to take sb's hat off; **il se décoiffa** he took his hat off **c** (*Tech*) [+ *obus*] to uncap

décoincement [dekwɛ̃smɑ̃] NM (*gén*) unjamming, loosening (**de** of); (*Tech*) removal of the wedge (**de** from)

décoincer [dekwɛ̃se] ▸ conjug 3 ◂ **1** VT (*gén*) to unjam, loosen; (*Tech*) **~ qn** to remove the wedge from sth; **~ qn*** to help sb to shake off their hang-ups* **2** **se décoincer** VPR [*objet*] to come loose; * [*personne*] to shake off one's hang-ups*

décolérer [dekɔleʀe] ▸ conjug 6 ◂ VI **ne jamais ~** to be always in a temper; **il ne décolère pas depuis hier** he hasn't calmed down since yesterday, he's still angry from yesterday

décollage [dekɔlaʒ] NM **a** [*avion*] takeoff; [*fusée*] lift-off; **au ~** at take off, at lift-off; **depuis le ~ économique de la région** since the region's economy took off; **le ~ de l'informatique n'a pas été facile** information technology had difficulty getting off the ground **b** [*timbre*] unsticking; [*papier peint*] stripping, peeling off

décollation [dekɔlasjɔ̃] NF decapitation, beheading

décollectivisation [dekɔlɛktivizasjɔ̃] NF [*agriculture, économie*] decollectivization

décollement [dekɔlmɑ̃] NM [*timbre*] unsticking; (*Méd*) [*rétine*] detachment; (*Coiffure*) **se faire faire un ~ de racines** to have one's hair volumized

décoller [dekɔle] ▸ conjug 1 ◂ **1** VT **a** (*gén*) to unstick; (*en trempant*) [+ *timbre*] to soak off; (*à la vapeur*) [+ *timbre*] to steam off; [+ *lettre*] to steam open; [+ *papier peint*] to steam off; **~ qn de*** [+ *livre, télévision*] to drag sb away from **b** * (= *se débarrasser de*) [+ *créanciers, poursuivants*] to shake off, get rid of; **je ne suis pas arrivé à m'en ~!** *ou* **le ~!** I couldn't manage to shake him off! *ou* get rid of him! **2** VI **a** [*avion, pays*] to take off; [*fusée*] to lift off (**de** from); [*industrie*] to take off, get off the ground **b** * (= *maigrir*) to lose weight **c** (* = *partir*) [*gêneur*] to budge, shift; [*drogué*] to get off*; **il n'a pas décollé (d'ici) pendant deux heures** he sat *ou* stayed here for two solid hours without budging*; (*Sport*) **~ du peloton** (*en avant*) to pull away from *ou* ahead of the pack; (*en arrière*) to fall *ou* drop behind the pack; **~ du réel** to escape from reality **3** **se décoller** VPR [*timbre*] to come unstuck; [*papier peint*] to peel; (*Méd*) [*rétine*] to become detached

décolletage [dekɔltaʒ] NM **a** (= *forme*) (low-cut) neckline, décolletage; [*robe*] (= *action*) cutting out of the neck **b** (*Agr*) topping; (*Tech*) cutting (from the bar)

décolleté, e [dekɔlte] (*ptp de* **décolleter**) **1** ADJ [*robe*] low-necked, low-cut; [*femme*] wearing a low-cut dress, décolleté (*attrib*);

[*chaussure*] low-cut; **robe ~e dans le dos** dress cut low at the back **2** NM [*robe*] low neck(line), décolletage; [*femme*] (bare) neck and shoulders; [*plongeant*] cleavage **3** COMP
► **décolleté bateau** bateau *ou* boat neck
► **décolleté en pointe** V-neck
► **décolleté rond** round-neck

décolleter [dekɔlte] ▸ conjug 4 ◂ VT **a** [+ *robe*] to cut out the neck of **b** (*Agr*) to top; (*Tech*) to cut (from the bar)

décolleuse [dekɔløz] NF [*papier peint*] steam stripper

décolonisateur, -trice [dekɔlɔnizatœʀ, tʀis] **1** ADJ decolonization (*épith*), decolonizing (*épith*) **2** NM,F decolonizer

décolonisation [dekɔlɔnizasjɔ̃] NF decolonization

décoloniser [dekɔlɔnize] ▸ conjug 1 ◂ VT to decolonize

décolorant, e [dekɔlɔʀɑ̃, ɑ̃t] **1** ADJ decolorizing (*épith*), bleaching (*épith*) **2** NM bleaching agent

décoloration [dekɔlɔʀasjɔ̃] NF (*gén*) discolouration (*Brit*), discoloration (*US*); [*tissu*] fading; [*cheveux*] bleaching, lightening; **se faire faire une ~** to have one's hair lightened; (*en blond*) to have one's hair bleached

décoloré, e [dekɔlɔʀe] (*ptp de* **décolorer**) ADJ [*vêtement*] faded; [*cheveux*] bleached, lightened; [*teint, lèvres*] pale, colourless (*Brit*), colorless (*US*); **une blonde ~e** a peroxide *ou* bleached *ou* bottle* blonde

décolorer [dekɔlɔʀe] ▸ conjug 1 ◂ **1** VT (*gén*) to discolour (*Brit*), discolor (*US*); [+ *tissu, soleil*] to fade; [*lavage*] to take the colour (*Brit*) *ou* color (*US*) out of, fade; [+ *cheveux*] (*gén*) to lighten; (*en blond*) to bleach **2** **se décolorer** VPR [*liquide*] to lose its colour (*Brit*) *ou* color (*US*); [*tissu*] to fade, lose its colour (*Brit*) *ou* color (*US*); **elle s'est décolorée ◊ elle s'est décoloré les cheveux** (*gén*) she has lightened her hair; (*en blond*) she has bleached her hair

décombres [dekɔ̃bʀ] NMPL rubble, debris *sg*

décommander [dekɔmɑ̃de] ▸ conjug 1 ◂ **1** VT [+ *marchandise*] to cancel (an order for); [+ *invités*] to put off; [+ *invitation*] to cancel **2** **se décommander** VPR to cancel one's appointment

décompensation [dekɔ̃pɑ̃sasjɔ̃] NF (*Méd*) (*physique*) decompensation; (*nerveuse*) (emotional) collapse

décompenser [dekɔ̃pɑ̃se] ▸ conjug 1 ◂ VI (*Méd*) (*physiquement*) to decompensate; (*nerveusement*) to collapse (emotionally)

décomplexer [dekɔ̃plɛkse] ▸ conjug 1 ◂ VT **~ qn** to rid sb of their complexes *ou* hang-ups

décomposable [dekɔ̃pozabl(ə)] ADJ (*Math*) [*nombre*] that can be factorized; (*Chim*) decomposable; (*Phys*) [*lumière*] that can be broken up, that can be split up; (*Tech*) [*forces*] resoluble

décomposer [dekɔ̃poze] ▸ conjug 1 ◂ **1** VT **a** (= *diviser*) (*gén*) to split up *ou* break up into its component parts; (*Math*) [+ *nombre*] to factorize, express as a product of prime factors; (*Chim*) to decompose; (*Phys*) [+ *lumière*] to break up, split up; (*Tech*) [+ *forces*] to resolve; (*Ling*) [+ *phrase*] to break down, split up; [+ *problème, idée*] to dissect, break down; **la prof de danse décomposa le mouvement devant nous** the dance teacher broke the movement up for us *ou* went through the movement slowly for us; **la phrase se décompose en trois propositions** the sentence can be broken down *ou* split up into three clauses **b** (= *altérer*) [+ *visage*] to contort, distort; **la douleur décomposait ses traits** his face was contorted with pain; **il était décomposé** he looked distraught **c** (= *putréfier*) [+ *viande*] to cause to decompose *ou* rot; **la chaleur décomposait les cada-**

vres the heat was causing the corpses to decompose *ou* to decay **2** **se décomposer** VPR **a** (= *pourrir*) [*viande*] to decompose, rot; [*cadavre*] to decompose, decay **b** (= *s'altérer*) [*visage*] to become distorted; **à cette nouvelle son visage se décomposa** when he heard this news his face fell **c** (= *se diviser*) to be divided; **se ~ en trois parties** to be divided *ou* broken up into three parts; **cela se décompose de la façon suivante ...** it breaks down *ou* is divided up in the following way ... **d** (= *se déstructurer*) [*société*] to break down; [*fédération*] to break up

décomposeur [dekɔ̃pozœʀ] NM (*Bio*) decomposer

décomposition [dekɔ̃pozisjɔ̃] NF **a** (= *division*) (*gén*) splitting up, breaking up; (*Math*) [*nombre*] factorization; (*Chim*) decomposition; (*Phys*) [*lumière*] breaking up, splitting up; (*Tech*) [*forces*] resolution; (*Ling*) [*phrase*] breaking down, splitting up; [*problème, idée*] dissection, breaking down; **le calcul de l'impôt nécessite la ~ du revenu en tranches** income needs to be divided up into bands for tax calculation purposes **b** (= *pourriture*) decomposition, decay; **cadavre en ~** corpse in a state of decomposition *ou* decay **c** (= *déstructuration*) [*société*] breakdown; [*fédération*] breakup; **société/système en complète ~** society/system in decay

décompresser [dekɔ̃pʀese] ▸ conjug 1 ◂ **1** VT (*Tech, Ordin*) to decompress **2** VI (* = *se détendre*) to unwind, relax

décompresseur [dekɔ̃pʀesœʀ] NM decompression tap; (*Aut*) decompressor

décompression [dekɔ̃pʀesjɔ̃] NF **a** (*Tech, Méd, Ordin*) decompression; **soupape/chambre de ~** decompression valve/chamber; **~ cardiaque** cardiac decompression **b*** (= *détente*) relaxation

décomprimer [dekɔ̃pʀime] ▸ conjug 1 ◂ VT to decompress

décompte [dekɔ̃t] NM **a** (= *calcul*) detailed account, breakdown **b** (= *déduction*) deduction; **faire le ~ des points** to count up *ou* tot up* (*surtout Brit*) the points; (*Pol*) **faire le ~ des voix** to count the votes; **vous voulez faire mon ~?** will you make out my bill? (*Brit*) *ou* check? (*US*)

décompter [dekɔ̃te] ▸ conjug 1 ◂ **1** VT (= *défalquer*) to deduct (**de** from) **2** VI [*horloge*] to strike *ou* chime at the wrong time

déconcentration [dekɔ̃sɑ̃tʀasjɔ̃] NF **a** [*personne*] loss of concentration **b** (*Admin*) devolution, decentralization; (*Ind*) dispersal; (*Chim*) deconcentration

déconcentré, e [dekɔ̃sɑ̃tʀe] (*ptp de* **déconcentrer**) ADJ **a** (*Admin*) devolved, decentralized; (*Ind*) dispersed **b** [*personne*] **être ~** to have lost (one's) concentration; **j'étais un peu/très ~** I wasn't really concentrating/wasn't concentrating at all

déconcentrer [dekɔ̃sɑ̃tʀe] ▸ conjug 1 ◂ **1** VT **a** (*Admin*) to devolve, decentralize; (*Ind*) to disperse **b** (= *distraire*) **ça m'a déconcentré** it made me lose (my) concentration **2** **se déconcentrer** VPR [*personne*] to lose (one's) concentration

déconcertant, e [dekɔ̃sɛʀtɑ̃, ɑ̃t] ADJ disconcerting

déconcerter [dekɔ̃sɛʀte] ▸ conjug 1 ◂ VT (= *décontenancer*) to disconcert; (†† = *déjouer*) to thwart, frustrate

déconditionner [dekɔ̃disjɔne] ▸ conjug 1 ◂ VT to decondition

déconfit, e [dekɔ̃fi, it] ADJ **a** (= *dépité*) [*personne, air, mine*] crestfallen, downcast; **avoir la mine ~e** to look downcast *ou* crestfallen **b** †† (= *battu*) defeated, discomfited†

déconfiture* [dekɔ̃fityʀ] NF (= *déroute*) (*gén*) failure, collapse; [*parti, armée*] defeat; (*financière*) (financial) collapse, ruin; **cette entreprise est en ~** the company is in a state of collapse

décongélation [dekɔ̃ʒelasjɔ̃] NF defrosting, unfreezing

décongeler [dekɔ̃ʒ(ə)le] ▶ conjug 5◀ ① VI [*aliment*] to defrost, thaw ② VT [+ *aliment*] to defrost, leave to thaw; [+ *sperme*] to thaw

décongestionnant, e [dekɔ̃ʒestjɔnɑ̃, ɑ̃t] ADJ [*gel, crème*] decongesting

décongestionner [dekɔ̃ʒestjɔne] ▶ conjug 1◀ VT (*Méd*) [+ *poumons, fosses nasales*] to decongest, relieve congestion in; [+ *malade*] to relieve congestion in; [+ *rue, centre-ville*] to relieve congestion in; [+ *service, aéroport, université, administration*] to relieve the pressure on

déconnade* [dekɔnad] NF **il aime la franche ~** he likes to mess around* *ou* to fool around*; **il se moquait d'elle pour la ~** he was teasing her for a laugh* *ou* just for the hell of it*

déconnecter [dekɔnekte] ▶ conjug 1◀ ① VT ⓐ (*Élec*) to disconnect ⓑ [+ *problème*] to dissociate (**de** from); **il est complètement déconnecté de la réalité/de son pays d'origine** he's completely out of touch with reality/with his native country ② VI* [*personne*] to switch off*

déconner* [dekɔne] ▶ conjug 1◀ VI [*personne*] (= *faire des bêtises*) to mess around*, fool around*; (= *dire des bêtises*) to talk nonsense; (= *plaisanter*) to joke, kid*; [*machine*] to act up*; **arrête de ~!** stop messing around!, quit fooling!; **sans ~, c'était super!** no joke*, it was great!; **faut pas ~!** come off it!*

déconneur* [dekɔnœʀ] NM fun-loving* *ou* crazy* guy

déconneuse* [dekɔnøz] NF fun-loving* *ou* crazy* girl

déconnexion [dekɔneksjɔ̃] NF disconnection

▼ **déconseiller** [dekɔ̃seje] ▶ conjug 1◀ VT to advise against; **~ qch à qn/à qn de faire qch** to advise sb against sth/sb against doing sth; **c'est déconseillé** it's not advisable, it's inadvisable; **dans ce régime, le beurre est déconseillé** butter is not recommended in this diet

déconsidération [dekɔ̃sideʀasjɔ̃] NF discredit, disrepute

déconsidérer [dekɔ̃sideʀe] ▶ conjug 6◀ VT to discredit; **il s'est déconsidéré en agissant ainsi** he has discredited himself *ou* brought discredit upon himself by acting thus

déconsigner [dekɔ̃sine] ▶ conjug 1◀ VT ⓐ [+ *valise*] to collect from the left luggage office (*Brit*) *ou* the baggage checkroom (*US*); [+ *bouteille*] to return the deposit on ⓑ [+ *troupes*] to release from confinement to barracks

déconsommation [dekɔ̃sɔmasjɔ̃] NF (*Écon*) drop in consumption (of consumer goods); **on observe une tendance à la ~ des ménages** there is a growing tendency for households to buy less consumer goods

déconstruction [dekɔ̃stʀyksjɔ̃] NF [*concept, système*] deconstruction; [*bâtiment*] dismantling

déconstruire [dekɔ̃stʀɥiʀ] ▶ conjug 38◀ VT [+ *concept, système*] to deconstruct; [+ *bâtiment*] to dismantle

décontamination [dekɔ̃taminasjɔ̃] NF decontamination

décontaminer [dekɔ̃tamine] ▶ conjug 1◀ VT to decontaminate

décontenancer [dekɔ̃t(ə)nɑ̃se] ▶ conjug 3◀ ① VT to disconcert, discountenance (*frm*) ② **se décontenancer** VPR to lose one's composure

décontract* [dekɔ̃tʀakt] ADJ INV laid-back*, cool*

décontractant, e [dekɔ̃tʀaktɑ̃, ɑ̃t] ① ADJ [*ambiance, massage, médicament*] relaxing ② NM relaxant

décontracté, e [dekɔ̃tʀakte] (*ptp de* **décontracter**) ADJ ⓐ [*muscles, corps*] relaxed ⓑ [*personne*] relaxed, laid-back*; (= *sans-gêne*) casual, offhand; [*atmosphère, attitude*] relaxed, laid-back*; [*vêtements, style*] casual

décontracter VT, **se décontracter** VPR [dekɔ̃tʀakte] ▶ conjug 1◀ to relax

décontraction [dekɔ̃tʀaksjɔ̃] NF ⓐ [*muscle, corps*] relaxation ⓑ (= *désinvolture*) relaxed *ou* laid-back* attitude; **sa ~ m'a étonné** I was amazed that he was so relaxed *ou* laid-back*

déconventionner [dekɔ̃vɑ̃sjɔne] ▶ conjug 1◀ VT [+ *établissement, médecin*] to strike off the register (*for financial misconduct*)

déconvenue [dekɔ̃v(ə)ny] NF (= *déception*) disappointment

décor [dekɔʀ] NM ⓐ (*Théât*) **le ~** ◊ **les ~s** the scenery (*NonC*), the décor (*NonC*); **~ de cinéma** film set; **on dirait un ~** *ou* **des ~s de théâtre** it looks like a stage setting *ou* a theatre set, it looks like scenery for a play; **tourner en ~s naturels** to shoot on location; **planter le ~** to set the scene; (*lit, fig*) **faire partie du ~** to be part of the furniture; **aller** *ou* **partir dans le ~*** *ou* **les ~s*** [*véhicule, conducteur*] to go off the road; **envoyer qn dans le ~*** *ou* **les ~s*** to force sb off the road → **changement, envers** ⓑ (= *paysage*) scenery; (= *arrière-plan*) setting; (= *intérieur de maison*) décor (*NonC*), decoration; **~ de montagnes** mountain scenery; **dans un ~ de verdure** in a green setting; **photographié dans son ~ habituel** photographed in his usual surroundings

décorateur, -trice [dekɔʀatœʀ, tʀis] NM,F ⓐ (*d'intérieur*) (interior) decorator → **peintre** ⓑ (*Théât* = *architecte*) stage *ou* set designer; (*TV, Ciné*) set designer

décoratif, -ive [dekɔʀatif, iv] ADJ [*ornement*] decorative, ornamental; [*arts, effet*] decorative; (*péj*) **elle a un rôle purement ~** she has a purely decorative role

décoration [dekɔʀasjɔ̃] NF ⓐ (= *action*) decoration ⓑ (*gén* = *ornement*) decorations; (= *ensemble des ornements*) decoration; **~s de Noël** Christmas decorations ⓒ (= *médaille*) decoration

décorder (se) [dekɔʀde] ▶ conjug 1◀ VPR (*Alpinisme*) to unrope

décoré, e [dekɔʀe] (*ptp de* **décorer**) ADJ ⓐ (= *orné*) decorated; **joliment ~** prettily decorated; **richement ~** ornate, richly decorated; **mur ~ de fresques** wall decorated with frescoes; **un vase très ~** an ornate vase ⓑ (= *récompensé*) wearing a (military) decoration (*ou* decorations), decorated; **un vieux monsieur très ~** an old man bedecked with medals and ribbons; **les ~s de la Première Guerre mondiale** soldiers awarded (military) decorations *ou* decorated during the First World War

décorer [dekɔʀe] ▶ conjug 1◀ VT ⓐ (= *embellir*: *gén*) to decorate; [+ *robe*] to trim; **~ une maison pour Noël** to decorate a house for Christmas; **l'ensemblier qui a décoré leur maison** the designer who did the (interior) decoration of their house ⓑ (= *médailler*) to decorate (**de** with); **on va le ~** (*gén*) he is to be decorated; (*Légion d'honneur*) he is to be made a member of the Legion of Honour

décorner [dekɔʀne] ▶ conjug 1◀ VT [+ *page*] to smooth out; [+ *animal*] to dehorn → **vent**

décorticage [dekɔʀtikaʒ] NM [*crevettes, amandes*] shelling; [*riz*] hulling, husking; [*texte*] dissection

décortication [dekɔʀtikasjɔ̃] NF (*Méd, Sylviculture*) decortication

décortiquer [dekɔʀtike] ▶ conjug 1◀ VT ⓐ [+ *crevettes, amandes*] to shell; [+ *riz*] to hull, husk; [+ *texte*] to dissect ⓑ (*Méd*) to decorticate ⓒ (*Sylviculture*) to remove the bark from

décorum [dekɔʀɔm] NM **le ~** (= *convenances*) decorum; (= *étiquette*) etiquette

décote [dekɔt] NF (*Fin*) [*devises, valeur*] below par rating; [*impôts*] tax relief

découcher [dekuʃe] ▶ conjug 1◀ VI to spend the night away from home

découdre [dekudʀ] ▶ conjug 48◀ ① VT ⓐ [+ *vêtement*] to take the stitches out of, unpick (*Brit*); [+ *bouton*] to take off; [+ *couture*] to take out, unpick (*Brit*) ⓑ **en ~** (*littér, hum* = *se battre*) to fight, do battle (**avec** with) ⓒ (*Chasse*) to gore, rip open ② **se découdre** VPR [*robe*] to come unstitched; [*bouton*] to come off; [*couture*] to come apart

découenné, e [dekwane] ADJ **jambon ~** rindless bacon

▼ **découler** [dekule] ▶ conjug 1◀ VI (= *dériver*) to ensue, follow (**de** from); **il découle de cela que ...** it ensues *ou* follows that ...

découpage [dekupaʒ] NM ⓐ [*papier, gâteau*] cutting up; [*viande*] carving; [*image, métal*] cutting out ⓑ (= *image*) cut-out; **un cahier de ~s** a cut-out book; **faire des ~s** to make cut-out figures ⓒ (*Ciné*) cutting ⓓ (*Pol*) **~ électoral** division into constituencies, distribution of constituencies (*Brit*), ≈ apportionment (*US*)

découpe [dekup] NF ⓐ (*Couture*) (= *coupe*) cut; (= *coupure*) cut-out ⓑ [*bois, verre, carrelage*] cutting to shape; **verre/bois à la ~** glass/wood cut to order

découpé, e [dekupe] (*ptp de* **découper**) ADJ [*relief, sommets, côte*] jagged, indented; [*feuille*] jagged, serrated

découper [dekupe] ▶ conjug 1◀ VT ⓐ (*Culin*) [+ *viande, volaille*] to carve, cut (up); [+ *gâteau*] to cut (up); **couteau/fourchette à ~** carving knife/fork ⓑ [+ *papier, tissu*] to cut up; [+ *bois, verre*] to cut to shape; [+ *images, métal*] to cut out; (*littér*) to indent; **~ un article dans un magazine** to cut an article out of a magazine; **« découpez suivant le pointillé »** "cut along the dotted line"; **les indentations qui découpent la côte** the indentations which cut into the coastline → **scie** ⓒ (= *se détacher*) **la montagne découpe ses aiguilles sur le ciel** the mountain's peaks stand out against the sky; **sa silhouette se découpait dans la lumière** his figure stood out *ou* was outlined against the light

découpeur, -euse [dekupœʀ, øz] ① NM,F (= *personne*) [*viande*] carver; [*métal*] cutter; [*bois*] jigsaw operator ② **découpeuse** NF (= *machine*: *gén*) cutting machine; [*bois*] fretsaw, jigsaw

découplage [dekuplaʒ] NM (*Élec*) decoupling; (= *dissociation*) delinking, decoupling; **le ~ croissance-emploi** the fact that there is no longer any connection between industrial growth and employment

découplé, e [dekuple] ADJ **bien ~** well-built

découpler [dekuple] ▶ conjug 1◀ VT (*Élec*) to decouple; (*Chasse*) to uncouple; (= *dissocier*) to delink, decouple (**de** from); **le pays n'a pas voulu ~ son économie de celles de ses partenaires** the country did not want to delink its economy from that of its partners

découpure [dekupyʀ] NF ⓐ (= *forme, contour*) jagged *ou* indented outline ⓑ **~s** (= *échancrures*) [*côte*] indentations; [*arête*] jagged *ou* indented edge *ou* outline; [*dentelle, guirlande*] scalloped edge ⓒ (= *morceau*) bit *ou* piece (*that has been cut out*); **~s de papier** cut-out bits of paper

décourageant, e [dekuʀaʒɑ̃, ɑ̃t] ADJ [*nouvelle*] disheartening, discouraging; [*élève, travail, situation*] disheartening

découragement [dekuʀaʒmɑ̃] NM discouragement, despondency

---

décourager [dekuraʒe] ▸ conjug 3 ◂ 1 VT a (= *démoraliser*) to discourage, dishearten; **il ne faut pas se laisser ~ par un échec** one must not be discouraged *ou* disheartened by failure b (= *dissuader*) to discourage, put off; **~ qn de qch/de faire qch** to discourage sb from sth/ from doing sth, put sb off sth/doing sth; **~ qn d'une entreprise** to discourage *ou* deter sb from an undertaking, put sb off an undertaking 2 **se décourager** VPR to lose heart, become disheartened *ou* discouraged; **ne nous décourageons pas** let's not lose heart

découronner [dekurɔne] ▸ conjug 1 ◂ VT [+ *roi*] to dethrone, depose; **arbre découronné par la tempête** tree that has had its topmost branches blown off by the storm

décours [dekur] NM a (*Astron*) wane; **au ~ de la lune** when the moon is (*ou* was) waning b (*Méd*) regression; **au ~ de la maladie** during the regression phase of the illness; **au ~ de la fièvre** when the fever is (*ou* was) abating

décousu, e [dekuzy] (*ptp de* **découdre**) 1 ADJ a (*Couture*) unstitched; **couture ~e** seam that has come unstitched *ou* unsewn; **ourlet ~** hem that has come down; **ta robe est ~e à la manche** your dress is coming apart at the sleeve b [*style*] disjointed, desultory; [*idées*] disconnected, unconnected; [*dissertation, travail*] scrappy, disjointed; [*paroles, conversation*] disjointed, desultory 2 NM [*style*] disjointedness, desultoriness; [*idées, raisonnement*] disconnectedness

découvert, e[1] [dekuvɛr, ɛrt] (*ptp de* **découvrir**) 1 ADJ a (= *mis à nu*) [*épaules, corps, tête*] bare, uncovered (*attrib*) ~ **visage** b (= *sans protection*) [*lieu*] open, exposed; [*piscine*] open-air (*épith*), outdoor (*épith*); **en terrain ~** in open country *ou* terrain; **allée ~e** open avenue 2 **à découvert** LOC ADV **être à ~ dans un champ** to be exposed *ou* without cover in a field; **la plage laissée à ~ par la marée** the beach left exposed by the tide; **mettre qch à ~** to expose sth, bring sth into the open; **parler à ~** to speak frankly *ou* openly; **agir à ~** to act openly 3 NM (*Fin*) [*firme, compte*] overdraft; [*caisse*] deficit; [*objet assuré*] uncovered amount *ou* sum; **~ du Trésor** Treasury deficit; **~ bancaire** bank overdraft; **~ budgétaire/de trésorerie** budget/cash deficit; **tirer de l'argent à ~** to overdraw one's account; **mon compte est/je suis à ~** my account is/I am overdrawn; **crédit à ~** unsecured credit; **vendre à ~** to sell short; **vente à ~** short sale

découverte[2] [dekuvɛrt] NF a (= *action*) discovery; [*objet*] find, discovery; **aller** *ou* **partir à la ~ de** to go in search of; **faire une ~** to make a discovery; **faire la ~ de** to discover; **montre-moi ta ~** show me what you've found; **ce n'est pas une ~!** that's hardly news!, so what's new?* b (*Art, Photo*) background

découvreur, -euse [dekuvrœr, øz] NM,F discoverer; **~ de talents** talent scout

découvrir [dekuvrir] ▸ conjug 18 ◂ 1 VT a (= *trouver*) [+ *trésor, loi scientifique, terre inconnue*] to discover; [+ *indices, complot*] to discover, unearth; [+ *cause, vérité*] to discover, find out, unearth; [+ *personne cachée*] to discover, find; **~ que ...** to discover *ou* find out that ...; **il veut ~ comment/pourquoi c'est arrivé** he wants to find out *ou* discover how/why it happened; **je lui ai découvert des qualités insoupçonnées** I have discovered some unsuspected qualities in him; **il a découvert l'amour à 50 ans** he found love at the age of 50; **faire ~ la musique/la peinture à qn** to introduce sb to music/painting; **il craint d'être découvert** (*percé à jour*) he is afraid of being found out;

(*trouvé*) he is afraid of being found *ou* discovered; **quand ils découvriront le pot aux roses*** when they find out what's been going on b (= *enlever ce qui couvre, protège*) [+ *plat, casserole*] to take the lid *ou* cover off; [+ *voiture*] to open the roof of; [+ *statue*] to unveil; (*Échecs*) [+ *roi*] to uncover; (*Mil*) [+ *frontière*] to expose, uncover; [+ *corps*] to uncover; [+ *membres, poitrine, épaules, tête*] to bare, uncover; (= *mettre à jour*) [+ *ruines*] to uncover; **elle enleva les housses et découvrit les meubles** she removed the dust sheets and uncovered the furniture; **il découvrit son torse/avant-bras** he bared *ou* uncovered his torso/forearm; **il resta découvert devant elle** he kept his hat off in her presence; (*Mil*) **ils découvrirent leur aile gauche** they exposed their left wing, they left their left wing open to attack c (= *laisser voir*) to reveal; **une robe qui découvre le dos** a dress cut low at the back; **son sourire découvre des dents superbes** when he smiles he shows his beautiful teeth d (= *voir*) to see, have a view of; (*Naut*) [+ *terre*] to sight; **du haut de la falaise on découvre toute la baie** from the top of the cliff you have a view of the whole bay e (= *révéler, dévoiler*) [+ *projets, intentions, motifs*] to reveal, disclose (**à qn** to sb); **~ son cœur** to lay bare *ou* open one's heart; (*lit, fig*) **~ son jeu** to show one's hand 2 VI [*mer*] to recede 3 **se découvrir** VPR a (= *ôter son chapeau*) to take off one's hat; (= *ôter ses habits*) to undress, take off one's clothes; (= *perdre ses couvertures*) to throw off the bedclothes, uncover o.s.; **en altitude on doit se ~ le moins possible** at high altitudes you must keep covered up as much as possible → **avril** b (*Boxe, Escrime*) to leave o.s. open; (*Mil, fig*) to expose o.s., leave o.s. open to attack c [*ciel, temps*] to clear; **ça va se ~** it will soon clear d (= *trouver*) **elle s'est découvert un cousin en Amérique/un talent pour la peinture** she found out *ou* discovered she had a cousin in America/a gift for painting; **c'est dans les épreuves qu'on se découvre** one finds *ou* discovers one's true self in testing situations

décrassage [dekrasaʒ] , **décrassement** [dekrasmã] NM [*objet boueux, graisseux*] cleaning; [*chaudière*] cleaning, cleaning-out; [*bougie de moteur*] cleaning-up; (* = *toilette*) **un bon ~** a good scrubbing-down *ou* clean-up

décrasser [dekrase] ▸ conjug 1 ◂ VT a [+ *enfant*] to scrub clean; [+ *objet boueux, graisseux*] to clean, get the mud (*ou* grease *etc*) off; (*en frottant*) to scrub; (*en trempant*) to soak the dirt out of; [+ *chaudière*] to clean out, clean; [+ *bougie de moteur*] to clean (up); **se ~** [*personne*] to give o.s. a good scrub, clean o.s. up; **se ~ le visage/les mains** to give one's face/hands a good clean; **le bon air, ça décrasse les poumons** fresh air cleans out the lungs; **rouler à cette vitesse, ça décrasse le moteur** driving at that speed gives the engine a good decoking (*Brit*) *ou* cleans the engine out well b (*fig = dégrossir*) to take the rough edges off

décrédibiliser [dekredibilize] ▸ conjug 1 ◂ VT [+ *personne, organisation*] to undermine the credibility of

décrêper [dekrepe] ▸ conjug 1 ◂ VT [+ *cheveux*] to straighten

décrépir [dekrepir] ▸ conjug 2 ◂ 1 VT [+ *mur*] to remove the roughcast from; **façade décrépie** peeling façade 2 **se décrépir** VPR [*mur*] to peel

décrépit, e [dekrepi, it] ADJ [*personne*] decrepit; [*maison, mur*] dilapidated, decrepit

décrépitude [dekrepityd] NF [*personne*] decrepitude; [*nation, institution, civilisation*] decay; **tomber en ~** [*personne*] to become decrepit; [*nation*] to decay

decrescendo [dekrefɛndo] 1 ADV (*Mus*) decrescendo; **sa réputation va ~** his reputation is declining *ou* waning 2 NM (*Mus*) decrescendo

décret [dekrɛ] NM (*Pol, Rel*) decree; **~ d'application** decree specifying how a law should be enforced; **gouverner par ~** to rule by decree; **~-loi** government decree; (*littér*) **les ~s de la Providence** the decrees of Providence

décréter [dekrete] ▸ conjug 6 ◂ VT [+ *mobilisation*] to order; [+ *état d'urgence*] to declare; [+ *mesure*] to decree; **le président a décrété la nomination d'un nouveau ministre** the president ordered the appointment of a new minister; **~ que** [*gouvernement, patron*] to decree *ou* order that; (*Rel*) to ordain *ou* decree that; **il a décrété qu'il ne mangerait plus de betteraves** he swore that he wouldn't eat beetroot any more; **j'ai décrété que je n'irai pas** I have decided that I won't go

décrier [dekrije] ▸ conjug 7 ◂ VT [+ *œuvre, mesure, principe, auteur*] to decry (*littér*), disparage, downcry (*US*); **la chasteté, une vertu si décriée de nos jours** chastity, a much disparaged virtue nowadays; **ces auteurs maintenant si décriés par la critique** these authors now so disparaged by the critics; **il décria fort ma conduite** he (strongly) censured my behaviour

décriminaliser [dekriminalize] ▸ conjug 1 ◂ VT to decriminalize

décrire [dekrir] ▸ conjug 39 ◂ VT a (= *dépeindre*) to describe b [+ *trajectoire*] to follow; [+ *cercle, ellipse*] to describe; **l'oiseau/l'avion décrivait des cercles au-dessus de nos têtes** the bird/plane flew in circles overhead; **la route décrit une courbe** the road makes *ou* follows a curve; **le satellite décrit une ellipse** the satellite follows *ou* makes *ou* describes an elliptical orbit

décrispation [dekrispasjɔ̃] NF (*Pol*) easing of tension (**entre** between); **il y a des signes de ~ politique** there are signs that the political tension is easing

décrisper [dekrispe] ▸ conjug 1 ◂ VT [+ *situation*] to defuse, de-escalate; [+ *personne*] to relax; **pour ~ les relations** to make relations less strained, ease relations

décrochage [dekrɔʃaʒ] NM a [*rideaux*] taking down, unhooking; [*wagon*] uncoupling b (*Mil*) **opérer un ~** to disengage, break off the action c (*Radio, TV*) switchover d (*Fin*) **le ~ du franc par rapport au mark** the decoupling *ou* unpegging of the franc from the mark e (*Aviat*) stalling; **faire un ~** to stall

décrochement [dekrɔʃmã] NM a [*wagon*] uncoupling b (*Géol*) thrust fault, slide c (*Constr*) (*en retrait*) recess; (*en saillie*) projection; **le mur présente un ~** (*en retrait*) the wall is recessed; (*en saillie*) the wall juts out d (*Fin*) = **décrochage**

décrocher [dekrɔʃe] ▸ conjug 1 ◂ 1 VT a (= *détacher*) [+ *tableau*] to take down; [+ *rideau*] to take down, unhook; [+ *vêtement*] to take down, take off the hook *ou* peg; [+ *fermoir*] to undo, unclasp; [+ *poisson*] to unhook; [+ *wagon*] to uncouple; **il n'a pas pu ~ son cerf-volant qui s'était pris dans l'arbre** he couldn't free *ou* unhook his kite which had got caught in the tree; (*Sport*) **~ le reste du peloton** to leave the pack behind; (*Fin*) **~ le franc du mark** to decouple *ou* unpeg the franc from the mark b [+ *téléphone*] (*pour répondre*) to pick up, lift; (*pour l'empêcher de sonner*) to take off the hook; (*sans complément*) to pick up *ou* lift the receiver; **ne décroche pas !** don't answer it!; **le téléphone est décroché** the telephone is off the hook c (* = *obtenir*) [+ *prix, contrat, poste, récompense*] to get, land*; **il a décroché une belle situation** he's landed (himself) a fine job*; (*lit, fig*) **~ le gros lot** *ou* **la timbale** to hit the jackpot → **lune, pompon**

2 VI **a** (*Mil*) to pull back, break off the action; [*coureur*] to fall behind

b * (= *abandonner, ne pas suivre*) to fall by the wayside, fail to keep up; (= *se désintéresser*) to drop out, opt out; (= *cesser d'écouter*) to switch off*

c (*arg Drogue*) to come off

d (*Fin = perdre du terrain*) **le franc a décroché du mark** the franc lost ground against the mark

e (*Radio, TV*) to go off the air

f (*Aviat*) to stall

3 **se décrocher** VPR [*tableau, vêtement*] to fall down *ou* off; [*rideau*] to fall down, come unhooked; [*fermoir*] to come undone; [*poisson*] to get unhooked; [*wagon*] to come uncoupled; **le cerf-volant pris dans l'arbre s'est finalement décroché** the kite which had been caught in the tree finally came free → **bâiller**

décroiser [dekʀwaze] ▶ conjug 1 ◀ VT [+ *jambes*] to uncross; [+ *bras*] to unfold; [+ *fils*] to untwine, untwist

décroissance [dekʀwasɑ̃s] NF (= *diminution*) decline, decrease (**de** in)

décroissant, e [dekʀwasɑ̃, ɑ̃t] ADJ (*gén*) decreasing, diminishing, declining; [*bruit*] fading; [*vitesse*] decreasing, falling; **par ordre ~** in decreasing *ou* descending order

décroissement [dekʀwasmɑ̃] NM [*jours*] shortening; [*lune*] waning

décroît [dekʀwa] NM [*lune*] **dans** *ou* **sur son ~** in its last quarter

décroître [dekʀwatʀ] ▶ conjug 55 ◀ VI [*nombre, population, intensité, pouvoir*] to decrease, diminish, decline; [*eaux, fièvre*] to subside, go down; [*popularité*] to decline, drop; [*vitesse*] to drop; [*force*] to decline, diminish, fail; [*revenus*] to get less, diminish; [*lune*] to wane; [*jours*] to get shorter; [*silhouette*] to get smaller and smaller; [*bruit*] to die away, fade; [*lumière*] to fade, grow fainter *ou* dimmer; **ses forces vont (en) décroissant** his strength is failing *ou* gradually diminishing *ou* declining; **cette ville a beaucoup décru en importance** this town has greatly declined in importance

décrotter [dekʀɔte] ▶ conjug 1 ◀ VT [+ *chaussures*] to scrape the mud off; (*fig*) [+ *rustre*] to take the rough edges off

décrottoir [dekʀɔtwaʀ] NM (= *lame*) mudscraper, shoescraper; (= *paillasson*) wire (door)mat

décrue [dekʀy] NF [*eaux, rivière*] fall *ou* drop in level (**de** of); [*taux d'intérêt*] drop (**de** in); [*popularité*] decline, drop (**de** in); **la ~ des eaux atteint deux mètres** the water level *ou* flood-level has fallen *ou* dropped by two metres; **au moment de la ~** when the water level drops

décryptage [dekʀiptaʒ], **décryptement** [dekʀiptəmɑ̃] NM deciphering; (*Ordin, TV*) decryption

décrypter [dekʀipte] ▶ conjug 1 ◀ VT (= *décoder*) [+ *message, code, génome*] to decipher; (*Ordin, TV*) to decrypt; (= *élucider*) **~ l'attitude de qn** to work sb out, understand sb's attitude

déçu, e [desy] (*ptp de* **décevoir**) ADJ disappointed; **j'ai été très ~ d'apprendre que ...** I was very disappointed to find out that ...; (*iro*) **elle ne va pas être ~e du voyage!** * she's going to be over the moon!* (*iro*)

de cujus [dekyʒys, dekujus] NM INV (*Jur*) **le ~** (*sans testament*) the deceased, the intestate; (*qui a fait un testament*) (*homme*) the testator; (*femme*) the testatrix

déculottée* [dekylɔte] NF (= *défaite*) clobbering*, hammering*; **prendre** *ou* **recevoir une ~** to get a hammering* *ou* clobbering*

déculotter [dekylɔte] ▶ conjug 1 ◀ VT **~** to take down sb's trousers **2** **se déculotter** VPR (*lit*) to take down one's trousers; (* = *s'humilier*) to lie down and take it*

déculpabilisation [dekylpabilizasjɔ̃] NF [*personne*] ridding of his (*ou* her) guilt; **la ~ du divorce** taking away the guilt associated with divorce

déculpabiliser [dekylpabilize] ▶ conjug 1 ◀ VT **~ qn** to rid sb of their guilt; **~ le divorce** to take away the guilt associated with divorce

déculturation [dekyltyʀasjɔ̃] NF loss of cultural identity

décuple [dekypl] **1** ADJ tenfold; **un revenu ~ du mien** an income ten times as large as mine **2** NM **20 est le ~ de 2** 20 is ten times 2; **il gagne le ~ de ce que je gagne** he earns ten times what I earn; **il me l'a rendu au ~** he paid me back tenfold

décuplement [dekypləmɑ̃] NM (*lit*) tenfold increase; **grâce au ~ de nos forces** thanks to our greatly increased strength

décupler [dekyple] ▶ conjug 1 ◀ VTI to increase tenfold; **la colère décuplait ses forces** anger gave him the strength of ten

dédaignable [dedɛɲabl] ADJ **ce n'est pas ~** it's not to be sniffed at

dédaigner [dedɛɲe] ▶ conjug 1 ◀ VT **a** (= *mépriser*) [+ *personne*] to despise, look down on, scorn; [+ *honneurs, richesse*] to scorn, despise, disdain; **il ne dédaigne pas de rire avec ses subordonnés** he doesn't consider it beneath him to joke with his subordinates; **il ne dédaigne pas un verre de vin de temps à autre** he's not averse to the occasional glass of wine **b** (= *négliger*) [+ *offre, adversaire*] to spurn; [+ *menaces, insultes*] to disregard, discount; **ce n'est pas à ~** (*honneur, offre*) it's not to be sniffed at; (*danger, adversaire*) it can't just be shrugged off; **il dédaigna de répondre/d'y aller** he did not deign to reply/go

dédaigneusement [dedɛɲøzmɑ̃] ADV disdainfully, scornfully, contemptuously

dédaigneux, -euse [dedɛɲø, øz] ADJ [*personne, air*] scornful, disdainful, contemptuous; **~ de** contemptuous *ou* scornful *ou* disdainful of; (*littér*) **il est ~ de plaire** he scorns to please

dédain [dedɛ̃] NM contempt, scorn, disdain (**de** for); **sourire de ~** disdainful *ou* scornful smile

dédale [dedal] NM **a** [*rues, idées, lois*] maze **b** (*Myth*) **Dédale** Daedalus

dedans [dədɑ̃] **1** ADV **a** (= *à l'intérieur*) inside; (= *pas à l'air libre*) indoors, inside; **voulez-vous dîner dehors ou ~?** do you want to have dinner outside or inside? *ou* outdoors or indoors?; **au-~** inside; **la maison est laide, mais ~** *ou* **au-~ c'est très joli** it's an ugly-looking house but it's lovely inside; **nous sommes restés ~ toute la journée** we stayed in *ou* inside *ou* indoors all day; **elle cherche son sac, tout son argent est ~** she is looking for her bag — it's got all her money in it; **prenez ce fauteuil, on est bien ~** have this chair, you'll be comfortable in it *ou* you'll find it comfortable; **de** *ou* **du ~ on n'entend rien** you can't hear a sound from inside; **passez par ~ pour aller au jardin** go through the house to get to the garden; **la crise? on est en plein ~!** the crisis? we're right in the middle of it! **b** **en ~** (= *à l'intérieur*) **fleur blanche en dehors et jaune en ~** a flower that's white (on the) outside and yellow (on the) inside; (= *vers l'intérieur*) **ces volets s'ouvrent en ~** these shutters open inwards; **avoir** *ou* **marcher les pieds en ~** to be pigeon-toed; **ne marche pas les pieds en ~** don't walk with your feet turned in

c (*loc: Cartes*) **être ~** to lose (**de** by); **mettre*** *ou* **ficher*** *ou* **foutre** **qn ~** to get sb confused, make sb get it wrong; **il s'est fait mettre ~** he got himself put away; **il a mis ~** put inside*; **il s'est fichu*** *ou* **foutu** **~** he got it all wrong*; **un bus lui est rentré ~** * a bus hit him *ou* ran into him*; **il a dérapé, il y avait un arbre, il est ren-** tré *ou* entré **~** * he skidded, there was a tree and he ran *ou* went *ou* crashed straight into it → **rentrer**

2 NM [*objet, bâtiment*] inside; **le coup a été préparé du ~** it's an inside job

dédicace [dedikas] NF **a** (*imprimée*) dedication; (*manuscrite*) [*livre, photo*] dedication, inscription (**à** to) **b** (*église*) consecration, dedication

dédicacer [dedikase] ▶ conjug 3 ◀ VT [+ *livre, photo*] (= *signer*) to sign, autograph (**à qn** for sb); (= *dédier*) to dedicate (**à** to)

dédicataire [dedikatɛʀ] NMF dedicatee

dédicatoire [dedikatwaʀ] ADJ dedicatory, dedicative

dédié, e [dedje] (*ptp de* **dédier**) ADJ (*Élec*) [*équipement, ordinateur*] dedicated

dédier [dedje] ▶ conjug 7 ◀ ◆ **dédier à** VT (*Rel*) to consecrate to, dedicate to; **~ ses efforts à** to devote *ou* dedicate one's efforts to; **~ un livre à** to dedicate a book to

dédire (se) [dedir] ▶ conjug 37 ◀ VPR **a** (= *manquer à ses engagements*) to go back on one's word; **se dédire d'une promesse** to go back on a promise **b** (= *se rétracter*) to retract, recant; **se dédire d'une affirmation** to withdraw a statement, retract (a statement) → **cochon**

dédit [dedi] NM **a** (*Comm = somme*) forfeit, penalty; **un ~ de 30 000 F** a 30,000 franc penalty **b** (= *rétractation*) retraction; (= *manquement aux engagements*) failure to keep one's word; (= *non-paiement*) default; **en cas de ~ il faut payer un supplément** in case of default a supplement must be paid

dédommagement [dedɔmaʒmɑ̃] NM compensation; **en ~, je lui ai donné une bouteille de vin** in compensation *ou* to make up for it, I gave him a bottle of wine; **en ~ des dégâts** *ou* **à titre de ~ pour les dégâts, on va me donner 500 F** they will give me 500 francs in compensation for the damage; **en ~ du mal que je vous donne** to make up for the trouble I'm causing you

dédommager [dedɔmaʒe] ▶ conjug 3 ◀ VT (= *indemniser*) **~ qn** to compensate sb (**de** for), give sb compensation (**de** for); **je l'ai dédommagé en lui donnant une bouteille de vin** I gave him a bottle of wine in compensation *ou* to make up for it; **~ qn d'une perte** to compensate sb for a loss, make good sb's loss; **comment vous ~ du dérangement que je vous cause?** how can I ever make up for the trouble I'm causing?; **le succès le dédommage de toutes ses peines** his success is compensation *ou* compensates for all his troubles

dédoré, e [dedɔʀe] (*ptp de* **dédorer**) ADJ [*bijou, tableau*] which has lost its gilt, tarnished; (*fig*) [*noblesse*] faded

dédorer [dedɔʀe] ▶ conjug 1 ◀ VT to remove the gilt from

dédouanage [dedwanaʒ], **dédouanement** [dedwanmɑ̃] NM (*Comm*) clearing *ou* clearance through customs, customs clearance; * [*personne*] clearing (the name of), putting in the clear*

dédouaner [dedwane] ▶ conjug 1 ◀ VT (*Comm*) to clear through customs; (* = *réhabiliter*) [+ *personne*] to clear (the name of), put in the clear*; **marchandises dédouanées** duty-paid goods; **se ~** to clear one's name

dédoublement [dedubləmɑ̃] NM [*classe*] dividing *ou* splitting in two; [*ongles*] splitting; **le ~ d'un train** the running of a relief train; (*Psych*) **le ~ de la personnalité est un trouble grave** having a split *ou* dual personality is a serious illness; **souffrir d'un ~ de la personnalité** to suffer from a split *ou* dual personality

dédoubler [deduble] ▶ conjug 1 ◀ **1** VT **a** [+ *manteau*] to remove the lining of **b** [+ *classe*] to split *ou* divide in two; [+ *ficelle*] to separate the strands of; **~ un train** to run *ou* put on a relief train; **pour Noël on a dû ~ tous les trains** at Christmas they had to run additional trains on all services [c] [+ *couverture*] to unfold, open out [2] **se dédoubler** VPR (= *se déplier*) to unfold, open out; [*ongles*] to split; **dans les cas où la personnalité se dédouble** in cases of split *ou* dual personality; **je ne peux pas me ~*** I can't be in two places at once; **l'image se dédoublait dans l'eau** there was a double outline reflected in the water

dédramatisation [dedramatizasjɔ̃] NF (= *minimisation*) [*événement*, *situation*] playing down the importance of; **au gouvernement, le ton est à la ~** the government is trying to play things down; **le patient fait un travail de ~ de sa maladie** the patient tries to come to terms with his illness

dédramatiser [dedramatize] ▸ conjug 1 ◂ VT [+ *examen*, *opération*] to make less alarming *ou* awesome; [+ *problème*] to play down the importance of; [+ *débat*] to take the heat out of; **il faut ~ la situation** we mustn't overdramatize the situation

déductible [dedyktibl] ADJ (*Fin*) [*frais*, *somme*] deductible (**de** from); **~ du revenu imposable** tax-deductible; **dépenses non ~s** non-deductible expenses

déductif, -ive [dedyktif, iv] ADJ deductive

déduction [dedyksjɔ̃] NF [a] (*Comm*) deduction; **~ fiscale** tax deduction; **~ forfaitaire** standard deduction; **~ faite de** after deducting, after deduction of; **ça entre en ~ de ce que vous nous devez** that's deductible from what you owe us, that'll be taken off what you owe us [b] (= *forme de raisonnement*) deduction, inference; (= *conclusion*) conclusion, inference

déduire [dedɥiʀ] ▸ conjug 38 ◂ VT (*Comm*) to deduct (**de** from); (= *conclure*) to deduce, infer (**de** from); **tous frais déduits** after deduction of expenses

déesse [deɛs] NF goddess; **elle a un corps/port de ~** she's got the body/bearing of a goddess

de facto [defakto] LOC ADV [*reconnaissance*, *gouvernement*] de facto; **reconnaître qch ~** to give de facto recognition to sth; **~, il devient président** he becomes de facto president

défaillance [defajɑ̃s] [1] NF [a] (= *évanouissement*) blackout; (= *faiblesse physique*) feeling of weakness *ou* faintness; (= *faiblesse morale*) weakness, failing; **avoir une ~** (= *évanouissement*) to faint, have a blackout; (*faiblesse*) to feel faint *ou* weak; **l'athlète a eu une ~ au troisième kilomètre** the athlete seemed to be in difficulty *ou* to be weakening at the third kilometre; **il a eu plusieurs ~s ces derniers jours** he has had several weak spells these last few days; **faire son devoir sans ~** to do one's duty without flinching [b] (= *mauvais fonctionnement*) (mechanical) fault, failure, breakdown (**de** in); **l'accident était dû à une ~ de la machine** the accident was caused by a fault in the machine [c] (= *insuffisance*) weakness; **élève qui a des ~s (en histoire)** pupil who has certain shortcomings *ou* weak points (in history); **devant la ~ du gouvernement** faced with the weakness of the government *ou* the government's failure to act; **mémoire sans ~** faultless memory [d] (*Jur*) default; **~ d'entreprise** bankruptcy [2] COMP ▸ **défaillance cardiaque** heart failure ▸ **défaillance mécanique** mechanical fault ▸ **défaillance de mémoire** lapse of memory

défaillant, e [defajɑ̃, ɑ̃t] ADJ [a] (= *affaibli*) [*forces*] failing, declining; [*santé*, *mémoire*, *raison*] failing; [*courage*, *volonté*] faltering, weakening; [*cœur*] weak [b] (= *tremblant*) [*voix*, *pas*] unsteady, faltering; [*main*] unsteady [c] (= *près de s'évanouir*) [*personne*] weak, faint (**de** with) [d] [*matériel*, *installation*] faulty; [*pouvoir*, *gouvernement*] shaky [e] (*Jur*) [*partie*, *témoin*]

defaulting; **client ~** client who defaults *ou* has defaulted; **candidat ~** candidate who fails (*ou* who has failed) to appear

défaillir [defajiʀ] ▸ conjug 13 ◂ VI [a] (= *s'évanouir*) to faint; **elle défaillait de bonheur/de faim** she felt faint with happiness/hunger [b] [*forces*] to weaken, fail; [*courage*, *volonté*] to falter, weaken; [*mémoire*] to fail; **faire son devoir sans ~** to do one's duty without flinching

défaire [defɛʀ] ▸ conjug 60 ◂ [1] VT [a] [+ *échafaudage*] to take down, dismantle; [+ *installation électrique*] to dismantle; [+ *sapin de Noël*] to take down [b] [+ *couture*, *tricot*] to undo, unpick (*Brit*); [+ *écheveau*] to undo, unravel, unwind; [+ *corde*, *nœud*, *ruban*] to undo, untie; [+ *courroie*, *fermeture*, *robe*] to undo, unfasten; [+ *valise*] to unpack; [+ *cheveux*, *nattes*] to undo; **~ ses bagages** to unpack (one's luggage) [c] **~ le lit** (*pour changer les draps*) to strip the bed; (*pour se coucher*) to pull back the sheets; (*mettre en désordre*) to unmake *ou* rumple the bed [d] [+ *mariage*] to break up; [+ *contrat*, *traité*] to break; **cela défit tous nos plans** it ruined all our plans; **il (faisait et) défaisait les rois** he (made and) unmade kings; **elle se plaît à ~ tout ce que j'essaie de faire pour elle** she takes pleasure in undoing everything I try to do for her [e] (= *miner*) **la maladie l'avait défait** his illness had left him shattered; **la douleur défaisait ses traits** his face was contorted with pain [f] (*littér*) [+ *ennemi*, *armée*] to defeat [g] (*littér*) **~ qn de** [+ *liens*, *gêneur*] to rid sb of, relieve sb of, deliver sb from (*littér*); [+ *habitude*] to break sb of, cure sb of, rid sb of; [+ *défaut*] to cure sb of, rid sb of

[2] **se défaire** VPR [a] [*nœud*, *ficelle*, *coiffure*] to come undone; [*couture*] to come undone *ou* apart; [*légumes*, *viande*] (*à la cuisson*) to fall to pieces, disintegrate; [*mariage*, *amitié*] to break up [b] (= *se déformer*) **ses traits se défirent** ◊ **son visage se défit** his face crumpled, his face twisted with grief (*ou* pain *etc*) [c] **se ~ de** (= *se débarrasser de*) [+ *gêneur*, *vieillerie*, *odeur*] to get rid of; [+ *image*, *idée*] to put *ou* get out of one's mind; [+ *habitude*] to break *ou* cure o.s. of, get rid of; [+ *défaut*] to cure o.s. of; [+ *souvenir*] to part with

défait, e[1] [defɛ, ɛt] (*ptp de* **défaire**) ADJ [a] [*visage*] ravaged, haggard; [*cheveux*] tousled, dishevelled; **il était complètement ~** he looked terribly haggard [b] [*lit*] unmade, rumpled [c] [*armée*] defeated

défaite[2] [defɛt] NF (*Mil*) defeat; (= *échec*) defeat, failure; **la ~ de notre équipe** our team's defeat; **~ électorale** electoral defeat

défaitisme [defetism] NM defeatism

défaitiste [defetist] ADJ, NMF defeatist

défalcation [defalkasjɔ̃] NF deduction; **~ faite des frais** after deduction of expenses

défalquer [defalke] ▸ conjug 1 ◂ VT to deduct

défatigant, e [defatigɑ̃, ɑ̃t] ADJ [*lait*, *lotion*] soothing

défausse [defos] NF discarding, throwing out *ou* away

défausser (se) [defose] ▸ conjug 1 ◂ VPR (*Cartes*) to discard, throw out *ou* away; **se défausser (d'une carte)** to discard; **il s'est défaussé à trèfle** he discarded a club

défaut [defo] [1] NM [a] [*pierre précieuse*, *métal*] flaw; [*étoffe*, *verre*] flaw, fault; [*machine*] defect, fault; [*bois*] blemish; [*roman*, *tableau*, *système*] flaw, defect; **sans ~** flawless, faultless [b] [*personne*] fault, failing; [*caractère*] defect, fault, failing (**de** in); **chacun a ses petits ~s** we've all got our little faults *ou* our shortcomings *ou* failings; **il n'a aucun ~** he's perfect, he hasn't a single failing; **la gourmandise n'est pas un gros ~** greediness isn't such a bad

fault → **curiosité** [c] (= *désavantage*) drawback; **ce plan/cette voiture a ses ~s** this plan/car has its drawbacks; **le ~ de** *ou* **avec* cette voiture, c'est que ...** the trouble *ou* snag* *ou* drawback with this car is that ... [d] (= *manque*) **~ de** [+ *raisonnement*] lack of; [+ *main-d'œuvre*] shortage of [e] **faire ~** [*temps*, *argent*, *talent*] to be lacking; (*Jur*) [*prévenu*, *témoin*] to default; **la patience/le temps lui fait ~** he lacks patience/time; **le courage lui a finalement fait ~** his courage failed him in the end; **ses amis lui ont finalement fait ~** his friends let him down in the end; **si ma mémoire ne me fait pas ~** if my memory serves me right [f] **à ~ de** for lack *ou* want of; **à ~ de vin, il boira du cidre** if there's no wine, he'll drink cider; **elle cherche une table ovale, ou, à ~, ronde** she is looking for an oval table, or, failing that, a round one (will do) [g] **être en ~** to be at fault *ou* in the wrong; **se mettre en ~** to put o.s. in the wrong; **prendre qn en ~** to catch sb out; (*Chasse*) **mettre les chiens en ~** to put the dogs off the scent; **c'est votre mémoire qui est en ~** it's your memory that's at fault [h] **par ~** by default; (*Jur*) **condamner/juger qn par ~** to sentence/judge sb in absentia; (*Math*) **calculer qch par ~** to calculate sth to the nearest decimal point; **il pèche par ~** he doesn't try hard enough; (*Ordin*) **le lecteur par ~** the default drive

[2] COMP ▸ **défaut de comparution** (*Jur*) default, non-appearance, failure to appear ▸ **le défaut de la cuirasse** (*lit*, *fig*) the chink in the armour ▸ **défaut d'élocution** = **défaut de prononciation** ▸ **le défaut de l'épaule** the hollow beneath the shoulder ▸ **défaut de fabrication** manufacturing defect ▸ **défaut de masse** (*Phys*) mass defect ▸ **défaut de paiement** (*Jur*) default in payment, non-payment ▸ **défaut de prononciation** speech impediment *ou* defect

défaut-congé (*pl* **défauts-congés**) [defokɔ̃ʒe] NM (*Jur*) dismissal of case through non-appearance of plaintiff

défaveur [defavœʀ] NF disfavour (*Brit*), disfavor (*US*) (**auprès de** with); **être en ~** to be out of favour (*Brit*) *ou* favor (*US*), be in disfavour; **s'attirer la ~ de** to incur the disfavour of

défavorable [defavɔʀabl] ADJ unfavourable (*Brit*), unfavorable (*US*) (**à** to); **voir qch d'un œil ~** to view sth with disfavour (*Brit*) *ou* disfavor (*US*)

défavorablement [defavɔʀabləmɑ̃] ADV unfavourably

défavoriser [defavɔʀize] ▸ conjug 1 ◂ VT (= *désavantager*) [*décision*, *loi*] to penalize; [*défaut*, *timidité*] to put at a disadvantage; [*examinateur*, *patron*] to put at an unfair disadvantage; **il a défavorisé l'aîné** he treated the eldest less fairly (than the others); **j'ai été défavorisé par rapport aux autres candidats** I was put at an unfair disadvantage with respect to the other candidates; **aider les couches plus défavorisées de la population** to help the most underprivileged *ou* disadvantaged sections of the population

défécation [defekasjɔ̃] NF (*Physiol*) defecation; (*Chim*) defecation, purification

défectif, -ive [defɛktif, iv] ADJ [*verbe*] defective

défection [defɛksjɔ̃] NF [*amis*, *alliés politiques*] desertion, defection; [*troupes*] failure to give *ou* lend assistance; [*candidats*] failure to attend *ou* appear; [*invités*] failure to appear; **faire ~** [*partisans*] to fail to lend support; [*invités*] to fail to appear *ou* turn up; **il y a eu plusieurs ~s** (*membres d'un parti*) a number of people have withdrawn their support; (*invités*, *candidats*) several people failed to appear

défectueux, -euse [defɛktɥø, øz] ADJ [*matériel*] faulty, defective; [*raisonnement*] faulty

défectuosité [defɛktɥozite] NF (= *état*) defectiveness, faultiness; (= *défaut*) imperfection, (slight) defect *ou* fault (**de** in)

défendable [defɑ̃dabl] ADJ (= *soutenable*) [*conduite*] defensible, justifiable; (= *soutenable*) [*position*] tenable, defensible; **il n'est pas ~** (*gén*) he has no excuse; (*Jur*) he cannot be defended

défendant [defɑ̃dɑ̃] → **corps**

défendeur, -deresse [defɑ̃dœʀ, dʀɛs] NM,F (*Jur*) defendant; **~ en appel** respondent

défendre [defɑ̃dʀ] ▸ conjug 41 ◂ **1** VT **a** (= *protéger*, *gén*, *Jur*, *Mil*) to defend; (= *soutenir*) [+ *personne*, *opinion*] to stand up for, defend (**contre** against); [+ *cause*] to champion, defend (**contre** against); **ville défendue par deux forts** town defended *ou* protected by two forts; (*fig*) **~ son bifteck*** to stand up for one's rights, defend one's livelihood **b** (= *interdire*) **~ qch à qn** to forbid sb sth; **~ à qn de faire qch** *ou* **qu'il fasse qch** to forbid sb to do sth; **le médecin lui défend le tabac/la mer** the doctor has forbidden him *ou* won't allow him to smoke/to go to the seaside; **il m'en a défendu l'accès** he forbade me access to it; **~ sa porte à qn** to bar one's door to sb, refuse to allow sb in; **ne fais pas ça, c'est défendu** don't do that, it's not allowed *ou* it's forbidden; **il est défendu de fumer** smoking is prohibited *ou* not allowed; **il est défendu de parler** talking is not allowed → **fruit**[1]

2 se défendre VPR **a** (= *se protéger*) (*gén*, *Jur*, *Mil*) to defend o.s. (**contre** against); (*contre brimades*, *critiques*) to stand up for o.s., defend o.s. (**contre** against); **se ~ du froid/de la pluie** to protect o.s. from the cold/rain **b** * (= *se débrouiller*) to manage, get along *ou* by; **elle se défend au tennis/au piano** she's not bad at tennis/on the piano; **il se défend bien/mal en affaires** he gets on *ou* does quite well/he doesn't do very well in business; **il se défend** he gets along *ou* by, he can hold his own (quite well) **c** (= *se justifier*) **se ~ d'avoir fait qch** to deny doing *ou* having done sth; **il se défendit d'être vexé/jaloux** he denied being *ou* that he was annoyed/jealous; **sa position/son point de vue se défend** his position/point of view is quite defensible; **ça se défend!** (*raisonnement*) it holds *ou* hangs together; **il dit que ce serait trop cher, ça se défend** he says it would be too expensive and he has a point *ou* it's a fair point **d** **se ~ de** (= *s'empêcher de*) to refrain from; **il ne pouvait se ~ d'un sentiment de pitié/gêne** he couldn't help feeling pity/embarrassment; **elle ne put se ~ de sourire** she could not refrain from smiling, she couldn't suppress a smile

défenestration [defənɛstʀasjɔ̃] NF defenestration

défenestrer [defənɛstʀe] ▸ conjug 1 ◂ **1** VT to throw out of the (*ou* a) window, defenestrate (*frm*) **2 se défenestrer** VPR to throw o.s. out of a window

défense[1] [defɑ̃s] NF **a** (*contre agression: gén*, *Mil*) defence (*Brit*), defense (*US*); **~s** (= *fortifications*) defences; **~ nationale/antiaérienne** *ou* **contre avions/passive** national/anti-aircraft/civil defence; **le budget de la ~ (nationale)** the (national) defence budget; **les ~s d'une frontière** border defences; **la ~ du pays** the country's defence *ou* protection; **ligne de ~** line of defence; **ouvrage de ~** fortification; **prendre la ~ de qn** to stand up for sb, defend sb **b** (= *protection*) [*droits*, *environnement*] protection; **la ~ des opprimés** the defence *ou* protection of the oppressed; **la ~ de l'emploi** job protection **c** (= *résistance*) defence (*Brit*), defense (*US*);

opposer une ~ courageuse to put up a brave defence; (*Physiol*, *Psych*) **mécanisme/instinct de ~** defence mechanism/instinct; **moyens de ~** means of defence; **~s immunitaires** immune defence system; **sans ~** (= *trop faible*) defenceless; (= *non protégé*) unprotected; **sans ~ contre les tentations** helpless *ou* defenceless against temptation → **légitime** **d** (*Sport*) defence (*Brit*), defense (*US*); **jouer en ~** to play in defence **e** (*Jur*) defence (*Brit*), defense (*US*); (= *avocat*) counsel for the defence (*Brit*), defense attorney (*US*); **assurer la ~ d'un accusé** to conduct the case for the defence; **la parole est à la ~** (*the counsel for*) the defence may now speak; **qu'avez-vous à dire pour votre ~?** what have you to say in your defence? **f** (= *interdiction*) **« ~ d'entrer »** "no entrance", "no entry", "no admittance"; **« propriété privée, ~ d'entrer »** "private property, no admittance *ou* keep out"; **« danger: ~ d'entrer »** "danger — keep out"; **« ~ de fumer/stationner »** "no smoking/parking", "smoking/parking prohibited"; **« ~ d'afficher »** "(stick *ou* post) no bills"; **~ d'en parler à quiconque** it is forbidden to speak of it to anyone; **il est sorti malgré ma ~** he went out in spite of the fact that I'd told him not to *ou* in spite of my having forbidden him to do so

défense[2] [defɑ̃s] NF [*éléphant*, *morse*, *sanglier*] tusk

défenseur [defɑ̃sœʀ] NM (*gén*, *Mil*, *Sport*) defender; [*cause*] champion, defender; [*doctrine*] advocate; (*Jur*) counsel for the defence (*Brit*), defense attorney (*US*); **l'accusé et son ~** the accused and his counsel; **~ de l'environnement** conservationist, preservationist → **veuf**

défensif, -ive [defɑ̃sif, iv] **1** ADJ (*Mil*, *fig*) defensive **2 défensive** NF **la défensive** the defensive; **être** *ou* **se tenir sur la défensive** to be on the defensive

déféquer [defeke] ▸ conjug 6 ◂ **1** VT (*Chim*) to defecate, purify **2** VI (*Physiol*) to defecate

déférence [deferɑ̃s] NF deference; **par ~ pour** in deference to

déférent, e [deferɑ̃, ɑ̃t] ADJ deferential, deferent → **canal**

déférer [defere] ▸ conjug 6 ◂ VT **a** (*Jur*) **~ une affaire** to refer a case to the court; **~ un coupable à la justice** to hand a guilty person over to the law **b** (= *céder*) to defer (**à** to) **c** † (= *conférer*) to confer (**à** on, upon)

déferlante [defɛʀlɑ̃t] ADJ F, NF (**vague**) **~** breaker; **la ~ de films américains/de produits nouveaux** the flood of American films/of new products

déferlement [defɛʀləmɑ̃] NM [*vagues*] breaking; [*violence*] surge, spread; [*véhicules*, *touristes*] flood; **ils étaient impuissants devant le ~ des troupes** they were powerless before the advancing tide of troops; **ce ~ d'enthousiasme le surprit** this sudden wave of enthusiasm surprised him; **le ~ de haine/des sentiments anti-catholiques dans tout le pays** the hatred/anti-Catholic feeling which has engulfed the country *ou* swept through the country

déferler [defɛʀle] ▸ conjug 1 ◂ VI [*vagues*] to break; **la violence/haine déferla sur le pays** violence/hatred swept through the country; **les touristes déferlaient sur les plages** tourists were streaming onto the beaches; **la foule déferla dans la rue/sur la place** the crowd flooded into the street/over the square **2** VT [+ *voile*, *pavillon*] to unfurl

déferrer [defeʀe] ▸ conjug 1 ◂ VT [+ *cheval*] to unshoe; [+ *porte*] to remove the iron plates from

défi [defi] NM (*gén*) challenge; (= *bravade*) defiance; **lancer un ~ à qn** to challenge sb; **relever un ~** to take up *ou* accept a challenge; **mettre qn au ~** to challenge *ou* defy sb (**de faire** to do); **c'est un ~ au bon sens** it defies common

sense, it goes against common sense; **d'un air** *ou* **d'un ton de ~** defiantly

défiance [defjɑ̃s] NF mistrust, distrust; **avec ~** with mistrust *ou* distrust, mistrustingly, distrustingly; **sans ~** [*personne*] unsuspecting; [*agir*, *s'abandonner*] unsuspectingly; **mettre qn en ~** to arouse sb's mistrust *ou* suspicions, make sb suspicious

défiant, e [defjɑ̃, ɑ̃t] ADJ mistrustful, distrustful

défibrillateur [defibʀijatœʀ] NM defibrillator

défibrillation [defibʀijasjɔ̃] NF defibrillation

déficeler [defis(ə)le] ▸ conjug 4 ◂ **1** VT to untie **2 se déficeler** VPR [*paquet*] to come untied *ou* undone

déficience [defisjɑ̃s] NF (*Méd*, *fig*) deficiency; **~ musculaire** muscular insufficiency; **~ immunitaire** immunodeficiency; **~ de mémoire** lapse of memory; **~ mentale** *ou* **intellectuelle** mental deficiency; **les ~s du système de production** the deficiencies in *ou* shortcomings of the production system

déficient, e [defisjɑ̃, ɑ̃t] **1** ADJ (*Méd*) [*force*, *intelligence*] deficient; [*raisonnement*] weak; [*matériel*] faulty, defective; **enfant ~ (intellectuellement)** mentally deficient child; **(physiquement)** child with a physical disability, physically disabled *ou* handicapped child **2** NM,F **~ mental/visuel** mentally/visually handicapped person; **~ moteur** person with motor deficiencies

déficit [defisit] NM **a** (*Fin*) deficit; **être en ~** to be in deficit; **le ~ budgétaire** the budget deficit; **le ~ de notre commerce extérieur** the deficit in our foreign trade; **~ de la balance des paiements** balance of payments deficit; **~ commercial/d'exploitation** trade/operating deficit; **~ de trésorerie** cash deficit; **les ~s sociaux** the social security budget deficit **b** [*manque*] **~ de ressources** resource(s) gap; **~ en main d'œuvre** labour (*Brit*) *ou* labor (*US*) shortage; (*Méd*) **~ en magnésium** magnesium deficiency; **~ psychologique/intellectuel** psychological/mental defect; **~ immunitaire** immunodeficiency

déficitaire [defisitɛʀ] ADJ (*Fin*) in deficit (*attrib*); [*récolte*] poor; [*année*] poor (**en** in), bad (**en** for); **~ en** [*main-d'œuvre*] short of, deficient in; **année ~ en blé** year showing a wheat shortage

défier [defje] ▸ conjug 7 ◂ **1** VT **a** [+ *adversaire*] to challenge (**à** to); **~ qn en combat singulier** to challenge sb to single combat; **~ qn du regard** to give sb a challenging look; **~ qn de faire qch** to defy *ou* challenge sb to do sth; **je t'en défie!** I dare *ou* challenge you (to)! **b** [+ *mort*, *adversité*] to defy, brave; [+ *opinion publique*] to fly in the face of, defy; [+ *autorité*] to defy, challenge; **ça défie l'imagination!** it defies the imagination!*; **à des prix qui défient toute concurrence** at absolutely unbeatable prices **2 se défier** VPR (*littér*) **se ~ de** to distrust, mistrust; **je me défie de moi-même** I don't trust myself; **défie-toi de ton caractère impulsif** beware of your impulsiveness; **défie-toi de lui!** beware of him!, be on your guard against him!

défigurement [defigyʀmɑ̃] NM [*vérité*] distortion; [*texte*, *tableau*] mutilation; [*visage*] disfigurement

défigurer [defigyʀe] ▸ conjug 1 ◂ VT **a** [*blessure*, *maladie*] to disfigure; [*bouton*, *larmes*] [*visage*] to spoil; **l'acné qui la défigurait** the acne that spoiled her looks **b** (= *altérer*) [+ *pensée*, *réalité*, *vérité*] to distort; [+ *texte*, *tableau*] to mutilate, deface; [+ *monument*] to deface; [+ *paysage*] to disfigure, mar, spoil

défilé [defile] NM **a** (= *cortège*) procession; (= *manifestation*) march; (*Mil*) march-past, parade; **~ de mode** *ou* **de mannequins** fashion show; (*Mil*) **~ aérien** flypast (*Brit*), flyover (*US*) **b** (= *succession*) [*visiteurs*] procession, stream;

[*voitures*] stream; [*impressions, pensées*] stream, succession ⃞c (*Géog*) (narrow) gorge, defile

défilement [defilmɑ̃] NM [*film*] projection; [*bande magnétique*] unreeling, unwinding; (*Ordin*) scrolling; (*Ciné*) **vitesse de ~** projection speed; (*Ordin*) **~ horizontal/vertical** horizontal/vertical scrolling

défiler [defile] ▶conjug 1◀ ⃞1 VT ⃞a [+ *aiguille, perles*] to unthread; [+ *chiffons*] to shred ⃞b [*Mil*] [+ *troupes*] to put under cover (*from the enemy's fire*)
⃞2 VI ⃞a (*Mil*) to march past, parade; [*manifestants*] to march (**devant** past) ⃞b [*bande magnétique*] to unreel, unwind; [*texte de téléprompteur*] to scroll; (*Ordin*) **faire ~ un document** to scroll a document; **faire ~ une bande magnétique** (*vers l'avant*) to (fast-)forward a tape; (*vers l'arrière*) to rewind a tape; **les souvenirs défilaient dans sa tête** a stream of memories passed through his mind; **les visiteurs défilaient devant le mausolée** the visitors filed past the mausoleum; **la semaine suivante tous les voisins défilèrent chez nous** the following week we were visited by all the neighbours one after the other; **nous regardions le paysage qui défilait devant nos yeux** we watched the scenery pass by ou (*plus vite*) flash by
⃞3 **se défiler** VPR ⃞a [*aiguille*] to come unthreaded; [*perles*] to come unstrung ou unthreaded
⃞b (*Mil*) to take cover (*from the enemy's fire*)
⃞c * [*personne*] (= *s'éclipser*) to slip away ou off; (= *se dérober*) **il s'est défilé** he wriggled ou ducked out of it

défini, e [defini] (*ptp de définir*) ADJ ⃞a (= *déterminé*) [*but*] definite, precise; **terme bien ~** well-defined term ⃞b (*Gram*) [*article*] definite; **passé ~** preterite

définir [definir] ▶conjug 2◀ VT [+ *idée, sentiment, position*] to define; (*Géom, Gram*) to define; [+ *personne*] to define, characterize; [+ *conditions*] to specify, define; **il se définit comme un humaniste** he defines himself as a humanist; **notre politique se définit comme étant avant tout pragmatique** our policies can be defined as being essentially pragmatic

définissable [definisabl(ə)] ADJ definable

▶ **définitif, -ive** [definitif, iv] ⃞1 ADJ ⃞a (= *final*) [*résultat, destination, résolution*] final; [*mesure, installation, victoire, fermeture*] permanent, definitive; [*solution*] definitive, final; [*étude, édition*] definitive; [*prix*] set, fixed; **son départ était ~** he was leaving for good, his departure was final; **les bâtiments provisoires sont vite devenus ~s** the temporary buildings quickly became permanent ⃞b (= *sans appel*) [*décision*] final; [*refus*] definitive, decisive; [*argument*] conclusive; **un jugement ~** a final judgment; **et c'est ~!** and that's that! ou that's final! ⃞2 **en définitive** LOC ADV (= *à la fin*) eventually; (= *somme toute*) in fact, when all is said and done

définition [definisjɔ̃] NF ⃞a [*concept, mot*] definition; [*mots croisés*] clue; **par ~** by definition; **~ de poste** job description ⃞b (*TV*) definition; **la haute ~** high definition; **(de) haute ~** high-definition (*épith*)

définitivement [definitivmɑ̃] ADV [*partir*] for good; [*résoudre*] conclusively, definitively; [*exclure, s'installer*] for good, permanently; [*refuser, décider, savoir*] definitely, positively; [*nommer*] on a permanent basis, permanently

définitoire [definitwar] ADJ (*Ling*) [*vocabulaire*] defining (*épith*)

défiscalisation [defiskalizasjɔ̃] NF tax exemption

défiscaliser [defiskalize] ▶conjug 1◀ VT to exempt from tax(ation)

déflagration [deflagrasjɔ̃] NF (*gén*) explosion; (*Chim*) deflagration

déflagrer [deflagre] ▶conjug 1◀ VI to deflagrate

déflation [deflɑsjɔ̃] NF (*Écon, Fin*) deflation; [*effectifs*] reduction, cut (**de** in); **~ salariale** declining wage trend

déflationniste [deflɑsjɔnist] ⃞1 ADJ [*politique, effets*] deflationary; [*économiste*] deflationist ⃞2 NMF deflationist

déflecteur [deflektœr] NM (*Aut*) quarter-light (*Brit*), vent (*US*); (*Tech*) jet deflector; (*Naut*) deflector

défleurir [deflœrir] ▶conjug 2◀ (*littér*) ⃞1 VT [+ *buisson*] to remove the blossom from ⃞2 VI [*buisson*] to shed its flowers ou its blossom

déflexion [defleksjɔ̃] NF deflection

déflocage [deflɔkaʒ] NM (*Tech*) removal of asbestos; **le ~ de l'immeuble a duré 6 mois** it took six months to remove the asbestos from the building

défloraison [deflɔrezɔ̃] NF (*Bot, littér*) falling of blossoms

défloration [deflɔrasjɔ̃] NF [*jeune fille*] defloration

déflorer [deflɔre] ▶conjug 1◀ VT. [+ *jeune fille*] to deflower; (*littér*) [+ *sujet, moments*] to spoil the charm of, deflower (*littér*)

défoliant [defɔljɑ̃] NM defoliant

défoliation [defɔljasjɔ̃] NF defoliation

défolier [defɔlje] ▶conjug 7◀ VTI to defoliate

défonçage [defɔ̃saʒ] NM, **défoncement** [defɔ̃smɑ̃] NM [*caisse, barque*] staving in; [*porte, clôture*] smashing in ou down, staving in; [*sommier, fauteuil*] breaking; [*route, terrain*] (*par bulldozers, camions*) ripping ou ploughing ou breaking up; (*Agr*) deep-ploughing

défonce [defɔ̃s] NF (*arg Drogue*) getting high*; **~ à la colle/aux solvants** getting high on glue/solvents; **il était en pleine ~** he was completely out of it*

défoncé, e [defɔ̃se] (*ptp de défoncer*) ⃞1 ADJ ⃞a [*canapé, fauteuil*] sagging; [*chemin, route*] full of potholes (*attrib*); **un vieux fauteuil tout ~** an old sunken armchair; **sur des routes ~es** on roads full of potholes ⃞b (*arg Drogue*) high*; **il était complètement ~** he was completely out of it*, he was as high as a kite* ⃞2 NM,F (= *drogué*) junkie*, drug addict; **un ~ au crack** a crack addict

défoncer [defɔ̃se] ▶conjug 3◀ ⃞1 VT [+ *caisse, barque*] to stave in, knock ou smash the bottom out of; [+ *porte, clôture*] to smash in ou down, stave in; [+ *sommier, fauteuil*] to break ou burst the springs of; [+ *route, terrain*] [*bulldozers, camions*] to rip ou plough ou break up; (*Agr*) to plough deeply, deep-plough; **il a eu le crâne défoncé** his skull was smashed in ⃞2 **se défoncer** VPR ⃞a* (= *travailler dur*) to work like a dog*, work flat out*; **se ~ pour qn/pour faire qch** to work like a dog* for sb/to do sth ⃞b (*arg Drogue*) to get high* (**à** on)

déforcer [defɔrse] ▶conjug 3◀ VT (*Belg*) to dishearten

déforestation [defɔrestasjɔ̃] NF deforestation

déformant, e [defɔrmɑ̃, ɑ̃t] ADJ [*miroir*] distorting; [*rhumatisme*] crippling

déformation [defɔrmasjɔ̃] NF ⃞a [*objet, métal*] bending (out of shape), distortion; [*bois*] warping; [*visage, image, vision*] distortion; [*vérité, pensée*] distortion, misrepresentation; [*esprit*] warping; **par une curieuse ~ d'esprit, il...** by a strange twist in his character, he...; **désolé, c'est de la ~ professionnelle** sorry, I can't help it, it's my job; **par ~ professionnelle** as a result of being so conditioned by one's job ⃞b (*Méd*) deformation; **souffrir d'une ~ de la hanche** to have a hip deformity

déformer [defɔrme] ▶conjug 1◀ ⃞1 VT [+ *objet, métal*] to bend (out of shape), distort; [+ *bois*] to warp; [+ *chaussures, vêtements*] to stretch out of shape; [+ *corps*] to deform; [+ *visage,*

image, vision] to distort; [+ *vérité, pensée*] to distort, misrepresent; [+ *esprit*] to warp; **vieillard au corps déformé** old man with a deformed ou misshapen body; **veste déformée** jacket which has lost its shape ou has gone out of shape; **pantalon (tout) déformé** trousers that have gone all baggy; **traits déformés par la douleur** features contorted ou distorted by pain; **mes propos ont été déformés** (*involontairement*) I've been misquoted; (*volontairement*) my words have been twisted; **il est déformé par son métier** he has been conditioned by his job → **chaussée**
⃞2 **se déformer** VPR [*objet*] to be bent (out of shape), lose its shape; [*métal*] to be bent (out of shape), be distorted; [*bois*] to warp; [*vêtement*] to lose its shape

défoulement [defulmɑ̃] NM [*instincts, sentiments*] (psychological) release; **moyen de ~** (psychological) outlet ou means of release; **après les examens on a besoin de ~** after the exams you need some kind of (psychological) release ou you need to let off steam*

défouler [defule] ▶conjug 1◀ ⃞1 VT **j'ai crié des injures, ça m'a défoulé** I shouted some abuse, it helped relieve my feelings ou helped me to get it out of my system*; **ça (vous) défoule de courir** running helps you unwind ou relax ⃞2 **se défouler** VPR (= *se libérer de tensions*) to let off steam*; (= *se relaxer*) to relax, unwind; **se ~ sur qn/qch** to take it out on sb/sth

défourailler* [defuraje] ▶conjug 1◀ VI to draw (one's gun)

défourner [defurne] ▶conjug 1◀ VT [+ *pain*] to take out of the oven; [+ *poteries*] to take out of the kiln

défragmentation [defragmɑ̃tasjɔ̃] NF (*Ordin*) [*disque dur*] defragmention

défragmenter [defragmɑ̃te] ▶conjug 1◀ VT (*Ordin*) [+ *disque dur*] to defragment

défraîchi, e [defreʃi] (*ptp de défraîchir*) ADJ [*article*] shopsoiled; [*fleur, couleur*] faded; [*tissu*] (= *passé*) faded; (= *usé*) worn; [*humour, idée*] dated, stale (*péj*)

défraîchir [defreʃir] ▶conjug 2◀ ⃞1 VT to take the freshness from ⃞2 **se défraîchir** VPR [*fleur, couleur*] to fade; [*tissu*] (= *passer*) to fade; (= *s'user*) to become worn

défraiement [defremɑ̃] NM payment ou settlement of expenses; **vous avez droit à un ~** you can claim expenses

défrayer [defreje] ▶conjug 8◀ VT ⃞a (= *payer*) **qn** to pay ou settle sb's expenses ⃞b (= *être en vedette*) **~ la conversation** to be the main topic of conversation; **~ la chronique** to be widely talked about, be in the news

défrichage [defriʃaʒ] NM, **défrichement** [defriʃmɑ̃] NM [*forêt, terrain*] clearing (*for cultivation*); **le ~ d'un sujet** the spadework (done) on a subject

défricher [defriʃe] ▶conjug 1◀ VT [+ *forêt, terrain*] to clear (*for cultivation*); [+ *sujet, question*] to open up, do the spadework on; (*fig*) **~ le terrain** to prepare the ground ou way (*fig*), clear the way (*fig*)

défricheur [defriʃœr] NM (*lit*) land-clearer; (*fig*) pioneer

défriper [defripe] ▶conjug 1◀ VT to smooth out

défriser [defrize] ▶conjug 1◀ VT ⃞a [+ *cheveux*] to straighten ⃞b (* = *contrarier*) [+ *personne*] to bug*; **ce qui me défrise** what bugs* ou gets* me; **et alors! ça te défrise?*** so (what)?*, what's it to you?*

défroisser [defrwase] ▶conjug 1◀ VT to smooth out

défroque [defrɔk] NF (= *frusques*) old cast-offs; (= *accoutrement*) getup*; [*moine*] effects (left by a dead monk)

défroqué, e [defrɔke] (*ptp de défroquer*)

défroquer

1 ADJ defrocked, unfrocked **2** NM defrocked *ou* unfrocked priest (*ou* monk)

défroquer [defʀɔke] ▸ conjug 1 ◂ **1** VT to defrock, unfrock **2** VI, **se défroquer** VPR to give up the cloth, renounce one's vows

défunt, e [defœ̃, œ̃t] **1** ADJ (*frm*) [*personne*] late (*épith*); (*littér*) [*espoir, année*] which is dead and gone; (*littér*) [*assemblée, projet*] defunct; **son ~ père** his late father **2** NM,F deceased

dégagé, e [degaʒe] (*ptp de* **dégager**) **1** ADJ **a** [*route*] clear; [*ciel*] clear, cloudless; [*espace, site*] open, clear; [*vue*] wide, open; [*front, nuque*] bare; **c'est un peu trop ~ autour des oreilles** it's a bit short around the ears **b** [*air, allure, manières*] casual, jaunty; [*ton*] airy, casual **2** NM (*Danse*) dégagé

dégagement [degaʒmɑ̃] NM **a** (= *action de libérer*) [*personne*] freeing, extricating; [*objet, main*] freeing; (*Mil*) [*troupe, ville*] relief; [*crédits, titres*] release (*for a specific purpose*); [*objet en gage*] redemption; **ils ont procédé au ~ des blessés enfouis sous les décombres** they began to free the injured from the rubble; **le ~ d'une promesse** going back on a promise **b** (*à l'accouchement*) expulsion, delivery; **~ de la tête** crowning **c** (= *production*) [*fumée, gaz, chaleur*] emission, emanation; [*énergie*] release; **un ~ de vapeurs toxiques** a discharge *ou* an emission of toxic fumes **d** (*Escrime*) disengagement; (*Ftbl, Rugby*) clearance; **faire un ~ au pied/au poing** to kick/knock a ball clear; **coup de pied de ~** kick downfield; (*en touche*) kick to touch **e** (= *espace libre*) [*forêt*] clearing; [*appartement*] (*gén*) open space; (= *couloir*) passage; (*Tech*) [*camion*] clearance, headroom (**de** above)

dégager [degaʒe] ▸ conjug 3 ◂ **1** VT **a** (= *libérer*) [*personne*] to free, extricate; [*objet, main*] to free; (*Mil*) [*troupe, ville*] to relieve, bring relief to; (*Fin*) [*crédits, titres*] to release (*for a specific purpose*); [*objet en gage*] to redeem, take out of pawn; **cela devrait se ~ facilement** it should come free easily; **on a dû ~ les blessés au chalumeau** the injured had to be cut loose *ou* free (from the wreckage); **~ qn de sa promesse/d'une obligation** to release *ou* free sb from his promise/an obligation; **~ qn d'une dette** to cancel sb's debt; **sa responsabilité d'une affaire** to disclaim *ou* deny (all) responsibility in a matter; **col/robe qui dégage le cou/les épaules** collar/dress which leaves the neck/shoulders bare **b** [+ *place, passage, table*] to clear (**de** of); (*Méd*) [+ *gorge, nez, poitrine*] to clear; (*chez le coiffeur*) **je voudrais que ce soit bien dégagé derrière les oreilles** cut it nice and short around the ears; **dégagez s'il vous plaît !** move away please!; **dégage !**‡ clear off!‡, buzz off!‡; **toutes ces vieilleries, à ~**‡ all these old things can go *ou* can be chucked out* **c** (= *exhaler*) [+ *odeur, fumée, gaz, chaleur*] to give off, emit; [+ *enthousiasme*] to radiate; **la maison dégageait une impression de tristesse** there was an aura of gloom about the house, the house had a gloomy feel about it **d** (= *extraire*) [+ *conclusion*] to draw; [+ *idée, sens*] to bring out; [+ *bénéfice, marge*] to show; (*Math*) **~ l'inconnue** to isolate the unknown quantity; **l'idée principale qu'on peut ~ de ce rapport** the main idea that can be drawn *ou* derived from this report; **je vous laisse ~ la morale de cette histoire** I'll let you guess what the moral of the story is **e** (*Escrime*) [+ *épées*] to disengage; (*Ftbl, Rugby*) [+ *ballon*] to clear; **~ (le ballon) en touche** to clear the ball into touch, kick (the ball) into touch **f** (*Danse*) to do a dégagé

2 se dégager VPR **a** [*personne*] to free *ou* extricate o.s., get free; (*Mil*) [*troupe*] to extricate itself (**de** from); **se ~ de** [+ *dette*] to free

o.s. of; [+ *obligation*] to free *ou* release o.s. from; [+ *affaire*] to get *ou* back out of; [+ *promesse*] to go back on; **il s'est dégagé d'une situation très délicate** he extricated himself from a very tricky situation; **j'ai une réunion mais je vais essayer de me ~** I have a meeting but I'll try to get out of it **b** [*ciel, rue, nez*] to clear; **le sommet/la silhouette se dégagea du brouillard** the summit/the outline loomed up out of the fog **c** [*odeur, fumée, gaz, chaleur*] to emanate, be given off; [*enthousiasme*] to emanate, radiate; [*impression*] to emanate (**de** from); **il se dégage d'elle une telle vitalité** she exudes such vitality **d** [*conclusion*] to be drawn; [*impression, idée, sens*] to emerge; [*morale*] to be drawn, emerge (**de** from); **il se dégage de tout cela que ...** from all this it emerges that ...

dégaine* [degɛn] NF **il a une drôle de ~** he's got an odd look about him; **je n'aime pas leur ~** I don't like the look of them

dégainer [degene] ▸ conjug 1 ◂ **1** VT [+ *épée*] to unsheathe, draw; [+ *pistolet*] to draw **2** VI to draw one's sword (*ou* gun)

déganter (se) [degɑ̃te] ▸ conjug 1 ◂ VPR to take off one's gloves; **main dégantée** ungloved hand

dégarni, e [degaʀni] ADJ [*front, arbre, salle, rayon*] bare; [*compte en banque*] low; [*portefeuille*] empty; [*magasin*] low in stock; [*tête, personne*] balding; **il est un peu ~ sur le dessus** he's a bit thin on top

dégarnir [degaʀniʀ] ▸ conjug 2 ◂ **1** VT [+ *maison, salle, vitrine*] to empty, clear; [+ *compte en banque*] to drain, draw heavily on; (*Mil*) [+ *ville, place*] to withdraw troops from; **il faut ~ un peu le sapin de Noël** we should take some of the decorations off the Christmas tree **2 se dégarnir** VPR [*salle*] to empty; [*personne*] to go bald; [*arbre*] to lose its leaves; [*bois*] to become sparse; (*Comm*) [*rayons*] to be cleaned out *ou* cleared; (*Comm*) [*stock*] to run out, be cleaned out; **il se dégarnit sur le dessus/au niveau des tempes** he's getting a bit thin on top/he has a receding hairline

dégât [dega] NM damage (*NonC*); **causer *ou* faire beaucoup de ~(s)** [*grêle, inondation, personne etc*] to cause *ou* do a lot of damage; [*alcool*] to do a lot of *ou* great harm; (*Assurances*) **~ des eaux** water damage → **limiter**

dégauchir [degoʃiʀ] ▸ conjug 2 ◂ VT [+ *bois*] to surface; [+ *pierre*] to dress

dégauchissage [degoʃisaʒ], **dégauchissement** [degoʃismɑ̃] NM [*bois*] surfacing; [*pierre*] dressing

dégauchisseuse [degoʃisøz] NF surface-planing machine

dégazage [degazaʒ] NM [*pétrolier*] degassing, emptying of tanks

dégazer [degaze] ▸ conjug 1 ◂ **1** VT to degas **2** VI [*navire*] to empty its tanks

dégel [deʒɛl] NM (*lit, fig*) thaw; **tu attends le ~ ou quoi ?*** what on earth are you waiting for?, are you waiting for Christmas or what? → **barrière**

dégelée* [deʒ(ə)le] NF (= *coups*) thrashing, hiding, beating; (= *défaite*) thrashing*; **recevoir une ~** (*coups*) to get a hiding; (*défaite*) to be thrashed*

dégeler [deʒ(ə)le] ▸ conjug 5 ◂ **1** VT **a** [+ *lac, terre*] to thaw (out); [+ *glace*] to thaw, melt; * [+ *pieds, mains*] to thaw **b** [+ *invité, réunion*] to thaw (out); **pour ~ l'atmosphère** to break the ice **c** (*Fin*) to unfreeze **2** VI **a** [*neige, lac*] to thaw (out) **b** (*Culin*) **faire ~** to thaw, leave to thaw **3** VB IMPERS **ça dégèle** it's thawing **4 se dégeler** VPR [*personne*] (*lit*) to warm up, get o.s. warmed up; (*fig*) to thaw (out); [*public*] to warm up

dégénératif, -ive [deʒeneʀatif, iv] ADJ [*affection, maladie*] degenerative, wasting

dégénéré, e [deʒeneʀe] (*ptp de* **dégénérer**) **1** ADJ **a** (= *abâtardi*) degenerate; (*Psych†*) defective; **t'es complètement ~ !*** you're such a moron!* **2** NM,F degenerate; (*Psych†*) defective; (*, péj*) moron*

dégénérer [deʒeneʀe] ▸ conjug 6 ◂ VI **a** (= *s'abâtardir*) [*race*] to degenerate; [*qualité*] to deteriorate **b** (= *mal tourner*) to degenerate (**en** into); **leur dispute a dégénéré en rixe** their quarrel degenerated into a brawl; **un coup de froid qui dégénère en grippe** a chill which develops into flu; **ça a rapidement dégénéré** [*débat, manifestation*] it soon got out of hand

dégénérescence [deʒeneʀesɑ̃s] NF **a** [*personne*] (*morale*) degeneracy; (*physique, mentale*) degeneration **b** [*moralité, race*] degeneration, degeneracy; [*qualité*] deterioration (**de** in) **c** (*Méd, Bio, Phys*) degeneration

dégénérescent, e [deʒeneʀesɑ̃, ɑ̃t] ADJ (*Méd*) degenerating, deteriorating

dégermer [deʒeʀme] ▸ conjug 1 ◂ VT to degerm, remove the germ from

dégingandé, e* [deʒɛ̃gɑ̃de] ADJ gangling, lanky

dégivrage [deʒivʀaʒ] NM [*réfrigérateur*] defrosting; [*avion, pare-brise*] de-icing; **~ automatique** auto-defrost

dégivrer [deʒivʀe] ▸ conjug 1 ◂ VT [+ *réfrigérateur*] to defrost; [+ *avion, pare-brise*] to de-ice; **rétroviseur dégivrant** heated *ou* de-icer rearview mirror

dégivreur [deʒivʀœʀ] NM [*réfrigérateur*] defroster; [*avion, pare-brise*] de-icer

déglaçage [deglasaʒ], **déglacement** [deglasmɑ̃] NM **a** (*Culin*) deglazing; **~ à la crème** deglazing with cream **b** (*Tech*) [*papier*] removal of the glaze (**de** from) **c** [*route*] removal of the ice (**de** from)

déglacer [deglase] ▸ conjug 3 ◂ VT **a** (*Culin*) to deglaze; **déglacez au vinaigre** deglaze with vinegar **b** (*Tech*) [+ *papier*] to remove the glaze from **c** [+ *route*] to remove the ice from

déglingue* [deglɛ̃g] NF dilapidation, decay; **il est au bord de la ~** he's on his last legs*

déglingué, e* [deglɛ̃ge] (*ptp de* **déglinguer**) ADJ [*mécanisme*] kaput*; [*valise*] battered, broken; [*banlieue, ville*] dilapidated, run-down; **la chaise était toute ~e** the chair was falling apart; **une voiture toute ~e** a ramshackle car; **nous vivons dans une société ~e** we live in a society that is coming apart at the seams *ou* that is falling apart

déglinguer* [deglɛ̃ge] ▸ conjug 1 ◂ **1** VT [+ *objet, appareil*] to bust* **2 se déglinguer** VPR [*appareil*] to be on the blink*; [*chaise*] to fall to pieces, fall *ou* come apart; [*serrure, robinet*] to go bust*; **se ~ l'estomac/la santé** to ruin one's stomach/one's health

déglutir [deglytiʀ] ▸ conjug 2 ◂ VTI (*Méd*) to swallow

déglutition [deglytisjɔ̃] NF (*Méd*) swallowing, deglutition (*SPEC*)

dégobiller* [degɔbije] ▸ conjug 1 ◂ VTI (= *vomir*) to puke‡

dégoiser* [degwaze] ▸ conjug 1 ◂ **1** VT [+ *boniments, discours*] to spout*; **qu'est-ce qu'il dégoise ?** what is he rattling on about?* **2** VI (= *parler*) to rattle on*, go on (and on)*; (= *médire*) **~ sur le compte de qn** to gossip about sb

dégommer* [degɔme] ▸ conjug 1 ◂ VT **a** (= *dégrader*) to demote; (= *détrôner*) to unseat; (= *renvoyer*) to give the push to*, fire, sack* (*Brit*); **se faire ~** to get the push*, be fired* *ou* sacked* (*Brit*) **b** [+ *avion*] to down*; [+ *quille*] to knock flying*; [+ *bille*] to knock out of the way; [+ *cible sur écran*] to zap*; [+ *cible sur stand de tir*] to hit

dégonflage [degɔ̃flaʒ] NM **a** [*pneu*] deflating **b*** (= *lâcheté*) chickening out*; **j'appelle ça**

du ~! that's what I call being chicken!*, that's what I call chickening out!*

dégonflard, e¤ [degɔ̃flaʀ, aʀd] NM,F (= *lâche*) chicken*, yellow-belly*

dégonflé, e [degɔ̃fle] (*ptp de* **dégonfler**) ① ADJ ⓐ [+ *pneu*] flat ⓑ¤ (= *lâche*) chicken* (*attrib*), yellow(-bellied)* ② NM,F yellow-belly*, chicken*

dégonflement [degɔ̃fləmɑ̃] NM [*ballon, pneu*] deflation; [*enflure*] reduction

dégonfler [degɔ̃fle] ▶ conjug 1 ◀ ① VT [+ *pneu*] to let down, let the air out of, deflate; [+ *ballon*] to deflate, let the air out of; [+ *enflure*] to reduce, bring down; [+ *chiffres, statistiques*] to reduce, bring down; [+ *effectif*] to reduce; [+ *mythe*] to debunk ② VI [*chiffre, effectifs*] to go down, fall; **ses yeux/jambes ont dégonflé** the swelling in his eyes/legs has gone down ③ **se dégonfler** VPR ⓐ [*ballon, pneu*] to deflate, go down; [*enflure*] to go down; **se ~ comme une baudruche** [*espoir, illusion, promesse*] to fade (away); [*mouvement politique, parti*] to fizzle out ⓑ¤ (= *avoir peur*) to chicken out*

dégorgement [degɔʀʒəmɑ̃] NM ⓐ (= *débouchage*) [*évier, égout*] clearing out ⓑ (= *évacuation*) [*eau, bile*] discharge ⓒ (= *écoulement*) [*égout, rivière*] discharge; [*gouttière*] discharge, overflow ⓓ [*Tech = lavage*] [*cuir*] cleaning; [*laine*] scouring

dégorgeoir [degɔʀʒwaʀ] NM (= *conduit d'évacuation*) overflow duct *ou* pipe; (*Pêche*) disgorger

dégorger [degɔʀʒe] ▶ conjug 3 ◀ ① VT ⓐ (= *déboucher*) [+ *évier, égout*] to clear out ⓑ (= *déverser*) [*tuyau*] [+ *eau*] to discharge, pour out; [*rue, rivière*] [+ *personnes*] to disgorge, pour forth *ou* out (**dans** into) ⓒ [*Tech = laver*] [+ *cuir, étoffe*] to clean; [+ *laine*] to scour ② VI ⓐ [*étoffe*] to soak (*to release impurities*); (*Culin*) [*viande*] to soak; **faire ~** [+ *étoffe, viande*] to soak; [+ *escargots*] *to clean by soaking in salted water*; **faites ~ le concombre** sprinkle the cucumber with salt and leave to drain ⓑ ~ **dans** [*égout, gouttière*] to discharge into; [*rivière*] to discharge itself into ③ **se dégorger** VPR [*eau*] to be discharged, pour out (**dans** into); [*foule*] to pour forth *ou* out (**dans** into)

dégot(t)er [degɔte] ▶ conjug 1 ◀ VT (= *trouver*) to dig up*, unearth, find

dégoulinade [degulinad] NF trickle

dégoulinement [degulinmɑ̃] NM (*en filet*) trickling; (*goutte à goutte*) dripping

dégouliner [deguline] ▶ conjug 1 ◀ VI (*en filet*) to trickle; (*goutte à goutte*) to drip; **ça me dégouline dans le cou** it's dripping *ou* trickling down my neck; **je dégoulinais (de sueur)*** I was dripping with sweat; **gâteau dégoulinant de crème** cake oozing with cream; **mélodrame dégoulinant de sentimentalité** melodrama full of treacly sentiment, cloyingly sentimental melodrama

dégoulinure [degulinyʀ] NF = **dégoulinade**

dégoupiller [degupije] ▶ conjug 1 ◀ VT [+ *grenade*] to pull the pin out of; **grenade dégoupillée** unpinned grenade, grenade with the pin pulled out

dégourdi, e* [deguʀdi] (*ptp de* **dégourdir**) ① ADJ (= *malin*) smart, resourceful, bright; **il n'est pas très ~** he's pretty clueless* ② NM,F **c'est un ~** he knows what's what*, he's on the ball*; (*iro*) **quel ~ tu fais !** you're a smart one! *ou* a bright one! *ou* a bright spark!* (*Brit*)

dégourdir [deguʀdiʀ] ▶ conjug 2 ◀ ① VT [+ *membres*] (*ankylosés*) to bring the circulation back to; (*gelés*) to warm up; (= *donner plus d'aisance à*) [+ *personne*] to knock the rough edges off, teach a thing or two to*; (= *réchauffer*) [*eau*] to warm (up); **le service militaire/habiter à Paris le dégourdira** military service/living in Paris will knock him into shape *ou* teach him a thing or two*; **~ qn en**

anglais/en physique to teach sb the basics of English/physics ② **se dégourdir** VPR **il est sorti pour se ~ un peu (les jambes)** he went out to stretch his legs a bit; **elle s'est un peu dégourdie depuis l'an dernier** she seems to have learnt a thing or two* since last year

dégoût [degu] NM ⓐ (*NonC* = *répugnance*) disgust (*NonC*), distaste (*NonC*) (**pour, de** for); **j'éprouve un certain ~ pour son comportement** I feel somewhat disgusted at his behaviour; **avoir du ~ pour** to feel disgust *ou* distaste for; **j'ai pris les épinards en ~** I don't like spinach these days, I've gone right off spinach (*Brit*); **je peux manger des cerises jusqu'au ~** I can eat cherries till they come out of my ears; **il fit une grimace de ~** he screwed up his face in disgust *ou* distaste; **ce ~ de la vie m'étonnait** such world-weariness surprised me ⓑ (= *aversion*) dislike; **ses ~s** the things he dislikes

dégoûtant, e [degutɑ̃, ɑ̃t] ① ADJ ⓐ (= *sale*) disgusting, filthy; (= *répugnant*) [*manie, image*] revolting ⓑ (= *scandaleux, injuste*) disgusting; **il a été ~ avec elle** the way he treated her was disgusting ⓒ (= *obscène, vicieux*) disgusting; **il est vraiment ~ ce type !** he's so disgusting! ② NM,F (= *personne sale*) (dirty) pig*; (= *personne injuste*) (*homme*) swine*; (*femme*) cow*; **espèce de vieux ~ !*** (*sale*) you messy old pig!*; (*vicieux*) you disgusting *ou* filthy old beast!*, you dirty old man!*

dégoûtation* [degutasjɔ̃] NF (= *dégoût*) disgust; (= *saleté*) **quelle ~!** what a disgusting *ou* filthy mess!

dégoûté, e [degute] (*ptp de* **dégoûter**) ① ADJ **je suis ~!** (*scandalisé*) I'm disgusted!; (*lassé*) I'm sick and tired of it!; **~ de la vie** weary *ou* sick of life; **il leur jeta un regard ~** he looked at them in disgust; (*hum*) **il n'est pas ~!** he's not (too) fussy! *ou* choosy!* ② NM,F **il a fait le ~** (*devant un mets, une offre*) he turned his nose up at it; **ne fais pas le ~!** don't be so fussy!

dégoûter [degute] ▶ conjug 1 ◀ ① VT ⓐ (= *écœurer*) **cet homme me dégoûte** that man disgusts me *ou* fills me with disgust, I find that man disgusting *ou* revolting; **ce plat me dégoûte** I find this food disgusting *ou* revolting; **la vie me dégoûte** I'm weary *ou* sick of life ⓑ **~ qn de qch** (= *ôter l'envie de*) to put sb (right) off sth; (= *remplir de dégoût pour*) to make sb feel disgusted with sth; **c'est à vous ~ d'être honnête** it's enough to put you (right) off being honest; **si tu n'aimes pas ça, n'en dégoûte pas les autres** if you don't like it, don't put the others off; **je suis dégoûté par ces procédés** I'm disgusted *ou* revolted by this behaviour; **ça m'a dégoûté de fumer** it put me (right) off smoking ② **se dégoûter** VPR **se ~ de qn/qch** to get sick of sb/sth; **elle s'est dégoûtée du tabac** she's gone right off smoking; **je me dégoûte d'avoir dit ça !** I'm disgusted with myself for having said that!

dégoutter [degute] ▶ conjug 1 ◀ VI to drip; **dégouttant de sueur** dripping with sweat; **l'eau qui dégoutte du toit** the water dripping down from *ou* off the roof; **dégouttant de pluie** dripping wet

dégradant, e [degʀadɑ̃, ɑ̃t] ADJ degrading

dégradation [degʀadasjɔ̃] NF ⓐ (*Mil*) demotion; (*Jur*) **~ civique** loss of civil rights ⓑ (= *avilissement*) [*personne*] degradation, debasement; [*qualité*] debasement; [*beauté*] defiling, debasement ⓒ (= *détérioration*) [*mur, bâtiment*] (*par le vandalisme*) damage; (*par la pluie*) erosion; [*monument, façade*] defacement; (*Géol*) [*roches*] erosion; (= *dégâts*) **~s** damage (*NonC*); **les ~s causées au bâtiment** the damage caused to the building; **la ~ des données** the corruption of the data ⓓ (*Art*) [*couleurs*] shading-off, gradation; [*lu-*

mière] gradation; ⓔ (= *avilissement moral*) degradation, debasement; (= *afaiblissement physique*) weakening ⓕ (= *détérioration*) [*relations, situation, qualité, santé, bâtiment*] deterioration; [*valeurs morales, forces*] decline; [*temps*] worsening; [*marché*] decline; (= *baisse*) [*monnaie, pouvoir d'achat*] weakening, erosion ⓖ (*Phys*) **la ~ de l'énergie** the degradation *ou* dissipation of energy

dégradé [degʀade] NM [*couleurs*] gradation; [*lumière*] (gradual) moderation; (*Ciné*) grading; (*Coiffure*) layers, layered cut; **couper en ~** to layer; **un ~ de rouges** a gradation of reds

dégrader [degʀade] ▶ conjug 1 ◀ ① VT ⓐ (*Mil* = *destituer*) ⓞ officier] to demote ⓑ (= *avilir*) [+ *personne*] to degrade, debase; [+ *qualité*] to debase; [+ *beauté*] to defile, debase ⓒ (= *détériorer*) [+ *mur, bâtiment*] [*vandales*] to damage, cause damage to; [*pluie*] to erode, cause to deteriorate; [+ *monument, façade*] to deface, damage; (*Géol*) [+ *roches*] to erode, wear away; [+ *relations*] to damage; **ils ont dégradé le matériel** they damaged the equipment; **les quartiers dégradés** the rundown areas ⓓ (*Art*) [+ *couleurs*] to shade off; [+ *lumière*] to subdue; **tons dégradés** shaded tones ⓔ [+ *cheveux*] to layer, cut in layers ② **se dégrader** VPR ⓐ [*personne*] (= *s'avilir moralement*) to degrade o.s., debase o.s.; (= *s'affaiblir physiquement*) to lose one's physical powers ⓑ [*relations, situation, qualité, santé, bâtiment*] to deteriorate; [*valeurs morales, forces*] to decline; [*mémoire*] to fail; [*marché*] to weaken; [*monnaie*] to grow weaker; [*pouvoir d'achat*] to shrink; **le temps se dégrade** the weather is deteriorating, there's a change for the worse in the weather ⓒ (*Art*) [*couleurs*] to shade off; [*lumière*] to become subdued ⓓ (*Sci*) [*énergie*] to become dissipated *ou* degraded

dégrafer [degʀafe] ▶ conjug 1 ◀ ① VT [+ *vêtement*] to unfasten, unhook, undo; [+ *bracelet, ceinture, collier*] to unfasten, undo; [+ *papiers*] to unstaple; **tu peux me ~?** can you undo me? ② **se dégrafer** VPR (*accidentellement*) [*vêtement, collier*] to come undone; [*papiers*] to come apart; (*volontairement*) [*personne*] to unfasten *ou* unhook *ou* undo one's dress *etc*

dégrafeur [degʀafœʀ] NM staple remover

dégraissage [degʀesaʒ] NM ⓐ **le ~ d'un vêtement** dry-cleaning a garment; **le ~ du bouillon** skimming (the fat off) the broth; **«~ et nettoyage à sec»** "dry cleaning" ⓑ (*Écon*) [*effectifs*] cutback, rundown (**de** in); **opérer un ~ ou des ~s** to slim down *ou* cut back the workforce

dégraissant [degʀesɑ̃] NM (= *produit*) spot remover

dégraisser [degʀese] ▶ conjug 1 ◀ ⓐ [+ *vêtement*] to dry-clean ⓑ (*Culin*) [+ *bouillon*] to skim (the fat off); [+ *viande*] to remove the fat from, cut the fat off; **jambon dégraissé** extra-lean ham ⓒ (*Menuiserie*) [+ *bois*] to trim the edges of ⓓ (*Écon*) [+ *personnel, effectifs*] to cut back, slim down

degré [dəgʀe] NM ⓐ (*gén* = *niveau*) degree; (= *stade de développement*) stage; (*Admin* = *échelon*) grade; **c'est le ~ zéro de la civilisation/ politique** it's civilisation/politics in its most basic form; **haut ~ de civilisation** high degree *ou* level of civilization; **à un ~ avancé de** at an advanced stage of; (*Alpinisme*) **mur de 6ème ~** grade 6 wall; **avare au plus haut ~** miserly in the extreme; **jusqu'à un certain ~** to some *ou* a certain extent *ou* degree, to a degree; **à un ~ moindre** ◊ **à un moindre ~** to a lesser degree *ou* extent; **par ~(s)** by degrees; **c'est le dernier ~ de la perfection/passion** it's the height of

perfection/passion; **il s'est montré grossier au dernier ~** he was extremely rude
[b] (*Gram, Mus, Sci*) degree; **équation du 1er/ 2ème ~** equation of the 1st/2nd degree; **il fait 20 ~s dans la chambre** it's 20 degrees (centigrade) in the room; **la température a baissé/ est montée de 2 ~s** the temperature has dropped/risen 2 degrees; **~ centigrade/ Fahrenheit/Celsius** degree centigrade/Fahrenheit/Celsius
[c] (= *proportion*) **~ d'alcool d'une boisson** proof of an alcoholic drink; **~ en alcool d'un liquide** percentage of alcohol in a liquid; **alcool à 90 ~s** 90% proof alcohol, surgical spirit (*Brit*); **du cognac à 40 ~s** 70° proof cognac; **ce vin fait (du) 11 ~s** this wine is 11° (*on Gay-Lussac scale*); **~ Baumé** degree Baumé
[d] (*dans un classement*) degree; (*Méd*) **brûlure du premier/deuxième ~** first/second degree burn; (*Sociol*) **~ de parenté** degree of (family) relationship *ou* of kinship (*frm*); **cousins au premier ~** first cousins; **parents au premier/ deuxième ~** relatives of the first/second degree; **prendre qch au premier ~** to take sth literally; **prendre qch au deuxième *ou* second ~** to look below the surface of sth; **c'est de l'humour au second ~** it's tongue-in-cheek (humour); **c'est à prendre au second ~** it's not to be taken literally
[e] (*Scol*) **enseignement du premier/second ~** primary/secondary education; **enseignant du premier/second ~** primary/secondary schoolteacher
[f] (*littér = marche*) step; **les ~s de l'échelle sociale** the rungs of the social ladder

dégressif, -ive [degʀesif, iv] ADJ [*impôt*] degressive; **appliquer un tarif ~** to use a sliding scale of charges

dégressivité [degʀesivite] NF [*impôt*] degression

dégrèvement [degʀɛvmɑ̃] NM **[a]** (*Fin*) **fiscal ◊ ~s fiscaux** tax exemption *ou* relief; **le ~ d'un produit** reduction of tax(es) on a product; **le ~ d'une industrie** reduction of the tax burden on an industry; **le ~ d'un contribuable** granting tax relief to a taxpayer **[b]** (*Jur*) [*hypothèque*] disencumbrance

dégrever [degʀəve] ▶conjug 5◀ VT [+ *produit*] to reduce the tax(es) on; [+ *industrie*] to reduce the tax burden on; [+ *contribuable*] to grant tax relief to; [+ *immeuble*] to disencumber

dégriffé, e [degʀife] **1** ADJ **robe ~e** unlabelled designer dress **2** NM **magasin de ~s** designer seconds store; **ils vendent du ~** they sell designer seconds

dégringolade [degʀɛ̃gɔlad] NF [*personne, objet*] fall; [*prix, firme*] tumble; (*Bourse*) [*cours, monnaie*] collapse; **pour stopper la ~ des prix** to stop prices (from) collapsing; **après son divorce, ça a été la ~** after his divorce he went downhill

dégringoler [degʀɛ̃gɔle] ▶conjug 1◀ **1** VI **[a]** [*personne, objet*] to tumble (down), fall; **il a dégringolé jusqu'en bas** he tumbled all the way down, he came *ou* went tumbling down; **elle a dégringolé du toit** she tumbled *ou* fell off the roof; **elle a fait ~ toute la pile de livres** she toppled the whole pile of books over *ou* brought the whole pile of books (crashing) down; **ça dégringole !*** [*pluie*] it's pouring (down) *ou* tipping down* (*Brit*) **[b]** [*monnaie, prix*] to collapse, take a tumble; [*firme, réputation*] to tumble, take a tumble; **il a dégringolé (jusqu')à la 15ème place/dans les sondages** he tumbled to 15th place/in the polls **2** VT [+ *escalier, pente*] (*en courant*) to rush *ou* tear down; (*en tombant*) to fall down

dégrippant [degʀipɑ̃] NM penetrating oil

dégripper [degʀipe] ▶conjug 1◀ VT to unblock, unchoke

dégrisement [degʀizmɑ̃] NM (*lit, fig*) sobering up

dégriser [degʀize] ▶conjug 1◀ **1** VT (*lit*) to sober up; (*fig*) to sober up, bring back down to earth **2** **se dégriser** VPR (*lit*) to sober up; (*fig*) to sober up, come back down to earth

dégrossir [degʀosiʀ] ▶conjug 2◀ VT **[a]** [+ *bois*] to trim, cut down to size; [+ *marbre*] to rough-hew **[b]** [+ *projet, travail*] to rough out, work out roughly, do the spadework on **[c]** [+ *personne*] to knock the rough edges off, polish up; **individu mal dégrossi** coarse *ou* unpolished *ou* unrefined individual; **il s'est un peu dégrossi** he has lost some of his rough edges

dégrossissage [degʀosisaʒ] NM [*bois*] trimming; [*marbre*] rough-hewing

dégrouiller (se)* [degʀuje] ▶conjug 1◀ VPR (= *se dépêcher*) to hurry up, get a move on*; **allez, dégrouille(-toi) !** come on, hurry up! *ou* get a move on!*; **se dégrouiller de *ou* pour faire qch** to hurry to do sth

dégroupement [degʀupmɑ̃] NM putting *ou* dividing into groups

dégrouper [degʀupe] ▶conjug 1◀ VT to put *ou* divide into groups

déguenillé, e [deg(ə)nije] **1** ADJ ragged, tattered **2** NM,F ragamuffin

déguerpir* [degɛʀpiʀ] ▶conjug 2◀ VI (= *s'enfuir*) to clear off*, scarper* (*Brit*); **faire ~** [+ *ennemi*] to scatter; [+ *voleur*] to chase *ou* drive off

dégueu: [degø] ADJ ABRÉV = **dégueulasse**

dégueulasse: [degœlas] **1** ADJ **[a]** (= *crasseux, sale*) disgusting, filthy **[b]** (= *mauvais, injuste*) lousy*, rotten*; **il a fait un temps ~** the weather was lousy*; **c'est ~ de faire ça** that's a lousy* *ou* rotten* thing to do; **il a vraiment été ~ avec elle** he was really rotten* to her; **c'est pas ~** it's not bad at all **[c]** (= *vicieux*) disgusting; **il est vraiment ~, ce type** he's a filthy swine: **2** NMF [*personne*] (*sale*) dirty pig:; (*mauvais, vicieux*) rotten: *ou* horrible swine:; (*femme*) bitch, cow: (*Brit*); **c'est un gros ~** he's a lousy *ou* rotten swine:; **c'est un vieux ~** he's a dirty old man:

dégueulasser: [degœlase] ▶conjug 1◀ VT [+ *vêtement, feuille, tapis*] to muck up*, mess up*, make mucky*

dégueuler: [degœle] ▶conjug 1◀ VTI (= *vomir*) to throw up:, spew (up):, puke (up):; **c'est à ~** it's enough to make you throw up: *ou* spew (up): *ou* puke (up):

dégueulis: [degœli] NM puke:

déguisé, e [degize] (*ptp de* **déguiser**) ADJ **[a]** (*pour tromper*) in disguise (*attrib*), disguised (**en** as); (*pour s'amuser*) in fancy dress (*Brit*), in costume (*US*); **~ en Zorro** dressed up as Zorro **[b]** [*voix, écriture, subvention, chômage*] disguised; [*ambition, sentiment*] disguised, masked, veiled; [*prêt, accord*] backdoor (*épith*); **non ~** unconcealed, undisguised; **il parlait avec une hostilité à peine ~e** he spoke with thinly veiled *ou* disguised hostility; **les taxes ont augmenté sous une forme ~e** there have been hidden tax increases

déguisement [degizmɑ̃] NM (*pour tromper*) disguise; (*pour s'amuser*) disguise, fancy dress (*Brit*), costume (*US*); (*littér*) **sans ~** without disguise, openly

déguiser [degize] ▶conjug 1◀ **1** VT (*gén*) [+ *voix, écriture, visage*] to disguise; [+ *pensée, ambition, vérité*] to disguise, mask, veil; [+ *poupée, enfant*] to dress up (**en** as); **je ne puis vous ~ ma surprise** I cannot conceal my surprise from you **2** **se déguiser** VPR (*pour tromper*) to disguise o.s.; (*pour s'amuser*) to dress up, to put on fancy dress (*Brit*); **se ~ en Zorro** to dress up as Zorro; **se ~ en courant d'air*** to make o.s. scarce*

dégurgiter [degyʀʒite] ▶conjug 1◀ VT [+ *nourriture*] to vomit *ou* bring back (up); [+ *leçon*] to parrot, regurgitate

dégustateur, -trice [degystatœʀ, tʀis] NM,F [*vin*] wine taster

dégustation [degystasjɔ̃] NF [*coquillages, fromages*] sampling; **une ~ de vin(s)** a wine-tasting session; « **ici, ~ d'huîtres à toute heure** » "oysters available *ou* served at all times"

déguster [degyste] ▶conjug 1◀ **1** VT [+ *vins*] to taste; [+ *coquillages, fromages*] to sample; [+ *repas, café, spectacle*] to enjoy, savour; **as-tu fini ton café ? — non, je le déguste** have you finished your coffee? — no, I'm enjoying it *ou* savouring it **2** VI* (= *souffrir*) **il a dégusté !** he didn't half have a rough time!*; **j'ai une rage de dents, je déguste !** I've got toothache and I'm in agony!* *ou* and it's killing me!*

déhanché, e [deɑ̃ʃe] (*ptp de* **déhancher**) ADJ [*démarche*] swaying; [*infirme*] lop-sided; **il se tenait légèrement ~** he was standing with his weight on one leg

déhanchement [deɑ̃ʃmɑ̃] NM (= *démarche*) swaying walk; [*infirme*] lop-sided walk; (= *posture*) standing with one's weight on one hip

déhancher (se) [deɑ̃ʃe] ▶conjug 1◀ VPR **[a]** (*en marchant*) to sway one's hips **[b]** (*immobile*) to stand with *ou* lean one's weight on one hip

dehors [dəɔʀ] **1** ADV **[a]** (= *à l'extérieur*) outside; (= *à l'air libre*) outside, outdoors, out of doors; (= *pas chez soi*) out; **attendez-le ~** wait for him outside; **je serai ~ toute la journée** I'll be out all day; **par beau temps, les enfants passent la journée ~** when it's fine, the children spend the day outdoors *ou* out of doors *ou* outside; **il fait plus frais dedans que ~** it is cooler inside than out(side) *ou* indoors than out(doors); **cela ne se voit pas de ~** it can't be seen from (the) outside; **passez par ~ pour aller au jardin** go round the outside (of the house) to get to the garden; **dîner ~** (*dans le jardin*) to eat out of doors *ou* outside; (*au restaurant*) to eat *ou* dine out; **jeter *ou* mettre *ou* ficher* *ou* foutre: qn** (*gén*) to throw *ou* kick: *ou* chuck: sb out; [*patron*] to sack* *ou* fire* sb; **mettre le nez *ou* le pied ~** to set foot outside; **il fait un temps à ne pas mettre le nez ~** it's weather for staying indoors
[b] **au ~** : **au ~, elle paraît calme, mais c'est une nerveuse** outwardly she looks relaxed, but actually she's quite highly strung; **au ~, la situation est tendue** outside the country, the situation is tense
[c] **en ~** : **avoir les pieds en ~** to have turned-out feet, be splay-footed; **marcher les pieds en ~** to walk with one's feet *ou* toes turned out, walk splay-footed; **en ~ de** (*lit*) outside; (*fig*) (= *sans rapport avec*) outside, irrelevant to; (= *excepté*) apart from; **ce passage est en ~ du sujet** this passage is outside the subject *ou* is irrelevant (to the subject); **en ~ de cela, il n'y a rien de neuf** apart from that *ou* beyond that *ou* otherwise there's nothing new; **cette tâche est en ~ de ses possibilités** this task is beyond his capabilities; **il a voulu rester en ~ de cette affaire** he didn't want to get involved; **en ~ de tout contrôle** [*fabriquer, exporter*] without any form of control

2 NM **[a]** (= *extérieur*) outside; **on n'entend pas les bruits du ~** you can't hear the noise from outside; **l'air du ~** the fresh air; **les détenus n'avaient aucune communication avec le ~** the prisoners had no contact with the outside world; **ce sont certainement des gens du ~ qui ont commis ce vol** it must be outsiders *ou* people from outside who are responsible for the theft

3 **dehors** NMPL (= *apparences*) **les ~ sont trompeurs** appearances are deceptive; **sous des ~ aimables, il est dur** under his friendly exterior, he's a hard man

déhoussable [deusabl] ADJ with loose covers (*attrib*)

déicide [deisid] **1** ADJ deicidal **2** NMF deicide **3** NM (= *crime*) deicide

déictique [deiktik] NM (Ling) deictic

déification [deifikasjɔ̃] NF deification

déifier [deifje] ▸ conjug 7 ◂ VT to deify

déisme [deism] NM deism

déiste [deist] 1 ADJ deistic, deist 2 NMF deist

déité [deite] NF (littér) deity

déjà [deʒa] ADV a (= dès maintenant, dès ce moment) already; **il a ~ fini** he has finished already, he has already finished; **est-il ~ rentré ?** has he come home yet?; (surprise) has he come home already?; **à trois heures il avait ~ écrit trois lettres** he'd already written three letters by three o'clock; **~ à cette époque** even then; **j'aurais ~ fini si tu ne me dérangeais pas tout le temps** I would have finished by now ou already if you didn't keep bothering me all the time; **je l'aurais ~ dit si je n'avais pas craint de le vexer** I would have said it before now ou by now ou already if I hadn't been afraid of offending him
b (= auparavant) before, already; **je suis sûr de l'avoir ~ rencontré** I'm sure I've met him before, I'm sure I've already met him; **j'ai ~ fait ce genre de travail** I've done that sort of work before, I've already done that sort of work; **c'est du ~-vu** we've seen it all before, it's old hat*; **impression de ~-vu** sense ou feeling of déjà vu
c (intensif) **1000 F, c'est ~ pas mal*** 1,000 francs, that's not bad at all; **30 tonnes, c'est ~ un gros camion** 30 tons, that's quite a big truck ou that's a fair-sized truck; **il est ~ assez paresseux** he's lazy enough as it is; **enfin, c'est ~ quelque chose !** anyway, it's better than nothing! ou it's a start!; **~ que* je ne suis pas riche, s'il faut encore payer une amende ...** I'm not rich as it is but if I have to pay a fine as well ...
d (* : interrogatif) **qu'est-ce qu'il a dit, ~ ?** what was it he said again?, what did he say again?; **c'est combien, ~ ?** how much is it again?, how much did you say it was again? → **ores**

déjanté, e: [deʒɑ̃te] (ptp de **déjanter**) ADJ **tu es complètement ~ !** you're off your rocker* ou trolley* (Brit)!

déjanter [deʒɑ̃te] ▸ conjug 1 ◂ 1 VT [pneu] to remove from its rim 2 VI* (= devenir fou) to go crazy*; **non mais tu déjantes !** you must be off your rocker!* ou trolley!* (Brit) 3 **se déjanter** VPR [pneu] to fall off its rim

déjection [deʒɛksjɔ̃] NF a (Méd) evacuation; **~s** faeces, excrement b (Géol) **~s** ejecta (SPÉC), ejectamenta (SPÉC) → **cône**

déjeté, e [deʒ(ə)te] ADJ [position, mur, arbre, infirme] lop-sided, crooked; [colonne vertébrale] twisted; **il est tout ~** he's all lop-sided ou misshapen

déjeuner [deʒœne] ▸ conjug 1 ◂ 1 VI a (gén : à midi) to have lunch; **nous avons déjeuné de fromage et de pain** we had bread and cheese for lunch; **inviter qn à ~** to invite sb to lunch; **rester à ~ chez qn** to stay and have lunch with sb, stay for ou to lunch at sb's; **viens ~ avec nous demain** come and have lunch with us tomorrow, come to lunch with us tomorrow; **nous avons déjeuné sur l'herbe** we had a picnic lunch; **ne pars pas sans ~** don't go before you've had your lunch
b (Belg, Helv = le matin) to (have) breakfast → **pouce**
2 NM a (= repas de midi : gén) lunch, luncheon (frm); **~ d'affaires** business lunch; **~ de travail** working lunch; **~ sur l'herbe** picnic lunch; **prendre son ~** to have lunch; **j'ai eu du poulet à ~** I had chicken for lunch; **j'ai ma mère à ~** I've got my mother coming for lunch
b (Belg, Helv : du matin) breakfast
c (= tasse et soucoupe) breakfast cup and saucer
d (loc) **ça a été un vrai ~ de soleil** (vêtement,

tissu) it didn't take long to fade; (objet) it soon gave up the ghost*, it didn't last long; (résolution) it was a flash in the pan, it didn't last long

déjouer [deʒwe] ▸ conjug 1 ◂ VT [+ complot] to foil, thwart; [+ plan] to thwart, frustrate; [+ ruse] to outsmart; [+ surveillance] to elude; **~ les plans de l'ennemi** to frustrate the enemy in his plans, confound the enemy's plans; **j'ai déjoué ses plans** I thwarted his plans, I outwitted him

déjuger (se) [deʒyʒe] ▸ conjug 3 ◂ VPR to go back on ou reverse one's decision

de jure [deʒyre] LOC ADJ, LOC ADV de jure

delà [dəla] 1 ADV a **au-~** beyond; **au-~ il y a l'Italie** beyond that is Italy; **il a eu ce qu'il voulait et bien au-~** he had all he wanted and more (besides); **vous avez droit à dix bouteilles et pas au-~/mais au-~ vous payez une taxe** you're entitled to ten bottles and no more/but above that you pay duty; **n'allez pas au-~** (somme, prix) don't go beyond ou over that figure (ou sum etc), don't exceed that figure (ou sum etc); **mes connaissances ne vont pas au-~** that's as far as my knowledge goes, that's the extent of my knowledge
b **par(-)delà** beyond; **devant eux il y a le pont et par(-)delà l'ennemi** in front of them is the bridge and beyond that the enemy ou and on the other ou far side of it, the enemy
c **en ~** beyond, outside; **la clôture était à 20 mètres et il se tenait un peu en ~** the fence was 20 metres away and he was standing just beyond it ou outside it
d (littér) **de ~ les mers** from beyond ou over the seas → **deçà**
2 PRÉP **au ~ de** [+ lieu, frontière] beyond, on the other side of; [+ somme, limite] over, above; (littér) **au ~ des mers** overseas, beyond ou over the seas; **ceci va au ~ de tout ce que nous espérions** this goes (far) beyond anything we hoped for; **au ~ de la conscience/douleur** beyond consciousness/pain; **aller au ~ de ses forces/moyens** to go beyond ou exceed one's strength/means
b **par ~** beyond; **par ~ les mers** overseas, beyond ou over the seas; **par ~ les apparences** beneath the surface (fig); **par ~ les siècles** across the centuries → **par-delà**

délabré, e [delabre] (ptp de **délabrer**) ADJ [maison] dilapidated, ramshackle (épith), tumbledown (épith); [mobilier, matériel] broken-down; [santé] ruined; [mur] crumbling, in ruins (attrib); [affaires] in a poor ou sorry state (attrib); [fortune] depleted

délabrement [delabrəmɑ̃] NM [maison] dilapidation, decay, ruin; [santé, affaires] poor ou sorry state; [vêtements] raggedness; [mobilier, matériel, mur] decay, ruin; [fortune] depletion; **état de ~** dilapidated state, state of decay ou ruin

délabrer [delabre] ▸ conjug 1 ◂ 1 VT [+ maison] to ruin; [+ mobilier, matériel] to spoil, ruin; [+ santé] to ruin, impair 2 **se délabrer** VPR [maison, mur, matériel] to fall into decay; [santé] to break down; [affaires] to go to rack and ruin

délacer [delase] ▸ conjug 3 ◂ 1 VT [+ chaussures] to undo (the laces of); [+ corset] to unlace 2 **se délacer** VPR [chaussures] to come undone

▾ **délai** [dele] 1 NM a (= temps accordé) time limit; **c'est un ~ trop court pour ...** it's too short a time for ...; **je vous donne trois mois, c'est un ~ impératif** I'll give you three months and that's the absolute limit; **avant l'expiration du ~** before the deadline; **dans le ~ imparti ou prescrit** within the allotted ou prescribed time, within the time laid down ou allotted; **dans un ~ de six jours** within (a period of) six days; (sur facture) **livrable dans un ~ de quinze jours** allow two weeks for delivery; **vous êtes dans les ~s** you're within the time

limit; **ce sera fait dans les ~s** it'll be done within the time limit ou allotted time; **observer ou respecter ou tenir les ~s** [travail] to keep ou meet the deadline; [livraison] to keep ou meet delivery dates; **prolonger un ~** to extend a time limit ou a deadline
b (= période d'attente) waiting period; **il faut compter un ~ de huit jours** you'll have to allow a week, there'll be a week's delay
c (= sursis) extension; **un dernier ~ de dix jours** a final extension of ten days; **accorder des ~s successifs** to allow further extensions; **il va demander un ~ pour achever le travail** he's going to ask for more time to finish off the job
d (loc) **à bref ~** [prévenir] at short notice; (= très bientôt) shortly, very soon; **dans le(s) plus bref(s) ~(s)** ◊ **dans les meilleurs ~s** as soon ou as quickly as possible; **il faut payer avant le 15, dernier ~** it must be paid by the 15th at the latest, the 15th is the deadline for payment; **15 octobre, dernier ~ pour les inscriptions** 15th October is the closing ou final date for registration, registration must be completed by 15th October at the latest; **sans ~** without delay, immediately
2 COMP ► **délai de carence** (Fin, Jur) waiting period (before receiving social security payments) ► **délai d'exécution** (pour un travail) turnaround time ► **délai de prescription** (Jur) limitation period ► **délai de grâce** (Fin, Jur) grace period; **un ~ de grâce de cinq jours** five days' grace ► **délai de fabrication** production time ► **délai de livraison** delivery time ou period ► **délai de paiement** term of payment, time for payment ► **délai de préavis** term ou period of notice ► **délai de réflexion** (avant réponse) time to think; (avant sanctions) cooling-off period; (Comm) right-to-cancel period ► **délai de rigueur** final deadline; **à remettre avant le 15 mai, ~ de rigueur** to be handed in before the final deadline of May 15th

délai-congé (pl **délais-congés**) [delɛkɔ̃ʒe] NM term ou period of notice

délaissement [delɛsmɑ̃] NM (= action) abandonment, desertion; (= état) neglect, state of neglect ou abandonment; (Jur) relinquishment ou renunciation (of a right)

délaisser [delese] ▸ conjug 1 ◂ VT a (= abandonner) [+ famille, ami] to abandon, give up; [+ travail] to give up, quit; **épouse délaissée** deserted wife b (= négliger) [+ famille, ami, travail] to neglect; **c'est un métier délaissé par les jeunes** young people don't go in for this kind of work; **épouse/fillette délaissée** neglected wife/little girl c (Jur) [+ droit] to relinquish

délassant, e [delasɑ̃, ɑ̃t] ADJ [massage, bain] relaxing; [lecture] entertaining

délassement [delasmɑ̃] NM (= état) relaxation, rest; (= distraction) relaxation

délasser [delase] ▸ conjug 1 ◂ 1 VT (= reposer) [+ membres] to refresh; (= divertir) [+ personne, esprit] entertain; **un bon bain, ça délasse** a good bath is very relaxing; **c'est un livre qui délasse** it's an entertaining sort of book 2 **se délasser** VPR (= se détendre) to relax (en faisant qch by doing sth)

délateur, -trice [delatœr, tris] NM,F (frm) informer

délation [delasjɔ̃] NF (frm) denouncement, informing; **lettre de ~** denunciatory letter

délavage [delavaʒ] NM a [aquarelle] watering down; [tissu, inscription] fading b [terre] waterlogging

délavé, e [delave] (ptp de **délaver**) ADJ a [tissu] faded; [inscription] washed-out; **jeans ~s** prewashed jeans; **un ciel ~ après la pluie** a watery ou washed-out (blue) sky after rain b [terre] waterlogged

délaver [delave] ▸ conjug 1 ◂ VT a [+ aquarelle] to water down; [+ tissu, inscription] to (cause to) fade (*by the action of water*) b [+ *terre*] to waterlog

Delaware [dəlawɛʀ] NM Delaware

délayage [delejaʒ] NM [*couleur*] thinning down; (*Culin*) [*farine, poudre*] mixing (*to a certain consistency*) (**dans** with); (*fig péj*) [*idée*] dragging out, spinning out; [*texte, exposé*] padding out; (*péj*) **faire du ~** [*personne, écrivain*] to waffle*; **son commentaire est un pur ~** his commentary is pure waffle*

délayer [deleje] ▸ conjug 8 ◂ VT [+ *couleur*] to thin down; (*Culin*) [+ *farine, poudre*] to mix (*to a certain consistency*) (**dans** with); (*péj*) [+ *idée*] to drag out, spin out; [+ *exposé*] to pad out; **~ 100 g de farine dans un litre d'eau** mix 100 g of flour with a litre of water; **quelques idées habilement délayées** a few ideas cleverly spun out

Delco® [dɛlko] NM distributor → **tête**

deleatur [deleatyʀ] NM INV delete mark *ou* sign, deleatur (*SPÉC*)

délectable [delɛktabl] ADJ delectable

délectation [delɛktasjɔ̃] NF delight, delectation (*littér*); (*Rel*) delight; **avec ~** [*écouter*] with delight; [*boire*] with relish; **~ morose** delectatio morosa

délecter (se) [delɛkte] ▸ conjug 1 ◂ [1] VT (*littér*) to delight [2] **se délecter** VPR **se ~ de qch/à faire** to delight *ou* revel *ou* take delight in sth/in doing; **il se délectait** he was thoroughly enjoying it

délégataire [delegatɛʀ] NMF proxy

délégation [delegasjɔ̃] NF a (= *groupe*) delegation; (= *commission*) commission; **ils sont allés en ~ voir le patron** they went as a delegation to see the boss b (= *mandat*) delegation; **quand il est absent, sa secrétaire signe le courrier par ~** when he is away his secretary signs his letters on his authority; **il agit par ~** *ou* **en vertu d'une ~** he is acting on somebody's authority; (*Jur*) **~ de créance** assignment *ou* delegation of debt; **~ de pouvoirs** delegation of powers; (*Mil*) **~ de solde** assignment of pay (*to relatives*) c (*Admin* = *succursale*) branch, office(s); **Délégation générale pour l'armement** state organization responsible for armament programmes; **Délégation à l'aménagement du territoire et à l'action régionale** state organization for regional development

délégué, e [delege] (*ptp de* **déléguer**) [1] ADJ delegated (à to); **membre ~** delegate; (*Ciné*) **producteur ~** associate producer; **~ à qch** [*adjoint, directeur*] responsible for sth → **administrateur, juge, ministre** [2] NM,F (= *représentant*) representative; (à *une réunion, une conférence*) delegate; (*Scol*) **~ rectoral** ≈ temporary teacher; (*Scol*) **~ de classe/de parents d'élèves** class/parents' representative; **~ du personnel** staff representative; **~ général** [*parti politique*] deputy leader; [*association, organisme*] chief representative; **~ syndical** union representative

---

DÉLÉGUÉS

At the start of the new school year in state "collèges" and "lycées", pupils elect two class representatives known as "délégués de classe", as well as two deputies. The role of the **délégués** is to represent the interest of the class as a whole by liaising with teachers and the school administration. At the end-of-term "Conseils de classe", for example, the **délégués** are consulted during discussions on whether borderline pupils should move up to the next year, leave school or repeat the year. The **délégués** of the whole school elect two "délégués d'établissement" who attend the "Conseil d'établissement", where they participate in discussions on the general running of the school and vote on decisions to be made.

---

déléguer [delege] ▸ conjug 6 ◂ VT a (= *transmettre*) [+ *compétence, pouvoirs, responsa-*

bilité] to delegate (à to); (*Jur*) [+ *créance*] to assign, delegate; **il faut savoir ~** it's important to be able to delegate b (= *mandater*) [+ *personne*] to (appoint as a) delegate (à to)

délestage [delɛstaʒ] NM (*Élec*) power cut; (*Aut*) diversion; [*ballon, navire*] removal of ballast (**de** from), unballasting; **établir un itinéraire de ~** to set up a relief route

délester [delɛste] ▸ conjug 1 ◂ [1] VT [+ *navire, ballon*] to remove ballast from, unballast; (*Élec*) to cut off power from; (*Aut*) **on a délesté la N4** a diversion has been set up on the N4 to relieve traffic congestion; **~ qn d'un fardeau** to relieve sb of a burden; (* = *voler qn*) **~ qn de qch** to relieve sb of sth [2] **se délester** VPR [*bateau, ballon*] to jettison ballast; (*Aviat*) **se ~ de ses bombes** (*en cas de panne*) to jettison its bombs; (*sur l'objectif*) to release its bombs; **elle se délesta de ses colis** she put down *ou* dropped her parcels; **se ~ de ses responsabilités sur qn** to offload one's responsibilities on sb

délétère [deletɛʀ] ADJ [*émanations, gaz*] noxious, deleterious; [*influence, propagande*] pernicious, deleterious

délétion [delesjɔ̃] NF (*Bio*) deletion

Delhi [deli] N Delhi

déliassage [deljasaʒ] NM (*Ordin*) decollation

déliasser [deljase] ▸ conjug 1 ◂ VT (*Ordin*) to decollate

délibérant, e [delibeʀɑ̃, ɑ̃t] ADJ deliberative

délibératif, -ive [delibeʀatif, iv] ADJ [*assemblée, conseil*] deliberative; **avoir voix délibérative** to have voting rights

délibération [delibeʀasjɔ̃] NF a (= *débat*) deliberation, debate; **~s** proceedings, deliberations; **mettre une question en ~** to debate *ou* deliberate (over *ou* upon) an issue; **après ~ du jury** after the jury's due deliberation b (= *réflexion*) deliberation, consideration c (= *décision*) decision, resolution; **~s** resolutions; **par ~ du jury** on the jury's recommendation

délibéré, e [delibeʀe] a (*ptp de* **délibérer**) [1] ADJ (= *intentionnel*) deliberate; (= *assuré*) resolute, determined → **propos** [2] NM (*Jur*) deliberation (*of court at end of trial*); **mettre une affaire en ~** to deliberate on a matter; **mise en ~** deliberation

délibérément [delibeʀemɑ̃] ADV (= *volontairement*) deliberately, intentionally; (= *après avoir réfléchi*) with due consideration; (= *résolument*) resolutely

délibérer [delibeʀe] ▸ conjug 6 ◂ [1] VI a (= *débattre*) (*gén*) to deliberate; [*jury*] to confer, deliberate; (= *réfléchir*) to deliberate, consider; **après avoir mûrement délibéré** after having pondered the matter, after duly considering the matter; **~ sur une question** to deliberate (over *ou* upon) an issue [2] **délibérer de** VT INDIR (= *décider*) **~ de qch** to deliberate sth; **~ de faire qch** to decide *ou* resolve to do sth (after deliberation)

délicat, e [delika, at] ADJ a (= *fin*) [*dentelle, parfum, forme, couleur*] delicate; [*fil, voile, facture, travail*] fine; [*mets*] dainty; **un objet gravé de facture ~e** an intricately engraved object b (= *fragile*) [*tissu, fleur, enfant, santé*] delicate; **il a la peau très ~e** he has very delicate *ou* sensitive skin; **lotion pour peaux ~es** lotion for sensitive skins c (= *difficile*) [*situation, question, opération*] delicate, tricky; [*sujet*] delicate, sensitive; **c'est ~!** it's rather delicate! *ou* tricky!; **c'est ~ de lui dire ça** it's a bit awkward to tell him that d (*gén nég* = *scrupuleux*) [*personne, conscience*] scrupulous; **des procédés peu ~s** unscrupulous *ou* dishonest methods; **il ne s'est pas montré très ~ envers vous** he hasn't behaved very fairly *ou* decently towards you e (= *raffiné*) [*sentiment, goût, esprit, style*] refined, delicate; [*attention*] thoughtful; [*geste*]

delicate, thoughtful; **ces propos conviennent peu à des oreilles ~es** this conversation isn't suitable for delicate *ou* sensitive ears; **avoir le palais ~** to have a discerning palate f (= *précis*) [*nuance*] subtle, fine, delicate; [*oreille*] sensitive, fine; [*travail*] fine, delicate g (= *léger*) [*toucher, touche*] gentle, delicate; **prendre qch d'un geste ~** to take sth gently *ou* delicately h (= *plein de tact*) tactful (**envers** to, towards) i (= *exigeant*) fussy, particular; **il est ~ pour manger** he's fussy *ou* particular about his food; **faire le ~** (*nourriture*) to be particular *ou* fussy; (*spectacle*) to be squeamish; (*propos*) to act shocked

délicatement [delikatmɑ̃] ADV a (= *finement*) **tableau ~ coloré** finely *ou* delicately coloured painting; **dentelle ~ ouvragée** finely *ou* delicately worked lace; **mets ~ préparé** daintily *ou* delicately prepared dish b (= *avec précision*) delicately, finely; **nuance ~ exprimée** subtly *ou* finely *ou* delicately expressed shade of meaning c (= *avec légèreté*) [*poser, saisir*] gently, delicately d (= *avec raffinement*) delicately; **sentiment ~ exprimé** delicately expressed feeling

délicatesse [delikatɛs] NF a (= *finesse*) [*dentelle, parfum, couleur, forme*] delicacy; [*mets*] daintiness; [*fil, voile, facture, travail*] fineness b (= *fragilité*) [*peau*] sensitiveness; [*tissu*] delicacy c (= *scrupules*) [*personne, procédés*] scrupulousness; **sa manière d'agir manque de ~** his behaviour is somewhat unscrupulous d (= *raffinement*) [*sentiment, goût, esprit, style*] refinement, delicacy; [*geste*] delicacy e (= *tact*) tact; (= *attentions*) thoughtfulness; **par ~ il se retira** he withdrew tactfully *ou* out of politeness f (= *précision*) [*nuance*] subtlety, fineness, delicacy; [*oreille*] sensitivity, fineness; [*travail*] fineness, delicacy g (= *légèreté*) gentleness; **il prit le vase avec ~** he picked up the vase gently *ou* delicately h (= *caractère complexe*) [*situation, question, opération*] delicacy; (*frm*) **être en ~ avec qn/la justice** to be at odds with sb/the law i (= *prévenances*: *gén pl*) consideration (*NonC*), (kind) attentions; **avoir des ~s pour qn** to show consideration for sb

délice [delis] NM (= *plaisir*) delight; **quel ~ de s'allonger au soleil!** what a delight to lie in the sun!; **se plonger dans l'eau avec ~** to jump into the water with sheer delight; **ce dessert est un vrai ~** this dessert is quite delightful *ou* delicious

délices [delis] NFPL (*littér* = *plaisirs*) delights; **les ~ de l'étude** the delights of study; **toutes les ~ de la terre se trouvaient réunies là** every earthly delight was to be found there; **faire ses ~ de qch** to take delight in sth; **cette vie rustique ferait les ~ de mon père** this country life would delight my father

délicieusement [delisjøzmɑ̃] ADV [*chanter*] delightfully, exquisitely; [*beau, parfumé*] exquisitely; **s'enfoncer ~ dans les couvertures** to snuggle down under the covers with delight

délicieux, -ieuse [delisjø, jøz] ADJ [*fruit*] delicious, delightful; [*goût*] delicious, delightful; [*lieu, personne, sensation, anecdote*] charming, delightful

délictuel, -elle [deliktɥɛl] ADJ [*action*] criminal

délictueux, -euse [deliktɥø, øz] ADJ (*Jur*) criminal; **fait ~** criminal act

délié, e [delje] (*ptp de* **délier**) [1] ADJ a (= *agile*) [*doigts*] nimble, agile; [*esprit*] astute, penetrating; **avoir la langue ~e** to be very talkative b (= *fin*) [*taille*] slender; [*fil, écriture*] fine [2] NM [*lettre*] (thin) upstroke; **les pleins et les ~s** the downstrokes and the upstrokes (*in* handwriting); (Mus) **avoir un bon ~** to have a flowing ou an even touch

délier [delje] ▸ conjug 7 ◂ **1** VT **a** [+ corde, paquet, prisonnier] to untie; [+ gerbe] to unbind; **déliez-lui les mains** untie his hands; **~ la langue de qn** to loosen sb's tongue → **bourse b ~ qn de** [+ obligation, serment] to free ou release sb from; (Rel) [+ péché] to absolve sb from **2 se délier** VPR **a** [lien] to come untied; [prisonnier] to untie o.s., get (o.s.) free; [langue] to loosen; **sous l'effet de l'alcool les langues se délient** alcohol loosens people's tongues **b se ~ d'un serment** to free ou release o.s. from an oath

délimitation [delimitasjɔ̃] NF [terrain, frontière] delimitation; [sujet, rôle] definition, delimitation; [responsabilités, attributions] determination

délimiter [delimite] ▸ conjug 1 ◂ VT [+ terrain, frontière] to delimit; [+ sujet, rôle] to define (the scope of), delimit; [+ responsabilités, attributions] to determine

délinquance [delɛ̃kɑ̃s] NF criminality; **~ juvénile** juvenile delinquency; **~ financière** financial crime; **~ routière** reckless driving; **la petite/la grande ~** petty/serious crime; **acte de ~** crime; **il a sombré dans la ~** he slid into crime

délinquant, e [delɛ̃kɑ̃, ɑ̃t] **1** ADJ delinquent; **la jeunesse ~e** juvenile delinquents ou offenders **2** NM,F delinquent, offender; **~ primaire** first offender

déliquescence [delikesɑ̃s] NF **a** (Chim = action) deliquescence **b** (= décadence) decay; **en ~** [régime, structure] in decline; **société en complète ~** society in a state of total decay; **tomber en ~** to fall into decay ou decline

déliquescent, e [delikesɑ̃, ɑ̃t] ADJ **a** (Chim) deliquescent **b** (= décadent) [régime, mœurs, société] decaying; [atmosphère] devitalizing; [esprit] enfeebled; [personne] decrepit

délirant, e [delirɑ̃, ɑ̃t] ADJ **a** (Méd) [malade] delirious; **crise ~e** bout ou spell of delirium **b** (= enthousiaste) [foule] delirious; [accueil] rapturous; **un public ~** a frenzied audience; **tu n'es pas d'un optimisme ~ !** you're not exactly overflowing with optimism! **c** (= extravagant) [idée, architecture] extraordinary, wild; [prix, propos] outrageous; [comédie, film] whacky*; **ce projet est complètement ~ !*** this project is completely off the wall!*

délire [delir] **1** NM **a** (Méd) delirium; **dans un accès de ~** in a fit of delirium; **être en plein ~** to be totally delirious **b** (= frénésie) frenzy; **sa passion allait jusqu'au ~** his passion was almost frenzied; **dans le ~ de son imagination** in his wild ou frenzied imagination; **une foule en ~** a frenzied crowd; **quand l'acteur parut, ce fut le ou du ~*** when the actor appeared the crowd went crazy **c** (= chose extravagante) **c'est du ~ !*** it's sheer madness! ou lunacy!; **aux heures de pointe, c'est du ~ dans cette ville** it's absolute chaos ou sheer madness in the city at rush hour **2** COMP ▸ **délire alcoolique** alcoholic mania ▸ **délire de grandeur** delusions of grandeur ▸ **délire hallucinatoire** hallucinatory delirium ▸ **délire de persécution** persecution mania ▸ **délire poétique** (Littérat) poetic frenzy

délirer [delire] ▸ conjug 1 ◂ VI (Méd) to be delirious; **~ de joie** to be delirious with joy; **il délire !*** he's raving!*, he's out of his mind!*

delirium tremens [delirjɔmtremɛ̃s] NM delirium tremens

délit [deli] NM (gén) crime, offence; (Jur) (criminal) offence, misdemeanor (US); **commettre un ~** to commit an offence; **~ de fuite** failure to report an accident, hit-and-run offence; **il a été arrêté pour ~ de faciès/de sale gueule** they arrested him because of the colour of his skin/because they didn't like the look of him; **~ financier** financial crime; **~**

d'ingérence abuse of office; **~ d'initié** insider dealing ou trading; **~ de presse** violation of the press laws; **~ sexuel** sexual offence ou crime; **être poursuivi pour ~ d'opinion** to be prosecuted for one's beliefs ou convictions → **corps, flagrant**

déliter [delite] ▸ conjug 1 ◂ **1** VT [+ pierre] to cleave **2 se déliter** VPR (lit) to disintegrate (because of exposure to moisture); [certitudes, valeurs] to crumble; [État, structure] to fall apart

délivrance [delivrɑ̃s] NF **a** [prisonniers] release; [pays] deliverance, liberation **b** (= soulagement) relief; **il est parti, quelle ~ !** he's gone — what a relief! **c** [passeport, reçu] issue, delivery; [ordonnance] issue; [lettre, marchandise] delivery; (Jur) **~ d'un brevet** issue of a patent **d** (Méd, littér = accouchement) delivery

délivrer [delivre] ▸ conjug 1 ◂ **1** VT **a** [+ prisonnier, esclave] to set free; **~ qn de** [+ rival] to relieve ou rid sb of; [+ liens, obligation] to free sb from, relieve sb of; [+ crainte] to relieve sb of; **être/se sentir délivré d'un grand poids** to be/feel relieved of a great weight **b** [+ passeport, reçu] to issue, deliver; [+ lettre, marchandise] to deliver; [+ ordonnance] to give, issue; [+ médicament] [pharmacien] to dispense; (Admin) to sell → **ordonnance 2 se délivrer** VPR [personne] to free o.s. (de from)

délocalisation [delɔkalizasjɔ̃] NF relocation

délocaliser [delɔkalize] ▸ conjug 1 ◂ VT [+ activités, entreprise, emplois] to relocate; **l'entreprise va se ~ à l'étranger** the company is going to relocate abroad

déloger [delɔʒe] ▸ conjug 3 ◂ **1** VT [+ locataire] to turn ou throw out; [+ fugitif] to flush out; [+ lièvre] to start; [+ objet, ennemi] to dislodge (de from) **2** VI **a** (= déguerpir) to clear out; **délogez de là !** clear out of there!* **b** (Belg = découcher) to spend the night away from home

déloquer (se): [delɔke] ▸ conjug 1 ◂ VPR (= se déshabiller) to strip off

déloyal, e (mpl -aux) [delwajal, o] ADJ [ami] unfaithful, disloyal (envers towards); [adversaire] underhand; [conduite] disloyal, underhand; [procédé] unfair; (Comm) **concurrence ~e** unfair competition; (Sport) **un coup ~** a foul

déloyalement [delwajalmɑ̃] ADV disloyally

déloyauté [delwajote] NF (NonC) [ami, conduite] disloyalty (envers towards); [adversaire] underhandedness, unfairness; [procédé] unfairness; **actes de ~** disloyal acts

Delphes [dɛlf] N Delphi

delphinarium [dɛlfinarjɔm] NM dolphinarium

delphinium [dɛlfinjɔm] NM delphinium

delta [dɛlta] NM (Géog, Ling) delta; **le ~ du Mékong** the Mekong delta; (Phys) **rayon ~** delta ray; (Aviat) **à ailes (en) ~** delta-winged → **aile**

deltaïque [dɛltaik] ADJ deltaic, delta (épith)

deltaplane® [dɛltaplan] NM (= appareil) hang-glider; (= sport) hang-gliding; **faire du ~** to hang-glide, go hang-gliding

deltoïde [dɛltɔid] ADJ, NM (Méd) deltoid

déluge [delyʒ] NM (= pluie) downpour, deluge; [larmes, paroles, injures] flood; [compliments, coups] shower; (Bible) **le ~** the Flood, the Deluge; **ça date du ~ ◊ ça remonte au ~** it's ancient history; **après moi le ~ !** I don't care what happens after I'm gone!, après moi le déluge!

déluré, e [delyre] (ptp de **délurer**) ADJ **a** (= débrouillard) smart, resourceful **b** (= impertinent: gén) forward; [fille] saucy, sassy* (US); **sa sœur est un peu ~e** his sister is a bit wild

délurer [delyre] ▸ conjug 1 ◂ VT (= dégourdir) to make smart ou resourceful, teach a thing or two to*; (péj) to make forward ou pert

2 se délurer VPR (= se dégourdir) to become smart ou resourceful; (péj) to become forward; **il s'est déluré au régiment** he learnt a thing or two* in the army

démagnétisation [demaɲetizasjɔ̃] NF demagnetization

démagnétiser [demaɲetize] ▸ conjug 1 ◂ VT, **se démagnétiser** VPR to demagnetize

démago* [demago] **1** ADJ ABRÉV = **démagogique 2** NMF ABRÉV = **démagogue**

démagogie [demagɔʒi] NF demagogy, demagoguery

démagogique [demagɔʒik] ADJ [discours, réforme] popularity-seeking, demagogic

démagogue [demagɔg] **1** NMF demagogue **2** ADJ **être ~** to be a demagogue

démaillage [demajaʒ] NM [bas] laddering (Brit), running (US); [tricot] undoing, unravelling

démailler [demaje] ▸ conjug 1 ◂ VT [+ bas] to ladder (Brit), run (US); [+ filet] to undo (the mesh of); [+ tricot] to undo, unravel; [+ chaîne] to unlink, separate the links of; **ses bas sont démaillés** her stockings are laddered (Brit) ou have got ladders (Brit) ou have runs (US) in them **2 se démailler** VPR [bas] to ladder (Brit), run (US); [tricot, filet] to unravel, come unravelled; **la chaîne s'est démaillée** the links of the chain have come apart

démailloter [demajɔte] ▸ conjug 1 ◂ VT [+ enfant] to take the swaddling clothes off

demain [d(ə)mɛ̃] ADV **a** (= dans un jour) tomorrow; **~ matin** tomorrow morning; **~ soir** tomorrow evening ou night; **~ en huit/en quinze** a week/two weeks tomorrow; **à dater ou à partir de ~** from tomorrow, from tomorrow on; **~ il fera jour** tomorrow is another day; **ce n'est pas ~ la veille ◊ ce n'est pas pour ~*** that won't happen in a hurry; **~ on rase gratis !*** it's jam tomorrow!; **à ~** (gén) see you tomorrow; (= je téléphonerai) I'll talk to you tomorrow; **d'ici (à) ~ tout peut changer** everything might be different by tomorrow → **remettre b** (= l'avenir) **le monde de ~** the world of tomorrow, tomorrow's world; **de quoi ~ sera-t-il fait ?** what will tomorrow's world hold for us?

démanché, e [demɑ̃ʃe] (ptp de **démancher**) **1** ADJ [bras] out of joint (attrib), dislocated; * [objet] loose; [meuble] rickety; **le marteau est ~** the hammer has no handle ou has lost its handle **2** NM (Mus) shift

démancher [demɑ̃ʃe] ▸ conjug 1 ◂ **1** VT [+ outil] to take the handle off; (* = disloquer) [+ meuble] to knock a leg off; [+ bras] to put out of joint, dislocate **2** VI (Mus) to shift **3 se démancher** VPR [outil] to lose its handle; [bras] to be put out of joint, be dislocated; * [meuble, objet] to fall to bits ou pieces; **se ~ le bras** to dislocate one's shoulder; **se ~ le cou pour voir qch*** to crane one's neck to see sth

demande [d(ə)mɑ̃d] NF **a** (= requête) request (de qch for sth); (= revendication) claim, demand (de for); (Admin) [autorisation, naturalisation] application (de for); [remboursement, dédommagement] claim (de for); [renseignement] enquiry; (Cartes) bid; (gén) **faire une ~** to make a request; **faire une ~ de remboursement** to put in ou make a claim for reimbursement ou a refund (à qn to sb), claim reimbursement ou a refund (à qn from sb); **adressez votre ~ au ministère** apply to the ministry; **remplir une ~** (= formulaire) to fill in a claim form (de for); **~ d'adhésion** application for membership; **~ d'asile** request ou application for asylum; **~ de rançon** ransom demand; **~ d'emploi** job application; (rubrique de journal) **« ~s d'emploi »** "situations wanted"; **~ (en mariage)** proposal (of marriage); **faire sa ~ (en mariage)** to propose; **à ou sur la ~ de qn** at sb's request; **à la ~ ◊ sur ~** (gén) on request;

(Admin) on application; **et maintenant, à la ~ générale ...** and now, by popular request ...

b (Écon) la ~ demand; **pour répondre à la ~ (de pétrole/de fruits)** to meet the demand (for oil/fruit); **il y a une forte ~ de produits importés** imported goods are in great demand, there is a great ou high demand for imported goods

c (Jur) ~ **en divorce** divorce petition; ~ **en renvoi** request for remittal; ~ **principale/accessoire/subsidiaire** chief/secondary/contingency petition

d (= besoins) [malade, enfant] needs; **d'affection** need for affection

demandé, e [d(ə)mɑ̃de] (ptp de **demander**) ADJ (Comm) (in demand) **cet article est très ~** this item is very much in demand, there is a great demand for this item; **il est très ~** [médecin, chanteur] he is very much in demand; **c'est une destination très ~e** it's a very popular destination

▼ **demander** [d(ə)mɑ̃de] ▸ conjug 1 ◂ **1** VT **a** (= solliciter) [+ chose, conseil, réponse, entrevue] to ask for, request (frm); [+ volontaire] to call for, ask for; (Admin, Jur) [+ délai, emploi, divorce] to apply for; [+ indemnité, remboursement] to claim; [+ réunion, enquête] to call for, ask for; ~ **qch à qn** to ask sb for sth; ~ **un service** ou **une faveur à qn** to ask sb a favour; ~ **la paix** to sue for peace; (Mil) ~ **une permission** to ask for ou request (frm) leave; ~ **la permission de faire qch** to ask ou request (frm) permission to do sth; ~ **aide et assistance** to request aid (à from); ~ **à voir qn/à parler à qn** to ask to see sb/to speak to sb; **il a demandé à partir plus tôt** he has asked to leave earlier; ~ **à qn de faire** ou **qu'il fasse qch** to ask ou request (frm) sb to do sth; **puis-je vous ~ (de me passer) du pain?** would you mind passing me some bread?; **vous n'avez qu'à ~** ◊ **il n'y a qu'à ~** you only have to ask; (hum) **que demande le peuple?** what more could you ask for? → **aumône, charité, pardon**

b (= appeler) [+ médecin, prêtre, plombier] to send for; **le blessé demande un prêtre** the injured man is asking ou calling for a priest

c (au téléphone, au bureau etc) [+ personne, numéro] to ask for; (au téléphone) **demandez-moi M. Leblanc** get me Mr Leblanc; **qui demandez-vous?** who do you wish to speak to?; **on le demande au bureau/au téléphone** he is wanted at the office/on the phone, someone is asking for him at the office/on the phone; **le patron vous demande** ou **demande après* vous** the boss wants to see you ou speak to you, the boss is asking to see you

d (= désirer) to be asking for, want; **ils demandent 60 F de l'heure et une semaine de congé** they are asking (for) 60 francs an hour and a week's holiday; **le chat miaule, il demande son lait** the cat's mewing — he's asking for his milk; **je demande à voir!*** I'll believe it when I see it!; **il ne demande qu'à apprendre/à se laisser convaincre** all he wants is to learn/to be convinced, he's more than willing to learn/be convinced; **il demande qu'on le laisse partir** he wants us to ou is asking us to let him go; **tout ce que je demande, c'est qu'il vienne** all (that) I ask is that he should come; **je ne demande pas mieux!** ou **que ça!** I'll be ou I'm only too pleased!; **il ne demandera pas mieux que de vous aider** he'll be only too pleased to help you

e (= s'enquérir de) [+ heure, nom, chemin] to ask; ~ **l'heure à qn** to ask sb the time; **je lui ai demandé son nom** I asked him his name; ~ **un renseignement à qn** to ask sb for some information; ~ **quand/comment/pourquoi c'est arrivé** to ask when/how/why it happened; ~ **des nouvelles de qn** ◊ ~ **après qn*** to enquire ou ask after sb; **«où est-il?» demanda-t-elle** "where is he?", she asked; **va ~!** go and ask!; **je ne t'ai rien demandé** I didn't ask you; **je ne te demande rien** I'm not asking you; **on ne t'a**

pas demandé l'heure (qu'il est)* ou **ton avis*** who asked you?, who rattled your cage?*; (excl) **je vous le demande!** ◊ **je vous demande un peu!** honestly!*

f (= nécessiter) [travail, décision] to require, need; **ça demande un effort** it requires an effort; **ces plantes demandent beaucoup d'eau/à être arrosées** these plants need ou require a lot of water/watering; **ce travail va (lui) ~ six heures** the job will take (him) 6 hours ou will require 6 hours, he'll need 6 hours to do the job; **cette proposition demande réflexion** this proposal needs thinking over; **cette proposition demande toute votre attention** this proposal calls for ou requires your full attention

g (= exiger) ~ **qch à** ou **de qn** to ask sth of sb; ~ **beaucoup à** ou **de la vie/ses élèves** to ask a lot of life/of one's pupils; **il ne faut pas trop lui en ~!** you mustn't ask too much of him!

h (Comm) **ils (en) demandent 500 F** they are asking ou want 500 francs (for it); **ils m'en ont demandé 500 F** they asked (me) for 500 francs for it; **ils demandent une vendeuse** (= ils en cherchent une) they're looking for a shop assistant; **ils demandent 3 vendeuses** (par annonce) they are advertising for ou they want 3 shop assistants; **on demande beaucoup de vendeuses en ce moment** shop assistants are very much in demand ou are in great demand just now; **«on demande: électricien»** "electrician wanted ou required"; **comme vous l'avez demandé dans votre lettre du 25 janvier** as requested in your letter of 25th January

2 **se demander** VPR **a** (= hésiter, douter) to wonder; **on peut vraiment se ~** ou **c'est à se ~ s'il a perdu la tête** it makes you wonder if he isn't out of his mind; **il se demande où aller/ce qu'il doit faire** he is wondering where to go/what to do; **il se demanda: suis-je vraiment aussi bête?** he asked himself ou wondered: am I really so stupid?; **ils se demandent bien pourquoi il a démissionné** they can't think why he resigned, they really wonder why he resigned

b (sens passif) **ça ne se demande pas!** that's a stupid question!

demandeur[1], **-deresse** [d(ə)mɑ̃dœʀ, dʀɛs] NM,F (Jur) plaintiff, complainant; (en divorce) petitioner; ~ **en appel** appellant; **la partie demanderesse** the moving party

demandeur[2], **-euse** [d(ə)mɑ̃dœʀ, øz] NM,F ~ **d'emploi** person looking for work, job-seeker; (Admin) **le nombre des ~s d'emploi a baissé** the number of job seekers has fallen; ~ **d'asile** asylum seeker; ~ **de visa** visa applicant; **ils sont très ~s (de nos produits)** our goods are very popular with them; **s'il existe un bon dictionnaire, je suis ~** if there's a good dictionary I'm interested

démangeaison [demɑ̃ʒɛzɔ̃] NF itching (NonC), itching sensation; **avoir des ~s** to be itching; **j'ai des ~s dans le dos** my back is itching; **j'ai une ~** I've got an itch

démanger [demɑ̃ʒe] ▸ conjug 3 ◂ VT **a** (= gratter) **son dos/son coup de soleil le** ou **lui démange** his back/sunburn itches ou is itching; **où est-ce que ça (vous) démange?** where does it itch?; **ça (me) démange** it itches, it's making me itch **b** (fig) **ses poings le démangent** he's itching* for a fight; **la main me démange** I'm itching* ou dying to hit him (ou her etc); **la langue me démange** I'm itching* ou dying to say something; **ça me démange de faire ...** ◊ **l'envie me démange de faire ...** I'm dying to do ...

démantèlement [demɑ̃tɛlmɑ̃] NM (Mil) [forteresse] demolition, demolishing; [armes, missiles, centrale nucléaire, entreprise, service] dismantling; [gang, réseau d'espionnage, de trafiquants] breaking up; [empire] dismantling, break-up

démanteler [demɑ̃t(ə)le] ▸ conjug 5 ◂ VT (Mil) [+ forteresse] to demolish; [+ armes, missiles,

centrale nucléaire, entreprise, service] to dismantle; [+ gang, réseau d'espionnage, de trafiquants] to break up; [+ empire] to dismantle, break up

démantibuler* [demɑ̃tibyle] ▸ conjug 1 ◂ **1** VT [+ objet] to demolish, break up **2** **se démantibuler** VPR to fall apart; **se ~ le bras** to dislocate one's shoulder

démaquillage [demakijaʒ] NM removal of make-up; **elle commença son ~** she started to take off ou remove her make-up

démaquillant, e [demakijɑ̃, ɑ̃t] **1** ADJ **lait** (ou **gel**) ~ make-up remover **2** NM make-up remover; ~ **pour les yeux** eye make-up remover

démaquiller [demakije] ▸ conjug 1 ◂ **1** VT [+ yeux, visage] to remove the make-up from, take the make-up off; ~ **qn** to take off ou remove sb's make-up **2** **se démaquiller** VPR to take one's make-up off, remove one's make-up; **se ~ les yeux** to remove one's eye make-up

démarcage [demaʀkaʒ] NM = **démarquage**

démarcatif, -ive [demaʀkatif, iv] ADJ demarcating

démarcation [demaʀkasjɔ̃] NF demarcation (**de, entre** between) → **ligne**[1]

démarchage [demaʀʃaʒ] NM (Comm) door-to-door ou doorstep selling; (Pol) ~ **électoral** canvassing; **faire du ~** (Comm) to do door-to-door selling; (Pol) to canvass

démarche [demaʀʃ] NF **a** (= façon de marcher) gait, walk; **avoir une ~ pesante/gauche** to have a heavy/an awkward gait ou walk, walk heavily/awkwardly **b** (= intervention) step, move; **faire une ~ auprès de qn (pour obtenir qch)** to approach sb (to obtain sth); **entreprendre des ~s auprès d'un service** to apply to a department; **toutes nos ~s n'ont échoué** none of the steps we took came to anything; **les ~s nécessaires pour obtenir qch** the necessary ou required procedures ou steps to obtain sth; **l'idée de (faire) cette ~ m'effrayait** I was frightened at the idea of taking this step ou of making this move **c** [raisonnement, pensée] reasoning; ~ **intellectuelle** intellectual reasoning; **expliquez-moi votre ~** explain your reasoning to me

démarcher [demaʀʃe] ▸ conjug 1 ◂ VT [+ clients] to canvass; [+ produit] to sell door-to-door

démarcheur, -euse [demaʀʃœʀ, øz] NM,F (= vendeur) door-to-door salesman (ou saleswoman); (Pol) (door-to-door) canvasser

démarier [demaʀje] ▸ conjug 7 ◂ VT (Agr) to thin out

démarquage [demaʀkaʒ] NM [linge, argenterie] removal of the identifying mark(s) (**de** on); [auteur, œuvre] copying (**de** from); (Sport) **le ~ d'un joueur** the drawing away of a player's marker; **cet ouvrage est un ~ grossier** this work is a crude plagiarism ou copy

démarque [demaʀk] NF (Comm) [article] markdown, marking-down; ~ **inconnue** shortfall (in stock)

démarqué, e [demaʀke] (ptp de **démarquer**) ADJ (Sport) [joueur] unmarked; **robe ~e** unlabelled designer dress

démarquer [demaʀke] ▸ conjug 1 ◂ **1** VT **a** [+ linge, argenterie] to remove the (identifying) mark(s) from; (Comm) (= solder) to mark down; (= retirer l'étiquette de) to remove the (designer) label from **b** [+ œuvre, auteur] to plagiarize, copy **c** (Sport) [+ joueur] to draw a marker away from **2** **se démarquer** VPR **a** (Sport) to lose ou shake off one's marker **b** **se ~ de** (= marquer sa différence avec) to distinguish ou differentiate o.s. from

démarrage [demaʀaʒ] **1** NM **a** (= départ) [véhicule] moving off (NonC); ~ **en trombe** shooting off (NonC); **il a calé au ~** he stalled as he moved off; **secoués à chaque ~ du bus** shaken about every time the bus moved off **b** (= début) [affaire, campagne, élève, débutant] start; **l'excellent/le difficile ~ de la campagne**

> GRAMMAIRE ACTIVE: **demander** 28.2, 43.1, 53.6

électorale the excellent/difficult start to the electoral campaign `c` (Sport = accélération) [coureur] pulling away (NonC); **il a placé un ~ à 100 m de l'arrivée** he put on a burst of speed ou he pulled away 100 metres from the finishing line `d` (Naut) casting off, unmooring `e` (= mise en marche) [véhicule] starting; **le ~ d'une affaire/campagne** getting a deal/a campaign started ▶ COMP ▶ **démarrage en côte** hill start ▶ **démarrage à la manivelle** crank-starting

démarrer [demaʀe] ▶conjug 1◀ `1` VI `a` [moteur, conducteur] to start (up); [véhicule] to move off; [affaire, campagne] to get under way, get off the ground; [économie] to take off; [élève, débutant] to start off; **l'affaire a bien démarré** the deal got off to a good start ou started off well; **~ en trombe** to shoot off; **faire ~** [+ véhicule] to start, get started; [+ affaire, campagne] to get under way, get off the ground; **il a bien démarré en latin** he got off to a good start in Latin, he started off well in Latin → **froid**
`b` (= accélérer) [coureur] to pull away
`c` (Naut) to cast off, unmoor
`2` **démarrer de** VT INDIR (= démordre de) [+ idée, projet] to let go of; **il ne veut pas ~ de son idée** he just won't let go of his idea
`3` VT [+ véhicule] to start, get started; (Naut) [+ embarcation] to cast off, unmoor; * [+ travail] to get going on*; **~ une affaire/une campagne** to get a deal/a campaign started; **~ qn en anglais** to get sb started in English

démarreur [demaʀœʀ] NM (Aut) starter

démasquer [demaske] ▶conjug 1◀ `1` VT `a` (= dévoiler) [+ imposteur, espion, hypocrisie] to unmask; [+ plan] to unveil, uncover `b` (= enlever le masque de) to unmask `2` **se démasquer** VPR [imposteur] to drop one's mask; [personne déguisée] to take off one's mask

démâtage [demataʒ] NM dismasting

démâter [demate] ▶conjug 1◀ `1` VT (involontairement) to dismast; (volontairement) to unstep the mast(s) of `2` VI [bateau] to lose its mast(s), be dismasted; **j'ai démâté** my boat lost its mast(s)

dématérialisation [demateʀjalizasjɔ̃] NF dematerialization

dématérialiser (se) [demateʀjalize] ▶conjug 1◀ VPR [transaction] to dematerialize; **les frontières de l'Europe se dématérialisent** Europe's borders are becoming less and less visible

démazouter [demazute] ▶conjug 1◀ VT [+ plage] to remove the oil from

d'emblée [dɑ̃ble] LOC ADV → **emblée**

démêlage [demɛlaʒ] NM (lit, fig) disentangling, untangling

démêlant, e [demɛlɑ̃, ɑ̃t] `1` ADJ (hair) conditioning `2` NM (hair) conditioner

démêlé [demele] NM (= dispute) dispute, quarrel; (= ennuis) **~s** problems; **il a eu des ~s avec la justice** he has fallen foul of the law ou has had some problems ou trouble with the law; **il risque d'avoir des ~s avec l'administration** he's likely to have some trouble with the authorities

démêlement [demɛlmɑ̃] NM = **démêlage**

démêler [demele] ▶conjug 1◀ `1` VT `a` [+ ficelle, écheveau] to disentangle, untangle; [+ cheveux] to untangle; (avec un peigne) to comb out `b` [+ problème, situation] to untangle, sort out; [+ intentions, machinations] to unravel, get to the bottom of; **~ qch d'avec ou de** to distinguish ou tell sth from; **~ le vrai du faux** to sort the truth out from the lies `c` (littér = débattre) **~ qch avec qn** to dispute sth with sb; **je ne veux rien avoir à ~ avec lui** I do not wish to have to contend with him `2` **se démêler de**† VPR (littér = se tirer de) [+ embarras, difficultés] to disentangle o.s. from, extricate o.s. from

démêloir [demɛlwaʀ] NM (large-toothed) comb

démêlures [demɛlyʀ] NFPL combings

démembrement [demɑ̃bʀəmɑ̃] NM `a` [animal] dismemberment `b` [pays, empire] dismemberment, break-up; [entreprise] asset-stripping

démembrer [demɑ̃bʀe] ▶conjug 1◀ VT `a` [+ animal] to dismember `b` [+ pays, empire] to dismember, break up; [+ entreprise] to asset-strip

déménagement [demenaʒmɑ̃] NM `a` [meubles] moving, removal (Brit); [pièce] emptying (of furniture) (NonC); **camion de ~** removal (Brit) ou moving (US) van; **le ~ du mobilier s'est bien passé** moving the furniture ou the removal of the furniture went well; **le ~ du laboratoire a posé des problèmes** moving the furniture out of the laboratory ou emptying the laboratory of (its) furniture proved to be no easy matter; **ils ont fait quatre ~s en trois jours** they did four moves ou removals (Brit) in three days `b` (= changement de domicile) move, moving (house) (NonC); (= changement de bureau) move, moving (offices) (NonC); **faire un ~** to move (house); **on a dû perdre ça pendant le ~** we must have lost it during the move; **trois ~s en une année, c'est trop** three moves in one year is too much, moving (house) three times in one year is too much

déménager [demenaʒe] ▶conjug 3◀ `1` VT [+ meubles, affaires] to move; [+ maison, pièce] to move the furniture out of, empty (of furniture) `2` VI `a` (= changer de maison) to move (house); (= changer d'appartement) to move (into a new flat); (= changer de locaux) to move (offices); **~ à la cloche de bois** to sneak off in the middle of the night, do a moonlight flit* (Brit) `b`* (= partir) to clear off*; **allez, déménage !** buzz ou clear off!*; **il nous a fait ~** he sent us packing*; **avec elle, les dossiers ça déménage*** she gets things through files like nobody's business* `c`* (= être fou) to be off one's rocker* `d`* (= être excellent) **il/ça déménage !** he's/it's brill!* (Brit) ou awesome!* (US)

déménageur [demenaʒœʀ] NM (= entrepreneur) furniture remover (Brit), moving company (US); (= ouvrier) removal man (Brit), (furniture) mover (US); **il a une carrure de ~** he's built like a tank

démence [demɑ̃s] NF (Méd) dementia; (Jur) mental disorder; (gén) madness, insanity; (fig) **c'est de la ~** it's (sheer) madness ou lunacy, it's insane; (Méd) **~ précoce** dementia praecox; (Méd) **~ sénile** senile dementia

démener (se) [dem(ə)ne] ▶conjug 5◀ VPR (= se débattre) to thrash about, struggle (violently); (= se dépenser) to exert o.s.; **se démener comme un beau diable** (pour se sauver) to thrash about ou struggle violently; (pour obtenir qch) to make a tremendous effort, go to great lengths; **si on se démène un peu on aura fini avant la nuit** if we put our backs into it a bit* we'll finish before nightfall; **ils se démenèrent tant et si bien que ...** they exerted themselves to such an extent that ..., they made such a great effort that ...; **il faut que tu te démènes si tu veux des billets** you'll have to get a move on* if you want tickets

dément, e [demɑ̃, ɑ̃t] `1` ADJ (= fou) mad, insane, crazy; (= incroyable) incredible, unbelievable; (* = extravagant) [type, musique] way-out*, weird*; [prix, projet] mad, crazy `2` NM,F (Méd) lunatic, demented person

démenti [demɑ̃ti] NM (= déclaration) denial, refutation; (apporté par les faits, les circonstances) refutation; **opposer un ~ à** [+ nouvelle, allégations, rumeurs] to deny formally; **publier un ~** to publish a denial; **sa version des faits reste sans ~** his version of the facts remains uncontradicted ou unchallenged;

son expression opposait un ~ à ses paroles his expression belied his words

démentiel, -ielle [demɑ̃sjɛl] ADJ `a` (Méd) dementia (épith) `b` [projet, prix] mad, crazy

démentir [demɑ̃tiʀ] ▶conjug 16◀ `1` VT `a` [personne] [+ nouvelle, rumeur] to deny, refute; [+ personne] to contradict; **il dément ses principes par son attitude** his attitude contradicts his principles `b` [faits] [+ témoignage] to refute; [+ apparences] to belie; [+ espoirs] to disappoint; **la douceur de son sourire est démentie par la dureté de son regard** the hardness in her eyes belies the sweetness of her smile; **les résultats ont démenti les pronostics** the results have contradicted the predictions `2` **se démentir** VPR (nég = cesser) **son amitié/sa fidélité ne s'est jamais démentie** his friendship/loyalty has never failed; **c'est un roman dont le succès ne s'est jamais démenti** the novel has always maintained its popularity; **leur intérêt pour ces mystères, qui ne s'est jamais démenti** their unfailing ou never-failing interest in these mysteries

démerdard, e‡ [demɛʀdaʀ, aʀd] `1` NM,F **c'est un ~** he knows how to look after himself `2` ADJ **il est ~** he's a smart customer*, there are no flies on him (Brit); **il n'est pas ~ pour deux sous** he's really clueless*, he hasn't (got) a clue*; **dans la vie il faut être ~** you have to learn to look out for yourself in life

démerde‡ [demɛʀd] `1` ADJ = **démerdard** `2` NF **la ~** (= ingéniosité) resourcefulness; (= astuce) smartness; **c'est le roi de la ~** he always knows how to wangle* things

démerder (se)‡ [demɛʀde] ▶conjug 1◀ VPR `a` (= se débrouiller) to manage; **il sait se démerder dans la vie** he knows how to look after himself all right*; **elle se démerde (pas mal) au ski/en peinture** she's pretty good at skiing/painting; **si je m'étais mieux démerdé, j'aurais gagné** if I'd known how to handle things better, I'd have won; **il s'est démerdé pour avoir une permission** he wangled himself some leave*, he wangled it so that he got some leave* `b` (= se tirer d'affaire) to get out of a mess; **il a voulu y aller, maintenant qu'il se démerde tout seul** he wanted to go so now he can get out of his own bloody‡ (Brit) ou damn‡ mess

démérite [demeʀit] NM (littér) demerit (littér), fault; **où est son ~, dans ce cas ?** where is he at fault in this matter?, wherein lies his fault in this matter? (littér)

démériter [demeʀite] ▶conjug 1◀ `1` **démériter de** VT INDIR [+ patrie, institution] to show o.s. unworthy of `2` VI (Rel) to deserve to fall from grace; **en quoi a-t-il démérité ?** how was he to blame?; **il n'a pas démérité** he hasn't done anything blameworthy; **l'équipe perdante n'a cependant pas démérité** the losing team nevertheless put up a creditable performance

démesure [dem(ə)zyʀ] NF [personnage] excessiveness, immoderation; [propos, exigences, style] outrageousness, immoderateness; **je hais la ~** I hate excess

démesuré, e [dem(ə)zyʀe] ADJ [orgueil, ambition, prétentions] inordinate, immoderate; [taille] disproportionate; [territoire, distances] vast, enormous; [membres] enormous

démesurément [dem(ə)zyʀemɑ̃] ADV [exagérer] immoderately, inordinately; [augmenter] disproportionately; **~ long** disproportionately ou inordinately long

démettre [demɛtʀ] ▶conjug 56◀ `1` VT `a` (= disloquer) [+ articulation] to dislocate `b` (= révoquer) **~ qn de ses fonctions/son poste** to dismiss sb from his duties/post `c` (Jur) **~ qn de son appel** to dismiss sb's appeal `2` **se démettre** VPR `a` (frm = démissionner) to resign, hand in one's resignation; **se ~ de ses fonctions/son poste** to resign (from) one's duties/post [b] (= se disloquer) **se ~ le poignet/ la cheville** to dislocate one's wrist/ankle, put one's wrist/ankle out of joint

demeurant [d(ə)mœrɑ̃] ◆**au demeurant** LOC ADV incidentally, by the way

demeure [d(ə)mœʀ] NF [a] (= maison) residence; (littér = domicile) residence, dwelling place (littér) → **dernier** [b] (loc) **à ~** [installations] permanent; [domestique] live-in, resident; **s'installer à ~ dans une ville** to make one's permanent home ou settle permanently in a town; **il ne faudrait pas qu'ils y restent à ~** they mustn't stay there permanently; **mettre qn en ~ de faire qch** to instruct ou order sb to do sth; (Jur) **mettre qn en ~ de payer/de partir** to give sb notice to pay/to quit ou leave; **mise en ~** formal demand, notice

demeuré, e [d(ə)mœʀe] (ptp de **demeurer**) [1] ADJ half-witted; **il est complètement ~** he's an absolute half-wit [2] NM,F half-wit

demeurer [d(ə)mœʀe] ▸conjug 1◂ VI [a] (avec aux avoir) **~ quelque part** (= habiter) to live somewhere; (= séjourner) to stay somewhere; **il demeure au 24 rue d'Ulm** he lives at number 24 (in the) rue d'Ulm [b] (frm: avec aux être, avec attrib ou adv de lieu) (= rester, = subsister) to remain; **~ fidèle/quelque part** to remain faithful/somewhere; **il lui faut ~ couché** he must remain in bed; **l'odeur demeurait dans la pièce** the smell lingered in the room; **la conversation en est demeurée là** the conversation was taken no further ou was left at that [c]† (= être transmis) **~ à qn** to be left to sb; **la maison leur est demeurée de leur mère** the house was left to them by their mother, they inherited the house from their mother

demi¹ [d(ə)mi] ADV half; **~ plein/nu** half-full/-naked; **il n'était qu'à ~ rassuré** he was only half reassured; **il ne te croit qu'à ~** he only half believes you; **il a fait le travail à ~** he has (only) done half the work, he has (only) half done the work; **je ne fais pas les choses à ~** I don't do things by halves; **ouvrir une porte à ~** to half open a door, open a door halfway

demi², e [d(ə)mi] [1] ADJ (après n: avec et, nominal) **une livre/heure et ~e** one and a half pounds/hours, a pound/an hour and a half; **un centimètre/kilo et ~** one and a half centimetres/kilos, one centimetre/kilo and a half; **à six heures et ~e** at half past six; **deux fois et ~ plus grand/autant** two and a half times greater/as much → **malin**

[2] ADV, PRÉF [a] (avant n = moitié) **une ~-livre/ -douzaine/-journée** half a pound/dozen/day, a half-pound/half-dozen/half-day; **un ~-tour de clé** half a turn of the key, a half turn of the key

[b] (avant n = incomplet) **c'est un ~-succès** it's a partial success; **une ~-vérité** a half-truth; **~-cécité** partial blindness; **~-pouvoir** partial power; **~-circulaire** [canal] semicircular

[3] NM,F (fonction pronominale) **un ~** (a) half; **une bouteille? — non, une ~e** one bottle? — no, (a) half ou no, half a bottle ou no, a half-bottle; **deux ~s font un entier** two halves make a whole

[4] NM [a] (= bière) glass of beer, ≈ half-pint, ≈ half* (Brit)

[b] (Sport) half-back; **~ gauche/droit** left/right half; (Rugby) **~ de mêlée** scrum half; (Rugby) **~ d'ouverture** stand-off half

[5] **demie** NF (à l'horloge) **la ~e** the half-hour; **la ~e a sonné** the half-hour has struck; **c'est déjà la ~e** it's already half past; **on part à la ~e** we're leaving at half past; **le bus passe à la ~e** the bus comes by at half past (the hour), the bus comes by on the half-hour; **la pendule sonne les heures et les ~es** the clock strikes the hours and the halves ou the half-hours

demiard [dəmjaʀ] NM (Can) half-pint, 0.284 litre

demi-botte [d(ə)mibɔt] NF calf-length boot

demi-bouteille [d(ə)mibutɛj] NF half-bottle

demi-canton (pl **demi-cantons**) [d(ə)mikɑ̃tɔ̃] NM (en Suisse) demicanton (Swiss territorial subdivision comprising half of a canton)

demi-cercle [d(ə)misɛʀkl] NM (= figure) semicircle; (= instrument) protractor; **en ~** semicircular; **se mettre en ~** to make a semicircle, stand (ou sit) in a semicircle

demi-colonne [d(ə)mikɔlɔn] NF semicolumn, demi-column, half-column

demi-deuil [d(ə)midœj] NM half-mourning; (Culin) **poularde ~** chicken served in a white sauce with black truffles

demi-dieu (pl **demi-dieux**) [d(ə)midjø] NM demigod

demi-douzaine [d(ə)miduzɛn] NF **une ~** half-a-dozen, a half-dozen; **une ~ d'œufs** half-a-dozen eggs, a half-dozen eggs; **une bonne ~ de voitures** a good half-a-dozen cars; **cette ~ de joueurs** these half-a-dozen players

demi-droite [d(ə)midʀwat] NF half-line, half-ray

demi-écrémé [dəmiekʀeme] ADJ M, NM (lait) **~** semi-skimmed milk

demi-fin, e [d(ə)mifɛ̃, fin] ADJ [petit pois] small; [aiguille] medium; [or] 12-carat

demi-finale [d(ə)mifinal] NF semifinal; **arriver en ~** to reach the semifinals; **éliminé en ~** eliminated in the semifinal

demi-finaliste [d(ə)mifinalist] NMF semifinalist

demi-fond [d(ə)mifɔ̃] NM (= discipline) **le ~** medium-distance ou middle-distance running; (= épreuve) medium-distance ou middle-distance race; **coureur de ~** medium-distance ou middle-distance runner

demi-frère [d(ə)mifʀɛʀ] NM half-brother

demi-gros [d(ə)migʀo] NM INV (Comm) retail-wholesale

demi-heure [d(ə)mijœʀ, dəmjœʀ] NF **une ~** half an hour, a half-hour; **la première ~ a passé très lentement** the first half-hour went very slowly

demi-jour (pl **demi-jour(s)**) [d(ə)miʒuʀ] NM (gén) half-light; (= le soir) twilight

demi-journée [d(ə)miʒuʀne] NF **une ~** half a day, a half-day; **faire des ~s de ménage/ couture** to work half-days cleaning/sewing; **il travaille deux ~s par semaine** he works two half-days a week

démilitarisation [demilitaʀizasjɔ̃] NF demilitarization

démilitariser [demilitaʀize] ▸conjug 1◂ VT to demilitarize

demi-litre [d(ə)militʀ] NM **un ~ (de)** half a litre (of), a half-litre (of); **versez ce ~ de lait sur ...** pour this half-litre of milk over ...

demi-longueur [d(ə)milɔ̃gœʀ] NF (Sport) **une ~** half a length, a half-length; **la ~ d'avance qui lui a valu le prix** the half-length lead that won him the prize

demi-lune [d(ə)milyn] [1] NF (Mil) demilune; (Rail) relief line; **en ~** semicircular, half-moon (épith) [2] ADJ [table, console] semicircular; **lunettes ~** half-moon glasses

demi-mal (pl **demi-maux**) [d(ə)mimal, d(ə)mimo] NM **il n'y a que** ou **ce n'est que ~** it could have been worse, there's no great harm done

demi-mesure [d(ə)mim(ə)zyʀ] NF [a] (= compromis) half-measure; **ils ne se contenteront pas de ~s** they won't be satisfied with half-measures; **elle n'aime pas les ~s** she doesn't do things by halves [b] (Habillement) **la ~** semifinished clothing; **s'habiller en ~** to buy semifinished clothing

demi-mondaine† [dəmimɔ̃dɛn] NF demimondaine

demi-monde† [d(ə)mimɔ̃d] NM demi-monde

demi-mot [d(ə)mimo] ◆**à demi-mot** LOC ADV without having to spell things out; **se faire comprendre à ~** to make o.s. understood without having to spell it out; **ils se comprenaient à ~** they didn't have to spell things out to each other

déminage [deminaʒ] NM [terrain] mine clearance; [eaux] minesweeping; **équipe de ~** (pour mines) mine-clearing team; (pour bombes) bomb disposal unit; **opérations de ~** mine-clearing operations

déminer [demine] ▸conjug 1◂ VT to clear of mines (ou bombs)

déminéralisation [demineʀalizasjɔ̃] NF (Tech) demineralization

déminéraliser [demineʀalize] ▸conjug 1◂ [1] VT (Tech) to demineralize; (Méd) to make deficient in essential minerals; **eau déminéralisée** distilled ou demineralized water [2] **se déminéraliser** VPR (Méd) to become deficient in essential minerals

démineur [deminœʀ] NM [mines] mine-clearing expert; [bombes] bomb disposal expert

demi-pause [d(ə)mipoz] NF (Mus) minim (Brit) ou half-note (US) rest

demi-pension [d(ə)mipɑ̃sjɔ̃] NF (à l'hôtel) half-board (Brit), bed and breakfast with an evening meal (Brit), modified American plan (US); (Scol) half-board; (Scol) **être en ~** to take school lunches

demi-pensionnaire [d(ə)mipɑ̃sjɔnɛʀ] NMF day pupil; **être ~** to take school lunches

demi-place [d(ə)miplas] NF (Transport) half-fare; (Ciné, Théât etc) half-price ticket ou seat

demi-point (pl **demi-points**) [d(ə)mipwɛ̃] NM (Écon) half point; **abaisser un taux d'un ~** to lower a rate by a half point ou by half a point

demi-pointe (pl **demi-pointes**) [d(ə)mipwɛ̃t] NF (Danse = position) demi-pointe; (chausson de) **~** ballet shoe; **faire des ~s** to dance on points

demi-portion* [d(ə)mipɔʀsjɔ̃] NF (péj) weed*, weedy person*

demi-queue [d(ə)mikø] ADJ, NM (piano) **~** baby grand (piano)

demi-reliure [d(ə)miʀəljyʀ] NF half-binding

démis, e [demi, iz] (ptp de **démettre**) ADJ [membre] dislocated

demi-saison [d(ə)misɛzɔ̃] NF spring (ou autumn), cool season; **un manteau de ~** a spring (ou an autumn) coat

demi-sang (pl **demi-sang(s)**) [d(ə)misɑ̃] NM (= cheval) half-breed (horse)

demi-sel [d(ə)misɛl] [1] ADJ INV slightly salted; (fromage) **~** slightly salted cream cheese [2] NM† (arg Crime) small-time crook*

demi-siècle (pl **demi-siècles**) [d(ə)misjɛkl] NM half-century; **l'organisation fête son ~ d'existence** the organization is celebrating its fiftieth anniversary; **les grands enjeux médicaux de ce dernier ~** the big medical issues of the last fifty years ou half-century

demi-sœur [d(ə)misœʀ] NF half-sister

demi-solde [d(ə)misɔld] NF (Mil) half-pay

demi-sommeil [d(ə)misɔmɛj] NM half-sleep; **dans un ~ il entendit des rires** in his half-sleep, he heard laughter; (Écon) **le marché est en ~** the market is rather sluggish

demi-soupir [d(ə)misupiʀ] NM (Mus) quaver (Brit) ou eighth note (US) rest

démission [demisjɔ̃] NF (d'un poste) resignation; (de ses responsabilités) abdication; **donner sa ~** to hand in ou tender (frm) one's resignation; **la ~ des politiques/de la police** the politicians'/the police's failure to take responsibility; **la ~ des parents** the abdication of parental responsibility

démissionnaire [demisjɔnɛʀ] [1] ADJ (= en train de démissionner) resigning; (= qui a *démissionné)* who has resigned [2] NMF person resigning

démissionner [demisjɔne] ▸conjug 1◂ [1] VI [*employé*] to resign, hand in one's notice; (= *abandonner*) [*parents, enseignants*] to give up; **il a démissionné de ses fonctions de président** he resigned from his post as president [2] VT **~ qn*** to give sb his cards* (*Brit*) *ou* his pink slip* (*US*); **on l'a démissionné** they persuaded him to resign

demi-tarif [d(ə)mitaʀif] NM half-price; (*Transport*) half-fare; **billet d'avion (à) ~** half-price *ou* half-fare plane ticket; **voyager à ~** to travel (at) half-fare

demi-teinte [d(ə)mitɛ̃t] NF (*Art*) halftone; **en ~** (= *nuancé, discret*) [*film, déclaration, humour*] low-key; (= *mitigé*) **notre équipe a eu une saison en ~** our team had a season with mixed results

demi-ton [d(ə)mitɔ̃] NM (*Mus*) semitone, half step (*US*), half-tone (*US*)

demi-tonneau (*pl* **demi-tonneaux**) [d(ə)mitɔno] NM (*Aviat*) half flick roll (*Brit*), snap roll (*US*)

demi-tour [d(ə)mituʀ] NM [a] (*lit, fig*) about-turn, U-turn; (*Aut*) U-turn; (*lit*) **faire un ~** to make an about-turn *ou* a U-turn; (*fig*) **faire ~** to do a U-turn, make an about-turn [b] (= *moitié d'un tour*) **le coureur a fini dernier, à un ~ de ses concurrents** the athlete finished last, half a lap behind the other competitors; **il avait déjà bouclé un ~ du monde** he had already completed half of a world tour, he had already travelled halfway round the world

démiurge [demjyʀʒ] NM demiurge

demi-vie [d(ə)mivi] NF [*radiation*] half-life

demi-vierge† [d(ə)mivjɛʀʒ] NF virgin in name only

demi-volée [d(ə)mivɔle] NF half-volley

demi-volte (*pl* **demi-voltes**) [d(ə)mivɔlt] NF (*Équitation*) demivolt(e)

démo* [demo] NF ABRÉV = **démonstration**

démobilisateur, -trice [demɔbilizatœʀ, tʀis] ADJ [*discours, mesure*] demobilizing, disarming

démobilisation [demɔbilizasjɔ̃] NF (*Mil*) demobilization, demob* (*Brit*); (= *apathie*) apathy, demobilization

démobiliser [demɔbilize] ▸conjug 1◂ VT (*Mil*) to demobilize, demob* (*Brit*); (= *démotiver*) to demobilize; **se ~** to become demobilized *ou* apathetic

démocrate [demɔkʀat] [1] ADJ democratic [2] NMF democrat

démocrate-chrétien, -ienne (*mpl* **démocrates-chrétiens**) [demɔkʀatkʀetjɛ̃, jɛn] ADJ, NM,F Christian Democrat

démocratie [demɔkʀasi] NF democracy; **~ directe/représentative** direct/representative democracy; **~ populaire** people's democracy; **~ parlementaire/présidentielle** parliamentary/presidential democracy

démocratique [demɔkʀatik] ADJ democratic; (*Can*) **le Nouveau Parti Démocratique** the New Democratic Party

démocratiquement [demɔkʀatikmɑ̃] ADV democratically

démocratisation [demɔkʀatizasjɔ̃] NF democratization

démocratiser [demɔkʀatize] ▸conjug 1◂ [1] VT to democratize [2] **se démocratiser** VPR to become (more) democratic

démodé, e [demɔde] (*ptp de* **se démoder**) ADJ [*vêtement, style*] old-fashioned; [*procédé, théorie*] outmoded, old-fashioned

démoder [demɔde] ▸conjug 1◂ [1] VT [+ *principe*] to make obsolete; [+ *vêtement*] to make old-fashioned [2] **se démoder** VPR [*vêtement, style*] to go out of fashion, become old-fashioned; [*procédé, théorie*] to become outmoded *ou* old-fashioned

démodulateur [demɔdylatœʀ] NM demodulator

démographe [demɔgʀaf] NMF demographer, demographist

démographie [demɔgʀafi] NF demography; **~ galopante** massive population growth

démographique [demɔgʀafik] ADJ demographic; **poussée ~** increase in population, population increase

demoiselle [d(ə)mwazɛl] [1] NF [a] (*frm, hum*) (*jeune*) young lady; (*d'un certain âge*) single lady, maiden lady; (*dial:* = *fille*) **votre ~*** your daughter [b] (*Hist* = *noble*) young noblewoman [c] (*Zool*) dragonfly [d] (*Tech*) rammer [2] COMP ▸ **demoiselle de compagnie** (lady's) companion ▸ **demoiselle d'honneur** (*à un mariage*) bridesmaid; (*d'une reine*) maid of honour

démolir [demɔliʀ] ▸conjug 2◂ VT [a] (= *détruire*) [+ *maison, quartier*] to demolish, pull down; **on démolit beaucoup dans le quartier** they are pulling down *ou* demolishing a lot of houses *ou* they are doing a lot of demolition in the area [b] (= *abîmer*) [+ *jouet, radio, voiture*] to wreck, demolish, smash up*; **cet enfant démolit tout !** that child wrecks *ou* demolishes everything!; **ces boissons vous démolissent l'estomac/la santé*** these drinks play havoc with *ou* ruin your stomach/health [c] [+ *autorité, influence*] to destroy; [+ *doctrine*] to demolish, crush; [+ *espoir*] to crush, shatter; [+ *foi*] to shatter, destroy [d]* [+ *personne*] (= *épuiser*) to do for*, do in*; (= *frapper*) to bash up*, duff up* (*Brit*); (= *critiquer*) to tear to pieces, slam*, slate* (*Brit*); **ce travail/cette maladie l'avait démoli** this work/this illness had just about done for him*; **je vais lui ~ le portrait** I'm going to smash his face in*; **cette marche m'a complètement démoli** I'm whacked* *ou* shattered* (*Brit*) after that walk, that walk has done for me* *ou* shattered me* (*Brit*)

démolissage* [demɔlisaʒ] NM (= *critique*) panning*, slating* (*Brit*)

démolisseur, -euse [demɔlisœʀ, øz] NM,F (= *ouvrier*) demolition worker; (= *entrepreneur*) demolition contractor; [*doctrine*] demolisher

démolition [demɔlisjɔ̃] NF [a] [*immeuble, quartier*] demolition, pulling down; [*doctrine, idéal*] demolition, crushing; **entreprise de ~** (*lit*) demolition company; [*droits, institution*] demolition job (**de** on); **l'immeuble est en ~** the building is (in the course of) being demolished → **chantier** [b] **~s** (= *décombres*) debris *sg*, ruins

démon [demɔ̃] NM [a] (*Rel*) demon, fiend; (= *enfant*) devil, demon; **sa femme est un vrai ~** his wife is a real harpy; **le ~** the Devil; **le ~ de midi** middle-aged lust; **le ~ du jeu** gambling fever; **le ~ de l'alcool** the demon drink; **le ~ de la luxure/de la curiosité** the demon of lechery/curiosity; **réveiller les vieux ~s du racisme** to reawaken the old demons of racism → **possédé** [b] (*Myth*) genius, daemon; **écoutant son ~ familier/son mauvais ~** listening to his familiar/evil spirit

démonétisation [demɔnetizasjɔ̃] NF (*Fin*) demonetization, demonetarization

démonétiser [demɔnetize] ▸conjug 1◂ VT [a] (*Fin*) to demonetize, demonetarize [b] [+ *théorie*] to devalue, discredit; [+ *personne*] to discredit

démoniaque [demɔnjak] [1] ADJ diabolical, fiendish [2] NMF person possessed by the devil *ou* by an evil spirit

démonisme [demɔnism] NM demonism

démonologie [demɔnɔlɔʒi] NF demonology

démonstrateur, -trice [demɔ̃stʀatœʀ, tʀis] NM,F demonstrator (*of commercial products*)

démonstratif, -ive [demɔ̃stʀatif, iv] [1] ADJ [a] [*personne, caractère*] demonstrative; **peu ~** undemonstrative [b] [*argument, preuve*] demonstrative, illustrative [c] (*Gram*) demonstrative [2] NM (*Gram*) demonstrative

démonstration [demɔ̃stʀasjɔ̃] NF [a] (*gén, Math*) [*vérité, loi*] demonstration; [*théorème*] proof; **cette ~ est convaincante** this demonstration is convincing [b] (*Comm*) [*fonctionnement, appareil*] demonstration; **faire une ~** to give a demonstration; **faire la ~ d'un appareil** to demonstrate an appliance; **appareil de ~** demonstration model; (*Ordin*) **disquette de ~** demo disk [c] (= *manifestation*) [*joie, tendresse*] demonstration, show, display; **accueillir qn avec des ~s d'amitié** to welcome sb with a great show of friendship; (*Mil*) **~ de force** show of force; (*Mil*) **~ aérienne/navale** display of air/naval strength

démontable [demɔ̃tabl] ADJ (*gén*) that can be dismantled; **armoire ~** wardrobe that can be dismantled *ou* taken to pieces, knockdown wardrobe (*US*)

démontage [demɔ̃taʒ] NM [a] [*installation, échafaudage, étagères*] taking down, dismantling; [*tente*] taking down; [*moteur, arme*] stripping; [*armoire, appareil, horloge*] dismantling, taking to pieces, taking apart; **pièces perdues lors de ~s successifs** parts lost during successive dismantling operations; **le ~ de la tente se fait en 5 minutes** it takes 5 minutes to take the tent down [b] [*pneu, porte*] taking off [c] [*raisonnement*] dissection, taking apart; (*pour contrecarrer*) demolishing

démonté, e [demɔ̃te] (*ptp de* **démonter**) ADJ [*mer*] raging, wild; [*personne*] (= *déconcerté*) disconcerted

démonte-pneu (*pl* **démonte-pneus**) [demɔ̃t(ə)pnø] NM tyre lever (*Brit*), tire iron (*US*)

démonter [demɔ̃te] ▸conjug 1◂ [1] VT [a] (= *désassembler*) [+ *installation, échafaudage, étagères*] to take down, dismantle; [+ *tente*] to take down; [+ *moteur, arme*] to strip down; [+ *armoire, appareil, horloge*] to dismantle, take to pieces, take apart; [+ *circuit électrique*] to dismantle [b] (= *enlever*) [+ *pneu, porte*] to take off [c] (= *déconcerter*) to disconcert; **ça m'a complètement démonté** I was completely taken aback by that, that really disconcerted me; **il ne se laisse jamais ~** he never gets flustered, he always remains unruffled [d] [+ *argumentation, raisonnement*] to dissect, take apart; (*pour contrecarrer*) to demolish [e] (= *désarçonner*) [+ *cavalier*] to throw, unseat [2] **se démonter** VPR [a] [*assemblage, pièce*] (*accidentellement*) to come apart *ou* to pieces; **est-ce que ça se démonte ?** can it be dismantled *ou* taken apart? [b] (= *perdre son calme:* *gén nég*) to get flustered; **répondre sans se ~** to reply without getting flustered *ou* without losing one's cool; **il ne se démonte pas pour si peu** he's not that easily flustered, it takes more than that to ruffle him

démontrable [demɔ̃tʀabl] ADJ demonstrable

▾ **démontrer** [demɔ̃tʀe] ▸conjug 1◂ VT (= *prouver*) [+ *loi, vérité*] to demonstrate; [+ *théorème*] to prove; (= *expliquer*) [+ *fonctionnement*] to demonstrate; (= *faire ressortir*) [+ *urgence, nécessité*] to show, demonstrate; **~ l'égalité de deux triangles** to demonstrate *ou* prove *ou* show that two triangles are equal; **sa hâte démontrait son inquiétude** his haste clearly indicated his anxiety; **tout cela démontre l'urgence de ces réformes** all this shows *ou* demonstrates the urgency of these reforms → **a**

démoralisant, e [demɔʀalizɑ̃, ɑ̃t] ADJ demoralizing

démoralisateur, -trice [demɔʀalizatœʀ, tʀis] ADJ demoralizing

démoralisation [demɔʀalizasjɔ̃] NF demoralization

démoraliser [demɔralize] ▸conjug 1◀ **1** VT to demoralize **2** **se démoraliser** VPR to lose heart, become demoralized

démordre [demɔrdr] ▸conjug 41◀ VI **il ne démord pas de son avis/sa décision** he is sticking to ou standing by his opinion/decision; **il ne veut pas en ~** he won't budge an inch, he's sticking to his guns

Démosthène [demɔsten] NM Demosthenes

démotivant, e [demɔtivã, ãt] ADJ demotivating

démotivation [demɔtivasjɔ̃] NF loss of motivation, demotivation

démotiver [demɔtive] ▸conjug 1◀ VT **~ qn** to demotivate sb, take sb's motivation away; **je suis totalement démotivé** I've lost all my motivation, I am ou I feel completely demotivated

démoucheté, e [demuʃte] ADJ [fleuret] unbuttoned

démoulage [demulaʒ] NM [statue] removal from the mould; [flan, gâteau] turning out; **procédez au ~ du gâteau** turn out the cake

démouler [demule] ▸conjug 1◀ VT [+ statue] to remove from the mould; [+ flan, gâteau] to turn out

démoustiquer [demustike] ▸conjug 1◀ VT to clear ou rid of mosquitoes

démultiplicateur, -trice [demyltiplikatœr, tris] **1** ADJ reduction (épith), reducing (épith) **2** NM reduction system

démultiplication [demyltiplikasjɔ̃] NF (= procédé) reduction; (= rapport) reduction ratio

démultiplier [demyltiplije] ▸conjug 7◀ VT [+ force] to reduce, gear down; [+ moyens] to increase

démuni, e [demyni] (ptp de **démunir**) ADJ **a** (= sans ressources) destitute; **nous sommes ~s** (sans argent) we are destitute; (sans défense) we are powerless (**devant** in the face of) **b** (= privé de) **~ de** without, lacking in; **~ d'ornements** unornamented, unadorned; **~ de protection** unprotected; **~ de talents/d'attraits** without talent/attraction, devoid of talent/ charm; **~ d'intérêt** devoid of ou without interest, uninteresting; **~ de tout** destitute; **~ d'argent** penniless, without money; **~ de papiers d'identité** without identity papers

démunir [demynir] ▸conjug 2◀ **1** VT **~ qn de** [+ vivres] to deprive sb of; [+ ressources, argent] to divest sb of; **~ qch de** to divest sth of **2** **se démunir** VPR (financièrement) to part with one's money; (= se défaire de) **se ~ de** to part with, give up

démystification [demistifikasjɔ̃] NF [personne] enlightenment; (= banalisation) demystification

démystifier [demistifje] ▸conjug 7◀ VT (= détromper) to enlighten, disabuse; (= banaliser) to demystify, take the mystery out of

démythification [demitifikasjɔ̃] NF demythologization, demystification

démythifier [demitifje] ▸conjug 7◀ VT to demythologize, demystify

dénasalisation [denazalizasjɔ̃] NF denasalization

dénasaliser [denazalize] ▸conjug 1◀ VT to denasalize

dénatalité [denatalite] NF fall ou decrease in the birth rate

dénationalisation [denasjɔnalizasjɔ̃] NF denationalization

dénationaliser [denasjɔnalize] ▸conjug 1◀ VT to denationalize

dénatter [denate] ▸conjug 1◀ VT [+ cheveux] to unplait

dénaturation [denatyrasjɔ̃] NF (Tech) denaturation

dénaturé, e [denatyre] (ptp de **dénaturer**) ADJ **a** (Tech) [alcool, sel] denatured **b** [goût, mœurs, parents] unnatural

dénaturer [denatyre] ▸conjug 1◀ VT **a** [+ vérité, faits] to distort, misrepresent; [+ propos] to distort, twist; [+ intentions] to misrepresent **b** (Tech) [+ alcool, substance alimentaire] to denature; (= altérer) [+ goût, aliment] to alter completely, change the nature of

dénazification [denazifikasjɔ̃] NF denazification

dendrite [dɑ̃drit, dɛ̃drit] NF (Géol, Anat) dendrite

dénébuliser [denebylize], **dénébuler** [denebyle] ▸conjug 1◀ VT to dispel the fog from

dénégation [denegasjɔ̃] NF (gén, Jur) denial

déneigement [denɛʒmɑ̃] NM snow-clearing (operation), snow removal

déneiger [deneʒe] ▸conjug 3◀ VT [+ objet] to clear of snow, clear the snow from

déni [deni] NM denial; (Jur) **~ de justice** denial of justice; (Psych) **~ (de la réalité)** denial

déniaiser [denjeze] ▸conjug 1◀ VT **~ qn** (= dégourdir qn) to teach sb a thing or two; (= dépuceler qn) to take away sb's innocence; **se ~** to learn about life, lose one's innocence

dénicher [deniʃe] ▸conjug 1◀ **1** VT **a*** (= trouver) [+ objet] to unearth; [+ magasin, restaurant] to discover; [+ personne] to track ou hunt down **b** (= débusquer) [+ fugitif, animal] to drive out (of hiding), flush out **c** (= enlever du nid) [+ œufs, oisillons] to take out of the nest **2** VI [oiseau] to leave the nest

dénicheur, -euse [deniʃœr, øz] NM,F **a** (hum) **c'est un vrai ~ d'objets rares** he's really good at finding rare objects; **~ de talents** talent scout **b** (d'oiseaux) bird's-nester

denier [dənje] **1** NM **a** (= monnaie) (Hist romaine) denarius; (Hist française) denier; **ça ne leur a pas coûté un ~†** it didn't cost them a farthing (Brit) ou a cent (US); **l'ayant payé de ses propres ~s** having paid for it out of his own pocket; **les trente ~s de Judas** Judas's thirty pieces of silver **b** (Tex = unité de poids) denier; **bas de 30 ~s** 30-denier stockings **2** COMP ▸ **le denier du culte** the contribution to parish costs (paid yearly) ▸ **les deniers publics** ou **de l'État** public moneys ou monies

dénier [denje] ▸conjug 7◀ VT **a** [+ responsabilité] to deny, disclaim; [+ faute] to deny **b** (= refuser) **~ qch à qn** to deny ou refuse sb sth

dénigrement [denigrəmɑ̃] NM denigration, defamation; **ce mot s'emploie par ~** this word is used disparagingly; **campagne de ~** smear campaign

dénigrer [denigre] ▸conjug 1◀ VT to denigrate, run down

denim [dənim] NM denim

dénivelé NM, **dénivelée** NF [deniv(ə)le] difference in height (**entre** between)

déniveler [deniv(ə)le] ▸conjug 4◀ VT (= rendre inégal) to make uneven; (= abaisser) to lower, put on a lower level

dénivellation [denivelasjɔ̃] NF, **dénivellement** [denivelmɑ̃] NM **a** (NonC) (= fait de rendre inégal) making uneven; (= abaissement) lowering, putting on a lower level **b** (= pente) slope; (= cassis, creux) unevenness (NonC), dip **c** (= différence de niveau) difference in level ou altitude

dénombrable [denɔ̃brabl] ADJ countable; (Ling) **nom ~** countable ou count noun; **non ~** uncountable

dénombrement [denɔ̃brəmɑ̃] NM counting; **~ de la population** population census ou count

dénombrer [denɔ̃bre] ▸conjug 1◀ VT (= compter) to count; (= énumérer) to enumerate,

list; **on dénombre trois morts et cinq blessés** there are three dead and five wounded

dénominateur [denɔminatœr] NM (Math) denominator; (Math, fig) (**plus petit**) **~ commun** (lowest) common denominator

dénominatif, -ive [denɔminatif, iv] ADJ, NM denominative

dénomination [denɔminasjɔ̃] NF (= nom) designation, appellation (frm), denomination (frm); (= action) denomination (frm), naming

dénommé, e [denɔme] (ptp de **dénommer**) ADJ (parfois péj) **le ~ X** a certain X, the man called X; **on m'a présenté un ~ Dupont** I was introduced to a certain Mr Dupont, I was introduced to someone by the name of Dupont

dénommer [denɔme] ▸conjug 1◀ VT (frm = donner un nom à) to denominate (frm), name; (= désigner) to designate, denote; (Jur) to name

dénoncer [denɔ̃se] ▸conjug 3◀ **1** VT **a** (= révéler) [+ coupable] to denounce; [+ forfait, abus] to expose; **sa hâte l'a dénoncé** his haste gave him away ou betrayed him; **~ qn à la police** to inform against sb, give sb away to the police **b** (= signaler publiquement) [+ danger, injustice] to denounce **c** (= annuler) [+ contrat, traité] to denounce **d** (littér = dénoter) to announce, indicate **2** **se dénoncer** VPR [criminel] to give o.s. up, come forward; **se ~ à la police** to give o.s. up to the police

dénonciateur, -trice [denɔ̃sjatœr, tris] **1** ADJ denunciatory, accusatory **2** NM,F [criminel] denouncer, informer; [forfait] exposer; **les ~s d'injustices/de malhonnêtetés** those who denounce injustices/dishonesty

dénonciation [denɔ̃sjasjɔ̃] NF [criminel] denunciation; [forfait, abus] exposure (NonC); [traité] denunciation, denouncement; [contrat] termination; **emprisonné sur la ~ de qn** imprisoned on the strength of a denunciation by sb

dénotatif, -ive [denɔtatif, iv] ADJ (Ling) denotative

dénotation [denɔtasjɔ̃] NF (Ling) denotation

dénoter [denɔte] ▸conjug 1◀ VT (= révéler) to indicate, denote; (Ling) to denote

dénouement [denumɑ̃] NM (Théât) dénouement; [affaire, aventure, intrigue] outcome, conclusion; **~ heureux** [film] happy ending

dénouer [denwe] ▸conjug 1◀ **1** VT **a** [+ nœud, lien] to untie, undo; [+ cravate] to undo; [+ cheveux] to let down, undo; **les cheveux dénoués** with her hair (falling) loose **b** [+ situation] to untangle, resolve; [+ difficultés, intrigue] to untangle, unravel **2** **se dénouer** VPR **a** [lien, nœud] to come untied, come undone; [cheveux] to come undone, come down → **langue** **b** [intrigue, situation] to be resolved

dénoûment [denumɑ̃] NM = **dénouement**

dénoyautage [denwajotaʒ] NM [fruit] stoning (Brit), pitting (US)

dénoyauter [denwajote] ▸conjug 1◀ VT [+ fruit] to stone (Brit), pit (US)

dénoyauteur [denwajotœr] NM stoner (Brit), pitter (US)

denrée [dɑ̃re] NF commodity, foodstuff, produce (NonC); **~s alimentaires** foodstuffs; **~s de base** basic foods; **~s de consommation courante** basic consumer goods; **~s périssables** perishable foods ou foodstuffs; (fig) **l'honnêteté devient une ~ rare** honesty is becoming a rare commodity

dense [dɑ̃s] ADJ (Phys) dense; [foule] dense, tightly packed; [feuillage, brouillard] dense, thick; [circulation] heavy; [texte] dense; [style] compact, condensed

densifier [dɑ̃sifje] ▸conjug 7◀ **1** VT [+ bois] to make denser **2** **se densifier** VPR [population, trafic] to get denser

densimètre [dɑ̃simɛtr] NM densimeter

densité [dãsite] NF (*Démographie, Phys*) density; [*brouillard*] denseness, thickness; [*circulation*] heaviness; [*foule*] denseness; **région à forte/faible ~ de population** densely/sparsely populated area, area with a high/low population density; (*Ordin*) **~ d'implantation** packing density

dent [dã] NF [a] [*homme, animal*] tooth; **~s du haut/du bas/de devant/du fond** upper/lower/front/back teeth; **~ de lait/de sagesse** milk *ou* baby/wisdom tooth; **~ définitive** *ou* **de remplacement** permanent *ou* second tooth; **donner un coup de ~ à** to bite into, take a bite at → **arracher, brosse, faux²**
[b] [*herse, fourche, fourchette*] prong; [*râteau*] tooth, prong; [*scie, peigne*] tooth; [*roue, engrenage*] tooth, cog; [*feuille*] serration; [*arête rocheuse*] jag; [*timbre*] perforation; **en ~s de scie** [*couteau*] serrated; [*montagne*] jagged; **graphique/carrière en ~s de scie** switchback graph/career
[c] (*loc*) **avoir la ~*** to be hungry; **avoir la ~ dure** to be scathing (in one's comments) (**envers** about); **avoir/garder une ~ contre qn** to have/hold a grudge against sb; **avoir les ~s longues** (= *être ambitieux*) to be very ambitious, have one's sights fixed high; (*hum*) **avoir les ~s qui rayent le parquet** to have one's sights fixed high, want it all*; (*lit, fig*) **montrer les ~s** to bare one's teeth; **être sur les ~s** (*fébrile*) to be keyed up; (*très occupé*) to be under great pressure; **faire** *ou* **percer ses ~s** to teethe, cut (one's) teeth; **il vient de percer une ~** he has just cut a tooth; **se faire les ~s** [*animal*] to cut its teeth; (*fig = s'exercer*) to cut one's teeth (**sur** on); **croquer/manger qch à belles ~s** to bite into sth/eat sth with gusto; **manger du bout des ~s** to eat half-heartedly, pick at one's food; **parler/marmotter entre ses ~s** to talk/mumble between one's teeth; **ils n'ont rien à se mettre sous la ~** they have nothing to eat; **on voudrait bien quelque chose à se mettre sous la ~** we wouldn't say no to a bite to eat *ou* something to eat; **il mange tout ce qui lui tombe sous la ~** he eats everything he can lay his hands on → **armé, casser**

dentaire [dãtɛʀ] ADJ dental; **faire (l'école) ~*** to study dentistry → **fil, formule, prothèse**

dental, e (*mpl* **-aux**) [dãtal, o] (*Ling*) [1] ADJ dental [2] **dentale** NF dental

dent-de-lion (*pl* **dents-de-lion**) [dãdəljõ] NF dandelion

denté, e [dãte] ADJ (*Tech*) toothed; (*Bot*) dentate → **roue**

dentelé, e [dãt(ə)le] (*ptp de* **denteler**) ADJ [*arête*] jagged; [*timbre*] perforated; [*contour, côte*] indented, jagged; (*Bot*) dentate; (*Anat*) serrate

denteler [dãt(ə)le] ▶conjug 4◀ VT (*Tech*) [+ *timbre-poste*] to perforate; (*fig = découper*) **l'érosion avait dentelé la côte** erosion had indented the coastline *ou* had given the coast a jagged outline; **les pics qui dentelaient l'horizon** the peaks that stood in a jagged line along the horizon

dentelle [dãtɛl] NF lace (*NonC*); **de** *ou* **en ~** lace (*épith*); **~ à l'aiguille** *ou* **au point** needle-point lace; **~ au(x) fuseau(x)** bobbin lace; **de papier** lacy paper; **~ de pierre** (stone) filigree; **crêpe ~** thin pancake; **il ne fait pas dans la ~*** he's not particular about details

dentellerie [dãtɛlʀi] NF (= *fabrication*) lacemaking; (*Comm*) lace manufacture

dentellier, -ière [dãtəlje, jɛʀ] [1] ADJ [*industrie*] lace (*épith*) [2] NM,F lacemaker [3] **dentellière** NF (= *machine*) lacemaking machine

dentelure [dãt(ə)lyʀ] NF [*timbre-poste*] perforations; [*feuille*] serration; [*arête*] jagged outline; **les ~s d'une côte** the indentations *ou* jagged outline of a coastline

dentier [dãtje] NM denture, dental plate; **porter un ~** to wear dentures

dentifrice [dãtifʀis] [1] NM toothpaste [2] ADJ **eau ~** mouthwash; **poudre ~** tooth powder; **pâte ~** toothpaste

dentine [dãtin] NF (*Anat*) dentine

dentiste [dãtist] NMF dentist → **chirurgien**

dentisterie [dãtistʀi] NF dentistry

dentition [dãtisjõ] NF (= *dents*) teeth *pl*; (= *croissance*) dentition; **~ de lait** milk *ou* baby teeth, deciduous dentition (*SPÉC*); **~ définitive** permanent teeth *ou* dentition (*SPÉC*)

denture [dãtyʀ] NF (= *humaine*) teeth *pl*, set of teeth, dentition (*SPÉC*); (*Tech*) [*roue*] teeth *pl*, cogs

dénucléarisation [denykleaʀizasjõ] NF denuclearization

dénucléariser [denykleaʀize] ▶conjug 1◀ VT to denuclearize; **zone dénucléarisée** nuclear-free zone

dénudé, e [denyde] (*ptp de* **dénuder**) ADJ (*gén*) bare; [*crâne*] [*colline*] bare, bald

dénuder [denyde] ▶conjug 1◀ [1] VT [a] (*Tech*) [+ *fil*] to bare, strip; (*Méd*) [+ *os*] to strip [b] [+ *arbre, sol, colline*] to bare, strip [c] [+ *bras, dos*] [*robe*] to leave bare; [*mouvement*] to bare [2] **se dénuder** VPR [a] [*personne*] to strip (off) [b] [*colline, arbre*] to become bare, be bared; [*crâne*] to be balding, be going bald

dénué, e [denɥe] (*ptp de* **dénuer**) ♦ **dénué de** ADJ devoid of; **~ de bon sens** senseless, devoid of sense; **~ d'intérêt** devoid of interest; **~ de talent/d'imagination** lacking in *ou* without talent/imagination, untalented/unimaginative; **~ de tout** destitute; **~ de tout fondement** completely unfounded *ou* groundless, entirely without foundation

dénuement [denymã] NM [*personne*] destitution; **le ~ de la recherche/du système de soins** the impoverished state of research/of the care system; **dans le ~ le plus total** in utter destitution

dénuer (se) [denɥe] ▶conjug 1◀ VPR (*littér*) to deprive o.s. (**de** of)

dénûment [denymã] NM = **dénuement**

dénutri, e [denytʀi] ADJ (*Méd*) [*enfant*] malnourished; **bébé gravement ~** severely malnourished baby

dénutrition [denytʀisjõ] NF undernutrition, undernourishment

déo* [deo] NM ABRÉV = **déodorant**

déodorant [deodoʀã] ADJ M, NM (**produit**) **~** deodorant; **~ (corporel)** deodorant

déontologie [deõtɔlɔʒi] NF professional code of ethics, deontology (*SPÉC*)

déontologique [deõtɔlɔʒik] ADJ ethical, deontological (*SPÉC*)

dép. ABRÉV = **département** [a] [*organisme, entreprise*] dept [b] (= *division du territoire*) → **département**

dépailler [depaje] ▶conjug 1◀ VT [+ *chaise*] to remove the straw seating from

dépannage [depanaʒ] NM [*véhicule, appareil*] fixing, repairing; **camion de ~** breakdown lorry (*Brit*), tow truck (*US*); **service de ~** (*pour véhicules*) breakdown service; (*pour appareils*) repair service; **ils ont fait trois ~s aujourd'hui** (*de véhicules*) they've fixed three breakdowns today; (*d'appareils*) they've done three repair jobs today; **c'est une lampe/une bouilloire de ~*** it's a spare lamp/kettle

dépanner [depane] ▶conjug 1◀ VT [a] (= *réparer*) [+ *véhicule, appareil*] to fix, repair; [+ *automobiliste*] to fix the car of; **j'ai dû me faire ~ sur l'autoroute** I had to call the breakdown service on the motorway [b]* (= *tirer d'embarras*) [+ *personne*] to help out; **~ qn d'un ticket restaurant** to help sb out with a luncheon voucher; **il m'avait donné 100 F pour me ~*** he gave me 100 francs to tide me over *ou* to help me out; **tu peux me ~ d'une cigarette ?** can you spare me a cigarette?

dépanneur [depanœʀ] NM (*gén*) repairman; (*Aut*) breakdown mechanic; (*TV*) television engineer *ou* repairman; (*Can* = *épicerie*) convenience store

dépanneuse [depanøz] NF breakdown lorry (*Brit*), tow truck (*US*), wrecker (*US*)

dépaqueter [depak(ə)te] ▶conjug 4◀ VT to unpack

déparasiter [depaʀazite] ▶conjug 1◀ VT [+ *poste de radio*] to fit a suppressor to; [+ *animal, local*] to rid of parasites

dépareillé, e [depaʀeje] (*ptp de* **dépareiller**) ADJ [*collection*] incomplete; [*objet*] odd (*épith*); (*Comm*) **articles ~s** oddments; (*Comm*) **couverts ~s** odd cutlery

dépareiller [depaʀeje] ▶conjug 1◀ VT [+ *collection, service de table*] to make incomplete, spoil; **en cassant cette assiette tu as dépareillé le service** you've spoilt the set now that you've broken that plate

déparer [depaʀe] ▶conjug 1◀ VT [+ *paysage*] to spoil, disfigure, mar; [+ *visage*] to disfigure; [+ *beauté, qualité*] to detract from, mar; **cette pièce ne déparerait pas ma collection** this piece would go well in my collection; **cette lampe ne déparerait pas dans la chambre** this lamp wouldn't look bad in the bedroom

déparié, e [depaʀje] (*ptp de* **déparier**) ADJ [*chaussures, gants*] odd (*épith*)

déparier [depaʀje] ▶conjug 7◀ VT [+ *chaussures, gants*] to split up

départ¹ [depaʀ] NM [a] [*voyageur, véhicule, excursion*] departure; [*fusée*] launch; (= *endroit*) point of departure; **observer le ~ du train** to watch the train leave; **le ~ est à huit heures** the train (*ou* coach *etc*) leaves at eight o'clock; **fixer l'heure/le jour de son ~** to set a time/day for one's departure; **être sur le ~** to be about to leave *ou* go; **excursions au ~ de Chamonix** excursions (leaving *ou* departing) from Chamonix, (day) trips from Chamonix; (*Rail*) **« ~ des grandes lignes »** "main-line departures"; **dès son ~ j'ai ...** as soon as he had left I ...; **mon ~ de l'hôtel** my departure from *ou* my leaving the hotel; **peu après mon ~ de l'hôtel** soon after I had left the hotel, soon after my departure from the hotel; **c'est bientôt le ~ en vacances** we'll soon be off on holiday (*Brit*) *ou* vacation (*US*), we'll soon be leaving on our holidays (*Brit*) *ou* on vacation (*US*); **alors, c'est pour bientôt le grand ~ ?** when's the big trip then?; **le ~ du train/bateau est imminent** the train/boat will be leaving any time now *ou* is about to depart; **son ~ précipité** his hasty departure; **il a essayé de reculer son ~ à l'armée** he tried to put off leaving for the army; **la levée du matin est à sept heures et le ~ du courrier se fait à neuf heures** the morning collection is at seven and the mail leaves town at nine o'clock → **tableau**
[b] (*Sport*) start; (*lit, fig*) **un faux ~** a false start; **~ lancé/arrêté** flying/standing start; **~ décalé** staggered start; **donner le ~ aux coureurs** to give the runners the starting signal, start the race; **les coureurs se rassemblent au ~** the runners are assembling at the start; **être au ~ d'une course ◊ prendre le ~ d'une course** to take part in a race; **47 concurrents ont pris le ~** 47 competitors took part in the race; (*lit, fig*) **prendre un bon/mauvais ~** to get off to a good/bad start
[c] [*salarié, ministre*] leaving (*NonC*), departure; **le ministre annonça son ~** the minister announced that he was going to quit *ou* that he was leaving; **demander le ~ d'un fonctionnaire** to demand the resignation of a civil servant; **réduire le personnel par ~s naturels** to reduce the staff gradually by natural wastage; **indemnité de ~** severance pay; **en préretraite** early retirement; **~ à la retraite** retirement; **~ volontaire** *ou* **négocié** voluntary redundancy

d (= *origine*) [*processus, transformation*] start; **au ~** at the start *ou* outset; **de ~** [*hypothèse*] initial; **salaire de ~** starting salary; **de la langue de ~ à la langue d'arrivée** from the source language to the target language; **il y a eu plusieurs ~s de feu** fire broke out in several places → **point**[1]

départ[2] [depar] NM (*littér*) distinction (**entre** between); **faire le ~ entre le vrai et le faux** to draw *ou* make a distinction between truth and falsehood

départager [departaʒe] ▶ conjug 3 ◀ VT [+ *concurrents*] to decide between; [+ *votes*] to settle, decide; (*littér*) [+ *opinions*] to decide between; (*littér*) [+ *camps opposés*] to separate; **~ l'assemblée** to settle the voting in the assembly

département [departamã] NM [*organisme, université, entreprise*] department; (= *division du territoire*) département; (= *administrative division*), ≈ county (*Brit*); **~ (ministériel)** ministry, department; (*aux USA*) **le ~ d'État** the State Department; **~ d'outre-mer** French overseas département

---
DÉPARTEMENT

Since 1790, France has been divided into 95 metropolitan **départements** *and four overseas* **départements**. *Each is run by its own local council, the "conseil général", which has its headquarters in the principal town ("le chef-lieu du département"). Every* **département** *has a code number which appears as the first two figures of postcodes and the last two figures on vehicle registration plates.* → ARRONDISSEMENT ; CANTON ; COMMUNE ; RÉGION ; DOM-TOM

---

départemental, e (*mpl* **-aux**) [departamãtal, o] ADJ (*gén*) departmental; (= *ministériel*) ministerial; (*Admin*) **d'un département** ; **(route) ~e** secondary road, ≈ B-road (*Brit*)

départementalisation [departamãtalizasjɔ̃] NF (*Admin*) [*territoire*] giving the status of département to; [*compétence*] devolution to the départements; **la ~ des services judiciaires** basing legal services in the départements

départir [departir] ▶ conjug 16 ◀ **1** VT (†, *littér* = *attribuer*) [+ *tâche*] to assign; [+ *faveur*] to accord (*frm*) **2** **se départir** VPR **se ~ de** (*gén nég* = *abandonner*) [+ *ton, attitude*] to abandon, depart from; [+ *sourire*] to drop; **sans se ~ de sa prudence/sa bonne humeur** without abandoning his caution/his good humour; **il a répondu sans se ~ de son calme** he answered without losing his composure

départiteur [departitœr] NM **(juge) ~** arbitrator

dépassé, e [depase] (*ptp de* **dépasser**) ADJ (= *périmé*) outmoded, old-fashioned, out of date; (* = *désorienté*) out of one's depth (*attrib*)

dépassement [depasmã] NM **a** (*Aut*) passing (*NonC*), overtaking (*Brit*) (*NonC*); **tout ~ est dangereux** overtaking is always dangerous, it is always dangerous to overtake; **« ~ interdit »** "no overtaking"; **après plusieurs ~s dangereux ...** after perilously overtaking several vehicles ... **b** [*limite, prix*] (= *action*) exceeding; (= *excès*) excess; **~ d'honoraires** charge exceeding the statutory fee; **faire des ~s d'honoraires** to charge more than the statutory fee; **il a eu une amende pour ~ de vitesse** *ou* **de la vitesse autorisée** he was fined for speeding *ou* for exceeding the speed limit **c** (*Fin*) (= *de crédit*) overspending (*NonC*); **un ~ de crédit de 5 millions** overspending by 5 million francs; **~ budgétaire** overspend on budget, overspending **d** **~ (de soi-même)** surpassing of oneself

dépasser [depase] ▶ conjug 1 ◀ **1** VT **a** (= *aller plus loin que*) [+ *endroit*] to pass, go past; (*Aviat*) [+ *piste*] to overshoot; (= *distancer*) [+ *véhicule, personne*] to pass, overtake (*Brit*); **dépassez les feux et prenez la première rue à gauche** take

the first on the left after the lights **b** (= *déborder de*) [+ *alignement*] (*horizontalement*) to jut out over, overhang; (*verticalement*) to jut out above, stand higher than; **son succès a dépassé les frontières** his success has reached beyond *ou* transcended national boundaries **c** (= *excéder*) [+ *limite, quantité mesurable*] to exceed; **~ qch en hauteur/largeur** to be higher *ou* taller/wider than sth, exceed sth in height/width; **il a dépassé son père (de 10 cm) maintenant** he's (10 cm) taller than his father now; **cette plante a dépassé l'autre** this plant has outgrown the other one *ou* is now taller than the other one; **~ en nombre** to outnumber; **tout colis qui dépasse 20 kg/la limite (de poids)** all parcels in excess of *ou* exceeding *ou* over 20 kg/the (weight) limit; **~ le nombre prévu** to be more than expected; **la réunion ne devrait pas ~ trois heures** the meeting shouldn't go on longer than *ou* last longer than three hours, the meeting shouldn't exceed three hours (in length); **il ne veut pas ~ 500 F** he won't go above *ou* over 500 francs; **ça va ~ 100 F** it'll be more than *ou* over 100 francs; **elle a dépassé la quarantaine** she is over forty, she has turned forty; **« ne pas ~ la dose prescrite »** "do not exceed the prescribed dose"; **le prix de cette maison dépasse nos moyens** this house is beyond our means *ou* is more than we can afford **d** (= *surpasser*) [+ *valeur, prévisions*] to exceed; [+ *réputation*] to outshine; [+ *rival*] to outmatch, outstrip; **~ qn en violence/intelligence** to be more violent/intelligent than sb, surpass sb in violence/intelligence; **pour la paresse/l'appétit il dépasse tout le monde** he beats everybody for laziness/appetite; **il dépasse tous ses camarades** he is ahead of *ou* he surpasses all his friends; **sa bêtise dépasse tout ce qu'on peut imaginer** his stupidity beggars belief, he's more stupid than you could possibly imagine; **les résultats ont dépassé notre attente** the results exceeded *ou* surpassed our expectations; **cela dépasse toutes mes espérances** it is beyond my wildest dreams, it is better than anything I had ever hoped for **e** (= *outrepasser*) [+ *moyens, instructions*] to go beyond; [+ *attributions*] to go beyond, overstep; [+ *crédits*] to exceed; **cela dépasse les bornes** *ou* **les limites** *ou* **la mesure** that's the absolute limit, that's going too far; **il a dépassé les bornes** *ou* **la mesure** he has really gone too far *ou* overstepped the mark *ou* passed over the bounds (*US*); **cela a dépassé le stade de la plaisanterie** it has gone beyond a joke; **les mots ont dû ~ sa pensée** he must have got carried away; **cela dépasse mes forces/ma compétence** it's beyond my strength/capabilities; **cela me dépasse** it's beyond me; **il a dépassé ses forces** he has overtaxed himself *ou* overdone it **f** (= *dérouter*) **cela/cet argument me dépasse !** it/this argument is beyond me!; **être dépassé (par les événements)** to be overtaken by events

2 VI **a** (*Aut*) to overtake (*Brit*), pass (*US*); **« défense de ~ »** "no overtaking" (*Brit*), "no passing" (*US*) **b** (= *faire saillie*) [*bâtiment, tour*] to stick out; [*planche, balcon, rocher*] to stick out, jut out, protrude; [*clou*] to stick out; [*jupon*] to show (**de, sous** below); [*chemise*] to be hanging out (**de** of), be untucked; **il y a quelque chose qui dépasse du tiroir** something's sticking out *ou* hanging out of the drawer; **leur chien a toujours un bout de langue qui dépasse** their dog always has the end of his tongue hanging out

3 **se dépasser** VPR to surpass o.s., excel o.s.

dépassionner [depasjɔne] ▶ conjug 1 ◀ VT [+ *débat*] to take the heat out of

dépatouiller (se)* [depatuje] ▶ conjug 1 ◀ VPR **se dépatouiller de** [+ *situation difficile*] to get out of; **laisse-le se dépatouiller !** leave him to *ou* let him get out of it on his own!; **savoir se dépatouiller** to (manage to) get by

dépavage [depavaʒ] NM removal of the cobbles *ou* cobblestones (**de** from)

dépaver [depave] ▶ conjug 1 ◀ VT to dig up the cobbles *ou* cobblestones from

dépaysant, e [depeizã, ãt] ADJ **j'ai passé un séjour très ~ en Inde** my stay in India provided me with a complete change of scene; **restaurant au décor ~** restaurant with an exotic décor

dépaysé, e [depeize] (*ptp de* **dépayser**) ADJ (*gén*) disoriented; **je me sens très ~ ici** I feel very much like a fish out of water here, I feel very disoriented here, I don't feel at home at all here; **il ne sera pas ~ dans notre service** he'll feel quite at home *ou* he won't feel at all out of place in our department

dépaysement [depeizmã] NM (= *changement salutaire*) change of scene *ou* scenery; (= *désorientation*) disorientation, feeling of strangeness; **partez en Inde, c'est le ~ assuré !** go to India, you're guaranteed exotic new surroundings!

dépayser [depeize] ▶ conjug 1 ◀ VT (= *désorienter*) to disorientate, disorient; (= *changer agréablement*) to give a change of scenery to, give a welcome change of surroundings to; **ce séjour m'a dépaysé** this stay has given me a change of scenery *ou* a welcome change of surroundings

dépeçage [depəsaʒ], **dépècement** [depɛsmã] NM [*animal*] (*par un boucher*) cutting up; (*par un fauve*) dismembering; [*territoire, état*] carving up, dismembering; [*groupe, entreprise*] carving up

dépecer [depəse] ▶ conjug 5 ◀ VT [+ *animal*] [*boucher*] to cut up; [*fauve*] to dismember, tear limb from limb; [+ *territoire, état*] to carve up, dismember; [+ *groupe, entreprise*] to carve up

dépêche [depɛʃ] NF **a** (*Admin*) dispatch; **~ diplomatique** diplomatic dispatch **b** (*Téléc*) **~ (télégraphique)** telegram, wire (*US*); **envoyer une ~ à qn** to send sb a telegram *ou* wire (*US*), telegraph sb, wire sb (*US*) **c** (*Journalisme*) **~ (d'agence)** dispatch, agency *ou* wire (*US*) story; **je reçois à l'instant une ~ de notre correspondant** I've just received a dispatch *ou* story from our correspondent

dépêcher [depeʃe] ▶ conjug 1 ◀ **1** VT to dispatch, send (**auprès de** to) **2** **se dépêcher** VPR to hurry; **il se dépêchait (en marchant, courant)** he was hurrying (along); (*en travaillant*) he was hurrying; **dépêche-toi !** hurry (up)!, (be) quick!; **se ~ de faire qch** to hurry to do sth; **dépêche-toi de les commander, il n'y en aura bientôt plus** hurry up and order them or there soon won't be any left

dépeigner [depeɲe] ▶ conjug 1 ◀ VT **~ qn** to make sb's hair untidy, ruffle sb's hair; **dépeigné par le vent** with windswept hair; **elle entra toute dépeignée** she came in with tousled *ou* dishevelled hair

dépeindre [depɛ̃dr] ▶ conjug 52 ◀ VT to depict

dépenaillé, e [dep(ə)naje] ADJ [*personne, vêtements*] (= *débraillé*) messy; (= *en haillons*) tattered, ragged; [*drapeau, livre*] tattered

dépénalisation [depenalizasjɔ̃] NF [*délit, drogue*] decriminalization

dépénaliser [depenalize] ▶ conjug 1 ◀ VT to decriminalize

dépendance [depãdãs] NF **a** (= *interdépendance*) dependence (*NonC*), dependency; **la ~ de qch vis-à-vis de qch d'autre** the dependence of sth (up)on sth else; **un réseau subtil de ~s** a subtle network of dependencies *ou* interdependencies **b** (= *asservissement, subordination*) subordination (**à l'égard de** to); **la ~ de qn vis-à-vis de qn d'autre** the subordination of sb to sb else; **être sous** ou **dans la ~ de qn** to be subordinate to sb [c] (= *bâtiment*) [*hôtel, château, ferme*] outbuilding, outhouse [d] (*Hist, Pol = territoire*) dependency [e] (*à une drogue, à l'alcool*) dependence, dependency (**à** on), addiction (**à** to) [f] (*Ling*) dependency

dépendant, e [depãdã, ãt] ADJ [a] (= *non autonome*) dependent (**de** (up)on); **personnes âgées ~es** elderly dependants [b] [*drogué*] dependent (**à** on), addicted (**à** to)

▼ **dépendre** [depãdR] ▶ conjug 41 ◀ [1] **dépendre de** VT INDIR [a] [*employé*] to be answerable to, to be responsible to; [*organisation*] to be dependent (up)on; [*territoire*] to be dependent (up)on, be a dependency of; **~ (financièrement) de ses parents** to be financially dependent (up)on one's parents; **ce pays dépend économiquement de la France** this country is economically dependent (up)on France; **je ne veux ~ de personne** I don't wish to be dependent (up)on anyone ou to have to depend (up)on anyone; **ce terrain dépend de leur domaine** this piece of land is part of ou belongs to their property; **ne ~ que de soi-même** to be answerable only to oneself [b] [*décision, résultat, phénomène*] to depend (up)on, be dependent (up)on; **ça va ~ du temps** it'll (all) depend on the weather; **— ça dépend** — it (all) depends; **il dépend de vous/de ceci que ...** it depends ou rests (up)on you/this whether ...; **il ne dépend que de vous que ...** it depends ou rests entirely (up)on you whether ..., it's entirely up to you whether ...; **il dépend de toi de réussir** it depends on you ou it's up to you whether you succeed (or not)

[2] VT [+ *lustre, guirlandes, pendu*] to take down

dépens [depã] NMPL [a] (*Jur*) costs; **être condamné aux ~** to be ordered to pay costs, have costs awarded against one [b] **aux ~ de** at the expense of; **rire aux ~ de qn** to (have a) laugh at sb's expense; **vivre aux ~ de qn** to live off sb; **je l'ai appris à mes ~** I learnt this to my cost ou at my expense; **notre équipe s'est qualifiée aux ~ de Toulon** our team qualified after ou by beating Toulon

dépense [depãs] NF [a] (= *argent dépensé, frais*) spending (*NonC*), expense, expenditure (*NonC*); (= *sortie*) outlay, expenditure (*NonC*); **une ~ de 1 000 F** an outlay ou expenditure of 1,000 francs; **les ~s du ménage** household expenses; **contrôler les ~s de qn** to control sb's expenditure ou spending; **je n'aurais pas dû faire cette ~** I shouldn't have spent that money; **j'hésite, c'est une grosse ~** I can't decide, it's a large outlay ou it's a lot to lay out; **calculer ~s et recettes** to calculate expenditure and receipts; **~s diverses** sundries; **~s publiques** public ou government expenditure ou spending; **les ~s de santé/militaires** health/military expenditure ou spending; **~ d'investissement** ou **d'équipement** capital expenditure (*NonC*); **pousser qn à la ~** to make sb spend some money; **faire la ~ d'une voiture** to lay out money ou spend money on a car; **ne pas regarder à la ~** to spare no expense [b] [*électricité, essence*] consumption; **~ physique** (physical) exercise

dépenser [depãse] ▶ conjug 1 ◀ [1] VT [a] [+ *argent*] to spend; [+ *électricité, essence*] to use; **~ sans compter** to spend without counting the cost, spend lavishly; **elle dépense peu pour la nourriture** she doesn't spend much on food, she spends little on food [b] [+ *forces, énergie*] to expend, use up; [+ *temps, jeunesse*] to spend, use up; **~ son trop-plein d'énergie** to use up one's surplus energy; **vous dépensez inutilement votre salive** you're wasting your breath [2] **se dépenser** VPR (= *faire des efforts*) to exert o.s.; (= *se défouler*) to let off steam*; **se ~ en démarches inutiles** to waste one's energies in useless procedures; **pour ce projet il s'est dépensé sans compter** he has put all his energy ou energies into this project; **les**

▶ GRAMMAIRE ACTIVE: **dépendre** 52.6

enfants ont besoin de se ~ physiquement children need to expend their energy

dépensier, -ière [depãsje, jɛR] ADJ, NM,F extravagant; **c'est une dépensière** ◊ **elle est dépensière** she's a spendthrift

déperdition [depɛRdisjɔ̃] NF (*Sci, gén*) loss

dépérir [depeRiR] ▶ conjug 2 ◀ VI [*personne*] to fade away, waste away; [*santé, forces*] to fail, decline; [*plante*] to wither; [*commerce*] to (be on the) decline, fall off; [*affaire, région, économie*] to be in decline, go downhill

dépérissement [depeRismã] NM [*personne*] fading away, wasting away; [*santé, forces*] failing, decline; [*plante*] withering; [*commerce*] decline, falling off; [*affaire, région, économie*] decline

dépersonnalisation [depɛRsɔnalizasjɔ̃] NF depersonalization

dépersonnaliser [depɛRsɔnalize] [1] VT to depersonalize [2] **se dépersonnaliser** VPR [*relations, débat*] to become impersonal ou depersonalized; (*Psych*) to become depersonalized

dépêtrer [depetRe] ▶ conjug 1 ◀ VT [1] [+ *bourbier, ronces, harnachement*] to extricate sb from, free sb from; [+ *situation*] to extricate sb from, get sb out of [2] **se dépêtrer** VPR (*lit, fig*) to extricate o.s., free o.s.; **se ~ de** [+ *ronces, situation*] to extricate ou free o.s. from, get out of; [+ *liens*] to free o.s. from; [+ *gêneur*] to get rid of

dépeuplement [depœplemã] NM [*région, ville*] depopulation; **le ~ de la rivière** the depletion of fish stocks in the river; **le ~ des forêts** the disappearance of wildlife from forests

dépeupler [depœple] ▶ conjug 1 ◀ [1] VT [a] [+ *région, ville*] to depopulate; **zones rurales dépeuplées** depopulated rural areas [b] [+ *rivière*] to deplete the fish stocks in; [+ *forêt*] to kill off the wildlife in [2] **se dépeupler** VPR [a] [*région, ville*] to be depopulated; **les campagnes se dépeuplent** the countryside is becoming depopulated [b] [*rivière*] to be depleted of fish; [*région, forêt*] to be emptied of wildlife

déphasage [defazaʒ] NM (*Phys*) phase difference; (* = *perte de contact*) being out of touch; **il y a ~ entre les syndicats et leurs dirigeants** the unions and their leaders are out of phase ou step

déphasé, e [defaze] (*ptp de* **déphaser**) ADJ [a] (*Phys*) out of phase [b]* (= *désorienté*) out of phase ou step (*attrib*), not with it* (*attrib*)

déphaser [defaze] ▶ conjug 1 ◀ VT [a] (*Phys*) to cause a phase difference in [b]* (= *désorienter*) to put out of touch

dépiauter* [depjote] ▶ conjug 1 ◀ VT [+ *animal*] to skin; [+ *paquet*] to undo; [+ *texte*] to pull to pieces

dépigmentation [depigmãtasjɔ̃] NF depigmentation

dépilation [depilasjɔ̃] NF (*Méd*) hair loss

dépilatoire [depilatwaR] [1] ADJ depilatory, hair-removing (*épith*) [2] NM depilatory ou hair-removing cream

dépiler [depile] ▶ conjug 1 ◀ VT (*Méd*) to cause hair loss to; (*Tech*) [+ *peaux*] to grain

dépiquer [depike] ▶ conjug 1 ◀ VT (*Couture*) to unstitch, unpick (*Brit*); (*Agr*) [+ *laitue*] to transplant; [+ *blé*] to thresh; [+ *riz*] to hull

dépistage [depistaʒ] NM [*maladie, virus, dopage*] screening (**de** for); **centre de ~ du sida** HIV testing centre; **examen** ou **test de ~** screening test; **test de ~ du sida** AIDS test

dépister [depiste] ▶ conjug 1 ◀ VT [a] (*Méd*) [+ *maladie, virus, dopage*] to detect; (= *faire passer un test à*) to screen [b] (= *détecter*) [+ *gibier, criminel*] to track down; [+ *influence, cause*] to unearth, detect

dépit [depi] NM [a] (= *amertume*) pique, (great) vexation; **causer du ~ à qn** to vex sb greatly; **il en a conçu du ~** he was very piqued at it; **il l'a fait par ~** he did it out of pique ou in a fit of pique; **par ~ amoureux elle a épousé le premier venu** she married the first man she met on the rebound* [b] **en ~ de** in spite of, despite; **faire qch en ~ du bon sens** to do sth any old how

dépité, e [depite] (*ptp de* **dépiter**) ADJ (greatly) vexed, piqued

dépiter [depite] ▶ conjug 1 ◀ VT to vex

dépitonner [depitɔne] ▶ conjug 1 ◀ VTI (*Alpinisme*) to depeg

déplacé, e [deplase] (*ptp de* **déplacer**) ADJ [*présence*] uncalled-for; [*intervention, scrupule*] misplaced, out of place (*attrib*); [*remarque, propos*] uncalled-for, out of place (*attrib*) → **personne**

déplacement [deplasmã] NM [a] [*objet, meuble*] moving, shifting [b] (*Méd*) [*articulation, os*] displacement; **~ de vertèbre** slipped disc; **~ d'organe** organ displacement [c] [*usine, fonctionnaire*] transfer; [*collectivité*] moving; **le ~ forcé des populations** the forced movement ou transfer of people; **j'ai demandé le ~ du rendez-vous** I asked for the appointment to be changed [d] (= *mouvement*) [*pièce mobile*] movement; [*substance*] movement, displacement; **~ d'air** displacement of air; **~ de troupes** movement of troops [e] (= *voyage*) trip; **les ~s coûtent cher** travelling ou travel is expensive; **être en ~ (pour affaires)** to be away on business; **ça vaut le ~*** it's worth the trip → **frais²** [f] (*Naut*) displacement; **~ de 10 000 tonnes** 10,000-ton displacement [g] (*Psych*) displacement

déplacer [deplase] ▶ conjug 3 ◀ [1] VT [a] (= *bouger*) [+ *objet, meuble*] to move, shift; (*hum*) **il déplace beaucoup d'air** he's all talk (and no action); **~ des montagnes** to move mountains [b] (*Méd*) [+ *articulation, os*] to displace [c] [+ *usine, fonctionnaire*] to transfer, move; [+ *collectivité*] to move; [+ *rendez-vous*] to change; (*Pol, Mil*) **personnes déplacées** displaced persons [d] (= *attirer*) **le spectacle a déplacé plus de 60 000 personnes** the show brought in ou drew more than 60,000 people [e] [+ *problème, question*] to shift the emphasis of [f] (*Naut*) to displace; **navire qui déplace 10000 tonnes** ship with a 10,000-ton displacement [2] **se déplacer** VPR [a] [*pièce mobile*] to move; [*air, substance*] to move, be displaced [b] [*animal*] to move (along); [*personne*] to move; (= *circuler*) to move (around); **il ne se déplace qu'avec peine** he has difficulty getting about; **il est interdit de se ~ pendant la classe** no moving around during class; **pouvez-vous vous ~ sur la droite ?** can you move (over) to the right? [c] (= *se déranger*) [*médecin*] to come out; **avec le téléachat on peut faire ses courses sans se ~** teleshopping means you can do your shopping in the comfort of your own home; **il ne s'est même pas déplacé pour le mariage de sa sœur** he didn't even bother to go to his sister's wedding [d] (= *voyager*) to travel; **il ne se déplace qu'en avion** he only travels by air; **il se déplace fréquemment** he travels a lot, he's a frequent traveller [e] (*Méd*) [*os*] to be displaced; **se ~ une articulation** to put a joint out, displace a joint; **se ~ une vertèbre** to slip a disc

déplafonnement [deplafɔnmã] NM [*crédit*] derestriction; **ils réclament le ~ des cotisations** they are asking for the ceiling on contributions to be lifted

déplafonner [deplafɔne] ▶ conjug 1 ◀ VT [+

déplaire

crédit] to derestrict; [+ *cotisations*] to lift the ceiling on

▼ **déplaire** [deplɛʀ] ▶conjug 54◀ ① VT INDIR [a] (= *n'être pas aimé de*) **il déplaît à tout le monde** he is disliked by everyone; **cette mode/ville/femme me déplaît** I dislike *ou* I don't like *ou* I don't care for this fashion/ town/woman; **au bout d'un moment, cela risque de ~** after a while it can become disagreeable *ou* unpleasant; **ça ne me déplairait pas de le faire** I wouldn't mind doing it; (*frm*) **il me déplaît de faire …** I dislike doing …; (*frm*) **il me déplairait d'avoir à vous renvoyer** I would be sorry to have to dismiss you [b] (= *irriter*) **~ à qn** to displease sb; **il fait tout pour nous ~** he does all he can to displease us; **ceci a profondément déplu** this gave profound *ou* great displeasure; **il cherche à ~** he is trying to be disagreeable *ou* unpleasant [c] († *ou hum*) **c'est, ne t'en déplaise, beaucoup plus pratique** whether you like it or not, it's more practical; **j'irai la voir, n'en déplaise à votre père** whatever your father's views on the matter, I shall go and see her

② **se déplaire** VPR **elle se déplaît ici/à la campagne** she dislikes it *ou* doesn't like it here/in the country; **se ~ dans son nouvel emploi** to be unhappy in one's new job, dislike one's new job; **ils se sont déplu dès leur première rencontre** they disliked each other right from the start

déplaisant, e [deplɛzɑ̃, ɑ̃t] ADJ disagreeable, unpleasant

déplaisir [deplɛziʀ] NM (= *contrariété*) displeasure, annoyance; **je le ferai sans ~** I'm quite willing *ou* happy to do it, I don't mind doing it; **faire qch avec (le plus grand) ~** to do sth with (the greatest) displeasure

déplantage [deplɑ̃taʒ] NM, **déplantation** [deplɑ̃tasjɔ̃] NF [*plante*] transplanting; [*plate-bande*] digging up; [*piquet*] pulling out

déplanter [deplɑ̃te] ▶conjug 1◀ VT [a] [+ *plante*] to transplant; [+ *plate-bande*] to dig up; [+ *piquet*] to pull out [b] [+ *ordinateur*] to get going again

déplâtrage [deplɑtʀaʒ] NM (*Constr*) **le ~ d'un mur** stripping the plaster off a wall; (*Méd*) **le ~ d'un membre** taking a limb out of plaster *ou* out of its (plaster) cast, taking a (plaster) cast off a limb

déplâtrer [deplɑtʀe] ▶conjug 1◀ VT (*Constr*) to strip the plaster off; (*Méd*) to take out of plaster, take the (plaster) cast off; **je me fais ~ lundi** I'm going to have my cast taken off on Monday

déplétion [deplesjɔ̃] NF depletion

dépliage [deplijaʒ] NM [*serviette, vêtement*] unfolding; [*carte, journal, canapé-lit*] opening out, unfolding

dépliant, e [deplijɑ̃, ijɑ̃t] ① ADJ extendible ② NM (= *prospectus*) leaflet; (= *grande page*) fold-out page; **~ touristique** travel brochure

déplier [deplije] ▶conjug 7◀ ① VT [a] [+ *serviette, vêtement*] to unfold; [+ *carte routière, journal, canapé-lit*] to open out, unfold; **~ les jambes** to stretch one's legs out [b]† (= *déballer*) [+ *paquet*] to open out, open up; **~ sa marchandise** to spread (out) one's wares ② **se déplier** VPR [*carte routière*] to open out; [*feuille d'arbre*] to open out, unfold; **ça peut se ~ ◊ ça se déplie** it unfolds *ou* opens out, it can be unfolded; **le canapé se déplie pour faire lit** the sofa opens out *ou* unfolds into a bed

déplissage [deplisaʒ] NM [*étoffe plissée*] taking the pleats out of; (= *défroissage*) flattening (out), smoothing (out)

déplisser [deplise] ▶conjug 1◀ ① VT (= *défaire les plis de*) to take the pleats out of; (= *défroisser*) to flatten (out), smooth (out); (*littér*) [+ *front*] to smooth ② **se déplisser** VPR [*jupe*] to come unpleated, lose its pleats

déploiement [deplwamɑ̃] NM [*voile, drapeau*] unfurling; [*ailes*] spreading; [*troupes*] deployment; [*richesses, forces, amabilité, talents*] display; **~ de force** deployment of troops (*ou* police)

déplomber [deplɔ̃be] ▶conjug 1◀ VT [+ *colis, compteur*] to unseal; [+ *dent*] to remove the filling from, take the filling out of; (*Ordin*) to hack into, gain unauthorized access to

déplorable [deplɔʀabl] ADJ [a] (= *regrettable*) [*incident, situation*] deplorable [b] (= *très mauvais*) [*conduite, gestion, notes*] appalling, deplorable; **il faisait un temps ~** the weather was appalling *ou* atrocious; **sa chambre est dans un état ~** his room is in an appalling *ou* a terrible state

déplorablement [deplɔʀabləmɑ̃] ADV deplorably, disgracefully; **il se conduit ~** he behaves appallingly *ou* deplorably

déploration [deplɔʀasjɔ̃] NF (*Art*) lamentation

déplorer [deplɔʀe] ▶conjug 1◀ VT (= *trouver fâcheux*) to deplore; (*littér* = *s'affliger de*) to lament

déployer [deplwaje] ▶conjug 8◀ ① VT [a] [+ *carte, tissu*] to open out, spread out; [+ *voile, drapeau*] to unfurl; [+ *ailes*] to spread [b] [+ *troupes, forces de police*] to deploy; [+ *assortiment, échantillons*] to spread out, lay out; **il a déployé ses troupes en éventail** he made his troops fan out [c] [+ *richesses, fastes*] to make a display of, display; [+ *talents, ressources, forces*] to display, exhibit [d] **~ beaucoup d'activité** to be very active; **~ beaucoup d'efforts/d'énergie** to expend a lot of effort/energy → **rire** ② **se déployer** VPR [*voile, drapeau*] to unfurl; [*ailes*] to spread; [*troupes*] to deploy; [*cortège*] to spread out

déplumé, e [deplyme] (*ptp de* **déplumer**) ADJ [a] [*oiseau*] featherless, that has lost its feathers [b]* (= *chauve*) bald; **il est un peu ~ sur le dessus** he's a bit thin on top; **son crâne ~** his bald *ou* hairless head [c]* (= *démuni*) broke*, skint* (*Brit*); **il s'est retrouvé complètement ~** he ended up completely skint* (*Brit*) *ou* with no money at all

déplumer [deplyme] ▶conjug 1◀ ① VT† to pluck ② **se déplumer** VPR [*oiseau*] to moult, lose its feathers; (* = *perdre ses cheveux*) to go bald, lose one's hair

dépoétiser [depɔetize] ▶conjug 1◀ VT to take the romance out of, make prosaic

dépoitraillé, e [depwatʀaje] ADJ (*péj*) **il était tout ~** his shirt was open, revealing his chest

dépolarisant, e [depɔlaʀizɑ̃, ɑ̃t] ① ADJ depolarizing ② NM depolarizer

dépolarisation [depɔlaʀizasjɔ̃] NF depolarization

dépolariser [depɔlaʀize] ▶conjug 1◀ VT to depolarize

dépoli, e [depɔli] (*ptp de* **dépolir**) ADJ → **verre**

dépolir [depɔliʀ] ▶conjug 2◀ ① VT [+ *argent, étain*] to tarnish; [+ *verre*] to frost ② **se dépolir** VPR to tarnish

dépolissage [depɔlisaʒ] NM [*argent, étain*] tarnishing; [*verre*] frosting

dépolitisation [depɔlitizasjɔ̃] NF depoliticization

dépolitiser [depɔlitize] ▶conjug 1◀ ① VT to depoliticize ② **se dépolitiser** VPR to become depoliticized

dépolluant, e [depɔlɥɑ̃, ɑ̃t] ① ADJ [*produit*] depolluting, anti-pollutant ② NM depollutant, anti-pollutant

dépolluer [depɔlɥe] ▶conjug 1◀ VT to clean up, rid *ou* clear of pollution

dépollution [depɔlysjɔ̃] NF getting rid of pollution (**de** from); **la ~ des plages souillées par le mazout** the cleaning (up) of oil-polluted beaches

déponent, e [depɔnɑ̃, ɑ̃t] ① ADJ (*Ling*) deponent ② NM deponent (verb)

déposséder

dépopulation [depɔpylasjɔ̃] NF depopulation

déportation [depɔʀtasjɔ̃] NF (= *exil*) deportation, transportation; (= *internement*) imprisonment (in a concentration camp); **ils sont morts en ~** they died in the (Nazi concentration) camps

déporté, e [depɔʀte] (*ptp de* **déporter**) NM,F (= *exilé*) deportee; (= *interné*) prisoner (in a concentration camp)

déportement [depɔʀtəmɑ̃] NM [a] (= *embardée*) **~ vers la gauche** swerve to the left [b] **~s** († = *écarts de conduite*) misbehaviour (*Brit*), misbehavior (*US*)

déporter [depɔʀte] ▶conjug 1◀ VT [a] [+ *personne*] (= *exiler*) to deport, transport; (= *interner*) to send to a concentration camp [b] (= *faire dévier*) to carry off course; **le vent l'a déporté** the wind carried *ou* blew him off course; (*Aut*) **se ~ sur la gauche** to swerve to the left

déposant, e [depozɑ̃, ɑ̃t] NM,F (= *épargnant*) depositor; (*Jur*) bailor; (= *témoin*) deponent

dépose [depoz] NF [*tapis*] lifting, taking up; [*serrure, moteur*] taking out, removal; [*rideau*] taking down

déposer [depoze] ▶conjug 1◀ ① VT [a] (= *poser*) to lay down, put down, set down; [+ *ordures*] to dump; **« défense de ~ des ordures »** "no dumping", "no tipping" (*Brit*); **~ les armes** to lay down (one's) arms; (*littér*) **~ un baiser sur le front de qn** to plant a kiss on sb's forehead [b] (= *laisser*) [+ *chose*] to leave; [+ *personne*] to drop; **~ sa carte** to leave one's card; **on a déposé une lettre/un paquet pour vous** somebody left a letter/a parcel for you, somebody dropped a letter/a parcel in for you; **~ une valise à la consigne** to deposit *ou* leave a suitcase at the left-luggage office (*Brit*) *ou* baggage check (*US*); **je te dépose à la gare** I'll drop you (off) at the station; **l'autobus le déposa à la gare** the bus dropped him *ou* set him down at the station; **est-ce que je peux vous ~ quelque part?** can I give you a lift (*Brit*) *ou* ride (*US*) anywhere?, can I drop you anywhere? [c] (*Fin*) [+ *argent, valeur*] to deposit; **~ de l'argent sur un compte** to put money into an account, deposit money in an account [d] (*Admin, Jur*) [+ *plainte*] to lodge; [+ *réclamation*] to file; [+ *conclusions*] to present; [+ *brevet, marque de fabrique*] to register; [+ *projet de loi*] to bring in, table (*Brit*); [+ *rapport*] to send in, file; **~ son bilan** to go into (voluntary) liquidation; **~ un préavis de grève** to give notice of strike action → **marque** [e] (= *destituer*) [+ *souverain*] to depose [f] [*eau, vin*] [+ *sable, lie*] to deposit [g] (= *démonter*) [+ *tenture*] to take down; [+ *tapis*] to take up, lift; [+ *serrure, moteur*] to take out, remove

② VI [a] [*liquide*] to form a sediment *ou* a deposit; **laisser ~** to leave to settle [b] (*Jur*) to give evidence, testify

③ **se déposer** VPR [*poussière, lie*] to settle

dépositaire [depoziteʀ] NMF [a] [*objet confié*] depository; [*secret, vérité*] possessor, guardian; (*Jur*) bailee; (*Jur*) **~ public** ≈ authorized depository; (*Fin*) **~ légal** escrow agent [b] (*Comm* = *agent*) agent (**de** for); **~ exclusif** sole agent (**de** for); **nous ne sommes pas ~s** we are not agents for them, it's not a line we carry

déposition [depozisjɔ̃] NF [a] (*Jur*) (*à un procès*) evidence (*NonC*); (*écrite*) (sworn) statement, deposition; **faire une ~** (*à un procès*) to give evidence; (*écrite*) to write a statement; **signer sa ~** to sign one's statement *ou* deposition [b] [*souverain*] deposition, deposing [c] (*Art*) **~ de croix** Deposition

déposséder [depɔsede] ▶conjug 6◀ VT **~ qn de** [+ *terres*] to dispossess sb of; [+ *place, biens*] to deprive sb of; [+ *charge*] to divest *ou* deprive

▶ GRAMMAIRE ACTIVE: **déplaire** 34.3

sb of; **ils se sentaient dépossédés** they felt dispossessed

dépossession [depɔsesjɔ̃] NF (*de terres*) dispossession; (*d'une place, de biens*) deprivation; (*d'une charge*) divesting; **leur sentiment de ~** their feeling of being dispossessed; (*littér*) **~ de soi** loss of a sense of self

dépôt [depo] [1] NM [a] (= *action de déposer*) [*argent, valeurs*] deposit(ing); **le ~ des manteaux au vestiaire est obligatoire** coats must be left *ou* deposited in the cloakroom; **le ~ d'une marque de fabrique** the registration of a trademark; **~ de bilan** (voluntary) liquidation; (*Jur*) **~ légal** registration of copyright; (*Fin*) **en ~ fiduciaire** in escrow → **mandat** [b] (= *garde*) **avoir qch en ~** to hold sth in trust; **confier qch en ~ à qn** to entrust sth to sb [c] (= *chose confiée*) **restituer un ~** to return what has been entrusted to one; **~ sacré** sacred trust; (*Fin*) **~ (bancaire)** (bank) deposit; (*Fin*) **~ à vue** deposit on current account (*Brit*), checking deposit (*US*); **~ à terme** fixed term deposit → **banque, compte** [d] (= *garantie*) deposit; **~ préalable** advance deposit; **verser un ~** to put down *ou* pay a deposit [e] (= *sédiment*) [*liquide, lie*] sediment, deposit; **~ de sable** silt (*NonC*); **~ de tartre** layer of sediment, fur (*Brit*) (*NonC*); **l'eau a formé un ~ calcaire dans la bouilloire** the water has formed a layer of sediment on the kettle *ou* has furred up the kettle (*Brit*) [f] (= *entrepôt*) warehouse, store; [*autobus*] depot, garage; [*trains*] depot, shed; (*Mil*) depot [g] (*Comm* = *point de vente*) **il y a un ~ de pain/de lait à l'épicerie** bread/milk can be bought at the grocer's [h] (= *prison*) jail, prison; **il a passé la nuit au ~** he spent the night in the cells *ou* in jail [2] COMP ▸ **dépôt d'essence** (*Aut*) petrol (*Brit*) *ou* gasoline (*US*) depot ▸ **dépôt de marchandises** goods (*Brit*) *ou* freight (*US*) depot *ou* station ▸ **dépôt de munitions** ammunition *ou* munitions dump ▸ **dépôt d'ordures** (rubbish) dump *ou* tip (*Brit*), garbage dump (*US*)

dépotage [depɔtaʒ], **dépotement** [depɔtmã] NM [*plante*] transplanting; [*liquide*] decanting

dépoter [depɔte] ▸ conjug 1 ◂ VT [+ *plante*] to take out of the pot; [+ *liquide*] to decant

dépotoir [depɔtwaʀ] NM [a] (*lit, fig* = *décharge*) dumping ground, (rubbish) dump *ou* tip (*Brit*), garbage dump (*US*); **classe ~** class of rejects; **c'est devenu une banlieue ~** it's become a suburban dumping ground [b] (= *usine*) sewage works

dépôt-vente (*pl* **dépôts-ventes**) [depovãt] NM second-hand shop (*Brit*) *ou* store (*US*) (*where items are sold on commission*)

dépouille [depuj] NF [a] (= *peau*) skin, hide; (*Zool : de mue*) cast; [*serpent*] slough [b] (*littér = cadavre*) **~ (mortelle)** (mortal) remains [c] (*littér = butin*) plunder, spoils; (*Pol US*) **système des ~s** spoils system

dépouillé, e [depuje] (*ptp de* **dépouiller**) ADJ [*décor*] bare; [*style*] bald; **~ de** [*poésie*] lacking in; [*ornements*] shorn *ou* stripped of

dépouillement [depujmã] NM [a] (= *examen*) [*comptes, journal documents, courrier*] going through, perusal (*frm*); [*auteur*] going through, studying; **le ~ du courrier a pris trois heures** it took three hours to go through the mail; **le ~ du scrutin** counting the votes; **lors du ~** when the votes are (*ou* were) being counted, during the count; **pendant le ~ des données** while sifting through the data [b] (= *ascèse, pauvreté*) asceticism; (= *sobriété*) spareness, sobriety; **vivre dans le ~** to lead an ascetic life [c] (= *spoliation*) stripping

dépouiller [depuje] ▸ conjug 1 ◂ [1] VT [a] (= *examiner en détail*) [+ *comptes, documents,*

---

courrier] to go through, peruse; [+ *auteur*] to go through, study (in detail); **~ un scrutin** to count the votes [b] (= *écorcher*) to skin; (= *écorcer*) to bark, strip the bark from [c] **~ qn de** [+ *vêtements*] to strip sb of; [+ *économies, honneurs*] to strip *ou* divest sb of; [+ *droits*] to strip *ou* deprive sb of [d] **~ qch de** [+ *ornements*] to strip *ou* divest *ou* denude sth of; [+ *feuilles, fleurs*] to strip *ou* denude sth of; **un livre qui dépouille l'amour de son mystère** a book that strips *ou* divests love of its mystery [e] (*littér = dénuder*) to strip, denude; **le vent dépouille les arbres** the wind strips *ou* denudes the trees (of their leaves); **l'hiver dépouille les champs** winter lays the fields bare; **~ un autel** to remove the ornaments from an altar, strip an altar (of its ornaments); **~ son style** to strip one's style of all ornament [f] (*littér = spolier*) **~ un voyageur** to despoil (*littér*) *ou* strip a traveller of his possessions; **~ un héritier** to deprive *ou* divest an heir of his inheritance; **il a dépouillé ses enfants** he's deprived *ou* stripped his children of everything; **ils ont dépouillé le pays** they have plundered the country *ou* laid the country bare

[2] **se dépouiller** VPR [a] (*littér*) **se ~ de** [+ *vêtements*] to shed, divest o.s. of; [+ *possessions*] to divest *ou* deprive o.s. of; [+ *arrogance*] to cast off *ou* aside, divest o.s. of; [*arbre*] [+ *feuilles, fleurs*] to shed; [*pré*] [+ *verdure, fleurs*] to become stripped *ou* denuded of; **les arbres se dépouillent (de leurs feuilles)** the trees are shedding their leaves; **la campagne se dépouille (de son feuillage** *ou* **de sa verdure)** the countryside is losing *ou* shedding its greenery; **son style s'était dépouillé de toute redondance** his style had been stripped *ou* shorn of all unnecessary repetition [b] [*animal qui mue*] to shed its skin

dépourvu, e [depuʀvy] [1] ADJ **~ de** (*gén*) lacking *ou* wanting in, without; [+ *intérêt, qualités, bon sens*] devoid of, lacking *ou* wanting in; [+ *méchanceté, mauvaises intentions*] devoid of, without; **~ d'ornements** bare of ornaments, without ornaments; **~ d'argent** penniless, without money; **ce récit n'est pas ~ d'intérêt/de qualités** this story is not devoid of interest/qualities *ou* not without interest/its qualities; **des gens ~s (de tout)** destitute people [2] NM **prendre qn au ~** to catch sb off their guard; **il a été pris au ~ par cette question inattendue** he was caught off his guard by this unexpected question

dépoussiérage [depusjeʀaʒ] NM (*lit*) dusting (**de** of); (*fig*) [*administration, parti*] revamping (**de** of)

dépoussiérant [depusjeʀã] NM anti-static furniture polish

dépoussiérer [depusjeʀe] ▸ conjug 6 ◂ VT (*lit*) to dust; (*fig*) [+ *texte, institution*] to blow *ou* brush away the cobwebs from; **~ l'image d'un parti** to revamp a party's image, get rid of a party's old-fashioned image

dépravation [depʀavasjɔ̃] NF (= *état*) depravity

dépravé, e [depʀave] (*ptp de* **dépraver**) [1] ADJ depraved [2] NM,F depraved person

dépraver [depʀave] ▸ conjug 1 ◂ VT to deprave; **les mœurs se dépravent** morals are becoming depraved

dépréciateur, -trice [depʀesjatœʀ, tʀis] NM,F disparager

dépréciatif, -ive [depʀesjatif, iv] ADJ [*propos, jugement*] depreciatory, disparaging; [*mot, sens*] derogatory, disparaging

dépréciation [depʀesjasjɔ̃] NF depreciation

déprécier [depʀesje] ▸ conjug 7 ◂ [1] VT (= *faire perdre de la valeur à*) to depreciate; (= *dénigrer*) to belittle, disparage, depreciate [2] **se déprécier** VPR [*monnaie, objet*] to depreciate; [*personne*] to belittle o.s., put o.s. down

---

déprédateur, -trice [depʀedatœʀ, tʀis] [1] ADJ (= *voleur*) plundering (*épith*); (= *destructeur*) [*personne*] destructive; **insectes ~s** insect pests [2] NM,F (= *pilleur*) plunderer; (= *escroc*) embezzler; (= *vandale*) vandal

déprédation [depʀedasjɔ̃] NF [a] (*gén pl*) (= *pillage*) plundering (*NonC*), depredation (*frm*); (= *dégâts*) damage (*NonC*), depredation (*frm*); **commettre des ~s** to cause damage [b] (*Jur = détournement*) misappropriation, embezzlement

déprendre (se) [depʀãdʀ] ▸ conjug 58 ◂ VPR (*littér*) **se déprendre de** [+ *personne, chose*] to lose one's fondness for; [+ *habitude*] to lose

dépressif, -ive [depʀesif, iv] ADJ, NM,F depressive

dépression [depʀesjɔ̃] NF [a] **~ (de terrain)** depression; (*petite*) dip [b] (*Mét*) **~ (atmosphérique)** (atmospheric) depression, low; **une ~ centrée sur le nord** an area of low pressure in the north [c] (*Psych* = *état*) depression; **~ (nerveuse)** (nervous) breakdown; **il a fait une ~** he had a (nervous) breakdown; **elle fait de la ~** she suffers from depression [d] (*Écon*) **~ (économique)** (economic) depression *ou* slump

dépressionnaire [depʀesjɔnɛʀ] ADJ (*Mét*) **zone ~** area of low pressure

dépressurisation [depʀesyʀizasjɔ̃] NF (*Astron, Aviat*) depressurization; **en cas de ~ de la cabine** should the pressure drop in the cabin

dépressuriser [depʀesyʀize] ▸ conjug 1 ◂ VT (*Astron, Aviat*) to depressurize

déprimant, e [depʀimã, ãt] ADJ (*moralement*) depressing; (*physiquement*) enervating, debilitating

déprime* [depʀim] NF depression; **faire de la ~** to be depressed; **c'est la ~ dans les milieux financiers** financial circles are depressed; **période de ~** low period

déprimé, e [depʀime] (*ptp de* **déprimer**) ADJ [a] [*personne*] (*moralement*) depressed, low (*attrib*) [b] [*terrain*] low-lying

déprimer [depʀime] ▸ conjug 1 ◂ [1] VT [a] (*moralement*) to depress; (*physiquement*) to debilitate, enervate [b] (= *enfoncer*) to depress [2] VI* to be depressed, feel down*

De profundis [depʀofɔ̃dis] NM de profundis

déprogrammation [depʀogʀamasjɔ̃] NF cancellation

déprogrammer [depʀogʀame] ▸ conjug 1 ◂ VT (*TV*) (*définitivement*) to take off the air; (*temporairement*) to cancel; [+ *magnétoscope*] to cancel the programming on; [+ *rendez-vous, visite*] to cancel

déprotéger [depʀoteʒe] ▸ conjug 6 et 3 ◂ VT (*Ordin*) to remove the write protection from

dépucelage* [depys(ə)laʒ] NM **~ d'une fille/ d'un garçon** taking of a girl's/boy's virginity

dépuceler* [depys(ə)le] ▸ conjug 4 ◂ VT [+ *fille*] (*hum*) [+ *garçon*] to take the virginity of; **se faire ~** to lose one's virginity *ou* one's cherry*; **c'est lui qui l'a dépucelée** she lost it to him*

depuis [dəpɥi] [1] PRÉP [a] (*point de départ dans le temps*) since, ever since (*intensif*); **il attend ~ hier/ce matin** he has been waiting (ever) since yesterday/this morning; **il attendait ~ lundi/le 3 mars** he had been waiting (ever) since Monday/since March 3rd; **~ leur dispute ils ne se parlent/parlaient plus** they haven't/ hadn't spoken to each other (ever) since their quarrel *ou* (ever) since they quarrelled; **ils ont toujours habité la même maison ~ leur mariage** they've lived in the same house (ever) since they were married; **je ne l'ai pas vue ~ qu'elle/~ le jour où elle s'est cassé la jambe** I haven't seen her since she/since the day she broke her leg; **elle joue du violon ~ son plus jeune âge** she has played the violin since *ou* from early childhood, she has been playing *ou* has played the violin (ever) since she was very small; **~ cette affaire il est très méfiant** (ever) since that affair he has been very suspicious; **~ quand le connaissez-vous ?** how long have you known him?, how long is it that you've known him?; **~ quelle date êtes-vous ici ?** since when have you been here?, when did you arrive here?; **~ cela** (*littér*) ◊ **~ lors** since then *ou* that time, from that time forward (*littér*), ever since; (*iro*) **~ quand es-tu (devenu) expert sur la question ?** since when have you been an expert on the matter? (*iro*); **~ le matin jusqu'au soir** from morning till night

b (*durée*) for; **il est malade ~ une semaine** he has been ill for a week (now); **~ combien de temps êtes-vous/travaillez-vous ici ? — je suis/travaille ici — cinq ans** how long have you been here/been working here? — I've been here/been working here (for) five years *ou* for the last five years; **il est parti/mort ~ deux ans** he has been gone/dead (for) two years; **~ ces derniers jours/mois il a bien changé** he has changed a great deal in *ou* over the last *ou* past few days/months; **elle cherche du travail ~ plus d'un mois** she's been looking for a job for over *ou* more than a month; **il dormait ~ une heure quand le réveil sonna** he had been sleeping *ou* asleep for an hour when the alarm went off; **mort ~ longtemps** long since dead; **tu le connais ~ longtemps ? — toujours** have you known him long? *ou* for a long time? — I've known him all my life *ou* I've always known him; **je la connaissais ~ peu quand elle est partie** I hadn't known her long *ou* I had known her (for) only a short time when she left; **nous n'avons pas été au théâtre ~ des siècles** we haven't been to the theatre for *ou* in ages; **~ peu elle a recommencé à sortir** lately *ou* recently *ou* of late she has started going out again

c (*lieu = à partir de*) from; **nous roulons/roulions sous la pluie ~ Londres** it's been raining/it rained all the way from London; **~ Nice il a fait le plein trois fois** he's filled up three times since Nice; **le concert est retransmis ~ Paris/nos studios** the concert is broadcast from Paris/our studios

d (*rang, ordre, quantité*) from; **~ le simple soldat jusqu'au général** from private (right up) to general; **~ le premier jusqu'au dernier** from the first to the last; **robes ~ 200 F jusqu'à ...** dresses from 200 francs to ..., dresses starting at 200 francs (and) going up to ...; **~ 5 grammes jusqu'à ...** from 5 grammes (up) to ...; **ils ont toutes les tailles ~ le 36** they have all sizes from 36 upwards, they have all sizes starting at 36

2 ADV ever since, since (then); **~, nous sommes sans nouvelles** we have been without news ever since; **nous étions en vacances ensemble, je ne l'ai pas revu ~** we were on holiday together and I haven't seen him since (then)

3 depuis (le temps) que LOC CONJ **~ qu'il habite ici, il n'a cessé de se plaindre** he hasn't stopped complaining (ever) since he's lived here; **~ qu'il est ministre il ne nous parle plus** now that he is *ou* since he became a minister he doesn't speak to us any more; **~ qu'il avait appris son succès il désirait la féliciter** he had wanted to congratulate her ever since he had heard of her success; **~ que le monde est monde** since the beginning of time, from time immemorial; **~ le temps qu'il apprend le français, il devrait pouvoir le parler** considering how long *ou* for all the time he's been learning French, he ought to be able to speak it; **~ le temps qu'il est ici, il ne nous a jamais dit un mot** in all the time he has been here he has never said a word to us; **~ le temps qu'on ne s'était pas vus !** it's ages since we (last) saw each other!, long time no see!*; **~ le temps que je voulais voir ce film !** I had been want-

ing to see that film for ages! *ou* for such a long time!; **~ le temps que je dis que je vais lui écrire !** I've been saying I'll write to him for ages!; **~ le temps qu'il essaie !** he has been trying long enough!; **~ le temps que je te le dis !** I've told you often enough!

dépuratif, -ive [depyʀatif, iv] ADJ, NM depurative

députation [depytɑsjɔ̃] NF (= *envoi, groupe*) deputation, delegation; (= *mandat de député*) post of deputy; **candidat à la ~** parliamentary candidate; **se présenter à la ~** to stand (*Brit*) *ou* run (*US*) for parliament

député [depyte] NM **a** (*au parlement*) deputy; (*en Grande-Bretagne*) Member of Parliament; (*aux États-Unis*) ≈ Congressman; **elle a été élue ~ de Metz** she has been elected (as) deputy *ou* member for Metz; **~ au Parlement européen** Member of the European Parliament, MEP; **le ~-maire de Rouen** the deputy and mayor of Rouen; **~ en exercice** present incumbent, sitting member (*Brit*) **b** (= *envoyé d'un prince*) envoy; (= *envoyé d'une assemblée*) delegate

---

☐ DÉPUTÉ

*577 **députés**, elected in the "élections législatives" held every five years, make up the lower house of the French parliament (the "Assemblée nationale"). Each **député** represents a constituency ("circonscription"). Their role is comparable to that of Members of Parliament in Britain and Congressmen and women in the United States.*
→ ASSEMBLÉE NATIONALE ; ÉLECTIONS ; MAIRE

---

députer [depyte] ▸conjug 1◂ VT **~ qn pour faire/aller** to delegate sb to do/go; **~ qn à** *ou* **auprès d'une assemblée/auprès de qn** to send sb (as representative) to an assembly/to sb

déqualification [dekalifikasjɔ̃] NF deskilling; (*Écon*) **la ~ est de plus en plus courante** more and more people are being given jobs for which they are overqualified *ou* which don't match their qualifications

déqualifié, e [dekalifje] (*ptp de* **déqualifier**) ADJ [*personnel, emploi*] deskilled

déqualifier [dekalifje] ▸conjug 7◂ VT [+ *personnel, emploi*] to deskill

der [dɛʀ] NF ABRÉV = **dernière** (*Cartes*) **dix de ~** ten points awarded for the last trick taken in belote; **la ~ des ~s** (*gén*) the very last one; (= *guerre de 1914-1918*) the war to end all wars

déracinable [deʀasinabl] ADJ [*préjugé*] eradicable; **difficilement ~** difficult to eradicate

déracinement [deʀasinmɑ̃] NM [*arbre, personne*] uprooting; [*erreur, préjugé*] eradication; **il a souffert de ce ~** he suffered as a result of being uprooted like this

déraciner [deʀasine] ▸conjug 1◂ VT [+ *arbre, personne*] to uproot; [+ *erreur*] to eradicate; [+ *préjugé*] to root out, eradicate; **toute ma vie, je serai un déraciné** I'll always be rootless, I'll never belong anywhere

déraillement [deʀajmɑ̃] NM derailment

dérailler [deʀaje] ▸conjug 1◂ VI **a** [*train*] to be derailed, go off *ou* leave the rails; **faire ~ un train** to derail a train; **faire ~ le processus de paix/les négociations** to derail the peace process/the negotiations **b*** (= *divaguer*) to talk nonsense *ou* twaddle* (*Brit*); (= *mal fonctionner*) to be on the blink*, be up the spout* (*Brit*); **tu dérailles !** (= *tu es fou*) you're nuts!*, you're off your rocker!*; (= *tu te trompes*) you're talking through your hat!*, you're talking nonsense!; (= *être gâteux*) **son père déraille complètement** his father is completely gaga* *ou* has lost his marbles*

dérailleur [deʀajœʀ] NM [*bicyclette*] derailleur; (*Rail*) derailer, derailing stop

déraison [deʀezɔ̃] NF (*littér*) insanity

déraisonnable [deʀezɔnabl] ADJ unreasonable

déraisonnablement [deʀezɔnabləmɑ̃] ADV unreasonably

déraisonner [deʀezɔne] ▸conjug 1◂ VI (*littér*) (= *dire des bêtises*) to talk nonsense; (= *être fou*) to rave

dérangé, e [deʀɑ̃ʒe] (*ptp de* **déranger**) **1** ADJ **a*** (= *fou*) crazy; **il est complètement ~ !** he's a real head case!*, he's nuts!*; **il a le cerveau** *ou* **l'esprit ~** he's deranged *ou* unhinged **b** (= *malade*) **il a l'estomac ~** he has an upset stomach *ou* a stomach upset; **il est (un peu) ~** he has (a bit of) diarrhoea, his bowels are (a bit) loose **c** [*coiffure*] dishevelled, untidy; **mes papiers étaient tout ~s** my papers were all in a mess **2** NM,F* nutcase*

dérangeant, e [deʀɑ̃ʒɑ̃, ɑ̃t] ADJ disturbing

▼ **dérangement** [deʀɑ̃ʒmɑ̃] NM **a** (= *gêne*) trouble; **(toutes) mes excuses pour le ~** my apologies for the trouble I'm causing *ou* for the inconvenience **b** (= *déplacement*) **pour vous éviter un autre ~** to save you another trip; **voilà 50 F pour votre ~** here's 50 francs for coming *ou* for taking the trouble to come **c** (= *bouleversement*) [*affaires, papiers*] disorder (**de** in); **en ~** [*machine, téléphone*] out of order

▼ **déranger** [deʀɑ̃ʒe] ▸conjug 3◂ **1** VT **a** (= *déplacer*) [+ *papiers*] to disturb, mix *ou* muddle up; [+ *coiffure*] to ruffle, mess up; [+ *vêtements*] to rumple, disarrange **b** (= *gêner, importuner*) to trouble, bother; (= *surprendre*) [+ *animal, cambrioleur*] to disturb; **ne vous dérange pas ?** am I disturbing you?, I hope I'm not disturbing you?; **les cambrioleurs ont été dérangés** the burglars were disturbed; **elle viendra vous voir demain, si cela ne vous dérange pas** she'll come and see you tomorrow, if that's all right by you* *ou* if that's no trouble to you; **elle ne veut pas ~ le médecin inutilement** she doesn't want to bother the doctor unnecessarily; **ne me dérangez pas toutes les cinq minutes** don't come bothering me every five minutes; **~ qn dans son sommeil** to disturb sb's sleep; **on le dérange toutes les nuits en ce moment** he is disturbed every night at the moment; **ça vous dérange si je fume ?** do you mind *ou* will it bother you if I smoke?; **cela vous dérangerait-il de venir ?** would you mind coming?; **alors, ça te dérange ?*** what does it matter to you?, what's it to you?*; **«ne pas ~»** "do not disturb"; **ses films dérangent** his films are disturbing **c** (= *dérégler*) [+ *projets, routine*] to disrupt, upset; [+ *machine*] to put out of order; **les essais atomiques ont dérangé le temps** the nuclear tests have unsettled *ou* upset the weather; **ça lui a dérangé l'esprit** this has unsettled his mind

2 se déranger VPR **a** [*médecin, réparateur*] to come out **b** (*pour une démarche, une visite*) to go along, come along; **sans vous ~, sur simple appel téléphonique, nous vous renseignons** without leaving your home, you can obtain information simply by telephoning us; **je me suis dérangé pour rien, c'était fermé** it was a waste of time going *ou* it was a wasted trip *ou* journey (*Brit*) — it was closed **c** (= *changer de place*) to move; **il s'est dérangé pour me laisser passer** he moved *ou* stepped aside to let me pass; **surtout, ne vous dérangez pas pour moi** please don't put yourself out *ou* go to any inconvenience on my account

dérapage [deʀapaʒ] NM **a** [*véhicule*] skid; (*Ski*) sideslipping; (*Aviat*) sideslip; **faire un ~** to skid; **faire un ~ contrôlé** to do a controlled skid; (*Ski*) **descendre une piste en ~** to sideslip down a slope **b** [*prix*] unexpected increase; (= *maladresse*) blunder, faux pas; **~s budgétaires** overspending; **~ verbal** slip, ver-

---

▶ GRAMMAIRE ACTIVE: **dérangement** 27.7 **déranger** 36.1

bal faux pas; **pour éviter tout ~ inflationniste** to prevent inflation from getting out of control

déraper [deʀape] ▸ conjug 1 ◂ VI [a] [*véhicule*] to skid; [*piéton, semelles, échelle*] to slip; (*Ski*) to sideslip; **ça dérape** [*chaussée*] it's slippery [b] [*ancre*] to drag; [*bateau*] to trip her anchor [c] [*prix, salaires*] to get out of hand, soar; [*conversation*] to veer onto slippery ground; [*personne*] to make a faux pas

dératé, e [deʀate] NM,F → **courir**

dératisation [deʀatizasjɔ̃] NF rat extermination

dératiser [deʀatize] ▸ conjug 1 ◂ VT **~ un lieu** to exterminate the rats in a place, rid a place of rats

derby [dɛʀbi] NM (*Ftbl, Rugby*) derby; (*Équitation*) Derby; (= *chaussure*) kind of lace-up shoe, blucher (*US*)

derche⁕ [dɛʀʃ] NM arse⁕ (*Brit*), ass⁕ (*US*); **c'est un faux ~** he's a two-faced bastard⁕

derechef [dəʀəʃɛf] ADV (†† *ou littér*) once more, once again

déréférencement [deʀefeʀɑ̃smɑ̃] NM (*Comm*) [*produit*] withdrawal from sale

déréférencer [deʀefeʀɑ̃se] ▸ conjug 3 ◂ VT (*Comm*) [+ *produit*] to withdraw from sale

déréglé, e [deʀegle] (*ptp de* **dérégler**) ADJ [a] (= *détraqué*) [*mécanisme*] out of order (*attrib*); [*esprit*] unsettled; [*habitudes, temps*] upset, unsettled; [*estomac, appétit, pouls*] upset; **les élucubrations de son imagination ~e** the ravings of his wild *ou* disordered imagination [b] (= *corrompu*) [*vie, mœurs*] dissolute

dérèglement [deʀɛgləmɑ̃] NM [*machine, mécanisme*] disturbance; [*pouls, estomac, temps*] upset; [*esprit*] unsettling (*NonC*); [*mœurs*] dissoluteness (*NonC*); (*littér*) **~s** (= *dépravations*) dissoluteness

déréglementation [deʀɛgləmɑ̃tasjɔ̃] NF deregulation

déréglementer [deʀɛgləmɑ̃te] ▸ conjug 1 ◂ VT to deregulate

dérégler [deʀegle] ▸ conjug 6 ◂ [1] VT [a] (= *détraquer*) [+ *mécanisme*] to throw out, disturb; [+ *machine*] to disturb the mechanism of, put out of order; [+ *esprit*] to unsettle; [+ *habitudes, temps*] to upset, unsettle; [+ *estomac, appétit, pouls*] to upset; [+ *métabolisme*] to disrupt, upset [b] (= *corrompre*) [+ *vie, mœurs*] to make dissolute [2] **se dérégler** VPR [a] [*mécanisme, machine, appareil*] to go wrong; [*pouls, estomac, temps*] to be upset; [*esprit*] to become unsettled; **cette montre se dérègle tout le temps** this watch keeps going wrong [b] (= *se corrompre*) [*mœurs*] to become dissolute

dérégulation [deʀegylasjɔ̃] NF [*marché, secteur*] deregulation; **~ économique/sociale** economic/social deregulation

déréguler [deʀegyle] ▸ conjug 1 ◂ VT [+ *marché, secteur*] to deregulate

déréliction [deʀeliksjɔ̃] NF (*Rel, littér*) dereliction

déremboursement [deʀɑ̃buʀsmɑ̃] NM (*Admin*) **le ~ des médicaments** cutting back on the reimbursement of medicines by the French Social Security system; **le gouvernement a annoncé des mesures de ~** the government have announced measures to cut back on the reimbursement of medicines

déresponsabiliser [deʀɛspɔ̃sabilize] ▸ conjug 1 ◂ VT [+ *personne*] to take away responsibility from

dérider [deʀide] ▸ conjug 1 ◂ [1] VT [+ *personne*] to brighten up; [+ *front*] to uncrease [2] **se dérider** VPR [*personne*] to cheer up; [*front*] to uncrease

dérision [deʀizjɔ̃] NF derision, mockery; **par ~** derisively, mockingly; **de ~** [*parole, sourire*] of derision, derisive; **esprit de ~** sense of mock-

ery *ou* ridicule; **tourner en ~** (= *ridiculiser*) to ridicule; (= *minimiser*) to make a mockery of

dérisoire [deʀizwaʀ] ADJ (*gén*) derisory, pathetic, laughable; **pour une somme ~** for a derisory sum

dérisoirement [deʀizwaʀmɑ̃] ADV pathetically

dérivant [deʀivɑ̃] ADJ M **filet ~** drift net

dérivatif, -ive [deʀivatif, iv] [1] ADJ derivative [2] NM distraction; **dans son travail il cherche un ~ à sa douleur** he throws himself into his work to try and take his mind off his grief

dérivation [deʀivasjɔ̃] NF [a] [*rivière*] diversion; [*circulation routière*] diversion (*Brit*), detour (*US*) → **canal** [b] (*Ling, Math*) derivation; **~ régressive** back formation [c] (*Élec*) shunt [d] (*Aviat, Naut*) drift, deviation

dérive [deʀiv] NF [a] (= *déviation*) drift, leeway; (= *errance*) drift; **~ sur bâbord** drift to port; **navire en ~** ship adrift; **~ des continents** continental drift; **~ nord-atlantique** North Atlantic Drift; **à la ~** adrift; (*fig*) **tout va à la ~** everything is going to the dogs *ou* is going downhill; **partir à la ~** to go drifting off; **être à la ~** [*personne*] to be adrift, be drifting [b] (= *dispositif*) (*Aviat*) fin, vertical stabilizer (*US*); (*Naut*) centre-board (*Brit*), center-board (*US*) [c] (= *abus*) excess, abuse; (= *évolution*) drift; **~ droitière/totalitaire** drift towards the right/towards totalitarianism

dérivé, e [deʀive] (*ptp de* **dériver**) [1] ADJ (*gén, Chim, Math*) derived [2] NM (*Chim, Ling, Math*) derivative; (= *produit*) by-product [3] **dérivée** NF (*Math*) derivative

dériver [deʀive] ▸ conjug 1 ◂ [1] VT [a] [+ *rivière, circulation*] to divert [b] (*Chim, Ling, Math*) to derive [c] (*Élec*) to shunt [d] (*Tech* = *dériveter*) to unrivet [2] **dériver de** VT INDIR to derive *ou* stem from; (*Ling*) to derive from, be derived from, be a derivative of [3] VI (*Aviat, Naut*) to drift; [*orateur*] to wander *ou* drift (away) from the subject; [*marginal*] to be adrift, be drifting; **la conversation a dérivé sur …** the conversation drifted onto …

dériveur [deʀivœʀ] NM (= *voile*) storm sail; (= *bateau*) sailing dinghy (*with centre-board*)

dermabrasion [dɛʀmabʀazjɔ̃] NF (*Méd*) dermabrasion

dermatite [dɛʀmatit] NF = **dermite**

dermato⁕ [dɛʀmato] [1] NF ABRÉV = **dermatologie** [2] NMF ABRÉV = **dermatologiste** *ou* **dermatologue**

dermatologie [dɛʀmatɔlɔʒi] NF dermatology

dermatologique [dɛʀmatɔlɔʒik] ADJ dermatological

dermatologue [dɛʀmatɔlɔg], **dermatologiste** [dɛʀmatɔlɔʒist] NMF dermatologist, skin specialist

dermatose [dɛʀmatoz] NF dermatosis

derme [dɛʀm] NM dermis

dermique [dɛʀmik] ADJ dermic, dermal

dermite [dɛʀmit] NF dermatitis

dernier, -ière [dɛʀnje, jɛʀ] [1] ADJ [a] (*dans le temps*: *gén*) last; **arriver ~** to come in last; **arriver bon ~** to come in a long way behind the others; **durant les ~s jours du mois** in the last few days of the month; **l'artiste, dans ses dernières œuvres …** the artist, in his final *ou* last works …; **les dernières années de sa vie** the last few years of his life [b] (*dans l'espace*) [*étage*] top (*épith*); [*rang*] back (*épith*); [*branche*] upper (*épith*), highest; **la dernière marche de l'escalier** (*en bas*) the bottom step; (*en haut*) the top step; **le ~ mouchoir de la pile** (*dessus*) the top handkerchief in the pile; (*dessous*) the bottom handkerchief in the pile; (*Presse*) **en dernière page** on the back page; **les 100 dernières pages** the last 100 pages → **jugement, premier** [c] (*dans une hiérarchie, un ordre*) [*élève*] bottom, last; **être reçu ~** to come last *ou* bottom

(à in); **il est toujours ~ (en classe)** he's always bottom (of the class), he's always last (in the class); **c'est bien la dernière personne à qui je demanderais !** he's the last person I'd ask! [d] (= *le plus récent*: *gén avant n*) last, latest; **son ~ roman** his latest *ou* last novel; **ces ~s mois/jours** (during) the last *ou* past couple of *ou* few months/days; **ces ~s incidents/événements** these latest *ou* most recent incidents/events → **temps** [e] (= *précédent*) last, previous; **les ~s propriétaires sont partis à l'étranger** the last *ou* previous owners went abroad; **le ~ détenteur du record était américain** the last *ou* previous record holder was American; **l'an/le mois ~** last year/month; **samedi ~** last Saturday [f] (= *extrême*) **il a protesté avec la dernière énergie** he protested most vigorously *ou* with the utmost vigour; **examiner qch dans les ~s détails** to study sth in the most minute *ou* in the minutest detail; **c'est du ~ ridicule** it's utterly ridiculous, it's ridiculous in the extreme; **c'est du ~ chic** it's the last word in elegance; **c'est de la dernière importance** it is of the utmost importance; **il est du ~ bien avec le patron** he's on the best of terms with his boss [g] (= *pire*) [*qualité*] lowest, poorest; **c'était la dernière chose à faire !** that was the last thing to do! [h] (*évoquant la mort*) last; **ses ~s moments** *ou* **instants** his last *ou* dying moments; **jusqu'à mon ~ jour** until the day I die, until my dying day; **je croyais que ma dernière heure était venue** I thought my last *ou* final hour had come; **à sa dernière heure** on his deathbed; **dans les ~s temps il ne s'alimentait plus** towards the end he stopped eating; (*littér*: *frm*) **rendre les ~s devoirs** to pay one's last respects (à to); **accompagner qn à sa dernière demeure** to accompany sb to his final resting place; **les dernières dispositions du défunt** the deceased's last will and testament → **soupir** [i] (= *final, ultime*) [*échelon, grade*] top, highest; **après un ~ regard/effort** after one last *ou* final look/effort; **on prend un ~ verre ?** one last drink?, one for the road? [2] NM,F [a] (*dans le temps*) last (one); **parler/sortir le ~** to speak/leave last; **les ~s arrivés n'auront rien** the last ones to arrive or the last arrivals will get nothing; **~ entré, premier sorti** last in, first out; **tu seras servi le ~** you'll be served last, you'll be the last to get served; **elle a tendance à gâter son (petit) ~** she's inclined to spoil her youngest (child) [b] (*dans une hiérarchie, un ordre*) **il est le ~ de sa classe/de la liste** he's (at the) bottom of the class/list; **il a été reçu dans les ~s** he was nearly bottom among those who passed the exam; **ils ont été tués jusqu'au ~** they were all killed (right down) to the last man, every single one of them was killed; **c'est la dernière à qui vous puissiez demander un service** she's the last person you can ask a favour of; **il est le ~ à pouvoir** *ou* **qui puisse faire cela** he's the last person to be able to do that → **souci** [c] (*péj*: *intensif*) **le ~ des imbéciles** an absolute imbecile, a complete and utter fool; **le ~ des filous** an out-and-out scoundrel; **c'est le ~ des ~s !** he's the lowest of the low! [d] **ce ~** ◊ **cette dernière** the latter; **enseignants et chercheurs étaient présents; ces ~s …** there were teachers and researchers there; the latter … **Luc, Marc et Jean étaient là et ce ~ a dit que …** Luc, Marc and Jean were there, and Jean said that …; **Paul, Pierre et Maud sont venus; cette dernière …** Paul, Pierre and Maud came; she … [3] NM [a] (= *dernier étage*) top floor *ou* storey (*Brit*) *ou* story (*US*) [b] (*dans un ordre*) **en ~** [*acheter, arriver*] last; **j'ai été servi en ~** I was served last, I was the last to be served

4 **dernière** NF [a] (*Théât*) last performance [b] (* : = *nouvelle*) **vous connaissez la dernière ?*** have you heard the latest?

dernièrement [dɛʀnjɛʀmɑ̃] ADV (= *il y a peu de temps*) recently; (= *ces derniers temps*) lately, recently, of late

dernier-né, dernière-née (*mpl* **derniers-nés**) [dɛʀnjene, dɛʀnjɛʀne] NM,F (= *enfant*) last-born, youngest child; (= *œuvre*) latest *ou* most recent creation; **le ~ de leurs logiciels** the latest in their line of software

dérobade [deʀɔbad] NF evasion; (*Équitation*) refusal; **~ fiscale** tax evasion

dérobé, e [deʀɔbe] (*ptp de dérober*) **1** ADJ [*escalier, porte*] secret, hidden **2** **à la dérobée** LOC ADV secretly, surreptitiously; **regarder qn à la ~e** to give sb a surreptitious *ou* stealthy glance

dérober [deʀɔbe] ▶ conjug 1 ◀ **1** VT [a] (= *voler*) to steal; **~ qch à qn** to steal sth from sb; **~ un baiser (à qn)** to steal a kiss (from sb) [b] (= *cacher*) **~ qch à qn** to hide *ou* conceal sth from sb; **une haie dérobait la palissade aux regards** a hedge hid *ou* screened the fence from sight, a hedge concealed the fence; **~ qn à la justice/au danger/à la mort** to shield sb from justice/danger/death [c] (*littér* = *détourner*) [+ *regard, front*] to turn away **2** **se dérober** VPR [a] (= *refuser d'assumer*) to shy away; **se ~ à son devoir/à ses obligations** to shy away from *ou* shirk one's duty/obligations; **se ~ à une discussion** to shy away from a discussion; **je lui ai posé la question mais il s'est dérobé** I put the question to him but he evaded *ou* side-stepped it [b] (= *se cacher de*) to hide, conceal o.s.; **se ~ aux regards** to hide from view; **se ~ à la justice** to hide from justice; **pour se ~ à la curiosité dont il était l'objet** in order to escape the curiosity surrounding him [c] (= *se libérer*) to slip away; **se ~ à l'étreinte de qn** to slip out of sb's arms; **il voulut la prendre dans ses bras mais elle se déroba** he tried to take her in his arms but she shrank *ou* slipped away [d] (= *s'effondrer*) [*sol*] to give way; **ses genoux se dérobèrent (sous lui)** his knees gave way (beneath him) [e] (*Équitation*) to refuse

dérocher [deʀɔʃe] ▶ conjug 1 ◀ **1** VI **se dérocher** VPR [*alpiniste*] to fall off (a rock face) **2** VT [+ *métal*] to pickle; [+ *terrain*] to clear of rocks

dérogation [deʀɔɡasjɔ̃] NF (special) dispensation; **ceci constitue une ~ par rapport à la loi** this constitutes a departure from the law; **aucune ~ ne sera permise** no exemption will be granted, no special dispensation will be allowed; **il a obtenu ceci par ~** he obtained this by special dispensation

dérogatoire [deʀɔɡatwaʀ] ADJ dispensatory, exceptional; **appliquer un régime ~ à** to apply exceptional arrangements to *ou* in respect of; **à titre ~** by special dispensation

déroger [deʀɔʒe] ▶ conjug 3 ◀ VI [a] (= *déchoir*) (*gén*) to lower o.s., demean o.s.; (*Hist*) to lose rank and title [b] (= *enfreindre*) **~ à qch** to go against sth, depart from sth; **~ aux règles** to depart from the rules; **ce serait ~ à la règle établie** that would go against the established order *ou* procedure

dérouillée: [deʀuje] NF thrashing, belting*; **recevoir une ~** (*coups*) to get a thrashing *ou* belting*; (*défaite*) to get a thrashing* *ou* hammering*

dérouiller [deʀuje] ▶ conjug 1 ◀ **1** VT [a] [+ *métal*] to remove the rust from; [+ *mémoire*] to refresh; **je vais me ~ les jambes** I'm going to stretch my legs [b]: (= *battre*) to give a thrashing *ou* belting* to, thrash **2** VI: (= *souffrir*) to have a hard time of it, go through it* (*surtout Brit*); (= *se faire battre*) to catch it*,

cop it: (*Brit*); **j'ai une rage de dents, qu'est-ce que je dérouille !** I've got toothache, it's agony!* *ou* it's driving me mad! *ou* it's killing me!*

déroulement [deʀulmɑ̃] NM [a] (= *fait de se passer*) **de carrière** career development; **rappelez-moi le ~ des événements** go over the sequence of events for me again; **pendant le ~ des opérations** during the course of (the) operations, while the operations were in progress; **pendant le ~ du film** while the film was on, during the film; **rien n'est venu troubler le ~ de la manifestation** the demonstration went off *ou* passed off without incident, nothing happened to disturb the course of the demonstration; **veiller au bon ~ des élections** to make sure the elections go smoothly [b] [*fil, bobine, film, bande magnétique*] unwinding; [*cordage*] uncoiling; [*carte*] unrolling

dérouler [deʀule] ▶ conjug 1 ◀ **1** VT [a] [+ *fil, bobine, pellicule, ruban*] to unwind; [+ *cordage*] to uncoil; [+ *carte, parchemin*] to unroll; [+ *tapis*] to roll out; [+ *store*] to roll down; **~ le tapis rouge à qn** to roll out the red carpet for sb; **la rivière déroule ses méandres** the river snakes *ou* winds along its tortuous course [b] (*Tech*) [+ *tronc d'arbre*] to peel a veneer from [c] (= *passer en revue*) **il déroula dans son esprit les événements de la veille** in his mind he went over *ou* through the events of the previous day **2** **se dérouler** VPR [a] (= *avoir lieu*) (*comme prévu*) to take place; (*accidentellement*) to happen, occur; **la ville où la cérémonie s'est déroulée** the town where the ceremony took place [b] (= *progresser*) [*histoire*] to unfold, develop; **à mesure que l'histoire se déroulait** as the story unfolded *ou* developed [c] (= *se passer*) to go (off); **la manifestation s'est déroulée dans le calme** the demonstration went off peacefully; **comment s'est déroulé le match ?** how did the match go?; **ça s'est bien déroulé** it went well; **son existence se déroulait, calme et morne** his life went on *ou* pursued its course, dreary and uneventful; **c'est là que toute ma vie s'est déroulée** that was where I spent my whole life [d] [*fil, bobine, pellicule, ruban*] to unwind, come unwound; [*bande magnétique*] to unwind; [*cordage*] to unreel, uncoil; [*carte, drapeau, parchemin*] to unroll, come unrolled; [*tapis*] to unroll; [*store*] to roll down; **le paysage se déroulait devant nos yeux** the landscape unfolded before our eyes

dérouleur [deʀulœʀ] NM [*papier*] holder; (*Ordin*) **~ de bande magnétique** magnetic tape drive

dérouleuse [deʀuløz] NF (*Tech*) winding machine

déroutant, e [deʀutɑ̃, ɑ̃t] ADJ disconcerting

déroute [deʀut] NF [*armée, équipe*] rout; [*régime, entreprise*] collapse; **armée en ~** routed army; **mettre en ~** [+ *armée*] to rout, put to rout *ou* flight; [+ *adversaire*] to rout

déroutement [deʀutmɑ̃] NM (*Aviat, Naut*) rerouting, diversion

dérouter [deʀute] ▶ conjug 1 ◀ VT [+ *avion, navire*] to reroute, divert; [+ *candidat, orateur*] to disconcert, throw*; [+ *poursuivants, police*] to throw *ou* put off the scent

derrick [deʀik] NM derrick

derrière [deʀjɛʀ] **1** PRÉP [a] (= *à l'arrière de, à la suite de*) behind; **il se cache ~ le fauteuil** he's hiding behind the armchair; **il avait les mains ~ le dos** he had his hands behind his back; **sors de ~ le lit** come out from behind the bed; **passe (par) ~ la maison** go round the back of *ou* round behind the house; **marcher l'un ~ l'autre** to walk one behind the other; (*lit, fig*) **il a laissé les autres loin ~ lui** he left the others far *ou* a long way behind (him);

disparaître ~ une colline to disappear behind a hill [b] (*fig*) behind; **il faut chercher ~ les apparences** you must look beneath (outward) appearances; **~ sa générosité se cache l'intérêt le plus sordide** behind his generosity lurks *ou* his generosity hides the most sordid self-interest; **faire qch ~ (le dos de) qn** to do sth behind sb's back; **dire du mal ~ (le dos de) qn** to say (unkind) things behind sb's back; **il a laissé trois enfants ~ lui** he left three children; **le président avait tout le pays ~ lui** the president had the whole country behind him *ou* had the backing of the whole country; **ayez confiance, je suis ~ vous** take heart, I'll support you *ou* back you up *ou* I'm on your side; **il laisse tout le monde ~ (lui) pour le talent/le courage** his talent/courage puts everyone else in the shade; **il laisse tout le monde ~ en chimie** he's head and shoulders above *ou* miles ahead of the others in chemistry; **il faut toujours être ~ lui** *ou* **son dos** you've always got to keep an eye on him; **un vin de ~ les fagots*** an extra-special (little) wine; **une bouteille de ~ les fagots*** a bottle of the best → **idée** [c] (*Naut*) (*dans le bateau*) aft, abaft; (*sur la mer*) astern of

2 ADV [a] (= *en arrière*) behind; **vous êtes juste ~** you're just *ou* right behind (it *ou* us *etc*); **on l'a laissé (loin) ~** we (have) left him (far *ou* a long way) behind; **il est assis trois rangs ~** he's sitting three rows back *ou* three rows behind (us *ou* them *etc*); (*Aut*) **il a préféré monter ~** he preferred to sit in the back; **chemisier qui se boutonne ~** blouse which buttons up *ou* does up at the back; **passe le plateau ~** pass the tray back; **regarde ~, on nous suit** look behind (you) *ou* look back — we're being followed; **il est ~** he's behind (us *ou* them *etc*); **regarde ~** (*au fond de la voiture*) look in the back; (*derrière un objet*) look behind (it); **arrêtez de pousser, ~ !** stop pushing back there!; (*fig*) **tu peux être sûr qu'il y a quelqu'un ~** you can be sure that there's somebody behind it (all) [b] (*Naut*) (*dans le bateau*) aft, abaft; (*sur la mer*) astern

3 **par-derrière** LOC ADV **c'est fermé, entre** *ou* **passe par-~** it's locked, go in by the back *ou* go in the back way; **attaquer par-~** [+ *ennemi*] to attack from behind *ou* from the rear; [+ *adversaire*] to attack from behind; **dire du mal de qn par-~** to say (unkind) things behind sb's back; **il fait tout par-~** he does everything behind people's backs *ou* in an underhand way

4 NM [a] [*personne*] bottom, behind*; [*animal*] hindquarters, rump; **donner un coup de pied au ~** *ou* **dans le ~ de qn** to give sb a kick in the behind* *ou* up the backside* *ou* in the pants*; **quand j'ai eu 20 ans mon père m'a chassé à coups de pied dans le ~** when I was 20 my father sent me packing *ou* kicked me out* → **botter** [b] [*objet*] back; [*maison*] back, rear; **le ~ de la tête** the back of the head; **habiter sur le ~** to live at the back (of the house); **roue de ~** back *ou* rear wheel; **porte de ~** [*maison*] back door; [*véhicule*] back *ou* rear door → **patte**

5 **derrières**† NMPL [*édifice*] back, rear; [*armée*] rear

derviche [dɛʀviʃ] NM dervish; **~ tourneur** whirling dervish

des [de] → **de¹, de²**

dès [dɛ] **1** PRÉP [a] (*dans le temps*) from; **dimanche il a commencé à pleuvoir ~ le matin** on Sunday it rained from the morning onwards *ou* it started raining in the morning; **~ le 15 août nous ne travaillerons plus qu'à mi-temps** (as) from August 15th we will only be working half-time; **~ le début** from the (very) start *ou* beginning, right from the start *ou* beginning; **~ son retour il fera le nécessaire** as soon as he's back *ou* immediately upon his return he'll do what's necessary; **~ son retour il commença à se plaindre** as soon as he was back *ou* from the moment he was back he started complaining; **il se précipita vers la sortie ~ la fin du spectacle** as soon as *ou* immediately the performance was over he rushed towards the exit; **~ l'époque romaine on connaissait le chauffage central** as early as *ou* as far back as Roman times people used central heating; **~ son enfance il a collectionné les papillons** he has collected butterflies from (his) childhood *ou* ever since he was a child; **on peut dire ~ maintenant** *ou* **à présent** it can be said here and now; **~ l'abord/ce moment** from the very beginning *ou* the outset/that moment

b (*dans l'espace*) **~ Lyon il se mit à pleuvoir** we ran into rain *ou* it started to rain as *ou* when we got to Lyons; **~ Lyon il a plu sans arrêt** it never stopped raining from Lyons onwards *ou* after Lyons; **~ l'entrée vous êtes accueillis par des slogans publicitaires** advertising slogans hit you as soon as *ou* immediately you walk in the door; **~ le seuil je sentis qu'il se passait quelque chose** as I walked in at the door I sensed that something was going on

c (*dans une gradation*) **~ sa première année il brilla en anglais** he was good at English right from the first year; **~ le premier verre il roula sous la table** after the (very) first glass he collapsed under the table; **~ la troisième chanson elle se mit à pleurer** at the third song she started to cry

2 dès que LOC CONJ as soon as, immediately; **~ qu'il aura fini il viendra** as soon as *ou* immediately he's finished he'll come

3 dès lors LOC ADV (= *depuis lors*) from that moment (on), from that time on, from then on; (= *conséquemment*) that being the case, consequently; **~ lors il ne fuma plus** from that time *ou* moment on he stopped smoking; **~ lors il décida de ne plus fumer** from that moment he decided he wouldn't smoke any more; **vous ne pouvez rien prouver contre lui, ~ lors vous devez le relâcher** you can prove nothing against him and that being the case *ou* and so you'll have to release him

4 dès lors que LOC CONJ (*temporel*) as soon as; (*relation de conséquence*) (= *si*) from the moment that; (= *puisque*) since, as; **~ lors que vous décidez de partir, nous ne pouvons plus rien pour vous** from the moment (that) you choose to go, we can do nothing more for you; **~ lors qu'il a choisi de démissionner, il n'a plus droit à rien** since *ou* as he has decided to hand in his notice he is no longer entitled to anything; **peu m'importe, ~ lors qu'ils sont heureux** I don't mind so long as they are happy

désabonnement [dezabɔnmɑ̃] NM non-renewal *ou* cancellation of one's subscription

désabonner [dezabɔne] ▸conjug 1◂ **1** VT **~ qn d'un journal** to cancel sb's subscription to a newspaper **2 se désabonner** VPR to cancel one's subscription, not to renew one's subscription

désabusé, e [dezabyze] (*ptp de* **désabuser**) ADJ [*personne, air*] disenchanted, disillusioned; († = *détrompé*) disabused, undeceived (*frm*); **geste ~** gesture of disillusion; **«non» dit-il d'un ton ~** "no" he said in a disillusioned voice

désabusement [dezabyzmɑ̃] NM disillusionment

désabuser [dezabyze] ▸conjug 1◂ VT to disabuse (**de** of), undeceive (*frm*) (**de** of)

désacclimater [dezaklimate] ▸conjug 1◂ VT to disacclimatize

désaccord [dezakɔʀ] NM **a** (= *mésentente*) discord; **être en ~ avec sa famille/son temps** to be at odds *ou* at variance with one's family/ time **b** (= *divergence*) (*entre personnes, points de vue*) disagreement; (*entre idées, intérêts*) conflict, clash; **le ~ qui subsiste entre leurs intérêts** their unresolved conflict *ou* clash of interests; **leurs intérêts sont en ~ avec les nôtres** their interests conflict *ou* clash with ours **c** (= *contradiction*) discrepancy; **~ entre la théorie et la réalité** discrepancy between theory and reality; **les deux versions de l'accident sont en ~ sur bien des points** the two versions of the accident conflict *ou* diverge on many points; **ce qu'il dit est en ~ avec ce qu'il fait** he says one thing and does another, there is a discrepancy between what he says and what he does

désaccordé, e [dezakɔʀde] (*ptp de* **désaccorder**) ADJ [*piano*] out of tune

désaccorder [dezakɔʀde] ▸conjug 1◂ **1** VT [+ *piano*] to put out of tune **2 se désaccorder** VPR to go out of tune

désaccoupler [dezakuple] ▸conjug 1◂ VT [+ *wagons, chiens*] to uncouple; (*Élec*) to disconnect

désaccoutumance [dezakutymɑ̃s] NF **~ de qch** losing the habit of (doing) sth; **méthode utilisée dans les cures de ~ du tabac** method used in breaking nicotine dependency *ou* to wean smokers off nicotine

désaccoutumer [dezakutyme] ▸conjug 1◂ **1** VT **~ qn de qch/de faire** to get sb out of the habit of sth/of doing, disaccustom sb from sth/from doing (*frm*) **2 se désaccoutumer** VPR **se ~ de qch/de faire** to lose the habit of sth/of doing

désacralisation [desakʀalizasjɔ̃] NF **la ~ d'une institution/d'une profession** the removal of the sacred aura surrounding an institution/a profession

désacraliser [desakʀalize] ▸conjug 1◂ VT [+ *institution, profession*] to take away the sacred aura of; **la médecine se trouve désacralisée** medicine has lost its sacred aura; **il désacralise tout** he debunks everything, nothing escapes his cynicism

désactiver [dezaktive] ▸conjug 1◂ VT (= *neutraliser*) [+ *engin explosif*] to deactivate; [+ *réseau d'espionnage*] to break up; (*Chim*) to deactivate; (*Phys Nucl*) to decontaminate; (*Ordin*) to disable

désadapté, e [dezadapte] ▸conjug 1◂ ADJ **personne ~e** misfit; **le système judiciaire est ~ par rapport à son époque** the legal system has not moved with the times

désaffectation [dezafɛktasjɔ̃] NF [*lieu*] closing down; [*somme d'argent*] withdrawal

désaffecté, e [dezafɛkte] (*ptp de* **désaffecter**) ADJ [*usine, gare*] disused; [*église*] deconsecrated

désaffecter [dezafɛkte] ▸conjug 1◂ VT [+ *lieu*] to close down; [+ *somme d'argent*] to withdraw; **l'école a été désaffectée pour en faire une prison** the school was closed down and converted into a prison

désaffection [dezafɛksjɔ̃] NF (*gén*) loss of interest (**pour** in); (*Pol*) disaffection (**pour** with)

désaffectionner (se) † [dezafɛksjɔne] ▸conjug 1◂ VPR **se désaffectionner de** to lose one's affection *ou* fondness for

désagréable [dezagʀeabl] ADJ unpleasant, disagreeable

désagréablement [dezagʀeabləmɑ̃] ADV unpleasantly, disagreeably

désagrégation [dezagʀegasjɔ̃] NF [*roche*] crumbling; [*État*] breakup; (*Psych*) disintegration (of the personality)

désagréger [dezagʀeʒe] ▸conjug 3 et 6◂ **1** VT [+ *roches*] to crumble; **pour ~ la cellulite** to break down cellulite; **ça a désagrégé leur couple** it was the end of *ou* it broke up their relationship **2 se désagréger** VPR **a** [*cachet, sucre*] to break up, disintegrate; [*roche*] to

crumble **b** [*amitié, État*] to break up; [*couple*] to break *ou* split up

désagrément [dezagʀemɑ̃] NM **a** (*gén pl* = *inconvénient, déboire*) annoyance, inconvenience, trouble (*NonC*); **malgré tous les ~s que cela entraîne** despite all the annoyances *ou* trouble it involves; **c'est un des ~s de ce genre de métier** it's one of the inconveniences of *ou* it's part of the trouble with this kind of job; **cette voiture m'a valu bien des ~s** this car has given me a great deal of trouble; **« la direction vous prie d'excuser les ~s causés par les travaux »** "the management apologizes for any inconvenience caused to customers during renovations" **b** (*frm* = *déplaisir*) displeasure; **causer du ~ à qn** to cause sb displeasure

désaimantation [dezɛmɑ̃tasjɔ̃] NF demagnetization

désaimanter [dezɛmɑ̃te] ▸conjug 1◂ VT to demagnetize

désaisonnaliser [desezɔnalize] ▸conjug 1◂ VT to make seasonal adjustments to; **le chiffre du chômage, en données désaisonnalisées** the seasonally adjusted unemployment figure

désalper [dezalpe] ▸conjug 1◂ VI (*Helv*) *to come down from the high mountain pastures*

désaltérant, e [dezalteʀɑ̃, ɑ̃t] ADJ thirst-quenching

désaltérer [dezalteʀe] ▸conjug 6◂ **1** VT to quench *ou* slake the thirst of; **le vin ne désaltère pas** wine does not quench your thirst, wine is not a thirst-quenching drink **2 se désaltérer** VPR to quench *ou* slake one's thirst

désambiguïsation [dezɑ̃biɡɥizasjɔ̃] NF disambiguation

désambiguïser [dezɑ̃biɡɥize] ▸conjug 1◂ VT to disambiguate

désamiantage [dezamjɑ̃taʒ] NM (*Tech*) removal of asbestos; **le ~ du bâtiment a pris 3 mois** it took 3 months to remove the asbestos from the building

désamianter [dezamjɑ̃te] ▸conjug 1◂ VT (*Tech*) [+ *bâtiment*] to remove asbestos from

désamorçage [dezamɔʀsaʒ] NM **a** [*fusée, pistolet*] removal of the primer (**de** from); [*bombe, situation, conflit*] defusing **b** [*dynamo*] failure

désamorcer [dezamɔʀse] ▸conjug 3◂ VT **a** [+ *fusée, pistolet*] to remove the primer from; [+ *bombe*] to defuse **b** [+ *pompe*] to drain **c** [+ *situation explosive, crise*] to defuse; [+ *mouvement de revendication*] to forestall

désamour [dezamuʀ] NM (*gén*) disenchantment; (*entre deux amoureux*) falling out of love; **le ~ des citoyens vis-à-vis de la politique** people's disillusionment *ou* disenchantment with politics; **il a quitté son amie par ~** he left his girlfriend because he no longer loved her *ou* because he had fallen out of love with her

désaper* [dezape] ▸conjug 1◂ **1** VT to undress **2 se désaper** VPR to peel off one's clothes*, get undressed

désapparié, e [dezapaʀje] (*ptp de* **désapparier**) ADJ = **déparié**

désapparier [dezapaʀje] ▸conjug 7◂ VT = **déparier**

désappointé, e [dezapwɛ̃te] (*ptp de* **désappointer**) ADJ disappointed

désappointement [dezapwɛ̃tmɑ̃] NM disappointment

désappointer [dezapwɛ̃te] ▸conjug 1◂ VT to disappoint

désapprendre [dezapʀɑ̃dʀ] ▸conjug 58◂ VT (*littér*) to forget; (*volontairement*) to unlearn; **~ à faire qch** to forget how to do sth; **ils ont dû ~ à être exigeants** they had to learn not to be so demanding

désapprobateur, -trice [dezapʀɔbatœʀ, tʀis] ADJ disapproving

désapprobation [dezaprɔbasjɔ̃] NF disapproval, disapprobation (frm)

▼ **désapprouver** [dezapRuve] ▶conjug 1◀ VT [+ acte, conduite] to disapprove of; **je le désapprouve de les inviter** I disagree with his inviting them, I disapprove of his inviting them; **elle désapprouve qu'il vienne** she disapproves of his coming; **le public désapprouva** the audience showed its disapproval

désarçonner [dezaRsɔne] ▶conjug 1◀ VT (= faire tomber) [cheval] to throw, unseat; [adversaire] to unseat, unhorse; (= déconcerter) [argument] to throw*, baffle; **son calme/sa réponse me désarçonna** I was completely thrown* ou nonplussed by his calmness/reply

désargenté, e [dezaRʒɑ̃te] (ptp de **désargenter**) ADJ a (= terni) **couverts ~s** cutlery with the silver worn off b * (= sans un sou) broke* (attrib), penniless; **je suis ~ en ce moment** I'm a bit short of cash ou a bit strapped for cash* at the moment

désargenter [dezaRʒɑ̃te] ▶conjug 1◀ VT a [+ métal] to rub ou wear the silver off; **cette fourchette se désargente** the silver is wearing off this fork b **~ qn*** to leave sb broke* ou penniless

désarmant, e [dezaRmɑ̃, ɑ̃t] ADJ disarming

désarmé, e [dezaRme] (ptp de **désarmer**) ADJ [pays, personne] unarmed; (fig = démuni) helpless (**devant** before)

désarmement [dezaRməmɑ̃] NM a [personne, forteresse] disarming; [pays] disarmament b [navire] laying up

désarmer [dezaRme] ▶conjug 1◀ 1 VT a [+ adversaire, pays] to disarm b [+ mine] to disarm, defuse; [+ fusil] to unload; (= mettre le cran de sûreté) to put the safety catch on c (Naut) to lay up d (= émouvoir) [sourire, réponse] to disarm 2 VI [pays] to disarm; [haine] to yield, abate; **il ne désarme pas contre son fils** he is unrelenting in his attitude towards his son; **il ne désarme pas et veut intenter un nouveau procès** he won't give in and wants a new trial

désarrimage [dezaRimaʒ] NM shifting (of the cargo)

désarrimer [dezaRime] ▶conjug 1◀ VT to shift, cause to shift

désarroi [dezaRwa] NM [personne] (feeling of) helplessness; [armée, équipe] confusion; **ceci l'avait plongé dans le ~ le plus profond** this had left him feeling totally helpless and confused; **être en plein ~** [personne] (= être troublé) to be utterly distraught; (= se sentir impuissant) to feel quite helpless; [marché, pays] to be in total disarray; **sa mort laisse le pays en plein ~** his death has left the nation numb with grief, the entire nation is deeply distressed by his death

désarticulation [dezaRtikylasjɔ̃] NF [membre] dislocation; (Chir) disarticulation

désarticuler [dezaRtikyle] ▶conjug 1◀ 1 VT [+ membre] (= déboîter) to dislocate; (= amputer) to disarticulate; [+ mécanisme] to upset; **il s'est désarticulé l'épaule** he dislocated his shoulder 2 **se désarticuler** VPR [acrobate] to contort o.s.

désassemblage [dezasɑ̃blaʒ] NM dismantling

désassembler [dezasɑ̃ble] ▶conjug 1◀ VT to dismantle, take apart

désassorti, e [dezasɔRti] (ptp de **désassortir**) ADJ [service de table] unmatching, unmatched; [+ assiettes etc] odd (épith); [magasin, marchand] poorly stocked

désassortir [dezasɔRtiR] ▶conjug 2◀ VT [+ service de table] to break up, spoil

désastre [dezastR] NM (lit, fig) disaster; **courir au ~** to be heading (straight) for disaster; **les ~s causés par la tempête** the damage caused by the storm

désastreusement [dezastRøzmɑ̃] ADV disastrously

désastreux, -euse [dezastRø, øz] ADJ [erreur, décision, récolte, influence] disastrous; [bilan, conditions, temps] terrible, appalling

désavantage [dezavɑ̃taʒ] NM (= handicap) disadvantage, handicap; (= inconvénient) disadvantage, drawback; **avoir un ~ sur qn** to be at a disadvantage compared to sb; **cela présente bien des ~s** it has many disadvantages ou drawbacks; **être/tourner au ~ de qn** to be/turn to sb's disadvantage; **malgré le ~ du terrain, ils ont gagné** they won even though the ground put them at a disadvantage

désavantager [dezavɑ̃taʒe] ▶conjug 3◀ VT to disadvantage, put at a disadvantage; **cette mesure nous désavantage par rapport aux autres** this measure puts us at a disadvantage compared to the others; **cela désavantage les plus pauvres** this penalizes the very poor; **nous sommes désavantagés par rapport à eux dans le domaine économique** in the economic field we are handicapped ou at a disadvantage compared to them; **se sentir désavantagé par rapport à son frère** to feel unfavourably treated by comparison with one's brother, feel one is treated less fairly than one's brother; **les couches sociales les plus désavantagées** the most under-privileged ou disadvantaged sectors of society

désavantageusement [dezavɑ̃taʒøzmɑ̃] ADV unfavourably, disadvantageously

désavantageux, -euse [dezavɑ̃taʒø, øz] ADJ unfavourable, disadvantageous

désaveu [dezavø] NM (= rétractation) retraction; (= reniement) [opinion, propos] disowning, disavowal (frm); (= blâme) repudiation, disowning; [signature] disclaiming, repudiation; **encourir le ~ de qn** to be disowned by sb; (Jur) **~ de paternité** repudiation ou denial of paternity

désavouer [dezavwe] ▶conjug 1◀ VT a (= renier) [+ livre, opinion, propos] to disown, disavow (frm); [+ signature] to disclaim; [+ paternité] to disclaim, deny b (= blâmer) [+ personne, action] to disown

désaxé, e [dezakse] (ptp de **désaxer**) 1 ADJ [personne] unhinged 2 NM,F lunatic; **ce crime est l'œuvre d'un ~** this crime is the work of a lunatic ou a psychotic

désaxer [dezakse] ▶conjug 1◀ VT [+ roue] to put out of true; [+ personne, esprit] to unbalance, unhinge

descellement [desɛlmɑ̃] NM [pierre] freeing; [grille] pulling up; [acte] unsealing, breaking the seal on ou of

desceller [desele] ▶conjug 1◀ 1 VT (= arracher) [+ pierre] to (pull) free; [+ grille] to pull up; (= ouvrir) [+ acte] to unseal, break the seal on ou of 2 **se desceller** VPR [objet] to come loose

descendance [desɑ̃dɑ̃s] NF (= enfants) descendants, issue (frm); (= origine) descent, lineage (frm)

descendant, e [desɑ̃dɑ̃, ɑ̃t] 1 ADJ [direction, chemin] downward, descending; (Mus) [gamme] falling, descending; (Mil) [garde] coming off duty (attrib); (Rail) [voie, train] down (épith); [bateau] sailing downstream; **marée ~e** ebb tide; **à marée ~e** when the tide is going out ou on the ebb 2 NM,F descendant (**de** of)

descendeur, -euse [desɑ̃dœR, øz] 1 NM,F (Ski, Cyclisme) downhill specialist ou racer, downhiller 2 NM (Alpinisme) descender, abseil device

descendre [desɑ̃dR] ▶conjug 41◀ 1 VI (avec aux être) a (= aller vers le bas) [personne] (vu d'en haut) to come down; (vu d'en bas) to come down (**à**, **vers** to, **dans** into); [fleuve] to flow down; [oiseau] to fly down; [avion] to come down, descend; **descends me voir** come down

and see me; **descends le prévenir** go down and warn him; **aidez-la à ~** (de sa chaise) help her down; (dans l'escalier) help her downstairs; **~ à pied/à bicyclette/en voiture/en parachute** to walk/cycle/drive/parachute down; **on descend par un sentier étroit** the way down is by a narrow path; **~ en courant/en titubant** to run/stagger down; **~ en train/par l'ascenseur** to go down by train/in the lift (Brit) ou elevator (US); **~ par la fenêtre** to get down through the window; **nous sommes descendus en dix minutes** we got down in 10 minutes; **~ à Marseille** to go down to Marseilles; **~ en ville** to go into town → **arène**, **rappel**, **rue**

b (d'un lieu élevé) **~ de** [+ toit, rocher, arbre] to climb ou come down from; [+ balançoire, manège] to get off; **il descendait de l'échelle** he was climbing ou coming down the ladder; **il est descendu de sa chambre** he came down from his room; **~ de la colline** to come ou climb ou walk down the hill; **fais ~ le chien du fauteuil** get the dog (down) off the armchair; **descends de ton nuage!*** come back (down) to earth!

c (d'un moyen de transport) **~ de voiture/du train** to get out of the car/off ou out of the train, alight from the car/train (frm); **« tout le monde descend! »** "all change!"; (dans le métro, le bus) **vous descendez (à la prochaine)?** are you getting off (at the next stop)?; **beaucoup de passagers sont descendus à Lyon** a lot of people got off at Lyons; **ça descend pas mal à Châtelet** a lot of people get off at Châtelet; **~ à terre** to go ashore; **~ de cheval** to dismount; **~ de bicyclette** to get off one's bicycle

d (= atteindre) [habits, cheveux] **~ à** ou **jusqu'à** to come down to; **son manteau lui descendait jusqu'aux chevilles** his coat came down to his ankles

e (= loger) **~ dans un hôtel** ou **à l'hôtel** to stay at ou put up at a hotel; **~ chez des amis** to stay with friends

f (= s'étendre de haut en bas) [colline, route] **~ en pente douce** to slope gently down; **~ en pente raide** to drop ou fall away sharply; **la route descend en tournant** ou **en lacets** the road winds downwards

g (= s'enfoncer) **le puits descend à 60 mètres** the well goes down 60 metres

h (= tomber) [obscurité, neige] to fall; [soleil] to go down, sink; **le brouillard descend sur la vallée** the fog is coming down over the valley; **le soleil descend sur l'horizon** the sun is going down on the horizon; **le soir descendait** night was falling; **les impuretés descendent au fond** the impurities fall ou drop to the bottom; **la neige descend en voltigeant** the snow is fluttering down; **qu'est-ce que ça descend!** ◊ **qu'est-ce qu'il descend!*** [pluie] it's pouring, it's tipping it down!* (Brit); [neige] it's snowing really hard

i (= baisser) [baromètre, température] to fall, drop; [mer, marée] to go out, ebb; [prix] to come down, fall, drop; [valeurs boursières, cote de popularité] to fall; **il est descendu à la dixième place** he's fallen back into tenth position; **l'équipe est descendue en seconde division** the team moved down into the second division; **~ dans l'échelle sociale** to move down the social scale; **faire ~ le taux d'inflation/le nombre des chômeurs** to bring down the inflation rate/the number of unemployed; **dans le 200 m, il est descendu en dessous de** ou **sous les 21 secondes** in the 200 metres he brought his time down to less than 21 seconds; **ma voix ne descend pas plus bas** my voice doesn't ou won't go any lower

j (= s'abaisser) **~ dans l'estime de qn** to go down in sb's estimation; **il est descendu bien bas/jusqu'à mendier** he has stooped very low/to begging

k (= faire irruption) **la police est descendue dans cette boîte de nuit** the police raided the

➤ GRAMMAIRE ACTIVE: désapprouver 41

night club, there was a police raid on the night club

1 (* = être avalé ou digéré) [vin, repas] **ça descend bien** that goes down well, that goes down a treat* (Brit); **se promener pour faire ~ son déjeuner** to take a walk in order to help digest one's lunch; **il a bu une bière pour faire ~ son sandwich** he washed his sandwich down with a beer

2 **descendre de** VT INDIR (= avoir pour ancêtre) to be descended from; **l'homme descend du singe** man is descended from the apes

3 VT (avec aux avoir) **a** (= parcourir vers le bas) [+ escalier, colline, pente] to go down, descend (frm); **l'escalier/les marches précipitamment** to dash downstairs/down the steps; **la péniche descend le fleuve** the barge goes down the river; **une rivière en canoë** to go down a river in a canoe, canoe down a river; **~ la rue en courant** to run down the street; **~ une piste en slalom** to slalom down a slope; (Mus) **~ la gamme** to go down the scale
b (= porter, apporter en bas) [+ valise] to get down, take down, bring down; [+ meuble] to take down, bring down; **faire ~ ses bagages** to have one's luggage brought ou taken down; **tu peux me ~ mes lunettes?** can you bring my glasses down for me?; **il faut ~ la poubelle tous les soirs** the rubbish (Brit) ou garbage (US) has to be taken down every night; **~ des livres d'un rayon** to reach ou take books down from a shelf; **je te descends en ville** I'll take ou drive you into town, I'll give you a lift into town; **le bus me descend à ma porte** the bus drops me right outside my front door
c (= baisser) [+ étagère, rayon] to lower; **descends les stores** pull the blinds down, lower the blinds; **~ une étagère d'un cran** to lower a shelf (by) a notch, take a shelf down a notch
d (* = abattre) [+ avion] to bring down, shoot down; (= tuer) [+ personne] to do in*, bump off*; **le patron du bar s'est fait ~** the bar owner got himself done in* ou bumped off*; (fig) **l'auteur s'est fait ~ en beauté (par la critique)** the author was shot down in flames (by the critics) → **flamme**
e (* = boire) [+ bouteille] to down*; **qu'est-ce qu'il descend!** he drinks like a fish!*

descente [desɑ̃t] **1** NF **a** (= action) going down (NonC); (Aviat, Alpinisme) descent; **la ~ dans le puits est dangereuse** it's dangerous to go down the well; **en montagne, la ~ est plus fatigante que la montée** in mountaineering, coming down ou the descent is more tiring than going up ou the climb; **le téléphérique est tombé en panne dans la ~** the cable-car broke down on the ou its way down; (Aviat) **~ en vol plané** gliding descent; (Aviat) **~ en feuille morte** falling leaf; (Aviat) **~ en tire-bouchon** spiral dive; **~ en parachute** parachute drop; (Ski) **la ~ ◊ l'épreuve de ~** the downhill (race); **~ en slalom** slalom descent; (Alpinisme) **~ en rappel** abseiling, roping down; **accueillir qn à la ~ du train/bateau** to meet sb off the train/boat; **à ma ~ de voiture** as I got out of the car → **tuyau**
b (= raid, incursion) raid; **~ de police** police raid; **faire une ~ sur** ou **dans** to raid, make a raid on; **les enfants ont fait une ~ dans le frigidaire*** the children have raided the fridge
c (en portant) **la ~ des bagages prend du temps** it takes time to bring down the luggage; **pendant la ~ du tonneau à la cave** while taking the barrel down to the cellar
d (= partie descendante) (downward) slope, incline; **s'engager dans la ~** to go off on the downward slope; **la ~ est rapide** it's a steep (downward) slope; **freiner dans les ~s** to brake going downhill ou on the downhill; **les freins ont lâché au milieu de la ~** the brakes went halfway down (the slope); **la ~ de la cave** the stairs ou steps down to the cellar; **la**

~ du garage the slope down to the garage; **il a une bonne ~** * he can really knock it back* ou put it away*

2 COMP ► **descente de croix** (Art, Rel) Deposition ► **descente aux enfers** (Rel, fig) descent into hell ► **descente de lit** bedside rug ► **descente d'organe** (Méd) prolapse of an organ

déscolarisé, e [deskɔlaRize] ADJ [enfant] who is outside the school system

descriptible [dɛskRiptibl] ADJ **ce n'est pas ~** it's indescribable

descriptif, -ive [dɛskRiptif, iv] **1** ADJ descriptive **2** NM (= brochure) explanatory leaflet; [travaux] specifications, specification sheet; [projet] outline

description [dɛskRipsjɔ̃] NF description; **faire la ~ de** to describe

descriptivisme [dɛskRiptivism] NM descriptivism

descriptiviste [dɛskRiptivist] NMF descriptivist

désectorisation [desɛktɔRizasjɔ̃] NF (Scol) removal of catchment area (Brit) ou school district (US) boundaries

désectoriser [desɛktɔRize] ► conjug 1 ◄ VT (Scol) **~ une région** to remove a region's catchment area (Brit) ou school district (US) boundaries

déségrégation [desegRegasjɔ̃] NF desegregation

désembourber [dezɑ̃buRbe] ► conjug 1 ◄ VT to get out of the mud

désembourgeoiser [dezɑ̃buRʒwaze] ► conjug 1 ◄ **1** VT to make less bourgeois **2** **se désembourgeoiser** VPR to become less bourgeois, lose some of one's bourgeois habits ou attitudes

désembouteiller [dezɑ̃buteje] ► conjug 1 ◄ VT (Aut) to unblock; [+ lignes téléphoniques] to unjam

désembuage [dezɑ̃byaʒ] NM demisting

désembuer [dezɑ̃bɥe] ► conjug 1 ◄ VT [+ vitre] to demist

désemparé, e [dezɑ̃paRe] (ptp de **désemparer**) ADJ **a** [personne, air] helpless, distraught **b** [navire] crippled

désemparer [dezɑ̃paRe] ► conjug 1 ◄ **1** VI **sans ~** without stopping **2** VT (Naut) to cripple

désemplir [dezɑ̃pliR] ► conjug 2 ◄ **1** VT to empty **2** VI **le magasin ne désemplit jamais** the shop is never empty ou is always full **3** **se désemplir** VPR to empty (de of)

désencadrer [dezɑ̃kadRe] ► conjug 1 ◄ VT **a** [+ tableau] to take out of its frame **b** (Écon) **~ le crédit** to ease credit controls

désenchaîner [dezɑ̃ʃene] ► conjug 1 ◄ VT to unchain, unfetter (frm)

désenchantement [dezɑ̃ʃɑ̃tmɑ̃] NM (= désillusion) disillusionment, disenchantment

désenchanter [dezɑ̃ʃɑ̃te] ► conjug 1 ◄ VT **a** [+ personne] to disillusion, disenchant **b** (littér) [+ activité] to dispel the charm of; (†† = désensorceler) to free from a ou the spell, disenchant

désenclavement [dezɑ̃klavmɑ̃] NM [région, quartier, ville] opening up; **cela a permis le ~ de la région** this has opened up the region

désenclaver [dezɑ̃klave] ► conjug 1 ◄ VT [+ région, quartier] to open up

désencombrement [dezɑ̃kɔ̃bRəmɑ̃] NM clearing

désencombrer [dezɑ̃kɔ̃bRe] ► conjug 1 ◄ VT [+ passage] to clear

désencrasser [dezɑ̃kRase] ► conjug 1 ◄ VT to clean out

désencroûter* [dezɑ̃kRute] ► conjug 1 ◄ **1** VT **~ qn** to get sb out of the ou a rut, shake sb up* **2** **se désencroûter** VPR to get (o.s.) out of the ou a rut, shake o.s. up*

désendettement [dezɑ̃dɛtmɑ̃] NM [entreprise, pays] reduction in debt; **l'entreprise poursuit son ~** the company is progressively clearing its debts; **une politique de ~ de l'État** a policy of reducing the national debt

désendetter [dezɑ̃dete] ► conjug 1 ◄ **1** VT (= annuler la dette de) to get out of debt; (= réduire la dette) to reduce the debt of **2** **se désendetter** VPR to get (o.s.) out of debt

désenfiler [dezɑ̃file] ► conjug 1 ◄ VT [+ aiguille] to unthread; [+ perles] to unstring; **mon aiguille s'est désenfilée** my needle has come unthreaded

désenfler [dezɑ̃fle] ► conjug 1 ◄ VI to go down, become less swollen

désengagement [dezɑ̃gaʒmɑ̃] NM (gén, Mil) withdrawal, disengagement; (Fin) disinvestment; **le ~ progressif des forces militaires** the gradual withdrawal of military forces; **le ~ de l'État** the withdrawal of state funding

désengager [dezɑ̃gaʒe] ► conjug 3 ◄ **1** VT [+ troupes] to disengage, withdraw; **~ qn d'une obligation** to free sb from an obligation **2** **se désengager** VPR [troupes] to disengage, withdraw; [entreprise, État] to withdraw, pull out (de from)

désengorger [dezɑ̃gɔRʒe] ► conjug 3 ◄ VT [+ tuyau] to unblock; [+ route] to relieve the traffic congestion on; [+ service] to relieve

désenivrer [dezɑ̃nivRe] ► conjug 1 ◄ VTI to sober up

désennuyer [dezɑ̃nɥije] ► conjug 8 ◄ **1** VT **~ qn** to relieve sb's boredom; **la lecture désennuie** reading relieves (one's) boredom **2** **se désennuyer** VPR to relieve the ou one's boredom

désensabler [dezɑ̃sable] ► conjug 1 ◄ VT [+ voiture] to dig out of the sand; [+ chenal] to dredge

désensibilisation [desɑ̃sibilizasjɔ̃] NF (Méd, Photo, fig) desensitization

désensibiliser [desɑ̃sibilize] ► conjug 1 ◄ VT (Méd, Photo, fig) to desensitize; (Méd) **se faire ~ au pollen** to be desensitized to pollen; **des enfants totalement désensibilisés à la violence** children totally inured to violence

désensorceler [desɑ̃sɔRsəle] ► conjug 4 ◄ VT to free ou release from a ou the spell

désentortiller [dezɑ̃tɔRtije] ► conjug 1 ◄ VT to disentangle, unravel

désentraver [dezɑ̃tRave] ► conjug 1 ◄ VT to unshackle

désenvaser [dezɑ̃vaze] ► conjug 1 ◄ VT (= sortir) to get out of the mud; (= nettoyer) to clean the mud off; [+ port, chenal] to dredge

désenvenimer [dezɑ̃vnime] ► conjug 1 ◄ VT [+ plaie] to take the poison out of; [+ relations] to take the bitterness out of; **pour ~ la situation** to defuse ou take the heat out of the situation

désenvoûtement [dezɑ̃vutmɑ̃] NM release from a ou the spell

désenvoûter [dezɑ̃vute] ► conjug 1 ◄ VT to free ou release from a ou the spell

désépaissir [dezepesiR] ► conjug 2 ◄ VT [+ cheveux] to thin (out); [+ sauce] to thin (down), make thinner

déséquilibrant, e [dezekilibRɑ̃, ɑ̃t] ADJ destabilizing

déséquilibre [dezekilibR] NM (= manque d'assise) unsteadiness; (dans un rapport de forces, de quantités) imbalance (entre between); (mental, nerveux) unbalance, disequilibrium (frm); **l'armoire est en ~** the cupboard is unsteady; **le budget est en ~** the budget is not balanced; **~ commercial** trade gap ou imbalance

déséquilibré, e [dezekilibRe] (ptp de **déséquilibrer**) **1** ADJ [budget] unbalanced; [esprit] disordered, unhinged **2** NM,F unbalanced ou mentally disturbed person

déséquilibrer [dezekilibʀe] ▸conjug 1◂ VT (*lit*) to throw off balance; [+ *esprit, personne*] to unbalance; [+ *budget*] to create an imbalance in

désert, e [dezɛʀ, ɛʀt] [1] ADJ deserted → **île** [2] NM (*Géog*) desert; (*fig*) desert, wilderness; **~ de Gobi/du Kalahari/d'Arabie** Gobi/Kalahari/Arabian Desert; **~ culturel** cultural desert → **prêcher, traversée**

déserter [dezɛʀte] ▸conjug 1◂ [1] VT [+ *lieu*] to desert, abandon; **village déserté par ses habitants** village deserted *ou* abandoned by its inhabitants [2] VI (*Mil, fig*) to desert

déserteur [dezɛʀtœʀ] [1] NM deserter [2] ADJ M deserting

désertification [dezɛʀtifikasjɔ̃] NF [a] (*Écol, Géog*) desertification [b] (*fig*) [*campagnes, région*] depopulation; **la ~ rurale** *ou* **des campagnes** rural depopulation

désertifier (se) [dezɛʀtifje] ▸conjug 7◂ VPR [a] (*Écol, Géog*) to turn into a desert; **zone désertifiée** desertified area [b] [*campagnes, région*] to become depopulated; **région désertifiée** depopulated area

désertion [dezɛʀsjɔ̃] NF (*Mil: fig*) desertion

désertique [dezɛʀtik] ADJ [*lieu*] (= *de sable*) desert (*épith*); (= *aride*) barren; [*climat, plante*] desert (*épith*)

désescalade [dezeskalad] NF (*Écon*) [*taux*] de-escalation

désespérance [dezɛspeʀɑ̃s] NF (*littér*) desperation, desperateness

désespérant, e [dezɛspeʀɑ̃, ɑ̃t] ADJ [*lenteur, nouvelle, bêtise*] appalling; [*enfant*] hopeless; [*temps*] depressing; **d'une naïveté ~e** hopelessly naïve

désespéré, e [dezɛspeʀe] (*ptp de* **désespérer**) [1] ADJ [*personne*] in despair (*attrib*), desperate; [*situation*] desperate, hopeless; [*cas*] hopeless; [*tentative*] desperate; **appel/regard ~** cry/look of despair, desperate cry/look; (*sens affaibli*) **je suis ~ d'avoir à le faire** I'm desperately sorry to have to do it [2] NM,F desperate person, person in despair; **la ~e s'est jetée dans la Seine** the woman committed suicide by jumping into the Seine

désespérément [dezɛspeʀemɑ̃] ADV (= *avec acharnement*) desperately; (= *sans espoir de changement*) hopelessly; **la salle restait ~ vide** the room remained hopelessly empty

désespérer [dezɛspeʀe] ▸conjug 6◂ [1] VT (= *décourager*) to drive to despair; **il désespère ses parents** he drives his parents to despair, he is the despair of his parents [2] VI (= *se décourager*) to despair, lose hope, give up hope; **c'est à ~** it's enough to drive you to despair, it's hopeless [3] **désespérer de** VT INDIR to despair of; **je désespère de toi/de la situation** I despair of you/of the situation; **je désespère de son succès** I despair of his (ever) being successful; **~ de faire qch** to have lost (all) hope *ou* have given up (all) hope of doing sth, despair of doing sth; **il désespère de leur faire entendre raison** he has lost all hope of making them see reason, he despairs of (ever) making them see reason; **je ne désespère pas de les amener à signer** I haven't lost hope *ou* given up hope of getting them to sign [4] **se désespérer** VPR to despair; **elle passe ses nuits à se ~** her nights are given over to despair

désespoir [dezɛspwaʀ] [1] NM (= *perte de l'espoir*) despair; (= *chagrin*) despair, despondency; **il fait le ~ de ses parents** he is the despair of his parents; **sa paresse fait mon ~** his laziness drives me to despair *ou* to desperation; **sa supériorité fait le ~ des autres athlètes** his superiority is the despair of the other athletes; **être au ~** to be in despair; (*sens affaibli*) **je suis au ~ de ne pouvoir venir** I'm desperately sorry that I can't come; **en ~ de**

cause, on fit appel au médecin in desperation, we called in the doctor [2] COMP ▸ **désespoir des peintres** (*Bot*) London pride, saxifrage

désétatisation [dezetatizasjɔ̃] NF denationalization

désétatiser [dezetatize] ▸conjug 1◂ VT to denationalize

désexualiser [deseksɥalize] ▸conjug 1◂ VT to desexualize

déshabillage [dezabijaʒ] NM undressing

déshabillé [dezabije] NM négligé

déshabiller [dezabije] ▸conjug 1◂ [1] VT to undress; (*fig*) **~ Pierre pour habiller Paul** to rob Peter to pay Paul [2] **se déshabiller** VPR to undress, take off one's clothes; (* = *ôter son manteau, sa veste*) to take off one's coat; **déshabillez-vous dans l'entrée** leave your coat *ou* things in the hall

déshabituer [dezabitɥe] ▸conjug 1◂ [1] VT **~ qn de (faire) qch** to get sb out of the habit of (doing) sth, break sb of the habit of (doing) sth [2] **se déshabituer** VPR **se ~ de qch/de faire qch** (*volontairement*) to get (o.s.) out of the habit *ou* break o.s. of the habit of sth/of doing sth; (*par inaction, inertie*) to get out of *ou* lose the habit of sth/of doing sth

désherbage [dezɛʀbaʒ] NM weeding

désherbant [dezɛʀbɑ̃] NM weed-killer

désherber [dezɛʀbe] ▸conjug 1◂ VT to weed

déshérence [dezeʀɑ̃s] NF escheat; **tomber en ~** to escheat

déshérité, e [dezeʀite] (*ptp de* **déshériter**) [1] ADJ (= *désavantagé*) [*quartier, région*] deprived; [*famille, population*] destitute, deprived, underprivileged; **l'enfance ~e** deprived children [2] NM,F **les ~s** the underprivileged

déshériter [dezeʀite] ▸conjug 1◂ VT [+ *héritier*] to disinherit

déshonnête [dezɔnɛt] ADJ (*littér* = *impudique*) unseemly, immodest

déshonnêteté [dezɔnɛtte] NF (*littér* = *impudeur*) unseemliness, immodesty

déshonneur [dezɔnœʀ] NM disgrace, dishonour (*Brit*), dishonor (*US*); **il n'y a pas de ~ à avouer son échec** there's no disgrace in admitting one's failure

déshonorant, e [dezɔnɔʀɑ̃, ɑ̃t] ADJ dishonourable (*Brit*), dishonorable (*US*), degrading

déshonorer [dezɔnɔʀe] ▸conjug 1◂ [1] VT [a] (= *discréditer*) [+ *profession*] to disgrace, dishonour (*Brit*), dishonor (*US*); [+ *personne, famille*] to dishonour (*Brit*), dishonor (*US*), be a disgrace to, bring disgrace on; **il se croirait déshonoré de travailler** he would think it beneath him to work [b]† [+ *femme*] to dishonour (*Brit*), dishonor (*US*) [2] **se déshonorer** VPR to disgrace o.s.

déshumaniser [dezymanize] ▸conjug 1◂ VT to dehumanize

déshumidificateur [dezymidifikatœʀ] NM dehumidifier

déshydratation [dezidʀatasjɔ̃] NF dehydration

déshydraté, e [dezidʀate] (*ptp de* **déshydrater**) ADJ [*peau, aliment*] dehydrated

déshydrater VT, **se déshydrater** VPR [dezidʀate] ▸conjug 1◂ to dehydrate

déshydrogénation [dezidʀɔʒenasjɔ̃] NF dehydrogenation, dehydrogenization

déshydrogéner [dezidʀɔʒene] ▸conjug 6◂ VT to dehydrogenate, dehydrogenize

déshypothéquer [dezipɔteke] ▸conjug 6◂ VT to free from mortgage

desiderata [deziderata] NMPL (= *souhaits*) wishes, desiderata (*frm*)

design [dizajn] [1] NM **le ~** (= *activité*) design; (= *style*) the designer look; (= *mobilier*) design-

er furniture; **le ~ industriel** industrial design [2] ADJ INV designer

désignation [deziɲasjɔ̃] NF (= *appellation*) name, designation (*frm*); (= *élection*) naming, appointment, designation

designer [dizajnœʀ] NM (= *décorateur*) designer

désigner [deziɲe] ▸conjug 1◂ VT [a] (= *montrer*) to point out, indicate; **~ qn du doigt** to point sb out; **ces indices le désignent clairement comme coupable** these signs point clearly to his guilt; **~ qch à l'attention de qn** to draw *ou* call sth to sb's attention; **~ qch à l'admiration de qn** to point sth out for sb's admiration [b] (= *nommer*) to name, appoint, designate; **le gouvernement a désigné un nouveau ministre** the government has named *ou* appointed a new minister; **~ qn pour remplir une mission** to designate sb to undertake a mission; **~ qn à un poste** to appoint sb to a post; **que des volontaires se désignent!** volunteers step forward!, could we have some volunteers!; **membre/successeur désigné** member/successor elect *ou* designate [c] (= *qualifier*) to mark out; **sa hardiesse le désigne pour (faire) cette tentative** his boldness marks him out for this attempt; **c'était le coupable désigné/la victime désignée** he was the classic culprit/victim; **être tout désigné pour faire qch** [*personne*] to be cut out to do sth, be altogether suited to doing sth; **l'endroit est tout désigné pour ce genre de festival** the place is perfect for this kind of festival [d] (= *dénommer*) to designate, refer to; **~ qn par son nom** to refer to sb by (their) name; **on désigne sous ce nom toutes les substances toxiques** this name designates all toxic substances; **ces métaphores désignent toutes le héros** these metaphors all refer to the hero; **les mots qui désignent des objets concrets** the words which denote *ou* designate concrete objects

désillusion [dezi(l)lyzjɔ̃] NF disillusion

désillusionnement [dezi(l)lyzjɔnmɑ̃] NM disillusionment

désillusionner [dezi(l)lyzjɔne] ▸conjug 1◂ VT to disillusion

désincarcération [dezɛ̃kaʀseʀasjɔ̃] NF **la ~ des victimes a pris deux heures** it took two hours to cut the victims (free) from the wreckage

désincarcérer [dezɛ̃kaʀseʀe] ▸conjug 6◂ VT [+ *accidenté*] to free (*from a wrecked vehicle*)

désincarné, e [dezɛ̃kaʀne] ADJ (*Rel*) [*âme*] disembodied; (*fig*) **on dirait qu'il est ~** you'd think he wasn't flesh and blood

désincrustant, e [dezɛ̃kʀystɑ̃, ɑ̃t] [1] ADJ [a] (*Tech*) (de)scaling [b] [*crème, masque*] (deep) cleansing (*épith*) [2] NM (*Tech*) (de)scaling agent

désincruster [dezɛ̃kʀyste] ▸conjug 1◂ VT [+ *chaudière*] to descale, remove the fur (*Brit*) *ou* sediment (*US*) from; [+ *peau*] to cleanse

désindexation [dezɛ̃dɛksasjɔ̃] NF de-indexation

désindexer [dezɛ̃dɛkse] ▸conjug 1◂ VT to de-index

désindustrialisation [dezɛ̃dystʀijalizasjɔ̃] NF de-industrialization

désindustrialiser [dezɛ̃dystʀijalize] ▸conjug 1◂ VT to de-industrialize

désinence [dezinɑ̃s] NF (*Ling*) ending, inflexion

désinentiel, -ielle [dezinɑ̃sjɛl] ADJ inflexional

désinfectant, e [dezɛ̃fɛktɑ̃, ɑ̃t] ADJ, NM disinfectant

désinfecter [dezɛ̃fɛkte] ▸conjug 1◂ VT to disinfect

désinfection [dezɛ̃fɛksjɔ̃] NF disinfection

désinflation [dezɛ̃flasjɔ̃] NF = **déflation**

désinformation [dezɛ̃fɔrmasjɔ̃] NF disinformation

désinformer [dezɛ̃fɔrme] ▸conjug 1◂ VT to give false information to

désinhiber [dezinibe] ▸conjug 1◂ VT ~ **qn** to rid sb of his (ou her) inhibitions

désinhibition [dezinibisjɔ̃] NF loss of inhibitions

désinsectisation [dezɛ̃sɛktizasjɔ̃] NF spraying ou treatment with insecticide, ≈ pest control

désinsectiser [dezɛ̃sɛktize] ▸conjug 1◂ VT to rid of insects, spray ou treat with insecticide

désinsertion [dezɛ̃sɛrsjɔ̃] NF **la ~ sociale provoquée par le chômage** the way unemployment turns people into social outcasts

désinstaller [dezɛ̃stale] ▸conjug 1◂ VT (Ordin) [+ logiciel] to deinstall

désintégration [dezɛ̃tegrasjɔ̃] NF [groupe] splitting-up, breaking-up; [État] disintegration, breakup; [roche] disintegration, breaking-up; [fusée] self-destructing; (Phys Nucl) [atome] splitting; **la ~ de la matière** the disintegration of matter

désintégrer [dezɛ̃tegre] ▸conjug 6◂ **1** VT [+ groupe] to split up, break up; [+ État, roche] to break up, disintegrate; (Phys Nucl) [+ atome, matière] to disintegrate **2 se désintégrer** VPR [groupe] to split up, break up; [État] to break up, disintegrate; [roche] to break up, disintegrate, crumble, break up; [fusée] to self-destruct; (Phys Nucl) to disintegrate

désintéressé, e [dezɛ̃terese] (ptp de **désintéresser**) ADJ (= généreux) disinterested, unselfish; (= impartial) disinterested; **elle n'était pas complètement ~e en l'invitant** she had an ulterior motive in inviting him

désintéressement [dezɛ̃teresmɑ̃] NM **a** (= générosité) unselfishness, selflessness; (= impartialité) disinterestedness; **avec ~** unselfishly **b** (Fin) [créancier] paying off; [associé] buying out

désintéresser [dezɛ̃terese] ▸conjug 1◂ **1** VT [+ créancier] to pay off; [+ associé] to buy out **2 se désintéresser** VPR **se ~ de** to lose interest in

désintérêt [dezɛ̃terɛ] NM disinterest, lack of interest (**pour** in)

désintoxication [dezɛ̃tɔksikasjɔ̃] NF (Méd) [alcoolique] detoxification, treatment for alcoholism; [drogué] detoxification, treatment for drug addiction; **il fait une** ou **est en cure de ~** [alcoolique] he's undergoing treatment for alcoholism, he's in detox*; [drogué] he's undergoing treatment for drug addiction, he's in detox*; **centre de ~** detoxification centre (Brit) ou center (US)

désintoxiqué, e [dezɛ̃tɔksike] (ptp de **désintoxiquer**) ADJ [ancien alcoolique] dried out, detoxed*; [ancien drogué] clean, detoxed*

désintoxiquer [dezɛ̃tɔksike] ▸conjug 1◂ VT **a** (Méd) [+ alcoolique] to treat for alcoholism, detoxify, dry out*; [+ drogué] to treat for drug addiction, detoxify; **il s'est fait ~** [alcoolique] he was treated for alcoholism; [drogué] he was treated for drug addiction **b** [+ citadin, gros mangeur] to cleanse the system of **c** (= désaccoutumer) **tu veux un café ? — non, j'essaie de me ~** do you want a coffee? — no, I'm trying to give it up; **pour ~ les enfants de la télévision** to wean children off ou from the television; (= déconditionner) **il faut ~ l'opinion publique** the record has to be set straight with the public

désinvestir [dezɛ̃vɛstir] ▸conjug 2◂ **1** VI **a** (Écon) to disinvest (**dans** in); **la société a désinvesti dans le secteur immobilier** the company has disinvested in ou withdrawn its investments from the real estate market **b** (Psych) to cease to invest o.s. in **2** VT (Mil) to lift the siege of **3 se désinvestir** VPR to lose

interest (**de** in); **elle s'est complètement désinvestie de sa relation amoureuse/de son travail** she has completely lost interest in her relationship/her work, she no longer puts anything into her relationship/her work

désinvestissement [dezɛ̃vɛstismɑ̃] NM **a** (Écon) disinvestment, withdrawal of investments; **la société a procédé à des ~s dans ces secteurs** the company began to disinvest in ou to withdraw its investments from these areas **b** (Psych) loss of interest; **on note chez certains cadres un grand ~** some managers are putting less and less of themselves into their jobs ou are less and less committed to their jobs

désinvolte [dezɛ̃vɔlt] ADJ (= sans gêne) casual, offhand, airy; (= à l'aise) casual, relaxed

désinvolture [dezɛ̃vɔltyr] NF casualness; **avec ~** casually, in an offhand way

désir [dezir] NM **a** (= souhait) wish, desire (**de qch** for sth); **le ~ de faire qch** the desire to do sth; **vos ~s sont des ordres** your wish is my command; **selon le ~ de qn** in accordance with sb's wishes; **prendre ses ~s pour des réalités** to indulge in wishful thinking, delude o.s. **b** (= convoitise, sensualité) desire (**de qch** for sth); **yeux brillants de ~** eyes burning with desire; **éprouver du ~ pour qn** to feel desire for sb

désirabilité [dezirabilite] NF desirability

désirable [dezirabl] ADJ desirable; **peu ~** undesirable

▸ **désirer** [dezire] ▸conjug 1◂ VT **a** (= vouloir) to want; **~ faire qch** to want ou wish to do sth; **que désirez-vous ?** (dans un magasin) what would you like?, what can I do for you?; **désirez-vous prendre du café ?** would you care for ou would you like some coffee?; **Madame désire ?** (dans une boutique) can I help you, madam?; (domestique) yes, madam?; **il désire que tu viennes tout de suite** he wants you to come at once; **désirez-vous qu'on vous l'envoie ?** would you like it sent to you?, do you wish to have it sent to you? **b** (sexuellement) to desire **c** (loc) **se faire ~*** to play hard-to-get*; **la cuisine/son travail laisse à ~** the food/his work leaves something to be desired ou is not (quite) up to the mark* (Brit); **ça laisse beaucoup à ~** it leaves much ou a lot to be desired; **la décoration ne laisse rien à ~** the decor is all that one could wish for ou leaves nothing to be desired

désireux, -euse [deziro, øz] ADJ **~ de faire** anxious to do, desirous of doing (frm); **il est très ~ de faire votre connaissance** he is most anxious to make your acquaintance; **ils sont peu ~ d'entamer les négociations** they aren't very eager to ou they are reluctant to start negotiations; **~ de qch** avid for sth, desirous of sth (frm)

désistement [dezistmɑ̃] NM (Jur, Pol) withdrawal

désister (se) [deziste] ▸conjug 1◂ VPR **a** (Pol) to withdraw, stand down (Brit) (**en faveur de qn** in sb's favour) **b** (Jur) **se désister de** [+ action, appel] to withdraw

désobéir [dezɔbeir] ▸conjug 2◂ VI to be disobedient, disobey; **~ à qn/à un ordre** to disobey sb/an order; **il désobéit tout le temps** he's always being disobedient

désobéissance [dezɔbeisɑ̃s] NF disobedience (NonC) (**à** to); **~ civile** civil disobedience

désobéissant, e [dezɔbeisɑ̃, ɑ̃t] ADJ disobedient

désobligeamment [dezɔbliʒamɑ̃] ADV (frm) [répondre, se conduire] disagreeably

désobligeance [dezɔbliʒɑ̃s] NF (frm) disagreeableness

désobligeant, e [dezɔbliʒɑ̃, ɑ̃t] ADJ disagreeable

désobliger [dezɔbliʒe] ▸conjug 3◂ VT (frm) to offend

désocialisation [desɔsjalizasjɔ̃] NF **la ~ des chômeurs de longue durée** the way the long-term unemployed are turned into social misfits ou outcasts

désocialiser [desɔsjalize] ▸conjug 1◂ VT [+ personne] to turn into a social misfit ou outcast

désodé, e [desɔde] ADJ [régime] sodium-free

désodorisant, e [dezɔdɔrizɑ̃, ɑ̃t] **1** ADJ [savon] deodorizing (épith), deodorant (épith); [filtre] deodorizing (épith); **bombe ~e** air freshener **2** NM (pour le corps) deodorant; (pour l'air) air freshener

désodoriser [dezɔdɔrize] ▸conjug 1◂ VT to deodorize

désœuvré, e [dezœvre] ADJ idle; **il restait ~ pendant des heures** he did nothing ou he sat idle for hours on end; **le voyant ~, elle lui a demandé de l'aider** seeing that he was at a loose end, she asked him to help her; **pour occuper les ~s** to occupy people with nothing to do

désœuvrement [dezœvrəmɑ̃] NM idleness; **lire par ~** to read for something to do ou for want of anything better to do

désolant, e [dezɔlɑ̃, ɑ̃t] ADJ [nouvelle, situation, spectacle] distressing; **cet enfant est vraiment ~** this child is absolutely hopeless; **ce serait ~ qu'elle ne puisse pas venir** it would be a terrible shame ou such a pity if she couldn't come; **il est ~ de bêtise/paresse** he's hopelessly ou desperately stupid/lazy

désolation [dezɔlasjɔ̃] NF **a** (= consternation) distress, grief; **être plongé dans la ~** to be plunged in grief; **il fait la ~ de sa mère** he causes his mother great distress, he breaks his mother's heart **b** (= dévastation) desolation, devastation

▸ **désolé, e** [dezɔle] (ptp de **désoler**) ADJ **a** [endroit] desolate **b** [personne, air] distressed; (= contrit) sorry; **(je suis) ~ de vous avoir dérangé** (I'm) sorry to have disturbed you; **~, je dois partir** (very) sorry, I have to go; **je suis ~ d'avoir appris que vous avez perdu votre mari** I am sorry to hear that you have lost your husband

désoler [dezɔle] ▸conjug 1◂ **1** VT **a** (= affliger) to distress, grieve, sadden; (= contrarier) to upset; **cet enfant me désole !** I despair of that child! **b** (littér = dévaster) to desolate, devastate **2 se désoler** VPR to be upset; **inutile de vous ~** it's no use upsetting yourself

désolidariser [desɔlidarize] ▸conjug 1◂ **1** VT (gén) to divide; (Tech) to separate **2 se désolidariser** VPR [syndicats] to go in different directions; **se ~ de** to dissociate o.s. from

désopilant, e [dezɔpilɑ̃, ɑ̃t] ADJ screamingly funny*, hilarious

désordonné, e [dezɔrdɔne] ADJ **a** [pièce, personne] untidy; [mouvements] uncoordinated; [combat, fuite] disorderly; [esprit] muddled, disorganized; **être ~ dans son travail** to be disorganized in one's work **b** [littér] [vie] disorderly; [dépenses, imagination] reckless, wild

désordre [dezɔrdr] **1** NM **a** (= état) [pièce, vêtements, cheveux] untidiness; [affaires publiques, service] disorderliness, disorder; **il ne supporte pas le ~** he can't bear disorder ou untidiness; **quel ~ !** what a mess!; **il régnait dans la pièce un ~ indescriptible** the room was in a terrible mess; **être en ~** [pièce, affaires] to be untidy ou in disorder ou in a mess; [cheveux, vêtements] to be untidy ou in a mess; **mettre une pièce en ~** ou **◊ mettre du ~ dans une pièce** to mess up a room, make a room untidy; **jeter quelques idées en ~ sur le papier** to jot down a few random ideas; **les mauvaises herbes sur la terrasse, ça fait ~*** the weeds on the terrace are rather unsightly, the terrace looks messy with weeds growing all over it; **un service sans chef, ça fait ~*** it doesn't look good, having a department without a manager; **dans le ~** in no particular order → **tiercé** [b] (= *agitation*) disorder; **des agitateurs ont semé le ~ dans l'armée** agitators spread unrest in the army; **faire du ~ (dans la classe/dans un lieu public)** to cause a commotion *ou* a disturbance (in class/in a public place); **arrêté pour ~ sur la voie publique** arrested for disorderly conduct; **jeter le ~ dans les esprits** to throw people's minds into confusion; **c'est un facteur de ~** it's a disruptive influence [c] (*littér = débauche*) dissoluteness, licentiousness; **mener une vie de ~** to lead a dissolute *ou* licentious life; **regretter les ~s de sa jeunesse** to regret the dissolute *ou* licentious ways of one's youth [d] (*Méd*) **~ fonctionnel/hépatique** functional/liver disorder [2] **désordres** NMPL (= *émeutes*) disturbances, disorder (*NonC*); **de graves ~s ont éclaté** serious disturbances have broken out, there have been serious outbreaks of violence; (= *perturbations*) **~s monétaires/politiques** monetary/political chaos

désorganisation [dezɔʀɡanizasjɔ̃] NF disorganization

désorganiser [dezɔʀɡanize] ▸conjug 1◂ VT (*gén*) to disorganize; [+ *projet, service*] to disrupt, disorganize; **à cause de la grève, nos services sont désorganisés** our services have been disrupted by the strike

désorientation [dezɔʀjɑ̃tasjɔ̃] NF disorientation

désorienté, e [dezɔʀjɑ̃te] (*ptp de* **désorienter**) ADJ (= *égaré*) disorientated; (= *déconcerté*) bewildered, confused (**par** by)

désorienter [dezɔʀjɑ̃te] ▸conjug 1◂ VT (= *égarer*) to disorientate; (= *déconcerter*) to bewilder, confuse

désormais [dezɔʀmɛ] ADV (*au présent*) from now on, henceforth (*frm*); (*au passé*) from then on, henceforth (*frm*)

désossé, e [dezose] (*ptp de* **désosser**) ADJ [*viande*] boned; (*fig*) [*personne*] supple

désossement [dezosmɑ̃] NM [*viande*] boning

désosser [dezose] ▸conjug 1◂ VT [+ *viande*] to bone; [+ *objet, texte*] to take to pieces; [+ *voiture*] to strip (down); **acrobate qui se désosse** acrobat who can twist himself in every direction

désoxydant, e [dezɔksidɑ̃, ɑ̃t] [1] ADJ deoxidizing [2] NM deoxidizer

désoxyder [dezɔkside] ▸conjug 1◂ VT to deoxidize

désoxyribonucléique [dezɔksiʀibɔnykleik] ADJ desoxyribonucleic

desperado [dɛsperado] NM desperado

despote [dɛspɔt] [1] ADJ despotic [2] NM (*lit, fig*) despot, tyrant

despotique [dɛspɔtik] ADJ despotic

despotiquement [dɛspɔtikmɑ̃] ADV despotically

despotisme [dɛspɔtism] NM (*lit, fig*) despotism, tyranny

desquamation [dɛskwamasjɔ̃] NF desquamation

desquamer [dɛskwame] ▸conjug 1◂ [1] VT to remove (*in scales*) [2] VI, **se desquamer** VPR to flake off, desquamate (*SPÉC*)

desquels, desquelles [dekel] → **lequel**

DESS [deɛsɛs] NM (ABRÉV = **diplôme d'études supérieures spécialisées**) → **diplôme**

dessaisir [desezir] ▸conjug 2◂ [1] VT (*Jur*) **~ un tribunal d'une affaire** to remove a case from a court; **être dessaisi du dossier** to be taken off the case [2] **se dessaisir** VPR **se ~ de** to give up, part with, relinquish

dessaisissement [desezismɑ̃] NM **~ d'un tribunal/juge (d'une affaire)** removal of a case from a court/judge

dessalage [desalaʒ] NM [a] (= *chavirement*) capsizing, turning turtle* [b] = **dessalement**

dessalé, e* [desale] (*ptp de* **dessaler**) ADJ (= *déluré*) **il est drôlement ~ depuis qu'il a fait son service militaire** he has really learnt a thing or two* since he did his military service

dessalement [desalmɑ̃] NM [*eau de mer*] desalination; [*poisson*] soaking

dessaler [desale] ▸conjug 1◂ [1] VT [a] [+ *eau de mer*] to desalinate; [+ *poisson*] to soak (*to remove the salt*); **faire ~** *ou* **mettre à ~ de la viande** to put meat to soak [b]* (= *délurer*) **~ qn** to teach sb a thing or two*, teach sb about life; **il s'était dessalé au contact de ses camarades** he had learnt a thing or two* *ou* learnt about life through contact with his friends [2] VI (*Naut*) to capsize, turn turtle*

dessangler [desɑ̃ɡle] ▸conjug 1◂ VT [+ *cheval*] to ungirth; [+ *paquetage*] to unstrap

dessaouler* [desule] ▸conjug 1◂ VTI = **dessoûler**

desséchant, e [deseʃɑ̃, ɑ̃t] ADJ [*vent*] parching, drying; [*travail*] soul-destroying

dessèchement [deseʃmɑ̃] NM (= *action*) drying (out *ou* up), parching; (= *état*) dryness; (= *amaigrissement*) emaciation

dessécher [deseʃe] ▸conjug 6◂ [1] VT [a] [+ *terre, végétation*] to dry out, parch; [+ *plante, feuille*] to wither, dry out; **le vent dessèche la peau** the wind dries (out) the skin; **la soif me dessèche la bouche** my mouth is dry *ou* parched; **lèvres desséchées** parched lips; **cheveux desséchés** dry and damaged hair [b] (*volontairement*) [+ *aliments*] to dry, dehydrate, desiccate [c] (= *racornir*) [+ *cœur*] to harden; **l'amertume/la vie lui avait desséché le cœur** bitterness/life had hardened his heart *ou* left him stony-hearted; **desséché par l'étude** fossilized by years of study [2] **se dessécher** VPR [*terre*] to dry out, become parched; [*plante, feuille*] to wither, dry out; [*aliments*] to dry out, go dry; [*bouche, lèvres*] to go dry, become parched; [*peau*] to dry out

dessein [desɛ̃] NM (*littér*) (= *intention*) intention, design; (= *projet*) plan; **son ~ est** *ou* **il a le ~ de faire** he intends *ou* means to do; **former le ~ de faire qch** to make up one's mind to do sth, form a plan to do sth; **avoir des ~s sur qn** to have designs on sb; **c'est dans ce ~ que** it is with this in mind *ou* with this intention that; **il est parti dans le ~ de** *ou* **à ~ de faire fortune** he went off meaning *ou* intending to make his fortune *ou* with the intention of making his fortune; **faire qch à ~** to do sth intentionally *ou* deliberately *ou* on purpose

desseller [desele] ▸conjug 1◂ VT to unsaddle

desserrage [deseʀaʒ] NM [*vis, écrou*] unscrewing, undoing, loosening; [*câble*] loosening, slackening; [*frein*] releasing; [*crédit*] relaxation

desserré, e [deseʀe] (*ptp de* **desserrer**) ADJ [*vis, écrou*] loose, undone (*attrib*); [*ficelle*] loose, slack; [*cravate, ceinture, nœud*] loose; [*frein*] off (*attrib*), released (*attrib*)

desserrement [deseʀmɑ̃] NM [*ficelle, câble*] loosening, slackening; [*nœud, écrou, étau*] loosening; [*frein*] releasing; [*étreinte, contrainte*] relaxation; **~ de la politique monétaire** relaxation of *ou* in monetary policy

desserrer [deseʀe] ▸conjug 1◂ [1] VT [a] [+ *nœud, ceinture, ficelle, écrou*] to loosen; [+ *poing, dents*] to unclench; [+ *frein*] to release, take off; [+ *étreinte*] to relax, loosen; [+ *objets alignés, mots, lignes*] to space out; **~ sa ceinture de 2 crans** to let one's belt out 2 notches; (*fig*) **~ les cordons de la bourse** to loosen the purse strings; **il n'a pas desserré les dents de toute la soirée** he didn't say a word *ou* open his mouth all evening; **~ l'étau** (*lit*) to loosen the vice; (*fig*) to loosen one's grip (**autour de** on) [b] (*Écon*) [+ *contrainte, politique monétaire*] to relax, ease [2] **se desserrer** VPR [*ficelle, câble*] to come loose, slacken; [*nœud*] to come

loose; [*écrou*] to work *ou* come loose; [*frein*] to release itself; [*étreinte*] to relax

dessert [desɛʀ] NM dessert, pudding (*Brit*), sweet (*Brit*); **ils en sont au ~** they're on to the dessert

desserte [desɛʀt] NF [a] (= *meuble*) sideboard [b] (*Transport*) **la ~ d'une localité par bateau** the servicing of an area by water transport; **la ~ de la ville est assurée par un car** there is a bus service to the town; **cette compagnie aérienne assure une ~ quotidienne entre ces deux villes** the airline operates a daily scheduled flight between these two cities [c] [*prêtre*] cure

dessertir [desɛʀtiʀ] ▸conjug 2◂ VT to unset, remove from its setting

desservant [desɛʀvɑ̃] NM priest in charge

desservir¹ [desɛʀviʀ] ▸conjug 14◂ VT [a] [+ *repas, plat*] to clear away; **vous pouvez ~ (la table)** you can clear away, you can clear the table [b] (= *nuire à*) [+ *personne, cause*] to do a disservice to; [+ *intérêts*] to harm; **son mauvais caractère le dessert** his bad temper goes against him *ou* doesn't do him any favours; **il m'a desservi auprès de mes amis** he turned my friends against me

desservir² [desɛʀviʀ] ▸conjug 14◂ VT [a] (*Transport*) to serve; **le village est desservi par 3 autobus chaque jour** there is a bus service from the village *ou* a bus runs from the village 3 times daily; **le village est desservi par 3 lignes d'autobus** the village is served by *ou* has 3 bus services; **ville bien desservie** town well served by public transport [b] [*porte, couloir*] to lead to [c] [*prêtre*] to serve; **~ une paroisse** to minister to a parish

dessiccatif, -ive [desikatif, iv] [1] ADJ desiccative [2] NM desiccant

dessiccation [desikasjɔ̃] NF (*Chim*) desiccation; [*aliments*] drying, desiccation, dehydration

dessiller [desije] ▸conjug 1◂ VT (*fig*) **~ les yeux de** *ou* **à qn** to open sb's eyes (*fig*); **mes yeux se dessillèrent** my eyes were opened, the scales fell from my eyes (*Brit*)

dessin [desɛ̃] NM [a] (= *image*) drawing; **il a fait un (joli) ~** he drew a (nice) picture, he did a (nice) drawing; **il passe son temps à faire des ~s** he spends his time drawing; **il fait toujours des petits ~s** he's always doodling on his exercise book; **~ à la plume/au fusain/au trait** pen-and-ink/charcoal/line drawing; **~ animé** cartoon (*film*); **~ humoristique** cartoon (*in a newspaper or magazine*); **~ publicitaire/de mode** advertisement/fashion drawing; (*hum*) **il n'a rien compris, fais lui donc un ~ !*** he hasn't understood a word — explain it in words of one syllable *ou* you'll have to spell it out for him → **carton** [b] (= *art*) drawing; **il est doué pour le ~** he has a gift for drawing; **école de ~** (*Art*) art school; (*technique*) technical college (for draughtsmen); **professeur de ~** art teacher; **~ technique** technical drawing; **~ de mode** fashion design; **~ industriel** draughtsmanship (*Brit*), draftsmanship (*US*); **table/planche à ~** drawing table/board; **~ assisté par ordinateur** computer-aided design [c] (= *motif*) pattern, design; **tissu avec des ~s jaunes** material with a yellow pattern on it; **le ~ des veines sur la peau** the pattern of the veins on the skin [d] (= *contour*) outline, line; **la bouche a un joli ~** the mouth has a good line *ou* is finely delineated

dessinateur, -trice [desinatœʀ, tʀis] NM,F (= *artiste*) drawer; (= *technicien*) draughtsman (*Brit*), draftsman (*US*); (= *technicienne*) draughtswoman (*Brit*), draftswoman (*US*); **~ humoristique** cartoonist; **~ de mode** fashion designer; **~ industriel** draughtsman (*Brit*), draftsman (*US*); **~ de publicité** commercial artist; **~-cartographe** cartographic designer, cartographer; **~ concepteur** designer

dessiner [desine] ▸conjug 1◂ 1 VT a (Art) to draw; **il dessine bien** he's good at drawing, he draws well; **~ qch à grands traits** to draw a broad outline of sth; **~ au pochoir** to stencil; **~ au crayon/à l'encre** to draw in pencil/ink b (= faire le plan, la maquette de) [+ véhicule, meuble] to design; [+ plan d'une maison] to draw; [+ jardin] to lay out, landscape; (fig) **une bouche/oreille bien dessinée** a finely delineated mouth/ear c [chose] to make, form; **les champs dessinent un damier** the fields form ou are laid out like a checkerboard ou (a) patchwork; **un vêtement qui dessine bien la taille** a garment that shows off the waist well 2 **se dessiner** VPR a [contour, forme] to stand out, be outlined; **des collines se dessinaient à l'horizon** hills stood out on the horizon b [tendance] to become apparent; [projet] to take shape; **on voit se ~ une tendance à l'autoritarisme** a tendency towards authoritarianism is becoming apparent ou is emerging; **un sourire se dessina sur ses lèvres** a smile played ou formed on his lips

dessouder [desude] ▸conjug 1◂ 1 VT a (Tech) to unsolder b (arg Crime = tuer) to bump off*, do in* 2 **se dessouder** VPR (Tech) to come unsoldered; **leur couple s'est dessoudé** they broke up

dessoûler* [desule] ▸conjug 1◂ VTI to sober up; **il n'a pas dessoûlé depuis 2 jours** he's been drunk for the past 2 days, he's been on a bender* for the past 2 days

dessous [d(ə)su] 1 ADV a (= sous) [placer, passer, suspendre] underneath; (= plus bas) below; **mettez votre valise ~** put your suitcase underneath (it) ou under it; **soulevez ces dossiers, la liste est ~** lift up those files — the list is underneath (them) ou under them ou beneath them; **passez (par) ~** go underneath (it) ou under it; **tu as mal lu, il y a une note ~** you misread it — there's a note underneath; **retirer qch de ~ le lit/la table** to get sth from under(neath) ou beneath the bed/table; **ils ont pris le buffet par (en) ~** they took hold of the sideboard from underneath b **au-~** below; **au-~ de** (lit) below, underneath; [+ possibilités, limite] below; (= indigne de) beneath; **ils habitent au-~** they live downstairs; **sa jupe lui descend au-~ du genou** her skirt comes down to below her knees ou reaches below her knees; **les enfants au-~ de 7 ans ne paient pas** children under 7 don't pay, the under-sevens don't pay; **20° au-~ (de zéro)** 20° below (zero); **des articles à 100 F et au-~** items at 100 francs and less ou below; **il considère que c'est au-~ de lui de faire la vaisselle** he considers it beneath him to do the dishes; (incapable) **il est au-~ de sa tâche** he's not up to the job; **il est au-~ de tout !** he's the absolute limit!, he's the end!; **le service est au-~ de tout** the service is hopeless ou a disgrace c **en ~** (= sous) underneath; (= plus bas) below; (= hypocritement) in an underhand ou underhanded (US) manner; **en ~ de** below; **il s'est glissé en ~** he slid underneath; **les locataires d'en ~** the people who rent the flat below ou downstairs; **jeter un coup d'œil en ~ à qn** ◊ **regarder qn en ~** to give sb a shifty look; **faire qch en ~** to do sth in an underhand ou underhanded (US) manner; **il est très en ~ de la moyenne** he's well below (the) average 2 NM a [objet] bottom, underside; [pied] sole; [avion, voiture, animal] underside; [tissu] wrong side; [tapis] back; **le ~ de la table est poussiéreux** the table is dusty underneath; **du ~** [feuille, drap] bottom; **les voisins du ~** the downstairs neighbours, the people below (us ou them etc), the people downstairs (from us ou them etc); **à l'étage du ~** on the floor be-

low; **les fruits du ~ sont moisis** the fruit at the bottom ou the fruit underneath is mouldy; **avoir le ~** to get the worst of it, come off worst b (= côté secret) **le ~ de l'affaire** ou **l'histoire** the hidden side of the affair; **les ~ de la politique** the unseen ou hidden side of politics; **connaître le ~ des cartes** to have inside information c (Habillement) undergarment; **les ~** underwear, undies* 3 COMP ▸ **dessous de caisse** (Aut) underbody ▸ **dessous de robe** slip, petticoat ▸ **dessous de verre** coaster

dessous-de-bouteille [d(ə)sud(ə)butɛj] NM INV bottle mat

dessous-de-bras [d(ə)sud(ə)bʀɑ] NM INV dress shield

dessous-de-plat [d(ə)sud(ə)pla] NM INV table mat (for hot serving dishes), hot pad (US)

dessous-de-table [d(ə)sud(ə)tabl] NM INV bribe, under-the-counter payment, backhander*

▼ **dessus** [d(ə)sy] 1 ADV a (= sur) [placer, poser, monter] on top (of it); [coller, écrire, fixer] on it; [passer, lancer] over it; (= plus haut) above; **mettez votre valise ~** put your suitcase on top (of it); **regardez ces dossiers, la liste doit être ~** have a look at those files — the list must be on top (of them); **il n'y a pas de timbre ~** there's no stamp on it; **c'est écrit ~** it's written on it; **montez ~** [+ tabouret, échelle] get up on it; **passez (par) ~** go over it; **il a sauté par ~** he jumped over it; **ôter qch de ~ la table** to take sth (from) off the table; **il n'a même pas levé la tête de ~ son livre** he didn't even look up from his book, he didn't even take his eyes off his book; **il lui a tapé/tiré ~** he hit him/shot at him; **il nous sont arrivés** ou **tombés ~ à l'improviste** they dropped in on us unexpectedly b **au-~** above; (= à l'étage supérieur) upstairs; (= posé sur) on top; (= plus cher) over, above; **au-~ de** (= plus haut que, plus au nord que) above; (= sur) on top of; [+ prix, limite] over, above; [+ possibilités] beyond; **la valise est au-~ de l'armoire** the suitcase is on top of the wardrobe; **les enfants au-~ de 7 ans paient** children over 7 pay, the over-sevens pay; **20° au-~ (de zéro)** 20° above (zero); **il n'y a pas d'articles au-~ de 100 F** there are no items over 100 francs; (prix) **c'est au-~ de ce que je peux mettre** it's beyond my means, it's more than I can afford; **cette tâche est au-~ de ses capacités** this task is beyond his capabilities; **c'est au-~ de mes forces** it's too much for me; **il ne voit rien au-~ de son fils** he thinks no one can hold a candle to his son; **il est au-~ de ces petites mesquineries** he's above this kind of pettiness; **être au-~ de tout soupçon/reproche** to be above suspicion/beyond reproach; **pour le confort, il n'y a rien au-~** there's nothing to beat it for comfort 2 NM a [objet, pied, tête] top; [tissu] right side; **du ~** [feuille, drap] top; **le ~ de la table est en marbre** the table-top ou the top of the table is marble; **les voisins du ~** the upstairs neighbours, the people above (us ou them etc) ou upstairs (from us ou them etc); **à l'étage du ~** on the floor above; **les fraises du ~ sont plus belles** the strawberries on top are nicer; **le ~ du panier** (= les meilleurs) the pick of the bunch; (= l'élite sociale) the upper crust; **elle portait deux pulls, celui du ~ était bleu** she was wearing two jumpers and the top one was blue b (loc) **avoir/prendre le ~** to have/get the upper hand; **reprendre le ~** to get over it; **il a été très malade/déprimé mais il a repris le ~ rapidement** he was very ill/depressed but he soon got over it 3 COMP ▸ **dessus de cheminée** (= ta-

blette) mantlepiece; (= bibelots) mantlepiece ornaments ▸ **dessus de table** table runner

dessus-de-lit [d(ə)syd(ə)li] NM INV bedspread

dessus-de-porte [d(ə)syd(ə)pɔʀt] NM INV overdoor

DEST [dɛaɛstə] NM (ABRÉV = **diplôme d'études supérieures techniques**) → **diplôme**

déstabilisant, e [destabilizɑ̃, ɑ̃t], **déstabilisateur, -trice** [destabilizatœʀ, tʀis] ADJ [influence, événement] destabilizing

déstabilisation [destabilizasjɔ̃] NF destabilization

déstabiliser [destabilize] ▸conjug 1◂ VT to destabilize

déstalinisation [destalinizasjɔ̃] NF destalinization

déstaliniser [destalinize] ▸conjug 1◂ VT to destalinize

destin [destɛ̃] NM (= fatalité, sort) fate; (= existence, avenir, vocation) destiny; **le ~ contraire** ill-fortune; **elle connut un ~ tragique** she met with a tragic end; **c'est le ~ !** it was meant to be!

destinataire [destinatɛʀ] NMF [lettre] addressee; [marchandise] consignee; [mandat] payee; (Ling) person addressed; **remettre une lettre à son ~** to hand a letter to the person it is addressed to

destinateur [destinatœʀ] NM (Ling) speaker

destination [destinasjɔ̃] NF a (= direction) destination; **à ~ de** [avion, train, bateau] to, bound for; [voyageur] travelling to; [lettre] sent to; **arriver à ~** to reach one's ou its destination, arrive (at one's ou its destination); **train/vol 702 à ~ de Paris** train number 702/flight (number) 702 to ou for Paris; **partir pour une ~ inconnue/lointaine** to leave for an unknown/a faraway destination b (= usage) [appareil, édifice, somme d'argent] purpose; **quelle ~ comptez-vous donner à cette somme/pièce ?** to what purpose do you intend to put this money/room?, what do you intend to use this money/room for?; **on a rendu à ce local sa ~ première** these premises have been restored to their original purpose

destiné, e[1] [destine] (ptp de **destiner**) ADJ a (= prévu pour) **~ à faire qch** intended ou meant to do sth; **ces mesures sont ~es à freiner l'inflation** these measures are intended ou meant to curb inflation; **cette pommade est ~e à guérir les brûlures** this ointment is intended for healing burns; **livre ~ aux enfants** book (intended ou meant) for children; **édifice ~ au culte** building intended for worship b (= voué à) **~ à qch** destined for sth; **~ à faire** destined to do; **il était ~ à une brillante carrière** he was destined for a brilliant career; **elle était ~e à mourir jeune** she was destined ou fated ou doomed to die young

destinée[2] [destine] NF (= fatalité, sort) fate; (= existence, avenir, vocation) destiny; **unir sa ~ à celle de qn** to unite one's destiny with sb's; **promis à de hautes ~s** destined for great things

destiner [destine] ▸conjug 1◂ VT a (= attribuer) **~ sa fortune à qn** to intend ou mean sb to have one's fortune, intend that sb should have one's fortune; **il vous destine ce poste** he intends ou means you to have this post; **~ une allusion à qn** to intend an allusion for sb; **~ un coup à qn** to aim a blow at sb; **nous destinons ce livre à tous ceux qui souffrent** this book is intended ou meant for all who are suffering, we have written this book with all those who are suffering in mind; **il ne put attraper le ballon qui lui était destiné** he couldn't catch the ball thrown to him; **sans deviner le sort qui lui était destiné** not knowing what fate had in store for him; **cette lettre t'était/ne t'était pas destinée** this letter was/was not (meant ou intended) for you

[b] (= *affecter*) ~ **une somme à l'achat de qch** to intend to use a sum to buy sth, earmark a sum for sth; ~ **un local à un usage précis** to intend a place to be used for a specific purpose, have a specific use in mind for a place; **les fonds seront destinés à la recherche** the money will be devoted to *ou* used for research
[c] (= *vouer*) to destine; ~ **qn à une fonction** to destine sb for a post; **sa famille la destinait à être médecin/à un vicomte** her family wanted her to be a doctor/wanted to marry her off to a viscount; **sa bravoure le destinait à mourir de mort violente** his boldness marked him out *ou* destined him to die a violent death; (*littér*) **je vous destine ma fille** I intend that my daughter should marry you; **il se destine à l'enseignement/à être ingénieur** he intends to go into teaching/to be an engineer, he has set his sights on teaching/being an engineer

destituer [dɛstitɥe] ▸conjug 1◂ VT (+ *ministre*) to dismiss; [+ *roi*] to depose; [+ *officier*] to discharge; ~ **un officier de son commandement** to relieve an officer of his command; ~ **qn de ses fonctions** to relieve sb of his duties

destitution [dɛstitysjɔ̃] NF [*ministre, fonctionnaire*] dismissal; [*officier*] discharge; [*roi*] deposition

déstockage [destɔkaʒ] NM destocking; (*dans une vitrine*) « ~ **massif** » "massive clearance sale"

déstocker [destɔke] ▸conjug 1◂ [1] VT [+ *produit, or*] to sell off; **vêtements déstockés** end-of-line garments [2] VI to reduce stocks, destock

destrier [dɛstrije] NM (*Hist*) charger

destroy* [dɛstrɔj] ADJ INV [*musique*] wild; **il avait une allure complètement ~** he looked wild and wasted

destroyer [dɛstrwaje] NM (*Naut*) destroyer

destructeur, -trice [dɛstryktœr, tris] [1] ADJ destructive; **produits ~s d'ozone** products that deplete *ou* destroy the ozone layer, ozone-depleting *ou* -destroying products [2] NM,F destroyer

destructible [dɛstryktibl] ADJ destructible

destructif, -ive [dɛstryktif, iv] ADJ destructive, destroying (*épith*)

destruction [dɛstryksjɔ̃] NF (*gén*) destruction (*NonC*); [*rats, insectes*] extermination (*NonC*); **les ~s causées par la guerre** the destruction caused by the war

déstructuration [destryktyrasjɔ̃] NF [*texte*] taking apart, deconstruction; (*Psych*) **pour empêcher la ~ de l'esprit** to prevent the mind from becoming destructured; **la ~ de la société** the breakdown of social structures

déstructurer [destryktyre] ▸conjug 1◂ [1] VT [+ *société, organisation*] to dismantle the structure of; [+ *texte*] to take apart, deconstruct; **veste déstructurée** unstructured jacket; ~ **l'emploi** to dismantle traditional job structures; **des gens déstructurés par le chômage** people who have been devastated by unemployment [2] **se déstructurer** VPR [*société*] to disintegrate, come apart at the seams; [*esprit, personnalité*] to become destructured

désuet, -ète [dezɥɛ, ɛt] ADJ (*gén*) outdated, antiquated, outmoded; [*charme*] old-fashioned, quaint; [*vêtement*] old-fashioned; [*mode*] outdated

désuétude [desɥetyd] NF disuse, obsolescence, desuetude (*littér*); **tomber en ~** [*loi*] to fall into abeyance; [*expression, coutume*] to become obsolete, fall into disuse

désuni, e [dezyni] (*ptp de* **désunir**) ADJ [*couple, famille*] divided, disunited; [*mouvements*] uncoordinated; [*coureur, cheval*] off his stride (*attrib*); (*Sport*) **l'équipe était un peu ~e** the team wasn't really working together

désunion [dezynjɔ̃] NF [*couple, parti*] disunity, dissension (**de** in)

désunir [dezynir] ▸conjug 2◂ [1] VT (+ *famille, couple*] to divide, disunite, break up; [+ *pierres, planches*] to separate [2] **se désunir** VPR [*athlète*] to lose one's stride; [*cheval*] to lose its stride; [*équipe*] to lose its coordination

désynchronisation [desɛ̃krɔnizasjɔ̃] NF de-synchronization

désynchroniser [desɛ̃krɔnize] ▸conjug 1◂ VT to de-synchronize

désyndicalisation [desɛ̃dikalizasjɔ̃] NF decrease in (trade) union membership

détachable [detaʃabl] ADJ detachable

détachage [detaʃaʒ] NM (= *nettoyage*) stain removal

détachant [detaʃɑ̃] [1] ADJ stain-removing (*épith*) [2] NM stain remover

détaché, e [detaʃe] (*ptp de* **détacher**) ADJ [a] (= *indifférent*) detached; **« peut-être », dit-il d'un ton ~** "maybe", he said with detachment; **elle prit un air ~** she assumed an indifferent air [b] (*Admin*) [*fonctionnaire*] on temporary assignment (**auprès de** to), on secondment (*Brit*) (**auprès de** to) [c] (*Mus*) detached → **pièce**

détachement [detaʃmɑ̃] NM [a] (= *indifférence*) detachment (**envers, à l'égard de** from); **regarder/dire qch avec ~** to look at/say sth with (an air of) detachment; **le ~ qu'il montrait pour les biens matériels** the disregard he showed for material goods [b] (*Mil*) detachment [c] [*fonctionnaire*] temporary assignment, secondment (*Brit*); **être en ~** to be on a temporary assignment *ou* on secondment; **en ~ à l'ambassade de France** on a temporary assignment at *ou* on secondment to the French embassy

détacher¹ [detaʃe] ▸conjug 1◂ [1] VT [a] (= *délier*) [+ *chien, cheval*] to untie, let loose; [+ *prisonnier*] to untie, unbind; [+ *paquet, objet*] to undo, untie; [+ *wagon, remorque*] to take off, detach; ~ **un wagon d'un convoi** to detach a carriage (*Brit*) *ou* car (*US*) from a train; **il détacha la barque/le prisonnier de l'arbre** he untied the boat/the prisoner from the tree [b] (= *dénouer*) [+ *vêtement, ceinture*] to undo, unfasten; [+ *lacet, nœud*] to undo, untie; [+ *chaussure, chaîne*] to unfasten, undo; **il détacha la corde du poteau** he untied *ou* removed the rope from the post [c] (= *ôter*) [+ *peau, écorce*] to remove (**de** from), take off; [+ *papier collé*] to remove, unstick (**de** from); [+ *rideau, tableau*] to take down (**de** from); [+ *épingle*] to take out (**de** of), remove; [+ *reçu, bon*] to tear out (**de** of), detach (**de** from); **l'humidité avait détaché le papier** the paper had come unstuck because of the damp; ~ **des feuilles d'un bloc** to tear *ou* take some sheets out of a pad, detach some sheets from a pad; ~ **un morceau de plâtre du mur** to remove a piece of plaster from the wall, take a piece of plaster from *ou* off the wall; **il détacha une pomme de l'arbre** he took an apple from the tree, he picked an apple off the tree; **détachez bien les bras du corps** keep your arms well away from your body; **il ne pouvait ~ son regard du spectacle** he could not take his eyes off the sight; (*sur un coupon*) **« partie à ~ »** "tear off (this section)"; **« ~ suivant le pointillé »** "tear off along the dotted line" [d] (= *envoyer*) [+ *personne*] to send, dispatch; (*Admin* = *affecter : à un ministère, une organisation*) to assign temporarily, second (*Brit*) (**à** to); **il a été détaché auprès du Premier ministre** he was temporarily assigned *ou* was seconded (*Brit*) to work with the Prime Minister [e] (= *mettre en relief*) [+ *lettres*] to separate; [+ *syllabes, mots*] to articulate, separate; (*Peinture*) [+ *silhouette, contour*] to bring out, make stand out; (*Mus*) [+ *notes*] to detach [f] (= *éloigner*) ~ **qn de qch/qn** to turn sb away from sth/sb; **son cynisme a détaché de lui**

tous ses amis his cynicism has turned his friends away from him
[2] **se détacher** VPR [a] (= *se délier*) [*chien*] to free itself, get loose (**de** from); [*prisonnier*] to free o.s., get loose; [*paquet*] to come undone *ou* untied; [*barque*] to come untied, loose itself (**de** from); [*wagon*] to come off, detach itself (**de** from); **la boule s'était détachée de l'arbre de Noël** the bobble had fallen off the Christmas tree [b] (= *se dénouer*) [*ceinture, chaussure*] to come undone *ou* unfastened; [*lacet, ficelle*] to come undone *ou* untied [c] (= *se séparer*) [*fruit, ficelle*] to come off; [*page*] to come loose, come out; [*peau, écorce*] to come off; [*papier collé*] to come unstuck, come off; [*épingle*] to come out, fall out; [*rideau*] to come down; **le papier s'était détaché à cause de l'humidité** the paper had come unstuck because of the damp; **un bloc de pierre se détacha du rocher** a block of stone broke away from *ou* detached itself from the rock; **l'écorce se détachait de l'arbre** the bark was coming off the tree *ou* was coming away from the tree; **la capsule spatiale s'est détachée de la fusée** the space capsule has separated from *ou* come away from the rocket [d] (*Sport*) [*coureur*] to pull *ou* break away (**de** from); **un petit groupe se détacha du reste des manifestants** a small group broke away from *ou* detached itself from the rest of the demonstrators [e] (= *ressortir*) to stand out; **la forêt se détache sur le ciel clair** the forest stands out against the clear sky [f] **se ~** (= *renoncer à*) to turn one's back on, renounce; (= *se désintéresser de*) to grow away from; **se ~ des plaisirs de la vie** to turn one's back on *ou* renounce the pleasures of life; **ils se sont détachés l'un de l'autre** they have grown apart

détacher² [detaʃe] ▸conjug 1◂ VT to remove the stains from, clean; **donner une robe à ~** to take a dress to be cleaned *ou* to the cleaner's; ~ **au savon/à la benzine** to clean with soap/benzine

détail [detaj] NM [a] (= *particularité*) detail; **dans les (moindres) ~s** in (minute) detail; **se perdre dans les ~s** to lose o.s. in details; **entrer dans les ~s** to go into detail(s) *ou* particulars; **je n'ai pas remarqué ce ~** I didn't notice that detail *ou* point; **c'est un ~ !** that's just a minor detail! → **revue**
[b] (= *description précise*) [*facture, compte*] breakdown; **examiner le ~ d'un compte** to examine a breakdown of *ou* the particulars of an account; **pourriez-vous nous faire le ~ de la facture/de ce que l'on vous doit** could you give us a breakdown of the invoice/of what we owe you?; **il nous a fait le ~ de ses aventures** he gave us a detailed account *ou* a run-down* of his adventures; **en ~ ◊ dans le ~** in detail; **il ne fait pas de** *ou* **le ~ !*** he doesn't make any exceptions!, he doesn't discriminate!
[c] (*Comm*) retail; **commerce/magasin/prix de ~** retail business/shop *ou* store/price; **vendre au ~** [+ *marchandise, vin*] to (sell) retail; [+ *articles, couverts*] to sell separately; **il fait le gros et le ~** he deals in wholesale and retail

détaillant, e [detajɑ̃, ɑ̃t] NM,F retailer, retail dealer

détaillé, e [detaje] (*ptp de* **détailler**) ADJ [*récit, plan, explications*] detailed; [*facture*] itemized

détailler [detaje] ▸conjug 1◂ VT [a] (*Comm*) [+ *articles*] to sell separately; [+ *marchandise*] to (sell) retail; **nous détaillons les services de table** we sell dinner services in separate pieces; **est-ce que vous détaillez cette pièce de tissu ?** do you sell lengths of this piece of material? [b] (= *passer en revue*) [+ *plan*] to detail, explain in detail; [+ *facture*] to itemize; [+ *récit*] to tell in detail; [+ *incidents, raisons*] to detail, give details of; **il m'a détaillé (de la tê-**

te aux pieds) he examined me *ou* looked me over (from head to foot)

détaler [detale] ▸ conjug 1 ◂ VI [*lapin*] to bolt; * [*personne*] to take off*, clear off*; **il a détalé comme un lapin** he bolted*, he skedaddled*

détartrage [detartraʒ] NM [*dents*] scaling; [*chaudière*] descaling; [*lave-vaisselle, WC*] removal of limescale from; **se faire faire un ~** to have one's teeth scaled (and polished)

détartrant [detartrɑ̃] 1 ADJ descaling 2 NM descaling agent

détartrer [detartre] ▸ conjug 1 ◂ VT [+ *dents*] to scale (and polish); [+ *chaudière*] to descale; [+ *lave-vaisselle, WC*] to remove limescale from

détaxation [detaksasjɔ̃] NF (= *réduction*) reduction in tax; (= *suppression*) removal of tax (**de** from)

détaxe [detaks] NF (= *réduction*) reduction in tax; (= *suppression*) removal of tax (**de** from); (= *remboursement*) tax refund; **~ à l'exportation** duty-free for export; **marchandises en ~** duty-free *ou* tax-free goods

détaxer [detakse] ▸ conjug 1 ◂ VT (= *réduire*) to reduce the tax on; (= *supprimer*) to remove the tax on, take the tax off; **produits détaxés** duty-free *ou* tax-free goods

détectable [detɛktabl] ADJ detectable, detectible

détecter [detɛkte] ▸ conjug 1 ◂ VT to detect

détecteur, -trice [detɛktœr, tris] 1 ADJ [*dispositif*] detecting (*épith*), detector (*épith*); [*lampe, organe*] detector (*épith*) 2 NM detector; **~ d'approche** intrusion-detection device; **~ de faux billets** forged banknote detector; **~ de fumée/de métaux** metal/smoke detector; **~ de mensonges** polygraph, lie detector; **~ de mines/particules** mine/particle detector

détection [detɛksjɔ̃] NF detection; **~ sous-marine/électromagnétique** underwater/electromagnetic detection

détective [detɛktiv] NM **~ (privé)** private detective *ou* investigator, private eye*

déteindre [detɛ̃dr] ▸ conjug 52 ◂ 1 VT [*personne, produit*] to take the colour out of; [*soleil*] to fade, take the colour out of 2 VI (*au lavage*) [*étoffe*] to run, lose its colour; [*couleur*] to run, come out; (*par l'humidité*) [*couleur*] to come off; (*au soleil*) [*étoffe*] to fade, lose its colour; [*couleur*] to fade; **~ sur** [*couleur*] to run into; (= *influencer*) [*trait de caractère*] to rub off on; **elle a déteint sur sa fille** something of her character rubbed off on her daughter; **le pantalon a déteint sur la chemise** some of the colour has come out of the trousers onto the shirt

dételer [det(ə)le] ▸ conjug 4 ◂ 1 VT [+ *bœufs*] to unyoke; [+ *chevaux*] to unharness; [+ *voiture*] to unhitch; [+ *wagon*] to uncouple, unhitch 2 VI* (= *arrêter de travailler*) to knock off*; **sans ~** [*travailler, faire qch*] without a break, non-stop

détendeur [detɑ̃dœr] NM [*bouteille de gaz, installation frigorifique*] regulator

détendre [detɑ̃dr] ▸ conjug 41 ◂ 1 VT [+ *ressort*] to release; [+ *corde*] to slacken, loosen; (*Phys*) [+ *gaz*] to release the pressure of; [+ *corps, esprit*] to relax; **~ ses jambes** to unbend one's legs; **je vais me ~ les jambes** I'm going to stretch my legs; **ces vacances m'ont détendu** this holiday has made me more relaxed; **pour ~ un peu ses nerfs** to calm *ou* soothe his nerves a little; **pour ~ la situation/les relations** to relieve *ou* ease the situation/the tension in relations; **il n'arrivait pas à ~ l'atmosphère** he couldn't ease the strained *ou* tense atmosphere; **~ le climat social** to defuse social unrest 2 **se détendre** VPR a [*ressort*] to lose its tension; [*corde*] to become slack, slacken; (*Phys*) [*gaz*] to be reduced in pressure b [*visage, esprit, corps*] to relax; [*nerfs*] to calm down; [*atmosphère*] become less tense; **aller à**

la campagne pour se **~** to go to the country to relax *ou* to unwind; **détendez-vous !** relax!; **la situation internationale s'est détendue** the international situation has grown less tense *ou* has relaxed; **pour que leurs rapports se détendent** to make their relations less strained, to ease the tension in their relations

détendu, e [detɑ̃dy] (*ptp de* **détendre**) ADJ [*personne, visage, atmosphère*] relaxed; [*câble*] slack; [*ressort*] unextended

détenir [det(ə)nir] ▸ conjug 22 ◂ VT a [+ *record, grade, titres*] to hold; [+ *secret, objets volés*] to hold, be in possession of, have in one's possession; [+ *moyen*] to have (in one's possession); **~ le pouvoir** to be in power, have *ou* hold the power; **il détient la clé de l'énigme** he holds the key to the enigma; **il détient 25% du capital de l'entreprise** he holds 25% of the company's capital b [+ *prisonnier*] to detain; [+ *otage*] to hold; **il a été détenu dans un camp** he was held prisoner in a camp

détente [detɑ̃t] NF a (= *délassement*) relaxation; **avoir besoin de ~** to need to relax *ou* unwind; **ce voyage a été une (bonne) ~** this trip has been (very) relaxing b (= *décrispation*) [*relations*] easing (**dans** of); (*Pol*) **la ~** détente c (= *élan*) [*sauteur*] spring; [*lanceur*] thrust; **ce sauteur a de la ~** *ou* **une bonne ~** this jumper has plenty of spring *ou* a powerful spring; **d'une ~ rapide, il bondit sur sa victime** with a swift bound he leaped upon his victim d (= *relâchement*) [*ressort, arc*] release; [*corde*] slackening, loosening e (*lit, fig* = *gâchette*) trigger → **dur** f (*Tech*) [*pendule*] catch; [*gaz*] reduction in pressure; [*moteur à explosion*] expansion

détenteur, -trice [detɑ̃tœr, tris] NM,F [*secret*] holder, keeper; [*record, titres, objet volé*] holder

détention [detɑ̃sjɔ̃] NF a (= *possession*) [*armes, drogue, faux passeport*] possession; [*titres*] holding; (*Jur*) [*bien*] holding b (= *captivité*) detention; (*Jur*) **en ~ préventive** *ou* **provisoire** remanded in custody, on remand; **mettre** *ou* **placer qn en ~ préventive** to remand in custody, put on remand

détenu, e [det(ə)ny] (*ptp de* **détenir**) NM,F prisoner; **~ politique/de droit commun** political/ordinary prisoner

détergent, e [detɛrʒɑ̃, ɑ̃t] ADJ, NM detergent

détérioration [deterjɔrasjɔ̃] NF [*objet*] damaging (**de** of), damage (**de** to); [*matériel, bâtiment, santé, temps*] deterioration (**de** in); [*relations, situation*] deterioration (**de** in), worsening (**de** in); **la ~ irréversible des muscles** the progressive wasting of the muscles; **la ~ du niveau de vie** the deterioration *ou* decline in living standards; **la ~ du climat économique** the deterioration in the economic climate

détériorer [deterjɔre] ▸ conjug 1 ◂ 1 VT [+ *objet*] to damage, spoil; [+ *santé, bâtiment, relations*] to damage 2 **se détériorer** VPR [*matériel, bâtiment, santé, temps*] to deteriorate; [*relations, situation, climat économique*] to deteriorate, worsen

déterminable [detɛrminabl] ADJ determinable

déterminant, e [detɛrminɑ̃, ɑ̃t] 1 ADJ (= *décisif*) determining (*épith*), deciding (*épith*); **ça a été ~** that was the deciding *ou* determining factor (**dans** in) 2 NM (*Ling*) determiner; (*Math, Bio*) determinant

déterminatif, -ive [detɛrminatif, iv] 1 ADJ determinative; [*proposition*] defining (*épith*) 2 NM determiner, determinative

détermination [detɛrminasjɔ̃] NF a [*cause, sens*] determining, establishing; [*date, quantité*] determining, fixing b (= *résolution*) decision, resolution c (= *fermeté*) determination; **il le regarda avec ~** he looked at him determinedly *ou* with (an air of) determination d (*Philo*) determination

▾ **déterminé, e** [detɛrmine] (*ptp de* **déterminer**) 1 ADJ a [*personne, air*] determined, resolute b (= *précis*) [*but, intentions*] specific, definite; (= *spécifique*) [*quantité, distance, date*] determined, given (*épith*) c (*Philo*) [*phénomènes*] predetermined 2 NM (*Gram*) determinatum

déterminer [detɛrmine] ▸ conjug 1 ◂ VT a (= *préciser*) [+ *cause, distance, sens d'un mot*] to determine, establish; [+ *date, lieu, quantité*] to determine, fix; **~ par des calculs où une météorite va tomber** to calculate *ou* work out where a meteorite will fall b (= *décider*) to decide, determine; **~ qn à faire qch** to decide *ou* determine sb to do sth; **ils se sont déterminés à agir** they have made up their minds *ou* resolved to act c (= *motiver*) [+ *chose*] to determine; **c'est ce qui a déterminé mon choix** that's what decided me; **ceci a déterminé d'importants retards** this brought about *ou* caused long delays d (*Gram*) to determine

déterminisme [detɛrminism] NM determinism

déterministe [detɛrminist] 1 ADJ determinist(ic) 2 NMF determinist

déterré, e [detɛre] (*ptp de* **déterrer**) NM,F (*péj*) **avoir une tête** *ou* **une mine de ~** to look deathly pale *ou* like death warmed up* (*Brit*) *ou* warmed over* (*US*)

déterrer [detɛre] ▸ conjug 1 ◂ VT [+ *objet enfoui*] to dig up, unearth; [+ *arbre*] to uproot, dig up; [+ *mort*] to dig up, disinter; * [+ *vieil objet, bouquin*] to dig out*, unearth

détersif, -ive [detɛrsif, iv] ADJ, NM detergent, detersive

détersion [detɛrsjɔ̃] NF cleaning

détestable [detɛstabl] ADJ [*personne*] detestable; [*attitude*] appalling, dreadful; [*habitude, caractère*] foul; **leur image de marque est ~** their public image is appalling; **cela a fait une impression ~** it made a dreadful impression

détestablement [detɛstabləmɑ̃] ADV [*jouer, chanter*] appallingly *ou* dreadfully badly

détestation [detɛstasjɔ̃] NF (*littér* = *haine*) abhorrence; **avoir de la ~ pour qn/qch** to abhor sb/sth

▾ **détester** [detɛste] ▸ conjug 1 ◂ VT to hate, detest; **il déteste la peinture/les enfants/le fromage** he hates *ou* detests painting/children/cheese; **elle déteste attendre** she hates *ou* detests *ou* can't bear having to wait; **il déteste qu'on range son bureau/qu'on l'appelle Michou** he hates other people tidying his desk/being called Michou; **il ne déteste pas le chocolat** he is not averse to chocolate; **il ne déteste pas (de) faire parler de lui** he's not averse to having people talk about him

déthéiné, e [deteine] ADJ decaffeinated

détonant, e [detɔnɑ̃, ɑ̃t] ADJ **cocktail** *ou* **mélange ~** (*lit, fig*) explosive mixture

détonateur [detɔnatœr] NM (*Tech*) detonator; (*fig*) **être le ~ de** to trigger off

détonation [detɔnasjɔ̃] NF [*bombe, obus*] detonation, explosion; [*fusil*] report, bang

détoner [detɔne] ▸ conjug 1 ◂ VI to detonate, explode

détonner [detɔne] ▸ conjug 1 ◂ VI a [*couleurs*] to clash (with each other); [*meuble, bâtiment, personne*] to be out of place; **ses manières vulgaires détonnent dans ce milieu raffiné** his vulgar manners are out of place in this refined milieu b (*Mus*) (= *sortir du ton*) to go out of tune; (= *chanter faux*) to sing out of tune

détordre [detɔrdr] ▸ conjug 41 ◂ VT to untwist; **le câble s'est détordu** the cable came untwisted

détortiller [detɔrtije] ▸ conjug 1 ◂ VT to untwist

détour [detur] NM a (= *sinuosité*) bend, curve; **la rivière fait des ~s** the river meanders; **ce sentier est plein de ~s** this path is

➤ GRAMMAIRE ACTIVE: **déterminé** 35.2   **détester** 34.3

full of twists and turns, it's a very winding path; **au ~ du chemin** at the bend in the path; **on devine au ~ d'une phrase ...** you begin to guess as you are reading ... [b] (= *déviation*) detour; **au ~ de la conversation** in the course of the conversation; **faire un ~** to make a detour (*par* via); **le musée valait le ~** the museum was worth the detour *ou* was worth seeing → **tour²** [c] (= *moyen indirect*) roundabout means; (= *circonlocution*) circumlocution; **explique-toi sans ~(s)** just say straight out what you mean; **user de longs ~s** *ou* **prendre beaucoup de ~s pour demander qch** to ask for sth in a very roundabout way; **il ne s'embarrasse pas de ~s pour arriver à ses fins** he doesn't shilly-shally when it comes to getting what he wants

détourné, e [deturne] (*ptp de* **détourner**) ADJ [*chemin*] roundabout (*épith*); [*moyen*] roundabout (*épith*), indirect; [*reproche*] indirect, oblique; **je l'ai appris de façon ~e** I heard it in a roundabout way *ou* indirectly

détournement [deturnəmã] NM [*rivière*] diversion, rerouting; **~ d'avion** hijacking, skyjacking*; **~ de fonds** embezzlement, misappropriation of funds; **~ de mineur** corruption of a minor; **~ de pouvoir** abuse of power

détourner [deturne] ▸conjug 1◂ [1] VT [a] (= *dévier*) [+ *route, ruisseau, circulation, convoi*] to divert, reroute; [+ *bus*] [*pirate*] to hijack; [+ *avion*] [*pirate de l'air*] to hijack, skyjack*; [+ *soupçon*] to divert (*sur* on to); [+ *coup*] to parry, ward off; (*Sport*) [+ *ballon, tir au but*] to deflect; **~ l'attention de qn** to divert *ou* distract sb's attention; **~ la conversation** to change the subject; **pour ~ leur colère** to ward off *ou* avert their anger [b] (= *tourner d'un autre côté*) to turn away; **~ les yeux** *ou* **le regard** to look away, avert one's gaze; **~ la tête** to turn one's head away [c] (= *écarter*) to divert; **~ qn de sa route** *ou* **de son chemin** to divert sb, take sb out of his way; (*à un conducteur*) **si ça ne te détourne pas (de ton chemin) ...** if it's not out of your way ...; **~ qn d'un projet/de faire qch** to dissuade sb from a plan/from doing sth, put sb off a plan/off doing sth; **~ qn de qn** to put sb off sb, turn sb away from sb; **~ qn du droit chemin** to lead sb astray, lead sb off the straight and narrow; **~ qn de son devoir** to lead sb away *ou* divert sb from his duty; **pour le ~ de ses soucis** to divert him from his worries, to take his mind off his worries [d] (= *modifier l'objectif de*) [+ *loi, réglementation*] to twist; **elle a détourné le sens de mes paroles** she twisted my words; **il a su ~ le système à son profit** he managed to work the system to his advantage; **~ un médicament de son usage normal** to use a drug for something it wasn't meant for [e] (= *voler*) [+ *fonds*] to embezzle, misappropriate; [+ *marchandises*] to misappropriate

[2] **se détourner** VPR to turn away (**de** from); **se ~ de sa route** (*pour aller ailleurs*) to make a detour *ou* diversion; (*par erreur*) to go off the right road; **il s'est détourné de tous ses amis** he has turned away *ou* aside from all his friends; **le public s'est détourné de ce produit** the public have turned their backs on *ou* spurned this product

détracteur, -trice [detraktœr, tris] [1] ADJ disparaging [2] NM,F detractor

détraqué, e [detrake] (*ptp de* **détraquer**) ADJ [*machine*] broken down; * [*personne*] unhinged, cracked*; [*temps*] unsettled; [*nerfs, santé*] shaky; [*imagination*] unbalanced; **cette horloge est ~e** this clock is on the blink* *ou* is bust*; **il a l'estomac ~** he's got an upset stomach; **avoir le cerveau ~*** to be unhinged *ou* cracked*, have a screw loose*; **c'est un ~*** he's a headcase*, he's off his head*; **c'est un ~ sexuel** he's a pervert

détraquement [detrakmã] NM [*machine*] breakdown; [*santé, nerfs*] shakiness; [*économie*] shakiness, instability; **à cause du ~ du temps** because of the unsettled weather

détraquer [detrake] ▸conjug 1◂ [1] VT [+ *machine*] to put out of order; [+ *personne*] (*physiquement*) to put out of sorts; [+ *estomac*] to upset; [+ *nerfs*]* to shake up, upset; **ces orages ont détraqué le temps** these storms have unsettled the weather; **ce drame lui a détraqué le cerveau*** *ou* **l'a détraqué*** this tragedy unhinged him *ou* sent him out of his mind* [2] **se détraquer** VPR [*machine*] to go wrong, break down; [*estomac*] to be upset; [*économie*] to become unstable; **le temps se détraque*** the weather is becoming unsettled; **tout, dans sa vie, s'est soudain détraqué** suddenly everything started going wrong for him

détrempe¹ [detrãp] NF (*Peinture*) (= *substance*) (*gén*) distemper; (*à base d'œuf*) tempera; (= *tableau*) distemper *ou* tempera painting; **peindre en** *ou* **à la ~** to paint in tempera *ou* distemper

détrempe² [detrãp] NF (*Tech*) [*acier*] softening

détremper¹ [detrãpe] ▸conjug 1◂ VT (= *délayer*) [+ *terre, pain*] to soak; [+ *couleurs*] to dilute, water down; [+ *chaux*] to mix with water, slake; [+ *mortier*] to mix with water, temper; **chemins détrempés** sodden *ou* waterlogged paths; **ma chemise est détrempée** my shirt is soaking (wet) *ou* soaked

détremper² [detrãpe] ▸conjug 1◂ VT (*Tech*) [+ *acier*] to soften

détresse [detrɛs] NF [a] (= *sentiment*) distress; **son cœur en ~** his anguished heart [b] (= *situation*) distress; **être dans la ~** to be in distress; **bateau/avion en ~** boat/plane in distress; **entreprise en ~** business in dire straits; **envoyer un appel/un signal de ~** to send out a distress call/signal → **feu¹**

détriment [detrimã] ✦**au détriment de** LOC PRÉP to the detriment of

détritique [detritik] ADJ [*roche*] detrital

détritivore [detritivɔr] ADJ [*bactérie, insecte*] detritivorous

détritus [detrity(s)] NMPL litter (*NonC*), rubbish (*NonC*) (*Brit*); (*Méd*) detritus (*NonC*)

détroit [detrwa] NM (*Géog*) strait; **le ~ de Gibraltar/du Bosphore** the Strait of Gibraltar/of the Bosphorus; **le ~ de Magellan** the Magellan Strait

détromper [detrãpe] ▸conjug 1◂ [1] VT [+ *personne*] to disabuse (**de** of); **je croyais cette histoire mais son frère m'a détrompé** I believed that story but his brother put me right [2] **se détromper** VPR **détrompez-vous, il n'est pas venu** you're quite mistaken, he didn't come; **si tu crois que je vais accepter, détrompe-toi !** if you think I'm going to accept, you've got another think coming* *ou* you'll have to think again!

détrôner [detrone] ▸conjug 1◂ VT [+ *souverain*] to dethrone, depose; (= *supplanter*) [+ *champion*] to oust, dethrone; [+ *mode, produit*] to supplant

détrousser [detruse] ▸conjug 1◂ VT († *ou hum*) **~ qn** to relieve sb of his money (*ou* luggage *etc*) (*hum*), rob sb

détrousseur [detrusœr] NM († *ou hum*) bandit, footpad† (*Brit*)

détruire [detryir] ▸conjug 38◂ VT [a] (= *ravager*) to destroy; **un incendie a détruit l'hôtel** the hotel was burnt (*Brit*) *ou* burned (*US*) down, the hotel was destroyed by fire; **la ville a été complètement détruite** the town was wiped out *ou* razed to the ground *ou* completely destroyed; **cet enfant détruit tout** this child wrecks *ou* ruins everything *ou* smashes everything up; **la tempête a détruit les récoltes** the storm has ruined the crops [b] (= *tuer*) [+ *armée*] to wipe out; [+ *animaux, in-*

sectes] to destroy, exterminate; **il a essayé de se ~** he tried to do away with himself [c] (= *ruiner*) [+ *empire*] to destroy; [+ *santé, réputation*] to ruin, wreck; [+ *sentiment*] to destroy, kill; [+ *espoir, théorie, projet*] to ruin, wreck, put paid to (*Brit*); **les effets se détruisent** the effects cancel each other out; **cela détruit tous ses beaux arguments** that destroys *ou* puts paid to (*Brit*) all his fine arguments

dette [dɛt] NF [a] (*Fin*) debt; **avoir des ~s** to be in debt, have debts; **faire des ~s** to get into debt, run up debts; **avoir 10 000 F de ~s** to be 10,000 francs in debt, be in debt to the tune of 10,000 francs; **~ de jeu** *ou* **d'honneur** a gambling *ou* gaming debt is a debt of honour; **la ~ publique** *ou* **de l'État/extérieure** the national/foreign debt [b] (*morale*) debt; **~ d'amitié/de reconnaissance** debt of friendship/gratitude; **je suis en ~ envers vous** I am indebted to you; **il a payé sa ~ envers la société** he has paid his debt to society; **j'ai une ~ de reconnaissance envers vous** I am eternally grateful to you

DEUG [døg] NM (ABRÉV = **diplôme d'études universitaires générales**) → **diplôme**

DEUG, DEUST

French students sit their **DEUG** *or their* **DEUST** *after two years of university study. Students can leave university after the* **DEUG** *or* **DEUST***, which may be awarded with distinction, or proceed to the "licence". The certificate obtained specifies the principle subject area studied.* → [DIPLÔMES]

---

deuil [dœj] NM [a] (= *perte*) bereavement; **il a eu un ~ récemment** he was recently bereaved, he recently suffered a bereavement (*frm*), there has been a death in his family [b] (= *affliction*) mourning (*NonC*), grief; **cela nous a plongés dans le ~** it has plunged us into mourning *ou* grief; **si nous pouvons vous réconforter dans votre ~** if we can comfort you in your grief *ou* sorrow; **décréter un ~ national de trois jours** to declare three days of national mourning [c] (= *vêtements*) mourning (clothes); **en grand ~** in deep mourning; **être/se mettre en ~** to be in/go into mourning; **quitter le ~** to come out of mourning; **prendre/porter le ~ d'un ami** to go into/be in mourning for a friend; **porter le ~ de ses espoirs/illusions** to grieve for one's lost hopes/illusions; (*littér*) **la nature/la forêt est en ~** nature/the forest is in mourning [d] (= *durée*) mourning; **le ~ du président dura un mois** the mourning for the president lasted a month [e] (= *cortège*) funeral procession; **conduire** *ou* **mener le ~** to head the funeral procession, be (the) chief mourner [f] * **faire son ~ de qch** to kiss sth goodbye*, say goodbye to sth*; **les vacances sont annulées, j'en ai fait mon ~** the holidays have been cancelled but I'm resigned to it *ou* it's no use crying about it

deus ex machina [deusɛksmakina] NM deus ex machina

deusio* [døzjo] ADV = **deuzio**

DEUST [døst] NM (ABRÉV = **diplôme d'études universitaires scientifiques et techniques**) → **diplôme**

deutérium [døterjɔm] NM deuterium

Deutéronome [døteronɔm] NM Deuteronomy

deux [dø] [1] ADJ INV [a] (= *nombre*) two; **les ~ yeux/mains** etc both eyes/hands *etc*; **ses ~ jambes** both his legs, his two legs; **montrez-moi les ~** show me both (of them) *ou* the two of them; **~ fois** twice; **il ne peut être en ~ endroits/aux ~ endroits à la fois** he can't be in two places/in both places at once; **je les ai vus tous (les) ~** I saw them both, I saw both of them, I saw the two of them; **inflation à ~ chiffres** double-figure *ou* two-figure inflation; **des ~ côtés de la rue** on both sides *ou* on either side of the street; **tous les ~ jours/mois** every other *ou* every second day/month, every two days/months; **habiter** *ou* **vivre à ~** to live together as a couple; **~ t/l** (*gén*) two t's/l's; (*en épelant*) double t/l

[b] (= *quelques*) a couple, a few; **c'est à ~ pas/à ~ minutes d'ici** it's only a short distance/just a few minutes from here, it's only a stone's throw/only a couple of minutes from here; **pouvez-vous attendre ~ (ou trois) minutes ?** could you wait two (or three) minutes? *ou* a couple of minutes?; **vous y serez en ~ secondes** you'll be there in no time (at all); **j'ai ~ mots à vous dire** I want to have a word with you

[c] (= *deuxième*) second; **volume/acte ~** volume/act two; **le ~ janvier** the second of January; **Jacques II** James the Second; *pour autres locutions voir* **six**

[d] (*Mus*) **mesure à ~~/à ~-quatre/à ~-huit** two-two/two-four/two-eight time

[e] (*loc*) **essayer et réussir, cela fait ~** to try is one thing but to succeed is another thing altogether, to try and to succeed are two (entirely) different things; **pris entre ~ feux** caught in the crossfire; **lui et les maths, ça fait ~ !** he hasn't got a clue about maths; **lui et la tendresse, ça fait ~ !** he doesn't know the meaning of tenderness; **faire** *ou* **avoir ~ poids ~ mesures** to have double standards *ou* two sets of rules; **être assis** *ou* **avoir le cul** entre ~ **chaises** to be caught between two stools ■(*PROV*) **~ précautions valent mieux qu'une** better safe than sorry (*PROV*); **~ avis valent mieux qu'un** two heads are better than one (*PROV*); **en ~ temps, trois mouvements il l'a réparé** he repaired it in no time *ou* before you could say Jack Robinson* (*hum*); **il ne reste pas les ~ pieds dans le même sabot** he doesn't just sit back and wait for things to happen

[2] NM INV (= *chiffre*) two; (*Cartes, Dés*) **le ~** the two, the deuce; **couper en ~** to cut in two *ou* in half; **marcher ~ par ~** *ou* **à ~** to walk two by two *ou* in pairs *ou* two abreast; **à nous ~** (= *parlons sérieusement*) let's talk; (= *je m'occupe de vous*) I'm all yours; (*à un ennemi*) now let's fight it out!; (*à un appareil à réparer*) now let's see what we can do with you, now let's get you fixed; **quand il y en a pour ~, il y en a pour trois** there's always enough to go around; **il cuisine comme pas ~*** he's a hell of a cook*; **elle est rapide comme pas ~*** she's damn quick*; **quel bricoleur/gardien de but de mes ~ !** what a crap* *ou* lousy* handyman/goalie!; *pour autres locutions voir* **six** *et* **moins, pas**

deuxième [døzjɛm] [1] ADJ, NMF second; *pour locutions voir* **sixième** [2] COMP ▶ **le Deuxième Bureau** (*Admin*) the intelligence branch *ou* service

▼ **deuxièmement** [døzjɛmmɑ̃] ADV second(ly)

deux-mâts [døma] NM INV (*Naut*) two-master

deux-pièces [døpjɛs] NM INV [a] (= *ensemble*) two-piece suit; (= *maillot*) two-piece (swimsuit) [b] (= *appartement*) two-room flat (*Brit*) *ou* apartment (*US*); « **à louer : ~ cuisine** » "for rent: two-room flat with separate kitchen"

deux-points [døpwɛ̃] NM INV colon

deux-ponts [døpɔ̃] ADJ, NM INV (*Naut*) two-decker; (*Aviat*) double-decker

deux-roues [døʀu] NM INV two-wheeled vehicle; ▶ **motorisé** motorcycle

deux-temps [døtɑ̃] [1] ADJ INV (*Aut*) two-stroke [2] NM INV (= *moteur*) two-stroke (engine); (*Mus*) half-common time

deuzio* [døzjo] ADV secondly

dévaler [devale] ▶conjug 1◀ [1] VT (*en courant*) to tear down, hurtle down; (*en tombant*) to tumble down; **il a dévalé les escaliers quatre à**

quatre he tore *ou* hurtled down the stairs four at a time, he came tearing *ou* hurtling down the stairs four at a time [2] VI [*rochers*] to hurtle down; [*lave*] to rush down, gush down; [*terrain*] to fall away sharply; **il a dévalé dans les escaliers et s'est cassé le bras** he tumbled down the stairs and broke his arm

dévaliser [devalize] ▶conjug 1◀ VT [+ *maison*] to burgle, burglarize (*US*); [+ *banque*] to rob; **~ qn** to strip sb of what he has on him; **~ un magasin** [*voleurs*] to burgle *ou* burglarize (*US*) a shop; [*clients*] to buy up a shop; **~ le réfrigérateur** to raid the fridge

dévalorisant, e [devalɔʀizɑ̃, ɑ̃t] ADJ [*emploi, tâche*] demeaning; **cette expérience a été très ~e pour lui** this experience was very damaging to his sense of self-worth

dévalorisation [devalɔʀizasjɔ̃] NF depreciation

dévaloriser [devalɔʀize] ▶conjug 1◀ [1] VT [+ *marchandises, collection*] to reduce the value of; [+ *monnaie, diplôme*] to undermine the value of; **son patron le dévalorise sans cesse** his boss is forever running *ou* putting him down; **ce type de publicité dévalorise les femmes** this type of advertising degrades women; **cette situation le dévalorise aux yeux de sa famille** this situation undermines his standing *ou* status in the eyes of his family [2] **se dévaloriser** VPR [*monnaie, marchandise*] to fall in value, depreciate; [*personne*] to run o.s. down; **ce métier s'est dévalorisé** this profession has lost its prestige

dévaluation [devalɥasjɔ̃] NF devaluation

dévaluer [devalɥe] ▶conjug 1◀ [1] VT [+ *monnaie, métier, diplôme*] to devalue, devaluate (*US*); [+ *rôle, statut*] to undermine [2] **se dévaluer** VPR [*monnaie*] to devalue, be devalued, fall in value

devancement [d(ə)vɑ̃smɑ̃] NM ▶ **d'une échéance** payment in advance *ou* before time; (*Mil*) ~ **d'appel** enlistment before call-up

devancer [d(ə)vɑ̃se] ▶conjug 3◀ VT [a] (= *distancer*) [+ *coureur*] to get ahead of, get in front of; [+ *concurrent, rival*] to get ahead of, forestall; **il m'a devancé de 3 minutes/de 3 points** he beat me by 3 minutes/3 points, he was 3 minutes/3 points ahead of me [b] (= *précéder*) to arrive before, arrive ahead of; **il m'a devancé au carrefour** he got to the crossroads before me; **~ son siècle** to be ahead of *ou* in advance of one's time [c] (= *aller au devant de*) [+ *question, objection, désir*] to anticipate; **j'allais le faire mais il m'a devancé** I was going to do it but he did it first *ou* got there first [d] (= *faire qch en avance*) (*Mil*) **~ l'appel** to enlist before call-up; (*Fin*) **~ la date d'un paiement** to make a payment before it is due

devancier, -ière [d(ə)vɑ̃sje, jɛʀ] NM,F predecessor

devant [d(ə)vɑ̃] [1] PRÉP [a] (*position = en face de*) in front of, before (*littér*); (*mouvement = le long de*) past; **ma voiture est ~ la porte** my car is (just) outside *ou* at the door; **~ nous se dressait un vieux chêne** before us *ou* in front of us stood an old oak tree; **le bateau est ancré ~ le port** the boat is anchored outside the port; **il est passé ~ moi sans me voir** he walked past me *ou* he passed me *ou* he went right by me without seeing me; **elle était assise ~ la fenêtre** she was sitting at *ou* by the window; **il est passé** *ou* **a filé ~ nous comme une flèche** he shot past us (like an arrow), he flashed past us; **va-t-en de ~ la vitrine** move away from (in front of) the window; **va-t-en de ~ la lumière** get out of the *ou* my light

[b] (= *en avant de*) (*proximité*) in front of; (*distance*) ahead of; **il marchait ~ moi** he was walking in front of *ou* ahead of me; **il est loin ~ nous** he is a long way ahead of us; **regarde ~ toi** look in front of you *ou* straight ahead (of you); **il est ~ moi en classe** (*banc*) he sits

in front of me at school; (*résultats*) he is ahead of me at *ou* in school; **fuir ~ qn** to flee before *ou* from sb; **(droit) ~ nous se dressait la muraille** the wall rose up (straight) in front of *ou* ahead of us; **allez droit ~ vous, vous trouverez le village** go straight on *ou* ahead and you'll come to the village; (*fig*) **aller droit ~ soi** (*sans s'occuper des autres*) to go straight on (regardless of others); **passe ~ moi si tu es pressé** you go first *ou* in front of me if you're in a hurry; **elle est passée ~ moi chez le boucher** she pushed (in) in front of me at the butcher's; **avoir du temps/de l'argent ~ soi** to have time/money to spare; **il avait du temps ~ lui** he had time to spare, he had time on his hands; **il a toute la vie ~ lui** he has his whole life ahead of him

[c] (= *en présence de*) before, in front of; **s'incliner ~ qn** to bow before sb; **comparaître ~ ses juges** to appear before one's judges; **ne dis pas cela ~ les enfants/tout le monde** don't say that in front of the children/everyone; **cela s'est passé juste ~ nous** *ou* **nos yeux** it happened before *ou* in front of our very eyes; **imperturbable ~ le malheur d'autrui** unmoved by *ou* in the face of other people's misfortune; **reculer ~ ses responsabilités** to shrink from one's responsibilities; (*Jur*) **par-~ notaire/Maître Durand** in the presence of a notary/Maître Durand

[d] (= *face à*) faced with, in the face of; (= *étant donné*) in view of, considering; **~ la gravité de la situation** in view of *ou* considering the gravity of the situation; **rester ferme ~ le danger** to stand fast in the face of danger; **il ne sut quelle attitude prendre ~ ces faits** he did not know what line to adopt when faced *ou* confronted with these facts; **tous égaux ~ la loi** everyone (is) equal in the eyes of the law

[2] ADV [a] (*position*) in front; **vous êtes juste ~** you're right in front of it; **vous êtes passé ~** you came past *ou* by it; **je suis garé juste ~** I'm parked just out at the front *ou* just outside; **en passant ~, regarde si la boutique est ouverte** see if the shop is open as you go past; **corsage qui se boutonne (par-)devant** blouse which buttons up *ou* does up at the front; **tu as mis ton pull ~ derrière** you've put your sweater on back-to-front (*Brit*) *ou* backwards (*US*); **entre par-~, le jardin est fermé** go in the front, the garden gate is locked

[b] (= *en avant*) ahead, in front; **il est parti ~** he went on ahead *ou* in advance; **il est loin ~** he's a long way ahead; (*Naut*) **attention, obstacle (droit) ~ !** stand by, hazard ahead!; **il est assis 3 rangs ~** he's sitting 3 rows in front (of us); **fais passer le plateau ~** pass the tray forward; **il a pris des places ~** he has got front seats *ou* seats at the front *ou* up front*; (*Aut*) **il a préféré monter ~** he preferred to sit in (the) front; **marchez ~, les enfants** walk in front, children; **passe ~, je te rejoindrai** go on ahead and I'll catch up with you; **passe ~, il roule trop lentement** go past him *ou* overtake him (*Brit*), he's going too slowly; **passez ~, je ne suis pas pressé** after you *ou* you go first *ou* you go in front of me, I'm in no hurry

[3] NM [a] [*maison, voiture, objet*] front; [*bateau*] fore, bow(s); **habiter sur le ~** to live at the front (of the house *etc*); **de ~** [*roue, porte*] front → **patte, point²**

[b] **je l'ai vu de loin et je suis allé au-~ de lui** I saw him in the distance and went (out) to meet him; **aller au-~ des désirs de qn** to anticipate sb's wishes; **courir au-~ du danger** to court danger; **aller au-~ des ennuis** *ou* **difficultés** to be asking for trouble; **nous avons bien assez de problèmes sans aller au-~** we've got enough problems as it is without asking for more

[4] **devants** NMPL **voyant qu'il hésitait, j'ai pris les ~s pour lui parler** as he was hesitating I made the first move *ou* took the initiative

and spoke to him; **nous étions plusieurs sur cette affaire, j'ai dû prendre les ~s en offrant un contrat plus intéressant** there were several of us after the job so I had to pre-empt *ou* forestall the others and offer a more competitive contract; *(Mil)* **prendre les ~s en attaquant** to launch a pre-emptive strike *ou* attack

devanture [d(ə)vɑ̃tyʀ] NF [a] (= *étalage*) display; (= *vitrine*) shop *ou* store *(US)* window; **à la** *ou* **en ~** on display; (*dans la vitrine*) in the window [b] (= *façade*) (shop *ou* store) front

dévastateur, -trice [devastatœʀ, tʀis] ADJ [*torrent, orage*] devastating; [*passion*] destructive

dévastation [devastasjɔ̃] NF devastation; **les ~s de la guerre/de la tempête** the ravages of war/the storm, the devastation *ou* havoc wreaked by war/the storm

dévasté, e [devaste] (*ptp de* **dévaster**) ADJ [*pays, ville, cultures*] devastated; [*maison*] ruined; [*visage*] ravaged

dévaster [devaste] ▶conjug 1◀ VT [+ *pays, ville, cultures*] to devastate, lay waste; [+ *esprit, cœur*] to devastate, ravage

déveine* [deven] NF rotten luck*; **être dans la ~** to be down on one's luck *ou* out of luck; **avoir la ~ de** to have the rotten luck to*; **quelle ~!** what rotten luck!*

développable [dev(ə)lɔpabl] ADJ (*gén, Géom*) developable

développé, e [dev(ə)lɔpe] (*ptp de* **développer**) [1] ADJ [*pays*] developed; [*sens, intuition, musculature*] well-developed; **bien/peu ~** well-developed/underdeveloped; **sens olfactif très ~** highly developed sense of smell [2] NM (*Haltérophilie*) press; (*Danse*) développé

développement [dev(ə)lɔpmɑ̃] NM [a] (= *croissance*) [*intelligence, corps, science, maladie*] development; [*économie, affaire, commerce, région*] development, expansion, growth; [*chômage*] growth; **une affaire en plein ~** a fast-expanding *ou* fast-developing business; **l'entreprise a connu un ~ important** the firm has expanded *ou* developed greatly *ou* has undergone a sizeable expansion; **la crise a connu un ~ inattendu** the crisis has taken an unexpected turn, there has been an unexpected development in the crisis; (*Écol*) **principe du ~ durable** principle of sustainable development → **pays¹**
[b] **~s** (= *prolongements*) [*affaire, enquête*] developments; **cette affaire pourrait connaître de nouveaux ~s** there could be some new developments in this affair
[c] [*sujet*] exposition; (*Mus*) [*thème*] development; **entrer dans des ~s inutiles** to go into unnecessary details, develop the subject unnecessarily
[d] (*Ind* = *mise au point*) development; **on évalue le ~ de ce missile à 4 milliards de francs** it is estimated that it will cost 4 billion francs to develop this missile
[e] (*Photo*) developing, development, processing; **appareil/photo à ~ instantané** instant camera/photograph
[f] (*Cyclisme*) **choisir un grand/petit ~** to choose a high/low gear
[g] (*Géom*) [*solide*] development; (*Algèbre*) [*fonction*] development; [*expression algébrique*] simplification

▼**développer** [dev(ə)lɔpe] ▶conjug 1◀ [1] VT
[a] [+ *corps, muscle, intelligence, stratégie*] to develop; [+ *commerce, industrie*] to develop, expand; **~ le goût de l'aventure chez les enfants** to bring out *ou* develop adventurousness in children; **il faut ~ les échanges entre les pays** exchanges between countries must be developed
[b] [+ *récit, argument, projet*] to develop, enlarge (up)on, elaborate upon; **il faut ~ ce paragraphe** this paragraph needs developing *ou* expanding

[c] (*Photo*) [+ *film*] to develop; **envoyer une pellicule à ~** to send a film to be developed *ou* processed
[d] (*Méd*) [+ *maladie*] to develop
[e] (= *déballer*) [+ *paquet*] to unwrap
[f] (= *déployer*) [+ *parchemin*] to unroll; [+ *coupon de tissu*] to unfold; [+ *armée, troupes*] to deploy
[g] (*Math*) [+ *solide, fonction, série*] to develop; [+ *expression algébrique*] to simplify
[h] **vélo qui développe 6 mètres** bicycle which moves forward 6 metres for every complete revolution of the pedal

[2] **se développer** VPR [a] [*personne, intelligence, plante*] to develop, grow; [*entreprise*] to expand, develop, grow; [*pays, région*] to develop
[b] [*armée*] to spread out
[c] [*habitude*] to spread
[d] [*maladie, symptôme*] to develop

développeur [dev(ə)lɔpœʀ] NM (*Photo, Ordin*) developer

devenir [dəv(ə)niʀ] ▶conjug 22◀ [1] VI [a] (= *passer d'un état à un autre*) to become; **~ capitaine/médecin** to become a captain/a doctor; **que veux-tu ~ dans la vie?** what do you want to do *ou* be in life?; **cet enfant maladif est devenu un homme solide** that sickly child has turned out *ou* turned into *ou* has become a strong man; **il est devenu tout rouge** he turned *ou* went quite red; **il devient de plus en plus agressif** he's becoming *ou* growing *ou* getting more and more aggressive; **~ vieux/grand** to grow *ou* get old/tall; **arrête, tu deviens grossier** stop it, you're starting to be rude; **c'est à ~ fou!** it's enough to drive you mad!
[b] (= *advenir de*) **bonjour, que devenez-vous?*** hullo, how are you doing?* *ou* getting on? (*Brit*) *ou* getting along? (*US*); **et Chantal, qu'est-ce qu'elle devient?** how's Chantal *ou* what's Chantal up to these days?; **qu'étais-tu devenu? nous te cherchions partout** where *ou* wherever had you gone? *ou* got to? (*Brit*) we were looking for you everywhere; **que sont devenues mes lunettes?** where *ou* wherever have my glasses gone? *ou* got to? (*Brit*); **que sont devenus tes grands projets?** what has become of your great plans?; **que deviendrais-je sans toi?** what(ever) would I do *ou* what(ever) would become of me without you?; **qu'allons-nous ~?** what is going to happen to us?, what will become of us?

[2] NM (= *progression*) evolution; (= *futur*) future; **quel est le ~ de l'homme?** what is man's destiny?; **en ~** constantly evolving

déverbal (*pl* **-aux**) [devɛʀbal, o] NM deverbal, deverbative

dévergondage [devɛʀgɔ̃daʒ] NM licentious *ou* loose living

dévergondé, e [devɛʀgɔ̃de] (*ptp de* **se dévergonder**) [1] ADJ [*femme*] shameless, loose; [*homme*] wild; [*conversation*] licentious, bawdy; **vie ~e** licentious *ou* loose living [2] NM,F **c'est une ~e** she's a shameless hussy; **c'est un ~** he leads a wild life

dévergonder [devɛʀgɔ̃de] ▶conjug 1◀ [1] VT [+ *personne*] to debauch [2] **se dévergonder** VPR to run wild, get into bad ways

déverrouillage [devɛʀujaʒ] NM [a] [*porte*] unbolting [b] [*mécanisme, arme à feu*] unlocking

déverrouiller [devɛʀuje] ▶conjug 1◀ VT [a] [+ *porte*] to unbolt; (*avec un verrou*) to unbolt; (*avec une serrure*) to unlock [b] [+ *mécanisme*] to unlock, release; [+ *arme à feu*] to release the bolt of; [+ *train d'atterrissage*] to release; **ils déverrouillent la grille des salaires** they are introducing greater flexibility into the salary structure; **pour tenter de ~ le débat** to try and break the deadlock in the debate

devers [dəvɛʀ] → **par-devers**

dévers [devɛʀ] NM [*route*] banking; [*mur*] slant

déversement [devɛʀsəmɑ̃] NM [*liquide*] pouring (out); [*sable, ordures*] tipping (out); [*bombes*] unloading; **~ accidentel de pétrole** oil spill; **le ~ en mer de déchets toxiques** the dumping of toxic waste at sea; **le ~ de produits sur le marché européen** the dumping of goods onto the European market

déverser [devɛʀse] ▶conjug 1◀ [1] VT [a] [+ *liquide*] to pour (out); **la rivière déverse ses eaux dans le lac** the river flows into the lake; **une fenêtre ouverte déversait des flots de musique** strains of music wafted from an open window
[b] [+ *sable, ordures*] to tip (out); [+ *bombes*] to unload; **~ des produits sur un marché** to dump *ou* unload products onto a market; **le train déversa des milliers de banlieusards** the train disgorged *ou* discharged thousands of commuters; **des tonnes de pommes de terre ont été déversées sur la route** tons of potatoes were dumped on the road
[c] (= *épancher*) **il déversa toute sa colère sur moi** he poured out *ou* vented his anger on me; **~ des injures sur qn** to shower abuse on sb; **~ sa bile sur qn** to vent one's spleen on sb
[2] **se déverser** VPR to pour (out); **la rivière se déverse dans le lac** the river flows into *ou* pours its waters into the lake; **de l'orifice se déversaient des torrents d'eaux boueuses** torrents of muddy water poured out of the hole; **les produits qui se déversent sur le marché européen** the products being dumped *ou* unloaded onto the European market

déversoir [devɛʀswaʀ] NM [*canal*] overflow; [*réservoir*] spillway, overflow; (*fig*) outlet

dévêtir [devetiʀ] ▶conjug 20◀ [1] VT [+ *personne, poupée*] to undress; **~ un enfant** to undress a child, take a child's clothes off [2] **se dévêtir** VPR to undress, get undressed, take one's clothes off

déviance [devjɑ̃s] NF (*Psych*) deviancy, deviance

déviant, e [devjɑ̃, jɑ̃t] [1] ADJ [*comportement*] deviant; [*discours, opinion*] dissenting [2] NM,F deviant; **~ sexuel** sexual deviant

déviation [devjasjɔ̃] NF [a] [*projectile, navire, aiguille aimantée*] deviation; [*circulation*] diversion [b] (*Aut* = *détour obligatoire*) diversion (*Brit*), detour (*US*) [c] (*Méd*) [*organe*] inversion; [*utérus*] displacement; [*colonne vertébrale*] curvature [d] (= *changement*) deviation; **~ par rapport à la norme** departure from the norm; **le parti l'a accusé de ~** he was accused of deviating from the party line; **il n'admettra aucune ~ par rapport à ses objectifs** he will not be deflected from his goals

déviationnisme [devjasjɔnism] NM deviationism; **faire du ~ de droite** to veer to the right

déviationniste [devjasjɔnist] ADJ, NMF deviationist

dévidage [devidaʒ] NM (= *déroulement*) [*pelote, bobine*] unwinding; (= *mise en pelote*) [*fil*] reeling

dévider [devide] ▶conjug 1◀ VT [a] (= *dérouler*) [+ *pelote, bobine*] to unwind; [+ *cordage, câble*] to unreel; **~ son chapelet** to tell one's beads; **~ un chapelet de clichés** to reel off a string of clichés; **elle m'a dévidé tout son chapelet*** she gave me a catalogue of her woes [b] (= *mettre en pelote*) [+ *fil*] to wind into a ball *ou* skein; [+ *écheveau*] to wind up

dévidoir [devidwaʀ] NM [*fil, tuyau*] reel; [*câbles*] drum, reel

dévier [devje] ▶conjug 7◀ [1] VI [a] [*aiguille magnétique*] to deviate; [*ballon, bateau, projectile*] to veer (off course), turn (off course); **le ballon a dévié vers la gauche** the ball veered to the left; **le poteau a fait ~ le ballon** the post deflected the ball; **le vent nous a fait ~ (de notre route)** the wind blew us off course

▶ GRAMMAIRE ACTIVE: **développer** 53.2

ou made us veer off course; **nous avons dévié par rapport à notre route** we've gone off course, we're off course [b] [*doctrine*] to alter; [*conversation*] to turn (**sur** (on)to); **voyant que la conversation déviait dangereusement** seeing that the conversation was taking a dangerous turn; **il fit ~ la conversation vers des sujets plus neutres** he turned *ou* diverted the conversation onto more neutral subjects; **nous avons dévié par rapport au projet initial** we have moved away *ou* departed from the original plan; **on m'accuse de ~ de ma ligne politique** I'm accused of straying from my political principles; **rien ne me fera ~ de mes principes** nothing will turn me away from my principles [2] VT [+ *route, circulation*] to divert (*Brit*), detour (*US*); [+ *projectile, coup*] to deflect, divert; **avoir la colonne vertébrale déviée** to have curvature of the spine

devin, devineresse [dəvɛ̃, dəvin(ə)ʀɛs] NM,F soothsayer, seer; **je ne suis pas ~!** I don't have second sight, I can't see into the future

devinable [d(ə)vinabl] ADJ [*résultat*] foreseeable; [*énigme*] solvable; [*secret, raison*] that can be guessed, guessable

deviner [d(ə)vine] ▸conjug 1◂ VT [a] [+ *secret, raison*] to guess; [+ *énigme*] to solve; [+ *avenir*] to foresee, foretell; **devine pourquoi/qui** guess why/who; **vous ne devinez pas?** can't you guess?; **tu devines le reste** you can imagine the rest; (*littér*) **~ qn** to read sb's mind; **je crois ~ où il veut en venir** I think I know *ou* I think I can guess what he's getting at; **rien ne laissait ~ leur liaison** nothing hinted that they were having an affair [b] (= *apercevoir*) to make out; **je devinais son sourire dans la pénombre** I could make out his smile in the darkness; **sa robe laissait ~ son corps souple** you could make out the contours of her lithe body through her dress; **une silhouette se devinait à la place du conducteur** you could just make out a figure in the driver's seat; **ses véritables sentiments se devinaient derrière son apparente indifférence** his true feelings showed through his apparent indifference

devineresse [dəvin(ə)ʀɛs] NF → **devin**

devinette [d(ə)vinɛt] NF riddle, conundrum; **poser une ~ à qn** to ask *ou* set sb a riddle; **jouer aux ~s** (*lit*) to play at riddles; **arrête de jouer aux ~s** stop playing guessing games *ou* talking in riddles

déviriliser [deviʀilize] ▸conjug 1◂ VT **~ qn** to emasculate sb, make sb look less manly

devis [d(ə)vi] NM estimate, quotation, quote; **~ descriptif/estimatif** detailed/preliminary estimate; **faire faire des réparations sur ~** to have repairs carried out on the basis of an estimate; **il a établi un ~ de 3 000 F** he drew up *ou* made out an estimate for 3,000 francs

dévisager [deviʒaʒe] ▸conjug 3◂ VT to stare at, look hard at

devise [dəviz] NF [a] (*Hér*) (= *formule*) motto, watchword; (= *figure emblématique*) device [b] [*maison de commerce*] slogan; [*parti*] motto, slogan; **simplicité est ma ~** simplicity is my motto [c] (*Fin* = *monnaie*) currency; **~ forte** hard *ou* strong currency; **~ faible** soft *ou* weak currency; **~s étrangères** foreign currency; **~ convertible** convertible currency; **payer en ~s** to pay in foreign currency → **cours**

deviser [dəvize] ▸conjug 1◂ VI (*littér*) to converse (**de** about, on)

dévissage [devisaʒ] NM [a] [*bouchon, couvercle, boulon*] unscrewing, undoing; [*ampoule électrique*] unscrewing [b] [*alpiniste*] fall

dévisser [devise] ▸conjug 1◂ [1] VT [+ *bouchon, couvercle, boulon*] to unscrew, undo; [+ *ampoule électrique*] to unscrew; (*fig*) **se ~ la tête** *ou* **le cou** to crane one's neck [2] VI [*alpiniste*] to fall

de visu [devizy] LOC ADV **s'assurer/se rendre compte de qch ~** to make sure of sth/see sth for o.s.

dévitalisation [devitalizasjɔ̃] NF **~ d'une dent** removal of a nerve from a tooth, devitalization (*SPÉC*) of a tooth

dévitaliser [devitalize] ▸conjug 1◂ VT [+ *dent*] to remove the nerve from, devitalize (*SPÉC*)

dévoiement [devwamɑ̃] NM (*littér*) [*personne*] leading astray; [*idéal, principe*] corruption; **ils réprouvaient les ~s du régime établi** they condemned the corrupt behaviour of the regime in power; **il voit dans cette expérience un ~ pervers de la science** he regards this experiment as a perverse misuse of science

dévoilement [devwalmɑ̃] NM [a] [*statue, plaque commémorative*] unveiling [b] [*intentions, secret, vérité, identité, date*] revelation, disclosure; [*projet*] unveiling, revealing; [*complot, scandale*] exposure

dévoiler [devwale] ▸conjug 1◂ VT [a] [+ *statue, plaque commémorative*] to unveil; (*hum*) **~ ses charmes** to reveal one's charms [b] [+ *intentions, secret, vérité, identité, date*] to reveal, disclose; [+ *projet*] to unveil, reveal; [+ *complot, scandale*] to expose, uncover; **~ son vrai visage** to show one's true face; **le mystère s'est dévoilé** the mystery has been revealed *ou* unfolded

▼ **devoir** [d(ə)vwaʀ]

▸conjug 28◂

[1] VERBE TRANSITIF	[4] NOM MASCULIN
[2] VERBE AUXILIAIRE	[5] NOM MASCULIN PL
[3] VERBE PRONOMINAL	

[1] VERBE TRANSITIF

[a] **= avoir à payer** [+ *chose, somme d'argent*] to owe; **~ qch à qn** to owe sb sth; **elle (lui) doit 200 F/2 jours de travail** she owes (him) 200 francs/2 days' work; **il réclame seulement ce qui lui est dû** he is asking only for what he's owed *ou* for what is owing to him

[b] **= être redevable de** **~ qch à qn** to owe sth to sb, owe sb sth; **c'est à son courage qu'elle doit la vie** she owes her life to his courage, it's thanks to his courage that she's alive; **je dois à mes parents d'avoir réussi** I have my parents to thank for my success, I owe my success to my parents; **c'est à lui que l'on doit cette découverte** we have him to thank for this discovery, it is to him that we owe this discovery; MAIS **à qui doit-on ce délicieux gâteau?** who do we have to thank for this delicious cake?; **à qui doit-on la découverte du radium?** who discovered radium?; **il ne veut rien ~ à personne** he doesn't want to be indebted to anyone; **sa réussite ne doit rien au hasard** his success has nothing to do with luck

[c] **= être tenu à** **~ (l')obéissance à qn** to owe sb obedience; **les enfants doivent le respect à leurs parents** children ought to respect their parents; **il lui doit bien cela!** it's the least he can do for him!; **avec les honneurs dus à son rang** with honours befitting his rank

[2] VERBE AUXILIAIRE

[a] obligation

Lorsque **devoir** *exprime une obligation, il se traduit généralement par* **have to** *ou la forme plus familière* **have got to** *lorsqu'il s'agit de contraintes extérieures; notez que* **have got to** *ne s'utilise qu'au présent. Le verbe* **must** *a généralement une valeur plus impérative;* **must** *étant défectif, on utilise* **have to** *aux temps où il ne se conjugue pas.*

elle doit (absolument) partir ce soir she (really) has to *ou* she (really) must go tonight, she's (really) got to go tonight; **il avait promis, il devait le faire** he'd promised, so he had to do it; **dois-je lui écrire tout de suite?** must I *ou* do I have to *ou* have I got to write to him immediately?; **vous ne devez pas entrer sans**

frapper you are not to *ou* must not come in without knocking; MAIS **il a cru ~ accepter** he thought he should accept; **dois-je comprendre par là que ...** am I to understand from this that ...

[b] conseil, suggestion

Lorsque **devoir** *est au conditionnel et qu'il a donc un sens proche du conseil, de la suggestion ou qu'il introduit ce qu'il est raisonnable de supposer, il se traduit par* **should** *ou* **ought to**.

tu devrais t'habiller plus chaudement you should *ou* ought to dress more warmly; **il aurait dû la prévenir** he should have *ou* ought to have warned her; **il devrait maintenant connaître le chemin** he ought to *ou* should know the way by now

[c] fatalité

Lorsque **devoir** *exprime une fatalité ou le caractère très vraisemblable d'un événement, il se traduit généralement par* **have to** *ou* **be bound to**.

nos chemins devaient se croiser un jour ou l'autre our paths were bound to *ou* had to cross some time; **cela devait arriver!** it was bound to happen!, it (just) had to happen!; **on doit tous mourir un jour** we all have to die some time; MAIS **les choses semblent ~ s'arranger/empirer** things seem to be sorting themselves out/getting worse

Notez l'emploi de **be to** *dans les exemples suivants.*

elle ne devait pas les revoir vivants she was never to see them alive again; **il devait devenir premier ministre trois mois plus tard** he was to become prime minister three months later

[d] prévision

Lorsque **devoir** *exprime une prévision, il est souvent traduit par* **be going to**.

elle doit vous téléphoner demain she's going to ring you tomorrow; **il devait acheter une moto mais c'était trop cher** he was going to buy a motorbike but it was too expensive

Notez l'emploi de **be due to** *et* **be supposed to** *dans les contextes où la notion de temps est importante.*

son train doit *ou* **devrait arriver dans cinq minutes** his train is due to arrive in five minutes; **il devait partir à 6 heures mais ...** he was supposed to be leaving at 6 but ...; **elle doit nous rejoindre ce soir** she's supposed to be joining us this evening; **nous ne devions pas arriver avant 8 heures** we weren't supposed to come before 8

[e] probabilité, hypothèse

Lorsque **devoir** *exprime une probabilité, une hypothèse, il se traduit généralement par* **must** *dans les phrases affirmatives.*

il doit faire froid ici en hiver it must be cold here in winter; **vous devez vous tromper** you must be mistaken; **il a dû se tromper** *ou* **il doit s'être trompé de chemin** he must have lost his way; **il devait être 6 heures quand il est sorti** it must have been 6 when he went out

Au conditionnel, on utilise **should** *ou* **ought to**.

ça devrait pouvoir se faire it should be *ou* ought to be feasible; **ça devrait tenir dans le coffre** it should go *ou* ought to go in the boot

Dans les phrases négatives, on utilise généralement **can't**.

elle ne doit pas être bête, vous savez she can't be stupid, you know; **il ne devait pas être loin du sommet quand il a abandonné** he can't have been far from the top when he gave up

[f] supposition **dussé-je** (*frm*) **perdre de l'argent, j'irai jusqu'au procès** I'll go to court even if it means losing money

Notez l'emploi possible de **be to**.

même s'il devait *ou* **dût-il** (*littér*) **être condamné, il refuserait de parler** even if he were (to be) found guilty he would refuse to talk

3 **se devoir** VERBE PRONOMINAL

a réciproque les époux se doivent (mutuellement) fidélité husband and wife have a duty to be faithful to one another; nous nous devons la vérité we owe it to each other to tell the truth

b
◆ **se devoir à qn/qch** : il se doit à sa famille he has a duty to his family; quand on gagne un salaire pareil, on se doit à son métier when you earn that much, you've got to be committed to your job

c
◆ **se devoir de** + infinitif (= être obligé de) nous nous devons de le lui dire it is our duty ou we are duty bound to tell him; l'ONU se devait de réagir/prendre des sanctions the UN was duty bound to react/to introduce sanctions; je me devais de la prévenir I owed it to myself to warn her; je me devais d'essayer I had to try for my own sake; nos deux pays se doivent de coopérer davantage our two countries must cooperate more; nous nous devons de satisfaire nos clients we must satisfy our customers; pour être acceptée, la nouvelle procédure se devait d'être simple the new procedure had to be simple if it was going to be accepted

◆ **comme il se doit/se devait** : j'en ai informé mon chef, comme il se doit I informed my boss, of course; il a convié le ministre, comme il se devait he invited the minister to attend, as was right and proper; on a fêté l'événement, comme il se doit and naturally ou of course, we celebrated the event; le premier tome est consacré, comme il se doit, au Moyen Âge not surprisingly, the first volume is devoted to the Middle Ages; comme il se doit en pareil cas, on a procédé à un vote as is usual in these cases, we put it to a vote; ils ont été punis comme il se doit they were duly punished; (hum) et il est arrivé en retard, comme il se doit ! and naturally he arrived late!

4 NOM MASCULIN

a (= obligation) duty; agir par ~ to act from a sense of duty; un homme de ~ a man of conscience ou with a sense of duty; accomplir ou faire ou remplir son ~ to carry out ou do one's duty (envers towards); les ~s du citoyen/d'une charge the duties of a citizen/a post; se faire un ~ de faire qch to make it one's duty to do sth; il est de mon/ton/son etc ~ de ... it is my/ your/his etc duty to ...; croire de son ~ de faire qch to think ou feel it one's duty to do sth; ~s religieux religious duties

◆ **se mettre en devoir de** + infinitif (frm) il se mit en ~ de répondre à la lettre he proceeded to reply to the letter; il se mit immédiatement en ~ de le faire he set about doing it immediately

b Scol (= dissertation) essay, paper; (= exercice) (fait à la maison) homework (NonC); (fait en classe) exercise; faire ses ~s to do one's homework; ~s de vacances holiday homework; ~ (à la) maison homework (NonC); ~ sur table ou surveillé (written) test

5 **devoirs** NMPL († ou hum = hommages) respects; présenter ses ~s à qn to pay one's respects to sb

---

dévoisé, e [devwaze] ADJ (Ling) [consonne] devoiced

dévoisement [devwazmɑ̃] NM (Ling) devoicing

dévolter [devɔlte] ▶conjug 1◀ VT to reduce the voltage of

dévolu, e [devɔly] **1** ADJ être ~ à qn [succession, droits] to be devolved upon ou to sb; [charge] to be handed down ou passed on to sb; le budget qui a été ~ à la recherche the funds that have been allotted ou granted to research; la part de gâteau qui m'avait été ~e the piece of cake that had been allotted to

me; c'est à moi qu'il a été ~ de commencer it fell to me to start; le sort qui lui sera ~ the fate that is in store for him **2** NM jeter son ~ sur qn/qch to set one's heart on sb/sth

dévolution [devɔlysjɔ̃] NF devolution

dévonien, -ienne [devɔnjɛ̃, jɛn] **1** ADJ Devonian **2** NM le ~ the Devonian

dévorant, e [devɔrɑ̃, ɑ̃t] ADJ [faim] raging (épith); [curiosité, soif] burning (épith); [passion] devouring (épith), consuming (épith); (littér) [flammes] all-consuming

dévorer [devɔre] ▶conjug 1◀ VT **a** (= manger) [fauve] to devour; [personne] to devour, wolf down*; des limaces ont dévoré mes laitues my lettuces have been eaten by slugs; cet enfant dévore ! this child has a huge appetite!; on est dévoré par les moustiques ! we're being eaten alive by mosquitoes!; ~ un livre to devour a book; ~ qch à belles dents to wolf sth down*; ~ qn/qch du regard ou des yeux to eye sb/sth greedily ou hungrily; ~ qn de baisers to smother sb with kisses; la barbe qui lui dévorait les joues the beard that covered his face → **loup**

b (= consumer) to consume; le feu dévore le bâtiment the building is being consumed by fire; il a dévoré sa fortune he has consumed his (whole) fortune; voiture qui dévore les kilomètres ou la route car which eats up the miles; c'est une tâche qui dévore tous mes loisirs it's a task which takes up ou swallows up all my free time

c (littér = tourmenter) [jalousie, remords, soucis] to consume, devour; [maladie] to consume; la soif le dévorait he had a burning ou raging thirst; être dévoré de remords/jalousie to be eaten up with ou consumed with ou devoured by remorse/jealousy; dévoré par l'ambition consumed with ambition

d (frm = cacher) ~ ses larmes to choke back ou gulp back one's tears

dévoreur, -euse [devɔrœr, øz] NM,F devourer; un ~ de livres an avid reader; ce projet est un gros ~ de crédits this project eats up money ou is a great drain on funds

dévot, e [devo, ɔt] **1** ADJ (gén) devout, pious; (péj = bigot) sanctimonious, churchy* **2** NM,F (gén) deeply religious person; (péj) sanctimonious person; (péj) une vieille ~e a churchy* ou sanctimonious old woman → **faux²**

dévotement [devɔtmɑ̃] ADV devoutly, piously

dévotion [devɔsjɔ̃] **1** NF **a** (= piété) devoutness, religious devotion → **faux²** **b** (= culte) devotion; avoir une ~ pour qn to worship sb; être à la ~ de qn to be totally devoted to sb; il avait à sa ~ plusieurs employés he had several totally devoted employees **2** **dévotions** NFPL devotions; faire ses ~s to perform one's devotions

dévoué, e [devwe] (ptp de se dévouer) ADJ [employé] devoted, dedicated; [époux, ami] devoted; être ~ à qn/qch to be devoted to sb/sth; (†† : formule de lettre) votre ~ serviteur your devoted servant → **croire**

dévouement [devumɑ̃] NM [mère, ami, voisin] devotion; [infirmière, sauveteur, soldat] devotion, dedication; ~ à un parti devotion to a party; avec ~ devotedly; avoir un ~ aveugle pour qn to be blindly devoted to sb; elle a fait preuve d'un grand ~ pour lui/à leur cause she showed great devotion to him/to their cause

dévouer (se) [devwe] ▶conjug 1◀ VPR **a** (= se sacrifier) to sacrifice o.s.; il se dévoue pour les autres he sacrifices himself for others; c'est toujours moi qui me dévoue ! it's always me who makes the sacrifices!; (hum) personne ne veut le manger ? bon, je me dévoue so nobody wants to eat it? all right, I'll be a martyr (hum) **b** (= se consacrer à) se ~ à qn/qch to devote o.s. ou dedicate o.s. to sb/sth

dévoyé, e [devwaje] (ptp de dévoyer) **1** ADJ [personne] depraved; un nationalisme ~

warped nationalism **2** NM,F corrupt individual; une bande de jeunes ~s a gang of young delinquents

dévoyer [devwaje] ▶conjug 8◀ **1** VT to lead astray **2** **se dévoyer** VPR to go astray

dextérité [dɛksterite] NF skill, dexterity; avec ~ skilfully, dextrously, with dexterity

dextre [dɛkstr] **1** ADJ [coquille] dextral; (Hér) dexter **2** NF (††, hum) right hand

dextrine [dɛkstrin] NF dextrin(e)

dey [dɛ] NM dey

DG [deʒe] **1** NM (ABRÉV = **directeur général**) → directeur **2** NF (ABRÉV = **direction générale**) (= siège social) head office; (de l'UE) DG

dg (ABRÉV = **décigramme**) dg

DGA [deʒea] **1** NM (ABRÉV = **directeur général adjoint**) → directeur **2** NF (ABRÉV = **Délégation générale pour l'armement**) → délégation

DGE [deʒeə] NF (ABRÉV = **dotation globale d'équipement**) state contribution to local government budget

DGI [deʒei] NF (ABRÉV = **Direction générale des impôts**) ≈ IR (Brit), ≈ IRS (US)

DGSE [deʒeəɛs] NF (ABRÉV = **Direction générale de la sécurité extérieure**) ≈ MI6 (Brit), ≈ CIA (US)

Dhaka [daka] N Dhaka

dia [dja] EXCL → **hue**

diabète [djabɛt] NM diabetes sg; avoir du ~ to have diabetes; ~ insipide/sucré diabetes insipidus/mellitus; ~ gras maturity-onset diabetes; ~ maigre insulin-dependent ou juvenile-onset diabetes

diabétique [djabetik] ADJ, NMF diabetic

diabétologie [djabetɔlɔʒi] NF study of diabetes

diabétologue [djabetɔlɔg] NMF diabetes specialist

diable [djabl] NM **a** (Myth, Rel) devil; le ~ the Devil; s'agiter comme un beau ~ to thrash about like the (very) devil; j'ai protesté comme un beau ~ I protested for all I was worth ou as loudly as I could; il a le ~ au corps he's the very devil; faire le ~ à quatre † to create the devil* of a rumpus; que le ~ l'emporte ! the devil take him!*; le ~ m'emporte si j'y comprends quelque chose ! the devil take me† ou the deuce† if I understand any of it!, I'll be damned if I understand it!*; c'est bien le ~ si on ne trouve pas à les loger it would be most surprising if we couldn't find anywhere for them to stay; ce n'est pas le ~ it's not that bad; (fait) à la ~ (done) any old how; tirer le ~ par la queue† to live from hand to mouth, be on one's uppers (Brit); se démener comme un ~ dans un bénitier to be like a cat on a hot tin roof ou on hot bricks (Brit) → avocat¹, île

b (dans excl) Diable !† c'est difficile ! it's dashed ou deuced difficult!†; ~ oui/non ! good gracious yes/no!; ~ si je le sais ! the devil take me† ou the deuce† if I know!; allons, du courage que ~ ! cheer up, dash it!* †; où/ quand/qui/pourquoi ~ ...? where/when/who/ why the blazes* ou the devil* ...?

c (loc) être situé/habiter au ~ (vauvert) to be/live miles from anywhere ou at the back of beyond (Brit); envoyer qn au ~ to tell sb to go to the devil*; il peut aller au ~ ! ◊ qu'il aille au ~ ! he can go to the devil!*; au ~ l'avarice ! hang the expense!; au ~ le percepteur ! the devil take the tax collector!*

d (* = enfant) devil, rogue; (* = personne) pauvre ~ poor devil ou wretch; grand ~ tall fellow; c'est un bon/ce n'est pas un mauvais ~ he's a nice/he's not a bad sort* ou fellow

e (en intensif) il fait un froid du ~ ou de tous les ~s it's fearfully ou fiendishly cold; il faisait un vent du ~ ou de tous les ~s there was the ou a devil* of a wind; on a eu un mal du ~ à le faire avouer we had the ou a devil* of a job making him own up; il est menteur en ~ he is a deuced† *ou* damned* liar; **il est courageux/ robuste en ~** he is devilishly brave/strong; **ce ~ d'homme** that wretched fellow; **cette ~ d'affaire** this wretched business; **avec ce ~ de temps on ne peut pas sortir** we can't go out in this wretched weather

f (= *chariot*) hand truck; (= *jouet*) ~ **(à ressort)** jack-in-the-box

g (= *casserole*) earthenware braising pot

h (*Culin*) **à la ~** in a piquant sauce, à la diable

diablement* [djablǝmɑ̃] ADV (= *très*) darned*; **il y a ~ longtemps que ...** it's a heck* of a long time since ...; **il m'a ~ surpris** he gave me a heck* of a surprise

diablerie [djablǝʀi] NF a (= *espièglerie*) roguishness; (= *acte*) mischief (*NonC*); **leurs ~s me feront devenir folle** their mischief will drive me mad b †† (= *machination*) machination, evil intrigue c †† (= *sorcellerie*) devilry d (*Théât*) mystery play featuring devils

diablesse [djablɛs] NF (= *diable femelle*) she-devil; († = *mégère*) shrew, vixen; (* = *bonne femme*) wretched woman; **cette enfant est une vraie ~** that child is a little devil

diablotin [djablɔtɛ̃] NM (*lit, fig*) imp; (= *pétard*) (Christmas) cracker (*Brit*), favor (*US*)

diabolique [djabɔlik] ADJ diabolic(al), devilish

diaboliquement [djabɔlikmɑ̃] ADV diabolically

diabolisation [djabɔlizasjɔ̃] NF [*adversaire, ennemi*] demonization; **la ~ du cannabis** the way cannabis is portrayed as an evil *ou* dangerous drug

diaboliser [djabɔlize] ▸conjug 1◂ VT [+ *personne, État*] to demonize

diabolo [djabɔlo] NM (= *jouet*) diabolo; (= *boisson*) **~ grenadine/menthe** grenadine/mint (cordial) and lemonade

diachronie [djakʀɔni] NF diachrony

diachronique [djakʀɔnik] ADJ diachronic

diaclase [djaklaz] NF (*Géol*) joint (*in rock*)

diaconal, e (*mpl* -aux) [djakɔnal, o] ADJ diaconal

diaconat [djakɔna] NM diaconate

diaconesse [djakɔnɛs] NF deaconess

diacre [djakʀ] NM deacon

diacritique [djakʀitik] ADJ diacritic(al); **(signe) ~** diacritic (mark)

diadème [djadɛm] NM (*lit, fig = couronne*) diadem; (= *bijou*) tiara

diagnostic [djagnɔstik] NM [*médecin, expert*] diagnosis; **~ prénatal** prenatal *ou* antenatal diagnosis; **faire** *ou* **poser un ~** to make a diagnosis; **erreur de ~** error in diagnosis; **il a un bon ~** he's a good diagnostician; **le ~ des économistes est pessimiste** the economists' diagnosis *ou* prognosis is pessimistic

diagnostique [djagnɔstik] ADJ diagnostic

diagnostiquer [djagnɔstike] ▸conjug 1◂ VT (*lit, fig*) to diagnose

diagonal, e (*mpl* -aux) [djagɔnal, o] 1 ADJ diagonal 2 **diagonale** NF diagonal; **couper un tissu dans la ~e** to cut a fabric on the bias *ou* on the cross (*Brit*); **en ~e** diagonally, crosswise; **tirer un trait en ~e** to draw a line across the page; **lire** *ou* **parcourir en ~e** to skim through

diagonalement [djagɔnalmɑ̃] ADV diagonally

diagramme [djagʀam] NM (= *schéma*) diagram; (= *courbe, graphique*) chart, graph; **~ à barres** *ou* **à bâtons** *ou* **en tuyaux d'orgue** bar chart *ou* graph; **~ sagittal/en arbre** sagittal/tree diagram; **~ en secteurs** pie chart

dialectal, e (*mpl* -aux) [djalɛktal, o] ADJ dialectal, dialectic(al)

dialecte [djalɛkt] NM dialect

dialecticien, -ienne [djalɛktisjɛ̃, jɛn] NM,F dialectician

dialectique [djalɛktik] 1 ADJ dialectic(al) 2 NF dialectics *sg*

dialectiquement [djalɛktikmɑ̃] ADV dialectically

dialectologie [djalɛktɔlɔʒi] NF dialectology

dialogue [djalɔg] NM (*gén*) dialogue, dialog (*US*); **le ~ social** the dialogue between employers (*ou* government) and trade unions; **c'est un ~ de sourds** it's a dialogue of the deaf; **c'est un ~ de sourds entre le syndicat et la direction** the union and the management are not listening to each other; **sa volonté de ~** his willingness to engage in dialogue; **c'est un homme de ~** he is a man who is open to dialogue *ou* who is prepared to discuss matters; **il faut établir un ~ entre parents et enfants** it's important to get parents and children to talk to each other *ou* to get a dialogue going between parents and children

dialoguer [djalɔge] ▸conjug 1◂ 1 VT [+ *roman*] to put into dialogue (form) 2 VI to have talks, enter into dialogue (*Brit*) *ou* dialog (*US*); **~ avec un ordinateur** to interact with a computer; **il veut faire ~ syndicats et patronat** he wants to get unions and employers to enter into dialogue

dialoguiste [djalɔgist] NMF dialogue writer, screen writer

dialyse [djaliz] NF dialysis; **~ rénale** kidney dialysis; **être en ~** to be on dialysis; **subir une ~** to have dialysis; **patient sous ~** dialysis patient

dialyser [djalize] ▸conjug 1◂ VT to dialyse (*Brit*), dialyze (*US*); **(malade) dialysé** dialysis patient

dialyseur [djalizœʀ] NM dialyser (*Brit*), dialyzer (*US*)

diam* [djam] NM (ABRÉV = **diamant**) rock*, diamond

diamant [djamɑ̃] NM (*gén*) diamond; (*fig*) **le ~ noir** the truffle → **croqueuse**

diamantaire [djamɑ̃tɛʀ] NM (= *tailleur*) diamond-cutter; (= *vendeur*) diamond merchant

diamanté, e [djamɑ̃te] ADJ (*Tech*) diamond-tipped; (*littér*) [*eau, lumière*] glittering

diamantifère [djamɑ̃tifɛʀ] ADJ diamantiferous

diamétral, e (*mpl* -aux) [djametral, o] ADJ diametral, diametric(al)

diamétralement [djametralmɑ̃] ADV (*Géom*) diametrally, diametrically; **points de vue ~ opposés** diametrically opposite *ou* opposed views

diamètre [djamɛtʀ] NM diameter; **10 m de ~** 10 m in diameter

Diane [djan] NF Diane, Diana; **~ chasseresse** Diana the Huntress

diane [djan] NF (*Mil*†) reveille; **sonner/battre la ~** to sound/beat the reveille

diantre [djɑ̃tʀ] EXCL† (*aussi hum*) by Jove!† (*aussi hum*), by gad!† (*aussi hum*); **qui/ pourquoi/comment ~ ...?** who/why/how the deuce ...?† *ou* the devil ...?*

diantrement [djɑ̃tʀǝmɑ̃] ADV (†, *hum*) devilish†, deuced†

diapason [djapazɔ̃] NM a (*Mus*) (= *registre*) compass, range, diapason; (= *instrument*) (*en métal*) tuning fork, diapason; (*à vent*) pitch pipe, diapason; **~ de Scheibler** tonometer b (*fig*) **être au ~ d'une situation** to be in tune with a situation; **se mettre au ~ de qn** to get in tune with sb, get onto sb's wavelength; **il s'est vite mis au ~** he soon fell *ou* got in step *ou* tune with the others

diaphane [djafan] ADJ [*tissu*] diaphanous, filmy; [*parchemin, porcelaine*] translucent; [*mains*] diaphanous

diaphragme [djafʀagm] NM (*Anat, Bot, Tech*) diaphragm; (= *contraceptif*) diaphragm; (*Photo*) aperture; (*Photo*) **ouvrir de deux ~s** to open two stops

diaphragmer [djafʀagme] ▸conjug 1◂ VI (*Photo*) to adjust the aperture

diaphyse [djafiz] NF (*Anat*) shaft

diapo* [djapo] NF ABRÉV = **diapositive**

diaporama [djapɔrama] NM slide show

diapositive [djapozitiv] NF slide, transparency (*Brit*); **passer** *ou* **projeter des ~s** to show slides *ou* transparencies (*Brit*)

diapré, e [djapʀe] (*ptp de* **diaprer**) ADJ mottled, variegated

diaprer [djapʀe] ▸conjug 1◂ VT (*littér*) to mottle, variegate

diaprure [djapʀyʀ] NF (*NonC*: *littér*) variegation, mottled effect

diarrhée [djare] NF diarrhoea (*Brit*) (*NonC*), diarrhea (*US*) (*NonC*); **avoir la ~** *ou* **des ~s** to have diarrhoea (*Brit*) *ou* diarrhea (*US*); (*péj*) **~ verbale*** verbal diarrhoea*

diarrhéique [djareik] ADJ diarrh(o)eal, diarrh(o)eic

diarthrose [djartroz] NF (*Anat*) hinge joint; **~ rotatoire** pivot joint

diaspora [djaspɔra] NF (*gén*) diaspora; **la Diaspora (juive)** the (Jewish) Diaspora

diastase [djastaz] NF diastase

diastasique [djastazik] ADJ diastatic, diastasic

diastole [djastɔl] NF diastole

diathermie [djatɛrmi] NF diathermy, diathermia

diatomique [djatɔmik] ADJ diatomic

diatonique [djatɔnik] ADJ diatonic

diatribe [djatrib] NF diatribe; **se lancer dans une longue ~ contre qn** to launch into a long diatribe against sb

dichotomie [dikɔtɔmi] NF (*Bot, littér*) dichotomy

dichotomique [dikɔtɔmik] ADJ dichotomous, dichotomic

dichromatique [dikrɔmatik] ADJ dichromatic

dico* [diko] NM ABRÉV = **dictionnaire**

dicotylédone [dikɔtiledɔn] 1 ADJ dicotyledonous 2 NF dicotyledon

Dictaphone® [diktafɔn] NM Dictaphone®

dictateur [diktatœʀ] NM dictator; **ton/allure de ~** dictatorial tone/manner

dictatorial, e (*mpl* -iaux) [diktatɔrjal, jo] ADJ dictatorial

dictature [diktatyʀ] NF dictatorship; **la ~ du prolétariat** dictatorship of the proletariat; **~ militaire** military dictatorship; **sous la ~ de** under the dictatorship of; (*fig*) **c'est de la ~!** this is tyranny!

dictée [dikte] NF (= *action*) dictating, dictation; (= *exercice*) dictation; **écrire qch sous la ~** to take down a dictation of sth; **écrire sous la ~ de qn** to take down sb's dictation *ou* what sb dictates; **~ musicale** musical dictation; (*littér*) **les ~s de son cœur** the dictates of his heart

dicter [dikte] ▸conjug 1◂ VT [+ *lettre, action*] to dictate; **ils nous ont dicté leurs conditions** they laid down *ou* dictated their conditions to us; **les mesures que nous dicte la situation** the steps that the situation imposes upon us; **il m'a dicté sa volonté** he imposed his will upon me; **sa réponse (lui) est dictée par sa femme/par la peur** his reply was dictated by his wife/by fear; **je n'aime pas qu'on me dicte ce que je dois faire!** I won't be dictated to!; **une paix dictée par l'ennemi** peace on the enemy's terms

diction [diksjɔ̃] NF (= *débit*) diction, delivery; (= *art*) speech production; **professeur/leçons de ~** speech production teacher/lessons

dictionnaire [diksjɔnɛʀ] NM dictionary; **~ analogique** thesaurus; **~ de langue/de rimes** language/rhyme dictionary; (*Ordin*) **~ de**

données data directory *ou* dictionary; **~ électronique** electronic dictionary; **~ encyclopédique/étymologique** encyclopaedic/etymological dictionary; **~ géographique** gazetteer; **~ des synonymes** dictionary of synonyms; **c'est un vrai ~** *ou* **un ~ vivant** he's a walking encyclopaedia

dicton [diktɔ̃] NM saying, dictum; **il y a un ~ qui dit ...** there's a saying that goes ...

didacticiel [didaktisjɛl] NM educational software (NonC), piece of educational software; **des ~s** educational software

didactique [didaktik] **1** ADJ **a** (= destiné à instruire) [ouvrage] educational; [exposé, style] didactic; **matériel ~** teaching aids **b** (= savant) [mot, terme] technical **c** (Psych) **psychanalyse ~** training analysis **2** NF didactics *sg*

didactiquement [didaktikmɑ̃] ADV didactically

didactisme [didaktism] NM didacticism

didascalie [didaskali] NF (Théât) stage direction

Didon [didɔ̃] NF Dido

dièdre [djɛdʀ] **1** ADJ [angle] dihedral **2** NM dihedron, dihedral; (Alpinisme) dièdre, corner

diérèse [djeʀɛz] NF (Ling) di(a)eresis

dièse [djɛz] NM (gén) hash mark *ou* sign; (Mus) sharp; **fa/sol ~** F/G sharp

diesel [djezɛl] NM diesel; **(moteur/camion) ~** diesel engine/lorry (Brit) *ou* truck

diéser [djeze] ▸conjug 6◂ VT (Mus) to sharpen, make sharp

diète¹ [djɛt] NF (Méd) (= jeûne) starvation diet; (= régime) diet; **lactée/végétale** milk/vegetarian diet; **mettre qn à la ~** to put sb on a starvation diet; **il est à la ~** he has been put on a starvation diet

diète² [djɛt] NF (Hist) diet

diététicien, -ienne [djetetisjɛ̃, jɛn] NM,F dietician, dietitian

diététique [djetetik] **1** ADJ [restaurant, magasin] health-food (épith) **2** NF dietetics *sg*

dieu [djø] (pl **dieux**) NM **a** (= divinité) god; **les ~x de l'Antiquité** the gods of Antiquity; **le ~ Chronos** the god Chronos **b** (dans le monothéisme) **Dieu** God; **le Dieu des chrétiens/musulmans** the God of the Christians/Muslims; **Dieu le père** God the Father; (hum) **c'est Dieu le père dans l'entreprise** he's God *ou* he's the big white chief in the company; **une société/génération sans Dieu** a godless society/generation; **le bon Dieu** the good *ou* dear Lord; **donner/recevoir le bon Dieu** to offer/receive the Lord (in Sacrament); **on lui donnerait le bon Dieu sans confession** he looks as if butter wouldn't melt in his mouth; **faire de qn son ~** to idolize *ou* worship sb, put sb on a pedestal; **il n'a ni ~ ni maître** he has neither lord nor master → **âme, homme** **c** (= idole) god **d** (loc) **mon Dieu!** my God!, my goodness!; **(grand) Dieu!** ◊ **grands Dieux!** good God!, good heavens!; **Dieu qu'il est beau/bête!** he's so good-looking/stupid!; **mon Dieu oui, on pourrait ...** well yes, we could ...; **Dieu vous bénisse!** God bless you!; **à Dieu ne plaise!** ◊ **Dieu m'en garde!** God forbid!; **Dieu vous entende/aide!** may God hear your prayer/help you!; **Dieu seul le sait** God only *ou* alone knows; **Dieu sait s'il est généreux/si nous avons essayé!** God knows he's generous/we've tried!; **Dieu sait pourquoi elle l'a épousé** heaven *ou* God (only) knows why she married him; **Dieu merci** ◊ **Dieu soit loué!** (frm) thank God!, praise the Lord!; **Dieu merci, il n'a pas plu** it didn't rain, thank goodness *ou* thank God *ou* thank heaven(s); **c'est pas Dieu possible!*** that's just not possible; **à-Dieu-vat!**† (entreprise risquée) it's in God's hands; (départ) Godspeed; **Dieu m'est témoin que je**

n'ai jamais ... as God is my witness I have never ...; **tu vas te taire bon Dieu!*** for Christ's sake! *ou* sakes! (US) will you be quiet! → **amour, grâce, plaire**

diffamant, e [difamɑ̃, ɑ̃t] ADJ [propos] slanderous, defamatory; [écrits] libellous, defamatory

diffamateur, -trice [difamatœʀ, tʀis] **1** ADJ [propos] slanderous, defamatory; [écrit] libellous, defamatory **2** NM,F slanderer

diffamation [difamasjɔ̃] NF **a** (NonC) (gén) defamation (of character); (en paroles) slander; (par écrit) libel; **campagne de ~** smear campaign; **procès en ~** action for slander (ou libel); **engager des poursuites en ~ contre qn** to sue sb for slander (ou libel); **il a été condamné pour ~ envers X** he was found guilty of slander (ou libel) against X *ou* of slandering (ou libelling) X **b** (= propos) slander (NonC); (= pamphlet) libel (NonC); **les ~ des journaux** the libellous reports in the newspapers

diffamatoire [difamatwaʀ] ADJ (gén) defamatory; [propos] slanderous; [écrit] libellous; **avoir un caractère ~** to be slanderous (ou libellous)

diffamer [difame] ▸conjug 1◂ VT (en paroles) to slander, defame; (par écrit) to libel, defame

différé, e [difeʀe] (ptp de **différer**) **1** ADJ (TV) (pre-)recorded **2** NM **(émission en) ~** (pre-)recorded programme, recording; **le match sera retransmis en ~** the match will be broadcast at a later time

différemment [difeʀamɑ̃] ADV differently

▼**différence** [difeʀɑ̃s] NF **a** (gén) difference; **~ d'opinion** difference of opinion; **~ d'âge/de prix** difference in age/price, age/price difference; **ils ont neuf ans de ~** there are nine years between them; **quelle ~ avec les autres!** what a difference from the others!; **ne pas faire de ~** to make no distinction (**entre** between); **ils savent faire la ~ entre vérité et mensonge** they can tell the difference *ou* distinguish between truth and falsehood; (Tennis) **c'est son service qui a fait la ~** it was his serve that made all the difference; **il fait des ~s entre ses enfants** he doesn't treat all his children in the same way *ou* equally; **tu auras à payer la ~** you will have to make up *ou* pay the difference; (Ftbl) **~ de buts** goal difference **b** (= identité) **marquer sa ~** to assert one's (ou its) distinctive identity; **il fait entendre sa ~ au sein du parti** he voices his dissent in the party **c** (loc) **à la ~ de** unlike; **à la ~ ou à cette ~ que** except (for the fact) that

différenciateur, -trice [difeʀɑ̃sjatœʀ, tʀis] ADJ differentiating, differential

différenciation [difeʀɑ̃sjasjɔ̃] NF differentiation

différencié, e [difeʀɑ̃sje] (ptp de **différencier**) ADJ (Bio) [cellule, tissu] differentiated; (Sociol) [groupe ethnique] diverse; (Scol) [enseignement, filières] specialized

▼**différencier** [difeʀɑ̃sje] ▸conjug 7◂ **1** VT to differentiate **2** **se différencier** VPR (= être différent de) to differ (**de** from); (= devenir différent) to become differentiated (**de** from); (= se rendre différent) to differentiate o.s. (**de** from)

différend [difeʀɑ̃] NM difference of opinion, disagreement; (Jur, Fin) controversy; **avoir un ~ avec qn** to have a difference of opinion with sb

▼**différent, e** [difeʀɑ̃, ɑ̃t] ADJ **a** (= dissemblable) different (**de** from); **dans des circonstances ~es, je vous aurais aidé** if things had been different *ou* in other *ou* different circumstances, I would have helped you; **chercher des solutions ~es** to try to find alternative *ou* other solutions **b** (pl, gén avant n = divers) different, various; **à ~es reprises** on several different *ou* various occasions; **à ~es heures de la journée** at different times of the day; **pour**

~es raisons for various *ou* diverse (frm) reasons

différentiation [difeʀɑ̃sjasjɔ̃] NF (Math) differentiation

différentiel, -ielle [difeʀɑ̃sjɛl] **1** ADJ, NM (gén) differential; **~ d'inflation** inflation differential **2** **différentielle** NF differential

différentier [difeʀɑ̃sje] ▸conjug 7◂ VT (Math) to differentiate

différer [difeʀe] ▸conjug 6◂ **1** VI **a** (= être dissemblable) to differ, be different (**de** from, **en, par** in); **leur politique ne diffère en rien de celle de leurs prédécesseurs** their policy is no different *ou* is in no way different from their predecessors **b** (= diverger) to differ; **elle et moi différons sur ou en tout** she and I differ about everything **c** (= varier) to differ, vary; **la mode diffère de pays à pays** fashions differ *ou* vary from one country to the next **2** VT [+ travail] to postpone, put off; [+ jugement, paiement, départ] to defer, postpone; **~ une décision** to defer *ou* postpone making *ou* put off making a decision; **à quoi bon ~ plus longtemps?** why delay any longer?; (frm) **~ de ou à faire qch** to delay *ou* defer *ou* postpone doing sth → **crédit**

▼**difficile** [difisil] ADJ **a** (= ardu) [travail, problème] difficult; **il nous est ~ de prendre une décision tout de suite** it is difficult *ou* hard for us *ou* we find it difficult *ou* hard to make a decision straight away; **il a eu un moment ~ lorsque sa femme est morte** he went through a difficult *ou* hard time when his wife died; **il a trouvé l'expédition ~** he found the expedition hard going *ou* heavy going; **~ à faire** difficult *ou* hard to do; **morceau ~ (à jouer)** *ou* **d'exécution ~** difficult *ou* hard piece to play **b** (= délicat) [position, situation] difficult, awkward; **ils ont des fins de mois ~s** they have a hard time making ends meet **c** [personne] (= contrariant) difficult, trying; (= exigeant) hard *ou* difficult to please (attrib), fussy; **un enfant ~** a difficult *ou* a problem child; **elle a un caractère ~** she's difficult *ou* awkward; **elle est ~ pour ce qui est de ou en ce qui concerne la propreté** she's a stickler for cleanliness, she's very fussy *ou* particular about cleanliness; **être ou se montrer ~ sur la nourriture** to be difficult *ou* fussy *ou* finicky about one's food; **il ne faut pas être trop ~ ou (trop) faire le ~** it's no good being too fussy *ou* over-fussy; **cette chambre ne vous plaît pas? vous êtes vraiment ~!** don't you like this room? you really are hard *ou* difficult to please!; **elle est ~ dans le choix de ses amis** she's very selective *ou* choosy* about her friends → **vivre** **d** [banlieue, quartier] tough

difficilement [difisilmɑ̃] ADV [marcher, s'exprimer] with difficulty; **c'est ~ visible/croyable** it's difficult *ou* hard to see/believe; **il gagne ~ sa vie** he finds it difficult *ou* hard to earn a living

difficulté [difikylte] NF **a** (NonC) difficulty; **selon la ~ du travail** depending on how difficult the work is, according to the difficulty of the work; **faire qch avec ~** to do sth with difficulty; **avoir ou éprouver de la ~ à faire qch** to have difficulty (in) doing sth, find it difficult *ou* hard to do sth; **j'ai eu beaucoup de ~ à trouver des arguments** I had great difficulty finding *ou* I was hard put to find any arguments; **être ou se trouver en ~** [personne] to find o.s. in difficulty, be in difficulties *ou* in trouble; [entreprise] to be having difficulties; **avion/navire en ~** aircraft/ship in distress; **couple en ~** couple with problems; **enfant en ~** (Scol) child with learning difficulties; (Psych) child with emotional difficulties; **mettre qn en ~** to put sb in a difficult position; **notre gardien de but a été plusieurs fois en ~** our goalkeeper ran into trouble several times

b (= *embarras, obstacle*) difficulty, problem; [*texte, morceau de musique*] difficult passage, difficulty; **avoir des ~s pour faire qch** to have some difficulty (in) doing sth; **enfant qui a des ~s (à l'école/en orthographe)** child who has difficulty *ou* difficulties (at school/with spelling); **avoir des ~s financières** to be in financial difficulties *ou* straits; **il s'est heurté à de grosses ~s** he has come up against grave difficulties; **ils ont des ~s avec leurs enfants** they have problems *ou* trouble with their children; **cela ne fait** *ou* **ne présente aucune ~** that presents no problem; **il y a une ~** there's a problem *ou* hitch* *ou* snag*; **c'est là la ~** that's where the trouble lies, that's the difficulty; **il a fait des ~s pour accepter nos conditions** he made *ou* raised difficulties about accepting our conditions; **il n'a pas fait de ~s pour nous suivre** he followed us without protest *ou* fuss; **sans ~** easily, without any difficulty; **en cas de ~** in case of difficulty

difficultueux, -euse† [difikyltɥø, øz] ADJ difficult, awkward

difforme [difɔʀm] ADJ [*corps, membre, visage*] deformed, misshapen; [*arbre*] twisted

difformité [difɔʀmite] NF deformity; **présenter des ~s** to have deformities, be deformed

diffracter [difʀakte] ▶conjug 1◀ VT to diffract

diffraction [difʀaksjɔ̃] NF diffraction → **réseau**

diffus, e [dify, yz] ADJ (*gén*) diffuse; [*douleur*] diffuse, not localized

diffuser [difyze] ▶conjug 1◀ **1** VT **a** [+ *lumière, chaleur*] to diffuse **b** [+ *rumeur, idée, nouvelle*] to spread; [+ *connaissances*] to disseminate, spread; **la police a diffusé le signalement du ravisseur** the police have issued a description of the kidnapper **c** (*Radio, TV*) [+ *émission*] to broadcast; **le concert était diffusé en direct/en différé** the concert was broadcast live/was pre-recorded; **des slogans diffusés par haut-parleur** slogans broadcast over a loudspeaker **d** (= *distribuer*) [+ *livres, revues*] to distribute; [+ *tracts*] to distribute, circulate; **hebdomadaire diffusé à 80 000 exemplaires** weekly magazine with a circulation of 80,000 **2** VI (*Sci*) to diffuse **3** **se diffuser** VPR [*chaleur, lumière*] to be diffused; [*rumeur, idée, nouvelle, phénomène*] to spread

diffuseur [difyzœʀ] NM (*Aut, Tech* = *appareil*) diffuser; (*Presse* = *distributeur*) distributor; (*fig* = *propagateur*) diffuser, spreader; **~ de parfum** diffuser (for room fragrance); **~ d'insecticide** electric mosquito killer

diffusion [difyzjɔ̃] NF **a** [*lumière, chaleur*] diffusion **b** [*rumeur, idée, nouvelle*] spreading; [*connaissances*] dissemination, diffusion **c** (*Radio, TV*) [*émission*] broadcasting; **des films en première ~** films being shown *ou* broadcast for the first time on television; **~ numérique** digital broadcasting **d** (= *distribution*) [*livres, revues*] distribution; [*tracts*] distribution, circulation; **journal de grande ~** large *ou* wide circulation paper; [*rapport*] **pour ~ restreinte** (*gén*) restricted; (*secret d'État*) classified **e** (*Méd*) [*maladie, virus*] spread, spreading

digérer [diʒeʀe] ▶conjug 6◀ VT **a** [+ *aliment, connaissance*] to digest; **je l'ai bien/mal digéré** I had no trouble/I had trouble digesting it; **c'est du Marx mal digéré** it's ill-digested Marx **b*** (= *supporter*) [+ *insulte, attitude*] to stomach*, put up with; [+ *échec, choc*] to accept, come to terms with; **je ne peux plus ~ son insolence** I won't put up with *ou* stand for his insolence any longer

digest [daʒɛst, diʒɛst] NM digest

digeste [diʒɛst] ADJ [*aliment*] easily digested, easily digestible; **c'est un livre peu ~*** this book's rather heavy going

digestibilité [diʒɛstibilite] NF digestibility

digestible [diʒɛstibl] ADJ easily digested, easily digestible

digestif, -ive [diʒɛstif, iv] **1** ADJ digestive → **tube** **2** NM (*Méd*) digestive; (= *liqueur*) liqueur

digestion [diʒɛstjɔ̃] NF digestion; **j'ai une ~ difficile** I have trouble digesting, I have digestive problems

digicode® [diʒikɔd] NM (press-button) door-entry system; **y a-t-il un ~ pour entrer chez toi ?** do you have a door code?

digit [diʒit] NM (*Ordin*) (= *chiffre*) digit; (= *caractère*) character

digital, e¹ [*mpl* -**aux**] [diʒital, o] ADJ (*gén*) digital → **empreinte²**

digitale² [diʒital] NF digitalis; **~ pourprée** foxglove

digitaline [diʒitalin] NF digitalin

digitaliser [diʒitalize] ▶conjug 1◀ VT [+ *données, images*] to digitize; **son digitalisé** digital sound

diglossie [diglɔsi] NF diglossia

digne [diɲ] ADJ **a** (= *auguste*) dignified; **il avait un air très ~** he had a very dignified air (about him) **b** (= *qui mérite*) **~ de** [+ *admiration, intérêt*] worthy of, deserving (of); **~ de ce nom** worthy of the name; **~ d'être remarqué** noteworthy; **~ d'éloges** praiseworthy; **~ de foi** trustworthy; **~ de pitié** pitiable; **~ d'envie** enviable; **vous devez vous montrer ~s de représenter la France** you must show that you are fit *ou* worthy to represent France; **livre à peine ~ d'être lu** book which is scarcely worth reading *ou* which scarcely deserves to be read; **il n'est pas ~ de vivre** he's not fit to live; (*littér*) **je ne suis pas ~ que vous m'offriez votre soutien** I am not worthy of your offering me your support (*littér*) **c** (= *à la hauteur*) worthy; **son ~ fils/père/représentant** his worthy son/father/representative; (*lit, péj*) **tu es le ~ fils** *ou* **tu es ~ de ton père** you're fit to be your father's son, you take after your father; **avoir un adversaire ~ de soi** to have an opponent worthy of oneself; **œuvre ~ de son auteur** work worthy of its author; **avec une attitude peu ~ d'un juge** with an attitude little befitting a judge *ou* unworthy of a judge; **un dessert ~ d'un si fin repas** a fitting dessert for such a fine meal

dignement [diɲ(ə)mɑ̃] ADV **a** (= *noblement*) with dignity; **garder le silence** to maintain a dignified silence **b** (= *justement*) fittingly, justly; **être ~ récompensé** to receive a fitting *ou* just reward, be fittingly *ou* justly rewarded

dignitaire [diɲitɛʀ] NM dignitary

dignité [diɲite] NF **a** (= *noblesse*) dignity; **la ~ du travail** the dignity of labour; **la ~ de la personne humaine** human dignity; **avoir de la ~** to be dignified, have dignity; **manquer de ~** to be lacking in dignity, be undignified; (*hum*) **c'est contraire à sa ~** it is beneath his dignity; **elle entra, pleine de ~** she came in with great dignity **b** (= *fonction*) dignity; **être élevé à la ~ de juge** to be promoted to the dignity *ou* rank of judge

digramme [digʀam] NM digraph

digression [digʀesjɔ̃] NF digression; **faire une ~** to digress, make a digression

digue [dig] NF (*gén*) dyke, dike; (*pour protéger la côte*) sea wall; (*fig*) barrier; **élever des ~s contre qch** to erect barriers against sth

diktat [diktat] NM diktat

dilapidateur, -trice [dilapidatœʀ, tʀis] **1** ADJ wasteful **2** NM,F spendthrift, squanderer; **~ des fonds publics** embezzler of public funds

dilapidation [dilapidasjɔ̃] NF [*héritage, fortune*] squandering; [*fonds publics, biens*] embezzlement, misappropriation

dilapider [dilapide] ▶conjug 1◀ VT [+ *héritage, fortune*] to squander; [+ *énergie*] to waste; [+ *fonds publics, biens*] to embezzle, misappropriate

dilatabilité [dilatabilite] NF dilatability

dilatable [dilatabl] ADJ [*corps*] dilatable

dilatant, e [dilatɑ̃, ɑ̃t] **1** ADJ dilative **2** NM dilat(at)or

dilatateur, -trice [dilatatœʀ, tʀis] **1** ADJ dilative **2** NM (**muscle**) **~** dilat(at)or, dilater

dilatation [dilatasjɔ̃] NF [*pupille, narine, vaisseau, col de l'utérus*] dilation, dilatation; [*estomac*] distension; [*métal, gaz, liquide*] expansion; [*pneu*] swelling, distension; **une ~ d'estomac** to have a distended stomach

dilater [dilate] ▶conjug 1◀ **1** VT [+ *pupille, narine, vaisseau, col de l'utérus, cœur*] to dilate; [+ *estomac*] to distend; [+ *métal, gaz, liquide*] to cause to expand; [+ *pneu*] to cause to swell **2** **se dilater** VPR [*pupille, narine*] to dilate; [*estomac*] to distend; [*métal, gaz, liquide*] to expand; [*pneu*] to swell; **se ~ les poumons** to open one's lungs; **pupilles dilatées** dilated pupils; **pores dilatés** enlarged pores; **se ~ la rate**† to split one's sides (laughing)*

dilatoire [dilatwaʀ] ADJ **manœuvres** *ou* **moyens ~s** delaying *ou* stalling tactics; **donner une réponse ~** to play for time

dilemme [dilɛm] NM dilemma; **sortir du ~** to resolve the dilemma; **enfermer qn dans un ~** to put sb in a dilemma

dilettante [diletɑ̃t] NMF (= *amateur d'art*) dilettante; (*péj* = *amateur*) dilettante, dabbler; **faire qch en ~** (*en amateur*) to dabble in sth; (*péj*) to do sth in an amateurish way

dilettantisme [diletɑ̃tism] NM amateurishness; **faire qch avec ~** to do sth in an amateurish way *ou* amateurishly

diligemment [diliʒamɑ̃] ADV (*littér*) (= *avec soin*) diligently; (= *avec célérité*) promptly, speedily

diligence [diliʒɑ̃s] NF **a** (†, *littér* = *empressement*) haste, dispatch; **faire ~** to make haste, hasten; **en ~** posthaste†, speedily **b** (*littér* = *soin*) diligence, conscientiousness; (*Jur*) **à la ~ du ministre** at the minister's behest (*littér*) *ou* request **c** (*Hist* = *voiture*) diligence, stagecoach

diligent, e [diliʒɑ̃, ɑ̃t] ADJ (*littér*) **a** (= *actif*) [*serviteur*] prompt **b** (= *assidu*) [*employé, travail*] diligent, conscientious; [*soins, attention*] diligent, sedulous (*frm*)

diligenter [diliʒɑ̃te] ▶conjug 1◀ VT (*Admin*) [+ *enquête*] to expedite, hasten

diluant [dilɥɑ̃] NM thinner

diluer [dilɥe] ▶conjug 1◀ VT **a** [+ *liquide*] to dilute; [+ *peinture*] to thin (down); (*péj*) [+ *discours*] to pad out; **alcool dilué** alcohol diluted with water; **ce médicament se dilue dans l'eau** this medicine should be diluted with water **b** [+ *force, pouvoir*] to dilute, weaken **c** (*Fin*) [+ *participation, capital, bénéfice*] to dilute; **capital dilué** diluted capital

dilution [dilysjɔ̃] NF **a** [*liquide*] dilution; [*peinture*] thinning (down); (*péj*) [*discours*] padding out; **à haute ~** highly diluted **b** [*force, pouvoir*] dilution, weakening **c** (*Fin*) dilution

diluvien, -ienne [dilyvjɛ̃, jɛn] ADJ [*pluie*] torrential; (*Bible*) [*époque*] diluvian

dimanche [dimɑ̃ʃ] NM Sunday; **le ~ des Rameaux/de Pâques** Palm/Easter Sunday; **le ~ de Noël** the Sunday after Christmas; **les ~s de l'Avent/de Carême** the Sundays in Advent/Lent; **mettre son costume** *ou* **ses habits du ~** to put on one's Sunday clothes *ou* one's Sunday best; **promenade/journal du ~** Sunday walk/(news)paper; (*péj*) **peintre/sportif du ~** amateur *ou* spare-time painter/sportsman; **chauffeur du ~** Sunday driver; **sauf ~ et jours fériés** Sundays and holidays excepted; **ici,**

c'est pas tous les jours ~! life isn't always much fun here!; **allez, encore un verre, c'est pas tous les jours ~!** go on, have another, it's not every day we have an excuse for celebrating!; *pour autres locutions voir* **samedi**

dîme [dim] NF (*Hist*) tithe; **lever une ~ sur qch** to tithe sth; **payer la ~ du vin/des blés** to pay tithes *ou* the tithe on wine/corn; (*fig*) **le grossiste/l'État prélève sa ~ (sur la marchandise)** the wholesaler takes his/the State takes its cut (on the goods)

dimension [dimɑ̃sjɔ̃] NF **a** (= *taille*) [*pièce, terrain*] size; **avoir la même ~** to be the same size, have the same dimensions; **de grande/petite ~** large/small-sized, of large/small dimensions; **faire une étagère à la ~ d'un recoin** to make a shelf to fit (into) an alcove **b** (= *mesure*) **~s** dimensions; **quelles sont les ~s de la pièce?** what are the dimensions *ou* measurements of the room?, what does the room measure?; **ce placard est fait aux ~s du mur** the cupboard has been built to the dimensions of the wall *ou* built to fit the wall; **mesurez-le dans la plus grande ~** measure it at the widest *ou* longest point; **prendre la ~ de qn/d'un problème** to size sb/a problem up **c** (= *importance*) **une entreprise de ~ internationale** a company of international standing; **une erreur de cette ~** a mistake of this magnitude; **un repas à la ~ de son appétit** a meal commensurate with one's appetite; **une tâche à la ~ de son talent** a task equal to *ou* commensurate with one's talent; **il n'a pas la ~ d'un premier ministre** he hasn't got what it takes to be a prime minister **d** (*Philo, Phys*) dimension; **la troisième/quatrième ~** the third/fourth dimension; **à ou en 2/3 ~s** 2-/3-dimensional

dimensionner [dimɑ̃sjɔne] ▸conjug 1◂ VT to proportion; **objet bien dimensionné** well-proportioned object

diminué, e [diminɥe] (*ptp de* **diminuer**) ADJ **a** (= *affaibli*) **il est (très)** *ou* **c'est un homme (très) ~ depuis son accident** he's not (at all) the man he was since his accident; **très ~ physiquement** in very poor health; **très ~ mentalement** mentally much less alert **b** (*Mus*) diminished; (*Tricot*) [*vêtement*] fully-fashioned; [*rang de tricot*] decreased

diminuer [diminɥe] ▸conjug 1◂ **1** VT **a** (= *réduire*) [+ *longueur, largeur, quantité, vitesse*] to reduce; [+ *durée, volume, nombre*] to reduce, decrease; [+ *prix, impôts, consommation, valeur*] to reduce, bring down; [+ *son*] to lower, turn down; [+ *ardeur*] to dampen; [+ *chances de succès, intérêt*] to lessen, reduce, diminish; **~ les effectifs** to cut back on numbers, reduce *ou* cut back the numbers; **~ le plaisir de qn** to take away from sb's pleasure; **~ les forces de qn** to diminish sb's strength **b** (= *affaiblir*) [+ *personne*] to weaken; **ça l'a beaucoup diminué physiquement/moralement** it greatly weakened him physically/mentally **c** (= *rabaisser*) [+ *personne*] to belittle; [+ *mérite, talent*] to belittle, depreciate; **il cherche toujours à se ~** he's always putting himself down **d** (*Tricot*) to decrease

2 VI **a** [*violence, intensité*] to diminish, lessen; [*lumière*] to fade; [*bruit*] to die down; [*pluie*] to let up; [*orage*] to die down, subside; [*intérêt, ardeur*] to die down, decrease, diminish; **l'attaque/le bruit diminue d'intensité** the attack/noise is dying down *ou* is decreasing in intensity **b** [*effectifs, nombre, valeur, pression*] to decrease, diminish, fall; [*provisions*] to diminish, run low; [*forces*] to decline, diminish; **~ de longueur/largeur** to grow shorter/narrower, decrease in length/width; **le (prix du) beurre a diminué** butter has gone *ou* come down *ou* dropped in price; **ça a diminué de volume** it has got smaller; **les jours diminuent** the days are growing shorter *ou* drawing in (*Brit*)

diminutif, -ive [diminytif, iv] **1** ADJ [*suffixe*] diminutive **2** NM (*Ling*) diminutive; (= *petit nom*) pet name (**de** for), diminutive (**de** of)

diminution [diminysjɔ̃] NF **a** [*longueur, largeur, vitesse*] reduction, decreasing; [*durée, volume, nombre, quantité*] reduction, decreasing; [*prix, impôts, consommation, valeur*] reduction, bringing down, cutting back; **il nous a consenti une petite ~** he gave us a small reduction; **une ~ très nette du nombre des accidents** a marked decrease *ou* drop *ou* fall-off in the number of accidents; **être en nette ~** to be falling rapidly **b** [*chances de succès, plaisir, intérêt*] lessening, reduction; [*violence, intensité*] diminishing, lessening **c** [*lumière, bruit*] fading, diminishing; [*circulation*] dying down; [*pluie*] letting up, diminishing; [*orage*] dying down, dying away, subsiding; [*ardeur*] dying down, diminishing, decrease (**de** in) **d** (*Tricot*) decreasing; **faire une ~** to decrease; **commencer les ~s** to begin decreasing

dimorphe [dimɔrf] ADJ dimorphous, dimorphic

dimorphisme [dimɔrfism] NM dimorphism

DIN [din] NM INV (ABRÉV = **Deutsche Industrie Norm**) DIN; **les ~ et les ASA** DIN and ASA standards

dinanderie [dinɑ̃dri] NF (= *commerce*) copperware trade; (= *articles*) copperware

dinandier [dinɑ̃dje] NM copperware manufacturer and retailer

dinar [dinar] NM dinar

dînatoire [dinatwar] ADJ (*frm*) **goûter ~** substantial afternoon meal, ≈ high tea (*Brit*); **buffet ~** ≈ buffet dinner

dinde [dɛ̃d] NF **a** (*Zool*) turkey hen; (*Culin*) turkey; **~ rôtie/de Noël** roast/Christmas turkey **b** (*péj = fille stupide*) silly little goose

dindon [dɛ̃dɔ̃] NM **a** (*gén*) turkey; (*mâle*) turkey cock **b** * (= *homme sot*) **être le ~ (de la farce)** to be the fall guy* → **pavaner**

dindonneau (*pl* **dindonneaux**) [dɛ̃dɔno] NM (*Zool*) turkey poult; (*Culin*) turkey

dîner [dine] ▸conjug 1◂ **1** VI **a** (*le soir*) to have dinner, dine; **~ aux chandelles** to have dinner *ou* to dine by candlelight; **~ d'une tranche de pain** to have a slice of bread for dinner; **avoir qn à ~** to have sb (round) to dinner → **dormir** **b** (*Can, Helv, Belg*) to have lunch **2** NM **a** (= *repas du soir*) dinner; **ils donnent un ~ demain** they are having a dinner party tomorrow; **~ de famille/d'affaires** family/business dinner; **~ en ville** (formal) dinner party; **avant le ~** before dinner **b** (*Can, Helv, Belg*) lunch

dînette [dinɛt] NF **a** (= *jeu d'enfants*) doll's tea party; **jouer à la ~** to play at having a tea party; **venez à la maison, on fera (la) ~*** come round and we'll have a bite to eat **b** (= *jouet*) **~ de poupée** doll's tea set, toy tea set

dîneur, -euse [dinœr, øz] NM,F diner

ding [diŋ] EXCL ding; **~ dong!** ding dong!

dingo¹ [dɛ̃go] NM (= *chien*) dingo

dingue* [dɛ̃g], **dingo²***† [dɛ̃go] **1** ADJ [*personne*] nuts*, crazy*, barmy* (*Brit*); **il y avait un bruit ~** it was incredibly noisy; **tu verrais les prix, c'est ~!** you should see the prices, they're crazy *ou* incredible!; **un film ~** a really way-out* film; **un vent ~** a hell of* a wind, an incredible wind; **il est ~ de cette fille/de ce chanteur** he's crazy* *ou* nuts* *ou* mad* about that girl/singer **2** NMF nutcase*, loony*; **on devrait l'envoyer chez les ~s** he ought to be locked up *ou* to be sent to the loony bin*; **c'est un ~ de la voiture/de la guitare** he's crazy* *ou* nuts* *ou* mad* about cars/guitar-playing

dinguer* [dɛ̃ge] ▸conjug 1◂ VI **aller ~** [*personne*] to fall flat on one's face, go sprawling; [*chose*] to go crashing down, go flying*; **envoyer ~ qn** (= *faire tomber*) to send sb flying*; (= *chasser*)

to tell sb to buzz off* *ou* push off*; **envoyer ~ qch** to send sth flying*

dinguerie* [dɛ̃gri] NF craziness, stupidity; **toutes ces ~s** all these stupidities

dinosaure [dinozɔr] NM (*Zool, fig*) dinosaur

diocésain, e [djɔsezɛ̃, ɛn] ADJ, NM,F diocesan

diocèse [djɔsɛz] NM diocese

diode [djɔd] NF diode

Diogène [djɔʒɛn] NM Diogenes

dionysiaque [djɔnizjak] ADJ Dionysian, Dionysiac; **les ~s** the Dionysia

Dionysos [djɔnizɔs] NM Dionysus, Dionysos

dioptrie [djɔptri] NF dioptre

dioptrique [djɔptrik] **1** ADJ dioptric(al) **2** NF dioptrics *sg*

diorama [djɔrama] NM diorama

dioxine [djɔksin] NF dioxin

dioxyde [djɔksid] NM dioxide

diphasé, e [difaze] ADJ diphase, diphasic, two-phase

diphtérie [difteri] NF diphtheria

diphtérique [difterik] ADJ diphther(it)ic, diphtherial

diphtongaison [diftɔ̃gɛzɔ̃] NF diphthongization

diphtongue [diftɔ̃g] NF diphthong

diphtonguer VT, **se diphtonguer** VPR [diftɔ̃ge] ▸conjug 1◂ to diphthongize

diplodocus [diplɔdɔkys] NM diplodocus

diplômant, e [diploma, ɑ̃t] ADJ **formation ~e** course leading to a qualification, ≈ certificate course

diplomate [diplɔmat] **1** ADJ diplomatic **2** NMF (= *ambassadeur, personne habile*) diplomat **3** NM (*Culin*) ≈ trifle; **~ au chocolat** ≈ chocolate charlotte russe

diplomatie [diplɔmasi] NF (*Pol, fig*) diplomacy; **le personnel de la ~** the diplomatic staff; **faire preuve de ~ envers qn** to treat sb diplomatically, be diplomatic towards sb; **entrer dans la ~** to enter the diplomatic service

diplomatique [diplɔmatik] ADJ (*gén*) diplomatic; **c'est une maladie ~** it's a face-saving illness → **valise**

diplomatiquement [diplɔmatikmɑ̃] ADV (*Pol, fig*) diplomatically

diplôme [diplom] NM (= *titre*) (*gén*) diploma, certificate; (*Univ*) ≈ degree; **avoir des ~s** to have qualifications; **~ d'études universitaires générales** diploma taken after two years at university; **~ d'études approfondies** post-graduate diploma taken before completing a PhD, ≈ all but dissertation (*US*); **~ d'études supérieures spécialisées** one-year post-graduate diploma in an applied subject; **~ d'études supérieures techniques** university post-graduate technical degree; **~ d'études universitaires scientifiques et techniques** science diploma taken after two years at university; **~ universitaire de technologie** two-year diploma taken at a technical college after the baccalauréat

┌─────────────────────────────────────┐
DIPLÔMES

The initial university qualifications in France are the DEUG or DEUST (taken after two years, the latter in science and technology), and the "licence", taken after three years. The one-year "maîtrise" follows the "licence", and is assessed on the basis of a written dissertation known as a "mémoire". Higher postgraduate study usually begins with a "DEA", a preparatory research qualification that precedes the "doctorat".
└─────────────────────────────────────┘

diplômé, e [diplome] (*ptp de* **diplômer**) **1** ADJ qualified **2** NM,F holder of a diploma; **il est ~ d'Harvard** he has a Harvard degree, he has a degree from Harvard

diplômer [diplome] ▸conjug 1◂ VT to award a diploma to

diplopie [diplɔpi] NF double vision, diplopia (SPÉC)

dipôle [dipol] NM (*Phys*) dipole; (*Élec*) dipole (aerial)

dipsomane [dipsɔman] **1** ADJ dipsomaniacal **2** NMF dipsomaniac

dipsomanie [dipsɔmani] NF dipsomania

diptère [diptɛʀ] **1** ADJ [*temple*] dipteral; [*insecte*] dipterous, dipteran **2** NM (*Zool*) dipteran; **les ~s** dipterans, the Diptera (SPÉC)

diptyque [diptik] NM (*Hist* = *tablette, Art*) diptych; (= *roman, film*) work in two parts

dir. ABRÉV = **direction**

dircom* [diʀkɔm] NMF ABRÉV = **directeur, -trice de la communication**

▼ **dire** [diʀ]

▶ conjug 37 ◀
1 VERBE TRANSITIF   **3** NOM MASCULIN
2 VERBE PRONOMINAL

1 VERBE TRANSITIF

a gén = **déclarer** to say; **avez-vous quelque chose à ~?** have you got anything to say?; **«j'ai froid», dit-il** "I'm cold", he said; **on peut commencer?** — **elle a dit oui can we start?** — she said yes *ou* she said we could; **~ bonjour/quelques mots à qn** to say hello/a few words to sb; **il m'a dit: «je comprends»** he said to me, "I understand"; **que dites-vous? ◊ qu'est-ce que vous dites?** (I beg your) pardon?, what did you say?; **comment dit-on ça en anglais?** what's the English for that?, how do you say that in English?; **comme disent les spécialistes** as the experts say; **~ ce que l'on pense** to speak one's mind, say what one thinks; **je ne fais que ~ tout haut ce que tout le monde pense tout bas** I'm only saying aloud what everyone else is thinking; **je ne savais plus quoi ~** I was at a loss for words; **il n'a pas dit un mot** he didn't say *ou* utter a (single) word; **l'argent ne fait pas le bonheur, dit-on** money can't buy you happiness, as the saying goes *ou* as they say; **qu'est-ce que les gens vont ~? ◊ qu'en dira-t-on?** whatever will people *ou* they say?; **il sait ce qu'il dit** he knows what he's talking about; **il ne sait pas ce qu'il dit** (= *il déraisonne*) he doesn't know what he's saying; (= *il ne sait pas de quoi il parle*) he doesn't know what he's talking about; **à** *ou* **d'après ce qu'il dit** according to him, according to what he says; **tu ne crois pas si bien ~!** you don't know how right you are!; **ce n'est pas une chose à ~** some things are better left unsaid; **où va-t-il? — il ne l'a pas dit** where's he going? — he didn't say; (*Cartes*) **c'est à vous de ~** your call → **bien, mal, parler**

◆ **ceci** *ou* **cela dit** (*avec restriction*) nevertheless, having said this; (= *à ces mots*) thereupon, having said this

◆ **cela va sans dire** it goes without saying; **il va sans ~ que c'était faux** needless to say it was wrong

◆ **comme on dit ◊ comme dire** *ou* **dirait l'autre*** as they say, so to speak

◆ **comme qui dirait*** as you might say; **j'entends comme qui dirait des grognements** I can hear what sounds like groans; **cette maison c'est comme qui dirait un énorme cube** the house looks a bit like a huge cube

◆ **comment dirais-je?** how shall I put it?

◆ **je ne te** *ou* **vous dis que ça!*** that's all I can say!; (*admiratif*) **il nous a fait un dîner, je ne te dis que ça!** he made us one hell of a dinner!*

◆ **pour ne pas dire**: **il est gros, pour ne pas ~ obèse** he's fat, not to say obese

◆ **soit dit en passant** by the way, let me say in passing, incidentally

b

◆ **dire que** to say that; **~ à qn que ...** to tell sb that ..., say to sb that ...; **il dit qu'il nous a écrit ◊ il dit nous avoir écrit** he says that he wrote to us; **il a bien dit qu'il ne rentrerait pas**

he did say that he would not be coming home; **est-ce qu'il doit venir? — elle dit que oui/que non** is he coming? — she says he is/he isn't *ou* she says so/not; **la radio et les journaux avaient dit qu'il pleuvrait** the radio and the papers had said it would rain; **vous nous dites dans votre lettre que ...** you tell us *ou* you say in your letter that ...; **votre lettre/la loi dit clairement que ...** your letter/the law says clearly that *ou* clearly states that ...; **qu'est-ce qui me dit que c'est vrai?** how can I tell it's the truth?, how am I to know *ou* how do I know it's the truth?

◆ **on dit que ...** rumour has it that ..., they say that ...

◆ **que dis-je**: **il a au moins 70 ans, que dis-je, plutôt 80** he must be at least 70 — what am I saying? — more like 80; **il est très économe, que dis-je, il est avare!** he's very thrifty, not to say mean!

c = **communiquer** [+ *mensonges, nouvelle, adresse, nom*] to tell; [+ *sentiment*] to tell of, express; **~ qch à qn** to tell sb sth; **il m'a dit quelque chose qui m'a fait rire** he told me something *ou* he said something to me that made me laugh; **j'ai quelque chose à vous ~** there's something I want to tell you *ou* say to you; **~ des bêtises** to talk nonsense; **il nous a dit sa joie/son soulagement** he told us how happy/how relieved he was; **je ne te le dirai pas deux fois** I won't tell you again; **je suis sûr, je te dis!*** I'm certain, I tell you!; **je vous l'avais bien dit!** I told you so!, didn't I tell you?; **quelque chose me dit que ...** something tells me (that) ..., I've got the feeling (that) ... → **aventure**

◆ **entre nous soit dit ◊ soit dit entre nous** (just) between the two of us, between you and me

◆ **pour mieux dire**: **sa franchise, ou pour mieux ~ son manque de tact** his frankness, or rather his tactlessness

◆ **pour tout dire** actually, in fact; **pour tout ~, ce film m'a paru sans intérêt** actually, I found the film totally uninteresting; **il n'est pas bricoleur, pour tout ~ il a horreur des travaux manuels** he's not much of a handyman - in fact he hates manual work

d = **ordonner, prévenir** to tell; **dites-lui de partir/qu'il parte ce soir** tell him to leave/that he must leave tonight; **il a dit de venir tôt** he said we were to come *ou* he said to come* early, he told us to come early; **fais ce qu'on te dit!** do as *ou* what you are told!; **ça suffit, j'ai dit!** I said that's enough!; **on nous a dit de l'attendre** we were told to wait for him → **envoyer**

e = **objecter** to say (à, contre against); **que veux-tu que je dise à ou contre ça?** what can I say against that?; **je n'ai rien à ~ sur son travail** I can't complain about his work; **tu n'as rien à ~, tu aurais fait la même chose!** you can talk! you would have done exactly the same thing!; **tais-toi, tu n'as rien à ~!** be quiet, you're in no position to comment!; **tu n'as rien à ~, tu es bien servi** you can't complain, you've done very well out of it

◆ **c'est pas pour dire***: **c'est pas pour ~, mais je l'ai bien réussi, ce gâteau!** I don't mean to boast, but I made a really good job of that cake!; **c'est pas pour ~, mais il aurait pu m'inviter!** I don't mean to complain, but he could have invited me!

◆ **il n'y a pas à dire* ◊ on ne peut pas dire*** there's no doubt about it, there's no getting away from it

f = **réciter** [+ *poèmes*] to say, recite; [+ *prière*] to say; [+ *rôle*] to speak; **~ la messe** to say mass; **l'acteur a très mal dit ce passage** the actor spoke the lines very badly → **chapelet**

g = **plaire** **ça vous dit de sortir?** do you feel like going out?, do you fancy (*Brit*) going out?; **ça ne me dit rien** I don't feel like it at all, it doesn't appeal to me at all, I don't fancy (*Brit*) it at all; **il y a des fraises mais ça ne me dit**

pas there are strawberries but I don't fancy them (*Brit*) *ou* I'm not in the mood for them; **rien ne me dit en ce moment** I'm not in the mood for anything *ou* I don't feel like doing anything just now; **si le cœur vous en dit** if you feel like it, if you feel so inclined

h = **penser** to think; **qu'est-ce que tu dis de ma robe?** what do you think of *ou* how do you like my dress?; **qu'est-ce que vous dites de ça?** what do you think *ou* how do you feel about it?, what are your feelings on the subject?; **qu'est-ce que vous diriez d'une promenade?** what would you say to a walk?, how about a walk?; **on dirait qu'il n'aime pas cette ville** he doesn't seem to like this town; **on dirait qu'il le fait exprès!** you'd almost think he does it on purpose!; **qui aurait dit qu'elle allait gagner?** who would have thought (that) she would win?; **on dirait qu'il va pleuvoir** it looks like rain; **on dirait qu'il va pleurer** he looks as though he is going to cry; **cette eau est noire, on dirait de l'encre** this water is black — it looks like ink; **on dirait du poulet** it tastes like *ou* it's like chicken; **on dirait du Brahms** it sounds like *ou* it's like Brahms; **on dirait du parfum** it's like *ou* it smells like perfume; **on dirait de la soie** it's like *ou* it feels like silk; **qui l'eût dit!** who'd have thought it!

◆ **dire que ...!** (*dans une phrase exclamative*) et **~ qu'il aurait pu se tuer!** to think he might have killed himself!

i = **supposer, prétendre** **on le dit malade/à Londres** he's rumoured to be ill/in London; **des gens dits cultivés** supposedly educated people

j = **décider** **venez bientôt, disons demain** come soon, let's make it tomorrow *ou* (let's) say tomorrow; **tout n'est pas dit** the last word has not been said, it isn't all over yet; **il est dit** *ou* **il a été dit que je ne gagnerai jamais** I'm destined *ou* fated never to win; **bon, c'est dit** *ou* **voilà qui est dit** right, that's settled *ou* it's all arranged; **ce qui est dit est dit** what's said is said; **à l'heure dite** at the appointed time *ou* hour; **au jour dit** on the appointed day → **aussitôt, facile, tenir**

k = **admettre** to say, admit; **il faut bien ~ que ...** I must say *ou* admit that ...; **disons-le, il nous ennuie** let's be frank *ou* let's face it*, we find him boring

l = **évoquer** **ce nom me dit quelque chose** this name rings a bell; **ça ne me dit rien du tout** that doesn't mean a thing to me

m * = **avoir tel aspect** **et tes plantations, qu'est-ce que ça dit?** how are your plants doing?; **pour l'instant, ça ne dit rien†, mais attendez que ce soit fini!** for the moment it doesn't look up to much*, but just wait until it's finished!

n = **indiquer** to say, show; **ma montre dit 6 heures** my watch says 6 o'clock, it's 6 o'clock by my watch; **son visage disait sa déception** his face gave away his disappointment, disappointment was written all over his face → **long**

o

◆ **faire dire**: **faire ~ qch à qn** to send word of sth to sb; **faire ~ à qn de venir** to send for sb; **faire ~ à qn qu'on a besoin de lui** to let sb know that he is needed; **faire ~ à qn des choses (qu'il n'a pas dites)** to put words in sb's mouth; **je ne vous le fais pas ~!** you said it!; **il ne se l'est pas fait ~ deux fois** he didn't need *ou* have to be told twice; **elle partit sans se le faire ~ deux fois** she left without having to be told twice; **sous la torture, on fait ~ aux gens ce qu'on veut** people can be made to say *ou* you can make people say anything under torture

p

◆ **laisser dire** to let people talk; **laisse ~!** let them talk!, never mind what they say!; **je me suis laissé ~ que ...** I heard that ..., I was told that ...

◆ **vouloir dire** (= *signifier*) to mean; **qu'est-ce que ça veut ~?** [*mot, texte*] what does that mean?; [*attitude de qn*] what does that imply? *ou* mean?; **cette phrase ne veut rien ~** this sentence doesn't mean a thing; **que veux-tu ~ par là?** what do you mean?; **ça ne veut pas ~ qu'il viendra** it doesn't mean (to say) that *ou* it doesn't follow that he'll come; **ça veut tout ~!** that says it all!; **ça dit bien ce que ça veut ~** it means exactly *ou* just what it says; (*reproche*) **non mais, qu'est-ce que ça veut ~ de crier comme ça?** what on earth is all this shouting about?

[r] [loc] **tu me l'envoies, dis, cette lettre?** you will send me that letter, won't you?; **dis Papa, quand est-ce qu'on part?** hey daddy, when are we going?; **dis** *ou* **dites donc!** (= *à propos*) by the way; (= *holà*) hey!, say!; (*US*) **c'est joli dis donc!** oh, isn't that pretty!; **ça lui a rapporté 100 000 F — ben dis donc!** that earned him 100,000 francs — goodness me *ou* well I never!* (*Brit*); **tu l'as dit (bouffi*)!** how right you are!, you said it!; **quand je vous le disais!** I told you so!, what did I tell you!; **c'est moi qui vous le dis** take my word for it; **c'est ce que je te dis** *ou* **dites** that's what YOU say; **c'est (vous) ~ s'il est content/s'il a eu peur** that just shows you how pleased he is/how frightened he was; **c'est beaucoup/trop ~** that's saying a lot/too much; **c'est peu ~** that's an understatement; **et ce n'est pas peu ~!** ◊ **ce qui n'est pas peu ~!** and that's really saying something!; **une superproduction hollywoodienne, c'est tout ~!** it's a Hollywood spectacular, which says it all!; **est-ce à ~ que ...?** does that mean (that) ...?; **qu'est-ce à ~?** (*frm*) what does that mean?; **que tu dis (ou qu'il dit etc)!** that's YOUR (*ou* HIS *etc*) story!, that's what YOU say (*ou* HE says *etc*)!; **qui dit argent, dit problèmes** money means problems; **à qui le dites-vous!** don't I know it!*, you're telling me!*; (*aux enchères*) **qui dit mieux?** any advance?; **il a fait 50 % de bénéfice, qui dit mieux?** he made a 50% profit, you can't get much better than that, can you?

[2] **se dire** VERBE PRONOMINAL

[a] [= *penser*] to say to o.s; **il se dit qu'il était inutile de rester** he said to himself that there was no point in staying; **je me dis que j'aurais dû l'acheter** I feel now *ou* I'm thinking now that I should have bought it; **il faut bien se ~ que ...** one has to realize *ou* accept that ...

[b] [= *se prétendre*] to claim to be; **il se dit malade** he claims to be ill *ou* that he is ill; **elle se dit sa cousine** she claims to be his cousin, she says she is his cousin

[c] [= *se croire*] **on se dirait en Grèce/au Moyen Âge** you'd think we were in Greece/back in the Middle Ages

[d] [mutuellement] **elles se dirent au revoir** they said goodbye (to each other)

[e] [= *être dit*] **ça ne se dit pas** (*inusité*) you don't say that; (*impoli*) it's not polite; **cela ne se dit plus en français** the expression is no longer used *ou* in use in French; **ça se dit de la même façon en anglais et en français** it's the same in English and in French; **comment ça se dit en français?** how do you say that in French?; (*dans un dictionnaire*) **se dit d'un objet/d'une personne** *etc* of an object/a person *etc*

[3] NOM MASCULIN

[= *déclaration*] statement; **d'après** *ou* **selon ses ~s** according to him *ou* to what he says; **au ~ de** ◊ **aux ~s de** according to; **au ~ de** *ou* **selon le ~ de tous** by all accounts; (*Jur*) **leurs ~s ne concordent pas** their statements do not agree

---

direct, e [diʀɛkt] [1] ADJ [a] (= *sans détour*) [*route, personne, reproche, regard*] direct; [*question*] direct, straight; [*allusion*] direct, pointed (*épith*); **c'est le chemin le plus ~** it's the most

direct route; **c'est ~ en bus** there's a bus that goes direct; **il m'a parlé de manière très ~e** ◊ **il a été très ~** he spoke to me in a very direct *ou* straightforward way, he didn't beat about the bush

[b] (= *sans intermédiaire*) (*gén*) direct; [*cause, conséquence*] immediate, direct; [*Jur*) [*action*] direct; **ses chefs ~s** his immediate superiors; **vente ~e** direct selling; **ligne téléphonique ~e** (*privée*) private *ou* direct line; (*automatique*) automatic dialling system; **être en rapport** *ou* **en contact ~** *ou* **en relations ~es avec** to deal directly *ou* be in direct contact with; **se mettre en rapport ~ avec qn** to contact sb *ou* make contact with sb directly; **il n'y a pas de rapport** *ou* **lien ~ entre les deux faits** there is no direct connection *ou* link between the two facts; **il a pris une part très ~e à cette affaire** he was directly involved in the deal

[c] (= *absolu*) **en contradiction/opposition ~e avec** in direct contradiction/opposition to

[d] (*Astron*) direct; (*Ling*) [*style, discours, objet*] direct; (*Logique*) [*proposition*] positive → **complément**

[e] (*Transport*) [*train*] through (*épith*), non-stop (*épith*); [*vol*] direct, non-stop (*épith*); **ce train est ~ jusqu'à Paris** this is a through *ou* non-stop train to Paris

[2] NM [a] (*Rail*) express (train), fast *ou* non-stop train; **le ~ Paris-Dijon** the Paris-Dijon express

[b] (*Boxe*) jab; **~ du gauche/du droit** straight left/right, left/right jab; **il lui a envoyé un ~ dans l'estomac** he delivered a punch straight to his stomach

[c] (*Radio, TV*) **c'est du ~** it's live; **émission en ~ live broadcast; **parler/faire un reportage en ~ de New York** to be speaking/reporting live from New York; **ce sont les risques du ~** those are the risks of live broadcasting *ou* of broadcasting live

[3] ADV* straight; **tu fais la traduction ~?** do you translate straight off?; **on l'a emmené ~ à l'hôpital** he was taken straight to hospital

directement [diʀɛktəmɑ̃] ADV [a] (= *immédiatement*) straight, right away, straight away (*Brit*); **il est allé se coucher ~** he went straight *ou* directly to bed, he went to bed right *ou* straight (*Brit*) away; **en rentrant il est allé ~ au réfrigérateur** when he came home he went straight to the fridge *ou* he made a beeline for the fridge

[b] (= *sans détour*) straight, directly; **cette rue mène ~ à la gare** this street leads straight to the station; **cet escalier communique ~ avec la cave** this staircase leads straight *ou* directly to the cellar; **il est entré ~ dans le vif du sujet** he came straight to the point

[c] (= *personnellement*) directly; **il m'a très ~ accusé de ce crime** he accused me of the crime straight out; **sa bonne foi est ~ mise en cause** it's a direct challenge to his good faith; **tout ceci ne me concerne pas ~ mais ...** none of this concerns me directly *ou* personally but ... none of this is of any direct *ou* immediate concern to me but ...; **les secteurs les plus ~ touchés par la crise** the sectors most directly *ou* immediately affected by the crisis

[d] (= *sans intermédiaire*) direct, straight; **adressez-vous ~ au patron** apply to the boss direct *ou* in person, go straight to the boss; **j'ai été ~ le trouver pour le lui demander** I went straight to him to ask him about it; **~ du producteur au consommateur** direct *ou* straight from the producer to the consumer; **colis expédié ~ à l'acheteur** parcel sent direct to the buyer

[e] (= *diamétralement*) (*lit*) directly; (*fig*) completely, utterly, directly; **la maison ~ en face** the house directly *ou* straight opposite

directeur, -trice [diʀɛktœʀ, tʀis] [1] ADJ (= *dirigeant*) directing; (= *principal*) [*idée*] principal, main; [*principe*] guiding; [*force*] guiding,

driving; (*Tech*) [*bielle*] driving; [*roue*] front; **le taux ~ de la Banque de France** the Bank of France's key interest rate → **comité, ligne¹, plan¹**

[2] NM [a] (= *responsable, gérant*) [*banque, usine*] manager; (*Admin*) head; (*Police*) ≈ chief constable (*Brit*), ≈ police chief (*US*); (*Ciné, TV*) director; **~ général** [*entreprise*] general manager; (*au conseil d'administration*) managing director, chief executive officer (*US*); [*organisme international*] director general; **~ général adjoint** assistant general manager; (*Univ*) **le ~ de l'UFR d'anglais** the head of the English department; (*Comm*) **des achats** *ou* **d'achat** chief buyer, purchasing manager

[b] (= *administrateur, propriétaire*) director

[c] **~ (d'école)** headmaster, principal (*US*)

[3] COMP ► **directeur administratif et financier** financial and administrative director ► **directeur artistique** artistic director ► **directeur de cabinet** (*d'un ministre*) principal private secretary ► **directeur commercial** commercial manager ► **directeur de la communication** head of communications ► **directeur de conscience** spiritual adviser ► **directeur financier** financial director ► **directeur gérant** managing director ► **directeur de journal** newspaper editor ► **directeur de la photographie** director of photography ► **directeur de prison** prison governor (*Brit*), head warden (*US*) ► **directeur des programmes** (*Radio, TV*) programme (*Brit*) *ou* program (*US*) director ► **directeur des ressources humaines** human resources manager ► **directeur spirituel** = directeur de conscience ► **directeur de théâtre** theatre (*Brit*) *ou* theater (*US*) manager ► **directeur de thèse** (*Univ*) supervisor (*Brit*), (dissertation) director (*US*) ► **directeur des ventes** sales manager

directif, -ive¹ [diʀɛktif, iv] ADJ managerial

direction [diʀɛksjɔ̃] NF [a] (= *sens*) direction; (= *route, chemin*) direction, way; **vous n'êtes pas dans** *ou* **vous n'avez pas pris la bonne ~** you're not going the right way, you're going in the wrong direction; **dans quelle ~ est-il parti?** which way did he go?; **aller dans la ~ de** *ou* **en ~ de Paris** ◊ **prendre la ~ de Paris** to go towards *ou* in the direction of Paris; (*métro*) **prendre la ~ Châtelet** take the line that goes to Châtelet; **train/avion en ~ de ...** train/plane for *ou* going to ...; **bateau en ~ de ...** ship bound for *ou* heading for ...; **nous devons chercher dans une autre ~** we must look in some other *ou* a different direction; **l'enquête a pris une nouvelle ~** the inquiry has taken a new turn; **dans toutes les ~s** in all directions; (*Aut*) **« autres ~s »** "all other routes"; **« toutes ~s »** "all routes"

[b] (= *action de diriger*) [*entreprise, usine, théâtre*] management, running; [*journal, pays, gouvernement, parti*] running; [*orchestre*] conducting; (*Ciné, Théât, TV*) [*acteurs*] directing; [*opération, manœuvre*] supervision; **il a été chargé de** *ou* **on lui a confié la ~ de l'enquête/des travaux** he has been put in charge of the inquiry/the work; **prendre la ~ de** [+ *service*] to become head of, take over the running of; [+ *usine, entreprise*] to become manager of, take over the running *ou* management of; [+ *équipe, travaux*] to take charge of, take over the supervision of; [+ *mouvement, pays*] to become leader of, take over the leadership of; [+ *débats*] to take control of; [+ *journal*] to take over the editorship of; **~ par objectifs** management by objectives; **prendre la ~ des opérations** to take charge *ou* control (of operations); **sous sa ~** under his leadership (*ou*

management *etc*); **il a travaillé sous la ~ d'un spécialiste** he has worked under the supervision of an expert; **il a fait ses études sous la ~ de M. Borel** he studied under M. Borel; (*Mus*) **orchestre (placé) sous la ~ de Luc Petit** orchestra conducted by Luc Petit

[c] (= *fonction de responsable*) post of manager, managership; (= *fonction d'administrateur*) post of director, directorship; [*école*] headship, post of head *ou* principal (*US*); [*journal*] editorship, post of editor; [*pays, gouvernement, parti*] leadership; **on lui a offert la ~ de l'usine/d'une équipe de chercheurs** he was offered the post of factory manager/of head of a research team; **on lui a donné la ~ générale** he was given the director-generalship

[d] (= *personnel dirigeant*) [*usine, service, équipe*] management; [*journal*] editorial board; **la ~ générale/commerciale** the general/sales management; **se plaindre à la ~** to make a complaint to the board *ou* the management; **la ~ décline toute responsabilité** the management accepts no responsibility → **changement**

[e] (= *bureau*) [*usine*] manager's (*ou* director's) office; [*école*] headmaster's (*ou* headmistress's) office, principal's office (*US*); [*journal*] editor's office

[f] (= *service*) department; **la ~ des ressources humaines** the human resources department; **adressez-vous à la ~ du personnel** apply to the personnel department; **notre ~ générale est à Paris** our head office is in Paris; (*de l'UE*) **Direction générale** Directorate General; **la Direction de la surveillance du territoire** the counter-espionage services, ≈ MI5 (*Brit*), ≈ the CIA (*US*); **Direction départementale de l'action sanitaire et sociale** ≈ social services; **Direction générale des impôts** ≈ Inland Revenue (*Brit*), ≈ Internal Revenue Service (*US*)

[g] (*Aut* = *mécanisme*) steering; **~ assistée** power-steering; **il n'y a plus de ~** the steering has gone → **rupture**

directionnel, -elle [diʀɛksjɔnɛl] ADJ (*Tech*) directional

directive² [diʀɛktiv] NF (*gén pl*) directive, order, instruction; **~ communautaire/européenne** Community/European directive

directoire [diʀɛktwaʀ] NM [a] (*Comm etc*) board of directors *ou* management; **membre/président du ~** member/chairman of the board (of directors); [b] (*Hist*) **le Directoire** the (French) Directory, the Directoire; **fauteuil/table ~** Directoire chair/table

directorat [diʀɛktɔʀa] NM [*administration*] directorship; [*entreprise*] managership; [*école*] headship, principalship (*US*)

directorial, e (*mpl* **-iaux**) [diʀɛktɔʀjal, jo] ADJ [*fonction, responsabilité*] (*Comm, Ind*) managerial; (*Admin*) of directors; (*Scol*) of headmaster (*ou* headmistress), of principal (*US*); **fauteuil/bureau ~** manager's (*ou* director's *ou* head's *ou* principal's (*US*)) chair/office

directrice [diʀɛktʀis] NF → **directeur**

dirham [diʀam] NM dirham

dirigeable [diʀiʒabl] ADJ, NM (**ballon**) **~** dirigible, airship

dirigeant, e [diʀiʒɑ̃, ɑ̃t] [1] ADJ [*classe*] ruling [2] NM,F [*parti, syndicat, pays*] leader; (= *monarque, dictateur*) ruler; **~ d'entreprise** company director; (*salarié*) company manager

diriger [diʀiʒe] ▶conjug 3◀ [1] VT [a] [+ *service*] to run, be in charge of; [+ *entreprise, usine, théâtre*] to manage, run; [+ *journal*] to run, edit; [+ *pays*] (*gén*) to lead; [*dictateur, monarque*] to rule; [+ *mouvement, parti*] to lead; [+ *orchestre*] to conduct; **mal ~ une entreprise** to mismanage a business, run a business badly; **savoir ~** to be a good manager *ou* leader; **équipe bien/mal dirigée** team under good/poor leadership *ou* management, well-/badly-run team → **économie**

[b] (= *superviser*) [+ *opération, manœuvre*] to direct, be in charge of; [+ *recherches, travaux*] to

supervise, oversee, be in charge of

[c] (= *mener*) [+ *enquête, procès*] to conduct; [+ *débat*] to conduct, lead; **a-t-il bien su ~ sa vie ?** did he manage to run his life properly?; **cette idée dirige toute notre politique** this idea guides *ou* determines our whole policy; **l'ambition dirige tous ses actes** he is entirely ruled by ambition

[d] (*Mil*) **~ le tir** to direct the firing

[e] (= *piloter*) [+ *voiture*] to steer; [+ *avion*] to pilot, fly; [+ *bateau*] to steer, navigate; (= *guider*) [+ *cheval*] (*de trait*) to steer; (*de selle*) to guide; **bateau qui se dirige facilement** boat which is easy to steer

[f] (= *acheminer*) [+ *marchandises, convoi*] to send (**vers, sur** to)

[g] (= *orienter*) [+ *personnes*] to direct, send (**sur, vers** to); **on m'a mal dirigé** I was misdirected *ou* sent the wrong way; **~ ses pas vers un lieu** to make for *ou* make one's way to *ou* head for a place; **la flèche est dirigée vers la gauche** the arrow is pointing left *ou* to(wards) the left; **on devrait ~ ce garçon vers les sciences** we should advise this boy to specialize in science, we should guide this boy towards the sciences; **cet élève a été mal dirigé** this pupil has been badly advised *ou* guided; **nous dirigeons notre enquête/nos travaux dans une voie nouvelle** we are conducting *ou* directing our inquiry/carrying out *ou* directing our work along new lines; **~ un article/une allusion contre qn/qch** to aim *ou* direct an article/an allusion at sb/sth; **~ une critique contre qn/qch** to aim *ou* direct *ou* level a criticism at sb/sth; **les poursuites dirigées contre lui** the proceedings brought against him

[h] (= *braquer*) **~ une arme sur** to point *ou* level *ou* aim a weapon at; **~ un canon/télescope sur** to train a gun/telescope on, point a gun/telescope at; **~ une lampe de poche/lumière sur** to shine a torch/light on; **le pompier dirigea sa lance vers les flammes** the fireman aimed *ou* pointed his hose at *ou* trained his hose on the flames; **~ son attention sur qn/qch** to turn one's attention to *ou* on sb/sth; **~ son regard *ou* ses yeux sur *ou* vers qch** to look towards *ou* in the direction of sth; **son regard se dirigea vers elle** he turned his gaze towards *ou* on her

[i] (*Ciné, Théât, TV*) [+ *acteurs*] to direct

[2] **se diriger** VPR [a] **se ~ vers** (= *aller, avancer vers*) to make for, head for, make one's way towards; **il se dirigea vers la sortie** he made his way towards *ou* made for the exit; **le bateau/la voiture semblait se ~ vers le port** the boat/car seemed to be heading *ou* making for the harbour; **l'avion se dirigea vers le nord** the plane flew *ou* headed northwards; **se ~ droit sur qch/qn** to make a beeline *ou* make straight for sth/sb; **nous nous dirigeons vers une solution/un match nul** we seem to be heading towards a solution/a draw; (*Scol*) **se ~ vers les sciences** to specialize in science; **se ~ vers une carrière juridique** to opt for *ou* be headed for a career in law

[b] (= *se guider*) to find one's way; **se ~ sur les étoiles/le soleil** to navigate *ou* sail by the stars/the sun; **se ~ au radar** to navigate by radar; **il n'est pas facile de se ~ dans le brouillard** it isn't easy to find one's way in the fog

dirigisme [diʀiʒism] NM (*Écon*) interventionism, state intervention

dirigiste [diʀiʒist] ADJ, NMF interventionist

dirlo [diʀlo] NMF (ABRÉV = **directeur, -trice**) (*arg Scol*) head

disant [dizɑ̃] → **soi-disant**

discal, e (*mpl* **-aux**) [diskal, o] ADJ (*Méd*) of the intervertebral discs → **hernie**

discernable [disɛʀnabl] ADJ discernible, detectable

discernement [disɛʀnəmɑ̃] NM [a] (= *sagesse*) judgment, discernment; **manquer de ~** to be

lacking in judgment *ou* discernment; **agir sans ~** to act without proper judgment [b] (= *action*) distinguishing, discriminating, distinction; **sans ~** without (making a) distinction

discerner [disɛʀne] ▶conjug 1◀ VT [a] (= *distinguer*) [+ *forme*] to discern, make out, perceive; [+ *bruit*] to detect, hear, make out; [+ *nuance*] to discern, detect [b] (= *différencier*) to distinguish, discriminate (**entre** between); **~ une couleur d'une *ou* d'avec une autre/le vrai du faux** to distinguish *ou* tell one colour from another/truth from falsehood

disciple [disipl] NM (= *élève*) disciple; (= *adepte*) follower, disciple

disciplinable [disiplinabl] ADJ disciplinable

disciplinaire [disiplinɛʀ] ADJ disciplinary

disciplinairement [disiplinɛʀmɑ̃] ADV in a disciplinary way

discipline [disiplin] NF [a] (= *règle*) discipline; **une ~ de fer** an iron discipline; **~ de vote d'un parti** party discipline; (*Pol Brit*) party whip; **elle n'a aucune ~** she has no self-discipline; **il s'entraîne tous les matins avec ~** he makes himself train every morning; **il fait régner la ~ dans sa classe** he imposes discipline on his class; **s'imposer une ~ alimentaire** to be very strict *ou* careful about what one eats → **compagnie, conseil** [b] (= *matière*) (*Scol, Univ*) subject, discipline; (*Sport*) sport; **~ olympique** Olympic sport; **c'est le meilleur dans sa ~** he's the best in his field

discipliné, e [disipline] (*ptp de* **discipliner**) ADJ (well-)disciplined

discipliner [disipline] ▶conjug 1◀ VT [+ *soldats, élèves*] to discipline; [+ *impulsions*] to discipline, control; [+ *cheveux*] to control, keep tidy; **cheveux difficiles à ~** unruly *ou* unmanageable hair; **il faut apprendre à se ~** one must learn self-discipline *ou* to discipline oneself

disc-jockey (*pl* **disc-jockeys**) [disk(ə)ʒɔke] NM disc jockey, DJ

disco [disko] [1] ADJ [*musique*] disco [2] NM **le ~** disco music

discobole [diskɔbɔl] NM discus thrower; (*Antiq*) discobolus

discographie [diskɔgʀafi] NF discography; **sa ~ est abondante** he's made a lot of records

discoïde [diskɔid] ADJ discoid(al), disc- *ou* disk-shaped

discontinu, e [diskɔ̃tiny] [1] ADJ (*Ling, Math*) discontinuous; (= *intermittent*) [*trait*] broken; [*bruit, effort*] intermittent; (*sur route*) **bande *ou* ligne blanche ~e** broken white line [2] NM (*Philo*) discontinuity; **en ~** intermittently

discontinuer [diskɔ̃tinye] ▶conjug 1◀ VTI (*littér*) to discontinue, cease, stop; **sans ~** without stopping, without a break; **pendant deux heures sans ~** for two hours at a stretch *ou* without stopping *ou* without a break

discontinuité [diskɔ̃tinyite] NF discontinuity

disconvenir [diskɔ̃v(ə)niʀ] ▶conjug 22◀ VI (*littér* = *nier*) **je n'en disconviens pas** I don't deny it; **il ne peut ~ que ce soit vrai** he cannot deny the truth of it *ou* that it's true

discophile [diskɔfil] NMF record collector

discordance [diskɔʀdɑ̃s] NF [a] [*caractères*] conflict, clash; [*opinions*] difference, conflict; [*sons*] discord (*NonC*), discordance, dissonance; [*couleurs*] clash(ing) (*NonC*); **leurs déclarations présentent des ~s graves** there were major discrepancies between their statements [b] (*Géol*) unconformability, discordance

discordant, e [diskɔʀdɑ̃, ɑ̃t] ADJ [a] [*caractères, opinions, témoignages*] conflicting; [*sons, cris, bruits*] discordant, harsh; [*instruments*] out of tune; [*couleurs*] clashing, discordant; **elle a une voix ~e** she has a harsh *ou* grating voice, her voice grates b (*Géol*) unconformable, discordant

discorde [diskɔʀd] NF (*littér*) discord, dissension; **mettre** *ou* **semer la ~** to sow discord, cause dissension (**chez, parmi** among) → **pomme**

discorder [diskɔʀde] ▶ conjug 1 ◀ VI [*sons*] to be discordant; [*couleurs*] to clash; [*témoignages*] to conflict

discothécaire [diskɔtekeʀ] NMF record librarian

discothèque [diskɔtɛk] NF (= *collection*) record collection; (= *meuble*) record cabinet; (= *bâtiment*) record library; (= *club*) discotheque

discount [diskunt] NM (= *rabais*) discount; **billets/vols en ~** discount tickets/flights; (**magasin**) **~** discount store *ou* shop; **à des prix ~** at discount prices

discounter[1] [diskunte] ▶ conjug 1 ◀ VT to discount, sell at a discount; **tout est discounté** everything is cut-price *ou* is at a discount price

discounter[2], **discounteur** [diskuntœʀ] NM discount dealer

discoureur, -euse [diskuʀœʀ, øz] NM,F (*péj*) speechifier, windbag*

discourir [diskuʀiʀ] ▶ conjug 11 ◀ VI a (= *faire un discours*) to discourse (*frm*), expatiate (*frm*) (**sur, de** (up)on); (*péj*) to hold forth (**sur, de** on), speechify b (= *bavarder*) to talk (away)

discours [diskuʀ] NM a (= *allocution*) speech; **~ d'ouverture/de clôture** opening/closing speech *ou* address; **~ inaugural** inaugural address *ou* speech; **~ d'investiture** nomination speech; **~-programme** keynote speech; **~ du trône** Queen's (*ou* King's) speech, speech from the throne; (*US Pol*) **~ sur l'état de l'Union** State of the Union Address; **faire** *ou* **prononcer un ~** to make *ou* deliver a speech; **prononcer un ~ sur la tombe de qn** to deliver a funeral oration for sb

b (*péj*) talking (*NonC*), chatter (*NonC*); **tous ces beaux ~ n'y changeront rien** all these fine words *ou* all this fine talk won't make any difference; **suis-moi sans faire de ~!** follow me and don't argue!; **que de ~!** what a lot of fuss (about nothing); **perdre son temps en ~** to waste one's time talking; **assez de ~, des faits!** that's enough talk, let's see some action!; **elle me tenait des ~ sans fin sur la morale/la politique** she gave me endless lectures on morality/politics, she lectured me endlessly on morality/politics; **il aime tenir de grands ~** he likes to hold forth; **elle m'a tenu des ~ à n'en plus finir** she went on and on as if she was never going to stop; **un dessin vaut mieux qu'un long ~** a picture is worth a thousand words

c (= *idées exprimées*) views; **le ~ des intellectuels/des extrémistes** the views expressed by intellectuals/extremists; **le ~ dominant** the prevailing attitude *ou* view; **c'est le ~ officiel** it's the official line; **leur ~ rassurant/optimiste** their reassuring/optimistic views; **changer de ~** to change one's position; **il tient rarement ce ~ en public** he seldom expresses these views in public; **ce parti tient un ~ nouveau** the party is taking a new line; **il m'a déjà tenu ce ~** he's already told me that; **ils tiennent tous le même ~** they all say the same thing

d **le ~** (= *expression verbale*) speech; (*Ling, Rhétorique*) discourse; (*Philo* = *raisonnement*) discursive reasoning *ou* thinking; (*Ling*) (**au**) **~ direct/indirect** (in) direct/indirect *ou* reported speech; **les parties du ~** (*Ling*) the parts of speech; (*Rhétorique*) the parts of discourse

e (*Philo* = *traité*) discourse, treatise; **« Le Discours de la méthode »** "the Discourse on Method"

discourtois, e [diskuʀtwa, waz] ADJ discourteous

discourtoisie [diskuʀtwazi] NF (*littér*) discourtesy

discrédit [diskʀedi] NM [*personne*] discredit, disfavour; [*idée, théorie, œuvre*] discredit, disrepute; **tomber dans le ~** to fall into disrepute; **être en ~** to be discredited *ou* in disrepute; **jeter le ~ sur qch/qn** to discredit sth/sb

discréditer [diskʀedite] ▶ conjug 1 ◀ VT [+ *personne*] to discredit; [+ *théorie, œuvre*] to discredit, bring into disrepute; **c'est une opinion tout à fait discréditée de nos jours** it is an opinion which has gone right out of favour *ou* which is quite discredited nowadays ② **se discréditer** VPR [*idée, théorie*] to become discredited, fall into disrepute; [*personne*] to bring discredit upon o.s., discredit o.s. (**aux yeux de qn, auprès de qn** in sb's eyes)

discret, -ète [diskʀe, ɛt] ADJ a (= *réservé, retenu*) [*personne, attitude*] discreet, reserved; [*allusion, reproche, compliment*] discreet; **soyez ~, ne lui parlez pas de sa défaite** be tactful *ou* discreet and don't mention his defeat to him b (= *qui n'attire pas l'attention*) [*personne, manière*] unassuming, unobtrusive; [*parfum, maquillage*] discreet, light; [*vêtement*] sober, plain, simple; [*couleur*] quiet; [*lumière*] subdued; [*endroit*] quiet, secluded; [*parole, regard*] discreet; **il lui remit un paquet sous emballage ~** he handed her a plainly wrapped parcel; **« envoi ~ »** "sent under plain cover"; **n'y a-t-il pas une façon plus discrète de m'avertir?** isn't there a more discreet *ou* less conspicuous way of warning me?

c (= *qui garde les secrets*) discreet d [*Math*] [*quantité*] discrete; (*Phys*) [*fonction*] discontinuous; (*Ling*) [*unité*] discrete

discrètement [diskʀetmɑ̃] ADV a (= *avec tact*) [*se tenir à l'écart, parler, reprocher*] discreetly, quietly; **il a ~ fait allusion à ...** he gently hinted at ..., he made a discreet allusion to ... b (= *pour ne pas se faire remarquer*) discreetly; [*se maquiller*] lightly; [*s'habiller*] plainly, simply; **il s'est éclipsé ~** he made a discreet exit, he slipped away *ou* out quietly; **parler ~ à l'oreille de qn** to have a quiet word in sb's ear, have a discreet word with sb

discrétion [diskʀesjɔ̃] NF a (= *art de garder un secret*) discretion; **« ~ assurée »** "discretion assured"; **j'aimerais que vous gardiez la plus grande ~ sur le sujet** I'd appreciate it if you could be as discreet as possible about this; **ils se sont mariés dans la plus grande ~** they had a very quiet wedding b (= *réserve*) [*personne*] discretion, tact; **sa ~ est exemplaire** he's a model of discretion *ou* tact c (= *modération*) [*maquillage, parfum*] lightness; [*vêtement*] plainness, simpleness; **avec ~** [*s'habiller*] soberly, plainly, simply; [*se conduire*] discreetly, unobtrusively; [*parler*] discreetly d (*littér* = *discernement*) discretion e (*loc*) **vin/pain à ~** unlimited wine/bread, as much wine/bread as you want; (*littér*) **être à la ~ de qn** to be in sb's hands

discrétionnaire [diskʀesjɔneʀ] ADJ discretionary

discriminant, e [diskʀiminɑ̃, ɑ̃t] ① ADJ discriminating, distinguishing ② NM (*Math*) discriminant

discrimination [diskʀiminasjɔ̃] NF discrimination (**contre, à l'égard de, envers** against); **~ raciale/sexuelle** race *ou* racial/sex *ou* sexual discrimination; **sans ~ d'âge ni de sexe** regardless of age or sex; **ce métier est accessible à tous sans ~** this profession is open to everyone without discrimination; **tirer sans ~ (dans la foule)** to fire indiscriminately (into the crowd); **~ positive** affirmative action

discriminatoire [diskʀiminatwaʀ] ADJ [*mesures*] discriminatory, discriminating

discriminer [diskʀimine] ▶ conjug 1 ◀ VT a (*littér* = *distinguer*) to distinguish; **apprendre à ~ les méthodes** to learn how to discriminate *ou*

distinguish between methods b (*surtout ptp*) [+ *personnes*] to discriminate against

disculpation [diskylpasjɔ̃] NF exoneration, exculpation (*frm*)

disculper [diskylpe] ▶ conjug 1 ◀ ① VT to exonerate, exculpate (*frm*) (**de** from) ② **se disculper** VPR to exonerate o.s., vindicate o.s., exculpate o.s. (*frm*) (**auprès de qn** in sb's eyes)

discursif, -ive [diskyʀsif, iv] ADJ discursive

discussion [diskysjɔ̃] NF a [*problème*] discussion (**de** of); [*projet de loi*] debate (**de** on), discussion (**de** of); **mettre une question en ~** to bring a matter up for discussion; **le projet de loi est en ~** the bill is being debated *ou* is under discussion b (= *débat*) discussion, debate; (= *pourparlers, échanges de vues*) discussion(s), talks; (= *conversation*) discussion, talk; **les délégués sont en ~** the delegates are in conference; **sans ~ possible** indisputably, undoubtedly ■ (*PROV*) **de la ~ jaillit la lumière** truth is reached through discussion c [*querelle*] argument, quarrel; **avoir une violente ~ avec qn** to have a violent disagreement *ou* quarrel *ou* argument with sb; **suis-moi et pas de ~s** follow me and don't argue *ou* no argument

discutable [diskytabl] ADJ [*solution, théorie*] debatable, questionable, arguable; [*goût*] doubtful, questionable; **il est compétent — c'est tout à fait ~** he's competent — that's debatable

discutailler* [diskytaje] ▶ conjug 1 ◀ VI (*péj*) (= *bavarder*) to chat (away), natter (away)* (*Brit*); (= *débattre sans fin*) to argue (**sur** over), go on* (**sur** about); (= *ergoter*) to wrangle, quibble (**sur** over); **~ dans le vide** to argue *ou* quibble over nothing

discuté, e [diskyte] (*ptp de* **discuter**) ADJ (= *contesté*) **ministre très ~** very controversial minister; **question très ~e** vexed question, much debated *ou* disputed question; **théorie très ~e** very *ou* highly controversial theory

discuter [diskyte] ▶ conjug 1 ◀ ① VT a (= *débattre*) [+ *problème*] to discuss; [+ *projet de loi*] to debate, discuss; [+ *prix*] to argue about, haggle over; **cette question se discute actuellement au Parlement** this issue is now being debated *ou* discussed in Parliament b (= *contester*) [+ *ordre, droits de qn*] to question, dispute; **ça se discute ◊ ça peut se ~** that's debatable; **cela ne se discute pas** the question doesn't even arise c **~ le coup*** (= *bavarder*) to have a chat *ou* natter* (*Brit*); (= *parlementer*) to argue away

② VI a (= *être en conférence*) to have a discussion, confer (**avec** with); (= *parler*) to talk (**avec** with); (= *parlementer*) to argue (**avec** with); **~ de** *ou* **sur qch** to discuss sth; **~ (de) politique/(d') affaires** to discuss *ou* talk politics/business; **on ne peut pas ~ avec lui!** you just can't argue with him!, there's no arguing with him! b (= *protester*) to argue; **suivez-moi sans ~** follow me and don't argue *ou* no argument; **il a obéi sans ~** he obeyed without question; **pour moi c'est décidé, il n'y a pas à ~** my mind's made up about it and that's that *ou* and that's final *ou* and there's nothing further to be said

c (= *débattre*) **~ de** *ou* **sur** [+ *question, problème*] to discuss, debate; **ensuite, nous avons discuté du prix** then we discussed the price; **~ sur le cas de qn** to discuss *ou* debate sb's case; **j'en ai discuté avec lui et il est d'accord** I have discussed the matter *ou* talked the matter over with him and he agrees; **vous discutez sur des points sans importance** you are arguing about *ou* niggling over trifles; (*hum*) **~ du sexe des anges** to discuss futilities, discuss how many angels can dance *ou* sit on the head of a pin (*hum*)

disert, e [dizɛʀ, ɛʀt] ADJ (frm, hum) talkative; **il s'est montré peu ~ sur ses intentions** he was less than ou not very forthcoming about his intentions

disette [dizɛt] NF [a] (= manque) [vivres, idées] scarcity, shortage, dearth [b] (= famine) food shortage, scarcity (of food)

diseur, -euse [dizœʀ, øz] NM,F **diseuse de bonne aventure** fortuneteller; **~ de bons mots** wit, wag

disgrâce [disgʀɑs] NF [a] (= défaveur, déchéance) disgrace; **encourir** ou **mériter la ~ de qn** to incur sb's disfavour (Brit) ou disfavor (US) ou displeasure; **être en ~ auprès de** to be out of favour (Brit) ou favor (US) with; **tomber en ~** to fall into disgrace [b]† (= malheur) misfortune; **pour comble de ~** most unfortunately of all

disgracié, e [disgʀasje] (ptp de **disgracier**) ADJ (= en disgrâce) in disgrace, disgraced; (frm = laid) ill-favoured (Brit) ou -favored (US), ugly

disgracier [disgʀasje] ▸ conjug 7 ◀ VT to disgrace, dismiss from favour (Brit) ou favor (US)

disgracieux, -ieuse [disgʀasjø, jøz] ADJ [geste] inelegant, awkward; [démarche] inelegant, awkward, ungainly; [visage] ugly; [forme, objet] unsightly

disharmonie [dizaʀmɔni, disaʀmɔni] NF disharmony

disjoindre [disʒwɛ̃dʀ(ə)] ▸ conjug 49 ◀ [1] VT [+ planches, tôles, tuiles] to take apart, separate; [+ tuyaux] to disconnect, take apart; [+ pierres] to break apart; [+ problèmes] to separate, split; (Jur) [+ causes] to deal with ou hear separately [2] **se disjoindre** VPR [planches, tôles, tuiles] to come apart ou loose, separate; [tuyaux, pierres] to come apart

disjoint, e [disʒwɛ̃, wɛ̃t] (ptp de **disjoindre**) ADJ **ces deux questions sont ~es** these two matters are not connected; **planches/tuiles ~es** planks/tiles which are coming apart ou loose, loose planks/tiles; **tuyaux ~s** pipes which have come apart ou undone

disjoncter [disʒɔ̃kte] ▸ conjug 1 ◀ [1] VT [+ courant] to cut off, disconnect [2] VI [a] (Élec) **ça a disjoncté** the trip-switch has gone [b]* [personne] to crack up*, lose it*; **cette musique la fait carrément ~** she really goes crazy* when she listens to that music

disjoncteur [disʒɔ̃ktœʀ] NM (Élec) circuit-breaker, cutout

disjonctif, -ive [disʒɔ̃ktif, iv] [1] ADJ disjunctive [2] **disjonctive** NF disjunctive

disjonction [disʒɔ̃ksjɔ̃] NF (gén, Logique) disjunction; (Jur) separation

dislocation [dislɔkasjɔ̃] NF [a] (Méd) [articulation] dislocation [b] [machine, meuble] (= démontage) dismantling; (= casse) smashing, breaking up [c] [rassemblement, cortège] dispersal, breaking up; [troupes] dispersal, scattering [d] [pays, empire] dismantling, breaking up; **~ de la cellule familiale** breakdown of the family unit [e] (Géol) fault

disloquer [dislɔke] ▸ conjug 1 ◀ [1] VT [a] (Méd) [+ articulation] to dislocate, put out of joint; **avoir l'épaule disloquée** to have a dislocated shoulder [b] (= démonter) [+ machine, meuble] to dismantle, take apart ou to pieces; (= casser) to smash, break up; **la chaise est toute disloquée** the chair's completely broken [c] (= disperser) [+ rassemblement, cortège] to disperse, break up; [+ troupes] to disperse, scatter [d] (= démembrer) [+ pays, empire] to dismantle, break up; **les familles disloquées par la guerre** families broken up ou torn apart by war [2] **se disloquer** VPR [a] **se ~ le bras** to dislocate one's arm, put one's arm out of joint; **son épaule s'est disloquée** he has dislocated his shoulder

[b] [meuble] to come apart, fall to pieces [c] [troupes] to disperse, scatter; [cortège] to disperse, break ou split up [d] [empire] to break up, disintegrate

disparaître [dispaʀɛtʀ] ▸ conjug 57 ◀ VI [a] (= s'en aller, devenir invisible) to disappear, vanish; **il disparut au coin de la rue/dans la foule** he disappeared ou vanished round the corner of the street/into the crowd; **~ discrètement** to slip away quietly; **~ furtivement** to sneak away ou out; **je ne veux pas le voir, je disparais** I don't want to see him so I'll just slip away ou so I'll be off; **le voilà, disparais !** there he is, make yourself scarce!*; **~ aux regards** to vanish out of sight, disappear from view; **~ à l'horizon** [soleil] to disappear ou vanish ou sink below the horizon; [bateau] to vanish ou disappear over the horizon; **l'arbre disparut dans le brouillard** the tree vanished ou was swallowed up in the fog; **le bâtiment disparaît sous le lierre** the building is (half-)hidden under the ivy

[b] (= être porté manquant) [personne] to disappear, go missing (Brit); [objet] to disappear; **il a disparu de son domicile** he is missing ou has gone missing (Brit) ou has disappeared from home; **trois voitures ont disparu (du garage)** three cars have disappeared ou are missing ou have gone (from the garage); **~ sans laisser de traces** to disappear ou vanish without trace; **il a disparu de la circulation*** he dropped out of circulation

[c] (= passer, s'effacer) [joie, crainte, sourire] to disappear, vanish, evaporate; [rougeur, douleur, cicatrice] to disappear, vanish, go away; (graduellement) to fade; [jeunesse] to vanish, be lost; [brouillard] to lift

[d] (= mourir) [race, civilisation] to die (out), vanish; [coutume] to die out, disappear; [personne] to die; (= se perdre) [navire] to sink, be lost; **si je venais à ~, tu n'aurais pas de soucis matériels** if I were to die, you wouldn't have any financial worries; **tout le charme de la Belle Époque disparaît avec elle** all the charm of the Belle Époque dies ou vanishes with her; **~ en mer** to be lost at sea; (Naut) **~ corps et biens** to go down with all hands

[e] **faire ~** [+ objet] (gén) to remove, hide away ou out of sight; [prestidigitateur] to make vanish ou disappear; [+ document] to dispose of, get rid of; [+ tache, trace, obstacle, difficulté] to remove; [+ personne] to eliminate, get rid of, do away with*; [+ crainte] to dispel, eliminate; **cela a fait ~ la douleur/la rougeur** it made the pain/red mark go away, it got rid of the pain/all trace of the red mark; **le voleur fit ~ le bijou dans sa poche** the thief concealed the jewel ou hid the jewel in his pocket; **il prenait de gros morceaux de pain qu'il faisait ~ dans sa bouche** he was taking large hunks of bread and cramming them into his mouth; **ils firent ~ toute trace de leur passage** they destroyed ou removed all trace of their visit; **faire ~ une inscription** [temps] to erase ou efface ou wear away an inscription; [personne] to erase ou wipe out ou remove an inscription

disparate [dispaʀat] ADJ [éléments] disparate; [objets, mobilier] disparate, ill-assorted; [couple, couleurs] ill-assorted, badly matched

disparité [dispaʀite] NF [éléments, salaires] disparity (de in); [objets, couleurs] mismatch (NonC) (de of)

disparition [dispaʀisjɔ̃] NF [a] [personne] disappearance; [cicatrice, rougeur] (gén) disappearance; (graduelle) fading; [brouillard] lifting; [soleil] sinking, setting; [tache, obstacle] disappearance, removal; **la ~ de la douleur sera immédiate** the pain will be relieved ou will go away ou vanish immediately [b] (= mort, perte) [personne] death; [espèce] extinction, disappearance; [coutume, langue] disappearance, dying out; [objet, bateau] loss, disappearance; **menacé** ou **en voie de ~** [espèce] endangered; [civilisation, langue, tradition] dying, fast disappearing; [emploi, métier] dying; **cette espèce est en voie de ~** (animaux) this species is becoming extinct ou is dying out, this is an endangered species; (fig) they're a dying breed

disparu, e [dispaʀy] (ptp de **disparaître**) [1] ADJ [a] (= révolu) [monde, époque] bygone (épith), vanished; [bonheur, jeunesse] lost [b] (= effacé) **une lueur menaçante, aussitôt ~e, brilla dans ses yeux** a dangerous gleam flickered and died in his eyes, his eyes glinted dangerously for a brief moment; **un sentiment d'espoir, bientôt ~, l'anima un court instant** hope filled him for a brief moment only to fade again [c] (= mort) [personne] dead, deceased; [espèce] extinct; [race, coutume, langue] vanished, dead, extinct; (= dont on est sans nouvelles) [victime] missing; **il a été porté ~** (Mil) he has been reported missing; (dans une catastrophe) he is missing, believed dead; **marin ~ en mer** sailor lost at sea [2] NM,F (= mort) dead person; (= dont on a perdu la trace) missing person; **le cher ~** the dear departed; **l'incendie a fait cinq morts et trois ~s** the fire left five people dead and three unaccounted for

dispatcher¹ [dispatʃe] ▸ conjug 1 ◀ VT to dispatch

dispatcher², dispatcheur [dispatʃœʀ] NM dispatcher

dispatching [dispatʃiŋ] NM (gén) dispatching; [courrier] routing, dispatching

dispendieusement [dispɑ̃djøzmɑ̃] ADV (frm) [vivre] extravagantly, expensively

dispendieux, -ieuse [dispɑ̃djø, jøz] ADJ (frm) [goûts, luxe] extravagant, expensive

dispensaire [dispɑ̃sɛʀ] NM community (Brit) ou free (US) clinic, health centre (Brit) ou center (US), people's dispensary

dispensateur, -trice [dispɑ̃satœʀ, tʀis] (littér) [1] ADJ dispensing [2] NM,F dispenser

dispense [dispɑ̃s] NF [a] (= exemption, Rel) exemption (de from), dispensation (de from) [b] (= permission) special permission; **~ d'âge pour passer un examen** permission to sit an exam under the statutory age limit; (pour un chômeur) **~ de recherche d'emploi** exemption from the actively seeking work rule; **~ du service militaire/d'un examen** exemption from military service/from an exam

dispenser [dispɑ̃se] ▸ conjug 1 ◀ [1] VT [a] (= exempter) to exempt, excuse (de faire from doing, de qch from sth); (Rel) **~ qn d'un vœu** to release sb from a vow; **je vous dispense de vos réflexions** I can do without your comments, you can spare me your comments; (frm) **dispensez-moi d'en dire plus** spare me the necessity of saying any more; **se faire ~** to get exempted; **il est dispensé de gymnastique** he's excused from gym [b] (littér = distribuer) [+ bienfaits] to dispense; [+ charme] to radiate; [+ lumière] to give out; **~ des soins à un malade** to give medical care to a patient [2] **se dispenser** VPR **se ~ de** [+ corvée] to avoid, get out of; [+ remarque] to refrain from; **se ~ de faire qch** to get out of doing sth, not to bother doing sth; **il peut se ~ de travailler** he doesn't need to work, he has no need to work; **je me dispenserais bien d'y aller** I'd gladly save myself the bother of going if I could; (iro) **il s'est dispensé de s'excuser** he didn't see any necessity for excusing himself

dispersant, e [dispɛʀsɑ̃, ɑ̃t] [1] ADJ dispersive [2] NM dispersant

dispersé, e [dispɛʀse] (ptp de **disperser**) ADJ [habitat, famille] scattered; **en ordre ~** in a disorganised manner; **leur actionnariat est très ~** they have many small shareholders; **nos efforts sont trop ~s** our efforts aren't focused enough

disperser [dispɛʀse] ▸ conjug 1 ◂ 1 VT a [+ *papiers, feuilles*] to scatter; [+ *brouillard, pétrole*] to disperse, break up; [+ *collection*] to break up; ~ **les cendres de qn** to scatter sb's ashes b [+ *forces*] to dissipate; [+ *foule, ennemi*] to scatter, disperse; ~ **l'attention de qn** to distract sb; **il ne faut pas ~ tes efforts** you shouldn't spread yourself too thin; **tous nos amis sont maintenant dispersés** all our friends are now scattered 2 **se disperser** VPR [*foule*] to scatter, disperse, break up; [*élève, artiste*] to overdiversify; **ne vous dispersez pas trop!** don't spread yourself too thin!, don't attempt to do too many things at once!

dispersion [dispɛʀsjɔ̃] NF a (*Chim, Phys, Stat*) dispersion; [*papiers, feuilles*] scattering; [*brouillard, pétrole*] dispersal, breaking up; [*collection*] breaking up b [*forces*] dissipation; [*foule, ennemi*] scattering, dispersal; **évitez la ~ dans votre travail** don't attempt to do too many things at once

disponibilité [dispɔnibilite] NF a [*choses*] availability; (*Jur*) ~ **des biens** (*faculté du possesseur*) ability to transfer one's property; (*caractère des possessions*) transferability of property; **en fonction des ~s ou de la ~ de chacun** depending on each person's availability b (*Fin*) ~s available funds, liquid assets c **mettre en ~** [+ *fonctionnaire*] to free from duty temporarily, grant leave of absence to; [+ *officier*] to place on reserve; **mise en ~** [*fonctionnaire*] leave of absence; [*officier*] transfer to reserve duty d [*élève, esprit, auditoire*] alertness, receptiveness; ~ **d'esprit** alertness *ou* receptiveness of mind

▼ **disponible** [dispɔnibl] 1 ADJ a [*appartement, fonds, produit*] available; **avez-vous des places ~s pour ce soir?** are there any seats (available) for this evening?; **il n'y a plus une seule place ~** there's not a single seat left *ou* not one spare seat; **ce soir** I'm not free tonight; **elle est toujours ~ pour écouter ses amis** she's always ready to listen to her friends; (*Jur*) **biens ~s** transferable property b (*Admin*) **fonctionnaire ~** civil servant on leave of absence *ou* temporarily freed from duty; **officier ~** officer on reserve c [*élève, esprit, auditoire*] alert, receptive 2 NM (*Fin*) available assets *ou* funds

dispos, e [dispo, oz] ADJ [*personne*] refreshed, in good form (*attrib*), full of energy (*attrib*); **avoir l'esprit ~** to have a fresh mind → **frais¹**

disposé, e [dispoze] (*ptp de* **disposer**) ADJ a (= *prêt*) **être ~ à faire** to be willing *ou* prepared *ou* disposed (*frm*) to do; **être peu ~ à faire** to be unwilling to do, not to be prepared *ou* disposed to do b **bien/mal ~** in a good/bad mood; **bien/mal ~ à l'égard de** *ou* **pour** *ou* **envers qn** well-disposed/ill-disposed towards sb c [*terrain*] situated, sited; **bâtiments ~s face à la mer** buildings facing the sea; **pièces bien/mal ~es** well/badly laid-out rooms

disposer [dispoze] ▸ conjug 1 ◂ 1 VT a (= *arranger*) [+ *personnes, meubles, fleurs*] to arrange; [+ *couverts*] to set, lay; ~ **des troupes sur le terrain** to draw up *ou* range troops on the battlefield; ~ **des objets en ligne/en cercle** to place *ou* lay *ou* arrange things in a row/in a circle; **on avait disposé le buffet dans le jardin** they had laid out *ou* set out the buffet in the garden b ~ **qn à faire/à qch** (= *engager à*) to incline *ou* dispose (*frm*) sb to do/towards sth; (*frm = préparer à*) to prepare sb to do/for sth; **cela ne dispose pas à l'optimisme** it doesn't exactly make you feel optimistic 2 VI (*frm = partir*) to leave; **vous pouvez ~** you may leave *ou* go (now), that will be all 3 **disposer de** VT INDIR a (= *avoir l'usage de*) to have (at one's disposal); ~ **d'une voiture** to have a car (at one's disposal), have the use of a car; ~ **d'une somme d'argent** to have a sum of money at one's disposal *ou* available

(for one's use); **il disposait de quelques heures pour visiter Lille** he had a few hours free *ou* to spare in which to visit Lille; **il peut ~ de son temps** his time is his own, he can do what he likes with his time; **avec les moyens dont il dispose** with the means at his disposal *ou* available to him; **si vous voulez vous pouvez en ~** if you wish you can use it; (*Jur*) ~ **d'un domaine (par testament)** to dispose of an estate (in one's will); **il se croit autorisé à ~ de ses amis** he thinks his friends are just there to do his bidding; **droit des peuples à ~ d'eux-mêmes** right of nations to self-determination; **le droit de chacun à ~ de son corps** (*pendant sa vie*) the individual's right to own and control his own body; (*après sa mort*) the individual's right to determine what shall be done to his body 4 **se disposer** VPR **se ~ à faire** (= *se préparer à*) to prepare to do, be about to do; **il se disposait à quitter le bureau** he was about to *ou* was getting ready to leave the office

dispositif [dispozitif] NM a (= *mécanisme*) device, mechanism; ~ **d'alarme** alarm *ou* warning device; ~ **de contrôle** control mechanism; ~ **de sécurité** safety device; (*Opéra, Théât*) ~ **scénique** set; (*Méd*) ~ **intra-utérin** intra-uterine (contraceptive) device, IUD b (= *moyens prévus*) plan (of action); (*Mil*) ~ **d'attaque** plan of attack; (*Mil*) ~ **de contrôle** control system; (*Mil*) ~ **de défense** defence (*Brit*) *ou* defense (*US*) system; ~ **législatif** legislation, laws; ~ **de lutte contre le chômage** measures to combat unemployment; ~ **de lutte contre l'incendie** fire-fighting system *ou* arrangements; **renforcer/alléger le ~ militaire** to increase/decrease the military presence; **un important ~ de sécurité a été mis en place à la frontière** a major security operation has been mounted on the border; ~ **de surveillance** surveillance *ou* monitoring system c (*Jur*) [*jugement*] pronouncement; [*loi*] purview

▼ **disposition** [dispozisjɔ̃] 1 NF a (= *arrangement*) (= *action*) arrangement, arranging, placing; (= *résultat*) arrangement, layout; **selon la ~ des pions/des joueurs** according to how the pawns/players are placed; **ils ont changé la ~ des objets dans la vitrine** they have changed the arrangement *ou* layout of the things in the window; **la ~ des lieux/pièces** the layout of the premises/rooms b (= *usage*) disposal; (*Jur*) **avoir la libre ~ de qch** to have free disposal of sth, be free to dispose of sth; **mettre qch/être à la ~ de qn** to put sth/be at sb's disposal; **la maison/la bibliothèque est à votre ~** the house/library is at your disposal, you can have the run of the house/library; **les moyens (mis) à notre ~ sont insuffisants** we have insufficient means at our disposal; **je me mets** *ou* **tiens à votre entière ~ pour de plus amples renseignements** I am entirely at your disposal *ou* service should you require further information; (*Jur*) **il a été mis à la ~ de la justice** he was handed over to the law c (= *mesure*) measure; ~s (= *préparatifs*) arrangements, preparations; (= *précautions*) measures, precautions, steps; **prendre des** *ou* **ses ~s pour que qch soit fait** to make arrangements *ou* take steps to have sth done *ou* for sth to be done; **prendre ses ~s pour partir** to make arrangements *ou* prepare for one's departure; **nous avons prévu des ~s spéciales** we have arranged for special steps *ou* measures *ou* precautions to be taken d (= *manière d'être*) mood, humour, frame of mind; **être dans de bonnes/mauvaises ~s** to be in a good/bad mood, be in (a) good/bad humour; **être dans de bonnes ~s pour faire qch** to be in the right mood to do sth, be in the right frame of mind for doing sth; **être dans**

les meilleures ~s to be in the best of moods; **être dans de bonnes/de mauvaises/les meilleures ~s à l'égard de qn** to feel well-disposed/ill-disposed/very well-disposed towards sb; **est-il toujours dans les mêmes ~s à l'égard de ce projet/candidat?** does he still feel the same way about this plan/candidate?; ~ **d'esprit** mood, state *ou* frame of mind e (= *tendance*) [*personne*] predisposition, tendency; [*objet*] tendency (à to); **avoir une ~ au rhumatisme** to have a tendency to rheumatism; **ce bateau a une curieuse/fâcheuse ~ à ...** this boat has a strange/an annoying tendency to ... f (*Jur*) clause; ~**s testamentaires** provisions of a will, testamentary provisions → **dernier** 2 **dispositions** NFPL (= *inclinations, aptitudes*) bent, aptitude, natural ability; **avoir des ~s pour la musique/les langues/le tennis** to have a special aptitude for *ou* a gift for music/languages/tennis

disproportion [dispʀɔpɔʀsjɔ̃] NF disproportion (**entre** between, **de** in)

disproportionné, e [dispʀɔpɔʀsjɔne] ADJ disproportionate (**par rapport à, avec** to), out of (all) proportion (**par rapport à, avec** to, with); **il a une tête ~e** his head is out of proportion with his body

dispute [dispyt] NF a (= *querelle*) argument, quarrel; ~ **d'amoureux** lovers' tiff *ou* quarrel; **tu cherches la ~!** you're looking for an argument!; **c'est leur principal sujet de ~** it's a major bone of contention between them b †† (= *débat polémique*) debate, dispute

disputé, e [dispyte] (*ptp de* **disputer**) ADJ **très ~** [*match*] close, closely fought; [*course, élection, siège de député*] hotly *ou* closely contested

disputer [dispyte] ▸ conjug 1 ◂ 1 VT a (= *contester*) ~ **qch/qn à qn** to fight with sb for *ou* over sth/sb; ~ **la victoire/la première place à son rival** to fight for victory/for first place with one's rival, fight one's rival for victory/first place; **elle essaya de lui ~ la gloire de son invention** she tried to rob him of the glory of his invention; (*littér*) **le ~ en beauté/en grandeur à qn** to vie with *ou* rival sb in beauty/greatness; ~ **le terrain** (*Mil*) to fight for every inch of ground; (*fig*) to fight every inch of the way b (= *livrer*) [+ *combat*] to fight; [+ *match*] to play; **le match a été disputé** *ou* **s'est disputé en Angleterre** the match was played *ou* took place in England c (= *gronder*) to tell off*, tick off* (*Brit*); **se faire ~ par son père** to get a telling-off* *ou* ticking-off* (*Brit*) from one's father 2 **se disputer** VPR a (= *se quereller*) to quarrel, argue, have a quarrel *ou* an argument (**avec** with); **il s'est disputé avec son oncle** (= *s'est querellé avec lui*) he quarrelled *ou* had a quarrel *ou* an argument with his uncle; (= *s'est brouillé avec lui*) he fell out with his uncle b (= *se battre pour*) **se ~ qch** to fight over sth, contest sth; **deux chiens se disputent un os** two dogs are fighting over a bone; **deux candidats se disputent un siège à l'Académie** there are two contenders for *ou* two candidates are contesting a seat at the Academy

disquaire [diskɛʀ] NMF (= *commerçant*) record dealer

disqualification [diskalifikasjɔ̃] NF (*Sport*) disqualification

disqualifier [diskalifje] ▸ conjug 7 ◂ VT a (*Sport* = *exclure*) to disqualify b (= *discréditer*) to dishonour (*Brit*), dishonor (*US*), bring discredit on; **il s'est disqualifié aux yeux de l'opinion** he has destroyed people's trust in him *ou* people's good opinion of him

disque [disk] NM a (*gén, Méd, Photo*) disc, disk (*surtout US*); ~ **d'embrayage** clutch plate; ~ **de stationnement** parking disc; ~ **à démaquiller** make-up remover pad → **frein**

▶ GRAMMAIRE ACTIVE: disponible 46.3 disposition 46.3

[b] (*Sport*) discus [c] (*Mus*) (*gén, en vinyle*) record; **~ compact** compact disc, CD; **~ (compact) audio/interactif/laser/vidéo** audio (compact)/interactive/laser/video disc; **~ d'or/de platine** gold/platinum disc; **mettre/passer un ~** (*vinyle*) to put on/play a record; (*compact*) to put on/play a CD; **ça vient de sortir en ~ compact** it's just come out on compact disc *ou* CD → **changer** [d] (*Ordin*) disk, disc; **~ dur/souple/optique** hard/floppy/optical disk; **~ optique compact** compact optical disk; **~ optique numérique** digital optical disk

disquette [diskɛt] NF (*Ordin*) floppy (disk *ou* disc), diskette

dissection [disɛksjɔ̃] NF dissection; **de ~** [*instrument, table*] dissecting, dissection

dissemblable [disɑ̃blabl] ADJ dissimilar, different (**de** from, to)

dissemblance [disɑ̃blɑ̃s] NF dissimilarity, difference (**de** in)

dissémination [diseminasjɔ̃] NF [a] (= *action*) [*graines*] scattering; [*troupes, maisons, usines*] scattering, spreading; [*idées*] dissemination [b] (= *état*) [*maisons, points de vente*] scattered layout *ou* distribution; **à cause de la ~ de notre famille** because our family is scattered

disséminer [disemine] ▶conjug 1◀ [1] VT [+ *graines*] to scatter; [+ *troupes, maisons*] to scatter, spread (out); [+ *idées*] to disseminate; **les points de vente sont très disséminés** the (sales) outlets are widely scattered *ou* thinly distributed [2] **se disséminer** VPR [*graines*] to scatter; [*personnes*] to spread (out); **les pique-niqueurs se disséminèrent aux quatre coins de la forêt** the picnickers spread out *ou* scattered to the four corners of the forest

dissension [disɑ̃sjɔ̃] NF dissension (**entre, au sein de** between, within)

dissentiment [disɑ̃timɑ̃] NM disagreement, difference of opinion

disséquer [diseke] ▶conjug 6◀ VT [+ *cadavre, plante*] to dissect; [+ *texte, problème*] to dissect

dissert [disɛʀt] NF (ABRÉV = **dissertation**) (*arg Scol*) paper

dissertation [disɛʀtasjɔ̃] NF (*Scol, hum*) essay; (*péj, ††* = *traité*) dissertation

disserter [disɛʀte] ▶conjug 1◀ VI [a] (*Scol*) **~ sur** (= *parler*) to speak on, discourse upon (*frm*); (= *écrire*) to write an essay on [b] (*péj*) to hold forth (**de, sur** about, on)

dissidence [disidɑ̃s] NF (= *sécession*) (*Pol*) dissidence, rebellion; (*Rel*) dissent; (= *dissidents*) dissidents, rebels; (*littér* = *divergence*) disagreement, dissidence; **entrer en ~ contre** [+ *régime*] to rebel against; [+ *parti*] to break away from; **rejoindre la ~** to join the dissidents *ou* the rebels

dissident, e [disidɑ̃, ɑ̃t] [1] ADJ (*Pol*) dissident; (*Rel*) dissenting; **groupe ~** breakaway *ou* splinter group; **une fraction ~e de cette organisation terroriste** a dissident minority in this terrorist organization; **une voix ~e à l'intérieur du parti** a dissenting voice within the party; **un candidat socialiste ~** a socialist candidate who has broken away from the party [2] NM,F (*Pol*) dissident, rebel; (*Rel*) dissenter

dissimilitude [disimilityd] NF dissimilarity

dissimulateur, -trice [disimylatœʀ, tʀis] [1] ADJ dissembling [2] NM,F dissembler

dissimulation [disimylasjɔ̃] NF (*NonC*) (= *duplicité*) dissimulation, dissembling; (= *cachotterie*) dissimulation (*NonC*), dissembling (*NonC*); (= *action de cacher*) concealment; **agir avec ~** to act in an underhand way; (*Jur*) **~ d'actif** (fraudulent) concealment of assets; (*Jur*) **~ de salariés** non-declaration of workers; **~ de preuve(s)** withholding of evidence

dissimulé, e [disimyle] (*ptp de* **dissimuler**) ADJ **sentiments mal ~s** ill-concealed feelings; **avec un plaisir non ~** with undisguised glee *ou* pleasure

dissimuler [disimyle] ▶conjug 1◀ [1] VT (= *cacher*) [+ *objet, personne, sentiment, difficulté*] to conceal, hide (**à qn** from sb); (*Fin*) [+ *bénéfices*] to conceal; **son visage dissimulé par un foulard** her face hidden by a scarf; **ces arbustes dissimulent la cabane** the shrubs hide the shed from view; **il sait bien ~** he's good at pretending *ou* dissembling (*frm*); **il parvenait mal à ~ son impatience/son envie de rire** he had great difficulty concealing *ou* hiding his annoyance/his urge to laugh; **je ne vous dissimulerai pas qu'il y a de gros problèmes** I won't disguise *ou* conceal the fact that there are serious problems

[2] **se dissimuler** VPR to conceal *ou* hide o.s.; **il essaie de se ~ la vérité/qu'il a tort** he's trying to close his eyes to the truth/to the fact that he's wrong, he's trying to conceal the truth from himself/to conceal from himself the fact that he's wrong

dissipateur, -trice [disipatœʀ, tʀis] NM,F (*littér*) spendthrift, squanderer (*Brit*)

dissipation [disipasjɔ̃] NF [a] (= *indiscipline*) misbehaviour (*Brit*), misbehavior (*US*), unruliness; (*littér* = *débauche*) dissipation; **une vie de ~** a dissipated life, a life of dissipation [b] (= *dilapidation*) [*fortune*] squandering, dissipation; (= *folle dépense*) extravagance [c] [*fumée, nuage*] dissipation, dispersal; [*brouillard*] clearing, lifting; [*craintes*] dispelling; **après ~ des brouillards matinaux** after the early morning fog has lifted *ou* cleared

dissipé, e [disipe] ADJ [*élève*] undisciplined, unruly; [*vie*] dissolute, dissipated

dissiper [disipe] ▶conjug 1◀ [1] VT [a] (= *chasser*) [+ *brouillard, fumée*] to dispel, disperse, clear away; [+ *nuage*] to break up, disperse; [+ *soupçon, crainte*] to dissipate, dispel; [+ *malentendu*] to clear up [b] (= *dilapider*) [+ *fortune*] to squander, fritter away, dissipate; (*littér*) [+ *jeunesse*] to waste, dissipate, idle away [c] **~ qn** to lead sb astray *ou* into bad ways; **il dissipe ses camarades en classe** he is a distracting influence on *ou* he distracts his classmates [d] (*Sci*) to dissipate [2] **se dissiper** VPR [a] (= *disparaître*) [*fumée*] to drift away, disperse; [*nuages*] to break (up), disperse; [*brouillard*] to clear, lift, disperse; [*inquiétude*] to vanish, melt away; [*malaise, fatigue*] to disappear, go away, wear off [b] [*élève*] to become undisciplined *ou* unruly, misbehave

dissociable [disɔsjabl] ADJ [*molécules*] dissociable, separable; [*problèmes*] separable

dissociation [disɔsjasjɔ̃] NF [*molécules, problèmes*] dissociation, separation

dissocier [disɔsje] ▶conjug 7◀ [1] VT [+ *molécules, problèmes*] to dissociate [2] **se dissocier** VPR [*éléments, groupe, équipe*] to break up, split up; **nous tenons à nous ~ de ces groupes/vues** we are anxious to dissociate ourselves from these groups/views

dissolu, e [disɔly] ADJ dissolute

dissolution [disɔlysjɔ̃] NF [a] (*Jur*) [*assemblée, gouvernement, mariage*] dissolution; [*association, groupe, parti*] dissolution, disbanding; **prononcer la ~ de** [+ *mariage*] to dissolve; [+ *parti, groupement*] to disband [b] (= *désagrégation*) [*groupe, association*] breaking-up, splitting-up; [*empire*] crumbling, decay, dissolution; **l'unité nationale est en pleine ~** national unity is crumbling *ou* disintegrating *ou* falling apart [c] [*sucre*] dissolving; **jusqu'à ~ complète du cachet** until the tablet has completely dissolved [d] (= *colle*) rubber solution [e] (*littér* = *débauche*) dissoluteness, dissipation

dissolvant, e [disɔlvɑ̃, ɑ̃t] [1] ADJ solvent, dissolvent [2] NM (= *produit*) solvent; (*pour les ongles*) **~ (gras)** nail polish *ou* varnish remover

dissonance [disɔnɑ̃s] NF (*Mus* = *intervalle*) dissonance, discord; [*couleurs, styles*] mismatch; (*fig*) clash; (= *manque d'harmonie*) discord, dissonance; **des ~s de tons dans un tableau** clashes of colour in a painting

dissonant, e [disɔnɑ̃, ɑ̃t] ADJ [*sons, accord*] dissonant, discordant; [*couleurs*] clashing (*épith*)

dissoudre [disudʀ] ▶conjug 51◀ [1] VT [a] [+ *sel*] to dissolve; **(faire) ~ du sucre** to dissolve sugar [b] (*Jur, Pol*) [+ *assemblée, gouvernement*] to dissolve; [+ *parti, groupement, association*] to disband; [+ *mariage*] to dissolve [2] **se dissoudre** VPR [a] [*sel, sucre*] to dissolve, be dissolved [b] [*association*] to disband

dissuader [disɥade] ▶conjug 1◀ VT [*personne*] to dissuade (**de qch** from sth, **de faire** from doing); [*circonstances*] to deter (**de faire** from doing); **il m'a dissuadé d'y aller** he talked me out of going, he persuaded me not to go

dissuasif, -ive [disɥazif, iv] ADJ [a] [*argument*] dissuasive; [*mesures, sanction*] deterrent (*épith*); **avoir un effet ~ sur** to have a deterrent effect on; **à un prix ~** at a prohibitive price; **c'est une procédure très dissuasive** it's a very off-putting procedure [b] (*Mil*) [*arme, force, stratégie*] deterrent (*épith*)

dissuasion [disɥazjɔ̃] NF (*gén*) dissuasion; (*Mil*) deterrence; **la ~ nucléaire** nuclear deterrence; **de ~** [*mesures, force, stratégie*] deterrent

dissyllabe [disi(l)lab] [1] ADJ disyllabic [2] NM disyllable

dissyllabique [disi(l)labik] ADJ disyllabic

dissymétrie [disimetʀi] NF dissymmetry

dissymétrique [disimetʀik] ADJ dissymmetric(al)

distance [distɑ̃s] NF [a] (= *éloignement, intervalle, trajet*) distance; **à quelle ~ est la gare ?** how far (away) is the station?, what's the distance to the station?; **parcourir de grandes/petites ~s** to cover great/small distances; (*Sport*) **il est meilleur sur les grandes ~s** he's better over long distances; **habiter à une grande ~/à quelques kilomètres de ~** to live a great distance away *ou* a long way away/a few kilometres away (**de** from); **à grande ~** [*détection*] long-range (*épith*), at long range; [*apercevoir*] from a long way off *ou* away; **téléphone/communication/vol longue ~** long-distance (tele)phone/call/flight; **entendre un bruit/distinguer qch à une ~ de 30 mètres** to hear a noise/make out sth from a distance of 30 metres *ou* from 30 metres away; **~ de freinage** braking distance; **respectez les ~s (de freinage)** keep your distance; **à deux ou trois ans de ~ je m'en souviens encore** two or three years later I can still remember it; **nés à quelques années de ~** born within a few years of one another, born a few years apart; **quelle ~ parcourue depuis son dernier roman !** what a long way *ou* how far he has come since his last novel!

[b] (= *écart*) gap; **la ~ qui sépare deux générations/points de vue** the gap between *ou* which separates two generations/points of view; **la guerre a mis une grande ~ entre ces deux peuples** the war has left a great gulf between these two nations

[c] (*loc*) **garder ses ~s** to keep one's distance (**vis à vis de** from); **prendre ses ~s** (*Mil*) to form open order; (*Scol etc*) to space out; (*fig*) to stand aloof (**à l'égard de** from), distance o.s. (**par rapport à** from); **les syndicats ont pris leurs ~s vis-à-vis du gouvernement** the unions have distanced themselves from the government; **tenir qn à ~** to keep sb at a distance *ou* at arm's length; **se tenir à ~** to keep one's distance, stand aloof; **tenir qn à une ~ respectueuse** to keep sb at arm's length; **se tenir à une ~ respectueuse de** to keep *ou* stay a respectful distance from; **tenir la ~** [*coureur*] to go *ou* do *ou* cover the distance, last *ou* stay the course; [*conférencier*] to stay *ou* last the course; **de ~ en ~** at intervals, here and there; **à ~** (*dans l'espace*) at *ou* from a distance, from afar; (*dans le temps*) at *ou* from a distance; **le**

prestidigitateur fait bouger des objets à ~ the conjurer moves objects from a distance; **mettre en marche à ~** [+ *appareil*] to switch on by remote control; (*Photo*) **~ focale** focal length → **commande**

distancer [distɑ̃se] ▶conjug 3◀ VT a [+ *coureur*] to outrun, outdistance, leave behind; [+ *voiture*] to outdistance, leave behind; [+ *concurrent, élève*] to outstrip, outclass, leave behind; **se laisser** *ou* **se faire ~** to be left behind, be outdistanced (**par** by); **ne nous laissons pas ~** let's not fall behind *ou* be left behind b (*Sport* = *disqualifier*) to disqualify

distanciation [distɑ̃sjasjɔ̃] NF distance; **sa ~ par rapport aux événements** the way he has distanced himself from events

distancier (se) [distɑ̃sje] ▶conjug 7◀ VPR to distance o.s. (**de** from)

distant, e [distɑ̃, ɑ̃t] ADJ a [*lieu*] far-off, far-away, distant; [*événement*] distant, far-off; **~ de la gare** far away from the station; **une ville ~e de 10 km** a town 10 km away; **deux villes ~es de 10 km (l'une de l'autre)** two towns 10 km apart *ou* 10 km away from one another b [*attitude*] distant, aloof; [*voix*] distant; **il s'est montré très ~** he was very stand-offish

distendre [distɑ̃dʀ] ▶conjug 41◀ 1 VT [+ *peau*] to distend; [+ *corde, pull, col*] to stretch 2 **se distendre** VPR [*lien*] to slacken, become looser; [*ventre, peau*] to distend, become distended *ou* bloated

distendu, e [distɑ̃dy] (*ptp de* **distendre**) ADJ [*ventre*] distended, bloated; [*corde*] slack, loose; [*élastique, ressort*] slack

distension [distɑ̃sjɔ̃] NF [*peau, estomac*] distension; [*corde*] slackening, loosening

distillat [distila] NM (*Chim*) distillate

distillateur [distilatœʀ] NM (= *personne*) distiller

distillation [distilasjɔ̃] NF distillation, distilling

distiller [distile] ▶conjug 1◀ 1 VT [+ *alcool*] to distil; [+ *suc*] to elaborate; [+ *ennui*] to exude; **eau distillée** distilled water 2 VI (*Sci*) to distil

distillerie [distilʀi] NF (= *usine*) distillery; (= *industrie*) distilling

distinct, e [distɛ̃(kt), ɛ̃kt] ADJ a (= *indépendant*) distinct, separate (**de** from) b (= *net*) distinct, clear

distinctement [distɛ̃ktəmɑ̃] ADV distinctly, clearly

distinctif, -ive [distɛ̃ktif, iv] ADJ distinctive

distinction [distɛ̃ksjɔ̃] NF a (= *différentiation*) distinction; **faire la ~ entre** to make a distinction between; **sans ~** without distinction; **sans ~ de race/d'âge** irrespective of race/age, without distinction of race/age b (= *décoration, honneur*) distinction c (= *raffinement*) distinction, refinement; **il a de la ~** he is very distinguished *ou* refined, he has great distinction d (= *éminence*) distinction, eminence; (*frm*) **un pianiste de la plus haute ~** a pianist of the highest distinction

distinguable [distɛ̃gabl] ADJ distinguishable (**de** from)

distingué, e [distɛ̃ge] (*ptp de* **distinguer**) ADJ a (= *élégant, bien élevé*) [*personne*] distinguished; [*allure*] elegant, refined, distinguished; **il a l'air très ~** he looks very distinguished, he has a very distinguished look about him; **ça fait très ~** it's very distinguished → **agréer** b (= *illustre*) distinguished, eminent; **notre ~ collègue, le professeur X** our distinguished *ou* eminent colleague, Professor X

distinguer [distɛ̃ge] ▶conjug 1◀ 1 VT a (= *percevoir*) [+ *objet, bruit*] to make out, distinguish, perceive; [+ *ironie*] to distinguish, perceive; **~ qn dans la foule** to pick out *ou* spot sb in the crowd; **on commença à ~ les collines à travers la brume** the hills began to be visible

through the mist, you could begin to make out the hills through the mist; **il distingue mal sans lunettes** he can't see very well without his glasses b (= *différencier*) to distinguish; **~ une chose d'une autre** *ou* **d'avec une autre** to distinguish *ou* tell one thing from another; **savoir ~ les oiseaux/plantes** to be able to distinguish different species of birds/plants; **les deux sœurs sont difficiles à ~ (l'une de l'autre)** the two sisters are difficult to tell apart; **~ le bien du mal/un Picasso d'un** *ou* **d'avec un Braque** to tell good from evil/a Picasso from a Braque, distinguish between good and evil/between a Picasso and a Braque; **tu la distingueras à sa veste rouge** you will recognize her *ou* pick her out by her red jacket; **distinguons, il y a chanteur et chanteur** we must make a distinction, there are good singers and bad singers c (= *rendre différent*) to distinguish, set apart (**de** from), mark off; **c'est son accent qui le distingue des autres** it is his accent which distinguishes him from *ou* makes him different from the others *ou* which sets him apart d (*frm*) (= *choisir*) to single out; (= *honorer*) to honour (*Brit*), honor (*US*); **on l'a distingué pour faire le discours d'adieu** he was singled out to make the farewell speech; **l'Académie française a distingué X pour son œuvre poétique** the Académie Française has honoured X for his works of poetry

2 **se distinguer** VPR a (= *différer*) to distinguish o.s., be distinguished (**de** from); **ces objets se distinguent par** *ou* **grâce à leur couleur** these objects can be distinguished by their colour; **les deux frères se distinguent (l'un de l'autre) par leur taille** you can tell the two brothers apart by their (different) height; **il se distingue par son accent/sa démarche** his accent/his walk makes him stand out *ou* makes him seem quite different b (= *se signaler, réussir*) to distinguish o.s.; **se ~ (pendant une guerre) par son courage** to distinguish o.s. (in a war) by one's courage; **il s'est distingué par ses découvertes en physique** he has become famous for *ou* from his discoveries in physics, he's made a name for himself by his discoveries in physics; (*hum*) **il se distingue par son absence** he is noticeable *ou* conspicuous by his absence; **il s'est particulièrement distingué en latin** he has done particularly well *ou* he has particularly distinguished himself in Latin

distinguo [distɛ̃go] NM (= *nuance*) distinction; **faire le ~ entre X et Y** to make a distinction between X and Y

distique [distik] NM distich

distordre VT, **se distordre** VPR [distɔʀdʀ] ▶conjug 41◀ to twist, distort

distorsion [distɔʀsjɔ̃] NF a (*gén, Anat, Téléc*) distortion; **la ~ des faits/de la réalité** distortion of the facts/of reality; (*Écon*) **~ de concurrence** distortion of competition; **~ du temps** time warp b (= *déséquilibre: entre des chiffres, salaires, taux*) imbalance (**entre** between); (= *décalage*) **la ~ entre les textes et la réalité** the discrepancy between the texts and reality

distractif, -ive [distraktif, iv] ADJ distractive (*frm*), recreational

distraction [distraksjɔ̃] NF a (= *inattention*) absent-mindedness, lack of attention; **j'ai eu une ~** my concentration lapsed, my attention wandered; **cette ~ lui a coûté la vie** this one lapse in concentration cost him his life; **les ~s proverbiales des savants** the proverbial absent-mindedness of scientists b (= *passe-temps*) leisure *ou* recreational activity, pastime; **ça manque de ~** there's not much in the way of entertainment; **c'est sa seule ~** it's his only form of entertainment c (*Jur* = *vol*) abstraction; **~ de fonds** misappropriation of funds

distraire [distʀɛʀ] ▶conjug 50◀ 1 VT a (= *divertir*) to entertain, amuse b (= *déranger*) to distract, divert (**de** from); **~ l'attention de qn** to distract sb's attention; (*Scol*) **il distrait ses camarades** he distracts his friends; **se laisser facilement ~ de son travail** to be easily distracted from one's work; **~ qn de ses soucis** to take sb's mind off his worries c (*frm* = *voler*) to abstract (**de** from); **~ des fonds** to misappropriate funds 2 **se distraire** VPR to amuse o.s., enjoy o.s.; **je vais au cinéma, j'ai besoin de me ~** I'm going to the cinema, I need to take my mind off things; **je lis des romans pour me ~** I read novels for entertainment

distrait, e [distʀɛ, ɛt] (*ptp de* **distraire**) ADJ [*personne, caractère*] absent-minded; **d'un air ~** absent-mindedly, abstractedly; **il n'y a prêté qu'une attention ~e** he wasn't really paying attention, he was only half paying attention; **d'une oreille ~e** with only half an ear, abstractedly; **je l'ai lu d'un œil ~** I glanced through it

distraitement [distʀɛtmɑ̃] ADV absent-mindedly, abstractedly

distrayant, e [distʀɛjɑ̃, ɑ̃t] ADJ entertaining, diverting; **les romans policiers sont d'une lecture ~e** detective novels make pleasant light reading

distribuer [distʀibɥe] ▶conjug 1◀ VT a (= *donner*) [+ *objets*] to distribute, give out, hand out; [+ *vivres*] to distribute, share out; [+ *courrier*] to deliver; [+ *récompense*] to present; (*Fin*) [+ *actions*] to allot; [+ *travail*] to distribute; [+ *argent, dividendes*] to distribute, hand out; [+ *cartes*] to deal (out); [+ *ordres*] to hand out, deal out; [+ *coups*] to deal, deliver; [+ *saluts, sourires, enseignement*] to dispense (**à** to); **~ les rôles d'une pièce** to cast a play; **~ des claques à qn** to slap sb b (= *répartir*) to distribute, arrange; (*Typo*) [+ *caractères*] to distribute; **on distribue ces plantes en quatre espèces** these plants are divided into four species; **savoir ~ son temps** to know how to allocate *ou* divide (up) one's time; **comment les pièces sont-elles distribuées?** how are the rooms set out? *ou* laid out?; **~ les masses dans un tableau** to arrange *ou* distribute the masses in a picture; **mon emploi du temps est mal distribué** my schedule is badly arranged c (= *amener*) to distribute, carry; **~ l'eau dans les villages** to distribute *ou* carry *ou* supply water to villages; **le sang est distribué dans tout le corps par le cœur** blood is pumped *ou* carried round the body by the heart; **chaîne de télévision distribuée par câble** cable television channel d (*Comm*) [+ *film, produit*] to distribute

distributeur, -trice [distʀibytœʀ, tʀis] 1 ADJ [*compagnie, entreprise*] distributing; **société distributrice de films** film distribution company, film distributor 2 NM,F (= *agent commercial*) distributor; **~ d'essence** petrol company; **~ de films** film distributor 3 NM (= *appareil*) machine; [*savon, papier absorbant*] dispenser; (*Aut*) distributor; **~ (automatique)** vending machine; **~ de boissons/préservatifs** drinks/condom(-vending) machine, drinks/condom dispenser; **~ (automatique) de billets** (*Banque*) cash dispenser *ou* machine, automatic *ou* automated teller machine; (*Rail*) (automatic) ticket machine; (*Agr*) **~ d'engrais** manure- *ou* muck-spreader

distributif, -ive [distʀibytif, iv] ADJ distributive

distribution [distʀibysjɔ̃] NF a [*objets*] distribution, giving out, handing out; [*vivres*] distribution, sharing out; [*argent, dividendes*] distribution; [*cartes*] deal; [*courrier*] delivery; (*Fin*) [*actions*] allotment; **la ~ du travail sera faite suivant l'âge** the work will be shared out *ou* allotted *ou* allocated according to age; **~ gra-**

tuite free gifts; (**jour de la**) ~ **des prix** prize giving (day) [b] (= *répartition*) distribution, arrangement; (*Ling*) distribution; **la** ~ **des mots dans une phrase** the distribution of words in a sentence; **la** ~ **des meubles dans une pièce** the arrangement of the furniture in a room; **cet appartement a une bonne/mauvaise** ~ (**des pièces**) the flat is well/badly laid out; (*fig*) **ce résultat a conduit à une nouvelle** ~ **des cartes** this result has shifted *ou* altered the balance of power *ou* has put a new complexion on the situation [c] (*Ciné, Théât* = *acteurs*) cast; ~ **par ordre d'entrée en scène** cast *ou* characters in order of appearance; **qui est responsable de la** ~ **de cette pièce ?** who's in charge of casting this play? [d] (= *acheminement*) [*eau, électricité*] supply; (*TV*) ~ **par câble/par satellite** cable/satellite distribution [e] (*Comm*) [*livres, films*] distribution; **réseau de** ~ distribution network; **la grande** ~ mass marketing [f] (*Aut, Tech*) distribution

distributionnel, -elle [distʀibysjɔnɛl] ADJ distributional

distributivement [distʀibytivmɑ̃] ADV distributively

distributivité [distʀibytivite] NF distributiveness

district [distʀikt] NM district

dit, e [di, dit] (*ptp de* **dire**) [1] ADJ [a] (= *appelé*) **Louis XIV,** ~ **le Roi Soleil** Louis XIV, known as the Sun King; **Jean Petit,** ~ **le Chacal** Jean Petit, also known as the Jackal *ou* aka *ou* alias the Jackal; **une émission** ~**e culturelle** a so-called cultural programme [b] (= *fixé*) **à l'heure** ~**e** at the appointed time *ou* hour; **le jour** ~ on the appointed day [2] NM (*Psych*) **le** ~ **et le non-**~ what is said and what is left unsaid

dithyrambe [ditiʀɑ̃b] NM (= *poème*) dithyramb; (= *éloge*) panegyric, eulogy

dithyrambique [ditiʀɑ̃bik] ADJ [*paroles*] laudatory, eulogistic; [*éloges*] extravagant; (*Littérat*) dithyrambic; **une critique** ~ a rave review

dito [dito] ADV (*Comm*) ditto

DIU [deiy] NM (ABRÉV = **dispositif intra-utérin**) IUD

diurèse [djyʀɛz] NF (*Physiol*) diuresis

diurétique [djyʀetik] ADJ, NM diuretic

diurne [djyʀn] ADJ diurnal

diva [diva] NF († *aussi hum*) diva, prima donna; **elle a des caprices de** ~ she's a bit of a prima donna

divagation [divagasjɔ̃] NF (*gén pl*) (= *délire*) wandering, rambling; (= *bêtises*) raving

divaguer [divage] ▶conjug 1◀ VI (= *délirer*) to ramble; (= *dire des bêtises*) to rave; **il commence à** ~ he's beginning to ramble; **tu divagues !** you're off your head!•

divan [divɑ̃] NM (= *siège*) divan; (*Hist*) divan; **le** ~ **du psychanalyste** the psychoanalyst's couch

dive [div] ADJ F (*allusion littéraire*) **la** ~ **bouteille** the bottle, drink; **il aime la** ~ **bouteille** he likes his drink

divergence [divɛʀʒɑ̃s] NF [a] [*opinions*] divergence, difference; [*témoignages*] discrepancy [b] (*Opt, Phys Nucl*) divergence

divergent, e [divɛʀʒɑ̃, ɑ̃t] ADJ [a] [*opinions*] divergent, differing; [*témoignages*] differing [b] (*Opt, Phys Nucl*) divergent → **strabisme**

▼ **diverger** [divɛʀʒe] ▶conjug 3◀ VI [a] [*opinions*] to diverge, differ; [*témoignages*] to differ [b] [*chemins, rayons*] to diverge [c] (*Phys Nucl*) to go critical

divers, e [divɛʀ, ɛʀs] ADJ [a] (*pl*) (= *varié*) [*couleurs, coutumes, opinions*] diverse, varied; (= *différent*) [*sens d'un mot, moments, occupations*] different, various; **frais** ~ ◊ **dépenses** ~**es** sundries, miscellaneous expenses; **ses dons/écrits** ~ **et variés** his many and various talents/ writings; (*hum*) **elle a suivi des traitements** ~ **et variés** she has undergone all manner of treatments → **fait¹** [b] (*pl* = *plusieurs*) various, several; ~**es personnes m'en ont parlé** various *ou* several people have spoken to me about it [c] (*littér* = *changeant*) [*spectacle*] varied, changing (*épith*)

diversement [divɛʀsəmɑ̃] ADV in various ways, in diverse ways; **son livre a été** ~ **accueilli** his book has had a varied *ou* mixed reception; **son discours a été** ~ **apprécié** there were mixed reactions to his speech

diversification [divɛʀsifikasjɔ̃] NF diversification; **l'entreprise poursuit la** ~ **de ses activités** the company is continuing to diversify (its activities)

diversifier [divɛʀsifje] ▶conjug 7◀ [1] VT [+ *méthodes, exercices*] to vary; [+ *activités, centres d'intérêt, production*] to diversify; **une économie/une gamme de produits diversifiée** a varied *ou* diversified economy/range of products [2] **se diversifier** VPR [*entreprise*] to diversify; [*activités*] to be diversified; [*clientèle, public*] to become more diverse; **nous devons nous** ~ **davantage** we must diversify more

diversion [divɛʀsjɔ̃] NF (*Mil, littér*) diversion; **faire** ~ to create a diversion

diversité [divɛʀsite] NF (= *grand nombre*) [*opinions, possibilités*] range, variety; [*sujet, spectacle*] variety, diversity; (= *divergence : entre deux opinions etc*) diversity, difference, divergence

divertir [divɛʀtiʀ] ▶conjug 2◀ [1] VT [a] (= *amuser*) to amuse, entertain [b] (*Jur* = *détourner*) ~ **des fonds/une succession** to misappropriate funds/an inheritance [2] **se divertir** VPR (= *se distraire*) to amuse o.s.; (= *prendre du bon temps*) to enjoy o.s.; (*littér*) **se** ~ **de qn** to make fun of sb, laugh at sb

divertissant, e [divɛʀtisɑ̃, ɑ̃t] ADJ (= *qui fait rire*) amusing; (= *qui occupe agréablement*) entertaining

divertissement [divɛʀtismɑ̃] NM [a] (*NonC = action de distraire*) entertainment; **la boxe est un** ~ **populaire** boxing is a popular form of entertainment; **le spectacle est organisé pour le** ~ **des touristes** the show is put on to entertain the tourists; **émission de** ~ light-entertainment programme; **film de divertissement** film for entertainment [b] (= *distraction, passe-temps*) recreation; **les** ~**s sont rares dans ce village** there isn't much to do in this village, not much goes on in this village [c] (*Mus*) divertimento, divertissement [d] (††, *Philo*) distraction

dividende [dividɑ̃d] NM (*Fin, Math*) dividend; ~ **sous forme d'actions** share *ou* stock dividend; ~ **prioritaire** preferential *ou* preference dividend; **avec** ~ cum div(idend), dividend on (*US*); **sans** ~ ex div(idend), dividend off (*US*)

divin, e [divɛ̃, in] ADJ [a] [*caractère, justice, service*] divine; **la loi** ~**e** divine law, the law of God; **le** ~ **Achille** the divine Achilles; **la** ~**e Providence** divine Providence; **notre** ~ **Sauveur** the divine saviour; **notre** ~ **Père** our heavenly Father; **l'amour** ~ divine *ou* heavenly love; **le sens du** ~ the sense of the divine → **bonté, droit³** [b] (= *excellent*) [*poésie, beauté, mets, robe, temps*] divine, heavenly

divinateur, -trice [divinatœʀ, tʀis] [1] ADJ divining, foreseeing [2] NM,F †† diviner, soothsayer

divination [divinasjɔ̃] NF divination

divinatoire [divinatwaʀ] ADJ [*science*] divinatory

divinement [divinmɑ̃] ADV divinely

divinisation [divinizasjɔ̃] NF deification

diviniser [divinize] ▶conjug 1◀ VT to deify

divinité [divinite] NF (= *essence divine*) divinity; (*lit, fig* = *dieu*) deity, divinity

diviser [divize] ▶conjug 1◀ [1] VT [a] (= *fractionner : gén*) to divide; [+ *tâche, ressources*] to share out, split up; [+ *gâteau*] to cut up, divide up; ~ **une somme en trois/en trois parties** to divide *ou* split a sum of money in three/ into three parts; ~ **une somme entre plusieurs personnes** to share (out) *ou* divide (out) a sum among several people; **le pays est divisé en deux par des montagnes** the country is split *ou* divided in two by mountains; ~ **un groupe en plusieurs équipes** to split a group up into several teams [b] (= *désunir*) [+ *famille, adversaires*] to divide, set at variance; **« ~ pour (mieux) régner »** "divide and rule"; **une famille divisée** a broken family; **les historiens sont très divisés à ce sujet** historians are very divided on this subject; **l'opinion est divisée en deux par cette affaire** opinion is split *ou* divided over this affair [c] † (= *séparer*) to divide, separate; **un rideau divise la chambre d'avec le salon** *ou* **du salon** a curtain separates the bedroom (off) from the drawing room [d] (*Math*) to divide; ~ **4 par 2** to divide 4 by 2 [2] **se diviser** VPR [a] (= *se scinder*) [*groupe, cellules*] to split up, divide (**en** into) [b] (= *se ramifier*) [*route*] to fork, divide; [*tronc d'arbre*] to fork; **ce livre se divise en plusieurs chapitres** this book is divided into several chapters

diviseur [divizœʀ] NM [a] (*Math*) divisor; **nombre/fraction** ~ divisor number/fraction; **plus grand commun** ~ highest common factor; (*Élec*) ~ **de fréquence** frequency divider [b] (= *personne*) divisive force *ou* influence

divisibilité [divizibilite] NF divisibility

divisible [divizibl] ADJ divisible; **le nombre est** ~ **par 2** the number is divisible by *ou* can be divided by 2

division [divizjɔ̃] NF [a] (= *fractionnement*) division; (= *partage*) sharing out, division (**en** into); ~ **du travail** division of labour; ~ **cellulaire** cellular division [b] (= *désaccord*) division; **il y a une** ~ **au sein du parti** there's a split *ou* rift within the party; **semer la** ~ to sow discord (**entre** among) [c] (*Math*) division; **faire une** ~ to do a division (sum) [d] (*Admin, Mil*) division; ~ **blindée/d'infanterie** armoured/infantry division → **général** [e] (*Ftbl etc*) division; ~ **d'honneur** 4th division; **club de première/deuxième** ~ first/ second division club; **ils sont montés en première** ~ they've gone up to *ou* have been promoted to the first division [f] (= *graduation, compartiment*) division [g] (= *partie*) [*livre, discours, exposé*] division; (= *branche*) [*science*] division

divisionnaire [divizjɔnɛʀ] [1] ADJ divisional [2] NM († *Mil*) major-general; (*Police*) (**commissaire**) ~ ≈ chief superintendent (*Brit*), ≈ police chief (*US*)

divorce [divɔʀs] NM (*lit, fig*) divorce (**avec, d'avec** from, **entre** between); **demander le** ~ (*gén*) to ask for a divorce; (*Jur*) to sue for (a) divorce; **obtenir le** ~ to obtain *ou* get a divorce; ~ **par consentement mutuel** divorce by consent (*Brit*), no-fault divorce (*US*); **les enfants du** ~ children of divorced parents *ou* of divorce

divorcé, e [divɔʀse] (*ptp de* **divorcer**) [1] ADJ (*lit, fig*) divorced (**de** from) [2] NM,F divorcee

divorcer [divɔʀse] ▶conjug 3◀ VI (*Jur*) to get a divorce, be *ou* get divorced; ~ **d'avec sa femme/son mari** to divorce one's wife/one's husband [b] (*fig*) to break (**d'avec, de** with)

divulgateur, -trice [divylgatœʀ, tʀis] NM,F divulger

divulgation [divylgasjɔ̃] NF disclosure

➤ GRAMMAIRE ACTIVE: **diverger** 39.1

divulguer [divylge] ▶conjug 1◀ VT to divulge, disclose

dix [dis] ADJ INV, NM INV ten; **les ~ commandements** the Ten Commandments; (*Scol*) **elle a eu ~ sur ~** she got ten out of ten, she got full marks (*Brit*); **avoir ~ dixièmes à chaque œil** to have twenty-twenty vision; **répéter/ recommencer ~ fois la même chose** to repeat/ start the same thing over and over (again); *pour autres locutions voir* **six**

dix-huit [dizyit] ADJ INV, NM INV eighteen; **un (golf) ~ trous** an eighteen-hole golf course

dix-huitième [dizyitjɛm] ADJ, NMF eighteenth; **un fauteuil fin ~** a late eighteenth-century armchair

dixième [dizjɛm] ADJ, NMF tenth; **je ne sais pas le ~ de ce qu'il sait** I don't know one tenth *ou* a tenth of the things he knows

dixièmement [dizjɛmmã] ADV tenthly, in (the) tenth place

dixit [diksit] LOC VERB dixit

dix-neuf [diznœf] ADJ INV, NM INV nineteen

dix-neuvième [diznœvjɛm] ADJ, NMF nineteenth; **les romans du ~** nineteenth-century novels

dix-sept [di(s)sɛt] ADJ INV, NM INV seventeen

dix-septième [di(s)sɛtjɛm] ADJ, NMF seventeenth; **les auteurs du ~** seventeenth-century writers

dizain [dizɛ̃] NM ten-line poem

dizaine [dizɛn] NF (= *dix*) ten; (= *quantité voisine de dix*) about ten, ten or so; **des ~s et des ~s de fois** over and over (again), countless times, hundreds* *ou* thousands* of times

DJ [didʒi] NM (ABRÉV = **disque-jockey**) DJ

Djakarta [dʒakarta] N Jakarta, Djakarta

djebel [dʒebɛl] NM jebel

djellaba [dʒe(l)laba] NF jellaba

Djibouti [dʒibuti] NM Djibouti, Djibouti

djiboutien, -ienne [dʒibusjɛ̃, jɛn] [1] ADJ of *ou* from Djibouti [2] **Djiboutien(ne)** NM,F inhabitant *ou* native of Djibouti

djihad [dʒi(j)ad] NF jihad, jehad; **le Djihad islamique** Islamic Jihad

djinn [dʒin] NM jinn, djinn

dl (ABRÉV = **décilitre**) dl

DM (ABRÉV = **Deutsche Mark**) DM

dm (ABRÉV = **décimètre**) dm

do [do] NM INV (*Mus*) (= *note*) C; (*en chantant la gamme*) doh; **le do du milieu du piano** middle C

doberman [dɔbɛRman] NM Doberman pinscher

doc* [dɔk] NF ABRÉV = **documentation**

docile [dɔsil] ADJ [*personne, caractère*] docile, meek, obedient; [*animal*] docile; [*cheveux*] manageable

docilement [dɔsilmã] ADV docilely, obediently

docilité [dɔsilite] NF docility, obedience

docimologie [dɔsimɔlɔʒi] NF (statistical) analysis of test *ou* exam results

dock [dɔk] NM [a] (= *bassin*) dock; (= *cale de construction*) dockyard; **~ de carénage/flottant** dry/floating dock [b] (= *hangar, bâtiment*) warehouse

docker [dɔkɛR] NM docker, stevedore

docte [dɔkt] ADJ (*littér, hum*) learned

doctement [dɔktəmã] ADV (*littér, hum*) learnedly

docteur [dɔktœR] NM (*gén, Univ*) doctor (**ès, en** of); (*Méd*) doctor; **~ en médecine** doctor of medicine; (*Méd*) **le ~ Lebrun** Dr Lebrun; **aller chez le ~** to go to the doctor's; (*Univ*) **maintenant que tu es ~** now you've got your doctorate *ou* Ph.D.; **Monsieur Leroux, ~ ès lettres** Dr Leroux, Ph.D.; (*Rel*) **les ~s de l'Église** the Doctors of the Church

doctoral, e (*mpl* **-aux**) [dɔktɔral, o] ADJ (*Univ*) doctoral; (*péj* = *pédant*) [*ton*] pompous, bombastic

doctorant, e [dɔktɔrã, ãt] NM,F doctoral student

doctorat [dɔktɔra] NM doctorate (**ès, en** in); **~ de 3ᵉ cycle** ◊ **~ d'État** doctorate, Ph.D. → DIPLÔMES

doctoresse [dɔktɔRɛs] NF woman *ou* lady doctor

doctrinaire [dɔktRinɛR] [1] ADJ (= *dogmatique*) doctrinaire; (= *sentencieux*) pompous, sententious [2] NMF doctrinarian

doctrinal, e (*mpl* **-aux**) [dɔktRinal, o] ADJ doctrinal

doctrine [dɔktRin] NF doctrine

docudrame [dɔkydRam] NM docudrama

document [dɔkymã] NM document; **nous avons des ~ le prouvant** we have documentary evidence, we have documents to prove it; **~s de travail** working documents; **~ de référence** *ou* **d'information** background paper; **~s d'expédition** dispatch documents; (*Ciné, TV*) **~s d'archives** archive footage (*NonC*) *ou* material (*NonC*); **~ administratif unique** Single Administrative Document

documentaire [dɔkymãtɛR] [1] ADJ [*intérêt*] documentary; **à titre ~** for your (*ou* his *etc*) information; **logiciel ~** documentation software (*NonC*) [2] NM (= *film*) documentary (film)

documentaliste [dɔkymãtalist] NMF (*Presse, TV*) researcher; (*Scol*) librarian

documentariste [dɔkymãtaRist] NMF documentary maker

documentation [dɔkymãtasjɔ̃] NF (= *brochures*) documentation, literature, information; (*Presse, TV* = *service*) research department

documenter [dɔkymãte] ▶conjug 1◀ [1] VT [+ *personne, livre*] to document; (**bien**) **documenté** [+ *personne*] well-informed; [+ *livre, thèse*] well-documented [2] **se documenter** VPR to gather information *ou* material (**sur** on, about)

dodécaèdre [dɔdekaɛdR] NM dodecahedron

dodécagonal, e (*mpl* **-aux**) [dɔdekagɔnal, o] ADJ dodecagonal

dodécagone [dɔdekagɔn] NM dodecagon

dodécaphonique [dɔdekafɔnik] ADJ dodecaphonic

dodécaphonisme [dɔdekafɔnism] NM dodecaphony

dodécaphoniste [dɔdekafɔnist] [1] ADJ [*compositeur, œuvre*] dodecaphonic [2] NMF dodecaphonist

dodeliner [dɔd(ə)line] ▶conjug 1◀ VI **il dodelinait de la tête** his head was nodding gently; **sa tête dodelinait par instants** his head would nod every now and again

dodo¹ [dodo] NM (*langage enfantin*) (= *sommeil*) beddy-byes (*langage enfantin*), sleep; (= *lit*) bed; **faire au ~** *ou* **d'aller au ~** to be asleep; **il est temps d'aller au ~** *ou* **d'aller faire ~** it's time to go to beddy-byes (*langage enfantin*); (**fais**) **~ !** come on, sleepy-time!; **un bon gros/un petit ~** a nice long/a short sleep

dodo² [dodo] NM (*Orn*) dodo

Dodoma [dodoma] N Dodoma

dodu, e [dɔdy] ADJ [*personne, poule, bras*] plump; [*enfant, joue*] chubby

doge [dɔʒ] NM doge

dogmatique [dɔgmatik] ADJ dogmatic

dogmatiquement [dɔgmatikmã] ADV dogmatically

dogmatiser [dɔgmatize] ▶conjug 1◀ VI to dogmatize

dogmatisme [dɔgmatism] NM dogmatism

dogme [dɔgm] NM (*lit, fig*) dogma; (*Rel*) **le ~** the dogma

dogon [dɔgɔ̃] [1] ADJ [*art, pays*] Dogon [2] **Dogon** NMF Dogon; **les Dogons** the Dogon people

dogue [dɔg] NM (*Zool*) **~ (anglais)** mastiff; **~ allemand** German mastiff

doigt [dwa] NM [a] [*main, gant*] finger; [*animal, mal*] digit; **~ de pied** toe; **le petit ~** the little finger; **se mettre** *ou* **se fourrer* les ~s dans le nez** to pick one's nose; **le ~ de Dieu** the hand of God; **montrer qn du ~** (*lit*) to point sth out; (*fig*) to point the finger at sb; **désigner qn d'un ~ accusateur** to point an accusing finger at sb → **bague, bout, compter** *etc* [b] (= *mesure*) **raccourcir une jupe de 2/3 ~s** to shorten a skirt by 1 inch/2 inches; **un ~ de vin** a drop of wine; **un ~ de whisky/vodka** a finger of whisky/vodka [c] (*loc*) **avoir des ~s de fée** [*couturière, tricoteuse*] to have nimble fingers; [*infirmière*] to have gentle hands; **il ne fait rien de ses dix ~s** he's an idle *ou* a lazy good-for-nothing, he's bone idle (*Brit*); **il ne sait rien faire de ses dix ~s** he's useless; **faire marcher** *ou* **mener qn au ~ et à l'œil** to keep a tight rein on sb; **avec lui, ils obéissent au ~ et à l'œil** with him, they have to toe the line; **le (petit) ~ sur la couture du pantalon** (*lit*) standing to attention; (*fig*) **c'est devenu un employé modèle, le petit ~ sur la couture du pantalon** he's become a model employee, always ready to jump to attention; **mon petit ~ me l'a dit** a little bird told me; **se mettre** *ou* **se fourrer* le ~ dans l'œil (jusqu'au coude)** to be kidding o.s.*; **là tu te mets** *ou* **te fourres* le ~ dans l'œil** you've got another think coming*; **il n'a pas levé** *ou* **bougé** *ou* **remué le petit ~ pour nous aider** he didn't lift a finger to help us; **mettre le ~ sur le problème** to put one's finger on the problem; (*fig*) **mettre le ~ sur la plaie** to touch a raw nerve; **toucher du ~** (*lit*) to touch sth (with one's finger); [+ *réalité, sentiment, difficulté*] to grasp fully; (*fig*) **faire toucher du ~ qch (à qn)** to bring sth home to sb); **mettre le ~ dans l'engrenage** to get involved; **filer** *ou* **glisser entre les ~s de qn** to slip through sb's fingers; **ils sont unis comme les (deux) ~s de la main** they're joined at the hip*, they're very close; **je le ferais les ~s dans le nez*** I could do it standing on my head *ou* with my eyes closed; **il a gagné les ~s dans le nez*** he won hands down*; **avoir un morceau de musique dans les ~s** to know a piece of music like the back of one's hand; **avoir les ~s de pied en éventail*** to have one's feet up; **être à deux ~s** *ou* **un ~ de faire** to come very close to doing; **il a été à deux ~s de se tuer/de la mort/de réussir** he was within an ace *ou* an inch of being killed/of death/of succeeding; **la balle est passée à un ~ de sa tête** the bullet passed within a hairbreadth *ou* an inch of his head

doigté [dwate] NM [a] (*Mus*) (= *jeu des doigts*) fingering technique; (= *position des doigts*) fingering [b] [*chirurgien, dactylo, pianiste*] touch; (= *tact*) diplomacy, tact; **avoir du ~** (*lit*) to be nimble-fingered; (*fig*) to be tactful; (*lit, fig*) **manquer de ~** to be heavy-handed; **il faudra du ~ pour mener à bien cette négociation** a certain amount of diplomacy will be needed to bring these negotiations to a successful conclusion

doigter [dwate] ▶conjug 1◀ VTI (*Mus*) to finger

doigtier [dwatje] NM fingerstall

doit [dwa] NM debit; **~ et avoir** debit and credit

dojo [dɔʒo] NM dojo

dol [dɔl] NM (*Jur*) fraud, wilful misrepresentation (*SPÉC*)

dolby® [dɔlbi] NM Dolby®

dolce vita [dɔltʃevita] NF dolce vita

doléances [dɔleãs] NFPL (= *plaintes*) complaints; (= *réclamations*) grievances

dolent, e [dɔlã, ãt] ADJ (*littér*) doleful, mournful

doline [dɔlin] NF doline

dollar [dɔlaʀ] NM dollar; **~ australien/canadien** Australian/Canadian dollar; **~ titre** security dollar

dollarisation [dɔlaʀizasjɔ̃] NF [économie, échanges] dollarization

dolman [dɔlmã] NM (Hist = veste) dolman

dolmen [dɔlmɛn] NM dolmen

dolomie [dɔlɔmi], **dolomite** [dɔlɔmit] NF dolomite; **les Dolomites** the Dolomites

dolomitique [dɔlɔmitik] ADJ dolomitic

DOM [dɔm] NM (ABRÉV = **département d'outre-mer**) → **département**

Dom [dɔ̃] NM (= titre) Dom

domaine [dɔmɛn] NM a (= propriété) estate, property; **le ~ de la couronne** Crown lands ou property; (Jur) **le ~ (de l'État)** (= propriété) state(-owned) property; (= service) state property department; **dans le ~ public/privé** in the public/private domain, in public/private ownership; **ses œuvres sont maintenant tombées dans le ~ public** his works are now out of copyright; **la salle de jeux est le ~ des enfants** the playroom is the children's domain, the playroom belongs to the children → **skiable** b (= sphère) domain, sphere; **ce n'est pas (de) mon ~** it's not my field ou sphere; **dans tous les ~s** in every domain ou field; (Gestion) **d'activité stratégique** strategic business unit; (fig) **~ réservé** preserve c (dans un dictionnaire) field; **indication de ~** field label

domanial, e [dɔmanjal, jo] (mpl **-iaux**) ADJ (= d'un domaine privé) belonging to a private estate; (= d'un domaine public) national (épith), state (épith)

dôme [dom] NM (= voûte) dome; (= cathédrale) cathedral; (littér) **le ~ du ciel** the vault of heaven; (fig) **un ~ de verdure** a canopy of foliage ou greenery; (Géog) **~ volcanique** volcanic dome

domestication [dɔmɛstikasjɔ̃] NF (= action) domestication, domesticating; (= résultat) domestication

domesticité [dɔmɛstisite] NF a (= condition de domestique) domestic service b (= personnel) (domestic) staff, household; **une nombreuse ~** a large staff of servants c (animal) domesticity

domestique [dɔmɛstik] 1 NMF servant, domestic; **les ~s** the servants, the staff (of servants); **je ne suis pas ton ~ !** I'm not your servant! 2 ADJ a (= ménager) [travaux] domestic, household (épith); [soucis, querelle] domestic, family (épith); **accidents ~s** accidents in the home; **déchets ~s** kitchen waste ou wastes (US); **les dieux ~s** the household gods b (Comm) [marché, consommation] domestic, home (épith) c (Zool) domestic; **animal ~** domestic animal

domestiquer [dɔmɛstike] ▶ conjug 1 ◀ VT [+ animal] to domesticate; [+ peuple] to subjugate; [+ énergie solaire, marée, vent] to harness

domicile [dɔmisil] NM place of residence, home, domicile (Admin); (Jur) [société] registered address; (sur formulaire) address; **~ légal** official domicile; **~ conjugal/parental** marital/parental home; **dernier ~ connu** last known address; **je vous l'apporterai à ~** I'll bring it to your home; **le travail à ~** home-working; **il cherche du travail à ~** he's looking for work at home; **travailler à ~** to work at ou from home; **« réparations à ~ »** "home repairs carried out"; (Sport) **jouer à ~** to play at home → **élire, sans, violation**

domiciliaire [dɔmisiljɛʀ] ADJ domiciliary, house (épith)

domiciliataire [dɔmisiljatɛʀ] NM paying agent

domiciliation [dɔmisiljasjɔ̃] NF domiciliation

▶ GRAMMAIRE ACTIVE: **dommage** 45.3

domicilier [dɔmisilje] ▶ conjug 7 ◀ VT [+ facture] to pay by banker's order; **être domicilié** to be domiciled (Admin), have one's home (à in); **je me suis fait ~ à Lyon** I gave Lyons as my official address ou place of residence; **faire ~ ses factures** to have one's bills paid by banker's order

dominance [dɔminãs] NF [gène] dominance

dominant, e [dɔminã, ãt] 1 ADJ [pays, rôle] dominant; [idéologie, opinion, vent] prevailing (épith); [idée, trait] dominant, main (épith); [passion] ruling (épith); [problème, préoccupation] main (épith), chief (épith); [position] dominating (épith), leading (épith); (Bio, Jur) dominant 2 **dominante** NF (= caractéristique) dominant characteristic; (= couleur) dominant ou predominant colour; (Mus) dominant; **tableau à ~e rouge** painting with red as the dominant ou predominant colour; (Mus) **septième de ~e** dominant seventh chord

dominateur, -trice [dɔminatœʀ, tʀis] 1 ADJ [personne, caractère] domineering, overbearing; [voix, geste, regard] imperious; [pays] dominating (épith); [passion] ruling (épith) 2 NM,F (littér) ruler

domination [dɔminasjɔ̃] NF a (Pol = autorité) domination; (fig = emprise) domination, influence; **la ~ de la Gaule (par Rome)** the domination of Gaul (by Rome); **la ~ de Rome (sur la Gaule)** Roman rule ou domination (over Gaul); **les pays sous (la) ~ britannique** countries under British rule ou domination ou dominion; **tomber sous la ~ de** to fall ou come under the domination of; **exercer sa ~ sur qn** to exert one's influence on sb, hold sway over sb; **exercer une ~ morale sur qn** to exert a moral influence on sb; **un besoin insatiable de ~** an insatiable need to dominate; **~ de soi-même** self-control, self-possession b (Rel) **~s** dominations

dominer [dɔmine] ▶ conjug 1 ◀ 1 VT a (= être maître de) [+ personne, pays] to dominate; **il voulait ~ le monde** he wanted to rule the world; **ces enfants sont dominés par leur père** these children are kept down ou dominated by their father; **il se laisse ~ par sa femme** he's dominated by his wife, he's under his wife's sway; **se laisser ~ par ses passions** to let one's be ruled by one's passions; **elle ne sait pas ~ ses élèves** she can't keep her pupils in order ou under control, she can't keep control over her pupils b (= surpasser) [+ adversaire, concurrent] to outclass, tower above; **il domine de loin les autres étudiants** he is way ahead of the other students; **écrivain qui domine son siècle** writer who dominates his century; **se faire ~ par l'équipe adverse** to be dominated ou outclassed by the opposing team; **parler fort pour ~ le bruit de la rue** to speak loudly to be heard above the noise from the street; **chez lui cette passion domine toutes les autres** this is his overriding passion; **le problème de la pollution domine tous les autres** the problem of pollution overshadows all others c (= être le meilleur dans) [+ course, match, marché] to dominate d (= maîtriser) [+ sentiment] to control, master, overcome; [+ problème] to overcome, master; [+ sujet] to master; [+ situation] to dominate, master; **elle ne put ~ son trouble** she couldn't overcome her confusion e (= diriger, gouverner) to dominate, govern; **l'idée maîtresse/la préoccupation qui domine toute son œuvre** the key idea/the main concern which dominates his whole work f (= surplomber) to tower above, dominate; **rocher/terrasse qui domine la mer** rock/terrace which overlooks the sea; **la tour domine la ville** the tower dominates the town; **il dominait la foule de sa haute taille** he towered above the crowd with his great height; **de là-haut on domine la vallée** from up there you look down over the whole valley

2 VI a (= être le meilleur) [nation] to hold sway; [orateur, concurrent] to be in the dominant position; (Sport) [équipe] to be in the dominant position, be on top; [coureur] to be in a commanding position; **l'Angleterre a dominé sur les mers pendant des siècles** England ruled the seas ou held dominion over the seas for centuries; **dans les débats, il domine nettement** in debates, he clearly has the edge on everyone else ou he's definitely the strongest speaker; **leur équipe a dominé pendant tout le match** their team was on top throughout the match; **ce coureur a dominé pendant les premiers kilomètres** this runner was out in front for the first few kilometres; (fig) **~ de la tête et des épaules** to be head and shoulders above the others b (= prédominer) [caractère, défaut, qualité] to predominate; [idée, théorie] to prevail; [préoccupation, intérêt] to be dominant, predominate; [parfum] to predominate; [couleur] to stand out, predominate; **c'est l'ambition qui domine chez lui** ambition is his dominant characteristic; **c'est le jaune qui domine** it is yellow which stands out ou which is the predominant colour

3 **se dominer** VPR to control o.s., keep o.s. under control; **il ne sait pas se ~** he has no self-control

dominicain, e [dɔminikɛ̃, ɛn] 1 ADJ (Géog, Rel) Dominican; **République ~e** Dominican Republic 2 **Dominicain(e)** NM,F a (Rel) Dominican b (Géog) Dominican

dominical, e [dɔminikal, o] (mpl **-aux**) ADJ Sunday (épith) → **repos**

dominion [dɔminjɔn] NM (Pol Brit) dominion (of the British Commonwealth)

Dominique [dɔminik] NF (Géog) **la ~** Dominica

domino [dɔmino] NM a (Habillement, Jeux) domino; (Élec) connecting block b **les ~s** dominoes sg; **un jeu de ~s** a domino set; (Pol) **la théorie des ~s** the domino theory; **l'effet ~** the domino effect

▼ **dommage** [dɔmaʒ] 1 NM a (= préjudice) harm (NonC), injury; **causer un ~ à qn** to cause ou do sb harm; **pour réparer le ~ que je vous ai causé** to repair the injury I've done you; **s'en tirer sans ~(s)** to emerge ou escape unscathed; (Jur) **~ causé avec intention de nuire** malicious damage b (loc) **c'est ~ ! ◊ quel ~ !** what a pity! ou shame!; **c'est vraiment ~ ...** it's such a pity ou it's a great pity that ...; (c'est ou quel) **~ que tu ne puisses pas venir** it's a ou what a pity ou shame (that) you can't come; **le spectacle était formidable, ~ pour les absents !** the show was fantastic, too bad for those who missed it!; (iro) **ça ne te plaît pas ? c'est bien ~ !** you don't like it? well, that really is a shame! (iro)

2 **dommages** NMPL (= ravages) damage (NonC); **causer des ~s aux récoltes** to damage ou cause damage to the crops; **les ~s sont inestimables** there is incalculable damage

3 COMP ▶ **dommage(s) corporel(s)** physical injury ▶ **dommages de guerre** war damages ▶ **dommages et intérêts** damages; **il réclame 5 000 F de ~s et intérêts** he is claiming 5,000 francs (in) damages ▶ **dommage(s) matériel(s)** material damage

dommageable [dɔmaʒabl] ADJ prejudicial, harmful, injurious (à to)

dommages-intérêts [dɔmaʒɛ̃teʀɛ] NMPL (Jur) damages

domotique [dɔmɔtik] NF home automation

domptable [dɔ̃(p)tabl] ADJ tam(e)able

domptage [dɔ̃(p)taʒ] NM taming

dompter [dɔ̃(p)te] ▶ conjug 1 ◀ VT [+ fauve] to tame; [+ cheval] to break in; [+ enfant insoumis] to subdue; [+ rebelles] to put down, subdue; [+

sentiments, passions] to master, control, overcome; [+ *nature, fleuve*] to tame

dompteur, -euse [dɔ̃(p)tœʀ, øz] NM,F (*gén*) tamer, trainer; ~ **(de lions)** liontamer

DOM-TOM [dɔmtɔm] NMPL (ABRÉV = **départements et territoires d'outre-mer**) French overseas departments and territories

---
DOM-TOM

There are four "Départements d'outre-mer": Guadeloupe, Martinique, La Réunion and French Guyana ("Guyane"). They are run in the same way as metropolitan "départements" and their inhabitants are French citizens.

The "Territoires d'outre-mer" include French Polynesia, Wallis-and-Futuna, New Caledonia and polar territories. They are independent, but each is supervised by a representative of the French government.

Don [dɔ̃] NM **a** (*Géog*) Don **b** (= *titre*) Don

don [dɔ̃] NM **a** (= *aptitude*) gift, talent; **~s littéraires** literary gifts ou talents; **avoir un ~ pour** to have a gift ou talent for; **avoir le ~ des maths** to have a gift for maths; **avoir des ~s** to be gifted ou talented; **elle a le ~ de m'énerver** she has a knack ou a genius for getting on my nerves; **cette proposition n'a pas eu le ~ de lui plaire** this proposal was not destined to ou didn't happen to please him **b** (= *cadeau*) gift; (= *offrande*) donation; **~ en argent** cash donation; **~ en nature** donation in kind; **~ d'organes** donation of organs; (*littér*) **les ~s de la terre** the gifts of the earth; **faire ~ de** [+ *fortune, maison*] to donate; **je lui ai fait ~ de ce livre** I made him a present ou gift of that book, I gave him that book as a gift; **cette tâche exige le ~ de soi** this task demands real self-sacrifice; **faire (le) ~ de sa vie pour sauver qn** to give one's life to save sb, lay down one's life for sb; (*fig*) **c'est un ~ du ciel** it's a godsend

Doña [dɔɲa] NF Doña

donataire [dɔnatɛʀ] NMF donee

donateur, -trice [dɔnatœʀ, tʀis] NM,F donor

donation [dɔnasjɔ̃] NF (*Jur*) ≈ settlement; **faire une ~ à qn** to make a settlement on sb; **~ entre vifs** donation inter vivos

donation-partage (*pl* **donations-partages**) [dɔnasjɔ̃paʀtaʒ] NF (*Jur*) inter vivos settlement, deed of gift

▼ **donc** [dɔ̃k *en tête de proposition ou devant voyelle; ailleurs*, dɔ̃] CONJ **a** (= *par conséquent*) therefore, so, thus; (= *après une digression*) so, then; **il partit ~ avec ses amis et ...** so he left with his friends and ...; **je n'étais pas d'accord, ~ j'ai refusé** I didn't agree (and) so I refused ou and I therefore refused; **j'ai raté le train, ~ je n'ai pas pu venir** I missed the train and was thus not able to come ou and so I couldn't come; **si ce n'est pas la variole c'est ~ la rougeole** if it's not smallpox then it's measles **b** (*intensif: marque la surprise*) then, so; **c'était ~ un espion ?** he was a spy then?, so he was a spy?; **voilà ~ ce dont il s'agissait** that's what it was (all) about then, so that's what it was (all) about **c** (*de renforcement*) **allons ~ !** come on!, come now!; **écoute-moi ~** do listen to me; **demande-lui ~** go on, ask him; **tais-toi ~ !** do be quiet!; **regarde ~ ça comme c'est joli** just look at that, isn't it pretty?; **pensez ~ !** just imagine ou think!; **comment ~ ?** how do you mean?; **quoi ~ ?** what was that?, what did you say?; **dis ~ ◇ dites ~** (*introduit une question*) tell me, I say; (*introduit un avertissement, une injonction*) look (here) ...; (*ton indigné*) well really ...; **non mais dis ~, ne te gêne pas !** well, don't mind me!; **dites ~, où l'avez-vous mis ?** I say, where did you put it?; **tiens ~ !** well, well!, I say!

dondon [dɔ̃dɔ̃] NF big ou fat woman (ou girl); **une grosse ~** a big lump* of a woman (ou girl)

donjon [dɔ̃ʒɔ̃] NM keep, donjon

don Juan [dɔ̃ʒɥɑ̃] NM Don Juan

donjuanesque [dɔ̃ʒɥanɛsk] ADJ of Don Juan, typical of Don Juan

donjuanisme [dɔ̃ʒɥanism] NM Don Juanism

donnant-donnant, donnant, donnant [dɔnɑ̃dɔnɑ̃] **1** NM quid pro quo; **stratégie/principe du ~** strategy/principle of quid pro quo; **les belligérants ont insisté sur le ~** the belligerents insisted on a quid pro quo arrangement **2** LOC ADV **avec lui, c'est donnant, donnant** he always wants something in return; **donnant, donnant : je te prête mon livre, tu me prêtes ton stylo** fair's fair — I lend you my book and you lend me your pen

donne [dɔn] NF (*Cartes*) deal; (*fig* = *situation*) order; **à vous la ~** your deal; **faire la ~** to deal (out) the cards; **il y a fausse ~** it's a misdeal; **la nouvelle ~ politique** the new political order

▼ **donné, e** [dɔne] (*ptp de* **donner**) **1** ADJ **a** (= *déterminé*) [*lieu, date*] given, fixed → **moment** **b** (*loc*) **étant ~ la situation** in view of ou given ou considering the situation; **étant ~ que tu es parti** seeing ou given that you left **c*** (= *pas cher*) (*dirt*) cheap* **2** NM **le ~, c'est ...** the facts of the situation are ... **3** **donnée** NF **a** (*Math, Sci*) [*problème*] datum; **~es** data; (*Écon*) **selon les ~es corrigées des variations saisonnières** according to the seasonally adjusted figures; **le taux de chômage en ~es corrigées des variations saisonnières** the seasonally adjusted unemployment rate **b** (= *chose connue*) piece of information; **~es facts**, particulars; **manquer de ~es** to be short of facts; **modifier les ~es du problème** to redefine the problem

---
donner [dɔne]

► conjug 1 ◄

1 VERBE TRANSITIF	**3** VERBE PRONOMINAL
2 VERBE INTRANSITIF	

1 VERBE TRANSITIF

a = **offrir** [+ qch à qn to give sth to sb, give sb sth; **je le lui ai donné** I gave it to him; **~ son cœur/son amitié (à qn)** to give one's heart/one's friendship (to sb); **~ à manger/boire à qn** to give sb something to eat/drink; **~ son corps à la science** to donate one's body to science; **il a donné ses tableaux au Louvre** he donated his paintings to the Louvre; **~ sa vie/son temps pour une cause** to give (up) one's life/one's time for a cause; **~ qch pour ou contre qch d'autre** to give sth in exchange for sth else, exchange sth for sth else; **en ~ à qn pour son argent** to give sb their money's worth; **on ne les vend pas, on les donne** we're not selling them, we're giving them away; **j'ai déjà donné !** (*lit*) I've already made a donation!; (*hum* = *on ne m'y reprendra plus !*) I've been there! ■ (*PROV*) **c'est ~ ~** (, **reprendre c'est voler**) a gift is a gift ■ (*PROV*) **qui donne aux pauvres prête à Dieu** charity will be rewarded in heaven → **change, matière, sang**

b = **remettre, confier** to give, hand; [+ *copie d'examen*] to hand in, give in; **~ quelque chose à faire à qn** to give sb something to do; **je donnerai la lettre au concierge** I shall give the letter to the caretaker; **donnez-moi les outils** give me ou hand me ou pass me the tools; **donnez-moi un kilo d'oranges** I'd like a kilo of oranges; **~ ses chaussures à ressemeler/au cordonnier** to take one's shoes (in) to be resoled/to the shoe-repair shop

c = **accorder** [+ *moyen, occasion*] to give; [+ *permission, interview*] to grant, give; [+ *prix, décoration, subvention*] to award, give; **donnez-moi le temps d'y réfléchir** give me time to think about it; **on lui a donné 24 heures pour quitter le pays** he was given 24 hours to leave the country; **le médecin lui donne trois mois (à**

vivre) the doctor has given him three months (to live); **~ sa fille en mariage à qn** to give one's daughter to sb in marriage; **il m'a été donné d'assister à cet événement historique** I was privileged enough to be there when this historic event took place; **il ou ça n'est pas donné à tout le monde de ...** not everyone is lucky ou fortunate enough to ...; **l'intelligence n'est pas donnée à tout le monde** not everyone is gifted with intelligence; **je vous le donne en cent ou en mille !*** you'll never guess (in a million years)! → **dieu**

d = **administrer** [+ *médicament, bain*] to give; (*Rel*) [+ *communion*] to give; [+ *sacrement*] to administer; **~ une punition à qn** to punish sb; **~ un baiser/un coup de pied à qn** to give sb a kiss/a kick; **~ un coup de balai à la pièce** to give the room a quick sweep; **~ un coup de chiffon à la pièce** to flick a duster over the room, give the room a quick dust

e = **céder** [+ *vieux vêtements*] to give away; **~ sa place à une dame** to give up one's seat to a lady; **je donnerais beaucoup pour savoir** I would give a lot to know → **langue**

f = **distribuer** to hand out, give out; [+ *cartes*] to deal (out); (*Cartes*) **c'est à vous de ~** it's your deal

g = **communiquer, indiquer** [+ *description, détails, idée, avis*] to give; [+ *sujet de devoir*] to set; **il lui a donné l'ordre de partir** he has ordered him to go; **pouvez-vous me ~ l'heure ?** can you tell me the time? → **alarme, alerte**

h = **causer** [+ *plaisir, courage*] to give (à to); [+ *peine, mal*] to cause, give (à to); **ça donne chaud/froid/soif/faim** it makes you (feel) hot/cold/thirsty/hungry; **~ le vertige/le mal de mer (à qn)** to make sb (feel) giddy/seasick; **ça donne des maux de tête** it causes headaches ou gives you headaches; **mangez ça, ça va vous ~ des forces** eat this, it'll give you some energy ou it'll make you feel stronger; **rajoute des fines herbes, ça donnera du goût** add some herbs to give it some flavour → **appétit**

◆ **donner à** + *infinitif* (= *faire*) **cela m'a donné à penser que ...** it made me think that ...; **tout donne à croire que ...** everything points to the fact that ...; **ces événements nous ont donné (beaucoup) à réfléchir** these events have given us (much) food for thought ou have really set us thinking; **c'est ce qu'on m'a donné à entendre** that's what I was given to understand ou led to believe; **~ à rire** to be laughable

i = **organiser** [+ *réception, bal*] to give, hold (à to); [+ *film*] to show; [+ *pièce*] to perform, put on

k = **conférer** [+ *poids, valeur*] to add, give; [+ *importance*] to give; **le brouillard donne un air triste à la ville** the fog makes the town look really dismal

l = **attribuer** **quel âge lui donnez-vous ?** how old would you say he was?; **je lui donne 50 ans** I'd say he was 50 → **raison, tort**

m
◆ **donner qch/qn pour** (= *présenter comme*) **~ un fait pour certain** to present a fact as a certainty; **on le donne pour un homme habile** he is said ou made out to be a clever man; **il se donne pour un tireur d'élite** he makes himself out ou claims to be a crack shot; **on l'a donné pour mort** he was given up for dead; **on m'a dit qu'il démissionnait, je te le donne pour ce que ça vaut*** for what it's worth, somebody told me he's resigning

n Mus [+ *le la, la note, le ton*] to give

o = **produire** [+ *fruits, récolte*] to yield; [+ *résultat*] to produce; **cette vigne donne un très bon vin** this vine produces a very good wine; **elle lui a donné un fils** she gave ou bore him a son; **cet écrivain donne un livre tous les ans** this writer produces a book every year; **cette méthode ne donne rien** this method is totally ineffective; **j'ai essayé de le convaincre, mais ça**

► GRAMMAIRE ACTIVE: **donc** 44.1   **donné** 44.1

n'a pas donné grand-chose I tried to convince him, but without much success; **qu'est-ce que ça donne ?*** (= *qu'en penses-tu*) how's that?, what do you think?; (= *comment ça se passe*) how's it going?; **essaie la robe, pour que je voie ce que ça donne** try the dress on so I can see what it looks like

[P] **⁎ = dénoncer** [+ complice] to squeal ou grass on⁎, shop⁎ (Brit)

[2] VERBE INTRANSITIF
[a] **= frapper** le voilier est allé ~ sur les rochers the boat ran onto ou struck the rocks; **le soleil donne en plein sur la voiture** the sun is beating down on ou shining right onto the car; ~ **de la tête contre une porte** to knock ou bump one's head against a door; **je ne sais plus où ~ de la tête** I don't know which way to turn
[b]
♦ **donner dans** (= *tomber dans*) [+ piège] to fall into; [+ défaut] to lapse into; ~ **dans le snobisme** to be rather snobbish, have a tendency to be snobbish → **panneau**
[c]
♦ **donner sur** (= *s'ouvrir sur*) [pièce, porte] to give onto, open onto; [fenêtre] to overlook, open onto, look onto; **la maison donne sur la mer** the house faces ou looks onto the sea
[d] **= attaquer** to attack; **l'artillerie va ~** the artillery is going to fire; **faites ~ la garde !** send in the guards!
[e] **= produire** to yield; **les pommiers ont bien donné cette année** the apple trees have produced a good crop ou given a good yield this year; **cet arbre ne donnera pas avant trois ans** this tree won't bear fruit for three years; **les tomates donnent à plein** it is the height of the tomato season; (fig) **la radio donne à plein** the radio is turned right up; (fig) **ça donne !⁎** (= *l'ambiance est fantastique*) it's cool⁎ ou magic⁎ ou brill!⁎

[3] **se donner** VERBE PRONOMINAL
[a] **= se consacrer** se ~ **à** [+ cause, parti, travail] to devote o.s. to
[b] **= agir avec énergie** il s'est donné à fond he gave his all; **il se donne pour réussir dans la vie** he works hard to succeed in life
[c] **sexuellement** elle s'est donnée à lui† she gave herself to him
[d] **= donner à soi-même** donne-toi un coup de peigne give your hair a quick comb, run a comb through your hair; **se ~ bien du mal** ou **de la peine** to go to a lot of trouble; **il s'est donné la peine de me prévenir** he took the trouble to warn me; **se ~ bonne conscience** to ease ou soothe one's conscience; **elle se donne des airs de jeune fille naïve** she makes herself out to be an innocent young thing; **se ~ un maire/un président** to choose a mayor/a president; **il s'est donné 6 mois pour fonder son entreprise** he gave ou allowed himself 6 months to set up the company → **mort, temps** etc
♦ **s'en donner⁎ (à cœur joie)** to have a whale of a time⁎, have the time of one's life → **cœur**
[e] **= échanger** ils se donnaient des baisers they were kissing each other; **ils se sont donné des coups/des nouvelles** they exchanged blows/news → **main, rendez-vous** etc
[f] **= être joué, montré** [pièce] to be on; [film] to be on, be showing

donneur, -euse [dɔnœʀ, øz] NM,F [a] (gén) giver; (Cartes) dealer; (Comm) ~ **d'ordre** principal; (péj) ~ **de leçons** sermonizer (péj) [b]⁎ (= dénonciateur) squealer⁎, grass⁎, informer [c] (Méd) donor; ~ **de sang/de sperme** blood/sperm donor; ~ **universel** universal donor

Don Quichotte [dɔ̃kiʃɔt] NM Don Quixote
don-quichottisme [dɔ̃kiʃɔtism] NM quixotism

dont [dɔ̃] PRON REL [a] (provenant d'un complément de nom : indique la possession, la qualité etc)

whose, of which; (antécédent humain) whose; **la femme ~ vous apercevez le chapeau** the woman whose hat you can see; **c'est un pays ~ j'aime le climat** it's a country whose climate I like ou which has a climate I like; **un vagabond ~ les chaussures laissaient voir les doigts de pied** a tramp whose toes showed through his shoes; **les enfants ~ la mère travaille sont plus indépendants** children whose mothers go out to work ou children with working mothers are more independent; **l'histoire, ~ voici l'essentiel, est ...** the story, of which these are the main points, is ...
[b] (indiquant la partie d'un tout) **il y a eu plusieurs blessés, ~ son frère** there were several casualties, among which ou among whom was his brother ou including his brother; **des livres ~ j'ai lu une dizaine environ/~ une dizaine sont reliés** books of which I have read about ten/of which about ten are bound; **ils ont trois filles ~ deux sont mariées** they have three daughters, two of whom are married ou of whom two are married, they have three daughters, two of them married; **il a écrit deux romans ~ un est autobiographique** he has written two novels one of which is autobiographical
[c] (indique la manière, la provenance) **la façon ~ elle marche/s'habille** the way (in which) she walks/dresses, her way of walking/dressing; **la pièce ~ il sort** the room (which) he is coming out of ou out of which he is coming; **mines ~ on extrait de l'or** mines from which gold is extracted, mines (that) gold is extracted from; **la classe sociale ~ elle est issue** the social class (which) she came from → **de¹**
[d] (provenant d'un complément prépositionnel d'adjectif, de verbe : voir aussi les adjectifs et verbes en question) **l'outil ~ il se sert** the tool (which) he is using; **la maladie ~ elle souffre** the illness she suffers from ou from which she suffers; **le vase ~ la maison m'a fait cadeau** the vase (which) the firm gave me, the vase with which the firm presented me; **le film/l'acteur ~ elle parle tant** the film/actor she talks so much about ou about which/whom she talks so much; **voilà ce ~ il faut vous assurer** that is what you must make sure of ou about; **l'accident ~ il a été responsable** the accident he was responsible for ou for which he was responsible; **le collier/l'enfant ~ elle est si fière** the necklace/child she is so proud of ou of which/whom she is so proud

donzelle [dɔ̃zɛl] NF (péj) young madam (péj)
dopage [dɔpaʒ] NM [athlète] (illegal) drug use, drug abuse; [cheval] doping; **l'athlète a été disqualifié pour ~** the athlete was disqualified for drug abuse ou after failing a drug ou dope test
dopamine [dɔpamin] NF dopamine
dopant, e [dɔpɑ̃, ɑ̃t] [1] ADJ produit ~ drug [2] NM drug
dope [dɔp] NF (arg Drogue) dope (arg)
doper [dɔpe] ▶conjug 1◀ [1] VT [+ athlète, cheval] to dope; [+ économie, ventes] to boost; (Tech) **semi-conducteur dopé** doped semiconductor [2] **se doper** VPR to take drugs; **il se dope aux amphétamines** he takes amphetamines
doping [dɔpiŋ] NM = **dopage**
Doppler [dɔplɛʀ] NM Doppler test; **se faire faire un ~** to have a Doppler test; **effet ~(-Fizeau)** Doppler effect
dorade [dɔʀad] NF = **daurade**
doré, e [dɔʀe] (ptp de **dorer**) [1] ADJ [a] (= couvert d'une dorure) gilt, gilded; ~ **sur tranche** gilt-edged, with gilded edges [b] (= couleur d'or) [peau] bronzed, tanned; [blé, cheveux, lumière] golden; [gâteau, viande] browned; (fig) **des rêves ~s** golden dreams; ~ **comme les blés** golden-blond, flaxen → **jeunesse** [2] NM [a] (= dorure) gilt, gilding; **le ~ du vase s'en va** the gilt ou gilding is coming off the vase

[b] (Can = poisson) yellow pike, wall-eyed pike
[3] **dorée** NF John Dory, dory
dorénavant [dɔʀenavɑ̃] ADV (dans le futur) from now on, henceforth (frm), henceforward (frm); (dans le passé) from then on, henceforth (frm), henceforward (frm)
dorer [dɔʀe] ▶conjug 1◀ [1] VT [a] (= couvrir d'or) [+ objet] to gild; **faire ~ un cadre** to have a frame gilded; (fig) ~ **la pilule à qn⁎** to sugar ou sweeten the pill for sb [b] (Culin) [+ gâteau] to glaze (with egg yolk); **le four dore bien la viande** the oven browns the meat well [c] [+ peau] to bronze, tan; (littér) **le soleil dore les blés** the sun turns the corn gold; **le soleil dore les dunes** the sun tinges the dunes with gold; **se ~ au soleil** ◊ **se ~ la pilule⁎** to lie (and get brown) in the sun, sunbathe [2] VI (Culin) [rôti] to brown; **faire ~ un poulet** to brown a chicken
d'ores et déjà [dɔʀzedeʒa] ADV → **ores**
doreur, -euse [dɔʀœʀ, øz] NM,F gilder
dorien, -ienne [dɔʀjɛ̃, jɛn] [1] ADJ (Géog) Dorian, Doric; [dialecte] Doric; (Mus) [mode] Dorian [2] NM (Ling) Doric (dialect)
dorique [dɔʀik] ADJ, NM Doric
dorlotement [dɔʀlɔtmɑ̃] NM pampering, (molly)coddling, cosseting
dorloter [dɔʀlɔte] ▶conjug 1◀ [1] VT to pamper, (molly)coddle, cosset; **il est trop dorloté** he's mollycoddled; **se faire ~** to be pampered ou (molly)coddled ou cosseted [2] **se dorloter** VPR to pamper o.s.
dormance [dɔʀmɑ̃s] NF (Bot, Méd) dormancy; **la ~ cancéreuse** dormancy of cancer cells
dormant, e [dɔʀmɑ̃, ɑ̃t] [1] ADJ [eau] still; (Tech) [châssis] fixed; (Jur, Fin) **compte ~** dormant account; (Espionnage) **agent ~** sleeper [2] NM [porte, châssis] casing, frame; (Naut) standing end
dormeur, -euse [dɔʀmœʀ, øz] [1] ADJ [poupée] with eyes that shut [2] NM,F sleeper; (péj) sleepyhead⁎; **c'est un gros ou grand ~** he likes his sleep, he's a real sleepyhead⁎ [3] NM (= crabe) (common ou edible) crab [4] **dormeuse** NF† (= boucle d'oreille) stud (earring)
dormir [dɔʀmiʀ] ▶conjug 16◀ VI [a] (gén) to sleep; (= être en train de dormir) to be asleep, be sleeping; ~ **d'un sommeil léger/lourd** to sleep lightly/heavily; **parler en dormant** to talk in one's sleep; **il dormait d'un sommeil agité** he was tossing and turning in his sleep; **je n'ai pas dormi de la nuit/de trois jours** I haven't slept a wink (all night)/for three days; **avoir envie de ~** to feel sleepy; **essayez de ~ un peu** try to get some sleep; **ça m'empêche de ~** [café] it keeps me awake; [soucis] I'm losing sleep over it; **ce n'est pas ça qui va m'empêcher de ~** I'm not going to lose any sleep over that; **il n'en dort pas** ou **plus** he's losing sleep over it, he can't sleep for thinking of it [b] (= rester inactif) [eau] to be still; [argent, capital] to lie idle; [machines] to be ou lie idle; [nature, forêt] to be still, be asleep; **tout dormait dans la maison/ville** everything was quiet ou still in the house/town; **la brute qui dormait en lui** the beast within ou inside; **investis ton capital plutôt que de le laisser ~** invest your capital rather than leave it idle; **ce n'est pas le moment de ~ !** this is no time for slacking ou idling!; **il dormait sur son travail** he wasn't concentrating on his work; **voilà six ans que le projet dort dans un tiroir** the project has been lying dormant ou has been in mothballs⁎ for six years → **pire**
[c] (loc) **je dors debout** I'm asleep on my feet, I can't keep my eyes open; **une histoire à ~ debout** a cock-and-bull story; (frm) ~ **(de) son dernier sommeil** to sleep one's last sleep; ~ **comme un bienheureux** to sleep like a baby; ~ **comme un loir** ou **une marmotte** ou **une souche** ou **un sonneur** to sleep like a log; **ne ~ que d'un œil** to sleep with one eye open; **il dort à**

poings fermés he is sound *ou* fast asleep, he's dead to the world*; **cette nuit je vais ~ à poings fermés** I'm going to sleep very soundly tonight; **~ du sommeil du juste** to sleep the sleep of the just; *(fig)* **~ tranquille** *ou* **sur ses deux oreilles** *(sans soucis)* to sleep soundly; *(sans danger)* to sleep safely (in one's bed) ■ *(PROV)* **qui dort dîne** he who sleeps forgets his hunger

dormitif, -ive [dɔʀmitif, iv] ADJ soporific

dorsal, e *(mpl* **-aux**) [dɔʀsal, o] **1** ADJ *(gén)* dorsal; *[douleur]* back *(épith)* → **épine**, **parachute** **2** **dorsale** NF **a** *(Ling)* dorsal consonant **b** *(Géog)* ridge; *(Mét)* **~e barométrique** ridge of high pressure

dortoir [dɔʀtwaʀ] NM dormitory; **banlieue(-) dortoir** dormitory *ou* bedroom *(US)* suburb

dorure [dɔʀyʀ] NF **a** *(= couche d'or)* gilt, gilding; **uniforme couvert de ~s** uniform covered in gold decorations **b** *(= action)* gilding

doryphore [dɔʀifɔʀ] NM Colorado beetle

DOS, Dos ® [dɔs] NM *(ABRÉV = **Disc Operating System**)* DOS®

dos [do] **1** NM **a** *(être animé, main, vêtement, siège, page)* back; *[livre]* spine; *[lame, couteau]* blunt edge; **avoir le ~ rond** to be round-shouldered; **couché sur le ~** lying on one's *(ou* its*)* back; **écrire au ~ d'une lettre/enveloppe** to write on the back of a letter/an envelope; **robe décolletée dans le ~** low-backed dress; **« voir au ~ »** "see over *ou* overleaf"; **aller à ~ d'âne/de chameau** to ride on a donkey/a camel; **les vivres sont portés à ~ de chameau/d'homme** the supplies are carried by camel/men; **ils partirent, sac au ~** they set off (with) their rucksacks on their backs; **avoir les cheveux dans le ~** to wear one's hair loose; **(vu) de ~ il a une allure jeune** (seen) from behind *ou* from the back he looks quite young; **le chat fait le gros ~** the cat is arching its back **b** *(= nage)* **~ (crawlé)** backstroke **c** *(loc)* **il s'est mis tout le monde à ~** he has turned everybody against him; **être ~ à ~** to be back to back; **renvoyer deux adversaires ~ à ~** to send away *ou* dismiss two opponents without pronouncing in favour of either; *(fig)* **le train/ta mère a bon ~*** (that's right) blame the train/your mother *(iro)*; **il n'y a pas avec le ~ de la cuiller*** he certainly doesn't go in for half-measures*, there are no half-measures with him; **faire qch dans** *ou* **derrière le ~ de qn** to do sth behind sb's back; **nous avions la mer/l'ennemi dans le ~** we had the sea/the enemy behind us *ou* at our back(s); **on l'a dans le ~!*** we've had it!*; *(fig)* **j'ai toujours mon patron sur le ~** my boss is always breathing down my neck *ou* is always standing over me; **mettre qch sur le ~ de qn** [+ *responsabilité*] to saddle sb with sth, make sb shoulder the responsibility for sth; [+ *accusation*] to pin sth on sb; **il s'est mis une sale affaire sur le ~** he has got himself mixed up in a nasty bit of business; **faire des affaires sur le ~ de qn** to do a bit of business at sb's expense; **il a tout pris sur le ~*** he bore the brunt of the whole thing; **je n'ai rien à me mettre sur le ~** I haven't a thing to wear; **tomber sur le ~ de qn** *(= arriver à l'improviste)* to drop in on sb, pay sb an unexpected visit; *(= attaquer) (physiquement)* to fall on sb, go for sb; *(en paroles)* to jump down sb's throat, go for sb; **tourner le ~ à** to turn one's back on; **avoir le ~ tourné à la mer/à la porte** to have one's back to the sea/door; **dès qu'il a le ~ tourné** as soon as his back is turned → **froid**, **laine**, **plein**

2 COMP ► **dos brisé** *(Reliure)* hollow *ou* open *ou* loose back

dosage [dozaʒ] NM **a** *[ingrédient, élément]* measuring out; *[remède]* dosage **b** *[mélange]* correct proportioning, mixture; **se tromper dans le ~ d'un cocktail/d'une solution chimique** to mix a cocktail/a chemical solution in

the wrong proportions **c** *(= équilibre)* **tout est question de ~** it's all a matter of striking a balance *ou* the right balance; **un savant ~ de prudence et d'audace** a judicious combination of caution and audacity

dos-d'âne [dodan] NM INV hump; **pont en ~** humpback bridge

dose [doz] NF **a** *(Pharm)* dose; **~ mortelle** lethal dose; **absorber une ~ excessive de barbituriques** to take an overdose of barbiturates; **s'en tenir à la ~ prescrite** to keep to the prescribed dose *ou* dosage **b** *(= proportion)* *[ingrédient, élément]* amount, quantity; *(hum)* **il a eu sa ~ quotidienne** he has had his daily dose *ou* fix* *(hum)*; **en avoir sa ~*** to have had more than one's share of it; *(fig)* **forcer la ~** to overdo it, overstep the mark; **introduire une petite ~ d'ironie dans un récit** to introduce a touch of irony into a story; **pour faire cela, il faut une ~ de courage peu commune** you need an extraordinary amount of courage to do that; **affligé d'une forte ~ de stupidité** afflicted with more than one's fair share of stupidity; **j'aime bien la poésie/ce chanteur mais seulement par petites ~s** *ou* **à petites ~s** I like poetry/that singer but only in small doses; *(hum)* **le travail, c'est bien mais à ~ homéopathiques** work's fine but only in small doses

doser [doze] ▶ conjug 1 ◀ VT **a** *(= mesurer)* [+ *ingrédient, élément*] to measure out; [+ *remède*] to measure out a dose of **b** *(= proportionner)* [+ *mélange*] to proportion correctly, mix in the correct proportions; **mal ~ un cocktail/une solution chimique** to mix a cocktail/a chemical solution in the wrong proportions; **gélules dosées à 100 mg** 100 mg capsules; **pilule faiblement dosée (en œstrogènes)** low-dose (oestrogen) pill **c** *(= équilibrer)* to strike a balance between; [+ *exercices, difficultés*] to grade; **il faut savoir ~ compréhension et sévérité** you must strike a balance *ou* the right balance between understanding and severity; **~ ses efforts** to pace o.s.; **cet auteur sait ~ l'ironie** this author has a gift for using irony in just the right amounts

doseur [dozœʀ] NM measure; **bouchon ~** measuring cap; **flacon ~** pump dispenser

dosimètre [dozimetʀ] NM dosimeter

dossard [dosaʀ] NM *(Sport)* number *(worn by competitor)*; **avec le ~ numéro 9** wearing number 9

dossier [dosje] NM **a** *[siège]* back **b** *(= documents)* file, dossier; *(Scol, Univ)* **~ d'inscription** registration forms; **~ médical** medical file *ou* records; **~ de presse** press kit; **~ scolaire** school record, student file *(US)*; **constituer un ~ sur qn** to draw up a file on sb; **connaître** *ou* **posséder ses ~s** to know what one is about, know what's what; **être sélectionné sur ~** to be selected on the basis of one's application **c** *(Jur)* *(= affaire)* case; *(= papiers)* case file; **il n'y a rien dans le ~** the case has no substance; **ils ont fermé le ~** they closed the case; **verser une pièce au ~** to add a piece of evidence to the case file **d** *(= question à traiter)* issue, question; *(Scol, Univ = travail de recherche)* project; **le ~ agricole** the agriculture issue; **le ~ brûlant de l'immigration** the burning *ou* highly sensitive issue of immigration; **ils ont un ~ à faire sur les ours** they've got to do a project on bears **e** *(Presse = article)* special report *(sur* on*)*, survey *(sur* of*)*; *(TV)* **~ spécial sur la Mafia** special programme *(Brit) ou* program *(US)* on the Mafia **f** *(= classeur)* file, folder

dot [dɔt] NF *[mariage]* dowry; *(Rel)* (spiritual) dowry; **apporter qch en ~** to bring a dowry of sth, bring sth as one's dowry → **coureur**

dotal, e *(mpl* **-aux**) [dɔtal, o] ADJ dotal, dowry *(épith)*

dotation [dɔtasjɔ̃] NF *(Jur)* *[institution]* endowment; *(Hist)* *[fonctionnaire, dignitaire]* emolument; *(Admin = allocation)* grant; **l'État a diminué les ~s en capital des entreprises publiques** the government has reduced subsidies to state-owned companies

doter [dɔte] ▶ conjug 1 ◀ VT **a** *(Jur)* [+ *fille à marier*] to provide with a dowry; [+ *institution*] to endow; *(Hist)* [+ *fonctionnaire, dignitaire*] to endow with an emolument; *(Admin)* [+ *université, organisme*] to grant money to, give a grant to; **doté de** *[équipement, matériel, dispositif]* equipped with; *[talent, courage, pouvoir]* endowed with; **richement dotée** *[fille]* with a handsome dowry; *[compétition]* with big prize-money **b** **~ qn/qch (de** *(= pourvoir de)* to equip *ou* provide sb/sth with; **la nature l'avait doté d'un grand talent** nature had endowed him with great talent, nature had bestowed great talent upon him

douaire [dwɛʀ] NM dower

douairière [dwɛʀjɛʀ] NF dowager

douane [dwan] NF **a** *(= service)* Customs; **les ~s britanniques** Customs and Excise, British Customs; **il est employé aux ~s** *ou* **à la ~** he's employed in the Customs department; **marchandises (entreposées) en ~** bonded goods, goods in bond; **zone/port sous ~** zone/port under the authority of the Customs **b** *(à la frontière)* customs; **poste** *ou* **bureau de ~** customs house; *(à l'aéroport etc)* **passer (à) la ~** to go through customs; *(dans le train)* **la visite de la ~** the customs check; **il s'est fait contrôler à la ~** he was stopped by customs (officers) *ou* at customs, he had his baggage checked *ou* examined by customs (officers) **c** *(droits de)* **~** customs duty *ou* dues, duty; **exempté de ~** duty-free, non-dutiable

douanier, -ière [dwanje, jɛʀ] **1** ADJ customs *(épith)* → **barrière**, **union** **2** NM,F customs officer

doublage [dublaʒ] NM **a** *[fil]* doubling; *[revêtement]* doubling, laying; *[couverture]* doubling, folding (in half) **b** *[film]* dubbing; **le ~ d'un acteur** *(voix)* dubbing an actor; *(rôle)* using a double for an actor **c** *[vêtement, paroi, boîte, tableau]* lining; *(Naut)* *[coque]* sheathing **d** *[somme, quantité, lettre]* doubling

double [dubl] **1** ADJ **a** *[consonne, longueur, épaisseur, fleur]* double; *[inconvénient, avantage]* double, twofold; **feuille ~** double sheet (of paper); **~ whisky** double *ou* large whisky; **le prix est ~ de ce qu'il était** the price is double *ou* twice what it was; **vous avez fait une ~ erreur** you have made two mistakes; **faire qch en ~ exemplaire** to make two copies of sth, do sth in duplicate; **à ~ action** *[rasoir]* dual-action; *[crème]* double-acting; *[shampooing]* two-in-one; **ustensile à ~ usage** dual-purpose utensil; **faire ~ emploi** to be redundant; **cet appareil fait maintenant ~ emploi avec l'ancien** this appliance makes the old one redundant; **« à vendre voiture, cause ~ emploi »** "for sale: car, surplus to requirements"; **fermer une porte à ~ tour** to double-lock a door; **enfermer qn à ~ tour** to put sb under lock and key; *(lit, fig)* **à ~ tranchant** double-edged, two-edged; **boîte/valise à ~ fond** box/case with a false bottom; **foyer à ~ revenu** dual-income *ou* double-income household; **mettre un fil (en) ~** to use a double thread; **mettre une couverture (en) ~** to put a blanket on double; **en ~ aveugle** double-blind *(épith)* → **bouchée²**, **coup** **b** *(= qui a des aspects opposés)* *[vie, aspect]* double; **à ~ face** *[tissu]* reversible; *[adhésif]* double-sided; **accusé de jouer un ~ jeu** accused of double-dealing *ou* of playing a double game *(Brit)*; **phrase à ~ sens** *ou* **entente** sentence with a double meaning; **mener une ~ vie** to lead a double life; **personnage à personnalité ~** person with a dual personality *ou* a Jekyll-and-Hyde personality → **agent**

2 NM **a** (= *quantité*) **manger/gagner le ~ (de qn)** to eat/earn twice as much (as sb) *ou* double the amount (that sb does); **il pèse le ~ de vous** he's twice your weight, he weighs twice as much as you do; **4 est le ~ de 2** 4 is two times *ou* twice 2; **c'est le ~ du prix normal** it is twice *ou* double the normal price; **c'est le ~ de la distance Paris-Lyon** it's twice *ou* double the distance from Paris to Lyons; **hier il a mis le ~ de temps à faire ce travail** yesterday he took twice as long *ou* double the time to do this job; **nous attendons le ~ de gens** we expect twice as many people *ou* double the number of people; **plier qch en ~** to fold sth in half *ou* in two → **quitte**
b (= *copie, duplicata*) [*facture, acte*] copy; [*timbre*] duplicate, double; [*personne*] double; [*objet d'art*] replica, exact copy; **se faire faire un ~ de clé** to have a second key cut; **avoir des timbres en ~** to have duplicates *ou* doubles *ou* two of a stamp; **il a tous les documents/toutes les photos en ~** he has copies of all the documents/all the photos; **on a tout en ~, pour plus de sûreté** we have two of everything to be on the safe side
c (*Sport*) [*jeu*] doubles; **le ~ dames/messieurs/mixte** the ladies'/men's/mixed doubles; **faire un ~** ◊ **jouer en ~** to play a doubles match
d (*Jeux*) [*dés, dominos*] double; **faire un ~** to throw a double; **~-six** double six; **~-blanc** double blank
3 ADV [*payer, compter*] double
4 COMP ► **double allumage** (*Tech*) NM dual ignition ► **double barre** (*Mus*) NF double bar ► **doubles cordes** (*Mus*) NFPL double stopping ► **double dièse** (*Mus*) NM double sharp ► **double fenêtre** NF double window ► **double nœud** NM double knot ► **double page** NF double page (spread) ► **doubles rideaux** NMPL double curtains (*Brit*) *ou* drapes (*US*)

doublé, e [duble] (*ptp de* **doubler**) **1** ADJ [*vêtement*] lined (**de** with); **~ de cuir/cuivre** [*boîte, paroi*] lined with leather/copper; **non ~** unlined; **~ de fourrure** fur-lined; **~ (de) coton/nylon** cotton/nylon-lined, lined with cotton/nylon **2** NM **a** (*Sport, fig* = *victoire, réussite*) double; (*Chasse* = *coup double*) right and left **b** (*Orfèvrerie*) rolled gold **c** (*Mus*) turn

double-crème (*pl* **doubles-crèmes**) [dubləkʀɛm] NM cream cheese

double-croche (*pl* **doubles-croches**) [dubləkʀɔʃ] NF semiquaver (*Brit*), sixteenth note (*US*)

double-décimètre (*pl* **doubles-décimètres**) [dub`ldesimɛtʀ] NM (20 cm) rule

doublement [dubləmã] **1** ADV (= *pour deux raisons*) for two reasons; (= *à un degré double*) doubly **2** NM **a** [*somme, quantité, lettre*] doubling **b** [*feuille*] doubling, folding (in half); [*fil*] doubling **c** [*véhicule*] passing, overtaking (*Brit*)

double-mètre (*pl* **doubles-mètres**) [dubləmɛtʀ] NM two-metre (*Brit*) *ou* -meter (*US*) rule

doubler [duble] ▶conjug 1◀ **1** VT **a** (= *augmenter*) [+ *fortune, dose, longueur, salaire*] to double; **~ le pas** to quicken one's pace, speed up; **il a doublé son poids** he has doubled in weight
b (= *mettre en double*) [+ *fil, ficelle*] to double; [+ *revêtement*] to double, lay double; [+ *couverture*] to double, fold (in half)
c (*Scol*) [+ *classe, année*] to repeat
d (*Ciné*) [+ *film, acteur*] to dub; **~ (la voix de) qn** to dub sb, dub sb's voice
e (*Théât, Ciné* = *remplacer*) to understudy, act as an understudy for; (*dans une scène dangereuse*) to stand in for; **il s'est fait ~ par un cascadeur** a stuntman stood in for him
f (= *revêtir*) [+ *boîte, paroi, tableau, veste*] to line (**de** with); **~ une veste de fourrure** to line

a jacket with fur
g (= *dépasser*) [+ *véhicule*] to pass, overtake (*Brit*); (*Naut*) [+ *cap*] to round; (*fig*) **il a doublé ce cap important** he has got over this important hurdle *ou* turned this important corner; **~ le cap des 50 ans** to turn 50, pass the 50 mark
h * (= *tromper*) **~ qn** to pull a fast one on sb*, double-cross sb
2 VI **a** (= *augmenter*) [*nombre, quantité, prix*] to double, increase twofold; **~ de poids/valeur** to double in weight/value; **le nombre des crimes a doublé** the number of crimes has doubled *ou* increased twofold
b (*Aut*) to pass, overtake (*Brit*)
3 se doubler VPR se **~ de** to be coupled with; **chez lui le sens de l'honneur se double de courage** with him a sense of honour is coupled with *ou* goes hand in hand with courage; **ce dispositif se double d'un système d'alarme** this device works *ou* functions in conjunction with an alarm system; **c'est un savant doublé d'un pédagogue** he's a teacher as well as a scholar

doublet [duble] NM **a** (*Ling*) doublet **b** (*Orfèvrerie*) doublet

doublon [dublɔ̃] NM **a** (= *monnaie*) doubloon **b** (= *redondance*) duplication **c** (*Typo*) double

doublure [dublyʀ] NF **a** (= *étoffe*) lining **b** (*Théât*) understudy; (*Ciné*) stand-in; (*pour scènes dangereuses*) stuntman (*ou* stuntwoman)

douce [dus] ADJ F, NF → **doux**

douceâtre [dusɑtʀ] ADJ [*saveur*] sickly sweet; (*péj*) [*air, sourire*] sickly sweet, mawkish

doucement [dusmã] **1** ADV **a** (= *légèrement*) [*toucher, prendre, soulever*] gently; [*frapper, parler*] gently, softly; [*éclairer*] softly; **marcher ~** to tread carefully *ou* softly; **allez-y ~!** * easy *ou* gently does it!*, go easy!* **b** (= *graduellement*) [*monter, progresser*] gently, gradually; (= *lentement*) [*rouler, avancer*] slowly; [*démarrer*] smoothly; **la route monte/descend ~** the road climbs/descends gradually *ou* goes gently up/down; **la température monte/descend ~** the temperature is slowly *ou* gradually rising/falling **c** * (= *plus ou moins bien*) so-so*; **comment allez-vous ? — (tout) ~** how are you? — so-so* **d** * (= *en cachette*) **s'amuser ~ de voir qn dans l'embarras** to have a quiet laugh* (to o.s.) at seeing sb in difficulties; **ça me fait ~ rigoler!** it makes me want to laugh! **2** EXCL gently!, easy!; **~ avec le whisky !** go easy on the whisky!*, careful with the whisky!; **~ les basses !** ‡ take it easy!*, go easy!*

doucereux, -euse [dus(ə)ʀø, øz] ADJ [*goût, saveur*] sickly sweet; (*péj*) [*ton, paroles*] sugary, honeyed; (*péj*) [*personne, manières*] suave, smooth*

doucet, -ette [dusɛ, ɛt] **1** ADJ† meek, mild **2** **doucette** NF (*Bot*) corn-salad, lamb's lettuce

doucettement* [dusɛtmã] ADV [*commercer, avancer*] gently; [*vivre*] quietly

douceur [dusœʀ] **1** NF **a** [*peau, tissu*] softness, smoothness; [*matelas, brosse, suspension*] softness
b [*temps, climat, température, saison*] mildness; [*brise*] gentleness
c (= *goût sucré*) [*fruit, liqueur, saveur*] sweetness; (= *goût faible*) [*fromage, tabac, moutarde, piment*] mildness
d [*son, musique, voix*] sweetness, gentleness; [*parfum*] sweetness; [*lumière, couleur*] softness
e (= *modération*) [*pente*] gentleness
f (= *affabilité, gentillesse*) [*caractère, personne, sourire, geste*] gentleness; **c'est un homme d'une grande ~** he's a very gentle man; **elle est d'une ~ angélique** she's as sweet as an angel; **prendre qn par la ~** to deal gently with sb; (*pour convaincre*) to use gentle persuasion

on sb; **~ de vivre** gentle way of life
g (*gén pl*) (= *sucrerie*) sweet; (= *flatterie*) sweet talk (*NonC*); **les ~s de l'amitié** the (sweet) pleasures of friendship
2 **en douceur** LOC ADJ, LOC ADV [*démarrage*] smooth; [*démarrer*] smoothly; [*commencer, manœuvrer*] gently; **il faut y aller en ~** we must go about it gently; **ça s'est passé en ~** it went off smoothly → **atterrissage**

Douchanbe [duʃãbe] N Dushanbe

douche [duʃ] **1** NF **a** (= *jet, système*) shower; **prendre une ~** to have *ou* take a shower; **passer à la ~** to go for a shower; **il est sous la ~** he's in the *ou* having a shower **b** (= *salle*) **~s** shower room, showers **c** * (= *déception*) let-down*, bummer‡; (= *réprimande*) (good) telling-off* *ou* ticking-off* (*Brit*); (= *averse, arrosage*) soaking, drenching; **on a pris une bonne ~** we got drenched *ou* soaked; **ça nous a fait l'effet d'une ~ (froide)** quand nous l'avons appris it was a real let-down* when we found out **2** COMP ► **douche écossaise** (*lit*) alternately hot and cold shower; (* *fig*) **ça a été la ~ écossaise** it came as a bit of a blow *ou* shock

doucher [duʃe] ▶conjug 1◀ **1** VT **a** **~ qn** to give sb a shower; **se faire ~** (*par l'averse*) to get a soaking, get soaked *ou* drenched; (*, †* = *se faire réprimander*) to get a (good) telling-off* *ou* ticking-off* (*Brit*) **b** [+ *espoirs, enthousiasme*] to dampen; * **ce qu'il m'a dit, ça m'a douché** what he said really knocked me back* **2** se doucher VPR to have *ou* take a shower

douchette [duʃɛt] NF [*douche*] shower rose; (*pour codes-barres*) bar-code reader *ou* scanner

doudou¹ * [dudu] NF (*terme des Antilles*) (= *femme*) woman; (= *jeune fille*) girl

doudou² [dudu] NM (*langage enfantin*) ≈ security blanket

doudoune [dudun] NF **a** (= *anorak*) down jacket **b** * (= *sein*) boob‡, breast

doué, e [dwe] (*ptp de* **douer**) ADJ **a** (= *talentueux*) gifted, talented (**en** in); **être ~ pour** to have a gift for; (*iro*) **il n'est pas ~*** he's not exactly bright *ou* clever; **~ sur le plan scolaire** academically able **b** (= *pourvu de*) **~ de** [+ *vie, raison*] endowed with; [+ *intelligence, talent, mémoire*] blessed with, endowed with

douer [dwe] ▶conjug 1◀ VT ♦ **douer qn de** [+ *vie, raison*] to endow sb with; [+ *intelligence, talent, mémoire*] to bless sb with, endow sb with

douille [duj] NF [*cartouche*] (cartridge) case, cartridge; [*fil électrique*] (electric light) socket; [*manche*] socket; (*Culin*) piping socket; (*Élec*) **~ à vis/à baïonnette** screw/bayonet socket

douiller‡ [duje] ▶conjug 1◀ VI (= *payer cher*) to pay through the nose*, fork out* a lot; **ça douille** it's damn expensive *ou* pricey‡

douillet, -ette [dujɛ, ɛt] **1** ADJ **a** (= *sensible à la douleur*) [*personne*] soft (*péj*); **je ne suis pas ~** I can take it **b** (= *confortable*) [*maison, atmosphère*] cosy, snug; [*nid, lit, vie*] soft, cosy **2** **douillette**† NF (*ecclésiastique*) (clerical) overcoat; [*bébé*] quilted coat

douillettement [dujɛtmã] ADV cosily, snugly

▼ **douleur** [dulœʀ] **1** NF **a** (*physique*) pain; **~s rhumatismales** rheumatic pains; **~s dorsales** backache (*NonC*), back pains; **les ~s (de l'accouchement)** labour (*Brit*) *ou* labor (*US*) pains; **j'ai une ~ dans le bras** I have a sore arm, I have a pain in my arm, my arm hurts; **mes vieilles ~s me font souffrir** my old aches and pains are bothering me → **accouchement**
b (*morale*) grief, distress; **il a eu la ~ de perdre son frère** he had the distress of *ou* had to suffer the grief of losing his brother; **«nous avons la ~ de vous faire part du décès de ... »** "it is our sad duty to tell you *ou* it is with great sorrow that we have to tell you of the death of ..."; **«nous avons la ~ d'apprendre que ... »** "it is with great sorrow that we've

learned that ..."; (fig) **j'ai compris ma ~*** I realized my mistake, I could have kicked myself* ■ (PROV) **les grandes ~s sont muettes** great sorrow is often silent

douloureusement [dulurøzmɑ̃] ADV (= *physiquement*) painfully; (= *moralement*) grievously

douloureux, -euse [dulurø, øz] **1** ADJ **[a]** [*sensation, maladie, opération, membre*] painful **[b]** [*perte*] grievous, distressing; [*décision, spectacle*] painful, distressing, harrowing; [*séparation, circonstances, moment*] painful, distressing; [*regard, expression*] sorrowful **2** **douloureuse*** NF (*hum*) (= *addition*) bill (*Brit*), check (*US*); (= *facture*) bill; **apportez-nous la douloureuse** what's the damage?*, let's hear the worst*

douma [duma] NF duma

▼ **doute** [dut] NM **[a]** (= *état d'incertitude*) doubt, uncertainty; (*Philo, Rel*) doubt; **être dans le ~** to be doubtful ou uncertain; **laisser qn dans le ~** to leave sb in a state of uncertainty; **être dans le ~ au sujet de qch** to be in doubt ou doubtful ou uncertain about sth; **le ~ n'est plus permis quant à** there is no more room for doubt concerning; **un air de ~** a doubtful air **[b]** (= *soupçon, perplexité*) doubt; **je n'ai pas le moindre ~ à ce sujet** I haven't the slightest doubt about it; **avoir des** ou **ses ~s sur** ou **au sujet de qch/qn** to have misgivings ou (one's) doubts about sth/sb; **malgré tout, j'ai des ~s** nevertheless, I have my doubts; **il a émis des ~s à propos de ...** he expressed (his) doubts ou misgivings about ...; **un ~ plane sur l'affaire** a certain amount of ou an element of doubt hangs over the matter **[c]** (*loc*) ■ (PROV) **dans le ~, abstiens-toi** when in doubt, don't!; **sans ~** (= *vraisemblablement*) doubtless, no doubt, probably; **sans ~ s'est-il trompé** he's doubtless ou no doubt mistaken; **tu viendras demain ? — sans ~** are you coming tomorrow — yes, probably ou most likely; **sans (aucun** ou **nul) ~** (= *incontestablement*) without (a) doubt, undoubtedly; **il ne fait aucun ~ que ...** there is (absolutely) no doubt that ..., there is no question that ...; **ceci ne fait aucun ~** there is no doubt ou question about it; **il est hors de ~ qu'il a raison** he's undoubtedly right, it's beyond doubt that he's right; **mettre hors de ~** [+ *authenticité*] to prove beyond doubt; **nul ~ que ...** (there is) no doubt that ...; **mettre en ~** [+ *affirmation, honnêteté de qn*] to question, challenge, cast doubt on; **mettre en ~ que ...** to question whether ... → **ombre¹**

▼ **douter** [dute] ▸conjug 1◂ **1** **douter de** VT INDIR **[a]** (*sentiment d'incertitude*) [+ *identité, authenticité, existence de qch*] to doubt, question, have doubts as to; [+ *réussite*] to be doubtful of; **au débat il le croyait, maintenant il doute** in the debate he believed it, now he's questioning it ou now he's doubting it; **il le dit mais j'en doute** he says so but I have my doubts ou but I doubt it; **il a dit la vérité, n'en doutez pas** he's telling the truth, you can be sure of that ou there's no doubt about that; **je doute d'avoir jamais fait/dit cela** I doubt that I ever did/said that; **je n'ai jamais douté du résultat** I never had any doubts about ou as to the result; **je doute qu'il vienne** I doubt (if ou whether) he'll come; **je ne doute pas qu'il le fera** ou **ne le fasse** I doubt not ou I dare say that he'll do it; **à n'en pas ~** (= *sans aucun doute*) without (a) doubt; (= *vraisemblablement*) doubtless, no doubt; (*littér*) **~ si** to doubt whether **[b]** (*Philo, Rel*: *esprit de réfutation*) **~ de** [+ *dogme*] to have ou entertain (*frm*) doubts about, doubt; **mieux vaut ~ que tout accepter** it is better to doubt than to accept everything **[c]** (*sentiment de méfiance*) **~ de** [+ *allié, sincérité de qn*] to have (one's) doubts about, doubt; **je**

n'ai jamais douté de vous I never doubted you, I never had any doubts about you; **~ de la parole de qn** to doubt sb's word; **il ne doute de rien!*** he's got some nerve!*; **il doute de lui(-même)** he has feelings of self-doubt; **je te dis que c'était lundi — ah, tu me fais ~ de moi, j'étais sûr que c'était mardi** I tell you it was Monday — oh, I was sure it was Tuesday, but now you're making me wonder **2** **se douter** VPR **se ~ de qch** to suspect sth; **je me doute de son inquiétude quand il apprendra la nouvelle** I can (just) imagine his anxiety when he learns the news; **je ne m'en suis jamais douté** I never guessed ou suspected it for a moment; **ça, je m'en doutais depuis longtemps** I've thought so ou thought as much ou suspected as much for a long time; **j'étais (bien) loin de me ~ que ...** little did I know that ...; **se ~ que** to suspect that, have an idea that; **il ne se doutait pas qu'elle serait là** he had no idea ou hadn't suspected (that) she would be there; **je me doute qu'il a dû accepter** I expect ou imagine that he must have accepted; **qu'il soit fâché, je m'en doute** I can well imagine that he's angry; **on s'en serait douté !*** surprise, surprise! (*iro*)

douteux, -euse [dutø, øz] ADJ **[a]** (= *incertain*) [*fait*] doubtful, questionable, uncertain; [*résultat, issue*] doubtful, uncertain; [*sens, date, réponse*] doubtful; **il est ~ que ...** it is doubtful ou questionable that ou whether ...; **il n'est pas ~ que ...** there is no doubt that ...; **d'origine douteuse** of uncertain ou doubtful origin **[b]** (*péj*) (= *médiocre*) [*raisonnement, propreté, qualité, mœurs*] doubtful, dubious, questionable; (= *peu solide* ou *peu propre*) [*vêtements, individu, aliment*] dubious-looking; [*amarrage, passerelle*] shaky, dubious-looking; **d'un goût ~** [*décoration, cravate, plaisanterie*] in doubtful ou questionable ou dubious taste

douve¹ [duv] NF **[a]** (*Agr*) drainage ditch; (*Équitation*) water jump; [*château*] **~(s)** moat **[b]** [*tonneau*] stave

douve² [duv] NF (*Vét, Zool*) fluke; **~ du foie** liver fluke

Douvres [duvʀ] N Dover

doux, douce [du, dus] **1** ADJ **[a]** (= *lisse, souple*) [*peau, tissu*] soft, smooth; [*matelas, suspension, brosse*] soft → **fer, lime [b]** [*eau*] (= *non calcaire*) soft; (= *non salé*) fresh **[c]** (= *clément*) [*temps, climat, température*] mild; [*brise, chaleur*] gentle; **il fait ~ aujourd'hui** it's mild today **[d]** (*au goût*) (= *sucré*) [*fruit, saveur, liqueur*] sweet; (= *pas fort*) [*moutarde, fromage, tabac, piment*] mild; **~ comme le miel** as sweet as honey → **orange, patate [e]** (*à l'ouïe, la vue*) [*son, musique, accents*] sweet, gentle; [*voix*] soft, gentle; [*lumière, couleur*] soft, mellow, subdued; **un nom aux consonances douces** a mellifluous ou sweet-sounding name **[f]** (= *modéré*) [*pente, montée*] gentle, gradual; **en pente douce** gently sloping; **nous pratiquons des prix très ~** our prices are easy on the pocket → **drogue, feu, médecine** etc **[g]** (= *non brutal, gentil*) [*caractère, manières, reproche*] mild, gentle; [*personne, sourire*] gentle; [*punition*] mild; **il a l'air ~** he looks gentle; **elle a eu une mort douce** she died peacefully; **il est ~ comme un agneau** he's as gentle ou meek (*Brit*) as a lamb; **d'un geste très ~** very gently → **œil [h]** (*gén avant nom* = *agréable*) [*victoire, revanche, repos, tranquillité*] sweet; [*parfum, souvenirs, pensées*] sweet, agreeable, pleasant; **cette pensée lui était douce** this thought gave him great pleasure; **qu'il m'était ~ de repenser à ces moments** what pleasure it gave me ou how pleasant ou agreeable for me to think over those moments → **billet, couler, folie**

2 **en douce*** LOC ADV on the quiet, on the q.t.* **3** **tout doux** LOC ADV **ça va tout ~*** things are going so-so*; († ou *hum*) **tout ~!** gently (now)!, careful (now)! → **filer 4** NM,F (*parfois péj* = *personne douce*) mild(-natured) person **5** **douce** NF († *aussi hum*) (= *amoureuse*) sweetheart†

doux-amer, douce-amère (*mpl* **doux-amers**, *fpl* **douces-amères**) [du(z)amɛʀ, dusamɛʀ] **1** ADJ (*lit, fig*) bittersweet **2** **douce-amère** NF (*Bot*) woody nightshade, bittersweet

douzain [duzɛ̃] NM (*Poésie*) twelve-line poem; (*Hist* = *monnaie*) douzain

douzaine [duzɛn] NF (= *douze*) dozen; (= *environ douze*) **une ~** about twelve, a dozen (or so); **une ~ d'huîtres/d'œufs** a dozen oysters/eggs; **il y a une ~ d'années** about twelve years ago, twelve or so years ago; **elle a une ~ d'années** she's about twelve; **vendre qch à la ~** to sell sth by the dozen; (*fig*) **il y en a à la ~** there are dozens of them → **treize**

douze [duz] **1** ADJ INV twelve; (*Comm*) **~ douzaines** a gross, twelve dozen; *pour autres locutions voir* **six 2** NM INV twelve; (*Hist*) **les Douze** the Twelve; *pour autres locutions voir* **six**

douzième [duzjɛm] ADJ, NMF twelfth; *pour locutions voir* **sixième**

douzièmement [duzjɛmmɑ̃] ADV in twelfth place, twelfthly

Dow Jones [dodʒɔns] NM (*Bourse*) **le ~ ◊ l'indice ~** the Dow Jones (index)

doyen, -enne [dwajɛ̃, jɛn] NM,F (*Rel, Univ*) = dean; [*équipe, groupe*] most senior member; [*assemblée, corps constitué*] = (**d'âge**) most senior member, doyen; **la doyenne des Français** France's oldest citizen

doyenné [dwajene] **1** NM (*Rel*) (= *circonscription*) deanery; (= *charge*) deanery, deanship **2** NF (= *poire*) **~ (du comice)** comice (pear)

DPLG [depeɛlʒe] (ABRÉV = **diplômé par le gouvernement**) **ingénieur ~** (state) certified engineer

Dr (ABRÉV = **docteur**) Dr

drachme [dʀakm] NF drachma

draconien, -ienne [dʀakɔnjɛ̃, jɛn] ADJ [*loi*] draconian; [*mesure*] drastic, draconian; [*régime alimentaire*] strict

dragage [dʀagaʒ] NM (*pour nettoyer*) dredging; (*pour trouver qch*) dragging; **~ des mines** minesweeping

dragée [dʀaʒe] NF **[a]** (= *friandise*) sugared almond, dragée; (*Méd*) sugar-coated pill, dragée (*SPÉC*) **[b]** (= *plomb de chasse*) small shot; (* = *balle*) slug*, bullet **[c]** (*Agr*) dredge **[d]** (*loc*) **tenir la ~ haute à qn** to hold out on sb

dragéifier [dʀaʒeifje] ▸conjug 7◂ VT to sugar, coat with sugar; **comprimé dragéifié** sugared ou sugar-coated tablet

drageon [dʀaʒɔ̃] NM (*Bot*) sucker

dragon [dʀagɔ̃] NM **[a]** (*Myth, fig*) dragon; **~ volant** flying lizard ou dragon; **~ de Komodo** Komodo dragon; (*fig*) **un ~ de vertu** a dragon of virtue **[b]** (*Hist Mil*) dragoon

dragonnade [dʀagɔnad] NF (*Hist*) dragonnade

dragonne [dʀagɔn] NF [*épée*] sword-knot; [*parapluie*] loop (*for wrist*); [*bâton de ski*] wrist-strap; (*Alpinisme*) wrist loop

dragonnier [dʀagɔnje] NM dragon tree

dragster [dʀagstɛʀ] NM dragster

drague [dʀag] NF **[a]** (*Pêche*) dragnet **[b]** (*Tech*) (= *machine*) dredge; (= *navire, ponton*) dredger **[c]** (*: *pour séduire*) **la ~** trying to pick people up*, chatting people up* (*Brit*)

draguer [dʀage] ▸conjug 1◂ **1** VT **[a]** (*Tech*) [+ *rivière, port, canal*] (*pour nettoyer*) to dredge; (*pour trouver qch*) to drag; [+ *mines*] to sweep

b (*Pêche*) to dredge for **c** (*Naut*) [*ancre*] **~ (le fond)** to drag **d** (* : *pour séduire*) **~ qn** to try and pick sb up*, chat sb up* (*Brit*); **elle s'est fait ~ par un mec** some guy tried to pick her up* **2** VI* to try and pick up* girls (*ou* guys), chat up* (*Brit*) girls (*ou* guys), be on the pull* (*Brit*) *ou* make* (*US*); **~ en voiture** to go cruising*, go kerb-crawling; **~ dans les boîtes** (*gén*) to go to night-clubs to try and pick somebody up; [*homosexuel*] to go cruising (in night-clubs)*

dragueur¹ [dʀagœʀ] NM (= *pêcheur*) dragnet fisherman; (= *ouvrier*) dredger; (= *bateau*) dredger; **~ de mines** minesweeper

dragueur², -euse* [dʀagœʀ, øz] NM,F **c'est un sacré ~** he's a great one for trying to pick up* girls *ou* women; **quelle dragueuse !** she's always trying to pick up guys

drain [dʀɛ̃] NM (*Agr*) (underground) drain; (*Méd*, *Élec*) drain; **poser un ~ à qn** to insert a drain in sb

drainage [dʀenaʒ] NM **a** [*marais, sol*] drainage **b** (*Méd*) drainage; **~ lymphatique** lymphatic drainage **c** [*main-d'œuvre, capitaux*] drain

draine [dʀɛn] NF mistlethrush

drainer [dʀene] ▶ conjug 1 ◀ VT **a** [+ *marais, sol*] to drain **b** (*Méd*) [+ *plaie, rein*] to drain **c** (= *attirer*) [+ *main-d'œuvre, capitaux*] to bring in; [+ *public, clientèle*] to attract; **~ l'épargne vers l'immobilier** to encourage savers to invest in real estate

draisienne [dʀezjɛn] NF (*Hist*) dandy horse

draisine [dʀezin] NF (*Rail*) track motorcar (*Brit*), gang car (*US*), handcar (*US*)

drakkar [dʀakaʀ] NM longship

Dralon® [dʀalɔ̃] NM Dralon®

dramatique [dʀamatik] **1** ADJ **a** (= *tragique*) tragic; **ce n'est pas ~ !** it's not the end of the world! **b** (*Théât*) **artiste ~** stage actor (*ou* actress); **auteur ~** playwright, dramatist; **centre ~** drama school; **critique ~** drama critic → **art**, **comédie c** (= *épique*) [*récit, puissance, intensité*] dramatic **2** NF (*TV*) **~** (television) play *ou* drama

dramatiquement [dʀamatikmɑ̃] ADV (= *de façon épique*) dramatically; (= *tragiquement*) tragically

dramatisation [dʀamatizasjɔ̃] NF dramatization

dramatiser [dʀamatize] ▶ conjug 1 ◀ VT to dramatize; **il ne faut pas ~ (la situation)** you shouldn't dramatize things

dramaturge [dʀamatyʀʒ] NMF dramatist, playwright

dramaturgie [dʀamatyʀʒi] NF (= *art*) dramatic art; (= *traité*) treatise on dramatic art

drame [dʀam] NM **a** (*Théât*) (= *genre littéraire*) drama; (= *œuvre*) play, drama **b** (= *événement tragique*) drama, tragedy; **~ de la jalousie** drama of jealousy; **la farce tournait au ~** the joke was going tragically wrong; **faire un ~ de qch** to make a drama out of sth; **n'en faites pas un ~** don't make such a fuss *ou* to-do* about it; **ce n'est pas un ~ !** it's not the end of the world!

drap [dʀa] NM **a** (= *tissu*) woollen cloth **b** (= *pièce de tissu*) **~ (de lit)** sheet; **~s de soie/nylon** silk/nylon sheets; **~ de dessus/dessous** top/bottom sheet; **~ de bain** bath sheet; **~ de plage** beach towel; **~ mortuaire** *ou* **funéraire** pall; **être dans les ~s** to be between the sheets; (*fig*) **être dans de beaux** *ou* **sales ~s** to be in a right fix* *ou* mess*; **tu m'as mis dans de beaux ~s** you got me in a right fix*, you really landed me in it*

drapé, e [dʀape] (*ptp de* **draper**) **1** ADJ draped; **tambours ~s** muffled drums **2** NM **le ~ d'un rideau** *etc* the hang *ou* drape of a curtain *etc*

drapeau (*pl* **drapeaux**) [dʀapo] NM **a** (*gén*) flag; **le ~ tricolore** the (French) tricolour; **le ~ blanc/rouge** the white/red flag; **hisser le ~ blanc** to wave the white flag; (*Courses*) **à damier** chequered (*Brit*) *ou* checkered (*US*) flag; (*Golf*) **~ de trou** pin; **le respect du ~** respect for the flag; **être sous les ~x** to be doing one's military service; **le ~ de la liberté** the flag of liberty; (*fig*) **mettre son ~ dans sa poche** to keep one's views well hidden **b** (*Aviat, Naut*) **en ~** feathered; **mettre une hélice en ~** to feather a propeller

draper [dʀape] ▶ conjug 1 ◀ **1** VT to drape; (*Tex*) [+ *laine*] to process; **un foulard de soie drapait ses épaules** a silk scarf was draped over her shoulders, her shoulders were draped in a silk scarf **2** **se draper** VPR **se ~ dans** to drape o.s. in; **se ~ dans sa dignité** to stand on one's dignity; **se ~ dans sa vertu/son honnêteté** to cloak o.s. in one's virtue/one's honesty

draperie [dʀapʀi] NF (= *tenture*) drapery, hanging; (*Comm*) drapery, cloth; (*Art*) drapery

drap-housse (*pl* **draps-housses**) [dʀaus] NM fitted sheet

drapier, -ière [dʀapje, jɛʀ] **1** ADJ **industrie drapière** clothing industry; **ouvrier ~** cloth-worker **2** NM (= *fabricant*) (woollen) cloth manufacturer; (**marchand**) **~** clothier, draper (*Brit*)

drastique [dʀastik] ADJ (*Méd, gén*) drastic

drave* [dʀav] NF (*Can Hist*) [*bois*] drive, rafting

draver* [dʀave] ▶ conjug 1 ◀ VT (*Can Hist*) [+ *bois*] to drive, raft

draveur* [dʀavœʀ] NM (*Can Hist*) (log *ou* timber) driver, raftsman

dravidien, -ienne [dʀavidjɛ̃, jɛn] ADJ, NM Dravidian

Dresde [dʀɛzd] N Dresden

dressage [dʀesaʒ] NM **a** [*animal sauvage*] taming; [*jeune cheval*] breaking in; (*pour le cirque*) [*chien, cheval*] training; * [*recrue*] knocking *ou* licking into shape*; (*Équitation*) **épreuve de ~** dressage event **b** [*tente*] pitching; [*échafaudage*] erection, putting up **c** [*pierre, planche, tôle*] dressing

dresser [dʀese] ▶ conjug 1 ◀ **1** VT **a** (= *établir*) [+ *inventaire, liste*] to draw up, make out; [+ *plan, carte*] to draw up; **~ un acte** to draw up a deed; **il a dressé un bilan encourageant de la situation** he gave an encouraging review of the situation *ou* an encouraging run-down* on the situation
b (= *ériger*) [+ *monument, statue, échafaudage*] to put up, erect; [+ *barrière, échelle*] to put up, set up; [+ *tente*] to pitch, put up; [+ *mât*] to raise, put up, erect; [+ *lit*] to put up; **nous avons dressé un buffet dans le jardin** we laid out a buffet in the garden; **~ le couvert** *ou* **la table** to lay *ou* set the table; (*Culin*) **dressez les filets sur un plat** arrange the fillets on a dish
c (= *lever*) [+ *tête*] to raise, lift; [+ *menton*] to stick out; (*fig*) **~ l'oreille** to prick up one's ears; [*chien*] **~ l'oreille** *ou* **ses oreilles** to prick up *ou* cock (up) its ears; **faire ~ les cheveux sur la tête à qn** to make sb's hair stand on end; **une histoire à faire ~ les cheveux sur la tête** a spine-chilling *ou* spine-tingling tale, a tale to make your hair stand on end
d (= *braquer*) **~ qn contre** to set sb against
e (= *dompter*) [+ *animal sauvage*] to tame; [+ *jeune cheval*] to break (in); (*pour le cirque*) [+ *chien, cheval*] to train; **~ un chien à rapporter** to train a dog to retrieve
f * (= *mater*) [+ *recrue*] to knock *ou* lick into shape*; **ça le dressera !** that will knock *ou* lick him into shape*; **~ un enfant** to teach a child his place; **les enfants/les élèves, ça se dresse !** children/pupils should be taught their place!; **enfant mal dressé** badly brought-up child
g (*Tech*) [+ *pierre, planche, tôle*] to dress

2 **se dresser** VPR **a** [*personne*] (*debout*) to stand up; (*assis*) to sit up (straight); **se ~ sur la pointe des pieds** to stand on tiptoe; **se ~ de toute sa taille** to draw o.s. up to one's full height; **se ~ sur ses pattes de derrière** [*cheval*] to rear (up); [*autre animal*] to stand up on its hind legs → **ergot**
b [*cheveux*] to stand on end; [*oreille*] to prick up
c [*statue, bâtiment, obstacle*] to stand; (*de façon imposante, menaçante*) to tower (up); **un navire se dressa soudain dans le brouillard** a ship suddenly loomed (up) out of the fog
d (= *s'insurger*) to rise up (**contre**, **face à** against)

dresseur, -euse [dʀesœʀ, øz] NM,F (*gén*) trainer; [*animaux sauvages*] tamer; **~ de lions** lion tamer; **~ de chevaux** (*débourrage*) horse-breaker; (*dans un cirque*) horse-trainer

dressing [dʀesiŋ], **dressing-room** (*pl* **dressing-rooms**) [dʀesiŋʀum] NM dressing room

dressoir [dʀeswaʀ] NM dresser

dreyfusard, e [dʀefyzaʀ, aʀd] **1** ADJ (*Hist*) supporting *ou* defending Dreyfus **2** NM,F supporter *ou* defender of Dreyfus

DRH [deeʀaʃ] **1** NF (ABRÉV = **direction des ressources humaines**) → **direction 2** NMF (ABRÉV = **directeur, -trice des ressources humaines**) → **directeur, -trice**

dribble [dʀibl] NM (*Sport*) dribble

dribbler [dʀible] ▶ conjug 1 ◀ (*Sport*) **1** VI to dribble **2** VT [+ *ballon*] to dribble; [+ *joueur*] to dribble past *ou* round

drill¹ [dʀil] NM (*Zool*) drill

drill² [dʀil] NM (*Scol etc* = *exercice*) drill

drille¹ [dʀij] NM† **bon** *ou* **joyeux ~** jolly fellow, cheerful character

drille² [dʀij] NF (*Tech*) hand-drill

dring [dʀiŋ] EXCL, NM ding, ding-a-ling

drisse [dʀis] NF (*Naut*) halyard

drive [dʀajv] NM (*Golf, Ordin*) drive

driver¹ [dʀajve, dʀive] ▶ conjug 1 ◀ **1** VT [*jockey*] to drive **2** VI (*Golf*) to drive

driver², driveur [dʀajvœʀ, dʀivœʀ] NM (*Équitation, Golf, Ordin*) driver

drogue [dʀɔg] NF **a** (= *stupéfiant*) drug; **la ~** drugs; **une ~ dure/douce** a hard/soft drug → **trafic b** (*Pharm, fig*) drug; (*péj*) patent medicine, quack remedy (*péj*)

drogué, e [dʀɔge] (*ptp de* **droguer**) NM,F drug addict

droguer [dʀɔge] ▶ conjug 1 ◀ **1** VT **a** (*péj*) [+ *malade*] to dose up (*péj*); (*Méd†*) to give drugs to **b** [+ *victime*] to drug **2** **se droguer** VPR **a** (*péj: de médicaments*) to dose o.s. (up) (**de** with) **b** (*de stupéfiants*) to take drugs; **il se drogue** he's on drugs, he takes drugs; **se ~ à la cocaïne** to be on *ou* take cocaine

droguerie [dʀɔgʀi] NF (= *commerce*) hardware trade; (= *magasin*) hardware shop

droguet [dʀɔge] NM (*Tex*) drugget

droguiste [dʀɔgist] NMF owner *ou* keeper of a hardware shop

▼**droit¹, e¹** [dʀwa, dʀwat] **1** ADJ (*après nom : opposé à gauche*) [*main, bras, jambe*] right; [*poche, chaussure*] right(-hand); **du côté ~** on the right-hand side → **bras, centre, main**
2 NM (*Boxe* = *coup*) right; (= *poing*) direct du **~** straight right; **crochet du ~** right hook
3 droite NF **a** (*opposé à la gauche*) **la ~e** the right (side), the right-hand side; **à ~e** on the right; (*direction*) to the right; **troisième rue à ~e** third street on the right; **à ma/sa ~e** on my/his right (hand), on my/his right(-hand) side; **le tiroir/chemin de ~e** the right-hand drawer/path; **il ne connaît pas sa ~e de sa gauche** he can't tell (his) right from (his) left; **à ~e de la fenêtre** to the right of the window; **de ~e à gauche** from right to left; **à ~e et à gauche ◊ de ~e et de gauche** this way and

that; **il a couru à ~e et à gauche pour se renseigner** he tried everywhere *ou* all over the place to get some information; **c'est ce qu'on entend dire de ~e et de gauche** that's what one hears from all sides *ou* quarters

[b] (*Aut*) **la ~e** the right; **rouler à ~e** to drive on the right (-hand side of the road); **garder** *ou* **tenir sa ~e** to keep to the right → **conduite**

[c] (*Pol*) **la ~e** the right (wing); **candidat/idées de ~e** right-wing candidate/ideas; **un homme de ~e** a man of the right; **membre de la ~e** right-winger; **elle est très à ~e** she's very right-wing; **la ~e est divisée** the right wing is split → **extrême**

[d] (*Boxe = coup*) right

droit², **e²** [drwa, drwat] [1] ADJ [a] (= *sans déviation, non courbe*) [*barre, ligne, route, nez*] straight; **ça fait 4 km en ligne ~e** it's 4 km as the crow flies; (*fig*) **cela vient en ~e ligne de ...** that comes straight *ou* direct from ...; (*Rel*) **le ~ chemin** the straight and narrow; (*Couture*) **le ~ fil** straight grain; (*fig*) **cette décision s'inscrit dans le ~ fil de leur politique** this decision is totally in keeping with *ou* in line with their policy → **coup**

[b] (= *vertical, non penché*) [*arbre, mur*] upright, straight; (*Géom*) [*prisme, cylindre, cône*] right; [*écriture*] upright; **ce tableau n'est pas ~** this picture isn't (hanging) straight; **est-ce que mon chapeau est ~?** is my hat (on) straight?; **jupe ~e** straight skirt; **veston ~** single-breasted jacket; **tiens ta tasse ~e** hold your cup straight *ou* level; (*péj, hum*) **être ~ comme un pieu** *ou* **un piquet** to be as stiff as a poker *ou* ramrod (*péj*); **être ~ comme un i** to have a very upright posture, hold o.s. very erect; **se tenir ~ comme un i** to stand bolt upright *ou* very erect; **tiens-toi ~** (*debout*) stand up (straight); (*assis*) sit up (straight) → **angle**

[c] (= *honnête, loyal*) [*personne*] upright, straight(forward)

[d] (= *sensé*) [*jugement*] sound, sane

[2] **droite** NF (*Géom*) (*ligne*) **~e** straight line

[3] ADV [*viser, couper, marcher*] straight; **aller/ marcher ~ devant soi** to go/walk straight ahead; **écrire ~** to have upright handwriting; **c'est ~ devant vous** it's straight ahead of you *ou* right in front of you; **aller ~ à la faillite** to be heading *ou* headed straight for bankruptcy; (*fig*) **aller ~ au but** *ou* **au fait** to go straight to the point; (*fig*) **cela lui est allé ~ au cœur** it went straight to his heart → **marcher**

droit³ [drwa] [1] NM [a] (= *prérogative*) right; **~ de pêche/chasse** fishing/hunting rights; **~ du sang/du sol** *right to nationality based on parentage/on place of birth*; (*fig*) **les ~s du sang** rights of kinship; **le ~ des peuples à disposer d'eux-mêmes** the right of peoples to self-determination; **le ~ à l'enfant** the right to have a child; **la ~ du plus fort** the law of the jungle; **avoir le ~ de faire** (*gén : simple permission, possibilité*) to be allowed to do; (*Admin, Jur : autorisation*) to have the right to do; **avoir le ~ pour soi** to have right on one's side; **avoir ~ à** [+ *allocation*] to be entitled to, be eligible for; [+ *critique*] to come in for; (*hum*) **il a eu ~ à une bonne raclée*/réprimande** he got *ou* earned himself a good hiding/telling-off*; **avoir (le) ~ de vie ou de mort sur** to have (the) power of life and death over; **avoir ~ de regard sur** [+ *documents*] to have the right to examine *ou* to inspect; [+ *affaires, choix, décision*] to have a say in; (*Fin, Jur*) **avoir ~ de regard dans la comptabilité** to be entitled to have access to the books and records; **avoir des ~s sur** to have rights over; **il n'a aucun ~ sur ce terrain** he has no right to this land; **cette carte vous donne ~ à des places gratuites** this card entitles you to free seats; **être en ~ de faire** to have a *ou* the right to do, be entitled to do; (*fig*) **on est en ~ de se demander pourquoi ...** one has every right *ou* one is entitled to wonder why ...; **être dans son (bon) ~** to be (quite) within one's rights; **faire ~ à** [+

requête] to grant, accede to; **l'humour ne perd jamais ses ~s** there is always a place for humour; **c'est (bien) votre ~** you've every right to do so, you are perfectly entitled to do so, you're perfectly within your rights; **à bon ~** with good reason, legitimately; **membre de ~ ex officio** member; **monarque de ~ divin** monarch by divine right; **cela lui revient de ~** it's his by right(s), it is rightfully his; **de quel ~ est-il entré?** what right did he have *ou* what gave him the right to come in?; **de ~ comme de fait** both legitimately and effectively; **être membre de plein ~** to be a fully-fledged member; **réclamer qch de plein ~** to claim sth as one's right → **force, qui**

[b] (*Jur*) **le ~** law; (*Univ*) **faire son ~** to study law; **~ civil/pénal** civil/criminal law; **~ constitutionnel/international** constitutional/ international law; **~ canon** canon law; **~ romain** Roman law; **~ privé/public** private/ public law; **~ coutumier** (= *concept*) customary law; (= *lois*) common law; **~ écrit** statute law; **~ administratif/commercial/fiscal/du travail** administrative/commercial/tax/employment law; **~ des affaires** company *ou* corporate law; **le ~ des gens** the law of nations; **~ de la famille** family law; **une société de ~ anglais** a firm that comes under English law

[c] (*gén pl = taxe*) duty, tax; (*d'inscription etc*) fee(s); **~ d'entrée** entrance (fee); **~s d'inscription/d'enregistrement** enrolment/ registration fee(s); (*Comm*) **~s portuaires** *ou* **de port** harbour fees *ou* dues; **exempt de ~s** duty-free; **passible de ~s** liable to duty, dutiable

[2] COMP ► **droit d'aînesse** birthright ► **droit d'asile** right of asylum ► **droit d'auteur** (= *propriété artistique, littéraire*) copyright ► **droits d'auteur** (= *rémunération*) royalties ► **droit de cité** (*fig*) **avoir ~ de cité parmi/dans** to be established among/in ► **droits civils** civil rights ► **droits civiques** civic rights ► **droit commun**: **condamné/délit de ~ commun** common law criminal/delict ► **droits compensatoires** (*Fin*) countervailing duties ► **droit de cuissage** (*Hist*) droit du seigneur; (*hum*) *right to subject employees to sexual harassment* ► **droits de douane** customs duties ► **les droits de la femme** women's rights; **les ~s de la femme mariée** the rights of married women *ou* a married woman ► **droit de gage** (*Jur*) lien ► **droit de garde** [*enfant*] custody ► **droit de grâce** right of reprieve ► **le droit de grève** the right to strike ► **les droits de l'homme** human rights ► **droit d'initiative** (*Pol*) citizens' right to initiate legislation (in Switzerland etc) ► **droit de mutation** (*Fin*) transfer tax ► **les droits naturels** natural rights ► **droit de passage** right of way, easement (*US*) ► **droit de propriété** right of property; **nous avons un ~ de propriété sur notre corps** we should have jurisdiction over our own bodies ► **droit réel** (*Jur*) title ► **droit de réponse** right of reply ► **droits de reproduction** reproduction rights; **« tous ~s (de reproduction) réservés »** "all rights reserved" ► **droit de souscription** application right ► **droits de succession** inheritance tax ► **droit de timbre** stamp duty ► **droits de tirage spéciaux** special drawing rights ► **droit d'usage** (*Jur*) right of user ► **droit de visite** (*Jur*) (right of) access ► **le droit de vote** the right to vote, the vote, franchise

droitement [drwatmɑ̃] ADV [*agir, parler*] uprightly, honestly; [*juger*] soundly

droitier, -ière [drwatje, jɛʀ] [1] ADJ (= *non gaucher*) right-handed; (*Pol*) right-wing [2] NM,F right-handed person; (*Pol*) right-winger; (*Tennis etc*) **c'est un ~** he's a right-handed player *ou* a right-hander

droiture [drwatyʀ] NF [*personne*] uprightness,

honesty; [*conscience*] honesty; **~ de caractère** uprightness, rectitude (of character)

drolatique [drɔlatik] ADJ (*littér*) comical, droll

drôle [drol] [1] ADJ [a] (= *amusant*) [*situation, accoutrement*] funny, comical, amusing; (= *spirituel*) [*personne*] funny, amusing; **je ne trouve pas ça ~** I don't find that funny *ou* amusing; **la vie n'est pas ~** life's no joke; **tu es ~, je ne pouvais pourtant pas l'insulter!*** you must be joking *ou* kidding — I could hardly insult him! → **histoire**

[b] (= *bizarre*) funny, strange; **c'est ~, j'aurais juré l'avoir rangé** that's funny *ou* strange, I could have sworn I had put it away; **avoir un ~ d'air** to look funny *ou* peculiar *ou* strange; **un ~ de type** a strange *ou* peculiar fellow, an oddbod*; **c'est un ~ de numéro** he's a bit of a character; **une ~ d'idée/d'odeur** a funny *ou* strange *ou* peculiar idea/smell; **il a fait une ~ de tête!** he pulled a wry *ou* funny face!; (*Hist*) **la ~ de guerre** the Phoney War; **se sentir tout ~** to feel funny *ou* strange *ou* peculiar; **ça me fait (tout) ~ (de le voir)*** it gives me a funny *ou* strange *ou* odd feeling (to see him)

[c] (*: intensif*) **un ~ d'orage** a fantastic* *ou* terrific* storm; **de ~s de muscles/progrès** fantastic* *ou* terrific* muscles/progress; **une ~ de correction** a hell of a punishment*; **on en a vu de ~s pendant la guerre** we had a hard time (of it) during the war

[2] NM (*dial = gamin*) child, kid*; († *péj = coquin*) scamp, rascal

drôlement [drolmɑ̃] ADV [a] (= *bizarrement*) strangely, peculiarly; **il m'a regardé ~** he gave me a strange *ou* funny look [b]* (= *extrêmement*) **~ bon/sage** awfully *ou* terribly good/well-behaved; **il fait ~ froid** it's awfully *ou* terribly cold, it isn't half cold*; **il est ~ musclé** he's really muscular, he's got a lot of muscle*; **il est ~ culotté** he's got some cheek*, he hasn't half got a cheek* (*Brit*); **il a ~ changé** he really has changed, he's changed an awful lot*; **ça lui a fait ~ plaisir** it pleased him no end* [c] (= *spirituellement*) funnily, comically, amusingly

drôlerie [drolʀi] NF [a] (*NonC*) funniness, drollness; **la ~ de la situation m'échappe** I don't see *ou* I fail to see what's so funny *ou* amusing; **c'est d'une ~!** it's so funny *ou* comical! [b] (= *propos, action*) funny *ou* amusing thing (to say *ou* do)

drôlesse† [droles] NF (*péj*) hussy† (*péj*)

dromadaire [dromadɛʀ] NM dromedary

dronte [drɔ̃t] NM dodo

drop [drɔp], **drop-goal** (*pl* **drop-goals**) [drɔpgol] NM (= *coup de pied*) drop kick; (= *but*) drop goal; **passer un ~** to score a drop goal

drosophile [drozɔfil] NF (*Zool*) fruit fly, drosophila (*SPÉC*)

drosser [drose] ▸conjug 1◂ VT (*Naut*) [*vent, courant*] to drive (*contre* onto, against)

dru, e [dry] [1] ADJ [*herbe*] thick; [*barbe*] thick, bushy; [*haie*] thick, dense; [*pluie*] heavy [2] ADV [*pousser*] thickly, densely; [*tomber*] [*pluie*] heavily, fast; [*coups*] thick and fast

drug(-)store (*pl* **drug(-)stores**) [drœgstɔʀ] NM drugstore

druide [drɥid] NM druid

druidesse [drɥides] NF druidess

druidique [drɥidik] ADJ druidic

druidisme [drɥidism] NM druidism

drupe [dryp] NF drupe

druze [dryz] [1] ADJ Drusean, Drusian [2] **Druzes** NMPL **les Druzes** the Druse *ou* Druze

dryade [drijad] NF (*Myth*) dryad, wood-nymph; (*Bot*) dryas

DST [deeste] NF (ABRÉV = **Direction de la surveillance du territoire**) ≈ MI5 (*Brit*), ≈ CIA (*US*)

DT [dete] NM (ABRÉV = **diphtérie, tétanos**) *vaccine against diphtheria and tetanus*

du [dy] **1** ART PARTITIF → **de²** **2** PRÉP + ART DÉF → **de¹**

▼ **dû, due** [dy] (*ptp de* **devoir**) **1** ADJ **a** (= *à restituer*) owing, owed; (= *arrivé à échéance*) due; **la somme due** the sum owing *ou* owed, the sum due; **la somme qui lui est due** the sum owing *ou* owed *ou* due to him → **chose, port²** **b** **dû** **à** due to; **ces troubles sont dus à ...** these troubles are due to ... **c** (*Admin, Jur*) **en (bonne et) due forme** in due form **2** NM due; (= *somme d'argent*) dues

dual, e [dɥal] ADJ [*économie, système*] dual; **société ~e** two-tier society

dualisme [dɥalism] NM dualism

dualiste [dɥalist] **1** ADJ dualistic **2** NMF dualist

dualité [dɥalite] NF duality

Dubaï, Dubay [dybaj] N Dubai

dubitatif, -ive [dybitatif, iv] ADJ doubtful, dubious; **d'un air ~** doubtfully, dubiously

dubitativement [dybitativmã] ADV doubtfully, dubiously

Dublin [dyblɛ̃] N Dublin

dublinois, e [dyblinwa, waz] **1** ADJ of *ou* from Dublin **2** **Dublinois(e)** NM,F Dubliner

duc [dyk] NM duke

ducal, e [mpl **-aux**] [dykal, o] ADJ ducal

ducasse [dykas] NF (*Belg*) fair

ducat [dyka] NM ducat

duché [dyʃe] NM (= *fonction*) dukedom; (= *territoire*) dukedom, duchy

duchesse [dyʃɛs] NF **a** (= *noble*) duchess; (*péj*) **elle fait la** *ou* **sa ~** she's playing the grand lady *ou* putting on airs **b** **(poire) ~** Duchesse pear

ductile [dyktil] ADJ ductile

ductilité [dyktilite] NF ductility

dudit [dydi], **de ladite** [dəladit] (*mpl* **desdits** [dedi]) (*fpl* **desdites** [dedit]) ADJ (*Jur, hum*) of the aforementioned, of the said; **le propriétaire ~** **édifice/chien** the owner of the aforementioned *ou* said building/dog

duègne [dɥɛɲ] NF duenna

duel¹ [dɥɛl] NM duel; **provoquer qn en ~** to challenge sb to a duel; **se battre en ~** to fight a duel (**avec** with); (*hum*) **deux malheureux bouts de viande se battaient en ~ au fond du plat** there were just two measly bits of meat on the plate; **~ oratoire** verbal duel *ou* battle; **~ d'artillerie** artillery battle

duel² [dɥɛl] NM (*Ling*) dual (number)

duelliste [dɥelist] NM duellist

duettiste [dɥetist] NMF duettist

duffle-coat (*pl* **duffle-coats**), **duffel-coat** (*pl* **duffel-coats**) [dœfœlkot] NM duffel coat

dugong [dygɔ̃g] NM dugong

dulcinée [dylsine] NF († *aussi hum*) ladylove† (*aussi hum*)

dum-dum [dumdum] NF INV **(balle) ~** dumdum (bullet)

dûment [dymã] ADV duly

dumping [dœmpiŋ] NM (*Écon*) dumping; **faire du ~** to dump goods; **~ social** social dumping

dune [dyn] NF dune; **~ de sable** sand dune

dunette [dynɛt] NF (*Naut*) poop deck

Dunkerque [dœ̃kɛʀk] N Dunkirk

duo [dɥo] NM (*Mus*) duet; (*Théât*) double act, duo; [*plaisantins*] pair, duo; (= *dialogue*) exchange; **chanter en ~** to sing a duet; (*sur menu*) **~ de poissons sur lit de poireaux** two fish on a bed of leeks

duodécimal, e (*mpl* **-aux**) [dɥodesimal, o] ADJ duodecimal

duodénal, e (*mpl* **-aux**) [dɥodenal, o] ADJ duodenal

duodénum [dɥodenɔm] NM duodenum

duopole [dɥɔpɔl] NM duopoly

dupe [dyp] **1** NF dupe; **prendre pour ~** to fool, take in, dupe; **être la ~ de qn** to be taken in *ou* fooled by sb → **jeu, marché** **2** ADJ **être ~ (de)** to be taken in (by), be fooled (by); **je ne** *ou* **n'en suis pas ~** I'm not taken in (by it), he (*ou* it *etc*) doesn't fool me

duper [dype] ▸conjug 1◂ VT to dupe, deceive, fool; **se ~ (soi-même)** to deceive o.s.

duperie [dypʀi] NF (= *tromperie*) dupery (*NonC*), deception

duplex [dyplɛks] **1** ADJ INV (*Téléc*) duplex, two-way **2** NM (= *appartement*) split-level apartment, duplex (*US*); (*Can*) duplex (house), maisonette; (*Téléc*) (**émission en**) **~** link-up

duplicata [dyplikata] NM INV (*Admin, Jur*) duplicate

duplicateur [dyplikatœʀ] NM duplicator, duplicating machine

duplication [dyplikasjɔ̃] NF (*Math*) duplication; (*Bio*) doubling; [*ADN*] replication; [*enregistrement*] duplication

duplicité [dyplisite] NF duplicity

dupliquer [dyplike] ▸conjug 1◂ VT to duplicate

dur, e [dyʀ] **1** ADJ **a** [*roche, métal, lit, crayon, sol*] hard; [*carton, col, brosse*] stiff; [*viande*] tough; [*porte, serrure, levier*] stiff; **être ~ d'oreille** ◊ **être ~ de la feuille*** ◊ **avoir l'oreille ~e†** to be hard of hearing; **~ comme le roc** as hard as (a) rock, rock-hard → **blé, œuf, pain** *etc*
b [*problème, travail, parcours*] hard, stiff, tough; **~ à manier/digérer/croire** hard to handle/digest/believe; **leur fils est un enfant très ~** their son is a very difficult child; **être ~ à la détente*** (= *avare*) to be tight-fisted*; (= *difficile à persuader*) to be pigheaded; (= *obtus*) to be slow on the uptake*
c [*climat, lumière, punition, combat*] harsh, hard; [*couleur, épreuve*] harsh; [*leçon*] hard; (= *âpre*) [*vin, cidre*] harsh; (= *calcaire*) [*eau*] hard; **il lui est ~ d'avoir à partir** it's hard for him to have to leave; **ce sont des vérités ~es à avaler** *ou* **digérer*** these are hard truths to take; (*souvent hum*) **la vie est ~e** it's a hard life, life's no bed of roses; **~ !*** *ou* **~, ~ !*** not easy!; (*souvent hum*) **les temps sont ~s** times are hard; **il nous mène la vie ~e** he makes life difficult for us, he gives us a hard time; **le plus ~ est passé** the worst is over → **coup**
d (= *sévère*) [*personne, voix, regard, traits, visage*] hard, harsh, severe; [*loi, critique*] harsh, severe; **être ~ avec** *ou* **pour** *ou* **envers qn** to be harsh with sb, be hard on sb → **dent, école**
e (= *insensible, cruel*) [*personne*] hard(-hearted); **il a le cœur ~** he's a hard-hearted man, he has a heart of stone
f (= *endurant*) **être ~ au mal** *ou* **à la douleur** to be tough; **être ~ à la peine** *ou* **à l'ouvrage** to be a tireless *ou* hard worker → **peau**
g (= *sans concession*) uncompromising; **le gouvernement adopte une ligne ~e sur le commerce international** the government is taking a hard line on *ou* a hardline stance on international trade → **pur**
2 ADV* [*travailler, frapper*] hard; **le soleil tape ~** the sun is beating down; **le vent souffle ~** the wind is blowing hard *ou* strongly; **croire à qch ~ comme fer** to have a blind belief in sth
3 NM **a** (* = *résistant*) tough one; (= *meneur, casseur*) tough nut*, tough guy*; (*gén, Pol* = *intransigeant*) hard-liner; **c'est un ~ au cœur tendre** his bark is worse than his bite; **c'est un ~ à cuire** *ou* **un ~ de ~*** he's a hard nut to crack*; **jouer les ~s** to act the tough guy*, act tough
b (*loc*) **construire en ~** to build a permanent structure; **une construction en ~** a permanent structure; **un court (de tennis) en ~** a hard court; **c'est du ~*** it's solid *ou* tough stuff, it's

sturdy
c [*corde*] tension; (*Alpinisme*) **~ !** pull tight!
4 **dure** NF **a*** **c'est une ~** (= *résistante*) she's a tough one; (= *meneuse*) she's a hard one
b (*loc*) **être élevé à la ~e** to be brought up the hard way; **vivre à la ~e** to live rough; **coucher sur la ~e** to sleep on the ground, sleep rough (*surtout Brit*)
c * (= *paroles, actions*) **en dire de ~es à qn** to give sb a good telling-off* *ou* ticking-off* (*Brit*); (= *reproches*) **en entendre de ~es** to get a good telling-off* *ou* ticking-off* (*Brit*); **en voir de ~es** to have a hard time (of it)*; **en faire voir de ~es à qn** to give sb a hard time (of it)*

durabilité [dyʀabilite] NF (*gén*) durability; [*produit*] life span

durable [dyʀabl] ADJ [*croissance, développement, reprise*] lasting; [*solution, paix*] lasting, durable; [*bonheur, monument, souvenir, succès*] lasting, enduring; [*emploi*] long-term (*épith*) → **bien**

durablement [dyʀabləmã] ADV [*s'installer*] on a long-term basis; **bâtir ~** to build something to last; **bâti ~** built to last

duraille* [dyʀaj] ADJ [*problème*] tough, hard; [*matelas, viande*] hard

duralumin® [dyʀalymɛ̃] NM Duralumin®

durant [dyʀã] PRÉP (*gén* = *pendant*) for; (= *au cours de*) during, in the course of; **il peut rêvasser ~ des heures** *ou* **des heures ~** he can daydream for hours (on end); **deux heures ~** for (a full *ou* whole) two hours; **des années ~** for years (and years); **sa vie ~** throughout his life, for as long as he lived (*ou* lives); **~ le spectacle** during the show; **il a plu ~ la nuit** it rained in the night *ou* during the night

duratif, -ive [dyʀatif, iv] ADJ durative

durcir [dyʀsiʀ] ▸conjug 2◂ **1** VT [+ *attitude*] to harden; [+ *contrôle, embargo, sanctions*] to tighten; **~ ses positions** to take a tougher stand; **~ un mouvement de grève** to step up strike action; **il a durci son discours** he has taken a tougher stand **2** VI, **se durcir** VPR [*sol, colle, visage, attitude, ton*] to harden; [*mouvement de grève*] to become more firmly entrenched; [*conflit*] to become more serious

durcissement [dyʀsismã] NM [*attitude, positions*] hardening; [*sanctions, embargo*] tightening; [*mouvements de grève*] stepping up of strike action

durcisseur [dyʀsisœʀ] NM hardener

durée [dyʀe] NF **a** [*spectacle, opération*] duration, length; [*bail*] term; [*prêt*] period; [*matériau, pile, ampoule*] life; (*Mus*) [*note*] value; **la ~ d'une mode dépend de ...** how long a fashion lasts depends on ...; **je m'étonne de la ~ de ce spectacle** I'm amazed at how long this show is; **pour une ~ illimitée** for an unlimited length of time, for an unlimited period; **pendant une ~ d'un mois** for (the period of) one month; **pour la ~ des négociations** while negotiations continue, for the duration of the negotiations; **pendant la ~ des réparations** for the duration of repairs, while repairs are being carried out; **de courte ~** [*séjour*] short; [*bonheur, répit*] short-lived; **(de) longue ~** [*effet*] long-lasting (*épith*); [*contrat, chômage, visa*] long-term (*épith*); [*pile*] long-life (*épith*), long-lasting (*épith*); **~ de vie utile** useful life
b (= *permanence*) continuance; **il n'osait croire à la ~ de cette prospérité** he didn't dare to believe that this prosperity would last *ou* to believe in the continuance of this prosperity
c (*Philo*) duration

durement [dyʀmã] ADV **a** (= *sévèrement*) harshly, severely; (= *brutalement*) harshly; **élever qn ~** to bring sb up the hard way; **parler ~ à qn** to speak harshly *ou* sharply to sb; **la manifestation a été ~ réprimée** the demonstration was suppressed using force **b** (= *cruellement*) [*éprouvé, ressenti*] sorely; **région ~**

touchée par la crise region hard hit by the recession

dure-mère (pl **dures-mères**) [dyʀmɛʀ] NF (Anat) dura mater

durer [dyʀe] ▶ conjug 1 ◀ VI **a** (= avoir une durée de) to last; **combien de temps cela dure-t-il?** how long does it last?; **l'effet dure deux minutes/mois** the effect lasts (for) two minutes/months; **le festival dure (pendant) deux semaines** the festival lasts (for) two weeks **b** (= se prolonger) [mode, maladie, tempête] to last; **la fête a duré toute la nuit/jusqu'au matin** the party went on ou lasted all night/until morning; **sa maladie dure depuis deux mois** he has been ill for two months (now), his illness has lasted for two months (now); **ça fait deux mois que ça dure** it has been going on ou it has lasted for two months (now); **ça n'a que trop duré!** it's gone on too long already!; **ça va ~ longtemps, cette plaisanterie?** how much longer is this joke going to go on? ou continue?; **ça durera ce que ça durera** I don't know if it'll last, it might last and it might not; **ça ne peut plus ~!** this can't go on (any longer)!; **elle dure, leur conversation!** they've been talking for ages!; **faire ~ un travail** to prolong ou spin out* (Brit) a job; (iro) **faire ~ le plaisir** to prolong the agony; (littér) **le temps me dure** time hangs heavy on my hands; (littér) **l'inaction me dure** I am growing impatient at this inactivity → **pourvu²** **c** (littér = subsister) [coutume] to linger on; (péj) [mourant] to hang on (péj), linger on **d** (= se conserver) [matériau, vêtement, outil] to last; **faire ~ des chaussures** to make shoes last; **cette somme doit te ~ un mois** this money will have to last you a month

dureté [dyʀte] NF **a** [roche, métal, lit, crayon] hardness; [carton, col, brosse] stiffness; [viande] toughness **b** [problème, travail, parcours] hardness, stiffness, toughness; **la ~ des temps** the hard times we live in; **la ~ de la vie quotidienne** the harshness of daily life **c** [climat, lumière, punition, combat] harshness, hardness; [vin, cidre] harshness **d** (= sévérité) [personne, voix, regard, traits, visage] hardness, harshness, severity; [loi, critique] harshness, severity; **sa ~ de ton m'a surpris** his harsh tone surprised me **e** (= insensibilité, cruauté) ~ **(de cœur)**

hard-heartedness; **traiter qn avec ~** to treat sb harshly **f** [eau] hardness; **tester la ~ de l'eau** to test how hard the water is

durillon [dyʀijɔ̃] NM (aux mains) callus, hard skin (NonC); (aux pieds) callus, corn

durit®, **durite** [dyʀit] NF (Aut) (radiator) hose

DUT [deyte] NM (ABRÉV = **diplôme universitaire de technologie**) → **diplôme**

duty-free [djutifʀi] **1** ADJ duty-free **2** NM duty-free (shop); **en ~** duty-free; **j'ai acheté du parfum en ~** I bought some duty-free perfume, I bought some perfume in the duty-free

duvet [dyvɛ] NM **a** [oiseau, fruit, joues] down **b** (= sac de couchage) (down-filled) sleeping bag

duveté, e [dyv(ə)te] ADJ [pêche, joue] downy; **elle avait la lèvre ~e** she had a faint moustache

duveter (se) [dyv(ə)te] ▶ conjug 5 ◀ VPR to become downy

duveteux, -euse [dyv(ə)tø, øz] ADJ downy

dynamique [dinamik] **1** ADJ (Phys, gén) dynamic → **cadre** **2** NF **a** (Phys, Mus) dynamics sg; (Sociol) **la ~ de groupe** group dynamics **b** (fig) dynamic; **créer une ~ de croissance/d'évolution technologique** to create a dynamic of growth/technological change; **accélérer la ~ de paix** to speed up the peace process; **la ~ en cours** the dynamic current

dynamiquement [dinamikmã] ADV dynamically

dynamisant, e [dinamizã, ãt] ADJ [effet, changement] stimulating

dynamisation [dinamizasjɔ̃] NF [secteur, marché] stimulation

dynamiser [dinamize] ▶ conjug 1 ◀ VT [+ économie, marché] to stimulate, give a boost to; [+ personnel] to energize; [+ affiche, image de marque] to make more dynamic; (Méd) [+ médicament] to potentiate (SPÉC)

dynamisme [dinamism] NM (Philo, gén) dynamism

dynamitage [dinamitaʒ] NM dynamiting

dynamite [dinamit] NF dynamite; **faire sauter qch à la ~** to blow sth up with dynamite; (fig) **c'est de la ~!** it's dynamite!

dynamiter [dinamite] ▶ conjug 1 ◀ VT (lit) to dynamite, blow up with dynamite; [+ certitudes, mythe] to explode

dynamiteur, -euse [dinamitœʀ, øz] NM,F dynamiter

dynamo [dinamo] NF dynamo

dynamoélectrique [dinamoelɛktʀik] ADJ dynamoelectric

dynamogène [dinamɔʒɛn], **dynamogénique** [dinamɔʒenik] ADJ dynamogenic

dynamographe [dinamɔgʀaf] NM dynamograph

dynamomètre [dinamɔmɛtʀ] NM dynamometer

dynamométrique [dinamɔmetʀik] ADJ dynamometric → **clé**

dynastie [dinasti] NF dynasty

dynastique [dinastik] ADJ dynastic, dynastical

dyne [din] NF dyne

dysenterie [disɑ̃tʀi] NF dysentery

dysentérique [disɑ̃teʀik] ADJ dysenteric

dysfonctionnement [disfɔksjɔnmã] NM (Méd) dysfunction; [organisation, service] poor running (NonC); **il y a des ~s dans la gestion du service** there are problems in the management of the department

dysgraphie [disgʀafi] NF dysgraphia

dysharmonie [disaʀmɔni] NF = **disharmonie**

dyslexie [disleksi] NF dyslexia, word-blindness

dyslexique [disleksik] ADJ, NMF dyslexic

dysménorrhée [dismenɔʀe] NF dysmenorrhoea

dyspareunie [dispaʀøni] NF dyspareunia

dyspepsie [dispɛpsi] NF dyspepsia

dyspepsique [dispɛpsik], **dyspeptique** [dispɛptik] ADJ, NMF dyspeptic

dysphasie [disfazi] NF dysphasia

dysplasie [displazi] NF (Méd) dysplasia

dyspnée [dispne] NF dyspnoea (Brit), dyspnea (US)

dysprosium [dispʀozjɔm] NM dysprosium

dystrophie [distʀɔfi] NF **~ musculaire progressive** muscular dystrophy

E

E¹, **e** [ə] NM (= *lettre*) E, e; **e dans l'o** o and e joined together, o and e ligature

E² (ABRÉV = **Est**) E

EAO [əao] NM (ABRÉV = **enseignement assisté par ordinateur**) CAI, CAL

EAU [əay] NMPL (ABRÉV = **Émirats arabes unis**) UAE

eau (pl **eaux**) [o] **1** NF **a** (*gén, Méd*) water; (= *pluie*) rain; **sans ~** [*alcool*] neat, straight; **cuire à l'~** to boil; **se passer les mains à l'~** to rinse one's hands, give one's hands a quick wash; **passer qch sous l'~** to give sth a quick rinse; **laver à grande ~** [+ *sol*] to wash *ou* sluice down; (*avec un tuyau*) to hose down; [+ *légumes*] to wash thoroughly; **port en ~ profonde** deep-water port; (*hum*) **que d'~**, **que d'~** ! it's coming down in buckets* *ou* in torrents!

b (*Bijouterie*) water; **diamant de la plus belle ~** diamond of the first water; **un escroc de la plus belle ~** an out-and-out crook; (*fig*) **de la même ~** of the same ilk

c (*loc*) **tout cela apporte de l'~ à son moulin** it's all grist to his mill; (*Naut*) **aller sur l'~** (= *flotter*) to be buoyant; (= *naviguer*) to sail; **aller à l'~** to go for a dip; **j'en avais l'~ à la bouche** my mouth was watering, it made my mouth water; **être en ~** to be bathed in perspiration *ou* sweat; (*Naut, Rail*) **faire de l'~** to take on (a supply of) water; **faire ~ (de toutes parts)** to leak (like a sieve); (*Naut*) **mettre à l'~** to launch; **mise à l'~** launch, launching; **se mettre à l'~** (= *nager*) to get into the water; (= *être sobre*) to go on the wagon*, keep off alcohol; **mettre de l'~ dans son vin** (*lit*) to put water down one's wine; (*fig*) (= *modérer ses prétentions*) to climb down; (= *faire des concessions*) to make concessions; [*chaussures*] **prendre l'~** to leak, let in water; **il passera** *ou* **coulera beaucoup d'~ sous les ponts avant que ...** it will be a long time before ...; ■ (*PROV*) **porter de l'~ à la rivière** to carry coals to Newcastle (*PROV*); ■ (*PROV*) **l'~ va à la rivière** money makes money, to him that has shall more be given; **s'en aller** *ou* **tourner en ~ de boudin*** to flop; **notre projet est (tombé) à l'~** our project has fallen through; **il y a de l'~ dans le gaz*** things aren't running too smoothly; **ils sont comme l'~ et le feu** they're as different as night and day *ou* as chalk and cheese (*Brit*)

2 **eaux** NFPL **a** [*fleuve*] **hautes ~x** high water; **basses ~x** (*lit*) low water; **pendant les basses ~x** when the waters are low, when the water level is low; (*fig*) **en période de basses ~x** when the economy is at a low ebb, during a period of economic stagnation; (*Naut*) **être dans les ~x d'un navire** to be in the wake of a ship; (*fig*) **nager** *ou* **naviguer en ~x troubles** to move in shady circles; **dans ces ~x-là*** or thereabouts; **entre deux ~x** just below the surface; (*fig*) **nager entre deux ~x** to keep a foot in both camps, to run with the hare and hunt with the hounds

b (*Méd*) **elle a perdu les ~x** her waters have broken

c (†,* = *station thermale*) **prendre les ~x** to

take the waters → **ville**

d (*Admin*) **la Compagnie des Eaux et de l'Ozone** the French water utility

3 COMP ► **eau bénite** holy water ► **eau blanche** lead acetate, sugar of lead ► **eau de Cologne** eau de Cologne, cologne ► **eau courante** running water ► **eau de cuisson** cooking water ► **eau douce** fresh water ► **eau écarlate**® (liquid) stain remover ► **eau d'érable** maple sap (*Can*) ► **eau de fleur d'oranger** orange-flower water ► **les Eaux et Forêts** ≈ the Forestry Commission (*Brit*), ≈ the Forest Service (*US*) ► **eau gazeuse** sparkling (mineral) water ► **eaux grasses** swill, slops ► **eaux internationales** international waters ► **eau de javel** bleach ► **eau lourde** heavy water ► **eau de mélisse** melissa water ► **eaux ménagères** (household) waste water ► **eau de mer** sea water ► **eaux mères** mother liquids ► **eau minérale** mineral water ► **eau oxygénée** hydrogen peroxide ► **eau de parfum** eau de parfum ► **eau plate** plain *ou* still water ► **eau de pluie** rainwater ► **eau potable** drinking water ► **eaux profondes** deep waters ► **eau de refroidissement** cooling water ► **eaux résiduaires** waste water ► **eau du robinet** tap water ► **eau de rose** rose water; **roman/histoire à l'~ de rose** sentimental *ou* schmaltzy* novel/story ► **eau rougie** wine and water ► **eau salée** salt water ► **eau savonneuse** soapy water ► **eau de Seltz** soda (water), seltzer water (*US*) ► **eau de source** spring water ► **eaux superficielles** surface water(s) ► **eaux territoriales** territorial waters; **dans les ~x territoriales françaises** in French (territorial) waters ► **eaux thermales** thermal springs *ou* waters ► **eau de toilette** eau de toilette, toilet water ► **eaux usées** waste water ► **eau de vaisselle** dishwater, washing-up (*Brit*) water

eau-de-vie (pl **eaux-de-vie**) [od(ə)vi] NF ≈ brandy; **~ de prune/poire** plum/pear brandy; **cerises à l'~** cherries in brandy

eau-forte (pl **eaux-fortes**) [ofɔʀt] NF (*Art*) etching; (*Chim*) aqua fortis

eaux-vannes [ovan] NFPL effluent (*NonC*)

ébahi, **e** [ebai] (*ptp de* **ébahir**) ADJ dumbfounded, flabbergasted, astounded

ébahir [ebaiʀ] ▶conjug 2◀ **1** VT to dumbfound, flabbergast, astound **2** **s'ébahir** VPR to wonder (**de voir** at seeing)

ébahissement [ebaismã] NM astonishment, amazement

ébarber [ebaʀbe] ▶conjug 1◀ VT [+ *papier, poisson*] to trim; [+ *métal*] to (de)burr, trim; [+ *plante*] to clip, trim

ébats [eba] NMPL frolics; **~ amoureux** *ou* **sexuels** lovemaking

ébattre (s') [ebatʀ] ▶conjug 41◀ VPR [*animaux*] to frolic, frisk, gambol (about); [*enfants*] to play *ou* romp about, frolic

ébaubi, **e** [ebobi] (*ptp de* **s'ébaubir**) ADJ (†, *hum*) bowled over, flabbergasted (**de** at); **être tout ~** to be agog (**devant** at)

ébaubir (s') [ebobiʀ] ▶conjug 2◀ VPR (†, *hum*) to wonder (**de voir** at seeing)

ébauche [eboʃ] NF [*livre*] skeleton, outline; [*tableau, dessin*] draft, sketch; [*statue*] rough shape; [*projet, roman*] (rough) outline; **l'~ d'une amitié** the beginnings of a friendship; **une ~ de sourire** the ghost of a smile; **l'~ d'un geste** a slight movement; **ce n'est que la première ~** this is just a rough draft; **c'est encore à l'état d'~** it's still in the early stages

ébaucher [eboʃe] ▶conjug 1◀ **1** VT [+ *livre, plan, tableau*] to sketch out; [*statue*] to rough out; [+ *programme d'action*] to outline; [+ *poutre*] to rough-hew; [+ *pierre*] to rough-hew, boast; [+ *diamant*] to begin to cut; [+ *amitié, conversation*] to start up; [+ *relations*] to open up; **~ un sourire** to give a faint smile; **~ un geste** to start to make a movement **2** **s'ébaucher** VPR [*plan*] to form, take shape *ou* form; [*livre*] to take shape *ou* form; [*amitié*] to form; [*conversation*] to start; [*relations*] to open up; **une solution s'ébauche lentement** a solution is gradually taking shape; **une idée à peine ébauchée** the bare bones *ou* the mere outline of an idea

ébaudir VT, **s'ébaudir** VPR [ebodiʀ] ▶conjug 2◀ (†, *hum*) to rejoice (**de, à** over, at)

ébène [eben] NF ebony; **cheveux/table d'~** ebony hair/table → **bois**

ébénier [ebenje] NM ebony (tree) → **faux²**

ébéniste [ebenist] NMF cabinetmaker

ébénisterie [ebenist(ə)ʀi] NF (= *métier*) cabinetmaking; (= *façon, meuble*) cabinetwork

éberlué, **e** [ebɛʀlɥe] (*ptp de* **éberluer**) ADJ flabbergasted, dumbfounded; **il avait un regard ~** he looked dazed

éberluer [ebɛʀlɥe] ▶conjug 1◀ VT to astound, flabbergast, dumbfound; **elle était un peu éberluée de** *ou* **par ce qui lui arrivait** she was dazed by what was happening to her

éblouir [ebluiʀ] ▶conjug 2◀ VT (*lit, fig*) to dazzle

éblouissant, **e** [ebluisã, ãt] ADJ (*lit, fig*) dazzling; **~ de talent/de beauté** dazzlingly talented/beautiful

éblouissement [ebluismã] NM **a** [*lampe*] dazzle **b** (= *émerveillement*) bedazzlement; (= *spectacle*) dazzling sight **c** (*Méd*) **avoir un ~** to have a dizzy spell

ébonite [ebɔnit] NF vulcanite, ebonite

éborgner [ebɔʀɲe] ▶conjug 1◀ VT **a** **~ qn** to blind sb in one eye, put *ou* poke sb's eye out; **j'ai failli m'~ contre la cheminée*** I nearly put *ou* poked my eye out on the corner of the mantelpiece **b** (*Agr*) to disbud

éboueur [ebwœʀ] NM dustman (*Brit*), refuse collector (*Brit Admin*), garbage man *ou* collector (*US*), sanitation man (*US Admin*)

ébouillanter [ebujãte] ▶conjug 1◀ **1** VT (*gén*) to scald; [+ *légumes*] to scald, blanch; [+ *théière*] to warm **2** **s'ébouillanter** VPR to scald o.s.

éboulement [ebulmã] NM **a** [*falaise*] (*progressif*) crumbling; (*soudain*) collapsing; [*mur, toit*] falling in, caving in; **~ de rochers**

rock fall; **~ de terrain** landslide, landslip [b] (= *éboulis*) heap *ou* mass of rocks (*ou* earth)

ébouler [ebule] ▶conjug 1◀ [1] VT to cause to collapse *ou* crumble, bring down [2] VI, **s'ébouler** VPR [*pente, falaise*] (*progressivement*) to crumble; (*soudainement*) to collapse; [*mur, toit*] to fall in, cave in; [*terre*] to slip, slide

éboulis [ebuli] NM mass of fallen rocks (*ou* earth); **pente couverte d'~** scree-covered slope

ébouriffant, e* [eburifɑ̃, ɑ̃t] ADJ [*vitesse, prix*] hair-raising

ébouriffé, e [eburife] (*ptp de* **ébouriffer**) ADJ [*cheveux*] tousled, dishevelled; [*plumes, poils*] ruffled; [*personne*] dishevelled; **il était tout ~** his hair was all tousled *ou* ruffled *ou* dishevelled

ébouriffer [eburife] ▶conjug 1◀ VT [a] [+ *cheveux*] to tousle, ruffle; [+ *plumes, poil*] to ruffle [b]* (= *surprendre*) to amaze, astound

ébrancher [ebrɑ̃ʃe] ▶conjug 1◀ VT to prune, lop (the branches off)

ébranchoir [ebrɑ̃ʃwar] NM billhook

ébranlement [ebrɑ̃lmɑ̃] NM [a] (= *tremblement*) shaking [b] (= *affaiblissement*) [*confiance, gouvernement*] weakening [c] (= *choc*) shock; **l'~ provoqué par cette nouvelle** the shock caused by the news

ébranler [ebrɑ̃le] ▶conjug 1◀ [1] VT [a] (= *faire trembler*) [+ *vitres, mur, sol*] to shake [b] (= *affaiblir*) [+ *nerfs*] to shake; [+ *santé*] to weaken; [+ *esprit*] to disturb, unhinge; [+ *résolution, confiance, gouvernement*] to shake, weaken; **ça a fortement ébranlé ses nerfs/sa santé** it has shattered his nerves/health; **le monde entier a été ébranlé par cette nouvelle** the whole world was shaken *ou* shattered by the news; **ces paroles l'ont ébranlé** he was very shaken by what he heard; **se laisser ~ par qch** to allow o.s. to be swayed by sth [2] **s'ébranler** VPR [*train, véhicule, cortège*] to move off, set off; [*cloche*] to start swinging

ébrécher [ebreʃe] ▶conjug 6◀ VT [+ *assiette*] to chip; [+ *lame*] to nick; [+ *fortune, personne*] to break into; [*achat*] to make a hole *ou* a dent in

ébréchure [ebreʃyr] NF [*assiette*] chip; [*lame*] nick

ébriété [ebrijete] NF (*frm*) intoxication, inebriation; **en état d'~** intoxicated, inebriated

ébrouement [ebrumɑ̃] NM [*cheval*] snort

ébrouer (s') [ebrue] ▶conjug 1◀ VPR [a] [*cheval*] to snort [b] [*personne, chien, oiseau*] to shake o.s.

ébruitement [ebrɥitmɑ̃] NM [*nouvelle, rumeur*] spreading; [*secret*] divulging, disclosing

ébruiter [ebrɥite] ▶conjug 1◀ [1] VT [+ *nouvelle, rumeur*] to spread; [+ *secret*] to divulge, disclose [2] **s'ébruiter** VPR **il ne faut pas que ça s'ébruite** people mustn't get to know about this; **pour que rien ne s'ébruite** so that nothing leaks out; **l'affaire s'est ébruitée** news of the affair got out

ébullition [ebylisjɔ̃] NF [*eau*] boiling; (= *agitation*) turmoil; **au moment de/avant l'~** as/before boiling point is reached; (*dans une recette*) **porter à ~** bring to the boil; **maintenir à ~ trois minutes** boil for three minutes; **être en ~** [*liquide*] to be boiling; [*ville, pays, maison*] to be in turmoil; [*personne*] (*par la surexcitation*) to be bubbling over with excitement; (*par la colère*) to be seething (with anger) → **point¹**

écaillage [ekajaʒ] NM [a] [*poisson*] scaling [b] [*huîtres*] opening [c] [*peinture*] flaking, peeling

écaille [ekaj] NF [*poisson, reptile, bourgeon, pomme de pin*] scale; [*tortue, huître*] shell; [*oignon*] layer, scale; [*peinture sèche*] flake; **lunettes (à monture) d'~** tortoiseshell *ou* horn-rimmed glasses; **en ~** tortoiseshell (*épith*);

(*frm*) **les ~s lui sont tombées des yeux** the scales fell from his eyes; **chat ~** tortoiseshell (cat)

écaillé, e [ekaje] (*ptp de* **écailler¹**) ADJ [*peinture, surface*] chipped, flaking; [*façade*] peeling, flaking; [*baignoire*] chipped; [*poisson*] scaled

écailler¹ [ekaje] ▶conjug 1◀ [1] VT [a] [+ *poisson*] to scale [b] [+ *huîtres*] to open [c] [+ *peinture*] to chip [2] **s'écailler** VPR [*peinture*] to flake (off), peel (off), chip; [*vernis à ongles*] to chip

écailler², -ère [ekaje, jɛr] NM,F (= *marchand*) oyster seller; (= *restaurateur*) owner of an oyster bar

écailleux, -euse [ekajø, øz] ADJ [*poisson, peau*] scaly; [*peinture, ardoise*] flaky, flaking

écaillure [ekajyr] NF [a] (= *morceau de peinture*) chip, flake; (= *surface écaillée*) chipped *ou* flaking patch [b] [*poisson*] scales

écale [ekal] NF [*noix*] husk

écaler [ekale] ▶conjug 1◀ VT [+ *noix*] to husk; [+ *œuf dur*] to peel

écarlate [ekarlat] [1] ADJ scarlet; (*fig : de honte*) **devenir ~** to turn scarlet *ou* crimson (*de* with) → **eau** [2] NF scarlet

écarquiller [ekarkije] ▶conjug 1◀ VT **les yeux** to stare wide-eyed (**devant** at)

écart [ekar] [1] NM [a] [*objets*] distance, space, gap; [*dates*] interval, gap; [*chiffres, températures*] difference; [*opinions*] difference, divergence; [*explications*] discrepancy, disparity (**entre** between); **~ par rapport à la règle** deviation *ou* departure from the rule; **il y a un ~ important de prix entre ...** there's a big difference in price between ...; **il y a un gros d'âge entre eux** there's a big age gap *ou* age difference between them; **ils ont 11 ans d'~** there are 11 years between them; (*lit, fig*) **réduire l'~ entre** to narrow *ou* close the gap between; (*Sport*) **réduire l'~ à la marque** to narrow *ou* close the gap; **faire un ~** [*cheval apeuré*] to shy; [*voiture*] to swerve; [*personne surprise*] to jump out of the way, leap aside; **faire un ~ de régime** to allow o.s. a break *ou* a lapse in one's diet; **grand ~** (*Gym, Danse*) splits *sg*; (*fig*) balancing act; **faire le grand ~** (*lit*) to do the splits; (*fig*) to do a balancing act [b] (*Cartes*) discard [c] (*Admin* = *hameau*) hamlet

[2] **à l'écart** LOC ADJ, LOC ADV **être à l'~** [*hameau*] to be out of the way *ou* isolated; **tirer qn à l'~** to take sb aside *ou* to one side; **mettre** *ou* **tenir qn à l'~** (= *empêcher de participer*) to keep sb in the background, keep sb out of things; (= *empêcher d'approcher*) to keep *ou* hold sb back; **se tenir** *ou* **rester à l'~** (= *s'isoler*) to stand *ou* remain aloof, stand apart; (= *ne pas approcher*) to stay in the background, keep out of the way; (= *ne pas participer*) to stay on the sidelines, keep out of things

[3] **à l'écart de** LOC PRÉP **la maison est à l'~ de la route** the house is (well) off the road; **ils habitent un peu à l'~ du village** they live just outside the village; **tenir qn à l'~ d'un lieu** to keep sb (well) away from a place; **tenir qn à l'~ d'une affaire** to keep sb out of a deal; **se tenir** *ou* **rester à l'~ des autres** to keep out of the way of *ou* well away from other people; **se tenir** *ou* **rester à l'~ d'une affaire/de la politique** to steer clear of *ou* keep out of an affair/out of politics

[4] COMP ► **écart de conduite** misdemeanour ► **écart d'inflation** inflation differential ► **écart de jeunesse** youthful misdemeanour ► **écart de langage** strong *ou* bad language (*NonC*); **faire un ~ de langage** to use unacceptable language ► **écart type** standard deviation

écarté, e [ekarte] (*ptp de* **écarter**) [1] ADJ [*lieu, hameau*] remote, isolated, out-of-the-way; [*yeux*] set far apart; **chemin ~** lonely road;

avoir les dents ~es to have gap(py) teeth, have gaps between one's teeth; **il se tenait debout, les jambes ~es/les bras ~s** he stood with his legs ~es *ou* feet apart/with his arms outspread *ou* with outspread arms [2] NM (*Cartes*) écarté

écartelé, e [ekartəle] (*ptp de* **écarteler**) ADJ (*Hér*) [*écu*] quartered

écartèlement [ekartɛlmɑ̃] NM (*Hist* = *supplice*) quartering; (= *tiraillement*) agonizing struggle

écarteler [ekartəle] ▶conjug 5◀ VT (*Hist* = *supplicier*) to quarter; (= *tirailler*) to tear apart; **écartelé entre ses obligations familiales et professionnelles** torn between family and professional obligations

écartement [ekartəmɑ̃] NM space, distance, gap (**de, entre** between); (*Rail*) **~ (des rails)** gauge; (*Aut*) **~ des essieux** wheelbase

écarter [ekarte] ▶conjug 1◀ [1] VT [a] (= *séparer*) [+ *objets*] to move apart, move away from each other; [+ *bras, jambes*] to open, spread; [+ *doigts*] to spread (open), part; [+ *rideaux*] to draw (back); **il écarta la foule pour passer** he pushed his way through the crowd [b] (= *exclure*) [+ *objection, solution*] to dismiss, set *ou* brush aside; [+ *idée*] to dismiss, rule out; [+ *candidature*] to dismiss, turn down; [+ *personne*] (*d'une liste*) to remove, strike off; (*d'une équipe*) to remove, exclude (**de** from) [c] (= *éloigner*) [+ *meuble*] to move away, push away *ou* back; [+ *foule, personne*] to push back (**de** from), push aside; (= *brouiller*) **elle essaie d'~ son mari de ses parents** she's trying to cut her husband off from his parents; **~ qn de la tentation** to keep sb (away) from temptation; **tout danger est maintenant écarté** the danger's passed now; **ce chemin nous écarte du village** this road takes *ou* leads us away from the village; **ça nous écarte de notre propos** this is taking *ou* leading us off the subject *ou* away from the issue; **ça l'écarte de l'étude** it distracts him from his studies [d] (*Cartes*) to discard

[2] **s'écarter** VPR [a] (= *se séparer*) [*foule*] to draw aside, part; [*nuages*] to part; **la foule s'écarta pour le laisser passer** the crowd drew aside *ou* parted to let him through [b] (= *s'éloigner*) to withdraw, move away, step back (**de** from); **la foule s'écarta du lieu de l'accident** the crowd moved away from the scene of the accident; **écartez-vous!** (move) out of the way!; **s'~ de sa route** to stray *ou* wander from one's path; **avec ce chemin nous nous écartons** this path is taking us out of our way; **les deux routes s'écartent l'une de l'autre** the two roads diverge; (*fig*) **s'~ du droit chemin** to wander from the straight and narrow; **le mur s'écarte dangereusement de la verticale** the wall is dangerously out of plumb; **s'~ de la norme** to deviate *ou* depart from the norm; **s'~ d'un sujet** to stray *ou* wander from a subject; **nous nous écartons!** we are getting away from the point!

écarteur [ekartœr] NM (*Méd*) retractor

ecchymose [ekimoz] NF bruise, ecchymosis (*SPÉC*)

Ecclésiaste [eklezjast] NM **(le livre de) l'~** (the Book of) Ecclesiastes

ecclésiastique [eklezjastik] [1] ADJ [*vie, charge*] ecclesiastical; [*revenus*] church (*épith*) → **habit** [2] NM ecclesiastic, clergyman

écervelé, e [esɛrvəle] [1] ADJ (= *étourdi*) scatterbrained, birdbrained [2] NM,F scatterbrain, birdbrain

échafaud [eʃafo] NM [a] (*pour l'exécution*) scaffold; **monter à l'~** to mount the scaffold; **finir sur l'~** to die on the scaffold; **tu finiras sur l'~†** you'll end up on the gallows; **il risque l'~** he's risking his neck [b]†† (= *estrade*) platform, stand

échafaudage [eʃafodaʒ] NM [a] (*Constr*) scaffolding (*NonC*); **ils ont mis un ~** they have put up scaffolding **b** (= *pile*) [*objets*] heap, pile **c** (= *élaboration*) [*fortune*] building up, amassing; [*théorie*] building up, construction; **l'~ financier de cette affaire** the financial framework of the deal

échafauder [eʃafode] ▸conjug 1◂ **1** VT **a** [+ *fortune*] to build (up), amass; [+ *projet*] to construct, build; [+ *théorie*] to construct, build up; **il a échafaudé toute une histoire pour ne pas venir** he made up *ou* fabricated a whole story so he wouldn't have to come **b** (= *empiler*) to pile up, stack up **2** VI (*Tech*) to put up *ou* erect scaffolding

échalas [eʃala] NM (= *perche*) stake, pole; (* = *personne*) beanpole*

échalier [eʃalje] NM (= *échelle*) stile; (= *clôture*) gate

échalote [eʃalɔt] NF shallot

échancré, e [eʃɑ̃kre] (*ptp de* **échancrer**) ADJ [*côte*] indented, jagged; [*feuille*] serrated, jagged; **robe ~e dans le dos** dress cut low in the back; **robe très ~e sur le devant** dress with a plunging neckline

échancrer [eʃɑ̃kre] ▸conjug 1◂ VT [+ *robe*] (*devant*) to cut (out) a neckline in; (*dans le dos*) to cut (out) the back of; [+ *manche*] to widen the top of, widen at the top

échancrure [eʃɑ̃kryr] NF [*robe*] neckline; [*côte*] indentation; [*feuille*] serration

▼**échange** [eʃɑ̃ʒ] **1** NM **a** (*gén, Échecs, Sci*) exchange (**avec** with); (= *troc*) swap, trade off (**entre** between); **~ de prisonniers** exchange of prisoners; **programme d'~ de seringues** needle *ou* syringe exchange scheme; **~ de vues** exchange of views; **~s de coups avec la police** scuffles with the police; **de vifs ~s entre des orateurs** heated exchanges between speakers; **c'est un ~ de bons procédés** it's an exchange of favours, one good turn deserves another; **~ standard** standard part replacement; (*Aut*) **faire l'~ standard d'un moteur** to replace an engine by a standard one **b** **faire (l')échange de qch** to swap *ou* exchange sth; **on a fait ~** we've done a swap *ou* an exchange; **ils ont fait (l')échange de leurs maisons** they've swapped houses; (*Échecs*) **faire ~** to exchange pieces **c** (= *relations*) exchange; **~ culturel** cultural exchange; **~ scolaire/universitaire** school/ university *ou* academic exchange **d** **en ~** (= *par contre*) on the other hand; (= *en guise de troc*) in exchange; (= *pour compenser*) to make up for it; **en ~ de** in exchange for, in return for **e** (*Tennis, Ping-Pong*) rally; **faire des ~s** to have a knock-up, knock up **2** NMPL (*Écon*) **~s (commerciaux)** trade, trading; **le volume des ~s** the volume of trade; **~s extérieurs/internationaux** foreign/international trade; (*Fin*) **dès les premiers ~s entre banques** as soon as trading between banks got under way

échangeabilité [eʃɑ̃ʒabilite] NF exchangeability

échangeable [eʃɑ̃ʒabl] ADJ exchangeable (**contre** for)

échanger [eʃɑ̃ʒe] ▸conjug 3◂ VT **a** (= *troquer*) to exchange, swap (**contre** for, **avec** with); (*Comm*) **« articles ni repris ni échangés »** "goods can neither be returned nor exchanged"; (*Bourse*) **le mark s'échangeait à 3,55 F** the mark was trading at 3.55 francs **b** [+ *idées, regards, lettres, coups*] to exchange; [+ *injures*] to trade, exchange; **ils ont échangé des remerciements** they thanked one another; (*Tennis, Ping-Pong*) **~ des balles** to have a knock-up, knock up

échangeur [eʃɑ̃ʒœr] NM **a** (*Aut* = *route*) interchange **b** (*Tech*) **~ (de chaleur** *ou* **thermique)** heat exchanger; (*Chim*) **~ d'ions** ion exchanger

▸ GRAMMAIRE ACTIVE: échange 44.1

échangisme [eʃɑ̃ʒism] NM (*gén*) partner-swapping; (*d'épouses*) wife-swapping

échangiste [eʃɑ̃ʒist] **1** ADJ [*club, soirée*] partner-swapping; **couples ~s** couples who engage in partner-swapping, swingers* **2** NMF partner-swapper, swinger*

échanson [eʃɑ̃sɔ̃] NM (*Hist*) cupbearer; (*hum*) wine waiter

échantillon [eʃɑ̃tijɔ̃] NM (*Stat, Ordin*) sample; [*parfum, crème*] (*pour tester*) tester; (*en cadeau*) sample; (*fig*) example; **~ de tissu** fabric sample, swatch (of material); **choisir un tissu sur ~** to choose a material from a sample *ou* swatch; (*Méd*) **~ de sang** blood sample *ou* specimen; **~ représentatif** [*personnes sondées*] cross-section, representative sample; **prendre** *ou* **prélever des ~s de** to take samples of, sample

échantillonnage [eʃɑ̃tijɔnaʒ] NM **a** (= *collection*) range *ou* selection of samples; **~ d'outils** selection of tools; **~ de tissus** swatch; **le festival représente un ~ intéressant du jeune cinéma français** the festival brings together an interesting cross-section of young French film directors **b** (*Stat, Ordin, Mus*) sampling; [*population*] sampling; **~ par couches** *ou* **par strates** stratified sampling; **~ au hasard** random sampling; **l'~ de la population a été fait de manière rigoureuse** the population samples were very carefully selected

échantillonner [eʃɑ̃tijɔne] ▸conjug 1◂ VT (*Stat, Ordin, Mus*) to sample; [+ *population à sonder*] to take a sample of

échappatoire [eʃapatwar] NF (= *faux-fuyant*) way out; **sa réponse n'était qu'une ~** his answer was just a way of evading the issue; **il nous faut trouver une ~** we need to find some way of getting out of this *ou* a way out; **il n'y a pas d'~ à la guerre** there's no way of avoiding war → **clause**

échappé, e [eʃape] (*ptp de* **échapper**) **1** NM,F **a** (*Sport*) breakaway; **les ~s** the breakaway group **b** (†† *ou hum*) **~ de l'asile** bedlamite† **2** **échappée** NF **a** (*Sport*) breakaway; **échappée solitaire** solo breakaway; **il ne faisait pas partie de l'échappée** he wasn't in the breakaway group; **faire une échappée de 100 km** to be ahead of the pack for 100 km **b** (= *vue*) vista; (= *rayon de soleil*) gleam **c** [*escalier*] headroom

échappement [eʃapmɑ̃] NM **a** (*Aut*) exhaust (system); **rouler en ~ libre** to drive without a silencer (*Brit*) *ou* a muffler (*US*); **soupape d'~** exhaust valve → **pot b** (*Horlogerie, Tech*) escapement **c** (*Ordin*) escape

échapper [eʃape] ▸conjug 1◂ **1** VI **a** **~ à** [+ *danger, destin, punition, mort*] to escape; [+ *poursuivants*] (*en fuyant*) to escape (from), get away from; (*par ruse*) to evade, elude; [+ *obligations, responsabilités*] to evade; [+ *corvée*] to get out of; [+ *ennuis*] to avoid; **~ aux recherches** to escape detection; (*Écon*) **~ à l'impôt** (*par privilège*) to be exempt from tax; (*illégalement*) to evade *ou* dodge* tax, avoid paying tax; **~ à la règle** to be an exception to the rule; **cela échappe à toute tentative de définition** it defies definition; **il échappe à tout contrôle** he is beyond (any) control; (*Jur*) **cela échappe à notre juridiction** it is outside *ou* beyond our jurisdiction; **tu ne m'échapperas pas !** (*lit*) you won't get away from me!; (*fig*) you won't get off as easily as that!, I'll get you yet!; (*fig*) **son fils lui échappe** (*gén*) her son is slipping from her clutches; (*en grandissant*) her son is growing away from her; **essaie d'~ pour quelques jours à ton travail** try and get away from work for a few days; **~ à la vue** *ou* **aux regards de qn** to escape sb's notice; (*hum*) **nous n'échapperons pas à une tasse de thé** we won't get away without having a cup of tea

b (*être oublié*) **~ à l'esprit de qn** to escape sb; **son nom m'échappe** his name escapes me *ou*

has slipped my mind; **ce détail m'avait échappé** this detail had escaped my attention, I had overlooked this detail; **ce détail ne lui a pas échappé** this detail was not lost on him; **ce qu'il a dit m'a échappé** (= *je n'ai pas entendu*) I didn't catch what he said; (= *je n'ai pas compris*) I didn't understand what he said; **ça a échappé à mon attention** it escaped my notice; **l'opportunité d'une telle mesure m'échappe** I can't see *ou* I fail to see the point of such a measure; **rien ne lui échappe** (= *il voit tout*) nothing escapes him, he doesn't miss a thing

c **~ des mains de qn** to slip out of *ou* slip from sb's hands; **~ des lèvres de qn** [*cri, parole*] to burst from sb's lips; **un cri de douleur lui échappa** he let out *ou* gave a cry of pain; **un gros mot lui a échappé** he let slip *ou* let out a swearword; **je ne voulais pas le dire mais ça m'a échappé** I didn't mean to say it but it just slipped out

d **il l'a échappé belle** he had a narrow escape, it was a close shave (for him)

e **laisser ~** [+ *gros mot*] to let out, let slip; [+ *cri*] to let out, give; [+ *objet*] to drop; [+ *secret*] to let out; [+ *occasion*] to let slip, let go; [+ *détail, faute*] to overlook; **laisser ~ un prisonnier** to let a prisoner escape *ou* get away

f **faire ~ un prisonnier** to help a prisoner (to) escape *ou* get out; **il a fait ~ l'oiseau** he let the bird out

2 **s'échapper** VPR **a** [*prisonnier*] to escape (**de** from), break out (**de** of); [*cheval*] to get out (**de** of); [*oiseau*] to fly away; [*cri*] to escape, burst (**de** from); **l'oiseau s'est échappé de la cage** the bird got out of *ou* escaped from the cage; **la voiture réussit à s'~ malgré la foule** the car got away in spite of the crowd; **je m'échappe un instant pour préparer le dîner** I'll slip away for a moment *ou* I must leave you for a moment to get dinner ready; **j'ai pu m'~ du bureau de bonne heure** I managed to get away *ou* slip out early from the office; (*Sport*) **le coureur s'est échappé dans la côte** the runner drew ahead *ou* pulled away on the uphill stretch

b [*gaz*] to escape, leak; [*odeur, lumière*] to come, issue (*littér*) (**de** from); **de la fumée s'échappait de la cheminée** smoke was coming from *ou* out of the chimney; **l'eau s'est échappée de la casserole** the water boiled over; **des flammes s'échappaient du toit** flames were coming out of the roof

écharde [eʃard] NF splinter

écharpe [eʃarp] NF (= *cache-nez*) scarf; (= *bandage*) sling; [*maire*] sash; **porter** *ou* **avoir le bras en ~** to have one's arm in a sling; **prendre une voiture en ~** to hit a car broadside *ou* sideways on (*Brit*)

écharper [eʃarpe] ▸conjug 1◂ VT (*lit, fig*) to tear to pieces; **se faire ~** to be torn to pieces

échasse [eʃas] NF (= *objet, oiseau*) stilt; **marcher avec des ~s** to walk on stilts; (*hum*) **être monté sur des ~s** to have long legs

échassier [eʃasje] NM wading bird, wader (*Brit*)

échauder [eʃode] ▸conjug 1◂ VT **a** (= *faire réfléchir*) **~ qn** to teach sb a lesson; **se faire ~** to burn one's fingers, get one's fingers burnt → **chat b** (= *laver à l'eau chaude*) to wash in hot water; (= *ébouillanter*) to scald; [+ *théière*] to warm

échauffant, e† [eʃofɑ̃, ɑ̃t] ADJ (= *constipant*) constipating

échauffement [eʃofmɑ̃] NM **a** (*Sport*) warm-up; **exercices/séance d'~** warm-up exercises/session **b** [*terre*] heating; [*moteur*] overheating **c**† (= *constipation*) constipation; (= *inflammation*) inflammation; [*sang*] overheating

échauffer [eʃofe] ▸conjug 1◂ **1** VT **a** [+ *moteur, machine*] to overheat; **il était échauffé par la course** ◊ **la course l'avait échauffé** he was hot after the race [b] [+ *imagination*] to fire, excite; **cette remarque a échauffé le débat** this remark made for a heated discussion; **après une heure de discussion les esprits étaient très échauffés** after arguing for an hour people were getting very heated *ou* worked up*; **tu commences à m'~* (les oreilles** *ou* **la bile**†) you're getting on my nerves *ou* wick* (*Brit*) [c]† (*Méd*) **~ la peau** to inflame the skin; **je suis un peu échauffé** I'm a bit constipated [2] **s'échauffer** VPR [a] (*Sport*) warm up [b] (= *s'animer*) [*personne*] to become heated, get worked up*; [*conversation*] to become heated

échauffourée [eʃofuʀe] NF (*avec la police*) brawl, clash; (*Mil*) skirmish

échauguette [eʃoɡɛt] NF bartizan, watchtower

èche [ɛʃ] NF (*Pêche*) bait

échéance [eʃeɑ̃s] NF [a] (= *date limite*) [*délai*] expiration *ou* expiry (*Brit*) date; [*bon, action*] maturity date; [*traite, emprunt*] redemption date; [*loyer*] date of payment; [*facture, dette*] due date, settlement date; (*Bourse*) settling day; **~s politiques** elections; (*Jur, Fin, Comm*) **payable à l'~** payable when due; **venir à ~** to fall due [b] (= *règlements à effectuer*) **l'~ de fin de mois** the end-of-month payments; **faire face à ses ~s** to meet one's financial obligations *ou* commitments; **avoir de lourdes ~s** to be heavily committed, have heavy financial commitments [c] (= *laps de temps*) term; **à longue ~** in the long run *ou* term; **à courte ou brève ~** before long; **à plus ou moins brève** *ou* **longue ~** sooner or later; **à longue/courte ~** [*traite*] long-/short-term (*épith*); [*bon*] long-/short-dated

échéancier [eʃeɑ̃sje] NM [*effets*] billbook; [*emprunt*] schedule of repayments; [*travaux*] schedule

échéant [eʃeɑ̃, ɑ̃t] ADJ M→ **cas**

échec¹ [eʃɛk] NM [a] (= *insuccès*) failure; (= *défaite*) defeat; (= *revers*) setback; **subir un ~** (*gén*) to suffer a setback; (*Mil*) to suffer a defeat; **son troisième ~ dans une élection** his third defeat in an election; **l'~ des pourparlers** the breakdown in *ou* the failure of the talks; **après l'~ des négociations** after negotiations broke down; **sa tentative s'est soldée par un ~** his attempt has failed *ou* has ended in failure; **voué à l'~** bound to fail, doomed to failure; (*Psych*) **avoir une conduite d'~** to be self-defeating; **être/mettre qn en situation** *ou* **position d'~** to be in/put sb in a hopeless *ou* no-win situation; **l'~ scolaire** academic failure; **jeunes en situation d'~ scolaire** young people who have failed in their school career [b] (*loc*) **tenir qn en ~** to hold sb in check; **faire ~ à qn** to foil *ou* frustrate *ou* thwart sb

échec² [eʃɛk] NM (*Jeux*) **les ~s** chess; **jeu d'~s** (= *échiquier*) chessboard; (= *pièces*) chessmen; **jouer aux ~s** to play chess; **mettre/être en ~** to put/be in check; **faire ~ au roi** to put the king in check; **~ au roi!** check!; **~ et mat** checkmate; **faire ~ et mat** to checkmate

échelle [eʃɛl] [1] NF [a] (= *objet*) ladder; (= *appui*) **courte ~** leg up, boost (*US*); **faire la courte ~ à qn** to give sb a leg up *ou* a boost (*US*); **la grande ~ (des pompiers)** the (firemen's) turntable ladder; (*fig*) **faire grimper** *ou* **monter qn à l'~** to pull sb's leg*, have sb on* (*Brit*); **il a grimpé à** *ou* **est monté à l'~*** he fell for it, he was taken in (by it); (*hum*) **il n'y a plus qu'à tirer l'~** we may as well give it up; **après lui, il n'y a plus qu'à tirer l'~** nobody can hold a candle to him, he's the best by a long shot [b] (= *dimension*) scale; **à l'~ (de) 1/100 000** on a scale of 1 to 100,000; **croquis à l'~** scale drawing; **le dessin est/n'est pas à l'~** the drawing is/is not to scale; **carte à grande/petite ~** large-/small-scale map; **sur une grande ~** on a large scale; **à l'~ nationale/**

mondiale on a national/world(wide) scale; **un monde à l'~ de l'homme** a world on a human scale; **à l'~ de la firme** (*et non d'une seule usine*) at the level of the firm as a whole; (*en rapport avec son importance*) in proportion to the firm's size (*ou* requirements *etc*) [c] [*bas, collant*] run, ladder (*Brit*) [d] (*dans les cheveux*) **faire des ~s à qn** to cut sb's hair all unevenly [e] (= *gradation, Mus*) scale; (= *hiérarchie*) ladder, scale; **être au sommet de l'~** [*poste*] to be at the top of the ladder; [*salaire*] to be at the top of the scale

[2] COMP ► **les échelles de Barbarie** the Ports of the Barbary Coast ► **échelle de Beaufort** Beaufort scale ► **échelle chromatique** (*Mus*) chromatic scale ► **échelle de corde** rope ladder ► **échelle coulissante** extending *ou* extension ladder ► **échelle de coupée** accommodation ladder ► **échelle d'incendie** fire escape ► **échelle double** high stepladder ► **échelle de gravité** [*accidents nucléaires*] international nuclear event scale ► **l'échelle de Jacob** (*Bible*) Jacob's ladder ► **les échelles du Levant** the Ports of the Levant ► **échelle de meunier** (wooden) step ladder ► **échelle mobile** [*pompier*] extending ladder; (*Écon*) sliding scale ► **échelle de Richter** Richter scale ► **échelle des salaires** salary scale ► **échelle à saumons** salmon ladder ► **échelle sociale** social scale *ou* ladder ► **échelle des traitements** = **échelle des salaires** ► **échelle des valeurs** scale of values

échelon [eʃ(ə)lɔ̃] NM [a] [*échelle*] rung; [*hiérarchie*] step, grade; (*Admin*) **fonctionnaire au 8ème ~** official on grade 8 of the salary scale); (*Admin*) **être au dernier/premier ~** to be on the highest *ou* top/on the lowest *ou* bottom grade; **monter d'un ~ dans la hiérarchie** to go up one step *ou* grade *ou* rung in the hierarchy; **grimper rapidement les ~s** to climb the career ladder quickly, get quick promotion [b] (= *niveau*) level; **à l'~ national** at the national level; (*lit, fig*) **à tous les ~s** at every level [c] (*Mil* = *troupe*) echelon

échelonnement [eʃ(ə)lɔnmɑ̃] NM [a] [*objets*] spacing out, spreading out [b] [*paiements*] spreading (**sur** over); [*congés, vacances*] staggering (**sur** over) [c] [*exercices*] (*dans la complexité*) grading; (*dans le temps*) gradual introduction

échelonner [eʃ(ə)lɔne] ▸ conjug 1 ◂ VT [a] [+ *objets*] to space out, spread out, place at intervals (**sur** over); **les bouées sont échelonnées à 50 mètres l'une de l'autre** the buoys are spaced *ou* placed 50 metres apart; **les membres du service d'ordre sont échelonnés tout au long du parcours** the police are positioned *ou* stationed at intervals all along the route; **les bâtiments s'échelonnent sur 3 km** the buildings are spaced out over 3 km [b] [+ *paiements*] to spread (out) (**sur** over); [+ *congés, vacances*] to stagger (**sur** over) [c] [+ *exercices, difficultés*] (*dans la complexité*) to grade; (*dans le temps*) to introduce gradually [d] (*Mil*) to place in echelon, echelon

échenilloir [eʃ(ə)nijwaʀ] NM billhook, pruning hook

écheveau (*pl* **écheveaux**) [eʃ(ə)vo] NM skein, hank; (*fig*) tangle, web

échevelé, e [eʃəv(ə)le] (*ptp de* **écheveler**) ADJ [*course, danse, rythme*] wild, frenzied; **il était tout ~** his hair was tousled *ou* dishevelled

écheveler [eʃəv(ə)le] ▸ conjug 4 ◂ VT (*littér*) [+ *personne*] to ruffle *ou* tousle *ou* dishevel the hair of

échevin [eʃ(ə)vɛ̃] NM (*Hist*) alderman, principal county magistrate; (*en Belgique*) deputy burgomaster; (*au Canada*) municipal councillor, alderman

échiffer* [eʃife] ▸ conjug 1 ◂ VT (*Can*) to tease, unravel

échine [eʃin] NF [a] (*Anat*) backbone, spine; (*Culin*) loin, chine; **côte de porc dans l'~** pork loin chop; (*fig*) **il a l'~ souple** he kowtows to his superiors, he's a bit of a doormat; **plier** *ou* **courber l'~** to submit (**devant** to) [b] (*Archit*) echinus

échiner (s') [eʃine] ▸ conjug 1 ◂ VPR (= *travailler dur*) to work o.s. to death *ou* into the ground (**à faire qch** doing sth); **s'~ à répéter/écrire qch** to wear o.s. out repeating/writing sth

échiquier [eʃikje] NM (*Échecs*) chessboard; **l'~ politique/économique** the political/economic scene; **notre place sur l'~ mondial** our place in the field *ou* on the scene of world affairs; **en ~** in a chequered pattern; (*Pol Brit*) **l'Échiquier** the Exchequer

écho [eko] NM [a] (*lit*) echo; **~ simple** echo; **~ multiple** multiple echo; **il y a de l'~** (*lit, fig*) there's an echo; **« toujours », répondit-il en ~** "always", he echoed [b] (= *rumeur*) rumour, echo; (= *témoignage*) account, report; (= *réponse*) response; **avez-vous eu des ~s de la réunion?** did you get any inkling of what went on at the meeting?, did anything come back to you from the meeting?; **se faire l'~ de** [+ *souhaits, opinions, inquiétudes*] to echo, repeat; [+ *rumeurs*] to repeat, spread; **sa proposition est restée sans ~** his suggestion wasn't taken up, nothing further came of his suggestion; **l'~ donné par les médias à cette nouvelle** the coverage *ou* publicity given to this news item by the media; **cette nouvelle n'a eu aucun ~ dans la presse** this item got no coverage *ou* was not mentioned in the press; **trouver un ~ (chez)** to find an echo (among) [c] (*Presse* = *nouvelle*) miscellaneous news item, item of gossip; (**rubrique des**) **~s** gossip column

échographie [ekɔɡʀafi] NF (= *technique*) ultrasound; (= *examen*) ultrasound (scan), echography, sonogram (*US*); **passer une ~** to have an ultrasound (scan) *ou* an echography *ou* a sonogram (*US*)

échographier [ekɔɡʀafje] ▸ conjug 1 ◂ VT **~ qn** to give sb an ultrasound (scan)

échographique [ekɔɡʀafik] ADJ [*étude, compte rendu*] ultrasound (*épith*), ultrasonographic; **guidage ~** ultrasound guidance

échoir [eʃwaʀ] VI [a] (*littér*) **~ (en partage) à qn** to fall to sb's share *ou* lot; **il vous échoit de ...** it falls to you to ... [b] [*loyer, dettes*] to fall due; [*délai*] to expire

échoppe† [eʃɔp] NF (= *boutique*) workshop; (*sur un marché*) stall, booth

échotier, -ière [ekɔtje, jɛʀ] NM,F gossip columnist

échouage [eʃwaʒ], **échouement** [eʃumɑ̃] NM (*Naut*) (= *état*) state of being aground; (= *action*) grounding, running aground

échouer [eʃwe] ▸ conjug 1 ◂ [1] VI [a] [*personne*] to fail; **~ à un examen/dans une tentative** to fail an exam/in an attempt [b] [*tentative*] to fail; [*plan*] to fail, fall through [c] **faire ~** [+ *complot*] to foil; [+ *projet*] to wreck, ruin; **faire ~ les plans de l'ennemi** to foil the enemy's plans, thwart the enemy in his plans; **on a fait ~ leur tentative** they were foiled in their attempt [d] (= *aboutir*) to end up; **nous avons échoué dans un petit hôtel** we ended up *ou* landed up in a small hotel [e] (*Naut*) [*bateau*] to run aground; [*débris d'épave*] to be washed up; [*baleine*] to be beached; **le bateau s'est échoué** *ou* **a échoué sur un écueil** the boat ran onto a reef; **le bateau s'est échoué** *ou* **a échoué sur un banc de sable** the boat ran aground on *ou* ran onto a sandbank; **bateau échoué** boat lying high and dry

2 VT (*Naut*) (*accidentellement*) to ground; (*volontairement*) to beach; **il a échoué sa barque sur un écueil** he ran his boat onto a reef

3 **s'échouer** VPR → **1e**

échu, e [efy] (*ptp de* **échoir**) ADJ (*Fin*) due, outstanding; **intérêts ~s** outstanding interest; **billets ~s** bills overdue; **obligations ~es** matured bonds; **effet non ~** unmatured bill; **à terme ~** at the expiry date, when the fixed period has expired; **les loyers sont versés à terme ~** rents are paid at the end of each rental period

écimer [esime] ▸conjug 1◂ VT [+ *arbre*] to pollard, poll

éclaboussement [eklabusmã] NM splash

éclabousser [eklabuse] ▸conjug 1◂ VT to splash, spatter; **~ de sang** to spatter with blood; **ils ont été éclaboussés par le scandale** their name has been smeared *ou* sullied *ou* tarnished by the scandal; **~ qn de son luxe** (*éblouir*) to dazzle sb with a show of wealth; (*humilier*) to overwhelm sb with a show of wealth

éclaboussure [eklabusyʀ] NF [*boue*] splash; [*sang*] spatter; (*sur la réputation*) stain, smear, blot; **il y a des ~s sur la glace** there are smears *ou* spots on the mirror

éclair [eklɛʀ] **1** NM **a** (*Mét*) flash of lightning; (*Photo*) flash; **il y a des ~s** there's lightning, there are flashes of lightning; **~s de chaleur** summer lightning; **~ de magnésium** magnesium flash

b [*intelligence, génie*] flash, spark; **~ de malice** mischievous glint; **dans un ~ de lucidité** in a moment *ou* flash of lucidity; **ses yeux lançaient des ~s (de colère)** her eyes blazed with anger

c (*loc*) **comme un ~** like a flash, like greased lightning*; **passer comme un ~** [*coureur*] to dart *ou* flash past *ou* by; [*moment*] to fly *ou* flash past *ou* by; **en un ~** in a flash, in a split second → **rapide**

d (*Culin*) éclair

2 ADJ INV [*attaque, victoire*] lightning (*épith*); [*visite*] lightning (*épith*), flying (*épith*); [*Échecs, partie*] lightning (*épith*); **voyage ~** flying visit; **raid ~** (*Aviat*) blitz raid; (*Mil*) hit-and-run raid; **son passage ~ au pouvoir** his brief spell in power → **fermeture, guerre**

éclairage [eklɛʀaʒ] NM **a** (*artificiel*) lighting; (= *niveau de luminosité*) light (level); **sous cet ~** in this light; **à l'électricité** electric lighting; **~ au néon** neon lighting; **~ direct/indirect/ d'ambiance** direct/indirect *ou* concealed/ subdued lighting; **l'~ est insuffisant pour faire une bonne photo** there isn't enough light to take a good photograph; (*Théât, Ciné*) **les ~s** (= *projecteurs*) the lights; (= *effets de lumière*) the lighting effects; (*Art*) **l'~ ou les ~s du Tintoret** Tintoretto's use of light

b (= *action d'éclairer*) lighting; **l'~ public ou des rues** street lighting

c (= *point de vue*) light; **sous cet ~** in this light; **donner ou apporter un nouvel ~ à qch** to shed *ou* cast new light on sth; **apporter un ~ intéressant/différent sur qch** to give an interesting/different perspective to sth; **ces informations apportent un premier ~ sur ce qui s'est passé** this information provides us with a first indication of what happened

éclairagiste [eklɛʀaʒist] NMF (*Théât*) electrician; (*Ciné*) lighting engineer

éclairant, e [eklɛʀã, ãt] ADJ (*lit*) [*pouvoir, propriétés*] lighting (*épith*); (*fig*) illuminating, enlightening → **fusée**

éclaircie [eklɛʀsi] NF **a** (*Mét*) bright interval, sunny spell; **b** (*dans la vie*) bright spot *ou* interval; (*dans une situation*) upturn, upswing **c** [*arbres*] thinning

éclaircir [eklɛʀsiʀ] ▸conjug 2◂ **1** VT **a** [+ *teinte*] to lighten; [+ *pièce*] to brighten up,

---

make brighter; **cela éclaircit le teint** it brightens the complexion **b** (= *désépaissir*) [+ *soupe*] to make thinner, thin (down); [+ *plantes*] to thin (out); [+ *arbres, cheveux*] to thin **c** [+ *mystère*] to clear up, solve; [+ *question, pensée, situation*] to clarify, make clear; [+ *meurtre*] to solve; **pouvez-vous nous ~ sur ce point ?** can you enlighten us on this point?

2 **s'éclaircir** VPR **a** [*ciel*] to clear; [*temps*] to clear up; **s'~ la voix ou la gorge** to clear one's throat **b** [*arbres, foule*] to thin out; [*cheveux*] to thin, get *ou* grow thin *ou* thinner; **les rangs de leurs alliés se sont éclaircis** their allies are getting thin on the ground **c** [*idées, situation*] to grow *ou* become clearer; [*mystère*] to be solved *ou* explained

éclaircissant, e [eklɛʀsisã, ãt] ADJ **shampooing ~** shampoo for lightening the hair

éclaircissement [eklɛʀsismã] NM **a** [*mystère*] solving, clearing up; [*texte obscur*] clarification; (= *explication*) explanation; **j'exige des ~s sur votre attitude** I demand some explanation of your attitude; (*Jur*) **demande d'~** request for clarification **b** [*cheveux*] **se faire faire un ~** to have one's hair lightened

éclairé, e [eklɛʀe] (*ptp de* **éclairer**) ADJ [*public, minorité, avis, despote*] enlightened

éclairement [eklɛʀmã] NM (*Phys*) illumination

éclairer [eklɛʀe] ▸conjug 1◂ **1** VT **a** [*lampe*] to light (up); [*soleil*] to shine (down) on; **une seule fenêtre était éclairée** there was a light in only one window, only one window was lit up; **café éclairé au néon** café with neon lights; **une grande baie éclairait l'entrée** a large bay window brought light into the hall; **ce papier peint éclaire le couloir** this wallpaper makes the passage look lighter *ou* brighter; (*littér*) **deux grands yeux éclairaient son visage** her large eyes seemed to light up her face; **un sourire éclaira son visage** a smile lit up his face; **bien/mal éclairé** well-/badly-lit **b** [+ *problème, situation*] to throw *ou* shed light on, clarify; [+ *auteur, texte*] to throw light on; **~ qch d'un jour nouveau** to shed *ou* cast new light on sth **c** **~ qn** (= *montrer le chemin*) to light the way for sb; (= *renseigner*) to enlighten sb (*sur* about); **~ la lanterne de qn** to put sb in the picture* **d** (*Mil*) **~ le terrain** to reconnoitre (*Brit*) *ou* reconnoiter (*US*) the area, scout the area; **~ un régiment** to reconnoitre (*Brit*) *ou* reconnoiter (*US*) for a regiment; **~ la route** (*Mil*) to scout out the route

2 VI **bien/mal** to give a good/poor light

3 **s'éclairer** VPR **a** [*rue*] to be lit; [*visage*] to light up, brighten (up) **b** [*situation*] to get clearer; **tout s'éclaire !** it's all becoming clear! **c** **s'~ à l'électricité** to have electric light; **s'~ à la bougie** to use candlelight; **prends une lampe pour t'~** take a lamp to light the way

éclaireur [eklɛʀœʀ] NM (*Mil*) scout; **avion ~** reconnaissance plane; **partir en ~** (*lit*) to go and scout around; (*fig*) to go on ahead **b** (*Scoutisme*) (boy) scout

éclaireuse [eklɛʀøz] NF (girl) guide (*Brit*), girl scout (*US*)

éclat [ekla] NM **a** [*os, verre*] splinter, fragment; [*bois*] splinter, sliver; [*grenade, pierre*] fragment; **~ d'obus** piece of shrapnel; **des ~s d'obus** shrapnel → **voler***

b [*lumière, métal, soleil*] brightness, brilliance; (*aveuglant*) glare; [*diamant, pierreries*] flash, brilliance, sparkle; [*couleur*] brightness, vividness; [*braise*] glow; [*vernis*] shine, gloss; [*satin, bronze*] sheen; [*perle*] lustre; (*Aut*) **l'~ des phares** the glare of the headlights; (*Théât*) **l'~ (des lumières) de la rampe** the blaze *ou* glare of the footlights

c [*yeux*] brightness, sparkle; [*teint, beauté*] ra-

---

diance; **dans tout l'~ de sa jeunesse** in the full radiance *ou* bloom of her youth; **perdre son ~** [*personne*] to lose one's sparkle; **pour retrouver l'~ de votre sourire** to put the sparkle back into your smile

d [*cérémonie*] glamour (*Brit*), glamor (*US*), splendour (*Brit*), splendor (*US*); [*nom*] fame; [*richesse, époque*] brilliance, glamour (*Brit*), glamor (*US*); [*personnage*] glamour (*Brit*), glamor (*US*); **donner de l'~ à qch** to lend glamour to sth; **réception donnée avec ~** sumptuous *ou* dazzling reception; **ça s'est déroulé sans ~** it passed off quietly *ou* without fuss; [*personnalité, interprétation*] **sans ~** lacklustre (*Brit*), lackluster (*US*); (= *exploit*) **coup ou action d'~** (glorious) feat

e (= *scandale*) fuss (*NonC*), commotion (*NonC*); **faire un ~ ou un coup d'~** to make *ou* cause a fuss, create a commotion

f (= *bruit*) **~s de voix** shouts; **sans ~ de voix** without voices being raised; **avec un soudain ~ de colère** in a sudden blaze of anger; **~ de rire** roar *ou* burst of laughter; **on l'accueillit avec des ~s de rire** his arrival was greeted with roars *ou* shouts of laughter; **« oui », dit-il dans un ~ de rire** "yes", he said with a peal of laughter

éclatant, e [eklatã, ãt] ADJ **a** [*lumière*] bright, brilliant; (= *aveuglant*) glaring; [*couleur*] bright, vivid; [*feu, soleil*] blazing; [*blancheur*] dazzling **b** [*teint*] blooming, radiant; [*beauté*] radiant, dazzling; [*sourire*] sparkling, dazzling; **~ de santé** radiant with health **c** [*succès*] dazzling, resounding; [*revanche*] shattering, devastating; [*victoire*] resounding; [*gloire*] shining; [*vérité*] manifest, self-evident; [*exemple*] striking, shining; [*mensonge*] blatant **d** [*rire, bruit*] loud; [*voix*] loud, ringing; [*musique*] blaring (*péj*), loud **e** [*fête, musique*] super, fab* (*Brit*)

éclaté, e [eklate] **1** ADJ [*initiatives, marché*] fragmented; [*paysage politique*] confused, fragmented **2** NM exploded view

éclatement [eklatmã] NM [*bombe, mine*] explosion; [*obus*] bursting, explosion; [*pneu, ballon*] bursting; [*veine*] rupture (*de* of); [*parti*] break-up, split (*de* in); **à cause de l'~ d'un pneu** as a result of a burst tyre; **l'~ d'une bombe/d'un obus le couvrit de terre** an exploding bomb/shell covered him with earth

éclater [eklate] ▸conjug 1◂ **1** VI **a** [*mine, bombe*] to explode, blow up; [*obus*] to burst, explode; [*veine*] to rupture; [*bourgeon*] to burst open; [*pneu, chaudière*] to burst; [*verre*] to splinter, shatter; [*parti, ville, services, structures familiales*] to break up; **j'ai cru que ma tête allait ~** I thought my head was going to burst **b** [*incendie, épidémie, guerre*] to break out; [*orage, scandale, nouvelle*] to break; **la nouvelle a éclaté comme un coup de tonnerre** the news came as *ou* was a bolt from the blue, the news was a real bombshell **c** (= *retentir*) **des cris ont éclaté** shouts were raised; **une détonation éclata** there was an explosion; **une fanfare éclata** there was a sudden flourish of trumpets; **un coup de fusil a éclaté** there was the crack of a rifle; **un coup de tonnerre éclata** there was a sudden peal of thunder; **des rires/des applaudissements ont éclaté** there was a roar of laughter/a burst of applause, laughter/applause broke out **d** (= *se manifester*) [*vérité, bonne foi*] to shine out, shine forth (*littér*); [*mauvaise foi*] to be blatant; **sa joie ou la joie éclate dans ses yeux/sur son visage** his eyes are/face is shining with joy **e** **~ de rire** to burst out laughing; **il éclata (de rage)** he exploded (with rage); **~ en menaces ou en reproches** to inveigh (*contre* against), rail (*contre* at, against); **~ en sanglots** to burst into tears; **nous avons éclaté en protestations devant sa décision** we protested angrily at his decision **f** **faire ~** [+ *mine*] to detonate, blow up; [+

bombe, obus] to explode; [+ *poudrière*] to blow up; [+ *pétard*] to let *ou* set off; [+ *ballon*] to burst; [+ *tuyau*] to burst, crack; [+ *verre*] to shatter, splinter; **cette remarque l'a fait ~ (de colère)** he exploded at this remark; **faire** *ou* **laisser ~ sa joie** to give free rein to one's joy; **faire** *ou* **laisser ~ sa colère** to give vent *ou* give free rein to one's anger

2 VT* (= *frapper*) **je vais l'~** ◊ **je vais lui ~ la tête** I'm going to smash his face in‡

3 **s'éclater** VPR (= *se défouler*) to have a ball*; **s'~ à faire** *ou* **en faisant qch** to get one's kicks* doing sth

éclateur [eklatœʀ] NM (*Élec*) spark gap

éclectique [eklɛktik] ADJ eclectic

éclectisme [eklɛktism] NM eclecticism

éclipse [eklips] NF (*Astron, fig*) eclipse; **~ partielle/totale (de soleil/lune)** partial/total eclipse (of the sun/moon); **~ annulaire** annular eclipse; **carrière à ~s** career with ups and downs; **personnalité à ~s** public figure who comes and goes, figure who is in and out of the public eye

éclipser [eklipse] ▸conjug 1 ◂ **1** VT (*Astron*) to eclipse; [*événement, gloire*] to eclipse, overshadow; [*personne*] to eclipse, overshadow, outshine **2** **s'éclipser** VPR [*personne*] to slip away, slip out

écliptique [ekliptik] ADJ, NM ecliptic

éclisse [eklis] NF (*Méd*) splint; (*Rail*) fishplate; [*violon*] rib; (*à fromage*) wicker tray

éclisser [eklise] ▸conjug 1 ◂ VT (*Méd*) to splint, put in splints; (*Rail*) to join with fishplates

éclopé, e [eklɔpe] **1** ADJ [*personne*] limping, lame; [*cheval*] lame **2** NM,F (*hum*) (*dans une bagarre*) (slightly) wounded person; (*dans un accident*) (slightly) injured person

éclore [eklɔʀ] ▸conjug 45 ◂ VI **a** [*œuf*] to hatch; [*poussin, larve*] to hatch (out); **faire ~** [+ *œuf*] to hatch **b** [*plan, idée*] to take form; [*association, secte*] to appear **c** [*fleur*] to open; [*littér*] [*amour, talent, jour*] to be born; **fleur à peine éclose/fraîche éclose** budding/fresh-blown flower; **faire ~** [+ *sentiment*] to kindle; [+ *qualités*] to draw forth

éclosion [eklozjɔ̃] NF **a** [*œuf, poussin, larve*] hatching **b** [*idée*] forming; [*association, secte*] appearance **c** [*fleur*] opening; (*littér*) [*amour, talent, jour*] birth, dawn

écluse [eklyz] NF (*Naut*) lock; **porte d'~** lock gate; (*fig*) **lâcher** *ou* **ouvrir les ~s*** to turn on the waterworks*

éclusée [eklyze] NF sluice (*amount of water contained in a lock*)

écluser [eklyze] ▸conjug 1 ◂ VT **a**‡ (= *boire*) to down*, knock back‡; **qu'est-ce qu'il a éclusé !** he really knocked it back!‡ **b** (*Tech*) [+ *canal*] to lock, sluice; [+ *bateau*] to lock

éclusier, -ière [eklyzje, jɛʀ] NM,F lock keeper

écobilan [ekobilɑ̃] NM life-cycle analysis

écodéveloppement [ekodevlɔpmɑ̃] NM ecodevelopment

écœurant, e [ekœʀɑ̃, ɑ̃t] ADJ [*conduite*] disgusting, sickening; [*personne*] loathsome; [*gâteau, boisson*] sickly (sweet); [*goût*] sickly, cloying; [*richesse*] obscene; [*talent, succès*] sickening; **elle a une chance ~e** she is so lucky it makes you sick *ou* it's sickening

écœurement [ekœʀmɑ̃] NM (= *dégoût*) (*lit*) nausea; (*fig*) disgust; (= *lassitude*) disillusionment, discouragement; **manger/boire jusqu'à ~** to eat/drink o.s. sick; **manger de la crème jusqu'à ~** to eat cream until one feels sick

écœurer [ekœʀe] ▸conjug 1 ◂ VT **~ qn** [*gâteau, boisson*] to make sb feel sick; [*conduite, personne*] to disgust sb, nauseate sb, make sb sick; [*avantage, chance*] to make sb sick, sicken sb; [*échec, déception*] to discourage sb, sicken sb

éco-industrie (*pl* **éco-industries**) [ekoɛ̃dystʀi] NF green-technology industry

école [ekɔl] **1** NF **a** (= *établissement*) school; **avion-/navire-~** training plane/ship; **ferme-~** teaching farm; **l'~ reprend dans une semaine** school starts again in a week's time; **aller à l'~** [*élève*] to go to school; [*visiteur*] to go to the school; **envoyer** *ou* **mettre un enfant à l'~** to send a child to school; **grande ~** (*Univ*) prestigious higher education institute with competitive entrance examination; (*école primaire*) **il va/est à la grande ~** he is at primary school **b** (= *enseignement*) schooling; (= *système scolaire*) school system; **l'~ gratuite** free education; **l'~ en France** the French school system; **les partisans de l'~ laïque** the supporters of secular state education; **elle fait l'~ depuis 15 ans**†† she's been teaching for 15 years **c** (*Art, Philo*) school; **un tableau/peintre de l'~ florentine** a painting/painter of the Florentine School; **querelle d'~s** petty quarrel between factions; **son œuvre est une ~ de courage/de vertu** his work presents us with an inspiring model of courage/virtue; **la lexicographie est une ~ de rigueur** you learn to be very rigorous when doing lexicography **d** (*loc*) **être à bonne ~** to be in good hands; **il a été à dure** *ou* **rude ~** he learned about life the hard way; **à l'~ de qn** under sb's guidance; **apprendre la vie à l'~ de la pauvreté** to be schooled by poverty; **faire l'~ buissonnière** to play truant (*Brit*) *ou* hooky (*US*); **faire ~** [*personne*] to acquire a following; [*théorie*] to gain widespread acceptance; **il est de la vieille ~** he belongs to *ou* is one of the old school

2 COMP ▸ **école de l'air** flying school ▸ **école d'application** (*Mil*) officers' training school ▸ **école des Beaux-Arts** ≈ art college ▸ **École centrale (des arts et manufactures)** prestigious college of engineering ▸ **école de commerce** business school; **elle a fait une ~ de commerce** she went to business school ▸ **école de conduite** driving school ▸ **école de danse** (*gén*) dancing school; (*classique*) ballet school ▸ **école de dessin** art school ▸ **école élémentaire** elementary school ▸ **école hôtelière** catering school, hotel management school ▸ **école libre** sectarian *ou* denominational school ▸ **école militaire** military academy ▸ **École nationale d'administration** prestigious college training senior civil servants ▸ **École nationale supérieure de chimie** national college of chemical engineering ▸ **École nationale supérieure d'ingénieurs** national college of engineering ▸ **école de neige** ski school ▸ **École normale** ≈ teacher training college ▸ **École normale supérieure** grande école for training of teachers ▸ **école de pensée** school of thought ▸ **école de police** police academy ▸ **école de secrétariat** secretarial college → **haut** ; → GRANDES ÉCOLES

ÉCOLE NATIONALE D'ADMINISTRATION

The "École nationale d'administration" or "ÉNA", in Strasbourg (formerly in Paris), is a competitive-entrance college training top civil servants such as diplomats, "préfets" and "inspecteurs des finances". Because so many ministers and high-ranking decision-makers are "énarques" (ex-students of ÉNA), the school has often been criticized for exercising too much influence, and French political life is perceived by some as being monopolised by the so-called "énarchie". → CONCOURS

écolier [ekɔlje] NM schoolboy; †† scholar†; (= *novice*) novice; **papier (format) ~** exercise (book) paper → **chemin**

écolière [ekɔljɛʀ] NF schoolgirl

écolo* [ekɔlo] **1** ADJ (ABRÉV = **écologique, écologiste**) **il est très ~** he's very ecology-minded, he's an eco-freak* **2** NMF (ABRÉV = **écologiste**) ecologist

écologie [ekɔlɔʒi] NF ecology

écologique [ekɔlɔʒik] ADJ **a** [*catastrophe*] ecological, environmental; [*équilibre*] ecological **b** [*produit*] eco-friendly, environmentally friendly **c** (*Pol*) [*association*] ecological, environmentalist; [*discours, politique*] on ecological issues; [*conscience, préoccupation*] ecological; **mouvement ~** ecological *ou* ecology *ou* green movement, ecomovement; **la cause ~** the green cause

écologisme [ekɔlɔʒism] NM environmentalism

écologiste [ekɔlɔʒist] **1** ADJ [*candidat*] green (*épith*), ecological (*épith*), ecologist (*épith*); [*vote*] green (*épith*); [*action, idée*] green (*épith*), ecologist (*épith*), ecology (*épith*); **militant ~** green *ou* ecology activist; **mouvement ~** ecological *ou* ecology *ou* green movement, ecomovement **2** NMF (= *spécialiste d'écologie*) ecologist, environmentalist; (*Pol*) ecologist; (= *partisan*) environmentalist

écologue [ekɔlɔg] NMF ecology expert; **ingénieur ~** ecological engineer

écomusée [ekomyze] NM eco-museum

éconduire [ekɔ̃dɥiʀ] ▸conjug 38 ◂ VT [+ *visiteur*] to dismiss; [+ *soupirant*] to reject; [+ *solliciteur*] to turn away

éconocroques‡ [ekonokʀɔk] NFPL savings

économat [ekonoma] NM (= *fonction*) bursarship, stewardship; (= *bureau*) bursar's office, steward's office; (= *magasin*) staff cooperative *ou* store

économe [ekonɔm] **1** ADJ thrifty; **elle est très ~** she's very careful with money; **être ~ de son temps/ses efforts** to be sparing of one's time/efforts; **il n'est jamais ~ de conseils** he's always full of advice; **une production de plus en plus ~ de main-d'œuvre** a system of production which requires less and less manpower **2** NMF bursar, steward **3** NM (**couteau**) **~** (vegetable) peeler, paring knife

économétricien, -ienne [ekonometʀisjɛ̃, jɛn] NM,F econometrician

économétrie [ekonometʀi] NF econometrics *sg*

économétrique [ekonometʀik] ADJ econometric

économie [ekonɔmi] **1** NF **a** (= *science*) economics *sg*; (*Pol* = *système*) economy; **~ politique/monétaire** political/cash economy; **~ de troc** barter economy; **~ dirigée** state-controlled *ou* centrally-planned economy; **~ de marché** free market *ou* free enterprise economy; (*Scol*) **~ domestique** home economics **b** (*NonC* = *épargne*) economy, thrift; **par ~** for the sake of economy; **il a le sens de l'~** he's careful with money, he's thrifty **c** (= *gain*) saving; **faire une ~ de temps/d'argent** to save time/money; **représenter une ~ de temps** to represent a saving in time; **procédé permettant une ~ de temps/de main-d'œuvre** time-saving/labour-saving process; **elle fait l'~ d'un repas par jour** she goes *ou* does without one meal a day; **j'ai fait l'~ d'une visite** I've saved myself a visit; **avec une grande ~ de moyens** with very restricted *ou* limited means; **~ d'échelle** economy of scale **d** [*livre*] arrangement; [*projet*] organization

2 **économies** NFPL (= *gains*) savings; **avoir des ~s** to have (some) savings, have some money saved up; **faire des ~s** to save up, put money by; **faire des ~s de chauffage** to economize on heating; **les ~s d'énergie sont nécessaires** energy conservation is essential; **réaliser d'importantes ~s d'énergie** to make significant energy savings *ou* make significant savings on one's fuel *ou* heating bills; **~s budgétaires** budget savings; **il n'y a pas de petites ~s** every little helps, look after the pennies and the pounds will look after themselves (*Brit*) (*PROV*); (*péj*) **faire des ~s de bouts**

de chandelle to make cheeseparing economies

économique [ekɔnɔmik] ADJ [a] (*Écon*) economic [b] (= *bon marché*) economical; (*Aut*) fuel-efficient; **cycle ~** [*machine à laver*] economy cycle; (*Aviat*) **classe ~** economy class

économiquement [ekɔnɔmikmɑ̃] ADV economically; (*Admin*) **les ~ faibles** the lower-income groups

économiser [ekɔnɔmize] ▶ conjug 1 ◀ VT [+ *électricité*] to economize on, save on; [+ *énergie*] to conserve, save; [+ *temps*] to save; [+ *argent*] to save up, put aside; **~ ses forces** to save one's strength; **~ sur le chauffage** to economize on *ou* cut down on heating; **économise ta salive** *ou* **tes paroles** don't waste your breath

économiseur [ekɔnɔmizœʀ] NM (*Aut*) **~ (de carburant)** fuel-saving device; (*Ordin*) **~ d'écran** screen saver

économisme [ekɔnɔmism] NM economism

économiste [ekɔnɔmist] NMF economist

écope [ekɔp] NF (*Naut*) bailer, baler, scoop

écoper [ekɔpe] ▶ conjug 1 ◀ VT (*Naut*) to bail *ou* bale (out) [b] (* = *prendre*) **~ (d')une punition** to catch it*, get it*, cop it* (*Brit*); **~ de trois ans de prison*** to get a three-year sentence, be sent down for three years*; **c'est moi qui ai écopé** I was the one that took the rap*; **il a écopé pour les autres** he took the rap for the others*

écoproduit [ekɔpʀɔdɥi] NM environmentally-friendly *ou* eco-friendly product

écorce [ekɔʀs] NF [*arbre*] bark; [*orange*] peel, skin; (*Géol*) **l'~ terrestre** the earth's crust; (*Can*) **canot d'~** bark canoe

écorcer [ekɔʀse] ▶ conjug 3 ◀ VT [+ *fruit*] to peel; [+ *arbre*] to bark, strip the bark from

écorché [ekɔʀʃe] NM (*Anat*) écorché; (*Tech*) cut-away (diagram); (*fig*) **c'est un ~ vif** he's a tormented soul

écorchement [ekɔʀʃəmɑ̃] NM [*animal*] skinning

écorcher [ekɔʀʃe] ▶ conjug 1 ◀ VT [a] (= *dépecer*) [+ *animal*] to skin; **écorché vif** flayed alive [b] (= *égratigner*) [+ *peau, visage*] to scratch, graze; [+ *genoux*] to graze, scrape; **il s'est écorché les genoux** he grazed his knees [c] (*par frottement*) to chafe, rub; [+ *cheval*] to gall [d] [+ *mot, nom*] to mispronounce; **il écorche l'allemand** his German's terrible [e]† (= *escroquer*) **~ le client** to fleece* one's customers [f] **~ les oreilles de qn** [*bruit*] to grate on sb's ears; [*personne*] to hurt sb's ears

écorchure [ekɔʀʃyʀ] NF [*peau, visage*] scratch, graze; [*genou*] graze

éco-recharge (*pl* **éco-recharges**) [ekɔ(ʀ)ə)ʃaʀʒ] NF eco-refill

écorner [ekɔʀne] ▶ conjug 1 ◀ VT [+ *meuble*] to chip the corner of; [+ *livre*] to turn down the corner of; [+ *économies, fortune*] to make a hole *ou* a dent in; **livre tout écorné** dog-eared book

écornifler*† [ekɔʀnifle] ▶ conjug 1 ◀ VT to cadge, scrounge (**chez qn** from sb)

écornifleur, -euse*† [ekɔʀniflœʀ, øz] NM,F cadger, scrounger

écossais, e [ekɔsɛ, ɛz] [1] ADJ (*gén*) Scottish, Scots (*épith*); [*whisky*] Scotch; [*tissu*] tartan → **douche** [2] NM [a] **Écossais** Scot, Scotsman; **les Écossais** the Scots [b] (*Ling*) (= *dialecte anglais*) Scots; (= *dialecte gaélique*) Gaelic [c] (= *tissu*) tartan (cloth) [3] **Écossaise** NF Scot, Scotswoman

Écosse [ekɔs] NF Scotland

écosser [ekɔse] ▶ conjug 1 ◀ VT to shell, pod; **petits pois à ~** peas in the pod → **haricot**

écosystème [ekɔsistɛm] NM ecosystem

écot [eko] NM (= *quote-part*) share (of a bill);

chacun de nous a payé son ~ we all paid our share

écotaxe [ekotaks] NF green tax, environment tax

écoulement [ekulmɑ̃] NM [a] [*eau*] flow; **tuyau/fossé d'~** drainage pipe/ditch; **~ d'air** air flow [b] [*humeur, pus*] discharge; **~ de sang** flow of blood, bleeding [c] [*foule*] dispersal; [*temps*] passage, passing; **l'~ des voitures** the flow of traffic [d] (*Comm*) selling; **articles d'~ facile** quick-selling *ou* fast-moving articles

écouler [ekule] ▶ conjug 1 ◀ [1] VT (*Comm*) to sell; **~ des faux billets** to get rid of *ou* dispose of counterfeit money; **on n'arrive pas à ~ ce stock** this stock isn't moving *ou* selling, we can't shift this stock; **nous avons écoulé tout notre stock** we've cleared all our stock

[2] **s'écouler** VPR [a] [*liquide*] (= *suinter*) to seep *ou* ooze (out); (= *fuir*) to leak (out); (= *couler*) to flow (out); [*pus*] to ooze out; **s'~ à grands flots** to pour out

[b] [*temps*] to pass (by), go by; [*argent*] to disappear, melt away; [*foule*] to disperse, drift away; **en réfléchissant sur sa vie écoulée** thinking over his past life; **10 ans s'étaient écoulés** 10 years had passed *ou* had elapsed *ou* had gone by; **les fonds s'écoulent vite** (the) funds are soon spent *ou* exhausted

[c] (*Comm*) to sell; **marchandise qui s'écoule bien** quick-selling *ou* fast-moving item; **nos produits se sont bien écoulés** our products have sold well

écourter [ekuʀte] ▶ conjug 1 ◀ VT [+ *bâton*] to shorten; [+ *visite, attente, supplice, adieux*] to cut short, shorten; [+ *texte, discours*] to shorten, cut down; [+ *queue*] to dock

écoutant, e [ekutɑ̃, ɑ̃t] NM,F telephone counsellor

écoute [ekut] NF [a] (= *attention*) **ces personnes recherchent un réconfort, une ~** what these people are looking for is some consolation and a sympathetic ear; **une ~ attentive du patient peut ...** listening attentively to what the patient has to say can ...; **être à l'~ de** [+ *opinion publique, pays*] to be in touch with, listen to; [+ *enfant, revendications*] to listen to; [+ *marché*] to have one's finger on the pulse of; **il faut être à l'~ de son corps** you should listen to what your body is telling you

[b]† **être aux ~s** to be listening (**de** to); (= *épier*) to listen in, eavesdrop (**de** on); (= *être aux aguets*) to be on the look-out (**de** for), keep one's ears open (**de** for)

[c] (*Radio*) listening (**de** to); **être à l'~ de** to be tuned in to, be listening to; **se mettre à** *ou* **prendre l'~** to tune in; **nous restons à l'~** we are staying tuned; **reprendre l'~** to retune; **heures de grande ~** (*Radio*) peak listening hours; (*TV*) prime time, peak viewing hours; (*Radio, TV*) **avoir une grande ~** to have a large audience; **avoir une grande ~ féminine** to have a large female audience *ou* a large number of women listeners (*Radio*) *ou* viewers (*TV*); **indice d'~** audience ratings

[d] (*Mil, Police*) **~s téléphoniques** phone-tapping; **ils sont sur ~(s)** their phone is being tapped; **mettre qn sur ~(s)** to tap sb's phone; **la mise sur ~(s) du ministre** tapping the minister's phone → **table**

[e] (*Mus*) **pour une meilleure ~** for better sound quality → **confort**

[f] (*Naut*) sheet

[g] [*sanglier*] **~s** ears

écouter [ekute] ▶ conjug 1 ◀ VT [a] [+ *discours, chanteur, radio, disque*] to listen to; **écoute !** listen!; (*au téléphone*) **(allô, oui) j'écoute** hello!; **j'ai été ~ sa conférence** I went to hear his lecture; **écoutons ce qu'il dit** let's listen to *ou* hear what he has to say; **~ qn jusqu'au bout** to hear sb out; **~ qch/qn secrètement** to eavesdrop on sth/sb; **~ qn parler** to hear sb speak; **savoir ~** to be a good listener; **~**

aux portes to eavesdrop; **~ de toutes ses oreilles** to be all ears, listen with both ears; **n'~ que d'une oreille** to listen with only half an ear; **faire ~ un disque/une chanson à qn** to play sb a record/a song

[b] [+ *justification, confidence*] to listen to; (*Jur, Rel*) to hear; **écoute-moi au moins !** at least listen to *ou* hear what I have to say!

[c] [+ *conseil*] to listen to, take notice of; **écoute-moi** listen to me; **refuser d'~ un conseil** to turn a deaf ear to advice, disregard a piece of advice; **bon, écoute !** look!, listen!; **aide-moi, écoute !** come on — help me!; **écoute, c'est bien simple** look *ou* listen — it's quite simple; **il se fait ~ du ministre** he has the ear of the minister; **c'est quelqu'un de très écouté** his opinion is highly valued; **ses conseils sont très écoutés** his advice is greatly valued *ou* greatly sought after

[d] (= *obéir à*) to listen to; **~ ses parents** to listen to *ou* obey one's parents; **vas-tu (m')écouter!** will you listen to me!; **faire ~ qn** to get sb to listen; **son père saura le faire ~** his father will get him to do as he's told; **il sait se faire ~** he's good at getting people to do what he says; **~ ses envies/son cœur** to be guided by one's desires/one's heart; **il faut apprendre à ~ son corps** you must listen to what your body is telling you; **n'écoutant que son courage** letting (his) courage be his only guide

[2] **s'écouter** VPR [*malade*] **elle s'écoute trop** she coddles herself; **si je m'écoutais je n'irais pas** if I were to take my own advice I wouldn't go; **s'~ parler** to savour one's words; **il aime s'~ parler** he loves the sound of his own voice

écouteur, -euse [ekutœʀ, øz] [1] NM,F (*littér* = *personne*) (*attentif*) listener; (*indiscret*) eavesdropper [2] NM [*téléphone*] earpiece; (*Radio*) **~s** earphones, headphones

écoutille [ekutij] NF (*Naut*) hatch(way)

écouvillon [ekuvijɔ̃] NM [*fusil*] swab; [*bouteille*] (bottle-)brush; [*boulanger*] scuffle

écouvillonner [ekuvijɔne] ▶ conjug 1 ◀ VT [+ *fusil*] to swab; [+ *bouteille, four*] to clean

écrabouiller* [ekʀabuje] ▶ conjug 1 ◀ VT to squash, crush; **se faire ~ par une voiture** to get flattened *ou* crushed by a car

écran [ekʀɑ̃] NM [a] (*gén*) screen; **ce mur fait ~ et nous isole du froid/du bruit** this wall screens *ou* shields us from the cold/noise, this wall acts as a screen *ou* shield against the cold/noise; **faire ~ à qn** (= *abriter*) to screen *ou* shelter sb; (= *gêner*) to get in sb's way; (= *éclipser*) to stand in sb's way; **son renom me fait ~** he puts me in the shade because he's so famous; **~ de fumée/de protection** smoke/protective screen; **~ de verdure** screen of foliage; **~ publicitaire** advertising slot; **~ solaire** (= *crème*) sun screen; **~ total** total sunblock

[b] (*Ordin, TV*) screen; **télévision grand ~** large-screen television; **~ cathodique** cathode-ray screen; **~ de contrôle** monitor (screen); **~ plat** flat screen; (*Ordin*) **pleine page** full page display; **~ vidéo** video screen; **~ de visualisation** (visual) display screen; **~ tactile** touch-sensitive screen; **~ 16/9ᵉ** wide screen; **le petit ~** (= *télévision*) the small screen, television; **une vedette du petit ~** a television *ou* TV star; (*Ordin*) **travailler sur ~** to work on screen

[c] (*Ciné*) **~ (de cinéma)** (= *toile*) screen; **~ de projection** projector screen; **sur ~ géant** on a giant screen; **porter un roman à l'~** to adapt a novel for the screen; **prochainement sur vos ~s** coming soon to a cinema near you; **ce film sera la semaine prochaine sur les ~s londoniens** this film will open *ou* be showing next week in London; **le grand ~** (= *le cinéma*) the big *ou* silver screen; **sur grand ~** on the big screen; **une vedette de l'~** *ou* **du grand ~** a star of the silver screen, a film *ou* movie (*US*) star

écrasant, e [ekʀazɑ̃, ɑ̃t] ADJ [*impôts, mépris, poids*] crushing; [*preuve, responsabilité, nombre*]

overwhelming; [*travail*] gruelling, back-breaking; [*défaite, supériorité*] crushing, overwhelming; [*chaleur*] overpowering, overwhelming; (*Pol*) **majorité/victoire ~e** landslide *ou* crushing majority/victory

écrasé, e [ekʀɑze] (*ptp de* **écraser**) ADJ [*nez*] flat, squashed; [*perspective, relief*] dwarfed

écrasement [ekʀɑzmɑ̃] NM **a** [*objet, révolte, ennemi*] crushing **b** (*Ordin*) [*données, fichier*] overwriting

écraser [ekʀɑze] ▸conjug 1◂ **1** VT **a** (*gén*) to crush; [+ *mouche*] to squash; [+ *mégot*] to stub out; (*en purée*) to mash; (*en poudre*) to grind (**en** to); (*au pilon*) to pound; (*pour le jus*) to squeeze; (*en aplatissant*) to flatten (out); (*en piétinant*) to trample down; (*Tennis*) [+ *balle*] to flatten, kill; **~ sous la dent** [+ *biscuit*] to crunch; [+ *noix*] to crush between one's teeth; **écrasé par la foule** squashed *ou* crushed in the crowd; **aïe, vous m'écrasez les pieds!** ouch, you're standing *ou* treading on my feet!; **~ la pédale d'accélérateur** to step on it* **b** (= *tuer*) [*voiture, train*] to run over; [*avalanche*] to crush; **il s'est fait ~ par une voiture** he was run over by a car **c** (= *accabler*) to crush; **nous sommes écrasés d'impôts** we are overburdened *ou* crushed by taxation; **il nous écrase de son mépris** he crushes us with his scornful attitude; **écrasé de chaleur** overcome by the heat; **écrasé de sommeil/de douleur** overcome by sleep/with grief; **écrasé de travail** snowed under with* *ou* overloaded with work **d** (= *vaincre*) [+ *ennemi*] to crush; [+ *rébellion*] to crush, suppress, put down; **notre équipe a été écrasée** *ou* **s'est fait ~** we were hammered* *ou* we were beaten hollow (*Brit*) **e** (*Ordin*) [+ *données, fichiers*] to overwrite **2** VI **a** * (= *ne pas insister*) to drop the subject; **oh écrase!** oh shut up!* *ou* belt up!‡ (*Brit*) **b** (= *dormir*) **en ~**‡ to sleep like a log* **3 s'écraser** VPR **a** [*avion, voiture*] to crash (**contre** into, against, **sur** on); [*objet, corps*] to be crushed (**contre** on, against) **b** [*foule*] to be *ou* get crushed (**dans** in); **on s'écrase pour en acheter** they're falling over each other *ou* they're rushing to buy them; **on s'écrase devant les cinémas** there's a great crush to get into the cinemas **c** ‡ (= *ne pas protester*) to pipe down*; **il s'écrase toujours devant son chef** he never says a word when the boss is around; **il a intérêt à s'~!** he'd better keep quiet!

écraseur, -euse* [ekʀɑzœʀ, øz] NM,F road-hog*

écrémage [ekʀemaʒ] NM **a** [*lait*] skimming **b** (*fig*) creaming off

écrémer [ekʀeme] ▸conjug 6◂ VT **a** [+ *lait*] to skim; **lait écrémé** skimmed milk **b** [+ *candidats*] to cream off the best from

écrémeuse [ekʀemøz] NF creamer, (cream) separator

écrêter [ekʀete] ▸conjug 1◂ VT (= *niveler*) to lop

écrevisse [ekʀəvis] NF (freshwater) crayfish (*Brit*), crawfish (*US*) → **rouge**

écrier (s') [ekʀije] ▸conjug 7◂ VPR to exclaim, cry out

écrin [ekʀɛ̃] NM case, box; [*bijoux*] casket; (*littér*) **niché dans un ~ de verdure** nestling in a green setting

▾**écrire** [ekʀiʀ] ▸conjug 39◂ **1** VT **a** (*gén*) [+ *mots, livres*] to write; (= *orthographier*) to spell; (= *inscrire, marquer*) to write down; **je lui ai écrit que je viendrais** I wrote and told him I would be coming; **~ des commentaires au crayon** to pencil in comments, make notes *ou* comments in pencil **b** (*loc*) **c'était écrit** it was bound to happen, it was inevitable; **il est écrit que je ne pourrai jamais y arriver!** I'm fated *ou* doomed never to succeed!; **c'est écrit sur sa figure** it's written all over his face; **c'est écrit noir sur blanc** *ou*

en toutes lettres it's written in black and white **2** VI (*gén*) to write; (= *être écrivain*) to be a writer, write; **vous écrivez très mal** your writing is really bad; **~ gros/fin** [*personne*] to have large/small (hand)writing; [*stylo*] to have a thick/fine nib; **~ au crayon/à l'encre** to write in pencil/in ink **3 s'écrire** VPR [*personnes*] to write to each other; **comment ça s'écrit?** how do you spell it?; **ça s'écrit comme ça se prononce** it's spelt how it sounds, you write it the same way as you pronounce it

écrit, e [ekʀi, it] (*ptp de* **écrire**) **1** ADJ (*Scol*) **épreuve ~e** written exam *ou* paper; **le texte/scénario est très ~** it's a very carefully written *ou* crafted text/script **2** NM (= *ouvrage*) piece of writing, written work; (= *examen*) written exam *ou* paper; (*Jur*) document; **par ~** in writing; (*Scol*) **être bon à l'~** to do well in the written papers

écriteau (*pl* **écriteaux**) [ekʀito] NM notice, sign

écritoire [ekʀitwaʀ] NF writing case

écriture [ekʀityʀ] **1** NF **a** (= *à la main*) (hand)writing (*NonC*); **il a une belle ~** he has beautiful (hand)writing; **~ de chat** spidery (hand)writing **b** (= *alphabet*) writing (*NonC*), script; **~ hiéroglyphique** hieroglyphic writing; **~ phonétique** phonetic script **c** (*littér* = *style*) writing (*NonC*) **d** (= *rédaction*) writing; **se consacrer à l'~ (de romans)** (*Littérat*) to devote one's time to writing (novels); **~ automatique** automatic writing **e** (*Fin*) entry; **passer une ~** to make an entry **f** (*Rel*) **les (Saintes) Écritures** *ou* **l'Écriture (sainte)** Scripture, the Scriptures, (the) Holy Writ **2 écritures** NFPL (*Comm*) accounts, books; **employé aux ~s** ledger clerk; **tenir les ~s** to do the bookkeeping *ou* the accounts *ou* the books

écrivailler [ekʀivaje] ▸conjug 1◂ VI (*péj*) to scribble

écrivailleur, -euse [ekʀivajœʀ, øz] NM,F, **écrivaillon** [ekʀivajɔ̃] NM (*péj*) scribbler

écrivain [ekʀivɛ̃] NM writer; **femme-~** woman writer; **~ public** (public) letter-writer

écrivassier, -ière [ekʀivasje, jɛʀ] NM,F = **écrivailleur, -euse**

écrou [ekʀu] NM **a** (*Tech*) nut; **~ à ailettes** wing nut **b** (*Jur*) commitment, committal, mittimus (*SPÉC*); **mettre qn sous ~** to enter sb on the prison register; **mise sous ~** entering on the prison register → **levée²**

écrouelles †† [ekʀuɛl] NFPL scrofula

écrouer [ekʀue] ▸conjug 1◂ VT (= *incarcérer*) to imprison, lock away (in prison); **il a été écroué sous le numéro 3489** he was entered on the prison register under the number 3489

écroulé, e [ekʀule] (*ptp de* **s'écrouler**) ADJ **a** [*maison, mur*] ruined; **à moitié ~** half-ruined, tumbledown (*épith*), dilapidated **b** **être ~*** (**de rire**) to be doubled up with laughter

écroulement [ekʀulmɑ̃] NM [*mur, édifice*] collapse; [*empire, entreprise*] collapse, fall; [*espoir, théorie, projet, prix*] collapse; **l'explosion a provoqué l'~ du toit** the explosion caused the roof to collapse *ou* cave in

écrouler (s') [ekʀule] ▸conjug 1◂ VPR **a** [*mur*] to fall (down), collapse; [*rocher*] to fall; [*toit*] to collapse, cave in, fall in; (*Rugby*) [*mêlée*] to collapse **b** [*empire*] to collapse, crumble; [*entreprise*] to collapse, crash; [*prix, cours*] to collapse, plummet; [*espoir, projet, théorie*] to collapse, crumble; **tous nos projets s'écroulent** all our plans are crumbling *ou* falling apart **c** [*personne*] (= *tomber*) to collapse; (* = *s'endormir*) to fall fast asleep; [*coureur, candidat*] to collapse; **s'~ de sommeil/de fatigue** to be overcome with *ou* collapse with sleepiness/weariness; **il s'écroula dans un fau-**

teuil* he flopped down *ou* slumped down *ou* collapsed into an armchair; **être près de s'~** to be on the verge of collapse

écru, e [ekʀy] ADJ [*tissu*] raw, in its natural state; [*vêtement*] ecru; **couleur ~e** ecru; **toile ~e** unbleached linen; **soie ~e** raw silk (*before dyeing*)

ectoplasme [ɛktoplasm] NM ectoplasm

écu [eky] NM **a** (= *monnaie ancienne, papier*) crown; (= *monnaie européenne*) ecu; (*Hér, Hist* = *bouclier*) shield

écubier [ekybje] NM hawse-hole

écueil [ekœj] NM (*lit*) reef, shelf; (= *pierre d'achoppement*) stumbling block; (= *piège, danger*) pitfall

écuelle [ekɥɛl] NF (= *assiette creuse*) (*pour chien*) bowl; (= *contenu*) bowlful; (*Hist*) platter

éculé, e [ekyle] (*ptp de* **éculer**) ADJ [*chaussure*] down-at-heel; [*plaisanterie*] hackneyed, worn; [*mot*] overused

éculer [ekyle] ▸conjug 1◂ **1** VT [+ *chaussure*] to wear down at the heel **2 s'éculer** VPR [*plaisanterie*] to wear thin; [*mot*] to be overused

écumage [ekymaʒ] NM skimming

écumant, e [ekymɑ̃, ɑ̃t] ADJ [*mer, torrent, vague*] foamy; [*lait*] frothy; [*bouche*] foaming

écume [ekym] NF [*mer*] foam; [*bouche, bière*] foam, froth; [*métal*] dross; [*confiture, bouillon*] scum; [*savon, cheval*] lather; **pipe en ~ de mer** meerschaum pipe; (*péj*) **l'~ de la société** the scum *ou* dregs of society

écumer [ekyme] ▸conjug 1◂ **1** VT **a** [+ *bouillon*] to skim; [+ *confiture*] to take the scum off, skim; [+ *métal*] to scum **b** (= *piller*) to clean out, plunder; **~ les mers** to scour the seas; **~ la ville à la recherche de** to scour the town in search of **2** VI [*mer, confiture*] to foam; [*métal*] to scum; [*bouche, liquide*] to froth, foam; [*cheval*] to lather; **~ (de rage)** to foam *ou* froth at the mouth (*fig*), foam with rage

écumeur [ekymœʀ] NM (*Hist, hum*) **~ des mers** pirate, buccaneer

écumeux, -euse [ekymø, øz] ADJ foamy, frothy

écumoire [ekymwaʀ] NF skimmer; **troué comme une ~** riddled with holes

écureuil [ekyʀœj] NM squirrel; **~ roux/gris** red/grey squirrel; **~ de Corée** chipmunk; **~ volant** flying squirrel

écurie [ekyʀi] NF [*chevaux, cyclistes etc*] stable; (*péj* = *endroit sale*) pigsty; **mettre un cheval à l'~** to stable a horse; **~ de course** racing stable; **nettoyer les ~s d'Augias** to clean the Augean stables → **sentir**

écusson [ekysɔ̃] NM (= *insigne*) badge; (*Mil*) tab; (*Hér*) escutcheon; [*serrure*] escutcheon; [*insecte*] scutellum; (*Agr*) **(greffe en) ~** shield-graft

écuyer [ekɥije] NM **a** (= *cavalier*) rider, horseman; (= *professeur d'équitation*) riding master; **~ de cirque** circus rider **b** (*Hist*) (*d'un chevalier*) squire; (*à la cour*) equerry

écuyère [ekɥijɛʀ] NF rider, horsewoman; **~ de cirque** circus rider; **bottes à l'~** riding boots

eczéma [ɛgzema] NM eczema; **avoir** *ou* **faire de l'~** to have eczema

eczémateux, -euse [ɛgzematø, øz] ADJ eczematous, eczema (*épith*)

édam [edam] NM (*Culin*) Edam

edelweiss [ɛdɛlvɛs, edɛlvajs] NM edelweiss

Éden [edɛn] NM **l'~** ◊ **le jardin d'~** (the garden of) Eden

édénique [edenik] ADJ (*littér*) Edenic

édenté, e [edɑ̃te] (*ptp de* **édenter**) **1** ADJ (*totalement*) toothless; (*partiellement*) gap-toothed **2** NM edentate mammal; **les ~s** edentate mammals, the Edentata (*SPÉC*)

édenter [edɑ̃te] ▸conjug 1◂ VT to break the teeth of

▶ **GRAMMAIRE ACTIVE:** écrire 48.1, 48.2

EDF [ədɛf] NF (ABRÉV = **Électricité de France**) **l'~** the French Electricity Board; **l'~-GDF** the French Electricity and Gas Board

édicter [edikte] ▸conjug 1◂ VT [+ *loi*] to enact, decree; [+ *peine*] to decree

édicule [edikyl] NM (*hum* = *cabinets*) public lavatory *ou* convenience (*Brit*), (public) rest room (*US*); (= *kiosque*) kiosk

édifiant, e [edifjɑ̃, jɑ̃t] ADJ [*livre, conduite*] edifying

édification [edifikasjɔ̃] NF [*bâtiment*] erection, construction; [*personne*] edification (*frm*), enlightenment

édifice [edifis] NM building, edifice (*frm*); **~ public** public building; **l'~ social** the social structure *ou* fabric

édifier [edifje] ▸conjug 7◂ VT **a** [+ *maison*] to build, construct, erect; [+ *fortune, empire*] to build (up); [+ *système*] to build, develop **b** (*moralement*) to edify (*frm*), enlighten

édile [edil] NM (*frm, hum*) (town) councillor

Édimbourg [edɛ̃buʁ] N Edinburgh

édit [edi] NM (*Hist*) edict; **l'Édit de Nantes** the Edict of Nantes

éditer [edite] ▸conjug 1◂ VT (= *publier*) to publish; [+ *disques*] to produce; (= *annoter, présenter*) to edit

éditeur, -trice [editœʁ, tʁis] **1** NM,F (= *annotateur*) editor **2** NM **a** (= *qui publie*) publisher; **~ de disques** record producer **b** (*Ordin*) **~ de textes** text editor

édition [edisjɔ̃] NF **a** (= *action de publier*) publishing; [*disques*] production; **travailler dans l'~** to be in publishing *ou* in the publishing business; **l'~ électronique** electronic publishing **b** (= *livre, journal*) edition; **~ spéciale** (*journal*) special edition; (= *magazine*) special issue; (*cri du vendeur*) **«~ spéciale!»** "extra! extra!"; (= *journal*) **~ de 5 heures** five o'clock edition; (*Radio, TV* = *informations*) **notre ~ de 13 heures** our 1 o'clock news bulletin; **dernière ~** (*Presse*) late edition; (*TV*) late news bulletin; (*hum*) **deuxième/troisième ~!** for the second/third time! **c** (= *annotation*) editing; (= *texte*) edition; **établir l'~ critique d'un texte** to produce a critical edition of a text; **~ revue et corrigée/revue et augmentée** revised/revised and enlarged edition **d** (*Ordin*) editing

édito* [edito] NM ABRÉV = **éditorial**

éditorial, e (*mpl* **-iaux**) [editɔʁjal, jo] **1** NM leading article, leader, editorial **2** ADJ [*comité, politique, projet*] editorial; **il y a un superbe travail ~** it's beautifully edited

éditorialiste [editɔʁjalist] NMF leader *ou* editorial writer

Édouard [edwaʁ] NM Edward; **~ le Confesseur** Edward the Confessor

édredon [edʁədɔ̃] NM eiderdown

éducable [edykabl] ADJ educable, teachable

éducateur, -trice [edykatœʁ, tʁis] **1** ADJ educational **2** NM,F (*gén*) teacher; (*en prison*) tutor, instructor; (= *théoricien*) educationalist; **~ spécialisé** (*gén*) teacher of children with special needs; [*maison de jeunes*] youth worker

éducatif, -ive [edykatif, iv] ADJ [*rôle, valeur, processus*] educational, educative; [*chaîne, programme, jeu*] educational; **système ~** education system; **équipe éducative** (*Scol*) teaching staff; [*services sociaux*] (social services) support team

éducation [edykasjɔ̃] NF **a** (= *enseignement*) education; **les problèmes de l'~** educational problems; **il faut faire l'~ politique des masses** the masses must be educated politically; **j'ai fait mon ~ à Paris** I was educated *ou* I went to school in Paris; **j'ai fait mon ~ musicale à Paris** I studied music in Paris; **il a reçu une bonne ~** he had a good education; **il a reçu une ~ religieuse** he had a religious upbringing; (*hum*) **toute une ~ à refaire!** you've got a few things

to learn!; **~ manuelle et technique** technical education (*Brit*), industrial arts (*US*); **l'Éducation nationale** (= *système*) state education; (= *ministère*) the Ministry (*Brit*) *ou* Department (*US*) of Education; **~ religieuse** religious education; **~ civique** civic education, civics *sg*; **~ permanente** continuing education; **~ physique et sportive** physical training *ou* education, P.E.; **~ sexuelle** sex education; **le roman raconte l'~ sentimentale d'un jeune homme** the novel recounts a young man's first experience of love → **maison, ministère** *etc* **b** (= *discipline familiale*) upbringing; **avoir de l'~** (*bonnes manières*) to be well-mannered *ou* well-bred *ou* well brought up; **manquer d'~** to be ill-mannered *ou* ill-bred, be badly brought up; **sans ~** ill-mannered, ill-bred, uncouth **c** [*goût, volonté*] training

⌐ **ÉDUCATION NATIONALE** ⌐

The French state education system is the responsibility of the "Ministre de l'Éducation nationale". Schools administration at local level is the responsibility of the "recteur d'académie".

State education in France is divided into four levels: "maternelle" (for children 2-6 years old), "primaire" (including "école élémentaire" and "école primaire", for 7 to 11-year-olds), "secondaire" (including "collège" and "lycée", for 12 to 18-year-olds) and "supérieur" (universities and other higher education establishments).

State education as a whole is designed to follow key republican principles, the concept of "laïcité" (secular education) being of particular significance. Private education (mainly in Catholic schools) is structured in a similar way to the state system. → ACADÉMIE ; COLLÈGE ; CONCOURS ; DIPLÔMES ; LYCÉE

édulcorant, e [edylkɔʁɑ̃, ɑ̃t] **1** ADJ sweetening **2** NM sweetener; **sans ~** unsweetened

édulcorer [edylkɔʁe] ▸conjug 1◂ VT **a** (= *expurger*) [+ *doctrine, propos*] to water down; [+ *texte osé*] to tone down; **ils ont adopté une version édulcorée des thèses de l'extrême droite** they have adopted a toned-down version of the ideas of the far right; **il a beaucoup édulcoré les passages violents du livre** he has really toned down the violent parts of the book **b** (*Pharm*) to sweeten

éduquer [edyke] ▸conjug 1◂ VT [+ *enfant*] (*à l'école*) to educate; (*à la maison*) to bring up, raise; [+ *peuple*] to educate; [+ *goût, volonté, œil, oreille*] to train; **bien éduqué** well-mannered, well-bred, well brought up; **mal éduqué** ill-mannered, ill-bred, badly brought up

EEE [əəə] NM (ABRÉV = **espace économique européen**) EEA

effaçable [efasabl] ADJ [*inscription*] erasable

effacé, e [efase] (*ptp de* **effacer**) ADJ **a** [*couleur*] (= *qui a passé*) faded; (= *sans éclat*) subdued **b** [*personne, manières*] unassuming, self-effacing; [*vie*] retiring; [*rôle*] unobtrusive **c** [*menton*] receding; [*poitrine*] flat; (*Escrime*) **en position ~e** sideways (on)

effacement [efasmɑ̃] NM **a** [*inscription, faute, souvenir*] obliteration, effacing; [*bande magnétique*] erasing; [*craintes*] dispelling; (*Ling*) deletion; (*Escrime*) **~ du corps/des épaules** drawing o.s./one's shoulders in; **l'~ progressif des frontières** the gradual elimination of borders **b** [*personne*] (*par modestie*) unassuming *ou* self-effacing manner; (*devant un rival*) **son ~ progressif au profit du jeune sous-directeur** the way in which he was gradually being eclipsed by the young deputy director

effacer [efase] ▸conjug 3◂ **1** VT **a** (= *enlever*) [+ *inscription, traces*] to erase, obliterate, efface; [+ *bande magnétique*] to erase; [+ *tableau noir*] to clean, wipe; (*à la gomme*) to erase, rub out (*Brit*); (*à l'éponge*) to wipe off, sponge off; (*en lavant*) to wash off *ou* out; (*au chiffon*) to wipe

off, rub out; (*Ling*) to delete; **cette gomme efface bien** this is a good rubber (*Brit*) *ou* eraser (*US*), this rubber (*Brit*) *ou* eraser (*US*) works well; **prends un chiffon pour ~** use a cloth to rub it out *ou* wipe it off; **un chemin à demi effacé** a barely distinguishable track **b** [+ *mauvaise impression, souvenir*] to erase, efface; [+ *faute*] to erase, obliterate; [+ *craintes*] to dispel; **pour ~ vos rides** to smooth out your wrinkles; **on efface tout et on recommence** (*on oublie le passé*) we'll let bygones be bygones, we'll wipe the slate clean; (*on reprend à zéro*) let's go back to square one, let's make a fresh start; **tenter d'~ son passé** to try to blot out one's past; **le temps efface tout** everything fades in *ou* with time; **ce moyen de communication efface les frontières** this means of communication cuts across borders **c** (= *éclipser*) to outshine, eclipse **d** (*Escrime*) **~ le corps** to stand sideways on; (*gén*) to draw o.s. in; **effacez les épaules!** shoulders back!; **effacez le ventre!** stomach in!

2 **s'effacer** VPR **a** [*inscription*] to wear away; [*couleurs*] to fade; [*sourire*] to fade, die; **le crayon s'efface mieux que l'encre** it is easier to erase *ou* rub out (*Brit*) pencil than ink, pencil erases *ou* rubs out (*Brit*) more easily than ink; **les frontières s'effacent** borders are coming down *ou* disappearing **b** [*crainte, impression, souvenir*] to fade, diminish; **tout s'efface avec le temps** everything fades in *ou* with time; **un mauvais souvenir qui s'efface difficilement** an unpleasant memory that is hard to forget *ou* that is slow to fade **c** (= *s'écarter*) to move aside, step back *ou* aside; (= *se faire discret*) to keep in the background; (= *se retirer*) to withdraw; **l'auteur s'efface derrière ses personnages** the author hides behind his characters; **elle s'efface le plus possible** she keeps (herself) in the background as much as possible; **s'~ devant** *ou* **au profit de qn** to step aside in favour of sb; **le romantisme s'efface devant** *ou* **derrière le réalisme** romanticism is giving way to realism

effaceur [efasœʁ] NM **~ d'encre** (ink) eraser pen

effarant, e [efaʁɑ̃, ɑ̃t] ADJ [*prix*] outrageous; [*vitesse*] alarming, breathtaking; [*bêtise*] astounding, incredible

effaré, e [efaʁe] (*ptp de* **effarer**) ADJ alarmed (*attrib*) (**de** by, at), aghast (*attrib*) (**de** at); **son regard ~** his wild eyes, his look of alarm

effarement [efaʁmɑ̃] NM alarm, trepidation

effarer [efaʁe] ▸conjug 1◂ VT (= *alarmer*) to alarm; (= *stupéfier*) **cette bêtise/hausse des prix m'effare** I find such stupidity/this rise in prices most alarming

effaroucher [efaʁuʃe] ▸conjug 1◂ **1** VT (= *alarmer*) [+ *animal*] to frighten away *ou* off, scare away *ou* off; [+ *personne timide*] to frighten, scare; (= *choquer*) to shock, upset **2** **s'effaroucher** VPR (*par timidité*) [*animal, personne*] to shy (**de** at), take fright (**de** at); (*par pudeur*) to be shocked *ou* upset (**de** by)

effectif, -ive [efɛktif, iv] **1** ADJ [*aide*] real (*épith*), positive (*épith*); [*travail*] effective, actual (*épith*), real (*épith*); (*Fin*) [*capital*] real (*épith*); **le couvre-feu sera ~ à partir de 22 heures** the curfew will take effect *ou* become effective as from 10 p.m.

2 NM [*armée*] strength (*NonC*); [*classe*] size, (total) number of pupils; [*parti*] size; [*entreprise*] staff, workforce; (*Mil*) **~s** numbers, strength; **l'école n'a jamais atteint son ~** *ou* **l'~ prévu** the school has never reached its full complement; **l'~ de la classe a triplé en deux ans** the (total) number of pupils in the class has *ou* the (size of the) class has trebled in two years; (*Mil*) **l'~ est au complet** we are at full strength *ou* up to strength; **augmenter ses**

~s [parti, lycée] to increase its numbers; [entreprise] to increase its workforce; **l'usine a un ~ de 70 personnes** the factory has 70 people on the payroll ou has a staff ou workforce of 70; (Ind) **maintenir le niveau des ~s** to keep up manning levels

effectivement [efɛktivmã] ADV [a] (= concrètement) [aider, travailler] effectively; **contribuer ~ à qch** to make a real ou positive contribution to sth [b] (= réellement) actually, really; **cet incident s'est ~ produit** the incident really did happen ou actually happened [c] (= en effet) actually, in fact; (dans une réponse = oui) quite, indeed; **c'est ~ plus rapide** it's true that it's faster, it is in fact faster; **n'y a-t-il pas risque de conflit? — ~!** isn't there a risk of conflict? — there is indeed!; **~, quand ce phénomène se produit ...** indeed ou in fact, when this phenomenon occurs ...

effectivité [efɛktivite] NF (frm) [action, démarche, aide, travail] effectiveness, efficacy

effectuer [efɛktɥe] ▸conjug 1◂ [1] VT [+ manœuvre, opération, mission, réparation] to carry out; [+ expérience] to carry out, perform; [+ mouvement, geste] to make; [+ paiement] to make, effect; [+ trajet] to make, complete; [+ reprise économique] to undergo, stage; **le franc/ le coureur a effectué une remontée spectaculaire** the franc/the runner made ou staged a spectacular recovery [2] **s'effectuer** VPR **le trajet s'effectue en 2 heures** the journey takes 2 hours (to complete); **le paiement peut s'~ de deux façons** payment may be made in two ways; **le rapatriement des prisonniers s'est effectué sans incident** the repatriation of the prisoners went off without a hitch; **la rentrée scolaire s'est effectuée dans de bonnes conditions** the new school year got off to a good start

efféminé, e [efemine] (ptp de **efféminer**) ADJ effeminate

efféminer [efemine] ▸conjug 1◂ VT [+ personne] to make effeminate; [+ peuple, pensée] to emasculate; **s'~** to become effeminate

effervescence [efɛrvesãs] NF (lit) effervescence; (fig) agitation; **mettre la ville en ~** to plunge the town into a turmoil; **être en ~** to be bubbling with excitement; **l'~ révolutionnaire** the stirrings of revolution

effervescent, e [efɛrvesã, ãt] ADJ (lit) effervescent; (fig) agitated, in turmoil (attrib)

effet [efɛ] [1] NM [a] (= résultat) [action, médicament] effect; **~ pervers** negative effect; **c'est un ~ de son inexpérience** it is because of ou a result of his inexperience; **c'est l'~ du hasard** it's pure chance, it is the result of chance; **avoir ou produire beaucoup d'~/l'~ voulu** to have ou produce a considerable effect/the desired effect; **ces livres ont un ~ nocif sur la jeunesse** these books have a harmful effect on young people; **créer un ~ de surprise** to create a surprise; **il espérait créer un ~ de surprise** he was hoping to surprise them (ou us etc); **avoir pour ~ de faire qch** to have the effect of doing sth; **avoir pour ~ une augmentation/ diminution de** to result in an increase/decrease in; [médicament] **faire ~** to take effect; **ce médicament (me) fait de l'~/a fait son ~** this medicine is effective ou works (on me)/has taken effect ou has worked; **la bière me fait beaucoup d'~** beer goes straight to my head; **la bière ne me fait aucun ~** beer has no effect on me; **être ou rester sans ~** to be ineffective, have no effect; **ces mesures sont demeurées sans ~** these measures had no effect ou were ineffective → **relation**
[b] (= impression) impression; **faire ou produire un ~ considérable/déplorable (sur qn)** to make a great/dreadful impression (on sb); **il a fait ou produit son petit ~** he managed to cause a bit of a stir ou a minor sensation; **il aime faire de l'~** he likes to create a stir; **c'est tout l'~ que ça te fait?** is that all it means to you?, is

that all you feel about it?; **quel ~ ça te fait d'être revenu?** what does it feel like ou how does it feel to be back?; **ça m'a fait un drôle d'~ de le revoir après si longtemps** I found it strange seeing him again after so long; **cela m'a fait de l'~ de le voir dans cet état** it really affected me ou it gave me quite a turn to see him in that state; **faire bon/mauvais ~ sur qn** to make a good/bad impression on sb; **il m'a fait bon ~** he made a good impression on me, I was favourably impressed by him; **ce tableau fait bon ~/beaucoup d'~ ici** this picture is quite/very effective here; **il me fait l'~ d'(être) une belle crapule** he strikes me as being a real crook, he seems like a real crook to me → **bœuf**
[c] (= artifice, procédé) effect; **~ de contraste/de style/comique** contrasting/stylistic/comic effect; **~ d'optique** visual effect; **~ facile** facile effect; **~s de lumière** (au théâtre) lighting effects; (naturels, sur l'eau) play of light (NonC); (Ciné) **~s spéciaux** special effects; **rechercher les ~s** ou **l'~** to strive for effect; **soigner ses ~s** to take great trouble over one's effects; **elle lui a coupé ses ~s** she stole his thunder; **manquer** ou **rater son ~** [personne] to spoil one's effect; [plaisanterie] to fall flat, misfire; **faire des ~s de voix** to use one's voice to dramatic effect, make dramatic use of one's voice; **il fait des ~s de manches** [avocat] he waves his arms about in a most dramatic fashion
[d] (Phys, Tech) effect; **machine à simple/ double ~** single-/double-effect machine; **~ de serre** greenhouse effect; **~ de souffle** [bombe, explosif] blast; (Math) **~ papillon** butterfly effect; **~ tunnel** tunnel effect → **boomerang, larsen, placebo, secondaire**
[e] (Sport) spin; **donner de l'~ à une balle** to put spin on a ball; **tu as mis trop d'~** you've put too much spin on the ball
[f] (Admin, Jur) **augmentation de salaire avec ~ rétroactif au 1er janvier** payrise backdated to the 1st January, retrospective payrise from 1st January; **prendre ~ à la date de** to take effect from, be operative from; (Jur) **à l'~ de** in order to
[g] (Comm = valeur) **~ bancaire** ◊ **~ de commerce** bill of exchange; **~ à vue** sight bill, demand note; **~ au porteur** bill payable to bearer; **~s à payer** notes payable; **~s à recevoir** bills receivable; **~s publics** government securities
[h] (loc) **mettre à ~** to put into operation ou effect; **à cet ~** ◊ **pour cet ~†** for this purpose, to this effect ou end
[2] **effets** NMPL (= affaires, vêtements) things, clothes; **~s personnels** personal effects
[3] **en effet** LOC ADV [a] (introduit une explication) because; **cette voiture me plaît beaucoup, en ~, elle est rapide et confortable** I like this car very much because it's fast and comfortable
[b] (= effectivement) **cela me plaît beaucoup, en ~ yes** (indeed), I like it very much; **c'est en ~ plus rapide** it's true that it's faster
[c] (dans une réponse) **étiez-vous absent mardi dernier? — en ~, j'avais la grippe** were you absent last Tuesday? — yes (I was) ou that's right, I had flu; **tu ne travaillais pas? — en ~** you weren't working? — no, I wasn't as it happens
[4] **sous l'effet de** LOC PRÉP [+ alcool] under the effect(s) ou influence of; [+ drogue] under the effect(s) of; **sous l'~ de la colère il me frappa** in his anger he hit me; **il était encore sous l'~ de la colère** his anger hadn't worn off yet, he was still angry

effeuillage [efœjaʒ] NM (Agr) thinning-out of leaves; (hum) striptease

effeuiller [efœje] ▸conjug 1◂ [1] VT [+ arbre, branche] [arboriculteur] to thin out the leaves of; [vent] to blow the leaves off; (par jeu) **~ une branche/une fleur** to pull ou pick the

leaves off a branch/the petals off a flower; **~ la marguerite** to play "she-loves-me, she-loves-me-not" [2] **s'effeuiller** VPR [arbre] to shed ou lose its leaves

effeuilleuse [efœjøz] NF (hum = strip-teaseuse) stripper

efficace [efikas] ADJ [remède, mesure] effective; [personne, machine] efficient → **grâce**

efficacement [efikasmã] ADV efficiently, effectively

efficacité [efikasite] NF [remède, mesure] effectiveness; [personne, machine] efficiency

efficience [efisjãs] NF efficiency

efficient, e [efisjã, jãt] ADJ efficient

effigie [efiʒi] NF effigy; **à l'~ de** bearing the effigy of; **en ~** in effigy

effilé, e [efile] (ptp de **effiler**) [1] ADJ [doigt, silhouette] slender; [pointe, outil] highly-sharpened; [carrosserie] streamlined; [tissu] frayed; **amandes ~es** flaked almonds; **poulet ~** oven-ready chicken [2] NM [jupe, serviette] fringe

effiler [efile] ▸conjug 1◂ [1] VT [a] [+ objet] to taper; [+ lignes, forme] to streamline [b] [+ étoffe] to fray; [+ cheveux] to thin (out) [2] **s'effiler** VPR [objet] to taper; [étoffe] to fray

effilochage [efilɔʃaʒ] NM fraying

effilocher [efilɔʃe] ▸conjug 1◂ [1] VT [+ tissu] to fray [2] **s'effilocher** VPR to fray; **veste effilochée** frayed jacket

efflanqué, e [eflãke] ADJ raw-boned; **c'était un cheval ~** the horse was just skin and bones

effleurement [eflœrmã] NM (= frôlement) light touch; (Ordin) touch; **elle sentit sur son bras l'~ d'une main** she felt the light touch of a hand on her arm, she felt a hand brush against her arm; **massage par ~** effleurage

effleurer [eflœre] ▸conjug 1◂ VT [a] (= frôler) to touch lightly, brush (against); (= érafler) to graze; [+ sujet] to touch (lightly) on ou upon, skim over; (Ordin) to touch; **les oiseaux effleuraient l'eau** the birds skimmed (across) the water; **une idée lui effleura l'esprit** an idea crossed his mind; **ça ne m'a pas effleuré** it didn't cross my mind, it didn't occur to me; **ayant oublié le désir qui l'avait effleuré** having forgotten his fleeting desire [b] [+ cuir] to buff

efflorescence [eflɔresãs] NF (Bot, Chim) efflorescence

efflorescent, e [eflɔresã, ãt] ADJ (Bot, Chim) efflorescent

effluent, e [eflyã, ãt] [1] ADJ effluent [2] NM (Géog) effluent; **~ urbain** urban effluent; **~s radioactifs** radioactive effluent (NonC) ou discharges

effluves [eflyv] NMPL (littér) (agréables) fragrance; (désagréables) smell, effluvia (frm)

effondré, e [efɔ̃dre] (ptp de **s'effondrer**) ADJ (gén = abattu) shattered, crushed (de by); **~ de douleur** prostrate with grief; **les parents ~s** the grief-stricken parents

effondrement [efɔ̃drəmã] NM [a] [mur, édifice] collapse; **ça a provoqué l'~ du plancher** it caused the floor to cave in ou collapse [b] [empire, entreprise] collapse, fall; [prix, marché] collapse [c] (= abattement) utter dejection

effondrer [efɔ̃dre] ▸conjug 1◂ [1] VT (Rugby) [+ mêlée] to collapse [2] **s'effondrer** VPR [a] [toit, plancher] to collapse, cave in, fall in; [mur] to collapse, fall down; [terre] to fall away, collapse; [pont] to collapse; (Rugby) [mêlée] to collapse [b] [empire, projet] to collapse; [prix, marché] to collapse, plummet; [argument] to collapse, fall to pieces; [espoirs] to be dashed; [rêves] to come to nothing [c] [personne] to collapse; (fig) [accusé] to break down; **elle s'est effondrée en larmes** she dissolved ou collapsed into tears, she broke down and wept; **effondré sur sa chaise** slumped on his chair

efforcer (s') [efɔrse] ▸conjug 3◂ VPR **s'~ de faire qch** to try hard ou endeavour to do sth, do one's best to do sth; *(littér)* **il s'efforçait à une politesse dont personne n'était dupe** he was striving to remain polite but he convinced nobody; *(littér)* **ils s'efforçaient en vain** they were striving in vain

effort [efɔʀ] NM a (*physique, intellectuel*) effort; **après bien des ~s** after much exertion *ou* effort; **la récompense de nos ~s** the reward for our efforts; **nécessiter un (gros) ~ financier** to require a (large) financial outlay; **faire un ~ financier en faveur des petites entreprises** to give financial help to small businesses; **l'~ financier de la France dans le domaine de l'énergie** France's investment in the field of energy; **~ de guerre** war effort; **~ de volonté** effort of will; **cela demande un ~ de réflexion** that requires careful thought; **faire un ~ de mémoire** to make an effort *ou* try hard to remember; **cela demande un ~ d'attention** you have to make an effort to concentrate; **tu dois faire un ~ d'imagination** you should try to use your imagination
b (*Tech*) stress, strain; (*Vét*) strain; **~ de torsion** torsional stress; **~ de traction** traction, pull; **l'~ que subissent les fondations** the strain on the foundations
c (*loc*) **faire un ~** to make an effort; **faire de gros ~s pour réussir** to make a great effort *ou* great efforts to succeed, try very hard to succeed; **faire un ~ sur soi-même pour rester calme** to make an effort *ou* force o.s. to stay calm; **faire l'~ de** to make the effort to; **faire porter son ~ sur** to concentrate one's efforts (**sur** on); **plier sous l'~** to bend with the effort; *(Sport)* **il est resté en deçà de son ~** he didn't go all out, he didn't stretch himself to his limit; **encore un ~** just a little more effort; **sans ~** effortlessly, easily; **avec ~** with some effort → **moindre**

effraction [efʀaksjɔ̃] NF (*Jur*) breaking and entering; **entrer par ~** to break in; **ils sont entrés par ~ dans la maison** they broke into the house; **~ informatique** (computer) hacking → **vol²**

effraie [efʀɛ] NF (**chouette**) **~** barn-owl

effrangé, e [efʀɑ̃ʒe] (*ptp de* **effranger**) ADJ fringed; (= *effiloché*) frayed

effranger [efʀɑ̃ʒe] ▶conjug 3 ◀ 1 VT to fringe (*by fraying*) 2 **s'effranger** VPR to fray; **ces manches s'effrangent** these sleeves are fraying (at the edges)

effrayant, e [efʀɛjɑ̃, ɑ̃t] ADJ (= *qui fait peur*) frightening; (= *alarmant*) alarming

effrayé, e [efʀeje] (*ptp de* **effrayer**) ADJ frightened, scared; **il me regarda d'un air ~** he looked at me in alarm

effrayer [efʀeje] ▶conjug 8 ◀ 1 VT (= *faire peur à*) to frighten, scare 2 **s'effrayer** VPR to be frightened *ou* scared *ou* afraid (**de** of)

effréné, e [efʀene] ADJ [*course*] wild, frantic; [*passion, luxe*] unbridled, unrestrained, wild

effritement [efʀitmɑ̃] NM [*roche*] crumbling; [*valeurs morales, majorité*] crumbling; [*monnaie*] erosion; [*fortune, valeurs boursières*] dwindling; [*relation*] disintegration

effriter [efʀite] ▶conjug 1 ◀ 1 VT [+ *biscuit, sucre*] to crumble; [+ *roche, falaise*] to cause to crumble 2 **s'effriter** VPR [*roche*] to crumble (*away*); [*valeurs morales*] to crumble (away), disintegrate; [*majorité électorale*] to crumble; [*monnaie*] to be eroded, decline in value; [*fortune, valeurs boursières*] to dwindle; [*relation*] to disintegrate, fall apart; (*Sport*) **son avance s'effrite** he's losing his lead

effroi [efʀwa] NM (*littér*) terror, dread; **saisi d'~** terror-stricken

effronté, e [efʀɔ̃te] 1 ADJ [*personne, air, réponse*] insolent, impudent, cheeky (*Brit*), sassy (*US*); [*mensonge, menteur*] barefaced (*épith*), shameless 2 NM,F insolent *ou* impudent person; **petit ~!** you insolent *ou* impudent *ou* cheeky (*Brit*) *ou* sassy (*US*) little thing!

effrontément [efʀɔ̃temɑ̃] ADV [*mentir*] brazenly; [*sourire*] impudently, cheekily (*Brit*)

effronterie [efʀɔ̃tʀi] NF [*réponse, personne*] insolence, impudence, cheek (*Brit*); [*mensonge*] shamelessness, effrontery

effroyable [efʀwajabl] ADJ appalling, horrifying

effroyablement [efʀwajabləmɑ̃] ADV appallingly, horrifyingly

effusion [efyzjɔ̃] NF [*tendresse*] outpouring; **après ~s** after all this effusiveness; **remercier qn avec ~** to thank sb effusively; **~ de sang** bloodshed

égailler (s') [egaje] ▶conjug 1 ◀ VPR to scatter, disperse

▼**égal, e** (*mpl -aux*) [egal, o] 1 ADJ a (= *de même valeur*) equal (**à** to); **de poids ~** of equal weight; **à poids ~** weight for weight; **à nombre/prix ~** for the same number/price; **égaux en nombre** equal in numbers; **à ~e distance de deux points** equidistant *ou* exactly halfway between two points; **Orléans est à ~e distance de Tours et de Paris** Orléans is equidistant from Tours and Paris *ou* is the same distance from Tours as from Paris; **Tours et Paris sont à ~e distance d'Orléans** Tours and Paris are the same distance from *ou* are equidistant from Orléans; **d'adresse/d'audace ~e** of equal skill/boldness, equally skilful/bold; **toutes choses ~es par ailleurs** all *ou* other things being equal → **signe**
b (= *sans variation*) [*justice*] even, unvarying; [*climat*] equable, unchanging; [*terrain*] even, level; [*bruit, rumeur, vent*] steady; **de caractère ~** even-tempered; **marcher d'un pas ~** to walk with a regular *ou* an even step
c (*loc*) **ça m'est ~** (= *je n'y attache pas d'importance*) I don't mind, it's all one *ou* the same to me; (= *je m'en fiche*) I don't care; **pense ce que tu veux, ça m'est bien ~** you can think what you like, I really don't care; **tout lui est ~** he doesn't feel strongly about anything; **c'est ~, il aurait pu m'écrire** all the same *ou* be that as it may, he might have written; **sa probité n'a d'~e que sa générosité** his integrity is matched *ou* equalled only by his generosity; **rester ~ à soi-même** to remain true to form → **arme, jeu**
2 NM,F a (= *personne*) equal; **il ne fréquente que ses égaux** he only associates with his equals
b (*loc*) **il a traité d'~ à ~ avec moi** he treated me as his *ou* an equal; **nous parlions d'~ à ~** we talked to each other as equals; **sa probité est à l'~ de sa générosité** his generosity is equalled *ou* matched by his integrity; **c'est une vraie mégère à l'~ de sa mère** she's a real shrew just like her mother; **sans ~** [*beauté, courage*] matchless, unequalled, peerless

égalable [egalabl] ADJ **difficilement ~** difficult to equal *ou* match

également [egalmɑ̃] ADV (= *sans aspérités*) evenly; (= *sans préférence*) equally; (= *aussi*) also, too, as well; **elle lui a ~ parlé** (*elle aussi*) she also *ou* too spoke to him; (*à lui aussi*) she spoke to him as well *ou* too

égaler [egale] ▶conjug 1 ◀ 1 VT a [+ *personne, record*] to equal (**en** in); (*Math*) **2 plus 2 égalent 4** 2 plus 2 equals 4; **personne ne l'a encore égalé en adresse** so far there has been no one to equal *ou* match his skill, so far no one has matched him for skill; **son intégrité égale sa générosité** his generosity is matched *ou* equalled by his integrity, his integrity matches *ou* equals his generosity b (= *comparer*) **~ qn à** to rank sb with; **c'est un bon compositeur mais je ne l'égalerais pas à Ravel** he's a good composer but I wouldn't rank him with *ou* put him beside Ravel c† (= *rendre égal*) **la mort égale tous les êtres** death is the great leveller 2 **s'égaler** VPR **s'~ à** (= *se montrer l'égal de*) to equal, be equal to; (= *se comparer à*) to liken o.s. to, compare o.s. to

égalisateur, -trice [egalizatœʀ, tʀis] ADJ equalizing (*Brit*), tying (*US*); (*Sport*) **le but ~** the equalizer (*Brit*), the tying goal (*US*); (*Tennis*) **le jeu ~** the game which evened (up) the score

égalisation [egalizasjɔ̃] NF (*Sport*) equalization (*Brit*), tying (*US*); [*sol, revenus*] levelling; (*Sport*) **c'est l'~** they've scored the equalizer (*Brit*) *ou* the tying goal (*US*), they've equalized (*Brit*) *ou* tied (*US*)

égaliser [egalize] ▶conjug 1 ◀ 1 VT [+ *chances*] to equalize, make equal; [+ *cheveux*] to straighten up; [+ *sol, revenus*] to level (out) 2 VI (*Sport*) to equalize (*Brit*), tie (*US*) 3 **s'égaliser** VPR [*chances*] to become (more) equal; [*sol*] to level (out), become (more) level

égaliseur [egalizœʀ] NM **~ graphique** graphic equalizer

égalitaire [egalitɛʀ] ADJ egalitarian

égalitarisme [egalitaʀism] NM egalitarianism

égalitariste [egalitaʀist] ADJ, NMF egalitarian

▼**égalité** [egalite] NF a [*hommes*] equality; (*Math*) identity; (*Gram*) **comparatif d'~** comparative of similar degree; **à ~ de qualification on prend le plus âgé** in the case of equal qualifications we take the oldest; **~ des chances** equal opportunities, equality of opportunity b [*climat*] equableness, equability; [*pouls*] regularity; [*surface*] evenness, levelness; **~ d'humeur** evenness of temper, equableness; **~ d'âme** equanimity c (*Sport*) **être à ~** (*après un but*) to be equal; (*fin du match*) to draw (*Brit*), tie (*US*); (*Tennis : à 40/40*) to be at deuce; (*Sport*) **ils sont à ~** the score is *ou* the scores are even; (*Tennis*) **«~!»** "deuce!" → **pied**

égard [egaʀ] NM a (= *respect*) **~s** consideration; **il la reçut avec de grands ~s** he welcomed her with every *ou* great consideration; **être plein d'~s pour qn** ◊ **avoir beaucoup d'~s pour qn** to be very considerate towards sb, show great consideration for sb; **manquer d'~s envers qn** to be inconsiderate to(wards) sb, show a lack of consideration for sb; **vous n'avez aucun ~ pour votre matériel** you have no respect for your equipment
b (*loc*) **avoir ~ à qch** to take sth into account *ou* consideration; **eu ~ à** in view of, considering; **par ~ pour** out of consideration for; **sans ~ pour** without regard for, without considering; **à bien des ~s** (*frm*) in many respects; **à tous (les) ~s** in all respects; **à certains ~s** in certain respects; **à cet/aucun ~** in this/no respect
c **à l'~ de** (*envers*) aimable à l'~ des enfants friendly towards children; (*contre*) **des mesures ont été prises à son ~** measures have been taken against him; **à l'~ de ce que vous me dites ...** (*en ce qui concerne*) concerning *ou* regarding *ou* with regard to what you're saying ...

égaré, e [egaʀe] (*ptp de* **égarer**) ADJ a [*voyageur*] lost; [*animal*] stray (*épith*), lost → **brebis** b [*air, regard*] distraught, wild

égarement [egaʀmɑ̃] 1 NM (*littér* = *trouble affectif*) distraction; **dans un moment d'~** in a moment of distraction 2 **égarements** NMPL (*littér* = *dérèglements*) aberrations; **elle est revenue de ses ~s** she's seen the error of her ways

égarer [egaʀe] ▶conjug 1 ◀ 1 VT a [+ *voyageur*] to lead out of his way; [+ *enquêteurs*] to mislead; (*moralement*) [+ *jeunes, esprits*] to lead astray; (*frm*) **la douleur vous égare** you are distraught *ou* distracted with grief
b [+ *objet*] to mislay
2 **s'égarer** VPR a [*voyageur*] to lose one's way, get lost; [*animal*] to get lost; (*du troupeau*) to stray; [*colis, lettre*] to get lost, go astray; [*discussion, auteur*] to wander from the point; **ne nous égarons pas!** let's stick to the point!, let's not wander from the point!; **il s'égare dans des détails** he loses himself *ou*

---

he gets lost in details; **une espèce d'original égaré dans notre siècle** an eccentric individual who seems out of place in the age we live in; *(fig, Rel)* **s'~ du droit chemin** to wander *ou* stray from the straight and narrow; **quelques votes d'extrême droite se sont égarés sur ce candidat socialiste** a few votes from the far right have been lost to the socialist candidate [b] (= *perdre la raison*) to lose one's reason; **mon esprit s'égare à cette pensée** the thought of it makes me feel quite distraught

égayement [egɛjmɑ̃] NM = **égaiement**

égayer [egeje] ▸ conjug 8 ◂ [1] VT [+ *personne*] to cheer up; [+ *pièce*] to brighten up; [+ *conversation*] to enliven [2] **s'égayer** VPR **s'~ aux dépens de qn** to amuse o.s. at sb's expense; **s'~ à voir ...** to be highly amused *ou* entertained at seeing ...

Égée [eʒe] ADJ **la mer ~** the Aegean Sea; **les îles de la mer ~** the Aegean Islands

égéen, -enne [eʒeɛ̃, ɛn] ADJ [*peuples*] Aegean

égérie [eʒeʀi] NF [a] [*poète*] oracle; [*voleurs*] mastermind; **la police a arrêté l'~ de la bande** the police have arrested the woman who was the brains behind the gang [b] **Égérie** *(Hist)* Egeria

égide [eʒid] ♦ **sous l'égide de** LOC PRÉP under the aegis of

églantier [eglɑ̃tje] NM wild *ou* dog rose

églantine [eglɑ̃tin] NF wild *ou* dog rose, eglantine

églefin [egləfɛ̃] NM = **aiglefin**

église [egliz] NF [a] (= *bâtiment*) church; **aller à l'~** to go to church; **il est à l'~** (*pour l'office*) he's at *ou* in church; (*en curieux*) he's in the church; **se marier à l'~** to get married in church, have a church wedding; **à l'~ Ste Marie** at St Mary's (church) [b] **l'Église** (= *secte, clergé*) the Church; **l'Église anglicane** the Church of England, the Anglican Church; **l'Église catholique** the Church of Rome, the Roman Catholic Church; **l'Église réformée** the Reformed Church; **l'Église orthodoxe** the Orthodox Church; **l'Église de France/Rome** The Church of France/Rome; **l'Église militante/triomphante/souffrante** the Church militant/triumphant/expectant → **gens¹, homme**

églogue [eglɔg] NF eclogue

ego [ego] NM (*Philo, Psych*) ego; **il a un ~ démesuré** he has an inflated ego

égocentrique [egosɑ̃tʀik] [1] ADJ egocentric, self-centred [2] NMF egocentric *ou* self-centred person

égocentrisme [egosɑ̃tʀism] NM (*gén*) egocentricity, self-centredness; (*Psych*) egocentricity

égocentriste [egosɑ̃tʀist] ADJ, NMF = **égocentrique**

égoïne [egɔin] NF (*scie*) **~** handsaw

égoïsme [egɔism] NM selfishness, egoism

égoïste [egɔist] [1] ADJ selfish, egoistic [2] NMF selfish person, egoist

égoïstement [egɔistəmɑ̃] ADV selfishly, egoistically

égorgement [egɔʀʒəmɑ̃] NM **l'~ d'un mouton** slitting *ou* cutting a sheep's throat

égorger [egɔʀʒe] ▸ conjug 3 ◂ VT (*lit*) to slit *ou* cut the throat of; * [+ *débiteur, client*] to bleed white

égorgeur, -euse [egɔʀʒœʀ, øz] NM,F cutthroat

égosiller (s') [egozije] ▸ conjug 1 ◂ VPR (= *crier*) to shout o.s. hoarse; (= *chanter fort*) to sing at the top of one's voice *ou* lungs (*US*)

égotisme [egɔtism] NM egotism

égotiste [egɔtist] (*littér*) [1] ADJ egotistic(al) [2] NMF egotist

égout [egu] NM sewer; **réseau** *ou* **système d'~s** sewerage system; **eaux d'~** sewage; [*eaux*

---

usées] **aller à l'~** to go down the drain; **~ pluvial** storm drain *ou* sewer

égoutier [egutje] NM sewer worker

égoutter [egute] ▸ conjug 1 ◂ [1] VT [+ *légumes*] (*avec une passoire*) to strain; [+ *linge*] (*en le tordant*) to wring out; [+ *fromage*] to drain [2] VI [*vaisselle*] to drain; [*linge, eau*] to drip; **faire ~ l'eau** to drain off the water; **mettre le linge à ~** to hang up the washing to drip; **ne l'essore pas, laisse-le ~** don't wring it out, leave it to drip dry [3] **s'égoutter** VPR [*arbre, linge, eau*] to drip; [*vaisselle*] to drain

égouttoir [egutwaʀ] NM [*vaisselle*] (*intégré dans l'évier*) draining (*Brit*) *ou* drain (*US*) board; (*mobile*) draining rack (*Brit*), drainer (*US*), dish rack (*US*); [*légumes*] strainer, colander

égratigner [egratiɲe] ▸ conjug 1 ◂ VT [+ *peau*] to scratch, graze; [+ *genou*] to graze, scrape; (*fig*) [+ *adversaire*] to have a dig at; **il s'est égratigné le genou** he grazed his knee; **le film/l'auteur s'est fait ~ par la critique** the film/the author was given a bit of a rough ride by the critics

égratignure [egratiɲyʀ] NF [*peau*] scratch, graze; [*genou*] graze, scrape; **il s'en est sorti sans une ~** he came out of it without a scratch; **ce n'était qu'une ~ faite à son amour-propre** it just dented his self-esteem

égrènement [egrɛnmɑ̃] NM **l'~ des heures/minutes** marking out the hours/minutes; (*littér*) **l'~ des hameaux le long de la vallée** the hamlets dotted along the valley

égrener [egrəne] ▸ conjug 5 ◂ [1] VT [a] [+ *pois*] to shell, pod; [+ *blé, maïs, épi*] to shell; [+ *coton*] to gin; [+ *grappe*] to pick grapes off; **~ des raisins** to pick grapes off the bunch [b] (*fig*) **~ son chapelet** to tell one's beads† (*aussi littér*), say the rosary; **la pendule égrène les heures** the clock marks out the hours [2] **s'égrener** VPR [*raisins*] to drop off the bunch; [*blé*] to drop off the stalk; [*rire*] to break out; **les maisons s'égrenaient le long de la route** the houses were dotted along the road; **les notes du piano s'égrenaient dans le silence** the notes of the piano fell one by one in the silence

égreneuse [egrənøz] NF [*céréales*] cornsheller; [*coton*] gin

égrillard, e [egrijaʀ, aʀd] ADJ [*ton, regard*] ribald; [*plaisanterie, rire, propos*] ribald, bawdy

Égypte [eʒipt] NF Egypt; **la basse/haute ~** Lower/Upper Egypt; **la République arabe d'~** the Arab Republic of Egypt

égyptien, -ienne [eʒipsjɛ̃, jɛn] [1] ADJ Egyptian [2] **Égyptien(ne)** NM,F Egyptian

égyptologie [eʒiptɔlɔʒi] NF Egyptology

égyptologue [eʒiptɔlɔg] NMF Egyptologist

eh [e] EXCL hey!; **~ oui!/non!** I'm afraid so!/not!; **~ bien** well

éhonté, e [eɔ̃te] ADJ [*action*] shameless, brazen; [*menteur, mensonge*] shameless, barefaced, brazen

eider [edɛʀ] NM eider

einsteinien, -ienne [ɛnstajnjɛ̃, jɛn] ADJ Einsteinian

einsteinium [ɛnstɛnjɔm] NM einsteinium

Eire [ɛʀ] NF Eire

éjaculateur [eʒakylatœʀ] NM **être un ~ précoce** to suffer from premature ejaculation, be a premature ejaculator

éjaculation [eʒakylasjɔ̃] NF (*Physiol*) ejaculation; **~ précoce** premature ejaculation

éjaculatoire [eʒakylatwaʀ] ADJ (*Physiol*) ejaculatory

éjaculer [eʒakyle] ▸ conjug 1 ◂ VI (*Physiol*) to ejaculate

éjectable [eʒɛktabl] ADJ → **siège¹**

éjecter [eʒɛkte] ▸ conjug 1 ◂ [1] VT [a] (*Tech*) to eject [b] [+ *personne*] (*accidentellement*) to throw out; **le choc l'a éjecté de la voiture** he was thrown out of the car [c] * (= *congédier*) to

---

sack*; (= *expulser*) to kick out*; **se faire ~** (*de son travail*) to get the sack*; (*d'une boîte de nuit*) to get kicked out* [2] **s'éjecter** VPR [*pilote*] to eject

éjection [eʒɛksjɔ̃] NF [a] (*Tech*) ejection [b] (= *licenciement*) sacking*

élaboration [elabɔʀasjɔ̃] NF [*plan, système*] working-out, elaboration; [*bile, sève, aliments*] elaboration

élaboré, e [elabɔʀe] (*ptp de* **élaborer**) ADJ (= *sophistiqué*) [*théorie, savoir*] elaborate; [*cuisine, coiffure, système*] elaborate, sophisticated

élaborer [elabɔʀe] ▸ conjug 1 ◂ VT [+ *plan, système, solution*] to work out, elaborate; [+ *document*] to draw up; [+ *bile, sève, aliments*] to elaborate

élagage [elagaʒ] NM (*lit, fig*) pruning

élaguer [elage] ▸ conjug 1 ◂ VT (*lit, fig*) to prune

élagueur, -euse [elagœʀ, øz] NM,F pruner

élan¹ [elɑ̃] NM (*Zool*) elk, moose

élan² [elɑ̃] NM [a] (= *début de course*) run up; **prendre son ~** to take a run up; **saut avec/sans ~** running/standing jump; (*littér*) **l'~ du clocher vers le ciel** the thrust of the steeple towards the sky [b] (= *vitesse acquise*) momentum; **prendre de l'~** [*coureur*] to gather speed; **perdre son ~** to lose one's momentum; **il a continué dans** *ou* **sur son ~** he continued to run at the same pace *ou* speed; **rien ne peut arrêter son ~** nothing can check *ou* stop his pace *ou* momentum; **emporté par son propre ~** (*lit*) carried along by his own impetus *ou* momentum; (*fig*) carried away on *ou* by the tide of his own enthusiasm [c] (= *poussée, transport*) **~ de** [+ *enthousiasme, colère*] surge *ou* rush of; **dans un ~ de générosité** in a surge of generosity; **les ~s de l'imagination** flights of fancy; **les rares ~s (de tendresse) qu'il avait vers elle** the few surges *ou* rushes of affection he felt for her; **les ~s lyriques de l'orateur** the lyrical outbursts of the speaker; **maîtriser les ~s de son cœur** to control the impulses of one's heart; **dire qch avec ~** to say sth with fervour *ou* passion [d] (= *ardeur*) vigour (*Brit*), vigor (*US*), spirit, élan; **~ patriotique** patriotic fervour; **l'~ des troupes** the vigour *ou* spirit of the troops [e] (= *dynamisme*) boost; **redonner de l'~** *ou* **donner un nouvel ~ à une politique/une institution/l'économie** to give new impetus to a policy/an institution/the economy; **~ vital** life force

élancé, e [elɑ̃se] (*ptp de* **élancer**) ADJ [*clocher, colonne, taille, personne*] slender

élancement [elɑ̃smɑ̃] NM (*Méd*) shooting *ou* sharp pain

élancer [elɑ̃se] ▸ conjug 3 ◂ [1] VT (*littér*) **le clocher élance sa flèche vers le ciel** the church steeple soars up *ou* thrusts upwards into the sky [2] VI [*blessure*] to give shooting *ou* sharp pains; **mon doigt m'élance** I get shooting *ou* sharp pains in my finger [3] **s'élancer** VPR [a] (= *se précipiter*) to rush forward; (= *prendre son élan*) to take a run up; **s'~ au-dehors** to rush *ou* dash outside; **s'~ comme une flèche vers** to dart towards; **s'~ d'un bond sur** to leap onto; **s'~ au secours de qn** to rush *ou* dash to help sb; **s'~ à la poursuite de qn** to rush off in pursuit of sb, dash after sb; **s'~ vers qn** to leap *ou* dash towards sb; **s'~ sur qn** to hurl *ou* throw o.s. at sb, rush at sb; **s'~ à l'assaut d'une montagne/forteresse** to launch an attack on a mountain/fortress [b] (*littér* = *se dresser*) to soar *oú* thrust (upwards); **la tour s'élance vers le ciel** the tower soars *ou* thrusts up into the sky

élargir [elaʀʒiʀ] ▸ conjug 2 ◂ [1] VT [a] (*pour agrandir*) [+ *rue*] to widen; [+ *robe*] to let out; [+ *chaussures*] to stretch, widen; (= *déformer*) [+ *vêtement, chaussures*] to stretch; **ça lui**

élargit la taille it makes her look bigger round the waist; **une veste qui élargit les épaules** a jacket that makes the shoulders look broader *ou* wider b [+ *débat, connaissances*] to broaden, widen; (*Pol*) **majorité élargie** increased majority; **~ son horizon** to enlarge *ou* widen one's horizons; **~ son champ d'action** to extend one's field of operations c (*Jur = libérer*) to release, free 2 **s'élargir** VPR [*vêtement*] to stretch; [*route*] to widen, get wider; [*esprit, débat*] to broaden; [*idées*] to broaden, widen

élargissement [elaʀʒismɑ̃] NM a (= *agrandissement*) [*rue*] widening; [*robe*] letting out; [*chaussures*] stretching, widening b [*débat, connaissances*] broadening, widening; **elle réclame un ~ de ses pouvoirs** she wants her powers to be extended c (*Jur = libération*) release, freeing

élasthanne [elastan] NM spandex®, elastane® (*Brit*)

élasticité [elastisite] NF a [*objet*] elasticity; [*démarche*] springiness; (*Écon*) [*offre, demande*] elasticity b [*sens, esprit, principes*] flexibility; (*péj*) [*conscience*] accommodating nature; [*règlement*] elasticity, flexibility

élastine [elastin] NF elastin

élastique [elastik] 1 ADJ a [*objet*] elastic; [*démarche*] springy; (*Écon*) [*offre, demande*] elastic; (*Couture*) **taille ~** elasticated (*Brit*) *ou* elasticized (*US*) waist b [*sens, esprit, principes*] flexible; (*péj*) [*conscience*] accommodating; [*règlement*] elastic, flexible 2 NM a (*de bureau*) elastic *ou* rubber band → **lâcher** b [*pour couture, jeu etc*] elastic (*NonC*); (*Sport*) bungee cord; **en ~** elasticated, elastic → **saut**

élastiqué, e [elastike] ADJ [*encolure, ceinture, manche, taille*] elasticated (*Brit*), elasticized (*US*); [*pantalon*] with an elasticated (*Brit*) *ou* elasticized (*US*) waist

élastomère [elastɔmɛʀ] NM elastomer; **en ~** [*chaussures*] man-made

Elbe [ɛlb] N **l'île d'~** (the island of) Elba; (= *fleuve*) **l'~** the Elbe

Eldorado [ɛldɔʀado] NM El Dorado

électeur, -trice [elɛktœʀ, tʀis] NM,F a (*Pol, gén*) voter, elector; (*dans une circonscription*) constituent; **le député et ses ~s** ≈ the member of parliament and his constituents; (*corps électoral*) **les ~s** the electorate, the voters; **grand ~** (*en France*) *elector who votes in the elections for the French Senate*; (*aux USA*) presidential elector b (*Hist*) **Électeur** Elector; **Électrice** Electress → SÉNAT

électif, -ive [elɛktif, iv] ADJ (*Pol*) elective

élection [elɛksjɔ̃] NF a (*Pol, gén*) election; **jour des ~s** polling *ou* election day; **se présenter aux ~s** to stand (*Brit*) *ou* run (*US*) as a candidate (in the election); **~ présidentielle** presidential election; **~ partielle** ≈ by(e)-election; **~s législatives** legislative elections, ≈ general election; **~s municipales/cantonales** municipal/cantonal elections; **~s régionales** regional elections b (*littér = choix*) choice; **lieu/patrie d'~** place/country of one's (own) choosing *ou* choice; **la France est une patrie *ou* terre d'~ pour les poètes** France is a country much favoured by poets; (*Jur*) **de domicile** choice of residence

---
ÉLECTIONS

Presidential elections are held in France every seven years, while legislative elections (for the "députés" who make up the "Assemblée nationale") take place every five years. Elections for one third of the "Sénat" are held every seven years, but these are collegiate and only "grands électeurs" (high-ranking officials and party representatives) vote in them.

There are two kinds of local election in France, and both are held every six years. They are the "élections cantonales" in which people vote for the "Conseil régional" and "Conseil général", and the

"élections municipales" for the "Conseil municipal" (or the "Conseil d'arrondissement" in Paris, Marseille and Lyon).

All public elections take place on a Sunday in France, usually in school halls and "mairies". → CANTON; COMMUNE; DÉPARTEMENT etc

électoral, e (*mpl* **-aux**) [elɛktɔʀal, o] ADJ [*affiche, réunion*] election (*épith*); **campagne ~e** election *ou* electoral campaign; **pendant la période ~e** during election time, during the run-up to the election; **il m'a promis son soutien ~** he promised me his backing in the election → **agent, circonscription, corps**

électoralisme [elɛktɔʀalism] NM electioneering

électoraliste [elɛktɔʀalist] ADJ electioneering

électorat [elɛktɔʀa] NM a (= *électeurs*) electorate; (*dans une circonscription*) constituency; (= *droit de vote*) franchise; **l'~ socialiste** the voters for the socialist party, the socialist vote b (*Hist = principauté*) electorate

Électre [elɛktʀ] NF Electra

électricien, -ienne [elɛktʀisjɛ̃, jɛn] NM,F electrician

électricité [elɛktʀisite] NF electricity; **allumer l'~** to turn *ou* switch *ou* put the light on; **ça marche à l'~** it runs on electricity, it's electrically operated; **refaire l'~** to rewire the house (*ou* shop etc); **être sans ~** (*gén*) to have no electricity; (*suite à une panne, à une grève*) to be without power; **~ statique** static electricity; **l'~ d'origine nucléaire** nuclear(-generated) electricity; **~ atmosphérique** atmospherics; **il y a de l'~ dans l'air*** the atmosphere is electric → **panne¹**

électrification [elɛktʀifikasjɔ̃] NF electrification

électrifier [elɛktʀifje] ▸conjug 7◂ VT to electrify; **~ un village** to bring electricity *ou* electric power to a village

électrique [elɛktʀik] ADJ (*lit*) electric(al); (*fig*) electric; **atmosphère ~** highly-charged atmosphere; **bleu ~** electric blue; **j'ai les cheveux ~s*** I've got static (electricity) in my hair

électriquement [elɛktʀikmɑ̃] ADV electrically

électrisable [elɛktʀizabl] ADJ [*foule*] easily roused; [*substance*] chargeable, electrifiable

électrisant, e [elɛktʀizɑ̃, ɑ̃t] ADJ [*discours, contact*] electrifying

électrisation [elɛktʀizasjɔ̃] NF [*substance*] charging, electrifying

électriser [elɛktʀize] ▸conjug 1◂ VT [+ *substance*] to charge, electrify; [+ *public*] to electrify

électroacoustique, électro-acoustique (*pl* **électro-acoustiques**) [elɛktʀoakustik] 1 ADJ electroacoustic 2 NF acoustoelectronics *sg*, electroacoustics *sg*

électro-aimant (*pl* **électro-aimants**) [elɛktʀoɛmɑ̃] NM electromagnet

électrocardiogramme [elɛktʀokaʀdjɔgʀam] NM electrocardiogram; **faire un ~ à qn** to give sb an electrocardiogram *ou* an ECG

électrocardiographe [elɛktʀokaʀdjɔgʀaf] NM electrocardiograph

électrocardiographie [elɛktʀokaʀdjɔgʀafi] NF electrocardiography

électrochimie [elɛktʀoʃimi] NF electrochemistry

électrochimique [elɛktʀoʃimik] ADJ electrochemical

électrochoc [elɛktʀoʃɔk] NM (= *procédé*) electric shock treatment, electroconvulsive therapy (*SPÉC*); **on lui a fait des ~s** he was given electric shock treatment *ou* ECT; **sa proposition a provoqué un ~** his proposal sent shock waves through the country

électrocuter [elɛktʀokyte] ▸conjug 1◂ 1 VT to electrocute 2 **s'électrocuter** VPR to electrocute o.s.

électrocution [elɛktʀokysjɔ̃] NF electrocution

électrode [elɛktʀɔd] NF electrode

électrodynamique [elɛktʀodinamik] 1 ADJ electrodynamic 2 NF electrodynamics *sg*

électro-encéphalogramme (*pl* **électro-encéphalogrammes**) [elɛktʀoɑ̃sefalogʀam] NM electroencephalogram

électro-encéphalographie (*pl* **électro-encéphalographies**) [elɛktʀoɑ̃sefalogʀafi] NF electroencephalography

électrogène [elɛktʀɔʒɛn] ADJ (*Zool*) electric → **groupe**

électrolyse [elɛktʀoliz] NF electrolysis

électrolyser [elɛktʀolize] ▸conjug 1◂ VT to electrolyse

électrolyseur [elɛktʀolizœʀ] NM electrolyser

électrolyte [elɛktʀolit] NM electrolyte

électrolytique [elɛktʀolitik] ADJ electrolytic(al)

électromagnétique [elɛktʀomaɲetik] ADJ electromagnetic

électromagnétisme [elɛktʀomaɲetism] NM electromagnetism

électromécanicien, -ienne [elɛktʀomekanisjɛ̃, jɛn] NM,F electromechanical engineer

électromécanique [elɛktʀomekanik] 1 ADJ electromechanical 2 NF electromechanical engineering

électroménager [elɛktʀomenaʒe] 1 ADJ **appareil ~** (household *ou* domestic) electrical appliance 2 NM **l'~** (= *appareils*) (household *ou* domestic) electrical appliances; (= *industrie*) the electrical goods industry; **le petit/gros ~** small/large electrical appliances; **magasin d'~** electrical goods shop (*Brit*) *ou* store (*US*)

électrométallurgie [elɛktʀometalyʀʒi] NF electrometallurgy

électrométallurgique [elɛktʀometalyʀʒik] ADJ electrometallurgical

électromètre [elɛktʀomɛtʀ] NM electrometer

électromoteur, -trice [elɛktʀomotœʀ, tʀis] 1 ADJ electromotive 2 NM electric motor, electromotor

électron [elɛktʀɔ̃] NM electron

électronégatif, -ive [elɛktʀonegatif, iv] ADJ electronegative

électronicien, -ienne [elɛktʀonisjɛ̃, jɛn] NM,F electronics engineer

électronique [elɛktʀonik] 1 ADJ (*gén*) electronic; [*microscope*] electron (*épith*); **groupe/industrie ~** electronics group/industry → **adresse, autoroute, courrier, dictionnaire** 2 NF electronics *sg*

électronucléaire [elɛktʀonykleɛʀ] 1 ADJ nuclear power (*épith*) 2 NM **l'~** nuclear power

électrophone [elɛktʀofɔn] NM record player

électropositif, -ive [elɛktʀopozitif, iv] ADJ electropositive

électrostatique [elɛktʀostatik] 1 ADJ electrostatic 2 NF electrostatics *sg*

électrotechnicien, -ienne [elɛktʀoteknisjɛ̃, jɛn] NM,F electrotechnician

électrotechnique [elɛktʀoteknik] 1 ADJ electrotechnical; **institut ~** institute of electrical engineering *ou* of electrotechnology 2 NF (= *science*) electrical engineering, electrotechnology, electrotechnics *sg*; (= *secteur*) electrical engineering

électrothérapie [elɛktʀoteʀapi] NF electrotherapy

élégamment [elegamɑ̃] ADV elegantly

élégance [elegɑ̃s] NF a [*personne, toilette*] elegance, stylishness b [*conduite*] generosity; [*solution*] elegance, neatness; **~s (de style)** ornaments (of style); **perdre avec ~** to be gracious in defeat *ou* a graceful loser; **l'~ féminine** feminine elegance; **concours d'~** *parade of elegant women in beautiful cars*; **il aurait pu avoir l'~ de s'excuser** he might have had the good grace to apologize

élégant, e [elegɑ̃, ɑ̃t] 1 ADJ a [*personne, toilette*] elegant, stylish; **tu es très ~ habillé comme ça** you're looking very elegant b [*conduite*] generous; [*solution*] elegant, neat; **user de procédés peu ~s** to use crude methods; **c'était une façon ~e de le remettre à sa place** it was a neat way of putting him in his place 2 NM† (= *dandy*) elegant *ou* stylish man, man of fashion **élégante**† NF elegant *ou* stylish woman, woman of fashion

élégiaque [eleʒjak] ADJ elegiac

élégie [eleʒi] NF elegy

élément [elemɑ̃] 1 NM a [*structure, ensemble*] element, component; [*problème*] element; [*mélange*] ingredient, element; [*réussite*] factor, element; [*appareil*] part, component; **~ comique (d'un roman)** comic element (of a novel)
b (= *meuble*) unit; **~s de rangement** storage units; **~s de cuisine/de bibliothèque** kitchen/ bookshelf units
c (*Mil*) **~s blindés/aéroportés** armoured/ airborne units
d (*Chim*) element; **l'~ hydrogène** the element hydrogen
e (*Tech*) [*pile*] cell
f (= *fait*) fact; **nous manquons d'~s** we lack information *ou* facts; **aucun ~ nouveau n'est survenu** there have been no new developments, no new facts have come to light; (*Mil*) **~s de tir** range data
g (*Comptab, Fin*) item; **après/hors ~s exceptionnels** after/before extraordinary items
h (= *individu*) **c'est le meilleur ~ de ma classe** he's the best pupil in my class; **bons et mauvais ~s** good and bad elements; **~s subversifs/ ennemis** subversive/hostile elements
i (= *milieu*) element; **les quatre ~s** the four elements; **les ~s (naturels)** the elements; **l'~ liquide** the liquid element; **quand on parle d'électronique il est dans son ~** when you talk about electronics he's in his element; **parmi ces artistes il ne se sentait pas dans son ~** he didn't feel at home *ou* he felt like a fish out of water among those artists
2 **éléments** NMPL (= *rudiments*) basic principles, rudiments, elements; **il a quelques ~s de chimie** he has some elementary knowledge of chemistry; (*titre d'ouvrage*) « **Éléments de Mécanique** » "Elementary Mechanics"

élémentaire [elemɑ̃tɛR] ADJ a (= *facile*) [*problème*] elementary; (= *de base*) [*notion*] elementary, basic; [*forme*] rudimentary, basic; (*Scol*) [*cours, niveau*] elementary; (= *évident*) [*précaution*] elementary, basic; **c'est ~!** it's elementary!; **la plus ~ courtoisie/discrétion veut que ...** elementary *ou* basic *ou* simple courtesy/discretion demands that ...; **mon cher Watson!** elementary, my dear Watson! b (*Chim*) elemental; (*Phys Nucl*) **particules ~s** elementary *ou* fundamental particles

Éléonore [eleɔnɔR] NF Eleanor

éléphant [elefɑ̃] NM elephant; **~ femelle** cow elephant; **~ d'Asie/d'Afrique** Indian/African elephant; **~ de mer** sea elephant, elephant seal; **comme un ~ dans un magasin de porcelaine** like a bull in a china shop; (*fig*) **les ~s du parti** the party old guard

éléphanteau (*pl* **éléphanteaux**) [elefɑ̃to] NM elephant calf, baby elephant

éléphantesque [elefɑ̃tɛsk] ADJ (= *énorme*) elephantine, gigantic

éléphantiasis [elefɑ̃tjazis] NM elephantiasis

élevage [el(ə)vaʒ] NM a [*bétail*] rearing, breeding; [*chiens, porcs, chevaux, vers à soie*] breeding; [*volailles*] farming; **l'~ (du bétail)** cat-

tle breeding *ou* rearing; **l'~ des abeilles** beekeeping; **~ intensif de porcs/poulets** intensive farming of pigs/chickens; **faire de l'~** to breed *ou* rear cattle; **faire l'~ de** [+ *bétail*] to rear, breed; [+ *chiens, porcs, chevaux, vers à soie*] to breed; [+ *abeilles*] to keep; **région** *ou* **pays d'~** cattle-rearing *ou* -breeding area; **truite/saumon d'~** farmed trout/salmon b (= *ferme*) [*bétail*] cattle farm; **~ de poulets/de truites** poultry/ trout farm; **~ de chiens** breeding kennels

élévateur, -trice [elevatœR, tRis] ADJ, NM,F (*muscle*) **~** elevator; (*appareil*) **~** elevator; (*Élec*) (*appareil* *ou* *transformateur*) **~ de tension** step-up transformer → **chariot**

élévation [elevasjɔ̃] NF a (= *action d'élever*) [*rempart, statue*] putting up, erection; [*objet, niveau*] raising; [*pensée, âme*] elevation; (*Math*) **~ d'un nombre au carré** squaring of a number; (*Math*) **~ d'un nombre à une puissance** raising of a number to a power; **son ~ au rang de capitaine** his being raised *ou* elevated to the rank of captain, his elevation to the rank of captain b (= *action de s'élever*) [*température, niveau*] rise (**de** in) c (*Rel*) **l'~** the Elevation d (= *tertre*) elevation, mound; **~ de terrain** rise e (*Archit, Géom* = *coupe, plan*) elevation f (= *noblesse*) [*pensée, style*] elevation, loftiness

élevé, e [el(ə)ve] (*ptp de* **élever**) ADJ a [*prix, niveau, température*] high; [*pertes*] heavy; **peu ~** [*prix, niveau*] low; [*pertes*] slight; (*Jur*) **dommages-intérêts ~s** substantial damages b [*cime, arbre*] tall; [*colline*] high c [*rang, grade*] high, elevated; (*frm*) **être de condition ~e** to be of high birth; **occuper une position ~e** to hold a high position, be high-ranking d (= *noble*) [*pensée, style*] elevated, lofty; [*conception*] exalted, lofty; [*principes*] high (*épith*) e (= *éduqué*) **bien ~** well-mannered; **mal ~** (= *rustre*) bad-mannered, ill-mannered; (= *impoli*) rude, impolite; **espèce de mal ~!** you rude thing!; **c'est mal ~ de parler en mangeant** it's bad manners *ou* it's rude to talk with your mouth full

élève [elɛv] NMF (*gén*) pupil, student; (*Grande École*) student; (*Mil*) cadet; **~ professeur** student teacher, trainee teacher; **~ infirmière** student nurse; **~ officier** officer cadet; **~-officier de réserve** officer cadet

élever [el(ə)ve] ▸ conjug 5 ◂ 1 VT a (= *éduquer*) [+ *enfant*] to bring up, raise; **il a été élevé dans du coton** he had a sheltered upbringing, he was wrapped (up) in cotton wool as a child (*Brit*); **elle a été élevée selon des principes stricts** she had a strict upbringing; **son fils est élevé maintenant** his son is grown-up now
b (= *faire l'élevage de*) [+ *bétail*] to rear, breed; [+ *chiens, porcs, chevaux, vers à soie*] to breed; [+ *abeilles*] to keep; [+ *volailles*] to farm; [+ *vin*] to produce; **vin élevé dans nos chais** wine matured in our cellars
c (= *dresser*) [+ *rempart, mur, statue*] to put up, erect, raise; (*littér*) **la maison élevait sa masse sombre** the dark mass of the house rose up *ou* reared up (*littér*); **~ des objections/ des protestations** to raise objections/a protest; **~ des critiques** to make criticisms
d (= *hausser*) [+ *édifice*] to raise, make higher; **~ une maison d'un étage** to raise a house by one storey, make a house one storey higher
e (= *lever, mettre plus haut*) [+ *poids, objet*] to lift (up), raise; [+ *niveau, taux, prix*] to raise; [+ *voix*] to raise; (*littér*) [+ *yeux, bras*] to raise, lift (up); **pompe qui élève l'eau** pump which raises water
f [+ *débat*] to raise the tone of; **musique qui élève l'âme** elevating *ou* uplifting music; (*Rel*) **élevons nos cœurs vers le Seigneur** let us lift up our hearts unto the Lord
g (= *promouvoir*) to raise, elevate; **il a été élevé au grade de capitaine** he was raised *ou* elevated to the rank of captain; **chez eux l'abstinence est élevée à la hauteur d'une**

institution they've given abstinence the status of an institution, they have made abstinence a way of life
h (*Math*) **~ une perpendiculaire** to raise a perpendicular; **~ un nombre à la puissance 5** to raise a number to the power of 5; **~ un nombre au carré** to square a number
2 **s'élever** VPR a (= *augmenter*) [*température, niveau, prix*] to rise, go up; **le niveau des élèves/de vie s'est élevé** the standard of the pupils/of living has risen *ou* improved
b (= *se dresser*) [*montagne, tour*] to rise; **la tour s'élève à 50 mètres au-dessus du sol** the tower rises *ou* stands 50 metres above the ground; **un mur s'élevait entre ces deux jardins** a wall stood between the two gardens; **la cime s'élève majestueusement au-dessus des forêts** the peak rises (up) *ou* towers majestically above the forests
c (= *monter*) [*avion*] to go up, ascend; [*oiseau*] to fly up, ascend; **l'avion s'élevait régulièrement** the plane was climbing *ou* ascending steadily; **la pensée s'élève vers l'absolu** thought soars *ou* ascends towards the absolute; **l'âme s'élève vers Dieu** the soul ascends to(wards) God; **le ton s'élève** ◊ **les voix s'élèvent** voices are beginning to rise; **s'~ au-dessus des querelles** to rise above petty quarrels
d [*objections, doutes*] to be raised, arise; **sa voix s'éleva dans le silence** his voice broke the silence; **aucune voix ne s'éleva en sa faveur** not a (single) voice was raised in his favour
e (*dans la société*) to rise; **s'~ jusqu'au sommet de l'échelle** to climb to the top of the ladder; **s'~ à la force du poignet/par son seul travail** to work one's way up unaided/by the sweat of one's brow
f (= *protester*) **s'~ contre** to rise up against
g (= *se bâtir*) to go up, be put up *ou* erected; **la maison s'élève peu à peu** the house is going up bit by bit *ou* is gradually going up
h (= *se monter*) **s'~ à** [*prix, pertes*] to total, add up to, amount to

éleveur, -euse [el(ə)vœR, øz] 1 NM,F (*Agr*) stockbreeder; [*vin*] producer; **~ (de bétail)** cattle breeder *ou* rearer; **~ de chiens/chevaux/ porcs** dog/horse/pig breeder; **~ de volailles** poultry farmer; **~ de vers à soie** silkworm breeder, sericulturist (*SPÉC*); **~ d'abeilles** beekeeper → **propriétaire** 2 **éleveuse** NF (*pour poussins*) brooder

elfe [ɛlf] NM elf

élider VT, **s'élider** VPR [elide] ▸ conjug 1 ◂ to elide; **article élidé** elided article

Élie [eli] NM Elijah

éligibilité [eliʒibilite] NF eligibility (**à** for)

éligible [eliʒibl] ADJ eligible (**à** for)

élimé, e [elime] (*ptp de* **élimer**) ADJ [*vêtement, tissu*] threadbare, worn; **manteau un peu ~** rather worn overcoat; **chemise ~e au col/aux poignets** shirt with a frayed collar/with frayed cuffs

élimer [elime] ▸ conjug 1 ◂ 1 VT [+ *vêtement, tissu*] to wear thin 2 **s'élimer** VPR [*vêtement, tissu*] to wear thin, become threadbare

élimination [eliminasjɔ̃] NF (*gén*) elimination; **procéder par ~** to work by a process of elimination

éliminatoire [eliminatwaR] 1 ADJ [*épreuve*] eliminatory (*épith*); [*note, temps*] disqualifying (*épith*) 2 NF (*Sport*) (eliminating *ou* preliminary) heat, eliminator

éliminer [elimine] ▸ conjug 1 ◂ VT (*gén, Math, Méd*) to eliminate; [+ *possibilité*] to rule out, eliminate; [+ *données secondaires*] to discard, eliminate; (*Pol*) **éliminé au second tour** eliminated in the second ballot; (*Scol*) **être éliminé à l'oral** to be eliminated in *ou* to fail (in) the oral; (*Jeux*) **éliminé!** you're out!; **éliminé en quart de finale** knocked out *ou* eliminated in the quarter finals; **les petits exploitants seront éliminés du marché** small farmers will be forced out of the market; **boire fait ~** drinking cleans out the system

élire [eliʀ] ▶conjug 43◀ VT to elect; **il a été élu président** he was elected president, he was voted in as president; **~ domicile** to take up residence (**à, dans** in)

Élisabeth [elizabɛt] NF Elizabeth

élisabéthain, e [elizabetɛ̃, ɛn] **1** ADJ Elizabethan **2** **Élisabéthain(e)** NM,F Elizabethan

Élisée [elize] NM Elisha

élision [elizjɔ̃] NF elision

élitaire [elitɛʀ] ADJ [club, festival] exclusive

élite [elit] NF **a** (= groupe) elite, élite; **l'~ de** the cream ou elite of; **les ~s (de la nation)** the elite (of the nation); **être** ou **personnalité d'~** exceptional person; (Mil) **corps/cavalerie d'~** crack corps/cavalry; **tireur d'~** crack shot; **troupe d'~** elite ou crack troops; **école d'~** elite school **b** (Imprim) **caractères ~** elite (type)

élitisme [elitism] NM elitism; **faire de l'~** to be elitist

élitiste [elitist] ADJ, NMF elitist

élixir [eliksiʀ] NM elixir; **~ de longue vie** elixir of life; **~ d'amour** love potion, elixir of love; **~ parégorique** paregoric (elixir)

elle [ɛl] PRON PERS F **a** (fonction sujet) (personne) she; (chose) it; (nation) it, she; (animal, bébé) she, it; **~s** they; **~ est couturière** she is a dressmaker; **prends cette chaise, ~ est plus confortable** have this chair — it's more comfortable; **je me méfie de sa chienne, ~ mord** I don't trust his dog — she ou it bites; **~, furieuse, a refusé** furious, she refused; **la Suisse a décidé qu'~ resterait neutre** Switzerland decided that it ou she would remain neutral; **qu'est-ce qu'ils ont dit ? — ~, rien** what did they say? — she said nothing; **il est venu mais pas ~/~s** he came but she/they didn't, he came but not her/them; **~ partie, j'ai pu travailler** with her gone ou after she had gone I was able to work; **~, ~ n'aurait jamais fait ça** she would never have done that; **~ renoncer ? ce n'est pas son genre** her give up? it wouldn't be like her → **même**

b (fonction objet, souvent emphatique) (personne) her; (chose) it; (nation) it, her; (animal) her, it; **~s** them; **il n'admire qu'~** he only admires her, she's the only one he admires; **je les ai bien vus, ~ et lui** I definitely saw both ou the two of them; **la revoir ~ ? jamais !** see her again? never!

c (emphatique avec qui, que) **c'est ~ qui me l'a dit** she was the one who ou that told me; **ce fut ~ qui lança le mouvement** she was the one ou it was her that launched the movement; **voilà la pluie, et ~ qui est sortie sans manteau !** here comes the rain and to think she has gone out without a coat! ou and there she is out without a coat!; **chasse cette chienne, c'est ~ qui m'a mordu** chase that dog away, it's the one that bit me; **c'est ~ que j'avais invitée** it was her I had invited; **c'est à ~ que je veux parler** it's her I want to speak to, I want to speak to her; **il y a une chouette dans le bois, c'est ~ que j'ai entendue cette nuit** there's an owl in the wood — that's what I heard last night

d (avec prép) (personne) her; (animal) her, it; (chose) it; **ce livre est à ~** this book belongs to her ou is hers; **ces livres sont à ~s** these books belong to them ou are theirs; **c'est à ~ de décider** it's up to her to decide, it's her decision; **c'est gentil à ~ d'avoir écrit** it was kind of her to write; **un ami à ~** a friend of hers, one of her friends; **~ ne pense qu'à ~** she only thinks of herself; **~ a une maison à ~** she has a house of her own; **ses enfants à ~** her children; **qu'est-ce qu'il ferait sans ~** what on earth would he do without her; **ce poème n'est pas d'~** this poem is not one of hers ou by her ou not one that she wrote; **il veut une photo d'~** he wants a photo of her

e (dans comparaisons) (sujet) she; (objet) her; **il est plus grand qu'~/~s** he is taller than she is/they are ou than her/them; **je le connais aussi bien qu'~** (aussi bien que je la connais) I know him as well as (I know) her; (aussi bien qu'elle le connaît) I know him as well as she does; **ne faites pas comme ~** don't do as ou what she does, don't do like her*

f (interrog, emphatique: gén non traduit) **Alice est-~ rentrée ?** is Alice back?; **sa lettre est-~ arrivée ?** has his letter come?; **les infirmières sont-~s bien payées ?** are nurses well paid?; **tu sais, ta tante, ~ n'est pas très aimable !** you know, your aunt isn't very nice!

ellébore [elebɔʀ] NM hellebore

elle-même (pl **elles-mêmes**) [ɛlmɛm] PRON → **même**

ellipse [elips] NF (Géom) ellipse; (Ling) ellipsis

ellipsoïdal, e (mpl **-aux**) [elipsɔidal, o] ADJ ellipsoidal

ellipsoïde [elipsɔid] **1** NM ellipsoid **2** ADJ (Géom) elliptical

elliptique [eliptik] ADJ (Géom) elliptic(al); (Ling) elliptical

elliptiquement [eliptikmã] ADV (Ling) elliptically

élocution [elɔkysjɔ̃] NF (= débit) delivery; (= clarté) diction; **défaut d'~** speech impediment ou defect; **professeur d'~** elocution teacher

éloge [elɔʒ] NM **a** (= louange) praise; **couvert d'~s** showered with praise; **digne d'~** praiseworthy, commendable; **faire des ~s à qn** to praise sb → **tarir** **b** (= apologie) praise; **faire l'~ de** to praise, speak (very) highly of; **son ~ n'est plus à faire** I do not need to add to the praise he has already received; **c'est le plus bel ~ à lui faire** it's the highest praise one can give him; **faire son propre ~** to sing one's own praises, blow one's own trumpet* (Brit) ou horn* (US); **l'~ que vous avez fait de cette œuvre** your praise ou commendation of this work **c** (littér = panégyrique) eulogy; **prononcer l'~ funèbre de qn** to deliver a funeral oration for sb

élogieusement [elɔʒjøzmã] ADV **parler ~ de qn** to speak very highly ou most favourably of

élogieux, -ieuse [elɔʒjø, jøz] ADJ laudatory, eulogistic(al); **parler de qn/qch en termes ~** to speak very highly of sb/sth, speak of sb/sth in the most laudatory terms

éloigné, e [elwaɲe] (ptp de **éloigner**) ADJ **a** (dans l'espace) distant, remote; **est-ce très ~ de la gare ? — oui, c'est très ~** is it very far ou a long way (away) from the station? — yes, it's a long way; **~ de 3 km** 3 km away; **le village est trop ~ pour qu'on puisse y aller à pied** the village is too far away to walk ou isn't within walking distance

b (dans le temps) [époque, événement, échéance] distant (**de** from), remote (**de** from); **dans un avenir peu ~** in the not-too-distant future, in the near future

c [parent] distant; [ancêtre] remote; **la famille ~e** distant relatives

d (fig) **être ~ de** to be far from, be a long way from; **sa version est très ~e de la vérité** his version is very far from the truth; **un sentiment pas très ~ de la haine** a feeling not far removed from hatred; **rien n'est plus ~ de mes pensées** nothing is ou could be further from my thoughts; **je ne suis pas très ~ de le croire** I almost believe him, I'm not far from believing him; **je suis fort ~ de ses positions** my point of view is very far removed from his

e **tenir ~ de** to keep away from; **cette conférence m'a tenu ~ de chez moi** the conference kept me away from home; **se tenir ~ du feu** to keep away from ou clear of the fire; **se tenir ~ du danger/des querelles** to steer ou keep clear of danger/of quarrels

éloignement [elwaɲmã] NM **a** (= action d'éloigner) [personne indésirable] taking away, removal; [soupçons] removal, averting; [échéance] putting off, postponement; **leur ~ de la cour, ordonné par le roi** their having been ordered away ou their banishment from the court by the king **b** (= action de s'éloigner) [être aimé] estrangement; **son ~ des affaires** his progressive disinvolvement with business **c** (= distance spatial, temporel) distance; **l'~ rapetisse les objets** distance makes objects (look) smaller; **notre ~ de Paris complique le travail** our being so far from Paris makes the work more complicated; **en amour, l'~ rapproche** absence makes the heart grow fonder (PROV); **le bruit est étouffé par l'~** the noise is muffled by distance; **avec l'~, on juge mieux les événements** it is easier to judge events from a distance

éloigner [elwaɲe] ▶conjug 1◀ **1** VT **a** [+ objet] to move away, take away (**de** from); **éloigne ce coussin du radiateur** move ou take that cushion away from the radiator; **la lentille éloigne les objets** the lens makes objects look further away than they really are

b [+ personne] (lit) to take away, remove (**de** from); (= exiler, écarter) to send away (**de** from); **~ les curieux du lieu d'un accident** to move onlookers ou bystanders away from the scene of an accident; **allumer du feu pour ~ les bêtes sauvages** to light a fire to keep off the wild animals; **~ qn de** [+ être aimé, compagnons] to estrange sb from; [+ activité] to take sb away from; [+ tentations, carrière] to take sb away from, remove sb from; **son penchant pour la boisson éloigna de lui ses amis** his drinking lost him his friends ou made his friends drift away from him; **ce chemin nous éloigne du village** this path takes ou leads us away from the village

c [+ souvenir, idée] to banish, dismiss; [+ crainte] to remove, dismiss; [+ danger] to ward off, remove; [+ soupçons] to remove, avert (**de** from)

d (= espacer) [+ visites] to make less frequent, space out

2 **s'éloigner** VPR **a** [objet, véhicule en mouvement] to move away; [cycliste] to ride away; [orage] to go away, pass; [bruit] to go away, grow fainter; **le village s'éloignait et finit par disparaître dans la brume** the village got further (and further) away ou grew more and more distant and finally disappeared in the mist

b [personne] (par prudence) to go away (**de** from); (par pudeur, discrétion) to go away, withdraw (**de** from); **s'~ en courant/en hâte** to run/hurry away ou off; **éloignez-vous, ça risque d'éclater !** move away ou stand back, it might explode!; **ne t'éloigne pas trop** don't go (too) far (away); **s'~ de** [+ être aimé, compagnons] to become estranged from, grow away from; [+ sujet traité] to wander from; [+ position prise] to move away from; [+ devoir] to swerve ou deviate from; **là vous vous éloignez (du sujet)** you're wandering from ou getting off the point ou subject; **je la sentais s'~ (de moi)** I felt her growing away from me, I felt her becoming more and more distant; **s'~ du droit chemin** to stray ou wander from the straight and narrow; **s'~ de la vérité** to wander from the truth

c [souvenir, échéance] to grow more (and more) distant ou remote; [danger] to pass, go away; [craintes] to go away

élongation [elɔ̃gasjɔ̃] NF **a** (Méd) strained ou pulled muscle; **les ~s font très mal** straining ou pulling a muscle is very painful, a pulled muscle is very painful; **se faire une ~** to strain ou pull a muscle; **je me suis fait une ~ à la jambe** I've strained ou pulled a muscle in my leg **b** (Astron) elongation; (Phys) displacement

éloquemment [elɔkamã] ADV eloquently

éloquence [elɔkɑ̃s] NF eloquence; **avec ~** eloquently; **il m'a fallu toute mon ~ pour la convaincre** I needed all the eloquence I could muster to convince her; **l'~ de ces chiffres rend tout commentaire superflu** these figures speak for themselves *ou* need no comment

éloquent, e [elɔkɑ̃, ɑ̃t] ADJ [*orateur, discours, geste*] eloquent; **ces chiffres sont ~s** these figures speak for themselves; **une étreinte plus ~e que toute parole** an embrace that spoke louder than any words, an embrace more eloquent *ou* meaningful than any words; **un silence ~** a silence that speaks volumes, a meaningful *ou* an eloquent silence

élu, e [ely] (*ptp de* **élire**) 1 ADJ (*Rel*) chosen; (*Pol*) elected 2 NM,F a (*Pol*) (= *député*) elected member, ≈ member of parliament, ≈ M.P. (*Brit*); (= *conseiller*) elected representative, councillor; **les nouveaux ~s** the newly elected members, the newly elected councillors; **les ~s locaux** the local *ou* town councillors; **les citoyens et leurs ~s** the citizens and their elected representatives b (*hum* = *fiancé*) **l'~ de son cœur** her beloved; **quelle est l'heureuse ~e?** who's the lucky girl? c (*Rel*) **les Élus** the Chosen ones, the Elect; **être l'~ de Dieu** to be chosen by God

élucidation [elysidasjɔ̃] NF elucidation

élucider [elyside] ▸ conjug 1 ◂ VT to clear up, elucidate

élucubrations [elykybʀasjɔ̃] NFPL (*péj*) wild imaginings

élucubrer [elykybʀe] ▸ conjug 1 ◂ VT (*péj*) to dream up

éluder [elyde] ▸ conjug 1 ◂ VT [+ *difficulté*] to evade, elude; [+ *loi, problème*] to evade, dodge

élusif, -ive [elyzif, iv] ADJ (*frm*) elusive

Élysée [elize] NM (*Myth*) **l'~** the Elysium; (**le palais de**) **l'~** the Élysée palace (*official residence of the French President*) → **champ¹**

élyséen, -enne [elizeɛ̃, ɛn] ADJ (*Myth*) Elysian; (*Pol française*) of the Élysée palace

élytre [elitʀ] NM wing case, elytron (*SPÉC*)

émaciation [emasjasjɔ̃] NF emaciation

émacié, e [emasje] ADJ [*corps, visage*] emaciated, wasted; [*personne*] emaciated

émacier [emasje] ▸ conjug 7 ◂ 1 VT to emaciate 2 **s'émacier** VPR to become emaciated *ou* wasted

émail (*pl* **-aux**) [emaj, o] NM (= *substance*) enamel; (= *objet*) piece of enamel, enamel; (*Hér*) colour; **en** *ou* **d'~** enamel(led); **cendrier en émaux** enamelled ashtray; **peinture sur ~** enamel painting; **faire des émaux** to do enamel work

émaillage [emajaʒ] NM enamelling

émaillé, e [emaje] (*ptp de* **émailler**) ADJ a (*lit*) enamelled b **~ de** (= *parsemé de*) [+ *étoiles*] spangled *ou* studded with; [+ *fautes, citations*] peppered *ou* dotted with; **voyage ~ d'incidents** journey punctuated by unforeseen incidents

émailler [emaje] ▸ conjug 1 ◂ VT a (*lit*) to enamel b (= *parsemer*) [*étoiles*] to stud, spangle; **~ un texte de citations/d'erreurs** to pepper a text with quotations/errors

émailleur, -euse [emajœʀ, øz] NM,F enameller, enamellist

émanation [emanasjɔ̃] NF a **~s** (= *odeurs*) smells, emanations; **~s fétides** fetid emanations; **~s volcaniques** volatiles; **~s toxiques** toxic fumes b (= *produit*) product; **le pouvoir est l'~ du peuple** power issues from the people, power is a product of the will of the people c (*Phys*) emanation; (*Rel*) procession

émancipateur, -trice [emɑ̃sipatœʀ, tʀis] 1 ADJ liberating, emancipatory 2 NM,F liberator, emancipator

émancipation [emɑ̃sipasjɔ̃] NF (*Jur*) emanci-

pation; [*colonie, femme*] liberation, emancipation

émancipé, e [emɑ̃sipe] (*ptp de* **émanciper**) ADJ emancipated, liberated

émanciper [emɑ̃sipe] ▸ conjug 1 ◂ 1 VT (*Jur*) to emancipate; [+ *femme*] to emancipate, liberate; [+ *esprit*] to liberate, (set) free 2 **s'émanciper** VPR [*femme*] to become emancipated *ou* liberated, liberate o.s.; [*esprit, art*] to become liberated, liberate *ou* free itself

émaner [emane] ▸ conjug 1 ◂ ◆ **émaner de** VT INDIR (*Pol, Rel*) [*pouvoir*] to issue from; [*ordres, note*] to come from, be issued by; [*chaleur, lumière, odeur*] to emanate *ou* issue *ou* come from; [*charme*] to emanate from

émargement [emaʀʒəmɑ̃] NM a (*NonC*) signing; (= *annotation*) annotating; **feuille d'~** (= *feuille de paye*) paysheet; (= *feuille de présence*) attendance sheet b (= *signature*) signature; (= *annotation*) annotation

émarger [emaʀʒe] ▸ conjug 3 ◂ 1 VT a (*frm*) (= *signer*) to sign; (= *mettre ses initiales*) to initial b (= *annoter*) to annotate c (*Typo*) to trim 2 VI a † (= *toucher son salaire*) to draw one's salary; **à combien émarge-t-il par mois?** what is his monthly salary? b (= *recevoir*) **~ d'une certaine somme à un budget** to receive a certain sum out of a budget

émasculation [emaskylasjɔ̃] NF (*lit, fig*) emasculation

émasculer [emaskyle] ▸ conjug 1 ◂ VT (*lit, fig*) to emasculate

emballage [ɑ̃balaʒ] NM a (= *action d'emballer*) (*dans un carton*) packing(-up), packaging; (*dans du papier*) wrapping(-up) b (*Comm*) (= *boîte, carton*) package, packaging (*NonC*); (= *papier*) wrapping (*NonC*); **carton d'~** ◊ **~ carton** cardboard packaging; **perdu** throwaway packaging; **produit sous ~ (plastique)** plastic-wrapped product

emballant, e* [ɑ̃balɑ̃, ɑ̃t] ADJ (*gén au nég*) thrilling; **ce n'est pas un film/un projet très ~** it's not a very inspiring film/project

emballement [ɑ̃balmɑ̃] NM a* (= *enthousiasme*) flight of enthusiasm; (= *colère*) flash of anger; (= *passade*) **méfiez-vous de ses ~s** beware of his (sudden) crazes* b [*moteur*] racing; [*cheval*] bolting c (*Écon*) **cela a provoqué l'~ du dollar/de l'économie** it caused the dollar/the economy to race out of control

emballer [ɑ̃bale] ▸ conjug 1 ◂ 1 VT a (= *empaqueter*) (*dans un carton, de la toile*) to pack (up); (*dans du papier*) to wrap (up); **emballé sous vide** vacuum-packed; (*fig*) **emballez, c'est pesé!*** it's a deal!* b‡ (= *arrêter*) to run in*, to nick‡ (*Brit*) c [+ *moteur*] to race d* (= *enthousiasmer*) [*idée, film*] to thrill to bits*; **je n'ai pas été très emballé par ce film** the film didn't do much for me*, I didn't go a bundle on the film* (*Brit*) e‡ (= *séduire*) [+ *personne*] to pick up*, get off with* 2 **s'emballer** VPR a* [*personne*] (*enthousiasme*) to get *ou* be carried away*, get worked up*; (*colère*) to fly off the handle* b [*moteur*] to race; [*cheval*] to bolt; **cheval emballé** runaway *ou* bolting horse c [*économie, monnaie*] to race out of control

emballeur, -euse [ɑ̃balœʀ, øz] NM,F packer

embarcadère [ɑ̃baʀkadɛʀ] NM landing stage, pier

embarcation [ɑ̃baʀkasjɔ̃] NF (small) boat, (small) craft *pl inv*

embardée [ɑ̃baʀde] NF (*Aut*) swerve; (*Naut*) yaw; **faire une ~** (*Aut*) to swerve; (*Naut*) to yaw

embargo [ɑ̃baʀgo] NM embargo (**à l'encontre de, contre** against); **~ économique/commercial/total** economic/trade/total embargo; **~ pétrolier/militaire** oil/military embargo; **mettre l'~ sur qch** to impose *ou* put an embargo on sth, embargo sth; **lever l'~ (mis sur qch/un pays)** to lift *ou* raise the embargo

(on sb/a country); **pays/marchandises sous ~** country/goods (placed) under embargo

embarquement [ɑ̃baʀkəmɑ̃] NM [*marchandises*] loading; [*passagers*] (*en bateau*) embarkation, boarding; (*en avion, en train*) boarding; **vol 134, ~ porte 9** flight 134 now boarding at gate 9; **carte d'~** boarding pass *ou* card

embarquer [ɑ̃baʀke] ▸ conjug 1 ◂ 1 VT a [+ *passagers*] to embark, take on board; **je l'ai embarqué dans le train*** I saw him onto the train, I put him on the train b [+ *cargaison*] (*en train, gén*) to load; (*en bateau*) to load, ship; **le navire embarque des paquets d'eau** the boat is taking in *ou* shipping water c ‡ (= *emporter*) to cart off*, lug off*; (= *voler*) to pinch*, nick‡ (*Brit*); (*pour emprisonner*) to cart off* *ou* away*; **se faire ~ par la police** to get picked up by the police* d* (= *entraîner*) **~ qn dans** to get sb mixed up *ou* involved in, involve sb in; **il s'est laissé ~ dans une sale histoire** he has got (himself) mixed up *ou* involved in a nasty bit of business; **une affaire bien/mal embarquée** an affair that has got off to a good/bad start 2 VI a (= *partir en voyage*) to embark; **il a embarqué** *ou* **il s'est embarqué hier pour le Maroc** he sailed for Morocco yesterday b (= *monter à bord*) to board, go aboard *ou* on board c (*Naut*) **le navire embarque** ◊ **la mer embarque** we are *ou* the boat is shipping water 3 **s'embarquer** VPR a → **2a** b **s'~ dans*** [+ *aventure, affaire*] to embark (up)on, launch into; [+ *affaire louche*] to get mixed up *ou* involved in

embarras [ɑ̃baʀa] NM a (= *ennui*) trouble; **cela constitue un ~ supplémentaire** that's yet another problem; **je ne veux pas être un ~ pour vous** I don't want to be a nuisance to you, I don't want to bother you; **causer** *ou* **faire toutes sortes d'~ à qn** to give *ou* cause sb no end* of trouble *ou* bother; **ne vous mettez pas dans l'~ pour moi** don't put yourself out *ou* go to any trouble for me b (= *gêne*) confusion, embarrassment; **dit-il avec ~** he said in some confusion *ou* with (some) embarrassment; **il remarqua mon ~ pour répondre** he noticed that I was at a loss for a reply *ou* that I was stuck* for a reply c (= *situation délicate*) predicament, awkward position; **mettre** *ou* **plonger qn dans l'~** to put sb in an awkward position *ou* on the spot*; **tirer qn d'~** to get *ou* help sb out of an awkward position *ou* out of a predicament; **être dans l'~** (*en mauvaise position*) to be in a predicament *ou* an awkward position; (*dans un dilemme*) to be in a quandary *ou* in a dilemma d (= *gêne financière*) **~ (d'argent** *ou* **financiers)** financial difficulties, money worries; **être dans l'~** to be in financial straits *ou* difficulties, be short of money e (*Méd*) **~ gastrique** upset stomach, stomach upset f † (= *encombrement*) **~ de circulation** *ou* **de voitures** (road) congestion (*NonC*), traffic holdup; **les ~ de Paris** the congestion in the streets of Paris g (= *chichis, façons*) **faire des ~** to make a fuss; **c'est un faiseur d'~** he's a fusspot*, he's always making a fuss h (*loc*) **avoir l'~ du choix** ◊ **n'avoir que l'~ du choix** to be spoilt for choice

embarrassant, e [ɑ̃baʀasɑ̃, ɑ̃t] ADJ a [*situation*] embarrassing, uncomfortable; [*problème*] awkward, thorny; **c'est ~ de devoir lui dire** it's embarrassing to have to tell him b [*paquets*] cumbersome, awkward; **ce que cet enfant peut être ~!** that child is always in the way!

embarrassé, e [ɑ̃baʀase] (*ptp de* **embarrasser**) ADJ a (= *gêné*) [*personne*] embarrassed, ill-at-ease (attrib); [sourire] embarrassed, uneasy; **être ~ de sa personne** to feel self-conscious; **je serais bien ~ de choisir entre les deux** I'd really be at a loss ou I'd be hard put to choose between the two **b** (= peu clair) [explication, phrase] muddled, confused **c** (Méd) **avoir l'estomac ~** to have an upset stomach; **j'ai la langue ~** my tongue is coated **d** (= encombré) [table, corridor] cluttered (up); **j'ai les mains ~es** my hands are full

embarrasser [ɑ̃baʀase] ▸conjug 1◂ **1** VT **a** (= encombrer) [paquets] to clutter (up); [vêtements] to hinder, hamper; **enlève ce manteau qui t'embarrasse** take that coat off — you'll be more comfortable without it; **je ne t'embarrasse pas au moins?** are you sure I'm not bothering you? ou I'm not in your way? **b** (= désorienter) **~ qn par des questions indiscrètes** to embarrass sb with indiscreet questions; **sa demande m'embarrasse** his request puts me in a predicament ou an awkward position ou on the spot*; **ça m'embarrasse de te le dire mais ...** I don't like to tell you this but ...; **il y a quelque chose qui m'embarrasse là-dedans** there's something about it that bothers ou worries me **c** (Méd) **~ l'estomac** to lie heavy on the stomach

2 **s'embarrasser** VPR **a** (= s'encombrer) **s'~ de** [+ paquets, compagnon] to burden o.s. with; (fig) **il s'embarrasse dans ses explications** he gets in a muddle with his explanations, he ties himself in knots* trying to explain things **b** (= se soucier) to trouble o.s. (**de** about), be troubled (**de** by); **sans s'~ des détails** without troubling ou worrying about the details; **il ne s'embarrasse pas de scrupules** he doesn't let scruples get in his way

embastillement [ɑ̃bastijmɑ̃] NM (††, hum) imprisonment

embastiller [ɑ̃bastije] ▸conjug 1◂ VT (††, hum) to imprison

embauche [ɑ̃boʃ] NF (= action d'embaucher) taking on, hiring; (= travail disponible) vacancy; **ils devront recourir à l'~ cet été** they will have to start taking people on ou hiring new staff this summer; **la surqualification peut être un obstacle à l'~** being overqualified can be an obstacle to finding employment; **est-ce qu'il y a de l'~?** are there any vacancies?, are you taking anyone on? ou hiring anyone?; **il n'y a pas d'~ (chez eux)** they're not hiring, they're not taking anybody on; **bureau d'~** employment office; **salaire d'~** starting salary; **chercher de l'~** to look for work; **aide(s) ou prime(s) à l'~** employment incentive(s); **le questionnaire leur est remis à l'~** they are given the questionnaire when they start work ou on their first day at work

embaucher [ɑ̃boʃe] ▸conjug 1◂ **1** VT to take on, hire; **il s'est fait ~ par l'entreprise** he was taken on ou hired by the company; **je t'embauche pour écosser les petits pois** I'll put you to work shelling the peas, you've got yourself a job shelling the peas; **s'~ comme peintre** to get o.s. taken on ou hired as a painter; **on embauche** [entreprise] we are recruiting new staff, we have vacancies (for new staff); **le nouvel embauché** the new recruit ou employee **2** VI (= commencer le travail) to start work

embaucheur, -euse [ɑ̃boʃœʀ, øz] NM,F employment ou labour (Brit) contractor

embauchoir [ɑ̃boʃwaʀ] NM shoetree

embaumé, e [ɑ̃bome] (ptp de **embaumer**) ADJ [air] fragrant, balmy (littér)

embaumement [ɑ̃bomɑ̃] NM embalming

embaumer [ɑ̃bome] ▸conjug 1◂ **1** VT **a** [+ cadavre] to embalm **b** (= parfumer) **le lilas embaumait l'air** the scent of lilac hung heavy in the air **c** (= avoir l'odeur de) to smell of; **l'air embaumait le lilas** the air was fragrant ou

balmy (littér) with the scent of lilac **2** VI [fleur] to give out a fragrance, be fragrant; [jardin] to be fragrant; [mets] to fill the air with a nice smell; [fromage] to smell strong; **ça n'embaume pas!*** it doesn't smell too sweet!

embaumeur, -euse [ɑ̃bomœʀ, øz] NM,F embalmer

embellie [ɑ̃beli] NF [temps] slight improvement (**de** in); [économie] slight improvement ou upturn (**de** in)

embellir [ɑ̃beliʀ] ▸conjug 2◂ **1** VT [+ personne, jardin] to beautify, make more attractive; [+ ville] to smarten up (Brit), give a face-lift to*; [+ vérité, récit] to embellish **2** VI [personne] to grow lovelier ou more attractive, grow in beauty (littér)

embellissement [ɑ̃belismɑ̃] NM [récit, vérité] embellishment; **les récents ~s de la ville** the recent improvements to the town, the recent face-lift the town has been given*

emberlificoter* [ɑ̃beʀlifikɔte] ▸conjug 1◂ **1** VT (= enjôler) to get round*; (= embrouiller) to mix up*, muddle (up); (= duper) to hoodwink*, bamboozle* **2** **s'emberlificoter** VPR (dans un vêtement) to get tangled ou caught up (**dans** in); **il s'emberlificote dans ses explications** he gets in a terrible muddle ou he gets himself tied up in knots* with his explanations*

embêtant, e [ɑ̃betɑ̃, ɑ̃t] ADJ (gén) annoying; [situation, problème] awkward, tricky; **c'est ~!** (ennuyeux) what a nuisance!, how annoying!; (alarmant) it's worrying!; **j'ai oublié de lui dire — ~!** I forgot to tell him — oh dear!

embêté, e [ɑ̃bete] (ptp de **embêter**) ADJ **je suis très ~** (= je ne sais pas quoi faire) I'm in a real state, I just don't know what to do; **elle a eu l'air ~ quand je lui ai demandé ça** she looked embarrassed when I asked her that; **je suis très ~, je ne pourrai vous donner la réponse que dans trois jours** I'm really sorry, I can't give you an answer for another three days

embêtement [ɑ̃betmɑ̃] NM problem, trouble; **causer des ~s à qn** to make trouble for sb; **ce chien/four ne m'a causé que des ~s** this dog/ oven has brought me nothing but trouble

embêter [ɑ̃bete] ▸conjug 1◂ **1** VT (= gêner, préoccuper) to bother, worry; (= importuner) to pester, bother; (= irriter) to annoy; (= lasser) to bore **2** **s'embêter** VPR **a** (= se morfondre) to be bored, be fed up*; **qu'est-ce qu'on s'embête ici!** it's so boring ou such a drag* here! **b** (= s'embarrasser) to bother o.s. (**à faire** doing); **ne t'embête pas avec ça** don't bother ou worry about that; **pourquoi s'~ à le réparer?** why go to all the trouble ou bother of repairing it?, why bother yourself repairing it?; **il ne s'embête pas!** (= il a de la chance) he does all right for himself!*; (= il ne se gêne pas) he's got a nerve!*

emblaver [ɑ̃blave] ▸conjug 1◂ VT to sow (with a cereal crop)

emblavure [ɑ̃blavyʀ] NF field (sown with a cereal crop)

emblée [ɑ̃ble] ♦ **d'emblée** LOC ADV straight-away, right away, at once; **détester qn d'~** to detest sb on sight, take an instant dislike to sb

emblématique [ɑ̃blematik] ADJ (lit) emblematic; (fig) symbolic; **c'est la figure ~ de l'opposition** he's the figurehead of the opposition

emblème [ɑ̃blɛm] NM (lit) emblem; (fig) symbol, emblem

embobiner* [ɑ̃bɔbine] ▸conjug 1◂ VT (= enjôler) to get round*; (= embrouiller) to mix up*, muddle (up); (= duper) to hoodwink*, bamboozle*; **elle sait ~ son père** she can twist her father round her little finger, she knows how to get round her father

emboîtement [ɑ̃bwatmɑ̃] NM fitting, interlocking

emboîter [ɑ̃bwate] ▸conjug 1◂ **1** VT **a** [+ pièces, parties] to fit together, fit into each other; [+ livre] to case; **~ qch dans** to fit sth into **b** **~ le pas à qn** (lit) to follow close behind sb ou close on sb's heels; (= imiter) to follow suit **2** **s'emboîter** VPR [pièces] to fit together, fit into each other; **ces deux pièces s'emboîtent exactement** these two parts fit together exactly; **des chaises qui peuvent s'~ pour le rangement** chairs that can be stacked (together) when not in use

embolie [ɑ̃bɔli] NF embolism; **~ gazeuse/ pulmonaire** air/pulmonary embolism; **faire une ~** to have an embolism

embonpoint [ɑ̃bɔ̃pwɛ̃] NM stoutness, portliness; **avoir/prendre de l'~** to be/become rather stout

embossage [ɑ̃bɔsaʒ] NM fore and aft mooring

embosser [ɑ̃bɔse] ▸conjug 1◂ VT **a** [+ navire] to moor fore and aft **b** [+ carte] to emboss

embouché, e [ɑ̃buʃe] (ptp de **emboucher**) ADJ **mal ~** (= grossier) foul-mouthed; (= de mauvaise humeur) in a foul mood

emboucher [ɑ̃buʃe] ▸conjug 1◂ VT [+ instrument] to raise to one's lips; **~ un cheval** to put the bit in a horse's mouth; (fig) **les trompettes de la victoire/du nationalisme** to launch into triumphalist/nationalist rhetoric

embouchure [ɑ̃buʃyʀ] NF [fleuve] mouth; [mors] mouthpiece; (Mus) mouthpiece, embouchure

embourber [ɑ̃buʀbe] ▸conjug 1◂ **1** VT **~ une voiture** to get a car stuck in the mud **2** **s'embourber** VPR [voiture] to get stuck in the mud, get bogged down (in the mud); **notre voiture s'est embourbée dans le marais** our car got stuck in ou got bogged down in the marsh; **s'~ dans** [+ détails] to get bogged down in; [+ monotonie] to sink into

embourgeoisement [ɑ̃buʀʒwazmɑ̃] NM [personne, parti] adoption of middle-class attitudes

embourgeoiser [ɑ̃buʀʒwaze] ▸conjug 1◂ **1** **s'embourgeoiser** VPR [parti, personne] to become middle-class, adopt a middle-class outlook; [quartier] to become middle-class **2** VT [+ personne] to make middle-class (in outlook)

embout [ɑ̃bu] NM [canne] tip, ferrule; [tuyau] nozzle

embouteillage [ɑ̃buteja ʒ] NM (Aut) traffic jam, (traffic) holdup; († = mise en bouteilles) bottling

embouteiller [ɑ̃buteje] ▸conjug 1◂ VT (Aut) to jam, block; (Téléc) [+ lignes] to block;† [+ vin, lait] to bottle; **les routes sont très embouteillées** the roads are very congested

emboutir [ɑ̃butiʀ] ▸conjug 2◂ VT [+ métal] to stamp; (Aut) to crash ou run into; **avoir une aile emboutie** to have a dented ou damaged wing; **il s'est fait ~ par une voiture** he was hit by another car

emboutisseur, -euse [ɑ̃butisœʀ, øz] **1** NM,F (= personne) stamper **2** **emboutisseuse** NF (= machine) stamping press ou machine

embranchement [ɑ̃brɑ̃ʃmɑ̃] NM **a** [voies, routes, tuyaux] junction; **à l'~ des deux routes** where the road forks **b** (= route) side road, branch road; (Rail = voie) branch line; (= tuyau) branch pipe; (= rivière) embranchment **c** (Bot, Zool = catégorie) branch

embrancher [ɑ̃brɑ̃ʃe] ▸conjug 1◂ **1** VT [+ tuyaux, voies] to join (up); **~ qch sur** to join sth (up) to **2** **s'embrancher** VPR [tuyaux, voies] to join (up); **s'~ sur** to join (up) to

embrasement [ɑ̃braz mɑ̃] NM **a** (littér = incendie) fire, conflagration (frm); **ce qui a provoqué l'~ de la maison** what set the house on fire; **l'~ du ciel au couchant** the blazing ou fiery sky at sunset; (lueurs) **des ~s soudains**

sudden blazes of light **b** [*pays*] unrest; **l'~ des esprits** the stirring *ou* rousing of people's passions

embraser [ɑ̃bʀaze] ▸conjug 1◂ **1** VT **a** (*littér*) [+ *maison, forêt*] to set ablaze, set fire to; [+ *ciel*] to set aglow *ou* ablaze; [+ *cœur*] to kindle, fire **b** [+ *pays*] to cause unrest in **2** **s'embraser** VPR **a** (*littér*) [*maison*] to blaze up, flare up; [*ciel*] to flare up, be set ablaze (**de** with); [*cœur*] to become inflamed, be fired (**de** with) **b** [*pays*] to be thrown into a state of unrest

embrassade [ɑ̃bʀasad] NF (*gén pl*) hugging and kissing (*NonC*)

embrasse [ɑ̃bʀas] NF tieback; **rideaux à ~s** curtains with tiebacks

embrassement [ɑ̃bʀasmɑ̃] NM (*littér*) = embrassade

▾ **embrasser** [ɑ̃bʀase] ▸conjug 1◂ **1** VT **a** (= *donner un baiser à*) to kiss; **~ qn à pleine bouche** to kiss sb (full) on the lips; (*en fin de lettre*) **je t'embrasse (affectueusement)** with love **b** († *ou frm*) (= *étreindre*) to embrace → **rime c** (*frm*) (= *choisir*) [+ *doctrine, cause*] to embrace, espouse (*frm*); [+ *carrière*] to take up, enter upon ▪(*PROV*) **qui trop embrasse mal étreint** you shouldn't bite off more than you can chew **d** (= *couvrir*) [+ *problèmes, sujets*] to encompass, embrace; (*littér*) **il embrassa la plaine du regard** he surveyed the plain **2** **s'embrasser** VPR to kiss (each other)

embrasure [ɑ̃bʀazyʀ] NF (*Constr* = *créneau*) embrasure; **il se tenait dans l'~ de la porte/la fenêtre** he stood in the doorway/the window

embrayage [ɑ̃bʀɛjaʒ] NM **a** (= *mécanisme*) clutch **b** (= *action*) engaging *ou* letting out (*Brit*) the clutch, clutching (*US*)

embrayer [ɑ̃bʀeje] ▸conjug 8◂ **1** VT (*Aut, Tech*) to put into gear **2** VI (*Aut*) to engage *ou* let out (*Brit*) the clutch, clutch (*US*); **~ sur** [+ *sujet*] to switch to

embrigadement [ɑ̃bʀigadmɑ̃] NM (= *endoctrinement*) indoctrination; (= *recrutement*) recruitment (**dans** into)

embrigader [ɑ̃bʀigade] ▸conjug 1◂ VT (*péj*) (= *endoctriner*) to indoctrinate; (= *recruter*) to recruit (**dans** into)

embringuer* [ɑ̃bʀɛ̃ge] ▸conjug 1◂ VT to mix up, involve; **il s'est laissé ~ dans une sale histoire** he got (himself) mixed up *ou* involved in some nasty business

embrocation [ɑ̃bʀɔkasjɔ̃] NF embrocation

embrocher [ɑ̃bʀɔʃe] ▸conjug 1◂ VT (*Culin*) (*sur broche*) to spit, put on a spit; (*sur brochette*) to skewer; (*fig*) **~ qn** (*avec une épée*) to run sb through; **il m'a embroché avec son parapluie** he ran into me with his umbrella

embrouillage [ɑ̃bʀujaʒ] NM = embrouillement

embrouillamini* [ɑ̃bʀujamini] NM muddle, jumble

embrouille* [ɑ̃bʀuj] NF **il y a de l'~ là-dessous** there's something funny at the bottom of this; **toutes ces ~s** all this carry-on*; **il y a eu une ~ administrative** there was an administrative mix-up*

embrouillé, e [ɑ̃bʀuje] (*ptp de* embrouiller) ADJ [*style, problème, idées*] muddled, confused; [*papiers*] muddled, mixed-up

embrouillement [ɑ̃bʀujmɑ̃] NM muddle; **l'~ de ses explications** his muddled explanations

embrouiller [ɑ̃bʀuje] ▸conjug 1◂ **1** VT **a** [+ *fils*] to tangle, snarl up; [+ *affaire, problème*] to muddle (up), confuse **b** [+ *personne*] to muddle, confuse, mix up **2** **s'embrouiller** VPR **a** [*idées, style, situation*] to become muddled *ou* confused **b** [*personne*] to get in a muddle, become confused *ou* muddled; **s'~ dans un discours/ses explications** to get in a muddle with a speech/with one's explanations

embroussaillé, e [ɑ̃bʀusaje] ADJ [*chemin*] overgrown; [*barbe, sourcils, cheveux*] bushy, shaggy

embrumer [ɑ̃bʀyme] ▸conjug 1◂ VT (*littér*) to mist over, cloud over (**de** with); (*fig*) to cloud (**de** with); **à l'horizon embrumé** on the misty *ou* hazy horizon; **l'esprit embrumé par l'alcool** his mind fuddled *ou* clouded with drink

embruns [ɑ̃bʀœ̃] NMPL sea spray (*NonC*), spindrift (*NonC*)

embryogenèse [ɑ̃bʀijoʒǝnɛz] NF embryogeny, embryogenesis

embryologie [ɑ̃bʀijɔlɔʒi] NF embryology

embryologique [ɑ̃bʀijɔlɔʒik] ADJ embryologic(al)

embryologiste [ɑ̃bʀijɔlɔʒist] NMF embryologist

embryon [ɑ̃bʀijɔ̃] NM (*lit, fig*) embryo; (*fig*) **à l'état d'~** in embryo, in an embryonic state; **un ~ de réseau/gouvernement** an embryonic network/government

embryonnaire [ɑ̃bʀijɔnɛʀ] ADJ (*Méd*) embryonic, embryonal; (*fig*) embryonic; (*fig*) **à l'état ~** in embryo, in an embryonic state

embûche [ɑ̃byʃ] NF pitfall, trap; **semé d'~s** treacherous, full of pitfalls *ou* traps

embuer [ɑ̃bɥe] ▸conjug 1◂ VT to mist (up), mist over; **vitre embuée** misted(-up) window pane; **yeux embués de larmes** eyes misted (over) *ou* clouded with tears

embuscade [ɑ̃byskad] NF ambush; **être** *ou* **se tenir en ~** to lie in ambush; **tendre une ~ à qn** to set (up) *ou* lay an ambush for sb; **tomber dans une ~** (*Mil*) to fall into an ambush; (*tendue par des brigands*) to fall into an ambush, be waylaid

embusqué [ɑ̃byske] (*ptp de* embusquer) **1** ADJ **être ~** [*soldats*] to lie *ou* wait in ambush **2** NM (*arg Mil*) shirker

embusquer (s') [ɑ̃byske] ▸conjug 1◂ VPR to lie *ou* wait in ambush

éméché, e* [emeʃe] ADJ tipsy*, merry*

émeraude [em(ǝ)ʀod] NF, ADJ INV emerald

émergence [emɛʀʒɑ̃s] NF (*gén*) emergence; **(point d')émergence d'une source** source of a spring

émergent, e [emɛʀʒɑ̃, ɑ̃t] ADJ (*Géol, Opt, Phys*) emergent; (*Écon*) **pays ~s** emerging countries

émerger [emɛʀʒe] ▸conjug 3◂ VI **a** (= *apparaître*) [*rocher, cime*] to emerge, rise up; [*vérité, astre*] to emerge, come out; [*fait, artiste*] to emerge; **il émergea de sa chambre** he emerged from his room; **le sommet émergea du brouillard** the summit rose out of *ou* emerged from the fog **b** (= *faire saillie*) [*rocher, fait, artiste*] to stand out **c** (*d'une situation difficile*) to begin to see light at the end of the tunnel

émeri [em(ǝ)ʀi] NM emery; **toile** *ou* **papier ~** emery paper → **bouché**

émerillon [em(ǝ)ʀijɔ̃] NM (*Orn*) merlin; (*Tech*) swivel

émérite [emeʀit] ADJ (= *chevronné*) highly skilled; **professeur ~** professor emeritus, emeritus professor

émersion [emɛʀsjɔ̃] NF emersion

émerveillement [emɛʀvɛjmɑ̃] NM (= *sentiment*) wonder; (= *vision, sons*) wonderful thing, marvel

émerveiller [emɛʀveje] ▸conjug 1◂ **1** VT to fill with wonder **2** **s'émerveiller** VPR to be filled with wonder; **s'~ de** to marvel at, be filled with wonder at

émétique [emetik] ADJ, NM emetic

émetteur, -trice [emetœʀ, tʀis] **1** ADJ **a** (*Radio*) transmitting → **poste², station b** (*Fin*) issuing (*épith*); **banque émettrice** issuing bank **2** NM (*Radio*) transmitter; **~ récepteur** transmitter-receiver, transceiver **3** NM,F (*Fin*) issuer

émettre [emɛtʀ] ▸conjug 56◂ VT **a** [+ *lumière*] [*lampe*] to give (out), send out; (*Phys*) to emit; [+ *son, radiation, liquide*] to give out, send out, emit; [+ *odeur*] to give off **b** (*Radio, TV*) to transmit; [+ *avion, bateau*] to send out; **son bateau n'émet plus** he's no longer sending out signals; **~ sur ondes courtes** to broadcast *ou* transmit on shortwave **c** (*Fin*) [+ *monnaie, actions*] to issue; [+ *emprunt*] to issue, float; [+ *chèque*] to draw **d** [+ *idée, hypothèse, doute*] to voice, put forward

émeu [emø] NM emu

émeute [emøt] NF riot; **~s** riots, rioting

émeutier, -ière [emøtje, jɛʀ] NM,F rioter

émiettement [emjɛtmɑ̃] NM [*pain, terre*] crumbling; [*territoire*] breaking up, splitting up; [*pouvoir, responsabilités*] dispersion; [*énergie, effort, temps*] dissipation; [*fortune*] frittering away

émietter [emjete] ▸conjug 1◂ **1** VT [+ *pain, terre*] to crumble; [+ *territoire*] to break up, split up; [+ *pouvoir, responsabilités*] to disperse; [+ *énergie, effort, temps*] to dissipate **2** **s'émietter** VPR [*pain, terre*] to crumble; [*pouvoir*] to disperse; [*énergie, existence*] to dissipate; [*fortune*] to be frittered *ou* whittled away

émigrant, e [emigʀɑ̃, ɑ̃t] NM,F emigrant

émigration [emigʀasjɔ̃] NF emigration

émigré, e [emigʀe] (*ptp de* émigrer) NM,F (*Hist*) émigré; (*Pol*) expatriate, émigré; (*Écon*) (**travailleur**) **~** migrant worker

émigrer [emigʀe] ▸conjug 1◂ VI to emigrate; (*Zool*) to migrate

émincé [emɛ̃se] NM (= *plat*) émincé; (= *tranche*) sliver, thin slice; **~ de veau/de foie de veau** émincé of veal/calves' liver

émincer [emɛ̃se] ▸conjug 3◂ VT to slice thinly, cut into slivers *ou* thin slices

éminemment [eminamɑ̃] ADV eminently

éminence [eminɑ̃s] NF **a** [*terrain*] knoll, hill; (*Méd*) protuberance **b** [*qualité, rang*] distinction, eminence **c** (= *cardinal*) Eminence; **Son/Votre Éminence** his/your Eminence; (*fig*) **l'~ grise** the power behind the throne, the éminence grise

éminent, e [eminɑ̃, ɑ̃t] ADJ distinguished, eminent; (*frm*) **mon ~ collègue** my learned *ou* distinguished colleague

éminentissime [eminɑ̃tisim] ADJ (*hum*) most distinguished *ou* eminent; (*Rel*) most eminent

émir [emiʀ] NM emir

émirat [emiʀa] NM emirate; **les Émirats arabes unis** the United Arab Emirates

émissaire [emisɛʀ] NM (*gén*) emissary → **bouc**

émission [emisjɔ̃] NF **a** (*Phys*) [*son, lumière, signaux*] emission; **source d'~ (de lumière/chaleur)** (emitting) source (of light/heat) **b** (*Radio, TV*) (= *transmission de sons, d'images*) broadcasting; (= *programme*) broadcast, programme (*Brit*), program (*US*); **~ télévisée/radiophonique** television/radio programme *ou* broadcast; **~ (de télévision) par câble** cablecast; **les ~s de la semaine** this week's programmes; **« nos ~s sont terminées »** "that's the end of today's broadcasts *ou* programmes *ou* broadcasting" **c** (*Fin*) [*monnaie, actions, emprunt*] issue, flotation; [*chèque*] drawing; **monopole d'~** monopoly of issue; **cours d'~** issue par; **prix d'~** offering price → **banque d** [*idée, hypothèse*] voicing, putting forward **e** (*Physiol*) **~ d'urine/de sperme** emission of urine/semen **f** (*Phon*) **~ de voix** utterance

emmagasiner [ɑ̃magazine] ▸conjug 1◂ VT (*gén* = *amasser*) to store up, accumulate; [+ *chaleur*] to store; [+ *souvenirs, connaissances*] to amass, accumulate; (*Comm*) to store, put into store, warehouse

emmailloter [ɑ̃majɔte] ▸conjug 1◂ VT [+ doigt, pied] to bind (up), bandage; [+ enfant] to wrap up

emmanché, e†‡ [ɑ̃mɑ̃ʃe] (ptp de **emmancher**) NM,F (= crétin) twit*, jerk*, berk‡ (Brit)

emmanchement [ɑ̃mɑ̃ʃmɑ̃] NM [outil] fitting of a handle (**de** to, on, onto)

emmancher [ɑ̃mɑ̃ʃe] ▸conjug 1◂ VT [+ pelle] to fix ou put a handle on; **~ une affaire*** to get a deal going, set up a deal; **l'affaire s'emmanche mal*** things are getting off to a bad start; **l'affaire est bien/mal emmanchée*** the deal has got off to a good/bad start

emmanchure [ɑ̃mɑ̃ʃyʀ] NF armhole

Emmaüs [emays] N Emmaus

<hr>
EMMAÜS

This is the name of a well-known charity founded in 1949 by l'Abbé Pierre that provides help for homeless people. It is partly financed by the proceeds of jumble sales organized by a community of volunteers known as "les Chiffonniers d'Emmaüs".
<hr>

emmêlement [ɑ̃mɛlmɑ̃] NM (= action) tangling; (= état) tangle, muddle

emmêler [ɑ̃mele] ▸conjug 1◂ VT [+ cheveux] to tangle (up), knot; [+ fil] to tangle (up), entangle, muddle up; [+ affaire] to confuse, muddle; **tes cheveux sont tout emmêlés** your hair is all tangled; (fig) **tu emmêles tout** you're getting everything mixed up ou muddled (up) ou confused ⟨2⟩ **s'emmêler** VPR [corde, cheveux] to tangle, get in a tangle; **s'~ les pieds dans le tapis** to get one's feet caught in the carpet; **s'~ dans ses explications** to get in a muddle with one's explanations; **s'~ les pieds* ou crayons* ou pinceaux* ou pédales*** to get all confused, to get in a right muddle* (Brit); **tout s'emmêle dans ma tête** everything's muddled up ou confused in my head

emménagement [ɑ̃menaʒmɑ̃] NM moving in (NonC); **au moment de leur ~ dans la nouvelle maison** when they moved into the new house

emménager [ɑ̃menaʒe] ▸conjug 3◂ VI to move in; **~ dans** to move into

emmener [ɑ̃m(ə)ne] ▸conjug 5◂ VT ⟨a⟩ [+ personne] (comme otage) to take away; (comme invité, compagnon) to take (along); **~ qn au cinéma** to take sb to the cinema; **~ qn en prison** to take sb (away ou off) to prison; **~ qn en promenade ou faire une promenade** to take sb (off) for a walk; **~ déjeuner qn** to take sb out to ou for lunch; **voulez-vous que je vous emmène (en voiture)?** shall I give you ou would you like a lift (Brit) ou ride (US)? ⟨b⟩* (= emporter) [+ chose] to take; **tu vas ~ cette grosse valise?** are you going to take that huge suitcase (with you)? ⟨c⟩ (Mil, Sport = guider) [+ équipe, troupe] to lead

emment(h)al [emɛtal] NM Emmenthal (cheese)

emmerdant, e‡ [ɑ̃mɛʀdɑ̃, ɑ̃t] ADJ ⟨a⟩ (= irritant, gênant) damned ou bloody (Brit) annoying‡; **elle n'est pas trop ~e** she isn't too much of a pain* ⟨b⟩ (= ennuyeux) damned ou bloody (Brit) boring‡; **qu'est-ce qu'il est ~ avec ses histoires** what a damned ou bloody (Brit) bore ou pain (in the neck) he is with his stories‡

emmerde‡ [ɑ̃mɛʀd] NF = **emmerdement**

emmerdement‡ [ɑ̃mɛʀdəmɑ̃] NM hassle*; **quel ~!** what a damned ou bloody (Brit) nuisance‡; **j'ai eu tellement d'~s avec cette voiture** that car has given me so much damned ou bloody (Brit) trouble‡; **je n'ai que des ~s en ce moment** it's just one damned ou bloody (Brit) hassle after the other at the moment; **ça risque de m'attirer des ~s** it's likely to get me into hot water* ou to land me in the shit‡‡

emmerder‡ [ɑ̃mɛʀde] ▸conjug 1◂ ⟨1⟩ VT **~ qn** (= irriter) to bug sb*, get on sb's nerves; (= préoccuper, contrarier) to bug sb*, bother sb; (= lasser) to bore the pants off sb‡, bore sb stiff* ou to death*; (= mettre dans l'embarras) to get sb into trouble, land sb in it*; **on n'a pas fini d'être emmerdé avec ça** we haven't heard the last of it; **je suis drôlement emmerdé** I'm in deep trouble*, I'm really in the shit‡‡; **il m'emmerde à la fin, avec ses questions** he really bugs me* ou gets up my nose‡ (Brit) with his questions; **ça m'emmerde qu'il ne puisse pas venir** it's a damned nuisance‡ ou a hell of a nuisance‡ that he can't come; **je les emmerde!** to hell with them!‡, bugger them!‡ (Brit) ⟨2⟩ **s'emmerder** VPR (= s'ennuyer) to be bored stiff* ou to death*; (= s'embarrasser) to put o.s. out; **ne t'emmerde pas avec ça** don't bother ou worry about that; **je me suis drôlement emmerdé à réparer ce poste!** I really put myself out repairing that damned‡ radio!; **on ne s'emmerde pas avec eux!** there's never a dull moment with them!; **tu ne t'emmerdes pas!** you've got a damn‡ nerve ou cheek!; **elle a trois voitures — dis donc, elle ne s'emmerde pas!** she has three cars — (it's) all right for some!*

emmerdeur, -euse‡ [ɑ̃mɛʀdœʀ, øz] NM,F damned nuisance‡, pain in the neck*

emmieller [ɑ̃mjele] ▸conjug 1◂ VT ⟨a⟩ [+ tisane] to sweeten with honey ⟨b⟩* (= ennuyer) **~ qn** to bug sb*; **je suis drôlement emmiellé** I'm in a bit of a fix*, I've run into a spot of bother* (Brit) ⟨c⟩ (= enjôler) [+ personne] to soft-soap*, cajole

emmitoufler [ɑ̃mitufle] ▸conjug 1◂ VT to wrap up (warmly), muffle up; **s'~ (dans un manteau)** to wrap o.s. up (in a coat)

emmouscailler‡† [ɑ̃muskaje] ▸conjug 1◂ VT **~ qn** (= irriter) to bug sb*; (= préoccuper) to bother sb; (= mettre dans l'embarras) to land sb in the soup*; **être bien emmouscaillé** to be in deep trouble* ou in a real mess; **s'~ à faire qch** to go to the bother of doing sth

emmurer [ɑ̃myʀe] ▸conjug 1◂ VT (lit) to wall up, immure (frm); **emmuré vivant** walled up alive; **s'~ dans** [+ silence, sentiment] to retreat into; **emmuré dans ses convictions** entrenched in his convictions

émoi [emwa] NM (littér) (= trouble) agitation, emotion; (de joie) excitement; (= tumulte) commotion; **doux ~** pleasant agitation; **l'affaire a suscité un grand ~ dans le pays** the affair plunged the country into turmoil; **dit-elle non sans ~** she said with some confusion; **en ~** [cœur] in a flutter (attrib); [sens] agitated, excited; **la rue était en ~** the street was in turmoil

émollient, e [emɔljɑ̃, jɑ̃t] ADJ, NM emollient

émoluments [emɔlymɑ̃] NMPL (Admin) [officier ministériel] fees, emoluments (frm); [employé] remuneration, emoluments (frm)

émondage [emɔ̃daʒ] NM [arbre] pruning, trimming

émonder [emɔ̃de] ▸conjug 1◂ VT [+ arbre] to prune, trim; [+ amandes] to blanch

émondeur, -euse [emɔ̃dœʀ, øz] NM,F (= personne) pruner

émondoir [emɔ̃dwaʀ] NM pruning hook

émotif, -ive [emɔtif, iv] ⟨1⟩ ADJ [personne, choc, réaction] emotional; (Ling) emotive; **charge émotive** emotional charge ⟨2⟩ NM,F emotional person; **c'est un ~** he's very emotional

émotion [emɔsjɔ̃] NF ⟨a⟩ (= sentiment) emotion; (= peur) fright; **ils ont évité l'accident mais l'~ a été grande** they avoided an accident but it gave them a bad fright; **ce scandale a suscité une vive ~ dans le pays** this scandal has caused a real stir in the country; **pour nous remettre de nos ~s ...** to get over all the excitement ou commotion ...; **pour les amateurs d'~s fortes** for those who are looking for thrills, for thrill-seekers; **grand moment d'~** very ou highly emotional moment; **c'est avec une grande ~ que nous recevons ...** it is with great pleasure that we welcome ... ⟨b⟩ (= sensibilité) emotion, feeling; **parler avec ~** to speak with emotion ou feeling, speak feelingly (de about); **se laisser gagner par l'~** to get emotional

émotionnel, -elle [emɔsjɔnɛl] ADJ emotional

émotionner* [emɔsjɔne] ▸conjug 1◂ ⟨1⟩ VT to upset; **j'en suis encore tout émotionné** it gave me quite a turn*, I'm still upset about it ⟨2⟩ **s'émotionner** VPR to get worked up*, get upset (de about)

émotivité [emɔtivite] NF emotionalism

émoulu, e [emuly] ADJ → **frais¹**

émoussé, e [emuse] (ptp de **émousser**) ADJ [couteau] blunt; [goût, sensibilité] blunted, dulled

émousser [emuse] ▸conjug 1◂ ⟨1⟩ VT [+ couteau] to blunt; [+ appétit] take the edge off; [+ souvenir, désir] to dull ⟨2⟩ **s'émousser** VPR [intérêt] to wane; [talent] to lose its fine edge

émoustillant, e* [emustijɑ̃, ɑ̃t] ADJ [présence] tantalizing, titillating; [propos] titillating

émoustiller* [emustije] ▸conjug 1◂ VT to titillate, tantalize

émouvant, e [emuvɑ̃, ɑ̃t] ADJ (nuance de compassion) moving, touching; (nuance d'admiration) stirring

émouvoir [emuvwaʀ] ▸conjug 27◂ ⟨1⟩ VT ⟨a⟩ [+ personne] (gén) to move, stir; (= perturber) to disturb; (= indigner) to rouse (the indignation of); (= effrayer) to disturb, worry, upset; **leur attitude ne l'émut/leurs menaces ne l'émurent pas le moins du monde** their attitude/threats didn't disturb ou worry ou upset him in the slightest; **plus ému qu'il ne voulait l'admettre par ce baiser** more aroused than he wished to admit by this kiss; **leur misère l'émouvait profondément** their wretchedness moved him deeply ou upset him greatly; **~ qn jusqu'aux larmes** to move sb to tears; **se laisser ~ par des prières** to be moved by entreaties, let o.s. be swayed by entreaties; **encore tout ému d'avoir frôlé l'accident/de cette rencontre** still very shaken ou greatly upset at having been so close to an accident/over that encounter ⟨b⟩ (littér) [+ colère] to arouse; **~ la pitié de qn** to move sb to pity, arouse sb's pity ⟨2⟩ **s'émouvoir** VPR (gén) to be moved, be stirred; (= être perturbé) to be disturbed; (= s'inquiéter) to be ou get worried, be ou get upset; **il ne s'émeut de rien** nothing upsets him; **dit-il sans s'~** he said calmly ou impassively; **s'~ à la vue de qch** to be moved at the sight of sth; **le pays entier s'est ému de l'affaire** the affair aroused the indignation of the whole country; **le gouvernement s'en est ému** the government was roused to action

empailler [ɑ̃paje] ▸conjug 1◂ VT [+ animal] to stuff; [+ chaise] to bottom (with straw)

empailleur, -euse [ɑ̃pajœʀ, øz] NM,F [chaise] chair-bottomer; [animal] taxidermist

empalement [ɑ̃palmɑ̃] NM impalement

empaler [ɑ̃pale] ▸conjug 1◂ ⟨1⟩ VT (= supplicier) to impale; (= embrocher) to stick on a spit ⟨2⟩ **s'empaler** VPR to impale o.s. (sur on)

empan [ɑ̃pɑ̃] NM (Hist = mesure) span

empanaché, e [ɑ̃panaʃe] ADJ plumed

empanner [ɑ̃pane] ▸conjug 1◂ VI (Naut) to gibe (Brit), jibe (US)

empaquetage [ɑ̃paktaʒ] NM (gén) wrapping (up); (Comm = conditionnement) packing, packaging

empaqueter [ɑ̃pakte] ▸conjug 4◂ VT (gén) to wrap (up); (Comm = conditionner) to pack, package

emparer (s') [ɑ̃paʀe] ▸conjug 1◂ VPR ⟨a⟩ **s'~ de** [+ objet] to seize ou grab (hold of); [+ butin] to seize, grab; [+ otage] to seize; [+ conversa-

tion, sujet] to take over; [+ *prétexte*] to seize (up)on; (*Mil*) [+ *ville, territoire, ennemi, pouvoir*] to seize; **s'~ des moyens de production/ d'information** to take over *ou* seize the means of production/the information networks; **ils se sont emparés du caissier** they grabbed (hold of) the cashier; (*Rugby*) **s'~ du ballon** to get possession (of the ball); **les journaux se sont emparés de l'affaire** the papers picked up the story **s'~ de** [*jalousie, colère, remords*] to take possession of, take *ou* lay hold of; **cette obsession s'empara de son esprit** his mind was taken over by this obsession; **une grande peur s'empara d'elle** she suddenly became very afraid

empâté, e [ɑ̃pate] (*ptp de* **empâter**) ADJ [*visage*] fleshy, bloated; [*personne, silhouette*] heavy; [*langue*] coated; [*voix*] slurred, thick

empâtement [ɑ̃patmɑ̃] NM [a] [*personne, silhouette, visage*] thickening-out, fattening-out; [*traits*] thickening [b] (*Peinture*) impasto

empâter [ɑ̃pate] ▸ conjug 1 ◂ [1] VT [+ *langue, bouche*] to coat, fur (up) (*Brit*); [+ *traits*] to thicken, coarsen; **la maladie l'a empâté** his illness has made him put on weight [2] **s'empâter** VPR [*personne, silhouette, visage*] to thicken out, fatten out; [*traits*] to thicken, grow fleshy; [*voix*] to become thick

empathie [ɑ̃pati] NF empathy

empathique [ɑ̃patik] ADJ empath(et)ic

empattement [ɑ̃patmɑ̃] NM (*Constr*) footing; (*Aut*) wheelbase; (*Typo*) serif

empêché, e [ɑ̃peʃe] (*ptp de* **empêcher**) ADJ [a] (= *retenu*) detained, held up; **~ par ses obligations, il n'a pas pu venir** because of his commitments he was prevented from coming [b] (= *embarrassé*) **avoir l'air ~** to look *ou* seem embarrassed *ou* ill-at-ease [c] † **tu es bien ~ de me le dire** you seem at a (complete) loss to know what to tell me; **je serais bien ~ de vous le dire** I'd be hard put (to it) to tell you, I'd be at a loss to know what to tell you

empêchement [ɑ̃peʃmɑ̃] NM (= *obstacle*) (unexpected) obstacle *ou* difficulty, hitch; (*Jur*) impediment; **il n'est pas venu, il a eu un ~** he couldn't come — something cropped up; **en cas d'~** if there's a hitch, if something crops up

empêcher [ɑ̃peʃe] ▸ conjug 1 ◂ [1] VT [a] [+ *chose, action*] to prevent, stop; **~ que qch (ne) se produise ◊ ~ qch de se produire** to prevent sth from happening, stop sth happening; **~ que qn (ne) fasse qch** to prevent sb from doing sth, stop sb (from) doing sth [b] **~ qn de faire qch** to prevent sb from doing sth, stop sb (from) doing sth; **rien ne nous empêche de partir** there's nothing stopping us (from) going *ou* preventing us from going; **~ qn de sortir/d'entrer** to prevent sb from going out *ou* coming in, keep sb in/out; **s'il veut le faire, on ne peut pas l'en ~ ou l'~** if he wants to do it, we can't prevent him (from doing it) *ou* stop him (doing it); **ça ne m'empêche pas de dormir** (*lit*) it doesn't prevent me from sleeping *ou* stop me sleeping *ou* keep me awake; (*fig*) I don't lose any sleep over it [c] (*loc*) **qu'est-ce qui empêche (qu'on le fasse)?** what's there to stop us (doing it)? *ou* to prevent us (from doing it)?, what's stopping us (doing it)?*; **qu'est-ce que ça empêche?*** what odds* *ou* difference does that make?; **ça n'empêche rien*** it makes no odds* *ou* no difference; (il) **n'empêche qu'il a tort** all the same *ou* be that as it may, he's wrong; **j'ai peut-être tort, n'empêche, il a un certain culot!*** maybe I'm wrong, but all the same *ou* even so he's got a nerve!* [2] **s'empêcher** VPR [a] (*littér*) **s'~ de faire qch** to stop o.s. (from) doing sth, refrain from doing sth; **par politesse, il s'empêcha de bâiller** out of politeness he stifled a yawn *ou* he stopped himself yawning

[b] **il n'a pas pu s'~ de rire** he couldn't help laughing, he couldn't stop himself (from) laughing; **je ne peux m'~ de penser que ...** I cannot help thinking that ...; **je n'ai pu m'en ~** I couldn't help it, I couldn't stop myself

empêcheur, -euse [ɑ̃peʃœʀ, øz] NM,F **~ de danser** *ou* **de tourner en rond** (= *trouble-fête*) spoilsport; (= *gêneur*) troublemaker

empeigne [ɑ̃pɛɲ] NF [*chaussure*] upper; (*péj*) **quelle gueule** *ou* **face d'~!*** what a jerk* *ou* a prat* (*Brit*)!

empennage [ɑ̃pɛnaʒ] NM (*Aviat*) stabilizer, tailplane (*Brit*); [*flèche*] (= *action*) feathering; (= *plumes*) feathers, fletchings

empenner [ɑ̃pɛne] ▸ conjug 1 ◂ VT [+ *flèche*] to feather, fledge

empereur [ɑ̃pʀœʀ] NM emperor; **l'~ à la barbe fleurie** Charlemagne

empesé, e [ɑ̃pəze] (*ptp de* **empeser**) ADJ [*col*] starched; (*péj*) [*personne, air*] stiff, starchy

empeser [ɑ̃pəze] ▸ conjug 5 ◂ VT to starch

empester [ɑ̃pɛste] ▸ conjug 1 ◂ VT (= *sentir*) [+ *odeur, fumée*] to stink of, reek of; (= *empuantir*) [+ *pièce*] to stink out (**de** with), make stink (**de** of); (*littér* = *empoisonner*) to poison, taint (**de** with); **ça empeste ici** it stinks in here, there's a foul smell in here

empêtrer (s') [ɑ̃petʀe] ▸ conjug 1 ◂ VPR **s'~ dans** (*lit*) to get tangled up in, get entangled in, get caught up in; [+ *mensonges*] to get o.s. tangled up in; [+ *affaire*] to get (o.s.) involved in, get (o.s.) mixed up in; **s'~ dans des explications** to tie o.s. up in knots trying to explain*, get tangled up in one's explanations

emphase [ɑ̃faz] NF [a] (= *pomposité*) bombast, pomposity; **avec ~** bombastically, pompously; **sans ~** in a straightforward manner, simply [b] † (= *force d'expression*) vigour

emphatique [ɑ̃fatik] ADJ [a] (= *grandiloquent*) bombastic, pompous [b] (*Ling*) emphatic

emphysémateux, -euse [ɑ̃fizematø, øz] [1] ADJ emphysematous [2] NM,F emphysema sufferer

emphysème [ɑ̃fizɛm] NM emphysema

empiècement [ɑ̃pjɛsmɑ̃] NM [*corsage*] yoke

empierrement [ɑ̃pjɛʀmɑ̃] NM [a] (= *action*) [*route*] metalling (*Brit*), gravelling (*US*); [*voie de chemin de fer*] ballasting; [*bassin, cour, fossé*] lining with stones [b] (= *pierres*) [*route*] roadbed, road metal (*Brit*); [*chemin de fer*] ballast

empierrer [ɑ̃pjɛʀe] ▸ conjug 1 ◂ VT [+ *route*] to metal (*Brit*), gravel (*US*); [+ *voie de chemin de fer*] to ballast; [+ *bassin, cour, fossé*] to line with stones

empiètement [ɑ̃pjɛtmɑ̃] NM (*sur territoire, mer, route*) encroachment (**sur** on); (*sur droits, libertés*) infringement (**sur** of), encroachment (**sur** on); (*sur des attributions*) trespassing (**sur** on)

empiéter [ɑ̃pjete] ▸ conjug 6 ◂ ◂ **empiéter sur** VT INDIR [+ *territoire, mer, route*] to encroach (up)on; [+ *droit, liberté*] to infringe, encroach (up)on; [+ *domaine, attributions*] to encroach (up)on, trespass on; (*Athlétisme*) **~ sur un couloir** to run into a lane

empiffrer (s')* [ɑ̃pifʀe] ▸ conjug 1 ◂ VPR to stuff one's face*, stuff o.s.* (**de** with)

empilable [ɑ̃pilabl] ADJ [*siège*] stackable

empilage [ɑ̃pilaʒ], **empilement** [ɑ̃pilmɑ̃] NM (= *action*) piling up, stacking up; (= *pile*) pile, stack

empiler [ɑ̃pile] ▸ conjug 1 ◂ [1] VT [a] (= *mettre en pile*) to pile (up), stack (up) [b]* (= *voler*) to rook*, do* (*Brit*); **se faire ~** to be had* *ou* done* (*Brit*) (**de** out of) [2] **s'empiler** VPR [a] (= *s'amonceler*) to be piled up (**sur** on) [b] (= *s'entasser*) **s'~ dans** [+ *local, véhicule*] to squeeze (*pile* into)

empire [ɑ̃piʀ] [1] NM [a] (*Pol, fig*) empire; **~ colonial/industriel/financier** colonial/industrial/financial empire; **pas pour un ~!** not for

all the tea in China!, not for all the world!; **premier/second Empire** First/Second Empire; **pendule Empire** Empire clock [b] (= *autorité, emprise*) influence, authority; **avoir de l'~ sur** to have influence *ou* a hold on *ou* over, hold sway over; **prendre de l'~ sur** to gain influence *ou* a hold over; **exercer son ~ sur** to exert one's authority over, use one's influence on *ou* over; **sous l'~ de** [*peur, colère*] in the grip of; [+ *jalousie*] possessed by; **sous l'~ de la boisson** under the influence of alcohol; **~ sur soi-même** self-control [2] COMP ▸ **l'Empire byzantin** the Byzantine Empire ▸ **l'Empire du Milieu** the Middle Kingdom ▸ **l'Empire romain d'Occident/d'Orient** the Western/Eastern Roman Empire ▸ **l'Empire du Soleil-Levant** the Land of the Rising Sun

empirer [ɑ̃piʀe] ▸ conjug 1 ◂ [1] VI to get worse, deteriorate [2] VT to make worse, worsen

empirique [ɑ̃piʀik] [1] ADJ (*Philo, Phys*) empirical; (†† *Méd*) empiric [2] NM (†† *Méd*) empiric

empiriquement [ɑ̃piʀikmɑ̃] ADV empirically

empirisme [ɑ̃piʀism] NM empiricism

empiriste [ɑ̃piʀist] ADJ, NMF (*Philo, Phys*) empiricist; (*Méd* ††) empiric

emplacement [ɑ̃plasmɑ̃] NM (= *endroit*) place; (= *site*) site; (*pour construire*) site, location; [*parking*] parking space; **à** *ou* **sur l'~ d'une ancienne cité romaine** on the site of an ancient Roman city; **pour indiquer l'~ du chemin** to show the location of the path; **~ publicitaire** (*sur un mur*) advertising site *ou* space (*NonC*); (*dans un journal*) advertising space (*NonC*)

emplafonner* [ɑ̃plafɔne] ▸ conjug 1 ◂ VT to slam* *ou* smash* into; **il s'est fait ~ par un camion** a lorry slammed* *ou* smashed* into his car *ou* him

emplâtre [ɑ̃plɑtʀ] NM (*Méd*) plaster; (*Aut*) patch; (* = *personne*) (great) lump*, clot*; **ce plat vous fait un ~ sur l'estomac*** this kind of food lies heavy on your stomach → **jambe**

emplette† [ɑ̃plɛt] NF purchase; **faire l'~ de qch** to purchase sth; **faire des** *ou* **quelques ~s** to do some shopping, make some purchases

emplir [ɑ̃pliʀ] ▸ conjug 2 ◂ [1] VT (†, *littér*) [+ *verre, récipient*] to fill (up) (**de** with) [b] [*foule, meubles*] to fill [2] **s'emplir** VPR **s'~ de** to fill with; **la pièce s'emplissait de lumière/de gens** the room was filling with light/people

emploi [ɑ̃plwa] NM [a] (= *usage*) use; **je n'en ai pas l'~** I have no use for it; **l'~ qu'il fait de son argent/temps** how he uses his money/time, the use he makes of his money/time; **sans ~** unused; **~ du temps** timetable, schedule; **~ du temps chargé** heavy *ou* busy timetable, busy schedule → **double** [b] (= *mode d'utilisation*) [*appareil, produit*] use; [*mot, expression*] use, usage; **un ~ nouveau de cet appareil** a new use for this piece of equipment; **divers ~s d'un mot** different uses of a word; **c'est un ~ très rare de cette expression** it's a very rare use *ou* usage of this expression → **mode** [c] (= *poste, travail*) job; (*Écon*) **l'~** employment; **créer de nouveaux ~s** to create new jobs; **être sans ~** to be unemployed; **la situation de l'~** the employment situation; **plein (-)~** full employment; **~s de service** service jobs → **demande, offre, proximité** [d] (*Théât* = *rôle*) role, part; **avoir le physique** *ou* **la tête de l'~*** to look the part

employabilité [ɑ̃plwajabilite] NF [*personne*] employability

employable [ɑ̃plwajabl] ADJ [*appareil, produit*] usable, employable; [*personne*] employable

employé, e [ɑ̃plwaje] (*ptp de* **employer**) NM,F employee; **~ de banque** bank employee *ou* clerk; **~ de commerce** business employee; **~ de bureau** office worker *ou* clerk; **~ municipal**

council worker *ou* employee; **~ des postes/ des chemins de fer/du gaz** postal/railway (*Brit*) *ou* railroad (*US*)/gas worker; **on a sonné, c'est l'~ du gaz** there's someone at the door — it's the gasman*; **~ de maison** domestic employee; **les ~s de cette firme** the staff *ou* employees of this firm

employer [ɑ̃plwaje] ▸conjug 8◂ 1 VT a (= *utiliser*) to use, employ; **~ toute son énergie à faire qch** to apply *ou* devote all one's energies to doing sth; **~ son temps à faire qch/à qch** to spend one's time doing sth/on sth; **~ son argent à faire qch/à qch** to spend *ou* use one's money doing sth/on sth; **bien ~** [+ *temps, argent*] to put to good use, make good use of; [+ *mot, expression*] to use properly *ou* correctly; **mal ~** [+ *temps, argent*] to misuse; [+ *mot, expression*] to misuse, use wrongly *ou* incorrectly; **ce procédé emploie énormément de matières premières** this process uses (up) huge amounts of raw materials b (= *faire travailler*) [+ *main-d'œuvre*] to employ; **l'emploient comme vendeur/à trier le courrier** they employ him as a salesman/to sort the mail; **il est mal employé à ce poste** he has been given the wrong sort of job *ou* is not suited to the post; **il est employé par cette société** he is employed by that firm, is on the staff of that firm

2 **s'employer** VPR **s'~ à faire qch/à qch** to apply *ou* devote o.s. to doing sth/to sth; **s'~ pour†** *ou* **en faveur de†** to go to great lengths *ou* exert o.s. on behalf of

▼**employeur, -euse** [ɑ̃plwajœʀ, øz] NM,F employer

emplumé, e [ɑ̃plyme] ADJ feathered, plumed

empocher* [ɑ̃pɔʃe] ▸conjug 1◂ VT (= *mettre en poche*) to pocket; (= *obtenir*) [+ *argent*] to pocket; [+ *prix*] to carry off; [+ *médaille*] to win

empoignade [ɑ̃pwaɲad] NF (= *bagarre*) fight; (= *altercation*) argument, row (*Brit*)

empoigne [ɑ̃pwaɲ] NF → **foire**

empoigner [ɑ̃pwaɲe] ▸conjug 1◂ VT a (= *saisir*) to grasp, grab (hold of) b (= *émouvoir*) to grip 2 **s'empoigner** VPR (= *se battre*) to fight, have a go at one another*

empois [ɑ̃pwa] NM starch (*for linen etc*)

empoisonnant, e* [ɑ̃pwazɔnɑ̃, ɑ̃t] ADJ (= *irritant*) irritating; (= *contrariant*) annoying, aggravating*; **il est ~ avec ses questions** he's so irritating *ou* he's such a nuisance *ou* such a pain* with his questions

empoisonnement [ɑ̃pwazɔnmɑ̃] NM (*Méd*) poisoning

empoisonner [ɑ̃pwazɔne] ▸conjug 1◂ 1 VT a (= *intoxiquer, tuer*) **~ qn** [*assassin*] to poison sb; [*aliments avariés*] to give sb food poisoning; **empoisonné à la strychnine** poisoned with strychnine; **flèches empoisonnées** poisoned arrows; **propos empoisonnés** poisonous words → **cadeau** b (= *empester*) [+ *relations, vie politique*] to poison; [+ *air*] to stink out; **elle empoisonne la vie de ses proches** she's making her family's life a misery c * (= *ennuyer*) **~ qn** [*gêneur*] to get on sb's nerves; [*contretemps*] to annoy sb, bug sb*; **il m'empoisonne avec ses jérémiades** he's so irritating *ou* such a nuisance *ou* such a pain* with his constant complaints; **il est bien empoisonné maintenant** he's in a real mess now*, he's really in the soup now*

2 **s'empoisonner** VPR a (*lit*) to poison o.s.; (*par intoxication alimentaire*) to get food poisoning b * (= *s'ennuyer*) to be bored stiff* *ou* to death*; **qu'est-ce qu'on s'empoisonne** this is such a drag*; (= *s'embarrasser*) **s'~ (l'existence) à faire qch** to go to the trouble *ou* bother of doing sth

empoisonneur, -euse [ɑ̃pwazɔnœʀ, øz]

NM,F a (*lit*) poisoner b * (= *gêneur*) pain in the neck*

empoissonner [ɑ̃pwasɔne] ▸conjug 1◂ VT to stock with fish

emporté, e [ɑ̃pɔʀte] (*ptp de* **emporter**) ADJ [*caractère, personne*] quick-tempered, hot-tempered; [*ton, air*] angry

emportement [ɑ̃pɔʀtəmɑ̃] NM fit of anger, rage, anger (*NonC*); **avec ~** angrily; (*littér*) **aimer qn avec ~** to love sb passionately, be madly in love with sb

emporte-pièce [ɑ̃pɔʀt(ə)pjɛs] NM INV (*Tech*) punch; (*Culin*) pastry cutter; **à l'~** [*déclaration, jugement*] cut-and-dried

emporter [ɑ̃pɔʀte] ▸conjug 1◂ 1 VT a (= *prendre comme bagage*) [+ *vivres, vêtements*] to take; **emportez des vêtements chauds** take warm clothes (with you); **j'emporte de quoi écrire** I'm taking something to write with; **si vous gagnez, vous pouvez l'~ (avec vous)** if you win, you can take it away (with you); **plats chauds/boissons à ~** take-away (*Brit*) *ou* take-out (*US*) hot meals/drinks, hot meals/drinks to go (*US*); **~ un secret dans la tombe** to take *ou* carry a secret to the grave; **il ne l'emportera pas en** *ou* **au paradis!** he'll soon be smiling on the other side of his face! b (= *enlever*) [+ *objet inutile*] to take away, remove; [+ *prisonniers*] to take away; [+ *blessés*] to carry *ou* take away; (* = *dérober*) to take; **emportez ces papiers/vêtements, nous n'en avons pas besoin** take those papers/clothes away, we don't need them any more; **ils ont emporté l'argenterie !** they've made off with* *ou* taken the silver! → **diable** c (= *entraîner*) [*courant, vent*] to sweep along, carry along; [*navire, train*] to carry along; [*imagination, colère*] to carry away; [*enthousiasme*] to carry away *ou* along, sweep along; **le courant emportait leur embarcation** the current swept *ou* carried their boat along; **emporté par son élan** carried *ou* borne along by his own momentum; **emporté par son imagination/enthousiasme** carried away by his imagination/enthusiasm; **se laisser ~ par la colère** to give way to (one's) anger, let one's anger get the better of one; **le train qui m'emportait vers de nouveaux horizons** the train which carried *ou* bore me away towards new horizons d (= *arracher*) [+ *jambe, bras*] to take off; [+ *cheminée, toit*] to blow away *ou* off; [+ *pont, berge*] to wash away, carry away; (*euph* = *tuer*) [*maladie*] to carry off; **l'obus lui a emporté le bras gauche** the shell blew off *ou* took off his left arm; **pont emporté par le torrent** bridge swept *ou* carried away by the flood; **la vague a emporté trois passagers** the wave washed *ou* swept three passengers overboard; **ça emporte la bouche** *ou* **la gueule!** it takes the roof of your mouth off* e (= *gagner*) [+ *prix*] to carry off; (*Mil*) [+ *position*] to take, win; **~ la décision** to carry *ou* win the day; **~ l'adhésion de qn** to win sb over f **l'~ (sur)** [*personne*] to gain *ou* get the upper hand (over); [*solution, méthode*] to prevail (over); **il a fini par l'~** he finally gained *ou* got the upper hand, he finally came out on top; **il va l'~ sur son adversaire** he's going to get the better of his opponent; **la modération/ cette solution finit par l'~** moderation/this solution prevailed in the end *ou* finally won the day; **cette méthode l'emporte sur l'autre** this method has the edge on the other one *ou* is more satisfactory than the other one; **cette voiture l'emporte sur ses concurrents sur tous les plans** this car outperforms its competitors on every score; **il l'emporte sur ses concurrents en adresse** he outmatches his opponents in skill, his opponents can't match *ou* rival him for skill

2 **s'emporter** VPR a (= *s'irriter*) to lose one's temper (**contre** with), blow up* (**contre**

at)

b (= *s'emballer*) [*cheval*] to bolt; **faire (s')~ son cheval** to make one's horse bolt

empoté, e* [ɑ̃pɔte] 1 ADJ awkward, clumsy 2 NM,F (*péj*) awkward lump*

empourprer [ɑ̃puʀpʀe] ▸conjug 1◂ 1 VT [+ *visage, ciel*] to turn crimson 2 **s'empourprer** VPR [*visage*] to flush, turn crimson; [*ciel*] to turn crimson

empoussiérer [ɑ̃pusjeʀe] ▸conjug 6◂ VT to cover with dust, make dusty

empreindre [ɑ̃pʀɛ̃dʀ] ▸conjug 52◂ (*littér*) 1 VT (= *imprimer*) to imprint; (*fig*) (= *marquer*) to stamp; (= *nuancer*) to tinge (**de** with) 2 **s'empreindre** VPR **s'~ de** [+ *mélancolie*] to be tinged with

empreint, e¹ [ɑ̃pʀɛ̃, ɛ̃t] (*ptp de* **empreindre**) ◆ **empreint de** ADJ [+ *regret, jalousie*] tinged with; [+ *bonté, autorité*] marked *ou* stamped with; [+ *menaces*] fraught *ou* heavy with

empreinte² [ɑ̃pʀɛ̃t] NF a (*lit, gén*) imprint, impression; [*animal*] track; **~ (de pas)** footprint; **~s (digitales)** (finger)prints; **~ génétique** genetic fingerprint; **~ vocale** voiceprint; **prendre l'~ d'une dent** to take an impression of a tooth; **relever** *ou* **prendre des ~s digitales** to take fingerprints b (= *influence*) stamp, mark; **laisser une ~ indélébile sur qn** to make a lasting impression on sb; **son œuvre laissera son ~ dans ce siècle** his work will leave its mark on this century

empressé, e [ɑ̃pʀese] (*ptp de* **s'empresser**) ADJ a (= *prévenant*) [*infirmière, serveur*] attentive; [*aide*] willing; (*gén péj*) [*admirateur, prétendant*] assiduous, overattentive; [*subordonné*] over-anxious to please (*attrib*), overzealous, (*péj*) **faire l'~ (auprès d'une femme)** to be overattentive (towards a woman) b (*littér* = *marquant de la hâte*) eager; **~ à faire qch** eager *ou* anxious to do sth

empressement [ɑ̃pʀɛsmɑ̃] NM a (= *prévenance*) [*infirmière, serveur*] attentiveness; [*aide*] willingness; (*gén péj*) [*admirateur, prétendant*] overzealousness, overattentiveness; [*subordonné*] overzealousness; **son ~ auprès des femmes** the way he fusses around women, his overattentiveness towards women; **il me servait avec ~** he waited upon me attentively b (= *hâte*) eagerness, anxiousness; **son ~ à partir me paraît suspect** his eagerness *ou* anxiousness to leave seems suspicious to me; **il montrait peu d'~ à ...** he seemed in no hurry to ..., he was obviously not anxious to ...; **il s'exécuta avec ~** he complied eagerly

empresser (s') [ɑ̃pʀese] ▸conjug 1◂ VPR a (= *s'affairer*) to bustle about; (*péj*) to fuss about *ou* around, bustle about *ou* around; **s'~ auprès** *ou* **autour de** [+ *blessé, invité*] to surround with attentions; [+ *femme courtisée*] to dance attendance upon, fuss around; **ils s'empressèrent autour de la victime** they rushed to help *ou* assist the victim; **ils s'empressaient auprès de l'actrice** they surrounded the actress with attentions b (= *se hâter*) **s'~ de faire qch** to hasten to do sth

emprise [ɑ̃pʀiz] NF a (= *influence*) hold, ascendancy (**sur** over); **avoir beaucoup d'~ sur qn** to hold sway over sb; **sous l'~ de la colère** in the grip of anger, gripped by anger; **sous l'~ de l'alcool/de la drogue** under the influence of alcohol/of drugs b (*Jur* = *mainmise*) expropriation

emprisonnement [ɑ̃pʀizɔnmɑ̃] NM imprisonment; **condamné à 10 ans d'~** sentenced to 10 years in prison, given a 10-year prison sentence

emprisonner [ɑ̃pʀizɔne] ▸conjug 1◂ VT a (*en prison*) to imprison, put in prison *ou* jail, jail; (*dans une chambre, un couvent*) to shut up, imprison b [*vêtement*] to confine; [*doctrine, milieu*] to trap; **ce corset lui emprisonne la taille** this corset grips her too tightly around the waist; **~ qn dans un système/un raisonnement**

to trap sb within a system/by a piece of reasoning; **emprisonné dans ses habitudes/la routine** imprisoned within *ou* a prisoner of his habits/routine

emprunt [ɑ̃pʀœ̃] NM [a] (= *action d'emprunter*) [*argent, objet*] borrowing; **ce n'était pas un vol, mais seulement un ~** it wasn't really stealing, only borrowing; (*Fin*) **recourir à l'~** to resort to borrowing *ou* to a loan [b] (= *demande, somme*) loan; **ses ~s successifs l'ont mis en difficulté** successive borrowing has *ou* his successive loans have put him in difficulty; **~ d'État/public** government/public loan; **~ du Trésor** (*américain*) (American *ou* US) Treasury bond; **~ à 5 %** loan at 5% (interest); **~s russes** Soviet loans; **faire un ~ d'un million à une banque** to take out a loan of one million from a bank, borrow a million from a bank; **faire un ~ pour payer sa voiture** to borrow money *ou* take out a loan to pay for one's car [c] (*Littérat, Ling*) borrowing; (= *terme*) loan word, borrowed word, borrowing; **c'est un ~ à l'anglais** it's a loan word *ou* borrowing from English [d] (*loc*) **d'~** [*nom, autorité*] assumed; [*matériel*] borrowed

emprunté, e [ɑ̃pʀœ̃te] (*ptp de* **emprunter**) ADJ [a] (= *gauche*) [*air, personne*] ill-at-ease (*attrib*), self-conscious, awkward [b] (= *artificiel*) [*gloire, éclat*] sham, feigned

emprunter [ɑ̃pʀœ̃te] ▸conjug 1◂ VT [a] [+ *argent, objet*] to borrow (**à** from) [b] [+ *mot, expression*] (*directement*) to borrow, take (**à** from); (*par dérivation*) to derive, take (**à** from); [+ *nom, autorité*] to assume, take on; [+ *idée*] to borrow, take (**à** from); **cette pièce emprunte son sujet à l'actualité** this play is based on a topical subject; **métaphores empruntées à la musique** metaphors derived from music; **mot emprunté à l'anglais** loan word from English [c] [+ *escalier, route*] to take; [+ *itinéraire*] to follow; **« empruntez le passage souterrain »** "use the underpass "; **les trains n'empruntent plus cette ligne** trains don't run on this line any more

emprunteur, -euse [ɑ̃pʀœ̃tœʀ, øz] NM,F borrower

empuantir [ɑ̃pɥɑ̃tiʀ] ▸conjug 2◂ VT to stink out (**de** with)

empyrée [ɑ̃piʀe] NM empyrean

EMT † [œmte] NF (ABRÉV = **éducation manuelle et technique**) → **éducation**

ému, e [emy] (*ptp de* **émouvoir**) ADJ [*personne*] (*compassion*) moved; (*gratitude*) touched; (*joie*) excited; (*timidité, peur*) nervous, agitated; [*air*] filled with emotion; [*voix*] emotional, trembling with emotion; [*souvenirs*] tender, touching; **~ jusqu'aux larmes** moved to tears (**devant** by); **très ~ lors de la remise des prix** very excited *ou* agitated at the prize giving; **encore tout ~, il la remercia** still quite overcome *ou* still (feeling) very touched, he thanked her; **dit-il d'une voix ~e** he said with emotion; **trop ~ pour les remercier/leur annoncer la nouvelle** too overcome to thank them/announce the news to them

émulateur [emylatœʀ] NM (*Ordin*) emulator

émulation [emylasjɔ̃] NF (*gén, Ordin*) emulation; **esprit d'~** spirit of competition, competitive spirit

émule [emyl] NMF (*littér*) (= *imitateur*) emulator; (= *égal*) equal; (*péj*) **ce fripon et ses ~s** this scoundrel and his like; **être l'~ de qn** to emulate sb; **il fait des ~s** people emulate him

émuler [emyle] ▸conjug 1◂ VT (*Ordin*) to emulate

émulsif, -ive [emylsif, iv] [1] ADJ (*Pharm*) emulsive; (*Chim*) emulsifying [2] NM emulsifier

émulsifiant, e [emylsifjɑ̃, jɑ̃t] [1] ADJ emulsifying [2] NM emulsifier

émulsion [emylsjɔ̃] NF emulsion

émulsionner [emylsjɔne] ▸conjug 1◂ VT to emulsify

EN (ABRÉV = **Éducation nationale**) → **éducation**

en¹ [ɑ̃]
PRÉPOSITION

> *Lorsque* **en** *se trouve dans des expressions figées telles que* **avoir confiance en qn, se mettre en tête de, couper qch en dés** *etc, reportez-vous à l'autre mot.*

[a] **dans l'espace** (*lieu où l'on est*) in; (*lieu où l'on va*) to; **vivre en France/Normandie** to live in France/Normandy; **aller** *ou* **partir en Angleterre/Normandie** to go to England/Normandy; **il habite en banlieue/ville** he lives in the suburbs/the town; **être en ville** to be in town; **aller en ville** to go (in)to town; **les objets en vitrine** the items in the window; *MAIS* **il voyage en Grèce/Corse** he's travelling around Greece/Corsica

[b]
♦ **en** + *pronom personnel*: **en lui-même, il n'y croit pas** deep down *ou* in his heart of hearts he doesn't believe it; **je me disais en moi-même que ...** I was thinking to myself that ...; **ce que j'aime en lui, c'est son courage** what I like about him is his courage; **on voit en lui un futur champion du monde** they see him as a future world champion

[c] **dans le temps** in; **en semaine** in *ou* during the week; **en soirée** in the evening; **en automne/été/mars/1999** in autumn/summer/March/1999; **il peut le faire en 3 jours** he can do it in 3 days; **en 6 ans je lui ai parlé deux fois** in (all of) 6 years I've spoken to him twice → **de¹**

[d] **avec moyen de transport** **en taxi/train/avion** by taxi/train *ou* rail/air; **faire une promenade en bateau/voiture** to go for a trip in a boat/car, go for a boat-/car-trip; **ils y sont allés en voiture** they went by car; **ils y sont allés en Rolls-Royce** they went in a Rolls-Royce; **ils sont arrivés en voiture** they arrived in a car; **je suis malade en bateau/en voiture** I get seasick/carsick; **il y est allé en pousse-pousse** he went there in a *ou* by rickshaw

> *Notez que l'anglais emploie souvent un verbe spécifique.*

aller à Londres en avion to fly to London; **ils ont remonté le fleuve en pirogue** they canoed up the river, they rowed up the river in a canoe

[e] **= habillé de** in; **être en noir/blanc** to be (dressed) in black/white, be wearing black/white; **elle est arrivée en manteau de fourrure** she arrived wearing *ou* in a fur coat; **la femme en manteau de fourrure** the woman in the fur coat *ou* with a fur coat on; **il était en chemise/pyjama** he was wearing a shirt/wearing pyjamas; **être en chaussettes** to be in one's stockinged feet; *MAIS* **elle était en bergère** she was disguised *ou* dressed as a shepherdess

[f] **description, présentation** in; **en cercle/rang** in a circle/row; **enregistré en stéréo** recorded in stereo; **ils y vont en groupe** they are going in a group; **l'œuvre de Proust en six volumes** Proust's works in six volumes; **une pièce en trois actes** a three-act play, a play in three acts; **ça se vend en boîtes de douze** they are sold in boxes of twelve; **c'est écrit en anglais/vers/prose/lettres d'or** it's written in English/verse/prose/gold letters; **image en trois dimensions** 3-D image, image in 3-D
♦ **en** + *adjectif*: **nous avons le même article en vert** we have the same item in green
♦ **en** + *comparatif*: **c'est son frère en mieux** he's like his brother, only better; **c'est son père en plus jeune/petit** he's just like his father only younger/smaller, he's a younger/smaller version of his father; **je veux la même valise en**

plus grand I want the same suitcase only bigger *ou* only in a bigger size

[g] **= composé de, fait de** **le plat est en or/argent** the dish is made of gold/silver; **l'escalier sera en marbre** the staircase will be (in *ou* made of) marble; **en quoi est-ce** *ou* **c'est fait ?** ◊ **c'est en quoi ?*** what's it made of?

> *Notez qu'en anglais le substantif est souvent utilisé en apposition comme adjectif.*

une bague en or/argent a gold/silver ring; **une table en acajou** a mahogany table; **une jupe en soie imprimée** a printed silk skirt, a skirt made (out) of printed silk

[h] **transformation** into; **se changer en** to change into; **convertir/transformer qch en** to convert/transform sth into; **traduire en italien** to translate into Italian; **casser qch en morceaux** to break sth in(to) pieces

[i] **= comme** **agir en tyran/lâche** to act like a tyrant/coward; **c'est en expert qu'il en a parlé** he spoke as an expert; **en bon politicien** (qu'il est), il ... good politician that he is, he ..., being the skilled politician he is, he ...; **je le lui ai donné en cadeau/souvenir** I gave it to him as a present/souvenir

[j] **= concernant** **en politique/art/musique** in politics/art/music; **en affaires, il faut de l'audace** you have to take risks in business; **je n'y connais rien en informatique** I don't know anything about computers; **ce que je préfère en musique, c'est ...** what I like best in the way of music is ...; **être bon** *ou* **fort en géographie** to be good at geography; **diplôme en droit/histoire** law/history degree

[k] **mesure** in; **mesurer en mètres** to measure in metres; **compter en francs** to reckon in francs; **ce tissu se fait en 140 (cm)** this material comes in 140 cm width; **nous avons ce manteau en trois tailles** we have this coat in three sizes

[l]
♦ **en** + *participe présent*
(*manière*) **il me regarda en fronçant les sourcils** he looked at me with a frown; **«je ne sais pas», dit-il en haussant les épaules** "I don't know" he said with a shrug; **endormir un enfant en le berçant/chantant** to rock/sing a child to sleep

> *Avec un verbe de mouvement ou d'énonciation, l'anglais préférera souvent un verbe suivi éventuellement d'une préposition.*

monter/entrer en courant to run up/in; **sortir en rampant/boitant** to crawl/limp out; **dire qch en murmurant/criant** to murmur/shout sth

> *Là où le français emploie* **en** *suivi d'un verbe au participe présent pour exprimer la simultanéité, l'anglais utilise une proposition temporelle ou une forme en* **ing**.

fermez la porte en sortant shut the door as *ou* when you go out; **elle est arrivée en chantant** she was singing when she arrived; **j'ai écrit une lettre (tout) en vous attendant** I wrote a letter while I was waiting for you; **il s'est endormi en lisant le journal** he fell asleep (while) reading the newspaper, he fell asleep over the newspaper; **il s'est coupé en essayant d'ouvrir une boîte** he cut himself trying to open a tin; **en apprenant la nouvelle, elle s'est évanouie** she fainted when she heard the news; **il a buté en montant dans l'autobus** he tripped as he got onto *ou* getting onto the bus; *MAIS* **il a fait une folie en achetant cette bague** it was very extravagant of him to buy this ring
(*nuance causale*) by; **en disant cela, il s'est fait des ennemis** he made enemies by saying that; **en refusant de coopérer, vous risquez de tout perdre** by refusing to cooperate, you risk losing everything

[m]
♦ **en être à**
(= *avoir atteint*) **en être à la page 9** to be at page 9, have reached page 9; **où en est-il de** *ou* **dans**

ses études? how far has he got with his studies?, what point has he reached in his studies?; **il en est à sa troisième année de méde-cine** he has reached his third year in medi-cine; **l'affaire en est là** that's how the matter stands, that's as far as it's got; (fig) **je ne sais plus où j'en suis** I don't know whether I am coming or going

(= se voir réduit à) **j'en suis à me demander si** I'm beginning to wonder if, I've come to wonder if, I've got to wondering if*; **il en est à mendier** he has come down to ou stooped to begging, he has been reduced to begging

en² [ã] PRON a (lieu) **quand va-t-il à Nice? — il en revient** when is he off to Nice? — he's just (come) back; **elle était tombée dans une cre-vasse, on a eu du mal à l'en sortir** she had fall-en into a crevasse and they had difficulty ou trouble (in) getting her out (of it); **le bénéfice qu'il en a tiré** the profit he got out of it ou from it; **il faut en tirer une conclusion** we must draw a conclusion (from it); **où en sommes-nous?** (livre, leçon) where have we got (up) to?, where are we?; (situation) where do we stand?

b (cause, agent, instrument) **je suis si inquiet que j'en dors pas** I can't sleep for worry-ing, I am so worried that I can't sleep; **il saisit sa canne et l'en frappa** he seized his stick and struck her with it; **ce n'est pas moi qui en per-drai le sommeil** I won't lose any sleep over it; **quelle histoire! nous en avons beaucoup ri** what a business! we had a good laugh over ou about it; **en mourir** (maladie) to die of it; (blessure) to die because of it ou as a result of it; **elle en est aimée** she is loved by him

c (complément de vb, d'adj, de n) **rendez-moi mon stylo, j'en ai besoin** give me back my pen — I need it; **qu'est-ce que tu en feras?** what will you do with it (ou them)?; **c'est une bonne classe, les professeurs en sont contents** they are a good class and the teach-ers are pleased with them; **elle, mentir! elle en est incapable** she couldn't lie if she tried; **elle a réussi et elle n'en est pas peu fière** she has been successful and she is more than a little proud of herself ou of it; **il ne fume plus, il en a perdu l'habitude** he doesn't smoke any more — he has got out of ou has lost the hab-it; **sa décision m'inquiète car j'en connais tous les dangers** her decision worries me because I am aware of all the dangers ou of all its pos-sible dangers; **je t'en donne/offre 10F** I'll give/offer you 10 francs for it

d (quantitatif, indéf) of it, of them (souvent omis); **si vous aimez les pommes, prenez-en plusieurs** if you like apples, take several; **il avait bien des lettres à écrire mais il n'en a pas écrit la moitié/beaucoup** he had a lot of let-ters to write but he hasn't written half of them/many (of them); **le vin est bon mais il n'y en a pas beaucoup** the wine is good but there isn't much (of it); **si j'en avais** if I had any; **voulez-vous du pain/des pommes? il y en a encore** would you like some bread/some apples? we have still got some (left); **il n'y en a plus** (pain) there isn't any left, there's none left; (pommes) there aren't any left, there are none left; **si vous cherchez un crayon, vous en trouverez des douzaines/un dans le tiroir** if you are looking for a pencil you will find dozens (of them)/one in the drawer; **élevé dans le village, j'en connaissais tous les habi-tants** having been brought up in the village I knew all its inhabitants; **a-t-elle des pou-pées? — oui, elle en a deux/trop/de belles** has she any dolls? — yes, she has two/too many/some lovely ones; **nous avons du vin, j'en ai acheté une bouteille hier** we have some wine, I bought a bottle yesterday; **des souris ici? nous n'en avons jamais vu** mice here? we've never seen any; **il en aime une autre** he loves another (littér), he loves somebody else

e (renforcement : non traduit) **il s'en souvien-dra de cette réception** he'll certainly remem-ber that party; **je n'en vois pas, moi, de places libres** well (I must say), I don't see any empty seats; **tu en as eu de beaux jouets à Noël!** well you did get some lovely toys ou what lovely toys you got for Christmas! → **accroire, aussi, entendre, venir** etc

ENA [ena]   NF (ABRÉV = **École nationale d'administration**) → **école**

enamouré, e [enamure]   (ptp de **s'enamourer**) ADJ [regard] adoring

enamourer (s')†† [enamure, ãnamure] ▸conjug 1◂ VPR **s'~ de** to become enamoured of

énarchie [enaʀʃi]   NF power of the énarques

énarque [enaʀk]   NMF énarque (student or for-mer student of the École nationale d'administration)

énarthrose [enaʀtʀoz]   NF socket joint

en-avant [ãnavã]   NM INV (Rugby) forward pass, knock on

en-but [ãby(t)]   NM INV (Rugby) in-goal area

encablure [ãkablyʀ]   NF cable's length; **à 3 ~s de ...** 3 cables' length away from ...

encadré [ãkadʀe]   (ptp de **encadrer**) NM box

encadrement [ãkadʀəmã]   NM a (NonC) [ta-bleau] framing; **« tous travaux d'~ »** "all fram-ing (work) undertaken" b (NonC) [étudiants, débutants, recrues] training, supervision c (= embrasure) [porte, fenêtre] frame; **il se tenait dans l'~ de la porte** he stood in the doorway d (= cadre) frame; **cet ~ conviendrait mieux au sujet** this frame would be more appropri-ate to the subject e (Admin) (= instructeurs) training personnel; (= cadres) managerial staff f (Écon) **~ du crédit** credit restriction

encadrer [ãkadʀe]   ▸conjug 1◂ 1 VT a [+ tableau] to frame; (iro) **c'est à ~!** that's price-less!, that's one to remember! b (= instruire) [+ étudiants, débutants, recrues] to train (and supervise); (= contrôler) [+ enfant] to take in hand; [+ équipe sportive, employés] to manage; (Écon) [+ crédit] to restrict; [+ prix, loyers] to control c (= entourer) [+ cour, plaine, visage] to frame, surround; [+ prisonnier] to surround; (par deux personnes) to flank; **les collines qui encadrent la plaine** the hills surrounding the plain; **encadré de ses gardes du corps** surrounded by his bodyguards; **l'accusé, encadré de deux gendarmes** the accused, flanked by two policemen d (:, gén nég = supporter) **je ne peux pas l'~** I can't stick* ou stand* him e (Mil) [+ objectif] to straddle f * (= heurter) [+ véhicule, maison] to smash into; **il s'est fait ~*** someone smashed into his car

2 **s'encadrer** VPR a (= apparaître) [visage, silhouette] to appear b * (en voiture) to crash one's car (dans into)

encadreur, -euse [ãkadʀœʀ, øz]   NM,F (pic-ture) framer

encager [ãkaʒe]   ▸conjug 3◂ VT [+ animal, oiseau] to cage (up); (fig) [+ personne] to cage in, cage up

encagoulé, e [ãkagule]   ADJ [moine] cowled; [pénitent] hooded, cowled; [bandit, visage] hooded, masked

encaissable [ãkesabl]   ADJ cashable, encash-able (Brit)

encaisse [ãkes]   NF cash in hand, cash bal-ance; **~ métallique** gold and silver reserves; **~ or** gold reserves

encaissé, e [ãkese]   (ptp de **encaisser**) ADJ [vallée] deep, steep-sided; [rivière] hemmed in by steep banks ou hills; [route] hemmed in by steep hills

encaissement [ãkesmã]   NM a [argent, loyer] collection, receipt; [facture] receipt of pay-

ment (de for); [chèque] cashing; [effet de com-merce] collection b [vallée] depth, steep-sidedness; **l'~ de la route/rivière faisait que le pont ne voyait jamais le soleil** the steep hills hemming in the road/river stopped the sun from ever reaching the bridge

encaisser [ãkese]   ▸conjug 1◂ VT a [+ argent, loyer] to collect, receive; [+ facture] to receive payment for; [+ chèque] to cash; [+ effet de commerce] to collect

b * [+ coups, affront, défaite] to take; **savoir ~** [boxeur] to be able to take a lot of beating ou punishment; (fig: dans la vie) to know how to roll with the punches; **qu'est-ce qu'il a encaissé!** (coups) what a hammering he got!*, what a beating he took!; (injures, réprimande) what a hammering he got!*, he certainly got what for!*; **qu'est-ce qu'on encaisse avec ces cahots!** we're taking a real hammering on these bumps!*

c (:, gén nég = supporter) **je ne peux pas ~ ce type** I can't stand* that guy; **il n'a pas encaissé cette décision** he couldn't stomach* the decision; **il n'a pas encaissé cette re-marque** he didn't appreciate that remark one little bit*

d (Tech) [+ route, fleuve, voie ferrée] to em-bank; **les montagnes qui encaissent la vallée** the mountains on either side of the valley; **la route s'encaisse entre les collines** the road is hemmed in by the hills

e [+ objets] to pack in(to) boxes; [+ plantes] to plant in boxes ou tubs

encaisseur [ãkesœʀ]   NM collector (of debts etc)

encalminé, e [ãkalmine]   ADJ [navire] be-calmed

encan [ãkã]   NM **mettre** ou **vendre à l'~** to sell off by auction

encanaillement [ãkanajmã]   NM mixing with the riffraff

encanailler (s') [ãkanaje]   ▸conjug 1◂ VPR (hum) to mix with the riffraff, slum it*; **son style/langage s'encanaille** his style/language is becoming vulgar

encapuchonner [ãkapyʃɔne]   ▸conjug 1◂ VT **~ un enfant** to put a child's hood up; **la tête encapuchonnée** hooded; **un groupe de bambins encapuchonnés** a group of toddlers snug in their hoods

encart [ãkaʀ]   NM (Typo) insert, inset; **~ publi-citaire** publicity ou advertising insert

encarté, e [ãkaʀte]   ADJ [Pol] [militant] card-carrying (épith); **être ~ à un parti** to be a card-carrying member of a party

encarter [ãkaʀte]   ▸conjug 1◂ VT (Typo) to in-sert, inset

en-cas [ãkɑ]   NM INV (= nourriture) snack

encaserner [ãkazɛʀne]   ▸conjug 1◂ VT to quar-ter ou lodge in barracks

encastrable [ãkastʀabl]   ADJ [four, lave-vaisselle] slot-in (Brit) (épith), ready to be in-stalled (US) (attrib)

encastré, e [ãkastʀe]   (ptp de **encastrer**) ADJ [four, placard] built-in; **spot ~ dans le plafond** recessed spotlight; **baignoire ~e (dans le sol)** sunken bath; **une église ~e entre deux gratte-ciel** a church hemmed ou boxed in be-tween two skyscrapers; **de gros blocs ~s dans la neige/le sol** great blocks sunk in ou embed-ded in the snow/ground

encastrement [ãkastʀəmã]   NM [interrupteur] flush fitting; [armoire, rayonnage] recessed fit-ting

encastrer [ãkastʀe]   ▸conjug 1◂ VT (dans un mur) to embed (**dans** in(to)), sink (**dans** into); [+ interrupteur] to fit flush (**dans** with); [+ rayonnage, armoire] to recess (**dans** into), fit (**dans** into); (dans un boîtier) [+ pièce] to fit (**dans** into); **tous les boutons sont encastrés dans le mur** all the switches are flush with the wall; **l'aquarium est encastré dans le mur** the aquarium is built into the wall; **la voiture s'est encastrée sous le train** the car jammed itself underneath the train; **ces pièces s'encastrent l'une dans l'autre/dans le boîtier** these parts fit exactly into each other/into the case

encaustique [ãkostik] NF wax polish

encaustiquer [ãkostike] ▸ conjug 1 ◂ VT to polish, wax

enceindre [ãsɛ̃dʀ] ▸ conjug 52 ◂ VT (gén ptp) to encircle, surround (de with); **enceint de** encircled ou surrounded by

enceinte¹ [ãsɛ̃t] ADJ F pregnant, expecting* (attrib); **tomber/se retrouver ~** to get ou become/find o.s. pregnant; **femme ~** pregnant woman, expectant mother; **~ de cinq mois** five months pregnant; **j'étais ~ de Paul** (= Paul était le bébé) I was pregnant with ou was expecting Paul; (= Paul était le père) I was pregnant by Paul; **il l'a mise ~** he got ou made her pregnant; **~ jusqu'aux yeux*** very pregnant*

enceinte² [ãsɛ̃t] NF ⓐ (= mur) wall; (= palissade) enclosure, fence; **une ~ de fossés défendait la place** the position was surrounded by defensive ditches ou was defended by surrounding ditches; **mur d'~** outer walls ⓑ (= espace clos) enclosure; [couvent] precinct; **dans l'~ de la ville** within ou inside the town; **dans l'~ du tribunal** in(side) the court room; **dans l'~ de cet établissement** within ou in(side) this establishment; **~ militaire** military area ou zone; (Phys) **~ de confinement** protective shield ⓒ **~ (acoustique)** speaker

encens [ãsã] NM incense; **l'~ des louanges/de leur flatterie** the heady wine of praise/of their flattery

encensement [ãsãsmã] NM ⓐ (Rel) incensing ⓑ (= louanges) praising (NonC) to the skies

encenser [ãsãse] ▸ conjug 1 ◂ VT ⓐ (Rel) to incense ⓑ (= louanger) to heap ou shower praise (up)on, praise to the skies

encenseur, -euse [ãsãsœʀ, øz] NM,F (Rel) thurifer, censer-bearer; (fig, †) flatterer

encensoir [ãsãswaʀ] NM censer, thurible; (péj) **manier l'~** to pour out flattery, heap on the praise; (fig) **coups d'~** excessive flattery

encéphale [ãsefal] NM encephalon

encéphalique [ãsefalik] ADJ encephalic

encéphalite [ãsefalit] NF encephalitis

encéphalogramme [ãsefalɔgʀam] NM encephalogram

encéphalopathie [ãsefalɔpati] NF encephalopathy; **~ bovine spongiforme** BSE, bovine spongiform encephalopathy (SPÉC)

encerclement [ãsɛʀkləmã] NM (par des murs) surrounding, encircling; (par l'armée, la police) surrounding

encercler [ãsɛʀkle] ▸ conjug 1 ◂ VT [murs] to surround, encircle; [armée, police] to surround

enchaîné [ãʃene] NM (Ciné) change → **fondu**

enchaînement [ãʃenmã] NM ⓐ (= suite logique) [épisodes, preuves] linking; **l'~ de la violence** the spiral of violence ⓑ [scènes, séquences] (= action) linking; (= résultat) link ⓒ (= série) [circonstances] sequence, series, string; **~ d'événements** chain ou series ou string ou sequence of events ⓓ (Danse) enchaînement; (Gym) **faire un ~** to do a sequence of movements; **un bel ~** a fluid sequence of movements; (Mus) **~ des accords** chord progression

enchaîner [ãʃene] ▸ conjug 1 ◂ ⓵ VT ⓐ (= lier) [+ animal] to chain up; [+ prisonnier] to put in chains, chain up; **~ qn à un arbre** to chain sb to a tree; **enchaînés l'un à l'autre** chained together
ⓑ (littér) [secret, souvenir, sentiment] to bind; **l'amour enchaîne les cœurs** love binds hearts

(together); **ses souvenirs l'enchaînaient à ce lieu** his memories tied ou bound ou chained him to this place
ⓒ (= asservir) [+ peuple] to enslave; [+ presse] to muzzle, gag; **~ la liberté** to put freedom in chains
ⓓ (= assembler) [+ faits, épisodes, séquences] to connect, link (together ou up); [+ paragraphes, pensées, mots] to link (together ou up), string together; **incapable d'~ deux pensées** incapable of stringing two thoughts together; **elle enchaînait réunion sur réunion** she had meeting after meeting ou one meeting after another; (Ciné) **~ (la scène suivante)** to change to ou move on to the next scene; (Ciné) **on va ~ les dernières scènes** we'll carry on with the last scenes, we'll go on to the last scenes

⓶ VI (Ciné, Théât) to move on ou carry on (Brit) (to the next scene); **sans laisser à Anne le temps de répondre, Paul enchaîna : « d'abord ... »** without giving Anne the time to reply, Paul went on ou continued: "first ..."; **on enchaîne ◊ enchaînons** (Théât) let's keep going ou carry on; (Ciné) let's keep rolling; (*: dans un débat) let's go on ou carry on, let's continue

⓷ **s'enchaîner** VPR [épisodes, séquences] to follow on from each other, be linked (together); [preuves, faits] to be linked (together); **tout s'enchaîne** it's all linked ou connected, it all ties up; **paragraphes/raisonnements qui s'enchaînent bien** well-linked paragraphs/pieces of reasoning

▾**enchanté, e** [ãʃãte] (ptp de **enchanter**) ADJ ⓐ (= ravi) enchanted (de by), delighted (de with); **~ (de vous connaître)** how do you do?, (I'm) very pleased to meet you ⓑ (= magique) [forêt, demeure] enchanted

enchantement [ãʃãtmã] NM ⓐ (= action) enchantment; (= effet) (magic) spell, enchantment; **comme par ~** as if by magic ⓑ (= ravissement) delight, enchantment; **ce spectacle fut un ~** it was an enchanting ou a delightful sight; **être dans l'~** to be enchanted ou delighted

enchanter [ãʃãte] ▸ conjug 1 ◂ ⓵ VT ⓐ (= ensorceler) to enchant, bewitch ⓑ (= ravir) to enchant, delight; **ça ne m'enchante pas beaucoup** I'm not exactly taken with it, it doesn't exactly thrill me ⓶ **s'enchanter** VPR (littér) to rejoice (de at)

enchanteur, -teresse [ãʃãtœʀ, tʀɛs] ⓵ ADJ enchanting, bewitching ⓶ NM (= sorcier) enchanter; (fig) charmer ⓷ **enchanteresse** NF enchantress

enchâssement [ãʃasmã] NM ⓐ [pierre] setting (dans in) ⓑ (Ling) embedding

enchâsser [ãʃase] ▸ conjug 1 ◂ VT (gén) to set (dans in); (Ling) to embed; (littér) **~ une citation dans un texte** to insert a quotation into a text ⓶ **s'enchâsser** VPR (l'un dans l'autre) to fit exactly together; **s'~ dans** to fit exactly into

enchère [ãʃɛʀ] ⓵ NF ⓐ (Comm = offre) bid; **faire une ~** to bid, make a bid; **faire monter les ~s** (lit) to raise ou push up the bidding; (fig) to raise ou up the stakes ou the ante; **les deux entreprises le veulent mais il laisse monter les ~s** the two companies want him but he's waiting for the highest possible bid ⓑ (Cartes) bid; **le système des ~s** the bidding system ⓶ **~s** NFPL (Comm) **mettre qch aux ~s (publiques)** to put sth up for auction; **le tableau a été mis aux ~s** the picture was put up for auction ou went under the hammer; **vendre aux ~s** to sell by auction; **acheté aux ~s** bought at an auction (sale) → **vente**

enchérir [ãʃeʀiʀ] ▸ conjug 2 ◂ VI ⓐ (Comm) **~ sur une offre** to make a higher bid; **~ sur qn** to bid higher than sb, make a higher bid than sb; **~ sur (l'offre d') une somme** to go higher than ou go above ou go over an amount

ⓑ (fig) **~ sur** to go further than, go beyond, go one better than ⓒ † (= augmenter) to become more expensive

enchérissement † [ãʃeʀismã] NM = **renchérissement**

enchérisseur, -euse [ãʃeʀisœʀ, øz] NM,F bidder

enchevêtrement [ãʃ(ə)vɛtʀəmã] NM [ficelles, branches] entanglement; [situation] confusion; **l'~ de ses idées** the confusion ou muddle his ideas were in; **un ~ de branches barrait la route** a tangle of branches blocked the way

enchevêtrer [ãʃ(ə)vɛtʀe] ▸ conjug 1 ◂ ⓵ VT [+ ficelle] to tangle (up), entangle, muddle up; [+ idées, intrigue] to confuse, muddle ⓶ **s'enchevêtrer** VPR ⓐ [ficelles] to get in a tangle, become entangled, tangle; [branches] to become entangled; **s'~ dans des cordes** to get caught up ou tangled up in ropes ⓑ [situations, paroles] to become confused ou muddled; **mots qui s'enchevêtrent les uns dans les autres** words that run into each other; **s'~ dans ses explications** to tie o.s. up in knots* explaining (something), get tangled up in one's explanations

enchifrené, e † [ãʃifʀəne] ADJ [nez] blocked up

enclave [ãklav] NF (lit, fig) enclave

enclavement [ãklavmã] NM (= action) enclosing, hemming in; (= état) **l'~ de la région par les montagnes** the way the region is enclosed by ou hemmed-in by mountains; **cette province souffre de son ~** this province suffers from its isolation ou from its hemmed-in position

enclaver [ãklave] ▸ conjug 1 ◂ VT ⓐ (= entourer) to enclose, hem in; **terrain complètement enclavé dans un grand domaine** piece of land completely enclosed within ou hemmed in by a large property; **pays enclavé** landlocked country ⓑ (= encastrer) **~ l'un dans l'autre** to fit together, interlock; **~ dans** to fit into ⓒ (= insérer) **~ entre** to insert between

enclenchement [ãklãʃmã] NM ⓐ (Tech) (= action) engaging; (= état) engagement; (= dispositif) interlock ⓑ (= début) start; **l'~ du processus de paix** the start of the peace process; **cela a provoqué l'~ d'une spirale déflationniste** this has set off a deflationary spiral

enclencher [ãklãʃe] ▸ conjug 1 ◂ ⓵ VT [+ mécanisme] to engage; [+ affaire, processus] to get under way, set in motion; (Aut) **j'ai laissé une vitesse enclenchée** I left the car in gear; **l'affaire est enclenchée** things are under way ⓶ **s'enclencher** VPR [mécanisme] to engage; [processus] to get under way

enclin, e [ãklɛ̃, in] ADJ **~ à qch/à faire qch** inclined ou prone to sth/to do sth

enclore [ãklɔʀ] ▸ conjug 45 ◂ VT to enclose, shut in; **~ qch d'une haie/d'une palissade/d'un mur** to hedge/fence/wall sth in

enclos [ãklo] NM (gén = terrain, clôture) enclosure; [chevaux] paddock; [moutons] pen, fold

enclume [ãklym] NF anvil; (Aut) engine block; (Anat) anvil (bone), incus (SPÉC)

encoche [ãkɔʃ] NF (gén) notch; [flèche] nock; **faire une ~ à ou sur qch** to notch sth, make a notch in sth

encocher [ãkɔʃe] ▸ conjug 1 ◂ VT (Tech) to notch; [+ flèche] to nock

encodage [ãkɔdaʒ] NM encoding

encoder [ãkɔde] ▸ conjug 1 ◂ VT to encode

encodeur [ãkɔdœʀ] NM encoder

encoignure [ãkɔɲyʀ] NF ⓐ (= coin) corner ⓑ (= meuble) corner cupboard

encoller [ãkɔle] ▸ conjug 1 ◂ VT to paste

encolure [ãkɔlyʀ] NF [cheval, personne, robe]

▶ GRAMMAIRE ACTIVE: **enchanté** 38.3

neck; (*Comm* = *tour de cou*) collar size; (*Équitation*) **battre d'une ~** to beat by a neck

encombrant, e [ãkɔ̃bʀã, ãt] ADJ [*paquet*] cumbersome, unwieldy, bulky; [*présence*] burdensome, inhibiting; **cet enfant est très ~** this child is a real nuisance

encombre [ãkɔ̃bʀ] **◆ sans encombre** LOC ADV without mishap *ou* incident

encombré, e [ãkɔ̃bʀe] (*ptp de* **encombrer**) ADJ [a] [*pièce*] cluttered (up); [*passage*] obstructed; [*lignes téléphoniques*] jammed, overloaded; [*profession*] overcrowded; [*marché*] glutted; **table ~e de papiers** table cluttered *ou* littered with papers; **les bras ~s de paquets** his arms laden with parcels; **j'ai les bronches ~es** my chest is congested; **le parking est très ~** the car park is very full [b] (= *embouteillé*) [*espace aérien, route*] congested

▼ **encombrement** [ãkɔ̃bʀǝmã] NM [a] (= *obstruction*) [*bronches*] congestion; **à cause de l'~ des lignes téléphoniques** because the telephone lines are jammed *ou* overloaded; **l'~ du couloir rendait le passage malaisé** all the clutter in the corridor made it difficult to get through; **un ~ de vieux meubles** a clutter *ou* jumble of old furniture [b] (= *embouteillage*) traffic jam, congestion (*NonC*); **être pris dans un ~** to be stuck in a traffic jam [c] (= *volume*) bulk; (= *taille*) size; [*ordinateur*] footprint; **objet de faible ~** compact *ou* small objet; **l'~ au sol de la tente est de 10 m²** the surface area of this tent is 10m²; (*Ordin*) **l'~ sur le disque/de la mémoire** the amount of space used on the disk/in the memory

encombrer [ãkɔ̃bʀe] ▶ conjug 1 ◀ [1] VT [a] [+ *pièce*] to clutter (up) (**de** with); [+ *couloir*] to obstruct (**de** with); [+ *rue*] to congest; [+ *lignes téléphoniques*] to jam; [+ *marché*] to glut (**de** with); (*Ordin*) **ces fichiers encombrent le disque** these files are using up too much space on the disk; **~ le passage** to block the way, be in the way; **toutes ces informations inutiles encombrent ma mémoire** my mind is cluttered (up) with all this useless information [b] [+ *personne*] **il m'encombre plus qu'il ne m'aide** he's more of a hindrance than a help (to me); **je ne veux pas vous ~** (*être à votre charge*) I don't want to be a burden to you; (*empiéter sur votre espace*) I don't want to get in your way; **ces boîtes m'encombrent** (*je les porte*) I'm loaded down with these boxes; (*elles gênent le passage*) these boxes are in my way

[2] **s'encombrer** VPR **s'~ de** [+ *paquets*] to load o.s. down with; [+ *enfants*] to burden *ou* saddle* o.s. with; **il ne s'encombre pas de scrupules** he's not overburdened with scruples, he's quite unscrupulous

encontre [ãkɔ̃tʀ] [1] **à l'encontre de** LOC PRÉP (= *contre*) against, counter to; (= *au contraire de*) contrary to; **aller à l'~ de** [+ *décision, faits*] to go against, run counter to; **je n'irai pas à l'~ de ce qu'il veut/fait** I won't go against his wishes/what he does; **cela va à l'~ du but recherché** it's counterproductive, it defeats the purpose; **action qui va à l'~ du but recherché** self-defeating *ou* counterproductive action; **à l'~ de ce qu'il dit, mon opinion est que ...** contrary to what he says, my opinion is that ... [2] **à l'encontre** LOC ADV in opposition, against it; **je n'irai pas à l'~** I won't go against it

encor [ãkɔʀ] ADV (††, *Poésie*) = **encore**

encorbellement [ãkɔʀbɛlmã] NM (*Archit*) corbelled construction; **fenêtre en ~** oriel window; **balcon en ~** corbelled balcony

encorder [ãkɔʀde] ▶ conjug 1 ◀ [1] VT to rope up [2] **s'encorder** VPR to rope up; **les alpinistes s'encordent** the climbers are roping themselves together *ou* are roping up

encore [ãkɔʀ] ADV [a] (= *toujours*) still; **il restait ~ quelques personnes** there were still a few people left; **il en était ~ au brouillon** he was still working on the draft; (*péj*) **tu en es ~ là!** haven't you got beyond *ou* past that yet!; **il n'est ~ qu'en première année/que caporal** he's still only in the first year/a corporal; **il n'est ~ que 8 heures** it's (still) only 8 o'clock; **le malfaiteur court ~** the criminal is still at large

[b] (*dans des phrases négatives*) **pas ~** ◊ **non ~** not yet; **il n'est pas ~ prêt** he's not ready yet, he's not yet ready; **ça ne s'était pas ~ vu** ◊ **ça ne s'était ~ jamais vu** it had never happened before; **il reste une question non ~ résolue** there remains one issue (that is) not yet resolved, there remains one issue still unresolved

[c] (= *pas plus tard que*) only; **~ ce matin** *ou* **ce matin ~, il semblait bien portant** only this morning he seemed quite well; **il me le disait ~ hier** *ou* **hier ~** he was saying that to me only yesterday

[d] (= *de nouveau*) again; **~ une fois** (once) again, once more, one more time; **~ une fois, je n'affirme rien** but there again, I'm not absolutely positive about it; **~ une fois non!** how many times do I have to tell you — no!; **ça s'est ~ défait** it has come undone (yet) again; **il a ~ laissé la porte ouverte** he has left the door open (yet) again; **elle a ~ acheté un nouveau chapeau** she has bought yet another new hat; **~ vous!** (not) you again!; **quoi ~ ?** ◊ **qu'y a-t-il ~ ?** what's the matter with you this time?, what is it this time *ou* now?

[e] (= *de plus, en plus*) more; **~ un!** yet another!, one more!; **~ un rhume** (yet) another cold; **~ une tasse ?** another cup?; **vous prendrez bien ~ quelque chose ?** *ou* **quelque chose ~ ?** surely you'll have something more? *ou* something else?; **~ un peu de thé ?** a little more tea?, (any) more tea?; **~ quelques gâteaux ?** (some *ou* any) more cakes?; **j'en veux ~** I want some more; **~ un mot, avant de terminer** (just) one more word before I finish; **que te faut-il ~ ?** what else *ou* more do you want?; **qu'est-ce que j'oublie ~ ?** what else have I forgotten?; **qui y avait-il ~ ?** who else was there?; **pendant ~ deux jours** for another two days, for two more days; **il y a ~ quelques jours avant de partir** there are a few (more) days to go before we leave; **un fou du volant! ~ un!** (yet) another roadhog!; **en voilà ~ deux** here are two more *ou* another two; **mais ~ ?** is that all?, what else?

[f] (*avec compar*) even; **il fait ~ plus froid qu'hier** it's even *ou* still colder than yesterday; **il fait ~ moins chaud qu'hier** it's even cooler than it was yesterday; **il est ~ plus grand que moi** he is even taller than I am; **ils veulent l'agrandir ~ (plus)** they want to make it even *ou* still larger, they want to enlarge it even further; **~ pire** ◊ **pire ~** even *ou* still worse, worse and worse; **~ autant** as much again (**que** as)

[g] (= *aussi*) too, also, as well; **tu le bats non seulement en force, mais ~ en intelligence** not only are you stronger than he is but you are more intelligent too *ou* as well

[h] (*valeur restrictive*) even then, even at that; **~ ne sait-il pas tout** even then he doesn't know everything, and he doesn't even know everything (at that); **il en est sûrement capable, ~ faut-il le faire** he's obviously capable, but whether he does it or not is another matter; **~ une chance** *ou* **heureux qu'il ne se soit pas plaint au patron** (still) at least he didn't complain to the boss, let's think ourselves lucky that he didn't complain to the boss; **on t'en donnera peut-être 100 F, et ~** they might give you 100 francs for it, if that *ou* and perhaps not even that; **c'est passable, et ~ !** it's passable but only just!; **et ~, ça n'a pas été sans mal** and even that wasn't easy; **si ~ if**

only; **si ~ je savais où ça se trouve, j'irais bien** if only I knew where it was, I would willingly go

[i] (*littér*) **~ que** (= *quoique*) even though; **~ que je n'en sache rien** though I don't really know

encorner [ãkɔʀne] ▶ conjug 1 ◀ VT to gore

encornet [ãkɔʀnɛ] NM squid

encourageant, e [ãkuʀaʒã, ãt] ADJ encouraging

encouragement [ãkuʀaʒmã] NM [a] (= *soutien*) encouragement; **message/mot d'~** message/word of encouragement; **il est arrivé sur scène sous les ~s du public** he came on stage to shouts of encouragement from *ou* to the cheers of the audience [b] (*Pol, Écon* = *avantage financier*) encouragement, incentive; **mesures d'~** incentive measures; **multiplier les ~s à l'épargne** to offer more incentives for people to save

encourager [ãkuʀaʒe] ▶ conjug 3 ◀ VT [a] (*gén*) to encourage (**à faire** to do); [+ *équipe*] to cheer; **~ qn au meurtre** to encourage sb to commit murder, incite sb to murder; **~ qn du geste et de la voix** to cheer sb on; **encouragé par ses camarades, il a joué un vilain tour au professeur** egged on *ou* encouraged by his classmates, he played a nasty trick on the teacher [b] (*Pol, Écon*) [+ *emploi, investissement, production*] to encourage

encourir [ãkuʀiʀ] ▶ conjug 11 ◀ VT [+ *amende, frais*] to incur; [+ *mépris, reproche, punition*] to bring upon o.s., incur

encours, en-cours [ãkuʀ] NM INV outstanding discounted bills

encrage [ãkʀaʒ] NM inking

encrassement [ãkʀasmã] NM [*arme*] fouling (up); [*cheminée, bougie de moteur*] sooting up; [*piston, poêle, tuyau, machine*] clogging (up), fouling up

encrasser [ãkʀase] ▶ conjug 1 ◀ [1] VT [a] [+ *arme*] to foul (up); [+ *cheminée, bougie de moteur*] to soot up; [+ *piston, poêle, tuyau, machine*] to clog (up), foul up [b] (= *salir*) to make filthy, (make) dirty; **ongles encrassés de cambouis** nails encrusted *ou* filthy with engine grease [2] **s'encrasser** VPR (*gén*) to get dirty; [*arme*] to foul (up); [*cheminée, bougie de moteur*] to soot up; [*piston, poêle, tuyau, machine*] to clog (up), foul up; [*filtre*] to clog up

encre [ãkʀ] [1] NF [a] (*pour écrire*) ink; **écrire à l'~** to write in ink; **d'un noir d'~** as black as ink, ink(y) black; (*littér*) **de sa plus belle ~** in his best style ▶ **bouteille, couler, sang** [b] (*Zool*) ink; (*Culin*) **calmars à l'~** squid cooked in ink [2] COMP ▶ **encre blanche** white ink ▶ **encre de Chine** Indian ink (*Brit*), India ink (*US*) ▶ **encre d'imprimerie** printing ink ▶ **encre sympathique** invisible ink

encrer [ãkʀe] ▶ conjug 1 ◀ VT to ink

encreur [ãkʀœʀ] ADJ M [*rouleau, tampon*] inking [2] NM inker

encrier [ãkʀije] NM (= *bouteille*) inkpot (*Brit*), ink bottle (*US*); (*décoratif*) inkstand; (*encastré*) inkwell

encroûté, e* [ãkʀute] (*ptp de* **encroûter**) ADJ **être ~** to stagnate, be in a rut; **quel ~ tu fais !** you're really stagnating!, you're really in a rut!

encroûtement [ãkʀutmã] NM [a] [*personne*] getting into a rut; **essayons de le tirer de son ~** let's try and get him out of his rut [b] [*objet*] encrusting, crusting over

encroûter [ãkʀute] ▶ conjug 1 ◀ [1] VT (= *entartrer*) to encrust, crust over [2] **s'encroûter** VPR [a]* [*personne*] to stagnate, get into a rut; **s'~ dans** [+ *habitudes, préjugés*] to become entrenched in; **s'~ dans la vie de province** to get into the rut of provincial life [b] [*objet*] to crust over, form a crust

enculé‼ [ɑ̃kyle] NM dickhead‼, sod‼ (Brit), bugger‼ (Brit)

enculer‼ [ɑ̃kyle] ▶conjug 1◀ VT to bugger‼ (Brit), ream‼ (US); **va te faire ~!** fuck off!‼; (fig) **ils enculent les mouches** they're nit-picking*

encyclique [ɑ̃siklik] ADJ, NF (lettre) ~ encyclical

encyclopédie [ɑ̃siklɔpedi] NF encyclopedia, encyclopaedia (Brit)

encyclopédique [ɑ̃siklɔpedik] ADJ encyclopedic, encyclopaedic (Brit)

encyclopédiste [ɑ̃siklɔpedist] NMF (Hist) encyclopedist, encyclopaedist (Brit)

endémie [ɑ̃demi] NF endemic disease

endémique [ɑ̃demik] ADJ (Méd, fig) endemic

endetté, e [ɑ̃dete] (ptp de **endetter**) ADJ in debt (attrib); **très ~** heavily ou deep in debt; **l'un des pays les plus ~s** one of the biggest ou largest debtor countries; (frm) **(très) ~ envers qn** (greatly) indebted to sb

endettement [ɑ̃dɛtmɑ̃] NM (= dette) debt; **notre ~ extérieur** our foreign debt; **causer l'~ d'une entreprise** to put a company in debt; **le fort ~ des ménages** the high level of household debt; **notre ~ envers la banque** our indebtedness to the bank

endetter [ɑ̃dete] ▶conjug 1◀ VT to put into debt; **l'entreprise est endettée à hauteur de 3 millions de francs** the company has a debt amounting to 3 million francs ② **s'endetter** VPR (particulier, entreprise) to get into debt; **s'~ sur dix ans** to take out a loan over ten years ou a ten-year loan

endeuiller [ɑ̃dœje] ▶conjug 1◀ VT (+ personne, pays) (= toucher par une mort) to plunge into mourning; (= attrister) to plunge into grief; (+ épreuve sportive, manifestation) to cast a pall over; (littér) (+ paysage) to make (look) dismal, give a dismal aspect to

endiablé, e [ɑ̃djable] ADJ (danse, rythme) boisterous, furious; (course) furious, wild; (personne) boisterous

endiguer [ɑ̃dige] ▶conjug 1◀ VT ⓐ (+ fleuve) to dyke (up) ⓑ (fig) (+ foule, invasion) to hold back, contain; (+ révolte) to check, contain; (+ sentiments, progrès) to check, hold back; (+ inflation, chômage) to curb

endimanché, e [ɑ̃dimɑ̃ʃe] (ptp de **s'endimancher**) ADJ (personne) (all done up) in one's Sunday best; (style) fancy, florid; (péj) **il a l'air ~** he's terribly overdressed

endimancher (s') [ɑ̃dimɑ̃ʃe] ▶conjug 1◀ VPR to put on one's Sunday best

endive [ɑ̃div] NF chicory (Brit) (NonC), endive (US); **cinq ~s** five pieces ou heads of chicory (Brit), five endives (US)

endocarde [ɑ̃dɔkaʀd] NM endocardium

endocardite [ɑ̃dɔkaʀdit] NF endocarditis

endocarpe [ɑ̃dɔkaʀp] NM endocarp

endocrine [ɑ̃dɔkʀin] ADJ **glande ~** endocrine (gland)

endocrinien, -ienne [ɑ̃dɔkʀinjɛ̃, jɛn] ADJ endocrinal, endocrinous

endocrinologie [ɑ̃dɔkʀinɔlɔʒi] NF endocrinology

endocrinologue [ɑ̃dɔkʀinɔlɔg], **endocrinologiste** [ɑ̃dɔkʀinɔlɔʒist] NMF endocrinologist

endoctrinement [ɑ̃dɔktʀinmɑ̃] NM indoctrination

endoctriner [ɑ̃dɔktʀine] ▶conjug 1◀ VT to indoctrinate

endoderme [ɑ̃dɔdɛʀm] NM endoderm

endogamie [ɑ̃dɔgami] NF endogamy

endogène [ɑ̃dɔʒɛn] ADJ endogenous

endolori, e [ɑ̃dɔlɔʀi] ADJ painful, aching, sore

endomètre [ɑ̃dɔmɛtʀ] NM endometrium

endométriose [ɑ̃dɔmetʀijoz] NF endometriosis

endommagement [ɑ̃dɔmaʒmɑ̃] NM damaging

endommager [ɑ̃dɔmaʒe] ▶conjug 3◀ VT to damage

endomorphine [ɑ̃dɔmɔʀfin] NF = **endorphine**

endormant, e [ɑ̃dɔʀmɑ̃, ɑ̃t] ADJ (deadly) boring, deadly dull, deadly*

endormeur, -euse [ɑ̃dɔʀmœʀ, øz] NM,F (péj = trompeur) beguiler

endormi, e [ɑ̃dɔʀmi] (ptp de **endormir**) ADJ ⓐ (lit) (personne) sleeping, asleep (attrib) ⓑ (fig) (= apathique) sluggish, languid; (= engourdi) numb; (= assoupi) (passion) dormant; (facultés) dulled; (ville, rue) sleepy, drowsy; **j'ai la main tout ~e** my hand has gone to sleep ou is completely numb; **à moitié ~** half asleep; **quel ~!** what a sleepyhead!

endormir [ɑ̃dɔʀmiʀ] ▶conjug 16◀ ① VT ⓐ (somnifère, discours) to put ou send to sleep; (en berçant) to send ou lull to sleep; **elle chantait pour l'~** she used to sing him to sleep ⓑ* (= ennuyer) to send to sleep*, bore stiff* ⓒ (= anesthésier) to put to sleep, put under*, anaesthetize; (= hypnotiser) to hypnotise, put under* ⓓ (= dissiper) (+ douleur) to deaden; (+ soupçons) to allay, lull ⓔ (= tromper) to beguile; **se laisser ~ par des promesses** to let o.s. be beguiled by promises ② **s'endormir** VPR ⓐ (personne) to go to sleep, fall asleep, drop off to sleep ⓑ (= se relâcher) to let up, slacken off; **ce n'est pas le moment de nous ~** now is not the time to slow up ou slacken off; **allons, ne vous endormez pas!** come on, don't go to sleep on the job!* → **laurier** ⓒ (rue, ville) to fall asleep; (passion, douleur) to subside, die down; (facultés) to go to sleep* ⓓ (euph = mourir) to go to sleep, pass away

endormissement [ɑ̃dɔʀmismɑ̃] NM **médicament qui facilite l'~** medicine which helps one to sleep, sleep-inducing medicine; **au moment de l'~** as one falls asleep

endorphine [ɑ̃dɔʀfin] NF endorphin

endos [ɑ̃do] NM endorsement

endoscope [ɑ̃dɔskɔp] NM endoscope

endoscopie [ɑ̃dɔskɔpi] NF endoscopy

endoscopique [ɑ̃dɔskɔpik] ADJ endoscopic

endosmose [ɑ̃dɔsmoz] NF endosmosis

endossable [ɑ̃dosabl] ADJ (Fin) endorsable

endossataire [ɑ̃dosatɛʀ] NMF endorsee

endossement [ɑ̃dosmɑ̃] NM endorsement

endosser [ɑ̃dose] ▶conjug 1◀ VT ⓐ (= revêtir) (+ vêtement) to put on; (fig) **l'uniforme/la soutane** to enter the army/the Church ⓑ (= assumer) (+ responsabilité) to take, shoulder (de for); **il a voulu me faire ~ son erreur** he wanted me to take ou shoulder the responsibility for his mistake ⓒ (Fin) to endorse

endosseur [ɑ̃dosœʀ] NM endorser

endothermique [ɑ̃dotɛʀmik] ADJ endothermic

endroit [ɑ̃dʀwa] ① NM ⓐ (= localité, partie du corps) place, spot; (= lieu de rangement, partie d'objet) place; **un ~ idéal pour le pique-nique/une usine** an ideal spot ou place for a picnic/a factory; **je l'ai mis au même ~** I put it in the same place; **manteau usé à plusieurs ~s** coat worn in several places, coat with several worn patches; **à ou en quel ~ ?** where(abouts)?, where exactly?; **les gens de l'~** the local people, the locals* → **petit** ⓑ (livre, récit) passage, part; **à quel ~ du récit t'es-tu arrêté?** what part of the story did you stop at?; **il arrêta sa lecture à cet ~** he stopped reading at that point ⓒ (loc) **à l'~ où** (lieu) (at the place) where; (dans un livre, un film) at the part ou bit where; **de/vers l'~ où** from/to (the place) where; **en quelque ~ que ce soit** wherever it may be; **en plusieurs ~s** in several places; **par ~s** in places; **au bon ~** in ou at the right place; (littér) **à l'~**

de (= à l'égard de) towards ⓓ (= bon côté) right side; (Tricot) **faites les diminutions sur l'~** decrease on the knit row ② **à l'endroit** LOC ADJ, LOC ADV (vêtement) the right way round; (objet posé) the right way round; (verticalement) the right way up; **remets tes chaussettes à l'~** put your socks on the right way out; (Tricot) **une maille à l'~, une maille à l'envers** knit one — purl one, one plain — one purl; (Tricot) **tout à l'~** knit every row

enduire [ɑ̃dɥiʀ] ▶conjug 38◀ VT ⓐ (personne, appareil) **~ une surface de** (+ peinture, vernis, colle) to coat a surface with; (+ huile, boue) to coat ou smear a surface with; **~ ses cheveux de brillantine** to grease one's hair with brilliantine, plaster brilliantine on one's hair; **surface enduite d'une substance visqueuse** surface coated ou smeared with a sticky substance; **s'~ de crème** to cover o.s. with cream ⓑ (substance) to coat; **la colle qui enduit le papier** the glue coating the paper

enduit [ɑ̃dɥi] NM (pour recouvrir, lisser) coating; (pour boucher) filler

endurable [ɑ̃dyʀabl] ADJ endurable, bearable

endurance [ɑ̃dyʀɑ̃s] NF (moral) endurance; (physique) stamina, endurance; **coureur qui a de l'~** runner with stamina ou staying power

endurant, e [ɑ̃dyʀɑ̃, ɑ̃t] ADJ tough, hardy; († = patient) **peu ou pas très ~** not very patient (avec with)

endurci, e [ɑ̃dyʀsi] (ptp de **endurcir**) ADJ (cœur) hardened; (personne) hardened, hard-hearted; **criminel ~** hardened criminal; **célibataire ~** confirmed bachelor

endurcir [ɑ̃dyʀsiʀ] ▶conjug 2◀ ① VT (physiquement) to toughen; (psychologiquement) to harden ② **s'endurcir** VPR (physiquement) to become tough; (moralement) to harden, become hardened; **s'~ à la douleur** to become hardened ou inured to pain

endurcissement [ɑ̃dyʀsismɑ̃] NM ⓐ (= action) (corps) toughening; (âme) hardening ⓑ (= état) (corps) toughness; (âme) hardness; **~ à la douleur** resistance to pain

endurer [ɑ̃dyʀe] ▶conjug 1◀ VT to endure, bear; **~ de faire qch** to bear to do sth; **il fait froid, on endure un pull** it's cold, you need a pullover

enduro [ɑ̃dyʀo] NM enduro, trial

Énée [ene] NM Aeneas

Énéide [eneid] NF **l'~** the Aeneid

énergéticien, -ienne [enɛʀʒetisjɛ̃, jɛn] NM,F energetics specialist

énergétique [enɛʀʒetik] ① ADJ ⓐ (Écon, Phys) (besoins, politique, ressources) energy (épith); **nos dépenses ~s** our fuel ou energy bill ⓑ (Physiol) (aliment) energy-giving, energizing; (valeur) energy (épith); **aliment très ~** high-energy food; **dépense ~** energy expenditure ② NF energetics sg

énergie [enɛʀʒi] NF ⓐ (= force physique) energy; **dépenser beaucoup d'~ à faire qch** to expend ou use up a great deal of energy doing sth; **j'ai besoin de toute mon ~** I need all my energy; **nettoyer/frotter avec ~** to clean/rub energetically; **être ou se sentir sans ~** to be ou feel lacking in energy, be ou feel unenergetic; **avec l'~ du désespoir** with the strength born of despair ⓑ (= fermeté, ressort moral) spirit, vigour (Brit), vigor (US); **protester/refuser avec ~** to protest/refuse energetically ou vigorously ou forcefully; **mobiliser toutes les ~s d'un pays** to mobilize all a country's resources; (littér) **l'~ de son style/d'un terme** the vigour ou energy of his style/of a term ⓒ (Écon, Phys) energy; (Tech) power, energy; **réaction qui libère de l'~** reaction that releases energy; **l'~ fournie par le moteur** the power supplied by the motor; **consommation d'~** (moteur, véhicule) power consumption;

[*industrie, pays*] energy consumption; **source d'~** source of energy

2 COMP ► **énergie atomique** atomic energy ► **énergie cinétique** kinetic energy ► **les énergies douces** alternative energy ► **énergie électrique** electrical power *ou* energy ► **énergie éolienne** wind power *ou* energy ► **les énergies fossiles** fossil fuels ► **énergie mécanique** mechanical power *ou* energy ► **énergies nouvelles** new energy sources ► **énergies renouvelables** renewable energy sources ► **les énergies de substitution** substitute fuels ► **énergie nucléaire** nuclear power *ou* energy ► **énergie potentielle** potential energy ► **énergie psychique** psychic energy ► **énergie solaire** solar energy *ou* power ► **énergie thermique** thermal energy ► **énergie vitale** vital energy *ou* force

énergique [enerʒik] ADJ a (*physiquement*) [*personne*] energetic; [*mouvement, geste, effort*] vigorous, energetic b (*moralement*) [*personne, style, voix*] vigorous, energetic; [*refus, protestation, intervention*] forceful, vigorous; [*mesures*] drastic, stringent; [*punition*] severe, harsh; [*médicament*] powerful, strong

énergiquement [enerʒikmã] ADV (*agir, parler*) energetically; [*refuser*] emphatically; [*condamner*] vigorously

énergisant, e [enerʒizã, ãt] 1 ADJ energizing 2 NM energizer, tonic

énergumène [energymɛn] NMF (*gén*) bizarre individual; (= *fou*) maniac; **qu'est-ce que c'est que cet ~ ?** who's that nutcase?*

énervant, e [enervã, ãt] ADJ (= *agaçant*) irritating, annoying

énervé, e [enerve] (*ptp de* **énerver**) ADJ (= *agacé*) irritated, annoyed; (= *agité*) nervous, edgy* (*Brit*)

énervement [enervǝmã] NM (= *agacement*) irritation, annoyance; (= *agitation*) nervousness, edginess* (*Brit*); **après les ~s du départ** after the upsets of the departure

énerver [enerve] ▸ conjug 1 ◂ 1 VT ▸ **qn** (= *agiter*) to overexcite sb; (= *agacer*) to irritate sb, annoy sb, get on sb's nerves*; **ça m'énerve** it really gets on my nerves*; **le vin blanc énerve** white wine is bad for your nerves 2 **s'énerver** VPR to get excited*, get worked up*; **ne t'énerve pas !** don't get all worked up!*, take it easy!; **ne t'énerve pas pour cela** don't let it get to you*

enfance [ãfãs] NF a (= *jeunesse*) childhood; [*garçon*] boyhood; [*fille*] girlhood; (*fig = début*) infancy; **petite ~** infancy; **science encore dans son ~** science still in its infancy; **c'est l'~ de l'art** it's child's play *ou* kid's stuff* → **retomber** b (= *enfants*) children *pl*; **la naïveté de l'~** the naivety of children *ou* of childhood; **l'~ déshéritée** deprived children

enfant [ãfã] 1 NMF a (*gén*) child; (= *garçon*) (little) boy; (= *fille*) (little) girl; **quand il était ~** when he was a child, as a child; **il se souvenait que, tout ~, il avait une fois ...** he remembered that, while still *ou* only a child, he had once ...; (*fig*) **c'est un grand ~** he's such a child, he's a big kid*; **il est resté très ~** he has remained very childlike; **faire l'~** to behave childishly, behave like a child; **ne faites pas l'~** don't be (so) childish, stop behaving like a child → **bon¹, bonne²**, **jardin**

b (= *descendant*) child; **sans ~** childless; **M. Leblanc, décédé sans ~** Mr Leblanc who died childless *ou* without issue (*frm*); **faire un ~ à une femme*** to get a woman pregnant; (*fig*) **faire un ~ dans le dos à qn*** to do the dirty on sb*; **ce livre est son ~** this book is his baby → **attendre**

c (= *originaire*) **c'est un ~ du pays/de la ville** he's a native of these parts/of the town; **~ de l'Auvergne/de Paris** child of the Auvergne/of Paris; **un ~ du peuple** a (true) child of the people

► GRAMMAIRE ACTIVE: enfin 53.2, 53.5

d * (= *adulte*) **les ~s !** folks*, guys*; **bonne nouvelle, les ~s !** good news, folks!* *ou* guys!*

2 COMP ► **enfant de l'amour** love child ► **enfant de la balle** child of the theatre (*ou* circus *etc*) ► **enfant bleu** (*Méd*) blue baby ► **enfant de chœur** (*Rel*) altar boy; (*ingénu*) **il me prend pour un ~ de chœur !** he thinks I'm still wet behind the ears!*; **ce n'est pas un ~ de chœur !** he's no angel!* ► **enfant gâté** spoilt child; **c'était l'~ gâté du service** he was the blue-eyed boy of the department ► **l'Enfant Jésus** (*Rel*) the baby Jesus ► **enfants de Marie** (*Rel*) children of Mary; **c'est une ~ de Marie** (*lit*) she's in the children of Mary; (**: ingénue*) she's a real innocent; **ce n'est pas une ~ de Marie !** she's no cherub!*, she's no innocent! ► **enfant naturel** natural child ► **enfant prodige** child prodigy ► **enfant prodigue** (*Bible, fig*) prodigal son ► **enfant terrible** (*lit*) unruly child; (*fig*) enfant terrible ► **enfant de troupe** child reared by the army ► **enfant trouvé** foundling ► **enfant unique** only child; **famille à ~ unique** one-child family, family with one child

enfantement [ãfãtmã] NM (†, *Bible* = *accouchement*) childbirth; (*littér, fig*) [*œuvre*] giving birth (**de** to)

enfanter [ãfãte] ▸ conjug 1 ◂ 1 VT (†, *Bible* = *mettre au monde*) to give birth to, bring forth (*littér, Bible*); (*littér, fig* = *élaborer*) to give birth to (*littér*) 2 VI to give birth, be delivered (*littér, Bible*)

enfantillage [ãfãtijaʒ] NM childishness (*NonC*); **se livrer à des ~s** to do childish things, behave childishly; **c'est de l'~** you're just being childish; **arrête ces ~s !** don't be so childish!

enfantin, e [ãfãtɛ̃, in] ADJ (= *typique de l'enfance*) [*joie, naïveté, confiance*] childlike, childish; (= *puéril*) [*attitude, réaction*] childish, infantile; (*facile*) **c'est ~** it's simple, it's child's play*, it's dead easy* (*Brit*); (*propre à l'enfant*) **rire/jeu ~** child's laugh/game; **ses amours ~es** his childhood loves → **classe, langage**

enfariné, e [ãfarine] ADJ (*lit*) dredged with flour; (*fig = poudré*) powdered; **arriver la gueule ~e** *ou* **le bec ~*** to breeze in*

enfer [ãfer] 1 NM a (*Rel*) **l'~** hell, Hell; (*Myth*) **les Enfers** Hell, the Underworld ■ (*PROV*) **l'~ est pavé de bonnes intentions** the road to hell is paved with good intentions (*PROV*) b (*fig*) hell; **cette usine est un ~** this factory is (absolute) hell; **cette vie est un ~** it's a hellish life; **l'~ de l'alcoolisme** the hellish world of alcoholism; **vivre un véritable ~** to go through a living hell c [*bibliothèque*] forbidden books department d **d'~** [*bruit, vision*] hellish, infernal; [*vie, rythme*] hellish; **feu d'~** raging fire; **jouer un jeu d'~** to play for very high stakes; **chevaucher à un train d'~** to ride hell (*Brit*) *ou* hellbent (*US*) for leather*; **rouler à un train d'~** to tear along at breakneck speed; **c'est d'~ !** it's magic!*; **sa copine est d'~*** his girlfriend is a real stunner* 2 EXCL ► **~ et damnation !** hell and damnation!*

enfermement [ãfermǝmã] NM (*lit*) confinement; (*fig*) **son ~ dans le silence** (*volontaire*) his retreat into silence; (*involontaire*) his silent isolation

enfermer [ãferme] ▸ conjug 1 ◂ 1 VT a (= *mettre sous clé*) [+ *enfant puni, témoin gênant*] to shut up, lock up; (*par erreur*) to lock in; [+ *prisonnier*] to shut up *ou* away, lock up; * [+ *aliéné*] to lock up*; [+ *objet précieux*] to lock away *ou* up; [+ *animaux*] to shut up (**dans** in); **~ qch dans** [+ *coffre*] to lock sth away *ou* up in; [+ *boîte, sac*] to shut sth up *ou* away in; **il est bon à ~*** he ought to be locked up* *ou* certified*, he's certifiable*; **ils ont dû l'~ à clé** they had to lock him in; **ne reste pas enfermé par ce beau temps** don't stay indoors *ou* in-

side in this lovely weather b (*fig = emprisonner*) to imprison; (*dans un dilemme*) to trap; **l'école enferme la créativité dans un carcan de conventions** school traps *ou* imprisons *ou* confines creativity in a straitjacket of convention; **~ le savoir dans des livres inaccessibles** to shut *ou* lock knowledge away in inaccessible books c (*littér = contenir, entourer*) to enclose, shut in; **les collines qui enfermaient le vallon** the hills that shut in *ou* enclosed the valley d (*Sport*) [+ *concurrent*] to hem *ou* box in 2 **s'enfermer** VPR a (*lit*) to shut o.s. up *ou* in; **il s'est enfermé dans sa chambre** he shut himself away *ou* up in his room; **zut, je me suis enfermé !** (*à l'intérieur*) damn, I've locked myself in!; (*à l'extérieur*) damn, I've locked myself out!; **il s'est enfermé à clé dans son bureau** he has locked himself (away) in his office; **ils se sont enfermés dans le bureau pour discuter** they have closeted themselves in the office *ou* shut themselves away in the office to have a discussion; **elle s'enferme toute la journée** she stays shut up indoors all day long b (*fig*) **s'~ dans** [+ *mutisme*] to retreat into; [+ *rôle, attitude*] to stick to; **s'~ dans sa décision** to keep *ou* stick stubbornly *ou* rigidly to one's decision; **s'~ dans un système** to lock o.s. into a rigid pattern of behaviour

enferrer (s') [ãfere] ▸ conjug 1 ◂ VPR a (= *s'embrouiller*) to tie o.s. up in knots*; **s'~ dans ses contradictions/ses mensonges** to tie *ou* tangle o.s. up in one's own contradictions/one's lies, ensnare o.s. in the mesh of one's own contradictions/lies; **s'~ dans une analyse/une explication** to tie o.s. up in knots* trying to make an analysis/trying to explain; **il s'enferre de plus en plus** he's getting himself in more and more of a mess *ou* into deeper and deeper water b (= *s'empaler*) to spike o.s. (**sur** on)

enfeu [ãfø] NM funereal recess

enfiévré, e [ãfjevre] (*ptp de* **enfiévrer**) ADJ [*atmosphère*] feverish; [*paroles*] impassioned

enfiévrer [ãfjevre] ▸ conjug 6 ◂ VT a [+ *imagination*] to fire, stir up; [+ *esprits*] to rouse; [+ *assistance*] to inflame, rouse b [+ *malade*] to make feverish; [+ *visage, joues*] to inflame

enfilade [ãfilad] NF (= *série*) **une ~ de** [*maisons*] a row *ou* string of; [*colonnes, couloirs*] a row *ou* series of; **pièces/couloirs en ~** series of linked rooms/corridors; **maisons en ~** houses in a row; (*Mil*) **prendre en ~** to rake, enfilade (*SPÉC*); [*conducteur*] **prendre les rues en ~** to go from one street to the next; (*Mil*) **tir d'~** raking, enfilading (*SPÉC*)

enfiler [ãfile] ▸ conjug 1 ◂ 1 VT a [+ *aiguille*] to thread; [+ *perles*] to string, thread; **on n'est pas là pour ~ des perles*** let's get on with it*, let's get down to it* *ou* to business; **~ des anneaux sur une tringle** to slip rings onto a rod b * (= *passer*) [+ *vêtement*] to slip on, put on c (= *fourrer*) **~ qch dans** *ou* **sur** to stick* *ou* shove* sth into sth d (= *s'engager dans*) [+ *ruelle, chemin*] to take; [+ *corridor*] to enter, take; **il tourna à gauche et enfila la rue de la Gare** he turned left into Rue de la Gare, he turned left and took the Rue de la Gare e (***: sexuellement*) to screw⋆⋆, shag⋆⋆ (*Brit*) 2 **s'enfiler** VPR a (= *s'engager dans*) **s'~ dans** [+ *escalier, couloir, ruelle*] to disappear into b ⋆ (= *consommer*) [+ *verre de vin*] to knock back⋆, down⋆; [+ *nourriture*] to wolf down*; [+ *corvée*] to land *ou* to stick o.s. with*, get lumbered with* *ou* landed with*

▼ **enfin** [ãfɛ̃] ADV a (= *à la fin, finalement*) at last, finally; **il y est ~ arrivé** he has finally succeeded, he has succeeded at last; **quand va-t-il ~ y arriver ?** when on earth is he going to manage it?; **~, après bien des efforts, ils y arrivèrent** eventually, after much effort, they managed it, after much effort they finally *ou* eventual-

ly managed it; **~ seuls !** alone at last!; **~, ils se sont décidés !** they've made up their minds at last!; **~ ça va commencer !** at long last it's going to begin!
[b] (= *en dernier lieu*) lastly, finally; **on y trouvait des noisetiers, des framboisiers, ~ des champignons de toutes sortes** there were hazel trees, raspberry bushes and all kinds of mushrooms as well; **~, je voudrais te remercier pour ...** finally, I'd like to thank you for ...; **... ensuite des manuels et des ouvrages de référence, ~ et surtout, des dictionnaires** ... and next manuals and reference works, and last but not least *ou* and last but by no means least, dictionaries
[c] (= *en conclusion*) in short, in a word; **rien n'était prêt, ~ (bref), la vraie pagaille !** nothing was ready — in actual fact, it was absolute chaos. *ou* it was absolute chaos, in fact!
[d] (*restrictif = disons, ou plutôt*) well; **elle était assez grosse, ~, potelée** she was rather fat, well, chubby; **pas exactement, ~, dans un sens, oui** not exactly, well — in a way, yes
[e] (= *somme toute*) after all; **c'est un élève qui, ~, n'est pas bête** he's not a stupid pupil after all; **c'est une méthode qui, ~, a fait ses preuves** it's a well-tried method after all
[f] (= *toutefois*) still; **~, si ça vous plaît/si vous le voulez, prenez-le** still, if you like it/if you want it, take it; **moi je veux bien, ~ ...!** I don't mind, but ...! *ou* still ...!
[g] (*valeur exclamative*) **~ ! que veux-tu y faire !** anyway *ou* still, what can you do!; **~, tu aurais pu le faire !** all the same *ou* even so, you could have done it!; **(mais) ~ ! je viens de te le dire !** but I've just told you!, (but) for goodness sake*, I've just told you!; **~ ! un grand garçon comme toi !** oh, come on, a big boy like you!; **c'est son père, ~ !** he is his father, after all!
[h] mais ~ but; **j'irai, mais ~ ce ne sera pas de gaieté de cœur** I'll go, but not willingly; **car ~** because *ou* since (after all)

enflammé, e [ɑ̃flame] (*ptp de* **enflammer**) ADJ **[a]** [*allumette, torche*] burning, blazing, ablaze (*attrib*); [*ciel*] ablaze (*attrib*), blazing, flaming **[b]** [*visage, yeux*] blazing, ablaze (*attrib*); [*caractère*] fiery, ardent, passionate; [*esprit*] afire (*attrib*), burning, on fire (*attrib*); [*paroles*] inflamed, fiery, ardent; [*déclaration*] impassioned, passionate, ardent **[c]** [*plaie*] inflamed

enflammer [ɑ̃flame] ▶ conjug 1 ◀ **[1]** VT **[a]** (= *mettre le feu à*) [+ *bois*] to set on fire, set fire to; [+ *allumette*] to strike; (*fig littér*) [+ *ciel*] to set ablaze **[b]** (= *exciter*) [+ *visage, regard*] to set ablaze; [+ *colère, désir, foule*] to inflame; [+ *imagination*] to fire, kindle; [+ *esprit*] to set on fire **[c]** [+ *plaie*] to inflame **[2]** **s'enflammer** VPR **[a]** (= *prendre feu*) to catch fire, ignite; **le bois sec s'enflamme bien** dry wood catches fire *ou* ignites *ou* kindles easily **[b]** [*visage, regard*] to blaze; [*sentiment, désir*] to flare up; [*imagination*] to be fired; [*orateur*] to become inflamed *ou* impassioned; **s'~ (de colère)** to flare up (in anger)

enflé, e [ɑ̃fle] (*ptp de* **enfler**) **[1]** ADJ [*membre*] swollen; [*style*] bombastic, turgid **[2]** NM,F* (= *imbécile*) jerk*, twit* (*Brit*), clot* (*Brit*)

enfler [ɑ̃fle] ▶ conjug 1 ◀ **[1]** VT **[a]** [+ *membre*] to cause to swell (up), make swell (up); (*littér*) [+ *voiles*] to fill, swell; (*littér*) [+ *fleuve*] to (cause to) swell; [+ *voix*] to raise; [+ *addition, facture*] to inflate; **~ son style** to adopt a bombastic *ou* turgid style **[b]** (** = *voler*) **~ qn** to diddle* *ou* do* sb (**de** out of); **se faire ~ de 10 F*** to be done out of 10 francs* **[2]** VI (*lit*) [*membre*] to become swollen, swell (up); (** = *prendre du poids*) to fill out **[3]** **s'enfler** VPR **[a]** [*voix*] to rise; [*style*] to become bombastic *ou* turgid; [*son*] to swell (up); (*littér*) [*fleuve*] to swell, become swollen; [*vagues*] to surge, swell; [*voiles*] to fill (out), swell (out)

enflure [ɑ̃flyR] NF **[a]** (*Méd*) swelling **[b]** [*style*]

turgidity **[c]*** (= *imbécile*) jerk*, twit* (*Brit*), clot* (*Brit*)

enfoiré, e* [ɑ̃fware] NM,F stupid jerk*, silly sod* (*Brit*)

enfoncé, e [ɑ̃fɔ̃se] (*ptp de* **enfoncer**) ADJ [*yeux*] deep-set; [*recoin*] deep; **il avait la tête ~e dans les épaules** his head was sunk between his shoulders

enfoncement [ɑ̃fɔ̃smɑ̃] NM **[a]** (= *action d'enfoncer*) [*pieu*] driving in; [*porte*] breaking down *ou* open; [*lignes ennemies*] breaking through; (*Méd*) **il souffre d'un ~ de la cage thoracique/de la boîte crânienne** he has crushed ribs/a fractured skull **[b]** (= *action de s'enfoncer*) [*sol*] giving way; [*fondations*] sinking; **cet ~ progressif dans le vice/la misère** this gradual slide into vice/poverty **[c]** (= *recoin*) [*mur*] recess, nook; **dissimulé dans un ~ de la muraille** hidden in a recess *ou* nook in the wall; **chalet dissimulé dans un ~ du vallon** chalet tucked away in a corner of the valley

enfoncer [ɑ̃fɔ̃se] ▶ conjug 3 ◀ **[1]** VT **[a]** (= *faire pénétrer*) [+ *pieu, clou*] to drive (well) in; [+ *épingle, punaise*] to stick (well) in, push (well) in; **~ un pieu dans** to drive a stake in(to); **~ une épingle dans** to stick *ou* push a pin in(to); **~ un couteau dans** to thrust *ou* plunge a knife into; **~ qch à coups de marteau** to hammer sth in, knock sth in with a hammer; (*fig*) **~ le clou** to hammer it in, drive the point home **[b]** (= *mettre*) **~ les mains dans ses poches** to thrust *ou* dig one's hands (deep) into one's pockets; **~ son chapeau jusqu'aux yeux** to ram *ou* pull one's hat (right) down over one's eyes; **il lui enfonça sa canne dans les côtes** he prodded *ou* poked *ou* stuck him in the ribs with his walking stick; **qui a bien pu lui ~ ça dans le crâne ?** *ou* **la tête ?** who on earth put that idea into his head?; **ça les a enfoncés davantage dans les frais** it involved them in even greater expense
[c] (= *défoncer*) [+ *porte*] to break open *ou* down; [+ *véhicule*] to smash in; [+ *lignes ennemies*] to break through; **~ le plancher** to make the floor give way *ou* cave in, cause the floor to give way *ou* cave in; **le choc lui a enfoncé les côtes** the blow smashed his rib cage *ou* his ribs; **il a eu les côtes enfoncées** he had his ribs broken, his ribs were broken *ou* smashed; **le devant de sa voiture a été enfoncé** the front of his car has been smashed *ou* bashed* in; (*fig*) **~ une porte ouverte** *ou* **des portes ouvertes** to state the obvious; **c'est ~ une porte ouverte que d'affirmer ...** it's stating the obvious to say ...
[d] * (= *battre*) to beat hollow*, hammer*; (= *surpasser*) to lick*; **ils se sont fait ~ !** they got beaten hollow!*, they got hammered!*; **il les enfonce tous** he's got them all licked*; (*causer la perte de*) **~ son complice** to put all the blame on one's accomplice; **~ un candidat** to destroy a candidate
[2] VI **[a]** (= *pénétrer*) to sink in; **attention, on enfonce ici** careful, you'll sink in here; **on enfonçait dans la neige jusqu'aux cuisses** we sank up to our thighs in the snow
[b] (= *céder*) [*sol*] to yield, give way; **ça enfonce sous le poids du corps** it yields beneath the weight of the body
[3] **s'enfoncer** VPR **[a]** [*lame, projectile*] **s'~ dans** to plunge *ou* sink into; **l'éclat d'obus s'enfonça dans le mur** the shell fragment embedded itself in the wall
[b] (= *disparaître: dans l'eau, la vase etc*) to sink (**dans** into, in); **s'~ dans** [+ *forêt, rue, brume*] to disappear into; [+ *fauteuil, coussins*] to sink deep into, sink back in(to); [+ *misère*] to sink into, be plunged into; [+ *vice, rêverie*] to plunge into, sink into; **chemin qui s'enfonce dans les bois** path which disappears into the woods; **je le regardais s'~, impuissant à le secourir** I watched him sinking (in), powerless to help him; **s'~ sous les couvertures** to bury o.s. under *ou* snuggle down under the covers;

il s'est enfoncé jusqu'au cou dans une sale histoire he's up to his neck in a nasty bit of business; **à mentir, tu ne fais que t'~ davantage** by lying, you're just getting yourself into deeper and deeper water *ou* into more and more of a mess
[c] (= *céder*) to give way; **le sol s'enfonce sous nos pas** the ground is giving way *ou* caving in beneath us; **les coussins s'enfoncèrent sous son poids** the cushions sank under his weight
[d] (= *faire pénétrer*) **s'~ une arête dans la gorge** to get a bone stuck in one's throat; **s'~ une aiguille dans la main** to stick *ou* run a needle into one's hand; **enfoncez-vous bien ça dans le crâne*** now get this firmly into your head

enfonceur, -euse [ɑ̃fɔ̃sœʀ, øz] NM,F (*hum*) **c'est un ~ de porte(s) ouverte(s)** he's always stating the obvious

enfouir [ɑ̃fwiʀ] ▶ conjug 2 ◀ **[1]** VT (*gén*) to bury (**dans** in); **il l'a enfoui dans sa poche** he tucked it (away) in his pocket; **chalet enfoui dans la neige** chalet buried beneath the snow; **la photo était enfouie sous des livres** the photo was buried under *ou* beneath a pile of books **[2]** **s'enfouir** VPR **s'~ dans/sous** to bury o.s. (*ou* itself) in/under; **s'~ sous les draps** to bury o.s. *ou* burrow beneath the covers

enfouissement [ɑ̃fwismɑ̃] NM burying; **site d'~ de déchets industriels** landfill site for industrial waste

enfourcher [ɑ̃fuʀʃe] ▶ conjug 1 ◀ VT [+ *cheval, bicyclette*] to mount, get on; **~ son dada** to get on one's hobby-horse

enfourner [ɑ̃fuʀne] ▶ conjug 1 ◀ **[1]** VT **[a]** [+ *plat*] to put in the oven; [+ *poterie*] to put in the kiln **[b]*** (= *avaler*) to guzzle down, gulp down, wolf down **[c]*** (= *enfoncer*) **~ qch dans qch** to shove* *ou* stuff* sth into sth **[2]** **s'enfourner** VPR **s'~ dans** [*personne*] to dive into; [*foule*] to rush into

enfreindre [ɑ̃fʀɛ̃dʀ] ▶ conjug 52 ◀ VT (*frm*) to infringe, break

enfuir (s') [ɑ̃fɥiʀ] ▶ conjug 17 ◀ VPR (= *se sauver*) to run away, run off, flee (**chez, dans** to); (= *s'échapper*) to run away, escape (**de** from); (*littér*) [*temps, souffrance*] to fly away (*littér*), flee (*littér*)

enfumer [ɑ̃fyme] ▶ conjug 1 ◀ VT [+ *pièce*] to fill with smoke; [+ *personne, renard, ruche*] to smoke out; **atmosphère/pièce enfumée** smoky atmosphere/room; **tu nous enfumes avec ta cigarette** you're smoking us out

enfutailler [ɑ̃fytaje], **enfûter** [ɑ̃fyte] ▶ conjug 1 ◀ VT to cask

engagé, e [ɑ̃gaʒe] (*ptp de* **engager**) **[1]** ADJ **[a]** [*écrivain, littérature*] (politically) committed; (*Pol*) **non ~** uncommitted **[b]** (*Archit*) [*colonne*] engaged **[2]** NM (*Mil* = *soldat*) enlisted man; **~ volontaire** volunteer **[b]** (*Sport*) (= *coureur*) entrant, competitor; (= *cheval*) runner

engageant, e [ɑ̃gaʒɑ̃, ɑ̃t] ADJ [*air, sourire*] engaging, winning, appealing; [*proposition*] attractive, appealing, tempting; [*repas, gâteau*] tempting, inviting; **elle a eu des paroles ~es** what she said sounded most appealing

engagement [ɑ̃gaʒmɑ̃] NM **[a]** (= *promesse*) commitment, promise; (= *accord*) agreement, undertaking; **sans ~ de votre part** without obligation *ou* commitment on your part; **signer un ~** to sign an undertaking *ou* agreement; **prendre l'~ de** to make a commitment to, undertake to; **manquer à ses ~s** to fail to keep one's promises; **faire face à/tenir** *ou* **honorer ses ~s** to fulfil/honour one's commitments *ou* promises
[b] (= *embauche*) [*ouvrier*] taking on, engaging; (= *recrutement*) [*soldats*] enlistment; **lettre d'~** letter of appointment
[c] (*Théât*) (= *contrat*) engagement; (*Sport*

= inscription pour un match, un combat) entry; **artiste sans ~** out-of-work actor

d (*Fin*) [*capitaux*] investing; [*dépenses*] incurring; **~s financiers** financial commitments *ou* liabilities; **cela a nécessité l'~ de nouveaux frais** this incurred further expenses; **faire face à ses ~s (financiers)** to meet one's (financial) commitments

e (= *amorce*) [*débat, négociations*] opening, start

f (*Sport*) (= *coup d'envoi*) kick-off; (*Boxe*) attack; (*Escrime*) engagement; (*Ping-Pong*) service

g (*Mil*) [*combat*] engaging; [*troupes fraîches*] throwing in, engaging; **tué dans un ~** killed in an engagement

h (= *prise de position*) commitment (**dans** to); **~ personnel/politique/militaire** personal/political/military commitment; **politique de non-~** policy of non-commitment

i (= *mise en gage*) [*montre*] pawning

j (= *encouragement*) encouragement; **c'est un ~ à persévérer** it encourages one to persevere

k (= *introduction*) [*clé*] introduction, insertion (**dans** in, into); [*voiture*] entry (**dans** into)

l (*Méd*) [*fœtus*] engagement

▼ **engager** [ɑ̃gaʒe] ▸ conjug 3 ◂ 1 VT a (= *lier*) to bind, commit; **nos promesses nous engagent** we are bound to honour our promises, we are bound by our promises; **ça l'engagerait trop** that would commit him too far; **ça n'engage à rien** it doesn't commit you to anything; **~ sa parole** *ou* **son honneur** to give one's word (of honour)

b (= *embaucher*) [+ *ouvrier*] to take on, hire; **je vous engage (à mon service)** you've got the job, you're hired

c (= *entraîner*) to involve; **ça l'a engagé dans de gros frais/dans une affaire louche** it involved him in great expense/in a shady deal; **le pays est engagé dans une politique d'inflation** the country is pursuing an inflationary policy

d (= *encourager*) **~ qn à faire qch** to urge *ou* encourage sb to do sth; **je vous engage à la circonspection** I advise you to be very cautious

e (= *introduire*) to insert (**dans** in, into); (*Naut*) [+ *ancre*] to foul; **il engagea sa clé dans la serrure** he fitted *ou* inserted his key into the lock; **~ sa voiture dans une ruelle** to enter a lane, drive into a lane; (*Aut*) **c'était à lui de passer puisqu'il était engagé** it was up to him to go since he had already pulled out; (*Escrime*) **~ le fer** to engage, cross blades

f (= *amorcer*) [+ *discussion*] to open, start (up); [+ *négociations*] to enter into; [+ *procédure, poursuites*] to institute (**contre** against); **~ la conversation** to engage in conversation, start up a conversation (**avec** with); **l'affaire semble bien/mal engagée** things seem to have got off to a good/bad start

g (= *mettre en gage*) to pawn, put in pawn; (= *investir*) to invest, lay out; **les frais engagés** the expenses incurred

h (*Sport*) [+ *concurrents*] to enter; **15 chevaux sont engagés dans cette course** 15 horses are running in this race; **~ la partie** to begin the match; **la partie est bien engagée** the match is well under way

i (*Mil*) [+ *recrues*] to enlist; [+ *troupes fraîches*] to throw in, bring in, engage; **~ le combat contre l'ennemi** to engage the enemy, join battle with the enemy†; **~ toutes ses forces dans la bataille** to throw all one's troops into the battle

2 **s'engager** VPR a (= *promettre*) to commit o.s.; **s'~ à faire qch** to commit o.s. to doing sth, undertake *ou* promise to do sth; **il n'a pas voulu s'~ trop** he didn't want to commit himself (too far) *ou* to stick his neck out too far*; **sais-tu à quoi tu t'engages?** do you know what you're letting yourself in for? *ou* what

you're committing yourself to?

b (= *s'embaucher*) to take a job (**chez** with); **il s'est engagé comme garçon de courses** he took a job as an errand boy, he got himself taken on as an errand boy

c **s'~ dans** (+ *frais*) to incur; [+ *discussion, pourparlers*] to enter into; [+ *affaire, entreprise*] to become involved in; **le pays s'engage dans une politique dangereuse** the country is embarking on a dangerous policy *ou* is steering a dangerous course

d (= *s'emboîter*) **s'~ dans** to engage into, fit into; (= *pénétrer*) **s'~ dans** [*véhicule*] to enter, turn into; [*piéton*] to take, turn into; **s'~ sur la chaussée** to step (out) onto the road; **la voiture s'engagea sous le pont** the car drove under the bridge; **j'avais la priorité puisque je m'étais engagé (dans la rue)** I had (the) right of way since I had already pulled out (into the street)

e (= *s'amorcer*) [*pourparlers*] to begin, start (up), get under way; **une conversation s'engagea entre eux** they struck up a conversation

f (*Sport*) to enter (one's name) (**dans** for)

g (*Mil*) [*recrues*] to enlist; **s'~ dans l'armée de l'air** to join the air force; **le combat s'engagea avec vigueur** the fight began briskly; **s'~ dans la bataille** to join in the fighting

h (*Littérat, Pol* = *prendre position*) to commit o.s.

engazonner [ɑ̃gazɔne] ▸ conjug 1 ◂ VT (= *recouvrir*) to turf; (= *ensemencer*) to plant with grass

engeance† [ɑ̃ʒɑ̃s] NF (*péj*) mob, crew; **quelle ~!** they're such a pain!*

engelure [ɑ̃ʒ(ə)lyʀ] NF chilblain

engendrement [ɑ̃ʒɑ̃dʀəmɑ̃] NM [*enfant*] begetting, fathering

engendrer [ɑ̃ʒɑ̃dʀe] ▸ conjug 1 ◂ VT a (*frm*) [+ *enfant*] to beget, father b (*Ling, Math, Phys*) to generate c [+ *colère, dispute*] to breed, create; [+ *malheurs*] to breed, create, engender (*frm*); **ils n'engendrent pas la mélancolie** they're (always) a good laugh*

engin [ɑ̃ʒɛ̃] 1 NM (= *machine*) machine; (= *outil*) instrument, tool; (*Aut*) heavy vehicle; (*Aviat*) aircraft; (* = *objet*) contraption*, gadget; (= *bombe*) bomb, device; **«attention: sortie d'~s»** "heavy plant crossing", "beware — lorries turning" (*Brit*) 2 COMP ► **engin balistique** ballistic missile ► **engin blindé** armoured vehicle ► **engin explosif** explosive device ► **engins de guerre**† engines of war† (*aussi littér*) ► **engin spatial** space vehicle ► **engins (spéciaux)** missiles ► **engin de terrassement** earth-mover

englober [ɑ̃glɔbe] ▸ conjug 1 ◂ VT (= *inclure*) to include, encompass (**dans** in); (= *annexer*) to take in, incorporate

engloutir [ɑ̃glutiʀ] ▸ conjug 2 ◂ 1 VT [+ *nourriture*] to gobble up, gulp *ou* wolf down; [+ *navire*] to engulf, swallow up; [+ *fortune*] [*personne*] to squander; [*dépenses*] to eat *ou* swallow up; **qu'est-ce qu'il peut ~!** it's amazing what he puts away!*; **la ville a été engloutie par un tremblement de terre** the town was swallowed up *ou* engulfed by an earthquake 2 **s'engloutir** VPR [*navire*] to be engulfed

engloutissement [ɑ̃glutismɑ̃] NM [*nourriture*] gobbling up; [*navire*] engulfing; [*fortune*] squandering

engluer [ɑ̃glye] ▸ conjug 1 ◂ 1 VT [+ *arbre, oiseau*] to lime 2 **s'engluer** VPR [*oiseau*] to get caught *ou* stuck in (bird) lime; **s'~ les doigts** to get one's fingers sticky; **s'~ dans ses problèmes/une situation** to get bogged down in one's problems/a situation

engoncer [ɑ̃gɔ̃se] ▸ conjug 3 ◂ VT to restrict, cramp; **ce manteau l'engonce** he looks cramped in that coat, that coat restricts his movements; **engoncé dans ses vêtements** (looking) cramped in his clothes; **le cou engoncé dans un gros col** his neck (stiffly) encased in a big collar; **engoncé dans cette peti-**

te vie bourgeoise cooped up in this petty middle-class life

engorgement [ɑ̃gɔʀʒəmɑ̃] NM [*tuyau*] obstruction, clogging, blocking (**de** of); (*Méd*) engorgement; (*Comm*) glut (**de** in)

engorger [ɑ̃gɔʀʒe] ▸ conjug 3 ◂ 1 VT [+ *tuyau*] to obstruct, clog, block; (*Méd*) to engorge; (*Comm*) to glut, saturate 2 **s'engorger** VPR [*tuyau*] to become blocked; [*route*] to get congested; (*Comm*) [*marché*] to become glutted *ou* saturated

engouement [ɑ̃gumɑ̃] NM (*pour qn*) infatuation, fancy (**pour** for); (*pour qch*) fad, craze (**pour** for); **~ passager** passing fancy, brief craze

engouer (s') [ɑ̃gwe] ▸ conjug 1 ◂ VPR **s'~ de** *ou* **pour qch** to develop a passion for sth; **s'~ de qn** to become infatuated with sb

engouffrer [ɑ̃gufʀe] ▸ conjug 1 ◂ 1 VT [+ *charbon*] to shovel (**dans** into); * [+ *fortune*] to swallow up, devour; * [+ *nourriture*] to gobble up, gulp down, wolf down; **qu'est-ce qu'il peut ~!** it's amazing what he puts away!* 2 **s'engouffrer** VPR [*vent*] to rush, sweep; [*flot, foule*] to surge, rush; [*personne*] to rush, dive; [*navire*] to sink (**dans** into)

engoulevent [ɑ̃gul(ə)vɑ̃] NM **~ (d'Europe)** nightjar, goatsucker (*US*); **~ (d'Amérique)** nighthawk

engourdi, e [ɑ̃guʀdi] (*ptp de* **engourdir**) ADJ [*membre*] numb; [*esprit*] dull, dulled

engourdir [ɑ̃guʀdiʀ] ▸ conjug 2 ◂ 1 VT a [+ *membres*] to numb, make numb; **être engourdi par le froid** [+ *membre*] to be numb with cold; [+ *animal*] to be sluggish with the cold; **j'ai la main engourdie** my hand is numb *ou* has gone to sleep *ou* gone dead b [+ *esprit*] to dull, blunt; [+ *douleur*] to deaden, dull; **la chaleur et le vin l'engourdissaient** the heat and the wine were making him sleepy *ou* drowsy 2 **s'engourdir** VPR [*corps*] to become *ou* go numb; [*bras, jambe*] to become *ou* go numb, go to sleep, go dead; [*esprit*] to grow dull *ou* sluggish

engourdissement [ɑ̃guʀdismɑ̃] NM a [*membre, corps*] numbness; [*esprit*] (= *torpeur*) sleepiness, drowsiness; (= *affaiblissement*) dullness b (= *action*) [*membre*] numbing; [*esprit*] dulling

engrais [ɑ̃gʀɛ] NM a (*chimique*) fertilizer; (*animal*) manure; **~ vert** green manure; **~ azoté** nitrogen fertilizer b (= *engraissement*) **mettre un animal à l'~** to fatten up an animal

engraissement [ɑ̃gʀɛsmɑ̃], **engraissage** [ɑ̃gʀɛsaʒ] NM [*bœufs*] fattening (up); [*volailles*] cramming

engraisser [ɑ̃gʀɛse] ▸ conjug 1 ◂ 1 VT [+ *animal*] to fatten (up); [+ *terre*] to manure, fertilize; * [+ *personne*] to fatten up; **quel pique-assiette, c'est nous qui devons l'~** we seem to be expected to feed this scrounger* *ou* provide for this scrounger*; **~ l'État*** to enrich the state 2 VI* [*personne*] to get fat(ter), put on weight 3 **s'engraisser** VPR **l'État s'engraisse sur le dos du contribuable** the state grows fat at the taxpayer's expense

engrangement [ɑ̃gʀɑ̃ʒmɑ̃] NM [*foin*] gathering in, garnering (*littér*)

engranger [ɑ̃gʀɑ̃ʒe] ▸ conjug 3 ◂ VT [+ *foin, moisson*] to gather *ou* get in, garner (*littér*); [+ *bénéfices*] to reap, rake in*; [+ *connaissances*] to amass, store (up)

engrenage [ɑ̃gʀənaʒ] NM gears, gearing; [*événements*] chain; **~ à chevrons** double helical gearing; (*fig*) **quand on est pris dans l'~** when one is caught up in the system; **l'~ de la violence** the spiral of violence → **doigt**

engrener [ɑ̃gʀəne] ▸ conjug 5 ◂ 1 VT a [+ *roues dentées*] to engage; (*fig*) [+ *personne*] to catch up (**dans** in), draw (**dans** into); (*fig*) **~ l'affaire** to set things in motion b (= *remplir de grain*) to feed *ou* fill with grain 2 **s'engre-**

ner VPR [*roues dentées*] to mesh (**dans** with), gear (**dans** into)

engrosser: [ãgʀose] ▸conjug 1◂ VT **~ qn** to knock sb up******, get sb pregnant; **se faire ~** to get (o.s.) knocked up******, get (o.s.) pregnant (**par** by)

engueulade: [ãgœlad] NF (= *dispute*) row, slanging match* (*Brit*); (= *réprimande*) bawling out*****, rocket***** (*Brit*); **passer une ~ à qn** to bawl sb out*****, give sb a rocket***** (*Brit*); **avoir une ~ avec qn** to have a screaming match *ou* a row *ou* slanging match* (*Brit*) with sb; **lettre d'~** stinking letter*****

engueuler: [ãgœle] ▸conjug 1◂ [1] VT **~ qn** to bawl sb out*****, give sb a rocket***** (*Brit*); **se faire ~** to get bawled out*****, get a rocket***** (*Brit*) ▸ **poisson** [2] **s'engueuler** VPR to have a row *ou* slanging match* (*Brit*) (**avec** with)

enguirlander [ãgiʀlãde] ▸conjug 1◂ VT [a] (= *disputer*) **~ qn** to give sb a telling-off* *ou* ticking-off* (*Brit*), tear sb off a strip***** (*Brit*); **se faire ~** to get a telling-off* *ou* ticking-off* (*Brit*), get torn off a strip***** (*Brit*) [b] (= *orner*) to garland

enhardir [ãaʀdiʀ] ▸conjug 2◂ [1] VT to make bolder; **enhardi par** emboldened by [2] **s'enhardir** VPR to become *ou* get bolder; **s'~ (jusqu')à dire** to make so bold as to say, be bold enough to say

enharmonique [ãnaʀmɔnik] ADJ enharmonic

énième [ɛnjɛm] ADJ = **n-ième**

énigmatique [enigmatik] ADJ enigmatic

énigmatiquement [enigmatikmã] ADV enigmatically

énigme [enigm] NF (= *mystère*) enigma, riddle; (= *jeu*) riddle, puzzle; **tu es une ~ pour moi** you are an enigma to *ou* for me; **trouver la clé** *ou* **le mot de l'~** to find the key *ou* clue to the puzzle *ou* riddle; **parler par ~s** to speak in riddles

enivrant, e [ãnivʀã, ãt] ADJ [*parfum, vin, succès*] heady, intoxicating; [*beauté*] intoxicating; [*vitesse*] intoxicating, dizzying

enivrement [ãnivʀamã] NM († = *ivresse*) intoxication; (*fig* = *exaltation*) exhilaration; **l'~ du succès** the intoxication of success

enivrer [ãnivʀe] ▸conjug 1◂ [1] VT (*lit*) to intoxicate, make drunk; (*fig*) to intoxicate; **le parfum m'enivrait** I was intoxicated by the perfume [2] **s'enivrer** VPR (*lit*) to get drunk (**de** on), become intoxicated (**de** with); (*fig*) to become intoxicated (**de** with); **il passe son temps à s'~** he spends all his time getting drunk; **s'~ de mots** to get drunk on words; **enivré de succès** intoxicated with *ou* by success

enjambée [ãʒãbe] NF stride; **d'une ~** in a stride; **faire de grandes ~s** to stride out, take big *ou* long strides; **il allait à grandes ~s vers ...** he was striding (along) towards ...

enjambement [ãʒãbmã] NM (*Littérat*) enjambement; (*Bio*) crossing-over

enjamber [ãʒãbe] ▸conjug 1◂ VT [+ *obstacle*] to stride *ou* step over; [+ *fossé*] to step *ou* stride across; [+ *pont*] to span, straddle, stretch across; **il enjamba la rampe et s'assit dessus** he sat down astride the banister

enjeu (*pl* **enjeux**) [ãʒø] NM [*pari, guerre*] stake, stakes (**de** in); **quel est l'~ de la bataille ?** what is at stake in the battle?, what are the battle stakes?

enjoindre [ãʒwɛ̃dʀ] ▸conjug 49◂ VT (*frm*) **~ à qn de faire** to enjoin *ou* charge sb to do (*frm*)

enjôlement [ãʒolmã] NM bewitching

enjôler [ãʒole] ▸conjug 1◂ VT (= *ensorceler*) to bewitch; (= *amadouer*) to get round; **elle a si bien su l'~ qu'il a accepté** she coaxed *ou* wheedled *ou* cajoled him into accepting it

enjôleur, -euse [ãʒolœʀ, øz] [1] ADJ [*sourire, paroles*] coaxing, wheedling, winning [2] NM,F (= *charmeur*) coaxer, wheedler; (= *escroc*)

twister [3] **enjôleuse** NF (= *séductrice*) wily woman

enjolivement [ãʒɔlivmã] NM [a] (= *action*) [*objet*] embellishment; [*réalité, récit*] embroidering, embellishment [b] (= *ornement*) embellishment, adornment; **les ~s apportés aux faits par le narrateur** the narrator's embellishment of the facts

enjoliver [ãʒɔlive] ▸conjug 1◂ VT [+ *objet*] to embellish; [+ *réalité, récit*] to embroider, embellish

enjoliveur [ãʒɔlivœʀ] NM (*Aut*) hub cap

enjolivure [ãʒɔlivyʀ] NF = **enjolivement**

enjoué, e [ãʒwe] ADJ cheerful; **d'un ton ~** cheerfully, in a cheerful way

enjouement [ãʒumã] NM cheerfulness

enkystement [ãkistamã] NM encystment

enkyster (s') [ãkiste] ▸conjug 1◂ VPR to encyst

enlacement [ãlasmã] NM (= *étreinte*) embrace; (= *enchevêtrement*) intertwining, interlacing

enlacer [ãlase] ▸conjug 3◂ [1] VT [a] (= *étreindre*) to embrace, clasp, hug; **le danseur enlaça sa cavalière** the dancer ran his arm round his partner's waist [b] (= *enchevêtrer*) [+ *fils*] to intertwine, interlace [c] (= *entourer*) [*lianes*] to wind round, enlace, entwine [2] **s'enlacer** VPR [a] [*amants*] to embrace, hug each other; [*lutteurs*] to take hold of each other, clasp each other; **amoureux enlacés** lovers clasped in each other's arms *ou* clasped in a fond embrace [b] (= *s'entrecroiser*) to intertwine, interlace; **fils inextricablement enlacés** hopelessly tangled threads [c] [*lianes*] **s'~ autour de** to twine round, wind round

enlaidir [ãlediʀ] ▸conjug 2◂ [1] VT [+ *personne*] to make look ugly; [+ *paysage*] to deface, ruin; **cette coiffure l'enlaidit** that hair style makes her look very plain *ou* rather ugly [2] VI [*personne*] to become ugly [3] **s'enlaidir** VPR to make o.s. look ugly

enlaidissement [ãledismã] NM **l'~ du paysage** the way the countryside is being defaced *ou* ruined

enlevé, e [ãl(ə)ve] (*ptp de* **enlever**) ADJ [*récit*] spirited; [*scène, morceau de musique*] played with spirit *ou* brio → **trot**

enlèvement [ãlɛvmã] NM [a] [*personne*] kidnapping, abduction; **~ de bébé** babysnatching; (*Art*) **«l'Enlèvement des Sabines»** "the Rape of the Sabine Women" [b] [*meuble, objet*] removal, taking *ou* carrying away; [*tache*] removal; [*organe*] removal; [*ordures*] collection, clearing (away); [*bagages, marchandises*] collection; [*voiture en infraction*] towing away [c] (*Mil*) [*position*] capture, taking

enlever [ãl(ə)ve] ▸conjug 5◂ [1] VT [a] (*gén*) to remove; [+ *couvercle*] to remove, lift (off); [+ *meuble*] to remove, take away; [+ *étiquette, housse*] to remove, take off; [+ *tache*] to remove; (*en frottant au lavant etc*) to brush *ou* wash *etc* out *ou* off; [+ *tapis*] to take up, remove; [+ *lustre, tableau*] to take down; [+ *peau de fruit*] to take off, peel off, remove; [+ *mauvaises herbes*] to clear, remove; [+ *organe*] to remove, take out; **se faire ~ une dent** to have a tooth out *ou* pulled (*US*); **enlève tes mains de tes poches/de là** take your hands out of your pockets/off there, remove your hands from your pockets/from there; **~ le couvert** to clear the table; **enlève tes coudes de la table** take your elbows off the table [b] [+ *vêtements*] to take off, remove; **il enleva son chapeau pour dire bonjour** he raised his hat in greeting; **j'enlève ma robe pour mettre quelque chose de plus confortable** I'll just slip out of this dress into something more comfortable, I'll just take off this dress and put on something more comfortable [c] **~ à qn** [+ *courage*] to rob sb of; [+ *espoir*] to

deprive sb of, rob sb of; [+ *objet, argent*] to take (away) from sb; **on lui a enlevé son commandement** he was relieved of his command; **on lui a enlevé la garde de l'enfant** the child was taken *ou* removed from his care; **ça lui enlèvera peut-être le goût de recommencer** perhaps that'll cure him of trying that again, perhaps that'll make him think twice before he does it again; **ça n'enlève rien à son mérite** that doesn't in any way detract from his worth; **pour vous ~ tout scrupule** in order to dispel your misgivings; **enlève-toi cette idée de la tête** get that idea out of your head [d] (= *emporter*) [+ *objet, meuble*] to take away, carry away, remove; [+ *ordures*] to collect, clear (away); [+ *voiture en infraction*] to tow away; **il a fait ~ ses vieux meubles** he had his old furniture taken away; **il fut enlevé dans les airs** he was borne (up) *ou* lifted (up) into the air; (*frm*) **il a été enlevé par un mal foudroyant** he was borne off by a sudden illness; (*littér*) **la mort nous l'a enlevé** death has snatched *ou* taken him from us [e] (= *kidnapper*) to kidnap, abduct; **se faire ~ par son amant** to elope with one's lover, be carried off by one's lover; (*hum*) **je vous enlève votre femme pour quelques instants** I'll just steal *ou* borrow your wife for a moment (if I may) (*hum*) [f] (= *remporter*) [+ *siège d'élu, victoire*] to win; [+ *titre de champion*] to win, take; (*Mil*) [+ *position*] to capture, take; **il a facilement enlevé la course** he won the race easily; **elle enlève tous les suffrages** she wins everyone's sympathies, she wins everyone over; **~ la décision** to carry the day; **~ une affaire** (*tractation*) to pull off a deal; (*commande*) to get secure an order; [*marchandise*] to carry off *ou* get away with a bargain; **ça a été vite enlevé** (*marchandise*) it sold *ou* went quickly, it was snapped up; (*: *travail*) it was done in no time *ou* in a jiffy* [g] (*Mus*) [+ *morceau, mouvement*] to play with spirit *ou* brio [h] (*Sport*) [+ *cheval*] to urge on [i] (= *enthousiasmer*) [+ *public*] to fill with enthusiasm [2] **s'enlever** VPR [a] [*tache*] to come out, come off; (*en brossant ou lavant etc*) to brush *ou* wash *etc* out *ou* off; [*peinture, peau, écorce*] to peel off, come off; **enlève-toi de là** get out of the way*, mind out of the way!* (*Brit*); **comment est-ce que ça s'enlève ?** [*étiquette, housse*] how do you remove it *ou* take it off?; [*vêtement*] how do you get out of it *ou* take it off? [b] (*Sport* = *sauter*) **le cheval s'enlève sur l'obstacle** the horse takes off to clear the obstacle [c] † (= *se vendre*) to sell

enlisement [ãlizmã] NM **causer l'~ d'un bateau** to cause a ship to get stuck in the mud (*ou* sand *etc*)

enliser [ãlize] ▸conjug 1◂ [1] VT **~ sa voiture** to get one's car stuck in the mud (*ou* sand *etc*) [2] **s'enliser** VPR [a] (*dans le sable*) to sink (**dans** into), get stuck (**dans** in) [b] (*dans les détails*) to get bogged down (**dans** in); **s'~ (dans la monotonie**) to sink into *ou* get bogged down in a monotonous routine; **en mentant, tu t'enlises davantage** you're getting in deeper and deeper (water) with your lies

enluminer [ãlymine] ▸conjug 1◂ VT [+ *manuscrit*] to illuminate

enlumineur, -euse [ãlyminœʀ, øz] NM,F illuminator

enluminure [ãlyminyʀ] NF illumination

enneigé, e [ãneʒe] ADJ [*pente, montagne*] snowy, snow-covered; [*sommet*] snow-capped; [*maison*] snowbound, snowed up (*attrib*); [*col, route*] blocked by snow, snowed up (*attrib*), snowbound

enneigement [ɑ̃nɛʒmɑ̃] NM snow coverage; **à cause du faible ~** because of the poor snow coverage; **bulletin d'~** snow report; **conditions d'~** snow conditions

ennemi, e [ɛn(ə)mi] **1** ADJ (Mil) enemy (épith); (= hostile) hostile; **en pays ~** in enemy territory **2** NM,F **a** (= adversaire) enemy, foe† (aussi littér); **se faire des ~s** to make enemies (for o.s.); **se faire un ~ de qn** to make an enemy of sb; **passer à l'~** to go over to the enemy; **~ public numéro un** public enemy number one **b** **être ~ de qch** to be opposed to sth, be against sth; **être ~ de la poésie/de la musique** to be strongly averse to poetry/music; **la hâte est l'ennemie de la précision** speed and accuracy don't mix ou don't go together, more haste less speed (PROV) → **mieux**

ennoblir [ɑ̃nɔblir] ▶conjug 2◀ VT (moralement) to ennoble

ennoblissement [ɑ̃nɔblismɑ̃] NM (moral) ennoblement

ennuager (s') [ɑ̃nɥaʒe] ▶conjug 3◀ VPR (littér) [ciel] to cloud over; **ennuagé** cloudy, clouded

ennui [ɑ̃nɥi] NM **a** (= désœuvrement) boredom; (littér = spleen) ennui (littér), world-weariness; (= monotonie) tedium, tediousness; **écouter avec ~** to listen wearily; **c'est à mourir d'~** it's enough to bore you to tears ou death* ou to bore you stiff* **b** (= tracas) trouble, worry, problem; **avoir des ~s** to have problems, be in difficulty; **il a eu des ~s avec la police** he's been in trouble with the police; **avoir des ~s de santé** to be troubled with bad health, have problems with one's health; **~s d'argent** money worries; **elle a des tas d'~s** she has a great many worries, she has more than her share of troubles; **faire** ou **créer** ou **causer des ~s à qn** to make trouble for sb; **ça peut lui attirer des ~s** that could get him into trouble ou hot water*; **j'ai eu un ~ avec mon vélo** I had some trouble ou bother with my bike, something went wrong with my bike; **si ça vous cause le moindre ~** if it is in any way inconvenient to you; **l'~, c'est que ...** the trouble ou the hitch is that ... **c** (littér, †† = peine) grief

ennuyant, e [ɑ̃nɥijɑ̃, ɑ̃t] ADJ (†, Can) = **ennuyeux**

ennuyé, e [ɑ̃nɥije] (ptp de **ennuyer**) ADJ (= préoccupé) worried, bothered (de about); (= contrarié) annoyed, put out (de at, about)

▼ **ennuyer** [ɑ̃nɥije] ▶conjug 8◀ **1** VT **a** (= lasser) to bore, weary; **ce spectacle m'a profondément ennuyé** I was thoroughly bored by the show; **cela (vous) ennuie à force** it palls (on you) ou it gets boring in the long run **b** (= préoccuper) to worry; (= importuner) to bother, put out; **il y a quelque chose qui m'ennuie là-dedans** there's something that worries ou bothers me about it; **ça m'ennuierait beaucoup de te voir fâché** I should be really upset to see you cross; **ça m'ennuie de le dire, mais ...** I'm sorry to have to tell you but ..., I hate to say it but ...; **ça m'ennuierait beaucoup d'y aller** it would really put me out to go; **si cela ne vous ennuie pas trop** if it wouldn't put you to any trouble ou inconvenience, if you wouldn't mind; **je ne voudrais pas vous ~** I don't want to put you to any trouble ou inconvenience, I don't want to bother you ou put you out; **ça m'ennuie, ce que tu me demandes de faire** what you're asking me to do is rather awkward ou a nuisance **c** (= irriter) **~ qn** to annoy sb, get on sb's nerves; **tu m'ennuies avec tes jérémiades** I'm tired of your constant complaints, you're getting on my nerves with your constant complaints

2 **s'ennuyer** VPR **a** (= se morfondre) to be bored (de, à with); **il s'ennuie à faire un travail monotone** he's getting bored doing a humdrum job; **s'~ à mourir** to be bored to tears ou to death*, be bored stiff*; **on ne s'ennuie jamais avec lui** there's never a dull moment when he's around **b** **s'~ de qn** to miss sb

ennuyeux, -euse [ɑ̃nɥijø, øz] ADJ **a** (= lassant) [personne, spectacle, livre] boring, tedious; [travail] boring, tedious, wearisome; **~ comme la pluie** deadly dull, dull as ditchwater (Brit) **b** (= qui importune) annoying, tiresome; (= préoccupant) worrying; **ce qui t'arrive est bien ~** this is a very annoying ou tiresome thing to happen to you

énoncé [enɔ̃se] NM **a** (= termes) [sujet scolaire] wording; [problème] terms; [loi] terms, wording; **pendant l'~ du sujet** while the subject is being read out **b** (Ling) utterance

énoncer [enɔ̃se] ▶conjug 3◀ VT **a** (+ idée) to express; [+ faits, conditions] to state, set out, set forth; (littér) **pour m'~ plus clairement**† to express myself more clearly, to put it more clearly → **concevoir**

énonciatif, -ive [enɔ̃sjatif, iv] ADJ (Ling) [phrase] enunciative

énonciation [enɔ̃sjasjɔ̃] NF [faits] statement; (Ling) enunciation

enorgueillir [ɑ̃nɔrgœjir] ▶conjug 2◀ **1** VT to make proud **2** **s'enorgueillir** VPR **s'~ de** (= être fier de) to pride o.s. on, boast about; (= avoir) to boast; **la ville s'enorgueillit de deux opéras** the town boasts two opera houses

énorme [enɔrm] ADJ enormous, tremendous, huge; (Météo) [mer] phenomenal; **mensonge ~** enormous ou whopping* lie, whopper*; **ça lui a fait un bien ~** it's done him a great deal ou a world ou a power* (Brit) of good; **il a accepté, c'est déjà ~** he has accepted and that's quite something; **c'est un type ~ !*** he's a terrific* ou a tremendous* ou a great* guy!

énormément [enɔrmemɑ̃] ADV **a** (= beaucoup) enormously, tremendously, hugely; **ça m'a ~ amusé** I was greatly ou hugely amused by it; **ça m'a ~ déçu** it greatly disappointed me, I was tremendously ou greatly disappointed by it; **il boit ~** he drinks a tremendous ou an enormous ou a huge ou a terrific* amount **b** **~ de** (argent, eau, bruit] a tremendous ou an enormous ou a huge amount of, a great deal of; **~ de gens** a great many people

énormité [enɔrmite] NF **a** [poids, somme] hugeness; [demande, injustice] enormity **b** (= propos inconvenant) outrageous remark; (= erreur) big blunder, howler*

enquérir (s') [ɑ̃kerir] ▶conjug 21◀ VPR to inquire, enquire, ask (de about); **s'~ (de la santé) de qn** to ask ou inquire after sb ou after sb's health; **je m'en suis enquis à la mairie** I inquired at the town hall about it; **je m'en suis enquis auprès de lui** I asked him about it

enquête [ɑ̃kɛt] NF (gén, Jur) inquiry, enquiry; (après un décès) inquest; (Police) investigation; (Comm, Sociol = sondage) survey, (opinion) poll; (Jur) **ouvrir une ~** to set up ou open an inquiry; **faire une ~** (Police) to make an investigation, make investigations, investigate; (Comm, Sociol) to do ou conduct a survey (sur on); (Police) **mener** ou **conduire une ~** to be in charge of ou lead an investigation; **j'ai fait** ou **mené ma petite ~** I've done a little investigating (myself), I've done a little private investigation; **~ administrative** public inquiry (into planning proposals etc); **~ parlementaire** parliamentary inquiry (by parliamentary committee); **~ statistique** statistical survey; (Presse) **« notre grande ~ »** "our big investigation ou survey ou inquiry"

enquêter [ɑ̃kete] ▶conjug 1◀ VI (Jur) to hold an inquiry (sur on); (Police) to investigate; (Comm, Sociol) to conduct a survey (sur on); **ils vont ~ sur l'origine de ces fonds** they'll investigate the origin of these funds ou carry out an investigation into the origin of these funds

enquêteur [ɑ̃kɛtœr] NM **a** (Police) officer in charge of ou leading the investigation; **les ~s poursuivent leurs recherches** the police are continuing their investigations; **les ~s sont aidés par la population du village** the police are being helped in their inquiries ou investigations by the villagers; **un des ~s a été abattu** one of the officers involved in the investigation was shot dead **b** (Comm, Sociol) investigator; (pour sondages) pollster, interviewer; **des ~s sont venus dans le village** some people doing ou conducting a survey came to the village

enquêteuse [ɑ̃kɛtøz] NF (Police) officer in charge of ou leading an investigation; (Sociol) = **enquêtrice**

enquêtrice [ɑ̃kɛtris] NF (Comm, Sociol) investigator; (pour sondages) pollster, interviewer → **enquêteur**

enquiquinant, e* [ɑ̃kikinɑ̃, ɑ̃t] ADJ (= qui importune) annoying, irritating; (= préoccupant) worrying; (= lassant) boring

enquiquinement* [ɑ̃kikinmɑ̃] NM **quel ~ !** what a darned ou flipping (Brit) nuisance!*; **j'ai eu tellement d'~s avec cette voiture** I had so many darned ou flipping (Brit) problems with that car*

enquiquiner* [ɑ̃kikine] ▶conjug 1◀ **1** VT (= importuner) to annoy, bother; (= préoccuper) worry; (= lasser) to bore **2** **s'enquiquiner** VPR (= se morfondre) to be fed up*, be bored; (= se donner du mal) **s'~ à faire** to go to a heck of a lot of trouble to do*, put o.s. out to do; **ne t'enquiquine pas avec ça** don't bother (yourself) with that

enquiquineur, -euse* [ɑ̃kikinœr, øz] NM,F pest*, darned nuisance*, pain in the neck*

enracinement [ɑ̃rasinmɑ̃] NM **a** [idée, arbre] taking root **b** [immigrant] settling

enraciner [ɑ̃rasine] ▶conjug 1◀ **1** VT [+ arbre] to root; [+ idée] to fix, cause to take root; **solidement enraciné** [+ préjugé] deep-rooted, firmly ou deeply entrenched; [+ famille] firmly rooted ou fixed; [+ arbre] well-rooted **2** **s'enraciner** VPR [arbre, préjugé] to take root; [importun] to settle o.s. down; [immigrant] to put down roots, settle

enragé, e [ɑ̃raʒe] (ptp de **enrager**) ADJ **a*** (= passionné) [chasseur, joueur] keen; **être ~ de** to be mad* ou crazy about*, be mad keen on* (Brit); **un ~ de la voiture** a car fanatic **b** (= en colère) furious; **les ~s de mai 68** the rebels of May '68 **c** (Vét) rabid → **vache**

enrageant, e [ɑ̃raʒɑ̃, ɑ̃t] ADJ annoying, infuriating; **c'est vraiment ~ de devoir partir si tôt** it's a real pain* ou it's really annoying having to leave so early

enrager [ɑ̃raʒe] ▶conjug 3◀ VI **a** **faire ~ qn*** (= taquiner) to tease sb; (= importuner) to pester sb **b** (frm) to be furious, be in a rage; **j'enrage d'avoir fait cette erreur** I'm furious at having made this mistake; **il enrageait dans son coin** he was fretting and fuming

enraiement [ɑ̃rɛmɑ̃] NM = **enrayement**

enrayage [ɑ̃rɛjaʒ] NM [machine, arme] jamming

enrayement [ɑ̃rɛjmɑ̃] NM [maladie, évolution] checking; [chômage, inflation] checking, curbing

enrayer [ɑ̃reje] ▶conjug 8◀ **1** VT **a** [+ maladie, évolution] to check; [+ chômage, inflation] to check, curb; [+ machine, arme] to jam **b** [+ roue] to spoke **2** **s'enrayer** VPR [machine, arme] to jam

enrégimenter [ɑ̃reʒimɑ̃te] ▶conjug 1◀ VT **a** (péj: dans un parti) to enlist, enrol; **se laisser ~ dans** [+ parti] to let o.s. be dragooned into **b** († Mil) to enlist

enregistrable [ɑ̃r(ə)ʒistrabl] ADJ [CD, disquette] recordable

enregistrement [ɑ̃ʀ(ə)ʒistʀəmɑ̃] NM [a] (fait, son, souvenir) recording [b] (= disque, bande) recording; ~ **vidéo/magnétique** video/tape recording [c] (Jur) [acte] registration; **l'Enregistrement** the Registration Department (for legal transactions); **droits** ou **frais d'~** registration fees [d] (Transport) ~ **des bagages** (à l'aéroport) check-in; (à la gare) registration of luggage; **se présenter à l'~** to go to the check-in desk; **comptoir d'~** check-in desk

enregistrer [ɑ̃ʀ(ə)ʒistʀe] ▸ conjug 1 ◂ VT [a] (sur bande) to record, tape; (sur CD, en studio) to record; (sur magnétoscope) to record, video(-tape); (Téléc) **vous écoutez un message enregistré** this is a recorded message [b] (Jur) [+ acte, demande] to register; (Comm) [+ commande] to enter, book [c] (Fin, Comm) [+ profit, perte] to show; **nous avons enregistré de bonnes ventes** we've had good sales; **ils ont enregistré un bénéfice de 5 millions** they showed a profit of 5 million; **le PIB a enregistré une hausse de 12%** the GDP has shown ou recorded an increase of 12% [d] (= constater) **on enregistre une progression de l'épidémie** the epidemic is spreading; **on enregistre une amélioration de la situation** we have seen ou there has been an improvement in the situation; **la plus forte hausse enregistrée** the biggest rise recorded ou on record [e] (= mémoriser) [+ information] to take in; **d'accord, j'enregistre*** ou **c'est enregistré*** all right, I'll make ou I've made a mental note of it ou I'll bear it in mind [f] (Transport) **(faire) ~ ses bagages** (à l'aéroport) to check in (one's luggage); (à la gare) to register one's luggage

enregistreur, -euse [ɑ̃ʀ(ə)ʒistʀœʀ, øz] [1] ADJ [appareil] recording → **caisse** [2] NM (= instrument) recorder, recording device; ~ **de vol** flight recorder; ~ **de temps** time recorder

enrhumé, e [ɑ̃ʀyme] (ptp de **enrhumer**) ADJ **être ~** to have a cold; **je suis un peu/très ~** I have a bit of a cold/a terrible ou bad cold

enrhumer [ɑ̃ʀyme] ▸ conjug 1 ◂ [1] VT to give a cold to; **être enrhumé** to have a cold [2] **s'enrhumer** VPR to catch a cold

enrichi, e [ɑ̃ʀiʃi] (ptp de **enrichir**) ADJ [a] (péj) nouveau riche [b] [pain] enriched; [lessive] improved (**de** with); **shampooing formule ~e** enriched formula shampoo → **uranium**

enrichir [ɑ̃ʀiʃiʀ] ▸ conjug 2 ◂ [1] VT [+ œuvre, esprit, langue, collection] to enrich; [+ catalogue] to expand; (financièrement) to make rich [2] **s'enrichir** VPR (financièrement) to get ou grow rich; [esprit] to grow richer (**de** in); [collection] to be enriched (**de** with); **leur collection s'enrichit d'année en année** their collection is becoming richer from year to year

enrichissant, e [ɑ̃ʀiʃisɑ̃, ɑ̃t] ADJ enriching

enrichissement [ɑ̃ʀiʃismɑ̃] NM enrichment (NonC)

enrobage [ɑ̃ʀɔbaʒ], **enrobement** [ɑ̃ʀɔbmɑ̃] NM coating

enrobé, e [ɑ̃ʀɔbe] (ptp de **enrober**) ADJ (= empâté) [personne] plump

enrober [ɑ̃ʀɔbe] ▸ conjug 1 ◂ VT [+ bonbon] to coat (**de** with); [+ paroles] to wrap up (**de** in)

enrochement [ɑ̃ʀɔʃmɑ̃] NM rip-rap

enrôlé [ɑ̃ʀole] NM recruit

enrôlement [ɑ̃ʀolmɑ̃] NM (Mil) enlistment; (dans un parti) enrolment, signing up

enrôler VT, **s'enrôler** VPR [ɑ̃ʀole] ▸ conjug 1 ◂ (Mil) to enlist; (dans un parti) to enrol, sign up

enroué, e [ɑ̃ʀwe] (ptp de **enrouer**) ADJ **être ~** to be hoarse, have a hoarse ou husky voice; **j'ai la voix ~e** my voice is hoarse ou husky

enrouement [ɑ̃ʀumɑ̃] NM hoarseness, huskiness

enrouer [ɑ̃ʀwe] ▸ conjug 1 ◂ [1] VT (froid, cris) to make hoarse [2] **s'enrouer** VPR (par le froid) to go hoarse ou husky; (en criant) to make o.s. hoarse; **s'~ à force de chanter** to sing o.s. hoarse

enroulement [ɑ̃ʀulmɑ̃] NM [a] (NonC) [tapis] rolling up; [cheveux] coiling; [corde, ruban, fil] winding (**sur, autour de** round); [bobine] winding [b] (Archit, Art) volute, scroll, whorl [c] (Élec) coil

enrouler [ɑ̃ʀule] ▸ conjug 1 ◂ [1] VT [+ tapis] to roll up; [+ cheveux] to coil; [+ corde, ruban, fil] to wind (**sur, autour de** round); [+ bobine] to wind; ~ **une feuille autour de/dans** to roll a sheet of paper round/up in [2] **s'enrouler** VPR [serpent] to coil up; [film, fil] to wind; **s'~ dans une couverture** to wrap ou roll o.s. up in a blanket

enrouleur, -euse [ɑ̃ʀulœʀ, øz] [1] ADJ [mécanisme, cylindre] winding [2] NM [tuyau d'arrosage] drum; (galet) ~ idle pulley, idler; ~ **(automatique) de cordon** automatic flex rewind; **laisse à ~** retractable lead → **ceinture**

enrubanner [ɑ̃ʀybane] ▸ conjug 1 ◂ VT to decorate ou trim with ribbon(s); (en attachant) to tie up ou do up with (a) ribbon

ENS [eenes] NF (ABRÉV = **École normale supérieure**) → **école**

ensablement [ɑ̃sɑbləmɑ̃] NM [a] [port] silting-up; [tuyau] choking ou blocking (with sand); [bateau] stranding; [voiture] getting stuck (in the sand) [b] (= tas de sable) (formé par le vent) (sand) dune; (formé par l'eau) sandbank

ensabler [ɑ̃sɑble] ▸ conjug 1 ◂ [1] VT [+ port] to silt up, sand up; [+ tuyau] to choke ou block with sand; [+ bateau] to strand (on a sandbank); [+ voiture] to get stuck (in the sand) [2] **s'ensabler** VPR [port] to silt up; [bateau, voiture] to get stuck in the sand; **je m'étais ensablé jusqu'aux essieux** my car had sunk into the sand up to the axles

ensacher [ɑ̃saʃe] ▸ conjug 1 ◂ VT to bag, pack (into bags)

ensanglanter [ɑ̃sɑ̃glɑ̃te] ▸ conjug 1 ◂ VT [+ visage] to cover with blood; [+ vêtement] to soak with blood; **manche ensanglantée** blood-soaked sleeve; ~ **un pays** to bathe a country in blood; **l'accident qui a ensanglanté la course** the accident which cast a tragic shadow over the race; **l'attentat qui a ensanglanté la visite du président** the terrorist attack which brought an element of bloodshed to the president's visit

enseignant, e [ɑ̃seɲɑ̃, ɑ̃t] [1] ADJ teaching → **corps** [2] NM,F teacher; **~-chercheur** teacher and researcher; **poste d'~** teaching position ou post ou job

enseigne [ɑ̃seɲ] [1] NF [a] (Comm) (shop) sign; ~ **lumineuse** neon sign; (restaurant) **«à l'~ du Lion Noir»** "the Black Lion"; **loger à l'~ du Lion Noir††** to put up at (the sign of) the Black Lion†; [b] (Mil, Naut) ensign; **(défiler) ~s déployées** (to march) with colours flying [c] (littér) **à telle(s) ~(s) que ...** so much so that ... [2] NM [a] (Hist) ensign [b] ~ **de vaisseau** (de 1re classe) lieutenant; (de 2e classe) sub-lieutenant (Brit), ensign (US)

enseignement [ɑ̃seɲ(ə)mɑ̃] NM [a] (= cours, leçons) education, instruction; **recevoir un ~ dans une discipline** to receive instruction in a subject; ~ **musical** musical education; ~ **agricole** agricultural training; ~ **assisté par ordinateur** computer-aided ou computer-assisted learning ou instruction; ~ **des langues** language teaching; ~ **ménager** home economics sg; ~ **par correspondance** correspondence courses; **à distance** distance learning; ~ **professionnel** professional ou vocational training; ~ **programmé** programmed learning; ~ **spécialisé** special education ou schooling; ~ **technique** technical education, industrial arts (US)

[b] (= système scolaire) education; **l'~ en France** (the system of) education in France; ~ **primaire** ou **du premier degré/secondaire** ou **du second degré** primary/secondary education; ~ **supérieur/universitaire** higher/university education; ~ **libre/privé/public** denominational/private/state education; **l'~ public et gratuit** free public education → ÉDUCATION NATIONALE [c] (= art d'enseigner) teaching; ~ **moderne** modern (methods of) teaching [d] (= carrière) **l'~** the teaching profession, teaching; **entrer dans l'~** to enter the teaching profession, go into teaching; **être dans l'~** to be a teacher, be a member of the teaching profession [e] (= leçon donnée par l'expérience) teaching, lesson; **on peut en tirer plusieurs ~s** it has taught us several things, we can draw several lessons from it; **les ~s du Christ** the teachings of Christ

enseigner [ɑ̃seɲe] ▸ conjug 1 ◂ VT to teach; ~ **qch à qn** to teach sb sth; ~ **à qn à faire qch** to teach sb (how) to do sth

ensemble¹ [ɑ̃sɑ̃bl] ADV [a] (= l'un avec l'autre) together; **ils sont partis ~** they left together; **tous ~** all together [b] (= simultanément) (deux personnes) together, both at once; (plusieurs) together, at the same time; **ils ont répondu ~** (deux) they both answered together ou at once; (plusieurs) they all answered together ou at the same time, they answered all together [c] (littér = à la fois) **tout ~** (deux) both, at once; (plus de deux) at (one and) the same time; **il était tout ~ triste et joyeux** he was both ou at once sad and happy [d] **aller ~** [objets] to go together; [idées] to go together ou hand in hand; **aller bien ~** [couple] to be well-matched; [escrocs] to make a pretty ou a fine pair; (plus de deux) to make a fine bunch; **l'armoire et la table ne vont pas (bien)** ou **vont mal ~** the wardrobe and the table don't go (very well) together [e] [personnes] **être bien ~** to get along ou on (Brit) well (together); **ils sont mal ~** they don't get along ou on (Brit) (well) (together)

ensemble² [ɑ̃sɑ̃bl] NM [a] (= totalité) whole; **former un ~ harmonieux** to form a harmonious whole; **l'~ du personnel** the entire ou whole staff; **on reconnaît cette substance à l'~ de ses propriétés** you can identify this substance from all its various properties [b] (= groupement) [personnes] set, group, body; [objets, poèmes] set, collection; [faits] set, series; [meubles] suite; [lois] body, corpus; **tout un ~ de choses** a whole combination of things; **bel ~ architectural** fine architectural grouping; ~ **immobilier de 500 logements** residential complex with 500 housing units; **grand ~** high-rise estate [c] (Mus) ensemble; ~ **instrumental/vocal** instrumental/vocal ensemble [d] (Math) set; ~ **vide** empty set; **théorie des ~s** set theory [e] (Couture) outfit, suit, ensemble; ~ **de ville** town suit; ~ **de voyage** travelling outfit; ~ **de plage** beach ensemble ou outfit; ~ **pantalon** trouser suit, pantsuit [f] (loc) **avec ~** [répondre] as one man, with one accord; **dans l'~** on the whole, in the main, by and large; **dans l'~ nous sommes d'accord** basically we agree; **les spectateurs dans leur ~** the audience as a whole; **examiner la question dans son ~** to examine the question in its entirety ou as a whole; **d'~** [vue, étude] overall, comprehensive, general; [impression] overall, general; **mouvement d'~** ensemble movement

ensemblier [ɑ̃sɑ̃blije] NM (= décorateur) interior designer; (Ciné) assistant (set) designer; (= entreprise) factory design consultancy

ensemencement [ɑ̃s(ə)mɑ̃smɑ̃] NM sowing

ensemencer [ɑ̃s(ə)mɑ̃se] ▸ conjug 3 ◂ VT (Agr) to sow (**de, en** with); (Bio) to culture

enserrer [ãseʀe] ▸conjug 1◂ VT [*vêtement*] to hug tightly; (*dans ses bras*) to hold, clasp; **vallée enserrée par des montagnes** valley shut in *ou* hemmed in by mountains

ensevelir [ãsəv(ə)liʀ] ▸conjug 2◂ VT (*frm* = *enterrer*) to bury; (*d'un linceul*) to shroud (**de** in); [+ *peine, honte*] to hide, bury; [*avalanche, décombres*] to bury; **enseveli sous la neige/la lave** buried beneath the snow/lava

ensevelissement [ãsəv(ə)lismã] NM (*gén*) burying; (*dans un linceul*) shrouding

ENSI [ãsi] NF (ABRÉV = **École nationale supérieure d'ingénieurs**) → **école**

ensilage [ãsilaʒ] NM ensilage

ensiler [ãsile] ▸conjug 1◂ VT to ensilage, ensile

en-soi [ãswa] NM (*Philo*) en-soi

ensoleillé, e [ãsɔleje] (*ptp de* **ensoleiller**) ADJ sunny

ensoleillement [ãsɔlejmã] NM (= *durée*) period *ou* hours of sunshine; **l'~ est meilleur sur le versant est** there is more sun(shine) on the eastern side

ensoleiller [ãsɔleje] ▸conjug 1◂ VT (*lit*) to fill with *ou* bathe in sunshine *ou* sunlight; (*fig*) to brighten, light up

ensommeillé, e [ãsɔmeje] ADJ sleepy, drowsy; **il a les yeux ~s** he is heavy-eyed with sleep, he is drowsy- *ou* sleepy-eyed

ensorcelant, e [ãsɔʀsəlã, ãt] ADJ [*regard, sourire*] bewitching; [*personne*] bewitching, captivating; [*paroles, roman, œuvre, rythme, musique*] spellbinding

ensorceler [ãsɔʀsəle] ▸conjug 4◂ VT (*lit, fig*) to bewitch, put *ou* cast a spell on *ou* over

ensorceleur, -euse [ãsɔʀsəlœʀ, øz] **1** ADJ bewitching, spellbinding **2** NM (*lit*) sorcerer, enchanter; (*fig*) charmer **3** **ensorceleuse** NF (*lit*) witch, enchantress, sorceress; (*fig* = *femme*) enchantress; (*hum* = *enfant*) charmer

ensorcellement [ãsɔʀsɛlmã] NM (= *action*) bewitching, bewitchment; (= *charme*) charm, enchantment

▾**ensuite** [ãsɥit] ADV (= *puis*) then, next; (= *par la suite*) afterwards, later; **il nous dit ~ que ...** then *ou* next he said that ...; **d'accord mais ~?** all right but what now? *ou* what next? *ou* then what?; **il se mit à crier, ~ de quoi il claqua la porte** he started shouting, after which *ou* and after that he slammed the door; **je le reçois d'abord et je vous verrai ~** I'll meet him first and I'll see you after *ou* afterwards

ensuivre (s') [ãsɥivʀ] ▸conjug 40◂ VPR to follow, ensue; **il s'ensuit que** it follows that; **et tout ce qui s'ensuit** and all that goes with it; **torturé jusqu'à ce que mort s'ensuive** tortured to death

ensuqué, e* [ãsyke] ADJ droopy

entablement [ãtabləmã] NM entablature

entacher [ãtaʃe] ▸conjug 1◂ VT [+ *honneur*] to soil, sully, taint; [+ *joie*] to taint, blemish; (*Jur*) **entaché de nullité** null and void; **entaché d'erreurs** spoilt *ou* marred by mistakes

entaille [ãtaj] NF **a** (*sur le corps*) (*gén*) cut; (*profonde*) gash; (*petite*) nick; **se faire une ~** to cut o.s. **b** (*sur un objet*) notch; (*allongée*) groove; (*dans une falaise*) gash

entailler [ãtaje] ▸conjug 1◂ VT [+ *corps*] (*gén*) to cut; (*profondément*) to gash; (*légèrement*) to nick; [+ *objet*] to notch; **carrière qui entaille la colline** quarry which cuts a gash in the hill; **s'~ la main** to cut *ou* gash one's hand

entame [ãtam] NF (= *tranche*) first slice; (*Cartes*) first card

entamer [ãtame] ▸conjug 1◂ VT **a** [+ *pain, jambon*] to start (on); [+ *tonneau*] to broach, tap; [+ *bouteille, boîte, sac*] to start, open; [+ *tissu*] to cut into; [+ *patrimoine*] to make a hole in, dip into; **mes économies sont bien entamées** it has made a big dent *ou* hole in my savings; **la boîte est à peine entamée** the box has hardly been touched

b (= *inciser*) [+ *chair, tissu*] to cut (into); [+ *métal*] to cut *ou* bite into

c (= *amorcer*) [+ *journée, livre*] to start; [+ *travail*] to start on; [+ *négociations, discussion*] to start, open; [+ *poursuites*] to institute, initiate; **la journée est déjà bien entamée** we are already well into the day, the day is already quite far advanced

d (= *ébranler*) [+ *résistance*] to wear down, break down; [+ *conviction*] to shake, weaken; [+ *optimisme, moral*] to wear down

e (= *salir*) [+ *réputation*] to damage, harm, cast a slur on

f (*Cartes* = *commencer*) **~ la partie** to open the game; **c'est à toi d'~** it's you to lead; **~ d'un pique** (*enchères*) to open (with) one spade; (*partie*) to lead a spade

entartrage [ãtaʀtʀaʒ] NM [*chaudière, tuyau, bouilloire*] scaling, furring-up (*Brit*); [*dents*] scaling

entartrer [ãtaʀtʀe] ▸conjug 1◂ **1** VT [+ *chaudière, tuyau, bouilloire*] to scale, fur up (*Brit*); [+ *dents*] to scale **2** **s'entartrer** VPR [*chaudière, tuyau, bouilloire*] to scale, fur up (*Brit*); [*dents*] to get covered in tartar

entassement [ãtasmã] NM **a** (= *action*) [*objets*] piling up, heaping up; [*personnes*] cramming in, packing together **b** (= *tas*) pile, heap

entasser [ãtase] ▸conjug 1◂ **1** VT **a** (= *amonceler*) [+ *objets, arguments*] to pile up, heap up (**sur** onto) **b** (= *tasser*) [+ *personnes, objets*] to cram, pack (**dans** into) **2** **s'entasser** VPR (= *s'amonceler*) [*déchets, erreurs*] to pile up; [*personnes*] to cram, pack (**dans** into); **ils s'entassent à 10 dans cette pièce** there are 10 of them crammed *ou* packed into that room; **s'~ sur la plage** to pack onto the beach

ente [ãt] NF (*Agr*) graft

entendement [ãtãdmã] NM (*Philo*) understanding; **cela dépasse l'~** that's beyond all understanding *ou* comprehension; (*frm*) **perdre l'~** to lose one's reason

entendeur [ãtãdœʀ] NM **à bon ~, salut** a word to the wise is enough

entendre [ãtãdʀ] ▸conjug 41◂ **1** VT **a** (= *percevoir*) [+ *voix, bruit*] to hear; **il entendit du bruit** he heard a noise; **il entend mal de l'oreille droite** he can't hear very well with his right ear; (*fig*) **il ne l'entend pas de cette oreille** he's not prepared to accept that; **il entendit parler quelqu'un** he heard somebody speak; **j'entendais quelqu'un parler** *ou* **parler quelqu'un** I heard *ou* could hear somebody talking; **faire ~ un son** to make a sound; **elle fit ~ sa voix mélodieuse** ◊ **sa voix mélodieuse se fit ~** her sweet voice was heard; **faire ~ sa voix** *ou* **se faire ~ dans un débat** to make oneself heard in a debate; **qu'est-ce que j'entends?** what did you say?, am I hearing right?; (*menace*) **tu vas être sage, tu entends!** you're to be good, do you hear (me)!; **ce qu'il faut ~ tout de même!*** really — the things you hear! *ou* the things people say!; **il vaut mieux ~ ça que d'être sourd!*** really, the things you hear!* → **voler¹**

b (*par ouï-dire*) **~ parler de qn/qch** to hear of *ou* about sb/sth; **j'en ai vaguement entendu parler** I did vaguely hear something about *ou* of it; **on n'entend plus parler de lui** you don't hear anything of them these days, you never hear of him any more; (*fig*) **il ne veut pas en ~ parler** he won't hear of it; **~ dire que ...** to hear it said that ...; **d'après ce que j'ai entendu dire** from what I have heard, by all accounts; **on entend dire que ...** it is said *ou* rumoured that ..., rumour has it that ...; **on entend dire des choses étranges** there are strange rumours going about; **je l'ai entendu dire que ...** I heard him say that ...

c (= *écouter*) to hear, listen to; **le patron a entendu les syndicats pendant une heure** the

boss listened to *ou* heard the unions for an hour; **j'ai entendu son discours jusqu'au bout** I listened right to the end of his speech; (*Jur*) **~ les témoins** to hear the witnesses; **à l'~, c'est lui qui a tout fait** to hear him talk *ou* to listen to him you'd think he had done everything; **il ne veut rien ~** he doesn't want to hear *ou* know about it, he just won't listen; **il raconte à qui veut l'~ que c'est lui qui l'a quittée** he tells anyone who'll listen that he's the one who left her; (*menace*) **si ça continue, il va m'~!** if he doesn't stop I'll give him a piece of my mind! → **messe, raison**

d (*frm* = *comprendre*) to understand; **oui, j'entends bien, mais ...** yes, I fully *ou* quite understand but ...; **je vous entends** I see what you mean, now I understand (you); **il n'entend rien à la musique** he doesn't know the first thing *ou* he doesn't have the first idea about music; † **il n'entend pas la plaisanterie** he can't take a joke, he doesn't know how to take a joke; **laisser ~ à qn que ...; ◊ donner à ~ à qn que ...** (= *faire comprendre*) to give sb to understand that ...; (= *donner l'impression que ...*) to let it be understood that ..., give sb the impression that ... → **malice, pire**

e (*frm avec infin* = *vouloir*) to intend, mean; **j'entends bien y aller** I certainly intend *ou* mean to go; **faites comme vous l'entendez** do as you see fit *ou* think best; **j'entends être obéi** *ou* **qu'on m'obéisse** I intend *ou* mean to be obeyed, I will be obeyed; **j'entends ne pas céder** ◊ **je n'entends pas céder** I have no intention of giving in

f (= *vouloir dire*) to mean; **qu'entendez-vous par là?** what do you mean by that?; **entendez-vous par là que ...?** are you trying to say that ...?, do you mean that ...?

2 **s'entendre** VPR **a** (*soi-même*) **je me suis entendu à la radio** I heard myself on the radio; **tu ne t'entends pas!** you don't know what you're saying!

b (= *être d'accord, s'accorder*) to agree; **ils se sont entendus sur plusieurs points** they have agreed on several points; **hier tu m'as dit le contraire, il faudrait s'~!** yesterday you told me exactly the opposite, make up your mind!

c (= *sympathiser*) to get on; **ils ne s'entendent pas** they don't get along *ou* on (*Brit*) (together *ou* with each other); **ils s'entendent à merveille** they get along *ou* on (*Brit*) extremely well (together *ou* with each other), they get on like a house on fire (*Brit*) → **larron**

d (= *s'y connaître*) **s'y ~ pour** *ou* **s'~ à** (*frm*) **faire qch** to be very good at doing sth; **il s'y entend!** he knows what he's doing!, he knows his onions!* (*Brit*) *ou* stuff!*

e (= *se comprendre*) **quand je dis magnifique, je m'entends, disons que c'est très joli** when I say it's magnificent, what I really mean is that it's very attractive; **il le fera, moyennant finances, (cela) s'entend** he will do it — for a fee, of course *ou* naturally; **entendons-nous bien!** let's be quite clear about *ou* on this, let's make quite sure we understand one another; **ça peut s'~ différemment suivant les contextes** that can be taken to mean different things depending on the context

f (= *être entendu*) **le bruit s'entendait depuis la route** the noise could be heard *ou* was audible from the road; (*fig*) **cette expression ne s'entend plus guère** that phrase is hardly ever used *ou* heard nowadays, you hardly ever hear that phrase nowadays; **on ne s'entend plus ici** you can't hear yourself think in here

entendu, e [ãtãdy] (*ptp de* **entendre**) ADJ **a** (= *convenu*) agreed; **étant ~ que** it being understood *ou* agreed that, since; **il est bien ~ que vous n'en dites rien** of course it's understood *ou* it must be understood that you make no mention of it; **c'est (bien) ~, n'est-ce pas?** that's (all) agreed, isn't it?; **(c'est) ~!** right!, agreed!, right-oh!* (Brit) b (= évidemment) **bien ~!** of course!; **(comme de) bien ~*, tu dormais!** as I might have known ou expected (you to be), you were asleep! c (concessif) all right, granted, so we all agree; **c'est ~ ou c'est une affaire ~e**, il t'a **poussé** all right, so he pushed you d (= complice) [sourire, air] knowing; **d'un air ~** with a knowing look, knowingly e †† (= habile) competent

enténébrer [ātenebʀe] ▶ conjug 6 ◀ VT (littér) [+ salle] to make dark ou gloomy; [+ vie, voyage] to cast a shadow over

entente [ātɑ̃t] NF a (= amitié) harmony, understanding; (= alliance) understanding; **politique d'~ avec un pays** policy of friendship with a country; **l'Entente cordiale** the Entente Cordiale; **la Triple Entente** the Triple Alliance; **vivre en bonne ~** to live in harmony ou harmoniously; **vivre en bonne ~ avec les voisins** to be on good terms with the neighbours b (= accord) agreement, understanding; (Écon = cartel) combine; **~s illicites** illegal agreements ou arrangements; **faire une demande d'~ préalable** to request the Social Security to agree to help with costs before one is treated c (= connaissance) grasp, understanding; (= habileté) skill → **double**

enter [āte] ▶ conjug 1 ◀ VT (Agr) to graft

entérinement [āteʀinmā] NM ratification, confirmation

entériner [āteʀine] ▶ conjug 1 ◀ VT to ratify, confirm

entérite [āteʀit] NF enteritis

enterrement [āteʀmā] NM a (= action) [mort] burial; [espoir] end, death b (= cérémonie) funeral, burial (service); (= convoi) funeral procession; **~ civil/religieux** non-religious/religious burial (service) ou funeral; **faire ou avoir une tête ou mine d'~*** to look down in the mouth*, look gloomy ou glum; (hum) **il a eu un ~ de première classe** [politicien, cadre] he was shunted off into the wings

enterrer [āteʀe] ▶ conjug 1 ◀ VT a (= inhumer) to bury, inter (frm); **hier il a enterré sa mère** yesterday he attended his mother's burial ou funeral; **on l'enterre ce matin** he is being buried this morning; **tu nous enterreras tous!** you'll outlive us all!; **s'~ dans un trou perdu** to bury o.s. in the sticks ou in the back of beyond (Brit) b (= enfouir) [+ os, trésor] to bury c (= oublier) [+ projet] to lay aside, forget about; [+ scandale] to hush up; [+ espoir] to forget about; **enterrons cette querelle** (let's) let bygones be bygones; **c'est une querelle enterrée depuis longtemps** that quarrel has long since been (dead and) buried; **~ son passé** to put one's past behind one; **~ sa vie de garçon** to have ou throw a stag party (before one's wedding)

entêtant, e [ātetā, āt] ADJ [vin, parfum] heady (épith), which goes to the head

en-tête (pl **en-têtes**) [ātɛt] NM heading; (Ordin) header; **papier à lettres à ~** headed notepaper

entêté, e [ātete] (ptp de **entêter**) 1 ADJ stubborn, pigheaded* 2 NM,F mule, stubborn individual; **quel ~ tu fais!** you're so stubborn!

entêtement [ātetmā] NM (= obstination) stubbornness, pigheadedness*; (= persévérance) doggedness

entêter [ātete] ▶ conjug 1 ◀ 1 VT [vin, parfum] to go to the head of; **ce parfum entête** this perfume goes to your head 2 **s'entêter** VPR to persist (**dans qch** in sth, **à faire qch** in doing sth)

enthousiasmant, e [ātuzjasmā, āt] ADJ [spectacle, livre, idée] exciting, exhilarating

▼ **enthousiasme** [ātuzjasm] NM enthusiasm; **avec ~** enthusiastically, with enthusiasm; **avoir des ~s soudains** to have sudden fits of enthusiasm ou sudden crazes

▼ **enthousiasmer** [ātuzjasme] ▶ conjug 1 ◀ 1 VT to fill with enthusiasm 2 **s'enthousiasmer** VPR to be enthusiastic (**pour** about, over); **il s'enthousiasma tout de suite pour ...** he was immediately enthusiastic about ou over ..., he was immediately filled with enthusiasm for ...; **c'est quelqu'un qui s'enthousiasme facilement** he's easily carried away (**pour** by)

enthousiaste [ātuzjast] 1 ADJ enthusiastic (**de** about, over) 2 NMF enthusiast

entichement [ātiʃmā] NM (pour une personne) infatuation (**pour, de** for, with); (pour une chose) passion, craze (**de, pour** for)

enticher (s') [ātiʃe] ▶ conjug 1 ◀ VPR (frm, péj) **s'~ de** [+ personne] to become infatuated ou besotted (Brit) with; [+ activité, théorie] to get completely hooked* on; **il est entiché de vieux livres** he has a passion for old books

entier, -ière [ātje, jɛʀ] 1 ADJ a (= total) [quantité, prix] whole, full; [surface, endroit, année] whole, entire; **boire une bouteille entière** to drink a whole ou full ou an entire bottle; **payer place entière** (Théât) to pay the full price; (Rail) to pay the full fare ou price; **une heure entière** a whole hour; **des heures entières** for hours (on end ou together); **dans le monde ~** in the whole ou entire world, in the whole of the world, throughout the world; **dans la France entière** throughout France, in the whole of France → **nombre** b **tout ~** entirely, completely; **se donner tout ~ à une tâche** to devote o.s. wholeheartedly ou entirely ou wholly to a task; **il était tout ~ à son travail** he was completely wrapped up in ou engrossed in his work c (= intact) [objet, vertu] intact; (Vét = non châtré) entire; **aucune assiette n'était entière** there wasn't one unbroken plate; **la question reste entière** the question still remains unresolved; **c'est un miracle qu'il en soit sorti ~** it's a miracle he escaped unscathed ou in one piece d (= absolu) [liberté, confiance] absolute, complete; **mon accord plein et ~** my full ou entire (and) wholehearted agreement; **donner entière satisfaction** to give complete satisfaction e (= sans demi-mesure) [personne, caractère] unyielding, unbending; [opinion] strong, positive f (Culin) → **lait**
2 NM (Math) whole, integer; (Ordin) integer; **deux demis font un ~** two halves make a whole; **la nation dans son ~** the nation as a whole, the entire nation
3 **en entier** LOC ADV totally, in its entirety; **occupé en ~ par des bureaux** totally occupied by offices, occupied in its entirety by offices; **boire une bouteille en ~** to drink a whole ou a full ou an entire bottle; **lire/voir qch en ~** to read/see the whole of sth, read/watch sth right through

entièrement [ātjɛʀmā] ADV entirely, completely, wholly; **je suis ~ d'accord avec vous** I fully ou entirely agree with you; **la ville a été ~ détruite** the town was wholly ou entirely destroyed

entièreté [ātjɛʀte] NF entirety

entité [ātite] NF entity

entoiler [ātwale] ▶ conjug 1 ◀ VT [+ estampe] to mount on canvas; [+ vêtement] to stiffen (with canvas)

entôler: [ātole] ▶ conjug 1 ◀ VT to con‡, fleece* (**de** of), do* (Brit) (**de** out of)

entomologie [ātɔmɔlɔʒi] NF entomology

entomologique [ātɔmɔlɔʒik] ADJ entomological

entomologiste [ātɔmɔlɔʒist] NMF entomologist

entonner [ātɔne] ▶ conjug 1 ◀ VT **une chanson** to break into song, strike up a song, start singing; **~ des louanges au sujet de qn** to start singing sb's praises; **~ un psaume** to strike up a psalm, start singing a psalm

entonnoir [ātɔnwaʀ] NM (Culin) funnel; (Géog) swallow hole, doline; (= trou) [obus] shell-hole; [bombe] crater; [forme, conduit] **en ~** funnel-shaped

entorse [ātɔʀs] NF a (Méd) sprain; **se faire une ~ au poignet** to sprain one's wrist b [loi] infringement (**à** of); **faire une ~ à** [+ vérité] to twist; [+ habitudes, régime] to break; **faire une ~ au règlement** to bend ou stretch the rules

entortillement [ātɔʀtijmā] NM (= action) twisting, winding, twining; (= état) entwinement

entortiller [ātɔʀtije] ▶ conjug 1 ◀ 1 VT a [+ ruban] to twist, twine, wind; [+ bonbons] to wrap (up) b* (= enjôler) to get round, wheedle, cajole; (= embrouiller) to mix up, muddle (up); (= duper) to hoodwink 2 **s'entortiller** VPR [liane] to twist, wind, twine; **s'~ dans ses réponses** to tie o.s. in knots* with one's answers; **s'~ dans les couvertures** (volontairement) to wrap ou roll o.s. up in the blankets; (involontairement) to get caught up ou tangled up ou entangled in the blankets

entour [ātuʀ] NM (littér) **les ~s de qch** the surroundings of sth; **à l'~ de qch** around sth

entourage [ātuʀaʒ] NM a (= famille) family circle; (= compagnie: gén) set, circle; [roi, président] entourage; **les gens de son ~/dans l'~ du président** people around him/around the president b (= bordure) [fenêtre] frame, surround (Brit); [massif floral] border, surround (Brit)

entouré, e [ātuʀe] (ptp de **entourer**) ADJ a (= admiré) popular; **cette jeune femme est très ~e** this young woman is the centre of attraction; **pendant cette épreuve il était très ~** during this difficult time many people rallied around (him); (Bourse) **c'est un titre très ~** everyone's rallying around that stock b (= encerclé) **~ de** surrounded with ou by

entourer [ātuʀe] ▶ conjug 1 ◀ 1 VT a (= mettre autour) **~ de** to surround with; **~ un champ d'une clôture** to put a fence round a field, surround a field with a fence; **il entoura ses épaules d'un châle** he put ou wrapped a shawl (a)round her shoulders; **~ qn de ses bras** to put one's arms (a)round sb b (= être autour: gén) to surround; [cadre] to frame, surround; [couverture, écharpe] to be round; [soldats] to surround, encircle; **le monde qui nous entoure** the world around ou about us, the world that surrounds us c (= soutenir) [+ personne souffrante] to rally round; **~ qn de son affection** to surround sb with love
2 **s'entourer** VPR **s'~ de** [+ amis, gardes du corps, luxe] to surround o.s. with; **s'~ de mystère** to surround o.s. with ou shroud o.s. in mystery; **s'~ de précautions** to take elaborate precautions; **nous voulons nous ~ de toutes les garanties** we wish to have ou avail ourselves of all possible guarantees

entourloupe* [ātuʀlup], **entourloupette*** [ātuʀlupɛt] NF mean ou rotten* trick; **faire une ~ à qn** to play a (rotten* ou mean) trick on sb

entournure [ātuʀnyʀ] NF armhole → **gêné**

entracte [ātʀakt] NM a (= pause) (Théât) interval, interlude, intermission (US); (Ciné) interval, intermission; (fig = interruption) interlude, break b (Théât = divertissement) entr'acte, interlude

entraide [ātʀɛd] NF mutual aid; **~ judiciaire internationale** international judicial cooperation; (Admin) **service d'~** support service

entraider (s') [ātʀede] ▶ conjug 1 ◀ VPR to help one another ou each other

▶ **GRAMMAIRE ACTIVE:** enthousiasme 40.2   enthousiasmer 34.3

entrailles [ɑ̃tʀaj] NFPL [a] [*animaux*] entrails, guts [b] (*littér*) [*personne*] entrails; (= *ventre maternel*) womb; (*fig*) **sans ~** heartless, unfeeling; **la faim le mordait aux ~** hunger gnawed at him *ou* at his guts; **spectacle qui vous prend aux ~** *ou* **qui vous remue les ~** sight that shakes your very soul *ou* shakes you to the core [c] (*littér*) [*édifice, terre*] bowels, depths

entrain [ɑ̃tʀɛ̃] NM [*personne*] spirit, drive; [*réunion*] spirit, liveliness, go; **avec ~** [*répondre, travailler*] enthusiastically; [*manger*] with gusto, heartily; **sans ~** [*travailler*] half-heartedly, unenthusiastically; **être plein d'~** ◊ **avoir de l'~** to have plenty of *ou* be full of drive *ou* go*; **ça manque d'~** (*soirée*) it's dragging, it's not exactly lively, it's a bit dead*

entraînant, e [ɑ̃tʀɛnɑ̃, ɑ̃t] ADJ [*paroles, musique*] stirring, rousing; [*rythme*] brisk, lively

entraînement [ɑ̃tʀɛnmɑ̃] NM [a] (= *action*) [*roue, bielle*] driving; [*athlète*] training, coaching; [*cheval*] training; **~ à chaîne** chain drive [b] (= *impulsion, force*) [*passions*] (driving) force, impetus; [*habitude*] force; **des ~s dangereux** dangerous impulses [c] (*Sport = préparation, exercice*) training (*NonC*); **deux heures d'~ chaque matin** two hours of training every morning; **course/terrain d'~** training course/ground; **manquer d'~** to be out of training; **il a de l'~** he's highly trained; **il est à l'~** he's in a training session, he's training; **il est à l'~ de rugby** he's at rugby practice; **il s'est blessé à l'~** he hurt himself at *ou* while training *ou* during a training session; (*hum*) **j'ai de l'~!** I've had lots of practice!

entraîner [ɑ̃tʀene] ▸ conjug 1 ◂ [1] VT [a] (*lit*) (= *charrier*) [+ *épave, objets arrachés*] to carry *ou* drag along; (*Tech* = *mouvoir*) [+ *machine*] to drive; (= *tirer*) [+ *wagons*] to pull; **le courant les entraîna vers les rapides** the current carried *ou* dragged *ou* swept them along towards the rapids; **le poids de ses habits l'entraîna vers le fond** the weight of his clothes dragged him (down) towards the bottom; **il entraîna son camarade dans sa chute** he pulled *ou* dragged his friend down in his fall [b] (= *emmener*) [+ *personne*] to take (off) (**vers** towards); **il m'entraîna vers la sortie/dans un coin** he dragged *ou* took me (off) towards the exit/into a corner; **il les entraîna à sa suite vers ...** he took them (along *ou* off) with him towards ... [c] (= *influencer*) to lead; **~ qn à voler qch** to get sb to steal sth; **~ ses camarades à boire/dans la débauche** to lead one's friends into drinking/bad ways; **se laisser ~ par ses camarades** to let o.s. be led by one's friends; **cela l'a entraîné à de grosses dépenses** that meant great expense for him, that led him into great expense [d] (= *causer*) to bring about, lead to; (= *impliquer*) to entail, mean; **ceci a entraîné des compressions budgétaires** this has brought about *ou* led to budgetary restraints; **si je vous comprends bien, ceci entraîne la perte de nos avantages** if I understand you, this will mean *ou* will entail the loss of our advantages [e] (= *emporter*) [*rythme*] to carry along; [*passion, enthousiasme*] to carry away; **son enthousiasme l'a entraîné trop loin** his enthusiasm carried him too far; **se laisser ~ (par ses passions)** to (let o.s.) get *ou* be carried away (by one's passions) [f] (= *préparer*) [+ *athlète*] to train, coach; [+ *cheval*] to train (**à** for)

[2] **s'entraîner** VPR [a] (*Sport*) to train; **où est-il? — il s'entraîne au stade** where is he? — he's (doing some) training at the stadium; **s'~ à la course/pour le championnat** to get in training *ou* to train for running/for the championship; **s'~ à faire un certain mouvement** to practise a certain movement, work on a certain movement [b] (*gén*) **s'~ à faire qch** to train o.s. to do sth;

s'~ à la discussion/à l'art de la discussion to train o.s. for discussion/in the art of discussion; **il s'entraîne à parler en public** he is training himself to speak in public

entraîneur [ɑ̃tʀɛnœʀ] NM [*cheval*] trainer; [*équipe, coureur, boxeur*] coach, trainer; (*littér*) **un ~ d'hommes** a leader of men

entraîneuse [ɑ̃tʀɛnøz] NF [*bar*] hostess; (*Sport*) coach, trainer

entrant, e [ɑ̃tʀɑ̃, ɑ̃t] NM,F (*gén pl*) **les ~s** the people coming (*ou* going) in

entrapercevoir [ɑ̃tʀapɛʀsəvwaʀ] ▸ conjug 28 ◂ VT to catch a (brief) glimpse of

entrave [ɑ̃tʀav] NF [a] (= *obstacle*) hindrance (**à** to); **~ à la circulation** hindrance to traffic; **~ à la liberté d'expression** constraint upon *ou* obstacle to freedom of expression; [*liberté, bonheur*] **sans ~** total; **vivre sans ~s** to lead an unfettered existence [b] [*animal*] hobble, fetter, shackle; [*prisonnier*] **~s** chains, fetters (*littér*); (*littér*) **se débarrasser des ~s de la rime** to free o.s. from the shackles *ou* fetters of rhyme (*littér*)

entravé, e [ɑ̃tʀave] (*ptp de* **entraver**) ADJ [*voyelle*] checked; **jupe ~e** pencil skirt

entraver [ɑ̃tʀave] ▸ conjug 1 ◂ VT [a] (= *gêner*) [+ *circulation*] to hold up; [+ *mouvements*] to hamper, hinder; [+ *action, plans, processus*] to hinder, hamper, impede; **~ la carrière de qn** to hinder sb in his career [b] [+ *animal*] to hobble, shackle, fetter; [+ *prisonnier*] to chain (up), fetter (*littér*) [c]* (= *comprendre*) to get*; **je n'y entrave que couic** *ou* **que dalle** I just don't get it*, I don't twig (it) at all* (*Brit*)

entre [ɑ̃tʀ] PRÉP [a] (= *à mi-chemin de, dans l'intervalle de*) [+ *objets, dates, opinions*] between; **~ le vert et le jaune** between green and yellow; **~ la vie et la mort** between life and death; **~ ciel et terre** between heaven and earth; **vous l'aimez saignant, à point ou ~ les deux?** do you like it rare, medium or between the two? *ou* or in-between?; **la vérité est ~ les deux** the truth is somewhere between the two *ou* somewhere in between → **lire¹** [b] (= *entouré par*) [+ *murs*] within, between; [+ *montagnes*] among, between; (*fig*) **enfermé ~ quatre murs** shut in; **encaissé ~ les hautes parois** enclosed between the high walls [c] (= *au milieu de, parmi*) [+ *objets épars, personnes*] among, amongst; **il aperçut un objet brillant ~ les pierres** he saw an object shining among(st) the stones; **choisir ~ plusieurs choses** to choose from among *ou* between several things; **il hésita ~ plusieurs routes** he hesitated between several roads; (*frm*) **je le compte ~ mes amis** I number him among my friends; **lui, ~ autres, n'est pas d'accord** he, for one *ou* among others, doesn't agree; **~ autres (choses)** among other things; **~ autres (personnes)** among others; **l'un d'~ eux** one of them; **plusieurs d'~ nous** several of us, several of our number (*frm*); **intelligent ~ tous** supremely intelligent; **problème difficile ~ tous** inordinately *ou* particularly difficult problem; **cette heure ~ toutes** this (hour) of all hours; **je le reconnaîtrais ~ tous** I would know *ou* recognize him anywhere; **c'est le meilleur ~ tous mes amis** he's the best friend I have; **il l'a partagé ~ tous ses amis** he shared it out among all his friends [d] (= *dans*) in, into; **j'ai eu ce livre ~ les mains** I had that book in my (very) hands; **prendre ~ ses bras** to take in one's arms; **ma vie est ~ vos mains** my life is *ou* lies in your hands; **tomber ~ les mains de l'ennemi/d'escrocs** to fall into the hands of the enemy/of crooks [e] (= *à travers*) through, between; **je l'ai aperçu ~ les branches** I saw it through *ou* between the branches [f] (*indiquant une relation*) (*deux choses*) between; (*plus de deux*) among; **rapports ~ deux personnes/choses** relationship between two

people/things; **nous sommes ~ nous** *ou* **~ amis** we're all friends here, we're among friends; **~ nous** between you and me, between ourselves; **~ nous c'est à la vie, à la mort** we are *ou* shall be friends for life; **~ eux 4** among the 4 of them; **qu'y a-t-il exactement ~ eux?** what exactly is there between them?; **il n'y a rien de commun ~ eux** they have nothing in common *ou* no common ground; **ils se marient ~ eux** they intermarry; **ils préfèrent rester ~ eux** they prefer to keep (themselves) to themselves *ou* to be on their own; **ils se sont entendus ~ eux** they reached a mutual agreement; **entendez-vous ~ vous** sort it out among yourselves; **ils se sont disputés ~ eux** they have quarrelled (with each other *ou* with one another); **laissons-les se battre ~ eux** let's leave them to fight it out (between *ou* among themselves); **on ne va pas se battre ~ nous** we're not going to fight (among ourselves)

entrebâillement [ɑ̃tʀəbajmɑ̃] NM **dans/par l'~ de la porte** in/through the half-open door

entrebâiller [ɑ̃tʀəbaje] ▸ conjug 1 ◂ VT to half-open; **la porte est entrebâillée** the door is ajar *ou* half-open

entrebâilleur [ɑ̃tʀəbajœʀ] NM door chain

entrechat [ɑ̃tʀəʃa] NM (*Danse*) entrechat; (*hum* = *saut*) leap, spring; **faire des ~s** (*Danse*) to do entrechats; (*hum*) to leap about

entrechoquement [ɑ̃tʀəʃɔkmɑ̃] NM (*gén*) knocking, banging; [*verres*] clinking; [*dents*] chattering; [*épées*] clashing

entrechoquer [ɑ̃tʀəʃɔke] ▸ conjug 1 ◂ [1] VT (*gén*) to knock *ou* bang together; [+ *verres*] to clink *ou* chink (together) [2] **s'entrechoquer** VPR (*gén*) to knock *ou* bang together; [*verres*] to clink *ou* chink (together); [*dents*] to chatter; [*épées*] to clash *ou* clang together; [*idées, mots*] to jostle together

entrecôte [ɑ̃tʀəkot] NF entrecôte steak, rib steak

entrecouper [ɑ̃tʀəkupe] ▸ conjug 1 ◂ [1] VT **~ de** [+ *citations*] to intersperse *ou* pepper with; [+ *rires, sarcasmes*] to interrupt with; [+ *haltes*] to interrupt with, break with; **voix entrecoupée de sanglots** voice broken with sobs; **parler d'une voix entrecoupée** to speak in a broken voice, have a catch in one's voice as one speaks [2] **s'entrecouper** VPR [*lignes*] to intersect, cut across each other

entrecroisement [ɑ̃tʀəkʀwazmɑ̃] NM [*fils, branches*] intertwining; [*lignes, routes*] intersecting

entrecroiser VT, **s'entrecroiser** VPR [ɑ̃tʀəkʀwaze] ▸ conjug 1 ◂ [*fils, branches*] to intertwine; [*lignes, routes*] to intersect

entre-déchirer (s') [ɑ̃tʀədeʃiʀe] ▸ conjug 1 ◂ VPR (*littér*) to tear one another *ou* each other to pieces

entre-deux [ɑ̃tʀədø] NM INV [a] (= *intervalle*) intervening period, period in between [b] (*Sport*) jump ball [c] (*Couture*) **~ de dentelle** lace insert

entre-deux-guerres [ɑ̃tʀədøgɛʀ] NM INV **l'~** the interwar years *ou* period; **pendant l'~** between the wars, in *ou* during the interwar years *ou* period

entre-dévorer (s') [ɑ̃tʀədevɔʀe] ▸ conjug 1 ◂ VPR (*littér*) to tear one another *ou* each other to pieces

entrée [ɑ̃tʀe] [1] NF [a] (= *arrivée*) [*personne*] (*gén*) entry, entrance; (*dans pays, ville*) entry; [*véhicule, bateau, armée occupante*] entry; **à son ~, tous se sont tus** as he came *ou* walked in *ou* entered, everybody fell silent; **à son ~ dans le salon** as he came *ou* walked into *ou* entered the lounge; **elle a fait une ~ remarquée** she made quite an entrance, she made a dramatic entrance; **faire son ~ dans le salon** to enter the lounge; **l'~ en gare du train** the train's entry into the station; **l'~ au port du navire** the

ship's entry into the port; **~ illégale dans un pays** illegal entry into a country
b (*Théât*) **faire son ~** to make one's entry *ou* entrance; (*Théât*) **rater son ~** (*sur scène*) to miss one's entrance; (*première réplique*) to miss one's cue
c (= *accès*) entry, admission (**de, dans** to); (*sur pancarte*) "way in"; «**~ libre**» (*dans boutique*) "come in and look round"; (*dans musée*) "admission free"; «**~ interdite**» "no admittance", "no entry"; «**~ interdite à tout véhicule**» "vehicles prohibited"; **l'~ est gratuite/payante** there is no admission charge/there is an admission charge; **on lui a refusé l'~ de l'amphithéâtre** he was refused admission *ou* entrance *ou* entry to the lecture hall
d (*Comm*) [*marchandises*] entry; (*Fin*) [*capital*] inflow; **droits d'~** import duties
e (*dans un domaine, un milieu*) entry; (*dans un club*) entry, admission; **l'~ de la Finlande dans l'Union européenne** Finland's entry into *ou* admission to the European Union; **se voir refuser son ~ dans un club/une école** to be refused admission *ou* entry to a club/school, be rejected by a club/school; **l'~ des jeunes dans la vie active est souvent difficile** young people often find it difficult to enter the job market; **ce parti a fait une ~ fracassante sur la scène politique** this party burst onto the political scene; **ce produit/l'entreprise a fait une ~ discrète sur le marché** the product/company has crept onto the market; **il a fait une ~ discrète au gouvernement** he entered the government unobtrusively; **faire son ~ dans le monde†** [*débutante*] to come out†, make one's début in society → **concours, examen**
f (= *billet*) ticket; **j'ai pris 2 ~s** I got 2 tickets; **billet d'~** entrance ticket; **les ~s couvriront tous les frais** the receipts *ou* takings will cover all expenses; **ils ont fait 10 000 ~s** they sold 10,000 tickets
g (= *porte, portail*) entry, entrance; [*tunnel, port, grotte*] entry, entrance, mouth; **~ principale** main entrance
h (= *vestibule*) entrance (hall)
i (*Tech*) [*fluide, air*] entry
j (= *début*) outset; (*Mus* = *motif*) entry; **à l'~ de l'hiver/de la belle saison** as winter/the warm weather set *ou* sets *etc*) in, at the onset *ou* beginning of winter/the warm weather; **d'~ de jeu** from the outset
k (*Culin*) [= *mets*] first course, starter (*Brit*); (*sur menu*) entrée (*Brit*), appetizer (*US*)
l (*Comm, Stat*) entry; (*Lexicographie* = *mot*) headword (*Brit*), entry word (*US*); **tableau à double ~** double-entry table
m (*Ordin*) input; **~-sortie** input-output

2 entrées NFPL **avoir ses ~s auprès de qn** to have free *ou* easy access to sb; **il a ses ~s au gouvernement** he has privileged access to government ministers

3 COMP ► **entrée d'air** (*Tech*) air inlet ► **entrée des artistes** stage door ► **entrée de service** [*hôtel*] service *ou* tradesmen's entrance; [*villa*] tradesmen's entrance

entre-égorger (s') [ãtregɔRʒe] ▸ conjug 3 ◂ VPR to cut each other's *ou* one another's throats

entrefaites [ãtRəfɛt] ♦ **sur ces entrefaites** LOC ADV (= *à ce moment-là*) at that moment, at this juncture

entrefer [ãtRəfɛR] NM air-gap

entrefilet [ãtRəfilɛ] NM (= *petit article*) paragraph

entregent [ãtRəʒã] NM savoir-faire; **avoir de l'~** to have a good manner with people

entrejambe [ãtRəʒãb] NM (*Couture, euph*) crotch

entrelacement [ãtRəlasmã] NM (= *action, état*) intertwining, interlacing; **un ~ de branches** a network *ou* crisscross of branches

entrelacer VT, **s'entrelacer** VPR [ãtRəlase] ▸ conjug 3 ◂ to intertwine, interlace; **lettres entrelacées** intertwined *ou* interlaced letters; **intrigues entrelacées** intertwined *ou* interwoven plots; **voluptueusement entrelacés** locked in a sensual embrace; (*Ordin*) **écran à balayage entrelacé/non entrelacé** screen with interleaved *ou* interlaced scanning/non-interleaved *ou* non-interlaced scanning

entrelacs [ãtRəla] NM (*Archit*) interlacing (*NonC*); (*Peinture*) interlace (*NonC*)

entrelardé, e [ãtRəlaRde] (*ptp de* **entrelarder**) ADJ (= *gras*) [*viande*] streaked with fat

entrelarder [ãtRəlaRde] ▸ conjug 1 ◂ VT (*Culin*) to lard; **~ de citations** to (inter)lard *ou* intersperse with quotations

entremêler [ãtRəmele] ▸ conjug 1 ◂ **1** VT **a** [+ *choses*] to (inter)mingle, intermix; **~ des scènes tragiques et des scènes comiques** to (inter)mingle *ou* intermix tragic and comic scenes **b** (= *truffer de*) **~ un récit de** to intersperse *ou* pepper a tale with **2 s'entremêler** VPR [*branches, cheveux*] to become entangled (**à** with); [*idées*] to become intermingled

entremets [ãtRəmɛ] NM dessert (*made with cream*)

entremetteur [ãtRəmetœR] NM **a** (*péj*) (*gén*) go-between; (= *proxénète*) procurer, go-between **b** (= *intermédiaire*) mediator, go-between

entremetteuse [ãtRəmetøz] NF (*péj*) (*gén*) go-between; (= *proxénète*) procuress, go-between

entremettre (s') [ãtRəmetR] ▸ conjug 56 ◂ VPR **a** (*dans une querelle*) to act as mediator, mediate, intervene (**dans** in); (*péj*) to interfere (**dans** in) **b** (= *intercéder*) to intercede (**auprès de** with)

entremise [ãtRəmiz] NF intervention; **offrir son ~** to offer to act as mediator *ou* to mediate; **grâce à son ~** thanks to his intervention; **apprendre qch par l'~ de qn** to hear about sth through sb

entrepont [ãtRəpɔ̃] NM (*Naut*) steerage; **dans l'~** in steerage

entreposage [ãtRəpozaʒ] NM storing, storage

entreposer [ãtRəpoze] ▸ conjug 1 ◂ VT (*gén*) to store, put into storage; (*en douane*) to put into a bonded warehouse

entrepôt [ãtRəpo] NM (*gén*) warehouse; (*Douane*) bonded warehouse; (= *ville, port*) entrepôt

entreprenant, e [ãtRəpRənã, ãt] ADJ (*gén*) enterprising; (*sexuellement*) forward

entreprendre [ãtRəpRãdR] ▸ conjug 58 ◂ VT **a** (= *commencer*) to begin *ou* start (upon); [+ *travail, démarche*] to set about; [+ *voyage*] to set out (up)on; [+ *procès*] to start up **b** (= *se lancer dans*) [+ *voyage, travail, recherches*] to undertake, embark upon, launch upon; **~ de faire qch** to undertake to do sth; [+ *peur d'~* the fear of undertaking things **c** [+ *personne*]† (= *courtiser*) to woo†, court†; (*pour raconter une histoire*) to buttonhole, collar*; (*pour poser des questions*) to tackle; **il m'entreprit sur le sujet de ...** he tackled me on the question of ...

entrepreneur, -euse [ãtRəpRənœR, øz] NM,F **a** (= *patron*) businessman; (*en menuiserie etc*) contractor; **~ (en** *ou* **de bâtiment)** building contractor; **~ de travaux publics** civil engineering contractor; **~ de transports** haulage contractor (*Brit*), trucking firm (*US*); **~ de pompes funèbres** undertaker, funeral director (*Brit*), mortician (*US*) **b** (= *brasseur d'affaires*) entrepreneur

entrepreneurial, e (*mpl* **-iaux**) [ãtRəpRənœRjal, jo] ADJ entrepreneurial

▼ **entreprise** [ãtRəpRiz] NF **a** (= *firme*) firm, company; **la grande ~ se porte mieux en France** big companies *ou* firms are doing bet-

ter in France; **~ agricole/familiale** farming/family business; **~ de construction** building firm; **~ de camionnage** *ou* **de transport** haulage firm (*Brit*), trucker (*US*); **~ de déménagement** removal (*Brit*) *ou* moving (*US*) firm; **~ de pompes funèbres** undertaker's (*Brit*), funeral director's (*Brit*), funeral parlor (*US*); **~ publique** state-owned company; **~ de service public** public utility; **~ de travaux publics** civil engineering firm → **chef¹, concentration**
b (= *secteur d'activité*) **l'~** business; **le monde de l'~** the business world **c** (= *dessein*) undertaking, venture, enterprise; **se livrer à une ~ de démoralisation** to set out to demoralize sb → **esprit, libre d** (*hum*: *envers une femme*) **~s** advances

entrer [ãtRe] ▸ conjug 1 ◂ **1** VI (*avec aux être*) **a** (*lit, gén*) (*vu du dehors*) to go in, enter; (*vu du dedans*) to come in, enter; (*à pied*) to walk in; (*en voiture*) to drive in; [*véhicule*] to drive in, go *ou* come in, enter; **~ dans** [+ *pièce, jardin*] to go *ou* come into, enter; [+ *voiture*] to get in(to); [+ *région, pays*] [*voyageurs*] to go *ou* come into, enter; [*armée*] to enter; **entrez !** come in!; **entre donc !** come on in!; **qu'il entre !** tell him to come in, show him in; **entrons voir** let's go in and see; **je ne fais qu'~ et sortir** I can't stop; **les gens entraient et sortaient** people were going *ou* coming in and out; **c'est à gauche en entrant** it's on the left as you go in; **il entra discrètement** he came in *ou* entered discreetly, he slipped in; **~ en gare/au port** to come into *ou* enter the station/harbour; **~ chez qn** to come (*ou* go) into sb's house; **je suis entré chez eux en passant** I called in *ou* dropped in at their house; **je suis entré chez le fleuriste** I went to *ou* I called in at the florist's; **~ en courant** to run in, come running in; **~ en boitant** to limp in, come limping in, come in limping; **~ en scène** (*lit*) to come (*ou* go) on (to the stage); (*fig*) to come on *ou* enter the scene; (*Théât*) «**entrent trois gardes**» "enter three guards"; **ils sont entrés par la porte de la cave/par la fenêtre** they got in *ou* entered by the cellar door/the window; **~ sans payer** to get in without paying; **entrez sans frapper** come *ou* go *ou* walk straight in (without knocking)
b (*Comm*) [*marchandises, devises*] to enter; **tout ce qui entre (dans le pays) est soumis à une taxe** everything entering (the country) is subject to duty; (*Ordin*) **~ dans un fichier/système** (*légalement*) to enter a file/system; (*illégalement*) to hack into a file/system
c (= *s'enfoncer*) **la boule est entrée dans le trou** the ball went into the hole; **le tenon entre dans la mortaise** the tenon fits into the mortice; **la balle est entrée dans le poumon gauche/le montant de la porte** the bullet went into *ou* lodged itself in the left lung/the doorframe; **son coude m'entrait dans les côtes** his elbow was digging into my ribs; **l'eau entre (à l'intérieur) par le toit** the water gets *ou* comes in through the roof; **l'air/la lumière entre dans la pièce** air/light comes into *ou* enters the room; **pour que l'air/la lumière puisse ~** to allow air/light to enter *ou* get in; **le vent entre de partout** the wind blows in everywhere; **~ dans l'eau** [*baigneur*] to get into the water; (*en marchant*) to wade into the water; [*embarcation*] to enter the water; **~ dans le bain** to get into the bath; **~ dans le brouillard** [*randonneurs, avion*] to enter *ou* hit* fog; **la rage/jalousie est entrée dans son cœur** his heart filled with rage/jealousy; **l'argent entre dans les caisses** money is coming in; **à force d'explications ça finira par ~*** explain it for long enough and it'll sink in; **alors ces maths, ça entre ?*** are you getting the hang of maths then?* → **beurre**
d (= *tenir*) **ça n'entre pas dans la boîte** it won't go *ou* fit into the box; **ça n'entre pas** it

► GRAMMAIRE ACTIVE: entreprise 46.1

won't go *ou* fit in; **nous n'entrerons jamais tous dans ta voiture** we're never all going to get *ou* fit into your car; **il faut que je perde 3 kg pour ~ dans cette robe** I'll have to lose 3 kilos if I want to get *ou* fit into this dress
[e] (= *devenir membre de*) **~ dans** [+ *club, parti, entreprise*] to join; [+ *groupe*] to go *ou* come into; [+ *métier*] to go into; **~ dans l'Union européenne** to join the European Union; **~ dans la magistrature** to become a magistrate, enter the magistracy; **~ dans l'armée** to join the army; **~ dans les affaires** to go into business; **~ à l'hôpital/en maison de retraite** to go into hospital/a retirement home; **~ en religion** to become a monk (*ou* a nun); **on l'a fait comme serveur/livreur** he's been found a job as *ou* they got him taken on as a waiter/delivery boy; (*Scol*) **elle entre en dernière année** she's just going into her final year; **~ à l'université/au lycée** to go to university *ou* college/secondary school; **~ au service de qn** to enter sb's service; **~ dans l'histoire** to go down in history → **jeu, légende, scène, usage**
[f] (= *heurter*) **~ dans** [+ *arbre, poteau*] to go *ou* crash into
[g] (= *être une composante de*) **~ dans** [+ *catégorie*] to fall into, come into; [+ *mélange*] to go into; **les substances qui entrent dans ce mélange** the substances which go into *ou* make up this mixture; **on pourrait faire ~ ceci dans la catégorie suivante** one might put this into the following category; **tous ces frais entrent dans le prix de revient** all these costs (go to) make up the cost price; **il y entre un peu de jalousie** a bit of jealousy comes into it; **votre avis est entré pour beaucoup dans sa décision** your opinion counted for a good deal in his decision; **ça n'entre pas dans mes intentions** I don't have any intention of doing so → **ligne[1]**
[h] (= *partager*) **~ dans** [+ *vues, peines de qn*] to share; (*frm*) **~ dans les sentiments de qn** to share sb's *ou* enter into sb's feelings, sympathize with sb → **peau**
[i] (*fig* = *commencer*) **~ dans** [+ *phase, période*] to enter (into); **~ dans une profonde rêverie/une colère noire** to go (off) into a deep daydream/a towering rage; **~ dans la vie active ◊ ~ dans le monde du travail** to begin one's working life; **~ dans la cinquantaine** to turn fifty → **danse**
[j] (= *commencer à être*) **~ en effervescence** to reach a state of effervescence (*frm*), begin to effervesce; **~ en ébullition** to reach boiling point, begin to boil; **~ en guerre** to go to war (**contre** against) → **contact, fonction, relation, vigueur**
[k] (*fig* = *aborder*) **~ dans** [+ *sujet, discussion*] to enter into; **il s'agit d'~ véritablement dans la discussion** one must enter into the discussion properly; **sans ~ dans les détails/ces considérations** without going into details/these considerations; **il entra dans des considérations futiles** he went off into some futile considerations → **vif**
[l] **laisser ~** [+ *visiteur, intrus*] to let in; [+ *lumière, air*] to let in, allow in; (*involontairement*) [+ *eau, air, poussière*] to let in; **ne laisse ~ personne** don't let anybody in; **laisser ~ qn dans** [+ *pièce*] to let sb into; [+ *pays*] to let sb into *ou* enter, allow sb into *ou* to enter; **on l'a laissé ~ au parti/club/dans l'armée** they've let him into *ou* let him join the party/club/army
[m] **faire ~** (= *introduire*) [+ *invité, visiteur, client*] to show in; [+ *pièce, tenon, objet à emballer*] to fit in; (*en fraude*) [+ *marchandises, immigrants*] to smuggle in, take *ou* bring in; [+ *accusé, témoin*] to bring in, call; **faire ~ la voiture dans le garage** to get the car into the garage; **faire ~ une clé dans la serrure** to insert *ou* fit a key in the lock; **il m'a fait ~ dans leur club/au jury** (*m'a persuadé*) he had me join *ou* got me to join their club/the panel; (*a fait jouer son influence*) he got me into their club/onto the panel, he helped me join their club/the pan-

el; (*m'a contraint*) he made me join their club/the panel; **il me fit ~ dans la cellule** he showed me into the cell; **faire ~ qch de force dans un emballage** to force *ou* stuff sth into a package
[2] VT (*avec aux avoir; plus gén: faire entrer*)
[a] [+ *marchandises*] (*par la douane*) to take *ou* bring in, import; (*en contrebande*) to take *ou* bring in, smuggle in
[b] (= *faire pénétrer*) **~ les bras dans les manches** to put one's arms into the sleeves
[c] (= *faire s'ajuster*) [+ *pièce*] to make fit (**dans qch** in sth); **comment allez-vous ~ cette armoire dans la chambre ?** how are you going to get that wardrobe into the bedroom?
[d] (*Ordin*) [+ *données*] to key in

entresol [ɑ̃tʀəsɔl] NM entresol, mezzanine (*between ground floor and first floor*)

entre-temps [ɑ̃tʀətɑ̃] [1] ADV meanwhile, (in the) meantime [2] NM **dans l'~** meanwhile, (in the) meantime

entretenir [ɑ̃tʀət(ə)niʀ] ▸ conjug 22 ◂ [1] VT
[a] (= *conserver en bon état*) [+ *propriété, bâtiment*] to maintain, see to the upkeep of, look after; [+ *vêtement*] to look after; [+ *route, machine*] to maintain; **~ un jardin** to look after *ou* see to the upkeep of a garden; **ce meuble s'entretient facilement** it's easy to look after this piece of furniture; **maison difficile à ~** house which is difficult to keep
[b] (= *faire vivre*) [+ *famille*] to support, keep, maintain; [+ *maîtresse*] to keep, support; [+ *armée*] to keep, maintain; [+ *troupe de théâtre*] to support; **se faire ~ par qn** to be kept *ou* supported by sb
[c] (= *faire durer*) [+ *souvenir*] to keep alive; [+ *amitié*] to keep alive, keep going; [+ *haine*] to fuel; **j'entretiens de grands espoirs** I have high hopes; **~ l'inquiétude de qn** to keep sb feeling uneasy, keep sb in a state of anxiety; **~ des rapports suivis avec qn** to be in constant contact with sb; **~ une correspondance suivie avec qn** to keep up a regular correspondence with sb, correspond regularly with sb; **~ l'illusion que ...** to maintain the illusion that ...; **l'air marin entretient une perpétuelle humidité** the sea air maintains a constant state of humidity; **~ le feu** to keep the fire going *ou* burning; **il m'a entretenu dans l'erreur** he didn't disabuse me (of it); **j'entretiens des craintes à son sujet** I am somewhat anxious about him; **~ sa forme** to keep o.s. in (good) shape, keep (o.s.) fit
[d] (*frm* = *converser*) **~ qn** to converse with *ou* speak to sb; **il m'a entretenu pendant une heure** we conversed for an hour, he conversed with me for an hour; **il a entretenu l'auditoire de ses voyages** he addressed the audience *ou* spoke to the audience about his travels
[2] **s'entretenir** VPR [a] (= *converser*) **s'~ avec qn** to converse with *ou* speak to sb (**de** about); **ils s'entretenaient à voix basse** they were conversing in hushed tones
[b] (= *pourvoir à ses besoins*) to support o.s., be self-supporting; **il s'entretient tout seul maintenant** he is completely self-supporting now, he supports himself entirely on his own now
[c] (= *prendre soin de soi*) **s'~ (en bonne forme)** to keep o.s. in (good) shape, keep (o.s.) fit

entretenu, e [ɑ̃tʀət(ə)ny] (*ptp de* entretenir) ADJ [*personne*] kept (*épith*); **jardin bien/mal ~** well-/badly-kept garden, well-/badly-tended garden; **maison bien ~e** (*propre et rangée*) well-kept house; (*en bon état*) house in a good state of repair, well-maintained house; **maison mal ~e** (*sale et mal rangée*) badly-kept house; (*en mauvais état*) house in a bad state of repair, badly-maintained house

▼ **entretien** [ɑ̃tʀətjɛ̃] NM [a] (= *conservation*) [*jardin, maison*] upkeep; [*route*] maintenance, upkeep; [*machine*] maintenance; **cher à l'~** expensive to maintain; **d'un ~ facile** [*vêtement*]

easy to look after; [*surface*] easy to clean; [*voiture, appareil*] easy to maintain; **visite d'~** service; **agent d'~** cleaning operative; **l'~ ◊ le service d'~** (*maintenance*) the maintenance services; (*nettoiement*) the cleaning service → **produit**
[b] (= *aide à la subsistance*) [*famille, étudiant*] keep, support; [*armée, corps de ballet*] maintenance, keep; **pourvoir à l'~ de** [+ *famille*] to keep, support, maintain; [+ *armée*] to keep, maintain
[c] (= *conversation*) conversation; (= *entrevue*) interview; (= *discussion*) discussion; (*Pol*) **~(s)** talks, discussions; **~ télévisé** televised interview; **~ téléphonique** telephone conversation; **~ d'embauche** job interview; **passer un ~** to have an interview; **nous aurons un ~ à Francfort avec nos collègues** we shall be having discussions in Frankfurt with our colleagues; **il est en ~** (*gén*) he's seeing someone, he's with someone; (*avec un candidat*) he's interviewing

entretoise [ɑ̃tʀətwaz] NF [*charpente*] diagonal *ou* angle brace, cross strut *ou* tie; [*machine*] cross arm

entre(-)tuer (s') [ɑ̃tʀətɥe] ▸ conjug 1 ◂ VPR to kill one another *ou* each other

entrevoir [ɑ̃tʀəvwaʀ] ▸ conjug 30 ◂ VT [a] (= *voir indistinctement*) to make out; (= *pressentir*) [+ *objections, solutions, complications*] to foresee, anticipate; [+ *amélioration*] to glimpse; **je commence à ~ la vérité** I'm beginning to see the truth, I'm beginning to have an inkling of the truth; (*lit, fig*) **~ la lumière au bout du tunnel** to see (the) light at the end of the tunnel [b] (= *apercevoir brièvement : gén*) to catch a glimpse of, catch sight of; [+ *visiteur*] to see briefly; **vous n'avez fait qu'~ les difficultés** you have only half seen the difficulties

entrevue [ɑ̃tʀəvy] NF (= *discussion*) meeting; (= *audience*) interview; (*Pol*) talks, discussions, meeting; **se présenter à** *ou* **pour une ~** to come for *ou* to an interview

entrisme [ɑ̃tʀism] NM entryism

entriste [ɑ̃tʀist] ADJ, NMF entryist

entropie [ɑ̃tʀɔpi] NF entropy

entrouvert, e [ɑ̃tʀuvɛʀ, ɛʀt] (*ptp de* entrouvrir) ADJ (*gén*) half-open; [*fenêtre, porte*] ajar (*attrib*), half-open; **ses lèvres ~es** her parted lips

entrouvrir [ɑ̃tʀuvʀiʀ] ▸ conjug 18 ◂ [1] VT to half-open [2] **s'entrouvrir** VPR (*gén*) to half-open; [*lèvres*] to part

entuber: [ɑ̃tybe] ▸ conjug 1 ◂ VT (= *duper*) to con:, do* (*Brit*); **se faire ~** to be conned: *ou* be done* (*Brit*); **il m'a entubé de 50 F** he did *ou* diddled* me out of 50 francs

enturbanné, e [ɑ̃tyʀbane] ADJ turbaned

énucléation [enykleasjɔ̃] NF (*Méd*) enucleation; [*fruit*] pitting, stoning (*Brit*)

énucléer [enyklee] ▸ conjug 1 ◂ VT (*Méd*) to enucleate; [+ *fruit*] to pit, stone

énumératif, -ive [enymeʀatif, iv] ADJ enumerative

énumération [enymeʀasjɔ̃] NF enumeration, listing

énumérer [enymeʀe] ▸ conjug 6 ◂ VT to enumerate, list

énurésie [enyʀezi] NF enuresis

énurétique [enyʀetik] [1] ADJ enuretic [2] NMF enuretic person

env. (ABRÉV = **environ**) approx.

envahir [ɑ̃vaiʀ] ▸ conjug 2 ◂ VT [a] (*Mil, gén*) to invade, overrun; [*douleur, sentiment*] to overcome, sweep through; **le sommeil l'envahissait** he was overcome by sleep, sleep was creeping *ou* stealing over him; **le jardin est envahi par les orties** the garden is overrun *ou* overgrown with nettles; **la foule envahit la place** the crowd swarmed *ou* swept into the square; **cette mode a déjà envahi le pays** this fashion has already swept across the country *ou* tak-

➤ GRAMMAIRE ACTIVE: **entretien** 46.3, 46.5

en the country by storm; **leurs produits enva-hissent notre marché** our market is becoming flooded *ou* overrun with their products ⓑ (*gén hum* = *déranger*) **~ qn** to invade sb's privacy, intrude on sb's privacy

envahissant, e [ãvaisã, ãt] ADJ [*personne, présence*] intrusive; [*enfant*] demanding; [*passion*] all-consuming; [*odeur, goût*] strong, pervasive

envahissement [ãvaismã] NM invasion

envahisseur [ãvaisœʀ] ① ADJ M invading ② NM invader

envasement [ãvazmã] NM [*port*] silting up

envaser [ãvaze] ▸ conjug 1 ◂ ① VT [+ *port*] to silt up ② **s'envaser** VPR [*port*] to silt up; [*bateau*] to stick in the mud; [*épave*] to sink in(to) the mud

enveloppant, e [ãv(ə)lɔpã, ãt] ADJ enveloping (*épith*); (*Mil*) surrounding (*épith*), encircling (*épith*); **mouvement ~** encircling movement

enveloppe [ãv(ə)lɔp] NF ⓐ (= *pli postal*) envelope; **~ gommée/autocollante** *ou* **auto-adhésive** stick-down/self-seal envelope; **~ rembourrée** *ou* **matelassée** padded bag; **à fenêtre** window envelope; **sous ~** [*envoyer*] under cover; **mettre une lettre sous ~** to put a letter in an envelope ⓑ (= *emballage*) (*gén*) covering; (*en papier, toile*) wrapping; (= *gaine*) [*graine*] husk; [*organe*] covering membrane; [*pneu*] cover, casing; [*dirigeable*] envelope; [*chaudière*] lagging, jacket; **dans une ~ de métal** in a metal casing ⓒ (= *apparence*) outward appearance, exterior; **un cœur d'or sous une rude ~** a heart of gold beneath a rough exterior ⓓ (*littér* = *corps*) **il a quitté son ~ mortelle** he has shuffled off *ou* shed his mortal coil (*littér*) ⓔ (*Math*) envelope ⓕ (= *somme d'argent*) sum of money; (= *crédits*) budget; **toucher une ~** (*pot-de-vin*) to get a bribe; (*gratification*) to get a bonus; (*départ en retraite*) to get a golden handshake; **~ de départ** gratuity; **~ budgétaire** budget; **l'~ de la recherche** the research budget; **le projet a reçu une ~ de 10 millions** the project was budgeted at 10 million

enveloppement [ãv(ə)lɔpmã] NM ⓐ (*Méd*) (= *action*) packing; (= *emplâtre*) pack; **~ d'algues** seaweed wrap ⓑ (*Mil*) [*ennemi*] surrounding, encirclement; **manœuvre d'~** pincer *ou* encircling movement

envelopper [ãv(ə)lɔpe] ▸ conjug 1 ◂ ① VT ⓐ [+ *objet, enfant*] to wrap (up); **voulez-vous que je vous l'enveloppe ?** shall I wrap it up for you?; (*hum*) **elle est assez enveloppée** she's well-padded*; (*propos*) **c'était très bien enveloppé** it was phrased nicely ⓑ (= *voiler*) [+ *pensée, parole*] to veil ⓒ (*gén littér* = *entourer*) [*brume*] to envelop, shroud; **le silence enveloppe la ville** the town is wrapped *ou* shrouded in silence; **la lumière enveloppe la campagne** the countryside is bathed in light; **événement enveloppé de mystère** event shrouded *ou* veiled in mystery; **~ qn du regard** to gaze at sb; **il l'enveloppa d'un regard tendre** he gave her a long loving look; **il enveloppa la plaine du regard** he took in the plain with his gaze, his eyes swept the plain; **~ qn de son affection** to envelop sb in one's affection, surround sb with one's affection; **~ dans sa réprobation†** to include in one's disapproval ⓓ (*Mil*) [+ *ennemi*] to surround, encircle ② **s'envelopper** VPR (*dans une couverture, un châle*) to wrap o.s. (**dans** in); **il s'enveloppa dans une cape** he wrapped *ou* swathed himself in a cape; (*hum*) **il s'enveloppa dans sa dignité** he assumed an air of dignity

envenimement [ãv(ə)nimmã] NM [*plaie*] poisoning; [*querelle*] embittering; [*situation*] worsening

envenimer [ãv(ə)nime] ▸ conjug 1 ◂ ① VT [+ *plaie*] to make septic, poison; [+ *querelle*] to inflame, fan the flames of; [+ *situation*] to inflame, aggravate ② **s'envenimer** VPR [*plaie*] to go septic, fester; [*querelle, situation*] to grow more bitter *ou* acrimonious

envergure [ãvɛʀgyʀ] NF ⓐ [*oiseau, avion*] wingspan; [*voile*] breadth ⓑ [*personne*] calibre; [*entreprise*] scale, scope; [*intelligence*] scope, range; **d'~ ◊ de grande ~** [*entreprise*] large-scale (*épith*); [*auteur, politicien*] of great stature; [*projet, réforme*] far-reaching; [*opération*] large-scale (*épith*), ambitious; **projet d'~ européenne** project of European dimensions; **prendre de l'~** [*entreprise, projet*] to expand; **ce projet manque d'~** this project is not far-reaching enough; **personnage sans ~** insignificant figure; **il a l'~ d'un chef d'État** he has the calibre *ou* stature of a head of state

envers[1] [ãvɛʀ] PRÉP towards, to; **cruel/traître ~ qn** cruel/a traitor to sb; **~ et contre tous** *ou* **tout** in the face of *ou* despite all opposition; **son attitude ~ moi** his attitude towards *ou* to me; **son dédain ~ les biens matériels** his disdain for *ou* of material possessions; **sa patience ~ elle** his patience with her

envers[2] [ãvɛʀ] NM ⓐ [*étoffe*] wrong side; [*vêtement*] wrong side, inside; [*papier*] back; [*médaille*] reverse (side); [*feuille d'arbre*] underside; [*peau d'animal*] (*Tricot*) **sur l'~** on the wrong side; **l'~ et l'endroit** the wrong (side) and the right side; (*fig*) **quand on connaît l'~ du décor** *ou* **du tableau** when you know what is going on underneath it all, when you know the other side of the picture ⓑ **à l'~** (*verticalement*) upside down, wrong side up; (*dans l'ordre inverse*) backwards; **mettre sa chemise à l'~** (*devant derrière*) to put one's shirt on back to front; (*dedans dehors*) to put one's shirt on inside out; **il a mis la maison à l'~*** he turned the house upside down *ou* inside out; **tout marche** *ou* **va à l'~** everything is haywire *ou* is upside down *ou* is going wrong; (*fig*) **faire qch à l'~** (*à rebours*) to do sth the wrong way round; (*mal*) to do sth all wrong; (*fig*) **elle avait la tête à l'~** her mind was in a whirl → **maille, monde**

envi [ãvi] **◆ à l'envi** LOC ADV (*littér*) [*répéter*] over and over again; **ils dénoncent ces abus à l'~** they ceaselessly condemn these abuses; **je pourrais multiplier les exemples à l'~** I could reel off a whole string of examples

enviable [ãvjabl] ADJ enviable; **peu ~** unenviable

▾ **envie** [ãvi] NF ⓐ (= *désir*) desire (**de qch** for sth); (*plus fort*) craving, longing (**de qch** for sth); **cette ~ de changement lui passa vite** he soon lost this desire *ou* longing for change; **avoir ~ de qch/qn** to want sth/sb; **j'ai ~ de ce livre** I want *ou* would like that book; **je n'ai pas ~ de lui** I don't want him; **avoir une ~ de chocolat** to have a craving *ou* longing for chocolate; **avoir des ~s de vacances** to feel like a holiday; **j'ai des ~s de meurtre** I could kill somebody, I feel like killing somebody; **des ~s de femme enceinte** pregnant woman's cravings; (*fig*) **elle a des ~s de femme enceinte** she has sudden cravings; **ce gâteau me fait ~** I like the look of that cake, I fancy (*Brit*) that cake; **si ça te fait ~** if you like, if you feel like it; **je vais lui faire passer l'~ de recommencer*** I'll make sure he won't feel like doing that again in a hurry; **l'~ l'a pris de** *ou* **il lui a pris l'~ d'y aller** he suddenly felt like *ou* fancied (*Brit*) going there, he suddenly felt the urge to go there ⓑ **avoir ~ de faire qch** to want to do sth, feel like doing sth; **j'ai ~ d'y aller** I feel like going, I would like to go; **je n'ai aucune ~ de le revoir** I have absolutely no desire to see him again; **avoir bien/presque ~ de faire qch** to have a good *ou* great mind/half a mind to do sth; **avoir ~ de rire** to feel like laughing; **avoir ~ de vomir** to feel sick, feel like vomiting; **cela lui a**

donné (l')~ de rire it made him want to laugh; **j'ai ~ qu'il s'en aille** I would like him to go away, I wish he would go away → **mourir** ⓒ (*euph*) **avoir ~*** to need the toilet *ou* the loo* (*Brit*); **être pris d'une ~ pressante** to have a sudden urge to go to the toilet, be taken short* (*Brit*) → **pisser** ⓓ (= *convoitise*) envy; **mon bonheur lui fait ~** he envies my happiness, my happiness makes him envious (of me); **ça fait ~** it makes you envious; **regarder qch avec (un œil d')~ ◊** **jeter des regards d'~ sur qch** to look enviously at sth, cast envious eyes *ou* glances at sth; **digne d'~** enviable ■ (*PROV*) **il vaut mieux faire ~ que pitié** (*gén*) it's better to be envied than pitied; (*pour personne grosse*) it's better to be a bit on the plump side than too thin ⓔ (*Anat*) (*sur la peau*) birthmark; (*autour des ongles*) hangnail

envier [ãvje] ▸ conjug 7 ◂ VT [+ *personne, bonheur*] to envy, be envious of; **je vous envie votre maison** I envy you your house, I wish I had a house like yours; **je vous envie (de pouvoir le faire)** I envy you *ou* I'm envious of you (being able to do it); **ce pays n'a rien à ~ au nôtre** (*il est mieux*) that country has no cause to be jealous of us; (*il est aussi mauvais*) that country is just as badly off as we are, there's nothing to choose between that country and ours

envieusement [ãvjøzmã] ADV enviously

envieux, -ieuse [ãvjø, jøz] ① ADJ envious; **être ~ de** to be envious of, envy ② NM,F envious person; **faire des ~** to excite *ou* arouse envy

environ [ãviʀɔ̃] ① ADV about, or thereabouts, or so; **c'est à 100 km ~ d'ici** it's about 100 km from here, it's 100 km or so from here; **il était ~ 3 heures** it was about 3 o'clock, it was 3 o'clock or thereabouts ② **les environs** NMPL ⓐ [*ville*] (*gén*) surroundings; (= *la banlieue*) outskirts; **les ~s sont superbes** the surrounding area is gorgeous; **dans les ~s** in the vicinity *ou* neighbourhood (**de** of); **qu'y a-t-il à voir dans les ~s?** what is there to see around about here? ⓑ (= *estimation*) **aux ~s de 3 heures** 3 o'clock or thereabouts, some time around 3 o'clock, (round) about (*Brit*) 3 o'clock; **aux ~s de 1 000 F** in the region of 1,000 francs

environnant, e [ãviʀɔnã, ãt] ADJ surrounding

environnement [ãviʀɔnmã] NM (*gén, Écol, Ordin*) environment; **~ économique/international/fiscal** economic/international/tax environment; **~ familial** family background

environnemental, e (*pl* -**aux**) [ãviʀɔnmãtal, o] ADJ environmental

environnementaliste [ãviʀɔnmãtalist(ə)] NMF environmentalist

environner [ãviʀɔne] ▸ conjug 1 ◂ VT to surround, encircle; **s'~ d'experts** to surround o.s. with experts

envisageable [ãvizaʒabl] ADJ conceivable

▾ **envisager** [ãvizaʒe] ▸ conjug 3 ◂ VT ⓐ (= *considérer*) to view, envisage, contemplate; **il envisage l'avenir de manière pessimiste** he views *ou* contemplates the future with pessimism, he has a pessimistic view of the future ⓑ (= *prévoir*) to envisage, consider; **~ de faire** to be thinking of doing, consider *ou* contemplate doing; **nous envisageons des transformations** we are thinking of *ou* envisaging changes; **nous n'avions pas envisagé cela** we hadn't envisaged that; **on ne peut raisonnablement ~ qu'il accepte** he cannot reasonably be expected to accept

envoi [ãvwa] NM ⓐ (*NonC*) [*colis, lettre*] sending (off); [*vœux, amitiés, message radio*] sending; (*Comm*) [*marchandises*] dispatching, sending off; (*par bateau*) shipment; [*argent*] sending, remittance; **faire un ~ de vivres** to send (a consignment of) supplies; **faire un ~ de fonds**

to remit cash; **~ contre remboursement** cash on delivery; **l'~ des couleurs** the hoisting of the colours; **coup d'~** (*Sport*) kick-off; [*festival*] start, opening; [*série d'événements*] start, beginning; **le spectacle qui donnera le coup d'~ du festival** the show which will kick off *ou* open the festival **b** (= *colis*) parcel; **~ de bouteilles** consignment of bottles; **«~ en nombre »** "mass mailing" **c** (*Littérat*) envoi

envol [ɑ̃vɔl] NM [*oiseau*] taking flight *ou* wing; [*avion*] takeoff; [*âme, pensée*] flight; **prendre son ~** [*oiseau*] to take flight *ou* wing; [*avion*] to take off; [*pensée*] to soar, take off

envolée [ɑ̃vɔle] NF **a** (*dans un discours, un texte*) flight; **~ oratoire/poétique** flight of oratory/poetry; **dans une belle ~ lyrique, il a décrit les vertus du système** he waxed lyrical about the virtues of the system **b** (= *augmentation*) [*chômage, prix, monnaie*] surge (**de** in); **l'~ de leur parti dans les sondages** their party's dramatic *ou* meteoric rise in the polls **c** [*oiseaux*] flight

envoler (s') [ɑ̃vɔle] ▶ conjug 1 ◀ VPR **a** [*oiseau*] to fly away; [*avion*] to take off; **je m'envole pour Tokyo dans deux heures** my flight leaves *ou* I take off for Tokyo in two hours **b** (= *être emporté*) [*chapeau*] to blow off, be blown off; [*fumée, feuille, papiers*] to blow away **c** (= *passer*) [*temps*] to fly (past *ou* by); [*espoirs*] to vanish (into thin air); (* = *disparaître*) [*portefeuille, personne*] to disappear *ou* vanish (into thin air) **d** (= *augmenter*) [*prix, cours, chômage*] to soar; **il s'est envolé dans les sondages** his popularity rating has soared in the opinion polls

envoûtant, e [ɑ̃vutɑ̃, ɑ̃t] ADJ entrancing, bewitching, spellbinding

envoûtement [ɑ̃vutmɑ̃] NM bewitchment

envoûter [ɑ̃vute] ▶ conjug 1 ◀ VT to bewitch, cast a spell on; **être envoûté par qn** to be under sb's spell

envoûteur [ɑ̃vutœʀ] NM sorcerer

envoûteuse [ɑ̃vutøz] NF witch, sorceress

envoyé, e [ɑ̃vwaje] (*ptp de* **envoyer**) **1** ADJ [*remarque, réponse*] **(bien) ~** well-aimed, sharp; **ça, c'est ~ !** well said!, well done! **2** NM,F (*gén*) messenger; (*Pol*) envoy; (*Presse*) correspondent; (*Presse*) **notre ~ spécial** our special correspondent; **un ~ du ministère** a government official; **vous êtes l'~ du ciel!** you're heaven-sent!

▼**envoyer** [ɑ̃vwaje] ▶ conjug 8 ◀ **1** VT **a** (= *expédier*) [+ *colis, lettre*] to send (off); [+ *vœux, amitiés, message radio*] to send; (*Comm*) [+ *marchandises*] to dispatch, send off; (*par bateau*) to ship; [+ *argent*] to send, remit (*Admin*); **~ sa démission** to send in one's resignation; **~ sa candidature** to send in one's *ou* an application; **n'envoyez pas d'argent par la poste** do not send money by post; **envoie-moi un mot** drop me a line* **b** [+ *personne*] (*gén*) to send; (*en vacances, en courses*) to send (off) (**chez, auprès de** to); (*en mission*) [+ *émissaire, troupes*] to dispatch, send out; (*chez le médecin à un malade*) to refer; **envoie David à l'épicerie/aux nouvelles** send David to the grocer's/to see if there's any news; **ils l'avaient envoyé chez sa grand-mère pour les vacances** they had sent him (off) to his grandmother's for the holidays; (*fig*) **~ qn à la mort** to send sb to their death → **monde** **c** (= *lancer*) [+ *objet*] to throw, fling; (*avec force*) to hurl; [+ *obus*] to fire; [+ *signaux*] to send (out); (*Sport*) [+ *ballon*] to send; **~ des baisers à qn** to blow sb kisses; **~ des sourires à qn** to smile at sb; **~ des coups de pied/poing à qn** to kick/punch sb; **ne m'envoie pas ta fumée dans les yeux** don't blow (your) smoke in(to) my eyes; **il le lui a envoyé dans les dents** ou **les gencives** he really let him have it!*; (*Ftbl*) **~ le ballon au fond des filets** to put *ou* send the ball into the back of the net; **~ qn à terre** *ou* **au tapis** to knock sb down, knock

sb to the ground, floor sb; **~ un homme sur la Lune** to send a man to the moon; (*Naut*) **~ par le fond** to send down *ou* to the bottom **d** (*Mil*) **~ les couleurs** to run up *ou* hoist the colours **e** (*loc*) **~ chercher qn/qch** to send for sb/sth; **~ promener qn*** *ou* **balader qn*** ◇ **~ qn coucher*** ◇ **~ qn sur les roses*** to send sb packing*, send sb about their business; **~ valser** *ou* **dinguer qch*** to send sth flying*; **il a tout envoyé promener*** he chucked the whole thing in; **il ne le lui a pas envoyé dire*** he gave it to him straight*, he told him straight to his face

2 **s'envoyer*** VPR (= *subir, prendre*) [+ *corvée*] to get stuck* *ou* landed* with; [+ *bouteille*] to knock back*; [+ *nourriture*] to scoff*; **je m'enverrais des gifles*** I could kick myself*; **s'~ une fille/un mec** to have it off (*Brit*) *ou* get off (*US*) with a girl/a guy*; make it with a girl/a guy*; **s'~ en l'air** to have it off* (*Brit*), get some* (*US*)

envoyeur, -euse [ɑ̃vwajœʀ, øz] NM,F sender → **retour**

enzymatique [ɑ̃zimatik] ADJ enzymatic, enzymic

enzyme [ɑ̃zim] NM *ou* F enzyme; **~ de restriction** restriction enzyme

éocène [eɔsɛn] **1** ADJ Eocene **2** NM **l'~** the Eocene

Éole [eɔl] NM Aeolus

éolien, -ienne [eɔljɛ̃, jɛn] **1** ADJ wind (*épith*), aeolian (*littér*) → **énergie, harpe** **2** **éolienne** NF windmill, windpump

EOR [eɔɛʀ] NM (ABRÉV = **élève officier de réserve**) → **élève**

éosine [eɔzin] NF eosin

épagneul, e [epaɲœl] NM,F spaniel; **~ breton** Brittany spaniel

épais, -aisse [epɛ, ɛs] **1** ADJ **a** (*gén*) [*chevelure, peinture*] thick; [*neige*] thick, deep; [*barbe*] bushy, thick; [*silence*] deep; [*personne, corps*] thickset; [*nuit*] pitch-black; **cloison épaisse de 5 cm** partition 5 cm thick; **j'ai la langue épaisse** my tongue is coated *ou* furred up (*Brit*); **au plus ~ de la forêt** in the depths of the forest; **tu n'es pas bien ~** you're not exactly fat **b** (*péj = inhabile*) [*esprit*] dull; [*personne*] dense, thick(headed); [*mensonge, plaisanterie*] clumsy **2** ADV **semer ~** to sow thick *ou* thickly; **il n'y en a pas ~!** there's not much of it!

épaisseur [epesœʀ] NF **a** (*gén*) thickness; [*neige, silence*] depth; **la neige a un mètre d'~** there is a metre of snow, the snow is a metre deep; **creuser une niche dans l'~ d'un mur** to hollow out a niche in a wall **b** (= *couche*) layer, thickness; **prenez deux ~s de tissu** take two thicknesses *ou* a double thickness of material; **plier une couverture en double ~** to fold a blanket double **c** (= *richesse*) [*œuvre*] substance, depth; [*personne*] depth; **ce personnage manque d'~** this character lacks depth *ou* is rather flat

épaissir [epesiʀ] ▶ conjug 2 ◀ **1** VT [+ *substance*] to thicken; [+ *mystère*] to deepen; **l'air était épaissi par les fumées** the air was thick with smoke; **l'âge lui épaissit les traits** his features are becoming coarse with age; **ce manteau m'épaissit beaucoup** this coat makes me look much broader *ou* fatter **2** VI to get thicker, thicken; **il a beaucoup épaissi** he has filled out a lot **3** **s'épaissir** VPR [*substance, brouillard*] to thicken, get thicker; [*chevelure, feuillage*] to get thicker; [*ténèbres*] to deepen; **sa taille s'épaissit** his waist is getting thicker, he's getting stouter around the waist; **le mystère s'épaissit** the mystery deepens, the plot thickens

épaississant, e [epesisɑ̃, ɑ̃t] **1** ADJ thickening **2** NM thickener

épaississement [epesismɑ̃] NM thickening

épanchement [epɑ̃ʃmɑ̃] NM [*sang*] effusion; [*sentiments*] outpouring; (*Méd*) **avoir un ~ de synovie** to have water on the knee

épancher [epɑ̃ʃe] ▶ conjug 1 ◀ **1** VT [+ *sentiments*] (*irrités*) to give vent to, vent; (*tendres*) to pour forth **2** **s'épancher** VPR [*personne*] to open one's heart, pour out one's feelings (**auprès de** to); [*sang*] to pour out

épandage [epɑ̃daʒ] NM (*Agr*) manure spreading, manuring → **champ**

épandre [epɑ̃dʀ] ▶ conjug 41 ◀ **1** VT (†, *littér*) [+ *liquide, tendresse*] to pour forth (*littér*); (*Agr*) [+ *fumier*] to spread **2** **s'épandre** VPR (*littér*) to spread

épanoui, e [epanwi] (*ptp de* **épanouir**) ADJ [*fleur*] in full bloom (*attrib*); [*visage, sourire*] radiant, beaming (*épith*); [*personne*] totally fulfilled (*attrib*); **c'est quelqu'un de très ~** he's very much at one with himself *ou* with the world

épanouir [epanwiʀ] ▶ conjug 2 ◀ **1** VT (*littér*) [+ *fleur*] to open out; [+ *branches, pétales*] to open *ou* spread out; [+ *visage*] to light up; **la maternité l'a épanouie** she really blossomed when she became a mother **2** **s'épanouir** VPR [*fleur*] to bloom, come out, open up *ou* out; [*visage*] to light up; [*personne*] to blossom, bloom; [*vase*] to open out, curve outwards; **à cette nouvelle il s'épanouit** his face lit up at the news; **s'~ dans sa profession** to find one's profession very fulfilling

épanouissant, e [epanwisɑ̃, ɑ̃t] ADJ totally fulfilling

épanouissement [epanwismɑ̃] NM [*fleur*] blooming, coming out, opening up *ou* out; [*visage*] lighting up; [*personne*] blossoming, blooming; **c'est une industrie en plein ~** it's a booming industry

épargnant, e [epaʀɲɑ̃, ɑ̃t] NM,F saver, investor; **petits ~s** small savers *ou* investors

épargne [epaʀɲ] NF (= *somme*) savings; (= *action d'épargner*) **l'~** saving; **~ de temps/d'argent** saving of time/money; **~ forcée/longue/ liquide** forced/long-term/liquid savings; **~ logement** home-buyers' savings scheme; **~ retraite** retirement savings scheme → **caisse, compte, plan¹**

épargner [epaʀɲe] ▶ conjug 1 ◀ VT **a** (= *économiser*) [+ *argent, nourriture, temps, forces*] to save; **~ 10 F sur une somme** to save 10 francs out of a sum; **~ sur la nourriture** to save *ou* make a saving on food; **ils n'ont pas épargné le poivre !*** they haven't stinted *ou* skimped on the pepper!; **~ pour ses vieux jours** to save (up) for one's old age, put something aside for one's old age; **je n'épargnerai rien pour le faire** I'll spare nothing to get it done; **il n'a pas épargné sa peine** he spared no effort (**pour** to) **b** (= *éviter*) **~ qch à qn** to spare sb sth; **je vous épargne les détails** I'll spare you the details; **pour t'~ des explications inutiles** to save giving you *ou* to spare you useless explanations; **pour m'~ la peine de venir** to save *ou* spare myself the bother of coming **c** (= *ménager*) [+ *ennemi*] to spare; **l'épidémie a épargné cette région** that region was spared the epidemic

éparpillement [epaʀpijmɑ̃] NM (= *action*) [*objets*] scattering; [*troupes*] dispersal; [*points de vente*] distribution, scattering; [*efforts, talent*] dissipation; (= *état*) [*troupes, succursales*] dispersal; **les maisons rendait les communications très difficiles** the fact that the houses were so scattered made communications difficult

éparpiller [epaʀpije] ▶ conjug 1 ◀ **1** VT [+ *objets, cendres*] to scatter; [+ *troupes*] to disperse; [+ *points de vente*] to distribute, scatter; [+ *efforts, talent*] to dissipate **2** **s'éparpiller** VPR **a** [*feuilles, foule*] to scatter; **maisons qui s'éparpillent dans la campagne** houses dotted about the countryside **b** [*personne*] **il**

s'éparpille beaucoup trop he spreads himself too thin; **tu t'es trop éparpillé dans tes lectures/recherches** you've spread yourself too thin in your reading/research

épars, e [epar, aRs] ADJ (littér) scattered

épatant, e*† [epatɑ̃, ɑ̃t] ADJ splendid*

épate* [epat] NF (péj) **l'~** showing off*; **faire de l'~** to show off*

épaté, e [epate] (ptp de **épater**) ADJ [vase] flat-bottomed; [nez] flat

épatement [epatmɑ̃] NM [a] [nez] flatness [b]* (= surprise) amazement

épater [epate] ▸conjug 1 ◂ [1] VT* (= étonner) to amaze, stagger*; (= impressionner) to impress; **pour ~ le bourgeois** to shake ou shock middle-class attitudes; **ça t'épate, hein!** how about that!*, what do you think of that! → **galerie** [2] **s'épater** VPR [objet, colonne] to spread out

épaulard [epolar] NM killer whale

épaule [epol] NF (Anat, Culin) shoulder; **large d'~s** broad-shouldered; **~ d'agneau** shoulder of lamb; **donner un coup d'~ à qn** to knock ou bump sb with one's shoulder; **tout repose sur vos ~s** everything rests on your shoulders; (fig) **il n'ont pas les ~s assez larges ou solides** (financièrement) they are not in a strong enough financial position → **hausser**, **tête**

épaulé-jeté (pl **épaulés-jetés**) [epole ʒ(ə)te] NM clean-and-jerk; **il soulève 150 kg à l'~** he can do a clean-and-jerk using 150 kg

épaulement [epolmɑ̃] NM (= mur) retaining wall; (= rempart) breastwork, epaulement; (Géol) escarpment

épauler [epole] ▸conjug 1 ◂ VT [a] [+ personne] to back up, support; **il faut s'~ dans la vie** people must help ou support each other in life; **il a été bien épaulé par son frère** his brother gave him a lot of help ou support [b] [+ fusil] to raise (to the shoulder); **il épaula puis tira** he took aim ou he raised his rifle and fired [c] (Tech) [+ mur] to support, retain [d] (Couture) [+ vêtement] to add shoulder pads to

épaulette [epolɛt] NF (Mil) epaulette; (= bretelle) shoulder strap; (= rembourrage d'un vêtement) shoulder pad

épave [epav] NF [a] (= navire, voiture) wreck; (= débris) piece of wreckage, wreckage (NonC); (= restes) flotsam (and jetsam) (NonC) [b] (Jur = objet perdu) derelict [c] (= restes) ruins; (= loque humaine) human wreck

épée [epe] NF [a] (= arme) sword; (Escrime) épée; **~ de Damoclès** Sword of Damocles; **l'~ nue ou à la main** with drawn sword; **c'est un coup d'~ dans l'eau** it's a complete waste of time → **cape, noblesse, rein** [b] (= escrimeur) swordsman; (= escrimeuse) swordswoman

épeiche [epɛʃ] NF great spotted woodpecker

épeichette [epɛʃɛt] NF lesser-spotted woodpecker

épeire [epɛR] NF garden spider

épéiste [epeist] NMF épéeist

épeler [ep(ə)le] ▸conjug 4 ou 5 ◂ VT [+ mot] to spell; [+ texte] to spell out

épépiner [epepine] VT to deseed, seed; **raisins épépinés** seedless grapes

éperdu, e [epɛRdy] ADJ [a] [personne] distraught, overcome; **~ de douleur/de terreur** distraught ou frantic ou out of one's mind with grief/terror; **~ de joie** overcome ou beside o.s. with joy [b] [gratitude] boundless; [regard] wild, distraught; [amour] passionate; [fuite] headlong, frantic; **désir/besoin ~ de bonheur** frantic desire/need of happiness

éperdument [epɛRdymɑ̃] ADV [crier, travailler] frantically, desperately; [aimer] passionately, madly; **je m'en moque ~** I just don't care less

éperlan [epɛRlɑ̃] NM (Zool) smelt

éperon [ep(ə)Rɔ̃] NM [cavalier, coq, montagne] spur; (Naut) [galère] ram; [pont] cutwater; **~ rocheux** rocky outcrop ou spur

éperonner [ep(ə)Rɔne] ▸conjug 1 ◂ VT [+ cheval] to spur (on); [+ navire] to ram; [+ personne] to spur on

épervier [epɛRvje] NM [a] (Orn) sparrowhawk [b] (= filet) cast(ing) net

éphèbe [efɛb] NM (Hist) ephebe; (iro, péj) beautiful young man

éphémère [efemɛR] [1] ADJ [bonheur, succès] fleeting, short-lived, ephemeral (frm); [moment] fleeting; [mouvement, règne, publication] short-lived; **le caractère ~ de la gloire** the transient nature of fame; **~ ministre, il ... ** having made a brief appearance as a minister, he ... [2] NM mayfly, ephemera (SPÉC)

éphéméride [efemeRid] NF [a] (= calendrier) block calendar, tear-off calendar [b] (Astron = tables) **~s** ephemeris sg

épi [epi] NM [a] [blé, maïs] ear; [fleur] spike; [cheveux] tuft; **les blés sont en ~s** the corn is in the ear [b] (= jetée) breakwater, groyne, groin [c] (Aut) **être garé en ~** to be parked at an angle to the kerb [d] **~ de faîtage** finial

épice [epis] NF spice; **quatre ~s** allspice → **pain**

épicé, e [epise] (ptp de **épicer**) ADJ [viande, plat] highly spiced, spicy; [goût] spicy; [histoire] spicy, juicy*

épicéa [episea] NM spruce

épicentre [episɑ̃tR] NM epicentre

épicer [epise] ▸conjug 3 ◂ VT [+ mets] to spice; [+ histoire] to add spice to

épicerie [episRi] NF (= magasin) grocery, grocer's (shop (Brit) ou store (US)); (= nourriture) groceries; (= métier) grocery trade; **rayon ~** grocery stand ou counter; **aller à l'~** to go to the grocer's ou grocery; **~ fine** ≈ delicatessen

épicier, -ière [episje, jɛR] NM,F (gén) grocer; (en fruits et légumes) greengrocer (Brit), grocer (US); (péj) **d'~** [idées, mentalité] small-town (épith), parochial

Épicure [epikyR] NM Epicurus

épicurien, -ienne [epikyRjɛ̃, jɛn] ADJ, NM,F (= gourmet) epicurean; (Philo) Epicurean

épicurisme [epikyRism] NM epicureanism

épidémie [epidemi] NF epidemic; **~ de grippe** flu epidemic

épidémiologie [epidemjɔlɔʒi] NF epidemiology

épidémiologique [epidemjɔlɔʒik] ADJ epidemiological

épidémique [epidemik] ADJ (lit) epidemic; (fig) contagious, catching (attrib)

épiderme [epidɛRm] NM epidermis (SPÉC), skin; **elle a l'~ délicat** she has delicate skin

épidermique [epidɛRmik] ADJ [a] (Anat) skin (épith), epidermal (SPÉC), epidermic (SPÉC); **blessure ~** (surface) scratch, skin wound [b] (fig) [réaction] instinctive, visceral; **je le déteste, c'est ~** I hate him, I just can't help it

épididyme [epididim] NM epididymis

épier [epje] ▸conjug 7 ◂ VT [+ personne] to spy on; [+ geste] to watch closely; [+ bruit] to listen out for; [+ occasion] to be on the look-out for, look (out) for, watch for

épieu [epjø] NM spear

épigastre [epigastR] NM epigastrium

épiglotte [epiglɔt] NF epiglottis

épigone [epigɔn] NM (Littérat) epigone

épigramme [epigRam] NF epigram

épigraphe [epigRaf] NF epigraph; **mettre un vers en ~** to use a line as an epigraph

épigraphique [epigRafik] ADJ epigraphic

épilateur [epilatœR] NM hair remover

épilation [epilasjɔ̃] NF removal of (unwanted) hair; [sourcils] plucking; **~ à la cire** waxing; **~ électrique** hair removal by electrolysis

épilatoire [epilatwaR] ADJ depilatory, hair-removing (épith)

épilepsie [epilɛpsi] NF epilepsy

épileptique [epilɛptik] ADJ, NMF epileptic

épiler [epile] ▸conjug 1 ◂ [1] VT [+ jambes] to remove the hair from; [+ sourcils] to pluck; **se faire ~ les aisselles** to have one's underarm hair removed [2] **s'épiler** VPR **elle s'épilait les jambes** she was removing the hair(s) from her legs; **s'~ les jambes à la cire** to wax one's legs; **s'~ les sourcils** to pluck one's eyebrows

épilogue [epilɔg] NM (Littérat) epilogue; (fig) conclusion, dénouement

épiloguer [epilɔge] ▸conjug 1 ◂ VI (parfois péj) to hold forth (**sur** on), go on* (**sur** about), expatiate (frm) (**sur** upon)

épinard [epinaR] NM (Bot) spinach; (Culin) **~s** spinach (NonC) → **beurre**

épine [epin] NF [a] [buisson] thorn, prickle; [hérisson, oursin] spine, prickle; [porc-épic] quill; **~ dorsale** backbone; **vous m'enlevez une belle ~ du pied** you have got me out of a spot* [b] (= arbre) thorn bush; **~ blanche** hawthorn; **~ noire** blackthorn

épinette [epinɛt] NF [a] (Mus) spinet [b] (Can) spruce; **~ blanche/noire** white/black spruce; **~ rouge** tamarack, hackmatack [c] (Agr) coop

épineux, -euse [epinø, øz] [1] ADJ [plante] thorny, prickly; [problème] thorny, tricky, ticklish; [situation] tricky, ticklish, sensitive; [caractère] prickly, touchy [2] NM prickly shrub ou bush

épinglage [epɛ̃glaʒ] NM pinning

épingle [epɛ̃gl] NF pin; **~ à chapeau** hatpin; **~ à cheveux** hairpin; **virage en ~ à cheveux** hairpin bend (Brit) ou curve (US); **~ de cravate** tie clip, tiepin; **~ à linge** clothes peg (Brit) ou pin (US); **~ de nourrice** ou **de sûreté** safety pin; (grand modèle) nappy (Brit) ou diaper (US) pin; **tirer son ~ du jeu** (= bien manœuvrer) to play one's game well; (= s'en sortir à temps) to extricate o.s. → **monter²**, **quatre**

épingler [epɛ̃gle] ▸conjug 1 ◂ VT [a] (= attacher) to pin (on) (**à, sur** to); **~ ses cheveux** to pin up one's hair; (Couture) **~ une robe** to pin up a dress [b]* (= arrêter) to nab*, nick* (Brit); **se faire ~** to get nabbed* ou nicked* (Brit) [c] (= dénoncer) to slam*, criticize (severely); **il a épinglé le gouvernement** he laid into* ou slammed* the government, he took a swipe at the government

épinglette [epɛ̃glɛt] NF lapel badge

épinière [epinjɛR] ADJ F → **moelle**

épinoche [epinɔʃ] NF stickleback

Épiphanie [epifani] NF **l'~** Epiphany, Twelfth Night; **à l'~** at Epiphany, on ou at Twelfth Night

épiphénomène [epifenɔmɛn] NM epiphenomenon

épiphyse [epifiz] NF epiphysis

épiphyte [epifit] [1] ADJ epiphytic(al), epiphytal [2] NM epiphyte

épique [epik] ADJ (lit, fig) epic; (hum) epic, dramatic

épiscopal, e (mpl **-aux**) [episkɔpal, o] ADJ episcopal; **palais ~** Bishop's ou episcopal palace

épiscopalien, -ienne [episkɔpaljɛ̃, jɛn] ADJ episcopalian; **l'Église épiscopalienne** the Episcopal Church

épiscopat [episkɔpa] NM episcopate, episcopacy

épiscope [episkɔp] NM episcope (Brit), opaque projector (US)

épisiotomie [epizjɔtɔmi] NF episiotomy

épisode [epizɔd] NM episode; **roman/film à ~s** serial, serialized novel/film; (Méd) **~ dépressif/infectieux** depressive/infectious phase

épisodique [epizɔdik] ADJ [a] (= occasionnel) [événement] occasional; [rôle] fleeting, transitory; **de façon ~** occasionally; **nous avons eu une relation ~ pendant deux ans** we had an on-off relationship for two years; **faire des apparitions ~s** to show up from time to time *ou* once in a while **b** (= *secondaire*) [*événement*] minor, of secondary importance; [*personnage*] minor, secondary

épisodiquement [epizɔdikmɑ̃] ADV occasionally

épisser [epise] ▶conjug 1◀ VT to splice

épissoir [episwaʀ] NM marlin(e) spike, splicing fid

épissure [episyʀ] NF splice; **on a dû faire une ~** we had to splice the two bits together

épistémologie [epistemɔlɔʒi] NF (*Philo*) epistemology; (*Sci*) epistemics *sg*

épistémologique [epistemɔlɔʒik] ADJ epistemological

épistolaire [epistɔlɛʀ] ADJ [*style*] epistolary; **être en relations ~s avec qn** to correspond with sb, be in correspondence with sb

épistolier, -ière [epistɔlje, jɛʀ] NM,F (*littér*) letter writer

épitaphe [epitaf] NF epitaph

épithélial, e (*mpl* **-iaux**) [epiteljal, jo] ADJ epithelial

épithélium [epiteljɔm] NM epithelium

épithète [epitɛt] NF **a** (*Gram*) attribute; **adjectif ~** attributive adjective **b** (= *qualificatif*) epithet

épître [epitʀ] NF epistle

épizootie [epizɔɔti, epizooti] NF epizootic (disease)

éploré, e [eplɔʀe] ADJ (*littér*) [*visage*] bathed in tears; [*personne*] tearful, weeping, in tears (*attrib*); [*voix*] tearful

épluchage [eplyʃaʒ] NM **a** [*fruits, légumes, crevettes*] peeling; [*salade, radis*] cleaning **b** [*journaux, comptes*] dissection

épluche-légumes [eplyʃlegym] NM INV (potato) peeler

éplucher [eplyʃe] ▶conjug 1◀ VT **a** [+ *fruits, légumes, crevettes*] to peel; [+ *salade, radis*] to clean **b** [+ *journaux, comptes*] to go over with a fine-tooth comb, dissect

épluchette [eplyʃɛt] NF (*Can*) corn-husking bee *ou* party

éplucheur, -euse [eplyʃœʀ, øz] **1** ADJ, NM (**couteau**) **~** (potato) peeler **2** NM,F (= *personne*) peeler; (*péj*) faultfinder **3** **éplucheuse** NF (= *machine*) potato-peeler

épluchure [eplyʃyʀ] NF **~ de pomme de terre** *etc* piece of potato *etc* peeling; **~s** peelings

épointer [epwɛ̃te] ▶conjug 1◀ VT [+ *aiguille*] to blunt; **crayon épointé** blunt pencil

éponge [epɔ̃ʒ] NF **a** (*Zool, gén*) sponge; **passer un coup d'~ sur qch** to give sth a (quick) sponge, wipe sth with a sponge; (*fig*) **passons l'~!** let's let bygones be bygones!, let's forget all about it!; **passons l'~ sur cette vieille querelle!** let's forget all about that old quarrel!, let's put that old quarrel behind us!; (*Boxe, fig*) **jeter l'~** to throw in the sponge *ou* towel; **~ métallique** scouring pad, scourer; **~ végétale** loofah (*Brit*), luffa (*US*) → **boire b** (*Tex*) (**tissu**) **~** (terry) towelling **c*** (= *ivrogne*) drunk*, drunkard

éponger [epɔ̃ʒe] ▶conjug 3◀ VT [+ *liquide*] to mop *ou* sponge up; [+ *plancher, visage*] to mop; [+ *dette*] to soak up, absorb; **s'~ le front** to mop one's brow

éponyme [epɔnim] **1** ADJ (*frm*) eponymous (*frm*); **le héros ~ de la pièce** the play's eponymous hero; **la chanson ~ de l'album** the title track of the album **2** NM eponym

épopée [epɔpe] NF (*lit, fig*) epic

époque [epɔk] NF **a** (*gén*) time; **les chansons de l'~** the songs of the time *ou* day; **j'étais jeune à l'~** I was young at the time; **à cette ~(-là)** at that time; **à l'~ où nous sommes** in this day and age; **être de son ~** to be in tune with one's time; **quelle ~!** what times these are!; **nous vivons une drôle d'~** these are strange times we're living in; **l'accordéon, les bals po-**pulaires, toute une ~!** accordions, open-air dances - a bygone era!

b (*Hist*) age, era, epoch; **chaque ~ a ses problèmes** every era has its problems; **l'~ révolutionnaire** the revolutionary era *ou* age *ou* epoch; **à l'~ des Grecs** at the time of *ou* in the age of the Greeks; **la Belle Époque** the Belle Époque, ≈ the Edwardian era; **cette invention a fait ~** it was an epoch-making invention; **il s'est trompé d'~** he was born in the wrong century; **à toutes les ~s** in every era; **documents d'~** contemporary (historical) documents; (*Mus*) **sur instruments d'~** on period *ou* authentic instruments

c (*Géol*) period; **à l'~ glaciaire** in the glacial period *ou* epoch

d (*Art* = *style*) period; **tableaux de la même ~** pictures of *ou* from the same period; **meubles d'~** antique *ou* period furniture; **ce vase n'est pas d'~** this vase isn't a genuine antique

épouiller [epuje] ▶conjug 1◀ VT to delouse

époumoner (s') [epumɔne] ▶conjug 1◀ VPR (*lit, fig*) to shout *ou* s.o. hoarse; **il s'époumonait à chanter** he was singing himself hoarse

épousailles [epuzaj] NFPL († *ou hum*) nuptials† (*aussi hum*)

épouse [epuz] NF wife, spouse (*frm ou hum*); **voulez-vous prendre pour ~ Jeanne Dumont?** do you take Jeanne Dumont to be your lawful wedded wife?

épousée [epuze] NF († *ou dial*) bride

épouser [epuze] ▶conjug 1◀ **1** VT **a** [+ *personne*] to marry, wed†; [+ *idée*] to embrace, espouse (*frm*); [+ *cause*] to espouse (*frm*), take up; **~ une grosse fortune** to marry into money **b** [*vêtement*] to mould, hug; [*route, tracé*] to follow; (*étroitement*) to hug; **cette robe épouse parfaitement les formes du corps** this dress moulds the curves of the body perfectly **2** **s'épouser** VPR (*littér*) [*personnes*] to marry, wed (*littér*)

épousseter [epuste] ▶conjug 4◀ VT (= *nettoyer*) to dust; (= *enlever*) to dust *ou* flick off

époustouflant, e* [epustuflɑ̃, ɑ̃t] ADJ staggering, amazing

époustoufler* [epustufle] ▶conjug 1◀ VT to stagger, flabbergast

épouvantable [epuvɑ̃tabl] ADJ (*gén*) terrible, dreadful; (= *très choquant*) appalling; **il a un caractère ~** he has a foul temper

épouvantablement [epuvɑ̃tabləmɑ̃] ADV terribly, dreadfully

épouvantail [epuvɑ̃taj] NM **a** (*à oiseaux*) scarecrow **b** (= *spectre*) spectre; **l'~ de la guerre/du chômage** the spectre of war/unemployment; **ils se servaient du communisme comme d'un ~** they were raising the bogeyman of communism **c** (*péj* = *personne*) scruff*; **j'ai l'air d'un ~ dans cette robe** I look a fright (*Brit*) *ou* like a scarecrow in this dress

épouvante [epuvɑ̃t] NF terror, (great) fear; **saisi d'~** terror-stricken; **il voyait arriver ce moment avec ~** he saw with dread the moment approaching; **roman/film d'~** horror story/film

épouvanter [epuvɑ̃te] ▶conjug 1◀ VT to terrify, appal, frighten; **s'~ de qch** to be appalled *ou* horrified by sth

époux [epu] NM husband, spouse (*frm ou hum*); **les ~** the (married) couple, the husband and wife; **les ~ Durand** the Durands, Mr and Mrs Durand; **voulez-vous prendre pour ~ Jean Legrand?** do you take Jean Legrand to be your lawful wedded husband?

époxy [epɔksi] ADJ INV epoxy

époxyde [epɔksid] NM epoxide

éprendre (s') [epʀɑ̃dʀ] ▶conjug 58◀ VPR (*littér*) **s'~ de** to fall in love with, become enamoured of (*littér*)

épreuve [epʀœv] NF **a** (= *essai*) test; **~ de résistance** strength test; **~ de résistance au choc/la chaleur** impact/heat test; **~ de force**trial of strength, confrontation; **~ de vérité** litmus *ou* acid test (*fig*); **faire l'~ d'un métal** to test a metal → **rude**

b (= *malheur*) ordeal, trial, hardship; **subir de rudes ~s** to suffer great hardships, undergo great trials *ou* ordeals; **savoir réagir dans l'~** to cope well in the face of adversity

c (*Scol*) test; **corriger les ~s d'un examen** to mark the examination papers; **~ orale** oral test; **~ écrite** written test *ou* paper

d (*Sport*) event; **~ de sélection** heat; **~ contre la montre** time trial; **~s sur piste** track events; **~ d'endurance** [*personne*] test of endurance, endurance test; (*Aut*) endurance test

e (*Typo*) proof; **premières/secondes ~s** first/second proofs; **corriger les ~s d'un livre** to proofread a book, correct the proofs of a book

f (*Photo*) print; (= *gravure*) proof; **~ (par) contact** contact print; (*Ciné*) **~s (de tournage)** rushes

g (*Hist*: *initiatique*) ordeal; **~ du feu** ordeal by fire

h **à l'~**: **mettre à l'~** to put to the test; (*Jur*) **mise à l'~** ≈ probation

i **à l'~ de gilet à l'~ des balles** bulletproof vest; **à l'~ du feu** fireproof; **résister à l'~ du temps** to stand the test of time

j **à toute ~** [*amitié, foi*] staunch; [*mur*] solid as a rock; **il a un courage à toute ~** he has unfailing courage, his courage is equal to anything

épris, e [epʀi, iz] (*ptp de* **s'éprendre**) ADJ (*frm*: *d'une personne*) smitten (**de** with), enamoured (*littér*) (**de** of), in love (**de** with); **être ~ de justice/liberté** to have a great love of justice/liberty; **~ d'histoire** enamoured of history

éprouvant, e [epʀuvɑ̃, ɑ̃t] ADJ [*travail, climat*] trying, testing; **~ pour les nerfs** nerve-racking

éprouvé, e [epʀuve] (*ptp de* **éprouver**) ADJ (= *sûr*) [*moyen, remède*] well-tried, proven; [*spécialiste, qualités*] (well-)proven; [*ami*] staunch, true, steadfast

éprouver [epʀuve] ▶conjug 1◀ VT **a** (= *ressentir*) [+ *sensation, sentiment*] to feel, experience **b** (= *subir*) [+ *perte*] to suffer, sustain; [+ *difficultés*] to meet with, experience **c** (= *tester*) [+ *métal*] to test; [+ *personne*] to put to the test, test **d** (*frm* = *affliger*) to afflict, distress; **très éprouvé par la maladie** sorely afflicted by illness (*frm*); **la ville a été durement éprouvée pendant la guerre** the city suffered greatly during the war

éprouvette [epʀuvɛt] NF test tube → **bébé**

EPS [əpees] NF (ABRÉV = **éducation physique et sportive**) PE, PT

epsilon [epsilɔn] NM epsilon

épuisant, e [epɥizɑ̃, ɑ̃t] ADJ exhausting

épuisé, e [epɥize] (*ptp de* **épuiser**) ADJ [*personne, cheval, corps*] exhausted, worn-out; (*Comm*) [*article*] sold out (*attrib*); [*stocks*] exhausted (*attrib*); [*livre*] out of print; **~ de fatigue** exhausted, tired out, worn-out

épuisement [epɥizmɑ̃] NM (*gén*) exhaustion; **devant l'~ de ses finances** seeing that his money had run out; **jusqu'à ~ des stocks** while stocks last; **jusqu'à l'~ du filon** until the seam is (*ou* was) worked out; **faire marcher qn jusqu'à (l')épuisement** to make sb walk till he drops (with exhaustion); **dans un grand état d'~** in a completely *ou* an utterly exhausted state, in a state of complete *ou* utter exhaustion

épuiser [epɥize] ▶conjug 1◀ **1** VT [+ *personne*] to exhaust, tire out, wear out; [+ *terre, sujet*] to exhaust; [+ *réserves, munitions*] to use up, exhaust; [+ *filon*] to exhaust, work out; [+ *patience*] to wear out, exhaust **2** **s'épuiser** VPR [*réserves*] to run out; [*source*] to dry up; [*personne*] to exhaust o.s., wear o.s. out, tire o.s. out (**à faire qch** doing sth); **les stocks s'étaient épuisés** the stocks had run out; **ses forces s'épuisent peu à peu** his strength is gradually failing; **je m'épuise à vous le répéter** I'm sick and tired of telling you

épuisette [epµizɛt] NF (*Pêche*) landing net; (*à crevettes*) shrimping net

épurateur [epyʀatœʀ] NM (*Tech*) purifier

épuration [epyʀasjɔ̃] NF [*eau, huile*] purification; [*langue, goût, style*] refinement, refining; (*Pol*) purge; **station d'~ des eaux** water purification plant

épure [epyʀ] NF working drawing

épurer [epyʀe] ▶conjug 1◀ VT [+ *eau, huile*] to purify; [+ *langue, goût, style*] to refine; (*Pol*) to purge

équanimité [ekwanimite] NF (*frm*) equanimity

équarrir [ekaʀiʀ] ▶conjug 2◀ VT a [+ *pierre, tronc*] to square (off); **poutre mal équarrie** rough-hewn beam b [+ *animal*] to cut up

équarrissage [ekaʀisaʒ] NM a [*pierre, tronc*] squaring (off) b [*animal*] quartering, cutting up; **envoyer un animal à l'~** to send an animal to the abattoir

équarrisseur [ekaʀisœʀ] NM (*gén*) renderer; [*chevaux*] knacker (*Brit*)

Équateur [ekwatœʀ] NM (= *pays*) **(la république de l') ~** (the Republic of) Ecuador

équateur [ekwatœʀ] NM equator; **sous l'~** at ou on the equator

équation [ekwasjɔ̃] NF a (*Math*) equation; **~ du premier/second degré** simple/quadratic equation; **mettre en ~** to put in an equation b (*fig*) equation; **l'~ politique** the political equation; (*Psych*) **~ personnelle** personal equation

équatorial, e (*mpl* **-iaux**) [ekwatɔʀjal, jo] 1 ADJ equatorial 2 NM (*Astron*) equatorial (telescope)

équatorien, -ienne [ekwatɔʀjɛ̃, jɛn] 1 ADJ Ecuadorian, Ecuadoran 2 **Équatorien(ne)** NM,F Ecuadorian, Ecuadoran

équerre [ekeʀ] NF (*pour tracer*) (set) square; (*de soutien*) brace; **double ~** T-square; **en ~** at right angles; **ce tableau n'est pas d'~** this picture isn't straight ou level

équestre [ekɛstʀ] ADJ [*statue, activités*] equestrian; **centre ~** riding school; **le sport ~** equestrian sport, horse-riding

équeuter [ekøte] ▶conjug 1◀ VT [+ *cerises*] to remove the stalk from, pull the stalk off; [+ *fraises*] to hull

équi(-) [ekµi] PRÉF equi(-); **équi possible** equally possible

équidé [ekide] NM member of the horse family; **les ~s** the Equidae (*SPÉC*)

équidistance [ekµidistɑ̃s] NF equidistance; **à ~ de Paris et de Dijon** half-way between Paris and Dijon

équidistant, e [ekµidistɑ̃, ɑ̃t] ADJ equidistant (**de** between)

équilatéral, e (*mpl* **-aux**) [ekµilateʀal, o] ADJ (*lit*) equilateral; **ça m'est complètement ~†‡** I don't give a damn‡

équilibrage [ekilibʀaʒ] NM (*Aut*) [*roues*] balancing

équilibrant, e [ekilibʀɑ̃, ɑ̃t] ADJ stabilizing (*épith*); **shampooing ~** shampoo which restores the hair's natural balance

équilibre [ekilibʀ] NM a (*gén*) [*corps, objet*] balance, equilibrium; **perdre/garder l'~** to lose/keep one's balance; **avoir le sens de l'~** to have a (good) sense of balance; **se tenir** ou **être en ~ (sur)** [*personne*] to balance (on); [*objet*] to be balanced (on); **mettre qch en ~** to balance sth (**sur** on); **~ stable/instable** stable/unstable equilibrium; **en ~ instable sur le bord du verre** precariously balanced on the edge of the glass; **exercice/tour d'~** balancing exercise/act b (*Psych*) **~ (mental)** (mental) equilibrium, (mental) stability; **il manque d'~** he's rather unstable

c (= *harmonie*) [*couple*] harmony; [*activités*] balance, equilibrium d (*Écon, Pol*) balance; [*course aux armements*] parity; **~ budgétaire/économique** balance in the budget/economy; **budget en ~** balanced budget; **atteindre l'~ financier** to break even (financially); **~ des pouvoirs** balance of power; **~ politique** political balance; **l'~ du monde** the world balance of power; **~ de la terreur** balance of terror e (*Sci*) equilibrium; (*Chim*) **solution en ~** balanced solution f (*Archit, Mus, Peinture*) balance

équilibré, e [ekilibʀe] (*ptp de* **équilibrer**) ADJ [*personne*] stable, well-balanced, level-headed; [*régime alimentaire*] (well-)balanced; [*esprit*] well-balanced; [*vie*] well-regulated, regular; **mal ~** unstable, unbalanced

équilibrer [ekilibʀe] ▶conjug 1◀ VT a (= *contrebalancer*) [+ *forces, poids, poussée*] to counterbalance; **les avantages et les inconvénients s'équilibrent** the advantages and the disadvantages counterbalance each other ou cancel each other out b (= *mettre en équilibre*) [+ *balance*] to equilibrate, balance; [+ *charge, embarcation, avion, roues*] to balance; (*Archit, Art*) to balance c (= *harmoniser*) [+ *emploi du temps, budget, pouvoirs*] to balance; (*fig*) **~ qn** to restore sb's mental equilibrium

équilibriste [ekilibʀist] NMF (= *funambule*) tightrope walker

équille [ekij] NF sand eel

équin, e [ekɛ̃, in] ADJ (*gén*) equine; (*Méd*) **pied bot ~** talipes equinus

équinoxe [ekinɔks] NM equinox; **marée d'~** equinoctial tide; **~ de printemps/d'automne** spring/autumn equinox

équinoxial, e (*mpl* **-iaux**) [ekinɔksjal, jo] ADJ equinoctial

équipage [ekipaʒ] NM a (*Aviat*) (air)crew; (*Naut*) crew → **homme, rôle** b* (= *attirail*) gear* (*NonC*) c† (*seigneur, chevaux*) equipage†; **à deux/à quatre chevaux** carriage and pair/and four; **en grand ~** in state, in grand ou great style d (*Tech*) equipment (*NonC*), gear (*NonC*)

équipe [ekip] NF a (*Sport*) team; [*rameurs*] crew; **jeu** ou **sport d'~** team game; **jouer en** ou **par ~s** to play in teams; **il joue en ~ de France** he plays for the French team → **esprit** b (= *groupe*) team; **~ de chercheurs** research team, team of researchers; **~ de secours** ou **de sauveteurs** ou **de sauvetage** rescue party ou squad ou team; **~ pédagogique** teaching staff; (*Ind*) **l'~ de jour/de 8 heures** the day/8 o'clock shift; **travailler en** ou **par ~s** to work in teams; (*sur un chantier*) to work in gangs; (*Ind*) to work in shifts; **on travaille en ~** we work as a team; **faire ~ avec** to team up with → **chef** c (* = *bande*) team; (*péj*) bunch*, crew*; **c'est la fine ~** they're a right bunch*

équipée [ekipe] NF [*prisonnier*] escape, flight; [*aventurier*] undertaking, venture; [*promeneur, écolier*] jaunt; **aller là-bas, c'est tout une ~** it's quite a palaver getting there; **la folle ~ des terroristes** the mad dash of the terrorists

équipement [ekipmɑ̃] NM a (= *matériel*) equipment; **l'~ complet du skieur** a complete set of skiing equipment b (= *aménagement*) **~ électrique** electrical fittings; **~ hôtelier** hotel facilities ou amenities; **~ industriel** industrial plant; (*Admin*) **~s collectifs** community facilities ou amenities; **prime** ou **subvention d'~** equipment grant c (= *action*) equipping; **assurer l'~ de qch** to equip sth

équipementier [ekipmɑ̃tje] NM components manufacturer; **~ automobile** car ou auto (*US*) parts manufacturer

équiper [ekipe] ▶conjug 1◀ 1 VT [+ *troupe*] to equip (**de** with); [+ *local*] to equip, fit out (**de** with); [+ *usine*] to tool up; [+ *ville, pays*] to equip, provide (**de** with); [+ *sportif*] to equip,

fit out, kit out (*Brit*) (**de** with); **cuisine tout équipée** fully equipped kitchen; **~ une machine d'un dispositif de sécurité** to fit a machine with a safety device 2 **s'équiper** VPR [*usine*] to tool up; [*personne*] to equip o.s. (**de, en** with); [*sportif*] to equip o.s., kit o.s. out (*Brit*), get o.s. kitted out (*Brit*); **l'école s'équipe en micro-ordinateurs** the school is acquiring some computers

équipier, -ière [ekipje, jɛʀ] NM,F (*Sport*) team member; (= *rameur*) crew member

équiprobable [ekµipʀɔbabl] ADJ equiprobable

équitable [ekitabl] ADJ [*partage, jugement*] equitable, fair; [*personne*] impartial, fair (-minded)

équitablement [ekitabləmɑ̃] ADV equitably, fairly

équitation [ekitasjɔ̃] NF (horse-)riding, equitation (*frm*); **faire de l'~** to go horse-riding; **école d'~** riding school

équité [ekite] NF equity; **avec ~** equitably, fairly

équivalence [ekivalɑ̃s] NF (*gén*) equivalence; (*Univ*) **diplômes étrangers admis en ~** recognized foreign diplomas; **demande d'~** request for an equivalent rating of one's degree; **j'ai eu ma licence par ~** I obtained my degree by being granted an equivalent rating of my qualifications ou by transfer of credits

▼**équivalent, e** [ekivalɑ̃, ɑ̃t] 1 ADJ equivalent (**à** to); **ces solutions sont ~es** these solutions are equivalent; **à prix ~, ce produit est meilleur** for the same ou equivalent price this is the better product 2 NM (= *chose semblable, mot*) equivalent (**de** of); **vous ne trouverez l'~ nulle part** you won't find the ou its like ou equivalent anywhere; **~ pétrole** fuel oil equivalent

équivaloir [ekivalwaʀ] ▶conjug 29◀ 1 VI (*lit*) [*quantité*] to be equivalent (**à** to); [*effet*] to be equivalent (**à** to), amount (**à** to); **ça équivaut à dire que ...** it amounts to ou is equivalent ou tantamount to saying that ... 2 **s'équivaloir** VPR to be the same; **ça s'équivaut** it amounts to the same thing

équivoque [ekivɔk] 1 ADJ (= *ambigu*) equivocal, ambiguous; (= *louche*) dubious, questionable 2 NF (= *ambiguïté*) equivocation, ambiguity; (= *incertitude*) doubt; (= *malentendu*) misunderstanding; **conduite sans ~** unequivocal ou unambiguous behaviour; **pour lever l'~** to remove any doubt (on the matter)

érable [eʀabl] NM maple (tree); **~ du Canada** ou **à sucre** silver maple

érablière [eʀabljɛʀ] NF maple grove

éradication [eʀadikasjɔ̃] NF eradication

éradiquer [eʀadike] ▶conjug 1◀ VT to eradicate

éraflement [eʀafləmɑ̃] NM scratching

érafler [eʀafle] ▶conjug 1◀ VT [+ *peau, genou*] to scratch, graze; [+ *surface*] to scratch, scrape

éraflure [eʀaflyʀ] NF (*sur peau*) scratch, graze; (*sur objet*) scratch, scrape (mark)

éraillé, e [eʀaje] (*ptp de* **érailler**) ADJ [*voix*] rasping, hoarse, croaking (*épith*)

éraillement [eʀajmɑ̃] NM [*voix*] hoarseness

érailler [eʀaje] ▶conjug 1◀ VT [+ *voix*] to make hoarse; (= *rayer*) [+ *surface*] to scratch; **s'~ la voix** to ruin one's voice

Érasme [eʀasm] NM **~ (de Rotterdam)** Erasmus

erbium [ɛʀbjɔm] NM erbium

ère [ɛʀ] NF era; **400 avant notre ~** 400 B.C.; **en l'an 1600 de notre ~** in the year of our Lord 1600, in the year 1600 A.D.; **l'~ chrétienne** the Christian era; **~ secondaire/tertiaire** secondary/tertiary era; **les ~s géologiques** the geological eras; **une ~ nouvelle commence** it's the beginning ou dawn of a new era; **l'~ Mitterrand/Thatcher** the Mitterrand/Thatcher era; **l'~ atomique/glaciaire/spatiale** the atomic/ice/space age

▶ GRAMMAIRE ACTIVE: **équivalent** 32.4

érectile [erektil] ADJ erectile

érection [ereksjɔ̃] NF [a] [monument] erection, raising; (fig) establishment, setting-up [b] (Physiol) erection; **avoir une ~** to have an erection

éreintant, e [erɛ̃tɑ̃, ɑ̃t] ADJ [travail] exhausting, backbreaking

éreintement [erɛ̃tmɑ̃] NM (= épuisement) exhaustion; (= critique) savage attack (**de** on), panning*, slating* (Brit)

éreinter [erɛ̃te] ▸ conjug 1 ◂ VT [a] (= épuiser) [+ animal] to exhaust; * [+ personne] to shatter*, wear out; **être éreinté** to be shattered* ou all in* ou worn out; **s'~ à faire qch** to wear o.s. out doing sth [b] (= critiquer) [+ auteur, œuvre] to pull to pieces, pan*, slate* (Brit)

érémiste ['eremist] NMF person receiving welfare payment, ≈ person on income support (Brit), ≈ person on welfare (US)

érésipèle [erezipɛl] NM = **érysipèle**

Erevan [ərəvã] N Yerevan

erg [erg] NM (Géog, Phys) erg

ergatif, -ive [ergatif, iv] ADJ, NM (Gram) ergative

ergol [ergɔl] NM propellant

ergonome [ergɔnɔm] NMF ergonomist

ergonomie [ergɔnɔmi] NF ergonomics sg

ergonomique [ergɔnɔmik] ADJ ergonomic(al)

ergonomiste [ergɔnɔmist] NMF ergonomist

ergot [ergo] NM [a] [coq] spur; [chien] dewclaw; (fig) **monter** ou **se dresser sur ses ~s** to get one's hackles up [b] [blé] ergot [c] (Tech) lug

ergotage [ergɔtaʒ] NM quibbling (NonC), cavilling (NonC), petty argument

ergoter [ergɔte] ▸ conjug 1 ◂ VI to quibble (**sur** about), cavil (**sur** at)

ergoteur, -euse [ergɔtœr, øz] NM,F quibbler, hairsplitter

ergothérapeute [ergoterapøt] NMF occupational therapist

Érié [erje] N **le lac ~** Lake Erie

ériger [eriʒe] ▸ conjug 3 ◂ VT (frm) [+ monument, bâtiment] to erect; [+ société] to set up, establish; **~ le dogmatisme en vertu** to make a virtue of dogmatism; **~ un criminel en héros** to set a criminal up as a hero; **il s'érige en maître/juge** he sets himself up as a master/judge

ermitage [ermitaʒ] NM (d'ermite) hermitage; (fig) retreat

ermite [ermit] NM hermit

éroder [erɔde] ▸ conjug 1 ◂ VT to erode

érogène [erɔʒɛn] ADJ erogenous

Éros [erɔs] NM (Myth) Eros; (Psych) **l'éros** Eros

érosif, -ive [erɔzif, iv] ADJ erosive

érosion [erɔzjɔ̃] NF (lit, fig) erosion; **~ monétaire** (monetary) depreciation

érotique [erɔtik] ADJ erotic

érotiquement [erɔtikmɑ̃] ADV erotically

érotisation [erɔtizasjɔ̃] NF eroticization

érotiser [erɔtize] ▸ conjug 1 ◂ VT to eroticize

érotisme [erɔtism] NM eroticism

érotomane [erɔtɔman] NMF erotomaniac

errance [erɑ̃s] NF (littér) wandering, roaming

errant, e [erɑ̃, ɑ̃t] ADJ (gén) wandering; **chien ~** stray dog → **chevalier, juif**

errata [erata] NM PL errata

erratique [eratik] ADJ (Géol, Méd) erratic

erratum [eratɔm] (pl **errata** [erata]) NM erratum

erre [er] NF [a] (Naut) headway (made after the engines have stopped); (fig) **se laisser glisser sur son ~** ◊ **courir sur son ~** to drift along [b] (Vénerie) **~s** tracks

errements [ermɑ̃] NMPL (littér) erring ways, bad habits

errer [ere] ▸ conjug 1 ◂ VI (littér) [a] [voyageur] to wander, roam; [regard] to rove, roam, wander (**sur** over); [pensée] to wander, stray; (littér) **un sourire errait sur ses lèvres** a smile played on his lips [b] (= se tromper) to err

▾ **erreur** [erœr] NF [a] (gén) mistake, error; (Stat) error; **~ matérielle** technical error; **~ d'écriture** clerical error; **~ de calcul** mistake in calculation, miscalculation; **faire une ~ de date** to make a mistake in ou be mistaken about the date; **~ d'impression** ◊ **typographique** misprint, typographical error; **~ de sens** wrong meaning; **~ de traduction** mistranslation; **~ (de) tactique** tactical error; **~ de jugement** error of judgment

[b] (loc) **par suite d'une ~** due to an error ou a mistake; **sauf ~** unless I'm (very much) mistaken; **sauf ~ ou omission** errors and omissions excepted; **par ~** by mistake; **~ profonde !** ◊ **grave ~ !** not at all!, absolutely not!; **commettre ou faire une ~** ◊ **tomber dans l'~** to make a mistake ou an error (**sur** about); **faire ~** ◊ **être dans l'~** to be wrong ou mistaken; **vous faites ~** (Téléc) you've got the wrong number; **il y a ~** there's been a mistake ou there's some mistake; **il n'y a pas d'~ (possible)** there's no mistake!; **ce serait une ~ de croire que ...** it would be a mistake ou be wrong to think that ..., you would be mistaken in thinking that ...; **il n'a pas droit à l'~** he's got to get it right; **l'~ est humaine** to err is human; **il y a ~ sur la personne** you've etc got the wrong person

[c] (= dérèglements) **~s** errors, lapses; **~s de jeunesse** youthful indiscretions; **retomber dans les ~s du passé** to lapse (back) into bad habits

[d] (Jur) **~ judiciaire** miscarriage of justice

erroné, e [erɔne] ADJ erroneous

ersatz [erzats] NM (lit, fig) ersatz, substitute; **~ de café** ersatz coffee

erse¹ [ers] NM, ADJ (Ling) Erse

erse² [ers] NF (Naut) grommet

éructation [eryktasjɔ̃] NF (frm) eructation (frm)

éructer [erykte] ▸ conjug 1 ◂ VI (frm) to eructate (frm)

érudit, e [erydi, it] [1] ADJ erudite, learned, scholarly [2] NM,F erudite ou learned person, scholar

érudition [erydisjɔ̃] NF erudition, scholarship

éruptif, -ive [eryptif, iv] ADJ eruptive

éruption [erypsjɔ̃] NF [a] (Géol) eruption; **~ (solaire)** solar flare; **volcan en ~** erupting volcano; **entrer en ~** to erupt [b] (Méd) **~ de boutons** outbreak of spots; **~ cutanée** skin rash, skin eruption [c] (= manifestation) **~ de violence** outbreak ou outburst of violence

érysipèle [erizipɛl] NM erysipelas

érythème [eritɛm] NM rash; **~ fessier** nappy (Brit) ou diaper (US) rash; **~ solaire** sunburn

Érythrée [eritre] NF Eritrea

érythrocyte [eritrɔsit] NM erythrocyte

érythromycine [eritrɔmisin] NF erythromycin

ès [es] PRÉP **licencié ès lettres/sciences** ≈ Bachelor of Arts/Science; **docteur ès lettres** ≈ Ph.D.; **ès qualités** [agir, être invité] in one's official capacity; **membre ès qualités** ex officio member

Ésaü [ezay] NM Esau

esbigner (s')‡† [esbiɲe] ▸ conjug 1 ◂ VPR to skedaddle*, clear off*

esbroufe* [esbruf] NF **faire de l'~** to show off; **il essaie de nous la faire à l'~** he's shooting us a line*, he's bluffing

esbroufeur, -euse* [esbrufœr, øz] NM,F big talker*

escabeau (pl **escabeaux**) [eskabo] NM (= tabouret) (wooden) stool; (= échelle) stepladder, pair of steps (Brit); **tu me prêtes ton ~ ?** can I borrow your stepladder? ou your steps (Brit)?

escadre [eskadr] NF (Naut) squadron; **~ (aérienne)** wing

escadrille [eskadrij] NF flight, ≈ squadron; **~ de chasse** fighter squadron

escadron [eskadrɔ̃] NM (Mil) squadron; (= bande) bunch*, crowd; **~ de gendarmerie** platoon of gendarmes; **~ de la mort** death squad

escagasser* [eskagase] ▸ conjug 1 ◂ VT (terme du Midi) (= assommer) to knock senseless, stun; (= ennuyer, agacer) to bore to death*; **ils l'ont escagassé d'un grand coup sur la tête** they landed him a blow to the head that knocked him senseless; **tu m'escagasses avec tes questions** you're boring me to death* ou you're being a real pain* with your questions

escalade [eskalad] NF [a] (= action) [montagne, rocher] climbing; [mur] climbing, scaling; (Hist) [forteresse] scaling; **partir faire l'~ d'une montagne** to set off to climb a mountain [b] (Sport) **l'~** (rock) climbing; **~ libre** free climbing; **~ artificielle** aid ou peg ou artificial climbing; **une belle ~** a beautiful climb; **faire de l'~** to go (rock) climbing [c] (= aggravation) escalation; **on craint une ~ de la violence en France** an escalation of violence is feared in France; **pour éviter l'~** to stop things getting out of control

escalader [eskalade] ▸ conjug 1 ◂ VT [+ montagne, rocher] to climb; [+ mur] to climb, scale; (Hist) [+ forteresse] to scale

escalator [eskalatɔr] NM escalator

escale [eskal] NF [a] (= endroit) (Naut) port of call; (Aviat) stop; **faire ~ à** (Naut) to call at, put in at; (Aviat) to stop over at [b] (= temps d'arrêt) (Naut) call; (Aviat) stop(over); (brève) touchdown; **vol sans ~** nonstop flight; **faire une ~ à Marseille** (Naut) to put in at Marseilles; (Aviat) to stop (over) at Marseilles; (Aviat) **~ technique** refuelling stop

escalier [eskalje] [1] NM (= marches) stairs; (à l'extérieur) stairs, steps; (= cage) staircase, stairway; **assis dans l'~** sitting on the stairs; **grand ~** main staircase; **~ en colimaçon** spiral staircase; (Ski) **montée en ~** side-stepping (NonC); **il m'a fait des ~s dans les cheveux*** he's cut my hair all unevenly → **esprit** [2] COMP
► **escalier d'honneur** grand staircase
► **escalier mécanique** ou **roulant** escalator
► **escalier de secours** fire escape
► **escalier de service** [maison] backstairs, servants' stairs; [hôtel] service stairs

escalope [eskalɔp] NF escalope

escamotable [eskamɔtabl] ADJ [train d'atterrissage, antenne] retractable; [lit, siège] collapsible, foldaway (épith); [escalier] foldaway (épith)

escamotage [eskamɔtaʒ] NM [a] [cartes] conjuring away [b] [difficulté] evading, getting ou skirting round; [question] dodging, evading; [mot] skipping [c]* [portefeuille] filching*, pinching* [d] [train d'atterrissage] retraction

escamoter [eskamɔte] ▸ conjug 1 ◂ VT [a] (= faire disparaître) [+ cartes etc] to conjure away [b] [+ difficulté] to evade, get round, skirt round; [+ question] to dodge, evade; [+ mot, repas] to skip [c]* (= voler) [+ portefeuille] to filch*, pinch* [d] [+ train d'atterrissage] to retract

escamoteur, -euse† [eskamɔtœr, øz] NM,F (= prestidigitateur) conjurer

escampette* [eskɑ̃pɛt] NF → **poudre**

escapade [eskapad] NF [écolier] **faire une ~** to run away ou off, do a bunk* (Brit); **on a fait une petite ~ ce week-end** we went for a little trip this weekend; (Tourisme) **~ de trois jours** three-day break

escarbille [eskarbij] NF bit of grit

escarboucle [eskarbukl] NF (= pierre) carbuncle

escarcelle [eskarsɛl] NF (†† = *portefeuille*) moneybag; (*hum*) **tomber dans l'~ de qn** [*argent, prime*] to wind up in sb's pocket; [*entreprise*] to get caught in sb's net

escargot [eskargo] NM (*Zool*) snail; (* = *lambin*) slowcoach* (*Brit*), slowpoke* (*US*); **avancer comme un ~** ou **à une allure d'~** to go at a snail's pace; **~ de mer** whelk; (= *manifestation*) **opération ~** go-slow (*Brit*), slow-down (*US*)

escargotière [eskargɔtjɛr] NF (= *parc*) snail farm; (= *plat*) snail-dish

escarmouche [eskarmuʃ] NF (*lit, fig*) skirmish

escarpé, e [eskarpe] ADJ steep

escarpement [eskarpəmã] NM (= *côte*) steep slope, escarpment (*SPÉC*); (= *raideur*) steepness; (*Géol*) **~ de faille** fault scarp

escarpin [eskarpɛ̃] NM low-fronted shoe, court shoe (*Brit*), pump (*US*)

escarpolette† [eskarpɔlɛt] NF (= *balançoire*) swing; (*Alpinisme*) etrier (*Brit*), stirrup (*US*)

escarre [eskar] NF bedsore, decubitus ulcer (*SPÉC*)

Escaut [esko] NM **l'~** the Scheldt

eschatologie [eskatɔlɔʒi] NF eschatology

Eschyle [eʃil] NM Aeschylus

escient [esjã] NM **à bon ~** advisedly; **à mauvais ~** ill-advisedly

esclaffer (s') [esklafe] ▶conjug 1 ◀ VPR to burst out laughing, guffaw

esclandre [esklãdr] NM (= *scandale*) scene; (*public*) scandal; **faire** ou **causer un ~** (*scandale*) to make a scene; (*public*) to cause ou create a scandal

esclavage [esklavaʒ] NM slavery, bondage (*littér*); **réduire en ~** to enslave; **tomber en ~** to become enslaved; (*fig*) **c'est de l'~!** it's sheer slavery!

esclavagisme [esklavaʒism] NM proslavery

esclavagiste [esklavaʒist] 1 ADJ proslavery (*épith*); **États ~s** slave states 2 NMF person in favour of slavery; (*fig*) slave driver

esclave [esklav] NMF slave (**de qn/qch** to sb/ sth); **vie d'~** slave's life, life of slavery; **être ~ de la mode/d'une habitude** to be a slave of fashion/to habit; **devenir l'~ de qn** to become enslaved to sb; **se rendre ~ de qch** to become a slave to sth

escogriffe [eskɔgrif] NM **(grand) ~** (great) beanpole*, string bean* (*US*)

escomptable [eskɔ̃tabl] ADJ (*Banque*) discountable

escompte [eskɔ̃t] NM (*Banque*) discount; **présenter à l'~** to tender ou remit for discount

escompter [eskɔ̃te] ▶conjug 1 ◀ VT (*Banque*) to discount; (*fig*) to expect; **~ faire qch** to expect to do sth, reckon ou count on doing sth

escompteur [eskɔ̃tœr] NM discounter

escopette† [eskɔpɛt] NF blunderbuss

escorte [eskɔrt] NF (*gén, Mil, Naut*) escort; (= *suite*) escort, retinue; (*fig*) **(toute) une ~ de** a whole train ou suite of; **sous bonne ~** under escort; **faire ~ à** to escort

escorter [eskɔrte] ▶conjug 1 ◀ VT to escort; **il est toujours escorté de jolies femmes** he's always surrounded by pretty women

escorteur [eskɔrtœr] NM (*navire*) **~** escort (ship)

escouade [eskwad] NF (*Mil*) squad; [*ouvriers*] gang, squad; (= *groupe de gens*) group, squad

escrime [eskrim] NF fencing; **faire de l'~** to fence

escrimer (s')* [eskrime] ▶conjug 1 ◀ VPR **s'~ à faire qch** to wear ou knock* o.s. out doing sth; **s'~ sur qch** to struggle away at sth

escrimeur, -euse [eskrimœr, øz] NM,F (*Sport*) fencer

escroc [eskro] NM crook, swindler, con man*

escroquer [eskrɔke] ▶conjug 1 ◀ VT to swindle, con*; **~ qn de qch** to swindle sb out of sth, swindle ou con* sth out of sb; **se faire ~ par qn** to be swindled ou conned* by sb

escroquerie [eskrɔkri] NF (*gén*) swindle, swindling (*NonC*); (*Jur*) fraud; **être victime d'une ~** (*gén*) to be swindled; (*Jur*) to be a victim of fraud; **50 F pour un café, c'est de l'~** 50 francs for a coffee, it's a rip-off* ou it's daylight (*Brit*) ou highway (*US*) robbery; **~ intellectuelle** intellectual fraud

escudo [eskydo] NM escudo

Esculape [eskylap] NM Aesculapius

esgourde†* [esgurd] NF ear, lug* (*Brit*); **ouvre bien tes ~s** pin back your lugholes* (*Brit*), listen up

Ésope [ezɔp] NM Aesop

ésotérique [ezɔterik] ADJ esoteric

ésotérisme [ezɔterism] NM esotericism

espace[1] [espas] NM [a] (*Art, Philo, Phys, Typo, gén*) space; **~-temps** space-time; **avoir assez d'~ pour bouger/vivre** to have enough room to move/live; **manquer d'~** to lack space, be short of space ou room, be cramped for space; **~s verts** parks; **l'Espace économique européen** the European Economic Area; (*Ordin*) **~ disque** disk space; **la musique est pour moi un ~ de liberté** music is an area in which I can express myself freely; **~ vital** (*Pol*) lebensraum; (*fig*) personal space [b] (= *intervalle*) space; **~ de temps** space of time, interval (of time); **laisser de l'~** to leave some space; **laisser un ~** to leave a space ou gap (**entre** between); **en l'~ de trois minutes** within the space of three minutes; **~ parcouru** distance covered

espace[2] [espas] NF (*Typo*) (= *tige*) quad; (= *blanc*) space

espacé, e [espase] (*ptp de* **espacer**) ADJ [*arbres, objets*] spaced (out); **elle a mis des bibelots sur l'étagère, bien ~s** she placed ornaments on the shelves, setting them neatly apart; **des crises assez régulièrement ~es** attacks occurring at fairly regular intervals; **ses visites sont très ~es ces temps-ci** his visits are few and far between these days; **réunions ~es de huit à dix jours** meetings taking place every eight to ten days

espacement [espasmã] NM (= *action*) spacing out; (= *résultat*) spacing; **devant l'~ de ses visites** in view of the growing infrequency of his visits

espacer [espase] ▶conjug 3 ◀ 1 VT [+ *objets*] to space out; [+ *visites*] to space out, make less frequent 2 **s'espacer** VPR [*visites, symptômes*] to become less frequent

espadon [espadɔ̃] NM swordfish

espadrille [espadrij] NF espadrille

Espagne [espaɲ] NF Spain → **château, grand**

espagnol, e [espaɲɔl] 1 ADJ Spanish 2 NM [a] (*Ling*) Spanish [b] **Espagnol** Spanish man, Spaniard; **les Espagnols** the Spanish, the Spaniards 3 **Espagnole** NF Spanish woman, Spaniard

espagnolette [espaɲɔlɛt] NF (window) catch; **fenêtre fermée à l'~** window resting on the catch

espalier [espalje] NM (*Agr*) espalier; (*Sport*) wall bars; **arbre en ~** espalier (tree)

espar [espar] NM (*Naut*) spar

espèce [espɛs] NF [a] (*Bio*) species; **~s** species; **~ humaine** human race; **~ animale/végétale** animal/plant species → **propagation** [b] (= *sorte*) sort, kind, type; **de toute ~** of all kinds ou sorts ou types; **ça n'a aucune ~ d'importance** that is of absolutely no importance ou not of the slightest importance; **c'est une ~ de boîte** it's a kind ou sort of box; **un voyou de la pire ~** a hoodlum of the worst kind ou sort → **cas** [c] (*, péj*) **une** ou **un ~ d'excentrique est venu** some eccentric turned

up; **qu'est-ce que c'est que cette** ou **cet ~ de crétin?** who's this stupid twit?* ou idiot?; **~ de maladroit!** you clumsy oaf!* ou clot!* (*Brit*) [d] (*Fin*) **~s** cash; **versement en ~s** payment in cash ou in specie (*SPÉC*); (†, *hum*) **en ~s sonnantes et trébuchantes** in coin of the realm (*hum*) [e] (*Philo, Rel*) species; **les Saintes Espèces** the Eucharistic ou sacred species → **communier** [f] (*frm*) **en l'~** in the case in point; **sous les ~s de** in the form of

espérance [esperãs] NF [a] (= *espoir*) hope, expectation(s); (*Rel, gén*) **l'~** hope; **contre toute ~** against all expectations ou hope, contrary to expectation(s); **~s trompeuses** false hopes; **donner de grandes ~s** to be very promising, show great promise; **avoir de grandes ~s** to have great prospects; **bâtir** ou **fonder des ~s sur** to build ou found one's hopes on; **mettre son ~** ou **ses ~s en** ou **dans** to pin one's hopes on [b] (= *sujet d'espoir*) hope; **c'est là toute mon ~** it is my greatest hope, it's what I hope for most; **vous êtes toute mon ~** you are my only hope [c] (*Sociol*) **~ de vie** life expectancy, expectation of life [d] († ou *hum* = *héritage*) **~s** expectations; **il a de belles ~s du côté de sa tante** he has great expectations of an inheritance from his aunt

espérantiste [esperãtist] ADJ, NMF Esperantist

espéranto [esperãto] NM Esperanto

▼ **espérer** [espere] ▶conjug 6 ◀ 1 VT (= *souhaiter*) [+ *succès, récompense, aide*] to hope for; **~ réussir** to hope to succeed; **~ que** to hope that; **nous ne vous espérions plus** we'd given up (all) hope of seeing you, we'd given up on you; **je n'en espérais pas tant** I wasn't hoping ou I hadn't dared to hope for as much; **viendra-t-il? — je l'espère (bien)** ou **j'espère (bien)** will he come? — I (certainly) hope so; **ceci (nous) laisse** ou **fait ~ un succès rapide** this gives us hope ou makes us hopeful of quick success; **n'espérez pas qu'il change d'avis** there is no point in hoping he'll change his mind; **j'espère bien n'avoir rien oublié** I hope I haven't forgotten anything 2 VI (= *avoir confiance*) to have faith; **il faut ~** you must have faith; **~ en** [+ *Dieu, honnêteté de qn, bienfaiteur*] to have faith in, trust in

esperluette [esperlɥɛt] NF ampersand

espiègle [espjɛgl] 1 ADJ [*enfant*] mischievous, impish; [*air*] roguish, mischievous 2 NMF imp, monkey*

espièglerie [espjɛgləri] NF [a] (= *caractère*) [*enfant*] mischievousness, impishness; [*air*] roguishness, mischievousness [b] (= *tour*) piece of mischief, prank

espion, -ionne [espjɔ̃, jɔn] NM,F spy

espionite [espjɔnit] NF spy mania

espionnage [espjɔnaʒ] NM espionage, spying; **film/roman d'~** spy film/novel ou thriller; **~ industriel** industrial espionage

espionner [espjɔne] ▶conjug 1 ◀ VT [+ *personne, actions*] to spy (up)on, keep a close watch on; **~ pour le compte de qn** to spy for sb

espionnite [espjɔnit] NF = **espionite**

esplanade [esplanad] NF esplanade

espoir [espwar] NM [a] (= *espérance*) hope; **~s chimériques** wild hopes; **dans l'~ de vous voir bientôt** hoping to see you soon, in the hope of seeing you soon; **avoir l'~/le ferme ~ que** to be hopeful/very hopeful that; **il n'y a plus d'~** all hope is lost ou there's no longer any hope; **avoir bon ~ de faire/que** to have great hopes of doing/that, be confident of doing/that; **reprendre ~** to (begin to) feel hopeful again, take heart once more; **sans ~** [*amour, situation*] hopeless; **aimer sans ~** to love without hope; **l'~ fait vivre** (*gén*) hope keeps us going; (*hum*) there's always hope; **tous les ~s sont permis** there's no limit to what we can hope for → **lueur, rayon**

▶ GRAMMAIRE ACTIVE: **espérer** 31, 35.2

b (= *personne*) hope; **vous êtes mon dernier ~** you are my last hope; **les jeunes ~s du ski/de la chanson** the young hopefuls of the skiing/singing world; **un des grands ~s de la boxe française** one of the great hopes in French boxing, one of France's great boxing hopes

esprit [ɛspʀi] **1** NM **a** (*gén*, = *pensée*) mind; **l'~ humain** the mind of man, the human mind *ou* intellect; **se reporter en ~ ou par l'~ à** to cast one's mind back to; **avoir l'~ large/étroit** to be broad-/narrow-minded; **avoir l'~ vif/lent** to be quick-/slow-witted; **vivacité/lenteur d'~** quickness/slowness of wit *ou* mind; **avoir l'~ clair** to have a clear head *ou* mind; **avoir l'~ mal tourné** to have a dirty mind, have that sort of mind (*Brit*); **il a l'~ ailleurs** his mind is elsewhere *ou* on other things; **où ai-je l'~ ?** what am I thinking of?; **j'ai l'~ plus libre maintenant** my mind is freer now; **il n'a pas l'~ à ce qu'il fait** his mind is not on what he's doing; **je n'ai pas l'~ à rire** I'm not in the mood for laughing; **dans mon ~ ça voulait dire ...** to my mind it meant ...; (*hum*) **l'~ est fort ou prompt, mais la chair est faible** the spirit is willing but the flesh is weak; **il m'est venu à l'~ que ...** it crossed my mind that ..., it occurred to me that ... ◾ (*PROV*) **un ~ sain dans un corps sain** a healthy *ou* sound mind in a healthy body → **aventure, disposition, état, faible**
b (= *humour*) wit; **avoir de l'~** to be witty; **faire de l'~** to try to be witty *ou* funny; **manquer d'~** to lack sparkle *ou* wit → **femme, mot, trait**
c (= *être humain*) **son pouvoir sur les ~s/jeunes ~s** his power over people's minds/young minds; **il joue les ~s forts** he claims to be a rational man; **c'est un ~ subtil** he is a shrewd man, he has a shrewd mind; **un des plus grands ~s du siècle** one of the greatest minds of the century; **bel ~** wit; **faire le bel ~** to show off one's wit; **les grands ou beaux ~s se rencontrent** great minds think alike
d (*Rel, Spiritisme*) spirit; **~, es-tu là ?** is (there) anybody there?; **je ne suis pas un pur ~** I'm flesh and blood (and I have to eat)
e [*loi, époque, texte*] spirit
f (= *aptitude*) **avoir l'~ mathématique/d'analyse/d'entreprise** to have a mathematical/an analytical/an enterprising mind; **avoir l'~ critique** to be critical, have a critical mind; **avoir l'~ de critique** to like criticizing for its own sake; **avoir l'~ de synthèse** to have a global approach; **avoir le bon ~ de** to have enough sense to, have the (good) sense to
g (= *attitude*) spirit; **l'~ de cette classe ou qui règne dans cette classe** the (general) attitude of this class; **~ de révolte/sacrifice** spirit of rebellion/sacrifice; **dans un ~ de conciliation** in a spirit of conciliation; **comprenez l'~ dans lequel je le dis** you must understand the spirit in which I say it; **avoir mauvais ~** to be negative about things; **faire du mauvais ~** to make snide remarks
h (*Ling*) **~ doux/rude** smooth/rough breathing

2 COMP ► **esprits animaux** († *Méd*) animal spirits ► **esprit de caste** class consciousness ► **esprits chagrins** (*péj*) faultfinders; **il y aura toujours des ~s chagrins pour critiquer** there'll always be miserable people who'll find fault ► **esprit de chapelle** cliquishness ► **esprit de clan** clannishness ► **esprit de clocher** parochialism; **avoir l'~ de clocher** to have a small-town mentality ► **esprit de compétition** competitive spirit ► **esprit de contradiction** argumentativeness; **il a l'~ de contradiction** he likes to contradict people just for the sake of it ► **esprit de corps** esprit de corps ► **esprit d'équipe** team spirit ► **esprit d'escalier** : **tu as l'~ d'escalier** you never think of an answer until it's too late ► **esprit de famille** family feeling; (*péj*)

clannishness ► **esprit frappeur** poltergeist ► **esprit malin** *ou* **du mal** evil spirit ► **l'Esprit saint** (*Rel*) the Holy Spirit *ou* Ghost ► **esprit de suite** consistency (*of thought*) ► **esprit de système** methodical *ou* systematic mind

esprit-de-bois [ɛspʀidbwa] NM wood alcohol

esprit-de-sel [ɛspʀidsɛl] NM spirits of salt

esprit-de-vin [ɛspʀidvɛ̃] NM spirits of wine

esquif [ɛskif] NM (*littér*) boat; **frêle ~** frail barque (*littér*)

esquille [ɛskij] NF splinter (of bone)

esquimau, -aude (*mpl* **esquimaux**) [ɛskimo, od] **1** ADJ Eskimo; **chien ~** husky **2** **a** (*Ling*) Eskimo **b** ® (= *glace*) choc-ice (*Brit*), ice-cream bar (*US*) **3** **Esquimau(de)** NM,F Eskimo

esquintant, e * [ɛskɛ̃tɑ̃, ɑ̃t] ADJ exhausting

esquinter * [ɛskɛ̃te] ► conjug 1 ◀ **1** VT **a** (= *abîmer*) [+ *objet*] to mess up*; [+ *yeux*] to do in*, ruin; [+ *santé*] to ruin; [+ *adversaire*] to beat up, bash up*; [+ *voiture*] to smash up; **se faire ~ par une voiture** [*automobiliste*] to have *ou* get one's car bashed* *ou* smashed into by another; [*cycliste, piéton*] to get badly bashed up* by a car; (*Aut*) **aile esquintée** damaged *ou* dented wing; **vieux râteau tout esquinté** battered old rake **b** (= *critiquer*) [+ *film, livre*] to pull to pieces, pan*, slate* (*Brit*) **2** **s'esquinter** VPR (= *se fatiguer*) to tire *ou* knock* o.s. out; (= *se blesser*) to hurt o.s.; **s'~ le bras** to hurt one's arm; **s'~ à travailler** to work o.s. to death, work o.s. into the ground; **s'~ à étudier** to wear o.s. out studying, work o.s. into the ground studying; **s'~ les yeux (à lire)** to strain one's eyes (reading)

esquisse [ɛskis] NF (*Peinture*) sketch; [*projet*] outline, sketch; [*geste, sourire*] beginnings, suggestion

esquisser [ɛskise] ► conjug 1 ◀ VT (*Peinture*) to sketch (out); [+ *projet*] to outline, sketch; **~ un geste** to make a slight *ou* vague gesture, half-make a gesture; **~ un pas de danse** to have a quick dance, have a quick twirl*; **un sourire à peine esquissé** the ghost of a smile, the faintest of smiles; **un certain progrès commence à s'~** one can begin to detect some progress

esquive [ɛskiv] NF (*Boxe*) dodge; (*en politique*) evasion, sidestepping (*NonC*); **il est passé maître dans l'art de l'~** he's a past master in the art of sidestepping *ou* dodging his opponents (*ou* the issue)

esquiver [ɛskive] ► conjug 1 ◀ **1** VT [+ *coup, question*] to dodge, evade; [+ *personne*] to elude, evade; [+ *obligation*] to shirk, dodge; [+ *difficulté*] to evade, get round, skirt round **2** **s'esquiver** VPR to slip *ou* sneak away

essai [ɛse] NM **a** (= *mise à l'épreuve*) [*produit*] testing; [*voiture*] trying out, testing; **faire l'~ de** [+ *produit*] to try out; [+ *nouvelle voiture*] to test drive, try (out) → **banc, bout**
b (= *test*) test; **~s nucléaires** nuclear tests; (*Aut, Aviat* = *tests techniques*) **~s** trials; **~s de résistance** resistance tests; (*Course automobile*) **~s** practice
c (= *tentative*) attempt, try; (*Sport*) attempt; **coup d'~** first attempt; **faire plusieurs ~s** to have several tries, make *ou* have several attempts; **faire des ~s infructueux** to make fruitless attempts; **où en sont tes ~s de plantations ?** how are your efforts at growing things *ou* your attempts at gardening progressing?; **ce n'est pas mal pour un premier ~** that's not bad for a first try *ou* attempt *ou* go; [*compagnie pétrolière*] **se livrer à des forages d'~** to test drill
d (*Rugby*) try; **marquer un ~** to score a try
e (*Littérat*) essay
f (*Tech*) [*or, argent*] assay
g **à l'~** : **être à l'~** [*personne*] to be on trial; **c'est à l'~** [*procédé*] it's being tried out *ou* test-

ed; **prendre qn à l'~** to take sb on for a trial period *ou* on a trial basis; **mettre à l'~** to test (out), put to the test

essaim [esɛ̃] NM (*lit, fig*) swarm; **~ de jeunes filles** bevy *ou* gaggle of girls

essaimage [esɛmaʒ] NM [*abeilles*] swarming; [*famille*] scattering; [*firme*] (= *développement*) spreading, expansion; (= *séparation*) hiving off

essaimer [esɛme] VI [*abeilles*] to swarm; [*famille*] to scatter; [*firme*] (= *se développer*) to spread, expand; (= *se séparer*) to hive off

essayage [esɛjaʒ] NM (*Couture*) fitting, trying on → **cabine, salon**

essayer [esɛje] ► conjug 8 ◀ **1** VT **a** (= *mettre à l'épreuve*) [+ *produit*] to test (out), try (out); [+ *médicament, vaccin*] to try out; [+ *voiture*] to test; **venez ~ notre nouveau modèle** come and test drive *ou* try (out) our new model; **~ sa force/son talent** to try *ou* test one's strength/skill
b (= *utiliser pour la première fois*) [+ *voiture, produit*] to try (out); **avez-vous essayé le nouveau boucher ?** * have you tried the new butcher('s)? → **adopter**
c [+ *vêtement*] to try on; **il faut que je vous l'essaie** I must try it on you
d (= *tenter*) [+ *méthode*] to try; **~ de faire** to try *ou* attempt to do; **as-tu essayé les petites annonces ?** have you tried the classified ads?; **essaie de le faire** try to do it, try and do it; **il a essayé de s'échapper** he attempted *ou* tried to run away; **je vais ~** I'll try, I'll have a go *ou* a try *ou* a shot (at it); **essaie un coup*** have a crack at it*, have a bash (at it)*; **essaie un peu pour voir** (*si tu y arrives*) have a try *ou* a go and see; (* *si tu l'oses*) just you try!*, just let me see you try it!; **n'essaie pas de ruser avec moi** don't try being clever with me, don't try it on with me* (*Brit*)
e (*Tech*) [+ *or, argent*] to assay
2 **s'essayer** VPR **s'~ à qch/à faire** to try one's hand at sth/at doing, have a go at sth/at doing

essayeur, -euse [esɛjœʀ, øz] NM,F (*Couture*) fitter; (*Tech*) assayer

essayiste [esɛjist] NMF essayist

esse [es] NF (= *crochet*) hook; (= *goupille*) linchpin; [*violon*] sound-hole

ESSEC [esɛk] NF (ABRÉV = **École supérieure des sciences économiques et commerciales**) *grande école for management and business students*

essence [esɑ̃s] NF **a** (= *carburant*) petrol (*Brit*), gas(oline) (*US*); (= *solvant*) spirit; **~ minérale** mineral oil; **~ ordinaire** two-star petrol (*Brit*), regular gas (*US*); **~ sans plomb** unleaded petrol (*Brit*), unleaded gas (*US*); **~ de térébenthine** turpentine; **à ~** petrol-driven (*Brit*), gasoline-powered (*US*); **prendre ou faire* de l'~** to get petrol (*Brit*) *ou* gas (*US*), fill up with petrol (*Brit*) *ou* gas (*US*) → **distributeur, panne**[1]
b (= *extrait*) [*plantes*] essential oil, essence; [*aliments*] essence; **~ de vanille/de violette/de café** vanilla/violet/coffee essence; **~ de citron/de rose** lemon/rose oil; **~ de lavande** lavender essence *ou* oil **c** (= *fondement*) [*conversation, question, doctrine*] gist, essence; [*livre*] gist; (*Philo*) essence; (*littér*) **par ~** in essence, essentially **d** (= *espèce*) [*arbres*] species; **~ à feuilles persistantes** evergreen species; (*littér*) **se croire d'une ~ supérieure** to think of o.s. as a superior being *ou* as of a superior species

▼ **essentiel, -elle** [esɑ̃sjɛl] **1** ADJ **a** (= *indispensable*) essential; **ces formalités sont essentielles** these formalities are essential (**à** to, **pour** for) **b** (= *de base*) essential, basic, main (*épith*); **~ à** essential to → **huile 2** NM **a** **l'~** (= *objets nécessaires*) the basic essentials; (= *points principaux*) the essentials, the essential *ou* basic points; **c'est l'~** that's the main thing; **l'~ est de ...** the main *ou* important thing is to ... **b** **l'~ de** [+ *conversation*] the main part of; [+ *fortune*] the best *ou* main part of, the bulk of; **l'~ de ce qu'il dit** most of what he says; **l'~ de leur temps** the best part of their time

essentiellement [esɑ̃sjelmɑ̃] ADV (*gén*) basically, essentially, mainly; (= *en majorité*) essentially, mainly; (*Philo*) essentially; **c'est ~ grâce à .../dû à ...** it is basically *ou* essentially thanks to .../due to ...

esseulé, e [esœle] ADJ (*littér*) forsaken (*littér*), forlorn (*littér*)

essieu (*pl* **essieux**) [esjø] NM axle(-tree)

essor [esɔʀ] NM (*frm* = *envol*) [*oiseau, imagination*] flight; (= *croissance*) [*entreprise, pays*] rapid development *ou* expansion; [*art, civilisation*] blossoming; **entreprise en plein ~** firm in full expansion; **prendre son ~** [*oiseau*] to soar up into the sky; [*société*] to develop *ou* expand rapidly; **le cinéma connaît un nouvel ~** the cinema is enjoying a new boom

essorage [esɔʀaʒ] NM (*avec essoreuse à rouleaux*) wringing; (*à la main*) wringing out; (*par la force centrifuge*) spin-drying; **mettre sur la position « ~ »** to put on "spin"; **~ court/doux** *ou* **léger** short/gentle spin

essorer [esɔʀe] ▸ conjug 1 ◂ VT [a] (*avec essoreuse à rouleaux*) to wring; (*à la main*) to wring out; (*par la force centrifuge*) to spin-dry [b] (*Hér*) **oiseau essoré** soaring bird

essoreuse [esɔʀøz] NF (*à rouleaux*) wringer, mangle; (*à tambour*) spin-dryer; **~ à salade** salad spinner

essoufflement [esuflɑ̃mɑ̃] NM breathlessness (*NonC*), shortness of breath (*NonC*); [*mouvement*] running out of steam

essouffler [esufle] ▸ conjug 1 ◂ [1] VT to make breathless, wind; **il était essoufflé** he was out of breath *ou* winded *ou* puffed* (*Brit*) [2] **s'essouffler** VPR [*coureur*] to get out of breath, get puffed* (*Brit*); [*roman, travail*] to tail off, fall off; [*romancier*] to exhaust o.s. *ou* one's talent, dry up*; [*reprise économique, mouvement de grève*] to run out of steam

essuie [esɥi] NM (*Belg*) (*pour les mains*) hand towel; (= *serviette de bain*) bath towel; (= *torchon*) cloth

essuie-glace (*pl* **essuie-glaces**) [esɥiglas] NM windscreen (*Brit*) *ou* windshield (*US*) wiper; **~ arrière** rear windscreen wiper; **~ à balayage intermittent** intermittent wiper

essuie-mains [esɥimɛ̃] NM INV hand towel

essuie-meuble(s) (*pl* **essuie-meubles**) [esɥimœbl] NM duster

essuie-tout [esɥitu] NM INV kitchen paper (*Brit*), paper towels (*US*), Scott towels® (*US*)

essuie-verre(s) (*pl* **essuie-verres**) [esɥivɛʀ] NM glass cloth

essuyage [esɥijaʒ] NM [*objet mouillé, assiettes*] wiping, drying; [*sol, surface mouillée*] wiping, mopping; [*tableau noir*] cleaning, wiping; [*surface poussiéreuse*] dusting; [*liquide*] wiping up, mopping up

essuyer [esɥije] ▸ conjug 8 ◂ [1] VT [a] (= *nettoyer*) [+ *objet mouillé, assiettes*] to wipe, dry; [+ *sol, surface mouillée*] to wipe, mop; [+ *tableau noir*] to clean, wipe; [+ *surface poussiéreuse*] to dust; [+ *liquide*] to wipe up, mop up; **essuie-toi les pieds** *ou* **essuie tes pieds avant d'entrer** wipe your feet before you come in; **~ la vaisselle** to dry the dishes, do the drying-up (*Brit*); **le tableau est mal essuyé** the blackboard hasn't been cleaned *ou* wiped properly; **nous avons essuyé les plâtres*** we had all the initial problems to put up with [b] (= *subir*) [+ *pertes, reproches, échec, insultes*] to endure; [+ *refus*] to meet with; [+ *tempête*] to weather, ride out; **~ le feu de l'ennemi** to come under enemy fire; **~ un coup de feu** to be shot at [2] **s'essuyer** VPR [*personne*] to dry o.s.; **s'~ les mains** to wipe one's hands (dry), dry one's hands; **s'~ la bouche** to wipe one's mouth; **s'~**

le torse/les pieds après un bain to dry one's body/feet after a bath

est [ɛst] [1] NM [a] (= *point cardinal*) east; **le vent d'~** the east wind; **un vent d'~** an east(erly) wind, an easterly (*Naut*); **le vent tourne/est à l'~** the wind is veering east(wards) *ou* towards the east/is blowing from the east; **regarder vers l'~** to look east(wards) *ou* towards the east; **le soleil se lève à l'~** the sun rises in the east; **à l'~ de** east of, to the east of; **la maison est exposée plein ~** the house faces *ou* looks due east; **d'~ en ouest** from east to west [b] (= *régions orientales*) east; (*Pol*) **l'Est** the East; **la France de l'Est ◊ l'~ (de la France)** the East (of France); **les pays/le bloc de l'Est** the Eastern countries/bloc; **l'Europe de l'Est** Eastern Europe [2] ADJ INV [*région, partie*] eastern; [*entrée, paroi*] east; [*versant, côté*] east(ern); [*côté*] east(ward); [*direction*] eastward, easterly → **longitude**

estacade [ɛstakad] NF landing stage

estafette [ɛstafɛt] NF (*Mil*) courier; (= *camionnette*) van

estafilade [ɛstafilad] NF gash, slash

est-allemand, e (*mpl* **est-allemands**) [ɛstalmɑ̃, ɑ̃d] (*Hist*) [1] ADJ East German [2] **Est-Allemand(e)** NM,F East German

estaminet† [ɛstaminɛ] NM tavern; (*péj*) pothouse† (*péj*), (low) dive (*péj*)

estampage [ɛstɑ̃paʒ] NM [a] (†,* = *escroquerie*) fleecing, swindling; **c'est de l'~** it's a plain swindle [b] (*Tech*) stamping

estampe [ɛstɑ̃p] NF (= *image*) engraving, print; (= *outil*) stamp; **~ japonaise** Japanese print; (*euph, hum*) **venez voir mes ~s japonaises** you must let me show you my etchings (*hum*)

estamper [ɛstɑ̃pe] ▸ conjug 1 ◂ VT [a] (†,* = *voler*) to fleece, swindle; **se faire ~** to be fleeced *ou* swindled [b] (*Tech*) to stamp

estampeur, -euse [ɛstɑ̃pœʀ, øz] NM,F [a]* swindler, shark* [b] (*Tech*) stamper

estampillage [ɛstɑ̃pijaʒ] NM stamping, marking

estampille [ɛstɑ̃pij] NF stamp

estampiller [ɛstɑ̃pije] ▸ conjug 1 ◂ VT to stamp

estarie [ɛstaʀi] NF (*Naut*) lay-days

ester¹ [ɛste] VI **~ en justice** [*plaignant*] to go to court; [*accusé*] to appear

ester² [ɛstɛʀ] NM (*Chim*) ester; **~ de colza** rape methyl ester

esthète [ɛstɛt] NMF aesthete (*Brit*), esthete (*US*)

esthéticien, -ienne [ɛstetisjɛ̃, jɛn] NM,F (*de salon de beauté*) beautician; (*Art*) aesthetician (*Brit*), esthetician (*US*)

esthétique [ɛstetik] [1] ADJ [*jugement, sentiment*] aesthetic (*Brit*), esthetic (*US*); [*pose, carrosserie*] attractive, aesthetically pleasing; **sens ~** aesthetic sense; **ce bâtiment n'a rien d'~** there is nothing attractive about this building, this building has no attractive features → **chirurgie, soin** [2] NF [*visage, pose*] aesthetic (*Brit*) *ou* esthetic (*US*) quality, attractiveness; (= *discipline*) **l'~** aesthetics *sg*, esthetics (*US*) *sg*; **l'~ industrielle** industrial design; **juste pour l'~** just for overall effect

esthétiquement [ɛstetikmɑ̃] ADV aesthetically (*Brit*), esthetically (*US*)

esthétisant, e [ɛstetizɑ̃, ɑ̃t] ADJ (*péj*) [*caractère, film*] mannered

esthétisme [ɛstetism] NM aestheticism (*Brit*), estheticism (*US*)

estimable [ɛstimabl] ADJ [a] (*frm* = *digne d'estime*) estimable (*frm*), worthy (*frm*), respectable; (*assez bon*) honest, sound [b] (= *déterminable*) assessable, calculable; **ces dégâts sont difficilement ~s** it is difficult to assess the extent of this damage

estimatif, -ive [ɛstimatif, iv] ADJ [*coût, valeur*]

estimated, appraised; **état ~** estimated statement

estimation [ɛstimasjɔ̃] NF [a] (= *évaluation*) [*objet*] appraisal, valuation; [*dégâts, prix*] assessment, estimation; [*distance, quantité*] estimation, reckoning; [*propriété*] valuation, assessment [b] (= *chiffre donné*) estimate, estimation; **d'après mes ~s** according to my estimations *ou* reckonings; **~ des coûts** cost estimate [c] (= *sondage d'opinion, prévision*) **~s** projections

▾ **estime** [ɛstim] NF [a] (= *considération*) esteem, respect, regard; **jouir d'une grande ~** to be highly respected *ou* regarded, be held in high esteem *ou* regard; **il a baissé dans mon ~** he has gone down in my estimation *ou* in my esteem; **ce succès mérite l'~ de tous** this success deserves the respect of everyone; **avoir de l'~ pour** to have (a) great esteem *ou* respect *ou* great regard for; **tenir en piètre ~** to have little regard *ou* respect for → **succès** [b] **naviguer à l'~** (*Naut*) to sail by dead reckoning; (*fig*) to sail in the dark; **calculer à l'~** to make a rough estimate

estimer [ɛstime] ▸ conjug 1 ◂ VT [a] (= *expertiser*) [+ *objet, propriété*] to appraise, value, assess; [+ *dégâts*] to assess, estimate, evaluate (**à** at); **faire ~ un bijou** to have a piece of jewellery valued *ou* appraised; **cette bague est estimée à 3 000 F** this ring is valued at 3,000 francs [b] (= *calculer approximativement*) [+ *prix*] to assess, estimate, evaluate (**à** at); [+ *distance, quantité*] to estimate, reckon; **les pertes sont estimées à 2 000 morts** 2,000 people are estimated to have died, an estimated 2,000 people have died, the number of those dead is estimated at *ou* put at 2,000; **j'estime sa vitesse à 80 km/h** I reckon his speed to be 80 km/h, I would put his speed at 80 km/h [c] (= *respecter*) [+ *personne*] to esteem, hold in esteem *ou* high esteem *ou* regard, respect; **estimé de tous** respected *ou* esteemed *ou* highly regarded by everyone; **notre estimé collègue** our esteemed colleague; **savoir se faire ~** to know how to win people's respect *ou* regard *ou* esteem [d] (= *faire cas de*) [+ *qualité*] to appreciate; **j'estime beaucoup sa loyauté** I greatly value his loyalty; **c'est un plat très estimé** this dish is considered a great delicacy [e] (= *considérer*) **~ que ...** to consider *ou* judge *ou* reckon that ...; **j'estime qu'il est de mon devoir de ...** I consider it *ou* judge it *ou* deem it† (to be) my duty to ...; **il estime que vous avez tort de faire cela** he considers it wrong for you to do that; **il estime avoir raison** he considers he is right *ou* in the right; **nous estimons nécessaire de dire/que** we consider it *ou* judge it *ou* deem it† necessary to say/ that; **~ inutile de faire** to see no point in doing, consider it pointless to do; **s'~ heureux d'avoir/que** to consider o.s. fortunate to have/that

estivage [ɛstivaʒ] NM *summering of cattle on mountain pastures*

estival, e (*mpl* **-aux**) [ɛstival, o] ADJ (*lit*) summer (*épith*); (= *agréable*) [*temps, température*] summery; **station ~e** summer resort; **la période ~e** the summer season *ou* months

estivant, e [ɛstivɑ̃, ɑ̃t] NM,F holiday-maker (*Brit*), vacationer (*US*), summer visitor

est-nord-est [ɛstnɔʀɛst] ADJ INV, NM INV east-north-east

estoc [ɛstɔk] NM → **frapper**

estocade [ɛstɔkad] NF (*Tauromachie*) death-blow, final thrust; **donner l'~ à un taureau** to deal a bull the death-blow; **donner l'~ à une personne/un projet** to give *ou* deal the finishing blow to a person/a plan

estomac [ɛstɔma] NM [a] (= *organe*) stomach; **avoir mal à l'~** to have (a) stomach ache *ou* tummy ache*; **partir l'~ creux** *ou* **vide** to set off on an empty stomach; **avoir l'~ plein** *ou* bien rempli to be full (up), have eaten one's fill; **j'ai l'~ dans les talons** I'm starving ou famished; **avoir un ~ d'autruche** to have a cast-iron stomach; **prendre de l'~*** to develop a paunch → **aigreur, creux, rester** b **:** avoir de l'~ (= *avoir du culot*) to have a nerve; (= *avoir du courage*) to have guts*; **il la lui a fait à l'~** he bluffed him

estomaquer* [ɛstɔmake] ▶conjug 1◀ VT to flabbergast, stagger

estompe [ɛstɔ̃p] NF (*Art*) stump

estompé, e [ɛstɔ̃pe] (*ptp de* **estomper**) ADJ (= *voilé*) [*couleurs, image*] blurred, soft

estomper [ɛstɔ̃pe] ▶conjug 1◀ 1 VT (*Art*) [+ *dessin*] to stump (*SPÉC*), shade off (*with a stump*); (= *voiler*) [+ *contours, souvenir*] to blur, dim, soften 2 **s'estomper** VPR [*contours, souvenir*] to fade; [*différences*] to become less marked; **la côte s'estompait dans la brume** the coastline became blurred ou hazy ou indistinct in the mist

Estonie [ɛstɔni] NF Estonia

estonien, -ienne [ɛstɔnjɛ̃, jɛn] 1 ADJ Estonian 2 NM (*Ling*) Estonian 3 **Estonien(ne)** NM,F Estonian

estouffade [ɛstufad] NF (*Culin*) **~ de bœuf** ≈ beef stew; (*fig*) **c'est de l'~** it's very stodgy

estourbir* [ɛsturbiʀ] ▶conjug 2◀ VT (= *assommer*) to stun; (= *tuer*) to do in*, bump off*

estrade [ɛstrad] NF platform

estradiol [ɛstradjɔl] NM = **œstradiol**

estragon [ɛstʀagɔ̃] NM tarragon

estran [ɛstʀɑ̃] NM foreshore

estrapade [ɛstʀapad] NF strappado

estrogène [ɛstʀɔʒɛn] NM → **œstrogène**

estropié, e [ɛstʀɔpje] (*ptp de* **estropier**) NM,F cripple, maimed person

estropier [ɛstʀɔpje] ▶conjug 7◀ VT a [+ *personne*] to cripple, disable, maim b [+ *texte, citation*] to twist, distort, mangle; [+ *nom*] to mutilate, mangle; [+ *langue étrangère, morceau de musique*] to mangle, murder

est-sud-est [ɛstsydɛst] ADJ INV, NM INV east-south-east

estuaire [ɛstɥɛʀ] NM estuary; (*en Écosse*) firth; **l'~ de la Seine** the Seine estuary

estudiantin, e [ɛstydjɑ̃tɛ̃, in] ADJ student (*épith*)

esturgeon [ɛstyʀʒɔ̃] NM sturgeon

et [e] CONJ a (*lie des termes*) and; **c'est vert et rouge** it's green and red; **pour piano et orchestre** for piano and orchestra; **je n'ai rien vu, et toi ?** I didn't see anything, did you? ou what about you?; **j'aime beaucoup ça, et vous ?** I'm very fond of that, aren't you? ou what about you?, I like that very much — do you?; **je n'aime pas ça et lui non plus** I don't like that and nor does he ou and he doesn't either; (*littér*) **Chantal y alla, et Madeleine** Chantal went, as did Madeleine; **une belle et grande maison** a beautiful, big house; (*littér*) **il y a mensonge et mensonge** there are lies and lies, there's lying and lying; **je suis né à Genève et mes parents aussi** I was born in Geneva and so were my parents, I was born in Geneva, as were my parents
 b (*lie des propositions*) and; **j'ai payé et je suis parti** I paid and left; **il est travailleur et ne boit pas** he works hard and (he) doesn't drink; **lui et moi nous nous entendons bien** he and I get along well; **et lui et vous l'avez dit** he and you have both said so, both he and you have said so; **2 et 2 font 4** 2 and 2 make 4; **il ne peut et ne doit pas y aller** he cannot and must not go; (*répétition*) **il a ri et ri/pleuré et pleuré** he laughed and laughed/cried and cried; **je ne l'approuve pas et ne l'approuverai jamais** I don't approve of it and (I) never shall ou will; **plus j'en mange et plus j'en ai envie** the more of it I eat the more I want

 c (*valeur emphatique*) **et alors/ensuite/après ?** and so/then/afterwards?; **et alors ?** (= *peu importe*) so (what)?*; **et moi alors ?** (and) what about me then?; **et puis** and then; **et puis (après) ?*** so (what)?*; **et moi, je peux venir ?** can I come too?; (*indignation*) **et vous osez revenir ?** and you dare (to) come back?; **et lui alors qu'est-ce qu'il va dire ?** what's he going to say?; **et ces livres que tu devais me prêter ?** what about these books (then) ou and what's happened to these books that you were supposed to lend me?; **et vous, vous y allez ?** and what about you, are you going?; **et si nous y allions aussi ?** what about (us) going as well?, why don't we go too?; **et voilà !** and there you are!; **et voilà que le voisin revient ...** and then the next-door neighbour comes back ...; **et voici qu'arrive notre ami** (and) along comes our friend; **et alors eux, voyant cela, ils sont partis** (and) so, seeing that, they left; (*littér*) **et lui de sourire/se fâcher** whereupon he smiled/grew angry; **et d'un il est paresseux, et de deux il est menteur** for one thing he's lazy, and for another thing he's a liar
 d **vingt/trente et un** twenty-/thirty-one; **à midi/deux heures et quart** at (a) quarter past twelve/two; **le vingt et unième** the twenty-first → **mille**[1]

étable [etabl] NF cowshed

établi [etabli] NM (*work*) bench

établir [etabliʀ] ▶conjug 2◀ 1 VT a (= *installer dans un lieu*) [+ *immeuble*] to put up, erect; [+ *usine*] to set up; [+ *liaisons, communications*] to establish, set up; [+ *empire*] to build, found; **~ son domicile** ou **sa demeure à** to set up house in, make one's home in; **l'ennemi a établi son camp/son quartier général dans le village** the enemy has pitched camp/has set up its headquarters in the village
 b (= *instaurer*) [+ *usage*] to establish, institute; [+ *gouvernement*] to form, set up; [+ *impôt*] to introduce, bring in; [+ *règlement*] to lay down, establish; [+ *normes*] to establish
 c (= *donner un emploi à*) to set up, establish; **~ un fonctionnaire dans une charge** to set a civil servant up in a position; **il a cinq enfants à ~** he has five children to set up in life; **il a établi son fils médecin** he has set his son up ou established his son in medical practice
 d (= *asseoir*) [+ *démonstration*] to base (**sur** on); [+ *réputation*] to found, base (**sur** on); [+ *droits*] to establish; [+ *fortune*] to found (**sur** on); **~ son pouvoir sur la force** to found ou base one's power on force
 e (= *faire régner*) [+ *autorité, paix*] to establish (**sur** over); **~ son pouvoir sur un pays** to get control of a country, establish control over a country
 f (= *dresser*) [+ *liste, devis*] to draw up, make out; [+ *programme*] to arrange; [+ *facture, chèque*] to make out; [+ *plans*] to draw up, draft; [+ *prix*] to fix, work out
 g (= *montrer*) [+ *fait, comparaison*] to establish; **~ l'innocence de qn** to establish sb's innocence; **il est établi que ...** it's an established fact that ...
 h (= *nouer*) [+ *relations*] to establish; **ils ont établi une amitié solide** they have established a firm friendship
 i (*Sport*) **~ un record** to set (up) ou establish a record

 2 **s'établir** VPR a (= *s'installer dans un lieu*) [*jeune couple*] to settle; **une usine s'est établie dans le village** a factory has been set up ou they've set up a factory in the village; **l'ennemi s'est établi sur la colline** the enemy has taken up position on the hill
 b (= *s'instaurer*) **l'usage s'est établi de ...** it has become customary to ...
 c (= *prendre un emploi*) **s'~ boulanger** to set o.s. up as a baker; **il s'est établi médecin** he has established himself ou set himself up in medical practice; **s'~ à son compte** to set up one's own business

 d (= *régner*) [*pouvoir, régime*] to become established; **son pouvoir s'est établi sur le pays** his rule has become (firmly) established throughout the country; **un grand silence s'établit** ◊ **il s'établit un grand silence** there was a great silence, a great silence fell; **un consensus a fini par s'~** a consensus was eventually reached
 e (= *se nouer*) [*amitié, contacts*] to develop, be established; **une amitié solide s'est établie entre eux** ◊ **il s'est établi entre eux une solide amitié** a firm friendship has developed ou has been established between them

établissement [etablismɑ̃] NM a (= *bâtiment*) establishment; (= *société*) establishment, firm, company; (= *institution*) institution; **~ (scolaire)** school; **~ hospitalier** hospital; **~ pénitentiaire** prison; **~ religieux** religious institution; **~ bancaire** bank; **avec les compliments des ~s Minot** with the compliments of Minot and Co.
 b (= *mise en place*) [*immeuble*] putting up, erecting; [*empire*] building, founding; [*programme*] arranging; [*relations, autorité, paix*] establishing (**sur** over); [*fortune*] founding (**sur** on); [*réputation*] founding, basing; [*usine, liaisons, communications*] setting up, establishing; [*impôt*] introduction, bringing in; [*usage*] establishing, institution; [*gouvernement*] setting up, forming; [*règlement*] laying down, establishing, institution; [*droits*] establishing; [*liste*] drawing up, making out; [*facture, chèque*] making out; [*plans*] drawing up, drafting; [*prix*] fixing, working out; [*fait, comparaison*] establishing; [*personne*] (*dans un emploi*) setting up, establishing; (*dans un lieu*) settling; [*pouvoir, régime*] establishment; [*amitié, contacts*] development, establishment
 c (= *colonie*) settlement

étage [etaʒ] NM a [*bâtiment*] floor, storey (*Brit*), story (*US*); **au premier ~** (*en France*) on the first floor (*Brit*), on the second floor (*US*), (*au Canada*) on the ground floor (*Brit*), on the first floor (*US*); **maison à** ou **de deux ~s** three-storeyed (*Brit*) ou -storied (*US*) house, house with three floors; **monter à l'~** to go upstairs; **monter à l'~ supérieur** to go to the next floor up; **il grimpa trois ~s** he went up ou walked up three floors ou flights; **les trois ~s de la tour Eiffel** the three levels of the Eiffel Tower
 b [*fusée*] stage; [*mine*] level; [*jardin*] terrace, level; [*gâteau*] tier; (*Géog*) **~s de végétation** levels of vegetation; (*Tech*) **~ de pression** pressure stage c **de bas ~** († = *humble*) lowborn; (*péj* = *médiocre*) poor, second-rate; **ce sont des trafiquants de bas ~** they are low-level ou common dealers

étagement [etaʒmɑ̃] NM [*vignobles*] terracing

étager [etaʒe] ▶conjug 3◀ 1 VT [+ *objets*] to set out in tiered rows, lay out in tiers 2 **s'étager** VPR [*jardins, maisons*] to rise in tiers ou terraces; **la foule s'étage sur les gradins** the crowd is gathered on the terraces ou the steps; **vignobles étagés sur la colline** vines in terraced rows on the hillside

étagère [etaʒɛʀ] NF (= *tablette, rayon*) shelf; (= *meuble*) **~s** shelves

étai [etɛ] NM (= *support*) stay, prop, strut; (*Naut* = *cordage*) stay

étaiement [etɛmɑ̃] NM = **étayage**

étain [etɛ̃] NM (*Min*) tin; (*Orfèvrerie*) (= *matière*) pewter; (= *objet*) piece of pewterware, pewterware (*NonC*); **pot en** ou **d'~** pewter pot → **papier**

étal (*pl* **étals**) [etal] NM [*boucherie, marché*] stall

étalage [etalaʒ] NM a (*Comm*) (= *action*) display, displaying; (= *devanture*) shop window, show window, display window; (= *tréteaux*) stall, stand; (= *articles exposés*) display; **présentation de l'~** window dressing; **disposer l'~** to dress the window, do the window display; **chemise qui a fait l'~** shop-soiled shirt; **droit d'~** stallage → **vol**[2] b (= *déploiement*) [*luxe,* connaissances] display, show; **faire ~ de** [+ *luxe, savoir*] to flaunt, show off, parade; [+ *malheurs*] to make a show of ⊂ (*Métal*) **~s bosh** d (*Tex*) roving

étalagiste [etalaʒist] NMF (= *décorateur*) window dresser; († = *marchand*) stallkeeper

étale [etal] 1 ADJ [*mer*] slack; [*vent, situation*] steady; **navire ~** becalmed ship 2 NF [*mer*] slack (water)

étalement [etalmã] NM a [*papiers, objets*] spreading (**sur** over); [*journal, tissu*] spreading out (**sur** on); (*Comm*) [*marchandise*] displaying, laying out, spreading out (**sur** on) b [*beurre*] spreading (**sur** on); [*peinture, crème solaire*] application c [*paiements*] spreading, staggering (**sur** over); [*vacances*] staggering (**sur** over); [*travaux, opération*] spreading (**sur** over)

étaler [etale] ▸conjug 1◂ 1 VT a (= *déployer*) [+ *papiers, objets*] to spread (**sur** over); [+ *journal, tissu*] to spread out (**sur** on); (*Comm*) [+ *marchandise*] to display, lay out, spread out (**sur** on); (*Cartes*) **~ son jeu** *ou* **ses cartes** to display *ou* lay down one's hand *ou* one's cards b (= *étendre*) [+ *beurre, colle*] to spread (**sur** on); [+ *peinture*] to apply, put on; [+ *crème solaire*] to apply, smooth on; (*Culin*) [+ *pâte*] to roll out; **une peinture qui s'étale bien** paint that is easy to apply c (= *répartir*) [+ *paiements*] to spread, stagger (**sur** over); [+ *vacances*] to stagger (**sur** over); [+ *travaux, opération*] to spread (**sur** over); (*Poste*) **étalez vos envois** space out your consignments; **les vacances/paiements s'étalent sur quatre mois** holidays/payments are staggered *ou* spread over a period of four months d [+ *luxe, savoir, richesse*] to parade, flaunt, show off; [+ *malheurs*] to make a show of; [+ *secrets*] to give away, disclose; **il faut toujours qu'il étale sa science** he doesn't miss an opportunity to display his knowledge; **il aime à en ~*** he likes to cause a stir e (* = *frapper*) to floor, lay out; **se faire ~ à un examen** to flunk* an exam; (*Sport*) **on s'est fait ~** we got a real hammering*

 2 **s'étaler** VPR a [*plaine, cultures*] to stretch out, spread out; **le titre s'étale sur trois colonnes** the headline is spread *ou* splashed across three columns b [*richesse, vanité*] to be flaunted; [*vaniteux*] to flaunt o.s.; **son ignominie s'étale au grand jour** his ignominy is plain for all to see c (= *se vautrer*) **s'~ sur un divan** to sprawl *ou* lounge on a divan; **étalé sur le tapis** sprawling on *ou* stretched out on the carpet; **tu t'étales! je n'ai plus de place sur la table!** stop spreading yourself, you're not leaving me any room on the table! d * (= *tomber*) **s'~ (par terre)** to fall flat on the ground, come a cropper* (*Brit*); **attention, tu vas t'~!** look out, you're going to fall flat on your face!* e * (= *échouer*) **s'~ à un examen/en chimie** to flunk* an exam/one's chemistry exam

étalon[1] [etalɔ̃] NM (= *cheval*) stallion

étalon[2] [etalɔ̃] NM = *mesure*) (*Comm, Fin*) standard; (*fig*) yardstick; **kilogramme/balance ~** standard kilogram/scales; (*Écon*) **~-or** gold standard; **c'est devenu l'~ de la beauté** it has become the yardstick by which we measure beauty; (*Ciné*) **copie ~** master print → **mètre**

étalonnage [etalɔnaʒ], **étalonnement** [etalɔnmã] NM a (= *graduation*) calibration b (= *vérification*) standardization

étalonner [etalɔne] ▸conjug 1◂ VT a (= *graduer*) to calibrate b (= *vérifier*) to standardize c [+ *test*] to set the standards for

étambot [etãbo] NM stern-post

étamer [etame] ▸conjug 1◂ VT (*gén*) to tin, tinplate; [+ *glace*] to silver; **cuivre étamé** tinned copper

étameur [etamœʀ] NM tinsmith

étamine [etamin] NF (*Bot*) stamen; (= *tissu*) muslin; (*pour laitage*) cheesecloth, butter muslin (*Brit*)

étanche [etɑ̃ʃ] ADJ [*vêtements, chaussures*] waterproof; [*montre*] waterproof, water-resistant; [*bateau, compartiment*] watertight; [*cuve*] leakproof; [*toit, mur*] impervious, impermeable; (*fig*) watertight; **~ à l'air** airtight; **enduit ~** sealant → **cloison**

étanchéité [etɑ̃ʃeite] NF (à *l'eau*) [*bateau, compartiment*] watertightness; **pour assurer son ~** [*vêtement, montre*] to make sure it is waterproof; **tester l'~ d'une montre** to test how waterproof *ou* water-resistant a watch is; **~ (à l'air)** airtightness

étancher [etɑ̃ʃe] ▸conjug 1◂ VT a [+ *sang*] to staunch, stem; [*littér*] [+ *larmes*] to dry, stem; (*littér*) [+ *soif*] to quench, slake; (*Naut*) [+ *voie d'eau*] to stop (up) b (= *rendre étanche*) to make watertight; [+ *écoulement, source*] to dam up, stem

étançon [etɑ̃sɔ̃] NM (*Tech*) stanchion, shore, prop

étançonner [etɑ̃sɔne] ▸conjug 1◂ VT to shore up, prop up

étang [etɑ̃] NM pond

étape [etap] NF a (= *trajet*) (*gén, Sport*) stage, leg; (= *lieu d'arrêt*) (*gén*) stop, stopping place; (*Sport*) stopover point, staging point; **faire ~ à** to stop off at, break the journey at (*Brit*); **par petites ~s** in easy stages; **~ de ravitaillement** staging post; **ville-~** (*Cyclisme*) stopover town; **Valence est une ville-~ entre Lyon et Nice** Valence is a stopping-off point *ou* place between Lyons and Nice b (= *phase*) stage; (= *palier*) stage, step; **les ~s de sa vie** the various stages of his life → **brûler**

état [eta] 1 NM a (= *condition physique*) state, condition; **dans un tel ~ d'épuisement** in such a state of exhaustion; **bon ~ général** good general state of health; **~ (de santé)** health; **en ~ d'ivresse** *ou* **d'ébriété** under the influence (of alcohol); **il n'est pas en ~ de le faire** he's in no condition *ou* (fit) state to do it; **dans quel ~ es-tu! tu saignes!** what a state you're in! you're bleeding!; **être dans un triste ~** to be in a sad *ou* sorry state b (= *condition psychique*) state; **être dans un grand ~ de nervosité** to be in a state of extreme nervousness, be extremely nervous; **il ne faut pas te mettre dans un ~ pareil** *ou* **des ~s pareils** you mustn't get yourself into such a state; **être dans tous ses ~s** to be beside o.s. (with anger *ou* anxiety *etc*), be all worked up*, be in a terrible state; **ça l'a mis dans tous ses ~s** that got him all worked up* *ou* into a terrible state; **il n'était pas dans son ~ normal** he wasn't his usual *ou* normal self; **être dans un ~ second** to be in a trance, be spaced out*; **je ne suis pas en ~ de le recevoir** I'm in no fit state to receive him c [*chose abstraite*] state; (*Chim*) [*corps*] state; **~ liquide/solide/gazeux** liquid/solid/gaseous state; **dans l'~ actuel de nos connaissances** in the present state of our knowledge, as our knowledge stands at (the) present; **dans l'~ actuel des choses** as things stand at present; **réduit à l'~ de cendres** reduced to cinders; **quel est l'~ de la question?** how do things stand? d [*objet, article d'occasion*] condition, state; **en bon/mauvais ~** in good/poor *ou* bad condition; **en ~** in (working) order; **en ~ de naviguer** sea-worthy; **en (parfait) ~ de marche** in (perfect) working order; **remettre en ~** [+ *voiture*] to repair, do up*; [+ *maison*] to renovate, do up*; **tenir en ~** [+ *voiture*] to maintain in good order, keep in good repair; [+ *maison*] to keep in good repair, look after; **sucre/pétrole à l'~ brut** sugar/oil in its raw *ou* unrefined *ou* crude state; **à l'~ (de) neuf** as good as new; **remettre qch en l'~** to put sth back *ou* leave sth as it was

 e (= *nation*) **État** state; **un État de droit** a constitutional state; **être un État dans l'État** to be a law unto itself; **les États pontificaux** *ou* **de l'Église** the Papal States; **coup d'État** coup (d'État); **l'État-patron** the state as an employer; **l'État-providence** the welfare state → **affaire, chef**[1]

 f † (= *métier*) profession, trade; (= *statut social*) station; **l'~ militaire** the military profession; **boucher/tailleur de son ~** a butcher/tailor by trade; **donner un ~ à qn** to set sb up in a trade; **honteux de son ~** ashamed of his station in life†

 g (= *registre, comptes*) statement, account; (= *inventaire*) inventory; **faire un ~ des recettes** to draw up a statement *ou* an account of the takings; **~ appréciatif** evaluation, estimation; **~ vérifié des comptes** audited statement of accounts

 h (*loc*) **faire ~ de** [+ *ses services*] to instance; [+ *craintes, intentions*] to state; [+ *conversation, rumeur*] to report; **(mettre) en ~ d'arrestation** (to put) under arrest; **en tout ~ de cause** anyway, in any case; **c'est un ~ de fait** it is an established *ou* irrefutable fact; (*hum*) **dans un ~ intéressant** in an interesting condition, in the family way*; **à l'~ latent** in a latent state; (*Rel*) **en ~ de péché (mortel)** in a state of mortal sin

 2 COMP ▸ **état d'alerte** (*Mil*) state of alert ▸ **état d'âme** mood, frame of mind; **avoir des ~s d'âme** (*scrupules*) to have scruples *ou* qualms; (*hésitation*) to have uncertainties ▸ **état d'apesanteur** weightlessness; **être en ~ d'apesanteur** to be weightless; **expérience en ~ d'apesanteur** experiment carried out under conditions of weightlessness ▸ **état de choc** : **être en ~ de choc** to be in (a state of) shock ▸ **état de choses** state of affairs, situation ▸ **(le bureau de) l'état civil** the registry office (*Brit*), the Public Records Office (*US*) ▸ **état de conscience** (*Psych*) state of consciousness ▸ **état de crise** state of crisis ▸ **état d'esprit** frame *ou* state of mind ▸ **les états** *ou* **États généraux** (*Hist*) the States General; (*fig*) **réunir les États généraux de l'université/de la santé** to organize a convention on university/health issues ▸ **état de grâce** (*Rel*) state of grace; (*fig*) **en ~ de grâce** inspired ▸ **état de guerre** state of war ▸ **état des lieux** inventory of fixtures ▸ **l'état de nature** the natural state ▸ **états de service** service record ▸ **état de siège** state of siege ▸ **État tampon** buffer state ▸ **état d'urgence** state of emergency; **décréter l'~ d'urgence** to declare a state of emergency ▸ **état de veille** waking state

étatique [etatik] ADJ [*structure, monopole, intervention*] state (*épith*); **système ~** system of state control

étatisation [etatizasjɔ̃] NF (= *doctrine*) state control; **~ d'une entreprise** placing of a concern under direct state control, takeover of a concern by the state

étatiser [etatize] ▸conjug 1◂ VT to establish state control over, put *ou* bring under state control; **économie/entreprise étatisée** state-controlled economy/firm

étatisme [etatism] NM state socialism, state *ou* government control

étatiste [etatist] 1 ADJ [*système, doctrine*] of state control 2 NMF partisan of state control, state socialist

état-major (*pl* **états-majors**) [etamaʒɔʀ] NM a (*Mil*) (= *officiers*) staff; (= *bureaux*) staff headquarters; **officier d'~** staff officer → **chef**[1] b [*parti politique*] administrative staff; [*entreprise*] top *ou* senior management

État-nation (*pl* **États-nations**) [etanasjɔ̃] NM nation-state

États-Unis [etazyni] NMPL **les ~ (d'Amérique)** the United States (of America); **les ~ d'Europe** the United States of Europe

étau (*pl* **étaux**) [eto] NM (*Tech*) vice; **~ limeur** shaper; **l'~ se resserre (autour des coupables)** the noose is tightening (around the guilty men); **se trouver pris (comme) dans un ~** to find o.s. caught in a stranglehold; **j'ai la tête comme dans un ~** I feel like my head's in a vice

étayage [etɛjaʒ], **étayement** [etejmã] NM [a] [*mur*] propping up, shoring up [b] [*théorie*] support(ing), backing up [c] [*régime, société*] support(ing), propping up

étayer [eteje] ▶conjug 8◀ VT [a] [+ *mur*] to prop up, shore up [b] [+ *théorie*] to support, back up [c] [+ *régime, société*] to support, prop up

etc [ɛtsetera] LOC (ABRÉV = **et cætera**) etc

et cætera, et cetera [ɛtsetera] LOC etcetera, and so on (and so forth)

été [ete] NM summer(time); **~ de la Saint-Martin** ◊ **~ indien** (*Can*) ◊ **~ des Indiens** Indian summer; **~ comme hiver** summer and winter alike; **en ~** in (the) summer(time); **jour d'~** summer's day; **mois d'~** summer month; **résidence d'~** summer residence

éteignoir [etɛɲwaʀ] NM [a] [*bougie*] extinguisher [b]† (= *rabat-joie*) wet blanket, killjoy

▼**éteindre** [etɛ̃dʀ] ▶conjug 52◀ [1] VT [a] [+ *incendie, poêle*] to put out, extinguish; [+ *bougie*] to blow out, snuff out, extinguish; [+ *cigarette*] to stub out, put out, extinguish [b] [+ *gaz, lampe*] to switch off, put out, turn off; [+ *électricité, chauffage, radio*] to turn off, switch off; **éteins dans la cuisine** put the kitchen light(s) out, switch out *ou* off the light(s) in the kitchen; **tous feux éteints** without lights [c] [+ *pièce, endroit*] to put out *ou* turn off the lights in; **sa fenêtre était éteinte** his window was dark, there was no light at *ou* in his window [d] [+ *colère*] to subdue, quell; [+ *amour, envie*] to kill; [+ *soif*] to quench, slake [e] [+ *dette*] to extinguish [2] **s'éteindre** VPR [a] [*cigarette, feu, gaz*] to go out; **la fenêtre s'est éteinte** the light in the window went out, the window went dark [b] [*agonisant*] to pass away, die; **famille qui s'est éteinte** family which has died out [c] [*colère*] to abate, evaporate; [*amour, envie*] to die, fade

éteint, e [etɛ̃, ɛ̃t] (*ptp de* **éteindre**) ADJ [*couleur*] faded; [*race, volcan*] extinct; [*regard*] dull, lacklustre; [*voix*] feeble, faint, dying; (* = *épuisé*) exhausted, tired out; **chaux ~e** slaked lime; **c'est un homme ~ maintenant** his spirit is broken now, he's a broken man now

étendard [etãdaʀ] NM [a] (= *drapeau, fig*) standard; **brandir** *ou* **lever l'~ de la révolte** to raise the standard of revolt [b] (*Bot*) standard, vexillum (*SPÉC*)

étendoir [etãdwaʀ] NM (= *corde*) clothes *ou* washing line; (*sur pied*) clotheshorse

étendre [etãdʀ] ▶conjug 41◀ [1] VT [a] (= *étaler*) [+ *journal, tissu*] to spread out, open out; [+ *tapis*] to roll out; [+ *beurre*] to spread; [+ *pâte*] to roll out; [+ *bras, jambes, blessé*] to stretch out; [+ *ailes*] to spread; (*Ling*) [+ *sens*] to stretch, extend; **~ le linge** (*sur un fil*) to hang out the washing; **veux-tu ~ le bras pour me passer ...** would you mind reaching out and passing me ...; **le cadavre, étendu sur le sol** the corpse, stretched (out) on the ground [b] * [+ *adversaire*] (= *frapper*) to floor, lay out; (= *vaincre*) to thrash*, knock out; [+ *candidat*] (*Scol*) to fail, clobber*; [+ *candidat*] (*Pol*) to hammer*; **se faire ~** [*adversaire*] to be laid out cold, be flattened*; [*candidat*] (*Scol*) to flunk it*; (*Pol*) to be hammered*; **il s'est fait ~ en anglais** he flunked* his English exam [c] (= *agrandir*) [+ *pouvoirs*] to extend (**sur** over); [+ *fortune*] to increase; [+ *connaissances, cercle d'amis, recherches*] to broaden; **~ ses activités** [*firme*] to expand; **~ son action à d'autres domaines** to extend *ou* widen one's action to

➤ GRAMMAIRE ACTIVE: **éteindre** 51.4

other fields; **~ une idée à une autre** to extend one idea to (cover) another, apply one idea to another [d] (= *diluer*) [+ *vin*] to dilute; [+ *sauce*] to thin (**de** with); **étendu d'eau** watered down [2] **s'étendre** VPR [a] (= *s'allonger*) to stretch out (**sur** on); (= *se reposer*) to lie down, have a lie down (*Brit*); (*en expliquant*) to elaborate; **s'~ sur son lit** to stretch out *ou* lie down on one's bed; **s'~ sur un sujet** to elaborate on *ou* enlarge on a subject; **ne nous étendons pas là-dessus** let's not dwell on that [b] (= *occuper un espace, une période*) [*côte, forêt*] to stretch (out), extend; [*cortège*] to stretch (out) (**jusqu'à** as far as, to); [*vacances, travaux*] to stretch, extend (**sur** over); **la plaine s'étendait à perte de vue** the plain stretched (away) as far as the eye could see [c] (= *augmenter*) [*brouillard, épidémie*] to spread; [*parti politique*] to expand; [*ville*] to spread, expand; [*pouvoirs, domaine, fortune*] to increase, expand; [*cercle d'amis*] to expand, widen; [*recherches*] to broaden in scope; [*connaissances, vocabulaire*] to increase, widen [d] (= *s'appliquer*) [*loi, avis*] to apply (**à** to); **sa bonté s'étend à tous** his kindness extends to everyone; **cette mesure s'étend à tous les citoyens** this measure applies *ou* is applicable to *ou* covers all citizens; **la domination romaine s'est étendue sur tout le monde méditerranéen** Roman rule spread *ou* expanded throughout the Mediterranean world [e] (= *s'étaler*) [*substance*] to spread; **cette peinture s'étend facilement** this paint goes on *ou* spreads easily

étendu, e¹ [etãdy] (*ptp de* **étendre**) ADJ [a] (= *vaste*) [*ville*] sprawling (*épith*), spread out (*attrib*); [*domaine*] extensive, large; [*connaissances, pouvoirs*] extensive, wide, wide-ranging; [*vue*] wide, extensive; [*vocabulaire*] wide, large, extensive; [*sens d'un mot*] broad (*épith*), wide; [*dégâts*] extensive, widespread; [*famille*] extended [b] (= *allongé*) [*personne, jambes*] stretched out; **~ sur l'herbe** lying *ou* stretched out on the grass; **~ les bras en croix** spreadeagled

étendue² [etãdy] NF [a] (= *surface*) area, expanse; **pays d'une grande ~** country with a large surface area *ou* which covers a large area; **sur une ~ de 16 km** over an expanse *ou* area of 16 km; **sur toute l'~ de la province** throughout the whole province, throughout the length and breadth of the province; **grande ~ de sable** large stretch *ou* expanse of sand; **surpris par l'~ de ce territoire** amazed at the sheer size *ou* extent of the territory [b] (= *durée*) duration, length; **sur une ~ de trois ans** over a period of three years [c] (= *importance*) [*pouvoir, dégâts*] extent; [*connaissances, recherches*] range, scope, extent; **pouvoir/culture d'une grande ~** wide *ou* wide-ranging *ou* extensive power/culture; **devant l'~ du désastre** faced with the scale of the disaster [d] (*Mus*) [*voix*] compass, range; [*instrument*] range [e] (*Philo*) [*matière*] extension, extent

éternel, -elle [etɛʀnɛl] [1] ADJ [a] (*Philo, Rel*) eternal; **je ne suis pas ~ !** I won't live forever!; **la vie éternelle** eternal *ou* everlasting life [b] (= *sans fin*) eternal, everlasting, endless; **ma reconnaissance sera éternelle** I'll be eternally grateful to you → **neige** [c] (= *perpétuel*) perpetual, eternal; **c'est un ~ insatisfait** he's never happy with anything, he's perpetually *ou* eternally dissatisfied; **c'est l'~ problème de ...** it's the eternal problem of ... [d] (* = *inamovible : avant n*) inevitable; **il était là, son ~ chapeau sur la tête** there he was, wearing the same old hat [2] NM [a] (*Rel*) **l'Éternel** the Eternal, the Everlasting; (*Bible*) the Lord; (*hum*) **grand joueur devant l'Éternel** inveterate gambler [b] **l'~ féminin** the eternal feminine *ou* woman

éternellement [etɛʀnɛlmã] ADV (*gén, Rel*) eternally; [*attendre, durer, rester*] forever; **~ jeune** forever young

éterniser [etɛʀnize] ▶conjug 1◀ [1] VT [a] [+ *débats, supplice, situation*] to drag out, draw out [b] (*littér*) [+ *nom, mémoire*] to immortalize, perpetuate [2] **s'éterniser** VPR [*situation, débat, attente*] to drag on, go on and on; [*visiteur*] to stay *ou* linger too long, linger on; **le jury s'éternise** the jury is taking ages; **on ne peut pas s'~ ici** we can't stay here for ever; **ne nous éternisons pas sur ce sujet** let's not dwell forever on that subject

éternité [etɛʀnite] NF eternity; **cela fait une ~ ou des ~s que je ne l'avais rencontré** it's ages *ou* donkey's years* (*Brit*) since I'd met him, I hadn't met him in ages; **il y a des ~s que tu m'as promis cela** you promised me that ages ago, it's ages since you promised me that; **ça a duré une ~** it lasted for ages; **ça va durer une ~** it'll take forever; **de toute ~** from the beginning of time, from time immemorial; **pour l'~** for all eternity, eternally

éternuement [etɛʀnymã] NM sneeze

éternuer [etɛʀnɥe] ▶conjug 1◀ VI to sneeze

étêter [etete] ▶conjug 1◀ VT [+ *arbre*] to pollard, poll; [+ *clou, poisson*] to cut the head off

éthane [etan] NM ethane

éthanol [etanɔl] NM ethanol

éther [etɛʀ] NM (*Chim*) ether

éthéré, e [etere] ADJ (*Chim, littér*) ethereal

éthéromane [eteʀɔman] NMF ether addict

éthéromanie [eteʀɔmani] NF addiction to ether

Éthiopie [etjɔpi] NF Ethiopia

éthiopien, -ienne [etjɔpjɛ̃, jɛn] [1] ADJ Ethiopian [2] **Éthiopien(ne)** NM,F Ethiopian

éthique [etik] [1] ADJ ethical [2] NF (*Philo*) ethics *sg*; (= *code moral*) moral code, code of ethics

ethmoïde [ɛtmɔid] NM ethmoid

ethnicité [ɛtnisite] NF ethnicity

ethnie [ɛtni] NF ethnic group

ethnique [ɛtnik] ADJ ethnic; **minorité ~** ethnic minority; **nettoyage** *ou* **purification ~** ethnic cleansing

ethnocentrisme [ɛtnɔsãtrism] NM ethnocentrism

ethnographe [ɛtnɔgraf] NMF ethnographer

ethnographie [ɛtnɔgrafi] NF ethnography

ethnographique [ɛtnɔgrafik] ADJ ethnographic(al)

ethnolinguistique [ɛtnɔlɛ̃gɥistik] NF ethnolinguistics *sg*

ethnologie [ɛtnɔlɔʒi] NF ethnology

ethnologique [ɛtnɔlɔʒik] ADJ ethnologic(al)

ethnologue [ɛtnɔlɔg] NMF ethnologist

ethnomusicologie [ɛtnɔmyzikɔlɔʒi] NF ethnomusicology

ethnomusicologue [ɛtnɔmyzikɔlɔg] NMF ethnomusicologist

éthologie [etɔlɔʒi] NF ethology

éthologique [etɔlɔʒik] ADJ ethological

éthologiste [etɔlɔʒist] NMF ethologist

éthologue [etɔlɔg] NMF ethologist

éthyle [etil] NM ethyl

éthylène [etilɛn] NM ethylene

éthylique [etilik] [1] ADJ [*coma*] alcoholic; [*délire*] alcohol-induced; **alcool ~** ethyl alcohol; **gastrite ~** alcoholic gastritis [2] NMF alcoholic

éthylisme [etilism] NM alcoholism; **crise d'~** alcoholic fit

éthylomètre [etilɔmɛtʀ] NM = **éthylotest**

éthylotest [etilɔtɛst] NM Breathalyser ® (*Brit*), Breathalyzer ® (*US*)

étiage [etjaʒ] NM (= *baisse*) low water (*NonC*)

(of a river); (= niveau) low-water level; (= marque) low-water mark

étincelant, e [etɛ̃s(ə)lɑ̃, ɑ̃t] ADJ [a] [lame, métal] gleaming; [étoile] glittering, twinkling; [diamant] sparkling, glittering; ~ **de propreté** sparkling clean [b] [yeux] (de colère) flashing; (de joie) shining [c] [conversation] scintillating, brilliant; **il a été ~** he was brilliant

étinceler [etɛ̃s(ə)le] ▶ conjug 4 ◀ VI [a] [lame, métal] to gleam; [étoile] to glitter, twinkle; [diamant] to sparkle, glitter; **la mer étincelle au soleil** the sea is sparkling ou glittering in the sun; (littér) ~ **de mille feux** [soleil, nuit, bague] to glitter with a myriad lights (littér) [b] [yeux] ~ **de colère** to glitter ou flash with anger; ~ **de joie** to sparkle ou shine with joy [c] [conversation, esprit, intelligence] to sparkle; [beauté] to sparkle, shine

étincelle [etɛ̃sɛl] NF [a] (= parcelle incandescente) spark; ~ **électrique** electric spark; **jeter des ~s** to throw out sparks; (fig) **c'est l'~ qui a mis le feu aux poudres** it was this which sparked off ou touched off the incident; (= se distinguer) **faire des ~s*** to scintillate, shine; (= exploser) **ça va faire des ~s*** sparks will fly [b] [lame, regard] flash, glitter; **jeter ou lancer des ~s** [diamant, regard] to flash [c] [raison, intelligence] gleam, flicker, glimmer; ~ **de génie** spark ou flash of genius

étincellement [etɛ̃sɛlmɑ̃] NM [a] [lame] gleam (NonC); [étoile] glitter (NonC), twinkling (NonC); [diamant] sparkle (NonC), glitter (NonC) [b] [yeux] (de colère) flashing (NonC); (de joie) sparkle (NonC), shining (NonC)

étiolement [etjɔlmɑ̃] NM [a] [plante] blanching, etiolation (SPÉC) [b] [personne, intelligence] decline

étioler (s') [etjɔle] ▶ conjug 1 ◀ VT [a] [+ plante] to blanch, etiolate (SPÉC) [b] [+ personne] to weaken, make sickly [2] **s'étioler** VPR [a] [plante] to wilt [b] [personne] to languish, decline; [intelligence] to decline

étiologie [etjɔlɔʒi] NF etiology

étiologique [etjɔlɔʒik] ADJ etiological

étique [etik] ADJ skinny, bony

étiquetage [etik(ə)taʒ] NM [paquet] labelling; [prix] marking, labelling

étiqueter [etik(ə)te] ▶ conjug 4 ◀ VT [+ paquet] to label; [+ prix] to mark, label; [+ personne] to label, classify (**comme** as); **il étiquette toujours les gens** he's always putting people in little boxes, he's always pigeonholing people (Brit)

étiquette [etikɛt] NF [a] (sur paquet, Ordin) label; (de prix) price tag; ~ **autocollante** self-stick ou self-adhesive ou stick-on label; ~ **politique** political label; (Pol) **les sans ~** the independents; (fig) **mettre une ~ à qn** to label sb, stick a label on sb, pigeonhole sb (Brit) [b] (= protocole) **l'~** etiquette

étirable [etirabl] ADJ → **film**

étirement [etirmɑ̃] NM stretching; **exercice d'~** stretching exercise; **faire des ~s** to do stretching exercises ou stretches

étirer [etire] ▶ conjug 1 ◀ [1] VT [+ peaux] to stretch; [+ métal, verre] to draw (out); ~ **ses membres** to stretch one's limbs [2] **s'étirer** VPR [personne] to stretch; [vêtement] to stretch; [convoi] to stretch out; [route] to stretch out ou away

Etna [etna] NM **l'~** Etna, Mount Etna

étoffe [etɔf] NF [a] (Tex) material, fabric; [livre] material, stuff [b] (fig) **avoir l'~ de** to have the makings of, be cut out to be; **avoir l'~ d'un héros** to be of the stuff heroes are made of, have the makings of a hero; **il a de l'~** [personne] he has a strong personality; [roman] it's really meaty; **manquer d'~** [personne] to lack personality; [roman] to lack substance

étoffé, e [etɔfe] (ptp de **étoffer**) ADJ [personne] fleshy; [discours] meaty; [catalogue, bibliothèque, palmarès] substantial; [équipe]

beefed up*, strengthened; **carnet de commandes bien ~** full order book; (Bourse) **le volume des échanges est resté très ~** trading continued heavy; **dans un marché ~ de 404 600 titres** in a market buoyed up ou bolstered by 404 600 bonds

étoffer [etɔfe] ▶ conjug 1 ◀ [1] VT [+ style] to enrich; [+ discours, personnage] to fill out, flesh out; [+ équipe] to beef up*, strengthen (**de** with); [+ carnet de commandes] to fill out; ~ **ses sourcils au crayon** to fill out one's eyebrows with eyebrow pencil [2] **s'étoffer** VPR [personne] to fill out; [carnet de commandes] to thicken, get thicker

étoile [etwal] [1] NF [a] (Astron) star; ~ **filante** shooting star; ~ **polaire** pole star, north star; ~ **du berger** ou **du soir** evening star; ~ **du matin** morning star, daystar; ~ **de David** star of David; (Hist) ~ **jaune** yellow star; **semé d'~s** starry, star-studded; **sans ~s** starless; **à la clarté des ~s** by starlight; **dormir** ou **coucher à la belle ~** to sleep out in the open, sleep under the stars [b] (= dessin, objet) star; (= fêlure) crack; **général à deux ~s** two-star general; **trois ~s** (cognac, restaurant) three-star (épith); **un trois ~s** (= restaurant) a three-star restaurant; (= hôtel) a three-star hotel; **moteur en ~** radial engine [c] (Ciné, Danse) star; ~ **du cinéma** film star, movie star (US); ~ **de la danse** dancing star; ~ **montante** rising ou up-and-coming star [d] (= destinée) **avoir foi en son ~** to trust one's lucky star, trust to one's luck; **être né sous une bonne/mauvaise ~** to be born under a lucky/an unlucky star; **son ~ a pâli** his star has faded [2] COMP ▶ **étoile de mer** starfish ▶ **étoile d'argent** (Bot) edelweiss

étoiler [etwale] ▶ conjug 1 ◀ VT [a] (= parsemer) to stud (**de** with); **nuit étoilée** starry ou starlit night; **ciel étoilé** starry ou star-studded sky [b] (= fêler: gén) to crack; [+ pare-brise] to craze

étole [etɔl] NF (Rel, gén) stole

étonnamment [etɔnamɑ̃] ADV surprisingly, amazingly, astonishingly

étonnant, e [etɔnɑ̃, ɑ̃t] [1] ADJ [a] (= surprenant) surprising, amazing, astonishing; **rien d'~ à cela** ◊ **cela n'a rien d'~** no wonder, there's nothing (so) surprising about that; **vous êtes ~** you're incredible ou amazing, you're the absolute limit* [b] (= remarquable) [personne] amazing, fantastic, incredible [2] NM **l'~ est que** the astonishing ou amazing thing ou fact is that, what's astonishing ou amazing is that

étonné, e [etɔne] (ptp de **étonner**) ADJ surprised; **il a pris un air ~** ou **a fait l'~ quand je lui ai dit** he acted surprised when I told him; **je ne serais pas autrement ~** I wouldn't be that surprised; **j'ai été très ~ de l'apprendre** I was really surprised ou I was amazed to hear that; **sous les yeux ~s du public** before the astonished gaze of the audience; **il a été le premier ~ de sa réussite/de réussir** nobody was more surprised than he was at his success/to have succeeded

étonnement [etɔnmɑ̃] NM surprise, amazement, astonishment

étonner [etɔne] ▶ conjug 1 ◀ [1] VT to surprise, amaze, astonish; **ça m'étonne que ...** I am surprised that ..., it surprises me that ...; **ça ne m'étonne pas** I'm not surprised, I don't wonder, it doesn't surprise me (**que** that); **vous serez étonnés du résultat** you'll be surprised by ou at the result; **ça m'étonnerait** I should be very surprised; (iro) **tu m'étonnes!*** you don't say!* (iro) [2] **s'étonner** VPR to be amazed, wonder, marvel (**de qch** at sth, **de voir** at seeing); **je m'étonne que ...** I am surprised that ..., it surprises me that ...; **il ne faut pas s'~ si** it's hardly surprising that

étouffant, e [etufɑ̃, ɑ̃t] ADJ stifling

étouffe-chrétien* [etufkretjɛ̃] NM INV **c'est de l'~** ou **un ~** it's stodgy

étouffée [etufe] ◆ **à l'étouffée** [1] LOC ADV **cuire à l'~** [poisson, légumes, viande] to steam [2] LOC ADJ [poisson, légumes, viande] steamed

étouffement [etufmɑ̃] NM [a] (= mort) suffocation; **tuer qn par ~** to kill sb by suffocating ou smothering him; **mourir d'~** to die of suffocation [b] (Méd) **sensation d'~** feeling of suffocation ou breathlessness; **avoir des ~s** to have fits of breathlessness [c] (= action) [scandale] hushing-up; [rumeurs] suppression, stifling; [révolte] quelling, suppression; [scrupules] stifling, overcoming [d] [pas] muffling

étouffer [etufe] ▶ conjug 1 ◀ [1] VT [a] [assassin] to suffocate, smother; [chaleur, atmosphère] to suffocate, stifle; [sanglots, colère, aliment] to choke; (fig) to stifle, suffocate; **mourir étouffé** to die of suffocation, suffocate to death; ~ **qn de baisers** to smother sb with kisses; **les scrupules ne l'étouffent pas** he isn't hampered ou overburdened by scruples, he doesn't let scruples cramp his style; **ce n'est pas la politesse qui l'étouffe!*** politeness is not his forte! ou his strong suit!; **ça l'étoufferait de dire merci** it would kill him to say thank you; **plantes qui étouffent les autres** plants which choke ou smother others [b] [+ bruit] to muffle, deaden; [+ bâillement] to stifle, smother, suppress; [+ sanglots, cris] to smother, choke back, stifle; ~ **un juron** to stop o.s. swearing; **rires étouffés** suppressed ou smothered laughter; **dit-il d'une voix étouffée** he said in a low ou hushed tone; **voix étouffées** (discrètes) subdued voices; (confuses) muffled voices [c] [+ scandale, affaire] to hush up, keep quiet; [+ rumeurs, scrupules, sentiments] to smother, suppress, stifle; [+ révolte] to put down, quell, suppress [d] [+ flammes] to smother, extinguish, quench (littér); ~ **un feu** to put out ou smother a fire [2] VI (= mourir étouffé) to die of suffocation, suffocate to death; (= être mal à l'aise) to feel stifled, suffocate; ~ **de colère/de rire** to choke with anger/with laughter; ~ **de chaleur** to be stifled, be overcome with the heat; **on étouffe dans cette pièce** it's stifling in here, the heat is suffocating ou overpowering in here [3] **s'étouffer** VPR (gén) to suffocate; **s'~ en mangeant** to choke on something

étouffoir [etufwar] NM (Mus) damper; **quel ~ ici!*** it's very stuffy in here!

étoupe [etup] NF (de lin, chanvre) tow; (de cordages) oakum

étourderie [eturdəri] NF (= caractère) absent-mindedness; (= bévue) (**faute d')étourderie** careless mistake ou blunder; **agir par ~** to act without thinking ou carelessly

étourdi, e [eturdi] (ptp de **étourdir**) [1] ADJ [personne, action] scatterbrained, absent-minded [2] NM,F scatterbrain; **agir en ~** to act without thinking ou carelessly

étourdiment [eturdimɑ̃] ADV carelessly, rashly

étourdir [eturdir] ▶ conjug 2 ◀ [1] VT [a] (= assommer) to stun, daze [b] ~ **qn** [bruit] to deafen sb; [succès, parfum, vin] to go to sb's head; **l'altitude m'étourdit** heights make me dizzy ou giddy, I've no head for heights (Brit); **ce vacarme m'étourdit** this row is deafening; **ce mouvement m'étourdit** this movement makes my head spin ou makes me feel quite dizzy [2] **s'étourdir** VPR **il s'étourdit par la boisson** he drowns his sorrows in drink; **il s'étourdit par les plaisirs** he tries to forget ou to deaden his sorrows by living a life of pleasure; **il s'étourdit pour oublier** he keeps up a whirl of activity to forget; **s'~ de paroles** to get drunk on words, be carried away by the sound of one's own voice

étourdissant, e [eturdisɑ̃, ɑ̃t] ADJ [bruit] deafening, earsplitting; [succès] staggering, stunning; [beauté] stunning; **à un rythme ~** at a tremendous ou breakneck pace; **~ de beauté** stunningly beautiful

étourdissement [eturdismɑ̃] NM **a** (= syncope) blackout; (= vertige) dizzy spell, fit of giddiness; **ça me donne des ~s** it makes me feel dizzy, it makes my head swim* ou spin **b** (littér = surprise) surprise **c** (littér = griserie) exhilaration, intoxication

étourneau (pl étourneaux) [eturno] NM **a** (Orn) starling **b** * (= distrait) scatterbrain, featherbrain (Brit), birdbrain (US)

étrange [etrɑ̃ʒ] **1** ADJ strange, odd, peculiar; **et chose ~** strangely ou funnily enough, the odd thing is; **aussi ~ que cela puisse paraître** strange as it may seem; **cela n'a rien d'~** there is nothing strange about ou in that **2** NM **l'~** the bizarre; **l'~ dans tout cela, c'est que ...** the odd ou strange ou funny thing is that ...

étrangement [etrɑ̃ʒmɑ̃] ADV (= bizarrement) strangely, oddly, peculiarly; (= étonnamment) surprisingly, amazingly; **ressembler ~ à** to be surprisingly ou amazingly ou suspiciously like

étranger, -ère [etrɑ̃ʒe, ɛr] **1** ADJ **a** (= d'un autre pays) foreign; (Pol) [politique, affaires] foreign; **être ~ au pays** to be a foreigner; **visiteurs ~s** foreign visitors, visitors from abroad **b** (= d'un autre groupe) strange, unknown (à to); **être ~ à un groupe** not to belong to a group, be an outsider; **il est ~ à notre famille** he is not a relative of ours, he is not a member of our family; **« entrée interdite à toute personne étrangère à l'établissement** ou **au service »** "no entry for unauthorized persons", "no unauthorized entry" **c** (= inconnu) [nom, usage, milieu] strange, unfamiliar (à to); [idée] strange, odd; **son nom/ son visage ne m'est pas ~** his name/face is not unknown ou not unfamiliar to me; **cette personne/technique lui est étrangère** this person/technique is unfamiliar ou unknown to him, he is unfamiliar ou unacquainted with this person/technique; **ce sentiment ne lui est pas ~** this feeling is not unknown to him → **corps** **d** (= extérieur) [donnée, fait] extraneous (à to); **~ au sujet** irrelevant (to the subject), beside the point; **il est ~ au complot** he is not involved ou mixed up in the plot, he has nothing to do with the plot

2 NM,F **a** (d'un autre pays) foreigner; (péj, Admin) alien; **une étrangère** a foreign lady ou woman; **c'est une étrangère** she's a foreigner **b** (= inconnu) stranger; (à un groupe) outsider, stranger

3 NM (= pays) **l'~** foreign countries, foreign parts; **vivre/voyager à l'~** to live/travel abroad; **rédacteur pour l'~** foreign editor; (Journalisme) **nouvelles de l'~** news from abroad

étrangeté [etrɑ̃ʒte] NF (= caractère) [conduite] strangeness, oddness; (= fait ou événement bizarre) odd ou strange fact (ou event etc)

étranglé, e [etrɑ̃gle] (ptp de étrangler) ADJ **a** [voix] tight, strangled; **elle a poussé un petit cri ~** she let out a strangled little cry **b** (= resserré) **taille ~e** tightly constricted waist

étranglement [etrɑ̃gləmɑ̃] NM **a** [victime] strangulation; (Hist = supplice) garotting; [presse, libertés] stifling **b** [vallée] neck; [rue] bottleneck, narrowing; [taille, tuyau] constriction **c** [voix] strain, tightness **d** (Méd) strangulation **e** (Sport) stranglehold; **faire un ~ à qn** to get sb in a stranglehold

étrangler [etrɑ̃gle] ▸ conjug 1 ◂ **1** VT **a** (= tuer) [+ personne] to strangle, choke, throttle; [+ poulet] to wring the neck of; (Hist = supplicier) to garotte; **mourir étranglé (par son écharpe)** to be strangled (by one's scarf); **cette cravate m'étrangle** this tie is choking ou

throttling me → **hernie** **b** [rage] to choke; **la fureur l'étranglait** he was choking with rage; **voix étranglée par l'émotion** voice choking ou strained ou tight with emotion **c** [+ presse, libertés] to stifle; **taxes qui étranglent les commerçants** taxes which cripple shopkeepers **d** (= resserrer) to squeeze (tightly)

2 s'étrangler VPR **a** [personne] to strangle o.s.; **elle s'est étranglée accidentellement** she was strangled accidentally, she accidentally strangled herself; **s'~ de rire/colère** to choke with laughter/anger; **s'~ en mangeant** to choke on something **b** [voix, sanglots] to catch in one's throat; **un cri s'étrangla dans sa gorge** a cry caught ou died in his throat **c** [rue, couloir] to narrow (down), make a bottleneck

étrangleur, -euse [etrɑ̃glœr, øz] **1** ADJ M **collier ~** choke chain **2** NM,F strangler

étrave [etrav] NF (Naut) stem

être [etr]

▸ conjug 61 ◂

1 VERBE COPULE   **4** VERBE IMPERSONNEL
2 VERBE AUXILIAIRE   **5** NOM MASCULIN
3 VERBE INTRANSITIF

*Pour les expressions figées telles que **être sur le point de**, **être en colère**, **étant donné que**, **il est de règle de** etc, reportez-vous au nom ou au verbe; pour les expressions telles que **c'est à relire**, **être en robe**, **en être à**, **être pour faire qch** etc, reportez-vous à la préposition.*

1 VERBE COPULE

a pour qualifier — to be; **le ciel est bleu** the sky is blue; **elle veut ~ médecin** she wants to be a doctor; **soyez sages!** be good!; **tu n'es qu'un enfant** you are only a child; **si j'étais vous, je lui parlerais** if I were you I'd speak to him; **il est tout pour elle** he's everything to her, he means the world to her; **il n'est plus rien pour moi** he doesn't mean anything to me any more; MAIS **nous sommes dix à vouloir partir** ten of us want to go

b pour indiquer la date — **nous sommes** ou **on est le 12 janvier** it's the 12th of January; **on était en juillet** it was (in) July; **quel jour sommes-nous?** (date) what's the date today?, what's today's date?; (jour) what day is it (today)?

c appartenance, participation à une activité
♦ **être de**: **nous sommes de la même religion** we are of the same faith; **~ de la fête/de l'expédition** to take part in the celebration/in the expedition; **je ne serai pas du voyage** I won't be going; **elle est des nôtres** (= elle vient avec nous) she's coming with us; (= elle appartient à notre groupe, à la même communauté d'esprit) she's one of us; **je ne pourrai pas ~ des vôtres jeudi** I won't be able to come on Thursday; **serez-vous des nôtres demain?** will you be coming tomorrow?
♦ **en être**: **vous en êtes?** are you taking part?; **il y avait une conférence, et bien sûr le en était** there was a conference, and of course she was there; (péj = homosexuel) **il en est*** ◊ **c'en est une*** he's one of them* (péj)

2 VERBE AUXILIAIRE

a

*être se traduit par **have** pour former les temps composés de verbes intransitifs ou pronominaux; ne pas oublier toutefois qu'un passé composé peut être rendu par un prétérit en anglais.*

est-il déjà passé? has he been already?; **nous étions montés** we had gone upstairs; **il est passé hier** he came yesterday; **elle serait tombée** she would ou might have fallen; **il s'est assis** he sat down; **ils s'étaient écrit** they had written to each other

b

*être se traduit par **be** pour former le passif; notez l'emploi du present perfect pour rendre certains présents français.*

~ donné/fabriqué par ... to be given/made by ...; **il est soutenu par son patron** he is backed up by his boss; **l'eau est changée tous les jours** the water is changed every day; **il a été blessé dans un accident** he was injured in an accident; **elle n'a pas été invitée** she hasn't been invited; **le contrat est signé** the contract has been signed; **la maison est vendue** the house has been sold

3 VERBE INTRANSITIF

a = exister — to be; **je pense, donc je suis** I think, therefore I am; **elle n'est plus** she is no more; **le temps n'est plus où ...** the time is past when ...; **que la lumière soit** let there be light; **un menteur s'il en est** a liar if ever there was one; MAIS **le meilleur homme qui soit** the kindest man imaginable

b = se trouver — to be; **il est maintenant à Lille/ au Japon** he is now in Lille/in Japan; **le village est à 10 km d'ici** the village is 10 km from here; **les verres étaient dans le placard** the glasses were in the cupboard; **où étais-tu?** where were you?; MAIS **je suis à la page 25** I've got to ou reached page 25, I'm up to page 25

c

*La tournure familière **avoir été** signifiant **être allé** est rendue par **be** sauf lorsque l'on a un prétérit en anglais; dans ce cas, on utilise **go**.*

il n'avait jamais été à Londres he'd never been to London; **as-tu déjà été à l'étranger?** — **oui j'ai été en Italie l'an dernier** have you ever been abroad? — yes I went to Italy last year; **elle a été lui téléphoner** (elle est partie) she's gone to phone him; (elle est revenue) she's been to phone him; **elle a été lui téléphoner à 3 heures** she went to phone him at 3 o'clock; **il a été dire que c'était de ma faute** he went and said that it was my fault

d littér **il s'en fut la voir** he went to see her; **elle s'en fut, furieuse** she left in a terrible rage

4 VERBE IMPERSONNEL

♦ **il est** + adjectif: **il est étrange que ...** it's odd that ...; **il fut facile de le convaincre** it was easy to convince him; **il serait très agréable de voyager** it would be very nice to travel

b pour dire l'heure — **quelle heure est-il?** what time is it?; **il est 10 heures** it's 10 o'clock; **il n'était pas encore 8 heures quand il est arrivé** it wasn't (even) 8 o'clock when he arrived; **il n'était pas encore 10 heures que la place était pleine de monde** it wasn't (even) 10 o'clock and the square was already full of people

c littér = il y a
♦ **il est** + nom singulier — there is
♦ **il est** + nom pluriel — there are
il est un pays où ... there is a country where ...; **il est des gens qui ...** there are people who ...; MAIS **il n'est pas un jour sans que ...** not a single day passes without ...; **il était une fois ...** once upon a time there was ...

d
♦ **c'est, ce sont** + nom ou pronom: **c'est le médecin** (en désignant) he's ou that's the doctor; (au téléphone, à la porte) it's the doctor; **c'est la plus intelligente de la classe** she's the most intelligent girl in the class; **c'est la camionnette du boucher** it's ou that's the butcher's van; **c'est une voiture rapide** it's a fast car; **ce sont des mannequins/de bons souvenirs** they are models/happy memories; **je vais acheter des pêches, ce n'est pas cher en ce moment** I am going to buy some peaches — they're quite cheap just now

*Notez l'emploi possible d'un auxiliaire en anglais pour traduire les propositions tronquées. Pour la forme **qui est-ce qui**, reportez-vous à **qui.**
qui a crié? — **c'est lui** who shouted? — he did*

ou it was him; **qui le fera ? — c'est moi** who'll do it? — I will

e ◆ **c'est** + *adjectif* it is; **c'est impossible** it's impossible; **c'était bruyant/formidable** it was noisy/wonderful; **c'est vrai** it's *ou* that's true; **ça c'est vrai !** that's true; **c'est vrai que ...** it's true that ...

f

Pour traduire des tournures emphatiques mettant en relief un sujet ou un complément, on peut employer soit un pronom suivi d'une relative, soit l'accent tonique.

◆ **c'est ... qui** : **c'est le vent qui a emporté la toiture** it was the wind that blew the roof off; **c'est eux*** *ou* **ce sont eux** *ou* **c'étaient eux qui mentaient** they are the ones who *ou* it's they who were lying; **c'est toi qui le dis !** that's what YOU say!; **c'est lui qui me l'a dit** he's the one who told me, he told me; **c'est elle qui a voulu** SHE wanted it; **c'est moi qu'on attendait** I was the one they were waiting for, it was me they were waiting for

◆ **c'est ... que** : **c'est une bonne voiture que vous avez là** that's a good car you've got there; **c'est ici que je l'ai trouvé** this is where I found it; **c'était elle que je voulais rencontrer** she was the one I wanted to meet; **ne partez pas, c'est à vous que je veux parler** don't go, it's you I want to talk to

Notez que l'anglais n'emploie pas de tournure avec le sujet réel antéposé.

un hôtel pas cher, c'est difficile à trouver it's not easy to find a cheap hotel, a cheap hotel isn't easy to find; **voler, c'est quelque chose que je ne ferai jamais** stealing is something I'll never do

◆ **c'est que** (*pour expliquer*) **quand il écrit, c'est qu'il a besoin d'argent** when he writes, it's because he needs money; **c'est qu'elle n'entend rien, la pauvre !** but the poor woman can't hear a thing!, but she can't hear, poor woman!; **c'est que je le connais bien !** I know him so well!; **c'est qu'elle n'a pas d'argent** it's because *ou* just that she has no money; (*exclamatif*) **mais elle n'a pas d'argent !** but she has no money!

◆ **ce n'est pas que** : **ce n'est pas qu'il soit beau !** it's not that he's good-looking!; **ce n'est pas qu'elle soit bête, mais elle est paresseuse** it's not that she's stupid, she's just lazy

g

La forme interrogative est-ce que est rendue en anglais par l'auxiliaire suivi du pronom.

est-ce que tu m'entends ? can you hear me?; **est-ce que c'est/c'était vrai ?** is/was it true?; **est-ce que vous saviez ?** did you know?; **est-ce que c'est toi qui l'as battu ?** was it you who beat him?; **quand est-ce que ce sera réparé ?** when will it be fixed?; **où est-ce que tu l'as mis ?** where have you put it?

h

La forme interrogative n'est-ce pas, qui demande une confirmation, est rendue en anglais par l'auxiliaire suivi du pronom ; cette tournure est négative si la proposition est affirmative et inversement.

vous viendrez, n'est-ce pas ? you will come, won't you?, you are coming, aren't you?; **n'est-ce pas qu'il a promis ?** he did promise, didn't he?; **il fait beau, n'est-ce pas ?** it's a lovely day, isn't it?; **elle n'est pas partie, n'est-ce pas ?** she hasn't left, has she?

Notez les traductions possibles de la valeur intensive de n'est-ce pas.

le problème, n'est-ce pas, reste entier you see the problem still hasn't been solved; **ce n'est pas moi, n'est-ce pas, qui vais lui dire** I'm certainly not going to tell him; **mais moi, n'est-ce pas, je ne suis qu'un raté** but I'm just a failure, aren't I?

i **pour exprimer la supposition** **si ce n'était** were it not for, if it were not for, but for; (*littér*) **n'était son orgueil** were it not for *ou* but for his pride, if it were not for his pride; **ne serait-ce que pour quelques jours** if (it were) only for a few days; **ne serait-ce que pour nous ennuyer** if only to annoy us

5 NOM MASCULIN

a **gén** (*Sci*) being; **~ humain/animé/vivant** human/animate/living being

b **= individu** person; **les ~s qui nous sont chers** our loved ones, those who are dear to us; **un ~ cher** a loved one; **c'était un ~ merveilleux** he was a wonderful person

c **= âme** **il l'aimait de tout son ~** he loved her with all his heart; **au plus profond de notre ~** deep down in our hearts; **tout son ~ se révoltait** his whole being rebelled

d **Philo** **l'~** being; **l'~ et le néant** being and nothingness; **l'Être suprême** the Supreme Being

étreindre [etʀɛ̃dʀ] ▸ conjug 52 ◂ VT **a** (*frm*) (*dans ses bras*) [+ *ami*] to embrace, hug, clasp in one's arms; [+ *ennemi*] to seize, grasp; (*avec les mains*) to clutch, grip, grasp; **les deux amis s'étreignirent** the two friends embraced each other → **embrasser** **b** [*douleur*] to grip

étreinte [etʀɛ̃t] NF (*frm*) [*ami*] embrace, hug; [*ennemi*] stranglehold, grip; [*main, douleur*] clutch, grip, grasp; **l'armée resserre son ~ autour de ...** the army is tightening its grip round ...

étrenner [etʀene] ▸ conjug 1 ◂ **1** VT to use (*ou* wear *etc*) for the first time **2** VI (†,* = *écoper*) to catch it*, cop it* (*Brit*), get it*

étrennes [etʀɛn] NFPL (*à un enfant*) New Year's gift, Christmas present; (*au facteur etc*) ≈ Christmas box; **que veux-tu pour tes ~ ?** what would you like for Christmas? *ou* as a Christmas present?; **donner ses ~ à la femme de ménage** to give a Christmas box to the cleaning lady

étrier [etʀije] NM (*Équitation, Constr, Méd*) stirrup; (*Anat*) stirrup bone, stapes (*SPÉC*); (*Alpinisme*) étrier (*Brit*), stirrup (*US*); **boire le coup de l'~*** (*gén*) to have one for the road*; [*cavalier*] to have a stirrup cup → **pied, vider**

étrille [etʀij] NF (= *brosse*) currycomb; (= *crabe*) velvet swimming crab

étriller [etʀije] ▸ conjug 1 ◂ VT [+ *cheval*] to curry(-comb); (†, *hum* = *rosser*) to trounce†

étripage [etʀipaʒ] NM gutting

étriper [etʀipe] ▸ conjug 1 ◂ **1** VT [+ *lapin*] to disembowel, gut; [+ *volaille*] to draw; [+ *poisson*] to gut; * [+ *adversaire*] to cut open, hack about (*Brit*) **2 s'étriper*** VPR to make mincemeat of each other*, tear each other's guts out*

étriqué, e [etʀike] (*ptp de* **étriquer**) ADJ [*habit*] tight; [*esprit*] narrow; [*vie*] narrow, cramped; **il fait tout ~ dans son manteau** he looks cramped in his coat, his coat looks too small for him

étriquer [etʀike] ▸ conjug 1 ◂ VT **ce vêtement l'étrique** this garment is too tight-fitting for him

étrivière [etʀivjɛʀ] NF stirrup leather

étroit, e [etʀwa, wat] **1** ADJ **a** [*rue, fenêtre, ruban*] narrow; [*espace*] narrow, cramped, confined; [*vêtement, chaussure*] tight; **nous avons une marge de manœuvre très ~e** we have very little room for manoeuvre; **être ~ des hanches** *ou* **du bassin** to have narrow hips **b** (= *borné*) [*vues*] narrow, limited; **être d'esprit** to be narrow-minded **c** (= *intime*) [*amitié*] close (*épith*); [*liens*] close (*épith*), intimate (*épith*); **en collaboration ~e avec ...** in close collaboration with ... **d** (= *strict*) [*surveillance*] close (*épith*), strict (*épith*); [*coordination, subordination*] strict (*épith*) **e** (*Ling*) [*acception*] narrow (*épith*), strict

(*épith*), restricted; **au sens ~ du terme** in the narrow *ou* strict sense of the term **f** (= *serré*) [*nœud, étreinte*] tight **2** **à l'étroit** LOC ADV cramped; **vivre** *ou* **être logé à l'~** to live in cramped *ou* confined conditions; **être à l'~ dans ses vêtements** to be wearing clothes that are too small, be bursting out of one's clothes; **il se sent un peu à l'~** (*dans un département, un parti*) he feels a bit cramped

étroitement [etʀwatmã] ADV [*lier, unir*] closely; [*obéir*] strictly; [*surveiller*] closely, strictly; [*tenir*] tightly; **être ~ logé** to live in cramped *ou* confined conditions

étroitesse [etʀwates] NF **a** [*rue, fenêtre, espace, hanches*] narrowness; **à cause de l'~ de ce logement** because of the cramped accommodation here **b** [*vues*] narrowness; **~ (d'esprit)** narrow-mindedness

étron [etʀɔ̃] NM (*hum*) (piece of) excrement, turd**

Étrurie [etʀyʀi] NF Etruria

étrusque [etʀysk] **1** ADJ Etruscan **2** NM (*Ling*) Etruscan **3 Étrusque** NMF Etruscan

étude [etyd] NF **a** (= *action*) (*gén*) study; (*Mus*) **l'~ d'un instrument** the study of an instrument, learning to play an instrument; **ce projet est à l'~** this project is under consideration *ou* is being studied; **mettre un projet à l'~ ◊ procéder à l'~ d'un projet** to investigate *ou* go into *ou* study a project; **avoir le goût de l'~** to like study *ou* studying; **une ~ gratuite de vos besoins** a free assessment of your needs; **voyage/frais d'~** study trip/costs; (*Écon*) **~ de marché** market research (*NonC*); **~ de cas** case study; (*Fin*) **~ complémentaire** follow-up study → **bureau** **b** (*Scol, Univ*) **~s** studies; **~s secondaires/supérieures** secondary/higher education; **faire ses ~s à Paris** to study in Paris, be educated in Paris; **travailler pour payer ses ~s** to work to pay for one's education; **faire des ~s de droit** to study law; **quand je faisais mes ~s** when I was studying **c** (= *ouvrage*) study; (*Écon, Sci*) paper, study; (*Littérat*) study, essay; (*Art*) **~s de fleurs** studies of flowers; (*Mus*) **~s pour piano** studies *ou* études for (the) piano **d** (*Scol*) (**salle d'**)**étude** study *ou* prep room, private study room (*Brit*), study hall (*US*); **l'~ (du soir)** preparation, prep* (*Brit*); **~ surveillée** (supervised) study period (*Brit*), study hall (*US*); **être en ~** to have a study period; **mettre des élèves en ~** to leave pupils to study on their own **e** (*Jur*) (= *bureau*) office; (= *charge, clientèle*) practice

étudiant, e [etydjã, jãt] **1** ADJ [*vie, problèmes, allures*] student (*épith*) **2** NM,F student; **~ en médecine/en lettres** medical/arts student; **~ de première année** first-year student *ou* undergraduate, fresher (*Brit*), freshman (*US*); **~ de troisième cycle** post-graduate (student)

étudié, e [etydje] (*ptp de* **étudier**) ADJ **a** (= *calculé*) [*jeu de scène*] studied; [*coupe, conception*] carefully designed; [*prix*] competitive, keen (*épith*) (*Brit*); **à des prix très ~s** at the lowest possible *ou* the keenest (*Brit*) prices; **maison d'une conception très ~e** very carefully *ou* thoughtfully designed house **b** (= *affecté*) [*allure*] studied; [*sentiments*] affected, assumed

▾ **étudier** [etydje] ▸ conjug 7 ◂ **1** VT **a** (= *apprendre*) [+ *matière*] (*gén*) to study; (*Univ*) to study, read (*Brit*); [+ *instrument*] to study, learn to play; (*Scol*) [+ *leçon*] to learn; [+ *texte, auteur*] to study; **s'amuser au lieu d'~** to have a good time instead of studying **b** (= *examiner*) [+ *projet, possibilités*] to study, examine, go into; [+ *dossier, cas*] to study, examine; **une proposition sous tous ses aspects** to study a proposal from every angle; **~ qch de près** to study sth closely, make a close study of sth, take a close look at sth

▸ GRAMMAIRE ACTIVE: **étudier** 53.2

c (= *observer*) [+ *terrain, adversaire*] to study, observe closely; [+ *visage*] to study, examine; **je sentais qu'il m'étudiait constamment** I sensed that he was observing me all the time **d** (= *concevoir*) [+ *procédé, dispositif*] to devise; [+ *machine, coupe*] to design; **c'est étudié pour*** that's what it's for **e** (= *calculer*) [+ *gestes, ton, effets*] to study, calculate **2 s'étudier** VPR (= *s'analyser*) to analyse o.s., be introspective; (= *se regarder*) to study o.s. *ou* one's appearance; **les deux adversaires s'étudiaient** the two opponents studied *ou* observed each other closely

étui [etɥi] NM [*violon, cigares*] case; [*parapluie*] cover; [*revolver*] holster; **~ à lunettes** spectacle *ou* glasses case

étuve [etyv] NF (= *bains*) steamroom; (*de désinfection*) sterilizer; (= *incubateur*) incubator; (*fig*) **quelle ~ !** it's like a sauna in here!

étuvée [etyve] ♦ **à l'étuvée** **1** LOC ADV **cuire à l'~** [+ *poisson, légumes, viande*] to braise **2** LOC ADJ [*poisson, légumes, viande*] braised

étuver [etyve] ▶ conjug 1 ◀ VT **a** [+ *poisson, légumes*] to steam; [+ *viande*] to braise **b** (= *stériliser*) to sterilize

étymologie [etimɔlɔʒi] NF etymology
étymologique [etimɔlɔʒik] ADJ etymological
étymologiquement [etimɔlɔʒikmɑ̃] ADV etymologically
étymologiste [etimɔlɔʒist] NMF etymologist
étymon [etimɔ̃] NM etymon

E.-U.(A.) (ABRÉV = **États-Unis (d'Amérique)**) US(A)

eucalyptus [økaliptys] NM eucalyptus
eucharistie [økaristi] NF **l'Eucharistie** ◊ **l'~** the Eucharist
eucharistique [økaristik] ADJ eucharistic
Euclide [øklid] NM Euclid
euclidien, -ienne [øklidjɛ̃, jɛn] ADJ Euclidean
eudiomètre [ødjɔmɛtʀ] NM eudiometer
eugénique [øʒenik] **1** NF eugenics *sg* **2** ADJ eugenic
eugénisme [øʒenism] NM eugenics *sg*
euh [ø] EXCL er
eunuque [ønyk] NM eunuch
euphémique [øfemik] ADJ euphemistic(al)
euphémiquement [øfemikmɑ̃] ADV euphemistically
euphémisme [øfemism] NM euphemism
euphonie [øfɔni] NF euphony
euphonique [øfɔnik] ADJ euphonious, euphonic
euphoniquement [øfɔnikmɑ̃] ADV euphoniously, euphonically
euphonium [øfɔnjɔm] NM euphonium
euphorbe [øfɔʀb] NF euphorbia, spurge
euphorie [øfɔʀi] NF euphoria
euphorique [øfɔʀik] ADJ euphoric
euphorisant, e [øfɔʀizɑ̃, ɑ̃t] **1** ADJ [*nouvelle*] exhilarating **2** NM (**médicament**) **~** antidepressant, pep pill*
euphoriser [øfɔʀize] ▶ conjug 1 ◀ VT to make exhilarated
Euphrate [øfʀat] NM **l'~** the Euphrates
eurafricain, e [øʀafʀikɛ̃, ɛn] **1** ADJ Eurafrican **2** NM,F **Eurafricain(e)** Eurafrican
eurasiatique [øʀazjatik] **1** ADJ Eurasian **2** **Eurasiatique** NMF Eurasian
Eurasie [øʀazi] NF Eurasia
eurasien, -ienne [øʀazjɛ̃, jɛn] **1** ADJ Eurasian **2 Eurasien(ne)** NM,F Eurasian
EURATOM [øʀatɔm] (ABRÉV = **European Atomic Energy Commission**) EURATOM
eurêka [øʀeka] EXCL eureka!
Euripide [øʀipid] NM Euripides
euristique [øʀistik] ADJ, NF = **heuristique**
euro [øʀo] NM (*Fin*) euro

euro-américain, e (*pl* **euro-américains**) [øʀoamerikɛ̃, ɛn] ADJ Euro-American; **alliance de défense ~e** Euro-American defence alliance

eurocentrisme [øʀosɑ̃tʀism] NM (*péj*) Eurocentrism; **nous sommes accusés d'~** we are accused of being Eurocentric *ou* of Eurocentrism

eurochèque [øʀoʃɛk] NM Eurocheque
eurocommunisme [øʀokɔmynism] NM Eurocommunism
Eurocorps [øʀokɔʀ] NM **l'~** the Eurocorps
eurocrate [øʀokʀat] NMF Eurocrat
eurocratie [øʀokʀasi] NF Eurocracy
eurodéputé [øʀodepyte] NM Euro-MP
eurodevise [øʀodəviz] NF Eurocurrency
eurodollar [øʀodɔlaʀ] NM Eurodollar
eurofranc [øʀofʀɑ̃] NM (*Fin*) eurofranc
euromissile [øʀomisil] NM European missile
euro-obligations [øʀoɔbligasjɔ̃] NF Eurobond

Europe [øʀɔp] NF Europe; **l'~ centrale/occidentale** central/Western Europe; **l'~ de l'est** Eastern Europe; **l'~ des quinze** the fifteen countries of the European Union; **l'~ politique** political union in Europe; **l'~ verte** European agriculture; **il faut construire l'~ sociale** we must strive to build a Europe with a common social policy

européanisation [øʀopeanizasjɔ̃] NF Europeanization
européaniser [øʀopeanize] ▶ conjug 1 ◀ **1** VT to Europeanize **2 s'européaniser** VPR to become Europeanized
européen, -enne [øʀopeɛ̃, ɛn] **1** ADJ European; **les (élections) européennes** the European elections **2 Européen(ne)** NM,F (*Géog*) European; (= *partisan de l'Union européenne*) European, pro-European
europessimisme [øʀopesimism] NM Europessimism
euroscepticisme [øʀoseptisism] NM Euroscepticism
eurosceptique [øʀoseptik] **1** ADJ Eurosceptic(al) **2** NMF Eurosceptic
Eurostar® [øʀostaʀ] NM Eurostar®; **voyager en ~** to travel by Eurostar
Eurovision [øʀovizjɔ̃] NF Eurovision
Eurydice [øʀidis] NF Eurydice
eurythmie [øʀitmi] NF (*Mus*) eurhythmy; (*Méd*) eurhythmia
Eustache [østaʃ] NM Eustace → **trompe**
euthanasie [øtanazi] NF euthanasia
eutrophisation [øtʀofizasjɔ̃] NF eutrophication

eux [ø] PRON PERS **a** (*sujet*) they; **si j'étais ~** if I were *ou* was them, if I were they (*frm*); **nous y allons, ~ non** *ou* **pas ~** we are going but they aren't *ou* they're not *ou* not them; **~ mentir ? ce n'est pas possible** them tell a lie? I can't believe it; **ce sont ~ qui répondront** they are the ones who will reply, they'll reply; **~ ils n'ont rien à dire** they've got nothing to say; **ils l'ont bien fait, ~** they did it all right; **~, pauvres innocents, ne l'ont jamais su** they, poor fools, never knew → **même** **b** (*objet*) them; **il n'obéit qu'à ~** they are the only ones he obeys, he'll only obey them; **les aider, ~ ? jamais !** help them? never! **c** (*avec prép*) **à ~ tout seuls, ils ont tout acheté** they bought everything all on their own; **cette maison est-elle à ~ ?** does this house belong to them?, is this house theirs?; **ils ont cette grande maison pour ~ seuls** they have this big house all to themselves; **ils ne pensent qu'à ~, ces égoïstes** these selfish people only think of themselves

eux-mêmes [ømɛm] PRON → **même**
E.V. [əve]† (ABRÉV = **en ville**) "by hand"

évacuateur, -trice [evakɥatœʀ, tʀis] **1** ADJ evacuation (*épith*) **2** NM sluice
évacuation [evakɥasjɔ̃] NF [*pays, personnes*] evacuation; [*liquide*] draining; (*Méd*) evacuation; **procéder à l'~ de** to evacuate
évacué, e [evakɥe] (*ptp de* **évacuer**) NM,F evacuee
évacuer [evakɥe] ▶ conjug 1 ◀ VT [+ *pays, ville, population*] to evacuate; [+ *salle, maison*] to evacuate, clear; (*Méd*) to evacuate, discharge; [+ *liquide*] to drain (off); * [+ *problème*] to dispose of; **faire ~** [+ *salle, bâtiment*] to clear
évadé, e [evade] (*ptp de* **s'évader**) NM,F escapee, escaped prisoner
évader (s') [evade] ▶ conjug 1 ◀ VPR **a** [*prisonnier*] to escape (**de** from); **faire ~ qn** to help sb (to) escape **b** (*pour se distraire*) **s'~ de la réalité** to escape from reality; **la musique me permet de m'~** music is an escape for me; (= *partir*) **j'ai besoin de m'~** I need to get away from it all
évaluable [evalɥabl] ADJ assessable; **difficilement ~** difficult to assess *ou* evaluate
évaluation [evalɥasjɔ̃] NF **a** (= *expertise*) [*maison, bijou*] appraisal, evaluation, assessment, valuation; [*dégâts, prix*] assessment, evaluation **b** (*approximative*) [*fortune, nombre, distance*] estimation, assessment **c** (= *appréciation*) [*besoins, risques, conséquences*] assessment **d** [*élève*] assessment; (*en entreprise*) **entretien d'~** appraisal
évaluer [evalɥe] ▶ conjug 1 ◀ VT **a** (= *expertiser*) [+ *maison, bijou*] to appraise, evaluate, assess, value (**à** at); [+ *dégâts, prix*] to assess, evaluate (**à** at); **faire ~ qch par un expert** to have sth valued *ou* appraised by an expert **b** (= *juger approximativement*) [+ *fortune, nombre, distance*] to estimate, assess (**à** at); **on évalue à 60 000 le nombre des réfugiés** there are an estimated 60,000 refugees, the number of refugees is estimated at *ou* put at 60,000 **c** (= *apprécier*) [+ *risques, besoins, conséquences*] to assess; **bien/mal ~ qch** to be correct/mistaken in one's assessment of sth; **j'ai mal évalué la distance** I misjudged the distance **d** [+ *élève, employé*] to assess
évanescence [evanesɑ̃s] NF evanescence
évanescent, e [evanesɑ̃, ɑ̃t] ADJ (*littér*) evanescent
évangélique [evɑ̃ʒelik] ADJ evangelic(al)
évangélisateur, -trice [evɑ̃ʒelizatœʀ, tʀis] **1** ADJ evangelistic **2** NM,F evangelist
évangélisation [evɑ̃ʒelizasjɔ̃] NF evangelization
évangéliser [evɑ̃ʒelize] ▶ conjug 1 ◀ VT to evangelize
évangélisme [evɑ̃ʒelism] NM evangelicalism, evangelism
évangéliste [evɑ̃ʒelist] NM evangelist; (*Bible*) Evangelist
évangile [evɑ̃ʒil] NM **a** (*Rel*) **l'Évangile** the Gospel; **l'Évangile selon saint Jean** the Gospel according to St John; **l'~ du jour** the gospel for the day, the day's reading from the gospel; **les Évangiles synoptiques** the synoptic Gospels **b** (*fig*) gospel; **c'est parole d'~** it's (the) gospel truth, it's gospel
évanoui, e [evanwi] (*ptp de* **s'évanouir**) ADJ [*blessé*] unconscious; **tomber ~** to faint, pass out
évanouir (s') [evanwiʀ] ▶ conjug 2 ◀ VPR [*personne*] to faint (**de** from), pass out (**de** with), black out*; [*rêves, apparition, craintes*] to vanish, disappear
évanouissement [evanwismɑ̃] NM **a** (= *syncope*) fainting fit, blackout **b** [*rêves, apparition, craintes*] disappearance, fading
évaporation [evapɔʀasjɔ̃] NF evaporation
évaporé, e [evapɔʀe] (*ptp de* **évaporer**) **1** ADJ (*péj*) [*personne*] giddy, scatterbrained, feather-

brained (*Brit*) [2] NM,F scatterbrain, feather-brain (*Brit*), birdbrain

évaporer [evapɔʀe] ▸conjug 1◂ [1] VTI (**faire**) **~** to evaporate [2] **s'évaporer** VPR (*lit*) to evaporate; (* = *disparaître*) to vanish *ou* disappear (into thin air)

évasé, e [evaze] (*ptp de* **évaser**) ADJ [*vallée, conduit*] which widens *ou* opens out; [*manches, jupe, pantalon*] flared; **verre à bords ~s** glass with a curving *ou* bell-shaped rim

évasement [evazmã] NM [*passage, tuyau*] opening out; [*manche, jupe*] flare; **à cause de l'~ de la vallée** because of the way the valley opens out

évaser [evaze] ▸conjug 1◂ [1] VT [+ *tuyau, ouverture*] to widen, open out; [+ *manche, jupe*] to flare [2] **s'évaser** VPR [*passage, tuyau*] to open out; [*manche, jupe*] to flare

évasif, -ive [evazif, iv] ADJ evasive

évasion [evazjɔ̃] [1] NF [a] [*prisonnier*] escape (**de** from) [b] (= *divertissement*) **l'~** escape; (= *tendance*) escapism; **littérature d'~** escapist literature; **besoin d'~** need to escape; **rechercher l'~ dans la drogue** to seek escape in drugs [2] COMP ▸ **évasion des capitaux** flight of capital ▸ **évasion fiscale** tax evasion

évasivement [evazivmã] ADV evasively

Ève [ɛv] NF Eve; (*hum*) **en tenue d'~** in the altogether*, in one's birthday suit → **connaître**

évêché [eveʃe] NM (= *région*) bishopric; (= *palais*) bishop's palace; (= *ville*) cathedral town

éveil [evɛj] NM (*littér*) [*dormeur, intelligence*] awakening; [*amour*] awakening, dawning; [*soupçons, jalousie*] arousing; **être en ~** [*personne*] to be on the alert *ou* on the qui vive; [*sens*] to be alert *ou* wide awake, be aroused; **donner l'~** to raise the alarm *ou* alert; **mettre qn en ~ ◊ donner l'~ à qn** to alert *ou* arouse sb's suspicions, put sb on his guard; (*Scol*) **activités d'~** early-learning activities

éveillé, e [eveje] (*ptp de* **éveiller**) ADJ (= *alerte*) [*enfant, esprit, air*] alert, sharp, bright; (= *à l'état de veille*) (wide-)awake → **rêve**

éveiller [eveje] ▸conjug 1◂ [1] VT [a] (*littér = réveiller*) to awaken, waken; **tenir qn éveillé** to keep sb awake [b] (= *faire naître*) [+ *curiosité, sentiment, souvenirs*] to arouse, awaken; [+ *passion*] to kindle, arouse; **pour ne pas ~ l'attention** so as not to attract attention; **sans ~ les soupçons** without arousing suspicion [c] (= *développer*) [+ *esprit*] to stimulate; **~ l'intelligence de l'enfant** to awaken the child's intelligence [2] **s'éveiller** VPR [a] (= *se réveiller*) (*lit*) to wake up, awaken, waken; (*fig*) [*ville, nature*] to come to life, wake (up) [b] (= *naître*) [*sentiment, curiosité, soupçons*] to be aroused; [*amour*] to dawn, be aroused *ou* born [c] (= *se développer*) [*intelligence, esprit*] to develop [d] (*littér = ressentir*) **s'~ à** [+ *amour*] to awaken to

événement, évènement [evenmã] NM [a] (*gén*) event; **semaine chargée en ~s** eventful week, action-packed week; **l'~ de la semaine** the main story *ou* news of the week; **faire ou créer l'~** [*personne, film*] to make a splash, be big news; (*hum*) **c'est un véritable ~ quand il dit merci** it's quite an event *ou* occasion when he says thank you; **les ~s de mai 68** the events of May 1968; **les ~s d'Algérie** the Algerian war of independence; **livre(-)/film(-)-événement** blockbuster → **dépasser, heureux, tournure** [b] (*Ordin*) event

événementiel, -ielle [evenmãsjɛl] ADJ factual; **histoire événementielle** factual history

évent [evã] NM [*baleine*] blowhole, spout (hole), spiracle (*SPÉC*)

éventail [evãtaj] NM [a] (= *instrument*) fan; **en ~** [*objet*] fan-shaped; [*plusieurs objets*] fanned out; (*Mil*) **se déployer en ~** to fan out → **doigt, voûte** [b] (= *gamme*) [*produits, prix, mesures*] range; **~ des salaires** salary range, wage range *ou* spread (*US*); **l'~ politique** the

political spectrum; **il y a tout un ~/un large ~ de possibilités** there is a whole range/a wide range of possibilities

éventaire [evãtɛʀ] NM (= *corbeille*) tray, basket; (= *étalage*) stall, stand

éventé, e [evãte] (*ptp de* **éventer**) ADJ [a] (= *exposé au vent*) windy; **rue très ~e** very windy *ou* exposed street [b] [*parfum, vin*] stale, musty; [*bière*] stale, flat [c] (= *connu*) well-known; **c'est un truc*** ~ it's a well-known *ou* a rather obvious trick; **le secret est ~** the secret is out

éventer [evãte] ▸conjug 1◂ [1] VT [a] (= *rafraîchir*) to air; (*avec un éventail*) to fan [b] (= *découvrir*) [+ *secret, complot*] to discover, lay open [2] **s'éventer** VPR [a] [*bière*] to go flat; [*vin, parfum*] to go stale *ou* musty [b] (*avec éventail*) to fan o.s.; **s'~ avec un journal** to fan o.s. with a newspaper

éventration [evãtʀasjɔ̃] NF (*Méd*) rupture

éventrer [evãtʀe] ▸conjug 1◂ [1] VT [a] (*avec un couteau*) to disembowel; (*d'un coup de corne*) to gore [b] [+ *boîte, sac*] to tear open; [+ *muraille, coffre*] to smash open; [+ *matelas*] to rip open [2] **s'éventrer** VPR [*boîte, sac*] to burst open; [*personne*] to rip one's stomach open; **le bateau s'est éventré sur les rochers** the ship's hull was ripped open on the rocks

éventreur [evãtʀœʀ] NM ripper; **Jack l'Éventreur** Jack the Ripper

éventualité [evãtɥalite] NF [a] (= *hypothèse*) possibility; **dans cette ~** if this happens, should that arise; **dans l'~ d'un refus de sa part** should he refuse, in the event of his refusal [b] (= *circonstance*) eventuality, contingency, possibility; **pour parer à toute ~** to guard against all eventualities

éventuel, -elle [evãtɥɛl] ADJ [*départ, refus*] possible; [*client, revenu*] potential; **l'achat ~ d'un ordinateur** the possibility of buying a computer

éventuellement [evãtɥɛlmã] ADV possibly; **~, nous pourrions ...** we could possibly *ou* perhaps ...; **~ je prendrais ma voiture** if need be *ou* if necessary I'd take my car

évêque [evɛk] NM bishop; **~ suffragant** suffragan (bishop)

Everest [ev(ə)ʀɛst] NM **le mont ~ ◊ l'~** Mount Everest

évertuer (s') [evɛʀtɥe] ▸conjug 1◂ VPR (= *s'efforcer de*) **s'~ à faire** to strive to do, do one's utmost to do; **j'ai eu beau m'~ à lui expliquer...** no matter how hard I tried to explain to him ...

éviction [eviksjɔ̃] NF (*Jur*) eviction; [*rival*] ousting, supplanting; **procéder à l'~ de** [+ *locataires*] to evict; **~ scolaire** temporary suspension from school of a child with an infectious illness

évidage [evidaʒ], **évidement** [evidmã] NM hollowing-out, scooping-out

évidemment [evidamã] ADV (= *bien sûr*) of course, obviously; (*frm* = *d'une manière certaine*) plainly; **bien ~** of course

▾ **évidence** [evidãs] [1] NF [a] (= *caractère*) obviousness, evidence; **c'est l'~ même !** it's quite *ou* perfectly evident *ou* patently obvious!; **se rendre à l'~** to bow *ou* yield to facts *ou* to the evidence, face facts *ou* the evidence; **nier l'~** to deny the obvious *ou* the facts [b] (= *fait*) obvious fact; **trois ~s se dégagent de ce discours** this speech brings three obvious facts to light; **c'est une ~ que de dire** it's stating the obvious to say [2] **en évidence** LOC ADV (**être**) **en ~** [*personne*] (to be) conspicuous *ou* in evidence; [*objet*] (to be) conspicuous *ou* in evidence, (be) in a conspicuous *ou* prominent position; **mettre en ~** [+ *personne*] to bring to the fore; [+ *fait*] (= *souligner*) to bring to the fore, give prominence to, underscore; (= *révéler*) to reveal; [+ *objet*] to put in a prominent *ou* conspicuous position; **se mettre en ~** to make o.s.

conspicuous, make one's presence felt; **la lettre était bien en ~** the letter was (lying) there for all to see

[3] **de toute évidence** LOC ADV quite obviously *ou* evidently

évident, e [evidã, ãt] ADJ obvious, evident, self-evident; **il est ~** it is obvious *ou* evident that, it is plain for all to see that; **ce n'est pas ~ !** it's not that easy *ou* simple!

évider [evide] ▸conjug 1◂ VT to hollow out, scoop out

évier [evje] NM sink; **~ (à) un bac/deux bacs** single/double sink

évincement [evɛ̃smã] NM [*rival*] ousting, supplanting

évincer [evɛ̃se] ▸conjug 3◂ VT [+ *concurrent*] to oust, supplant; (*Jur*) [+ *locataire*] to evict

éviscérer [evisere] ▸conjug 6◂ VT to eviscerate

évitable [evitabl] ADJ avoidable; **difficilement ~** hard to avoid

évitage [evitaʒ] NM (*Naut*) (= *mouvement*) swinging; (= *espace*) swinging room

évitement [evitmã] NM [*risque, véhicule*] avoidance; (*Transport*) **voie d'~** loop line; **gare d'~** station with a loop line; (*Aut, Aviat*) **manœuvre d'~** evasive action; (*Bio, Psych*) **réaction ou comportement d'~** avoidance behaviour

▾ **éviter** [evite] ▸conjug 1◂ [1] VT [a] [+ *coup, projectile*] to avoid, dodge; [+ *obstacle, danger, maladie, situation*] to avoid, steer clear of; [+ *gêneur, créancier*] to avoid, keep clear of, evade; [+ *regard*] to avoid, evade; **~ qu'une situation n'empire** to prevent a situation from getting worse, avoid a deterioration in a situation; **~ d'être repéré** to escape detection, avoid being detected [b] [+ *erreur, méthode*] to avoid; **~ de faire qch** to avoid doing sth; **~ le sel** to avoid *ou* keep off salt; **on lui a conseillé d'~ la marche** he has been advised to avoid walking *ou* advised against walking; **évite de m'interrompre/de dire des bêtises** try not to interrupt me/say anything stupid [c] **~ qch à qn** to spare *ou* save sb sth; **ça lui a évité d'avoir à se déplacer** that spared *ou* saved him the bother *ou* trouble of going [2] VI (*Naut*) to swing [3] **s'éviter** VPR [a] (= *se fuir*) to avoid each other *ou* one another; **ils s'évitaient depuis quelque temps** they had been avoiding each other *ou* keeping clear of each other for some time [b] **s'~ qch** to avoid sth; **je voudrais m'~ le trajet** I'd rather not have to make the trip, I'd like to save myself the trip; **s'~ toute fatigue** to spare o.s. any fatigue, save o.s. from getting at all tired

évocateur, -trice [evɔkatœʀ, tʀis] ADJ evocative, suggestive (**de** of)

évocation [evɔkasjɔ̃] NF [a] [*souvenirs, faits*] evocation, recalling; [*scène, idée*] conjuring-up, evocation; **ces ~s la faisaient s'attendrir** she became more tender as she recalled these memories; **la simple ~ de cette question** the mere mention of this issue; **pouvoir ou puissance d'~ d'un mot** evocative *ou* suggestive power of a word [b] (*littér*) [*démons*] evocation, calling-up, conjuring-up

évolué, e [evɔlɥe] (*ptp de* **évoluer**) ADJ [*peuple, civilisation*] (highly) developed, advanced; [*personne*] broad-minded, enlightened; [*espèce animale*] evolved; [*procédé, industrie, technologie*] advanced; (*Ordin*) [*langage*] high-level; (*hum*) **jeune fille ~e** liberated young woman

évoluer [evɔlɥe] ▸conjug 1◂ VI [a] (= *changer*) [*civilisation, idées, marché, situation, technique*] to evolve, develop; [*personne, goûts*] to change; [*maladie, tumeur*] to develop; [*espèce*] to evolve; **la situation évolue/n'évolue pas dans le bon sens** the situation is/isn't moving in the right direction; **voyons comment les choses vont** ~ let's wait and see how things develop; **faire ~** [+ *situation, société*] to bring about some change in; [+ *réglementation*] to make changes to; (*Ordin*) [+ *matériel*] to upgrade **b** (*professionnellement*) [*personne*] to advance **c** (= *se mouvoir*) [*danseur*] to move about; [*avion*] to fly around, wheel about; [*bateau à voile*] to sail around; [*troupes*] to manoeuvre (*Brit*), maneuver (*US*); **le monde dans lequel il évolue** the world in which he moves

évolutif, -ive [evɔlytif, iv] ADJ (*gén, Bio*) evolutionary, evolutional; (*Méd*) progressive; [*poste*] with potential (for advancement *ou* promotion) → **ski**

évolution [evɔlysjɔ̃] **1** NF **a** (= *changement*) [*civilisation, idées, situation, technique*] evolution, development; [*goûts*] change; [*maladie, tumeur*] development; [*espèce*] evolution; **il faut tenir compte de l'~ du marché/des prix** market/price trends have to be taken into account; **~ positive** (*gén*) positive development; (*économique*) improvement; (*Bio*) **théorie de l'~** theory of evolution **b** (*professionnelle*) **~ de carrière** career advancement **2** **évolutions** NFPL (= *mouvements*) movements; **il regardait les ~s du danseur/de l'avion** he watched the dancer as he moved about gracefully/the plane as it wheeled *ou* circled overhead; **les ~s des troupes** troop manoeuvres (*Brit*) *ou* maneuvers (*US*)

évolutionnisme [evɔlysjɔnism] NM evolutionism

évolutionniste [evɔlysjɔnist] **1** ADJ evolutionary **2** NMF evolutionist

évolutivité [evɔlytivite] NF (*Méd*) [*maladie*] progressive nature; **pour évaluer l'~ du cancer** to assess to what extent the cancer is likely to progress *ou* develop

évoquer [evɔke] ▸ conjug 1 ◂ VT **a** (= *remémorer*) [+ *souvenirs*] to recall, call up, evoke; [+ *fait, événement*] to evoke, recall; [+ *mémoire d'un défunt*] to recall **b** (= *faire penser à*) [+ *scène, idée*] to call to mind, evoke, conjure up; **ça évoque mon enfance** it reminds me of my childhood **c** (= *effleurer*) [+ *problème, sujet*] to touch on, bring up **d** (*littér* = *invoquer*) [+ *démons*] to evoke, call up, conjure up **e** (*Jur*) to transfer to a higher court

evzone [evzɔn, ɛvzɔn] NM evzone

ex. (ABRÉV = **exemple**) eg, e.g.

ex* [ɛks] NMF ex*

ex- [ɛks] PRÉF ex-; **l'~URSS** former soviet Union

exacerbation [ɛgzasɛʁbasjɔ̃] NF [*tensions*] exacerbation; [*concurrence*] intensification; **pour éviter l'~ nationaliste** to prevent the heightening *ou* exacerbation of nationalist tensions

exacerber [ɛgzasɛʁbe] ▸ conjug 1 ◂ **1** VT [+ *douleur*] to aggravate, exacerbate; [+ *émotion, passion*] to intensify, heighten; [+ *problème, tensions*] to exacerbate; [*concurrence*] to intensify; **sensibilité exacerbée** heightened sensibility **2** **s'exacerber** VPR [*concurrence, passion*] to become more intense, intensify; [*tensions*] to increase, be heightened; [*polémique*] to become more intense

exact, e [ɛgza(kt), ɛgzakt(ə)] ADJ **a** (= *fidèle*) [*reproduction, compte rendu*] exact, accurate; **réplique ~e** exact *ou* faithful replica; **c'est l'~e vérité** that's the absolute truth **b** (= *correct*) [*définition, raisonnement*] correct, exact; [*réponse, calcul*] correct, right; **ce n'est pas le terme** ~ that's not the right word; **est-il ~ que ... ?** is it right *ou* correct *ou* true that ...?; **ce n'est pas tout à fait ~** that's not quite right *ou* accurate, that's not altogether correct; **~ !** absolutely!, exactly! **c** (= *précis*) [*dimension, nombre, valeur*] exact, precise; [*donnée*] accurate, precise, correct; [*pendule*] accurate, right; **l'heure ~e** the right *ou* exact *ou* correct time; **la nature ~e de son travail** the precise nature of his work →

science

d (= *ponctuel*) punctual, on time; **c'est quelqu'un de très ~ d'habitude** he's usually on time *ou* very punctual; **être ~ à un rendez-vous** to arrive at an appointment on time, arrive punctually for an appointment **e** (*littér*) [*discipline*] exact, rigorous, strict; [*obéissance*] rigorous, strict, scrupulous

▾ **exactement** [ɛgzaktəmɑ̃] ADV **a** (*gén*) exactly; **c'est à 57 km ~** it's exactly *ou* precisely 57 km away; **au troisième top, il sera ~ huit heures** at the third stroke, it will be eight o'clock precisely; **c'est ~ ce que je pensais** that's exactly *ou* just *ou* precisely what I was thinking; (*hum*) **ce n'est pas ~ un expert** he's not exactly an expert **b** (= *tout à fait*) exactly; **oui, ~ !** yes, exactly! *ou* precisely!

exaction [ɛgzaksjɔ̃] **1** NF (*littér* = *extorsion*) exaction **2** **exactions** NFPL (= *abus de pouvoir*) abuses (of power); (= *violences*) acts of violence, violent acts

exactitude [ɛgzaktityd] NF **a** (= *fidélité*) [*reproduction, compte rendu*] exactness, exactitude (*frm*), accuracy **b** (= *justesse*) [*définition, raisonnement*] correctness, exactness; [*réponse, calcul*] correctness; **je ne mets pas en doute l'~ de vos informations** I'm not saying your information is wrong **c** (= *précision*) [*dimension, nombre, valeur*] exactness, precision; [*donnée*] accuracy, precision, correctness; [*pendule*] accuracy **d** (= *ponctualité*) punctuality ■ (*PROV*) **l'~ est la politesse des rois** punctuality is the essence of courtesy **e** (*littér* = *minutie*) exactitude

ex æquo [ɛgzeko] **1** ADJ INV (*Scol, Sport*) placed equal (*attrib*); **ils sont ~** they tied **2** NM INV **les ~** those who are (*ou* were) placed equal; **il y a deux ~ pour la deuxième place** there is a tie for second place **3** ADV **être (classé) premier ~** to be placed first equal *ou* joint first, tie for first place

exagération [ɛgzaʒeʁasjɔ̃] NF (*gén*) exaggeration; **on peut dire sans ~ que ...** one can say without any exaggeration *ou* without exaggerating that ...; **il est sévère sans ~** he's severe without taking it to extremes; **on lui a reproché des ~s dans sa biographie** he has been accused of exaggerating in his biography

exagéré, e [ɛgzaʒeʁe] (*ptp de* **exagérer**) ADJ (= *excessif*) [*dépenses, optimisme*] excessive; (= *surfait, amplifié*) [*commentaires*] exaggerated; **donner une importance ~e à** to exaggerate the importance of; **je suis peut-être d'un optimisme ~** maybe I'm being overly optimistic; **venir se plaindre après ça, c'est un peu ~** it was too much *ou* a bit much* (*Brit*) to come and complain after all that; **il serait ~ de dire** it would be an exaggeration *ou* an overstatement to say, it would be going too far to say; **la polémique a pris des proportions ~es** the controversy has been blown out of all proportion

exagérément [ɛgzaʒeʁemɑ̃] ADV [*cher*] excessively; [*optimiste, méfiant, simpliste*] overly, excessively

▾ **exagérer** [ɛgzaʒeʁe] ▸ conjug 6 ◂ **1** VT (*gén*) to exaggerate; **on a beaucoup exagéré leur rôle** their role has been hugely exaggerated; **sans ~, ça a duré trois heures** without any exaggeration *ou* I'm not exaggerating, it lasted three hours; **quand même il exagère !** really he goes too far *ou* oversteps the mark!; **500 F pour ça ? — ils exagèrent !** 500 francs for that? — they must be joking! *ou* that's a bit steep!; **n'exagérons rien !** let's not exaggerate!; **joue le personnage plus passionné, mais sans ~** make the character more passionate but don't overdo it **2** **s'exagérer** VPR [+ *difficultés*] to exaggerate; [+ *plaisirs, avantages*] to exaggerate, overrate

exaltant, e [ɛgzaltɑ̃, ɑ̃t] ADJ [*vie, aventure*] exciting, thrilling

exaltation [ɛgzaltasjɔ̃] NF **a** (= *surexcitation*) intense excitement; (*joyeuse*) elation; (*Psych*) overexcitement; **~ mystique** exaltation **b** (*littér* = *glorification*) extolling, praising, exalting **c** (*Rel*) **~ de la Sainte Croix** Exaltation of the Cross

exalté, e [ɛgzalte] (*ptp de* **exalter**) **1** ADJ [*imagination*] wild, vivid; [*esprit*] excited **2** NM,F (= *impétueux*) hothead; (= *fanatique*) fanatic

exalter [ɛgzalte] ▸ conjug 1 ◂ **1** VT **a** (= *surexciter*) [+ *esprit, imagination*] to fire; **exalté par cette nouvelle** (*très excité*) excited by *ou* keyed up with excitement over this piece of news; (*euphorique*) elated *ou* overjoyed by *ou* at this piece of news **b** (= *glorifier*) [*praise, exalt* **2** **s'exalter** VPR to get excited, get carried away

exam* [ɛgzam] NM (ABRÉV = **examen**) exam

▾ **examen** [ɛgzamɛ̃] **1** NM **a** (= *action d'étudier, d'analyser*: *gén*) examination; [*question, demande, cas, projet de loi*] examination, consideration; [*possibilité*] examination, investigation; **l'~ détaillé ou minutieux du rapport ...** detailed *ou* close examination of the report ...; **la question est à l'~** the matter is under consideration; **son argument ne résiste pas à l'~** his argument doesn't stand up to scrutiny; **procéder à l'~ de** [+ *demande, question*] to consider, look into; [+ *ordre du jour*] to go through **b** (*Jur*) **mettre qn en ~** to indict sb (**pour** for); **mise en ~** indictment; **il a demandé la mise en ~ de Luc Dufour** he asked that Luc Dufour be indicted **c** (*Méd*) **~ (médical)** [*patient*] (medical) examination; (= *analyse de sang etc*) (medical) test; **l'~ clinique** clinical examination; **se faire faire des ~s** to have some tests done *ou* taken; **subir un ~ médical complet** to undergo *ou* have a complete *ou* thorough checkup, have a thorough medical examination **d** (*Scol*) exam, examination; **~ écrit/oral** written/oral examination; **passer un ~** to take *ou* sit (*Brit*) an exam → **rattrapage** **2** COMP ▸ **examen blanc** (*Scol*) mock exam (*Brit*), practice test (*US*) ▸ **examen de conscience** self-examination; (*Rel*) examination of conscience; **faire son ~ de conscience** to examine one's conscience, take stock of o.s. ▸ **examen de passage** (*Scol*) end-of-year exam (*Brit*), final exam (*US*); (*fig*) ultimate test; **il a réussi son ~ de passage** he has proved himself, he has passed the ultimate test ▸ **examen prénuptial** (*Méd*) pre-marital examination ▸ **examen de santé** (medical) check-up ▸ **examen spécial d'entrée à l'université** university entrance examination ▸ **examen spectroscopique** (*Sci*) spectroscopic examination ▸ **examen de la vue** (*Méd*) eye *ou* sight test; **passer un ~ de la vue** to have one's eyes tested

examinateur, -trice [ɛgzaminatœʁ, tʁis] NM,F examiner; **~ extérieur/à l'oral** external/oral examiner

▾ **examiner** [ɛgzamine] ▸ conjug 1 ◂ **1** VT **a** (= *analyser*) [+ *document, faits, situation*] to examine, take a look at; [+ *possibilité*] to examine, investigate; [+ *question, demande, cas*] to consider, look into; [+ *comptes, dossier*] to examine, go through; [+ *projet de loi*] to consider; **~ qch dans le** *ou* **en détail** to examine sth in detail; **~ qch de près** to look closely at sth, take a close look at sth; **~ qch de plus près** to take a closer look at sth **b** (= *regarder*) [+ *objet, personne, visage*] to examine; [+ *ciel, horizon*] to scan; [+ *appartement, pièce*] to look over, have a (close) look round (*Brit*); **~ les lieux** to look over the place, have a look round (*Brit*); **~ qn de la tête aux pieds** to look sb up and down (contemptuously) **c** (*Méd*) [+ *malade*] to examine; **se faire ~ par un spécialiste** to be examined by a specialist

s'examiner VPR [*personne*] to examine o.s.; **s'~ devant la glace** to examine o.s. in the mirror; **ils s'examinaient à la dérobée** they were looking at each other furtively

exanthème [ɛgzɑ̃tɛm] NM exanthem

exarque [ɛgzaʀk] NM exarch

exaspérant, e [ɛgzaspeʀɑ̃, ɑ̃t] ADJ exasperating

exaspération [ɛgzaspeʀasjɔ̃] NF exasperation

exaspérer [ɛgzaspeʀe] ▸ conjug 6 ◂ VT **a** (= *irriter*) to exasperate **b** (*littér* = *aviver*) [+ *douleur*] to exacerbate, aggravate; [+ *émotion, désir*] to exacerbate

exaucement [ɛgzosmɑ̃] NM [*vœu*] fulfilment, granting; [*prière*] granting

exaucer [ɛgzose] ▸ conjug 3 ◂ VT [+ *vœu*] to fulfil, grant; (*Rel*) [+ *prière*] to grant, answer; **~ qn** to grant sb's wish, answer sb's prayer

ex cathedra [ɛkskatedʀa] ADV ex cathedra

excavateur [ɛkskavatœʀ] NM (= *machine*) excavator, mechanical digger (*Brit*), steam shovel (*US*)

excavation [ɛkskavasjɔ̃] NF (= *trou*) excavation; **~ naturelle** natural hollow (*ou cave etc*); (= *creusement*) excavation

excavatrice [ɛkskavatʀis] NF = **excavateur**

excaver [ɛkskave] ▸ conjug 1 ◂ VT to excavate

excédant, e [ɛksedɑ̃, ɑ̃t] ADJ (= *énervant*) exasperating, infuriating

excédent [ɛksedɑ̃] NM surplus (**sur** over); **~ de la balance des paiements** balance of payments surplus; **~ budgétaire/commercial** budget/trade surplus; **~ (du commerce) extérieur** foreign trade surplus, external surplus; **~ de trésorerie** cash surplus; **~ de poids/bagages** excess weight/luggage *ou* baggage; **il y a 2 kg d'~** *ou* **en ~** it's 2 kg over (weight); **budget en ~** surplus budget; **payer 30 F d'~** to pay 30 francs excess charge → **recette**

excédentaire [ɛksedɑ̃tɛʀ] ADJ [*production*] excess (*épith*), surplus (*épith*); **budget ~** surplus budget; **la production est ~** production is over target; **ils ont une balance commerciale ~** they have an active trade balance

excéder [ɛksede] ▸ conjug 6 ◂ VT **a** (= *dépasser*) [+ *longueur, temps, prix*] to exceed, be greater than; **le prix excédait (de beaucoup) ses moyens** the price was (way *ou* far) beyond *ou* far exceeded his means; **les avantages excèdent les inconvénients** the advantages outweigh the disadvantages; **l'apprentissage n'excède pas trois ans** the apprenticeship doesn't last more than three years *ou* lasts no more than *ou* does not exceed three years **b** (= *outrepasser*) [+ *pouvoir, droits*] to overstep, exceed, go beyond; [+ *forces*] to overtax **c** (= *accabler*: *gén pass*) to exhaust, weigh down, weary; **excédé de fatigue** overcome by tiredness, exhausted, tired out; **excédé de travail** overworked **d** (= *agacer*: *gén pass*) to exasperate, irritate, infuriate; **je suis excédé** I'm furious; **tu m'excèdes avec tes jérémiades !** your whining irritates me!, you exasperate me with your moaning!

excellemment [ɛkselamɑ̃] ADV (*littér*) excellently

excellence [ɛkselɑ̃s] NF **a** (*littér*) excellence; **il est le poète surréaliste par ~** he is the surrealist poet par excellence; **il aime la musique par ~** he loves music above all else **b** **Son Excellence** His (*ou* Her) Excellency; **merci (Votre) Excellence** thank you, Your Excellency

excellent, e [ɛkselɑ̃, ɑ̃t] ADJ excellent

exceller [ɛksele] ▸ conjug 1 ◂ VI to excel (**dans** *ou* **en qch** at *ou* in sth, **à faire** in doing)

excentré, e [ɛksɑ̃tʀe] ADJ **a** [*quartier, région*] outlying (*épith*); **le magasin est trop ~ pour fidéliser une clientèle** the shop is (located) too far out (of town) to attract regular cus-

tomers **b** (*Tech*) [*pièce*] off-centre (*Brit*), off-center (*US*)

excentricité [ɛksɑ̃tʀisite] NF (*gén, Math, Astron*) eccentricity; [*quartier*] outlying location

excentrique [ɛksɑ̃tʀik] **1** ADJ [*personne*] (*Math*) [*cercle*] eccentric; [*quartier*] outlying (*épith*) **2** NMF eccentric, crank (*péj*)

excentriquement [ɛksɑ̃tʀikmɑ̃] ADV (*gén*) eccentrically

excepté, e [ɛksɛpte] (*ptp de* **excepter**) **1** ADJ **il n'a plus de famille sa mère ~e** he has no family left apart from *ou* aside from (*US*) *ou* except his mother, excluding his mother he has no family left **2** PRÉP except, but for, apart from, aside from (*US*); **~ quand** except *ou* apart from when; **~ que** except that; **tous ~ sa mère** everyone but his mother, everyone except for *ou* aside from (*US*) his mother

excepter [ɛksɛpte] ▸ conjug 1 ◂ VT to except (**de** from), make an exception of; **sans ~ personne** without excluding anyone, no one excepted

exception [ɛksɛpsjɔ̃] NF **a** (= *dérogation*) exception; **à quelques ~s près** with a few exceptions; **c'est l'~ qui confirme la règle** it's the exception which proves the rule; **d'~** [*tribunal*] special; [*régime, mesure*] special, exceptional **b** (*Jur*) objection, plea; **~ péremptoire** ≈ demurrer **c** (*loc*) **faire une ~ à** [+ *règle*] to make an exception to; **faire ~ (à la règle)** to be an exception (to the rule); **faire ~ de** to make an exception of; **à faire de ◊ à l'~ de** except for, apart from, aside from (*US*), with the exception of; **sans ~** without exception; **sauf ~** allowing for exceptions → **titre**

exceptionnel, -elle [ɛksɛpsjɔnɛl] **1** ADJ (= *rare*) exceptional; (*Comm*) **offre exceptionnelle** special offer, special (*US*); **fait ~, il a accepté** he accepted for once; **d'un talent ~** exceptionally talented → **élément** **2** NM **l'~** the exceptional

exceptionnellement [ɛksɛpsjɔnɛlmɑ̃] ADV **a** (= *à titre d'exception*) **ils se sont réunis ~ un dimanche** contrary to their general practice *ou* in this particular instance they met on a Sunday; **le magasin sera ~ ouvert dimanche** the store will open on Sunday just for this week *ou* for this week only; **~, je vous recevrai lundi** just this once I will see you on Monday **b** [*difficile, élevé, fort*] exceptionally

excès [ɛksɛ] **1** NM **a** (= *surplus*) [*argent*] excess, surplus; [*marchandises, produits*] glut, surplus; **il y a un ~ d'acide** (= *il en reste*) there is some acid left over *ou* some excess acid; (= *il y en a trop*) there is too much acid; **~ de cholestérol dans le sang** excess of cholesterol in the blood; **~ de précautions** excessive care *ou* precautions; **~ de zèle** overzealousness → **pécher** **b** (*gén, Méd, Pol* = *abus*) excess; **des ~ de langage** extreme *ou* immoderate language; **tomber dans l'~** to go to extremes; **tomber dans l'~ inverse** to go to the opposite extreme; **~ de boisson** overindulgence in drink, intemperance; **des ~ de table** overindulgence at (the) table, surfeit of (good) food; **faire des ~ de table** to overindulge, eat too much; **se laisser aller à des ~** to go overboard*; **je me suis trompé, par ~ de confiance en moi/d'optimisme** I made a mistake by being overconfident/over-optimistic **c** (*loc littér*) **à l'~ ◊ jusqu'à l'~** to excess, excessively, inordinately; **généreux à l'~** inordinately generous, overgenerous, generous to a fault; **avec ~** to excess, excessively; **il fait tout avec ~** he does everything to excess, he is excessive in everything he does; **boire avec ~** to drink to excess *ou* excessively; **dépenser avec ~** to be excessive in one's spending; **il est sévère, mais sans ~** he's strict, but not excessively so ■ (*PROV*) **l'~ en tout est un défaut** everything in moderation

2 COMP ▸ **excès de pouvoir** (*Jur*) abuse of power, actions ultra vires (*SPÉC*) ▸ **excès de vitesse** (*Aut*) breaking *ou* exceeding the speed limit, speeding; **coupable de plusieurs ~ de vitesse** guilty of having broken *ou* of exceeding the speed limit on several occasions

excessif, -ive [ɛksesif, iv] ADJ **a** [+ *colère, enthousiasme, prix*] excessive; [+ *fierté*] excessive, inordinate; **des horaires de travail ~s** excessively long working hours; **300 F, c'est ~ !** 300 francs, that's far too much!; **500 F, ce n'est vraiment pas ~ !** 500 francs isn't what you'd call expensive! **b** [+ *personne*] **elle est excessive (en tout)** she's a woman of extremes, she takes everything to extremes *ou* too far

excessivement [ɛksesivmɑ̃] ADV (*gén*) excessively; [*cher, fier*] excessively, inordinately; **~ difficile/grave** extremely difficult/serious

exciper [ɛksipe] ▸ **exciper de** VT INDIR (*frm*) [+ *bonne foi, précédent*] to plead

excipient [ɛksipjɑ̃] NM excipient

exciser [ɛksize] ▸ conjug 1 ◂ VT to excise

excision [ɛksizjɔ̃] NF excision

excitabilité [ɛksitabilite] NF (*Bio*) excitability

excitable [ɛksitabl] ADJ excitable, easily excited

excitant, e [ɛksitɑ̃, ɑ̃t] **1** ADJ **a** (= *enthousiasmant*) [*idée, livre, projet*] exciting; **ce n'est pas très ~ !** it's not very exciting! **b** (= *stimulant*) [*effet, substance*] stimulating **c** (*sexuellement*) arousing, sexy **2** NM stimulant

excitation [ɛksitasjɔ̃] NF **a** (*Méd*) [*nerf, muscle*] excitation, stimulation; (*Élec*) [*électro-aimant*] excitation **b** (*Jur* = *incitation*) **~ à** incitement to; **~ de mineurs à la débauche** incitement of minors to immoral behaviour **c** (= *enthousiasme, nervosité*) excitement; **dans un état de grande ~** in a state of great excitement *ou* arousal; (= *désir*) **~ (sexuelle)** (sexual) excitement *ou* arousal

excité, e [ɛksite] (*ptp de* **exciter**) **1** ADJ **a*** (= *enthousiasmé*) excited; **il ne semblait pas très ~ à l'idée de me revoir*** he didn't seem too thrilled at the idea of *ou* too wild* about seeing me again → **puce** **b** (= *nerveux*) [*animal*] restless; [*enfant*] hyped-up*; **des soldats, très ~s, ont commencé à tirer** some of the soldiers were very jumpy* and started to shoot **c*** (= *irrité*) worked-up **d** (*sexuellement*) excited **2** NM,F* (= *nerveux*) hothead; (= *fanatique*) fanatic; **une poignée d'~s** a bunch of hotheads; **ne fais pas attention, c'est un ~** don't take any notice, he gets carried away

exciter [ɛksite] ▸ conjug 1 ◂ **1** VT **a** (= *provoquer*) [+ *intérêt, désir*] to (a)rouse; [+ *curiosité*] to rouse, excite; [+ *imagination*] to stimulate, fire, stir; [+ *appétit*] to whet; **tous ses sens étaient excités** all his senses were aroused **b** (= *aviver*) [+ *colère, douleur, ardeur*] to intensify, increase; **cela ne fit qu'~ sa colère** that only increased *ou* intensified his anger, that only made him even more angry **c** (= *enthousiasmer*) [+ *personne*] to thrill; **ça ne m'excite guère d'y aller** I'm not exactly thrilled at the thought of going **d** (= *rendre nerveux*) **~ un animal/un enfant** to get an animal/a child excited; **le vent les excite** the wind makes them restless; **le café, ça m'excite trop** coffee makes me too nervous *ou* hyper* **e** (*sexuellement*) to arouse *ou* excite (sexually) **f** * (= *irriter*) [*situation, réunion*] to get worked-up; **il commence à m'~** he's getting on my nerves **g** (= *encourager*) to urge on, spur on; **excitant ses chiens de la voix** urging on *ou* spurring on his dogs with shouts, shouting to urge on his dogs; **~ qn contre qn** to set sb against sb

boxed[h] (= *inciter*) **à** to exhort to, incite to, urge to; **~ qn à faire qch** to push sb into doing sth, provoke *ou* urge sb to do sth; **~ des soldats au combat** to incite *ou* exhort soldiers to combat *ou* battle
boxed[i] (*Méd*) [+ *nerf, muscle*] to stimulate, excite; (*Élec, Phys*) [+ *électro-aimant, noyau*] to excite

2 s'exciter VPR boxed[a]* (= *s'enthousiasmer*) to get excited (**sur, à propos de** about, over), get carried away; (= *devenir nerveux*) to get worked up*, get in a flap*; (= *se fâcher*) to get angry *ou* annoyed, get hot under the collar*; **pas la peine de t'~** (*bêtement*) it's no use getting hot under the collar*
boxed[b] (*sexuellement*) to become (sexually) excited, be (sexually) aroused

exclamatif, -ive [ɛksklamatif, iv] ADJ exclamatory

exclamation [ɛksklamasjɔ̃] NF exclamation → **point[1]**

exclamer (s') [ɛksklame] ▸conjug 1◂ VPR to exclaim; **« dommage !» s'exclama-t-il** "what a pity!", he exclaimed; (*littér*) (= *de colère/d'admiration*) to exclaim *ou* cry out in anger/admiration; (*littér = protester*) **s'~ sur qch** to shout *ou* make a fuss about sth

exclu, e [ɛkskly] **1** ADJ boxed[a] (= *non accepté*) [*personne*] excluded; **se sentir ~ de la société** to feel excluded from society boxed[b] (= *excepté*) **tous les jours, mardi ~** every day, except Tuesday boxed[c] (= *hors de question*) **c'est tout à fait ~** it's completely out of the question; **aucune hypothèse n'est ~e** no possibility has been ruled out; **il n'est pas ~ que ...** it is not impossible that ...; **une défaite n'est pas ~e** defeat cannot be ruled out **2** NM,F **les ~s (de la société)** (social) outcasts; **les ~s de la croissance économique** those left out of the economic boom

exclure [ɛksklyʀ] ▸conjug 35◂ **1** VT boxed[a] (= *chasser*) (*d'un parti, d'une équipe*) to expel; (*d'un club*) to expel, ban; (*temporairement*) to suspend; (*d'une école*) to expel, exclude; (*temporairement*) to suspend, exclude; (*d'une université*) to expel, send down (*Brit*) (**de** from) boxed[b] (= *écarter*) [+ *solution*] to exclude, rule out; [+ *hypothèse*] to dismiss, rule out; **~ qch de son régime** to cut sth out of one's diet boxed[c] (= *être incompatible avec*) [*fait*] to preclude **2 s'exclure** VPR **s'~ mutuellement** [*idées*] to be mutually exclusive; [*actions, mesures*] to be (mutually) incompatible

exclusif, -ive[1] [ɛksklyzif, iv] ADJ boxed[a] [*privilège*] exclusive (*épith*); **à l'usage/au profit ~ de** for the sole use/benefit of; **pour mon usage ~** for my use alone; **dans le but ~ de faire ...** with the sole *ou* exclusive aim of doing ... boxed[b] (*Comm*) [*droits, distributeur*] sole (*épith*), exclusive (*épith*); [*représentant*] sole (*épith*); [*photo, reportage, fabrication*] exclusive (*épith*) boxed[c] (*Math, Logique*) exclusive; **le ou ~** the exclusive or boxed[d] (*dans ses sentiments*) **il lui porte un amour ~** he loves her to the exclusion of all others, he loves her alone; **elle est exclusive en amour** she's a one-man woman; **il a un caractère (trop) ~** he's (too) exclusive in his relationships; **très ~ dans ses amitiés** very selective *ou* exclusive in his friendships; **très ~ dans ses goûts** very selective in his tastes

exclusion [ɛksklyzjɔ̃] NF boxed[a] (= *expulsion*) [*parti, équipe, club*] expulsion; (*temporaire*) suspension; [*école*] expulsion, exclusion; (*temporaire*) suspension, exclusion (**de** from) → **zone** boxed[b] (= *marginalisation*) **l'~ (sociale)** social exclusion; **personne en voie d'~** person who is in danger of becoming a social outcast boxed[c] **à l'~ de** (= *en écartant*) to the exclusion of; (= *sauf*) with the exclusion *ou* exception of; **aimer les pommes à l'~ de tous les autres fruits** to love apples to the exclusion of all other fruit; **il peut manger de tous les fruits à l'~ des pommes** he can eat any fruit excluding ap-

ples *ou* with the exclusion *ou* exception of apples

exclusive[2] [ɛksklyziv] NF (*frm*) bar, debarment; **tous sans ~** with none debarred; **frapper qn d'~** ◊ **prononcer l'~ contre qn** to debar sb

exclusivement [ɛksklyzivmɑ̃] ADV boxed[a] (= *seulement*) exclusively, solely; **~ réservé au personnel** reserved for staff only boxed[b] (= *non inclus*) **du 10 au 15 du mois ~** from the 10th to the 15th exclusive boxed[c] (*littér = de manière entière ou absolue*) exclusively

exclusivité [ɛksklyzivite] NF boxed[a] (*Comm*) exclusive rights; **avoir l'~ de la couverture d'un événement** to have (the) exclusive coverage of an event; **avoir l'~ de la distribution de qch** to have exclusive distribution rights to sth; (*fig*) **il n'en a pas l'~** he's not the only one to have it, he hasn't (got) a monopoly on it*; **contrat d'~** exclusive contract; **en ~ dans notre journal** exclusive to our paper; **films en première ~** new releases; **ce film passe en ~** this film is showing only *ou* exclusively at boxed[b] (= *reportage*) (*gén*) exclusive; (*à sensation*) scoop; **c'est une ~ de notre maison** it's made (*ou* sold) exclusively by our company, it's exclusive to our company boxed[c] [*sentiment*] **l'~ en amour est rare** it is rare for somebody to love one person alone

excommunication [ɛkskɔmynikasjɔ̃] NF excommunication

excommunier [ɛkskɔmynje] ▸conjug 7◂ VT to excommunicate

excrément [ɛkskʀemɑ̃] NM excrement (*NonC*); **~s** excrement, faeces

excrémenteux, -euse [ɛkskʀemɑ̃tø, øz], **excrémentiel, -elle** [ɛkskʀemɑ̃sjɛl] ADJ excremental, excrementitious

excréter [ɛkskʀete] ▸conjug 6◂ VT to excrete

excréteur, -trice [ɛkskʀetœʀ, tʀis] ADJ excretory

excrétion [ɛkskʀesjɔ̃] NF excretion; **~s** excreta

excrétoire [ɛkskʀetwaʀ] ADJ = **excréteur**

excroissance [ɛkskʀwasɑ̃s] NF (*Méd*) excrescence, outgrowth; (*fig*) outgrowth, development

excursion [ɛkskyʀsjɔ̃] NF (*en car*) excursion, (sightseeing) trip; (*en voiture*) drive; (*à vélo*) ride; (*à pied*) walk, hike; **~ en mer** boat trip; **~ de trois jours** three-day tour *ou* (sightseeing) trip; **partir en ~** *ou* **faire une ~** (*en car*) to go on an excursion *ou* a trip; (*en voiture*) to go for a drive; (*à vélo*) to go for a ride; (*à pied*) to go on a walk *ou* hike, go walking *ou* hiking

excursionner [ɛkskyʀsjɔne] ▸conjug 1◂ VI to go on an excursion *ou* trip

excursionniste [ɛkskyʀsjɔnist] NMF (*en car*) (day) tripper (*Brit*), traveler (*US*); (*à pied*) hiker, walker

excusable [ɛkskyzabl] ADJ [*acte*] excusable, forgivable; **il n'est pas ~** what he did is unforgivable

▼ **excuse** [ɛkskyz] NF boxed[a] (= *prétexte*) excuse; **bonne/mauvaise ~** good/poor *ou* lame excuse; **sans ~** inexcusable; **il a pris pour ~ qu'il avait à travailler** he made *ou* gave the excuse that he had work to do, he used his work as an excuse; (*Jur*) **~s légales** lawful *ou* legal excuses; (*iro*) **la belle ~ !** that's a fine excuse! (*iro*) → **mot** boxed[b] **~s** (= *regrets*) apology; **faire des ~s** ◊ **présenter ses ~s** to apologize, offer one's apologies (**à** to); **je vous dois des ~s** I owe you an apology; **exiger des ~s** to demand an apology; **mille ~s** do forgive me, I'm so sorry; (* *ou hum*) **faites ~** excuse me, 'scuse me* boxed[c] (*Tarot*) excuse

▼ **excuser** [ɛkskyze] ▸conjug 1◂ **1** VT boxed[a] (= *pardonner*) [+ *personne, faute*] to excuse, forgive; **veuillez ~ mon retard** please excuse my being late *ou* my lateness, I do apologize for being late; **je vous prie de l'~** please excuse *ou* forgive him; (*frm*) **veuillez m'~** ◊ **je vous prie**

de m'~ I beg your pardon, please forgive me (**pour avoir fait** for having done); **excusez-moi** excuse me, I'm sorry; **je m'excuse*** (I'm) sorry; **excusez-moi de vous le dire mais ...** excuse *ou* forgive *ou* pardon my saying so but ...; **excusez-moi de ne pas venir** excuse my not coming, I'm sorry I can't come; **vous êtes tout excusé** please don't apologize, you are quite forgiven; **ils ont invité 500 personnes, excusez du peu !*** they invited 500 people if you please!*; **vous invitez 500 personnes ? excusez du peu !*** you're inviting 500 people? is that all? (*iro*)
boxed[b] (= *justifier*) to excuse; **cette explication n'excuse rien** this explanation is no excuse boxed[c] (= *dispenser*) to excuse; **il a demandé à être excusé pour la réunion de demain** he asked to be excused from tomorrow's meeting; **se faire ~** to ask to be excused; **« M. Dupont : (absent) excusé »** "Mr Dupont has sent an apology", "apologies for absence received from Mr Dupont"

2 s'excuser VPR to apologize (**de qch** for sth); (*aller*) **s'~ auprès de qn** to apologize to sb ■ (*PROV*) **qui s'excuse s'accuse** apologizing is a way of admitting one's guilt

exécrable [ɛgzekʀabl] ADJ atrocious, execrable

exécrablement [ɛgzekʀabləmɑ̃] ADV atrociously, execrably

exécration [ɛgzekʀasjɔ̃] NF boxed[a] (*littér = haine*) execration, loathing; **avoir qch en ~** to hold sth in abhorrence boxed[b] †† (= *imprécation*) curse

exécrer [ɛgzekʀe] ▸conjug 6◂ VT to loathe, abhor, execrate

exécutable [ɛgzekytabl] ADJ [*tâche*] possible, manageable; [*projet*] workable, feasible; (*Ordin*) [*fichier*] executable

exécutant, e [ɛgzekytɑ̃, ɑ̃t] NM,F (*Mus*) performer, executant; (*péj = agent*) underling; **il n'est qu'un ~** he just carries out (his) orders, he's just an underling

exécuter [ɛgzekyte] ▸conjug 1◂ **1** VT boxed[a] (= *accomplir*) [+ *plan, ordre, mouvements*] to execute, carry out; [+ *projet, mission*] to execute, carry out, accomplish; [+ *promesse*] to fulfil, carry out; [+ *travail*] to do, execute; [+ *tâche*] to execute, discharge, perform; **travail exécuté à la hâte** work done in a hurry; **il a fait ~ des travaux dans sa maison** he had some work done on his house
boxed[b] (= *réaliser*) [+ *objet*] to make; [+ *tableau*] to paint, execute boxed[c] (= *préparer*) [+ *ordonnance*] to make up; [+ *commande*] to fulfil, carry out; **faire ~ une ordonnance** to have a prescription made up boxed[d] (*Mus*) [+ *morceau*] to perform, play; **brillamment exécuté** brilliantly executed *ou* played boxed[e] (= *tuer*) to execute boxed[f] (= *vaincre*) to trounce; (= *critiquer*) to demolish boxed[g] (*Jur*) [+ *traité, loi, décret*] to enforce; [+ *contrat*] to perform; [+ *débiteur*] to distrain upon boxed[h] (*Ordin*) [+ *programme*] to run; [+ *instruction*] to carry out

2 s'exécuter VPR (*en s'excusant*) to comply; (*en payant*) to pay up; **je lui demandai de s'excuser et il finit par s'~** I asked him to apologize and finally he complied *ou* did; **au moment de l'addition, il s'exécuta de mauvaise grâce** when the time came to settle the bill he paid up with bad grace

exécuteur, -trice [ɛgzekytœʀ, tʀis] **1** NM,F [*arrêt, décret*] enforcer **2** NM (*Hist*) **~ (des hautes œuvres)** executioner; (*péj = homme de main*) **~ des basses œuvres** henchman; (*Jur*) **~ (testamentaire)** (= *homme*) executor; (= *femme*) executrix

exécutif, -ive [ɛgzekytif, iv] **1** ADJ **pouvoir ~** executive power **2** NM **l'~** the executive

exécution [ɛgzekysjɔ̃] NF [a] (= *accomplissement*) [*plan, ordre, mouvement*] execution; [*projet, mission*] execution, accomplishment; [*promesse*] fulfilment; [*travail, tâche*] execution; **l'~ des travaux a été ralentie** the work has been slowed down *ou* delayed; **~ !** get on with it!; **mettre à ~** [+ *projet, idées, menaces*] to carry out; **mise à ~** [*loi*] implementation, enforcement; **pour empêcher la mise à ~ de cette menace** to prevent the threat from being carried out → **voie**
[b] (= *réalisation*) [*objet*] production; [*tableau*] execution
[c] (= *préparation*) [*commande*] fulfilment, carrying out; [*ordonnance*] making up
[d] (*Mus*) [*morceau*] performance; **d'une ~ difficile** difficult to play
[e] (= *mise à mort*) execution; **~ capitale/sommaire** capital/summary execution
[f] (*Jur*) [*traité, loi, décret*] enforcement; [*contrat*] performance; **en ~ de la loi** in compliance *ou* accordance with the law
[g] (*Ordin*) [*programme*] running; [*instruction*] carrying out

exécutoire [ɛgzekytwaʀ] ADJ (*Jur*) executory, enforceable; **mesure ~ pour chaque partie contractante** measure binding on each contracting party

exégèse [ɛgzeʒɛz] NF exegesis; **faire l'~ d'un discours politique** to analyse a political speech

exégète [ɛgzeʒɛt] NM exegete

exemplaire [ɛgzɑ̃plɛʀ] [1] ADJ [*mère*] model (*épith*), exemplary; [*punition*] exemplary; **infliger une punition ~ à qn** to make an example of sb (by punishing him) [2] NM [a] [*livre, formulaire*] copy; **en deux ~s** in duplicate; **en trois ~s** in triplicate; **25 ~s de cet avion ont été vendus** 25 aeroplanes of this type have been sold → **tirer** [b] (= *échantillon*) specimen, example

exemplairement [ɛgzɑ̃plɛʀmɑ̃] ADV exemplarily

exemplarité [ɛgzɑ̃plarite] NF exemplary nature

▼ **exemple** [ɛgzɑ̃pl] NM [a] (= *modèle*) example; **l'~ de leur faillite/de sa sœur lui sera bien utile** their failure/his sister will be a useful example for him; **il est l'~ de la vertu/l'honnêteté** he sets an example of virtue/honesty, he is a model of virtue/honesty; **citer qn/qch en ~** to quote sb/sth as an example; **donner l'~ de l'honnêteté/de ce qu'il faut faire** to give *ou* set an example of honesty/of what to do; **donner l'~** to set an example; **suivre l'~ de qn** to follow sb's example; **prendre ~ sur qn** to take sb as a model; **servir d'~ à qn** to serve as an example to sb; **à l'~ de son père** just like his father, following in his father's footsteps; **faire un ~ de qn** (*punir*) to make an example of sb; **il faut absolument faire un ~** we must make an example of somebody; **il faut les punir pour l'~** they must be punished as an example *ou* as a deterrent to others → **prêcher**
[b] (= *cas, spécimen*) example; **un bel ~ du gothique flamboyant** a fine example of flamboyant gothic; **~ typique** typical example; **le seul ~ que je connaisse** the only example *ou* instance I know of *ou* am aware of; **être d'une bêtise/avarice sans ~** to be of unparalleled stupidity/meanness; **il en existe plusieurs : ~, le rat musqué** there are several, for example *ou* for instance the muskrat
[c] (*Lexicographie*) example, illustrative phrase
[d] **par ~** (*explicatif*) for example *ou* instance; **(ça) par ~ !** (*surprise*) well I never!, my word!; (*indignation*) honestly!, well really!; (* = *par contre*) **c'est assez cher, par ~ on y mange bien** it's pretty expensive but on the other hand *ou* but there again the food is good

exemplification [ɛgzɑ̃plifikasjɔ̃] NF exemplification

exemplifier [ɛgzɑ̃plifje] ▸ conjug 1 ◂ VT to exemplify

exempt, e [ɛgzɑ̃, ɑ̃(p)t] [1] ADJ [a] (= *dispensé de*) **~ de** [+ *service militaire, corvée, impôts*] exempt from; **~ de taxes** tax-free, duty-free; **~ de TVA** zero-rated for VAT [b] (= *dépourvu de*) **~ de** [+ *vent, dangers, arrogance, erreurs*] free from; **entreprise ~e de dangers** danger-free undertaking, undertaking free from all danger; **d'un ton qui n'était pas ~ d'humour** in a voice which was not without humour, with the faintest tinge of humour in his voice [2] NM (*Hist : Mil, Police*) exempt

exempté [ɛgzɑ̃(p)te] NM (*Mil*) man who is exempt from military service

exempter [ɛgzɑ̃(p)te] ▸ conjug 1 ◂ VT [a] (= *dispenser*) to exempt (**de** from) [b] (= *préserver de*) **~ qn de** [+ *soucis*] to save sb from

exemption [ɛgzɑ̃psjɔ̃] NF exemption

exerçant, e [ɛgzɛʀsɑ̃, ɑ̃t] ADJ **médecin ~** practising doctor

exercé, e [ɛgzɛʀse] (*ptp de* **exercer**) ADJ [*œil, oreille*] keen, trained; [*personne*] experienced

exercer [ɛgzɛʀse] ▸ conjug 3 ◂ [1] VT [a] (= *pratiquer*) [+ *métier*] to have; [+ *fonction*] to fulfil, exercise; [+ *talents*] to exercise; [*littér*] [+ *charité, hospitalité*] to exercise, practise; **dans le métier que j'exerce** [*médecin, avocat*] in my profession *ou* job; **il exerce encore** he's still practising *ou* in practice
[b] [+ *droit, pouvoir*] to exercise (**sur** over); [+ *contrôle, influence*] to exert, exercise (**sur** over); [+ *représailles*] to take (**sur** on); [+ *poussée, pression*] to exert (**sur** on); **~ des pressions sur qn** to bring pressure to bear on sb, exert pressure on sb; **~ ses sarcasmes contre qn** to use one's sarcasm on sb, make sb the butt of one's sarcasm; **les forces qui s'exercent sur le levier** the force exerted on *ou* brought to bear on the lever; **~ des poursuites contre qn** to bring an action against sb
[c] (= *aguerrir*) [+ *corps, esprit, mémoire, voix*] to train, exercise (**à** to, for); **~ des élèves à lire** *ou* **à la lecture** to get pupils to practise their reading; **~ un chien à rapporter le journal** to train a dog to bring back the newspaper
[d] (= *éprouver*) [+ *sagacité, habileté*] to tax; [+ *patience*] to try, tax
[2] **s'exercer** VPR [*pianiste, sportif*] to practise; **s'~ à** [+ *technique, mouvement*] to practise; **s'~ à la patience** to train o.s. to be patient; **s'~ à faire qch** to train o.s. to do sth

exercice [ɛgzɛʀsis] [1] NM [a] (= *pratique*) [*métier*] practice; [*droit*] exercising; [*facultés*] exercise; **l'~ du pouvoir** the exercise of power; **après 40 ans d'~** after 40 years in practice; **condamné pour ~ illégal de la médecine** sentenced for practising medicine illegally *ou* for the illegal practice of medicine; **dans l'~ de ses fonctions** in the exercise *ou* execution *ou* discharge of his duties
[b] **en ~ : être en ~** [*médecin*] to be in practice; [*juge, fonctionnaire*] to be in *ou* hold office; **juge en ~** sitting judge; **président en ~** serving chairman; **entrer en ~** to take up *ou* assume one's duties
[c] (= *activité physique*) **l'~ (physique)** (physical) exercise; **prendre†** *ou* **faire de l'~** to take some exercise
[d] (*Mil*) **l'~** exercises, drill; **aller à l'~** to go on exercises; **faire l'~** to drill, be at drill
[e] (*Mus, Scol, Sport* = *travail d'entraînement*) exercise; **~ pour piano** piano exercise; **~ de pronunciation** pronunciation exercise *ou* drill; **~ d'application** practise *ou* application exercise; (*Gym*) **~ au sol** floor exercises; **~ d'évacuation** fire drill; **l'interview est un ~ difficile** interviewing is a difficult business → **cahier**
[f] (*Admin, Fin* = *période*) year; **l'~ 1996** the 1996 fiscal *ou* tax year
[2] COMP ▸ **exercices d'assouplissement** limbering up exercises, bending and stretching exercises ▸ **exercice budgétaire** budg-

etary year ▸ **exercice comptable** accounting year ▸ **exercice du culte** religious worship ▸ **exercice fiscal** fiscal *ou* tax year ▸ **exercice de style** (*Littérat*) stylistic composition; (*fig*) exercise in style ▸ **exercices de tir** (*Mil*) shooting drill *ou* practice

exerciseur [ɛgzɛʀsizœʀ] NM (*gén*) exercise machine; (*pour poitrine*) chest expander

exergue [ɛgzɛʀg] NM [*texte*] **porter qch en ~** to bear sth as an epigraph; **cette médaille porte en ~ l'inscription ...** (*lit*) this medal is inscribed below ...; **mettre en ~** (= *mettre en évidence*) [+ *idée, phrase*] to bring out, underline; **mettre une citation en ~ à un chapitre** to head a chapter with a quotation, put in a quotation as (an) epigraph to a chapter; **mettre un proverbe en ~ à un tableau** to inscribe a painting with a proverb

exfoliant, e [ɛksfɔljɑ̃, jɑ̃t] ADJ exfoliating (*épith*)

exfoliation [ɛksfɔljasjɔ̃] NF exfoliation

exfolier [ɛksfɔlje] ▸ conjug 7 ◂ [1] VT [+ *peau*] to exfoliate [2] **exfolier (s')** VPR [*peau, os, roche, bois*] to exfoliate

exhalaison [ɛgzalezɔ̃] NF (*littér*) (*désagréable*) exhalation; (*agréable*) fragrance, exhalation

exhalation [ɛgzalasjɔ̃] NF (*Physiol*) exhalation

exhaler [ɛgzale] ▸ conjug 1 ◂ [1] VT (*littér*) [a] [+ *odeur, vapeur*] to exhale, give off [b] [+ *soupir*] to breathe; [+ *plainte*] to utter, give forth (*littér*); [+ *joie, douleur*] to give vent *ou* expression to [c] (*Physiol* = *souffler*) to exhale [2] **s'exhaler** VPR [*odeur*] to rise (up) (**de** from); **un soupir s'exhala de ses lèvres** a sigh rose from his lips

exhaussement [ɛgzosmɑ̃] NM raising

exhausser [ɛgzose] ▸ conjug 1 ◂ VT [+ *construction*] to raise (up); **~ une maison d'un étage** to add a floor to a house

exhausteur [ɛgzostœʀ] NM **~ de goût** *ou* **de saveur** flavour enhancer

exhaustif, -ive [ɛgzostif, iv] ADJ exhaustive

exhaustivement [ɛgzostivmɑ̃] ADV exhaustively

exhaustivité [ɛgzostivite] NF exhaustiveness

exhiber [ɛgzibe] ▸ conjug 1 ◂ [1] VT [a] (*frm* = *produire*) [+ *document, passeport*] to present, show, produce [b] (= *montrer au public*) [+ *animal*] to show, exhibit [c] (*péj*) [+ *partie du corps*] to show off, display; [+ *savoir, richesse, diplômes*] to display, show off, flaunt [2] **s'exhiber** VPR [a] (*péj* = *parader*) to show o.s. off (in public), parade around [b] [*exhibitionniste*] to expose o.s.

exhibition [ɛgzibisjɔ̃] NF [a] (*Sport*) **match d'~** exhibition match [b] [*partie du corps*] showing off [c] [*animal*] exhibiting, showing; (= *concours*) show [d] (= *comportement*) outrageous behaviour (*NonC*) [e] (*frm*) [*document, passeport*] presentation, production

exhibitionnisme [ɛgzibisjɔnism] NM exhibitionism

exhibitionniste [ɛgzibisjɔnist] NMF exhibitionist; **il est un peu ~** he's a bit of an exhibitionist

exhortation [ɛgzɔʀtasjɔ̃] NF exhortation

exhorter [ɛgzɔʀte] ▸ conjug 1 ◂ VT to exhort (**à faire** to do, **à qch** to sth), urge (**à faire** to do)

exhumation [ɛgzymasjɔ̃] NF [*corps*] exhumation; [*ruines, vestiges*] excavation; [*faits, vieux livres*] unearthing, digging up *ou* out; [*souvenirs*] recollection, recalling

exhumer [ɛgzyme] ▸ conjug 1 ◂ VT [+ *corps*] to exhume; [+ *ruines, vestiges*] to excavate; [+ *faits, vieux livres*] to unearth, dig up *ou* out; [+ *souvenirs*] to recall

exigeant, e [ɛgziʒɑ̃, ɑ̃t] ADJ [*client, hôte*] particular (*attrib*), demanding, hard to please (*attrib*); [*enfant, amant*] demanding, hard to please (*attrib*); [*parents, patron, travail, amour*] demanding, exacting; **je ne suis pas ~**,

▸ GRAMMAIRE ACTIVE: **exemple** 53.1, 53.5

donnez-moi 100 F I'm not asking for much — give me 100 francs; **il est très ~ envers lui-même** he sets very high standards for himself

exigence [ɛgziɑ̃s] NF a (= caractère) [client] particularity; [maître] strictness; **il est d'une ~ insupportable** he's impossibly demanding ou particular; **son ~ de rigueur** his requirement ou demand for accuracy b (gén pl = revendication, condition) demand, requirement; **produit satisfaisant à toutes les ~s** product which meets all requirements; **les ~s du marché** the demands of the market; **~s (salariales)** salary expectations

▼ **exiger** [ɛgziʒe] ▶ conjug 3 ◀ VT a (= réclamer) to demand, require (**qch de qn** sth of ou from sb), insist on (**qch de qn** sth from sb); **j'exige de le faire** I insist on doing it; **j'exige que vous le fassiez** I insist on your doing it, I demand ou insist that you do it; **j'exige (de vous) des excuses** I demand an apology (from you), I insist on an apology (from you); **la loi l'exige** the law requires ou demands it; **des titres universitaires sont exigés pour ce poste** university degrees are required ou needed ou are a requirement for this post; **trop ~ de ses forces** to overtax one's strength b (= nécessiter) to require, call for; **cette plante exige beaucoup d'eau** this plant needs ou requires a lot of water

exigibilité [ɛgziʒibilite] NF [dette] payability; **~s** current liabilities

exigible [ɛgziʒibl] ADJ [dette] payable, due for payment; **~ le 15 mai** payable ou due on May 15

exigu, -uë [ɛgziɡy] ADJ [lieu] cramped, exiguous (littér); [ressources] scanty, meagre, exiguous (littér); [délais] short; (Écon) [marché] limited

exiguïté [ɛgziɡyite] NF [lieu] crampedness, exiguity (littér); [ressources] scantiness, meagreness, exiguity (littér); [délais] shortness; (Écon) [marché] limited size

exil [ɛgzil] NM exile; **~ volontaire** voluntary ou self-imposed exile; **deux années d'~** two years in ou of exile; **lieu d'~** place of exile; **en ~** [personne] in exile (attrib), exiled; [vivre] in exile; **envoyer qn en ~** to send sb into exile, exile sb

exilé, e [ɛgzile] (ptp de **exiler**) NM,F exile (de from); **~ politique/volontaire** political/voluntary exile

exiler [ɛgzile] ▶ conjug 1 ◀ 1 VT a (Pol) to exile b (littér) to banish; **se sentir exilé (loin de)** to feel like an outcast ou exile (far from); **une note exilée en bas de page** a note tucked away at the bottom of the page 2 **s'exiler** VPR a (Pol) to go into exile b (fig) **s'~ à la campagne** to bury o.s. in the country; **s'~ en Australie** to exile o.s. to Australia, take o.s. off to Australia; **s'~ loin du monde** to cut o.s. off from the world

existant, e [ɛgzistɑ̃, ɑ̃t] 1 ADJ [coutume, loi, prix] existing 2 NM **l'~** (= stock) the existing stock; (= circonstances) the existing circumstances

existence [ɛgzistɑ̃s] NF a (Philo, Rel = présence) existence b (= vie quotidienne) existence, life; **dans l'~** in life; **cette coutume a plusieurs siècles d'~** this custom has existed ou has been in existence for several centuries → **moyen**

existentialisme [ɛgzistɑ̃sjalism] NM existentialism

existentialiste [ɛgzistɑ̃sjalist] ADJ, NMF existentialist

existentiel, -ielle [ɛgzistɑ̃sjɛl] ADJ existential

exister [ɛgziste] ▶ conjug 1 ◀ 1 VI a (= vivre) to exist; (péj) **il se contente d'~** he is content with just getting by ou just existing b (= être réel) to exist, be; **pour lui, la peur n'existe pas** there is no such thing as fear ou fear doesn't exist as far as he is concerned;

---

quoi que vous pensiez, le bonheur ça existe whatever you may say, there is such a thing as happiness c (= se trouver) to be, be found; **la vie existe-t-elle sur Mars ?** is there life on Mars?; **produit qui existe en magasin** product (to be) found in shops; **ce modèle existe-t-il en rose ?** is this model available in pink?; **le costume régional n'existe plus guère** regional dress is scarcely ever (to be) found ou seen these days; **les bateaux à aubes n'existent plus/existent encore** paddle steamers no longer/still exist; **il existe encore une copie** there is still one copy extant ou in existence; **pourquoi monter à pied ? les ascenseurs ça existe !** why walk up? there are lifts, you know! (iron) lifts have been invented!; (hum) **si Hélène/la machine à café n'existait pas, il faudrait l'inventer !** if Hélène/the coffee machine didn't exist, we would have to invent her/it! 2 VB IMPERS (= il y a) **il existe** (avec sg) there is; (avec pl) there are; **il n'existe pas de meilleur exemple** there is no better example; **il existe des bégonias de plusieurs couleurs** begonias come ou are found in several colours

exit [ɛgzit] VI, NM (Théât) exit; (hum) **~ le directeur** out goes the manager, exit the manager; (hum) **~ les pauses-café** no more coffee breaks, that's the end of the coffee breaks

ex-libris [ɛkslibris] NM INV ex-libris

ex nihilo [ɛksniilo] ADV ex nihilo

exocet [ɛgzɔsɛ] NM a (= poisson) flying fish b ® (= missile) exocet®

exode [ɛgzɔd] NM (lit, fig) exodus; (Hist) **l'~** the flight of civilians from the north of France during the German invasion in 1940; (Bible) **l'Exode** the Exodus; **(le livre de) l'Exode** (the Book of) Exodus; **~ rural** drift from the land, rural exodus; **~ des cerveaux** brain drain; **~ des capitaux** flight ou outflow of capital

exogame [ɛgzɔgam] ADJ exogamous, exogamic

exogamie [ɛgzɔgami] NF exogamy

exogène [ɛgzɔʒɛn] ADJ exogenous

exonération [ɛgzɔneʁasjɔ̃] NF (Fin) exemption (de from); **~ fiscale** ou **d'impôt** tax exemption

exonérer [ɛgzɔneʁe] ▶ conjug 6 ◀ VT (Fin) to exempt (de from); **placement à 3,5% exonéré d'impôts** investment at 3.5% free of tax; **les plus-values seront fiscalement exonérées** capital gains will be tax-exempt ou will be exempted from tax

exorbitant, e [ɛgzɔʁbitɑ̃, ɑ̃t] ADJ [prix, demande, prétention] exorbitant, inordinate, outrageous

exorbité, e [ɛgzɔʁbite] ADJ [yeux] bulging (de with)

exorcisation [ɛgzɔʁsizasjɔ̃] NF exorcizing

exorciser [ɛgzɔʁsize] ▶ conjug 1 ◀ VT to exorcize

exorciseur [ɛgzɔʁsizœʁ] NM exorcizer

exorcisme [ɛgzɔʁsism] NM exorcism

exorciste [ɛgzɔʁsist] NM exorcist

exorde [ɛgzɔʁd] NM introduction, exordium (SPÉC)

exosmose [ɛgzɔsmoz] NF exosmosis

exotique [ɛgzɔtik] ADJ [pays, plante] exotic

exotisme [ɛgzɔtism] NM exoticism; **aimer l'~** to love all that is exotic

expansé, e [ɛkspɑ̃se] ADJ expanded

expansibilité [ɛkspɑ̃sibilite] NF expansibility

expansible [ɛkspɑ̃sibl] ADJ expansible

expansif, -ive [ɛkspɑ̃sif, iv] ADJ a (de caractère) expansive, out-going; **il s'est montré peu ~** he was not very forthcoming ou communicative b (Phys) expansionary

expansion [ɛkspɑ̃sjɔ̃] NF a (= extension) expansion; **l'~ d'une doctrine** the spreading of a doctrine; **économie en pleine ~** booming ou fast-expanding economy; **univers en ~** ex-

---

panding universe b (= effusion) expansiveness (NonC), effusiveness (NonC); **avec de grandes ~s** expansively, effusively

expansionnisme [ɛkspɑ̃sjɔnism] NM expansionism

expansionniste [ɛkspɑ̃sjɔnist] 1 ADJ (Écon, Math, Phys) expansionary; (Pol: péj) expansionist 2 NMF (Pol) expansionist

expansivité [ɛkspɑ̃sivite] NF expansiveness

expatriation [ɛkspatʁijasjɔ̃] NF expatriation

expatrié, e [ɛkspatʁije] (ptp de **expatrier**) NM,F expatriate

expatrier [ɛkspatʁije] ▶ conjug 7 ◀ 1 VT to expatriate 2 **s'expatrier** VPR to expatriate o.s., leave one's country

expectative [ɛkspɛktativ] NF (= incertitude) state of uncertainty; (= attente prudente) cautious approach; **être** ou **rester dans l'~** (incertitude) to be still waiting ou hanging on (to hear ou see etc); (attente prudente) to hold back, wait and see

expectorant, e [ɛkspɛktɔʁɑ̃, ɑ̃t] ADJ, NM expectorant

expectoration [ɛkspɛktɔʁasjɔ̃] NF expectoration

expectorer [ɛkspɛktɔʁe] ▶ conjug 1 ◀ VTI to expectorate

expédient, e [ɛkspedjɑ̃, jɑ̃t] 1 ADJ (frm) expedient 2 NM expedient, makeshift; **vivre d'~s** [personne] to live by one's wits; [pays] to resort to short-term measures

▼ **expédier** [ɛkspedje] ▶ conjug 7 ◀ VT a [+ lettre, paquet] to send, dispatch; **~ par la poste** to send through the post ou mail; **~ par le train** to send by rail ou train; **~ par bateau** [+ lettres, colis] to send surface mail; [+ matières premières] to ship, send by sea; **je l'ai expédié en vacances chez sa grand-mère*** I sent ou packed* him off to his grandmother's for the holidays → **monde** b* [+ client, visiteur] to dismiss; **~ une affaire** to dispose of ou dispatch a matter, get a matter over with; **~ son déjeuner en cinq minutes** to polish off* one's lunch in five minutes c (Admin) **~ les affaires courantes** to dispose of ou dispatch day-to-day matters

expéditeur, -trice [ɛkspeditœʁ, tʁis] 1 ADJ dispatching, forwarding 2 NM,F [courrier] sender, addresser, addressor; [marchandises] consignor, shipper → **retour**

expéditif, -ive [ɛkspeditif, iv] ADJ [personne] quick, expeditious; [méthode, solution] expeditious; [justice, licenciement, procès] summary

expédition [ɛkspedisjɔ̃] NF a (= action) [lettre, vivres, renforts] dispatch; [colis] dispatch, shipping; (par bateau) shipping; **notre service ~** our shipping department b (= paquet) consignment, shipment; (par bateau) shipment c (Mil, Sport, Sci) expedition; **~ de police** police raid; (fig) **quelle ~ !** what an expedition!, what a palaver! d (Admin) **l'~ des affaires courantes** the dispatching of day-to-day matters e (Jur = copie) exemplified copy

expéditionnaire [ɛkspedisjɔnɛʁ] 1 ADJ (Mil) expeditionary 2 NMF (Comm) forwarding agent; (Admin) copyist

expéditivement [ɛkspeditivmɑ̃] ADV expeditiously

▼ **expérience** [ɛksperjɑ̃s] NF a (= pratique) experience; **avoir de l'~** to have experience, be experienced (en in); (frm) **avoir l'~ du monde** to have experience of the world, know the ways of the world; **sans ~** inexperienced; **il est sans ~ de la vie** he has no experience of life; **savoir par ~** to know by ou from experience; **il a une longue ~ de l'enseignement** he has a lot of teaching experience b (= aventure humaine) experience; **~ amoureuse** ou **sexuelle** sexual experience; **tente l'~, tu verras bien** try it and see; **faire l'~ de qch** to experience sth; **ils ont fait une ~ de vie communautaire** they experimented with communal liv-

---

ing [c] (= *essai scientifique*) experiment; **vérité/ fait d'~** experimental truth/fact; **faire une ~ sur un cobaye** to do *ou* carry out an experiment on a guinea-pig

expérimental, e (*mpl* **-aux**) [ɛkspeʀimãtal, o] ADJ experimental; **à titre ~** on a trial *ou* an experimental basis

expérimentalement [ɛkspeʀimãtalmã] ADV experimentally

expérimentateur, -trice [ɛkspeʀimãtatœʀ, tʀis] NM,F (*gén*) experimenter; (*Sci*) bench scientist

expérimentation [ɛkspeʀimãtasjɔ̃] NF experimentation; **~ animale** (= *pratique*) animal experimentation; (= *expériences, tests*) animal experiments

expérimenté, e [ɛkspeʀimãte] (*ptp de* **expérimenter**) ADJ experienced (**en, dans** in)

expérimenter [ɛkspeʀimãte] ▸ conjug 1 ◂ VT [+ *appareil*] to test; [+ *remède*] to experiment with, try out; [+ *méthode*] to test out, try out; **~ en laboratoire** to experiment *ou* do experiments in a laboratory

expert, e [ɛkspeʀ, ɛʀt] [1] ADJ [*personne*] expert, skilled (**en in, à** at); [*mains*] expert; **être ~ en la matière** to be skilled *ou* (an) expert in the subject [2] NM (= *connaisseur*) expert (**en** in, at), connoisseur (**en** in, of); (= *spécialiste*) expert; (*d'assurances après dégâts*) assessor; (*d'objet de valeur*) valuer, assessor; (*Naut*) surveyor; **médecin(-)~** medical expert; **géomètre(-)~** ≈ chartered surveyor

expert-comptable, experte-comptable [ɛkspeʀkɔ̃tabl] (*mpl* **experts-comptables**) NM,F chartered accountant (*Brit*), certified public accountant (*US*)

expertise [ɛkspeʀtiz] NF [a] (= *évaluation*) [*bijou*] valuation; [*dégâts*] assessment; **~ d'avarie** damage survey; **~ comptable** chartered accountancy (*Brit*); **~ psychiatrique** psychiatric examination; **(rapport d')~** valuer's *ou* assessor's *ou* expert's report [b] (= *compétence*) expertise; **notre ~ technique dans ce domaine** our technical expertise in this field

expertiser [ɛkspeʀtize] ▸ conjug 1 ◂ VT [+ *bijou*] to value, evaluate; [+ *dégâts*] to assess, evaluate; **faire ~ un diamant** to have a diamond valued

expiable [ɛkspjabl] ADJ expiable

expiation [ɛkspjasjɔ̃] NF expiation (**de** of), atonement (**de** for); **en ~ de ses crimes** in expiation *ou* atonement for his crimes

expiatoire [ɛkspjatwaʀ] ADJ expiatory

expier [ɛkspje] ▸ conjug 7 ◂ VT [+ *péchés, crime*] to expiate, atone for; (*fig*) **~ une imprudence** to pay for an imprudent act

expirant, e [ɛkspiʀɑ̃, ɑ̃t] ADJ dying

expiration [ɛkspiʀasjɔ̃] NF [a] (= *terme*) expiration, expiry (*Brit*); **venir à ~** to expire; **à l'~ du délai** when the deadline expires [b] (= *respiration*) expiration, exhalation; **une profonde ~** a complete exhalation

expirer [ɛkspiʀe] ▸ conjug 1 ◂ [1] VT [+ *air*] to breathe out, exhale, expire (*SPÉC*) [2] VI [a] [*délai, passeport*] to expire; **le contrat/la carte expire le 5 mai** the contract/the card expires on May 5th [b] (*frm = mourir*) to expire [c] (= *respirer*) to exhale, breathe out; **expirez lentement !** breathe out slowly!

explétif, -ive [ɛkspletif, iv] [1] ADJ expletive, expletory; **le ne ~** "ne" used as an expletive [2] NM expletive

explicable [ɛksplikabl] ADJ explicable, explainable; **difficilement ~** difficult to explain

explicatif, -ive [ɛksplikatif, iv] ADJ explanatory, explicative; (*Gram*) **proposition relative explicative** non-restrictive relative clause

▾ **explication** [ɛksplikasjɔ̃] NF [a] [*méthode, phénomène*] explanation (**de** of); (= *marche à suivre*) **~s** instructions [b] (= *justification*) explanation (**de** for); **votre conduite demande**

des ~s your conduct requires some explanation; **j'exige des ~s** I demand an explanation [c] (= *discussion*) discussion; (= *dispute*) argument; (= *bagarre*) fight; **j'ai eu une petite ~ avec lui** I had a bit of an argument with him [d] (*Scol*) [*auteur, passage*] commentary (**de** on), analysis (**de** of); **~ de texte** critical analysis *ou* appreciation of a text, textual analysis

explicitation [ɛksplisitasjɔ̃] NF [*symbole*] making explicit, explaining, clarifying; **faire un effort d'~** to try to explain in more detail

explicite [ɛksplisit] ADJ [*clause, terme*] explicit; **il n'a pas été très ~ sur ce point** he wasn't very clear on that point

explicitement [ɛksplisitmã] ADV explicitly

expliciter [ɛksplisite] ▸ conjug 1 ◂ VT [+ *clause*] to make explicit; [+ *pensée*] to explain, clarify

expliquer [ɛksplike] ▸ conjug 1 ◂ [1] VT [a] (= *faire comprendre*) to explain; **il m'a expliqué comment faire** he told me *ou* explained to me how to do it; **je lui ai expliqué qu'il avait tort** I pointed out to him *ou* explained to him that he was wrong; **explique-moi comment/ pourquoi** explain how/why, tell me how/ why; **il m'a expliqué le pourquoi du comment** he explained to me the how and the why of it
[b] (= *rendre compte de*) to account for, explain; **cela explique qu'il ne soit pas venu** that explains why he didn't come, that accounts for his not coming
[c] (*Scol*) [+ *texte*] to comment on, criticize, analyse; **~ un passage de Flaubert** to give a critical analysis *ou* a critical appreciation *ou* a critical interpretation of a passage from Flaubert

[2] **s'expliquer** VPR [a] (= *donner des précisions*) to explain o.s., make o.s. clear; **je m'explique** let me explain, let me make myself clear; **le président s'explique** the president gives his reasons; **s'~ sur ses projets** to talk about *ou* explain one's plans; **s'~ devant qn** to justify o.s. to sb, explain one's actions to sb
[b] (= *comprendre*) to understand; **je ne m'explique pas bien qu'il soit parti** I can't see *ou* understand *ou* it isn't at all clear to me why he should have left
[c] (= *être compréhensible*) **son retard s'explique par le mauvais temps** his lateness is explained by the bad weather, the bad weather accounts for *ou* explains his lateness; **leur attitude s'explique : ils n'ont pas reçu notre lettre** that explains their attitude: they didn't get our letter; **tout s'explique !** it's all clear now!, I see it all now!
[d] (= *parler clairement*) **s'~ bien/mal** to express o.s. well/badly; **je me suis peut-être mal expliqué** perhaps I have expressed myself badly, perhaps I didn't make myself (quite) clear
[e] **s'~ avec qn** (= *discuter*) to have a talk with sb; (= *se disputer, se battre*) to have it out with sb*; **va t'~ avec lui** go and sort it out with him; **après longuement expliqués ils sont tombés d'accord** after having discussed the matter *ou* after having talked the matter over for a long time they finally reached an agreement; **ils sont allés s'~ dehors*** they went to fight it out outside *ou* to finish it off outside; **s'~ à coups de fusil** to shoot it out

exploit [ɛksplwa] NM exploit, feat, achievement; **quel ~ !** what a feat! *ou* an achievement!; **~s amoureux** amorous exploits; **~ sportif** sporting achievement *ou* feat; **il a réussi l'~ d'arriver le premier** he came first, which was quite an achievement; **~ d'huissier** writ

exploitable [ɛksplwatabl] ADJ (*gén*) exploitable

exploitant, e [ɛksplwatã, ãt] NM,F [a] (= *fermier*) **~ (agricole)** farmer; **petit ~ (agricole)** small farmer, smallholder (*Brit*); **~ forestier**

forestry developer [b] (*Ciné*) (= *propriétaire*) cinema owner; (= *gérant*) cinema manager

exploitation [ɛksplwatasjɔ̃] NF [a] (= *action*) [*mine, sol*] working, exploitation; [*entreprise*] running, operating; **mettre en ~** [+ *domaine, ressources*] to exploit, develop; **frais/méthodes d'~** running *ou* operating costs/methods; **satellite en ~** working satellite; (*Ciné*) **copie d'~** release print → **visa** [b] (= *entreprise*) **~ familiale** family business; **~ (agricole)** farm; **petite ~ (agricole)** small farm, smallholding (*Brit*); **~ vinicole** vineyard; **~ commerciale/industrielle** business/industrial concern; **~ minière** mine; **~ forestière** forestry site [c] [*idée, situation, renseignement*] exploiting, using; **la libre ~ de l'information** the free use of information [d] (= *abus*) exploitation; **l'~ de l'homme par l'homme** man's exploitation of man *ou* of his fellow man; **l'~ sexuelle des enfants** sexual exploitation of children

exploité, e [ɛksplwate] (*ptp de* **exploiter**) [1] ADJ [*personne*] exploited; **terres non ~es** unfarmed land; **richesses non ~es** unexploited *ou* untapped riches; **un créneau peu ~** a niche in the market that has not been fully tapped *ou* exploited [2] NM,F exploited person

exploiter [ɛksplwate] ▸ conjug 1 ◂ VT [a] [+ *mine*] to work, exploit; [+ *sol, terres*] to farm, work; [+ *entreprise*] to run, operate; [+ *ligne aérienne, réseau*] to operate; [+ *brevet*] to use; [+ *ressources*] to exploit [b] [+ *idée, situation*] to exploit, make the most of; [+ *don*] to make use of; [+ *personne, bonté, crédulité*] to exploit; [+ *avantage*] to capitalize on, exploit; **ils exploitent la xénophobie à des fins politiques** they're capitalizing on *ou* exploiting xenophobia for political ends

exploiteur, -euse [ɛksplwatœʀ, øz] NM,F exploiter

explorateur, -trice [ɛksplɔʀatœʀ, tʀis] NM,F (= *personne*) explorer

exploration [ɛksplɔʀasjɔ̃] NF (*gén*) exploration; [*possibilité, problème*] investigation, examination, exploration; (*Méd*) exploration; **~ spatiale** space exploration

exploratoire [ɛksplɔʀatwaʀ] ADJ exploratory

explorer [ɛksplɔʀe] ▸ conjug 1 ◂ VT (*gén*) to explore; [+ *possibilité, problème*] to investigate, examine, explore; (*Méd*) to explore

exploser [ɛksploze] ▸ conjug 1 ◂ VI [a] [*bombe, chaudière*] to explode, blow up; [*gaz*] to explode; **j'ai cru que ma tête allait ~** I thought my head was going to explode *ou* burst; **faire ~** [+ *bombe*] to explode, detonate; [+ *bâtiment*] to blow up; [+ *monopole, système, coalition*] to break up; [+ *contraintes*] to sweep away [b] [*sentiments*] **~ (de colère)** to blow up, explode (with anger); **laisser ~ sa colère** to give vent to one's anger; **~ de joie** to go wild with joy [c] (= *augmenter*) [*chômage, demande, production, prix*] to soar, rocket; [*marché*] to boom [d] (* = *abîmer*) [+ *objet*] to smash up; **il s'est explosé le genou** he did his knee in*; **je vais lui ~ la gueule**** I'm going to smash his face in*

explosible [ɛksplozibl] ADJ [*mélange*] explosive

explosif, -ive [ɛksplozif, iv] [1] ADJ [*charge, situation*] explosive; **dossier ~** highly sensitive file [2] NM explosive

explosion [ɛksplozjɔ̃] NF [a] [*bombe, gaz, chaudière*] explosion → **moteur¹** [b] [*joie, violence*] outburst, explosion; [*dépenses, nombre*] explosion, dramatic rise (**de** in); **~ de colère** angry outburst, explosion of anger; **~ démographique** population explosion; **~ sociale** outburst *ou* explosion of social unrest

expo* [ɛkspo] NF ABRÉV = **exposition**

exponentiel, -ielle [ɛkspɔnɑ̃sjɛl] ADJ exponential

export [ɛkspɔʀ] NM (ABRÉV = **exportation**) export; **se lancer dans l'~** to go into exports; **les**

▸ GRAMMAIRE ACTIVE: **explication** 53.4

bénéfices réalisés à l'~ profits earned on exports

exportable [εkspɔʀtabl] ADJ exportable

exportateur, -trice [εkspɔʀtatœʀ, tʀis] **1** ADJ export (épith), exporting; **pays ~** exporting country; **être ~ de** to export, be an exporter of **2** NM,F exporter; **~ de pétrole** oil exporter

exportation [εkspɔʀtasjɔ̃] NF (= action) export, exportation; (= produit) export; **faire de l'~** to be in the export business; **produit d'~** export product

exporter [εkspɔʀte] ▶conjug 1◀ VT (Comm, Ordin) to export; **notre mode s'exporte bien/mal** our fashions are popular/not very popular abroad

exposant, e [εkspozɑ̃, ɑ̃t] **1** NM,F [foire, salon] exhibitor **2** NM (Math) exponent; **chiffre en ~** superscript number

exposé [εkspoze] NM (= action) account, statement, exposition (frm); (= conférence) talk; (Scol) (oral) presentation; (écrit) (written) paper; **faire un ~ oral sur** to give a presentation on; **faire un ~ de la situation** to give an account ou overview of the situation; (Jur) **~ des motifs** preamble (in bill, stating grounds for its adoption)

exposer [εkspoze] ▶conjug 1◀ **1** VT **a** (= exhiber) [+ marchandises] to put on display, display; [+ tableaux] to exhibit, show; **ce peintre expose dans cette galerie** that painter shows ou exhibits at that gallery; **exposé en vitrine** on display; **les œuvres exposées** the works on show; (frm) **son corps est exposé dans l'église** he is lying in state in the church **b** (= expliquer) [+ faits, raisons] to set out, state; [+ griefs] to air; [+ idées, théories] to expound, set out; [+ situation] to explain **c** (= mettre en danger) [+ personne] to expose (à to); [+ vie, réputation] to risk; **c'est une personnalité très exposée** his position makes him an easy target for criticism; **sa conduite l'expose à des reproches** his behaviour lays him open to censure **d** (= orienter, présenter) to expose; (Photo) to expose; **~ au soleil/aux regards** to expose to sunlight/to view; **maison exposée au sud** house facing (due) south, house with a southern aspect; **maison bien exposée** house with a good aspect; **endroit très exposé** (au vent, à l'ennemi) very exposed place **e** (Littérat) [+ action] to set out; (Mus) [+ thème] to introduce **f** (Hist) [+ enfant] to expose **2** **s'exposer** VPR to expose o.s.; **s'~ à** [+ danger, reproches, poursuites] to expose o.s. to, lay o.s. open to; **s'~ au soleil** to expose o.s. to the sun

exposition [εkspozisjɔ̃] NF **a** [marchandises] display; [faits, raisons, situation, idées] exposition; [condamné, enfant] exposure; (au danger, à la chaleur) exposure (**à** to); (Comm) **grande ~ de blanc** special linen week ou event **b** (= foire, salon) exhibition, show; **l'Exposition universelle** the World Fair; **faire une ~** (visiteur) to go to an exhibition; (artiste) to put on an exhibition **c** (Photo) exposure **d** (Littérat, Mus) exposition; **scène d'~** expository ou introductory scene **e** (= orientation) [maison] aspect

exposition-vente (pl **expositions-ventes**) [εkspozisjɔ̃vɑ̃t] NF [artisanat, art] show (with goods on display for sale)

expo-vente+ (pl **expos-ventes**) [εkspovɑ̃t] NF ABRÉV = **exposition-vente**

▼ **exprès[1]** [εkspʀε] ADV (= spécialement) specially; (= intentionnellement) on purpose, deliberately, intentionally; **venir (tout) ~ pour** to come specially to; **il l'a fait ~** he did it on purpose ou deliberately ou intentionally; **il ne l'a pas fait ~** he didn't do it on purpose, he didn't mean to do it; **c'est fait ~** it's meant to be like that, it's deliberate; **comme par un fait ~** almost as if it was meant to happen

exprès[2], -esse [εkspʀεs] **1** ADJ [interdiction, ordre] formal, express; (Jur) [clause] express **2** NM, ADJ INV (**lettre/colis**) **~** express (Brit) ou special delivery (US) letter/parcel; (**messager**) **~†** express messenger; **envoyer qch en ~** to send sth by express post (Brit) ou special delivery (US), send sth express (Brit)

express [εkspʀεs] ADJ, NM **a** (**train**) **~** fast train **b** (= café) espresso (coffee)

expressément [εkspʀesemɑ̃] ADV (= formellement) [dire, interdire] expressly; (= spécialement) [fait, conçu] specially; **il ne l'a pas dit ~** he didn't say it in so many words

expressif, -ive [εkspʀesif, iv] ADJ [geste, regard] expressive, meaningful; [physionomie] expressive; [langage] expressive, vivid; [silence] eloquent

expression [εkspʀesjɔ̃] NF **a** (gén) expression; **au-delà de toute ~** beyond (all) expression, inexpressible; **visage plein d'~/sans ~** expressive/expressionless face; **jouer avec beaucoup d'~** to play with great feeling ou expression; **~ corporelle** music and movement; **journal d'~ française/anglaise** French/English-language newspaper → **agréer, liberté, moyen, réduire b** (Math = formule) expression; (Gram = locution) phrase, expression; **~ figée** set ou fixed expression, set phrase; **~ toute faite** stock phrase; **~ nominale** nominal; **réduit à sa plus simple ~** reduced to its simplest terms ou expression

expressionnisme [εkspʀesjɔnism] NM expressionism

expressionniste [εkspʀesjɔnist] **1** ADJ expressionist (épith), expressionistic **2** NMF expressionist

expressivement [εkspʀesivmɑ̃] ADV expressively

expressivité [εkspʀesivite] NF expressiveness

expresso [εkspʀeso] NM (= café) espresso; **machine/cafetière (à) ~** espresso machine/coffee maker

exprimable [εkspʀimabl] ADJ expressible

exprimer [εkspʀime] ▶conjug 1◀ **1** VT **a** (= signifier) to express; [+ pensée] to express, give expression ou utterance to (frm); [+ opinion] to voice, express; **mots qui expriment un sens** words which express ou convey a meaning; **regards qui expriment la colère** looks which express ou indicate anger; **œuvre qui exprime parfaitement l'artiste** work which expresses the artist completely **b** (Écon, Math) to express; **somme exprimée en francs** sum expressed in francs; **le signe + exprime l'addition** the sign + indicates ou stands for addition **c** (littér) [+ jus] to press ou squeeze out **2** **s'exprimer** VPR to express o.s.; **s'~ par gestes** to use gestures to express o.s.; **je me suis peut-être mal exprimé** perhaps I have expressed myself badly, I may not have made myself clear; **il ne peux m'~ ainsi** if I may put it like that; **il faut permettre au talent de s'~** talent must be allowed free expression ou to express itself; **la joie s'exprima sur son visage** (his) joy showed in his expression, his face expressed his joy

expropriation [εkspʀɔpʀijasjɔ̃] NF (= action) expropriation, compulsory purchase (Brit); (= arrêté) expropriation order, compulsory purchase order (Brit)

exproprier [εkspʀɔpʀije] ▶conjug 7◀ VT [+ propriété] to expropriate, place a compulsory purchase order on (Brit); **ils ont été expropriés** their property has been expropriated, they have had a compulsory purchase order made on their property

expulsable [εkspylsabl] ADJ [locataire] liable to be evicted; [immigré clandestin] liable to be deported

expulser [εkspylse] ▶conjug 1◀ VT **a** (gén) [+ élève] to expel (**de** from); [+ étranger] to de-

port, expel (**de** from); [+ locataire] to evict (**de** from), throw out (**de** of); (Sport) [+ joueur] to send off; [+ manifestant] to eject (**de** from), throw out, turn out (**de** of) **b** (Anat) [+ déchets] to evacuate, excrete; [+ placenta] to deliver

expulsion [εkspylsjɔ̃] NF **a** (gén) [élève] expulsion (**de** from); [étranger] deportation, expulsion (**de** from); [locataire] eviction (**de** from); [joueur] sending off; [manifestant] ejection (**de** from) **b** (Anat) [déchets] evacuation, excretion; [placenta] delivery

expurger [εkspyʀʒe] ▶conjug 3◀ VT to expurgate, bowdlerize; **version expurgée** sanitized ou expurgated ou bowdlerized version

exquis, -ise [εkski, iz] ADJ [plat, choix, politesse] exquisite; [personne, temps] delightful; (Méd) [douleur] exquisite

exsangue [εksɑ̃g] ADJ [visage, lèvres] bloodless; [littérature] anaemic; **les guerres ont laissé le pays ~** wars have bled the country white

exsudation [εksydasjɔ̃] NF (frm) exudation (frm)

exsuder [εksyde] VTI (frm, lit) to exude; **son visage exsude la joie** his face radiates joy

extase [εkstaz] NF (Rel) ecstasy; (sexuelle) climax; (fig) ecstasy, rapture; **il est en ~ devant sa fille** he is rapturous about his daughter, he goes into raptures over his daughter; **tomber/rester en ~ devant un tableau** to go into ecstasies at/stand in ecstasy before a painting

extasié, e [εkstazje] (ptp de **s'extasier**) ADJ ecstatic, enraptured

extasier (s') [εkstazje] ▶conjug 7◀ VPR to go into ecstasies ou raptures (**devant, sur** over)

extatique [εkstatik] ADJ ecstatic, enraptured

extenseur [εkstɑ̃sœʀ] **1** ADJ (**muscle**) **~** extensor **2** NM (Sport) chest expander

extensibilité [εkstɑ̃sibilite] NF extensibility

extensible [εkstɑ̃sibl] ADJ [matière] extensible; [définition] extendable; **le budget de l'État n'est pas ~ à l'infini** the state budget is not inexhaustible

extensif, -ive [εkstɑ̃sif, iv] ADJ (Agr) [culture] extensive; [sens] wide, extensive

extension [εkstɑ̃sjɔ̃] NF **a** (= étirement) [ressort] stretching; [membre] (gén) stretching, extension; (Méd) traction; **le ressort atteint son ~ maximum** the spring is fully stretched ou is stretched to its maximum; **être en ~** [personne] to be stretching; [bras] to be stretched out ou extended **b** (= augmentation) [épidémie, grève, incendie] extension, spreading; [commerce, domaine] expansion; [pouvoirs] extension, expansion; **prendre de l'~** [épidémie] to spread; [entreprise] to expand **c** (= élargissement) [loi, mesure, sens d'un mot] extension (**à** to); (Logique) extension; **par ~ (de sens)** by extension → **carte**

exténuant, e [εkstenyɑ̃, ɑ̃t] ADJ exhausting

exténuer [εkstenye] ▶conjug 1◀ **1** VT to exhaust, tire out **2** **s'exténuer** VPR to exhaust o.s., tire o.s. out (**à faire qch** doing sth)

extérieur, e [εksteʀjœʀ] **1** ADJ **a** (à un lieu) [paroi] outer, outside, exterior; [escalier, W.-C.] outside; [quartier, cour, boulevard] outer; [bruit] external, outside; [décoration] exterior, outside; [collaborateur] outside; **apparence ~e** [personne] outward appearance; [maison] outside **b** (à l'individu) [monde, influences] external, outside; [activité, intérêt] outside; [réalité] external; **manifestation ~e de colère** outward show ou display of anger **c** (= étranger) [commerce, vente] external, foreign; [politique, nouvelles] foreign **d** (= superficiel) [amabilité] surface (épith), superficial; **sa gaieté est toute ~e** his gaiety is all on the surface ou all an outward display **e** (= sans relation avec) **être ~ à une question** to be external to ou outside a question, be beyond the scope of a question; **c'est tout à fait ~ à moi** it has nothing to do with me, it doesn't concern me in the least; **rester ~ à un conflit** to stay *ou* keep out of a conflict; **« interdit à toute personne ~e à l'usine/au chantier »** "factory employees/site workers only", "no entry for unauthorized personnel" ⬚**f** (*Géom*) [*angle*] exterior

⬚**2** NM ⬚**a** [*objet, maison*] outside, exterior; [*piste, circuit*] outside; **il l'a débordé par l'~** [*joueur*] he overtook him on the outside ⬚**b** **à l'~** (= *au dehors*) outside; **travailler à l'~** (*hors de chez soi*) to work outside the home; **il a été recruté à l'~** (*de l'entreprise*) he was recruited from outside; **téléphoner à l'~** to make an outside *ou* external call; **jouer à l'~** to play an away match, play away; **c'est à l'~** (*de la ville*) it's outside (the town); (*fig*) **juger qch de l'~** (*d'après son apparence*) to judge sth by appearances; (*en tant que profane*) to judge sth from the outside ⬚**c** **l'~** (*gén*) the outside world; (= *pays étrangers*) foreign countries; **vendre beaucoup à l'~** to sell a lot abroad *ou* to foreign countries; **nouvelles de l'~** news from abroad ⬚**d** (*frm* = *apparence*) exterior, (outward) appearance

⬚**3** **extérieurs** NMPL (*Ciné*) location shots; **tourner en ~s** to shoot on location

extérieurement [ɛksterjœrmɑ̃] ADV ⬚**a** (= *du dehors*) on the outside, externally ⬚**b** (= *en apparence*) on the surface, outwardly

extériorisation [ɛksterjɔrizasjɔ̃] NF [*sentiment*] display, outward expression; (*Psych*) externalization, exteriorization

extérioriser [ɛksterjɔrize] ▶conjug 1◀ VT ⬚**1** [*+ sentiment*] to show, express; (*Psych*) to exteriorize, externalize ⬚**2** **s'extérioriser** VPR [*personne*] to express o.s.; [*sentiment*] to be expressed

extériorité [ɛksterjɔrite] NF (*Philo*) exteriority

exterminateur, -trice [ɛksterminatœr, tris] ⬚**1** ADJ exterminating → **ange** ⬚**2** NM,F exterminator

extermination [ɛksterminasjɔ̃] NF extermination → **camp**

exterminer [ɛkstermine] ▶conjug 1◀ VT (*lit, fig*) to exterminate, wipe out

externalisation [ɛksternalizasjɔ̃] NF [*activité, service*] outsourcing

externaliser [ɛksternalize] ▶conjug 1◀ VT [*+ activité, service*] to outsource

externat [ɛksterna] NM (*Scol*) day school; (*Méd*) **faire son ~** to be a non-resident student *ou* an extern (*US*) at

externe [ɛkstern] ⬚**1** ADJ [*surface*] external, outer; [*angle*] exterior; [*candidature, recrutement, croissance*] external ⬚**2** NMF (= *élève*) day pupil; **~ (des hôpitaux)** non-resident student at a teaching hospital, extern (*US*)

exterritorialité [ɛksteritɔrjalite] NF exterritoriality

extincteur, -trice [ɛkstɛ̃ktœr, tris] ⬚**1** ADJ extinguishing ⬚**2** NM (fire) extinguisher

extinction [ɛkstɛ̃ksjɔ̃] NF [*incendie, lumières*] extinction, extinguishing, putting out; [*peuple*] extinction, dying out; [*dette, droit*] extinguishment; **~ de voix** loss of voice, aphonia (*SPÉC*); **avoir une ~ de voix** to lose one's voice; (*Mil, fig*) **avant l'~ des feux** before lights out; **espèce en voie d'~** endangered species

extirpation [ɛkstirpasjɔ̃] NF (*littér*) [*abus, vice*] eradication; (*Chir*) extirpation; [*plante*] uprooting, pulling up

extirper [ɛkstirpe] ▶conjug 1◀ ⬚**1** VT (*littér*) [*+ abus, vice*] to eradicate, root out; (*Chir*) to extirpate; [*+ herbes*] to uproot, pull up; **elle a extirpé un chéquier de son sac*** she rooted around in her handbag and pulled out a chequebook; **impossible de lui ~ une parole !***

it's impossible to drag *ou* get a word out of him!; **~ qn de son lit*** to drag *ou* haul sb out of bed ⬚**2** **s'extirper** VPR **s'~ de son manteau** to extricate o.s. from one's coat; **s'~ du lit** to drag o.s. out of bed

extorquer [ɛkstɔrke] ▶conjug 1◀ VT [*+ argent*] to extort; [*+ aveu, promesse*] to extract, extort (**à qn** from sb); **ils lui ont extorqué une signature** they forced a signature out of him

extorqueur, -euse [ɛkstɔrkœr, øz] NM,F extortioner

extorsion [ɛkstɔrsjɔ̃] NF extortion; **~ de fonds** extortion of money

extra [ɛkstra] ⬚**1** NM (= *serveur*) catering assistant; (= *gâterie*) (special) treat; **s'offrir un ~** to give o.s. a treat, treat o.s. to something special ⬚**2** ADJ INV (*Comm* = *supérieur*) [*fromage, vin*] first-rate, extra-special; [*tissu*] top-quality; (* = *excellent*) [*film, personne, week-end*] fantastic, terrific*, great*; **de qualité ~** of the finest *ou* best quality

extraconjugal, e (*mpl* **-aux**) [ɛkstrakɔ̃ʒygal, o] ADJ extramarital

extracteur [ɛkstraktœr] NM extractor

extractif, -ive [ɛkstraktif, iv] ADJ [*industrie*] extractive, mining

extraction [ɛkstraksjɔ̃] NF ⬚**a** [*pétrole*] extraction; [*charbon*] mining; [*marbre*] quarrying ⬚**b** (*Math, Méd*) extraction ⬚**c** †† (= *origine*) extraction (*frm*); **de haute/basse ~** of high/low birth

extrader [ɛkstrade] ▶conjug 1◀ VT to extradite

extradition [ɛkstradisjɔ̃] NF extradition

extrafin, e, **extra-fin, e** [ɛkstrafɛ̃, fin] ADJ [*haricots, petits pois*] super-fine; [*aiguille*] extra fine

extrafort, extra-fort, e [ɛkstrafɔr, fɔrt] ⬚**1** ADJ [*carton, moutarde*] extra-strong ⬚**2** NM (*Couture*) binding

extraire [ɛkstrer] ▶conjug 50◀ ⬚**1** VT ⬚**a** [*+ minerai, pétrole*] to extract; [*+ charbon*] to mine; [*+ marbre*] to quarry ⬚**b** [*+ gaz, jus*] to extract; (*en pressant*) to squeeze out; (*en tordant*) to wring out ⬚**c** [*+ dent*] to extract, pull out; [*+ clou*] to pull out; [*+ racine carrée*] to extract; [*+ balle*] to extract, remove (**de** from) ⬚**d** **~ de** [*+ placard, poche*] to take *ou* bring out of; [*+ avalanche, prison*] to rescue from, get out of; **passage extrait d'un livre** passage taken from a book ⬚**2** **s'extraire** VPR **s'~ de son manteau** to extricate o.s. from one's coat; **s'~ de sa voiture** to climb out of one's car

extrait [ɛkstre] NM ⬚**a** [*discours, journal*] extract; [*auteur, film, livre*] extract, excerpt; [*chanson*] excerpt; **~ de naissance/baptême** birth/baptismal certificate; **~ de compte** abstract of accounts; **un court ~ de l'émission** a clip from the programme ⬚**b** [*plante*] essence; **~ de viande** meat extract

extrajudiciaire [ɛkstraʒydisjer] ADJ (*Jur*) [*exécution*] extrajudicial

extralégal, e (*mpl* **-aux**) [ɛkstralegal, o] ADJ extra-legal

extralinguistique [ɛkstralɛ̃gɥistik] ADJ extralinguistic

extra-lucide, extralucide [ɛkstralysid] ADJ, NMF clairvoyant

extra-marital, e (*mpl* **-aux**) [ɛkstramarital, o] ADJ extra-marital

extra-muros [ɛkstramyros] ⬚**1** ADJ INV extramural; **un campus ~** a campus outside town; **Paris ~** outer Paris ⬚**2** ADV outside the town

extraordinaire [ɛkstraɔrdiner] ADJ ⬚**a** (= *étrange*) [*costume, événement, opinions*] extraordinary; **l'~, c'est que ...** the extraordinary thing is that ... ⬚**b** (= *exceptionnel*) [*beauté, force*] extraordinary, exceptional, outstanding; [*succès*] resounding; **ce roman n'est pas ~** this isn't a particularly great novel, this novel

isn't up to much* (*Brit*) ⬚**c** (*Pol*) [*assemblée, mesures, moyens*] extraordinary, special → **ambassadeur** ⬚**d** **si par ~** if by some unlikely chance; **quand par ~** on those rare occasions when

extraordinairement [ɛkstraɔrdinermɑ̃] ADV (= *exceptionnellement*) extraordinarily, exceptionally; (= *d'une manière étrange*) extraordinarily

extraparlementaire [ɛkstraparləmɑ̃ter] ADJ extra-parliamentary

extraplat, e [ɛkstrapla, at] ADJ [*télévision, montre, calculatrice*] slimline

extrapolation [ɛkstrapɔlasjɔ̃] NF extrapolation

extrapoler [ɛkstrapɔle] ▶conjug 1◀ VTI to extrapolate (**à partir de** from)

extrascolaire [ɛkstraskɔler] ADJ [*activités*] extracurricular

extrasensible [ɛkstrasɑ̃sibl] ADJ extrasensible (*frm*), that cannot be perceived by the senses

extrasensoriel, -ielle [ɛkstrasɑ̃sɔrjel] ADJ [*perception*] extrasensory

extrasystole [ɛkstrasistɔl] NF extrasystole

extraterrestre [ɛkstraterestr] ⬚**1** ADJ extra-terrestrial ⬚**2** NMF extra-terrestrial, alien

extraterritorialité [ɛkstrateritɔrjalite] NF extraterritoriality

extra-utérin, e (*mpl* **extra-utérins**) [ɛkstrayterɛ̃, in] ADJ extrauterine; **grossesse ~e** ectopic pregnancy

extravagance [ɛkstravagɑ̃s] NF ⬚**a** (= *caractère*) [*costume, conduite*] eccentricity, extravagance ⬚**b** (= *acte*) eccentric *ou* extravagant behaviour (*NonC*); **dire des ~s** to talk wildly *ou* extravagantly

extravagant, e [ɛkstravagɑ̃, ɑ̃t] ADJ [*idée, théorie*] extravagant, wild, crazy; [*prix*] outrageous, excessive

extraversion [ɛkstraversjɔ̃] NF extroversion

extraverti, e [ɛkstraverti] ADJ, NM,F extrovert

extrême [ɛkstrem] ⬚**1** ADJ ⬚**a** (*le plus éloigné*) extreme, furthest; **à l'~ bout de la table** at the far *ou* furthest end of the table, at the very end of the table; **dans son ~ jeunesse** in his very young days, in his earliest youth; **à l'~ opposé** at the opposite extreme (**de** of); (*Pol*) **l'~ droite/gauche** the far right/left ⬚**b** (*le plus intense*) extreme, utmost; **dans la misère ~** in extreme *ou* the utmost poverty; **c'est avec un plaisir ~ que** it is with the greatest *ou* the utmost pleasure that; **il m'a reçu avec une ~ amabilité** he received me in the friendliest possible way *ou* with the utmost kindness; **il fait une chaleur ~** it is extremely hot; **d'une pâleur/difficulté ~** extremely pale/difficult → **rigueur, urgence** ⬚**c** (*après n* = *excessif, radical*) [*théories, moyens*] extreme; **ça l'a conduit à des mesures ~s** that drove him into taking drastic *ou* extreme steps; **il a un caractère ~** he tends to go to extremes, he is an extremist by nature

⬚**2** NM ⬚**a** (= *opposé*) extreme; **les ~s se touchent** extremes meet; **passer d'un ~ à l'autre** to go from one extreme to the other *ou* to another ⬚**b** (*Math*) **~s** extremes

⬚**3** **à l'extrême** LOC ADV **jusqu'à l'~** in the extreme, to an extreme degree; **cela lui répugnait à l'~** he was extremely loath to do it; **noircir une situation à l'~** to paint the blackest possible picture of a situation; **scrupuleux à l'~** scrupulous to a fault

extrêmement [ɛkstremmɑ̃] ADV extremely, exceedingly

extrême-onction (*pl* **extrêmes-onctions**) [ɛkstremɔ̃ksjɔ̃] NF Extreme Unction

Extrême-Orient [ɛkstremɔrjɑ̃] NM INV Far East

extrême-oriental, e (*mpl* **extrême-orientaux**) [ɛkstremɔrjɑ̃tal, o] ⬚**1** ADJ far eastern, oriental

2 **Extrême-Oriental(e)** NM,F person from the Far East, Oriental (*parfois péj*)

extrémisme [εkstremism] NM extremism

extrémiste [εkstremist] ADJ, NMF extremist

extrémité [εkstremite] NF a (= *bout*: *gén*) end; [*aiguille*] point; [*objet mince*] tip; [*village, île*] extremity, limit; [*péninsule*] head b (*frm = situation critique*) plight, straits; **être dans la pénible ~ de devoir** to be in the unfortunate necessity of having to; **réduit à la dernière ~** in the most dire plight *ou* straits; **être à toute ~ ◊ être à la dernière ~** to be on the point of death c (*frm = action excessive*) extremes, extreme lengths; **se porter à une ~** *ou* **à des ~s** to go to extremes; **pousser qn à une ~** *ou* **à des ~s** to push *ou* drive sb to extremes *ou* into taking extreme action; **se livrer à des ~s (sur qn)** to assault sb; **d'une ~ dans l'autre** from one extreme to another d (= *pieds et mains*) **~s** extremities

extrinsèque [εkstrɛ̃sɛk] ADJ extrinsic

extruder [εkstryde] ▶ conjug 1 ◀ VT to extrude

extrusion [εkstryzjɔ̃] NF extrusion

exubérance [εgzyberɑ̃s] NF (= *caractère*) exuberance (*NonC*); (= *action*) exuberant behaviour (*NonC*) (*ou* talk (*NonC*) *etc*); **parler avec ~** to speak exuberantly

exubérant, e [εgzyberɑ̃, ɑ̃t] ADJ (*gén*) exuberant

exultation [εgzyltasjɔ̃] NF exultation

exulter [εgzylte] ▶ conjug 1 ◀ VI to exult

exutoire [εgzytwar] NM (*Tech*) outlet; (= *dérivatif*) outlet (**à** for)

ex-voto [εksvɔto] NM INV thanksgiving *ou* commemorative plaque

eye-liner (*pl* **eye-liners**) [ajlajnœr] NM eye-liner

Ézéchiel [ezekjεl] NM Ezekiel; **(le livre d') ~** (the Book of) Ezechiel

F

F¹, f [ɛf] NM (= *lettre*) F, f; (= *appartement*) **un F2** a 2-roomed flat (*Brit*) *ou* apartment (*surtout US*)

F² a (ABRÉV = **franc**) F, fr b (ABRÉV = **Fahrenheit**) F c ABRÉV = **frère**

fa [fa] NM INV (*Mus*) F; (*en chantant la gamme*) fa → **clé**

FAB [efabe] (ABRÉV = **franco à bord**) FOB

fable [fabl] NF (= *genre*) fable; (= *légende*) fable, legend; (= *mensonge*) tale, story; **quelle ~ va-t-il inventer?** what yarn will he spin?; **cette rumeur est une pure ~** this rumour is completely unfounded *ou* untrue; **être la ~ de toute la ville†** to be the laughing stock of the whole town

fabliau (*pl* **fabliaux**) [fablijo] NM fabliau

fablier [fablije] NM book of fables

fabricant, e [fabrikɑ̃, ɑ̃t] NM,F manufacturer; **un gros ~ d'ordinateurs** a big computer manufacturer; **~ de pneus** tyre-maker (*Brit*), tire-maker (*US*)

fabricateur, -trice [fabrikatœr, tris] NM,F [*fausse monnaie, faux papiers*] counterfeiter, forger; [*fausses nouvelles*] fabricator

fabrication [fabrikasjɔ̃] NF a (*industrielle*) manufacture, manufacturing; (*artisanale, personnelle*) making; **la ~ industrielle/en série** factory *ou* industrial/mass production; **~ par lots** batch production; **de ~ française** made in France, French-made; **de ~ étrangère** foreign-made; **de ~ locale** made locally; **c'est une ~ maison*** it's home-made; **de bonne ~** well-made, of good *ou* high-quality workmanship; **~ assistée par ordinateur** computer-aided manufacturing; **une robe de sa ~** a dress of her own making, a dress she made herself → **artisanal, défaut, procédé** *etc* b (*faux*) forging; [*fausses nouvelles*] fabricating, making up; **~ de fausse monnaie** counterfeiting *ou* forging money

fabrique [fabrik] NF a (= *établissement*) factory; **~ de gants** glove factory; **~ de papier** paper mill → **marque, prix** b (*littér* = *facture*) workmanship; **de bonne ~** well-made, of good *ou* high-quality workmanship c (*Rel*) **la ~** the fabric

fabriquer [fabrike] ▸ conjug 1 ◂ VT a (*industriellement*) to manufacture; (*de façon artisanale, chez soi*) to make; [+ *cellules, anticorps*] to make, produce; [+ *faux document*] to forge; [+ *fausses nouvelles, fausses preuves*] to fabricate, make up; [+ *incident, histoire*] to invent, make up; **~ de la fausse monnaie** to counterfeit *ou* forge money; **~ en série** to mass-produce; **~ industriellement** to manufacture, produce industrially; **~ de façon artisanale** to handcraft, make *ou* produce on a small scale; **c'est une histoire fabriquée de toutes pièces** this story is made up from start to finish *ou* is a complete fabrication; **il s'est fabriqué un personnage de prophète** he created *ou* invented a prophet-like character for himself; **il s'est fabriqué un poste de radio/une cabane** he built *ou* made himself a radio set/a shed

b (= *faire*) to do; **qu'est-ce qu'il fabrique?** what (on earth) is he doing? *ou* is he up to?*; **quelquefois, je me demande ce que je fabrique ici!** sometimes I wonder what on earth I'm doing here!

fabulateur, -trice [fabylatœr, tris] 1 ADJ **faculté fabulatrice** faculty for fantasizing; **tendance fabulatrice** tendency to fabricate *ou* spin stories 2 NM,F storyteller

fabulation [fabylasjɔ̃] NF (= *fait d'imaginer*) fantasizing; (= *fait de mentir*) storytelling; (= *fable*) tale, fable; (= *mensonge*) story, yarn, tale

fabuler [fabyle] ▸ conjug 1 ◂ VI make up *ou* invent stories

fabuleusement [fabyløzmɑ̃] ADV fabulously, fantastically

fabuleux, -euse [fabylø, øz] ADJ a (*littér*) (= *des temps anciens, de la mythologie*) mythical, legendary; (= *de la légende, du merveilleux*) fabulous b (= *prodigieux*) [*richesse, exploits, vitesse*] fabulous, fantastic

fabuliste [fabylist] NM writer of fables *ou* tales

fac* [fak] NF (ABRÉV = **faculté**) → **faculté a**

façade [fasad] NF a (= *devant de maison*) (*gén*) façade, front, frontage; (*Archéol*) façade; (= *côté de maison*) side; [*magasin*] front, frontage; **~ latérale** side wall; **~ ouest** west side *ou* wall; **la ~ arrière de la maison** the back of the house; **les ~s des magasins** the shop fronts; **3 pièces en ~** 3 rooms at *ou* facing the front; (*Mét*) **sur la ~ atlantique** along the Atlantic shoreline

b (= *apparence*) façade, appearance; (= *couverture*) cover; **~ de respectabilité/de vertu** façade *ou* outward show *ou* appearance of respectability/virtue; **ce n'est qu'une ~** it's just a front *ou* façade, it's a mere façade *ou* pretence; **de ~** [*luxe*] apparent; [*optimisme*] fake; **maintenir une unité de ~** to preserve an appearance *ou* outward show of unity; **pour la ~** for the sake of appearances, for appearances' sake; **ce restaurant est une ~ qui cache un tripot clandestin** this restaurant is a cover for an illegal dive*

c (‡ = *visage*) **se refaire la ~** (= *se maquiller*) to redo one's face*; (= *se faire faire un lifting*) to have a face-lift; **il va te démolir la ~**‡ he's going to smash your face in‡

face [fas] 1 NF a (*frm, Méd* = *visage*) face; **les blessés de la ~** people with facial injuries; **tomber ~ contre terre** to fall flat on the ground *ou* flat on one's face; **se prosterner ~ contre terre** to prostrate o.s. with one's face to the ground; **~ de rat/de singe**‡ rat/monkey face‡; **sauver/perdre la ~** to save/lose face; **opération destinée à sauver la ~** face-saving move → **voiler¹**

b (= *côté*) [*objet, organe*] side; [*médaille, pièce de monnaie*] front, obverse; (*Math*) [*cube, figure*] side, face; (*Alpinisme*) face, wall; **~ A/B** [*disque*] A-/B-side; **la ~ interne des cuisses** the inner thighs; **la ~ cachée de la lune** the dark side of the moon; **examiner un objet/une question sous** *ou* **sur toutes ses ~s** to examine an object/a problem from all sides; **question**

à **double ~** two-sided question; **la pièce est tombée sur ~** *ou* **côté ~** the coin fell face up; (*jeu de pile ou face*) **~!** heads! → **pile**

c (= *aspect*) face; **la ~ changeante des choses** the changing face of things; **changer la ~ du monde** to change the face of the world; **le monde a changé de ~** (the face of) the world has changed

d (*littér* = *surface*) **la ~ de la terre** *ou* **du globe** the face of the earth; **la ~ de l'océan** the surface of the ocean

e (*loc*) **faire ~** to face up to things; **faire ~ à** [+ *lieu, objet, personne*] to face, be opposite; [+ *épreuve, adversaire, obligation*] to face (up to); [+ *dette, engagement*] to meet; **se faire ~** [*maisons*] to be facing *ou* opposite each other; [*adversaires*] to be face to face; **il a dû faire ~ à des dépenses élevées** he has been faced with *ou* he has had to face considerable expense

2 **à la face de** LOC PRÉP **il éclata de rire à la ~ de son professeur** he laughed in his teacher's face; **proclamer à la ~ de l'univers** *ou* **du monde** to proclaim to the whole world *ou* to the world at large

3 **en face** LOC ADV a (= *de l'autre côté de la rue*) across the street, opposite, over the road; **j'habite en ~** I live across the street *ou* over the road *ou* opposite; **la maison d'en ~** the house across the street *ou* over the road *ou* opposite; **le trottoir d'en ~** the opposite pavement; **la dame d'en ~** the lady (from) across the street *ou* (from) over the road, the lady opposite

b (= *directement, ouvertement*) **regarder qn (bien) en ~** to look sb (straight) in the face; **je lui ai dit en ~ ce que je pensais d'elle** I told her to her face what I thought of her; **regarder la mort en ~** to look death in the face; **il faut voir les choses en ~** one must see things as they are, one must face facts; **avoir le soleil en ~** to have the sun in one's eyes

4 **en face de** LOC PRÉP (= *en vis-à-vis de*) opposite; (= *en présence de*) in front of; **au banquet, on les a mis l'un en ~ de l'autre** *ou* **en ~ l'un de l'autre** they were placed opposite each other *ou* facing each other at the banquet; **les deux ennemis étaient maintenant l'un en ~ de l'autre** the two enemies now stood facing each other *ou* were now face to face; **il n'ose rien dire en ~ de son patron** he daren't say anything in front of his boss; **ne te mets pas en ~ de moi/de ma lumière** don't stand in my way/in my light; **se trouver en ~ d'un danger/problème** to be confronted *ou* faced with a danger/problem; (*fig*) **en ~ de cela** on the other hand

5 **de face** LOC ADJ, LOC ADV [*portrait*] full-face; [*nu, portrait en pied*] full-frontal; [*attaque*] (full-)frontal; [*place*] (*au théâtre*) in the centre (*Brit*) *ou* center (*US*); **un personnage/cheval de ~** the front view of a person/horse; **avoir une vue de ~ sur qch** to have a front view of sth; **voir qn de ~** to see sb face on; **vu/filmé de ~** seen/filmed from the front; **attaquer de ~** to make a (full-)frontal attack on, attack from

the front; **avoir le vent de ~** to have the wind in one's face

6 **face à** LOC PRÉP facing; **il se dressa ~ à l'ennemi** he positioned himself facing the enemy; **~ à ces problèmes, il se sentait impuissant** faced with *ou* in the face of such problems, he felt helpless

7 **face à face** LOC ADV [*lieux, objets*] opposite *ou* facing each other; [*personnes, animaux*] face to face, facing each other; **~ à ~ avec** [+ *lieu, objet*] opposite, facing; [+ *personne, animal*] face to face with; **~ à ~ avec une difficulté** faced with *ou* up against a difficulty

face-à-face [fasafas] NM INV (= *rencontre*) (face-to-face) meeting *ou* encounter; (= *rivalité*) showdown; (= *conflit*) confrontation; **~ télévisé** one-to-one *ou* face-to-face TV debate; (*Sport*) **le ~ Bordeaux-Nantes** the encounter between Bordeaux and Nantes

face-à-main (*pl* **faces-à-main**) [fasamɛ̃] NM lorgnette

facétie [fasesi] NF (= *drôlerie*) joke; (= *farce*) prank, trick; **faire des ~s** to play pranks *ou* tricks; **dire des ~s** to crack jokes

facétieusement [fasesjøzmɑ̃] ADV mischievously

facétieux, -ieuse [fasesjø, jøz] ADJ [*personne, caractère*] mischievous

facette [fasɛt] NF (*lit, fig*) facet; **à ~s** [*pierre*] faceted; [*caractère, personnage*] multi-faceted, many-sided; [*histoire, réalité*] multifaceted; **yeux à ~s** compound eyes; **étudier un problème sous toutes ses ~s** to examine a problem from every angle

facetter [fasete] ▸ conjug 1 ◂ VT to facet

fâché, e [faʃe] (*ptp de* **fâcher**) ADJ **a** (= *en colère*) angry, cross (*surtout Brit*) (**contre** with); **elle a l'air ~(e)** she looks angry *ou* cross (*surtout Brit*); **tu n'es pas ~, au moins?** you're not angry *ou* cross (*surtout Brit*), are you? **b** (= *brouillé*) **ils sont ~s** they have fallen out; **elle est ~e avec moi** she has fallen out with me; **nous sommes ~s à mort** we can't stand the sight of each other, we are mortal enemies; (*hum*) **il est ~ avec les chiffres** he's hopeless with numbers; (*hum*) **il est ~ avec l'orthographe** he can't spell to save his life; (*hum*) **il est ~ avec son peigne** his hair has never seen a comb **c** (= *contrarié*) sorry (**de qch** about sth); (*frm*) **je suis ~ de ne pas pouvoir vous aider** I'm sorry that I can't help you; **je ne suis pas ~ d'avoir fini ce travail** I'm not sorry to have finished this job; (*hum*) **je ne serais pas ~ que vous me laissiez tranquille** I wouldn't mind being left alone ou in peace, I wouldn't object to a bit of peace and quiet

fâcher [faʃe] ▸ conjug 1 ◂ **1** VT **a** (= *mettre en colère*) to anger, make angry, vex; **tu ne réussiras qu'à le ~ davantage** you will only make him more angry *ou* angrier **b** (*frm* = *contrarier*) to grieve (*frm*), distress; **cette triste nouvelle me fâche beaucoup** this sad news grieves me (*frm*) *ou* greatly distresses me **2** **se fâcher** VPR **a** (= *se mettre en colère*) to get angry *ou* cross (*surtout Brit*), lose one's temper; **se ~ contre qn/pour/au sujet de qch** to get angry *ou* annoyed with sb/about *ou* over sth; **va au lit ou je me fâche!** go to bed or I'll get angry!; (*hum*) **si tu continues, je vais me ~ tout rouge*** if you go on like that, I'll get really angry *ou* cross (*surtout Brit*) **b** (= *se brouiller*) to quarrel, fall out (**avec** with)

fâcherie [faʃri] NF (= *brouille*) quarrel

fâcheusement [faʃøzmɑ̃] ADV [*survenir*] (most) unfortunately *ou* awkwardly; **~ surpris** (most) unpleasantly surprised

fâcheux, -euse [faʃø, øz] **1** ADJ [*exemple, décision, coïncidence, situation*] unfortunate, regrettable; **il est ~ qu'il ait cru devoir s'abstenir** it's unfortunate *ou* a pity that he felt it necessary to abstain; **le ~ dans tout ça c'est que ...**

---

the unfortunate *ou* annoying *ou* tiresome thing about it (all) is that ... **2** NM,F (*littér* = *importun*) bore

facho* [faʃo] ADJ, NMF (ABRÉV = **fasciste**) (*péj*) fascist; **il est un peu ~** he's a bit of a fascist

facial, e (*mpl* **facials** *ou* **-iaux**) [fasjal, jo] ADJ facial → **angle**

faciès [fasjɛs] NM **a** (= *visage*) features; (*Ethnol, Méd*) facies → **délit** **b** (*Bot, Géog*) facies

facile [fasil] **1** ADJ **a** (= *aisé*) [*travail, problème, succès, proie*] easy; **un livre ~ à lire** an easy book to read; **c'est** *ou* **il est ~ de ...** it's easy to ...; **~ d'emploi** ◊ **~ à utiliser** easy to use; **~ d'accès** ◊ **d'accès** ◊ **~** easy to reach *ou* get to, of easy access; **avoir la vie ~** to have an easy life; **ils ne lui rendent pas la vie ~** they don't make life easy for him; **c'est ~ à dire!** that's easy to say!; **plus ~ à dire qu'à faire** easier said than done; **c'est trop ~ de s'indigner** it's too easy to get indignant; **ce n'est pas si ~** it's not as simple as that; **~ comme tout*** *ou* **comme bonjour*** (as) easy as pie*, dead easy* **b** (= *spontané*) **avoir la parole ~** (= *parler aisément*) to be a fluent *ou* an articulate speaker; (= *parler volontiers*) to have a ready tongue *ou* the gift of the gab*; **il a la plume ~** (= *écrire aisément*) he has an eloquent pen; (= *être toujours prêt à écrire*) he finds it easy to write, writing comes easily to him; **avoir la larme ~** to be quick to cry, be easily moved to tears; **il a l'argent ~*** he's very casual about money, money just slips through his fingers; **l'argent ~** easy money; **avoir la gâchette ~** to be trigger-happy; **il a le couteau ~** he's all too quick to use his knife, he's very ready with his knife **c** (*péj* = *superficiel*) **effet/ironie ~** facile effect/irony; **littérature ~** cheap literature **d** [*caractère*] easy-going; **il est d'humeur ~** he's easy-going; **il est ~ à vivre/contenter** he's easy to get along with *ou* on with (*Brit*)/to please; **il n'est pas ~ tous les jours** he's not always easy to get along with *ou* on with (*Brit*); **il n'est pas ~ en affaires** he's a tough businessman, he drives a hard bargain; **ce n'est pas un adversaire ~** he's a formidable adversary; **c'est un bébé très ~** he's a very easy baby **e** (*péj*) [*femme*] loose (*épith*); **une fille ~** a woman of easy virtue

2 ADV* (= *facilement*) easily; (= *au moins*) at least, easily; **il y est arrivé ~** he managed it easily; **il fait du 200 km/h ~** he's doing at least 200 km/h; **elle a 50 ans ~** she's at least *ou* easily 50

facilement [fasilmɑ̃] ADV (*gén*) easily; **médicament ~ toléré par l'organisme** medicine easily *ou* readily tolerated by the body; **il se fâche ~** he loses his temper easily, he's quick to lose his temper, he's quick-tempered; **on met ~ 10 jours*** it takes 10 days easily *ou* at least 10 days

facilité [fasilite] NF **a** (= *simplicité*) [*devoir, problème, travail*] easiness; **aimer la ~** to like things that are easy *ou* simple; **tâche d'une grande ~** extremely easy *ou* straightforward task; **d'une grande ~ d'emploi** [*outil*] very easy to use; [*logiciel*] very user-friendly **b** (= *aisance*) [*succès, victoire*] ease; [*expression, style*] fluency, ease; **il a choisi la ~ en ne venant pas** he took the easy way out by not coming; **réussir qch avec ~** to manage sth with ease *ou* easily; **la ~ avec laquelle il a appris le piano** the ease with which he learnt the piano; **il travaille avec ~** he works with ease; **il s'exprime avec ~** *ou* **avec une grande ~ de parole** he expresses himself with (great) fluency *ou* ease *ou* fluently → **solution** **c** (= *aptitude*) ability, aptitude; **cet élève a beaucoup de ~** this pupil has great ability *ou* aptitude; **il a beaucoup de ~ pour les langues** he has a great aptitude *ou* facility for languages

---

d (*gén pl = possibilité*) facility; **avoir la ~/ toutes (les) ~s de** *ou* **pour faire qch** to have the/every opportunity to do sth *ou* of doing sth; **~s de transport** transport facilities; **~s d'accès à un lieu/à des services** easy access *ou* ease of access to a place/services; **~s de crédit** credit facilities *ou* terms; **~s de paiement** easy terms; **consentir des ~s de caisse** to grant an overdraft facility

e (= *tendance*) tendency; **il a une certaine ~ à se mettre en colère** he has a tendency to lose his temper

f (*littér* = *complaisance*) readiness; **il a une grande ~ à croire ce que l'on raconte/à se plier à une règle** he has a great tendency *ou* is very ready to believe what people tell him/to comply with the rules

faciliter [fasilite] ▸ conjug 1 ◂ VT (*gén*) to make easier, facilitate; **ça ne va pas ~ les choses** that's not going to make matters *ou* things (any) easier, that's not going to ease matters; **pour lui ~ sa mission/la tâche** to make his mission/work easier, make the mission/work easier for him

façon [fasɔ̃] **1** NF **a** (= *manière*) way, manner; **voilà la ~ dont il procède** this is how *ou* the way he does it; **il s'y prend de** *ou* **d'une ~ curieuse** he has a strange way of going about things; **de quelle ~ est-ce arrivé?** how did it happen?; **il faut le faire de la ~ suivante** you must do it in the following way *ou* as follows; **je le ferai à ma ~** I shall do it my own way; **il raconte l'histoire à sa ~** he tells the story in his own way; **à la ~ de** like; **à la ~ d'un enfant** like a child, as a child would do; **sa ~ d'agir/ de répondre** the way he behaves/answers, his way of behaving/answering; **c'est une ~ de parler** it's (just) a figure of speech; **je vais lui dire ma ~ de penser** (*point de vue*) I'll tell him what I think about it *ou* how I feel about it; (*colère*) I'll give him a piece of my mind, I'll tell him what I think about it; **c'est une ~ de voir (les choses)** it's one way of seeing things *ou* of looking at things ■ (*PROV*) **la ~ de donner vaut mieux que ce qu'on donne** it's the thought that counts

b (*loc*) **rosser qn de (la) belle ~** †† to give sb a sound thrashing; **d'une certaine ~, c'est vrai** it is true in a way *ou* in some ways; **d'une ~ générale** generally speaking, as a general rule; **de la même ~** in the same way; **il a réagi de la même ~ que l'an dernier** he reacted (in the same way) as he did last year; **il n'a pas réagi de la même ~ que son frère** he didn't react in the same way as his brother, his reaction was different from his brother's; **de toute(s) ~(s)** in any case, at any rate, anyway; **de cette ~,tu n'auras rien à payer** that way, you won't have to pay anything; **d'une ~ ou d'une autre** somehow or other, one way or another; **en aucune ~** in no way; **de quelque ~ qu'il s'y prenne** however *ou* no matter how he goes about it; **je vais lui jouer un tour de ma ~** I'm going to play a trick of my own on him; **un poème de ma ~** a poem written by me; **un plat de ma ~** a dish of my own making *ou* made by me; **de telle ~ que ...** in such a way that ...; **de ~ à ne pas le déranger** so as not to disturb him; **de ~ à ce qu'il puisse regarder** ◊ **de (telle) ~ qu'il puisse regarder** so that he can see; **accepter sans ~** to accept without fuss; **il est sans ~** he's unaffected; **merci, sans ~** no thanks, really *ou* honestly; **repas sans ~** simple *ou* unpretentious meal; **et sans plus de ~s** and without further ado

c (*Couture*) [*robe*] cut, making-up (*Brit*); **payer la ~** to pay for the tailoring *ou* making-up (*Brit*); **le travail à ~** tailoring, dressmaking; **travailler à ~** to (hand) tailor *ou* make up (*Brit*) customers' own material; **tailleur à ~** bespoke tailor (*Brit*), custom tailor (*US*); **vêtement à ~** tailor-made garments, bespoke garments (*Brit*)

[d] (= *imitation*) **veste ~ daim/cuir** jacket in imitation suede/leather; **châle ~ cachemire** cashmere-style shawl; **bijoux ~ antique** old-fashioned *ou* antique style jewellery; **gigot ~ chevreuil** leg of lamb cooked like *ou* done like venison

[e] (*Agr*) tillage; **donner une ~ à la terre** to till the land

[f] (*Artisanat*) (= *fabrication*) making, crafting; (= *facture*) workmanship, craftmanship; **payer la ~** to pay for the workmanship

[g] † (= *genre*) **une ~ de maître d'hôtel** a head waiter of sorts; **une ~ de roman** a novel of sorts

[2] **façons** NFPL manners, behaviour (*Brit*), behavior (*US*); **ses ~s me déplaisent profondément** I find his manners extremely unpleasant, I don't like his behaviour at all; **en voilà des ~s!** what a way to behave!, that's no way to behave!; **faire des ~s** (*minauderies*) to put on airs and graces; (*chichis*) to make a fuss

faconde [fakɔd] NF (*littér*) loquaciousness; **avoir de la ~** to be very loquacious; **quelle ~!** what a talker!, he's (*ou* she's) got the gift of the gab!*

façonnage [fasɔnaʒ] NM [a] [*argile, métal*] shaping, fashioning; [*tronc d'arbre, bloc de pierre*] hewing, shaping [b] [*pièce, clé*] (*industriel*) manufacturing; (*artisanal*) making, crafting; [*chapeau, robe, statuette*] fashioning, making [c] [*Imprim*] forwarding

façonnement [fasɔnmɑ̃] NM [*esprits, caractère*] moulding (*Brit*), molding (*US*), shaping, forming

façonner [fasɔne] ▸ conjug 1 ◂ VT [a] [+ *argile, métal*] to shape, fashion; [+ *tronc d'arbre, bloc de pierre*] to hew, shape; [+ *terre*] to till [b] [+ *pièce, clé*] (*industriellement*) to manufacture; (*artisanalement*) to make, craft; [+ *chapeau, robe, statuette*] to fashion, make [c] [+ *caractère, personne*] to mould (*Brit*), mold (*US*), shape, form; **l'éducation puritaine qui a façonné son enfance** the puritanical upbringing that shaped his childhood

façonnier, -ière [fasɔnje, jɛʀ] ADJ (= *maniéré*) affected, over-refined; **elle est façonnière** she puts on airs and graces, she's affected

fac-similé (*pl* **fac-similés**) [faksimile] NM facsimile

factage [faktaʒ] NM (= *transport*) cartage, forwarding; **entreprise de ~** parcel delivery company, transport company; **frais de ~** cartage, delivery charge, carriage

facteur [faktœʀ] NM [a] (*Poste*) postman (*Brit*), mailman (*US*) → **factrice** [b] (= *élément, Math*) factor (**de, dans** in); **le ~ chance/prix/humain** the chance/price/human factor; **~ de risque** risk factor; **~ de croissance** (*Méd*) growth factor; (*Écon*) **le libre-échange a été un ~ de croissance** free trade has been a factor in economic growth; (*Math, gén*) **commun** common factor; **mettre en ~s** to factorize; **mise en ~s** factorization; **~ Rhésus** Rhesus *ou* Rh factor [c] (= *fabricant*) **~ de pianos** piano maker; **~ d'orgues** organ builder

factice [faktis] [1] ADJ [*marbre, beauté*] artificial; [*cuir, bijou*] imitation (*épith*), artificial; [*barbe*] false; [*bouteilles, articles exposés*] dummy (*épith*); [*enthousiasme, amabilité*] false, feigned, sham; **tout semblait ~, le marbre du sol et la civilité des employés** everything seemed phoney* *ou* artificial, from the marble floor to the politeness of the employees [2] NM (= *objet*) dummy

factieux, -ieuse [faksjø, jøz] [1] ADJ factious, seditious [2] NM,F seditionary

faction [faksjɔ̃] NF [a] (= *groupe factieux*) faction [b] (= *garde*) [*sentinelle*] sentry duty, guard duty; [*soldat*] guard duty; [*personne qui attend*] long watch; **être de** *ou* **en ~** [*soldat*] to be on guard (duty), stand guard; [*sentinelle*] to be on guard (duty) *ou* (sentry) duty, stand guard; [*personne qui attend*] to keep *ou* stand

watch; **mettre qn de ~** to put sb on guard (duty)

factionnaire [faksjɔnɛʀ] NM (= *sentinelle, garde*) sentry *ou* guard (on duty)

factitif, -ive [faktitif, iv] ADJ (*Ling*) factitive, causative

factoriel, -ielle [faktɔʀjɛl] [1] ADJ (*Math*) factorial; **analyse factorielle** factor analysis [2] **factorielle** NF (*Math*) factorial

factoring [faktɔʀiŋ] NM factoring

factorisation [faktɔʀizasjɔ̃] NF factorization

factoriser [faktɔʀize] ▸ conjug 1 ◂ VT to factorize

factotum [faktɔtɔm] NM (= *homme à tout faire*) odd-job man, general handyman, (general) factotum (*hum*); (*péj* = *larbin*) gofer*, (general) dogsbody (*Brit, péj*)

factrice [faktʀis] NF (*Poste*) postwoman (*Brit*), mailwoman (*US*)

factuel, -elle [faktɥɛl] ADJ factual

factum [faktɔm] NM (*littér*) lampoon

facturation [faktyʀasjɔ̃] NF (= *opération*) invoicing, billing; (= *bureau*) invoice office; **~ détaillée** itemized billing

▼ **facture** [faktyʀ] NF [a] (= *note*) (*gén*) bill; (*Comm*) invoice; **~ d'électricité/de téléphone** electricity/(tele)phone bill; (*Écon*) **notre ~ pétrolière/énergétique** the nation's oil/energy bill; **fausse ~** false invoice; (*Pol*) **l'affaire des fausses ~s** scandal involving the use of false invoices to fund French political parties; **établir une ~** to make out a bill *ou* an invoice; (*fig*) **qui va payer la ~?** who will foot the bill? → **pro forma** [b] (= *manière, style*) [*objet*] workmanship, craftmanship; [*roman, symphonie*] construction; [*artiste*] technique; **roman de ~ classique/originale** classic/original novel; **meubles de bonne/belle ~** well-made/beautifully made furniture, furniture of good/beautiful workmanship [c] [*instrument de musique*] making

facturer [faktyʀe] ▸ conjug 1 ◂ VT (= *établir une facture pour*) to invoice; (= *compter*) to charge (for), put on the bill, include in the bill; **~ qch 200 F (à qn)** to charge *ou* bill (sb) 200 francs for sth; **~ l'emballage** to charge for the packing, include the packing in the bill

facturette [faktyʀɛt] NF credit card slip

facturier [faktyʀje] NM (= *registre*) invoice register; (= *employé*) invoice clerk

facturière [faktyʀjɛʀ] NF (= *employée*) invoice clerk; (= *machine*) invoicing machine, biller (*US*)

facultatif, -ive [fakyltatif, iv] ADJ [*travail, cours*] optional; [*halte, arrêt*] request (*épith*); **matière facultative** optional subject, elective (subject) (*US*)

facultativement [fakyltativmɑ̃] ADV optionally

faculté [fakylte] NF [a] (*Univ*) faculty; **la ~ des Lettres/de Médecine** the Faculty of Arts/Medicine, the Arts/Medical Faculty (*Brit*), the School *ou* College of Arts/Medicine (*US*); (*Can*) **Faculté des Arts/Sciences** Faculty of Arts/Science; (*au Québec*) **Faculté des études supérieures** graduate and postgraduate studies; **quand j'étais en ~** *ou* **à la ~** when I was at university *ou* college *ou* school (*US*); **professeur de ~** university professor; (*hum*) **la Faculté me défend le tabac** I'm not allowed to smoke on doctor's orders [b] (= *don*) faculty; (= *pouvoir*) power; (= *propriété*) property; **avoir une grande ~ de concentration** to have great powers of concentration *ou* a great faculty for concentration; **avoir la ~ de marcher/de la préhension** to have the ability to walk/grasp, have the power of walking/grasping; (= *aptitudes intellectuelles*) **~s** faculties; **ce problème dépasse mes ~s** this problem is beyond my powers; **jouir de** *ou* **avoir toutes ses ~s** to be

in full possession of one's faculties, have all one's faculties [c] (= *droit*) right, option; (= *possibilité*) power, freedom, possibility; **le propriétaire a la ~ de vendre son bien** the owner has the right to sell *ou* the option of selling his property; **je te laisse la ~ de choisir** I'll give you the freedom to choose *ou* the possibility *ou* option of choosing; (*frm*) **le Premier ministre a la ~ de révoquer certains fonctionnaires** the Prime Minister has the faculty *ou* power of dismissing certain civil servants; **l'acheteur aura la ~ de décider** the buyer shall have the option to decide

fada* [fada] [1] ADJ (*dial* = *fou*) cracked*, crackers* (*attrib*), barmy* (*Brit*) [2] NM crackpot*

fadaise [fadɛz] NF (*littér: gén pl*) (= *bagatelle*) trifle; (= *platitude*) **dire des ~s** to mouth insipid *ou* empty phrases

fadasse [fadas] ADJ (*péj*) [*plat, boisson*] tasteless, insipid; [*couleur, style, propos*] wishy-washy, insipid

fade [fad] ADJ [*soupe, cuisine*] tasteless, insipid; [*goût*] insipid, bland; [*lumière, teinte*] dull; [*compliment, plaisanterie*] tame, insipid; [*décor, visage, individu, conversation, style*] dull, insipid; [*politesses, amabilité*] insipid; **l'odeur ~ du sang** the sickly smell of blood; **des cheveux d'un blond ~** dull blond hair

fadé, e ‡ [fade] ADJ (*iro*) first-class, priceless; **il est drôlement ~** he's a prize specimen*

fader (se)* [fade] ▸ conjug 1 ◂ VPR [+ *corvée, personne*] to get landed with*, get lumbered with* (*Brit*)

fadeur [fadœʀ] NF [a] [*soupe, cuisine*] tastelessness, insipidness; [*goût*] insipidness, blandness; [*lumière, teinte*] dullness; [*compliment, plaisanterie, conversation, style*] dullness, insipidness; [*politesses, amabilité*] insipidness; [*odeur*] sickliness [b] † (= *platitude*) **~s** sweet nothings, bland compliments; **dire des ~s à une dame** to say sweet nothings to *ou* pay bland compliments to a lady

fading [fadiŋ] NM (*Radio*) fading

faf* [faf] ADJ, NMF (*ABRÉV* = *fasciste*) (*péj*) fascist

fafiots‡ [fafjo] NMPL (= *billets*) (bank)notes

fagot [fago] NM bundle of sticks *ou* firewood → **derrière, sentir**

fagoter [fagɔte] ▸ conjug 1 ◂ [1] VT (*péj* = *accoutrer*) [+ *enfant*] to dress up, rig out* (*Brit*); **il est drôlement fagoté** (*déguisé*) he's wearing the strangest getup* *ou* rig-out* (*Brit*); (*mal habillé*) he's really oddly dressed [2] **se fagoter** VPR to dress o.s., rig o.s. out* (*Brit*) (**en** as a)

Fahrenheit [faʀɛnajt] ADJ, NM Fahrenheit; **32 degrés ~** 32 degrees Fahrenheit

faiblard, e* [feblaʀ, aʀd] [1] ADJ (*péj*) (*en classe*) weak, on the slow *ou* weak side (*attrib*); (*physiquement*) (rather) weakly; [*argument, démonstration*] feeble, weak, on the weak side (*attrib*) [2] NM,F weakling

▼ **faible** [fɛbl] [1] ADJ [a] (*physiquement*) weak; [*monnaie*] weak, soft; **je me sens encore très ~ sur mes jambes** I still feel very shaky on my legs; **avoir le cœur ~** to have a weak heart → **économiquement, sexe** [b] (*moralement*) weak; **il est ~ de caractère** he has a weak character; **il est trop ~ avec elle/ses élèves** he's too soft with her/with his pupils [c] (*en importance*) [*rendement, revenu, demande*] low, poor; [*marge*] small; [*débit*] slow; [*quantité*] small, slight; [*écart, différence*] slight, small; [*espoir*] faint, slight, slender; [*avantage*] slight; **il a de ~s chances de s'en tirer** (*optimiste*) he has a slight chance of pulling through; (*pessimiste*) his chances of pulling through are slight *ou* slim; **à une vitesse plus ~** more slowly; **à une ~ hauteur** low down, not very high up; **à une ~ profondeur** not far below the surface; (*Pol*) **à une ~ majo-**

rité by a narrow *ou* slight majority; **pays à ~ natalité** country with a low birth rate

d (*en qualité*) [*élève*] weak; [*expression, devoir, style*] weak, poor; [*raisonnement, argument*] weak, poor, feeble; **il est ~ en français** he's weak *ou* poor at *ou* in French; **le côté ~ de ce raisonnement** the weak side of this argument → **esprit, point¹, temps¹**

e (*en intensité*) [*pouls, voix*] weak, faint, feeble; [*lumière*] dim, weak, faint; [*bruit, odeur*] faint, slight; [*résistance, protestation*] mild, weak; [*vent*] light, faint; **vent ~ à modéré** wind light to moderate; **~ en alcool** low in alcohol; **à ~ teneur en sucre/cuivre** with a low sugar/copper content; **c'est un escroc, et le terme est ~** he's a crook, and that's putting it mildly *ou* and that's an understatement; **vous n'avez qu'une ~ idée de sa puissance** you have only a slight *ou* faint idea of his power

f (*Ling*) [*conjugaison, verbe*] weak

2 NM **a** (= *personne*) weak person; **les ~s et les opprimés** the weak *ou* feeble and the oppressed; **un ~ d'esprit** a feeble-minded person; **c'est un ~, elle en fait ce qu'elle veut** he's a weakling — she does what she wants with him

b † (= *déficience*) weak point; **le ~ de ce livre, ce sont les dialogues** the dialogues are the weak point in this book

c (= *penchant*) weakness; **il a un ~ pour le chocolat** he has a weakness for chocolate; **il a un ~ pour sa fille** he has a soft spot for his daughter

faiblement [fɛbləmɑ̃] ADV **a** (= *avec peine*) weakly; **la demande reprend ~** demand is picking up slightly **b** (= *peu*) [*éclairer*] dimly; [*augmenter*] slightly; **~ alcoolisé/gazéifié** slightly alcoholic/gaseous; **~ éclairé** dimly *ou* poorly lit; **zones ~ peuplées** sparsely populated areas

faiblesse [fɛblɛs] NF **a** (*physique*) weakness; **sa ~ de constitution** his weak *ou* frail constitution; **il a une ~ dans le bras gauche** he has a weakness in his left arm

b (*morale*) weakness; **sa ~ de caractère** his weak character, his weakness of character; **avoir la ~ d'accepter** to be weak enough to accept; **sa ~ à l'égard de son frère** his softness *ou* weakness towards his brother; **chacun a ses petites ~s** we all have our little foibles *ou* weaknesses *ou* failings

c (= *niveau peu élevé*) **la ~ de la demande** the low level of demand; **la ~ du revenu par habitant** the low per capita income

d (*Bourse*) [*monnaie, cours, marché*] weakness

e (= *médiocrité*) [*argument, raisonnement*] feebleness, weakness; [*œuvre*] weakness; **sa ~ en anglais est un vrai problème** the fact that he's so weak in English is a real problem

f (= *défaut*) weak point, weakness; **le film/l'intrigue présente quelques ~s** the film/the plot has several weak points *ou* weaknesses

faiblir [fɛbliʀ] ▶ conjug 2 ◀ VI **a** [*malade, branche*] to get weaker, weaken; [*cœur, vue, intelligence*] to fail; [*forces, courage*] to fail, flag, give out; [*influence*] to wane, fall off; [*résolution, autorité*] to weaken; **elle a faibli à la vue du sang/à sa vue** she felt weak *ou* faint when she saw the blood/when she saw him; **il a faibli devant leurs prières** he weakened *ou* relented in the face of their pleas; **pièce qui faiblit au 3ᵉ acte** play that falls off *ou* weakens in the 3rd act; **la première ligne a faibli sous le choc** the front line weakened under the impact; **ce n'est pas le moment de ~!** don't give up now!

b [*voix*] to weaken, get weaker *ou* fainter; [*bruit, protestation*] to die down; [*lumière*] to dim, get dimmer *ou* fainter; [*pouls*] to weaken, get weaker; [*vent*] to drop, abate; [*rendement*] to slacken (off); [*intensité, espoir*] to diminish, decrease; [*résistance, demande, chances*] to weaken, run

out; **l'écart faiblit entre eux** the gap is closing *ou* narrowing between them

faïence [fajɑ̃s] NF (= *substance*) (glazed) earthenware; (= *objets*) crockery (NonC), earthenware (NonC); (= *vase, objet*) piece of earthenware, earthenware (NonC); **assiette en/carreau de ~** earthenware plate/tile; **~ fine** china; **~ de Delft** delft, delftware → **chinois**

faïencerie [fajɑ̃sʀi] NF earthenware factory

faïencier, -ière [fajɑ̃sje, jɛʀ] **1** ADJ earthenware (*épith*) **2** NM,F (= *fabricant*) earthenware maker; (= *marchand*) earthenware seller

faignant, e [fɛɲɑ̃, ɑ̃t] ADJ, NM,F = **fainéant, e**

faille¹ [faj] NF (*Géol*) fault; (*fig = point faible*) flaw, weakness; (= *cassure*) rift; **il y a une ~ dans votre raisonnement** there's a flaw in your argument; **ce qui a causé une ~ dans leur amitié ...** what caused a rift in their friendship ... *ou* a rift between them ...; **sans ~** [*fidélité, soutien*] unfailing, unwavering; [*organisation*] faultless, impeccable; [*volonté, détermination*] unfailing → **ligne¹**

faille² [faj] → **falloir**

failli¹ [faji] *ptp de* **faillir**

failli², e [faji] ADJ, NM,F (*Comm*) bankrupt; **~ concordataire/réhabilité** certified/discharged bankrupt

faillibilité [fajibilite] NF fallibility

faillible [fajibl] ADJ fallible

faillir [fajiʀ] VI **a** (= *manquer*) **j'ai failli tomber/réussir** I almost *ou* very nearly fell/succeeded, I all but fell/succeeded; **il a failli se faire écraser** he almost *ou* very nearly got run over, he narrowly missed getting run over; (*iro*) **j'ai failli attendre** I hope you didn't rush on my account (*iro*) **b** (*frm*) **~ à** (= *manquer à*) [+ *engagement, mission*] to fail in; [+ *promesse, parole*] to fail to keep; **il a failli/n'a pas failli à la tradition** he broke with/kept with *ou* to tradition; **il n'a pas failli à sa parole** he was true to *ou* kept his word; **le cœur lui faillit**† his heart missed a beat; **le cœur *ou* le courage lui faillit**† his courage failed him; **il résista jusqu'au bout sans ~** he resisted unfailingly *ou* unflinchingly to the end; **ne pas ~ à sa réputation** to live up to one's reputation **c**† (= *fauter*) to lapse

faillite [fajit] **1** NF **a** (*Comm*) bankruptcy **b** (= *échec*) [*espoir, tentative, méthode*] collapse, failure; **la ~ du gouvernement en matière économique** the government's failure on the economic front **c** (*loc*) **en ~** [*entreprise*] bankrupt; **être en ~** (*Comm*) to be bankrupt; **faire ~** (*Comm*) to go bankrupt; (*fig*) to collapse; **faire une ~ de 800 000 F** to go bankrupt with debts of 800,000 francs; **déclarer/mettre qn en ~** to declare *ou* adjudge/make sb bankrupt; **se déclarer en ~** to file (a petition) for bankruptcy **2** COMP ▶ **faillite frauduleuse** fraudulent bankruptcy ▶ **faillite personnelle** personal bankruptcy ▶ **faillite simple** bankruptcy

faim [fɛ̃] NF **a** (= *envie de manger*) hunger; **avoir (très) grand**†) **~** to be (very) hungry; **j'ai une ~ de loup *ou* une de ces ~s** I'm ravenous *ou* famished *ou* starving*; **je n'ai plus ~** (*après un repas*) I'm (quite) full; (*plus envie de manger*) I'm not hungry any more; **manger sans ~** (*sans besoin réel*) to eat for the sake of eating; (*sans appétit*) to pick at one's food, toy with one's food; **manger à sa ~** to eat one's fill; **ça m'a donné ~** it made me hungry; **il fait ~** we're hungry; **la ~ dans le monde** world hunger ■(*PROV*) **la ~ fait sortir *ou* chasse le loup du bois** hunger will drive him out → **crever, mourir** etc

b (= *besoin*) hunger; **avoir ~ de** [+ *honneur, tendresse, justice*] to hunger for, crave (for); **sa ~ de richesses** his hunger *ou* yearning for wealth; **son discours a laissé les journalistes sur leur ~** his speech left the journalists hungry for more *ou* unsatisfied → **rester**

faîne [fɛn] NF beechnut; **~s (tombées)** beechmast (NonC)

fainéant, e [fɛneɑ̃, ɑ̃t] **1** ADJ lazy, idle, bone idle* → **roi** **2** NM,F idler, loafer, lazybones*

fainéanter [fɛneɑ̃te] ▶ conjug 1 ◀ VI to idle *ou* loaf about

fainéantise [fɛneɑ̃tiz] NF laziness, idleness

faire [fɛʀ]

▶ conjug 60 ◀
1 VERBE TRANSITIF	**4** VERBE SUBSTITUT
2 VERBE INTRANSITIF	**5** VERBE AUXILIAIRE
3 VERBE IMPERSONNEL	**6** VERBE PRONOMINAL

Lorsque **faire** *est suivi d'un nom dans une expression figée telle que* **faire une faute, faire une promesse, se faire des idées** *etc, cherchez sous le nom.*

1 VERBE TRANSITIF

a

Lorsque **faire** *est utilisé pour parler d'une activité non précisée, ou qu'il remplace un verbe plus spécifique, il se traduit par* do.

que fais-tu ce soir? what are you doing tonight?; **j'ai beaucoup/je n'ai rien à ~** I have a lot/nothing to do; **ils sont en retard, qu'est-ce qu'ils peuvent bien ~?** they're late — what on earth are they doing? *ou* what are they up to?*; **que voulez-vous qu'on y fasse?** what do you expect us to do (about it)?; **~ ses chaussures/l'argenterie/la chambre** to do one's shoes/the silver/the bedroom

b

Lorsque **faire** *veut dire* **créer, être l'auteur de**, *il se traduit souvent par* make *ou par un verbe plus spécifique; cherchez sous le nom.*

~ un film to make *ou* do a film; **~ un tableau** to do a painting, paint a picture; **~ un plan** to make *ou* draw a map; **fais-moi un joli chat** (*dessin*) do a nice cat for me; (*pâte à modeler*) make a nice cat for me

c = **fabriquer, produire** [+ *meuble, voiture*] to make; [+ *mur, nid*] to make, build; [+ *maison*] to build; [+ *blé, betteraves*] to grow; **ils font du mouton*** they raise sheep; **cette école fait de bons ingénieurs** the school turns out good engineers

d Culin

Dans le sens de **préparer, confectionner**, **faire** *peut se traduire par* do *de façon assez vague, mais* make *est beaucoup plus courant.*

~ de la confiture/du vin/un cocktail to make jam/wine/a cocktail; **elle fait du lapin ce soir** she's doing rabbit tonight; **je vais ~ quelques pommes de terre** I'll do a few potatoes

e Sport [+ *football, tennis, rugby*] to play; [+ *sport de combat*] to do → **natation, ski** *etc*

f Scol [+ *matière, roman, auteur*] to do; **~ l'école hôtelière** to go to a catering school

g Mus (= *jouer*) to play; (= *s'entraîner*) to practise; **~ du piano/du violon** to play the piano/the violin; **va ~ ton piano*** go and practise your piano

h Méd [+ *diabète, tension*] to have; **il m'a encore fait une otite** he's gone and got another ear infection*

i = **parcourir, visiter** to do; **~ 10 km** to do *ou* cover 10 km; **~ 100 km/h** to do 100 km/h; **~ Rome/la Grèce en trois jours** to do Rome/Greece in three days; **on a fait Lyon-Paris en cinq heures** we did Lyons to Paris in five hours

j = **chercher dans** **j'ai fait tous les placards/toutes les pièces, je ne l'ai pas trouvé** I looked in all the cupboards/in every room but I didn't find it; **il a fait toute la ville pour en trouver** he's been all over town looking for some; **j'ai fait toutes les librairies mais sans succès** I went round all the bookshops but I didn't have any luck

|k| = **vendre** ~ l'épicerie to sell groceries; **nous ne faisons pas les boutons/cette marque** we don't do ou stock ou carry (US) buttons/that make; **je vous fais ce fauteuil (à) 700 F** I'll let you have this armchair for 700 francs

|l| = **mesurer, peser, coûter** la cuisine fait 6 mètres de large the kitchen is 6 metres wide; **il fait 23 degrés** it is 23 degrees; **ce rôti fait bien 3 kg** this joint weighs ou is a good 3 kg; **ça fait encore loin jusqu'à Paris** it's still a long way to Paris; **combien fait cette chaise ?** how much is this chair?; **cette table fera un bon prix** this table will go for ou will fetch a high price; **ça nous fera 1 000 F** (dépense) it will cost us 1,000 francs; (gain) it will give ou bring us 1,000 francs

|m| dans un calcul to make; **24 en tout, ce qui en fait 2 chacun** 24 altogether, which makes 2 each; **deux et deux font quatre** two and two make four; **cela fait combien en tout ?** how much does that make altogether?

|n| Gram « canal » fait « canaux » au pluriel the plural of "canal" is "canaux"; **qu'est-ce ça fait au subjonctif ?** what's the subjunctive?

|o| = **imiter** il a fait celui qui ne comprenait pas he pretended not to understand; **ne fais pas l'enfant/l'idiot** don't be so childish/so stupid; **il fait bien le train** he does a really good imitation of a train

|p| = **faire fonction de, servir de** [personne] to be; (Théât) to play; [objet] to be used as, serve as; **tu fais l'arbitre ?** will you be referee?; **il fait le fantôme dans « Hamlet »** he plays the ghost in "Hamlet"; **une vieille malle faisait table basse** an old trunk was being used as a coffee table; **la cuisine fait salle à manger** the kitchen doubles as ou is used as ou serves as a dining room; MAIS **cette branche fera une bonne canne** this branch will make a nice walking stick; **cet hôtel fait aussi restaurant** the hotel has its own restaurant; **cette montre fait aussi boussole** this watch doubles as a compass

|q| = **être, constituer** **quel imbécile je fais !** what a fool I am!; **ils font un beau couple** they make such a lovely couple; **il veut ~ médecin** he wants to be a doctor; **il fera un bon musicien** he'll make a good musician

|r| = **avoir la forme de, ressembler à** to look like; **ça fait comme une cloche** it looks a bit like a bell

|s| = **représenter** to make out; **on le fait plus riche qu'il n'est** he's made out ou people make him out to be richer than he is

|t| = **dire** to say; **« vraiment ? » fit-il** "really?", he said; **il fit un « ah » de surprise** "ah", he said, surprised; **le chat fait miaou** the cat goes ou says miaow

|u| = **agir sur** **qu'est-ce qu'on lui fait à l'hôpital ?** what's he gone into hospital for?; **qu'est-ce que tu as fait à ton frère ?** what have you been doing to your brother?; **ils ne peuvent rien me ~** they can't do anything to me; **on ne me la fait pas à moi !*** I wasn't born yesterday!

|v| = **constituer** to make; **cela fait la richesse du pays** that's what makes the country rich; **c'est ce qui fait tout son charme** that's what makes him so charming

|w| = **importer** **qu'est-ce que cela peut bien te ~ ?** what's it to you?; **qu'est-ce que ça fait ?** so what?; **la mort de son père ne lui a rien fait** he was completely unaffected by his father's death; **cela ne vous ferait rien de sortir ?** would you mind leaving the room?

♦ **faire + de + complément** |a| = **utiliser** to do with; **qu'as-tu fait de ta vie ?** what have you done with your life?; **je ne sais pas quoi ~ de mon temps libre** I don't know what to do with my spare time

|b| = **oublier, laisser quelque part** (à la forme interrogative directe ou indirecte) to do with; **qu'avez-vous fait de votre sac/de vos enfants ?** what have you done with your bag/your

children?; **qu'ai-je bien pu ~ de mes lunettes ?** what on earth have I done with my glasses?

|c| = **transformer** la vie a fait de lui un aigri life has made him a bitter man; **il a fait d'une grange une demeure agréable** he has turned ou made a barn into a comfortable home; **il veut en ~ un avocat** he wants to make a lawyer of him

♦ **ne faire que**
(constamment) **il ne fait que se plaindre** he's always ou forever complaining; **il ne fait que bavarder** he won't stop chattering, he does nothing but chatter
(seulement) **je ne fais que dire la vérité** I'm only telling the truth; **je ne fais que passer** I'm just passing
(récemment) **je ne fais que d'arriver** I've only just come

♦ **n'avoir que faire de : je n'ai que ~ de vos conseils !** I don't need your advice!; **je n'ai que ~ de gens comme lui !** I have no use for people like him!

|2| VERBE INTRANSITIF

|a| = **agir, procéder** ~ vite to act quickly; **faites vite !** be quick (about it)!; (aussi hum) **faites comme chez vous** make yourself at home

|b| = **durer** **ce chapeau (me) fera encore un hiver** this hat will do ou last me another winter

|c| = **paraître** to look; **ce vase fait bien sur la table** the vase looks nice on the table; [personne] ~ **vieux/jeune** to look old/young (for one's age); **elle fait très femme** she looks very grown-up

|d| * **besoins naturels** [personne] to go; [animal] to do its business; **as-tu fait ce matin ?** have you been this morning?

|3| VERBE IMPERSONNEL

Lorsque faire est suivi d'une expression de temps et exprime une durée écoulée, on utilise généralement since ou for ; for se construit avec le present perfect ou le pluperfect.

cela fait deux ans/très longtemps que je ne l'ai pas vu it's two years/a very long time since I last saw him, I haven't seen him for two years/for a very long time; **ça fait trois ans qu'il est parti** it's three years since he left, he's been gone (for) three years

♦ **ce qui fait que ... ◊ ça fait que ...** (= ce qui implique que) that means ...; **ça fait que nous devons partir** that ou which means we have to go; **et ça fait qu'il est arrivé en retard** and that meant he arrived late

|4| VERBE SUBSTITUT

to do; **il travaille mieux que je ne fais** he works better than I do; **as-tu payé la note ? — non, c'est lui qui l'a fait** did you pay the bill? — no, he did; **puis-je téléphoner ? — faites, je vous en prie** could I use the phone? — (yes) please do ou (yes) by all means; **n'en faites rien !** (please) don't!; **je n'en ferai rien !** I'll do nothing of the sort!

|5| VERBE AUXILIAIRE

♦ **faire + infinitif** |a| = **provoquer un acte, une situation** to make; **l'idée m'a fait sourire** the thought made me smile; **ça m'a fait pleurer** it made me cry; **ma mère me faisait manger des épinards quand j'étais petit** my mother made me eat spinach when I was little; **il lui a fait boire du whisky** (pour la remonter) he got her to drink some whisky, he made her drink some whisky; (pour qu'elle goûte) he gave her some whisky to drink; MAIS **ce genre de musique me fait dormir** that kind of music puts me to sleep; **j'ai fait démarrer la voiture** I got the car going ou started

|b| = **aider** to help; ~ **traverser la rue à un aveugle** to help a blind man across the road; **je lui ai fait ~ ses devoirs** I helped him with his homework; MAIS ~ **manger un patient** to feed a patient

|c| = **laisser volontairement** ~ **entrer qn** (qn que l'on attendait) to let sb in; (qn que l'on attendait

pas) to ask sb in; ~ **venir** [+ employé] to send for; [+ médecin] to call; ~ **entrer/sortir le chien** to let the dog in/out; **faites entrer le patient** ask the patient to come in

|d|

Lorsque faire signifie laisser involontairement, sa traduction dépend étroitement du contexte ; reportez-vous au second verbe.

il a fait déborder le lait he let the milk boil over; **elle a fait s'échapper le chien** she let the dog out; **il a fait glisser son frère** he (accidentally) made his brother slip over; **elle a fait tomber une tasse** she dropped a cup ~ **qch par qn** to have sth done (ou made) by sb; ~ ~ **qch à qn** (gén) to get sb to do (ou to make) sth, have sb do (ou make) sth (surtout US); (en le forçant) to make sb do sth; (se) ~ **une robe** to have a dress made; ~ **réparer une voiture/une montre** to have a car/a watch repaired; ~ ~ **la vaisselle à qn** to get sb to do ou have sb do (surtout US) the dishes; **elle a fait lire les enfants** she made the children read, she got the children to read; **il m'a fait ouvrir le coffre-fort** he made me open the safe

|6| **se faire** VERBE PRONOMINAL

|a| **pour soi** **il se fait la cuisine** he cooks for himself; **il s'est fait beaucoup d'amis/d'ennemis** he has made himself a great many friends/enemies; **on s'est fait un restaurant/un film*** we went to a restaurant/the cinema

|b| * = **gagner** to make; **il se fait 20 000 F par mois*** he makes 20,000 francs a month

|c| = **mûrir, évoluer** [fromage] to ripen, mature; [vin] to mature; [personne] **il s'est fait tout seul** he's a self-made man

|d| = **être accompli** **les choses finissent toujours par se ~** things always get done in the end; **rien ne se fera sans son aide** nothing will get done without his help; **si ça doit se ~, ça se fera sans moi** if it's going to happen, it'll happen without me

|e| = **convenir** **ça se fait d'offrir des fleurs à un homme ?** is it done ou OK to give flowers to a man?; **cela ne se fait pas** it's not done; **mais tu sais, ça se fait de vivre ensemble sans être marié !** people do live together without being married, you know!

|f| = **être courant, à la mode** **les jupes longues se font beaucoup cette année** long skirts are in this year ou are being worn a lot this year; **ça se fait encore ce style-là ?** are people still wearing that style?; **ça se fait de plus en plus, ces chaussures** more and more people are wearing these shoes

|g| **sexuellement** se ~ **qn‡** to have sb‡

|h| ‡ = **agresser** to get‡; **un jour, je me le ferai !** I'll get him one of these days*

|i| * = **cambrioler** [+ banque, bijouterie] to do*

|j| = **se passer** (gén avec subjonctif) **il peut/il pourrait se ~ qu'il pleuve** it may/it might (well) rain; **comment se fait-il qu'il soit absent ? ◊ comment ça se fait qu'il est absent ?*** how come he's not here?*

♦ **se faire + adjectif**
(= devenir involontairement) to get, become; **se ~ vieux** to be getting old; **il se faisait tard** it was getting late; **il se fit violent** he became violent
(= devenir volontairement) **se ~ beau** to make o.s. beautiful; **il se fit menaçant** he became threatening; **elle se fit implorante** she started pleading; **sa voix se fit plus douce** his voice became softer
(= faire semblant d'être) to make o.s. out to be; **il se fait plus bête qu'il n'est** he makes himself out to be more stupid than he really is

♦ **se faire + infinitif**

Lorsque cette tournure implique un ordre, elle se traduit généralement par have + verbe ; lorsqu'elle implique une demande polie, elle se traduit par ask ou get + verbe.

il se faisait apporter le journal tous les matins he had the paper brought to him every morning; **il s'est fait ouvrir par le voisin** he got his neighbour to let him in; **elle s'est fait apporter un sandwich** she got somebody to bring her a sandwich; **fais-toi expliquer le règlement** ask someone to explain the rules to you

Notez les différentes traductions possibles et en particulier l'emploi de la forme passive en anglais lorsque se faire + infinitif *exprime une action subie par quelqu'un; reportez-vous à l'autre verbe.*

il s'est fait frapper par deux jeunes he was hit by two youths, two youths hit him; **elle s'est fait renvoyer** she was sacked; **tu vas te ~ gronder** you'll get yourself into trouble, you'll get yourself told off*

◆ **se faire à** (= *s'habituer à*) to get *ou* become used to; **il ne peut pas se ~ au climat** he can't get used to the climate

◆ **(il) faut se le/la/les faire!**: (il) faut se le ~! [+ *travail*] it's a hell of a chore!*, it's really heavy going!*; [+ *personne*] he's a real pain in the neck!*

◆ **s'en faire** (= *s'angoisser*) to worry; **il ne s'en fait pas** he doesn't worry; **il ne s'en fait pas!** (= *a du culot*) he's got a nerve!; **je viens de m'acheter un bateau — dis donc, tu t'en fais pas toi!** I've just bought a boat — you lucky devil!*

---

faire-part [fɛʀpaʀ] NM INV announcement (of birth *ou* marriage *ou* death); **~ de mariage** wedding announcement; (*avec carton d'invitation*) wedding invitation

faire-valoir [fɛʀvalwaʀ] NM INV **a** (*Agr*) farming, working (of land); **~ direct/indirect** farming by the owner/tenant **b** (= *personne*) foil; (*dans une comédie*) stooge; **son mari lui sert de ~** her husband serves as a foil to her

fair-play [fɛʀplɛ] **1** NM INV fair play **2** ADJ INV **être ~** to play fair; **c'est un joueur ~** he plays fair

faisabilité [fəzabilite] NF feasibility; **étude de ~** feasibility study

▼ **faisable** [fəzabl] ADJ feasible; **est-ce ~ en deux jours?** can it be done in two days?; **est-ce ~ à pied?** can it be done on foot?

faisan [fəzɑ̃] NM **a** (= *oiseau*) (*gén*) pheasant; (*mâle*) cock pheasant; **~ doré** golden pheasant **b**† (= *escroc*) shark

faisandé, e [fəzɑ̃de] (*ptp de* faisander) ADJ **a** (*Culin*) well hung; (*désagréablement*) high; **je n'aime pas le ~** I don't like high game; **viande trop ~e** meat which has hung for too long **b** (*péj†*) [*littérature, société*] corrupt, decadent; [*milieu*] crooked

faisandeau (*pl* faisandeaux) [fəzɑ̃do] NM young pheasant

faisander [fəzɑ̃de] ▸ conjug 1 ◂ **1** VTI (*Culin*) (**faire** *ou* **laisser**) **~** to hang **2** **se faisander** VPR to become high

faisanderie [fəzɑ̃dʀi] NF pheasantry

faisane [fəzan] NF, ADJ F (**poule**) **~** hen pheasant

faisceau (*pl* faisceaux) [fɛso] **1** NM **a** (= *fagot*) bundle; (= *réseau*) **~ de preuves** body of evidence; **~ de faits/raisons** range of facts/reasons; **nouer en ~x** to tie into bundles **b** (*Mil*) **~x (d'armes)** stack (of arms); **mettre en ~x** [*fusils*] to stack; **former/rompre les ~x** to stack/unstack arms **c** (*Phys*) beam **d** (*Antiq, Hist* = *emblème*) **~x** fasces **2** COMP ▸ **faisceau d'électrons** *ou* **électronique** electron beam ▸ **faisceau hertzien** electromagnetic wave ▸ **faisceau laser** laser beam ▸ **faisceau lumineux** *ou* **de lumière** beam of light ▸ **faisceau musculaire** fasciculus *ou* fascicule of muscle fibres ▸ **faisceau nerveux** fasciculus *ou* fascicule of nerve fibres ▸ **faisceau de particules** particle beam

faiseur, -euse [fəzœʀ, øz] **1** NM,F **~ de**† [+ *monuments, meubles*] maker of; (*hum, péj*)

[+ *romans, tableaux, opéras*] producer of **2** NM (†*péj* = *hâbleur*) show-off; (= *escroc*) shark; (*frm* = *tailleur*) (**bon**) **~** good tailor **3** COMP ▸ **faiseuse d'anges** backstreet abortionist ▸ **faiseur de bons mots** punster, wag ▸ **faiseur d'embarras** fusspot (*Brit*), fussbudget (*US*) ▸ **faiseur d'intrigues** (*péj*) schemer ▸ **faiseur de littérature** (*péj*) scribbler ▸ **faiseur de marché** (*Bourse*) market maker ▸ **faiseur de mariages** matchmaker ▸ **faiseur de miracles** miracleworker ▸ **faiseur de phrases** (*péj*) speechifier ▸ **faiseur de vers** (*péj*) poetaster (*péj*), versifier

faisselle [fɛsɛl] NF (= *passoire*) cheese strainer; (= *fromage*) fromage frais (*packed in its own strainer*)

▼ **fait¹** [fɛ] **1** NM **a** (= *événement*) event, occurrence; (= *donnée*) fact; (= *phénomène*) phenomenon; **il s'agit d'un ~ courant/rare** this is a common/rare occurrence *ou* event; **aucun ~ nouveau n'est survenu** no new facts have come to light, there have been no new developments; **il me faut des ~s concrets** I must have facts *ou* concrete evidence; (*Jur*) **reconnaissez-vous les ~s?** do you accept the facts?; (*Jur*) **les ~s qui lui sont reprochés** the charges (brought) against him; **ces ~s remontent à 3 ans** these events go back 3 years; **il s'est produit un ~ curieux** a strange thing has happened; **s'incliner devant les ~s** to bow to (the) facts → **erreur, incriminer** **b** (= *acte*) **le ~ de manger/bouger** the fact of eating/moving, eating/moving; (*Jur, Mil*) **être puni pour ~ d'insoumission** to be punished for (an act of) insubordination → **haut** **c** (= *cause*) **c'est le ~ du hasard** it's the work of fate; **c'est le ~ de son inexpérience** it's because of *ou* owing to his inexperience, it comes of his inexperience; **par le ~** in fact; **par ce ~** by this very fact; **par le ~ même que/de** by the very fact that/of; **par le (simple) ~ de** by the simple fact of; **par le ~ même de son obstination** because of *ou* by his very obstinacy, by the very fact of his obstinacy **d** (*loc*) **au ~** (= *à propos*) by the way; **au ~!** (= *à l'essentiel*) come to the point!; **aller droit/en venir au ~** to go straight/get to the point; **au ~ de** (= *au courant*) conversant *ou* acquainted with, informed of; **mettre qn au ~ (d'une affaire)** to acquaint *ou* familiarize sb with the facts (of a matter), inform sb of the facts (of a matter); (= *en fait*) in fact; **il est de ~ que** it is a fact that; **de ce ~** therefore, for this reason; **du ~ de sa démission/qu'il a démissionné** on account of *ou* as a result of his resignation/his having resigned; **en ~** in (actual) fact, in point of fact, as a matter of fact; **en ~ de** (= *en guise de*) by way of; (= *en matière de*) as regards, in the way of; **en ~ de repas on a eu droit à un sandwich** we were allowed a sandwich by way of a meal; **en ~ de spécialiste, c'est plutôt un charlatan!** as for being a specialist...— charlatan more like!*; **le ~ est que** the fact is that; **le ~ que** the fact that; **les ~s sont là** *ou* **sont têtus** there's no denying the facts, the facts speak for themselves; **le ~ est là** that's the fact of the matter; **être le ~ de** (= *être typique de*) to be typical *ou* characteristic of; (= *être le résultat de*) to be the result of; **de son (propre) ~** through *ou* by his (own) doing; **c'est un ~** that's a fact; **c'est un ~ que** it's a fact that; **dire son ~ à qn** to tell sb what's what, talk straight to sb, give sb a piece of one's mind; **prendre ~ et cause pour qn** to fight for sb's cause, take up the cudgels for sb, take sides with sb → **sur¹, sûr, tout, voie**

2 COMP ▸ **fait accompli** fait accompli; **mettre qn devant le ~ accompli** ◊ **pratiquer avec qn la politique du ~ accompli** to present sb with a fait accompli ▸ **fait d'armes** feat of arms ▸ **fait divers** (= *nouvelle*) (short)

news item; (= *événement insignifiant*) trivial event; (= *rubrique*) «~s divers» "(news) in brief" ▸ **faits et gestes** actions, doings; **~ s et gestes de qn** to watch sb's every move ▸ **faits de guerre** acts of war ▸ **fait de langue** fait de langue, language event ▸ **fait de parole** fait de parole, speech event ▸ **le fait du prince** the government fiat; **c'est le ~ du prince** there's no going against authority ▸ **faits de résistance** acts of resistance

fait², **faite** [fɛ, fɛt] (*ptp de* faire) ADJ **a** **être ~ pour** to be made *ou* meant for; **voitures ~es pour la course** cars (specially) made *ou* designed *ou* conceived for racing; **ces chaussures ne sont pas ~es pour la marche** these are not proper walking shoes, these shoes are not suitable *ou* designed for walking in; **c'est ~ pour*** that's what it's for; **ce que tu lui as dit l'a énervé — c'était ~ pour*** what you said annoyed him — it was meant to; **ceci n'est pas ~ pour lui plaire** this is not going to *ou* is not likely to please him; **ce discours n'est pas ~ pour le rassurer** this is not the kind of speech to reassure him, this sort of speech isn't likely to reassure him; **il est ~ pour être médecin** he's got the makings of a doctor; **il n'est pas ~ pour être professeur** he's not cut out to be a teacher; **ils sont ~s l'un pour l'autre** they are made for each other **b** (= *fini*) **c'en est ~ de notre vie calme** that's the end of our quiet life, it's goodbye to peace and quiet; **c'en est ~ de moi** I'm done for*, I've had it*; **c'est toujours ça de ~** that's one job done, that's one thing out of the way **c** (= *constitué*) **bien ~** [*femme*] shapely; [*homme*] well-built; **avoir la jambe/main bien ~e** to have shapely *ou* nice legs/pretty *ou* nice hands; **le monde est ainsi ~** that's the way of the world; **les gens sont ainsi ~s que** people are such that; **comment est-il ~?** what is he like?, what does he look like?; **regarde comme tu es ~!*** look at the state of you!*, what a sight you are! **d** (= *mûr*) [*personne*] mature; [*fromage*] ripe; **fromage ~ à cœur** fully ripened cheese **e** (= *maquillé*) made-up; **avoir les yeux ~s** to have one's eyes made up; **avoir les ongles ~s** to have painted nails **f** **tout ~** [*objet, idée, solution*] ready-made; **vêtements tout ~s** ready-made *ou* ready-to-wear clothes → **expression, phrase** **g** (*loc*) **il est ~ (comme un rat)*** he's in for it now*, he's cornered; **c'est bien ~ pour toi!** it serves you right!, you asked for it!*; **c'est bien ~ (pour eux)!** it serves them right!; **ce n'est ni ~ ni à faire** it's a botched job* → **vite**

faîtage [fɛtaʒ] NM (= *poutre*) ridgepole; (= *couverture*) roofing; (*littér* = *toit*) roof

faîte [fɛt] NM **a** (= *poutre*) ridgepole **b** (= *sommet*) [*montagne*] summit; [*arbre*] top; [*maison*] rooftop; **~ du toit** rooftop → **ligne¹** **c** (= *summum*) **~ de la gloire** pinnacle *ou* height of glory; **parvenu au ~ des honneurs** having attained the highest honours

faîtière [fɛtjɛʀ] ADJ F, NF (**tuile**) **~** ridge tile; **lucarne ~** skylight

faitout NM, **fait-tout** NM INV [fɛtu] stewpot

faix [fɛ] NM (†*ou littér*) burden; **sous le ~** under the weight *ou* burden (**de**)

fakir [fakiʀ] NM (*Rel*) fakir; (*Music-Hall*) wizard

fakirisme [fakiʀism] NM (*Rel*) practice of a fakir; (*fig*) **c'est du ~!** (*divination*) it's prophecy!; (*pouvoir magique*) it's wizardry!

falaise [falɛz] NF cliff

falbalas [falbala] NMPL frills and flounces, furbelows; (*péj*) frippery (*NonC*) (*péj*), furbelows (*péj*)

Falkland(s) [folklɑ̃d] NPL **les (îles) ~** the Falkland Islands, the Falklands; **la guerre des ~** the Falklands war

---

fallacieusement [fa(l)lasjøzmɑ̃] ADV [*promettre*] deceptively

fallacieux, -ieuse [fa(l)lasjø, jøz] ADJ [*promesse, apparence, appellation*] deceptive; [*arguments, raisonnement*] fallacious; [*espoir*] illusory, delusive

▼**falloir** [falwaʀ]

  ▶ conjug 29 ◀
  1 VERBE IMPERSONNEL   2 VERBE PRONOMINAL

1 VERBE IMPERSONNEL
  a besoin, nécessité

Lorsque **falloir** *exprime un besoin ou une nécessité, il se traduit généralement par* need; *il a alors pour sujet la personne, exprimée ou non en français, qui a besoin de quelque chose; si l'on ne veut ou ne peut pas mentionner cette personne en anglais,* **falloir** *se traduit le plus souvent par* take.

♦ **falloir** + *nom ou pronom*: il va ~ 10 000 F we're going to need 10,000 francs; il faut du temps/ de l'argent pour faire cela it takes time/money to do that, you need time/money to do that; faut-il aussi de l'ail? do we need *ou* want garlic as well?; c'est juste ce qu'il faut (*outil etc*) that's just what we need *ou* want; (*en quantité*) that's just the right amount; c'est plus qu'il n'en faut that's more than we need; trois mètres de tissu? — oui, il faudra au moins ça three metres of material? — yes, we'll need *ou* want at least that much; trois heures? — oh oui, il faut bien ça three hours? — yes, it'll take at least that long; il n'en faut pas beaucoup pour qu'il se mette à pleurer it doesn't take much to make him cry; il lui faut quelqu'un pour l'aider he needs somebody to help him; une bonne fessée, voilà ce qu'il lui faut! what he needs *ou* wants is a good hiding!; il ne me faut pas plus de dix minutes pour y aller it won't take me more than ten minutes to get there; et avec ça, vous faut-il autre chose? (is there) anything else?; s'il le faut if necessary, if need be; il vous le faut pour quand? when do you need it for?; il t'en faut combien? how many (*ou* much) do you need?; MAIS il a fait ce qu'il fallait pour la rendre heureuse/pour l'énerver he did just the right thing to make her happy/to annoy her; il me faudrait trois steaks, s'il vous plaît I'd like three steaks, please; il me le faut absolument *ou* à tout prix I absolutely must have it, I've absolutely got to have it

♦ **falloir** + *infinitif*: faut-il réserver à l'avance? do you have to *ou* need to book in advance?, is it necessary to book in advance?; il vous faut tourner à gauche ici you need *ou* want to turn left here; il faudrait avoir plus de temps we need more time, if it faut bien vivre/manger you have to live/eat

  b obligation

Lorsque **falloir** *exprime une obligation, il se traduit généralement par* have to *ou la forme plus familière* have got to *lorsqu'il s'agit de contraintes extérieures. Le verbe* must *a généralement une valeur plus impérative; attention,* must *étant un verbe défectif, on utilise* have to *aux temps où il ne se conjugue pas.*

tu pars déjà? — il le faut are you leaving already? — I have to *ou* I've got to; je le ferai s'il le faut I'll do it if I have to *ou* if I must; il a bien fallu! I (*ou* we *etc*) had to!

♦ **falloir** + *infinitif*: il va ~ le faire we'll have to do it, it'll have to be done; il faut opérer they're (*ou* we're *etc*) going to have to operate; il m'a fallu obéir I had to do as I was told; que vous fallait-il faire? (*frm*) what did you have to do?; c'est dans le règlement, il faut le faire those are the rules, you must do it; à l'époque, il fallait porter l'uniforme in those days you had to wear a uniform; que faut-il leur dire? what should I (*ou* we *etc*) tell them?

♦ **falloir que** + *subjonctif*: il va ~ qu'il parte bientôt he'll have to go soon; allez, il faut que je parte! right, I must go!; il faut que tu y ailles, c'était ce qu'on avait prévu you have to go *ou*

---

you must go, that was the arrangement; il faudra bien que tu me le dises un jour you'll have to tell me some time

  c suggestion, conseil, exhortation

Lorsque **falloir** *est utilisé pour exprimer une suggestion, un conseil ou une exhortation au présent, il se traduit souvent par* must; *au passé, au conditionnel ou dans une phrase négative, il se traduit généralement par* should *ou* ought to.

il faut voir ce spectacle you must see this show; il faut m'excuser, je ne savais pas you must excuse me, I didn't know; il faut que vous veniez nous voir à Toulouse! you must come and see us in Toulouse!; il faut vous dire que ... I must *ou* I have to tell you that ...; il faut éviter de tirer des conclusions hâtives it's important to *ou* we must avoid jumping to conclusions; dans pareil cas, il faut surtout rester calme in cases like these, it's very important to stay calm *ou* you must above all stay calm; des fleurs! il ne fallait pas! flowers! you shouldn't have!; il fallait me le dire you ought to *ou* should have told me; il ne fallait pas faire ça, c'est tout you shouldn't have done it and that's all there is to it; il aurait fallu lui téléphoner you (*ou* we *etc*) should have phoned him; MAIS il s'est mis en colère — il faut le comprendre he got angry — that's understandable; il faudrait que tu viennes m'aider I'm going to need your help; faudrait pas qu'il essaie* he'd better not try*

  d probabilité, hypothèse

Lorsque **falloir** *exprime une probabilité, une hypothèse, il se traduit généralement par* must *dans les phrases affirmatives;* must *étant défectif, on utilise* have to *aux temps où il ne se conjugue pas.*

♦ **falloir** + *infinitif*: il faut être fou pour parler comme ça (*ou* he *etc*) must be mad to talk like that; il fallait être désespéré pour faire ça they must have been desperate to do something like that; MAIS il ne faut pas être intelligent pour dire ça that's a pretty stupid thing to say; faut-il donc être bête! some people are so *ou* really stupid!; faut (pas) être gonflé!* it takes some nerve!*

♦ **falloir que** + *subjonctif*: il faut que tu te sois trompé you must have made a mistake; faut-il qu'il soit bête! he must be so *ou* really stupid!

  e dans des exclamatives   (*exprimant l'admiration ou l'agacement*) il faut entendre ce qu'ils disent sur elle! you should hear the sort of things they say about her!; il faut l'entendre chanter! you should hear him sing!; faut dire qu'il est culotté* you've got to *ou* you must admit he's got a nerve; (il) faut le voir (*admiratif*) that takes some doing!; * (*péj*) that takes some beating!; ce qu'il faut entendre! the things you hear!; quand faut y aller faut y aller!* a man's gotta do what a man's gotta do!*

  f fatalité

♦ **falloir que** + *subjonctif*: il a fallu qu'elle l'apprenne she would have to hear about it; il a fallu qu'il arrive à ce moment-là of course, he had to arrive just then; il fallait bien que ça arrive it was bound to happen; il faut toujours qu'elle se trouve des excuses she always has to find some excuse; faut-il toujours que tu te plaignes? do you always have to complain?

  g loc: hum   elle a ce qu'il faut* she's got what it takes*; il faut ce qu'il faut* you've got to do things properly; il faut de tout pour faire un monde it takes all sorts to make a world

♦ **il faut/fallait/faudrait voir**: il faut voir! (*réserve*) we'll have to see!; elle danse superbement, il faut (la) voir! you should see her dance, it's wonderful!; (il) faut le voir pour le croire it has to be seen to be believed; faudrait voir à voir!* come on!*, come off it!*; (il) faudrait voir à faire/ne pas faire ...* make sure you do/don't do ...; son travail est fait faut voir (comme)!* *ou* (il) faut voir comment!* you should see what a job he's made

---

of it!; il faut voir comment tu t'y prends, aussi! look at how you're going about it though!; il faut voir comment s'habille! you should see the way he dresses!; (il) faudrait voir à ne pas nous ennuyer!* you'd better see you don't cause us any trouble!*

2 s'en falloir VERBE PRONOMINAL

♦ **s'en falloir de**: j'ai raté le train, il s'en est fallu de 5 minutes I missed the train by 5 minutes; il ne s'en fallait que de 100 F pour qu'il ait la somme he was only *ou* just 100 francs short of the full amount; il s'en est fallu de peu (pour) que ça (n')arrive it came very close to happening, it very nearly happened; elle ne l'a pas injurié, mais il s'en est fallu de peu she very nearly insulted him

♦ **loin s'en faut! ◊ tant s'en faut! ◊ il s'en faut (de beaucoup)!** far from it!; il s'en faut de beaucoup qu'il soit heureux he is far from being happy, he is by no means happy

♦ **peu s'en faut**: il a fini, *ou* peu s'en faut he has as good as finished, he has just about finished; ça m'a coûté 500 F *ou* peu s'en faut it cost me the best part of 500 francs, it cost me very nearly 500 francs; peu s'en est fallu (pour) qu'il pleure he almost wept, he very nearly wept

falot¹ [falo] NM a (= *lanterne*) lantern b (*arg Mil = tribunal militaire*) court martial

falot², e [falo, ɔt] ADJ [*personne*] colourless (*Brit*), colorless (*US*); [*lumière*] wan, pale

falsifiable [falsifjabl] ADJ [*document, papiers d'identité, signature*] forgeable; [*écriture*] that can be copied easily

falsificateur, -trice [falsifikatœʀ, tʀis] NM,F [*document, signature*] forger; **les ~s de l'histoire** those who distort history, the distorters of history

falsification [falsifikasjɔ̃] NF [*comptes, faits, document*] falsification; [*signature*] forgery, forging; [*aliment*] doctoring, adulteration

falsifier [falsifje] ▶ conjug 7 ◀ VT [+ *comptes, faits, document*] to falsify; [+ *signature*] to forge; [+ *aliment*] to doctor, adulterate

falzar [falzaʀ] NM bags* (*Brit*), (pair of) trousers, (pair of) pants (*US*)

famé, e [fame] ♦ **mal famé** LOC ADJ disreputable

famélique [famelik] ADJ scrawny, scraggy, rawboned

fameusement [famøzmɑ̃] ADV (= *très*) remarkably, really; **c'est ~ bon** it's remarkably *ou* really good

fameux, -euse [famø, øz] ADJ a (*: après n = de qualité*) [*mets, vin*] first-rate, first-class b **pas ~** [*mets, travail, temps*] not too good, not so great*; [*roman, auteur*] no great shakes*, not up to much* (*Brit*); **et le temps pour demain? — pas ~** and tomorrow's weather? — not all that good *ou* not up to much* (*Brit*); **il n'est pas ~ en latin** he's not too good *ou* not all that good at Latin c (*avant n: intensif*) real; **c'est un ~ trajet/ problème/travail** it's quite a *ou* one hell of a* journey/problem/piece of work; **c'est une fameuse erreur/raclée** it's quite a *ou* it's a real mistake/thrashing; **un ~ salaud** a downright *ou* an out-and-out *ou* a real bastard*; **une fameuse assiettée** a huge *ou* great plateful; **c'est un ~ gaillard** (*bien bâti*) he's a strapping fellow; (*chaud lapin*) he's one for the ladies, he's a bit of a lad* (*Brit*) d (*avant n = bon*) [*idée, voiture*] first-rate, great*, fine; **c'est une fameuse aubaine** a real *ou* great stroke of luck; **il a fait un ~ travail** he's done a first-class *ou* first-rate *ou* fine job; **elle était fameuse, ton idée!** what a bright *ou* great* idea you had! e (*: avant n = fonction de référence*) famous; **quel est le nom de cette fameuse rue?** what's the name of that (famous) street?; **ah, c'est ce ~ Paul dont tu m'as tant parlé** so this is the fa-

▶ GRAMMAIRE ACTIVE: **falloir** 37.1, 37.2

mous Paul you've told me so much about; **c'est ça, sa fameuse honnêteté** so this is his much-vaunted honesty

[f] (*après n = célèbre*) famous (**pour, par** for)

familial, e (*mpl* **-iaux**) [familjal, jo] [1] ADJ [*problème*] family (*épith*), domestic (*épith*); [*liens, vie, entreprise, ambiance*] family (*épith*); [*boîte, paquet*] family-size(d); [*modèle de voiture*] family (*épith*) → **aide, allocation** [2] **familiale** NF (family) estate car (*Brit*), station wagon (*US*)

familiarisation [familjaʀizasjɔ̃] NF familiarization

familiariser [familjaʀize] ▶ conjug 1 ◀ [1] VT ~ **qn avec** to familiarize sb with, get sb used to [2] **se familiariser** VPR to familiarize o.s. with; **se ~ avec** [+ *lieu, personne, méthode, langue*] to familiarize o.s. with, get to know, become acquainted with; [+ *bruit, danger*] to get used *ou* accustomed to; **ses pieds, peu familiarisés avec le sol rocailleux** his feet, unused *ou* unaccustomed to the stony ground

familiarité [familjaʀite] NF [a] (= *bonhomie*) familiarity; (= *désinvolture*) offhandedness, (*over*)familiarity [b] (= *privautés*) **~s** familiarities; **cessez ces ~s** stop these familiarities, stop taking liberties [c] (= *habitude*) **~ avec** [+ *langue, auteur, méthode*] familiarity with [d] (= *atmosphère amicale*) informality; (*littér*) **dans la ~ de** on familiar terms with

familier, -ière [familje, jɛʀ] [1] ADJ [a] (= *bien connu*) [*problème, spectacle, objet*] familiar; **sa voix/cette technique m'est familière** I'm familiar with his voice/this technique, his voice/this technique is familiar *ou* well-known to me; **la langue anglaise lui est devenue familière** he has become (thoroughly) familiar with *ou* at home with the English language [b] (= *routinier*) [*tâche*] familiar; **cette attitude lui est familière** this is a typical attitude of his; **le mensonge lui était devenu ~** lying had become quite a habit of his *ou* had become almost second nature to him [c] (= *amical*) [*entretien, atmosphère*] informal, friendly, casual [d] (= *désinvolte*) [*personne*] (*over*)familiar; [*surnom*] familiar; [*ton, remarque*] (*over*)familiar, offhand; [*attitude, manières*] offhand; **il devient vite ~** he soon gets too familiar; **(trop) ~ avec ses supérieurs/ses clients/les femmes** overfamiliar with his superiors/his customers/women [e] (= *non recherché*) [*mot*] informal, colloquial; [*style, registre*] informal, conversational, colloquial; **expression familière** colloquialism, colloquial phrase *ou* expression [f] [*divinités*] household (*épith*) → **démon** [2] NM [*club, théâtre*] regular visitor (**de** to); **le crime a été commis par un ~ (de la maison)** the crime was committed by a very good friend of the household *ou* by a regular visitor to the house

familièrement [familjɛʀmɑ̃] ADV (= *amicalement*) [*s'entretenir*] informally; (= *cavalièrement*) [*se conduire*] familiarly; (= *sans recherche*) [*s'exprimer*] informally, colloquially; **comme on dit ~** as you say colloquially *ou* in conversation; **le ficus elastica, ~ appelé caoutchouc** ficus elastica, commonly known as the rubber plant; **il te parle un peu (trop) ~** he's being a bit too familiar with you

famille [famij] NF [a] (*gén*) family; **~ éloignée/ proche** distant/close family *ou* relations *ou* relatives; **avez-vous de la ~ à Londres ?** do you have any family *ou* relations *ou* relatives in London?; **on a prévenu la ~** the relatives *ou* the next of kin (*Admin*) have been informed; **~ d'accueil** host family; **~ nombreuse** large family; **la ~ étendue/nucléaire** the extended/nuclear family; **elle promenait (toute) sa petite ~** she was taking her (entire) brood* for a walk; **comment va la petite ~ ?** how are the

little ones?; **entrer dans une ~** to become part of a family; **leur mariage a consacré son entrée dans la ~** their marriage made him an official member of the family; **elle fait partie de la ~** ◊ **elle est de la ~** she is part *ou* one of the family; **c'est une ~ de musiciens** they're a family of musicians → **monoparental** [b] [*plantes, langues*] family; **la ~ des cuivres** the brass family; **~ de mots** word family; **~ de produits** family of products, product family; **ils sont de la même ~ politique** they're of the same political persuasion [c] (*loc*) [*possessions, réunion, dîner*] family (*épith*); **tableau de ~** (= *peinture*) family portrait; (= *spectacle*) family scene; (*légué par les ancêtres*) family heirloom; **de bonne ~** from a good family *ou* background; **c'est de ~** ◊ **ça tient de ~** it runs in the family; **en ~** (= *avec la famille*) with the family; (= *comme une famille*) as a family; **tout se passe en ~** it's all kept in the family; **il vaut mieux régler ce problème en ~** it's best to sort this problem out within the family; **passer ses vacances en ~** to spend one's holidays with the family; **il est sans ~** he has no family; **un (petit) bridge des ~s*** a quiet *ou* cosy little game of bridge; **il est très ~*** he's very family-oriented, he's a real family man → **air², caveau, chef¹, sept**

famine [famin] NF (= *épidémie*) famine, starvation (*NonC*); **nous allons à la ~** we are heading for starvation, we are going to starve; **crier ~** to complain that the wolf is at the door → **salaire**

fan* [fan] NM (= *admirateur*) fan

fana* [fana] ABRÉV = **fanatique** [1] ADJ crazy* (**de** about), mad keen* (*Brit*) (**de** on) [2] NMF fanatic; **~ de ski/de varappe** skiing/rock-climbing fanatic; **~ d'informatique/de cinéma** computer/cinema buff*; **~ d'écologie** eco-freak*

fanage [fanaʒ] NM tossing, turning, tedding

fanal (*pl* **-aux**) [fanal, o] NM (= *feu*) [*train*] headlight, headlamp; [*mât*] lantern; (= *phare*) beacon, lantern; (= *lanterne à main*) lantern, lamp

fanatique [fanatik] [1] ADJ fanatical (**de** about) [2] NMF (*gén, Sport*) fanatic; (*Pol, Rel*) fanatic, zealot; **~ du ski/du football/des échecs** skiing/football/chess fanatic

fanatiquement [fanatikmɑ̃] ADV fanatically

fanatisation [fanatizasjɔ̃] NF rousing to fanaticism, fanaticization (*frm*)

fanatiser [fanatize] ▶ conjug 1 ◀ VT to rouse to fanaticism, fanaticize (*frm*)

fanatisme [fanatism] NM fanaticism

fan-club (*pl* **fan-clubs**) [fanklœb] NM [*vedette*] fan club; (*hum*) **il fait partie de mon ~** he's one of my fans

fane [fan] NF (*surtout pl*) [*légume*] top; **~s de carottes/radis** carrot/radish tops; **~s de haricots/pommes de terre** bean/potato haulms

fané, e [fane] (*ptp de* **faner**) ADJ [*fleur, bouquet*] withered, wilted; [*couleur, teint, beauté, étoffe*] faded

faner [fane] ▶ conjug 1 ◀ [1] VI (*littér*) to make hay [2] VT [a] [+ *herbe*] to toss, turn, ted; **on fane (l'herbe) après la fauchaison** the tossing *ou* turning of the hay *ou* the tedding is done after the mowing [b] (*littér*) [+ *couleur, beauté*] to fade; **femme que l'âge a fanée** woman whose looks have faded [3] **se faner** VPR [*plante*] to fade, wither, wilt; [*peau*] to wither; [*teint, beauté, couleur*] to fade

faneur, -euse [fanœʀ, øz] [1] NM,F (= *ouvrier*) haymaker [2] **faneuse** NF (= *machine*) tedder

fanfare [fɑ̃faʀ] NF [a] (= *orchestre*) brass band; **la ~ du régiment** the regimental band [b] (= *musique*) fanfare; **~ de clairons** fanfare of bugles; **~ de trompettes** flourish *ou* fanfare of trumpets; **des ~s éclatèrent** there was the sound of fanfares [c] (*loc*) **en ~** [*réveil, départ*] clamorous, tumultuous; [*réveiller, partir*] noisi-

ly, with a great commotion; **il est arrivé en ~** (*avec bruit*) he came in noisily *ou* with a great commotion; (*fièrement*) he came in triumphantly; **annoncer en ~** [+ *nouvelle, réforme*] to blazon *ou* trumpet forth, publicize widely

fanfaron, -onne [fɑ̃faʀɔ̃, ɔn] [1] ADJ [*personne, attitude*] boastful; [*air, propos*] bragging, boastful; **il avait un petit air ~** he was quite full of himself, he looked very pleased with himself [2] NM,F braggart; **faire le ~** to brag, boast, go around bragging *ou* boasting

fanfaronnade [fɑ̃faʀɔnad] NF bragging (*NonC*), boasting (*NonC*), boast; **arrête tes ~s** stop boasting

fanfaronner [fɑ̃faʀɔne] ▶ conjug 1 ◀ VI to brag, boast

fanfreluche [fɑ̃fʀəlyʃ] NF (*sur rideau, ameublement*) trimming; **robe ornée de ~s** dress trimmed with frills and flounces

fange [fɑ̃ʒ] NF (*littér*) mire (*littér*) → **traîner, vautrer**

fangeux, -euse [fɑ̃ʒø, øz] ADJ (*littér*) miry (*littér*)

fanion [fanjɔ̃] NM [*vélo, club, bateau*] pennant; (*Rugby*) flag; (*Ski*) pennant; (*Mil*) **~ de commandement** commanding officer's pennant

fanon [fanɔ̃] NM [a] [*baleine*] plate of whalebone *ou* baleen; (= *matière*) whalebone (*NonC*) [b] [*cheval*] fetlock [c] [*bœuf*] dewlap; [*dindon*] wattle [d] [*mitre*] lappet

fantaisie [fɑ̃tezi] NF [a] (= *caprice*) whim; **elle se plie à toutes ses ~s** ◊ **elle lui passe toutes ses ~s** she gives in to his every whim; **s'offrir une ~ en allant** *ou* **s'offrir la ~ d'aller au restaurant** to give o.s. a treat by having a meal out *ou* by eating out; **je me suis payé une petite ~** (*bibelot, bijou, gadget*) I bought myself a little present [b] (= *extravagance*) extravagance; **ces ~s vestimentaires** such extravagance *ou* extravagances of dress [c] (*littér = bon plaisir*) **il agit selon** *ou* **il n'en fait qu'à sa ~** he does as the fancy takes him; **il lui a pris la ~ de ...** he took it into his head to ...; **à votre ~** as it may please you [d] (= *imagination*) fancy, imagination; **être plein de ~** to be full of imagination *ou* very fanciful *ou* imaginative; **manquer de ~** [*vie*] to be monotonous *ou* uneventful; [*personne*] to be lacking in imagination *ou* unimaginative; **c'est de la ~ pure** that is sheer *ou* pure fantasy *ou* fancy ou imagination [e] (*en adj*) **boucles d'oreilles (de) ~** (*originales*) fancy *ou* novelty earrings; (*imitation*) imitation gold (*ou silver etc*) earrings; **bijoux (de) ~** costume jewellery; **rideaux ~** fancy curtains; **boutons ~** fancy *ou* novelty buttons; **kirsch ~** kirsch-flavoured brandy [f] (= *œuvre*) (*Littérat*) fantasy; (*Mus*) fantasia

fantaisiste [fɑ̃tezist] [1] ADJ [a] [*nouvelle, explication*] fanciful, whimsical; [*horaires*] unpredictable [b] [*personne*] (= *farceur*) whimsical; (= *capricieux*) fanciful; (= *peu sérieux*) unreliable; (= *bizarre*) eccentric, unorthodox [2] NMF [a] (*Théât*) variety artist *ou* entertainer [b] (= *original*) eccentric, oddball*

fantasmagorie [fɑ̃tasmagɔʀi] NF phantasmagoria

fantasmagorique [fɑ̃tasmagɔʀik] ADJ phantasmagorical

fantasmatique [fɑ̃tasmatik] ADJ [*rêve, vision*] fantastical

fantasme [fɑ̃tasm] NM fantasy; **il vit dans ses ~s** he lives in a fantasy world

fantasmer [fɑ̃tasme] ▶ conjug 1 ◀ [1] VI to fantasize (**sur** about) [2] VT to fantasize about

fantasque [fɑ̃task] ADJ (*littér*) [*personne, humeur*] whimsical, capricious; [*chose*] weird, fantastic

fantassin [fɑ̃tasɛ̃] NM foot soldier, infantryman; **2 000 ~s** 2,000 foot *ou* infantry

fantastique [fɑ̃tastik] [1] ADJ [a] (= étrange) [atmosphère] weird, eerie; [rêve] weird, fantastic; **conte ~** tale of fantasy ou of the supernatural; **roman ~** (gén) fantasy; (= romantique) Gothic novel; **film ~** fantasy film; **le cinéma ~** science fiction, horror and fantasy films [b]* (= excellent) fantastic*, terrific*, great*; (= énorme, incroyable) fantastic*, incredible [2] NM **le ~** the fantastic, the uncanny; (Littérat) (gén) fantasy, the fantastic; (romantique) Gothic literature; (Ciné) science fiction, horror and fantasy

fantastiquement [fɑ̃tastikmɑ̃] ADV fantastically

fantoche [fɑ̃tɔʃ] NM, ADJ puppet; **gouvernement ~** puppet government

fantomatique [fɑ̃tɔmatik] ADJ ghostly

fantôme [fɑ̃tom] [1] NM (= spectre) ghost, phantom; **les ~s du passé** ghosts from the past; (= personne amaigrie) **ce n'est plus qu'un ~** he's a shadow of his former self [2] ADJ [société] dummy, bogus; **salarié ~** ghost employee ou worker; **bateau ~** ghost ou phantom ship; **train/ville ~** ghost train/town; **étudiants ~s** students who do not attend classes; (Méd) **membre ~** phantom limb; (Phys) **image ~** ghost; (Pol) **cabinet/gouvernement ~** shadow cabinet/government → **vaisseau**

FAO [efao] NF [a] (ABRÉV = **fabrication assistée par ordinateur**) CAM [b] (ABRÉV = **Food and Agriculture Organization**) FAO

faon [fɑ̃] NM (Zool) fawn

faquin †† [fakɛ̃] NM wretch, rascal

far [faR] NM **~ (breton)** custard flan with prunes; **~ aux poires** custard flan with pears

farad [faRad] NM farad

faraday [faRadɛ] NM faraday

faramineux, -euse* [faRaminø, øz] ADJ [bêtise, inconscience] staggering*, fantastic*, mind-boggling*; [prix] astronomical*, sky-high* (attrib); **toi et tes idées faramineuses!** you and your brilliant ideas!

farandole [faRɑ̃dɔl] NF (= danse) farandole; **la ~ des desserts** a selection of desserts

faraud, e † [faRo, od] [1] ADJ boastful; **tu n'es plus si ~** you are no longer quite so boastful ou full of yourself ou pleased with yourself [2] NM,F braggart; **faire le ~** to brag, boast

farce[1] [faRs] NF [a] (= tour) practical joke, prank, hoax; **faire une ~ à qn** to play a practical joke ou a prank on sb; **~s (et) attrapes** (= objets) (assorted) tricks; **magasin de ~s-attrapes** joke and novelty) shop [b] (fig, Théât) farce; **grosse ~** slapstick comedy; **ce procès est une ~** this trial is a farce → **dindon**

farce[2] [faRs] NF (Culin) (gén) stuffing; (à la viande) forcemeat

farceur, -euse [faRsœR, øz] [1] NM,F (facétieux) (en actes) practical joker, prankster; (en paroles) joker, wag; (= fumiste) clown (péj); **va!** you're (ou he's etc) a sly ou crafty one! [2] ADJ (= espiègle) mischievous; **il est très ~** he likes playing tricks ou practical jokes

farcir [faRsiR] ▶ conjug 2 ◀ [1] VT [a] (Culin) to stuff; **tomates farcies** stuffed tomatoes [b] (fig) **farci de fautes** crammed ou littered with mistakes; **j'en ai la tête farcie** I've had about as much as I can take [2] **se farcir** VPR [a] (péj) **se ~ la mémoire** ou **la tête de** to fill one's head with [b] [+ lessive, travail, personne] to get stuck ou landed with*; [+ bouteille] to knock back*, polish off*; [+ gâteaux] to gobble down*, guzzle*, scoff* (Brit); **se ~ une fille/un mec** to make it with a girl/a guy, have it off with (Brit) a girl/a guy; **il faudra se ~ ton cousin pendant 3 jours** we'll have to put up with your cousin for 3 days; **il faut se le ~** importun) he's a real pain (in the neck)!*; [+ livre] it's really heavy going!; **je me suis farci le voyage à pied** I bloody well walked the whole way

fard [faR] NM (= maquillage) make-up; († = poudre) rouge†, paint; [acteur] **~ (gras)** greasepaint; **~ à joues** blusher; **~ à paupières** eye shadow; **sans ~** [parler] openly; [élégance] unpretentious, simple → **piquer**

fardage [faRdaʒ] NM [bilan, marchandise] dressing-up

fardé, e [faRde] (ptp de farder) ADJ [personne] wearing make-up; **elle est trop ~e** she's wearing too much make-up; **elle avait les paupières/joues ~es** she was wearing eye-shadow/blusher; **elle avait les lèvres ~es** she was wearing lipstick

fardeau (pl **fardeaux**) [faRdo] NM (lit) load, burden (littér); (fig) burden; **sous le ~** under the weight ou burden of; **il a traîné ou porté ce ~ toute sa vie** he carried ou bore this burden all his life

farder [faRde] ▶ conjug 1 ◀ [1] VT [a] (Théât) [+ acteur] to make up; †† [+ visage] to rouge†, paint [b] [+ bilan, marchandise] to dress up; (littér) [+ vérité] to disguise, mask, veil [2] **se farder** VPR (= se maquiller) to make (o.s.) up; († = se poudrer) to paint one's face†; [acteur] to make up

farfadet [faRfadɛ] NM sprite, elf

farfelu, e* [faRfəly] [1] ADJ [idée, projet] hare-brained; [personne, conduite] eccentric, scatty* (Brit) [2] NM,F eccentric

farfouiller* [faRfuje] ▶ conjug 1 ◀ VI to rummage about (**dans** in)

faribole [faRibɔl] NF (littér) (piece of) nonsense; **conter des ~s** to talk nonsense ou twaddle (Brit); **~s (que tout cela)!** (stuff and) nonsense!, fiddlesticks! † *, poppycock! † *

farine [faRin] [1] NF [blé] flour; (littér) **de (la) même ~** of the same ilk → **fleur, rouler** [2] COMP ▶ **farines animales** bone meal ▶ **farine d'avoine** oatmeal ▶ **farine de blé** = **farine de froment** ▶ **farine complète** wheatmeal ou whole wheat ou wholemeal (Brit) flour ▶ **farine de froment** wheat flour ▶ **farine à gâteaux** cake flour ▶ **farine de gruau** fine wheat flour ▶ **farine lactée** baby cereal ▶ **farine de lin** linseed meal ▶ **farine de maïs** cornflour (Brit), cornstarch (US) ▶ **farine de manioc** cassava, manioc flour ▶ **farine de moutarde** mustard powder ▶ **farine de poisson** fish meal ▶ **farine de riz** rice flour ▶ **farine de sarrasin** buckwheat flour ▶ **farine de seigle** rye flour

fariner [faRine] ▶ conjug 1 ◀ VT to flour; **moule beurré et fariné** buttered and floured tin (Brit) ou pan (US)

farineux, -euse [faRinø, øz] [1] ADJ [consistance, aspect, goût] floury, chalky; [chocolat] powdery, chalky; [fromage] chalky; [pomme de terre] floury; [pomme] dry, mushy [2] NM starchy food, starch; **les ~** starchy foods, starches

farniente [faRnjɛ̃te] NM idle life, idleness; **faire du ~ sur la plage** to lounge ou laze on the beach

farouche [faRuʃ] ADJ [a] (= timide) [personne, animal] shy; (= peu sociable) [voisin] unsociable; **ces daims ne sont pas ~s** these deer are not a bit shy ou timid ou are quite tame; **c'est une femme peu ~** she's not backwards in coming forwards, she's no shrinking violet [b] (= acharné) [opposition, attachement, adversaire] fierce; [volonté] unshakeable, inflexible; [énergie] irrepressible; [partisan, défenseur] staunch; [haine, ennemi] bitter; (= hostile) [regard] fierce, hostile [c] (= indompté) savage, wild

farouchement [faRuʃmɑ̃] ADV fiercely; **nier ~ qch** to deny sth fiercely ou vehemently

farsi [faRsi] NM Farsi

fart [faRt] NM (ski) wax; **~ de montée** climbing wax

fartage [faRtaʒ] NM [skis] waxing

farter [faRte] ▶ conjug 1 ◀ VT [+ skis] to wax

Far-West, Far West [faRwɛst] NM INV **le ~** the Wild West

fascicule [fasikyl] NM part, instalment, fascicule (SPÉC); **ce livre est vendu avec un ~ d'exercices** this book is sold with a manual of exercises; (Mil) **~ de mobilisation** instructions for mobilization

fascinant, e [fasinɑ̃, ɑ̃t] ADJ (gén) fascinating; [beauté] bewitching, fascinating

fascination [fasinasjɔ̃] NF fascination; **exercer une grande ~** to exert (a) great fascination (**sur** on, over), have (a) great fascination (**sur** for)

fascine [fasin] NF (= fagot) faggot (of brushwood); (Constr) fascine

fasciner[1] [fasine] ▶ conjug 1 ◀ VT (gén) to fascinate; (= soumettre à son charme) to bewitch; **se laisser ~ par des promesses** to allow o.s. to be bewitched by promises; **être fasciné par le pouvoir** to be fascinated ou mesmerized by power

fasciner[2] [fasine] ▶ conjug 1 ◀ VT (Constr) to line with fascines

fascisant, e [faʃizɑ̃, ɑ̃t] ADJ fascistic

fascisation [faʃizasjɔ̃] NF fascistization

fascisme [faʃism] NM fascism

fasciste [faʃist] ADJ, NMF fascist

faste[1] [fast] NM splendour (Brit), splendor (US), pomp; **sans ~** [cérémonie] simple, low-key; [célébrer] quietly, simply

faste[2] [fast] ADJ (littér) [année, période] (= de chance) lucky; (= prospère) prosperous; **jour ~** lucky day

fastes [fast] NMPL (= annales) annals

fast-food (pl **fast-foods**) [fastfud] NM (= restaurant) fast-food restaurant; (= restauration) fast food

fastidieusement [fastidjøzmɑ̃] ADV tediously, tiresomely, boringly

fastidieux, -ieuse [fastidjø, jøz] ADJ tedious, tiresome, boring

fastoche [fastɔʃ] ADJ dead easy*; **c'est vachement ~!** it's dead easy* ou a cinch!

fastueusement [fastɥøzmɑ̃] ADV sumptuously, luxuriously; **recevoir qn ~** (pour dîner) to entertain sb lavishly; (à son arrivée) to give sb a lavish reception

fastueux, -euse [fastɥø, øz] ADJ sumptuous, luxurious; **réception fastueuse** lavish reception; **mener une vie fastueuse** to lead a sumptuous ou luxurious existence, live a life of great luxury

fat † [fa(t), fat] [1] ADJ conceited, smug, complacent [2] NM conceited ou smug ou complacent person

fatal, e (mpl **fatals**) [fatal] ADJ [a] (= funeste) [accident, issue] fatal; [coup] fatal, deadly; **erreur ~e!** fatal error ou mistake!; **être ~ à qn** [chute, accident] to kill sb; [erreur, bêtise] to prove fatal ou disastrous for ou to sb [b] (= inévitable) inevitable; **c'était ~** it was inevitable, it was bound to happen; **il était ~ qu'elle le fasse** she was bound ou fated to do it, it was inevitable that she should do it [c] (= marqué par le destin) [instant, heure] fatal, fateful → **femme**

fatalement [fatalmɑ̃] ADV (= inévitablement) inevitably; **~, il est tombé!** inevitably, he fell!; **au début, ce fut ~ mauvais** at the beginning, it was inevitably ou unavoidably bad; **ça devait ~ arriver** it was bound ou fated to happen

fatalisme [fatalism] NM fatalism

fataliste [fatalist] [1] ADJ fatalistic [2] NMF fatalist

fatalité [fatalite] NF [a] (= destin) fate, fatality (littér); **être poursuivi par la ~** to be pursued by fate; **c'est la ~** it's fate [b] (= nécessité) **le chômage est-il une ~?** is unemployment inevitable?; **par quelle ~ se sont-ils rencontrés?** by what terrible ou unfortunate coincidence did they meet? **c** (= *caractère inévitable*) inevitability; **la ~ de la mort/de cet événement** the inevitability of death/this event

fatidique [fatidik] ADJ (= *lourd de conséquences*) [*décision, paroles, date*] fateful; (= *crucial*) [*moment*] fatal, fateful

fatigabilité [fatigabilite] NF [*personne*] fatigability

fatigant, e [fatigã, ãt] ADJ (= *épuisant*) tiring; (= *agaçant*) [*personne*] annoying, tiresome, tedious; [*conversation*] tiresome, tedious; **c'est ~ pour la vue** it's tiring *ou* a strain on the eyes; **c'est ~ pour le cœur** it's a strain on the heart; **tu es vraiment ~ avec tes questions** you really are annoying *ou* tiresome *ou* a nuisance with your questions; **c'est ~ de devoir toujours tout répéter** it's annoying *ou* tiresome *ou* a nuisance to have to repeat everything all the time

fatigue [fatig] NF **a** [*personne*] (*gén*) tiredness, fatigue; (*Méd*) fatigue; (*fig*) **tomber** *ou* **être mort de ~** to be dead tired*, be exhausted; **il a voulu nous épargner cette ~** he wanted to save *ou* spare us the strain; **dans un état d'extrême** *ou* **de grande ~** in a state of utter exhaustion; **se remettre des ~s du voyage** to get over the strain *ou* the tiring effects of the journey; **pour se reposer de la ~ du voyage** to rest after a tiring journey; **cette ~ dans le bras gauche** this weakness in the left arm; **~ oculaire** *ou* **visuelle** eyestrain → **recru** **b** (*Tech*) fatigue; **la ~ des métaux** metal fatigue

fatigué, e [fatige] (*ptp de* **fatiguer**) ADJ **a** [*personne, voix*] tired, weary; [*traits, membres*] tired; [*cœur*] strained, overworked; [*cerveau*] overtaxed, overworked; [*estomac, foie*] upset; **il a les bras ~s** his arms are tired; **j'ai les yeux ~s** my eyes are tired *ou* strained; **~ par le voyage** travel-worn, travel-weary, tired *ou* weary from *ou* after travelling; (*péj*) **il est né ~** he's bone-lazy *ou* bone-idle **b** **~ de** [+ *jérémiades, voiture, personne*] tired of; **~ de la vie** tired of life *ou* living **c** [*poutre, joint, moteur, habits*] worn

fatiguer [fatige] ▸conjug 1◂ **1** VT **a** (*physiquement*) **~ qn** [*maladie, effort, études*] to make sb tired *ou* weary, tire sb; [*professeur, patron*] to overwork sb; **ces efforts fatiguent, à la longue** all this effort tires *ou* wears you out in the end; **ça fatigue les yeux/le cœur/ l'organisme** it is *ou* puts a strain on the eyes/ heart/whole body; **se ~ les yeux/le cœur** to strain one's eyes/heart **b** [+ *cheval*] [*effort*] to tire, put a strain on; [*propriétaire*] to overwork; [+ *moteur*] [*effort*] to put (a) strain on, strain; [+ *poutre, pièce*] to put (a) strain on, strain; [+ *chaussures, vêtement*] to wear out; [+ *sol*] to exhaust, impoverish **c** (= *agacer*) to annoy; (= *lasser*) to wear out; **tu commences à me ~** you're beginning to annoy me; **il vous fatigue avec ses sermons** he wears you out *ou* he becomes a bit wearisome with his sermons **d** [+ *salade*] to toss **2** VI [*moteur*] to labour (*Brit*), labor (*US*), strain; [*poutre, pièce, joint*] to become strained, show (signs of) strain; [*personne*] to tire, grow tired *ou* weary; **je commence à ~** I'm starting to get tired **3** **se fatiguer** VPR **a** (*physiquement*) to get tired; **se ~ à faire qch** to tire o.s. out doing sth; (*iro*) **il ne s'est pas trop fatigué** he didn't overdo it, he didn't kill himself* **b** (= *se lasser de*) **se ~ de qch/de faire** to get tired *ou* weary of sth/of doing **c** (= *s'évertuer à*) **se ~ à répéter/expliquer** to wear o.s. out repeating /explaining; **ne te fatigue pas** *ou* **pas la peine de te ~, il est borné** he's just dim so don't waste your time *ou* your breath

fatras [fatra] NM [*choses*] jumble; [*idées*] jumble, hotchpotch (*Brit*), hodgepodge (*US*)

fatuité [fatɥite] NF self-complacency, self-conceit, smugness

fatwa [fatwa] NF fatwa; **prononcer une ~ contre qn** to declare *ou* issue a fatwa against sb

faubourg [fobur] NM (inner) suburb; **avoir l'accent des ~s** to have a working-class Paris accent

faubourien, -ienne [foburjẽ, jɛn] ADJ [*accent, manières*] working-class Paris

fauchage [foʃaʒ] NM [*blé*] reaping; [*champs, prés*] mowing; [*herbe*] (*avec une faux*) scything, mowing, cutting; (*mécanique*) mowing, cutting

fauchaison [foʃɛzɔ̃] NF **a** (= *époque*) [*pré*] mowing (time), reaping (time); [*blés*] reaping (time) **b** (= *action*) = **fauchage**

fauche [foʃ] NF **a*** (= *vol*) thieving; **il y a beaucoup de ~** a lot of thieving goes on; **lutter contre la ~ dans les supermarchés** to combat shoplifting *ou* thieving in supermarkets **b**†† = **fauchaison**

fauché, e* [foʃe] (*ptp de* **faucher**) ADJ (= *sans argent*) (flat *ou* dead) broke* (*attrib*), hard up*, stony-broke* (*Brit*) (*attrib*); **il est ~ comme les blés** he hasn't got a penny to his name, he hasn't got a bean* (*Brit*) *ou* a brass farthing (*Brit*); **c'est un éternel ~** he's permanently broke*, he never has a penny; (*iro*) **avec toi, on n'est pas ~!** you're a dead loss!*, you're a fat lot of good!* (*Brit*)

faucher [foʃe] ▸conjug 1◂ **1** VT **a** [+ *blé*] to reap; [+ *champs, prés*] to mow, reap; [+ *herbe*] (*avec une faux*) to scythe, mow, cut; (*mécanique*) to mow, cut **b** [+ *abattre*] [*vent*] to flatten; [*véhicule*] to knock over *ou* down, mow down; [*tir*] to mow down; [*explosion*] to flatten, blow over; (*Ftbl*) to bring down; **la mort l'a fauché en pleine jeunesse** he was cut down in his prime; **ils ont été fauchés par un obus de mortier** they were blown up by a shell; **avoir une jambe fauchée par un train** to have a leg cut off *ou* taken off by a train **c*** (= *voler*) to swipe*, pinch* (*Brit*), nick* (*Brit*); **elle fauche dans les magasins** she pinches* things from shops **2** VI [*cheval*] to dish

faucheur, -euse [foʃœr, øz] **1** NM,F (= *personne*) mower, reaper **2** NM = **faucheux** **3** **faucheuse** NF (= *machine*) reaper, mower; (*littér* = *mort*) **la Faucheuse** the (Grim) Reaper

faucheux [foʃø] NM harvestman (*Brit*), harvest spider, daddy-longlegs (*US*)

faucille [fosij] NF sickle; **la ~ et le marteau** the hammer and sickle

faucon [fokɔ̃] NM (*lit*) falcon, hawk; (*fig Pol*) hawk; **~ crécerelle** kestrel; **~ pèlerin** peregrine falcon; **chasser au ~** to hawk; **chasse au ~** hawking

fauconneau (*pl* **fauconneaux**) [fokono] NM young falcon *ou* hawk

fauconnerie [fokɔnri] NF (= *art*) falconry; (= *chasse*) hawking, falconry; (= *lieu*) hawk house

fauconnier [fokɔnje] NM falconer, hawker

faufil [fofil] NM tacking *ou* basting thread

faufilage [fofilaʒ] NM tacking, basting

faufiler [fofile] ▸conjug 1◂ **1** VT to tack, baste **2** **se faufiler** VPR **se ~ dans** to worm *ou* inch *ou* edge one's way into; **se ~ entre** to dodge in and out of, thread one's way through; **se ~ parmi la foule** to worm *ou* inch *ou* thread one's way through the crowd, slip through the crowd; **se ~ entre les** *ou* **au milieu des voitures** to nip *ou* dodge in and out of the traffic, thread one's way through the traffic; **il se faufila à l'intérieur/au dehors** he wormed *ou* inched *ou* edged his way in/out

faune¹ [fon] NM (*Myth*) faun

faune² [fon] NF (*Zool*) wildlife, fauna; (*péj* = *personnes*) bunch, crowd; **la ~ et la flore** the flora and fauna; **la ~ marine** marine fauna *ou* animal life

faunesque [fonɛsk] ADJ faunlike

faussaire [fosɛr] NMF forger

fausse [fos] ADJ F → **faux²**

faussement [fosmã] ADV [*accuser*] wrongly, wrongfully; [*croire*] wrongly, erroneously, falsely; **~ modeste** falsely modest; **~ intéressé** pretending to be interested; **d'un ton ~ indifférent** in a tone of feigned indifference, in a deceptively detached tone of voice

fausser [fose] ▸conjug 1◂ VT **a** [+ *calcul, statistique, fait*] to distort, alter; [+ *réalité, pensée*] to distort, pervert; [+ *sens d'un mot*] to distort; [+ *esprit*] to unsettle, disturb; [+ *jugement*] to distort **b** [+ *clé*] to bend; [+ *serrure*] to break; [+ *poulie, manivelle, charnière*] to buckle, bend; [+ *essieu, volant, hélice, lame*] to warp, buckle, bend; **soudain il se troubla, sa voix se faussa** suddenly he became flustered and his voice became strained **c** (*loc*) **~ compagnie à qn** to give sb the slip, slip *ou* sneak away from sb; **vous nous avez de nouveau faussé compagnie hier soir** you gave us the slip again last night, you sneaked *ou* slipped off again last night

fausset¹ [fosɛ] NM falsetto (voice); **d'une voix de ~** in a falsetto voice

fausset² [fosɛ] NM [*tonneau*] spigot

fausseté [foste] NF **a** [*idée, accusation, dogme*] falseness, falsity **b** [*caractère, personne*] duplicity, deceitfulness **c**† (= *propos mensonger*) falsity†, falsehood

Faust [fost] NM Faust

faustien, -ienne [fostjẽ, jɛn] ADJ Faustian, of Faust

faut [fo] → **falloir**

▼**faute** [fot] NF **1** **a** (= *erreur*) mistake, error; **faire** *ou* **commettre une ~** to make a mistake *ou* an error; **~ de grammaire** grammatical mistake *ou* error; **~ de ponctuation** mistake in punctuation, error of punctuation; **~ de prononciation** mispronunciation; **faire des ~s de prononciation** to mispronounce words; **dictée sans ~** error-free dictation **b** (= *mauvaise action*) misdeed; (*Jur*) offence; († = *péché de chair*) lapse (from virtue), sin (of the flesh); **commettre une ~** (*gén*) to commit a misdeed *ou* misdemeanour; († = *péché de chair*) to sin; **une ~ contre** *ou* **envers la religion** a sin *ou* transgression against religion **c** (*Sport*) foul; (*Tennis*) fault; **le joueur a fait une ~** the player committed a foul; **faire une ~ sur qn** to foul sb; (*Volley*) **faire une ~ de filet** to make contact with the net; **faire une ~ de main** to handle the ball; (*Basket*) **~ personnelle** personal foul; (*Tennis*) **~ de pied** foot fault; **faire une ~ de pied** to foot-fault; (*Tennis*) **faire une double ~** (*de service*) to serve a double fault, double-fault; **~!** (*pour un joueur*) foul!; (*pour la balle*) fault!; (*Tennis*) **la balle est ~** the ball was out → **parcours, sans-faute** **d** (= *responsabilité*) fault; **par la ~ de Richard/sa ~** because of Richard/him; **c'est (de) la ~ de** *ou* **à* Richard/(de) sa ~** it's Richard's fault/his fault; **la ~ lui en revient** the fault lies with him; **à qui la ~?** whose fault is it?, who is to blame?; **c'est la ~ à pas de chance*** it's just bad *ou* hard luck **e** (*loc*) **être/se sentir en ~** to be/feel at fault *ou* in the wrong; **prendre qn en ~** to catch sb out; (*littér*) **il ne se fait pas ~ de faire** he doesn't shy from *ou* at doing, he doesn't fail to do; (*littér*) **il ne se fit pas ~ d'en parler** he didn't miss a chance to talk about it; **~ de** for *ou* through lack of; **~ d'argent** for want of *ou* through lack of money; **~ de temps** for *ou* through lack of time; **~ de mieux** for lack of *ou* want of anything better; **~ de quoi** failing which, otherwise; **relâché** *ou* **~ de preuves** released for *ou* through lack of evidence; **~ de réponse sous huitaine** failing a reply within a week, if we receive no reply within a week; **~**

d'avis **contraire** unless otherwise informed; ~ d'y être allé, je ... since I didn't go, I ...; **je n'y suis pas arrivé, mais ce n'est pas ~ d'avoir essayé** I didn't manage to do it but it wasn't for want ou lack of trying; **le combat cessa ~ de combattants** the battle died down, there being nobody left to carry on the fight ▪ (PROV) **~ de grives, on mange des merles** you have to cut your coat according to your cloth (PROV), beggars can't be choosers (PROV), ▪ (PROV) **~ avouée est à demi** ou **à moitié pardonnée** a sin confessed is a sin half pardoned

2 COMP ► **faute d'accord** (Ling) mistake in (the) agreement ► **faute de calcul** miscalculation, error in calculation ► **faute de carres** (Ski) edging mistake ► **faute civile** (Jur) civil wrong ► **faute de conduite** (Aut) (= erreur) driving error; (= infraction) driving offence ► **faute d'étourderie** = **faute d'inattention** ► **faute de français** grammatical mistake (in French) ► **faute de frappe** typing error ► **faute de goût** error of taste ► **faute d'impression** misprint ► **faute d'inattention** careless ou thoughtless mistake ► **faute d'orthographe** spelling mistake ► **faute pénale** (Jur) criminal offence ► **faute professionnelle** professional misconduct (NonC) ► **faute de service** (Admin) act of (administrative) negligence

fauter† [fote] ▸ conjug 1 ◂ VI [femme] to sin

fauteuil [fotœj] 1 NM (gén) armchair; (avec dos rembourré, moderne) easy chair, armchair; [président] chair; [théâtre, académicien] seat; **occuper le ~** (= siéger comme président) to be in the chair; **il est arrivé dans un ~*** he romped home*, he walked in* (Brit)

2 COMP ► **fauteuil de balcon** (Théât) balcony seat, seat in the dress circle; **~s de balcon** (= région de la salle) dress circle ► **fauteuil à bascule** rocking chair ► **fauteuil club** (big) leather armchair ► **fauteuil crapaud** squat armchair ► **fauteuil de dentiste** dentist's chair ► **fauteuil de jardin** garden chair ► **fauteuil d'orchestre** (Théât) seat in the front ou orchestra stalls (Brit) ou the orchestra (US); **~s d'orchestre** (= région de la salle) front ou orchestra stalls (Brit), orchestra (US) ► **fauteuil à oreillettes** winged chair ► **fauteuil pivotant** swivel chair ► **fauteuil pliant** folding chair ► **fauteuil roulant** wheelchair ► **fauteuil tournant** = **fauteuil pivotant**; → **voltaire**

fauteur [fotœʀ] NM **~ de troubles** ou **de désordre** troublemaker, mischief-maker, rabble-rouser; **~ de guerre** warmonger

fautif, -ive [fotif, iv] 1 ADJ a [conducteur] at fault (attrib), in the wrong (attrib); [élève, enfant] guilty; **il se sentait ~** he felt he was at fault ou in the wrong, he felt guilty b [texte, liste, calcul] faulty, incorrect; [citation] incorrect, inaccurate; (littér) [mémoire] poor, faulty 2 NM,F **c'est moi le ~** I'm the one to blame ou the guilty one ou the culprit

fautivement [fotivmɑ̃] ADV by mistake, in error

fauve [fov] 1 ADJ a [tissu, couleur] tawny, fawn(-coloured (Brit) ou -colored (US)); (littér) [odeur] musky ◇ **bête** b (Art) **période ~** Fauvist period 2 NM a (= animal) wildcat; **la chasse aux ~s** big-game hunting; **les (grands) ~s** the big cats; **ça sent le ~ ici*** there's a strong smell of B.O. in here*, it really stinks (of sweat) here* b (= couleur) fawn c (Art) Fauvist, painter of the Fauvist school; **les Fauves** the Fauvists ou Fauves

fauverie [fovʀi] NF big-cat house

fauvette [fovɛt] NF warbler; **~ d'hiver** ou **des haies** hedge sparrow, dunnock; **~ des marais** sedge warbler; **~ des roseaux** reed warbler

fauvisme [fovism] NM Fauvism

faux¹ [fo] NF (Agr) scythe; (Anat) falx

▼ **faux²**, **fausse** [fo, fos] 1 ADJ a (= imité) [argent, billet] forged, fake; [marbre, bijoux, meuble] (= en toc) imitation (épith); (pour duper) false, fake; [documents, signature] false, fake, forged; [tableau] fake; **fausse pièce** forged ou fake coin, dud*; **une fausse carte** a trick card; **~ papiers** false papers, forged identity papers; **fausse monnaie** forged currency; **fausse perle** artificial ou imitation pearl; **c'est du ~ Renaissance** it's mock-Renaissance; **il peint des ~ Picasso** he does Picasso forgeries → **facture**

b (= postiche) [dent, nez] false c (= simulé) [bonhomie, colère, désespoir, modestie] feigned; **un ~ air de prude** an air of false modesty; **fausse dévotion** false piety d (= mensonger) [déclaration, promesse, prétexte] false, spurious (frm); **c'est ~** it's wrong ou untrue e (= prétendu) [médecin, policier, étudiant] bogus; [écrivain] sham (épith); **un ~ intellectuel/ savant** a pseudo-intellectual/-scientist; **~ chômeur** false claimant f (= fourbe) [personne, attitude] false, deceitful; [regard] deceitful g (= inexact) [calcul, numéro, rue] wrong; [idée] wrong, mistaken; [affirmation, faits] wrong, untrue; [instrument de mesure] inaccurate, faulty; [instrument de musique, voix] out of tune; [raisonnement, vers] faulty; **c'est ~** [résultat] that's wrong; [fait] that's wrong ou untrue; **il est ~ (de dire) qu'il y soit allé** it's wrong ou incorrect to say that he went, it's not true (to say) that he went; **dire quelque chose de ~** to say something (that's) wrong ou untrue; **faire fausse route** (lit) to go the wrong way, take the wrong road; (fig) to be on the wrong track; **faire un ~ pas** (lit) to trip (over), stumble; (fig) to make a foolish mistake; (par manque de tact) to make a faux pas; **avoir tout ~*** (gén = avoir tort) to get it all wrong; (à un examen) to get everything wrong h (= non fondé) [espoir, rumeur, soupçons, principe] false; **avoir de fausses craintes** to have groundless ou ill-founded fears i (= gênant, ambigu) [position, situation, atmosphère] awkward, false

2 NM a (= mensonge, Philo) **le ~** falsehood; **plaider** ou **prêcher le ~ pour savoir le vrai** to tell a lie (in order) to get at the truth b (= contrefaçon) forgery; (= tableau, meuble, document) fake, forgery; **faire un ~** to do a forgery; **pour ~ et usage de ~** for forgery and the use of forgeries; **~ en écriture** false entry → **inscrire**

3 ADV a [chanter, jouer] out of tune, off key → **sonner** b (loc) **tomber à ~** to come at the wrong moment; **accuser qn à ~** to accuse sb unjustly ou wrongly → **porter**

4 COMP ► **faux acacia** locust tree, false acacia ► **fausse alerte** false alarm ► **faux ami** (= traître) false friend; (Ling) false friend, faux ami, deceptive cognate ► **faux bond**: **faire ~ bond à qn** to let sb down, leave sb in the lurch ► **faux bourdon** (= insecte) drone ► **faux bruit** false rumour ► **faux chignon** hairpiece ► **faux col** [chemise] detachable collar; [bière] head ► **fausses côtes** false ribs ► **fausse couche** miscarriage; **faire une fausse couche** to have a miscarriage, miscarry ► **faux cul** (= homme) two-faced bastard**; (= femme) two-faced bitch** ► **faux départ** (lit, fig) false start ► **faux derche** = **faux-cul** ► **faux dévot, fausse dévote** NM,F pharisee ► **faux ébénier** laburnum ► **fausse fenêtre** blind window ► **fausse fourrure** fake ou faux fur ► **faux frais** PL extras, incidental expenses ► **faux frère** false friend ► **faux jeton*** two-faced person ► **fausse joie** vain joy ► **faux jour**: **il y a un ~ jour** there's a reflection that makes it difficult to see properly; **sous un ~ jour** in a false light ► **faux mouvement** awkward movement; **j'ai fait un**

~ mouvement et maintenant j'ai un torticolis I turned round too quickly and now I've got a crick in my neck ► **faux nom** false ou assumed name ► **fausse note** (Mus) wrong note; (fig) sour note; **sans une fausse note** (fig) without a sour note, smoothly ► **fausse nouvelle** false report ► **faux ongles** false nails ► **faux ourlet** false hem ► **fausse piste** (lit, fig) wrong track ► **faux plafond** false ceiling ► **faux plat** (= montée) slight incline; (= creux) dip (in the road) ► **faux pli** crease ► **fausse porte** false door ► **faux problème** non-problem, non-issue ► **fausse pudeur** false modesty ► **faux seins** falsies* ► **faux serment** false oath ► **fausse sortie** (Théât) sham exit; **il a fait une fausse sortie** (fig) he made a pretence of leaving ► **faux témoignage** (= déposition mensongère) false evidence (NonC); (= délit) perjury ► **faux témoin** lying witness

faux-bourdon (pl **faux-bourdons**) [fobuʀdɔ̃] NM (Mus) faux bourdon

faux-filet (pl **faux-filets**) [fofilɛ] NM sirloin

faux-fuyant (pl **faux-fuyants**) [fofɥijɑ̃] NM prevarication, evasion, equivocation; **assez de ~s** stop dodging ou evading the issue, stop hedging ou prevaricating; **user de ~s** to equivocate, prevaricate, evade the issue; **dire qch sans ~s** to say sth without beating about the bush

faux-monnayeur (pl **faux-monnayeurs**) [fomɔnejœʀ] NM forger, counterfeiter

faux-pont, **faux pont** (pl **faux(-)ponts**) [fopɔ̃] NM (Naut) orlop deck

faux-semblant (pl **faux-semblants**) [fosɑ̃blɑ̃] NM sham, pretence; **user de ~s** to put up a pretence

faux-sens, **faux sens** [fosɑ̃s] NM INV mistranslation

faux-titre, **faux titre** (pl **faux(-)titres**) [fotitʀ] NM half-title, bastard title

favela [favela] NF favela

▼ **faveur¹** [favœʀ] NF a (frm = gentillesse) favour (Brit), favor (US); **faites-moi la ~ de ...** would you be so kind as to ...; **fais-moi une ~** do me a favour; **obtenir qch par ~** to get sth as a favour; **par ~ spéciale (de la direction)** by special favour (of the management) b (= considération) favour (Brit), favor (US); (littér, hum) **avoir la ~ du ministre** to be in favour with the minister; **gagner/perdre la ~ du public** to win/lose public favour, find favour/fall out of favour with the public; (littér) **être en ~** to be in favour (auprès de qn with sb) c (littér, hum) **~s** favours (Brit), favors (US); **elle lui a refusé ses ~s** she refused him her favours; **elle lui a accordé ses dernières ~s** she bestowed her (ultimate) favours upon him (littér, aussi hum) d **de ~** [prix, taux] preferential, special; **billet de ~** complimentary ticket; **régime** ou **traitement de ~** preferential treatment; **avoir un tour de ~** to go in ahead of one's turn e **en ~ de** (= à cause de) in consideration of, on account of; (= au profit de) in favour of, for; (= dans un but charitable) in aid of, on behalf of, for; **en ma/sa ~** in my/his (ou her) favour f **à la ~ de** thanks to, owing to; **à la ~ de la nuit** under cover of darkness ou the night

faveur² [favœʀ] NF (= ruban) ribbon, favour (Brit), favor (US)

▼ **favorable** [favɔʀabl] ADJ a [moment, occasion] right, favourable (Brit), favorable (US); [terrain, position, vent] favourable (Brit), favorable (US); **par temps ~** in favourable weather; **avoir un préjugé ~ envers** to be biased in favour of, be favourably disposed towards; **jouir d'un préjugé ~** to be favourably thought of; **recevoir un accueil ~** to meet with a favourable reception; **se montrer sous un jour ~** to show o.s. in a favourable light; **prêter une oreille ~ à** to lend a sympathetic *ou* kindly ear to; **voir qch d'un œil ~** to view sth favourably *ou* with a favourable eye; **le change nous est ~** the exchange rate is in our favour [b] **être ~ à** [*personne*] to be favourable to

favorablement [favɔʀabləmɑ̃] ADV favourably (*Brit*), favorably (*US*)

▼ **favori, -ite** [favɔʀi, it] [1] ADJ favourite (*Brit*), favorite (*US*) [2] NM [a] (= *préféré, gagnant probable*) favourite; **le ~ des jeunes** the favourite with *ou* of young people; (*Sport*) **ils sont partis ~s** they started off favourites; **c'est le grand ~ de la course** he's the firm favourite for the race [b] (*Hist*) king's favourite (*Brit*) *ou* favorite (*US*) [3] **favoris** NMPL side whiskers, sideburns, sideboards (*Brit*) [4] **favorite** NF (*gén*) favourite (*Brit*), favorite (*US*); (*Hist*) king's favourite *ou* mistress

favorisant, e [favɔʀizɑ̃, ɑ̃t] ADJ (*Méd*) **facteurs ~s** predisposing factors

favoriser [favɔʀize] ▸ conjug 1 ◂ VT [a] (= *avantager, encourager*) [+ *candidat, ambitions, commerce, parti*] to favour (*Brit*), favor (*US*); **les événements l'ont favorisé** events favoured him *ou* were to his advantage; **la fortune le favorise** fortune favours him; **les classes les plus favorisées** the most fortunate *ou* favoured classes [b] (= *faciliter*) to further, favour (*Brit*), favor (*US*); **ceci a favorisé la rébellion/sa fuite** this furthered *ou* favoured the rebellion/his escape; **ces facteurs favorisent l'apparition du cancer** these factors contribute to the development of cancer

favorite [favɔʀit] NF → **favori**

favoritisme [favɔʀitism] NM favouritism (*Brit*), favoritism (*US*); **faire du ~** to show favouritism

fax [faks] NM (= *machine*) fax (machine); (= *document*) fax; **envoyer par ~** to send by fax, fax; **~-modem** fax modem

faxer [fakse] ▸ conjug 1 ◂ VT to fax

fayot [fajo] NM [a] (* *Culin*) bean [b] (‡ *péj = lèche-bottes*) bootlicker, crawler*, brown-nose‡ (*US*)

fayo(t)tage‡ [fajɔtaʒ] NM (*péj*) bootlicking, crawling*, brown-nosing‡ (*US*)

fayo(t)ter‡ [fajɔte] ▸ conjug 1 ◂ VI (*péj = faire du zèle*) to crawl*, suck up‡, brown-nose‡ (*US*)

FB (ABRÉV = **franc belge**) → **franc**

FBI [ɛfbiaj] NM (ABRÉV = **Federal Bureau of Investigation**) FBI

Fco ABRÉV = **franco**

féal, e [feal] (*mpl* **-aux**) [feal, o] [1] ADJ†† loyal, trusty [2] NM,F (*littér, hum*) loyal supporter

fébrifuge [febʀifyʒ] ADJ, NM febrifuge, antipyretic

fébrile [febʀil] ADJ (*lit, fig*) feverish, febrile (*frm*)

fébrilement [febʀilmɑ̃] ADV [*s'activer, attendre*] feverishly

fébrilité [febʀilite] NF feverishness

fécal, e [fekal] (*mpl* **-aux**) [fekal, o] ADJ faecal; **matières ~es** faeces

fèces [fɛs] NFPL faeces

fécond, e [fekɔ̃, ɔ̃d] ADJ [a] (= *non stérile*) [*femelle, fleur*] fertile [b] (= *prolifique*) [*auteur*] prolific [c] (= *fertile*) [*sujet, idée*] fruitful, creative, fertile; (*littér*) [*terre*] fruitful, rich, fecund (*littér*); **journées ~es en mésaventures/événements** days rich in *ou* abounding in mishaps/events

fécondable [fekɔ̃dabl(ə)] ADJ [*ovule*] capable of being fertilized; [*femme, femelle*] capable of becoming pregnant

fécondateur, -trice [fekɔ̃datœʀ, tʀis] ADJ (*littér*) fertilizing

fécondation [fekɔ̃dasjɔ̃] NF [*femme*] impregnation; [*animal*] insemination, fertilization; [*fleur*] pollination, fertilization; **~ in vitro** in vitro fertilization; **~ in vitro et transfert d'embryon** zygote intra-fallopian transfer

féconder [fekɔ̃de] ▸ conjug 1 ◂ VT [+ *femme*] to make pregnant, impregnate; [+ *animal*] to inseminate, fertilize; [+ *fleur*] to pollinate, fertilize; (*littér*) [+ *terre*] to make fruitful; (*littér*) [+ *esprit*] to enrich

fécondité [fekɔ̃dite] NF (*lit*) fertility, fecundity (*littér*); (*fig*) [*terre, sujet, idée*] fruitfulness, richness, fecundity (*littér*); **les pays à forte/faible ~** countries with a high/low fertility rate

fécule [fekyl] NF starch; **~ (de pommes de terre)** potato flour

féculent, e [fekylɑ̃, ɑ̃t] [1] ADJ starchy [2] NM starchy food, starch

FED [ɛfəde] NM (ABRÉV = **Fonds européen de développement**) EDF

fedayin [fedajin] NM (*surtout au pl*) fedayee

fédéral, e [mpl **-aux**] [federal, o] ADJ federal

fédéraliser [federalize] ▸ conjug 1 ◂ VT to federalize

fédéralisme [federalism] NM federalism

fédéraliste [federalist] ADJ, NMF federalist

fédérateur, -trice [federatœʀ, tʀis] [1] ADJ federative [2] NM,F unifier

fédératif, -ive [federatif, iv] ADJ federative

fédération [federasjɔ̃] NF federation; **~ syndicale** trade union; **Fédération syndicale mondiale** World Federation of Trade Unions; **la Fédération de Russie** the Russian Federation

fédéré, e [federe] (*ptp de* **fédérer**) ADJ federate

fédérer [federe] ▸ conjug 6 ◂ VT to federate

fée [fe] NF fairy; (*hum*) **une vraie ~ du logis** a real homebody; **la ~ Carabosse** the wicked fairy → **conte, doigt**

feed-back [fidbak] NM INV feedback

feeder [fidœʀ] NM (*Tech*) feeder

feeling [filiŋ] NM feeling; **faire qch au ~** to do sth intuitively

féerie [fe(e)ʀi] NF [a] (*Ciné, Théât*) extravaganza, spectacular (*incorporating features from pantomime*) [b] (*littér = vision enchanteresse*) **la ~ des soirées d'été/d'un ballet** the enchantment of summer evenings/of a ballet; **la ~ à jamais perdue de l'enfance** the irretrievable fairy-tale world of childhood

féerique [fe(e)ʀik] ADJ magical

feignant, e [fɛɲɑ̃, ɑ̃t] ADJ, NM,F = **fainéant, e**

feindre [fɛ̃dʀ] ▸ conjug 52 ◂ [1] VT (= *simuler*) [+ *enthousiasme, ignorance, innocence*] to feign; **~ la colère** to pretend to be angry, feign anger; **~ d'être/de faire** to pretend to be/do; **il feint de ne pas comprendre** he pretends not to understand; **~ de dormir** to feign sleep, pretend to be asleep [2] VI (*frm*) to dissemble, dissimulate; **inutile de ~ (avec moi)** no use pretending (with me)

feint, e[1] [fɛ̃, fɛ̃t] (*ptp de* **feindre**) ADJ [a] (*émotion, maladie*) feigned, affected; **non ~** [*plaisir, larmes*] genuine [b] (*Archit*) [*arcade, fenêtre, porte*] false

feinte[2] [fɛ̃t] NF [a] (= *manœuvre*) (*gén*) dummy move; (*Ftbl, Rugby*) dummy (*Brit*), fake (*US*); (*Boxe, Escrime*) feint; (*Rugby*) **faire une ~** to dummy (*Brit*), fake (*US*); (*Rugby*) **~ de passe** dummy (*Brit*) *ou* fake (*US*) pass; **~ de corps** dodge [b] (*littér = ruse*) sham (*NonC*), pretence; **agir/parler sans ~** to act/speak without dissimulation

feinter [fɛ̃te] ▸ conjug 1 ◂ [1] VT [a] (*Ftbl, Rugby*) to dummy (*Brit*) *ou* fake (*US*) (one's way past); (*Boxe, Escrime*) to feint at [b]‡ (= *duper*) to trick, fool, take in; **j'ai été feinté** I've been had* *ou* taken in [2] VI (*Escrime*) to feint

feldspath [fɛldspat] NM fel(d)spar

fêlé, e [fele] (*ptp de* **fêler**) [1] ADJ [a] [*assiette, voix*] cracked [b]* (= *fou*) **être ~** [*personne*] to be a bit cracked*; **elle est complètement ~e** she's completely nuts* *ou* cracked*; **il a le cerveau ~** *ou* **la tête ~e** he's cracked* *ou* crackers* [2] NM,F* (= *personne*) crackpot*, nutcase*

fêler [fele] ▸ conjug 1 ◂ [1] VT to crack [2] **se fêler** VPR to crack; **se ~ le bras** to crack a bone in one's arm

▼ **félicitations** [felisitasjɔ̃] NFPL congratulations (**pour** on); **~!** congratulations!; **faire ses ~ à qn pour** to congratulate sb on; (*Scol, Univ*) **avec les ~ du jury** highly commended, summa cum laude

félicité [felisite] NF (*littér, Rel*) bliss (*NonC*)

▼ **féliciter** [felisite] ▸ conjug 1 ◂ [1] VT to congratulate (**qn de** *ou* **sur qch** sb on sth); (*iro*) **je vous félicite!** congratulations!; (*iro*), well done! (*iro*); **eh bien je ne vous félicite pas** you don't get any praise for that [2] **se féliciter** VPR to congratulate o.s. (**de** on), be very glad *ou* pleased (**de** about); **je n'y suis pas allé et je m'en félicite** I didn't go and I'm glad *ou* very pleased I didn't; **il se félicitait d'avoir refusé d'y aller** he was congratulating himself on having refused to go

félidé [felide] NM feline, felid (*SPÉC*); **les ~s** the Felidae (*SPÉC*)

félin, e [felɛ̃, in] [1] ADJ [*race*] feline; [*allure, grâce*] feline, catlike [2] NM feline; **les ~s** felines, the cat family; **les grands ~s** the big cats

fellah [fela] NM fellah

fellation [felasjɔ̃] NF fellatio(n)

fellinien, -ienne [felinjɛ̃, jɛn] ADJ [*fantaisie*] Fellinesque; **des femmes à la silhouette fellinienne** full-bodied *ou* buxom women

félon, -onne [felɔ̃, ɔn] (*frm*) [1] ADJ perfidious (*frm*), disloyal, treacherous [2] NM (*aussi hum*) traitor [3] **félonne** NF (*aussi hum*) traitress

félonie [felɔni] NF (*frm*) (= *caractère*) perfidy (*frm*), disloyalty; (= *acte*) act of treachery, perfidy

felouque [fəluk] NF felucca

fêlure [felyʀ] NF (*lit, fig*) crack; (*affective*) rift

femelle [fəmɛl] [1] ADJ (*Bot, Tech, Zool*) female; **panthère ~** she-panther, female panther; **merle ~** hen-blackbird, female blackbird; **éléphant ~** cow-elephant, female elephant [2] NF (*Zool*) female; (‡ *péj = femme*) female* (*péj*)

féminin, e [feminɛ̃, in] [1] ADJ (*gén, Ling*) feminine; [*hormone, population, sexe*] female; [*silhouette*] womanly; [*mode, magazine, épreuve sportive, équipe*] women's; **elle est peu ~e** she's not very feminine; **elle est déjà très ~e** she's already quite a young woman; **il a des traits assez ~s** he has rather feminine features; **premier rôle ~** female lead; **ses conquêtes ~es** his conquests → **éternel, intuition, rime** etc [2] NM (*Ling*) feminine; **au ~** in the feminine; **ce mot est du ~** this word is feminine

féminisant, e [feminizɑ̃, ɑ̃t] ADJ feminizing

féminisation [feminizasjɔ̃] NF feminization

féminiser [feminize] ▸ conjug 1 ◂ [1] VT (*Bio*) to feminize; (*Ling*) to make feminine, put in the feminine; (= *rendre efféminé*) to make effeminate; **~ une profession** to increase the number of women in a profession; **profession féminisée** largely female profession; **c'est un secteur féminisé à 80%** women make up 80% of the workforce in this sector [2] **se féminiser** VPR (*Bio*) to feminize; (= *devenir efféminé*) to become effeminate; **la profession se féminise** an increasing number of women are entering the profession

féminisme [feminism] NM (*Sociol*) feminism

féministe [feminist] ADJ, NMF feminist

féminité [feminite] NF femininity

femme [fam] [1] NF [a] (= *individu*) woman; (= *espèce*) **la ~** woman; **une jeune ~** a young woman; **c'est la ~ de sa vie** she is his one true love *ou* the love of his life; **elle n'est pas à faire ceci** she's not the type (of woman) to do that; **ce que ~ veut ...** what a woman wants ...; **les ~s et les enfants d'abord!** women and children first!; **une ~-enfant** a childlike woman ▪ (*PROV*) **souvent ~ varie (bien fol est qui**

s'y fie) woman is fickle → **bon¹, bout, chercher, droit** *etc*
⟦**b**⟧ (= *épouse*) wife; **prendre qn pour ~†** to take sb as one's wife†; **chercher/prendre ~†** to seek/take a wife†
⟦**c**⟧ (*profession*) **~ médecin** woman *ou* lady doctor; **professeur ~** woman *ou* female teacher
⟦**d**⟧ (*Jur*) **la ~ Dupuis** Mrs Dupuis
⟦**2**⟧ ADJ INV **être/devenir ~** (*nubile*) to have reached *ou* attained/reach *ou* attain womanhood; (*n'être plus vierge*) to be/become a woman; **être très ~** (*féminine*) to be very much a woman, be very womanly
⟦**3**⟧ COMP ► **femme d'affaires** businesswoman ► **femme auteur** authoress ► **femme battue** battered woman ► **femme de chambre** (*dans un hôtel*) chambermaid; (*de qn*) (lady's) maid ► **femme de charge†** housekeeper ► **femme entretenue** († *péj*) kept woman ► **femme d'esprit** woman of wit and learning ► **femme fatale** femme fatale ► **la femme au foyer** the housewife, the woman (who stays) at home ► **femme galante†** loose woman, courtesan ► **femme d'intérieur** housewife; **être ~ d'intérieur** to take pride in one's home, be houseproud (*Brit*) ► **femme de lettres** woman of letters ► **femme de mauvaise vie†** loose woman ► **femme de ménage** domestic help, cleaning lady ► **femme du monde** society woman ► **femme de service** (*nettoyage*) cleaner; (*cantine*) dinner lady ► **femme soldat** woman soldier ► **femme de tête** strong-minded intellectual woman → **vertu**

femmelette [famlɛt] NF (*péj*) (= *homme*) weakling; (= *femme*) frail female

femme-objet (*pl* **femmes-objets**) [famɔbʒɛ] NF (woman as a) sex object; **elle refuse d'être une ~** she refuses to be treated as a sex object

fémoral, e (*mpl* **-aux**) [femɔral, o] ADJ femoral

fémur [femyʀ] NM thighbone, femur (*SPÉC*) → **col**

FEN [fɛn] NF (ABRÉV = **Fédération de l'éducation nationale**) *confederation of teachers' unions*

fenaison [fənɛzɔ̃] NF (= *époque*) haymaking time; (= *action*) haymaking

fendant [fɑ̃dɑ̃] NM Swiss white wine (*from the Valais region*)

fendard¹: [fɑ̃daʀ] NM (pair of) trousers, (pair of) pants (*US*)

fendard², e: [fɑ̃daʀ, aʀd] ADJ hilarious; **ce film est vraiment ~** that film's a real scream*

fendart: [fɑ̃daʀ] NM = **fendard¹**

fendillé, e [fɑ̃dije] (*ptp de* **fendiller**) ADJ [*glace, plâtre, porcelaine, terre, vernis*] crazed; [*bois*] sprung; [*lèvres, peau*] chapped

fendillement [fɑ̃dijmɑ̃] NM [*glace, plâtre, porcelaine, terre, vernis*] crazing; [*bois*] springing; [*lèvres, peau*] chapping

fendiller [fɑ̃dije] ▸ conjug 1 ◂ ⟦**1**⟧ VT [+ *glace, plâtre, porcelaine, terre, vernis*] to craze; [+ *bois*] to spring; [+ *lèvres, peau*] to chap ⟦**2**⟧ **se fendiller** VPR [*glace, plâtre, porcelaine, terre, vernis*] to craze (over); [*bois*] to spring; [*lèvres, peau*] to chap

fendoir [fɑ̃dwaʀ] NM chopper, cleaver

fendre [fɑ̃dʀ] ▸ conjug 41 ◂ ⟦**1**⟧ VT ⟦**a**⟧ [+ *personne*] (= *couper en deux*) [+ *bûche, ardoise*] to split; [+ *tissu*] to slit, slash; **~ du bois** to chop wood; **il lui a fendu le crâne** he split his skull open ⟦**b**⟧ [*éléments, cataclysme, accident*] [+ *rochers*] to cleave; [+ *mur, plâtre, meuble*] to crack; **cette chute lui a fendu le crâne** the fall cracked *ou* split his skull open → **geler** ⟦**c**⟧ (= *pénétrer*) to cut *ou* slice through, cleave through (*littér*); **~ les flots/l'air** to cleave through (*littér*) the waves/air; **le soc fend la terre** the ploughshare cuts through the earth; **~ la foule** to push *ou* cleave (*littér*) one's way through the crowd ⟦**d**⟧ (*Habillement*) [+ *jupe*] to put a slit in; [+

veste] to put a vent in; [+ *manche*] to put a slash in ⟦**e**⟧ (*loc*) **ce récit me fend le cœur** *ou* **l'âme** this story breaks my heart *ou* makes my heart bleed; **spectacle à vous ~ le cœur** heartrending *ou* heartbreaking sight; **soupirs à ~ l'âme** heartrending *ou* heartbreaking sighs ⟦**2**⟧ **se fendre** VPR ⟦**a**⟧ (= *se fissurer*) to crack ⟦**b**⟧ [+ *partie du corps*] **il s'est fendu le crâne** he has cracked his skull open; **se ~ la lèvre** to cut one's lip; **se ~ la pipe:** *ou* **la pêche:** *ou* **la poire:** *ou* **la gueule::** (= *rire*) to laugh one's head off, split one's sides*; (= *s'amuser*) to have a good laugh ⟦**c**⟧ (*Escrime*) to lunge ⟦**d**⟧ **:** **se ~ de** [+ *somme*] to shell out*; [+ *bouteille, cadeau*] to lash out on*; **il ne s'est pas fendu !** he didn't exactly break himself!*

fendu, e [fɑ̃dy] (*ptp de* **fendre**) ADJ ⟦**a**⟧ [*crâne*] cracked; [*lèvre*] cut; [*manche*] slashed; [*veste*] with a vent; [*jupe*] slit; **la bouche ~e jusqu'aux oreilles** grinning from ear to ear ⟦**b**⟧* (= *hilare*) **j'étais ~** I fell about (laughing)*, I cracked up*

fenestrage [fənɛstʀaʒ] NM = **fenêtrage**

fenestration [fənɛstʀasjɔ̃] NF (*Archit, Méd*) fenestration

fenêtrage [fənɛtʀaʒ] NM (*Archit*) windows, fenestration (*SPÉC*)

fenêtre [f(ə)nɛtʀ] NF ⟦**a**⟧ (*Archit*) window; **regarder/sauter par la ~** to look out of *ou* through/jump out of the window; **se mettre à la ~** (*se diriger vers*) to go to the window; (*s'asseoir*) to sit by the window; **coin ~** window seat, seat by the window; **~ à guillotine** sash window; **~ à battants** *ou* **meneaux** casement/mullioned window; **~ à croisillons** lattice window; **~ en saillie** bow window, bay window; **~ à tabatière** skylight; (*Ciné*) **~ d'observation** port, (projectionist's) window; (*fig*) **c'est une ~ ouverte sur ...** it's a window on ... → **faux** ⟦**b**⟧ [*enveloppe*] window; [*formulaire*] space ⟦**c**⟧ (*Ordin*) window; **~ de dialogue** dialogue box; **~ d'aide/d'édition** help/text-editing window ⟦**d**⟧ (*Anat: dans l'oreille*) fenestra ⟦**e**⟧ (*Espace*) **~ de lancement** launch window; (*Naut*) **~ météo** weather window

fenêtrer [fənɛtʀe] ▸ conjug 1 ◂ VT (*Archit*) to make windows in

fenil [fəni(l)] NM hayloft

fennec [fenɛk] NM fennec

fenouil [fənuj] NM fennel

fente [fɑ̃t] NF ⟦**a**⟧ [*mur, terre, rocher*] crack, fissure, cleft; [*bois*] crack, split ⟦**b**⟧ [*volet, palissade*] slit; [*boîte à lettres*] slot, opening; [*tirelire*] slit, slot; [*tête d'une vis*] groove, slot; [*jupe*] slit; [*veste*] vent; [*pèlerine, cape*] slit, armhole; (*Anat*) fissure ⟦**c**⟧ (*Escrime*) lunge

fenugrec [fənygʀɛk] NM fenugreek

féodal, e (*mpl* **-aux**) [feɔdal, o] ⟦**1**⟧ ADJ feudal ⟦**2**⟧ NM feudal lord

féodaliser [feɔdalize] ▸ conjug 1 ◂ VT to feudalize

féodalisme [feɔdalism] NM feudalism

féodalité [feɔdalite] NF (*Hist*) feudal system, feudalism

fer [fɛʀ] ⟦**1**⟧ NM ⟦**a**⟧ (= *métal*) iron; **de ~** (*lit, fig*) iron (*épith*); **volonté de ~** will of iron, iron will; **croire qch dur comme ~** to believe sth firmly, be absolutely convinced of sth → **âge, chemin, fil** *etc* ⟦**b**⟧ (= *barre, poutre*) iron girder; **~ en T/U** T/U girder ⟦**c**⟧ (= *embout*) [*cheval*] shoe; [*chaussure*] steel tip; [*club de golf*] iron; [*flèche, lance*] head, point; [*rabot*] blade, iron; **mettre un ~ à un cheval** to shoe a horse; **avoir plusieurs ~s au feu** to have several irons in the fire → **plaie, quatre** ⟦**d**⟧ (= *outil*) (*pour repasser*) iron; [*relieur*] blocking stamp; **donner un coup de ~ à qch** to run the iron over sth, give sth an iron; (*plus

soigneusement*) to press sth ⟦**e**⟧ (*fig = arme, Escrime*) **engager/croiser le ~** to engage/cross swords; **par le ~ et par le feu** by fire and sword ⟦**f**⟧ (†† = *chaînes*) **~s** chains, fetters, irons; **mettre un prisonnier aux ~s** to clap a prisoner in irons; (*littér*) **être dans les ~s** to be in chains *ou* irons ⟦**g**⟧ (†† *Méd*) **~s** forceps
⟦**2**⟧ COMP ► **fer à béton** (*Constr*) steel reinforcement bar ► **fer à cheval** (*lit, fig*) horseshoe; **en ~ à cheval** (*table, bâtiment*) horseshoe-shaped, U-shaped; **disposer qch en ~ à cheval** to arrange sth in a U-shape ► **fer doux** soft iron ► **fer forgé** wrought iron ► **fer à friser** curling tongs ► **fer à gaufrer** goffering iron ► **fer de lance** (*fig*) spearhead ► **fer à repasser** (*électrique*) (electric) iron; (*ancien modèle*) (flat) iron; (*: pour cartes bancaires*) credit-card machine → **nager** ► **fer rouge** brand, branding iron; **marquer au ~ rouge** to brand ► **fer à souder** soldering iron ► **fer à vapeur** steam iron

féra [feʀa] NF (*Zool*) féra, ferra

fer-blanc (*pl* **fers-blancs**) [fɛʀblɑ̃] NM tin(plate); **une boîte en** *ou* **de ~** a (tin) can

ferblanterie [fɛʀblɑ̃tʀi] NF (= *métier*) tinplate making; (= *produit*) tinware; (= *commerce*) tin trade; (= *boutique*) ironmonger's (shop) (*Brit*), hardware store (*US*)

ferblantier [fɛʀblɑ̃tje] NM (= *fabricant*) tinsmith; (= *vendeur*) ironmonger (*Brit*), hardware dealer (*US*); **ouvrier ~** tinplate worker

féria [feʀja] NF feria (*Spanish and Southern French festival*)

férié, e [feʀje] ADJ **jour ~** public holiday, official holiday; **le lundi suivant est ~** the following Monday is a holiday

férir [feʀiʀ] ♦ **sans coup férir** LOC ADV without meeting *ou* encountering any opposition

ferler [fɛʀle] ▸ conjug 1 ◂ VT (*Naut*) to furl

fermage [fɛʀmaʒ] NM (= *procédé*) tenant farming; (= *loyer*) (farm) rent

ferme¹ [fɛʀm] ⟦**1**⟧ ADJ ⟦**a**⟧ [*chair, fruit*] firm; [*sol*] firm, solid; **cette viande est un peu ~** this meat is a bit tough; **pour des cuisses plus ~s** to tone up the thigh muscles → **terre** ⟦**b**⟧ (= *assuré*) [*main, écriture*] steady, firm; [*voix*] firm; [*style, exécution, trait*] confident, assured; [*marché, cours*] steady; **être ~ sur ses jambes** to be steady on one's legs *ou* feet; **marcher d'un pas ~** to walk with a firm stride *ou* step; **rester ~ dans l'adversité** to remain steadfast in adversity ⟦**c**⟧ (= *déterminé*) [*personne, ton*] firm; [*décision, résolution, prise de position*] firm, definite; **avec la ~ intention de faire qch** with the firm intention of doing sth ⟦**d**⟧ (*Comm: = irrévocable*) [*achat, vente*] firm; [*acheteur, vendeur*] firm, definite; (*Bourse*) **prix ~s et définitifs** firm prices; **ces prix sont ~s** these prices are binding; **« prix : 200 000 F ~ »** "price: 200 000 francs (not negotiable)"
⟦**2**⟧ ADV ⟦**a**⟧* (*intensif*) [*travailler, cogner*] hard; **boire ~** to drink hard, be a hard drinker; **discuter ~** to discuss vigorously; **s'ennuyer ~** to be bored stiff* → **tenir** ⟦**b**⟧ (*Comm*) [*acheter, vendre*] definitely ⟦**c**⟧ (*Jur*) **condamné à sept ans (de prison) ~** sentenced to seven years imprisonment without remission

ferme² [fɛʀm] NF ⟦**a**⟧ (= *domaine*) farm; (= *habitation*) farmhouse; **~ collective** collective farm; **~ d'élevage** cattle(-breeding) farm; **~ marine** fish farm → **cour, fille, valet** ⟦**b**⟧ (*Jur: = contrat*) farm lease; (*Hist: = perception*) farming (of taxes); **donner à ~** [+ *terres*] to let, farm out; **prendre à ~** [+ *terres*] to farm (on lease)

ferme³ [fɛʀm] NF (*Constr*) roof timbers, truss

ferme⁴ [fɛʀm] EXCL **la ~ !:** shut up!:, shut your mouth!:, pipe down!* → **fermer**

fermé, e [fɛʀme] (*ptp de* **fermer**) ADJ [a] [*porte, magasin, valise*] shut, closed; [*col, route*] closed; [*espace*] closed-in; [*voiture*] locked; [*angle*] narrow; [*voyelle*] close(d), high; [*syllabe*] closed; [*série, ensemble*] closed; [*robinet*] off (*attrib*); [*chemise*] fastened (*attrib*), done up (*attrib*); **la porte est ~e à clé** the door is locked; **la station est ~e au public** the station is closed to the public; (*Ftbl*) **pratiquer un jeu ~** to play a tight game [b] [*milieu, club*] exclusive, select; **cette carrière lui est ~e** this career is not open to him *ou* is closed to him; **économie ~e** closed economy [c] [*visage, air*] inscrutable, impenetrable; [*caractère, personne*] uncommunicative [d] **être ~ à** [+ *sentiment, qualité*] to be impervious to *ou* untouched by *ou* closed to; [+ *science, art*] to have no interest in

fermement [fɛʀməmɑ̃] ADV (*lit, fig*) firmly

ferment [fɛʀmɑ̃] NM (= *micro-organisme*) ferment, fermenting agent, leaven (*NonC*); (*fig*) ferment (*NonC*); **~ lactique** starter culture

fermentation [fɛʀmɑ̃tasjɔ̃] NF fermentation; (*fig*) **devant la ~ des esprits** with feelings running so high; **en ~** (*lit*) fermenting; (*fig*) in a ferment

fermenté, e [fɛʀmɑ̃te] (*ptp de* **fermenter**) ADJ [*aliment, boisson*] fermented; **bière non ~e** unfermented beer; **cidre très peu ~** barely fermented cider

fermenter [fɛʀmɑ̃te] ▶ conjug 1 ◀ VI (*lit*) to ferment, work; (*fig littér*) [*esprits*] to be in a ferment; **faire ~** (*lit*) to ferment

fermer [fɛʀme] ▶ conjug 1 ◀ [1] VT [a] [+ *porte, fenêtre, tiroir, paquet*] to close, shut; [+ *rideaux*] to draw, close; [+ *store*] to pull down, close; [+ *magasin, café, musée*] (*le soir*) to shut, close; (*pour cause de vacances*) to shut (up), close; **~ à clé** [+ *porte*] to lock; [+ *chambre*] to lock (up); **~ au verrou** to bolt; **il ferma violemment la porte** he slammed the door (shut); **~ (la porte) à double tour** to double-lock the door; **~ la porte au nez de qn** to shut *ou* slam the door in sb's face; (*fig*) **~ sa porte** *ou* **sa maison à qn** to close one's door to sb; **maintenant, toutes les portes lui sont fermées** all doors are closed to him now; **~ la porte aux abus** to close the door to abuses; **va ~** go and close *ou* shut the door; **on ferme!** (it's) closing time!, we're closing!; **on ferme en juillet** we close in July, we're closed *ou* shut in July; **on ferme un jour par semaine** we close *ou* shut one day a week, we are closed *ou* shut one day a week → **parenthèse**
[b] [+ *yeux, bouche, paupières*] to close, shut; **la ferme!** **ferme-la*** shut *ou* belt up*; **je n'ai pas fermé l'œil de la nuit** I didn't get a wink of sleep *ou* I didn't sleep a wink all night; (*fig*) **~ les yeux** to turn a blind eye, look the other way; **~ les yeux sur** [+ *misère, scandale*] to close *ou* shut one's eyes to; [+ *abus, fraude, défaut*] to turn a blind eye to; **~ son cœur à la pitié** to close one's heart to pity
[c] [+ *canif, livre, éventail*] to close, shut; [+ *lettre*] to close; [+ *parapluie*] to close, shut; [+ *main, poing*] to close; [+ *manteau, gilet*] to do up, fasten
[d] (= *boucher*) [+ *chemin, passage*] to block, bar; [+ *accès*] to shut off, close off; **des montagnes fermaient l'horizon** mountains blocked off the horizon; **le champ était fermé par une haie** the field had a hedge round it; (*Sport*) **~ le jeu** to tighten up play
[e] (= *interdire l'accès de*) [+ *frontière, col, route*] to close; [+ *aéroport*] to close (down), shut (down)
[f] (= *cesser l'exploitation de*) [+ *magasin, restaurant, école*] to close (down), shut (down); **~ boutique** to close down, shut up shop; **obliger qn à ~ (boutique)** to put sb out of business; **ils ont dû ~ pour raisons financières** they had to close down *ou* cease trading because of financial difficulties
[g] (= *arrêter*) [+ *liste, souscription, compte en banque, débat*] to close; **~ la marche** to bring

up the rear; **~ le cortège** to bring up the rear of the procession
[h] [+ *gaz, électricité, radio*] to turn off, switch off; [+ *eau, robinet*] to turn off; [+ *lumière*] to turn off *ou* out, switch off; [+ *vanne*] to close
[2] VI [a] [*fenêtre, porte, boîte*] to close, shut; **cette porte/boîte ferme mal** this door/box doesn't close *ou* shut properly; **ce robinet ferme mal** this tap doesn't turn off properly [b] [*magasin*] (*le soir*) to close, shut; (*définitivement, pour les vacances*) to close down, shut down; **ça ferme à 7 heures** they close *ou* shut at 7 o'clock
[3] **se fermer** VPR [a] [*porte, fenêtre, livre*] to close, shut; [*fleur, coquillage*] to close (up); [*blessure*] to close (up); [*paupières, yeux*] to close, shut; **ça se ferme par devant** it does up *ou* fastens at the front; **l'avenir se fermait devant lui** the future was closing before him; **quand on essaie de lui expliquer ça, son esprit se ferme** when you try to explain it to him he closes his mind to it; **son cœur se fermait à la sœur de cette misère** he refused to be moved *ou* touched by the sight of this poverty; **son visage se ferma** his face became expressionless; **pays qui se ferme aux produits étrangers** country which closes its markets to foreign products
[b] [*personne*] **se ~ à la pitié/l'amour** to close one's heart *ou* mind to pity/love; **il se ferme tout de suite** he just clams up* *ou* closes up

fermeté [fɛʀmte] NF [a] [*chair, fruit, sol*] firmness [b] (= *assurance*) [*main, écriture*] steadiness, firmness; [*voix*] firmness; [*style, exécution, trait*] confidence, assurance [c] (= *détermination*) firmness; **avec ~** firmly, resolutely [d] (= *autorité*) firmness; **il manque de ~ avec son fils** he's not firm enough with his son; **elle lui a parlé avec beaucoup de ~** she spoke to him very firmly [e] (*Bourse*) firmness

fermette [fɛʀmɛt] NF (small) farmhouse

fermeture [fɛʀmətyʀ] NF [a] [*porte*] **la ~ est automatique** the doors close automatically; **« ne pas gêner la ~ des portes »** "do not obstruct the doors (when closing)" [b] [*magasin, musée, aéroport, route*] closing; **les jours de ~ du magasin** the days when the shop is closed; **~ annuelle** (*gén*) annual closure; (*sur la devanture*) closed for the holidays; **à (l'heure de) la ~** at closing time; **« ~ pour (cause de) travaux »** "closed for repairs (ou redecoration *ou* refurbishment etc)"; (*Comm*) **faire la ~** to close; (*clients d'un bar*) **on a fait la ~** we stayed until closing time; **la ~ de la chasse** the end of the hunting season [c] (= *cessation d'activité*) [*magasin, restaurant, école*] closing down, closure; **~ définitive** permanent closure [d] (*Comptab*) closing [e] (= *mécanisme*) [*coffre-fort*] catch, latch; [*vêtement*] fastener, fastening; [*sac*] fastener, catch, clasp; **~ à glissière ◊ ~ éclair**® zip (fastener) (*Brit*), zipper (*US*)

fermier, -ière [fɛʀmje, jɛʀ] [1] ADJ **poulet ~** ≈ free-range chicken, **~ farm** chicken; **beurre ~** dairy butter; **fromage ~** farmhouse cheese [2] NM [a] (= *cultivateur*) (*gén*) farmer; (= *locataire*) tenant farmer [b] (*Hist*) **~ général** farmer general [3] **fermière** NF farmer's wife; (*indépendante*) (woman) farmer

fermium [fɛʀmjɔm] NM fermium

fermoir [fɛʀmwaʀ] NM [*livre, collier, sac*] clasp

féroce [feʀɔs] ADJ [*animal, regard, personne*] ferocious, fierce; [*répression, critique*] fierce, savage; [*envie*] savage, raging; [*appétit*] ferocious, ravenous; [*concurrence*] fierce, harsh, cutthroat; **une satire ~ de la société** a ferocious social satire; **avec une joie ~** with savage joy → **bête**

férocement [feʀɔsmɑ̃] ADV ferociously; **un marché ~ compétitif** a ferociously competitive market

férocité [feʀɔsite] NF [*animal, regard, personne*] ferocity, ferociousness, fierceness; [*répression, critique*] fierceness, savagery; [*satire, appétit*] ferociousness; [*concurrence*] fierceness

Féroé [feʀɔe] N **les îles ~** the Fa(e)roe Islands

ferrage [feʀaʒ] NM [*cheval*] shoeing

ferraillage [feʀajaʒ] NM (*Constr*) (iron) framework

ferraille [feʀaj] NF [a] (= *déchets de fer*) scrap (iron), old iron; **tas de ~** scrap heap; **bruit de ~** clanking *ou* rattling noise; **mettre une voiture à la ~** to scrap a car, send a car for scrap; **bon à mettre à la ~** ≈ good *ou* fit for the scrap heap; **la voiture n'était plus qu'un amas de ~** the car was no more than a heap of twisted metal [b]* (= *monnaie*) small *ou* loose change

ferrailler [feʀaje] ▶ conjug 1 ◀ VI (*lit*) to clash swords; **~ contre** [+ *injustice, préjugés*] to fight against; **~ avec qn** (= *se disputer*) to cross swords with sb

ferrailleur [feʀajœʀ] NM [a] (= *marchand de ferraille*) scrap (metal) merchant [b] († *péj*) swashbuckler

Ferrare [feʀaʀ] NF Ferrara

ferrate [feʀat] NM ferrate

ferré, e [feʀe] (*ptp de* **ferrer**) ADJ [a] [*canne, bâton*] steel-tipped; [*chaussure*] hobnailed; [*lacet*] tagged; [*cheval*] shod; [*roue*] steel-rimmed; **à bout ~** [*canne, bâton*] with a steel *ou* metal tip, steel-tipped → **voie** [b]* (= *calé*) clued up* (**en, sur** about); **être ~ sur un sujet** to be well up* in a subject *ou* hot* at a subject, know a subject inside out

ferrement [feʀmɑ̃] NM [a] (= *garniture*) iron fitment [b] = **ferrage**

ferrer [feʀe] ▶ conjug 1 ◀ VT [a] [+ *cheval*] to shoe; [+ *roue*] to rim with steel; [+ *chaussure*] to nail; [+ *lacet*] to tag; [+ *bâton*] to tip, fit a metal tip to; [+ *porte*] to fit with iron corners [b] [+ *poisson*] to strike

ferret [feʀe] NM [a] [*lacet*] (metal) tag [b] (*Minér*) **~ d'Espagne** red haematite

ferreux, -euse [feʀø, øz] ADJ ferrous

ferrique [feʀik] ADJ ferric

ferrite [feʀit] NF ferrite

ferro- [feʀo] PRÉF (*Chim, Phys*) ferro-

ferro-alliage (*pl* **ferro-alliages**) [feʀoaljaʒ] NM iron alloy

ferronnerie [feʀɔnʀi] NF (= *atelier*) ironworks; (= *métier*) ironwork; (= *objets*) ironwork, ironware; **faire de la ~ d'art** to be a craftsman in wrought iron; **grille en ~** wrought-iron gate; **c'est un beau travail de ~** that's a fine piece of wrought iron work

ferronnier [feʀɔnje] NM (= *artisan*) craftsman in (wrought) iron; (= *commerçant*) ironware merchant; **~ d'art** craftsman in wrought iron

ferroutage [feʀutaʒ] NM (*Rail*) piggyback

ferrouter [feʀute] ▶ conjug 1 ◀ VT (*Rail*) to piggyback

ferroviaire [feʀɔvjɛʀ] ADJ [*réseau, trafic*] railway (*épith*) (*Brit*), railroad (*épith*) (*US*), rail (*épith*); [*transport*] rail (*épith*)

ferrugineux, -euse [feʀyʒinø, øz] ADJ [*roche*] ferruginous, iron-bearing; [*eau, source*] chalybeate, iron-bearing

ferrure [feʀyʀ] NF [a] (= *charnière*) (ornamental) hinge; [*porte*] **~s** (door) fittings [b] [*cheval*] shoeing

ferry (*pl* **ferries**) [feʀi] NM ABRÉV = **ferry-boat**

ferry-boat (*pl* **ferry-boats**) [feʀibot] NM [*voitures*] (car) ferry; [*trains*] (train) ferry

fertile [fɛʀtil] ADJ [*sol, région*] fertile, fruitful, productive; [*esprit, imagination*] fertile; **affaire ~ en rebondissements** affair which triggers off *ou* which spawns a whole series of new developments; **journée ~ en événements/en émotions** eventful/emotion-packed day

fertilisable [fɛʀtilizabl] ADJ fertilizable

fertilisant, e [fɛʀtilizɑ̃, ɑ̃t] ADJ fertilizing

fertilisation [fɛʀtilizasjɔ̃] NF fertilization
fertiliser [fɛʀtilize] ▸ conjug 1 ◂ VT to fertilize
fertilité [fɛʀtilite] NF (lit, fig) fertility
féru, e [feʀy] ADJ (frm) **être ~ de** to be very interested in ou keen on (Brit)
férule [feʀyl] NF (Hist Scol) ferula; **être sous la ~ de qn** (fig) to be under sb's (firm ou iron) rule
fervent, e [fɛʀvɑ̃, ɑ̃t] 1 ADJ fervent, ardent 2 NM,F devotee; **~ de musique** music lover, devotee of music
ferveur [fɛʀvœʀ] NF fervour (Brit), fervor (US), ardour (Brit), ardor (US); **avec ~** fervently, ardently
fesse [fɛs] NF a (Anat) buttock; **les ~s** the buttocks, the bottom, the backside*; **coup de pied aux ~s** kick up the backside* ou in the pants*; **gare à tes ~s** watch out or you'll get spanked; **le bébé a les ~s rouges** the baby's got a bit of nappy (Brit) ou diaper (US) rash; **on a les flics aux ~s** the cops are on our tail*; **où je pose mes ~s?** where can I park myself?* → **pousser, serrer** b (= sexe) **il y a de la ~ dans ce film** there's a lot of bare flesh ou there are a lot of tits and bums‡ in that film; **magazine de ~s** girlie ou porn magazine*; **histoire de ~s** dirty story
fessée [fese] NF spanking, smack on the bottom; **je vais te donner une ~** I'm going to smack your bottom
fesse-mathieu†† (pl **fesse-mathieux**) [fesmatjø] NM skinflint
fesser [fese] ▸ conjug 1 ◂ VT to give a spanking to, spank
fessier, -ière [fesje, jɛʀ] 1 ADJ [muscles] buttock (épith), gluteal (SPÉC); [poche] buttock 2 NM (Anat) gluteus (SPÉC); ‡ behind, backside*, ass‡ (US)
fessu, e* [fesy] ADJ with a big bottom (attrib), big-bottomed
festif, -ive [fɛstif, iv] ADJ festive
festin [fɛstɛ̃] NM feast; **c'était un vrai ~** it was a real feast
festival (pl **festivals**) [fɛstival] NM (Mus, Théât) festival; **ce fut un vrai ~ (de talents)!** what a brilliant display (of talent) it was!
festivalier, -ière [fɛstivalje, jɛʀ] NM,F festival-goer
festivités [fɛstivite] NFPL (gén) festivities; (* = repas joyeux) festivities, merrymaking; **les ~ du couronnement** the coronation festivities ou celebrations
festoiement [fɛstwamɑ̃] NM feasting
feston [fɛstɔ̃] NM (= guirlande, Archit) festoon; (Couture) scallop; **à ~** scalloped → **point²**
festonner [fɛstɔne] ▸ conjug 1 ◂ VT [+ façade] to festoon; [+ robe] to scallop
festoyer [fɛstwaje] ▸ conjug 8 ◂ VI to feast
feta [feta] NF feta (cheese)
fêtard, e* [fɛtaʀ, aʀd] NM,F (péj) reveller; **réveillé par une bande de ~s** woken up by a band of merrymakers ou revellers
fête [fɛt] 1 NF a (= commémoration) (religieuse) feast; (civile) holiday; **la Toussaint est la ~ de tous les saints** All Saints' Day is the feast of all the saints; **le 11 novembre est la ~ de la Victoire** November 11th is the day we celebrate the Victory (in the First World War); **Noël est la ~ des enfants** Christmas is for children
b (= jour du prénom) name day, saint's day; **la ~ de la Saint-Jean** Saint John's day; **souhaiter sa ou bonne ~ à qn** to wish sb a happy name day
c (= congé) holiday; **les ~s (de fin d'année)** the (Christmas and New Year) celebrations ou holidays; **demain c'est ~** tomorrow is a holiday
d (= foire) fair; (= kermesse) fête, fair; (= exposition, salon) festival, show; **~ paroissiale/ communale** parish/local fête ou fair; **~ de la**

bière/du jambon beer/ham festival; **~ de l'aviation** air show; **~ de la moisson** harvest festival; **~ de la vendange** festival of the grape harvest; **c'est la ~ au village** the fair is on in the village; **la ~ de la ville a lieu le premier dimanche de mai** the town festival takes place on the first Sunday in May → **comité, jour** etc
e (= réception) party; **donner une ~** to give ou throw a party; **faire une ~** to have (a birthday etc) party; **les ~s en l'honneur d'un souverain étranger** the celebrations in honour of a foreign monarch; (Art) **~s galantes** scenes of gallantry, fêtes galantes
f (= allégresse collective) **la ~** celebration; **c'est la ~!** everyone's celebrating!, everyone's in a festive mood!; **c'est la ~ chez nos voisins** our neighbours are celebrating; **toute la ville était en ~** the whole town was celebrating; **la foule en ~** the festive crowd; **air/atmosphère de ~** festive air/atmosphere
g (loc) **hier il était à la ~** he had a field day yesterday, it was his day yesterday; **je n'étais pas à la ~** it was no picnic (for me)*, I was feeling pretty uncomfortable; **il n'avait jamais été à pareille ~** he'd never had such a fine time, he was having the time of his life; **être de la ~** to be one of the party; **ça va être ta ~‡** you've got it coming to you*, you're going to get it in the neck; **faire sa ~ à qn‡** to bash sb up‡; **faire la ~*** to live it up*, have a wild time; **faire ~ à qn** to give sb a warm welcome ou reception; **le chien fit ~ à son maître** the dog made a fuss of its master; **elle se faisait une ~ d'y aller/de cette rencontre** she was really looking forward to going/to this meeting; **ce n'est pas tous les jours ~** it's not everyday that we have an excuse to celebrate
2 COMP ▸ **fête carillonnée** great feast day ▸ **fête de charité** charity bazaar ou fair ▸ **fête de famille** family celebration ▸ **fête fixe** fixed festival ▸ **fête foraine** fun fair ▸ **la fête du Grand Pardon** the Day of Atonement ▸ **fête légale** public holiday ▸ **la fête des Mères** Mother's Day, Mothering Sunday (Brit) ▸ **fête mobile** movable feast ▸ **la fête des Morts** All Souls' Day ▸ **fête nationale** (gén) national holiday; (en France) Bastille Day; (aux États-Unis) Independence Day; (au Canada) Confederation Day; (en Irlande) St Patrick's Day ▸ **la fête des Pères** Father's Day ▸ **la fête des Rois** Twelfth Night ▸ **la fête du travail** Labour Day ▸ **fête de village** village fête

┌─ **FÊTES LÉGALES** ─┐

Holidays to which employees are entitled in addition to their paid leave in France are as follows:
Religious holidays: *Christmas Day, New Year's Day, Easter Monday, Ascension Day, Pentecost, Assumption (15th August) and All Saints' Day (1st November).*
Other holidays: *1st May ("la fête du travail"), 8th May (commemorating the end of the Second World War), 14th July (Bastille Day) and 11th November (Armistice Day).*
When a holiday falls on a Tuesday or a Thursday, many people take an extra day off to fill in the gap before or after the weekend. Doing this is called "faire le pont".

Fête-Dieu (pl **Fêtes-Dieu**) [fɛtdjø] NF **la ~** Corpus Christi
fêter [fɛte] ▸ conjug 1 ◂ VT [+ anniversaire, victoire] to celebrate; [+ personne] to fête; **il faut ~ cela!** this calls for a celebration!
fétiche [fetiʃ] NM (lit) fetish; (fig = mascotte) mascot; **son acteur ~** his favourite actor; **film ~** cult film
fétichisme [fetiʃism] NM fetishism
fétichiste [fetiʃist] ADJ, NMF fetishist
fétide [fetid] ADJ fetid
fétidité [fetidite] NF fetidness

fétu [fety] NM **~ (de paille)** wisp of straw; **emporté comme un ~ (de paille)** [avion, pont] swept away as if it were weightless; [personne] swept along helplessly
fétuque [fetyk] NF ou M fescue (grass)

▾**feu¹** [fø]

| 1 NOM MASCULIN | 3 COMPOSÉS |
| 2 ADJECTIF INVARIABLE | |

1 NOM MASCULIN
a = source de chaleur fire; **~ de bois/tourbe** wood/peat fire; **allumer/faire un ~** to light/ make a fire; **faire du ~** to have ou make a fire; **jeter qch au ~** to throw sth on the fire; **un ~ d'enfer brûlait dans la cheminée** a fire blazed brightly ou a hot fire blazed in the fireplace; **sur un ~ de braises** on glowing embers; (pour un fumeur) **avez-vous du ~?** have you got a light?; **donner du ~ à qn** to give sb a light; (Rel) **le ~ éternel** eternal fire (and damnation); (Hist) **l'épreuve du ~** ordeal by fire; **une soirée du ~ de Dieu*** a fantastic evening; **avoir le ~ au derrière** ou **aux fesses*** ou **au cul‡*** (= être pressé) to be in a hell of a hurry*; (sexuellement) to be really horny*; (littér) **faire ~ des quatre fers** [cheval] to run like lightning, make the sparks fly; [personne] to go all out, pull out all the stops*; **faire ~ de tout bois** to use all available means ou all the means at one's disposal; **jeter** ou **lancer ~ et flammes** to breathe fire and fury, be in a towering rage; **pousser les ~x** (Naut) to stoke the boiler; (fig) **il faut pousser les ~x pour réduire les inégalités sociales** we must speed up the process of reducing social inequalities → **coin, long**
b = incendie fire; **mettre le ~ à qch** (lit) to set fire to sth, set sth on fire; (fig) **l'assassinat a mis le ~ au pays** the assassination has plunged the country into chaos ou turmoil; **ça a mis le ~ aux poudres** it sparked things off; **prendre ~** [maison, forêt] to catch fire; (fig) **il prend ~ facilement dans la discussion** he easily gets carried away in arguments; **le ~ a pris dans la grange** fire has broken out in the barn; **au ~!** fire!; **il y a le ~** there's a fire; **il y a le ~ au grenier!** the attic's on fire!; (fig) **il n'y a pas le ~ (au lac)!*** there's no panic!
♦ **à feu et à sang**: **mettre une ville à ~ et à sang** to put a town to fire and sword; **la région est à ~ et à sang** the region is being torn apart ou laid waste by war
♦ **en feu** on fire (attrib); **devant la maison en ~** in front of the burning house; **le piment m'a mis la bouche en ~** the chilli made my mouth burn; **il avait les joues en ~** his cheeks were on fire
c Culin = brûleur burner; (= plaque électrique) burner, ring (Brit); **cuisinière à trois ~x** stove with three burners ou rings (Brit); **faire cuire à ~ doux/vif** (sur brûleur ou plaque) to cook over ou on a low/high heat; (au four) to cook in a low/hot oven; **plat qui va au ~** ou **sur le ~** fireproof dish; **mettre qch/être sur le ~** to put sth/ be on the stove; (fig) **sur le ~** (= en préparation) in the pipeline
d
♦ **mettre à feu** [+ fusée] to fire off; [+ charge explosive, bombe] to set off, trigger; [+ moteur] to fire
♦ **mise à feu** [fusée, moteur] firing; [explosif, bombe] setting off, triggering; **au moment de la mise à ~ de la fusée** at blast-off
e = sensation de brûlure, de chaleur **j'ai le ~ aux joues** my cheeks are burning; **le ~ lui monta au visage** the blood rushed to his face; **le ~ du rasoir** shaving rash, razor burn; **le bébé a des ~x de dents** the baby's cutting a tooth ou teething
f = ardeur fire; **plein de ~** full of fire; **parler avec ~** to speak passionately; **un tempérament**

feu (suite)

de ~ a fiery temperament; **avoir du ~ dans les veines** to have fire in one's blood; **avoir le ~ sacré** to burn with zeal; **dans le ~ de l'action/de la discussion** in the heat of (the) action/the discussion

◆ **tout feu tout flamme** wildly enthusiastic, burning with enthusiasm

g Mil = tir fire; (= combat) action; **faire ~** to fire; **~ !** fire!; **~ à volonté !** fire at will!; **sous le ~ de l'ennemi** under enemy fire; **~ nourri/rasant/roulant** sustained/grazing/running fire; **un ~ roulant de questions** a barrage of questions; **des ~x croisés** crossfire; (lit, fig) **être pris entre deux ~x** to be caught in the crossfire; **aller au ~** to go to the firing line; **tué au ~** killed in action → arme, baptême

h

◆ **coup de feu**
(d'une arme) (gun)shot; **il a reçu un coup de ~** he has been shot; **faire le coup de ~ avec qn** to fight alongside sb
(fig = précipitation, bousculade) **c'est le coup de ~** it's all go*
(Culin) **ma pizza a eu un coup de ~** my pizza's a bit burnt

i = revolver (arg Crime) gun, shooter*, rod‡ (US)

j = signal lumineux (Aut, Aviat, Naut) light; **le ~ était (au) rouge** the lights were (on) red; **s'arrêter aux ~x** to stop at the lights; **naviguer/rouler tous ~x éteints** to sail/drive without lights; **les ~x de la côte** the lights of the shore

k = éclairage light; **les ~x de la rampe** the footlights; **pleins ~x sur ...** spotlight on ...; **être sous le ~ des projecteurs** (lit) to be in the glare of the spotlights; (fig) to be in the limelight; **les ~x de l'actualité sont braqués sur eux** they are under ou in the full glare of the media spotlight

l littér = éclat **les ~x d'une pierre précieuse** the fire of a precious stone; **les diamants jetaient mille ~x** the diamonds were sparkling; **le ~ de son regard** his fiery gaze

m littér = lumière **les ~x de la nuit** the lights in the night; **les ~x du couchant** the fiery glow of sunset; **les ~x de la ville** the lights of the town; (= chaleur) **les ~x de l'été** the summer heat

n ↑↑ = maison hearth†; **un hameau de 15 ~x** a hamlet of 15 homesteads

◆ **sans feu ni lieu** (littér) with neither hearth nor home†

2 ADJECTIF INVARIABLE
flame-coloured; **rouge ~** flame red; **chien noir et ~** black and tan dog

3 COMPOSÉS
► **feu antibrouillard** fog light ou lamp ► **feu arrière** tail light, rear light (Brit) ► **feu d'artifice** firework display, fireworks; **un beau ~ d'artifice** beautiful fireworks; **le texte est un ~ d'artifice d'images et de métaphores** the text is a virtuoso display of imagery and metaphor ► **feu de Bengale** Bengal light ► **feu de brouillard** = feu antibrouillard ► **feu de brousse** bush fire ► **feu de camp** campfire ► **feu de cheminée** (= flambée) fire; (= incendie) chimney fire ► **feu clignotant** flashing light ► **feux de croisement** dipped headlights (Brit), low beams (US) ► **feux de détresse** hazard (warning) lights ► **feu follet** (lit, fig) will-o'-the-wisp ► **feu de forêt** forest fire ► **feu grégeois** Greek fire ► **feu de joie** bonfire ► **feu orange** amber light (Brit), yellow light (US) ► **feu de paille** (fig) flash in the pan ► **feu de plancher*** (= pantalon) high-riders*, clam-diggers* ► **feu de position** sidelight ► **feux de recul** reversing lights (Brit), back-up lights (US) ► **feu rouge** (couleur) red light; (= objet) traffic light; **tournez au prochain ~ rouge** turn at the next set of traffic lights ► **feux de route** headlamps ou headlights on full beam ► **feux de la Saint-Jean** bonfires lit to celebrate the summer solstice ► **feux de signalisation** traffic lights ► **feux de stationnement** parking lights ► **feu de stop** stop ou brake light ► **feux tricolores** traffic lights ► **feu vert** green light; (fig) **donner le ~ vert à qn/qch** to give sb/sth the green light ou the go-ahead

feu², **e** [fø] ADJ (inv devant art ou adj poss : frm) ~ **ma tante** ◊ **ma ~e tante** my late aunt

feuillage [fœjaʒ] NM (sur l'arbre) foliage (NonC); (coupé) greenery (NonC); **les oiseaux gazouillaient dans le ~** ou **les ~s** the birds were twittering among the leaves ou the foliage

feuillaison [fœjɛzɔ̃] NF leafing, foliation (SPÉC); **à l'époque de la ~** when the trees come into leaf

feuille [fœj] **1** NF **a** [arbre, plante] leaf; (littér = pétale) petal; ~ **de laurier** bay leaf; **à ~s caduques/persistantes** deciduous/evergreen → trèfle, trembler

b [papier, plastique, bois, ardoise, acier] sheet; **les ~s d'un cahier** the leaves of an exercise book; **or en ~s** gold leaf; **doré à la ~ d'or** gilded with gold leaf; (Imprim) **bonnes ~s** advance sheets; **alimentation ~ à ~** sheet feed; (Culin) **une ~ d'aluminium** (a sheet of) aluminium foil

c (= bulletin) slip; (= formulaire) form; (= journal) paper; ~ **à scandales** scandal sheet; (Scol) ~ **d'appel** daily register (sheet) (Brit), attendance sheet (US)

d (Ordin) ~ **de programmation** work ou coding sheet; ~ **de style** style sheet; ~ **de calcul** spread sheet

e (* = oreille) ear, lug* (Brit); **dur de la ~** hard of hearing

2 COMP ► **feuille de chêne** (Bot) oak-leaf; (Mil) general's insignia ► **feuille de chou** (péj = journal) rag ► **feuille de garde** end-paper ► **feuille d'impôt** tax form ou slip ► **feuille de maladie** form given by doctor to patient for forwarding to the Social Security ► **feuille morte** dead leaf; (Aviat) **descendre en ~ morte** to do the falling leaf ► **feuille de paye** ou **paie** pay slip ► **feuille de présence** attendance sheet ► **feuille de route** (Mil) travel warrant ► **feuille de soins** = feuille de maladie ► **feuille de température** temperature chart ► **feuilles de thé** tea leaves ► **feuille de vigne** (Bot, Culin) vine leaf; (Sculp) fig leaf ► **feuille volante** loose sheet → oreille

feuille-morte [fœjmɔʀt] ADJ INV (= couleur) russet

feuillet [fœjɛ] NM **a** [cahier, livre] leaf, page; [bois] layer; (Bio) **~s embryonnaires** germ layers **b** [ruminants] omasum, manyplies

feuilleté, **e** [fœjte] (ptp de feuilleter) **1** ADJ [roche] foliated; [verre, pare-brise] laminated **2** NM (= pâtisserie) ≈ Danish pastry; ~ **au jambon/aux amandes** ham/almond pastry

feuilleter [fœjte] ⊳ conjug 4 ◄ VT **a** [+ pages, livre] to leaf ou flick ou flip through; (fig = lire rapidement) to leaf ou skim ou glance through **b** (Culin) [+ pâte] to turn and roll

feuilleton [fœjtɔ̃] NM (Presse, Radio, TV) serial; ~ **télévisé** television serial; (populaire et de longue durée) soap (opera); **publié en ~** serialized; **ses amours, c'est un véritable ~** his love life is like a soap opera

feuilletoniste [fœjtɔnist] NMF serial writer

feuillette [fœjɛt] NF cask, barrel (containing 114-140 litres)

feuillu, **e** [fœjy] **1** ADJ leafy **2** NM broadleaved tree

feuillure [fœjyʀ] NF rebate, rabbet

feulement [følmã] NM growl

feuler [føle] ⊳ conjug 1 ◄ VI to growl

feutrage [føtʀaʒ] NM felting

feutre [føtʀ] NM (Tex) felt; (= chapeau) felt hat, trilby (Brit), fedora (US); (= stylo) felt-tip (pen), felt pen

feutré, **e** [føtʀe] (ptp de feutrer) ADJ **a** [étoffe, surface] felt-like, felt (épith); [lainage] matted **b** (fig) [atmosphère, bruit] muffled; **marcher à pas ~s** to walk with a muffled tread, pad along ou about; **elle descendit l'escalier à pas ~s** she crept down the stairs

feutrer [føtʀe] ⊳ conjug 1 ◄ **1** VT to line with felt, felt; [+ lainage] to mat; (fig = amortir) to muffle **2** VI to felt **3** se feutrer VPR to felt, mat; **mon pull-over s'est feutré** my pullover has gone all matted ou has felted

feutrine [føtʀin] NF (lightweight) felt

fève [fɛv] NF **a** (Bot) broad bean; ~ **de cacao** cocoa bean **b** [galette] charm (hidden in cake for Twelfth Night) → LES ROIS **c** (* : Can) bean; **~s jaunes** wax beans; **~s vertes** string ou French beans; **~s au lard** pork and beans

février [fevʀije] NM February; pour locutions voir septembre

fez [fɛz] NM fez

FF **a** (ABRÉV = franc français) FF **b** (ABRÉV = frères) bros

FFI [ɛfɛfi] NFPL (ABRÉV = Forces françaises de l'intérieur) → force

FFL [ɛfɛfɛl] NFPL (ABRÉV = Forces françaises libres) → force

Fg ABRÉV = faubourg

fi [fi] EXCL (††, hum) bah!, pooh!; **faire ~ de** [+ loi, conventions, conseils] to flout; [+ danger] to snap one's fingers at

fiabilité [fjabilite] NF [chiffres] accuracy, reliability; [personnel] reliability, dependability; [machine] reliability

fiable [fjabl] ADJ [chiffres, méthode] accurate, reliable; [personnel] reliable, dependable; [machine] reliable

fiacre [fjakʀ] NM (hackney) cab ou carriage, hackney

▼ **fiançailles** [fjɑ̃saj] NFPL engagement, betrothal (littér); **ils m'ont invité à leurs ~** they invited me to their engagement party

▼ **fiancé**, **e** [fjɑ̃se] (ptp de fiancer) **1** ADJ engaged **2** NM (= homme) fiancé; (= couple) **les ~s** the engaged couple **3** fiancée NF fiancée

fiancer [fjɑ̃se] ⊳ conjug 3 ◄ **1** VT to betroth (littér) (avec, à to) **2** se fiancer VPR to become ou get engaged ou betrothed (littér) (avec, à to)

fiasco [fjasko] NM fiasco; **être un ~** to be a fiasco; **faire (un) ~** [personne] to fail miserably; [négociations, projet] to end in a fiasco

fiasque [fjask] NF wine flask

fibranne [fibʀan] NF bonded fibre

fibre [fibʀ] NF **a** (lit : gén) fibre (Brit), fiber (US); **dans le sens des ~s** with the grain; ~ **de bois/carbone** wood/carbon fibre; **~s musculaires** muscle fibres; **~s nerveuses** nerve fibres; ~ **de verre** fibreglass (Brit), fiberglass (US), Fiberglas® (US); ~ **optique** (= câble) optical fibre; (= procédé) fibre optics; **câble en ~s optiques** fibre-optic cable; **riche en ~s** (alimentaires) high in (dietary) fibre **b** (fig = âme) **avoir la ~ maternelle/militaire** to be a born mother/soldier; **faire vibrer la ~ patriotique** to play on ou stir patriotic feelings

fibreux, **-euse** [fibʀø, øz] ADJ [texture] fibrous; [viande] stringy

fibrillation [fibʀijasjɔ̃] NF fibrillation

fibrille [fibʀij] NF fibril, fibrilla

fibrine [fibʀin] NF fibrin

fibrinogène [fibʀinɔʒɛn] NM fibrinogen

fibroblaste [fibʀoblast] NM fibroblast

fibrociment® [fibʀosimã] NM fibrocement

fibromateux, **-euse** [fibʀomatø, øz] ADJ fibromatous

fibrome [fibʀom] NM fibroid, fibroma

fibroscope [fibʀɔskɔp] NM fibrescope (Brit), fiberscope (US)

fibroscopie [fibʀɔskɔpi] NF endoscopy produced by fibroscope

► GRAMMAIRE ACTIVE: fiançailles 51.2 fiancé 51.2

fibule [fibyl] NF (= broche) fibula

ficaire [fikɛʀ] NF lesser celandine, pilewort

ficelage [fis(ə)laʒ] NM (= action) tying (up); (= liens) string

ficeler [fis(ə)le] ▶conjug 4◀ VT **a** [+ paquet, rôti, prisonnier] to tie up; **ficelé comme un saucisson** tied up in a bundle **b** * (= habiller) to get up*, rig out* (Brit); **ta mère t'a drôlement ficelé!** that's some get-up* ou rig-out* (Brit) your mother has put you in!; **c'est bien ficelé** [scénario, film] it's well put together

ficelle [fisɛl] NF **a** (= matière) string; (= morceau) piece ou length of string; (= pain) stick (of French bread); (arg Mil) stripe (of officer) **b** (loc) **tirer les ~s** to pull the strings; **connaître les ~s du métier** to know the tricks of the trade, know the ropes; **la ~ est un peu grosse** you can see right through it

fichage [fiʃaʒ] NM **le ~ de la population** filing ou recording information on the population

fiche[1] [fiʃ] NF **a** (= carte) (index) card; (= feuille) sheet, slip; (= formulaire) form; **~ client** customer card; **~ d'état civil** record of civil status, ≈ birth and marriage certificate; **~ d'inscription** enrolment form; **~ perforée** perforated card; **~ cartonnée** index card; **~ de paye** ou **de paie** pay slip; **~ de police** police record; **~ technique** specification sheet; **mettre en ~** to index; **~cuisine/-tricot** [magazine] (pull-out) recipe/knitting pattern card → **signalétique** **b** (= cheville) pin, peg; (Élec) (= broche) pin; (= prise) plug

fiche[2]* [fiʃ] VB → **ficher**[2]

ficher[1] [fiʃe] ▶conjug 1◀ VT **a** (= mettre en fiche) [+ renseignements] to file; [+ suspects] to put on file; **tous les meneurs sont fichés à la police** the police have files on all subversives **b** (= enfoncer) to stick in, drive in; **~ qch en terre** to drive sth into the ground; **j'ai une arête fichée dans le gosier** I've got a fishbone stuck in my throat, a fishbone has got stuck in my throat

ficher[2]* [fiʃe] ▶conjug 1◀ **1** VT **a** (= faire) to do; **qu'est-ce qu'il fiche, il est déjà 8 heures** what on earth ou what the heck* is he doing ou is he up to* — it's already 8 o'clock; **qu'est-ce que tu as fichu aujourd'hui?** what have you been up to* ou what have you done today?; **il n'a rien fichu de la journée** he hasn't done a thing ou a stroke (Brit) all day*; **(pour) ce que j'en ai à fiche, de leurs histoires** I couldn't care less about what they're up to* **b** (= donner) to give; **~ une trempe à qn** to give sb a slap in the face; **ça me fiche la trouille** it gives me the jitters* ou the willies*; **cette odeur/musique me fiche la migraine** that smell/music is giving me a damn* ou blinking* (Brit) headache; **fiche-moi la paix!** leave me alone!; **eux, faire ça? je t'en fiche!** you think they'd do that? not a hope!* ou you'll be lucky!*; **ça va nous ~ la poisse** that'll bring us bad luck ou put a jinx* on us; **je vous fiche mon billet que ...** I bet you anything (you like) ou my bottom dollar that ...; **qui est-ce qui m'a fichu un idiot pareil!** how stupid can you get!*, of all the blinking (Brit) idiots!* **c** (= mettre) to put; **fiche-le dans le tiroir** stick* ou bung* (Brit) it in the drawer; **~ qn à la porte** to chuck* ou kick* sb out; **se faire ~ ou fiche à la porte** to get o.s. chucked* ou kicked* out, get the push* ou the sack* (Brit); **~ qch par la fenêtre/à la corbeille** to chuck* sth out of the window/in the wastebasket; **ce médicament me fiche à plat** this medicine knocks me right out* ou knocks me for six*; **il a fiche le vase par terre** (qui était posé) he knocked the vase off; (qu'il avait dans les mains) he dropped the vase; (fig) **ça fiche tout par terre** that mucks* ou messes everything up; **~ qn dedans** (= emprisonner) to put sb inside*; (= faire se tromper) to get sb all confused; **ça m'a fichu en colère** that made me really ou hop-

ping mad* → **air**[2]
d **~ le camp** to clear off*, shove off*, push off*; **fiche-moi le camp!** clear off!*, push off!*

2 **se ficher** VPR **a** (= se mettre) **attention, tu vas te ~ ce truc dans l'œil** careful, you're going to stick that thing in your eye; **se ~ qch dans le crâne** to get sth into one's head ou noddle*; **je me suis fichu dedans** I (really) boobed*; **se ~ par terre** to go sprawling, come a cropper* (Brit); **il s'est fichu en l'air avec sa voiture** he smashed himself up* in his car **b** **se ~ de qn** (= rire de) to make fun of sb; (= raconter des histoires à) to pull sb's leg; **se ~ de qch** to make fun of sth; (= être indifférent) **se ~ de qn/de qch/de faire qch** not to give a darn about sb/about sth/about doing sth*, not to care two hoots about sb/about sth/about doing sth*; **laisse-le tomber, tu vois bien qu'il se fiche de toi** it's perfectly obvious that he's leading you on* ou he couldn't care less about you; **ils se fichent de nous, 50 F pour une bière!** what (on earth) do they take us for ou they really must think we're idiots, 50 francs for a beer!; **il se fiche de nous, c'est la troisième fois qu'il se décommande** he's giving us the runaround* ou really messing us about* (Brit) — that's the third time he has cancelled his appointment; **il se fiche du monde!** he's the absolute limit!*; **là, ils ne se sont vraiment pas fichus de nous** they really did us proud!; **je m'en fiche pas mal!** I couldn't care less!, I don't give a damn!*; **il s'en fiche comme de sa première chemise ou comme de l'an quarante** he couldn't care two hoots* (about it), what the heck does he care!
c **va te faire fiche!** get lost!*, go to blazes!*, take a running jump!*; **j'ai essayé, mais je t'en fiche ou va te faire fiche!** ça n'a pas marché I did try but blow me* (Brit), it didn't work, I did try but I'll be darned* (US) if it worked

fichier [fiʃje] NM (gén, Ordin) file; [bibliothèque] catalogue (Brit), catalog (US); **~ d'adresses** mailing list; **~ ASCII** ASCII file; **~ (des) clients** customer file; **~ (informatisé)** data file; (Ordin) **~ de travail** scratch ou work file; **~ système** system file; **~ (de) texte** text file

fichiste† [fiʃist(ə)] NMF filing clerk

fichtre*† [fiʃtʀ] EXCL (étonnement, admiration) gosh!*, by Jove! †*; **~ non!** gosh* ou goodness, no!

fichtrement*† [fiʃtʀəmɑ̃] ADV darned*, dashed* (Brit); **ça a coûté ~ cher** it was darned ou dashed (Brit) expensive

fichu[1] [fiʃy] NM (head)scarf; (Hist : couvrant le corsage) fichu

fichu[2], **e*** [fiʃy] (ptp de ficher[2]) ADJ **a** (avant n) (= sale) [métier, idée] wretched*, lousy*; (= mauvais) rotten*, lousy*, foul*; (= sacré) one heck of a*, a heck of a*; **avec ce ~ temps on ne peut rien faire** with this lousy* ou wretched* weather we can't do a thing; **il fait un ~ temps** what rotten* ou lousy* ou foul* weather; **il a un ~ caractère** he's got a rotten* ou lousy* temper, he's a nasty piece of work* (Brit); **il y a une ~e différence** there's one heck of a ou a heck of a difference* **b** (après n = perdu, détruit) [malade, vêtement] done for*; [appareil] done for*, bust*; **il/ce veston est ~** he/this jacket has had it* ou is done for*; **avec ce temps, le pique-nique est ~** with weather like this, we've had it for the picnic* **c** (= habillé) got up*, rigged out* (Brit); **regarde comme il est ~!** look at the way he's got up!* ou rigged out!* (Brit); **~ comme l'as de pique** looking like a scarecrow **d** (= bâti, conçu) **elle est bien ~e** she's well put together*, she's got a nice body; **cet appareil/ce livre est bien ~** this is a clever little gadget/book; **cet appareil/ce livre est mal ~** this gadget/book is hopeless ou useless; **il est tout mal ~** he's a fright; **comment c'est ~ ce**

truc? how does this thing work?
e **être mal ~ ou pas bien ~** [malade] to feel rotten*, be under the weather* ou out of sorts*; (euph) [femme] to have the curse*, be on the rag* (US)
f (= capable) **il est ~ d'y aller, tel que je le connais** knowing him he's quite capable of going; **il n'est (même) pas ~ de réparer ça** he can't even mend the darned thing*

fictif, -ive [fiktif, iv] ADJ **a** (= imaginaire) [personnage, exemple] fictitious, imaginary; **naturellement, tout ceci est ~** of course this is all fictitious ou imagined ou imaginary **b** (= faux) [nom, adresse] fictitious, false; [emploi] fictitious; [promesse, sentiment] false; [concurrence] artificial **c** (Fin) [prêt, actifs, contrat] fictitious; **valeur fictive** [monnaie] face value

fiction [fiksjɔ̃] NF **a** (= imagination) fiction, imagination; **cette perspective est encore du domaine de la ~** this prospect still belongs in the realms of fiction; **livre de ~** work of fiction **b** (= fait imaginé) invention; (= situation imaginaire) fiction; (= roman) (work of) fiction, fictional work; (= film de télévision) TV drama; (= mensonge) illusion, myth; **heureusement, ce que je vous décris est une ~** fortunately all that I've been telling you is imaginary

fictivement [fiktivmɑ̃] ADV in fiction

ficus [fikys] NM ficus

fidéicommis [fideikɔmi] NM (= régime) trust; (= fonction) trusteeship

fidéicommissaire [fideikɔmisɛʀ] NM trustee

fidèle [fidɛl] **1** ADJ **a** (= loyal) (gén) faithful, loyal; [époux] faithful; **~ serviteur/épée** trusty ou loyal servant/sword; (lit, fig) **demeurer ~ au poste** to be loyal ou faithful to one's post; **rester ~ à** [+ personne] to remain faithful ou true to; [+ promesse] to be ou remain faithful to, keep; [+ principe, idée] to remain true ou faithful to, stand by; [+ habitude, mode] to keep to; [+ marque, produit] to remain loyal to, stay ou stick* with; **être ~ à soi-même** to be true to o.s.; **~ à lui-même ou à son habitude, il est arrivé en retard** true to form ou true to character he arrived late
b (= habituel) [lecteur, client] regular, faithful; **nous informons nos ~s clients que ...** we wish to inform our customers that ...
c (= exact) [historien, narrateur, son, reproduction] faithful; [souvenir, récit, portrait, traduction] faithful, accurate; [mémoire, appareil, montre] accurate, reliable; **sa description est ~ à la réalité** his description is a true ou an accurate picture of the situation

2 NMF **a** (Rel) believer; **les ~s** (= croyants) the faithful; (= assemblée) the congregation **b** (= client) regular (customer); (= lecteur) regular (reader); **je suis un ~ de votre émission depuis 10 ans** I have been a regular listener to (ou viewer of) your programme for 10 years **c** (= adepte) [doctrine, mode, écrivain] follower, devotee

fidèlement [fidɛlmɑ̃] ADV **a** (= loyalement) faithfully, loyally **b** (= régulièrement) faithfully, regularly; **j'écoute ~ vos émissions depuis 10 ans** I have been listening to your programmes regularly ou I have been a regular listener to your programmes for the past 10 years **c** (= scrupuleusement) faithfully **d** (= conformément à la réalité) faithfully, accurately; **combat ~ décrit dans un livre** fight which is accurately described in a book

fidélisation [fidelizasjɔ̃] NF **~ de la clientèle** development of customer loyalty

fidéliser [fidelize] ▶conjug 1◀ VT **~ sa clientèle/son personnel** to establish ou develop customer/staff loyalty; **~ un public** to build up a loyal audience

fidélité [fidelite] NF **a** (= loyauté) (gén) faithfulness, loyalty; [conjoint, lecteur, client] faithfulness; (à un produit, un parti) loyalty, fidelity; **la ~ (conjugale)** fidelity → **carte, jurer** **b** (= exactitude) [historien, narrateur, son, reproduction] faithfulness; [souvenir, récit, portrait, traduction] faithfulness, accuracy; [mémoire, appareil, montre] accuracy, reliability

Fidji [fidʒi] NFPL **les (îles) ~** Fiji, the Fiji Islands

fidjien, -ienne [fidʒjɛ̃, jɛn] **1** ADJ Fiji, Fijian **2 Fidjien(ne)** NM,F Fiji, Fijian

fiduciaire [fidysjɛʀ] **1** ADJ fiduciary; **circulation** ~ fiduciary circulation; **héritier** ~ heir, trustee; **monnaie** ~ fiat ou paper money; **société** ~ trust company **2** NM (Jur) trustee

fiducie [fidysi] NF trust; **société de** ~ trust company

fief [fjɛf] NM (Hist) fief; (fig = zone d'influence) [firme, organisation] preserve; [parti, secte] stronghold; (hum = domaine) private kingdom; ~ **(électoral)** electoral stronghold; (hum) **ce bureau est son** ~ this office is his kingdom

fieffé, e [fjefe] ADJ [menteur] arrant

fiel [fjɛl] NM (lit) gall; **propos pleins de** ~ words filled with venom ou gall

fielleux, -euse [fjɛlø, øz] ADJ venomous, spiteful

fiente [fjɑ̃t] NF [oiseau] droppings

fienter [fjɑ̃te] ▸ conjug 1 ◂ VI to make ou leave droppings

fier, fière [fjɛʀ] ADJ **a** (= arrogant) proud; ~ **comme Artaban** ou **comme un coq** ou **comme un paon** (as) proud as a peacock; **trop ~ pour accepter** too proud to accept; **faire le ~** (= être méprisant) to be aloof, give o.s. airs; (= faire le brave) to be full of o.s.; **c'est quelqu'un de pas ~*** he's not stuck-up*; **devant le danger, il n'était plus si ~** when he found himself faced with danger, he wasn't so full of himself any more → **fier-à-bras**
b (littér = noble) [âme, démarche] proud, noble; **avoir fière allure** to cut a fine figure, cut a dash
c ~ **de qch/de faire qch** proud of sth/to do sth; **elle est fière de sa beauté** she's proud of her beauty; **toute fière de sortir avec son papa** as proud as could be to be going out with her daddy; **il n'y a pas de quoi être ~** there's nothing to feel proud about ou to be proud of ou to boast about; **je n'étais pas ~ de moi** I didn't feel very proud of myself, I felt pretty small*; **elle est fière qu'il ait réussi** she's proud he has succeeded
d (intensif: avant n) ~† **imbécile** first-class ou prize† idiot; **fière†** **canaille** out-and-out ou downright scoundrel; **il a un ~ toupet** he has the devil of a nerve* ou cheek* (Brit); **je te dois une fière chandelle** I'm terribly indebted to you
e (littér = fougueux) [cheval] mettlesome; **le ~ Aquilon** the harsh ou chill north wind

fier (se) [fje] ▸ conjug 7 ◂ VPR **a** (loyauté) **se fier à** [+ allié, promesses, discrétion] to trust; **on ne peut pas se fier à lui** you can't trust him, he's not to be trusted, he can't be trusted; **ne vous fiez pas à ce qu'il dit** don't go by ou trust what he says; **il a l'air calme mais il ne faut pas s'y fier** he looks calm but that's nothing to go by **b** (fiabilité) **se fier à** [+ appareil, collaborateur, instinct, mémoire] to trust, rely on; [+ destin, hasard] to trust to; **ne te fie pas à ta mémoire, prends des notes** don't trust your memory, make notes

fier-à-bras (pl **fiers-à-bras**) [fjɛʀabʀɑ] NM braggart

fièrement [fjɛʀmɑ̃] ADV (= dignement) proudly; (*† = extrêmement) devilishly*†

fiérot, e* [fjeʀo, ɔt] ADJ cocky*; **faire le ~** to show off*; **tout ~** (d'avoir gagné/de son succès) as pleased as Punch (about winning/about ou at his success)

fierté [fjɛʀte] NF (gén) pride; (péj = arrogance) pride, haughtiness; **tirer ~ de** to get a sense of pride from; **sa ~ est d'avoir réussi tout seul** he takes pride in having succeeded all on his own; **son jardin est sa ~** his garden is his pride and joy; **je n'ai pas accepté son aide, j'ai** ma ~! I didn't accept his help — I have my pride!

fiesta* [fjɛsta] NF rave-up*; **faire la** ou **une ~** to have a rave-up*

fieu [fjø] NM († ou dial) son, lad

fièvre [fjɛvʀ] NF **a** (= température) fever, temperature; **accès de ~** bout of fever; **avoir (de) la ~/beaucoup de ~** to have ou run a temperature/a high temperature; **avoir 39 de ~** to have a temperature of 104(°F) ou 39(°C); **une ~ de cheval*** a raging fever; **il a les yeux brillants de ~** his eyes are bright with fever → **bouton**
b (= maladie) fever; ~ **jaune/typhoïde** yellow/typhoid fever; ~ **hémorragique** haemorrhagic fever; ~ **aphteuse** foot-and-mouth disease; ~ **quarte††** quartan fever ou ague; **avoir les ~†** to have marsh fever; (hum) ~ **acheteuse** compulsive shopping
c (= agitation) fever, excitement; **parler avec** ~ to speak excitedly; **dans la ~ du départ** in the heat of departure, in the excitement of going away; **la ~ de l'or/des élections** gold/election fever; **pays saisi par la ~ du nationalisme** country caught in the grip of nationalist fervour
d (= envie) fever; **être pris d'une ~ d'écrire** to be seized with a frenzied ou feverish urge to write

fiévreusement [fjevʀøzmɑ̃] ADV feverishly, excitedly

fiévreux, -euse [fjevʀø, øz] ADJ (Méd, fig) feverish

FIFA [fifa] NF (ABRÉV = **Fédération internationale de football association**) FIFA

fifille*† [fifij] NF (terme affectueux) **viens par ici,** ~ come here, my little girl ou sweetheart; (péj) ~ **à sa maman** mummy's (Brit) ou mommy's (US) little girl

fifre [fifʀ] NM (= instrument) fife; (= joueur) fife player

fifrelin† [fifʀəlɛ̃] NM **ça ne vaut pas un ~** it's not worth a brass farthing (Brit) ou nickel (US)

fifty-fifty* [fiftififti] LOC ADV **faire ~** to go fifty-fifty*, go Dutch*; **on partage, ~?** shall we go fifty-fifty* ou Dutch*?

figaro† [figaʀo] NM (hum) barber

figé, e [fiʒe] (ptp de **figer**) ADJ [style] stilted; [manières] stiff, constrained; [société, mœurs] rigid, ossified; [attitude, sourire] set, fixed; [forme, expression] set; **être ~ dans des structures anciennes** to be set rigidly in outdated structures

figement [fiʒmɑ̃] NM [huile, sauce] congealing; [sang] clotting, coagulation, congealing

figer [fiʒe] ▸ conjug 3 ◂ **1** VT [+ huile, sauce] to congeal; [+ sang] to clot, coagulate, congeal; **le cri le figea sur place** the scream froze ou rooted him to the spot; **figé par la peur** terror-stricken; **histoire à vous ~ le sang** bloodcurdling story, story to make one's blood run cold; **des corps figés par la mort** rigid corpses **2** VI [sauce, huile] to congeal; [sang] to clot, coagulate, congeal **3 se figer** VPR [sauce, huile] to congeal; [sang] to clot, coagulate, congeal; [sourire, regard] to freeze; [visage] to stiffen, freeze; **il se figea au garde-à-vous** he stood rigidly to attention; **son sang se figea dans ses veines** his blood froze in his veins

fignolage* [fiɲɔlaʒ] NM touching up, polishing; **on a pratiquement terminé, le reste c'est du ~** just a few more finishing touches and we'll be done

fignoler* [fiɲɔle] ▸ conjug 1 ◂ VT (= soigner) to polish up, put the finishing touches to; **c'est du travail fignolé** that's a really neat job

fignoleur, -euse [fiɲɔlœʀ, øz] NM,F meticulous worker, perfectionist

figue [fig] NF (Bot) fig; ~ **de Barbarie** prickly pear; ~ **de mer** (edible) sea squirt

figuier [figje] NM fig tree; ~ **de Barbarie** prickly pear; ~ **banian** banyan tree

figurant, e [figyʀɑ̃, ɑ̃t] NM,F (Ciné) extra; (Théât) walk-on, supernumerary; (fig) (= pantin) puppet, cipher; (= complice) stooge; **avoir un rôle de** ~ (dans un comité, une conférence) to play a minor part, be a mere onlooker; (dans un crime) to be a stooge; (Ciné) to be an extra; (Théât) to have a walk-on part

figuratif, -ive [figyʀatif, iv] **1** ADJ **a** (Art) representational, figurative **b** [plan, écriture] figurative **2** NM,F representational ou figurative artist

figuration [figyʀasjɔ̃] NF **a** (Théât) (= métier) playing walk-on parts; (= rôle) walk-on (part); (= figurants) walk-on actors; (Ciné) (= métier) working as an extra; (= rôle) extra part; (= figurants) extras; **faire de la ~** (Théât) to do walk-on parts; (Ciné) to work as an extra **b** (= représentation) representation

figurativement [figyʀativmɑ̃] ADV diagrammatically

figure [figyʀ] **1** NF **a** (= visage) face; (= mine) face, countenance (frm); **sa ~ s'allongea** his face fell; **elle lui a jeté** ou **lancé ses lettres à la ~** she threw his letters in his face; **il lui a jeté** ou **lancé à la ~ qu'elle en était incapable** he told her to her face that she wasn't up to it → **casser**
b (= personnage) figure; ~ **équestre** equestrian figure; **les grandes ~s de l'histoire** the great figures of history; (Cartes) **les ~s** the court ou face cards
c (= image) illustration, picture; (Danse, Ling, Patinage) figure; (Math = tracé) diagram, figure; ~ **géométrique** geometrical figure; **faire une ~** to draw a diagram
d (loc) **faire ~ de favori** to be generally thought of ou be looked on as the favourite; **faire ~ d'idiot** to look a fool; **faire ~ dans le monde††** to cut a figure in society†; **faire bonne ~** to put up a good show; **faire pâle ~** to pale into insignificance (à côté de beside, next to); **faire triste** ou **piètre ~** to cut a sorry figure, look a sorry sight; **il n'a plus ~ humaine** he is disfigured beyond recognition; **prendre ~** [construction, projet] to take shape

2 COMP ▸ **figure de ballet** balletic figure ▸ **figure chorégraphique** choreographic figure ▸ **figures imposées** (Patinage) compulsory figures; (fig) **ça fait partie des ~s imposées** it's part of the compulsory ritual ▸ **figures libres** (Patinage) freestyle (skating) ▸ **figure mélodique** figure ▸ **figure de proue** (Naut) figurehead; (fig = chef) key figure, figurehead ▸ **figure de rhétorique** rhetorical figure ▸ **figure de style** stylistic device

figuré, e [figyʀe] (ptp de **figurer**) ADJ [langage, style, sens] figurative; [prononciation] symbolized; [plan, représentation] diagrammatic; (Archit) figured; **mot employé au ~** word used figuratively ou in the figurative; **au propre comme au ~** both literally and figuratively, in the literal as well as the figurative sense

figurément [figyʀemɑ̃] ADV figuratively, metaphorically

figurer [figyʀe] ▸ conjug 1 ◂ **1** VT to represent; **le peintre l'avait figuré sous les traits de Zeus** the painter had shown ou represented him in the guise of Zeus; **la scène figure un palais** the scene is a palace; **la balance figure la justice** scales are the symbol of justice

2 VI **a** (= être mentionné) to appear; **mon frère figure parmi les gagnants** my brother is listed among the winners ou is in the list of winners; **son nom figure en bonne place/ne figure pas parmi les gagnants** his name is high up among/does not appear among the winners; ~ **sur une liste/dans l'annuaire** to appear on a list/in the directory; **cet article ne figure plus sur votre catalogue** this item is no longer featured ou listed in your catalogue

b (*Théât*) to have a walk-on part; (*Ciné*) to be an extra

3 se figurer VPR to imagine; **figurez-vous une grande maison** picture *ou* imagine a big house; **si tu te figures que tu vas gagner ... if** you think *ou* imagine you're going to win ...; **figurez-vous que j'allais justement vous téléphoner** it so happens I was just about to phone you; **je ne tiens pas à y aller, figure-toi !** believe it or not, I've no particular desire to go!; **tu ne peux pas te ~ comme il est bête** you wouldn't believe *ou* you can't imagine how stupid he is

figurine [figyʀin] NF figurine

fil [fil] **1** NM **a** (= *brin*) [*coton, nylon*] thread; [*laine*] yarn; [*cuivre, acier*] wire; [*haricot, marionnette*] string; [*araignée*] thread; [*appareil électrique*] cord; **haricots pleins de ~s/sans ~s** stringy/stringless beans; **~ de trame/de chaîne** weft/warp yarn; **tu as tiré un ~ à ton manteau** you have pulled a thread in your coat; **j'ai tiré un ~ à mon collant** I've laddered my tights (*Brit*), my hose have a run in them (*US*); (*fig*) **il suffit de tirer un ~ et on découvre l'ampleur du scandale** you only have to scratch the surface to see the true scale of the scandal; **n'avoir plus un ~ de sec** to be soaked through; **~ (à linge)** (washing *ou* clothes) line; **~ (à pêche)** (fishing) line

b (= *téléphone*) **j'ai ta mère au bout du ~** I have your mother on the line *ou* phone; **coup de ~*** (phone) call; **donner** *ou* **passer un coup de ~ à qn*** to give sb a ring *ou* call *ou* buzz*, call *ou* phone *ou* ring (*Brit*) sb (up); **il faut que je passe un coup de ~*** I've got to make a phone call

c (*Tex* = *matière*) linen; **chemise de ~** linen shirt; **chaussettes pur ~ (d'Écosse)** lisle socks

d (= *sens*) [*bois, viande*] grain; **couper dans le sens du ~** to cut with the grain; **dans le sens contraire du ~** against the grain → **droit²**

e (= *tranchant*) edge; **donner du ~ à un rasoir** to sharpen a razor; **être sur le ~ du rasoir** to be on the razor's edge *ou* on a razor-edge; **passer un prisonnier au ~ de l'épée** to put a prisoner to the sword

f (= *cours*) [*discours, pensée*] thread; **suivre/interrompre le ~ d'un discours/de ses pensées** to follow/interrupt the thread of a speech/of one's thoughts; **tu m'as interrompu et j'ai perdu le ~** you've interrupted me and I've lost the thread; **au ~ des jours/des ans** with the passing days/years, as the days/years go (*ou* went) by; **raconter sa vie au ~ de ses souvenirs** to reminisce about one's life; **suivre le ~ de l'eau** to follow the current; **le bateau/papier s'en allait au ~ de l'eau** the boat/paper was drifting away with the stream *ou* current

g (*loc*) **maigre** *ou* **mince comme un ~** (as) thin as a rake; **donner du ~ à retordre à qn** to make life difficult for sb; **avoir un ~ à la patte*** to be tied down; **ne tenir qu'à un ~** to hang by a thread; **de ~ en aiguille** one thing leading to another, gradually

2 COMP ▶ **fil d'Ariane** (*Myth*) Ariadne's thread; (*fig*) vital lead ▶ **fil conducteur** [*enquête*] vital lead; [*récit*] main theme *ou* thread ▶ **fil à coudre** (sewing) thread ▶ **fil à couper le beurre** cheesewire ▶ **fil dentaire** dental floss ▶ **fil électrique** electric wire; (*fig*) **avoir les jambes comme des ~s de fer** to have legs like matchsticks ▶ **fil de fer** wire; (*fig*) **avoir les jambes comme des ~s de fer** to have legs like matchsticks ▶ **fil de fer barbelé** barbed wire ▶ **fil à plomb** plumbline ▶ **fil rouge**: **le ~ rouge de ses émissions** the common theme linking his programmes ▶ **fil de soie** silk thread ▶ **fil dentaire** = fil dentaire ▶ **fil à souder** soldering wire ▶ **fil de terre** earth wire (*Brit*), ground wire (*US*) ▶ **fils de la vierge** gossamer (*NonC*), gossamer threads → **inventer**

fil-à-fil [filafil] NM INV (= *tissu*) pepper-and-salt (fabric)

filage [filaʒ] NM [*laine*] spinning; (*Ciné*) ghost image; (*Théât*) run-through

filaire [filɛʀ] NF (*Zool*) filaria

filament [filamɑ̃] NM (*Bio, Élec*) filament; [*glu, bave*] strand, thread

filamenteux, -euse [filamɑ̃tø, øz] ADJ filamentous

filandière [filɑ̃djɛʀ] NF (hand-)spinner

filandreux, -euse [filɑ̃dʀø, øz] ADJ [*viande, légume*] stringy; [*discours, explication*] long-winded

filant, e [filɑ̃, ɑ̃t] ADJ [*liquide*] free-flowing; (*Culin*) runny; (*Méd*) [*pouls*] very weak → **étoile**

filao [filao] NM beefwood

filasse [filas] **1** NF tow; **~ de chanvre/lin** hemp/flax tow **2** ADJ INV **cheveux (blond) ~** tow-coloured hair; **aux cheveux (blond) ~** tow-haired, tow-headed

filateur [filatœʀ] NM mill owner

filature [filatyʀ] NF **a** (*Tex* = *action*) spinning; (= *usine*) mill **b** (= *surveillance*) shadowing (*NonC*), tailing* (*NonC*); **prendre qn en ~** to shadow *ou* tail* sb

fildefériste, fil-de-fériste (*pl* **fil-de-féristes**) [fildeferist] NMF high-wire artist

file [fil] NF [*personnes, objets*] line; **~ (d'attente)** queue (*Brit*), line (*US*); **~ de voitures** (*en stationnement*) line *ou* stream of cars; (*roulant*) line *ou* stream of cars; (*Aut*) **se mettre sur** *ou* **prendre la ~ de gauche** to move into the left-hand lane; **se garer en double ~** to double-park; **il est en double ~** he's double-parked; **se mettre en ~** to line up; **se mettre à la ◊ prendre la ~** to join the queue (*Brit*) *ou* the line (*US*); **marcher à la ~** *ou* **en ~** to walk in line; **entrer/sortir en ~** *ou* **à la ~** to file in/out; **en ~ indienne** in single file; **chanter plusieurs chansons à la ~** to sing several songs in a row *ou* in succession *ou* one after the other → **chef¹**

filé [file] (*ptp de* **filer**) NM (*Tex*) thread, yarn; **~ d'or/d'argent** golden/silver thread

filer [file] ▸ conjug 1 ◂ **1** VT **a** [+ *laine, coton, acier, verre*] to spin; [*araignée, chenille*] to spin; **~ un mauvais coton** (*au physique*) to be in a bad way; (*au moral*) to get into bad ways; **verre/sucre filé** spun glass/sugar

b (= *prolonger*) [+ *image, métaphore*] to spin out, extend; [+ *son, note*] to draw out; **~ le parfait amour** to spin out love's sweet dream; **~ une pièce de théâtre** to run through a play

c (*Police* = *suivre*) to shadow, tail*; **~ le train à qn*** to be hard *ou* close on sb's heels; **j'ai quitté la salle et il m'a filé le train*** I left the room and he followed after me

d (*Naut*) [+ *amarre*] to veer out; **navire qui file 20 nœuds** ship doing 20 knots

e * (= *donner*) **~ qch à qn** to give sth to sb, give sb sth; **il m'a filé son rhume** he's given me his cold; **~ un coup de poing à qn** to punch sb, give sb a punch; **file-toi un coup de peigne** run a comb through your hair

f (= *démailler*) [+ *bas, collant*] to get a run in, ladder (*Brit*)

2 VI **a** [*liquide*] to run, trickle; [*fromage fondu*] to go stringy; [*sirop*] to thread; [*lampe, flamme*] to smoke; **il faisait ~ du sable entre ses doigts** he was running *ou* trickling sand through his fingers

b * (= *courir, passer*) [*personne*] to fly, dash; [*temps*] to fly (by); **~ bon train/comme le vent/à toute allure** to go at a fair speed/like the wind/at top speed; **il fila comme une flèche devant nous** he darted *ou* zoomed* straight past us; **~ à la poste/voir qn** to dash to the post office/to see sb

c * (= *s'en aller*) to go off; **le voleur avait déjà filé** the thief had already made off*; **il faut que je file** I must dash *ou* fly*; **file dans ta chambre** off to your room with you; **allez, file, garnement !** clear off, you little pest!*; **~ à l'anglaise** to run off *ou* away, take French leave (*Brit*); **~ entre les doigts de qn** [*poisson*]

to slip between sb's fingers; [*voleur, argent*] to slip through sb's fingers; **les billets de 100 F, ça file vite** 100 franc notes disappear in no time; **~ doux** to toe the line

d (= *se démailler*) [*maille*] to run; [*bas, collant*] to run, ladder (*Brit*); **mon collant a filé** I've got a run *ou* ladder in my tights (*Brit*), my hose have a run in them (*US*)

e [*monnaie*] to slide, slip; **laisser ~ le dollar** to let the dollar slide

filet [filɛ] NM **a** (= *petite quantité*) [*eau, sang*] dribble, trickle; [*fumée*] wisp; [*lumière*] (thin) shaft; (= *trait*) thin line; **il avait un ~ de voix** he had a reedy voice; **mettez un ~ de vinaigre** add a drop *ou* a dash of vinegar; **arrosez d'un ~ d'huile d'olive** drizzle with olive oil

b [*poisson*] fillet; [*viande*] fillet (*Brit*) ou filet (*US*) steak; **donnez-moi un rôti dans le ~** I'd like some fillet (*Brit*) ou filet (*US*) of beef; **~ mignon** (pork) tenderloin; (*Belg*) **~ américain** steak tartare

c (= *nervure*) [*langue*] frenum; [*pas de vis*] thread; (*Typo*) rule; (*Archit*) fillet, list(el); **~s nerveux** nerve endings

d (*Pêche, Sport*) net; **~ (à provisions)** string bag; **~ (à bagages)** (luggage) rack; **~ à crevettes/à papillons/à cheveux** shrimping/butterfly/hair net; **~ à poissons** *ou* **de pêche** fishing net, fishnet (*US*); **~ dérivant** drift net; (*Ftbl*) **envoyer la balle au fond des ~s** to send the ball into the back of the net; (*Tennis*) **~ !** let!; (*Tennis*) **envoyer la balle dans le ~** to put the ball into the net, net the ball; (*Tennis*) **monter au ~** to go up to the net; (*fig*) **il a dû monter au ~ pour défendre son projet** he had to stick his neck out to defend his proposal; **travailler sans ~** [*acrobates*] to perform without a safety net; (*fig*) to be out on one's own; **tendre un ~** [*chasseur*] to set a snare; [*police*] to set a trap; **le ~ se resserre** the net is closing in *ou* tightening; (*fig*) **coup de ~** haul; (*fig*) **attirer qn dans ses ~s** to ensnare sb

filetage [filtaʒ] NM (= *action*) thread cutting, threading; [*pas de vis*] thread

fileter [filte] ▸ conjug 5 ◂ VT **a** [+ *vis, tuyau*] to thread; (= *étirer*) [+ *métal*] to draw; **tissu violet fileté d'or** purple cloth shot through with gold threads **b** (*Culin*) [+ *poisson*] to fillet

fileur, -euse [filœʀ, øz] NM,F spinner

filial, e¹ (*mpl* **-iaux**) [filjal, jo] ADJ filial

filiale² [filjal] NF (*Comm*) **(société) ~** subsidiary (company); **~ commune** joint venture; **~ à 100%** wholly-owned subsidiary; **~ de distribution/vente** distribution/sales subsidiary

filiation [filjasjɔ̃] NF [*personnes*] filiation; [*idées, mots*] relation; **être issu de qn par ~ directe** to be a direct descendant of sb

filière [filjɛʀ] NF **a** (= *succession d'étapes*) [*carrière*] path; [*administration*] channels, procedures; **la ~ administrative** the administrative procedures *ou* channels; **passer par** *ou* **suivre la ~ pour devenir directeur** to work one's way up to become a director; **il a suivi la ~ classique pour devenir professeur** he followed the classic route into teaching; **de nouvelles ~s sont offertes aux jeunes ingénieurs** new paths are open to young engineers

b (*Scol, Univ* = *domaine d'études spécifique*) course, subjects; **~s technologiques/scientifiques/artistiques** technology/science/arts courses; **nouvelles ~s** new subjects; **suivre une ~ courte/longue** to do a short/long course

c (= *réseau*) network; **les policiers ont réussi à remonter toute la ~** the police have managed to trace the network right through to the man at the top; **de nouvelles ~s pour le passage de la drogue** new channels for drug trafficking

d (*Écon* = *secteur d'activité*) industry; **~ bois/pêche/agroalimentaire** timber/fishing/food-processing industry; **ce pays a choisi la ~ nucléaire** this country chose the nuclear(-

power) option *ou* opted to use nuclear power
e (*Phys Nucl*) ~ **à eau légère/à eau pressurisée** light-water/pressurised water reactor
technology
f (*Tech*) (*pour étirer*) drawplate; (*pour fileter*)
screwing die
g (*Zool*) [*araignée, chenille*] spinneret

filiforme [filifɔrm] ADJ [*antenne, patte*] threadlike, filiform (*SPÉC*); [*jambes*] long and slender; [*corps*] lanky; (*Méd*) [*pouls*] thready

filigrane [filigran] NM [*papier, billet*] watermark; [*objet*] filigree; **en** ~ (*lit*) as a watermark;
(*fig*) **ce projet apparaît** *ou* **est inscrit en** ~ **dans
le texte** this project is hinted at in the text;
sa haine apparaissait en ~ **dans ses paroles**
there was veiled hatred in his words; **cette
possibilité est inscrite en** ~ **dans la loi** this
possibility is implicit in the law

filigraner [filigrane] ▶conjug 1 ◀ VT [+ *papier,
billet*] to watermark; [+ *objet*] to filigree

filin [filɛ̃] NM rope

fille [fij] **1** NF **a** (*dans une famille*) daughter;
la ~ **de la maison** the daughter of the house;
(*souvent péj*) **la** ~ **Martin** the Martin girl; (*littér*)
la peur, ~ **de la lâcheté** fear, the daughter of
cowardice; (*Rel*) **oui, ma** ~ yes, my child; **c'est
bien la** ~ **de son père/de sa mère** she's very
much her father's/her mother's daughter,
she's just like her father/her mother → **jouer**
b (= *enfant*) girl; (= *femme*) woman; († =
vierge) maid†; **c'est une grande/petite** ~ she's
a big/little girl; **elle est belle** ~ she's a good-
looking girl; **c'est une bonne** *ou* **brave** ~ she's
a nice girl *ou* a good sort; **elle n'est pas** ~ **à se
laisser faire** she's not the type to let herself *ou*
the type of girl who lets herself be messed
about; **être encore/rester** ~† to be still/stay
unmarried; **mourir** ~† to die an old maid →
jeune, vieux
c († = *servante*) ~ **de ferme** farm girl; ~
d'auberge/de cuisine serving/kitchen maid;
ma ~†† my girl
d († *péj = prostituée*) whore; ~ **en carte** registered prostitute
2 COMP ▶ **fille d'Ève** daughter of Eve
▶ **fille d'honneur** (*Hist*) maid of honour
▶ **fille de joie** prostitute ▶ **fille publique**
streetwalker ▶ **fille des rues** streetwalker
▶ **fille de salle** (*restaurant*) waitress;
(*hôpital*) ward orderly ▶ **fille à soldats**
(*péj*) soldiers' whore ▶ **fille soumise**† registered prostitute

fille-mère† (*pl* **filles-mères**) [fijmɛr] NF unmarried mother

fillette [fijɛt] NF **a** (= *petite fille*) (little) girl;
rayon ~ girls' department; (*hum*) **elle chausse
du 42** ~* her feet are like boats* **b** (*=
bouteille*) ≈ (half-)bottle

filleul [fijœl] NM godson, godchild; ~ **de
guerre** adoptive son (in wartime)

filleule [fijœl] NF goddaughter, godchild

film [film] **1** NM **a** (*Ciné*) (= *pellicule*) film; (=
œuvre) film, movie (*surtout US*); (*genre*) **le** ~
fantastique/d'avant-garde fantasy/avant-garde
films; **le grand** ~† the feature (film); (*fig*) **repasser le** ~ **des événements de la journée** to
go over the sequence of the day's events; (*fig*)
il n'a rien compris au ~* he didn't get it at all
→ **métrage**
b (= *mince couche*) film; ~ **alimentaire** *ou* **étirable** (*transparent*) Clingfilm® (*Brit*), clingwrap (*Brit*), Saran Wrap® (*US*); ~ **plastique de
congélation** freezer film
2 COMP ▶ **film d'animation** animated film
▶ **film d'archives** archive film ▶ **film documentaire** documentary (film) ▶ **film
d'épouvante** = **film d'horreur** ▶ **film de
guerre** war film ▶ **film d'horreur** horror
film ▶ **film muet** silent film ▶ **film noir**
film noir ▶ **film parlant** talking film, talkie*
▶ **film policier** detective film ▶ **film publicitaire** (= *publicité*) advertising film; (= *film
promotionnel*) promotional film ▶ **film à**

sketches film made up of sketches → **action, aventure, espionnage**

filmage [filmaʒ] NM [*personne, paysage*] filming; [*film, scène*] filming, shooting

filmer [filme] ▶conjug 1 ◀ VT [+ *personne,
paysage*] to film; [+ *film, scène*] to film, shoot;
théâtre filmé film drama

filmique [filmik] ADJ film (*épith*), cinematic;
l'œuvre ~ **de Renoir** Renoir's film work

filmographie [filmɔgrafi] NF filmography

filmologie [filmɔlɔʒi] NF film studies

filoguidé, e [filogide] ADJ wire-guided

filon [filɔ̃] NM **a** (*Minér*) vein, seam, lode
b (* *fig = situation*) **trouver le** ~ to strike it
lucky *ou* rich; **il exploite ce** ~ **depuis des
années** he's worked that seam for years; **on
n'a pas fait de recherches sur ce sujet, c'est un
** ~ **qu'il faudrait exploiter** no research has been
done on that subject — it's a line worth developing; **nous tenons un bon** ~ we're on to a
good thing *ou* something good, we've struck
it rich; **c'est un bon** ~ [*métier*] it's a cushy
number*; [*secteur lucratif*] there's a lot of
money to be made in it

filou [filu] NM (= *escroc*) crook, swindler; (= *enfant espiègle*) rascal

filouter* [filute] ▶conjug 1 ◀ **1** VT [+ *personne*]
to cheat, do* (*Brit*), diddle* (*Brit*); [+ *argent, objets*] to snaffle*, filch*; **il m'a filouté (de) 10 F**
he's cheated *ou* diddled (*Brit*) me out of 10
francs* **2** VI (= *tricher*) to cheat; **il est difficile
de** ~ **avec le fisc** it's hard to cheat *ou* diddle
(*Brit*) the taxman*

filouterie [filutri] NF fraud (*NonC*), swindling
(*NonC*)

fils [fis] **1** NM **a** son; **le** ~ **de la maison** the son
of the house; **M. Martin** ~ young Mr Martin;
(*Comm*) **Martin** ~ Mr Martin junior; (*Comm*)
Martin et Fils Martin and Son (*ou* Sons); **le** ~
Martin the Martin boy; **elle est venue avec ses
deux** ~ she came with her two sons *ou* boys;
c'est bien le ~ **de son père** he's very much his
father's son, he's just like his father; (*frm*) **les**
~ **de la France/de Charlemagne** the sons of
France/of Charlemagne; (*frm*) **être le** ~ **de ses
œuvres** to be a self-made man; (*Rel*) **oui, mon**
~ yes, my son; (*Rel*) **le Fils de l'homme/de Dieu**
the Son of Man/of God **2** COMP ▶ **fils de
famille** young man of means *ou* with money
▶ **fils de garce‡†**, **fils de pute‡‡** son of a
bitch!‡ ▶ **fils spirituel** spiritual son → **papa**

filtrage [filtraʒ] NM [*liquide*] filtering; (*Élec*) filtration; [*nouvelles, spectateurs*] screening

filtrant, e [filtrã, ãt] ADJ [*substance*] filtering
(*épith*); [*verre*] filter (*épith*); **virus** ~ filterable virus; **le pouvoir** ~ **de ces lunettes de soleil** the
way these sunglasses filter sunlight

filtrat [filtra] NM filtrate

filtration [filtrasjɔ̃] NF [*liquide*] filtering, filtration

filtre [filtr] NM (*gén*) filter; [*cigarette*] filter tip;
~ **à café** coffee filter; **papier-**~ filter paper; **cigarette à bout** ~ filter-tipped cigarette; **~ avec
ou sans** ~ ? "tipped or plain?"; ~ **à air/huile/
essence** air/oil/fuel filter; ~ **anti-UV** UV filter;
~ **solaire** sunscreen

filtrer [filtre] ▶conjug 1 ◀ **1** VT [+ *liquide, lumière, son*] to filter; [+ *nouvelles, spectateurs, appels téléphoniques*] to screen **2** VI [*liquide*] to
filter (through), seep through; [*lumière, son*] to
filter through; [*information*] to leak out, filter
through; **rien n'a filtré de leur conversation**
none of their conversation got out

fin¹, fine¹ [fɛ̃, fin] **1** ADJ **a** (= *mince*) [*tranche,
couche, papier, tissu*] thin; [*cheveux, sable,
poudre, papier de verre*] fine; [*pointe, pinceau*]
fine; [*bec d'oiseau*] thin, pointed; [*lame*] sharp,
keen; [*écriture*] small; [*taille, doigt, jambe*] slender, slim; **plume** ~**e** fine-nibbed pen; **petits
pois** ~**s/très** ~**s** high-quality/top-quality garden peas; **une petite pluie** ~**e** a fine drizzle →
peigne, sel

b (= *raffiné, supérieur*) [*lingerie, porcelaine, travail*] fine, delicate; [*traits, visage, or, pierres*]
fine; [*silhouette, membres*] neat, shapely;
[*produits, aliments*] high-class, top-quality;
[*mets*] choice, exquisite; [*chaussures*] fine-
leather; **faire un repas** ~ to have a gourmet
meal; **vins** ~**s** fine wines; **perles** ~**es** real
pearls; ~**e fleur de froment** finest wheat flour;
la ~**e fleur de l'armée française** the pride *ou*
flower of the French army; **le** ~ **du** ~ the last
word *ou* the ultimate (**de** in) → **épicerie,
partie²**
c (= *très sensible*) [*vue, ouïe*] sharp, keen;
[*goût, odorat*] fine, discriminating; **avoir
l'oreille** *ou* **l'ouïe** ~**e** to have a keen ear, have
keen hearing → **nez**
d (= *subtil*) [*personne*] astute; [*esprit, observation*] shrewd, sharp; [*allusion, nuance*] subtle;
[*sourire*] wise, shrewd; **faire des plaisanteries
** ~**es sur qch** to joke wittily about sth; **il n'est
pas très** ~ he's not very bright; **ce n'est pas
très** ~ **de sa part** that's not very clever of him;
(*iro*) **comme c'est** ~! (that's) very clever! (*iro*);
(*iro*) **c'est** ~ **ce que tu as fait!** that was clever
of you! (*iro*); **il se croit plus** ~ **que les autres**
he thinks he's smarter than everybody else;
bien ~ **qui pourrait le dire!** who knows!; **tu as
l'air** ~! you look a right idiot!*; **jouer au plus** ~
avec qn to try to outsmart sb
e (*avant n* = *habile*) expert; ~ **connaisseur**
connoisseur; ~**e cuisinière** skilled cook; ~
gourmet ◊ ~**e bouche** *ou* **gueule*** gourmet; ~**e
lame** expert swordsman; ~ **stratège** expert
strategist; ~ **tireur** crack shot
f (*avant n : intensif*) **au** ~ **fond de la campagne** right in the heart of the country, in the
depths of the country; **au** ~ **fond du tiroir**
right at the back of the drawer; **du** ~ **fond de
ma mémoire** from the depths *ou* recesses of
my memory; **savoir le** ~ **mot de l'histoire** to
know the real story
2 ADV [*moudre, tailler*] finely; (*Billard*) fine;
écrire ~ to write small; ~ **prêt** quite *ou* all
ready; ~ **soûl** dead *ou* blind drunk*
3 COMP ▶ **fines herbes** (sweet) herbs, fines
herbes ▶ **fin limier** (keen) sleuth ▶ **fine
mouche, fin renard** sharp customer → **1e**

▼**fin²** [fɛ̃] **1** NF **a** (*gén*) end; [*année, réunion*]
end, close; [*compétition*] end, finish, close;
« **Fin** » [*film, roman*] "The End"; **vers** *ou* **sur la** ~
towards the end; **le quatrième en partant de**
ou **en commençant par la** ~ the fourth from
the end, the last but three (*Brit*); ~ **juin** ◊ **à la**
(**de**) **juin** at the end of June; (*Comm*) ~ **courant**
at the end of the current month; **jusqu'à la** ~
to the very end; **jusqu'à la** ~ **des temps** *ou* **des
siècles** until the end of time; **la** ~ **du monde**
the end of the world; **avoir des** ~**s de mois
difficiles** to have difficulty making ends
meet; **en** ~ **de semaine** towards *ou* at the end
of the week; **on n'en verra jamais la** ~ we'll
never see the end of this; **à la** ~ **il a réussi à se
décider** he eventually managed *ou* in the end
he managed to make up his mind; **tu
m'ennuies, à la** ~!* you're beginning to get on
my nerves!; **en** ~ **d'après-midi** towards the
end of the afternoon, in the late afternoon;
en ~ **de liste** at the end of the list; **en** ~ **de
compte** (= *tout bien considéré*) when all is said
and done, in the end, at the end of the day;
(= *en conclusion*) in the end, finally; **sans** ~
[*discussion, guerre, histoire*] endless, never-
ending; [*errer, tourner*] endlessly; **arriver en** ~
de course [*vis*] to screw home; [*piston*] to complete its stroke; [*batterie*] to wear out; *
[*personne*] to be worn out, come to the end of
the road; (*Bourse*) **en** ~ **de séance** at the close;
un chômeur en ~ **de droits** ◊ **un** ~ **de droits*** an
unemployed person no longer entitled to benefit;
prendre ~ [*réunion*] to come to an end;
[*contrat*] to terminate, expire (**le** on); **être sur
sa** ~ ◊ **toucher à** *ou* **tirer à sa** ~ to be coming to
an end, be drawing to a close; **on arrive à la** ~
du spectacle we're getting near the end of

the show; **mettre ~ à** to put an end to, end; **mettre ~ à ses jours** to put an end to one's life; **mener qch à bonne ~** to bring sth to a successful conclusion, carry sth off successfully; (= *se marier*) **faire une ~†** to settle down → **début**, **mot** etc

b (= *ruine*) end; **c'est la ~ de tous mes espoirs** that's the end of all my hopes; **c'est la ~ de tout!** ou **des haricots!*** that's the last straw!

c (= *mort*) end, death; **avoir une ~ tragique** to die a tragic death; **il a eu une belle ~** he had a fine end; **la ~ approche** the end is near

d (= *but*) end, aim, purpose; (*Philo*) end; **~ en soi** end in itself; **il est arrivé** ou **parvenu à ses ~s** he achieved his aim ou ends; **à cette ~** to this end, with this end ou aim in view; **à quelle ~ faites-vous cela?** what is your purpose ou aim in doing that?; **c'est à plusieurs ~s** it has a variety of uses; **à seule ~ de faire** for the sole purpose of doing; (*frm*) **à toutes ~s utiles** for your information; (*Jur*) **aux ~s de la présente loi** for the purposes of this Act ■ (*PROV*) **la ~ justifie les moyens** the end justifies the means

2 COMP ▶ **fin d'exercice** (*Comptab*) end of the financial year ▶ **fin de race** (*péj*) ADJ INV degenerate ◆ NM,F degenerate aristocrat ▶ **fin de section** [*autobus*] stage limit, fare stage ▶ **fin de semaine** (*Can*) weekend ▶ **fin de série** (*Comm*) end-of-line stock (*NonC*) ▶ **fin de siècle** (*péj*) ADJ INV decadent, fin de siècle → **non-recevoir**

final, e¹ (*mpl* **finals** ou **-aux**) [final, o] ADJ **a** (= *terminal*) final; **la scène ~e** the final ou last scene → **point¹** **b** (= *marquant la finalité : Ling, Philo*) final; (*Ling*) **proposition ~e** purpose ou final clause; **au** ou **en ~** in the end

finale² [final] NF **a** (*Sport*) final; **quart de ~** quarterfinal; **demi-~** semifinal; **huitième/seizième de ~** third/second round (*in a six-round tournament*) **b** (= *syllabe*) final ou last syllable; (= *voyelle*) final ou last vowel

finale³ [final] NM (*Mus*) finale

finalement [finalmɑ̃] ADV (*gén*) in the end, finally; (= *après tout*) **ce n'est pas si mal ~** it's not so bad after all; **~ je ne suis pas plus avancé** in the end ou finally I'm no further on

finalisation [finalizasjɔ̃] NF [*accord, contrat*] finalization; **un protocole en voie de ~** a protocol in the process of being finalized

finaliser [finalize] ▶ conjug 1 ◀ VT **a** (= *achever*) to finalize **b** (= *orienter*) to target

finalisme [finalism] NM finalism

finaliste [finalist] **1** ADJ (*Philo*) finalist **2** NM,F (*Philo, Sport*) finalist

finalité [finalite] NF (= *but*) end, aim; (= *fonction*) purpose, function

finance [finɑ̃s] NF **a** (*Pol* = *recettes et dépenses*) **~s** finances; **les Finances** (= *administration*) the Ministry of Finance, ≈ the Treasury, ≈ the Exchequer (*Brit*), ≈ the Treasury Department (*US*); **il est aux Finances** (*employé*) he works at the Ministry of Finance; (*ministre*) he is Minister of Finance; **~s publiques** public funds; **l'état de mes ~s*** the state of my finances, my financial state; **les** ou **mes ~s sont à sec*** I'm right out of funds* → **loi, ministre** **b** (*Fin*) finance; **la (haute) ~** (= *activité*) (high) finance; (= *personnes*) (top) financiers; **le monde de la ~** the financial world; **il est dans la ~** he's in banking ou finance → **moyennant**

financement [finɑ̃smɑ̃] NM financing; **plan de ~** financial plan; **~ à court/long terme** short-/long-term financing; **~-relais** bridge ou interim financing; **~ à taux fixe** fixed-rate financing; **~ par emprunt** debt financing

financer [finɑ̃se] ▶ conjug 3 ◀ **1** VT to finance, back, put up the money for **2** VI* to fork out*

financier, -ière [finɑ̃sje, jɛʀ] **1** ADJ **a** (*Fin*) financial; **soucis ~s** money ou financial worries → **place** **b** (*Culin*) **(sauce) financière** sauce financière **2** NM (*Fin*) financier; (*Culin*) almond sponge finger

financièrement [finɑ̃sjɛʀmɑ̃] ADV financially

finasser* [finase] ▶ conjug 1 ◀ VI to use trickery; **inutile de ~ avec moi!** there's no point trying to use your tricks on me!

finasserie* [finasʀi] NF trick, dodge*, ruse

finasseur, -euse [finasœʀ, øz], **finassier, -ière** [finasje, jɛʀ] NM,F trickster, dodger*

finaud, e [fino, od] **1** ADJ wily **2** NM,F **c'est un petit ~** he's a crafty one*, there are no flies on him*, he's nobody's fool

finauderie [finodʀi] NF **a** (= *caractère*) wiliness, guile; (= *action*) wile, dodge* (*Brit*)

fine² [fin] NF **a** (= *alcool*) liqueur brandy; **~ Champagne** fine champagne cognac **b** (= *huître*) **~ de claire** green oyster → HUÎTRES

finement [finmɑ̃] ADV [*ciselé, brodé*] finely, delicately; [*faire remarquer*] subtly; [*agir, manœuvrer*] cleverly, shrewdly

finesse [fines] **1** NF **a** (= *minceur*) [*cheveux, poudre, pointe*] fineness; [*lame*] keenness, sharpness; [*écriture*] smallness; [*taille*] slenderness, slimness; [*couche, papier*] thinness **b** (= *raffinement*) [*broderie, porcelaine, travail, traits*] delicacy, fineness; [*aliments, mets*] delicacy, choiceness; **son visage est d'une grande ~** he has very refined ou delicate features **c** (= *sensibilité*) [*sens*] sharpness, sensitivity; [*vue, odorat, goût, ouïe*] sharpness, keenness **d** (= *subtilité*) [*personne*] sensitivity; [*esprit, observation, allusion*] subtlety **2** **finesses** NFPL [*langue, art*] niceties, finer points; [*affaire*] ins and outs; **il connaît toutes les ~s** he knows all the ins and outs

finette [finet] NF brushed cotton

fini, e [fini] (*ptp de* **finir**) **1** ADJ **a** (= *terminé*) finished, over; **tout est ~ entre nous** it's all over between us, we're finished, we're through*; **~e la rigolade!*** the party* ou the fun is over!; (**c'est**) **~ de rire maintenant** the fun ou joke is over now; **ça n'est pas un peu ~ ce bruit?** will you stop that noise! **b*** (= *fichu*) [*acteur, homme politique, chose*] finished; **il est ~** he's finished, he's a has-been* **c** (= *usiné, raffiné*) finished; **costume bien/mal ~** well-/badly-finished suit **d** (*péj = complet*) [*menteur, escroc, salaud*] out-and-out, downright; [*ivrogne, bon à rien*] absolute, complete **e** (*Math, Philo, Ling*) finite; **grammaire à états ~s** finite state grammar **2** NM [*ouvrage*] finish; **ça manque de ~** it needs a few finishing touches

finir [finiʀ] ▶ conjug 2 ◀ **1** VT **a** (= *achever*) [+ *travail, études, parcours*] to finish, complete; (= *clôturer*) [+ *discours, affaire*] to finish, end, conclude; **finis ton travail** ou **de travailler avant de partir** finish your work before you leave; **il a fini ses jours à Paris** he ended his days in Paris; **~ son verre** to finish one's glass, drink up; **finis ton pain!** finish your bread!, eat up your bread!; **il finira (d'user) sa veste en jardinant** he can wear out his old jacket (doing the gardening); **il a fini son temps** [*soldat, prisonnier*] he has done ou served his time **b** (= *arrêter*) to stop (**de faire** doing); **finissez donc!** do stop it!; **finissez de vous plaindre!** stop complaining!; **vous n'avez pas fini de vous chamailler?** haven't you quite finished squabbling?; **tu as fini de m'embêter?** have you quite finished? **c** (= *parachever*) [+ *œuvre d'art, meuble, mécanisme*] to put the finishing touches to

2 VI **a** (= *se terminer*) to finish, end; **le cours finit à deux heures** the class finishes ou ends at two; **les vacances finissent demain** the holidays end ou are over tomorrow; **la réunion/le jour finissait** the meeting/the day was drawing to a close; **le sentier finit ici** the path ends ou comes to an end here; **il est temps que cela finisse** it is time (it was) stopped; **ce film finit bien** this film has a happy ending; **tout cela va mal ~** it will all end in disaster; **et pour ~ et finally** → **beauté** **b** [*personne*] to finish up, end up; **il finira mal** he will come to a bad end; **il a fini directeur/en prison** he ended up as (a) director/in prison; **~ dans la misère** to end one's days in poverty, end up in poverty; (*Sport*) **~ troisième/cinquième** finish third/fifth **c** (= *mourir*) to die; **il a fini dans un accident de voiture** he died in a car accident **d** **~ en qch** to end in sth; **ça finit en pointe/en chemin de terre** it ends in a point/in a dirt track; **mots finissant en** ou **par -ble** words ending in ou with -ble → **queue** **e** **~ par une dispute/un concert** to end in an argument/with a concert; **ils vont ~ par avoir des ennuis** they'll end up getting into trouble; **il a fini par se décider** he finally ou eventually made up his mind, he made up his mind in the end; **tu finiras par m'ennuyer** you're beginning to annoy me; **ça finira bien par s'arranger** it'll work out all right in the end ou eventually **f** **en ~ avec qch/qn** to have ou be done with sth/sb; **il faut en ~ avec cette situation** we'll have to put an end to this situation; **nous en aurons bientôt fini** we'll soon be finished with it, we'll soon have it over and done with; **quand en auras-tu fini avec tes jérémiades?** when will you ever stop moaning?; **je vais lui parler pour qu'on en finisse** I'll talk to him so that we can get the matter settled; **qui n'en finit pas** ◊ **à n'en plus ~** [*route, discours, discussion*] never-ending, endless; **elle n'en finit pas de se préparer** she takes ages to get ready; **on n'en aurait jamais fini de raconter ses bêtises** you could go on for ever talking about the stupid things he's done; **il a des jambes qui n'en finissent pas** he's all legs*

finish [finiʃ] NM (*Sport*) finish; **combat au ~** fight to the finish; **il a du ~** ou **un bon ~** he has good finish

finissage [finisaʒ] NM (*Couture, Tech*) finishing

finissant, e [finisɑ̃, ɑ̃t] ADJ [*règne, siècle*] that is (ou was) drawing to an end; [*pouvoir, monarchie*] declining; **la lumière du jour ~e** the dusky light; **le calme de l'été ~** the calm at the end of the summer, the end-of-summer calm

finisseur, -euse [finisœʀ, øz] NM,F **a** (*Couture, Tech*) finisher **b** (*Sport*) good ou strong finisher

finition [finisjɔ̃] NF (= *action*) finishing; (= *résultat*) finish; **la ~ est parfaite** the finish is perfect; **faire les ~s** (*Couture*) to finish off; (*Tricot*) to sew up; (*Constr*) **travaux de ~** finishing off

finitude [finityd] NF finiteness

finlandais, e [fɛ̃lɑ̃dɛ, ɛz] **1** ADJ Finnish **2** NM (*Ling*) Finnish **3** **Finlandais(e)** NM,F Finn

Finlande [fɛ̃lɑ̃d] NF Finland

finlandisation [fɛ̃lɑ̃dizasjɔ̃] NF Finlandization

finnois, e [finwa, waz] **1** ADJ Finnish **2** NM (*Ling*) Finnish

finno-ougrien, -ienne [finougʀijɛ̃, ijɛn] ADJ, NM (*Ling*) Finno-Ugric, Finno-Ugrian

fiole [fjɔl] NF (= *flacon*) phial, flask; (* = *tête*) face, mug*

fiord [fjɔʀ(d)] NM = **fjord**

fioriture [fjɔʀityʀ] NF [*dessin*] flourish; (*Mus*) fioritura; **~s de style** flourishes ou embellishments of style; **sans ~s** plain, unadorned, unembellished; [*répondre*] in no uncertain terms

fioul [fjul] NM = **fuel**

firmament [fiʀmamɑ̃] NM (*littér*) firmament (*littér*); (*fig*) **au ~ de** at the height of

firme [fiʀm] NF firm

FIS [fis] NM (ABRÉV = **Front islamique de** ou **du Salut**) FIS

fisc [fisk] NM tax department, ≈ Inland Revenue (Brit), ≈ Internal Revenue Service (US); **agent du ~** official of the tax department, ≈ Inland Revenue official (Brit), ≈ collector of the Internal Revenue Service (US); **avoir des ennuis avec le ~** to have problems with the taxman*, have tax problems

fiscal, e (mpl **-aux**) [fiskal, o] ADJ (gén) fiscal; [abattement, avantage] tax (épith); **l'année ~e** the tax ou fiscal year; **politique ~e** tax ou fiscal policy → **abri, fraude, paradis**

fiscalement [fiskalmã] ADV fiscally

fiscalisation [fiskalizasjɔ̃] NF [revenus] making subject to tax; [prestation sociale] funding by taxation

fiscaliser [fiskalize] ▶ conjug 1 ◀ VT [+ revenus] to make subject to tax; [+ prestation sociale] to fund by taxation

fiscaliste [fiskalist] NMF tax consultant ou adviser ou expert; **avocat ~** tax lawyer

fiscalité [fiskalite] NF (= système) tax system; (= impôts) taxation, taxes

fish-eye (pl **fish-eyes**) [fiʃaj, fiʃajz] NM fish-eye lens

fissa* [fisa] ADV **faire ~** to get a move on*

fissible [fisibl] ADJ fissile, fissionable

fissile [fisil] ADJ (Géol) tending to split; (Phys) fissile, fissionable

fission [fisjɔ̃] NF fission; **~ de l'atome** atomic fission, splitting of the atom

fissuration [fisyRasjɔ̃] NF fissuring, cracking, splitting

fissure [fisyR] NF (lit) crack, fissure; (fig) crack, (Anat) fissure

fissurer [fisyRe] ▶ conjug 1 ◀ [1] VT to crack, fissure; (fig) to split [2] **se fissurer** VPR to crack, fissure

fiston* [fistɔ̃] NM son; **dis-moi, ~** tell me, son ou sonny*

fistulaire [fistylɛR] ADJ fistular

fistule [fistyl] NF fistula

fistuleux, -euse [fistylø, øz] ADJ fistulous

fitness [fitnɛs] NM (Sport) fitness; **centre de ~** fitness centre ou club; **salle de ~** gym

FIV [ɛfive] NF (ABRÉV = **fécondation in vitro**) IVF

five o'clock† [fajvɔklɔk] NM (hum) (afternoon) tea

FIVETE, Fivete [fivet] NF (ABRÉV = **fécondation in vitro et transfert d'embryon**) ZIFT

fixage [fiksaʒ] NM (Art, Photo, Tex, Fin) fixing

fixateur [fiksatœR] NM (Art) fixative; (Coiffure) (= laque) hair spray; (= crème) hair cream; (avant la mise en plis) setting lotion; (Photo) fixer

fixatif [fiksatif] NM fixative; (Can = laque) hair spray

fixation [fiksasjɔ̃] NF [a] (Chim, Psych, Zool) fixation; (Photo) fixing; (Psych) **faire une ~ sur qch** to have a fixation about sth [b] (= attache) fastening; (Ski) **~s (de sécurité)** (safety) bindings; (Ski) **~s de randonnée** touring bindings [c] [peuple] settling [d] [salaires, date] fixing

fixe [fiks] [1] ADJ [a] (= immobile) [point, panneau] fixed; [personnel] permanent; [emploi] permanent, steady; [regard] vacant, fixed; **regarder qn les yeux ~s** to gaze ou look fixedly ou intently at sb; (commandement) **~!** eyes front! → **barre** [b] (= prédéterminé) [revenu, date] fixed, set; **à heure ~** at set times → **prix** [c] (= inaltérable) [couleur] fast, permanent; **encre bleu ~** permanent blue ink → **beau²**, **idée** [2] NM [a] (= salaire) basic ou fixed salary [b] (arg Drogue) fix; **se faire un ~** to get a fix

fixe-chaussette (pl **fixe-chaussettes**) [fiksəʃoset] NM garter, suspender (Brit)

fixement [fiksəmã] ADV [regarder] fixedly

fixer [fikse] ▶ conjug 1 ◀ [1] VT [a] (= attacher) to fix, fasten (**à**, **sur** to); **~ qch dans sa mémoire** to fix sth firmly in one's memory [b] (= décider) [+ date] to set, arrange, fix; **~ la date/l'heure d'un rendez-vous** to set ou arrange ou fix the date/the time for a meeting; **mon choix s'est fixé sur celui-ci** I settled ou decided on this one; **je ne suis pas encore fixé sur ce que je ferai** I haven't made up my mind what to do yet, I haven't got any fixed plans in mind yet; **avez-vous fixé le jour de votre départ?** have you decided what day you are leaving (on)?; **à l'heure fixée** at the agreed ou appointed time; **au jour fixé** on the appointed day [c] (+ regard, attention) to fix; **~ les yeux sur qn/qch** ◊ **~ qn/qch du regard** to stare at sb/sth; **il la fixa longuement** he stared at her, he looked hard at her; **mon regard se fixa sur lui** I fixed my gaze on him; **tous les regards étaient fixés sur lui** all eyes were on him; **~ son attention sur** to focus ou fix one's attention on [d] (= déterminer) [+ prix, impôt, délai] to set, fix; [+ règle, principe] to lay down, determine; [+ idées] to clarify, sort out; [+ conditions] to lay down, set; **les droits et les devoirs fixés par la loi** the rights and responsibilities laid down ou determined by law; **~ ses idées sur le papier** to set one's ideas down on paper; **mot fixé par l'usage** word fixed by usage; **l'orthographe s'est fixée** the spelling became fixed [e] (= renseigner) **~ qn sur qch*** to put sb in the picture about sth*, enlighten sb as to sth; **être fixé sur le compte de qn** to be wise to sb*, have sb weighed up* (Brit); **alors, tu es fixé maintenant?*** have you got the picture now?* [f] (= stabiliser) **~ qn** to make sb settle (down); **seul le mariage pourra le ~** marriage is the only thing that will make him settle down [g] (Photo) to fix [2] **se fixer** VPR [a] (= s'installer) to settle; **il s'est fixé à Lyon** he settled in Lyon [b] (= s'assigner) **se ~ un objectif** to set o.s. a target; **je me suis fixé fin mai pour terminer** I've decided the end of May is my deadline

fixing [fiksiŋ] NM (Fin) fixing

fixité [fiksite] NF [opinions] fixedness; [regard] fixedness, steadiness

fjord [fjɔR(d)] NM fiord, fjord

Fl (ABRÉV = **florin**) fl

flac [flak] EXCL splash!; **faire (un) ~** to splash

flaccidité [flaksidite] NF flabbiness, flaccidity

flacon [flakɔ̃] NM (small) bottle; (Chim) flask; **~ à parfum** perfume bottle

flafla* [flafla] NM **faire des ~s** to show off; **sans ~** without fuss (and bother)

flagada* [flagada] ADJ INV **être ~** to be washed-out*

flagellateur, -trice [flaʒelatœR, tRis] NM,F flogger, scourger, flagellator

flagellation [flaʒelasjɔ̃] NF (gén) flogging; (Rel) flagellation, scourging; (= pratique sexuelle) flagellation

flagelle [flaʒɛl] NM flagellum

flagellé, e [flaʒele] (ptp de **flageller**) ADJ, NM (Zool) flagellate; **les ~s** flagellates, Mastigophora, Flagellata

flageller [flaʒele] ▶ conjug 1 ◀ VT (gén) to flog; (Rel) to flagellate, scourge; (fig) to flay; **~ le vice** to castigate vice

flageolant, e [flaʒɔlã, ãt] ADJ shaky, trembling

flageoler [flaʒɔle] ▶ conjug 1 ◀ VI **il flageolait (sur ses jambes)** ◊ **ses jambes flageolaient** (de faiblesse, de fatigue) his legs were giving way, his legs were trembling ou shaking; (de peur) he was quaking at the knees, his legs were trembling ou shaking

flageolet [flaʒɔlɛ] NM [a] (Mus) flageolet [b] (Bot) flageolet, dwarf kidney bean

flagorner [flagɔRne] ▶ conjug 1 ◀ VT (frm, hum) to toady to, fawn upon

flagornerie [flagɔRnəRi] NF (frm, hum) toadying (NonC), fawning (NonC), sycophancy (NonC)

flagorneur, -euse [flagɔRnœR, øz] (frm, hum) [1] ADJ toadying, fawning, sycophantic [2] NM,F toady, sycophant

flagrance [flagRãs] NF (Jur) blatancy, flagrance

flagrant, e [flagRã, ãt] ADJ [mensonge] blatant; [erreur, injustice] flagrant, blatant, glaring; **prendre qn en ~ délit** to catch sb red-handed ou in the act ou in flagrante delicto (SPÉC); **pris en ~ délit de mensonge** caught lying

flair [flɛR] NM [chien] sense of smell, nose; [personne] intuition, sixth sense; **avoir du ~** [chien] to have a good nose; [personne] to have intuition ou a sixth sense; **pour les investissements, il a du ~** he has a (good) nose for investments

flairer [flɛRe] ▶ conjug 1 ◀ VT [a] (= humer) to smell (at), sniff (at); (Chasse) to scent [b] (= deviner) to sense; **il a tout de suite flairé que quelque chose n'allait pas** he immediately sensed that something wasn't right; **~ quelque chose de louche** to smell a rat; **~ le danger** to sense ou scent danger; **~ le vent** to see which way the wind is blowing, read the wind

flamand, e [flamã, ãd] [1] ADJ Flemish [2] NM [a] (Ling) Flemish [b] **Flamand** Fleming, Flemish man; **les Flamands** the Flemish [3] **Flamande** NF Fleming, Flemish woman

flamant [flamã] NM flamingo; **~ rose** pink flamingo

flambage [flãbaʒ] NM [a] [volaille] singeing; [instrument] sterilizing (in a flame) [b] (Tech) buckling

flambant, e [flãbã, ãt] ADJ (= qui brûle) burning; (* = superbe) great*; **~ neuf** brand new

flambart*†, flambard*† [flãbaR] NM swank-pot*; **faire le ou son ~** to swank*

flambé, e¹* [flãbe] (ptp de **flamber**) ADJ [personne] finished; **il est ~!** he's had it!*; **l'affaire est ~e!** it's all over!*

flambeau (pl **flambeaux**) [flãbo] NM [a] (= torche) (flaming) torch; **aux ~x** [dîner, défiler] by torchlight; **marche aux ~x** torchlight ou torchlit procession → **retraite** [b] (fig) torch; **passer le ~ à qn** to pass on ou hand on the torch to sb; **reprendre le ~** to take up the torch [c] (= chandelier) candlestick

flambée² [flãbe] NF [a] (= feu) blazing fire; **faire une ~ dans la cheminée** to make ou light a fire in the fireplace [b] (fig) [violence] outburst; [cours, prix] explosion; **~ de colère** angry outburst, flare-up; **la ~ de la Bourse** the sudden rise in the stock exchange

flambement [flãbmã] NM (Tech) buckling

flamber [flãbe] ▶ conjug 1 ◀ [1] VI [a] [bois] to burn; [feu, incendie] to blaze; **la maison a flambé en quelques minutes** in a few minutes the house was burnt to the ground [b]* [joueur] to gamble huge sums, play for high stakes [c] [cours, prix, Bourse] to shoot up, rocket [2] VT [a] (Culin) to flambé; **bananes flambées** bananas flambé [b] [+ volaille, cheveux] to singe; [+ aiguille, instrument de chirurgie] to sterilize (in a flame)

flambeur, -euse* [flãbœR, øz] NM,F big-time gambler

flamboiement [flãbwamã] NM [flammes] blaze, blazing; [lumière] blaze; [yeux] flash, gleam; **dans un ~ de couleurs** in a blaze of colour

flamboyant, e [flãbwajã, ãt] [1] ADJ [a] [feu, lumière, ciel, soleil] blazing; [yeux] flashing, blazing; [couleur] flaming; [regard] fiery; [épée, armure] gleaming, flashing [b] (Archit) flamboyant [2] NM [a] (*Archit*) flamboyant style [b] (*Bot*) flamboyant, royal poinciana

flamboyer [flɑ̃bwaje] ▶conjug 8◀ VI [*flamme, soleil, ciel*] to blaze; [*yeux*] to flash, blaze; [*couleur*] to flame; [*épée, armure*] to gleam, flash

flamenco [flamenko], **flamenca** [flamenka] [1] ADJ [*fête, chants*] flamenco; **guitare flamenca** *ou* ~ flamenco guitar [2] NM flamenco

flamiche [flamiʃ] NF leek pie

flamingant, e [flamɛ̃gɑ̃, ɑ̃t] [1] ADJ Flemish-speaking [2] **Flamingant(e)** NM,F Flemish speaker; (*Pol*) Flemish nationalist

flamme [flɑm] NF [a] (*lit*) flame; **être en ~s à la proie des ~s** to be ablaze *ou* on fire *ou* in flames; **dévoré par les ~s** consumed by fire *ou* the flames; **la ~ olympique** the Olympic flame; **les ~s de l'enfer** the flames *ou* fires of hell; **descendre (qch/qn) en ~s*** to shoot (sth/sb) down in flames [b] (= *ardeur*) fire, fervour (*Brit*), fervor (*US*); **discours plein de ~** passionate *ou* fiery speech; **jeune homme plein de ~** young man full of fire [c] (= *éclat*) fire, brilliance; **la ~ de ses yeux** *ou* **de son regard** his flashing *ou* blazing eyes [d] (*littér ouhum = amour*) love, ardour (*Brit*), ardor (*US*); **il lui a déclaré sa ~** he declared his undying love to her [e] (= *drapeau*) pennant, pennon [f] (*Poste*) postal logo

flammé, e [flɑme] ADJ [*céramique*] flambé

flammèche [flɑmɛʃ] NF (flying) spark

flan [flɑ̃] NM [a] (*Culin*) custard tart [b] (*Tech*) [*imprimeur*] flong; [*monnaie*] blank, flan; [*disque*] mould [c]* **c'est du ~!** it's a load of hooey!* → **rond**

flanc [flɑ̃] NM [a] [*personne*] side, flank; [*animal*] side, flank; (†, *littér*) **l'enfant qu'elle portait dans son ~** the child she was carrying in her womb; **être couché sur le ~** to be lying on one's side; **tirer au ~*** to shirk, skive* (*Brit*); **être sur le ~** (= *malade*) to be laid up; (= *fatigué*) to be all in*; **cette grippe m'a mis sur le ~** this flu has really knocked me out* → **battre** [b] [*navire*] side; [*armée, bastion, écu*] flank; [*montagne*] slope, side; **à ~ de coteau** *ou* **de colline** on the hillside; **prendre de ~** (*fig, Naut*) to catch broadside on; (*Mil*) to attack on the flank → **prêter**

flancher* [flɑ̃ʃe] ▶conjug 1◀ VI [*cœur*] to give out, pack up* (*Brit*); [*troupes*] to give way; **sa mémoire a flanché** his memory failed him; **c'est le moral qui a flanché** he lost his nerve; **il a flanché en math** he fell down *ou* came down in maths; **sans ~** without flinching; **ce n'est pas le moment de ~** this is no time for weakness

flanchet [flɑ̃ʃɛ] NM (*Boucherie*) flank

Flandre [flɑ̃dʀ] NF **la ~** ◊ **les ~s** Flanders

flandrin [flɑ̃dʀɛ̃] NM († †, *péj*) **grand ~** great gangling fellow

flanelle [flanɛl] NF (*Tex*) flannel; **~ de coton** cotton flannel; **pantalon de ~ grise** grey flannel trousers, grey flannels

flâner [flɑne] ▶conjug 1◀ VI to stroll; (*péj*) to hang about, lounge about; **va chercher du pain, et sans ~!** go and get some bread, and don't hang about! *ou* and be quick about it!

flânerie [flɑnʀi] NF stroll; (*péj*) **perdre son temps en ~s** to waste one's time lounging about

flâneur, -euse [flɑnœʀ, øz] [1] ADJ idle [2] NM,F stroller; (*péj*) idler, loafer

flanquer¹ [flɑ̃ke] ▶conjug 1◀ VT to flank; **la boutique qui flanque la maison** the shop adjoining *ou* flanking the house; **flanqué de ses gardes du corps** flanked by his bodyguards; (*péj*) **il est toujours flanqué de sa mère** he always has his mother in tow*

flanquer²* [flɑ̃ke] ▶conjug 1◀ [1] VT [a] (= *jeter*) ~ **qch par terre** (*lit*) to fling sth to the ground; (*fig*) to knock sth on the head*, put paid to

sth (*Brit*); ~ **qn par terre** to fling sb to the ground; ~ **qn à la porte** to chuck sb out*; (= *licencier*) to fire sb, sack sb* (*Brit*), give sb the sack* (*Brit*); ~ **tout en l'air** to chuck* *ou* pack it all in* (*Brit*) [b] (= *donner*) ~ **une gifle à qn** give sb a slap *ou* a clout* (*Brit*); ~ **la trouille à qn** to give sb a scare, put the wind up sb* (*Brit*) [2] **se flanquer** VPR **se ~ par terre** to fall flat on one's face

flapi, e* [flapi] ADJ washed-out*

flaque [flak] NF ~ **de sang/d'huile** pool of blood/oil; ~ **d'eau** (*petite*) puddle; (*grande*) pool of water

flash (*pl* **flashs** *ou* **flashes**) [flaʃ] NM [a] (*Photo*) flash; **au ~** using a flash, with a flash; ~ **anti-yeux rouges** flash with a red-eye reduction feature [b] (*Radio, TV*) ~ **(d'informations)** newsflash; (*Radio*) ~ **publicitaire** commercial break [c] **avoir un ~** (*arg Drogue*) to be on a high*; (= *se souvenir*) to have a flashback

flash-back (*pl* **flash-back** *ou* **flashs-back** *ou* **flashes-back**) [flaʃbak] NM flashback

flasher* [flaʃe] ▶conjug 1◀ VI **j'ai flashé pour** *ou* **sur cette robe** I fell in love with this dress; **à chaque fois que je le vois, je flashe** *ou* **il me fait ~** every time I see him I go weak at the knees *ou* my heart skips a beat

flashmètre [flaʃmɛtʀ] NM flash meter

flasque¹ [flask] ADJ [*peau*] flaccid, flabby; (*fig*) [*personne*] spineless, spiritless; [*style*] limp

flasque² [flask] NF (= *bouteille*) flask

flatté, e [flate] (*ptp de* **flatter**) ADJ [*portrait*] flattering

flatter [flate] ▶conjug 1◀ [1] VT [a] (= *flagorner*) to flatter; ~ **servilement** *ou* **bassement qn** to fawn on sb, toady to sb; **cette photo la flatte** this photo flatters her; **sans vous ~** without meaning to flatter you [b] (= *faire plaisir*) [*compliment, décoration*] to flatter, gratify; **je suis très flatté de cet honneur** I am most flattered by this honour; **cela le flatte dans son orgueil** ◊ **cela flatte son orgueil** it flatters his pride [c] (*frm = favoriser*) [+ *manie, goûts*] to pander to; [+ *vice, passion*] to encourage [d] (*littér = tromper*) ~ **qn d'un espoir** to hold out false hopes to sb [e] (= *charmer*) [+ *oreille, regard*] to delight, be pleasing to; [+ *goût*] to flatter; ~ **le palais** to delight the taste buds [f] (*frm = caresser*) to stroke [2] **se flatter** VPR (*frm*) [a] (= *prétendre*) **se ~ de faire qch** to claim *ou* profess to be able to do sth; **il se flatte de tout comprendre** he professes to understand everything; **je me flatte d'avoir quelque influence sur lui** I like to think that I have some influence over him; **je me flatte de m'y connaître un peu en informatique** I flatter myself that I know a little about computers [b] (= *s'enorgueillir*) **se ~ de qch** to pride o.s. on sth; **elle se flatte de son succès** she prides herself on her success; **et je m'en flatte!** and I'm proud of it! [c] (= *se leurrer*) to delude o.s.; **se ~ d'un vain espoir** to cherish a forlorn hope; **s'il croit réussir, il se flatte!** if he thinks he can succeed, he's deluding himself!

flatterie [flatʀi] NF flattery (*NonC*); (*littér, hum*) **vile ~** base flattery

flatteur, -euse [flatœʀ, øz] [1] ADJ flattering; **comparaison flatteuse** flattering comparison; **faire un tableau ~ de la situation** to paint a rosy picture of the situation; **ce n'est pas ~!** that's not very flattering! [2] NM,F flatterer; (*littér, hum*) **vil ~** base flatterer

flatteusement [flatøzmɑ̃] ADV flatteringly

flatulence [flatylɑ̃s] NF wind, flatulence

flatulent, e [flatylɑ̃, ɑ̃t] ADJ flatulent

flatuosité [flatɥozite] NF (*Méd*) flatus (*SPÉC*); **avoir des ~s** to have wind

fléau (*pl* **fléaux**) [fleo] NM [a] (= *calamité*) scourge, curse; **le chômage est un véritable ~** social unemployment is the scourge of society; **quel ~, ce type!*** that guy's such a pest!* [b] [*balance*] beam; (*Agr*) flail

fléchage [fleʃaʒ] NM signposting (*with arrows*)

flèche¹ [flɛʃ] [1] NF [a] (= *arme*) arrow; (*Ordin*) arrow; ~ **en caoutchouc** rubber-tipped dart; **les ~s de l'Amour** *ou* **de Cupidon** Cupid's darts *ou* arrows; **monter en ~** [*avion*] to soar; [*prix*] to soar, rocket; **il monte en ~** [*chanteur*] he's on the up and up, he's rocketing to fame; **les prix sont montés en ~** prices have soared *ou* shot up *ou* rocketed; **la montée en ~ des prix** the surge in prices; **partir comme une ~** to set off like a shot; **il est passé devant nous comme une ~** he shot past us; **ce n'est pas une ~!*** he's no Einstein!*; **se trouver en ~** *ou* **prendre une position en ~ dans un débat** to take up an extreme position in a debate; **leur équipe se trouve en ~ dans la recherche génétique** their team is at the cutting edge of genetic research [b] (= *critique*) **diriger ses ~s contre qn** to direct one's shafts against sb; **la ~ du Parthe** (*Hist*) the Parthian shot; (*fig*) **c'était la ~ du Parthe** it was his parting shot; **faire ~ de tout bois** to use all available means [c] (= *direction*) (direction) arrow, pointer [d] [*église*] spire; [*grue*] jib; [*mât*] pole; [*affût, canon*] trail; [*balance*] pointer, needle; [*charrue*] beam; [*attelage*] pole; **atteler en ~** to drive tandem; **cheval de ~** lead horse [2] COMP ▶ **flèche lumineuse** (*sur l'écran*) arrow; (= *torche*) arrow pointer

flèche² [flɛʃ] NF (*Culin*) flitch

fléché, e [fleʃe] (*ptp de* **flécher**) ADJ **parcours ~** arrowed course, course marked *ou* signposted with arrows; **croix ~e** crosslet → **mot**

flécher [fleʃe] ▶conjug 1◀ VT to mark (with arrows); **ils ont fléché le parcours** they marked the route (out) with arrows, they put arrows along the route

fléchette [fleʃɛt] NF dart; **jouer aux ~s** to play darts

fléchi, e [fleʃi] (*ptp de* **fléchir**) ADJ [a] (= *plié*) [*bras, jambe, genou*] bent, flexed; [*corps*] bent; **avec les jambes légèrement ~es** with the legs slightly bent *ou* flexed [b] (*Ling*) inflected

fléchir [fleʃiʀ] ▶conjug 2◀ [1] VT [a] (= *plier*) to bend; (*Méd*) [+ *articulation*] to flex; ~ **le genou devant qn** to go down on one knee in front of sb [b] (= *faire céder*) [+ *personne*] to sway; [+ *colère*] to soothe; **il s'est laissé ~** he let himself be swayed [2] VI [a] (= *plier*: *gén*) to bend; [*planches*] to sag, bend; [*poutre, genoux*] to sag; **ses jambes** *ou* **ses genoux fléchirent** his legs gave way [b] (= *faiblir*) [*armée*] to give ground, yield; [*volonté*] to weaken; **sans ~** with unflinching determination [c] (= *diminuer*) [*attention*] to flag; [*recettes, talent, nombre*] to fall off; [*cours de Bourse*] to ease, drop; [*monnaie*] to weaken, drop; **la courbe de l'inflation fléchit** there is a downturn in inflation; (*Bourse*) **les pétrolières ont fléchi en début de séance** oils were down *ou* dropped slightly in early trading [d] (= *céder*) to yield, soften; **il fléchit devant leurs prières** he yielded to their entreaties [e] (*Ling*) **forme fléchie** inflected form

fléchissement [fleʃismɑ̃] NM [a] [*objet, membre*] bending; (*Méd*) [*articulation*] flexing [b] [*armée*] yielding; [*volonté*] weakening [c] [*attention*] flagging; [*recettes, talent, nombre*] falling off; [*cours de Bourse*] easing off (**de** of), drop (**de** in); [*monnaie*] weakening, dropping (**de** of); [*natalité, exportations*] drop (**de** in)

fléchisseur [fleʃisœʀ] ADJ M, NM (*Anat*) **(muscle) ~** flexor

flegmatique [flɛgmatik] ADJ phlegmatic

flegmatiquement [flɛgmatikmɑ̃] ADV phlegmatically

flegme [flɛgm] NM composure, phlegm; **il perdit son ~** he lost his composure *ou* cool*; (*hum*) **le ~ britannique** the British stiff upper lip

flémingite* [flemeʒit] NF (*hum*) bone idleness; **il a une ~ aiguë** he's suffering from acute inertia (*hum*)

flemmard, e* [flemar, ard] [1] ADJ workshy, bone-idle* (*Brit*) [2] NM,F idler, lazybones

flemmarder* [flemarde] ▸ conjug 1 ◂ VI to loaf about, lounge about

flemmardise* [flemardiz] NF laziness, idleness

flemme* [flem] NF laziness; **j'ai la ~ de le faire** I can't be bothered; **tirer sa ~** to idle around, loaf about

fléole [fleɔl] NF **~ des prés** timothy

flet [flɛ] NM flounder

flétan [fletɑ̃] NM halibut

flétri, e [fletri] (*ptp de* **flétrir¹**) ADJ [*feuille, fleur*] withered, wilted; [*peau, visage*] withered; [*beauté*] faded

flétrir¹ [fletrir] ▸ conjug 2 ◂ [1] VT (= *faner*) to wither, fade; **l'âge a flétri son visage** his face is wizened with age [2] **se flétrir** VPR [*fleur*] to wither, wilt; [*beauté*] to fade; [*peau, visage*] to become wizened; [*cœur*] to wither

flétrir² [fletrir] ▸ conjug 2 ◂ VT [a] (= *stigmatiser*) [+ *personne, conduite*] to condemn; [+ *réputation*] to blacken [b] (*Hist*) to brand

flétrissement [fletrismɑ̃] NM [*fleur*] withering, wilting; [*peau*] withering; [*beauté*] fading

flétrissure¹ [fletrisyr] NF [*fleur, peau*] withering; [*teint*] fading

flétrissure² [fletrisyr] NF [a] [*réputation, honneur*] stain, blemish (**à** on) [b] (*Hist*) brand

fleur [flœr] [1] NF [a] (*Bot*) flower; [*arbre*] blossom; **en ~(s)** [*plante*] in bloom, in flower; [*arbre*] in blossom, in flower; **papier à ~s** flowered *ou* flower-patterned *ou* flowery paper; **assiette à ~s** flower-patterned *ou* flowery plate; **chapeau à ~s** flowery hat; **« ni ~s ni couronnes »** "no flowers by request" [b] [*cuir*] grain side; **cuir pleine ~** finest quality leather [c] (= *le meilleur*) **la ~ de** the flower of; **à** *ou* **dans la ~ de l'âge** in the prime of life, in one's prime; (†, *hum*) **perdre sa ~** to lose one's honour† (*aussi hum*) → **fin¹** [d] (*loc*) **comme une ~*** (= *sans effort*) without trying; (= *sans prévenir*) unexpectedly; **il est arrivé le premier comme une ~** he romped home; **à ~ de terre** just above the ground; **un écueil à ~ d'eau** a reef just above the water *ou* which just breaks the surface of the water; **j'ai les nerfs à ~ de peau** I'm all on edge, my nerves are all on edge; **il a une sensibilité à ~ de peau** he's very touchy; **avoir les yeux à ~ de tête** to have protruding eyes; **faire une ~ à qn*** to do sb a favour *ou* a good turn; (*fig*) **lancer des ~s à qn** ◊ **couvrir qn de ~s** to shower praise on sb; **s'envoyer des ~s** (*réfléchi*) to pat o.s. on the back*; (*réciproque*) to pat each other on the back*; (*hum*) **~ bleue** naïvely sentimental; **il est resté ~ bleue en vieillissant** even in his old age he is still a bit of a romantic; **ils sont partis la ~ au fusil** they went to battle full of innocent enthusiasm

[2] COMP ▸ **fleur de farine** fine wheat flour ▸ **fleurs de givre** frost patterns ▸ **fleur de lis** (*Hér*) fleur-de-lis ▸ **fleur(s) d'oranger** orange blossom ▸ **fleur(s) de pommier** apple blossom ▸ **fleurs de rhétorique** flowers of rhetoric ▸ **fleur de sel** *best quality unrefined salt* ▸ **fleur de soufre** flowers of sulphur (*Brit*) *ou* sulfur (*US*)

fleuraison [flœrɛzɔ̃] NF = **floraison**

fleurdelisé, e [flœrdəlize] [1] ADJ decorated

with fleurs-de-lis; **croix ~e** fleurettée *ou* fleurty cross [2] NM (*Can*) **le ~** the Quebec flag

fleurer [flœre] ▸ conjug 1 ◂ VT (*littér*) to have the scent of, smell of; **ça fleure bon le pain grillé** there's a lovely smell of toast; **~ bon la lavande** to smell (sweetly) of lavender; **sa musique fleure bon l'exotisme** his music has an exotic feel to it

fleuret [flœrɛ] NM (= *épée*) foil; **propos à ~s mouchetés** discussion full of barbed remarks

fleurette† [flœrɛt] NF (*hum*) floweret → **conter, crème**

fleuri, e [flœri] (*ptp de* **fleurir**) ADJ [a] [*fleur*] in bloom; [*branche*] in blossom; [*jardin, pré*] in flower *ou* bloom; [*tissu, papier*] flowered, flowery; [*appartement, table*] decorated *ou* decked with flowers; **à la boutonnière ~** (*avec une fleur*) wearing *ou* sporting a flower in his buttonhole; (*avec une décoration*) wearing a decoration on his lapel; **« Annecy, ville ~e »** "Annecy, town in bloom" [b] [*teint*] florid; [*style*] flowery, florid; (*hum*) **barbe ~e** flowing white beard [c] [*croûte de fromage*] mouldy

fleurir [flœrir] ▸ conjug 2 ◂ [1] VI [a] [*arbre*] to blossom, (come into) flower; [*fleur*] to flower, (come into) bloom; (*littér*) [*qualité, sentiment*] to blossom (*littér*); **un sourire fleurit sur ses lèvres** a smile appeared on his lips [b] (*imparfait florissait*) [*commerce, arts*] to flourish, prosper, thrive [2] VT [+ *salon*] to decorate *ou* deck with flowers; **~ une tombe/un mort** to put flowers on a grave/on sb's grave; **~ sa boutonnière** to put a flower in one's buttonhole; **un ruban fleurissait (à) sa boutonnière** he was wearing a decoration on his lapel; **fleurissez-vous, mesdames, fleurissez-vous!**† treat yourselves to some flowers, ladies!, buy yourselves a buttonhole (*Brit*) *ou* boutonnière (*US*), ladies!

fleuriste [flœrist] NMF (= *personne*) florist; (= *boutique*) florist's (shop), flower shop

fleuron [flœrɔ̃] NM [*couronne*] floweret; [*bâtiment*] finial; (*Bot*) floret; [*collection*] jewel; (*Écon*) flagship; **c'est le plus beau ~ de ma collection** it's the jewel of my collection; **l'un des ~s de l'industrie française** a flagship French industry

fleuve [flœv] [1] NM (*lit*) river (*flowing into the sea*); **~ de boue/de lave** river of mud/of lava; **le ~ Jaune** the Yellow River; **~ de larmes** flood of tears; **~ de sang** river of blood; (*hum*) **sa vie n'a pas été un long ~ tranquille** his life hasn't been a bed of roses [2] ADJ INV [*discours, film*] marathon (*épith*)

flexibilité [flɛksibilite] NF flexibility; **la ~ de l'emploi** flexibility in employment

flexible [flɛksibl] [1] ADJ [*métal*] flexible, pliable, pliant; [*branche, roseau*] pliable, pliant; [*caractère*] (= *accommodant*) flexible, adaptable; (= *malléable*) pliant, pliable; **taux de change ~** floating exchange rate; **atelier** *ou* **usine ~** flexible manufacturing system, FMS → **horaire** [2] NM (= *câble*) flexible coupling; (= *tuyau*) flexible tubing *ou* hose

flexion [flɛksjɔ̃] NF [a] (= *courbure*) [*ressort, lame d'acier*] flexion, bending; [*poutre, pièce*] bending, sagging; **résistance à la ~** bending strength [b] [*membre, articulation*] flexing (*NonC*), bending (*NonC*); (*Ski*) knee-bend; **faire plusieurs ~s du bras/du corps** to flex the arm/bend the body several times [c] (*Ling*) inflection, inflexion; **langue à ~** inflecting *ou* inflected language

flexionnel, -elle [flɛksjɔnɛl] ADJ [*désinence*] inflexional, inflectional, inflected; **langue flexionnelle** inflecting *ou* inflected language

flexueux, -euse [flɛksɥø, øz] ADJ flexuous, flexuose

flexuosité [flɛksɥozite] NF flexuosity

flexure [flɛksyr] NF flexure

flibuste [flibyst] NF (= *piraterie*) freebooting, buccaneering; (= *pirates*) freebooters, buccaneers

flibustier [flibystje] NM (= *pirate*) freebooter, buccaneer; (*‡* = *escroc*) swindler, crook

flic* [flik] NM cop*, policeman; **les ~s** the cops*, the police

flicage‡ [flikaʒ] NM [*quartier*] heavy policing; **le ~ des ouvriers par la direction** the way the management keeps tabs on the workers

flicaille‡ [flikaj] NF **la ~** the fuzz‡, the pigs‡, the filth‡ (*Brit*)

flicard‡ [flikar] NM cop*, pig‡

flic flac [flikflak] NM, EXCL plop, splash; **ses chaussures faisaient ~ dans la boue** his shoes went splash splash through the mud

flingue‡ [flɛ̃g] NM gun, rifle

flinguer‡ [flɛ̃ge] ▸ conjug 1 ◂ VT [a] (= *tuer*) [+ *personne*] to gun down, put a bullet in, shoot up* (*US*); **il y a de quoi se ~!** it's enough to make you want to shoot yourself! [b] (= *détruire*) [+ *appareil*] to bust‡; [+ *voiture*] to smash (up)‡, total* (*US*) [c] (= *critiquer*) to shoot down in flames* (*Brit*), shoot down* (*US*)

flingueur‡ [flɛ̃gœr] NM (= *tueur à gages*) hitman*, contract killer; **c'est un ~** (= *il a la gâchette facile*) he's trigger-happy*

flingueuse‡ [flɛ̃gøz] NF contract killer

flint(-glass) [flint(glas)] NM flint glass

flip¹* [flip] NM (*arg Drogue*) (fit of) depression; **un jour de ~** a day on a downer*

flip² [flip] NM **porto ~** egg flip (*with port*)

flippant, e‡ [flipɑ̃, ɑ̃t] ADJ [*situation, film*] grim*, depressing; [*personne*] depressing

flipper¹ [flipœr] NM (= *billard électrique*) pinball machine; **jouer au ~** to play pinball

flipper²* [flipe] ▸ conjug 1 ◂ VI (*fig, Drogue*) to freak out*; (= *être déprimé*) to feel down*; **son examen la fait ~** she's freaking out* at the thought of her exam

fliqué, e‡ [flike] ADJ [*endroit*] full of *ou* crawling with cops*; **le coin est très ~** the place is full of *ou* crawling with cops*

fliquer‡ [flike] ▸ conjug 1 ◂ VT [a] [*police*] [+ *quartier*] to bring the cops* into [b] [+ *personne*] to keep under close surveillance; **ma mère n'arrête pas de me ~** my mother watches my every move *ou* has always got her beady eye on me

flirt [flœrt] NM [a] (= *action*) flirting (*NonC*); (= *amourette*) flirtation, brief romance; (= *rapprochement*) flirtation; **avoir un ~ avec qn** to have a brief romance with sb [b] (= *amoureux*) boyfriend (*ou* girlfriend); **un de mes anciens ~s** an old flame of mine

flirter [flœrte] ▸ conjug 1 ◂ VI to flirt; (= *fréquenter*) **~ avec qn** to go around with sb; (*fig*) **~ avec** [+ *idée, parti*] to flirt with

flirteur, -euse† [flœrtœr, øz] [1] ADJ flirtatious [2] NM,F flirt

FLN [ɛfɛlɛn] NM (ABRÉV = **Front de libération nationale**) FLN

FLNC [ɛfɛlɛnse] NM (ABRÉV = **Front de libération nationale de la Corse**) → **front**

floc [flɔk] NM, EXCL plop, splash; **faire ~** to splash, (go) plop

flocage [flɔkaʒ] NM [a] (*Tex*) flocking [b] (*Tech*) **~ à l'amiante** asbestos fireproofing

flocon [flɔkɔ̃] NM [*écume*] fleck; [*laine*] flock; **~ de neige** snowflake; **~s d'avoine** oatflakes, rolled oats; **~s de maïs** cornflakes; **la neige tombe à gros ~s** the snow is falling in big flakes; **purée en ~s** instant mashed potato

floconneux, -euse [flɔkɔnø, øz] ADJ [*nuage, étoffe*] fluffy; [*écume, substance, liquide*] frothy

flonflons [flɔ̃flɔ̃] NMPL (*gén*) oompah, oompah-pah; **les ~ de la musique foraine** the pom-pom of the fairground music

flop* [flɔp] NM flop*; **sa tournée a fait un ~** his tour was a real flop*

flopée* [flɔpe] NF **une ~ de** loads of*, masses of; **il y a une ~** *ou* **des ~s de touristes** there are loads* *ou* masses of tourists; **elle a une ~ d'enfants** she's got loads* of children

floqué, e [flɔke] ADJ [*moquette, papier, tissu*] flock (*épith*), flocked; **plafond ~ à l'amiante** ceiling insulated with asbestos

floraison [flɔʀɛzɔ̃] NF a (*lit*) (= *épanouissement*) flowering, blossoming; (= *époque*) flowering time; **rosiers qui ont plusieurs ~s** rosebushes which have several flowerings *ou* which flower several times a year b [*talents*] flowering, blossoming; [*affiches, articles*] rash, crop

floral, e (*mpl* **-aux**) [flɔʀal, o] ADJ a (*gén*) flower (*épith*); **art ~** flower arranging; **composition ~e** flower arrangement; **exposition ~e** flower show; **parc ~** flower garden b (*Bot*) [*enveloppe, organes*] floral

floralies [flɔʀali] NFPL flower show

flore [flɔʀ] NF (= *plantes*) flora; (= *livre*) plant guide; **~ intestinale** intestinal flora

floréal [flɔʀeal] NM Floreal (*eighth month in the French Republican calendar*)

Florence [flɔʀɑ̃s] N (= *ville*) Florence

florentin [flɔʀɑ̃tɛ̃, in] 1 ADJ Florentine 2 NM (*Ling*) Florentine dialect 3 **Florentin(e)** NM,F Florentine

florès [flɔʀɛs] NM (*littér, hum*) **faire ~** [*personne*] to shine, enjoy great success; [*théorie*] to be in vogue

floriculture [flɔʀikyltyʀ] NF flower-growing, floriculture (*SPÉC*)

Floride [flɔʀid] NF Florida

florifère [flɔʀifɛʀ] ADJ (= *qui a des fleurs*) flower-bearing; **cette variété est très ~** this variety produces a lot of flowers *ou* flowers abundantly

florilège [flɔʀilɛʒ] NM anthology

florin [flɔʀɛ̃] NM florin

florissant, e [flɔʀisɑ̃, ɑ̃t] ADJ [*pays, économie, théorie*] flourishing; [*santé, teint*] blooming

flot [flo] NM a (*littér*) [*lac, mer*] **~s** waves; **les ~s** the waves, **voguer sur les ~s bleus** to sail the ocean blue b (= *grande quantité*) [*lumière, boue, sang, véhicules*] stream; [*paroles, informations, images*] stream, flood; [*souvenirs, larmes, lettres*] flood; **un ~ ou des ~s de rubans/dentelle** a cascade of ribbons/lace; **les ~s de sa chevelure** her flowing locks *ou* mane (*littér*) c (= *marée*) **le ~** the floodtide, the incoming tide d (*loc*) **à (grands) ~s** in streams *ou* torrents; **le vin coulait à ~s** the wine flowed like water; **l'argent coule à ~s** there's plenty of money around; **la lumière entre à ~s** light is streaming in *ou* flooding in *ou* pouring in; **être à ~** [*bateau*] to be afloat; [*entreprise*] to be on an even keel; [*personne*] to have one's head above water; **remettre à ~** [+ *bateau*] to refloat; [+ *entreprise*] to bring back onto an even keel; **ces mesures devraient permettre la remise à ~ de l'économie** these measures should help get the economy back onto an even keel; (*Scol*) **classes de remise à ~** remedial classes; (*lit, fig*) **mettre à ~** to launch; **la mise à ~ d'un bateau** the launching of a ship

flottabilité [flɔtabilite] NF buoyancy

flottable [flɔtabl] ADJ [*bois, objet*] buoyant; [*rivière*] floatable

flottage [flɔtaʒ] NM floating (*of logs down a river*)

flottaison [flɔtɛzɔ̃] NF a (*Naut*) **(ligne de) ~** waterline; **~ en charge** load line, Plimsoll line b (*Fin*) flotation, floatation

flottant, e [flɔtɑ̃, ɑ̃t] 1 ADJ a [*bois, glace, mine*] floating; [*brume*] drifting; (*Ordin*) [*virgule*] floating → **île** b [*cheveux, cape*] flowing; [*vêtement*] loose c [*capitaux, taux de change, dette*] floating; [*effectifs*] fluctuating; **électorat ~** floating voters d [*caractère, esprit*] irresolute, vacillating; **rester ~** to be unable to

---

make up one's mind (**devant** when faced with) e [*côte, rein*] floating 2 NM a (= *short*) shorts; **son ~ est usé** his shorts are worn out; **deux ~s** two pairs of shorts b (*Fin*) float

flotte [flɔt] NF a (*Aviat, Naut*) fleet; **~ aérienne** air fleet; **~ de guerre** naval fleet; **~ marchande** *ou* **de commerce** merchant fleet b* (= *pluie*) rain; (= *eau*) water; (*péj*) **son café, c'est de la ~** his coffee's like dishwater c (= *flotteur*) float

flottement [flɔtmɑ̃] NM a (= *hésitation*) wavering, hesitation; **on observa un certain ~ dans la foule** the crowd seemed to hesitate; **il y a eu un ~ électoral important** there was strong evidence *ou* a strong element of indecision among voters b (*Mil: dans les rangs*) swaying, sway c (= *relâchement*) (*dans une œuvre, copie*) vagueness, imprecision; (*dans le travail*) unevenness (**dans** in); **le ~ de son esprit/imagination** his wandering mind/ roving imagination d (= *ondulation*) [*fanion*] fluttering; **le ~ du drapeau dans le vent** the fluttering *ou* flapping of the flag in the wind e (*Fin*) floating

flotter [flɔte] ▶ conjug 1 ◀ 1 VI a (*sur l'eau*) to float; **faire ~ qch sur l'eau** to float sth on the water b [*brume*] to drift, hang; [*parfum*] to hang; [*cheveux*] to stream (out); [*drapeau*] to fly; [*fanion*] to flutter; **~ au vent** [*cape, écharpe*] to flap *ou* flutter in the wind; **un drapeau flottait sur le bâtiment** a flag was flying over *ou* from the building c (= *être trop grand*) [*vêtement*] to hang loose; **il flotte dans ses vêtements** his clothes are too big for him d (*littér = errer*) [*pensée, imagination*] to wander, rove; **un sourire flottait sur ses lèvres** a smile hovered on *ou* played about his lips e (= *hésiter*) to waver, hesitate f (*Fin*) [*devise*] to float 2 VB IMPERS* (= *pleuvoir*) to rain 3 VT [+ *bois*] to float (down a waterway)

flotteur [flɔtœʀ] NM [*filet, hydravion, carburateur, trimaran*] float; [*chasse d'eau*] ballcock (*Brit*), floater (*US*)

flottille [flɔtij] NF [*bateaux*] flotilla; [*avions*] squadron

flou, e [flu] 1 ADJ a [*dessin, trait*] blurred; [*image, contour*] hazy, vague; [*photo*] blurred, fuzzy, out of focus; [*couleur*] soft b [*robe*] loose(-fitting); [*coiffure*] soft c [*idée, pensée, théorie*] woolly, vague; [*logique*] fuzzy 2 NM [*photo, tableau*] fuzziness; [*couleur*] softness; [*robe*] looseness; [*contours*] haziness; **le ~ de son esprit** the vagueness of his mind; **le ~ artistique** (*lit*) soft focus; (*fig*) **c'est le ~ artistique** it's all very vague; **~ juridique** vagueness of the law; **sur ses intentions, il est resté dans le ~** he remained vague about his intentions

flouer*† [flue] ▶ conjug 1 ◀ VT (= *duper*) to swindle, diddle* (*Brit*); **se faire ~** to be had*

flouse‡†, flouze‡† [fluz] NM (= *argent*) bread‡, dough‡, lolly‡

fluctuant, e [flyktɥɑ̃, ɑ̃t] ADJ [*prix, monnaie*] fluctuating; [*humeur*] changing

fluctuation [flyktɥasjɔ̃] NF [*prix*] fluctuation; [*opinion publique*] swing, fluctuation (**de** in); **~s du marché** market fluctuations

fluctuer [flyktɥe] ▶ conjug 1 ◀ VI to fluctuate

fluet, -ette [flɥɛ, ɛt] ADJ [*corps*] slight, slender; [*personne*] slightly built, slender; [*taille, membre, doigt*] slender, slim; [*voix*] thin, reedy, piping

fluide [flɥid] 1 ADJ a [*liquide, substance*] fluid; [*style, mouvement*] fluid, flowing; [*ligne, silhouette, robe*] flowing; (*Écon*) [*main-d'œuvre*] flexible; **la circulation est ~** the traffic is moving freely; **la situation politique reste ~** the political situation remains fluid 2 NM a [*gaz, liquide*] fluid; **~ de refroidissement** coolant b (= *pouvoir*) (mysterious) power; **il a du ~** ◊ **il a un ~ magnétique** he has mysterious powers

---

fluidification [flɥidifikasjɔ̃] NF fluidification, fluxing

fluidifier [flɥidifje] ▶ conjug 7 ◀ VT to fluidify, flux

fluidité [flɥidite] NF [*liquide, style*] fluidity; [*ligne, silhouette*] flow; [*circulation*] free flow; (*Écon*) [*main-d'œuvre*] flexibility

fluo* [flyo] ADJ INV (ABRÉV = **fluorescent**) fluorescent; **vert/rose ~** fluorescent green/pink

fluor [flyɔʀ] NM fluorine; **dentifrice au ~** fluoride toothpaste

fluoré, e [flyɔʀe] ADJ [*dentifrice*] fluoride (*épith*); [*eau*] fluoridated

fluorescéine [flyɔʀesein] NF fluorescein

fluorescence [flyɔʀesɑ̃s] NF fluorescence

fluorescent, e [flyɔʀesɑ̃, ɑ̃t] ADJ fluorescent; **écran/tube ~** fluorescent screen/lamp

fluorine [flyɔʀin] NF fluorspar, fluorite, calcium fluoride

fluorure [flyɔʀyʀ] NM fluoride

flush [flœʃ] NM (*Cartes*) flush

flûte [flyt] 1 NF a (= *instrument*) flute; (= *verre*) flute (glass); (= *pain*) baguette, French stick (*Brit*); (*Mus*) **petite ~** piccolo; **une ~ de champagne** a flute of champagne → **bois** b (= *jambes*) **~s*** legs, pins* (*Brit*), gams* (*US*); **se tirer les ~s†‡** to leg it*, scarper* (*Brit*) → **jouer** c (*Hist = navire*) store ship 2 EXCL* drat!* 3 COMP ▶ **flûte basse** bass flute ▶ **flûte à bec** recorder ▶ **flûte à champagne** champagne flute ▶ **flûte de Pan** panpipes ▶ **flûte traversière** flute

flûté, e [flyte] ADJ [*voix*] fluty

flûteau (*pl* **flûteaux**) [flyto], **flûtiau** (*pl* **flûtiaux**) [flytjo] NM (= *flûte*) penny whistle, reed pipe; (= *mirliton*) kazoo

flûtiste [flytist] NMF flautist, flutist (*US*)

fluvial, e (*mpl* **-iaux**) [flyvjal, jo] ADJ [*eaux, pêche, navigation*] river (*épith*); [*érosion*] fluvial (*épith*)

fluvioglaciaire [flyvjoglasjɛʀ] ADJ fluvioglacial

flux [fly] NM a (= *grande quantité*) [*argent, paroles*] flood; [*récriminations*] spate; [*personnes*] influx; (*Écon*) **~ de capitaux** capital flow; **~ monétaire** flow of money; **~ de trésorerie** cash flow; (*Comm*) **travailler en ~ tendus** to use just-in-time methods b (= *marée*) **le ~** the floodtide, the incoming tide; **le ~ et le reflux** the ebb and flow c (*Phys*) flux, flow; **~ électrique/magnétique/lumineux** electric/magnetic/luminous flux d (*Méd*) **~ de sang** flow of blood; **~ menstruel** menstrual flow

fluxion [flyksjɔ̃] NF (*Méd*) swelling, inflammation; (*dentaire*) gumboil; **~ de poitrine** pneumonia

FM [ɛfɛm] 1 NM (ABRÉV = **fusil-mitrailleur**) MG 2 NF (ABRÉV = **fréquence modulée**) FM

FMI [ɛfɛmi] NM (ABRÉV = **Fonds monétaire international**) IMF

FN [ɛfɛn] NM (ABRÉV = **Front national**) → **front**

FNE [ɛfɛnə] NM (ABRÉV = **Fonds national de l'emploi**) → **fonds**

FNSEA [ɛfɛnɛsəa] NF (ABRÉV = **Fédération nationale des syndicats d'exploitants agricoles**) *French farmers' union*

FO [ɛfo] NF (ABRÉV = **Force ouvrière**) *French trade union*

foc [fɔk] NM jib; **grand/petit ~** outer/inner jib; **~ d'artimon** mizzen-topmast staysail

focal, e (*mpl* **-aux**) [fɔkal, o] 1 ADJ focal; **point ~** focal point 2 **focale** NF (*Géom, Opt*) focal distance *ou* length

focalisation [fɔkalizasjɔ̃] NF focus (**sur** on); **les raisons de la ~ de l'opinion publique sur le chômage** the reasons why public attention is focused on unemployment

focaliser [fɔkalize] ▶ conjug 1 ◀ 1 VT (*fig, Phys*) to focus (**sur** on) 2 **se focaliser** VPR [personne] to focus; [attention] to be focused (**sur** on)

foehn [føn] NM a (Mét) foehn b (Helv) hairdryer

foène, foëne [fwɛn] NF pronged harpoon, fishgig

fœtal, e (mpl -aux) [fetal, o] ADJ foetal, fetal

fœtus [fetys] NM foetus, fetus

fofolle [fɔfɔl] ADJ F → foufou

foi [fwa] NF a (= croyance) faith; **avoir la ~** to have faith; **perdre la ~** to lose one's faith; **il faut avoir la ~!** you've got to be (really) dedicated!; **il n'y a que la ~ qui sauve!** faith is a marvellous thing!; **la ~ transporte** ou **fait bouger les montagnes** faith can move mountains; **la ~ du charbonnier** blind faith; **sans ~ ni loi** fearing neither God nor man → **article, profession**

b (= confiance) faith, trust; **avoir ~ en Dieu** to have faith ou trust in God; **avoir ~ en qn/qch/l'avenir** to have faith in sb/sth/the future; **digne de ~** [témoin] reliable, trustworthy; [témoignage] reliable → **ajouter**

c (= assurance) word; **respecter la ~ jurée** to honour one's word; **~ d'honnête homme!** on my word as a gentleman!, on my word of honour!; **cette lettre en fait ~** this letter proves it; (Jur) **les deux textes feront** ~ both texts shall be deemed authentic; **sous la ~ du serment** under ou on oath; **sur la ~ de vagues rumeurs** on the strength of vague rumours; **sur la ~ des témoins** on the word ou testimony of witnesses; **en ~ de quoi j'ai décidé ...** (gén) on the strength of which I have decided ...; (Jur) in witness whereof I have decided ...; **être de bonne ~** to be sincere ou honest; **c'était de bonne ~** it was done (ou said etc) in good faith; **faire qch en toute bonne ~** to do sth in all good faith; **en toute bonne ~ je l'ignore** honestly I don't know; **la mauvaise ~** (gén) dishonesty; (Philo) bad faith, mauvaise foi; **tu es de mauvaise ~** you're being dishonest → **cachet**

d **ma ~ ... well ...; ma ~, c'est comme ça, mon vieux*** well, that's how it is, old man; **ça, ma ~, je n'en sais rien** well, I don't know anything about that; **c'est ma ~ vrai que ...** well it's certainly ou undeniably true that ...

foie [fwa] NM liver; **~ de veau/de volaille** calves'/chicken liver; **~ gras** foie gras; **avoir mal au ~** to have a stomach ache; **avoir une crise de ~** to have a bad stomach upset; **avoir les ~s*** to be scared to death*

foie-de-bœuf (pl **foies-de-bœuf**) [fwadbœf] NM beefsteak fungus

foil [fɔjl] NM (Naut) (hydro)foil

foin[1] [fwɛ̃] NM hay; **faire les ~s** to make hay; **à l'époque des ~s** in the haymaking season; **~ d'artichaut** choke; **faire du ~*** (= faire un scandale) to kick up a fuss; (= faire du bruit) to make a row ou racket → **rhume**

foin[2] [fwɛ̃] EXCL (††, hum) **~ des soucis d'argent/des créanciers!** a plague on money worries/on creditors!, the devil take money worries/creditors!

foire [fwaR] NF a (= marché) fair; (= exposition commerciale) trade fair; (= fête foraine) (fun) fair; **~ agricole** agricultural show; **~ aux bestiaux** cattle fair ou market; **~ exposition** exposition, expo → **larron** b (loc) **avoir la ~*†** to have the runs* ou trots*; **faire la ~*** to whoop it up*; **il aime faire la ~** he's a party animal*, he loves partying*; **c'est la ~ ici!** **c'est une vraie ~!*** it's bedlam in here!*; **~ d'empoigne** free-for-all

foirer [fwaRe] ▶ conjug 1 ◀ 1 VI* [vis] to slip; [obus] to fail to go off; ⁞ [projet] to fall through, bomb* (US); **il a tout fait ~** he ballsed (Brit) ou balled (US) everything up* 2 VT⁞ (= rater) to flunk*; **j'ai foiré l'histoire** I flunked history*

foireux, -euse⁞ [fwaRø, øz] ADJ († = peureux) yellow(-bellied)*, chicken* (attrib); (= raté) [idée, projet] useless; **ce projet/film est ~** this project/film is a washout*

fois [fwa] NF a (gén) time; **une ~** once; **deux ~** twice; **trois ~** three times; (aux enchères) **une ~, deux ~, trois ~, adjugé!** going, going, gone!; **pour la toute première ~** for the very first time; **quand je l'ai vu pour la première/dernière ~** when I first/last saw him, the first/last time I saw him; **cette ~-ci/-là** this/that time; **c'est bon** ou **ça va pour cette ~** I'll let you off this time ou (just) this once; **plusieurs ~** several times, a number of times; **peu de ~** on few occasions; **bien des ~ ◊ maintes (et maintes) ~** many a time, many times; **autant de ~ que** as often as, as many times as; **y regarder à deux** ou **à plusieurs ~ avant d'acheter qch** to think twice ou very hard before buying sth; **s'y prendre à** ou **en deux/plusieurs ~ pour faire qch** to take two/several attempts ou goes to do sth; **payer en plusieurs ~** to pay in several instalments; **frapper qn par deux/trois ~** to hit sb two/three times; **je suis trois ~ grand-père** I am a grandfather three times over; **vous avez mille ~ raison** you're absolutely right → **autre, cent¹, encore etc**

b (dans un calcul) **une ~** once; **deux ~** twice, two times; **trois/quatre ~** three/four times; **une ~ tous les deux jours** once every two days, every other ou second day; **trois ~ par an ◊ trois ~ l'an†** three times a year; **neuf ~ sur dix** nine times out of ten; **quatre ~ plus d'eau/de voitures** four times as much water/as many cars; **quatre ~ moins d'eau** four times less water, a quarter as much water; **quatre ~ moins de voitures** four times fewer cars, a quarter as many cars; (Math) **3 ~ 5** (font **15**) 3 times 5 (is ou makes 15); **il avait trois ~ rien** (argent) he had hardly any money; (blessure) there was hardly a scratch on him; **et encore merci! — oh, c'est trois ~ rien!** and thanks again! — oh, please don't mention it!

c **une ~** once; **il était une ~ ... ◊ il y avait une ~ ...** once upon a time there was ..., it doesn't do any harm once in a while; **pour une ~!** for once!; **en une ~** at ou in one go; **une (bonne) ~ pour toutes** once and for all; **il faudrait qu'il pleuve une bonne ~** what's needed is a good downpour; **une ~ (qu'il sera) parti** once he has left; **une ~ qu'il n'était pas là** once ou on one occasion when he wasn't there; (Belg) **viens une ~ ici** just come over here → (PROV) **une ~ n'est pas coutume** just the once won't hurt

d * **des ~** (= parfois) sometimes; **des ~, il est très méchant** he can be very nasty at times, sometimes he's pretty nasty; **si des ~ vous le rencontrez** if you should happen ou chance to meet him; **non mais, des ~!** (scandalisé) do you mind!; (en plaisantant) you must be joking!; **non mais des ~, pour qui te prends-tu?** look here, who do you think you are!; **des ~ que** (just) in case; **attendons, des ~ qu'il viendrait** let's wait in case he comes; **allons-y, des ~ qu'il resterait des places** let's go — there may be some seats left

e **à la ~** at once, at the same time; **ne répondez pas tous à la ~** don't all answer at once; **il était à la ~ grand et gros** he was both tall and fat; **il était à la ~ grand, gros et fort** he was tall, fat and strong; **faire deux choses à la ~** to do two things at once ou at the same time

foison [fwazɔ̃] NF **il y a du poisson/des légumes à ~** there is an abundance of fish/of vegetables, there is fish/there are vegetables in plenty; **il y en avait à ~ au marché** there was plenty of it (ou there were plenty of them) at the market

foisonnant, e [fwazɔnɑ̃, ɑ̃t] ADJ [végétation] luxuriant, lush; [documentation] abundant, lavish; **un roman ~** a novel crowded with incident

foisonnement [fwazɔnmɑ̃] NM a (= épanouissement) burgeoning; (= abondance) profusion, abundance b [chaux] expansion

foisonner [fwazɔne] ▶ conjug 1 ◀ VI a [idées, erreurs] to abound, proliferate; [gibier] to abound; **pays qui foisonne de** ou **en matières premières** country which abounds in raw materials; **pays qui foisonne de** ou **en talents** country which has a profusion ou an abundance of talented people ou which is teeming with talented people; **texte foisonnant d'idées/de fautes** text teeming with ideas/with mistakes b [chaux] to expand

fol [fɔl] ADJ M → **fou**

folâtre [fɔlɑtR] ADJ [enfant] playful, frolicsome; [jeux] lively; [caractère] lively, sprightly; (frm, hum) **il n'est pas d'humeur ~** he's not in a very playful mood

folâtrer [fɔlɑtRe] ▶ conjug 1 ◀ VI [enfants] to frolic, romp; [chiots, poulains] to gambol, frolic, frisk; **au lieu de tu ferais mieux de travailler** you should do some work instead of fooling around

folâtrerie [fɔlɑtRəRi] NF (littér) (NonC = caractère) playfulness; (= action) frolicking (NonC), romping (NonC), gambolling (NonC)

foldingue* [fɔldɛ̃g] 1 ADJ [personne] nuts*, crazy*; [soirée, musique] wild; **tu es complètement ~!** you're nuts!* ou crazy!* 2 NMF nutcase*; **les ~s de l'informatique** computer fanatics ou freaks*

foliacé, e [fɔljase] ADJ foliated, foliaceous

foliation [fɔljasjɔ̃] NF (= développement) foliation, leafing; (= disposition) leaf arrangement

folichon, -onne [fɔliʃɔ̃, ɔn] ADJ (gén nég) pleasant, interesting, exciting; **aller à ce dîner, ça n'a rien de ~** going to this dinner won't be much fun ou won't be very exciting; **la vie n'est pas toujours folichonne avec lui** life's not always fun with him

folie [fɔli] NF a (= maladie) madness, insanity, lunacy; **il a un petit grain de ~*** there's something eccentric about him; (Méd) **~ furieuse** raving madness; **c'est de la ~ douce** ou **pure** ou **furieuse** it's utter ou sheer madness ou lunacy; **~ meurtrière** killing frenzy; **c'était un coup de ~** it was a moment's madness; **avoir la ~ des grandeurs** to have delusions of grandeur; **il a la ~ des timbres-poste** he's mad* ou crazy* about stamps; **aimer qn à la ~** to be madly in love with sb, love sb to distraction; **il a eu la ~ de refuser** he was mad enough ou crazy enough to refuse; **c'est ~ d'y aller** it would be pure folly to go there; **les soldats en ~ ont tout saccagé** the soldiers went mad and ransacked the place; **un monde en ~** a world gone mad

b (= bêtise, erreur, dépense) extravagance; **il a fait des ~s dans sa jeunesse** he had his fling ou a really wild time in his youth; **des ~s de jeunesse** youthful indiscretions; **ils ont fait une ~ en achetant cette voiture** they were mad ou crazy to buy that car; **vous avez fait des ~s en achetant ce cadeau** you have been far too extravagant in buying this present; **il ferait des ~s pour elle** he would do anything for her; **il ferait des ~s pour la revoir** he'd give anything to see her again; (hum) **je ferais des ~s pour un morceau de fromage** I'd give ou do anything for a piece of cheese; **une nouvelle ~ de sa part** (dépense) another of his extravagances; (projet) another of his hare-brained schemes

c (Hist Archit) folly

folié, e [fɔlje] ADJ foliate

folingue* [fɔlɛ̃g] ADJ nuts*, crazy*

folio [fɔljo] NM folio

foliole [fɔljɔl] NF (Bot) leaflet

folioter [fɔljɔte] ▶ conjug 1 ◀ VT to folio

folique [fɔlik] ADJ **acide ~** folic acid

folk [fɔlk] [1] NM ABRÉV = **folk music** [2] ADJ **chanteur/musique ~** folk singer/music

folklo* [fɔlklo] ADJ (ABRÉV = **folklorique**) (= *excentrique*) weird, outlandish; **c'est un peu ~ chez lui** his house (*ou* apartment *etc*) is a bit weird; **cette soirée, c'était ~** it was a really way-out* *ou* whacky* party

folklore [fɔlklɔʀ] NM folklore; (*péj*) **c'est du ~!*** (*ridicule, dépassé*) it's all terribly quaint; (*péj*) **le ~ habituel des visites princières** the usual razzmatazz of royal visits

folklorique [fɔlklɔʀik] ADJ [a] [*chant, costume*] folk (*épith*) [b]* (= *excentrique*) [*personne, tenue, ambiance*] weird, outlandish; **la réunion a été assez ~** the meeting was pretty bizarre

folk song [fɔlksɔg] NM folk music

folle [fɔl] ADJ F, NF → **fou**

follement [fɔlmã] ADV [a] [*espérer, dépenser*] madly; **~ amoureux** madly in love, head over heels in love; **il se lança ~ à leur poursuite** he dashed after them in mad pursuit; **avant de te lancer ~ dans cette aventure** before rushing headlong into *ou* jumping feet first into this business [b] (= *énormément*) [*drôle, intéressant*] madly, wildly; **on s'est ~ amusé** we had a fantastic time*; **il désire ~ lui parler** he's dying* to speak to her, he desperately wants to speak to her

follet, -ette [fɔlɛ, ɛt] ADJ (= *étourdi*) scatter-brained → **feu¹, poil**

folliculaire [fɔlikylɛʀ] ADJ follicular

follicule [fɔlikyl] NM follicle

folliculine [fɔlikylin] NF oestrone

fomentateur, -trice [fɔmãtatœʀ, tʀis] NM,F troublemaker, agitator

fomentation [fɔmãtasjɔ̃] NF fomenting, fomentation

fomenter [fɔmãte] ▶ conjug 1 ◀ VT (*lit, fig*) to foment, stir up

foncé, e [fɔse] (*ptp de* **foncer²**) ADJ [*couleur*] (*gén*) dark; [*tons pastels*] deep; **à la peau ~e** dark-skinned

foncer¹ [fɔse] ▶ conjug 3 ◀ VI [a] (* = *aller à vive allure*) [*conducteur, voiture*] to tear* *ou* belt* (*Brit*) along; [*coureur*] to charge* *ou* tear* along; (*dans un tunnel*) to get a move on*; **maintenant, il faut que je fonce** I must dash *ou* fly* now; **fonce le chercher** go and fetch him straight away (*Brit*) *ou* right away (*US*); **il a foncé chez le directeur** he rushed off to see the manager; **allez, fonce!** come on, hurry up! [b] * (= *être dynamique*) to have drive; (= *aller de l'avant*) to go for it* [c] (= *se précipiter*) to charge (**vers** at, **dans** into); **~ sur** *ou* **vers l'ennemi/l'obstacle** to charge at *ou* make a rush at the enemy/the obstacle; **le camion a foncé sur moi** the truck drove straight at me; (*lit, fig*) **~ sur un objet** to make straight for *ou* make a beeline for an object; **~ dans la foule** [*taureau, police*] to charge into the crowd; [*camion*] to plough into the crowd; **~ (tête baissée) dans la porte/le piège** to walk straight into the door/straight *ou* headlong into the trap; (*fig*) **~ dans le brouillard** to forge ahead regardless *ou* in the dark; **la police a foncé dans le tas*** the police charged (into the crowd)

foncer² [fɔse] ▶ conjug 3 ◀ [1] VT [+ *couleur*] to make darker [2] VI [*liquide, couleur, cheveux*] to turn *ou* go darker

foncer³ [fɔse] ▶ conjug 3 ◀ VT [+ *tonneau*] to bottom; [+ *puits*] to sink, bore; (*Culin*) [+ *moule*] to line

fonceur, -euse* [fɔsœʀ, øz] NM,F go-getter*; **c'est un ~** he's a go-getter*, he's got tremendous drive

foncier, -ière [fɔsje, jɛʀ] [1] ADJ [a] [*impôt*] property (*épith*), land (*épith*); [*noblesse, propriété*] landed (*épith*); [*problème, politique*] (relating to) land ownership; **propriétaire ~**

property owner; **revenus ~s** income from property [b] [*qualité, différence*] fundamental, basic; **la malhonnêteté foncière de ces pratiques** the fundamental *ou* basic dishonesty of these practices; **être d'une foncière malhonnêteté** to be fundamentally dishonest [2] NM **le ~** real estate

foncièrement [fɔsjɛʀmã] ADV fundamentally, basically

fonction [fɔ̃ksjɔ̃] NF [a] (= *métier*) post, office; (= *tâches*) **~s** office, duties; **entrer en ~(s)** ◊ **prendre ses ~s** [*employé*] to take up one's post; [*maire, président*] to come into *ou* take office, take up one's post; **depuis son entrée en ~(s)** *ou* **sa prise de ~(s)** since he came into *ou* took office; **ça n'entre pas dans mes ~s** it's not part of my duties; **de par ses ~s** by virtue of his office; **être en ~** to be in office; **la ~ publique** the civil service; **logement de ~** (*gén*) company accommodation; [*concierge, fonctionnaire*] on-site accommodation (with low or free rent); **avoir une voiture de ~** (*gén*) to have a car that goes with one's job; (*firme privée*) to have a company car → **démettre, exercice** [b] (= *rôle*) (*gén, Gram, Ordin*) function; **~ biologique** biological function; **remplir une ~ to** fulfil a function; **cet organe a pour ~ de ... ◊ la ~ de cet organe est de ...** the function of this organ is to ...; (*Gram*) **avoir** *ou* **faire ~ de sujet** to function *ou* act as a subject; (*hum*) **la ~ crée l'organe** necessity is the mother of invention (*PROV*) [c] (*Math*) **~ (algébrique)** (algebraic) function; (*Chim*) **~ acide** acid(ic) function; (*Math*) **être ~ de** to be a function of [d] (*loc*) **faire ~ de directeur/d'ambassadeur** to act as manager/as ambassador; **il n'y a pas de porte, ce rideau en fait ~** there is no door but this curtain serves the purpose *ou* does instead; **sa réussite est ~ de son travail** his success depends on how well he works; **en ~ de** according to; **salaire en ~ des diplômes** salary according to *ou* commensurate with qualifications

┌─────────────────────────┐
│ ▪ **FONCTION PUBLIQUE** │
└─────────────────────────┘

The term **la fonction publique** *has great cultural significance in France, and covers a much broader range of activities than the English term 'civil service'. There are almost three million "fonctionnaires" (also known as "agents de l'État") in France. They include teachers, social services staff, post office workers and employees of the French rail service.*

Recruitment for jobs in the **fonction publique** *is by competitive examination, and successful candidates gain the official status of "titulaire". Because this status theoretically guarantees total job security, "fonctionnaires" are sometimes stereotyped as being unfairly privileged compared to private sector employees.* → [CONCOURS]

fonctionnaire [fɔ̃ksjɔnɛʀ] NMF (*gén*) state employee; (*dans l'administration*) [*ministère*] government official, civil servant; [*municipalité*] local government officer *ou* official; **haut ~** high-ranking *ou* top-ranking civil servant, senior official; **petit ~** minor (public) official; **les ~s de l'enseignement** state-employed teachers; **~ de (la) police** police officer, officer of the law; (*péj*) **il a une mentalité de ~** he has the mentality of a petty bureaucrat; **c'est un vrai ~** he's a petty bureaucrat *ou* a real jobsworth* (*Brit*)

fonctionnalisme [fɔ̃ksjɔnalism] NM functionalism

fonctionnaliste [fɔ̃ksjɔnalist] ADJ, NMF functionalist

fonctionnalité [fɔ̃ksjɔnalite] NF (*gén*) practicality; (*Ordin*) functionality

fonctionnariat [fɔ̃ksjɔnaʀja] NM state employee status

fonctionnarisation [fɔ̃ksjɔnaʀizasjɔ̃] NF **la ~ de la médecine** the state takeover of medicine; **le gouvernement propose la ~ des médecins** the government proposes taking doctors into the public service *ou* making doctors employees of the state

fonctionnariser [fɔ̃ksjɔnaʀize] ▶ conjug 1 ◀ VT **~ qn** to make sb an employee of the state; (*dans l'administration*) to take sb into the public service; **~ un service** to take over a service (to be run by the state)

fonctionnarisme [fɔ̃ksjɔnaʀism] NM (*péj*) officialdom; **c'est le règne du ~** bureaucracy rules, officialdom has taken over

fonctionnel, -elle [fɔ̃ksjɔnɛl] [1] ADJ functional; (*Ling*) **mot ~** function word [2] NM staff manager; **les ~s et les opérationnels** managers and operatives, staff and line

fonctionnellement [fɔ̃ksjɔnɛlmã] ADV functionally

fonctionnement [fɔ̃ksjɔnmã] NM [*appareil*] functioning; [*entreprise, institution*] operation, running; (*Méd*) [*organisme*] functioning; **expliquer le ~ d'un moteur** to explain how a motor works; **en parfait ~** in perfect working order; **pour assurer le (bon) ~ de l'appareil** to keep the machine in (good) working order; **pour assurer le (bon) ~ du service** to ensure the smooth running of the department; **panne due au mauvais ~ du carburateur** breakdown due to a fault *ou* a malfunction in the carburettor; **pendant le ~ de l'appareil** while the machine is in operation *ou* is running; **budget de ~** operating budget; **dépenses** *ou* **frais de ~** running costs; (*Ordin*) **~ en réseau** networking

fonctionner [fɔ̃ksjɔne] ▶ conjug 1 ◀ VI [*mécanisme, machine*] to work, function; [*entreprise*] to function, operate; * [*personne*] to function, operate; **faire ~** [+ *machine*] to operate; **je n'ai jamais vraiment compris comment il fonctionne*** I've never really understood what makes him tick*; **notre téléphone/télévision fonctionne mal** there's something wrong with our phone/television, our phone/television isn't working properly; **le courrier fonctionne mal** the mail isn't reliable; **ça ne fonctionne pas** it's out of order, it's not working; **sais-tu faire ~ la machine à laver?** do you know how to work the washing machine?; **~ au gaz/à l'énergie solaire/sur piles** to be gas-powered/solar-powered/battery-operated, run on gas/on solar power/on batteries

fond [fɔ̃] [1] NM [a] [*récipient, vallée*] bottom; [*armoire*] back; [*jardin*] bottom, far end; [*pièce*] far end, back; [*utérus*] fundus; (*Min*) **le ~** the (coal) face; (*Min*) **travailler au ~** to work at *ou* on the (coal) face; **être/tomber au ~ de l'eau** to be at/fall to the bottom of the water; **le ~ de la gorge** the back of the throat; **les mots lui sont restés au ~ de la gorge** the words stuck in his throat; **envoyer un navire par le ~** to send a ship to the bottom; **y a-t-il beaucoup de ~?** is it very deep?; **l'épave repose par 10 mètres de ~** the wreck is lying 10 metres down; **les grands ~s** the ocean depths; **à ~ de cale** (*Naut*) (down) in the hold; (*fig = *vite*) at top speed; **au ~ du couloir** at the far end of the corridor; **au ~ de la boutique** at the back of the shop; **ancré au ~ de la baie** anchored at the (far) end of the bay; **village perdu au ~ de la province** village in the depths *ou* heart of the country; **venir du ~ des âges** [*dynastie, réflexe, sagesse*] to be age-old; (*lit, fig*) **sans ~** bottomless → **double, fin¹** [b] (*fig* = *tréfonds*) **le ~ de son cœur est pur** deep down his heart is pure; **savoir lire au ~ des cœurs** to be able to see deep (down) into people's hearts; **merci du ~ du cœur** I thank you from the bottom of my heart; **il pensait au ~ de son cœur** *ou* **de lui(-même) que ...** deep down he thought that ..., in his heart of hearts he thought that ...; **vous avez deviné/je**

vais vous dire le ~ de ma pensée you have guessed/I shall tell you what I really think ou what my feelings really are; **regarder qn au ~ des yeux** to look deep into sb's eyes; **il a un bon ~** ◊ **il n'a pas un mauvais ~** he's basically a good person, he's a good person at heart ou bottom; **il y a chez lui un ~ d'honnêteté/de méchanceté** there's a streak of honesty/of maliciousness in him; **il y a un ~ de vérité dans ce qu'il dit** there's an element of truth in what he says; **toucher le ~** (lit) to touch the bottom; (fig) [personne] to hit rock bottom; [récession, productivité] to bottom out; **toucher le ~ de la douleur/misère** to be in ou plumb the depths of sorrow/misery

c (= essentiel) [affaire, question, débat] heart; **c'est là le ~ du problème** that's the heart ou root ou core of the problem; **aller au ~ du problème** to get to the heart ou root of the problem; **aller au ~ des choses** to do things thoroughly; **il faut aller jusqu'au ~ de cette histoire** we must get to the root of this business; **débat de ~** fundamental discussion; **problème de ~** basic ou fundamental problem; **ouvrage de ~** basic work; (Presse) **article de ~** feature article

d (= contenu) content; **le ~ et la forme** content and form; (Jur) **le ~ de l'affaire** the substance of the case

e (= arrière-plan) [tableau, situation] background; **~ sonore** ou **musical** background music; **blanc sur ~ noir** white on a black background; **avec cette sombre perspective pour ~** with this gloomy prospect in the background → **bruit, toile**

f (= petite quantité) drop; **versez-m'en juste un ~ (de verre)** pour me just a drop; **ils ont vidé les ~s de bouteilles** they emptied what was left in the bottles ou the dregs from the bottles; **il va falloir racler** ou **gratter** ou **faire les ~s de tiroirs** we'll have to scrape together what we can

g (= lie) sediment, deposit

h (Sport) **le ~** long-distance running; **de ~** [course, coureur] long-distance (épith) → **ski**

i (chapeau) crown; [pantalon] seat; **c'est là que j'ai usé mes ~s de culotte** that's where I spent my early school years

j (loc) **le ~ de l'air est frais** it's a bit chilly, there's a nip in the air; **au ~** ◊ **dans le ~** (= sous les apparences) basically, at bottom; (= en fait) basically, really, in fact; **il n'est pas méchant au ~** he's not a bad sort at heart; **il fait semblant d'être désolé, mais dans le ~ il est bien content** he makes out he's upset but he's quite pleased really ou but deep down he's quite pleased; **dans le ~** ou **au ~, ça ne change pas grand-chose** basically, it makes no great difference, it makes no great difference really; **ce n'est pas si stupide, au ~** it's not such a bad idea after all; **étudier une question à ~** to study a question thoroughly ou in depth; **il est soutenu à ~ par ses amis** his friends back him up all the way; **visser un boulon à ~** to screw a bolt (right) home; **respirer à ~** to breathe deeply; **à ~ de train** ◊ **à ~ les manettes*** at top speed; **de ~ en comble** [fouiller] from top to bottom; [détruire] completely, utterly; **ce retard bouleverse mes plans de ~ en comble** this delay throws my plans right out, this delay completely overturns my plans

2 COMP ▶ **fond d'artichaut** artichoke heart ▶ **fond de court** (Tennis) **jeu/joueur de ~ de court** baseline game/player ▶ **fond de magasin** (= invendus) leftover stock ▶ **les fonds marins** the sea bed ▶ **fond d'œil fundus; faire un ~ d'œil à qn** to look into the back of sb's eye, perform a funduscopy on sb (SPÉC) ▶ **fond de portefeuille** (Bourse) portfolio base ▶ **fond de robe** slip ▶ **fond de tarte** (= pâte) pastry base; (= crème) custard base ▶ **fond de teint** foundation (cream)

▼ **fondamental, e** (mpl -aux) [fɔ̃damɑ̃tal, o]
1 ADJ (= essentiel) [question, recherche, changement] fundamental, basic; [vocabulaire] basic; [couleurs] primary; (= foncier) [égoïsme, incompréhension] basic, inherent, fundamental; **son ~** ◊ **note ~e** fundamental (note); (Scol) **matière ~e** basic subject, core subject (Brit) 2 **fondamentale** NF (Mus) root, fundamental (note)

fondamentalement [fɔ̃damɑ̃talmɑ̃] ADV [vrai, faux] inherently, fundamentally; [modifier, opposer] radically, fundamentally; **méchant/généreux** basically ou fundamentally malicious/generous; **cela vient ~ d'un manque d'organisation** that arises from a basic ou an underlying lack of organization

fondamentalisme [fɔ̃damɑ̃talism] NM fundamentalism

fondamentaliste [fɔ̃damɑ̃talist] ADJ, NMF fundamentalist

fondant, e [fɔ̃dɑ̃, ɑ̃t] 1 ADJ [neige] thawing, melting; [fruit] luscious; [viande] tender, melt-in-the-mouth (épith); **température de la glace ~e** temperature of melting ice; **bonbon ~** fondant; **chocolat ~** high-quality plain chocolate 2 NM (Chim) flux; (= bonbon, Culin) fondant; (= gâteau) **~ au chocolat** chocolate fondant cake

fondateur, -trice [fɔ̃datœʀ, tʀis] 1 ADJ [mythe, texte, idée] founding 2 NM,F founder; (Jur, Fin) incorporator

fondation [fɔ̃dasjɔ̃] NF (= action, institut) foundation; (Constr) **~s** foundations

fondé, e [fɔ̃de] (ptp de **fonder**) 1 ADJ a [crainte, réclamation] well-founded, justified; **bien ~** well-founded, fully justified; **mal ~** ill-founded, groundless; **ce qu'il dit n'est pas ~** there are no grounds ou there is no justification for what he says; **~ sur des ouï-dire** based on hearsay b **être ~ à faire/croire/dire qch** to have good reason to do/believe/say sth, have (good) grounds for doing/believing/saying sth 2 NM **~ (de pouvoir)** (Jur) authorized representative; (= cadre bancaire) senior banking executive

fondement [fɔ̃dmɑ̃] NM a (= base) foundation; **~ d'une action en justice** cause of action; **sans ~** without foundation, unfounded, groundless; **jeter les ~s de qch** to lay the foundations of sth b (hum = derrière) posterior ou (hum), backside; (= fond de pantalon) trouser seat

fonder [fɔ̃de] ▶ conjug 1 ◀ 1 VT a (= créer) [+ ville, parti, prix littéraire] to found; (+ commerce) to set up; [+ famille] to start; **~ un foyer** to set up home and start a family; (Comm) « **maison fondée en 1850** » "Established 1850" b (= baser) to base, found (**sur** on); **~ sa richesse sur qch** to build one's wealth on sth; **~ une théorie sur qch** to base a theory on sth; **~ tous ses espoirs sur qch/qn** to place ou pin all one's hopes on sth/sb c (= justifier) [+ réclamation] to justify 2 **se fonder** VPR **se ~ sur** [personne] to go by, go on, base o.s. on; [théorie, décision] to be based on; **sur quoi vous fondez-vous pour l'affirmer?** what grounds do you have for saying this?

fonderie [fɔ̃dʀi] NF a (= usine d'extraction) smelting works; (= atelier de moulage) foundry b (= action) founding, casting

fondeur, -euse [fɔ̃dœʀ, øz] 1 NM,F (Ski) cross-country skier 2 NM (Métal) (= industriel) foundry owner; (= ouvrier) foundry worker

fondre [fɔ̃dʀ] ▶ conjug 41 ◀ 1 VT a (= liquéfier) [+ substance] to melt; [+ argenterie, objet de bronze] to melt down; [+ minerai] to smelt; [+ neige] to melt, thaw
b (= diminuer, attendrir) [+ dureté, résolution] to melt
c (= couler) [+ cloche, statue] to cast, found
d (= réunir) to combine, fuse together,

merge (**en** into)
e (Peinture) [+ couleur, ton] to merge, blend
2 VI a (à la chaleur) (gén) to melt; [neige] to melt, thaw; (dans l'eau) to dissolve; **faire ~** [+ beurre] to melt; [+ graisse] to render down; [+ sel, sucre] to dissolve; [+ neige] to melt, thaw; **ça fond dans la bouche** it melts in your mouth
b [colère, résolution] to melt away; [provisions, réserves] to vanish; **~ comme neige au soleil** to melt away; **l'argent fond entre ses mains** money runs through his fingers, he spends money like water; **cela fit ~ sa colère** at that his anger melted away; **~ en larmes** to dissolve ou burst into tears
c * (= maigrir) to slim down; **j'ai fondu de 5 kg** I've lost 5kg
d * (= s'attendrir) to melt; **j'ai fondu** my heart melted, I melted; **son sourire me fait ~** ◊ **je fonds devant son sourire** his smile makes me melt ou makes me go weak at the knees
e (= s'abattre) **~ sur qn** [vautour, ennemi] to swoop down on sb; [malheurs] to sweep down on sb
3 **se fondre** VPR a (= se réunir) [cortèges, courants] to merge (**en** into)
b (= disparaître) **se ~ dans la nuit/brume** to fade (away) ou merge into the night/mist; **se ~ dans la masse** ou **foule** [personne] to melt into the crowd; **ce détail se fond dans la masse** this detail is lost among the rest; **se ~ dans le décor** [personne] to melt into the background; [appareil, objet] to blend in with the decor

fondrière [fɔ̃dʀijeʀ] NF pothole

fonds [fɔ̃] NM a (Comm) **~ de commerce** (lit) business; (fig = source de revenus) money-maker; **il possède le ~ mais pas les murs** he owns the business but not the property; **vendre son ~** to sell up; **~ de terre** land (NonC)
b (= ressources) [musée, bibliothèque] collection; **ce pays a un ~ folklorique très riche** this country has a rich folk heritage; **~ de secours/de solidarité/d'amortissement** relief/solidarity/sinking fund; **~ de garantie** guarantee fund; **Fonds national de l'emploi** French state fund to provide retraining and redundancy payments for the unemployed; **Fonds européen de coopération monétaire** European Monetary Cooperation Fund; **Fonds européen de développement** European Development Fund; **Fonds social européen** European Social Fund; **le Fonds monétaire international** the International Monetary Fund
c (= organisme) **~ commun de placement** investment ou mutual fund; **~ de développement économique et social** fund for economic and social development; **~ de pension** pension fund; **~ de prévoyance** contingency fund ou reserve; **~ régulateur** buffer fund; **~ de stabilisation des changes** (currency) stabilization fund, Foreign Exchange Equalization Account (Brit)
d (Fin : souvent pl) (= argent) money; (= capital) funds, capital; (pour une dépense précise) funds; **pour transporter ce ~** to transport the money; **investir des ~ importants dans qch** to invest large sums of money ou a large amount of capital in sth; **réunir les ~ nécessaires à un achat** to raise the necessary funds for a purchase; **mise de ~** capital outlay; **faire une mise de ~** to lay out capital; **mise de ~ initiale** initial (capital) outlay; **ne pas être/être en ~** to be out of/be in funds; **je lui ai prêté de l'argent, ça a été à ~ perdus** I lent him some money, but I never saw it again ou but I never got it back; **~ de caisse** cash in hand; **~ de roulement** (gén) working capital; [syndic] contingency fund; **~ bloqués** frozen assets; **~ disponibles** liquid assets; **~ d'État** government securities; **~ propres** shareholders' equity, stockholders' equity (US), equity capital; **~ publics** (Bourse) government stock ou securities; (= recettes de l'État)

public funds *ou* money; **~ secrets** secret funds → **appel, bailleur, détournement**

fondu, e [fɔ̃dy] (*ptp de* **fondre**) **1** ADJ **a** (= *liquide*) [*beurre*] melted; [*métal*] molten; **neige ~e** slush → **fromage b** (*Métal = moulé*) **statue de bronze ~** cast bronze statue **c** (= *flou, estompé*) [*contours*] blurred, hazy; [*couleurs*] blending **d*** (= *fou*) nuts*, loopy*; **t'es complètement ~!** you're nuts!*, you're off your rocker!* **2** NM,F* (= *fanatique*) **c'est un ~ de jazz/télévision** he's a jazz/television freak* **3** NM **a** (*Peinture*) [*couleurs*] blend; **le ~ de ce tableau me plaît** I like the way the colours blend in this picture **b** (*Ciné*) **~ (enchaîné)** dissolve, fade in-fade out; **fermeture en ~ ◊ ~ en fermeture** fade-out; **ouverture en ~ ◊ ~ en ouverture** fade-in; **faire un ~ au noir** to fade to black **4 fondue** NF (*Culin*) **~e (savoyarde)** (cheese) fondue; **~e bourguignonne** fondue bourguignonne, meat fondue; **~e de poireaux/tomates** leek/tomato fondue

fongible [fɔ̃ʒibl] ADJ fungible

fongicide [fɔ̃ʒisid] **1** ADJ fungicidal **2** NM fungicide

fontaine [fɔ̃tɛn] NF (*ornementale*) fountain; (*naturelle*) spring; (*murale*) fountain; (= *distributeur d'eau potable*) (*à jet d'eau*) drinking fountain; (*avec gobelets*) water dispenser; (*hum*) **cette petite, c'est une vraie ~*** she's a real little crybaby ▪ (*PROV*) **il ne faut pas dire ~ je ne boirai pas de ton eau** never say never, you never know → **jouvence**

fontainier [fɔ̃tenje] NM hydraulic engineer

fontanelle [fɔ̃tanɛl] NF fontanel(le)

fonte [fɔ̃t] NF **a** (= *action*) [*substance*] melting; [*argenterie, objet de bronze*] melting down; [*minerai*] smelting; [*neige*] melting, thawing; [*cloche, statue*] casting, founding; **à la ~ des neiges** when the thaw comes, when the snow melts *ou* thaws **b** (= *métal*) cast iron; **~ brute** pig-iron; **en ~** [*tuyau, radiateur*] cast-iron (*épith*) **c** (*Typo*) fount **d** (*Agr*) **~ des semis** damping off

fontes [fɔ̃t] NFPL holsters (*on saddle*)

fonts [fɔ̃] NMPL **~ baptismaux** (baptismal) font; **tenir un enfant sur les ~ baptismaux** to be godfather (*ou* godmother) to a child

foot* [fut] NM ABRÉV = **football**

football [futbol] NM football (*Brit*), soccer; **~ américain** American football (*Brit*), football (*US*); **jouer au ~** to play football → **ballon**

footballeur, -euse [futbolœʀ, øz] NM,F footballer (*Brit*), football (*Brit*) *ou* soccer player

footballistique [futbolistik] ADJ soccer (*épith*), football (*épith*) (*Brit*)

footing [futiŋ] NM jogging (*NonC*); **faire du ~** to go jogging; **faire un (petit) ~** to go for a (little) jog

for [fɔʀ] NM **dans** *ou* **en mon ~ intérieur** in my heart of hearts, deep down inside

forage [fɔʀaʒ] NM [*roche, paroi*] drilling, boring; [*puits*] sinking, boring; **effectuer plusieurs ~s** to drill several bare holes; **se livrer à des ~s d'exploration** to test-drill; **faire des ~s de prospection pétrolière** to prospect for oil, wildcat (*US*)

forain, e [fɔʀɛ̃, ɛn] **1** ADJ fairground (*épith*), carnival (*US*) (*épith*) → **baraque, fête 2** NM (= *acteur*) (fairground) entertainer; (= *commerçant*) (**marchand**) **~** stallholder; (*fête foraine*) **les ~s** fairground people, carnies* (*US*)

forban [fɔʀbɑ̃] NM (*Hist* = *pirate*) pirate; (*fig* = *escroc*) shark, crook

forçage [fɔʀsaʒ] NM (*Agr*) forcing

forçat [fɔʀsa] NM (= *bagnard*) convict; (= *galérien, fig*) galley slave; **travailler comme un ~** to work like a slave; **c'est une vie de ~** it's sheer slavery

▼ **force** [fɔʀs] **1** NF **a** (= *vigueur*) strength; **avoir de la ~** to be strong; **avoir de la ~ dans les bras** to have strong arms; **je n'ai plus la ~ de**

parler I have no strength left to talk; **il ne connaît pas sa ~** he doesn't know his own strength; **à la ~ du poignet** [*grimper*] using only one's arms; [*obtenir qch, réussir*] by the sweat of one's brow; **cet effort l'avait laissé sans ~** the effort had left him completely drained; **c'est une ~ de la nature** he's a real Goliath; **dans la ~ de l'âge** in the prime of life; **~ morale/intellectuelle** moral/intellectual strength; **c'est ce qui fait sa ~** that is where his great strength lies; **bracelet** *ou* **poignet de ~** (leather) wristband → **bout, union**
b (= *violence*) force; **recourir/céder à la ~** to resort to/give in to force; **employer la ~/ la brutale** *ou* **brute** to use brute force; **la ~ prime le droit** might is right
c (= *ressources physiques*) **~s** strength; **reprendre des ~s** to get one's strength back, regain one's strength; **ses ~s l'ont trahi** his strength failed *ou* deserted him; **c'est au-dessus de mes ~s** it's too much for me, it's beyond me; **frapper de toutes ses ~s** to hit as hard as one can *ou* with all one's might; **désirer qch de toutes ses ~s** to want sth with all one's heart
d [*coup, vent*] force; [*argument*] strength, force; [*sentiment, alcool, médicament*] strength; **vent de ~ 4** force 4 wind; **dans toute la ~ du terme** in the fullest *ou* strongest sense of the word; **la ~ de l'évidence** the weight of evidence; **la ~ de l'habitude** force of habit; **par la ~ des choses** (*gén*) by force of circumstance; (= *nécessairement*) inevitably; **les ~s naturelles** *ou* **de la nature** the forces of nature; **les ~s aveugles du destin** the blind forces of fate; **les ~s vives du pays** the lifeblood of the country; **avoir ~ de loi** to have force of law → **cas, idée-force, ligne¹**
e (*Mil*) strength; **~s** forces; **notre ~ navale** our naval strength; (*Pol*) **les ~s de l'opposition** the opposition forces; **d'importantes ~s de police** large contingents *ou* numbers of police; **armée d'une ~ de 10 000 hommes** army with a strength of 10,000 men
f (= *valeur*) **les deux joueurs sont de la même ~** the two players are evenly *ou* well matched; **ces deux cartes sont de la même ~** these two cards have the same value; **il est de première ~ au bridge** he's a first-class bridge player, he's first-rate at bridge; **il est de ~ à le faire** he's equal to it, he's up to (doing) it*; **tu n'es pas de ~ à lutter avec lui** you're no match for him; **à ~s égales ◊ à égalité de ~s** on equal terms
g (*Phys*) force; **~ de gravité** force of gravity; **~ centripète/centrifuge** centripetal/centrifugal force
h (*Typo*) [*corps, caractère*] size
i (*loc*) **attaquer/arriver** *ou* **venir en ~** to attack/arrive in force; **la montée en ~ du chômage** the dramatic rise in unemployment; (*Sport*) **passer un obstacle en ~** to get past an obstacle by sheer effort; **faire entrer qch de ~ dans qch** to cram sth into sth; **faire entrer qn de ~** *ou* **par la ~ dans qch** to force sb into sth; **obtenir qch par ~** to get sth by *ou* through force; **enlever qch de ~ à qn** to remove sth forcibly from sb, take sth from sb by force; **entrer de ~ chez qn** to force one's way into *ou* force an entry into sb's house; **être en position de ~** to be in a position of strength; **coup de ~** takeover by force; **~ nous est/lui est d'accepter** we have/he has no choice but to accept, we are/he is forced to accept; **~ m'est de reconnaître que ...** I am forced *ou* obliged to recognize that ...; **affirmer avec ~** to insist, state firmly; **insister avec ~ sur un point** to emphasize a point strongly; **vouloir à toute ~** to want absolutely *ou* at all costs; **à ~ de chercher on va bien trouver** if we keep on looking we'll end up finding it; **à ~ de gentillesse** by dint of kindness; **à ~, tu vas le casser** you'll end up breaking it; (*Naut*) **faire ~ de rames** to ply the oars; (*Naut*) **faire ~ de voiles** to cram on sail → **tour²**

2 ADV († *hum*) many, a goodly number of (*hum*); **boire ~ bouteilles** to drink a goodly number of bottles; **avec ~ remerciements** with profuse thanks

3 COMP ▸ **force d'âme** fortitude, moral strength ▸ **la force armée** the army, the military ▸ **les forces armées** the armed forces ▸ **force de caractère** strength of character ▸ **force contre-électromotrice** back electromotive force ▸ **force de dissuasion** deterrent power ▸ **les Forces françaises de l'intérieur** Resistance forces operating within France during World War II ▸ **les Forces françaises libres** the Free French (Forces *ou* Army) ▸ **force de frappe** strike force ▸ **force d'inertie** force of inertia ▸ **force d'interposition** intervention force ▸ **forces d'intervention** (*Mil, Police*) rapid deployment force ▸ **forces de maintien de la paix** peace-keeping force(s) ▸ **force nucléaire stratégique** strategic nuclear force ▸ **les forces de l'ordre** the police ▸ **la force publique** the police ▸ **force de vente** sales force

forcé, e [fɔʀse] (*ptp de* **forcer**) ADJ **a** (= *imposé*) [*cours, mariage*] forced; (= *poussé*) [*comparaison*] forced; **atterrissage ~** forced *ou* emergency landing; **prendre un bain ~** to take an unintended dip; **conséquence ~e** inevitable consequence → **marche¹, travail¹ b** (= *feint*) [*rire, sourire*] forced; [*amabilité*] affected, put-on **c** (= *évident*:*) **c'est ~** there's no way round it, it's inevitable; **je suis malade — c'est ~, tu as mangé trop de chocolat!** I'm ill — of course you are, you've eaten too much chocolate!; **c'est ~ que tu sois en retard** it's obvious you're going to be late

forcement [fɔʀsəmɑ̃] NM forcing

forcément [fɔʀsemɑ̃] ADV inevitably; **ça devait ~ arriver** it was bound to happen, it was inevitable; **il le savait ~, puisqu'on le lui a dit** he obviously knew, because he'd been told; **il est enrhumé — ~, il ne se couvre pas** he's got a cold — of course he has, he doesn't dress warmly enough; **c'est voué à l'échec — pas ~** it's bound to fail — not necessarily

forcené, e [fɔʀsəne] **1** ADJ (= *fou*) deranged, out of one's wits (*attrib*) *ou* mind (*attrib*); (= *acharné*) [*ardeur, travail*] frenzied; (= *fanatique*) [*joueur, travailleur*] frenzied; [*partisan, critique*] fanatical **2** NM,F maniac; **travailler comme un ~** to work like a maniac*; (*hum*) **~ du travail** workaholic*; (*hum*) **les ~s du vélo/de la canne à pêche** cycling/angling fanatics

forceps [fɔʀsɛps] NM pair of forceps, forceps *pl*; **accouchement au ~** forceps delivery

forcer [fɔʀse] ▸ conjug 3 ◂ **1** VT **a** (= *contraindre*) to force, compel; **~ qn à faire qch** to force sb to do sth, make sb do sth; **il est forcé de garder le lit** he is forced to stay in bed; **il a essayé de me ~ la main** he tried to force my hand; **~ qn au silence/à des démarches/à la démission** to force sb to keep silent/to take action/to resign
b (= *faire céder*) [+ *coffre, serrure, barrage*] to force; [+ *porte, tiroir*] to force (open); [+ *blocus*] to run; [+ *ville*] to take by force; **~ le passage** to force one's way through; **~ la porte** to force one's way in; **~ la porte de qn** to force one's way into sb's home; **~ la consigne** to bypass orders; **sa conduite force le respect/ l'admiration** his behaviour commands respect/admiration; **il a réussi à ~ la décision** he managed to settle *ou* decide the outcome
c (= *traquer*) [+ *cerf, lièvre*] to run *ou* hunt down; [+ *ennemi*] to track down; **la police a forcé les bandits dans leur repaire** the police tracked the gangsters down to their hideout
d (= *pousser*) [+ *cheval*] to override; [+ *fruits, plantes*] to force; [+ *talent, voix*] to strain; [+ *allure*] to increase; [+ *destin*] to tempt, brave; **votre interprétation force le sens du texte** your interpretation stretches the meaning of the

▸ **GRAMMAIRE ACTIVE:** **force 43.4**

text; **~ sa nature** (*timidité*) to overcome one's shyness; (*volonté*) to force o.s.; **~ le pas** to quicken one's pace; **il a forcé la dose*** *ou* **la note*** he overdid it; **~ le trait** (= *exagérer*) to exaggerate

2 VI to overdo it; **j'ai voulu ~, et je me suis claqué un muscle** I overdid it and pulled a muscle; **il a gagné sans ~*** he had no trouble winning, he won easily; **ne force pas, tu vas casser la corde** don't force it or you'll break the rope; **arrête de tirer, tu vois bien que ça force** stop pulling, can't you see it's jammed?; **~ sur ses rames** to strain at the oars; **il force un peu trop sur l'alcool*** once he starts drinking he doesn't know when to stop; **il avait un peu trop forcé sur l'alcool*** he'd had a few too many*

3 **se forcer** VPR to force o.s., make an effort (**pour faire** to do); **il se force à travailler** he forces himself to work, he makes himself work; **elle se force pour manger** she forces herself to eat

forces [fɔʀs] NMPL (= *ciseaux*) shears

forcing [fɔʀsiŋ] NM (*gén*: *Boxe*) pressure (**auprès de** with); **faire le ~** to pile on the pressure; **on a dû faire le ~ pour avoir le contrat** we had to put on a lot of pressure *ou* we really had to push to get the contract; **on a dû faire le ~ pour combler notre retard** we had to pull out all the stops to make up the time; **négociations menées au ~** negotiations conducted under pressure

forcir [fɔʀsiʀ] ▶ conjug 2 ◀ VI [*personne*] to broaden out; [*vent*] to strengthen

forclore [fɔʀklɔʀ] ▶ conjug 45 ◀ VT (*Jur*) to debar; **il s'est laissé ~** he didn't make his claim within the prescribed time limit

forclusion [fɔʀklyzjɔ̃] NF (*Jur*) debarment

forer [fɔʀe] ▶ conjug 1 ◀ VT [+ *roche*, *paroi*] to drill, bore; [+ *puits*] to drill, sink, bore

forestier, -ière [fɔʀestje, jɛʀ] 1 ADJ [*région, végétation, chemin*] forest (*épith*); **exploitation forestière** (= *activité*) forestry, lumbering; (= *lieu*) forestry site; (*Culin*) **perdreau (à la) forestière** partridge (cooked) with mushrooms → **garde²** 2 NM forester

foret [fɔʀe] NM (= *outil*) drill

forêt [fɔʀe] NF (*lit, fig*) forest; **~ vierge** virgin forest; **~ tropicale** tropical (rain) forest; **~ domaniale** national *ou* state-owned forest; **~-galerie** gallery forest → **arbre, eau**

forêt-noire (*pl* **forêts-noires**) [fɔʀenwaʀ] NF a (*Culin*) Black Forest gâteau b **la Forêt-Noire** (*Géog*) the Black Forest

foreuse [fɔʀøz] NF drill

forfaire [fɔʀfɛʀ] ▶ conjug 60 ◀ VI (*frm*) **~ à qch** to be false to sth, betray sth; **~ à l'honneur** to forsake honour

forfait [fɔʀfɛ] NM a (*Comm*) (= *prix fixe*) fixed *ou* set price; (= *prix tout compris*) all-inclusive price; (= *ensemble de prestations*) package; **travailler au** *ou* **à ~** to work for a flat rate *ou* a fixed sum; **notre nouveau ~-vacances** our new package tour *ou* holiday (*Brit*); **~ avion-hôtel** flight and hotel package; **~ hôtelier** hotel package; **~-skieur(s)** ski-pass; (*impôts*) **être au (régime du) ~** to be taxed on estimated income b (*Sport* = *abandon*) withdrawal; **gagner par ~** to win by default; **déclarer ~** (*Sport*) to withdraw; (*fig*) to give up c (*littér* = *crime*) crime

forfaitaire [fɔʀfetɛʀ] ADJ (= *fixe*) fixed, set; (= *tout compris*) inclusive; **montant ~** lump *ou* fixed sum; **indemnité ~** inclusive payment, lump sum payment; **prix ~** fixed *ou* set price

forfaitairement [fɔʀfetɛʀmɑ̃] ADV [*payer, évaluer*] on an inclusive basis, inclusively

forfaiture [fɔʀfɛtyʀ] NF (*Jur*) abuse of authority; (*Hist*) felony; (*littér* = *crime*) act of treachery

forfanterie [fɔʀfɑ̃tʀi] NF (= *caractère*) boastfulness; (= *acte*) bragging (*NonC*)

forge [fɔʀʒ] NF (= *atelier*) forge, smithy; (= *fourneau*) forge; († = *fonderie*) **~s** ironworks → **maître**

forger [fɔʀʒe] ▶ conjug 3 ◀ 1 VT a (= *façonner*) [+ *métal*] to forge; (*littér*) **~ des liens** to forge links; (*littér*) **~ les fers** *ou* **les chaînes de qn** to enslave *ou* enchain sb ■ (*PROV*) **c'est en forgeant qu'on devient ~on** practice makes perfect (*PROV*) → **fer** b (= *aguerrir*) [+ *caractère*] to form, mould c (= *inventer*) [+ *mot*] to coin; [+ *exemple, prétexte*] to make up; [+ *histoire, mensonge, plan*] to concoct; **cette histoire est forgée de toutes pièces** this story is a complete fabrication 2 **se forger** VPR **il s'est forgé une réputation d'homme sévère** he has won *ou* earned himself the reputation of being a stern man; **se ~ un idéal** to create an ideal for o.s.; **se ~ des illusions** to build up illusions

forgeron [fɔʀʒəʀɔ̃] NM blacksmith, smith → **forger**

formalisation [fɔʀmalizasjɔ̃] NF formalization

formaliser [fɔʀmalize] ▶ conjug 1 ◀ 1 VT to formalize 2 **se formaliser** VPR to take offence (**de** at)

formalisme [fɔʀmalism] NM a (*péj*) formality; **pas de ~ ici** we don't stand on ceremony here; **s'encombrer de ~** to weigh o.s. down with formalities b (*Art, Philo, Math*) formalism

formaliste [fɔʀmalist] 1 ADJ a (*péj*) formalistic b (*Art, Philo*) formalist 2 NMF formalist

formalité [fɔʀmalite] NF (*Admin*) formality; **les ~s à accomplir** *ou* **à remplir** the necessary procedures, the procedures involved; **pas de ~s entre nous, appelle-moi Maud** no need to be formal, call me Maud; (*fig*) **ce n'est qu'une ~** it's a mere formality; (*fig*) **sans autre ~** without any more *ou* further ado

formant [fɔʀmɑ̃] NM (*Ling, Phon*) formant

format [fɔʀma] NM [*livre*] format, size; [*papier, objet*] size; (*Ordin*) format; **papier ~ A4** A4 paper; (*Ordin*) **~ portrait** *ou* **à la française** portrait; **~ paysage** *ou* **à l'italienne** landscape; (*Ordin*) **~ de données** data format; **photo (en) petit ~** small format print; **enveloppe grand ~** large envelope; **les petits/grands ~s** (*livres*) small/large format books; (*fig hum*) **il aime les blondes et préfère les petits ~s** he likes blondes, preferably of the petite variety → **poche**

formatage [fɔʀmataʒ] NM formatting

formater [fɔʀmate] ▶ conjug 1 ◀ VT (*Ordin*) to format

formateur, -trice [fɔʀmatœʀ, tʀis] 1 ADJ [*élément, expérience*] formative; [*stage*] training 2 NM,F trainer

formatif, -ive [fɔʀmatif, iv] 1 ADJ [*langue*] inflected, flexional; [*préfixe*] formative 2 **formative** NF (*Ling*) formative

formation [fɔʀmasjɔ̃] NF a (= *développement*) [*gouvernement, croûte, fruits*] formation, forming; **à (l'époque de) la ~** [*fruit*] when forming; [*enfant*] at puberty; **en voie** *ou* **en cours de ~** being formed, in the process of formation; **la ~ des mots** word formation; **la ~ du caractère** the forming *ou* moulding of character b (= *apprentissage*) training; (= *stage, cours*) training course; **il a reçu une ~ littéraire** he received a literary education; **~ des maîtres** ◊ **~ pédagogique** teacher training, teacher education (*US*); **sa ~ d'ingénieur** his training as an engineer; **je suis juriste de ~** I trained as a lawyer; **~ professionnelle** vocational training; **~ permanente** *ou* **continue** continuing education; **~ continue (au sein de l'entreprise)** (in-house) training; **~ alternée** *ou* **en alternance** [*salarié*] ≈ block-release training; [*élève en apprentissage*] school course combined with work experience; **~**

courte/longue short/long training course; **stage de ~ accélérée** intensive (training) course, crash course; **centre de ~** training centre; **suivre une ~ en informatique** to do a computer (training) course → **tas** c (*gén, Mil* = *groupe*) formation; **voler en ~** to fly in formation; **~ serrée** close formation; **~ musicale** music group; **~ politique** political grouping *ou* formation

forme [fɔʀm] 1 NF a (= *contour, apparence*) form, shape; **cet objet est de ~ ronde/carrée** this object is round/square (in shape); **en ~ de poire/cloche** pear-/bell-shaped; **elle a des ~s gracieuses** she has a graceful figure; **elle prend des ~s** she's filling out; **vêtement qui moule les ~s** clinging *ou* figure-hugging garment; **une ~ apparut dans la nuit** a form *ou* figure *ou* shape appeared out of the darkness; **n'avoir plus ~ humaine** to be unrecognizable; **sans ~** [*chapeau*] shapeless; [*pensée*] formless; **prendre la ~ d'un rectangle** to take the form *ou* shape of a rectangle; **prendre la ~ d'un entretien** to take the form of an interview; **prendre ~** [*statue, projet*] to take shape; **sous ~ de comprimés** in tablet form; **sous la ~ d'un vieillard** in the guise of *ou* as an old man; **sous toutes ses ~s** in all its forms b (= *genre*) [*civilisation, gouvernement*] form; **~ d'énergie** form of energy; **~ de vie** (= *présence effective*) form of life, life form; (= *coutumes*) way of life; **une ~ de pensée différente de la nôtre** a way of thinking different from our own; **les animaux ont-ils une ~ d'intelligence ?** do animals have a form of intelligence? c (*Art, Jur, Littérat, Philo*) form; **soigner la ~** to be careful about form; **mettre en ~** [+ *texte*] to finalize the presentation *ou* layout of; [+ *idées*] to formulate; **poème à ~ fixe** fixed-form poem; **poème en ~ d'acrostiche** poem forming an acrostic; **de pure ~** [*aide, soutien*] token (*épith*), nominal; **remarques de pure ~** purely formal remarks; **pour la ~** as a matter of form, for form's sake; **en bonne (et due) ~** in due form; **faites une réclamation en ~** put in a formal request; **sans autre ~ de procès** without further ado → **fond, vice** d (*Ling*) form; **mettre à la ~ passive** to put in the passive; **~ contractée** contracted form; **~ de base** base form e (= *moule*) mould; (*Typo*) forme (*Brit*), form (*US*); [*cordonnier*] last; [*couturier*] (dress) form; (= *partie de chapeau*) crown; (*Typo*) **mise en ~** imposition f (*gén, Sport*) **~ (physique)** form, fitness; **être en (pleine ou grande) ~** *ou* ◊ **tenir la ~*** (*gén*) to be in (great) form, be in *ou* on top form; (*physiquement*) to be very fit; **il n'est pas en ~** *ou* ◊ **il n'a pas la ~*** (*gén*) he's not on form, he's off form; (*physiquement*) he's not very fit, he's unfit; **baisse de ~** loss of form; **retrouver la ~** to get back into shape, get fit again; **ce n'est pas la grande ~*** I'm (*ou* he's *etc*) not feeling too good*; **centre de remise en ~** ≈ health spa → **péter** g (*Mus*) **~ sonate** sonata form h (*Naut*) **~ de radoub** *ou* **sèche** dry *ou* graving dock 2 **formes** NFPL (= *convenances*) proprieties, conventions; **respecter les ~s** to respect the proprieties *ou* conventions; **refuser en y mettant des ~s** to decline as tactfully as possible; **faire une demande dans les ~s** to make a request in the correct form

formé, e [fɔʀme] (*ptp de* **former**) ADJ a [*jeune fille*] pubescent; [*fruit, épi*] formed; **cette jeune fille est ~e maintenant** this girl is fully developed now b (*goût, jugement*) (well-)developed; **son jugement n'est pas encore ~** his judgment is as yet unformed

formel, -elle [fɔʀmɛl] ADJ a (= *catégorique*) definite, positive; **dans l'intention formelle de refuser** with the definite intention of refusing; **il a l'obligation formelle de le faire** he is obliged to do so; **interdiction formelle d'en**

parler à quiconque you mustn't talk about this to anyone; **je suis ~!** I'm absolutely sure! [b] (*Art, Philo*) formal [c] (= *extérieur*) [*politesse*] formal

formellement [fɔʀmɛlmɑ̃] ADV [a] (= *catégoriquement*) [*démentir, contester*] categorically; [*identifier*] positively; [*interdire*] strictly [b] (= *officiellement*) [*demander*] formally; [*condamner*] officially [c] (*Art, Philo*) formally

former [fɔʀme] ▸ conjug 1◂ [1] VT [a] [+ *gouvernement*] to form; [+ *entreprise, équipe*] to set up; [+ *liens d'amitié*] to form, create; [+ *croûte, dépôt*] to form; **il s'est formé des liens entre nous** bonds have formed *ou* been created between us; **le cône que forme la révolution d'un triangle** the cone formed by the revolution of a triangle [b] [+ *collection*] to form, build up; [+ *convoi*] to form; [+ *forme verbale*] to make up; **~ correctement ses phrases** to form proper sentences; **phrase bien formée** well-formed sentence; **phrase mal formée** ill-formed sentence; **le train n'est pas encore formé** they haven't made up the train yet [c] (= *être le composant de*) to make up, form; **article formé de trois paragraphes** article made up of *ou* consisting of three paragraphs; **ceci forme un tout** this forms a whole; **ils forment un beau couple** they make a nice couple [d] (= *dessiner*) to make, form; **ça forme un rond** it makes *ou* forms a circle; **la route forme des lacets** the road winds; **il forme bien/mal ses lettres** he forms his letters well/badly [e] (= *éduquer*) [+ *soldats, ingénieurs*] to train; [+ *intelligence, caractère, goût*] to form, develop; **les voyages forment la jeunesse** travel broadens the mind; **le personnel est peu formé** the staff is relatively untrained [f] **~ l'idée** *ou* **le projet de faire qch** to form *ou* have the idea of doing sth; **nous formons des vœux pour votre réussite** we wish you every success

[2] **se former** VPR [a] (= *se rassembler*) to form, gather; **des nuages se forment à l'horizon** clouds are forming *ou* gathering on the horizon; **se ~ en cortège** to form a procession; **il s'est formé un attroupement** a crowd gathered *ou* formed; **l'armée se forma en carré** *ou* **forma le carré** the army took up a square formation [b] [*dépôt, croûte*] to form [c] (= *apprendre un métier*) to train o.s.; (= *éduquer son goût, son caractère*) to educate o.s. [d] (= *se développer*) [*goût, caractère, intelligence*] to form, develop; [*fruit*] to form; **les fruits commencent à se ~ sur l'arbre** the fruit is beginning to form on the tree

Formica® [fɔʀmika] NM Formica®; **table en ~** Formica table

formidable [fɔʀmidabl] ADJ [a] (= *très important*) [*coup, obstacle, bruit*] tremendous [b]* (= *très bien*) fantastic*, great* [c]* (= *incroyable*) incredible; **c'est tout de même ~ qu'on ne me dise jamais rien!** it's a bit much* that nobody ever tells me anything!; **il est ~:** il convoque une réunion et il est en retard! he's marvellous (*iro*) *ou* incredible — he calls a meeting and then he's late! [d] (*littér* = *effrayant*) fearsome

formidablement [fɔʀmidabləmɑ̃] ADV (= *très bien*) fantastically*; **on s'est ~ amusé** we had a fantastic time*; **comment ça a marché? — ~!** how did it go? — great!* *ou* fantastic!*

formique [fɔʀmik] ADJ formic

formol [fɔʀmɔl] NM formalin, formol

formosan, e [fɔʀmozɑ̃, an] [1] ADJ Formosan [2] **Formosan(e)** NM,F Formosan

Formose [fɔʀmoz] NF Formosa

formulable [fɔʀmylabl] ADJ which can be formulated; **difficilement ~** difficult to formulate

formulaire [fɔʀmylɛʀ] NM [a] (à *remplir*) form;

~ de demande application form; **~ E111** form E111 [b] [*pharmaciens, notaires*] formulary

formulation [fɔʀmylasjɔ̃] NF [*plainte, requête*] formulation, wording; [*sentiment*] formulation, expression; [*ordonnance, acte notarié*] drawing up; (*Chim, Math*) formulation; **changer la ~ d'une demande** to change the way an application is formulated, change the wording of an application

formule [fɔʀmyl] NF [a] (*Chim, Math*) formula; **~ dentaire** dentition, dental formula [b] (= *expression*) phrase, expression; (*magique, prescrite par l'étiquette*) formula; **~ heureuse** happy turn of phrase; **~ de politesse** polite phrase; (*en fin de lettre*) letter ending; **~ publicitaire** advertising slogan; **~ toute faite** ready-made phrase; **~ incantatoire** incantation → **consacré** [c] (= *méthode*) system, way; **~ de paiement** method of payment; **~ de vacances** holiday programme *ou* schedule; **trouver la bonne ~** to hit on *ou* find the right formula; **c'est la ~ idéale pour des vacances avec de jeunes enfants** it's the ideal solution for going on holiday with young children; (*dans un restaurant*) **~ à 89 F** 89 franc menu; **ils proposent différentes ~s de location/de crédit** they offer several different rental/credit options [d] (= *formulaire*) form; **~ de chèque/de télégramme** cheque/telegram form [e] (*Aut*) **la ~ 1/2/3** Formula One/Two/Three; **une (voiture de) ~ 1** a Formula-One car

formuler [fɔʀmyle] ▸ conjug 1◂ VT [+ *plainte, requête*] to set out, word, formulate (*frm*); [+ *critiques, sentiment*] to express; [+ *ordonnance, acte notarié*] to draw up; (*Chim, Math*) to formulate; **il a mal formulé sa question** he didn't word *ou* phrase his question very well

fornicateur, -trice [fɔʀnikatœʀ, tʀis] NM,F (*littér, hum*) fornicator

fornication [fɔʀnikasjɔ̃] NF (*littér, hum*) fornication

forniquer [fɔʀnike] ▸ conjug 1◂ VI (*littér, hum*) to fornicate

FORPRONU, Forpronu [fɔʀpʀɔny] NF (ABRÉV = **Force de protection des Nations unies**) **la ~** Unprofor

fors †† [fɔʀ] PRÉP save, except

forsythia [fɔʀsisja] NM forsythia

fort¹, e¹ [fɔʀ, fɔʀt]

[1] ADJECTIF	[2] ADVERBE

[1] ADJECTIF

[a] = **puissant** [*personne, État, lunettes*] strong; **il est ~ comme un bœuf** *ou* **un Turc** he's as strong as an ox *ou* a horse; **il est de ~e constitution** he has a strong constitution; **le dollar est une monnaie ~e** the dollar is a strong *ou* hard currency; (*Cartes*) **la dame est plus ~e que le valet** the queen is higher than the jack; **c'est plus ~ que moi** I can't help it; **il est ~ en gueule*** he's loud-mouthed* *ou* a loudmouth* → **partie**

♦ **fort de**: **une armée ~e de 20 000 hommes** an army 20,000 strong; **une équipe ~e de 15** personnes a team of 15 people; **~ de leur soutien/de cette garantie** armed with their support/with this guarantee; **~ de son expérience, il ...** wiser for this experience, he ...; **être ~ de son bon droit** to be confident of one's rights

[b] **euph = gros** [*personne*] stout, large; [*hanches*] broad, wide, large; [*poitrine*] large, ample; **il s'habille au rayon (pour) hommes ~s** he gets his clothes from the outsize department; **elle est un peu ~e des hanches** she has rather wide *ou* broad *ou* large hips, she's a bit broad in the beam*

[c] = **solide, résistant** [*carton*] strong, stout; [*colle*] strong → **château, place**

[d] = **intense** [*lumière, rythme, battements*] strong; [*bruit, voix*] loud; [*sentiments*] strong,

intense; [*dégoût, crainte*] great; [*impression*] great, strong; [*colère, douleur, chaleur*] great, intense; [*fièvre*] high; **une ~e grippe** a bad bout of flu; **une œuvre ~e** a powerful work; **il y a quelques moments ~s dans son film** there are some powerful scenes in his film; **au sens ~ du terme** in the strongest sense of the term; **génie? le terme est un peu ~!** a genius? I wouldn't go so far as to say that! → **envie, temps¹**

[e] = **marqué** [*pente*] pronounced, steep; [*accent*] strong, marked, pronounced; [*goût, odeur, moutarde, café*] strong

[f] = **violent** [*secousse, coup*] hard; [*houle, pluies*] heavy; [*vent*] strong, high; (*Mét Naut*) **mer ~e/très ~e** rough/very rough sea

[g] = **excessif** **c'est trop ~!** that's too much!, that's going too far!; **c'est un peu ~ (de café)*** that's a bit much*, that's going a bit (too) far*; (*hum*) **elle est ~e celle-là!*** ◊ **c'est plus ~ que de jouer au bouchon!*** that beats everything!*, that takes the biscuit!* (*Brit*); **et le plus ~ ou et ce qu'il y a de plus ~, c'est que ...** and the best (part) of it is that ...

[h] = **important** [*somme*] large, great; [*hausse, baisse, différence*] big, great; [*dose, augmentation*] large, big; [*consommation*] high; **vin ~ en alcool** strong wine, wine with a high alcohol content → **prix**

[i] = **courageux, obstiné** [*personne*] strong; **être ~ dans l'adversité** to be strong *ou* to stand firm in (the face of) adversity; **âme ~e** steadfast soul; **esprit ~†** freethinker; **c'est une ~e tête** he (*ou* she) is a rebel

[j] = **doué** good (**en, à** at), able; **il est ~ en histoire/aux échecs** he's good at history/at chess; **il est très ~!** he's very good (at it)!; **être ~ sur un sujet** to be well up on* *ou* good at a subject; **il a trouvé plus ~ que lui** he has (more than) found *ou* met his match; **quand il s'agit de critiquer, il est ~!** he can criticize all right!, he's very good at criticizing!; **ce n'est pas très ~ (de sa part)*** that's not very clever *ou* bright of him; **c'est trop ~ pour moi** it's beyond me → **point¹**

[k] **Ling** **consonne ~e** hard consonant; **forme ~e** strong form → **verbe**

[2] ADVERBE

[a] = **intensément** [*lancer, serrer, souffler*] hard; **frapper ~** (*bruit*) to knock loudly; (*force*) to knock *ou* hit hard; **sentir ~** to have a strong smell, smell strong; **respirez bien ~** breathe deeply, take a deep breath; **son cœur battait très ~** his heart was pounding *ou* was beating hard; **le feu marche trop ~** the fire is burning too fast; **tu y vas un peu ~ tout de même*** even so, you're overdoing it a bit* *ou* going a bit far*; **tu as fait ~!*** that was a bit much!*

[b] = **bruyamment** [*parler, crier*] loudly, loud; **parlez plus ~** speak up *ou* louder; **mets la radio moins/plus ~** turn the radio down/up

[c] **littér = beaucoup** greatly; **cela me déplaît ~** that displeases me greatly *ou* a great deal; **j'en doute ~** I very much doubt it; **il y tient ~** he sets great store by it; **j'ai ~ à faire avec lui** I have a hard job with him, I've got my work cut out with him

[d] **frm = très** [*simple, différent, rare, ancien*] extremely, very; [*aimable*] most; [*mécontent, intéressant*] most, highly; **il est ~ apprécié de ses chefs** he is highly regarded by his bosses; **il est ~ inquiet** he is very *ou* most anxious; **c'est ~ bon** it is very *ou* exceedingly good, it is most excellent; **il y avait ~ peu de monde** there were very few people → **aise**

♦ **fort bien** [*dessiné, dit, conservé*] extremely well; **tu sais bien que ...** you know very well *ou* full well that ...; **nous avons été ~ bien accueillis** we were made most welcome; **je peux ~ bien le faire moi-même/m'en passer** I can quite easily do it myself/do without it

(*excl*) **~ bien!** very good!, excellent!; **tu refu-**

ses? ~ bien, tu l'auras voulu you refuse? very well, on your own head be it

e

◆ **se faire fort de** + *infinitif*: **nos champions se font ~ de gagner** our champions are confident they will win *ou* confident of winning; **je me fais ~ de le réparer** I'm (quite) sure I can mend it, I can mend it, don't worry *ou* you'll see

fort² [fɔʀ] 1 NM a (= *forteresse*) fort b (= *personne*) **le ~ l'emporte toujours contre le faible** the strong will always win against the weak; (*péj Scol*) **un ~ en thème** an egghead*, a swot* (*Brit*) → **raison** c (= *spécialité*) strong point, forte; **l'amabilité n'est pas son ~** kindness is not his strong point *ou* his forte 2 **au fort de** LOC PRÉP (*littér*) [+ *été*] at the height of; [+ *hiver*] in the depths of; **au plus ~ du combat** (*lieu*) in the thick of the battle; (*intensité*) when the battle was at its most intense, at the height of the battle 3 COMP ► **fort des Halles** market porter

Fort-de-France [fɔʀdəfʀɑ̃s] N Fort-de-France

forte² [fɔʀte] ADV (*Mus*) forte

fortement [fɔʀtəmɑ̃] ADV [*conseiller*] strongly; [*tenir*] fast, tight(ly); [*frapper*] hard; [*serrer*] hard, tight(ly); **il est ~ probable que ...** it is highly *ou* most probable that ...; **~ marqué/attiré** strongly marked/attracted; **il en est ~ question** it is being seriously considered; **j'espère ~ que vous le pourrez** I very much hope that you will be able to; **boiter ~** to have a pronounced limp, limp badly; **il est ~ intéressé par l'affaire** he is highly *ou* most interested in the matter

forteresse [fɔʀtəʀɛs] NF (*lit*) fortress, stronghold; (*fig*) stronghold; **~ volante** flying fortress

fortiche* [fɔʀtiʃ] ADJ [*personne*] terrific*, great* (**en** at)

fortifiant, e [fɔʀtifjɑ̃, jɑ̃t] 1 ADJ [*médicament, boisson*] fortifying; [*air*] invigorating, bracing; (*littér*) [*exemple, lecture*] uplifting 2 NM (*Pharm*) tonic

fortification [fɔʀtifikasjɔ̃] NF fortification

fortifier [fɔʀtifje] ▸conjug 7◂ 1 VT [+ *corps, âme*] to strengthen, fortify; [+ *position, opinion, impression*] to strengthen; [+ *ville*] to fortify; **l'air marin fortifie** (the) sea air is invigorating *ou* bracing; **cela m'a fortifié dans mes résolutions** that strengthened my resolve 2 **se fortifier** VPR (*Mil*) to fortify itself; [*opinion, amitié, position*] to grow stronger, be strengthened; [*santé*] to grow more robust

fortin [fɔʀtɛ̃] NM (small) fort

fortiori [fɔʀsjɔʀi] → **a fortiori**

fortran [fɔʀtʀɑ̃] NM Fortran, FORTRAN

fortuit, e [fɔʀtɥi, it] ADJ [*événement, circonstance, remarque, rencontre*] fortuitous, chance (*épith*); [*coïncidence*] fortuitous; [*découverte*] fortuitous, chance (*épith*), accidental

fortuitement [fɔʀtɥitmɑ̃] ADV fortuitously, by chance

fortune [fɔʀtyn] NF a (= *richesse*) fortune; **situation de ~** financial situation; **ça vaut** *ou* **coûte une (petite) ~** it costs a fortune; **cet homme est l'une des plus grosses ~s de la région** that man has one of the largest fortunes *ou* that man is one of the wealthiest in the area; **avoir de la ~** to be independently wealthy; **faire ~** to make one's fortune (**dans** in); **le mot a fait ~** the word has really become popular *ou* has really caught on → **impôt, revers**

b (= *chance*) luck (*NonC*), fortune (*NonC*); (= *destinée*) fortune; **chercher ~** to seek one's fortune; **connaître des ~s diverses** (*sujet pluriel*) to enjoy varying fortunes; (*sujet singulier*) to have varying luck; **il a eu la (bonne) ~ de le rencontrer** he was fortunate enough to meet him, he had the good fortune to meet him; **ayant eu la mauvaise ~ de le rencontrer** having had the misfortune *ou* the ill-fortune to meet him; **faire contre mauvaise ~ bon cœur** to make the best of it; **venez dîner à la ~ du pot** come to dinner and take pot luck with us; (*Jur, Naut*) **~s de mer** sea risks, perils of the sea ■ (*PROV*) **la ~ sourit aux audacieux** fortune favours the brave

c **de ~** [*abri, embarcation, réparation, moyen*] makeshift; [*installation*] makeshift, rough-and-ready; [*compagnon*] chance (*épith*); **mât/gouvernail de ~** jury mast/rudder

d (*Naut*) **~ (carrée)** crossjack

fortuné, e [fɔʀtyne] ADJ (= *riche*) wealthy, well-off; (*littér* = *heureux*) fortunate

forum [fɔʀɔm] NM (= *place, colloque*) forum

fosse [fos] 1 NF (= *trou*) pit; (= *tombe*) grave; (*Sport*: *pour le saut*) (sand)pit; (*Anat*) fossa 2 COMP ► **fosse d'aisances** cesspool ► **fosse commune** common *ou* communal grave ► **fosse à fumier** manure pit ► **fosse aux lions** (*lit, fig*) lions' den ► **fosse marine** ocean trench ► **fosses nasales** nasal fossae ► **fosse d'orchestre** orchestra pit ► **fosse aux ours** bear pit ► **fosse à purin** slurry pit ► **fosse septique** septic tank

fossé [fose] NM a (*lit*) ditch; **~ d'irrigation** irrigation channel *ou* ditch; **~ antichar** anti-tank ditch b (*fig*) gulf, gap; **un ~ les sépare** a gulf lies between them; **~ culturel** cultural gap; **le ~ des** *ou* **entre les générations** the generation gap

fossette [fosɛt] NF dimple

fossile [fosil] 1 NM (*lit, fig*) fossil 2 ADJ fossil (*épith*), fossilized → **rayonnement**

fossilifère [fosilifɛʀ] ADJ fossiliferous

fossilisation [fosilizasjɔ̃] NF fossilization

fossiliser [fosilize] ▸conjug 1◂ (*lit, fig*) 1 VT to fossilize 2 **se fossiliser** VPR to fossilize, become fossilized

fossoyeur [foswajœʀ] NM gravedigger; (*fig*) destroyer

fou, folle [fu, fɔl] (*m*: *devant voyelle ou h muet* **fol**) 1 ADJ a (*Méd*) mad, insane; (*gén*) mad, crazy; **~ à lier** ◊ **~ furieux** raving mad; **il est devenu subitement ~** he suddenly went mad *ou* crazy; (*lit, fig*) **ça l'a rendu ~** it drove him mad *ou* crazy; **c'est à devenir ~** it's enough to drive you mad *ou* crazy; **~ de colère/de désir/de chagrin** out of one's mind with anger/with desire/with grief; **~ de joie** delirious *ou* out of one's mind with joy; **~ d'amour (pour)** ◊ **amoureux ~ (de)** madly in love (with); **elle est folle de lui/de ce musicien** she's mad* *ou* crazy* about him/about that musician; **tu es complètement ~ de refuser** you're completely mad *ou* absolutely crazy to refuse; **y aller? (je ne suis) pas si ~!** go there?, I'm not that crazy!; **pas folle, la guêpe*** he's (*ou* she's) no fool!; (*hum*) **elle est folle de son corps*** she's sex-mad*

b (= *insensé*) [*terreur, rage, course*] mad, wild; [*amour, joie, espoir*] mad, insane; [*idée, désir, tentative, dépense*] mad, insane, crazy; [*audace*] insane; [*imagination*] wild, insane; [*regard, gestes*] wild, crazed; **avoir le ~ rire** to have the giggles; (*Comm*) **prix ~s sur les chemises** shirts at give-away prices; (†, *hum*) **folle jeunesse** wild youth; **folle enchère** irresponsible bid

c * (= *énorme*) [*courage, énergie, succès*] fantastic*, terrific, tremendous; [*peur*] terrific, tremendous; **j'ai un mal de tête ~** I've got a splitting headache*, my head's killing me*; **j'ai une envie folle de chocolat/d'y aller** I'm dying for some chocolate/to go; **j'ai eu un mal ~ pour venir** I had a terrific *ou* terrible job* getting here; **tu as mis un temps ~** it took you ages*; **gagner/dépenser un argent ~** to earn/spend loads of money*; **payer un prix ~** to pay a ridiculous *ou* an astronomical price; **rouler à une vitesse folle** to drive at a tremendous speed; **il y a un monde ~** it's really crowded; **c'est ~ ce qu'il y a comme monde** it's incredible how many people there are; **c'est ~ ce qu'on s'amuse!** we're having such a great *ou* fantastic time!*; **c'est ~ ce qu'il a changé** it's incredible *ou* unbelievable how much he has changed

d (= *déréglé*) [*boussole, aiguille*] erratic; [*camion, cheval*] runaway (*épith*); [*mèche de cheveux*] stray, unruly; **elle a les cheveux ~s** her hair's all over the place; **folle avoine** wild oats → **herbe, patte**

2 NM a (*Méd, fig*) madman, lunatic; **courir comme un ~** to run like a madman *ou* lunatic; **travailler comme un ~** to work like mad* *ou* crazy*; **arrêtez de faire les ~s** stop messing *ou* fooling about*; **ce jeune ~** this young lunatic; **espèce de vieux ~** you silly old fool → **histoire, maison, plus**

b * (= *fanatique*) fanatic; **c'est un ~ de jazz/tennis** he's a jazz/tennis fanatic

c (*Échecs*) bishop

d (*Hist* = *bouffon*) jester, fool; **le ~ du roi** the king's fool, the court jester

e (*Zool*) **~ (de Bassan)** gannet

3 **folle** NF a (*Méd, fig*) madwoman, lunatic; **cette vieille folle** that old madwoman, that mad old woman; (*littér*) **la folle du logis** the imagination

b (‡ *péj* = *homosexuel*) **(grande) folle** queen‡, fag‡ (*US*)

foucade [fukad] NF (*littér*) caprice, whim, passing fancy; (= *emportement*) outburst

foudre¹ [fudʀ] 1 NF (*Mét*) lightning; (*Myth*) thunderbolt; **frappé par la ~** struck by lightning; **la ~ est tombée sur la maison** the house was struck by lightning; **comme la ~** ◊ **avec la rapidité de la ~** like lightning, as quick as a flash; **ce fut le coup de ~** it was love at first sight; **j'ai eu le coup de ~ pour Julie** I fell head over heels in love with Julie; **elle a eu le coup de ~ pour l'Écosse** she fell in love with Scotland 2 NFPL (= *colère, Rel*) **~s** anathema *sg*; **il s'est attiré les ~s de l'opposition** he provoked an angry response from the opposition

foudre² [fudʀ] NM (†, *hum*) **~ de guerre** outstanding *ou* great leader (in war); **ce n'est pas un ~ de guerre** he's no firebrand; **~ d'éloquence** brilliant orator

foudre³ [fudʀ] NM (= *tonneau*) tun

foudroiement [fudʀwamɑ̃] NM striking (by lightning)

foudroyant, e [fudʀwajɑ̃, ɑ̃t] ADJ [*progrès, vitesse, attaque*] lightning (*épith*); [*poison, maladie*] violent (*épith*); [*mort*] instant; [*succès*] stunning (*épith*); **une nouvelle ~e** a devastating piece of news; **il lui lança un regard ~** he looked daggers at him

foudroyer [fudʀwaje] ▸conjug 8◂ VT [*foudre*] to strike; [*coup de feu, maladie, malheur*] to strike down; **il a été foudroyé** he was struck by lightning; **la décharge électrique la foudroya** the electric shock killed her; **cette nouvelle le foudroya** he was thunderstruck by the news; **~ qn du regard** to look daggers at sb, glare at sb; **dans le champ il y avait un arbre foudroyé** in the field was a tree that had been struck by lightning

fouet [fwɛ] NM a (= *cravache*) whip; (*Culin* = *batteur*) whisk; **donner le ~ à qn** to give sb a whipping *ou* flogging; **coup de ~** (*lit*) lash; (*fig*) boost; **donner un coup de ~ à l'économie** to stimulate the economy, give the economy a boost, kick-start the economy; **le café/la douche froide lui a donné un coup de ~** the coffee/the cold shower perked him up → **plein** b (*Zool*) [*aile, queue*] tip

fouettard [fwetaʀ] ADJ → **père**

fouetté, e [fwete] (*ptp de* **fouetter**) 1 ADJ **crème ~e** whipped cream 2 NM (*Danse*) fouetté

fouettement [fwɛtmɑ̃] NM [*pluie*] lashing

fouetter [fwete] ▸conjug 1◂ 1 VT a [+ *personne*] to whip, flog; [+ *cheval*] to whip;

(Culin) [+ crème] to whip; [+ blanc d'œuf] to whisk; **la pluie fouettait les vitres** the rain lashed against the window panes; **le vent le fouettait au visage** the wind whipped his face; (hum) **fouette cocher!** don't spare the horses! (hum) → **chat** b (= stimuler) [+ imagination] to fire; [+ désir] to whip up; **l'air frais fouette le sang** fresh air is a real tonic 2 VI a **la pluie fouettait contre les vitres** the rain lashed against the window panes b (= avoir peur) to be scared stiff* ou to death* c (= puer) to reek, stink; **ça fouette ici!** there's one hell of a stench ou stink in here!‡

foufou, fofolle* [fufu, fɔfɔl] ADJ crazy, scatty* (Brit)

foufoune‡ [fufun], **foufounette‡** [fufunɛt] NF pussy*‡, fanny*‡ (Brit)

fougasse [fugas] NF (= galette) wheat pancake; (= pain brioché) ≈ brioche

fougère [fuʒɛʀ] NF fern; ~ **arborescente** tree fern; ~ **aigle** bracken; **clairière envahie de ~(s)** clearing overgrown with bracken

fougue [fug] NF [personne] spirit; [discours, attaque] fieriness; **plein de ~** [orateur, réponse] fiery; [cheval] mettlesome, fiery; **la ~ de la jeunesse** the hotheadedness of youth; **avec ~** spiritedly

fougueusement [fugøzmɑ̃] ADV spiritedly; **se ruer ~ sur qn** to hurl o.s. impetuously at sb

fougueux, -euse [fugø, øz] ADJ [réponse, tempérament, orateur] fiery; [jeunesse] hotheaded, fiery; [cheval] mettlesome, fiery; [attaque] spirited

fouille [fuj] NF a [personne] searching, frisking; [maison, bagages] search, searching; **corporelle** body search b (Archéol) ~**s** excavation(s), dig*; **faire des ~s** to carry out excavations c (Constr) (= action) excavation; (= lieu) excavation (site) d (‡ = poche) pocket; **s'en mettre plein les ~s** (= gagner de l'argent) to make a packet*

fouillé, e [fuje] (ptp de **fouiller**) ADJ [analyse, étude] detailed, in-depth (épith), thorough; **fronton fouillé** finely detailed pediment

fouille-merde‡ [fujmɛʀd] NMF INV muckraker, shit-stirrer*‡

fouiller [fuje] ▶ conjug 1 ◀ 1 VT [+ pièce, mémoire] to search; [+ personne] to search, frisk; [+ poches] to search, go ou rummage through; [+ région, bois] to search, scour, comb; [+ question] to go (deeply) into; [+ sol] to dig; [+ terrain] to excavate, dig up; [+ bas-relief] to undercut; **on a fouillé mes bagages à la frontières** my bags were searched at the border; **il fouillait l'horizon avec ses jumelles** he scanned ou searched the horizon with his binoculars; **il fouilla l'obscurité des yeux** he peered into the darkness; **il le fouilla du regard** he gave him a searching look; **étude/ analyse très fouillée** very detailed study/ analysis; **rinceaux très fouillés** finely detailed mouldings

2 VI ~ **dans** [+ tiroir, armoire] to rummage in, dig about in; [+ poches, bagages] to go ou rummage through; [+ mémoire] to delve into, search; **qui a fouillé dans mes affaires?** who's been rummaging about in my things?; ~ **dans les archives** to delve into the files; ~ **dans le passé de qn** to delve into sb's past

3 **se fouiller** VPR to go through one's pockets; **tu peux toujours te ~!**‡ no way!*, nothing doing!*

fouilleur, -euse [fujœʀ, øz] 1 NM,F a (Archéol) digger b (Police) searcher, frisker* 2 **fouilleuse** NF (Agr) subsoil plough (Brit) ou plow (US)

fouillis [fuji] NM [papiers, objets] jumble, muddle; [branchages] tangle; [idées] jumble, hotchpotch (Brit), hodgepodge (US); **faire du ~** (dans une pièce) [personne] to make a mess; [objets] to look a mess, look messy; **sa chambre est en ~** his room is a dreadful mess; **il régnait un ~**

indescriptible everything was in an indescribable mess; **il est très ~*** he's very untidy; **un exposé ~*** a muddled account

fouinard, e* [fwinaʀ, aʀd] ADJ, NM,F = **fouineur, -euse**

fouine [fwin] NF (Zool) stone marten; (fig) **c'est une vraie ~** he's a real snoop(er)* (péj); **visage** ou **tête de ~** weasel face

fouiner [fwine] ▶ conjug 1 ◀ VI (péj) to nose around ou about; **je n'aime pas qu'on fouine dans mes affaires** I don't like people nosing ou ferreting about in my things; **il est toujours à ~ partout** he's always poking his nose into things

fouineur, -euse [fwinœʀ, øz] (péj) 1 ADJ prying, nosey* 2 NM,F nosey parker*, snoop(er)*

fouir [fwiʀ] ▶ conjug 2 ◀ VT to dig

fouisseur, -euse [fwisœʀ, øz] 1 ADJ burrowing, fossorial (SPÉC) 2 NM burrower, fossorial animal (SPÉC)

foulage [fulaʒ] NM [raisin] pressing; [drap] fulling; [cuir] tanning

foulant, e* [fulɑ̃, ɑ̃t] ADJ **ce n'est pas trop ~** it won't kill you (ou him etc)* → **pompe¹**

foulard [fulaʀ] NM a (= écharpe) (carré) (head)scarf; (long) scarf; ~ **islamique** chador b (= tissu) foulard

foule [ful] NF a (gén) crowd; (péj = populace) mob; **la ~** (= le peuple) the masses; **une ~ hurlante** a howling mob; **la ~ et l'élite** the masses and the élite; **la ~ des badauds** the crowd of onlookers → **psychologie** b (loc) **il y avait ~ à la réunion** there were lots of people at the meeting; **il n'y avait pas ~!** there was hardly anyone there!; **une ~ de** [+ livres, questions] masses* ou loads* of; **il y avait une ~ de gens** there was a crowd ou there were crowds of people; **une ~ de gens pensent que c'est faux** lots ou masses* of people think it's wrong; **j'ai une ~ de choses à te dire** I've got loads* ou masses* (of things) to tell you; **ils vinrent en ~ à l'exposition** they flocked to the exhibition; **les idées me venaient en ~** my head was teeming with ideas

foulée [fule] NF [cheval, coureur] stride; [animal sauvage] spoor; (Sport) **suivre qn dans la ~** ◊ **être dans la ~ de qn** to follow (close) on sb's heels; **courir à petites ~s** to jog ou trot along; **dans la ~ je vais repeindre le couloir** I'll paint the corridor while I'm at it

fouler [fule] ▶ conjug 1 ◀ 1 VT [+ raisins] to press; [+ drap] to full; [+ cuir] to tan; (littér) **le sol de sa patrie** to walk upon ou tread (upon) native soil; ~ **aux pieds quelque chose de sacré** to trample something sacred underfoot, trample on something sacred 2 **se fouler** VPR a **se ~ la cheville/le poignet** to sprain one's ankle/one's wrist b* (= travailler dur) **il ne se foule pas beaucoup** ◊ **il ne se foule pas la rate** he doesn't exactly overtax himself ou strain himself; **ils ne se sont pas foulés!** they didn't exactly go to a lot of trouble!

fouleur, -euse [fulœʀ, øz] NM,F [drap] fuller; [cuir] tanner

fouloir [fulwaʀ] NM [drap] fulling mill; [cuir] tanning drum

foulon [fulɔ̃] NM → **terre**

foulque [fulk] NF coot

foultitude* [fultityd] NF **une ~ de** heaps of*, loads of*, masses of*; **j'ai une ~ de choses à faire** I've got a thousand and one things to do heaps* ou masses* of things to do

foulure [fulyʀ] NF sprain

four [fuʀ] 1 NM a [boulangerie, cuisinière] oven; [potier] kiln; [usine] furnace; ~ **à céramique/à émaux** pottery/enamelling kiln; **cuire au ~** [+ gâteau] to bake; [+ viande] to roast; **plat allant au ~** ovenproof ou fireproof dish; **poisson cuit au ~** baked fish; **il a ouvert la bouche comme un ~*** he opened his great

cavern of a mouth; **je ne peux pas être au ~ et au moulin** I can't be in two places at once → **banal²**, **noir** b (Théât) flop, fiasco; **cette pièce est** ou **a fait un ~** the play is a complete flop c (= gâteau) (**petit**) ~ small pastry, petit four; **petits ~s frais** miniature pastries; **petits ~s salés** savoury appetizers (bite-size pizzas, quiches etc)

2 COMP ► **four à chaleur tournante** fan(-assisted) oven ► **four à chaux** lime kiln ► **four crématoire** [crématorium] crematorium ou crematory (furnace); (Hist) **les ~s crématoires** the ovens (in Nazi concentration camps) ► **four électrique** (gén) electric oven; (Ind) electric furnace ► **four à pain** baker's oven ► **four solaire** solar furnace → **micro-onde**

fourbe [fuʀb] ADJ [personne, caractère, air, regard] deceitful, treacherous; **c'est un ~** he's deceitful ou treacherous

fourberie [fuʀbəʀi] NF (littér) (= nature) deceitfulness, treachery; (= acte, geste) deceit, treachery; **à cause de ses ~s** because of his treachery ou deceit

fourbi* [fuʀbi] NM (= attirail) gear* (NonC), clobber* (NonC) (Brit); (= fouillis) mess; **canne à pêche, hameçons et tout le ~** fishing rod, hooks and all the rest of the gear; **partir en vacances avec le bébé, ça va en faire du** ou **un ~** going on holiday with the baby will mean taking a whole heap of gear* with us

fourbir [fuʀbiʀ] ▶ conjug 2 ◀ VT [+ arme] to polish, furbish; (fig) ~ **ses armes** to prepare for battle, get ready for the fray

fourbissage [fuʀbisaʒ] NM polishing, furbishing

fourbu, e [fuʀby] ADJ exhausted

fourche [fuʀʃ] NF a (pour le foin) pitchfork; (pour bêcher) fork b [arbre, chemin, bicyclette] fork; [pantalon, jambes] crotch; [cheveu] split end; **la route faisait une ~** the road forked c (Hist) **les Fourches Caudines** the Caudine Forks; (fig) **passer sous les ~s Caudines** to admit defeat d (Belg = temps libre) break

fourcher [fuʀʃe] ▶ conjug 1 ◀ VI [arbre, chemin] † to fork; **avoir les cheveux qui fourchent** to have split ends; **ma langue a fourché** it was a slip of the tongue

fourchette [fuʀʃɛt] NF a (pour manger) fork; ~ **à gâteaux/à huîtres** pastry/oyster fork; (hum) **manger avec la ~ d'Adam** to eat with one's fingers; **il a une bonne ~** ou **un bon coup de ~** he has a hearty appetite, he's a good ou hearty eater b [oiseau] wishbone; [cheval] frog; (Aut) selector fork; (Tech) fork; (Anat) ~ **vulgaire** fourchette; (Anat) ~ **sternale** suprasternal notch c (Stat) margin; **la ~ se rétrécit** the margin is narrowing; ~ **d'âge** age bracket; ~ **d'imposition** tax bracket ou band; ~ **de prix** price range d (Échecs) fork; (Cartes) **prendre la dame en ~** to finesse the queen

fourchu, e [fuʀʃy] ADJ [arbre, chemin] forked; [menton] jutting (épith); **animal au pied ~** cloven-hoofed animal; **elle a les cheveux ~s** she's got split ends → **langue**

fourgon [fuʀgɔ̃] NM (= wagon) wag(g)on; (= camion) (large) van, lorry (Brit); (= diligence) coach, carriage; (= tisonnier) poker; ~ **à bagages** luggage van; ~ **à bestiaux** cattle truck; ~ **blindé** armoured van; ~ **cellulaire** prison ou police van (Brit), patrol wagon (US); ~ **de déménagement** removal (Brit) ou moving (US) van; ~ **funéraire** ou **mortuaire** hearse; ~ **de munitions** munitions wagon; ~ **postal** mail van; ~ **de queue** rear brake van; (Mil) ~ **de vivres** supply wagon

fourgonner [fuʀgɔne] ▶ conjug 1 ◀ 1 VT [+ poêle, feu] to poke, rake 2 VI (*: parmi des objets) to rummage about, poke about; **je l'entendais qui fourgonnait dans la cuisine/**

dans le placard I heard him rummaging *ou* poking about in the kitchen/in the cupboard

fourgonnette [fuʀɡɔnɛt] NF (small) van, delivery van

fourgue[1] [fuʀɡ] (*arg Crime*) **1** NM (= *personne*) fence* **2** NF (= *trafic*) fencing*; (= *marchandise*) fenced goods*

fourguer* [fuʀɡe] ▶conjug 1◀ VT (= *vendre*) [+ *mauvaise marchandise*] to flog* (**à** to), unload* (**à** onto); (= *donner*) to unload (**à** onto); (*arg Crime* = *dénoncer*) **il m'a fourgué aux flics*** he squealed on me to the cops*

fouriérisme [fuʀjeʀism] NM Fourierism

fouriériste [fuʀjeʀist] **1** ADJ Fourieristic **2** NMF Fourierist, Fourierite

fourme [fuʀm] NF *type of French blue-veined cheese*

fourmi [fuʀmi] NF **a** (*Zool*) ant; (= *personne affairée*) beaver; **~ noire/rouge/volante** black/red/flying ant; **~ maçonne** builder *ou* worker ant; **avoir des ~s dans les jambes** to have pins and needles in one's legs; **vus de si haut les gens ont l'air de ~s** seen from so high up the people look like ants; **elle s'affaire comme une ~** she bustles about as busy as a bee → **travail**[1] **b** (*arg Drogue*) small-time runner, mule (*arg*)

fourmilier [fuʀmilje] NM anteater

fourmilière [fuʀmiljɛʀ] NF (= *monticule*) ant-hill; (= *nid*) ants' nest; (*fig*) hive of activity; **cette ville/ce bureau est une (vraie) ~** this town/this office is a hive of activity

fourmilion [fuʀmiljɔ̃] NM antlion, doodlebug (*US*)

fourmillant, e [fuʀmijɑ̃, jɑ̃t] ADJ [*foule*] milling, swarming; [*cité*] teeming

fourmillement [fuʀmijmɑ̃] NM **a** [*insectes, personnes*] swarming; **le ~ de la rue** the swarming *ou* milling crowds in the street; **un ~ d'insectes** a mass of swarming insects; **un ~ d'idées** a welter of ideas **b** (*gén pl* = *picotement*) **~s** pins and needles

fourmiller [fuʀmije] ▶conjug 1◀ VI [*insectes, personnes*] to swarm; **dissertation où fourmillent les erreurs** essay riddled with mistakes; **~ de** [+ *insectes, personnes*] to be swarming *ou* crawling *ou* teeming with; [+ *idées, erreurs*] to be teeming with

fournaise [fuʀnɛz] NF (= *feu*) blaze, blazing fire; (= *endroit surchauffé*) furnace, oven

fourneau (*pl* **fourneaux**) [fuʀno] NM **a**† (= *cuisinière, poêle*) stove; **être aux ~x** to do the cooking **b** [*forge, chaufferie*] furnace; [*pipe*] bowl; **~ de mine** blast hole → **haut**

fournée [fuʀne] NF (*lit, fig*) batch

fourni, e [fuʀni] (*ptp de* **fournir**) ADJ [*herbe*] luxuriant, lush; [*cheveux*] thick, abundant; [*barbe, sourcils*] bushy, thick; **chevelure peu ~e** sparse *ou* thin head of hair; **carte bien ~e** extensive *ou* full menu; **boutique bien ~e** well-stocked shop

fournil [fuʀni] NM bakery, bakehouse

fourniment* [fuʀnimɑ̃] NM gear* (*NonC*), clobber‡ (*NonC*) (*Brit*); **il va falloir emporter tout un ~** we'll have to take a whole heap of gear* *ou* stuff*

fournir [fuʀniʀ] ▶conjug 2◀ **1** VT **a** (= *approvisionner*) [+ *client, restaurant*] to supply; **~ qn en viande/légumes** to supply sb with meat/vegetables **b** (= *procurer*) [+ *matériel, main-d'œuvre*] to supply, provide; [+ *preuves, secours*] to supply, furnish; [+ *renseignements*] to supply, provide, furnish; [+ *pièce d'identité*] to produce; [+ *prétexte, exemple*] to give, supply; **~ qch à qn** to supply *ou* provide sb with sth; **~ à qn l'occasion/les moyens de faire qch** to provide sb with the opportunity of doing sth/the means to do sth; **~ du travail à qn** to provide sb with work; **~ le vivre et le couvert** to provide board and lodging **c** (= *produire*) [+ *effort*] to put in; [+ *prestation*]

to give; [+ *récolte*] to supply; **~ un gros effort** to put in a lot of effort, make a great deal of effort

d (*Cartes*) **~ (une carte)** to follow suit; **~ à cœur** to follow suit in hearts

2 fournir à† VT INDIR [+ *besoins*] to provide for; [+ *dépense, frais*] to defray; **ses parents fournissent à son entretien** his parents give him his keep *ou* provide for his maintenance

3 se fournir VPR to provide o.s. (**de** with); **se ~ en** *ou* **de charbon** to get (in) supplies of coal; **je me fournis toujours chez le même épicier** I always buy *ou* get my groceries from the same place, I always shop at the same grocer's

fournisseur [fuʀnisœʀ] NM (*Comm, Ind*) supplier; (= *détaillant*) retailer, stockist (*Brit*); **~ exclusif** sole supplier; **~ de viande/papier** supplier *ou* purveyor (*frm*) of meat/paper, meat/paper supplier; (*Internet*) **~ d'accès** access provider; **les pays ~s de la France** countries that supply France (with goods *ou* imports); **les ~s de l'armée** army contractors; **chez votre ~ habituel** at your local retailer('s) *ou* stockist('s) (*Brit*); **nos ~s manquent de matière première** our suppliers are out of raw materials

fourniture [fuʀnityʀ] NF **a** (= *action*) [*matériel, marchandises*] supply(ing), provision **b** (= *objet*) **~s (de bureau)** office supplies, stationery; **~s scolaires** school stationery

fourrage [fuʀaʒ] NM (*Agr*) fodder, forage; **~ vert** silage

fourrager[1] [fuʀaʒe] ▶conjug 3◀ ♦ **fourrager dans** VT INDIR [+ *papiers, tiroir*] to rummage through, dig about in

fourrager[2]**, -ère**[1] [fuʀaʒe, ɛʀ] ADJ **plante/betterave/culture fourragère** fodder plant/beet/crop; **céréales fourragères** feed grains

fourragère[2] [fuʀaʒɛʀ] NF **a** (*Mil*) fourragère **b** (= *champ*) fodder *ou* forage field; (= *charrette*) haywagon

fourre [fuʀ] NF (*Helv*) (= *taie*) pillowcase, pillowslip; [*édredon*] cover; (= *chemise cartonnée ou plastifiée*) folder; [*livre*] (dust) jacket *ou* cover; [*disque*] sleeve, jacket (*US*)

fourré[1] [fuʀe] NM thicket; **se cacher dans les ~s** to hide in the bushes

fourré[2]**, e** [fuʀe] (*ptp de* **fourrer**) ADJ [*bonbon, chocolat*] filled; [*manteau, gants*] fur-lined; (= *molletonné*) fleecy-lined; **~ d'hermine** ermine-lined; **chocolats ~s** chocolate creams; **gâteau ~ à la crème** cream(-filled) cake; **tablette de chocolat ~ à la crème** bar of cream-filled chocolate; (*fig*) **coup ~** underhand trick

fourreau (*pl* **fourreaux**) [fuʀo] NM **a** [*épée*] sheath, scabbard; [*parapluie*] cover; **mettre au/tirer du ~ son épée** to sheathe/unsheathe one's sword **b** (*robe*) **~** sheath dress

fourrer* [fuʀe] ▶conjug 1◀ VT **a** (= *enfoncer*) to stick*, shove*, stuff*; (= *mettre*) to stick*; **où ai-je bien pu le ~?** where on earth *ou* the heck* have I put it?; **~ ses mains dans ses poches** to stuff* *ou* stick* *ou* shove* one's hands in one's pockets; **~ qch dans un sac** to stuff* *ou* shove* sth into a bag; **qui t'a fourré ça dans le crâne?** who put that (idea) into your head?; **~ son nez partout/dans les affaires des autres** to poke *ou* stick* one's nose into everything/into other people's business; **~ qn dans le pétrin** to land sb in the soup* *ou* in it* (*Brit*); **~ qn en prison** to stick sb in prison* **b** [+ *gâteau*] to fill; [+ *manteau*] to line (with fur)

2 se fourrer* VPR **a** **se ~ une idée dans la tête** to get an idea into one's head; **il s'est fourré dans la tête que ...** he has got it into his head that ...

b **se ~ dans un coin** to go into a corner; **se ~ sous la table** to get under the table; **où a-t-il encore été se ~?** where has he got to now?; **il ne savait plus où se ~** he didn't know where

to put himself; **tu es toujours fourré dans mes pattes!** you're always getting under my feet!; **il est toujours fourré chez eux** he's always round at their place; **son ballon est allé se ~ dans la niche du chien** his ball ended up in *ou* landed in the dog kennel → **doigt, guêpier**

fourre-tout [fuʀtu] NM INV (= *pièce*) junk room; (= *placard*) junk cupboard; (= *sac*) holdall; **sa chambre est un vrai ~** his bedroom is an absolute dump* *ou* tip* (*Brit*); (*péj*) **sa dissertation/son livre est un vrai ~** his essay/his book is a real hotchpotch (*Brit*) *ou* hodge-podge (*US*) of ideas; **un discours/une loi ~** a rag-bag of a speech/law

fourreur [fuʀœʀ] NM furrier

fourrier [fuʀje] NM (*Hist Mil*) (*pour le logement*) harbinger; (*pour les vivres*) quartermaster; (*fig: littér*) forerunner, harbinger (*littér*) → **sergent**[1]

fourrière [fuʀjɛʀ] NF (*gén, Aut*) pound; [*chiens*] dog pound; **emmener une voiture à la ~** to tow away a car, impound a car

fourrure [fuʀyʀ] NF (= *pelage*) coat; (= *matériau, manteau*) fur

fourvoiement [fuʀvwamɑ̃] NM (*littér*) mistake

fourvoyer [fuʀvwaje] ▶conjug 8◀ **1** VT **~ qn** [*personne*] to get sb lost, mislead sb; [*mauvais renseignement*] to mislead sb; [*mauvais exemple*] to lead sb astray **2 se fourvoyer** VPR (= *s'égarer*) to lose one's way; (= *se tromper*) to go astray; **se ~ dans un quartier inconnu** to stray into an unknown district (by mistake); **dans quelle aventure s'est-il encore fourvoyé?** what has he got involved in now?; **il s'est complètement fourvoyé en faisant son problème** he has gone completely wrong *ou* completely off the track with his problem

foutaise‡ [futɛz] NF (**des**) **~s!** ◊ **(c'est de la) ~!** (that's) bullshit!‡, that's crap!‡; **dire des ~s** to talk bullshit‡ *ou* crap‡; **se disputer pour une ~** *ou* **des ~s** to quarrel over nothing

foutoir‡ [futwaʀ] NM damned‡ *ou* bloody‡ (*Brit*) shambles *sg*; **sa chambre est un vrai ~** his bedroom is a pigsty *ou* a dump* *ou* a bloody shambles‡ (*Brit*)

foutre[1]**‡** [futʀ] **1** VT **a** (= *faire*) to do; **qu'est-ce qu'il fout, il est déjà 8 heures** what the hell‡ is he doing *ou* up to — it's already 8 o'clock; **il n'a rien foutu de la journée** he hasn't done a damned‡ *ou* bloody‡ (*Brit*) thing all day, he's done damn all‡ *ou* bugger all‡** (*Brit*) today; **j'en n'ai rien à ~ de leurs histoires** I don't give a damn‡ about what they're up to; **qu'est-ce que ça peut me ~?** ◊ **qu'est-ce que j'en ai à ~?** what the hell do I care?‡

b (= *donner*) **~ une raclée à qn** to beat the hell out of sb‡; **~ une gifle à qn** to belt sb one*; **ça me fout la trouille** it gives me the willies* *ou* creeps*; **fous-moi la paix!‡**, bugger off!‡** (*Brit*) **je croyais qu'il avait compris mais je m'en fous!** I thought he'd understood but he damn well hadn't!‡; **qu'est-ce qui m'a foutu un idiot pareil!** of all the flaming idiots!*; **je t'en foutrai des amis comme ça!** who the hell needs friends like that?‡; **je t'en foutrai, moi, du champagne!** I'll give you goddam‡ *ou* bloody‡ (*Brit*) champagne!

c (= *mettre*) **fous-le là/dans ta poche** shove* it in here/in your pocket; **c'est lui qui a foutu le feu** he was the one who set fire to the place; **~ qn à la porte** to give sb the boot*, kick sb out*; **il a foutu le vase par terre** (*qui était posé*) he knocked the vase off, he sent the vase flying* (*Brit*); (*qu'il avait dans les mains*) he dropped the vase; **ça fout tout par terre** that screws‡* *ou* buggers‡* (*Brit*) everything up; **ça l'a foutu en rogne** that made him as mad as hell*; **ça la fout mal** it looks pretty bad* → **bordel, merde**

d **~ le camp** [*personne*] to split*, bugger off‡** (*Brit*); [*bouton, rimmel, vis*] to come off; **fous-moi le camp!** get lost!‡, bugger off!‡** (*Brit*),

sod off!** (Brit); **tout fout le camp** everything's falling apart ou going to hell*
 2 **se foutre** VPR **a** (= se mettre) **je me suis foutu dedans** I really screwed up**; **tu vas te ~ par terre** you're going to fall flat on your face; **se ~ dans une sale affaire** to get mixed up in a messy business; **ils se sont foutu sur la gueule** they beat (the) hell out of each other*
 b (= se moquer) **se ~ de qn/qch** to take the mickey* ou piss** (Brit) out of sb/sth; (= être indifférent) not to give a damn about sb/sth*; (= dépasser les bornes) **se ~ de qn** to mess* ou muck* (Brit) sb about; **100 F pour ça, ils se foutent du monde** ou **du monde** 100 francs for that! — what the hell do they take us for!*; **ça, je m'en fous pas mal** I couldn't give a damn* about that; **je me fous qu'il parte** ou **qu'il reste** I couldn't give a damn* whether he goes or stays; **tu te fous de ma gueule ?** (= tu te moques de moi) are you making fun of me?, are you taking the piss?* (Brit); (= tu me fais marcher) are you putting me on?*; **quelle belle bague ! il s'est pas foutu de toi !** what a beautiful ring! he really treats you right!*; **du champagne et du caviar ! elle ne s'est pas foutue de nous !** champagne and caviar! she's really done us proud!
 c ** **va te faire ~** fuck off!**, fuck you!**, bugger off!** (Brit), get stuffed!* (Brit); **je lui ai bien demandé, mais va te faire ~ : il n'a jamais voulu** I did ask him but no fucking** way would he do it
 d **se ~ à faire qch** to start to do sth; **il s'est foutu à chialer** he started to blubber*
 foutre² †* [futʀ] NM come*, spunk** (Brit)
 foutre³ †* [futʀ] EXCL, ADV damnation!*, bloody hell!* (Brit); **je n'en sais ~ rien !** I haven't got a fucking** clue!
 foutrement* [futʀəmɑ̃] ADV damn*, bloody* (Brit); **il s'est ~ bien défendu** he stood up for himself damn well* ou bloody well* (Brit)
 foutriquet †* [futʀikɛ] NM (péj) nobody, little runt*
 foutu, e* [futy] (ptp de **foutre**) ADJ **a** (avant n : intensif) [objet, appareil, personne] damned*, bloody* (Brit); (= mauvais) [temps, pays, travail] damned awful*, bloody awful (Brit); **il a un ~ caractère** he's got one hell of a temper*
 b (après n) [malade, vêtement] done for* (attrib); [appareil] bust*, buggered* (Brit); **il est ~** he's had it*; **c'est ~ pour mon avancement** there ou bang* goes my promotion **c** (= habillé) got up*, rigged out* **d** (= bâti, conçu) **bien/mal ~** [appareil, émission, documentaire] well-/badly-made; [manuel] well-/badly-written; **montre-moi comment c'est ~** show me what it looks like; **elle est bien ~e** she's well put together*, she's got a nice body
 e (= malade) **être mal** ou **pas bien ~** to feel lousy*, feel bloody* (Brit) awful* **f** (= capable) **il est ~ de le faire** he's quite likely ou liable to go and do it; **il est même pas ~ de réparer ça** he can't even mend the damned thing*
 fox(-terrier) (pl **fox(-terriers)**) [fɔks(tɛʀje] NM fox terrier
 fox(-trot) [fɔks(tʀɔt] NM INV foxtrot
 fox-hound (pl **fox-hounds**) [fɔksaund] NM foxhound
 foyer [fwaje] NM **a** (frm) (= maison) home; (= famille) family; **~ uni** close ou united family; **les joies du ~** the joys of family life; **revenir au ~** to come back home; **un jeune ~** a young couple; **~ fiscal** household (as defined for tax purposes) → **femme, fonder, renvoyer**
 b [locomotive, chaudière] firebox; (= âtre) hearth, fireplace; (= dalle) hearth(stone)
 c (= résidence) [vieillards, soldats] home; [jeunes] hostel; [étudiants] hostel, hall; **~ éducatif** special (residential) school; **~ socio-éducatif** community home; **~ d'étudiants** students' hall (of residence) ou hostel
 d (= lieu de réunion) [jeunes, retraités] club; (Théât) foyer; **~ des artistes** greenroom; **~ des**

jeunes youth club
 e (Math, Opt, Phys) focus; **à ~ variable** variable-focus (épith); **verres à double ~** bifocal lenses
 f **~ de** [+ incendie] seat of, centre of; [+ lumière, infection] source of; [+ agitation] centre of; **~ d'extrémistes** centre of extremist activities
 FP (ABRÉV = **franchise postale**) → **franchise**
 FR3 † [ɛfɛʀtʀwa] (ABRÉV = **France Régions 3**) former name of the third French television channel (now called France 3)
 frac [fʀak] NM tails, tail coat; **être en ~** to be in tails, be wearing a tail coat
 fracas [fʀaka] NM [objet qui tombe] crash; [train, tonnerre, vagues] roar; [bataille] din; **tomber avec ~** to fall with a crash, come crashing down; **la nouvelle a été annoncée à grand ~** the news was announced amid a blaze of publicity; **démissionner avec ~** to resign dramatically; **ils ont quitté la conférence avec ~** they stormed out of the conference → **perte**
 fracassant, e [fʀakasɑ̃, ɑ̃t] ADJ [bruit] thunderous, deafening; [nouvelle] shattering, staggering, sensational; [déclaration] sensational; [succès] resounding, thundering (épith)
 fracasser [fʀakase] ▸conjug 1◂ **1** VT [+ objet, mâchoire, épaule] to smash, shatter; [+ porte] to smash (down), shatter **2** **se fracasser** VPR **se ~ contre** ou **sur qch** [vagues] to crash against sth; [bateau, véhicule] to be smashed (to pieces) against sth; **la voiture est allée se ~ contre l'arbre** the car smashed ou crashed into the tree
 fractal, e [fʀaktal] **1** ADJ fractal **2** **fractale** NF fractal
 fraction [fʀaksjɔ̃] NF (Math) fraction; [groupe, somme, terrain] part; **en une ~ de seconde** in a fraction of a second, in a split second; **par ~ de 3 jours/de 10 unités** for every 3-day period/10 units; **une ~ importante du groupe** a large proportion of the group
 fractionnaire [fʀaksjɔnɛʀ] ADJ [nombre] fractional; (Comm) **livre ~** day book
 fractionné, e [fʀaksjɔne] (ptp de **fractionner**) ADJ (Chim) [distillation, cristallisation] fractional; [groupe de personnes] fragmented; **mon emploi du temps est trop ~** my timetable is too disjointed ou fragmented; **paiement ~** payment in instalments (Brit) ou installments, installment payment (US)
 fractionnel, -elle [fʀaksjɔnɛl] ADJ [attitude, menées] divisive
 fractionnement [fʀaksjɔnmɑ̃] NM splitting up, division; (Bourse) **~ d'actions** stock splitting
 fractionner [fʀaksjɔne] ▸conjug 1◂ **1** VT [+ groupe, somme, travail] to divide (up), split up **2** **se fractionner** VPR [groupe] to split up, divide
 fracture [fʀaktyʀ] NF **a** (Géol, Méd) fracture; **~ du crâne** fractured skull; **~ ouverte** open fracture; **~s multiples** multiple fractures **b** (fig, Pol) split (entre between); **la ~ sociale** the gap between the haves and the have-nots
 fracturer [fʀaktyʀe] ▸conjug 1◂ VT (Géol, Méd) to fracture; [+ serrure] to break (open); [+ coffre-fort, porte] to break open; **il s'est fracturé la jambe** he's fractured his leg
 fragile [fʀaʒil] ADJ [corps, vase] fragile, delicate; [organe, peau, tissu] delicate; [cheveux] brittle; [santé] fragile, delicate, frail; [surface, revêtement] easily damaged; [construction, économie, preuve, argument] flimsy, frail; [équilibre] delicate, shaky; [bonheur, paix] frail, flimsy, fragile; [gloire] fragile; (sur étiquette) «attention ~» "fragile, handle with care"; **ne soyez pas trop brusque, elle est encore ~** (physiquement, affectivement) don't be too rough with her — she's still (feeling) rather fragile ou delicate; **~ comme du verre** as deli-

cate as porcelain ou china; **avoir l'estomac ~ ◊ être ~ de l'estomac** to have a weak stomach; **être de constitution ~** to have a weak constitution
 fragilisation [fʀaʒilizasjɔ̃] NF [position, gouvernement, secteur] weakening; **cela entraîne la ~ des familles** this puts a great strain on the family unit; **c'est un facteur de ~ de l'entreprise** this is a factor that might undermine the company ou that might lead to the weakening of the company
 fragiliser [fʀaʒilize] ▸conjug 1◂ VT [+ position, secteur] to weaken; [+ régime politique] to undermine, weaken; **des familles fragilisées par la récession** families made vulnerable by the recession
 fragilité [fʀaʒilite] NF [corps, vase] fragility; [organe, peau] delicacy; [cheveux] brittleness; [santé] fragility, delicacy, frailty; [construction, économie, preuve, argument] flimsiness, frailty; [bonheur, paix] frailty, flimsiness, fragility; [gloire] fragility; [pouvoir, prospérité] fragility, flimsiness
 fragment [fʀagmɑ̃] NM **a** [vase, roche, papier] fragment, bit, piece; [os, vitre] fragment, splinter, bit **b** [conversation] bit, snatch; [chanson] snatch; [lettre] bit, part; [roman] (= bribe) fragment; (= extrait) passage, extract
 fragmentaire [fʀagmɑ̃tɛʀ] ADJ [connaissances] sketchy, patchy, fragmentary; [étude, exposé] sketchy, fragmentary; [effort, travail] sketchy, fragmented; **nous avons une vue très ~ des choses** we have only a sketchy ou an incomplete picture of the situation
 fragmentation [fʀagmɑ̃tasjɔ̃] NF [matière] breaking up, fragmentation; [État, terrain] fragmentation, splitting up, breaking up; [étude, travail, livre, somme] splitting up, division → **bombe**
 fragmenter [fʀagmɑ̃te] ▸conjug 1◂ **1** VT [+ matière] to break up, fragment; [+ État, terrain] to fragment, split up, break up; [+ étude, travail, livre, somme] to split up, divide (up); **avoir une vision fragmentée du monde** to have a fragmented view of the world; **ce travail est trop fragmenté** this work is too fragmented **2** **se fragmenter** VPR [roches] to fragment, break up
 fragrance [fʀagʀɑ̃s] NF (littér) fragrance
 frai [fʀɛ] NM (= œufs) spawn; (= alevins) fry; (= époque) spawning season; (ponte) spawning
 fraîche [fʀɛʃ] NF → **frais¹**
 fraîchement [fʀɛʃmɑ̃] ADV **a** (= récemment) freshly, newly; **~ arrivé** newly ou just arrived; **fruit ~ cueilli** freshly picked fruit; **amitié ~ nouée** newly-formed friendship **b** (= froidement) [accueillir] coolly; **comment ça va ? — ~ !** how are you? — a bit chilly!*
 fraîcheur [fʀɛʃœʀ] NF **a** [boisson] coolness; [pièce] (agréable) coolness; (trop froid) chilliness; **la ~ du soir/de la nuit** the cool of the evening/of the night; **chercher un peu de ~** to look for a cool spot ou place; **ce déodorant procure une agréable sensation de ~** this deodorant leaves you feeling pleasantly cool **b** [accueil] coolness, chilliness **c** [âme] purity; [sentiment, jeunesse, teint] freshness; [couleurs] freshness, crispness **d** [aliment] freshness; **de première ~** very fresh
 fraîchir [fʀɛʃiʀ] ▸conjug 2◂ VI [temps, température] to get cooler; [vent] to freshen
 frais¹, fraîche [fʀɛ, fʀɛʃ] **1** ADJ **a** (= légèrement froid) [eau, endroit] cool; [vent] cool, fresh; (Mét Naut) **vent ~** strong breeze **b** (= sans cordialité) [accueil] chilly, cool **c** (= sain, éclatant) [couleur] fresh, clear, crisp; [joues, teint] fresh; [parfum] fresh; [haleine] fresh, sweet; [voix] clear; [joie, âme, histoire d'amour] pure; **ses vêtements ne sont plus très ~** his clothes don't look very fresh; **un peu d'air ~** a breath of ou a little fresh air **d** (= récent) [plaie] fresh; [traces, souvenir] re-

cent, fresh; [*peinture*] wet, fresh; [*nouvelles*] recent; **l'encre est encore fraîche** the ink is still wet → **date**

e (*opposé à sec, en conserve*) [*poisson, légumes, lait, pâtes*] fresh; [*œuf*] fresh, new-laid; [*pain*] new, fresh → **chair**

f (= *jeune, reposé*) [*troupes*] fresh; **~ et dispos** fresh (as a daisy); **~ comme un gardon** bright as a button; **je ne suis pas très ~ ce matin** I'm feeling a bit seedy this morning; **fraîche comme une rose** ou **la rosée** as fresh as a daisy; **elle est encore très fraîche pour son âge** she's very young-looking for her age

g (*Comm*) **argent ~** (*disponible*) ready cash; (*à investir*) fresh money

h * (= *en difficulté*) **eh bien, on est ~!** ou **nous voilà ~!** well, we're in a fine mess now!*

2 ADV a **il fait ~** (*agréable*) it's cool; (*froid*) it's chilly; **en été, il faut boire ~** in summer you need cool ou cold drinks; «**servir ~ »** "serve cold ou chilled"

b (= *récemment*) newly; **herbe ~** ou **fraîche coupée** newly ou freshly cut grass; **~ émoulu de l'université** fresh from ou newly graduated from university; **~ débarqué de sa province** fresh ou newly up from the country; **habillé/rasé de ~** freshly changed/shaven

3 NM a (= *fraîcheur*) **prendre le ~** to take a breath of fresh air; (*lit*) **mettre (qch) au ~** to put (sth) in a cool place; (*fig*) **mettre qn au ~*** to put sb in the cooler*; **le linge sent le ~** the linen smells lovely and fresh

b (*Mét, Naut*) **joli** ou **bon ~** strong breeze; **grand ~** near gale

c (*Comm*) **le ~** fresh produce

4 **fraîche** NF (*sortir*) **à la fraîche** (to go out) in the cool of evening

frais² [fʀɛ] 1 NMPL a (*gén* = *débours*) expenses, costs; (*facturés*) charges; (*Admin* = *droits*) charges, fee(s); **tous ~ compris** inclusive of all costs; **voyage d'affaires tous ~ payés** business trip with all expenses paid; (*Comm*) **tous ~ payés** after costs; **faire de grands ~** to go to great expense; **ça m'a fait beaucoup de ~** it cost me a great deal of money; **avoir de gros ~** to have heavy outgoings → **arrêter, faux²**

b (*loc*) **se mettre en ~** (*lit*) to go to great expense; **se mettre en ~ pour qn/pour recevoir qn** to put o.s. out for sb/to entertain sb; **faire les ~ de la conversation** (*parler*) to keep the conversation going; (*en être le sujet*) to be the (main) topic of conversation; **nous ne voulons pas faire les ~ de cette erreur** we do not want to have to pay for this mistake; **rentrer dans** ou **faire ses ~** to recover one's expenses; **j'ai essayé d'être aimable mais j'en ai été pour mes ~** I tried to be friendly but I might just as well have spared myself the trouble ou but I was wasting my time; **aux ~ de la maison** at the firm's expense; **à ses ~** at one's own expense; **aux ~ de la princesse*** (*de l'État*) at the taxpayer's expense; (*de l'entreprise*) at the firm's expense; (= *gratuitement*) with all expenses paid; **à grands ~** at great expense; **il se l'est procuré à grands ~** he acquired it at great expense, he paid a great deal for it; **il se l'est procuré à moindre(s) ~** it didn't cost him a lot, he paid very little for it; **à peu de ~** cheaply, at little cost; **il s'en est tiré à peu de ~** he got off lightly

2 COMP ▶ **frais d'agence** agency fees ▶ **frais d'avocats** solicitors' ou legal fees ▶ **frais bancaires** banking charges ▶ **frais de démarrage** start-up costs ▶ **frais de déplacement** travelling expenses ou costs ▶ **frais divers** miscellaneous expenses, sundries ▶ **frais d'encaissement** collection charges ▶ **frais d'enregistrement** registration fee(s) ▶ **frais d'entretien** [*jardin, maison*] (cost of) upkeep; [*machine, équipement*] maintenance costs ▶ **frais d'envoi, frais d'expédition** forwarding charges ▶ **frais d'exploitation** running

costs ▶ **frais financiers** (*gén*) interest charges; [*crédit*] loan charges ▶ **frais fixes** fixed ou standing charges ou expenses ou costs ▶ **frais de fonctionnement** running ou upkeep costs ▶ **frais de garde** [*enfant*] childminding fees ou costs; [*malade*] nursing fees; (*Fin*) management charges ▶ **frais généraux** overheads (*Brit*), overhead (*US*) ▶ **frais de gestion** (= *charges*) running costs; (= *prix d'un service*) management fees; (*Fin*) management charges ▶ **frais d'hébergement** accommodation costs ou expenses ou fees ▶ **frais d'hospitalisation** hospital fees ou expenses ▶ **frais d'hôtel** hotel expenses ▶ **frais d'inscription** registration fees ▶ **frais de justice** (legal) costs ▶ **frais de logement** accommodation expenses ou costs ▶ **frais de main-d'œuvre** labour costs ▶ **frais de manutention** handling charges ▶ **frais médicaux** medical costs ou expenses ou fees ▶ **frais de notaire** legal fees ▶ **frais de personnel** staff(ing) costs ▶ **frais de port et d'emballage** postage and packing ▶ **frais de premier établissement** start-up costs, organization expenses ▶ **frais professionnels** business expenses ▶ **frais réels** [*Impôts*] allowable expenses ▶ **frais de représentation** entertainment expenses ▶ **frais de scolarité** (*à l'école, au lycée*) school fees (*Brit*), tuition fees (*US*); (*pour un étudiant*) tuition (fees) ▶ **frais de timbre** stamp charges ▶ **frais de transport** transportation costs → **étude, installation**

fraisage [fʀezaʒ] NM (*pour agrandir*) reaming; (*pour mettre une vis*) countersinking; (*pour usiner*) milling

fraise [fʀez] 1 NF a (= *fruit*) strawberry; **~ des bois** wild strawberry → **sucrer** b (*Tech*) (*pour agrandir un trou*) reamer; (*pour trou de vis*) countersink (bit); [*métallurgiste*] milling-cutter; [*dentiste*] drill c (*Boucherie*) **~ de veau/de porc** calf's/pig's caul d (*Hist* = *col*) ruff, fraise; (*Zool* = *caroncule*) wattle e (*Méd*) strawberry mark f * (= *visage*) face → **ramener** 2 ADJ INV [*couleur*] strawberry pink

fraiser [fʀeze] ▸ conjug 1 ◂ VT (= *agrandir*) to ream; (*pour mettre une vis*) to countersink; (= *usiner*) to mill; **à tête fraisée** countersunk

fraiseur [fʀezœʀ] NM milling-machine operator

fraiseuse [fʀezøz] NF a (= *machine*) milling machine b (= *ouvrière*) (woman) milling-machine operator

fraisier [fʀezje] NM a (*Bot*) strawberry plant b (*Culin*) strawberry gateau

fraisure [fʀezyʀ] NF countersink, countersunk hole

framboise [fʀɑ̃bwaz] NF (= *fruit*) raspberry; (= *liqueur*) raspberry liqueur

framboisier [fʀɑ̃bwazje] NM a (*Bot*) raspberry bush; **~s** raspberry canes ou bushes b (*Culin*) raspberry gateau

franc¹, franche [fʀɑ̃, fʀɑ̃ʃ] 1 ADJ a (= *loyal*) [*personne*] frank, straightforward; [*réponse*] frank, straight(forward), plain; [*regard, entretien*] frank, candid; [*rire*] hearty; [*gaieté*] open; [*entrevue*] frank, candid; **pour être ~ avec vous** to be frank with you; **~ comme l'or** ◊ **~ du collier** straight as a die → **jouer** b (= *net*) [*situation*] clear-cut, unequivocal; [*différence*] clear(-cut); [*cassure*] clean; [*hostilité, répugnance*] unequivocal; [*couleur*] clear, pure; **accord ~ et massif** overwhelming ou unequivocal acceptance; (*Jur*) **5 jours ~s** 5 clear days c (*péj* = *total*) [*imbécile*] utter, downright, absolute; [*canaille*] downright, out-and-out, absolute; [*ingratitude*] downright, sheer; **c'est une franche comédie/grossièreté** it's downright ou utterly hilarious/rude, it's sheer comedy/rudeness d (= *libre*) [*zone, ville, port*] free; **boutique**

franche duty-free shop; (*Comm*) **~ de** free of; (*livré*) **~ de port** [*marchandises*] carriage-paid; [*paquet*] post-free, postage paid; **~ d'avaries communes/particulières** free of general/particular average → **corps, coudée, coup** e (*Agr*) (**arbre**) **~ (de pied)** cultivar; **greffer sur ~** to graft onto a cultivar

2 ADV **à vous parler ~** to be frank with you; **je vous le dis tout ~** I'm being frank ou candid with you

franc² [fʀɑ̃] NM (= *monnaie*) franc; **ancien/nouveau ~** old/new franc; **~ lourd** revalued franc; **~ constant** constant ou inflation-adjusted franc; **~ courant** franc at the current rate; **~ belge/français/suisse** Belgian/French/Swiss franc; **~ CFA** CFA franc (*unit of currency used in certain African states*); **le ~ fort** the strong franc; **demander/obtenir le ~ symbolique** to demand/obtain token damages; **racheter une entreprise pour le** ou **un ~ symbolique** to buy up a company for a nominal ou token sum; **ça coûte/il gagne trois ~s six sous** it costs/he earns peanuts* ou next to nothing

franc³, franque [fʀɑ̃, fʀɑ̃k] 1 ADJ Frankish 2 **Franc** NM Frank 3 **Franque** NF Frank

français, e [fʀɑ̃sɛ, ɛz] 1 ADJ French 2 ADV **acheter ~** to buy French (products); **boire/rouler ~** to buy French wine/cars 3 NM a (*Ling*) French; **tu ne comprends pas le ~ ?*** ≈ don't you understand (plain) English?; **c'est une faute de ~** ≈ it's a grammatical mistake b **Français** Frenchman; **les Français** (= *gens*) the French, French people; (= *hommes*) Frenchmen; **le Français moyen** the average Frenchman, the man in the street 4 **française** NF **Française** Frenchwoman b **à la ~e** [*démocratie, socialisme, capitalisme*] French-style, à la française; [*humour*] French → **jardin**

franc-bord (*pl* **francs-bords**) [fʀɑ̃bɔʀ] NM (*Naut*) freeboard

France [fʀɑ̃s] NF France; **histoire/équipe/ambassade de ~** French history/team/embassy; **le roi de ~** the King of France; (*Hist*) **la ~ libre** free France; (*TV*) **2/3** state-owned channels on French television → **profond, vieux**

┌─────────────────────┐
│ **FRANCE TÉLÉVISION** │
└─────────────────────┘

There are two state-owned television channels in France: France 2 (still often known by its former name of "Antenne 2"), and France 3, a regionally-based channel formerly known as "FR3". Broadly speaking, France 2 is a general-interest and light entertainment channel, while France 3 offers more cultural and educational viewing.

Francfort [fʀɑ̃kfɔʀ] N Frankfurt; **~-sur-le-Main** Frankfurt am Main → **saucisse**

franchement [fʀɑ̃ʃmɑ̃] ADV a (= *honnêtement*) [*parler, répondre*] frankly; [*agir*] openly; **pour vous parler ~** to be frank (with you); **avouez ~ que ...** you've got to admit that ...; **~ !** **j'en ai assez!** quite frankly, I've had enough!; **il y a des gens, ~ !** really! ou honestly! some people!; **~ non** frankly no b (= *sans hésiter*) [*entrer, frapper*] boldly; **il entra ~** he strode in, he walked straight ou boldly in; **appuyez-vous ~ sur moi** put all your weight on me, lean hard on me; **allez-y ~** (*explication*) get straight to the point, say it straight out; (*manœuvre*) go right ahead c (= *sans ambiguïté*) clearly; (= *nettement*) definitely; **je lui ai posé la question ~** I put the question to him straight; **dis-moi ~ ce que tu veux** tell me straight out ou clearly what you want; **c'est ~ rouge** it's clearly ou quite obviously red; **c'est ~ au-dessous de la moyenne** it's definitely ou well below average d (*intensif* = *tout à fait*) [*mauvais, laid*] utterly, downright, really; [*bon*] really; [*impossible*] downright, utterly; [*irréparable*] completely, absolutely; **ça m'a ~ dégoûté** it really ou utterly disgusted me; **ça s'est ~ mal passé** it went really badly; **on s'est ~ bien amusé** we really *ou* thoroughly enjoyed ourselves; **c'est ~ trop (cher)** it's much *ou* far too expensive

franchir [fʀɑ̃ʃiʀ] ▸conjug 2◂ VT [+ *obstacle*] to clear, get over; [+ *fossé*] to clear, jump over; [+ *rue, rivière, ligne d'arrivée*] to cross; [+ *seuil*] to cross, step across; [+ *porte*] to go through; [+ *distance*] to cover; [+ *mur du son*] to break (through); [+ *difficulté*] to get over, surmount; [+ *borne, limite*] to overstep, go beyond; (*littér*) **~ les mers** to cross the sea; **~ le Rubicon** to cross the Rubicon; **il lui reste 10 mètres à ~** he still has 10 metres to go; **~ le cap de la soixantaine** to turn sixty, pass the sixty mark; **le pays vient de ~ un cap important** the country has just passed an important milestone; **ne pas réussir à ~ la barre de ...** [*chiffres, vote*] to be *ou* fall short of ...; **sa renommée a franchi les frontières** his name has spread far and wide; **l'historien, franchissant quelques siècles ...** the historian, passing over a few centuries ...

franchisage [fʀɑ̃ʃizaʒ] NM franchising

franchise [fʀɑ̃ʃiz] NF [a] [*personne, réponse*] frankness, straightforwardness, candour (*Brit*), candor (*US*); [*regard*] candour (*Brit*), candor (*US*), openness; **en toute ~** quite frankly [b] (= *exemption*) (*gén*) exemption; (*Hist*) [*ville*] franchise; **~ fiscale** tax exemption; **~ (douanière)** exemption from (customs) duties; **colis en ~** duty-free parcel; **importer qch en ~** to import sth duty-free; **« ~ postale »** ≈ "official paid"; **~ de bagages** baggage allowance [c] (*Assurances*) excess (*Brit*), deductible (*US*) [d] (*Comm*) franchise; **agent/magasin en ~** franchised dealer/shop (*Brit*) *ou* store (*US*)

franchisé, e [fʀɑ̃ʃize] [1] ADJ **boutique ~e** franchised outlet [2] NM,F franchisee

franchiser [fʀɑ̃ʃize] ▸conjug 1◂ VT to franchise

franchiseur [fʀɑ̃ʃizœʀ] NM franchisor

franchissable [fʀɑ̃ʃisabl] ADJ surmountable

franchissement [fʀɑ̃ʃismɑ̃] NM [*obstacle*] clearing; [*rivière, seuil*] crossing; [*limite*] overstepping

franchouillard, e* [fʀɑ̃ʃujaʀ, aʀd] (*péj*) [1] ADJ typically French [2] NM typically narrow-minded Frenchman [3] **franchouillarde** NF typically narrow-minded French woman

francilien, -ienne [fʀɑ̃siljɛ̃, jɛn] [1] ADJ from *ou* of the Île-de-France [2] **Francilien(ne)** NM,F inhabitant of the Île-de-France [3] **Francilienne** NF **la Francilienne** (= *autoroute*) motorway that encircles the Parisian region

francique [fʀɑ̃sik] NM Frankish

francisation [fʀɑ̃sizasjɔ̃] NF (*Ling*) gallicizing, Frenchifying; (*Naut*) [*navire*] registration as French

franciscain, e [fʀɑ̃siskɛ̃, ɛn] ADJ, NM,F Franciscan

franciser [fʀɑ̃size] ▸conjug 1◂ VT (*Ling*) to gallicize, Frenchify; (*Naut*) to register as French; **il a francisé son nom** he made his name sound more French, he Frenchified his name

francisque [fʀɑ̃sisk] NF francisc

francité [fʀɑ̃site] NF Frenchness

francium [fʀɑ̃sjɔm] NM francium

franc-jeu [fʀɑ̃ʒø] NM (*Sport*) fair-play; (*fig*) **jouer ~** to play fair

franc-maçon, -onne [fʀɑ̃masɔ̃, ɔn] (*mpl* **francs-maçons**, *fpl* **franc-maçonnes**) [1] NM,F freemason [2] ADJ **loge ~ne** masonic lodge, freemasons' lodge; **la solidarité ~ne** freemason solidarity

franc-maçonnerie (*pl* **franc-maçonneries**) [fʀɑ̃masɔnʀi] NF freemasonry

franco [fʀɑ̃ko] ADV (*Comm*) **~ (de port)** [*marchandise*] carriage-paid; [*colis*] postage paid; **~ de port et d'emballage** free of charge;

~ à bord/sur wagon free on board/on rail; **~ (le) long du bord** free alongside ship; **~ (le long du) quai** free alongside quay; **y aller ~*** (*explication*) to go straight to the point, come straight out with it*; (*coup, manœuvre*) to go right ahead

franco- [fʀɑ̃ko] PRÉF Franco-; **les relations ~britanniques** Franco-British relations; **le sommet ~allemand** the Franco-German summit

franco-canadien, -ienne [fʀɑ̃kokanadjɛ̃, jɛn] ADJ, NM,F French Canadian

franco-français, e [fʀɑ̃kofʀɑ̃sɛ, ɛz] ADJ purely French; (*péj*) typically French

François [fʀɑ̃swa] NM Francis; **saint ~ d'Assise** Saint Francis of Assisi

francophile [fʀɑ̃kofil] ADJ, NMF francophile

francophilie [fʀɑ̃kofili] NF francophilia

francophobe [fʀɑ̃kofɔb] ADJ, NMF francophobe

francophobie [fʀɑ̃kofɔbi] NF francophobia

francophone [fʀɑ̃kofɔn] [1] ADJ French-speaking; (*Can*) primarily French-speaking [2] NMF (native) French speaker; (*Can*) Francophone (*Can*)

francophonie [fʀɑ̃kofɔni] NF French-speaking world

franco-québécois [fʀɑ̃kokebekwa] NM (*Ling*) Quebec French

franc-parler [fʀɑ̃paʀle] NM INV outspokenness; **avoir son ~** to speak one's mind, be outspoken

franc-tireur (*pl* **francs-tireurs**) [fʀɑ̃tiʀœʀ] NM [a] (*Mil*) (= *combattant*) irregular, franc tireur; (= *tireur isolé*) sniper [b] (*fig*) maverick; **un ~ de la politique** a maverick politician; **faire qch/agir en ~** to do sth/act independently *ou* off one's own bat (*Brit*)

frange [fʀɑ̃ʒ] NF [a] [*tissu*] fringe; [*cheveux*] fringe (*Brit*), bangs (*US*); **une ~ de lumière** a band of light; **~s d'interférence** interference fringes; **~s synoviales** synovial folds *ou* fringes [b] (= *limite*) [*conscience, sommeil*] threshold [c] (= *minorité*) fringe (group); **toute une ~ de la population** a whole swathe *ou* chunk of the population

franger [fʀɑ̃ʒe] ▸conjug 3◂ VT (*gén ptp*) to fringe (**de** with)

frangin* [fʀɑ̃ʒɛ̃] NM brother

frangine* [fʀɑ̃ʒin] NF sister

frangipane [fʀɑ̃ʒipan] NF (*Culin*) almond paste, frangipane; **gâteau fourré à la ~** frangipane (pastry)

frangipanier [fʀɑ̃ʒipanje] NM frangipani (tree)

franglais [fʀɑ̃glɛ] NM Franglais

franque [fʀɑ̃k] ADJ, NF → **franc³**

franquette* [fʀɑ̃kɛt] ◆**à la bonne franquette** LOC ADV [*inviter*] informally; [*recevoir*] without any fuss; **venez déjeuner, ce sera à la bonne ~** come and have lunch with us — it'll be a simple meal *ou* it won't be anything special; **on a dîné à la bonne ~** we had an informal *ou* a potluck (*US*) dinner

franquisme [fʀɑ̃kism] NM Francoism

franquiste [fʀɑ̃kist] [1] ADJ pro-Franco [2] NMF Franco supporter

fransquillon [fʀɑ̃skijɔ̃] NM (*Belg péj*) French Belgian

frap(p)adingue* [fʀapadɛ̃g] [1] ADJ nutty*, loopy* [2] NMF nutcase*

frappant, e [fʀapɑ̃, ɑ̃t] ADJ striking → **argument**

frappe [fʀap] NF [a] [*monnaie, médaille*] (= *action*) striking; (= *empreinte*) stamp, impression [b] [*dactylo, pianiste*] touch; [*machine à écrire*] (= *souplesse*) touch; (= *impression*) typeface; **la lettre est à la ~** the letter is being typed (out); **c'est la première ~** it's the top copy → **faute**; **vitesse** [c] (*péj* = *voyou*) **petite ~** young hood-

lum *ou* thug [d] (*Sport*) [*boxeur*] punch; [*footballeur*] kick; [*joueur de tennis*] stroke; **il a une bonne ~ de balle** [*footballeur*] he kicks the ball well, he has a good kick; [*joueur de tennis*] he strikes *ou* hits the ball well [e] (*Mil*) (military) strike; **~ aérienne** airstrike; **~ en second** second strike → **chirurgical, force**

frappé, e [fʀape] (*ptp de* **frapper**) ADJ [a] (= *saisi*) struck; **~ de panique** panic-stricken; **~ de stupeur** thunderstruck; **j'ai été (très) ~ d'entendre/de voir que ...** I was (quite) amazed to hear/to see that ... [b] [*velours*] embossed → **coin** [c] [*champagne, café*] iced; **boire un vin bien ~** to drink a wine well chilled [d]* (= *fou*) touched* (*attrib*), crazy*

frappement [fʀapmɑ̃] NM striking

frapper [fʀape] ▸conjug 1◂ [1] VT [a] (= *cogner*) [+ *personne, surface*] (*avec le poing, un projectile*) to hit, strike; (*avec un couteau*) to stab, strike; [+ *cordes, clavier*] to strike; **~ qn à coups de poing/de pied** to punch/kick sb; **~ le sol du pied** to stamp (one's foot) on the ground; (*Hist*) **~ d'estoc et de taille** to cut and thrust; (*Théât*) **~ les trois coups** to give *ou* sound the three knocks (*to announce the start of a performance*); **la pluie/la lumière frappait le mur** the rain lashed (against)/the light fell on the wall; (*fig*) **~ un grand coup** to pull out all the stops; **frappé à mort** fatally *ou* mortally wounded [b] [*maladie*] to strike (down); [*coincidence, détail*] to strike; **frappé par le malheur** stricken by misfortune; **ce deuil le frappe cruellement** this bereavement is a cruel blow to him; **il a frappé tout le monde par son énergie** ◊ **son énergie a frappé tout le monde** everybody was struck by his energy; **cela l'a frappé de stupeur** he was thunderstruck *ou* dumbfounded at this; **cette découverte le frappa de panique/d'horreur** he was panic-/horror-stricken at this discovery, this discovery filled him with panic/horror; **~ l'imagination** to catch *ou* fire the imagination; **ce qui (me) frappe** what strikes me; **ce qui a frappé mon regard/mon oreille** what caught my eye/reached my ears [c] [*mesures, impôts*] to hit; **cet impôt frappe lourdement les petits commerçants** this tax is hitting small businesses hard; **~ qn d'une amende/d'un impôt** to impose a fine/a tax on sb; **la loi doit ~ les coupables** the law must punish the guilty; **ils ont frappé le tabac d'un impôt supplémentaire** they have put *ou* slammed* an extra tax on tobacco; **contrat/jugement frappé de nullité** contract/judgment declared null and void [d] [+ *monnaie, médaille*] to strike [e] (= *glacer*) [+ *champagne, vin*] to put on ice, chill; [+ *café*] to ice

[2] VI to strike (**sur** on, **contre** against); **~ du poing sur la table** to bang one's fist on the table; **~ sur la table avec une règle** to tap the table with a ruler; (*plus fort*) to bang on the table with a ruler; **~ dans ses mains** to clap one's hands; **~ du pied** to stamp (one's foot); (*lit, fig*) **~ à la porte** to knock on *ou* at the door; **on a frappé** there was a knock at the door; **frappez avant d'entrer** knock before you go in *ou* enter; **~ à toutes les portes** to try every door; **~ dur ou fort ou sec*** to hit hard; (*fig*) **~ fort** (*pour impressionner*) to pull out all the stops → **entrer**

[3] **se frapper** VPR [a] **se ~ la poitrine** to beat one's breast; **se ~ le front** to tap one's forehead [b] * (= *se tracasser*) to get (o.s.) worked up, get (o.s.) into a state*

frappeur, -euse [fʀapœʀ, øz] [1] ADJ **esprit ~** poltergeist [2] NM,F [*monnaie*] striker

frasil [fʀazi(l)] NM (*Can*) frazil (*Can*)

frasque [fʀask] NF (*gén pl*) escapade; **faire des ~s** to get up to mischief; **~s de jeunesse** youthful indiscretions

Antoine; **les ~s maçons** *ou* **trois-points*** the Freemasons; **on l'a mis en pension chez les ~s** he has been sent to a Catholic boarding school

frérot* [fʀeʀo] NM kid brother*, little brother; **salut ~!** hello little brother!

fresque [fʀɛsk] NF (*Art*) fresco; (*Littérat*) portrait; (*fig = description*) panorama; **peindre à ~** to paint in fresco; **ce film est une ~ historique** the film is a sweeping historical epic

fresquiste [fʀɛskist] NMF fresco painter

fret [fʀɛ(t)] NM (= *prix*) (*Aviat, Naut*) freight(age); (*Aut*) carriage; (= *cargaison*) (*Aviat, Naut*) freight, cargo; (*Aut*) load; ~ **d'aller** outward freight; ~ **de retour** inward *ou* home *ou* return freight; ~ **aérien** air freight; **prendre à ~** to charter

fréter [fʀete] ▸conjug 6◂ VT (*gén = prendre à fret*) to charter; (*Naut = donner à fret*) to freight

fréteur [fʀetœʀ] NM (*Naut*) owner; ~ **et affréteur** owner and charterer

frétillant, e [fʀetijɑ̃, ɑ̃t] ADJ [*poisson*] wriggling; [*personne*] lively; ~ **d'impatience** fidgeting *ou* quivering with impatience

frétillement [fʀetijmɑ̃] NM [*poisson*] wriggling (*NonC*); ~ **d'impatience** quiver of impatience

frétiller [fʀetije] ▸conjug 1◂ VI [*poisson*] to wriggle; [*personne*] to wriggle, fidget; **le chien frétillait de la queue** the dog was wagging its tail; ~ **d'impatience** to fidget *ou* quiver with impatience; ~ **de joie** to be quivering *ou* quiver with joy; (*hum, péj*) **elle frétille de l'arrière-train** she's wiggling her bottom (*hum*)

fretin [fʀətɛ̃] NM (= *poissons*) fry; (= *personnes, choses négligeables*) small fry → **menu²**

frette [fʀɛt] NF (*Mus*) fret; (*Tech*) reinforcing band

freudien, -ienne [fʀødjɛ̃, jɛn] ADJ, NM,F Freudian

freudisme [fʀødism] NM Freudianism

freux [fʀø] NM (*Orn*) rook

friabilité [fʀijabilite] NF [*roche, sol*] crumbly nature, flakiness, friability (*SPÉC*)

friable [fʀijabl] ADJ [*roche, sol*] crumbly, flaky, friable (*SPÉC*); (*Culin*) [*pâte*] crumbly

friand, e [fʀijɑ̃, ɑ̃d] **1** ADJ ~ **de** [+ *lait, miel, bonbons*] partial to, fond of; [+ *compliments*] fond of **2** NM (= *pâté*) (minced) meat pie, ≈ sausage roll (*Brit*); (*sucré*) small almond cake; ~ **au fromage** cheese puff

friandise [fʀijɑ̃diz] NF titbit, delicacy, sweetmeat†; (= *bonbons*) ~s sweets (*Brit*), candy (*NonC*) (*US*)

fric* [fʀik] NM (= *argent*) money, cash*; **il a du ~** he's loaded*; **elle se fait beaucoup de ~** she makes a packet*; **je n'ai plus de ~** (*temporairement*) I'm out of cash*; (*définitivement*) I'm broke*

fricandeau (*pl* **fricandeaux**) [fʀikɑ̃do] NM fricandeau

fricassée [fʀikase] NF fricassee; ~ **de poulet** chicken fricassee; **faire cuire en ~** to fricassee

fricasser [fʀikase] ▸conjug 1◂ VT to fricassee

fricative [fʀikativ] ADJ F, NF fricative

fric-frac†* (*pl* **fric-frac(s)**) [fʀikfʀak] NM break-in

friche [fʀiʃ] NF fallow land (*NonC*); (*lit*) **en ~** (lying) fallow; **être en ~** (*Agr*) to lie fallow; [*talent, intelligence*] to go to waste; [*économie, pays*] to be neglected; **laisser qch en ~** (*Agr*) to let sth lie fallow; [*talent, intelligence*] to let sth go to waste; [*économie, pays*] to neglect; **le projet est resté en ~ pendant 5 ans** the project has been shelved *ou* has been on ice for 5 years; ~ **industrielle** industrial wasteland

frichti*, **fricot**†* [fʀiʃti, fʀiko] NM food, grub* (*NonC*); **préparer son ~** to do the cooking

fricoter* [fʀikɔte] ▸conjug 1◂ **1** VT (*lit, fig*) to cook up*; **qu'est-ce qu'il fricote?** what's he cooking up?*, what's he up to?* **2** VI (=

trafiquer) to get involved in some shady business; ~ **avec qn** (= *s'associer*) to have dealings with sb; (= *avoir une liaison*) to sleep with sb

friction [fʀiksjɔ̃] NF **a** (*Phys, Tech, Ling*) friction; (= *massage*) rub, rubdown; (*chez le coiffeur*) scalp massage; (*Jeux*) **voiture à ~** friction car **b** (= *conflit*) friction; (*lit, fig*) **point de ~** point of friction; **les taux d'intérêt, éternel point de ~ entre ces deux pays** interest rates, an eternal bone of contention between the two countries

frictionner [fʀiksjɔne] ▸conjug 1◂ VT to rub; **se ~ après un bain** to rub o.s. down after a bath

fridolin†‡ [fʀidɔlɛ̃] NM (*injurieux = Allemand*) Fritz‡ (*injurieux*), Jerry‡ (*injurieux*)

frigidaire® [fʀiʒidɛʀ] NM refrigerator, fridge

frigide [fʀiʒid] ADJ frigid

frigidité [fʀiʒidite] NF frigidity

frigo* [fʀigo] NM fridge, refrigerator

frigorifier [fʀigɔʀifje] ▸conjug 7◂ VT (*lit*) to refrigerate; (*fig = pétrifier*) to petrify, freeze to the spot; **être frigorifié** (= *avoir froid*) to be frozen stiff

frigorifique [fʀigɔʀifik] ADJ [*mélange*] refrigerating (*épith*); [*camion, wagon*] refrigerator (*épith*) → **armoire**

frigoriste [fʀigɔʀist] NMF refrigeration engineer

frileusement [fʀiløzmɑ̃] ADV ~ **serrés l'un contre l'autre** huddled close together to keep warm *ou* against the cold; ~ **enfouis sous les couvertures** huddled under the blankets to keep warm

frileux, -euse [fʀilø, øz] ADJ **a** [*personne*] sensitive to (the) cold; [*geste, posture*] shivery; **il est très ~** he feels the cold easily, he is very sensitive to (the) cold; **elle se couvrit de son châle d'un geste ~** with a shiver she pulled her shawl around her **b** (= *trop prudent*) [*boursier*] overcautious; [*marché*] nervous

frilosité [fʀilozite] NF **a** [*personne*] sensitivity to the cold **b** [*boursier*] overcautiousness; [*marché*] nervousness

frimaire [fʀimɛʀ] NM Frimaire (*third month in the French Republican calendar*)

frimas [fʀima] NMPL (*littér*) wintry weather

frime* [fʀim] NF **c'est de la ~** it's all put on*; **c'est pour la ~** it's all *ou* just for show

frimer* [fʀime] ▸conjug 1◂ VI to show off*

frimeur, -euse* [fʀimœʀ, øz] NM,F show-off*; **il est très ~** he's a real show-off*

frimousse* [fʀimus] NF (*sweet*) little face

fringale* [fʀɛ̃gal] NF (= *faim*) raging hunger; (= *désir*) **une ~ de** a craving for; **j'ai la ~** I'm ravenous* *ou* famished *ou* starving*

fringant, e [fʀɛ̃gɑ̃, ɑ̃t] ADJ [*cheval*] frisky, high-spirited; [*personne, allure*] dashing

fringue* [fʀɛ̃g] NF garment; **je me suis acheté une ~** I bought myself something to wear; **des ~s** clothes, togs*, threads* (*US*); **elle a toujours de belles ~s** she always has such great clothes* *ou* such fantastic gear*

fringué, e* [fʀɛ̃ge] (*ptp de* **(se) fringuer**) ADJ dressed, done up*; **bien/mal ~** well-/badly-dressed; **vise un peu comme elle est ~e!** look what she's got on!, look what she's done up in!*

fringuer* [fʀɛ̃ge] ▸conjug 1◂ **1 se fringuer** VPR (= *s'habiller*) to get dressed; (= *s'habiller élégamment*) to doll (o.s.) up*, do o.s. up*; **il ne sait pas se ~** he's got no dress sense **2** VT to dress

fripe* [fʀip] **1** NF **la ~** (= *commerce*) the clothing trade, the rag trade* (*Brit*); (*d'occasion*) secondhand clothes business **2 fripes** NFPL (= *vêtements*) clothes; (*d'occasion*) secondhand clothes

friper [fʀipe] ▸conjug 1◂ VT to crumple (up), crush; **ça se fripe facilement** it crumples *ou*

crushes easily; **des habits tout fripés** badly crumpled *ou* rumpled clothes; **visage tout fripé** crumpled face

friperie [fʀipʀi] NF (= *boutique*) secondhand clothes shop (*Brit*) *ou* store (*US*)

fripier, -ière [fʀipje, jɛʀ] NM,F secondhand clothes dealer

fripon, -onne [fʀipɔ̃, ɔn] **1** ADJ [*air, allure, yeux*] mischievous, cheeky (*Brit*); [*nez*] saucy, pert **2** NM,F († = *gredin*) knave†, rascally fellow†; (*: *nuance affectueuse*) rascal, rogue; **petit ~!** you little rascal!

friponnerie [fʀipɔnʀi] NF (= *acte*) mischief (*NonC*), prank; **les ~s de ce gamin** the mischief this little imp gets up to

fripouille [fʀipuj] NF (*péj*) rogue, scoundrel; (*nuance affectueuse*) **petite ~!*** you little devil!*

fripouillerie [fʀipujʀi] NF roguishness

friqué, e‡ [fʀike] ADJ loaded*, filthy rich*; **je ne suis pas très ~ en ce moment** I'm not exactly loaded* at the moment, I'm a bit hard-up* at the moment

frire [fʀiʀ] VTI **(faire) ~** to fry; (*en friteuse*) to deep-fry → **pâte, poêle**

frisbee® [fʀizbi] NM Frisbee®

frise [fʀiz] NF (*Archit, Art*) frieze; (*Théât*) border → **cheval**

frisé, e [fʀize] (*ptp de* **friser**) **1** ADJ [*cheveux*] (very) curly; [*personne, animal*] curly-haired; **il est tout ~** he has very curly hair; ~ **comme un mouton** curly-headed *ou* -haired, frizzy-haired → **chou¹ 2** NM (‡ *injurieux = Allemand*) Fritz‡ (*injurieux*), Jerry‡ (*injurieux*) **3 frisée** NF (= *chicorée*) curly endive

friselis [fʀizli] NM slight trembling (*NonC*)

friser [fʀize] ▸conjug 1◂ **1** VT **a** [+ *cheveux*] to curl; [+ *moustache*] to twirl; ~ **qn** to curl sb's hair → **fer b** (= *frôler*) [+ *surface*] to graze, skim; [+ *catastrophe, mort*] to be within a hair's breadth of, be within an ace of; [+ *insolence, ridicule*] to border on, verge on; ~ **la soixantaine** to be getting on for sixty, be close to sixty **2** VI [*cheveux*] to curl, be curly; [*personne*] to have curly hair; **faire ~ ses cheveux** to make one's hair go curly; (*chez le coiffeur*) to have one's hair curled **3 se friser** VPR to curl one's hair; **se faire ~** (*par un coiffeur*) to have one's hair curled

frisette [fʀizɛt] NF **a** (= *cheveux*) little curl, little ringlet **b** (= *lambris*) panel; ~ **de pin** pine panel

frison¹ [fʀizɔ̃] NM **a** (= *mèche*) little curl *ou* ringlet (*around face or neck*) **b** (= *copeaux*) ~s wood shavings (*used for packing*)

frison², -onne [fʀizɔ̃, ɔn] **1** ADJ Frisian, Friesian **2** NM (*Ling*) Frisian, Friesian **3 Frison(ne)** NM,F Frisian, Friesian **4 frisonne** NF (*vache*) **frisonne** Frisian, Friesian (*cow*)

frisottant, e [fʀizɔtɑ̃, ɑ̃t] ADJ frizzy, tightly curled

frisotter [fʀizɔte] ▸conjug 1◂ **1** VT to crimp, frizz **2** VI to frizz; **ses cheveux frisottent quand il pleut** his hair goes all frizzy when it rains

frisquet, -ette* [fʀiskɛ, ɛt] ADJ [*vent*] chilly; **il fait ~** it's chilly, there's a chill *ou* nip in the air

frisson [fʀisɔ̃] NM [*froid, fièvre*] shiver; [*répulsion, peur*] shudder, shiver; [*volupté*] thrill, shiver, quiver; **elle fut prise** *ou* **saisie d'un ~** a sudden shiver ran through her; **la fièvre me donne des ~s** this fever is making me shiver *ou* is giving me the shivers*; **ça me donne le ~** *ou* **des ~s** it gives me the creeps* *ou* the shivers*, it makes me shudder; **le ~ des herbes sous le vent** the quivering of the grass in the wind; (*hum*) **ça a été le grand ~** (*gén*) it was a real thrill*; (*sexuel*) the earth moved

frissonnement [fʀisɔnmɑ̃] NM **a** (*de peur*) quaking, trembling, shuddering; (*d'horreur*) shuddering, shivering; (*de fièvre, de froid*) shivering; (*de volupté, de désir*) quivering, trembling; **un long ~ parcourut son corps** a shiver ran the length of his body [b] [*feuillage*] quivering, trembling, rustling; [*lac*] rippling

frissonner [fʀisɔne] ▸ conjug 1 ◂ VI [a] (*de peur*) to quake, tremble, shudder; (*d'horreur*) to shudder, shiver; (*de fièvre, froid*) to shiver; (*de volupté, désir*) to quiver, tremble (**de** with); **le vent le fit ~** the wind made him shiver [b] [*feuillage*] to quiver, tremble, rustle; [*lac*] to ripple

frit, e[1] [fʀi, fʀit] (*ptp de frire*) ADJ (*Culin*) fried; (: = *fichu, perdu*) **ils sont ~s** they've had it*, their goose is cooked*, their number's up*

frite[2] [fʀit] NF [a] (*Culin : gén pl*) **(pommes) ~s** French fries, chips (*Brit*), fries (*surtout US*) [b]: (= *forme*) **avoir la ~** to be feeling great*, be full of beans* (*Brit*); **en ce moment, elle n'a pas la ~** she's a bit down* at the moment; **ça va te donner la ~** that'll perk you up *ou* put the wind back in your sails* [c]: (= *tape*) **faire une ~ à qn** to slap sb on the bottom

friter (se): [fʀite] ▸ conjug 1 ◂ VPR [*personnes*] (= *se disputer*) to have a row; (= *se battre*) to have a set-to* *ou* scrap*; **il adore provoquer et se friter** he loves provoking people and getting into scraps*

friterie [fʀitʀi] NF (= *boutique*) ≈ chip shop (*Brit*), ≈ hamburger stand (*US*)

friteuse [fʀitøz] NF deep fryer, chip pan (*Brit*); **~ électrique** electric fryer

fritillaire [fʀitilɛʀ] ADJ fritillary

friture [fʀityʀ] NF [a] (*Culin*) (= *méthode*) frying; (= *graisse*) (deep) fat (for frying); (= *poisson, mets*) fried fish (*NonC ou pl*); **(petite) ~** small fish; **~ de goujons** (dish of) fried gudgeon [b]* (*Radio*) crackle, crackling (*NonC*); (*Téléc*) **il y a de la ~ sur la ligne** there's interference on the line, the line is a bit scratchy

fritz: [fʀits] NM INV (*injurieux* = *Allemand*) Fritz: (*injurieux*), Jerry: (*injurieux*)

frivole [fʀivɔl] ADJ [*personne*] frivolous; [*occupation, argument*] frivolous, trivial

frivolement [fʀivɔlmɑ̃] ADV frivolously

frivolité [fʀivɔlite] NF [a] [*personne*] frivolity, frivolousness; [*occupation, argument*] frivolousness, triviality [b] (*Comm* = *articles*) **~s** † fancy goods

froc [fʀɔk] NM [a] (*Rel*) frock, habit; **porter le ~** to be a monk, wear the habit of a monk; **jeter le ~ aux orties** to leave the priesthood [b]* (= *pantalon*) (pair of) trousers, (pair of) pants (*US*) [c] (*: loc*) **faire dans son ~** to be shitting:* *ou* wetting: o.s.; **baisser son ~** to take it lying down*; **ils baissent leur ~ devant le chef** they just lie down and take it from the boss*

froid, e [fʀwa, fʀwad] [1] ADJ [*personne, repas, décor, couleur, moteur*] cold; [*manières, accueil*] cold, chilly; [*détermination, calcul*] cold, cool; **colère ~e** cold *ou* controlled anger; **il fait assez ~** it's rather cold; **d'un ton ~** coldly; **ça me laisse ~** it leaves me cold; **garder la tête ~e** to keep cool, keep a cool head; **~ comme le marbre** as cold as marble; **à table! ça va être ~** come and get it! it's getting cold → **battre, sueur** *etc*

[2] **à froid** LOC ADV **laminer à ~** to cold-roll; **souder à ~** to cold-weld; **« laver *ou* lavage à ~ »** "wash in cold water"; **démarrer à ~** to start (from) cold; **démarrage à ~** cold start *ou* starting (*US*); **opérer à ~** (*Méd*) to perform cold surgery; (*fig*) to let things cool down before acting; (*fig*) **parler à ~ de qch** to speak coldly *ou* coolly of sth; (*fig*) **prendre *ou* cueillir qn à ~** to catch sb unawares *ou* off guard → **ciseau**

[3] NM [a] **le ~** (= *gén*) the cold; (= *industrie*) refrigeration; **j'ai ~** I'm cold; **j'ai ~ aux pieds** my feet are cold; **il fait ~/un ~ de canard*** *ou* **de loup*** it's cold/freezing cold *ou* perishing*; **ça**

me donne ~ it makes me (feel) cold; **ça me fait ~ dans le dos** (*lit*) it gives me a cold back, it makes my back cold; (*fig*) it sends shivers down my spine; **prendre *ou* attraper (un coup de) ~** to catch cold *ou* a chill; **vague *ou* coup de ~** cold spell; **les grands ~s** the cold of winter; **n'avoir pas ~ aux yeux** [*homme d'affaires, aventurier*] to be venturesome *ou* adventurous; [*enfant*] to have plenty of pluck → **craindre, jeter, mourir**

[b] (= *brouille*) coolness (*NonC*); **malgré le ~ qu'il y avait entre eux** despite the coolness that existed between them; **nous sommes en ~** things are a bit strained between us

froidement [fʀwadmɑ̃] ADV [*accueillir, remercier*] coldly, coolly; [*calculer, réfléchir*] coolly; [*tuer*] cold-bloodedly, in cold blood; **il me reçut ~** I got a cold *ou* chilly reception (from him), he greeted me coldly; **meurtre accompli ~** cold-blooded murder; (*hum*) **comment vas-tu ? — ~ !** how are you? — cold!

froideur [fʀwadœʀ] NF [*personne, sentiments*] coldness; [*manières, accueil*] coldness, chilliness; **recevoir qn avec ~** to give sb a cold *ou* chilly *ou* cool reception, greet sb coldly; **contempler qch avec ~** to contemplate sth coldly *ou* coolly; (*littér*) **la ~ de son cœur** her coldness of heart

froidure †† [fʀwadyʀ] NF cold

froissement [fʀwasmɑ̃] NM [a] [*tissu*] crumpling, creasing [b] (= *bruit*) rustle, rustling (*NonC*); **des ~s soyeux** the sound of rustling silk [c] (*Méd*) **~ (d'un muscle)** (muscular) strain [d] (*littér* = *vexation*) **~ (d'amour-propre)** blow to sb's pride

froisser [fʀwase] ▸ conjug 1 ◂ [1] VT [a] [+ *tissu*] to crumple, crease; [+ *habit*] to crumple, rumple, crease; [+ *papier*] to screw up, crumple; [+ *herbe*] to crush; **il froissa la lettre et la jeta** he screwed up the letter and threw it away [b] [+ *personne*] to hurt, offend; **ça l'a froissé dans son orgueil** that wounded *ou* hurt his pride [2] **se froisser** VPR [*tissu*] to crease, crumple; [*personne*] to take offence, take umbrage (**de** at); (*Méd*) **se ~ un muscle** to strain a muscle

frôlement [fʀolmɑ̃] NM (= *contact*) light touch, light contact (*NonC*); (= *bruit*) rustle, rustling (*NonC*); **le ~ des corps dans l'obscurité** the light contact of bodies brushing against each other in the darkness

frôler [fʀole] ▸ conjug 1 ◂ [1] VT [a] (= *toucher*) to brush against; (= *passer près de*) to skim; **le projectile le frôla** the projectile skimmed past him; **l'automobiliste frôla le réverbère** the driver just missed the lamppost; **le dollar a frôlé la barre des 10 F** the dollar came very close to the 10 franc mark; **la mort/la catastrophe** to come within a hair's breadth *ou* an ace of death/a catastrophe; **~ la victoire** to come close to victory; **le thermomètre a frôlé les 40 degrés** temperatures were in the upper 30's [b] (= *confiner à*) to verge *ou* border on; **ça frôle l'indécence** it verges on the indecent [2] **se frôler** VPR [*personnes*] to brush against one another; **les deux voitures se sont frôlées** the two cars just missed each other

fromage [fʀɔmaʒ] [1] NM cheese; **biscuit/omelette/soufflé au ~** cheese biscuit/omelette/soufflé; **nouilles au ~** pasta with cheese; (*fig*) **trouver un (bon) ~*** to find a cushy job* *ou* cushy number* (*Brit*), get on the gravy train* (*US*); **il en a fait tout un ~*** he made a great song and dance *ou* a big fuss about it → **cloche, plateau, poire** [2] COMP
► **fromage blanc** fromage blanc
► **fromage de chèvre** goat's milk cheese
► **fromage à la crème** cream cheese
► **fromage fermenté** fermented cheese
► **fromage fondu** cheese spread
► **fromage frais** fromage frais ► **fromage gras** full-fat cheese ► **fromage maigre** low-fat cheese ► **fromage à pâte cuite** cooked cheese ► **fromage à pâte dure**

hard cheese ► **fromage à pâte molle** soft cheese ► **fromage à pâte persillée** veined cheese ► **fromage râpé** grated cheese ► **fromage à tartiner** cheese spread ► **fromage de tête** pork brawn, head-cheese (*US*)

fromager, -ère [fʀɔmaʒe, ɛʀ] [1] ADJ [*industrie, commerce, production*] cheese (*épith*); **association fromagère** cheese producers' association [2] NM [a] (= *fabricant*) cheese maker; (= *marchand*) cheese seller [b] (*Bot*) kapok tree

fromagerie [fʀɔmaʒʀi] NF cheese dairy

froment [fʀɔmɑ̃] NM wheat

from(e)ton: [fʀɔmtɔ̃] NM cheese

fronce [fʀɔ̃s] NF gather; **~s** gathers, gathering (*NonC*); **faire des ~s à une jupe** to gather a skirt; **ça fait des ~s** it's all puckered

froncement [fʀɔ̃smɑ̃] NM **~ de sourcils** frown

froncer [fʀɔ̃se] ▸ conjug 3 ◂ VT (*Couture*) to gather; **~ les sourcils** to frown, knit one's brows

frondaison [fʀɔ̃dɛzɔ̃] NF (= *feuillage*) foliage (*NonC*)

fronde[1] [fʀɔ̃d] NF (= *arme*) sling; (= *jouet*) catapult (*Brit*), slingshot (*US*)

fronde[2] [fʀɔ̃d] NF (= *révolte*) revolt; **esprit/vent de ~** spirit/wind of revolt *ou* insurrection; (*Hist*) **la Fronde** the Fronde

fronde[3] [fʀɔ̃d] NF (*Bot*) frond

fronder [fʀɔ̃de] ▸ conjug 1 ◂ VT (= *railler*) to lampoon, satirize

frondeur, -euse [fʀɔ̃dœʀ, øz] ADJ [*attitude, mentalité*] recalcitrant, anti-authority, rebellious; [*propos*] anti-authority

front [fʀɔ̃] NM [a] (*Anat*) forehead, brow; (*fig* = *tête*) head; (*littér* = *visage*) brow (*littér*), face; (*littér*) [*bâtiment*] façade, front; **il peut marcher le ~ haut** he can hold his head (up) high; (*littér*) **la honte sur son ~** the shame on his brow (*littér*) *ou* face; **~ de mer** (sea) front → **courber, frapper**

[b] (*Mét, Mil, Pol*) front; **aller *ou* monter au ~** to go to the front, go into action; **tué au ~** killed in action; **le ~ ennemi** the enemy front; **le Front populaire** the Popular Front; **le Front national** the National Front; **le Front de libération nationale de la Corse** the Corsican liberation front

[c] (*Min*) **~ (de taille)** (*gén*) face; [*houillère*] coalface

[d] (*loc*) **attaque de ~** frontal attack; **choc de ~** head-on crash; (*lit, fig*) **attaquer qn de ~** to attack sb head-on; **se heurter de ~** (*lit*) to collide head-on; (*fig*) to clash head-on; **marcher (à) trois de ~** to walk three abreast; **mener plusieurs tâches de ~** to have several tasks in hand *ou* on the go (at one time); **aborder de ~ un problème** to tackle a problem head-on; **il va falloir faire ~** you'll (*ou* we'll *etc*) have to face up to it *ou* to things; **faire ~ à l'ennemi/aux difficultés** to face up *ou* stand up to the enemy/difficulties; **faire ~ commun contre qn/qch** to join forces against sb/sth, take a united stand against sb/sth; (*littér*) **avoir le ~ de faire** to have the effrontery *ou* front to do

frontal, e (*mpl* -**aux**) [fʀɔ̃tal, o] [1] ADJ [*collision, concurrence*] head-on; [*attaque*] frontal, head-on; (*Anat, Géom*) frontal; **lave-linge à chargement ~** front-loader, front-loading washing machine; **choc ~** (*lit*) head-on crash *ou* collision; (*fig*) head-on clash [2] NM (*os*) **~** frontal (bone)

frontalier, -ière [fʀɔ̃talje, jɛʀ] [1] ADJ [*ville, zone*] border (*épith*), frontier (*épith*); **travailleurs ~s** people who cross the border every day to work [2] NM,F inhabitant of the border *ou* frontier zone

frontière [fʀɔ̃tjɛʀ] [1] NF (*Géog, Pol*) frontier, border; **à l'intérieur et au-delà de nos ~s** at home and abroad; **~ naturelle/linguistique** natural/linguistic boundary; **faire reculer les ~s du savoir/d'une science** to push back the frontiers of knowledge/of a science; **à la ~ du**

rêve et de la réalité on the borders of dream and reality, on the borderline between dream and reality → **incident** [2] ADJ INV **ville/zone** → frontier *ou* border town/zone → **garde¹, poste²**

frontispice [fʀɔ̃tispis] NM frontispiece

fronton [fʀɔ̃tɔ̃] NM (*Archit*) pediment; (*à la pelote basque*) (front) wall

frottement [fʀɔtmɑ̃] NM (= *action*) rubbing; (= *bruit*) rubbing (*NonC*), rubbing noise, scraping (*NonC*), scraping noise; (*Tech* = *friction*) friction; (= *désaccord*) **il y a des ~s entre eux** there's friction between them

frotter [fʀɔte] ▸conjug 1◂ [1] VT [a] (*gén*) [+ *peau, membre*] to rub; [+ *cheval*] to rub down; **frotte tes mains avec du savon** scrub your hands with soap; **~ son doigt sur la table** to rub one's finger on the table; **~ une allumette** to strike a match; **pain frotté d'ail** bread rubbed with garlic
[b] (*pour nettoyer*) [+ *cuivres, meubles*] to rub (up), shine; [+ *plancher, casserole, linge, pomme de terre*] to scrub; [+ *chaussures*] (*pour cirer*) to rub (up), shine; (*pour enlever la terre*) to scrape
[c] (†, *hum*) **~ les oreilles à qn** to box sb's ears; **je vais te ~ l'échine** I'm going to beat you black and blue
[2] VI to rub, scrape; **la porte frotte (contre le plancher)** the door is rubbing *ou* scraping (against the floor)
[3] **se frotter** VPR [a] (= *se laver*) to rub o.s.; (*lit, fig*) **se ~ les mains** to rub one's hands [b] **se ~ à** (= *fréquenter*) **se ~ à la bonne société** to rub shoulders with high society; (= *attaquer*) **se ~ à qn** to cross swords with sb; **il vaut mieux ne pas s'y ~** I wouldn't cross swords with him ■ (*PROV*) **qui s'y frotte s'y pique** if you cross swords with him you do so at your peril

frottis [fʀɔti] NM (*Méd*) smear; (*Art*) scumble; **se faire faire un ~ (cervico-)vaginal** to have a cervical *ou* Pap (*US*) smear

frottoir [fʀɔtwaʀ] NM (*à allumettes*) friction strip; (*pour le parquet*) (long-handled) brush

froufrou [fʀufʀu] NM [a] (= *bruit*) rustle, rustling (*NonC*), swish (*NonC*); **faire ~** to rustle, swish [b] (= *dentelles*) **des ~s** frills

froufroutant, e [fʀufʀutɑ̃, ɑ̃t] ADJ rustling, swishing

froufroutement [fʀufʀutmɑ̃] NM rustle, rustling (*NonC*), swish (*NonC*)

froufrouter [fʀufʀute] ▸conjug 1◂ VI to rustle, swish

froussard, e* [fʀusaʀ, aʀd] (*péj*) [1] ADJ chicken* (*attrib*), yellow-bellied* (*épith*) [2] NM,F chicken*, coward

frousse* [fʀus] NF fright; **avoir la ~** to be scared (to death) *ou* scared stiff*; **quand il a sonné j'ai eu la ~** when he rang I really got a fright *ou* the wind up* (*Brit*); **ça lui a fichu la ~** that really gave him a fright *ou* put the wind up him* (*Brit*)

fructidor [fʀyktidɔʀ] NM Fructidor (*twelfth month in the French Republican calendar*)

fructifère [fʀyktifɛʀ] ADJ fruit-bearing, fructiferous

fructification [fʀyktifikasjɔ̃] NF fructification

fructifier [fʀyktifje] ▸conjug 7◂ VI [*arbre*] to bear fruit; [*terre*] to be productive; [*idée*] to bear fruit; [*investissement*] to yield a profit; **faire ~ son argent** to make one's money work for one

fructose [fʀyktoz] NM fructose

fructueusement [fʀyktɥøzmɑ̃] ADV fruitfully, profitably

fructueux, -euse [fʀyktɥø, øz] ADJ [*lectures, spéculation*] fruitful, profitable; [*collaboration, recherches*] fruitful; [*commerce*] profitable

frugal, e (*mpl* **-aux**) [fʀygal, o] ADJ frugal

frugalement [fʀygalmɑ̃] ADV frugally

frugalité [fʀygalite] NF frugality

fruit¹ [fʀɥi] [1] NM [a] (*gén*) fruit (*NonC*); **il y a des ~s/trois ~s dans la coupe** there is some fruit/there are three pieces of fruit in the bowl; **passez-moi un ~** pass me some fruit *ou* a piece of fruit
[b] (= *espèce*) fruit; **l'orange et la banane sont des ~s** the orange and the banana are kinds of fruit *ou* are fruits → **pâte, salade**
[c] (*littér* = *produit*) fruit(s); **les ~s de la terre/ de son travail** the fruits of the earth/of one's work; (= *résultat*) **c'est le ~ de l'expérience/ d'un gros travail** it is the fruit of experience/of much work; **cet enfant est le ~ de leur union** this child is the fruit of their union (*littér*); **porter ses ~s** to bear fruit; **avec ~** fruitfully, profitably, with profit; **sans ~** fruitlessly, to no avail
[2] COMP ▸ **fruits des bois** fruits of the forest ▸ **fruits confits** candied *ou* glacé fruits ▸ **fruit défendu** (*fig, Bible*) forbidden fruit ▸ **fruits déguisés** *prunes ou dates stuffed with marzipan* ▸ **fruits de mer** seafood(s) ▸ **fruit de la passion** passion fruit ▸ **fruits rafraîchis** fresh fruit salad ▸ **fruits rouges** red berries ▸ **fruit sec** (*séché*) dried fruit (*NonC*); (*fig* = *raté*) failure

fruit² [fʀɥi] NM [*mur*] batter; **donner du ~ à** to batter

fruité, e [fʀɥite] ADJ fruity

fruiterie [fʀɥitʀi] NF fruit (and vegetable) store, fruiterer's (shop) (*Brit*)

fruiticulteur, -trice [fʀɥitikyltœr, tʀis] NM,F fruit farmer

fruitier, -ière [fʀɥitje, jɛʀ] [1] ADJ fruit (*épith*) [2] NM,F (= *marchand de fruits*) fruit seller, fruiterer (*Brit*), greengrocer (*Brit*); (= *fromager*) cheese maker [3] NF (= *fromagerie*) cheese dairy (*in Savoy, Jura*)

frusques [fʀysk] NFPL (*péj*) (= *vêtements*) gear* (*NonC*), togs*, clobber* (*NonC*) (*Brit*); (= *vieux vêtements*) rags

fruste [fʀyst] ADJ [*art, style*] crude, unpolished; [*manières, personne*] coarse

frustrant, e [fʀystʀɑ̃, ɑ̃t] ADJ frustrating

frustration [fʀystʀasjɔ̃] NF (*Psych*) frustration

frustré, e [fʀystʀe] (*ptp de* **frustrer**) ADJ, NM,F (*gén, Psych*) frustrated; **c'est un ~** he's frustrated

frustrer [fʀystʀe] ▸conjug 1◂ VT [a] (= *priver*) **~ qn de** [+ *satisfaction*] to deprive sb of, do sb out of*; (*Jur*) [+ *biens*] to defraud sb of; **~ qn dans ses espoirs/efforts** to thwart *ou* frustrate sb's hopes/efforts, thwart sb in his hopes/ efforts; (*Jur*) **~ qn au profit d'un autre** to defraud one party by favouring another [b] (= *décevoir*) [+ *attente, espoir*] to thwart, frustrate [c] (*Psych*) to frustrate

FS (*ABRÉV* = **franc suisse**) SF

FSE [ɛfɛsə] NM (*ABRÉV* = **Fonds social européen**) ESF

fuchsia [fyʃja] NM, ADJ INV fuchsia

fuchsine [fyksin] NF fuchsin(e)

fucus [fykys] NM wrack, fucus (*SPÉC*); **~ vésiculeux** bladderwrack

fuel [fjul] NM (= *carburant*) fuel oil; **~ domestique** domestic *ou* heating oil

fugace [fygas] ADJ [*parfum, impression, lueur*] fleeting; [*beauté, fraîcheur*] fleeting, transient; [*bonheur*] transient

fugacité [fygasite] NF [*parfum, impression, lueur*] fleetingness; [*beauté, fraîcheur*] fleetingness, transience

fugitif, -ive [fyʒitif, iv] [1] ADJ (= *en fuite*) [*esclave, prisonnier*] fugitive (*épith*), runaway (*épith*); (= *fugace*) [*vision, forme, impression*] fleeting; [*calme*] momentary; [*beauté, bonheur*] fleeting, transient, short-lived; (*littér*) [*jours, années*] fleeting [2] NM,F fugitive

fugitivement [fyʒitivmɑ̃] ADV [*entrevoir*] fleetingly

fugue [fyg] NF [a] (= *fuite*) running away (*NonC*); **faire une ~** to run away, abscond (*Admin*); **il a fait plusieurs ~s** he ran away several times; **~ amoureuse** elopement [b] (*Mus*) fugue

fuguer* [fyge] ▸conjug 1◂ VI to run away *ou* off

fugueur, -euse [fygœʀ, øz] NM,F absconder (*Admin*), runaway; **élève ~** pupil who keeps running away

fuir [fɥiʀ] ▸conjug 17◂ [1] VT [a] (= *éviter*) [+ *personne, danger*] to avoid, shun; [+ *obligation, responsabilité*] to evade, shirk; **~ qn/qch comme la peste** to avoid sb/sth like the plague; **le sommeil/la tranquillité me fuit** sleep/quiet eludes me; (*littér*) **~ le monde** to flee society, withdraw from the world; (*littér*) **l'homme se fuit** man flees from his inner self
[b] (= *s'enfuir de*) [+ *patrie, bourreaux*] to flee from, run away from, fly from (*littér*)
[2] VI [a] (= *s'enfuir*) [*prisonnier*] to run away, escape; [*troupes*] to take flight, flee (*devant* from); [*femme*] (*avec un amant*) to run off; (*pour se marier*) to elope (*avec* with); **faire ~** (= *mettre en fuite*) to put to flight; (= *chasser*) to chase off *ou* away; **laid à faire ~** repulsively ugly; **~ devant** [+ *danger, obligations*] to run away from; **il a fui chez ses parents** he has fled to his parents
[b] (*littér* = *passer rapidement*) [*esquif*] to speed along, glide swiftly along; [*heures, saison*] to fly by, slip by; [*horizon, paysage*] to recede; **l'été a fui si rapidement** the summer flew by
[c] (= *s'échapper*) [*gaz*] to leak, escape; [*liquide*] to leak; (= *n'être pas étanche*) [*récipient, robinet*] to leak

fuite [fɥit] NF [a] [*fugitif*] flight, escape; [*prisonnier*] escape; [*amants*] flight; (*pour se marier*) elopement; **~ des capitaux** flight of capital; **~ des cerveaux** brain drain; **dans sa ~** as he ran away; **la ~ des galaxies** the flight of the galaxies; **chercher la ~ dans le sommeil** to seek escape in sleep; **la ~ en avant du gouvernement dans le domaine économique** the government's blind *ou* headlong pursuit of its economic policy, the government's decision to forge ahead regardless in economic matters; **sa ~ devant toute responsabilité** his evasion of all responsibility; **prendre la ~** [*personne*] to run away, take flight; [*conducteur, voiture*] to drive away; **mettre qn en ~** to put sb to flight; **les prisonniers sont en ~** the prisoners are on the run; **renversé par un automobiliste qui a pris la ~** knocked down by a hit-and-run driver → **délit**
[b] (*littér* = *passage rapide*) [*esquif*] swift passage; [*temps, heures, saisons*] (swift) passage *ou* passing
[c] (= *perte de liquide*) leak, leakage; **~ de gaz/ d'huile** gas/oil leak; **avaries dues à des ~s** damage due to *ou* caused by leakage
[d] (= *indiscrétion*) leak; **il y a eu des ~s à l'examen** some exam questions have been leaked
[e] (= *trou*) [*récipient, tuyau*] leak
[f] (*Art*) **point de ~** vanishing point

Fuji-Yama [fuʒijama] NM Mount Fuji, Fujiyama, Fuji-san

fulgurance [fylgyʀɑ̃s] NF (*frm*) [*progrès, processus*] lightning *ou* dazzling speed; [*plaisir, douleur*] searing intensity

fulgurant, e [fylgyʀɑ̃, ɑ̃t] ADJ [*vitesse, progrès*] lightning (*épith*), dazzling; [*succès, carrière*] dazzling; [*ascension*] meteoric; [*réplique*] lightning (*épith*); [*regard*] blazing (*épith*), flashing (*épith*); **une douleur ~e me traversa le corps** a searing pain flashed *ou* shot through my body; **une clarté ~e illumina le ciel** a blinding flash lit up the sky

fulguration [fylgyʀasjɔ̃] NF (= *éclair*) flash (of lightning); (= *thérapie*) fulguration; **il revit son enfance dans une ~** childhood memories flashed through his mind

fulgurer [fylgyʀe] ▸conjug 1◂ VI to flash

fuligineux, -euse [fyliʒinø, øz] ADJ (*littér*) [*couleur, flamme*] sooty

fuligule [fyligyl] NM **~ (morillon)** tufted duck

full [ful] NM (*Cartes*) full house; **~ aux as/rois** full house to aces/kings

fulmar [fylmaʀ] NM fulmar

fulminant, e [fylminɑ̃, ɑ̃t] ADJ a [*personne*] enraged, livid; [*lettre, réponse, regard*] angry and threatening; **~ de colère** enraged, livid (with anger) b (= *détonant*) [*mélange*] explosive; **poudre ~e** fulminating powder; **capsule ~e** percussion cap; **sels ~s** explosive salts (of fulminic acid)

fulminate [fylminat] NM fulminate

fulmination [fylminasjɔ̃] NF a (= *malédictions*) **~s** fulminations b (= *colère*) fulmination

fulminer [fylmine] ▸conjug 1◂ 1 VT [+ *reproches, insultes*] to thunder forth; (*Rel*) to fulminate 2 VI a (= *pester*) to thunder forth; **~ contre** to fulminate *ou* thunder forth against b (*Chim*) to fulminate, detonate

fulminique [fylminik] ADJ **acide ~** fulminic acid

fumage [fymaʒ] NM (*Culin*) [*saucissons*] smoking, curing (by smoking); (*Agr*) [*terre*] manuring, dunging

fumant, e [fymɑ̃, ɑ̃t] ADJ a (= *chaud*) [*cendres, cratère*] smoking; [*soupe, corps, naseaux*] steaming; (*Chim*) fuming; (*fig*) **un coup ~** a master stroke b * (= *en colère*) [*patron*] fuming (*attrib*); **~ de colère** fuming with anger*

fumasse [fymas] ADJ (= *en colère*) fuming* (*attrib*)

fumé, e[1] [fyme] (*ptp de fumer*) ADJ [*jambon, saumon, verre*] smoked; [*lunettes*] **verres ~s** tinted lenses; **aimer le ~** to like smoked food → **lard**

fume-cigare (*pl* **fume-cigares**) [fymsigaʀ] NM cigar holder

fume-cigarette (*pl* **fume-cigarettes**) [fymsigaʀɛt] NM cigarette holder

fumée[2] [fyme] NF a [*combustion*] smoke; **~ de tabac/de cigarettes** tobacco/cigarette smoke; **la ~ ne vous gêne pas?** do you mind my smoking?; **sans ~** [*combustible*] smokeless *ou* **avaler, noir, rideau** b (= *vapeur*) [*soupe, étang, corps, naseaux*] steam; **les ~s de l'alcool** *ou* **de l'ivresse** the vapours of alcohol c (*loc*) **partir** *ou* **s'en aller en ~** to go up in smoke, fizzle out ■ (*PROV*) **il n'y a pas de ~ sans feu** there's no smoke without fire (*PROV*)

fumer [fyme] ▸conjug 1◂ 1 VI a [*volcan, cheminée, cendres, lampe*] to smoke; [*soupe, étang, corps*] to steam; [*produit chimique*] to emit *ou* give off fumes, fume b * (= *être en colère*) to be fuming*; **il fumait de rage** he was fuming with rage* c [*fumeur*] to smoke; **~ comme un sapeur** *ou* **un pompier** *ou* **une locomotive** to smoke like a chimney → **défense**[1] 2 VT a [+ *tabac, hachisch*] to smoke; **~ la cigarette/le cigare/la pipe** to smoke cigarettes/cigars/a pipe; **elle est allée en ~ une dehors*** she went outside to have a cigarette *ou* a smoke*; **il fumait cigarette sur cigarette** he was chainsmoking b (*Culin*) [+ *aliments*] to smoke, cure (by smoking) c (*Agr*) [+ *sol, terre*] to manure

fumerie [fymʀi] NF **~ (d'opium)** opium den

fumerolle [fymʀɔl] NF (*gén pl*) (= *gaz*) smoke and gas (emanating from a volcano); (= *fumée*) wisp of smoke

fumet [fyme] NM [*plat, viande*] aroma, [*vin*] bouquet, aroma; (*Vénerie*) scent

fumeterre [fymtɛʀ] NF fumitory

fumette* [fymɛt] NF (= *drogue*) smoke*; **la ~** (= *action*) smoking*

fumeur, -euse [fymœʀ, øz] NM,F smoker; (*Rail*) (**compartiment**) **~s** smoking compartment (*Brit*) *ou* car (*US*), smoker; **~ d'opium/de pipe** opium/pipe smoker

fumeux, -euse [fymø, øz] ADJ a (= *confus*) [*idées, explication*] hazy, woolly; [*esprit*] woolly; [*théoricien*] woolly-minded b (*avec de la fumée*) [*flamme, clarté*] smoky; (*avec de la vapeur*) [*horizon, plaine*] hazy, misty

fumier [fymje] NM a (= *engrais*) dung, manure; **~ de cheval** horse-dung *ou* -manure; **tas de ~** dunghill, dung *ou* muck *ou* manure heap b (** péj = salaud*) bastard**, shit**

fumigateur [fymigatœʀ] NM (*Agr, Méd* = *appareil*) fumigator

fumigation [fymigasjɔ̃] NF fumigation

fumigatoire [fymigatwaʀ] ADJ fumigating, fumigatory

fumigène [fymiʒɛn] ADJ [*engin, grenade*] smoke (*épith*); (*Agr*) (**appareil**) **~** smoke apparatus

fumiste [fymist] 1 NM (= *réparateur, installateur*) heating mechanic; (= *ramoneur*) chimney sweep 2 NMF (** péj = paresseux*) shirker, skiver* (*Brit*) 3 ADJ [*attitude*] (*de paresseux*) shirking; (*de plaisantin*) phoney*; **il est un peu ~ (sur les bords)** he's a bit of a shirker *ou* skiver* (*Brit*)

fumisterie [fymistəri] NF a (*péj*) **c'est une** *ou* **de la ~** it's a fraud *ou* a con* b (= *établissement*) (heating mechanic's) workshop; (= *métier*) stove-building

fumoir [fymwaʀ] NM (= *salon*) smoking room; (*Ind*) smokehouse

fumure [fymyʀ] NF manuring; (= *substance*) manure (*NonC*)

fun[1]*** [fœn] 1 ADJ (= *amusant, excitant*) fun (*épith*); **c'est ~!** it's fun! 2 NM (= *amusement*) **le ~** fun; **je suis mannequin, c'est le ~!** I'm a model, it's great fun!; **ils ont tout cassé, juste pour le ~** they smashed up everything, just for the fun *ou* hell* of it

fun[2] [fœn] NM ABRÉV = **funboard**

Funafuti [funafuti] N Funafuti

funambule [fynɑ̃byl] NMF tightrope walker, funambulist (*SPÉC*)

funambulesque [fynɑ̃bylɛsk] ADJ (*lit*) [*prouesse, art*] of tightrope walking; (*fig = bizarre*) [*idée, organisation*] fantastic, bizarre

funboard [fœnbɔʀd] NM (= *planche*) short windsurfing board *ou* sailboard; (= *sport*) windsurfing

funèbre [fynɛbʀ] ADJ a (= *de l'enterrement*) [*service, marche, oraison*] funeral (*épith*); [*cérémonie, éloge, discours*] funeral (*épith*), funerary (*épith*); **air ~** dirge → **entrepreneur, pompe**[2]**, veillée** b (= *lugubre*) [*mélodie*] mournful, doleful; [*ton, silence, allure*] lugubrious, funereal; [*atmosphère, couleur, décor*] gloomy, dismal

funérailles [fyneʀaj] NFPL (*frm = enterrement*) funeral, obsequies (*littér*)

funéraire [fyneʀɛʀ] ADJ [*dalle, monument, urne*] funeral (*épith*), funerary (*épith*); **pierre ~** gravestone; (*Can*) **salon ~** funeral home, funeral parlour (*Brit*) *ou* parlor (*US*)

funérarium [fyneʀaʀjɔm] NM funeral home, funeral parlour (*Brit*) *ou* parlor (*US*)

funeste [fynɛst] ADJ a (= *désastreux*) [*erreur*] disastrous, grievous; [*conseil, décision*] disastrous, harmful; [*influence*] baleful, baneful, harmful; [*suite, conséquence*] dire, disastrous; **le jour ~ où je l'ai rencontré** the fateful *ou* ill-fated day when I met him; **politique ~ aux intérêts du pays** policy harmful to the country's interests b (= *de mort*) [*pressentiment, vision*] deathly (*épith*), of death c (*littér = mortel*) [*accident*] fatal; [*coup*] fatal, lethal, deadly, mortal

funiculaire [fynikylɛʀ] NM funicular (railway)

funk [fœnk] 1 ADJ funk (*épith*), funky 2 NM funk

funky [fœnki] ADJ funky

fur [fyʀ] 1 **au fur et à mesure** LOC ADV [*classer, nettoyer*] as one goes along; [*dépenser*] as fast as one earns; **il vaut mieux leur donner leur argent de poche au ~ et à mesure qu'en une fois** it's better to give them their pocket money in dribs and drabs* *ou* as they need it rather than all in one go; **le frigo se vidait au ~ et à mesure** the fridge was emptied as fast as it was stocked up; **passe-moi les assiettes au ~ et à mesure** pass the plates to me as you go along 2 **au fur et à mesure que** LOC CONJ **donnez-les-nous au ~ et à mesure que vous les recevez** give them to us as (soon as) you receive them; **nous dépensions tout notre argent au ~ et à mesure que nous le gagnions** we spent all our money as fast as we earned it 3 **au fur et à mesure de** LOC PRÉP **au ~ et à mesure de leur progression** as they advanced, the further they advanced; **prenez-en au ~ et à mesure de vos besoins** take some as and when you need them, help yourselves as you find you need them

furax* [fyʀaks] ADJ INV (= *furieux*) livid* (*attrib*), hopping mad* (*attrib*) (*Brit*)

furet [fyʀɛ] NM (= *animal*) ferret; (= *jeu*) pass-the-slipper

fureter [fyʀ(ə)te] ▸conjug 5◂ VI (= *regarder*) to nose *ou* ferret about; (= *fouiller*) to rummage (about)

fureteur, -euse [fyʀ(ə)tœʀ, øz] 1 ADJ [*regard, enfant*] prying, inquisitive 2 NM,F snooper

fureur [fyʀœʀ] NF a (= *colère*) fury; (= *accès de colère*) fit of rage; **crise** *ou* **accès de ~** fit of rage, furious outburst; **être pris de ~** to fly into a rage (**contre qn** at sb); **être/entrer en ~** to be/become infuriated *ou* enraged; **être/entrer dans une ~ noire** to be in/go *ou* fly into a towering rage; **mettre en ~** to infuriate, enrage; **se mettre dans des ~s folles** to have mad fits of rage, fly into wild fits of anger b (= *violence*) [*passion*] violence, fury; [*combat, attaque*] fury, fierceness, furiousness; [*tempête, flots, vents*] fury c (= *passion*) **la ~ du jeu** a passion *ou* mania for gambling; **il a la ~ de la vitesse/de lire** he has a mania for speed/reading; **la ~ de vivre** the lust *ou* passion for life d (*littér = transe*) frenzy; **~ prophétique** prophetic frenzy; **~ poétique** poetic ecstasy *ou* frenzy e (*loc*) **avec ~** (= *avec rage*) furiously; (= *à la folie*) wildly, madly, passionately; **faire ~** to be all the rage

furibard, e* [fyʀibaʀ, aʀd] ADJ livid* (*attrib*), hopping mad* (*attrib*) (*Brit*)

furibond, e [fyʀibɔ̃, ɔ̃d] ADJ [*personne*] furious, livid* (*attrib*); [*colère*] wild, furious; [*ton, voix, yeux*] enraged, furious; **il lui a lancé un regard ~** he glared at him

furie [fyʀi] NF a (*péj = mégère*) shrew, termagant; (*Myth*) Fury b (= *violence*) [*attaque, combat*] fury, fierceness, furiousness; [*tempête, flots*] fury; [*passions*] violence, fury c (= *passion*) **la ~ du jeu** a passion *ou* mania for gambling d (= *colère*) fury e (*loc*) **en ~** [*personne*] infuriated, enraged, in a rage (*attrib*); [*mer*] raging; [*tigre*] raging; **mettre qn en ~** to infuriate sb, enrage sb

furieusement [fyʀjøzmɑ̃] ADV (= *avec fureur*) [*attaquer*] furiously; [*répondre*] angrily; (*gén hum = extrêmement*) [*ressembler*] amazingly, tremendously; **j'ai ~ envie d'une glace à la fraise** I'm simply dying for* *ou* I've got a terrible craving for a strawberry ice cream

furieux, -ieuse [fyʀjø, jøz] ADJ a (= *violent*) [*combat, résistance*] furious, fierce; [*tempête*] raging, furious, violent; **avoir une furieuse envie de faire qch** to be dying to do sth* → **folie, fou** b (= *en colère*) [*personne*] furious (**contre** with, at); [*ton, geste*] furious; **taureau ~** raging bull; **rendre qn ~** to infuriate *ou* enrage sb; **le taureau, rendu ~ par la foule** the bull, driven wild by the crowd; **elle est fu-**

rieuse de n'avoir pas été invitée she's furious that she wasn't invited *ou* at not having been invited; **il est ~ que je lui aie menti** he is furious with *ou* at me for having lied to him [c] (*gén hum = fort*) [*envie, coup*] almighty* (*épith*), tremendous

furoncle [fyʀɔ̃kl] NM boil, furuncle (*SPÉC*)

furonculose [fyʀɔ̃kyloz] NF (recurrent) boils, furunculosis (*SPÉC*)

furtif, -ive [fyʀtif, iv] ADJ [*coup d'œil, geste*] furtive, stealthy; [*joie*] secret → **avion**

furtivement [fyʀtivmɑ̃] ADV furtively, stealthily

fusain [fyzɛ̃] NM (= *crayon*) charcoal (crayon); (= *croquis*) charcoal (drawing); (= *arbrisseau*) spindle-tree; **tracé au ~** charcoal(-drawn), (drawn) in charcoal

fusant, e [fyzɑ̃, ɑ̃t] ADJ **obus ~** time shell; **tir ~** air burst

fuseau (*pl* **fuseaux**) [fyzo] [1] NM [a] [*fileuse*] spindle; [*dentellière*] bobbin [b] **(pantalon) ~** ◊ **~x** stretch ski pants (*Brit*), stirrup pants (*US*) [c] (*Anat, Bio*) spindle [d] (*loc*) **en (forme de) ~** [*colonne*] spindle-shaped; [*cuisses, jambes*] slender; **arbuste taillé en ~** shrub shaped into a cone [e] **~ horaire** time zone; **changer de ~ horaire** to cross time zones

fusée [fyze] [1] NF [a] (*spatiale*) (space) rocket; (*missile*) rocket, missile; **~ air-air/sol-air** air-to-air/ground-to-air missile [b] [*feu d'artifice*] rocket; [*mine, mine*] fuse; **partir comme une ~** to set off like a rocket, whizz off [c] (*Tech*) [*essieu*] spindle; (*Aut*) stub axle; [*montre*] fusee [2] COMP ▸ **fusée antichar** anti-tank rocket ▸ **fusée de détresse** distress rocket ▸ **fusée éclairante** flare ▸ **fusée à étages** multi-stage rocket ▸ **fusée interplanétaire** (interplanetary) space rocket ▸ **fusée de lancement** launch vehicle

fusée-engin (*pl* **fusées-engins**) [fyzeɑ̃ʒɛ̃] NF rocket shell

fusée-sonde (*pl* **fusées-sondes**) [fyzesɔ̃d] NF rocket-powered space probe

fuselage [fyz(ə)laʒ] NM [*avion*] fuselage

fuselé, e [fyz(ə)le] ADJ [*colonne*] spindle-shaped; [*doigts*] tapering, slender; [*cuisses, jambes*] slender

fuser [fyze] ▸ conjug 1 ◂ VI [a] [*cris, rires*] to burst forth; [*questions*] to come from all sides; [*liquide, vapeur*] to gush *ou* spurt out; [*étincelles*] to fly (out); [*lumière*] to stream out *ou* forth; **les plaisanteries fusaient** the jokes came thick and fast; **les insultes fusaient de toutes parts** insults were flying from all sides [b] (*Tech*) [*bougie*] to run; [*pile*] to sweat; [*poudre*] to burn out

fusible [fyzibl] [1] ADJ fusible [2] NM (= *fil*) fuse(-wire); (= *fiche*) fuse; (*fig* = *personne*) fall guy; **les ~s ont sauté** the fuses have blown

fusiforme [fyzifɔʀm] ADJ spindle-shaped, fusiform (*SPÉC*)

fusil [fyzi] [1] NM [a] (= *arme*) (*de guerre, à canon rayé*) rifle, gun; (*de chasse, à canon lisse*) shotgun, gun; (*fig*) **c'est un bon ~** he's a good shot; († *Mil*) **un groupe de 30 ~s** a group of 30 riflemen *ou* rifles; (*fig*) **changer son ~**

d'épaule to have a change of heart; **coup de ~** gun shot, rifle shot; (*fig*) **c'est le coup de ~** the prices are extortionate, you pay through the nose* [b] (= *allume-gaz*) gas lighter; (= *instrument à aiguiser*) steel [2] COMP ▸ **fusil à air comprimé** airgun ▸ **fusil d'assaut** assault rifle ▸ **fusil automatique** automatic rifle ▸ **fusil à canon rayé** rifle, rifled gun ▸ **fusil à canon scié** sawn-off (*Brit*) *ou* sawed-off (*US*) shotgun ▸ **fusil de chasse** shotgun, hunting gun ▸ **fusil à deux coups** double-barrelled *ou* twin-barrel rifle ▸ **fusil de guerre** army rifle ▸ **fusil à harpon** harpoon gun ▸ **fusil à lunette** rifle with telescopic sight ▸ **fusil à pompe** pump-action shotgun ▸ **fusil à répétition** repeating rifle ▸ **fusil sous-marin** (underwater) speargun

fusilier [fyzilje] NM rifleman, fusilier; (*Hist*) fusilier; **les ~s** (= *régiment*) the rifles; (*Hist*) the fusiliers; **~ marin** marine

fusillade [fyzijad] NF (= *bruit*) fusillade (*frm*), gunfire (*NonC*), shooting (*NonC*); (= *combat*) shoot-out, shooting battle; (= *exécution*) shooting

fusiller [fyzije] ▸ conjug 1 ◂ VT [a] (= *exécuter*) to shoot; **~ qn du regard** to look daggers at sb [b]* (= *casser*) to bust* [c]* (= *dépenser*) to blow*

fusilleur [fyzijœʀ] NM member of a firing squad

fusil-mitrailleur (*pl* **fusils-mitrailleurs**) [fyzimitʀajœʀ] NM machine gun

fusion [fyzjɔ̃] NF [a] [*métal*] melting, fusion; [*glace*] melting, thawing; **en ~** [*métal*] molten; **au moment de l'entrée en ~** when melting point is reached [b] (*Bio, Phys*) fusion; **~ nucléaire/chromosomique** nuclear/chromosome fusion [c] (= *union*) [*cœurs, esprits, races*] fusion; [*partis*] merging, combining; [*systèmes, philosophies*] blending, merging, uniting [d] (*Comm*) [*sociétés*] merger, amalgamation; (*Ordin*) [*fichiers*] merging; **~ absorption** take-over; **~ acquisition** acquisition and merger

fusionnel, -elle [fyzjɔnɛl] ADJ (*Psych*) [*rapport*] intensely close; [*amour*] based on a very close bond; **une relation trop fusionnelle avec la mère** a relationship with the mother that is too close *ou* too intense

fusionnement [fyzjɔnmɑ̃] NM (*Comm*) merger, amalgamation; (*Pol*) merging, combining

fusionner [fyzjɔne] ▸ conjug 1 ◂ VTI (*Comm*) to merge, amalgamate; (*Pol*) to merge, combine; (*Ordin*) to merge

fustanelle [fystanɛl] NF fustanella

fustigation [fystigasjɔ̃] NF [a] (*littér*) [*adversaire*] flaying; [*pratiques, mœurs*] censuring, denouncing, denunciation [b]†† (= *flagellation*) birching, thrashing

fustiger [fystiʒe] ▸ conjug 3 ◂ VT [a] (*littér*) [+ *adversaire*] to flay; [+ *pratiques, mœurs*] to censure, denounce; **ses sketches fustigent la société actuelle** his sketches are a scathing attack on modern society [b]†† (= *fouetter*) to

birch, thrash

fut* [fyt] NM (ABRÉV = **futal**) trousers (*Brit*), pants (*US*)

fût [fy] NM [a] [*arbre*] bole, trunk; [*colonne*] shaft; [*fusil*] stock [b] (= *tonneau*) barrel, cask

futaie [fyte] NF (= *groupe d'arbres*) cluster of (tall) trees; (= *forêt*) forest (of tall trees); (*Sylviculture*) plantation of trees (for timber); **haute ~** mature (standing) timber; **arbre de haute ~** mature tree

futaille [fytaj] NF (= *barrique*) barrel, cask

futaine [fyten] NF (*Tex*) fustian

futal* (*pl* **futals**) [fytal], **fute*** [fyt] NM trousers (*Brit*), pants (*US*)

futé, e [fyte] ADJ wily, crafty, cunning, sly; **c'est une petite ~e** she's a crafty *ou* sly little minx; **il n'est pas très ~** he's not very bright

fute-fute* [fytfyt] ADJ **il n'est pas (très) ~** he's not very bright

futile [fytil] ADJ [*entreprise, tentative*] futile, pointless; [*raison, souci, occupation, propos*] trifling, trivial, futile; [*personne, esprit*] frivolous; **l'univers ~ de la mode** the frivolous world of fashion

futilement [fytilmɑ̃] ADV (= *frivolement*) frivolously

futilité [fytilite] NF [a] [*entreprise, tentative*] futility, pointlessness; [*raison, souci, occupation, propos*] triviality, futility; [*personne, esprit*] triviality, frivolousness [b] (= *propos, action*) **~s** trivialities; **dire des ~s** to talk about trivia; **ils ont passé leur journée à des ~s** they frittered the day away

futon [fytɔ̃] NM futon

futur, e [fytyʀ] [1] ADJ (= *prochain*) [*génération, désastres, besoins*] future (*épith*); (*Rel*) **dans la vie ~e** in the afterlife, in the hereafter; **~ mari** husband-to-be; **les ~s époux** the bride-and-groom-to-be; **tout pour la ~e maman** everything for the mother-to-be; **~ collègue/directeur** future colleague/director; **~ client** prospective customer; (*en herbe*) **~ président/champion** budding *ou* future president/champion [2] NM [a] (= *avenir*) future [b] (*Ling*) **le ~ (simple)** the future (tense); **le ~ proche** the immediate future; **le ~ antérieur** *ou* **du passé** the future perfect *ou* anterior [c]† (= *fiancé*) fiancé, husband-to-be, intended† [3] **future** NF († = *fiancée*) fiancée, wife-to-be, intended†

futurisme [fytyʀism] NM futurism

futuriste [fytyʀist] [1] NMF futurist [2] ADJ futuristic

futurologie [fytyʀɔlɔʒi] NF futurology

futurologue [fytyʀɔlɔg] NMF futurist, futurologist

fuyant, e [fɥijɑ̃, ɑ̃t] ADJ [a] (= *insaisissable*) [*regard, air*] evasive; [*personne, caractère*] elusive, evasive [b] (= *en retrait*) [*menton, front*] receding (*épith*) [c] (*littér* = *fugitif*) [*ombre, vision*] fleeting (*épith*) [d] (*Art*) [*vues, lignes*] receding (*épith*), vanishing (*épith*); [*perspective*] vanishing (*épith*)

fuyard, e [fɥijaʀ, aʀd] NM,F runaway

G

G¹, g¹ [ʒe] NM (= *lettre*) G, g; **le G-8** the G8 nations, the Group of Eight; (*Anat*) **point G** G spot

G² [a] (ABRÉV = **Giga**) G [b] (= *constante de gravitation*) G

g² [a] (ABRÉV = **gramme**) g [b] (*Phys* = *accélération*) g

gabardine [gabaʀdin] NF (= *tissu*) gabardine; (= *manteau*) gabardine (raincoat)

gabarit [gabaʀi] NM [a] (= *dimension*) [*objet, véhicule*] size [b]* [*personne*] (= *taille*) size, build; (= *valeur*) calibre (*Brit*), caliber (*US*); **ce n'est pas le petit ~!** he's not exactly small!, he's rather on the large side!; **du même ~** of the same build; **il n'a pas le ~ d'un directeur commercial** he hasn't got what it takes *ou* he isn't of the right calibre to be a sales manager [c] (*Tech* = *appareil de mesure*) gauge, gage (*US*); (= *maquette*) template; (*Rail*) **~ de chargement** loading gauge

gabegie [gabʒi] NF (*péj*) (= *gâchis*) waste (*due to bad management*); (= *désordre*) chaos; **c'est une vraie ~!** it's a real mess!, it's total chaos!

gabelle [gabɛl] NF (*Hist* = *impôt*) salt tax, gabelle

gabelou [gablu] NM (*Hist*) salt-tax collector; (*péj*) customs officer

gabier [gabje] NM (*Naut*) topman

Gabon [gabɔ̃] NM **le ~** (the) Gabon

gabonais, e [gabɔnɛ, ɛz] [1] ADJ Gabonese [2] **Gabonais(e)** NM,F Gabonese

Gabriel [gabʀijel] NM Gabriel

gâchage [gɑʃaʒ] NM [a] [*plâtre*] tempering; [*mortier*] mixing [b] [*argent, talent, temps*] wasting

gâche [gɑʃ] NF [a] [*maçon*] (plasterer's) trowel [b] [*serrure*] striking plate, strike (plate)

gâcher [gɑʃe] ▶conjug 1◀ VT [a] [+ *plâtre*] to temper; [+ *mortier*] to mix [b] [+ *argent, temps*] to waste, fritter away; [+ *nourriture, occasion, talent*] to waste; [+ *travail*] to botch; **~ sa vie** to fritter away *ou* waste one's life; **une vie gâchée** a wasted *ou* misspent life [c] (= *gâter: gén*) to spoil; [+ *jeunesse, séjour, chances*] to ruin; **il nous a gâché le** *ou* **notre plaisir** he spoiled it for us; **je ne veux pas lui ~ sa joie** I don't want to spoil his happiness; **il gâche le métier** he spoils it for others (*by selling cheap or working for a low salary*)

gâchette [gɑʃɛt] NF [*arme*] trigger; [*serrure*] tumbler; **appuyer** *ou* **presser sur la ~** to pull the trigger; **il a la ~ facile** he's trigger-happy; (= *tireur*) **une bonne ~** a good shot; **la meilleure ~ de l'Ouest** the fastest gun in the West

gâcheur, -euse [gɑʃœʀ, øz] [1] ADJ wasteful [2] NM,F [a] [*matériel*] wasteful person; [*argent*] spendthrift; [*travail*] bungler, botcher [b] (*péj* = *snob*) fusspot (*Brit*), fussbudget (*US*), fussy person [3] NM (= *ouvrier*) builder's helper *ou* mate (*Brit*) (*who mixes cement or tempers plaster*)

gâchis [gɑʃi] NM [a] (= *désordre*) mess; **tu as fait un beau ~!** you've made a real mess of it!

[b] (= *gaspillage*) [*argent, nourriture, sentiments*] waste (*NonC*); **je ne supporte pas le ~** I hate waste *ou* wastefulness; **quel ~!** what a waste! [c] (*Tech*) mortar

gadget [gadʒɛt] NM (= *chose*) thingummy* (*Brit*), gizmo* (*US*); (= *jouet, ustensile*) gadget; (= *procédé, trouvaille*) gimmick; **cette loi n'est qu'un ~** that law is just a token measure

gadgétiser [gadʒetize] ▶conjug 1◀ VT to equip with gadgets

gadin* [gadɛ̃] NM **prendre** *ou* **ramasser un ~** to fall flat on one's face, come a cropper* (*Brit*)

gadoue [gadu] NF (= *boue*) mud, sludge; (= *neige*) slush; (= *engrais*) night soil

GAEC [gaɛk] NM (ABRÉV = **groupement agricole d'exploitation en commun**) → **groupement**

gaélique [gaelik] [1] ADJ Gaelic [2] NM (*Ling*) Gaelic

gaffe [gaf] NF [a] (= *bévue*) blunder, boob* (*Brit*); **faire une ~** (*action*) to make a blunder *ou* a boob* (*Brit*); (*parole*) to put one's foot in it*, say the wrong thing, drop a clanger* (*Brit*) [b] (= *perche*) (*Naut*) boat hook; (*Pêche*) gaff [c]* **faire ~** (= *être attentionné*) to pay attention (à to); **fais ~!** watch out!, be careful!; **fais ~ à toi** watch yourself

gaffer [gafe] ▶conjug 1◀ [1] VI (*bévue*) to blunder, boob* (*Brit*); (*paroles*) to put one's foot in it*, drop a clanger* (*Brit*); **j'ai gaffé ?** have I put my foot in it?, did I say the wrong thing? [2] VT [a] (*Naut*) to hook; (*Pêche*) to gaff [b] (†,* = *regarder*) **gaffe un peu la fille !** get a load of her!*

gaffeur, -euse [gafœʀ, øz] NM,F blunderer, blundering idiot; **il est drôlement ~!** he's always putting his foot in it!*, he's a blundering idiot!

gag [gag] NM (*gén, Ciné, Théât*) gag; **ce n'est pas un ~** it's not a joke; **le ~, c'est qu'il va falloir s'en servir** the funniest part of it is that we'll have to use it

gaga* [gaga] ADJ [*vieillard*] gaga*, senile; **sa fille le rend ~** he's putty in his daughter's hands, his daughter can wind him round her little finger; **être ~ de qn** to be crazy* *ou* nuts* about sb

gage [gaʒ] NM [a] (à un créancier, arbitre) security; (à un prêteur) pledge; **mettre qch en ~ (chez un prêteur)** to pawn sth (at the pawnbroker's); **laisser qch en ~** to leave sth as (a) security → **prêteur** [b] (= *garantie*) guarantee; **sa bonne forme physique est un ~ de succès** his fitness will guarantee him success *ou* assure him of success [c] (= *témoignage*) proof (*NonC*), evidence (*NonC*); **donner des ~s de sa sincérité/de son talent** to give proof *ou* evidence of one's sincerity/one's talent; **donner des ~s de (sa) bonne volonté** to make several gestures of goodwill; **donner à qn un ~ d'amour/de fidélité** to give sb a token of one's love/of one's faithfulness; **en ~ de notre amitié/de ma bonne foi** as a token *ou* in token of our friendship/of my good faith

[d] (*Jeux*) forfeit; **avoir un ~** to have a forfeit [e] († = *salaire*) **~s** wages; **être aux ~s de qn** (*gén*) to be employed by sb; (*péj*) to be in the pay of sb → **tueur**

gager [gaʒe] ▶conjug 3◀ VT [a] (*frm* = *parier*) **~ que** to wager that, bet that; **gageons que ... ◊ je gage que ...** I bet (you) that ... [b] [+ *emprunt*] to guarantee

gageure [gaʒyʀ] NF [a] (= *entreprise difficile*) **c'est une véritable ~ que de vouloir tenter seul cette ascension** it's attempting the impossible to try to do this climb alone; **il a réussi la ~ de faire cette ascension tout seul** he achieved the impossible — he managed to do the climb on his own, despite the odds he managed to do the climb on his own [b] †† (= *pari*) wager

gagnable [gaɲabl] ADJ winnable

gagnant, e [gaɲɑ̃, ɑ̃t] [1] ADJ [*numéro, combinaison, point*] winning (*épith*); **on donne ce concurrent ~** this competitor is the favourite to win *ou* is expected to win; **il joue** *ou* **part ~ dans cette affaire** he's bound to win *ou* come out on top in this deal; **tu es ~** you can't lose (out); (*Jur*) **la partie ~e** the prevailing party [2] NM,F winner

gagne* [gaɲ] NF (*Sport*) **la ~** the will *ou* drive to win; **ce joueur est venu pour la ~** this player has come intent on winning

gagne-pain* [gaɲpɛ̃] NM INV source of income; **c'est son ~** it's his bread and butter*

gagne-petit [gaɲpəti] NM INV (= *qui gagne peu*) low wage earner; (*péj*) small-time racketeer; **c'est un ~** he doesn't earn much (money)

gagner [gaɲe] ▶conjug 1◀ [1] VT [a] (= *acquérir par le travail*) to earn; **~ sa vie** to earn one's living (**en faisant** (by) doing); **elle gagne mal sa vie** she doesn't earn much; **elle gagne bien sa vie** she earns a good living; **elle gagne bien*** she earns good money*; **~ son pain** to earn one's daily bread; **~ de l'argent** (*par le travail*) to earn *ou* make money; (*dans une affaire*) to make money; **~ de quoi vivre** to earn a living; **~ gros** to make a lot of money; **il ne gagne pas des mille et des cents*** he doesn't exactly earn a fortune; **~ sa croûte*** *ou* son **bifteck*** to earn one's crust *ou* one's bread and butter; **il gagne bien sa croûte dans cet emploi*** he earns a good wage in that job; (*iro*) **j'ai gagné ma journée** that really made my day (*iro*) [b] (= *mériter*) to earn; **il a bien gagné ses vacances** he's really earned his holiday [c] (= *acquérir par le hasard*) [+ *prix, somme*] to win; (*lit, fig*) **~ le gros lot** to hit *ou* win the jackpot [d] (= *obtenir*) [+ *réputation*] to gain; [+ *parts de marché*] to win; **avoir tout à ~ et rien à perdre** to have everything to gain and nothing to lose; **vous n'y gagnerez rien** you'll gain nothing by it; **vous n'y gagnerez rien de bon** you'll get nothing out of it; **vous y gagnerez d'être tranquille** at least you'll get some peace and quiet that way; **chercher à ~ du temps** (= *aller* *plus vite*) to try to save time; (= *temporiser*) to play for time, try to gain time; **cela fait ~ beaucoup de temps** it saves a lot *ou* a great deal of time, it's very time-saving; **ce à la place** to save space; **c'est toujours ça de gagné!** that's always something!; **c'est toujours 10 F de gagné** at least that's 10 francs saved *ou* that's saved us 10 francs; **en jouant sur l'épaisseur, on peut ~ sur la quantité** by adjusting the thickness, we can gain in quantity; **à sortir par ce temps, vous y gagnerez un bon rhume** you'll get nothing but a bad cold going out in this weather; **je n'y ai gagné que des ennuis** I only made trouble for myself, I only succeeded in making things difficult for myself; **s'il dit oui, c'est gagné** if he says yes, then everything will be all right

[e] (= *augmenter de*) **~ dix centimètres** [*plante, enfant*] to grow ten centimetres; **l'indice CAC 40 gagne 4 points** the CAC 40 index is up 4 points; **il gagne 3 points dans les sondages** he gains 3 points in the opinion polls

[f] (= *être vainqueur de*) [+ *élection, bataille, procès, pari, course*] to win; (*arg Sport*) [+ *joueur*] to beat; **le match/procès n'est pas gagné** the match/trial hasn't been won yet; **ce n'est pas gagné d'avance** it's far from certain; **~ haut la main** to win hands down; **~ qn aux échecs** to beat sb at chess; **~ qn de vitesse** to catch up on sb

[g] (= *se concilier*) [+ *gardiens, témoins*] to win over; **~ l'estime/le cœur de qn** to win sb's esteem *ou* regard/heart; **~ la confiance de qn** to win *ou* gain sb's confidence; **savoir se ~ des amis/des partisans** to know how to win friends/supporters; **se laisser ~ par les prières de qn** to be won over by sb's prayers; **~ qn à une cause** to win sb over to a cause; **~ qn à sa cause** to win sb over

[h] (= *envahir*) to spread to; **le sommeil les gagnait** sleep was creeping over them *ou* was gradually overcoming them; **la gangrène gagne la jambe** the gangrene is spreading to his leg; **le froid les gagnait** they were beginning to feel the cold; **le feu gagna rapidement les rues voisines** the fire quickly spread to the neighbouring streets; **l'eau/l'ennemi gagne du terrain** the water/the enemy is gaining ground; **la grève gagne tous les secteurs** the strike is gaining ground in *ou* is spreading to all sectors

[i] (= *atteindre*) [+ *lieu, frontière, refuge*] to reach; **~ le port** to reach port; (*Naut*) **~ le large** to get out into the open sea

[2] VI [a] (= *être vainqueur*) to win; **~ aux courses** to win on the horses *ou* at the races; **il a gagné aux courses hier** he won on the horses *ou* had a win at the races yesterday; **il gagne sur tous les tableaux** he's winning all the way *ou* on all fronts; (*iro*) **eh bien, tu as gagné!** well, you got what you asked for!*

[b] (= *trouver un avantage*) **vous y gagnez** it's in your interest, it's to your advantage; **vous gagnerez à ce que personne ne le sache** it'll be to your advantage *ou* it will be better for you if nobody knows about it; **qu'est-ce que j'y gagne?** what do I get out of it? *ou* gain from it?, what's in it for me?; **vous gagneriez à partir en groupe** you'd be better off going in a group; **tu aurais gagné à te taire!** you would have done better to keep quiet!; **elle a gagné au change** she ended up better off

[c] (= *s'améliorer*) **~ en hauteur** to increase in height; **son style gagne en force ce qu'il perd en élégance** his style gains in vigour what it loses in elegance; **ce vin gagnera à vieillir** this wine will improve with age; **il gagne à être connu** he improves on acquaintance; **ce roman gagne à être relu** this novel gains by a second reading, this novel is better at a second reading

[d] (= *s'étendre*) [*incendie, épidémie*] to spread, gain ground; **la mer gagne sur les falaises** the sea is encroaching *ou* advancing on the cliffs

gagneur, -euse [gaɲœʀ, øz] [1] NM,F (= *battant*) go-getter*; **avoir un tempérament de ~** to be a born winner [2] **gagneuse:** NF (= *prostituée*) whore:, hooker:

gai, e [ge] [1] ADJ [a] [*personne, vie*] cheerful, happy; [*voix, visage*] cheerful, happy, cheery; [*caractère, roman, conversation, musique*] cheerful; **le ~ Paris** gay Paris; **c'est un ~ luron** he's a cheery *ou* happy fellow; **~ comme un pinson** happy as a lark; **tu n'as pas l'air (bien) ~** you don't look too happy [b] (*euph* = *ivre*) merry, tipsy → **vin** [c] [*robe*] bright; [*couleur, pièce*] bright, cheerful; **on va peindre la chambre en jaune pour faire ~** we're going to paint the bedroom yellow to brighten it up [d] (*iro* = *amusant*) **j'ai oublié mon parapluie, c'est ~!** that's great*, I've forgotten my umbrella! (*iro*) **ça va être ~, un week-end avec lui!** the week-end's going to be great fun with him around! (*iro*) [e] (= *homosexuel*) gay [2] NM (= *homosexuel*) gay

gaiement [gemã] ADV [a] (= *joyeusement*) cheerfully, merrily [b] (= *avec entrain*) **allons-y ~!** come on then, let's get on with it!; **il va recommencer ~ à faire les mêmes bêtises** he'll blithely *ou* gaily start the same old tricks again

gaieté [gete] NF [*personne, caractère, roman, conversation*] cheerfulness, gaiety; [*couleur*] brightness; **plein de ~** cheerful; **perdre/retrouver sa ~** to lose/recover one's good spirits; **ses films sont rarement d'une ~ folle** his films are not exactly cheerful; **ce n'est pas de ~ de cœur qu'il accepta** he wasn't exactly happy about accepting, it was with some reluctance that he accepted; (*iro*) **voilà les ~s de la province** those are the joys *ou* delights of living in a provincial town (*iro*)

gaillard¹, e [gajaʀ, aʀd] [1] ADJ [a] (= *alerte*) [*personne*] strong; [*allure*] lively, springy, sprightly; **vieillard encore ~** sprightly *ou* spry old man [b] (= *grivois*) [*propos*] bawdy, ribald [2] NM [a] (= *costaud*) (**robuste** *ou* **grand** *ou* **beau**) **~** strapping fellow *ou* lad [b]* (= *type*) fellow, guy*, chap* (*Brit*); **toi, mon ~, je t'ai à l'œil!** I've got my eye on you, chum!* *ou* mate!* (*Brit*) [3] **gaillarde** NF (= *femme forte*) strapping wench* *ou* woman; (= *femme hardie*) **c'est une sacrée ~e!** she's quite a woman!

gaillard² [gajaʀ] NM (*Naut*) **~ d'avant** forecastle (head), fo'c'sle; **~ d'arrière** quarter-deck

gaillardement [gajaʀdəmã] ADV (= *avec bonne humeur*) cheerfully; (= *sans faiblir*) bravely, gallantly; **ils attaquèrent la côte ~** they set off energetically *ou* stoutly up the hill; **il porte sa soixantaine ~** he's a sprightly *ou* vigorous sixty-year-old

gaillardise [gajaʀdiz] NF bawdy *ou* ribald remark

gaîment [gemã] ADV = **gaiement**

gain [gɛ̃] NM [a] (= *salaire*: *gén*) earnings; [*ouvrier*] earnings, wages, wage; **pour un ~ modeste** for a modest wage

[b] (= *lucre*) **le ~** gain → **appât**

[c] (= *bénéfice*) [*société*] profit; (*au jeu*) winnings; (*à la Bourse*) profit; **faire un ~ de 2 milliards** to make a profit of 2 billion; **se retirer sur son ~** (*au jeu*) to pull out with one's winnings intact; (*spéculation*) to retire on one's profits *ou* with what one has made

[d] (= *économie*) saving; **le ~ d'argent/de place est énorme** it saves a considerable amount of money/space; **ça permet un ~ de temps** it saves time; **ce procédé permet un ~ de 50 minutes/d'électricité** this procedure saves 50 minutes/electricity

[e] (= *avantage matériel*) gain; **~ de productivité** productivity gain; **~ de pouvoir d'achat** increase in purchasing power; **~s territoriaux** territorial gains

[f] (= *obtention*) [*match, bataille, procès*] winning; [*fortune, voix d'électeurs*] gaining; **~ de poids** weight gain; **ce ~ de trois sièges leur donne la majorité** winning *ou* gaining these three seats has given them a majority; **l'action a terminé la séance sur un ~ de 2 points** the share was up (by) 2 points at close of trading

[g] (*Élec*) gain, amplification; **contrôle automatique de ~** automatic gain control

[h] (*loc*) **avoir** *ou* **obtenir ~ de cause** (*Jur*) to win the case; (*fig*) to be proved right; **on ne voulait pas me rembourser mais j'ai fini par avoir ~ de cause** they didn't want to reimburse me but in the end I won my claim; **donner ~ de cause à qn** (*Jur*) to decide in sb's favour; (*fig*) to pronounce sb right

gainant, e [genã, ãt] ADJ [*collant, culotte*] body-shaping

gaine [gɛn] NF [a] (*Habillement*) girdle; **~ culotte** panty girdle [b] (= *fourreau*: *Anat*), (*Bot*) sheath; [*obus*] priming tube; **~ d'aération** *ou* **de ventilation** ventilation shaft [c] (= *piédestal*) plinth

gainer [gene] ▸conjug 1◂ VT (*gén*) to cover; [+ *fil électrique*] to sheathe; (= *mouler*) to put into a sailbag; **jambes gainées de soie** legs sheathed in silk; **objet gainé de cuir** leather-covered *ou* -cased object

gaîté [gete] NF = **gaieté**

gala [gala] NM official reception; (*pour collecter des fonds*) fund-raising reception; **~ de bienfaisance** charity gala; **de ~** [*soirée, représentation*] gala (*épith*); **tenue de ~** full evening dress

Galaad [galaad] NM Galahad

galactique [galaktik] ADJ galactic

galactogène [galaktɔʒɛn] ADJ galactagogue (*SPÉC*); **glande ~** milk gland

galactomètre [galaktɔmɛtʀ] NM lactometer

galactophore [galaktɔfɔʀ] ADJ **canal/glande ~** milk duct/gland

galactose [galaktoz] NM galactose

Galalithe® [galalit] N Galalith®

galamment [galamã] ADV courteously, gallantly; **se conduire ~** to behave courteously *ou* gallantly *ou* in a gentlemanly fashion

galandage [galãdaʒ] NM (brick) partition

galant, e [galã, ãt] [1] ADJ [a] (= *courtois*) gallant, courteous, gentlemanly; **soyez ~, ouvrez-lui la porte** be a gentleman and open the door for her; **c'est un ~ homme** he is a gentleman; (*péj*) **femme ~e†** courtesan [b] [*ton, humeur, propos*] flirtatious, gallant; [*scène, tableau*] amorous, romantic; [*conte*] racy, spicy; [*poésie*] amorous, courtly; **en ~e compagnie** [*homme*] with a lady friend; [*femme*] with a gentleman friend; **rendez-vous ~** tryst [2] NM (††, *hum* = *soupirant*) gallant ††, suitor ††, admirer† (*aussi hum*)

galanterie [galãtʀi] NF (= *courtoisie*) gallantry, chivalry; (= *propos*) gallant remark

galantine [galãtin] NF galantine

Galapagos [galapagɔs] NFPL **les (îles) ~** the Galapagos (Islands)

galapiat† [galapja] NM (= *polisson*) rapscallion†, scamp

Galatée [galate] NF Galatea

Galates [galat] NMPL (*Bible*) Galatians

galaxie [galaksi] NF (*Astron*) galaxy; (*fig* = *monde, domaine*) world, universe; **la Galaxie** the Galaxy

galbe [galb] NM [*meuble, visage, cuisse*] curve; **cuisses d'un ~ parfait** shapely thighs

galbé, e [galbe] (*ptp de* **galber**) ADJ [*meuble*] with curved outlines; [*mollet*] rounded; **bien ~** [*corps*] curvaceous, shapely; [*objet*] beautifully shaped

galber [galbe] ▸conjug 1◂ VT to shape (*into curves*), curve

gale [gal] NF [a] (*Méd*) scabies, itch; (*Vét*) [*chien, chat*] mange; [*mouton*] scab; (*Bot*) scab; (*hum*) **tu peux boire dans mon verre, je n'ai pas la ~!** you can drink out of my glass, you won't catch anything from me! ou I haven't got the plague! [b] (= *personne*) nasty character, nasty piece of work*; **il est mauvais** ou **méchant comme la ~** he's a really nasty piece of work*

galée [gale] NF (*Typo*) galley

galéjade [galeʒad] NF tall story

galéjer [galeʒe] ▸ conjug 6 ◂ VI to spin a yarn; **oh, tu galèjes!** that's a tall story!

galène [galɛn] NF galena, galenite

galère [galɛʀ] NF [a] (*Hist* = *bateau*) galley; **~ réale** royal galley; **envoyer/condamner qn aux ~s** to send/sentence sb to the galleys; **qu'est-il allé faire dans cette ~?** why on earth did he have to get involved in that business?; **dans quelle ~ me suis-je embarqué!** whatever have I let myself in for? → **voguer** [b]* = *ennui, problème*) **quelle ~!** ◊ **c'est (la) ~!** what a drag* ou **pain*!**; **rien n'allait dans ma vie, c'était (vraiment) la ~** nothing was going right for me, it was hell* ou it was the pits*; **j'ai connu des années de ~** I went through some difficult years ou years of hardship

galérer* [galeʀe] ▸ conjug 1 ◂ VI [a] (= *travailler dur*) to sweat blood*, slog* (*Brit*) [b] (= *avoir des difficultés*) to have a lot of hassle*, have a hard time of it*; **il a galéré pendant des années avant d'être reconnu** he struggled for years before gaining recognition

galerie [galʀi] [1] NF [a] (= *couloir*: *gén*) gallery; [*mine*] gallery, level; [*fourmilière*] gallery; [*taupinière*] tunnel [b] (*Art* = *magasin*) gallery; (= *salle de musée*) room, gallery; (= *collection*) collection [c] (*Théât* = *balcon*) circle; **premières/deuxièmes ~s** dress/upper circle; **les troisièmes ~s** the gallery, the gods* (*Brit*) [d] (= *public*) gallery, audience; **il a dit cela pour la ~** he said that for appearances' sake; **pour épater la ~** to show off* ou impress people → **amuser** [2] (*Aut*) roof rack; (*Archit* = *balustrade*) gallery [2] COMP ▸ **galerie d'art** art gallery ▸ **la galerie des Glaces** (*Archit*) the Hall of Mirrors ▸ **galerie marchande** shopping arcade, shopping mall (*US*) ▸ **galerie de peinture** picture ou art gallery ▸ **galerie de portraits** (*Littérat*) collection of pen portraits ▸ **galerie de tableaux = galerie de peinture**

galérien [galeʀjɛ̃] NM (*Hist*) galley slave; **travailler comme un ~** to work like a (galley) slave

galeriste [galeʀist] NMF gallery owner

galet [galɛ] NM [a] (= *pierre*) pebble; **~s** shingle, pebbles; **plage de ~s** shingle ou shingly beach [b] (*Tech*) wheel, roller

galetas [galta] NM (= *mansarde*) garret; (= *taudis*) hovel

galette [galɛt] NF [a] (*Culin*) (= *gâteau*) round, flat biscuit; (*Naut*) ship's biscuit; (= *crêpe*) **~ (de sarrasin)** (buckwheat) pancake; **~ de maïs** tortilla; **~ de pommes de terre** potato pancake; **~ des Rois** cake eaten in France on Twelfth Night → **plat¹**; → **LES ROIS** [b] (*Ciné*) roll [c]* (= *argent*) dough*, bread*, lolly* (*Brit*); **il a de la ~** he's loaded*, he's rolling in money*

galeux, -euse [galø, øz] [1] ADJ [a] [*personne*] affected with scabies, scabious (*SPEC*); [*chien*] mangy; [*mouton, plante, arbre*] scabby; [*plaie*] caused by scabies ou the itch; [*éruption*] scabious; **il m'a traité comme un chien ~** he treated me like dirt ou as if I was the scum of the earth → **brebis** [b] (= *sordide*) [*murs*] peeling, flaking; [*pièce, quartier*] squalid, dingy, seedy [2] NM,F (= *personne méprisable*) scum; **pour lui je suis un ~** as far as he's concerned I'm the lowest of the low ou the scum of the earth

galhauban [galobɑ̃] NM backstay

Galien [galjɛ̃] NM Galen

Galilée¹ [galile] NM Galileo

Galilée² [galile] NF Galilee; **la mer de ~** the Sea of Galilee

galiléen¹, -enne¹ [galileɛ̃, ɛn] [1] ADJ (*Géog*) Galilean [2] **Galiléen(ne)** NM,F Galilean

galiléen², -enne² [galileɛ̃, ɛn] ADJ (*Phys, Astron*) Galilean; **satellites ~s** Galilean satellites ou moons

galimatias [galimatja] NM (= *propos*) gibberish (*NonC*), twaddle (*Brit*) (*NonC*); (= *écrit*) tedious nonsense (*NonC*), twaddle (*Brit*) (*NonC*)

galion [galjɔ̃] NM galleon

galipette* [galipɛt] NF (= *cabriole*) somersault; **~s** (*hum* = *ébats*) bedroom romps (*hum*); **faire des ~s** (*cabrioles*) to somersault, do somersaults; (*hum*: *ébats*) to have a romp

galle [gal] NF gall; **~ du chêne** oak apple → **noix**

Galles [gal] NFPL → **pays¹, prince**

gallican, e [ga(l)likã, an] ADJ, NM,F Gallican

gallicanisme [ga(l)likanism] NM Gallicanism

gallicisme [ga(l)lisism] NM (= *idiotisme*) French idiom; (*dans une langue étrangère* = *calque*) gallicism

gallinacé, e [galinase] [1] ADJ gallinaceous [2] NM gallinacean

gallique [galik] ADJ gallic

gallium [galjɔm] NM gallium

gallois, e [galwa, waz] [1] ADJ Welsh [2] NM [a] (*Ling*) Welsh [b] **Gallois** Welshman; **les Gallois** the Welsh [3] **Galloise** NF Welshwoman

gallon [galɔ̃] NM gallon; (*Can*) **~ canadien** ou **impérial** Imperial gallon (*4.545 litres*); **~ américain** US gallon (*3.785 litres*)

gallo-romain, e (*mpl* **gallo-romains**) [ga(l)loʀɔmɛ̃, ɛn] [1] ADJ Gallo-Roman [2] **Gallo-Romain(e)** NM,F Gallo-Roman

galoche [galɔʃ] NF [a] (= *sabot*) clog; (= *chaussure*) wooden-soled shoe → **menton** [b] (*Naut*) snatch block

galon [galɔ̃] NM [a] (*Couture*) braid (*NonC*), piece of braid; (*Mil*) stripe; **il a gagné ses ~s d'homme d'État/de professeur en faisant ...** he earned ou won his stripes as a statesman/as a teacher doing ...; **prendre du ~** to get promotion (*US*), get a promotion (*US*), move upstairs* [b] (*Can*) measuring tape, tape measure

galonné, e [galɔne] (*ptp de* **galonner**) [1] ADJ (*Mil*) [*manche, uniforme*] with stripes on [2] NM (*Mil*) **un ~*** a brass hat*

galonner [galɔne] ▸ conjug 1 ◂ VT (*Couture*) to trim with braid; **robe galonnée d'or** dress trimmed with gold braid

galop [galo] NM [a] (*gén*) gallop; **~ d'essai** (*lit*) trial gallop; (*fig*) trial run; **j'ai fait un ~ de quelques minutes** I galloped for a few minutes; **cheval au ~** galloping horse; **prendre le ~** ◊ **se mettre au ~** to break into a gallop; **mettre son cheval au ~** to put one's horse into a gallop; **partir au ~** [*cheval*] to set off at a gallop; [*personne*] to take off like a shot; **nous avons dîné au ~** we bolted down our dinner; **va chercher tes affaires au ~!** go and get your things at (*Brit*) ou on (*US*) the double! and make it snappy!*; **au petit ~** at a canter; **au grand ~** at full gallop; **au triple ~** [*partir, arriver*] at top speed; **elle a rappliqué au triple ~*** she came in like a shot* [b] (= *danse*) gallopade

galopade [galɔpad] NF (*Équitation*) hand gallop; (= *course précipitée*) stampede

galopant, e [galɔpɑ̃, ɑ̃t] ADJ (*inflation*) galloping, runaway; **démographie ~e** population explosion → **phtisie**

galoper [galɔpe] ▸ conjug 1 ◂ VI [*cheval*] to gallop; [*imagination*] to run wild, run riot; [*enfant*] to run; **~ ventre à terre** to gallop flat out*, go at full gallop; **les enfants galopent dans les couloirs** the children are charging ou haring* (*Brit*) along the corridors; **j'ai galopé toute la journée!*** I've been rushing around ou haring* (*Brit*) around all day!; **faire ~ qn** (= *presser qn*) to rush sb

galopin* [galɔpɛ̃] NM (= *polisson*) urchin, ragamuffin; **petit ~!** you little rascal! ou ragamuffin!

galuchat [galyʃa] NM shagreen

galure* [galyʀ], **galurin*** [galyʀɛ̃] NM (= *chapeau*) hat, headgear* (*NonC*)

galvanique [galvanik] ADJ galvanic

galvanisation [galvanizasjɔ̃] NF galvanization

galvaniser [galvanize] ▸ conjug 1 ◂ VT (*Tech*) to galvanize; (= *stimuler*) to galvanize (into action)

galvanisme [galvanism] NM (*Méd*) galvanism

galvanomètre [galvanɔmɛtʀ] NM galvanometer

galvanoplastie [galvanoplasti] NF (= *reproduction*) electrotyping, galvanoplasty; (= *dépôt*) electroplating

galvanoplastique [galvanoplastik] ADJ galvanoplastic

galvanotype [galvanotip] NM electrotype

galvanotypie [galvanotipi] NF electrotyping

galvaudage [galvodaʒ] NM [*nom, réputation*] tarnishing, sullying; [*talent*] prostituting

galvaudé, e [galvode] (*ptp de* **galvauder**) ADJ [*expression*] trite, hackneyed; [*mot*] overused

galvauder [galvode] ▸ conjug 1 ◂ [1] VT [+ *réputation, image*] to tarnish, sully; [+ *nom*] to bring into disrepute; [+ *talent*] to prostitute; [+ *expression*] to make trite ou hackneyed; [+ *mot*] to overuse, overwork [2] **se galvauder** VPR (= *s'avilir*) to demean o.s., lower o.s., compromise o.s.; [*expression*] to become hackneyed; [*mot*] to become trivialized (through overuse)

galvaudeux, -euse† [galvodø, øz] NM,F (= *vagabond*) tramp; (= *bon à rien*) good-for-nothing

gambade [gɑ̃bad] NF leap, caper; **faire des ~s** [*personne, enfant*] to leap (about), caper (about), prance about; [*animal*] to gambol, leap (about), frisk about

gambader [gɑ̃bade] ▸ conjug 1 ◂ VI [*animal*] to gambol, leap (about), frisk about; [*personne, enfant*] to leap (about), caper (about), prance about; [*esprit*] to flit ou jump from one idea to another; **~ de joie** to jump for joy

gambas [gɑ̃bas] NFPL Mediterranean prawns, gambas

gambe [gɑ̃b] NF → **viole**

gamberge* [gɑ̃bɛʀʒ] NF **la ~** (= *réflexion*) hard thinking; (= *soucis*) brooding

gamberger* [gɑ̃bɛʀʒe] ▸ conjug 3 ◂ VI (= *réfléchir*) to think hard; (= *se faire du souci*) to brood; **ça gamberge là-dedans!** your brain is really working overtime!*

gambette* [gɑ̃bɛt] [1] NF* (= *jambe*) leg; **jouer des ~s** to run away, take to one's heels [2] NM (*Zool*) redshank

Gambie [gɑ̃bi] NF **la ~** (= *pays*) The Gambia; (= *fleuve*) the Gambia

gambien, -ienne [gɑ̃bjɛ̃, jɛn] [1] ADJ Gambian [2] **Gambien(ne)** NM,F Gambian

gambiller* † [gɑ̃bije] ▸ conjug 1 ◂ VI to dance, jig*

gambit [gɑ̃bi] NM (*Échecs*) gambit

gamelle [gamɛl] NF [*soldat*] mess tin (*Brit*) ou kit (*US*); [*ouvrier, campeur*] billy-can, billy; [*chien*] bowl, dish; (*hum* = *assiette*) dish, plate; **(se) ramasser** ou **(se) prendre une ~*** to fall flat on one's face, come a cropper* (*Brit*)

gamète [gamɛt] NM gamete

gamin, e [gamɛ̃, in] [1] ADJ (= *espiègle*) mischievous, playful; (= *puéril*) childish [2] NM,F*

(= *enfant*) kid*; **quand j'étais ~** when I was a kid*; **~ des rues/de Paris** street/Paris urchin

gaminerie [gaminRi] NF (= *espièglerie*) playfulness (*NonC*); (= *puérilité*) childishness (*NonC*); (= *farce*) prank; **faire des ~s** to play (mischievous) pranks, be childish; **arrête tes ~s** stop being so childish

gamma [ga(m)ma] NM gamma → **rayon**

gammaglobulines [ga(m)maglɔbylin] NFPL gamma globulins

gamme [gam] NF a (= *série*) [*couleurs, articles*] range; [*sentiments*] gamut, range; **toute la ~**⁎ the whole lot; **produit d'entrée/de milieu de ~** bottom-of-the-range/middle-of-the-range product; **haut/bas de ~** upmarket/downmarket, top-of-the-range/bottom-of-the-range; **voiture haut/bas de ~** car at the top/lower end of the range, upmarket/downmarket car; **le très haut de ~ en chaînes hi-fi** the very top of the range in sound systems b (*Mus*) scale; **faire des ~s** to practise scales; (*fig*) **~ chromatique/ascendante/descendante** chromatic/rising/falling scale

gammée [game] ADJ f → **croix**

ganache [ganaʃ] NF a (*⁎† = imbécile*) **(vieille) ~** (old) fool, (old) duffer* b [*cheval*] lower jaw c (*Culin*) ganache

Gand [gɑ̃] N Ghent

gandin† [gɑ̃dɛ̃] NM (*péj*) dandy

gang [gɑ̃g] NM gang (*of crooks*)

Gange [gɑ̃ʒ] NM **le ~** the Ganges

gangétique [gɑ̃ʒetik] ADJ gangetic

ganglion [gɑ̃glijɔ̃] NM ganglion; **~ lymphatique** lymph node; **il a des ~s** he has swollen glands

ganglionnaire [gɑ̃glijɔnɛR] ADJ ganglionic

gangrène [gɑ̃gRɛn] NF a (*Méd*) gangrene; **avoir la ~** to have gangrene b (= *corruption*) corruption, canker (*fig*); **la ~ de la corruption** the cancer *ou* blight of corruption

gangrener [gɑ̃gRəne], **gangréner** [gɑ̃gRene] ▸conjug 5◂ VT a (*Méd*) to gangrene; **blessure qui se gangrène** wound which is going gangrenous; **membre gangrené** gangrenous limb b (= *corrompre*) to blight; **société gangrenée** society in decay; **la corruption gangrène tout le système** corruption is eating away at *ou* poisoning the entire system

gangreneux, **-euse** [gɑ̃gRənø, øz], **gangréneux**, **-euse** [gɑ̃gRenø, øz] ADJ gangrenous

gangster [gɑ̃gstɛR] NM (= *criminel*) gangster, mobster (*US*); (*péj* = *escroc*) shark, swindler, crook

gangstérisme [gɑ̃gsteRism] NM gangsterism

gangue [gɑ̃g] NF [*minerai, pierre*] gangue; (= *carcan*) strait jacket; **~ de boue** coating *ou* layer of mud

ganse [gɑ̃s] NF (*Habillement*) braid (*NonC*)

ganser [gɑ̃se] ▸conjug 1◂ VT to braid; **veste gansée de noir** jacket with black braiding

gant [gɑ̃] 1 NM a (*gén*) glove; **~s de caoutchouc** rubber gloves b (*loc*) **remettre les ~s**⁎ to take up boxing again; **cette robe lui va comme un ~** that dress fits her like a glove; **ton idée/ce rôle lui va comme un ~** your idea/this role suits him down to the ground; **je ne vais pas prendre des ~s avec lui** I'm not going to pull my punches with him; **tu ferais mieux de prendre des ~s avec lui** you'd better handle him with kid gloves; **il va falloir prendre des ~s pour lui annoncer la nouvelle** we'll have to break the news to him gently; (*lit, fig*) **jeter/relever le ~** to throw down/take up the gauntlet → **main, retourner** 2 COMP ► **gants de boxe** boxing gloves ► **gants de chirurgien** surgical gloves ► **gant de crin** massage glove ► **gant de cuisine** oven glove ► **gant de jardinage** gardening glove ► **gant de toilette** ≈ facecloth (*Brit*), (face) flannel (*Brit*), ≈ wash cloth (*US*)

gantelet [gɑ̃t(ə)lɛ] NM (*Mil, Sport*) gauntlet; (*Tech*) hand leather

ganter [gɑ̃te] ▸conjug 1◂ 1 VT [+ *main, personne*] to fit with gloves, put gloves on; **ganté de cuir** wearing leather gloves; **main gantée de cuir** leather-gloved hand 2 VI **~ du 7** to take (a) size 7 in gloves 3 **se ganter** VPR to put on one's gloves

ganterie [gɑ̃tRi] NF (= *usine*) glove factory; (= *magasin*) glove shop; (= *commerce*) glove trade; (= *industrie*) glove-making industry

gantier, -ière [gɑ̃tje, jɛR] NM,F glover

garage [gaRaʒ] 1 NM garage; **as-tu mis la voiture au ~?** have you put the car in the garage? *ou* away? 2 COMP ► **garage d'autobus** bus depot *ou* garage ► **garage d'avions** hangar ► **garage de *ou* à bicyclettes** bicycle shed ► **garage de canots** boathouse → **voie**

garagiste [gaRaʒist] NMF (= *propriétaire*) garage owner; (= *mécanicien*) garage mechanic; **le m'a dit que ...** the man at the garage *ou* the mechanic told me that ...; **emmener sa voiture chez le ~** to take one's car to the garage

garance [gaRɑ̃s] 1 NF (= *plante, teinture*) madder 2 ADJ INV madder(-coloured)

garant, e [gaRɑ̃, ɑ̃t] 1 NM,F (*gén*) (= *personne, état*) guarantor (**de** for); (= *chose*) guarantee (**de** of); **servir de ~ à qn** [*personne*] to stand surety for sb, act as guarantor for sb; [*honneur, parole*] to be sb's guarantee; **être ou se porter ~ de qch** (*Jur*) to be answerable *ou* responsible for sth; (*gén = assurer*) to vouch for sth, guarantee sth 2 NM (*Naut*) fall

garanti, e¹ [gaRɑ̃ti] (*ptp de* **garantir**) ADJ guaranteed; **~ étanche/trois ans** guaranteed waterproof/for three years; **~ pièces et main-d'œuvre** guaranteed for parts and labour; **~ pure laine** warranted *ou* guaranteed pure wool; **c'est ~ pour cinq ans** it carries a five-year guarantee, it is guaranteed for five years; **il va refuser, c'est ~ (sur facture)**⁎ he'll refuse — it's for sure *ou* it's a cert* (*Brit*), you can bet your life he'll refuse*; **c'est la migraine ~e**⁎ you're bound to get *ou* it's a surefire way of getting* a headache

garantie² [gaRɑ̃ti] 1 NF a (*Comm*) guarantee; **sous ~** under guarantee → **bon**², **contrat** b (= *assurance*) guarantee, guaranty (*SPÉC*); (= *gage*) security, surety; (= *protection*) safeguard; **ils nous ont donné leur ~ que ...** they gave us their guarantee that ...; **si on a la ~ qu'ils se conduiront bien** if we have a guarantee *ou* a firm undertaking (*Brit*) that they'll behave; **servir de ~** [*bijoux*] to act as a surety *ou* security *ou* guarantee; [*otages*] to be used as a security; [*honneur*] to be a guarantee; **donner des ~s** to give guarantees; **il faut prendre des ~s** we have to find sureties *ou* get guarantees; **cette entreprise présente toutes les ~s de sérieux** there is every indication that the firm is reliable; **c'est une ~ de succès** it's a guarantee of success; **c'est une ~ contre le chômage/l'inflation** it's a safeguard against unemployment/inflation c (= *caution*) **donner sa ~ à** to guarantee, stand security *ou* surety for, be guarantor for d [*police d'assurance*] cover (*NonC*) e (*loc*) **je vous dis ça, mais c'est sans ~** I can't vouch for what I'm telling you, I can't guarantee that what I'm telling you is right; **j'essaierai de le faire pour jeudi mais sans ~** I'll try and get it done for Thursday but I can't guarantee it *ou* I'm not making any promises; **ils ont bien voulu essayer de le faire, sans ~ de succès** they were quite willing to try and do it, but they couldn't guarantee success 2 COMP ► **garantie constitutionnelle** constitutional guarantee ► **garantie de l'emploi** job security ► **garantie d'exécution** performance bond ► **garanties individuelles** guarantees of individual liberties ► **garantie d'intérêt** guaranteed inter-

est ► **garantie de paiement** guarantee of payment

▼ **garantir** [gaRɑ̃tiR] ▸conjug 2◂ VT a (*gén = assurer*) to guarantee; [+ *emprunt*] to guarantee, secure; **~ que** to assure *ou* guarantee that; **se ~ contre** [+ *vol, incendie, risque*] to insure *ou* cover o.s. against; **je te garantis que ça ne se passera pas comme ça!**⁎ I can assure you things won't turn out like that!; **le poulet sera tendre, le boucher me l'a garanti** the chicken will be tender — the butcher assured me it would be; **je te garantis le fait** I can vouch for the fact b (= *protéger*) **~ qch de** to protect sth from; **se ~ les yeux (du soleil)** to protect one's eyes (from the sun); **se ~ contre la pollution/dévaluation** to guard against pollution/currency devaluation

garce⁎ [gaRs] NF (*péj*) (= *méchante*) bitch⁑; (= *dévergondée*) slut⁑, tart⁑ (*Brit*); **qu'est-ce que tu es ~!** you're such a bitch!⁑; **~ de tondeuse!** damned *ou* bloody! (*Brit*) mower!

garçon [gaRsɔ̃] 1 NM a (= *enfant, fils*) boy; **tu es un grand ~ maintenant** you're a big boy now; **traiter qn comme un petit ~** to treat sb like a child *ou* a little boy; **à côté d'eux, on est des petits ~s** compared with them we're only beginners; **cette fille est un ~ manqué** *ou* **un vrai ~** this girl is a real tomboy b (= *jeune homme*) young man; **il est beau** *ou* **joli ~** he's good looking, he's a good-looking guy* *ou* young man; (*hum*) **eh bien mon ~ ...** well my boy ...; **c'est un brave ~** he's a good sort *ou* a nice fellow; **ce ~ ira loin** that young man will go far → **mauvais** c (= *commis*) (shop) assistant; **~ boulanger/boucher** baker's/butcher's assistant; (= *jeune homme*) baker's/butcher's boy; **~ coiffeur** hairdresser's assistant *ou* junior d (= *serveur*) waiter e (*† = célibataire*) bachelor; **être/rester ~** to be/remain single *ou* a bachelor; **vivre en ~** to lead a bachelor's life → **enterrer, vie, vieux** 2 COMP ► **garçon d'ascenseur** lift (*Brit*) *ou* elevator (*US*) attendant; (= *jeune homme*) lift (*Brit*) *ou* elevator (*US*) boy ► **garçon de bureau**† office assistant; (= *jeune homme*) office boy ► **garçon de cabine** cabin boy ► **garçon de café** waiter ► **garçon de courses** messenger; (= *jeune homme*) errand boy ► **garçon d'écurie** stable boy *ou* lad (*Brit*) ► **garçon d'étage** boots *sg* (*Brit*), bellhop (*US*) ► **garçon de ferme** farm hand ► **garçon d'honneur** best man ► **garçon de laboratoire** laboratory assistant ► **garçon livreur** delivery man; (= *jeune homme*) delivery boy ► **garçon de recettes** bank messenger ► **garçon de salle** waiter

garçonne [gaRsɔn] ♦ **à la garçonne** LOC ADJ, LOC ADV **coupe** *ou* **coiffure à la ~** urchin cut; **être coiffée à la ~** to have an urchin cut

garçonnet [gaRsɔnɛ] NM small boy; **taille ~** boy's size; **rayon ~** boys' department

garçonnier, -ière¹ [gaRsɔnje, jɛR] ADJ [*fille*] tomboyish; **une fille à l'allure garçonnière** a tomboy-looking girl; **c'est un jeu trop ~ pour elle** it's too much of a boy's game for her

garçonnière² [gaRsɔnjɛR] NF bachelor flat (*Brit*) *ou* apartment (*US*)

Garde [gaRd] N **le lac de ~** Lake Garda

garde¹ [gaRd] 1 NF a (= *surveillance*) **on lui avait confié la ~ des bagages/des prisonniers** he had been put in charge of the luggage/the prisoners, he had been given the job of looking after *ou* of guarding the luggage/the prisoners; **il s'est chargé de la ~ des bagages/des prisonniers** he undertook to look after *ou* to guard *ou* to keep an eye on the luggage/the prisoners; **la ~ des frontières est assurée par ...** the task *ou* job of guarding the frontiers is carried out by ...; **confier qch/qn à la ~ de qn** to entrust sth/sb to sb's care, leave sth/sb in sb's care; **prendre en ~** [+ *enfant, animal*] to take into one's care, look after; **il nous ont laissé leur enfant en ~** they left their child in our care; **Dieu vous ait en sa (sainte) ~** (may) God be with you; **être sous la ~ de la police** to be under police guard; **être/mettre qn sous bonne ~** to be/put sb under guard

b (*Jur: après divorce*) custody; **elle a eu la ~ des enfants** she got *ou* was given (the) custody of the children; **~ alternée/conjointe** alternating/joint custody

c (= *veille*) [*soldat*] guard duty; [*infirmière*] ward duty; [*médecin*] duty period; **sa ~ a duré douze heures** (*soldat*) he was on guard duty for 12 hours; (*médecin, infirmier*) he was on duty for 12 hours; **assurer 15 ~s par mois** [*médecin*] to be on call *ou* on duty 15 times a month; **(être) de ~** [*infirmière, sentinelle*] (to be) on duty; [*médecin, pharmacien*] (to be) on call *ou* on duty; **pharmacie de ~** duty chemist (*Brit*) *ou* pharmacist (*US*); **quel est le médecin de ~?** who is the doctor on call? → **chien, monter**[1], **poste**[2]

d (= *conservation*) **être de bonne ~** [*aliment, boisson*] to keep well; **vin de ~** wine for laying down, wine that will benefit from being kept

e (= *groupe, escorte*) guard; **~ rapprochée** [*président*] personal bodyguard; **~ descendante/montante** old/relief guard → **corps, relever** *etc*

f (= *infirmière*) nurse; **~ de jour/de nuit** day/night nurse

g (*Boxe, Escrime*) guard; (*Escrime*) **~s** positions; **en ~!** on guard!; **se mettre en ~** to take one's guard; **avoir/tenir la ~ haute** to have/keep one's guard up; **fermer/ouvrir sa ~** to close/open one's guard; **baisser sa ~** (*lit*) to lower one's guard; (*fig*) to drop one's guard

h [*épée*] hilt, guard; (*lit*) **jusqu'à la ~** (up) to the hilt

i (*Typo*) **(page de) ~** flyleaf

j [*serrure*] **~s** wards

k (*Aut*) **~ au sol** ground clearance; **~ au toit** headroom; **laisser une ~ suffisante à la pédale** to allow enough play on the pedal; **~ d'embrayage** clutch linkage *ou* pedal play

l (*Cartes*) **avoir la ~ à cœur** to have a stop (*Brit*) *ou* covering card (*US*) in hearts

m (*loc*) **mettre qn en ~** to put sb on his guard, warn sb (**contre** against); **mise en ~** warning; (*littér*) **n'avoir ~ de faire** to take good care not to do, make sure one doesn't do; **faire bonne ~** to keep a close watch; **prendre ~ de** *ou* **à ne pas faire** to be careful *ou* take care not to do; **prends ~ de (ne pas) tomber** be careful *ou* take care you don't fall *ou* not to fall, mind you don't fall (*Brit*); **prends ~!** (*exhortation*) watch out!; (*menace*) watch it!*; **prends ~ à toi** watch yourself, take care; **prends ~ aux voitures** be careful of *ou* watch out for *ou* mind the cars; **sans prendre ~ au danger** without considering *ou* heeding the danger; **sans y prendre ~** without realizing it; **être/se mettre/se tenir sur ses ~s** to be/put o.s./stay on one's guard

2 COMP ► **garde d'enfants** (= *personne*) child minder (*Brit*), day-care worker (*US*); (= *activité*) child minding (*Brit*), day care (*US*) ► **garde d'honneur** guard of honour ► **garde impériale** Imperial Guard ► **garde judiciaire** legal surveillance (*of impounded property*) ► **garde juridique** legal liability ► **garde mobile** anti-riot police ► **garde municipale** *municipal guard* ► **garde pontificale** Papal Guard ► **garde républicaine** Republican Guard ► **garde à vue** ≈ police custody; **être mis** *ou* **placé en ~ à vue** ≈ to be kept in police custody, ≈ to be held for questioning

garde[2] [gaʀd] **1** NM **a** [*locaux, prisonnier*] guard; [*domaine, château*] warden (*Brit*), keeper (*US*); [*jardin public*] keeper **b** (*Mil* = *soldat*)

guardsman; (*Hist*) guard, guardsman; (= *sentinelle*) guard **2** COMP ► **garde champêtre** rural policeman ► **garde du corps** bodyguard ► **garde forestier** forest warden (*Brit*), (park) ranger (*US*), forester ► **garde impérial** imperial guard *ou* guardsman ► **garde maritime** coastguard ► **garde mobile** member of the anti-riot police ► **garde municipal** municipal guard *ou* guardsman ► **garde pontifical** papal guard *ou* guardsman ► **garde républicain** Republican guard *ou* guardsman, member of the Republican Guard ► **garde rouge** Red Guard ► **Garde des Sceaux** French Minister of Justice, ≈ Lord Chancellor (*Brit*), ≈ Attorney General (*US*); (*Hist*) ≈ Keeper of the Seals → **garder**

gardé, e [gaʀde] (*ptp de* **garder**) ADJ **passage à niveau ~/non ~** manned/unmanned level crossing; (*Alpinisme*) **cabane ~e/non ~e** hut with/without resident warden → **chasse**[1], **proportion**

garde-à-vous [gaʀdavu] NM INV (*Mil*) (= *action*) standing to attention (*NonC*); (= *cri*) order to stand to attention; **~ fixe!** attention!; **ils exécutèrent des ~ impeccables** they stood to attention faultlessly; (*Mil, fig*) **rester/se mettre au ~** to stand at/stand to attention

garde-barrière (*pl* **gardes-barrières**) [gaʀd(ə)baʀjeʀ] NMF level-crossing keeper

garde-boue [gaʀdəbu] NM INV mudguard (*Brit*), fender (*US*)

garde-chasse (*pl* **gardes-chasse(s)**) [gaʀdəʃas] NM gamekeeper

garde-chiourme (*pl* **gardes-chiourme**) [gaʀdəʃjuʀm] NM (*Hist*) warder (*of galley slaves*); (*fig*) martinet

garde-corps [gaʀdəkɔʀ] NM INV (*Naut*) lifeline, manrope; (= *rambarde*) (*en fer*) railing; (*en pierre*) parapet

garde-côte (*pl* **garde-côtes**) [gaʀdəkot] NM (= *navire*) (*Mil*) coastguard ship; (= *vedette garde-pêche*) fisheries protection launch *ou* craft; (*personne*) coastguard

garde-feu (*pl* **garde-feu(x)**) [gaʀdəfø] NM fireguard

garde-fou (*pl* **garde-fous**) [gaʀdəfu] NM (*en fer*) railing; (*en pierre*) parapet; (*fig*) safeguard

garde-frein (*pl* **gardes-frein(s)**) [gaʀdəfʀɛ̃] NM guard, brakeman

garde-frontière (*pl* **gardes-frontières**) [gaʀd(ə)-fʀɔ̃tjeʀ] NMF border guard

garde-magasin (*pl* **gardes-magasins**) [gaʀd(ə)-magazɛ̃] NM (*Mil*) ≈ quartermaster; (= *magasinier*) warehouseman

garde-malade (*pl* **gardes-malades**) [gaʀd(ə)-malad] NMF home nurse

garde-manger [gaʀd(ə)mɑ̃ʒe] NM INV (= *armoire*) meat safe (*Brit*), cooler (*US*); (= *pièce*) pantry, larder

garde-meuble (*pl* **garde-meubles**) [gaʀdə-mœbl] NM furniture depository (*Brit*); **mettre une armoire au ~** to put a wardrobe in storage *ou* in store (*Brit*)

gardénal® [gaʀdenal] NM phenobarbitone (*Brit*), phenobarbital (*US*), Luminal®

gardénia [gaʀdenja] NM gardenia

garde-pêche [gaʀdəpɛʃ] **1** NM (= *personne*) water bailiff (*Brit*), fish (and game) warden (*US*) **2** NM INV (= *frégate*) fisheries protection vessel; **vedette ~** fisheries protection launch *ou* craft

garde-port (*pl* **gardes-ports**) [gaʀdəpɔʀ] NM wharf master, harbour master

garder [gaʀde] ▶ conjug 1 ◀ **1** VT **a** (= *surveiller*) [+ *enfants, magasin*] to look after, mind; [+ *bestiaux*] to look after, guard; [+ *bagages*] to look after, watch over; [+ *trésor, prisonnier*] to guard, watch over; (= *défendre*)

[+ *frontière, passage, porte*] to guard; **le chien garde la maison** the dog guards the house; **~ des enfants** (*métier*) to be a child minder (*Brit*) *ou* day-care worker (*US*); **garde ma valise pendant que j'achète un livre** look after *ou* keep an eye on my suitcase while I buy a book; **on n'a pas gardé les cochons ensemble!*** you've got a nerve(, we hardly know each other)!*; **toutes les issues sont gardées** all the exits are guarded, a watch is being kept on all the exits; **une statue gardait l'entrée** a statue stood at the entrance *ou* guarded the entrance

b (= *ne pas quitter*) **~ la chambre** to stay in *ou* keep to one's room; **~ le lit** to stay in bed; **un rhume lui a fait ~ la chambre** he stayed in his room because of his cold, his cold kept him at home *ou* in his room

c [+ *denrées, marchandises, papiers*] to keep; **gardez la monnaie** keep the change; **ces fleurs ne gardent pas leur parfum** these flowers lose their scent; **il garde tout** he holds on to everything, he never throws anything out; **il ne peut rien ~** (*gén*) he can't keep anything; (= *il vomit*) he can't keep anything down

d (= *conserver sur soi*) [+ *vêtement*] to keep on; **gardez donc votre chapeau** do keep your hat on

e (= *retenir*) [+ *personne, employé, client*] to keep; [*police*] [+ *personne*] to detain; (*Jur*) **~ qn à vue** to keep sb in custody; **~ qn à déjeuner** to have sb stay for lunch; **~ un élève en retenue** to keep a pupil in, keep a pupil in detention; **il m'a gardé une heure au téléphone** he kept me on the phone for an hour

f (= *mettre de côté*) to keep, put aside *ou* to one side; (= *réserver*) [+ *place*] (*pendant absence*) to keep (**à, pour** for); (*avant l'arrivée d'une personne*) to save, keep (**à, pour** for); **je lui ai gardé une côtelette pour ce soir** I've kept *ou* saved a chop for him for tonight; **j'ai gardé de la soupe pour demain** I've kept *ou* saved *ou* I've put aside some soup for tomorrow; **~ le meilleur pour la fin** to keep the best till the end; **~ une poire pour la soif** to keep *ou* save something for a rainy day → **chien, dent**

g (= *maintenir*) to keep; **~ les yeux baissés/la tête haute** to keep one's eyes down/one's head up; **~ un chien enfermé/en laisse** to keep a dog shut in/on a leash

h (= *ne pas révéler*) to keep; **~ le secret** to keep the secret; **~ ses pensées pour soi** to keep one's thoughts to oneself; **gardez cela pour vous** keep it to yourself, keep it under your hat*; **gardez vos réflexions** *ou* **remarques pour vous** keep your comments to yourself

i (= *conserver*) [+ *souplesse, élasticité, fraîcheur*] to keep, retain; [+ *jeunesse, droits, facultés*] to retain; [+ *habitudes, apparences*] to keep up; [+ *emploi*] to keep; **il a gardé toutes ses facultés** *ou* **toute sa tête** he still has all his faculties, he's still in full possession of his faculties; **~ le jeûne** to observe *ou* keep the fast; **~ son calme** to keep *ou* remain calm; **~ la tête froide** to keep a cool head, keep one's head; **~ ses distances** to keep one's distance; **~ un bon souvenir de qch** to have happy memories of sth; **~ sa raison** to keep one's sanity; **~ le silence** to keep silent *ou* silence; **~ l'espoir** to keep hoping; **~ l'anonymat** to remain anonymous; **~ la ligne** to keep one's figure; **~ rancune à qn** to bear sb a grudge; **j'ai eu du mal à ~ mon sérieux** I had a job keeping *ou* to keep a straight face; **~ les idées claires** to keep a clear head

j (= *protéger*) **~ qn de l'erreur/de ses amis** to save sb from error/from his friends; **ça vous gardera du froid** it'll protect you from the cold; **Dieu** *ou* **le Ciel vous garde** God be with you; **la châsse qui garde ces reliques** the shrine which houses these relics

2 **se garder** VPR a [*denrées*] to keep; **ça se garde bien** it keeps well
b **se ~ de qch** (= *se défier de*) to beware of *ou* be wary of sth; (= *se protéger de*) to protect o.s. from sth, guard against sth; **gardez-vous de décisions trop promptes/de vos amis** beware *ou* be wary of hasty decisions/of your own friends; **se ~ de faire qch** to be careful not to do sth; **elle s'est bien gardée de le prévenir** she was very careful not to tell him, she carefully avoided telling him; **vous allez lui parler? — je m'en garderai bien!** are you going to speak to him? — that's one thing I won't do! *ou* that's the last thing I'd do!

garderie [gardəri] NF a **~ (d'enfants)** (*jeunes enfants*) day nursery (*Brit*), day-care center (*US*); (*Scol*) ≈ after-school club (*Brit*), ≈ after-school center (*US*) (*child-minding service operating outside school hours while parents are working*) b (= *étendue de bois*) forest ranger's appointed area

garde-robe (*pl* garde-robes) [gardərɔb] NF (= *habits*) wardrobe; **il faut que je renouvelle ma ~** I need a whole new wardrobe

gardeur, -euse [gardœr, øz] NM, F **~ de troupeaux** herdsman; **~ de vaches** cowherd; **~ de chèvres** goatherd; **~ de cochons** swineherd

garde-voie (*pl* gardes-voies) [gardəvwa] NM (*Rail*) line guard

gardian [gardjã] NM herdsman (*in the Camargue*)

gardien, -ienne [gardjɛ̃, jɛn] 1 NM,F a [*prisonnier*] guard; [*propriété, château*] warden (*Brit*), keeper (*US*); [*usine, locaux*] guard; [*hôtel*] attendant; [*cimetière*] caretaker, keeper; [*jardin public, zoo*] keeper; [*réserve naturelle*] warden; [*bovins*] cowherd ◆ (= *défenseur*) guardian, protector; **la constitution, gardienne des libertés** the constitution, protector *ou* guardian of freedom; (*fig*) **~ du temple** keeper of the flame; **les ~s de l'ordre public** the keepers of public order → **ange**
2 COMP ► **gardien de but** goalkeeper, goalie* ► **gardienne (d'enfants)** child minder (*Brit*), day-care worker (*US*) ► **gardien d'immeuble** caretaker (*of a block of flats*) (*Brit*), (apartment house) manager (*US*) ► **gardien de musée** museum attendant ► **gardien de nuit** night watchman ► **gardien de la paix** policeman, (police) constable, patrolman (*US*) ► **gardien de phare** lighthouse keeper ► **gardien (de prison)** prison officer *ou* warder (*Brit*) *ou* guard (*US*) ► **gardienne (de prison)** prison officer *ou* wardress (*Brit*) *ou* guard (*US*)

gardiennage [gardjɛnaʒ] NM [*immeuble*] caretaking; [*locaux*] guarding; [*port*] security; **~ électronique** electronic surveillance; **société de ~ et de surveillance** security company

gardon [gardɔ̃] NM roach → **frais¹**

gare¹ [gar] 1 NF (*Rail*) station; **~ d'arrivée/de départ** station of arrival/of departure; **~ de marchandises/de voyageurs** goods (*Brit*) *ou* freight (*US*)/passenger station; **le train entre/est en ~** the train is coming in/is in; **l'express de Dijon entre en ~ sur la voie 6** the express from Dijon is now approaching platform 6; (*péj*) **littérature/roman de ~** pulp literature/novel → **chef¹** 2 COMP ► **gare fluviale** canal *ou* river basin ► **gare de fret** cargo terminal ► **gare maritime** harbour station ► **gare routière** [*camions*] haulage depot; [*autocars*] coach (*Brit*) *ou* bus (*US*) station ► **gare de triage** marshalling yard

gare² [gar] EXCL (= *attention*) **~ à toi!** ◊ **~ à tes fesses!¹** (just) watch it!*; **~ à toi** *ou* **à tes fesses¹ si tu recommences!** you'll be in for it if you do that again!*; **~ au premier qui bou-**

---

ge! whoever makes the first move will be in trouble!, the first one to move will be for it!* (*Brit*); **et fais ce que je dis, sinon ~!** and do what I say, or else!*; **~ à ne pas recommencer!** just make sure you don't do it again!; **la porte est basse, ~ à ta tête** it's a low door so (be) careful you don't bang your head *ou* mind (*Brit*) (you don't bang) your head; **~ aux conséquences/à ce type** beware of the consequences/of him → **crier**

garenne [garɛn] 1 NF rabbit warren → **lapin** 2 NM wild rabbit

garer [gare] ▸conjug 1◂ 1 VT [+ *véhicule*] to park; [+ *train*] to put into a siding; [+ *embarcation*] to dock; [+ *récolte*] (put into) store 2 **se garer** VPR a [*automobiliste*] to park b (= *se ranger de côté*) [*véhicule, automobiliste*] to draw into the side, pull over; [*piéton*] to move aside, get out of the way c* (= *éviter*) **se ~ de qch/qn** to avoid sth/sb, steer clear of sth/sb

Gargantua [gargɑ̃tɥa] NM Gargantua; **c'est un ~** he has a gargantuan *ou* gigantic appetite

gargantuesque [gargɑ̃tɥɛsk] ADJ [*appétit, repas*] gargantuan, gigantic

gargariser (se) [gargarize] ▸conjug 1◂ VPR to gargle; (*péj* = *se vanter de*) **se gargariser de** to crow over *ou* about; **se gargariser de grands mots** to revel in big words

gargarisme [gargarism] NM gargle; **se faire un ~** to gargle

gargote [gargɔt] NF (*péj*) cheap restaurant *ou* eating-house, greasy spoon*, greasy Joe's* (*Brit*)

gargotier, -ière [gargɔtje, jɛr] NM,F (= *aubergiste*) owner of a greasy spoon*

gargouille [garguj] NF (*Archit*) gargoyle; (*Constr*) waterspout

gargouillement [gargujmɑ̃] NM = **gargouillis**

gargouiller [garguje] ▸conjug 1◂ VI [*eau*] to gurgle; [*intestin*] to rumble

gargouillis [garguji] NM (*gén pl*) [*eau*] gurgling (*NonC*); [*intestin*] rumbling (*NonC*); **faire des ~** [*eau*] to gurgle; [*intestin*] to rumble

gargoulette [gargulɛt] NF (= *vase*) earthenware water jug

garnement [garnəmɑ̃] NM (= *gamin*) (young) imp; (= *adolescent*) tearaway (*Brit*), hellion (*US*); **petit ~!** you little rascal!

garni, e [garni] (*ptp de* **garnir**) 1 ADJ a (= *rempli*) **bien ~** [*réfrigérateur, bibliothèque*] well-stocked; [*bourse*] well-lined; [+ *portefeuille*] well-filled, well-lined; **il a encore une chevelure bien ~e** he has still got a good head of hair b [*plat, viande*] (*de légumes*) served with vegetables; (*de frites*) served with French fries *ou* chips (*Brit*); **cette entrecôte est bien ~e** there's a generous helping of French fries *ou* chips (*Brit*) with this steak → **bouquet¹, choucroute** c† (= *meublé*) [*chambre*] furnished 2 NM† furnished accommodation *ou* rooms (*for renting*)

garnir [garnir] ▸conjug 2◂ 1 VT a (= *protéger, équiper*) **~ de** to fit out with; **~ une porte d'acier** to fit *ou* reinforce a door with steel plate; **~ une canne d'un embout** to put a tip on the end of a walking stick; **~ une muraille de canons** to range cannons along a wall; **~ une boîte de tissu** to line a box with material; **~ un mur de pointes** to arm a wall with spikes, set spikes along a wall; **mur garni de canons/pointes** wall bristling with cannons/spikes
b [*chose*] (= *couvrir*) **l'acier qui garnit la porte** the steel plate covering the door; **les canons qui garnissent la muraille** the cannons lining the wall *ou* ranged along the wall; **des pointes garnissent le mur** there are spikes set in the wall; **le cuir qui garnit la poignée** the leather covering the handle; **coffret garni de velours** casket lined with velvet, velvet-lined

---

casket c (= *approvisionner*) [+ *boîte, caisse*] to fill (**de** with); [+ *réfrigérateur*] to stock (**de** with); [+ *chaudière*] to stoke (**de** with); [+ *hameçon*] to bait (**de** with); **le cuisinier garnissait les plats de charcuterie** the cook was setting out *ou* putting (slices of) cold meat on the plates; **~ de livres une bibliothèque** to stock *ou* fill (the shelves of) a library with books; (*Mil*) **~ les remparts** to garrison the ramparts
d (= *remplir*) [+ *boîte*] to fill; (= *recouvrir*) [+ *surface, rayon*] to cover, fill; **une foule dense garnissait les trottoirs** a dense crowd covered *ou* packed the pavements; **les chocolats qui garnissaient la boîte** the chocolates which filled the box; **boîte garnie de chocolats** box full of chocolates; **plats garnis de tranches de viande** plates filled with *ou* full of slices of meat
e [+ *siège*] (= *canner*) to cane; (= *rembourrer*) to pad
f (= *enjoliver*) [+ *vêtement*] to trim; [+ *étagère*] to decorate; [+ *aliment*] to garnish (**de** with); **~ une jupe d'un volant** to trim a skirt with a frill; **~ une table de fleurs** to decorate a table with flowers; **les bibelots qui garnissent la cheminée** the trinkets which decorate the mantelpiece; **des plats joliment garnis de charcuterie** plates nicely laid out with cold meat; **des côtelettes garnies de cresson/de mayonnaise** chops garnished with cress/with mayonnaise
2 **se garnir** VPR [*salle, pièce*] to fill up (**de** with); **la salle commençait à se ~** the room was beginning to fill up

garnison [garnizɔ̃] NF (= *troupes*) garrison; **(ville de) ~** garrison town; **vie de ~** garrison life; **être en ~ à** ◊ **tenir ~ à** to be stationed *ou* garrisoned at

garniture [garnityr] 1 NF a (= *décoration*) [*robe, chapeau*] trimming (*NonC*); [*table*] set of table linen; [*coffret*] lining; (*Aut*) **~ intérieure** upholstery, interior trim
b (*Culin*) (= *légumes*) vegetables; (= *sauce à vol-au-vent*) filling; **servi avec ~** served with vegetables, vegetables included; **pour la ~, vous avez des carottes ou des pois** you have a choice of carrots or peas as a vegetable
c (*Typo*) furniture
d (*Tech* = *protection*) [*chaudière*] lagging (*NonC*); [*boîte*] covering (*NonC*); **avec ~ de caoutchouc/cuir** with rubber/leather fittings *ou* fitments; **~ d'embrayage/de frein** clutch/brake lining; **changer les ~s de freins** to reline the brakes, change the brake linings
2 COMP ► **garniture de cheminée** mantelpiece ornaments ► **garniture de foyer** (set of) fire irons ► **garniture de lit** (set of) bed linen ► **garniture périodique** sanitary towel (*Brit*) *ou* napkin (*US*) ► **garniture de toilette** toilet set

Garonne [garɔn] NF **la ~** the Garonne

garrigue [garig] NF garrigue, scrubland

garrot [garo] NM [*cheval*] withers; (*Méd*) tourniquet; (= *supplice*) garrotte; **poser un ~** to apply a tourniquet (**à qn** to sb)

garrotter [garɔte] ▸conjug 1◂ VT (= *attacher*) to tie up; († = *censurer*) [+ *presse*] to gag

gars* [ga] NM a (= *enfant, fils*) boy, lad (*Brit*); **les petits ~ du quartier** the local youths; **dis-moi mon ~** tell me son *ou* sonny* (*Brit*) b (= *type*) guy*, bloke* (*Brit*); **un drôle de ~** an odd guy *ou* customer; **allons-y, les ~!** come on, guys* *ou* lads* (*Brit*)!

Gascogne [gaskɔɲ] NF Gascony → **golfe**

gascon, -onne [gaskɔ̃, ɔn] 1 ADJ Gascon 2 NM (*Ling*) Gascon 3 **Gascon(ne)** NM,F Gascon → **promesse**

gasconnade [gaskɔnad] NF (*littér* = *vantardise*) boasting (*NonC*), bragging (*NonC*)

gasoil, gas-oil [gazwal, gazɔjl] NM diesel oil

gaspacho [gaspatʃo] NM gazpacho

gaspillage [gaspijaʒ] NM (= *action*) wasting; (= *résultat*) waste; **quel ~!** what a waste!; **un immense ~ des ressources naturelles** an enormous waste of natural resources

gaspiller [gaspije] ▸ conjug 1 ◂ VT [+ *eau, nourriture, temps, ressources*] to waste; [+ *fortune, argent, dons, talent*] to waste, squander; **il gaspille inutilement ses forces/son énergie** he's wasting his strength/energy; **qu'est-ce que tu gaspilles!** you're so wasteful!

gaspilleur, -euse [gaspijœʀ, øz] [1] ADJ wasteful [2] NM,F [*eau, nourriture, temps, dons*] waster; [*fortune*] squanderer; **quel ~** he's so wasteful

gastéropode [gasteʀɔpɔd] NM gastropod, gasteropod; **~s** Gastropoda (SPÉC)

gastralgie [gastʀalʒi] NF stomach pains, gastralgia (SPÉC)

gastralgique [gastʀalʒik] ADJ gastralgic

gastrine [gastʀin] NF gastrin

gastrique [gastʀik] ADJ gastric → **embarras**

gastrite [gastʀit] NF gastritis

gastro-duodénal, e (*mpl* **-aux**) [gastʀodɥɔdenal, o] ADJ gastro-duodenal

gastroentérite [gastʀoɑ̃teʀit] NF gastroenteritis (NonC)

gastroentérologie [gastʀoɑ̃teʀɔlɔʒi] NF gastroenterology

gastroentérologue [gastʀoɑ̃teʀɔlɔg] NMF gastroenterologist

gastro-intestinal, e (*mpl* **-aux**) [gastʀoɛ̃testinal, o] ADJ gastrointestinal

gastronome [gastʀɔnɔm] NMF gourmet, gastronome

gastronomie [gastʀɔnɔmi] NF gastronomy

gastronomique [gastʀɔnɔmik] ADJ gastronomic → **menu¹, restaurant**

gâté, e [gate] (*ptp de* **gâter**) ADJ [*enfant, fruit*] spoilt; **dent ~e** bad tooth; **avoir les dents ~es** to have bad teeth

gâteau (*pl* **gâteaux**) [gato] [1] NM [a] (= *pâtisserie*) (au caramel) gateau; (Helv = *tarte*) tart; **~ d'anniversaire/aux amandes** birthday/almond cake; **~x (à) apéritif** (small) savoury biscuits, appetizers; **~x secs** biscuits (Brit), cookies (US); **~ de semoule/de riz** semolina/rice pudding → **petit** [b]* (= *butin, héritage*) loot*; **se partager le ~** to share out the loot*; **vouloir sa part du ~** to want one's share of the loot* *ou* a fair share of the cake *ou* a piece of the pie* (US) [c] **c'est du ~*** it's a piece of cake* *ou* a doddle* (Brit), it's a snap* (US); **pour lui, c'est du ~*** it's a piece of cake for him*, that's pie* to him (US); **c'est pas du ~*** it's no picnic* [d] (*de plâtre*) cake; **~ de miel** *ou* **de cire** honeycomb [2] ADJ INV* (= *indulgent*) soft; **c'est un papa ~** he's a real softie* of a dad

gâter [gate] ▸ conjug 1 ◂ [1] VT [a] (= *abîmer*) [+ *paysage, visage, plaisir, goût*] to ruin, spoil; [+ *esprit, jugement*] to have a harmful effect on; **la chaleur a gâté la viande** the heat has made the meat go bad *ou* go off (Brit); **tu vas te ~ les dents** you'll ruin your teeth; **et, ce qui ne gâte rien, elle est jolie** and she's pretty to boot, and she's pretty, which is an added bonus *ou* is even better [b] (= *choyer*) [+ *enfant*] to spoil; **nous avons été gâtés cette année, il a fait très beau** we've been really lucky *ou* we've been spoilt this year — the weather's been lovely; (*iro*) **il pleut, on est gâté!** just our luck! — it's raining!; **il n'est pas gâté par la nature** he hasn't been blessed by nature; **la vie ne l'a pas gâté** life hasn't been very kind to him

[2] **se gâter** VPR [*viande*] to go bad, go off (Brit); [*fruit*] to go bad; [*temps*] to change (for the worse), take a turn for the worse; * [*ambiance, relations*] to take a turn for the worse; **le temps va se ~** the weather's going to

change for the worse *ou* going to break; **ça commence** *ou* **les choses commencent à se ~ (entre eux)** things are beginning to go wrong (between them); **mon père vient de rentrer, ça va se ~!** my father has just come in and there's going to be trouble! *ou* things are going to turn nasty!

gâterie [gatʀi] NF little treat; **je me suis payé une petite ~** (*objet*) I've treated myself to a little something, I've bought myself a little present; (*sucrerie*) I've bought myself a little treat

gâte-sauce (*pl* **gâte-sauces**) [gatsos] NM (= *apprenti*) kitchen boy; (*péj*) bad cook

gâteux, -euse [gatø, øz] [1] ADJ (= *sénile*) [*vieillard*] senile, gaga*, doddering; **il l'aime tellement qu'il en est ~** he's really quite besotted with her, he's dotty* (Brit) about her; **son petit-fils l'a rendu ~** he's gone soft* over his grandson [2] NM (*vieux*) **~** (= *sénile*) dotard, doddering old man; (*péj* = *radoteur, imbécile*) silly old duffer* [3] NF (**vieille**) **gâteuse** (= *sénile*) doddering old woman; (*péj*) silly old bag* *ou* woman

gâtifier* [gatifje] ▸ conjug 1 ◂ VI to go soft in the head*

gâtisme [gatism] NM [*vieillard*] senility; [*personne stupide*] idiocy, stupidity

GATT [gat] NM (ABRÉV = **General Agreement on Tariffs and Trade**) GATT

gauche¹ [goʃ] [1] ADJ (*après nom*) [*bras, chaussure, côté, rive*] left; **du côté ~** on the left(-hand) side; **habiter au troisième ~** to live on the third floor on the left → **arme, lever, main, marier**

[2] NM (*Boxe*) (= *coup*) left; (= *poing*) **direct du ~** straight left; **crochet du ~** left hook

[3] NF [a] (= *côté*) **la ~** the left (side), the left-hand side; **à ~** on the left; (*direction*) to the left; **à ma/sa ~** on my/his left, on my/his left-hand side; **le tiroir/chemin de ~** the left-hand drawer/path; **rouler à ~** *ou* **sur la ~** to drive on the left; **de ~ à droite** from left to right; **mettre de l'argent à ~†*** to put money aside (on the quiet) → **conduite, jusque**; *pour autres locutions voir* **droit¹**

[b] (*Pol*) **la ~** the left; **la ~ caviar** champagne socialists; **les ~s** the parties of the left; **homme de ~** man of the left, left-winger; **candidat/idées de ~** left-wing candidate/ideas; **elle est très à ~** she's very left-wing

gauche² [goʃ] ADJ [a] (= *maladroit*) [*personne, style, geste*] awkward, clumsy; (= *emprunté*) [*air, manière*] awkward, gauche [b] (= *tordu*) [*planche, règle*] warped; (*Math* = *courbe*) [*surface*] skew

gauchement [goʃmɑ̃] ADV clumsily, awkwardly

gaucher, -ère [goʃe, ɛʀ] [1] ADJ left-handed [2] NM,F left-handed person; (*Sport*) left-hander; **~ contrarié** left-handed person forced to use his right hand

gaucherie [goʃʀi] NF [*allure*] awkwardness (NonC); [*action, expression*] clumsiness (NonC); (= *acte*) awkward *ou* clumsy behaviour (NonC); (*Méd*) sinistral tendency; **une ~ de style** a clumsy turn of phrase

gauchir [goʃiʀ] ▸ conjug 2 ◂ [1] VT [a] (*Aviat, Menuiserie*) to warp [b] [+ *idée, fait*] to distort, misrepresent; [+ *esprit*] to warp [c] (*Pol*) **~ sa position** to swing further to the left; **elle a gauchi son discours** she's become more left-wing in what she says [2] VI, **se gauchir** VPR (= *se déformer*) to warp

gauchisant, e [goʃizɑ̃, ɑ̃t] ADJ [*auteur*] with left-wing *ou* leftist tendencies; [*théorie*] with a left-wing *ou* leftish bias

gauchisme [goʃism] NM leftism

gauchissement [goʃismɑ̃] NM [a] (*Aviat, Menuiserie*) warping [b] [*idée, fait*] distortion, misrepresentation; [*esprit*] warping

gauchiste [goʃist] [1] ADJ leftist (*épith*) [2] NMF leftist

gaucho¹* [goʃo] (*Pol*) [1] ADJ left-wing (*épith*) [2] NMF lefty*, left-winger

gaucho² [go(t)ʃo] NM (= *gardien de troupeaux*) gaucho

gaudriole* [godʀijɔl] NF [a] (= *débauche*) **il aime la ~** he likes a bit of slap and tickle* [b] (= *propos*) broad *ou* blue* joke

gaufrage [gofʀaʒ] NM [*papier, cuir*] (*en relief*) embossing (NonC); (*en creux*) figuring (NonC); [*tissu*] goffering (NonC)

gaufre [gofʀ] NF (*Culin*) waffle; (*en cire*) honeycomb → **moule¹**

gaufrer [gofʀe] ▸ conjug 1 ◂ VT [+ *papier, cuir*] (*en relief*) to emboss; (*en creux*) to figure; [+ *tissu*] to goffer; **papier gaufré** embossed paper → **fer**

gaufrerie [gofʀəʀi] NF (*Can*) waffle shop

gaufrette [gofʀɛt] NF wafer

gaufrier [gofʀije] NM waffle iron

gaufrure [gofʀyʀ] NF [*papier, cuir*] (*en relief*) embossing (NonC), embossed design; (*en creux*) figuring (NonC); [*papier*] goffering (NonC)

Gaule [gol] NF Gaul

gaule [gol] NF (= *perche*) (long) pole; (*Pêche*) fishing rod

gauler [gole] ▸ conjug 1 ◂ VT [+ *arbre*] to beat (using a long pole to bring down the fruit or nuts); [+ *fruits, noix*] to bring down, shake down (with a pole); **se faire ~*** to get caught; (*par la police*) to get nabbed* *ou* nicked* (Brit)

gaullien, -ienne [goljɛ̃, jɛn] ADJ de Gaullian

gaullisme [golism] NM Gaullism

gaulliste [golist] ADJ, NMF Gaullist

gaulois, e [golwa, waz] [1] ADJ [a] (= *de Gaule*) Gallic; (*hum* = *français*) French [b] (= *grivois*) bawdy; **esprit ~** (broad *ou* bawdy) Gallic humour [2] NM (*Ling*) Gaulish [3] **Gaulois(e)** NM,F Gaul → **moustache** [4] **gauloise** ♦ **Gauloise** ® NF (= *cigarette*) Gauloise

gauloisement [golwazmɑ̃] ADV bawdily

gauloiserie [golwazʀi] NF (= *propos*) broad *ou* bawdy story (*ou* joke); (= *caractère grivois*) bawdiness

gauss [gos] NM (*Phys*) gauss

gausser (se) [gose] ▸ conjug 1 ◂ VPR (*littér* = *se moquer*) to laugh (and make fun), mock; **vous vous gaussez!** you jest!; **se gausser de** to deride, make mock of (*littér*), poke fun at

gavage [gavaʒ] NM (*Agr*) force-feeding; (*Méd*) forced feeding, gavage

gave [gav] NM mountain stream (*in the Pyrenees*)

gaver [gave] ▸ conjug 1 ◂ [1] VT [+ *animal*] to force-feed; [+ *personne*] to fill up (**de** with); **je suis gavé!** I'm full (up)!, I'm full to bursting!*; **on les gave de connaissances inutiles** they cram their heads with useless knowledge; **on nous gave de séries télévisées/de publicité** we're fed a non-stop diet of television serials/of advertisements [2] **se gaver** VPR **se ~ de** [+ *nourriture*] to stuff o.s. with, gorge o.s. on; [+ *romans*] to devour; **il se gave de films** he's a real film buff* *ou* addict; **si tu te gaves maintenant, tu ne pourras plus rien manger au moment du dîner** if you go stuffing yourself* *ou* filling yourself up now, you won't be able to eat anything at dinner time

gaveur, -euse [gavœʀ, øz] [1] NM,F (= *personne*) force-feeder [2] **gaveuse** NF (= *machine*) automatic force-feeder

gavial [gavjal] NM gavial, g(h)arial

gavotte [gavɔt] NF gavotte

gavroche [gavʀɔʃ] NM street urchin (*in Paris*)

gay* [gɛ] ADJ, NM gay

gaz [gaz] [1] NM INV [a] (*Chim*) gas; [*boisson*] fizz; **le ~ (domestique)** (domestic) gas (NonC); (*Mil*) **les ~** gas; **l'employé du ~** the gasman; **se chauffer au ~** to have gas(-fired) heating;

s'éclairer au ~ to have ou use gas lighting; **faire la cuisine au ~** to cook with gas; **vous avez le ~ ?** do you have gas?, are you on gas? (Brit); **il s'est suicidé au ~** he gassed himself; **suicide au ~** (suicide by) gassing; **mettre les ~*** (Aut) to put one's foot down* (Brit), step on the gas* (US); (Aviat) to throttle up; **rouler (à) pleins ~*** to drive flat out*; (Aviat) **remettre les ~** to pull ou nose up; **on prend une bière mais vite fait sur le ~*** let's have a beer but a quick one* ou a quickie* → **bec, chambre, eau**

[b] (euph = pet) wind (NonC); **avoir des ~** to have wind

[2] COMP ► **gaz d'admission** (Aut) air-fuel mixture ► **gaz asphyxiant** poison gas ► **gaz en bouteille** bottled gas ► **gaz carbonique** carbon dioxide ► **gaz de combat** poison gas (for use in warfare) ► **gaz d'échappement** exhaust gas ► **gaz d'éclairage†** = gaz de ville ► **gaz hilarant** laughing gas ► **gaz des houillères** firedamp (NonC) ► **gaz lacrymogène** teargas ► **gaz des marais** marsh gas ► **gaz moutarde** (Mil) mustard gas ► **gaz naturel** natural gas ► **gaz neurotoxique** nerve gas ► **gaz parfait** perfect ou ideal gas ► **gaz de pétrole liquéfié** liquid petroleum gas ► **gaz poivre** pepper gas ► **gaz propulseur** propellant ► **gaz rare** rare gas ► **gaz sulfureux** sulphur dioxide ► **gaz de ville** town gas

Gaza [gaza] N **la bande** ou **le territoire de ~** the Gaza Strip

gazage [gazaʒ] NM (Mil, Tex) gassing

gaze [gaz] NF gauze; **compresse de ~** gauze (compress)

gazé, e [gaze] (ptp de **gazer**) [1] ADJ (Mil) gassed [2] NM,F gas victim; **les ~s de 14-18** the (poison) gas victims of the 1914-18 war

gazéification [gazeifikasjɔ̃] NF (Chim) gasification; [eau minérale] aeration

gazéifier [gazeifje] ▸ conjug 7 ◂ VT (Chim) to gasify; [+ eau minérale] to aerate; **eau minérale gazéifiée** sparkling mineral water

gazelle [gazɛl] NF gazelle; **c'est une vraie ~ !** she's so graceful and lithe! → **corne**

gazer [gaze] ▸ conjug 1 ◂ [1] VI (* = aller, marcher) **ça gaze ?** (affaires, santé) how's things?*, how goes it?*; (travail) how goes it?*, how's it going?*; **ça gaze avec ta belle-mère ?** how's it going with your mother-in-law?*; **ça va tu are you getting on OK with your mother-in-law?*; **ça a/ça n'a pas gazé ?** did it/didn't it go OK?*; **ça ne gaze pas fort** (santé) I'm not feeling so ou too great*; (affaires) things aren't going too well; **il y a quelque chose qui ne gaze pas** there's something slightly fishy about it, there's something wrong somewhere [2] VT (Mil, Tex) to gas

gazetier, -ière [gaz(ə)tje, jɛʀ] NM,F (†† ou hum) journalist

gazette [gazɛt] NF (††, hum, littér) newspaper; (hum) **c'est dans la ~ locale** it's in the local rag; **c'est une vraie ~** he's a mine of information about the latest (local) gossip; **faire la ~** to give a rundown* (de on)

gazeux, -euse [gazø, øz] ADJ (Chim) gaseous; **boisson gazeuse** fizzy drink (Brit), soda (US), pop (US) → **eau**

gazier, -ière [gazje, jɛʀ] [1] ADJ gas (épith) [2] NM (= employé) gasman; (*† = type) guy*, geezer* (Brit)

gazinière [gazinjɛʀ] NF gas cooker

gazoduc [gazodyk] NM gas main, gas pipeline

gazogène [gazɔʒɛn] NM gas generator

gazole [gazɔl] NM diesel oil

gazoline [gazɔlin] NF gasoline, gasolene

gazomètre [gazɔmɛtʀ] NM gasholder, gasometer

gazon [gazɔ̃] NM (= pelouse) lawn; (= herbe) **le**

~ turf (NonC), grass (NonC); **motte de ~** turf, sod; (pelouse) **~ anglais** well-kept lawn

gazonné, e [gazɔne] (ptp de **gazonner**) ADJ grassy

gazonner [gazɔne] ▸ conjug 1 ◂ VT [+ talus, terrain] to plant with grass, turf

gazouillement [gazujmɑ̃] NM [oiseau] chirping (NonC); [ruisseau] babbling (NonC); [bébé] gurgling (NonC); **j'entendais le ~ des oiseaux/du bébé** I could hear the birds chirping/the baby gurgling; **bercé par le ~ du ruisseau** lulled by the babbling brook

gazouiller [gazuje] ▸ conjug 1 ◂ VI [oiseau] to chirp, warble; [ruisseau] to babble; [bébé] to babble, gurgle

gazouilleur, -euse [gazujœʀ, øz] ADJ [oiseau] chirping, warbling; [ruisseau] babbling; [bébé] babbling, gurgling

gazouillis [gazuji] NM [oiseau] chirping, warbling; [ruisseau] babbling; [bébé] babbling, gurgling

GB [ʒebe] (ABRÉV = **Grande-Bretagne**) GB

gdb* [ʒedebe] NF (ABRÉV = **gueule de bois**) **avoir la ~** to have a hangover

GDF [ʒedeef] NM (ABRÉV = **Gaz de France**) French gas company

geai [ʒɛ] NM jay

géant, e [ʒeɑ̃, ɑ̃t] [1] ADJ [objet] gigantic; [animal, plante] gigantic, giant (épith); [paquet, carton] giant-size (épith), giant (épith); [étoile, écran] giant (épith); **c'est ~ !*** it's great!* ou magic!* [2] NM (= homme, firme) giant; (Pol) giant power; **les ~s de la route** the great cycling champions → **pas'** [3] **géante** NF (= femme) giantess; (= étoile) giant star; **~e rouge** red giant

géhenne [ʒeɛn] NF (Bible = enfer) Gehenna

geignard, e* [ʒeɲaʀ, aʀd] [1] ADJ [personne] moaning; [voix] whingeing, whining; [musique] whining [2] NM,F moaner

geignement [ʒeɲmɑ̃] NM moaning (NonC)

geindre [ʒɛ̃dʀ] ▸ conjug 52 ◂ VI [a] (= gémir) to groan, moan (de with) [b]* (= pleurnicher) to moan; **il geint tout le temps** he never stops moaning ou complaining [c] (littér) [vent, instrument de musique] to moan; [parquet] to creak; **le vent faisait ~ les peupliers/le gréement** the poplars/the rigging groaned ou moaned in the wind

geisha [geʃa] NF geisha (girl)

gel [ʒɛl] NM [a] (= temps) frost; **un jour de ~** one frosty day; **plantes tuées par le ~** plants killed by (the) frost [b] (= glace) frost; **« craint le ~ »** "keep away from extreme cold" [c] [crédits, licenciements] freeze; **~ des terres** set-aside; **protester contre le ~ des salaires** to protest against the wage freeze; **ils réclament le ~ du programme nucléaire** they are calling for a freeze on the nuclear programme [d] (= substance) gel; **~ (de) douche** shower gel; **~ coiffant** ou **structurant** hair (styling) gel

gélatine [ʒelatin] NF gelatine

gélatineux, -euse [ʒelatinø, øz] ADJ jelly-like, gelatinous

gelé, e¹ [ʒ(ə)le] (ptp de **geler**) ADJ [a] [eau, rivière] frozen, iced-over; [sol, tuyau] frozen [b] [membre] frostbitten; [plante] nipped ou damaged by frost; **ils sont morts ~s** they froze to death, they died of exposure [c] (= très froid) [eau] ice-cold; **j'ai les mains ~es** my hands are frozen ou freezing; **je suis ~** I'm frozen (stiff) ou freezing [d] [crédits, prix, projet] frozen; [négociations] suspended

gelée² [ʒ(ə)le] NF [a] (= gel) frost; **~ blanche** white frost, hoarfrost [b] (Culin) [fruits, viande, volaille] jelly; **poulet/œuf en ~** chicken/egg in aspic ou jelly; **~ de framboises** raspberry jelly (Brit) ou Jell-O® (US) ou jello (US); **~ royale** royal jelly

geler [ʒ(ə)le] ▸ conjug 5 ◂ [1] VT [a] [+ eau, rivière] to freeze (over); [+ buée] to turn to ice; [+ sol, tuyau] to freeze [b] (= endommager) **le froid a gelé les bourgeons** the buds were nipped ou damaged by frost; **le froid lui a gelé les mains** he got frostbite in both hands [c] [+ prix, crédits, salaires, projet] to freeze; [+ terres] to set aside; [+ négociations] to suspend [d] (= mettre mal à l'aise) [+ assistance] to chill, send a chill through

[2] **se geler*** VPR (= avoir froid) to freeze; **on se gèle ici** we're ou it's freezing here; **on se les gèle*** it's damned* ou bloody* (Brit) freezing, it's brass monkey weather* (Brit); **vous allez vous ~, à l'attendre** you'll get frozen stiff waiting for him

[3] VI [a] [eau, lac] to freeze (over), ice over; [sol, linge, conduit] to freeze; [récoltes] to be attacked ou blighted ou nipped by frost; [doigt, membre] to be freezing, be frozen; **les salades ont gelé sur pied** the lettuces have frozen on their stalks [b] (= avoir froid) to be frozen, be freezing; **on gèle ici** we're ou it's freezing here [c] (dans un jeu) **je chauffe ? — non, tu gèles** am I getting warmer? — no, you're freezing

[4] VB IMPERS **il gèle** it's freezing; **il a gelé dur** ou **à pierre fendre** (littér) it froze hard, there was a hard frost; **il a gelé blanc** there was a white icy frost

gélifiant [ʒelifjɑ̃] NM gelling agent

gélifier [ʒelifje] ▸ conjug 7 ◂ [1] VT **~ qch** to make sth gel [2] **se gélifier** VPR to gel

gélinotte [ʒelinɔt] NF ~ **(des bois)** hazel grouse, hazel hen; **~ d'Écosse** red grouse; **~ blanche** willow grouse

gélose [ʒeloz] NF agar-agar

gélule [ʒelyl] NF (Pharm) capsule

gelure [ʒ(ə)lyʀ] NF (Méd) frostbite (NonC)

Gémeaux [ʒemo] NMPL (Astron) Gemini; **il est (du signe des) ~** he's (a) Gemini

gémellaire [ʒemelɛʀ] ADJ twin (épith)

gémellité [ʒemelite, ʒemɛlite] NF twinship; **taux de ~** incidence of twin births; **les cas de vraie/fausse ~** cases of identical twin/non-identical twin births

gémination [ʒeminasjɔ̃] NF gemination

géminé, e [ʒemine] [1] ADJ (Ling) [consonne] geminate; (Archit) twin (épith), gemeled (SPÉC); (Bio) geminate [2] **géminée** NF (Ling) geminate

gémir [ʒemiʀ] ▸ conjug 2 ◂ VI [a] (= geindre) to groan, moan (de with); **~ sur son sort** to bemoan one's fate; (littér) **~ sous l'oppression** to groan under oppression [b] (= grincer) [ressort, gonds, plancher] to creak; [vent] to moan; **les gonds de la porte gémissaient horriblement** the door hinges made a terrible creaking noise [c] [colombe] to coo

gémissant, e [ʒemisɑ̃, ɑ̃t] ADJ [voix] groaning, moaning; [gonds, plancher] creaking

gémissement [ʒemismɑ̃] NM [voix] groan, moan; (prolongé) groaning (NonC), moaning (NonC); [meuble] creaking (NonC); [vent] moaning (NonC); [colombe] cooing

gemmage [ʒemaʒ] NM tapping (of pine trees)

gemmail (pl **-aux**) [ʒemaj, o] NM non-leaded stained glass

gemme [ʒɛm] NF [a] (Minér) gem(stone) → **sel** [b] (= résine de pin) (pine) resin

gemmé, e [ʒeme] ADJ (littér) gemmed, studded with precious stones

gemmer [ʒeme] ▸ conjug 1 ◂ VT to tap (pine trees)

gémonies [ʒemɔni] NFPL (littér) **vouer** ou **traîner qn/qch aux ~** to subject sb/sth to ou hold sb/sth up to public obloquy

gênant, e [ʒenɑ̃, ɑ̃t] ADJ [a] (= irritant) **tu es/c'est vraiment ~** you're/it's a real nuisance; **ce**

n'est pas ~ it's OK, it doesn't matter [b] (= *embarrassant*) [*situation, moment, témoin*] awkward, embarrassing; [*révélations, regard, présence*] embarrassing; [*meuble, talons*] awkward; [*handicap*] bothersome

gencive [ʒɑ̃siv] NF (*Anat*) gum; **il a pris un coup dans les ~s*** he got a sock on the jaw* *ou* a kick in the teeth*; **prends ça dans les ~s!*** take that!; **il faut voir ce qu'elle lui a envoyé dans les ~s!*** you should have heard the way she let fly at him!; **je lui ai envoyé dans les ~s que ...** I told him to his face that ...

gendarme [ʒɑ̃daʀm] NM [a] (= *policier*) policeman, police officer; (*en France*) gendarme; (*Hist, Mil*) horseman; (= *soldat*) soldier, man-at-arms; **faire le ~** to play the role of policeman; (*hum*) **sa femme est un vrai ~** his wife's a real battle-axe*; **jouer aux ~s et aux voleurs** to play cops and robbers; **~ mobile** member of the anti-riot police; **le ~ de la Bourse** the French stock exchange watchdog → **chapeau, peur** [b] (*Zool* = *punaise*) fire bug; (*Alpinisme*) gendarme (*SPÉC*), pinnacle [c] (*†* = *hareng*) bloater (*Brit*), salt herring (*US*) [d] (*Aut*) **~ couché** speed bump, sleeping policeman (*Brit*)

gendarmer (se) [ʒɑ̃daʀme] ▶conjug 1◀ VPR **il faut se gendarmer pour qu'elle aille se coucher/pour la faire manger** you really have to take quite a strong line (with her) *ou* you really have to lay down the law to get her to go to bed/to eat

gendarmerie [ʒɑ̃daʀməʀi] NF (= *police*) police force, constabulary (*in countryside and small towns*); (*en France*) Gendarmerie; (= *bureaux*) police station (*in countryside and small town*); (= *caserne*) gendarmes' *ou* Gendarmerie barracks, police barracks; (*Hist, Mil* = *cavalerie*) heavy cavalry *ou* horse; (= *garde royale*) royal guard; **~ mobile** anti-riot police; **la ~ nationale** the national Gendarmerie; **~ maritime** coastguard

gendre [ʒɑ̃dʀ] NM son-in-law

gêne [ʒɛn] NF [a] (= *malaise physique*) discomfort; **~ respiratoire** breathing *ou* respiratory problems; **il ressentait une certaine ~ à respirer** he experienced some *ou* a certain difficulty in breathing [b] (= *désagrément, dérangement*) trouble, bother; **je ne voudrais vous causer aucune ~** I wouldn't like to put you to any trouble *ou* bother, I wouldn't want to be a nuisance; (*péj*) some people only think of their own comfort; **« nous vous prions de bien vouloir excuser la ~ occasionnée durant les travaux »** "we apologize to customers for any inconvenience caused during the renovations" ■ (*PROV*) **où il y a de la ~, il n'y a pas de plaisir** comfort comes first, there's no sense in being uncomfortable [c] (= *manque d'argent*) financial difficulties *ou* straits; **vivre dans la ~/dans une grande ~** to be in financial difficulties *ou* straits/in great financial difficulties *ou* dire (*financial*) straits [d] (= *confusion, trouble*) embarrassment; **un moment de ~** a moment of embarrassment; **j'éprouve de la ~ devant lui** I feel embarrassed *ou* self-conscious in his presence; **il éprouva de la ~ à lui avouer cela** he felt embarrassed admitting *ou* to admit that to her

gêné, e [ʒene] (*ptp de* **gêner**) ADJ [a] (= *à court d'argent*) short (of money) (*attrib*); **être ~ aux entournures*** to be short of money *ou* hard up* [b] (= *embarrassé*) [*personne, sourire, air*] embarrassed, self-conscious; [*silence*] uncomfortable, embarrassed, awkward; **j'étais ~!** I was (so) embarrassed!, I felt (so) awkward! *ou* uncomfortable!; **il n'est pas ~!** he's got a nerve!*; (*hum*) **ce sont les plus ~s qui s'en vont!** if you want to leave, no one's stopping you! [c] (*physiquement*) uncomfortable; **êtes-vous ~ pour respirer?** do you have trouble

(in) breathing?; **je suis ~e dans cette robe** I'm uncomfortable in this dress

gène [ʒɛn] NM gene; **~ dominant/récessif** dominant/recessive gene

généalogie [ʒenealɔʒi] NF [*famille*] ancestry, genealogy; [*animaux*] pedigree; (*Bio*) [*espèces*] genealogy; (= *sujet d'études*) genealogy; **faire** *ou* **dresser la ~ de qn** to trace sb's ancestry *ou* genealogy

généalogique [ʒenealɔʒik] ADJ genealogical → **arbre**

généalogiste [ʒenealɔʒist] NMF genealogist

génépi [ʒenepi] NM (= *plante*) wormwood, absinthe; (= *liqueur*) absinth(e)

gêner [ʒene] ▶conjug 1◀ [1] VT [a] (*physiquement*) [*fumée, bruit*] to bother; [*vêtement étroit, obstacle*] to hamper; **cela vous gêne-t-il si je fume?** do you mind if I smoke?, does it bother you if I smoke?; **~ le passage** to be in the way; **ça me gêne** *ou* **c'est gênant pour respirer/pour écrire** it hampers my breathing/hampers me when I write; **le bruit me gêne pour travailler** noise bothers me *ou* disturbs me when I'm trying to work; **son complet le gêne aux entournures*** his suit is uncomfortable *ou* constricting; **ces papiers me gênent** these papers are in my way; **ces travaux gênent la circulation** these roadworks are disrupting the (flow of) traffic [b] (= *déranger*) [+ *personne*] to bother, put out; [+ *projet*] to hamper, hinder; **je crains de ~** I am afraid to bother people *ou* put people out, I'm afraid of being a nuisance; **je ne voudrais pas (vous) ~** I don't want to bother you *ou* put you out *ou* be in the way; **j'espère que ça ne vous gêne pas d'y aller** I hope it won't inconvenience you *ou* put you out to go; **cela vous gênerait de ne pas fumer?** would you mind not smoking?; **ce qui me gêne (dans cette histoire), c'est que ...** what bothers me (in this business) is that...; **et alors, ça te gêne?*** so what?*, what's it to you?* [c] (*financièrement*) to put in financial difficulties; **ces dépenses vont les ~ considérablement** *ou* **vont les ~ aux entournures*** these expenses are really going to put them in financial difficulties *ou* make things tight for them *ou* make them hard up* [d] (= *mettre mal à l'aise*) to make feel ill-at-ease *ou* uncomfortable; **ça me gêne de vous dire ça mais ...** I hate to tell you but ...; **ça me gêne de me déshabiller chez le médecin** I find it embarrassing to get undressed at the doctor's; **sa présence me gêne** I feel uncomfortable when he's around, his presence *ou* he makes me feel uncomfortable; **son regard la gênait** his glance made her feel ill-at-ease *ou* uncomfortable; **cela le gêne qu'on fasse tout le travail pour lui** it embarrasses him to have all the work done for him, he feels awkward about having all the work done for him [2] **se gêner** VPR [a] (= *se contraindre*) to put o.s. out; **ne vous gênez pas pour moi** don't mind me, don't put yourself out for me; (*iro*) **ne vous gênez pas!** do you mind!; **il ne faut pas vous ~ avec moi** don't stand on ceremony with me; **non mais! je vais me ~!** why shouldn't I!; **il y en a qui ne se gênent pas!** some people just don't care!; **il ne s'est pas gêné pour le lui dire** he told him straight out, he made no bones about telling him [b] (*dans un lieu*) **on se gêne à trois dans ce bureau** this office is too small for the three of us

général¹, e (*mpl* -**aux**) [ʒeneʀal, o] [1] ADJ [a] (= *d'ensemble*) [*vue*] general; (= *vague*) [*idée*] general; **un tableau ~ de la situation** a general *ou* an overall picture of the situation; **remarques d'ordre très ~** comments of a very general nature; **se lancer dans des considérations ~es sur le temps** to venture some general remarks about the weather; **d'une façon** *ou* **manière ~e** in general, generally; (*précédant*

une affirmation) generally *ou* broadly speaking → **règle** [b] (= *total, global*) [*assemblée, grève*] general; (= *commun*) **dans l'intérêt ~** in the general *ou* common interest; **cette opinion est devenue ~e** this is now a widely shared *ou* generally held opinion; **devenir ~** [*crise, peur*] to become widespread; **la mêlée devint ~e** the fight turned into a free-for-all; **à l'indignation/la surprise ~e** to everyone's indignation/surprise; **à la demande ~e** in response to popular demand → **concours, état, médecine** [c] **en ~** (= *habituellement*) usually, generally, in general; (= *de façon générale*) generally, in general; **je parle en ~** I'm speaking in general terms *ou* generally [d] (*Admin* = *principal*) general (*épith*) → **directeur, fermier, président, secrétaire** [2] NM (*Philo*) **le ~** the general; **aller du ~ au particulier** to go from the general to the particular [3] **générale** NF [a] (*Théât*) (*répétition*) ~e dress rehearsal [b] (*Mil*) **battre** *ou* **sonner la ~e** to call to arms

général², e (*mpl* -**aux**) [ʒeneʀal, o] [1] NM (*Mil*) general; **oui mon ~** yes sir *ou* general [2] **générale** NF (= *épouse*) general's wife → **Madame** [3] COMP ▶ **général d'armée** general; (*Aviat*) air chief marshal (*Brit*), general (*US*) ▶ **général de brigade** brigadier (*Brit*), brigadier general (*US*) ▶ **général de brigade aérienne** air commodore (*Brit*), brigadier general (*US*) ▶ **général en chef** general-in-chief, general-in-command ▶ **général de corps aérien** air marshal (*Brit*), lieutenant general (*US*) ▶ **général de corps d'armée** lieutenant-general ▶ **général de division** major general ▶ **général de division aérienne** air vice marshal (*Brit*), major general (*US*)

▼ **généralement** [ʒeneʀalmɑ̃] ADV generally; **il est ~ chez lui après 8 heures** he's generally *ou* usually at home after 8 o'clock; **coutume assez ~ répandue** fairly widespread custom; **plus ~, ce genre de phénomène s'accompagne de ...** more generally *ou* commonly *ou* usually, this type of phenomenon is accompanied by ...

généralisable [ʒeneʀalizabl] ADJ [*mesure, observation*] which can be applied generally

généralisateur, -trice [ʒeneʀalizatœʀ, tʀis] ADJ **tendance généralisatrice** tendency to generalize *ou* towards generalization; **il a un esprit ~** he is given to generalizing

généralisation [ʒeneʀalizasjɔ̃] NF [a] (= *extension*) [*infection, corruption, pratique*] spread; **la ~ du cancer** the spread of the cancer; **il y a un risque de ~ du conflit** there's a risk that the conflict might become widespread [b] (= *énoncé*) generalization; **~s hâtives/abusives** sweeping/excessive generalizations

généraliser [ʒeneʀalize] ▶conjug 1◀ [1] VT [a] (= *étendre*) [+ *méthode*] to put *ou* bring into general *ou* widespread use; **l'usage d'un produit** to bring a product into general use [b] (= *globaliser*) to generalize; **il ne faut pas ~** we mustn't generalize [2] **se généraliser** VPR [*infection*] to spread, become generalized; [*corruption*] to become widespread; [*conflit*] to spread; [*procédé*] to become widespread, come into general use; **l'usage du produit s'est généralisé** the use of this product has become widespread, this product has come into general use; **crise généralisée** general crisis; **il a un cancer généralisé** the cancer has spread throughout his whole body; **infection généralisée** systemic infection

généralissime [ʒeneʀalisim] NM generalissimo

généraliste [ʒeneʀalist] [1] ADJ [*radio, télévision*] general-interest (*épith*); [*formation*] general; [*ingénieur*] non-specialized [2] NM (**méde-**

cin) ~ general *ou* family practitioner, G.P. (*Brit*)

généralité [ʒeneralite] **1** NF a (= *presque totalité*) majority; **ce n'est pas une ~** that's not the case in general; **dans la ~ des cas** in the majority of cases, in most cases b (= *caractère général*) [*affirmation*] general nature **2** **généralités** NFPL (= *introduction*) general points; (*péj* = *banalités*) general remarks, generalities

générateur, -trice [ʒeneratœʀ, tʀis] **1** ADJ [*force*] generating; [*fonction*] generative, generating; **facteur ~ de désordres** factor which creates disruption; **secteur ~ d'emplois** job-generating sector; **activité génératrice de profits** profit-making activity, activity that generates profit **2** NM (*Tech*) generator; **~ électrique/de particules/de programme** electric/particle/program generator; **~ de vapeur** steam boiler **3** **génératrice** NF a (*Élec*) generator b (*Math*) generating line, generatrix

génératif, -ive [ʒeneʀatif, iv] ADJ (*Ling*) generative; **grammaire générative** generative grammar

génération [ʒeneʀasjɔ̃] NF generation; **depuis des ~s** for generations; **la ~ actuelle/montante** the present-day/rising generation; **la jeune ~** the younger generation; **~ spontanée** spontaneous generation; **ordinateur/immigré de la deuxième/troisième ~** second-/third-generation computer/immigrant

générer [ʒeneʀe] ▸conjug 6◂ VT [+ *froid, emplois, chômage*] to generate; (*Ling, Math, Ordin*) to generate

généreusement [ʒeneʀøzmɑ̃] ADV generously; **accueilli ~** warmly welcomed

généreux, -euse [ʒeneʀø, øz] ADJ a (= *large*) [*personne, pourboire*] generous; **être ~ de son temps** to be generous with one's time; **c'est très ~ de sa part** it's very generous of him; **se montrer ~ envers qn** to be generous with sb; **faire le ~** to act generously* b (= *noble, désintéressé*) [*acte, caractère*] generous; [*âme, sentiment, idée*] generous, noble; [*adversaire*] generous, magnanimous c (= *riche*) [*sol*] productive, fertile d [*vin*] generous, full-bodied e [*poitrine*] ample; **formes généreuses** generous curves

générique [ʒeneʀik] **1** ADJ generic; [*produit*] unbranded, no-name (*épith*); [*médicament*] generic; (*Ling*) **terme ~** generic term **2** NM (*Ciné*) credit titles, credits, cast (and credits) (*US*); **être au ~** to feature *ou* be in the credits

générosité [ʒeneʀozite] NF a (= *libéralité*) [*pourboire, personne*] generosity; **avec ~** generously b (= *noblesse*) [*acte, caractère*] generosity; [*âme, sentiment*] nobility; [*adversaire*] generosity, magnanimity; **avoir la ~ de** to be generous enough to, have the generosity to c (= *largesses*) **~s** kindnesses

Gênes [ʒɛn] N Genoa

genèse [ʒənɛz] NF (= *élaboration*) genesis; **(le livre de) la Genèse** (the Book of) Genesis

genet [ʒ(ə)nɛ] NM (= *cheval*) jennet

genêt [ʒ(ə)nɛ] NM (= *plante*) broom

généticien, -ienne [ʒenetisjɛ̃, jɛn] NM,F geneticist

génétique [ʒenetik] **1** ADJ genetic; **carte ~** genetic *ou* gene map; **affection d'origine ~** genetically-transmitted disease → **manipulation 2** NF genetics *sg*; **~ des populations** population genetics

génétiquement [ʒenetikmɑ̃] ADV genetically

genette [ʒ(ə)nɛt] NF genet(te)

gêneur, -euse [ʒɛnœʀ, øz] NM,F (= *importun*) intruder; (= *représentant un obstacle*) **supprimer un ~** to do away with a person who is *ou* stands in one's way

Genève [ʒ(ə)nɛv] N Geneva

genevois, e [ʒən(ə)vwa, waz] **1** ADJ Genevan **2** **Genevois(e)** NM,F Genevan

genévrier [ʒənevʀije] NM juniper

génial, e [ʒenjal, jo] ADJ a (= *inspiré*) [*écrivain*] of genius; [*plan, idée, invention*] inspired; **plan d'une conception ~e** inspired idea, brilliantly thought out idea b (* = *formidable*) [*atmosphère, soirée*] fantastic*, great*; [*personne*] great*; [*plan*] brilliant*, great*; **c'est ~!** that's great!* *ou* fantastic!*; **il n'est pas ~ mais** ... he's not up to much physically but ...; **ce n'est pas ~!** (*idée*) that's not very clever!; (*film*) it's not brilliant!*

génialement [ʒenjalmɑ̃] ADV with genius, brilliantly

génie [ʒeni] **1** NM a (= *aptitude supérieure*) genius; **avoir du ~** to have genius; **éclair *ou* trait de ~** stroke of genius; **de ~** [*découverte*] brilliant; **homme de ~** man of genius; **idée de ~** brainwave, brilliant idea b (= *personne*) genius; **ce n'est pas un ~!** he's no genius!; **~ méconnu** unrecognized genius c (= *talent*) genius; **avoir le ~ des affaires** to have a genius for business; **avoir le ~ du mal** to have an evil bent; **il a le ~ de *ou* pour dire ce qu'il ne faut pas** he has a genius for saying the wrong thing d (= *spécificité*) genius (*frm*); **le ~ de la langue française** the genius of the French language e (= *allégorie, être mythique*) spirit; [*contes arabes*] genie; **le ~ de la liberté** the spirit of liberty; **le ~ de la lampe** the genie of the lamp; **~ des airs/des eaux** spirit of the air/waters; **être le bon/mauvais ~ de qn** to be sb's good/evil genius f (*Mil*) **le ~** ≈ the Engineers; **soldat du ~** sapper, engineer; **faire son service dans le ~** to do one's service in the Engineers g (= *technique*) engineering; **~ atomique/chimique/électronique** atomic/chemical/electronic engineering

2 COMP ▸ **génie civil** (*branche*) civil engineering; (*corps*) civil engineers ▸ **génie génétique** genetic engineering ▸ **génie industriel** industrial engineering ▸ **génie informatique** computer engineering ▸ **génie logiciel** software engineering ▸ **génie maritime** (*branche*) marine engineering; (*corps*) marine engineers (*under state command*) ▸ **génie mécanique** mechanical engineering ▸ **génie militaire** (*branche*) military engineering; (*corps*) ≈ Engineers ▸ **génie rural** agricultural engineering → **ingénieur**

genièvre [ʒənjɛvʀ] NM (= *boisson*) Dutch gin, Hollands (gin) (*Brit*), genever (*Brit*); (= *arbre*) juniper; (= *fruit*) juniper berry; **grains de ~** juniper berries

génique [ʒenik] ADJ gene (*épith*); **thérapie ~** gene therapy

génisse [ʒenis] NF heifer

génital, e (*mpl* -aux) [ʒenital, o] ADJ genital; **organes génitaux** ◊ **parties ~es** genitals, genital organs, genitalia

géniteur, -trice [ʒenitœʀ, tʀis] **1** NM,F (*hum* = *parent*) parent **2** NM (*Zool* = *reproducteur*) sire

génitif [ʒenitif] NM genitive (case); **au ~** in the genitive; **~ absolu** genitive absolute

génito-urinaire (*pl* **génito-urinaires**) [ʒenitoyʀinɛʀ] ADJ genito-urinary

génocide [ʒenɔsid] NM genocide

génois, e [ʒenwa, waz] **1** ADJ Genoese **2** **Génois(e)** NM,F Genoese **3** NM (*Naut*) genoa (jib) **4** **génoise** NF (*Culin*) sponge cake; (*Archit*) eaves consisting of decorative tiles

génome [ʒenom] NM genom(e); **~ humain** human genome

génotype [ʒenotip] NM genotype

genou (*pl* **genoux**) [ʒ(ə)nu] **1** NM a (*Anat, Habillement, Zool*) knee; **avoir les ~x cagneux *ou* rentrants** to be knock-kneed; **mes ~x se dé-**

robèrent sous moi my legs gave way under me; **des jeans troués aux ~x** jeans with holes at the knees, jeans that are out at the knees; **dans la vase jusqu'aux ~x** up to one's knees *ou* knee-deep in mud b (= *cuisses*) **~x** lap; **avoir/prendre qn sur ses ~x** to have/take sb on one's knee *ou* lap; **écrire sur ses ~x** to write on one's lap c (*loc*) **il me donna un coup de ~ dans le ventre** he kneed me in the stomach; **il me donna un coup de ~ pour me réveiller** he nudged me with his knee to wake me up; **faire du ~ à qn** to play footsie with sb*; **tomber aux ~x de qn** to fall at sb's feet, go down on one's knees to sb; (*littér*) **fléchir *ou* plier *ou* ployer le ~ devant qn** to bend the knee to sb; **mettre (un) ~ à terre** to go down on one knee d (*Tech*) ball and socket joint

2 **à genoux** LOC ADV **il était à ~x** he was kneeling, he was on his knees; (*fig*) **être à ~x devant qn** to idolize *ou* worship sb; **se mettre à ~x** to kneel down, go down on one's knees; (*fig*) **se mettre à ~x devant qn** to go down on one's knees to sb; **c'est à genoux à ~x!*** it's out of this world!*; **tomber/se jeter à ~x** to fall/throw o.s. to one's knees; **demander qch à (deux) ~x** to ask for sth on bended knee, go down on one's knees for sth; **je te demande pardon à ~x** I beg you to forgive me

3 **sur les genoux*** LOC ADV **être sur les ~x** [*personne*] to be ready to drop; [*pays*] to be on its knees*; **ça m'a mis sur les ~x** it wore me out

genouillère [ʒ(ə)nujɛʀ] NF (*Méd*) knee support; (*Sport*) kneepad, kneecap

▾ **genre** [ʒɑ̃ʀ] NM a (= *espèce*) kind, type, sort; **~ de vie** lifestyle, way of life; **elle n'est pas du ~ à se laisser faire** she's not the type *ou* kind *ou* sort to let people push her around; **ce n'est pas son ~ de ne pas répondre** it's not like him not to answer; **donner des augmentations, ce n'est pas leur ~** it's not their style to give pay rises; **c'est bien son ~!** that's just like him!; **tu vois le ~!** you know the type *ou* sort!; **les rousses, ce n'est pas mon ~** redheads aren't my type; **c'est le ~ grognon*** he's the grumpy sort*; **un type (du) ~ homme d'affaires*** a businessman type; **une maison ~ chalet*** a chalet-style house; **il n'est pas mal dans son ~** he's quite attractive in his own way; **ce qui se fait de mieux dans le ~** the best of its kind; **réparations en tout ~ *ou* en tous ~s** all kinds of repairs *ou* repair work undertaken; **quelque chose de ce ~ *ou* du même ~** something of the kind, that sort of thing; **des remarques de ce ~** remarks *ou* comments like that *ou* of that nature; **il a écrit un ~ de roman** he wrote a novel of sorts *ou* a sort of novel; **plaisanterie d'un ~ douteux** doubtful joke; **dans le ~ film d'action ce n'est pas mal** as action films go, it's not bad → **unique**

b (= *allure*) appearance; **avoir bon/mauvais ~** to look respectable/disreputable; **je n'aime pas son ~** I don't like his style; **il a un drôle de ~** he's a bit weird; **avoir le ~ bohème/artiste** to be a bohemian/an arty type; **avoir un ~ prétentieux** to have a pretentious manner; **faire du ~** to stand on ceremony; **c'est un ~ qu'il se donne** it's (just) something *ou* an air he puts on; **il aime se donner un ~** he likes to stand out *ou* to be a bit different; **ce n'est pas le ~ de la maison*** that's just not the way we (*ou* they *etc*) do things

c (*Art, Littérat, Mus*) genre; (*Peinture*) **tableau de ~** genre painting; **œuvre dans le ~ ancien/italien** work in the old/Italian style *ou* genre; **ses tableaux/romans sont d'un ~ un peu particulier** the style of his paintings/novels is slightly unusual

d (*Gram*) gender; **s'accorder en ~** to agree in gender

e (*Philo, Sci*) genus; **le ~ humain** mankind, the human race

▸ GRAMMAIRE ACTIVE: **genre** 34.3

gens¹ [ʒɑ̃] **①** NMPL **ⓐ** (*gén*) people; **il faut savoir prendre les ~** you've got to know how to handle people; **les ~ sont fous!** people are crazy (at times)!; **les ~ de la ville** townspeople, townsfolk; **les ~ du pays** *ou* **du coin*** the local people, the locals*; **ce ne sont pas ~ à raconter des histoires** they're not the kind *ou* type *ou* sort of people to tell stories → **droit³, jeune, monde**

ⓑ (*loc, avec accord féminin de l'adjectif antéposé*) **ce sont de petites ~** they are people of modest means; **vieilles/braves ~** old/good people *ou* folk*; **honnêtes ~** honest people; (*hum*) **écoutez bonnes ~** harken, ye people (*hum*)

ⓒ († *hum* = *serviteurs*) servants; **il appela ses ~** he called his servants

② COMP ► **gens d'armes** (*Hist*) men-at-arms† ► **les gens d'Église** the clergy ► **gens d'épée** (*Hist*) soldiers (*of the aristocracy*) ► **gens de lettres** men of letters ► **les gens de loi**† the legal profession ► **gens de maison** domestic servants ► **gens de mer** sailors, seafarers ► **les gens de robe** (*Hist*) the legal profession ► **gens de service** = **gens de maison** ► **les gens de théâtre** the acting profession, theatrical people ► **les gens du voyage** (= *gitans*) travellers

gens² [ʒɛ̃s] NF (*Antiq*) gens

gent [ʒɑ̃(t)] NF (†† *ou hum*) race, tribe; **la ~ canine** the canine race; **la ~ féminine** the fair sex; **la ~ masculine** the male *ou* masculine sex

gentiane [ʒɑ̃sjan] NF gentian

▼**gentil, -ille** [ʒɑ̃ti, ij] **①** ADJ **ⓐ** (= *aimable*) kind, nice (**avec, pour** to); **il a toujours un mot ~ pour chacun** he always has a kind word for everyone *ou* to say to everyone; **vous serez ~ de me le rendre** would you mind giving it back to me; **c'est ~ à toi** *ou* **de ta part de** ... it's very kind *ou* nice *ou* good of you to ...; **tu es ~ tout plein*** you're so sweet; **tout ça, c'est bien ~ mais** ... that's (all) very nice *ou* well but ...; **elle est bien gentille avec ses histoires mais** ... what she has to say is all very well *ou* nice but ...; **sois ~, va me le chercher** be a dear and go and get it for me

ⓑ (= *sage*) good; **il n'a pas été ~** he hasn't been a good boy; **sois ~, je reviens bientôt** be good, I'll be back soon

ⓒ (= *gracieux*) [*visage, endroit*] nice, pleasant; **une gentille petite robe/fille** a nice little dress/girl; **c'est ~ comme tout chez vous** you've got a lovely little place; **c'est ~ sans plus** it's OK but it's nothing special

ⓓ (= *rondelet*) [*somme*] tidy, fair

② NM (*Hist, Rel*) gentile

gentilé [ʒɑ̃tile] NM gentilic

gentilhomme [ʒɑ̃tijɔm] (*pl* **gentilshommes** [ʒɑ̃tizɔm]) NM (*Hist, fig*) gentleman; **~ campagnard** country squire

gentilhommière [ʒɑ̃tijɔmjɛʀ] NF (small) country seat, (small) manor house

gentillesse [ʒɑ̃tijɛs] NF **ⓐ** (= *amabilité*) kindness; **être d'une grande ~** to be very kind (**avec qn** to sb); **me ferez-vous** *ou* **auriez-vous la ~ de faire** ... would you be kind as to do *ou* kind enough to do ... **ⓑ** (= *faveur*) favour (*Brit*), favor (*US*), kindness; **remercier qn de toutes ses ~s** to thank sb for all his kindness(es); **une ~ en vaut une autre** one good turn deserves another; **il me disait des ~s** he said kind *ou* nice things to me

gentillet, -ette [ʒɑ̃tijɛ, ɛt] ADJ **c'est ~** (= *mignon*) [*appartement*] it's a nice little place; (*péj = insignifiant*) [*film, roman*] it's nice enough (but it's nothing special)

gentiment [ʒɑ̃timɑ̃] ADV (= *aimablement*) kindly; (= *gracieusement*) nicely; **ils jouaient ~** they were playing nicely *ou* like good children; (*iro*) **on m'a ~ fait comprendre que** ... they made it quite clear to me that ...

► GRAMMAIRE ACTIVE: gentil 49, 52.4

gentleman [ʒɑ̃tləman] (*pl* **gentlemen** [dʒɑ̃tləmɛn]) NM gentleman; **~-farmer** gentleman-farmer

gentleman's agreement [dʒɛntləmans-agʀimɛnt], **gentlemen's agreement** [dʒɛntləmɛnsagʀimɛnt] NM gentleman's *ou* gentlemen's agreement

génuflexion [ʒenyflɛksjɔ̃] NF (*Rel*) genuflexion; **faire une ~** to make a genuflexion, genuflect

géo [ʒeo] NF (*arg Scol*) ABRÉV = **géographie**

géocentrique [ʒeosɑ̃tʀik] ADJ geocentric

géocentrisme [ʒeosɑ̃tʀism] NM geocentrism

géochimie [ʒeoʃimi] NF geochemistry

géode [ʒeɔd] NF (*Minér*) geode; (*Spectacle*) geodesic dome

géodésie [ʒeɔdezi] NF geodesy

géodésique [ʒeɔdezik] **①** ADJ geodesic; **point ~** triangulation point; **ligne ~** geodesic line **②** NF geodesic

géodynamique [ʒeɔdinamik] **①** ADJ geodynamic **②** NF geodynamics *sg*

géographe [ʒeɔgʀaf] NMF geographer

géographie [ʒeɔgʀafi] NF geography; **~ humaine/économique/physique** human/economic/physical geography

géographique [ʒeɔgʀafik] ADJ geographic(al) → **dictionnaire**

géographiquement [ʒeɔgʀafikmɑ̃] ADV geographically

geôle [ʒol] NF (*littér*) jail, gaol (*Brit*)

geôlier, -ière [ʒolje, jɛʀ] NM,F (*littér*) jailer, gaoler (*Brit*)

géologie [ʒeɔlɔʒi] NF geology

géologique [ʒeɔlɔʒik] ADJ geological

géologue [ʒeɔlɔg] NMF geologist

géomagnétique [ʒeomaɲetik] ADJ geomagnetic

géomagnétisme [ʒeomaɲetism] NM geomagnetism

géomancie [ʒeomɑ̃si] NF geomancy

géomancien, -ienne [ʒeomɑ̃sjɛ̃, jɛn] NM,F geomancer

géométral, e (*mpl* **-aux**) [ʒeometʀal, o] ADJ plane (*not in perspective*)

géomètre [ʒeomɛtʀ] NM **ⓐ** (= *arpenteur*) surveyor **ⓑ** (= *phalène*) emerald, geometrid (*SPÉC*)

géométrie [ʒeometʀi] NF (= *science*) geometry; (= *livre*) geometry book; **~ descriptive/plane/analytique** descriptive/plane/analytical geometry; **~ dans l'espace** solid geometry; **à ~ variable** (*Aviat*) swing-wing; [*politique*] which changes with the wind; **c'est une justice à ~ variable** it's one rule for one and one rule for another

géométrique [ʒeometʀik] ADJ geometric(al) → **lieu¹, progression**

géométriquement [ʒeometʀikmɑ̃] ADV geometrically

géomorphologie [ʒeomɔʀfɔlɔʒi] NF geomorphology

géophage [ʒeofaʒ] **①** ADJ geophagous **②** NMF geophagist

géophysicien, -ienne [ʒeofizisjɛ̃, jɛn] NM,F geophysicist

géophysique [ʒeofizik] **①** ADJ geophysical **②** NF geophysics *sg*

géopolitique [ʒeopolitik] **①** ADJ geopolitical **②** NF geopolitics *sg*

Georges [ʒɔʀʒ] NM George

Georgetown [ʒɔʀʒtaun] N Georgetown

georgette [ʒɔʀʒɛt] NF → **crêpe²**

Géorgie [ʒeɔʀʒi] NF Georgia; **~ du Sud** South Georgia

géorgien, -ienne [ʒeɔʀʒjɛ̃, jɛn] **①** ADJ Georgian **②** NM (*Ling*) Georgian **③** **Géorgien(ne)** NM,F Georgian

géorgique [ʒeɔʀʒik] ADJ (*Hist Littérat*) georgic

géosciences [ʒeosjɑ̃s] NFPL geosciences

géostationnaire [ʒeostasjɔnɛʀ] ADJ geostationary

géostratégie [ʒeostʀateʒi] NF geostrategy

géostratégique [ʒeostʀateʒik] ADJ geostrategic

géosynchrone [ʒeosɛ̃kʀɔn] ADJ geosynchronous

géosynclinal (*pl* **-aux**) [ʒeosɛ̃klinal, o] NM geosyncline

géothermie [ʒeotɛʀmi] NF geothermal science

géothermique [ʒeotɛʀmik] ADJ geothermal

gérable [ʒeʀabl] ADJ manageable; **difficilement ~** hard to handle

gérance [ʒeʀɑ̃s] NF [*commerce, immeuble*] management; **il assure la ~ d'une usine** he manages a factory; **au cours de sa ~** while he was manager; **prendre un commerce en ~** to take over the management of a business; **il a mis son commerce en ~** he has appointed a manager for his business; **être en ~ libre** [*entreprise*] to be run by a manager; **~ salariée** salaried management

géranium [ʒeʀanjɔm] NM geranium; **~-lierre** ivy(-leaved) geranium

gérant [ʒeʀɑ̃] NM [*usine, café, magasin, banque*] manager; [*immeuble*] managing agent, factor (*Écos*); [*journal*] managing editor; **~ de portefeuilles** portfolio manager

gérante [ʒeʀɑ̃t] NF [*usine, café, magasin, banque*] manageress; [*immeuble*] managing agent; [*journal*] managing editor

gerbage [ʒɛʀbaʒ] NM **ⓐ** (*Agr*) binding, sheaving **ⓑ** (*Tech*) [*tonneaux*] stacking, piling; **« ~ interdit »** "do not stack"

gerbe [ʒɛʀb] NF [*blé*] sheaf; [*osier*] bundle; [*fleurs*] spray; [*étincelles*] shower, burst; [*écume*] shower, flurry; **déposer une ~ sur une tombe** to place a spray of flowers on a grave; **~ d'eau** spray *ou* shower of water; **~ de flammes** *ou* **de feu** jet *ou* burst of flame

gerber [ʒɛʀbe] ► conjug 1 ◄ **①** VT **ⓐ** (*Agr*) to bind into sheaves, sheave **ⓑ** (*Tech*) [+ *tonneaux*] to stack, pile **②** VI* (= *vomir*) to throw up*, puke (up)*; **il me fait ~, ce mec** that guy makes me want to throw up*

gerbera [ʒɛʀbeʀa] NM gerbera

gerbeur [ʒɛʀbœʀ] NM stacking *ou* pallet truck

gerbille [ʒɛʀbij] NF gerbil

gerboise [ʒɛʀbwaz] NF jerboa

gercer [ʒɛʀse] ► conjug 3 ◄ **①** VT [+ *peau, lèvres*] to chap, crack; [+ *sol*] to crack; **avoir les lèvres toutes gercées** to have badly chapped lips; **j'ai les mains gercées** my hands are all cracked **②** VI, **se gercer** VPR [*peau, lèvres*] to chap, crack; [*sol*] to crack

gerçure [ʒɛʀsyʀ] NF (*gén*) (small) crack; **pour éviter les ~s** to avoid chapping

gérer [ʒeʀe] ► conjug 6 ◄ VT [+ *entreprise, projet*] to manage, run; [+ *pays*] to run; [+ *carrière, budget, temps, données, biens, fortune*] to manage; **il gère bien ses affaires** he manages his affairs well; **il a mal géré son affaire** he has mismanaged his business, he has managed his business badly; (*Pol*) **~ la crise** to handle *ou* control the crisis

gerfaut [ʒɛʀfo] NM gyrfalcon

gériatre [ʒeʀjatʀ] NMF geriatrician

gériatrie [ʒeʀjatʀi] NF geriatrics *sg*

gériatrique [ʒeʀjatʀik] ADJ geriatric

germain, e [ʒɛʀmɛ̃, ɛn] **①** ADJ **ⓐ** → **cousin¹** **ⓑ** (*Hist*) German **②** NM,F (*Hist*) **Germain(e)** German

Germanie [ʒɛʀmani] NF (*Hist*) Germania

germanique [ʒɛʀmanik] **①** ADJ Germanic **②** NM (*Ling*) Germanic **③** **Germanique** NMF Germanic

germanisant, e [ʒɛʀmanizɑ̃, ɑ̃t] NM,F = **germaniste**

germanisation [ʒɛʀmanizasjɔ̃] NF germanization

germaniser [ʒɛʀmanize] ▶conjug 1◀ VT to germanize

germanisme [ʒɛʀmanism] NM (Ling) germanism

germaniste [ʒɛʀmanist] NMF German scholar, germanist

germanium [ʒɛʀmanjɔm] NM germanium

germanophile [ʒɛʀmanɔfil] ADJ, NMF germanophil(e)

germanophilie [ʒɛʀmanɔfili] NF germanophilia

germanophobe [ʒɛʀmanɔfɔb] 1 ADJ germanophobic 2 NMF germanophobe

germanophobie [ʒɛʀmanɔfɔbi] NF germanophobia

germanophone [ʒɛʀmanɔfɔn] 1 ADJ [personne] German-speaking; [littérature] German-language (épith), in German (attrib) 2 NMF German speaker

germe [ʒɛʀm] NM a (Bio) [embryon, graine] germ; [œuf] germinal disc; [pomme de terre] eye; **~s de blé** wheatgerm (NonC); **~s de soja** (soya) bean sprouts; **~ dentaire** tooth bud → **porteur** b (= source) [maladie, erreur, vie] seed; **~ d'une idée** germ of an idea; **avoir** ou **contenir en ~** to contain in embryo, contain the seeds of; **l'idée était en ~ depuis longtemps** the idea had existed in embryo for a long time c (Méd = microbe) germ; **~s pathogènes** pathogenic bacteria

germer [ʒɛʀme] ▶conjug 1◀ VI [bulbe, graine] to sprout, germinate; [idée] to form, germinate (frm); **pommes de terre germées** sprouting potatoes; **l'idée a commencé à ~ dans ma tête** the idea began to form in my mind

germicide [ʒɛʀmisid] 1 ADJ germicidal 2 NM germicide

germinal¹, e (mpl **-aux**) [ʒɛʀminal, o] ADJ germinal

germinal² [ʒɛʀminal] NM Germinal (seventh month in the French Republican calendar)

germinateur, -trice [ʒɛʀminatœʀ, tʀis] ADJ germinative

germinatif, -ive [ʒɛʀminatif, iv] ADJ germinal

germination [ʒɛʀminasjɔ̃] NF (Bot, fig) germination

germoir [ʒɛʀmwaʀ] NM (Agr) seed tray; [brasserie] maltings sg

gérondif [ʒeʀɔ̃dif] NM (Ling) (latin) (avec être) gerundive; (complément de nom) gerund; (français) gerund

gérontocratie [ʒeʀɔ̃tɔkʀasi] NF gerontocracy

gérontocratique [ʒeʀɔ̃tɔkʀatik] ADJ gerontocratic

gérontologie [ʒeʀɔ̃tɔlɔʒi] NF gerontology

gérontologique [ʒeʀɔ̃tɔlɔʒik] ADJ gerontological

gérontologiste [ʒeʀɔ̃tɔlɔʒist], **gérontologue** [ʒeʀɔ̃tɔlɔg] NMF gerontologist

gérontophile [ʒeʀɔ̃tɔfil] NMF gerontophile, gerontophiliac

gérontophilie [ʒeʀɔ̃tɔfili] NF gerontophilia

gésier [ʒezje] NM gizzard

gésine [ʒezin] NF **être en ~†** (= accoucher) to be in labour (Brit) ou labor (US)

gésir [ʒeziʀ] VI [personne] to be lying (down), lie (down); [arbres, objets] to lie; **il gisait sur le sol** he was lying ou lay on the ground; **là gît le problème** therein lies the problem; (fig) **c'est là que gît le lièvre** there's the rub

gestaltisme [ɡɛʃtaltism] NM Gestalt (psychology)

gestation [ʒɛstasjɔ̃] NF gestation; **en ~** (lit) in gestation; **être en ~** [roman, projet] to be in preparation, be in the pipeline

geste¹ [ʒɛst] NM a (= mouvement) gesture; **~ d'approbation/d'effroi** gesture of approval/of terror; **~ maladroit** ou **malheureux** clumsy gesture ou movement; **pas un ~ ou je tire!** one move and I'll shoot!; **quelle précision dans le ~ de l'horloger** what precision there is in every move of the watchmaker's hand; (Tennis) **le ~ du service** the service action; **il parlait en faisant de grands ~s** he waved his hands about as he spoke; **il refusa d'un ~** he made a gesture of refusal, he gestured his refusal; **il le fit entrer d'un ~** he motioned ou gestured ou waved to him to come in; **il lui indiqua la porte d'un ~** with a gesture he showed him the door; **faire un ~ de la main** to gesture with one's hand, give a wave (of one's hand); **s'exprimer par ~s** to use one's hands to express o.s.; (fig) **il ne fit pas un ~ pour l'aider** he didn't lift a finger ou make a move to help him; (fig) **tu n'as qu'un ~ à faire pour qu'il revienne** just say the word ou you only have to say the word and he'll come back; (fig) **avoir le ~ large** to be generous → **fait¹, joindre** b (= action) gesture, act; **~ de défi/de conciliation** gesture of defiance/of reconciliation; **~ politique** political gesture; **beau ~** noble gesture ou deed; **dans un ~ de désespoir** in sheer despair, out of sheer desperation; **faire un (petit) ~** to make a (small) gesture

geste² [ʒɛst] NF (Littérat) gest(e) → **chanson**

gesticulation [ʒɛstikylasjɔ̃] NF gesticulation, gesticulating (NonC)

gesticuler [ʒɛstikyle] ▶conjug 1◀ VI to gesticulate

gestion [ʒɛstjɔ̃] NF [entreprise, projet] management, [pays] running; [biens, carrière, temps, déchets] management; **mauvaise ~** mismanagement, bad management; **~ administrative** administration, administrative management; **~ de portefeuilles** portfolio management; **~ des ressources humaines** human resources management; **~ des stocks** inventory (US) ou stock (Brit) control; **~ de fichiers/ mémoire/base de données** file/memory/database management; **~ de la production assistée par ordinateur** computer-assisted production management; **la ~ quotidienne de l'entreprise** the day-to-day running of the company; **la ~ des affaires publiques** the conduct of public affairs

gestionnaire [ʒɛstjɔnɛʀ] 1 ADJ administrative, management (épith) 2 NMF administrator; **~ de portefeuilles** portfolio manager 3 (Ordin) manager; **~ de base de données/de fichiers/de programmes** database/ file/program manager; **~ de mémoire/de réseau** memory/network manager; **~ d'écran** screen monitor; **~ d'impression** print monitor ou manager; **~ de périphériques** device driver

gestuel, -elle [ʒɛstyɛl] 1 ADJ gestural 2 **gestuelle** NF body movements

Gethsemani [ɡɛtsemani] N Gethsemane

geyser [ʒezɛʀ] NM geyser

Ghana [ɡana] NM Ghana

ghanéen, -enne [ɡaneɛ̃, ɛn] 1 ADJ Ghanaian 2 **Ghanéen(ne)** NM,F Ghanaian

ghetto [ɡeto] NM (lit, fig) ghetto; **cité-~** inner-city ghetto; **banlieue-~** run-down suburban area

ghilde [ɡild] NF = **guilde**

GI [dʒiaj] NM (ABRÉV = **Government Issue**) (= soldat américain) GI

gibbeux, -euse [ʒibø, øz] ADJ (Astron, littér) gibbous, gibbose

gibbon [ʒibɔ̃] NM gibbon

gibbosité [ʒibozite] NF (Astron, Méd, littér) hump, gibbosity (SPÉC)

gibecière [ʒib(ə)sjɛʀ] NF (gén) (leather) shoulder bag; [chasseur] gamebag;† [écolier] satchel

gibelin [ʒiblɛ̃] NM (Hist) Ghibelline

gibelotte [ʒiblɔt] NF fricassee of game in wine

giberne [ʒibɛʀn] NF cartridge pouch

gibet [ʒibɛ] NM gibbet, gallows; (Hist) **condamner qn au ~** to condemn sb to death by hanging, condemn sb to the gallows

gibier [ʒibje] NM a (Chasse) game; **gros/menu ~** big/small game; **~ d'eau** waterfowl; **~ à poil** game animals; **~ à plume** game birds b (= personne) prey; **les policiers attendaient leur ~** the policemen awaited their prey; **~ de potence** gallows bird; **le gros ~** big game

giboulée [ʒibule] NF (sudden) shower, sudden downpour; **~ de mars** ≈ April shower

giboyeux, -euse [ʒibwajø, øz] ADJ [pays, forêt] abounding in game, well-stocked with game

Gibraltar [ʒibʀaltaʀ] NM Gibraltar

gibus [ʒibys] NM opera hat

GIC [ʒeise] NM (ABRÉV = **grand invalide civil**) **macaron ~** disabled sticker → **invalide**

giclée [ʒikle] NF spurt, squirt

gicler [ʒikle] ▶conjug 1◀ VI a (= jaillir) to spurt, squirt; **faire ~ de l'eau d'un robinet** to squirt water from a tap; **le véhicule a fait ~ de l'eau à son passage** the vehicle sent up a spray of water as it went past b (= être expulsé) [+ personne] to be given the bum's rush*, get the boot*; [+ objet] to be tossed (out) ou chucked* (out)

gicleur [ʒiklœʀ] NM (Aut) jet; **~ de ralenti** idle, slow-running jet (Brit)

GIE [ʒeiə] NM (ABRÉV = **groupement d'intérêt économique**) → **groupement**

gifle [ʒifl] NF (lit) slap (in the face), smack (on the face); (fig) slap in the face; **donner ou filer* ou flanquer* ou allonger* une ~ à qn** to slap sb in the face, give sb a slap in the face

gifler [ʒifle] ▶conjug 1◀ VT to slap (in the face); **~ qn** to slap ou smack sb's face, slap sb in the face; **visage giflé par la grêle** face lashed by (the) hail

GIG [ʒeiʒe] NM (ABRÉV = **grand invalide de guerre**) → **invalide**

giga... [ʒiga] PRÉF giga...; **~octet** gigabyte; **~watt** gigawatt

gigantesque [ʒigɑ̃tɛsk] ADJ [taille, objet, entreprise] gigantic, huge; [bêtise] immense

gigantisme [ʒigɑ̃tism] NM (Méd) gigantism; (= grandeur) gigantic size ou proportions; **ville/entreprise atteinte de ~** city/firm that suffers from overexpansion on a gigantic scale

GIGN [ʒeiʒeɛn] NM (ABRÉV = **Groupe d'intervention de la Gendarmerie nationale**) special task force of the Gendarmerie, ≈ SAS (Brit), ≈ SWAT (US)

gigogne [ʒigɔɲ] ADJ → **lit, poupée, table**

gigolette [ʒigɔlɛt] NF (Culin) **~ de canard/de dinde** leg of duck/of turkey

gigolo* [ʒigɔlo] NM gigolo

gigot [ʒigo] NM **~ de mouton/d'agneau** leg of mutton/lamb; **~ de chevreuil** haunch of venison; **une tranche de ~** a slice off the leg of mutton ou lamb etc., a slice off the joint; **elle a de bons ~s*** she has nice sturdy legs → **manche¹**

gigoter* [ʒigɔte] ▶conjug 1◀ VI to wriggle (about)

gigoteuse [ʒigɔtøz] NF sleeper, Babygro® (Brit)

gigue [ʒig] NF (Mus) gigue; (= danse) jig; **~s*** (= jambes) legs; (péj = fille) **grande ~** bean-pole* (Brit), string bean* (US); **~ de chevreuil** haunch of venison

gilde [ʒild] NF = **guilde**

gilet [ʒilɛ] NM (de complet) waistcoat (Brit), vest (US); (= cardigan) cardigan; **~ de corps ou de peau** vest (Brit), undershirt (US); **~ pare-balles** bulletproof jacket, flak jacket*; **~ de sauvetage** (gén) life jacket; (Aviat) life vest → **pleurer**

giletier, -ière [ʒil(ə)tje, jɛʀ] NM,F waistcoat (*Brit*) *ou* vest (*US*) maker

gin [dʒin] NM gin; **~ tonic** gin and tonic

gingembre [ʒɛ̃ʒɑ̃bʀ] NM ginger; **racine de ~** root ginger (*NonC*), ginger root (*NonC*)

gingival, e (*mpl -aux*) [ʒɛ̃ʒival, o] ADJ gingival; **pâte ~e** gum ointment

gingivite [ʒɛ̃ʒivit] NF inflammation of the gums, gingivitis (*SPÉC*)

ginkgo [ʒiŋko] NM gingko

ginseng [ʒinsɛŋ] NM ginseng

girafe [ʒiʀaf] NF (*Zool*) giraffe; (*péj = personne*) beanpole* (*Brit*), string bean* (*US*); (*Ciné*) boom → **peigner**

girafeau [ʒiʀafo], **girafon** [ʒiʀafɔ̃] NM baby giraffe

girandole [ʒiʀɑ̃dɔl] NF (= *chandelier*) candelabra, girandole; (= *feu d'artifice, guirlande lumineuse*) girandole

girasol [ʒiʀasɔl] NM girasol

giration [ʒiʀasjɔ̃] NF gyration

giratoire [ʒiʀatwaʀ] ADJ gyrating, gyratory → **sens**

girelle [ʒiʀɛl] NF rainbow wrasse

girl [gœʀl] NF chorus girl

girofle [ʒiʀɔfl] NM clove → **clou**

giroflée [ʒiʀɔfle] NF wallflower, gillyflower; (*vivace*) stock; * (= *gifle*) **~ à cinq feuilles** slap in the face

giroflier [ʒiʀɔflije] NM clove tree

girolle [ʒiʀɔl] NF chanterelle

giron [ʒiʀɔ̃] NM [a] (= *genoux*) lap; (= *sein*) bosom; (*fig*) **rentrer dans le ~ de l'Église** to return to the fold, return to the bosom of the Church; **enfant élevé dans le ~ maternel** child reared in the bosom of his family [b] (*Hér*) giron [c] (*Archit*) stair's width

Gironde [ʒiʀɔ̃d] NF **la ~** the Gironde

gironde† [ʒiʀɔ̃, ɔ̃d] ADJ F buxom, well-padded*

girondin, e [ʒiʀɔ̃dɛ̃, in] [1] ADJ (*Géog*) from the Gironde; (*Hist*) Girondist [2] NM,F (*Géog*) inhabitant *ou* native of the Gironde [3] NM (*Hist*) Girondist

girouette [ʒiʀwɛt] NF weather vane *ou* cock; (*fig*) **c'est une vraie ~** he changes (his mind) with the weather, he changes his mind depending on which way the wind is blowing

gisait, gisaient [ʒizɛ] → **gésir**

gisant, e [ʒizɑ̃, ɑ̃t] [1] ADJ lying [2] NM (*Art*) recumbent statue (*on tomb*)

gisement [ʒizmɑ̃] NM [a] (*Minér*) deposit; **~ de pétrole** oilfield; **~ houiller** coal seam [b] [*clientèle*] pool; **~ d'emplois** source of jobs *ou* employment; **~ d'informations** mine of information [c] (*Naut*) bearing

gisent [ʒiz], **gît** [ʒi] → **gésir**

gitan, e [ʒitɑ̃, an] [1] ADJ gipsy (*épith*) [2] **Gitan(e)** NM,F gipsy [3] **gitane ♦ Gitane®** NF (= *cigarette*) Gitane (*cigarette*)

gîte¹ [ʒit] NM [a] (= *abri*) shelter; († = *maison*) home; (*Tourisme*) gîte, self-catering cottage *ou* flat; **rentrer au ~** to return home; **ils lui donnent le ~ et le couvert** they give him room and board *ou* board and lodging (*Brit*); (*pour randonneurs*) **~ d'étape** lodge; **~ rural** (*country*) gîte, self-catering cottage (in the country) [b] (*Chasse*) [*lièvre*] form [c] (*Boucherie*) **~ (à la noix)** topside (*Brit*), bottom round (*US*); **~~ shin** (*Brit*), shank (*US*) [d] (*Minér*) deposit

gîte² [ʒit] NF (*Naut* = *emplacement d'épave*) bed (*of a sunken ship*); **donner de la ~** to list, heel

gîter [ʒite] ▸ conjug 1 ◂ VI (*littér*) to lodge; (*Naut*) (= *pencher*) to list, heel; (= *être échoué*) to be aground

givrage [ʒivʀaʒ] NM (*Aviat*) icing

givrant, e [ʒivʀɑ̃, ɑ̃t] ADJ → **brouillard**

givre [ʒivʀ] NM [a] (= *gelée blanche*) (hoar) frost, rime (*SPÉC*) → **fleur** [b] (*Chim*) crystallization

givré, e [ʒivʀe] (*ptp de* **givrer**) ADJ [a] [*arbre*] covered in frost; [*fenêtre, hélice*] iced-up; [*verre*] frosted; **orange ~e** orange sorbet served in the (orange) skin [b]* (= *ivre*) plastered‡; (= *fou*) cracked*, nuts*, bonkers‡ (*Brit*); **devenir complètement ~** to go completely off one's head *ou* rocker‡

givrer VT, **se givrer** VPR [ʒivʀe] ▸ conjug 1 ◂ [*pare-brise, aile d'avion*] to ice up

glabre [glabʀ] ADJ (= *imberbe*) hairless; (= *rasé*) clean-shaven; (*Bot*) glabrous

glaçage [glasaʒ] NM [*viande, papier, étoffe*] glazing; [*gâteau*] (*au sucre*) icing; (*au blanc d'œuf*) glazing

glaçant, e [glasɑ̃, ɑ̃t] ADJ [*attitude, accueil, ton*] frosty, chilly; [*humour*] icy

glace¹ [glas] [1] NF [a] (= *eau congelée*) ice (*NonC*); **~ pilée** crushed ice; **sports de ~** ice sports; (*lit, fig*) **briser** *ou* **rompre la ~** to break the ice → **compartiment, hockey, saint** *etc* [b] **de ~** (= *insensible, peu chaleureux*) [*accueil*] icy, frosty; [*expression, visage*] stony, frosty; **rester de ~** to remain unmoved [c] (*Culin*) (= *dessert*) ice cream; (*pour pâtisserie* = *glaçage*) royal icing, frosting (*US*); **~ à l'eau** water ice (*Brit*), sherbet (*US*); **~ à la crème** dairy ice cream; **~ à la vanille/au café** vanilla/coffee ice cream; **~ à l'italienne** soft ice cream → **sucre** [2] **glaces** NFPL (*Géog*) ice sheet(s), ice field(s); **~s flottantes** drift ice, ice floe(s); **canal bloqué par les ~s** canal blocked with ice *ou* with ice floes; **bateau pris dans les ~s** ice-bound ship

glace² [glas] NF [a] (= *miroir*) mirror; **~ à main** hand mirror → **armoire, tain** [b] (= *verre*) plate glass (*NonC*); (= *plaque*) sheet of (plate) glass; **la ~ d'une vitrine** the glass of a shop window [c] [*véhicule*] (= *vitre*) window [d] (*Bijouterie*) white speckle

glacé, e [glase] (*ptp de* **glacer**) ADJ [*neige, lac*] frozen; [*vent, eau, chambre*] icy, freezing; [*boisson*] icy, ice-cold; [*cuir, tissu*] glazed; [*fruit*] glacé; [*accueil, attitude, sourire*] frosty, chilly; **je suis ~** I'm frozen (stiff), I'm chilled to the bone; **j'ai les mains ~es** my hands are frozen *ou* freezing; **à servir ~** to be served iced *ou* ice-cold; **café/chocolat ~** iced coffee/chocolate → **crème, marron¹, papier**

glacer [glase] ▸ conjug 3 ◂ [1] VT [a] [+ *liquide*] (= *geler*) to freeze; (= *rafraîchir*) to chill, ice; **mettre des boissons à ~** to put some drinks to chill [b] [+ *personne, membres*] to make freezing, freeze; **ce vent glace les oreilles** your ears freeze with this wind; **ce vent vous glace** it's a freezing *ou* perishing (*Brit*) (cold) wind, this wind chills you to the bone [c] **~ qn** (= *intimider*) to turn sb cold, chill sb; (= *paralyser*) to make sb's blood run cold; **cela l'a glacé d'horreur** *ou* **d'épouvante** he was frozen with terror at this; **~ le sang de qn** to make sb's blood run cold, chill sb's blood; (*littér*) **cette réponse lui glaça le cœur** this reply turned his heart to ice; **son attitude vous glace** he has a chilling way about him [d] [+ *viande, papier, étoffe*] to glaze; [+ *gâteau*] (*au sucre*) to ice; (*au blanc d'œuf*) to glaze [2] **se glacer** VPR [*eau*] to freeze; **mon sang se glaça dans mes veines** my blood ran cold *ou* my blood froze in my veins; **son sourire/son expression se glaça** his smile/expression froze

glaceuse [glasøz] NF glazing machine

glaciaire [glasjɛʀ] [1] ADJ [*période, calotte*] (*épith*); [*relief, régime, vallée, érosion*] glacial [2] NM **le ~** the glacial, the ice age

glacial, e (*mpl* **glacials** *ou* **glaciaux**) [glasjal, jo] ADJ [a] [*froid*] icy, freezing (*épith*); [*nuit, pluie, vent*] icy, freezing (cold) → **océan** [b] [*accueil, silence, regard*] frosty, icy; **c'est quelqu'un de ~**

he's a real cold fish, he's a real iceberg; **« non », dit-elle d'un ton ~** "no", she said frostily *ou* icily

glaciation [glasjasjɔ̃] NF glaciation

glacier [glasje] NM [a] (*Géog*) glacier [b] (= *fabricant*) ice-cream maker; (= *vendeur*) ice-cream man → **pâtissier**

glacière [glasjɛʀ] NF icebox, cool box; **c'est une vraie ~ ici !** it's like a fridge *ou* an icebox here!

glaciologie [glasjɔlɔʒi] NF glaciology

glaciologique [glasjɔlɔʒik] ADJ glaciological

glaciologue [glasjɔlɔg] NMF glaciologist

glacis [glasi] NM [a] (*Art*) glaze [b] (*Archit*) weathering; (*Géog, Mil*) glacis

glaçon [glasɔ̃] NM [*rivière*] block of ice; [*toit*] icicle; [*boisson*] ice cube; (*péj = personne*) cold fish; **avec ou sans ~ ?** (*boisson*) with or without ice?; **mes pieds sont comme des ~s** my feet are like blocks of ice

gladiateur [gladjatœʀ] NM gladiator

glagla* [glagla] **♦ à glagla** LOC EXCL it's freezing!

glaïeul [glajœl] NM gladiola, gladiolus

glaire [glɛʀ] NF [*œuf*] white; (*Méd*) phlegm; **~ cervicale** cervical mucus

glaireux, -euse [glɛʀø, øz] ADJ slimy

glaise [glɛz] NF clay → **terre**

glaiseux, -euse [glɛzø, øz] ADJ clayey

glaisière [glɛzjɛʀ] NF clay pit

glaive [glɛv] NM two-edged sword; (*littér*) **le ~ de la justice** the sword of justice; **le ~ et la balance** the sword and the scales

glamour [glamuʀ] [1] ADJ [*personne, tenue*] glamorous; [*émission*] glitzy*, glossy [2] NM **le ~** glamour

glanage [glanaʒ] NM gleaning

gland [glɑ̃] NM (*Bot*) acorn; (*Anat*) glans; (= *ornement*) tassel; (** = *imbécile*) **quel ~ !** what a prick!**

glande [glɑ̃d] NF gland; (*Méd*) **avoir des ~s** to have swollen glands; **avoir les ~s‡** (= *être en colère*) to be really *ou* hopping (*Brit*) mad*; (= *être anxieux*) to be all wound-up*

glander‡ [glɑ̃de] ▸ conjug 1 ◂ VI (= *traînailler*) to fart around** (*Brit*), footle about* (*Brit*), screw around‡ (*US*); (= *attendre*) to hang around*, kick one's heels* (*Brit*); **j'en ai rien à ~** I don't give *ou* care a damn‡; **qu'est-ce que tu glandes ?** what the hell are you doing?‡

glandeur, -euse‡ [glɑ̃dœʀ, øz] NM,F layabout*, shirker; **c'est un vrai ~** he's a lazy bastard** *ou* slob‡

glandouiller‡ [glɑ̃duje] ▸ conjug 1 ◂ VI = **glander**

glandulaire [glɑ̃dylɛʀ] ADJ glandular

glane [glan] NF [a] (= *glanage*) gleaning [b] (= *chapelet*) **~ d'oignons/d'ail** string of onions/of garlic

glaner [glane] ▸ conjug 1 ◂ VT (*lit, fig*) to glean

glaneur, -euse [glanœʀ, øz] NM,F gleaner

glapir [glapiʀ] [1] VI [*renard, chien*] to yap, yelp; (*péj*) [*personne*] to yelp, squeal [2] VT [+ *insultes*] to scream

glapissement [glapismɑ̃] NM [*renard, chien*] yapping, yelping; (*péj*) [*personne*] yelping, squealing

glas [glɑ] NM knell (*NonC*), toll (*NonC*); **on sonne le ~** the bell is tolling, they are tolling the knell (*ou* bell); (*fig*) **sonner le ~ de** to toll *ou* sound the knell of

glasnost [glasnɔst] NF (*Hist*) glasnost; **le parti est en train de faire sa ~** the party is pursuing a policy of glasnost *ou* openness

glaucome [glokom] NM glaucoma

glauque [glok] ADJ [a] (= *vert-bleu*) blue-green [b] (*, péj* = *louche*) [*quartier, hôtel*] shabby; [*atmosphère*] murky; [*individu*] shifty, shady [c] (= *lugubre*) dreary completely warped [2] **se gondoler** VPR [a] [*papier*] to crinkle; [*planche*] to warp; [*tôle*] to buckle [b]* (= *rire*) to split one's sides laughing*, crease up*

gondolier, -ière [gɔ̃dɔlje, jɛʀ] NM,F (= *batelier*) gondolier; (*dans un supermarché*) shelf stocker

gonfalon [gɔ̃falɔ̃] NM gonfalon

gonfalonier [gɔ̃falɔnje] NM gonfalonier

gonflable [gɔ̃flabl] ADJ [*ballon, matelas, piscine*] inflatable; (*Aut*) **coussin** *ou* **sac ~** air bag → **poupée**

gonflage [gɔ̃flaʒ] NM inflating (*NonC*), inflation (*NonC*); **vérifier le ~ des pneus** to check the air in the tyres (*Brit*) *ou* tires (*US*)

gonflant, e [gɔ̃flɑ̃, ɑ̃t] [1] ADJ [a] [*coiffure*] bouffant [b]* (= *irritant*) damned‡ *ou* bloody‡ (*Brit*) irritating; **il est ~ avec ses histoires** he's a real pain (in the neck)* the way he goes on [2] NM **donner du ~ à ses cheveux** to give one's hair (some) body

gonflé, e [gɔ̃fle] (*ptp de* **gonfler**) ADJ [a] [*yeux, visage, pieds, chevilles*] puffy, swollen; [*ventre*] (*par la maladie*) distended, swollen; (*par un repas*) blown-out, bloated; **il a les joues bien ~es** he has chubby *ou* plump cheeks; **je me sens un peu ~** I feel a bit bloated [b]* **il est ~!** (= *courageux*) he's got some nerve!*; (= *impertinent*) he's got a nerve!* *ou* a cheek!* (*Brit*); **être ~ à bloc** to be raring to go*

gonflement [gɔ̃fləmɑ̃] NM [*ballon, pneu*] inflation; [*visage, ventre*] swelling; [*prix, résultats*] inflation; [*effectifs*] (= *augmentation*) swelling; (= *exagération*) exaggeration; **le ~ de son estomac m'inquiétait** his swollen stomach worried me; **le ~ de la masse monétaire** the increase in the money supply; **le ~ de la dette publique** the expansion of *ou* the increase in the public debt

gonfler [gɔ̃fle] ▸conjug 1◂ [1] VT [a] [+ *pneu, ballon*] (*avec une pompe*) to pump up, inflate; (*en soufflant*) to blow up, inflate; [+ *aérostat*] to inflate; [+ *joues, narines*] to puff out; [+ *poumons*] to fill (**de** with); **les pluies ont gonflé la rivière** the rain has swollen the river *ou* caused the river to swell; **le vent gonfle les voiles** the wind fills (out) *ou* swells the sails; **un paquet gonflait sa poche** his pocket was bulging with a package; **un soupir gonflait sa poitrine** he heaved a great sigh; **éponge gonflée d'eau** sponge swollen with water; **la bière me gonfle** *ou* **me fait ~ l'estomac** beer blows out my stomach, beer makes me feel bloated *ou* makes my stomach bloated; **il avait les yeux gonflés par le manque de sommeil** his eyes were puffy *ou* swollen with lack of sleep

[b] (= *dilater*) to swell; **ses succès l'ont gonflé d'orgueil** his successes have made his head swell *ou* made him puffed up (with pride); **l'orgueil gonfle son cœur** his heart is swollen with pride; **l'espoir/le chagrin lui gonflait le cœur** his heart was swelling *ou* bursting with hope/was heavy with sorrow; **cœur gonflé de joie/d'indignation** heart bursting with joy/ indignation; **il nous les gonfle!**‡ he's a pain in the neck* *ou* butt!‡ (*surtout US*)

[c] (= *grossir*) [+ *prix, résultat*] to inflate; [+ *effectif*] (= *augmenter*) to swell; (= *exagérer*) to exaggerate; [+ *moteur*] to soup up*; **on a gonflé l'importance de l'incident** the incident has been blown up out of (all) proportion, they have exaggerated the importance of the incident; **chiffres gonflés** inflated *ou* exaggerated figures

[2] VI (= *enfler*) [*genou, cheville*] to swell (up); [*bois*] to swell; (*Culin*) [*pâte*] to rise; **faire ~ le riz/les lentilles** to leave the rice/lentils to swell, soak the rice/lentils; **faire ~ ses cheveux** to give one's hair body

[3] **se gonfler** VPR [a] [*rivière*] to swell; [*poitrine*] to swell, expand; [*voiles*] to swell, fill (out)

[b] **se ~ (d'orgueil)** to be puffed up (with pride), be bloated with pride; **son cœur se gonfle de tristesse/d'espoir** his heart is heavy (with sorrow)/is bursting with hope

gonflette* [gɔ̃flɛt] NF (*péj*) body building (exercises); **faire de la ~** (*Sport*) to pump iron*; (*fig* = *exagérer*) to exaggerate, lay it on thick*

gonfleur [gɔ̃flœʀ] NM air pump

gong [gɔ̃g] NM (*Mus*) gong; (*Boxe*) bell → **sauver**

goniomètre [gɔnjɔmɛtʀ] NM goniometer

goniométrie [gɔnjɔmetʀi] NF goniometry

goniométrique [gɔnjɔmetʀik] ADJ goniometric(al)

gonococcie [gɔnɔkɔksi] NF gonorrhoea (*Brit*), gonorrhea (*US*)

gonocoque [gɔnɔkɔk] NM gonococcus

gonzesse‡ [gɔ̃zɛs] NF (*péj*) bird‡ (*Brit*), chick* (*US*); (*péj: efféminé*) **c'est une vraie ~** he's a real sissy*

gordien [gɔʀdjɛ̃] ADJ M → **nœud**

goret [gɔʀɛ] NM piglet; (*à un enfant*) **petit ~!** you dirty little pig!*, you mucky (little) pup!* (*Brit*)

gorge [gɔʀʒ] NF [a] [*personne*] (= *cou, gosier*) throat; (*littér* = *seins*) breast, bosom (*littér*); [*oiseau*] (= *poitrine*) breast; (= *gosier*) throat; **rire à pleine ~** *ou* **à ~ déployée** to roar with laughter, laugh heartily; **chanter à pleine ~** *ou* **à ~ déployée** to sing at the top of one's voice → **chat, couteau** etc

[b] (= *vallée, défilé*) gorge; **les ~s du Tarn** the gorges of the Tarn

[c] (= *rainure*) [*moulure, poulie*] groove; [*serrure*] tumbler

[d] (*loc*) **prendre qn à la ~** [*créancier*] to put a gun to sb's head; [*agresseur*] to grab sb by the throat; [*fumée, odeur*] to catch *ou* get in sb's throat; [*peur*] to grip sb by the throat; **tenir qn à la ~** (*lit*) to hold sb by the throat; (*fig* = *avoir à sa merci*) to have a stranglehold on sb, have sb by the throat; **l'os lui est resté dans la** *ou* **en travers de la ~** the bone (got) stuck in his throat; (*fig*) **ça lui est resté dans la** *ou* **en travers de la ~** (= *il n'a pas aimé*) he found it hard to take *ou* swallow; (= *il n'a pas osé le dire*) it *ou* the words stuck in his throat; **faire des ~s chaudes de qch** to laugh sth to scorn; **je lui enfoncerai** *ou* **ferai rentrer ses mots dans la ~** I'll make him eat his words; **faire rendre ~ à qn** to force sb to give back ill-gotten gains

gorge-de-pigeon [gɔʀʒ(ə)dəpiʒɔ̃] ADJ INV dapple-grey

gorgée [gɔʀʒe] NF mouthful; **boire à petites ~s** to take little sips; **boire à grandes ~s** to drink in gulps; **boire son vin à grandes/petites ~s** to gulp down/sip one's wine; **vider un verre d'une seule ~** to empty a glass in one gulp, down a glass in one*

gorger [gɔʀʒe] ▸conjug 3◂ [1] VT (*gén*) to fill (**de** with); [+ *animal*] to force-feed; **~ qn de pâtisseries** to fill sb up *ou* stuff* sb with cakes; **terre/éponge gorgée d'eau** earth/ sponge saturated with *ou* full of water; **fruits gorgés de soleil** sun-kissed fruit [2] **se gorger** VPR **se ~ de nourriture** to gorge o.s., stuff o.s.* (with food); **se ~ de gâteaux** to gorge o.s. on *ou* with cakes; **éponge qui se gorge d'eau** sponge which soaks up water

Gorgone [gɔʀgɔn] NF (*Myth*) Gorgon; (*Zool*) **gorgone** gorgonia

gorille [gɔʀij] NM (*Zool*) gorilla; (* = *garde du corps*) bodyguard, heavy*

Gorki [gɔʀki] NM Gorky

gosier [gozje] NM (*Anat*) throat; (* = *gorge*) throat, gullet; **crier à plein ~** to shout at the top of one's voice, shout one's head off; **chanter à plein ~** to sing at the top of one's voice; **avoir le ~ sec*** to be parched*; **ça m'est resté en travers du ~*** (*lit*) it (got) stuck in my

throat; (*fig*) I found it hard to take, it stuck in my craw* (*US*) → **humecter**

gospel [gɔspɛl] NM gospel (music)

gosse* [gɔs] NMF kid*; **sale ~** little brat*; **elle est restée très ~** she's still a kid at heart*; **~ des rues** street urchin; (*péj*) **~ de riche(s)** (spoilt) rich kid *ou* brat*; **il est beau ~*** he's a good-looker*

Goth [gɔt] NMF Goth

gotha [gɔta] NM (= *aristocratie*) high society; (*fig*) **le ~ de la finance/de la publicité** the financial/advertising bigwigs*

gothique [gɔtik] [1] ADJ [*architecture, style*] Gothic; **écriture ~** Gothic script [2] NM **le ~** the Gothic; **le ~ flamboyant** Flamboyant style

gotique [gɔtik] NM (*Ling*) Gothic

gouache [gwaʃ] NF (= *matière*) gouache, poster paint; (= *tableau*) gouache

gouaille [gwaj] NF cheeky *ou* cocky* humour

gouailleur, -euse [gwajœʀ, øz] ADJ cheeky, cocky*

gouape* [gwap] NF thug

Goudjerate [gudʒeʀat] NM = Guj(a)rât

goudron [gudʀɔ̃] NM tar; **~ de houille** coal tar; **~ végétal** *ou* **de bois** wood tar; (*sur un paquet de cigarettes*) **« ~s: 15 mg »** ≈ "15 mg tar"

goudronnage [gudʀɔnaʒ] NM tarring

goudronner [gudʀɔne] ▸conjug 1◂ VT [+ *route, toile*] to tar

goudronneux, -euse [gudʀɔnø, øz] ADJ tarry

gouffre [gufʀ] NM (*Géog*) abyss, gulf, chasm; **un ~ nous sépare** there's a gulf between us; **le ~ de l'oubli** the depths of oblivion; **c'est un ~ d'ignorance/de bêtise** he's abysmally ignorant/utterly stupid; **c'est un ~ (financier)** it just swallows up money, it's a bottomless pit; **nous sommes au bord du ~** we are on the brink of the abyss

gouge [guʒ] NF gouge

gougnafier* [guɲafje] NM bungling idiot*

gouine‡ [gwin] NF dyke*

goujat [guʒa, at] [1] ADJ boorish, churlish [2] NM boor, churl

goujaterie [guʒatʀi] NF boorishness

goujon [guʒɔ̃] NM (= *poisson*) gudgeon; (*Tech* = *cheville*) pin

goulache, goulasch [gulaʃ] NM *ou* F goulash

goulafre* [gulafʀ] ADJ, NMF (*Belg*) **il est ~** ◊ **c'est un ~** he's a greedy pig*

goulag [gulag] NM Gulag

goule [gul] NF ghoul

goulée [gule] NF [*liquide*] gulp; [*solide*] big mouthful; **prendre une ~ d'air frais** (*gorgée*) to take in a lungful of fresh air; (* : *bol d'air*) to get some fresh air

goulet [gulɛ] NM (*Naut*) narrows, bottleneck (*at entrance of harbour*); (*Géog*) gully; **~ d'étranglement** bottleneck

gouleyant, e [gulɛjɑ̃, ɑ̃t] ADJ lively

goulot [gulo] NM [*bouteille*] neck; **boire au ~** to drink straight from the bottle; **~ d'étranglement** bottleneck

goulotte [gulɔt] NF (*Archit*) channel; (*Tech*) chute, inclined flute

goulu, e [guly] [1] ADJ [*personne*] greedy, gluttonous; [*regards*] greedy [2] NM,F glutton

goulûment [gulymɑ̃] ADV greedily, gluttonously

goumier [gumje] NM (*Hist*) Moroccan soldier in the French army

goupil †† [gupi(l)] NM fox

goupille [gupij] NF (*Tech*) pin

goupillé, e* [gupije] (*ptp de* **goupiller**) ADJ (= *arrangé*) **bien/mal ~** [*machine, plan, procédé*] well/badly thought out; **comment est-ce ~, ce mécanisme?** how does this thing work?

goupiller [gupije] ▸conjug 1◂ [1] VT **a*** (= *combiner*) to fix*; **il a bien goupillé son affaire**

he did alright for himself there* **b** (Tech) to pin **2** **se goupiller*** VPR (= s'arranger) **comment est-ce que ça se goupille pour demain?** what's the setup ou gen (Brit) ou dope (US) for tomorrow?*; **ça s'est bien/mal goupillé, notre plan** our plan came off* (all right)/didn't come off*; **ça se goupille plutôt mal, cette histoire de déménagement** this removal business is a bit of a shambles* ou cock-up‡

goupillon [gupijɔ̃] NM (Rel) (holy water) sprinkler, aspergillum; (à bouteille) bottle brush → **sabre**

gourance‡ [guʀɑ̃s], **gourante‡** [guʀɑ̃t] NF cock-up‡, boob* (Brit); **faire une ~** to make a cock-up‡ ou a boob* (Brit), goof up‡ (US)

gourbi [guʀbi] NM (arabe) shack; (* = taudis) slum

gourd, e[1] [guʀ, guʀd] ADJ (par le froid) numb (with cold); (= maladroit, mal à l'aise) awkward

gourde[2] [guʀd] **1** NF a (Bot) gourd; [eau, alcool] flask **b*** (= empoté) dope*, clot* (Brit), dumbbell* (US) **2** ADJ* (= bête) dopey*, gormless* (Brit); (= maladroit) clumsy

gourde[3] [guʀd] NF (Fin) gourde

gourdin [guʀdɛ̃] NM club, bludgeon; **assommer qn à coups de ~** to club ou bludgeon sb

gourer (se)‡ [guʀe] ▶ VPR to boob* (Brit), goof up‡ (US); **se gourer de jour** to get the day wrong; **je me suis gouré de numéro de téléphone** I dialled the wrong number; **on s'est gouré de rue** we went to the wrong street; **je me suis gouré dans mes calculs** I made a cock-up in‡ ou I goofed up‡ (US) my calculations

gourgandine†† [guʀgɑ̃din] NF hussy† *

gourmand, e [guʀmɑ̃, ɑ̃d] **1** ADJ (lit, fig) [personne] greedy; **il est ~ comme un chat** he likes good food but he's fussy about what he eats; **je suis très ~** (gén) I'm very fond of my food; (pour les sucreries) I've got a sweet tooth; **être ~ de** [+ sucreries] to be fond of, be partial to; [+ nouveautés] to be avid for; **jeter un œil ~ sur qch** to eye sth greedily; **cette voiture est (très) ~e** this car's a gas-guzzler, this car's heavy on petrol (Brit) ou gas (US); (Agr) **branche ~e** sucker **2** NM,F gourmand (frm); **c'est une ~e** she's very fond of her food; (pour les sucreries) she's got a sweet tooth; (enfant) **tu n'es qu'un ~!** you greedy thing! **3** NM (Agr) sucker

gourmander [guʀmɑ̃de] ▶ conjug 1 ◀ VT (littér) to rebuke, berate (littér)

gourmandise [guʀmɑ̃diz] **1** NF a (gén) fondness of food; (péj) greed, greediness; (Rel = péché) gluttony; **elle regardait le gâteau avec ~** she eyed the cake greedily **2** **gourmandises** NFPL delicacies, sweetmeats†

gourme [guʀm] NF (†: Méd) impetigo; (Zool) strangles sg; **jeter sa ~** to sow one's wild oats

gourmé, e [guʀme] ADJ (littér) starchy, stiff

gourmet [guʀmɛ] NM gourmet, epicure → **fin[1]**

gourmette [guʀmɛt] NF [cheval] curb chain; [poignet] chain bracelet

gourou [guʀu] NM guru

gousse [gus] NF [vanille, petits pois] pod; **~ d'ail** clove of garlic

gousset [gusɛ] NM [gilet, pantalon] fob; [slip] gusset; (Tech = pièce d'assemblage) gusset → **montre[1]**

goût [gu] NM a (= sens) taste; **amer au ~** bitter to the taste **b** (= saveur) taste; **cela a un ~ de moisi** it tastes mouldy; **ça a bon/mauvais ~** it tastes good/nasty, it has a nice/bad taste; **la soupe a un ~** the soup tastes funny ou has a funny taste; **plat sans ~** tasteless ou flavourless dish; **ça a un ~ de fraise** it tastes of strawberries; **yaourt ~ vanille** vanilla-flavoured yoghurt; [épice, condiment] **donner du ~ à qch** to add (a

bit of) flavour to sth; **la vie n'a plus de ~ pour lui** he no longer has any taste for life, he has lost his taste for life; **ses souvenirs ont un ~ amer** he has bitter memories; **cette rétrospective a un ~ de nostalgie** this retrospective has a nostalgic feel ou flavour; **ça a un ~ de revenez-y*** it makes you want seconds, it's very more-ish* (Brit) **c** (= jugement) taste; **(bon) ~** (good) taste; **avoir du/manquer de ~** to have/lack taste; **avoir un ~ vulgaire** to have vulgar tastes; **le ~ ne s'apprend pas** taste is something you're born with; **faire qch sans/avec ~** to do something tastelessly/tastefully; **elle s'habille avec beaucoup de ~** she has very good taste in clothes, she has very good dress sense; **homme/femme de ~** man/woman of taste → **faute** **d** [vêtement, ameublement] **de bon ~** tasteful, in good taste (attrib); **de mauvais ~** tasteless, in bad ou poor taste (attrib); **c'est une plaisanterie de mauvais ~** this joke is in bad taste; **il serait de mauvais ~/d'un ~ douteux de faire** it would be in bad ou poor/doubtful taste to do; (hum) **il serait de bon ~ d'y aller/qu'il se mette à travailler** it mightn't be a bad idea to go/if he started doing some work **e** (= penchant) taste, liking (de, pour for); **salez à votre ~** salt (according) to taste; **il a peu de ~ pour ce genre de travail** this sort of work is not to his taste ou liking ou is not his cup of tea*; **il n'a aucun ~ pour les sciences** science subjects don't appeal to him; **il a le ~ de l'ordre** he likes order; **il a le ~ du risque** he likes taking risks; **faire qch par ~** to do sth from inclination ou because one has a taste for it; **prendre ~ à qch** to get ou acquire a taste for sth, get to like sth; **elle a repris ~ à la vie/la danse** she has started to enjoy life/dancing again; **il n'avait ~ à rien** he didn't feel like doing anything; **à mon/son ~** for my/his liking ou taste(s); **ce n'est pas du ~ de chacun** it's not to everybody's taste; **ses déclarations n'ont pas été du ~ de ses alliés politiques** what he said didn't go down well with his political allies, his political allies didn't like the sound of what he said; **cela m'a mis en ~** that gave me a taste for it; **est-ce à votre ~?** is it to your taste?; **c'est tout à fait à mon ~** this is very much to my taste; **il la trouve à son ~** she suits his taste; **faire passer le ~ du pain à qn*** to wipe the smile off sb's face; (= tuer) to do sb in*, bump sb off* → **chacun** **f** (= tendances) **~s** tastes; **avoir des ~s de luxe/modestes** to have expensive/simple tastes ■ (PROV) **des ~s et des couleurs (on ne discute pas)** there's no accounting for taste(s) ■ (PROV) **tous les ~s sont dans la nature** it takes all sorts to make a world **g** (= style) style; **dans le ~ classique/de X** in the classical style/the style of X; **ou quelque chose dans ce ~-là*** or something of that sort; **au ~ du jour** in keeping with the style of the day ou with current tastes; **il s'est mis au ~ du jour** he has brought himself into line with current tastes; **chanson remise au ~ du jour** song brought up to date

goûter[1] [gute] ▶ conjug 1 ◀ **1** VT a [+ aliment] to taste; **goûte-le, pour voir si c'est assez salé** taste it and see if there's enough salt **b** [+ repos, spectacle] to enjoy, savour (Brit), savor (US) **c** (littér) [+ écrivain, œuvre, plaisanterie] to appreciate; **il ne goûte pas l'art abstrait** he doesn't appreciate abstract art, abstract art isn't to his taste **d** (Belg) [aliment] to taste of

2 **goûter à** VT INDIR [+ aliment, plaisir] to taste, sample; [+ indépendance, liberté] to taste; **il y a à peine goûté** he's hardly touched it; **voulez-vous ~ à mon gâteau?** would you like to try ou sample my cake?; **goûtez-y** [+ vin] have a sip ou taste, taste it; [+ plat] have a taste, taste it

3 **goûter de** VT INDIR (= faire l'expérience de) to have a taste of, taste; **il a goûté de la vie militaire/de la prison** he has had a taste of army/prison life, he has tasted army/prison life

4 VI a (= faire une collation) to have tea (Brit), have an afterschool snack (US); **emporter à ~** to take an afterschool snack; **inviter des enfants à ~** to ask children to tea (Brit), invite children for a snack (US) **b** (Belg) [aliment] to taste good

goûter[2] [gute] NM [enfants] (afterschool) snack; [adultes] afternoon tea; **donner un ~ d'enfants** to give ou have a children's (tea) party (Brit), invite children for a snack (US); **l'heure du ~** (afternoon) snack time

goûteur, -euse [gutœʀ, øz] NM,F **~ d'eau/de vin** water/wine taster

goûteux, -euse [gutø, øz] ADJ [vin, viande] flavoursome (Brit), flavorful (US)

goutte [gut] **1** NF a (lit, fig) drop; **~ de rosée** dewdrop; **~ de sueur** bead of sweat; **suer à grosses ~s** to be streaming with sweat; **pleuvoir à grosses ~s** to rain heavily; **il est tombé quelques ~s** there were a few spots ou drops of rain; **du lait? — une ~** milk? — just a drop; **tomber ~ à ~** to drip **b** (Pharm) **~s** drops; **~s pour les yeux/le nez** eye/nose drops **c*** (= eau-de-vie) brandy **d** (††, hum = rien) **vois/entends** ~ I see/hear not a thing† (aussi hum) **e** (Méd) gout **f** (loc) **avoir la ~ au nez** to have a dripping ou runny nose; **passer entre les ~s** (pluie) to run between the drops; (fig) to come through without a scratch **2** COMP ▶ **goutte d'eau** drop of water; (Bijouterie) drop, droplet; **c'est une ~ d'eau dans la mer** it's a drop in the ocean (Brit) ou in the bucket (US); **c'est la ~ (d'eau) qui fait déborder le vase** it's the last straw, it's the straw that breaks the camel's back → **ressembler**

goutte-à-goutte [gutagut] NM INV (Méd) drip (Brit), IV (US); **alimenter qn au ~** to put sb on a drip (Brit) ou on an IV (US), drip-feed sb (Brit)

gouttelette [gut(ə)lɛt] NF droplet

goutter [gute] ▶ conjug 1 ◀ VI to drip (de from)

goutteux, -euse [gutø, øz] ADJ (Méd) gouty

gouttière [gutjɛʀ] NF (horizontale) gutter; (verticale) drainpipe; (Aut) rain gutter; (Méd) (plaster) cast; (Anat: sur os) groove → **chat**

gouvernable [guvɛʀnabl] ADJ governable; **difficilement ~** difficult to govern

gouvernail [guvɛʀnaj] NM (= pale) rudder; (= barre) helm, tiller; **~ de direction** rudder; **~ de profondeur** elevator; (fig) **tenir le ~** to be at the helm

gouvernant, e[1] [guvɛʀnɑ̃, ɑ̃t] **1** ADJ [parti, classe] ruling (épith), governing (épith) **2** NMPL (Pol) **les ~s** the rulers, those in power; **les gouvernés et les ~s** the citizens and those who govern them

gouvernante[2] [guvɛʀnɑ̃t] NF (= institutrice) governess; (= dame de compagnie) housekeeper

gouverne [guvɛʀn] NF **a** (frm) **pour ta ~** for your guidance **b** (Naut = pilotage) steering **c** (Aviat) (= surface) control surface; (= dispositif) **~ de profondeur** elevator; **~ latérale** aileron

gouverné [guvɛʀne] NM (gén pl) citizen

gouvernement [guvɛʀnəmɑ̃] NM (= administration, régime) government; (= cabinet) Cabinet, Government; **former un ~** to set up ou form a government; **soutenir le ~** to back the government; **il est au ~** he's a member of ou he's in the government; **les gens du ~** members of the government; **sous un ~ socialiste** under socialist rule ou government; **ça a eu lieu sous le ~ de Thatcher** it happened during the Thatcher government ou during Thatcher's government; **~ de cohabitation** cohabitation government

gouvernemental, e (mpl **-aux**) [guvɛrnəmãtal, o] ADJ [député] of the governing party; [organe, politique] government (épith), governmental (épith); [journal] pro-government; [troupes] government (épith); **le parti ~** the governing ou ruling party, the party in office; **l'équipe ~e** the government

gouverner [guvɛrne] ▶conjug 1◀ 1 VT **a** (Pol) to govern, rule; **le parti qui gouverne** the party in office, the governing ou ruling party; **droit des peuples à se ~** (eux-mêmes) right of peoples to self-government **b** (littér) [+ passions] to control; **savoir ~ son cœur** to have control over one's heart; **se laisser ~ par l'ambition/par qn** to let one's self be ruled ou governed by ambition/by sb; **il sait fort bien se ~** he is well able to control himself; **l'intérêt gouverne le monde** self-interest rules the world **c** (Naut) to steer, helm; **~ vers tribord** to steer to(wards) starboard **d** (Gram) to govern, take 2 VI (Naut) to steer; **le bateau gouverne bien/mal** the boat steers well/badly; **~ sur son ancre/sa bouée** to steer towards one's anchor/one's buoy

gouverneur [guvɛrnœr] NM **a** (Admin, Pol) governor; **le Gouverneur de la Banque de France** the Governor of the Bank of France; **~ militaire** military governor; (Can) **~ général** governor general **b** (Hist = précepteur) tutor

gouzi-gouzi* [guziguzi] NM INV tickle; **faire des ~ à qn** to tickle sb

goy [gɔj] 1 ADJ goyish 2 NMF goy

goyave [gɔjav] NF (= fruit) guava

goyavier [gɔjavje] NM (= arbre) guava

GPAO [ʒepeao] NF (ABRÉV = **gestion de la production assistée par ordinateur**) → **gestion**

GPL [ʒepeel] NM (ABRÉV = **gaz de pétrole liquéfié**) LPG

GPS [ʒepees] NM (ABRÉV = **global positioning system**) (système) ~ GPS (system)

GQG [ʒekyʒe] NM (ABRÉV = **Grand Quartier Général**) GHQ

GR [ʒeɛr] NM (ABRÉV = (**sentier de**) **grande randonnée**) **emprunter un GR** to take an official hiking trail → **randonnée**

Graal [gral] NM Grail; **la quête du ~** the quest for the Holy Grail

grabat [graba] NM pallet, mean bed

grabataire [grabatɛr] 1 ADJ bedridden 2 NMF bedridden invalid

grabuge* [grabyʒ] NM **il va y avoir du ~** there'll be ructions* (Brit) ou a ruckus* (US) ou a rumpus*; **faire du ~** to create havoc

▼ **grâce** [gras] NF **a** (= charme) [personne, geste] grace; [chose, paysage] charm; **plein de ~** graceful; **visage sans ~** plain face; **avec ~** [danser] gracefully; [s'exprimer] elegantly; **faire des ~s** to put on airs (and graces) **b** (= faveur) favour (Brit), favor (US); **demander une ~ à qn** to ask a favour of sb; **accorder une ~ à qn** to grant sb a favour; **trouver ~ auprès de ou aux yeux de qn** to find favour with sb; (frm, hum) **il nous a fait la ~ d'accepter** he did us the honour of accepting; **elle nous a fait la ~ de sa présence ou d'être présente** she graced ou honoured us with her presence; **être en ~** to be in favour; **rentrer en ~** to come back into favour; **être dans les bonnes ~s de qn** to be in favour with sb, be in sb's good graces ou good books*; **chercher/gagner les bonnes ~s de qn** to seek/gain sb's favour; **délai de ~** days of grace; **donner à qn une semaine de ~** to give sb a week's grace **c** (loc) **bonne/mauvaise ~** good/bad grace; **faire qch de ou avec bonne/mauvaise ~** to do sth with (a) good/bad grace, do sth willingly/grudgingly; **il y a mis de la mauvaise ~** he did it very reluctantly; **il a eu la bonne ~ de reconnaître ...** he had the good grace to admit ...; **il aurait mauvaise ~ à refuser** it would be bad form ou in bad taste for him to refuse

d (= miséricorde) mercy; (Jur) pardon; **~ royale/présidentielle** royal/presidential pardon; **demander ou crier ~** to beg ou cry for mercy; **demander ~ pour qn** to appeal for clemency on sb's behalf; **~!** (have) mercy!; **de ~, laissez-le dormir** for pity's sake ou for goodness' sake, let him sleep; **je vous fais ~ des détails/du reste** I'll spare you the details/the rest; **donner/recevoir le coup de ~** to give/receive the coup de grâce ou deathblow → **droit³, recours**

e (= reconnaissance) **dire les ~s** to give thanks (after a meal); **~ à qn/qch** thanks to sb/sth; **~ à Dieu!** thank God!, thank goodness! → **action, jour, rendre**

f (Rel) grace; **à la ~ de Dieu!** it's in God's hands!; **nous réussirons par la ~ de Dieu** with God's blessing we shall succeed; **~ efficace/suffisante/vivifiante** efficacious/sufficient/life-giving grace → **an, état**

g (= don, inspiration) gift; **avoir la ~** to have a gift; **il a été touché par la ~** he has been inspired; **c'est la ~ que nous lui souhaitons** that is what we wish for him

h (= déesse) **les trois Grâces** the three Graces

i (= titre) **Sa Grâce ...** (homme) His Grace ...; (femme) Her Grace ...

gracier [grasje] ▶conjug 7◀ VT to grant a pardon to, pardon; **il a été gracié par le président** he was granted a presidential pardon

gracieusement [grasjøzmã] ADV (= élégamment) gracefully; (= aimablement) amiably, kindly; (= gratuitement) free of charge; **ceci vous est ~ offert par la société Leblanc** Messrs Leblanc offer you this with their compliments, please accept this with the compliments of Messrs Leblanc; **documents ~ prêtés par l'Institut Pasteur** documentation kindly loaned by the Pasteur Institute

gracieuseté [grasjøzte] NF (littér) (= amabilité) amiability; (= geste élégant) graceful gesture; (= cadeau) free gift; (iro) **je vous remercie de vos ~s** so kind of you to say so (iro)

gracieux, -ieuse [grasjø, jøz] ADJ **a** (= élégant) [gestes, silhouette, personne] graceful **b** (= aimable) [sourire, abord, personne] amiable, kindly; [enfant] amiable; (frm) **notre gracieuse souveraine** our gracious sovereign (frm) **c** (frm = gratuit) [aide, service] gratuitous (frm) → **recours, titre**

gracile [grasil] ADJ [personne, corps, tige] slender; [cou] slender, swanlike

gracilité [grasilite] NF slenderness

Gracques [grak] NMPL **les ~** the Gracchi

gradation [gradasjɔ̃] NF gradation

grade [grad] NM **a** (Admin, Mil) rank; **monter en ~** to be promoted; **en prendre pour son ~*** to be hauled over the coals, get a proper dressing-down* **b** (= titre: Univ) degree; **~ de licencié** (first) degree, bachelor's degree **c** (Math) grade **d** (Tech) [huile] grade

gradé, e [grade] NM,F (Mil) (gén) officer; (= subalterne) N.C.O., non-commissioned officer; (Police) officer, ≈ (police) sergeant (Brit)

gradient [gradjã] NM gradient

gradin [gradɛ̃] NM (Théât) tier; [stade] step (of the terracing); (Agr) terrace; [stade] **les ~s** the terraces; **dans les ~s** on the terraces; **en ~s** terraced; **la colline s'élevait/descendait en ~s** the hill went up/down in steps ou terraces

graduation [graduasjɔ̃] NF [instrument] graduation

gradué, e [gradɥe] (ptp de **graduer**) ADJ [exercices] graded; [règle, thermomètre] graduated; **verre/pot ~** measuring glass/jug

graduel, -elle [gradɥel] 1 ADJ [progression, amélioration, augmentation] gradual; [difficultés] progressive 2 NM (Rel) gradual

graduellement [gradɥelmã] ADV gradually

graduer [gradɥe] ▶conjug 1◀ VT [+ exercices] to increase in difficulty; [+ difficultés, efforts] to

step up ou increase gradually; [+ règle, thermomètre] to graduate

graffiter [grafite] ▶conjug 1◀ VT to write graffiti on

graffiteur, -euse [grafitœr, øz] NM,F (gén) graffitist; (= artiste) graffiti artist

graffiti (pl **graffiti(s)**) [grafiti] NM graffiti (NonC); **un ~** a piece of graffiti

graille* [graj] NF grub*, nosh* (Brit), chow* (US); **à la ~!** come and get it!*, grub's up!* (Brit)

grailler [graje] ▶conjug 1◀ VI **a*** (= manger) to nosh* (Brit), chow down* (US) **b** [corneille] to caw **c** (= parler) to speak in a throaty ou hoarse voice

graillon [grajɔ̃] NM (péj = déchet) bit of burnt fat; **ça sent le ~** there's a smell of burnt fat

graillonner* [grajɔne] ▶conjug 1◀ VI (= tousser) to cough; (= parler) to speak in a throaty ou hoarse voice

grain [grɛ̃] 1 NM **a** [blé, riz, maïs, sel] grain; (= céréales) [de blé, etc] the grain; **~ d'orge** grain of barley, barleycorn; **donner du ~ aux poules** to give grain to the chickens; **alcool ou eau-de-vie de ~(s)** grain alcohol; (Rel) **le bon ~** the good seed; **cela leur a donné du ~ à moudre** (matière à réflexion) it gave them food for thought, it gave them something to chew over; (travail) it kept them occupied ou busy for a while; **mettre son ~ de sel*** to put ou stick one's oar in* (Brit), to put in one's two cents* (US); → **poulet, séparer**

b [café] bean; **café en ~s** coffee beans, unground coffee; **~ de raisin** grape; **~ de cassis** blackcurrant; **~ de poivre** peppercorn; **poivre en ~s** whole pepper, peppercorns; **moutarde en ~s** whole grain mustard

c [collier, chapelet] bead; (Méd = petite pilule) pellet

d (= particule) [sable, farine, pollen] grain; [poussière] speck; (fig) **~ de sable** blip*, glitch*; **il suffit d'un ~ de sable pour tout bloquer** one blip* ou glitch* is enough to bring everything grinding to a halt

e **un ~ de** (= un peu de) [+ fantaisie] a touch of; [+ bon sens] a grain ou an ounce of; **il n'y a pas un ~ de vérité dans ce qu'il dit** there's not a grain ou scrap of truth in what he says; **il a un (petit) ~*** he's a bit touched*, he's not quite all there*; **il faut parfois un petit ~ de folie** it sometimes helps to have a touch of madness ou to be a bit eccentric

f (= texture) [peau] texture; (Photo) grain; **à ~ fin** [bois, roche] fine-grained; **à gros ~s** coarse-grained; **travailler dans le sens du ~** to work with the grain

g (= averse brusque) heavy shower; (Naut = bourrasque) squall; **essuyer un ~** to run into a squall → **veiller**

h (†† = poids) grain (0.0647 gramme)

2 COMP ▶ **grain de beauté** mole, beauty spot ▶ **grain de plomb** leadshot (NonC)

graine [grɛn] NF (Agr) seed; **~s de radis** radish seeds; **~s germées** sprouting seeds; **~s pour oiseaux** birdseed (NonC); **monter en ~** [plante] to go ou run to seed, bolt; (hum) [enfant] to shoot up; **tu vois ce qu'a fait ton frère, prends-en de la ~*** you've seen what your brother has done so take a leaf out of his book*; **c'est de la ~ de voleur** he has the makings of a thief; **la petite ~** the precious seed (hum), sperm → **casser, mauvais**

grainer [grene] ▶conjug 1◀ VT, VI = **grener**

graineterie [grɛntri] NF (= commerce) seed trade; (= magasin) seed shop, seed merchant's (shop)

grainetier, -ière [grɛntje, jɛr] NM,F seed merchant; (= homme) seedsman

graissage [grɛsaʒ] NM [machine] greasing, lubricating; **faire faire un ~ complet de sa voitu-**

re to take one's car in for a complete lubricating job

graisse [gʀɛs] ① NF ⓐ [animal, personne] fat; (Culin) fat; [viande cuite] dripping (Brit), drippings (US); (= lubrifiant) grease; **~(s) végétale(s)/animale(s)** animal/vegetable fat; [animal] **prendre de la ~** to put on fat → **bourrelet** ⓑ (Typo) weight ② COMP ► **graisse de baleine** (whale) blubber ► **graisse de phoque** seal blubber ► **graisse de porc** lard

graisser [gʀese] ▸ conjug 1 ◂ ① VT (= lubrifier) (gén) to grease; [+ chaussures] to wax; (= salir) to get grease on, make greasy; (= donner un aspect gras à) [+ cheveux, peau] to make greasy; **cette lotion ne graisse pas** this lotion is non-greasy; **~ la patte à qn*** to grease ou oil sb's palm* ② VI [cheveux] to get greasy

graisseur [gʀesœʀ] NM (= objet) lubricator; **dispositif ~** lubricating ou greasing device; **(pistolet) ~** grease gun

graisseux, -euse [gʀeso, øz] ADJ [main, objet] greasy; [papiers] grease-stained, greasy; [nourriture] greasy, fatty; [bourrelet] fatty, of fat; [tissu, tumeur] fatty

graminacée [gʀaminase] NF = **graminée**

graminée [gʀamine] NF **une ~** a grass; **les ~s** grasses, graminae (SPÉC)

grammaire [gʀa(m)mɛʀ] NF (= science, livre) grammar; **faute de ~** grammatical mistake; **règle de ~** grammatical rule, rule of grammar; **exercice/livre de ~** grammar exercise/book; **~ des cas** case grammar; **~ (de structure) syntagmatique** phrase structure grammar; **~ de surface** surface grammar

grammairien, -ienne [gʀa(m)mɛʀjɛ̃, jɛn] NM,F grammarian

grammatical, e (mpl -aux) [gʀamatikal, o] ADJ (gén) grammatical; **exercice ~** grammar exercise; **phrase ~e** well-formed ou grammatical sentence → **analyse**

grammaticalement [gʀamatikalmɑ̃] ADV grammatically

grammaticalisation [gʀamatikalizasjɔ̃] NF grammaticalization

grammaticalité [gʀamatikalite] NF grammaticality

gramme [gʀam] NM gram(me); **je n'ai pas pris/perdu un ~** (de mon poids) I haven't put on/lost an ounce; **il n'a pas un ~ de jugeote** he hasn't got an ounce of commonsense

gramophone®† [gʀamɔfɔn] NM gramophone†

grand, e [gʀɑ̃, gʀɑ̃d] ① ADJ ⓐ (= de haute taille) [personne, verre] tall; [arbre, échelle] high, big, tall

ⓑ (= plus âgé, adulte) **son ~ frère** his older ou elder ou big* brother; **il a un petit garçon et deux ~es filles** he has a little boy and two older ou grown-up daughters; **ils ont deux ~s enfants** they have two grown-up children; **quand il sera ~** [enfant] when he grows up, when he's grown-up; [chiot] when it's big, when it's fully grown; **il est assez ~ pour savoir** he's big enough ou old enough to know; **tu es ~/~e maintenant** you're a big boy/girl now

ⓒ (en dimensions: gén) big, large; [hauteur, largeur] great; [bras, distance, voyage, enjambées] long; [avenue, marge] wide; **aussi/plus ~ que nature** as large as/larger than life; **ouvrir de ~s yeux** to open one's eyes wide; **ouvrir la fenêtre/la bouche toute ~e** to open the window/one's mouth wide; **l'amour avec un ~ A** love with a capital L

ⓓ (en nombre, en quantité) [vitesse, poids, valeur, puissance] great; [nombre, quantité] large, great; [famille] large, big; [foule] large, great, big; [dépense] great; [fortune] great, large; **la ~e majorité des gens** the great ou vast majority of people; **une ~e partie de ce**

qu'il a a great ou large proportion of what he has

ⓔ (= intense, violent) [bruit, cri] loud; [froid] severe, intense; [chaleur] intense; [vent] strong, high; [effort, danger, plaisir, déception] great; [pauvreté] great, dire (épith); [soupir] deep, big; **l'incendie a causé de ~s dégâts** the fire has caused extensive damage ou a great deal of damage; **avec un ~ rire** with a loud ou big laugh; **~ chagrin** deep ou great sorrow; **à ma ~e surprise/honte** much to my surprise/shame, to my great surprise/shame

ⓕ (= riche, puissant) [pays, firme, banquier, industriel] leading, big; **les ~s trusts** the big trusts; **un ~ personnage** an important person → **train**

ⓖ (= important) [aventure, progrès, intelligence] great; [différence, appétit, succès] great, big; [ville, travail] big; **je t'annonce une ~e nouvelle!** I've got some great news!; **le ~ moment approche** the big ou great moment is coming; **c'est un ~ jour/honneur pour nous** this is a great day/honour for us

ⓗ (= principal) main; **c'est la ~e nouvelle du jour** it's the main news of the day; **les ~s points de son discours** the main points of his speech; **les ~s fleuves du globe** the major ou main ou great rivers of the world; **la ~e difficulté consiste à ...** the main ou major difficulty lies in ...

ⓘ (intensif) [travailleur] great, hard; [collectionneur] great, keen; [buveur] heavy, hard; [mangeur] big; [fumeur] heavy; [ami, rêveur] great, big; [menteur] big; **c'est un ~ ennemi du bruit** he can't stand ou abide noise; **un ~ amateur de musique** a great music lover; **~ lâche/sot!** you big coward/fool!; **~e jeunesse** extreme youth; **un ~ mois/quart d'heure** a good month/quarter of an hour; **rester un ~ moment** to stay a good while; **un ~ kilomètre** a good kilometre; **un ~ verre d'eau** a large glass of water; **un ~ panier de champignons** a full basket of mushrooms; **les ~s malades** the very ill ou sick; **un ~ invalide** a seriously disabled person

ⓙ (= remarquable) [champion, œuvre, savant, civilisation] great; **un ~ vin/homme** a great wine/man; **une ~e année** a vintage ou great year; **le ~ Molière** the great Molière; **c'est du ~ jazz*** it's jazz at its best; **une ~e figure de l'Histoire** a major historical figure

ⓚ (= de gala) [réception, dîner] grand; **en ~e cérémonie/pompe** with great ceremony/pomp

ⓛ (= noble) [âme] noble, great; [pensée, principe] high, lofty; **se montrer ~ (et généreux)** to be big-hearted ou magnanimous

ⓜ (= exagéré) **faire de ~es phrases** to trot out high-flown sentences; **tous ces ~s discours** all these high-flown speeches; **faire de ~s gestes** to wave one's arms about → **cheval, mot**

ⓝ (= beaucoup de) **cela te fera (le plus) ~ bien** it'll do you a great deal of ou the world of good; **j'en pense le plus ~ bien** I think most highly of him; **~ bien vous fasse!** much good may it do you!; **il n'y a pas ~ danger** there's no great danger; **cela lui fera ~ tort** it'll do him a lot of harm

② ADV ⓐ (en taille) **ces sandales chaussent ~** these sandals are big-fitting (Brit) ou run large (US); **ce n'est pas une maquette, il l'a réalisé en ~** it's not a model, he made it full scale

ⓑ (= largement) **ouvrir (en) ~** [+ porte] to open wide; [+ robinet] to turn full on; **la fenêtre était ~(e) ouverte** the window was wide open; **voir ~** to think big; **il a vu trop ~** he was over-ambitious; **dix bouteilles? tu as vu ~!** ten bottles? you don't do things by halves!; **il fait toujours les choses en ~** he always does things on a large scale

③ NM ⓐ (Scol) older ou bigger boy, senior boy ou pupil; **jeu pour petits et ~s** game for

old and young alike ou for the young and the not-so-young; **il va à l'école tout seul comme un ~** he goes to school on his own like a big boy

ⓑ (terme d'affection) **mon ~** son, my lad (Brit)

ⓒ (= personne puissante) **les ~s de ce monde** men in high places; (Pol) **les quatre Grands** the Big Four; **les cinq ~s de l'électronique** the five big ou major electronics companies; **Pierre/Alexandre/Frédéric le Grand** Peter/Alexander/Frederick the Great

④ **grande** NF ⓐ (Scol) older ou bigger girl, senior girl ou pupil; **elle parle comme une ~e** she talks like a big girl

ⓑ (terme d'affection) **ma ~e** (my) dear

⑤ COMP ► **la grande Bleue** ou **bleue** the Med*, the Mediterranean ► **grand d'Espagne** Spanish grandee ► **le grand huit**† [fête foraine] the scenic railway† ► **grand œuvre** (= réalisation très importante) great work; (Alchimie) **le Grand Œuvre** the Great Work ► **le Grand Orient** the Grand Lodge of France ► **grande personne** grown-up ► **la grande vie** the good life; **mener la ~e vie** to live in style, live the good life

---

GRANDES ÉCOLES

The **grandes écoles** are competitive-entrance higher education establishments where engineering, business administration and other subjects are taught to a very high standard. The most prestigious include "l'École Polytechnique" (engineering), the three "Écoles normales supérieures" (humanities), "l'ÉNA" (the civil service college), and "HEC" (business administration).

Pupils prepare for entrance to the **grandes écoles** after their "baccalauréat" in two years of "classes préparatoires" (nicknamed "hypokhâgne" and "khâgne" for humanities and "hypotaupe" and "taupe" for science).

→ CLASSES PRÉPARATOIRES ; CONCOURS ; ÉCOLE NATIONALE D'ADMINISTRATION

---

grand-angle (pl grands-angles) [gʀɑ̃tɑ̃gl, gʀɑ̃zɑ̃gl], **grand-angulaire** (pl grands-angulaires) [gʀɑ̃tɑ̃gylɛʀ, gʀɑ̃zɑ̃gylɛʀ] NM wide-angle lens; **faire une photo au ~** to take a picture with a wide-angle lens, take a wide-angle shot

grand-chose [gʀɑ̃ʃoz] ① PRON INDÉF **pas ~** not much; **on ne sait pas ~ à son sujet** we don't know very much about him; **cela ne vaut pas ~** it's not worth much, it's not up to much* (Brit), it's no great shakes*; **es-tu blessé? — ce n'est pas ~** are you hurt? — it's nothing much; **il n'y a plus ~ dans ce magasin** there isn't much ou there's nothing much left in this shop; **il n'y a pas ~ à dire** there's not a lot to say, there's nothing much to say; **il n'en sortira pas ~ de bon** not much good will come (out) of this, I can't see much good coming (out) of this; **sans changer ~ au plan** without altering the plan much ② NMF INV (péj) **c'est un pas ~** he's a good-for-nothing

grand-croix (pl grands-croix) [gʀɑ̃kʀwa] ① NM holder of the Grand Cross ② NF INV Grand Cross (of the Légion d'honneur)

grand-duc (pl grands-ducs) [gʀɑ̃dyk] NM ⓐ (= personne) grand duke → **tournée²** ⓑ (= hibou) eagle owl

grand-ducal, e (mpl -aux) [gʀɑ̃dykal, o] ADJ (= du grand-duc) grand-ducal; (= du grand-duché de Luxembourg) of Luxembourg

grand-duché (pl grands-duchés) [gʀɑ̃dyʃe] NM grand duchy; **le ~ de Luxembourg** the grand duchy of Luxembourg

Grande-Bretagne [gʀɑ̃dbʀətaɲ] NF **la ~** Great Britain

grande-duchesse (pl grandes-duchesses) [gʀɑ̃ddyʃɛs] NF grand duchess

grandement [gʀɑ̃dmɑ̃] ADV [a] (= tout à fait) se tromper ~ to be greatly mistaken; **avoir ~ raison/tort** to be absolutely right/wrong [b] (= largement) [aider, contribuer] a great deal, greatly; **il a ~ le temps** he has plenty of time; **il y en a ~ assez** there's plenty of it *ou* easily enough (of it); **être ~ logé** to have plenty of room *ou* ample room (in one's house); **nous ne sommes pas ~ logés** we haven't got (very) much room; **je lui suis ~ reconnaissant** I'm deeply *ou* extremely grateful to him; **il est ~ temps de partir** it's high time we went [c] (= généreusement) [agir] nobly; **faire les choses ~** to do things lavishly in grand style

grandesse [gʀɑ̃dɛs] NF Spanish grandeeship

grandeur [gʀɑ̃dœʀ] [1] NF [a] (= dimension) size; **c'est de la ~ d'un crayon** it's the size of *ou* as big as a pencil; **ils sont de la même ~** they are the same size; ~ **nature** [statue] life-size (épith); [expérience] in real conditions; **en vraie ~** [maquette] full-size (épith), full-scale (épith) → **haut, ordre[1]** [b] (= importance) [œuvre, sacrifice, amour] greatness; **avoir des idées de ~** to have delusions of grandeur → **délire** [c] (= dignité) greatness; (= magnanimité) magnanimity; **faire preuve de ~** to show magnanimity; **la ~ humaine** the greatness of man; ~ **d'âme** generosity of spirit [d] (= gloire) greatness; ~ **et décadence de** rise and fall of; **politique de ~** politics of national grandeur [e] (Astron) magnitude; (Math) ~ **variable** variable magnitude; **de première ~** [étoile] of first magnitude; (fig) of the first order [f] † (= titre) **Sa Grandeur l'évêque de Lyon** (the) Lord Bishop of Lyons; **oui, Votre Grandeur** yes, my Lord [2] NFPL (= honneurs) ~s glory → **folie**

Grand-Guignol [gʀɑ̃giɲɔl] NM Grand Guignol; (fig) **c'est du ~** it's all blood and thunder

grand-guignolesque (pl **grand-guignolesques**) [gʀɑ̃giɲɔlɛsk] ADJ [situation, événement, pièce de théâtre] gruesome, blood-curdling

grandiloquence [gʀɑ̃dilɔkɑ̃s] NF grandiloquence, bombast

grandiloquent, e [gʀɑ̃dilɔkɑ̃, ɑ̃t] ADJ grandiloquent, bombastic

grandiose [gʀɑ̃djoz] ADJ [œuvre, spectacle, paysage] imposing, grandiose; **le ~ d'un paysage** the grandeur of a landscape

grandir [gʀɑ̃diʀ] ▸ conjug 2 ◂ [1] VI [a] [plante, enfant] to grow; [ombre portée] to grow (bigger); **il a grandi de 10 cm** he has grown 10 cm; **je le trouve grandi** he has grown since I last saw him; **en grandissant tu verras que …** as you grow up you'll see that …; **il a grandi dans mon estime** he's gone up in my estimation, he has grown *ou* risen in my esteem; **enfant grandi trop vite** lanky *ou* gangling child [b] [sentiment, influence, foule] to increase, grow; [bruit] to grow (louder), increase; [firme] to grow, expand; **l'obscurité grandissait** (the) darkness thickened, it grew darker and darker; **son pouvoir va grandissant** his power grows ever greater *ou* constantly increases; ~ **en sagesse** to grow *ou* increase in wisdom [2] VT [a] (= faire paraître grand) [microscope] to magnify; **les dangers/difficultés** to exaggerate the dangers/difficulties; **ces chaussures te grandissent** those shoes make you (look) taller; **il se grandit en se mettant sur la pointe des pieds** he made himself taller by standing on tiptoe [b] (= rendre prestigieux) **cette épreuve l'a grandi** this ordeal has made him grow in stature; **il sort grandi de cette épreuve** he has come out of this ordeal with increased stature; **la France n'en est pas sortie grandie** it did little for France's reputation

grandissant, e [gʀɑ̃disɑ̃, ɑ̃t] ADJ [foule, bruit, sentiment] growing; **nombre/pouvoir (sans cesse) ~** (ever-)growing *ou* (ever-)increasing number/power

grandissement† [gʀɑ̃dismɑ̃] NM (Opt) magnification

grandissime [gʀɑ̃disim] ADJ (hum = très grand) tremendous

grand-livre (pl **grands-livres**) [gʀɑ̃livʀ] NM († Comm) ledger

grand-maman (pl **grands-mamans**) [gʀɑ̃mamɑ̃] NF granny*, grandma

grand-mère (pl **grands-mères**) [gʀɑ̃mɛʀ] NF (= aïeule) grandmother; (* = vieille dame) (old) granny*

grand-messe (pl **grands-messes**) [gʀɑ̃mɛs] NF (Rel) high mass; (Pol) powwow*, ritual gathering; ~ **médiatique** media jamboree; **la ~ catholique** *ou* **du journal de 20 heures** the 8 o'clock TV news ritual

grand-oncle (pl **grands-oncles**) [gʀɑ̃tɔ̃kl, gʀɑ̃zɔ̃kl] NM great-uncle

grand-papa (pl **grands-papas**) [gʀɑ̃papa] NM grandpa, grandad*

grand-peine ◆**à grand-peine** LOC ADV with great difficulty

grand-père (pl **grands-pères**) [gʀɑ̃pɛʀ] NM (= aïeul) grandfather; (* = vieux monsieur) old man; (péj) **avance, ~!*** get a move on, grandad!*

grand-route (pl **grand-routes**) [gʀɑ̃ʀut] NF main road

grand-rue (pl **grand-rues**) [gʀɑ̃ʀy] NF **la ~** the high street (Brit), the main street (US)

grands-parents [gʀɑ̃paʀɑ̃] NMPL grand-parents

grand-tante (pl **grands-tantes**) [gʀɑ̃tɑ̃t] NF great-aunt

grand-vergue (pl **grands-vergues**) [gʀɑ̃vɛʀg] NF main yard

grand-voile (pl **grands-voiles**) [gʀɑ̃vwal] NF mainsail

grange [gʀɑ̃ʒ] NF barn

granit(e) [gʀanit] NM granite

granité, e [gʀanite] [1] ADJ granite-like (épith); **papier ~** grained paper [2] NM (= tissu) pebbleweave (cloth); (= glace) granita (Italian ice cream)

graniteux, -euse [gʀanitø, øz] ADJ (Minér) granitic

granitique [gʀanitik] ADJ (Minér) granite (épith), granitic

granivore [gʀanivɔʀ] [1] ADJ grain-eating, granivorous (SPÉC) [2] NM grain-eater, granivore (SPÉC)

granny smith [gʀanismis] NF INV Granny Smith (apple)

granulaire [gʀanylɛʀ] ADJ (Sci) granular

granulat [gʀanyla] NM aggregate

granulation [gʀanylasjɔ̃] NF [a] (= grain) grainy effect; ~s granular *ou* graining surface; ~s **cytoplasmiques** cytoplasmic granules [b] (Tech = action) granulation [c] (Photo) graininess

granule [gʀanyl] NM granule; (Pharm) small pill; ~ **homéopathique** homeopathic pill

granulé, e [gʀanyle] (ptp de **granuler**) [1] ADJ [surface] granular [2] NM granule

granuler [gʀanyle] ▸ conjug 1 ◂ VT [+ métal, poudre] to granulate

granuleux, -euse [gʀanylø, øz] ADJ (gén) granular; [peau] grainy

grape(-)fruit (pl **grape(-)fruits**) [gʀɛpfʀut] NM grapefruit

graphe [gʀaf] NM (Écon, Math) graph

graphème [gʀafɛm] NM grapheme

grapheur [gʀafœʀ] NM graphics application package, graphics software (NonC)

graphie [gʀafi] NF written form; **il y a plusieurs ~s pour ce mot** there are several written forms of this word *ou* several ways of spelling this word; ~ **phonétique** phonetic spelling

graphique [gʀafik] [1] ADJ (gén) graphic; (Ordin) [application, écran] graphics (épith); [environnement] graphic; [interface] graphical; **l'industrie ~** the computer graphics industry [2] NM (= courbe) graph, chart; ~ **en barres** *ou* **à colonnes** *ou* **à tuyaux d'orgue** bar chart *ou* graph; ~ **à secteurs** pie chart

graphiquement [gʀafikmɑ̃] ADV graphically

graphisme [gʀafism] NM [a] (= technique) (Design) graphics sg; (Art) graphic arts [b] (= style) [peintre, dessinateur] style of drawing [c] (= écriture individuelle) hand, handwriting; (= alphabet) script

graphiste [gʀafist] NMF graphic designer

graphitage [gʀafitaʒ] NM graphitization

graphite [gʀafit] NM graphite

graphiter [gʀafite] ▸ conjug 1 ◂ VT to graphitize; **lubrifiant graphité** graphitic lubricant

graphiteux, -euse [gʀafitø, øz] ADJ graphitic

graphologie [gʀafɔlɔʒi] NF graphology

graphologique [gʀafɔlɔʒik] ADJ of handwriting, graphological

graphologue [gʀafɔlɔg] NMF graphologist

grappe [gʀap] NF [fleurs] cluster; [groseilles] bunch; ~ **de raisin** bunch of grapes; **en** *ou* **par ~s** in clusters; ~s **humaines** clusters of people; **les ~s de la cytise** the laburnum flowers

grappillage [gʀapijaʒ] NM [a] [grains] gathering; [fruits, fleurs] picking, gathering; (après la vendange) gleaning [b] [idées] lifting; [argent] fiddling*; **ses ~s se montaient à quelques centaines de francs** his pickings amounted to several hundred francs; **pour limiter les ~s** to reduce fiddling*

grappiller [gʀapije] ▸ conjug 1 ◂ [1] VI (après la vendange) to glean; (= picorer) **arrête de ~, prends la grappe** stop picking at it and take the whole bunch; **elle ne mange pas, elle grappille** she doesn't eat, she just nibbles [2] VT [a] [+ grains] to gather; [+ fruits, fleurs] to pick, gather [b] [+ connaissances, nouvelles] to pick up; [+ renseignements, informations] to glean; [+ idées] to lift; [+ objets] to pick up (here and there); ~ **quelques sous** to fiddle* *ou* pick up a little extra on the side; **réussir à ~ quelques voix/sièges** to manage to pick up a few votes/seats; (péj) **il a beaucoup grappillé chez d'autres auteurs** he's lifted a lot from other authors

grappin [gʀapɛ̃] NM [bateau] grapnel; [grue] grab (Brit), drag (US); **mettre le ~ sur qn*** to grab sb, collar sb*; (pour l'épouser) **elle lui a mis le ~ dessus*** she's got her claws into him*; **mettre le ~ sur qch*** to get one's claws on *ou* into sth*

gras, grasse [gʀa, gʀas] [1] ADJ [a] [substance, aliment, bouillon] fatty; [huître] fat; **fromage ~** full fat cheese; **crème grasse pour la peau** rich moisturizing cream → **chou[1], corps, matière** [b] (= gros) [personne, animal, visage, main] fat; [bébé] podgy (Brit), pudgy (US); [volaille] plump; **être ~ comme un chanoine** *ou* **un moine** ◊ **être ~ à lard**† to be as round as a barrel; (péj) **être ~ du bide*** to have a bit of a belly* *ou* of a corporation* (Brit); (par excès de boisson) to have a beer-gut* *ou* a beer-belly*; (péj) **un ~ du bide*** a fat slob* → **vache, veau** [c] (= graisseux, huileux) [mains, cheveux, surface] greasy; [pavé, rocher] slimy; [boue, sol] sticky, slimy → **houille** [d] (= épais) [trait, contour] thick → **caractère, crayon, plante[1]** [e] [toux] loose, phlegmy; [voix, rire] throaty [f] (= vulgaire) [mot, plaisanterie] coarse, crude [g] (= abondant) [pâturage] rich, luxuriant; [récompense] fat* (épith); **la paye n'est pas grasse** the pay is rather meagre, it's not much of a salary; **j'ai touché 200 F, ce n'est pas ~*** I earned 200 francs, which is hardly a fortune; **il n'y a pas ~ à manger*** there's not much to eat

▸ **h** (loc) **faire la grasse matinée** to have a lie in, sleep in

▸ **2** NM **a** (Culin) fat; [baleine] blubber; (Théât) greasepaint; **j'ai les mains couvertes de ~** my hands are covered in grease ▸ **b** (= partie charnue) [jambe, bras] **le ~ de** the fleshy part of ▸ **c** (Typo) **c'est imprimé en (caractères) ~** it's printed in bold (type) ▸ **d** * (= profit) profit

▸ **3** ADV **a** **manger ~** to eat fatty foods; (Rel) **faire ~** to eat meat ▸ **b** **il tousse ~** he has a loose ou phlegmy cough; **parler/rire ~*** to speak/laugh coarsely

gras-double (pl **gras-doubles**) [gʀadubl] NM (Culin) tripe

grassement [gʀasmã] ADV **a** (rétribuer) generously, handsomely; (péj) **vivre ~** to live off the fat of the land; **~ payé** highly ou well paid ▸ **b** [parler, rire] coarsely

grasseyant, e [gʀasɛjã, ãt] ADJ [voix] guttural

grasseyement [gʀasɛjmã] NM guttural pronunciation

grasseyer [gʀasɛje] ▸ conjug 1 ◂ VI to have a guttural pronunciation; (Ling) to use a fricative ou uvular (Parisian) R

grassouillet, -ette* [gʀasujɛ, ɛt] ADJ podgy (Brit), pudgy (US), plump

gratifiant, e [gʀatifjã, jãt] ADJ [expérience, travail] rewarding, gratifying

gratification [gʀatifikasjɔ̃] NF **a** (Admin = prime) bonus; **~ de fin d'année** Christmas bonus ▸ (Brit) **b** (Psych = satisfaction) gratification

gratifier [gʀatifje] ▸ conjug 7 ◂ VT **~ qn de** [+ récompense, avantage] to present sb with; [+ sourire, bonjour] to favour (Brit) ou favor (US) ou grace sb with; (iro) [+ amende] to present sb with; (iro) [+ punition] to give sb; **il nous gratifia d'un long sermon** he favoured ou honoured us with a long sermon; (Psych) **se sentir gratifié** to feel gratified

gratin [gʀatɛ̃] NM **a** (Culin) (= plat) cheese (-topped) dish, gratin; (= croûte) cheese topping, gratin; **~ de pommes de terre** potatoes au gratin; **chou-fleur au ~** cauliflower cheese; **~ dauphinois** gratin Dauphinois ▸ **b** (= haute société) **le ~*** the upper crust*, the swells* (US); **tout le ~ de la ville était là** everybody who's anybody was there, all the nobs* (Brit) ou swells* (US) of the town were there

gratiné, e [gʀatine] (ptp de **gratiner**) **1** ADJ **a** (Culin) au gratin ▸ **b** (*: intensif) [épreuve, amende] (really) stiff; [aventures, plaisanterie] (really) wild; **il m'a passé une engueulade ~e** he gave me a heck of a telling-off*, he didn't half give me a telling-off* (Brit); **c'est un examen ~** it's a tough* ou stiff exam; **comme film érotique, c'est plutôt ~** as erotic films go, it's pretty hot stuff* ou spicy; **comme imbécile il est ~** he's a prize idiot **2** **gratinée** NF French onion soup

gratiner [gʀatine] ▸ conjug 1 ◂ VT (Culin) [+ pommes de terre] to cook au gratin **2** VI (= dorer) to brown, turn golden

gratis [gʀatis] **1** ADJ free **2** ADV free, for nothing

gratitude [gʀatityd] NF gratitude, gratefulness

gratos* [gʀatos] ADJ, ADV = **gratis**

gratouiller* [gʀatuje] ▸ conjug 1 ◂ VT **a** (= démanger) **~ qn** to make sb itch ▸ **b** **~ sa guitare** to strum on one's guitar

grattage [gʀataʒ] NM **a** [surface] (avec un ongle, une pointe) scratching; (avec un outil) scraping; **j'ai gagné au ~** I won on the scratch cards ▸ **b** (pour enlever) [tache] scratching off; [inscription] scratching out; [boue, papier peint]

scraping off; **après un ~ à la toile émeri** after rubbing with emery cloth

gratte [gʀat] NF **a** * (= petit bénéfice illicite) pickings; **faire de la ~** to make a bit on the side* ▸ **b** * (= guitare) guitar

gratte-ciel (pl **gratte-ciel(s)**) [gʀatsjɛl] NM skyscraper

gratte-cul (pl **gratte-culs**) [gʀatky] NM (Bot) rose hip

gratte-dos [gʀatdo] NM INV backscratcher

grattement [gʀatmã] NM scratching

gratte-papier (pl **gratte-papier(s)**) [gʀatpapje] NM (péj) penpusher (Brit), pencil pusher (US)

gratte-pieds [gʀatpje] NM INV shoe-scraper

gratter [gʀate] ▸ conjug 1 ◂ **1** VT **a** [+ surface] (avec un ongle, une pointe) to scratch; (avec un outil) to scrape; [+ guitare] to strum; [+ allumette] to strike; **gratte-moi le dos** scratch my back for me; **pour gagner, il suffit de ~ le ticket** to win you just have to scratch the card ▸ **b** (= enlever) [+ tache] to scratch off; [+ inscription] to scratch out; [+ boue, papier peint] to scrape off; **si on gratte un peu (le vernis) on se rend compte qu'il n'est pas très cultivé** if you scratch the surface you'll find he's not very educated ▸ **c** (= irriter) **ce drap me gratte** this sheet's really scratchy; **ça (me) gratte** I've got an itch; **la laine me gratte** wool makes me itch; **il y a quelque chose qui me gratte la gorge** I've got a tickly throat, my throat's tickly; **vin qui gratte la gorge** rough wine → **poil** ▸ **d** * (= grappiller) **~ quelques francs** to fiddle a few pounds* (Brit), pick up a little extra on the side; **il n'y a pas grand-chose à ~** there's not much to be made on that → **fond** ▸ **e** * (Sport = dépasser) to overtake; (Écon) **on s'est fait ~ par nos concurrents** we were overtaken by our competitors

2 VI **a** [plume] to scratch; [drap] to be scratchy; **ça gratte !** it's really itchy! ▸ **b** * (= économiser) to scrimp and save; **il gratte sur tout** he skimps on everything ▸ **c** * (= travailler) to slave away*, slog away* (Brit) ▸ **d** * (= écrire) to scribble ▸ **e** (= frapper) **~ à la porte** to scratch at the door

3 **se gratter** VPR to scratch (o.s.); **se ~ la tête** to scratch one's head; **tu peux toujours te ~ !*** you can whistle for it!*

gratteur, -euse [gʀatœʀ, øz] NM,F [guitare] strummer; (péj) **~ de papier** penpusher (Brit), pencil pusher (US)

grattoir [gʀatwaʀ] NM scraper

grattons [gʀatɔ̃] NMPL (Culin) ≈ pork scratchings

grattouiller [gʀatuje] VT = **gratouiller**

gratuit, e [gʀatɥi, ɥit] ADJ **a** (= non payant) free; **entrée ~e** admission free; **appel ~ au ...** call free on ..., ring Freefone (Brit) ..., call toll-free on (US) ...; **journal ~** free sheet; **le premier exemplaire est ~** the first copy is free, no charge is made for the first copy; (frm) **à titre ~** free of charge ou **crédit, enseignement** ▸ **b** (= non motivé) [supposition, affirmation] unwarranted; [accusation] unfounded, groundless; [cruauté, insulte, violence] gratuitous, wanton; [geste] gratuitous, unmotivated; [meurtre] motiveless, wanton; **c'est une hypothèse purement ~e** it's pure speculation → **acte c** (littér = désintéressé) disinterested

gratuité [gʀatɥite] NF **a** (= caractère non payant) **grâce à la ~ de l'éducation/des soins médicaux** thanks to free education/medical care ▸ **b** (= supposition, affirmation) unwarranted nature; [cruauté, insulte] wantonness; [geste] gratuitousness, unmotivated nature ▸ **c** (littér) [geste] disinterestedness

gratuitement [gʀatɥitmã] ADV **a** (= gratis) [entrer, participer, soigner] free (of charge) ▸ **b**

sans raison) [détruire] wantonly, gratuitously; [agir] gratuitously, without motivation; **supposer ~ que ...** to make the unwarranted supposition that ...

gravats [gʀava] NMPL (Constr) rubble

grave [gʀav] **1** ADJ **a** (= solennel) [air, ton, personne] grave, solemn; [assemblée] solemn ▸ **b** (= important) [raison, opération, problème, avertissement, responsabilité] serious; **s'il n'en reste plus, ce n'est pas ~ !** if there's none left, it doesn't matter! ▸ **c** (= alarmant) [maladie, situation, accident, nouvelle, blessure, menace] serious; [danger] serious, grave; **l'heure est ~** it is a serious moment; **il a de très ~s ennuis** he has very serious problems; **c'est très ~ ce que vous m'annoncez là** what you've told me is most alarming; **il n'y a rien de ~** it's nothing serious ▸ **d** (= bas) [note] low; [son, voix] deep, low-pitched → **accent** ▸ **e** (*: péj) **il est vraiment ~** he's the pits*; **t'es ~ vous're a case***

2 NM (Ling) grave (accent); (Mus) low register; (Radio) **« ~-aigu »** "bass-treble"; (Radio) **appareil qui vibre dans les ~s** set that vibrates at the bass tones; (Mus) **les ~s et les aigus** (the) low and high notes, the low and high registers

graveleux, -euse [gʀav(ə)lø, øz] ADJ **a** (= grivois) smutty ▸ **b** [terre] gravelly; [fruit] gritty

gravelle †† [gʀavɛl] NF (Méd) gravel †

gravelure [gʀavlyʀ] NF smut (NonC)

gravement [gʀavmã] ADV **a** [parler, regarder] gravely, solemnly ▸ **b** (= de manière alarmante) [blesser, offenser] seriously; **être ~ compromis** to be seriously compromised; **être ~ menacé** to be under a serious threat; **être ~ coupable** to be seriously involved in an offence ou crime; **être ~ malade** to be gravely ou seriously ill

graver [gʀave] ▸ conjug 1 ◂ VT **a** [+ signe, inscription] (sur métal, papier) to engrave; (sur pierre, bois) to carve, engrave; **~ à l'eau-forte** to etch; **c'est à jamais gravé dans sa mémoire** it's imprinted ou engraved forever on his memory; (fig) **c'est gravé sur son front** it's written all over his face ▸ **b** [+ médaille, monnaie] to engrave ▸ **c** [+ disque, CD] to cut ▸ **d** (= imprimer) to print; **faire ~ des cartes de visite** to get some visiting cards printed

graveur, -euse [gʀavœʀ, øz] **1** NM,F (sur pierre, métal, papier) engraver; (sur bois) (wood) engraver, woodcutter; **~ à l'eau-forte** etcher **2** NM (= machine) [disque] embossed groove recorder; **~ de CD (ROM)** CD writer ou recorder

gravide [gʀavid] ADJ [animal, utérus] gravid (SPÉC); **truie ~** sow in pig

gravier [gʀavje] NM **a** (= caillou) (little) stone, bit of gravel ▸ **b** (Géol = revêtement) gravel (NonC); **allée de ou en ~** gravel ou gravelled path; **recouvrir une allée de ~(s)** to gravel a path

gravière [gʀavjɛʀ] NF gravel pit

gravillon [gʀavijɔ̃] NM **a** (= petit caillou) bit of grit ou gravel ▸ **b** (= revêtement) **du ~ ◇ des ~s** gravel, loose chippings (Brit)

gravillonner [gʀavijɔne] ▸ conjug 1 ◂ VT to gravel; **~ une route** to gravel a road, put loose chippings (Brit) on a road

gravimétrie [gʀavimetʀi] NF gravimetry

gravimétrique [gʀavimetʀik] ADJ gravimetric(al)

gravir [gʀaviʀ] ▸ conjug 2 ◂ VT [+ montagne] to climb (up); [+ escalier] to climb; **~ péniblement une côte** to struggle up a slope; **~ les échelons de la hiérarchie** to climb the rungs of the (hierarchical) ladder

gravissime [gʀavisim] ADJ extremely ou most serious

gravitation [gʀavitasjɔ̃] NF gravitation

gravitationnel, -elle [gʀavitasjɔnɛl] ADJ gravitational; **la force gravitationnelle** the force of gravity

gravité [gʀavite] NF **a** [air, ton, personne] gravity, solemnity; [assemblée] solemnity; **plein de ~** very solemn **b** [erreur, problème, maladie, situation, danger, moment] seriousness, gravity; [accident, blessure, menace] seriousness; **c'est un accident sans ~** it was a minor accident, it wasn't a serious accident; **cela n'a ou ne présente aucun caractère de ~** it's not at all serious **c** [note] lowness; [son, voix] deepness **d** (Phys, Rail) gravity; **les lois de la ~** the laws of gravity → **centre**, **force**

graviter [gʀavite] ▶ conjug 1 ◀ VI **a** (= tourner) [astre] to revolve (**autour de** round, about); [personne] to hover, revolve (**autour de** round); **cette planète gravite autour du soleil** this planet revolves around ou orbits the sun; **il gravite dans les milieux diplomatiques** he moves in diplomatic circles; **pays satellite qui gravite dans l'orbite d'une grande puissance** country that is the satellite of a major power **b** (= tendre vers) [astre] **~ vers** to gravitate towards

gravois† [gʀavwa] NMPL = **gravats**

gravure [gʀavyʀ] **1** NF **a** [signe, inscription, médaille, monnaie] engraving **b** [disque] cutting **c** (= estampe) engraving **d** (= reproduction) (dans une revue) plate; (au mur) print, engraving **2** COMP ▶ **gravure sur bois** (= technique) woodcutting, wood engraving; (= dessin) woodcut, wood engraving ▶ **gravure en creux** intaglio engraving ▶ **gravure sur pierre** stone carving ▶ **gravure sur métaux** metal engraving ▶ **gravure sur cuivre** copperplate (engraving) ▶ **gravure directe** hand-cutting ▶ **gravure en relief** embossing ▶ **gravure à l'eau-forte** etching ▶ **gravure de mode** fashion plate ▶ **gravure à la pointe sèche** dry-point engraving ▶ **gravure en taille douce** line-engraving

gré [gʀe] NM **a** [personnes] **à mon/votre ~** (goût) to my/your liking ou taste; (désir) as I/you like ou please ou wish; (choix) as I/you like ou prefer ou please; (avis) **c'est trop moderne, à mon ~** it's too modern for my liking ou to my mind; **c'est à votre ~?** is it to your liking? **agir ou** (en) **faire à son ~** to do as one likes ou pleases ou wishes; **venez à votre ~ ce soir ou demain** come tonight or tomorrow, as you like ou prefer ou please; **on a fait pour le mieux, au ~ des uns et des autres** we did our best to take everyone's wishes into account; **contre le ~ de qn** against sb's will **b** (loc) **de ~ à ~** by mutual agreement; **il le fera de ~ ou de force** he'll do it whether he likes it or not, he'll do it willy-nilly; **de son plein ~** of one's own free will, of one's own accord; **de bon ~** willingly; **de mauvais ~** reluctantly, grudgingly; **bon ~ mal ~** whether you (ou they etc) like it or not, willy-nilly → **savoir** **c** [choses] **flottant au ~ de l'eau** drifting wherever the water carries (ou carried) it, drifting (along) on ou with the current; **volant au ~ du vent** [chevelure] flying in the wind; [plume, feuille] carried along by the wind; [planeur] gliding wherever the wind carries (ou carried) it; **au ~ des événements** [décider, agir] according to how ou the way things go ou develop; **ballotté au ~ des événements** tossed about by events; **il décorait sa chambre au ~ de sa fantaisie** he decorated his room as the fancy took him; **son humeur change au ~ des saisons** his mood changes with ou according to the seasons

grèbe [gʀɛb] NM grebe; **~ huppé** great-crested grebe; **~ castagneux** dabchick, little grebe

grec, grecque [gʀɛk] **1** ADJ [île, personne, langue] Greek; [habit, architecture, vase] Gre-

cian, Greek; [profil, traits] Grecian → **renvoyer** **2** NM (Ling) Greek **3** **Grec(que)** NM,F Greek **4** **grecque** NF (= décoration) (Greek) fret; (Culin) **champignons à la grecque** mushrooms à la grecque

Grèce [gʀɛs] NF Greece

gréco- [gʀeko] PRÉF Greek(-); **~catholique** Greek Catholic; **~macédonien** Greek Macedonian; **~turc** Greek-Turkish, greco-turkish

gréco-latin, e (mpl **gréco-latins**) [gʀekolatɛ̃, in] ADJ Graeco-Latin (Brit), Greco-Latin (US)

gréco-romain, e (mpl **gréco-romains**) [gʀekoʀɔmɛ̃, ɛn] ADJ Graeco-Roman (Brit), Greco-Roman (US)

gredin† [gʀədɛ̃] NM (= coquin) scoundrel†, rascal

gréement [gʀemɑ̃] NM (Naut) (= équipement) rigging; (= disposition) rig; **le voilier a un ~ de cotre/ketch** the yacht is cutter-rigged/ketch-rigged; **les vieux ~s** (= voiliers) tall ships, old sailing ships

green [gʀin] NM (Golf) green

gréer [gʀee] ▶ conjug 1 ◀ VT (Naut) to rig

greffage [gʀefaʒ] NM (Bot) grafting

greffe¹ [gʀef] NF **a** (Méd) [organe] transplant; [tissu] graft; **~ du cœur/rein** heart/kidney transplant; **on lui a fait une ~ de la cornée** he was given a corneal transplant; **la ~ a pris** (lit) the graft has taken; (fig) things have turned out fine **b** (Bot) (= action) grafting; (= pousse) graft

greffe² [gʀef] NM (Jur) Clerk's Office

greffé, e [gʀefe] (ptp de **greffer**) NM,F **~ (du cœur)** (récent) heart transplant patient; (ancien) person who has had a heart transplant

greffer [gʀefe] ▶ conjug 1 ◀ **1** VT **a** (Méd) [+ organe] to transplant; [+ tissu] to graft; **on lui a greffé un rein** he was given a kidney transplant **b** (Bot) to graft **2** **se greffer** VPR **se ~ sur** [problèmes] to come on top of

greffier, -ière [gʀefje, jɛʀ] **1** NM,F (Jur) clerk (of the court) **2** NM (*† = chat) malkin†

greffon [gʀefɔ̃] NM **a** (Méd) (= organe) transplant, transplanted organ; (= tissu) graft; **~ de rein** transplanted kidney **b** (Bot) graft

grégaire [gʀegɛʀ] ADJ (Zool) gregarious; (péj) **instinct ~** herd instinct; **avoir l'instinct ~** (péj) to go with the crowd, be easily led; (= aimer la société) to like socialising, be the sociable type

grégarisme [gʀegaʀism] NM gregariousness

grège [gʀɛʒ] **1** ADJ [soie] raw, greyish-beige **2** NM raw silk

grégeois [gʀeʒwa] ADJ M → **feu¹**

grégorien, -ienne [gʀegɔʀjɛ̃, jɛn] **1** ADJ Gregorian **2** NM (chant) **~** Gregorian chant, plainsong

grêle¹ [gʀɛl] ADJ [jambes, silhouette, tige] spindly; [personne] lanky; [son, voix] shrill → **intestin¹**

grêle² [gʀɛl] NF hail; **averse de ~** hail storm; **~ de coups/de pierres** hail ou shower of blows/stones

grêlé, e [gʀele] (ptp de **grêler**) ADJ [visage] pockmarked; [région] damaged by hail

grêler [gʀele] ▶ conjug 1 ◀ **1** VB IMPERS **il grêle** it is hailing **2** VT **la tempête a grêlé les vignes** the hail storm has damaged the vines

grêlon [gʀelɔ̃] NM hailstone

grelot [gʀəlo] NM (little spherical) bell; **avoir les ~s*** to be shaking in one's shoes*

grelottant, e [gʀəlɔtɑ̃, ɑ̃t] ADJ [personne] shivering

grelottement [gʀəlɔtmɑ̃] NM (= tremblement) shivering; (= tintement) jingling

grelotter [gʀəlɔte] ▶ conjug 1 ◀ VI **a** (= trembler) to shiver (**de** with); **~ de froid/de fièvre/peur** to shiver with cold/fever/fear **b** (= tinter) to jingle

greluche: [gʀəlyʃ] NF (péj = fille) bird: (Brit), chick: (US)

Grenade [gʀənad] **1** N (= ville) Granada **2** (= État) Grenada

grenade [gʀənad] NF **a** (Bot) pomegranate **b** (= explosif) grenade; **~ à fusil/main** rifle/hand grenade; **~ lacrymogène/fumigène** teargas/smoke grenade; **~ sous-marine** depth charge **c** (= insigne) badge (on soldier's uniform etc)

grenadier [gʀənadje] NM **a** (Bot) pomegranate tree **b** (Mil) grenadier

grenadin¹ [gʀənadɛ̃] NM **a** (Bot) grenadin(e) **b** (Culin) **~ de veau** (small) veal medallion

grenadin², e¹ [gʀənadɛ̃, in] **1** ADJ Grenadian **2** **Grenadin(e)** NM,F Grenadian

grenadine² [gʀənadin] NF (= sirop) grenadine

grenaille [gʀənaj] NF **de la ~** (= projectiles) shot; (pour poules) middlings; **~ de plomb** lead shot; **~ de fer** iron filings

grenaison [gʀənɛzɔ̃] NF seeding

grenat [gʀəna] **1** NM garnet **2** ADJ INV dark red, garnet-coloured (Brit) ou -colored (US)

grené, e [gʀəne] (ptp de **grener**) **1** ADJ [cuir, peau] grainy; [dessin] stippled **2** NM [gravure, peau] grain

greneler [gʀənle] ▶ conjug 4 ◀ VT [+ cuir, papier] to grain

grener [gʀəne] ▶ conjug 5 ◀ **1** VT [+ sel, sucre] to granulate, grain; [+ métal, glace] to grain **2** VI (Agr) [plante] to seed

grenier [gʀənje] NM attic; (pour conserver le grain) loft; **~ à blé** (lit) corn loft (Brit), wheat loft (US); (fig) granary; **~ à foin** hayloft; **~ à sel** salt storehouse

grenouillage [gʀənujaʒ] NM (Pol péj) shady dealings, jiggery-pokery (Brit)

grenouille [gʀənuj] NF frog; (péj) **~ de bénitier** churchy old man (ou woman) (péj), Holy Joe* (Brit) (péj); **manger ou bouffer la ~*** to make off with the takings; **avoir des ~s dans le ventre*** to have a rumbling stomach

grenouiller* [gʀənuje] ▶ conjug 1 ◀ VI (péj) to indulge in ou be involved in shady dealings

grenouillère [gʀənujɛʀ] NF (= pyjama) sleepsuit

grenu, e [gʀəny] ADJ [peau] coarse-grained; [cuir, papier] grained; [roche] granular

grenure [gʀənyʀ] NF graining

grès [gʀɛ] NM **a** (Géol) sandstone **b** (Poterie) stoneware; **cruche/pot de ~** stoneware pitcher/pot

gréseux, -euse [gʀezø, øz] ADJ sandstone (épith)

grésil [gʀezil] NM (Mét) (fine) hail

grésillement [gʀeziljmɑ̃] NM **a** [beurre, friture] sizzling, sputtering; [poste de radio, téléphone] crackling **b** [grillon] chirruping, chirping

grésiller¹ [gʀezije] ▶ conjug 1 ◀ VI **a** [beurre, friture] to sizzle, sputter; [poste de radio, téléphone] to crackle **b** [grillon] to chirrup, chirp

grésiller² [gʀezije] ▶ conjug 1 ◀ VB IMPERS **il grésille** fine hail is falling, it's hailing

gressin [gʀesɛ̃] NM (small) bread stick

grève [gʀɛv] **1** NF **a** (= arrêt du travail) strike; **se mettre en ~** to go on strike, strike, take strike ou industrial action; **être en ~ ◊ faire ~** to be on strike, be striking; **usine en ~** striking factory; **~ des cheminots/des transports** train/transport strike → **briseur**, **droit³**, **piquet** **b** (= rivage) [mer] shore, strand (littér); [rivière] bank, strand (littér); (Hist) **la place de Grève** the Place de Grève **2** COMP ▶ **grève d'avertissement** warning strike ▶ **grève de la faim** hunger strike; **faire la ~ de la faim** to go (ou be) on hunger strike ▶ **grève générale** general ou all-out strike ▶ **grève illimitée** indefinite strike ▶ **grève de l'impôt** non-payment of taxes

► **grève partielle** partial strike ► **grève patronale** lockout ► **grève perlée** ≈ go-slow (Brit), ≈ slowdown (strike) (US); **faire une ~ perlée** ≈ to go slow (Brit), slowdown (US) ► **grève de protestation** protest strike ► **grève sauvage** wildcat strike ► **grève de solidarité** sympathy strike; **faire une ~ de solidarité** to strike ou come out (Brit) in sympathy ► **grève surprise** lightning strike ► **grève sur le tas** sit-down strike ► **grève totale** all-out strike ► **grève tournante** strike by rota (Brit), staggered strike (US) ► **grève du zèle** ≈ work-to-rule; **faire la ~ du zèle** to work to rule

grever [gʀəve] ▶ conjug 5 ◀ VT [+ budget] to put a strain on; [+ économie, pays] to burden; **la hausse des prix grève sérieusement le budget des ménagères** the rise in prices puts a serious strain on the housewife's budget; **grevé d'impôts** weighed down with ou crippled by taxes; **maison grevée d'hypothèques** house mortgaged down to the last brick

gréviste [gʀevist] **1** ADJ [mouvement] strike (épith) **2** NMF striker; **les employés ~s** the striking employees; **~ de la faim** hunger striker

gribiche [gʀibiʃ] ADJ **sauce ~** vinaigrette sauce with chopped boiled eggs, gherkins, capers and herbs

gribouillage [gʀibujaʒ] NM (= écriture) scrawl (NonC), scribble; (= dessin) doodle, doodling (NonC)

gribouille† [gʀibuj] NM short-sighted idiot, rash fool; **politique de ~** short-sighted policy

gribouiller [gʀibuje] ▶ conjug 1 ◀ **1** VT (= écrire) to scribble, scrawl; (= dessiner) to scrawl **2** VI (= dessiner) to doodle

gribouilleur, -euse [gʀibujœʀ, øz] NM,F (péj) (= écrivain) scribbler; (= dessinateur) doodler

gribouillis [gʀibuji] NM = **gribouillage**

grièche [gʀijɛʃ] ADJ → **pie-grièche**

grief [gʀijɛf] NM grievance; **faire ~ à qn de qch** to hold sth against sb; **ils me font ~ d'être parti** ou **de mon départ** they reproach me ou they hold it against me for having left

grièvement [gʀijɛvmɑ̃] ADV **~ blessé** (very) seriously injured

griffade [gʀifad] NF scratch

griffe [gʀif] NF **a** [mammifère, oiseau] claw; **le chat fait ses ~s** the cat is sharpening its claws; (lit, fig) **sortir** ou **montrer/rentrer ses ~s** to show/draw in one's claws; **elle l'attendait, toutes ~s dehors** she was waiting, ready to pounce on him; **tomber sous la ~/arracher qn des ~s d'un ennemi** to fall into/snatch sb from the clutches of an enemy; **les ~s de la mort** the jaws of death; **coup de ~** (lit) scratch; (fig) dig; **donner un coup de ~ à qn** (lit) to scratch sb; (plus fort) to claw sb; (fig) to have a dig at sb **b** (= signature) signature; (= tampon) signature stamp; (= étiquette de couturier) maker's label (inside garment); (fig = empreinte) [auteur, peintre] stamp; **l'employé a mis sa ~ sur le document** the clerk stamped his signature on the document **c** (Bijouterie) claw **d** (Bot) [asperge] crown

griffé, e [gʀife] ADJ [accessoire, vêtement] designer (épith), with a designer label; **tous ses tailleurs sont ~s** all her suits have designer labels

griffer [gʀife] ▶ conjug 1 ◀ VT **a** [chat] to scratch; (avec force) to claw; [ronces] to scratch; **elle lui griffa le visage** she clawed ou scratched his face **b** (Haute Couture) to put one's name to

griffon [gʀifɔ̃] NM (= chien) griffon; (= vautour) griffon vulture; (Myth) griffin

griffonnage [gʀifɔnaʒ] NM (= écriture) scribble; (= dessin) hasty sketch

griffonner [gʀifɔne] ▶ conjug 1 ◀ **1** VT (= écrire) to scribble, jot down; (= dessiner) to sketch

hastily **2** VI (= écrire) to scribble; (= dessiner) to sketch hastily

griffu, e [gʀify] ADJ (lit, péj) **pattes** ou **mains ~es** claws

griffure [gʀifyʀ] NF scratch, claw mark

grignotage [gʀiɲɔtaʒ] NM [personne] snacking (NonC); [salaires, espaces verts, majorité] (gradual) erosion, eroding, whittling away

grignotement [gʀiɲɔtmɑ̃] NM [souris] nibbling, gnawing

grignoter [gʀiɲɔte] ▶ conjug 1 ◀ **1** VT **a** [personne] to nibble (at); [souris] to nibble (at), gnaw (at) **b** (= réduire) [+ salaires, espaces verts, libertés] to eat away (at), erode gradually, whittle away; [+ héritage] to eat away (at); (= obtenir) [+ avantage, droits] to win gradually; **~ du terrain** to gradually gain ground; **il a grignoté son adversaire*** he gradually made up on ou gained ground on his opponent; **il n'y a rien à ~ dans cette affaire** there's nothing much to be gained in that business **2** VI (= manger peu) to nibble (at one's food), pick at one's food; **~ entre les repas** to snack between meals

grigou* [gʀigu] NM (= avare) penny-pincher*, skinflint

grigri, gri-gri (pl **gris-gris**) [gʀigʀi] NM (gén) charm; [indigène] grigri

gril [gʀil] NM **a** (Culin) steak pan, grill pan; (= supplice) **saint Laurent a subi le supplice du ~** Saint Laurence was roasted alive; **être sur le ~*** to be on tenterhooks, be like a cat on hot bricks (Brit) ou on a hot tin roof (US); **faire cuire au ~** to grill **b** (Anat) **~ costal** rib cage

grill [gʀil] NM → **grill-room**

grillade [gʀijad] NF (= viande) grill; (= morceau de porc) pork steak; **~ d'agneau/de thon** grilled lamb/tuna

grillage¹ [gʀijaʒ] NM **a** (Culin) [pain, amandes] toasting; [poisson, viande] grilling; [café, châtaignes] roasting **b** (Tech) [minerai] roasting; [coton] singeing

grillage² [gʀijaʒ] NM (= treillis métallique) wire netting (NonC); (très fin) wire mesh (NonC); (= clôture) wire fencing (NonC); **entouré d'un ~** surrounded by a wire fence

grillager [gʀijaʒe] ▶ conjug 3 ◀ VT (avec un treillis métallique) to put wire netting on; (très fin) to put wire mesh on; (= clôturer) to put wire fencing around; **à travers la fenêtre grillagée on voyait le jardin** through the wire mesh covering ou over the window we could see the garden; **un enclos grillagé** an area fenced off with wire netting

grille [gʀij] NF **a** [parc] (= clôture) railings; (= portail) (metal) gate; [magasin] shutter **b** (= claire-voie) [cellule, fenêtre] bars; [comptoir, parloir] grille; [château-fort] portcullis; [égout, trou] (metal) grate, (metal) grating; [radiateur de voiture] grille, grid; [poêle à charbon] grate **c** (= répartition) [salaires, tarifs] scale; [programmes de radio] schedule; [horaires] grid, schedule **d** (= codage) (cipher ou code) grid; **~ de mots croisés** crossword puzzle (grid); **~ de loto** loto card; **appliquer une ~ de lecture freudienne à un roman** to interpret a novel from a Freudian perspective **e** (Élec) grid **f** (Sport Aut) **~ de départ** starting grid

grillé, e* [gʀije] (ptp de **griller**) ADJ (= discrédité) **tu es ~!** you're finished!; **il est ~** (= gén) his name is mud*, he's finished; (espion) his cover's been blown*; **je suis ~ avec Gilles/chez cet éditeur** my name is mud* with Gilles/at that publisher's

grille-pain [gʀijpɛ̃] NM INV toaster

griller [gʀije] ▶ conjug 1 ◀ **1** VT **a** (Culin) [+ pain, amandes] to toast; [+ poisson, viande] to grill; [+ café, châtaignes] to roast **b** [+ visage, corps] to burn; **se ~ les pieds devant le feu** to toast one's feet in front of the fire; **se ~ au soleil** to roast in the sun **c** [+ plantes, cultures] to scorch

d [+ fusible, lampe] (court-circuit) to blow; (trop de courant) to burn out; [+ moteur] to burn out; **une ampoule grillée** a dud bulb **e** * (= fumer) **~ une cigarette** ◊ **en ~ une** to have a smoke* **f** * (= dépasser) **~ qn à l'arrivée** to pip sb at the post* (Brit), beat sb (out) by a nose (US); **se faire ~** to be outstripped **g** * (= discréditer) **elle m'a grillé auprès de lui** I've got no chance with him thanks to her **h** * (= ne pas respecter) **~ un feu rouge** to go through a red light, jump the lights* (Brit), run a stoplight (US); **~ un arrêt** [autobus] to miss out ou go past a stop; **~ les étapes** to go too far too fast **i** (Tech) [+ minerai] to roast **2** VI **a** (Culin) **faire ~** [+ pain] to toast; [+ viande] to grill; [+ café] to roast; **on a mis les steaks à ~** we've put the steaks on to grill ou on the grill **b** * [personne] **on grille ici !** we're ou it's roasting ou boiling in here!*; **ils ont grillé dans l'incendie** they were roasted alive in the fire; **~ (d'impatience ou d'envie) de faire qch** to be burning ou itching to do sth; **~ de curiosité** to be burning with curiosity

grillon [gʀijɔ̃] NM cricket

grill-room [gʀilʀum] NM ≈ steakhouse

grimaçant, e [gʀimasɑ̃, ɑ̃t] ADJ [visage, bouche] (de douleur, de colère) twisted, grimacing; (sourire figé) grinning unpleasantly ou sardonically

grimace [gʀimas] NF **a** (de douleur) grimace; (pour faire rire, effrayer) grimace, (funny) face; **l'enfant me fit une ~** the child made a face at me; **s'amuser à faire des ~s** to make ou pull (funny) faces, grimace; **il eut ou fit une ~ de dégoût/de douleur** he gave a grimace of disgust/pain, he grimaced with disgust/pain, his face twisted with disgust/pain; **avec une ~ de dégoût/de douleur** with a disgusted/pained expression; **il eut ou fit une ~** he pulled a wry face, he grimaced; **il a fait la ~ quand il a appris la décision** he pulled a long face when he learned of the decision → **apprendre, soupe** **b** (= hypocrisies) **~s** posturings; **toutes leurs ~s me dégoûtent** I find their posturings ou hypocritical façade quite sickening **c** (= faux pli) pucker; **faire une ~** to pucker

grimacer [gʀimase] ▶ conjug 3 ◀ **1** VI **a** (par contorsion) **~ (de douleur)** to grimace with pain, wince; **~ (de dégoût)** to pull a wry face (in disgust); **~ (sous l'effort)** to grimace ou screw one's face up (with the effort); **le soleil le faisait ~** the screwed his face up in the sun; **à l'annonce de la nouvelle il grimaça** he pulled a wry face ou he grimaced when he heard the news **b** (= sourire) [personne] to grin unpleasantly ou sardonically; [portrait] to wear a fixed grin **c** [vêtement] to pucker **2** VT (littér) **~ un sourire** to force ou manage a smile

grimacier, -ière [gʀimasje, jɛʀ] ADJ (= affecté) affected; (= hypocrite) hypocritical

grimage [gʀimaʒ] NM (Théât) (= action) making up; (= résultat) (stage) make-up

grimer [gʀime] ▶ conjug 1 ◀ **1** VT (Théât = maquiller) to make up; **on l'a grimé en vieille dame** he was made up as an old lady **2** **se grimer** VPR to make (o.s.) up

grimoire [gʀimwaʀ] NM **a** (inintelligible) piece of mumbo jumbo; (illisible) illegible scrawl (NonC), unreadable scribble **b** (= livre de magie) (vieux) ~ book of magic spells

grimpant, e [gʀɛ̃pɑ̃, ɑ̃t] ADJ **plante ~e** climbing plant, climber; **rosier ~** climbing rose, rambling rose

grimpe* [gʀɛ̃p] NF rock-climbing

grimpée [gʀɛ̃pe] NF (= montée) (steep) climb

grimper [gʀɛ̃pe] ▶ conjug 1 ◀ **1** VI **a** [personne, animal] to climb (up); (avec difficulté) to clamber up; (dans la société) to climb; [chat] **~ aux**

rideaux to climb up the curtains; **ça le fait ~ aux rideaux*** (de colère) it drives him up the wall*; (sexuellement) it makes him horny‡ ou randy (Brit)*; **~ aux arbres** to climb trees; **~ à l'échelle** to climb (up) the ladder; **~ à la corde** to shin up ou climb a rope, pull o.s. up a rope; **~ sur** ou **dans un arbre** to climb up ou into a tree; **~ le long de la gouttière** to shin up ou climb up the drain pipe; **~ dans un taxi*** to jump ou leap into a taxi; (dans une voiture) **allez, grimpe!** come on, get in!; **grimpé sur la table/le toit** having climbed ou clambered onto the table/roof

[b] [route, plante] to climb; **ça grimpe dur!** it's a hard ou stiff ou steep climb!

[c] * [fièvre] to soar; [prix] to rocket, soar

[2] VT [+ montagne, côte] to climb (up), go up; **~ l'escalier** to climb (up) the stairs; **~ un étage** to climb up a ou one floor

[3] NM [Athlétisme] (rope-)climbing (NonC)

grimpereau (pl **grimpereaux**) [gʀɛ̃pʀo] NM **~ (des bois)** tree creeper; **~ (des jardins)** short-toed tree creeper

grimpette* [gʀɛ̃pɛt] NF (steep little) climb

grimpeur, -euse [gʀɛ̃pœʀ, øz] [1] ADJ, NM (oiseaux) **~s** climbing ou scansorial (SPÉC) birds, scansores (SPÉC) [2] NM,F (= varappeur) (rock-)climber; (= cycliste) hill specialist, climber; **c'est un bon/mauvais ~** (cycliste) he's good/bad on hills, he's a good/bad climber

grinçant, e [gʀɛ̃sɑ̃, ɑ̃t] ADJ [comédie] darkly humorous; [charnière, essieux] grating; [porte] creaking; **ironie ~e** dark irony

grincement [gʀɛ̃smɑ̃] NM [objet métallique] grating; [plancher, porte, ressort, sommier] creaking; [freins] squealing; [plume] scratching; [craie] squeaking; **il ne l'a pas accepté sans ~s de dents** he accepted it only with much gnashing of teeth

grincer [gʀɛ̃se] ▸ conjug 3 ◂ VI [a] [objet métallique] to grate; [plancher, porte, ressort, sommier] to creak; [freins] to squeal; [plume] to scratch; [craie] to squeak [b] **~ des dents (de colère)** to grind ou gnash one's teeth (in anger); **ce bruit vous fait ~ les dents** that noise really sets your teeth on edge

grincheux, -euse [gʀɛ̃ʃø, øz] [1] ADJ (= acariâtre) grumpy; **humeur grincheuse** grumpiness [2] NM,F grumpy person, misery

gringalet [gʀɛ̃galɛ] [1] ADJ M (péj = chétif) puny [2] NM (péj) **(petit) ~** puny little thing, (little) runt

gringo [gʀiŋgo] ADJ, NMF (péj) gringo

gringue* [gʀɛ̃g] NM **faire du ~ à qn** to chat sb up

griot [gʀijo] NM griot

griotte [gʀijɔt] NF (= cerise) Morello cherry; (Géol) griotte

grippage [gʀipaʒ] NM (Tech) jamming; **pour éviter le ~ de l'économie** to prevent the economy seizing up

grippal, e (mpl -aux) [gʀipal, o] ADJ flu (épith), influenzal (SPÉC); **médicament pour état ~** anti-flu drug

grippe [gʀip] NF flu, influenza (frm); **avoir la ~** to have (the) flu, have influenza; **il a une petite ~** he's got a touch of flu; **~ intestinale** gastric flu; **prendre qn/qch en ~** to take a sudden dislike to sb/sth

grippé, e [gʀipe] ADJ (Méd) **il est ~** he's got (the) flu; **rentrer ~** to go home with (the) flu; **les ~s** people with ou suffering from flu

gripper [gʀipe] ▸ conjug 1 ◂ [1] VT (Tech) to jam [2] VI (= se bloquer) [moteur] to jam, seize up; (= se froncer) [tissu] to bunch up [3] **se gripper** VPR [moteur] to jam, seize up; **le système judiciaire se grippe** the court system is seizing up

grippe-sou* (pl **grippe-sous**) [gʀipsu] NM (= avare) penny-pincher*, skinflint

gris, e [gʀi, gʀiz] [1] ADJ [a] [couleur, temps] grey (Brit), gray (US); **~ acier/anthracite/ardoise/fer/perle/souris** steel/anthracite/slate/iron/pearl/squirrel grey; **~-bleu/-vert** blue-/green-grey; **cheval ~ pommelé** dapple-grey horse; **~ de poussière** grey with dust, dusty; **aux cheveux ~** grey-haired; **il fait ~** it's a grey ou dull day → **ambre, éminence, matière** [b] (= morne) [vie] colourless (Brit), colorless (US), dull; [pensées] grey (Brit), gray (US) [c] (= éméché) tipsy* [d] (loc) **faire ~e mine** to pull a long face; **faire ~e mine à qn** to give sb a cool reception [2] NM [a] (= couleur) grey (Brit), gray (US) [b] (= tabac) shag [c] (Équitation) grey (Brit) ou gray (US) (horse)

grisaille [gʀizaj] NF [a] [vie] colourlessness (Brit), colorlessness (US), dullness; [ciel, temps, paysage] greyness (Brit), grayness (US) [b] (Art) grisaille; **peindre qch en ~** to paint sth in grisaille

grisant, e [gʀizɑ̃, ɑ̃t] ADJ (= stimulant) exhilarating; (= enivrant) intoxicating

grisâtre [gʀizɑtʀ] ADJ greyish (Brit), grayish (US)

grisbi [gʀizbi] NM (arg Crime) loot‡

grisé [gʀize] NM grey (Brit) ou gray (US) tint; **zone en ~** shaded area

griser [gʀize] ▸ conjug 1 ◂ [1] VT [alcool] to intoxicate, make tipsy; [air, vitesse, parfum] to intoxicate; **ce vin l'avait grisé** the wine had gone to his head ou made him tipsy*; **l'air de la montagne grise** the mountain air goes to your head (like wine); **se laisser ~ par le succès/des promesses** to let success/promises go to one's head; **se laisser ~ par l'ambition** to be carried away by ambition [2] **se griser** VPR [buveur] to get tipsy* (avec, de on); **se ~ de** [+ air, vitesse] to get drunk on; [+ émotion, paroles] to allow o.s. to be intoxicated by ou carried away by

griserie [gʀizʀi] NF (lit, fig) intoxication

grisette [gʀizɛt] NF (Hist) grisette

gris-gris [gʀigʀi] NM = **grigri**

**grison †† ** [gʀiz5] NM (= âne) ass

grisonnant, e [gʀizɔnɑ̃, ɑ̃t] ADJ greying (Brit), graying (US); **il avait les tempes ~es** he was greying ou going grey at the temples; **la cinquantaine ~e, il ...** a greying fifty-year-old, he ...

grisonnement [gʀizɔnmɑ̃] NM greying (Brit), graying (US)

grisonner [gʀizɔne] ▸ conjug 1 ◂ VI to be greying (Brit) ou graying (US), be going grey (Brit) ou gray (US)

Grisons [gʀiz5] NMPL **les ~** the Graubünden; **canton des ~** canton of Graubünden; (Culin) **viande des ~** dried beef served in thin slices

grisou [gʀizu] NM firedamp; **coup de ~** firedamp explosion

grisoumètre [gʀizumɛtʀ] NM firedamp detector

grive [gʀiv] NF (Orn) thrush; **~ musicienne** song thrush → **faute**

grivèlerie [gʀivɛlʀi] NF (Jur) offence of ordering food ou drink in a restaurant and being unable to pay for it

griveton* [gʀivt5] NM soldier

grivois, e [gʀivwa, waz] ADJ saucy

grivoiserie [gʀivwazʀi] NF (= mot) saucy expression; (= attitude) sauciness; (= histoire) saucy story

grizzli, grizzly [gʀizli] NM grizzly bear

grœnendael [gʀɔ(n)endal] NM Groenendael (sheepdog)

Groenland [gʀɔenlɑ̃d] NM Greenland

groenlandais, e [gʀɔenlɑ̃dɛ, ɛz] [1] ADJ of ou from Greenland, Greenland (épith) [2] **Groenlandais(e)** NM,F Greenlander

grog [gʀɔg] NM ≈ (hot) toddy (usually made with rum)

groggy* [gʀɔgi] ADJ INV (Boxe) groggy; **être ~** (d'émotion) to be in a daze; (de fatigue) to be completely washed out

grognard [gʀɔɲaʀ] NM (Hist) soldier of the old guard of Napoleon I

grognasse‡ [gʀɔɲas] NF (péj) old bag‡

grognasser* [gʀɔɲase] ▸ conjug 1 ◂ VI to grumble ou moan on (and on)

grogne* [gʀɔɲ] NF **la ~ des syndicats** the rumbling ou simmering discontent in the unions; **face à la ~ sociale** faced with rumbling ou simmering social discontent; **la ~ monte chez les étudiants** students are grumbling more and more ou are showing more and more signs of discontent

grognement [gʀɔɲmɑ̃] NM [personne] grunt; [cochon] grunting (NonC), grunt; [sanglier] snorting (NonC), snort; [ours, chien] growling (NonC), growl; **il m'a répondu par un ~** he growled in reply

grogner [gʀɔɲe] ▸ conjug 1 ◂ [1] VI [personne] to grumble, moan* (contre at); [cochon] to grunt; [sanglier] to snort; [ours, chien] to growl; **les syndicats grognent** there are rumblings of discontent among the unions [2] VT [+ insultes] to growl, grunt

grognon, -onne [gʀɔɲ5, ɔn] ADJ [air, expression, vieillard] grumpy, gruff; [attitude] surly; [enfant] grouchy; **elle est ~** ou **grognonne!** ◊ **quelle ~(ne)!** what a grumbler! ou moaner!*

groin [gʀwɛ̃] NM [animal] snout; (péj) [personne] ugly ou hideous face

grolle‡ [gʀɔl] NF shoe

grommeler [gʀɔm(ə)le] ▸ conjug 4 ◂ [1] VI [personne] to mutter (to o.s.), grumble to o.s.; [sanglier] to snort [2] VT [+ insultes] to mutter

grommellement [gʀɔmɛlmɑ̃] NM muttering, indistinct grumbling

grondement [gʀɔ̃dmɑ̃] NM [canon, train, orage] rumbling (NonC); [torrent] roar, roaring (NonC); [chien] growl, growling (NonC); [foule] (angry) muttering; [moteur] roar; **le ~ de la colère/de l'émeute** the rumbling of mounting anger/of the threatening riot; **le train passa devant nous dans un ~ de tonnerre** the train thundered past us

gronder [gʀɔ̃de] ▸ conjug 1 ◂ [1] VT (= réprimander) [+ enfant] to tell off, scold; **je vais me faire ~ si je rentre tard** I'll get told off if I get in late; (amicalement) **il faut que je vous gronde d'avoir fait ce cadeau** you're very naughty to have bought this present, I should scold you for buying this present [2] VI a [canon, train, orage] to rumble; [torrent, moteur] to roar; [chien] to growl; [foule] to mutter (angrily) [b] [émeute] to be brewing; **la colère gronde chez les infirmières** nursing staff are getting increasingly angry [c] (littér = grommeler) to mutter

gronderie [gʀɔ̃dʀi] NF scolding

grondeur, -euse [gʀɔ̃dœʀ, øz] ADJ [ton, humeur, personne] grumbling; [vent, torrent] rumbling; **d'une voix grondeuse** in a grumbling voice

grondin [gʀɔ̃dɛ̃] NM gurnard

groom [gʀum] NM (= employé) bellboy, bellhop (US); [porte] door closer; **je ne suis pas ton ~** I'm not your servant

gros, grosse [gʀo, gʀos]

[1] ADJECTIF	[4] ADVERBE
[2] NOM MASCULIN	[5] COMPOSÉS
[3] NOM FÉMININ	

[1] ADJECTIF

[a] dimension (gén) big, large; [lèvres, corde] thick; [chaussures] big, heavy; [personne] fat; [ventre, bébé] fat, big; [pull, manteau] thick, heavy; **le ~ bout** the thick end; **il pleut à grosses gouttes** it's raining heavily; **c'est ~ comme une tête d'épingle/mon petit doigt** it's

the size of *ou* it's no bigger than a pinhead/ my little finger; **des tomates grosses comme le poing** tomatoes as big as your fist; **un mensonge ~ comme une maison*** a gigantic lie, a whopper*; **je l'ai vu venir ~ comme une maison*** I could see it coming a mile off*

b **= important** [*travail*] big; [*problème, ennui, erreur*] big, serious; [*somme*] large, substantial; [*entreprise*] big, large; [*soulagement, progrès*] great; [*dégâts*] extensive, serious; (= *violent*) [*averse*] heavy; [*fièvre*] high; [*rhume*] heavy, bad; **une grosse affaire** a large business, a big concern; **les grosses chaleurs** the height of summer, the hot season; **les ~ consommateurs d'énergie** big energy consumers; **un ~ mensonge** a terrible lie, a whopper*; (*fig*) **c'est un ~ morceau*** (= *travail*) it's a big job; (= *livre*) it's a huge book; (= *obstacle*) it's a big hurdle (to clear) *ou* a big obstacle (to get over); **il a un ~ appétit** he has a big appetite; **la grosse industrie** heavy industry; **acheter par** *ou* **en grosses quantités** to buy in bulk, bulk-buy (*Brit*)

c **= houleux** [*mer*] heavy, (*Mét*) rough; (= *gonflé*) **la rivière est grosse** the river is swollen

d **= sonore** [*voix*] booming (*épith*); [*soupir*] big, deep → **rire**

e **= riche et important** big; **un ~ industriel/ banquier** a big industrialist/banker

f **intensif** **un ~ buveur** a heavy drinker; **un ~ mangeur** a big eater; **un ~ kilo/quart d'heure** a good kilo/quarter of an hour; **tu es un ~ paresseux*** you're such a lazybones; **~ nigaud !*** you big ninny!*

g **= rude** [*drap, laine, vêtement*] coarse; [*traits du visage*] thick, heavy; **le ~ travail** the heavy work; **son ~ bon sens est réconfortant** his down-to-earth *ou* plain commonsense is a comfort; **il aime les grosses plaisanteries** he likes obvious *ou* unsubtle *ou* inane jokes; **oser nous dire ça, c'est vraiment un peu ~** how dare he say that to us, it's a bit thick* *ou* a bit much*

h **† = enceinte** pregnant; **grosse de 6 mois** 6 months' pregnant

i **loc** **avoir les yeux ~ de larmes** to have eyes filled *ou* brimming with tears; **regard ~ de menaces** threatening *ou* menacing look, look full of menace; **l'incident est ~ de conséquences** the incident is fraught with consequences; **jouer ~ jeu** to play for big *ou* high stakes; **faire les ~ yeux (à un enfant)** to glower (at a child); **faire la grosse voix*** to speak gruffly *ou* sternly; **c'est une grosse tête*** he's brainy*, he's a brainbox*; (*fig*) **avoir la grosse tête*** to be big-headed; **faire une grosse tête à qn*** to bash sb up*, smash sb's face in*; **il me disait des « Monsieur »** **~ comme le bras** he was falling over himself to be polite to me and kept calling me "sir"

2 NOM MASCULIN

a **= personne corpulente** fat man; **un petit ~*** a fat little man; **mon ~*** old thing* → **pêche²**

b
♦ **les gros** (= *personnes importantes*) the rich and powerful, the big fish*

c **= principal** **le ~ du travail est fait** the bulk of *ou* the main part of the work is done; **le ~ des troupes** (*lit*) the main body of the army; (*fig*) the great majority; **le ~ de l'orage est passé** the worst of the storm is over; **faites le plus ~ d'abord** do the main things *ou* the essentials first

d **= milieu** **au ~ de l'hiver** in the depths of winter; **au ~ de l'été/de la saison** at the height of summer/of the season

e **Comm** (= *commerce de*) **~** the wholesale business; **il fait le ~ et le détail** he deals in *ou* trades in both wholesale and retail; **maison/ prix/marché de ~** wholesale firm/prices/market

f
♦ **en gros** (= *en grosses lettres*) **c'est écrit en ~** it's written

in big *ou* large letters
(*Comm*) **papetier en ~** wholesale stationer; **commande en ~** bulk order; **acheter/vendre en ~** to buy/sell wholesale → **marchand**
(= *dans les grandes lignes*) **évaluer en ~ la distance/le prix** to make a rough *ou* broad estimate of the distance/the price; **dites-moi, en ~, ce qui s'est passé** tell me roughly *ou* broadly what happened

3 **grosse** NF **= personne** fat woman; **ma grosse*** old girl*, old thing* (*Brit*); (*péj*) **c'est une bonne grosse*** she's a good-natured lump of a girl* → **grosse²**

4 ADVERBE

écrire ~ to write big, write in large letters; **il risque ~** he's risking a lot *ou* a great deal; **ça peut nous coûter ~** it could cost us a lot *ou* a great deal; **je donnerais ~ pour ...** I'd give a lot *ou* a great deal to ...; **il y a ~ à parier que ...** it's a safe bet that ...; **en avoir ~ sur le cœur** *ou* **sur la patate*** to be upset *ou* peeved*

5 COMPOSÉS
► **gros bétail** cattle ► **gros bonnet*** bigwig*, big shot* ► **gros bras*** muscleman; **jouer les ~ bras*** to play *ou* act the he-man* ► **grosse caisse** (*Mus*) big *ou* bass drum ► **grosse cavalerie*** heavy stuff* ► **grosse-gorge*** NF (*Can*) goitre ► **grosse légume*** = gros bonnet ► **gros mot** swearword; **il dit des ~ mots** he uses bad language, he swears ► **gros œuvre** (*Archit*) shell (*of a building*) ► **gros plan** (*Photo*) close-up; **une prise de vue en ~ plan** a shot in close-up, a close-up shot; (*fig = émission*) **~ plan sur ...** programme devoted to *ou* all about ... ► **gros poisson*** = gros bonnet ► **(avion) gros porteur** jumbo jet ► **gros rouge*** rough (red) wine, (red) plonk* (*Brit*), Mountain Red (wine) (*US*) ► **gros sel** cooking salt ► **gros temps** rough weather; **par ~ temps** in rough weather *ou* conditions → **gibier, intestin, lot** *etc*

gros-bec (*pl* **gros-becs**) [gʀobɛk] NM (*Orn*) hawfinch

gros-cul* (*pl* **gros-culs**) [gʀoky] NM juggernaut (*Brit*), eighteen-wheeler* (*US*)

groseille [gʀozɛj] **1** NF **~ (rouge)** red currant; **~ (blanche)** white currant; **~ à maquereau** gooseberry **2** ADJ INV (cherry-)red

groseillier [gʀozeje] NM currant bush; **~ rouge/blanc** red/white currant bush; **~ à maquereau** gooseberry bush

gros-grain (*pl* **gros-grains**) [gʀogʀɛ̃] NM (*Tex*) petersham

Gros-Jean [gʀoʒɑ̃] NM INV **il s'est retrouvé ~ comme devant** †* he found himself back where he started *ou* back at square one (*Brit*)

grosse² [gʀos] NF (*Jur*) engrossment; (*Comm*) gross

grossesse [gʀosɛs] NF pregnancy; **~ nerveuse** false pregnancy, phantom pregnancy; **~ gémellaire/extra-utérine/à risque** twin/ extrauterine/high-risk pregnancy → **robe**

grosseur [gʀosœʀ] NF **a** [*objet*] size; [*fil, bâton*] thickness; [*personne*] weight, fatness; **être d'une ~ maladive** to be unhealthily fat; **as-tu remarqué sa ~ ?** have you noticed how fat he is? **b** (= *tumeur*) lump

grossier, -ière [gʀosje, jɛʀ] ADJ **a** [*matière, tissu*] coarse; [*aliment*] unrefined; [*ornement, instrument*] crude
b (= *sommaire*) [*travail*] superficially done, roughly done; [*imitation*] crude, poor; [*dessin*] rough; [*solution, réparation*] rough-and-ready; [*estimation*] rough; **avoir une idée grossière des faits** to have a rough idea of the facts
c (= *lourd*) [*manières*] unrefined, crude; [*esprit, être*] unrefined; [*traits du visage*] coarse, thick; [*ruse*] crude; [*plaisanterie*] unsubtle, inane; [*erreur*] stupid, gross (*épith*); [*ignorance*] crass (*épith*)
d (= *bas, matériel*) [*plaisirs, jouissances*] base

e (= *insolent*) [*personne*] rude
f (= *vulgaire*) [*plaisanterie, geste, mots, propos*] coarse; [*personne*] coarse, uncouth; **il s'est montré très ~ envers eux** he was very rude to them; **~ personnage !** uncouth individual!; **il est ~ avec les femmes** he is coarse *ou* uncouth in his dealings with women

grossièrement [gʀosjɛʀmɑ̃] ADV **a** (= *de manière sommaire*) [*exécuter, réparer, dessiner*] roughly, superficially; [*façonner, imiter*] crudely; [*hacher*] roughly, coarsely; **pouvez-vous me dire ~ combien ça va coûter ?** can you tell me roughly how much that will cost? **b** (= *de manière vulgaire*) coarsely; (= *insolemment*) rudely **c** (= *lourdement*) **se tromper ~** to be grossly mistaken, make a gross error

grossièreté [gʀosjɛʀte] NF **a** (= *insolence*) rudeness **b** (= *vulgarité*) [*personne*] coarseness, uncouthness; [*plaisanterie, geste*] coarseness; **dire des ~s** to use coarse language; **une ~** a rude *ou* coarse remark **c** (= *rusticité*) [*fabrication*] crudeness; [*travail, exécution*] superficiality; [*étoffe*] coarseness **d** (*littér* = *manque de finesse*) [*personne*] lack of refinement; [*traits*] coarseness; **la ~ de ses manières** his unrefined *ou* crude manners

grossir [gʀosiʀ] ► conjug 2 ◄ **1** VI [*personne*] (*signe de déficience*) to get fat(ter), put on weight; (*signe de santé*) to put on weight; [*fruit*] to swell, grow; [*rivière*] to swell; [*tumeur*] to swell, get bigger; [*foule*] to grow (larger), swell; [*somme, économies*] to grow, get bigger; [*rumeur, nouvelle*] to spread; [*bruit*] to get louder, grow (louder), swell; **l'avion grossissait dans le ciel** the plane grew larger *ou* bigger in the sky; **~ des cuisses/des hanches** to put on weight on the thighs/the hips; **j'ai grossi de trois kilos** I've put on three kilos

2 VT **a** (= *faire paraître plus gros*) [+ *personne*] to make look fatter; **ce genre de vêtement (vous) grossit** clothing of this sort makes one look fatter
b [*microscope*] to magnify; [*lentille, lunettes*] to enlarge, magnify; [*imagination*] [+ *dangers, importance*] to magnify, exaggerate
c (= *exagérer volontairement*) [+ *fait, événement*] to exaggerate; **ils ont grossi l'affaire à des fins politiques** they've exaggerated *ou* blown up the issue for political reasons
d [+ *cours d'eau*] to swell; [+ *voix*] to raise
e [+ *somme*] to increase, add to; [+ *foule*] to swell; **~ les rangs/le nombre de** to add to *ou* swell the ranks/the numbers of

grossissant, e [gʀosisɑ̃, ɑ̃t] ADJ **a** [*lentille, verre*] magnifying, enlarging **b** [*foule, bruit*] swelling, growing

grossissement [gʀosismɑ̃] NM **a** [*tumeur*] swelling, enlarging **b** (= *pouvoir grossissant*) [*microscope*] magnification, (magnifying) power; **~ de 200 fois** magnification *ou* magnifying power of 200 times; **ceci peut être observé à un faible/fort ~** this can be seen with a low-power/high-power lens **c** [*objet*] magnification, magnifying; (= *exagération*) [*dangers*] magnification, exaggeration; [*faits*] exaggeration

grossiste [gʀosist] NMF wholesaler, wholesale dealer

grosso modo [gʀosomɔdo] ADV **a** (= *en gros*) more or less, roughly; **~, cela veut dire que ...** roughly speaking, it means that ...; **dis-moi ~ de quoi il s'agit** tell me roughly what it's all about **b** (= *tant bien que mal*) after a fashion

grotesque [gʀotɛsk] **1** ADJ **a** (= *ridicule*) [*personnage, accoutrement, allure*] ludicrous, ridiculous; [*idée, histoire*] grotesque; **c'est d'un ~ incroyable** it's absolutely ludicrous *ou* ridiculous **b** (*Art*) grotesque **2** NM (*Littérat*) **le ~** the grotesque **3** NF (*Art*) grotesque

grotesquement [gʀotɛskəmɑ̃] ADV grotesquely

grotte [gʀɔt] NF (*naturelle*) cave; (*artificielle*) grotto; **~ préhistorique** prehistoric cave

grouillant, e [gʀujɑ̃, ɑ̃t] ADJ [*foule, masse*] milling, swarming; **~ de** [+ *touristes, insectes*] swarming *ou* teeming *ou* crawling with; [+ *policiers*] bristling *ou* swarming with; **boulevard/café ~ (de monde)** street/café swarming *ou* teeming *ou* crawling with people, bustling street/café

grouillement [gʀujmɑ̃] NM [*foule, touristes*] milling, swarming; [*vers, insectes*] swarming

grouiller [gʀuje] ▶conjug 1◀ ① VI [*foule, touristes*] to mill about; [*café, rue*] to be swarming *ou* teeming with people; **~ de** [+ *touristes, insectes*] to be swarming *ou* teeming *ou* crawling with ② **se grouiller** VPR to get a move on*; **grouille-toi ou on va rater le train !** get your skates on* *ou* get a move on* or we'll miss the train!; **se ~ pour arriver à l'heure** to hurry so as not to be late

grouillot [gʀujo] NM messenger (boy)

groupage [gʀupaʒ] NM ⓐ (*Comm*) [*colis*] bulking ⓑ (*Méd*) **~ sanguin** blood grouping *ou* typing; **~ tissulaire** tissue typing

groupe [gʀup] ① NM ⓐ (*Art, Écon, Math, Pol, Sociol*) group; **~ de communication/de distribution/industriel** communications/ distribution/industrial group; **le ~ de la majorité** the deputies *ou* MPs (*Brit*) *ou* Congressmen (*US*) of the majority party; **psychologie de ~** group psychology
ⓑ [*personnes*] group; [*touristes*] party, group; [*musiciens*] band, group; **~ de rock** rock group *ou* band; **des ~s se formaient dans la rue** groups (of people) *ou* knots of people were forming in the street; **par ~s de trois ou quatre** in groups of three or four, in threes or fours; **travailler/marcher en ~** to work/walk in *ou* as a group; **travail/billet de ~** group work/ ticket
ⓒ [*objets*] **~ de maisons** cluster *ou* group of houses; **~ d'arbres** clump *ou* cluster *ou* group of trees
ⓓ (*Ling*) group, cluster; **~ nominal/verbal** noun/verb phrase, nominal/verbal group; **~ consonantique** consonant cluster
② COMP ▶ **groupe d'âge** age group ▶ **groupe armé** armed group ▶ **groupe de combat** fighter group ▶ **groupe électrogène** generating set, generator ▶ **groupe hospitalier** hospital complex ▶ **groupe d'intervention de la Gendarmerie nationale** crack force of the Gendarmerie ▶ **groupe de mots** word group, phrase ▶ **groupe parlementaire** parliamentary group ▶ **groupe de presse** (*gén*) publishing conglomerate; (*spécialisé dans la presse*) press group ▶ **groupe de pression** pressure group, ginger group (*Brit*), special interest group (*US*) ▶ **groupe sanguin** blood group ▶ **groupe de saut** [*parachutistes*] stick ▶ **groupe scolaire** school complex ▶ **le groupe des Sept (pays les plus industrialisés)** the Group of Seven (most industrialized countries) ▶ **groupe de tête** (*Sport*) (group of) leaders; (*Scol*) top pupils (in the class); (*Écon*) (group of) leading firms ▶ **groupe tissulaire** tissue type ▶ **groupe de travail** working party

groupement [gʀupmɑ̃] NM ⓐ (= *action*) [*personnes, objets, faits*] grouping; **~ de mots par catégories** grouping words by categories ⓑ (= *groupe*) group; (= *organisation*) organization; **~ révolutionnaire** band of revolutionaries, revolutionary band; (*Mil*) **~ tactique** task force; **~ d'achats** (commercial) bulk-buying organization; **~ de gendarmerie** squad of Gendarmes; **~ professionnel** professional organization; **~ d'intérêt économique** economic interest group; **~ agricole d'exploitation en commun** farmers' economic interest group ⓒ (*Chim*) group

grouper [gʀupe] ▶conjug 1◀ ① VT ⓐ [+ *personnes, objets, faits*] to group (together); (*Comm*) [+ *colis*] to bulk; [+ *efforts, ressources, moyens*] to pool; **~ des colis par destination** to bulk parcels according to their destination ⓑ (*Sport*) [+ *genoux*] to tuck → **saut** ② **se grouper** VPR [*foule*] to gather; (= *se coaliser*) to form a group; **groupez-vous par trois** get into threes *ou* into groups of three; **restez groupés** keep together, stay in a group; **les consommateurs doivent se ~ pour se défendre** consumers must band together to defend their interests; **se ~ en associations** to form associations; **on s'est groupé pour lui acheter un cadeau** we all got together *ou* chipped in* to buy him a present; (*fig*) **se ~ autour d'un chef** to rally round a leader; **le village groupé autour de l'église** the village clustered round the church

groupie [gʀupi] NMF [*chanteur*] groupie; * [*parti*] (party) faithful

groupuscule [gʀupyskyl] NM (*Pol péj*) small group

grouse [gʀuz] NF grouse

Groznyï [gʀɔzni] N Grozny

gruau [gʀyo] NM (= *graine*) hulled grain, groats; **pain de ~** fine wheaten bread

grue [gʀy] NF ⓐ (*Tech, TV*) crane; **~ flottante** floating crane; **~ de levage** wrecking crane ⓑ (*Orn*) **~ (cendrée)** crane; **~ couronnée** crowned crane → **pied** ⓒ (‡ *péj = prostituée*) hooker‡ (*péj*), tart‡ (*Brit*) (*péj*)

gruger [gʀyʒe] ▶conjug 3◀ VT ⓐ (*frm = duper*) to dupe; (= *escroquer*) to swindle; **se faire ~** (= *se faire duper*) to be duped, be had*; (= *se faire escroquer*) to be swindled ⓑ (*Can*) to nibble

grume [gʀym] NF (= *écorce*) bark (*left on timber*); **bois de ou en ~** undressed timber, rough lumber (*US*)

grumeau (*pl* **grumeaux**) [gʀymo] NM [*sel, sauce*] lump; **la sauce fait des ~x** the sauce is going lumpy; **pâte pleine de ~x** lumpy dough

grumeler (se) [gʀym(ə)le] ▶conjug 5◀ VPR [*sauce*] to go lumpy; [*lait*] to curdle

grumeleux, -euse [gʀym(ə)lø, øz] ADJ [*sauce*] lumpy; [*lait*] curdled; [*fruit*] gritty; [*peau*] bumpy, lumpy

grunge [gʀœnʒ] ① ADJ [*musique, mouvement*] grunge (*épith*) ② NM (*Mus*) grunge (music)

gruppetto [gʀupeto] (*pl* **gruppetti** [gʀupeti]) NM (*Mus*) gruppetto, turn

grutier, -ière [gʀytje, jɛʀ] NM,F crane driver *ou* operator

gruyère [gʀyjɛʀ] NM gruyère (cheese) (*Brit*), Swiss (cheese) (*US*)

GSM [ʒeesɛm] NM (ABRÉV = **Global System for Mobile Communication**) GSM; **réseau ~** GSM network

guacamole [gwakamɔle] NM (*Culin*) guacamole

Guadeloupe [gwadlup] NF Guadeloupe

guadeloupéen, -enne [gwadlupeɛ̃, ɛn] ① ADJ Guadelupian ② **Guadeloupéen(ne)** NM,F inhabitant *ou* native of Guadeloupe

Guam [gwam] NM Guam

guano [gwano] NM [*oiseau*] guano; [*poisson*] manure

guarani [gwaʀani] ① ADJ Guarani (*épith*) ② (*Ling*) Guarani; (= *monnaie*) guarani ③ **Guarani** NMF Guarani

Guatemala [gwatemala] NM Guatemala

guatémaltèque [gwatemaltɛk] ① ADJ Guatemalan ② **Guatémaltèque** NMF Guatemalan

gué [ge] NM ford; **passer (une rivière) à ~** to ford a river

guéable [geabl] ADJ fordable

guéer [gee] ▶conjug 1◀ VT to ford

guéguerre* [gegɛʀ] NF squabble; **c'est la ~ entre les représentants** the representatives are squabbling amongst themselves

guelfe [gɛlf] ① ADJ Guelphic ② NMF Guelph

guelte [gɛlt] NF (*Comm*) commission

guenille [gənij] NF (piece of) rag; **~s** (old) rags; **en ~s** in rags (and tatters)

guenon [gənɔ̃] NF (*Zool*) female monkey; (*péj* = *laideron*) fright, (ugly) hag

guépard [gepaʀ] NM cheetah

guêpe [gɛp] NF wasp → **fou, taille[1]**

guêpier [gepje] NM ⓐ (*Zool*) bee-eater ⓑ (= *piège*) trap; (= *nid*) wasp's nest; **se fourrer dans un ~** to land o.s. in the soup* *ou* in it* (*Brit*)

guêpière [gepjɛʀ] NF basque

guère [gɛʀ] ADV ⓐ (+ *adj*, + *adv*) (= *pas très, pas beaucoup*) hardly, scarcely; **elle ne va ~ mieux** she's hardly any better; **comment vas-tu, aujourd'hui ? — ~ mieux !** how are you feeling today? — much the same!; **il n'est ~ poli** he's not very polite; **le chef, ~ satisfait de cela, ...** the boss, little *ou* hardly satisfied with that, ...; **il n'y a ~ plus de 2 km** there is barely *ou* scarcely more than 2 km to go; **ça ne fera ~ moins de 100 F** it won't be (very) much less than 100 francs
ⓑ (+ *vb*) **ne ... ~** (= *pas beaucoup*) not much *ou* really; (= *pas souvent*) hardly *ou* scarcely ever; (= *pas longtemps*) not (very) long; **il n'a ~ d'argent/le temps** he has hardly any money/ time; **je n'aime ~ qu'on me questionne** I don't much like *ou* really care for being questioned; **il n'en reste plus ~** there's hardly any left; **cela ne te va ~** it doesn't really suit you; **ce n'est plus ~ à la mode** it's hardly fashionable at all nowadays; **il ne vient ~ nous voir** he hardly *ou* scarcely ever comes to see us; **cela ne durera ~** it won't last (for) very long; **il ne tardera ~** he won't be (very) long now; (*frm*) **l'aimez-vous ? — ~** do you like it? — not (very) much *ou* not really *ou* not particularly
ⓒ (+ *de, que*) **il n'y a ~ de monde** there's hardly *ou* scarcely anybody there; **il n'y a ~ que lui qui ...** he's about the only one who ..., there's hardly *ou* scarcely anyone but he who ...

guéret [geʀe] NM tillage (*NonC*)

guéridon [geʀidɔ̃] NM pedestal table

guérilla [geʀija] NF guerrilla war *ou* warfare (*NonC*); **~ urbaine** urban guerrilla warfare

guérillero, guérilléro [geʀijeʀo] NM guerrilla

guérir [geʀiʀ] ▶conjug 2◀ ① VT (= *soigner*) [+ *malade*] to cure, make better; [+ *maladie*] to cure; [+ *membre, blessure*] to heal; **je ne peux pas le ~ de ses mauvaises habitudes** I can't cure *ou* break him of his bad habits
② VI ⓐ (*Méd = aller mieux*) [*malade, maladie*] to get better, be cured; [*blessure*] to heal, mend; **sa main guérie était encore faible** his hand although healed was still weak; **il est guéri (de son angine)** he is cured (of his throat infection); **dépenser de telles sommes, j'en suis guéri !** you won't catch me spending money like that again!, that's the last time I spend money like that!
ⓑ [*chagrin, passion*] to heal
③ **se guérir** VPR [*malade, maladie*] to get better, be cured; **se ~ d'une habitude** to cure *ou* break o.s. of a habit; **se ~ par les plantes** to cure o.s. by taking herbs, cure o.s. with herbs; **se ~ d'un amour malheureux** to get over *ou* recover from an unhappy love affair

guérison [geʀizɔ̃] NF [*malade*] recovery; [*maladie*] curing (*NonC*); [*membre, plaie*] healing (*NonC*); **sa ~ a été rapide** he made a rapid recovery; **~ par la foi** faith healing → **voie**

guérissable [geʀisabl] ADJ [*malade, maladie*] curable; **sa jambe/blessure est ~** his leg/injury can be healed

guérisseur, -euse [geʀisœʀ, øz] NM,F healer; (*péj*) quack (doctor) (*péj*)

guérite [geʀit] NF ⓐ (*Mil*) sentry box ⓑ (*sur chantier*) workman's hut; (*servant de bureau*) site office

Guernesey [gɛʀn(ə)zɛ] NF Guernsey

guernesiais, e [gɛʀnəzjɛ, ɛz] **1** ADJ of *ou* from Guernsey, Guernsey (*épith*) **2** **Guernesiais(e)** NM,F inhabitant *ou* native of Guernsey

guerre [gɛʀ] **1** NF **a** (= *conflit*) war; **de ~** [*correspondant, criminel*] war (*épith*); **~ civile/sainte/atomique** civil/holy/atomic war; **~ de religion/de libération** war of religion/of liberation; **la ~ scolaire** *ongoing debate on church schooling versus state schooling*; **la Grande Guerre** the Great War (*Brit*), World War I; **la Première Guerre mondiale** the First World War, World War I; **la Seconde** *ou* **Deuxième Guerre mondiale** the Second World War, World War II; **entre eux c'est la ~ (ouverte)** it's open war between them

b (= *technique*) warfare; **la ~ atomique/psychologique/chimique** atomic/psychological/chemical warfare

c (*loc*) **en ~** (*lit, fig*) at war (**avec, contre** with, against); **dans les pays en ~** in the warring countries, in the countries at war; (*Mil*) **faire la ~ à** to wage war on *ou* against; **soldat qui a fait la ~** a soldier who was in the war; **ton chapeau a fait la ~*** your hat has been in the wars* (*Brit*) *ou* through the war (*US*); **elle lui fait la ~ pour qu'il s'habille mieux** she is constantly battling with him to get him to dress better; **faire la ~ aux abus/à l'injustice** to wage war against *ou* on abuses/injustice; **partir en ~ contre** (*lit*) to go to war against, wage war on; (*fig*) to wage war on; **de ~ lasse elle finit par accepter** she grew tired of resisting and finally accepted; **à la ~ comme à la ~** we'll just have to make the best of things; **c'est de bonne ~** that's fair enough → **entrer**

2 COMP ► **guerre bactériologique** bacteriological warfare ► **guerre biologique** biological warfare ► **guerre de Cent Ans** the Hundred Years' War ► **guerre de conquête** war of conquest ► **la guerre des Deux-Roses** the Wars of the Roses ► **guerre éclair** blitzkrieg, lightning war (*US*) ► **guerre économique** economic warfare ► **guerre électronique** electronic warfare ► **guerre d'embuscade** guerrilla warfare ► **la guerre des étoiles** Star Wars ► **guerre d'extermination** war of extermination ► **guerre froide** cold war ► **la guerre du Golfe** the Gulf War ► **la guerre du Mexique** the Mexican War ► **guerre mondiale** world war ► **guerre de mouvement** war of movement ► **guerre des nerfs** war of nerves ► **guerre nucléaire** nuclear war ► **guerre des ondes** battle for the airwaves ► **guerre à outrance** all-out war ► **guerre de position** war of position ► **guerre presse-bouton** push-button war ► **les guerres puniques** the Punic Wars ► **la guerre de quatorze** the 1914-18 war ► **la guerre de quarante** the Second World War ► **la guerre de Sécession** the American Civil War ► **guerre de succession** war of succession ► **guerre totale** total warfare, all-out war ► **guerre de tranchées** trench warfare ► **la guerre de Trente Ans** the Thirty Years War ► **la guerre de Troie** the Trojan War ► **guerre d'usure** war of attrition

guerrier, -ière [gɛʀje, jɛʀ] **1** ADJ [*nation, air*] warlike; [*danse, chants, exploits*] war (*épith*) **2** NM,F warrior

guerroyer [gɛʀwaje] ▸conjug 8◂ VI (*littér*) to wage war (**contre** against, on)

guet [gɛ] NM **a** **faire le ~** to be on (the) watch *ou* lookout; (*littér*) **avoir l'œil au ~** to keep one's eyes open *ou* peeled*; (*littér*) **avoir l'oreille au ~** to keep one's ears open **b** (*Hist* = *patrouille*) watch

guet-apens (*pl* **guets-apens**) [gɛtapɑ̃] NM (= *embuscade*) ambush, ambuscade (*frm*); (*fig*) trap; **attirer qn dans un ~** (*lit*) to lure sb into

an ambush; (*fig*) to lure sb into a trap; **tomber dans un ~** (*lit*) to be caught in an ambush; (*fig*) to fall into a trap

guêtre [gɛtʀ] NF gaiter → **traîner**

guêtré, e [getʀe] ADJ (*hum : Hist*) wearing gaiters *ou* spats

guetter [gete] ▸conjug 1◂ VT **a** (= *épier*) [+ *victime, ennemi*] to watch (intently); [+ *porte*] to watch **b** (= *attendre*) [+ *réaction, signal, occasion*] to watch out for, be on the lookout for; [+ *personne*] to watch (out) for; (*hostilement*) to lie in wait for; [+ *proie*] to lie in wait for; **~ le passage/l'arrivée de qn** to watch (out) for sb (to pass by)/(to come); **~ la sonnerie du téléphone** to be waiting for the telephone to ring; **~ le pas de qn** to listen out for sb; **ses fans guettent la sortie de son nouvel album** his fans are eagerly waiting for his new album **c** (= *menacer*) [*danger*] to threaten; **la crise cardiaque/la faillite le guette** he's heading for a heart attack/bankruptcy; **c'est le sort qui nous guette tous** it's the fate that's in store for all of us *ou* that's liable to befall all of us

guetteur [getœʀ] NM (*Mil, Naut*) lookout; (*Hist*) watch

gueulante [gœlɑ̃t] NF **pousser une** *ou* **sa ~** (*colère*) to kick up a stink*; (*douleur*) to give an almighty yell*

gueulard, e [gœlaʀ, aʀd] **1** ADJ **a** (= *braillard*) [*personne*] loud-mouthed; (*air, musique*) noisy **b** (= *criard*) [*couleur, vêtement*] gaudy, garish **c** (= *gourmand*) **être ~** to love one's food **2** NM,F **a** (= *braillard*) loud-mouth **b** (= *gourmand*) **c'est un ~** he really loves his food **3** NM (*Tech*) throat

gueule [gœl] **1** NF **a** (= *bouche*) mouth; (*ferme*) **ta ~!** shut your trap!; *ou* **face!**; **ça vous emporte** *ou* **brûle la ~** it takes the roof off your mouth; **il dépense beaucoup d'argent pour la ~** he spends a lot on feeding his face*; **s'en mettre plein la ~** to stuff o.s. one's face*; **tu peux crever la ~ ouverte** you can go to hell for all I care; **il nous laisserait bien crever la ~ ouverte** he wouldn't give a damn what happened to us; **donner un coup de ~*** to shout one's head off*; **il est connu pour ses coups de ~*** he's well known for being a loudmouth; **bourré** *ou* **rempli jusqu'à la ~** crammed to the gills*, jam-packed → **fin¹**

b (= *figure*) face; **il a une bonne/sale ~** I like/I don't like the look of him; **avoir une bonne/sale ~** [*aliment*] to look nice/horrible; **avoir la ~ de l'emploi** to look the part; **faire la ~** to sulk; **faire la ~ à qn** to be in a huff* with sb; **faire une ~ d'enterrement** to look really miserable; **il a fait une sale ~ quand il a appris la nouvelle** he didn't half pull a face when he heard the news; **bien fait pour sa ~** bully for him!; **un fort en ◊ une grande ~** a loudmouth; **cette bagnole a de la ~** that's a great-looking car!, that's some car!; **cette maison a une drôle de ~** that's a weird-looking house; **les vêtements achetés en boutique ont plus de ~** boutique clothes look much nicer *ou* better; (*péj*) **~ de raie** fish-face*; **~ d'empeigne** shithead → **casser, foutre, soûler**

c [*animal*] mouth; **se jeter** *ou* **se mettre dans la ~ du loup** to throw o.s. into the lion's jaws **d** (= *ouverture*) [*four*] mouth; [*canon*] muzzle

2 COMP ► **gueule de bois*** hangover; **avoir la ~ de bois** to have a hangover, be feeling the effects of the night before* ► **gueule cassée** *war veteran with severe facial injuries* ► **gueule noire** miner

gueule-de-loup (*pl* **gueules-de-loup**) [gœldəlu] NF (*Bot*) snapdragon

gueulement [gœlmɑ̃] NM (= *cri*) bawl; **pousser des ~s** (*douleur*) to yell one's head off*; (*colère*) to kick up a stink*

gueuler [gœle] ▸conjug 1◂ **1** VI [*chien*] to bark like mad*; [*personne*] (= *crier*) to shout; (=

parler fort) to bawl, bellow; (= *chanter fort*) to bawl; (= *hurler de douleur*) to howl, yell (one's head off*); (= *protester*) to kick up a stink*; **~ après qn** to bawl sb out*; **ça va ~** all hell will break loose, there'll be one hell of a row*. **b** [*poste de radio*] to blast out, blare out; **faire ~ sa télé** to turn one's TV up full blast* **2** VT [+ *ordres*] to bawl (out), bellow (out); [+ *chanson*] to bawl

gueules [gœl] NM (*Hér*) gules

gueuleton* [gœltɔ̃] NM blow-out* (*Brit*), chow-down; (*US*) **faire un ~** to have a blow-out* (*Brit*) *ou* a chow-down; (*US*)

gueuletonner* [gœltɔne] ▸conjug 1◂ VI to have a blow-out* (*Brit*) *ou* a chow-down; (*US*)

gueuse [gøz] NF **a** (†, *littér*) (= *mendiante*) beggarwoman; (= *coquine*) rascally wench → **courir** **b** (*fonte*) pig **c** (= *bière*) **~(-lambic)** gueuse beer

gueux [gø] NM (†, *littér*) (= *mendiant*) beggar; (= *coquin*) rogue, villain

gugusse [gygys] NM (= *clown*) ≈ Coco the clown; (* = *type*) guy*, bloke* (*Brit*); (* = *personne ridicule*) twit*

gui [gi] NM **a** (*Bot*) mistletoe **b** (*Naut*) boom

guibol(l)e* [gibɔl] NF (= *jambe*) leg

guiche [giʃ] NF (= *accroche-cœur*) kiss curl

guichet [giʃɛ] NM **a** (= *comptoir individuel*) window; (= *bureau*) **~(s)** [*banque, poste*] counter; [*théâtre*] box office, ticket office; [*gare*] ticket office, booking office (*Brit*); **adressez-vous au ~ d'à côté** inquire at the next window; **renseignez-vous au(x) ~(s)** [*banque, poste*] go and ask at the counter; [*théâtre, gare*] go and ask at the ticket office; (*à la poste, à la banque*) **« ~ fermé »** "position closed"; **on joue à ~s fermés** the performance is fully booked *ou* is booked out (*Brit*); **~ automatique (de banque)** cash dispenser, ATM **b** [*porte, mur*] wicket, hatch; (*grillagé*) grille

guichetier, -ière [giʃ(ə)tje, jɛʀ] NM,F [*banque*] counter clerk

guidage [gidaʒ] NM (*Min, Tech*) (= *mécanisme*) guides; (= *action*) guidance

guide [gid] **1** NM **a** (= *idée, sentiment*) guide; **l'ambition est son seul ~** ambition is his only guide **b** (= *livre*) guide(book); **~ pratique/touristique/gastronomique** practical/tourist/restaurant guide; **~ de voyage** travel guide **c** (*Tech* = *glissière*) guide; **~ de courroie** belt-guide **2** NMF (= *personne*) guide; **~ (de montagne)** (mountain) guide; **« n'oubliez pas le ~ »** "please remember the guide"; **« suivez le ~ ! »** "this way, please!"; **~-conférencier** lecturing guide; **~-interprète** tour guide and interpreter **3** **guides** NFPL (= *rênes*) reins **4** NF (= *éclaireuse*) ≈ (girl) guide (*Brit*), ≈ girl scout (*US*)

guider [gide] ▸conjug 1◂ VT (= *conduire*) [+ *voyageur, embarcation, cheval*] to guide; (*moralement*) to guide; **l'ambition le guide** he is guided by (his) ambition, ambition is his guide; **organisme qui guide les étudiants durant leur première année** organization that provides guidance for first-year students; **il m'a guidé dans mes recherches** he guided me through *ou* in my research; **se laissant ~ par son instinct** letting himself be guided by (his) instinct, letting (his) instinct be his guide; **se guidant sur les étoiles/leur exemple** guided by the stars/their example, using the stars/their example as a guide; **missile guidé par infrarouge** heat-seeking missile; **bombe guidée au** *ou* **par laser** laser-guided bomb → **visite**

guidon [gidɔ̃] NM **a** [*vélo*] handlebars **b** (= *drapeau*) guidon **c** [*mire*] foresight, bead

guigne¹ [giɲ] NF (= *cerise*) *type of cherry*; **il s'en soucie comme d'une ~** he doesn't care a fig about it

guigne²* [giɲ] NF (= *malchance*) rotten luck*; **avoir la ~** to be jinxed*; **porter la ~ à qn** to put a jinx on sb*; **quelle ~ !** what rotten luck!*

guigner [giɲe] ▸conjug 1◂ VT [+ *personne*] to eye surreptitiously; [+ *héritage, place*] to have one's eye on, eye

guignol [giɲɔl] NM [a] (*Théât*) (= *marionnette*) popular French glove puppet; (= *spectacle*) puppet show, ≈ Punch and Judy show; **aller au ~** to go to a puppet show; **c'est du ~!** it's a real farce! [b] (*péj* = *personne*) clown; **arrête de faire le ~!** stop clowning about!, stop acting the clown!

guignolet [giɲɔlɛ] NM cherry liqueur

guignon [giɲɔ̃] NM = **guigne²**

guilde [gild] NF (*Hist*) guild; (*Comm*) club

guili-guili* [giligili] NM tickle tickle*; **faire ~ à qn** to tickle sb

Guillaume [gijom] NM William; **~ le Roux** William Rufus; **~ Tell** William Tell; **~ d'Orange** William of Orange; **~ le Conquérant** William the Conqueror

guillaume [gijom] NM rabbet plane

guilledou [gij(ə)du] NM → **courir**

guillemet [gijmɛ] NM quotation mark, inverted comma (*Brit*); **ouvrez les ~s** quote, open quotation marks *ou* inverted commas (*Brit*); **fermez les ~s** unquote, close quotation marks *ou* inverted commas (*Brit*); **sa digne épouse, entre ~s** his noble spouse, quote unquote *ou* in inverted commas (*Brit*); **mettre un mot entre ~s** to put a word in quotation marks *ou* quotes *ou* inverted commas (*Brit*)

guillemot [gijmo] NM guillemot

guilleret, -ette [gijʀɛ, ɛt] ADJ [a] (= *enjoué*) [*personne, air*] perky, bright; **être tout ~** to be full of beans* [b] (= *leste*) [*propos*] saucy

guilloché, e [gijɔʃe] (*ptp de* **guillocher**) ADJ ornamented with guilloche

guillocher [gijɔʃe] ▸conjug 1◂ VT to ornament with guilloche

guillotine [gijɔtin] NF guillotine → **fenêtre**

guillotiner [gijɔtine] ▸conjug 1◂ VT to guillotine

guimauve [gimov] NF (*Bot*) marsh mallow; (*Culin*) marshmallow; (*péj*) **c'est de la ~** (*mou*) it's jelly; (*sentimental*) it's mush*, it's schmaltzy*; **chanson (à la) ~** mushy* *ou* schmaltzy* *ou* soppy* (*Brit*) song

guimbarde [gɛ̃baʀd] NF (*Mus*) Jew's harp; (* = *voiture*) **(vieille) ~** jalopy, old banger* (*Brit*), old crock* (*Brit*)

guimpe [gɛ̃p] NF (*Rel*) wimple; (= *corsage*) chemisette (*Brit*), dickey (*US*)

guincher* [gɛ̃ʃe] ▸conjug 1◂ VI (= *danser*) to dance

guindé, e [gɛ̃de] (*ptp de* **guinder**) ADJ [*personne, air*] stiff, starchy, uptight*; [*style*] stilted; **il est ~ dans ses vêtements** his clothes are too tight for him

guinder [gɛ̃de] ▸conjug 1◂ [1] VT [a] [+ *style*] to make stilted; [*vêtements*] **~ qn** to make sb look stiff and starchy [b] (= *hisser*) [+ *mât, charge*] to raise [2] **se guinder** VPR [*personne*] to become starchy; [*style*] to become stilted

Guinée [gine] NF Guinea

Guinée-Bissau [ginebiso] NF Guinea-Bissau

Guinée-Équatoriale [gineekwatɔʀjal] NF Equatorial Guinea

guinéen, -enne [gineɛ̃, ɛn] [1] ADJ Guinean [2] **Guinéen(ne)** NM,F native of Guinea, Guinean

guingois* [gɛ̃gwa] ADV (= *de travers*) **de ~** askew, skew-whiff* (*Brit*); **le tableau est (tout) de ~** the picture is askew *ou* skew-whiff* *ou* lop-sided; **il se tient tout de ~ sur sa chaise** he's sitting lop-sidedly *ou* skew-whiff* in his chair; **marcher de ~** to walk lop-sidedly; **tout va de ~** everything's going haywire*

guinguette [gɛ̃gɛt] NF open-air café *or* dance hall

guipure [gipyʀ] NF guipure

▾ **guise** [giz] NF [a] **n'en faire qu'à sa ~** to do as one pleases *ou* likes; **à ta ~!** as you wish! *ou* please! *ou* like! [b] (*loc*) **en ~ de** by way of; **en ~ de remerciement** by way of thanks; **en ~ de chapeau il portait un pot de fleurs** he was wearing a flowerpot by way of a hat *ou* for a hat

guitare [gitaʀ] NF guitar; **~ hawaïenne/électrique** Hawaiian/electric guitar; **~ basse/acoustique** *ou* **sèche/classique** bass/acoustic/classical guitar; **à la ~, Joe** on guitar, Joe

guitariste [gitaʀist] NMF guitarist, guitar player

guitoune* [gitun] NF tent

Guj(a)rât [gudʒ(a)ʀat] NM Gujarat

Gulf Stream [gœlfstʀim] NM Gulf Stream

guru [guʀu] NM = **gourou**

gus* [gys] NM (= *type*) guy*, bloke* (*Brit*)

gustatif, -ive [gystatif, iv] ADJ gustative, gustatory → **nerf, papille**

gustation [gystasjɔ̃] NF gustation

guttural, e (*mpl* **-aux**) [gytyʀal, o] [1] ADJ [*langue, son, consonne*] guttural; [*voix*] guttural, throaty [2] **gutturale** NF (*Phon*) guttural

Guyana [gɥijana] NM Guyana

guyanais, e [gɥijanɛ, ɛz] [1] ADJ Guyanese [2] **Guyanais(e)** NM,F Guyanese

Guyane [gɥijan] NF Guiana; **~ française** French Guiana; **~ hollandaise** Dutch Guyana; **~ britannique** (British) Guyana

guyot [gɥijo] NF (= *fruit*) guyot pear; (= *volcan*) guyot

gym* [ʒim] NF (ABRÉV = **gymnastique**) (*gén*) gym; (*Scol*) PE; **je vais à la ~** I go to the gym; **faire de la ~** (*sport*) to do gym; (*chez soi*) to do exercises

gymkhana [ʒimkana] NM rally; **~ motocycliste** motorcycle scramble; **il faut faire du ~ pour arriver à la fenêtre!** it's like an obstacle course to get to the window!

gymnase [ʒimnɑz] NM (*Sport*) gymnasium, gym; (*Helv* = *lycée*) secondary school (*Brit*), high school (*US*)

gymnaste [ʒimnast] NMF gymnast

gymnastique [ʒimnastik] [1] NF [a] (= *sport*) gymnastics *sg*; (*Scol*) physical education, gymnastics *sg*; **de ~** [*professeur, instrument*] physical education (*épith*), PE (*épith*); **faire de la ~** (*sport*) to do gymnastics; (*chez soi*) to do exercises → **pas¹** [b] (*fig*) gymnastics *sg*; **~ intellectuelle** *ou* **de l'esprit** mental gymnastics *sg*; **c'est toute une ~ pour attraper ce que l'on veut dans ce placard** it's a real juggling act *ou* you have to stand on your head to find what you want in this cupboard

[2] COMP ▸ **gymnastique acrobatique** acrobatics *sg* ▸ **gymnastique aquatique** aquaerobics *sg* ▸ **gymnastique chinoise** t'ai chi (ch'uan) ▸ **gymnastique corrective** remedial gymnastics ▸ **gymnastique douce** ≈ Callanetics® ▸ **gymnastique oculaire** eye exercises ▸ **gymnastique orthopédique** orthopaedic (*Brit*) *ou* orthopedic (*US*) exercises ▸ **gymnastique respiratoire** breathing exercises ▸ **gymnastique rythmique** eurhythmics *sg* ▸ **gymnastique rythmique et sportive** rhythmic gymnastics ▸ **gymnastique au sol** floor gymnastics ▸ **gymnastique suédoise**† callisthenics†

gymnique [ʒimnik] [1] ADJ gymnastic [2] NF gymnastics *sg*

gymnosperme [ʒimnospɛʀm] [1] ADJ gymnospermous [2] NF gymnosperm; **les ~s** gymnosperms, the Gymnospermae (*SPÉC*)

gynécée [ʒinese] NM [a] (*Hist*) gynaeceum; (*fig*) den of females [b] (*Bot*) gynoecium, gynecium (*US*)

gynéco* [ʒineko] [1] ADJ ABRÉV = **gynécologique** [2] NMF ABRÉV = **gynécologue** [3] NF ABRÉV = **gynécologie**

gynécologie [ʒinekɔlɔʒi] NF gynaecology (*Brit*), gynecology (*US*)

gynécologique [ʒinekɔlɔʒik] ADJ gynaecological (*Brit*), gynecological (*US*)

gynécologue [ʒinekɔlɔg] NMF gynaecologist (*Brit*), gynecologist (*US*); **~ obstétricien** obstetrician, ob-gyn* (*US*)

gypaète [ʒipaɛt] NM bearded vulture, lammergeyer

gypse [ʒips] NM gypsum

gypseux, -euse [ʒipsø, øz] ADJ gypseous

gypsophile [ʒipsɔfil] NF gypsophila

gyrocompas [ʒiʀokɔ̃pa] NM gyrocompass

gyrophare [ʒiʀofaʀ] NM revolving *ou* flashing light (*on vehicle*)

gyroscope [ʒiʀɔskɔp] NM gyroscope

gyroscopique [ʒiʀɔskɔpik] ADJ gyroscopic

gyrostat [ʒiʀɔsta] NM gyrostat

H

H, h [aʃ] NM (= *lettre*) H, h; **h aspiré** aspirate h; **h muet** silent *ou* mute h; **(à l')heure H** (at) zero hour → **bombe**

ha¹ ['a] EXCL oh!; (= *rire*) **ha, ha !** ha-ha!

ha² (ABRÉV = **hectare**) ha

habeas corpus [abeaskɔrpys] NM INV **l'~** habeas corpus

habile [abil] ADJ **a** [*mains, ouvrier, peintre, politicien*] skilful (*Brit*), skillful (*US*), skilled; [*écrivain*] clever; **il est ~ de ses mains** he's good *ou* clever with his hands; **être ~ à (faire) qch** to be clever *ou* skilful *ou* good at (doing) sth **b** [*film, intrigue, raisonnement, argument*] clever; [*manœuvre*] clever, deft; **ce n'était pas bien ~ de sa part** that wasn't very clever of him; **un ~ trucage vidéo** a clever video effect **c** (*Jur*) fit (à to)

habilement [abilmã] ADV [*manier un instrument*] skilfully (*Brit*), skillfully (*US*); [*manœuvrer*] skilfully (*Brit*), skillfully (*US*), cleverly; [*profiter, répondre, dissimuler*] cleverly; **il fit ~ remarquer que ...** he cleverly pointed out that ...; **il gère ~ sa carrière** he manages his career with skill

habileté [abilte] NF **a** [*ouvrier, peintre, politicien*] skill (**à faire** at doing); **~ manuelle** manual dexterity *ou* skill; **son ~ à travailler le bois** his woodworking skills; **faire preuve d'une grande ~ politique/technique** to show considerable political/technical skill **b** [*tactique, démarche*] skilfulness (*Brit*), skillfulness (*US*), cleverness; [*manœuvre*] cleverness, deftness **c** (*Jur*) = **habilité**

habilitation [abilitasjɔ̃] NF (*Jur*) capacitation; (*Univ*) **~ (à diriger des recherches)** authorization *ou* accreditation to supervise research

habilité [abilite] NF (*Jur*) fitness

habiliter [abilite] ▸conjug 1◂ VT (*Jur*) to capacitate; (*Univ*) to authorize, accredit; **être habilité à faire qch** (*Jur, Pol*) to be empowered to do sth; (*gén*) to be entitled *ou* authorized to do sth; **représentant dûment habilité** duly authorized officer

habillage [abijaʒ] NM **a** [*acteur, poupée*] dressing **b** [*montre*] assembly; [*bouteille*] labelling and sealing; [*marchandise*] packaging and presentation; [*machine*] casing; [*chaudière*] lagging; [*peaux*] dressing; (*Aut*) **~ intérieur** interior trim **c** (= *présentation*) **~ de bilan** window dressing (*of a balance sheet*); **ces contrats ne sont que l'~ juridique de primes occultes** these contracts are just a front for secret bonus payments; (*TV*) **le nouvel ~ de la chaîne devrait plaire** the channel's new format *ou* new look should go down well

habillé, e [abije] (*ptp de* **habiller**) ADJ **a** (= *chic*) [*robe*] smart, dressy; [*chaussures*] dress (*épith*), smart; **soirée ~e** formal occasion; **trop ~** [*costume*] too dressy; [*personne*] overdressed **b** (= *vêtu*) [*personne*] dressed; **chaudement ~** warmly dressed; **bien/mal ~** well/badly dressed; **~ de noir/d'un costume** dressed in *ou* wearing black/a suit; **elle était ~e en Chanel** she was wearing Chanel clothes *ou* a Chanel

outfit; **se coucher tout ~** to go to bed fully dressed *ou* with all one's clothes on

habillement [abijmã] NM (= *action*) dressing, clothing; (= *toilette, costume*) clothes, dress (*NonC*), outfit; (*Mil* = *uniforme*) outfit; (= *profession*) clothing trade, rag trade* (*Brit*), garment industry (*US*)

habiller [abije] ▸conjug 1◂ **1** VT **a** (+ *poupée, enfant*) (= *vêtir*) to dress (**de** in); (= *déguiser*) to dress up (**en** as); **cette robe vous habille bien** that dress really suits you *ou* looks good on you; **un rien l'habille** she looks good in anything, she can wear anything **b** (= *fournir en vêtements*) to clothe; (*Mil*) [+ *recrues*] to provide with uniforms; (*Couture*) **Mlle Lenoir est habillée par Givenchy** Miss Lenoir buys *ou* gets all her clothes from Givenchy's; (*dans un générique*) Miss Lenoir's wardrobe *ou* clothes by Givenchy **c** (= *recouvrir, envelopper*) [+ *mur, fauteuil, livre*] to cover (**de** with); [+ *bouteille*] to label and seal; [+ *marchandise*] to package; [+ *machine, radiateur*] to encase (**de** in); [+ *chaudière*] to lag (**de** with); **~ un fauteuil d'une housse** to put a loose cover on an armchair; **tableau de bord habillé de bois** wooden dashboard; **il faut ~ ce coin de la pièce** we must put something in *ou* do something with this corner of the room **d** (*Hort*) [+ *arbre*] to trim (for planting) **e** (*Typo*) [+ *image*] to set the text around **f** (*Tech*) [+ *montre*] to assemble; [+ *peaux, carcasse*] to dress **g** (= *enjoliver*) [+ *réalité, vérité*] to adorn; **ils ont habillé le bilan** they did some financial window-dressing **2** **s'habiller** VPR **a** (= *mettre ses habits*) to dress (o.s.), get dressed; (= *se déguiser*) to dress up (**en** as); **aider qn à s'~** to help sb on with their clothes, help sb get dressed; **s'~ chaudement** to dress warmly; **elle s'habille trop jeune/vieux** she wears clothes that are too young/old for her; **elle s'habille long/court** she wears long/short skirts, she wears her skirts long/short; **s'~ en Arlequin** to dress up as Harlequin; **faut-il s'~ pour la réception ?** do we have to dress (up) for the reception?; **comment t'habilles-tu ce soir ?** what are you wearing tonight?; **elle ne sait pas s'~** she has no clothes sense *ou* dress sense **b** (*Couture*) **s'~ chez un tailleur** to buy *ou* get one's clothes from a tailor; **s'~ sur mesure** to have one's clothes made to measure

habilleur, -euse [abijœr, øz] **1** NM (*Tech*) [*peaux*] dresser **2** NM,F (*Ciné, Théât*) dresser

habit [abi] **1** NM **a** **~s** clothes; **mettre/ôter ses ~s** to put on/take off one's clothes *ou* things; **~s de travail/de deuil** working/mourning clothes; **il portait ses ~s du dimanche** he was wearing his Sunday best *ou* Sunday clothes; **il était encore en ~s de voyage** he was still in his travelling clothes *ou* in the clothes he'd worn for the journey → **brosse** **b** (= *costume*) dress (*NonC*), outfit; **~ d'arlequin** Harlequin suit *ou* costume ■ (*PROV*) **l'~ ne fait pas le moine** appearances are sometimes

deceptive, one shouldn't judge by appearances **c** (= *jaquette*) morning coat; (= *queue-de-pie*) tail coat, tails; **en ~ (de soirée)** wearing tails, in evening dress; **l'~ est de rigueur** formal *ou* evening dress must be worn **d** (*Rel*) habit; **prendre l'~** [*homme*] to take (holy) orders, take the cloth; [*femme*] to take the veil; **quitter l'~** [*homme*] to leave the priesthood; [*femme*] to leave the Church; **lors de sa prise d'~** [*homme*] when he took (holy) orders *ou* the cloth; [*femme*] when she took the veil **2** COMP ► **habit de cheval** riding habit ► **habit de cour** court dress (*NonC*) ► **habit ecclésiastique** clerical dress (*NonC*); **porter l'~ ecclésiastique** (= *être prêtre*) to be a cleric ► **habit de gala** formal *ou* evening dress (*NonC*) ► **habit de lumière** bullfighter's costume ► **habit militaire** military dress (*NonC*) ► **habit religieux** (monk's) habit ► **habit de soirée** = **habit de gala** ► **habit vert** green coat of member of the *Académie française*

habitabilité [abitabilite] NF [*maison*] habitability, fitness for habitation; [*voiture, ascenseur*] capacity

habitable [abitabl] ADJ (in)habitable; **35 m² ~s ou de surface** = 35 m² living space; **la maison n'est pas encore ~** the house isn't fit to live in yet *ou* isn't habitable yet; **~ début mai** ready for occupation in early May

habitacle [abitakl] NM **a** (*Naut*) binnacle; (*Aviat*) cockpit; (*Aut*) passenger compartment *ou* cell; [*véhicule spatial*] cabin **b** (*Rel, littér*) dwelling place (*littér*), abode (*littér*)

habitant, e [abitã, ãt] NM,F **a** [*maison*] occupant, occupier; [*ville, pays*] inhabitant; **ville de 3 millions d'~s** town of 3 million inhabitants; **les ~s du village/du pays** the people who live in the village/country, the inhabitants of the village/country; **être** *ou* **loger chez l'~** [*touristes*] to stay with local people in their own homes; [*soldats*] to be billeted on *ou* with the local population; (*littér*) **les ~s des bois** the denizens (*littér*) of the wood **b** (*Can** = *fermier*) farmer; (*péj* = *rustre*) country bumpkin

habitat [abita] NM (*Bot, Zool*) habitat; (= *conditions de logement*) housing *ou* living conditions; (= *mode de peuplement*) settlement; **~ rural/sédentaire/dispersé** rural/fixed/scattered settlement; **~ individuel/collectif** detached/group housing

habitation [abitasjɔ̃] NF **a** (= *fait de résider*) living, dwelling (*littér*); **locaux à usage d'~** dwellings; **conditions d'~** housing *ou* living conditions; **impropre à l'~** unfit for human habitation, uninhabitable **b** (= *domicile*) residence, home, dwelling place (*littér*); **la caravane qui lui sert d'~** the caravan that serves as his home; **changer d'~** to change one's (place of) residence **c** (= *bâtiment*) house; **des ~s modernes** modern housing *ou* houses; **groupe d'~s** housing development *ou* estate (*Brit*); **~ à**

loyer modéré (= *appartement*) ≈ council flat (*Brit*), ≈ public housing unit (*US*); (= *immeuble*) ≈ (block of) council flats (*Brit*), ≈ housing project (*US*)

habité, e [abite] (*ptp de* **habiter**) ADJ [*château, maison*] lived-in, occupied; [*planète, région*] inhabited; [*vol, engin, station orbitale*] manned

habiter [abite] ▸conjug 1◂ **1** VT **a** [+ *maison, appartement*] to live in, occupy; [+ *ville, région*] to live in; [+ *planète*] to live on; **cette région a longtemps été habitée par les Celtes** for a long time, this region was inhabited by the Celts; **cette maison est-elle habitée?** does anyone live in this house?, is this house occupied? **b** (= *obséder*) [*sentiment*] to haunt; **habité d'idées sombres** haunted by gloomy thoughts; **habité par la jalousie/la peur** filled with jealousy/fear, in the grip of jealousy/ fear **2** VI to live (**en, dans** in); ~ **à la campagne/chez des amis/en ville** to live in the country/with friends/in town; **il habite (au) 17 (de la) rue Leblanc** he lives at number 17 rue Leblanc

habitude [abityd] NF **a** (= *accoutumance*) habit; **avoir/prendre l'~ de faire qch** to be/get used to doing sth; **avoir pour ~ de faire qch** to be in the habit of doing sth; **prendre de mauvaises ~s** to pick up *ou* get into bad habits; **perdre une ~** to get out of a habit; **faire perdre une ~ à qn** to break sb of a habit; **avoir une longue ~ de qch** to have long experience of sth; **ce n'est pas dans ses ~s de faire cela** he doesn't usually do that, he doesn't make a habit of (doing) that; **j'ai l'~!** I'm used to it!; **je n'ai pas l'~ de me répéter** I'm not in the habit of repeating myself; **je n'ai pas l'~ de cette voiture/de ces méthodes** I'm not used to this car/to these methods; **elle a une grande ~ des enfants** she's used to (dealing with) children ▪ (*PROV*) **l'~ est une seconde nature** habit is second nature; **avoir ses ~s dans un restaurant** to be a regular customer *ou* an habitué at a restaurant; **il a ses petites ~s** he has his own little ways *ou* his own little routine → **esclave, question** **b** (= *coutume*) ~**s** customs; **les ~s d'un pays** the customs of a country; **il a des ~s de bourgeois** he has a middle-class way of life **c** (*loc*) **d'~** usually, as a rule; **c'est meilleur que d'~** it's better than usual; **comme d'~** as usual; **par ~** out of habit, from force of habit; **selon** *ou* **suivant** *ou* **comme à son ~** as he usually does, as is his wont (*frm*)

habitué, e [abitɥe] (*ptp de* **habituer**) NM,F [*maison, musée, bibliothèque*] regular visitor, habitué(e); [*café, hôtel*] regular (customer), habitué(e); **les ~s du festival** (= *visiteurs*) regular visitors to the festival; (= *artistes*) regular performers at the festival; **ce metteur en scène est un ~ du festival de Cannes** this director makes regular appearances at *ou* is regularly featured at the Cannes film festival; **c'est un ~ des lieux** (*gén*) he knows his way round; (= *client*) he's a regular (customer); (*hum*) **c'est un ~ du chèque sans provision** he's a master of the rubber cheque* (*Brit*) *ou* check* (*US*); (*Sport*) **c'est un ~ des podiums** he knows what winning is all about

habituel, -elle [abitɥɛl] ADJ [*comportement*] usual, customary, habitual; [*réjouissances, formule de politesse*] customary, usual; **d'un geste qui lui était ~** with his usual gesture, with that typical gesture of his; **c'est l'histoire habituelle** it's the usual story

habituellement [abitɥɛlmã] ADV usually, generally, as a rule

habituer [abitɥe] ▸conjug 1◂ **1** VT ~ **qn à qch/à faire qch** (= *accoutumer*) to accustom sb to sth/to doing sth, get sb used to sth/to doing sth; (= *apprendre*) to teach sb sth/to do sth; **on m'a habitué à obéir** I've been taught to obey; **être habitué à qch/à faire qch** to be used *ou* accustomed to sth/to doing sth

2 s'habituer VPR **s'~ à qch/à faire qch** to get *ou* become *ou* grow used *ou* accustomed to sth/to doing sth; **je ne m'y habituerai jamais** I'll never get used to it

hâblerie [ˈɑbləʀi] NF (= *manière d'être*) bragging, boasting; (= *propos*) boast, big talk* (*NonC*)

hâbleur, -euse [ˈɑblœʀ, øz] **1** ADJ bragging, boasting, boastful **2** NM,F braggart, boaster

Habsbourg [ˈapsbuʀ] NMF Hapsburg

hachage [ˈaʃaʒ] NM (*au couteau*) chopping; (*avec un appareil*) mincing (*Brit*), grinding (*US*)

hache [ˈaʃ] NF axe, ax (*US*); ~ **d'armes** battle-axe; ~ **du bourreau** executioner's axe; ~ **de guerre** (*gén*) hatchet, axe; [*indien*] tomahawk; **déterrer/enterrer la ~ de guerre** to take up/ bury the hatchet; **casser qch/tuer qn à coups de** ~ to smash sth/kill sb with an axe; **abattre un arbre à coups de** ~ to chop a tree down; **visage taillé à la** ~ *ou* **à coups de** ~ angular *ou* roughly-hewn face; (*Can*) **mettre la ~ dans les dépenses** to cut expenses drastically

haché, e [ˈaʃe] (*ptp de* **hacher**) **1** ADJ **a** [*viande*] minced (*Brit*), ground (*US*); **bifteck ~** minced beef *ou* steak (*Brit*), (beef *ou* steak) mince (*Brit*), ground beef (*US*), hamburger (*US*) **b** [*style*] jerky; [*phrases*] jerky, broken **2** NM mince (*Brit*), minced meat (*Brit*), ground beef (*US*)

hache-légumes [ˈaʃlegym] NM INV vegetable-chopper

hachement [ˈaʃmã] NM = **hachage**

hache-paille [ˈaʃpaj] NM INV chaff-cutter

hacher [ˈaʃe] ▸conjug 1◂ VT **a** (= *couper*) (*au couteau*) to chop; (*avec un appareil*) to mince (*Brit*), grind (*US*); ~ **menu** to chop finely, mince; **il a été haché menu comme chair à pâté** they made mincemeat of him; **je me ferais ~ menu plutôt que d'accepter** I'd die rather than accept **b** (= *entrecouper*) [+ *discours, phrases*] to break up → **haché** **c** (*Art*) to hatch

hachette [ˈaʃɛt] NF hatchet

hache-viande [ˈaʃvjãd] NM INV (meat-)mincer (*Brit*), grinder (*US*)

hachich [ˈaʃiʃ] NM = **hachisch**

hachis [ˈaʃi] NM [*légumes*] chopped vegetables; [*viande*] mince (*Brit*), minced meat (*Brit*), hamburger (*US*), ground meat (*US*); (= *farce*) forcemeat (*NonC*); ~ **de porc** pork mince; ~ **Parmentier** ≈ shepherd's *ou* cottage pie (*Brit*)

hachisch [ˈaʃiʃ] NM hashish

hachoir [ˈaʃwaʀ] NM (= *couteau*) [*viande*] chopper, cleaver; [*légumes*] chopper; (= *planche*) chopping board; (= *appareil*) (meat-)mincer (*Brit*), grinder (*US*)

hachure [ˈaʃyʀ] NF (*Art*) hatching (*NonC*), hachure; (*Cartographie*) hachure

hachurer [ˈaʃyʀe] ▸conjug 1◂ VT (*Art*) to hatch; (*Cartographie*) to hachure

hacienda [asjɛnda] NF hacienda

haddock [ˈadɔk] NM smoked haddock

Hadrien [adʀijɛ̃] NM Hadrian

hadron [adʀɔ̃] NM hadron

Haendel [ˈɛndɛl] NM Handel

hagard, e [ˈagaʀ, aʀd] ADJ [*yeux*] wild; [*visage, air, gestes*] distraught, frantic, wild

hagiographe [aʒjɔgʀaf] NMF hagiographer

hagiographie [aʒjɔgʀafi] NF hagiography

hagiographique [aʒjɔgʀafik] ADJ hagiographic(al)

haie [ˈɛ] NF **a** (= *clôture*) hedge; ~ **d'aubépines** hawthorn hedge; ~ **vive** quickset hedge **b** (*Sport* = *obstacle*) [*coureur*] hurdle; [*chevaux*] fence; **course de ~s** (*coureur*) hurdles (race); (*chevaux*) steeplechase; **110 mètres ~s** 110 metres hurdles **c** (= *rangée*) [*spectateurs, policiers*] line, row; **faire une ~ d'honneur** to form a guard of honour; **faire la ~** to form a line

haïku [ˈajku, ˈaiku] NM haiku, hokku

haillon [ˈajɔ̃] NM rag; **en ~s** in rags *ou* tatters

haillonneux, -euse [ˈajɔnø, øz] ADJ (*littér*) in rags, in tatters, tattered and torn

Hainaut [ˈɛno] NM **le ~** Hainaut, Hainault

haine [ˈɛn] NF hatred (**de, pour** of, for); **cris/regards de ~** cries/looks of hatred *ou* hate; **incitation à la ~ raciale** incitement to racial hatred; **prendre qn en ~** to take a violent dislike *ou* a strong aversion to sb; **avoir de la ~ pour** to feel hatred for, be filled with hate *ou* hatred for; **par ~ de** out of *ou* through hatred of; **avoir la ~*** to be full of hatred *ou* aggro* (*Brit*)

haineusement [ˈɛnøzmã] ADV [*dire, regarder*] with hatred

haineux, -euse [ˈɛnø, øz] ADJ [*propos, personne*] full of hatred; **regard ~** look of hate *ou* hatred

haïr [ˈaiʀ] ▸conjug 10◂ VT to hate, detest; **elle me hait de l'avoir trompée** she hates me for having deceived her; **je hais ses manières affectées** I can't stand *ou* I hate *ou* I loathe his affected ways; **je hais d'être dérangé** I hate being *ou* to be disturbed; **ils se haïssent cordialement** they cordially detest one another

haire [ˈɛʀ] NF (= *chemise*) hair shirt

haïssable [ˈaisabl] ADJ detestable, hateful

Haïti [aiti] NM Haiti

haïtien, -ienne [aisjɛ̃, jɛn] **1** ADJ Haitian **2** Haïtien(ne) NM,F Haitian

halage [ˈalaʒ] NM (*Naut*) towing; (*Can*) timber hauling; **chemin de ~** towpath; **cheval de ~** towhorse

hâle [ˈɑl] NM (sun)tan

hâlé, e [ˈɑle] (*ptp de* **hâler**) ADJ (sun)tanned

haleine [alɛn] NF **a** (= *souffle*) breath; (= *respiration*) breathing (*NonC*); **avoir l'~ courte** to be short of breath *ou* short-winded; **retenir son ~** to hold one's breath; **être hors d'~** to be out of breath, be breathless; **perdre ~** to lose one's breath, get out of breath; **rire à perdre ~** to laugh until one's sides ache *ou* until one is out of breath; **reprendre ~** (*lit*) to get one's breath back; (*fig*) to get one's breath back, take a breather; **d'une seule ~** [*dire*] in one breath, in the same breath; [*faire*] (all) at one go; **il respirait d'une ~ régulière** his breathing was regular → **courir** **b** (= *air expiré*) breath; **avoir l'~ fraîche** to have fresh breath; **avoir mauvaise ~** *ou* **l'~ forte** to have bad breath; **j'ai senti à son ~ qu'il avait bu** I could smell drink on his breath, I could tell from his breath that he'd been drinking **c** (*loc*) **tenir qn en ~** (*attention*) to hold sb spellbound *ou* breathless; (*incertitude*) to keep sb in suspense *ou* on tenterhooks; **travail de longue ~** long-term job

haler [ˈale] ▸conjug 1◂ VT [+ *corde, ancre*] to haul in; [+ *bateau*] to tow

hâler [ˈale] ▸conjug 1◂ VT to (sun)tan

haletant, e [ˈal(ə)tã, ãt] ADJ [*personne*] (= *essoufflé*) panting, gasping for breath (*attrib*), out of breath (*attrib*); (= *assoiffé, effrayé*) panting (**de** with); (= *curieux*) breathless (**de** with); [*animal*] panting; [*poitrine*] heaving; [*voix*] breathless; [*roman policier*] suspenseful; **sa respiration était ~e** he was panting, his breath came in gasps

halètement [ˈalɛtmã] NM [*personne*] (*par manque d'air*) panting (*NonC*), gasping for breath (*NonC*); (*de soif, d'émotion*) panting (*NonC*); [*chien*] panting (*NonC*); [*moteur*] puffing (*NonC*)

haleter [ˈal(ə)te] ▸conjug 5◂ VI [*personne*] (= *manquer d'air*) to pant, gasp for breath; (*de soif, d'émotion*) to pant (**de** with); [*chien*] to pant; [*moteur, locomotive*] to puff; **son auditoire haletait** his audience listened with bated breath

haleur, -euse ['alœʀ, øz] [1] NM (= *remorqueur*) tug (boat) [2] NM,F (= *personne*) (boat) hauler

halieutique [aljøtik] [1] ADJ halieutic(al) [2] NF halieutics *sg*

hall ['ol] NM [*immeuble*] hall; [*hôtel*] foyer, lobby, hall; [*cinéma, théâtre*] foyer; [*gare, lycée, université*] concourse; (Aviat) **~ d'arrivée** arrivals lounge *ou* hall; (Aviat) **~ des départs** departure lounge; **~ d'entrée** entrance hall; **~ d'accueil** reception hall; **~ d'exposition** exhibition hall; **c'est un vrai ~ de gare!** it's like Piccadilly Circus (Brit) *ou* Grand Central Station (US) (here)!

hallali [alali] NM (*Chasse*) (= *mise à mort*) kill; (= *sonnerie*) mort; **sonner l'~** (*lit*) to blow the mort; (*fig*) to go in for the kill

halle ['al] [1] NF [a] (= *marché*) (covered) market; (= *grande salle*) hall; **~ au blé** corn exchange *ou* market; **~ aux vins** wine market [b] (*Belg* = *gymnase*) **~ de gymnastique** gymnasium, gym [2] **halles** NFPL (covered) market; (*alimentation en gros*) central food market → **fort²**

hallebarde ['albaʀd] NF halberd; **il pleut** *ou* **tombe des ~s*** it's bucketing (down)*, it's raining cats and dogs*

hallebardier ['albaʀdje] NM halberdier

hallier ['alje] NM thicket, brush (NonC), brushwood (NonC)

Halloween [alɔwin] NF (Can) Hallowe'en

hallucinant, e [a(l)lysinã, ãt] ADJ [*histoire, image, spectacle, ressemblance*] staggering*, incredible

hallucination [a(l)lysinasjɔ̃] NF hallucination; **~ collective** group hallucination; **avoir des ~s** to hallucinate; **tu as des ~s!*** you must be seeing things!

hallucinatoire [a(l)lysinatwaʀ] ADJ hallucinatory

halluciné, e [a(l)lysine] (*ptp de* **halluciner**) [1] ADJ [*malade*] suffering from hallucinations; [*yeux, regard*] haunted [2] NM,F (*Méd*) person suffering from hallucinations; (* = *fou, exalté*) lunatic*

halluciner [a(l)lysine] ▶ conjug 1 ◀ VI (*Méd*) to hallucinate; **j'hallucine!*** I must be seeing things!

hallucinogène [a(l)lysinɔʒɛn] [1] ADJ [*drogue*] hallucinogenic, mind-expanding **~ champignon** [2] NM hallucinogen, hallucinant

halo ['alo] NM (Astron, Tech = *auréole*) halo; (Photo) fogging, halation; **~ de lumière** halo of light; **~ de gloire** cloud of glory; **~ de mystère** aura of mystery

halogène [alɔʒɛn] [1] ADJ (*gén*) halogenous; [*lampe*] halogen (*épith*) [2] NM (Chim) halogen; (= *lampe*) halogen lamp

halte ['alt] NF [a] (= *pause, repos*) stop, break; (= *répit*) pause; **faire ~** to (make a) stop (**à** in) [b] (= *endroit*) stopping place; (Rail) halt [c] (*loc*) **~!** (*gén*) stop!; (Mil) halt!; **« ~ au feu!»** "no fires!"; **~ aux essais nucléaires!** no more atomic tests!; **dire ~ à un conflit** to call for a stop *ou* an end to a conflict; **~-là!** (Mil) halt! who goes there?; (*fig*) just a moment!, hold on!

halte-garderie (*pl* **haltes-garderies**) [alt(ə)gaʀdəʀi] NF crèche, ≈ day nursery

haltère [altɛʀ] NM [a] (Sport) (*à boules*) dumbbell; (*à disques*) barbell; **faire des ~s** to do weight lifting → **poids** [b] [*insecte*] halter(e), balancer

haltérophile [altɛʀɔfil] NMF weight lifter

haltérophilie [altɛʀɔfili] NF weight lifting; **faire de l'~** to do weight lifting

hamac ['amak] NM hammock; **accrocher** *ou* **suspendre un ~** to sling a hammock

hamadryade [amadʀijad] NF (Myth) hamadryad

hamamélis [amamelis] NM witch hazel

Hambourg ['ãbuʀ] N Hamburg

hamburger ['ãbuʀgœʀ] NM hamburger

hameau (*pl* **hameaux**) ['amo] NM hamlet

hameçon [amsɔ̃] NM (fish) hook → **mordre**

hammam ['amam] NM (= *établissement*) hammam; (*dans complexe sportif*) steam room, hammam

hampe¹ ['ãp] NF [*drapeau*] pole; [*lance*] shaft; [*lettre*] (*vers le bas*) downstroke; (*vers le haut*) upstroke; (Bot) scape

hampe² ['ãp] NF [*cerf*] breast; [*bœuf*] flank

hamster ['amstɛʀ] NM hamster

han ['ã] EXCL oof!; **il poussa un ~ et souleva la malle** he gave a grunt as he lifted the trunk

hanche ['ãʃ] NF [a] [*personne*] hip; [*cheval*] haunch; [*insecte*] coxa; **balancer** *ou* **rouler des ~s** to wiggle one's hips; **les mains sur les ~s, il ... arms akimbo** *ou* with his hands on his hips, he ... → **tour** [b] (Naut) quarter

hand· ['ãd] NM ABRÉV = **hand(-)ball**

hand(-)ball ['ãdbal] NM handball

handballeur, -euse ['ãdbalœʀ, øz] NM,F handball player

Händel ['ɛndɛl] NM = **Haendel**

handicap ['ãdikap] NM (*lit, fig*) handicap; **avoir un sérieux ~** to be seriously handicapped *ou* disadvantaged (**sur qn** in relation to sb)

handicapant, e ['ãdikapã, ãt] ADJ [*maladie*] crippling, disabling; (= *gênant*) **c'est assez ~** it's a bit of a handicap; **la fiscalité ne doit pas être ~e pour la croissance** taxation mustn't handicap *ou* cramp economic growth

handicapé, e ['ãdikape] (*ptp de* **handicaper**) [1] ADJ disabled, handicapped; **très ~** severely handicapped [2] NM,F disabled *ou* handicapped person; **~ mental/physique** mentally/physically handicapped person; **~ moteur** person with motor disability

handicaper ['ãdikape] ▶ conjug 1 ◀ VT (*lit, fig*) to handicap

handicapeur ['ãdikapœʀ] NM (Courses) handicapper

handisport ['ãdispɔʀ] ADJ [*tennis, basket-ball*] wheelchair (*épith*); [*natation*] for the disabled

hangar ['ãgaʀ] NM [*matériel, machines*] shed; [*fourrage*] barn; [*marchandises*] warehouse, shed; [*avions*] hangar; **~ à bateaux** boathouse

hanneton ['an(ə)tɔ̃] NM cockchafer, may bug *ou* beetle → **piqué**

Hannibal [anibal] NM Hannibal

Hanoi, Hanoï [anɔj] N Hanoi

Hanovre ['anɔvʀ] N Hanover

hanovrien, -ienne ['anɔvʀjɛ̃, jɛn] [1] ADJ Hanoverian [2] **Hanovrien(ne)** NM,F Hanoverian

Hanse ['ãs] NF (Hist) **la ~** Hanse

hanséatique [ãseatik] ADJ Hanseatic; **la ligue ~** the Hanseatic League

hanter ['ãte] ▶ conjug 1 ◀ VT [*fantôme, personne, souvenir*] to haunt; **~ les mauvais lieux** to haunt places of ill repute; **maison hantée** haunted house; **cette question hante les esprits** this question is preying on people's minds

hantise ['ãtiz] NF obsessive fear; **avoir la ~ de la maladie** to be haunted by a fear of illness, have an obsessive fear of illness; **vivre dans la ~ du chômage/de l'échec** to live in dread of unemployment/failure; **c'est ma ~!** I never stop worrying about it!

haoussa ['ausa] [1] ADJ Hausa [2] NM (Ling) Hausa [3] **Haoussa** NMF Hausa; **les Haoussas** the Hausa

happening ['ap(ə)niŋ] NM (Art, Théât) happening

happer ['ape] ▶ conjug 1 ◀ VT (*avec la gueule, le bec*) to snap up; (*avec la main*) to snatch, grab; **il le happa au passage** he grabbed him as he went past; **il a eu le bras happé par une machine** he got his arm caught in a piece of machinery; **être happé par une voiture** to be hit by a car; **happé par l'abîme** dragged down into the abyss; **ils ont été happés dans un engrenage d'emprunts** they got caught up in a spiral of debt

happy end (*pl* **happy ends**) ['apiɛnd] NM happy ending

happy few ['apifju] NMPL **les ~** the privileged *ou* select few

haptonomie [aptɔnɔmi] NF communication with a foetus through sensory stimulation

hara-kiri (*pl* **hara-kiris**) ['aʀakiʀi] NM hara-kiri, hari-kiri; **(se) faire ~** to commit hara-kiri

harangue ['aʀɑ̃g] NF harangue

haranguer ['aʀɑ̃ge] ▶ conjug 1 ◀ VT to harangue, hold forth to *ou* at

harangueur, -euse ['aʀɑ̃gœʀ, øz] NM,F mob orator, haranguer (*frm*)

Harare [aʀaʀe] N Harare

haras ['aʀa] NM stud farm

harassant, e ['aʀasã, ãt] ADJ exhausting, wearing

harassé, e ['aʀase] (*ptp de* **harasser**) ADJ exhausted, tired out, worn out; **~ de travail** overwhelmed with work

harassement ['aʀasmã] NM exhaustion

harasser ['aʀase] ▶ conjug 1 ◀ VT to exhaust

harcèlement ['aʀsɛlmã] NM [*personne*] harassment; **~ sexuel/policier** sexual/police harassment; (Mil) **opérations** *ou* **guerre de ~** guerrilla warfare; **il faut mener une guerre de ~ contre les dealers** we must keep hounding the drug dealers

harceler ['aʀsəle] ▶ conjug 5 ◀ VT [a] [+ *personne*] (*de critiques, d'attaques*) to harass, plague (**de** with); (*de questions, de réclamations*) to plague, pester (**de** with); **~ qn pour obtenir qch** to pester sb for sth; **elle a été harcelée de coups de téléphone anonymes** she has been plagued by anonymous phone calls [b] (Mil) [+ *ennemi*] to harass, harry [c] [+ *animal*] to worry; [+ *gibier*] to hunt down, harry

hard· ['aʀd] [1] NM [a] (Mus) hard rock [b] (= *pornographie*) hard porn* [c] (Ordin) hardware [2] ADJ [*film, revue*] porno*, hard-core; [*scène*] hard-core

harde ['aʀd] NF [*cerfs*] herd

hardes ['aʀd] NFPL (*littér, péj*) (= *vieux habits*) old clothes, rags

hardi, e ['aʀdi] ADJ [a] (= *audacieux*) [*initiative, personne, comparaison, métaphore*] bold, daring [b] (= *provocant*) [*décolleté*] daring; [*fille*] bold, brazen; [*plaisanterie*] daring, audacious; † [*mensonge*] brazen, barefaced (*épith*) [c] (*loc*) **~ les gars!** go to it, lads! (Brit) come on lads! (Brit) *ou* you guys! (US); **et ~ petit! les voilà qui poussent la voiture*** and heave-ho! there they are pushing the car

hardiesse ['aʀdjɛs] NF [a] (*littér* = *audace*) boldness, daring; **avoir la ~ de** to be bold *ou* daring enough to; **montrer une grande ~ de** to show great boldness *ou* daring [b] (= *effronterie*) [*personne*] audacity, effrontery, impudence; [*livre, plaisanterie*] audacity; **la ~ de son décolleté choqua tout le monde** everyone was shocked by her daring neckline [c] (= *originalité*) [*style, tableau, conception*] boldness [d] (= *libertés*) **~s** [*livre, pamphlet*] bold statements; [*domestique, soupirant*] liberties; **~s de langage/de style** bold language/turns of phrase

hardiment ['aʀdimã] ADV [a] (= *audacieusement*) [*innover*] boldly, daringly; **ne vous engagez pas trop ~** don't commit yourself rashly [b] (= *effrontément*) brazenly; **elle le dévisagea ~** she stared at him brazenly

hard-top (*pl* **hard-tops**) ['aʀdtɔp] NM hardtop

hardware ['aʀdwɛʀ] NM hardware

harem [ˈaʀɛm] NM harem; (hum) **entouré d'un véritable ~** surrounded by a bevy of girls

hareng [ˈaʀɑ̃] NM herring; **~ saur** smoked herring, kipper, bloater → **sec**, **serré**

harengère† [ˈaʀɑ̃ʒɛʀ] NF (péj) fishwife (péj)

harfang [ˈaʀfɑ̃] NM snowy owl

hargne [ˈaʀɲ] NF (= colère) spiteful anger; (= ténacité) fierce determination; **j'étais dans une telle ~!** I was so angry! ou mad!*; **avec ~** (= avec colère) spitefully

hargneusement [ˈaʀɲøzmɑ̃] ADV [répondre] bad-temperedly; [aboyer] ferociously

hargneux, -euse [ˈaʀɲø, øz] ADJ a [personne, caractère] bad-tempered, cantankerous; [animal] vicious, fierce; **un petit chien ~** a snappy little dog b [sportif] aggressive

haricot [ˈaʀiko] NM a (Bot) bean; **~ beurre** type of yellow French bean, wax bean (US); **~ blanc** haricot bean; **~ d'Espagne** scarlet runner; **~ grimpant** ou **à rame** runner bean; **~ rouge** red kidney bean; **~ vert** French bean; **~ sec** dried bean; **~s à écosser** fresh beans (for shelling) → **courir**, **fin²** b (Culin) **~ de mouton** lamb and bean stew, mutton stew c (= cuvette) kidney tray d (loc: †) **pour des ~s** for next to nothing

haridelle [ˈaʀidɛl] NF (péj = cheval) nag, jade

harissa [ˈaʀisa, aʀisa] NF harissa (hot chilli sauce)

harki [ˈaʀki] NM Algerian soldier loyal to the French during the Algerian War of Independence

harle [ˈaʀl] NM **~ bièvre** goosander; **~ huppé** red-breasted merganser

harmonica [aʀmɔnika] NM harmonica, mouth organ

harmoniciste [aʀmɔnisist] NMF harmonica player

harmonie [aʀmɔni] NF (Littérat, Mus, gén) harmony; (= section de l'orchestre) wind section; (= fanfare) wind band; (Mus) **~s** harmonies; (Littérat) **~ imitative** onomatopoeia; **être en ~ avec** to be in harmony ou in keeping with; **vivre en bonne ~** to live together harmoniously ou in harmony → **table**

harmonieusement [aʀmɔnjøzmɑ̃] ADV harmoniously

harmonieux, -ieuse [aʀmɔnjø, jøz] ADJ (gén) harmonious; **couleurs harmonieuses** well-matched ou harmonizing colours; **un couple ~** a well-matched couple

harmonique [aʀmɔnik] 1 ADJ (gén, Math, Mus) harmonic 2 NM (Mus) harmonic

harmonisation [aʀmɔnizasjɔ̃] NF [couleurs] matching, harmonization; [politiques, règlements] harmonization, standardization; **~ vocalique** vowel harmony

harmoniser [aʀmɔnize] ▶conjug 1◀ 1 VT [+ couleurs] to match, harmonize (avec with); [+ politiques, règlements] to harmonize, standardize; **il faut ~ nos règlements avec les normes européennes** we must bring our rules into line with European regulations; (Univ) **il faut ~ la notation** we have to make sure that grading is done consistently 2 **s'harmoniser** VPR [couleurs] to match, harmonize (avec with); [politiques] to be harmonized ou standardized

harmoniste [aʀmɔnist] NMF (Rel, Mus) harmonist; [orgue] organ tuner

harmonium [aʀmɔnjɔm] NM harmonium

harnachement [ˈaʀnaʃmɑ̃] NM a (= action) [cheval, bébé, cascadeur] harnessing b (= objets) [cheval de trait] harness; [cheval de monte] tack, saddlery; * [campeur, photographe] gear*

harnacher [ˈaʀnaʃe] ▶conjug 1◀ 1 VT [+ cheval de trait, alpiniste] to harness; [+ cheval de monte] to put the bridle and saddle on; (péj) **il était drôlement harnaché*** he was wearing the strangest gear* ou rig-out* (Brit) ou get-up* 2 **se harnacher** VPR [alpiniste, parachutiste] to put one's harness on; * [campeur] to put one's gear on*, rig o.s. out*

harnais [ˈaʀnɛ], **harnois**†† [ˈaʀnwa] NM [cheval de trait, bébé, alpiniste] harness; [cheval de monte] tack, saddlery; **~ (de sécurité)** (safety) harness; **~ d'engrenage** train of gear wheels

haro [ˈaʀo] EXCL (†† Jur) harrow!, haro!; (littér) **crier ~ sur qn/qch** to inveigh ou rail against sb/sth

harpagon [aʀpagɔ̃] NM skinflint, Scrooge

harpe [ˈaʀp] NF (Mus) harp; **~ éolienne** aeolian ou wind harp; **~ celtique** ou **irlandaise** Celtic ou Irish harp

harpie [ˈaʀpi] NF (Myth, péj) harpy; (Zool) harpy eagle

harpiste [ˈaʀpist] NMF harpist

harpon [ˈaʀpɔ̃] NM (Pêche) harpoon; (Constr) toothing stone → **fusil**, **pêche²**

harponnage [aʀpɔnaʒ], **harponnement** [aʀpɔnmɑ̃] NM harpooning

harponner [aʀpɔne] ▶conjug 1◀ VT [+ baleine] to harpoon; * [+ malfaiteur] to collar*, nab*; * [+ passant, voisin] to waylay, buttonhole*

harponneur [aʀpɔnœʀ] NM harpooner

hasard [ˈazaʀ] NM a (= événement fortuit) **un ~ heureux/malheureux** a stroke ou piece of luck/bad luck, a stroke of good fortune/ misfortune; **quel ~ de vous rencontrer ici !** what a coincidence meeting you here!, fancy meeting you here!*; **c'est un vrai** ou **pur ~ que je sois libre** it's quite by chance ou it's a pure coincidence that I'm free; **par un curieux ~** by a curious coincidence; **on l'a retrouvé par le plus grand des ~s** it was quite by chance ou it was a piece of sheer luck that they found him; **les ~s de la vie/de la carrière** the fortunes of life/one's career
b (= destin) **le ~** chance, fate, luck; (Stat) chance; **les caprices du ~** the whims of fate; **le ~ fait bien les choses !** what a stroke of luck!; **faire la part du ~** (= événements futurs) to allow for chance (to play its part); (événements passés) to admit that chance had a hand in it; **le ~ a voulu qu'il soit absent** as luck would have it he wasn't there; **c'est ça le ~!** that's the luck of the draw!*; **c'est un fait du ~** it's a matter of chance; **les lois du ~** the laws of fate → **jeu**
c (= risques) **~s** hazards; **les ~s de la guerre** the hazards of war
d **au ~** [aller] aimlessly; [agir] haphazardly, in a haphazard way; [tirer, choisir] at random; **j'ai répondu au ~** I gave an answer off the top of my head*; **voici des exemples au ~** here are some random examples ou some examples taken at random; **il a acheté ces livres au ~ des ventes/de ses voyages** he bought these books just as he happened to see them in the sales/on his trips; **faire confiance** ou **s'en remettre au ~** to trust to luck; **il ne laisse jamais rien au ~** he never leaves anything to chance
e **à tout ~** (= en cas de besoin) just in case; (= espérant trouver ce qu'on cherche) (just) on the off chance; **on avait emporté une tente à tout ~** we had taken a tent just in case; **je suis entré à tout ~** I looked in on the off chance
f **par ~** by chance, by accident; **je passais par ~** I happened to be passing by; **tu n'aurais pas par ~ 100 F à me prêter ?** you wouldn't by any chance have ou you wouldn't happen to have 100 francs to lend me?; **voudrais-tu par ~ m'apprendre mon métier ?** you wouldn't be trying to teach me my job by any chance?; **comme par ~ !** what a coincidence!; **il est arrivé comme par ~ au moment où on débouchait les bouteilles** he turned up as if by chance as we were opening the bottles; (iro) **comme par ~, il était absent** he just happened to be away (iro); **si par ~ tu le vois** if you happen to see him, if by chance you should see him

hasarder [ˈazaʀde] ▶conjug 1◀ 1 VT [+ vie, réputation] to risk; [+ remarque, hypothèse, démarche] to hazard, venture; [+ argent] to gamble, risk 2 **se hasarder** VPR **se ~ dans un endroit dangereux** to venture into a dangerous place; **se ~ à faire** to risk doing, venture to do; **à votre place je ne m'y hasarderais pas** if I were you I wouldn't risk it

hasardeux, -euse [ˈazaʀdø, øz] ADJ [entreprise] hazardous, risky; [hypothèse] dangerous, rash; **il serait bien ~ de** it would be dangerous ou risky to

has been* [ˈazbin] NM INV (péj) has-been*

hasch* [ˈaʃ] NM hash*, pot*, grass*

haschisch [ˈaʃiʃ] NM = **hachisch**

hase [ˈaz] NF doe (female hare)

hassidique [asidik] ADJ Hassidic

hâte [ˈat] NF a (= empressement) haste; (= impatience) impatience; **à la ~** hurriedly, hastily; **en (grande** ou **toute) ~** as fast as you (ou we etc) can, posthaste, with all possible speed; **elle est montée/descendue en toute ~** she hurried up/down the stairs; **mettre de la ~ à faire qch** to do sth speedily ou in a hurry ou hurriedly; **avoir ~ de faire** to be eager ou anxious to do; **je n'ai qu'une ~, c'est d'avoir terminé ce travail** I can't wait to get this work finished; **sans ~** unhurriedly

hâter [ˈate] ▶conjug 1◀ 1 VT [+ fin, développement] to hasten; [+ départ] to bring forward, hasten; [+ fruit] to bring on, force; **~ le pas** to quicken ou hasten one's pace ou step 2 **se hâter** VPR to hurry, hasten; **se ~ de faire** to hurry ou hasten ou make haste to do; **hâtez-vous** hurry up; **je me hâte de dire que** I hasten to say that; **hâte-toi lentement** more haste, less speed (PROV); **ne nous hâtons pas de juger** let's not be in a hurry to judge ou too hasty in our judgments

hâtif, -ive [ˈatif, iv] ADJ [développement] precocious; [fruit, saison] early; [travail] hurried; [décision, jugement] hasty; **ne tirons pas de conclusions hâtives** let's not rush to conclusions

hâtivement [ˈativmɑ̃] ADV hurriedly, hastily; **dire qch un peu/trop ~** to say sth rather/too hastily

hauban [ˈobɑ̃] NM (Naut) shroud; [pont] stay; **pont à ~s** cable-stayed bridge

haubaner [ˈobane] ▶conjug 1◀ VT [+ mât] to prop ou shore up with shrouds

haubert [ˈobɛʀ] NM (Hist) coat of mail, hauberk

hausse [ˈos] NF a [prix, niveau, température] rise, increase (de in); (Bourse) rise (de in); **~ de salaire** (pay) rise (Brit) ou raise (US); **être en ~** [monnaie, prix] to be going up ou rising; [actions, marchandises] to be going up (in price); (Bourse) **marché à la ~** bull(ish) market; **tendance à la ~** bullish ou upward trend; (fig) **sa cote est** ou **ses actions sont en ~** things are looking up for him, his popularity is increasing; (essence) **une ~ à la pompe** a rise in pump prices; **revoir** ou **réviser à la ~** [+ prévisions, chiffres, objectif] to revise upwards, scale up b [fusil] backsight adjuster

haussement [ˈosmɑ̃] NM **~ d'épaules** shrug; **il eut un ~ d'épaules** he shrugged (his shoulders); **elle eut un ~ des sourcils** she raised her eyebrows

hausser [ˈose] ▶conjug 1◀ 1 VT a (= élever) [+ barre, niveau, sourcil, ton, voix] to raise; [+ prix] to raise, increase; **~ les épaules** to shrug (one's shoulders) b [+ mur] to heighten, raise; [+ maison] to heighten, make higher; **~ une maison d'un étage** to add another floor to a house 2 **se hausser** VPR **se ~ sur la pointe des pieds** to stand up on tiptoe; **se ~ au niveau de qn** to raise o.s. up to sb's level; **se ~ du col** to show off

haussier, -ière [ˈosje, jɛʀ] 1 ADJ (Bourse) [marché] bullish, bull (épith); [prix, cours] rising; **tendance haussière** bullish trend 2 NM (Bourse) bull

haussmannien, -ienne [osmanjɛ̃, jɛn] ADJ [immeuble, façade] Haussmann (épith) (reflecting the opulent style of architecture typical of the period in the 1850s and 1860s when Paris was redeveloped by Baron Haussmann)

haut, e [ˈo, ˈot]

1 ADJECTIF	4 NOM FÉMININ
2 NOM MASCULIN	5 ADVERBE
3 NOM MASCULIN PL	6 COMPOSÉS

1 ADJECTIF

a = de taille élevée [mur, montagne] high; [herbe, arbre, édifice] tall, high; une ~e silhouette a tall figure; de ~e taille tall; un chien ~ sur pattes a long-legged dog; il a le front ~ he has a high forehead; ~ comme trois pommes* knee-high to a grasshopper*; un mur ~ de 3 mètres a wall 3 metres high; pièce ~e de plafond room with a high ceiling

b = situé en altitude [plafond, branche, nuage, plateau] high; le soleil était déjà ~ dans le ciel the sun was already high up in the sky; le plus ~ étage the top floor; dans les plus ~es branches de l'arbre in the topmost branches of the tree → montagne, ville

c = de niveau élevé [prix, température, rendement] high; [Élec] [fréquence, voltage] high; c'est (la) marée ~e ◊ la mer est ~e it's high tide, the tide is in; à marée ~e at high tide; pendant les ~es eaux (du fleuve) while the river is high, during high water

d Mus = aigu [note, ton] high, high-pitched

e = fort, bruyant son mari est si gentil — jamais un mot plus ~ que l'autre ! her husband is so nice — never an angry word!; pousser ou jeter les ou des ~s cris to make a terrible fuss → verbe, voix

f dans une hiérarchie = supérieur (gén avant n) [qualité, rang, précision] high; [âme, pensée] lofty, noble; avoir une ~e idée ou opinion de soi-même to have a high ou an exalted opinion of o.s.; c'est du plus ~ comique it's highly amusing ou comical, it's excruciatingly funny; ~ en couleur (= rougeaud) with a high colour ou a ruddy complexion; (= coloré, pittoresque) colourful; athlète/cadre de ~ niveau top athlete/executive; discussions au plus ~ niveau top-level discussions; (hum) ~s faits heroic deeds; les ~es cartes the high cards, the picture cards; la ~e cuisine/couture/coiffure haute cuisine/couture/coiffure; les ~es mathématiques higher mathematics; ~ personnage high-ranking person → lutte

g = ancien dans la plus ~e antiquité in earliest antiquity; le ~ Moyen Âge the Early Middle Ages; le ~ Empire the Early (Roman) Empire; (Ling) le ~ allemand Old High German

h Géog le Haut Rhin the Upper Rhine; la Haute Normandie Upper Normandy; la Haute-Égypte Upper Egypt; les ~es terres the highlands; (Hist Can) le Haut Canada Upper Canada

2 NOM MASCULIN

a = hauteur le mur a 3 mètres de ~ the wall is 3 metres high; combien fait-il de ~ ? how high is it?

b = partie haute [arbre, colline, armoire] top; au ~ de l'arbre at the top of the tree, high up in the tree; la colonne est évasée dans le ~ the column gets wider at the top; le ~ du visage the top part of the face; (sur un colis) « ~ » "top", "this way up", "this side up"; (fig) tenir le ~ du pavé to take pride of place

c = vêtement top

d expressions figées

♦ **au plus haut** : être au plus ~ (dans les sondages) [personne] to be riding high; [cote, popularité] to be at its peak; le prix de l'or est au plus ~ the price of gold has reached a peak ou maximum

♦ **de haut**

(= avec détachement) voir les choses de ~ to take a detached view of things

(= avec mépris) prendre qch de (très) ~ to react (most) indignantly to sth; le prendre de ~ avec ou à l'égard de qn ◊ prendre ou traiter qn de ~ to look down on sb, treat sb disdainfully → regarder, tomber

♦ **de haut en bas** [s'ouvrir] from the top downwards; regarder qn de ~ en bas to look sb up and down; frapper de ~ en bas to strike downwards; couvert de graffitis de ~ en bas covered in graffiti from top to bottom; ça se lit de ~ en bas it reads vertically (starting at the top); lissez le papier peint de ~ en bas smooth the wallpaper, starting at the top and working down → bas

♦ **d'en haut** : les chambres d'en ~ the upstairs bedrooms; (socialement) ceux ou les gens d'en ~ people at the top; (Rel) un signe d'en ~ a sign from on high; vu d'en ~ seen from above; des ordres qui viennent d'en ~ orders from on high ou from above

♦ **du haut** : les pièces du ~ the upstairs rooms; les voisins du ~ the neighbours ou people upstairs; l'étagère/le tiroir du ~ the top shelf/drawer; les dents du ~ the top teeth

♦ **du haut de** : du ~ d'un arbre from the top of a tree; tomber du ~ du 5e étage to fall from the 5th floor; parler du ~ d'une tribune/d'un balcon to speak from a platform/a balcony; (hum) il me dévisageait, du ~ de son mètre cinquante he looked down on me, which was quite something as he was all of five feet tall; il me regarda du ~ de sa grandeur he looked down his nose at me

♦ **du haut en bas** [couvrir, fouiller] from top to bottom; du ~ en bas de la hiérarchie/société at all levels of the hierarchy/of society

♦ **en haut** (= au sommet) at the top; (dans un immeuble) upstairs; il habite en ~/tout en ~ he lives upstairs/right at the top; écris l'adresse en ~ à gauche write the address in the top left-hand corner; manteau boutonné jusqu'en ~ coat buttoned right up ou (right) up to the top; les voleurs sont passés par en ~ the burglars came in from upstairs ou got in upstairs; en ~ de [+ immeuble, escalier, côte, écran] at the top of; en ~ de l'échelle sociale high up the social ladder

3 hauts NOM MASCULIN PL

a = périodes fastes des ~s et des bas ups and downs; il a connu des ~s et des bas he's had his ups and downs; elle gagne plus ou moins sa vie, il y a des ~s et des bas she makes a reasonable living but it's a bit up and down

b Géog les Hauts de Meuse/de Seine the upper reaches of the Meuse/Seine

c Naut topside

4 haute NF (les gens de) la ~e* the upper crust*, (Brit), the toffs‡ (Brit), the swells† *

5 ADVERBE

a monter, sauter, voler high; mettez vos livres plus ~ put your books higher up; c'est lui qui saute le plus ~ he can jump the highest; ~ les mains ! hands up!, stick 'em up!‡; ~ les cœurs ! take heart!

b = fort [parler] loudly; lire/penser tout ~ to read/think aloud ou out loud; mettez la radio plus ~ turn up the radio; j'ose le dire bien ~ I'm not afraid of saying it out loud; parle plus ~ ! speak up!

c Mus = dans les aigus monter ~ to hit the top notes; chanter trop ~ to sing sharp

d sur le plan social des gens ~ placés people in high places; arriver très ~ to reach a high position; viser ~ to aim high

e = en arrière, dans le temps aussi ~ qu'on peut remonter as far back as we can go; « voir plus ~ » "see above"; comme je l'ai dit plus ~ as I said above ou previously

6 COMPOSÉS

► **haut commandement** high command
► **le Haut Commissariat (de l'ONU) pour les réfugiés** the UN High Commission for Refugees ► **Haute Cour** high court (for impeachment of French President or Ministers)
► **haute école** (Équitation) haute école; (fig) c'est de la ~e école it's very advanced (stuff*)
► **haut fourneau** blast ou smelting furnace
► **haut lieu** : un ~ lieu de la culture/musique a Mecca for culture/music; en ~ lieu in high places ► **haute trahison** high treason
► **haut vol, haute volée** : de ~ vol ◊ de ~e volée [personne] high-flying; [opération, activité] far-reaching; un industriel/athlète de ~e volée a top-flight industrialist/athlete; un escroc de ~ vol a big-time swindler; une escroquerie de ~ vol a major swindle

hautain, e [ˈotɛ̃, ɛn] ADJ [personne] haughty; [air, manière] haughty, lofty

hautainement [ˈotɛnmɑ̃] ADV haughtily, loftily

hautbois [ˈobwa] NM (= instrument) oboe

hautboïste [ˈobɔist] NMF oboist, oboe player

haut-commissaire (pl **hauts-commissaires**) [ˈokɔmisɛr] NM high commissioner (à for); ~ des Nations unies pour les réfugiés United Nations High Commissioner for Refugees

haut-commissariat (pl **hauts-commissariats**) [ˈokɔmisarja] NM (= ministère) high commission (à of); (= grade) high commissionership

haut-de-chausse(s) (pl **hauts-de-chausse(s)**) [ˈod(ə)ʃos] NM (Hist) (knee) breeches, trunk hose

haut-de-forme (pl **hauts-de-forme**) [ˈod(ə)fɔrm] NM top hat

haute-contre (pl **hautes-contre**) [ˈotkɔ̃tr] 1 ADJ, NM counter tenor 2 NF counter tenor, alto

haute-fidélité (pl **hautes-fidélités**) [ˈotfidelite] 1 ADJ [chaîne, son] high-fidelity 2 NF high-fidelity

hautement [ˈotmɑ̃] ADV (= extrêmement) highly; (= ouvertement) openly; [personnel] ~ qualifié highly qualified

▼ **hauteur** [ˈotœr] NF **a** (= élévation verticale) [tour, montagne, astre, personne] height; [son] pitch; (Aut) [châssis] ground clearance; il se redressa de toute sa ~ he drew himself up to his full height; d'une ~ de 4 mètres (dimension) 4 metres high; (d'un point élevé) from a height of 4 metres; (Aut) ~ maximum ou libre 3 mètres headroom 3 metres; pièce de 3 mètres de ~ sous plafond room whose ceiling height is 3 metres; tomber de toute sa ~ [personne] to fall headlong ou flat, measure one's length (Brit); [armoire] to come crashing down; perdre de la ~ to lose height; prendre de la ~ (lit) to climb, gain height; (fig) to distance o.s.; ~ de vues ability to distance o.s.; à ~ d'appui at leaning height; à ~ des yeux at eye level; à ~ d'homme at the right height ou level for a man → saut

b (Géom) perpendicular height; (ligne) perpendicular; (Astron) altitude

c (plan horizontal) arriver à la ~ de qn to draw level with sb; la procession arrivait à sa ~ the procession was drawing level with him; nous habitons à la ~ de la mairie we live up by the town hall; (Naut) arriver à la ~ d'un cap to come abreast of a cape; un accident à la ~ de Tours an accident near Tours ou in the vicinity of ou neighbourhood of Tours

d (loc) être à la ~ de la situation to be equal to the situation; il s'est vraiment montré à la ~* he proved he was up to it*; ne pas se sentir à la ~* not to feel up to it*, not to feel equal to the task

e (= colline) height, hill; gagner les ~s to make for the heights ou hills

f (= noblesse) loftiness, nobility; la ~ de ses sentiments his noble ou lofty sentiments, the loftiness ou nobility of his sentiments

g (= arrogance) haughtiness, loftiness; parler avec ~ to speak haughtily ou loftily

➤ GRAMMAIRE ACTIVE: **hauteur** 42.4, 43.4

$\boxed{\text{h}}$ (*Écon*) **à (la) ~ de 10 000 F** up to 10,000 francs

Haute-Volta ['otvɔlta] NF Upper Volta

haut-fond (*pl* **hauts-fonds**) ['ofɔ̃] NM shallow, shoal

Haut-Karabakh ['okaʀabak] N Nagorno Karabakh

haut-le-cœur ['ol(ə)kœʀ] NM INV retch, heave; **avoir un ~** to retch, heave

haut-le-corps ['ol(ə)kɔʀ] NM INV (sudden) start, jump; **avoir un ~** to start, jump

haut-parleur (*pl* **haut-parleurs**) ['oparlœʀ] NM (loud)speaker; **~ aigu** tweeter; **~ grave** woofer; **une voiture ~** a loudspeaker car

haut-relief (*pl* **hauts-reliefs**) ['oʀəljef] NM high relief

hauturier, -ière ['otyʀje, jɛʀ] ADJ **navigation hauturière** ocean navigation; **pêche hauturière** deep-sea fishing; **pilote ~** deep-sea pilot

havage ['avaʒ] NM (mechanical) cutting

havanais, e ['avanɛ, ɛz] $\boxed{1}$ ADJ of *ou* from Havana $\boxed{2}$ **Havanais(e)** NM,F inhabitant *ou* native of Havana

havane ['avan] $\boxed{1}$ NM (= *tabac*) Havana tobacco; (= *cigare*) Havana cigar $\boxed{2}$ ADJ INV (*couleur*) tobacco brown $\boxed{3}$ **Havane** NF **la Havane** Havana

hâve ['αv] ADJ (= *émacié*) gaunt, haggard; (= *pâle*) wan

haveneau (*pl* **haveneaux**) ['av(ə)no] NM shrimping net

haver ['ave] ▶conjug 1◀ VT (*Tech*) to cut (*mechanically*)

haveuse ['avøz] NF coal cutter

havre ['avʀ] NM († *ou littér*) haven; **~ de paix** haven of peace

havresac ['avʀəsak] NM haversack, knapsack

Hawaï, Hawaii [awai] N Hawaii; **les îles ~** the Hawaiian Islands

hawaïen, -ïenne [awajɛ̃, jɛn] $\boxed{1}$ ADJ Hawaiian $\boxed{2}$ NM (*Ling*) Hawaiian $\boxed{3}$ **Hawaïen(ne)** NM,F Hawaiian

Haye ['ɛ] NF **La ~** The Hague

hayon ['ɛjɔ̃] NM (*camion, charrette*) tailboard; (*voiture*) **~ (arrière)** hatchback, tailgate; **modèle avec ~ arrière** hatchback (model); (*camion*) **~ élévateur** fork-lift

HCR ['aʃseɛʀ] NM (ABRÉV = **Haut Commissariat des Nations Unies pour les réfugiés**) UNHCR

hé ['e] EXCL (*pour appeler*) hey!; (*pour renforcer*) well; **hé ! hé !** well, well!, ha-ha!; **hé non !** not a bit of it!

heaume ['om] NM (*Hist*) helmet

heavy metal [evimetal] NM (*Mus*) heavy metal

hebdo* [ɛbdo] NM ABRÉV = **hebdomadaire**

hebdomadaire [ɛbdɔmadɛʀ] ADJ, NM weekly; **~ d'actualité** news weekly → **repos**

hebdomadairement [ɛbdɔmadɛʀmɑ̃] ADV weekly

hébergement [ebɛʀʒəmɑ̃] NM $\boxed{a}$ (= *lieu*) housing, accommodation; (*pendant un séjour*) accommodation; **le prix comprend l'~** the price includes accommodation; **~ d'urgence** emergency housing *ou* accommodation $\boxed{b}$ (= *action d'héberger*) (*ami*) putting up; (*réfugiés*) taking in; (*évadé*) harbouring → **centre**

héberger [ebɛʀʒe] ▶conjug 3◀ VT $\boxed{a}$ (= *loger*) (+ *touristes*) to accommodate; (+ *ami*) to put up; **pouvez-vous nous ~ ?** can you put us up?; **il est hébergé par un ami** he's staying with a friend $\boxed{b}$ (= *accueillir*) (+ *réfugiés*) to take in; (+ *évadé*) to harbour; **les sinistrés ont été hébergés chez des voisins** the victims were taken en *ou* given shelter by neighbours; **le musée va ~ une collection de meubles** the museum will house a collection of furniture

hébété, e [ebete] (*ptp de* **hébéter**) ADJ $\boxed{a}$ (= *étourdi*) (*regard, air, personne*) dazed; **être ~ de fatigue/de douleur** to be numbed with fatigue/pain; **~ par l'alcool** in a drunken stupor $\boxed{b}$* (= *stupide*) (*regard, air*) dumb*, vacant

hébétement [ebetmɑ̃] NM stupor

hébéter [ebete] ▶conjug 6◀ VT (*alcool*) to stupefy, besot (*Brit*); (*lecture, télévision*) to daze, numb; (*fatigue, douleur*) to numb

hébétude [ebetyd] NF (*littér*) stupor; (*Méd*) hebetude

hébraïque [ebʀaik] ADJ Hebrew (*épith*), Hebraic

hébraïsant, e [ebʀaizɑ̃, ɑ̃t] $\boxed{1}$ ADJ Hebraistical $\boxed{2}$ NM,F Hebraist, Hebrew scholar

hébraïser [ebʀaize] ▶conjug 1◀ VT to assimilate into Jewish culture

hébraïsme [ebʀaism] NM Hebraism

hébraïste [ebʀaist] NMF = **hébraïsant**

hébreu (*pl* **hébreux**) [ebʀø] $\boxed{1}$ ADJ M Hebrew $\boxed{2}$ NM (*Ling*) Hebrew; **pour moi, c'est de l'~*** it's all Greek *ou* double Dutch (*Brit*) to me!* $\boxed{3}$ **Hébreu** NM Hebrew

Hébrides [ebʀid] NFPL **les (îles) ~** the Hebrides

HEC ['aʃese] NF (ABRÉV = **(école des) Hautes études commerciales**) *top French business school* → GRANDES ÉCOLES

hécatombe [ekatɔ̃b] NF (= *tuerie*) slaughter; (*à un examen*) (wholesale) slaughter *ou* massacre; **quelle ~ sur les routes ce week-end !** it was absolute carnage on the roads this weekend!; **faire une ~ de** to slaughter

hectare [ɛktaʀ] NM hectare

hectique [ɛktik] ADJ (*Méd*) hectic

hecto... [ɛkto] PRÉF hecto...

hectogramme [ɛktɔgʀam] NM hectogram(me)

hectolitre [ɛktɔlitʀ] NM hectolitre; **3 millions d'~s** 300 million litres

hectomètre [ɛktɔmɛtʀ] NM hectometre

hectométrique [ɛktɔmetʀik] ADJ hectometre (*épith*)

hectopascal [ɛktɔpaskal] NM millibar

Hector ['ɛktɔʀ] NM Hector

hectowatt [ɛktɔwat] NM hectowatt, 100 watts

Hécube ['ekyb] NF Hecuba

hédonisme [edɔnism] NM hedonism

hédoniste [edɔnist] $\boxed{1}$ ADJ hedonist(ic) $\boxed{2}$ NMF hedonist

hégélianisme [egeljanism] NM Hegelianism

hégélien, -ienne [egeljɛ̃, jɛn] ADJ, NM,F Hegelian

hégémonie [eʒemɔni] NF hegemony

hégémonique [eʒemɔnik] ADJ hegemonic

hégémonisme [eʒemɔnism] NM (*pays*) hegemonism

hégire [eʒiʀ] NF **l'~** the Hegira

hein* ['ɛ̃] EXCL (*de surprise, pour faire répéter*) eh?*, what?; **qu'est-ce que tu feras, ~ ?** what are you going to do (then), eh?*; **tu veux partir, ~, tu veux t'en aller ?** you want to go, is that it, you want to leave?; **ça suffit, ~ !** that's enough, O.K.!?* *ou* all right?*; **~ que je te l'ai dit ?** didn't I tell you so?, I told you so, didn't I?; **arrête ~ !** stop it, will you!

hélas [elɑs] EXCL alas!; **~ non !** I'm afraid not!, unfortunately not; **~ oui !** I'm afraid so!, yes, unfortunately; **~, trois fois ~ !** alas, what a shame!; **mais ~, ils n'ont pas pu en profiter** but unfortunately *ou* sadly they were not able to reap the benefits of it

Hélène [elɛn] NF Helen, Helena; **~ de Troie** Helen of Troy

héler ['ele] ▶conjug 6◀ VT (+ *navire, taxi*) to hail; (+ *personne*) to call, hail

hélianthe [eljɑ̃t] NM helianthus, sunflower

hélianthine [eljɑ̃tin] NF helianthine, methyl orange

hélice [elis] NF (*Tech*) propeller, screw(-propeller); (*Archit, Géom*) helix; **escalier en ~** spiral staircase; **~ double** double helix

hélico* [eliko] NM (ABRÉV = **hélicoptère**) chopper*, copter*

hélicoïdal, e (*mpl* **-aux**) [elikɔidal, o] ADJ (*gén*) helical; (*Bot, Math*) helicoid

hélicoïde [elikɔid] ADJ, NM helicoid

hélicon [elikɔ̃] NM helicon

hélicoptère [elikɔptɛʀ] NM helicopter; **~ d'attaque** attack helicopter; **~ de combat** helicopter gunship; **transporter en ~** to transport by helicopter, helicopter; **amener/évacuer par ~** to take in/out by helicopter, helicopter in/out; **plateforme pour ~s** helipad

héligare [eligaʀ] NF helicopter station

héliographe [eljɔgʀaf] NM heliograph

héliographie [eljɔgʀafi] NF (*Astron, Typo*) heliography

héliogravure [eljɔgʀavyʀ] NF heliogravure

héliomarin, e [eljɔmaʀɛ̃, in] ADJ (*cure*) of sun and sea-air; **établissement ~** seaside sanatorium (*specializing in heliotherapy*)

héliostat [eljɔsta] NM heliostat

héliotrope [eljɔtʀɔp] NM (*Bot, Minér*) heliotrope

héliport [elipɔʀ] NM heliport

héliportage [elipɔʀtaʒ] NM helicopter transport

héliporté, e [elipɔʀte] ADJ (*troupes*) helicopter-borne; (*évacuation, opération*) helicopter (*épith*)

hélitreuiller [elitʀœje] ▶conjug 1◀ VT to winch up into a helicopter

hélium [eljɔm] NM helium

hélix [eliks] NM (*Anat, Zool*) helix

hellène [elɛn] $\boxed{1}$ ADJ Hellenic $\boxed{2}$ **Hellène** NMF Hellene

hellénique [elenik] ADJ (*gén*) Greek; (*Antiq*) Hellenic

hellénisant, e [elenizɑ̃, ɑ̃t] ADJ, NM,F (*juif*) **~** Hellenist, Hellenistic Jew; (*savant*) **~** Hellenist, Hellenic scholar

hellénisation [elenizasjɔ̃] NF Hellenization

helléniser [elenize] ▶conjug 1◀ VT to Hellenize

hellénisme [elenism] NM Hellenism

helléniste [elenist] NMF = **hellénisant**

hellénistique [elenistik] ADJ Hellenistic

hello* ['ɛllo] EXCL hello, hullo, hí*

Helsinki [ɛlzinki] N Helsinki

helvète [ɛlvɛt] $\boxed{1}$ ADJ Helvetian $\boxed{2}$ **Helvète** NMF Helvetian

Helvétie [ɛlvesi] NF Helvetia

helvétique [ɛlvetik] ADJ Swiss, Helvetian

helvétisme [ɛlvetism] NM (*Ling*) Swiss idiom

hem ['ɛm] EXCL (a)hem!, h'm!

hématie [emasi] NF red (blood) corpuscle

hématite [ematit] NF h(a)ematite

hématologie [ematɔlɔʒi] NF haematology (*Brit*), hematology (*US*)

hématologique [ematɔlɔʒik] ADJ haematological (*Brit*), hematological (*US*)

hématologiste [ematɔlɔʒist], **hématologue** [ematɔlɔg] NMF haematologist (*Brit*), hematologist (*US*)

hématome [ematom] NM bruise, haematoma (*Brit, SPÉC*), hematoma (*US, SPÉC*)

hématopoïèse [ematopɔjɛz] NF hæmatopoiesis, hæmatosis, hæmatogenesis

héméralope [emeralɔp] $\boxed{1}$ ADJ night-blind, nyctalopic (*SPÉC*) $\boxed{2}$ NMF person suffering from night-blindness *ou* nyctalopia (*SPÉC*)

héméralopie [emeralɔpi] NF night-blindness, nyctalopia (*SPÉC*)

hémicycle [emisikl] NM semicircle, hemicycle; (= *salle*) amphitheatre; **l'~ (de l'Assemblée nationale)** the benches of the French National Assembly, ≈ the benches of the Commons (*Brit*) *ou* House of Representatives (*US*)

hémiplégie [emipleʒi] NF paralysis of one side, hemiplegia (SPÉC)

hémiplégique [emipleʒik] [1] ADJ paralyzed on one side, hemiplegic (SPÉC) [2] NMF person paralyzed on one side, hemiplegic (SPÉC)

hémisphère [emisfɛʀ] NM (gén, Anat, Géog) hemisphere; ~ **sud** ou **austral/nord** ou **boréal** southern/northern hemisphere

hémisphérique [emisfeʀik] ADJ hemispheric(al)

hémistiche [emistiʃ] NM hemistich

hémodialyse [emodjaliz] NF haemodialysis (Brit), hemodialysis (US); **séance d'~** session of haemodialysis (Brit) ou hemodialysis (US) treatment

hémoglobine [emoglɔbin] NF haemoglobin (Brit), hemoglobin (US); **dans ce film, l'~ coule à flots*** this film is full of blood and gore

hémophile [emofil] [1] ADJ haemophilic (Brit), hemophilic (US) [2] NMF haemophiliac (Brit), hemophiliac (US)

hémophilie [emofili] NF haemophilia (Brit), hemophilia (US)

hémorragie [emɔʀaʒi] NF [a] (Méd) bleeding (NonC), haemorrhage (Brit), hemorrhage (US); **~ cérébrale** brain ou cerebral haemorrhage; **~ interne** internal bleeding (NonC) ou haemorrhage; **il a eu ou a fait une ~ interne** he suffered internal bleeding [b] (= fuite) [capitaux] massive outflow ou drain; [cadres, talents] mass exodus (**de** of); **pour stopper l'~ financière** to stem the massive outflow of money; **l'~ démographique** ou **de population** the population drain

hémorragique [emɔʀaʒik] ADJ haemorrhagic (Brit), hemorrhagic (US)

hémorroïdal, e [mpl **-aux**] [emɔʀɔidal, o] ADJ (Méd) haemorrhoidal (Brit), hemorrhoidal (US); (Anat) [artère] anorectal

hémorroïde [emɔʀɔid] NF (gén pl) haemorrhoid (Brit), hemorrhoid (US), pile; **avoir des ~s** to have haemorrhoids ou piles

hémostatique [emɔstatik] ADJ, NM haemostatic (Brit), hemostatic (US) → **crayon**

henné ['ene] NM henna; **se faire un ~** to henna one's hair; **cheveux teints au ~** hennaed hair

hennin ['enɛ̃] NM (Hist = bonnet) hennin; **~ à deux cornes** horned headdress

hennir ['eniʀ] ▸ conjug 2 ◂ VI to neigh, whinny; (fig péj) to bray

hennissement ['enismɑ̃] NM [cheval] neigh, whinny; (péj) [personne] braying (NonC)

Henri [ɑ̃ʀi] NM Henry

hep ['ɛp] EXCL hey!

héparine [epaʀin] NF heparin

hépatique [epatik] [1] ADJ (Méd) hepatic [2] NMF person suffering from a liver complaint [3] NF (Bot) liverwort, hepatic (SPÉC); **les ~s** the Hepaticae (SPÉC)

hépatite [epatit] NF hepatitis; **~ virale** viral hepatitis; **~ A/B/C** hepatitis A/B/C; **~ chronique/aiguë** chronic/acute hepatitis

hépatologie [epatɔlɔʒi] NF hepatology

heptaèdre [ɛptaɛdʀ(ə)] NM heptahedron

heptagonal, e [mpl **-aux**] [ɛptagɔnal, o] ADJ heptagonal

heptagone [ɛptagɔn] NM heptagon

heptasyllabe [ɛptasi(l)lab] [1] ADJ heptasyllabic [2] NM heptasyllable

heptathlon [ɛptatlɔ̃] NM heptathlon

Héra [eʀa] NF Hera

Héraclite [eʀaklit] NM Heraclitus

héraldique [eʀaldik] [1] ADJ heraldic [2] NF heraldry

héraldiste [eʀaldist] NMF heraldist, expert on heraldry

héraut ['eʀo] NM [a] (Hist) **~ (d'armes)** herald [b] (fig littér) herald, harbinger (littér)

herbacé, e [ɛʀbase] ADJ herbaceous

herbage [ɛʀbaʒ] NM (= herbe) pasture, pasturage; (= pré) pasture

herbager, -ère [ɛʀbaʒe, ɛʀ] [1] ADJ [paysage] grassy; [région] with lot of grazing land [2] NM,F grazier

herbe [ɛʀb] [1] NF [a] (= plante) grass (NonC); (= espèce) grass; **arracher une ~** to pull up a blade of grass; **terrain en ~** field under grass; **~s folles** wild grasses; **jardin envahi par les ~s** weed-infested garden, garden overrun with weeds; **dans les hautes ~s** in the long ou tall grass; **faire de l'~ pour les lapins** to cut grass for rabbits; (fig) **couper l'~ sous le pied de qn** to cut the ground ou pull the rug out from under sb's feet → **déjeuner, mauvais** [b] (Culin, Méd) herb; **~s médicinales/aromatiques/ potagères** medicinal/aromatic/pot herbs; **omelette/porc aux ~s** omelette/pork with herbs → **fin'** [c]* (= drogue) grass*, pot* [d] **en ~** [blé] in the blade (attrib); [écrivain, chimiste] budding [2] COMP ▸ **herbes de Provence** herbes de Provence, ≈ mixed herbs ▸ **herbe à chat** ou **aux chats** catmint, catnip ▸ **herbe au chantre** sisymbrium, hedge mustard

herbeux, -euse [ɛʀbø, øz] ADJ grassy

herbicide [ɛʀbisid] [1] ADJ herbicidal [2] NM weed-killer, herbicide

herbier [ɛʀbje] NM (= collection) herbarium; (= planches) set of illustrations of plants; (= banc d'algues) seagrass bed

herbivore [ɛʀbivɔʀ] [1] ADJ herbivorous [2] NM herbivore

herborisation [ɛʀbɔʀizasjɔ̃] NF (= action) collection of plants

herboriser [ɛʀbɔʀize] ▸ conjug 1 ◂ VI to collect plants, botanize

herboriste [ɛʀbɔʀist] NMF herbalist

herboristerie [ɛʀbɔʀistəʀi] NF (= commerce) herb trade; (= magasin) herbalist('s shop)

herbu, e [ɛʀby] ADJ grassy

Hercule [ɛʀkyl] NM (Myth) Hercules; **c'est un ~** he's a real Hercules; **hercule de foire** strongman → **travail**

herculéen, -enne [ɛʀkyleɛ̃, ɛn] ADJ Herculean

hercynien, -ienne [ɛʀsinjɛ̃, jɛn] ADJ Hercynian

hère ['ɛʀ] NM (frm) **pauvre ~** poor ou miserable wretch

héréditaire [eʀeditɛʀ] ADJ hereditary; (hum) **c'est ~** it runs in the family

héréditairement [eʀeditɛʀmɑ̃] ADV hereditarily; (Méd) **caractère ~ transmissible d'une maladie** hereditary nature of an illness

hérédité [eʀedite] NF [a] (Bio) heredity (NonC); **il a une lourde ~** ou **une ~ chargée** his family has a history of mental (ou physical) illness; (culturelle) **une ~ catholique/royaliste** a Catholic/Royalist heritage [b] (Jur) (= droit) right of inheritance; (= caractère héréditaire) hereditary nature

hérésiarque [eʀezjaʀk] NM heresiarch

hérésie [eʀezi] NF (Rel) heresy; (fig) sacrilege, heresy; (hum) **servir du vin rouge avec le poisson est une véritable ~!** it's absolute sacrilege to serve red wine with fish!

hérétique [eʀetik] [1] ADJ heretical [2] NMF heretic

hérissé, e ['eʀise] (ptp de **hérisser**) ADJ [a] (= dressé) [poils, cheveux] standing on end, bristling; [barbe] bristly [b] (= garni) **tête ~e de cheveux roux** head bristling with red hair; **~ de poils** bristling with hairs; **~ d'épines/de clous** spiked with thorns/nails; **toits ~s d'antennes** roofs bristling with aerials; **traduction ~e de difficultés** translation riddled with difficulties [c] (= garni de pointes) [cactus, tige] prickly

hérisser ['eʀise] ▸ conjug 1 ◂ [1] VT [a] [animal] **le chat hérisse ses poils** the cat bristles its coat ou makes its coat bristle; **le porc-épic hérisse ses piquants** the porcupine bristles its spines ou makes its spines bristle; **l'oiseau hérisse ses plumes** the bird ruffles its feathers [b] [vent, froid] **le vent hérisse ses cheveux** the wind makes his hair stand on end [c] (= armer) **~ une planche de clous** to spike a plank with nails; **~ une muraille de créneaux** to top ou crown a wall with battlements [d] (= garnir) **des clous hérissent la planche** the plank is spiked with nails; **les créneaux qui hérissent la muraille** the battlements crowning the wall; **de nombreuses difficultés hérissent le texte** numerous difficulties are scattered through the text [e] (= mettre en colère) **~ qn** to put ou get sb's back up*, make sb's hackles rise; **il y a une chose qui me hérisse (les poils*), c'est le mensonge** there's one thing that gets my back up* and that's lying [2] **se hérisser** VPR [a] [poils, cheveux] to stand on end, bristle; **ses poils se sont hérissés quand il a entendu ça** his hackles rose when he heard that [b] [animal] to bristle; **le chat se hérissa** the cat's fur stood on end ou bristled, the cat bristled [c] (= se fâcher) to bristle, get one's back up*; **il se hérisse facilement** it's easy to get his back up*

hérisson ['eʀisɔ̃] NM [a] (Zool) hedgehog; **~ de mer** sea urchin; (péj) **c'est un vrai ~** he's very prickly [b] [ramoneur] (chimney sweep's) brush, flue brush; (= égouttoir) draining rack (for bottles); (= herse) beater

héritage [eʀitaʒ] NM [a] (= action) inheritance [b] [argent, biens] inheritance, legacy; [coutumes, système] heritage, legacy; **faire un ~** to come into an inheritance; **laisser qch en ~ à qn** to leave sth to sb, bequeath sth to sb; **l'~ du passé** the heritage ou legacy of the past; **un tel déficit est un lourd ~** a deficit like that is a heavy burden to inherit

hériter [eʀite] ▸ conjug 1 ◂ VT, **hériter de** VT INDIR [+ maison, tradition, culture, qualités] to inherit; (hum) [+ punition] to get; **~ d'une fortune** to come into ou inherit a fortune; **~ de son oncle** to inherit ou come into one's uncle's property; **il a hérité de la maison de son oncle** he inherited his uncle's house; **qui hériterait?** who would benefit from the will?, who would inherit?; **impatient d'~, il ...** eager to come into ou gain his inheritance, he ...; (hum) **et maintenant un bateau? ils ont hérité!** and now they've got a boat? they must have won the lottery ou the pools (Brit)!; **il a hérité d'un vieux chapeau** he has fallen heir to ou he has inherited an old hat; **il a hérité d'un rhume** he's picked up a cold; **ils ont hérité d'une situation catastrophique** they inherited a disastrous situation

héritier [eʀitje] NM heir; **~ naturel** heir-at-law; **~ testamentaire** legatee; **~ légitime** legitimate heir; **~ présomptif de la couronne** heir apparent (to the throne); **~ d'une grande fortune/ d'une longue tradition** heir to a large fortune/a long tradition; (hum) **elle lui a donné un ~** she gave him an heir ou a son and heir

héritière [eʀitjɛʀ] NF heiress

hermaphrodisme [ɛʀmafʀɔdism] NM hermaphroditism

hermaphrodite [ɛʀmafʀɔdit] [1] ADJ hermaphrodite, hermaphroditic(al) [2] NM hermaphrodite

herméneutique [ɛʀmenøtik] [1] ADJ hermeneutic [2] NF hermeneutics sg

Hermès [ɛʀmɛs] NM Hermes

hermétique [ɛʀmetik] ADJ [a] (= étanche) [récipient] (à l'air) airtight; (à l'eau) watertight; **cela assure une fermeture ~ de la porte** this makes sure that the door closes tightly *ou* that the door is a tight fit [b] (= *impénétrable*) [*secret*] impenetrable; **visage ~** closed *ou* impenetrable expression; **être ~ à** to be impervious to; **il est ~ à ce genre de peinture** this kind of painting is a closed book to him [c] (= *obscur*) [*écrivain, livre*] abstruse, obscure [d] (*Alchimie, Littérat*) Hermetic

hermétiquement [ɛʀmetikmɑ̃] ADV [a] [*fermer, joindre*] tightly, hermetically; **emballage ~ fermé** hermetically sealed package; **pièce ~ close** sealed(-up) room [b] [*s'exprimer*] abstrusely, obscurely

hermétisme [ɛʀmetism] NM (*péj* = *obscurité*) abstruseness, obscurity; (*Alchimie, Littérat*) hermetism

hermine [ɛʀmin] NF [a] (*Zool*) (*brune*) stoat; (*blanche*) ermine [b] (= *fourrure, Hér*) ermine

herminette [ɛʀminɛt] NF adze

Hermione [ɛʀmjɔn] NF Hermione

herniaire [ɛʀnjɛʀ] ADJ hernial → **bandage**

hernie [ˈɛʀni] NF (*Méd*) hernia, rupture; [*pneu*] bulge; **~ discale** herniated (*SPÉC*) *ou* slipped disc; **~ étranglée** strangulated hernia

hernié, e [ˈɛʀnje] ADJ [*organe*] herniated

héro* [eʀo] NF (ABRÉV = **héroïne 2**) heroin, smack*

Hérode [eʀɔd] NM Herod → **vieux**

Hérodiade [eʀɔdjad] NF Herodias

Hérodote [eʀɔdɔt] NM Herodotus

heroïcomique [eʀɔikɔmik] ADJ mock-heroic

héroïne¹ [eʀɔin] NF (= *femme*) heroine

héroïne² [eʀɔin] NF (= *drogue*) heroin

héroïnomane [eʀɔinɔman] [1] ADJ addicted to heroin, heroin-addicted (*épith*) [2] NMF heroin addict

héroïnomanie [eʀɔinɔmani] NF heroin addiction

héroïque [eʀɔik] ADJ heroic; **l'époque ~** the pioneering days; **les temps ~s** the heroic age

héroïquement [eʀɔikmɑ̃] ADV heroically

héroïsme [eʀɔism] NM heroism; **manger ça, c'est de l'~!*** eating that is nothing short of heroic! *ou* of heroism!

héron [ˈeʀɔ̃] NM heron; **~ cendré** grey heron

héros [ˈeʀo] NM hero; **mourir en ~** to die the death of a hero *ou* a hero's death; **ils ont été accueillis en ~** they were given a hero's welcome; **~ national** national hero; **~ de la Résistance** hero of the (French) Resistance; **le ~ du jour** the hero of the day

herpès [ɛʀpɛs] NM (*gén*) herpes; **~ génital** genital herpes; (*autour de la bouche*) **avoir de l'~** to have a cold sore

herpétique [ɛʀpetik] ADJ herpetic

hersage [ˈɛʀsaʒ] NM (*Agr*) harrowing

herse [ˈɛʀs] NF (*Agr*) harrow; [*château*] portcullis; (*Théât*) batten

herser [ˈɛʀse] ▶ conjug 1 ◀ VT (*Agr*) to harrow

hertz [ɛʀts] NM hertz

hertzien, -ienne [ɛʀtsjɛ̃, jɛn] ADJ [*ondes*] Hertzian; [*chaîne, diffusion, télévision*] terrestrial; **réseau ~** (*TV*) terrestrial network; (*Radio*) radio-relay network

hésitant, e [ezitɑ̃, ɑ̃t] ADJ [*personne, début*] hesitant; [*caractère*] wavering, hesitant; [*voix, pas*] hesitant, faltering

hésitation [ezitasjɔ̃] NF hesitation; **marquer une ~** *ou* **un temps d'~** to hesitate; **j'accepte sans ~** I accept without hesitation *ou* unhesitatingly; **après bien des ~s** after much hesitation; **il eut un moment d'~ et répondit ...** he hesitated for a moment and replied ..., after a moment's hesitation he replied ...; **je n'ai plus d'~s** I shall hesitate no longer; **ses ~s continuelles** his continual hesitations *ou* dithering

▼ **hésiter** [ezite] ▶ conjug 1 ◀ VI [a] (= *balancer*) to hesitate; **tu y vas? — j'hésite** are you going? — I'm in two minds about it *ou* I'm not sure;

il n'y a pas à ~ you don't need to think twice about it; **sans ~** without hesitating, unhesitatingly; **~ à faire** to hesitate to do, be unsure whether to do; **j'hésite à vous déranger** I don't want to disturb you; **il hésitait sur la route à prendre** he hesitated as to which road to take, he dithered over which road to take (*Brit*); **~ sur une date** to hesitate over a date; **~ entre plusieurs possibilités** to hesitate *ou* waver between several possibilities [b] (= *s'arrêter*) to hesitate; **~ dans ses réponses** to be hesitant in one's replies; **~ en récitant sa leçon** to recite one's lesson falteringly *ou* hesitantly; **~ devant l'obstacle** to falter *ou* hesitate before an obstacle

Hespérides [ɛspeʀid] NFPL **les ~** the Hesperides

hétaïre [etaiʀ] NF (= *prostituée*) courtesan; (*Antiq*) hetaera

hétéro* [eteʀo] ADJ, NMF (ABRÉV = **hétérosexuel**) hetero* (*épith*), straight*

hétéroclite [eteʀɔklit] ADJ (= *disparate*) [*ensemble, roman, bâtiment*] heterogeneous; [*objets*] sundry, ill-assorted; **pièce meublée de façon ~** room filled with a miscellaneous *ou* an ill-assorted collection of furniture

hétérodoxe [eteʀɔdɔks] ADJ heterodox

hétérodoxie [eteʀɔdɔksi] NF heterodoxy

hétérogamie [eteʀɔgami] NF heterogamy

hétérogène [eteʀɔʒɛn] ADJ heterogeneous; **c'est un groupe très ~** it's a very mixed *ou* heterogeneous group

hétérogénéité [eteʀɔʒeneite] NF heterogeneousness

hétérosexualité [eteʀɔsɛksɥalite] NF heterosexuality

hétérosexuel, -elle [eteʀɔsɛksɥɛl] ADJ, NM,F heterosexual

hétérozygote [eteʀɔzigɔt] [1] ADJ heterozygous [2] NMF heterozygote

hêtraie [ˈɛtʀɛ] NF beech grove

hêtre [ˈɛtʀ] NM (= *arbre*) beech (tree); (= *bois*) beech (wood); **~ pourpre/pleureur** copper/weeping beech

heu [ø] EXCL (*doute*) h'm!, hem!; (*hésitation*) um!, er!

heur†† [œʀ] NM good fortune; (*littér, iro*) **je n'ai pas eu l'~ de lui plaire** I did not have the good fortune to please him, I was not fortunate enough to please him

heure [œʀ]
NOM FÉMININ

[a] = **mesure de durée** hour; **les ~s passaient vite/lentement** the hours went by quickly/slowly; **l'~ tourne** time passes; **j'ai attendu une bonne ~/une petite ~** I waited (for) a good hour/just under an hour; **j'ai attendu 2 ~s d'horloge** I waited 2 solid hours; **il a parlé des ~s** he spoke for hours; (*Scol*) **~ (de cours)** class, ≈ period (*Brit*); **j'ai deux ~s de français aujourd'hui** I've two periods of French today; **pendant les ~s de classe/de bureau** during school/office *ou* business hours; **gagner/coûter 80 F de l'~** to earn/cost 80 francs an hour *ou* per hour; **1 ~/3 ~s de travail** 1 hour's/3 hours' work; **cela représente 400 ~s de travail** *ou* **400 ~s-homme** it represents 400 hours of work *ou* 400 man-hours; **il me faut 12 ~s-machine** I need 12 hours' computer time; **faire beaucoup d'~s** to put in long hours; **lutter pour la semaine de 30 ~s (de travail)** to campaign for a 30-hour (working) week; **24 ~s sur 24** round the clock, 24 hours a day; **ce sera fait dans les 24 ~s/48 ~s** it'll be done within 24 hours/48 hours → **réception, supplémentaire**

♦ **à l'heure** : **être payé à l'~** [*travail*] to be paid by the hour; [*personne*] to be paid by the hour, get an hourly rate; (*Aut*) **faire du 100 (km) à l'~** to do 100 km an hour *ou* per hour

[b] = **mesure de distance** hour; **c'est à plus d'une ~ de Paris** it's more than an hour (away)

from Paris *ou* more than an hour's run from Paris; **c'est à 2 ~s de route** it's 2 hours (away) by road; **il y a 2 ~s de route** *ou* **voiture/train** it's a 2-hour drive/train journey, it takes 2 hours by car/train (to get there)

[c] = **divisions de la journée** savoir l'~ to know what time it is, know the time; **quelle ~ est-il?** what time is it?; **quelle ~ as-tu?** what time do you make it?; **avez-vous l'~?** have you got the time?; **tu as vu l'~ (qu'il est)?** do you realize what time it is?; **il est 6 ~s/6 ~s 10/6 ~s moins 10/6 ~s et demie** it is 6 (o'clock)/10 past *ou* after (*US*) 6/10 to *ou* of (*US*) 6/half past *ou* after (*US*) 6; **10 ~s du matin/du soir** 10 (o'clock) in the morning/at night, 10 a.m./p.m.; **à 16 ~s 30** at 4.30 p.m., at 16.30 (*Admin*); **il est 8 ~s passées** *ou* **sonnées** it's gone 8; **à 4 ~s pile*** *ou* **sonnant(es)** *ou* **tapant(es)*** *ou* **pétant(es)***₁ at exactly 4 (o'clock), at dead on 4 (o'clock)* (*Brit*), at 4 (o'clock) on the dot*; **à 4 ~s juste(s)** at 4 sharp; **je prendrai le train de 6 ~s** I'll take the 6 o'clock train; **les bus passent à l'~/à l'~ et à la demie** the buses come on the hour/on the hour and on the half hour; **à une ~ avancée (de la nuit)** late at night; **jusqu'à une ~ avancée (de la nuit)** late *ou* well into the night; **ils ont joué aux échecs jusqu'à pas*** *ou* **point*** (*hum*) **d'~** they played chess into the early hours; **se coucher à pas* d'~** to stay up till all hours; (*fig*) **demain, à la première ~** tomorrow at first light; **de la première ~** [*allié, partisan*] from the very beginning; **les ouvriers de la onzième** *ou* **dernière ~** people who turn up when the work is almost finished; **collaborateur/candidat de la dernière ~** last-minute helper/candidate → **demander**

♦ **de bonne heure** (*dans la journée*) early; (*dans la vie*) early in life → **lever**

♦ **d'heure en heure** with each passing hour, hour by hour; **le pays entier suit le sauvetage d'~ en ~** the whole country is following every minute of the rescue operation; **son inquiétude grandissait d'~ en ~** hour by hour *ou* as the hours went by he grew more (and more) anxious, he grew hourly more anxious

♦ **d'une heure à l'autre** (= *incessamment*) **nous l'attendons d'une ~ à l'autre** we are expecting him any time (now); (= *rapidement*) **la situation évolue d'une ~ à l'autre** the situation changes from one moment to the next

[d] = **l'heure fixée** time; **c'est l'~!** (*de rendre un devoir*) time's up!; **c'est l'~** (*de rentrer/d'aller au lit*)! it's time to go home!/for bed!; **avant l'~** before time, ahead of time, early; **un homme vieilli avant l'~** a man grown old before his time; (*fig*) **un cubiste avant l'~** a cubist before the term was ever invented; **après l'~** late; **venez quand vous voulez, je n'ai pas d'~** come when you like, I have no fixed timetable *ou* schedule, come when you like, any time suits me; **~ de Greenwich** Greenwich mean time; **~ légale/locale** standard/local time; **il est midi, ~ locale/~ de Paris** it's noon, local time/Paris time; **nous venons de passer à l'~ d'hiver** we have just put the clocks back; **~ d'été** (*Can*) ◊ **~ avancée** daylight saving(s) time, (British) summer time (*Brit*); **passer à l'~ d'été** to go over *ou* change to summer time; **l'~ militaire** the right *ou* exact time; **l'~ c'est l'~** ◊ **avant l'~ ce n'est pas l'~, après l'~ ce n'est plus l'~*** a minute late is a minute too late; (*hum*) **il n'y a pas d'~ pour les braves** any time is a good time → **laitier**

♦ **à l'heure** : **arriver/être à l'~** [*personne, train*] to arrive/be on time; **ma montre/l'horloge est toujours à l'~** my watch/the clock is always right *ou* keeps good time; **ma montre n'est pas à l'~** my watch is wrong; **mettre sa montre à l'~** to set *ou* put one's watch right → **remettre**

[e] = **moment** time, moment; **je n'ai pas une ~ à moi** I haven't a moment to myself; (*frm*) **l'~ est venue** the time has come; **nous avons passé ensemble des ~s merveilleuses** we spent many happy hours together; **l'~ du dé-**

➤ GRAMMAIRE ACTIVE: **hésiter** 36.2

jeuner lunchtime, time for lunch; **elle fait ses courses pendant son ~ de table** she does her shopping during the **ou** her lunch hour; **l'~ d'aller se coucher** bedtime, time for bed; **l'~ du biberon** (baby's) feeding time; **à l'~ ou aux ~s des repas** at mealtime(s); (*en maternelle*) **l'~ des mamans** home time; **à ~s fixes** at fixed times; **~s d'ouverture/de fermeture** opening/closing times; **l'~ de la sortie** (*écoliers, ouvriers*) time to go home; **travailler/rester jusqu'à l'~ de la sortie** to work/stay until it is time to go home; **les problèmes de l'~** the problems of the moment; **l'~ est grave** it is a grave moment; **à l'~ qu'il est ◊ à cette ~** at this moment in time, at present; **à l'~ qu'il est, nous ignorons encore ...** at present we still don't know ...; **à l'~ qu'il est, il devrait être rentré** he should be home by now; **selon les informations dont nous disposons à cette ~ ...** according to the latest information ...; **l'~ est à la concertation** it is now time for consultation and dialogue, dialogue is now the order of the day; **l'~ n'est pas à la rigolade*** this is no time for laughing **ou** for jokes; **« Paris à l'~ écossaise »** "Paris goes Scottish" → **actuel, creux, H**

• **à l'heure de** : **à l'~ du danger** in times of danger; **à l'~ de notre mort** at the hour of our death; (*fig*) **la France à l'~ de l'ordinateur** France in the computer age; **il faut mettre nos universités à l'~ de l'Europe** our universities have got to start thinking in terms of Europe **ou** start thinking European

• **à toute heure** at any time (of the day); **repas chauds à toute ~** hot meals all day; **à toute ~ du jour et de la nuit** at every hour of the day and night

• **pour l'heure** for the time being; **pour l'~, rien n'est décidé** nothing has been decided as yet **ou** for the time being

• **sur l'heure** (*littér*) at once; **il décommanda sur l'~ tous ses rendez-vous** he immediately cancelled all his meetings

[f]

• *adjectif possessif* + **heure** : **il est poète/aimable à ses ~s** he writes poetry/he can be quite pleasant when the fancy takes him **ou** when the mood is on him **ou** when he feels like it; **ce doit être Paul — c'est son ~** it must be Paul — it's his (usual) time; **votre ~ sera la mienne** name **ou** say a time; **elle a eu son ~ de gloire/de célébrité** she has had her hour of glory/fame; **il aura son ~** (*de gloire etc*) his hour **ou** time will come; **il attend son ~** he is biding his time **ou** waiting for the right moment; **son ~ viendra/est venue** (*de mourir*) his time will come/has come; **sa dernière ~ a sonné** his time has come **ou** is up

[g] [Rel] **~s canoniales** canonical hours; **Grandes/Petites ~s** night/daylight offices → **livre¹**

[h]

• **à la bonne heure !** (= *très bien*) that's fine!; (*iro*) that's a fine idea! (*iro*)

---

heureusement [øRøzmã] ADV [a] (= *par bonheur*) fortunately, luckily; **~, il n'y avait personne** fortunately, there was no one there [b] (= *tant mieux*) **~ pour lui !** fortunately **ou** luckily for him!; **il est parti, ~ !** ◊ **~ qu'il est parti*** thank goodness he's gone [c] (= *judicieusement*) happily; **mot ~ choisi** well **ou** felicitously (*frm*) chosen word; **phrase ~ tournée** cleverly turned sentence [d] (= *favorablement*) successfully; **l'entreprise fut ~ menée à terme** the task was successfully completed; **tout s'est ~ terminé** it all turned out well in the end

▼ **heureux, -euse** [øRø, øz] ADJ [a] (*gén après n*) (= *rempli de bonheur*) [*personne, souvenir, vie*] happy; **il a tout pour être ~** he has everything he needs to be happy **ou** to make him happy; (*dans un conte*) **ils vécurent ~** they lived happily ever after; **~ comme un poisson dans l'eau ou comme un roi ou comme un pape** happy as

---

Larry* (*Brit*) **ou** a sandboy (*Brit*) **ou** a clam (*US*); **~ celui qui ...!** happy is he who ...!; (*Bible*) **~ les simples d'esprit** blessed are the poor in spirit; **ces jouets vont faire des ~ !** these toys will make some children very happy!; **ne jette pas tes vieux livres, ça pourrait faire des ~** don't throw away your old books, some people might be glad of them **ou** glad to have them → **bon¹**

[b] (= *satisfait*) happy, pleased; **je suis très ~ d'apprendre la nouvelle** I am very glad **ou** happy **ou** pleased to hear the news; **M. et Mme Durand sont ~ de vous annoncer ...** Mr and Mrs Durand are happy **ou** pleased to announce ...; **je suis ~ de ce résultat** I am pleased **ou** happy with this result; **je suis ~ de cette rencontre** I am pleased **ou** glad about this meeting; **il sera trop ~ de vous aider** he'll be only too glad **ou** happy **ou** pleased to help you; **~ de vous revoir** nice **ou** good **ou** pleased to see you again; (*hum*) **alors, heureuse ?** how was it for you? (*hum*)

[c] (*gén avant n* = *qui a de la chance*) [*personne*] fortunate, lucky; **~ au jeu/en amour** lucky at cards/in love; **~ au jeu, malheureux en amour** lucky at cards, unlucky in love; **c'est ~ (pour lui) que** it is fortunate **ou** lucky (for him) that; **il accepte de venir — c'est encore ~ !** he's willing to come — it's just as well! **ou** I should think so too!; **encore ~ que je m'en sois souvenu !** it's just as well **ou** it's lucky **ou** it's a good thing that I remembered! → **élu, main**

[d] (*gén avant n* = *optimiste, agréable*) [*disposition, caractère*] happy, cheerful → **nature**

[e] (= *judicieux*) [*décision, choix*] fortunate, happy; [*formule, expression, effet, mélange*] happy, felicitous (*frm*); **un ~ mariage de styles** a successful combination of styles

[f] (= *favorable*) [*présage*] propitious, happy; [*résultat, issue*] happy; **par un ~ hasard** by a fortunate coincidence; **attendre un ~ événement** to be expecting a happy event

heuristique [øRistik] [1] ADJ heuristic [2] NF heuristics *sg*

heurt [œR] NM [a] (= *choc*) [*voitures*] collision; [*objets*] bump [b] (= *conflit*) clash; **il y a eu des ~s entre la police et les manifestants** there were clashes between the police and the demonstrators; **sans ~(s)** [*se passer*] smoothly; **la réforme ne se fera pas sans ~s** the reform will not have a smooth passage; **leur amitié ne va pas sans quelques ~s** their friendship has its ups and downs **ou** goes through occasional rough patches

heurté, e [œRte] (*ptp de* **heurter**) ADJ [*couleurs*] clashing; [*style, jeu, carrière*] jerky, uneven; [*discours*] jerky, halting

heurter [œRte] ▶ conjug 1 ◀ [1] VT [a] (= *cogner*) [+ *objet*] to strike, hit; [+ *personne*] to collide with; [+ *voiture*] to bump into; (= *bousculer*) to jostle; **~ qch du coude/du pied** to strike **ou** hit sth with one's elbow/foot; **la voiture a heurté un arbre** the car ran into **ou** struck a tree [b] (= *choquer*) [+ *personne, préjugés*] to offend; [+ *théorie, bon goût, bon sens, tradition*] to go against, run counter to; [+ *amour-propre*] to upset; [+ *opinions*] to conflict **ou** clash with; **~ qn de front** to clash head-on with sb

[2] VI **~ à** to knock at **ou** on; **~ contre qch** [*personne*] to stumble against sth; [*objet*] to knock **ou** bang against sth

[3] **se heurter** VPR [a] (= *s'entrechoquer*) [*passants, voitures*] to collide (with each other); [*objets*] to hit one another; **ses idées se heurtaient dans sa tête** his head was a jumble of ideas, ideas jostled about in his head [b] (= *s'opposer*) [*personnes, opinions, couleurs*] to clash (with each other) [c] (= *cogner contre*) **se ~ à ou contre qn/qch** to collide with sb/sth; **se ~ à un refus** to meet with **ou** come up against a refusal; **se ~ à un problème** to come up against a problem

---

heurtoir [œRtwaR] NM [*porte*] (door) knocker; (*Tech* = *butoir*) stop; (*Rail*) buffer

hévéa [evea] NM hevea

héxadécimal, e (*mpl* **-aux**) [egzadesimal, o] ADJ hexadecimal

hexaèdre [egzaedR] [1] ADJ hexahedral [2] NM hexahedron

hexaédrique [egzaedRik] ADJ hexahedral

hexagonal, e (*mpl* **-aux**) [egzagɔnal, o] ADJ [a] (*Géom*) hexagonal [b] (= *français*) [*politique, frontière*] national; (*péj*) [*conception*] chauvinistic

hexagone [egzagɔn] NM [a] (*Géom*) hexagon [b] **l'Hexagone** (metropolitan) France

hexamètre [egzametR] [1] ADJ hexameter (*épith*), hexametric(al) [2] NM hexameter

Hezbollah [ezbɔla] NM **le ~** Hezbollah

HF (ABRÉV = **haute fréquence**) HF, h.f.

hiatal, e (*mpl* **-aux**) [jatal, o] ADJ hiatal, hiatus (*épith*); **hernie ~e** hiatus hernia

hiatus [jatys] NM (*Anat, Ling*) hiatus; (= *incompatibilité*) gap, discrepancy (**entre** between)

hibernal, e (*mpl* **-aux**) [ibeRnal, o] ADJ winter (*épith*), hibernal (*frm*)

hibernation [ibeRnasjɔ̃] NF hibernation; (*Méd*) **~ artificielle** induced hypothermia

hiberner [ibeRne] ▶ conjug 1 ◀ VI to hibernate

hibiscus [ibiskys] NM hibiscus

hibou (*pl* **hiboux**) ['ibu] NM owl; (*péj*) (**vieux**) **~*** crusty old bird* **ou** beggar* **ou** devil*

hic* ['ik] NM **c'est là le ~** that's the snag **ou** the trouble; **il y a un ~** there's a snag **ou** slight problem

hic et nunc ['ikɛtnɔk] LOC ADV immediately, at once, there and then

hickory ['ikɔRi] NM hickory

hidalgo [idalgo] NM hidalgo; (*hum*) **un bel ~** a dark dashing Spaniard (**ou** Italian *etc*)

hideur ['idœR] NF (*littér*) hideousness (*NonC*)

hideusement ['idøzmã] ADV hideously

hideux, -euse ['idø, øz] ADJ hideous

hier [jɛR] ADV yesterday; **~ (au) soir** yesterday evening, last night **ou** evening; **toute la matinée d'~** all yesterday morning; **toute la journée d'~** all day yesterday; **il avait tout ~ pour se décider** he had all (day) yesterday to make up his mind; **je m'en souviens comme si c'était ~** I remember it as if it was **ou** were yesterday → **dater, naître**

hiérarchie ['jeRaRʃi] NF hierarchy; (= *supérieurs*) superiors

hiérarchique ['jeRaRʃik] ADJ hierarchic(al); **chef ou supérieur ~** superior, senior in rank **ou** in the hierarchy → **voie**

hiérarchiquement ['jeRaRʃikmã] ADV hierarchically

hiérarchisation ['jeRaRʃizasjɔ̃] NF (= *action*) organization into a hierarchy; (= *organisation*) hierarchical organization; **la ~ des tâches** the prioritization of tasks

hiérarchiser ['jeRaRʃize] ▶ conjug 1 ◀ VT [+ *structure*] to organize into a hierarchy; [+ *tâches*] to prioritize; **institution/société hiérarchisée** hierarchical institution/society; **hiérarchisons ces questions** let's sort out these questions in order of priority

hiératique ['jeRatik] ADJ hieratic

hiératisme ['jeRatism] NM hieratic quality

hiéroglyphe ['jeRɔglif] NM hieroglyph(ic); **~s** (= *plusieurs symboles*) hieroglyph(ic)s; (= *système d'écriture, aussi péj*) hieroglyphics

hiéroglyphique ['jeRɔglifik] ADJ hieroglyphic(al)

hi-fi ['ifi] ADJ INV, NF INV (ABRÉV = **high fidelity**) hi-fi

high-tech ['ajtɛk] ADJ INV, NM INV (ABRÉV = **high technology**) hi-tech, high-tech

hi-han ['iã] EXCL heehaw!

➤ GRAMMAIRE ACTIVE: **heureux** 30, 38.1, 38.3, 51.1, 51.2, 52.4

hi-hi [hihi] EXCL (*rire*) tee-hee!, hee-hee!; (*pleurs*) boo hoo!, sniff-sniff!

hilarant, e [ilaʀɑ̃, ɑ̃t] ADJ [*aventure*] hilarious, side-splitting → **gaz**

hilare [ilaʀ] ADJ [*personne*] smiling; [*visage*] beaming, smiling

hilarité [ilaʀite] NF hilarity, mirth; **provoquer** *ou* **déclencher l'~ générale** to cause great mirth

hile ['il] NM (*Anat, Bot*) hilum

hilote [ilɔt] NM = **ilote**

Himalaya [imalaja] NM **l'~** the Himalayas; **escalader un sommet de l'~** to climb one of the Himalayan peaks *ou* one of the peaks in the Himalayas

himalayen, -yenne [imalajɛ̃, jɛn] ADJ Himalayan

hindi [indi] NM (*Ling*) Hindi

hindou, e [ɛ̃du] 1 ADJ [*coutumes, dialecte*] Hindu, Hindoo; † [*nationalité*] Indian 2 **Hindou(e)** NM,F (= *croyant*) Hindu, Hindoo; († = *citoyen*) Indian

hindouisme [ɛ̃duism] NM Hinduism, Hindooism

hindouiste [ɛ̃duist] ADJ, NMF Hindu, Hindoo

Hindoustan [ɛ̃dustɑ̃] NM Hindustan

hindoustani [ɛ̃dustani] NM Hindustani

hip ['ip] EXCL **~ ~ ~ hourra !** hip hip hurray! *ou* hurrah!

hip(-)hop [ipɔp] NM (*Mus*) hip-hop

hippie ['ipi] ADJ, NMF hippy

hippique [ipik] ADJ horse (*épith*), equestrian; **chronique ~** racing news *sg*; **le sport ~** equestrian sport

hippisme [ipism] NM (horse) riding, equestrianism

hippo [ipo] NM (ABRÉV = **hippopotame**) hippo*

hippocampe [ipɔkɑ̃p] NM (*Anat, Myth*) hippocampus; (= *poisson*) sea horse

Hippocrate [ipɔkʀat] NM Hippocrates → **serment**

hippocratisme [ipɔkʀatism] NM (*Méd* = *doctrine*) Hippocratism; **~ digital** Hippocratic *ou* clubbed fingers

hippodrome [ipodʀom] NM (= *champ de courses*) racecourse (*Brit*), racetrack (*US*); (*Antiq*) hippodrome

hippogriffe [ipogʀif] NM hippogriff, hippogryph

Hippolyte [ipɔlit] NM Hippolytus

hippomobile [ipomɔbil] ADJ horse-drawn

hippophagique [ipofaʒik] ADJ **boucherie ~** horse(meat) butcher's

hippopotame [ipɔpɔtam] NM hippopotamus, hippo*; **c'est un vrai ~*** he (*ou* she) is like an elephant* *ou* a hippo*

hippy (*pl* hippies) ['ipi] ADJ, NMF = **hippie**

hirondelle [iʀɔdɛl] NF a (*Zool*) swallow; **~ de fenêtre/de rivage** house/sand martin; **~ de cheminée** barn swallow; **~ de mer** tern ▪ (*PROV*) **une ~ ne fait pas le printemps** one swallow doesn't make a summer (*PROV*) → **nid** b †* (= *policier*) (bicycle-riding) policeman

Hiroshima ['iʀɔʃima] N Hiroshima

hirsute [iʀsyt] ADJ a (= *ébouriffé*) [*tête*] tousled; [*gamin*] shaggy-haired; [*barbe*] shaggy; **un individu ~** a shaggy-haired *ou* hirsute individual b (*Méd*) hirsute

hirsutisme [iʀsytism] NM (*Méd*) hirsutism

hispanique [ispanik] ADJ Hispanic

hispanisant, e [ispanizɑ̃, ɑ̃t] NM,F (= *spécialiste*) hispanist; (= *étudiant*) Spanish scholar

hispanisme [ispanism] NM hispanicism

hispaniste [ispanist] NMF = **hispanisant**

hispano-américain, e (*mpl* **hispano-américains**) [ispanoameʀikɛ̃, ɛn] 1 ADJ

Spanish-American 2 NM (*Ling*) Latin American Spanish 3 **Hispano-Américain(e)** NM,F Spanish-American, Hispanic (*US*)

hispano-arabe (*mpl* **hispano-arabes**) [ispanoaʀab], **hispano-mauresque** (*mpl* **hispano-mauresques**) [ispanomɔʀesk] ADJ Hispano-Moresque

hispanophone [ispanɔfɔn] 1 ADJ Spanish-speaking; [*littérature*] Spanish-language (*épith*), in Spanish (*attrib*) 2 NMF Spanish speaker

hisse ['is] ♦**oh hisse** LOC EXCL heave ho!

hisser ['ise] ▸ conjug 1 ◂ 1 VT (*Naut*) to hoist; (= *soulever*) [+ *objet*] to hoist, haul up, heave up; [+ *personne*] to haul up, heave up; **~ les couleurs** to run up *ou* hoist the colours; **hissez les voiles !** up sails!; **~ qn au pouvoir** to hoist sb into a position of power 2 **se hisser** VPR to heave o.s. up, haul o.s. up; **se ~ sur un toit** to heave *ou* haul o.s. (up) onto a roof; **se ~ sur la pointe des pieds** to stand up *ou* raise o.s. on tiptoe; **se ~ à la première place/au pouvoir** to work one's way up to first place/a position of power

histamine [istamin] NF histamine

histaminique [istaminik] ADJ histaminic

histocompatibilité [istokɔ̃patibilite] NF histocompatibility

histogramme [istogʀam] NM histogram

histoire [istwaʀ] 1 NF a (= *science, événements*) **l'~** history; **l'~ jugera** posterity will be the judge; **laisser son nom dans l'~** to find one's place in history; **tout cela, c'est de l'~ ancienne*** all that's ancient history*; **~ naturelle** † natural history; **l'~ de France** French history, the history of France; **l'~ de l'art/de la littérature** art/literary history; **l'~ des sciences** the history of science; **l'Histoire sainte** Biblical *ou* sacred history; **la petite ~** the footnotes of history; **pour la petite ~** for the record, incidentally b (= *déroulement de faits*) history; **son ~ familiale** his family history; **raconter l'~ de sa vie** to tell one's life story *ou* the story of one's life c (*Scol*) (= *leçon*) history (lesson); († = *livre*) history book d (= *récit, conte*) story; **c'est toute une ~** it's a long story; **une ~ vraie** a true story; **~ de pêche/de revenants** fishing/ghost story; **~ d'amour** love story; **~ drôle** funny story, joke; **~ marseillaise** tall story *ou* tale, fisherman's tale (*Brit*); **~ à dormir debout** cock-and-bull story, tall story; **~ de fous** shaggy-dog story; **c'est une ~ de fous !** it's absolutely crazy!; **qu'est-ce que c'est que cette ~ ?** what on earth is all this about?, just what is all this about?; **le plus beau *ou* curieux de l'~ c'est que** the best part *ou* strangest part of it is that; **l'~ veut qu'il ait dit ...** the story goes that he said ... e * (= *mensonge*) story, fib*; **tout ça, ce sont des ~s** that's just a lot of fibs*, you've (*ou* they *etc*) made all that up; **tu me racontes des ~s** you're pulling my leg, come off it!* f * (= *affaire, incident*) business; **c'est une drôle d'~** it's a funny business; **il vient de lui arriver une curieuse ~/une drôle d'~** something odd/funny has just happened to him; **ils se sont disputés pour une ~ d'argent/de femme** they had a fight over money/about a woman; **se mettre dans une sale ~** *ou* ◊ **se mettre une sale ~ sur le dos** to get mixed up in some nasty business; **sa nomination va faire toute une ~** his appointment will cause a lot of fuss *ou* a great to-do, there will be quite a fuss *ou* to-do over his appointment; **c'est toujours la même ~ !** it's always the same old story!; **ça, c'est une autre ~ !** that's (quite) another story!; **j'ai pu avoir une place mais ça a été toute une ~** I managed to get a seat but it was a real struggle; **sans ~s** [*personne*] ordinary; [*se dérouler*] uneventfully g * (= *relation amoureuse*) (love) affair; (= *dispute*) falling-out; **pourquoi ne se parlent-ils**

pas ? — **il y a une ~ entre eux** why aren't they on speaking terms? — they fell out over something h (= *chichis*) fuss, to-do, carry-on* (*Brit*); **quelle ~ pour si peu !** what a to-do *ou* fuss *ou* carry-on* (*Brit*) over so little!; **faire un tas d'~s** to make a whole lot of fuss *ou* a great to-do; **au lit, et pas d'~s !** off to bed, and I don't want any fuss!; **il fait ce qu'on lui demande sans faire d'~s** he does what he is told without (making) a fuss i * (*loc*) **~ de faire** just to do; **~ de prendre l'air** just for a breath of (fresh) air; **~ de rire** just for a laugh*, just for fun; **il a essayé, ~ de voir/de faire quelque chose** he had a go just to see what it was like/just for something to do

2 **histoires*** NFPL (= *ennuis*) trouble; **faire** *ou* **chercher des ~s à qn** to make trouble for sb; **cela ne peut lui attirer** *ou* **lui valoir que des ~s** that's bound to get him into trouble, that will cause him nothing but trouble; **je ne veux pas d'~s avec la police/les voisins** I don't want any trouble with the police/the neighbours

histologie [istɔlɔʒi] NF histology

histologique [istɔlɔʒik] ADJ histological

historicisme [istɔʀisism] NM historicism

historicité [istɔʀisite] NF historicity

historié, e [istɔʀje] ADJ (*Art*) historiated

historien, -ienne [istɔʀjɛ̃, jɛn] NM,F (= *savant*) historian; (= *étudiant*) history student, historian

historiette [istɔʀjɛt] NF little story, anecdote

historiographe [istɔʀjɔgʀaf] NMF historiographer

historiographie [istɔʀjɔgʀafi] NF historiography

historiographique [istɔʀjɔgʀafik] ADJ [*tradition, courant, connaissance*] historiographical

historique [istɔʀik] 1 ADJ [*étude, vérité, roman, temps*] historical; [*personnage, événement, monument*] historic; (= *mémorable*) historic; **c'est une journée ~ pour notre équipe** it's a red letter day *ou* a historic day for our team 2 NM history; **faire l'~ de** [+ *problème, institution*] to trace the history of

historiquement [istɔʀikmɑ̃] ADV historically

histrion [istʀijɔ̃] NM a (*Hist Théât*) (wandering) minstrel, strolling player b (*péj* = *comédien*) ham (actor)

hit* [it] NM hit*

hitlérien, -ienne [itleʀjɛ̃, jɛn] ADJ, NM,F Hitlerian, Hitlerite

hitlérisme [itleʀism] NM Hitlerism

hit-parade (*pl* hit-parades) ['itpaʀad] NM (*Mus*) **le ~** the charts; **premier/bien placé au ~** number one/high up in the charts; **être en tête du ~** to be at the top of the charts; **figurer au ~ du chômage** to be in the list of countries with high unemployment; **être bien placé au ~ des hommes politiques** to be one of the most popular politicians

hittite ['itit] 1 ADJ Hittite 2 **Hittite** NMF Hittite

HIV [aʃive] NM (ABRÉV = **human immunodeficiency virus**) HIV; **virus ~** HIV virus

hiver [ivɛʀ] NM winter; **il fait un temps d'~** it's like winter, it's wintry weather; **~ nucléaire** nuclear winter; (*littér*) **à l'~ de sa vie** in the twilight of his (*ou* her) life

hivernage [ivɛʀnaʒ] NM a [*bateau, caravane, bétail*] wintering b (*Mét*) rainy season c (= *fourrage*) winter fodder

hivernal, e (*mpl* **-aux**) [ivɛʀnal, o] 1 ADJ [*lit* = *de l'hiver*] [*brouillard, pluies*] winter (*épith*), hibernal (*frm*); (*fig* = *comme en hiver*) [*atmosphère, température, temps*] wintry (*épith*); **il faisait une température ~e** it was as cold as (in) winter, it was like winter 2 **hivernale** NF (*Alpinisme*) winter ascent

hivernant, e [ivɛʀnɑ̃, ɑ̃t] NM,F winter visitor *ou* holiday-maker (*Brit*)

hiverner [ivɛʀne] ▸conjug 1◂ ① VI to winter ② VT [+ *bétail*] to winter; [+ *terre*] to plough before winter

HLA [aʃɛla] ADJ (ABRÉV = **human leucocyte antigens**) HLA; **système ~** HLA system

HLM [aʃɛlɛm] NM *ou* NF (ABRÉV = **habitation à loyer modéré**) **cité ~** council housing estate (*Brit*), public housing project (*US*) → **habitation**

ho [ʼo] EXCL (*appel*) hey (there)!; (*surprise, indignation*) oh!

hobby (*pl* **hobbies**) [ʼɔbi] NM hobby

hobereau (*pl* **hobereaux**) [ʼɔbʀo] NM (= *oiseau*) hobby; (*péj* = *seigneur*) local (country) squire

hochement [ʼɔʃmɑ̃] NM **~ de tête** (*affirmatif*) nod (of the head); (*négatif*) shake (of the head)

hochequeue [ʼɔʃkø] NM wagtail

hocher [ʼɔʃe] ▸conjug 1◂ VT **~ la tête** (*affirmativement*) to nod (one's head); (*négativement*) to shake one's head

hochet [ʼɔʃɛ] NM [*bébé*] rattle; (= *chose futile*) toy

Hô Chi Minh-Ville [oʃiminvil] N Ho Chi Minh City

hockey [ʼɔkɛ] NM hockey; **faire du ~** to play hockey; **~ sur glace** ice hockey, hockey (*US*); **~ sur gazon** hockey (*Brit*), field hockey (*US*)

hockeyeur, -euse [ʼɔkejœʀ, øz] NM,F hockey player

Hodgkin [ɔdʒkin] N (*Méd*) **maladie de ~** Hodgkin's disease

hoirie†† [waʀi] NF inheritance → **avancement**

holà [ʼɔla] ① EXCL (*pour attirer l'attention*) hello!; (*pour protester*) hang on a minute! ② NM **mettre le ~ à qch** to put a stop *ou* an end to sth

holding [ʼɔldiŋ] NM *ou* F holding company

hold-up [ʼɔldœp] NM INV hold-up; **faire un ~** to stage a hold-up; **condamné pour le ~ d'une banque** sentenced for having held up a bank *ou* for a bank hold-up

holisme [ʼɔlism] NM holism

holiste [ʼɔlist], **holistique** [ʼɔlistik] ADJ holistic

hollandais, e [ʼɔ(l)lɑ̃dɛ, ɛz] ① ADJ Dutch → **sauce** ② NM ⓐ (*Ling*) Dutch ⓑ **Hollandais** Dutchman; **les Hollandais** the Dutch ③ **hollandaise** NF ⓐ (= *vache*) Friesian (*Brit*), Holstein (*US*) ⓑ **Hollandaise** (= *femme*) Dutchwoman

Hollande [ʼɔ(l)lɑ̃d] NF Holland

hollande [ʼɔ(l)lɑ̃d] ① NF (= *toile*) holland; (= *porcelaine*) Dutch porcelain ② NM (= *fromage*) Dutch cheese; (= *papier*) Holland

Hollywood [ʼɔliwud] N Hollywood

hollywoodien, -ienne [ʼɔliwudjɛ̃, jɛn] ADJ Hollywood (*épith*)

holocauste [ɔlokost] NM ⓐ (*Rel, fig* = *sacrifice*) sacrifice, holocaust, burnt offering; (*Hist*) **l'Holocauste** the Holocaust; **offrir qch en ~** to offer sth up in sacrifice; (*littér*) **s'offrir en ~** to make a total sacrifice of one's life ⓑ (= *victime*) sacrifice

holocène [ɔlosɛn] ① ADJ Holocene ② NM **l'~** the Holocene (period)

hologramme [ɔlogʀam] NM hologram

holographe [ɔlogʀaf] ADJ holograph (*épith*)

holographie [ɔlogʀafi] NF holography

holographique [ɔlogʀafik] ADJ holographic(al)

holophrastique [ɔlofʀastik] ADJ holophrastic

homard [ʼɔmaʀ] NM lobster; **~ à l'armoricaine/à l'américaine/thermidor** lobster à l'armoricaine/à l'américaine/thermidor

home [ʼom] NM **~ d'enfants** children's home

homélie [ɔmeli] NF homily

homéopathe [ɔmeopat] NMF homoeopath(ist), homeopath(ist); **médecin ~** hom(o)eopathic doctor

homéopathie [ɔmeopati] NF hom(o)eopathy; **se soigner à l'~** to take hom(o)eopathic medicine

homéopathique [ɔmeopatik] ADJ homoeopathic; (*hum*) **à dose ~** in small doses

Homère [ɔmɛʀ] NM Homer

homérique [ɔmeʀik] ADJ Homeric → **rire**

home-trainer (*pl* **home-trainers**) [ʼomtʀɛnœʀ] NM exercise bike

homicide [ɔmisid] ① ADJ (†, *littér*) homicidal ② NMF (*littér* = *criminel*) homicide (*littér*), murderer (*ou* murderess) ③ NM (*Jur* = *crime*) murder, homicide (*US*); **~ volontaire** murder, voluntary manslaughter, first-degree murder (*US*); **~ involontaire** *ou* **par imprudence** manslaughter, second-degree murder (*US*)

hominidé [ɔminide] NM hominid; **les ~s** the Hominidae

hominien [ɔminjɛ̃] NM hominoid

hommage [ɔmaʒ] ① NM ⓐ (= *marque d'estime*) tribute; **rendre ~ à qn/au talent de qn** to pay homage *ou* tribute to sb/to sb's talent; **rendre ~ à Dieu** to pay homage to God; **rendre un dernier ~ à qn** to pay one's last respects to sb; **recevoir l'~ d'un admirateur** to accept the tribute paid by an admirer; **discours en ~ aux victimes de la guerre** speech paying homage *ou* tribute to the victims of the war ⓑ (= *don*) **acceptez ceci comme un ~** *ou* **en ~ de ma gratitude** please accept this as a mark *ou* token of my gratitude; **faire ~ d'un livre** to give a presentation copy of a book; **~ de l'auteur/de l'éditeur** with the author's/publisher's compliments ⓒ (*Hist*) homage; **~ lige** liege homage ② **hommages** NMPL (*frm* = *civilités*) respects; **mes ~s, Madame** my humble respects, madam; **présenter ses ~s à une dame** to pay one's respects to a lady; **présentez mes ~s à votre femme** give my regards to your wife

hommasse [ɔmas] ADJ mannish

homme [ɔm] ① NM ⓐ (= *espèce*) **l'~** man, mankind; **les premiers ~s** the first men on Earth ⓑ (= *individu*) man; **approche si tu es un ~!** come on if you're man enough *ou* if you dare!; **l'enfant devient ~** the child grows into *ou* becomes a man; **vêtements d'~** men's clothes; **montre/veste d'~** man's watch/jacket; **métier d'~** male profession; (*Comm*) **rayon ~s** men's *ou* menswear department; **voilà votre ~** (*que vous cherchez*) there's the man you're looking for; (*qu'il vous faut*) that's the man for you; **je suis votre ~!** I'm your man!; **elle a rencontré l'~ de sa vie** she's found Mr Right *ou* the man for her; **c'est l'~ de ma vie** he's the man of my life; **c'est l'~ du jour** he's the man of the moment *ou* hour; **c'est l'~ de la situation** he's the right man for the job; **l'~ fort du régime** the strongman of the regime; (*unité*) **heure-/journée-/mois-** *etc* **~** man-hour/-day/-month *etc* → **abominable, âge, mémoire**[1] ⓒ * (= *mari, compagnon*) man; **son ~** her man*; **voilà mon ~** here comes that man of mine* ⓓ (*loc*) **parler d'~ à ~** to speak man to man, have a man-to-man talk; **il n'est pas ~ à mentir** he's not one to lie *ou* a man to lie; **comme un seul ~** as one man; **il a trouvé son ~** (*un égal*) he has found his match ■ (*PROV*) **un ~ averti en vaut deux** forewarned is forearmed (*PROV*) ■ (*PROV*) **l'~ propose, Dieu dispose** man proposes, God disposes (*PROV*); (*Naut*) **un ~ à la mer!** man overboard! ② COMP ▸ **homme d'action** man of action ▸ **homme d'affaires** businessman

▸ **homme d'armes**†† man-at-arms† ▸ **homme de barre** helmsman ▸ **homme de bien**† good man ▸ **les hommes en blanc** (= *psychiatres*) men in white coats; (= *médecins*) doctors ▸ **homme des cavernes** cave man ▸ **l'homme de Cro-Magnon** Cro-Magnon man ▸ **homme d'Église** man of the Church ▸ **homme d'équipage** member of a ship's crew; **navire avec 30 ~s d'équipage** ship with a crew of 30 (men) ▸ **homme d'esprit** man of wit ▸ **homme d'État** statesman ▸ **homme à femmes** womanizer, ladies' man ▸ **homme au foyer** househusband ▸ **homme de lettres** man of letters ▸ **homme lige** liege man ▸ **homme de loi** man of law, lawyer ▸ **homme de main** hired man, henchman ▸ **homme de ménage** (*male*) domestic help ▸ **homme du monde** man about town, socialite; **c'est un parfait ~ du monde** he's a real gentleman ▸ **l'homme de Neandertal** Neanderthal man ▸ **homme de paille** man of straw (*used as a front*) ▸ **homme de peine** workhand ▸ **homme de plume** man of letters, writer ▸ **homme politique** politician ▸ **homme de quart** man *ou* sailor on watch ▸ **homme de robe**†† legal man, lawyer ▸ **l'homme de la rue** the man in the street ▸ **homme de science** man of science ▸ **homme à tout faire** odd-job man ▸ **homme de troupe** (*Mil*) private

homme-grenouille (*pl* **hommes-grenouilles**) [ɔmgʀənuj] NM frogman

homme-orchestre (*pl* **hommes-orchestres**) [ɔmɔʀkɛstʀ] NM (*Mus*) one-man band; (*fig*) one-man band, man of many parts; **c'est l'~ de l'entreprise** he's the man who looks after everything in the company

homme-sandwich (*pl* **hommes-sandwichs**) [ɔmsɑ̃dwitʃ] NM sandwich man

homo* [ɔmo] NM (ABRÉV = **homosexuel**) gay

homocentre [ɔmosɑ̃tʀ] NM common centre

homocentrique [ɔmosɑ̃tʀik] ADJ homocentric

homogène [ɔmoʒɛn] ADJ (*gén*) homogeneous; **pour obtenir une pâte ~** to obtain a mixture of an even consistency; **c'est une classe ~** they are all about the same level *ou* standard in that class; **texte peu ~** text that lacks consistency

homogénéisation [ɔmoʒeneizasjɔ̃] NF homogenization

homogénéiser [ɔmoʒeneize] ▸conjug 1◂ VT to homogenize

homogénéité [ɔmoʒeneite] NF homogeneity, homogeneousness; [*texte*] **manquer d'~** to lack consistency

homographe [ɔmogʀaf] ① ADJ homographic ② NM homograph

homologation [ɔmologasjɔ̃] NF (*Sport*) ratification; (*Jur*) approval, sanction; (*Admin*) authorization, approval; **~ de testament** probate of will

homologie [ɔmoloʒi] NF (*Sci*) homology; (*gén*) equivalence

homologue [ɔmolog] ① ADJ (*Sci*) homologous; (*gén*) equivalent, homologous (**de** to) ② NM (*Chim*) homologue; (= *personne*) counterpart, opposite number; **son ~ en Grande-Bretagne** his British counterpart, his opposite number in Britain

homologuer [ɔmologe] ▸conjug 1◂ VT (*Sport*) to ratify; (*Jur*) to approve, sanction; [+ *testament*] to grant probate of (*Brit*), probate (*US*); (*Admin*) [+ *appareil, établissement*] to approve; **tarif homologué** approved *ou* sanctioned rate; **record homologué** official record; **le record n'a pas pu être homologué** the record could not be made official

homoncule [ɔmɔ̃kyl] NM = **homuncule**

homonyme [ɔmɔnim] [1] ADJ homonymous [2] NM (Ling) homonym; (= personne) namesake

homonymie [ɔmɔnimi] NF homonymy

homonymique [ɔmɔnimik] ADJ homonymic

homophobe [ɔmɔfɔb] [1] ADJ [personne] homophobic [2] NMF homophobe

homophobie [ɔmɔfɔbi] NF homophobia

homophone [ɔmɔfɔn] [1] ADJ (Ling) homophonous; (Mus) homophonic [2] NM homophone

homophonie [ɔmɔfɔni] NF homophony

homosexualité [ɔmɔsɛksɥalite] NF homosexuality

homosexuel, -elle [ɔmɔsɛksɥɛl] ADJ, NM,F homosexual

homozygote [omozigɔt] [1] ADJ homozygous [2] NMF homozygote

homuncule [ɔmɔkyl] NM homunculus

Honduras ['ɔdyras] NM **le ~** Honduras; **le ~ britannique** British Honduras

hondurien, -ienne ['ɔdyrjɛ̃, jɛn] [1] ADJ Honduran [2] **Hondurien(ne)** NM,F Honduran

Hongkong, Hong-Kong ['ɔgkɔg] N Hong Kong

hongre ['ɔgʀ] [1] ADJ gelded [2] NM gelding

Hongrie ['ɔgʀi] NF Hungary

hongrois, e ['ɔgʀwa, waz] [1] ADJ Hungarian [2] (Ling) Hungarian [3] **Hongrois(e)** NM,F Hungarian

honnête [ɔnɛt] [1] ADJ [a] (= intègre) [personne] honest, decent; [conduite] decent; [procédés, intentions] honest; **ce sont d'~s gens** they are decent people ou folk*; **des procédés peu ~s** dishonest practices → **poli** [b] † (= vertueux) [femme] respectable [c] (= correct) [marché] fair; [prix, résultats] reasonable, fair; [repas] reasonable; **ce livre est ~** this book isn't bad ou is reasonable; **rester dans une ~ moyenne** to maintain a fair average; **un vin ~** an honest little wine [d] (= franc) honest, frank; **sois ~, tu aimerais bien le renvoyer** be honest, you'd love to sack him [2] COMP ▶ **honnête homme** (Hist) gentleman, man of breeding

honnêtement [ɔnɛtmã] ADV [a] (= avec intégrité) [agir] fairly, decently; [gérer] honestly; **gagner ~ sa vie** to make an honest living [b] (= correctement) reasonably; **c'est ~ payé** it's reasonably paid, you get a fair ou reasonable wage for it; **il s'en sort ~** he's managing fairly well ou reasonably well; **il gagne ~ sa vie** he makes a decent living [c] (= franchement) honestly, frankly; **il a ~ reconnu son erreur** he frankly admitted his error; **~, vous le saviez bien!** come on, you knew!; **~, qu'en penses-tu?** be honest, what do you think?

honnêteté [ɔnɛtte] NF [a] (= intégrité) [personne] honesty, decency; [conduite] decency; [procédés, intentions] honesty; **~ intellectuelle** intellectual honesty; **avec une ~ scrupuleuse** with scrupulous honesty [b] (= franchise) honesty; **en toute ~, je ne le crois pas** in all honesty ou to be perfectly frank, I don't believe it; **il a l'~ de reconnaître que...** he is honest enough to admit that... [c] † (= vertu) [femme] respectability

honneur [ɔnœʀ] [1] NM [a] (= réputation) honour (Brit), honor (US); **l'~ est sauf** our (ou their etc) honour is intact ou safe; **l'~ m'oblige à le faire** I am in honour bound to do it; **mettre son** ou **un point d'~ à faire qch** to make it a point of honour to do sth; **jurer/promettre sur l'~** to swear/promise on one's honour; **homme/femme d'~** man/woman of honour, man/woman with a sense of honour; **bandit d'~** outlaw (because of a blood feud) → **dette, manquer, parole** etc [b] (= mérite) credit; **avec ~** creditably; **il s'en est tiré avec ~** he made quite a creditable job of it; **c'est tout à son ~** it does him (great)

credit ou is much to his credit; **c'est à lui que revient l'~ d'avoir inventé ...** the credit is his for having invented ...; **être l'~ de sa profession** to be a credit ou an honour to one's profession; **cette décision vous fait ~** this decision does you credit ou is to your credit; **c'est trop d'~ que vous me faites** you're giving me too much credit → **tour²** [c] (= privilège, faveur) honour; **faire (à qn) l'~ de venir** to do sb the honour of coming; **me ferez-vous l'~ de danser avec moi?** may I have the pleasure of this dance?; **avoir l'~ de** to have the honour of; **j'ai eu l'~ de recevoir sa visite** he honoured me with a visit; **je suis ravi de vous rencontrer — tout l'~ est pour moi** delighted to meet you — the pleasure is (all) mine ou it is my pleasure; **qui commence à jouer? — à toi l'~** who is it to start? — it's you (to start); (formule épistolaire) **j'ai l'~ de solliciter ...** I am writing to ask ...; **j'ai l'~ de vous informer que** I am writing to inform you that, I beg to inform you that (frm); **garde/invité** ou **hôte d'~** guard/guest of honour; **président/membre d'~** honorary president/member → **baroud, champ, citoyen** etc [d] (Cartes) honour [e] (= titre) **votre Honneur** Your Honour [f] (loc) **~ aux vainqueurs!** hail the victors!, honour to the conquerors!; **~ aux dames** ladies first; **à toi ou vous l'~** after you; **être à l'~** [personne] to have the place of honour; [mode, style] to be to the fore, be much in evidence; **être en ~** [coutume] to be the done thing; [style, mode] to be in favour; **remettre en ~** to reintroduce; **en l'~ de nos hôtes/de cet événement** in honour of our guests/of this event; **à qui ai-je l'~?** to whom do I have the honour of speaking?; **que me vaut l'~ de votre visite?** to what do I owe the honour of your visit?; (iro) **en quel ~ toutes ces fleurs?** what are all these flowers in aid of?*; (iro) **en quel ~ t'appelle-t-il «mon bijou»?** what gives him the right to call you "my love"?; **faire ~ à** [+ engagements, signature] to honour; [+ traite] to honour, meet; [+ sa famille] to be a credit ou an honour to; [+ repas] to do justice to; **il a fini la partie pour l'~** he gallantly finished the game (for its own sake) → **bras** [2] **honneurs** NMPL (= marques de distinction) honours; **aimer/mépriser les ~s** to be fond of/despise honours; **couvert d'~s** covered in honours; **avec tous les ~s dus à son rang** with all the honours due to his rank; **~s militaires** military honours; **se rendre avec les ~s de la guerre** (Mil) to be granted the honours of war; (fig) to suffer an honourable defeat; **faire les ~s de la maison à qn** to (do the honours and) show sb round the house; **avoir les ~s de la première page** to make the front page; **avoir les ~s de la cimaise** to have one's works exhibited; **rendre les derniers ~s à qn** to pay one's last respects to sb

honnir ['ɔniʀ] ▶ conjug 2 ◀ VT (frm) to hold in contempt; **honni soit qui mal y pense** honi soit qui mal y pense

honorabilité [ɔnɔʀabilite] NF [personne, sentiments] worthiness; **soucieux d'~** anxious to be thought honourable

honorable [ɔnɔʀabl] ADJ [a] (= respectable) [personne, but, sentiment] honourable (Brit), honorable (US), worthy; **l'~ compagnie** this worthy company (frm, aussi hum); (frm, iro) **mon ~ collègue** my honourable ou esteemed colleague (frm, aussi iro); **à cet âge ~** at this grand old age; **une défaite ~** an honourable defeat [b] (= suffisant) [salaire, résultats] decent, respectable → **amende**

honorablement [ɔnɔʀabləmã] ADV [a] (= de façon respectable) honourably (Brit), honorably (US); **~ connu dans le quartier** known and respected in the district [b] (= convenablement) decently; **il gagne ~ sa vie** he makes a decent living; (Sport) **l'équipe s'est comportée ~** the

team put up a decent ou creditable performance

honoraire [ɔnɔʀɛʀ] [1] ADJ [membre, président] honorary; **professeur ~** professor emeritus, emeritus professor [2] **honoraires** NMPL [médecin, avocat] fees

honorer [ɔnɔʀe] ▶ conjug 1 ◀ [1] VT [a] (= glorifier) [+ savant, Dieu] to honour (Brit), honor (US); **~ la mémoire de qn** to honour the memory of sb [b] (littér = estimer) to hold in high regard ou esteem; **je l'honore à l'égal de ...** I have the same regard ou esteem for him as I do for ...; **mon honoré collègue** my esteemed ou respected colleague [c] (= gratifier) **~ qn de qch** to honour sb with sth; **il m'honorait de son amitié/de sa présence** he honoured me with his friendship/his presence; (iro) **il ne m'a pas honoré d'un regard** he did not honour me with so much as a glance (iro), he did not (even) deign to look at me; **je suis très honoré** I am highly ou greatly honoured [d] (= faire honneur à) to do credit to, be a credit to; **cette franchise l'honore** this frankness does him credit; **il honore sa profession/son pays** he's a credit ou an honour to his profession/country [e] [+ chèque, signature, promesse] to honour; [+ traite] to honour, meet; [+ médecin, notaire] to settle one's account with; († = lettre) **votre honorée du ...** yours of the ... [f] († ou hum) **~ sa femme** to fulfil one's conjugal duties (hum) [2] **s'honorer** VPR **s'~ de** to pride o.s. (up)on, take pride in

honorifique [ɔnɔʀifik] ADJ [fonction] honorary, ceremonial (US); **à titre ~** on an honorary basis

honoris causa [ɔnɔʀiskoza] ADJ **il a été nommé docteur ~** he has been awarded an honorary doctorate; **docteur ~ de l'université de Harvard** honorary doctor of the University of Harvard

honte ['ɔt] NF [a] (= déshonneur, humiliation) disgrace, shame; **couvrir qn de ~** to bring disgrace ou shame on sb, disgrace sb; **quelle ~** ou **c'est une ~ pour la famille!** what a disgrace to the family!, he brings shame upon the family!; **faire** ou **être la ~ de la famille/profession** to be the disgrace of one's family/profession; (littér) **~ à celui qui ...** shame upon him who ... (littér); **~ à toi!** shame on you!; **il n'y a aucune ~ à être ...** there's no shame ou disgrace in being ...; **c'est une ~!** that's disgraceful! ou a disgrace!; **c'est la ~!*** it's pathetic!*; **j'avais la ~!*** I felt so pathetic!* [b] (= sentiment de confusion, gêne) shame; **à ma (grande) ~** to my (great) shame; **sans ~** shamelessly; **sans fausse ~** quite openly; **avoir ~ (de qch/de faire)** to be ou feel ashamed (of sth/of doing); **tu devrais avoir ~!** you should be ashamed (of yourself)!; **pleurer/rougir de ~** to weep for/blush with shame; **mourir de ~** to die of shame; **elle n'a aucune ~** † she is utterly shameless, she has no shame; (frm) **avoir toute ~ bue** to be beyond shame; **tu me fais ~!** you're an embarrassment!, you make me feel so ashamed!; **faire ~ à qn de sa lenteur** to make sb (feel) ashamed of how slow they are; **il leur fait ~ par sa rapidité** he's so fast he puts them to shame → **court¹**

honteusement ['ɔtøzmã] ADV [a] (= scandaleusement: gén) shamefully; [exploiter] shamelessly [b] (= avec confusion) [cacher] in shame

honteux, -euse ['ɔtø, øz] ADJ [a] (= déshonorant) shameful; (= scandaleux) disgraceful, shameful; **c'est ~!** it's a disgrace!, it's disgraceful! ou shameful!; **il n'y a rien de ~ à cela** that's nothing to be ashamed of, there's nothing shameful about that → **maladie** [b] (= confus) ashamed (de of); **d'un**

air ~ shamefacedly; (= *cachant ses opinions*) **bourgeois/nationaliste ~** closet bourgeois/nationalist [c] (*Anat*) [*nerf, artère*] pudendal

hooligan ['uligan] NM hooligan

hooliganisme ['uliganism] NM hooliganism

hop ['ɔp] EXCL **~ (là)!** (*pour faire sauter*) hup!; (*pour faire partir*) off you go!; (*après un geste maladroit*) (w)oops!

hopi ['ɔpi] [1] ADJ [*village, indien*] Hopi [2] **Hopi** NMF Hopi; **les Hopis** the Hopis, the Hopi Indians

hôpital (*pl* **-aux**) [ɔpital, o] NM hospital; **être à l'~** [*patient*] to be in hospital (*Brit*), be in the hospital (*US*); [*médecin, visiteur*] to be at the hospital; **aller à l'~** to go to hospital; **entrer à l'~** to go into hospital; **~ militaire/psychiatrique** military/psychiatric hospital; **~ de jour** day (*Brit*) *ou* outpatient (*US*) hospital; **~ pour enfants** children's hospital; **l'~ public** (*institution*) state-run hospitals, ≈ NHS *ou* National Health (Service) hospitals (*Brit*); **c'est l'~ qui se moque de la charité** it's the pot calling the kettle black

hoquet ['ɔkɛ] NM [*personne*] hiccup; **~s** [*machine, véhicule*] spluttering (*NonC*); **avoir le ~** to have (the) hiccups; **il a eu un ~ de dégoût/peur** he gulped with distaste/fear; (= *dysfonctionnements*) **malgré quelques ~s, les négociations continuent** despite a few hiccups *ou* the occasional glitch*, the negotiations are continuing

hoqueter ['ɔk(ə)te] ▸ conjug 4 ◂ VI [*personne*] (= *avoir le hoquet*) to hiccup; (= *pleurer*) to gasp; [*machine, véhicule*] to splutter

Horace ['ɔras] NM Horatio; (= *le poète*) Horace

horaire [ɔʀɛʀ] [1] ADJ [a] [*débit, salaire, moyenne, coût*] hourly; **vitesse ~** speed per hour [b] (*Astron*) horary → **décalage, fuseau, tranche** [2] NM [a] [*personnel*] schedule, working hours; [*élèves*] timetable; **quand on est directeur, on n'a pas d'~** when you are a manager, you don't have any set working hours; **je ne suis tenu à aucun ~** I can keep my own hours, I'm not tied down to a fixed schedule; **~s de travail/bureau** working/office hours; **avoir des ~s flexibles** *ou* **variables** *ou* **à la carte** to have flexible working hours, work flexitime (*Brit*) *ou* flextime (*US*) [b] [*bus, train*] timetable; [*bateau, vols*] schedule, timetable; **~s de train** train times; **le train est en avance/en retard sur l'~ prévu** the train is ahead of/behind schedule; **il a 20 minutes de retard sur l'~ prévu** [*car, train*] it's running 20 minutes late; [*avion*] it's 20 minutes late *ou* behind schedule; (*Radio, TV*) **l'~** *ou* **les ~s de diffusion** the broadcasting schedule; **ce n'est pas un bon ~ de diffusion pour cette émission** it's not a good time-slot for this programme

horde ['ɔʀd] NF horde

horion ['ɔʀjɔ̃] NM († *ou hum*) (*gén pl*) blow, punch; **échanger des ~s avec la police** to exchange blows with the police

horizon [ɔʀizɔ̃] NM [a] (*Astron, Art*) horizon; **la ligne d'~** the horizon; **~ artificiel** artificial horizon; **un bateau sur** *ou* **à l'~** a boat on the horizon *ou* skyline; **disparaître à l'~** to disappear below the horizon; **personne à l'~?** *ou* **nu!** nobody around *ou* in sight? — let's go then!; (*lit, fig*) **se pointer** *ou* **se profiler** *ou* **poindre à l'~** to loom on the horizon [b] (= *paysage*) landscape, view; **on découvre un vaste ~/un ~ de collines** you come upon a vast panorama/a hilly landscape; **changer d'~** to have a change of scenery *ou* scene; **ce village était tout son ~** this village was his whole world *ou* the only world he knew; **voyager vers de nouveaux ~s** to make for new horizons; **venir d'~s divers** to come *ou* hail (*frm*) from different backgrounds [c] (= *avenir, perspective*) horizon; **ça lui a**

ouvert de nouveaux ~s it opened (up) new horizons *ou* vistas for him; **l'~ économique du pays** the country's economic prospects; **faire des prévisions pour l'~ 2020** to make forecasts for (the year) 2020; **à l'~ 2020** by (the year) 2020 → **tour²**

horizontal, e (*mpl* **-aux**) [ɔʀizɔ̃tal, o] [1] (*gén, Écon*) horizontal; **être en position ~e** to be lying down flat [2] **horizontale** NF (*gén, Géom*) horizontal; **placer qch à l'horizontale** to put sth horizontal *ou* in a horizontal position; **tendez vos bras à l'horizontale** stretch your arms out in front of you

horizontalement [ɔʀizɔ̃talmɑ̃] ADV (*gén*) horizontally; (*dans mots croisés*) across

horizontalité [ɔʀizɔ̃talite] NF horizontality, horizontalness

horloge [ɔʀlɔʒ] NF (*gén, Ordin*) clock; **avec une régularité de ~** as regular as clockwork; **avec la précision d'une ~** with clockwork precision; **il est 2 heures à l'~** it's 2 o'clock *ou* according to the clock; **l'~ parlante** the speaking clock (*Brit*), Time (*US*); **~ astronomique/atomique** astronomical/atomic clock; **~ normande** *ou* **de parquet** grandfather clock; **~ interne/biologique** internal/biological clock → **heure**

horloger, -ère [ɔʀlɔʒe, ɛʀ] [1] ADJ [*industrie*] watch-making (*épith*), clock-making (*épith*) [2] NM,F (*gén*) watchmaker; (*spécialement d'horloges*) clockmaker; **~ bijoutier** jeweller; (*specializing in clocks and watches*); (*littér*) **le grand ~** the Creator

horlogerie [ɔʀlɔʒʀi] NF (= *fabrication*) (*gén*) watch-making; [*horloges*] clock-making; (= *objets*) time-pieces; (= *magasin*) watchmaker's (shop), clockmaker's (shop); (= *technique, science*) horology; **~ bijouterie** jeweller's shop (*specializing in clocks and watches*); **pièces d'~** clock components → **mouvement**

hormis ['ɔʀmi] PRÉP (= *except for, apart from*; **personne ~ ses fils** nobody except for *ou* apart from his sons, nobody but *ou* save (*frm*) his sons

hormonal, e (*mpl* **-aux**) [ɔʀmɔnal, o] ADJ [*traitement*] hormonal, hormone (*épith*); [*contraception, déséquilibre*] hormonal

hormone [ɔʀmɔn] NF hormone; **~ de croissance/sexuelle** growth/sex hormone; **poulet/veau aux ~s** hormone-fed *ou* hormone-treated chicken/veal

hormonothérapie [ɔʀmɔnoteʀapi] NF hormone therapy

horodaté, e [ɔʀɔdate] ADJ [*stationnement*] pay and display (*épith*); [*ticket*] stamped with the hour and date (*attrib*)

horodateur [ɔʀɔdatœʀ] NM [*parking*] ticket machine, pay-and-display ticket machine (*Brit*)

horoscope [ɔʀɔskɔp] NM horoscope; **faire l'~ de qn** to cast *ou* do sb's horoscope; **regarder/lire son ~** to consult/read one's horoscope *ou* stars*

horreur [ɔʀœʀ] NF [a] (= *effroi, répulsion*) horror; **il était devenu pour elle un objet d'~** he had become an object of horror to her; **frappé** *ou* **saisi d'~** horror-stricken, horror-struck; **vision d'~** horrific *ou* horrendous *ou* horrifying sight; **l'~ d'agir/du risque qui le caractérise** the horror of acting/taking risks which is typical of him; **son ~ de la lâcheté** his horror *ou* loathing of cowardice; **je me suis aperçu avec ~ que ...** to my horror I realized that ... [b] (= *laideur*) [*crime, guerre*] horror; **l'esclavage dans toute son ~** slavery in all its horror [c] (= *chose*) **les ~s de la guerre** the horrors of war; **ce film/travail est une ~*** this film/piece of work is terrible *ou* awful *ou* dreadful; **c'est une ~*** [*tableau*] it's hideous *ou* ghastly*; [*personne laide*] he's (*ou* she's) hideous; [*personne méchante*] he's (*ou* she's) ghastly*; **quelle ~!** how dreadful! *ou* awful! → **film,**

musée

[d] * (= *actes, propos*) **~s** dreadful *ou* terrible things; **débiter des ~s sur qn** to say dreadful *ou* terrible things about sb
[e] (*loc*) **cet individu me fait ~** that fellow disgusts me; **le mensonge me fait ~** I loathe *ou* detest lying, I have a horror of lying; **la viande me fait ~** I can't stand *ou* bear meat, I loathe *ou* detest meat; **avoir qch/qn en ~** to loathe *ou* detest sth/sb; **j'ai ce genre de livre en ~** I loathe *ou* detest this type of book, I have a horror of this type of book; **prendre qch/qn en ~** to come to loathe *ou* detest sth/sb; **avoir ~ de qch/de faire qch** to loathe *ou* detest sth/doing sth

horrible [ɔʀibl] ADJ (= *effrayant*) [*crime, accident, blessure*] horrible; (= *extrême*) [*chaleur, peur*] terrible, dreadful; (= *laid*) [*chapeau, personne, tableau*] horrible, hideous; (= *mauvais*) [*temps*] terrible, ghastly*, dreadful; [*travail*] terrible, dreadful; (= *méchant*) [*personne, propos*] horrible, awful; **il a été ~ avec moi** he was horrible to me

horriblement [ɔʀibləmɑ̃] ADV (= *de façon effrayante*) horribly; (= *extrêmement*) horribly, terribly, dreadfully

horrifiant, e [ɔʀifjɑ̃, jɑ̃t] ADJ horrifying

horrifier [ɔʀifje] ▸ conjug 7 ◂ VT to horrify; **horrifié par la dépense** horrified at the expense

horrifique [ɔʀifik] ADJ (*hum*) blood-curdling, horrific

horripilant, e [ɔʀipilɑ̃, ɑ̃t] ADJ trying, exasperating

horripiler [ɔʀipile] ▸ conjug 1 ◂ VT **~ qn** to try sb's patience, exasperate sb

hors ['ɔʀ] [1] PRÉP (= *excepté*) except (for), apart from, save (*littér*), but; (*littér*) **~ que** save that (*littér*); **Arles ~ les murs** the outer parts of Arles (*beyond the city walls*) [2] **hors de** LOC PRÉP [a] (*position*) outside, out of, away from; (*changement de lieu*) out of; **vivre ~ de la ville** to live out of town *ou* outside the town; **vivre ~ de son pays** to live away from *ou* outside one's own country; **le choc l'a projeté ~ de la voiture** the impact threw him out of the car; **il est plus agréable d'habiter ~ du centre** it is more pleasant to live away from *ou* outside the centre; **vivre ~ de son temps/la réalité** to live in a different age/in a dream world; **~ de temps** [*personnage, univers*] timeless; **~ d'ici!** get out of here! ■ (*PROV*) **~ de l'Église, point de salut** without the Church there is no salvation; (*hum*) **~ de l'Europe, point de salut** without Europe there can be no salvation *ou* there is no hope [b] (*loc*) **il est ~ d'affaire** he is out of the wood (*Brit*) *ou* woods (*US*), he's over the worst; **mettre qn ~ d'état de nuire** to render sb harmless; **être ~ de soi** to be beside o.s. (with anger); **cette remarque l'a mise ~ d'elle** she was beside herself when she heard the remark → **atteinte, commun, portée** *etc*
[3] COMP ▸ **hors jeu** [*joueur*] offside; [*ballon*] out of play; (*Tennis*) out (of play); (*fig*) out of the running; **mettre qn ~ jeu** (*Sport*) to put sb offside; (*fig*) to put sb out of the running; **se mettre ~ jeu** to rule *ou* put o.s. out of the running ▸ **hors ligne** = **hors pair** ▸ **hors pair** outstanding, unparalleled, matchless ▸ **hors tout**: **longueur/largeur ~ tout** overall length/width → **circuit, course, service** *etc*

hors-bord ['ɔʀbɔʀ] NM INV (= *moteur*) outboard motor; (= *bateau*) speedboat (*with outboard motor*)

hors-cote ['ɔʀkɔt] NM INV over-the-counter market, unofficial market, off-board market (*US*)

hors-d'œuvre ['ɔʀdœvʀ] NM INV (*Culin*) hors d'œuvre; **~ variés** assorted cold meats and salads; (*fig*) **son discours n'était qu'un ~** his speech was just a taste of things to come

hors-jeu ['ɔrʒø] NM INV offside; **être en position de ~** to be offside → **hors**

hors-la-loi [ɔrlalwa] NMF INV outlaw

hors-piste ['ɔrpist] **1** ADV, ADJ INV off-piste **2** NM INV off-piste skiing; **faire du ~** to ski off piste

hors-série ['ɔrseri] NM INV (= *magazine*) special edition

hors-texte ['ɔrtɛkst] NM INV (= *gravure*) plate

hortensia [ɔrtɑ̃sja] NM hydrangea

horticole [ɔrtikɔl] ADJ horticultural

horticulteur, -trice [ɔrtikyltœr, tris] NM,F horticulturist

horticulture [ɔrtikyltyr] NF horticulture

hortillonnage [ɔrtijɔnaʒ] NM (= *marais*) marsh used for vegetable farming

hosanna [oza(n)na] NM hosanna

hospice [ɔspis] NM **a** (= *hôpital*) home; **~ de vieillards** old people's home; (*péj*) **mourir à l'~** to die in the poorhouse **b** [*monastère*] hospice

hospitalier, -ière [ɔspitalje, jɛr] **1** ADJ **a** [*service, personnel, médecine*] hospital (*épith*); **centre** ou **établissement ~** hospital **b** (= *accueillant*) hospitable **2** NM,F **a** (= *religieux*) (frère) ~ ◊ (sœur) hospitalière hospitaller **b** (= *infirmier*) nurse; **les ~s** hospital staff

hospitalisation [ɔspitalizasjɔ̃] NF hospitalization; **~ à domicile** home (medical) care

hospitaliser [ɔspitalize] ▶ conjug 1 ◀ VT to hospitalize, send to hospital; **malade hospitalisé** in-patient; **10% des malades hospitalisés** 10% of hospital patients ou cases; **être hospitalisé** to be admitted to hospital, be hospitalized; **elle a été hospitalisée d'urgence** she was rushed to hospital

hospitalisme [ɔspitalism] NM hospitalism

hospitalité [ɔspitalite] NF hospitality; **donner l'~ à qn** to give ou offer sb hospitality; **avoir le sens de l'~** to be hospitable

hospitalo-universitaire (*mpl* hospitalo-universitaires) [ɔspitaloyniversitɛr] ADJ **centre ~** teaching hospital

hostellerie† [ɔstɛlri] NF hostelry†

hostie [ɔsti] NF (*Rel*) host; (†† = *victime*) sacrificial victim

hostile [ɔstil] ADJ hostile; **~ à** [+ *projet*] opposed ou hostile to

hostilement [ɔstilmɑ̃] ADV hostilely

hostilité [ɔstilite] NF hostility (**à, envers** to, towards); **ouvrir/reprendre les ~s** to open/reopen hostilities

hosto* [ɔsto] NM hospital

hot(-)dog (*pl* hot(-)dogs) [ɔtdɔg] NM hot dog

hôte [ot] **1** NM (= *maître de maison*) host; († = *aubergiste*) landlord, host; (*Bio*) host; (*Ordin*) host computer; (*littér*) **les ~s du bois/du marais** the denizens (*littér*) of the wood/marsh → **chambre, table 2** NMF (= *invité*) guest; (= *client*) patron; (= *locataire*) occupant; **un ~ de marque** a distinguished guest; **~ payant** paying guest

hôtel [otɛl] **1** NM hotel; **vivre/coucher à l'~** to live/sleep in a hotel; **aller** ou **descendre à l'~** to put up at a hotel → **maître, rat 2** COMP ► **hôtel des impôts** tax office ► **hôtel meublé** (cheap) residential hotel ► **l'hôtel de la Monnaie** ≈ the Mint ► **hôtel particulier** town house, (private) mansion ► **hôtel de passe** hotel used by prostitutes ► **hôtel de police** police station ► **hôtel de tourisme** tourist hotel ► **hôtel des ventes** saleroom, salesroom (*US*) ► **hôtel de ville** town hall

hôtel-Dieu (*pl* hôtels-Dieu) [otɛldjø] NM general hospital

hôtelier, -ière [otəlje, jɛr] **1** ADJ [*chaîne, complexe, industrie, profession*] hotel (*épith*) → **école 2** NM,F hotelier, hotel-keeper; **restaurateur** hotel-and-restaurant owner

---

hôtellerie [otɛlri] NF (= *auberge*) inn, hostelry†; [*abbaye*] guest quarters, hospice†; (= *profession*) hotel business; (= *matière enseignée*) hotel management; **~ de plein air** camping and caravanning

hôtel-restaurant (*pl* hôtels-restaurants) [otɛlrɛstɔrɑ̃] NM hotel (with public restaurant)

hôtesse [otɛs] NF (= *maîtresse de maison*) hostess; († = *aubergiste*) landlady; **~ (de l'air)** stewardess, air hostess (*Brit*), flight attendant; **~ (d'accueil)** [*hôtel, bureau*] receptionist; [*exposition, colloque*] hostess

hotte ['ɔt] NF (= *panier*) basket (carried on the back); [*cheminée, laboratoire*] hood; [*cuisine*] **~ aspirante** ou **filtrante** extractor ou cooker (*Brit*) ou range (*US*) hood; **la ~ du Père Noël** Santa Claus's sack

hottentot, e ['ɔtɑ̃to, ɔt] **1** ADJ Hottentot **2** **Hottentot(e)** NM,F Hottentot

hou ['u] EXCL boo!

houblon ['ublɔ̃] NM (= *plante*) hop; (= *ingrédient de la bière*) hops

houblonnière ['ublɔnjɛr] NF hopfield

houe ['u] NF hoe

houille ['uj] NF coal; **~ blanche** hydroelectric power; **~ grasse/maigre** bituminous/lean coal

houiller, -ère ['uje, jɛr] **1** ADJ [*bassin, industrie*] coal (*épith*); [*terrain*] coal-bearing **2** **houillère** NF coalmine

houle ['ul] NF swell; **une forte ~** a heavy swell

houlette ['ulɛt] NF [*pâtre, évêque*] crook; [*jardinier*] trowel, spud; **sous la ~ de** under the leadership of

houleux, -euse ['ulø, øz] ADJ [*mer*] stormy; [*séance*] stormy, turbulent; [*salle, foule*] tumultuous, turbulent

houp ['up] EXCL = **hop**

houppe ['up] NF [*plumes, cheveux*] tuft; [*fils*] tassel; **~ à poudrer** powder puff

houppelande ['uplɑ̃d] NF (loose-fitting) greatcoat

houppette ['upɛt] NF powder puff

hourra ['ura] EXCL hurrah!; **pousser des ~s** to cheer, shout hurrah; **salué par des ~s** greeted by cheers → **hip**

house (music) [aus(mjuzik)] NF house (music)

houspiller ['uspije] ▶ conjug 1 ◀ VT (= *réprimander*) to scold, tell off, tick off* (*Brit*); († = *malmener*) to hustle

housse ['us] NF (*gén*) cover; [*meubles*] (*pour protéger temporairement*) dust cover; (*pour recouvrir à neuf*) loose cover; (*en tissu élastique*) stretch cover; **~ de couette** quilt cover; [*habits*] **~ (penderie)** hanging wardrobe

houx ['u] NM holly

hovercraft [ovœrkraft] NM hovercraft

hoverport [ovœrpɔr] NM hoverport

HS [aʃɛs] **1** ADJ INV **a*** (ABRÉV = **hors service**) [*appareil*] kaput*, bust* (*attrib*); [*personne*] (*par fatigue*) beat* (*attrib*), shattered* (*attrib*) (*Brit*); (*par maladie*) out of it* (*attrib*) **b** (*Tourisme*) (ABRÉV = **haute saison**) → **saison 2** NF (ABRÉV = **heure supplémentaire**) → **supplémentaire**

HT (ABRÉV = **hors taxe(s)**) → **taxe**

huard, huart ['yar] NM (*Can* = *oiseau*) diver (*Brit*), loon (*US*)

hublot ['yblo] NM [*bateau*] porthole; [*avion, machine à laver*] window; **~s*** (= *lunettes*) specs*

huche ['yʃ] NF (= *coffre*) chest; (= *pétrin*) dough ou kneading trough; **~ à pain** bread bin

hue ['y] EXCL **~ (cocotte)!** gee up!; **ils tirent tous à ~ et à dia** they are all pulling in opposite directions

huée ['ye] NF (*Chasse*) hallooing; (*de dérision*) **~s** boos, booing (*NonC*); **sous les ~s de la foule** to the boos of the crowd; **il est sorti de**

---

scène sous les ~s du public he was booed off the stage

huer ['ye] ▶ conjug 1 ◀ **1** VT (*Chasse*) to hallo; (*par dérision*) to boo **2** VI (*chouette*) to hoot

hugolien, -ienne [ygɔljɛ̃, jɛn] ADJ of Victor Hugo

huguenot, e ['yg(a)no, ɔt] ADJ, NM,F Huguenot

Hugues ['yg] NM Hugh; **~ Capet** Hugh ou Hughes Capet

huilage [ɥilaʒ] NM oiling, lubrication

huile [ɥil] **1** NF **a** (= *liquide*) oil; (*Tech* = *pétrole*) petroleum, crude (oil); (*Culin*) **cuit à l'~** cooked in oil; **sardines/thon à l'~** sardines/tuna in oil; (*Aut*) **vérifier le niveau d'~** to check the oil; **jeter** ou **verser de l'~ sur le feu** to add fuel to the flames ou fire; **mettre de l'~ dans les rouages** to oil the wheels; **mer d'~** glassy sea → **lampe, saint, tache b*** (= *notabilité*) bigwig*, big noise*, big shot*; **les ~s** the top brass*, the big shots* **c** (*Peinture*) (= *tableau*) oil painting; (= *technique*) oil painting, oils; **peint à l'~** painted in oils → **peinture 2** COMP ► **huile d'amandes douces** sweet almond oil ► **huile d'arachide** groundnut (*Brit*) ou peanut (*US*) oil ► **huile de bain** bath oil ► **huile de colza** rapeseed ou colza oil ► **huile de noix** walnut oil ► **huile de coude*** elbow grease* ► **huile essentielle** essential oil ► **huile de foie de morue** cod-liver oil ► **huile de friture** cooking ou frying oil ► **huile de graissage** lubricating oil ► **huile de lin** linseed oil ► **huile de maïs** corn oil ► **huile d'olive** olive oil ► **huile de paraffine** liquid paraffin ► **huile de ricin** castor oil ► **huile de sésame** sesame oil ► **huile de soja** soya oil ► **huile solaire** (sun)tan oil ► **huile de table** salad oil ► **huile de tournesol** sunflower oil ► **huile végétale** vegetable oil ► **huile de vidange** (*gén*) lubricating oil; (*usagée*) waste oil ► **huile vierge** virgin olive oil

huiler [ɥile] ▶ conjug 1 ◀ VT [+ *machine, serrure*] to oil, lubricate; [+ *récipient*] to oil; **papier huilé** oil-paper; (*fig*) **la mécanique est bien/parfaitement huilée** it's a well-oiled/perfectly smooth-running machine; **équipe bien huilée** slick team

huilerie [ɥilri] NF (= *usine*) oil factory; (= *commerce*) oil trade; (= *moulin*) oil-mill

huileux, -euse [ɥilø, øz] ADJ [*liquide, matière*] oily; [*aspect, surface*] oily, greasy

huilier [ɥilje] NM (oil and vinegar) cruet, oil and vinegar bottle

huis [ɥi] NM†† door; (*Jur*) **à ~ clos** in camera; (*Jur*) **ordonner le ~ clos** to order proceedings to be held in camera; **les négociations se poursuivent à ~ clos** the talks are continuing behind closed doors

huisserie [ɥisri] NF [*porte*] doorframe; [*fenêtre*] window frame

huissier [ɥisje] NM **a** (= *appariteur*) usher **b** (*Jur*) **~ (de justice)** ≈ bailiff

┌─────── **HUISSIER** ───────┐

*Although in some respects the role of **huissiers** is similar to that of bailiffs, their activities are not identical. The main function of a **huissier** is to carry out decisions made in the courts, for example evictions for non-payment of rent and seizure of goods following bankruptcy proceedings. Unlike bailiffs, **huissiers** can also be called upon to witness the signature of important documents, and to ensure that public competitions are judged fairly.*

└────────────────────────────┘

huit ['ɥi(t)] **1** ADJ INV eight; *pour autres locutions voir* **six 2** NM INV eight; (*en patinage*) figure of eight; (*en aviron*) eight; **lundi en ~** a week on (*Brit*) ou from (*US*) Monday, Monday week* (*Brit*) → **grand** [3] COMP ► **huit jours** (= *une semaine*) a week; **dans ~ jours** in a week, in a week's time (*Brit*); **donner ses ~ jours à un domestique**† to give a servant a week's notice

huitain [ɥitɛ̃] NM (= *poème*) octet, octave

huitaine [ɥitɛn] NF eight or so, about eight; **dans une ~ (de jours)** in a week or so; (*Jur*) **son cas a été remis à ~** the hearing has been postponed *ou* deferred for one week; **sans réponse sous ~** if no reply is received within seven days

huitante [ɥitɑ̃t] ADJ INV (*Helv*) eighty

huitième [ɥitjɛm] [1] ADJ, NMF eighth; **la ~ merveille du monde** the eighth wonder of the world; *pour autres locutions voir* **sixième** [2] NF (*Scol*) penultimate class of primary school, fifth grade (*US*) [3] NMPL (*Sport*) **~s de finale** second round in a five-round knock-out competition; **être en ~s de finale** to be in the last sixteen

huitièmement [ɥitjɛmmɑ̃] ADV eighthly

huître [ɥitʀ] NF (= *oyster*); **~ perlière** pearl oyster; **se (re)fermer comme une ~** to clam up

huit-reflets [ɥiʀ(ə)flɛ] NM INV silk top hat

huîtrier, -ière [ɥitʀije, ijɛʀ] [1] ADJ [*industrie*] oyster (*épith*) [2] NM (= *oiseau*) oyster catcher [3] **huîtrière** NF (= *banc*) oyster bed; (= *établissement*) oyster farm

hulotte [ylɔt] NF tawny owl

hululement [ylylmɑ̃] NM hooting, screeching

hululer [ylyle] ▶ conjug 1 ◀ VI to hoot, screech

hum [œm] EXCL hem!, h'm!

humain, e [ymɛ̃, ɛn] [1] ADJ (*gén*) human; (= *compatissant, compréhensif*) humane; **justice/ espèce/condition ~e** human justice/race/condition; **il n'avait plus figure ~e** he was disfigured beyond recognition; **se montrer ~** to show humanity, act humanely (*envers* towards); **il s'est sauvé — c'est ~** he ran away — it's only human → **respect, science, voix** *etc* [2] NM [a] (*Philo*) **l'~** the human element [b] (= *être humain*) human (being); **les ~s** humans, human beings

humainement [ymɛnmɑ̃] ADV (= *avec bonté*) humanely; (= *par l'homme*) humanly; **ce n'est pas ~ possible** it's not humanly possible; **~, on ne peut pas le renvoyer** it would be heartless to dismiss him; **une situation ~ intolérable** an unbearable situation for people to be in; **la restructuration a été ~ douloureuse** the human cost of the restructuring was high, the restructuring was painful in human terms

humanisation [ymanizasjɔ̃] NF humanization

humaniser [ymanize] ▶ conjug 1 ◀ [1] VT [+ *doctrine*] to humanize; [+ *conditions*] to make more humane, humanize [2] **s'humaniser** VPR [*personne*] to become more human; [*architecture*] to become less forbidding *ou* impersonal

humanisme [ymanism] NM humanism

humaniste [ymanist] [1] ADJ humanist, humanistic [2] NMF humanist

humanitaire [ymanitɛʀ] ADJ [*intervention, convoi*] humanitarian; **aide/action ~** humanitarian aid/relief; **association ~** humanitarian (aid) organization

humanitarisme [ymanitaʀism] NM (*péj*) unrealistic humanitarianism

humanitariste [ymanitaʀist] [1] ADJ (*péj*) unrealistically humanitarian [2] NMF unrealistic humanitarian

humanité [ymanite] [1] NF [a] (= *le genre humain*) **l'~** humanity, mankind [b] (= *bonté*) humaneness, humanity; **geste d'~** humane gesture [c] (*Philo, Rel*) humanity [2] **humanités** NFPL († *Scol*) classics, humanities; **faire ses ~s** to study *ou* read (*Brit*) classics

humanoïde [ymanɔid] ADJ, NM humanoid

humble [œbl(ə)] ADJ (= *modeste, pauvre*) humble; (= *obscur*) humble, lowly; **d'~ naissance** of humble *ou* lowly birth *ou* origins; **à mon ~ avis** in my humble opinion; **«je suis votre ~ serviteur»**† "I am your humble servant "†

humblement [œbləmɑ̃] ADV humbly

humecter [ymɛkte] ▶ conjug 1 ◀ VT [+ *linge, herbe*] to dampen; [+ *front*] to moisten, dampen; **la sueur humectait ses tempes** his brow was damp with sweat; **l'herbe humectée de rosée** the dewy *ou* dew-damp grass; **s'~ les lèvres** to moisten one's lips; **ses yeux s'humectèrent** his eyes grew moist (with tears), tears welled in his eyes; **s'~ le gosier*** to wet one's whistle*

humer [yme] ▶ conjug 1 ◀ VT [+ *plat*] to smell; [+ *air, parfum*] to inhale, breathe in

humérus [ymeʀys] NM humerus

humeur [ymœʀ] NF [a] (= *disposition momentanée*) mood, humour; **selon son ~** *ou* **l'~ du moment** according to the mood he was in; **se sentir d'~ à travailler** to feel in the mood for working *ou* for work *ou* to work; **de quelle ~ est-il aujourd'hui ?** what kind of mood is he in today?; **mettre/être de bonne ~** to put/be in a good mood *ou* humour, put/be in good spirits; **travailler dans la bonne ~** to work contentedly; **la bonne ~ régnait dans la maison** contentment reigned in the house; **roman/ film plein de bonne ~** good-humoured novel/film, novel/film full of good humour; **être de mauvaise ~** to be in a bad mood; **il est d'une ~ massacrante** *ou* **de chien** he's in a rotten* *ou* foul temper *ou* mood; **~ noire** black mood → **saute**

[b] (= *tempérament*) temper, temperament; **d'~ changeante** *ou* **inégale** moody; **d'~ égale** even-tempered, equable (*frm*); **être d'~** *ou* **avoir l'~ batailleuse** to be fiery-tempered; **être d'~ maussade** to be sullen, be a sullen type; **il y a incompatibilité d'~ entre eux** they are temperamentally unsuited *ou* incompatible

[c] (= *irritation*) bad temper, ill humour; **passer son ~ sur qn** to take out *ou* vent one's bad temper *ou* ill humour on sb; **accès** *ou* **mouvement d'~** fit of (bad) temper *ou* ill humour; **geste d'~** bad-tempered gesture; **agir par ~** to act in a fit of (bad) temper *ou* ill humour; **dire qch avec ~** to say sth ill-humouredly *ou* testily (*littér*)

[d] (*Méd*) secretion; **~ aqueuse/vitreuse** *ou* **vitrée de l'œil** aqueous/vitreous humour of the eye; **les ~s**†† the humours†

humide [ymid] ADJ [*mains, front, terre*] moist, damp; [*torchon, habits, mur, poudre, herbe*] damp; [*local, climat, région, chaleur*] humid; (= *plutôt froid*) damp; [*tunnel, cave*] dank, damp; [*saison, route*] wet; **yeux ~s d'émotion** eyes moist with emotion; **il lui lança un regard ~** he looked at her with moist eyes; **temps lourd et ~** muggy weather; **temps froid et ~** cold wet weather

humidificateur [ymidifikatœʀ] NM [*air*] humidifier

humidification [ymidifikasjɔ̃] NF humidification

humidifier [ymidifje] ▶ conjug 7 ◀ VT [+ *air*] to humidify; [+ *terre*] to moisten; [+ *linge*] to moisten, dampen

humidité [ymidite] NF [*air, climat*] humidity; (*plutôt froide*) dampness; [*sol, mur*] dampness; [*tunnel, cave*] dankness, dampness; (= *atmosphérique*) humidity (of the atmosphere); **air saturé d'~** air saturated with moisture; **dégâts causés par l'~** damage caused by (the) damp; **traces d'~ sur le mur** traces of moisture *ou* of damp on the wall; **taches d'~** damp patches, patches of damp; (*sur emballage*) **«craint l'~»** ◊ **«à protéger de l'~»** "to be kept dry", "keep in a dry place"

humiliant, e [ymiljɑ̃, jɑ̃t] ADJ humiliating

humiliation [ymiljasjɔ̃] NF (*gén*) humiliation; (*Rel*) humbling (*NonC*)

humilier [ymilje] ▶ conjug 7 ◀ VT (= *rabaisser*) to humiliate; (††, *Rel* = *rendre humble*) to humble; **s'~ devant** to humble o.s. before

humilité [ymilite] NF (= *modestie*) humility, humbleness; **ton d'~** humble tone; **en toute ~** with all humility

humoral, e (*mpl* -**aux**) [ymɔʀal, o] ADJ humoral

humoriste [ymɔʀist] [1] ADJ [*écrivain*] humorous [2] NMF humorist

humoristique [ymɔʀistik] ADJ humorous → **dessin**

humour [ymuʀ] NM humour; **~ noir** black humour; **~ à froid** deadpan humour; **l'~ anglais** *ou* **britannique** British humour; **manquer d'~** to have no sense of humour; **avoir de l'~/ beaucoup d'~** to have a sense of humour/a good *ou* great sense of humour; **faire de l'~** to try to be funny

humus [ymys] NM humus

Hun [œ̃] NM (*Hist*) Hun

hune [yn] NF top; **mât de ~** topmast; **grande ~** maintop

hunier [ynje] NM topsail; **grand ~** main topsail

huppe [yp] NF (= *oiseau*) hoopoe; (= *crête*) crest

huppé, e [ype] ADJ [a] (*Orn*) crested [b]* (= *riche*) posh*, swanky*

hure [yʀ] NF (= *tête*) head; (= *pâté*) pork brawn; **~ de sanglier** boar's head

hurlant, e [yʀlɑ̃, ɑ̃t] ADJ [*foule*] howling; [*enfant*] yelling; [*sirène*] wailing; [*couleurs*] clashing

hurlement [yʀləmɑ̃] NM [a] [*loup, chien*] howl, howling (*NonC*); [*personne*] yell, howl; **pousser des ~s** (*de rage*) to howl with rage; (*de douleur*) to howl with pain; (*de joie*) to whoop for *ou* with joy; **des ~s de rire** screams *ou* gales of laughter [b] [*vent*] howling (*NonC*); [*sirènes*] wailing (*NonC*); [*pneus, freins*] screeching (*NonC*), screech, squealing (*NonC*), squeal

hurler [yʀle] ▶ conjug 1 ◀ [1] VI [a] (= *crier*) [*personne*] (*de peur*) to shriek, scream; (*de douleur*) to scream, yell (out), howl; (*de rage*) to roar, bellow; [*foule*] to roar, yell (**de** with, in); **~ de rire** to roar *ou* bellow with laughter; **il hurlait comme si on l'égorgeait** he was screaming like a stuck pig; **elle hurlait après les enfants** she was yelling at the children; **cette réforme va faire ~ l'opposition** this reform will enrage the opposition

[b] (= *vociférer*) to yell

[c] [*chien, vent*] to howl; [*freins*] to screech, squeal; [*sirène*] to wail; [*radio*] to blare; **faire ~ sa télé** to have the TV on full blast*; **~ à la lune** *ou* **à la mort** to bay at the moon; (*fig*) **avec les loups** to follow the pack *ou* crowd

[d] [*couleurs*] to clash; **ce tableau jaune sur le mur vert, ça hurle !** that yellow picture really clashes with the green wall

[2] VT [+ *injures, slogans*] to yell, roar; [+ *ordres*] to bellow, yell; **il hurlait son désespoir** he gave vent to his despair

hurleur, -euse [yʀlœʀ, øz] [1] ADJ (= *braillard*) [*personne*] yelling (*épith*) [2] NM (**singe**) **~** howler (monkey)

hurluberlu, e [yʀlybɛʀly] NM,F crank

huron, -onne [yʀɔ̃, ɔn] [1] ADJ Huron; **le lac Huron** Lake Huron [2] NM (*Ling*) Huron [3] **Huron(ne)** NM,F Huron

hurrah [yʀa, huʀa] EXCL = **hourra**

husky (*pl* **huskies**) [œski] NM husky

hussard [ysaʀ] NM hussar

hussarde [ysaʀd] ◆ **à la hussarde** LOC ADV in a rough and ready way

hutte [yt] NF hut

hutu [uty] [1] ADJ Hutu [2] **Hutu** NMF Hutu; **les Hutus** the Hutus

hyacinthe [jasɛ̃t] NF (= *pierre*) hyacinth, jacinth; († = *fleur*) hyacinth

hybridation [ibʀidasjɔ̃] NF hybridization

hybride [ibʀid] ADJ, NM hybrid

hybrider [ibʀide] ▶ conjug 1 ◀ VT to hybridize

hybridisme [ibʀidism] NM hybridism

hydracide [idʀasid] NM hydracid

hydratant, e [idʀatɑ̃, ɑ̃t] 1 ADJ moisturizing 2 NM moisturizer

hydratation [idʀatasjɔ̃] NF (*Chim, Méd*) hydration; [*peau*] moisturizing

hydrate [idʀat] NM hydrate; **~ de carbone** carbohydrate

hydrater [idʀate] ▶ conjug 1 ◀ 1 VT (*gén*) to hydrate; [+ *peau*] to moisturize 2 **s'hydrater** VPR (*Chim*) to hydrate; (= *boire*) to take lots of fluids

hydraulicien, -ienne [idʀolisjɛ̃, jɛn] NMF hydraulics specialist

hydraulique [idʀolik] 1 ADJ [*circuit, énergie, frein, presse, travaux*] hydraulic; **station ~** waterworks *sg* 2 NF hydraulics *sg*

hydravion [idʀavjɔ̃] NM seaplane, hydroplane

hydre [idʀ(ə)] NF **a** (*Myth*) **l'~ de Lerne** the Lernean Hydra; **on voit resurgir l'~ du racisme** racism is rearing *ou* raising its ugly head again **b** (*Zool*) hydra; **~ d'eau douce** freshwater hydra

hydrique [idʀik] ADJ water (*épith*); **ressources ~s** water resources; (*Méd*) **diète ~** liquid diet

hydrocarbure [idʀokaʀbyʀ] NM hydrocarbon; **~s saturés/insaturés** saturated/unsaturated hydrocarbons

hydrocéphale [idʀosefal] 1 ADJ hydrocephalic, hydrocephalous 2 NMF person suffering from hydrocephalus

hydrocéphalie [idʀosefali] NF hydrocephalus

hydrocortisone [idʀokɔʀtizɔn] NF hydrocortisone

hydrocution [idʀokysjɔ̃] NF (*Méd*) immersion syncope

hydrodynamique [idʀodinamik] 1 ADJ hydrodynamic 2 NF hydrodynamics *sg*

hydro(-)électricité [idʀoelɛktʀisite] NF hydroelectricity

hydro(-)électrique [idʀoelɛktʀik] ADJ hydroelectric

hydrofoil [idʀofɔjl] NM hydrofoil (*boat*)

hydrofuge [idʀofyʒ] ADJ [*peinture*] waterrepellent

hydrogénation [idʀoʒenasjɔ̃] NF hydrogenation

hydrogène [idʀoʒɛn] NM hydrogen; **~ lourd** heavy hydrogen → **bombe**

hydrogéner [idʀoʒene] ▶ conjug 6 ◀ VT to hydrogenate, hydrogenize

hydroglisseur [idʀoglisœʀ] NM hydroplane, jet-foil

hydrographe [idʀogʀaf] NM hydrographer

hydrographie [idʀogʀafi] NF hydrography

hydrographique [idʀogʀafik] ADJ hydrographic(al)

hydrologie [idʀolɔʒi] NF hydrology

hydrologique [idʀolɔʒik] ADJ hydrologic(al)

hydrologiste [idʀolɔʒist], **hydrologue** [idʀolɔg] NMF hydrologist

hydrolyse [idʀoliz] NF hydrolysis

hydrolyser [idʀolize] ▶ conjug 1 ◀ VT to hydrolize

hydromel [idʀomɛl] NM mead

hydromètre [idʀomɛtʀ] NM (*Tech*) hydrometer

hydrométrie [idʀometʀi] NF hydrometry

hydrométrique [idʀometʀik] ADJ hydrometric(al)

hydrophile [idʀofil] ADJ [*lentilles cornéennes*] hydrophilic → **coton**

hydrophobe [idʀofɔb] ADJ, NMF hydrophobic

hydrophobie [idʀofɔbi] NF hydrophobia

hydropique [idʀopik] 1 ADJ dropsical, hydropic(al) 2 NMF person suffering from dropsy

hydropisie [idʀopizi] NF dropsy

hydroponique [idʀoponik] ADJ hydroponic; **culture ~** hydroponics *sg*, hydroponic gardening *ou* farming

hydroptère [idʀoptɛʀ] NM hydrofoil (*boat*)

hydrosoluble [idʀosolybl] ADJ water-soluble

hydrosphère [idʀosfɛʀ] NF hydrosphere

hydrostatique [idʀostatik] 1 ADJ hydrostatic 2 NF hydrostatics *sg*

hydrothérapie [idʀoteʀapi] NF (= *traitement*) hydrotherapy; (= *science*) hydrotherapeutics *sg*; **soins d'~** hydrotherapy treatments, water cures

hydrothérapique [idʀoteʀapik] ADJ [*traitement*] hydrotherapy (*épith*); [*science*] hydrotherapeutic

hydroxyde [idʀoksid] NM hydroxide

hyène [jɛn] NF hyena

hygiaphone® [iʒjafɔn] NM Hygiaphone® (*grill for speaking through at ticket counters etc*)

hygiène [iʒjɛn] NF hygiene; (= *science*) hygienics *sg*, hygiene; (*Scol*) health education; **ça manque d'~** it's not very hygienic; **~ corporelle** personal hygiene; [*femme*] **~ intime** personal hygiene; **~ mentale/publique** mental/public health; **~ du travail** industrial hygiene; **~ alimentaire** food hygiene; **pour une meilleure ~ de vie** for a healthier life; **il suffit d'avoir de l'~** you just need to be careful about hygiene; **n'avoir aucune ~** to have no sense of hygiene

hygiénique [iʒjenik] ADJ hygienic; **promenade ~** constitutional (walk) → **papier, seau, serviette**

hygiéniste [iʒjenist] NMF hygienist

hygromètre [igʀomɛtʀ] NM hygrometer

hygrométrie [igʀometʀi] NF hygrometry

hygrométrique [igʀometʀik] ADJ hygrometric

hygroscope [igʀoskɔp] NM hygroscope

hymen [imɛn] NM (*littér* = *mariage*) marriage; (*Anat*) hymen

hyménée [imene] NM (*littér*) marriage

hyménoptère [imenɔptɛʀ] NM hymenopteran; **les ~s** Hymenoptera

hymne [imn] NM (*Littérat, Rel*) hymn; **son discours était un ~ à la liberté** his speech was a hymn to liberty; **~ national** national anthem

hypallage [ipa(l)laʒ] NF hypallage

hyper(-)... [ipɛʀ] PRÉF **a** (*gén*) hyper(-)... **b** (*: + adj = très*) really; **hyper sympa*** really *ou* dead* nice; **hyper riche** mega* rich; **hyper important** really *ou* very important

hyper* [ipɛʀ] NM ABRÉV = **hypermarché**

hyperacidité [ipeʀasidite] NF hyperacidity

hyperactif, -ive [ipeʀaktif, iv] ADJ hyperactive

hyperactivité [ipeʀaktivite] NF hyperactivity

hyperbare [ipeʀbaʀ] ADJ hyperbaric

hyperbole [ipeʀbɔl] NF (*Math*) hyperbola; (*Littérat*) hyperbole

hyperbolique [ipeʀbɔlik] ADJ (*Math, Littérat*) hyperbolic

hyperboréen, -enne [ipeʀbɔʀeɛ̃, ɛn] ADJ hyperborean

hypercholestérolémie [ipeʀkɔlesteʀɔlemi] NF hypercholesterolaemia (*Brit*), hypercholesterolemia (*US*)

hypercorrect, e [ipeʀkɔʀɛkt] ADJ (*Ling*) hypercorrect

hypercorrection [ipeʀkɔʀɛksjɔ̃] NF (*Ling*) hypercorrection

hyperémotivité [ipeʀemɔtivite] NF excess emotionality

hyperespace [ipeʀɛspas] NM hyperspace

hyperesthésie [ipeʀestezi] NF hyperaesthesia (*Brit*), hyperesthesia (*US*)

hyperfocal, e (*mpl* -**aux**) [ipeʀfɔkal, o] ADJ hyperfocal

hyperfréquence [ipeʀfʀekɑ̃s] NF very *ou* ultra high frequency

hyperglycémie [ipeʀglisemi] NF hyperglycaemia (*Brit*), hyperglycemia (*US*)

hyperinflation [ipeʀɛ̃flasjɔ̃] NF hyperinflation

hypermarché [ipeʀmaʀʃe] NM hypermarket, superstore

hypermétrope [ipeʀmetʀɔp] 1 ADJ long-sighted, far-sighted (*US*), hypermetropic (*SPÉC*) 2 NMF long-sighted *ou* far-sighted (*US*) *ou* hypermetropic (*SPÉC*) person

hypermétropie [ipeʀmetʀɔpi] NF long-sightedness, far-sightedness (*US*), hypermetropia (*SPÉC*)

hypernerveux, -euse [ipeʀnɛʀvø, øz] ADJ very highly strung (*Brit*), very high strung (*US*)

hypernervosité [ipeʀnɛʀvozite] NF extreme nervous tension

hyperonyme [ipeʀonim] NM superordinate

hyperplasie [ipeʀplazi] NF hyperplasia

hyperréalisme [ipeʀʀealism] NM hyperrealism

hyperréaliste [ipeʀʀealist] ADJ, NMF hyperrealist

hypersécrétion [ipeʀsekʀesjɔ̃] NF hypersecretion

hypersensibilité [ipeʀsɑ̃sibilite] NF hypersensitivity, hypersensitiveness

hypersensible [ipeʀsɑ̃sibl] ADJ hypersensitive

hypersonique [ipeʀsonik] ADJ hypersonic

hypertendu, e [ipeʀtɑ̃dy] 1 ADJ suffering from high blood pressure *ou* from hypertension (*SPÉC*) 2 NM,F hypertensive

hypertension [ipeʀtɑ̃sjɔ̃] NF **~ (artérielle)** high blood pressure, hypertension (*SPÉC*); **faire de l'~** to suffer from *ou* have high blood pressure

hypertexte [ipeʀtɛkst] NM (*Ordin*) hypertext; **lien ~** hypertext link; **navigation en (mode) ~** browsing hypertext

hyperthermie [ipeʀtɛʀmi] NF hyperthermia; **traiter qn par ~** to give sb hyperthermia treatment

hyperthyroïdie [ipeʀtiʀoidi] NF hyperthyroidism

hypertrophie [ipeʀtʀofi] NF (*Méd*) hypertrophy; [*ville, secteur*] overdevelopment

hypertrophié, e [ipeʀtʀofje] ADJ [*muscle*] hypertrophied, abnormally enlarged; [*administration, bureaucratie, secteur*] overdeveloped, hypertrophied

hypertrophier [ipeʀtʀofje] ▶ conjug 7 ◀ 1 VT to hypertrophy 2 **s'hypertrophier** VPR (*Méd*) to hypertrophy; [*ville, secteur*] to become overdeveloped

hypertrophique [ipeʀtʀofik] ADJ hypertrophic

hypervitaminose [ipeʀvitaminoz] NF hypervitaminosis

hypnose [ipnoz] NF hypnosis; **sous ~** ◊ **en état d'~** under hypnosis

hypnotique [ipnotik] ADJ (*lit*) hypnotic; (*fig*) hypnotic, mesmeric, mesmerizing

hypnotiser [ipnotize] ▶ conjug 1 ◀ VT (*lit*) to hypnotize; (*fig*) to hypnotize, mesmerize

hypnotiseur [ipnotizœʀ] NM hypnotist

hypnotisme [ipnotism] NM hypnotism

hypo... [ipo] PRÉF hypo...

hypoallergénique [ipoalɛʀʒenik], **hypoallergique** [ipoalɛʀʒik] ADJ hypoallergenic

hypocagne [ipɔkaɲ] NF = **hypokhâgne**

hypocalorique [ipokalɔrik] ADJ [aliment, régime] low-calorie (épith)

hypocentre [iposɑ̃tr] NM hypocentre

hypocondriaque [ipɔkɔ̃drijak] ADJ, NM,F (Méd) hypochondriac

hypocondrie [ipɔkɔ̃dri] NF hypochondria

hypocrisie [ipɔkrizi] NF hypocrisy

hypocrite [ipɔkrit] 1 ADJ hypocritical 2 NMF hypocrite

hypocritement [ipɔkritmɑ̃] ADV hypocritically

hypodermique [ipɔdɛrmik] ADJ hypodermic

hypofertile [ipofɛrtil] ADJ [personne] suffering from low fertility

hypofertilité [ipofɛrtilite] NF [personne] low fertility

hypogastre [ipɔgastr] NM hypogastrium

hypogée [ipɔʒe] NM (Archéol) hypogeum

hypoglycémie [ipoglisemi] NF hypoglycaemia (Brit), hypoglycemia (US); **avoir** ou **faire une crise d'~** to suffer an attack of hypoglycaemia

hypoglycémique [ipoglisemik] 1 ADJ hypoglycaemic (Brit), hypoglycemic (US); **évanouissement/coma ~** fainting fit/coma brought on by an attack of hypoglycaemia 2 NMF person suffering from hypoglycaemia

hypokhâgne [ipokaɲ] NF first year of two-year preparatory course for the arts section of the École normale supérieure → GRANDES ÉCOLES ; CLASSES PRÉPARATOIRES ; CONCOURS

hyponyme [ipɔnim] NM hyponym

hypophysaire [ipofizɛr] ADJ pituitary, hypophyseal (SPÉC); **glande/hormone ~** pituitary gland/hormone; **nanisme d'origine ~** dwarfism caused by pituitary growth hormone deficiency

hypophyse [ipɔfiz] NF pituitary gland, hypophysis (SPÉC)

hyposodé, e [iposɔde] ADJ low-salt (épith), low in salt (attrib)

hypostase [ipostaz] NF (Méd, Rel) hypostasis

hypostyle [ipostil] ADJ hypostyle

hypotaupe [ipotop] NF first year of two-year preparatory course for the science section of the Grandes Écoles

hypotendu, e [ipotɑ̃dy] 1 ADJ suffering from low blood pressure ou from hypotension (SPÉC) 2 NM,F hypotensive

hypotension [ipotɑ̃sjɔ̃] NF low blood pressure, hypotension (SPÉC)

hypoténuse [ipotenyz] NF hypotenuse

hypothalamus [ipɔtalamys] NM hypothalamus

hypothécable [ipɔtekabl] ADJ mortgageable

hypothécaire [ipɔtekɛr] ADJ (gén) hypothecary; [marché, prêt] mortgage (épith); **garantie ~** mortgage security

hypothèque [ipɔtɛk] NF a (Jur) mortgage; **prendre une ~ sur l'avenir** to mortgage the future b (= obstacle) obstacle; (Pol) **lever l'~** to take away the obstacle

hypothéquer [ipɔteke] ▸ conjug 6 ◂ VT [+ maison] to mortgage; [+ créance] to secure (by mortgage); [+ avenir] to mortgage

hypothermie [ipɔtɛrmi] NF hypothermia

hypothèse [ipɔtɛz] NF (gén) hypothesis, assumption; (Sci) hypothesis; **émettre l'~ que** (gén) to suggest the possibility that; (Sci) to theorize that; **prenons comme ~ que** let's assume ou suppose that; **l'~ du suicide n'a pas été écartée** the possibility of suicide has not been ruled out; **en toute ~** in any case ou event, no matter what happens; **dans l'~ où ...** in the event that ...; **dans l'~ de leur victoire** in the event of their winning, should they win, supposing they win; **dans la meilleure/pire des ~s** at best/worst; **je le pense mais ce n'est qu'une ~** I think so but it's only a hypothesis ou I'm just hypothesizing; **en être réduit aux ~s** to be reduced to speculation ou guessing; **~ d'école** purely hypothetical case; **~ de travail** working hypothesis

hypothétique [ipɔtetik] ADJ hypothetical; (Jur) **cas ~** moot case

hypothétiquement [ipɔtetikmɑ̃] ADV hypothetically

hypovitaminose [ipovitaminoz] NF hypovitaminosis

hypoxie [ipɔksi] NF hypoxia; (Sport) **entraînement en ~** altitude training

hysope [izɔp] NF hyssop

hystérectomie [isterɛktɔmi] NF hysterectomy

hystérie [isteri] NF (Méd) hysteria; **~ collective** mass hysteria; **c'était l'~ dans le public** the audience went wild ou crazy; **faire** ou **avoir une crise d'~** (Méd) to have an attack of hysteria, have a fit of hysterics; (excitation) to become hysterical

hystérique [isterik] 1 ADJ hysterical 2 NMF (Méd) hysteric; (péj) **c'est un ~** he's the hysterical sort

hystérographie [isterɔgrafi] NF hysterography

Hz (ABRÉV = **hertz**) Hz

I

I, i [i] NM (= *lettre*) I, i → **droit²**, **point¹**

IAD [iade] NF (ABRÉV = **insémination artificielle avec donneur**) DI; **enfant né d'~** *ou* **par ~** DI baby, baby conceived by DI

iambe [jɑ̃b] NM (*Littérat*) (= *pied*) iambus, iambic; (= *vers*, *poème*) iambic

iambique [jɑ̃bik] ADJ iambic

IAO [iao] NF (ABRÉV = **ingénierie assistée par ordinateur**) CAE

ibère [ibɛʀ] **1** ADJ Iberian **2** **Ibère** NMF Iberian

ibérique [ibeʀik] **1** ADJ Iberian → **péninsule** **2** **Ibérique** NMF Iberian

ibid [ibid], **ibidem** [ibidɛm] ADV ibid, ibidem

ibis [ibis] NM ibis

Ibiza [ibiza] NF Ibiza

Icare [ikaʀ] NM Icarus

iceberg [ajsbɛʀg] NM iceberg; **la partie immergée** *ou* **cachée de l'~** (*lit*) the invisible part of the iceberg; (*fig*) the hidden aspects of the problem; (*lit, fig*) **la partie visible de l'~** the tip of the iceberg

icelui [isəlɥi], **icelle** [isɛl] (*mpl* **iceux** [isø]) (*fpl* **icelles** [isɛl]) PRON (††, *hum, Jur*) = **celui-ci, celle-ci, ceux-ci, celles-ci** ; → **celui**

ichtyologie [iktjɔlɔʒi] NF ichthyology

ichtyologique [iktjɔlɔʒik] ADJ ichthyologic(al)

ichtyologiste [iktjɔlɔʒist] NMF ichthyologist

ichtyosaure [iktjozɔʀ] NM ichthyosaur

ici [isi] ADV **a** (*dans l'espace*) here; (*à un chien*) **~!** here!; **loin/près d'~** far from/near here; **il y a 10 km d'~ à Paris** it's 10 km from here to Paris; **c'est à 10 minutes d'~** it's 10 minutes away (from here); **passez par ~** come this way; **par ~ s'il vous plaît** this way please; **par ~** (= *dans le coin*) around here; (*au marché*) **par ~, Mesdames, par ~ les belles laitues!** this way, ladies, lovely lettuces this way! *ou* over here!; **par ~ la sortie** this way out; **~ même** on this very spot, in this very place; **c'est ~ que ...** this is the place where ..., it is here that ...; **~ on est un peu isolé** we're a bit cut off (out) here; **le bus vient jusqu'~** the bus comes as far as this *ou* this far → **soupe**
b (*dans le temps*) **d'~ demain/la fin de la semaine** by tomorrow/the end of the week; **d'~ peu** before (very) long, shortly; **d'~ là** before then, in the meantime; **jusqu'~** (up) until now; (*dans le passé*) (up) until then; **d'~ (à ce) qu'il se retrouve en prison, ça ne va pas être long** it won't be long before he lands up in jail (again); **d'~ (à ce) qu'il accepte, ça risque de faire long** it might be (quite) some time before he says yes; **le projet lui plaît, mais d'~ à ce qu'il accepte!** he likes the plan, but there's a difference between just liking it and actually agreeing to it!; **d'~ à l'an 2050** by the year 2050
c (*loc*) **ils sont d'~ ou ne sont pas d'~** they are/ aren't local *ou* from around here; **les gens d'~** the local people; **je vois ça d'~!*** I can just see that!; **tu vois d'~ la situation/sa tête!*** you can (just) imagine the situation/the look on his

face!; **vous êtes ~ chez vous** please make yourself (quite) at home; **~ présent** here present; **«~ Chantal Barry»** (*au téléphone*) "Chantal Barry speaking *ou* here"; (*à la radio*) "this is Chantal Barry"; **~ et là** here and there; **~ comme ailleurs** *ou* **partout** here as anywhere else

ici-bas [isiba] ADV (*Rel, hum*) here below; **les choses d'~** things of this world *ou* of this life; **la vie (d')~** life here below

icône [ikon] NF (*Art, Ordin*) icon

iconoclasme [ikɔnɔklasm] NM iconoclasm

iconoclaste [ikɔnɔklast] **1** ADJ iconoclastic **2** NMF iconoclast

iconographe [ikɔnɔgʀaf] NMF iconographer

iconographie [ikɔnɔgʀafi] NF (= *étude*) iconography; (= *images*) (collection of) illustrations

iconographique [ikɔnɔgʀafik] ADJ iconographic(al)

ictère [iktɛʀ] NM icterus

id (ABRÉV = **idem**) ditto, idem

Idaho [idao] NM Idaho

idéal, e (*mpl* **-als** *ou* **-aux**) [ideal, o] **1** ADJ (= *imaginaire*) ideal; (= *rêvé, parfait*) [*maison, vacances*] ideal **2** NM **a** (= *modèle, aspiration*) ideal; (= *valeurs morales*) ideals; **il n'a pas d'~** he has no ideals **b** (= *le mieux*) **l'~ serait qu'elle l'épouse** the ideal thing *ou* solution would be for her to marry him, it would be ideal if she were to marry him *ou* if she married him; **ce n'est pas l'~** it's not ideal; **dans l'~ c'est ce qu'il faudrait faire** ideally that's what we should do

idéalement [idealmɑ̃] ADV ideally

idéalisation [idealizasjɔ̃] NF idealization

idéaliser [idealize] ▸ conjug 1 ◂ VT to idealize

idéalisme [idealism] NM idealism

idéaliste [idealist] **1** ADJ (*gén*) idealistic; (*Philo*) idealist **2** NMF idealist

▾**idée** [ide] **1** NF **a** (= *concept*) idea; **l'~ de nombre/de beauté** the idea of number/of beauty; **l'~ que les enfants se font du monde** the idea *ou* concept children have of the world; **c'est lui qui a eu le premier l'~ d'un moteur à réaction** it was he who first thought of *ou* conceived the idea of the jet engine, he was the first to hit upon the idea of the jet engine
b (= *pensée*) idea; **il a eu l'~** *ou* **l'~ lui est venue de faire** he had the idea *ou* hit upon the idea of doing; **l'~ ne lui viendrait jamais de nous aider** it would never occur to him to help us, he would never think of helping us; **ça m'a donné l'~ qu'il ne viendrait pas** that made me think that he wouldn't come; **à l'~ de faire qch/de qch** at the idea *ou* thought of doing sth/of sth; **tout est dans l'~ qu'on s'en fait** it's all in the mind; **avoir une ~ derrière la tête** to have something at the back of one's mind; **ça va lui remettre les ~s en place!** that'll teach him!; **~ directrice** driving principle → **changer, haut, ordre¹**
c (= *illusion*) idea; **tu te fais des ~s** you're im-

agining things; **ne te fais pas des ~s** don't get ideas into your head; **ça pourrait lui donner des ~s** it might give him ideas *ou* put ideas into his head; **quelle ~!** the (very) idea!, what an idea!; **il a de ces ~s!** the ideas he has!, the things he thinks up!

d (= *suggestion*) idea; **quelle bonne ~!** what a good idea!; **quelques ~s pour votre jardin** a few ideas *ou* suggestions for your garden; **de nouvelles ~s-vacances/-rangement** some new holiday/storage tips *ou* hints; **~-cadeau** gift idea; **~-recette** recipe idea

e (= *vague notion*) idea; **donner à qn/se faire une ~ des difficultés** to give sb/get an *ou* some idea of the difficulties; **avez-vous une ~** *ou* **la moindre ~ de l'heure/de son âge?** have you got any idea of the time/of his age?; **je n'en ai pas la moindre ~** I haven't the faintest *ou* least *ou* slightest idea; **vous n'avez pas ~ de sa bêtise** you've no idea how stupid he is; **on n'a pas ~ (de faire des choses pareilles)!*** it's incredible (doing things like that!); **j'ai (comme une) ~ qu'il n'acceptera pas** I (somehow) have an idea *ou* a feeling *ou* I have a sort of feeling that he won't accept; **j'ai mon ~** *ou* **ma petite ~ sur la question** I have my own ideas on the subject

f (= *opinion*) **~s** ideas, views; **~s politiques/ religieuses** political/religious ideas *ou* views; **avoir des ~s avancées** to have progressive ideas; **ce n'est pas dans ses ~s** he doesn't hold with these views; **avoir des ~s larges/ étroites** to be broad-minded/narrow-minded; (*péj*) **avoir les ~s courtes** to have limited ideas

g (= *goût, conception personnelle*) ideas; **juger selon** *ou* **à son ~** to judge in accordance with one's own ideas; **agir selon** *ou* **à son ~** to act *ou* do as one sees fit; **il n'en fait qu'à son ~** he just does as he likes; **pour être décorateur il faut de l'~** *ou* **un peu d'~** to be a decorator you have to have some imagination *ou* a few ideas; **il y a de l'~*** (*dessin, projet*) there's something in it; (*décoration intérieure*) it's got (a certain) something

h (= *esprit*) **avoir dans l'~ que** to have an idea that, have it in one's mind that; **il a dans l'~ de partir au Mexique** he's thinking of going to Mexico; **ça m'est sorti de l'~** it went clean* *ou* right out of my mind *ou* head; **cela ne lui viendrait jamais à l'~** it would never occur to him *ou* enter his head; **on ne m'ôtera pas de l'~ qu'il a menti** you won't get me to believe that he didn't lie; **il s'est mis dans l'~ de ...** he took *ou* got it into his head to ...

2 COMP ▸ **idée fixe** idée fixe, obsession ▸ **idée de génie, idée lumineuse** brilliant idea, brainwave ▸ **idées noires** black *ou* gloomy thoughts; **il a souvent des ~s noires** he suffers from depression ▸ **idée reçue** generally accepted idea, received idea

idée-force (*pl* **idées-forces**) [idefɔʀs] NF key idea

idem [idɛm] ADV ditto, idem; **il a mauvais caractère et son frère ~*** he's bad-tempered and so is his brother *ou* and his brother's the

▸ GRAMMAIRE ACTIVE: **idée** 28, 33.2, 53.1, 53.3, 53.5

same; **une bière — ~ pour moi*** a beer — (the) same for me

identifiable [idãtifjabl] ADJ identifiable

identificateur, -trice [idãtifikatœʀ, tʀis] 1 ADJ identifying (épith), identity (épith) 2 NM a (à la morgue) morgue employee b (Ling, Ordin) identifier

identification [idãtifikasjɔ̃] NF identification (**à, avec** with)

identifier [idãtifje] ▶conjug 7◀ 1 VT (= reconnaître) to identify; (= assimiler à) **~ qch/qn à** ou **avec** ou **et** to identify sth/sb with 2 **s'identifier** VPR **s'~ à** (= se mettre dans la peau de) [+ personnage, héros] to identify with; (= être l'équivalent de) to identify o.s. with, become identified with

identique [idãtik] ADJ identical (**à** to); **elle reste toujours ~ à elle-même** she never changes, she's always the same; **cette maison a été refaite à l'~** the house was rebuilt exactly as it was

identiquement [idãtikmã] ADV identically

identitaire [idãtitɛʀ] ADJ **crise ~** [individu] identity crisis; [pays] crisis surrounding issues of national ou ethnic identity; **quête ~** search for identity; **sentiment ~** sense of identity; **les revendications ~s des multiples ethnies** the various ethnic groups' demands for recognition

identité [idãtite] NF a (= similarité) identity, similarity; (Psych : = égalité) identity; **une ~ de goûts les rapprocha** (their) similar tastes brought them together; (Math) **~ (remarquable)** identity b (Admin) identity; **~ culturelle** cultural identity; **~ d'emprunt** assumed ou borrowed identity; **vérification/papiers d'~** identity check/papers; **l'Identité judiciaire** ≈ the Criminal Records Office → **carte, pièce**

idéogramme [ideɔgʀam] NM ideogram

idéographie [ideɔgʀafi] NF ideography

idéographique [ideɔgʀafik] ADJ ideographic(al)

idéologie [ideɔlɔʒi] NF ideology

idéologique [ideɔlɔʒik] ADJ ideological

idéologue [ideɔlɔg] NMF ideologist

ides [id] NFPL (Antiq) ides; **les ~ de mars** the ides of March

id est [idɛst] LOC CONJ id est

idiolecte [idjɔlɛkt] NM idiolect

idiomatique [idjɔmatik] ADJ idiomatic; **expression ~** idiom, idiomatic expression

idiome [idjom] NM (Ling) idiom

idiosyncrasie [idjosɛ̃kʀazi] NF idiosyncrasy

idiot, e [idjo, idjɔt] 1 ADJ [action, personne, histoire, erreur] idiotic, stupid; [accident] stupid; (†: Méd) idiotic; **dis-le moi, je ne veux pas mourir ~*** tell me, I don't want to go to my grave without knowing ou I don't want to die in ignorance 2 NM,F (gén) idiot, fool; (†: Méd) idiot; **ne fais pas l'~*** (= n'agis pas bêtement) don't be an idiot ou a fool; (= ne simule pas la bêtise) stop acting stupid*; **l'~ du village** the village idiot

idiotement [idjɔtmã] ADV idiotically, stupidly, foolishly

idiotie [idjɔsi] NF a [action, personne] idiocy, stupidity; (Méd) idiocy b (= action) idiotic ou stupid ou foolish thing to do; (= parole) idiotic ou stupid ou foolish thing to say; (= livre, film) trash (NonC), rubbish (NonC) (Brit); **ne va pas voir cette ~** ou **de telles ~s** don't go and see such trash ou rubbish (Brit); **et ne dis/fais pas d'~s** and don't say/do anything stupid ou idiotic

idiotisme [idjɔtism] NM idiom, idiomatic phrase

idoine [idwan] ADJ (Jur, hum = approprié) appropriate, fitting

idolâtre [idɔlɑtʀ] 1 ADJ (Rel) idolatrous (de

of); (fig) [public, foule] adulatory 2 NM (Rel) idolater 3 NF (Rel) idolatress

idolâtrer [idɔlɑtʀe] ▶conjug 1◀ VT to idolize

idolâtrie [idɔlɑtʀi] NF (Rel, fig) idolatry

idole [idɔl] NF (= personne, = artiste, Rel) idol; **il est devenu l'~ des jeunes** he's become a teenage idol

IDS [idees] NF (ABRÉV = **initiative de défense stratégique**) SDI

idylle [idil] NF (= poème) idyll; (= amour) romance, idyll; **ce n'est plus l'~ entre les patrons et les syndicats** the honeymoon is over between management and unions

idyllique [idilik] ADJ idyllic

i.e. (ABRÉV = **id est**) i.e.

if [if] NM a (= arbre) yew (tree); (= bois) yew b (= égouttoir à bouteilles) draining rack

IFOP [ifɔp] NM (ABRÉV = **Institut français d'opinion publique**) French public opinion research institute, ≈ MORI

IGF [iʒeɛf] NM (ABRÉV = **impôt sur les grandes fortunes**) → **impôt**

igloo [iglu] NM igloo

IGN [iʒeɛn] NM (ABRÉV = **Institut géographique national**) → **institut**

Ignace [iɲas] NM Ignatius; **saint ~ de Loyola** (St) Ignatius Loyola

igname [iɲam] NF yam

ignare [iɲaʀ] (péj) 1 ADJ ignorant 2 NMF ignoramus

igné, e [igne, iɲe] ADJ a (littér = ardent) fiery b (Géol) igneous

ignifugation [iɲifygasjɔ̃] NF fireproofing

ignifuge [iɲifyʒ] 1 ADJ [produit] fireproofing (épith), fire-retardant 2 NM fireproofing ou fire-retardant material ou substance

ignifugé, e [iɲifyʒe] (ptp de **ignifuger**) ADJ fireproof(ed)

ignifugeant, e [iɲifyʒã, ãt] 1 ADJ fireproofing (épith), fire-retardant 2 NM fireproofing ou fire-retardant material ou substance

ignifuger [iɲifyʒe] ▶conjug 3◀ VT to fireproof

ignoble [iɲɔbl] ADJ [conduite, personne] ignoble, vile, base; [crime] sordid, hideous; [breuvage, nourriture] vile, revolting; [temps] rotten, foul; [taudis] squalid; **c'est ~ !** it's appalling!; **il est ~ ! ◊ quel ~ individu !** he's disgusting!; **il a été ~ avec moi** he was horrible to me

ignoblement [iɲɔbləmã] ADV ignobly, vilely, basely

ignominie [iɲɔmini] NF a (= caractère) ignominy; (= acte) ignominious ou disgraceful act; **c'est une ~ !** it's a disgrace! b (= déshonneur) ignominy, disgrace

ignominieusement [iɲɔminjøzmã] ADV ignominiously

ignominieux, -ieuse [iɲɔminjø, jøz] ADJ ignominious

ignorance [iɲɔʀãs] NF a (= inculture) ignorance; (= méconnaissance) **~ de** ignorance of; **tenir qn/être dans l'~ de qch** to keep sb/be in ignorance of sth ou in the dark about sth; **dans l'~ des résultats** ignorant of the results; **d'une ~ crasse*** pig ignorant* b (= lacune) **de graves ~s en anglais/en matière juridique** serious gaps in his knowledge of English/of legal matters; **cet ouvrage permet de dissiper des ~s** this book helps to dispel people's ignorance → **pécher**

ignorant, e [iɲɔʀã, ãt] 1 ADJ (= ne sachant rien) ignorant (**en** about); (= ne connaissant pas) **~ de** ignorant ou unaware of; **~ des usages, il ...** ignorant ou unaware of the customs, he ..., not knowing the customs, he ... 2 NM,F ignoramus; **quel ~ tu fais !** what an ignoramus you are!; **ne fais pas l'~** stop pretending you don't know; **parler en ~** to speak from ignorance

ignoré, e [iɲɔʀe] (ptp de **ignorer**) ADJ [travaux, chercheurs, événement] unknown; **~ de tous** (inconnu) unknown to anybody; (boudé) ignored by all; **vivre ~** to live in obscurity

▼ **ignorer** [iɲɔʀe] ▶conjug 1◀ 1 VT a (= ne pas connaître) [+ incident] to be unaware of, not to know about ou of; [+ fait, artiste] not to know; **j'ignore comment/si ...** I don't know how/if ...; **vous n'ignorez certainement pas que .../ comment ...** you (will) doubtless know that .../how ..., you're no doubt well aware that .../how ...; **je l'ignore** I don't know; **j'ignore la réponse** I don't know the answer; **j'ignore tout de cette affaire** I don't know anything ou I know nothing about this business; **je n'ignorais pas ces problèmes** I was (fully) aware of these problems, I was not unaware of these problems; **j'ignore avoir dit cela** I am not aware of having said that → **nul** b (= être indifférent à) [+ personne, remarque, avertissement] to ignore c (= être sans expérience de) [+ plaisir, guerre, souffrance] not to know, to have had no experience of; (hum) **des gosses qui ignorent le savon** kids who have never seen (a cake of) soap ou who are unaware of the existence of soap; **des joues qui ignorent le rasoir** cheeks that never see a razor

2 **s'ignorer** VPR a (= se méconnaître) **une tendresse qui s'ignore** an unconscious tenderness; **c'est un poète qui s'ignore** he should have been a poet b (= être indifférents l'un à l'autre) to ignore each other

IGPN [iʒepeɛn] NF (ABRÉV = **Inspection générale de la police nationale**) → **inspection**

IGS [iʒeɛs] NF (ABRÉV = **Inspection générale des services**) → **inspection**

iguane [igwan] NM iguana

iguanodon [igwanɔdɔ̃] NM iguanodon

ikebana [ikebana] NM ikebana

il [il] PRON PERS M a (= personne) he; (= bébé, animal) it, he; (= chose) it; (= bateau, nation) she, it; **ils** they; **il était journaliste** he was a journalist; **prends ce fauteuil, il est plus confortable** have this chair — it's more comfortable; **je me méfie de son chien, il mord** I don't trust his dog — it bites; **l'insecte emmagasine la nourriture qu'il trouve** the insect stores the food it finds; **le Japon/le Canada a décidé qu'il n'accepterait pas** Japan/Canada decided she ou they ou it wouldn't accept → **avoir** b (impers) it; **il fait beau** it's a fine day; **il y a un enfant/trois enfants** there is a child/are three children; **il est vrai que ...** it is true that ...; **il faut que je le fasse** I've got to ou I must do it → **fois** c (interrog emphatique) **Paul est-il rentré ?** is Paul back?; **le courrier est-il arrivé ?** has the mail come?; **les enfants sont-ils bien couverts ?** are the children warmly wrapped up?; **il est si beau cet enfant/cet arbre** this child/tree is so beautiful; **tu sais, ton oncle, il est arrivé*** your uncle has arrived you know

île [il] 1 NF island, isle (littér); **~ corallienne** coral island; **~ déserte** desert island; **les Îles** (= Antilles) the (French) West Indies; **l'~ de Ré/Bréhat** the île de Ré/Bréhat; **vivre dans une ~** to live on an island

2 COMP ► **les îles Anglo-Normandes** the Channel Islands ► **l'île de Beauté** Corsica ► **les îles Britanniques** the British Isles ► **l'île de la Cité** the Île de la Cité ► **l'île du Diable** Devil's Island ► **les îles Féroé** the Faroe Islands ► **île flottante** (Culin) île flottante, floating island ► **île de glace** (Géog) large ice floe ► **les îles ioniennes** the Ionian Islands ► **l'île de Man** the Isle of Man ► **les îles Marshall** the Marshall Islands ► **l'île Maurice** Mauritius ► **l'île de Pâques** Easter Island ► **les îles Scilly** the Scilly Isles, the Scillies ► **les îles Shetland**

➤ GRAMMAIRE ACTIVE: **ignorer** 33.3, 43.1

the Shetland Islands, Shetland ► **les îles de la Sonde** the Sunda Islands ► **les îles Sorlingues** = **les îles Scilly** ► **l'île de la Tortue** Tortuga, La Tortue ► **l'île de Vancouver** Vancouver Island ► **les îles du Vent/Sous-le-Vent** the Windward/Leeward Islands ► **les îles Vierges** the Virgin Islands ► **l'île de Wight** the Isle of Wight

Île-de-France [ildəfʀɑ̃s] NF **l'~** the Île-de-France (*Paris and the surrounding departments*)

iléon [ileɔ̃] NM ileum

Iliade [iljad] NF [*Littérat*] « **l'Iliade** » "the Iliad"

iliaque [iljak] ADJ iliac; **os ~** hip bone, innominate bone (*SPÉC*)

îlien, îlienne [iljɛ̃, iljɛn] ① ADJ island (*épith*) ② NM,F islander

ilion [iljɔ̃] NM ilium

illégal, e (*mpl* **-aux**) [i(l)legal, o] ADJ illegal; (*Admin*) unlawful; [*organisation, société*] illegal, outlawed; **c'est ~** it's illegal, it's against the law

illégalement [i(l)legalmɑ̃] ADV illegally; (*Admin*) unlawfully

illégalité [i(l)legalite] NF [*action*] illegality; (*Admin*) unlawfulness; (= *acte illégal*) illegality; **vivre dans l'~** to live outside the law; **se mettre dans l'~** to break the law

illégitime [i(l)leʒitim] ADJ ⓐ [*enfant*] illegitimate ⓑ [*acte, gouvernement*] illegitimate, illicit ⓒ [*optimisme, colère, crainte, soupçon*] unwarranted, unfounded; [*prétention, revendication*] unjustified

illégitimement [i(l)leʒitimmɑ̃] ADV illegitimately

illégitimité [i(l)leʒitimite] NF illegitimacy

illettré, e [i(l)letʀe] ADJ, NM,F illiterate; **les ~s** illiterates, illiterate people

illettrisme [i(l)letʀism] NM illiteracy; **campagne contre l'~** literacy campaign

illicite [i(l)lisit] ADJ illicit

illicitement [i(l)lisitmɑ̃] ADV illicitly

illico [i(l)liko] ADV (= *tout de suite*) **~ (presto)** right away, at once, pronto*, straightaway (*surtout Brit*)

illimité, e [i(l)limite] ADJ [*moyen, domaine, ressource*] unlimited, limitless; [*confiance*] boundless, unbounded, limitless; [*congé, durée*] indefinite, unlimited

Illinois [ilinwa] NM Illinois

illisibilité [i(l)lizibilite] NF illegibility

illisible [i(l)lizibl] ADJ (= *indéchiffrable*) illegible, unreadable; (= *mauvais*) unreadable

illogique [i(l)lɔʒik] ADJ illogical

illogiquement [i(l)lɔʒikmɑ̃] ADV illogically

illogisme [i(l)lɔʒism] NM illogicality

illumination [i(l)lyminasjɔ̃] NF ⓐ (= *éclairage*) lighting, illumination; (*avec des projecteurs*) floodlighting ⓑ (= *lumières*) **~s** illuminations, lights; **les ~s de Noël** the Christmas lights ou illuminations ⓒ (= *inspiration*) flash of inspiration; (*Rel*) inspiration

illuminé, e [i(l)lymine] (*ptp de* **illuminer**) ① ADJ (= *éclairé*) lit up (*attrib*), illuminated; (*avec des projecteurs*) floodlit; **il est comme ~ de l'intérieur** he seems to have a kind of inner light ② NM,F (*péj* = *visionnaire*) visionary, crank (*péj*)

illuminer [i(l)lymine] ► conjug 1 ◄ ① VT ⓐ (= *éclairer*) to light up, illuminate; (*avec des projecteurs*) to floodlight ⓑ [*joie, foi, colère*] to light up; (*Rel*) [+ *prophète, âme*] to enlighten, illuminate; **le bonheur illuminait son visage** his face shone ou was aglow with happiness; **un sourire illumina son visage** a smile lit up her face; **ça va ~ ma journée** that will brighten up my day ② **s'illuminer** VPR [*visage, ciel*] to light up (**de** with); [*rue, vitrine*] to be lit up

illusion [i(l)lyzjɔ̃] NF illusion; **~ d'optique** optical illusion; **ne te fais aucune ~** don't be under any illusion, don't delude ou kid* your-

self; **tu te fais des ~s** you're deluding ou kidding* yourself; **ça lui donne l'~ de servir à quelque chose** ou **qu'il sert à quelque chose** it gives him the illusion ou it makes him feel that he's doing something useful; **cet imposteur/ce stratagème ne fera pas ~ longtemps** this impostor/tactic won't delude ou fool people for long; **il a perdu ses ~s** he's become disillusioned, he's lost his illusions → **bercer**

illusionner [i(l)lyzjɔne] ► conjug 1 ◄ ① **s'illusionner** VPR to delude o.s. (**sur qch** about sth); **s'~ sur qn** to delude o.s. ou be mistaken about sb ② VT (= *induire en erreur*) to delude

illusionnisme [i(l)lyzjɔnism] NM conjuring

illusionniste [i(l)lyzjɔnist] NMF conjurer, illusionist

illusoire [i(l)lyzwaʀ] ADJ (= *trompeur*) illusory, illusive

illusoirement [i(l)lyzwaʀmɑ̃] ADV deceptively, illusorily

illustrateur, -trice [i(l)lystʀatœʀ, tʀis] NM,F illustrator; (*TV, Ciné*) **~ sonore** music arranger

illustratif, -ive [i(l)lystʀatif, iv] ADJ illustrative

illustration [i(l)lystʀasjɔ̃] NF ⓐ (= *gravure, exemple*) illustration; (= *iconographie*) illustrations; **à l'~ abondante** copiously illustrated ⓑ (= *action, technique*) illustration; **l'~ par l'exemple** illustration by example

illustre [i(l)lystʀ] ADJ illustrious, renowned; (*frm, iro*) **l'~ M. Pinot** the illustrious Mr Pinot; (*hum*) **un ~ inconnu** a person of obscure repute (*hum*)

illustré, e [i(l)lystʀe] ① ADJ illustrated ② NM (= *journal*) comic

▼ **illustrer** [i(l)lystʀe] ► conjug 1 ◄ ① VT ⓐ (*avec images, notes*) to illustrate (**de** with); **ça illustre bien son caractère** that's a good example of what he's like ⓑ (*littér* = *rendre célèbre*) to bring fame to, render illustrious (*littér*) ② **s'illustrer** VPR [*personne*] to win fame ou renown, become famous (**par, dans** through)

illustrissime [i(l)lystʀisim] ADJ†† most illustrious

ILM [iɛlɛm] NM (ABRÉV = **immeuble à loyer moyen** ou **modéré**) → **immeuble**

îlot [ilo] NM ⓐ (= *île*) small island, islet ⓑ (= *petite zone*) island; **~ de fraîcheur/de verdure** oasis ou island of coolness/of greenery; **~ de résistance/prospérité** pocket of resistance/prosperity ⓒ (= *groupe d'habitations*) (housing) block ⓓ (*Comm*) gondola ⓔ (*dans une rue*) **~ directionnel** traffic island

îlotage [ilotaʒ] NM community policing

ilote [ilot] NMF (*Hist*) Helot; (*littér*) slave, serf

îlotier [ilotje] NM ≈ community policeman

image [imaʒ] ① NF ⓐ (= *dessin*) picture; (*Scol*) picture given to pupils as a reward for good work; **les ~s d'un film** the frames of a film; (*Audiov*) **l'~ et le son** picture and sound; (*Ciné, TV*) **l'~ est nette/floue** the picture is clear/fuzzy; **popularisé par l'~** popularized by the camera; **en ~s** on film, in pictures; (*TV*) **apparaître à l'~** to appear on screen → **chasseur, livre¹, sage**
ⓑ **~ de** (= *représentation*) picture of; (= *ressemblance*) image of; **l'~ du père** the father figure; **une ~ fidèle de la France** an accurate picture of France; **ils présentent l'~ du bonheur** they are the picture of happiness; **fait à l'~ de** made in the image of; **Dieu créa l'homme à son ~** God created man in his own image; **donner une ~ saisissante de la situation** to paint a vivid picture of the situation
ⓒ (= *métaphore*) image; **les ~s chez Blake** Blake's imagery; **s'exprimer par ~s** to express o.s. in images
ⓓ (= *reflet*) (*gén*) reflection, image; (*Phys*) image; **regarder son ~ dans l'eau** to gaze at one's reflection in the water; **~ réelle/virtuelle** real/virtual image
ⓔ (= *vision mentale*) image, picture; (= *réputa-*

tion*) image; **~ visuelle/auditive** visual/auditory image; **~ de soi** self-image; **se faire une ~ fausse/idéalisée de qch** to have a false/an idealized picture of sth; **le pays veut améliorer/soigner son ~ à l'étranger** the country wants to improve/enhance its image abroad
② COMP ► **l'image animée** : **les ~s animées** (*gén*) moving pictures; (*Ordin*) animated graphics ► **images d'archives** library pictures ► **image d'Épinal** (*lit*) popular 18th/19th century print depicting traditional scenes of French life; (*fig*) **cette réunion familiale était une touchante ~ d'Épinal** the family reunion was a touching scene of traditional family life ► **image fixe** (*Ciné*) still (frame); (*Ordin*) still image ► **image de marque** [*produit*] brand image; [*parti, firme, politicien*] public image ► **image pieuse** holy picture ► **image radar** radar image ► **image satellite** satellite picture ► **image de synthèse** computer-generated image ou picture; **~s de synthèse** (*domaine*) computer graphics; (*animées*) computer animation

┌─────────────────────┐
│ **IMAGES D'ÉPINAL** │
└─────────────────────┘

Distinctive prints depicting a variety of scenes in a realistic but stereotypical manner were produced in the town of Épinal, in the Vosges, in the early nineteenth century. The prints became so popular that the term image d'Épinal *has passed into the language, and is now used to refer to any form of stereotypical representation.*

imagé, e [imaʒe] (*ptp de* **imager**) ADJ [*poème, texte*] full of imagery (*attrib*); (*euph*) [*langage*] colourful

imager [imaʒe] ► conjug 3 ◄ VT [+ *style, langage*] to embellish with images

imagerie [imaʒʀi] NF (*Hist* = *commerce*) coloured-print trade; (= *images, gravures*) prints; (*Littérat*) **l'~ romantique** romantic imagery; **l'~ médicale** medical imaging; **~ par résonance magnétique/par ultrasons** magnetic resonance/ultrasound imaging

imagier [imaʒje] NM (*Hist* = *peintre*) painter of popular pictures; (= *sculpteur*) sculptor of figurines; (= *imprimeur*) coloured-print maker; (= *vendeur*) print seller

imaginable [imaʒinabl] ADJ conceivable, imaginable; **difficilement ~** hard to imagine; **un tel comportement n'était pas ~ il y a 50 ans** such behaviour was inconceivable 50 years ago → **possible**

imaginaire [imaʒinɛʀ] ① ADJ (= *fictif*) imaginary; [*monde*] make-believe, imaginary; **ces persécutés/incompris ~s** these people who (falsely) believe they are ou believe themselves persecuted/misunderstood → **malade, nombre** ② NM **l'~** the imagination; **dans l'~ de Joyce** in Joyce's imaginative world ou universe

imaginatif, -ive [imaʒinatif, iv] ADJ imaginative; **c'est un grand ~** he has a vivid imagination

imagination [imaʒinasjɔ̃] NF (= *faculté*) imagination; (= *chimère, rêve*) imagination (*NonC*), fancy; **tout ce qu'il avait vécu en ~** everything he had experienced in his imagination; **ce sont de pures ~s** that's sheer imagination, those are pure fancies; **monstres sortis tout droit de son ~** monsters straight out of his imagination; **avoir de l'~** to be imaginative, have a good imagination; **avoir trop d'~** to imagine things; **une ~ débordante** a lively ou vivid imagination; **avec un peu d'~ ...** with a little imagination ...; (*slogan*) **l'~ au pouvoir !** power to the imagination!

▼ **imaginer** [imaʒine] ► conjug 1 ◄ ① VT ⓐ (= *se représenter, supposer*) to imagine; **~ que** to imagine that; **tu imagines la scène !** you can imagine ou picture the scene!; **on imagine mal** leurs conditions de travail their working conditions are hard to imagine; **je l'imaginais plus vieux** I imagined him to be older, I pictured him as being older; **qu'allez-vous ~ là?** what on earth are you thinking of?; (*ton de défi*) **et tu vas t'y opposer, j'imagine?** and I imagine ou suppose you're going to oppose it? **b** (= *inventer*) [+ *système, plan*] to devise, dream up; **qu'est-il encore allé ~?*** now what has he dreamed up? ou thought up?; **il a imaginé d'ouvrir un magasin** he has taken it into his head to open up a shop, he has dreamed up the idea of opening a shop

2 s'imaginer VPR **a** (= *se figurer*) to imagine; **imagine-toi une île paradisiaque** imagine ou picture an island paradise; **je me l'imaginais plus jeune** I imagined him to be younger, I pictured him as being younger; **comme on peut se l'~ ...** as you can (well) imagine ...; **imagine-toi que je n'ai pas que ça à faire!** look, I've got other things to do! **b** (= *se voir*) to imagine o.s., picture o.s.; **s'~ à 60 ans/en vacances** to imagine ou picture o.s. at 60/on holiday **c** (= *croire à tort que*) **s'~ que** to imagine ou think that; **il s'imaginait pouvoir faire cela** he imagined ou thought he could do that; **si tu t'imagines que je vais te laisser faire!** don't think I'm going to let you get away with that!

imago [imago] NF (*Bio, Psych*) imago

imam [imam] NM ima(u)m

imbattable [ɛ̃batabl] ADJ [*prix, personne, record*] unbeatable; **il est ~ aux échecs** he is unbeatable at chess

imbécile [ɛ̃besil] **1** ADJ (= *stupide*) stupid, idiotic; (†: *Méd*) imbecilic (*SPÉC*), idiotic **2** NMF **a** (= *idiot*) idiot, imbecile; **faire l'~*** to act ou play the fool; **ne fais pas l'~*** (= *n'agis pas bêtement*) don't be an idiot* ou a fool; (= *ne simule pas la bêtise*) stop acting stupid*; **le premier ~ venu te le dira** any fool will tell you; **c'est un ~ heureux** he's living in a fool's paradise; **les ~s heureux** the blissfully ignorant **b** (†: *Méd*) imbecile, idiot

imbécillité [ɛ̃besilite] NF **a** [*action, personne*] idiocy; (†: *Méd*) imbecility, idiocy **b** (= *action*) idiotic ou stupid ou imbecile thing to do; (= *propos*) idiotic ou stupid ou imbecile thing to say; (= *film, livre*) trash (*NonC*), rubbish (*NonC*) (*Brit*); **tu racontes des ~s** you're talking nonsense ou rubbish (*Brit*); **ne va pas voir de telles ~s** don't go and see such trash ou rubbish (*Brit*)

imberbe [ɛ̃bɛʁb] ADJ [*personne*] beardless, smooth-cheeked; [*visage*] beardless

imbiber [ɛ̃bibe] ▸ conjug 1 ◂ **1** VT (= *imprégner*) **~ un tampon/une compresse de** to soak ou moisten ou impregnate a pad/compress with; **imbibé d'eau** [+ *chaussures, étoffe*] saturated (with water), soaked; [+ *terre*] saturated, waterlogged; **gâteau imbibé de rhum** cake soaked in rum; **être imbibé*** (= *ivre*) to be sloshed*; (= *alcoolique*) to be a lush* **2 s'imbiber** VPR **s'~ de** to become saturated ou soaked with

imbit(t)able** [ɛ̃bitabl] ADJ **a** (= *difficile à comprendre*) fucking** hard to understand; **cette équation est ~** I don't understand this fucking** equation **b** (= *insupportable*) **il est ~** he's a fucking pain in the arse** (*Brit*) ou ass** (*US*)

imbrication [ɛ̃bʁikasjɔ̃] NF [*problèmes, souvenirs, parcelles*] interweaving; [*plaques, tuiles*] overlapping, imbrication (*SPÉC*)

imbriqué, e [ɛ̃bʁike] (*ptp de* **imbriquer**) ADJ [*plaques, tuiles*] overlapping, imbricate(d) (*SPÉC*); [*problèmes*] interwoven, interlinked; [*récits, souvenirs*] interwoven; [*économies, politiques*] interlinked; **les deux cultures sont étroitement ~es l'une dans l'autre** the two cul-

tures are inextricably interlinked ou deeply enmeshed

imbriquer [ɛ̃bʁike] ▸ conjug 1 ◂ **1 s'imbriquer** VPR [*problèmes, affaires*] to be linked ou interwoven; [*plaques*] to overlap (each other), imbricate (*SPÉC*); **ça s'imbrique l'un dans l'autre** [*cubes*] they fit into each other; [*problèmes*] they are linked ou interwoven; **ce nouveau problème est venu s'~ dans une situation déjà compliquée** this new problem has arisen to complicate an already complex situation **2** VT [+ *cubes*] to fit into each other; [+ *plaques*] to overlap

imbroglio [ɛ̃bʁɔljo] NM (*Théât, gén*) imbroglio

imbu, e [ɛ̃by] ADJ **~ de lui-même** ou **de sa personne** pompous, full of himself, full of self-importance; **un peuple ~ de préjugés** a people steeped in prejudice

imbuvable [ɛ̃byvabl] ADJ [*boisson*] undrinkable; (* = *mauvais*) [*personne*] unbearable, insufferable; [*film, livre*] unbearably awful*

IME [iɛmə] NM (ABRÉV = **Institut monétaire européen**) EMI

imitable [imitabl] ADJ which can be imitated, imitable; **facilement ~** easy to imitate, easily imitated

imitateur, -trice [imitatœʁ, tʁis] **1** ADJ imitative **2** NM,F imitator; (*Théât*) [*voix, personne*] impersonator; [*bruits*] imitator

imitatif, -ive [imitatif, iv] ADJ imitative

imitation [imitasjɔ̃] NF **a** (= *reproduction*) [*bruit*] imitation; (= *parodie*) [*personnage célèbre*] imitation, impersonation; [*voix, geste*] imitation, mimicry; (= *sketch*) impression, imitation, impersonation; **avoir le don d'~** to have a gift for imitating people ou for mimicry; **à l'~ de** in imitation of **b** [*héros, style*] imitation, copying **c** (= *contrefaçon*) [*document, signature*] forgery **d** (= *copie*) [*bijou, fourrure*] imitation; [*meuble, tableau*] copy, reproduction; **c'est en ~ cuir** it's imitation leather **e** (*Mus*) imitation

imiter [imite] ▸ conjug 1 ◂ VT **a** [+ *bruit*] to imitate; [+ *personnage célèbre*] to imitate, impersonate, take off* (*Brit*); [+ *voix, geste, accent*] to imitate, mimic **b** (= *prendre pour modèle*) [+ *héros, style, écrivain*] to imitate, copy **c** [+ *document, signature*] to forge **d** (= *faire comme*) **il se leva et tout le monde l'imita** he got up and everybody did likewise ou followed suit **e** (= *avoir l'aspect de*) [*matière, revêtement*] to look like; **un lino qui imite le marbre** lino made to look like marble, marble-effect lino

immaculé, e [imakyle] ADJ [*linge, surface*] spotless, immaculate; [*blancheur*] immaculate; [*réputation*] spotless, unsullied, immaculate; **d'un blanc ~** spotlessly white; (*Rel*) **l'Immaculée Conception** the Immaculate Conception

immanence [imanɑ̃s] NF immanence

immanent, e [imanɑ̃, ɑ̃t] ADJ immanent (**à** in) → **justice**

immangeable [ɛ̃mɑ̃ʒabl] ADJ uneatable, inedible

immanquable [ɛ̃mɑ̃kabl] ADJ [*cible, but*] impossible to miss (*attrib*); **c'était ~!** it had to happen!, it was bound to happen!, it was inevitable!

immanquablement [ɛ̃mɑ̃kabləmɑ̃] ADV inevitably, without fail

immatérialité [i(m)materjalite] NF immateriality

immatériel, -elle [i(m)materjɛl] ADJ [*légèreté, minceur, plaisir*] ethereal; (*Philo*) immaterial

immatriculation [imatʁikylasjɔ̃] NF (*gén*) registration (**à** with); (*Helv* = *inscription à l'université*) enrolment (*Brit*), enrollment (*US*), registration → **numéro, plaque**

IMMATRICULATION

The last two digits on vehicle number plates in France refer to the code number of the département where they were registered (cars registered in the Dordogne bear the number 24, for example).

immatriculer [imatʁikyle] ▸ conjug 1 ◂ VT [+ *véhicule, personne*] to register; **faire ~** [+ *véhicule*] to register; **se faire ~** to register (**à** with); **voiture immatriculée dans le Vaucluse** car with a Vaucluse registration number (*Brit*) ou with a Vaucluse license plate (*US*); **une voiture immatriculée CM 75** a car with CM 75 on its number plate (*Brit*) ou its license plate (*US*); (*Helv*) **s'~ (à l'université)** to enrol at university, register (as a student)

immature [imatyʁ] ADJ immature

immaturité [imatyʁite] NF (*littér*) immaturity

immédiat, e [imedja, jat] **1** ADJ (*gén, Philo*) immediate; [*soulagement*] immediate, instant (*épith*); **en contact ~ avec le mur** in direct contact with the wall; **dans l'avenir ~** in the immediate future; **la mort fut ~e** death was instantaneous **2** NM **dans l'~** for the time being, for the moment

immédiatement [imedjatmɑ̃] ADV immediately, at once, directly; **~ après** immediately after, straight after

immédiateté [imedjatte] NF (*Philo*) immediacy

immémorial, e (*mpl* -**iaux**) [i(m)memɔʁjal, jo] ADJ age-old; **depuis des temps immémoriaux** (*littér*) ◊ **de temps ~** from time immemorial

immense [i(m)mɑ̃s] ADJ [*océan, espace, horizon, désert*] boundless, vast, immense; [*foule, fortune, pays*] vast, immense, huge; [*personne*] (*très grand*) gigantic, extremely tall; [*avenir, bonté, sagesse*] boundless; [*influence, avantage, succès, talent*] immense, tremendous, huge; [*chagrin*] immense; **l'~ majorité des électeurs** the overwhelming majority of voters; **dans l'~ majorité des cas** in the vast majority of cases **b** (= *talentueux*) **c'est un ~ acteur/écrivain** he's a hugely talented actor/writer

immensément [i(m)mɑ̃semɑ̃] ADV immensely, tremendously

immensité [i(m)mɑ̃site] NF [*océan, espace, horizon, désert*] immensity; [*fortune, pays*] vastness; (*littér*) **le regard perdu dans l'~** gazing into infinity

immergé, e [imɛʁʒe] (*ptp de* **immerger**) ADJ [*terres*] submerged; [*plantes*] immerged; (*Élec*) [*câble*] laid under water; **~ par 100 mètres de fond** lying 100 metres down; **rochers ~s** submerged ou underwater rocks, rocks under water; **la partie ~e de la balise** the part of the buoy which is under water ou which is submerged; **~ dans ses problèmes** engrossed in ou taken up with his own problems; **économie ~e** black ou underground economy → **iceberg**

immerger [imɛʁʒe] ▸ conjug 3 ◂ **1** VT [+ *objet*] to immerse, submerge; [+ *fondations*] to build under water; [+ *déchets*] to dump at sea, dispose of at sea; [+ *câble*] to lay under water; [+ *corps*] to bury at sea; (*Rel*) [+ *catéchumène*] to immerse **2 s'immerger** VPR [*sous-marin*] to dive, submerge; **s'~ dans un travail** to immerse o.s. in a piece of work

immérité, e [imerite] ADJ undeserved, unmerited

immersion [imɛʁsjɔ̃] NF **a** [*objet*] immersion, submersion; [*fondations*] building under water; [*déchets*] dumping ou disposal at sea; [*câble*] laying under water; [*corps*] burying at sea; **baptême par ~** baptism by immersion; **par ~ totale dans la langue** by immersing oneself totally in the language **b** [*sous-marin*] diving, submersion **c** (*Astron*) immersion, ingress

immettable [ɛ̃metabl] ADJ [vêtement] unwearable

immeuble [imœbl] **1** NM **a** (= bâtiment) building; (à usage d'habitation) block of flats (Brit), apartment building (US) **b** (Jur) real estate (NonC) **2** ADJ [biens] real, immovable **3** COMP ► **immeuble de bureaux** office block (Brit) ou building (US) ► **immeuble d'habitation** residential block, apartment building (US) ► **immeuble à loyer moyen**, **immeuble à loyer modéré** ≈ block of council flats (Brit), ≈ low-rent building (US) ► **immeuble de rapport** residential property (for renting), investment property ► **immeuble à usage locatif** block of rented flats (Brit), rental apartment building (US) → **copropriété**

immigrant, e [imigrã, ãt] ADJ, NM,F immigrant

immigration [imigʀasjɔ̃] NF immigration; (**les services de**) **l'~** the immigration department; **~ clandestine** illegal immigration

immigré, e [imigʀe] (ptp de **immigrer**) ADJ, NM,F immigrant; **~ de la deuxième génération** second-generation immigrant; **~ clandestin** illegal immigrant

immigrer [imigʀe] ▸conjug 1◂ VI to immigrate (**à, dans** into)

imminence [iminãs] NF imminence

imminent, e [iminã, ãt] ADJ [danger, crise, départ] imminent, impending (épith)

immiscer (s') [imise] ▸conjug 3◂ VPR **s'~ dans** to interfere in ou with

immixtion [imiksjɔ̃] NF interference (**dans** in, with)

immobile [i(m)mɔbil] ADJ **a** [personne, eau, air, arbre] motionless, still; [visage] immobile; [pièce de machine] fixed; **regard ~** fixed stare; **rester ~** to stay ou keep still **b** (littér) [dogme] immovable; [institutions] unchanging, permanent

immobilier, -ière [imɔbilje, jɛʀ] **1** ADJ [vente, crise] property (épith); [succession] in real estate (attrib); **marché ~** property market; **biens ~s** real estate, real property (Brit); **la situation immobilière est satisfaisante** the property situation is satisfactory → **agence, société 2** NM **l'~** (Comm) the property business, the real-estate business; (Jur) real estate immovables

immobilisation [imɔbilizasjɔ̃] NF **a** [membre blessé, circulation] immobilization; **cela a entraîné l'~ totale de la circulation** that brought the traffic to a complete standstill, that brought about the complete immobilization of traffic; **attendez l'~ complète du train/de l'appareil** wait until the train is completely stationary/the aircraft has come to a complete standstill ou stop; **la réparation nécessite l'~ de la voiture/l'avion** the car will have to be taken off the road/the plane will have to be grounded to be repaired **b** (Jur) [bien] conversion into an immovable **c** (Fin) [capitaux] immobilization, tying up; **~s fixed assets** **d** (Sport) hold

immobiliser [imɔbilize] ▸conjug 1◂ **1** VT [+ troupes, membre blessé] to immobilize; [+ circulation, affaires] to bring to a standstill, immobilize; [+ machine, véhicule] (= stopper) to stop, bring to a halt ou standstill; (= empêcher de fonctionner) to immobilize; (Aut : avec un sabot) to clamp; (Jur) [+ biens] to convert into immovables; (Fin) to immobilize, tie up; **ça l'immobilise à son domicile** it keeps him housebound; **avions immobilisés par la neige** aeroplanes grounded by snow; **la peur l'immobilisa** he was paralyzed with fear, he was rooted to the spot with fear **2** **s'immobiliser** VPR [personne] to stop, stand still; [machine, véhicule, échanges commerciaux] to come to a halt ou a standstill

immobilisme [imɔbilism] NM [gouvernement, entreprise] failure to act; **faire de/être partisan de l'~** to try to maintain/support the status quo

immobiliste [imɔbilist] ADJ [politique] designed to maintain the status quo; **c'est un ~** he is a supporter of the status quo, he is opposed to progress

immobilité [imɔbilite] NF [personne, foule, eau, arbre] stillness, motionlessness; [visage] immobility; [regard] fixedness; [institutions] unchanging nature, permanence; **le médecin lui a ordonné l'~ complète** the doctor ordered him not to move (at all); **~ forcée** forced immobility; **~ politique** lack of political change, political inertia

immodération [imɔdeʀasjɔ̃] NF immoderation

immodéré, e [imɔdeʀe] ADJ immoderate, inordinate

immodérément [imɔdeʀemã] ADV immoderately, inordinately

immodeste [imɔdɛst] ADJ immodest

immodestie [imɔdɛsti] NF immodesty

immolation [imɔlasjɔ̃] NF (Rel) immolation; (= suicide) **~ (par le feu)** self-immolation

immoler [imɔle] ▸conjug 1◂ **1** VT (= sacrifier) to immolate (littér), sacrifice (**à** to); (littér = massacrer) to slay (littér); **il a été immolé sur l'autel des intérêts nationaux** he was sacrificed on the altar of national interest **2** **s'immoler** VPR to sacrifice o.s. (**à** to); **s'~ par le feu** to set fire to o.s., immolate o.s.

immonde [i(m)mɔ̃d] ADJ [taudis] squalid; [langage, action, personne] base, vile; [crime] sordid, hideous; (* = laid) ugly, hideous; (Rel) unclean; **il est ~!** he's disgusting!

immondices [i(m)mɔ̃dis] NFPL (= ordures) refuse (NonC); (littér) **commettre/proférer des ~** to do/say unspeakable things

immoral, e [i(m)mɔʀal, o] ADJ immoral

immoralisme [i(m)mɔʀalism] NM immoralism

immoraliste [i(m)mɔʀalist] ADJ, NMF immoralist

immoralité [i(m)mɔʀalite] NF immorality

immortaliser [imɔʀtalize] ▸conjug 1◂ **1** VT to immortalize **2** **s'immortaliser** VPR to win immortality, win eternal fame (**par** thanks to)

immortalité [imɔʀtalite] NF immortality

immortel, -elle [imɔʀtɛl] **1** ADJ immortal **2** **Immortel(le)** NM,F member of the Académie française **3** **immortelle** NF (= fleur) everlasting flower

immotivé, e [i(m)mɔtive] ADJ [action, crime] unmotivated; [réclamation, crainte] groundless

immuabilité [imɥabilite] NF = **immutabilité**

immuable [imɥabl] ADJ [lois, passion] unchanging, immutable; [paysage, routine] unchanging; [sourire] unchanging, perpetual; **il est resté ~ dans ses convictions** he remained unchanged in his convictions; **vêtu de son ~ complet à carreaux** wearing that eternal checked suit of his

immuablement [imɥabləmã] ADV [fonctionner, se passer] immutably; [triste, grognon] perpetually; **ciel ~ bleu** permanently ou perpetually blue sky

immun, e [imœ̃, yn] ADJ immune; **réponse/réaction ~e** immune response/reaction

immunisation [imynizasjɔ̃] NF immunization

immuniser [imynize] ▸conjug 1◂ VT (Méd) to immunize (**contre** against); (fig) **je suis immunisé** it no longer has any effect on me; **être immunisé contre les tentations** to be immune to temptation; **ça l'immunisera contre le désir de recommencer** this'll stop him ever ou this'll cure him of ever wanting to do it again; **il s'est immunisé contre leurs critiques** he's become immune ou impervious to their criticism

immunitaire [imynitɛʀ] ADJ immune; [défenses] immunological; [réactions] immune

immunité [imynite] NF (Bio, Jur) immunity; **~ diplomatique/parlementaire** diplomatic/ parliamentary immunity; **~ fiscale** immunity from taxation, tax immunity; **~ cellulaire** cell-mediated immunity → **levée**

immunodéficience [imynodefisjãs] NF immunodeficiency → **syndrome, virus**

immunodéficitaire [imynodefisitɛʀ] ADJ immunodeficient

immunodépresseur [imynodepʀesœʀ] ADJ, NM immunosuppressant, immunodepressant

immunodépressif, -ive [imynodepʀesif, iv] ADJ immunosuppressive, immunodepressive

immunodéprimé, e [imynodepʀime] ADJ immunosuppressed, immunocompromised

immunogène [imynɔʒɛn] ADJ immunogenic

immunoglobuline [imynoglɔbylin] NF immunoglobulin

immunologie [imynɔlɔʒi] NF immunology

immunologique [imynɔlɔʒik] ADJ immunological

immunologiste [imynɔlɔʒist] NMF immunologist

immunostimulant, e [imynostimylã, ãt] **1** ADJ [substance, traitement] that stimulates the immune system **2** NM immunostimulant

immunosuppresseur [imynosypʀesœʀ] NM immunosuppressive drug, immunosuppressant (drug)

immunothérapie [imynoteʀapi] NF immunotherapy

immutabilité [i(m)mytabilite] NF immutability

impact [ɛ̃pakt] NM **a** (= heurt) impact (**sur** on); (= trace de heurt) **mur criblé d'~s de balles** wall riddled with bullet holes → **point¹** **b** (= effet) impact (**sur** on); **l'argument a de l'~** the argument has some impact; (Admin, Écon) **étude d'~** impact study

impair, e [ɛ̃pɛʀ] **1** ADJ [nombre] odd, uneven; [jour] odd; [page] odd-numbered; [vers] irregular (with uneven number of syllables); [organe] unpaired; **côté ~ d'une rue** side of the street where the buildings have odd numbers **2** NM **a** (= gaffe) blunder, faux pas; **commettre un ~** to (make a) blunder, make a faux pas **b** (Casino) **miser sur l'~** to put one's money on the impair ou odd numbers; **« ~ et manque »** "impair et manque"

impala [impala] NM impala

impalpable [ɛ̃palpabl] ADJ (= très fin) [cendre, poussière] extremely fine; (= immatériel) [barrière, frontière] intangible, impalpable

impaludation [ɛ̃palydasjɔ̃] NF infection with malaria

impaludé, e [ɛ̃palyde] ADJ [malade] suffering from malaria; [région] malaria-infected

imparable [ɛ̃paʀabl] ADJ **a** [coup, tir] unstoppable **b** [argument, riposte] unanswerable; [logique] unanswerable, implacable

impardonnable [ɛ̃paʀdɔnabl] ADJ [faute] unforgivable, unpardonable; **vous êtes ~ (d'avoir fait cela)** you cannot be forgiven (for doing that), it's unforgivable of you (to have done that)

imparfait, e [ɛ̃paʀfɛ, ɛt] **1** ADJ (gén) imperfect **2** NM (Ling) imperfect tense; **à l'~** in the imperfect (tense)

imparfaitement [ɛ̃paʀfɛtmã] ADV imperfectly; **connaître ~ qch** to have an imperfect knowledge of sth

impartial, e [mpl -iaux] [ɛ̃paʀsjal, jo] ADJ impartial, unbiased, unprejudiced

impartialement [ɛ̃paʀsjalmã] ADV impartially, without bias ou prejudice

impartialité [ɛ̃paʀsjalite] NF impartiality; **en toute ~** from a completely impartial standpoint; **faire preuve d'~ dans ses jugements** to show impartiality in one's judgements

impartir [ɛ̃paʀtiʀ] ▶conjug 2◀ VT (*littér* = *attribuer à*) ~ **des devoirs/une mission à qn** to assign duties/a mission to sb; ~ **des pouvoirs à** to invest powers in; (*Jur*) ~ **un délai à** to grant an extension to; **dans les délais impartis** within the time allowed; (*Jeux*) **le temps qui vous était imparti est écoulé** your time is up; **les dons que Dieu nous a impartis** the gifts God has bestowed upon us *ou* has endowed us with *ou* has imparted to us

impasse [ɛ̃pɑs] NF **a** (= *cul-de-sac*) dead end, cul-de-sac; (*sur panneau*) "no through road" **b** (= *situation sans issue*) impasse; **être dans l'~** (*négociations*) to have reached an impasse, have reached deadlock; [*personne*] to be at a dead end; [*relation*] to have reached a dead end; **pour sortir les négociations de l'~** to break the deadlock in the negotiations; **notre pays doit sortir de l'~** our country must get out of the rut it's in **c** (*Scol*, *Univ*) **j'ai fait 3 ~s en géographie** I skipped over *ou* missed out (*Brit*) 3 topics in my geography revision; **faire l'~ sur qch** to choose to overlook sth **d** (*Cartes*) finesse; **faire une ~** to (make a) finesse; **faire l'~ au roi** to finesse against the king **e** (*Fin*) ~ **budgétaire** budget deficit

impassibilité [ɛ̃pasibilite] NF impassiveness, impassivity

impassible [ɛ̃pasibl] ADJ impassive

impassiblement [ɛ̃pasibləmɑ̃] ADV impassively

impatiemment [ɛ̃pasjamɑ̃] ADV impatiently

impatience [ɛ̃pasjɑ̃s] NF impatience; **il était dans l'~ de la revoir** he was impatient to see her again, he couldn't wait to see her again; **il répliqua avec ~ que ...** he replied impatiently that ...; **avoir des ~s dans les jambes†** to have the fidgets*

impatiens [ɛ̃pasjɑ̃s] NF (*Bot*) Busy Lizzie, impatiens (*SPÉC*)

impatient, e [ɛ̃pasjɑ̃, jɑ̃t] **1** ADJ [*personne, geste, attente*] impatient; ~ **de faire** impatient *ou* eager to do; **je suis si ~ de vous revoir** I'm longing to see you again, I just can't wait to see you again*, I'm really looking forward to seeing you again; **quel ~!** what an impatient character! **2** **impatiente** NF = **impatiens**

impatienter [ɛ̃pasjɑ̃te] ▶conjug 1◀ **1** VT to irritate, annoy **2** **s'impatienter** VPR to grow *ou* get impatient, lose patience (**contre qn** with sb, **contre** *ou* **de qch** at sth)

impavide [ɛ̃pavid] ADJ (*littér*) unruffled, impassive, cool; ~ **devant le danger** cool *ou* unruffled in the face of danger

impayable* [ɛ̃pejabl] ADJ (= *drôle*) priceless*; **il est ~!** he's priceless!*, he's a scream!*

impayé, e [ɛ̃peje] **1** ADJ unpaid **2** **impayés** NMPL outstanding payments

impec* [ɛ̃pɛk] ADJ ABRÉV = **impeccable**

impeccable [ɛ̃pekabl] ADJ **a** (= *parfait*) [*travail, style, technique, service*] impeccable, perfect, faultless; [*employé*] perfect; [*diction*] impeccable; **parler un français ~** to speak impeccable French; (**c'est**) **~!** great!*, brilliant!*; **ça va? — ~!** is it OK? — it's fine! **b** (= *net*) [*personne*] impeccable, impeccably dressed; [*coiffure*] impeccable, immaculate; [*appartement, voiture*] spotless, spotlessly clean, impeccable

impeccablement [ɛ̃pekabləmɑ̃] ADV [*coiffé, habillé, maquillé, repassé*] impeccably, immaculately; [*rangé, coupé, entretenu*] beautifully; **une robe ~ finie** a beautifully finished dress

impécunieux, -ieuse [ɛ̃pekynjø, jøz] ADJ (*littér*) impecunious

impécuniosité [ɛ̃pekynjozite] NF (*littér*) impecuniousness

impédance [ɛ̃pedɑ̃s] NF (*Élec*) impedance

impedimenta [ɛ̃pedimɛ̃ta] NMPL (*Mil, fig*) impedimenta

impénétrabilité [ɛ̃penetrabilite] NF **a** [*forêt, secteur*] impenetrability **b** [*mystère, desseins*] unfathomableness, impenetrability **c** [*personnage, caractère*] inscrutability, impenetrability; [*visage*] inscrutability, impenetrability

impénétrable [ɛ̃penetrabl] ADJ **a** (= *inaccessible*) [*forêt*] impenetrable (**à** to, by); **un secteur quasi ~ pour les Européens** a market sector almost impossible for Europeans to break into **b** (= *insondable*) [*mystère, desseins*] unfathomable, impenetrable → **voie** **c** (= *énigmatique*) [*personnage, caractère, visage*] inscrutable, impenetrable; [*air*] inscrutable

impénitence [ɛ̃penitɑ̃s] NF unrepentance, impenitence

impénitent, e [ɛ̃penitɑ̃, ɑ̃t] ADJ unrepentant, impenitent; **fumeur ~** unrepentant smoker

▼**impensable** [ɛ̃pɑ̃sabl] ADJ [*événement hypothétique*] unthinkable; [*événement arrivé*] unbelievable

imper* [ɛ̃pɛʀ] NM (ABRÉV = **imperméable**) raincoat

impératif, -ive [ɛ̃peʀatif, iv] **1** ADJ (= *obligatoire, urgent*) [*besoin, consigne*] urgent, imperative; (= *impérieux*) [*geste, ton*] imperative, imperious, commanding; (*Jur*) [*loi*] mandatory; **il est ~ de .../que ...** it is absolutely essential *ou* it is imperative to .../that ... **2** NM **a** (*Ling*) imperative mood; **à l'~** in the imperative (mood) **b** (= *prescription*) [*fonction, charge*] requirement; [*mode*] demand; (= *nécessité*) [*situation*] necessity, (*Mil*) imperative; **des ~s d'horaire nous obligent à ...** we are obliged by the demands *ou* constraints of our timetable to ...; ~ **catégorique** (*Philo*) categorical imperative; (*fig*) essential requirement

impérativement [ɛ̃peʀativmɑ̃] ADV imperatively; **je le veux ~ pour demain** it is imperative that I have it for tomorrow, I absolutely must have it for tomorrow

impératrice [ɛ̃peʀatʀis] NF empress

imperceptibilité [ɛ̃pɛʀsɛptibilite] NF imperceptibility

imperceptible [ɛ̃pɛʀsɛptibl] ADJ **a** (= *non perceptible*) [*son, détail, nuance*] imperceptible (**à** to) **b** (= *à peine perceptible*) [*son, sourire*] faint, imperceptible; [*détail, changement, nuance*] minute, imperceptible

imperceptiblement [ɛ̃pɛʀsɛptibləmɑ̃] ADV imperceptibly

imperfectible [ɛ̃pɛʀfɛktibl] ADJ which cannot be perfected, unperfectible

imperfectif, -ive [ɛ̃pɛʀfɛktif, iv] **1** ADJ imperfective, continuous **2** NM imperfective

imperfection [ɛ̃pɛʀfɛksjɔ̃] NF (= *caractère imparfait*) imperfection; (= *défaut*) [*personne, caractère*] shortcoming, imperfection, defect; [*ouvrage, dispositif, mécanisme*] imperfection, defect; [*peau*] blemish

impérial, e [*mpl* **-iaux**] [ɛ̃peʀjal, jo] **1** ADJ imperial **2** **impériale** NF [*autobus*] top *ou* upper deck; **autobus à ~** ≈ double-decker (bus); **monter à l'impériale** to go upstairs *ou* on top **b** (= *barbe*) imperial **c** (*Jeux*) (**série**) ~**e** royal flush

impérialement [ɛ̃peʀjalmɑ̃] ADV imperially

impérialisme [ɛ̃peʀjalism] NM imperialism

impérialiste [ɛ̃peʀjalist] **1** ADJ imperialist(ic) **2** NMF imperialist

impérieusement [ɛ̃peʀjøzmɑ̃] ADV imperiously; **avoir ~ besoin de qch** to need sth urgently, have urgent need of sth

impérieux, -ieuse [ɛ̃peʀjø, jøz] ADJ (= *autoritaire*) [*personne, ton, caractère*] imperious; (= *pressant*) [*besoin, nécessité*] urgent, pressing; [*obligation*] pressing

impérissable [ɛ̃peʀisabl] ADJ [*œuvre*] imperishable; [*souvenir, gloire*] undying (*épith*), im-

perishable; [*monument, valeur*] permanent, lasting (*épith*)

impéritie [ɛ̃peʀisi] NF (*littér* = *incompétence*) incompetence

imperium [ɛ̃peʀjɔm] NM (*Hist*) imperium; (*fig*) dominion (**sur** over)

imperméabilisation [ɛ̃pɛʀmeabilizasjɔ̃] NF waterproofing

imperméabiliser [ɛ̃pɛʀmeabilize] ▶conjug 1◀ VT to waterproof; **tissu imperméabilisé** waterproofed material

imperméabilité [ɛ̃pɛʀmeabilite] NF **a** [*terrain*] impermeability; [*tissu*] waterproof qualities, impermeability **b** (*littér* = *insensibilité*) ~ **à** imperviousness to

imperméable [ɛ̃pɛʀmeabl] **1** ADJ **a** [*terrain, roches*] impermeable; [*revêtement, tissu*] waterproof; [*frontière*] impenetrable; ~ **à l'eau** waterproof; ~ **à l'air** airtight **b** (= *insensible*) ~ **à** impervious to **2** NM (= *manteau*) raincoat

impersonnalité [ɛ̃pɛʀsɔnalite] NF impersonality; (*Ling*) impersonal form

impersonnel, -elle [ɛ̃pɛʀsɔnɛl] **1** ADJ (*gén, Ling*) impersonal **2** NM (*Ling*) impersonal verb

impersonnellement [ɛ̃pɛʀsɔnɛlmɑ̃] ADV impersonally

impertinemment [ɛ̃pɛʀtinamɑ̃] ADV impertinently

impertinence [ɛ̃pɛʀtinɑ̃s] NF (= *caractère*) impertinence; (= *propos*) impertinent remark, impertinence; **répondre avec ~** to reply impertinently *ou* cheekily; **arrête tes ~s!** that's enough impertinence!, that's enough of your impertinent remarks!

impertinent, e [ɛ̃pɛʀtinɑ̃, ɑ̃t] ADJ impertinent, cheeky; **c'est un petit ~!** he's so impertinent!

imperturbabilité [ɛ̃pɛʀtyʀbabilite] NF imperturbability

imperturbable [ɛ̃pɛʀtyʀbabl] ADJ [*sang-froid, gaieté, sérieux*] unshakeable; [*personne, caractère*] imperturbable; **rester ~** to remain unruffled

imperturbablement [ɛ̃pɛʀtyʀbabləmɑ̃] ADV imperturbably; **il écouta ~** he listened imperturbably *ou* unperturbed *ou* unruffled

impétigo [ɛ̃petigo] NM impetigo

impétrant, e [ɛ̃petʀɑ̃, ɑ̃t] NM,F (*Jur*) applicant; (*Univ*) recipient (*of a qualification*)

impétueusement [ɛ̃petɥøzmɑ̃] ADV (*littér*) impetuously

impétueux, -euse [ɛ̃petɥø, øz] ADJ (*littér*) [*fougueux*] [*caractère, jeunesse*] impetuous, hotheaded; [*orateur*] fiery; [*rythme*] impetuous; [*torrent, vent*] raging

impétuosité [ɛ̃petɥozite] NF (*littér*) [*rythme, personne*] impetuousness, impetuosity; **méfiez-vous de l'~ des torrents de montagne** beware of raging mountain streams

impie [ɛ̃pi] **1** ADJ [*acte, parole*] impious, ungodly, irreligious **2** NMF ungodly *ou* irreligious person

impiété [ɛ̃pjete] NF († *ou littér*) (= *caractère*) impiety, ungodliness, irreligiousness; (= *parole, acte*) impiety

impitoyable [ɛ̃pitwajabl] ADJ (*gén*) merciless, pitiless, ruthless

impitoyablement [ɛ̃pitwajabləmɑ̃] ADV mercilessly, pitilessly, ruthlessly

implacabilité [ɛ̃plakabilite] NF implacability

implacable [ɛ̃plakabl] ADJ (= *impitoyable*) implacable

implacablement [ɛ̃plakabləmɑ̃] ADV implacably, relentlessly

implant [ɛ̃plɑ̃] NM (*Méd*) implant; ~ **capillaire** hair graft; ~ **dentaire** implant

implantation [ɛ̃plɑ̃tasjɔ̃] NF **a** [*usage, mode*] introduction; [*immigrants*] settlement; [*usine, industrie*] setting up; [*idée, préjugé*] implanta-

▶ GRAMMAIRE ACTIVE: **impensable** 39.2

tion |b| (= *présence*) **nous bénéficions d'une solide ~ à l'étranger** [*entreprise*] we have a number of offices abroad; **nous avons su renforcer notre ~ locale** we have reinforced our presence locally; **la forte ~ du parti dans la région** the party's strong presence in the region |c| (*Méd*) [*organe, prothèse, embryon*] implantation |d| (= *disposition*) [*dents*] arrangement; **l'~ des cheveux** the way the hair grows

implanter [ɛ̃plɑ̃te] ▸ conjug 1 ◂ |1| VT |a| (= *introduire*) [+ *usage, mode*] to introduce; **~ un produit sur le marché** to establish a product on the market |b| (= *établir*) [+ *usine, industrie*] to set up, establish; [+ *idée, préjugé*] to implant; **une société implantée dans la région depuis plusieurs générations** a company that has been established in the area for generations; **la gauche est fortement implantée ici** the left is well-established here |c| (*Méd*) [+ *organe, prothèse, embryon*] to implant |2| **s'implanter** VPR [*usine, industrie*] to be set up *ou* established; [*immigrants*] to settle; [*parti politique*] to establish itself, become established; **le parti est solidement implanté dans cette région** the party is well-established in this region

implémentation [ɛ̃plemɑ̃tasjɔ̃] NF (*Ordin*) implementation

implémenter [ɛ̃plemɑ̃te] ▸ conjug 1 ◂ VT (*Ordin*) to implement

implication [ɛ̃plikasjɔ̃] |1| NF |a| (= *relation logique*) implication |b| (= *mise en cause*) **~ dans** implication in; (= *participation à*) implication *ou* involvement in |2| **implications** NFPL (= *conséquences, répercussions*) implications

implicite [ɛ̃plisit] ADJ [*condition, foi, volonté*] implicit; (*Ling*) **connaissance ~** tacit knowledge

implicitement [ɛ̃plisitmɑ̃] ADV implicitly

impliquer [ɛ̃plike] ▸ conjug 1 ◂ |1| VT |a| (= *supposer*) to imply (**que** that) |b| (= *nécessiter*) to entail, involve |c| **~ qn dans** (= *mettre en cause*) to implicate sb in; (= *mêler à*) to implicate *ou* involve sb in |2| **s'impliquer** VPR **s'~ dans son travail/un projet** to get involved in one's work/a project; **s'~ beaucoup dans qch** to put a lot into sth, get heavily *ou* deeply involved in sth

implorant, e [ɛ̃plɔʀɑ̃, ɑ̃t] ADJ imploring, beseeching; **il me regarda d'un air ~** he looked at me imploringly *ou* beseechingly

imploration [ɛ̃plɔʀasjɔ̃] NF entreaty

implorer [ɛ̃plɔʀe] ▸ conjug 1 ◂ VT (= *supplier*) [+ *personne, Dieu*] to implore, beseech (*frm*); (= *demander*) [+ *faveur, aide*] to implore; **~ la clémence de qn** to beg sb for mercy; **~ le pardon de qn** to beg sb's forgiveness; **~ qn de faire** to implore *ou* beseech *ou* entreat sb to do

imploser [ɛ̃ploze] ▸ conjug 1 ◂ VI to implode

implosif, -ive [ɛ̃plozif, iv] ADJ implosive

implosion [ɛ̃plozjɔ̃] NF implosion

impoli, e [ɛ̃poli] ADJ impolite, rude (**envers** to)

impoliment [ɛ̃polimɑ̃] ADV impolitely, rudely

impolitesse [ɛ̃polites] NF (= *attitude*) impoliteness, rudeness; (= *remarque*) impolite *ou* rude remark; (= *acte*) impolite thing to do, impolite action; **répondre avec ~** to answer impolitely *ou* rudely; **c'est une ~ de faire** it is impolite *ou* rude to do

impolitique [ɛ̃politik] ADJ impolitic

impondérabilité [ɛ̃pɔ̃derabilite] NF imponderability

impondérable [ɛ̃pɔ̃derabl] |1| ADJ imponderable |2| NM imponderable, unknown (quantity)

impopulaire [ɛ̃pɔpylɛʀ] ADJ unpopular (**auprès de** with)

impopularité [ɛ̃pɔpylarite] NF unpopularity

import [ɛ̃pɔʀ] NM (ABRÉV = **importation**) import

importable [ɛ̃pɔʀtabl] ADJ (*Écon*) importable; [*vêtement*] unwearable

importance [ɛ̃pɔʀtɑ̃s] NF |a| [*problème, affaire, personne*] importance; [*événement, fait*] importance, significance; [*personne, question*] **avoir de l'~** to be important, be of importance; **ça a beaucoup d'~ pour moi** it's very important to me, it matters a great deal to me; **accorder** *ou* **attacher de l'~ à qch** to give *ou* lend importance to sth; **accorder beaucoup/peu d'~ à qch** to attach a lot of/little importance to sth; **sans ~** [*personne*] unimportant; [*problème, incident, détail*] unimportant, insignificant; **c'est sans ~** ◊ **ça n'a pas d'~** it doesn't matter, it's of no importance *ou* consequence; **(et alors,) quelle ~ ?** (so) does it really matter?; **de peu d'~** [*événement, fait*] of little importance; [*détail*] trifling, minor; [*retard*] slight; **d'une certaine ~** [*problème, événement*] fairly *ou* rather important; **de la plus haute ~** ◊ **de (la) première ~** [*problème, affaire, document*] of paramount *ou* of the highest importance; [*événement*] momentous |b| (= *taille*) [*somme, effectifs, entreprise*] size; (= *ampleur*) [*dégâts, désastre, retard*] extent; **d'une certaine ~** [*entreprise*] sizeable; [*dégâts*] considerable, extensive |c| (*loc*) **prendre de l'~** [*question*] to gain in importance, become more important; [*firme*] to increase in size; [*personne*] to become more important; (*péj*) **se donner de l'~** to act important *ou* in a self-important way; **l'affaire est d'~** this is no trivial matter, this is a matter of some seriousness; (*littér*) **tancer/rosser qn d'~** to give sb a thorough dressing-down/trouncing (*littér*)

▼**important, e** [ɛ̃pɔʀtɑ̃, ɑ̃t] |1| ADJ |a| [*personnage, question, rôle*] important; [*événement, fait*] important, significant; **peu ~** of little *ou* of no great importance, of little significance; **rien d'~** nothing important *ou* of importance; **quelqu'un d'~** somebody important |b| (*quantitativement*) [*somme*] large, considerable, substantial; [*différence*] big; [*retard*] considerable; [*dégâts*] extensive, considerable; **la présence d'un ~ service d'ordre** the presence of a considerable number *ou* a large contingent of police |c| (*péj*) [*airs*] (self-)important; [*personnage*] self-important |2| NM **l'~ est de ...** the important thing is to ...; **ce n'est pas le plus ~** that's not what's most important |3| NM,F (*péj*) **faire l'~(e)** to act important *ou* in a self-important way

importateur, -trice [ɛ̃pɔʀtatœʀ, tʀis] |1| ADJ importing; **pays ~ de blé** wheat-importing country |2| NM,F importer

importation [ɛ̃pɔʀtasjɔ̃] NF |a| (*Comm*) [*marchandises*] importing, importation; **produits/articles d'~** imported products/items |b| [*animal, plante, maladie*] introduction; **cette marque est d'~ récente** this brand is a recent import |c| (= *produit*) import

importer¹ [ɛ̃pɔʀte] ▸ conjug 1 ◂ VT (*Comm, Ordin*) to import; [+ *coutumes, danses*] to import, introduce (**de** from)

▼**importer²** [ɛ̃pɔʀte] ▸ conjug 1 ◂ VI |a| (= *être important*) to matter; **les conventions importent peu à ces gens-là** conventions don't matter much *ou* aren't very important *ou* matter little to those people; **ce qui importe, c'est d'agir vite** the important thing is *ou* what matters is to act quickly; **que lui importe le malheur des autres ?** what does he care about other people's unhappiness?, what does other people's unhappiness matter to him?; (*frm*) **il importe de faire** it is important to do; (*frm*) **il importe qu'elle connaisse les risques** it is important that she knows *ou* should know the risks |b| **peu importe** *ou* **qu'importe** (*littér*) **qu'il soit absent** what does it matter if he is absent?, it matters little that he is absent (*frm*); **peu importe le temps, nous sortirons** we'll go out whatever the weather *ou* no matter what the

weather is like; **peu m'importe** (= *je n'ai pas de préférence*) I don't mind; (= *je m'en moque*) I don't care; **que m'importe!** what do I care?, I don't care!; **achetez des pêches ou des poires, peu importe** buy peaches or pears — it doesn't matter which; **quel fauteuil veux-tu ? — oh, n'importe** which chair will you have? — it doesn't matter *ou* I don't mind *ou* any one will do; **il ne veut pas ? qu'importe!** doesn't he want to? what does it matter? *ou* it doesn't matter!; **les maisons sont chères, n'importe, elles se vendent!** houses are expensive, but no matter, they still sell ▪ (*PROV*) **qu'importe le flacon pourvu qu'on ait l'ivresse!** never mind the bottle, let's just drink it! |c| **n'importe comment** anyhow; **il a fait cela n'importe comment!** he did it any old how* (*Brit*) *ou* any which way* (*US*); **n'importe comment, il part ce soir** anyway, he's leaving tonight, he's leaving tonight in any case *ou* anyhow; **n'importe lequel d'entre nous** any (one) of us; **n'importe où** anywhere; **attention, n'allez pas vous promener n'importe où** be careful, don't go walking just anywhere; **n'importe quand** anytime; **entrez dans n'importe quelle boutique** go into any shop; **n'importe quel docteur vous dira la même chose** any doctor will tell you the same thing; **venez à n'importe quelle heure** come (at) any time; **il cherche un emploi, mais pas n'importe lequel** he's looking for a job, but not just any job; **n'importe qui** anybody, anyone; **ce n'est pas n'importe qui** he's not just anybody; **n'importe quoi** anything; **il fait/dit n'importe quoi!*** he has no idea what he's doing!/ saying!; **(c'est) n'importe quoi!*** what nonsense! *ou* rubbish! (*Brit*)

import-export (*pl* **imports-exports**) [ɛ̃pɔʀ-ɛkspɔʀ] NM import-export; **société d'~** import-export company; **entreprise d'~ de vins** import-export company dealing in wine; **faire de l'~** to be in the import-export business

importun, e [ɛ̃pɔʀtœ̃, yn] |1| ADJ (*frm*) [*curiosité, présence, pensée, plainte*] troublesome, importunate (*frm*); [*arrivée, visite*] inopportune, ill-timed; [*personne*] importunate (*frm*); **je ne veux pas être ~** (*déranger*) I don't wish to disturb you *ou* to intrude; (*irriter*) I don't wish to be importunate (*frm*) *ou* a nuisance; **se rendre ~ par** to make o.s. objectionable by |2| NM,F (= *gêneur*) irksome individual; (= *visiteur*) intruder

importunément [ɛ̃pɔʀtynemɑ̃] ADV (*frm*) (= *de façon irritante*) importunately (*frm*); (= *à un mauvais moment*) inopportunely

importuner [ɛ̃pɔʀtyne] ▸ conjug 1 ◂ VT (*frm*) [*représentant, mendiant*] to importune (*frm*), bother; [*insecte, bruit*] to trouble, bother; [*interruptions, remarques*] to bother; **je ne veux pas vous ~** I don't wish to put you to any trouble *ou* to bother you

importunité [ɛ̃pɔʀtynite] NF (*frm*) [*démarche, demande*] importunity (*frm*); (= *sollicitations*) **~s** importunities

imposable [ɛ̃pozabl] ADJ [*personne, revenu*] taxable

imposant, e [ɛ̃pozɑ̃, ɑ̃t] ADJ (= *majestueux*) [*personnage, stature*] imposing; [*allure*] stately; (= *impressionnant*) [*bâtiment*] imposing; (= *considérable*) [*majorité, mise en scène, foule*] imposing, impressive; (= *gros*) **une ~e matrone** a woman with an imposing figure; **la présence d'un ~ service d'ordre** the presence of an imposing number *ou* a large contingent of police

imposé, e [ɛ̃poze] (*ptp de* **imposer**) |1| ADJ (*Fin*) [*personne, revenu*] taxable; (*Sport*) [*exercices, figures*] compulsory; (*Comm*) **prix ~** set price; **tarif ~** set rate |2| NM (*Sport* = *exercice*) compulsory exercice |3| NM,F (= *contribuable*) taxpayer

imposer [ɛ̃poze] ▶conjug 1◀ **1** VT **a** (= *prescrire*) [+ *tâche, date*] to set; [+ *règle, conditions*] to impose, lay down; [+ *punition, taxe*] to impose (**à** on); [+ *prix*] to set, fix; **~ ses idées/sa présence à qn** to impose *ou* force one's ideas/one's company on sb; **~ des conditions à qch** to impose *ou* place conditions on sth; **~ un travail/une date à qn** to set sb a piece of work/a date; **~ un régime à qn** to put sb on a diet; **la décision leur a été imposée par les événements** the decision was forced *ou* imposed (up)on them by events; **il nous a imposé son candidat** he has imposed his candidate on us; **on lui a imposé le silence** silence has been imposed upon him → **loi**
b (= *faire connaître*) **~ son nom** [*candidat*] to come to the fore; [*artiste*] to make o.s. known, compel recognition; [*firme*] to establish itself, become an established name; **il impose/sa conduite impose le respect** he commands/his behaviour compels respect
c (*Fin* = *taxer*) [+ *marchandise, revenu, salariés*] to tax; **~ insuffisamment** to undertax
d (*Typo*) to impose
e (*Rel*) **~ les mains** to lay on hands
f **en ~ à qn** to impress sb; **il en impose** he's an imposing individual; **sa présence/son intelligence en impose** his presence/his intelligence is imposing; **ne vous en laissez pas ~ par ses grands airs** don't let yourself be impressed by his haughty manner
2 **s'imposer** VPR **a** (= *être nécessaire*) [*décision, action*] to be essential *ou* vital *ou* imperative; **dans ce cas, le repos s'impose** in this case rest is essential *ou* vital *ou* imperative; **c'est la solution qui s'impose** it's the obvious solution; **ces mesures ne s'imposaient pas** these measures were unnecessary; **quand on est à Paris une visite au Louvre s'impose** when in Paris, a visit to the Louvre is imperative *ou* is a must*
b (= *se contraindre à*) **s'~ une tâche** to set o.s. a task; **il s'est imposé un trop gros effort** he put himself under too much strain; **s'~ de faire** to make it a rule to do
c (= *montrer sa supériorité*) to assert o.s.; (= *avoir une personnalité forte*) to be assertive; **impose-toi !** assert yourself!; **s'~ par ses qualités** to stand out *ou* to compel recognition because of one's qualities; **il s'est imposé dans sa branche** he has made a name for himself in his branch; **il s'est imposé comme le seul susceptible d'avoir le prix** he emerged *ou* he established himself as the only one likely to get the prize; **le skieur s'est imposé dans le slalom géant** the skier dominated the giant slalom event; **le joueur canadien s'est imposé face au russe** the Canadian player outplayed the Russian
d (= *imposer sa présence à*) **s'~ à qn** to impose (o.s.) upon sb; **je ne voudrais pas m'~** I don't want to impose; **le soleil s'imposera peu à peu sur tout le pays** gradually sunshine will spread across the whole country

imposition [ɛ̃pozisjɔ̃] NF (*Fin*) taxation; (*Typo*) imposition; (*Rel*) **l'~ des mains** the laying on of hands; (*Fin*) **double ~** double taxation

▼ **impossibilité** [ɛ̃pɔsibilite] NF impossibility; **l'~ de réaliser ce plan** the impossibility of carrying out this plan; **en cas d'~** should it prove impossible; **y a-t-il ~ à ce qu'il vienne ?** is it impossible for him to come?; **être dans l'~ de faire qch** to be unable to do sth; **l'~ dans laquelle il se trouvait de ...** the fact that he was unable to ..., the fact that he found it impossible to ...; **se heurter à des ~s** to come up against insuperable obstacles

▼ **impossible** [ɛ̃pɔsibl] **1** ADJ **a** (= *irréalisable, improbable*) impossible; **~ à faire** impossible to do; **il est ~ de .../que ...** it is impossible to .../ that ...; **il est ~ qu'il soit déjà arrivé** he cannot possibly have arrived yet; **il m'est ~ de le faire** it's impossible for me to do it, I can't possibly do it; **pouvez-vous venir lundi ? — non,**

cela m'est ~ can you come on Monday? — no, I can't *ou* no, it's impossible; **ce n'est pas ~ ◊ ça n'a rien d'~** (= *ça peut arriver*) it may well happen; (= *ça peut être le cas*) it may well be the case; **est-ce qu'il va partir ? — ce n'est pas ~** is he going to leave? — he may well ▪ (*PROV*) **~ n'est pas français** there's no such word as "can't" → **vaillant**
b (= *pénible, difficile*) [*enfant, situation*] impossible; **rendre l'existence ~ à qn** to make sb's life impossible *ou* a misery; **elle a des horaires ~s** she has impossible *ou* terrible hours; **il mène une vie ~** he leads an incredible life
c (= *invraisemblable*) [*nom, titre*] ridiculous, impossible; **se lever à des heures ~s** to get up at an impossible *ou* a ridiculous time *ou* hour; **il lui arrive toujours des histoires ~s** impossible things are always happening to him
2 NM **a** the impossible; **demander/tenter l'~** to ask for/attempt the impossible; **je ferai l'~ (pour venir)** I'll do my utmost (to come) ▪ (*PROV*) **à l'~ nul n'est tenu** no one can be expected to do the impossible
b **par ~** by some miracle, by some remote chance; **si par ~ je terminais premier ...** if by some miracle *ou* some remote chance I were to finish first ...

imposte [ɛ̃pɔst] NF **a** (*Archit* = *moulure*) impost **b** (= *fenêtre*) fanlight (*Brit*), transom (window) (*US*)

imposteur [ɛ̃pɔstœʀ] NM impostor

imposture [ɛ̃pɔstyʀ] NF imposture, deception; **c'est une ~ !** it's all a sham!

impôt [ɛ̃po] **1** NM (= *taxe*) tax; **payer l'~** *ou* pay tax *ou* taxes; **les ~s** (*gén*) taxes; (= *service local*) the tax office; (= *service national*) the Inland Revenue (*Brit*), the Internal Revenue Service (*US*); **les ~s me réclament 10 000 F** the taxman* wants 10,000 francs from me; **payer des ~s** to pay tax; **je paye plus de 10 000 F d'~s** I pay more than 10,000 francs (in) tax; **frapper d'un ~** to put a tax on; **~ direct/indirect/déguisé** direct/indirect/hidden tax; **retenu à la source** tax deducted at source; **bénéfices avant ~** pre-tax profits; **faire un bénéfice de 10 000 F avant ~** to make a profit of 10,000 francs before tax → **assiette, déclaration, feuille** *etc*
2 COMP ▶ **impôt sur les bénéfices** tax on profits, ≈ corporation tax ▶ **impôt sur le chiffre d'affaires** tax on turnover ▶ **impôt foncier** ≈ land tax ▶ **impôt (de solidarité) sur la fortune, impôt sur les grandes fortunes**† wealth tax ▶ **impôts locaux** local taxes, ≈ council tax (*Brit*) ▶ **impôt sur les plus-values** ≈ capital gains tax ▶ **impôt sur le revenu (des personnes physiques)** income tax ▶ **impôt sur le transfert des capitaux** capital transfer tax ▶ **impôt du sang** (†, *littér*) blood tribute ▶ **impôt sécheresse** *tax levied to help farmers in case of drought* ▶ **impôt sur les sociétés** corporate tax

---

⬛ IMPÔTS

The main forms of taxation in France are income tax ("l'impôt sur le revenu"), value-added tax on consumer goods ("TVA"), local taxes funding public amenities ("les impôts locaux", which include "la taxe d'habitation" and "la taxe foncière") and two kinds of company tax ("la taxe professionnelle" and "l'impôt sur les sociétés").

Income tax for a given year is payable the following year and is calculated from information supplied in the "déclaration d'impôts". It can either be paid in three instalments (the first two, known as "tiers provisionnels", are estimates based on the previous year's tax, while the third makes up the actual tax due), or in monthly instalments (an option known as "mensualisation"). Late payment incurs a 10% penalty known as a "majoration".

---

impotence [ɛ̃pɔtɑ̃s] NF (*Méd*) infirmity; (*fig*) impotence

impotent, e [ɛ̃pɔtɑ̃, ɑ̃t] **1** ADJ disabled, crippled; **l'accident l'a rendu ~** the accident has disabled *ou* crippled him **2** NM,F disabled person, cripple

impraticable [ɛ̃pʀatikabl] ADJ [*idée*] impracticable, unworkable; [*tâche*] impracticable; (*Sport*) [*terrain*] unfit for play, unplayable; [*route, piste*] impassable; **~ pour les ou aux véhicules à moteur** unfit *ou* unsuitable for motor vehicles, impassable to motor vehicles

imprécateur, -trice [ɛ̃pʀekatœʀ, tʀis] NM,F (*littér*) doomsayer, prophet of doom

imprécation [ɛ̃pʀekasjɔ̃] NF imprecation, curse; **se répandre en ou lancer des ~s contre** to inveigh against

imprécatoire [ɛ̃pʀekatwaʀ] ADJ (*littér*) imprecatory (*littér*)

imprécis, e [ɛ̃pʀesi, iz] ADJ **a** [*souvenir, idée*] vague; [*contours*] vague, indistinct; **les causes du décès restent encore ~es** the cause of death remains unclear **b** [*estimation, plan, chiffre, résultat*] imprecise; [*tir*] inaccurate

imprécision [ɛ̃pʀesizjɔ̃] NF **a** [*souvenir, idée*] vagueness **b** [*estimation, plan, chiffre, résultat*] imprecision, lack of precision; [*tir*] inaccuracy; **ce texte comporte de nombreuses ~s** there are a number of inaccuracies in the text

imprégnation [ɛ̃pʀeɲasjɔ̃] NF **a** [*tissu, matière*] impregnation; [*pièce, air*] permeation; **taux d'~ alcoolique** blood alcohol level, level of alcohol in the blood **b** (= *assimilation*) [*esprit*] imbuing, impregnation; **pour apprendre une langue, rien ne vaut une lente ~** to learn a language there's nothing like gradually immersing oneself in it

imprégner [ɛ̃pʀeɲe] ▶conjug 6◀ **1** VT **a** [+ *tissu, matière*] (*de liquide*) to impregnate, soak (**de** with); (*d'une odeur, de fumée*) to impregnate (**de** with); [+ *pièce, air*] to permeate, fill (**de** with); **cette odeur imprégnait toute la rue** the smell filled the whole street; **maison imprégnée de lumière** house flooded with light; **un endroit imprégné d'histoire** a place steeped in history
b [+ *esprit*] to imbue, impregnate (**de** with); **l'amertume qui imprégnait ses paroles** the bitterness which pervaded his words; **imprégné des préjugés de sa caste** imbued with *ou* steeped in the prejudices of his class
2 **s'imprégner** VPR **s'~ de** [*tissu, substance*] (*de liquide*) to become impregnated *ou* soaked with; (*d'une odeur, de fumée*) to become impregnated with; [*pièce, air*] to become permeated *ou* filled with; [*esprits, élèves*] to become imbued with, absorb; **séjourner à l'étranger pour s'~ de la langue étrangère** to live abroad to immerse o.s. in *ou* to absorb the foreign language; **s'~ d'alcool** to soak up alcohol

imprenable [ɛ̃pʀənabl] ADJ [*forteresse*] impregnable; **vue ~** unrestricted view

impréparation [ɛ̃pʀepaʀasjɔ̃] NF lack of preparation

imprésario [ɛ̃pʀesaʀjo] NM [*acteur, chanteur*] manager; [*troupe de théâtre, ballet*] impresario, manager

imprescriptibilité [ɛ̃pʀeskʀiptibilite] NF **l'~ des crimes contre l'humanité** the non-applicability of statutory limitation to crimes against humanity

imprescriptible [ɛ̃pʀeskʀiptibl] ADJ [*crime*] to which the statute of limitations does not apply; [*droit*] inalienable

▼ **impression** [ɛ̃pʀesjɔ̃] NF **a** (= *sensation physique*) feeling, impression; (= *sentiment, réaction*) impression; **se fier à sa première ~** to trust one's first impressions; **ils échangèrent leurs ~s (de voyage)** they exchanged their impressions (of the trip); **quelles sont vos ~s sur la réunion ?** what was your impression *ou* what did you think of the meeting?; **l'~ que**

j'ai de lui my impression of him, the impression I have of him; **ça m'a fait peu d'/une grosse ~** that made little/a great impression upon me; **ça m'a fait une drôle d'~ de la revoir** it was really strange seeing her again; **faire bonne/mauvaise/forte ~** to make ou create a good/bad/strong impression; **avoir l'~ que ...** to have a feeling that ..., get ou have the impression that; **j'ai comme l'~ qu'il ne me dit pas toute la vérité** I have a feeling ou a hunch* that he's not telling me the whole truth; **créer/donner une ~ de ...** to create/give an impression of ...; **il ne me donne ou fait pas l'~ d'(être) un menteur** I don't get the impression that he's a liar, he doesn't give me the impression of being a liar; **faire ~** [film, orateur] to make an impression, have an impact

b [livre, tissu, motif] printing; **~ en couleur** colour printing; **~ laser** (= action) laser printing; (= feuille imprimée) laser print ou copy; (Ordin) **« ~ écran »** "print screen"; **ce livre en est à sa 3ᵉ ~** this book is at its 3rd impression ou printing; **le livre est à l'~** the book is with the printers; **l'~ de ce livre est soignée** this book is beautifully printed → **faute**

c (= motif) pattern; **tissu à ~s florales** floral pattern(ed) fabric, fabric with a floral pattern **d** (Peinture) **(couche d')~** undercoat

impressionnabilité [ɛ̃pʀesjɔnabilite] NF (= émotivité) impressionability, impressionableness

impressionnable [ɛ̃pʀesjɔnabl] ADJ [personne] impressionable

impressionnant, e [ɛ̃pʀesjɔnɑ̃, ɑ̃t] ADJ (= imposant) [somme, spectacle, monument] impressive; (= bouleversant) [scène, accident] upsetting; **elle était ~e de calme** her calmness was impressive

impressionner [ɛ̃pʀesjɔne] ▶ conjug 1 ◀ VT **a** (= frapper) to impress; (= bouleverser) to upset; **ne te laisse pas ~** don't let yourself be overawed; **cela risque d'~ les enfants** this may upset children; **tu ne m'impressionnes pas!** you don't scare me!, I'm not afraid of you! **b** (Opt) [+ rétine] to act on; (Photo) [+ pellicule] [image, sujet] to show up on; [photographe] to expose; **la pellicule n'a pas été impressionnée** the film hasn't been exposed

impressionnisme [ɛ̃pʀesjɔnism] NM impressionism

impressionniste [ɛ̃pʀesjɔnist] **1** ADJ impressionistic; (Art, Mus) impressionist **2** NMF impressionist

imprévisibilité [ɛ̃pʀevizibilite] NF unpredictability

imprévisible [ɛ̃pʀevizibl] ADJ unforeseeable, unpredictable; **elle est assez ~ dans ses réactions** her reactions are quite unpredictable

imprévoyance [ɛ̃pʀevwajɑ̃s] NF (= insouciance) lack of foresight; (en matière d'argent) improvidence

imprévoyant, e [ɛ̃pʀevwajɑ̃, ɑ̃t] ADJ (= insouciant) lacking (in) foresight; (en matière d'argent) improvident

imprévu, e [ɛ̃pʀevy] **1** ADJ [événement, succès, réaction] unforeseen, unexpected; [courage, geste] unexpected; [dépenses] unforeseen; **de manière ~e** unexpectedly **2** NM **a** **l'~** the unexpected, the unforeseen; **j'aime l'~** I like the unexpected; **un peu d'~** an element of surprise ou of the unexpected ou of the unforeseen; **vacances pleines d'~** holidays full of surprises; **en cas d'~** if anything unexpected ou unforeseen crops up; **sauf ~** barring any unexpected ou unforeseen circumstances, unless anything unexpected ou unforeseen crops up **b** (= incident) unexpected ou unforeseen event; **il y a un ~** something unexpected ou unforeseen has cropped up; **tous ces ~s nous ont retardés** all these unexpected ou unforeseen events have delayed us

imprimable [ɛ̃pʀimabl] ADJ printable

imprimant, e [ɛ̃pʀimɑ̃, ɑ̃t] **1** ADJ printing (épith) **2** **imprimante** NF printer; **~e matricielle/ligne par ligne/à jet d'encre** dot-matrix/line/ink-jet printer; **~e à marguerite/laser/feuille à feuille** daisywheel/laser/sheet-fed printer

imprimatur [ɛ̃pʀimatyʀ] NM INV imprimatur

imprimé, e [ɛ̃pʀime] **1** ADJ [tissu, feuille] printed **2** NM **a** (= formulaire) printed form; (Poste) **« ~s »** "printed matter"; **envoyer qch au tarif ~s** to send sth at the printed paper rate; **catalogue/section des ~s** catalogue/department of printed books; **~ publicitaire** advertising leaflet **b** (= tissu) **l'~** printed material ou fabrics, prints; **à fleur** floral print (fabric ou material); **l'~ et l'uni** printed and plain fabrics ou material

imprimer [ɛ̃pʀime] ▶ conjug 1 ◀ **1** VT **a** [+ livre, foulard, billets de banque, dessin] to print **b** (= apposer) [+ visa, cachet] to stamp (sur, dans on, in) **c** (= marquer) [+ rides, traces, marque] to imprint (dans in, on); **une scène imprimée dans sa mémoire** a scene imprinted on his memory **d** (= publier) [+ texte, ouvrage] to publish; [+ auteur] to publish the work of; **la joie de se voir imprimé** the joy of seeing o.s. ou one's work in print **e** (= communiquer) [+ impulsion] to transmit (à to); **la pédale imprime un mouvement à la roue** the movement of the pedal causes the wheel to turn; **~ une direction à** to give a direction to **f** (Peinture) [+ surface] to prime **2** VI (* = retenir) **je n'ai pas imprimé** it didn't sink in ou register

imprimerie [ɛ̃pʀimʀi] NF (= firme, usine) printing works; (= atelier) printing house; (= section) printery; (pour enfants) printing outfit ou kit; (= technique) **l'~** printing; **l'Imprimerie nationale** ≈ HMSO (Brit), ≈ the Government Printing Office (US); **écrire en caractères ou lettres d'~** to write in block capitals ou letters

imprimeur [ɛ̃pʀimœʀ] NM printer; **~-éditeur** printer and publisher; **~-libraire** printer and bookseller

impro* [ɛ̃pʀo] NF ABRÉV = **improvisation**

improbabilité [ɛ̃pʀɔbabilite] NF unlikelihood, improbability

improbable [ɛ̃pʀɔbabl] ADJ unlikely, improbable

improbité [ɛ̃pʀɔbite] NF (littér) lack of integrity

improductif, -ive [ɛ̃pʀɔdyktif, iv] **1** ADJ [travail, terrain] unproductive, non-productive; [capitaux] non-productive **2** NM,F inactive member of society

improductivité [ɛ̃pʀɔdyktivite] NF unproductiveness, lack of productivity

impromptu [ɛ̃pʀɔ̃pty] **1** ADJ (= improvisé) [départ] sudden (épith); [visite] surprise (épith); [repas, exposé] impromptu (épith); **faire un discours ~ sur un sujet** to speak off the cuff ou make an impromptu speech on a subject, extemporize on a subject **2** NM (Littérat, Mus) impromptu **3** ADV (= à l'improviste) [arriver] impromptu; (= sans préparation) [répondre] off the cuff, impromptu; **il arriva ~, un soir de juin** he arrived (quite) out of the blue one evening in June

imprononçable [ɛ̃pʀɔnɔ̃sabl] ADJ unpronounceable

impropre [ɛ̃pʀɔpʀ] ADJ **a** [terme] inappropriate **b** [outil, personne] **~ à** unsuitable for, unsuited to; **eau ~ à la consommation** water unfit for (human) consumption

improprement [ɛ̃pʀɔpʀəmɑ̃] ADV [appeler, qualifier] incorrectly, improperly

impropriété [ɛ̃pʀɔpʀijete] NF [forme] incorrectness, inaccuracy; **~ (de langage)** (language) error, mistake

improuvable [ɛ̃pʀuvabl] ADJ unprovable

improvisateur, -trice [ɛ̃pʀɔvizatœʀ, tʀis] NM,F improviser

improvisation [ɛ̃pʀɔvizasjɔ̃] NF improvisation; **faire une ~** to improvise; (Jazz) **~ collective** jam session; **j'adore l'~** I love doing things on the spur of the moment

improvisé, e [ɛ̃pʀɔvize] (ptp de **improviser**) ADJ (= de fortune) [réforme, table] improvised, makeshift; [solution] makeshift, ad hoc; [cuisinier, infirmier] acting, temporary; [équipe] scratch (épith); (= impromptu) [+ conférence de presse, pique-nique, représentation] impromptu, improvised; [discours] off-the-cuff (épith), improvised; [excuse] improvised, invented; **avec des moyens ~s** with whatever means are available ou to hand

improviser [ɛ̃pʀɔvize] ▶ conjug 1 ◀ **1** VT [+ discours, réunion, pique-nique] to improvise; [+ excuse] to improvise, invent **2** VI [organisateur] to improvise; [musicien] to extemporize, improvise; [acteur, orateur] to improvise, extemporize, ad-lib* **3** **s'improviser** VPR [secours, réunion] to be improvised **b** **s'~ cuisinier/infirmière** to act as cook/nurse; **on ne s'improvise pas menuisier ◊ être menuisier, ça ne s'improvise pas** you don't just suddenly become a carpenter, you don't become a carpenter just like that

improviste [ɛ̃pʀɔvist] **♦ à l'improviste** LOC ADV unexpectedly, without warning; **je lui ai fait une visite à l'~** I dropped in on him unexpectedly ou without warning; **prendre qn à l'~** to catch sb unawares

imprudemment [ɛ̃pʀydamɑ̃] ADV [circuler, naviguer] carelessly; [parler] unwisely, imprudently; **un inconnu qu'il avait ~ suivi** a stranger whom he had foolishly ou imprudently ou unwisely followed

imprudence [ɛ̃pʀydɑ̃s] NF **a** [conducteur, geste, action] carelessness **b** [remarque] imprudence, foolishness; [projet] foolishness, foolhardiness; **il a eu l'~ de mentionner ce projet** he was foolish ou unwise ou imprudent enough to mention the project; (Jur) **blessures par ~** injuries through negligence → **homicide c** (= étourderie, maladresse) **commettre une ~** to do something foolish ou imprudent; **(ne fais) pas d'~s** don't do anything foolish

imprudent, e [ɛ̃pʀydɑ̃, ɑ̃t] **1** ADJ **a** [conducteur, geste, action] careless **b** [remarque] imprudent, unwise, foolish; [projet] foolish, foolhardy; [politique] rash; **il est ~ de se baigner tout de suite après un repas** it's unwise to swim straight after a meal; **je vous trouve bien ~ de ne pas porter de casque** I think it's rather unwise ou foolish of you not to wear a helmet **2** NM,F careless person; **c'est un ~** he's very careless; **les ~s!** how careless of them!

impubère [ɛ̃pybɛʀ] **1** ADJ pre-pubescent **2** NMF (Jur) ≈ minor

impubliable [ɛ̃pyblijabl] ADJ unpublishable

impudemment [ɛ̃pydamɑ̃] ADV (frm) (= effrontément) impudently; (= cyniquement) brazenly, shamelessly

impudence [ɛ̃pydɑ̃s] NF (frm) **a** (= effronterie) impudence; (= cynisme) brazenness, shamelessness; **quelle ~!** what impudence!; **il a eu l'~ d'exiger des excuses!** he had the effrontery to demand an apology! **b** (= acte) impudent action; (= parole) impudent remark; **je ne tolérerai pas ses ~s** I won't put up with ou tolerate his impudent behaviour ou his impudence

impudent, e [ɛ̃pydɑ̃, ɑ̃t] (frm) **1** ADJ (= insolent) impudent; (= cynique) brazen, shameless **2** NM,F impudent person; **petite ~e!** impudent little girl!

impudeur [ɛ̃pydœʀ] NF immodesty, shamelessness

impudicité [ɛ̃pydisite] NF immodesty, shamelessness

impudique [ɛ̃pydik] ADJ [personne] immodest, shameless; [regard, pose, décolleté] immodest; [propos] shameless

impudiquement [ɛ̃pydikmɑ̃] ADV immodestly, shamelessly

impuissance [ɛ̃pɥisɑ̃s] NF a (= faiblesse) powerlessness, helplessness; **~ à faire** powerlessness ou incapacity to do; **réduire qn à l'~** to render sb powerless b (sexuelle) impotence

impuissant, e [ɛ̃pɥisɑ̃, ɑ̃t] 1 ADJ a [personne] powerless, helpless; **~ à faire** powerless to do, incapable of doing b (sexuellement) impotent 2 NM impotent man

impulser [ɛ̃pylse] ▶ conjug 1 ◀ VT (Écon) [+ secteur] to boost, stimulate; [+ politique, mouvement revendicatif] to boost, give impetus to, spur; **il est là pour écouter, ~** he's there to listen and to get things moving ou to make things happen

impulsif, -ive [ɛ̃pylsif, iv] 1 ADJ impulsive 2 NM,F impulsive person

impulsion [ɛ̃pylsjɔ̃] NF a (mécanique) impulse; (électrique) impulse, pulse; **radar à ~s** pulse(-modulated) radar; **~s nerveuses** nerve impulses b (= élan) impetus; **l'~ donnée à l'économie** the boost ou impetus given to the economy; **sous l'~ de leurs chefs/des circonstances** spurred on by their leaders/by circumstances; **réforme entreprise sous l'~ de l'Irlande** reform undertaken at Ireland's instigation; **sous l'~ de la colère** driven ou impelled by anger, under the impulse of anger c (= mouvement, instinct) impulse; **cédant à des ~s morbides** yielding to morbid impulses → **achat**

impulsivité [ɛ̃pylsivite] NF impulsiveness

impunément [ɛ̃pynemɑ̃] ADV with impunity; **on ne se moque pas ~ de lui** you can't make fun of him and (expect to) get away with it, one can't make fun of him with impunity

impuni, e [ɛ̃pyni] ADJ unpunished

impunité [ɛ̃pynite] NF impunity; **en toute ~** with complete impunity; **ils déplorent l'~ dont jouissent certains** they deplore the way people get off scot-free ou go unpunished

impur, e [ɛ̃pyʀ] ADJ a (= altéré) [liquide, air] impure; [race] mixed; (Rel) [animal] unclean b (= immoral) [geste, pensée, personne] impure

impureté [ɛ̃pyʀte] NF (gén) impurity; **vivre dans l'~** to live in a state of impurity; **~s** impurities

imputabilité [ɛ̃pytabilite] NF (Jur) imputability

imputable [ɛ̃pytabl] ADJ a [faute, accident] **~ à** imputable to, ascribable to, attributable to b (Fin) **~ sur** chargeable to

imputation [ɛ̃pytasjɔ̃] NF a (= accusation) imputation (frm), charge b (Fin) [somme] **~ à** ou **sur** charging to

imputer [ɛ̃pyte] ▶ conjug 1 ◀ VT a (= attribuer à) **~ à** to impute to, attribute to, ascribe to b (Fin) **~ à** ou **sur** to charge to

imputrescibilité [ɛ̃pytʀesibilite] NF rotproof nature, imputrescibility (SPÉC)

imputrescible [ɛ̃pytʀesibl] ADJ rotproof, imputrescible (SPÉC)

in †* [in] ADJ trendy*, in*

INA [ina] NM (ABRÉV = **Institut national de l'audiovisuel**) → **institut**

inabordable [inabɔʀdabl] ADJ [personne] unapproachable; [lieu] inaccessible; [prix] prohibitive, exorbitant; **les fruits sont ~s** fruit is terribly expensive

inabrogeable [inabʀɔʒabl] ADJ (Jur) unrepealable

in absentia [inapsɑ̃sja] LOC ADV in absentia

in abstracto [inapstʀakto] LOC ADV in the abstract

inaccentué, e [inaksɑ̃tɥe] ADJ unstressed, unaccented, unaccentuated

inacceptable [inakseptabl] ADJ [offre, plan, conduite, propos] unacceptable; **c'est ~** it's unacceptable

inaccessibilité [inaksesibilite] NF inaccessibility

inaccessible [inaksesibl] ADJ a [montagne, personne, but] inaccessible; [endroit] out-of-the-way (épith), inaccessible; [objet] inaccessible, out of reach (attrib) b [texte] (= obscur) obscure; (= incompréhensible) incomprehensible (à to) c (= insensible à) **~ à** impervious to

inaccompli, e [inakɔ̃pli] ADJ (littér) [vœux] unfulfilled; [tâche] unaccomplished

inaccomplissement [inakɔ̃plismɑ̃] NM (littér) [vœux] non-fulfilment; [tâche] non-execution

inaccoutumé, e [inakutyme] ADJ unusual; (littér) **~ à** unaccustomed to, unused to

inachevé, e [inaʃ(ə)ve] ADJ unfinished, uncompleted; **une impression d'~** a feeling of incompleteness ou incompletion

inachèvement [inaʃɛvmɑ̃] NM incompleteness, incompletion

inactif, -ive [inaktif, iv] 1 ADJ a [vie, personne, capitaux, machine] inactive, idle; (Bourse) [marché] slack; [population] non-working; [volcan] inactive, dormant b (= inefficace) [remède] ineffective, ineffectual 2 NMPL **les ~s** the non-working ou inactive population, those not in active employment

inaction [inaksjɔ̃] NF (= oisiveté) inactivity, idleness

inactivation [inaktivasjɔ̃] NF (Méd) inactivation; **~ virale** viral inactivation

inactiver [inaktive] ▶ conjug 1 ◀ VT [+ gène, hormone, virus] to inactivate; **produits inactivés** inactivated blood products; **vaccin inactivé** inactivated vaccine

inactivité [inaktivite] NF (= non-activité) inactivity; (Admin, Mil) **être en ~** to be out of active service

inactuel, -elle [inaktɥɛl] ADJ irrelevant to the present day

inadaptable [inadaptabl] ADJ [roman] impossible to adapt

inadaptation [inadaptasjɔ̃] NF maladjustment; **~ à** failure to adjust to ou adapt to; **~ d'un enfant à la vie scolaire** a child's inability to cope with school life

inadapté, e [inadapte] 1 ADJ [personne, enfance] maladjusted; [outil, moyens] unsuitable (à for); **~ à** not adapted ou adjusted to; **un genre de vie complètement ~ à ses ressources** a way of life quite unsuited to his resources; **enfant ~ (à la vie scolaire)** maladjusted child, child with (school) behavioural problems 2 NM,F (péj : = adulte) misfit; (Admin, Psych) maladjusted person; **les ~s (sociaux)** (social) misfits

inadéquat, e [inadekwa(t), kwat] ADJ inadequate

inadéquation [inadekwasjɔ̃] NF inadequacy

inadmissibilité [inadmisibilite] NF (Jur) inadmissibility

inadmissible [inadmisibl] ADJ a [comportement, négligence] inadmissible, intolerable; [propos] unacceptable; [situation] unacceptable, intolerable; **il est ~ de .../que ...** it is unacceptable to .../that ... b (Jur) [témoignage, preuve] inadmissible

inadvertance [inadvɛʀtɑ̃s] NF oversight; **par ~** inadvertently, by mistake

inaliénabilité [inaljenabilite] NF inalienability

inaliénable [inaljenabl] ADJ inalienable

inaltérabilité [inalteʀabilite] NF a [métal, substance] stability; [couleur] (au lavage) fastness; (à la lumière) fade-resistance; [vernis,

encre] permanence; **~ à l'air** stability in air, ability to resist exposure to the air; **~ à la chaleur** heat-resistance, ability to withstand heat; (littér) **l'~ du ciel** the unvarying blue(ness) of the sky b [sentiment] unchanging ou unfailing ou unshakeable nature; [principes, espoirs] steadfastness; **l'~ de son calme** his unchanging ou unshakeable calm(ness)

inaltérable [inalteʀabl] ADJ a [métal, substance] stable; [couleur] (au lavage) fast; (à la lumière) fade-resistant; [vernis, encre] permanent; [ciel, cycle] unchanging; **~ à l'air** unaffected by exposure to the air; **~ à la chaleur** heat-resistant b [sentiments] unchanging, unfailing, unshakeable; [bonne santé] unfailing; [principes, espoir] steadfast, unfailing; **il a fait preuve d'une ~ patience** he was unfailingly patient; **d'une humeur ~** even-tempered

inaltéré, e [inalteʀe] ADJ unchanged, unaltered

inamical, e (mpl **-aux**) [inamikal, o] ADJ unfriendly

inamovibilité [inamɔvibilite] NF (Jur) [fonction] permanence; [juge, fonctionnaire] irremovability

inamovible [inamɔvibl] ADJ a (Jur) [juge, fonctionnaire] irremovable; [fonction, emploi] from which one is irremovable b (= fixe) [plaque, panneau, capuche] fixed; **cette partie est ~** this part is fixed ou cannot be removed c (hum) [casquette, sourire] eternal; **il travaille toujours chez eux ? il est vraiment ~** is he still with them? — he's a permanent fixture ou he's part of the furniture (hum)

inanimé, e [inanime] ADJ [matière] inanimate; [personne, corps] (= évanoui) unconscious, senseless; (= mort) lifeless; (Ling) inanimate; **tomber ~** to fall senseless to the ground, fall to the ground unconscious

inanité [inanite] NF [conversation] inanity; [querelle, efforts] futility, pointlessness; [espoirs] vanity, futility; **dire des ~s** to come out with a lot of inane comments

inanition [inanisjɔ̃] NF exhaustion through lack of nourishment; **tomber/mourir d'~** to faint with/die of hunger

inapaisable [inapezabl] ADJ (littér) [colère, chagrin, désir] unappeasable; [soif] unquenchable

inapaisé, e [inapeze] ADJ (littér) [colère, chagrin, désir] unappeased; [soif] unquenched

inaperçu, e [inapɛʀsy] ADJ unnoticed; **passer ~** to pass ou go unnoticed; **le geste ne passa pas ~** the gesture did not go unnoticed ou unremarked

inapparent, e [inapaʀɑ̃, ɑ̃t] ADJ [maladie] with no visible symptoms; [tumeur] invisible; [motif] hidden

inappétence [inapetɑ̃s] NF (= manque d'appétit) lack of appetite, inappetence (frm); (littér = manque de désir) lack of desire, inappetence (frm)

inapplicable [inaplikabl] ADJ [loi] unenforceable; **dans ce cas, la règle est ~** in this case, the rule cannot be applied ou is inapplicable (à to)

inapplication [inaplikasjɔ̃] NF a [élève] lack of application b [loi] non-application, non-enforcement

inappliqué, e [inaplike] ADJ [méthode] not applied (attrib); [loi, règlement, traité] not enforced (attrib)

inappréciable [inapʀesjabl] ADJ a [précieux] [aide, service] invaluable; [avantage, bonheur] inestimable b (= difficilement décelable) [nuance, différence] inappreciable, imperceptible

inapproprié, e [inapʀɔpʀije] ADJ [terme, mesure, équipement] inappropriate

inapte [inapt] ADJ (= incapable) incapable; **~ aux affaires/à certains travaux** unsuited to ou

inaptitude [inaptityd] NF (*mentale*) inaptitude, incapacity; (*physique*) unfitness (**à qch** for sth, **à faire qch** for doing sth); (*Mil*) **~ (au service)** unfitness (for military service)

inarticulé, e [inaʀtikyle] ADJ [*mots, cris*] inarticulate

inassimilable [inasimilabl] ADJ [*notions, substance, immigrants*] that cannot be assimilated

inassimilé, e [inasimile] ADJ [*notions, immigrants, substance*] unassimilated

inassouvi, e [inasuvi] ADJ [*haine, colère, désir*] unappeased; [*faim*] unsatisfied, unappeased; (*lit, fig*) [*soif*] unquenched; **vengeance ~e** unappeased desire for revenge, unsated lust for revenge (*littér*); **soif ~e de puissance** unappeased *ou* unquenched lust for power

inassouvissement [inasuvismā] NM **l'~ de sa faim/son désir** (*action*) the failure to appease his hunger/quench his desire; (*résultat*) his unappeased hunger/desire

inattaquable [inatakabl] ADJ [*poste, position*] unassailable; [*preuve*] irrefutable; [*argument*] unassailable, irrefutable; [*conduite, réputation*] irreproachable, unimpeachable; [*personne*] (*par sa qualité*) beyond reproach (*attrib*); (*par sa position*) unassailable; [*métal*] corrosion-proof, rustproof

inatteignable [inatɛɲabl] ADJ [*objet, idéal, objectif*] unattainable

inattendu, e [inatɑ̄dy] **1** ADJ [*événement, réaction*] unexpected, unforeseen; [*visiteur, remarque*] unexpected **2** NM **l'~** the unexpected, the unforeseen; **l'~ d'une remarque** the unexpectedness of a remark

inattentif, -ive [inatɑ̄tif, iv] ADJ inattentive; **~ à** (*= ne prêtant pas attention à*) inattentive to; (*= se souciant peu de*) [*dangers, détails matériels*] heedless of, unmindful of

inattention [inatɑ̄sjɔ̄] NF **a** (*= distraction*) lack of attention, inattention; **(instant d')~** moment's inattention, momentary lapse of concentration; **(faute d')~** careless mistake **b** (*littér = manque d'intérêt pour*) **~ à** [+ *convenances, détails matériels*] lack of concern for

inaudible [inodibl] ADJ (*= non ou peu audible*) inaudible; (*péj = mauvais*) unbearable

inaugural, e [mpl -aux] [inogyʀal, o] ADJ [*séance, cérémonie*] inaugural; [*vol, voyage*] maiden (*épith*); **discours ~** [*député*] maiden *ou* inaugural speech; (*lors d'une inauguration*) inaugural speech; (*lors d'un congrès*) opening *ou* inaugural speech

inauguration [inogyʀasjɔ̄] NF **a** (*= action*) [*monument, plaque*] unveiling; [*route, bâtiment*] inauguration, opening; [*manifestation, exposition*] opening; **cérémonie/discours d'~** inaugural ceremony/lecture *ou* speech **b** (*= cérémonie*) [*monument, plaque*] unveiling ceremony; [*route, bâtiment, exposition*] opening ceremony

inaugurer [inogyʀe] ▶ conjug 1 ◀ VT **a** [+ *monument, plaque*] to unveil; [+ *route, bâtiment*] to inaugurate, open; [+ *manifestation, exposition*] to open; **~ les chrysanthèmes*** to be a mere figurehead **b** (*= commencer*) [+ *politique, période*] to inaugurate; [+ *procédé*] to pioneer; **nous inaugurions une période de paix** we were entering a time of peace; **~ la saison** [*spectacle*] to open *ou* begin the season **c** (*= étrenner*) [+ *raquette, bureau, chapeau*] to christen*

inauthenticité [inotātisite] NF inauthenticity

inauthentique [inotātik] ADJ [*document, fait*] not authentic (*attrib*); (*Philo*) [*existence*] unauthentic

inavouable [inavwabl] ADJ [*procédé, motifs,*

mœurs] shameful, too shameful to mention (*attrib*); [*bénéfices*] undisclosable

inavoué, e [inavwe] ADJ [*crime*] unconfessed; [*sentiments*] unconfessed, unavowed

INC [iɛnse] NM (ABRÉV = **Institut national de la consommation**) ≈ CA (*Brit*), ≈ CPSC (*US*)

inca [ɛ̄ka] **1** ADJ Inca **2** **Inca** NMF Inca

incalculable [ɛ̄kalkylabl] ADJ (*gén*) incalculable; **un nombre ~ de** countless numbers of, an incalculable number of

incandescence [ɛ̄kɑ̄desɑ̄s] NF incandescence; **en ~** white-hot, incandescent; **porter qch à ~** to heat sth white-hot *ou* to incandescence → **lampe, manchon**

incandescent, e [ɛ̄kɑ̄desɑ̄, ɑ̄t] ADJ [*substance, filament*] incandescent, white-hot; [*lave*] glowing; [*métal*] white-hot

incantation [ɛ̄kɑ̄tasjɔ̄] NF incantation

incantatoire [ɛ̄kɑ̄tatwaʀ] ADJ incantatory → **formule**

▼ **incapable** [ɛ̄kapabl] **1** ADJ **a** (*= inapte*) incapable, incompetent, useless* **b** **~ de faire** (*incompétence, impossibilité morale*) incapable of doing; (*impossibilité physique*) unable to do, incapable of doing; **j'étais ~ de bouger** I was unable to move, I was incapable of movement *ou* of moving; **elle est ~ de mentir** she's incapable of lying, she can't tell a lie **c** **~ d'amour** incapable of loving, unable to love; **~ de malhonnêteté** incapable of dishonesty *ou* of being dishonest; **~ du moindre effort** unable to make the least effort, incapable of making the least effort **d** (*Jur*) incapable, (legally) incompetent **2** NMF **a** (*= incompétent*) incompetent; **c'est un ~** he's useless* *ou* incapable, he's an incompetent **b** (*Jur*) incapable *ou* (legally) incompetent person

incapacitant, e [ɛ̄kapasitɑ̄, ɑ̄t] **1** ADJ incapacitating (*épith*) **2** NM incapacitant

incapacité [ɛ̄kapasite] NF **a** (*= incompétence*) incompetence, incapability **b** (*= impossibilité*) **~de faire** incapacity *ou* inability to do; **être dans l'~ de faire** to be unable to do, be incapable of doing **c** (*= invalidité*) disablement, disability; **~ totale/partielle/permanente** total/partial/permanent disablement *ou* disability; **~ de travail** industrial disablement *ou* disability **d** (*Jur*) incapacity, (legal) incompetence; **~ de jouissance** incapacity (*by exclusion from a right*); **~ d'exercice** incapacity (*by restriction of a right*); **~ civile** civil incapacity

incarcération [ɛ̄kaʀseʀasjɔ̄] NF incarceration, imprisonment

incarcérer [ɛ̄kaʀseʀe] ▶ conjug 6 ◀ VT to incarcerate, imprison; **il y est incarcéré depuis deux ans** he has been incarcerated *ou* held there for the past two years

incarnat, e [ɛ̄kaʀna, at] **1** ADJ [*teint*] rosy, pink; [*teinture*] crimson **2** NM [*teint, joues*] rosy hue, rosiness; [*tissu*] crimson tint

incarnation [ɛ̄kaʀnasjɔ̄] NF **a** (*Myth, Rel*) incarnation **b** (*= image, personnification*) **être l'~ de** to be the incarnation *ou* embodiment of

incarné, e [ɛ̄kaʀne] (*ptp de* **incarner**) ADJ **a** (*Rel*) incarnate **b** (*= personnifié*) incarnate, personified; **c'est la méchanceté ~e** he is wickedness incarnate *ou* personified, he is the embodiment of wickedness **c** [*ongle*] ingrown

incarner [ɛ̄kaʀne] ▶ conjug 1 ◀ **1** VT **a** (*Rel*) to incarnate **b** (*= représenter*) [*personne*] to embody, personify, incarnate; [*œuvre*] to embody; (*Théât*) [*acteur*] to play **2** **s'incarner** VPR **a** (*Rel*) to become *ou* be incarnate (*b = être représenté par*) **s'~ dans** *ou* **en** to be embodied in; **tous nos espoirs s'incarnent en vous** you embody all our hopes, you are the embodiment of all our hopes **c** [*ongle*] to become ingrown

incartade [ɛ̄kaʀtad] NF **a** (*= écart de conduite*) prank, escapade; **ils étaient punis à la moindre ~** they were punished for the slightest prank;

faire une ~ to go on an escapade **b** (*Équitation = écart*) swerve; **faire une ~** to shy

incassable [ɛ̄kasabl] ADJ unbreakable

incendiaire [ɛ̄sɑ̄djɛʀ] **1** NMF fire-raiser, arsonist **2** ADJ [*balle, bombe*] incendiary; [*discours, article*] inflammatory, incendiary; [*lettre d'amour, œillade*] passionate → **blond**

incendie [ɛ̄sɑ̄di] **1** NM **a** (*= sinistre*) fire, blaze, conflagration (*littér*); **un ~ s'est déclaré dans ...** a fire broke out in ... → **assurance, foyer, pompe¹ b** (*littér*) **l'~ du couchant** the blaze of the sunset, the fiery glow of the sunset; **l'~ de la révolte/de la passion** the fire of revolt/of passion **2** COMP ▶ **incendie criminel** arson (*NonC*), case of arson ▶ **incendie de forêt** forest fire ▶ **incendie volontaire** arson

incendié, e [ɛ̄sɑ̄dje] (*ptp de* **incendier**) ADJ [*bâtiment, voiture*] gutted (by fire), burned-out; [*village*] destroyed by fire

incendier [ɛ̄sɑ̄dje] ▶ conjug 7 ◀ VT **a** (*= mettre le feu à*) to set fire to, set on fire, set alight; (*= brûler complètement*) [+ *bâtiment*] to burn down; [+ *voiture*] to burn; [+ *ville, récolte, forêt*] to burn (to ashes) **b** [+ *imagination*] to fire; [+ *bouche, gorge*] to burn, set on fire; **la fièvre lui incendiait le visage** (*sensation*) fever made his face burn; (*apparence*) his cheeks were burning *ou* glowing with fever; (*littér*) **le soleil incendie le couchant** the setting sun sets the sky ablaze **c*** (*= réprimander*) **~ qn** to give sb a stiff telling-off* *ou* a rocket* (*Brit*); **tu vas te faire ~** you're in for it*, you'll get a rocket* (*Brit*); **elle l'a incendié du regard** she looked daggers at him, she shot him a baleful look

incertain, e [ɛ̄sɛʀtɛ̄, en] **1** ADJ **a** [*personne*] uncertain, unsure (**de qch** about *ou* as to sth); **~ de savoir la vérité, il ...** uncertain *ou* unsure as to whether he knew the truth, he ...; **encore ~ sur la conduite à suivre** still undecided *ou* uncertain about which course to follow **b** [*démarche*] uncertain, hesitant **c** [*temps*] uncertain, unsettled; [*contour*] indistinct, blurred; [*lumière*] dim, vague **d** [*avenir*] uncertain; [*résultat, entreprise, origine*] uncertain, doubtful; [*date, durée*] uncertain, unspecified; [*fait*] uncertain, doubtful **2** NM (*Fin*) **l'~** the exchange rate

▼ **incertitude** [ɛ̄sɛʀtityd] **1** NF **a** [*personne, résultat, fait*] uncertainty; **être dans l'~** to be in a state of uncertainty, feel uncertain; **être dans l'~ sur ce qu'on doit faire** to be uncertain as to the best course to follow **b** (*Math, Phys*) uncertainty; **principe d'~** uncertainty principle **2** **incertitudes** NFPL (*= hésitations*) doubts, uncertainties; (*= impondérables*) [*avenir, entreprise*] uncertainties

incessamment [ɛ̄sesamɑ̄] ADV (*= sans délai*) (very) shortly; **il doit arriver ~** he'll be here any minute now *ou* very shortly; (*hum*) **~ sous peu** any second now

incessant, e [ɛ̄sesɑ̄, ɑ̄t] ADJ [*efforts, activité*] ceaseless, incessant, unremitting; [*pluie, bruit, réclamations, coups de téléphone*] incessant, unceasing

incessibilité [ɛ̄sesibilite] NF non-transferability

incessible [ɛ̄sesibl] ADJ non-transferable

inceste [ɛ̄sɛst] NM incest

incestueux, -euse [ɛ̄sɛstɥø, øz] **1** ADJ [*relations, personne*] incestuous; [*enfant*] born of incest **2** NM,F (*Jur*) person guilty of incest

inchangé, e [ɛ̄ʃɑ̄ʒe] ADJ unchanged, unaltered; **la situation/son expression reste ~e** the situation/his expression remains unchanged *ou* the same *ou* unaltered

inchangeable [ɛ̄ʃɑ̄ʒabl] ADJ unchangeable

inchantable [ɛ̄ʃɑ̄tabl] ADJ unsingable

inchauffable [ɛ̄ʃofabl] ADJ impossible to heat (*attrib*)

inchavirable [ɛ̄ʃaviʀabl] ADJ uncapsizable, self-righting

> GRAMMAIRE ACTIVE: **incapable** 43.4   **incertitude** 43.1

inchoatif, -ive [ɛ̃kɔatif, iv] **1** ADJ inchoative, inceptive **2** NM inceptive

incidemment [ɛ̃sidamɑ̃] ADV (*gén*) in passing; (= *à propos*) by the way, incidentally

incidence [ɛ̃sidɑ̃s] NF (= *conséquence*) effect; (*Écon, Méd, Phys*, incidence); **avoir une ~ sur** to affect, have an effect (up)on; **cette réforme est sans ~ directe sur l'emploi** this reform will have no direct impact on employment → **angle**

incident, e [ɛ̃sidɑ̃, ɑ̃t] **1** ADJ (*frm, Jur* = *accessoire*) incidental; (*Phys*) incident; **il a évoqué ce fait de façon ~e** he mentioned this fact in passing; **je désirerais poser une question ~e** I'd like to ask a question in connection with this matter, I'd like to interpose a question **2** NM (*gén*) incident; (*Jur*) point of law; **la vie n'est qu'une succession d'~s** life is just a series of minor incidents; **~ imprévu** unexpected incident, unforeseen event; **c'est un ~ sans gravité** *ou* **sans importance** this incident is of no importance; **l'~ est clos** that's the end of the matter; **voyage sans ~(s)** uneventful journey; **se dérouler sans ~(s)** to go off without incident *ou* smoothly **3** **incidente** NF (*Ling*) (**proposition**) **~e** parenthesis, parenthetical clause **4** COMP ▸ **incident cardiaque** slight heart attack ▸ **incident diplomatique** diplomatic incident ▸ **incident de frontière** border incident ▸ **incident de paiement** (*Fin*) default in payment, nonpayment ▸ **incident de parcours** (*gén*) (minor *ou* slight) setback, hitch; (*santé*) (minor *ou* slight) setback ▸ **incident technique** (*lit, hum*) technical hitch

incinérateur [ɛ̃sineratœr] NM incinerator; **~ à ordures** refuse incinerator

incinération [ɛ̃sinerasjɔ̃] NF [*ordures, cadavre*] incineration; (*au crématorium*) cremation; **four d'~ d'ordures ménagères** incinerator for household waste → **usine**

incinérer [ɛ̃sinere] ▸ conjug 6 ◂ VT [+ *ordures, cadavre*] to incinerate; (*au crématorium*) to cremate; **se faire ~** to be cremated

incipit [ɛ̃sipit] NM INV incipit

incirconcis [ɛ̃sirkɔ̃si, iz] **1** ADJ M uncircumcised **2** NM uncircumcised male

incise [ɛ̃siz] NF (*Mus*) phrase; (*Ling*) (**proposition**) **~** interpolated clause

inciser [ɛ̃size] ▸ conjug 1 ◂ VT [+ *écorce, arbre*] to incise, make an incision in; [+ *peau*] to incise; [+ *abcès*] to lance

incisif, -ive [ɛ̃sizif, iv] **1** ADJ [*ton, style, réponse*] cutting, incisive; [*regard*] piercing; **il était très ~ dans ses questions** he was very incisive in his questioning, his questions were very incisive **2** **incisive** NF (= *dent*) incisor; **incisive supérieure/inférieure** upper/lower incisor

incision [ɛ̃sizjɔ̃] NF **a** (= *action*) [*écorce, arbre*] incising; [*peau*] incision; [*abcès*] lancing **b** (= *entaille*) incision; **pratiquer une ~ dans** to make an incision in, incise

incitateur, -trice [ɛ̃sitatœr, tris] NM,F instigator

incitatif, -ive [ɛ̃sitatif, iv] ADJ **mesure incitative** (= *aide*) incentive (à to); **aide incitative** incentive aid; **prix ~** attractive price

incitation [ɛ̃sitasjɔ̃] NF (*au meurtre, à la révolte*) incitement (à to); (*à l'effort, au travail*) incentive (à to, à faire to do); (*à la débauche, à la violence*) incitement; **~ à la haine raciale** incitement to racial hatred; **~ financière/fiscale** financial/tax incentive

inciter [ɛ̃site] ▸ conjug 1 ◂ ♦ **inciter à** VT INDIR **qn à faire qch** to encourage sb to do sth; **cela m'incite à la méfiance** that prompts me to be on my guard, that puts me on my guard; **cela les incite à la violence/la révolte** that incites

them to violence/revolt; **ça n'incite pas au travail** it doesn't (exactly) encourage one to work, it's no incentive to work

incivil, e [ɛ̃sivil] ADJ (*frm*) uncivil, rude

incivilité [ɛ̃sivilite] NF (*frm*) [*attitude, ton*] incivility, rudeness; (= *propos impoli*) uncivil *ou* rude remark; **ce serait commettre une ~ que de ...** it would be uncivil to ...

incivisme [ɛ̃sivism] NM lack of civic *ou* public spirit

inclassable [ɛ̃klasabl] ADJ which cannot be categorized, unclassifiable

inclémence [ɛ̃klemɑ̃s] NF inclemency

inclément, e [ɛ̃klemɑ̃, ɑ̃t] ADJ inclement

inclinable [ɛ̃klinabl] ADJ [*dossier de siège*] reclining; [*lampe*] adjustable; [*toit d'une voiture*] tilting

inclinaison [ɛ̃klinɛzɔ̃] **1** NF **a** (= *déclivité*) [*plan, pente*] incline; [*route, voie ferrée*] incline, gradient; [*toit*] slope, slant, pitch; [*barre, tuyau*] slope, slant; **toit à faible/forte ~** gently-sloping/steeply-sloping roof **b** (= *aspect*) [*mur*] lean; [*mât, tour*] lean, tilt; [*chapeau*] slant, tilt; [*appareil, tête*] tilt; [*navire*] list; **régler l'~ d'un siège** to adjust the angle of a seat **c** (*Géom*) [*droite, surface*] angle; (*Astron*) inclination → **angle** **2** COMP ▸ **inclinaison magnétique** (*Phys*) magnetic declination

inclination [ɛ̃klinasjɔ̃] NF **a** (= *penchant*) inclination; **suivre son ~** to follow one's (own) inclination; **son ~ naturelle au bonheur** his natural inclination *ou* tendency towards happiness; **~s altruistes** altruistic tendencies; **une certaine ~ à mentir** a certain inclination *ou* tendency *ou* propensity to tell lies; **avoir de l'~ pour la littérature** to have a strong liking *ou* a penchant for literature; **~ pour qn †** liking for sb **b** (= *mouvement*) **~ de (la) tête** (= *acquiescement*) nod; (= *salut*) inclination of the head; **~ (du buste)** bow

incliné, e [ɛ̃kline] (*ptp de* **incliner**) ADJ **a** (= *en pente raide*) [*toit*] steep, sloping **b** (= *penché*) [*tour, mur*] leaning; [*mât, table d'architecte*] at an angle, sloping; [*récipient, dossier de siège*] tilted; (*Géol*) inclined; **orbite ~e à 51 degrés** orbit inclined at 51 degrees → **plan** **c** (= *enclin*) **~ à** inclined to

incliner [ɛ̃kline] ▸ conjug 1 ◂ **1** VT **a** (= *pencher*) [+ *appareil, mât, bouteille, dossier de siège*] to tilt; (*littér* = *courber*) [+ *arbre*] to bend (over); (= *donner de l'inclinaison à*) [+ *toit, surface*] to slope; **le vent incline le navire** the wind heels the boat over; **~ la tête** *ou* **le front** (*pour saluer*) to give a slight bow, incline one's head; (*pour acquiescer*) to nod (one's head), incline one's head; **~ la tête de côté** to tilt *ou* incline one's head on one side; **~ le buste** (*saluer*) to bow, give a bow; **inclinez le corps plus en avant** lean *ou* bend forward more **b** (*littér*) **~ qn à l'indulgence** to encourage sb to be indulgent; **ceci m'incline à penser que** that makes me inclined to think that, that leads me to believe that **2** VI **a** **~ à** (= *tendre à*) to tend towards; (= *pencher pour*) to be *ou* feel inclined towards; **il incline à l'autoritarisme/à l'indulgence** he tends towards authoritarianism/indulgence, he tends to be authoritarian/indulgent; **il inclinait à la clémence/sévérité** he felt inclined to be merciful/severe, he inclined towards clemency/severity; **~ à penser/croire que ... to** be inclined to think/believe that ...; **j'incline à accepter cette offre** I'm inclined to accept this offer **b** (*littér*) [*mur*] to lean; [*arbre*] to bend; **la colline inclinait doucement vers la mer** the hill sloped gently (down) towards the sea **c** (= *modifier sa direction*) **~ vers** to veer (over) towards *ou* to **3** **s'incliner** VPR **a** (= *se courber*) to bow (**devant** before); **s'~ jusqu'à terre** to bow to

the ground **b** (= *rendre hommage à*) **s'~ devant qn** *ou* **devant la supériorité de qn** to bow before sb's superiority; **devant un tel homme, on ne peut que s'~** one can only bow (down) before such a man; **il est venu s'~ devant la dépouille mortelle du président** he came to pay his last respects at the coffin of the president **c** (= *céder*) **s'~ devant l'autorité/la volonté de qn** to yield *ou* bow to sb's authority/wishes; **s'~ devant un ordre** to accept an order; **puisque vous me l'ordonnez, je n'ai plus qu'à m'~** since you order me to do it, I can only accept it and obey **d** (= *s'avouer battu*) to admit defeat, give in; **le boxeur s'inclina (devant son adversaire) à la 3e reprise** the boxer admitted defeat in the 3rd round; **Marseille s'est incliné devant Saint-Étienne (par) 2 buts à 3** Marseilles lost to Saint-Étienne by 2 goals to 3 **e** [*arbre*] to bend over; [*mur*] to lean; [*navire*] to heel (over); [*chemin, colline*] to slope; [*toit*] to be sloping; **le soleil s'incline à l'horizon** the sun is sinking (down) towards the horizon

inclure [ɛ̃klyr] ▸ conjug 35 ◂ VT **a** (= *insérer*) [+ *clause*] to insert (**dans** in); [+ *nom*] to include (**dans** in); (= *joindre à un envoi*) [+ *billet, chèque*] to enclose (**dans** in) **b** (= *contenir*) to include; **ce récit en inclut un autre** this is a story within a story

inclus, e [ɛ̃kly, yz] (*ptp de* **inclure**) ADJ **a** (= *joint à un envoi*) enclosed **b** (= *compris*) [*frais*] included; **eux ~** including them; **jusqu'au 10 mars ~** until March 10th inclusive, up to and including March 10th; **jusqu'au 3e chapitre ~** up to and including the 3rd chapter; **les frais sont ~ dans la note** the bill is inclusive of expenses, expenses are included in the bill **c** (*Math*) [*ensemble*] **~ dans** included in; **A est ~ dans B** A is the subset of B **d** (*Bot*) [*étamines*] included; (*Méd*) **dent ~e** impacted tooth

inclusif, -ive [ɛ̃klyzif, iv] ADJ (*Gram, Logique*) inclusive

inclusion [ɛ̃klyzjɔ̃] NF **a** (*gén, Math*) inclusion (**dans** in) **b** (*Méd*) [*dent*] impaction **c** (= *élément inclus*) inclusion; **cette pierre présente des ~s de tourmaline** the stone contains streaks of tourmaline *ou* has tourmaline inclusions (*frm*) **d** (= *objet de décoration*) ornament set in acrylic

inclusivement [ɛ̃klyzivmɑ̃] ADV **jusqu'au 16e siècle ~** up to and including the 16th century; **jusqu'au 1er janvier ~** until January 1st inclusive, up to and including January 1st

incoercible [ɛ̃kɔɛrsibl] ADJ [*toux*] uncontrollable; [*besoin, désir, rire*] uncontrollable, irrepressible

incognito [ɛ̃kɔɲito] **1** ADV incognito **2** NM **garder l'~** ◊ **rester dans l'~** to remain incognito; **l'~ lui plaisait** he liked being incognito; **l'~ dont il s'entourait** the secrecy with which he surrounded himself

incohérence [ɛ̃kɔerɑ̃s] NF **a** (= *caractère illogique*) [*geste, propos, texte*] incoherence; [*comportement, politique*] inconsistency **b** (= *propos, acte*) inconsistency

incohérent, e [ɛ̃kɔerɑ̃, ɑ̃t] ADJ **a** [*geste, propos, texte*] incoherent; [*comportement, politique*] inconsistent **b** (*Phys*) [*lumière, vibration*] incoherent

incollable [ɛ̃kɔlabl] ADJ **a** (= *qui ne colle pas*) **riz ~** non-stick rice **b** (* = *imbattable*) unbeatable; [*candidat*] **il est ~** he's got all the answers, you can't catch him out* (*Brit*)

incolore [ɛ̃kɔlɔr] ADJ [*liquide, style*] colourless; [*verre, vernis*] clear; [*cirage*] neutral; **~, inodore et sans saveur** [*personne*] without an ounce of personality; [*film*] (totally) bland

incomber [ɛ̃kɔ̃be] ▸ conjug 1 ◂ ♦ **incomber à** VT INDIR (*frm*) [*devoirs, responsabilité*] to be incumbent (up)on; [*frais, réparations, travail*] to be the responsibility of; **il m'incombe de faire cela** (*gén*) it falls to me to do it, it is incumbent upon me to do it; (*responsabilité morale*) the onus is on me to do it; **ces frais leur incombent entièrement** these costs are to be paid by them in full *ou* are entirely their responsibility

incombustibilité [ɛ̃kɔ̃bystibilite] NF incombustibility

incombustible [ɛ̃kɔ̃bystibl] ADJ incombustible

incommensurabilité [ɛ̃kɔmɑ̃syrabilite] NF incommensurability

incommensurable [ɛ̃kɔmɑ̃syrabl] ADJ a (= *immense*: *gén*) immeasurable; [*bêtise, haine*] boundless b (= *sans commune mesure*: *Math, littér*) incommensurable (**avec** with)

incommensurablement [ɛ̃kɔmɑ̃syrabləmɑ̃] ADV immeasurably

incommodant, e [ɛ̃kɔmɔdɑ̃, ɑ̃t] ADJ [*odeur*] unpleasant, offensive; [*bruit*] annoying, unpleasant; [*chaleur*] uncomfortable

incommode [ɛ̃kɔmɔd] ADJ a (= *peu pratique*) [*pièce, appartement*] inconvenient; [*heure*] awkward, inconvenient; [*meuble, outil*] impractical b (= *inconfortable*) [*siège*] uncomfortable; [*position, situation*] awkward, uncomfortable

incommodément [ɛ̃kɔmɔdemɑ̃] ADV [*installé, assis*] awkwardly, uncomfortably; [*logé*] inconveniently; [*situé*] inconveniently, awkwardly

incommoder [ɛ̃kɔmɔde] ▶conjug 1 ◀ VT ~ **qn** [*bruit*] to disturb *ou* bother sb; [*odeur, chaleur*] to bother sb; [*comportement*] to make sb feel ill at ease *ou* uncomfortable; **être incommodé par** to be bothered by; **se sentir incommodé** to feel indisposed *ou* unwell

incommodité [ɛ̃kɔmɔdite] NF a [*pièce, appartement*] inconvenience; [*heure*] awkwardness; [*système, outil*] impracticability, awkwardness b [*position, situation*] awkwardness; **l'~ des sièges** the fact that the seating is so uncomfortable, the uncomfortable seats c (= *inconvénient*) inconvenience

incommunicabilité [ɛ̃kɔmynikabilite] NF incommunicability

incommunicable [ɛ̃kɔmynikabl] ADJ incommunicable

incommutabilité [ɛ̃kɔmytabilite] NF inalienability

incommutable [ɛ̃kɔmytabl] ADJ inalienable

incomparable [ɛ̃kɔ̃parabl] ADJ (= *remarquable*) incomparable, matchless; (= *dissemblable*) not comparable; **est-ce plus confortable ? — c'est ~ !** is it more comfortable? — there's no comparison !

incomparablement [ɛ̃kɔ̃parabləmɑ̃] ADV ~ **plus/mieux** incomparably more/better; **chanter ~** to sing exceptionally well

incompatibilité [ɛ̃kɔ̃patibilite] NF (*gén, Sci*) incompatibility; (*Jur*) ~ **d'humeur** (mutual) incompatibility; **il y a ~ d'humeur entre les membres de cette équipe** the members of this team are (temperamentally) incompatible; ~ **médicamenteuse** incompatibility of medications

incompatible [ɛ̃kɔ̃patibl] ADJ incompatible (**avec** with)

incompétence [ɛ̃kɔ̃petɑ̃s] NF (= *incapacité*) incompetence; (= *ignorance*) lack of knowledge; (*Jur*) incompetence; **il reconnaît volontiers son ~ en musique** he freely admits to his lack of knowledge of music *ou* that he knows nothing about music; **il a atteint son seuil d'~** he's reached his level of incompetence

incompétent, e [ɛ̃kɔ̃petɑ̃, ɑ̃t] 1 ADJ (= *incapable*) incompetent; (= *ignorant*) ignorant, inexpert; (*Jur*) incompetent; **en ce qui concerne la musique je suis ~** as far as music goes I'm not competent *ou* I'm incompetent to judge 2 NM,F incompetent

incomplet, -ète [ɛ̃kɔ̃plɛ, ɛt] ADJ incomplete

incomplètement [ɛ̃kɔ̃plɛtmɑ̃] ADV [*renseigné*] incompletely; [*rétabli, guéri*] not completely

incomplétude [ɛ̃kɔ̃pletyd] NF (*littér = insatisfaction*) non-fulfilment

incompréhensibilité [ɛ̃kɔ̃preɑ̃sibilite] NF incomprehensibility

incompréhensible [ɛ̃kɔ̃preɑ̃sibl] ADJ (*gén*) incomprehensible

incompréhensif, -ive [ɛ̃kɔ̃preɑ̃sif, iv] ADJ unsympathetic; **il s'est montré totalement ~** he (just) refused to understand, he was totally unsympathetic; **des parents totalement ~s** parents who show a total lack of understanding

incompréhension [ɛ̃kɔ̃preɑ̃sjɔ̃] NF (= *méconnaissance*) lack of understanding (**envers** of); (= *refus de comprendre*) unwillingness to understand; **leur ~ du texte** their failure to understand the text; **cet article témoigne d'une ~ totale du problème** the article shows a total lack of understanding of the problem; ~ **mutuelle** mutual incomprehension

incompressibilité [ɛ̃kɔ̃presibilite] NF (*Phys*) incompressibility; **l'~ du budget** the irreducibility of the budget

incompressible [ɛ̃kɔ̃presibl] ADJ (*Phys*) incompressible; (*Jur*) [*peine*] to be served in full; **nos dépenses sont ~s** our expenses cannot be reduced *ou* cut down

incompris, e [ɛ̃kɔ̃pri, iz] ADJ misunderstood; **il fut un grand ~ à son époque** he was never understood by his contemporaries

▼**inconcevable** [ɛ̃kɔ̃s(ə)vabl] ADJ (*gén*) inconceivable; **avec un toupet ~** with unbelievable *ou* incredible nerve

inconcevablement [ɛ̃kɔ̃s(ə)vabləmɑ̃] ADV inconceivably, incredibly

inconciliable [ɛ̃kɔ̃siljabl] ADJ, NM irreconcilable, incompatible (**avec** with); **concilier l'~** to reconcile the irreconcilable

inconditionnalité [ɛ̃kɔ̃disjɔnalite] NF unreservedness, whole-heartedness; **l'~ de son soutien au gouvernement** his wholehearted *ou* unreserved support for the government

inconditionnel, -elle [ɛ̃kɔ̃disjɔnɛl] 1 ADJ a (= *sans condition*) [*acceptation, ordre, soumission*] unconditional; **libération inconditionnelle** unconditional release b (= *absolu*) [*appui*] wholehearted, unconditional, unreserved; [*partisan, foi*] unquestioning 2 NM,F [*homme politique, doctrine*] unquestioning *ou* ardent supporter; [*écrivain, chanteur*] ardent admirer; **les ~s des sports d'hiver** winter sports enthusiasts *ou* fanatics; **c'est un ~ de l'informatique** he absolutely loves computers

inconditionnellement [ɛ̃kɔ̃disjɔnɛlmɑ̃] ADV [*soutenir, admirer*] whole-heartedly; [*accepter*] unconditionally, without conditions

inconduite [ɛ̃kɔ̃dɥit] NF (= *débauche*) loose living (*NonC*)

inconfort [ɛ̃kɔ̃fɔr] NM [*logement*] lack of comfort, discomfort; [*situation, position*] unpleasantness; **l'~ lui importait peu** discomfort didn't matter to him in the least; **vivre dans l'~** to live in uncomfortable surroundings

inconfortable [ɛ̃kɔ̃fɔrtabl] ADJ a (= *sans confort*) [*maison, meuble*] uncomfortable; [*position*] uncomfortable, awkward b (= *gênant*) [*situation*] awkward

inconfortablement [ɛ̃kɔ̃fɔrtabləmɑ̃] ADV uncomfortably

incongru, e [ɛ̃kɔ̃gry] ADJ a (= *déplacé*) [*attitude, bruit*] unseemly; [*remarque*] incongruous, ill-placed, ill-chosen b (= *bizarre, inattendu*) [*objet*] incongruous; [*personnage*] outlandish; [*situation*] strange, weird

incongruité [ɛ̃kɔ̃grɥite] NF a (= *caractère déplacé*) impropriety, unseemliness; [*propos*] incongruity, inappropriateness b (= *bizarrerie*) [*situation*] strangeness c (= *propos*) un-

seemly *ou* ill-chosen *ou* ill-placed remark; (= *acte*) unseemly action, unseemly behaviour (*NonC*)

incongrûment [ɛ̃kɔ̃grymɑ̃] ADV [*agir, parler*] in an unseemly way

inconnaissable [ɛ̃kɔnɛsabl] 1 ADJ unknowable 2 NM **l'~** the unknowable

inconnu, e [ɛ̃kɔny] 1 ADJ [*destination, fait*] unknown; [*odeur, sensation*] new, unknown; [*ville, personne*] unknown, strange (**de** to); **son visage m'était ~** his face was new *ou* unfamiliar to me, I didn't know his face; **une joie ~e l'envahit** he was seized with a strange joy *ou* a joy that was (quite) new to him; **on se sent très seul en pays ~** one feels very lonely in a strange country *ou* in a foreign country *ou* in strange surroundings; **s'en aller vers des contrées ~es** to set off in search of unknown *ou* unexplored *ou* uncharted lands; ~ **à cette adresse** not known at this address; **il est ~ au bataillon*** no one's ever heard of him → **père, soldat**
2 NM,F stranger, unknown person; **pour moi, ce peintre-là, c'est un ~** I don't know this painter, this painter is unknown to me; **le coupable n'était pas un ~ pour la police** the culprit was known *ou* was not unknown *ou* was no stranger to the police; **ne parle pas à des ~s** don't talk to strangers → **illustre**
3 NM **l'~** (= *ce qu'on ignore*) the unknown
4 **inconnue** NF (= *élément inconnu*) unknown factor *ou* quantity, unknown; (*Math*) unknown; **dans cette entreprise, il y a beaucoup d'inconnues** there are lots of unknowns *ou* unknown factors in this venture; **l'avenir du service reste la grande ~e** a big question mark hangs over the future of the department; **son attitude demeure la grande ~e** it's anybody's guess what line he'll take

inconsciemment [ɛ̃kɔ̃sjamɑ̃] ADV (= *involontairement*) unconsciously, unwittingly; (= *à la légère*) thoughtlessly, recklessly, rashly

inconscience [ɛ̃kɔ̃sjɑ̃s] NF a (*physique*) unconsciousness; **sombrer dans l'~** to lose consciousness, sink into unconsciousness b (*morale*) thoughtlessness, recklessness, rashness; **c'est de l'~ !** that's sheer madness ! *ou* stupidity ! c [*événements extérieurs*] unawareness

inconscient, e [ɛ̃kɔ̃sjɑ̃, jɑ̃t] 1 ADJ a (= *évanoui*) unconscious; (= *échappant à la conscience*) [*sentiment*] subconscious; (= *machinal*) [*mouvement*] unconscious, automatic; (= *irréfléchi*) [*décision, action, personne*] thoughtless, reckless, rash; (* : = *fou*) mad*, crazy; ~ **de** [*événements extérieurs*] unaware of, not aware of; [*conséquence, danger*] unaware of, not aware of, oblivious to 2 NM (*Psych*) **l'~** the subconscious, the unconscious; **l'~ collectif** the collective unconscious 3 NM,F reckless person; **c'est un ~ !** he must be mad !

inconséquence [ɛ̃kɔ̃sekɑ̃s] NF (= *manque de logique*) inconsistency, inconsequence (*NonC*); (= *légèreté*) thoughtlessness (*NonC*), fecklessness (*NonC*)

inconséquent, e [ɛ̃kɔ̃sekɑ̃, ɑ̃t] ADJ (= *illogique*) [*comportement, personne*] inconsistent, inconsequent; (= *irréfléchi*) [*démarche, décision, personne*] thoughtless

inconsidéré, e [ɛ̃kɔ̃sidere] ADJ [*action*] rash, reckless; [*promesse*] rash; [*démarche*] ill-considered; [*propos*] ill-considered, thoughtless; **l'usage ~ d'engrais** the indiscriminate use of fertilizers; **il fait des dépenses ~es** he's extravagant, he throws money around; **prendre des risques ~s** to take unnecessary risks

inconsidérément [ɛ̃kɔ̃sideremɑ̃] ADV thoughtlessly, rashly, without thinking

inconsistance [ɛ̃kɔ̃sistɑ̃s] NF a [*preuve, idée, espoir*] flimsiness; [*politique, argumentation, intrigue, personnage*] flimsiness, weakness; [*personne*] colourlessness (*Brit*), colorlessness

---

▶ GRAMMAIRE ACTIVE: inconcevable 43.3

(US); [caractère] weakness **b** [crème] runniness; [bouillie, soupe] watery ou thin consistency

inconsistant, e [ɛ̃kɔ̃sistã, ãt] ADJ **a** [preuve, idée, espoir] flimsy; [politique, argumentation, intrigue, personnage] flimsy, weak; [personne] colourless (Brit), colorless (US); [caractère] weak **b** [crème] runny; [bouillie, soupe] watery, thin

inconsolable [ɛ̃kɔ̃sɔlabl] ADJ [personne] disconsolate, inconsolable; [chagrin] inconsolable

inconsolé, e [ɛ̃kɔ̃sɔle] ADJ [personne] disconsolate; [chagrin] unconsoled

inconsommable [ɛ̃kɔ̃sɔmabl] ADJ unfit for consumption (attrib)

inconstance [ɛ̃kɔ̃stãs] NF **a** (= instabilité) fickleness **b** (littér) **~s** (dans le comportement) inconsistencies; (en amour) infidelities, inconstancies (frm)

inconstant, e [ɛ̃kɔ̃stã, ãt] ADJ fickle

inconstitutionnalité [ɛ̃kɔ̃stitysjɔnalite] NF unconstitutionality

inconstitutionnel, -elle [ɛ̃kɔ̃stitysjɔnɛl] ADJ unconstitutional

inconstructible [ɛ̃kɔ̃stryktibl] ADJ [zone, terrain] unsuitable for (building) development

incontestabilité [ɛ̃kɔ̃testabilite] NF incontestability

▼**incontestable** [ɛ̃kɔ̃testabl] ADJ (= indiscutable) incontestable, unquestionable, indisputable; **il a réussi, c'est ~** he's succeeded, there is no doubt about that, it's undeniable that he has succeeded; **il est ~ qu'elle est la meilleure** she is incontestably ou indisputably ou unquestionably the best

incontestablement [ɛ̃kɔ̃testabləmã] ADV incontestably, unquestionably, indisputably; **c'est prouvé? — ~** is it proved? — beyond any shadow of (a) doubt

incontesté, e [ɛ̃kɔ̃teste] ADJ [autorité, principe, fait] uncontested, undisputed; **le chef/maître ~** the undisputed chief/master; **le gagnant ~** the undisputed ou outright winner

incontinence [ɛ̃kɔ̃tinãs] **1** NF (Méd) incontinence; **~ urinaire** incontinence, enuresis (SPÉC); **~ nocturne** bedwetting, enuresis (SPÉC) **2** COMP ▶ **incontinence de langage** lack of restraint in speech ▶ **incontinence verbale** verbal diarrhoea*, garrulousness

incontinent¹, e [ɛ̃kɔ̃tinã, ãt] **1** ADJ (Méd) [personne] incontinent, enuretic (SPÉC); [vessie] weak **2** NM,F person suffering from incontinence ou enuresis (SPÉC)

incontinent²† [ɛ̃kɔ̃tinã] ADV (littér = sur-le-champ) forthwith† (littér)

incontournable [ɛ̃kɔ̃turnabl] ADJ [réalité, fait] inescapable; [date, délai] imperative; [argument, problème, artiste] that can't be ignored; [personnage, interlocuteur] key (épith); [œuvre d'art] major (épith); **c'est un livre ~** the book is essential reading; **ce produit est désormais ~** this product has become indispensable; (hum) **trois personnalités étaient invitées, dont l'~ Éliane Hotin** three celebrities were invited, including the inevitable Éliane Hotin

incontrôlable [ɛ̃kɔ̃trolabl] ADJ **a** (= non vérifiable) unverifiable, unable to be checked **b** (= irrépressible) [personne, colère] uncontrollable

incontrôlé, e [ɛ̃kɔ̃trole] ADJ **a** (= non réprimé) uncontrolled **b** (= non vérifié) [nouvelle, information] unverified

inconvenance [ɛ̃kɔ̃v(ə)nãs] NF **a** (= caractère) impropriety, unseemliness **b** (= acte) impropriety, indecorous ou unseemly behaviour (NonC); (= remarque) impropriety, indecorous ou unseemly language (NonC)

inconvenant, e [ɛ̃kɔ̃v(ə)nã, ãt] ADJ [comportement, parole] improper, indecorous, unseemly; [question] improper; [personne] ill-

mannered; **il serait ~ d'insister** it wouldn't be right to keep asking

▼**inconvénient** [ɛ̃kɔ̃venjã] NM **a** (= désavantage) [situation, plan] disadvantage, drawback, inconvenience; **les avantages et les ~s** the advantages and disadvantages (de of) **b** **~s** (= conséquences fâcheuses) [situation] (unpleasant) consequences, drawbacks **c** (= risque) risk; **n'y a-t-il pas d'~ à mettre ce plat en faïence au four?** is it (really) safe to put this earthenware plate in the oven?; **peut-on sans ~ prendre ces deux médicaments ensemble?** can one safely take ou is there any danger in taking these two medicines together? **d** (= obstacle) drawback; **l'~ c'est que je ne serai pas là** the snag ou the annoying thing ou the one drawback is that I won't be there; **il n'y a qu'un ~, c'est le prix!** there's only one drawback and that's the price; **pouvez-vous sans ~ vous libérer jeudi?** would it be convenient for you to get away on Thursday?, will you be able to get away on Thursday without any difficulty?; **voyez-vous un ~ ou y a-t-il un ~ à ce que je parte ce soir?** have you ou is there any objection to my leaving this evening?; **si vous n'y voyez pas d'~ ...** if you have no objections ...

inconvertibilité [ɛ̃kɔ̃vertibilite] NF (Fin) inconvertibility

inconvertible [ɛ̃kɔ̃vertibl] ADJ (Fin) inconvertible

incoordination [ɛ̃kɔɔrdinasjɔ̃] NF [idées, opération] lack of coordination; (Méd) incoordination, lack of coordination

incorporable [ɛ̃kɔrpɔrabl] ADJ incorporable (**dans** in, into)

incorporalité [ɛ̃kɔrpɔralite] NF incorporeality

incorporation [ɛ̃kɔrpɔrasjɔ̃] NF **a** (= mélange) [substance, aliment] mixing, blending **b** (= réunion) [territoire] incorporation; (= intégration) [chapitre] incorporation, insertion, integration **c** (Mil) (= appel) enlistment (**à** into); (= affectation) posting → **report, sursis** **d** (Psych) incorporation

incorporel, -elle [ɛ̃kɔrpɔrɛl] ADJ (= immatériel) incorporeal; (Fin) intangible

incorporer [ɛ̃kɔrpɔre] ▶conjug 1◀ VT **a** (= mélanger) [+ substance, aliment] to mix (**à, avec** with, into), blend (**à, avec** with) **b** (= intégrer) [+ territoire] to incorporate (**dans, à** into); [+ chapitre] to incorporate (**dans** in, into), insert (**dans** in); [+ personne] to incorporate, integrate (**dans, à** into); **il a très bien su s'~ à notre groupe** he fitted into our group very well; **appareil photo avec flash incorporé** camera with built-in flash **c** (Mil) (= appeler) to recruit; (= affecter) **~ qn dans** to enrol ou enlist sb into; **on l'a incorporé dans l'infanterie** he was recruited ou drafted into the infantry

incorrect, e [ɛ̃kɔrɛkt] ADJ **a** (= inadéquat) [terme] incorrect; [réglage, interprétation] faulty; [solution] incorrect, wrong **b** (= impoli) [paroles, manières] improper, impolite; [tenue] incorrect, indecent; [personne] discourteous, impolite; **il s'est montré très ~** he was very rude ou impolite → **politiquement** **c** (= déloyal) [personne, procédé] shabby; **être ~ avec qn** to treat sb shabbily

incorrectement [ɛ̃kɔrɛktəmã] ADV [prononcer, parler] incorrectly; [interpréter] wrongly; [se conduire] (= impoliment) discourteously, impolitely; (= indélicatement) shabbily

incorrection [ɛ̃kɔrɛksjɔ̃] NF **a** (= impropriété) [terme] impropriety; (= inconvenance) [tenue, personne, langage] impropriety, incorrectness; (= déloyauté) [procédés, concurrent] dishonesty, underhand nature **b** (= terme impropre) impropriety; (= action inconvenante) incorrect ou improper ou impolite behaviour (NonC); (=

remarque inconvenante) impolite ou improper remark

incorrigible [ɛ̃kɔriʒibl] ADJ [enfant, distraction] incorrigible; **cet enfant est ~!** this child is incorrigible!, this child will never learn!; **être d'une ~ paresse** to be incorrigibly lazy

incorruptibilité [ɛ̃kɔryptibilite] NF incorruptibility

incorruptible [ɛ̃kɔryptibl] **1** ADJ incorruptible **2** NMF incorruptible person; **c'est un ~** he's incorruptible

incrédule [ɛ̃kredyl] **1** ADJ **a** (= sceptique) incredulous; **d'un air ~** incredulously **b** (Rel) unbelieving **2** NMF (Rel) unbeliever, non-believer

incrédulité [ɛ̃kredylite] NF **a** (= scepticisme) incredulity; **avec ~** incredulously **b** (Rel) unbelief, lack of belief

incréé, e [ɛ̃kree] ADJ uncreated

incrément [ɛ̃kremã] NM (Ordin) increment

incrémentation [ɛ̃kremãtasjɔ̃] NF (Ordin) incrementation

incrémenter [ɛ̃kremãte] ▶conjug 1◀ VT (Ordin, Math) to increment

incrémentiel, -elle [ɛ̃kremãsjɛl] ADJ (Ordin) incremental

increvable [ɛ̃krəvabl] ADJ **a** [ballon] which cannot be burst, unburstable; [pneu] unpuncturable, puncture-proof **b*** (= infatigable) [animal, travailleur] tireless; (= indestructible) [moteur, chaussures] indestructible, which will never wear out

incriminer [ɛ̃krimine] ▶conjug 1◀ VT (= mettre en cause) [+ personne] to incriminate, accuse; [+ action, conduite] to bring under attack; [+ honnêteté, bonne foi] to call into question; **il cherche à m'~ dans cette affaire** he's trying to incriminate ou implicate me in this business; **après avoir analysé la clause incriminée du contrat ...** after having analysed the offending clause ou the clause in question ou at issue in the contract ...; **au moment des faits incriminés** at the time of the crime, when the crime was committed

incrochetable [ɛ̃krɔʃ(ə)tabl] ADJ [serrure] burglar-proof, which cannot be picked

incroyable [ɛ̃krwajabl] **1** ADJ (= invraisemblable) incredible, unbelievable; (= inouï) incredible, amazing; **~ mais vrai** incredible ou unbelievable but true; **c'est ~ ce qu'il fait chaud** it's unbelievably ou incredibly hot; **il est ~ d'arrogance** he's incredibly ou unbelievably arrogant; **il est ~, ce type!** that guy's unreal!* ou something else!* **2** NM **l'~** the unbelievable **b** (Hist = dandy) dandy

incroyablement [ɛ̃krwajabləmã] ADV (= étonnamment) incredibly, unbelievably, amazingly

incroyance [ɛ̃krwajãs] NF (Rel) unbelief; **il affirme son ~** he declares himself to be a non-believer

incroyant, e [ɛ̃krwajã, ãt] **1** ADJ unbelieving **2** NM,F unbeliever, non-believer

incrustation [ɛ̃krystasjɔ̃] NF **a** (Art) (= technique) inlaying; (= ornement) inlay; (dans un corsage, une nappe) inset, insert; **des ~s d'ivoire** inlaid ivory work, ivory inlays; **table à ~s d'ivoire/d'ébène** table inlaid with ivory/ebony **b** (TV) superimposition, overlay **c** (= croûte) (dans un récipient) fur (Brit), residue (US); (dans une chaudière) scale; (sur une roche) incrustation; **pour empêcher l'~** to prevent the formation of scale, to prevent furring (Brit)

incruste: [ɛ̃kryst] NF **taper l'~** to be a hanger-on* (péj); **c'est un champion de l'~** once he's made himself at home in a place it's impossible to get rid of him ou to shake him off

incruster [ɛ̃kryste] ▶conjug 1◀ **1** VT **a** (Art) (= insérer) **~ qch dans** to inlay sth into; (= décorer) **~ qch de** to inlay sth with; **incrusté**

dont souffre le pays the country's dire lack of resources b (= *médiocrité*) [*scénario*] mediocrity; **~ intellectuelle** intellectual poverty; **l'~ du débat intellectuel dans ce pays** the low level of intellectual debate in this country; **~ d'idées** dearth *ou* paucity of ideas

indigène [ɛ̃diʒɛn] 1 NMF (= *autochtone*) native; (*hum:* = *personne du pays*) local 2 ADJ a (= *autochtone*) [*coutume*] native; [*population*] native, indigenous; (*Bot, Zool* = *non importé*) indigenous, native b (= *local*) [*main-d'œuvre, population*] local

indigent, e [ɛ̃diʒɑ̃, ɑ̃t] 1 ADJ a (*matériellement*) [*personne*] destitute, poverty-stricken, indigent (*frm*) b (*intellectuellement*) [*film, roman*] poor; [*imagination, spectacle, architecture*] mediocre c [*végétation*] poor, sparse 2 NM,F pauper; **les ~s** the destitute, the poor, the indigent (*frm*)

indigeste [ɛ̃diʒɛst] ADJ (*lit, fig*) indigestible, difficult to digest (*attrib*)

indigestion [ɛ̃diʒɛstjɔ̃] NF a (*Méd*) attack of indigestion, indigestion (*NonC*); **il a eu une ~ de pâtisseries** he gave himself *ou* he got indigestion from eating too many cakes b (*fig*) **j'ai une ~ de films policiers** I've been OD'ing* on detective films *ou* I've been watching too many detective films; **j'en ai une ~, de toutes ces histoires*** I'm sick (and tired) of all these complications*, I'm fed up with all these complications*; **il nous répétait les mêmes conseils, jusqu'à l'~** he repeated the same advice to us ad nauseam

indignation [ɛ̃diɲasjɔ̃] NF indignation; **avec ~** indignantly; **à ma grande ~** to my great indignation; **devant l'~ générale, il changea d'avis** faced with a mood of general indignation, he changed his mind

indigne [ɛ̃diɲ] ADJ a (= *pas digne de*) **~ de** [+ *amitié, confiance, personne*] unworthy of, not worthy of; **il est ~ de vivre** he doesn't deserve to live, he's not fit to live; **ce livre est ~ de figurer dans ma bibliothèque** this book is not worthy of a place in my library; **c'est ~ de vous** [*travail, emploi*] it's beneath you; [*conduite, attitude*] it's unworthy of you; **empêcher les débats d'idées est ~ d'un démocrate** a democrat worthy of the name doesn't try to stifle intellectual debate b (= *abject*) [*acte*] shameful, disgraceful; [*mère, époux*] unworthy; [*fils*] ungrateful; **il a eu une attitude ~** he behaved disgracefully; **c'est un père ~** he's not fit to be a father

indigné, e [ɛ̃diɲe] (*ptp de* **indigner**) ADJ indignant (**par** at)

indignement [ɛ̃diɲmɑ̃] ADV shamefully

indigner [ɛ̃diɲe] ▶ conjug 1 ◀ 1 VT **~ qn** to make sb indignant 2 **s'indigner** VPR (= *se fâcher*) to become *ou* get indignant *ou* annoyed (**de** about, at, **contre** with, about, at); (= *être écœuré*) **s'~ que/de** ◊ **être indigné que/de** to be indignant that/about *ou* at; **je l'écoutais s'~ contre les spéculateurs** I listened to him waxing indignant *ou* going on* *ou* sounding off* indignantly about speculators; **je m'indigne de penser/voir que ...** it makes me indignant *ou* it fills me with indignation *ou* it infuriates me to think/see that ...

indignité [ɛ̃diɲite] NF a (= *caractère*) [*personne*] unworthiness; [*conduite*] baseness, shamefulness b (= *acte*) shameful act; **c'est une ~ !** it's a disgrace!, it's shameful!

indigo [ɛ̃digo] 1 NM (= *matière, couleur*) indigo 2 ADJ INV indigo (blue)

indigotier [ɛ̃digɔtje] NM (*Bot*) indigo (plant)

indiqué, e [ɛ̃dike] (*ptp de* **indiquer**) ADJ a (= *conseillé*) advisable; **ce n'est pas très ~** it's not really advisable, it's really not the best thing to do b (= *adéquat*) **prenons ça, c'est tout ~** let's take that — it's just the thing we need; **pour ce travail M. Legrand est tout ~** Mr Legrand is the obvious choice *ou* is

just the man we need for that job; **c'est le moyen ~** it's the best *ou* right way to do it; **c'était un sujet tout ~** it was obviously an appropriate *ou* a suitable subject c (= *prescrit*) [*médicament, traitement*] appropriate; **le traitement ~ dans ce cas est ...** the appropriate *ou* correct *ou* prescribed treatment in this case is ...; **ce remède est particulièrement ~ dans les cas graves** this drug is particularly appropriate *ou* suitable for serious cases

indiquer [ɛ̃dike] ▶ conjug 1 ◀ VT a (= *désigner*) to point out, indicate; **~ qch/qn du doigt** to point sth/sb out (**à qn** to sb), point to sth/sb; **~ qch de la main/de la tête** to indicate sth with one's hand/with a nod; **il m'indiqua du regard le coupable** his glance *ou* look directed me towards the culprit; **~ le chemin à qn** to give directions to sb, show sb the way; **~ la réception/les toilettes à qn** to direct sb to *ou* show sb the way to the reception desk/the toilets
b (= *montrer*) [*flèche, voyant, écriteau*] to show, indicate; **~ l'heure** [*montre*] to give *ou* show *ou* tell the time; **la petite aiguille indique les heures** the small hand shows *ou* marks the hours; **l'horloge indiquait 2 heures** the clock said *ou* showed it was 2 o'clock; **qu'indique la pancarte ?** what does the sign say?
c (= *recommander*) [+ *livre, hôtel, médecin*] to recommend
d (= *dire*) [*personne*] [+ *heure, solution*] to tell; [+ *dangers, désavantages*] to point out, show; **il m'indiqua le mode d'emploi/comment le réparer** he told me how to use it/how to fix it
e (= *fixer*) [+ *heure, date, rendez-vous*] to give, name; **à l'heure indiquée, je ...** at the time indicated *ou* stated, I ...; **au jour *ou* à l'heure *ou* au moment indiqué** at the agreed *ou* appointed time, I ...; **à la date indiquée** on the given *ou* agreed day; **au lieu indiqué** at the given *ou* agreed place
f (= *faire figurer*) [*étiquette, plan, cartographe*] to show; [*table, index*] to give, show; **est-ce indiqué sur la facture/dans l'annuaire ?** is it given *ou* mentioned on the invoice/in the directory?; **il a sommairement indiqué les fenêtres sur le plan** he quickly marked *ou* drew in the windows on the plan; **quelques traits pour ~ les spectateurs/ombres** a few strokes to give an impression of spectators/shadows; **quelques croquis pour ~ le jeu de scène** a few sketches to give a rough idea of the action
g (= *dénoter*) to indicate, point to; **tout indique que les prix vont augmenter** everything indicates that prices are going to rise, everything points to a forthcoming rise in prices; **cela indique une certaine négligence/hésitation de sa part** that shows *ou* points to a certain carelessness/hesitation on his part

indirect, e [ɛ̃diʀɛkt] ADJ (*gén*) indirect; (*Jur*) [*ligne, héritier*] collateral; **d'une manière ~e** in a roundabout *ou* an indirect way; **apprendre qch de manière ~e** to hear of sth in a roundabout way → **discours, éclairage, impôt**

indirectement [ɛ̃diʀɛktəmɑ̃] ADV (*gén*) indirectly; (= *de façon détournée*) [*faire savoir, apprendre*] in a roundabout way

indiscernable [ɛ̃disɛʀnabl] ADJ indiscernible, imperceptible

indiscipline [ɛ̃disiplin] NF (= *insubordination*) indiscipline, lack of discipline; **faire preuve d'~** to behave in an undisciplined *ou* unruly manner

indiscipliné, e [ɛ̃disipline] ADJ [*troupes, écolier*] undisciplined; [*cheveux*] unmanageable, unruly

indiscret, -ète [ɛ̃diskʀɛ, ɛt] ADJ a (= *trop curieux*) [*personne*] inquisitive; [*question*] indiscreet; [*regard, yeux*] inquisitive, prying; **à l'abri des regards ~s/des oreilles indiscrètes** away from prying *ou* inquisitive eyes/from eavesdroppers; **serait-ce ~ de vous demander ... ?** would it be indiscreet to ask you ...?; **mettre**

des documents à l'abri des ~s to put documents out of the reach of inquisitive people b (= *bavard*) [*personne*] indiscreet; **ne confiez rien aux ~s** don't confide in people who can't keep secrets

indiscrètement [ɛ̃diskʀɛtmɑ̃] ADV [*demander*] inquisitively; [*regarder*] indiscreetly

indiscrétion [ɛ̃diskʀesjɔ̃] NF a (= *curiosité*) [*question*] indiscreetness, indiscretion; [*personne, regard*] inquisitiveness; **excusez mon ~, mais quel âge avez-vous ?** I hope you don't mind me *ou* my asking, but how old are you?; **elle pousse l'~ jusqu'à lire mon courrier** she's so inquisitive she even reads my mail; **sans ~, peut-on savoir si ... ?** without wanting to be *ou* without being indiscreet, may we ask whether ...?; **sans ~, combien l'avez-vous payé ?** would you mind if I asked how much you paid for it? b (= *tendance à trop parler*) indiscretion; **il est d'une telle ~ !** he's so indiscreet! c (= *parole*) indiscreet word *ou* remark, indiscretion; (= *action*) indiscreet act, indiscretion; **commettre une ~** to commit an indiscretion; **les ~s de la presse à scandale** tabloid revelations

indiscutable [ɛ̃diskytabl] ADJ indisputable, unquestionable

▼ **indiscutablement** [ɛ̃diskytabləmɑ̃] ADV indisputably, unquestionably

indiscuté, e [ɛ̃diskyte] ADJ undisputed

▼ **indispensable** [ɛ̃dispɑ̃sabl] 1 ADJ essential; **cette lecture est ~** it's essential reading; **ces outils/précautions sont ~s** these tools/precautions are essential; **ce collaborateur m'est ~** this collaborator is indispensable to me, I can't do without this collaborator; **tu veux que je vienne ? — ce n'est pas ~** do you want me to come? — it's not necessary *ou* there's no need; **il est ~ que/de faire** it is essential *ou* absolutely necessary *ou* vital that/to do; **je crois qu'il est ~ qu'ils y aillent** I think it's vital *ou* essential that they (should) go; **emporter les vêtements ~s (pour le voyage)** to take the clothes which are essential *ou* indispensable (for the journey); **prendre les précautions ~s** to take the necessary precautions; **crédits/travaux ~s à la construction d'un bâtiment** funds/work essential *ou* vital for the construction of a building; **l'eau est un élément ~ à la vie** water is essential to life; **savoir se rendre ~** to make o.s. indispensable
2 NM **nous n'avions que l'~** we only had what was absolutely essential *ou* necessary *ou* indispensable; **faire l'~ d'abord** to do what is essential *ou* absolutely necessary first; **l'~ est de ...** it's absolutely necessary *ou* essential to ...

indisponibilité [ɛ̃disponibilite] NF unavailability

indisponible [ɛ̃disponibl] ADJ (*gén*) not available, unavailable (*attrib*), unavailable; (*Jur*) unavailable

indisposé, e [ɛ̃dispoze] (*ptp de* **indisposer**) ADJ (= *fatigué, malade*) indisposed, unwell; (*euph*) [*femme*] indisposed

indisposer [ɛ̃dispoze] ▶ conjug 1 ◀ VT (= *rendre malade*) [*aliment, chaleur*] to upset, indispose; (= *mécontenter*) [*personne, remarque*] to antagonize; **il a des allures qui m'indisposent** his way of behaving irritates me *ou* puts me off him* (*Brit*); **il indispose tout le monde (contre lui)** he antagonizes everybody; **tout l'indispose !** anything annoys him!, he takes a dislike to everything!; **cette scène trop violente risque d'~ les spectateurs** audiences are likely to find this very violent scene disturbing

indisposition [ɛ̃dispozisjɔ̃] NF (= *malaise*) (slight) indisposition, upset; (*euph* = *règles*) period

indissociable [ɛ̃disɔsjabl] ADJ [*éléments, problèmes*] indissociable (**de** from); **être un élément ~ de qch** to be an integral part of sth

▶ GRAMMAIRE ACTIVE: **indiscutablement** 53.6   **indispensable** 37.1

indissociablement [ɛ̃disɔsjabləmɑ̃] ADV inextricably

indissolubilité [ɛ̃disɔlybilite] NF indissolubility

indissoluble [ɛ̃disɔlybl] ADJ indissoluble

indissolublement [ɛ̃disɔlybləmɑ̃] ADV indissolubly; **~ liés** indissolubly ou inextricably linked

indistinct, e [ɛ̃distɛ̃(kt), ɛ̃kt] ADJ [forme, idée, souvenir] indistinct, vague; [rumeur, murmure] indistinct, confused; [lumière] faint; [couleurs] vague; **des voix ~es** a confused murmur of voices

indistinctement [ɛ̃distɛ̃ktəmɑ̃] ADV [a] (= confusément) indistinctly, vaguely; **des bruits provenaient ~ du jardin** I could hear confused noises coming from the garden [b] (= ensemble) indiscriminately; **tuant ~ femmes et enfants** killing women and children indiscriminately ou without distinction [c] (= indifféremment) **cette cuisinière marche ~ au gaz ou à l'électricité** this cooker runs either on gas or on electricity ou runs equally well on gas or on electricity; **il se méfie ~ de la gauche et de la droite** he has an equal mistrust of the left wing and the right wing

indium [ɛ̃djɔm] NM indium

individu [ɛ̃dividy] NM [a] (= unité: gén), (Bio) individual; **le conflit entre l'~ et la société** the conflict between the individual and society [b] (hum = corps) **dans la partie la plus charnue de son ~** in the fleshiest part of his anatomy [c] (péj = homme) fellow, individual, character; **un ~ l'aborda** someone came up to him; **il aperçut un drôle d'~/un ~ louche** he noticed an odd-looking/a shady-looking character ou individual

individualisation [ɛ̃dividɥalizasjɔ̃] NF individualization, personalization; **~ des salaires** wage negotiation on an individual basis; **~ de l'enseignement** tailoring education to suit individual ou particular needs; (Jur) **l'~ d'une peine** sentencing according to the characteristics of the offender

individualisé, e [ɛ̃dividɥalize] (ptp de **individualiser**) ADJ [caractères, groupe] distinctive; [objet personnel, voiture] personalized, customized; [formation, programme] individualized, personalized; **groupe fortement ~** highly distinctive group, group with a distinctive identity; **des solutions ~es selon les besoins** solutions which are tailored to suit individual ou particular requirements

individualiser [ɛ̃dividɥalize] ▶ conjug 1 ◀ [1] VT [a] (= personnaliser) [+ objet personnel, voiture] to personalize, customize; [+ solutions, horaire, enseignement] to tailor to suit individual ou particular needs; (Jur) [+ peine] to match with the characteristics of the offender [b] (= caractériser) to individualize [2] **s'individualiser** VPR [personne] to acquire an identity of one's own, become more individual; [groupe, région] to acquire an identity of its own

individualisme [ɛ̃dividɥalism] NM individualism

individualiste [ɛ̃dividɥalist] [1] ADJ individualistic [2] NMF individualist

individualité [ɛ̃dividɥalite] NF (= caractère individuel) individuality; (= personne) individual; (= personnalité) personality

individuation [ɛ̃dividɥasjɔ̃] NF individuation

individuel, -elle [ɛ̃dividɥɛl] ADJ [a] (= propre à l'individu) (gén) individual; [responsabilité, défaut, contrôle, livret] personal, individual; [ordinateur] personal; [caractères] distinctive, individual; [maison] detached; **propriété individuelle** personal ou private property; **liberté individuelle** personal freedom, freedom of the individual; **chambre individuelle** (dans un hôtel) single room; **voyager en ~** to travel alone; **parler à titre ~** to speak in a personal capacity [b] (= isolé) [fait] individual, isolated; [sachet]

individual; **les cas ~s seront examinés** individual cases ou each individual case will be examined [c] (Sport) individual; **épreuve individuelle** individual event

individuellement [ɛ̃dividɥɛlmɑ̃] ADV individually

indivis, e [ɛ̃divi, iz] ADJ (Jur) [propriété, succession] undivided, joint (épith); [propriétaires] joint (épith); **par ~** [posséder] jointly

indivisaire [ɛ̃divizɛʀ] NMF (Jur) tenant in common

indivisément [ɛ̃divizemɑ̃] ADV (Jur) jointly

indivisibilité [ɛ̃divizibilite] NF indivisibility

indivisible [ɛ̃divizibl] ADJ indivisible

indivisiblement [ɛ̃divizibləmɑ̃] ADV indivisibly

indivision [ɛ̃divizjɔ̃] NF (Jur) joint possession ou ownership; **propriété en ~** jointly-held property; **posséder qch en ~** to own sth jointly

Indochine [ɛ̃dɔʃin] NF Indo-China

indochinois, e [ɛ̃dɔʃinwa, waz] [1] ADJ Indo-Chinese [2] **Indochinois(e)** NM,F Indo-Chinese

indocile [ɛ̃dɔsil] ADJ [enfant] unruly; [mémoire] intractable

indocilité [ɛ̃dɔsilite] NF [enfant] unruliness; [mémoire] intractability

indo-européen, -enne [ɛ̃doøʀɔpeɛ̃, ɛn] [1] ADJ Indo-European [2] NM (Ling) Indo-European [3] **Indo-Européen(ne)** NM,F Indo-European

indolemment [ɛ̃dɔlamɑ̃] ADV indolently

indolence [ɛ̃dɔlɑ̃s] NF [élève] idleness, indolence; [pouvoirs publics] apathy, lethargy; [geste, regard] indolence, languidness

indolent, e [ɛ̃dɔlɑ̃, ɑ̃t] ADJ [élève] idle, indolent; [pouvoirs publics] apathetic, lethargic; [air, geste, regard] indolent, languid

indolore [ɛ̃dɔlɔʀ] ADJ painless

indomptable [ɛ̃dɔ̃(p)tabl] ADJ [animal, adversaire, peuple] (hum) [personne] untameable; [cheval] untameable, which cannot be broken ou mastered; [enfant] unmanageable, uncontrollable; [caractère, courage, volonté] indomitable, invincible; [passion, haine] ungovernable, invincible, uncontrollable

indompté, e [ɛ̃dɔ̃(p)te] ADJ [enfant, animal, peuple] untamed, wild; [cheval] unbroken, untamed; [courage] undaunted; [énergie] unharnessed, untamed; [passion] ungoverned, unsuppressed

Indonésie [ɛ̃dɔnezi] NF Indonesia

indonésien, -ienne [ɛ̃dɔnezjɛ̃, jɛn] [1] ADJ Indonesian [2] NM (Ling) Indonesian [3] **Indonésien(ne)** NM,F Indonesian

indou, e [ɛ̃du] ADJ, NM,F = **hindou**

in-douze [induz] ADJ INV, NM INV duodecimo, twelvemo

indu, e [ɛ̃dy] [1] ADJ [a] (= qui n'est pas dû) [somme, charges] not owed, unowed; [avantage] unwarranted, unjustified [b] (hum, littér = déraisonnable) undue; **sans optimisme ~** without undue optimism; **à une heure ~e** at an ou some ungodly hour [2] NM (Fin) unowed sum

indubitable [ɛ̃dybitabl] ADJ [preuve] indubitable, undoubted; **c'est ~** there is no doubt about it, it's beyond doubt, it's indubitable; **il est ~ qu'il a tort** he is undoubtedly wrong, there's no doubt (that) he's wrong

indubitablement [ɛ̃dybitabləmɑ̃] ADV (= assurément) undoubtedly, indubitably; **vous vous êtes ~ trompé** you have undoubtedly made a mistake

inductance [ɛ̃dyktɑ̃s] NF inductance

inducteur, -trice [ɛ̃dyktœʀ, tʀis] [1] ADJ (gén, Phys) inductive [2] NM (Chim, Phys) inductor

inductif, -ive [ɛ̃dyktif, iv] ADJ (gén: Phys) inductive

induction [ɛ̃dyksjɔ̃] NF (gén, Bio, Élec, Phys) induction; **raisonnement par ~** reasoning by induction; **~ magnétique** magnetic induction

induire [ɛ̃dɥiʀ] ▶ conjug 38 ◀ VT [a] **~ qn en erreur** to mislead sb, lead sb astray [b] († = inciter) **~ qn à** [+ péché, gourmandise] to lead sb into; **~ qn à faire** to induce sb to do [c] (= inférer) to infer, induce (de from); **j'en induis que** I infer from this that [d] (= occasionner) to lead to, result in [e] (Élec) to induce

induit, e [ɛ̃dɥi, it] [1] ADJ (= résultant) [avantage, risque] resulting; [effet induit] side-effect; (Écon) **emplois ~s** spinoff jobs [2] NM (Élec) armature

indulgence [ɛ̃dylʒɑ̃s] NF [a] (= bienveillance) [parent, critique, commentaire] indulgence; [juge, examinateur] leniency; **une erreur qui a rencontré l'~ du jury** a mistake for which the jury made allowances ou which the jury was prepared to overlook ou be lenient about; **il a demandé l'~ des jurés** he asked the jury to make allowances for ou to show leniency towards his client; **faire preuve d'~ envers** ou **à l'égard de** [parent] to be indulgent with; [juge, examinateur] to be lenient with; [critique] to be kind to; **avec ~** leniently; **d'une ~ excessive** overindulgent; **sans ~** [juge, jugement] stern; [portrait, critique] brutally frank; [punir] without leniency; [critiquer] with brutal frankness; **regard plein d'~** indulgent look [b] (Rel) indulgence

indulgent, e [ɛ̃dylʒɑ̃, ɑ̃t] ADJ [parent] indulgent, lenient; [juge, examinateur] lenient (**envers** towards); [critique, commentaire, regard] indulgent; **15, c'est une note trop ~e** 15 is (far) too lenient ou generous a mark; **se montrer ~** [juge] to show leniency; [examinateur, parent] to be lenient

indûment [ɛ̃dymɑ̃] ADV [protester] unduly; [détenir] without due cause ou reason, wrongfully; **s'ingérer ~ dans les affaires de qn** to interfere unnecessarily in sb's business

induration [ɛ̃dyʀasjɔ̃] NF induration (SPÉC), hardening

induré, e [ɛ̃dyʀe] (ptp de **indurer**) ADJ indurate (SPÉC), hardened

indurer [ɛ̃dyʀe] ▶ conjug 1 ◀ [1] VT to indurate (SPÉC), harden [2] **s'indurer** VPR to indurate (SPÉC), become indurate (SPÉC), harden

Indus [ɛ̃dys] NM **l'~** the Indus

industrialisation [ɛ̃dystʀijalizasjɔ̃] NF industrialization

industrialisé, e [ɛ̃dystʀijalize] (ptp de **industrialiser**) ADJ [pays, monde] industrialized; **région fortement ~e** heavily industrialized area; **région faiblement ~e** area without much industry ou with a low level of industry

industrialiser [ɛ̃dystʀijalize] ▶ conjug 1 ◀ [1] VT to industrialize [2] **s'industrialiser** VPR to become industrialized

industrialisme [ɛ̃dystʀijalism] NM industrialism

industrialiste [ɛ̃dystʀijalist] ADJ [politique] which favours ou encourages industrialization

industrie [ɛ̃dystʀi] [1] NF [a] (= activité, secteur, branche) industry; **~ légère/lourde** light/heavy industry; **la grande ~** big industry; **~ naissante** infant industry; **doter un pays d'une ~** to provide a country with an industrial structure → **ministère, pointe** [b] (= entreprise) industry, industrial concern; **petites et moyennes ~s** small businesses → **capitaine** [c] (littér, †) (= ingéniosité) ingenuity; (= ruse) cunning [d] (= activité: littér, hum) **il exerçait sa coupable ~** he plied his evil trade → **chevalier** [2] COMP ▶ **industrie aéronautique** aviation industry ▶ **industrie automobile** car ou automobile (US) industry ▶ **industrie alimentaire** food (processing) industry

► **industrie chimique** chemical industry
► **l'industrie cinématographique** *ou* **du cinéma** the film industry ► **l'industrie hôtelière** the hotel industry ► **industries de la langue** language industries ► **industries du livre** book-related industries ► **industrie de** *ou* **du luxe** luxury goods industry ► **industrie manufacturière** manufacturing industry ► **l'industrie du multimédia** the multimedia industry ► **industrie pharmaceutique** pharmaceutical *ou* drug industry ► **industrie de précision** precision tool industry ► **l'industrie du spectacle** the entertainment business, show business ► **industrie de transformation** processing industry

industriel, -elle [ɛ̃dystʀijɛl] ⓵ ADJ industrial; **aliments ~s** factory feedstuffs; **pain ~** factory-baked bread; **équipement à usage ~** heavy-duty equipment; **élevage ~** (= *système*) factory farming; (= *ferme*) factory farm → **quantité, zone** ⓶ NM (= *fabricant*) industrialist, manufacturer; **les ~s du textile/de l'automobile** textile/car *ou* automobile (*US*) manufacturers

industriellement [ɛ̃dystʀijɛlmɑ̃] ADV industrially; **poulets élevés ~** factory-farmed chickens

industrieux, -ieuse [ɛ̃dystʀijø, ijøz] ADJ (*littér* = *besogneux*) industrious

inébranlable [inebʀɑ̃labl] ADJ ⓐ [*adversaire, interlocuteur*] steadfast, unwavering; [*personne, foi, résolution*] unshakable, steadfast, unwavering; [*certitude*] unshakeable, unwavering; [*principes, conviction*] steadfast; **il était ~ dans sa conviction que ...** he was steadfast *ou* unshakeable *ou* unwavering in his belief that ... ⓑ [*objet pesant*] solid; [*objet encastré*] immovable, solidly *ou* firmly fixed

inébranlablement [inebʀɑ̃lablǝmɑ̃] ADV unshakeably

inécoutable [inekutabl] ADJ [*musique*] unbearable

inécouté, e [inekute] ADJ unheeded

inédit, e [inedi, it] ⓵ ADJ ⓐ (= *non publié*) [*texte, auteur*] (previously *ou* hitherto) unpublished; **ce film est ~ en France** this film has never been released *ou* distributed in France ⓑ (= *nouveau*) [*méthode, trouvaille*] novel, new, original; [*spectacle*] new ⓶ NM (= *texte*) (previously *ou* hitherto) unpublished material (*NonC*) *ou* work; (*hum*) **c'est de l'~!** that's never happened before!

inéducable [inedykabl] ADJ ineducable

ineffable [inefabl] ADJ ineffable

ineffaçable [inefasabl] ADJ indelible, ineffaceable

inefficace [inefikas] ADJ [*remède, mesure, traitement*] ineffective; [*employé, machine*] inefficient

inefficacement [inefikasmɑ̃] ADV (= *sans succès*) ineffectively; (= *de manière incompétente*) inefficiently

inefficacité [inefikasite] NF [*remède, mesure*] ineffectiveness; [*machine, employé*] inefficiency; **d'une totale ~** [*remède, mesure*] totally ineffective; [*employé, machine*] totally inefficient

inégal, e [*mpl* -**aux**] [inegal, o] ADJ ⓐ (= *différent*) unequal; **d'~e grosseur** of unequal size; **de force ~e** of unequal strength; **les hommes sont inégaux** all men are not equal ⓑ (= *irrégulier*) [*sol, pas, mouvement*] uneven; [*pouls*] irregular, uneven; [*artiste, sportif*] erratic; [*œuvre, jeu*] uneven; [*étalement, répartition*] uneven; [*humeur, caractère*] uneven, changeable; [*conduite*] changeable; **d'intérêt ~** of varying *ou* mixed interest; **de qualité ~e** of varying quality ⓒ (= *disproportionné*) [*lutte, partage*] unequal

inégalable [inegalabl] ADJ incomparable, matchless

inégalé, e [inegale] ADJ [*record*] unequalled, unbeaten; [*charme, beauté*] unrivalled

inégalement [inegalmɑ̃] ADV (= *différemment, injustement*) unequally; (= *irrégulièrement*) unevenly; **livre ~ apprécié** book which met (*ou* meets) with varying approval

inégalitaire [inegalitɛʀ] ADJ [*société, système*] unequal, inegalitarian (*frm*); [*traitement, loi*] unequal

inégalité [inegalite] NF ⓐ (= *différence*) [*hauteurs, volumes*] difference (**de** between); [*sommes, parts*] difference, disparity (**de** between); **~ des chances** inequality of opportunity; **l'~ de l'offre et de la demande** the difference *ou* disparity between supply and demand; **l'~ de traitement entre hommes et femmes** the unequal treatment of men and women; **les ~s sociales** social inequalities; **~s de revenus** disparities in income ⓑ (*Math*) inequality ⓒ (= *injustice*) inequality ⓓ (= *irrégularité*) [*sol, pas, rythme, répartition*] unevenness; [*humeur, caractère*] unevenness, changeability; **~s de terrain** unevenness of the ground, bumps in the ground; **~s d'humeur** moodiness

inélégamment [inelegamɑ̃] ADV inelegantly

inélégance [inelegɑ̃s] NF ⓐ [*geste, toilette, silhouette*] inelegance; [*allure*] inelegance, ungainliness ⓑ [*procédé*] discourtesy

inélégant, e [inelegɑ̃, ɑ̃t] ADJ ⓐ (= *disgracieux*) [*geste, toilette, silhouette*] inelegant; [*allure*] inelegant, ungainly ⓑ (= *indélicat*) [*procédé*] discourteous; **c'était très ~ de sa part** it was very discourteous of him

inéligibilité [ineliʒibilite] NF (*Pol*) ineligibility

inéligible [ineliʒibl] ADJ (*Pol*) ineligible

inéluctabilité [inelyktabilite] NF inescapability, ineluctability (*frm*)

▼ **inéluctable** [inelyktabl] ADJ, NM inescapable, ineluctable (*frm*)

inéluctablement [inelyktablǝmɑ̃] ADV inescapably, ineluctably (*frm*)

inemployable [inɑ̃plwajabl] ADJ [*procédé*] unusable; [*personnel*] unemployable

inemployé, e [inɑ̃plwaje] ADJ (= *inutilisé*) [*outil, argent*] unused; [*talent, capacités*] untapped; (= *gâché*) [*dévouement, énergie*] unchannelled, unchannelled

inénarrable [inenaʀabl] ADJ ⓐ (= *désopilant*) [*incident, scène*] hilarious, priceless*, too funny for words (*attrib*); [*vêtement, démarche*] incredibly funny, priceless*; **son ~ mari** her incredible husband* ⓑ (= *incroyable*) [*péripéties, aventure*] incredible

inentamé, e [inɑ̃tame] ADJ [*réserve d'essence, d'argent*] intact (*attrib*); [*victuailles*] intact (*attrib*), untouched; [*bouteille*] unopened; [*énergie, moral*] (as yet) intact (*attrib*)

inenvisageable [inɑ̃vizaʒabl] ADJ which cannot be considered, unthinkable

inéprouvé, e [inepʀuve] ADJ [*méthode, vertu, procédé*] untested, untried, not yet put to the test (*attrib*); [*émotion*] not yet experienced (*attrib*)

inepte [inɛpt] ADJ [*personne*] inept, useless*, hopeless*; [*histoire, raisonnement*] inept

ineptie [inɛpsi] NF ⓐ (= *caractère*) ineptitude ⓑ (= *acte, propos*) ineptitude; (= *idée, œuvre*) nonsense (*NonC*), rubbish (*Brit*) (*NonC*); **dire des ~s** to talk nonsense; **ce qu'il a fait est une ~** what he did was utterly stupid

inépuisable [inepɥizabl] ADJ inexhaustible; **il est ~ sur ce sujet** he could talk for ever on that subject; **source ~ de conflits** unending *ou* abiding source of conflict

inéquation [inekwasjɔ̃] NF inequation

inéquitable [inekitabl] ADJ inequitable

inerte [inɛʀt] ADJ (= *immobile*) [*corps, membre*] lifeless, inert; [*visage*] expressionless; (= *sans réaction*) [*personne*] passive, inert; [*esprit, élève*]

apathetic; (*Sci*) inert; **ne reste pas ~ sur ta chaise** don't just sit there

inertie [inɛʀsi] NF [*personne*] inertia, passivity, apathy; [*service administratif*] apathy, inertia; [*élève*] apathy; (*Phys*) inertia; (*Aviat*) **navigation par ~** inertial guidance *ou* navigation → **force**

inescompté, e [inɛskɔ̃te] ADJ unexpected, unhoped-for

inespéré, e [inɛspeʀe] ADJ unexpected, unhoped-for

inesthétique [inɛstetik] ADJ [*pylône, usine, cicatrice*] unsightly; [*démarche, posture*] ungainly

inestimable [inɛstimabl] ADJ [*aide*] inestimable, invaluable; [*valeur*] priceless, incalculable, inestimable; [*dommages*] incalculable

inévitable [inevitabl] ⓵ ADJ [*obstacle, accident*] unavoidable; (= *fatal*) [*résultat*] inevitable, inescapable; (*hum*) [*chapeau, cigare*] inevitable; **c'était ~!** it was inevitable!, it was bound to happen!, it had to happen! ⓶ NM **l'~** the inevitable

▼ **inévitablement** [inevitablǝmɑ̃] ADV inevitably

▼ **inexact, e** [inɛgza(kt), akt] ADJ ⓐ (= *faux*) [*renseignement, calcul, traduction, historien*] inaccurate, inexact; **non, c'est ~** no, that's not correct *ou* that's wrong ⓑ (= *sans ponctualité*) unpunctual; **être ~ à un rendez-vous** to be late for an appointment

inexactement [inɛgzaktǝmɑ̃] ADV [*traduire, relater*] inaccurately, incorrectly

inexactitude [inɛgzaktityd] NF ⓐ (= *manque de précision*) inaccuracy ⓑ (= *erreur*) inaccuracy ⓒ (= *manque de ponctualité*) unpunctuality (*NonC*)

inexaucé, e [inɛgzose] ADJ [*prière*] (as yet) unanswered; [*vœu*] (as yet) unfulfilled

inexcusable [inɛkskyzabl] ADJ [*faute, action*] inexcusable, unforgivable; **vous êtes ~ (d'avoir fait cela)** you had no excuse (for doing that), it was inexcusable *ou* unforgivable of you (to have done that)

inexécutable [inɛgzekytabl] ADJ [*projet, travail*] impractical, impracticable; [*musique*] unplayable; [*ordre*] which cannot be carried out *ou* executed

inexécution [inɛgzekysjɔ̃] NF [*contrat, obligation*] nonfulfilment

inexercé, e [inɛgzɛʀse] ADJ [*soldats*] inexperienced, untrained; [*oreille*] unpractised, untrained

inexistant, e [inɛgzistɑ̃, ɑ̃t] ADJ (= *absent*) [*service d'ordre, réseau téléphonique, aide*] nonexistent; (= *imaginaire*) [*difficultés*] imaginary, nonexistent; (*péj*) **quant à son mari, il est ~** as for her husband, he's a (complete) nonentity *ou* cipher

inexistence [inɛgzistɑ̃s] NF non-existence

inexorabilité [inɛgzɔʀabilite] NF [*destin, vieillesse*] inexorability; [*juge, arrêt, loi*] inflexibility, inexorability (*littér*)

inexorable [inɛgzɔʀabl] ADJ ⓐ (= *implacable*) [*destin, vieillesse*] inexorable; (= *inévitable*) **l'~ montée de la violence** the inexorable rise of violence ⓑ (= *impitoyable*) [*arrêt, loi*] inflexible, inexorable (*littér*); [*juge*] unyielding, inflexible, inexorable (*littér*); **il fut ~ à leurs prières** he was unmoved by their entreaties

inexorablement [inɛgzɔʀablǝmɑ̃] ADV inexorably

inexpérience [inɛkspeʀjɑ̃s] NF inexperience, lack of experience

inexpérimenté, e [inɛkspeʀimɑ̃te] ADJ [*personne*] inexperienced; [*mouvements, gestes*] inexpert; [*arme, produit*] untested

inexpiable [inɛkspjabl] ADJ inexpiable

inexpié, e [inɛkspje] ADJ unexpiated

inexplicable [inɛksplikabl(ǝ)] ADJ, NM inexplicable

► **GRAMMAIRE ACTIVE:** **inéluctable** 53.4   **inévitablement** 42.1   **inexact** 53.6

inexplicablement [inɛksplikabləmɑ̃] ADV inexplicably

inexpliqué, e [inɛksplike] ADJ unexplained

inexploitable [inɛksplwatabl] ADJ (gén) unexploitable; [filon] unworkable

inexploité, e [inɛksplwate] ADJ (gén) unexploited; [talent, ressources] untapped

inexplorable [inɛksplɔrabl] ADJ unexplorable

inexploré, e [inɛksplɔre] ADJ unexplored

inexplosible [inɛksplozibl] ADJ non-explosive

inexpressif, -ive [inɛkspresif, iv] ADJ [visage, regard] expressionless, inexpressive, blank; [style, mots] inexpressive

inexpressivité [inɛkspresivite] NF inexpressiveness, expressionlessness

inexprimable [inɛksprimabl] ADJ, NM inexpressible

inexprimé, e [inɛksprime] ADJ [sentiment] unexpressed; [reproches, doutes] unspoken

inexpugnable [inɛkspygnabl] ADJ [citadelle] impregnable, unassailable

inextensible [inɛkstɑ̃sibl] ADJ [matériau] that does not stretch, unstretchable; [étoffe] non-stretch

in extenso [inɛkstɛ̃so] 1 LOC ADV [écrire, publier, lire] in full, in extenso (frm) 2 LOC ADJ [texte, discours] full (épith)

inextinguible [inɛkstɛ̃gibl] ADJ (littér) [passion, feu] inextinguishable; [haine] undying; [besoin, soif] unquenchable; [rire] uncontrollable

in extremis [inɛkstremis] 1 LOC ADV [sauver, arriver] at the last minute 2 LOC ADJ [sauvetage, succès] last-minute (épith); **faire un mariage/testament ~** to marry/make a will on one's deathbed

inextricable [inɛkstrikabl] ADJ inextricable

inextricablement [inɛkstrikabləmɑ̃] ADV inextricably

infaillibilité [ɛ̃fajibilite] NF (gén, Rel) infallibility

infaillible [ɛ̃fajibl] ADJ [méthode, remède, personne] infallible; [instinct] unerring, infallible

infailliblement [ɛ̃fajibləmɑ̃] ADV (= à coup sûr) inevitably, without fail; (= sans erreur) infallibly

infaisable [ɛ̃fəzabl] ADJ impossible, impracticable, not feasible (attrib); **ce n'est pas ~** it's not impossible, it's (just about) feasible; **pourquoi serait-ce ~ en France?** why couldn't this be done in France?

infalsifiable [ɛ̃falsifjabl] ADJ [document] impossible to forge

infamant, e [ɛ̃famɑ̃, ɑ̃t] ADJ [acte] infamous, ignominious; [accusation] libellous; [propos] defamatory; [terme] derogatory; (Jur) **peine ~e** sentence involving exile or deprivation of civil rights

infâme [ɛ̃fam] ADJ (gén) vile, loathsome; [métier, action, trahison] unspeakable, vile, loathsome; [traître] infamous, vile; [complaisance, servilité] shameful, vile; [entremetteur, spéculateur] despicable; [nourriture, odeur, taudis] revolting, vile, disgusting

infamie [ɛ̃fami] NF a (= honte) infamy; **couvert d'~** disgraced b (= caractère infâme) [personne, acte] infamy c (= insulte) vile abuse (NonC); (= action infâme) infamous ou vile ou loathsome deed; (= ragot) slanderous gossip (NonC); **c'est une ~** it's absolutely scandalous, it's an absolute scandal; **dire des ~s sur le compte de qn** to make slanderous remarks about sb

infant [ɛ̃fɑ̃] NM infante

infante [ɛ̃fɑ̃t] NF infanta

infanterie [ɛ̃fɑ̃tri] NF infantry; **avec une ~ de 2 000 hommes** with 2,000 foot, with an infantry of 2,000 men; **~ légère/lourde** ou **de li-**

gne light/heavy infantry; **~ de marine** marines; **d'~** [régiment] infantry (épith)

infanticide [ɛ̃fɑ̃tisid] 1 ADJ infanticidal 2 NMF (= personne) infanticide, child-killer 3 NM (= acte) infanticide

infantile [ɛ̃fɑ̃til] ADJ [maladie] infantile; [médecine, clinique] child (épith); (= puéril) infantile, childish, babyish → **mortalité**

infantilisant, e [ɛ̃fɑ̃tilizɑ̃, ɑ̃t] ADJ [émission, livre] infantile, childish

infantilisation [ɛ̃fɑ̃tilizasjɔ̃] NF l'~ des personnes âgées/du public treating old people/the public like children

infantiliser [ɛ̃fɑ̃tilize] ▶conjug 1◀ VT to make into a child (ou children), infantilize

infantilisme [ɛ̃fɑ̃tilism] NM (Méd, Psych) infantilism; (= puérilité) infantile ou childish ou babyish behaviour; **c'est de l'~!** how childish!

infarctus [ɛ̃farktys] NM (Méd) infarction (SPÉC), infarct (SPÉC); **~ du myocarde** coronary thrombosis, myocardial infarction (SPÉC); **il a eu** ou **fait trois ~** he has had three coronaries

infatigable [ɛ̃fatigabl] ADJ [personne] indefatigable, tireless, untiring; [zèle] tireless

infatigablement [ɛ̃fatigabləmɑ̃] ADV indefatigably, tirelessly, untiringly

infatuation [ɛ̃fatɥasjɔ̃] NF (frm = vanité) self-conceit, self-importance

infatué, e [ɛ̃fatɥe] (ptp de s'infatuer) ADJ [air, personne] conceited, vain; **être ~ de son importance** to be full of one's own importance; **être ~ de son physique** to be vain ou conceited about one's looks; **~ de sa personne** ou **de lui-même** full of himself ou of self-conceit, self-important

infatuer (s') [ɛ̃fatɥe] ▶conjug 1◀ VPR a (= s'engouer de) **s'~ de** [+ personne, choses] to become infatuated with b (= tirer vanité de) **s'~ de son importance** to become full of one's own importance; **s'~ de son physique** to become vain ou conceited about one's looks; **s'~ (de soi-même)** to become full of o.s. ou of self-conceit

infécond, e [ɛ̃fekɔ̃, ɔ̃d] ADJ [terre, femme, animal] barren, sterile, infertile; [œuf] infertile; [esprit] infertile, sterile

infécondité [ɛ̃fekɔ̃dite] NF [terre, femme, animal] barrenness, sterility, infertility; [esprit] infertility, sterility

infect, e [ɛ̃fɛkt] ADJ [goût, nourriture, vin, attitude] revolting; [conduite, personne] obnoxious; [temps] filthy, foul, rotten; [taudis, chambre] squalid; [livre, film] (= très mauvais) rotten*, appalling; (= scandaleux) revolting; **odeur ~e** stench, vile ou foul smell; **il a été ~ avec moi** he was horrible to me

infectant, e [ɛ̃fɛktɑ̃, ɑ̃t] ADJ (Méd) [agent] infective; [contact, piqûre] causing infection

infecter [ɛ̃fɛkte] ▶conjug 1◀ 1 VT (gén) [+ atmosphère, eau] to contaminate; (Méd) [+ personne, plaie] to infect; (fig littér) to poison, infect; **cellules infectées par un virus** virus-infected cells 2 **s'infecter** VPR [plaie] to become infected, turn septic

infectieux, -ieuse [ɛ̃fɛksjø, jøz] ADJ (Méd) infectious

infection [ɛ̃fɛksjɔ̃] NF (Méd) infection; (= puanteur) stench; **~ généralisée** systemic infection; **~ microbienne/virale** bacterial/viral infection; **quelle ~!** ◊ **c'est une ~!** what a stench!

inféodation [ɛ̃feɔdasjɔ̃] NF (Pol) allegiance (à to); (Hist) infeudation, enfeoffment

inféoder [ɛ̃feɔde] ▶conjug 1◀ 1 VT (Hist) to enfeoff 2 **s'inféoder** VPR **s'~ à** to give one's allegiance to, pledge allegiance ou o.s. to; **être inféodé à** to be subservient to, be the vassal of

inférence [ɛ̃ferɑ̃s] NF inference

inférer [ɛ̃fere] ▶conjug 6◀ VT to infer, gather (de from); **j'infère de ceci que ... ◊ j'en infère que ...** I infer ou gather from this that ..., this leads me to conclude that ...

▼**inférieur, e** [ɛ̃ferjœr] 1 ADJ a (dans l'espace: gén) lower; [mâchoire, lèvre] lower, bottom; [planètes] inferior; **la partie ~e de l'objet** the bottom part of the object; **le feu a pris dans les étages ~s** fire broke out on the lower floors; **descendez à l'étage ~** go down to the next floor ou the floor below, go to the next floor down; **le cours ~ d'un fleuve** the lower course ou stretches of a river b (dans une hiérarchie) [classes sociales, animaux, végétaux] lower; **à l'échelon ~** on the next rung down; **d'un rang ~** of a lower rank, lower in rank c [qualité] inferior, poorer; [vitesse] lower; [nombre] smaller, lower; [quantité] smaller; [intelligence, esprit] inferior; **forces ~es en nombre** forces inferior ou smaller in number(s) d **~ à** [nombre] less ou lower ou smaller than, below; [somme] smaller ou less than; [production] inferior to, less ou lower than; **note ~e à 20** mark below 20 ou less than 20; **intelligence/qualité ~e à la moyenne** below average ou lower than average intelligence/quality; **travail d'un niveau ~ à ...** work of a lower standard than ..., work below the standard of ...; **roman/auteur ~ à un autre** novel/author inferior to another; **tu ne lui es ~ en rien** you're in no way inferior to him; **être hiérarchiquement ~ à qn** to be lower (down) than sb ou be below sb in the hierarchy; (fig) **il est ~ à sa tâche** he isn't equal to his task, he isn't up to the job

2 NM,F inferior

inférieurement [ɛ̃ferjœrmɑ̃] ADV (= moins bien) less well; **~ équipé** [armée, laboratoire, bateau] less well-equipped

inférioriser [ɛ̃ferjɔrize] ▶conjug 1◀ VT (= sous-estimer) to underestimate; (= complexer) to make feel inferior

infériorité [ɛ̃ferjɔrite] NF inferiority; **en état** ou **position d'~** in an inferior position, in a position of inferiority → **comparatif, complexe**

infermentescible [ɛ̃fɛrmɑ̃tesibl] ADJ which cannot be fermented

infernal, e (mpl -aux) [ɛ̃fɛrnal, o] ADJ a (= intolérable) [bruit, allure, chaleur, cadence] infernal; [enfant] impossible; **c'est ~!** it's unbearable!, it's sheer hell!; **les disputes/images se succèdent à un rythme ~** the arguments/images come thick and fast b (= satanique) [caractère, personne, complot] diabolical, infernal, devilish c (= effrayant) [vision, supplice] diabolical; [spirale, engrenage] vicious; **cycle ~** vicious circle → **machine** d (Myth) [divinité] infernal

infertile [ɛ̃fɛrtil] ADJ (lit, fig) infertile

infertilité [ɛ̃fɛrtilite] NF (lit, fig) infertility

infestation [ɛ̃fɛstasjɔ̃] NF (Méd) infestation

infester [ɛ̃fɛste] ▶conjug 1◀ VT (gén) to infest, overrun; (Méd) to infest; **infesté de moustiques** infested with mosquitoes, mosquito-infested ou -ridden; **infesté de souris/pirates** infested with ou overrun with ou by mice/pirates

infibulation [ɛ̃fibylasjɔ̃] NF infibulation

infichu, e* [ɛ̃fiʃy] ♦ **infichu de** LOC ADJ **~ de faire qch** totally incapable of doing sth; **je suis ~ de me rappeler où je l'ai mis** I can't remember where the hell I put it*

infidèle [ɛ̃fidɛl] 1 ADJ a [ami] unfaithful, disloyal (à qn to sb); [époux] unfaithful (à qn to sb); (littér) **être ~ à sa promesse** to be untrue to one's promise b [récit, traduction, traducteur] unfaithful, inaccurate; [mémoire] unreliable c (Rel) infidel 2 NMF (Rel) infidel

infidèlement [ɛ̃fidɛlmɑ̃] ADV [*traduire, raconter*] unfaithfully, inaccurately

infidélité [ɛ̃fidelite] NF [a] (= *inconstance*) [*ami*] disloyalty, unfaithfulness; [*époux*] infidelity, unfaithfulness (**à** to); (*littér*) **~ à une promesse** being untrue to a promise (*littér*) [b] (= *acte déloyal*) [*époux*] infidelity; **elle lui pardonna ses ~s** she forgave him his infidelities; **faire une ~ à qn** to be unfaithful to sb; **il a fait bien des ~s à sa femme** he has been unfaithful *ou* guilty of infidelity to his wife on many occasions; (*hum*) **faire des ~s à son boucher/éditeur** to be unfaithful to *ou* forsake one's butcher/publisher [c] (= *manque d'exactitude*) [*description, historien*] inaccuracy; [*mémoire*] unreliability [d] (= *erreur*) [*description, traducteur*] inaccuracy; **on trouve beaucoup d'~s dans cette traduction** we find many inaccuracies in this translation

infiltration [ɛ̃filtrasjɔ̃] NF [a] [*liquide*] percolation, infiltration; (*dans le sol*) seepage; [*hommes, idées*] infiltration; **il y a une ~ ou des ~s dans la cave** there are leaks in the cellar, water is leaking into the cellar [b] (*Méd* = *accumulation dans un tissu*) infiltration; (= *piqûre*) injection; **se faire faire des ~s** to have injections

infiltrer [ɛ̃filtre] ▸ conjug 1 ◂ [1] VT (= *noyauter*) [+ *groupe, réseau*] to infiltrate [2] **s'infiltrer** VPR [*liquide*] to percolate (through), seep in, infiltrate; [*lumière*] to filter through; [*hommes, idées*] to infiltrate; **s'~ dans** [*personne*] to infiltrate; [*idées*] to filter into, infiltrate (into); [*liquide*] to percolate (through), seep through, infiltrate; [*lumière*] to filter into; **s'~ dans un groupe/chez l'ennemi** to infiltrate a group/the enemy

infime [ɛ̃fim] ADJ (= *minuscule*) tiny, minute, minuscule; (= *inférieur*) lowly, inferior; **une ~ minorité** a tiny minority

in fine [infine] LOC ADV ultimately

infini, e [ɛ̃fini] [1] ADJ [a] (*Math, Philo, Rel*) infinite [b] (= *sans limites*) [*espace*] infinite, boundless; [*patience, bonté*] infinite, unlimited, boundless; [*douleur*] immense; [*prudence, soin, bêtise*] infinite, immeasurable; [*quantité*] infinite, unlimited; **avec d'~es précautions** with infinite *ou* endless precautions [c] (= *interminable*) [*luttes, propos*] interminable, never-ending; **un temps ~ me parut s'écouler** an eternity seemed to pass [2] NM **l'~** (*Philo*) the infinite; (*Math, Photo*) infinity; (*Photo*) **faire la mise au point à** *ou* **sur l'~** to focus to infinity; **l'~ des cieux** heaven's immensity, the infinity of heaven; **à l'~** [*discourir*] ad infinitum, endlessly; [*multiplier*] to infinity; [*se diversifier, faire varier*] infinitely; **les champs s'étendaient à l'~** the fields stretched away endlessly into the distance; **droite prolongée à l'~** straight line tending towards infinity

infiniment [ɛ̃finimɑ̃] ADV [a] (= *immensément*) infinitely [b] (*sens affaibli = beaucoup*) infinitely; **~ long/grand** immensely *ou* infinitely long/large; **je vous suis ~ reconnaissant** I am immensely *ou* extremely *ou* infinitely grateful (to you); **je regrette ~** I'm extremely sorry; **ça me plaît ~** I like it immensely, there's nothing I like more; **~ meilleur/plus intelligent** infinitely better/more intelligent; **avec ~ de soin/de tendresse** with infinite *ou* with the utmost care/tenderness [c] **l'~ grand** the infinitely great; **l'~ petit** the infinitesimal

infinité [ɛ̃finite] NF (*littér*) infinity; (= *quantité infinie*) **une ~ de** an infinite number of

infinitésimal, e (*mpl* **-aux**) [ɛ̃finitezimal, o] ADJ (*gén, Math*) infinitesimal

infinitif, -ive [ɛ̃finitif, iv] ADJ, NM infinitive; **~ de narration** historic infinitive; **à l'~** in the infinitive

infirmatif, -ive [ɛ̃firmatif, iv] ADJ (*Jur*) invali-

dating; **~ de** invalidating, annulling, quashing

infirmation [ɛ̃firmasjɔ̃] NF (*Jur*) invalidation, annulment, quashing (**de** of)

infirme [ɛ̃firm] [1] ADJ [*personne*] crippled, disabled; (*avec l'âge*) infirm; **l'accident l'avait rendu ~** the accident had left him crippled *ou* disabled; **il est ~ du bras droit** he's crippled in his right arm, he has a crippled *ou* disabled right arm; **être ~ de naissance** to be disabled from birth, be born disabled [2] NMF cripple, disabled person; **les ~s** the crippled *ou* disabled; **~ mental/moteur** mentally/physically handicapped *ou* disabled person; **~ du travail** industrially disabled person; **~ de guerre** disabled veteran, war cripple (*Brit*)

infirmer [ɛ̃firme] ▸ conjug 1 ◂ VT (= *démentir*) to invalidate; (*Jur*) [+ *décision, jugement*] to invalidate, annul, quash

infirmerie [ɛ̃firməri] NF (*gén*) infirmary; [*école*] sickroom, infirmary, sick bay (*Brit*); (*Univ*) health centre; [*navire*] sick bay

infirmier, -ière [ɛ̃firmje, jɛr] [1] ADJ nursing (*épith*); **personnel ~** nursing staff; **élève ~** student nurse [2] NM (male) nurse; **~ en chef** charge nurse (*Brit*), head nurse (*US*) [3] **infirmière** NF (*gén*) nurse; [*internat*] matron (*Brit*), nurse (*US*); **infirmière chef** (nursing) sister (*Brit*), charge nurse (*Brit*), head nurse (*US*); **infirmière diplômée** registered nurse; **infirmière diplômée d'État** ≈ state registered nurse; (*Mil*) **infirmière-major** matron; **infirmière visiteuse** visiting nurse; ≈ district nurse (*Brit*)

infirmité [ɛ̃firmite] NF [a] (= *invalidité*) disability; **~ motrice cérébrale** physical disability; **les ~s de la vieillesse** the infirmities of old age [b] († = *imperfection*) weakness, failing

infixe [ɛ̃fiks] NM (*Ling*) infix

inflammable [ɛ̃flamabl] ADJ inflammable, flammable

inflammation [ɛ̃flamasjɔ̃] NF (*Méd*) inflammation

inflammatoire [ɛ̃flamatwar] ADJ (*Méd*) inflammatory

inflation [ɛ̃flasjɔ̃] NF (*Écon*) inflation; **croissance de 4% hors ~** 4% growth over and above inflation; **une ~ de projets/candidatures** a marked increase in the number of projects/applications

inflationniste [ɛ̃flasjɔnist] [1] ADJ [*politique, économie*] inflationist; [*tendance, risque, pressions*] inflationary; [*craintes, menace*] of inflation [2] NMF inflationist

infléchi, e [ɛ̃fleʃi] (*ptp de* **infléchir**) ADJ [*voyelle*] inflected

infléchir [ɛ̃fleʃir] ▸ conjug 2 ◂ [1] VT [a] (*lit*) [+ *rayon*] to inflect, bend [b] (*fig*) [+ *politique*] (*légèrement*) to change *ou* shift the emphasis of; (*plus nettement*) to reorientate; [+ *tendance, stratégie, attitude*] to modify; [+ *position*] to soften; [+ *décision*] to affect; **pour ~ la courbe du chômage** to bring down unemployment [2] **s'infléchir** VPR [a] [*route*] to bend, curve round; [*poutre*] to sag; [*courbe*] (*vers le bas*) to dip, go down; (*vers le haut*) to climb, go up [b] (*fig*) [*politique*] to shift, change emphasis; (= *conjoncture*) to change; **cette tendance s'infléchit** this trend is becoming less marked

infléchissement [ɛ̃fleʃismɑ̃] NM [*politique*] (*léger*) (slight) shift (**de** in); (*plus marqué*) reorientation; [*stratégie, attitude*] shift (**de** in); [*position*] softening; **un net ~ des ventes** (*à la baisse*) a sharp drop *ou* fall in sales; (*à la hausse*) a sharp *ou* marked increase in sales

inflexibilité [ɛ̃fleksibilite] NF [*caractère, personne*] inflexibility, rigidity; [*volonté*] inflexibility; [*règle*] inflexibility, rigidity

inflexible [ɛ̃fleksibl] ADJ [*caractère, personne*] inflexible, rigid, unyielding; [*volonté*] inflexible; [*règle*] inflexible, rigid; **il demeura ~ dans sa résolution** he remained inflexible *ou* unyielding *ou* unbending in his resolve

inflexiblement [ɛ̃fleksibləmɑ̃] ADV inflexibly

inflexion [ɛ̃fleksjɔ̃] NF [a] [*voix*] inflexion, modulation; (*Ling*) **~ vocalique** vowel inflexion [b] (= *déviation*: *Sci*) [*rayon*] deflection; [*courbe*] inflexion [c] (*fig*) [*politique*] reorientation (**de** of)

infliger [ɛ̃fliʒe] ▸ conjug 3 ◂ VT [+ *défaite, punition, supplice*] to inflict (**à** on); [+ *amende, tâche*] to impose (**à** on); [+ *affront*] to deliver (**à** to); **~ de lourdes pertes à l'ennemi** to inflict heavy losses on the enemy; **~ sa présence à qn** to inflict one's presence *ou* o.s. on sb; (*Scol*) **~ un avertissement** *ou* **un blâme à qn** to give sb an order mark (*Brit*) *ou* a bad mark (*Brit*) *ou* a demerit point (*US*); **~ un démenti à qn** to give sb the lie; **il s'est infligé volontairement des blessures** he harmed himself deliberately

inflorescence [ɛ̃flɔresɑ̃s] NF inflorescence

influençable [ɛ̃flyɑ̃sabl] ADJ easily influenced

influence [ɛ̃flyɑ̃s] NF influence (**sur** on, upon); **c'est quelqu'un qui a de l'~** he's a person of influence, he's an influential person; **avoir beaucoup d'~ sur qn** ◊ **jouir d'une grande ~ auprès de qn** to have *ou* carry a lot of influence with sb; **avoir une ~ bénéfique/néfaste sur** [*climat, médicament*] to have a beneficial/harmful effect on; **ces fréquentations ont une mauvaise ~ sur ses enfants** these friends are a bad influence on her children; **sous l'~ de** under the influence of; **être sous ~** (* : *de l'alcool, d'une drogue*) to be under the influence*; (*de qn*) to be under somebody's control *ou* spell; **zone/sphère d'~** zone/sphere of influence → **trafic**

influencer [ɛ̃flyɑ̃se] ▸ conjug 3 ◂ VT (*gén*) to influence; (= *agir sur*) to act upon; **ne te laisse pas ~ par lui** don't let yourself be influenced by him, don't let him influence you

influent, e [ɛ̃flyɑ̃, ɑ̃t] ADJ influential

influenza [ɛ̃flyɑ̃za] NF influenza

influer [ɛ̃flye] ▸ conjug 1 ◂ ◆ **influer sur** VT INDIR to influence, have an influence on

influx [ɛ̃fly] NM [a] (*Méd*) **~ (nerveux)** (nerve) impulse [b] (*fig = fluide*) influx†, inflow†

info* [ɛ̃fo] NF [a] (ABRÉV = **information**) (*Presse, TV*) news item, piece of news; (= *renseignements*) info* (*NonC*); (*Presse, TV*) **les ~s** the news [b] (ABRÉV = **informatique**) (*Ordin*) computing; **il fait de l'~** (*en amateur*) he's into computing; (*professionnellement*) he's in computers

infographie® [ɛ̃fografi] NF computer graphics

infographique [ɛ̃fografik] ADJ **document ~** computer graphic picture; **création ~** computer graphics *sg*

infographiste [ɛ̃fografist] NMF computer graphics artist

in-folio [infoljo] ADJ INV, NM INV folio

infondé, e [ɛ̃fɔ̃de] ADJ [*critique, crainte, accusation*] unfounded, groundless; [*demande*] unjustified; [*rumeurs*] unfounded; **ces rumeurs ne sont peut-être pas totalement ~es** there may be some truth in these rumours, these rumours are perhaps not totally unfounded

informateur, -trice [ɛ̃fɔrmatœr, tris] NM,F (*gén*) informant; (*Police*) informer; (*Presse*) inside source

informaticien, -ienne [ɛ̃fɔrmatisjɛ̃, jɛn] NM,F (= *spécialiste*) computer scientist; (= *analyste-programmeur*) computer analyst; **elle est informaticienne** she's in computers

informatif, -ive [ɛ̃fɔrmatif, iv] ADJ [*brochure*] informative; **campagne de publicité informative pour un produit** advertising campaign giving information on a product

▼ **information** [ɛ̃fɔrmasjɔ̃] NF [a] (= *renseignement*) piece of information; (*Presse, TV = nouvelle*) news item, piece of news; **voilà une ~ intéressante** here's an interesting piece

> GRAMMAIRE ACTIVE: **information** 46.3

of information *ou* some interesting information; **recueillir des ~s sur** to gather information on; **voici nos ~s** here *ou* this is the news; **~s politiques** political news; **~s télévisées** television news; **écouter/regarder les ~s** to listen to/watch the news (bulletins); **c'était aux ~s de 10 heures** it was on the 10 o'clock news; **nous recevons une ~ de dernière minute** we've just received some last-minute *ou* late news; **bulletin/flash d'~s** news bulletin/flash; **aller aux ~s** to (go and) find out

b (= *diffusion de renseignements*) information; **pour votre ~, sachez que ...** for your (own) information you should know that ...; **pour l'~ des voyageurs** for the information of travellers; **assurer l'~ du public en matière d'impôts** to ensure that the public is informed *ou* has information on the subject of taxation; **réunion d'~** briefing; **journal d'~** serious newspaper

c (*Ordin, Sci*) **l'~** information; **traitement de l'~** data processing, processing of information; **théorie de l'~** information theory; **~ génétique** genetic information

d (*Jur*) **~ judiciaire** (judicial) inquiry; **ouvrir une ~** to start an initial *ou* a preliminary investigation; **~ contre X** inquiry against person *ou* persons unknown

informationnel, -elle [ɛ̃fɔʀmasjɔnɛl] ADJ [*système*] informational; **révolution informationnelle** information revolution; (*Bio*) **molécule informationnelle** information molecule

informatique [ɛ̃fɔʀmatik] **1** NF (= *science*) computer science, computing; (= *techniques*) data processing; **~ de bureau/de gestion** office/commercial computing; **il est dans l'~** he's in computers; **l'ère de l'~** the computer age **2** ADJ computer (*épith*); **l'industrie ~** the computer *ou* computing industry

informatiquement [ɛ̃fɔʀmatikmɑ̃] ADV **traiter qch ~** to process sth on a computer

informatisation [ɛ̃fɔʀmatizasjɔ̃] NF computerization

informatiser [ɛ̃fɔʀmatize] ▶ conjug 1 ◀ **1** VT to computerize **2** **s'informatiser** VPR to become computerized

informe [ɛ̃fɔʀm] ADJ [*masse, tas*] shapeless, formless; [*vêtement*] shapeless; [*visage, être*] misshapen, ill-shaped, ill-formed; [*projet*] rough, undefined

informé [ɛ̃fɔʀme] **1** ADJ [*personne*] well-informed **2** NM **journaux/milieux bien ~s** well-informed *ou* authoritative newspapers/circles → **jusque**

informel, -elle [ɛ̃fɔʀmɛl] ADJ (*gén, Art*) informal; **l'économie informelle** the informal *ou* unofficial economy

informer [ɛ̃fɔʀme] ▶ conjug 1 ◀ **1** VT **a** (*d'un fait*) to inform, tell (**de** of, about); (*d'un problème*) to inform (**sur** about); **m'ayant informé de ce fait** having informed *ou* told me of this fact, having acquainted me with this fact; **nous vous informons que nos bureaux ouvrent à 8 heures** we are pleased to inform you that *ou* for your information our offices open at 8 a.m.; **s'il vient, vous voudrez bien m'en ~** if he comes, please let me know *ou* inform me *ou* tell me; **on vous a mal informé** (*faussement*) you've been misinformed *ou* wrongly informed; (*imparfaitement*) you've been badly informed *ou* ill-informed; **nous ne sommes pas assez informés** we don't have enough information

b (*Philo*) **les concepts informent la matière** concepts impart *ou* give form to matter

2 VI (*Jur*) **~ sur un crime** to inquire into *ou* investigate a crime; **~ contre X** to start inquiries against person *ou* persons unknown

3 **s'informer** VPR (*d'un fait*) to inquire, find out, ask (**de** about); (*dans une matière*) to inform o.s. (**sur** about); **informez-vous s'il est arrivé** find out *ou* ascertain whether he has arrived; **où puis-je m'~ de l'heure/à ce sujet/si**

...? where can I inquire *ou* find out *ou* ask about the time/about this matter/whether ...?; **s'~ de la santé de qn** to ask after *ou* inquire after *ou* about sb's health

informulé, e [ɛ̃fɔʀmyle] ADJ unformulated

infortune [ɛ̃fɔʀtyn] NF (= *revers*) misfortune; (= *adversité*) ill fortune, misfortune; **~s conjugales** marital misfortunes; **le récit de ses ~s** the tale of his woes *ou* misfortunes; **compagnon/frère/sœur d'~** companion/brother/sister in misfortune

infortuné, e [ɛ̃fɔʀtyne] **1** ADJ [*personne*] hapless (*épith*), ill-fated, wretched; [*démarche, décision*] ill-fated **2** NM,F (poor) wretch

infoutu, e [ɛ̃futy] ♦**infoutu de** LOC ADJ **~ de faire quoi que ce soit** damn* *ou* bloody (*Brit*)‡ incapable of doing anything; **je suis ~ de m'en souvenir** I can't for the life of me remember*

infra [ɛ̃fʀa] ADV **voir ~** see below

infraction [ɛ̃fʀaksjɔ̃] NF (= *délit*) offence; **~ à** [+ *loi, règlement, sécurité*] breach of; **~ au code de la route** driving offence; (*Aut*) **être en ~** to be committing an offence, be breaking *ou* in breach of the law; **~ à la loi** breach *ou* violation *ou* infraction of the law; **~ fiscale** breach of the tax code; **toute ~ sera punie** all offenders will be prosecuted

infranchissable [ɛ̃fʀɑ̃ʃisabl] ADJ (*lit*) impassable; (*fig*) insurmountable, insuperable

infrangible [ɛ̃fʀɑ̃ʒibl] ADJ (*littér*) infrangible (*littér*)

infrarouge [ɛ̃fʀaʀuʒ] ADJ, NM infrared; **missile guidé par ~** heat-seeking missile

infrason [ɛ̃fʀasɔ̃] NM infrasonic vibration

infrastructure [ɛ̃fʀastʀyktyʀ] NF (*Constr*) substructure, understructure; (*Écon*) infrastructure; (*Aviat*) ground installations; **~ routière/de transports** road/transport infrastructure

infréquentable [ɛ̃fʀekɑ̃tabl] ADJ not to be associated with; **ce sont des gens ~s** they're people you just don't associate with *ou* mix with

infroissable [ɛ̃fʀwasabl] ADJ crease-resistant, non-crease (*épith*)

infructueux, -euse [ɛ̃fʀyktɥø, øz] ADJ [*tentative, effort, réunion*] fruitless, unsuccessful; [*démarche*] unsuccessful

infumable [ɛ̃fymabl] ADJ unsmokable

infus, e [ɛ̃fy, yz] ADJ (*littér*) innate, inborn (**à** in) → **science**

infuser [ɛ̃fyze] ▶ conjug 1 ◀ **1** VT (*littér*) [+ *idée, conviction*] to instil (**à** into); **~ un sang nouveau à qch/à qn** to infuse *ou* inject *ou* instil new life into sth/into sb **2** VI (**faire**) **~** [+ *tisane*] to infuse; [+ *thé*] to brew, infuse, steep (*US*); **laisser ~ le thé quelques minutes** leave the tea to brew *ou* infuse a few minutes; **le thé est-il assez infusé ?** has the tea brewed *ou* infused (long) enough?

infusion [ɛ̃fyzjɔ̃] NF **a** (= *tisane*) infusion, herb tea; **~ de tilleul** lime tea; **boire une ~** to drink some herb tea *ou* an infusion; **la verveine se boit en ~** verbena is drunk as an infusion **b** (= *action*) infusion; **préparé par ~** prepared by infusion

ingambe [ɛ̃gɑ̃b] ADJ spry, nimble

ingénier (s') [ɛ̃ʒenje] ▶ conjug 7 ◀ VPR **s'~ à faire** to strive (hard) to do, try hard to do; (*iro*) **dès que j'ai rangé, il s'ingénie à tout remettre en désordre** as soon as I've tidied things up, he goes out of his way *ou* he contrives to mess them up again

ingénierie [ɛ̃ʒeniʀi] NF engineering; **~ financière/informatique/génétique** financial/computer/genetic engineering

ingénieur [ɛ̃ʒenjœʀ] NM engineer; **~ chimiste/des mines/agronome** chemical/mining/agricultural engineer; **~ électricien/en génie civil** electrical/civil engineer; **~ système** system(s) engineer; **~ électronicien** electronic

engineer; **~ du son** sound engineer; **~ des eaux et forêts** forestry expert; **~ des travaux publics** construction *ou* civil engineer → **conseil**

ingénieusement [ɛ̃ʒenjøzmɑ̃] ADV ingeniously, cleverly

ingénieux, -ieuse [ɛ̃ʒenjø, jøz] ADJ ingenious, clever

ingéniosité [ɛ̃ʒenjozite] NF ingenuity, cleverness

ingénu, e [ɛ̃ʒeny] **1** ADJ ingenuous, artless, naïve **2** NM,F ingenuous *ou* artless *ou* naïve person **3** **ingénue** NF (*Théât*) ingénue; **jouer les ~es** to play ingénue roles; (*fig*) to pretend to be all sweet and innocent

ingénuité [ɛ̃ʒenɥite] NF ingenuousness, artlessness, naïvety

ingénument [ɛ̃ʒenymɑ̃] ADV ingenuously, artlessly, naïvely

ingérable [ɛ̃ʒeʀabl] ADJ unmanageable

ingérence [ɛ̃ʒeʀɑ̃s] NF interference, interfering (*NonC*), meddling (*NonC*) (**dans** in); (*Pol*) **le devoir d'~** the duty to interfere

ingérer [ɛ̃ʒeʀe] ▶ conjug 6 ◀ **1** VT to ingest **2** **s'ingérer** VPR **s'~ dans** to interfere in *ou* with, meddle in

ingestion [ɛ̃ʒɛstjɔ̃] NF ingestion

ingouvernable [ɛ̃guvɛʀnabl] ADJ (*Pol*) ungovernable; (*fig*) [*passion, sentiment*] uncontrollable; **dans la tempête, le voilier était ~** in the storm it was impossible to steer the yacht

ingrat, e [ɛ̃gʀa, at] **1** ADJ [*personne*] ungrateful (**envers** to, towards); [*tâche, métier, sujet*] thankless (*épith*), unrewarding; [*sol*] stubborn, barren, sterile; [*visage*] unprepossessing, unattractive; [*contrée*] bleak, hostile; [*mémoire*] unreliable, treacherous → **âge** **2** NM,F ungrateful person; **tu n'es qu'un ~!** how ungrateful of you!; **vous n'aurez pas affaire à un ~** I won't forget what you've done (for me)

ingratitude [ɛ̃gʀatityd] NF ingratitude, ungratefulness (**envers** to, towards); **avec ~** ungratefully

ingrédient [ɛ̃gʀedjɑ̃] NM [*recette, produit*] ingredient; [*situation, crise*] ingredient, component

inguérissable [ɛ̃geʀisabl] ADJ [*maladie, malade, blessure, paresse*] incurable; [*chagrin, amour*] inconsolable

inguinal, e (*mpl* **-aux**) [ɛ̃gɥinal, o] ADJ inguinal

ingurgitation [ɛ̃gyʀʒitasjɔ̃] NF ingurgitation

ingurgiter [ɛ̃gyʀʒite] ▶ conjug 1 ◀ VT [+ *nourriture*] to swallow, ingurgitate (*frm*); [+ *vin*] to gulp (down), swill (*péj*); (*fig*) to ingest, ingurgitate; **faire ~ de la nourriture/une boisson à qn** to make sb swallow food/a drink, force food/a drink down sb; **faire ~ aux téléspectateurs des émissions insipides** to feed television viewers a diet of dull programmes; **faire ~ des connaissances à qn** to force sb to take in facts, force *ou* stuff knowledge into sb; **faire ~ des données à un ordinateur** to feed data into a computer; **il a ingurgité le cours en trois jours** it took him three days to take all the coursework in

inhabile [inabil] ADJ (*littér*) **a** (= *peu judicieux*) [*discours, politicien*] inept; [*manœuvre*] inept, clumsy **b** (= *gauche*) [*apprenti*] unskilful, clumsy; [*gestes, mains, dessin, travail*] clumsy, awkward **c** (*Jur*) incapable; **~ à tester** incapable of making a will

inhabileté [inabilte] NF (*littér*) **a** [*politicien, discours*] ineptitude; [*manœuvre*] ineptitude, clumsiness **b** [*apprenti*] unskilfulness; [*gestes, mains, dessin, travail*] clumsiness, awkwardness

inhabilité [inabilite] NF (*Jur*) incapacity (**à** to)

inhabitable [inabitabl] ADJ uninhabitable; **cette maison est ~** it's impossible to live in this house, this house is uninhabitable

inhabité, e [inabite] ADJ [*région*] uninhabited; [*maison*] uninhabited, unoccupied; **la maison a l'air ~e** the house looks uninhabited *ou* unoccupied *ou* unlived-in

inhabituel, -elle [inabituɛl] ADJ unusual, unaccustomed

inhalateur [inalatœʀ] NM inhaler

inhalation [inalasjɔ̃] NF inhalation; (*Méd*) **faire des ~s** to use steam inhalations

inhaler [inale] ▸ conjug 1 ◂ VT (*Méd*) to inhale; (*littér*) to inhale, breathe (in)

inharmonieux, -ieuse [inaʀmɔnjø, jøz] ADJ (*littér*) inharmonious

inhérence [ineʀɑ̃s] NF (*Philo*) inherence

inhérent, e [ineʀɑ̃, ɑ̃t] ADJ inherent (**à** in, to)

inhibé, e [inibe] (*ptp de* **inhiber**) 1 ADJ inhibited 2 NM,F inhibited person

inhiber [inibe] ▸ conjug 1 ◂ VT (*Physiol, Psych*) to inhibit

inhibiteur, -trice [inibitœʀ, tʀis] 1 ADJ inhibitory, inhibitive 2 NM (*Chim, Méd*) inhibitor

inhibition [inibisjɔ̃] NF (*Chim, Physiol, Psych*) inhibition

inhospitalier, -ière [inɔspitalje, jɛʀ] ADJ inhospitable

inhumain, e [inymɛ̃, ɛn] ADJ inhuman

inhumainement [inymɛnmɑ̃] ADV (*littér*) inhumanly

inhumanité [inymanite] NF (*littér*) inhumanity

inhumation [inymasjɔ̃] NF burial, interment, inhumation (*frm*)

inhumer [inyme] ▸ conjug 1 ◂ VT to bury, inter → **permis**

inimaginable [inimaʒinabl] ADJ, NM unthinkable; (*sens affaibli*) unimaginable, unbelievable; **l'~ s'est produit** the unthinkable happened

inimitable [inimitabl] ADJ inimitable

inimitié [inimitje] NF enmity; **avoir de l'~ pour** *ou* **contre qn** to have hostile feelings towards sb

ininflammable [inɛ̃flamabl] ADJ nonflammable, noninflammable

inintelligence [inɛ̃teliʒɑ̃s] NF [*personne, esprit*] lack of intelligence, unintelligence; (= *incompréhension*) **l'~ du problème** the failure to understand the problem, the lack of understanding of the problem

inintelligent, e [inɛ̃teliʒɑ̃, ɑ̃t] ADJ unintelligent

inintelligibilité [inɛ̃teliʒibilite] NF unintelligibility

inintelligible [inɛ̃teliʒibl] ADJ unintelligible

inintelligiblement [inɛ̃teliʒibləmɑ̃] ADV unintelligibly

inintéressant, e [inɛ̃teʀesɑ̃, ɑ̃t] ADJ uninteresting

ininterrompu, e [inɛ̃teʀɔ̃py] ADJ [*suite, ligne*] unbroken; [*file de voitures*] unbroken, steady (*épith*), uninterrupted; [*flot, vacarme*] steady (*épith*), uninterrupted, nonstop; [*hausse, baisse*] steady; [*effort, travail*] unremitting, continuous, steady (*épith*); **12 heures de sommeil ~** 12 hours' uninterrupted *ou* unbroken sleep; **30 ans de succès ~** 30 years of continuous *ou* unbroken success; **programme de musique ~e** programme of continuous music

inique [inik] ADJ iniquitous

iniquité [inikite] NF (*gén, Rel*) iniquity

initial, e (*mpl* **-iaux**) [inisjal, jo] 1 ADJ initial → **vitesse** 2 **initiale** NF initial; **mettre ses ~es sur qch** to put one's initials on sth, initial sth

initialement [inisjalmɑ̃] ADV initially

initialisation [inisjalizasjɔ̃] NF (*Ordin*) initialization

initialiser [inisjalize] ▸ conjug 1 ◂ VT (*Ordin*) to initialize

initiateur, -trice [inisjatœʀ, tʀis] 1 ADJ innovatory 2 NM,F (= *maître, précurseur*) initiator; [*mode, technique*] innovator, pioneer; [*projet, mouvement artistique*] initiator, originator

initiation [inisjasjɔ̃] NF initiation (**à** into); (*titre d'ouvrage*) **~ à la linguistique** introduction to linguistics; **stage d'~ à l'informatique** introductory *ou* beginners' course in computing → **rite**

initiatique [inisjatik] ADJ [*rite, cérémonie*] initiation (*épith*), initiatory; [*roman, film*] rite(s)-of-passage (*épith*); **parcours** *ou* **voyage** *ou* **quête ~** initiatory voyage *ou* journey; **épreuves ~s** initiation rites

initiative [inisjativ] NF (*gén, Pol*) initiative; **prendre l'~ d'une action/de faire qch** to take the initiative for an action/in doing sth; **garder l'~** to keep the initiative; **avoir de l'~** to have initiative; **~ de paix** peace initiative; **~ de défense stratégique** Strategic Defense Initiative; **à** *ou* **sur l'~ de qn** on sb's initiative; **à l'~ de la France ...** following France's initiative ...; **conférence à l'~ des USA** conference initiated by the USA; **de sa propre ~** on his own initiative → **droit³, syndicat**

initié, e [inisje] (*ptp de* **initier**) 1 ADJ initiated; **le lecteur ~/non ~** the initiated/uninitiated reader 2 NM,F initiated person, initiate (*frm*); **les ~s** the initiated *ou* initiates (*frm*) → **délit**

initier [inisje] ▸ conjug 7 ◂ 1 VT a [+ *personne*] to initiate (**à** into); **~ qn aux joies de la voile** to introduce sb to the joys of sailing b [+ *enquête, dialogue, politique*] to initiate (*frm*) 2 **s'initier** VPR to become initiated, initiate o.s. (**à** into); **j'ai besoin d'un peu de temps pour m'~ à l'informatique** I need some time to get to know a bit about computers

injectable [ɛ̃ʒɛktabl] ADJ injectable

injecté, e [ɛ̃ʒɛkte] (*ptp de* **injecter**) ADJ (*Méd, Tech*) injected (**de** with); [*visage*] congested; **yeux ~s de sang** bloodshot eyes

injecter [ɛ̃ʒɛkte] ▸ conjug 1 ◂ VT (*Méd, Tech*) to inject; **elle s'est injecté de l'insuline** she injected herself with insulin; **~ des fonds dans une entreprise** to pump money into a project

injecteur, -trice [ɛ̃ʒɛktœʀ, tʀis] 1 ADJ injection (*épith*) 2 NM (*Astronautique, Tech*) injector

injection [ɛ̃ʒɛksjɔ̃] NF (*gén*) injection; (*Méd : avec une poire*) douche; **il s'est fait une ~ d'insuline** he injected himself with insulin; **~ d'argent frais** injection of fresh money, new injection of money; **à ~** [*seringue, tube*] injection (*épith*); [*moteur, système*] fuel-injection (*épith*); **à ~ électronique/directe** [*moteur*] with electronic/direct fuel injection

injoignable [ɛ̃ʒwaɲabl] ADJ impossible to contact

injonction [ɛ̃ʒɔ̃ksjɔ̃] NF injunction, command, order; **sur son ~** on his orders *ou* command; (*Jur*) **~ thérapeutique** probation order which stipulates that the offender complete a drug rehabilitation programme

injouable [ɛ̃ʒwabl] ADJ [*musique*] unplayable; [*pièce*] unperformable; (*Sport*) [*coup, match, terrain*] unplayable

injure [ɛ̃ʒyʀ] NF a (= *insulte*) abuse (*NonC*), insult; **« espèce de salaud » est une ~** "bastard" is a term of abuse *ou* an insult; **bordée d'~s** stream of abuse *ou* insults; (*Jur*) **l'~ et la diffamation** abuse and slander b (*littér = affront*) **faire ~ à qn** to offend sb, affront sb; **il m'a fait l'~ de ne pas venir** he insulted *ou* affronted me by not coming; **ce serait lui faire ~ que de le croire si naïf** it would be insulting to him *ou* an insult to him to think that he could be so naïve c (*littér = dommage*) **l'~ des ans/du sort** the injury *ou* assault of time/of fate (*littér*)

injurier [ɛ̃ʒyʀje] ▸ conjug 7 ◂ VT to abuse, insult, revile

injurieux, -ieuse [ɛ̃ʒyʀjø, jøz] ADJ [*termes, propos*] abusive, offensive; [*attitude, article*] insulting, offensive (**pour, à l'égard de** to)

injuste [ɛ̃ʒyst] ADJ (= *inéquitable*) unjust; (= *partial*) unfair (**avec, envers** to, towards); **ne sois pas ~ !** be fair!

injustement [ɛ̃ʒystəmɑ̃] ADV [*accuser, punir*] unfairly; **~ oublié** unjustly forgotten

injustice [ɛ̃ʒystis] NF a (= *iniquité*) injustice; (= *partialité*) unfairness; **il a éprouvé un sentiment d'~** he felt he had been treated unfairly; **lutter contre l'~ sociale** to fight against social injustice b (= *acte*) injustice; **réparer des ~s** to right wrongs; **il a été victime d'une ~** he was unfairly treated

injustifiable [ɛ̃ʒystifjabl] ADJ unjustifiable

▼ **injustifié, e** [ɛ̃ʒystifje] ADJ unjustified, unwarranted

inlandsis [inlɑ̃dsis] NM (= *calotte glaciaire*) icecap

inlassable [ɛ̃lɑsabl] ADJ [*personne*] tireless, untiring; [*zèle*] unflagging, tireless; [*patience*] inexhaustible

inlassablement [ɛ̃lɑsabləmɑ̃] ADV [*répéter*] tirelessly; **revenir ~** to keep (on) coming back

inné, e [i(n)ne] ADJ innate, inborn; **idées ~es** innate ideas

innervation [inɛʀvasjɔ̃] NF innervation

innerver [inɛʀve] ▸ conjug 1 ◂ VT to innervate

innocemment [inɔsamɑ̃] ADV innocently

innocence [inɔsɑ̃s] NF (*gén*) innocence; **l'~ de ces farces** the innocence *ou* harmlessness of these pranks; **il l'a fait en toute ~** he did it in all innocence, he meant no harm (by it); **tu n'as tout de même pas l'~ de croire que ...** come on, you're not so naïve as to believe that ...

▼ **innocent, e** [inɔsɑ̃, ɑ̃t] 1 ADJ (*gén, Jur, Rel*) innocent; **être ~ de qch** to be innocent of sth; **remarque/petite farce bien ~e** quite innocent *ou* harmless remark/little prank; **il est vraiment ~ !** he is a real innocent!; **~ comme l'enfant** *ou* **l'agneau qui vient de naître** as innocent as a new-born babe 2 NM,F a (*Jur*) innocent person b (= *candide*) innocent (person); (= *niais*) simpleton; **ne fais pas l'~** don't act *ou* play the innocent (with me); **don't come the innocent with me** (*Brit*); **quel ~ tu fais !** how innocent can you be?, how innocent you are!; **l'~ du village** the village simpleton *ou* idiot ▪ (*PROV*) **aux ~s les mains pleines** fortune favours the innocent → **massacre**

innocenter [inɔsɑ̃te] ▸ conjug 1 ◂ VT (*Jur = disculper*) to clear, prove innocent (**de** of); (= *excuser*) to excuse, justify

innocuité [inɔkɥite] NF (*frm*) innocuousness (*frm*), harmlessness

innombrable [i(n)nɔ̃bʀabl] ADJ [*détails, péripéties, variétés*] innumerable, countless; [*foule*] vast

innomé, e [i(n)nɔme] ADJ = **innommé**

innommable [i(n)nɔmabl] ADJ [*conduite, action*] unspeakable, loathsome, unmentionable; [*nourriture, ordures*] foul, vile

innommé, e [i(n)nɔme] ADJ (= *non dénommé*) unnamed; (= *obscur, vague*) nameless

innovant, e [inɔvɑ̃, ɑ̃t] ADJ innovative

innovateur, -trice [inɔvatœʀ, tʀis] 1 ADJ innovatory, innovative 2 NM,F innovator

innovation [inɔvasjɔ̃] NF innovation

innover [inɔve] ▸ conjug 1 ◂ VI to innovate; **~ en matière de mode/d'art** to break new ground *ou* innovate in the field of fashion/of art; **ce peintre innove par rapport à ses prédécesseurs** this painter is breaking new ground compared with his predecessors

inobservable [inɔpsɛʀvabl] ADJ unobservable

inobservance [inɔpsɛʀvɑ̃s] NF (littér) inobservance, non-observance

inobservation [inɔpsɛʀvasjɔ̃] NF (littér, Jur) non-observance, inobservance

inobservé, e [inɔpsɛʀve] ADJ (littér, Jur) unobserved

inoccupation [inɔkypasjɔ̃] NF (littér) inoccupation (littér), inactivity

inoccupé, e [inɔkype] ADJ **a** (= vide) [appartement] unoccupied, empty; [siège, emplacement, poste] vacant, unoccupied, empty **b** (= oisif) unoccupied, idle

in-octavo [inɔktavo] ADJ INV, NM INV octavo

inoculable [inɔkylabl] ADJ inoculable

inoculation [inɔkylasjɔ̃] NF (Méd) (volontaire) inoculation; (accidentelle) infection; **l'~ (accidentelle) d'un virus/d'une maladie dans l'organisme par blessure** the (accidental) infection of the organism by a virus/by disease as a result of an injury

inoculer [inɔkyle] ▸conjug 1◂ VT **a** (Méd) **~ un virus/une maladie à qn** (volontairement) to inoculate sb with a virus/a disease; (accidentellement) to infect sb with a virus/a disease; **~ un malade** to inoculate a patient (**contre** against) **b** (fig = communiquer) **~ une passion/son enthousiasme à qn** to infect ou imbue sb with a passion/one's enthusiasm; **~ un vice à qn** to pass on a vice to sb

inodore [inɔdɔʀ] ADJ [gaz] odourless; [fleur] scentless; (fig) [personne, film, livre] insipid → **incolore**

inoffensif, -ive [inɔfɑ̃sif, iv] ADJ [personne, plaisanterie] inoffensive, harmless, innocuous; [piqûre, animal, remède] harmless, innocuous

inondable [inɔ̃dabl] ADJ liable to flooding

inondation [inɔ̃dasjɔ̃] NF **a** (= débordement d'eau) flood; **la fuite a provoqué une ~ dans la salle de bains** the leak flooded the bathroom **b** (= afflux) flood, deluge; **une véritable ~ de produits allégés** a flood of low-fat products

inonder [inɔ̃de] ▸conjug 1◂ VT **a** (= submerger) [+ prés, cave] to flood; **populations inondées** flood victims, victims of flooding; **tu as inondé toute la cuisine** you've flooded the whole kitchen **b** (= envahir) [+ marché] to flood, swamp, inundate (**de** with); **la foule a inondé les rues** the crowd flooded onto the streets; **nous sommes inondés de lettres** we have been inundated with letters, we have received a flood of letters; **inondé de soleil** bathed in sunlight; **inondé de lumière** flooded with light; **la joie inonda son cœur** he was overcome with joy **c** (= tremper) to soak, drench; **se faire ~ (par la pluie)** to get soaked ou drenched (by the rain); **je suis inondé** I'm soaked (through) ou drenched ou saturated*; **~ ses cheveux de parfum** to saturate one's hair with scent; **la sueur/le sang inondait son visage** the sweat/blood was pouring ou streaming down his face; **inondé de larmes** [+ joues] streaming with tears; [+ yeux] full of tears

inopérable [inɔpeʀabl] ADJ inoperable

inopérant, e [inɔpeʀɑ̃, ɑ̃t] ADJ ineffectual, ineffective, inoperative

inopiné, e [inɔpine] ADJ [rencontre] unexpected; **mort ~e** sudden death

inopinément [inɔpinemɑ̃] ADV unexpectedly

inopportun, e [inɔpɔʀtœ̃, yn] ADJ [demande, remarque] ill-timed, inopportune, untimely; **le moment est ~** it's not the right ou best moment, it's not the most opportune moment

inopportunément [inɔpɔʀtynemɑ̃] ADV inopportunely

inopportunité [inɔpɔʀtynite] NF (littér) inopportuneness, untimeliness

inopposabilité [inɔpozabilite] NF (Jur) non-invocability

inopposable [inɔpozabl] ADJ (Jur) non-invocable

inorganique [inɔʀganik] ADJ inorganic

inorganisé, e [inɔʀganize] ADJ [compagnie, industrie] unorganized; [personne] disorganized, unorganized; (Sci) unorganized

inoubliable [inublijabl] ADJ unforgettable, never to be forgotten

inouï, e [inwi] ADJ [événement, circonstances] unprecedented, unheard-of; [nouvelle] extraordinary, incredible; [vitesse, audace, force] incredible, unbelievable; **c'est/il est ~!** it's/he's incredible! ou unbelievable!

inox [inɔks] ADJ, NM (ABRÉV = **inoxydable**) stainless steel; **couteau/évier (en) ~** stainless steel knife/sink

inoxydable [inɔksidabl] **1** ADJ [acier, alliage] stainless; [couteau] stainless steel (épith) **2** NM stainless steel

in petto [inpeto] LOC ADV **« quel idiot », se dit-il** "what a fool", he thought ou said to himself

input [input] NM (Écon, Ordin) input

inqualifiable [ɛ̃kalifjabl] ADJ [conduite, propos] unspeakable; **d'une ~ bassesse** unspeakably low

in-quarto [inkwarto] ADJ INV, NM INV quarto

inquiet, inquiète [ɛ̃kjɛ, ɛ̃kjɛt] ADJ [personne] (momentanément) worried, anxious; (par nature) anxious; [gestes] uneasy; [attente, regards] uneasy, anxious; [sommeil] uneasy, troubled; (littér) [curiosité, amour] restless; **je suis ~ de son absence** I'm worried at his absence, I'm worried ou anxious that he's not here; **je suis ~ de ne pas le voir** I'm worried ou anxious at not seeing him; **je suis ~ qu'il ne m'ait pas téléphoné** I'm worried that he hasn't phoned me; **c'est un (éternel) ~** he's a (perpetual) worrier

inquiétant, e [ɛ̃kjetɑ̃, ɑ̃t] ADJ [situation, tendance] worrying; [signe, expérience, phénomène] disturbing, disquieting (frm), unsettling; [propos, personnage] disturbing

inquiéter [ɛ̃kjete] ▸conjug 6◂ **1** VT **a** (= alarmer) to worry, disturb; **la santé de mon fils m'inquiète** I'm worried about my son's health, my son's health worries me; **le champion commence à ~ son adversaire** the champion is starting to get his opponent worried; (Sport) **ils n'ont jamais pu ~ leurs adversaires** they never presented a real threat to their opponents **b** (= harceler) [+ ville, pays] to harass; **l'amant de la victime ne fut pas inquiété (par la police)** the victim's lover wasn't troubled ou bothered by the police **2** s'inquiéter VPR **a** (= s'alarmer) to worry; **ne t'inquiète pas** don't worry; **il n'y a pas de quoi s'~** there's nothing to worry about ou get worried about; **t'inquiète !‡** (= ça ne te regarde pas) none of your business!‡, mind your own business!‡, keep your nose out of it!‡ **b** (= s'enquérir) **s'~ de** to inquire about; **s'~ de l'heure/de la santé de qn** to inquire what time it is/about sb's health **c** (= se soucier) **s'~ de** to worry about, trouble (o.s.) about, bother about; **ne t'inquiète pas de ça, je m'en occupe** don't (you) trouble yourself ou worry ou bother about that— I'll see to it; **sans s'~ des circonstances/conséquences** without worrying ou bothering about the circumstances/consequences; **sans s'~ de savoir si ...** without bothering to find out if ...; **je ne m'inquiète pas pour elle, elle se débrouille toujours** I'm not worried about her, she always manages somehow

inquiétude [ɛ̃kjetyd] NF anxiety; (littér = agitation) restlessness; **donner de l'~ ou des ~s à qn** to worry sb, give sb cause for worry ou anxiety; **avoir ou éprouver des ~s au sujet de** to feel anxious ou worried about, feel some anxiety about; **sujet d'~** cause for concern; **soyez sans ~** have no fear; **fou d'~** mad with worry

inquisiteur, -trice [ɛ̃kizitœʀ, tʀis] **1** ADJ inquisitive, prying **2** NM inquisitor; (Hist) **le Grand Inquisiteur** the Grand Inquisitor

inquisition [ɛ̃kizisjɔ̃] NF **a** (Hist) **l'Inquisition** the Inquisition; **la Sainte Inquisition** the Holy Office **b** (péj = enquête) inquisition

inquisitoire [ɛ̃kizitwaʀ] ADJ (Jur) **procédure ~** proceeding presided over by an interrogating judge

inquisitorial, e (mpl -iaux) [ɛ̃kizitɔʀjal, jo] ADJ inquisitorial

INRA [inʀa] NM (ABRÉV = **Institut national de la recherche agronomique**) → **institut**

inracontable [ɛ̃ʀakɔ̃tabl] ADJ (= trop osé) unrepeatable; (= trop compliqué) unrecountable

inratable* [ɛ̃ʀatabl] ADJ **ce plat est ~** you can't go wrong with this dish; **cet examen est ~** you'd have to be an idiot to make a mess* of this exam

INRI (ABRÉV = **Iesus Nazarenus Rex Iudaeorum**) INRI

insaisissabilité [ɛ̃sezisabilite] NF (Jur) non-distrainability

insaisissable [ɛ̃sezisabl] ADJ [fugitif, ennemi] elusive; [personnage] enigmatic, elusive; [nuance, différence] imperceptible, indiscernible; (Jur) [biens] not liable to seizure, non-distrainable

insalissable [ɛ̃salisabl] ADJ dirt-proof

insalubre [ɛ̃salybʀ] ADJ [climat] insalubrious, unhealthy; [logement, bâtiment] unfit for habitation; [profession] unhealthy

insalubrité [ɛ̃salybʀite] NF [climat] insalubrity, unhealthiness; [logement, bâtiment] insalubrity; [profession] unhealthiness; **l'immeuble a été démoli pour ~** the building was demolished because it was unfit for habitation

insanité [ɛ̃sanite] NF (= caractère) insanity, madness; (= acte) insane act; (= propos) insane talk (NonC); **proférer des ~s** to talk insanely

insatiabilité [ɛ̃sasjabilite] NF insatiability

insatiable [ɛ̃sasjabl] ADJ insatiable

insatiablement [ɛ̃sasjabləmɑ̃] ADV insatiably

insatisfaction [ɛ̃satisfaksjɔ̃] NF dissatisfaction

insatisfait, e [ɛ̃satisfɛ, ɛt] **1** ADJ [personne] (= non comblé) unsatisfied; (= mécontent) dissatisfied (**de** with); [désir, passion] unsatisfied **2** NM,F **c'est un éternel ~** he's never satisfied, he's perpetually dissatisfied; **les ~s** the malcontents

insaturé, e [ɛ̃satyʀe] ADJ (Chim) unsaturated

inscriptible [ɛ̃skʀiptibl] ADJ (gén) inscribable; (Ordin) writable

inscription [ɛ̃skʀipsjɔ̃] **1** NF **a** (= texte) inscription; **mur couvert d'~s** wall covered in writing ou inscriptions **b** (= action) **l'~ du texte n'est pas comprise dans le prix** the inscription ou engraving of the text is not included in the price; **l'~ d'une question à l'ordre du jour** putting ou placing a question on the agenda; **cela a nécessité l'~ de nouvelles dépenses au budget** this necessitated adding further expenditure to the budget **c** (= immatriculation) (gén) registration; (Univ) registration, enrolment (Brit), enrollment (US) (**à** at); **l'~ à un parti/club** joining a party/club; **l'~ des enfants à l'école est obligatoire** it is compulsory to enrol ou register children for school; **il y a déjà 20 ~s pour la sortie de jeudi** 20 people have already signed up for Thursday's outing; **les ~s (en faculté) seront closes le 30 octobre** the closing date for enrolment ou registration (at the university) is October 30th; **dossier d'~** (gén) registration form; (Univ) admission form, ≈ UCAS form (Brit); **votre ~ sur la liste dépend de ...** the inclusion of your name on the list depends on ...; **faire**

son ~ *ou* **prendre ses ~s†** **en faculté** to register *ou* enrol at university; **les ~s sont en baisse de 5%** enrolment *ou* intake (*Brit*) is down by 5%; **droits d'~** enrolment *ou* registration fees; **~ électorale** registration on the electoral roll (*Brit*), voter registration (*US*)
[d] (*Math*) inscribing
[2] COMP ► **inscription de faux** (*Jur*) challenge (*to validity of document*) ► **inscription hypothécaire** mortgage registration ► **inscription maritime** registration of sailors; **l'Inscription maritime** (= *service*) the Register of Sailors

inscrire [ɛ̃skʀiʀ] ► conjug 39◄ [1] VT [a] (= *marquer*) [+ *nom, date*] to note down, write down; (*Ftbl*) [+ *but*] to score, notch up; **~ des dépenses au budget** to list *ou* include expenses in the budget; **~ une question à l'ordre du jour** to put *ou* place a question on the agenda; **ce n'est pas inscrit à l'ordre du jour** it isn't (down) on the agenda; **~ qch dans la pierre/le marbre** to inscribe *ou* engrave sth on stone/marble; **c'est demeuré inscrit dans ma mémoire** it has remained inscribed *ou* etched on my memory; **sa culpabilité est inscrite sur son visage** his guilt is written all over his face *ou* on his face; **greffier, inscrivez (sous ma dictée)** clerk, take *ou* note this down; **le temple est inscrit au patrimoine mondial de l'humanité** the temple is listed as a World Heritage site; **son nom est** *ou* **il est inscrit sur la liste des gagnants** his name is (written) on the list of winners; **il a inscrit une quatrième victoire à son palmarès** he has added a fourth victory to his record
[b] (= *enrôler*) [+ *client*] to put down; [+ *soldat*] to enlist; [+ *patient*] to register, enrol; **~ qn sur une liste d'attente** to put sb down *ou* put sb's name down on a waiting list; **je ne peux pas vous ~ avant le 3 août** I can't put you down for an appointment *ou* I can't give you an appointment before August 3rd; **(faire) ~ un enfant à l'école** to put a child *ou* child's name down for school, enrol *ou* register a child for school; **(faire) ~ qn à la cantine/pour une vaccination** to register sb at the canteen/for a vaccination
[c] (*Math*) to inscribe
[2] **s'inscrire** VPR [a] (= *apparaître*) **un message s'inscrivit sur l'écran** a message came up *ou* appeared on the screen; **l'avion ennemi s'inscrivit dans le viseur** the enemy aircraft came up in the viewfinder; **la tour s'inscrivait tout entière dans la fenêtre** the tower was framed in its entirety by the window
[b] (= *s'enrôler*) (*gén*) to register; (*sur la liste électorale*) to put one's name down (**sur** on); (*à l'université*) to register, enrol (*Brit*), enroll (*US*) (**à** at); (*à une épreuve sportive*) to put o.s. down, put one's name down, enter (**à** for); **s'~ à un parti/club** to join a party/club; **je me suis inscrit pour des cours du soir** I've enrolled in *ou* for some evening classes; **s'~ au registre du commerce** ≈ to register with the Chamber of Commerce (*for a trade licence*)
[c] (= *s'insérer dans*) **ces réformes s'inscrivent dans le cadre de notre nouvelle politique** these reforms lie *ou* come *ou* fall within the scope *ou* framework of our new policy; **cette décision s'inscrit dans le cadre de la lutte contre le chômage** this decision is part of the general struggle against unemployment; **cette mesure s'inscrit dans un ensemble** the measure is part of a package
[d] (*Écon*) **s'~ en hausse/en baisse** [*indice, résultat, dépenses*] to be up/down; **l'indice de la Bourse s'inscrivait en baisse de 3 points à la clôture** the share index closed 3 points down
[e] (*Math*) to be inscribed (**dans** in)
[f] (*Jur*) **s'~ en faux** to lodge a challenge; **je m'inscris en faux contre de telles assertions** I strongly deny such assertions

inscrit, e [ɛ̃skʀi, it] (*ptp de* **inscrire**) [1] ADJ [a] [*étudiant*] registered, enrolled; [*candidat,*

électeur] registered [b] (*Math*) inscribed [2] NM,F (= *membre*) registered member; (= *étudiant*) registered student; (= *concurrent*) (registered) entrant; (= *candidat*) registered candidate; (= *électeur*) registered elector; **~ maritime** registered sailor

insécable [ɛ̃sekabl] ADJ indivisible, undividable; (*Typo*) **espace ~** hard space

insecte [ɛ̃sɛkt] NM insect

insecticide [ɛ̃sɛktisid] [1] NM insecticide [2] ADJ insecticide (*épith*), insecticidal

insectivore [ɛ̃sɛktivɔʀ] [1] NM insectivore; **~s** insectivores, Insectivorae (*SPÉC*) [2] ADJ insectivorous

insécurité [ɛ̃sekyʀite] NF insecurity

INSEE [inse] NM (ABRÉV = **Institut national de la statistique et des études économiques**) → **institut**

inséminateur, -trice [ɛ̃seminatœʀ, tʀis] [1] ADJ inseminating (*épith*) [2] NM,F inseminator

insémination [ɛ̃seminasjɔ̃] NF insemination; **~ artificielle** artificial insemination

inséminer [ɛ̃semine] ► conjug 1◄ VT to inseminate

insensé, e [ɛ̃sɑ̃se] ADJ [a] (= *fou*) [*projet, action, espoir*] insane; [*personne, propos*] insane, demented; [*guerre*] senseless, insane; [*risques, course, défi*] mad, insane; **vouloir y aller seul, c'est ~!** it's insane *ou* crazy to want to go alone!; **c'est un ~!** he's demented! *ou* insane!, he's a madman!; **cela demande un travail ~!** it takes an incredible *ou* a ridiculous amount of work! [b] (= *bizarre*) [*architecture, arabesques*] weird, extravagant [c] (= *incroyable*) [*somme*] enormous, extravagant; [*embouteillage*] impossible; [*personne, soirée*] crazy

insensibilisation [ɛ̃sɑ̃sibilizasjɔ̃] NF anaesthetization (*Brit*), anesthetization (*US*)

insensibiliser [ɛ̃sɑ̃sibilize] ► conjug 1◄ VT to anaesthetize (*Brit*), anesthetize (*US*); (*fig*) **nous sommes insensibilisés aux atrocités de la guerre** we've become insensitive *ou* inured to the atrocities of war

insensibilité [ɛ̃sɑ̃sibilite] NF (*morale*) insensitivity, insensibility; (*physique*) numbness; **~ au froid/à la douleur/aux reproches** insensitivity *ou* insensibility to cold/pain/blame

insensible [ɛ̃sɑ̃sibl] ADJ [a] (*moralement*) insensible, insensitive (**à** to); (*physiquement*) numb; **~ au froid/à la douleur/à la poésie** insensitive *ou* insensible to cold/pain/poetry; **à la critique** impervious *ou* immune to criticism; **il n'est pas resté ~ à son charme** he was not impervious to her charm [b] (= *imperceptible*) imperceptible, insensible

insensiblement [ɛ̃sɑ̃sibləmɑ̃] ADV imperceptibly

inséparable [ɛ̃separabl] [1] ADJ inseparable (**de** from); **ils sont ~s** they are inseparable [2] NM (*Zool*) **~s** lovebirds

inséparablement [ɛ̃separabləmɑ̃] ADV inseparably

insérable [ɛ̃seʀabl] ADJ insertable (**dans** into)

insérer [ɛ̃seʀe] ► conjug 6◄ [1] VT [+ *feuillet, clause, objet*] to insert (**dans** into, **entre** between); [+ *annonce*] to put, insert (**dans** in); (*Ciné, TV*) **ces séquences ont été insérées après coup** these scenes were edited in afterwards [2] **s'insérer** VPR [a] (= *faire partie de*) **s'~ dans** to fit into; **ces changements s'insèrent dans le cadre d'une restructuration de notre entreprise** these changes come within *ou* lie within *ou* fit into our overall plan for restructuring the firm [b] (= *s'introduire dans*) **s'~ dans** to filter into; **le rêve s'insère parfois dans la réalité** sometimes dreams invade reality [c] (= *être attaché*) to be inserted *ou* attached

INSERM [insɛʀm] NM (ABRÉV = **Institut national de la santé et de la recherche médicale**) ≈ MRC (*Brit*), ≈ NIH (*US*)

insert [ɛ̃sɛʀ] NM (*Ciné, Radio, TV*) insert, cut-in; **film comportant en ~ des images d'archives** film with archive footage edited into it; **~ (de cheminée)** enclosed (glass-fronted) room-heater

insertion [ɛ̃sɛʀsjɔ̃] NF (= *action*) insertion, inserting; (= *résultat*) insertion; (*Ordin*) (**mode d'**)**~** insert (mode); **~ sociale** social integration; **l'~ professionnelle des jeunes** the integration of young people into the world of work; **logements d'~** housing for the rehabilitation of homeless *ou* destitute people → **revenu**

insidieusement [ɛ̃sidjøzmɑ̃] ADV insidiously

insidieux, -ieuse [ɛ̃sidjø, jøz] ADJ [*maladie, question*] insidious

insigne¹ [ɛ̃siɲ] ADJ (= *éminent*) [*honneur*] distinguished; [*services*] notable, distinguished; [*faveur*] signal (*épith*), notable; (*iro*) [*maladresse, mauvais goût*] remarkable

insigne² [ɛ̃siɲ] NM (= *cocarde*) badge; (*frm* = *emblème*) **l'~ de** *ou* **les ~s de** the insignia of; **portant les ~s de sa fonction** wearing the insignia of his office

insignifiance [ɛ̃siɲifjɑ̃s] NF [a] (= *banalité*) [*personne, visage, œuvre*] insignificance [b] (= *médiocrité*) [*affaire, somme, propos, détails*] insignificance, triviality; [*dispute*] triviality

insignifiant, e [ɛ̃siɲifjɑ̃, jɑ̃t] ADJ [a] (= *quelconque*) [*personne, visage, œuvre*] insignificant [b] (= *dérisoire*) [*affaire, somme, détail*] insignificant, trivial, trifling; [*propos*] insignificant, trivial; [*dispute*] trivial

insincère [ɛ̃sɛ̃sɛʀ] ADJ (*littér*) insincere

insincérité [ɛ̃sɛ̃seʀite] NF (*littér*) insincerity

insinuant, e [ɛ̃sinɥɑ̃, ɑ̃t] ADJ [*façons, ton, personne*] ingratiating

insinuation [ɛ̃sinɥasjɔ̃] NF insinuation, innuendo

insinuer [ɛ̃sinɥe] ► conjug 1◄ [1] VT to insinuate, imply; **que voulez-vous ~?** what are you insinuating? *ou* implying? *ou* suggesting? [2] **s'insinuer** VPR **s'~ dans** [*personne*] to worm one's way into, insinuate o.s. into; [*eau, odeur*] to seep *ou* creep into; **l'humidité s'insinuait partout** the dampness was creeping in everywhere; **les idées qui s'insinuent dans mon esprit** the ideas that steal *ou* creep into my mind; **ces arrivistes s'insinuent partout** these opportunists worm their way in everywhere; **s'~ dans les bonnes grâces de qn** to worm one's way into *ou* insinuate o.s. into sb's favour

insipide [ɛ̃sipid] ADJ [a] [*plat, boisson*] insipid, tasteless [b] (*péj*) [*conversation, style*] insipid, vapid; [*écrivain, film, œuvre, vie*] insipid

insipidité [ɛ̃sipidite] NF [a] [*plat, boisson*] insipidness, insipidity, tastelessness [b] (*péj*) [*conversation, style*] insipidity, vapidity; [*écrivain, film, œuvre, vie*] insipidity

insistance [ɛ̃sistɑ̃s] NF insistence (**sur qch** on sth, **à faire qch** on doing sth); **avec ~** [*répéter, regarder*] insistently

insistant, e [ɛ̃sistɑ̃, ɑ̃t] ADJ insistent

insister [ɛ̃siste] ► conjug 1◄ VI [a] **~ sur** [+ *sujet, détail*] to stress, lay stress on; [+ *syllabe, note*] to accentuate, emphasize, stress; **j'insiste beaucoup sur la ponctualité** I lay great stress upon punctuality; **frottez en insistant (bien) sur les taches** rub hard, paying particular attention to stains; **c'est une affaire louche, enfin n'insistons pas** it's a shady business — however let us not dwell on it *ou* don't let us keep on about it*; **je préfère ne pas ~ là-dessus** I'd rather not dwell on it, I'd rather let the matter drop
[b] (= *s'obstiner*) to be insistent (**auprès de** with), insist; **il insiste pour vous parler** he is insistent about wanting to talk to you; **comme ça ne l'intéressait pas, je n'ai pas insisté** since it didn't interest him, I didn't push the matter *ou* I didn't insist; **sonnez encore, insistez, elle est un peu sourde** ring

again and keep (on) trying because she's a little deaf; **j'insiste, c'est très important !** I assure you it's very important!; **bon, je n'insiste pas, je m'en vais*** OK, I won't insist — I'll go

in situ [insity] ADV in situ

insociable [ɛ̃sɔsjabl] ADJ unsociable

insolation [ɛ̃sɔlasjɔ̃] NF [a] (= *malaise*) sunstroke (NonC), insolation (SPÉC); **attraper une ~** to get sunstroke; **j'ai eu une ~** I had a touch of sunstroke [b] (= *ensoleillement*) (period of) sunshine; **ces stations ont une ~ très faible** these resorts get very little sun(shine); **une ~ de 1 000 heures par an** 1,000 hours of sunshine a year [c] (= *exposition au soleil*) [personne] exposure to the sun; [pellicule] exposure (to the light), insolation (SPÉC)

insolemment [ɛ̃sɔlamɑ̃] ADV [a] (= *effrontément*) [parler, répondre] insolently [b] (= *outrageusement*) unashamedly, blatantly, brazenly [c] (littér = *avec arrogance*) arrogantly

insolence [ɛ̃sɔlɑ̃s] NF (= *impertinence*) insolence (NonC); (littér = *morgue*) arrogance; (= *remarque*) insolent remark; **répondre/rire avec ~** to reply/laugh insolently; **il a eu l'~ de la contredire** he was insolent enough to contradict her, he had the temerity to contradict her; **encore une ~ comme celle-ci et je te renvoie** one more insolent remark like that ou any more of your insolence and I'll send you out

insolent, e [ɛ̃sɔlɑ̃, ɑ̃t] ADJ [a] (= *impertinent*) [personne, attitude, réponse] insolent; **tu es un ~ !** don't be so insolent! [b] (= *inouï*) [luxe, succès] unashamed; [joie] brazen, unashamed; **il a une chance ~ e !** he has the luck of the devil! [c] (littér = *arrogant*) [parvenu, vainqueur] arrogant

insolite [ɛ̃sɔlit] [1] ADJ unusual, out of the ordinary (attrib) [2] NM **aimer l'~** to like things which are out of the ordinary, to like unusual things

insolubilité [ɛ̃sɔlybilite] NF insolubility

insoluble [ɛ̃sɔlybl] ADJ insoluble

insolvabilité [ɛ̃sɔlvabilite] NF insolvency

insolvable [ɛ̃sɔlvabl] ADJ insolvent

insomniaque [ɛ̃sɔmnjak] ADJ, NMF insomniac; **c'est un ~ ◊ il est ~** he's an insomniac

insomnie [ɛ̃sɔmni] NF insomnia (NonC); **nuit d'~** sleepless night; **ses ~s** his (periods of) insomnia

insondable [ɛ̃sɔ̃dabl] ADJ [gouffre, mystère, douleur] unfathomable; [stupidité] immense, unimaginable

insonore [ɛ̃sɔnɔʀ] ADJ soundproof

insonorisation [ɛ̃sɔnɔʀizasjɔ̃] NF soundproofing

insonoriser [ɛ̃sɔnɔʀize] ▸ conjug 1 ◂ VT to soundproof; **immeuble mal insonorisé** badly soundproofed building

insortable* [ɛ̃sɔʀtabl] ADJ **tu es ~ !** I (ou we etc) can't take you anywhere!*

insouciance [ɛ̃susjɑ̃s] NF (= *nonchalance*) unconcern, lack of concern; (= *manque de prévoyance*) heedless ou happy-go-lucky attitude; **vivre dans l'~** to live a carefree life

insouciant, e [ɛ̃susjɑ̃, jɑ̃t] ADJ (= *sans souci*) [personne, vie, humeur] carefree, happy-go-lucky; [rire, paroles] carefree; (= *imprévoyant*) heedless, happy-go-lucky; **quel ~ (tu fais) !** you're such a heedless ou happy-go-lucky person!; **~ du danger** heedless of (the) danger

insoucieux, -ieuse [ɛ̃susjø, jøz] ADJ carefree; **~ du lendemain** unconcerned about the future, not caring about what tomorrow may bring

insoumis, e [ɛ̃sumi, iz] [1] ADJ [caractère, enfant] refractory, rebellious, insubordinate; [tribu, peuple, région] undefeated, unsubdued; (Mil) **soldat ~** draft-dodger [2] NM (Mil) draft-dodger

insoumission [ɛ̃sumisjɔ̃] NF insubordination, rebelliousness; (Mil) absence without leave

insoupçonnable [ɛ̃supsɔnabl] ADJ [personne] above ou beyond suspicion (attrib); [cachette] impossible to find; [desseins] unsuspected

insoupçonné, e [ɛ̃supsɔne] ADJ unsuspected

insoutenable [ɛ̃sut(ə)nabl] ADJ [spectacle, douleur, chaleur, odeur] unbearable; [théorie] untenable; **d'une violence ~** unbearably violent

inspecter [ɛ̃spɛkte] ▸ conjug 1 ◂ VT (= *contrôler*) to inspect; (= *scruter*) to inspect, examine

inspecteur, -trice [ɛ̃spɛktœʀ, tʀis] NM,F (gén) inspector; **~ des finances** auditor at the Treasury (with special responsibility for the inspection of public finances); **~ des impôts** tax inspector; **~ de police (judiciaire)** ≈ detective (Brit), ≈ (police) lieutenant (US); **~ de police principal** detective chief inspector (Brit), (police) lieutenant (US); **~ du travail** factory inspector; **~ primaire** primary school inspector; **~ d'Académie** chief education officer; **~ pédagogique régional** ≈ inspector of schools (Brit); ≈ accreditation officer (US); **~ général de l'instruction publique** ≈ chief inspector of schools; (hum ou péj) **voilà l'~ des travaux finis !*** it's a bit late to start offering your advice!

inspection [ɛ̃spɛksjɔ̃] NF [a] (= *examen*) inspection; **faire l'~ de** to inspect; **soumettre qch à une ~ en règle** to give sth a good ou thorough inspection ou going-over* [b] (= *inspectorat*) inspectorship; (= *inspecteurs*) inspectorate; (= *service*) **~ académique** school inspectorate, ≈ education authority (Brit); **~ (générale) des Finances** department of the Treasury responsible for auditing public bodies; **~ du Travail** factory inspectorate; (Police) **l'Inspection générale des services** the police monitoring service, ≈ the Police Complaints Board (Brit); **Inspection générale de la police nationale** police disciplinary body, ≈ Complaints and Discipline Branch (Brit), ≈ Internal Affairs (US)

inspectorat [ɛ̃spɛktɔʀa] NM inspectorship

inspirateur, -trice [ɛ̃spiʀatœʀ, tʀis] [1] ADJ [idée, force] inspiring; (Anat) inspiratory [2] NM,F (= *animateur*) inspirer; (= *instigateur*) instigator; **le poète et son inspiratrice** the poet and the woman who inspires (ou inspired) him

inspiration [ɛ̃spiʀasjɔ̃] NF [a] (divine, poétique) inspiration; **avoir de l'~** to have inspiration, be inspired; **selon l'~ du moment** according to the mood of the moment, as the mood takes me (ou you etc); **Julie fut une source d'~ pour lui** Julie was an inspiration to him [b] (= *idée*) inspiration, brainwave*; **par une heureuse ~** thanks to a flash of inspiration; **j'eus la bonne/mauvaise ~ de refuser** I had the bright/bad idea of refusing [c] (= *instigation*) instigation; (= *influence*) inspiration; **sous l'~ de qn** at sb's instigation, prompted by sb; **tableau d'~ religieuse** picture inspired by a religious subject; **mouvement d'~ communiste** communist-inspired movement [d] (= *respiration*) inspiration

inspiré, e [ɛ̃spiʀe] (ptp de **inspirer**) ADJ [a] [poète, œuvre, air] inspired; (iro) **qu'est-ce que c'est que cet ~ ?** whoever's this cranky character? ou this weirdo?* (péj) [b] (* = *avisé*) **il serait bien ~ de partir** he'd be well advised ou he'd do well to leave; **j'ai été bien/mal ~ de refuser ou quand j'ai refusé** I was truly inspired/ill inspired when I refused [c] **~ de** inspired by; **mode ~e des années cinquante** style inspired by the Fifties

inspirer [ɛ̃spiʀe] ▸ conjug 1 ◂ [1] VT [a] [+ poète, prophète] to inspire; **sa passion lui a inspiré ce poème** his passion inspired him to write this poem; **cette idée ne m'inspire pas beaucoup*** I'm not very taken with that idea, I'm not all that keen on this idea* (Brit); **le sujet de dissertation ne m'a pas vraiment inspiré** I

didn't find the essay subject very inspiring [b] (= *susciter*) [+ acte, personne] to inspire; **~ un sentiment à qn** to inspire sb with a feeling; **~ le respect à qn** to command sb's respect; **sa santé m'inspire des inquiétudes** his health gives me cause for concern; **il ne m'inspire pas confiance** he doesn't inspire me with confidence, I don't really trust him; **cela ne m'inspire rien de bon** I don't like the sound (ou look) of it; **toute l'opération était inspirée par un seul homme** the whole operation was inspired by one man; **l'horreur qu'il m'inspire** the horror he fills me with; **sa réaction était inspirée par la crainte** his reaction sprang from fear [c] (= *insuffler*) **~ de l'air dans qch** to breathe air into sth [2] VI (= *respirer*) to breathe in, inspire (SPÉC) [3] **s'inspirer** VPR **s'~ d'un modèle** [artiste] to draw one's inspiration from a model, be inspired by a model; [mode, tableau, loi] to be inspired by a model

instabilité [ɛ̃stabilite] NF [a] (gén, Sci) instability; [meuble, échafaudage] unsteadiness; **l'~ du temps** the unsettled (nature of the) weather [b] (Psych) [personne, caractère] (emotional) instability

instable [ɛ̃stabl] ADJ [a] (gén, Sci) unstable; [meuble, échafaudage] unsteady; [temps] unsettled → **équilibre** [b] (Psych) [personne, caractère] (emotionally) unstable

installateur [ɛ̃stalatœʀ] NM fitter; **~ en chauffage central** central heating installation engineer; **~ de cuisine** kitchen fitter

installation [ɛ̃stalasjɔ̃] NF [a] (= *mise en service, pose*) [électricité, chauffage central, téléphone, eau courante] installation, installing, putting in; [applique] putting in; [rideaux, étagère] putting up; [tente] putting up, pitching; **l'~ du téléphone n'est pas gratuite** there's a charge for installing the telephone; **ils s'occupent aussi de l'~ du mobilier** they also take care of moving the furniture in ou of installing the furniture; **frais/travaux d'~** installation costs/work [b] (= *aménagement*) [pièce, appartement] fitting out; (= *meubles*) living arrangements, setup*; **ils ont une ~ provisoire** they have temporary living arrangements ou a temporary setup*; **qu'est-ce que vous avez comme ~ ?** what kind of a setup* do you have? [c] (= *établissement*) [artisan, commerçant] setting up; [dentiste, médecin] setting up one's practice; [usine] setting up; **il lui fallait songer à l'~ de son fils** he had to think about setting his son up [d] (dans un logement) settling; (= *emménagement*) settling in; **il voulait fêter son ~** he wanted to celebrate moving in; **leur ~ terminée, ils...** when they had finally settled in, they...; **ils sont en pleine ~** they're moving in at the moment [e] (= *équipement*) (gén pl) fittings, installations; (= *usine*) plant (NonC); **l'~ téléphonique** the phone system; **l'~ électrique est défectueuse** the wiring is faulty; **~(s) sanitaire(s)/électrique(s)** sanitary/electrical fittings ou installations; **~s sportives** sports facilities; **les ~s industrielles d'une région** the industrial installations ou plant of a region; **~s nucléaires** nuclear plant; **~s portuaires** port facilities; **le camping est doté de toutes les ~s nécessaires** the campsite has all the necessary facilities [f] (Art) installation

installé, e [ɛ̃stale] (ptp de **installer**) ADJ **aménagé] bien/mal ~** [appartement] well/badly fitted out; [atelier, cuisine] well/badly equipped ou fitted out; **ils sont très bien ~s** they have a comfortable ou nice home; **c'est un homme ~†** he is well-established

installer [ɛ̃stale] ▸ conjug 1 ◂ [1] VT [a] (= *mettre en service*) [+ électricité, chauffage central, téléphone, eau courante] to install, put in; [+ usine] to set up; **faire ~ le gaz/le téléphone** to have (the) gas/the telephone put in *ou* installed

b̲ (= *placer, poser*) [+ *rideaux, étagère*] to put up; [+ *applique*] to put in; [+ *meuble*] to put in, install; [+ *tente*] to put up, pitch; **où va-t-on ~ le lit?** where shall we put the bed?

c̲ (= *aménager*) [+ *pièce, appartement*] to fit out; **ils ont très bien installé leur appartement** they've got their flat (*Brit*) *ou* apartment (*US*) well fitted out; **ils ont installé leur bureau dans le grenier** they've turned the attic into a study, they've made a study in the attic; **comment la cuisine est-elle installée?** how is the kitchen laid out? *ou* fitted out?

d̲ (= *loger*) [+ *malade, jeune couple*] to get settled, settle; **ils installèrent leurs hôtes dans une aile du château** they installed *ou* put their guests in a wing of the château

e̲ (= *établir*) **il a installé son fils dentiste/à son compte** he set his son up as a dentist/in his own business

f̲ (= *nommer*) [+ *fonctionnaire, évêque*] to install; **il a été officiellement installé dans ses fonctions** he has been officially installed in his post

g̲ (*Ordin*) to install

2̲ **s'installer** VPR a̲ (= *s'établir*) [*artisan, commerçant*] to set o.s. up (**comme** as); [*dentiste, médecin*] to set up one's practice; **s'~ à son compte** to set up on one's own, set up one's own business; (= *se fixer*) **ils se sont installés à la campagne/à Lyon** they've settled *ou* they've set up house in the country/in Lyons

b̲ (= *se loger*) to settle; (= *emménager*) to settle in; **laisse-leur le temps de s'~** give them time to settle in; **pendant la guerre, ils s'étaient installés chez des amis** during the war they moved in *ou* lived with friends; **s'~ dans une maison abandonnée** to set up home in an abandoned house; **ils sont bien installés dans leur nouvelle maison** they have made themselves very comfortable in their new house

c̲ (*sur un siège, à un emplacement*) to settle down; **s'~ commodément** to settle (down) comfortably; **s'~ par terre/dans un fauteuil** to settle down on the floor/in an armchair; **installe-toi comme il faut** (*confortablement*) make yourself comfortable; (*tiens-toi bien*) sit properly; **installons-nous près de cet arbre** let's sit down near this tree; **partout où il va il s'installe comme chez lui** wherever he goes he makes himself at home; **les forains se sont installés sur un terrain vague** the fairground people have set themselves up on a piece of wasteland; **la fête s'est installée sur la place du marché** the fair has been set up *ou* has been set up in the marketplace

d̲ [*grève, maladie*] to take hold; [*personne*] **s'~ dans** [+ *inertie*] to sink into, be sunk in; [+ *malhonnêteté*] to entangle o.s. in, get entangled in; **s'~ dans la guerre** to settle into *ou* become accustomed to a state of war; **le doute s'installa dans mon esprit** I began to have doubts; **la peur s'était installée dans la ville** the town was gripped by fear

instamment [ɛ̃stamɑ̃] ADV insistently, earnestly; **il demande ~ au gouvernement de prendre une décision** he is urging the government to make a decision

instance [ɛ̃stɑ̃s] NF a̲ (= *autorité*) authority; **les ~s internationales/communautaires** the international/EEC authorities; **la plus haute ~ judiciaire du pays** the country's highest judicial body *ou* legal authority; **les plus hautes ~s du parti** the party leadership; **le conflit devra être tranché par l'~ supérieure** the dispute will have to be resolved by a higher authority; **les ~s dirigeantes du football** football's governing bodies

b̲ (*Jur*) (legal) proceedings; **introduire une ~** to institute (legal) proceedings; **en seconde ~** on appeal → **juge, tribunal**

c̲ (= *prière, insistance*) **demander qch avec ~** to ask for something with insistence, to make an earnest request for sth; **~s** entreaties; **sur** *ou* **devant les ~s de ses parents** in the face of his parents' entreaties

d̲ **en ~** (= *en cours*) **l'affaire est en ~** the matter is pending; **être en ~ de divorce** to be waiting for a divorce; **le train est en ~ de départ** the train is on the point of departure *ou* about to leave; **courrier en ~** mail ready for posting *ou* to be dispatched; **en dernière ~** in the final analysis, ultimately

e̲ (*Psych*) agency

instant¹ [ɛ̃stɑ̃] NM a̲ (= *moment*) moment, instant; **des ~s de tendresse** tender moments, moments of tenderness; **j'ai cru (pendant) un ~ que** I thought for a moment *ou* a second *ou* one instant that; **(attendez) un ~!** wait one instant!; **wait one instant!,** wait *ou* just a moment!, wait one instant!; **l'~ fatal** the final moment

b̲ (= *le présent*) **il faut vivre dans l'~** you must live in the present (moment)

c̲ (*loc*) **je l'ai vu à l'~** I've just this instant *ou* minute *ou* second seen him; **il faut le faire à l'~** we must do it this instant *ou* minute; **on me l'apprend à l'~ (même)** I've just been told, I've just heard about it; **à l'~ (présent)** at this very instant *ou* moment *ou* minute; **à l'~ où je vous parle** as I'm speaking to you now, as I speak; **à l'~ (même) où il sortit** just as he went out, (just) at the very moment *ou* instant he went out; **à chaque ~** (= *d'un moment à l'autre*) at any moment *ou* minute; (= *tout le temps*) all the time, every minute; **d'un ~ à l'autre** any minute now; **au même ~** at the (very) same moment *ou* instant; **d'~ en ~** from moment to moment, every moment; **dans l'~** (= *immédiatement*) there and then, immediately; **dans un ~** in a moment *ou* minute; **en un ~** in an instant, in no time (at all); **de tous les ~s** [*surveillance*] perpetual, constant; [*dévouement, attention*] constant; **par ~s** at times; **pour l'~** for the moment, for the time being; **je n'en doute pas un (seul) ~** I don't doubt it for a (single) moment; **dès l'~ où** *ou* **que vous êtes d'accord** (*puisque*) since you agree; **dès l'~ où je l'ai vu** (*dès que*) as soon as I saw him, from the moment I saw him

instant², e [ɛ̃stɑ̃, ɑ̃t] ADJ (*littér = pressant*) insistent, pressing, earnest

instantané, e [ɛ̃stɑ̃tane] 1̲ ADJ [*lait, café, soupe*] instant (*épith*); [*mort, réponse, effet*] instantaneous; (*littér = bref*) [*vision*] momentary 2̲ NM (*Photo*) snapshot, snap*; (*fig*) snapshot

instantanéité [ɛ̃stɑ̃taneite] NF instantaneousness, instantaneity; **cela favorise l'~ de l'accès à l'information** that enables us to have instant access to information

instantanément [ɛ̃stɑ̃tanemɑ̃] ADV instantaneously; **pour préparer ~ un bon café** to make good coffee instantly

instar [ɛ̃staR] ◆ **à l'instar de** LOC ADV (*frm*) (= *à l'exemple de*) following the example of, after the fashion of; (= *comme*) like

instauration [ɛ̃stɔRasjɔ̃] NF [*pratique*] institution; [*régime, dialogue*] establishment; [*taxe*] introduction; [*état d'urgence*] imposition

instaurer [ɛ̃stɔRe] ◆ conjug 1 ◀ VT [+ *usage, pratique*] to institute; [+ *paix, régime, dialogue*] to establish; [+ *méthode, quotas, taxe*] to introduce; [+ *couvre-feu, état d'urgence*] to impose; **la révolution a instauré la république** the revolution established the republic; **le doute s'est instauré dans les esprits** people have begun to have doubts

instigateur, -trice [ɛ̃stigatœR, tRis] NM,F instigator

instigation [ɛ̃stigasjɔ̃] NF instigation; **à l'~ de qn** at sb's instigation

instillation [ɛ̃stilasjɔ̃] NF instillation

instiller [ɛ̃stile] ◆ conjug 1 ◀ VT (*littér, Méd*) to instil (*Brit*), instill (*US*) (**dans** in, into); **il m'a**

instillé la passion du jeu he instilled the love of gambling in *ou* into me

instinct [ɛ̃stɛ̃] NM (*gén*) instinct; **~ maternel** maternal instinct; (*Psych*) **~ de mort** death wish; **~ de vie** will to live; **~ grégaire** gregarious *ou* herd instinct; **~ de conservation** instinct of self-preservation; **il a l'~ des affaires** he has an instinct for business; **faire qch d'~** *ou* **par ~** *ou* **à l'~** to do sth instinctively; **d'~, il comprit la situation** intuitively *ou* instinctively he understood the situation; **mon ~ me dit que** (my) instinct tells me that; **céder à ses (mauvais) ~s** to yield to one's (bad) instincts

instinctif, -ive [ɛ̃stɛ̃ktif, iv] ADJ (*gén*) instinctive, instinctual; **c'est un ~** he (always) acts on instinct

instinctivement [ɛ̃stɛ̃ktivmɑ̃] ADV instinctively

instit* [ɛ̃stit] NMF ABRÉV = **instituteur, -trice**

instituer [ɛ̃stitɥe] ◆ conjug 1 ◀ 1̲ VT [+ *règle, pratique, organisation*] to institute; [+ *relations commerciales*] to establish; [+ *impôt*] to introduce; [+ *évêque*] to institute; [+ *héritier*] to appoint, institute 2̲ **s'instituer** VPR [*relations commerciales*] to start up, be (*ou* become) established

institut [ɛ̃stity] 1̲ NM institute; (*Univ*) institute, school (*Brit*); **l'Institut (de France)** the Institut de France, ≈ the Royal Society (*Brit*); **membre de l'Institut** member of the Institut de France, ≈ Fellow of the Royal Society (*Brit*); **~ de beauté** beauty salon *ou* parlor (*US*); **~ de sondage** polling organization

2̲ COMP ► **Institut géographique national** *French geographical institute*, ≈ Ordnance Survey (*Brit*), ≈ United States Geological Survey (*US*), ≈ USGS (*US*) ► **Institut du Monde Arabe** *Arab cultural centre in Paris* ► **Institut monétaire européen** European Monetary Institute, EMI ► **Institut national de l'audiovisuel** *library of radio and television archives* ► **Institut national de la consommation** *consumer research organization*, ≈ Consumers' Association (*Brit*), ≈ Consumer Product Safety Commission (*US*) ► **Institut national de la propriété industrielle** ≈ Patent Office ► **Institut national de la recherche agronomique** *national institute for agronomic research* ► **Institut national de la santé et de la recherche médicale** *national institute for health and medical research*, ≈ Medical Research Council (*Brit*), ≈ National Institute of Health (*US*) ► **Institut national de la statistique et des études économiques** *French national institute of economic and statistical information* ► **Institut Pasteur** Pasteur Institute ► **Institut universitaire de formation des maîtres** *teacher training college* ► **Institut universitaire de technologie** ≈ polytechnic (*Brit*), ≈ technical school *ou* institute (*US*) → **médico-légal**

instituteur, -trice [ɛ̃stitytœR, tRis] 1̲ NM,F (primary school) teacher; **~ spécialisé** teacher in special school (for the handicapped) 2̲ **institutrice** NF (*Hist = gouvernante*) governess

institution [ɛ̃stitysjɔ̃] 1̲ NF a̲ (= *organisme, structure*) institution; (= *école*) private school; (*Pol*) **nos ~s sont menacées** our institutions are threatened; (*iro*) **ce présentateur est devenu une véritable ~** this TV presenter has become a national institution; (*iro*) **la mendicité est ici une véritable ~!** begging is a way of life here! b̲ (= *instauration*) [*pratique*] institution; [*relations*] establishment; [*impôt*] introduction; [*évêque*] institution 2̲ COMP ► **institution d'héritier** (*Jur*) appointment of an heir ► **institution religieuse** (*gén*) denominational school; (*catholique*) Catholic school, parochial school (*US*)

institutionnalisation [ɛ̃stitysjɔnalizasjɔ̃] NF institutionalization

institutionnaliser [ɛ̃stitysjɔnalize] ▸conjug 1◂ 1 VT to institutionalize 2 **s'institutionnaliser** VPR to become institutionalized

institutionnel, -elle [ɛ̃stitysjɔnɛl] ADJ institutional

institutrice [ɛ̃stitytʀis] NF → **instituteur**

instructeur [ɛ̃stʀyktœʀ] 1 NM instructor 2 ADJ **juge** ou **magistrat** ~ examining magistrate; **capitaine/sergent** ~ drill captain/sergeant

instructif, -ive [ɛ̃stʀyktif, iv] ADJ instructive

instruction [ɛ̃stʀyksjɔ̃] 1 NF a (= enseignement) education; **l'~ que j'ai reçue** the teaching ou education I received; **niveau d'~** academic standard; ~ **civique** civics sg; ~ **militaire** army training; ~ **religieuse** religious instruction ou education ou studies; **l'~ publique** state education

b (= culture) education; **avoir de l'~** to be well educated; **être sans ~** to have no education

c (Jur) pretrial investigation of a case; **ouvrir une** ~ to initiate an investigation into a crime → **juge**

d (Admin = circulaire) directive; ~ **ministérielle/préfectorale** ministerial/prefectural directive

e (Ordin) instruction; ~**s d'entrée-sortie** input-output instructions

2 **instructions** NFPL (= directives) instructions; (= mode d'emploi) instructions, directions; ~**s de lavage** (gén) washing instructions; (= étiquette) care label; **suivre les ~s données sur le paquet** to follow the instructions ou directions given on the packet; **conformément/contrairement à vos ~s** in accordance with/contrary to your instructions

instruire [ɛ̃stʀɥiʀ] ▸conjug 38◂ 1 VT a (= former: gén) to teach, educate; [+ recrue] to train; ~ **qn dans l'art oratoire** to educate ou instruct sb in the art of oratory; **c'est la vie qui m'a instruit** life has educated me, life has been my teacher; ~ **qn par l'exemple** to teach ou educate sb by example; **instruit par son exemple** having learnt from his example; **ces émissions ne visent pas à** ~ **mais à divertir** these broadcasts are not intended to teach ou educate ou instruct but to entertain

b (= informer) ~ **qn de qch** to inform ou advise sb of sth

c (Jur) [+ affaire, dossier] to conduct an investigation into; ~ **contre qn** to conduct investigations concerning sb

2 **s'instruire** VPR (= apprendre) to educate o.s.; (hum) **c'est comme ça qu'on s'instruit !** that's how you learn!; (hum) **on s'instruit à tout âge** it's never too late to learn; (frm) **s'~ de qch** (= se renseigner) to obtain information about sth, find out about sth; **s'~ de qch auprès de qn** to obtain information ou find out from sb about sth

instruit, e [ɛ̃stʀɥi, it] (ptp de **instruire**) ADJ educated; **peu** ~ uneducated

instrument [ɛ̃stʀymɑ̃] NM a (= objet) instrument; ~ **de musique/de chirurgie/de mesure/à vent** musical/surgical/measuring/wind instrument; ~**s aratoires** ploughing implements; ~ **de travail** tool; (Aviat) **les ~s de bord** the controls; (Aviat) **naviguer aux ~s** to fly on instruments b (= moyen) **être l'~ de qn** to be sb's tool; **le président fut l'~ de/servit d'~ à la répression** the president was the instrument ou tool of/served as an ou the instrument of repression; **elle a été l'~ de cette vengeance** she was ou served as the instrument of this revenge; **elle a été l'~ privilégié de sa réussite** she was the key ou principal instrument of his success; ~**s de paiement** means of payment; ~**s financiers** financial instruments

instrumental, e [mpl -aux] [ɛ̃stʀymɑ̃tal, o] 1 ADJ (Ling, Mus) instrumental 2 NM (Ling) instrumental

instrumentaliser [ɛ̃stʀymɑ̃talize] ▸conjug 1◂ VT [+ chose, événement, personne] to make use of, exploit; **toutes les nations instrumentalisent l'histoire** all countries use ou exploit history for their own ends; **la société instrumentalise l'individu** society turns people into robots

instrumentation [ɛ̃stʀymɑ̃tasjɔ̃] NF a (Mus) instrumentation, orchestration b (Tech) instrumentation

instrumenter [ɛ̃stʀymɑ̃te] ▸conjug 1◂ 1 VI (Jur) to draw up a formal document 2 VT a (Mus) to orchestrate b (Tech) to instrument

instrumentiste [ɛ̃stʀymɑ̃tist] NMF a (Mus) instrumentalist b (Chir) theatre nurse

insu [ɛ̃sy] ♦ **à l'insu de** LOC PRÉP a (= en cachette de) **à l'~ de qn** without sb's knowledge, without sb's knowing b (= inconsciemment) **à mon (ou ton etc)** ~ without my ou me (ou your ou you etc) knowing it; **je souriais à mon** ~ I was smiling without knowing it

insubmersible [ɛ̃sybmɛʀsibl] ADJ insubmersible, unsinkable

insubordination [ɛ̃sybɔʀdinasjɔ̃] NF (gén) insubordination, rebelliousness; (Mil) insubordination; **pour fait d'~** for insubordination

insubordonné, e [ɛ̃sybɔʀdɔne] ADJ (gén) insubordinate, rebellious; (Mil) insubordinate

insuccès [ɛ̃syksɛ] NM failure

insuffisamment [ɛ̃syfizamɑ̃] ADV (en quantité) insufficiently; (en qualité, intensité, degré) inadequately; **tu dors** ~ you're not getting adequate ou sufficient sleep; **pièce** ~ **éclairée** room with insufficient ou inadequate lighting, poorly-lit room

insuffisance [ɛ̃syfizɑ̃s] NF a (= médiocrité) inadequacy; (= manque) insufficiency, inadequacy; **l'~ de nos ressources** the inadequacy of our resources, the shortfall in our resources, our inadequate ou insufficient resources; **nous souffrons d'une grande ~ de moyens** we are suffering from a great inadequacy ou insufficiency ou shortage of means; **une ~ de personnel** a shortage of staff b (= faiblesses) ~**s** inadequacies; **avoir des ~s en maths** to be weak in ou at maths; **il y a des ~s dans son travail** his work is not adequate c (Méd) ~(**s**) **cardiaque(s)/thyroïdienne(s)** cardiac/thyroid insufficiency (NonC); ~ **rénale/respiratoire** kidney/respiratory failure

insuffisant, e [ɛ̃syfizɑ̃, ɑ̃t] 1 ADJ a (en quantité) insufficient; **ce qu'il nous donne est** ~ what he gives us is insufficient ou not enough; **nous travaillons avec un personnel** ~ we have insufficient staff; **nous sommes en nombre** ~ there aren't enough of us b (en qualité, intensité, degré) inadequate; (Scol: sur une copie) poor 2 NM (Méd) **les** ~**s cardiaques/respiratoires** people with cardiac/respiratory insufficiency; **les** ~**s rénaux** people suffering from kidney failure

insufflateur [ɛ̃syflatœʀ] NM (Méd) insufflator

insufflation [ɛ̃syflasjɔ̃] NF (Méd) insufflation

insuffler [ɛ̃syfle] ▸conjug 1◂ VT a (= inspirer, donner) ~ **le courage/le désir à qn** to inspire sb with courage/with desire, breathe courage/desire into sb; (Rel) ~ **la vie à** to breathe life into b (Méd) [+ air] to blow, insufflate (SPÉC) (dans into); **se faire** ~ to be insufflated (SPÉC)

insulaire [ɛ̃sylɛʀ] 1 ADJ [administration, population] island (épith); [conception, attitude] insular 2 NMF islander

insularité [ɛ̃sylaʀite] NF insularity

insuline [ɛ̃sylin] NF insulin

insulinodépendance [ɛ̃sylinodepɑ̃dɑ̃s] NF insulin-dependent diabetes

insulinodépendant, e [ɛ̃sylinodepɑ̃dɑ̃, ɑ̃t] ADJ [diabète, diabétique] insulin-dependent

insultant, e [ɛ̃syltɑ̃, ɑ̃t] ADJ insulting (pour to)

insulte [ɛ̃sylt] NF (= grossièreté) abuse (NonC), insult; (= affront) insult; (frm) **c'est me faire ~ que de ne pas me croire** you insult me by not believing me; **c'est une ~ ou c'est faire ~ à son intelligence** it's an insult ou affront to his intelligence

insulté, e [ɛ̃sylte] (ptp de **insulter**) 1 ADJ insulted 2 NM (en duel) injured party

insulter [ɛ̃sylte] ▸conjug 1◂ 1 VT (= faire affront à) to insult; (= injurier) to abuse, insult 2 **insulter à** VT INDIR (fig littér) to be an insult to 3 **s'insulter** VPR to insult one another

insulteur [ɛ̃syltœʀ] NM insulter

insupportable [ɛ̃sypɔʀtabl] ADJ [bruit, personne] unbearable, intolerable, insufferable; [situation, douleur, spectacle] unbearable, intolerable; [vie, solitude] unbearable

insupportablement [ɛ̃sypɔʀtabləmɑ̃] ADV unbearably, intolerably, insufferably

insupporter [ɛ̃sypɔʀte] ▸conjug 1◂ VT (hum) **cela m'insupporte/l'insupporte** I/he can't stand this

insurgé, e [ɛ̃syʀʒe] (ptp de **s'insurger**) ADJ, NM,F rebel, insurgent

insurger (s') [ɛ̃syʀʒe] ▸conjug 3◂ VPR (lit, fig) to rebel, rise up, revolt (contre against)

insurmontable [ɛ̃syʀmɔ̃tabl] ADJ a (= infranchissable) [difficulté, obstacle] insurmountable, insuperable b (= irrépressible) [peur, dégoût] unconquerable

insurpassable [ɛ̃syʀpasabl] ADJ unsurpassable, unsurpassed

insurrection [ɛ̃syʀɛksjɔ̃] NF (lit) insurrection, revolt, uprising; (fig) revolt; **mouvement/foyer d'~** movement/nucleus of revolt

insurrectionnel, -elle [ɛ̃syʀɛksjɔnɛl] ADJ [mouvement, gouvernement, force] insurrectionary; **climat** ~ atmosphere of open rebellion

intact, e [ɛ̃takt] ADJ [objet, réputation, argent] intact (attrib); **le vase est arrivé** ~ the vase arrived intact ou in one piece; **le mystère reste** ~ the mystery remains unsolved; **son enthousiasme reste** ~ he's still as enthusiastic as ever

intaille [ɛ̃taj] NF intaglio

intangibilité [ɛ̃tɑ̃ʒibilite] NF inviolability

intangible [ɛ̃tɑ̃ʒibl] ADJ (= impalpable) intangible; (= sacré) inviolable

intarissable [ɛ̃taʀisabl] ADJ (lit, fig) inexhaustible; **il est** ~ he could talk for ever (sur about)

intarissablement [ɛ̃taʀisabləmɑ̃] ADV inexhaustibly

intégrable [ɛ̃tegʀabl] ADJ that can be integrated

intégral, e [mpl -aux] [ɛ̃tegʀal, o] 1 ADJ complete, full; **le remboursement** ~ **de qch** the repayment in full of sth, the full ou complete repayment of sth; **publier le texte** ~ **d'un discours** to publish the text of a speech in full ou the complete text of a speech; (Ciné) **version** ~**e** uncut version; (Presse) **texte** ~ unabridged version; **« texte » »** "unabridged"; **le nu** ~ complete ou total nudity; **bronzage** ~ all-over suntan; **casque** ~ full-face helmet → **calcul** 2 **intégrale** NF (Math) integral; (Mus) (= série) complete series; (= œuvre) complete works; (= outil) single-purpose tool; **l'intégrale des symphonies de Sibelius** the complete symphonies of Sibelius

intégralement [ɛ̃tegʀalmɑ̃] ADV in full, fully; **le concert sera retransmis** ~ the concert will be broadcast in full

intégralité [ɛ̃tegʀalite] NF whole; **l'~ de la somme** the whole of the sum, the whole ou entire ou full sum ou amount; **la somme vous sera remboursée dans son** ~ the sum will be repaid to you in its entirety ou in toto ou in full; **le match sera retransmis dans son** ~ the match will be broadcast in full; **l'~ de mon salaire** the whole of my salary, my whole *ou* entire salary

intégrant, e [ɛ̃tegʀɑ̃, ɑ̃t] ADJ → **partie²**

intégrateur, -trice [ɛ̃tegʀatœʀ, tʀis] 1 ADJ **le rôle ~ de l'école** the role of schools in integrating children into society 2 **intégrateur** NM (*Ordin*) integrator

intégration [ɛ̃tegʀasjɔ̃] NF (*gén*) integration (**à, dans** into); **politique d'~ des immigrés** policy favouring the integration of immigrants; (*Univ*) **après son ~ à Polytechnique** after getting into *ou* being admitted to the École polytechnique; (*Ordin*) **~ à très grande échelle** very large-scale integration

intégrationniste [ɛ̃tegʀasjɔnist] ADJ, NMF integrationist

intégré, e [ɛ̃tegʀe] (*ptp de* **intégrer**) ADJ [*circuit, système*] integrated; [*lecteur CD-ROM*] built-in; **cuisine ~e** fitted kitchen; **populations bien ~es** well-assimilated populations

intègre [ɛ̃tegʀ] ADJ upright, honest

intégrer [ɛ̃tegʀe] ▸conjug 6◂ 1 VT a (*Math*) to integrate (**à** = *assimiler*) [+ *idées, personne*] to integrate (**à, dans** into) c (= *entrer dans*) [+ *entreprise, club*] to join 2 VI (*Univ*) **~ à ...** to get into ... 3 **s'intégrer** VPR to become integrated (**à, dans** into); **bien s'~ dans une société** to integrate well into a society; **cette maison s'intègre mal dans le paysage** this house doesn't really fit into the surrounding countryside

intégrisme [ɛ̃tegʀism] NM fundamentalism

intégriste [ɛ̃tegʀist] ADJ, NMF fundamentalist

intégrité [ɛ̃tegʀite] NF (= *totalité*) integrity; (= *honnêteté*) integrity, honesty, uprightness

intellect [ɛ̃telɛkt] NM intellect

intellectualisation [ɛ̃telɛktɥalizasjɔ̃] NF intellectualization

intellectualiser [ɛ̃telɛktɥalize] ▸conjug 1◂ VT to intellectualize

intellectualisme [ɛ̃telɛktɥalism] NM intellectualism

intellectualiste [ɛ̃telɛktɥalist] ADJ, NMF intellectualist

intellectualité [ɛ̃telɛktɥalite] NF (*littér*) intellectuality

intellectuel, -elle [ɛ̃telɛktɥel] 1 ADJ [*facultés, effort, supériorité*] mental, intellectual; [*fatigue*] mental; [*personne, mouvement, œuvre, vie*] intellectual; (*péj*) highbrow (*péj*), intellectual; **activité intellectuelle** mental *ou* intellectual activity, brainwork*; **les travailleurs ~s** non-manual workers; **les milieux ~s** intellectual circles → **quotient** 2 NM,F intellectual; (*péj*) highbrow (*péj*), intellectual; **les ~s de gauche** left-wing intellectuals

intellectuellement [ɛ̃telɛktɥelmɑ̃] ADV mentally, intellectually; **un enfant ~ très doué** an intellectually gifted child

intelligemment [ɛ̃teliʒamɑ̃] ADV (*agir*) intelligently, cleverly; **les gens consomment plus ~** people are consuming more intelligently; **c'est fait très ~** it's very intelligently *ou* cleverly done

intelligence [ɛ̃teliʒɑ̃s] 1 NF a (= *facultés mentales*) intelligence; **personne à l'~ vive** person with a sharp *ou* quick mind; **faire preuve d'~** to show intelligence; **avoir l'~ de faire** to have the intelligence *ou* the wit to do, be intelligent enough to do; **travailler avec ~/sans ~** to work intelligently/unintelligently; **il met beaucoup d'~ dans ce qu'il fait** he applies great intelligence to what he does; **c'est une ~ exceptionnelle** he has a great intellect *ou* mind *ou* brain; **les grandes ~s** great minds *ou* intellects; **~ artificielle** artificial intelligence b (= *compréhension*); **pour l'~ du texte** for a clear understanding of the text, in order to understand the text; **avoir l'~**

des affaires to have a good grasp *ou* understanding of business matters, have a good head for business c (= *complicité*) secret agreement; **agir d'~ avec qn** to act in (secret) agreement with sb; **signe/sourire d'~** sign/smile of complicity; **être d'~ avec qn** to have a (secret) understanding *ou* agreement with sb; **vivre en bonne/mauvaise ~ avec qn** to be on good/bad terms with sb 2 **intelligences** NFPL (= *relations secrètes*) secret relations *ou* contacts; **entretenir des ~s avec l'ennemi** to have secret dealings with the enemy

intelligent, e [ɛ̃teliʒɑ̃, ɑ̃t] ADJ a [*personne*] intelligent, clever, bright; [*visage, front, regard, animal*] intelligent; [*choix, réponse*] intelligent, clever; **supérieurement ~** of superior intelligence; (*iro*) **c'est ~ !** very clever! (*iro*); **son livre est ~** his book shows intelligence; **armes ~es** smart weapons; **ce n'était pas très ~ de sa part !** that wasn't very clever of him! b (*Ordin*) intelligent; **terminal ~** intelligent terminal

intelligentsia [ɛ̃teliʒɛnsja] NF **l'~** the intelligentsia

intelligibilité [ɛ̃teliʒibilite] NF intelligibility

intelligible [ɛ̃teliʒibl] ADJ intelligible; **à haute et ~ voix** loudly and clearly; **s'exprimer de façon peu ~** to express o.s. unintelligibly *ou* in an unintelligible way

intelligiblement [ɛ̃teliʒibləmɑ̃] ADV intelligibly

intello* [ɛ̃telo] ADJ, NMF (*péj*) highbrow (*péj*), intellectual; **c'est l'~ de la famille** he's the brains of the family; **il est du genre ~ rive gauche** he's the arty* intellectual type

intempérance [ɛ̃tɑ̃peʀɑ̃s] NF (*frm*) (= *gloutonnerie, ivrognerie*) intemperance (*frm*); (= *luxure*) overindulgence; **une telle ~ de langage** such excessive language

intempérant, e [ɛ̃tɑ̃peʀɑ̃, ɑ̃t] ADJ (*frm*) (= *glouton, ivrogne*) intemperate; (= *luxurieux*) overindulgent

intempéries [ɛ̃tɑ̃peʀi] NFPL bad weather; **affronter les ~** to brave the (bad) weather

intempestif, -ive [ɛ̃tɑ̃pɛstif, iv] ADJ untimely; **pas de zèle ~ !** no misplaced *ou* excessive zeal!

intempestivement [ɛ̃tɑ̃pɛstivmɑ̃] ADV at an untimely moment

intemporalité [ɛ̃tɑ̃pɔʀalite] NF (*littér*) (= *atemporalité*) timelessness; (= *immatérialité*) immateriality

intemporel, -elle [ɛ̃tɑ̃pɔʀɛl] ADJ (*littér*) (= *atemporel*) timeless; (= *immatériel*) immaterial

intenable [ɛ̃t(ə)nabl] ADJ (= *intolérable*) [*chaleur, situation*] intolerable, unbearable; [*personne*] unruly; (= *indéfendable*) [*position, théorie*] untenable

intendance [ɛ̃tɑ̃dɑ̃s] NF (*Mil*) (= *service*) Supply Corps; (= *bureau*) Supplies office; (*Scol*) (= *métier*) school management, financial administration; (= *bureau*) bursar's office; [*propriété*] (= *métier*) estate management; (= *bureau*) estate office; (*Hist* = *province*) intendancy; **les problèmes d'~** (*Mil*) the problems of supply; (*gén*) the day-to-day problems of running a house (*ou* a company *etc*); (*fig*) **l'~ suivra** all material support will be provided

intendant [ɛ̃tɑ̃dɑ̃] NM a (*Scol*) bursar b (*Mil*) quartermaster; (= *régisseur*) steward c (*Hist*) intendant

intendante [ɛ̃tɑ̃dɑ̃t] NF a (*Scol*) bursar; (= *régisseur*) stewardess b (*Rel*) Superior

intense [ɛ̃tɑ̃s] ADJ a [*lumière, moment, joie, activité, réflexion, match, chagrin*] intense; [*froid, douleur*] severe, intense; **une chemise d'un bleu ~** a vivid blue shirt; **ça demande un travail ~** it requires really hard work b [*circulation*] dense, heavy

intensément [ɛ̃tɑ̃semɑ̃] ADV intensely

intensif, -ive [ɛ̃tɑ̃sif, iv] 1 ADJ (*gén, Agr, Ling*) intensive → **cours, culture** 2 NM (*Ling*) intensive

intensification [ɛ̃tɑ̃sifikasjɔ̃] NF intensification; **l'~ du trafic aérien** the increase in air traffic

intensifier [ɛ̃tɑ̃sifje] ▸conjug 7◂ 1 VT [+ *coopération, concurrence, production*] to intensify; [+ *lutte, effort*] to intensify, step up 2 **s'intensifier** VPR [*combats, bombardements*] to intensify; [*concurrence*] to intensify, become keener; **le froid va s'~** it's going to get colder

intensité [ɛ̃tɑ̃site] NF a [*lumière, moment, activité*] intensity; [*froid, douleur*] severity, intensity; **un moment d'une grande ~** a very intense moment; **~ dramatique** dramatic intensity b [*circulation*] density c (*Ling*) accent **d'~** stress accent d (*Élec*) [*courant*] strength; (*Phys*) [*force*] intensity

intensivement [ɛ̃tɑ̃sivmɑ̃] ADV intensively

intenter [ɛ̃tɑ̃te] ▸conjug 1◂ VT **~ un procès contre** *ou* **à qn** to take sb to court, start *ou* institute proceedings against sb; **~ une action contre** *ou* **à qn** to bring an action against sb

▾ **intention** [ɛ̃tɑ̃sjɔ̃] NF a (*gén*) intention; **quelles sont vos ~s ?** what are your intentions?, what do you intend to do?; **bonnes ~s** good intentions; **agir dans une bonne ~** to act with good intentions; **elle l'a fait sans mauvaise ~** she didn't mean any harm; **c'est l'~ qui compte** it's the thought that counts; **il n'entre** *ou* **n'est pas dans ses ~s de démissionner** it's not his intention to resign, he has no intention of resigning; **à cette ~** with this intention, to this end; **avoir l'~ de faire** to intend *ou* mean to do, have the intention of doing; **avec** *ou* **dans l'~ de faire** with the intention of doing, with a view to doing; **avec** *ou* **dans l'~ de tuer** with intent to kill; (*Pol*) **~ de vote** voting intention; (*Pol*) **déclaration d'~** declaration of intent → **enfer, procès** b **à l'~ de qn** [*collecte*] for the benefit of sb, in aid of sb; [*renseignement*] for the benefit *ou* the information of sb; [*cadeau, prière, messe*] for sb; [*fête*] in sb's honour; **livre/film à l'~ des enfants** book/film aimed at children; **je l'ai acheté à votre ~** I bought it just *ou* specially for you

intentionnalité [ɛ̃tɑ̃sjɔnalite] NF intentionality

intentionné, e [ɛ̃tɑ̃sjɔne] ADJ **bien ~** well-meaning, well-intentioned; **mal ~** ill-intentioned

intentionnel, -elle [ɛ̃tɑ̃sjɔnɛl] ADJ intentional, deliberate

intentionnellement [ɛ̃tɑ̃sjɔnɛlmɑ̃] ADV intentionally, deliberately

inter¹† [ɛ̃tɛʀ] NM (*Téléc*) ABRÉV = **interurbain**

inter²† [ɛ̃tɛʀ] NM (*Sport*) **~ gauche/droit** inside-left/-right

inter(-)... [ɛ̃tɛʀ] PRÉF inter...; **~africain** inter-African; **~américain** inter-American; **~arabe** inter-Arab

interactif, -ive [ɛ̃tɛʀaktif, iv] ADJ interactive

interaction [ɛ̃tɛʀaksjɔ̃] NF interaction (**entre** between)

interactivement [ɛ̃tɛʀaktivmɑ̃] ADV (*gén, Ordin*) interactively

interactivité [ɛ̃tɛʀaktivite] NF interactivity

interagir [ɛ̃tɛʀaʒiʀ] ▸conjug 2◂ VI to interact (**avec** with)

interallemand, e [ɛ̃tɛʀalmɑ̃, ɑ̃d] ADJ [*frontière, relations*] between the two Germanies

interallié, e [ɛ̃tɛʀalje] ADJ inter-Allied

interarmées [ɛ̃tɛʀaʀme] ADJ INV (*Mil*) interservice; **forces ~ combinées** combined joint task forces; **chef d'état-major ~** commander of joint task forces

---

➤ GRAMMAIRE ACTIVE: **intention** 35, 45.1, 45.4

interarmes [ɛ̃tɛʀaʀm] ADJ INV [*opération*] combined-arms (*épith*), interservice (*épith*)

interbancaire [ɛ̃tɛʀbɑ̃kɛʀ] ADJ [*relations, marché*] interbank

intercalaire [ɛ̃tɛʀkalɛʀ] **1** ADJ **feuillet ~** inset, insert; **fiche ~** divider; **jour ~** intercalary day **2** NM (= *feuillet*) inset, insert; (= *fiche*) divider

intercalation [ɛ̃tɛʀkalasjɔ̃] NF [*mot, exemple*] insertion, interpolation; [*feuillet*] insertion; [*jour d'année bissextile*] intercalation

intercaler [ɛ̃tɛʀkale] ▶ conjug 1 ◀ **1** VT **a** [+ *mot, exemple*] to insert, interpolate; [+ *feuille*] to insert **b** [+ *jour d'année bissextile*] to intercalate; **~ quelques jours de repos dans un mois de stage** to fit a few days' rest into a month of training; **on a intercalé dans le stage des visites d'usines** the training course was interspersed with *ou* broken by visits to factories **2** **s'intercaler** VPR **s'~ entre** to come in between

intercéder [ɛ̃tɛʀsede] ▶ conjug 6 ◀ VI to intercede (**en faveur de** on behalf of, **auprès de** with)

intercellulaire [ɛ̃tɛʀselylɛʀ] ADJ intercellular

intercensitaire [ɛ̃tɛʀsɑ̃sitɛʀ] ADJ intercensal

intercepter [ɛ̃tɛʀsɛpte] ▶ conjug 1 ◀ VT **a** [+ *ballon, message, conversation téléphonique, personne*] to intercept **b** [+ *lumière, chaleur*] to cut *ou* block off

intercepteur [ɛ̃tɛʀsɛptœʀ] NM interceptor (plane)

interception [ɛ̃tɛʀsɛpsjɔ̃] NF [*ballon, message, personne*] interception; [*lumière, chaleur*] cutting *ou* blocking off; [*Mil*] **avion** *ou* **chasseur d'~** interceptor(-plane)

intercesseur [ɛ̃tɛʀsesœʀ] NM (*littér, Rel*) intercessor

intercession [ɛ̃tɛʀsesjɔ̃] NF (*littér, Rel*) intercession

interchangeabilité [ɛ̃tɛʀʃɑ̃ʒabilite] NF interchangeability

interchangeable [ɛ̃tɛʀʃɑ̃ʒabl] ADJ interchangeable

interclasse [ɛ̃tɛʀklas] NM (*Scol*) break (*between classes*)

interclubs [ɛ̃tɛʀklœb] ADJ INV [*tournoi*] inter-club

intercommunal, e (*mpl* -aux) [ɛ̃tɛʀkɔmynal, o] ADJ [*décision, stade*] shared by several French communes, ≈ intervillage, ≈ intermunicipal

intercommunalité [ɛ̃tɛʀkɔmynalite] NF intermunicipal links

intercommunautaire [ɛ̃tɛʀkɔmynotɛʀ] ADJ intercommunity, intercommunal

intercommunication [ɛ̃tɛʀkɔmynikasjɔ̃] NF intercommunication

interconnecter [ɛ̃tɛʀkɔnɛkte] ▶ conjug 1 ◀ VT (*Élec*) to interconnect

interconnexion [ɛ̃tɛʀkɔnɛksjɔ̃] NF interconnection

intercontinental, e (*mpl* -aux) [ɛ̃tɛʀkɔ̃tinɑtal, o] ADJ intercontinental

intercostal, e (*mpl* -aux) [ɛ̃tɛʀkɔstal, o] **1** ADJ intercostal **2** NMPL intercostal muscles, intercostals

intercours [ɛ̃tɛʀkuʀ] NM (*Scol*) break (*between classes*)

interculturel, -elle [ɛ̃tɛʀkyltyʀɛl] ADJ cross-cultural, intercultural

interdépartemental, e (*mpl* -aux) [ɛ̃tɛʀdepaʀtamɑtal, o] ADJ *shared by several French departments*

interdépendance [ɛ̃tɛʀdepɑdɑs] NF interdependence

interdépendant, e [ɛ̃tɛʀdepɑdɑ, ɑt] ADJ interdependent, mutually dependant

interdiction [ɛ̃tɛʀdiksjɔ̃] **1** NF **a** **~ de qch** (= *action*) banning of sth; (= *état*) ban on sth; **à cause de l'~ faite aux fonctionnaires de cumuler plusieurs emplois** because civil serv-

---

ants are not allowed to hold several positions; **l'~ de coller des affiches/de servir de l'alcool** the ban on the posting of bills/the serving of alcohol, the ban on posting bills/ serving alcohol; **« ~ de coller des affiches »** "(post *ou* stick *Brit*) no bills", "bill-posting *ou* bill-sticking (*Brit*) prohibited"; **« ~ (formelle *ou* absolue) de fumer »** "(strictly) no smoking", "smoking (strictly) prohibited"; **« ~ de tourner à droite »** "no right turn"; **« ~ de stationner »** "no parking"; **« ~ de déposer des ordures »** "no dumping"; **~ d'en parler à quiconque/de modifier quoi que ce soit** it is (strictly) forbidden to talk to anyone about it/to alter anything; **malgré l'~ d'entrer** despite not being allowed to enter; **renouveler à qn l'~ de faire** to reimpose a ban on sb's doing; **~ lui a été faite de sortir** he has been forbidden to go out **b** (= *interdit*) ban; **enfreindre/lever une ~** to break/lift a ban; **il a garé sa voiture malgré le panneau d'~** he parked his car in spite of the no parking sign **c** (= *suspension*) [*livre, film*] banning (**de** of), ban (**de** on); [*fonctionnaire*] banning from office; [*prêtre*] interdiction; (*Jur*) **~ légale** *suspension of a convict's civic rights* **2** COMP ▶ **interdiction de séjour** *order denying former prisoner access to specified places*; **~ bancaire** suspension of banking privileges; **~ de chéquier** withdrawal of chequebook facilities

interdigital, e (*mpl* -aux) [ɛ̃tɛʀdiʒital, o] ADJ interdigital

interdire [ɛ̃tɛʀdiʀ] ▶ conjug 37 ◀ **1** VT **a** (= *prohiber*) to forbid; [+ *stationnement, circulation*] to prohibit, ban; **~ l'alcool/le tabac à qn** to forbid sb alcohol/tobacco, forbid sb to drink/smoke; **~ à qn de faire qch** to tell sb not to do sth, forbid sb to do sth, prohibit (*frm*) sb from doing sth; **elle nous a interdit d'y aller seuls, elle a interdit que nous y allions seuls** she forbade us to go on our own; **on a interdit les camions dans le centre de la ville** lorries have been barred from *ou* banned from *ou* prohibited in the centre of the town **b** (= *empêcher*) [*contretemps, difficulté*] to preclude, prevent; [*obstacle physique*] to block; **son état de santé lui interdit tout travail/effort** his state of health does not allow *ou* permit him to do any work/to make any effort; **sa maladie ne lui interdit pas le travail** his illness does not prevent him from working; **la gravité de la crise (nous) interdit tout espoir** the gravity of the crisis leaves us no hope *ou* precludes all hope; **leur attitude interdit toute négociation** their attitude precludes *ou* prevents any possibility of negotiation; **une porte blindée interdisait le passage** an armoured door blocked *ou* barred the way **c** (= *frapper d'interdiction*) [+ *fonctionnaire*] to bar from office; [+ *prêtre*] to suspend; [+ *film, réunion, journal*] to ban; (*fig*) **on lui a interdit le club** he has been barred *ou* banned from the club; **~ sa porte aux intrus** to bar one's door to intruders **d** † (= *interloquer*) to dumbfound, take aback, disconcert **2** **s'interdire** VPR **s'~ toute remarque** to refrain *ou* abstain from making any remark; **nous nous sommes interdit d'intervenir** we have not allowed ourselves to intervene, we have refrained from intervening; **s'~ la boisson/les cigarettes** to abstain from drink *ou* drinking/smoking; **il s'interdit d'y penser** he doesn't let himself think about it *ou* allow himself to think about it; **il s'est interdit toute possibilité de revenir en arrière** he has (deliberately) denied himself *ou* not allowed himself any chance of going back on his decision

interdisciplinaire [ɛ̃tɛʀdisipliner] ADJ interdisciplinary

interdisciplinarité [ɛ̃tɛʀdisiplinaʀite] NF interdisciplinarity

---

▼ **interdit¹, e** [ɛ̃tɛʀdi, it] (*ptp de* **interdire**) **1** ADJ [*film, livre*] banned; **film ~ aux moins de 18 ans** ≈ 18 film (*Brit*), ≈ NC-17 film (*US*); **film ~ aux moins de 13 ans** ≈ PG film, ≈ PG-13 film (*US*); **passage/stationnement ~** no entry/parking; **il est strictement ~ de ...** it is strictly forbidden *ou* prohibited to ...; **(il est) ~ de fumer** no smoking, smoking (is) prohibited; **être ~ bancaire** to have one's banking privileges suspended; **être ~ de chéquier** to have chequebook facilities withdrawn; (*Aviat*) **~ de vol** grounded; (*Comm*) **~ de vente** banned; (*slogan*) **« il est ~ d'interdire »** forbidding is forbidden → **reproduction**

2 NM (= *interdiction*) (*gén*) ban; (*Rel*) interdict; (*social*) prohibition; (*Rel*) **~s alimentaires** dietary restrictions; (*Psych*) **transgresser les ~s** to break taboos; (*Comm, Écon*) **frapper d'~** to ban; **lever l'~** to lift the ban

3 COMP ▶ **interdit de séjour** (*Jur*) *person banned from entering specified areas*; (*fig*) persona non grata; **la violence est ~ de séjour sur les terrains de sport** violence is unacceptable in sports grounds

interdit², e [ɛ̃tɛʀdi, it] ADJ dumbfounded, taken aback (*attrib*), disconcerted; **la réponse le laissa ~** the answer took him aback, he was dumbfounded *ou* disconcerted by *ou* at the answer

interentreprises [ɛ̃tɛʀɑ̃tʀəpʀiz] ADJ [*crédit, coopération*] inter-company (*Brit*), inter-corporate (*US*)

▼ **intéressant, e** [ɛ̃teʀesɑ̃, ɑ̃t] ADJ **a** (= *captivant*) [*livre, détail, visage*] interesting; **peu ~** (= *ennuyeux*) [*conférencier*] uninteresting, dull; (*péj*) **personnage peu ~** worthless individual; (*péj*) **il faut toujours qu'il cherche à se rendre ~** *ou* **qu'il fasse son ~** he always has to draw attention to himself; (†, *hum*) **elle est dans une situation** *ou* **position ~e*** she is in an interesting condition (*hum*) *ou* in the family way* **b** (= *avantageux*) [*offre, affaire*] attractive, worthwhile; [*prix*] favourable, attractive; **ce n'est pas très ~ pour nous** it's not really worth our while, it's not really worth it for us; **ce serait (financièrement) plus ~ pour nous de prendre le train** we'd be better off taking the train, it would work out cheaper for us to take the train; **c'est une personne ~e à connaître** he's someone worth knowing

intéressé, e [ɛ̃teʀese] (*ptp de* **intéresser**) ADJ **a** (= *qui est en cause*) concerned, involved; **les ~s** ◊ **les parties ~es** the interested parties, the parties involved *ou* concerned; **dans cette affaire, c'est lui le principal** *ou* **premier ~** in this matter, he's the one who's most concerned **b** (= *qui cherche son intérêt personnel*) [*personne*] self-seeking, self-interested; [*motif*] interested; **visite ~e** visit motivated by self-interest; **rendre un service ~** to do a good turn out of self-interest; **ce que je vous propose, c'est très** ◊ my suggestion to you is strongly motivated by self-interest

intéressement [ɛ̃teʀesmɑ̃] NM (*Écon*: = *système*) profit-sharing (scheme); **l'~ des travailleurs aux bénéfices de l'entreprise** the workers' participation in *ou* sharing of the firm's profits

intéresser [ɛ̃teʀese] ▶ conjug 1 ◀ **1** VT **a** (= *captiver*) to interest; **~ qn à qch** to interest sb in sth; **cela m'intéresserait de faire** I would be interested to do *ou* in doing, it would interest me to do; **ça ne m'intéresse pas** I'm not interested, it doesn't interest me; **rien ne l'intéresse** he isn't interested *ou* he takes no interest in anything; **le film l'a intéressé** he found the film interesting, the film interested him; **ça pourrait vous ~** this might interest you *ou* be of interest to you; **cette question n'intéresse pas (beaucoup) les jeunes** this matter is of no (great) interest to *ou* doesn't (greatly) interest young people; **il ne sait pas ~ son public** he doesn't know how to interest his

---

▶ GRAMMAIRE ACTIVE: **interdire** 36.3, 37.4 **interdit** 37.4 **intéressant** 53.6

audience; (iro) **continue, tu m'intéresses!** do go on — I find that very interesting ou I'm all ears!*; **tes petites histoires n'intéressent personne** no one cares about your little problems

b (= concerner) to affect, concern; **la nouvelle loi intéresse les petits commerçants** the new law affects ou concerns small shopkeepers

c (Comm, Fin) **~ le personnel de l'usine aux bénéfices** to give the factory employees a share ou an interest in the profits, operate a profit-sharing scheme in the factory; **être intéressé dans une affaire** to have a stake ou a financial interest in a business

d (Jeux) **~ une partie** to stake money on a game

2 **s'intéresser** VPR **s'~ à qch/qn** to be interested in sth/sb, take an interest in sth/sb; **il s'intéresse vivement/activement à cette affaire** he is taking a keen/an active interest in this matter; **il ne s'intéresse pas à nos activités** he isn't interested in our activities; **il mérite qu'on s'intéresse à lui** he deserves one's ou people's interest; **il s'intéresse beaucoup à cette jeune fille** he is taking ou showing a great deal of interest in that girl

▼ **intérêt** [ɛ̃teRɛ] NM a (= attention) interest; **écouter avec ~/(un) grand ~** to listen with interest/with great interest; **prendre ~ à qch** to take an interest in sth; **il a perdu tout ~ à son travail** he has lost all interest in his work

b (= bienveillance) interest; **porter/témoigner de l'~ à qn** to take/show an interest in sb

c (= originalité) interest; **film dénué d'~ ou sans aucun ~** film devoid of interest; **tout l'~ réside dans le dénouement** the most interesting part is the ending, what is most interesting is the ending

d (= importance) significance, importance, relevance; **l'~ des recherches spatiales** the significance ou importance ou relevance of space research; **après quelques considérations sans ~** after a few unimportant ou minor considerations, after considerations of minor interest ou importance; **c'est sans ~ pour la suite de l'histoire** it's of no relevance ou consequence ou importance for the rest of the story; **une découverte du plus haut ~** a discovery of the greatest ou utmost importance ou significance ou relevance; **la nouvelle a perdu beaucoup de son ~** the news has lost much of its significance ou interest; **être déclaré d'~ public** to be officially recognized as being beneficial to the general public

e (= avantage) interest; **ce n'est pas (dans) leur ~ de le faire** it is not in their interest to do it; **agir dans/contre son ~** to act in/against one's own interests; **dans l'~ général** in the general interest; (Admin) **autorisation refusée dans l'~ du service** permission refused on administrative grounds ou for administrative reasons; **il y trouve son ~** he finds it to his (own) advantage, he finds it worth his while; **il sait où est son ~** he knows where his interest lies, he knows which side his bread is buttered; **il a (tout) ~ à accepter** it's in his interest to accept, he'd be well advised to accept, he'd do well to accept; **quel ~ aurait-il à faire cela?** why would he want to do that?; **tu aurais plutôt ~ à te taire!*** you'd be well advised ou you'd do very well to keep quiet!; **est-ce qu'il faut que je lui en parle? — (il) y a ~!*/t'as pas ~!*** should I talk to him about it? — you'd better!/you'd better not!; **y a-t-il un ~ quelconque à se réunir?** is there any point at all in getting together?

f (Fin) interest; **recevoir 7% d'~** to get 7% interest; **prêt à ~ élevé** high-interest loan; **prêter à ou avec ~** to lend at ou with interest; **~s simples/composés** simple/compound interest; **~s courus** accrued interest → **taux**

g (= recherche d'avantage personnel) self-interest; **agir par ~** to act out of self-interest → **mariage**

h **~s** interest(s); **la défense de nos ~s** the defence of our interests; (Écon, Fin) **il a des ~s dans l'affaire** he has a stake ou an interest ou a financial interest in the deal

interétatique [ɛ̃teRetatik] ADJ [accord, coopération] inter-state (épith)

interethnique [ɛ̃teRetnik] ADJ inter-ethnic

interface [ɛ̃teRfas] NF interface; **~ utilisateur/graphique** user/graphical interface; (fig) **servir d'~ entre** to liaise between, act as an interface between

interfacer VT, **s'interfacer** VPR [ɛ̃teRfase] ▸conjug 3◂ to interface (**avec** with)

interférence [ɛ̃teRfeRɑ̃s] NF a (Phys) interference b (fig) (= conjonction) conjunction; (= immixtion) [problème] intrusion (**dans** into); [personne, pays] interférence (NonC) (**dans** in); **l'~ des problèmes économiques et politiques** the conjunction of economic and political problems; **l'~ des problèmes économiques dans la vie politique** the intrusion of economic problems into political life; **il se produit des ~s entre les deux services** there's interference between the two services

interférent, e [ɛ̃teRfeRɑ̃, ɑ̃t] ADJ (Phys) interfering

interférer [ɛ̃teRfeRe] ▸conjug 6◂ VI to interfere (**avec** with, **dans** in); **les deux procédures interfèrent** the two procedures interfere with each other

interférométrie [ɛ̃teRfeRɔmetRi] NF interferometry

interféron [ɛ̃teRfeRɔ̃] NM interferon; **~ humain** human interferon

interfluve [ɛ̃teRflyv] NM interfluve

intergalactique [ɛ̃teRgalaktik] ADJ intergalactic

intergouvernemental, e (mpl **-aux**) [ɛ̃teRguveRnəmɑ̃tal, o] ADJ intergovernmental; (au Québec) **Affaires ~es** Intergovernmental Affairs

intergroupe [ɛ̃teRgRup] NM (Pol) [plusieurs partis] joint committee; [deux partis] bipartisan committee

intérieur, e [ɛ̃teRjœR] 1 ADJ a [paroi, escalier] inner, interior, inside; [cour] inner; **mer ~e** inland sea; **la poche ~e de son manteau** the inside pocket of his coat; **angle/point ~ à un cercle** angle/point interior to a circle → **conduite**

b [vie, monde, voix] inner; [sentiment] inner, inward → **for**

c [politique, dette] domestic, internal; [marché] home (épith), domestic, internal; [communication, réseau, navigation] inland; (Aviat) [vol] domestic; **le commerce ~** domestic trade; **les affaires ~es** internal ou domestic affairs

2 NM a [tiroir, piste, champ de course] inside; [maison] inside, interior; **l'~ de la maison était lugubre** the house was gloomy inside, the inside ou the interior of the house was gloomy; **l'~ de la ville** the inner town; **écrin avec un ~ de satin** case with a satin lining; **à l'~** inside; **je vous attends à l'~** I'll wait for you inside; **à l'~ de la ville** inside the town; **à l'~ de l'entreprise** [promotion, corruption] within the company; [stage, formation] in-house; **rester à l'~** (gén) to stay inside; (de la maison) to stay inside ou indoors; **vêtement/veste d'~** indoor garment/jacket; **chaussures d'~** indoor ou house shoes; **fermé/vu de l'~** locked/viewed from the inside; (Ciné) **scènes tournées en ~** interior scenes, interiors → **femme**

b (fig) [personne] **à l'~** within; **il paraissait calme, mais à l'~ les soucis le rongeaient** he appeared to be calm, but inwardly ou inside he was consumed with anxiety

c [pays] interior; **l'~ (du pays) est montagneux** the interior ou the inland part of the country is mountainous; **les villes de l'~** the inland cities ou towns, the cities ou towns of the interior; **la côte est riante mais l'~ est sau-**

vage the coast is pleasant, but it's wild further inland ou the hinterland is wild; **en allant vers l'~** going inland; **à l'~ de nos frontières** within ou inside our frontiers; **les ennemis de l'~** the enemies within (the country); (Mil) **le moral de l'~** the morale at home, the country's morale → **ministère, ministre**

d (= décor, mobilier) interior; **un ~ douillet** a cosy interior; **tableau d'~** interior (painting); (Aut) **~ cuir** leather trim

e (Ftbl) **~ gauche/droit** inside-left/-right

intérieurement [ɛ̃teRjœRmɑ̃] ADV inwardly; **rire ~** to laugh inwardly ou to o.s.

intérim [ɛ̃teRim] NM a (= période) interim period; **il prendra toutes les décisions dans ou pendant l'~** he will make all the decisions in the interim; **il assure l'~ en l'absence du directeur** he deputizes for the manager in his absence ou in the interim; **diriger une firme par ~** to be the interim manager of a company; **président/ministre par ~** acting ou interim president/minister b (= travail à temps partiel) temporary work, temping; **agence ou société d'~** temping agency; **faire de l'~** to temp

intérimaire [ɛ̃teRimeR] 1 ADJ [directeur, ministre] acting (épith), interim (épith); [secrétaire, personnel, fonctions] temporary; [mesure, solution] interim (épith), temporary; (Pol) [gouvernement, chef de parti] caretaker (épith) 2 NMF temporary worker (recruited from an employment agency); (= secrétaire) temporary secretary, temp, Kelly girl (US); (= fonctionnaire) deputy; (= médecin, prêtre) stand-in, locum (Brit); **travailler comme ~** to temp

interindividuel, -elle [ɛ̃teRɛ̃dividɥɛl] ADJ interpersonal; **psychologie interindividuelle** psychology of interpersonal relationships

intériorisation [ɛ̃teRjɔRizasjɔ̃] NF [conflit, émotion] internalization, interiorization; (Ling) [règles] internalization

intérioriser [ɛ̃teRjɔRize] ▸conjug 1◂ VT [+ conflit, émotion] to internalize, interiorize; (Ling) [+ règles] to internalize; **son jeu est très intériorisé** his acting is very introspective

intériorité [ɛ̃teRjɔRite] NF interiority

interjectif, -ive [ɛ̃teRʒektif, iv] ADJ interjectional

interjection [ɛ̃teRʒeksjɔ̃] NF (Ling) interjection; (Jur) lodging of an appeal

interjeter [ɛ̃teRʒəte] ▸conjug 4◂ VT (Jur) **~ appel** to lodge an appeal

interleukine [ɛ̃teRløkin] NF interleukin

interlignage [ɛ̃teRliɲaʒ] NM (Typo) interline spacing

interligne [ɛ̃teRliɲ] 1 NM (= espace) space between the lines; (= annotation) insertion between the lines; (Mus) space; **double ~** double spacing; **écrire qch dans l'~** to write ou insert sth between the lines; **taper un texte en double ~** to type a text in double spacing 2 NF (Typo) lead

interligner [ɛ̃teRliɲe] ▸conjug 1◂ VT (= espacer) to space; (= inscrire) to write between the lines

interlocuteur, -trice [ɛ̃teRlɔkytœR, tRis] NM,F speaker, interlocutor (frm); **son/mon ~** the person he/I was speaking to; (Pol) **~ valable** valid negotiator ou representative; **les syndicats sont les ~s privilégiés d'un gouvernement de gauche** the unions have a privileged relationship with a left-wing government; **c'est mon ~ privilégié** he's the person I liaise with

interlope [ɛ̃teRlɔp] ADJ a (= équivoque) shady b (= illégal) illicit, unlawful; **navire ~** ship carrying illicit merchandise

interloqué, e [ɛ̃teRlɔke] (ptp de **interloquer**) ADJ taken aback; **il a eu l'air un peu ~** he looked rather taken aback; **tout le monde**

▸ GRAMMAIRE ACTIVE: **intérêt** 28.1, 29.2

s'est tu, ~ everybody fell into a stunned silence

interloquer [ɛ̃tɛʀlɔke] ▶conjug 1◀ VT to take aback

interlude [ɛ̃tɛʀlyd] NM (*Mus, TV*) interlude

intermariage [ɛ̃tɛʀmaʀjaʒ] NM intermarriage

intermède [ɛ̃tɛʀmɛd] NM (= *interruption, Théât*) interlude

intermédiaire [ɛ̃tɛʀmedjɛʀ] 1 ADJ [*niveau, choix, position*] intermediate, middle (*épith*), intermediary; **couleur ~ entre** colour halfway between; **trouver/choisir une solution ~** to find/choose a compromise; **il n'y a pas de solution ~** there's no half-way house *ou* no compromise solution; **une date ~ entre le 25 juillet et le 3 août** a date midway between 25th July and 3rd August 2 NM **sans ~** [*vendre, négocier*] directly; **par l'~ de qn** through (the intermediary *ou* agency of) sb; **par l'~ de la presse** through the medium of the press 3 NMF (= *médiateur*) intermediary, mediator, go-between; (*Comm, Écon*) middleman

intermédiation [ɛ̃tɛʀmedjasjɔ̃] NF (*Fin*) (financial) intermediation

intermezzo [ɛ̃tɛʀmɛdzo] NM intermezzo

interminable [ɛ̃tɛʀminabl] ADJ [*conversation, série*] endless, interminable, never-ending; (*hum*) [*jambes, mains*] extremely long

interminablement [ɛ̃tɛʀminabləmɑ̃] ADV endlessly, interminably

interministériel, -elle [ɛ̃tɛʀministeʀjɛl] ADJ interdepartmental

intermission [ɛ̃tɛʀmisjɔ̃] NF (*Méd*) intermission

intermittence [ɛ̃tɛʀmitɑ̃s] NF a **par ~** [*travailler*] in fits and starts, sporadically, intermittently; [*pleuvoir*] on and off, sporadically, intermittently; **le bruit nous parvenait par ~** the noise reached our ears at (sporadic) intervals b (*Méd: entre deux accès*) remission; [*pouls, cœur*] irregularity c (*littér*) intermittence, intermittency

intermittent, e [ɛ̃tɛʀmitɑ̃, ɑ̃t] 1 ADJ [*fièvre, lumière*] intermittent; [*douleur*] sporadic, intermittent; [*travail, bruit*] sporadic, periodic; [*pouls*] irregular, intermittent; [*fontaine, source*] intermittent; **pluies ~es sur le nord** scattered showers in the north 2 NM,F contract worker; **les ~s du spectacle** *workers in the entertainment industry without steady employment*

intermoléculaire [ɛ̃tɛʀmɔlekylɛʀ] ADJ intermolecular

intermusculaire [ɛ̃tɛʀmyskylɛʀ] ADJ intermuscular

internat [ɛ̃tɛʀna] NM a (*Scol*) (= *établissement*) boarding school; (= *système*) boarding; (= *élèves*) boarders → **maître** b (*Méd*) (= *concours*) entrance examination (for hospital work); (= *stage*) hospital training (*as a doctor*), period *ou* time as a houseman (*Brit*) *ou* an intern (*US*), internship (*US*)

international, e (*mpl* **-aux**) [ɛ̃tɛʀnasjɔnal, o] 1 ADJ international 2 NM,F (*Ftbl, Tennis etc*) international player; (*Athlétisme*) international athlete 3 NM (*Écon*) **le tiers du chiffre d'affaires est réalisé à l'~** a third of all sales are on the international market 4 **Internationale** NF (= *association*) International; (= *hymne*) Internationale; **l'Internationale ouvrière** the International Workingmen's Association 5 **internationaux** NMPL (*Sport*) internationals; **les internationaux de France (de tennis)** the French Open

internationalement [ɛ̃tɛʀnasjɔnalmɑ̃] ADV internationally

internationalisation [ɛ̃tɛʀnasjɔnalizasjɔ̃] NF internationalization

internationaliser [ɛ̃tɛʀnasjɔnalize] ▶conjug 1◀ VT to internationalize

internationalisme [ɛ̃tɛʀnasjɔnalism] NM internationalism

internationaliste [ɛ̃tɛʀnasjɔnalist] NMF internationalist

internationalité [ɛ̃tɛʀnasjɔnalite] NF internationality

internaute [ɛ̃tɛʀnot] NMF net surfer, Internet surfer

interne [ɛ̃tɛʀn] 1 ADJ [*partie, politique, organe, hémorragie*] internal; [*oreille*] inner; [*angle*] interior; **médecine ~** internal medicine 2 NMF a (*Scol*) boarder; **être ~** to be at boarding school b (*Méd*) **~ (des hôpitaux)** house doctor (*Brit*), houseman (*Brit*), intern (*US*); **~ en médecine** house physician (*Brit*), intern (*US*); **~ en chirurgie** house surgeon (*Brit*), intern in surgery (*US*) c **travail réalisé en ~** work carried out in-house

interné, e [ɛ̃tɛʀne] (*ptp de* **interner**) NM,F (*Pol*) internee; (*Méd*) inmate (of a mental hospital)

internement [ɛ̃tɛʀnəmɑ̃] NM (*Pol*) internment; (*Méd*) confinement (to a mental hospital); **~ abusif** wrongful confinement

interner [ɛ̃tɛʀne] ▶conjug 1◀ VT (*Pol*) to intern; (*Méd*) **~ qn (dans un hôpital psychiatrique)** to confine sb to a mental hospital, institutionalize sb (*US*); **on devrait l'~** he ought to be locked up *ou* certified*, he's certifiable

Internet [ɛ̃tɛʀnɛt] NM (**l'**)**Internet** (the) Internet; **sur ~** on (the) Internet

interocéanique [ɛ̃tɛʀɔseanik] ADJ interoceanic

interosseux, -euse [ɛ̃tɛʀɔsø, øz] ADJ interosseous

interparlementaire [ɛ̃tɛʀpaʀləmɑ̃tɛʀ] ADJ interparliamentary

interpellateur, -trice [ɛ̃tɛʀpelatœʀ, tʀis] NM,F a (*Pol*) interpellator, questioner b (*dans un débat*) questioner; (= *perturbateur*) heckler

interpellation [ɛ̃tɛʀpelasjɔ̃] NF a (= *appel*) hailing (*NonC*) b (*dans un débat*) questioning; (*perturbatrice*) heckling (*NonC*); (*Pol*) interpellation, questioning (*NonC*) c (*Police*) **il y a eu une dizaine d'~s** about ten people were taken in for questioning

interpeller [ɛ̃tɛʀpəle] ▶conjug 1◀ VT a (= *appeler*) to call out to, shout out to, hail; (*impoliment*) to shout at; **les automobilistes se sont interpellés grossièrement** the motorists shouted insults at each other b (*au cours d'un débat*) to question; (*en chahutant*) to heckle; (*Pol*) to interpellate, question c (*Police*) to take in for questioning d (= *concerner*) [*problème, situation*] to concern, be of concern to; (*hum*) **ça m'interpelle (quelque part)** I can relate to that*

interpénétration [ɛ̃tɛʀpenetʀasjɔ̃] NF interpenetration

interpénétrer (s') [ɛ̃tɛʀpenetʀe] ▶conjug 6◀ VPR to interpenetrate

interpersonnel, -elle [ɛ̃tɛʀpɛʀsɔnɛl] ADJ interpersonal

interphone [ɛ̃tɛʀfɔn] NM intercom, interphone; [*immeuble*] entry phone

interplanétaire [ɛ̃tɛʀplanetɛʀ] ADJ interplanetary

Interpol [ɛ̃tɛʀpɔl] NM (ABRÉV = **International Criminal Police Organization**) Interpol

interpolation [ɛ̃tɛʀpɔlasjɔ̃] NF interpolation

interpoler [ɛ̃tɛʀpɔle] ▶conjug 1◀ VT to interpolate

interposé, e [ɛ̃tɛʀpoze] (*ptp de* **interposer**) ADJ **par personne ~e** through an intermediary *ou* a third party; **par service ~** through another department; **par journaux ~s** through the press

interposer [ɛ̃tɛʀpoze] ▶conjug 1◀ 1 VT (= *intercaler*) to interpose (**entre** between) 2 **s'interposer** VPR [*personne*] to intervene, interpose o.s. (*frm*) (**dans** in); **elle s'interposa**

entre le père et le fils she intervened between father and son

interposition [ɛ̃tɛʀpozisjɔ̃] NF a (= *intercalation*) interposition b (= *médiation*) intervention; (*Pol*) **force d'~** intervention force c (*Jur*) fraudulent use of a third party's identity

interprétable [ɛ̃tɛʀpʀetabl] ADJ interpretable

interprétariat [ɛ̃tɛʀpʀetaʀja] NM interpreting; **école d'~** interpreting school

interprétatif, -ive [ɛ̃tɛʀpʀetatif, iv] ADJ (*gén*) interpretative; (*Jur*) **émettre des réserves interprétatives sur un texte de loi** to express reservations about the possible interpretations of a bill; **ce texte requiert un gros travail ~** this text needs a lot of interpreting; (*Méd*) **délire ~** delusions of reference, referential delusion; (*hum*) **le délire ~ de certains critiques** the tendency of some critics to go overboard in their interpretations

interprétation [ɛ̃tɛʀpʀetasjɔ̃] NF a (*Théât, Ciné*) performance; (*Mus*) interpretation, rendering; **son ~ de Macbeth** his performance as Macbeth, his interpretation of the role of Macbeth b (= *explication*) interpretation; **donner une ~ fausse de qch** to give a false interpretation of sth; **l'~ des rêves** the interpretation of dreams; **c'est une erreur d'~** it's an error of *ou* a mistake in interpretation c (= *métier d'interprète*) interpreting; **~ simultanée** simultaneous translation

interprète [ɛ̃tɛʀpʀɛt] NMF a [*musique*] performer, interpreter; [*chanson*] singer; (*Théât*) performer; **les ~s par ordre d'entrée en scène ...** the cast in order of appearance ...; **l'un des plus grands ~s de Shakespeare** one of the greatest Shakespearean actors; **l'~ de Phèdre** the actress playing the part of Phèdre; **Paul était l'~ de cette sonate** Paul played this sonata; **Paul était l'~ de cette chanson** Paul was the singer of *ou* sang this song b (= *traducteur*) interpreter; **~ de conférence** conference interpreter; **faire l'~ ◊ servir d'~** to act as an interpreter c (= *porte-parole*) **servir d'~ à qn/aux idées de qn** to act *ou* serve as a spokesman for sb/for sb's ideas; **je me ferai votre ~ auprès du ministre** I'll speak to the minister on your behalf d (= *exégète*) [*texte*] interpreter, exponent; [*rêves, signes*] interpreter

▼ **interpréter** [ɛ̃tɛʀpʀete] ▶conjug 6◀ VT a [+ *musique*] to perform, play, interpret; [+ *chanson*] to sing; [+ *rôle*] to play; **il interprète superbement Hamlet** his (performance of) Hamlet is excellent; **je vais maintenant vous ~ un nocturne de Chopin** I'm now going to play one of Chopin's nocturnes for you b (= *comprendre*) to interpret; **comment ~ son silence ?** what does his silence mean?; **il a mal interprété mes paroles** he misinterpreted my words; **~ qch en bien/mal** to take sth the right/wrong way; **son attitude peut s'~ de plusieurs façons** there are several ways of interpreting his attitude c (= *traduire*) to interpret d (*Ordin*) to interpret; **langage interprété** interpreted language

interpréteur [ɛ̃tɛʀpʀetœʀ] NM (*Ordin*) interpreter

interprofession [ɛ̃tɛʀpʀɔfesjɔ̃] NF (*Écon*) joint-trade organization

interprofessionnel, -elle [ɛ̃tɛʀpʀɔfesjɔnɛl] ADJ [*réunion*] interprofessional → **salaire**

interracial, e (*mpl* **-iaux**) [ɛ̃tɛʀasjal, jo] ADJ interracial

interrégional, e (*mpl* **-aux**) [ɛ̃tɛʀeʒjɔnal, o] ADJ interregional

interrègne [ɛ̃tɛʀɛɲ] NM interregnum

interro* [ɛ̃tɛʀo] NF (ABRÉV = **interrogation**) (*Scol*) test

interrogateur, -trice [ɛ̃tɛʀɔgatœʀ, tʀis] 1 ADJ [*air, regard, ton*] questioning (*épith*), inquiring (*épith*); **d'un air** *ou* **ton ~** questioningly, inquiringly 2 NM,F (*oral*) examiner

3 NM (*Télec*) **~ à distance** remote access facility

interrogatif, -ive [ɛ̃teʀɔgatif, iv] **1** ADJ [*air, regard*] questioning (*épith*), inquiring (*épith*); (*Ling*) interrogative **2** NM interrogative; **mettre à l'~** to put into the interrogative **3** **interrogative** NF interrogative clause

interrogation [ɛ̃teʀɔgasjɔ̃] NF **a** (= *interrogatoire*) questioning; (*serrée, prolongée*) interrogation **b** [*élève*] testing, examination; **(écrite)** short (written) test (*Brit*), quiz (*US*); **~ (orale)** oral (test) **c** (*Ordin, Télec*) **système d'~ à distance** remote access system **d** (= *question*) question; (*Gram*) **~ directe/indirecte** direct/indirect question; **les sourcils levés, en signe d'~** his eyebrows raised questioningly *ou* inquiringly; **les yeux pleins d'une ~ muette** his eyes silently questioning → **point¹ e** (= *réflexions*) **~s** questioning; **ces ~s continuelles sur la destinée humaine** this continual questioning about human destiny **f** (= *examen*) [*conscience*] examination

interrogatoire [ɛ̃teʀɔgatwaʀ] NM (*Police*) questioning; (*au tribunal*) cross-examination, cross-questioning (*NonC*); (= *compte rendu*) statement; (*fig* = *série de questions*) cross-examination, interrogation; **subir un ~ en règle** to undergo a thorough *ou* detailed interrogation; **pendant l'~, elle s'est évanouie** while being cross-examined, she fainted

interrogeable [ɛ̃teʀɔʒabl] ADJ **répondeur ~ à distance** answering machine with a remote access facility; **compte en banque ~ par Minitel** bank account that can be accessed by Minitel

interroger [ɛ̃teʀɔʒe] ▶conjug 3◀ **1** VT **a** (= *questionner*) to question; (*pour obtenir un renseignement*) to ask; (*Police*) to interview, question; (*de manière serrée, prolongée*) to interrogate (**sur** about); (*sondage*) to poll; **15% des personnes interrogées** 15% of the people polled *ou* asked; **~ du regard** to give sb a questioning *ou* an inquiring look, look questioningly *ou* inquiringly at sb
b (*Scol, Univ*) **~ un élève** to test *ou* examine a pupil; **~ par écrit les élèves** to give the pupils a written test; **elle a été interrogée sur un sujet difficile** she was examined *ou* questioned on a difficult subject
c (= *examiner*) [+ *ciel, conscience*] to examine; [+ *mémoire*] to search
d [+ *base de données*] to query; **~ son répondeur** to check calls on one's answering machine
2 **s'interroger** VPR (= *se poser des questions*: *sur un problème*) to wonder (**sur** about); **s'~ sur la conduite à tenir** to wonder what course to follow

interrompre [ɛ̃teʀɔ̃pʀ] ▶conjug 41◀ **1** VT **a** (= *arrêter*) [+ *voyage, circuit électrique*] to break, interrupt; [+ *conversation*] (*gén*) to interrupt, break off; (*pour s'interposer*) to break into, cut into; [+ *études*] to break off, interrupt; [+ *émission*] to interrupt; [+ *négociations, traitement médical*] to break off; **il a interrompu la conversation pour téléphoner** he broke off *ou* interrupted his conversation to telephone; **elle a interrompu sa carrière pour voyager** she took a career break *ou* she interrupted her career to travel; **le match a été interrompu par la pluie** the match was stopped by rain; **sans ~ sa lecture** without looking up (from his *ou* her book); (*Méd*) **~ une grossesse** to terminate a pregnancy
b (= *couper la parole à, déranger*) **~ qn** to interrupt sb; **je ne veux pas qu'on m'interrompe (dans mon travail)** I don't want to be interrupted (in my work); **je ne veux pas ~ mais ...** I don't want to cut in *ou* interrupt but ...
2 **s'interrompre** VPR [*personne, conversation*] to break off; (*TV*) **nos émissions s'interrompront à 23 h 50** we will be going off the air *ou* closing down (*Brit*) at 11.50 pm

interrupteur, -trice [ɛ̃teʀyptœʀ, tʀis] **1** NM (*Élec*) switch **2** NM,F interrupter

---

interruption [ɛ̃teʀypsjɔ̃] NF (= *action*) interruption (**de** of); (= *état*) break (**de** in), interruption (**de** of, in); [*négociations*] breaking off (**de** of); **une ~ de deux heures** a break *ou* an interruption of two hours; **~ (volontaire) de grossesse** termination (of pregnancy); **~ thérapeutique de grossesse** *termination of pregnancy for medical reasons*; **il y a eu une ~ de courant** there has been a power cut; **après l'~ des hostilités** after hostilities had ceased; **sans ~** [*parler*] without a break *ou* an interruption, uninterruptedly, continuously; [*pleuvoir*] without stopping, without a break, continuously; **« ouvert sans ~ de 9h à 19h »** "open all day from 9 am to 7 pm"; **réélu sans ~ jusqu'en 1998** reelected to hold office until 1998; **un moment d'~** a moment's break

intersaison [ɛ̃teʀsɛzɔ̃] NF (*Sport*) close season; (*Tourisme*) low season; **à** *ou* **pendant l'~** (*Sport*) during the close season; (*Tourisme*) out of season

interscolaire [ɛ̃teʀskɔlɛʀ] ADJ inter-schools

intersection [ɛ̃teʀsɛksjɔ̃] NF [*lignes*] intersection; [*routes*] intersection, junction → **point¹**

intersession [ɛ̃teʀsesjɔ̃] NF (*Pol*) recess

intersexualité [ɛ̃teʀsɛksɥalite] NF intersexuality

intersexuel, -elle [ɛ̃teʀsɛksɥɛl] ADJ intersexual

intersidéral, e (*mpl* **-aux**) [ɛ̃teʀsideʀal, o] ADJ intersidereal

interstellaire [ɛ̃teʀstelɛʀ] ADJ interstellar

interstice [ɛ̃teʀstis] NM (*gén*) crack, chink, interstice; [*volet, cageot*] slit; **à travers les ~s des rideaux** through the cracks *ou* chinks in the curtains

interstitiel, -ielle [ɛ̃teʀstisjɛl] ADJ (*Anat, Méd*) interstitial

intersubjectif, -ive [ɛ̃teʀsybʒɛktif, iv] ADJ intersubjective

intersubjectivité [ɛ̃teʀsybʒɛktivite] NF intersubjectivity

intersyndical, e (*mpl* **-aux**) [ɛ̃teʀsɛ̃dikal, o] **1** ADJ interunion **2** **intersyndicale** NF interunion association, trade union group (*Brit*)

intertitre [ɛ̃teʀtitʀ] NM (*Presse*) subheading; (*Ciné*) title

intertropical, e (*mpl* **-aux**) [ɛ̃teʀtʀɔpikal, o] ADJ intertropical

interurbain, e [ɛ̃teʀyʀbɛ̃, ɛn] **1** ADJ **a** (*relations*) interurban **b** (*Télec*) long-distance **2** NM **l'~** the long-distance telephone service, the trunk call service (*Brit*)

intervalle [ɛ̃teʀval] NM **a** (= *espace*) space, distance; (*entre 2 mots, 2 lignes*) space; (= *temps*) interval; (*Mus*) interval; (*Math*) interval; **~ fermé/ouvert** closed/open interval **b** (*loc*) **c'est arrivé à 2 jours/mois d'~** it happened after a space or an interval of 2 days/months; **ils sont nés à 3 mois d'~** they were born 3 months apart; **à ~s réguliers/rapprochés** at regular/close intervals; **à ~s de 5 mètres** ◊ **à 5 mètres d'~** 5 metres apart; **par ~s** at intervals; **dans l'~** (*temporel*) in the meantime, meanwhile; (*spatial*) in between

intervenant, e [ɛ̃teʀvənɑ̃, ɑ̃t] NM,F (*Jur*) intervener; (= *conférencier*) contributor; (*Écon*) participant; **~ extérieur** outside contributor

intervenir [ɛ̃teʀvəniʀ] ▶conjug 22◀ VI **a** (= *entrer en action*) to intervene; (= *contribuer*) to play a part; (*dans une discussion*) **puis-je ~?** may I interrupt?, can I say something (here)?; **il est intervenu en notre faveur** he interceded *ou* intervened on our behalf; **~ militairement** to intervene militarily; **on a dû faire ~ l'armée** *ou* **l'armée a dû ~** the army had to intervene, the army had to be brought in *ou* called in; **les pompiers n'ont pas pu ~** the firemen were unable to help **b** (*Méd*) to operate **c** (= *survenir*) [*fait, événement*] to take place,

---

occur; [*accord*] to be reached, be entered into; [*décision, mesure*] to be taken; [*élément nouveau*] to arise, come up; **cette mesure intervient au moment où ...** this measure is being taken *ou* comes at a time when ... **d** (*Jur*) to intervene

intervention [ɛ̃teʀvɑ̃sjɔ̃] NF **a** (*gén, Jur*) intervention; (= *discours*) speech; **cela a nécessité l'~ de la police** the police had to be brought in *ou* to intervene; **son ~ en notre faveur** his intercession *ou* intervention on our behalf; **~ armée** armed intervention; **plusieurs ~s aériennes** several air strikes → **force b** (*Écon, Pol*) **~ de l'État** state intervention; **politique d'~** policy of intervention, interventionist policy; **prix d'~** intervention price; **beurre d'~** (*EEC*) subsidized butter **c** (*Méd*) operation; **~ chirurgicale** surgical operation

interventionnisme [ɛ̃teʀvɑ̃sjɔnism] NM interventionism

interventionniste [ɛ̃teʀvɑ̃sjɔnist] ADJ, NMF interventionist

interversion [ɛ̃teʀvɛʀsjɔ̃] NF inversion; **~ des rôles** reversal *ou* inversion of roles

intervertir [ɛ̃teʀvɛʀtiʀ] ▶conjug 2◀ VT to invert *ou* reverse the order of, invert; **~ les rôles** to reverse *ou* invert roles

interview [ɛ̃teʀvju] NF (*Presse, TV*) interview

interviewé, e [ɛ̃teʀvjuve] (*ptp de* **interviewer**) NM,F (*Presse, TV*) interviewee

interviewer¹ [ɛ̃teʀvjuve] ▶conjug 1◀ VT (*Presse, TV*) to interview

interviewer² [ɛ̃teʀvjuvœʀ] NMF (= *journaliste*) interviewer

intervocalique [ɛ̃teʀvɔkalik] ADJ intervocalic

intestat [ɛ̃testa] **1** ADJ (*Jur*) **mourir ~** to die intestate **2** NMF intestate

intestin¹ [ɛ̃testɛ̃] NM intestine; **~s** intestines, bowels; **~ grêle** small intestine; **gros ~** large intestine; **avoir l'~ fragile** *ou* **les ~s fragiles** to have an irritable bowel, have irritable bowel syndrome

intestin², e [ɛ̃testɛ̃, in] ADJ [*lutte, rivalité*] internecine, internal; **querelles ~es** internecine quarrels *ou* strife, infighting

intestinal, e (*mpl* **-aux**) [ɛ̃testinal, o] ADJ intestinal → **grippe**

Intifada [intifada] NF **l'~** the Intifada

intimation [ɛ̃timasjɔ̃] NF (*Jur*) (= *assignation*) summons *sg* (*before an appeal court*); (= *signification*) notification

intime [ɛ̃tim] **1** ADJ **a** (= *privé*) [*hygiène*] personal, intimate; [*vie*] private; [*chagrin, confidences*] intimate; [*secret*] close, intimate; [*cérémonie, mariage*] quiet; [*salon, atmosphère*] intimate, cosy; **dîner ~** (*entre amis*) dinner with (old) friends; (*entre amoureux*) romantic dinner
b (= *étroit*) [*mélange, relation, rapport*] intimate; [*union*] close; [*ami*] close, intimate, bosom (*épith*); **être ~ avec qn** to be intimate with *ou* close to sb; **avoir des relations** *ou* **rapports ~s avec qn** to be on intimate terms with sb, have close relations with sb
c (= *profond*) [*nature, structure*] intimate, innermost; [*sens, sentiment, conviction*] inner(most), inmost, intimate; **j'ai l'~ conviction que** it is my firm conviction that, I'm thoroughly convinced that
2 NMF close friend; **seuls les ~s sont restés dîner** only those who were close friends stayed to dinner; (*hum*) **Jo pour les ~s*** Jo to his friends *ou* buddies* (*hum*)

intimé, e [ɛ̃time] (*ptp de* **intimer**) NM,F (*Jur*) respondent, appellee

intimement [ɛ̃timmɑ̃] ADJ intimately; **~ persuadé** deeply *ou* firmly convinced; **être ~ mêlé à qch** to be closely involved in sth

intimer [ɛ̃time] ▶conjug 1◀ VT **a** **~ à qn (l'ordre) de faire** to order sb to do **b** (*Jur*) (= *as-*

signer) to summon (*before an appeal court*); (= signifier) to notify

intimidable [ɛ̃timidabl] ADJ easily intimidated

intimidant, e [ɛ̃timidɑ̃, ɑ̃t] ADJ intimidating

intimidateur, -trice [ɛ̃timidatœr, tris] ADJ intimidating

intimidation [ɛ̃timidasjɔ̃] NF intimidation; **manœuvre/moyens d'~** device/means of intimidation; **on l'a fait parler en usant d'~** they scared *ou* frightened him into talking

intimider [ɛ̃timide] ▸conjug 1◂ VT to intimidate; **ne te laisse pas ~ par lui** don't let him intimidate you, don't let yourself be intimidated by him

intimisme [ɛ̃timism] NM (*Art, Littérat*) intimism (SPÉC)

intimiste [ɛ̃timist] ADJ, NMF (*Art, Littérat*) intimist (SPÉC); **un roman/film ~** a novel/film *focusing on the private world of people's feelings and relationships*; **un peintre ~** a painter who specializes in interior scenes

intimité [ɛ̃timite] NF **a** (= vie privée) privacy; **dans l'~ c'est un homme très simple** in private life, he's a man of simple tastes; **nous serons dans l'~** there will only be a few of us *ou* a few close friends and relatives; **se marier dans l'~** to have a quiet wedding; **la cérémonie a eu lieu dans la plus stricte ~** the ceremony took place in the strictest privacy; **pénétrer dans l'~ de qn** to be admitted into sb's private life **b** (= familiarité) intimacy; **dans l'~ conjugale** in the intimacy of one's married life; **vivre dans l'~ de qn** to be on very intimate terms with sb **c** (= confort) [atmosphère, salon] cosiness, intimacy **d** (littér = profondeur) depths; **dans l'~ de sa conscience** in the depths of *ou* innermost recesses of one's conscience

intitulé [ɛ̃tityle] NM [livre, loi, jugement] title; [chapitre] heading, title; [sujet de dissertation] wording; [compte en banque] (= type de compte) type; (= coordonnées) name, address and account number

intituler [ɛ̃tityle] ▸conjug 1◂ **1** VT to entitle, call **2 s'intituler** VPR [livre, chapitre] to be entitled *ou* called; [personne] to call o.s., give o.s. the title of

▼ **intolérable** [ɛ̃tɔlerabl] ADJ (gén) intolerable, unbearable; [douleur] unbearable

intolérablement [ɛ̃tɔlerabləmɑ̃] ADV intolerably

intolérance [ɛ̃tɔlerɑ̃s] NF intolerance; **~ à un médicament** ◇ **médicamenteuse** inability to tolerate a drug

intolérant, e [ɛ̃tɔlerɑ̃, ɑ̃t] ADJ intolerant

intonation [ɛ̃tɔnasjɔ̃] NF (Ling, Mus) intonation; **voix aux ~s douces** soft-toned voice

intouchable [ɛ̃tuʃabl] ADJ, NMF untouchable

intox(e)* [ɛ̃tɔks] NF (ABRÉV = **intoxication**) (Pol) brainwashing, propaganda; (= désinformation) disinformation; **c'est de l'~!** it's pure propaganda!; **il nous fait de l'~ pour avoir un magnétoscope** he's trying to brainwash us into getting (him) a video recorder

intoxication [ɛ̃tɔksikasjɔ̃] NF **a** (= empoisonnement) poisoning (NonC); **~ alimentaire/au plomb** food/lead poisoning (NonC); **~ médicamenteuse** drug intoxication **b** (Pol) brainwashing, indoctrination

intoxiqué, e [ɛ̃tɔksike] (ptp de **intoxiquer**) NM,F (par la drogue) drug addict; (par l'alcool) alcoholic

intoxiquer [ɛ̃tɔksike] ▸conjug 1◂ **1** VT **a** (= empoisonner) [fumée, pollution] to intoxicate; **être intoxiqué par le tabac/l'alcool/la drogue** to be poisoned by the effects of tobacco/alcohol/drugs; **il y a eu 50 personnes intoxiquées** 50 people were intoxicated **b** (= corrompre) to brainwash, indoctrinate; **intoxiqué par la publicité** brainwashed by adver-

tisements **2 s'intoxiquer** VPR to be poisoned

intracellulaire [ɛ̃traselylɛr] ADJ intracellular

intracommunautaire [ɛ̃trakɔmynotɛr] ADJ (Pol) intra-Community (épith); **50% du commerce de l'UE est ~** 50% of EU trade is conducted between member states of the Community

intradermique [ɛ̃tradɛrmik] ADJ intradermal, intradermic, intracutaneous

intradermo(-)réaction [ɛ̃tradɛrmoreaksjɔ̃] NF INV skin test

intraduisible [ɛ̃traduizibl] ADJ [texte] untranslatable; [sentiment, idée] inexpressible; **il eut une intonation ~** his intonation was impossible to reproduce

intraitable [ɛ̃trɛtabl] ADJ uncompromising, inflexible; **il est ~ sur la discipline** he's a stickler for discipline, he's uncompromising *ou* inflexible about discipline

intra-muros [ɛ̃tramyros] ADV **habiter ~** to live inside the town; **Paris ~** inner Paris

intramusculaire [ɛ̃tramyskylɛr] **1** ADJ intramuscular **2** NF intramuscular injection

intransigeance [ɛ̃trɑ̃ziʒɑ̃s] NF intransigence; **faire preuve d'~** to be uncompromising *ou* intransigent

intransigeant, e [ɛ̃trɑ̃ziʒɑ̃, ɑ̃t] ADJ [personne, attitude] uncompromising, intransigent, inflexible; [morale] uncompromising; **se montrer ~ ou adopter une ligne de conduite ~ envers qn** to take a hard line with sb; **les ~s** the intransigents

intransitif, -ive [ɛ̃trɑ̃zitif, iv] ADJ, NM intransitive

intransitivement [ɛ̃trɑ̃zitivmɑ̃] ADV intransitively

intransitivité [ɛ̃trɑ̃zitivite] NF intransitivity, intransitiveness

intransmissibilité [ɛ̃trɑ̃smisibilite] NF intransmissibility; (Jur) untransferability, non-transferability

intransmissible [ɛ̃trɑ̃smisibl] ADJ intransmissible; (Jur) untransferable, non-transferable

intransportable [ɛ̃trɑ̃sportabl] ADJ [objet] untransportable; [malade] who is unfit *ou* unable to travel

intrant [ɛ̃trɑ̃] NM (Écon) input

intra-utérin, e [ɛ̃trayterɛ̃, in] ADJ (mpl intra-utérins) intra-uterine; **vie ~e** life in the womb, intra-uterine life (SPÉC)

intraveineux, -euse [ɛ̃travenø, øz] **1** ADJ intravenous **2 intraveineuse** NF intravenous injection

intrépide [ɛ̃trepid] ADJ (= courageux) intrepid, dauntless, bold; (= résolu) dauntless; [bavard] unashamed; [menteur] barefaced (épith), unashamed

intrépidement [ɛ̃trepidmɑ̃] ADV intrepidly, dauntlessly, boldly

intrépidité [ɛ̃trepidite] NF intrepidity, dauntlessness, boldness; **avec ~** intrepidly, dauntlessly, boldly

intrication [ɛ̃trikasjɔ̃] NF intrication, intricacy

intrigant, e [ɛ̃trigɑ̃, ɑ̃t] **1** ADJ scheming **2** NM,F schemer, intriguer

intrigue [ɛ̃trig] NF (= manœuvre) intrigue, scheme; (Ciné, Littérat, Théât) plot; **~ amoureuse ou sentimentale** (= liaison) (love) affair

intriguer [ɛ̃trige] ▸conjug 1◂ **1** VT to intrigue, puzzle **2** VI to scheme, intrigue

intrinsèque [ɛ̃trɛ̃sɛk] ADJ intrinsic

intrinsèquement [ɛ̃trɛ̃sɛkmɑ̃] ADV intrinsically

intriquer (s') [ɛ̃trike] ▸conjug 1◂ VPR (souvent ptp) [facteurs] to be interlinked (dans with); **les deux phénomènes sont étroitement intriqués** the two phenomena are closely interlinked

introducteur, -trice [ɛ̃trɔdyktœr, tris] NM,F (= initiateur) initiator (à to)

introductif, -ive [ɛ̃trɔdyktif, iv] ADJ **a** (gén) [article, chapitre, discours] introductory, opening (épith) **b** (Jur) **réquisitoire ~** opening speech for the prosecution

▼ **introduction** [ɛ̃trɔdyksjɔ̃] NF **a** (= présentation) **paroles/chapitre d'~** introductory words/chapter; **en (guise d')~** by way of introduction; **~, développement et conclusion** [dissertation, exposé] introduction, exposition, conclusion **b** (= recommandation) **lettre/mot d'~** letter/note of introduction **c** [objet] insertion, introduction; [liquide] introduction; [visiteur] admission, introduction **d** (= lancement) [mode, idée] launching; **~ en Bourse** stock market listing *ou* flotation **e** (Jur) [instance] institution **f** (Rugby) put-in

introduire [ɛ̃trɔduir] ▸conjug 38◂ **1** VT **a** (= faire entrer) [+ objet] to place (dans in), insert, introduce (dans into); [+ liquide] to introduce (dans into); [+ visiteur] to show in; **il introduisit sa clé dans la serrure** he put his key in the lock, he inserted his key into the lock; **on m'introduisit dans le salon/auprès de la maîtresse de maison** I was shown into *ou* ushered into the lounge/shown in *ou* ushered in to see the mistress of the house; (Rugby) **~ la balle en mêlée** to put the ball into the scrum **b** (= lancer) [+ mode] to launch, introduce; [+ idées nouvelles] to bring in, introduce; (Ling) [+ mot] to introduce (dans into); (Écon) **~ un produit sur le marché** to launch a product on the market; **~ des valeurs en Bourse** to list *ou* float shares on the stock market **c** (= présenter) [+ ami, protégé] to introduce; **il m'a introduit auprès du directeur/dans le groupe** he introduced me to the manager/to the group **d** (Jur) [+ instance] to institute **2 s'introduire** VPR **a** (= pénétrer) **s'~ dans un groupe** to work one's way into a group, be *ou* get o.s. admitted *ou* accepted into a group; **s'~ chez qn par effraction** to break into sb's home; **s'~ dans une pièce** to get into *ou* enter a room; **l'eau/la fumée s'introduisait partout** the water/smoke was getting in everywhere; **le doute s'introduisit dans son esprit** he began to have doubts **b** (= être adopté) [usage, mode, idée] to be introduced (dans into)

introduit, e [ɛ̃trɔdui, it] (ptp de **introduire**) ADJ (frm) **être bien ~ dans un milieu** to be well connected in a certain milieu; **bien ~ auprès du ministre** on good terms with the minister

intromission [ɛ̃trɔmisjɔ̃] NF intromission

intronisation [ɛ̃trɔnizasjɔ̃] NF [roi, pape] enthronement; (hum) **discours d'~** (président) acceptance speech

introniser [ɛ̃trɔnize] ▸conjug 1◂ VT [+ roi, pape] to enthrone; [+ président] to set up; **il a été intronisé (comme) chef du parti** he was set up as leader of the party

introspectif, -ive [ɛ̃trɔspɛktif, iv] ADJ introspective

introspection [ɛ̃trɔspɛksjɔ̃] NF introspection

introuvable [ɛ̃truvabl] ADJ which (ou who) cannot be found; **ma clé est ~** I can't find my key anywhere, my key is nowhere to be found; **l'évadé demeure toujours ~** the escaped prisoner has still not been found *ou* discovered, the whereabouts of the escaped prisoner remain unknown; **ces meubles sont ~s aujourd'hui** furniture like this is unobtainable *ou* just cannot be found these days; **l'accord reste ~ entre les deux pays** the two countries are still unable to reach an agreement

introversion [ɛ̃trɔvɛrsjɔ̃] NF introversion

introverti, e [ɛ̃trɔvɛrti] **1** ADJ introverted **2** NM,F introvert

intrus, e [ɛ̃tʀy, yz] **1** ADJ intruding, intrusive **2** NM,F intruder; *(jeu)* **cherchez l'~** find the odd one out

intrusion [ɛ̃tʀyzjɔ̃] NF *(gén, Géol)* intrusion; **~ dans les affaires de qn** interference *ou* intrusion in sb's affairs; **roches d'~** intrusive rocks

intubation [ɛ̃tybasjɔ̃] NF *(Méd)* intubation

intuber [ɛ̃tybe] ▸ conjug 1 ◂ VT *(Méd)* to intubate

intuitif, -ive [ɛ̃tɥitif, iv] **1** ADJ intuitive **2** NM,F intuitive person; **c'est un ~** he's very intuitive

intuition [ɛ̃tɥisjɔ̃] NF intuition; **avoir de l'~** to have intuition; **l'~ féminine** feminine intuition; **elle eut l'~ que .../de ...** she had an intuition that .../of ...; **mon ~ me dit que ...** instinct *ou* my intuition tells me that ...

intuitivement [ɛ̃tɥitivmɑ̃] ADV intuitively

intumescence [ɛ̃tymesɑ̃s] NF intumescence

intumescent, e [ɛ̃tymesɑ̃, ɑ̃t] ADJ intumescent

inuit, e [inɥit] **1** ADJ INV Inuit **2** **Inuit** NMF Inuit

inusable [inyzabl] ADJ *[vêtement]* hard-wearing

inusité, e [inyzite] ADJ *[mot]* uncommon, not in common use *(attrib)*; *[méthode]* no longer in use; **ce mot est pratiquement ~** this word is practically never used

inusuel, -elle [inyzɥɛl] ADJ *(littér)* unusual

in utero [inyteʀo] ADJ, ADV in utero

inutile [inytil] ADJ **a** (= *qui ne sert pas)* *[objet]* useless; *[effort, parole, démarche]* pointless; **connaissances ~s** useless knowledge; **sa voiture lui est ~ maintenant** his car is (of) no use *ou* is no good *ou* is useless to him now; **~ d'insister!** it's useless *ou* no use *ou* no good insisting!, there's no point *ou* it's pointless (insisting)!; **je me sens ~** I feel so useless; **vous voulez de l'aide? — non, c'est ~** do you want some help? — no, there's no need **b** (= *superflu)* *[paroles, crainte, travail, effort, dépense]* needless; *[bagages]* unnecessary; **évitez toute fatigue** avoid tiring yourself unnecessarily; **~ de vous dire que je ne suis pas resté** needless to say I didn't stay, I hardly need tell you I didn't stay → **bouche**

inutilement [inytilmɑ̃] ADV needlessly, unnecessarily

inutilisable [inytilizabl] ADJ unusable

inutilisé, e [inytilize] ADJ unused

inutilité [inytilite] NF *[objet]* uselessness; *[effort, paroles, travail, démarche]* pointlessness

invaincu, e [ɛ̃vɛ̃ky] ADJ *(gén)* unconquered, unvanquished, undefeated; *(Sport)* unbeaten, undefeated

invalidant, e [ɛ̃validɑ̃, ɑ̃t] ADJ *[maladie]* incapacitating, disabling

invalidation [ɛ̃validasjɔ̃] NF *[contrat, élection]* invalidation; *[député]* removal (from office)

invalide [ɛ̃valid] **1** NMF disabled person; **grand ~ civil** severely disabled person; **(grand) ~ de guerre** (severely) disabled ex-serviceman; **l'hôtel des Invalides ◊ les Invalides** the Invalides **2** ADJ *(Méd)* disabled; *(Jur)* invalid

invalider [ɛ̃valide] ▸ conjug 1 ◂ VT *(Jur)* to invalidate; *[+ député]* to remove from office; *[+ élection]* to invalidate; *(Méd)* to disable

invalidité [ɛ̃validite] NF disablement, disability → **assurance**

invariabilité [ɛ̃vaʀjabilite] NF invariability

invariable [ɛ̃vaʀjabl] ADJ *(gén, Ling)* invariable; *(littér)* unvarying

invariablement [ɛ̃vaʀjablmɑ̃] ADV invariably

invariance [ɛ̃vaʀjɑ̃s] NF invariance, invariancy

invariant, e [ɛ̃vaʀjɑ̃, jɑ̃t] ADJ, NM invariant

invasif, -ive [ɛ̃vazif, iv] ADJ *(Méd)* *[cancer, tumeur, traitement]* invasive; **chirurgie non invasive** non-invasive surgery

invasion [ɛ̃vazjɔ̃] NF invasion; **c'est l'~!** it's an invasion!

invective [ɛ̃vɛktiv] NF invective; **~s** abuse, invectives; **se répandre en ~s contre qn** to let loose a torrent *ou* stream of abuse against sb

invectiver [ɛ̃vɛktive] ▸ conjug 1 ◂ VT to hurl *ou* shout abuse at; **ils se sont violemment invectivés** they hurled *ou* shouted violent abuse at each other **2** VI to inveigh, rail **(contre** against)

invendable [ɛ̃vɑ̃dabl] ADJ *(gén)* unsaleable; *(Comm)* unmarketable

invendu, e [ɛ̃vɑ̃dy] **1** ADJ unsold **2** NM (= *objet)* unsold item; (= *magazine)* unsold copy; **ce magasin brade ses ~s** this shop is selling off its unsold stock

inventaire [ɛ̃vɑ̃tɛʀ] NM **a** *(gén, Jur)* inventory; **faire un ~** to make an inventory → **bénéfice** **b** *(Comm)* (= *liste)* stocklist *(Brit)*, inventory *(US)*; (= *opération)* stocktaking *(Brit)*, inventory *(US)*; *(Comm)* **faire un ~** to take stock, do the stocktaking *(Brit)* *ou* inventory *(US)*; **«fermé pour cause d'~»** "closed for stocktaking *(Brit)* *ou* inventory *(US)* " **c** *(fig* = *recensement)* *[monuments, souvenirs]* survey; **faire l'~ de** to assess, make an assessment of

inventer [ɛ̃vɑ̃te] ▸ conjug 1 ◂ **1** VT **a** (= *créer, découvrir: gén)* to invent; *[+ moyen, procédé]* to devise; **il n'a pas inventé la poudre** *ou* **le fil à couper le beurre** *ou* **l'eau chaude** he'll never set the world *ou* the Thames *(Brit)* on fire, he's no bright spark* **b** (= *imaginer, trouver)* *[+ jeu]* to think up, make up; *[+ mot]* to make up; *[+ excuse, histoire fausse]* to invent, make *ou* think up; **c'est lui qui a inventé le mot** he coined the word; **il ne sait plus quoi ~ pour échapper à l'école** he doesn't know what to think up *ou* dream up next to get out of school; **ils avaient inventé de faire entrer les lapins dans le salon** they had the bright idea of bringing the rabbits into the drawing room; **je n'invente rien** I'm not making anything up, I'm not inventing a thing; **qu'est-ce que tu vas ~ là!** whatever can you be thinking of! → **pièce** **c** *(Jur)* *[+ trésor]* to find **2** **s'inventer** VPR **ce sont des choses qui ne s'inventent pas** those are things people just don't make up; **s'~ une famille** to invent a family (for o.s.); **tu t'inventes des histoires!** you're imagining things!

inventeur, -trice [ɛ̃vɑ̃tœʀ, tʀis] NM,F inventor; *(Jur)* finder

inventif, -ive [ɛ̃vɑ̃tif, iv] ADJ *[esprit, solution, cuisine]* inventive; *[personne]* resourceful, inventive

invention [ɛ̃vɑ̃sjɔ̃] NF *(gén, péj)* invention; (= *ingéniosité)* inventiveness, spirit of invention; *(Jur)* *[trésor]* finding; **cette excuse est une pure** *ou* **de la pure ~** that excuse is a pure invention *ou* fabrication; **l'histoire est de son ~** the story was made up *ou* invented by him *ou* was his own invention; **un cocktail de mon ~** a cocktail of my own creation → **brevet**

inventivité [ɛ̃vɑ̃tivite] NF *[esprit, solution, cuisine]* inventiveness; *[personne]* resourcefulness, inventiveness

inventorier [ɛ̃vɑ̃tɔʀje] ▸ conjug 7 ◂ VT *(gén, Jur)* to make an inventory of; *(Comm)* to make a stocklist of

invérifiable [ɛ̃veʀifjabl] ADJ *(gén)* unverifiable; *[chiffres]* that cannot be checked

inverse [ɛ̃vɛʀs] **1** ADJ *(gén)* opposite; *(Logique, Math)* inverse; **arriver en sens ~** to arrive from the opposite direction; **l'image apparaît en sens ~ dans le miroir** the image is reversed in the mirror; **dans l'ordre ~** in (the) reverse order; **dans le sens ~ des aiguilles d'une montre** counterclockwise, anticlockwise *(Brit)* **2** NM **l'~** *(gén)* the opposite, the reverse; *(Philo)* the converse; **tu as fait l'~ de ce que je t'ai dit** you

did the opposite to *ou* of what I told you; **t'a-t-il attaqué ou l'~?** did he attack you or vice versa?, did he attack you or was it the other way round?; **à l'~** conversely; **cela va à l'~ de nos prévisions** that goes contrary to our plans; **à l'~ de sa sœur, il est très timide** unlike his sister, he is very shy

inversé, e [ɛ̃vɛʀse] *(ptp de inverser)* ADJ *[image]* reversed; *[relief]* inverted

inversement [ɛ̃vɛʀsəmɑ̃] ADV *(gén)* conversely; *(Math)* inversely; **~ proportionnel à** inversely proportional to; **... et/ou ~ ...** and/or vice versa

inverser [ɛ̃vɛʀse] ▸ conjug 1 ◂ VT *[+ ordre]* to reverse, invert; *[+ courant électrique]* to reverse; *[+ rôles]* to reverse

inverseur [ɛ̃vɛʀsœʀ] NM *(Élec, Tech)* reverser; *(Aéronautique)* **~ de poussée** thrust reverser

inversible [ɛ̃vɛʀsibl] ADJ *(Photo)* **film ~** reversal film

inversion [ɛ̃vɛʀsjɔ̃] NF **a** *(gén, Anat, Ling)* inversion; *(Élec)* reversal; *(Mét)* **~ thermique** temperature inversion; *(Aéronautique)* **~ de poussée** thrust reversal; *(Chim)* **~ du sucre** inversion of sucrose **b** *(Psych)* homosexuality, inversion *(SPÉC)*

invertébré, e [ɛ̃vɛʀtebʀe] ADJ, NM invertebrate; **~s** invertebrates, Invertebrata *(SPÉC)*

inverti, e [ɛ̃vɛʀti] *(ptp de invertir)* **1** ADJ *(Chim)* **sucre ~** invert sugar **2** NM,F† homosexual, invert†

invertir† [ɛ̃vɛʀtiʀ] ▸ conjug 2 ◂ VT to invert

investigateur, -trice [ɛ̃vɛstigatœʀ, tʀis] **1** ADJ *[technique]* investigative; *[esprit]* inquiring *(épith)*; *[regard]* searching *(épith)*, scrutinizing *(épith)* **2** NM,F investigator

investigation [ɛ̃vɛstigasjɔ̃] NF *(gén)* investigation; *(Méd)* examination; *(gén, Police)* **~s** investigations; **la police poursuit ses ~s** the police are continuing their investigations; **champ d'~** *[chercheur]* field of research; **journalisme d'~** investigative journalism

investir [ɛ̃vɛstiʀ] ▸ conjug 2 ◂ **1** VT **a** *(Fin)* *[+ capital]* to invest **(dans** in) **b** *[+ fonctionnaire]* to induct; *[+ évêque]* to invest; **~ qn de pouvoirs/droits** to invest *ou* vest sb with powers/rights, vest powers/rights in sb; **~ qn de sa confiance** to place one's trust in sb **c** *(Mil)* *[+ ville]* to surround, besiege; *(Police)* to surround, cordon off **2** **s'investir** VPR **s'~ dans son travail/une relation** to put a lot into one's work/a relationship; **s'~ beaucoup pour faire qch** to put a lot of effort into doing sth

investissement [ɛ̃vɛstismɑ̃] NM *(Écon, Méd, Psych)* investment; *(Mil)* investing; (= *efforts)* contribution

investisseur, -euse [ɛ̃vɛstisœʀ, øz] **1** ADJ investing *(épith)* **2** NM investor; **~s institutionnels** institutional investors

investiture [ɛ̃vɛstityʀ] NF *[candidat]* nomination; *[évêché]* investiture; **recevoir l'~ de son parti** *(gén)* to be endorsed by one's party; *(Pol US)* to be nominated by one's party; **discours d'~** inaugural speech

invétéré, e [ɛ̃vetere] ADJ *[fumeur, joueur]* inveterate, confirmed; *[menteur]* out-and-out, downright; *[habitude]* inveterate, deep-rooted

invincibilité [ɛ̃vɛ̃sibilite] NF *[adversaire, nation]* invincibility

invincible [ɛ̃vɛ̃sibl] ADJ *[adversaire, nation]* invincible, unconquerable; *[courage]* invincible, indomitable; *[charme]* irresistible; *[difficultés]* insurmountable, insuperable; *[argument]* invincible, unassailable

invinciblement [ɛ̃vɛ̃sibləmɑ̃] ADV invincibly

inviolabilité [ɛ̃vjɔlabilite] NF *[droit]* inviolability; *[serrure]* impregnability; *[parlementaire, diplomate]* immunity

inviolable [ɛ̃vjɔlabl] ADJ *[droit]* inviolable; *[serrure]* impregnable, burglar-proof; *[parlementaire, diplomate]* immune

inviolé, e [ɛ̃vjɔle] ADJ (*gén*) unviolated, inviolate (*frm*); [*tombe*] intact; [*paysage, île*] unspoilt

invisibilité [ɛ̃vizibilite] NF invisibility

invisible [ɛ̃vizibl] [1] ADJ (= *impossible à voir*) invisible; (= *minuscule*) barely visible (à to); (*Écon*) invisible; **~ à l'œil nu** invisible to the naked eye; **la maison était ~ derrière les arbres** the house was invisible *ou* couldn't be seen behind the trees; **danger ~** unseen *ou* hidden danger; **il est ~ pour l'instant** he can't be seen *ou* he's unavailable at the moment; **il est ~ depuis deux mois** he hasn't been seen (around) for two months [2] NM **l'~** the invisible; (*Écon*) **~s** invisibles

invisiblement [ɛ̃visibləmɑ̃] ADV invisibly

invitant, e [ɛ̃vitɑ̃, ɑ̃t] ADJ (*littér*) inviting; (*Pol*) **puissance ~e** host country

▼ **invitation** [ɛ̃vitasjɔ̃] NF invitation, invite* (à to); **carte** *ou* **carton d'~** invitation card; **lettre d'~** letter of invitation; **« sur ~ (uniquement) »** "by invitation only"; **~ à dîner** invitation to dinner; **faire une ~ à qn** to invite sb, extend an invitation to sb; **venir sans ~** to come uninvited *ou* without (an) invitation; **à** *ou* **sur son ~** at his invitation; **une ~ à déserter** an (open) invitation to desert; **cet événement est une ~ à réfléchir sur le sens de la vie** this event leads us to reflect on the meaning of life; **ses tableaux sont une ~ au voyage** his paintings make us dream of faraway places

invite [ɛ̃vit] NF (*littér*) invitation; **à son ~** at his invitation

invité, e [ɛ̃vite] (*ptp de* **inviter**) NM,F guest; **~ de marque** distinguished guest; **~ d'honneur** guest of honour

▼ **inviter** [ɛ̃vite] ▸conjug 1◂ VT [a] (= *convier*) to invite, ask (à to); **~ qn chez soi/à dîner** to invite *ou* ask sb to one's house/to *ou* for dinner; **elle ne l'a pas invité à entrer/monter** she didn't invite *ou* ask him (to come) in/up; **il s'est invité** he invited himself; **c'est moi qui invite** it's my treat, it's on me* [b] (= *engager*) **~ à** to invite to; **~ qn à démissionner** to invite sb to resign; **il l'invita de la main à s'approcher** he beckoned *ou* motioned (to) her to come nearer; **ceci invite à croire que ...** this induces *ou* leads us to believe that ..., this suggests that ...; **la chaleur invitait au repos** the heat tempted one to rest

in vitro [invitro] LOC ADJ, LOC ADV in vitro

invivable [ɛ̃vivabl] ADJ (*gén*) unbearable; [*personne*] unbearable, obnoxious

in vivo [invivo] LOC ADJ, LOC ADV in vivo

invocation [ɛ̃vɔkasjɔ̃] NF invocation (à to)

invocatoire [ɛ̃vɔkatwaR] ADJ (*littér*) invocatory (*littér*)

involontaire [ɛ̃vɔlɔ̃tɛR] ADJ [*sourire, mouvement*] involuntary; [*peine, insulte*] unintentional, unwitting; [*témoin, complice*] unwitting

involontairement [ɛ̃vɔlɔ̃tɛRmɑ̃] ADV [*sourire*] involuntarily; [*bousculer qn*] unintentionally, unwittingly; **l'accident dont je fus (bien) ~ le témoin** the accident to *ou* of which I was an *ou* the unintentional witness

involutif, -ive [ɛ̃vɔlytif, iv] ADJ (*Bio, Math*) involute; (*Méd*) [*processus*] ~ involution

involution [ɛ̃vɔlysjɔ̃] NF (*Bio, Méd, Math*) involution; (*Méd*) **~ utérine** involution of the uterus

invoquer [ɛ̃vɔke] ▸conjug 1◂ VT [a] (= *alléguer*) [+ *argument*] to put forward; [+ *témoignage*] to call upon; [+ *excuse, jeunesse, ignorance*] to plead; [+ *loi, texte*] to cite, refer to; (*Jur*) **~ les règles de compétence** to avail o.s. of the rules of jurisdiction; **les arguments de fait et de droit invoqués** the points of fact and law relied on; **les raisons invoquées** the reasons adduced [b] (= *appeler à l'aide*) [+ *Dieu*] to invoke, call upon; **~ le secours de qn** to call upon sb for help; **~ la clémence de qn** to beg sb *ou* appeal to sb for clemency

---

invraisemblable [ɛ̃vRɛsɑ̃blabl] ADJ [a] (= *peu plausible*) [*histoire, nouvelle*] unlikely, improbable; [*argument*] implausible [b] (= *inimaginable*) [*insolence, habit*] incredible; **aussi ~ que cela paraisse** incredible though it may seem; **c'est ~ !** it's incredible!

invraisemblablement [ɛ̃vRɛsɑ̃blabləmɑ̃] ADV incredibly

invraisemblance [ɛ̃vRɛsɑ̃blɑ̃s] NF [*fait, nouvelle*] unlikelihood (*NonC*), unlikeliness (*NonC*), improbability; [*argument*] implausibility; **plein d'~s** full of improbabilities *ou* implausibilities

invulnérabilité [ɛ̃vylneRabilite] NF invulnerability

invulnérable [ɛ̃vylneRabl] ADJ (*lit*) invulnerable; (*fig*) **~ à** [+ *maladie*] immune to; [+ *attaque*] invulnerable to, impervious to

iode [jɔd] NM iodine → **phare, teinture**

iodé, e [jɔde] ADJ [*air, sel*] iodized; **les huîtres ont un goût ~** oysters really taste of the sea

ioder [jɔde] ▸conjug 1◂ VT to iodize

iodler [jɔdle] ▸conjug 1◂ VT = **jodler**

iodoforme [jɔdɔfɔRm] NM iodoform

iodure [jɔdyR] NM iodide

ion [jɔ̃] NM ion

ionien, -ienne [jɔnjɛ̃, jɛn] [1] ADJ Ionian [2] NM (*Ling*) Ionic [3] **Ioniens** NMPL Ionians

ionique [jɔnik] [1] ADJ (*Archit*) Ionic; (*Sci*) ionic [2] NM (*Archit*) **l'~** the Ionic

ionisant, e [jɔnizɑ̃, ɑ̃t] ADJ ionizing

ionisation [jɔnizasjɔ̃] NF ionization

ioniser [jɔnize] ▸conjug 1◂ VT to ionize

ionosphère [jɔnɔsfɛR] NF ionosphere

iota [jɔta] NM iota; **je n'y ai pas changé un ~** I didn't change it one iota, I didn't change one *ou* an iota of it; (*lit, fig*) **il n'a pas bougé d'un ~** he didn't move an inch, he didn't budge

iourte [juRt] NF = **yourte**

Iowa [ajɔwa] NM Iowa

ipéca [ipeka] NM ipecacuanha, ipecac (*US*)

ipomée [ipɔme] NF ipomoea

IPR [ipeɛR] NM (ABRÉV = **inspecteur pédagogique régional**) → **inspecteur**

ipso facto [ipsofakto] LOC ADV ipso facto

IRA [iRa] NF (ABRÉV = **Irish Republican Army**) IRA

Irak [iRak] NM Iraq, Irak

irakien, -ienne [iRakjɛ̃, jɛn] [1] ADJ Iraqi [2] NM (*Ling*) Iraqi [3] **Irakien(ne)** NM,F Iraqi

Iran [iRɑ̃] NM Iran

iranien, -ienne [iRanjɛ̃, jɛn] [1] ADJ Iranian [2] NM (*Ling*) Iranian [3] **Iranien(ne)** NM,F Iranian

Iraq [iRak] NM = **Irak**

iraqien, -ienne [iRakjɛ̃, jɛn] ADJ, NM,F = **irakien**

irascibilité [iRasibilite] NF short- *ou* quick-temperedness, irascibility

irascible [iRasibl] ADJ short- *ou* quick-tempered, irascible

ire [iR] NF (*littér*) ire (*littér*)

iridacée [iRidase] NF iridaceous plant; **les ~s** iridaceous plants, the Iridaceae (*SPÉC*)

iridié, e [iRidje] ADJ iridic → **platine¹**

iridium [iRidjɔm] NM iridium

iris [iRis] NM (*Anat, Photo*) iris; (*Bot*) iris, flag; **~ jaune/des marais** yellow/water flag

irisation [iRizasjɔ̃] NF iridescence, irisation

irisé, e [iRize] ADJ (*ptp de* **iriser**) ADJ iridescent

iriser [iRize] ▸conjug 1◂ [1] VT to make iridescent [2] **s'iriser** VPR to become iridescent

irlandais, e [iRlɑ̃dɛ, ɛz] [1] ADJ Irish [2] NM [a] (*Ling*) Irish [b] **Irlandais** Irishman; **les Irlandais** the Irish; **les Irlandais du Nord** the Northern Irish [3] **Irlandaise** NF Irishwoman

Irlande [iRlɑ̃d] NF (= *pays*) Ireland; (= *État*) Irish Republic, Republic of Ireland; **l'~ du**

Nord Northern Ireland, Ulster; **de l'~ du Nord** Northern Irish; **~ du Sud** Southern Ireland

IRM [iɛRɛm] NF (ABRÉV = **imagerie par résonance magnétique**) MRI; **on m'a fait une ~** I had an MRI scan

Iroise [iRwaz] N **la mer d'~** the Iroise; **le pays d'~** the Iroise region (*in Western Brittany*)

ironie [iRɔni] NF (*lit, fig*) irony; **par une curieuse ~ du sort** by a strange irony of fate; **~ grinçante** bitter irony; **il sait manier l'~** he is a master of irony; **je le dis sans ~** I mean what I say

ironique [iRɔnik] ADJ ironic(al)

ironiquement [iRɔnikmɑ̃] ADV ironically

ironiser [iRɔnize] ▸conjug 1◂ VI to be ironic(al) (**sur** about); **ce n'est pas la peine d'~** there's no need to be ironic(al) (about it)

ironiste [iRɔnist] NMF ironist

iroquois, e [iRɔkwa, waz] [1] ADJ [*peuplade*] Iroquoian; (*Hist*) Iroquois [2] NM (*Ling*) Iroquoian [b] (= *coiffure*) Mohican (*Brit*), Mohawk (*US*) [3] **Iroquois(e)** NM,F Iroquoian, Iroquois

IRPP [iɛRpepe] NM (ABRÉV = **impôt sur le revenu des personnes physiques**) → **impôt**

irradiant, e [iRadjɑ̃, jɑ̃t] ADJ [*douleur*] radiant

irradiation [iRadjasjɔ̃] NF (= *action*) irradiation; (= *halo*) radiation; (= *rayons*) radiation, irradiation; (*Méd*) radiation

irradier [iRadje] ▸conjug 7◂ [1] VT (*Phys*) to irradiate; **les personnes irradiées** the people who were irradiated *ou* exposed to radiation; **combustible irradié** spent (nuclear) fuel, irradiated fuel; **un sourire irradiait son visage** a smile lit up his face [2] VI [*lumière*] to radiate, irradiate; [*douleur*] to radiate; (*fig*) to radiate

irraisonné, e [iRezɔne] ADJ irrational

irrationalisme [iRasjɔnalism] NM irrationalism

irrationalité [iRasjɔnalite] NF irrationality

irrationnel, -elle [iRasjɔnɛl] [1] ADJ (*gén, Math*) irrational [2] NM **l'~** the irrational

irrationnellement [iRasjɔnɛlmɑ̃] ADV irrationally

irrattrapable [iRatRapabl] ADJ [*bévue*] irretrievable

irréalisable [iRealizabl] ADJ (*gén*) unrealizable, unachievable; [*projet*] impracticable, unworkable; **c'est ~** it's not feasible, it's unworkable

irréalisé, e [iRealize] ADJ (*littér*) unrealized, unachieved

irréalisme [iRealism] NM lack of realism, unrealism

irréaliste [iRealist] ADJ unrealistic

irréalité [iRealite] NF unreality

irrecevabilité [iRəs(ə)vabilite] NF [a] [*argument, demande*] unacceptability [b] (*Jur*) inadmissibility

irrecevable [iRəs(ə)vabl] ADJ [a] (= *inacceptable*) [*argument, demande*] unacceptable [b] (*Jur*) inadmissible; **témoignage ~** inadmissible evidence; **leur plainte a été jugée ~** their claim was declared inadmissible

irréconciliable [iRekɔ̃siljabl] ADJ irreconcilable (**avec** with)

irrécouvrable [iRekuvRabl] ADJ irrecoverable

irrécupérable [iRekypeRabl] ADJ (*gén*) irretrievable; [*créance*] irrecoverable; [*ferraille, meubles*] unreclaimable; [*voiture*] beyond repair (*attrib*); **il est ~** [*personne*] he's beyond redemption

irrécusable [iRekyzabl] ADJ [*témoin, juge*] unimpeachable; [*témoignage, preuve*] incontestable, indisputable

irrédentisme [iRedɑ̃tism] NM irredentism

irrédentiste [iRedɑ̃tist] ADJ, NMF irredentist

irréductibilité [iRedyktibilite] NF [a] [*fait, élément*] irreducibility [b] (= *caractère invincible*) [*obstacle*] insurmountability, invincibility; [*volonté*] implacability [c] (*Chim, Math, Méd*) irreducibility

irréductible [iʀedyktibl] ADJ [a] (= *qui ne peut être réduit*) [*fait, élément*] irreducible [b] (= *invincible*) [*obstacle*] insurmountable, invincible; [*volonté, opposition, ennemi*] implacable; **les ~s du parti** the hard core of the party [c] (*Chim, Math, Méd*) irreducible

irréductiblement [iʀedyktiblǝmɑ̃] ADV implacably; **être ~ opposé à une politique** to be in out-and-out opposition to *ou* be implacably opposed to a policy

irréel, -elle [iʀeɛl] [1] ADJ unreal [2] NM **l'~** the unreal; (*Ling*) (*mode*) ~ *mood expressing unreal condition*; **l'~ du présent/passé** the hypothetical present/past

irréfléchi, e [iʀefleʃi] ADJ [*geste, paroles, action*] thoughtless, unconsidered; [*personne*] impulsive; [*courage, audace*] reckless, impetuous

irréflexion [iʀefleksjɔ̃] NF thoughtlessness

irréfutabilité [iʀefytabilite] NF irrefutability

irréfutable [iʀefytabl] ADJ [*preuve, logique*] irrefutable; [*signe*] undeniable; **de façon ~** irrefutably

irréfutablement [iʀefytablǝmɑ̃] ADV irrefutably

irréfuté, e [iʀefyte] ADJ unrefuted

irrégularité [iʀegylaʀite] NF [a] (= *asymétrie*) [*façade, traits, forme*] irregularity; [*écriture*] irregularity, unevenness; **les ~s du terrain** the unevenness of the ground; **les ~s de ses traits** his irregular features [b] (= *variabilité*) [*développement, horaire, pouls, respiration*] irregularity; [*rythme, courant, vitesse*] variation; [*sommeil, vent*] fitfulness; [*service, visites, intervalles*] irregularity [c] (= *inégalité*) [*travail, effort, qualité, résultats*] unevenness; [*élève, athlète*] erratic performance [d] (= *illégalité*) irregularity; **des ~s ont été commises lors du scrutin** irregularities occurred during the ballot [e] (*Ling*) [*verbe, pluriel*] irregularity

irrégulier, -ière [iʀegylje, jɛʀ] [1] ADJ [a] (= *asymétrique*) [*façade, traits, forme*] irregular; [*écriture*] irregular, uneven; [*terrain*] irregular, uneven [b] (= *variable*) [*développement, horaire*] irregular; [*rythme, courant, vitesse*] irregular, varying (*épith*); [*sommeil, pouls, respiration*] irregular, fitful; [*service, visites, intervalles*] irregular; [*vent*] fitful [c] (= *inégal*) [*travail, effort, qualité, résultats*] uneven; [*élève, athlète*] erratic [d] (= *illégal*) [*opération, situation, procédure*] irregular; [*détention*] illegal; [*agent, homme d'affaires*] dubious; (*Jur*) **absence irrégulière** unauthorized absence; **étranger en situation irrégulière** foreign national whose papers are not in order; **pour éviter de vous mettre en situation irrégulière** to avoid being in breach of the regulations; **il était en séjour ~** he was in the country illegally [e] (*Ling*) [*verbe, pluriel*] irregular [f] (*Mil*) irregular [2] NM (*Mil: gén pl*) irregular

irrégulièrement [iʀegyljɛʀmɑ̃] ADV (*gén*) irregularly; (= *sporadiquement*) sporadically; (= *illégalement*) illegally; **il ne paie son loyer que très ~** he only pays his rent at very irregular intervals; **ceux entrés ~ dans le pays** those who came into the country illegally

irréligieux, -ieuse [iʀeliʒjø, jøz] ADJ irreligious

irréligion [iʀeliʒjɔ̃] NF irreligiousness, irreligion

irrémédiable [iʀemedjabl] ADJ [a] (= *irréparable*) [*dommage, perte*] irreparable; **essayer d'éviter l'~** to try to avoid doing anything that can't be undone [b] (= *incurable*) [*mal, vice*] incurable, irremediable [c] (= *irréversible*) [*changement, tendance*] irreversible; **l'~ montée du chômage** the inexorable rise of unemployment

irrémédiablement [iʀemedjablǝmɑ̃] ADV irreparably, irremediably

irrémissible [iʀemisibl] ADJ (*littér*) irremissible

irrémissiblement [iʀemisiblǝmɑ̃] ADV (*littér*) irremissibly

irremplaçable [iʀɑ̃plasabl] ADJ irreplaceable ▪ (*PROV*) **nul** *ou* **personne n'est ~** everyone is replaceable

irréparable [iʀepaʀabl] ADJ [a] (= *hors d'état*) [*objet*] irreparable, unmendable, beyond repair (*attrib*); **la voiture est ~** the car is beyond repair *ou* is a write-off [b] (= *irrémédiable*) [*dommage, erreur, impair*] irreparable; **pour éviter l'~** to avoid doing something that can't be undone

irrépréhensible [iʀepʀeɑ̃sibl] ADJ (*littér*) irreprehensible

irrépressible [iʀepʀesibl] ADJ irrepressible

irréprochable [iʀepʀɔʃabl] ADJ [*technique, travail*] perfect, impeccable; [*alibi*] perfect; [*moralité, conduite, vie*] irreproachable, beyond reproach (*attrib*); [*tenue*] impeccable, faultless; **c'est une mère ~** she's the perfect mother

irréprochablement [iʀepʀɔʃablǝmɑ̃] ADV **~ pur/propre** impeccably pure/clean

irrésistible [iʀezistibl] ADJ [*personne, charme, plaisir, force*] irresistible; [*besoin, désir, preuve, logique*] compelling; **il est (d'un comique) ~!** (*amusant*) he's hilarious!

irrésistiblement [iʀezistiblǝmɑ̃] ADV irresistibly

irrésolu, e [iʀezɔly] ADJ [*personne*] irresolute, indecisive; [*problème*] unresolved, unsolved

irrésolution [iʀezɔlysjɔ̃] NF irresolution, irresoluteness, indecisiveness

irrespect [iʀɛspɛ] NM disrespect (**envers, de** for)

irrespectueusement [iʀɛspɛktɥøzmɑ̃] ADV disrespectfully

irrespectueux, -euse [iʀɛspɛktɥø, øz] ADJ disrespectful (**envers** to, towards)

irrespirable [iʀɛspiʀabl] ADJ [a] [*air*] (= *pénible à respirer*) unbreathable; (= *dangereux*) unsafe, unhealthy [b] [*ambiance*] oppressive, stifling

irresponsabilité [iʀɛspɔ̃sabilite] NF irresponsibility

irresponsable [iʀɛspɔ̃sabl] ADJ irresponsible (**de** for); **c'est un ~!** he's (totally) irresponsible!; **notre pays est entre les mains d'~s** this country is in irresponsible hands

irrétrécissable [iʀetʀesisabl] ADJ (*sur étiquette, publicité*) unshrinkable, nonshrink

irrévérence [iʀeveʀɑ̃s] NF (= *caractère*) irreverence; (= *propos*) irreverent word; (= *acte*) irreverent act

irrévérencieusement [iʀeveʀɑ̃sjøzmɑ̃] ADV irreverently

irrévérencieux, -ieuse [iʀeveʀɑ̃sjø, jøz] ADJ irreverent (**envers, à l'égard de** towards)

irréversibilité [iʀeveʀsibilite] NF irreversibility

irréversible [iʀeveʀsibl] ADJ irreversible

irréversiblement [iʀeveʀsiblǝmɑ̃] ADV irreversibly

irrévocabilité [iʀevɔkabilite] NF (*littér, Jur*) irrevocability

irrévocable [iʀevɔkabl] ADJ [*décision, choix, juge*] irrevocable; [*temps, passé*] beyond *ou* past recall (*attrib*), irrevocable; **l'~** the irrevocable

irrévocablement [iʀevɔkablǝmɑ̃] ADV irrevocably

irrigable [iʀigabl] ADJ irrigable

irrigation [iʀigasjɔ̃] NF (*Agr, Méd*) irrigation

irriguer [iʀige] ▸ conjug 1 ◂ VT (*Agr, Méd*) to irrigate

irritabilité [iʀitabilite] NF irritability

irritable [iʀitabl] ADJ irritable

irritant, e [iʀitɑ̃, ɑ̃t] [1] ADJ (= *agaçant*) irritating, annoying, irksome; (*Méd*) irritant [2] NM irritant

irritation [iʀitasjɔ̃] NF (= *colère*) irritation, annoyance; (*Méd*) irritation

irrité, e [iʀite] (*ptp de* **irriter**) ADJ [*gorge, yeux*] irritated, inflamed; [*geste, regard*] irritated, annoyed, angry; **être ~ contre qn** to be annoyed *ou* angry with sb

irriter [iʀite] ▸ conjug 1 ◂ [1] VT [a] (= *agacer*) to irritate, annoy, irk [b] (= *enflammer*) [+ *œil, peau, blessure*] to make inflamed, irritate; **il avait la gorge irritée par la fumée** the smoke irritated his throat [c] (*littér = aviver*) [+ *désir, curiosité*] to arouse [2] **s'irriter** VPR [a] (= *s'agacer*) **s'~ de qch/contre qn** to get annoyed *ou* angry at sth/with sb, feel irritated at sth/with sb [b] [*œil, peau, blessure*] to become inflamed *ou* irritated

irruption [iʀypsjɔ̃] NF (= *entrée subite ou hostile*) irruption (*NonC*); [*nouvelles technologies, doctrine*] sudden emergence; **pour empêcher l'~ des manifestants dans le bâtiment** to prevent the demonstrators from storming the building *ou* bursting into the building; **faire ~ (chez qn)** to burst in (on sb); **les eaux firent ~ dans les bas quartiers** the waters swept into *ou* flooded the low-lying parts of the town; **ils ont fait ~ dans le monde musical en 1996** they burst onto the music scene in 1996

Isaac [izak] NM Isaac

Isabelle [izabɛl] NF Isabel; **~ la Catholique** Isabella the Catholic

isabelle [izabɛl] [1] ADJ INV light-tan [2] NM light-tan horse

Isaïe [isai] NM Isaiah; (**le livre d'**)**Isaïe** (the Book of) Isaiah

isard [izaʀ] NM izard

isba [izba] NF isba

ISBN [iɛsbeɛn] ADJ, NM (*ABRÉV* = **International Standard Book Number**) ISBN

ischémie [iskemi] NF ischaemia (*Brit*), ischemia (*US*)

ischion [iskjɔ̃] NM ischium

Iseu(l)t [izø] NF Isolde → **Tristan**

ISF [iɛsɛf] NM (*ABRÉV* = **impôt de solidarité sur la fortune**) → **impôt**

Isis [izis] NF Isis

Islam [islam] NM **l'~** Islam

Islamabad [islamabad] N Islamabad

islamique [islamik] ADJ Islamic; **la République ~ de ...** the Islamic Republic of ...

islamisation [islamizasjɔ̃] NF Islamization

islamiser [islamize] ▸ conjug 1 ◂ VT to Islamize

islamisme [islamism] NM Islamism

islamiste [islamist] [1] ADJ Islamic [2] NMF Islamist

islandais, e [islɑ̃dɛ, ɛz] [1] ADJ Icelandic [2] NM (*Ling*) Icelandic [3] **Islandais(e)** NM,F Icelander

Islande [islɑ̃d] NF Iceland

ISO [izo] NM INV (*ABRÉV* = **International Standardization Organization**) **degré/norme/certification ~** ISO rating/standard/certification

isobare [izobaʀ] [1] ADJ isobaric [2] NF isobar

isocèle [izosɛl] ADJ isosceles

isochrone [izɔkʀɔn], **isochronique** [izɔkʀɔnik] ADJ isochronal, isochronous

isoglosse [izoglɔs] [1] ADJ isoglossal, isoglottic [2] NF isogloss

isolable [izolabl] ADJ isolable; **difficilement ~** difficult to isolate

isolant, e [izolɑ̃, ɑ̃t] [1] ADJ (*Constr, Élec*) insulating; (= *insonorisant*) soundproofing, sound-insulating; (*Ling*) isolating [2] NM insulator, insulating material; **~ thermique/électrique** heat/electrical insulator; **~ phonique** soundproofing material

isolat [izɔla] NM (*Bio, Chim, Ling*) isolate

isolateur, -trice [izɔlatœʀ, tʀis] **1** ADJ [*écran, gaine*] insulating **2** NM (= *support*) insulator

isolation [izɔlasjɔ̃] NF (*Élec*) insulation; **~ phonique** *ou* **acoustique** soundproofing, sound insulation; **~ thermique** thermal *ou* heat insulation

isolationnisme [izɔlasjɔnism] NM isolationism

isolationniste [izɔlasjɔnist] ADJ, NMF isolationist

isolé, e [izɔle] (*ptp de* **isoler**) **1** ADJ [*cas, personne, protestation, acte*] isolated; [*incident*] isolated, one-off; [*lieu*] isolated, remote; [*philosophe, tireur, anarchiste*] lone (*épith*); (*Élec*) insulated; **se sentir ~** to feel isolated; **vivre ~** to live in isolation; **phrase ~e de son contexte** sentence taken out of context; **quelques voix ~es se sont élevées pour dénoncer...** a few lone voices have been raised in protest against... **2** NM,F (= *personne délaissée*) lonely person; (= *personne qui agit seule*) loner; **le problème des ~s** the problem of the lonely *ou* isolated; **seuls quelques ~s l'ont encouragé** only a few isolated individuals encouraged him; **ce dissident n'est plus un ~** this dissident is no longer out on his own

isolement [izɔlmɑ̃] NM [*maison, théoricien, prisonnier, malade, pays*] isolation; (*Élec*) [*câble*] insulation; **leur pays tente de sortir de son ~ international** their country is trying to break out of its international isolation

isolément [izɔlemɑ̃] ADV in isolation, individually; **chaque élément pris ~** each element considered separately *ou* individually *ou* in isolation

isoler [izɔle] ▶conjug 1◀ **1** VT **a** [+ *prisonnier*] to place in solitary confinement; [+ *malade, citation, fait, mot*] to isolate (**de** from); [+ *lieu*] to cut off (**de** from), isolate; **ses opinions l'isolent** his opinions isolate him; **hameau isolé par l'inondation/la neige** village cut off by floods/snow **b** (*contre le froid, Élec*) to insulate; (*contre le bruit*) to soundproof, insulate **c** (*Bio, Chim*) to isolate **2 s'isoler** VPR (*dans un coin, pour travailler*) to isolate o.s.; **s'~ du reste du monde** to cut o.s. off *ou* isolate o.s. from the rest of the world; **pourrait-on s'~ quelques instants ?** could we go somewhere quiet for a few minutes?

isoloir [izɔlwaʀ] NM polling booth

isomère [izɔmɛʀ] **1** ADJ isomeric **2** NM isomer

isométrique [izɔmetʀik] ADJ (*Math, Sci*) isometric

isomorphe [izɔmɔʀf] ADJ (*Chim*) isomorphic, isomorphous; (*Math, Ling*) isomorphic

isomorphisme [izɔmɔʀfism] NM isomorphism

Isorel® [izɔʀɛl] NM hardboard

isotherme [izɔtɛʀm] **1** ADJ isothermal (*SPÉC*); **sac ~** cool *ou* insulated bag; **caisse ~** ice box; **camion ~** refrigerated lorry (*Brit*) *ou* truck (*US*) **2** NF isotherm

isotope [izɔtɔp] **1** ADJ isotopic **2** NM isotope

isotrope [izɔtʀɔp] ADJ isotropic, isotropous

Israël [isʀaɛl] NM Israel; **l'État d'~** the state of Israel

israélien, -ienne [isʀaeljɛ̃, jɛn] **1** ADJ Israeli **2** **Israélien(ne)** NM,F Israeli

israélite [isʀaelit] **1** ADJ Jewish **2** NM (*gén*) Jew; (*Hist*) Israelite **3** NF Jewess; (*Hist*) Israelite

ISSN [iɛsɛsɛn] ADJ, NM (ABRÉV = **International Standard Serial Number**) ISSN

issu, e¹ [isy] ♦**issu de** LOC ADJ [+ *parents*] born of; **être ~ de** (= *résulter de*) to stem from; (= *être né de*) [+ *parents*] to be born of; [+ *milieu familial*] to be born into → **cousin**

issue² [isy] NF **a** (= *sortie*) exit; [*eau, vapeur*] outlet; **voie sans ~** (*lit, fig*) dead end; (*panneau*) "no through road"; **~ de secours** (*lit*) emergency exit; (*fig*) fallback option; **il a su se ménager une ~** he has managed to leave himself a way out **b** (= *solution*) way out, solution; **la seule ~ possible** the only way out; **la situation est sans ~** there is no way out *ou* no solution to the situation; **un avenir sans ~** a future without prospects *ou* which leads nowhere; **ils n'ont pas d'autre ~ que la soumission** *ou* **que de se soumettre** there's no option left open to them but to submit, they've no option but to submit **c** (= *fin*) outcome; **heureuse ~** happy outcome; **~ fatale** fatal outcome; **à l'~ de** at the end of

Istanbul [istɑ̃bul] N Istanbul

isthme [ism] NM (*Anat, Géog*) isthmus; **l'~ de Corinthe/de Panama/de Suez** the Isthmus of Corinth/of Panama/of Suez

isthmique [ismik] ADJ isthmian

Istrie [istʀi] NF Istria

italianisant, e [italjanizɑ̃, ɑ̃t] **1** ADJ [*œuvre*] Italianate; [*artiste*] Italianizing (*épith*) **2** NM,F (*Univ*) Italianist; (= *artiste*) Italianizer

italianisme [italjanism] NM (*Ling*) Italianism

Italie [itali] NF Italy

italien, -ienne [italjɛ̃, jɛn] **1** ADJ Italian **2** NM (*Ling*) Italian **3** **Italien(ne)** NM,F Italian **4 à l'italienne** LOC ADJ [*cuisine, mobilier, situation politique*] Italian-style; [*théâtre*] *with a proscenium*; (*Ordin*) [*format*] landscape (*épith*); **la comédie à l'italienne** the commedia dell'arte

italique [italik] **1** NM **a** (*Typo*) italics; **mettre un mot en ~** to put a word in italics, italicize a word **b** (*Hist, Ling*) Italic **2** ADJ (*Typo*) italic; (*Hist, Ling*) Italic

item [item] **1** ADV (*Comm*) ditto **2** NM (*Ling, Psych*) item

itératif, -ive [iteratif, iv] ADJ (*gén, Gram, Ordin*) iterative; (*Jur*) reiterated, repeated

itération [iterasjɔ̃] NF iteration

Ithaque [itak] NF Ithaca

itinéraire [itineʀɛʀ] NM (= *chemin*) route, itinerary; (*Alpinisme*) route; **son ~ philosophique/ religieux** his philosophical/religious path; **~ bis** *ou* **de délestage** alternative route; **faire** *ou* **tracer un ~** to map out a route *ou* an itinerary

itinérant, e [itineʀɑ̃, ɑ̃t] ADJ itinerant, travelling; **vacances ~es** (*en voiture*) touring holiday (*Brit*) *ou* vacation (*US*); (*à pied*) rambling holiday (*Brit*) *ou* vacation (*US*); **ambassadeur ~** roving ambassador; **troupe ~e** (band of) strolling players; **exposition ~e** travelling exhibition; **bibliothèque ~e** mobile library, bookmobile (*US*)

itou*† [itu] ADV likewise; **et moi ~ !** (and) me too!*

IUFM [iyɛfɛm] NM (ABRÉV = **Institut universitaire de formation des maîtres**) → **institut**

IUP [iype] NM (ABRÉV = **Institut universitaire professionnalisé**) → **institut**

IUT [iyte] NM (ABRÉV = **Institut universitaire de technologie**) → **institut**

Ivan [ivɑ̃] NM Ivan; **~ le Terrible** Ivan the Terrible

IVG [iveʒe] NF (ABRÉV = **interruption volontaire de grossesse**) → **interruption**

ivoire [ivwaʀ] NM **a** [*éléphant*] (= *matière, objet*) ivory; **en** *ou* **d'~** ivory (*épith*); (*Tech*) **~ végétal** vegetable ivory, ivory nut → **côte, tour¹** **b** [*dent*] dentine

ivoirien, -ienne [ivwaʀjɛ̃, jɛn] **1** ADJ of *ou* from the Ivory Coast **2** **Ivoirien(ne)** NM,F inhabitant *ou* native of the Ivory Coast

ivraie [ivʀɛ] NF (*Bot*) rye grass → **séparer**

ivre [ivʀ] ADJ drunk, intoxicated (*frm*); **~ mort** dead *ou* blind drunk; **légèrement ~** slightly drunk, tipsy; **complètement ~** blind drunk*, completely drunk; **~ de joie/rage** wild with joy/rage, beside o.s. with joy/rage; **~ de vengeance** thirsting for revenge

ivresse [ivʀɛs] NF (= *ébriété*) drunkenness, intoxication; **dans l'~ du combat/de la victoire** in the exhilaration of the fight/of victory; **l'~ du plaisir** the (wild) ecstasy of pleasure; **l'~ de la vitesse** the thrill *ou* exhilaration of speed; **avec ~** rapturously, ecstatically; **instants/ heures d'~** moments/hours of rapture *ou* (wild) ecstasy; **~ chimique** drug dependence; (*Méd*) **~ des profondeurs** staggers → **état**

ivrogne [ivʀɔɲ] **1** NMF drunkard → **serment** **2** ADJ drunken (*épith*)

ivrognerie [ivʀɔɲʀi] NF drunkenness

J

J¹, j [ʒi] NM (= *lettre*) J, j → **jour**

J² (ABRÉV = **Joule**) J

j' [ʒ] → **je**

jabot [ʒabo] NM **a** [*oiseau*] crop **b** (*Habillement*) jabot

jacassement [ʒakasmɑ̃] NM [*pie*] chatter (*NonC*); (*péj*) [*personnes*] jabber(ing) (*NonC*), chatter(ing) (*NonC*)

jacasser [ʒakase] ▷ conjug 1 ◁ VI [*pie*] to chatter; (*péj*) [*personne*] to jabber, chatter

jachère [ʒaʃɛʀ] NF fallow (*NonC*); (= *procédé*) practice of fallowing land; **laisser une terre en ~** to leave a piece of land fallow, let a piece of land lie fallow; **rester en ~** to lie fallow

jacinthe [ʒasɛ̃t] NF hyacinth; **~ sauvage** *ou* **des bois** bluebell

jack [(d)ʒak] NM (*Téléc, Tex*) jack; (*Élec*) jack plug

jackpot [(d)ʒakpɔt] NM (= *combinaison*) jackpot; (= *machine*) slot machine; (*lit, fig*) **gagner** *ou* **ramasser** *ou* **toucher*** **le ~** to hit the jackpot; **c'est le ~ assuré!*** you're (*ou* we're *etc*) going to make a mint!*

Jacob [ʒakɔb] NM Jacob → **échelle**

jacobin, e [ʒakɔbɛ̃, in] **1** ADJ Jacobinic(al) **2** (*Hist*) Jacobin Jacobin

jacobinisme [ʒakɔbinism] NM Jacobinism

jacobite [ʒakɔbit] NM Jacobite

jacquard [ʒakaʀ] **1** ADJ [*pull*] Jacquard **2** NM (= *métier*) Jacquard loom; (= *tissu*) Jacquard (weave)

jacquerie [ʒakʀi] NF jacquerie

Jacques [ʒak] NM James; **faire le ~†*** to play *ou* act the fool, fool about → **maître**

jacquet [ʒakɛ] NM backgammon

Jacquot [ʒako] NM (= *prénom de perroquet*) Polly

jactance [ʒaktɑ̃s] NF **a** (*= bavardage*) chat; **il a de la ~!** he's got the gift of the gab!* **b** (*littér = vanité*) conceit

jacter* [ʒakte] ▷ conjug 1 ◁ VI to jabber, gas*; (*arg Police*) to talk, sing*

jacuzzi® [ʒakyzi] NM Jacuzzi®

jade [ʒad] NM (= *pierre*) jade; (= *objet*) jade object *ou* ornament; **de ~** jade (*épith*)

jadis [ʒadis] **1** ADV in times past, formerly, long ago; **mes amis de ~** my friends of long ago *ou* of old; **on se promenait dans ces jardins** in olden days *ou* long ago people used to walk in these gardens **2** ADJ **au temps ~** in days of old, in days gone by, once upon a time; **du temps ~** of times gone by, of yesteryear

jaguar [ʒagwaʀ] NM (= *animal*) jaguar

jaillir [ʒajiʀ] ▷ conjug 2 ◁ VI **a** [*liquide, sang*] (*par à-coups*) to spurt out; (*abondamment*) to gush forth; [*larmes*] to flow; [*geyser*] to spout up, gush forth; [*vapeur, source*] to gush forth; [*flammes*] to shoot up, spurt out; [*lumière*] to flash on (**de** from, out of); **faire ~ des étincelles** to make sparks fly; **un éclair jaillit dans l'obscurité** a flash of lightning split the darkness, lightning flashed in

the darkness
b (= *apparaître, s'élancer*) [*personne*] to spring out; [*voiture*] to shoot out; **des soldats jaillirent de tous côtés** soldiers sprang out *ou* leapt out from all sides; **le train jaillit du tunnel** the train shot *ou* burst out of the tunnel; **des montagnes jaillissaient au-dessus de la plaine** mountains towered above the plain; **des tours qui jaillissent de terre** soaring tower blocks; **des monstres jaillis de son imagination** monsters sprung from his imagination
c [*cris, rires, réponses*] to burst forth *ou* out
d [*idée*] to spring up; [*vérité, solution*] to spring (**de** from)

jaillissant, e [ʒajisɑ̃, ɑ̃t] ADJ [*eau*] spurting, gushing

jaillissement [ʒajismɑ̃] NM [*liquide, vapeur*] spurt, gush; [*idées*] outpouring

jais [ʒɛ] NM (*Minér*) jet; **de ~** *ou* **en ~** [*perles, bijou*] jet (*épith*); **cheveux de ~** jet-black hair → **noir**

Jakarta [dʒakaʀta] N Jakarta

jalon [ʒalɔ̃] NM **a** (= *piquet*) ranging-pole; [*arpenteur*] (surveyor's) staff **b** (= *point de référence*) landmark, milestone; **planter** *ou* **poser les premiers ~s de qch** to prepare the ground for sth, pave the way for sth; **il commence à poser des ~s** he's beginning to prepare the ground

jalonnement [ʒalɔnmɑ̃] NM [*route*] marking out

jalonner [ʒalɔne] ▷ conjug 1 ◁ VT **a** (= *déterminer le tracé de*) [+ *route, chemin de fer*] to mark out *ou* off **b** (= *border, s'espacer sur*) to line, stretch along; **des champs de fleurs jalonnent la route** fields of flowers line the road **c** (= *marquer*) [+ *vie*] to punctuate; **carrière jalonnée de succès/d'obstacles** career punctuated with successes/with obstacles

jalousement [ʒaluzmɑ̃] ADV jealously

jalouser [ʒaluze] ▷ conjug 1 ◁ VT to be jealous of

jalousie [ʒaluzi] NF **a** (*entre amants*) jealousy; (= *envie*) jealousy, envy; **~s mesquines** petty jealousies; **être malade de ~** ◊ **crever de ~*** [*amant*] to be mad *ou* sick with jealousy; [*envieux*] to be green with envy **b** (= *persienne*) slatted blind, jalousie

jaloux, -ouse [ʒalu, uz] ADJ **a** (*en amour*) jealous; **~ comme un tigre** madly jealous; **observer qn d'un œil ~** to keep a jealous eye on sb, watch sb jealously; **c'est un ~** he's the jealous type, he's a jealous man **b** (= *envieux*) jealous, envious; **~ de qn/de la réussite de qn** jealous of sb/of sb's success; **faire des ~** to make people jealous **c** (*littér*) **~ de** (= *désireux de*) intent upon, eager for; **~ de perfection** eager for perfection; (= *qui tient à*) **il est ~ de son indépendance/ses prérogatives** he jealously guards his independence/his privileges

jamaïcain, e, jamaïquain, e [ʒamaikɛ̃, ɛn] **1** ADJ Jamaican **2 Jamaïcain(e)** ◊ **Jamaïquain(e)** NM,F Jamaican

Jamaïque [ʒamaik] NF Jamaica

▼jamais [ʒamɛ] **1** ADV **a** (*avec ne* = *à aucun moment*) never, not ever; **il n'a ~ avoué** he never confessed; **n'a-t-il ~ avoué?** did he never confess?, didn't he ever confess?; **il n'a ~ autant travaillé** he's never worked as hard (before), he's never done so much work (before); **~ je n'ai vu un homme si égoïste** I've never met *ou* seen such a selfish man (before), never (before) have I met *ou* seen such a selfish man; **~ mère ne fut plus heureuse** there was never a happier mother; **il n'est ~ trop tard** it's never too late; **on ne l'a ~ encore entendu se plaindre** he's never yet been heard to complain; **ne dites ~ plus cela!** never say that again!, don't you ever say that again!; **il ne lui a ~ plus écrit** he's never *ou* he hasn't (ever) written to her since; **il partit pour ne ~ plus revenir** he left never to return; **nous sommes restés deux ans sans ~ recevoir de nouvelles** we were *ou* went two years without ever hearing any news, for two years we never (once) heard any news; **je n'ai ~ de ma vie vu un chien aussi laid** never in my life have I *ou* I have never in my life seen such an ugly dog; **~ au grand ~ on ne me reprendra à le faire** you'll never ever catch me doing it again; **~ de la vie je n'y retournerai** I shall never in my life go back there, I shall never ever go back there; **accepterez-vous? — ~ de la vie!** will you accept? — never! *ou* not on your life!*; **~ plus!** ◊ **plus ~!** never again!; **c'est ce que vous avez dit — ~!** that's what you said — never! *ou* I never did!*; **presque ~** hardly *ou* scarcely ever, practically never; **c'est maintenant ou ~** ◊ **c'est le moment ou** ~ it's now or never; **c'est le moment ou ~ d'acheter** now is the time to buy, if ever there was a time to buy it's now; **une symphonie ~ jouée/terminée** an unplayed/unfinished symphony; **il ne faut ~ dire ~** never say never; **~ deux sans trois!** (*choses agréables*) good things come *ou* happen in threes!; (*malheurs*) bad things come *ou* happen in threes!; **alors, ~ on ne dit «merci»?*** didn't anyone ever teach you to say "thank you"? → **mieux, savoir**
b (*sans ne: intensif*) **elle est belle comme ~** she's more beautiful than ever; **il travaille comme ~ (il n'a travaillé)** he's working harder than ever, he's working as he's never worked before
c (*sans ne* = *un jour, une fois*) ever; **a-t-il avoué?** did he ever confess?; **si ~ vous passez par Londres venez nous voir** if ever you're passing *ou* if ever you should pass through London come and see us; **si ~ j'avais un poste pour vous je vous préviendrais** if ever I had *ou* if I ever had a job for you I'd let you know; **si ~ tu rates le train, reviens** if by (any) chance you miss *ou* if you (should) happen to miss the train, come back; **si ~ tu recommences, gare!** don't you ever do that again or you'll be in trouble!; **il désespère d'avoir ~ de l'avancement** he despairs of ever getting promotion *ou* of ever being promoted
d (*avec que: intensif*) **je n'ai ~ fait que mon devoir** I've always just done my duty; **il n'a ~ fait que critiquer (les autres)** he's never done

▶ GRAMMAIRE ACTIVE: **jamais** 39.3

anything but criticize (others); **ça ne fait ~ que deux heures qu'il est parti** it's no more than two hours since he left; **ce n'est ~ qu'un enfant** he is only a child (after all)

[e] (avec comparatif) ever; **les œufs sont plus chers que ~** eggs are more expensive than ever (before); **c'est pire que ~** it's worse than ever; **avez-vous ~ vu ça?** have you ever seen ou did you ever see such a thing?; **c'est le plus grand que j'aie ~ vu** it's the biggest one I've ever seen

[2] **à jamais** LOC ADV for good, for ever; **leur amitié est à ~ compromise** their friendship will never be the same again

[3] **à tout jamais ◊ pour jamais** LOC ADV for ever (and ever), for evermore; **je renonce à tout ~ à le lui faire comprendre** I've given up ever trying to make him understand it

jambage [ʒɑ̃baʒ] NM [a] [lettre] downstroke, descender [b] (Archit) jamb

jambe [ʒɑ̃b] NF [a] (Anat, Habillement, Zool) leg; **fille aux longues ~s** ou **toute en ~s** girl with long legs, long-legged ou leggy* girl; **remonte ta ~ (de pantalon)** roll up your trouser leg; (Méd) **~ de bois/artificielle/articulée** wooden/ artificial/articulated leg

[b] (loc) **avoir les ~s comme du coton** ou **en coton** to have legs like jelly ou cotton wool (Brit); **n'avoir plus de ~s ◊ en avoir plein les ~s*** to be worn out ou on one's knees*; **avoir 20 km dans les ~s** to have walked 20 km; **je n'ai plus mes ~s de vingt ans!** I'm not as quick on my feet as I used to be!; **la peur/l'impatience lui donnait des ~s** fear/impatience lent new strength to his legs ou lent him speed; (iro) **ça me fait une belle ~!** a fat lot of good that does me!*; (Sport) **se mettre en ~s** to warm up, limber up; **mise en ~s** warming-up exercises; **tirer** ou **traîner la ~** (par fatigue) to drag one's feet, trudge along; (= boiter) to limp along; **elle ne peut plus (se) tenir sur ses ~s** her legs are giving way under her, she can hardly stand; **prendre ses ~s à son cou** to take to one's heels; **traiter qn/qch par-dessous** ou **par-dessus la ~*** to treat sb/deal with sth in a casual ou an offhand manner; **faire qch par-dessous** ou **par-dessus la ~*** to do sth carelessly ou in a slipshod way; **il m'a tenu la ~ pendant des heures*** he kept me hanging about talking for hours*; **tirer dans les ~s de qn*** to make life difficult for sb; **il s'est jeté dans nos ~s*** he got under our feet; **elle est toujours dans mes ~s*** she's always getting in my way, she's always under my feet; **j'en ai eu les ~s coupées*** it knocked me sideways* ou for six* ou for a loop* (US); **c'est un cautère** ou **un emplâtre sur une ~ de bois** it's no use at all → **s'engourdir, partie²**

[c] (Tech) [compas] leg; (= étai) prop, stay; **~ de force** (Constr) strut; (Aut) torque rod

jambier, -ière¹ [ʒɑ̃bje, jɛʀ] ADJ, NM **(muscle) ~** leg muscle

jambière² [ʒɑ̃bjɛʀ] NF (gén) legging, gaiter; (Sport) pad; [armure] greave; **~s (en laine)** leg-warmers

jambon [ʒɑ̃bɔ̃] NM [a] (Culin) ham; **~ blanc** ou **cuit** ou **de Paris** boiled ou cooked ham; **~ cru** ou **de pays** cured ham; **~ de Parme/d'York** Parma/York ham; **~ à l'os** ham on the bone; **~ au torchon** top-quality cooked ham; **un ~-beurre*** a ham sandwich (made from baguette) [b] (* péj = cuisse) thigh

jambonneau (pl **jambonneaux**) [ʒɑ̃bɔno] NM knuckle of ham

jamboree [ʒɑ̃bɔʀe] NM (Scoutisme) jamboree

janissaire [ʒanisɛʀ] NM janissary

jansénisme [ʒɑ̃senism] NM Jansenism; (fig) austere code of morals

janséniste [ʒɑ̃senist] ADJ, NMF Jansenist

jante [ʒɑ̃t] NF [bicyclette, voiture] rim; (Aut) **~s (en) alu/en alliage (léger)** aluminium (Brit) ou aluminum (US)/alloy wheels

Janus [ʒanys] NM Janus; **c'est un ~** he's two-faced

janvier [ʒɑ̃vje] NM January; pour locutions voir **septembre**

Japon [ʒapɔ̃] NM Japan

japonais, e [ʒapɔnɛ, ɛz] [1] ADJ Japanese [2] NM (Ling) Japanese [3] **Japonais(e)** NM,F Japanese

japonaiserie [ʒapɔnɛzʀi] NF Japanese curio

japonisant, e [ʒapɔnizɑ̃, ɑ̃t] [1] ADJ [décor, style] Japanese-inspired [2] NM,F expert on Japan

jappement [ʒapmɑ̃] NM yap, yelp

japper [ʒape] ▸conjug 1◂ VI to yap, yelp

jaquette [ʒakɛt] NF [a] [homme] morning coat; [femme] jacket; **il est de la ~ (flottante)†‡** he's one of them*, he's a poof‡ (Brit) ou a fag‡ (US) [b] [livre] (dust) jacket, (dust) cover; [cassette vidéo] (plastic) cover [c] [dent] crown

jardin [ʒaʀdɛ̃] [1] NM garden, yard (US); **rester au** ou **dans le ~** to stay in the garden ou yard (US); **faire le ~** to do the gardening; **siège/ table de ~** garden seat/table; (fig) **c'est mon ~ secret** those are my private secrets → **côté, cultiver, pierre**

[2] COMP ▸ **jardin d'acclimatation** zoological garden(s) ▸ **jardin d'agrément** ornamental ou pleasure garden ▸ **jardin anglais** ou **à l'anglaise** landscaped garden ▸ **jardin botanique** botanical garden(s) ▸ **jardin de curé** small enclosed garden ▸ **jardin d'enfants** kindergarten ▸ **jardin à la française** formal garden ▸ **le jardin des Hespérides** the garden of Hesperides ▸ **jardin d'hiver** [château] winter garden; [maison] conservatory ▸ **jardin japonais** Japanese garden ▸ **le jardin des Oliviers** (Bible) the Garden of Gethsemane ▸ **jardins ouvriers** small plots of land rented out for gardening, allotments (Brit) ▸ **jardin potager** vegetable ou kitchen garden ▸ **jardin public** (public) park, public gardens ▸ **jardin de rapport†** market garden ▸ **jardins suspendus** terraced gardens, hanging gardens; **les ~s suspendus de Babylone** the hanging gardens of Babylon ▸ **jardin zoologique = jardin d'acclimatation**

jardinage [ʒaʀdinaʒ] NM (gén) gardening; (Sylviculture) selective harvesting, selection; **faire du ~** to garden, do some gardening

jardiner [ʒaʀdine] ▸conjug 1◂ [1] VI to garden, do some gardening [2] VT [+ forêt] to manage

jardinerie [ʒaʀdinʀi] NF garden centre

jardinet [ʒaʀdinɛ] NM small garden; **les ~s des pavillons de banlieue** the small gardens ou the little patches of garden round suburban houses

jardinier, -ière [ʒaʀdinje, jɛʀ] [1] ADJ Japanese (épith); **culture jardinière** horticulture; **plantes jardinières** garden plants [2] NM,F gardener [3] **jardinière** NF [a] (= caisse à fleurs) window box; (d'intérieur) jardinière [b] (Culin) **jardinière (de légumes)** mixed vegetables, jardinière [c] (Scol) **jardinière d'enfants** kindergarten teacher

jargon [ʒaʀgɔ̃] NM [a] (= baragouin) gibberish (NonC), double Dutch* (NonC) (Brit) [b] (= langue professionnelle) jargon (NonC), lingo* (NonC); **~ administratif** officialese (NonC), official jargon; **~ informatique** computerese* (NonC); **~ journalistique** journalese (NonC); **~ médical** medical jargon; **~ de métier** trade jargon ou slang; (Jur) **~ du palais** legal jargon, legalese (NonC)

jargonner [ʒaʀgɔne] ▸conjug 1◂ VI (= utiliser un jargon) to talk in ou use jargon; (péj) to talk gibberish

Jarnac [ʒaʀnak] N **coup de ~** stab in the back

jarre [ʒaʀ] NF (earthenware) jar

jarret [ʒaʀɛ] NM (Anat) [homme] back of the knee, ham; [animal] hock; **avoir des ~s d'acier** to have strong legs [b] (Culin) **~ de veau** knuckle ou shin of veal, veal shank (US)

jarretelle [ʒaʀtɛl] NF suspender (Brit), garter (US)

jarretière [ʒaʀtjɛʀ] NF garter → **ordre¹**

jars [ʒaʀ] NM (Zool) gander

jaser [ʒaze] ▸conjug 1◂ VI [a] [enfant] to chatter, prattle; [personne] to chat away, chat on*; [oiseau] to chatter, twitter; [jet d'eau, ruisseau] to babble, sing; **on entend ~ la pie/le geai** you can hear the magpie/the jay chattering [b] (arg Police) to talk, sing‡; **essayer de faire ~ qn** to try to make sb talk [c] (= médire) to gossip; **cela va faire ~ les gens** that'll set tongues wagging, that'll set people talking ou gossiping

jaseur, -euse [ʒazœʀ, øz] [1] ADJ [enfant] chattering (épith), prattling (épith); [oiseau] chattering (épith), twittering (épith); [ruisseau, jet d'eau] babbling (épith), singing (épith); [personne] (= médisant) gossipy, tittle-tattling (épith) (Brit) [2] NM [a] (= bavard) gasbag*, chatterbox; (= médisant) gossip, tittle-tattle [b] (Zool) waxwing

jasmin [ʒasmɛ̃] NM (= arbuste) jasmine; (= parfum) **(essence de) ~** jasmine (perfume)

jaspe [ʒasp] NM (= pierre) jasper; (= objet) jasper ornament; **~ sanguin** bloodstone

jaspé, e [ʒaspe] ADJ mottled, marbled

jaspiner‡ [ʒaspine] ▸conjug 1◂ VI to chatter, natter* (Brit)

jatte [ʒat] NF (shallow) bowl, basin

jauge [ʒoʒ] NF [a] (= instrument) gauge; **~ d'essence** petrol gauge; **~ (de niveau) d'huile** (oil) dipstick [b] (= capacité) [réservoir] capacity; [navire] tonnage, burden; (Tex) tension [c] (Agr) trench; **mettre en ~** to heel in

jaugeage [ʒoʒaʒ] NM [navire, réservoir] gauging

jauger [ʒoʒe] ▸conjug 3◂ [1] VT [a] [+ réservoir] to gauge the capacity of; [+ navire] to measure the tonnage of [b] [+ personne] to size up; **il le jaugea du regard** he looked him up and down; **~ qn d'un coup d'œil** to size sb up at a glance [2] VI to have a capacity of; **navire qui jauge 500 tonneaux** ship with a tonnage of 500, ship of 500 tonnes ou tons burden

jaunasse* [ʒonas] ADJ (péj) yellowish, dirty yellow (épith)

jaunâtre [ʒonatʀ] ADJ [+ lumière, couleur] yellowish; [teint] sallow, yellowish

jaune [ʒon] [1] ADJ [couleur, dents] yellow; (littér) [blés] golden; **il a le teint ~** (mauvaise mine) he looks yellow ou sallow; (basané) he has a sallow complexion; **~ d'or** golden yellow; **~ comme un citron** ou **un coing** as yellow as a lemon → **corps, fièvre, nain, péril** [2] NM [a] (= couleur) yellow [b] (Culin) **~ (d'œuf)** (egg) yolk [c] (* = pastis) pastis [3] NMF [a] (*‡, injurieux) **Jaune** Asian; (= Chinoise) Chink‡‡ (injurieux); (= Japonaise) Jap‡‡ (injurieux), Nip‡‡ (injurieux) [b] (péj = non-gréviste) scab‡, blackleg (Brit)

jaunet, -ette [ʒonɛ, ɛt] [1] ADJ slightly yellow, yellowish [2] NM†† gold coin

jaunir [ʒoniʀ] ▸conjug 2◂ [1] VT [+ feuillage, vêtements] to turn yellow; **doigts jaunis par la nicotine** nicotine-stained fingers, fingers stained yellow with nicotine; **photos jaunies** yellowed photos [2] VI to yellow, turn ou become yellow

jaunissant, e [ʒonisɑ̃, ɑ̃t] ADJ (littér) [papier, feuillage] yellowing; [blé] ripening, yellowing (littér)

jaunisse [ʒonis] NF (Méd) jaundice; **en faire une ~*** (de dépit) to be pretty miffed*; (de jalousie) to be ou turn green with envy; **tu ne vas pas nous en faire une ~!*** you're not going to get all huffy*, are you?

jaunissement [ʒonismɑ̃] NM yellowing

Java [ʒava] NF Java

java [ʒava] NF (= *danse*) popular waltz; **faire la ~**‡ to live it up*, have a rave-up*‡ (*Brit*); **ils ont fait une de ces ~s** they had a really wild time* *ou* a real rave-up*‡ (*Brit*)

javanais, e [ʒavanɛ, ɛz] [1] ADJ Javanese [2] NM (*Ling*) Javanese; (= *argot*) *slang formed by adding "av" before each vowel of a word*; (= *charabia*) gibberish, double Dutch* (*Brit*) [3] **Javanais(e)** NM,F Javanese

Javel [ʒavɛl] NF (**eau de**) **~** bleach

javeline [ʒavlin] NF javelin

javelle [ʒavɛl] NF (*céréales*) swath; **mettre en ~s** to lay in swaths

javellisation [ʒavelizasjɔ̃] NF chlorination

javelliser [ʒavelize] ▶conjug 1◀ VT to chlorinate; **cette eau est trop javellisée** there's too much chlorine in this water; **eau très javellisée** heavily chlorinated water

javelot [ʒavlo] NM (*Mil, Sport*) javelin → **lancement**

jazz [dʒaz] NM jazz; **la musique (de) ~** jazz (music)

jazzman [dʒazman] (*pl* **jazzmen** [dʒazmɛn]) NM jazzman, jazz musician

jazzy [dʒazi] ADJ INV [*musique*] jazz-style (*épith*), jazzy; [*musicien*] jazz-style (*épith*); **une version ~ de leur chanson** a jazz version of their song

J.-C. (ABRÉV = **Jésus-Christ**) **en (l'an) 300 av./ap. ~** in (the year) 300 BC/AD

je, j' [ʒ(ə)] [1] PRON PERS I [2] NM **le je** (*Ling*) the I-form, the 1st person singular; (*Philo*) the I

Jean [ʒɑ̃] NM John; (**saint**) **~-Baptiste** (St) John the Baptist; (**saint**) **~ de la Croix** St John of the Cross; **~ sans Terre** John Lackland; **c'est ~ qui rit et ~ qui pleure** one minute he's laughing, the next minute he's crying

jean [dʒin] NM (= *tissu*) denim; (= *vêtement*) (pair of) jeans, (pair of) denims; **~ (de ou en) velours** cord(uroy) jeans; **blouson en ~ vert** green denim jacket; **être en ~(s)** to be wearing jeans

jean-foutre* [ʒɑ̃futʀ] NM INV (*péj*) jackass (*péj*)

Jeanne [ʒan] NF Jane, Joan, Jean; **~ d'Arc** Joan of Arc; **coiffure à la ~ d'Arc** page boy (haircut)

jeannette [ʒanɛt] NF [a] (**croix à la**) **~** gold cross (*worn around neck*) [b] (= *planche à repasser*) sleeve-board [c] (*Scoutisme*) Brownie (Guide)

Jeannot [ʒano] NM Johnny; **~ lapin** bunny (rabbit), Mr Rabbit

Jeep® [(d)ʒip] NF Jeep®

Jéhovah [ʒeova] NM Jehovah → **témoin**

jéjunum [ʒeʒynɔm] NM jejunum

je-m'en-fichisme* [ʒ(ə)mɑ̃fiʃism] NM (I-) couldn't-care-less attitude*

je-m'en-fichiste* (*pl* **je-m'en-fichistes**) [ʒ(ə)mɑ̃fiʃist] [1] ADJ couldn't-care-less* (*épith*); **il est trop ~** he's got too much of a couldn't-care-less* attitude [2] NMF couldn't-care-less type*

je-m'en-foutisme: [ʒ(ə)mɑ̃futism] NM (I-) couldn't-give-a-damn attitude*

je-m'en-foutiste: (*pl* **je-m'en-foutistes**) [ʒ(ə)mɑ̃futist] [1] ADJ (I-)couldn't-give-a-damn* (*épith*) [2] NMF (I-)couldn't-give-a-damn type*

je-ne-sais-quoi, je ne sais quoi [ʒə-n(ə)sɛkwa] NM INV (certain) something; **elle a un ~ qui attire** there's (a certain) something about her that's very attractive, she has a certain je-ne-sais-quoi *ou* a certain indefinable charm; **cette journée avait un ~ d'inhabituel** there was something unusual about today

jenny [ʒeni] NF spinning jenny

jérémiades* [ʒeʀemjad] NFPL moaning, whining

Jérémie [ʒeʀemi] NM (= *prophète*) Jeremiah

Jéricho [ʒeʀiko] N Jericho

jéroboam [ʒeʀɔbɔam] NM [a] (= *bouteille*) jeroboam (*bottle containing 3 litres*) [b] (*Bible*) **Jéroboam** Jeroboam

jerricane, jerrycan [(d)ʒeʀikan] NM jerry can

Jersey [ʒɛʀze] NF Jersey

jersey [ʒɛʀze] NM [a] (= *vêtement*) jersey top (*ou garment etc*), sweater, jumper (*Brit*) [b] (= *tissu*) (cloth); **~ de laine/de soie** jersey wool/silk; **point de ~** stocking stitch; **tricoter un pull en ~** to knit a jumper in stocking stitch

jersiais, e [ʒɛʀzje, jez] [1] ADJ Jersey (*épith*), of *ou* from Jersey; (*Agr*) **race ~e** Jersey breed; (**vache**) **~e** Jersey (cow) [2] **Jersiais(e)** NM,F inhabitant *ou* native of Jersey

Jérusalem [ʒeʀyzalɛm] N Jerusalem; **la ~ nouvelle/céleste** the New/Heavenly Jerusalem

jésuite [ʒezɥit] ADJ, NM (*Rel, péj*) Jesuit

jésuitique [ʒezɥitik] ADJ (*lit, péj*) Jesuitical

jésuitisme [ʒezɥitism] NM Jesuitism, Jesuitry

jésus [ʒezy] NM [a] **Jésus** (*prénom*) Jesus; **le petit Jésus** the baby *ou* infant Jesus; **Jésus-Christ** Jesus Christ; **en 300 avant/après Jésus-Christ** in 300 BC/AD; **doux Jésus !*** sweet Jesus!* [b] (= *statue*) statue of the infant Jesus [c] (= *terme d'affection*) **mon ~** (my) darling [d] (= *saucisson*) kind of pork sausage [e] (**papier**) **~** super royal (printing paper); (**papier**) **petit ~** super royal (writing paper)

jet¹ [ʒɛ] [1] NM [a] (= *jaillissement*) [*eau, gaz, flamme*] jet; [*sang*] spurt, gush; [*salive*] stream; [*pompe*] flow; **~ de lumière** beam of light [b] [*pierre, grenade*] (= *action*) throwing; (= *résultat*) throw; **à un ~ de pierre** a stone's throw away; **un ~ de 60 mètres au disque** a 60-metre discus throw; (*Boxe*) **il a gagné par ~ de l'éponge au troisième round** he won because his opponent's corner threw in the towel in the third round → **arme** [c] (*loc*) **premier ~** [*lettre, livre*] first *ou* rough draft; [*dessin*] first *ou* rough sketch; **du premier ~** at the first attempt; **écrire d'un (seul) ~** to write in one go; **à ~ continu** in a continuous *ou* an endless stream [d] (*Tech* = *coulage*) casting; **couler une pièce d'un seul ~** to produce a piece in a single casting [e] (*Bot* = *pousse*) main shoot; (= *rameau*) branch [2] COMP ▶ **jet d'eau** (= *fontaine*) fountain; (= *gerbe*) spray; (*au bout d'un tuyau*) nozzle; (*Archit*) weathering ▶ **jet à la mer** (*Naut*) jettison(ing)

jet² [dʒɛt] NM (*Aviat*) jet

jetable [ʒ(ə)tabl] ADJ [*briquet, mouchoir, rasoir*] disposable; (**appareil-photo**) **~** disposable camera

jeté, e¹ [ʒ(ə)te] [1] ADJ (‡ = *fou*) mad*, crazy* [2] NM (*Danse*) **~ (simple)** jeté; **~ battu** grand jeté [b] (*Sport*) jerk [c] (*Tricot*) **~ (simple)** make one; **faire un ~** to drop a stitch [3] COMP ▶ **jeté de canapé** throw ▶ **jeté de lit** bedspread ▶ **jeté de table** table runner

jetée² [ʒ(ə)te] NF jetty; (*grande*) pier; **~ flottante** floating bridge

jeter [ʒ(ə)te] ▶conjug 4◀ [1] VT [a] (= *lancer*) to throw; (*avec force*) to fling, hurl, sling; [+ *dés*] to throw; **~ qch à qn** (*pour qu'il l'attrape*) to throw sth to sb; (*agressivement*) to throw *ou* fling *ou* hurl sth at sb; **~ qn/qch à l'eau** (*de la rive*) to throw sb/sth into the water; (*d'un bateau*) to throw sb/sth overboard; (*Naut*) **le navire a été jeté à la côte** the ship was driven towards the coast; **elle lui a jeté son cadeau à la figure** *ou* **à la tête** she threw *ou* hurled his present at him; (*Naut*) **~ à la mer** *ou* **par-dessus bord** [+ *personne*] to throw overboard; [+ *objet*] to throw overboard, jettison; (*littér*) **~ bas** [+ *statue, gouvernement*] to topple; **~ qn à**

terre *ou* **à bas** [*cheval*] to throw sb; **il a jeté son camion contre un arbre** he crashed his truck *ou* lorry (*Brit*) into a tree, his truck *ou* lorry (*Brit*) careered into a tree; **~ dehors** *ou* **à la porte** [+ *visiteur*] to throw out, chuck out* (*Brit*); [+ *employé*] to fire, sack (*Brit*); **~ qn en prison** to throw *ou* cast sb into prison; **~ qch par la fenêtre** to throw sth out of the window; **~ sa cigarette/un papier par terre** to throw one's cigarette/a piece of paper on the ground; **il a jeté sa serviette/son sac par terre** he threw down his towel/his bag; **les gens qui jettent leurs papiers par terre** people who drop litter; **il a jeté son agresseur par** *ou* **à terre** he threw his attacker on the ground; **n'en jetez plus (la cour est pleine)!*** (*après compliments*) don't! *ou* stop it! you're embarrassing me!; (*après injures etc*) cut it out!*, pack it in!* (*Brit*) → **ancre, bébé, dévolu, rue** *etc*

[b] (= *mettre au rebut*) [+ *papiers, objets*] to throw away *ou* out; (*Cartes*) to discard; **~ qch au panier/à la poubelle/au feu** to throw sth into the wastepaper basket/in the dustbin/in *ou* on the fire; **jette l'eau sale dans l'évier** pour *ou* tip the dirty water down the sink; (*hum*) **il n'y a rien à ~*** it (*ou* he *etc*) can't be faulted; **se faire ~‡** (*d'une réunion, entreprise*) to get thrown out, get chucked‡ (*Brit*) (**de** of); (*lors d'une requête, déclaration d'amour*) to be sent packing* → **bon¹**

[c] (= *construire*) [+ *pont*] to throw (**sur** over, across); [+ *fondations*] to lay; (*fig*) **~ les bases d'une nouvelle Europe** to lay the foundations of a new Europe; (*Naut*) **jetez la passerelle !** set up the gangway!

[d] (= *émettre*) [+ *lueur*] to give out, cast, shed; [+ *ombre*] to cast; [+ *son*] to let out, give out; [+ *cri*] to utter, let out; **il en jette, dans son smoking !‡** he's a knockout* *ou* he looks a million dollars* in his dinner jacket!; **ce nouveau tapis dans le salon, ça en jette‡** the new carpet in the sitting room looks really great*; **elle (en) jette, cette voiture !*** that's some car!* → **feu¹**

[e] (= *mettre rapidement*) **~ des vêtements dans un sac** to sling *ou* throw some clothes into a bag; **va ~ cette carte à la boîte** go and pop* this card into the postbox; **~ une veste sur ses épaules** to slip a jacket over *ou* round one's shoulders; **~ une idée sur le papier** to jot down an idea

[f] (= *plonger*) to plunge, throw; **~ qn dans le désespoir** to plunge sb into despair; **~ qn dans l'embarras** to throw sb into confusion; **il a jeté son pays dans la guerre** he plunged his country into war

[g] (= *répandre*) to cast; **~ l'effroi chez/parmi** to sow alarm and confusion in/among; **~ le trouble dans les esprits** (= *perturber*) to disturb *ou* trouble people; (= *rendre perplexe*) to sow confusion in people's minds; **sa remarque a jeté un froid** his remark put a damper on things *ou* cast a chill over the company → **discrédit, sort**

[h] (= *dire* à *to*); **« dépêche-toi ! »**, **me jeta-t-il en passant** "hurry up!", he called out to me as he went by; **~ des remarques dans la conversation** to throw in *ou* toss in remarks; **~ des insultes/menaces** to hurl insults/threats; **je lui ai jeté la vérité/l'accusation à la figure** *ou* **à la tête** I hurled *ou* flung the truth/accusation at him; **il lui jeta à la tête qu'il n'était qu'un imbécile** he told him to his face that he was nothing but a fool; **il nous jette à la tête ses relations/ses diplômes** he's always trying to impress us with *ou* always harping on* to us about the important people he knows/all the qualifications he's got

[i] (*mouvement du corps*) **~ les épaules/la tête en avant** to throw *ou* thrust one's shoulders/one's head forward; **~ les bras autour du cou de qn** to throw *ou* fling one's arms round sb's

neck; **elle lui jeta un regard plein de mépris** she cast a withering look at him, she looked *ou* glanced witheringly at him → **œil**

2 **se jeter** VPR **a** (= *s'élancer*) **se ~ par la fenêtre/du douzième étage** to throw o.s. out of the window/from the twelfth floor; **se ~ à l'eau** (*lit*) to launch o.s. *ou* plunge into the water; (*fig*) to take the plunge; **se ~ à la tête de qn** to throw o.s. at sb; **se ~ dans les bras/aux pieds de qn** to throw o.s. into sb's arms/ at sb's feet; **sa voiture s'est jetée contre un arbre** his car crashed into a tree; **un chien s'est jeté sous mes roues** a dog rushed out under the wheels of my car; **il s'est jeté sous un train** he threw himself under *ou* in front of a train; **se ~ sur qn** to rush at sb; **se ~ sur sa proie** to swoop down *ou* pounce on one's prey; **il se jeta sur la nourriture comme un affamé** he fell (up)on the food like a starving man; **se ~ sur** [+ *lit*] to throw *ou* fling o.s. onto; [+ *téléphone*] to rush to; [+ *journal, roman*] to pounce on; [+ *occasion, solution*] to jump at; **se ~ dans la politique/les affaires** to launch o.s. into politics/business → **corps, cou, genou**

b (= *se déverser*) [*rivière*] to flow (dans into); **le Rhône se jette dans la Méditerranée** the Rhone flows into the Mediterranean

c (= *se lancer*) [+ *pierres, ballon*] to throw *ou* hurl at each other; **ils se jetèrent des injures à la tête** they hurled insults at each other

d (‡ = *boire*) **on va s'en ~ un (derrière la cravate)** we'll have a quick one*; **on va s'en ~ un dernier** we'll have one for the road*

e (*sens passif*) **ça se jette** it's disposable, you can throw it away (once you've used it)

jeteur [ʒ(ə)tœʀ] NM **~ de sort** wizard

jeteuse [ʒ(ə)tøz] NF **~ de sort** witch

jeton [ʒ(ə)tɔ̃] NM **a** (= *pièce*) (*gén*) token; (*Jeux*) counter; (*Roulette*) chip; **~ de téléphone** telephone token; **~ (de présence)** (= *argent*) director's fees; (= *objet*) token; (= *somme*) **toucher ses ~s** to draw one's fees → **faux‡ b** ‡ (= *coup*) bang; (= *marque*) dent; **ma voiture a pris un ~** my car was dented; **avoir les ~s** to have the jitters* *ou* the willies‡; **ça lui a fichu les ~s** it gave him the jitters* *ou* the willies‡

jet-set (*pl* **jet-sets**) [dʒɛsɛt] NM *ou* F, **jet-society** [dʒɛtsɔsajti] NF jet set; **membre de la ~** jet setter

jeu (*pl* **jeux**) [ʒø] **1** NM **a** (= *amusement, divertissement*) **le ~** play; **l'enfant s'éduque par le ~** the child learns through play; (*fig*) **le ~ du soleil sur l'eau** the play of the sunlight on the water; **c'est un ~ d'enfant** it's child's play, it's a snap* (*US*); **il s'est fait un ~ de résoudre ce problème** he made light work of the problem; **par ~** for fun; **il critiquait tout, comme par ~** he criticized everything as if it was some kind of game

b (*gén avec règles*) game; **~ d'intérieur/de plein air** indoor/outdoor game; **~ d'adresse** game of skill; **~ de cartes** card game; **~ d'échecs/de quilles** the game of chess/of skittles; (*Rugby*) **~ à 13/15** rugby league/union; **le ~ de la vérité** the truth game; **quel ~ de cons !** how bloody*! (*Brit*) *ou* goddam* (*US*) stupid!; **c'est le ~** it's fair (play); **ce n'est pas de *ou* du ~** that's not (playing) fair; **ce n'est qu'un ~** it's just a game; **ce n'est qu'un ~ de l'esprit** it's just a mental exercise; **le ~ n'en vaut pas la chandelle** the game is not worth the candle ▪ (*PROV*) **~x de main(s), ~x de vilain(s)!** stop fooling around or it will end in tears! → **jouer**

c (*Sport* = *partie*) game; (*Tennis*) **il mène (par) 5 ~x à 2** he leads (by) 5 games to 2; **« ~, set, et match »** "game, set and match"; **la pluie a ralenti le ~** the rain slowed down play (in the game); **faire ~ égal avec qn** to be evenly matched

d (*Sport* = *terrain*) **~ de boules** (*sur sol nu*) area *where boules is played*; (*sur gazon*) bowling green; **~ de quilles** skittle alley; **la balle est**

sortie du **~** the ball has gone out of play → **hors**

e (*Casino*) gambling; **il a perdu toute sa fortune au ~** he has gambled away his entire fortune, he lost his fortune (at) gambling; **« faites vos ~x »** "place your bets"; **les ~x sont faits** (*Casino*) les jeux sont faits; (*fig*) the die is cast; **~x de tirage** lotteries, draws; **~x de grattage** scratch-card games → **heureux**

f (= *ensemble des pions, boîte*) game, set; **~ d'échecs/de boules/de quilles** chess/bowls/ skittle set; **~ de 52 cartes** pack *ou* deck (*US*) of 52 cards

g (= *série complète*) [*clés, aiguilles*] set; **~ d'orgue(s)** organ stop

h (= *cartes*) hand; **il laisse voir son ~** he shows his hand; **je n'ai jamais de ~** I never have a good hand; **le grand ~** (*aux tarots*) the major arcana; (*fig*) **sortir le grand ~** to pull out all the stops; **il a beau ~ de protester maintenant** it's easy for him to complain now → **cacher**

i (= *façon de jouer*) (*Sport*) game; (*Mus*) technique, (manner of) playing; (*Ciné, Théât*) acting; (*Sport*) **il a un ~ rapide/lent/efficace** he plays a fast/a slow/an effective game; (*Rugby*) **pratiquer un ~ ouvert** to keep the game open; (*Mus*) **elle a un ~ saccadé/dur** she plays jerkily/harshly, her playing is jerky/harsh

j (= *fonctionnement*) (*Admin, Pol etc*) working, interaction, interplay; (*Tech*) play; **le ~ des pistons** the play of the pistons; **le ~ des alliances/des institutions** the interplay of alliances/of institutions; **le marché est régulé par le ~ de l'offre et de la demande** the market is regulated by (the interplay between) supply and demand; **fausser le ~ de la concurrence** to restrict *ou* hamper the free play of competition

k (= *stratégie, manège*) game; **j'ai compris son petit ~!** I know his little game *ou* what he's up to!; **à quel ~ joues-tu?** what are you playing at?; **c'est un ~ de dupes** it's a fool's *ou* mug's* (*Brit*) game; **entrer *ou* marcher dans le ~ de qn** to go *ou* play along with sb, play sb's game; **faire *ou* jouer le ~ de qn** to play into sb's hands; **je vois clair *ou* je lis dans son ~** I know his little game, I know what he's playing at *ou* what he's up to; **il s'est piqué *ou* pris au ~** he really got into it*, he got hooked*; **il a été pris à son propre ~** he was caught out at his own game → **bascule, double**

l (= *espace*) **donner du ~ à qch** to loosen sth up a bit; **la vis a pris du ~** the screw has worked loose; **la porte ne ferme pas bien, il y a du ~** the door isn't a tight fit

2 **en jeu** LOC ADV **a** (*Sport*) in play; **mettre *ou* remettre en ~** to throw in; **mise en ~** (*Tennis*) serve; (*Hockey*) bully-off; (*sur glace*) face-off; **remise en ~** throw-in

b (= *en action*) **les forces en ~** the forces at work; **entrer/mettre en ~** to come/bring into play; **mise en ~** [*facteur, élément*] bringing into play; [*mécanisme*] activation, bringing into operation

c (= *en cause*) **être en ~** to be at stake; **les intérêts/les sommes en ~ sont considérables** there are considerable interests/sums of money at stake; **il mettra tout en ~ pour nous aider** he'll risk everything *ou* stake his all to help us

3 COMP ► **jeu d'arcade** video game ► **jeu blanc** (*Tennis*) love game ► **jeux du cirque** (*Hist*) circus games ► **jeu de construction** building *ou* construction set ► **jeu décisif** (*Tennis*) tie-break, tiebreaker ► **jeux d'eau** fountains ► **jeu d'écritures** (*Comm*) dummy entry ► **jeu électronique** electronic game ► **jeu d'entreprise** business *ou* management game ► **jeu de hasard** game of chance ► **jeu de jambes** (*Sport*) footwork, leg movement ► **jeux de lumière** (*artificiels*) lighting effects; (*naturels*) play of light (*NonC*) ► **jeu de mains** [*pianiste*] playing, technique

► **jeu de massacre** (*à la foire*) Aunt Sally; (*fig*) wholesale massacre *ou* slaughter ► **jeu de mots** play on words (*NonC*), pun ► **jeu de l'oie** ≈ snakes and ladders ► **Jeux olympiques** Olympic games, Olympics; **les Jeux olympiques d'hiver** the Winter Olympics; **Jeux olympiques handisports *ou* pour handicapés** Paralympics ► **jeu de patience** puzzle ► **jeux de physionomie** facial expressions ► **jeu de piste** treasure hunt ► **jeu radiophonique** radio game ► **jeu de rôles** role play ► **jeu de scène** (*Théât*) stage business (*NonC*) ► **jeu des sept erreurs** (game of) spot the difference ► **jeu de société** (*charades, portrait etc*) parlour game; (*Monopoly, Scrabble etc*) board game ► **jeux du stade** (*Hist*) (ancient) Olympic games ► **jeu de stratégie** game of strategy ► **jeu télévisé** television game; (*avec questions*) (television) quiz ► **jeu vidéo** video game

jeu-concours (*pl* **jeux-concours**) [ʒøkɔ̃kuʀ] NM (*Presse, Radio, TV*) competition; (*avec questions*) quiz

jeudi [ʒødi] NM Thursday; **le ~ de l'Ascension** Ascension Day → **saint**; *pour autres locutions voir* **samedi**

jeun [ʒœ̃] ◆ **à jeun** LOC ADV **être à ~** (= *n'avoir rien mangé*) to have eaten nothing; (= *n'avoir rien bu*) to have drunk nothing; (= *ne pas être ivre*) to be sober; **boire à ~** to drink on an empty stomach; (*Méd*) **à prendre à ~** to be taken on an empty stomach; **venez à ~** don't eat or drink anything before you come

jeune [ʒœn] **1** ADJ **a** (*en années*) young; **homme ~** young man; **~ chien** young dog; **mes ~s années** the years of my youth; **dans mon ~ âge *ou* temps** in my youth, when I was young; **vu son ~ âge** in view of his youth; **il n'est plus tout *ou* très ~** he's not as young as he used to be, he's not in his first youth; **il est plus ~ que moi de cinq ans** he's five years younger than me, he's five years my junior; **ils font ~(s)** they look young; **il fait plus ~ que son âge** he doesn't look his age, he looks younger than he is; **cette coiffure la fait paraître plus ~** that hairstyle makes her look young

b (*après nom*) [*apparence, visage*] youthful; [*couleur, vêtement*] young, which makes one look young; **soyez/restez ~s!** be/stay young! *ou* youthful!; **être ~ d'allure** to be young-looking, be youthful in appearance; **être ~ de caractère *ou* d'esprit** (*puéril*) to have a childish outlook, be immature; (*dynamique*) to have a young *ou* youthful outlook; **être ~ de cœur** to be young at heart; **être ~ de corps** to have a youthful figure

c (= *récent*) [*industrie, science, vin*] young

d (= *inexpérimenté*) raw, inexperienced, green*; **il est encore bien ~** he's still very inexperienced; **être ~ dans le métier** to be new *ou* a newcomer to the trade

e (= *cadet*) junior; **mon ~ frère** my younger brother; **mon plus ~ frère** my youngest brother; **Durand ~** Durand junior

f (* = *insuffisant*) short, skimpy; **ça fait ~** ◊ **c'est un peu ~** [*temps*] it's cutting it a bit short *ou* fine; [*argent*] that's not much; [*tissu*] it's not (going to be) enough; [*boisson, nourriture*] there's not enough to go round

2 NM **a** (= *personne*) youngster, youth, young man; **un petit ~** a young lad; **les ~s de maintenant *ou* d'aujourd'hui** young people *ou* the young *ou* the youth of today; **club *ou* maison de ~s** youth club

b (= *animal*) young animal

c (*loc*) **donner un coup de ~ à** (* [+ *bâtiment, local*] to give a face-lift to, freshen up; [+ *émission*] to give a new look to; **ils ont donné un coup de ~ au cinéma australien** they've breathed new life into Australian cinema

3 NF girl; **une petite ~** a young girl

4 ADV **s'habiller ~** to dress young for one's age; **se coiffer ~** to have a young *ou* modern hairstyle

5 COMP ► **jeune femme** young woman ► **jeune fille** girl ► **jeune garçon** boy, young lad* ► **jeune génération** younger generation ► **jeunes gens** (*gén*) young people; (= *garçons*) boys ► **jeune homme** young man ► **jeune loup** (*gén*) go-getter; (= *politicien*) young Turk ► **jeune marié** bridegroom; **les ~s mariés** the newlyweds; **un couple de ~s mariés** a couple of newlyweds ► **jeune mariée** bride ► **jeune premier** (*Ciné, Théât*) romantic male lead; **il a un physique** *ou* **une tête de ~ premier** he has film-star looks; **il veut encore jouer les ~s premiers** he still thinks he can play young roles ► **jeune première** (*Ciné, Théât*) romantic female lead

jeûne [ʒøn] NM fast; **rompre le ~** to break one's fast; **jour de ~** fast day; **faire un ~ de trois jours** to fast for three days

jeûner [ʒøne] ▸ conjug 1 ◂ VI (*gén*) to go without food; (*Rel*) to fast; **faire ~ un malade** to make a sick person go without food; **laisser ~ ses enfants** to let one's children go hungry

jeunesse [ʒœnɛs] NF **a** (= *période*) youth; (*littér*) **la ~ du monde** the dawn of the world; **en pleine ~** in the prime of youth; **dans ma ~** in my youth, in my younger days; **folie/erreur/péché de ~** youthful prank/mistake/indiscretion; **je n'ai pas eu de ~** I didn't have much of a childhood; **en raison de son extrême ~** owing to his extreme youth; **il n'est plus de la première ~** he's not as young as he was *ou* as he used to be, he's not in the first flush of youth ■ (*PROV*) **il faut que ~ se passe** youth must have its fling → **œuvre**
b (= *qualité*) youth, youthfulness; **~ de cœur** youthfulness of heart; **la ~ de son visage/de son corps** his youthful face/figure; **avoir un air de ~** to have a youthful look; **~ d'esprit** youthfulness of mind
c (= *personnes jeunes*) youth, young people; **la ~ dorée** the young jet set; **la ~ ouvrière** (the) young workers; **la ~ étudiante/des écoles** young people at university/at school; **livres pour la ~** books for the young *ou* for young people; **la ~ est partie devant** the young ones *ou* the young people have gone on ahead ■ (*PROV*) **si ~ savait, si vieillesse pouvait** if youth but knew, if old age but could → **auberge, voyage**
d (**† = jeune fille*) (young) girl
e (*gén pl = groupe*) youth; **les ~s communistes** the Communist Youth Movement

jeunet, -ette* [ʒœnɛ, ɛt] ADJ (*péj*) rather young; **il est un peu ~ pour lire ce roman** he's rather young *ou* he's a bit on the young side to be reading this novel

jeûneur, -euse [ʒønœʀ, øz] NM,F person who fasts *ou* is fasting

jeunot, -otte* [ʒœno, ɔt] **1** ADJ = **jeunet 2** NM young fellow*

jf **a** (ABRÉV = **jeune fille**) → **jeune b** (ABRÉV = **jeune femme**) → **jeune**

jh (ABRÉV = **jeune homme**) → **jeune**

jihad [ʒi(j)ad] NM = **djihad**

jiu-jitsu [ʒjyʒitsy] NM jujitsu, jiujitsu

JO [ʒio] **1** NMPL (ABRÉV = **Jeux olympiques**) Olympics **2** NM (ABRÉV = **Journal officiel**) → **journal**

joaillerie [ʒɔajʀi] NF **a** (= *travail*) jewellery (*Brit*) *ou* jewelry (*US*) making; (= *commerce*) jewellery (*Brit*) *ou* jewelry (*US*) trade; **travailler dans la ~** to work in jewellery *ou* in the jewel trade **b** (= *marchandise*) jewellery (*Brit*), jewelry (*US*) **c** (= *magasin*) jeweller's (*Brit*), jeweler's (*US*) (shop)

joaillier, -ière [ʒɔaje, jɛʀ] NM,F jeweller

Job [ʒɔb] NM (*Rel*) Job → **pauvre**

job [ʒɔb] **1** NM (** = travail*) job; **il a trouvé un**

petit ~ pour l'été he's found a summer job **2** NF (*Can*) job

jobard, e* [ʒɔbaʀ, aʀd] **1** ADJ gullible **2** NM,F (= *dupe*) sucker*, mug* (*Brit*)

jobarderie* [ʒɔbaʀd(ə)ʀi], **jobardise*** [ʒɔbaʀdiz] NF gullibility

jobiste [(d)ʒɔbist] NMF (*Belg*) student who does part-time jobs

jockey [ʒɔkɛ] NM jockey → **régime**

Joconde [ʒɔkɔ̃d] NF **la ~** the Mona Lisa

jocrisse † [ʒɔkʀis] NM (= *niais*) simpleton

jodhpur(s) [dʒɔdpyʀ] NM(PL) jodhpurs

jodler [ʒɔdle] ▸ conjug 1 ◂ VT to yodel

joggeur, -euse [dʒɔɡœʀ, øz] NM,F jogger

jogging [dʒɔɡiŋ] NM (= *sport*) jogging; (= *survêtement*) jogging suit, sweatsuit (*surtout US*); **faire du ~** to go jogging; **il faisait son ~ dans le parc** he was jogging in the park; **je fais mon ~ tous les jours** I go for a jog *ou* I go jogging every day

▼ **joie** [ʒwa] **1** NF **a** (= *sentiment*) joy; (*sens diminué*) pleasure; **à ma grande ~** to my great joy *ou* delight; **fou** *ou* **ivre de ~** wild with joy; **la nouvelle le mit au comble de la ~** he was overjoyed at hearing the news *ou* to hear the news; **accueillir la nouvelle avec une ~ bruyante** to greet the news with great shouts of joy; **ses enfants sont sa plus grande ~** his children are his greatest delight *ou* joy; **c'était une ~ de le regarder** it was a joy *ou* delight to look at him, he was a joy to look at; **quand aurons-nous la ~ de vous revoir ?** when shall we have the pleasure of seeing you again?; **il accepta avec ~** he accepted with delight; **sauter** *ou* **bondir de ~** to jump for joy; (*souvent iro*) **on travaille dans la ~ et la bonne humeur ici** it's a real joy to work here → **cœur, feu¹, fille**
b (*loc*) **~ de vivre** joie de vivre, joy of life; **être plein de ~ de vivre** to be full of joie de vivre *ou* the joys of life; **cela le mit en ~** he was overjoyed; **ce livre a fait la ~ de tous** this book has delighted *ou* has given great pleasure to everyone; **le clown tomba pour la plus grande ~ des enfants** the clown fell over to the (great) delight of the children; **il se faisait une telle ~ d'y aller** he was so looking forward to going; **je me ferai une ~ de le faire** I shall be delighted *ou* too pleased to do it; **c'est pas la ~ !*** it's no fun!

2 joies NFPL **les ~s de la vie** the joys of life; (*Rel*) **les ~s du monde** *ou* **de la terre** worldly *ou* earthly pleasures *ou* joys; **les ~s du mariage** the joys of marriage; (*iro*) **encore une panne, ce sont les ~s de la voiture !** another breakdown, that's one of the joys *ou* delights of motoring! (*iro*)

joignable [ʒwaɲabl] ADJ **être difficilement ~** to be difficult to reach *ou* contact; **il est ~ à tous moments** he can be reached at any time

▼ **joindre** [ʒwɛ̃dʀ] ▸ conjug 49 ◂ **1** VT **a** (= *mettre ensemble*) to join, put together; **~ deux tables/planches** to put two tables/planks together; **~ un bout de ficelle à un autre** to join one piece of string to another; **~ les mains** to put *ou* bring one's hands together, clasp one's hands; **~ les talons/les pieds** to put one's heels/one's feet together; **les mains jointes** with his (*ou* her *etc*) hands together
b (= *relier*) to join, link; **une digue/un câble joint l'île au continent** a dyke/a cable links the island with the mainland
c (= *unir*) [+ *efforts*] to combine, join; **~ l'utile à l'agréable** to combine business with pleasure; **elle joint l'intelligence à la beauté** she combines intelligence and beauty; **~ le geste à la parole** to act in accordance with what one says, match one's action to one's words; **~ les deux bouts*** to make (both) ends meet
d (= *ajouter*) to add, attach (**à** to); (= *inclure*) [+ *timbre, chèque*] to enclose (**à** with); **les avantages joints à ce poste** the advantages at-

tached to this post, the fringe benefits of this post; **carte jointe à un bouquet/cadeau** card attached to a bouquet/a gift; **pièces jointes** [*lettre*] enclosures
e (= *contacter*) [+ *personne*] to get in touch with, contact; **essayez de le ~ par téléphone** try to get in touch with *ou* try to get hold of *ou* try to contact him by telephone

2 VI [*fenêtre, porte*] to shut, close; **ces fenêtres joignent mal** these windows don't shut *ou* close properly; **est-ce que ça joint bien ?** [*planches*] does it make a good join?, does it join well?

3 **se joindre** VPR **a** (= *s'unir à*) **se ~ à** to join; **se ~ à la procession** to join the procession; **se ~ à la foule** to mingle *ou* mix with the crowd; **voulez-vous vous ~ à nous ?** would you like to join us?; **se ~ à la discussion** to join in the discussion; **mon mari se joint à moi pour vous exprimer notre sympathie** my husband and I wish to express our sympathy, my husband joins me in offering our sympathy (*frm*)
b [*mains*] to join

joint¹ [ʒwɛ̃] NM **a** (*Anat, Géol, Tech*) (= *assemblage, articulation*) joint; (= *ligne de jonction*) join; (*en ciment*) pointing; **~ de cardan** cardan joint; **~ de culasse** cylinder head gasket; **~ d'étanchéité** seal; **~ de robinet** washer **b** (*loc*) **faire le ~*** (*en provisions*) to last *ou* hold out; (*en argent*) to bridge the gap (**jusqu'à** until); **chercher/trouver le ~*** to look (around) for/find the answer

joint²* [ʒwɛ̃] NM (*Drogue*) joint*, reefer*, spliff*; **se faire** *ou* **se rouler un ~** to roll (o.s.) a joint* *ou* a reefer* *ou* a spliff*

jointé, e [ʒwɛ̃te] ADJ **cheval court-~/long-~** short-/long-pasterned horse, horse with short/long pasterns

jointif, -ive [ʒwɛ̃tif, iv] ADJ joined, contiguous; [*planches*] butt-jointed; **(cloison) jointive** butt-jointed partition

jointoyer [ʒwɛ̃twaje] ▸ conjug 8 ◂ VT (*Tech*) to point; **des murs de pierre grossièrement jointoyés** stone walls with rather crudely-finished pointing

jointure [ʒwɛ̃tyʀ] NF **a** (*Anat*) joint; **~ du genou** knee joint; **à la ~ du poignet** at the wrist (joint); **faire craquer ses ~s** to crack one's knuckles; **à la ~ de deux os** at the joint between two bones; **~s** [*cheval*] fetlock-joints **b** (*Tech*) (= *assemblage*) joint; (= *ligne de jonction*) join

joint-venture, joint venture (*pl* **joint(-)ventures**) [dʒɔjntvɛntʃœʀ] NF joint venture

jojo* [ʒoʒo] **1** ADJ [*personne, objet*] **il est pas ~** he's (*ou* it's) not much to look at **2** NM **affreux ~** (= *enfant*) little horror; (= *adulte*) nasty piece of work*

jojoba [ʒɔʒɔba] NM jojoba; **huile de ~** jojoba oil

joker [(d)ʒɔkɛʀ] NM (*Cartes*) joker; (*Ordin*) wild card; **jouer** *ou* **sortir** *ou* **utiliser son ~** (*lit*) to play one's joker; (*fig*) to play one's trump card

joli, e [ʒɔli] ADJ **a** [*enfant, femme*] pretty, attractive; [*chanson, objet*] pretty, nice; [*pensée, promenade, appartement*] nice; **d'ici, la vue est très ~e** you get a very nice view from here; **~ comme un cœur** (as) pretty as a picture; **il est ~ garçon** he's quite good-looking
b (** = non négligeable*) [*revenu, profit*] nice (*épith*), good, handsome (*épith*); [*résultat*] nice (*épith*), good; **ça fait une ~e somme** it's quite a tidy sum; **il a une ~e situation** he has a good position
c (*iro*) **embarquez tout ce ~ monde !** take the whole nasty bunch *ou* crew away!; **un ~ coco*** *ou* **monsieur** a nasty character, a nasty piece of work*
d (*loc*) **tout ça c'est bien ~ mais ...** that's all very well *ou* fine but ...; (*iro*) **vous avez fait du**

~! you've made a fine mess of things!; (iro) **tu as encore menti, c'est du ~!** you've lied again — shame on you!*; **faire le ~ cœur** to play the ladykiller; **ce n'était pas ~ à voir** it wasn't a pretty sight!; (iro) **elle est ~e, votre idée!** that's a great idea! (iro); (iro) **c'est ~ de dire du mal des gens!** that's nice, spreading nasty gossip about people! (iro); **c'est pas ~~!*** (laid) it's not a pretty sight*; (méchant) that wasn't very nice*

joliesse [ʒɔljɛs] NF (littér) [personne] prettiness; [gestes] grace

joliment [ʒɔlimɑ̃] ADV **a** (= élégamment) [décoré, habillé] nicely; (iro) **il l'a ~ arrangé!** he sorted him out nicely ou good and proper!* **b** (* = très, beaucoup) really; **il était ~ content/en retard** he was really glad/late

Jonas [ʒɔnas] NM Jonah, Jonas

jonc [ʒɔ̃] NM **a** (= plante) rush, bulrush; (= canne) cane, rattan; **corbeille ou panier de ~** rush basket **b** (Aut) trim **c** ~ **(d'or)** (= bracelet) (plain gold) bangle; (= bague) (plain gold) ring

jonchée [ʒɔ̃ʃe] NF swath; **des ~s de feuilles mortes couvraient la pelouse** dead leaves lay in drifts on ou lay scattered ou strewn over the lawn

joncher [ʒɔ̃ʃe] ▸ conjug 1 ◂ VT [papiers] to litter, be strewn over; [cadavres, détritus, fleurs] to be strewn over; **jonché de** littered ou strewn with

jonchets [ʒɔ̃ʃɛ] NMPL jackstraws, spillikins

jonction [ʒɔ̃ksjɔ̃] NF (= action) joining, junction; (= état) junction; (Élec) junction; **à la ~ des deux routes** at the junction of the two roads, where the two roads meet; (Mil) **opérer une ~** to effect a junction, link up; **point de ~** junction, meeting point; (Jur) **~ d'instance** joinder

jongler [ʒɔ̃gle] ▸ conjug 1 ◂ VI (lit) to juggle (**avec** with); **~ avec** [+ dates, emplois du temps, chiffres] to juggle (with); [+ difficultés] to juggle

jonglerie [ʒɔ̃gləʀi] NF juggling

jongleur, -euse [ʒɔ̃glœʀ, øz] NM,F **a** (gén) juggler **b** (Hist) jongleur

jonque [ʒɔ̃k] NF (Naut) junk

jonquille [ʒɔ̃kij] **1** NF daffodil, jonquil **2** ADJ INV daffodil yellow

Jordanie [ʒɔʀdani] NF Jordan

jordanien, -ienne [ʒɔʀdanjɛ̃, jɛn] **1** ADJ Jordanian **2** **Jordanien(ne)** NM,F Jordanian

Joseph [ʒozɛf] NM Joseph

Josué [ʒozɥe] NM Joshua

jouable [ʒwabl] ADJ playable; **ce sera difficile, mais c'est ~** [projet] it'll be difficult, but it's worth a try ou a go

jouasse: [ʒwas] ADJ pleased as Punch*, chuffed* (Brit); **il n'était pas ~!** he wasn't too thrilled!

joue [ʒu] NF **a** (Anat) cheek; **~ contre ~** cheek to cheek; **tendre la ~** to offer one's cheek; **présenter ou tendre l'autre ~** to turn the other cheek; (Culin) **~ de bœuf** ox cheek **b** (Mil) **en ~!** take aim!; **coucher ou mettre une cible/qn en ~** to aim at ou take aim at a target/sb; **coucher ou mettre en ~ un fusil** to take aim with a rifle, aim a rifle; **tenir qn en ~** to keep one's gun trained on sb **c** (Naut) **~s d'un navire** bows of a ship

---

jouer [ʒwe]

▸ conjug 1 ◂

1 VERBE INTRANSITIF　　**3** VERBE TRANSITIF
2 VERBE TRANSITIF　　　**4** VERBE PRONOMINAL
　　INDIR

1 VERBE INTRANSITIF

a = s'amuser to play (**avec** with) **arrête, je ne joue plus** stop it, I'm not playing any more; **faire qch pour ~** to do sth for fun; (= manipuler) **elle jouait avec son crayon/son collier**

---

she was toying ou fiddling with her pencil/her necklace; **~ avec les sentiments de qn** to play ou trifle with sb's feelings; (= mettre en danger) **~ avec sa vie/sa santé** to gamble with one's life/one's health; **~ avec le feu** (lit, fig) to play with fire; (fig) **on ne joue pas avec ces choses-là** matters like these are not to be treated lightly → **cour**

♦ **jouer à** : **~ à la poupée** to play with one's dolls; **~ au golf/au ping-pong/aux cartes/aux échecs** to play golf/table tennis/cards/chess; **~ aux soldats/aux cowboys et aux Indiens** to play (at) soldiers/(at) cowboys and Indians; **~ au docteur (et au malade)** to play (at) doctors and nurses; **~ à qui sautera le plus loin** to see who can jump the furthest); (fig) **à quoi joues-tu ?** what are you playing at?; **n'essaie pas de ~ au plus fin ou malin avec moi** don't try to outsmart me; **~ au con:** to mess about*, arse around** (Brit) → **bille**

b = pratiquer un jeu, un sport **il joue bien/mal (au tennis)** he is a good/poor (tennis) player, he plays (tennis) well/badly; **il a vraiment bien joué** he played an excellent game, he played really well; **~ contre qn/une équipe** to play (against) sb/a team; **à qui de ~ ?** whose go ou turn is it?; **à vous** (ou **moi** etc) **de ~!** (lit, fig) your (ou my etc) go! ou turn!; (Échecs) your (ou my etc) move!; **bien joué!** (lit) well played!; (fig) well done!; (Tennis) **~ petit bras** to play underarm; **~ serré** to play (it) tight, play a close game; **~ perdant/gagnant** to play a losing/winning game

c Mus to play; **l'orchestre joue ce soir à l'opéra** the orchestra is playing at the opera this evening; **ce pianiste joue bien/mal** this pianist plays well/badly

d pour de l'argent (Casino) to gamble; **~ pair/impair** to play (on) the even/odd numbers; **~ aux courses** to bet on the horses; **~ à la ou en Bourse** to speculate ou gamble on the Stock Exchange

e Ciné, Théât, TV to act; **il joue dans « Hamlet »** he's acting ou he's in "Hamlet"; **il joue au théâtre des Mathurins** he's playing ou acting at the théâtre des Mathurins; **elle joue très bien/mal** she is a very good/bad ou poor actress, she acts very well/badly; **elle a très bien joué Juliette** she gave an excellent performance as Juliet; **la troupe va ~ à Avignon** the company is going to perform in Avignon → **guichet**

♦ **jouer sur** : **~ sur les mots** to play with words; (= spéculer sur) **ils ont joué sur votre inquiétude** they took advantage of the fact that you were worried; **~ sur l'effet de surprise** to use the element of surprise; **il joue sur la fibre nationaliste** he is playing on nationalist feeling ou exploiting nationalist sentiment; **il a réussi en jouant sur les différences de législations** he succeeded by exploiting differences in legislation → **velours**

g = fonctionner to work; **la clé joue dans la serrure** the key turns in the lock; **la clé joue mal dans la serrure** the key doesn't fit (in) the lock very well; **faire ~ un ressort** to activate ou trigger a spring; **la barque jouait sur son ancre** the boat bobbed about at anchor

h = joindre mal [pièce, cheville] to fit loosely, be loose; (= travailler) [bois] to warp

i = bouger [soleil, lumière] to play; **la lumière jouait au plafond** the light played ou danced on the ceiling

j = intervenir, s'appliquer to apply (pour to); **l'âge ne joue pas** age doesn't come into it ou is of no consequence; **cet argument joue à plein** this argument is entirely applicable; **cette augmentation joue pour tout le monde** this rise applies to ou covers everybody; **l'augmentation**

---

joue depuis le début de l'année the rise has been operative from ou since the beginning of the year; **ses relations ont joué pour beaucoup dans la décision** his connections counted for a lot in the decision; **cet élément a joué en ma faveur/contre moi** this factor worked in my favour/against me; **le temps joue contre lui** ou is not on his side; **faire ~** [+ clause de sauvegarde] to invoke; **les distributeurs font ~ la concurrence** the distributors are playing the competitors off against each other; **il a fait ~ ses appuis politiques pour obtenir ce poste** he made use of his political connections to get this post

2 **jouer de** VERBE TRANSITIF INDIR

a Mus **~ d'un instrument/du piano/de la guitare** to play an instrument/the piano/the guitar

b = manier to make use of, use; **~ de l'éventail** to play with one's fan; **ils durent ~ du couteau/du revolver pour s'enfuir** they had to use knives/revolvers to get away; **ils jouent trop facilement du couteau** they are too quick with their knives, they use knives too readily; (hum) **~ de la fourchette** to dig in*, tuck in* (Brit); (= se servir de) **~ des jambes*** ou **des flûtes:** to leg it:, hare off*; **~ des coudes pour arriver au buffet/pour entrer** to elbow one's way to the buffet/one's way in → **prunelle**

c = utiliser to use, make use of; **il sait ~ de l'espace et des couleurs** he knows how to use ou how to make use of space and colour; **~ de son influence/charme pour obtenir qch** to use ou make use of one's influence/charm to get sth; **il joue de sa maladie pour ne rien faire** he plays on his illness to get out of doing anything

d = être victime de **~ de malheur** ou **de malchance** to be dogged by ill luck

3 VERBE TRANSITIF

a Ciné, Théât [+ rôle] to play, act; [+ pièce, film] to put on, show; **on joue « Macbeth » ce soir** "Macbeth" is on ou is being played this evening; **elle joue toujours les soubrettes** she always plays the maid's part; (fig) **~ la fille de l'air** to vanish into thin air; (hum : reproche) **qu'est-ce que tu nous joues, là ?** what are you playing at? → **comédie, rôle**

b = simuler **~ les héros/les victimes** to play the hero/the victim; **~ la surprise/le désespoir** to pretend to be surprised/in despair, affect ou feign surprise/despair; **~ un double jeu** to play a double game

c

♦ **jouer un (mauvais) tour à qn** to play a (dirty) trick on sb; **mes yeux me jouent des tours** my eyes are playing tricks on me; **cela te jouera un mauvais** ou **vilain tour** you'll get your comeuppance*, you'll be sorry for it

d Mus [+ concerto, valse] to play; **il va ~ du Bach** he's going to play (some) Bach; **il joue très mal Chopin** he plays Chopin very badly

e Jeux, Sport [+ partie d'échecs, de tennis] to play; [+ carte] to play; [+ pion] to play, move; (Ftbl) **il est interdit de ~ le ballon à la main** it is forbidden to handle the ball; (Rugby) **il préfère ~ le ballon à la main** he prefers to run the ball; **jouez le ballon plutôt que l'adversaire** play the ball, not your opponent; **~ un coup facile/difficile** (Sport) to play an easy/a difficult shot; (Échecs) to make an easy/a difficult move; (fig) **~ la montre** to play for time, kill the clock (US); **il faut ~ le jeu** you've got to play the game; **ils ont refusé de ~ le jeu** they refused to play ball* ou to play the game; **~ franc jeu** to play fair → **atout**

f = mettre en jeu (Casino) [+ argent] to stake, wager; (Courses) [+ argent] to bet, stake (**sur** on); [+ cheval] to back, bet on; (fig) [+ fortune, possessions, réputation] to wager; **~ gros jeu** ou **un jeu d'enfer** to play for high stakes; **il ne joue que des petites sommes** he only places small bets ou plays for small stakes; **il a joué et perdu une fortune** he gambled away a fortune; (Pol) **~ son mandat/son ministère sur qch** to stake

jouet — 497 — jour

one's re-election prospects/one's ministerial position on sth; (fig) **dans cette histoire, il joue sa tête/sa réputation** he's risking his neck/his reputation in this affair; (fig) **rien n'est encore joué** (= décidé) nothing is settled ou decided yet, there's still everything to play for → gros, tout, va-tout

g Bourse = investir dans ~ **les financières/les pétrolières** to speculate in financials/oil

h frm = tromper [+ personne] to deceive, dupe

i = opter pour ~ **la prudence/la sécurité** to be cautious/play safe → carte

4 **se jouer** VERBE PRONOMINAL

a mutuellement **ils se jouent des tours** they're playing tricks on each other

b = être joué **ce jeu se joue à quatre** this is a game for four people, you need four people to play this game; **la pièce se joue au théâtre des Mathurins** the play is on at the théâtre des Mathurins; (fig) **le drame s'est joué très rapidement** the tragedy happened very quickly

c = être décidé **tout va se ~ demain** everything will be settled ou decided tomorrow; **l'avenir de l'entreprise va se ~ sur cette décision** the future of the company hinges ou depends on this decision; **c'est l'avenir de l'entreprise qui se joue** the future of the company is at stake; **son sort se joue en ce moment** his fate is hanging in the balance at the moment

d
♦ **se jouer de** (frm)
(= tromper) **se ~ de qn** to deceive sb, dupe sb
(= se moquer de) **se ~ des lois/de la justice** to scoff at the law/at justice
(= triompher facilement de) **se ~ des difficultés** to make light of the difficulties; (ellipt) **il fait tout cela (comme) en se jouant** he makes child's play of it all

e littér [vent, lumière] to play

jouet [ʒwɛ] NM **a** [enfant] toy **b** (= victime) plaything; **il n'était qu'un ~ entre leurs mains** he was just a plaything in their hands; **être le ~ des vagues/des événements/de rivalités politiques** to be at the mercy of the waves/of events/of rivalries between political parties; **être le ~ d'une hallucination** to be the victim of a hallucination

joueur, joueuse [ʒwœʀ, ʒwøz] **1** ADJ [enfant, animal] playful; **il a un tempérament ~** ◊ **il est très ~** [enfant, animal] he loves to play, he's very playful; [parieur] he loves to gamble, he's a keen gambler **2** NM,F (Échecs, Mus, Sport) player; (Jeux) gambler; **~ de cricket** cricketer; **~ de golf** golfer; **~ de cornemuse** (bag)piper; **~ de cartes** card player; **être beau/mauvais ~** to be a good/bad loser; **sois beau ~!** be a sport!; **il faut être beau ~** it's important to be a good loser

joufflu, e [ʒufly] ADJ [personne] chubby-cheeked, round-faced; [visage] chubby

joug [ʒu] NM **a** (Agr, fig) yoke; **tomber sous le ~ de** to come under the yoke of; **mettre sous le ~** to yoke, put under the yoke **b** [balance] beam **c** (Antiq) yoke

jouir [ʒwiʀ] ▶ conjug 2 ◀ **1** **jouir de** VT INDIR **a** (frm) [+ autorité, réputation, liberté] to enjoy; (Jur) [+ bien] to enjoy the use of; **~ de toutes ses facultés** to be in full possession of one's faculties; **la région jouit d'un bon climat** the region has ou enjoys a good climate; **cette pièce jouit d'une superbe vue** the room has a magnificent view **b** (= savourer) [+ vie] to enjoy; **il jouissait de leur embarras évident** he delighted in ou enjoyed their obvious embarrassment **2** VI **a** (*: plaisir sexuel) to have an orgasm, come*; **ça me fait ~ de les voir s'empoigner** I get a (real) kick out of seeing them at each other's throats* **b** (*: douleur) to suffer agonies; **on va ~!** we're going to

have a hell of a time!‡; **we aren't half going to have fun!*

jouissance [ʒwisɑ̃s] NF **a** (= volupté) pleasure, enjoyment, delight; (sensuelle) sensual pleasure; (= orgasme) orgasm, climax; (frm) **cela lui a procuré une vive ~** this afforded him intense pleasure **b** (Jur = usage) use, possession; [propriété, bien] use, enjoyment; **avoir la ~ de certains droits** to enjoy certain rights

jouisseur, -euse [ʒwisœʀ, øz] **1** ADJ sensual **2** NM,F sensualist

jouissif, -ive‡ [ʒwisif, iv] ADJ fun, great fun (attrib)

joujou (pl **joujoux**) [ʒuʒu] NM (langage enfantin) toy; (* = revolver) gun; **cette voiture est son nouveau ~** this car is his new toy; **faire ~ avec** to play with; (fig) **il ne faut pas faire ~ avec ça** that's not a toy

joule [ʒul] NM joule

jour [ʒuʀ]

| **1** NOM MASCULIN | **3** COMPOSÉS |
| **2** NOM MASCULIN PL | |

1 NOM MASCULIN

a = espace de temps day; **dans deux ~s** in two days' time, in two days; **c'était il y a deux ~s** it was two days ago; (à prendre) **trois fois par ~** (to be taken) three times a day; **des poussins d'un ~** day-old chicks; (fig) **d'un ~** [célébrité, joie] short-lived, fleeting; **c'est à deux ~s de marche/de voiture de ...** it's a two-day walk/drive from ...; **faire 30 ~s (de prison)** to do 30 days (in jail)* ■ (PROV) **les ~s se suivent et ne se ressemblent pas** time goes by and every day is different, the days go by and each is different from the last → compter, huit, quinze

♦ **au jour le jour** [existence, gestion] day-to-day (épith); (Fin) **taux d'intérêt ou loyer de l'argent au ~ le** call-money rate; **vivre au ~ le ~** (= sans soucis) to live from day to day; (= pauvrement) to live from hand to mouth; **il gère la situation au ~ le ~** he's dealing with the situation on a day-by-day basis

♦ **de jour en jour** day by day, from day to day

♦ **du jour au lendemain** overnight; **ça ne se fera pas du ~ au lendemain** it won't happen overnight

♦ **d'un jour à l'autre** (= incessamment) on l'attend d'un ~ à l'autre he's expected any day (now); (= très rapidement) **il change d'avis d'un ~ à l'autre** he changes his mind from one day to the next

♦ **jour après jour** day after day, day in day out

♦ **jour par jour** day by day

b = époque précise day; **quel ~ sommes-nous ?** what day is it today?; **ce ~-là** that day; **le ~ de Noël/de Pâques** Christmas/Easter Day; **par un ~ de pluie/de vent** on a rainy/windy day; **le ~ précédent ou d'avant** the day before, the previous day; **le ~ suivant ou d'après** the day after, the next day, the following day; **l'autre ~** the other day; **un ~ il lui écrivit** one day he wrote to her; **un beau ~** (passé) one (fine) day; (futur) one of these (fine) days, one (fine) day; **le grand ~ approche** the big day ou D-day is drawing nearer; **le ~ où tu sauras conduire, tu m'emmèneras** you can take me there the day you learn to drive; **un ~ viendra où ...** a day will come when ...; **le ~ n'est pas loin où ...** the day is not far off when ...; **premier ~** [vacances, mois etc] first day; [exposition] opening ou first day; (Philat) **enveloppe premier ~** first day cover; **ils s'aiment comme au premier ~** they're still as much in love as ever; **dès le premier ~** from day one, from the outset ou beginning; **être dans un bon/mauvais ~** to be in a good/bad mood; **il est dans (un de) ses bons ~s/ses mauvais ~s** he's having a good spell/a bad spell, it's one of his good/his bad days; (iro) **décidément c'est mon ~ !** I'm having

a real day of it today!, really it's just not my day today!; **il y a des ~s avec et des ~s sans** there are good days and bad days; **ce n'est vraiment pas le ~ !** you've (ou we've etc) picked the wrong day!; **prendre ~ avec qn** to fix a day with sb, make a date with sb → autre

♦ **à ce jour** to date; **il n'existe à ce ~ aucun traitement efficace** no effective treatment has been found to date ou up to now

♦ **au jour d'aujourd'hui** (†, hum) in this day and age

♦ **du jour**: **un œuf du ~** a new-laid egg, a freshly-laid egg; **les nouvelles du ~** the news of the day, the day's news; **le héros du ~** the hero of the day ou hour; **l'homme du ~** the man of the moment; **le mode du ~** the fashion of the day; **il a remis ces vieilles chansons au goût du ~** he's done modern versions of these old songs → cours, ordre, plat²

♦ **du jour où ...** from the day that ...; **du ~ où sa femme l'a quitté, il s'est mis à boire** he started drinking the day his wife left him

♦ **jour pour jour**: **il y a deux ans ~ pour ~** two years ago to the day

♦ **tous les jours** every day; **cela arrive tous les ~s** it happens every day, it's an everyday occurrence; **tous les deux ~s** every other day, every two days; **tous les ~s que (le bon) Dieu fait** every blessed day; **de tous les ~s** everyday (épith), ordinary; **la vie de tous les ~s** in everyday life; **mon manteau de tous les ~s** my everyday ou ordinary coat

♦ **un de ces jours** one of these (fine) days; **à un de ces ~s!** see you again sometime!, be seeing you!*

♦ **un jour ou l'autre** sometime or other, sooner or later

c
♦ **à jour**: **être/mettre/tenir à ~** [+ liste, comptes, notes] to be/bring/keep up to date; **remettre à ~ un catalogue** to update a catalogue, bring a catalogue up to date; **ce tarif n'est plus à ~** this price list is out of date; **se mettre à ~ dans son travail** to catch up with one's work; **mise à ~** (= action) updating; (= résultat) update; **la mise à ~ d'un compte/d'un dossier** the updating of an account/of a file; **la mise à ~ d'un dictionnaire** the revision ou updating of a dictionary; (Ordin) **programme de mise à ~** update routine; **il est/n'est pas à ~ de sa cotisation** he's up to date with/behind with his subscription

d = lumière day(light); **il fait ~** it's daylight; **demain, il fera ~ à 7 h** tomorrow it'll be ou it'll get light at 7; **un faible ~ filtrait à travers les volets** a faint light filtered through the shutters; **le ~ entra à flots** daylight streamed ou flooded in; **le ~ tombe ou baisse** it's getting dark; **avoir le ~ dans les yeux** to have the light in one's eyes; **tes deux enfants, c'est le ~ et la nuit** your two children are as different as night and day ou chalk and cheese (Brit); **ça va mieux avec le nouveau produit ? — c'est le ~ et la nuit !** is it better with this new product? — there's absolutely no comparison!

e = période où le soleil éclaire day(time); **de ~ comme de nuit** night and day; **je fais ça le ~** I do it during the day ou in the daytime; **se lever avant le ~** to get up ou rise before dawn ou daybreak ■ (PROV) **à la Sainte Luce, les ~s augmentent ou croissent du saut d'une puce** Lucy light, the shortest day and the longest night (PROV) → grand, lumière, plein

♦ **au petit jour** at dawn ou daybreak

♦ **de jour** [crème, équipe, service] day (épith); **hôpital de ~** (pour traitement) outpatient clinic; (Psych) day hospital; (pour activités) day-care centre; **être de ~** to be on day duty; **il travaille de ~, cette semaine** he's on day shifts ou he's working days this week; **voyager de ~** to travel by day

♦ **jour et nuit** night and day; **ils ont travaillé ~ et nuit pour préparer le bateau** they worked day and night ou night and day ou round the clock to get the boat ready

[f] [fig = éclairage] light; montrer/présenter/voir qch sous un ~ favorable/flatteur to show/present/see sth in a favourable/flattering light; jeter un ~ nouveau sur to throw (a) new light on; se présenter sous un ~ favorable [projet] to look promising ou hopeful; [personne] to show o.s. to advantage ou in a favourable light; nous voyons le problème sous un autre ~ we can see the problem in a different light; nous le voyons maintenant sous son véritable ~ now we see him in his true colours ou see what he is really like; mettre au ~ (= révéler) to bring to light; se faire ~ (= apparaître) to become clear, come out; la vérité se fit ~ dans mon esprit the truth dawned on me ou became clear to me → faux², grand

[g] [= symbole de de la naissance] donner le ~ à to give birth to, bring into the world; voir le ~ [enfant] to be born, come into the world; [projet] to see the light, come into being

[h] [= ouverture] [mur] gap, chink; [haie] gap; clôture à ~ openwork fence

[i] [Couture] ~ simple openwork, drawn-threadwork; drap à ~s sheet with an openwork border; faire des ~s dans un drap/dans un mouchoir to hemstitch a sheet/a handkerchief

2 jours NOM MASCULIN PL

[a] [= période] time, days; la fuite des ~s the swift passage of time; il faut attendre des ~s meilleurs we must wait for better times ou days; nous avons connu des ~s difficiles we've been through hard times; nous gardons cela pour les mauvais ~s we're keeping that for a rainy day ou for hard times; aux beaux ~s in (the) summertime; (fig) il y a encore de beaux ~s pour les escrocs there are good times ahead for crooks; (fig) ces vedettes ont fait les beaux ~s de Broadway these stars made Broadway what it was; (iro) comme aux plus beaux ~s de la dictature just like in the good old days of the dictatorship (iro); du Moyen Âge à nos ~s from the Middle Ages right up until today

♦ **ces jours-ci** (passé) il a fait très beau ces ~s-ci the weather's been very fine lately ou these last few days; (futur) elle doit arriver ces ~s-ci she'll be here any day now; (présent) ceux qui veulent prendre l'avion ces ~s-ci people wanting to fly now ou at this time

♦ **de nos jours** these days, nowadays, in this day and age

[b] [= vie] days, life; jusqu'à la fin de mes ~s until I die; finir ses ~s à l'hôpital to end one's days in hospital; attenter à/mettre fin à ses ~s to make an attempt on/put an end to one's life; nous gardons cela pour nos vieux ~s we're keeping that for our old age; sur ses vieux ~s, il était devenu sourd he had gone deaf in his old age → couler

3 COMPOSÉS

► le jour de l'An New Year's Day ► jour d'arrêt (Mil) day of detention; donner huit ~s d'arrêt to give a week's detention ► jour de congé day off, holiday ► jour de deuil day of mourning ► jour férié public holiday ► jour de fête feastday, holiday ► le jour J D-day ► jour de maladie day off sick ► jour mobile discretionary holiday (granted by company, boss etc) ► le jour des Morts All Souls' Day ► jour ouvrable weekday, working day ► jour ouvré working day ► jour des prix (†, Scol) prize (giving) day ► jour de réception (Admin) day of opening (to the public); [dame du monde] "at home" day; le ~ de réception du directeur est le lundi the director is available to see people on Mondays ► jour de repos [salarié] day off; après deux ~s de repos, il est reparti after taking a two-day break, he set off again ► le jour des Rois Epiphany, Twelfth Night ► le jour du Seigneur Sunday, the Sabbath† ► jour de sortie [domestique] day

off, day out; [élève] day out ► jour de travail working day

Jourdain [ʒuʀdɛ̃] NM (= fleuve) le ~ the (river) Jordan

journal (pl -aux) [ʒuʀnal, o] **1** NM [a] (Presse) (news)paper; (= magazine) magazine; (= bulletin) journal; (= bureaux) je suis passé au ~ I dropped by at the office ou paper; dans ou sur le ~ in the (news)paper; ~ local local paper; grand ~ national paper ou daily; ~ du matin/du soir morning/evening paper → papier
[b] (TV, Radio) news (bulletin); le ~ de 20 h the 8 o'clock news
[c] (= recueil) diary, journal; tenir un ou son ~ intime to keep a private ou personal diary

2 COMP ► journal de bord (Naut) (ship's) log, log book; (Aviat) flight log; (fig) record; tenir un ~ de bord to keep a log ► journal électronique electronic newspaper ► journal d'enfants ou pour enfants children's paper ► journal interne in-house newsletter ► journal littéraire literary journal ► journal lumineux electronic noticeboard ► journal de mode fashion magazine ► le Journal officiel (de la République française) official bulletin giving details of laws and official announcements, ≈ the Gazette (Brit), ≈ The Congressional Record (US) ► journal parlé (Radio) radio news ► journal sportif sports magazine ► journal télévisé (TV) television news

┌──────────────────┐
│ **JOURNAUX** │
└──────────────────┘

The main French national daily newspapers are Le Monde (centre-left), Libération (centre-left) and Le Figaro (right)."Le Canard Enchaîné" is an influential satirical weekly famous for uncovering political scandals. There is also a thriving regional press, with prominent newspapers published in all the major provincial cities. The best-selling newspaper in the country, Ouest-France, is a regional paper. Although some newspapers are tabloid format, the British and American "tabloid" press has no real equivalent in France.

journaleux* [ʒuʀnalø] NM (péj) hack (journalist) (péj), journo*

journalier, -ière [ʒuʀnalje, jɛʀ] **1** ADJ (= de chaque jour) [travail, trajet, production, pratique] daily (épith); (= banal) [existence] everyday (épith); c'est ~ it happens every day → indemnité **2** NM (Agr) day labourer

journalisme [ʒuʀnalism] NM (= métier, style) journalism; faire du ~ to be in journalism, be a journalist; ~ d'investigation investigative journalism

journaliste [ʒuʀnalist] NMF journalist; ~ sportif/parlementaire sports/parliamentary correspondent; ~ d'investigation investigative journalist; ~ de radio/de télévision radio/television reporter ou journalist; ~ de (la) presse écrite newspaper ou print journalist

journalistique [ʒuʀnalistik] ADJ journalistic; style ~ journalistic style; (péj) journalese

journée [ʒuʀne] NF [a] (= jour) day; dans ou pendant la ~ during the day, in the daytime; dans la ~ d'hier yesterday, in the course of yesterday; passer sa ~/toute sa ~ à faire qch to spend the day/one's entire day doing sth; passer des ~s entières à rêver to daydream for days on end; (= grève) une ~ d'action dans les transports publics a day of action organized by the public transport unions
[b] [ouvrier] ~ (de travail) day's work; ~ (de salaire) day's wages ou pay; faire de dures ~s to put in a heavy day's work; faire des ~s chez les autres† to work as a domestic help ou daily help (Brit); il se fait de bonnes ~s he gets a good day's wage; travailler/être payé à la ~ to work/be paid by the day; faire la ~ continue [bureau, magasin] to remain open over

lunch ou all day; [personne] to work over lunch; ~ de 8 heures 8-hour day; ~ de repos day off, rest day
[c] (= événement) day; ~s d'émeute days of rioting; (Mil) la ~ a été chaude ◊ ce fut une chaude ~ it was a hard struggle ou a stiff fight; ~ d'études (Pol) seminar
[d] (= distance) à trois ~s de voyage/de marche three days' journey/walk away; voyager à petites ~s† to travel in short ou easy stages

journellement [ʒuʀnɛlmɑ̃] ADV (= quotidiennement) daily, every day; (= souvent) all the time

joute [ʒut] NF [a] (Hist Naut) joust, tilt
[b] [politiciens] duel, contest; ~s politiques/électorales political/pre-election sparring ou jousting; ~ oratoire (= compétition) debate; (entre avocats, députés) verbal jousting ou sparring (NonC); ~ d'esprit battle of wits; ~s nautiques water jousting

jouter [ʒute] ▶conjug 1◀ VI (Hist) to joust, tilt; (fig, frm) to joust (contre against), spar (contre with)

jouteur [ʒutœʀ] NM jouster, tilter

jouvence [ʒuvɑ̃s] NF Fontaine de Jouvence Fountain of Youth; eau de ~ waters of youth → bain

jouvenceau (pl jouvenceaux) [ʒuvɑ̃so] NM (††, hum) stripling†, youth

jouvencelle [ʒuvɑ̃sɛl] NF (††, hum) damsel† (hum)

jouxter [ʒukste] ▶conjug 1◀ VT to adjoin, be next to

jovial, e (mpl -iaux ou jovials) [ʒɔvjal, jo] ADJ jovial, jolly; d'humeur ~e in a jovial mood

jovialement [ʒɔvjalmɑ̃] ADV jovially

jovialité [ʒɔvjalite] NF joviality, jollity

jovien, -ienne [ʒɔvjɛ̃, jɛn] ADJ Jovian

joyau (pl joyaux) [ʒwajo] NM (lit, fig) gem, jewel; les ~x de la couronne the crown jewels; ~ de l'art gothique jewel ou masterpiece of Gothic art

joyeusement [ʒwajøzmɑ̃] ADV [célébrer] merrily, joyfully; [accepter] gladly; [crier] joyfully; ils reprirent ~ le travail they cheerfully went back to work

joyeusetés [ʒwajøzte] NFPL (littér ou iro) ce sont les ~ de la vie en couple these are just some of the joys ou pleasures of living together

▼**joyeux, -euse** [ʒwajø, øz] ADJ [a] [personne, groupe] cheerful, merry, joyous; [repas] cheerful; [cris] merry, joyful; [musique] joyful, joyous; [visage] cheerful, joyful; [nouvelle] joyful; c'est un ~ luron ou drille he's a jolly fellow; être en joyeuse compagnie to be in merry company ou with a merry group; mener joyeuse vie to lead a merry life; être d'humeur joyeuse to be in a joyful mood; ils étaient partis ~ they had set out merrily ou in a merry group; il était tout ~ à l'idée de partir he was overjoyed ou (quite) delighted at the idea of going; (iro) ce sera ~!* great!* (iro), brilliant!* (iro); ce n'est pas ~!* [film] it's not very funny; [histoire triste] it's no joke!; le défilé progressait dans un ~ désordre the procession went along in an atmosphere of cheerful chaos
[b] (dans les souhaits) joyeuses fêtes! Happy Christmas! (ou New Year)!; (sur carte) Season's Greetings → anniversaire, noël

JT [ʒite] NM (ABRÉV = journal télévisé) → journal

jubé [ʒybe] NM (= clôture) jube, rood-screen; (= galerie) jube, rood-loft

jubilaire [ʒybilɛʀ] ADJ (Rel) jubilee (épith)

jubilation [ʒybilasjɔ̃] NF jubilation, exultation

jubilatoire [ʒybilatwaʀ] ADJ [spectacle, livre, expérience, humour] exhilarating; il observait leur dispute avec un enthousiasme quasi ~ he felt something akin to jubilation as he watched them quarrel

┌──┐
│ ► GRAMMAIRE ACTIVE: joyeux 50.2, 50.3 │
└──┘

jubilé [ʒybile] NM jubilee

jubiler* [ʒybile] ▶conjug 1◀ VI to be jubilant, gloat (péj)

jucher VT, **se jucher** VPR [ʒyʃe] ▶conjug 1◀ to perch (**sur** on, upon); **juchée sur les épaules de son père** perched on her father's shoulders; **juchée sur des talons aiguilles** teetering on stiletto heels

Juda [ʒyda] NM Judah

judaïque [ʒydaik] ADJ [loi] Judaic; [religion] Jewish

judaïsme [ʒydaism] NM Judaism

judas [ʒyda] NM [a] [porte] spyhole [b] (Bible) **Judas** Judas

Judée [ʒyde] NF Judaea, Judea

judéité [ʒydeite] NF Jewishness

judéo- [ʒydeɔ] PRÉF (dans les mots composés à trait d'union, le préfixe reste invariable) Jewish-; **~catholique** Jewish-Catholic

judéo-allemand, e [ʒydeɔalmɑ̃, ɑ̃d] ADJ German-Jewish

judéo-arabe [ʒydeɔaRab] ADJ, NMF Judeo-Arab, Judaeo-Arab (Brit)

judéo-chrétien, -ienne [ʒydeɔkʀetjɛ̃, jɛn] ADJ, NMF Judeo-Christian, Judaeo-Christian (Brit)

judéo-christianisme [ʒydeɔkʀistjanism] NM Judeo-Christianity, Judaeo-Christianity (Brit)

judiciaire [ʒydisjɛʀ] [1] ADJ judicial; **l'autorité ~** (= concept) the judiciary; (= tribunal) judicial authority; **pouvoir ~** judicial power; **poursuites ~s** judicial ou legal proceedings; **vente ~** sale by order of the court; **enquête ~** judicial inquiry; **actes ~s** judicial documents; **procédure ~** legal procedure; **cette affaire n'a pas eu de suites ~s** there were no legal repercussions to this affair; **de source ~ française, on apprend que ...** from a French legal source we have learned that ... → **casier, erreur, police** etc [2] NM **le ~** the judiciary

judiciairement [ʒydisjɛʀmɑ̃] ADV judicially

judicieusement [ʒydisjøzmɑ̃] ADV judiciously, wisely

judicieux, -ieuse [ʒydisjø, jøz] ADJ [choix, idée, remarque] wise, judicious; [conseils] wise, sound; **faire un emploi ~ de son temps** to use one's time wisely ou judiciously, make judicious use of one's time; **il serait plus ~ de ... il** would be wiser to ...; **ce choix s'est révélé peu ~** it proved (to be) an unfortunate choice, it was an unwise choice

judo [ʒydo] NM judo; **faire du ~** to do judo

judoka [ʒydɔka] NMF judoka

juge [ʒyʒ] [1] NM (Jur, Rel, Sport, fig) judge; **oui, Monsieur le Juge** yes, your Honour; **(madame)/(monsieur) le ~ Ledoux** Mrs/Mr Justice Ledoux; **prendre qn pour ~** to ask sb to be (the) judge; **être bon/mauvais ~** to be a good/bad judge (**en matière de** of); **être à la fois ~ et partie** to be both judge and judged; **je vous fais ~ de tout ceci** I'll let you be the judge (of all this); **se faire ~ de ses propres actes/de qch** to be the judge of one's own actions/of sth; **il est seul ~ en la matière** he is the only one who can judge; **aller devant le ~** to go before the judge; (Bible) **le livre des Juges** the Book of Judges

[2] COMP ▶ **juge de l'application des peines** judge responsible for overseeing the terms and conditions of a prisoner's sentence ▶ **juge aux affaires matrimoniales** divorce court judge ▶ **juge d'arrivée** (Sport) finishing judge ▶ **juge consulaire** judge in a commercial court ▶ **juge de faute de pied** (Tennis) foot-fault judge ▶ **juge des** ou **pour enfants** children's judge, ≈ juvenile court judge ▶ **juge de filet** (Tennis) net cord judge ▶ **juge d'instance** justice of the peace, magistrate ▶ **juge d'instruction** examining ou investigating magistrate ▶ **juge de ligne** (Tennis) (gén) line judge, linesman

(pour ligne de fond) foot-fault judge ▶ **juge de paix**† = juge d'instance ; (fig) **cette épreuve sera le ~ de paix** this test will be the determining factor ou will determine the outcome ▶ **juge de touche** (Rugby) touch judge, linesman; (Ftbl) linesman

jugé [ʒyʒe] ♦ **au jugé** LOC ADV (lit, fig) by guesswork; **tirer au ~** to fire blind; **faire qch au ~** to do sth by guesswork

jugeable [ʒyʒabl] ADJ (Jur) subject to judgment in court; (= évaluable) **difficilement ~** difficult to judge

juge-arbitre (pl **juges-arbitres**) [ʒyʒaRbitR] NM referee

jugement [ʒyʒmɑ̃] NM [a] (Jur = décision, verdict) [affaire criminelle] sentence; [affaire civile] decision, award; **prononcer** ou **rendre un ~** to pass sentence; **passer en ~** to be brought for ou stand trial; **faire passer qn en ~** to put sb on trial; **~ par défaut** judgment by default; **~ déclaratoire** declaratory judgment; **détention sans ~** detention without trial [b] (= opinion) judgment, opinion, **~ de valeur** value judgment; **exprimer/formuler un ~** to express/formulate an opinion; **porter un ~ (sur)** to pass judgment (on); **s'en remettre au ~ de qn** to defer to sb's judgment; **j'ai peur de son ~** I'm afraid of what he'll think (of me) [c] (= discernement) judgment; **avoir du/ manquer de ~** to have/lack (good) judgment; **on peut faire confiance à son ~** you can trust his judgment; **il a une grande sûreté de ~** he has very sound judgment [d] (Rel) judgment; **le ~ de Dieu** Divine Judgment; (Hist) the Ordeal; **le Jugement dernier** the Last Judgment; **le jour du Jugement dernier** Judgment Day, Doomsday; **le ~ de Salomon** the judgment of Solomon

jugeote* [ʒyʒɔt] NF common sense, gumption* (Brit); **manquer de ~** to lack common sense; **il n'a pas deux sous de ~** he hasn't got an ounce of common sense, he's got no gumption* (Brit); **sers-toi un peu de ~!** use your head! ou loaf!*, wise up!‡ (surtout US)

juger[1] [ʒyʒe] ▶conjug 3◀ [1] VT [a] (Jur) [+ affaire] to judge, try; [+ accusé] to try; **~ un différend** to arbitrate in a dispute; **le tribunal jugera** the court will decide; **être jugé pour meurtre** to be tried for murder; **le jury a jugé qu'il n'était pas coupable** the jury found him not guilty; **l'affaire doit se ~ à l'automne** the case is to come before the court ou is to be heard in the autumn; **l'histoire jugera** history will judge [b] (= décider, statuer) to judge, decide; **à vous de ~ (ce qu'il faut faire/si c'est nécessaire)** it's up to you to decide ou to judge (what must be done/whether ou if it's necessary) [c] (= apprécier) [+ livre, film, personne, situation] to judge; **~ qn d'après les résultats** to judge sb on his results; **il ne faut pas ~ d'après les apparences** you must not judge from ou go by appearances; **~ qch/qn à sa juste valeur** to judge sth/sb at its/his real value; **~ bien/mal les gens** to be a good/bad judge of character; **jugez combien j'étais surpris** ou **si ma surprise était grande** imagine how surprised I was ou what a surprise I got [d] (= estimer) **~ qch/qn ridicule** to consider ou find ou think sth/sb ridiculous; **~ que** to think ou consider that; **pourquoi est-ce que vous me jugez mal?** why do you think badly of me?, why do you have such a low opinion of me?; **si vous le jugez bon** if you see fit, if you think it's a good idea ou it's advisable; **~ bon/malhonnête de faire qch** to consider it a good thing ou advisable/dishonest to do sth; **il se jugea perdu** he thought ou considered himself lost; **il se juge capable de le faire** he thinks ou reckons he is capable of doing it; **je n'ai pas jugé utile de le prévenir** I didn't think it was worth telling him (about it)

[2] **juger de** VT INDIR to appreciate, judge; **si j'en juge par mon expérience** judging by ou if I (can) judge by my experience; **à en ~ par ...** judging by ..., to judge by ...; **à en ~ par ce résultat, il ...** if this result is any indication ou anything to go by, he ...; **lui seul peut ~ de l'urgence** only he can appreciate the urgency, only he can tell how urgent it is; **autant que je puisse en ~** as far as I can judge; **jugez de ma surprise !** imagine my surprise!

juger[2] [ʒyʒe] NM = **jugé**

jugulaire [ʒygylɛR] [1] ADJ [veines, glandes] jugular; (†, hum) **il est ~ ~** he's a stickler for the rules [2] NF [a] (Mil) chin strap [b] (Anat) jugular vein

juguler [ʒygyle] ▶conjug 1◀ VT [+ maladie] to arrest, halt; [+ envie, désirs] to suppress, repress; [+ inflation] to curb, stamp out; [+ révolte] to put down, quell

juif, juive [ʒyif, ʒyiv] [1] ADJ Jewish [2] NM Jew; (Littérat) **le Juif errant** the Wandering Jew [3] **juive** NF Jew, Jewish woman

juillet [ʒyije] NM July; **la révolution/monarchie de Juillet** the July revolution/monarchy; pour autres locutions voir **septembre** et **quatorze**

LE QUATORZE JUILLET

Bastille Day, commemorating the fall of the Bastille in 1789, is the most important day of national celebration in France. The festivities actually begin on 13th July, with dances ("bals") organized in the streets of large towns. On the day itself there is a large military parade in Paris in the morning, and firework displays take place throughout France in the evening.

juilletiste [ʒyijetist] NMF July holiday-maker (Brit) ou vacationer (US)

juin [ʒyɛ̃] NM June; pour autres locutions voir **septembre**

juive [ʒyiv] ADJ F, NF → **juif**

juiverie† [ʒyivRi] NF (injurieux) **la ~** the Jews, the Jewish people

jujube [ʒyʒyb] NM (= fruit, pâte) jujube

jujubier [ʒyʒybje] NM jujube (tree)

juke-box (pl **juke-boxes**) [ʒykbɔks] NM jukebox

julep [ʒylɛp] NM julep

jules [ʒyl] NM [a] (†* = amoureux) boyfriend, guy*, bloke* (Brit); (‡ = proxénète) pimp, ponce‡ (Brit) [b] (†* = vase de nuit) chamberpot, jerry‡ (Brit) [c] **Jules** Julius; **Jules César** Julius Caesar

julien, -ienne [ʒyljɛ̃, jɛn] [1] ADJ (Astron) Julian [2] **julienne** NF [a] (Culin) [légumes] julienne; [poisson] ling [b] (Bot) rocket

jumbo-jet (pl **jumbo-jets**) [ʒœmbodʒɛt] NM jumbo jet

jumeau, -elle[1] (mpl **jumeaux**) [ʒymo, ɛl] [1] ADJ [frère, sœur] twin; **c'est mon frère ~** he's my twin (brother); **fruits ~x** double fruits; **maison jumelle** semi-detached house (Brit), duplex (US); **muscles ~x** gastrocnemius sg [2] NM,F [a] (= personne) twin; **vrais/faux ~x** identical/fraternal twins [b] (= sosie) double; **c'est mon ~/ma jumelle** he's/she's my double; **j'aimerais trouver le ~ de ce vase** I'd like to find the partner to this vase [3] NM (Culin) clod of beef

jumelage [ʒym(ə)laʒ] NM twinning

jumelé, e [ʒym(ə)le] (ptp de **jumeler**) ADJ [colonnes, vergues, mât] twin; **roues ~es** double wheels; (Loterie) **billets ~s** double series ticket; **villes ~es** twin towns; **être ~ avec** [villes] to be twinned with; (Courses) **pari ~** dual forecast (for first and second place in the same race)

jumeler [ʒym(ə)le] ▶conjug 4◀ VT [+ villes] to twin; [+ efforts] to join; [+ mâts, poutres] to double up, fish (SPÉC)

jumelle[2] [ʒymɛl] NF [a] (Opt) **(paire de) ~s** (pair of) binoculars; **~s de spectacle** ou **théâ-**

tre opera glasses; **~ marine** binoculars; **observer qch à la ~** to look at sth through binoculars [b] [*mât*] fish; (*Aut*) **~ de ressort** shackle → **jumeau**

jument [ʒymɑ̃] NF mare

jumping [dʒœmpiŋ] NM (*gén*) jumping; (= *concours équestre*) show jumping

jungle [ʒɑ̃gl] NF (*lit, fig*) jungle; **~ urbaine** urban jungle → **loi**

junior [ʒynjɔʀ] [1] ADJ (*Comm, Sport, hum*) junior; **Dupont ~** Dupont junior; **équipe ~** junior team; **mode ~** young *ou* junior fashion; **~ entreprise** student organization that obtains contract work from businesses whose activities are related to the students' field of study [2] NMF (*Sport*) junior

junk bond (*pl* **junk bonds**) [(d)ʒœnkbɔ̃d] NM (*Fin*) junk bond

junkie [dʒœnki] ADJ, NMF (*Drogue*) junkie*

Junon [ʒynɔ̃] NF Juno

junte [ʒœt] NF junta

jupe [ʒyp] [1] NF (*Habillement, Tech*) skirt; **~ plissée/droite** pleated/straight skirt; **~s** skirts; **il est toujours dans les ~s de sa mère** he's still tied to his mother's apron strings; **il est toujours dans mes ~s** he's always under my feet [2] COMP ▸ **jupe portefeuille** wrap-around skirt

jupe-culotte (*pl* **jupes-culottes**) [ʒypkylɔt] NF culottes, divided skirt

jupette [ʒypɛt] NF (short) skirt

Jupiter [ʒypitɛʀ] NM (*Myth*) Jupiter, Jove; (*Astron*) Jupiter → **cuisse**

jupon [ʒypɔ̃] NM [a] (*Habillement*) petticoat, underskirt [b] (*fig†* = *femme*) bit of skirt*; **aimer le ~** to love anything in a skirt

juponné, e [ʒypɔne] ADJ [*robe*] with an underskirt

Jura [ʒyʀɑ] NM **le ~** (= *montagne*) the Jura (Mountains); (= *région*) the Jura

jurassique [ʒyʀasik] [1] ADJ Jurassic [2] NM **le ~** the Jurassic

juré, e [ʒyʀe] (*ptp de* **jurer**) [1] ADJ (= *qui a prêté serment*) sworn; **ennemi ~** sworn enemy; **promis ? — ~, craché !*** do you promise? — cross my heart (and hope to die)! [2] NM juror, juryman; **premier ~** foreman of the jury; **Mesdames et Messieurs les ~s apprécieront** the members of the jury will bear that in mind; **être convoqué comme ~** to be called for jury service *ou* duty [3] **jurée** NF juror, jurywoman

jurer [ʒyʀe] ▸conjug 1◂ [1] VT [a] (= *promettre*) to swear, vow; **~ fidélité/obéissance/amitié à qn** to swear *ou* pledge loyalty/obedience/friendship to sb; **~ la perte de qn** to swear to ruin sb *ou* bring about sb's downfall; **je jure que je me vengerai** I swear *ou* vow I'll get my revenge; **faire ~ à qn de garder le secret** to swear *ou* pledge sb to secrecy; **jure-moi que tu reviendras** swear (to me) you'll come back; **~ sur la Bible/sur la croix/devant Dieu** to swear on the Bible/on the cross/to God; **~ sur la tête de ses enfants** *ou* **de sa mère** to swear by all that one holds dear *ou* sacred, swear on one's children's *ou* one's mother's life; **il jurait ses grands dieux qu'il n'avait rien fait** he swore blind* *ou* by all the gods† that he hadn't done anything; **je vous jure que ce n'est pas facile** I can tell you *ou* assure you that it isn't easy; **ah ! je vous jure !** honestly!; **il faut de la patience, je vous jure, pour la supporter !** I swear you need a lot of patience to put up with her, you need a lot of patience to put up with her, I can tell you [b] (*admiration*) **on ne jure plus que par lui/par ce nouveau remède** everyone swears by him/ by this new medicine

[2] **jurer de** VT INDIR to swear to; **j'en jurerais** I could swear to it, I'd swear to it ▪ (*PROV*) **il ne faut ~ de rien** you never can tell

[3] VI [a] (= *pester*) to swear, curse; **~ après** *ou* **contre qch/qn** to swear *ou* curse at sth/sb; **~ comme un charretier** to swear like a trooper [b] [*couleurs*] to clash (**avec** with); [*propos*] to jar (**avec** with)

[4] **se jurer** VPR [a] (*à soi-même*) to vow to o.s., promise o.s.; **il se jura bien que c'était la dernière fois** he vowed it was the last time [b] (*réciproquement*) to pledge (to) each other, swear, vow; **ils se sont juré un amour éternel** they pledged *ou* vowed *ou* swore eternal love

juridiction [ʒyʀidiksjɔ̃] NF [a] (= *compétence*) jurisdiction; **hors de/sous sa ~** beyond/within his jurisdiction; **exercer sa ~** to exercise one's jurisdiction; **tombant sous la ~** falling *ou* coming within the jurisdiction of [b] (= *tribunal*) court(s) of law

juridictionnel, -elle [ʒyʀidiksjɔnɛl] ADJ jurisdictional; **pouvoir ~** power of jurisdiction; **fonctions juridictionnelles** judicial powers; **aide juridictionnelle** ≈ legal aid

juridique [ʒyʀidik] ADJ legal, juridical; **études ~s** law *ou* legal studies

juridiquement [ʒyʀidikmɑ̃] ADV juridically, legally

juridisme [ʒyʀidism] NM legalism

jurisconsulte [ʒyʀiskɔ̃sylt] NM jurisconsult

jurisprudence [ʒyʀispʀydɑ̃s] NF (= *source de droit*) ≈ case law, ≈ jurisprudence; (= *décisions*) (judicial) precedents; **faire ~** to set a precedent; **cas qui fait ~** test case

jurisprudentiel, -ielle [ʒyʀispʀydɑ̃sjɛl] ADJ jurisprudential; **décision jurisprudentielle** decision taken by a court that sets a legal precedent; **précédent ~** legal *ou* judicial precedent; **le droit ~** case law

juriste [ʒyʀist] NMF (= *auteur, légiste*) jurist; **~ d'entreprise** corporate lawyer

juron [ʒyʀɔ̃] NM oath, curse, swearword; **dire des ~s** to swear, curse

jury [ʒyʀi] NM [a] (*Jur*) jury; **~ populaire** civilian jury; **président du ~** foreman of the jury; **membre du ~** member of the jury, juror [b] (*Art, Sport*) panel of judges; (*Scol*) board of examiners, jury; **~ de thèse** Ph.D. examining board *ou* committee (*US*)

jus [ʒy] NM [a] (= *liquide*) juice; **~ de fruit** fruit juice; **~ de raisin** grape juice; **~ de viande** juice(s) from the meat, ≈ gravy; **plein de ~** juicy; **~ de la treille*** juice of the vine (*hum*), wine → **cuire**, **mijoter** [b] (* = *café*) coffee; **c'est un ~ infâme** it's a foul brew*; **au ~ !** coffee's ready!, coffee's up!!*; (*péj*) **~ de chaussette** dishwater (*fig*) [c] (* = *courant*) juice*; **prendre le ~** *ou* **un coup de ~** to get a shock [d]* (*loc*) **jeter/tomber au ~** *ou* **dans le ~** to throw/fall into the water *ou* drink*; **au ~ !** (*en poussant qn*) into the water with him!, in he goes!; (*en y allant*) here I come!; **ça valait le ~ !*** it was priceless!* [e] (*arg Mil*) **soldat de 1ᵉʳ ~** ≈ lance corporal (*Brit*); **soldat de 2ᵉ ~** ≈ private; **c'est du huit au ~** only a week to go (to the end of military service)

jusant [ʒyzɑ̃] NM ebb tide

jusqu'au-boutisme [ʒyskobutism] NM (= *politique*) hard-line policy; (= *attitude*) extremist attitude

jusqu'au-boutiste (*pl* **jusqu'au-boutistes**) [ʒyskobutist] [1] NMF extremist, hard-liner; **c'est un ~** he takes things to the bitter end, he always goes the whole hog* [2] ADJ [*attitude*] hardline (*épith*); [*théorie*] extremist

jusque [ʒysk(ə)] [1] PRÉP [a] (*lieu*) **jusqu'à la** ◊ **jusqu'au** to, as far as, (right) up to, all the way to; **j'ai couru jusqu'à la maison/l'école** I ran all the *ou* right the way home/to school; **j'ai marché jusqu'au village** I walked to *ou* as far as the village; **ils sont montés jusqu'à 2 000 mètres** they climbed up to 2,000 metres; **il s'est avancé jusqu'au bord du précipice** he walked (right) up to the edge of the precipice; **il a rampé jusqu'à nous** he crawled up to

us; **il avait de la neige jusqu'aux genoux** he had snow up to his knees, he was knee-deep in snow; **la nouvelle est venue jusqu'à moi** the news has reached me; **il menace d'aller jusqu'au ministre** he's threatening to take it to the minister

[b] (*temps*) **jusqu'à** ◊ **jusqu'en** until, till, up to; **jusqu'en mai** until May; **jusqu'à samedi** until Saturday; **du matin jusqu'au soir** from morning till night; **jusqu'à cinq ans il vécut à la campagne** he lived in the country until *ou* up to the age of five; **les enfants restent dans cette école jusqu'à (l'âge de) dix ans** (the) children stay at this school until they are ten *ou* until the age of ten; **marchez jusqu'à ce que vous arriviez à la mairie** walk until you reach the town hall, walk as far as the town hall; **rester jusqu'à la fin** to stay till *ou* to the end; **de la Révolution jusqu'à nos jours** from the Revolution (up) to the present day

[c] (*limite*) **jusqu'à 20 kg** up to 20 kg, not exceeding 20 kg; **véhicule transportant jusqu'à 15 personnes** vehicle which can carry up to *ou* as many as 15 people; **pousser l'indulgence jusqu'à la faiblesse** to carry indulgence to the point of weakness; **aller jusqu'à dire/faire qch** to go so far as to say/do sth; **j'irai jusqu'à 100** I'll go as far as *ou* up to 100; **je n'irais pas jusqu'à faire ça** I wouldn't go so far as to do that

[d] (= *y compris*) even; **il a mangé jusqu'aux arêtes** he ate everything including *ou* even the bones, he ate the lot (*Brit*) — bones and all (*Brit*); **ils ont regardé ~ sous le lit** they even looked under the bed; **tous jusqu'au dernier l'ont critiqué** every single *ou* last one of them criticized him

[e] (*avec prép ou adv*) **accompagner qn ~ chez lui** to take *ou* accompany sb (right) home; **veux-tu aller ~ chez le boucher pour moi ?** would you go (along) to the butcher's for me?; **jusqu'où ?** how far?; **jusqu'à quand ?** until when?, how long for?; **jusqu'à quand restez-vous ?** how long *ou* till when are you staying?, when are you staying till?; **jusqu'ici** (*temps présent*) so far, until now; (*au passé*) until then; (*lieu*) up to *ou* as far as here; **~-là** (*temps*) until then; (*lieu*) up to there; **j'en ai ~-là !** I'm sick and tired of it!, I've had about as much as I can take! *ou* I've had it up to here!; **jusqu'alors** ◊ **~s alors** until then; **jusqu'à maintenant** ◊ **jusqu'à présent** until now, so far; **~ (très) tard** until (very) late; **~ vers 9 heures** until about 9 o'clock → **mettre**

[f] (*loc*) **jusqu'au bout** to the (very) end; **jusqu'à concurrence de 100 F** to the amount of 100 francs; **vrai jusqu'à un certain point** true up to a certain point; **jusqu'au fond** to the (very) bottom; **elle a été touchée jusqu'au fond du cœur** she was deeply touched; (*Admin*) **jusqu'à nouvel ordre** until further notice; **jusqu'à plus ample informé** until further information is available, pending further information; **tu vois jusqu'à quel point tu t'es trompé** you see how wrong you were; **jusqu'au moment où** until, till; **jusqu'à la gauche** totally

[2] ADV **~(s) et y compris** up to and including; **jusqu'à** (= *même*) even; **j'ai vu jusqu'à des enfants tirer sur des soldats** I even saw children shooting at soldiers; **il n'est pas jusqu'au paysage qui n'ait changé** the very landscape *ou* even the landscape has changed

[3] **jusqu'à ce que** ◊ **jusqu'à tant que** LOC CONJ until; **sonnez jusqu'à ce que l'on vienne ouvrir** ring until someone answers the door; **il faudra le lui répéter jusqu'à ce** *ou* **jusqu'à tant qu'il ait compris** you'll have to keep on telling him until he understands

jusques [ʒysk(ə)] ADV, CONJ, PRÉP (*littér*) = **jusque**

jusquiame [ʒyskjam] NF henbane

justaucorps [ʒystokɔʀ] NM (*Hist*) jerkin; [*gymnaste*] leotard

▼ **juste** [ʒyst] **1** ADJ **a** (= *équitable*) [*personne, notation*] just, fair; [*sentence, guerre, cause*] just; **être ~ pour** *ou* **envers** *ou* **à l'égard de qn** to be fair to sb; **c'est un homme ~** he is a just man; **il faut être ~** one must be fair; **pour être ~ envers lui** in fairness to him, to be fair to him; **ce n'est pas ~!** it isn't fair!; **il n'est pas ~ de l'accuser** it is unfair to accuse him; **c'est un ~ retour des choses** it's poetic justice; **il finira par se faire renvoyer, et ce ne sera qu'un ~ retour des choses** he'll end up getting the sack, and it'll serve him right

b (= *légitime*) [*revendication, vengeance, fierté*] just; [*colère*] righteous, justifiable; **la ~ récompense de son travail** the just reward for his work

c (= *exact*) [*addition, réponse, heure*] right, exact; **à l'heure ~** right on time, dead on time*; **à 6 heures ~s** on the stroke of 6, at 6 o'clock sharp*; **apprécier qch à son ~ prix** *ou* **à sa ~ valeur** to appreciate the true worth of sth; **le ~ milieu** the happy medium, the golden mean; (*Pol*) the middle course *ou* way; **le mot ~** the right word, the mot juste

d (= *pertinent, vrai*) [*idée, raisonnement*] sound; [*remarque, expression*] apt; **il a dit des choses très ~s** he made some pertinent points, he said some very sound things; **très ~!** good point!, quite right!; **c'est ~** that's right, that's a fair point

e (= *précis, sûr*) [*appareil, montre*] accurate; [*esprit*] sound; [*balance*] accurate, true; [*oreille*] good

f (*Mus*) [*note*] right, true; [*voix*] true; [*instrument*] in tune (*attrib*), well-tuned; **il a une voix ~** he has a true voice, he sings in tune; **quinte ~** perfect fifth

g (= *trop court, étroit*) [*vêtement, chaussure*] tight; [*longueur, hauteur*] on the short side; **1 kg pour six, c'est un peu ~** 1 kg for six people, is barely enough *ou* is a bit on the short *ou* skimpy side; **trois heures pour faire cette traduction, c'est ~** three hours to do that translation is barely enough; **elle n'a pas raté son train mais c'était ~** she didn't miss her train but it was a close thing; **mon salaire est trop ~** my salary is inadequate, I don't earn enough; **je suis un peu ~ actuellement*** I'm a bit strapped for cash* *ou* things are a bit tight at the moment; **ses notes sont trop ~s** [*élève*] his marks aren't good enough

h (*excl*) **~ ciel!**† heavens (above)!; **~ Dieu!**† almighty God!, ye Gods!

2 à juste titre LOC ADV justly, rightly; **il en est fier, et à ~ titre** he's proud of it and rightly *ou* understandably so

3 ADV **a** (= *avec précision*) [*compter, viser*] accurately; [*raisonner*] soundly; [*deviner*] rightly, correctly; [*chanter*] in tune; **tomber ~** (= *deviner*) to hit the nail on the head, be (exactly) right; [*calculs*] to come out right; **division qui tombe ~** division which works out exactly; **~ à temps** [*arriver*] just in time; (*Écon*) **travailler en ~ à temps** to use the just-in-time system *ou* techniques

b (= *exactement*) just, exactly; **~ au-dessus** just above; **~ au coin** just on *ou* round the corner; **il a dit ~ ce qu'il fallait** he said exactly *ou* just what was needed; **c'est ~ le contraire** it's exactly *ou* just the opposite; **~ au moment où j'entrais** (just) at the very moment when I was coming in; **j'arrive ~** I've only just arrived; **je suis arrivé ~ quand/comme il sortait** I arrived just when/as he was leaving; **j'ai ~ assez** I have just enough; **3 kg ~** 3 kg exactly

c (= *seulement*) only, just; **j'ai ~ à passer un coup de téléphone** I only *ou* just have to make a telephone call; **il est parti il y a ~ un moment** he left just *ou* only a moment ago

d (= *pas assez*) (**un peu**) **~** [*compter, prévoir*] not quite enough, too little; **il est arrivé un peu ~** *ou* **bien ~** he cut it a bit too close *ou* fine* (*Brit*), he arrived at the last minute; **il a**

mesuré trop ~ he didn't allow quite enough

e (*loc*) **que veut-il au ~?** what exactly does he want? *ou* is he after?*, what does he actually want?; **au plus ~ prix** at the lowest *ou* minimum price; **calculer au plus ~** to work things out to the minimum; **comme de ~ il pleuvait!** and of course it was raining!; **tout ~** (= *seulement*) only just; (= *à peine*) hardly, barely; (= *exactement*) exactly; **c'est tout ~ s'il ne m'a pas frappé** he came this close to hitting me; **son livre vaut tout ~ la peine qu'on le lise** his book is barely worth reading; **c'est tout ~ passable** it's just *ou* barely passable

4 NM (*Rel*) just man; **les ~s** (*gén*) the just; (*Rel*) the righteous; **avoir la conscience du ~** to have a clear *ou* an untroubled conscience
→ **dormir**

justement [ʒystəmɑ̃] ADV **a** (= *précisément*) exactly, just, precisely; **il ne sera pas long, ~, il arrive** he won't be long, in fact he's just coming; **on parlait ~ de vous** we were just talking about you; **~, j'allais le dire** actually, that's what I was going to say **b** (= *à plus forte raison*) **puisque vous me l'interdisez ... eh bien, ~ je le lui dirai** since you say I mustn't ... just for that I'll tell him; **tu n'étais pas obligé d'accepter — si, ~!** you didn't have to accept — that's the problem, I did have to! **c** (= *avec justesse*) [*remarquer*] rightly; [*raisonner*] soundly; **comme l'a rappelé fort ~ Paul** as Paul has quite rightly pointed out **d** (= *à juste titre*) justly; **~ puni** justly punished; **~ inquiet/fier** justifiably anxious/proud

justesse [ʒystes] **1** NF **a** (= *exactitude*) [*appareil, montre, balance, tir*] accuracy, precision; [*calcul*] accuracy, correctness; [*réponse, comparaison, observation*] exactness; [*coup d'œil, oreille*] accuracy **b** [*note, voix, instrument*] accuracy **c** (= *pertinence*) [*idée, raisonnement*] soundness; [*remarque, expression*] aptness, appropriateness; **on est frappé par la ~ de son esprit** one is struck by the soundness of his judgment *ou* by how sound his judgment is **2 de justesse** LOC ADV just, barely; **gagner de ~** to win by a narrow margin; **rattraper qn/qch de ~** to catch sb/sth just in time; **j'ai évité l'accident de ~** I barely *ou* only just avoided having an accident; **il s'en est tiré de ~** he got out of it by the skin of his teeth; **il a eu son examen de ~** he only just passed his exam, he scraped through his exam

justice [ʒystis] NF **a** (= *équité*) fairness, justice; **en bonne ~** in all fairness; **on lui doit cette ~ que ...** it must be said in fairness to him that ...; **ce n'est que ~ qu'il soit récompensé** it's only fair that he should have his reward; **il a la ~ pour lui** justice is on his side; **traiter qn avec ~** to treat sb justly *ou* fairly; **~ sociale** social justice

b (= *fait de juger*) justice; **exercer/rendre la ~** to exercise/dispense justice; **passer en ~** to stand trial; **décision de ~** judicial decision; **aller en ~** to go to court; **demander/obtenir ~** to demand/obtain justice; **~ de paix**† court of first instance; (*Rel, Philo*) **~ immanente** immanent justice; (*fig*) **sans le vouloir, il s'est puni lui-même, il y a une sorte de ~ immanente** there's a sort of poetic justice in the fact that, without meaning to, he punished himself → **déni, palais, traduire** *etc*

c (= *loi*) **la ~** the law; **la ~ le recherche** he is wanted by the law; **il a eu des démêlés avec la ~** he's had a brush *ou* he's had dealings with the law; **la ~ de notre pays** the law of our country; **c'est du ressort de la ~ militaire** it comes under military law

d (*loc*) **faire ~ de qch** (= *récuser qch*) to refute sth; (= *réfuter qch*) to disprove sth; **il a pu faire ~ des accusations** he was able to refute the accusations; **se faire ~** (= *se venger*) to take the law into one's own hands, take (one's) revenge; (= *se suicider*) to take one's own life;

rendre ~ à qn to do sb justice, do justice to sb; **il faut lui rendre cette ~ qu'il n'a jamais cherché à nier** he's never tried to deny it, we must grant *ou* give him that, in fairness to him it must be said that he's never tried to deny it; **on n'a jamais rendu ~ à son talent** his talent has never had fair *ou* due recognition

justiciable [ʒystisjabl] **1** ADJ **a** (*Jur*) **criminel ~ de la cour d'assises** criminal subject to trial in a criminal court **b** (= *responsable*) **l'homme politique est ~ de l'opinion publique** politicians are accountable to the public *ou* are publicly accountable **c** (= *qui nécessite*) **situation ~ de mesures énergiques** situation where strong measures are indicated *ou* required, situation requiring strong measures **2** NMF (*Jur*) person subject to trial; **les ~s** those to be tried

justicier, -ière [ʒystisje, jɛʀ] NM,F **a** (*gén*) upholder of the law, dispenser of justice; (*dans les westerns*) lawman; **il veut jouer au ~** he wants to take the law into his own hands **b** (††: *Jur*) dispenser of justice

justifiable [ʒystifjabl] ADJ justifiable; **cela n'est pas ~** that is unjustifiable, that can't be justified

justificateur, -trice [ʒystifikatœʀ, tʀis] ADJ [*raison, action*] justificatory, justifying

justificatif, -ive [ʒystifikatif, iv] **1** ADJ [*démarche, document*] supporting, justificatory; **pièce justificative** (*officielle*) written proof; (= *reçu*) receipt **2** NM (= *pièce officielle*) written proof; (= *reçu*) receipt; **~ de domicile** proof of address

justification [ʒystifikasjɔ̃] NF **a** (= *explication*) justification; **cette mesure ne trouve guère de ~ économique** there is no economic justification for this measure; **fournir des ~s** to give some justification **b** (= *preuve*) proof **c** (*Typo*) justification

justifier [ʒystifje] ▶conjug 7◀ **1** VT **a** (= *légitimer*) [+ *personne, attitude, action*] to justify; **rien ne justifie cette colère** such anger is quite unjustified

b (= *donner raison*) [+ *opinion*] to justify, bear out, vindicate; [+ *espoir, inquiétude*] to justify; **ça justifie mon point de vue** it bears out *ou* vindicates my opinion; **~ qn d'une erreur** to clear sb of having made a mistake; **craintes parfaitement justifiées** perfectly justified fears

c (= *prouver*) to prove, justify; **pouvez-vous ~ ce que vous affirmez?** can you justify *ou* prove your assertions?

d (*Typo*) to justify; **~ à droite/gauche** to justify right/left, right(-)/left(-)justify

2 justifier de VT INDIR to prove; **~ de son identité** to prove one's identity; **~ de son domicile** to show proof of one's address; **cette quittance justifie du paiement** this receipt is evidence *ou* proof of payment

3 se justifier VPR to justify o.s.; **se ~ d'une accusation** to clear o.s. of an accusation

jute [ʒyt] NM jute → **toile**

juter [ʒyte] ▶conjug 1◀ VI [*fruit*] to be juicy, drip with juice; **pipe qui jute** dribbling pipe

juteux, -euse [ʒytø, øz] **1** ADJ [*fruit*] juicy; *[*affaire*] lucrative **2** NM (*arg Mil* = *adjudant*) adjutant

Juvénal [ʒyvenal] NM Juvenal

juvénile [ʒyvenil] ADJ [*allure*] young, youthful; **plein de fougue ~** full of youthful enthusiasm

juvénilité [ʒyvenilite] NF (*littér*) youthfulness

juxtalinéaire [ʒykstalineɛʀ] ADJ **traduction ~** line by line translation

juxtaposer [ʒykstapoze] ▶conjug 1◀ VT to juxtapose, place side by side; **propositions juxtaposées** juxtaposed clauses

juxtaposition [ʒykstapozisjɔ̃] NF juxtaposition

➤ GRAMMAIRE ACTIVE: **juste** 53.3, 53.6

K

K¹, k¹ [ka] NM (= *lettre*) K, k; (*Ordin*) K; **K 7** [*magnétophone, magnétoscope*] cassette, tape

K² (ABRÉV = **Kelvin**) K

k² (ABRÉV = **kilo**) k

kabbale [kabal] NF = **cabale**

kabbaliste [kabalist] NMF = **cabaliste**

kabbalistique [kabalistik] ADJ = **cabalistique**

Kaboul [kabul] N Kabul

kabuki [kabuki] NM Kabuki

Kabul [kabul] N = **Kaboul**

kabyle [kabil] 1 ADJ Kabyle 2 NM (*Ling*) Kabyle 3 **Kabyle** NMF Kabyle

Kabylie [kabili] NF Kabylia; **Grande/Petite ~** Great/Lesser Kabylia

kafkaïen, -ïenne [kafkajɛ̃, jɛn] ADJ [*univers*] Kafkaesque

kaiser [kɛzɛʀ, kajzɛʀ] NM Kaiser

kakatoès [kakatɔɛs] NM = **cacatoès**

kaki [kaki] 1 ADJ INV khaki, olive drab (*US*) 2 NM INV (= *couleur*) khaki, olive drab (*US*) 3 NM (= *fruit*) persimmon, sharon fruit

kalachnikov [kalaʃnikɔf] NF Kalashnikov

Kalahari [kalaaʀi] N **désert du ~** Kalahari Desert

kaléidoscope [kaleidɔskɔp] NM kaleidoscope

kaléidoscopique [kaleidɔskɔpik] ADJ kaleidoscopic

kamikaze [kamikaz] 1 ADJ (*lit, fig*) **opération ~** kamikaze *ou* suicide mission; **être ~*** [*personne*] to have a death wish; **ce serait ~ !** it would be suicidal *ou* suicide! 2 NM kamikaze

Kampala [kãpala] N Kampala

Kampuchea [kãputʃea] NM **~ (démocratique)** (Democratic) Kampuchea

kampuchéen, -enne [kãputʃeɛ̃, ɛn] 1 ADJ Kampuchean 2 **Kampuchéen(ne)** NM,F Kampuchean

kanak, e [kanak] ADJ, NM,F = **canaque**

kangourou [kãguʀu] NM kangaroo; **sac** *ou* **poche ~** baby carrier → **slip**

Kansas [kãsas] NM Kansas

kantien, -ienne [kãsjɛ̃, jɛn] ADJ Kantian

kantisme [kãtism] NM Kantianism

kaolin [kaɔlɛ̃] NM kaolin(e)

kapo [kapo] NM kapo, capo

kapok [kapɔk] NM kapok

kapokier [kapɔkje] NM kapok tree, silk cotton tree

Kaposi [kapozi] N **(maladie** *ou* **sarcome** *ou* **syndrome de) ~** Kaposi's sarcoma; **il a un (début de) ~** he is suffering from (the early stages of) Kaposi's sarcoma

kappa [kapa] NM kappa

kaput* [kaput] ADJ [*personne*] shattered*, bushed*, dead(-beat)*; [*machine*] kaput*

karaoké, karaoke [kaʀaɔke] NM karaoke; **bar (à) ~** karaoke bar; **faire un ~** to perform in a karaoke bar

karaté [kaʀate] NM karate

karatéka [kaʀateka] NMF karateka

karité [kaʀite] NM shea(-tree); **beurre de ~** shea butter

karma [kaʀma] NM karma

karstique [kaʀstik] ADJ karstic

kart [kaʀt] NM go-cart, kart

karting [kaʀtiŋ] NM go-carting, karting; **faire du ~** to go-cart, go karting

kascher [kaʃɛʀ] ADJ kosher

Katmandou [katmãdu] N Katmandu

kawa* [kawa] NM (= *café*) (cup of) coffee

kayak [kajak] NM [*esquimau*] kayak; [*sportif*] canoe, kayak; (= *sport*) canoeing; **faire du ~** to go canoeing

kayakiste [kajakist] NMF kayaker

kazakh [kazak] 1 ADJ kazakh 2 NM (*Ling*) Kazakh 3 **Kazakh** NMF Kazakh

Kazakhstan [kazakstã] N Kazakhstan

kebab [kebab] NM kebab

kéfié, keffieh [kefje] NM keffiyeh, kaffiyeh, kufiyah

kelvin [kelvin] NM kelvin

kendo [kendo] NM kendo

Kenya [kenja] NM Kenya; **le mont ~** Mount Kenya

kényan, -ane [kenjã, jan] 1 ADJ Kenyan 2 **Kényan(e)** NM,F Kenyan

képi [kepi] NM kepi

kératine [keʀatin] NF keratin

kératite [keʀatit] NF keratitis

kératose [keʀatoz] NF keratosis

Kerguelen [kɛʀgəlɛn] NFPL **les (îles) ~** the Kerguelen (Islands)

kermesse [kɛʀmɛs] NF (= *fête populaire*) fair; (= *fête de charité*) bazaar, charity fête; **~ paroissiale** church fête *ou* bazaar

kérosène [keʀozɛn] NM [*avion*] aviation fuel, kerosene (*US*); [*jet*] (jet) fuel; [*fusée*] (rocket) fuel

ketch [kɛtʃ] NM ketch

ketchup [kɛtʃœp] NM ketchup, catsup (*US*)

keuf* [kœf] NM cop*, pig*

kevlar® [kevlaʀ] NM kevlar®

keynésianisme [kenezjanism] NM Keynesianism, Keynesian economics *sg*

keynésien, -ienne [kenezjɛ̃, jɛn] ADJ Keynesian

kF [kaɛf] NM (ABRÉV = **kilofranc**) ≈ K*; **il gagne 240 kF** ≈ he earns 24 K*

kg (ABRÉV = **kilogramme**) kg

KGB [kaʒebe] NM (ABRÉV = **Komitet Gosudarstvennoy Bezopasnosti**) KGB

khâgne [kaɲ] NF (*arg Scol*) second year of a two-year preparatory course for the arts section of the École Normale Supérieure
→ CLASSES PRÉPARATOIRES ; GRANDES ÉCOLES

khâgneux, -euse [kaɲø, øz] NM,F (*arg Scol*) student in khâgne

khalife [kalif] NM = **calife**

khan [kã] NM khan

Khartoum [kaʀtum] N Khartoum

khat [kat] NM k(h)at

khédive [kediv] NM khedive

khi [ki] NM chi

khmer, -ère [kmɛʀ] 1 ADJ Khmer 2 NM (*Ling*) Khmer 3 **Khmer** NM Khmer; **les Khmers rouges** the Khmer Rouge

khôl [kol] NM kohl

kibboutz [kibuts] NM INV kibbutz

kick [kik] NM kick-start(er); **démarrer au ~** [*personne*] to kick-start one's motorbike; **la moto (se) démarre au ~** you have to kick-start the motorbike

kidnapper [kidnape] ▸ conjug 1 ◂ VT to kidnap, abduct

kidnappeur, -euse [kidnapœʀ, øz] NM,F kidnapper, abductor

kidnapping [kidnapiŋ] NM kidnapping, abduction

Kiev [kjev] N Kiev

kif¹ [kif] NM (= *haschich*) kif, kef

kif²* [kif] NM **c'est du ~** it's all the same, it makes no odds* (*Brit*)

kif-kif* [kifkif] ADJ INV **c'est ~ (bourricot)** it's all the same, it makes no odds* (*Brit*)

Kigali [kigali] N Kigali

kiki* [kiki] NM a (= *cou*) **serrer le ~ à qn** [*personne*] to throttle sb, grab sb by the throat; [*cravate, encolure*] to choke sb → **partir** b (*hum, langage enfantin = pénis*) willie* (*Brit*), peter* (*US*)

kikouyou, kikuyu [kikuju] 1 ADJ Kikuyu 2 **Kikouyou** NMF Kikuyu; **les Kikouyous** the Kikuyu

kil* [kil] NM **~ de rouge** bottle of cheap (red) wine *ou* plonk* (*Brit*)

Kilimandjaro [kilimãdʒaʀo] NM **le ~** Mount Kilimanjaro

kilo [kilo] NM kilo

kilo... [kilo] PRÉF kilo...

kilobar [kilɔbaʀ] NM kilobar

kilocalorie [kilokalɔʀi] NF kilocalorie

kilocycle [kilosikl] NM kilocycle

kilofranc [kilofʀã] NM thousand francs

kilogramme [kilɔgʀam] NM kilogramme

kilohertz [kilɔɛʀts] NM kilohertz

kilojoule [kilɔʒul] NM kilojoule

kilométrage [kilɔmetʀaʒ] NM a [*voiture, distance*] ≈ mileage; **voiture en** *ou* **à ~ illimité** car with unlimited mileage b [*route*] ≈ marking with milestones

kilomètre [kilɔmetʀ] NM a (= *distance*) kilometre (*Brit*), kilometer (*US*); **200 ~s à l'heure** *ou* **~s-heure** 200 kilometres an hour *ou* per hour; **bouffer du ~*** ≈ to eat up the miles*; **~-passager** passenger kilometre, ≈ passenger mile; (*Ski*) **~ lancé** speed-record trial; **d'ici à ce qu'il ne vienne pas, il n'y a pas des ~s*** I wouldn't be surprised if he didn't turn up b (*grande quantité*) **des ~s de** [+ *pellicule*] rolls and rolls of; [+ *tissu*] yards and yards of; **ils produisent des émissions au ~** they churn out one programme after another

kilométrer [kilɔmetʀe] ▶conjug 6◀ VT [+ *route*] ≈ to mark with milestones

kilométrique [kilɔmetʀik] ADJ **distance ~** distance in kilometres (*Brit*) *ou* kilometer (*US*); **borne ~** ≈ milestone; **indemnité ~** ≈ mileage allowance; **tarif ~** rate per kilometre

kilo-octet (*pl* **kilo-octets**) [kilɔɔktε] NM kilobyte

kilotonne [kilɔtɔn] NF kiloton

kilowatt [kilɔwat] NM kilowatt

kilowattheure [kilɔwatœʀ] NM kilowatt-hour

kilt [kilt] NM kilt; (*pour femme*) pleated *ou* kilted skirt

kimono [kimɔno] NM kimono → **manche**[1]

kinase [kinaz] NF kinase

kiné(si)* [kine(zi)] NMF (ABRÉV = **kinésithérapeute**) physio*

kinésithérapeute [kineziteʀapøt] NMF physiotherapist (*Brit*), physical therapist (*US*)

kinésithérapie [kineziteʀapi] NF physiotherapy (*Brit*), physical therapy (*US*)

kinesthésique [kinestezik] ADJ kinaesthetic

Kingston [kiŋstɔn] N Kingston

Kingstown [kiŋstaun] N Kingstown

Kinshasa [kinʃasa] N Kinshasa

kiosque [kjɔsk] NM **a** [*jardin*] pavilion, summerhouse; **~ à musique** bandstand **b** (= *étal*) kiosk, stall; **~ à journaux** newsstand, newspaper kiosk; **en vente en ~** on sale at newsstands **c** (*Téléc*) **~ télématique**® *information service provided by Minitel* **d** [*sous-marin*] conning tower; [*bateau*] wheelhouse

kiosquier, -ière [kjɔskje, jεʀ] NM,F newspaper seller (*at kiosk*)

kippa [kipa] NF kippa

kir [kiʀ] NM kir (*white wine with blackcurrant liqueur*); **~ royal** kir royal (*champagne with blackcurrant liqueur*)

kirghiz [kiʀgiz] **1** ADJ Kirghiz **2** NM (*Ling*) Kirghiz **3** **Kirghiz** NMF Kirghiz

Kirghizistan [kiʀgizistɑ̃], **Kirghizstan** [kiʀgistɑ̃] NM Kirghizia

Kiribati [kiʀibati] N Kiribati

kirsch [kiʀʃ] NM kirsch

kit [kit] NM kit; **en ~** in kit form

kit(s)ch [kitʃ] ADJ INV, NM kitsch

kitchenette [kitʃ(ə)nεt] NF kitchenette

kiwi [kiwi] NM **a** (= *oiseau*) kiwi **b** (= *arbre*) kiwi tree; (= *fruit*) kiwi (fruit), Chinese gooseberry

klaxon® [klaksɔn] NM (*Aut*) horn; **coup de ~** (*fort*) hoot; (*léger*) toot; **donner des coups de ~** to hoot (one's horn), sound one's horn

klaxonner [klaksɔne] ▶conjug 1◀ **1** VI (*gén*) to hoot (one's horn), sound one's horn; (*doucement*) to toot (the horn); **klaxonne, il ne t'a pas vu** hoot your horn *ou* give him a toot, he hasn't seen you **2** VT **~ qn** (*gén*) to hoot at sb; (*doucement*) to give sb a toot

kleb(s)* [klεp(s)] NM = **clebs**

Kleenex® [klinεks] NM tissue, paper hanky, Kleenex®

kleptomane [klεptɔman] ADJ, NMF kleptomaniac

kleptomanie [klεptɔmani] NF kleptomania

km (ABRÉV = **kilomètre(s)**) km

km/h (ABRÉV = **kilomètres/heure**) km/h, kph, ≈ mph

knickerbockers [knikeʀbɔkeʀs, nikœʀbɔkœʀ] NMPL knickerbockers

knock-out [nɔkaut] **1** ADJ (*Boxe,**) knocked out, out for the count*; **mettre qn ~** to knock sb out; **il est complètement ~** he's out cold* **2** NM knockout

knout [knut] NM knout

K.-O. [kao] ABRÉV = **knock out 1** NM (*Boxe*) KO; **perdre par ~** to be knocked out; **gagner par ~** to win by a knockout; **mettre ~** to KO*, knock out; **il a été mis ~ au 5ᵉ round** he was knocked out in round 5; **être ~** to be out for the count; **être ~debout** [*boxeur*] to be punch-drunk; (*vaincu*) to be knocked for six*; (*stupéfait*) to be stunned **2** ADJ (* = *fatigué*) shattered*, knackered‡

Ko (ABRÉV = **kilo-octet**) kb

koala [kɔala] NM koala (bear)

kola [kɔla] NM = **cola**

kolkhoze [kɔlkoz] NM kolkhoz, Russian collective farm

kolkhozien, -ienne [kɔlkozjɛ̃, jεn] ADJ, NM,F kolkhozian

kommandantur [kɔmɑ̃dɑ̃tuʀ] NF German military command

kopeck [kɔpεk] NM kopeck; **je n'ai plus un ~**†* I haven't got a penny left

korrigan, e [kɔʀigɑ̃, an] NM,F Breton goblin

kouglof [kuglɔf] NM kugelhopf (*kind of bun*)

koulak [kulak] NM kulak

Koweït [kɔwεt] NM Kuwait

koweïtien, -ienne [kɔwεtjɛ̃, jεn] **1** ADJ Kuwaiti **2** **Koweïtien(ne)** NM,F Kuwaiti

krach [kʀak] NM (*Bourse*) crash; **~ boursier** stock market crash

kraft [kʀaft] NM → **papier**

Kremlin [kʀεmlɛ̃] NM **le ~** the Kremlin

krill [kʀil] NM krill

krypton [kʀiptɔ̃] NM krypton

ksi [ksi] NM xi

Kuala Lumpur [kwalalumpuʀ] N Kuala Lumpur

Ku Klux Klan [kyklyksklɑ̃] NM Ku Klux Klan

kummel [kymεl] NM kümmel

kumquat [kɔmkwat] NM kumquat

kung-fu [kuŋfu] NM INV (= *art*) kung fu; (= *personne*) person who practises *ou* does kung fu

kurde [kyʀd] **1** ADJ Kurdish **2** NM (*Ling*) Kurdish **3** **Kurde** NMF Kurd

Kurdistan [kyʀdistɑ̃] NM Kurdistan

kW (ABRÉV = **kilowatt**) kW

K-way® [kawε] NM (lightweight nylon) cagoule

kWh (ABRÉV = **kilowattheure**) kWh

Kyoto [kjɔto] N Kyoto, Kioto

kyrie (eleison) [kiʀje(eleisɔn)] NM INV (*Rel*, *Mus*) Kyrie (eleison)

kyrielle [kiʀjεl] NF [*injures, réclamations*] string, stream; [*personnes*] crowd, stream; [*objets*] pile

kyste [kist] NM cyst; **~ de l'ovaire** *ou* **ovarien** ovarian cyst

kystique [kistik] ADJ cystic

L

L, l¹ [ɛl] NM (= *lettre*) L, l

l² (ABRÉV = **litre(s)**) l

l' [l] → **le¹**, **le²**

la¹ [la] → **le¹**, **le²**

la² [la] NM INV (*Mus*) A; (*en chantant la gamme*) lah; **donner le ~** (*lit*) to give an A; (*fig*) to set the tone ou the fashion

---

là [la]

1 ADVERBE	**3** LOC ADVERBIALE
2 LOC ADVERBIALE	**4** EXCLAMATION

1 ADVERBE

a par opposition à ici there; **là, on s'occupera bien de vous** you will be well looked after there; **je le vois là, sur la table** I can see it (over) there, on the table; **c'est là que** ou **c'est là où je suis né** that's where I was born → **çà, fait¹**

b = ici here, there; **ne restez pas là au froid** don't stand here ou there in the cold; **n'ayez pas peur, je suis là** don't be afraid, I'm here; **qui est là?** who's there?; **c'est là! je reconnais le portail!** there it is! ou here we are! I recognize the gate!; **M. Roche n'est pas là** Mr Roche isn't here ou in; **je suis là pour ça!** that's what I'm here for!; **ce monument est là pour nous rappeler que ...** this monument is here ou exists to remind us that ...; **c'est là qu'il est tombé** that's ou this is where he fell; **là où tu es/d'où tu viens** where you are/come from; **déjà là?** (are you) here already?; **qu'est-ce que tu fais là?** (*lit*) what are you doing here?; (*fig*) what are you up to? → **fait¹**

c dans le temps then, at this ou that moment; **c'est là qu'il comprit qu'il était en danger** that was when he realized ou it was then that he realized he was in danger; **ce qu'il propose là n'est pas bête** what he's just suggested isn't a bad idea → **ici, jusque**

d = dans cette situation **tout cela pour en arriver ou en venir là!** all that effort just for this!; **il faut s'en tenir ou en rester là** we'll have to leave it at that ou stop there; **les choses en sont là** that's how things stand at the moment, that's the state of play at present; **ils en sont là** (*lit*) that's how far they've got, that's the stage they've reached; (*péj*) that's how low they've sunk; **ils n'en sont pas encore là** they haven't got that far yet ou reached that stage yet; (*péj*) they haven't reached that stage yet ou come to that yet; **j'en étais là de mes réflexions quand ...** such was my state of mind when ...; **c'est bien là qu'on voit les paresseux!** that's where ou when you see who the lazy ones are!; **il a été courageux là où d'autres auraient eu peur** he was courageous where others would have been afraid → **loin**

e intensif **n'allez pas croire là que ...** don't get the idea that ..., don't go thinking that ...; **qu'est-ce que tu me racontes là?** what (on earth) are you saying to me?

f = en cela, dans cela **c'est là où** ou **que nous ne sommes plus d'accord** that's where I take issue ou start to disagree with you; **là, ils exagèrent!** now they're really going too far!; **je ne** vois là rien d'étonnant I don't see anything surprising in ou about that; **il y a là quelque chose d'inquiétant** there's something worrying about that; **tout est là** that's the whole question; **c'est là qu'est la difficulté** là est la difficulté that's where the difficulty lies; **il y a là une contradiction** there's a contradiction in that → **question**

g

♦ **ce** ou **cette ...-là** that ...; **ce jour-là** that day; **cet homme-là est détesté par tout le monde** everybody hates that man; **c'est à ce point-là?** it's as bad as that, is it?; **en ce temps-là** in those days

♦ **ces ...-là** those ...; **ces gens-là** those people → **ce¹**

h

♦ **celui-là** ◊ **celle-là** (= *objet, personne*) that one

♦ **ceux-là** ◊ **celles-là** (= *objets*) those; **je veux celui-là** I want that one; (= *personnes*) **certains le croient, Luc est de ceux-là** some people, including Luc, believe it; **celles-là, elles ne risquent rien** THEY're not in any danger; **celui-/celle-là alors!** (*irritation*) oh, that man/woman!; (*surprise*) how does he/she do it!; **il est marrant*, celui-là!** that guy's such a laugh! → **celui**

2 de là LOC ADVERBIALE

a dans l'espace **il est allé à Paris, et de là à Londres** he went to Paris, and from there to London ou and then (from there) on to London; **c'est à 3 km de là** it's 3 km away (from there)

b dans le temps **à partir de là** from then on, after that; **à quelques jours de là** a few days later ou after(wards)

c conséquence **il n'a pas travaillé, de là son échec** he didn't work, hence his failure ou which explains why he failed; **de là vient que nous ne le voyons plus** that's why we no longer see him; **de là à dire qu'il ment, il n'y a qu'un pas** there isn't much difference between saying that and saying he's lying, that's tantamount to saying he's a liar; **oui, mais de là à prétendre qu'il a tout fait seul!** there's a big difference between saying that and claiming that he did it all himself!

3 par là LOC ADVERBIALE

a dans l'espace (= *de ce côté*) **quelque part par là** somewhere around there ou near there; (= *par cet endroit*) **passez par là** go that way; **c'est par ici ou par là?** is it this way or that way?

b * = environ **il doit avoir 20 ans, par là** he must be about 20, he must be 20 or so

c loc **que veux-tu dire par là?** what do you mean by that?; **si tu (y) vas par là ...** if that's what you're saying ... → **entendre, passer**

4 EXCLAMATION

fiche-moi la paix, là!* leave me alone, will you!*; **hé là!** (*appel*) hey!; (*surprise*) good grief!; **là, là, du calme!** now, now, calm down!; **il est entré dans une rage, mais là, une de ces rages!** he flew into a rage, and what a rage!; **alors là** ou **oh là, ça ne m'étonne pas** (oh) now, that doesn't surprise me

♦ **oh là là (là là)!** (*surprise*) oh my goodness!; (*consternation*) oh dear! (oh dear!); **oh là là!, ce que j'ai froid!** God*, I'm so cold!; **oh là là! quel désastre!** oh dear! ou oh no! what a disaster!

---

là-bas [laba] ADV (over) there, yonder; **~ aux USA** over in the USA; **~ dans le nord** up (there) in the north; **~ dans la plaine** down there in the plain; **Serge a réapparu, tout ~** Serge reappeared way over there

labbe [lab] NM skua; **~ parasite** Arctic skua

label [label] NM (*Comm, Ordin*) label; **~ d'origine** label of origin; **~ de qualité** (*lit*) quality label; (*fig*) guarantee of quality; **~ rouge** quality label for meat; **~ politique** political label; **l'association a accordé son ~ à 80 projets** the association has given its seal of approval to 80 projects

labelliser [labelize] ▶ conjug 1 ◀ VT (*Comm*) to label, put a label on; [+ *projet*] to give one's seal of approval to

labeur [labœʀ] NM (*littér*) labour, toil (*NonC*); **c'est un dur ~** it's hard work

labial, e (*mpl* **-iaux**) [labjal, jo] **1** ADJ [*consonne*] labial; [*muscle*] lip (*épith*), labial (*SPÉC*) **2** **labiale** NF labial

labialisation [labjalizasjɔ̃] NF [*consonne*] labialization; [*voyelle*] labialization, rounding

labialiser [labjalize] ▶ conjug 1 ◀ VT [+ *consonne*] to labialize; [+ *voyelle*] to labialize, round

labié, e [labje] **1** ADJ labiate **2** NF labiate; **les ~es** labiates, Labiatae (*SPÉC*)

labiodental, e (*mpl* **-aux**) [labjodɑ̃tal, o] ADJ, NF labiodental

labo* [labo] NM (ABRÉV = **laboratoire**) lab*; **~ photo** photo lab

laborantin, e [labɔʀɑ̃tɛ̃, in] NM,F laboratory ou lab* assistant

laboratoire [labɔʀatwaʀ] NM (*gén*) laboratory; **~ spatial/de recherches** space/research laboratory; **~ d'analyses (médicales)** (medical) analysis laboratory; **~ (de) photo** photo laboratory; **~ de langue(s)** language laboratory; **~ d'essai** (*lit*) testing laboratory; (*fig*) testing ground; **simulation/essais en ~** laboratory simulation/trials

laborieusement [labɔʀjøzmɑ̃] ADV laboriously, with much effort; **gagner ~ sa vie** to struggle to earn a living, earn a living by the sweat of one's brow

laborieux, -ieuse [labɔʀjø, jøz] ADJ **a** (= *pénible*) laborious, painstaking; [*entreprise, recherches*] laborious; [*style, récit*] laboured, laborious; [*digestion*] heavy; **il s'exprimait dans un français ~** his French was very laboured; **il a enfin fini, ça a été ~!** he's finished at long last, he made heavy weather of it! **b** (= *travailleur*) hard-working, industrious; **les classes laborieuses** the working ou labouring classes; **une vie laborieuse** a life of toil ou hard work

labour [labuʀ] NM [a] (avec une charrue) ploughing (Brit), plowing (US); (avec une bêche) digging (over) → **cheval** [b] (= champ) ploughed (Brit) ou plowed (US) field

labourable [labuʀabl] ADJ (avec une charrue) ploughable (Brit), plowable (US); (avec une bêche) soft enough for digging; **terres ~s** arable land

labourage [labuʀaʒ] NM (avec une charrue) ploughing (Brit), plowing (US); (avec une bêche) digging (over)

labourer [labuʀe] ▶ conjug 1 ◀ VT [a] (avec une charrue) to plough (Brit), plow (US); (avec une bêche) to dig (over); **terre qui se laboure bien** land which ploughs well ou is easy to plough; (Naut) **~ le fond** [navire] to scrape ou graze the bottom; [ancre] to drag; **terrain labouré par les sabots des chevaux** ground churned ou ploughed up by the horses' hooves [b] **la balle lui avait labouré la jambe** the bullet had ripped into ou gashed his leg; **labouré de rides** lined ou furrowed with wrinkles; **ce corset me laboure les côtes** this corset is digging into my sides; **se ~ le visage/les mains** to tear at one's face/one's hands; **le chat lui a labouré le visage** the cat scratched his face really badly

laboureur [labuʀœʀ] NM ploughman (Brit), plowman (US); (Hist) husbandman

Labrador [labʀadɔʀ] NM (Géog) Labrador

labrador [labʀadɔʀ] NM (= chien) Labrador (retriever)

labradorite [labʀadɔʀit] NF (Minér) labradorite

labrit [labʀi] NM Pyrenean sheepdog

labyrinthe [labiʀɛ̃t] NM (lit, fig) maze, labyrinth; (Anat) labyrinth

labyrinthique [labiʀɛ̃tik] ADJ labyrinthine

lac [lak] NM ~ **de montagne** mountain lake; **le ~ Léman** ou **de Genève** Lake Geneva; **le ~ Majeur** Lake Maggiore; **les ~s écossais** the Scottish lochs; **les Grands Lacs** "the Great Lakes; (Mus) « Le Lac des Cygnes »** "Swan Lake"; (fig) **être (tombé) dans le ~*** to have fallen through, have come to nothing

laçage [lasaʒ] NM lacing(-up)

lacanien, -ienne [lakanjɛ̃, jɛn] ADJ (Psych) Lacanian

Lacédémone [lasedemɔn] N Lacedaemonia

lacédémonien, -ienne [lasedemɔnjɛ̃, jɛn] [1] ADJ Lacedaemonian [2] **Lacédémonien(ne)** NM,F Lacedaemonian

lacement [lasmɑ̃] NM = **laçage**

lacer [lase] ▶ conjug 3 ◀ VT [+ chaussure] to tie; [+ corset] to lace up; (Naut) [+ voile] to lace; **lace tes chaussures** ou **tes lacets** do up ou tie your shoelaces; **ça se lace (par) devant** it laces up at the front

lacération [laseʀasjɔ̃] NF [vêtement, affiche] ripping up, tearing up; [corps, visage] laceration; [tableau] slashing

lacérer [laseʀe] ▶ conjug 6 ◀ VT [+ affiche, papier, vêtement] to tear ou rip up, tear to shreds; [+ tableau] to slash; [+ corps, visage] to lacerate; **il avait été lacéré de coups de couteau** he had been slashed with a knife

lacet [lase] NM [a] [chaussure] (shoe)lace; [botte] (boot)lace; [corset] lace; **chaussures à ~** lace-ups, lace-up shoes; **faire** ou **nouer ses ~s** to do up ou tie one's laces [b] [route] (sharp) bend, twist; **en ~(s)** winding, twisty; **la route fait des ~s** ou **monte en ~s** the road twists ou winds steeply upwards [c] (= piège) snare; **prendre des lièvres au ~** to trap ou snare hares [d] (Couture) braid

lâchage* [lɑʃaʒ] NM (= abandon) desertion; **écœuré par le ~ de ses amis** disgusted at the way his friends had deserted him ou run out on him; **ils dénoncent le ~ du pays par l'ONU** they're denouncing the UN's abandonment of the country

lâche [lɑʃ] [1] ADJ [a] [corde, ressort] slack; [nœud] loose; [vêtement] loose(-fitting); [tissu] loosely-woven, open-weave (épith) [b] [discipline, morale] lax; [règlement, canevas] loose [c] (littér) [style, expression] loose, woolly; **dans ce roman, l'intrigue est un peu ~** the novel has quite a loose plot [d] [personne, fuite, attitude] cowardly; [attentat] vile, despicable; [procédé] low; **se montrer ~** to be a coward; **c'est assez ~ de sa part d'avoir fait ça** it was pretty cowardly of him to do that [e] (littér = faible) weak, feeble [2] NMF coward

lâchement [lɑʃmɑ̃] ADV [a] (= sans courage) in a cowardly way; **il a ~ refusé** like a coward, he refused; **il a été ~ assassiné** he was killed in the most cowardly way [b] [nouer] loosely

lâcher [lɑʃe] ▶ conjug 1 ◀ [1] VT [a] [+ ceinture] to loosen, let out, slacken; **~ la taille d'une jupe** to let a skirt out at the waist; (Pêche) **~ du fil** to let out some line [b] [+ main, proie] to let go of; [+ bombes] to drop, release; [+ pigeon, ballon] to release; [+ chien de garde] to unleash, set loose; [+ frein] to release, let out; [+ amarres] to cast off; (Chasse) [+ chien, faucon] to slip; **lâche-moi !** let go (of me)!; **attention ! tu vas ~ le verre** careful, you're going to drop the glass!; **le professeur nous a lâchés à 4 heures*** the teacher let us go ou let us out at 4; **~ un chien sur qn** to set a dog on sb; **s'il veut acheter ce tableau, il va falloir qu'il lâche*** ou **qu'il lâche ses sous*** if he wants this picture, he'll have to part with the cash*; **il les lâche difficilement*** he hates to part with his money [c] [+ bêtise, juron] to come out with; [+ pet] to let out;† [+ coup de fusil] to fire; **~ quelques mots** to say a few words; **voilà le grand mot lâché !** there's the fatal word!; **~ un coup de poing à qn**† to deal ou fetch (Brit) sb a blow with one's fist [d] (* = abandonner) [+ époux] to leave, walk out on; [+ amant] to jilt, drop, chuck* (Brit); [+ ami] to drop; [+ études, métier] to give up, pack in* (Brit), chuck in* (Brit); [+ avantage] to give up; **~ le peloton** to leave the rest of the field behind, build up a good lead (over the rest of the pack); **ne pas ~ qn** [poursuivant, créancier] to stick to sb; [importun, représentant] not to leave sb alone; [mal de tête] not to let up on sb*, not to leave sb; **il nous a lâchés en plein milieu du travail** he walked out on us right in the middle of the work; **il ne m'a pas lâché d'une semelle** he stuck close all the time, he stuck to me like a leech; **la communauté internationale nous a lâchés** the international community has abandoned us; **ma voiture m'a lâché** my car gave up on me*; **une bonne occasion, ça ne se lâche pas** ou **il ne faut pas la ~** you don't miss ou pass up* an opportunity like that [e] (loc) **~ prise** (lit) to let go; (fig) to loosen one's grip; **~ pied** to fall back, give way; **~ la bride** ou **les rênes à un cheval** to give a horse its head; (fig) **~ la bride à qn** to give sb more of a free rein; **tu me lâches !*** leave me alone!; **lâche-moi les baskets !*** ou **la grappe !*** get off my back!*, get off my case!* (US); **il les lâche avec des élastiques**‡ he's as stingy as hell‡, he's a tight-fisted so-and-so* [2] VI [corde] to break, give way; [frein] to fail [3] NM **~ de ballons** balloon release

lâcheté [lɑʃte] NF [a] (= couardise) cowardice, cowardliness; (= bassesse) lowness; **par ~** through ou out of cowardice; **je trouve ça d'une ~ !** that's so cowardly! [b] (= acte) cowardly act, act of cowardice [c] (littér = faiblesse) weakness, feebleness

lâcheur, -euse* [lɑʃœʀ, øz] NM,F unreliable ou fickle so-and-so*; **alors, tu n'es pas venu, ~ !** so you didn't come then — you're a dead loss!* ou **you old so-and-so!*; c'est une lâcheuse, ta sœur !** your sister's so unreliable!*

lacis [lasi] NM [ruelles] maze; [veines] network; [soie] web

laconique [lakɔnik] ADJ [personne, réponse] laconic; [style] terse

laconiquement [lakɔnikmɑ̃] ADV laconically, tersely

laconisme [lakɔnism] NM terseness

lacrymal, e (mpl **-aux**) [lakʀimal, o] ADJ lacrimal (SPÉC), lachrymal (SPÉC), tear (épith)

lacrymogène [lakʀimɔʒɛn] ADJ → **gaz, grenade**

lacs [lɑ] NMPL († littér) snare; **~ d'amour** lover's ou love knot

lactaire [laktɛʀ] [1] ADJ (Anat) lacteal [2] NM (Bot) milk cap

lactalbumine [laktalbymin] NF lactalbumin

lactase [laktɑz] NF lactase

lactation [laktasjɔ̃] NF lactation

lacté, e [lakte] ADJ [sécrétion] milky, lacteal (SPÉC); [couleur, suc] milky; [régime] milk (épith) → **voie**

lactifère [laktifɛʀ] ADJ lactiferous

lactique [laktik] ADJ lactic

lactogène [laktɔʒɛn] ADJ lactogenic

lactose [laktoz] NM lactose

lactosérum [laktoseʀɔm] NM whey

lacunaire [lakynɛʀ] ADJ (Bio) [tissu] lacunary, lacunal; [documentation] incomplete, deficient; **il a des connaissances ~s** there are gaps in his knowledge

lacune [lakyn] NF [a] [texte, mémoire, connaissances] gap; [manuscrit] lacuna; [loi] gap, loophole; **les ~s du système éducatif** the shortcomings of the education system; **elle a de grosses ~s en histoire** there are big gaps in her knowledge of history; **il y a de sérieuses ~s dans ce livre** this book has some serious deficiencies ou leaves out ou overlooks some serious points [b] (Anat, Bot) lacuna

lacustre [lakystʀ] ADJ lake (épith), lakeside (épith); **cité ~** lakeside village (on piles)

lad [lad] NM (Équitation) stable-boy, stable-lad

là-dedans [lad(ə)dɑ̃] ADV (lit) inside, in there; **il y a du vrai ~** there's some truth in that; **il n'a rien à voir ~** it's nothing to do with him; **il a voulu mettre de l'argent ~** he wanted to put some money into it; **quand il s'est embarqué ~** when he got involved in that ou in it; (admiratif) **(il) y en a ~ !*** you see, I'm (ou he's etc) not just a pretty face!; **et nous, ~, qu'est-ce qu'on devient ?*** and where do we fit into all this?

là-dessous [lad(ə)su] ADV underneath, under there, under that; (fig) **il y a quelque chose ~** there's something odd about it ou that, there's more to it than meets the eye

là-dessus [lad(ə)sy] ADV (= sur cet objet) on that, on there; (= sur ces mots) at that point, thereupon (frm); (= à ce sujet) about that, on that point; **~, il sortit** with that, he left; **vous pouvez compter ~** you can count on that; **il n'y a aucun doute ~** there's no doubt about it

ladite [ladit] ADJ → **ledit**

ladre [ladʀ] [1] ADJ (littér = avare) mean, miserly [2] NMF (littér) miser

ladrerie [ladʀəʀi] NF [a] (littér = avarice) meanness, miserliness [b] (Hist = hôpital) leper-house

lady [ledi] NF (= titre) **Lady** Lady; **c'est une vraie ~** she's a real lady

lagon [lagɔ̃] NM lagoon

lagopède [lagɔpɛd] NM **~ d'Écosse** (red) grouse; **~ blanc** willow grouse; **~ des Alpes** ptarmigan

Lagos [lagos] N Lagos

lagunaire [lagynɛʀ] ADJ lagoon (épith), of a lagoon

lagune [lagyn] NF lagoon

là-haut [lao] ADV (gén) up there; (= dessus) up on top; (= à l'étage) upstairs; (= au ciel) on high, in heaven above; **tout ~, au sommet de**

la **montagne** way up there, at the top of the mountain; ~ **dans les nuages** above in the clouds

lai[1] [lɛ] NM (*Poésie*) lay

lai[2], **e**[1] [lɛ] ADJ (*Rel*) lay; **frère** ~ lay brother

laïc [laik] ADJ, NM = **laïque**

laîche [lɛʃ] NF sedge

laïcisation [laisizasjɔ̃] NF secularization, laicization

laïciser [laisize] VT [+ *institutions*] to secularize, laicize

laïcité [laisite] NF (= *caractère*) secularity; (*Pol* = *système*) secularism

laid, e [lɛ, lɛd] ADJ **a** (*physiquement*) [*personne, visage, animal, meuble, dessin*] ugly; [*ville, région*] ugly, unattractive; [*bâtiment*] ugly, unsightly; ~ **comme un singe** *ou* **un pou** *ou* **un crapaud** *ou* **les sept péchés capitaux** *ou* **à faire peur** as ugly as sin; **il est très ~ de visage** he's got a terribly ugly face **b** (*moralement*) [*action*] despicable, low; [*vice*] ugly, loathsome; **c'est ~, ce que tu as fait** that was a nasty *ou* disgusting thing to do

laidement [lɛdmã] ADV (= *sans beauté*) in an ugly way; (*littér* = *bassement*) despicably

laideron [lɛdʀɔ̃] NM ugly girl *ou* woman; **c'est un vrai** ~ she's a real ugly duckling

laideur [lɛdœʀ] NF **a** (*physique*) [*personne, visage, animal, meuble, dessin*] ugliness; [*ville, région*] ugliness, unattractiveness; [*bâtiment*] ugliness, unsightliness; **c'est d'une ~!** it's so ugly! **b** (*morale*) [*action*] lowness, meanness; **la guerre/l'égoïsme dans toute sa ~** the full horror of war/of selfishness, war/selfishness in all its ugliness; **les ~s de la vie** the ugly side of life; **les ~s de la guerre** the ugliness of war

laie[2] [lɛ] NF (*Zool*) wild sow

laie[3] [lɛ] NF (= *sentier*) forest track *ou* path

lainage [lɛnaʒ] NM **a** (= *vêtement*) woollen *ou* woolen (*US*) garment, woolly*; **la production des ~s** the manufacture of woollens *ou* of woollen goods **b** (= *étoffe*) woollen material *ou* fabric; **beau ~** fine quality woollen material

laine [lɛn] **1** NF wool; **de ~** [*vêtement, moquette*] woollen, woolly; **tapis de haute ~** deep *ou* thick pile wool carpet; **il faut mettre une petite ~** (*vêtement*) you'll need a sweater; **il ne faut pas te laisser tondre** *ou* **manger la ~ sur le dos** you shouldn't let people walk all over you → **bas**[2] **2** COMP ► **laine d'acier** steel wool ► **laine à matelas** flock ► **laine peignée** [*pantalon, veston*] worsted wool; [*pull*] combed wool ► **laine de roche** rockwool ► **laine à tricoter** knitting wool ► **laine de verre** glass wool ► **laine vierge** new *ou* virgin wool

laineux, -euse [lɛnø, øz] ADJ [*tissu, plante*] woolly

lainier, -ière [lɛnje, jɛʀ] **1** ADJ [*industrie*] wool(len) (*épith*) **2** NM,F (= *marchand*) wool merchant; (= *ouvrier*) wool worker

laïque [laik] **1** ADJ [*tribunal*] lay, civil; [*vie*] secular; [*habit*] ordinary; [*collège*] non-religious, secular; **l'enseignement** *ou* **l'école ~** (*gén*) secular education; (*en France*) state education **2** NM layman; **les ~s** laymen, the laity **3** NF laywoman

laisse [lɛs] NF **a** (= *attache*) leash, lead; **tenir en ~** [+ *chien*] to keep on a leash *ou* lead; (*fig*) [+ *personne*] to keep a tight rein on, keep in check **b** (*Géog*) foreshore; ~ **de mer** tide mark; ~ **de haute/basse mer** high-/low-water mark **c** (*Poésie*) laisse

laissé-pour-compte, laissée-pour-compte (*mpl* **laissés-pour-compte**) [lesepuʀkɔ̃t] **1** ADJ **a** (*Comm*) (= *refusé*) rejected, returned; (= *invendu*) unsold, left over **b** [*personne*] rejected; [*chose*] rejected, discarded **2** NM **a** (*Comm*) (= *refusé*) reject;

(*invendu*) unsold article; **brader les laissés-pour-compte** to sell off old *ou* leftover stock cheaply **b** (= *personne*) **les laissés-pour-compte de la société** society's rejects; **ce sont les laissés-pour-compte du progrès** these people are the casualties of progress, progress has left these people out in the cold *ou* on the scrap heap

▼ **laisser** [lese] ▶ conjug 1 ◀ **1** VT **a** (= *abandonner*) [+ *place, fortune, personne, objet*] to leave; ~ **sa clé au voisin** to leave one's key with the neighbour, leave the neighbour one's key; **laisse-lui du gâteau** leave him some cake, leave some cake for him; **il m'a laissé ce vase pour 100 F** he let me have this vase for 100 francs; **laissez, je vais le faire/c'est moi qui paie** leave that, I'll do it/I'm paying; **laisse-moi le temps d'y réfléchir** give me time to think about it; **laisse-moi devant la banque** drop *ou* leave me at the bank; **il a laissé un bras dans l'accident** he lost an arm in the accident; **il y a laissé sa vie** it cost him his life; **elle l'a laissé de meilleure humeur** she left him in a better mood; **au revoir, je vous laisse** good-bye, I must leave you; **laisse-moi!** leave me alone!; **je l'ai laissé à son travail** (*accompagner*) I dropped him off at work; (*ne plus déranger*) I left him to get on with his work

b (= *faire demeurer*) [+ *trace, regrets, goût*] to leave; ~ **qn indifférent/dans le doute** to leave sb unmoved/in doubt; ~ **qn debout** to keep sb standing (up); **on lui a laissé ses illusions** ◊ **on l'a laissé à ses illusions** we didn't disillusion him; **elle m'a laissé une bonne impression** she made a good impression on me; **on l'a laissé dans l'erreur** we didn't tell him that he was mistaken; **il vaut mieux le ~ dans l'ignorance de nos projets** it is best to leave him in the dark *ou* not to tell him about our plans; ~ **un enfant à ses parents** (*gén*) to leave a child with his parents; (*Jur*) to leave a child in the custody of his parents; **vous laissez le village sur votre droite** you go past the village on your right; ~ **la vie à qn** to spare sb's life; **cette opération ne doit pas ~ de séquelles** this operation should leave *ou* have no after-effects

c (*loc: lit, fig*) ~ **la porte ouverte** to leave the door open; ~ **le meilleur pour la fin** to leave the best till last; **je te laisse à penser combien il était content** you can imagine *ou* I don't need to tell you how pleased he was → **champ, désirer, plan**[1]

d (*littér* = *manquer*) **il n'a pas laissé de me le dire** he didn't fail to tell me, he could not refrain from telling me; **cela n'a pas laissé de me surprendre** I couldn't fail to be surprised by *ou* at that; **cela ne laisse pas d'être vrai** it is true nonetheless

2 VB AUX ~ **(qn) faire qch** to let sb do sth; **laisse-le partir** let him go; **laisse-le monter/descendre** let him come *ou* go up/down; (*iro*) **laissez-moi rire!** don't make me laugh!; ~ **voir** (= *révéler*) to show, reveal; **il a laissé voir sa déception** he couldn't help showing his disappointment; ~ **voir ses sentiments** to let one's feelings show; **il n'en a rien laissé voir** he showed no sign of it, he gave no inkling of it; **laisse-le faire** (*sans l'aider*) let him do it himself; (*à sa manière*) let him do it his own way; (*ce qui lui plaît*) let him do as he likes *ou* wants; **il faut ~ faire le temps** we must let things take their course; **laisse faire!** never mind!, don't bother!; **j'ai été attaqué dans la rue et les gens ont laissé faire** I was attacked in the street and people did nothing *ou* people just stood by; **on ne va pas le ~ faire sans réagir!** we're not going to let him get away with that! → **courir, penser, tomber**

3 **se laisser** VPR **se ~ persuader/exploiter/duper** to let o.s. be persuaded/exploited/fooled; **il s'est laissé attendrir par leur pauvreté** he was moved by their poverty; **il ne faut**

pas se ~ décourager/abattre you mustn't let yourself become *ou* allow yourself to become discouraged/downhearted; **je me suis laissé surprendre par la pluie** I got caught in the rain; **ce petit vin se laisse boire*** this wine goes down well *ou* nicely; **se ~ aller** to let o.s. go; **se ~ aller à mentir** to stoop to telling lies; **je me suis laissé faire** I let myself be persuaded, I let myself be talked into it; **je n'ai pas l'intention de me ~ faire** I'm not going to let myself be pushed around; **laisse-toi faire!** (*à qn que l'on soigne*) come on, it won't hurt (you)!; (*à qn que l'on habille*) let me do it; (*en offrant une liqueur etc*) go on, be a devil!*; **laisse-toi faire, je vais te peigner** just let me comb your hair, keep still while I comb your hair; **et tu t'es laissé faire sans protester?** and you just let them do it without saying anything? → **conter, dire, vivre**

laisser-aller [leseale] NM INV (*gén*) casualness, carelessness; [*travail, langage, vêtements*] sloppiness, carelessness; **il y a beaucoup de ~ dans ce service** things are very lax in this department, this department is very slack

laisser-faire [lesefɛʀ] NM INV (*Écon*) laissez-faire (policy *ou* economics *sg*), non-interventionism

laissées [lese] NFPL wild boar droppings

laissez-passer [lesepase] NM INV (*gén*) pass; (*Douane*) transire

lait [lɛ] **1** NM **a** (*animal*) milk; ~ **de vache/de chèvre/d'ânesse** cow's/goat's/ass's milk; ~ **concentré sucré/non sucré** condensed/evaporated milk; ~ **entier** whole *ou* full cream (*Brit*) milk; ~ **cru** unpasteurized milk; **mettre qn au ~** to put sb on a milk diet; (*fig*) **boire du (petit)** ~ to lap it up; **cela se boit comme du petit ~** you don't notice you're drinking it; **frère/sœur de ~** foster brother/sister → **café, chocolat, cochon, dent b** (*végétal*) milk; ~ **d'amande/de coco/de soja** almond/coconut/soy(a) milk **c** (*Cosmétique*) lotion; ~ **de beauté** beauty lotion; ~ **démaquillant** cleansing milk; ~ **solaire** sun lotion

2 COMP ► **lait caillé** curds ► **lait de chaux** lime water ► **lait de croissance** vitamin-enriched milk (*for babies and young children*) ► **lait fraise** strawberry-flavoured milk ► **lait maternel** mother's milk, breast milk ► **lait maternisé** formula, baby milk (*Brit*) ► **lait en poudre** dried *ou* powdered milk ► **lait de poule** (*Culin*) eggflip, eggnog ► **lait végétal** latex

laitage [lɛtaʒ] NM (= *produit laitier*) dairy product

laitance [lɛtãs] NF soft roe

laiterie [lɛtʀi] NF (= *usine, magasin*) dairy; (= *industrie*) dairy industry

laiteux, -euse [lɛtø, øz] ADJ [*couleur, liquide, peau, huître*] milky; [*teint*] milky(-white), creamy; [*lumière*] pearly; [*chair*] creamy

laitier, -ière [lɛtje, jɛʀ] **1** ADJ [*industrie, produit*] dairy (*épith*); [*production, vache*] (*épith*), dairy (*épith*) **2** NM **a** (= *livreur*) milkman; (= *vendeur*) dairyman; **à l'heure du ~** at the crack of dawn, in the early hours **b** (*Ind*) slag **3** **laitière** NF (= *vendeuse*) dairywoman; (= *livreuse*) milkwoman; (= *vache*) dairy *ou* milk cow; **une bonne laitière** a good milker

laiton [lɛtɔ̃] NM (= *alliage*) brass; (= *fil*) brass wire

laitue [lety] NF lettuce; ~ **de mer** sea lettuce

laïus* [lajys] NM INV (= *discours*) long-winded speech; (= *verbiage*) verbiage (*NonC*), padding (*NonC*); **faire un ~** to hold forth at great length, give a long-winded speech

laïusser* [lajyse] ▶ conjug 1 ◀ VI to expatiate, hold forth, spout* (**sur** on)

lama [lama] NM (*Zool*) llama; (*Rel*) lama

lamaïsme [lamaism] NM Lamaism

lamaïste [lamaist] ADJ, NM,F Lamaist

lamantin [lamãtɛ̃] NM manatee

lamarckien, -ienne [lamaʀkjɛ̃, jɛn] ADJ (*Bio*) Lamarckian

lamaserie [lamazʀi] NF lamasery

lambada [lãbada] NF lambada

lambda [lãbda] 1 NM (= *lettre*) lambda 2 ADJ INV (= *quelconque*) [*spectateur, lecteur*] average; **le citoyen ~** the average citizen, the man in the street

lambeau (*pl* **lambeaux**) [lãbo] NM [*papier, tissu*] scrap; **~x de chair** strips of flesh; **en ~x** [*vêtements*] in tatters *ou* rags, tattered; [*affiche*] in tatters, tattered; **mettre en ~x** to tear to shreds *ou* bits; **tomber** *ou* **partir en ~x** to fall to pieces *ou* bits; **~x de conversation** scraps of conversation; **~x du passé** fragments *ou* remnants of the past

lambic(k) [lãbik] NM *kind of strong Belgian beer* → **gueuse**

lambin, e* [lãbɛ̃, in] 1 ADJ slow; **que tu es ~!** you're such a dawdler! *ou* slowcoach* (*Brit*) *ou* slowpoke!* (*US*) 2 NM,F dawdler*, slow-coach* (*Brit*), slowpoke* (*US*)

lambiner* [lãbine] ▸ conjug 1 ◂ VI to dawdle

lambourde [lãbuʀd] NF (*pour parquet*) backing strip (*on joists*); (*pour solive*) wall-plate

lambrequin [lãbʀəkɛ̃] NM [*fenêtre*] pelmet, lambrequin; [*ciel de lit*] valance; (= *ornement*) lambrequin; (*Hér*) **~s** lambrequin, mantling

lambris [lãbʀi] NM (*en bois*) panelling (*NonC*), wainscoting (*NonC*); (*en marbre*) marble wall panels; (*fig*) **sous les ~ dorés des ministères** in the corridors of power

lambrisser [lãbʀise] ▸ conjug 1 ◂ VT (*avec du bois*) to panel, wainscot; (*avec du marbre*) to panel; **lambrissé de pin** pine-panelled

lame [lam] 1 NF a [*métal, verre*] strip; [*bois*] strip, lath; (*Aut*) [*ressort*] leaf; [*store*] slat; [*pour microscope*] slide b [*couteau, tondeuse, scie*] blade; **visage en ~ de couteau** hatchet face c (*fig*) (= *épée*) sword; **une bonne** *ou* **fine ~** (= *escrimeur*) good swordsman (*ou* swordswoman) d (= *vague*) wave e [*partie de la langue*] blade 2 COMP ▸ **lame de fond** ground swell (*NonC*) ▸ **lame de parquet** floorboard, strip of parquet flooring ▸ **lame de rasoir** razor blade

lamé, e [lame] 1 ADJ lamé (*épith*); **robe ~e (d')or** gold lamé dress 2 NM lamé

lamelle [lamɛl] NF (*de métal, plastique*) (small) strip; [*persiennes*] slat; [*champignon*] gill; (*pour microscope*) coverglass; **~ de mica** mica flake; **couper en ~s** [+ *légumes*] to cut into thin strips *ou* slices

lamellé-collé (*pl* **lamellés-collés**) [lamelekɔle] NM glued laminated timber

lamellibranche [lamelibʀãʃ] NM bivalve, lamellibranch; **les ~s** lamellibranchia

lamentable [lamãtabl] ADJ a (= *mauvais*) [*conditions, résultat, état, comportement*] appalling, lamentable, awful; [*concurrent, spectacle*] appalling, awful; **cette émission est ~!** what a pathetic* programme! b (= *tragique*) [*sort*] miserable, pitiful; [*histoire*] dreadful, appalling

lamentablement [lamãtabləmã] ADV [*échouer*] miserably, lamentably; **il se traînait ~ dans la maison** he was moping around the house

lamentation [lamãtasjɔ̃] NF (= *cri de désolation*) lamentation, wailing (*NonC*); (*péj*) [*jérémiades*] moaning (*NonC*); (*Bible*) **le livre des Lamentations** (the Book of) Lamentations → **mur**

lamenter (se) [lamãte] ▸ conjug 1 ◂ VPR to moan, lament; **se lamenter sur qch** to moan over sth, bemoan sth; **se lamenter sur son sort** to bemoan *ou* bewail *ou* lament one's fate; **arrête de te lamenter sur ton propre sort** stop feeling sorry for yourself; **il se lamente d'avoir échoué** he is bemoaning his failure

lamento [lamɛnto] NM lament

laminage [laminaʒ] NM (*Tech*) lamination

laminaire [lamineʀ] NF (*Bot*) laminaria

laminer [lamine] ▸ conjug 1 ◂ VT a [+ *métal*] to laminate; **laminé à chaud/à froid** hot-/cold-rolled b (= *détruire*) **ses marges bénéficiaires ont été laminées par les hausses de prix** his profit margins have been eaten away *ou* eroded by price rises; **les petites formations politiques ont été laminées aux dernières élections** small political groupings were practically wiped out in the last election

lamineur, -euse [laminœʀ, øz] 1 ADJ M **cylindre ~** roller 2 NM,F rolling mill operator

laminoir [laminwaʀ] NM rolling mill; (*fig*) **passer au ~** to steamroller

lampadaire [lãpadɛʀ] NM [*intérieur*] standard lamp; [*rue*] street lamp; **(pied de) ~** [*intérieur*] lamp standard; [*rue*] lamppost

lampant [lãpã] ADJ M → **pétrole**

lamparo [lãpaʀo] NM [*pêche*] **pêche au ~** fishing by lamplight (*in the Mediterranean*)

lampe [lãp] 1 NF lamp, light; (= *ampoule*) bulb; (*Radio*) valve; **éclairé par une ~** lit by lamplight → **mettre** 2 COMP ▸ **lampe à acétylène** acetylene lamp (*Brit*) *ou* torch (*US*) ▸ **lampe à alcool** spirit lamp ▸ **lampe à arc** arc light *ou* lamp ▸ **lampe d'architecte** Anglepoise lamp® ▸ **lampe Berger**® Berger lamp® ▸ **lampe à bronzer** sun lamp ▸ **lampe de bureau** desk lamp *ou* light ▸ **lampe à carbure** carbide lamp ▸ **lampe de chevet** bedside lamp *ou* light ▸ **lampe électrique** flashlight, torch (*Brit*) ▸ **lampe à huile** oil lamp ▸ **lampe à incandescence** incandescent lamp ▸ **lampe de lecture** reading lamp ▸ **lampe de mineur** (miner's) safety lamp ▸ **lampe au néon** neon light ▸ **lampe à pétrole** paraffin (*Brit*) *ou* kerosene (*US*) *ou* oil lamp ▸ **lampe pigeon** (small) oil *ou* paraffin (*Brit*) *ou* kerosene (*US*) lamp ▸ **lampe de poche** flashlight, torch (*Brit*) ▸ **lampe à sodium** sodium light ▸ **lampe solaire** sun lamp ▸ **lampe à souder** (*lit*) blowtorch, blowlamp (*Brit*); (*arg Mil*) machine gun ▸ **lampe témoin** (*gén*) warning light; [*magnétoscope etc*] (indicator) light → **halogène**

lampée* [lãpe] NF gulp, swig*; **boire qch à grandes ~s** to gulp *ou* swig* sth down

lamper*† [lãpe] ▸ conjug 1 ◂ VT to gulp down, swig (down)*

lampe-tempête (*pl* **lampes-tempête**) [lãptãpɛt] NF storm lantern, hurricane lamp

lampion [lãpjɔ̃] NM Chinese lantern → **air³**

lampiste [lãpist] NM (*lit*) light (maintenance) man; (*, hum* = *subalterne*) underling, dogsbody* (*Brit*); **c'est toujours la faute du ~*** it's always the underling who gets the blame

lamproie [lãpʀwa] NF **~ (de mer)** lamprey; **~ de rivière** river lamprey, lampern

Lancastre [lãkastʀ(ə)] N Lancaster

lance [lãs] NF a (= *arme*) spear; [*tournoi*] lance; **frapper qn d'un coup de ~** to hit sb with one's lance → **fer**, **rompre** b (= *tuyau*) **(à eau)** hose; **~ d'arrosage** garden hose; **~ d'incendie** fire hose

lance-bombes [lãsbɔ̃b] NM INV bomb launcher

lancée [lãse] NF **être sur sa ~** to have got started; **continuer sur sa ~** to keep going; **il a encore travaillé trois heures sur sa ~** once he was under way *ou* he'd got going he worked for another three hours; **je peux encore courir deux km sur ma ~** now I'm in my stride I can run another two km; **je ne voulais pas t'interrompre sur ta ~** I didn't want to interrupt you in full flow

lance-engins [lãsãʒɛ̃] NM INV missile launch-

er; **sous-marin nucléaire ~** nuclear missile submarine

lance-flammes [lãsflɑm] NM INV flame-thrower

lance-fusées [lãsfyze] NM INV (*Mil*) rocket launcher; [*fusée éclairante*] flare gun

lance-grenades [lãsɡʀənad] NM INV grenade launcher; **fusil ~** shoulder-held grenade launcher

lancement [lãsmã] NM a [*entreprise*] launching, starting up; [*campagne*] launching; [*fusée*] launching, launch; [*processus*] starting (off); [*produit*] launching; [*emprunt*] issuing, floating; **lors du ~ du nouveau produit** when the new product was launched; **fenêtre** *ou* **créneau de ~** launch window b (*Sport*) throwing; **~ du disque/javelot/marteau** throwing the discus/javelin/hammer, discus/javelin/hammer throwing; **~ du poids** putting the shot, shot put

lance-missiles [lãsmisil] NM INV missile launcher; **sous-marin ~** ballistic missile submarine

lancéolé, e [lãseɔle] ADJ (*Bot*) lanceolate; (*Archit*) lanceted

lance-pierre (*pl* **lance-pierres**) [lãspjɛʀ] NM catapult; **manger avec un ~*** to grab a quick bite (to eat)*; **payer qn avec un ~*** to pay sb peanuts*

lancer¹ [lãse] ▸ conjug 3 ◂ 1 VT a (= *jeter*) (*gén*) to throw; (*violemment*) to hurl, fling; (*Sport*) [+ *disque, marteau, javelot*] to throw; **~ qch à qn** (*pour qu'il l'attrape*) to throw sth to sb, throw sb sth; (*agressivement*) to throw sth at sb; **lance-moi mes clés** throw me my keys; **~ une balle/son chapeau en l'air** to throw *ou* toss a ball/one's hat into the air *ou* up in the air; (*Pêche*) **~ sa ligne** to cast one's line; **il lança sa voiture dans la foule** he drove his car straight at the crowd; **~ son chien contre qn** to set one's dog on sb; (*Mil*) **~ ses hommes contre l'ennemi/à l'assaut** to launch one's men against the enemy/into the assault; **lance ta jambe en avant** kick your leg up; **~ un coup de poing** to throw a punch, lash out with one's fist; **~ un coup de pied** to kick out, lash out with one's foot; (*Sport*) **~ le poids** to put the shot; **il lance à 15 mètres** he can throw 15 metres; (*fig*) **~ un pont sur une rivière** to throw a bridge across a river; **la cathédrale lance sa flèche de pierre vers le ciel** the stone spire of the cathedral thrusts up into the sky

b (= *projeter*) [+ *flèche, obus*] to fire; [+ *bombe*] to drop; [+ *torpille*] to fire, launch; [+ *fumée*] to send up *ou* out; [+ *flammes, lave*] to throw out; **~ des éclairs** [*bijoux*] to sparkle; **ses yeux lançaient des éclairs** (*de colère*) his eyes blazed *ou* flashed with anger → **étincelle**

c (= *émettre*) [+ *accusations*] to level, hurl; [+ *menaces, injures*] to hurl; [+ *avertissement, proclamation, mandat d'arrêt*] to issue, put out; [+ *théorie*] to put forward, advance; [+ *appel*] to launch; [+ *SOS, signal*] to send out; [+ *fausse nouvelle, rumeur*] to put out; [+ *invitation*] to send off; [+ *hurlement*] to give out; **~ un cri** to cry out; **~ une plaisanterie** to crack a joke; **il lui lança un coup d'œil furieux** she flashed *ou* darted a furious glance at him; **« je refuse » lança-t-il fièrement** "I refuse," he retorted proudly; **« salut » me lança-t-il du fond de la salle** "hello," he called out to me from the far end of the room

d (= *faire démarrer*) [+ *fusée, satellite, navire*] to launch; [+ *affaire, entreprise*] to launch, start up; [+ *attaque, campagne électorale*] to launch; [+ *processus*] to start (off); [+ *emprunt*] to issue, float; [+ *projet*] to launch; (*Ordin*) [+ *programme, recherche, impression*] to start; **~ une souscription** to start a fund; **~ une discussion** to get a discussion going, start a discussion; **c'est lui qui a lancé l'idée du voyage** he's the one who came up with the idea of the trip on a lancé quelques idées we floated a few ideas; il a lancé son parti dans une aventure dangereuse he has launched his party into ou set his party off on a dangerous venture; ne le lancez pas sur son sujet favori don't set him off on ou don't let him get launched on his pet subject; une fois lancé, on ne peut plus l'arrêter! once he gets the bit between his teeth ou once he gets warmed up there's no stopping him!

e (= faire connaître ou adopter) [+ vedette] to launch; [+ produit] to launch, bring out; ~ une nouvelle mode to launch ou start a new fashion; ~ qn dans la politique/les affaires/le monde to launch sb into politics/in business/in society; c'est ce film qui l'a lancé it was this film that launched his career; il est lancé maintenant he has made a name for himself ou has made his mark now

f (= donner de l'élan) [+ moteur] to open up; [+ voiture] to get up to speed; [+ balançoire] to set going; ~ un cheval to give a horse its head; ~ le balancier d'une horloge to set the pendulum in a clock going; la moto était lancée à 140 quand elle l'a heurté the motorbike had reached ou had got up to a speed of 140 km/h when it hit him; une fois lancée, la voiture ... once the car gets up speed ou builds up speed, it ...

g (= faire mal à) ça me lance (dans le bras etc) I've got shooting pains (in my arm etc)

2 se lancer VPR a (mutuellement) [+ balle] to throw to each other; [+ injures, accusations] to hurl at each other, exchange; ils n'arrêtent pas de se ~ des plaisanteries they're always cracking jokes together

b (= sauter) to leap, jump; (= se précipiter) to dash, rush; dans le vide to leap ou jump into space; il faut sauter, n'hésite pas, lance-toi! you've got to jump, don't hesitate, just do it! ou let yourself go!; se ~ contre un obstacle to dash ou rush at an obstacle; se ~ en avant to dash ou rush ou run forward; se ~ à l'assaut to leap to the attack; se ~ à l'assaut d'une forteresse to launch an attack on a fortress; chaque week-end, des milliers de voitures se lancent sur les routes thousands of cars take to ou pour onto the roads every weekend

c (= s'engager) se ~ à la recherche de qn/qch to go off in search of sb/sth; il s'est lancé à la recherche d'un emploi he started looking for a job; l'entreprise se lance sur le marché the company is entering the market; il construit un bateau — dis donc, il se lance!! he's building a boat — wow, he's aiming high! ou he's thinking big!*; elle n'attend que toi! vas-y, lance-toi!* it's you she wants! go for it!*; se ~ dans [+ aventure] to embark on, set off on; [+ discussion] to launch into, embark on; [+ dépenses] to embark on, take on; [+ métier] to go into, take up; [+ travaux, grève] to embark on, start; [+ passe-temps] to take up; [+ bataille] to pitch into; se ~ dans la politique/les affaires to go into politics/business; se ~ dans la course au pouvoir/à l'audience to enter the race for power/the ratings battle; ils se sont lancés dans des opérations financières hasardeuses they got involved in some risky financial deals; se ~ dans la lecture d'un roman to set about ou begin reading a novel; se ~ dans la production/fabrication de qch to start producing/manufacturing sth

d (* = se faire une réputation) il cherche à se ~ he's trying to make a name for himself

lancer² [lɑ̃se] NM a (Sport) (gén) throw; il a droit à trois ~s he is allowed three attempts ou throws; ~ annulé no throw; (Basket) ~ franc free throw, charity toss (US); (Alpinisme) ~ de corde lassoing (NonC), lasso; le ~ du disque/du javelot/du marteau the discus/javelin/hammer; le ~ du poids putting the shot, the shot put b (Pêche) (pêche au) ~ casting; ~ léger spinning; ~ lourd bait-casting

lance-roquettes [lɑ̃srɔkɛt] NM INV rocket launcher

lance-satellites [lɑ̃ssatelit] NM INV satellite launcher

lance-torpilles [lɑ̃stɔrpij] NM INV torpedo tube

lancette [lɑ̃sɛt] NF (Archit, Méd) lancet

lanceur, -euse [lɑ̃sœʀ, øz] 1 NM,F a [disque, javelot, marteau, pierres] thrower; (Cricket) bowler; (Base-ball) pitcher; ~ de poids shot putter b ~ de mode trendsetter; le ~ du produit the company which launched the product 2 NM (Espace, Mil) launcher; ~ d'engins/de satellites missile/satellite launcher

lancier [lɑ̃sje] NM (Mil) lancer; les ~s (= danse) the lancers

lancinant, e [lɑ̃sinɑ̃, ɑ̃t] ADJ a [douleur] shooting (épith), piercing (épith) b [obsédant] [souvenir] haunting; [musique] insistent, monotonous; [problème, question] nagging; ce que tu peux être ~ à toujours réclamer* you are a real pain* ou you get on my nerves the way you're always asking for things

lanciner [lɑ̃sine] ▸ conjug 1 ◂ 1 VI to throb 2 VT [pensée] to obsess, haunt, plague; * il nous a lancinés pendant trois jours pour aller au cirque [enfant] he tormented ou plagued us ou he went on at us* for three days about going to the circus

lançon [lɑ̃sɔ̃] NM sand-eel

landau [lɑ̃do] NM (= voiture d'enfant) pram (Brit), baby carriage (US); (= carrosse) landau

lande [lɑ̃d] 1 NF moor, heath 2 Landes NFPL les Landes the Landes (region) (southwest France)

Landern(e)au [lɑ̃dɛʀno] NM (hum) dans le Landerneau littéraire/universitaire in the literary/academic fraternity

landgrave [lɑ̃dgʀav] NM (Hist) landgrave

langage [lɑ̃gaʒ] 1 NM a (Ling, gén) language; le ~ de l'amour/des fleurs the language of love/of flowers; en ~ administratif/technique in administrative/technical language; je n'aime pas que l'on me tienne ce ~ I don't like being spoken to like that; il m'a tenu un drôle de ~ he said some odd things to me; quel ~ me tenez-vous là? what do you mean by that?; il m'a parlé avec ou il m'a tenu le ~ de la raison he spoke to me with the voice of reason; tenir un double ~ to use double talk; il a dû changer de ~ he had to change his tune

b (Ordin) language; ~ évolué/naturel high-level/natural language; ~ de haut/bas niveau high-/low-level language; ~ de programmation programming language

2 COMP ▸ le langage des animaux the language of animals ▸ langage argotique slang ▸ langage chiffré cipher, code (language) ▸ langage courant everyday language ▸ langage enfantin childish ou children's language; [bébé] baby talk ▸ langage intérieur (Philo) inner language ▸ langage machine (Ordin) machine language ▸ langage parlé spoken language, speech ▸ langage populaire popular speech

langagier, -ière [lɑ̃gaʒje, jɛʀ] 1 ADJ linguistic, of language (épith) 2 NM,F (Can) linguist

lange [lɑ̃ʒ] NM (baby's) flannel blanket; ~s swaddling clothes; (fig) dans les ~s in (its) infancy

langer [lɑ̃ʒe] ▸ conjug 3 ◂ VT ~ un bébé = lui mettre une couche) to change a baby, change the nappy (Brit) ou diaper (US); (= l'emmailloter) to wrap a baby in swaddling clothes; table/matelas à ~ changing table/mat

langoureusement [lɑ̃guʀøzmɑ̃] ADV languorously

langoureux, -euse [lɑ̃guʀø, øz] ADJ languorous

langouste [lɑ̃gust] NF (Zool) spiny ou rock lobster, crayfish, crawfish; (Culin) lobster

langoustier [lɑ̃gustje] NM (= filet) crayfish net; (= bateau) fishing boat (for crayfish)

langoustine [lɑ̃gustin] NF langoustine, Dublin bay prawn

langue [lɑ̃g] 1 NF a (Anat) tongue; ~ de bœuf/veau ox/veal tongue; avoir la ~ blanche ou chargée ou pâteuse to have a coated ou furred tongue; tirer la ~ (au médecin) to stick out ou put out one's tongue (à qn for sb); (par impolitesse) to stick out ou put out one's tongue (à qn at sb); (= être dans le besoin) to have a rough time of it*; (* = être frustré) to be green with envy; (* = avoir soif) il tirait la ~ his tongue was hanging out*, he was dying of thirst*; coup de ~ lick; le chien lui a donné un coup de ~ the dog licked him

b (= organe de la parole) tongue; avoir la ~ déliée ou bien pendue to be a bit of a gossip, have a ready tongue; avoir la ~ bien affilée to have a quick ou sharp tongue; (hum) avoir la ~ fourchue to speak with a forked tongue; il a la ~ trop longue ◊ il ne sait pas tenir sa ~ he can't hold his tongue, he doesn't know when to hold his tongue; il n'a pas la ~ dans sa poche he's never at a loss for words; tu as avalé ou perdu ta ~? has the cat got your tongue?, have you lost your tongue?; tu as retrouvé ta ~? so we're talking again, are we?; délier ou dénouer la ~ à qn to loosen sb's tongue; donner sa ~ au chat to give in ou up; j'ai le mot sur (le bout de) la ~ the word is on the tip of my tongue; il faut tourner sept fois sa ~ dans sa bouche avant de parler you should count to ten before you say anything; prendre ~ avec qn† to make contact with sb; (hum) les ~s vont aller bon train tongues will start wagging ou will wag

c (= personne) mauvaise ou méchante ~ spiteful ou malicious gossip; je ne voudrais pas être mauvaise ~ mais ... I don't want to tittle-tattle ou to spread scandal but ...; (iro) les bonnes ~s diront que ... worthy ou upright folk will say that ...

d (Ling) language, tongue (frm); la ~ française/anglaise the French/English language; les gens de ~ anglaise/française English-speaking/French-speaking people; ~ maternelle mother tongue; ~ mère parent language; ~ vivante/morte/étrangère living/dead/foreign language; ~ officielle official language; ~ écrite/parlée written/spoken language; ~ source ou de départ/cible ou d'arrivée (en traduction) source/target language; ~ vernaculaire vernacular (language); la ~ de Shakespeare (gén) Shakespearian language, the language of Shakespeare; (= l'anglais) English, the language of Shakespeare; il parle une ~ très pure his use of the language is very pure, his spoken language is very pure; (lit, fig) nous ne parlons pas la même ~ we don't speak the same language

e (Géog) ~ glaciaire spur of ice; ~ de terre strip ou spit of land

2 COMP ▸ la langue du barreau legal parlance, the language of the courts ▸ langue de bois (péj) waffle*, cant ▸ la langue diplomatique the language of diplomacy ▸ langue de feu tongue of fire ▸ la langue journalistique journalistic language, journalese (péj) ▸ langue d'oc langue d'oc ▸ langue d'oïl langue d'oïl ▸ langue populaire (idiome) popular language; (usage) popular speech ▸ langue de serpent (Bot) adder's-tongue, ophioglossum (SPÉC) ▸ langue de spécialité specialist language ▸ langue de travail working language ▸ langue verte slang ▸ langue de vipère spiteful gossip; elle a une ~ de vipère she's got a vicious ou venomous tongue

langue-de-bœuf (pl **langues-de-bœuf**) [lɑ̃gdəbœf] NF (Bot) beefsteak fungus

langue-de-chat (pl **langues-de-chat**) [lɑ̃gdəʃa] NF (flat) finger biscuit, langue de chat

languette [lɑ̃gɛt] NF (bois, cuir) tongue; (papier) (narrow) strip; (orgue) languet(te), languid; (instrument à vent) metal reed; (balance) pointer

langueur [lɑ̃gœʀ] NF (personne) languidness, languor; (style) languidness; **regard plein de ~** languid ou languishing look → **maladie**

languide [lɑ̃gid] ADJ (littér) languid, languishing

languir [lɑ̃giʀ] ▶ conjug 2 ◀ VI **a** (= dépérir) to languish; **~ dans l'oisiveté/d'ennui** to languish in idleness/in boredom; **(se) ~ d'amour pour qn** to be languishing with love for sb **b** (conversation, intrigue) to flag; (affaires) to be slack **c** (littér = désirer) **~ après qn/qch** to languish for ou pine for sb/sth **d** (= attendre) to wait, hang around*; **je ne languirai pas longtemps ici** I'm not going to hang around here for long*; **faire ~ qn** to keep sb waiting; **ne nous fais pas ~, raconte !** don't keep us in suspense, tell us about it!

languissamment [lɑ̃gisamɑ̃] ADV (littér) languidly

languissant, e [lɑ̃gisɑ̃, ɑ̃t] ADJ (personne) languid, listless; (regard) languishing (épith); (conversation, industrie) flagging (épith); (récit, action) dull; (activité économique) slack

lanière [lanjɛʀ] NF (cuir) thong, strap; (étoffe) strip; (fouet) lash; (appareil photo) strap; (Culin) **découper qch en ~s** to cut sth into strips

lanoline [lanɔlin] NF lanolin

lansquenet [lɑ̃skənɛ] NM (Cartes, Hist) lansquenet

lanterne [lɑ̃tɛʀn] **1** NF (gén) lantern; (électrique) lamp, light; (Hist = réverbère) street lamp; (Archit) lantern; (Aut) **allumer ses ~s†** to switch on one's (side)lights; (fig) **éclairer la ~ de qn** to enlighten sb; **les aristocrates à la ~ !** string up the aristocracy! → **vessie** **2** COMP ▶ **lanterne d'Aristote** Aristotle's lantern ▶ **lanterne arrière†** (Aut) rear light ▶ **lanterne de bicyclette** bicycle lamp ▶ **lanterne magique** magic lantern ▶ **lanterne de projection** slide lantern ▶ **lanterne rouge** (convoi) rear ou tail light; (maison close) red light; (fig = être le dernier) **être la ~ rouge** to lag behind ▶ **lanterne sourde** dark lantern ▶ **lanterne vénitienne** paper lantern, Chinese lantern

lanterneau (pl **lanterneaux**) [lɑ̃tɛʀno] NM (coupole) lantern; (escalier, atelier) skylight

lanterner [lɑ̃tɛʀne] ▶ conjug 1 ◀ VI (= traîner) to dawdle; **sans ~** straight away; **faire ~ qn** to keep sb waiting around ou hanging about (Brit)

lanternon [lɑ̃tɛʀnɔ̃] NM = **lanterneau**

lanthane [lɑ̃tan] NM lanthanum

Laos [laos] NM Laos

laotien, -ienne [laosjɛ̃, jɛn] **1** ADJ Laotian **2** NM (Ling) Laotian **3** **Laotien(ne)** NM,F Laotian

Lao-Tseu [laotsø] NM Lao-tze

La Palice [lapalis] N **c'est une vérité de ~** it's stating the obvious, it's a truism; (hum) **avant d'être en panne, cette machine marchait — ~ n'aurait pas dit mieux !** this machine worked before it broke down — well, that's very observant of you! (hum)

lapalissade [lapalisad] NF statement of the obvious; **c'est une ~ de dire que ...** it's stating the obvious to say that ...

laparoscopie [lapaʀɔskɔpi] NF laparoscopy

laparotomie [lapaʀɔtɔmi] NF laparotomy

La Paz [lapaz] N La Paz

lapement [lapmɑ̃] NM (= bruit, action) lapping (NonC); (= gorgée) lap

laper [lape] ▶ conjug 1 ◀ **1** VT to lap up **2** VI to lap

lapereau (pl **lapereaux**) [lapʀo] NM young rabbit

lapidaire [lapidɛʀ] **1** ADJ **a** (musée, inscription) lapidary **b** (= concis) (style, formule) terse **2** NM (= artisan) lapidary

lapidation [lapidasjɔ̃] NF stoning

lapider [lapide] ▶ conjug 1 ◀ VT (= tuer) to stone (to death); (= attaquer) to stone, throw ou hurl stones at

lapin [lapɛ̃] NM (= animal) rabbit; (= fourrure) rabbit(skin); **manteau en ~** rabbitskin coat; **~ domestique/de garenne** domestic/wild rabbit; **on s'est fait tirer comme des ~s** they were taking potshots at us; **mon petit ~** (terme d'affection) my lamb, my sweetheart; **coup du ~*** rabbit punch; (dans un accident de voiture) whiplash; **faire le coup du ~ à qn*** to give sb a rabbit punch; **poser un ~ à qn*** to stand sb up* → **chaud, courir**

lapine [lapin] NF (doe) rabbit; (péj) **c'est une vraie ~** she has one baby after another

lapiner [lapine] ▶ conjug 1 ◀ VI to litter, give birth; (péj) **elle n'arrête pas de ~** (femme) she churns out babies one after another (péj)

lapinière [lapinjɛʀ] NF rabbit hutch

lapis(-lazuli) [lapis(lazyli)] NM INV lapis lazuli

lapon, e [lapɔ̃, ɔn] **1** ADJ Lapp, Lappish **2** NM (Ling) Lapp, Lappish **3** **Lapon(e)** NM,F Lapp, Laplander

Laponie [lapɔni] NF Lapland

laps [laps] NM **~ de temps** (gén) period of time; (écoulé) **au bout d'un certain ~ de temps** after a certain period ou length of time

lapsus [lapsys] NM (parlé) slip of the tongue; (écrit) slip of the pen; **~ révélateur** Freudian slip; **faire un ~** to make a slip of the tongue (ou of the pen)

laquage [lakaʒ] NM (support) lacquering

laquais [lakɛ] NM (= domestique) lackey, footman; (péj = personne servile) lackey (péj), flunkey (péj)

laque [lak] **1** NF (= produit brut) lac, shellac; (= vernis) lacquer; (pour les cheveux) hairspray, (hair) lacquer; (pour les ongles) nail varnish; (= peinture) ~ **(brillante)** gloss paint **2** NM ou F (de Chine) lacquer **3** NM (= objet d'art) piece of lacquerware

laqué, e [lake] (ptp de **laquer**) ADJ (cheveux) lacquered; (ongles) painted; (peinture) gloss (épith); **meubles (en) ~ blanc** furniture with a white gloss finish; **murs ~s (de) blanc** walls painted in white gloss; **ses ongles ~s de rouge** her red fingernails → **canard**

laquelle [lakɛl] → **lequel**

laquer [lake] ▶ conjug 1 ◀ VT (+ support) to lacquer; **se ~ les cheveux** to put hairspray ou lacquer on one's hair

larbin* [laʀbɛ̃] NM (péj) servant, flunkey (péj); **je ne suis pas ton ~ !** I'm not your slave!

larcin [laʀsɛ̃] NM (littér = vol) theft; (= butin) spoils, booty; **dissimuler son ~** to hide one's spoils ou what one has stolen

lard [laʀ] NM (= gras) fat (of pig); (= viande) bacon; **~ fumé** ≈ smoked bacon; **~ maigre ou petit ~** streaky bacon (usually diced or in strips); **(se) faire du ~*** to lie back ou sit around doing nothing; (fig) **un gros ~*** a fat lump*; **on ne sait jamais avec lui si c'est du ~ ou du cochon*** you never know where you are with him* → **rentrer, tête**

larder [laʀde] ▶ conjug 1 ◀ VT (+ viande) to lard; **~ qn de coups de couteau** to hack at sb with a knife; **texte lardé de citations** text larded ou crammed with quotations

lardoire [laʀdwaʀ] NF (Culin) larding-needle, larding-pin; (* = épée) sword, steel

lardon [laʀdɔ̃] NM **a** (= tranche de lard) lardon; **(petits) ~s** (cubes) diced bacon **b** (* = enfant) kid*

lares [laʀ] NMPL, ADJ PL (**dieux**) ~ lares

largable [laʀgabl] ADJ releasable

largage [laʀgaʒ] NM (amarres) casting off; (étage de fusée) jettisoning; (module, satellite) release; (parachutiste, bombe, vivres, tracts) dropping; **zone de ~** drop zone; **opération de ~** drop

large [laʀʒ] **1** ADJ **a** (rue, fleuve, lit, couloir, ouverture) wide; (lame, dos, visage, main, nez, front) broad; (jupe) full; (chemise) loose-fitting; (pantalon) baggy; **à cet endroit, le fleuve est le plus ~** at this point the river is at its widest; **~ de 3 mètres** 3 metres wide; **chapeau à ~s bords** broad-brimmed ou wide-brimmed hat; **décrire un ~ cercle** to describe a big ou wide circle; **ouvrir une ~ bouche** to open one's mouth wide; **d'un geste ~** with a broad ou sweeping gesture; **avec un ~ sourire** with a broad smile; **ce veston est trop ~** this jacket is too big across the shoulders; **être ~ d'épaules** (personne) to be broad-shouldered; (vêtement) to be big across the shoulders; **être ~ de dos/de hanches** (personne) to have a broad back/wide hips; (vêtement) to be big across the back/the hips **b** (= important) (concession, amnistie) broad, wide; (pouvoirs, diffusion) wide, extensive; (soutien) extensive; (choix, gamme) wide; **une ~ majorité** a big majority; **retransmettre de ~s extraits d'un match** to show extensive extracts of a match; **destiné à un ~ public** designed for a wide audience; **faire une ~ part à qch** to give great weight to sth; **dans une ~ mesure** to a great ou large extent; **il a une ~ part de responsabilité dans l'affaire** he must take a large share of the responsibility in this matter; **au sens ~ du terme** in the broad sense of the term **c** (= généreux) (personne) generous; **une vie ~** a life of ease **d** (= tolérant) (conscience) accommodating; **~s vues** liberal views; **il est ~ d'idées ou d'esprit ◊ il a les idées ~s ou l'esprit ~** he's very broad-minded

2 ADV **voir ~** to think big; **prends un peu plus d'argent, il vaut mieux prévoir ~** take a bit more money, it's better to allow a bit extra; **calculer/mesurer ~** to be generous ou allow a bit extra in one's calculations/measurements; (Aut) **prendre un virage ~** to take a bend wide; **s'habiller ~** to wear loose-fitting styles; **cette marque taille ou habille ~** the sizes in this brand tend to be on the large side; **chausser ~** to be wide-fitting → **mener**

3 NM **a** (= largeur) **une avenue de 8 mètres de ~** an avenue 8 metres wide ou 8 metres in width; **acheter une moquette en 2 mètres de ~** to buy a carpet in 2 metre widths; **cela se fait en 2 mètres et 4 mètres de ~** that comes in 2-metre and 4-metre widths; **être au ~** (= avoir de la place) to have plenty of room ou space; († = avoir de l'argent) to be well-provided for, have plenty of money → **long** **b** (Naut) **le ~** the open sea; **le grand ~** the high seas; **se diriger vers/gagner le ~** to head for/reach the open sea; **au ~ de Calais** off Calais; (fig) **se tenir au ~ de qch** to stay clear of sth; (fig) **prendre le ~*** to clear off*, make o.s. scarce, hop it* (Brit); **ils ont pris le ~ avec les bijoux*** they made off with the jewels → **appel, vent**

largement [laʀʒəmɑ̃] ADV **a** (= amplement) (écarter) widely; **~ espacés** (arbres, maisons) widely spaced, wide apart; **fenêtre ~ ouverte** wide open window; **robe ~ décolletée** dress with a very open ou very scooped neckline **b** (= sur une grande échelle) (répandre, diffuser) widely; **amnistie ~ accordée** wide ou widely extended amnesty; **idée ~ répandue** widespread ou widely held view; **bénéficier de pouvoirs ~ étendus** to hold greatly increased powers **c** (= de loin, de beaucoup) greatly; **ce succès dépasse ~ nos prévisions** this success greatly exceeds our expectations *ou* is far beyond our expectations; **ce problème dépasse ~ ses compétences** this problem is altogether beyond *ou* is way beyond* his capabilities; **vous débordez ► le sujet** you are going well beyond the limits of the subject; **elle vaut ~ son frère** she's every bit as *ou* at least as good as her brother; (*Pol, Sport*) **~ battu** heavily defeated

d (= *grandement*) **vous avez ~ le temps** you have ample time *ou* plenty of time; **c'est ~ suffisant** that's plenty, that's more than enough; **cela me suffit ~** that's plenty *ou* ample *ou* more than enough for me; **il est ~ temps de commencer** it's high time we started; **j'ai été ~ récompensé de ma patience** my patience has been amply rewarded; **ça vaut ~ la peine/la visite** it's well worth the trouble/the visit; **ce film est ~ inspiré de mon livre** this film is, to a great extent, inspired by my book

e (= *généreusement*) [*payer, donner*] generously; **ils nous ont servis/indemnisés ~** they gave us generous *ou* ample helpings/compensation; **vivre ~** to live handsomely

f (= *au moins*) easily, at least; **il gagne ~ 35 000 F par mois** he earns easily *ou* at least 35,000 francs a month; **tu as mis trois heures pour le faire? — oh oui, ~** you took three hours to do it? — yes, easily *ou* at least; **il a ~ 50 ans** he is well past 50, he is well into his fifties; **c'est à cinq minutes/cinq km d'ici, ~** it's a good 5 minutes/5 km from here

largesse [laʀʒɛs] NF a (= *caractère*) generosity; **avec ~** generously b (= *dons*) **~s** liberalities; **faire des ~s** to make generous gifts

largeur [laʀʒœʀ] NF a [*rue, fleuve, lit, couloir, ouverture*] width; [*lame, dos, visage, main, nez, front*] breadth; [*voie ferrée*] gauge; **sur toute la ~** right across, all the way across; **dans le sens de la ~** widthways, widthwise; **quelle est la ~ de la fenêtre?** how wide is the window?; **tissu en grande/petite ~** double-width/single-width material b [*idées*] broadness; **d'esprit** broad-mindedness; **~ de vues** broadness of outlook c (* : *loc*) **dans les grandes ~s** with a vengeance, well and truly; **il s'est trompé dans les grandes ~s** he's slipped up with a vengeance, he's boobed this time, and how!*; **cette fois on les a eus dans les grandes ~s** we had them well and truly this time*, we didn't half put one over on them this time* (*Brit*)

largo [laʀgo] ADV, NM largo

largue [laʀg] 1 ADJ [*cordage*] slack; [*vent*] quartering 2 NM (= *vent*) quartering wind; **adopter l'allure du grand ~** to start to sail off the wind *ou* to sail large

largué, e [laʀge] (*ptp de* **larguer**) ADJ **être ~*** to be all at sea; **être un peu ~** to be a bit lost

larguer [laʀge] ▶ conjug 1 ◀ VT a (*Naut*) [+ *cordage*] to loose, release; [+ *voile*] to let out, unfurl; [+ *amarres*] to cast off, slip b [+ *parachutiste, bombe, vivres, tracts*] to drop; [+ *carburant, étage de fusée*] to jettison; [+ *cabine spatiale, module, satellite*] to release c (* = *se débarrasser de*) [+ *ami*] to drop, dump*; [+ *amant*] to dump*, ditch*; [+ *collaborateur*] to drop, get rid of, dump*; [+ *emploi*] to quit*; [+ *objet*] to chuck out*, get rid of; [+ *principes*] to jettison, ditch*; **il s'est fait ~** he was dumped

larigot [laʀigo] NM → **tire-larigot**

larme [laʀm] 1 NF a (*Physiol*) tear; **en ~s** in tears; **~s de joie/de rage** tears of joy/of rage; **verser des ~s sur qch/qn** to shed tears over sth/sb; **avec des ~s dans la voix** with tears in his voice, with a tearful voice; **avoir les ~s aux yeux** to have tears in one's eyes; **ça lui a fait venir les ~s aux yeux** it brought tears to his eyes; **elle a la ~ facile** she is easily moved to tears; **y aller de sa (petite) ~*** to shed a tear, have a little cry; **avoir toujours la ~ à l'œil** to be a real cry-baby → **fondre, rire, vallée** *etc* b (* = *goutte*) [*vin*] drop 2 COMP ► **larmes**

de crocodile crocodile tears ► **larmes de sang** tears of blood

larmier [laʀmje] NM (*Archit*) dripstone; [*cerf*] tearpit; [*cheval*] temple

larmoiement [laʀmwamã] NM a (= *pleurnicherie*) whimpering (*NonC*), snivelling (*NonC*) b (*Physiol*) watering (of the eyes)

larmoyant, e [laʀmwajã, ãt] ADJ a [*yeux*] (*gén*) tearful; (= *toujours humides*) watery; [*personne*] in tears (*attrib*); **d'une voix ~e ◊ d'un ton ~** in a tearful voice *ou* tearfully b (*péj*) [*récit*] maudlin; [*scène*] tear-jerking; (*Théât*) **comédie ~e** sentimental comedy; **c'est un de ces mélos ~s** it's a real tear-jerker

larmoyer [laʀmwaje] ▶ conjug 8 ◀ VI a (= *pleurnicher*) to whimper, snivel b [*yeux*] to water, run

larron [laʀõ] NM (†, *Bible*) thief; **s'entendre comme ~s en foire** to be as thick as thieves → **occasion, troisième**

larsen [laʀsen] NM (**effet) Larsen** interference; **il y a du ~ dans les micros** there's interference in the mikes*

larvaire [laʀvɛʀ] ADJ (*Zool*) larval; (*fig*) embryonic

larve [laʀv] NF (*Zool*) larva; (= *asticot*) grub; (*péj*) **~ (humaine)** worm

larvé, e [laʀve] ADJ [*crise, conflit*] dormant, latent; [*racisme*] latent; (*Méd*) [*fièvre, maladie*] larvate (*SPÉC*)

laryngé, e [laʀɛʒe] ADJ laryngeal

laryngectomie [laʀɛʒɛktɔmi] NF laryngectomy

laryngien, -ienne [laʀɛʒjɛ, jɛn] ADJ = **laryngé**

laryngite [laʀɛʒit] NF laryngitis (*NonC*)

laryngologie [laʀɛgɔlɔʒi] NF laryngology

laryngologiste [laʀɛgɔlɔʒist], **laryngologue** [laʀɛgɔlɔg] NMF throat specialist, laryngologist

laryngoscope [laʀɛgɔskɔp] NM laryngoscope

laryngoscopie [laʀɛgɔskɔpi] NF laryngoscopy

laryngotomie [laʀɛgɔtɔmi] NF laryngotomy

larynx [laʀɛks] NM larynx, voice-box

las¹, lasse [lɑ, lɑs] ADJ (*frm*) weary, tired; **~ de qn/de faire qch/de vivre** tired *ou* weary of sb/of doing sth/of life → **guerre**

las²†† [lɑs] EXCL alas!

lasagne [lazaɲ] NF lasagna

lascar†* [laskaʀ] NM (= *type louche*) character; (= *malin*) rogue; (*hum* = *enfant*) terror; **~ (louche)** shady character*; (*malin*) real rogue, smart customer*; **je vous aurai, mes ~s !** (*à des adultes*) I'll get you yet, you old rogues!*; (*à des enfants*) I'll get you yet, you little *ou* young rascals!*

lascif, -ive [lasif, iv] ADJ lascivious

lascivement [lasivmã] ADV lasciviously

lasciveté [lasivte], **lascivité** [lasivite] NF lasciviousness

laser [lazɛʀ] NM laser; **~ de puissance** power laser; **disque/rayon ~** laser disc/beam; **au ~** [*nettoyer, détruire*] using a laser; **opération au ~** laser operation

lassant, e [lɑsã, ãt] ADJ (*frm*) wearisome, tiresome

lasser [lɑse] ▶ conjug 1 ◀ 1 VT [+ *auditeur, lecteur*] to weary, tire; **~ la patience/bonté de qn** to exhaust sb's patience/goodwill, stretch sb's patience/goodwill too far; **je suis lassée de ses mensonges** I'm tired of his lies; **sourire lassé** weary smile; **lassé de tout** weary of everything 2 **se lasser** VPR **se ~ de qch/de faire qch** to (grow) weary of sth/of doing sth, tire *ou* grow tired of sth/of doing sth; **parler sans se ~** to speak without tiring *ou* flagging; **on écoute 5 minutes, et puis on se lasse** you listen for 5 minutes and then you get tired of it

lassitude [lasityd] NF weariness (*NonC*), lassitude (*NonC*) (*frm*); **avec ~** wearily

lasso [laso] NM lasso; **prendre au ~** to lasso

lasure [lazyʀ] NF tint, stain

lasuré, e [lazyʀe] ADJ tinted, stained

latence [latãs] NF latency; **temps de ~** (*gén*) latent period; (*Comm*) lead time; **période de ~** latency period

latent, e [latã, ãt] ADJ (*gén*) latent; **à l'état ~** latent, in the latent state

latéral, e [lateʀal] (*mpl* -**aux**) 1 ADJ side (*épith*), lateral (*frm*) 2 **latérale** NF (*Phon*) lateral (consonant)

latéralement [lateʀalmã] ADV (*gén*) laterally; [*être situé*] on the side; [*arriver, souffler*] from the side; [*diviser*] sideways

latéralité [lateʀalite] NF laterality

latérite [lateʀit] NF laterite

latex [latɛks] NM INV latex; (*euph* = *préservatif*) condom, rubber*

latifundiaire [latifɔ̃djɛʀ] ADJ **propriétaire ~** owner of a latifundium; **propriété ~** latifundium

latifundium [latifɔ̃djɔm] NM (*pl* **latifundia** [latifɔ̃dja]) latifundium

latin, e [latɛ̃, in] 1 ADJ (*gén, Rel*) Latin; **langues ~es** romance *ou* Latin languages → **Amérique, quartier, voile** 2 NM (*Ling*) Latin; **~ vulgaire** vulgar Latin; (*péj*) **~ de cuisine** dog Latin; **j'y ou j'en perds mon ~** I can't make head nor tail of it → **bas¹** 3 **Latin(e)** NM,F Latin; **les Latins** the Latin people, Latins

latinisation [latinizasjɔ̃] NF latinization

latiniser [latinize] ▶ conjug 1 ◀ VTI to latinize

latinisme [latinism] NM latinism

latiniste [latinist] NMF (= *spécialiste*) latinist, Latin scholar; (= *enseignant*) Latin teacher; (= *étudiant*) Latin student

latinité [latinite] NF (*Ling* = *caractère*) latinity; (= *civilisation*) **la ~** the Latin world

latino* [latino] ADJ, NMF Latino

latino-américain, e [latinoameʀikɛ̃, ɛn] (*mpl* **latino-américains**) 1 ADJ Latin-American, Hispanic 2 **Latino-Américain(e)** NM,F Latin-American, Hispanic

latitude [latityd] 1 NF a (*Astron, Géog*) latitude; **Paris est à 48° de ~ Nord** Paris is situated at latitude 48° north b (= *pouvoir, liberté*) latitude, scope; **avoir toute ~ pour faire qch** to have a free hand *ou* have carte blanche to do sth; **laisser/donner toute ~ à qn** to allow/give sb full scope *ou* a free hand; **on a une certaine ~** we have some leeway *ou* latitude *ou* some freedom of movement 2 **latitudes** NFPL latitudes; **sous toutes les ~s** in all latitudes, in all parts of the world; **sous nos ~s** in our part of the world

latitudinaire [latitydinɛʀ] ADJ, NMF (*littér*) latitudinarian

latomies [latɔmi] NFPL latomies

lato sensu [latosɛ̃sy] LOC ADV in the broader sense of the word

latrines [latʀin] NFPL latrines

lattage [lataʒ] NM lathing

latte [lat] NF (*gén*) lath; [*plancher*] board; [*fauteuil, sommier*] slat; (*Ski*) **~s*** boards*; **donner un coup de ~ à qn*** to wack sb*

latté, e [late] (*ptp de* **latter**) 1 ADJ lathed 2 NM blockboard

latter [late] ▶ conjug 1 ◀ VT to lath

lattis [lati] NM lathing (*NonC*), lathwork (*NonC*)

laudanum [lodanɔm] NM laudanum

laudateur, -trice [lodatœʀ, tʀis] NM,F (*littér*) adulator, laudator (*frm*)

laudatif, -ive [lodatif, iv] ADJ laudatory; **parler de qn en termes ~s** to speak highly *ou* in laudatory terms of sb, be full of praise for sb

lauréat, e [lɔʀea, at] 1 ADJ (prize-)winning 2 NM,F (prize-)winner, award winner; **les ~s du prix Nobel** the Nobel prize-winners

Laurent [lɔʀɑ̃] NM Lawrence, Laurence; **~ le Magnifique** Lorenzo the Magnificent

laurier [lɔʀje] **1** NM (*Culin*) **~ (commun)** bay-tree, (sweet) bay; **feuille de ~** bayleaf; **mettre du ~** to put in some bayleaves **2** **lauriers** NMPL laurels; **s'endormir** *ou* **se reposer sur ses ~s** to rest on one's laurels; **être couvert de ~s** to be showered with praise

laurier-cerise (*pl* **lauriers-cerises**) [lɔʀjesəʀiz] NM cherry laurel

laurier-rose (*pl* **lauriers-roses**) [lɔʀjeʀoz] NM oleander, rosebay

laurier-sauce (*pl* **lauriers-sauce**) [lɔʀjesos] NM (sweet) bay, bay-tree

laurier-tin (*pl* **lauriers-tins**) [lɔʀjetɛ̃] NM laurustinus

lavable [lavabl] ADJ washable; **~ en machine** machine-washable; **papier peint ~ (et lessivable)** washable wallpaper

lavabo [lavabo] **1** NM washbasin, bathroom sink (*US*) **2** **lavabos** NMPL (*euph*) **les ~s** the toilets, the loo* (*Brit*)

lavage [lavaʒ] **1** NM **a** [*plaie*] bathing, cleaning; [*corps, cheveux*] washing; **~ d'intestin** intestinal wash; **on lui a fait un ~ d'estomac** he had his stomach pumped **b** (= *action*) [*mur, vêtement, voiture*] washing (*NonC*); (= *opération*) wash; **après le ~ vient le rinçage** after the wash comes the rinse; **pour un meilleur ~, utilisez ...** for a better wash, use ...; **« ~ à la main »** "hand wash only"; **« ~ en machine »** "machine wash"; **le ~ des sols à la brosse/à l'éponge** scrubbing/sponging (down) floors; **on a dû faire trois ~s** it had to be washed three times, it had to have three washes; **le ~ de la vaisselle** dish-washing, washing-up (*Brit*); **ça a rétréci/c'est parti au ~** it shrunk/came out in the wash; **ton chemisier est au ~** your blouse is in the wash → **froid, température c** (*Tech*) [*gaz, charbon, laine*] washing **2** COMP ▶ **lavage de cerveau** brainwashing; **on lui a fait subir un ~ de cerveau** he was brainwashed

lavallière [lavaljɛʀ] NF floppy necktie, lavallière

lavande [lavɑ̃d] **1** NF lavender; **(eau de) ~** lavender water **2** ADJ INV **(bleu) ~** lavender (blue)

lavandière [lavɑ̃djɛʀ] NF (= *laveuse*) washerwoman; (= *oiseau*) wagtail

lavandin [lavɑ̃dɛ̃] NM hybrid lavender

lavaret [lavaʀɛ] NM (= *poisson*) pollan

lavasse* [lavas] NF dishwater*; **ce café, c'est de la ~** *ou* **une vraie ~** this coffee tastes like dishwater*

lave [lav] NF lava (*NonC*)

lavé, e [lave] (*ptp de* **laver**) ADJ [*couleur*] watery, washy, washed-out; [*ciel*] pale, colourless (*Brit*), colorless (*US*); [*yeux*] pale; (*Art*) **dessin ~** wash drawing

lave-auto (*pl* **lave-autos**) [lavoto] NM (*Can*) car wash

lave-glace (*pl* **lave-glaces**) [lavglas] NM windscreen (*Brit*) *ou* windshield (*US*) washer, screen wash(er) (*Brit*)

lave-linge [lavlɛ̃ʒ] NM INV washing machine; **~ séchant** washer-dryer

lave-mains [lavmɛ̃] NM INV (small) washbasin (*Brit*) *ou* washbowl (*US*)

lavement [lavmɑ̃] NM (*Méd*) enema; **~ baryté** barium enema; (*Bible*) **le ~ des pieds** the washing of the feet

laver [lave] ▶ conjug 1 ◀ **1** VT **a** (*gén*) to wash; [+ *mur*] to wash (down); [+ *plaie*] to bathe, cleanse; [+ *tache*] to wash out *ou* off; [+ *intestin*] to wash out; **~ avec une brosse** to scrub (down); **~ avec une éponge** to wash with a sponge, sponge (down); **~ au jet** to hose down; **~ à grande eau** [+ *sol*] to wash down; [+ *trottoir, pont de navire*] to sluice

down; [+ *légume*] to wash *ou* rinse thoroughly; **~ la vaisselle** to do *ou* wash the dishes, wash up (*Brit*), do the washing-up (*Brit*); **il faut ~ son linge sale en famille** it doesn't do to wash one's dirty linen in public; (*fig*) **~ la tête à qn** to haul sb over the coals, give sb a dressing down* → **machine b** (*en emploi absolu*) [*personne*] to do the washing; **ce savon lave bien** this soap washes well **c** [+ *affront, injure*] to avenge; [+ *péchés, honte*] to cleanse, wash away; **~ qn d'une accusation/d'un soupçon** to clear sb of an accusation/of suspicion **d** (*Art*) [+ *couleur*] to dilute; [+ *dessin*] to wash **2** **se laver** VPR **a** [*personne*] to wash, have a wash; **se ~ la figure/les mains** to wash one's face/one's hands; **se ~ les dents** to clean *ou* brush one's teeth; **se ~ dans un lavabo/une baignoire** to have a stand-up wash/a bath, wash (o.s.) at the basin/in the bath **b** [*vêtement, tissu*] **ça se lave en machine** it's machine-washable; **ça se lave à la main** it has to be hand-washed; **ce tissu se lave bien** this material washes well; **le cuir ne se lave pas** leather isn't washable **c** **se ~ de** [+ *accusation*] to clear o.s. of; [+ *affront*] to avenge o.s. of; (*fig*) **je m'en lave les mains** I wash my hands of it

laverie [lavʀi] NF **a** (*pour linge*) laundry; **~ (automatique)** Launderette® (*Brit*), Laundromat® (*US*) **b** (*Ind*) washing *ou* preparation plant

lavette [lavɛt] NF **a** (= *chiffon*) dish cloth; (= *brosse*) dish mop; (*Belg, Helv* = *gant de toilette*) (face) flannel (*Brit*), washcloth (*US*) **b** (*péj* = *homme*) wimp*, drip*

laveur [lavœʀ] NM (= *personne*) washer; **~ de carreaux** *ou* **de vitres** window cleaner; **~ de voitures** car cleaner → **raton**

laveuse [lavøz] NF (= *personne*) **~ (de linge)** washerwoman; (*Can* = *lave-linge*) washing machine

lave-vaisselle [lavvɛsɛl] NM INV dishwasher

lavis [lavi] NM (= *procédé*) washing; **(dessin au) ~** wash drawing; **colorier au ~** to wash-paint

lavoir [lavwaʀ] NM (*découvert*) washing-place; (= *édifice*) wash house; (= *bac*) washtub; (*Tech*) (= *machine*) washer; (= *atelier*) washing plant

lavure [lavyʀ] NF [*minerai*] washing; **~s** washings

Lawrence [lɔʀɑ̃s] N **~ d'Arabie** Lawrence of Arabia

laxatif, -ive [laksatif, iv] ADJ, NM laxative

laxisme [laksism] NM (*Rel*) latitudinarianism; (= *indulgence*) laxness, laxity; **le gouvernement est accusé de ~ à l'égard des syndicats** the government is accused of being too soft *ou* lax with the trade unions

laxiste [laksist] **1** ADJ (*Rel*) latitudinarian; (= *indulgent*) lax **2** NMF (*Rel*) latitudinarian; (= *indulgent*) lax person

layette [lɛjɛt] NF baby clothes, layette; **rayon ~** [*magasin*] babywear department; **couleurs ~** baby *ou* pastel colours; **bleu/rose ~** baby blue/pink

layon [lɛjɔ̃] NM (forest) track *ou* trail

Lazare [lazaʀ] NM Lazarus

lazaret [lazaʀɛ] NM lazaret

lazulite [lazylit] NF lazulite

lazzi [la(d)zi] NM gibe; **être l'objet des ~(s) de la foule** to be gibed at *ou* heckled by the crowd

LCD [ɛlsede] ADJ (ABRÉV = **liquid crystal display**) (*Ordin*) [*écran*] LCD

le[1] [lə], **la** [la] (*pl* **les** [le]) ART DÉF (*contraction avec à, de : au, aux, du, des*) **a** (*détermination*) the; **le propriétaire de la voiture** the owner of the car; **la femme de l'épicier** the grocer's wife; **les parcs de la ville** the town parks, the parks in the town; **je suis inquiète, les enfants**

sont en retard I'm worried because the children are late; **le thé/le café que je viens d'acheter** the tea/the coffee I have just bought; **allons à la gare ensemble** let's go to the station together; **il n'a pas le droit/l'intention de le faire** he has no right to do it/no intention of doing it; **il n'a pas eu la patience/l'intelligence d'attendre** he didn't have the patience/the sense to wait; **il a choisi le tableau le plus original de l'exposition** he chose the most original picture in the exhibition; **le plus petit des deux frères est le plus solide** the smaller of the two brothers is the more robust *ou* the stronger; **le Paris de Balzac** Balzac's Paris; **l'Angleterre que j'ai connue** the England (that) I knew **b** (*dans le temps*) the (*souvent omis*); **venez le dimanche de Pâques** come on Easter Sunday; **l'hiver dernier/prochain** last/next winter; **l'hiver 1998** the winter of 1998; **le premier/dernier lundi du mois** the first/last Monday of *ou* in the month; **il ne travaille pas le samedi** he doesn't work on Saturdays *ou* on a Saturday; **elle travaille le matin** she works mornings *ou* in the morning; **vers les cinq heures** at about five o'clock; **il est parti le 5 mai** (*à l'oral*) he left on the 5th of May *ou* on May the 5th; (*à l'écrit, dans une lettre*) he left on May 5th *ou* 5th May (*Brit*); **il n'a pas dormi de la nuit** he didn't sleep a wink all night **c** (*distribution*) a, an; **50 F le mètre/le kg/le litre/la pièce** 50 francs a metre/a kg/a litre/each *ou* a piece; **60 km à l'heure** 60 km an *ou* per hour; **deux fois la semaine/l'an** twice a week/a year **d** (*fraction*) a, an; **le tiers/quart** a third/quarter; **j'en ai fait à peine la moitié/le dixième** I have barely done (a) half/a tenth of it **e** (*dans les généralisations, les abstractions : gén non traduit*) **le hibou vole surtout la nuit** owls fly *ou* the owl flies mainly at night; **l'enfant n'aime pas** *ou* **les enfants n'aiment pas l'obscurité** children don't like the dark; **le thé et le café sont chers** tea and coffee are expensive; **j'aime la musique/la poésie/la danse** I like music/poetry/dancing; **le beau/grotesque** the beautiful/grotesque; **les riches** the rich; **aller au concert/au restaurant** to go to a concert/out for a meal **f** (*possession : gén adj poss, parfois art indéf*) **elle ouvrit les yeux/la bouche** she opened her eyes/her mouth; **elle est sortie le manteau sur le bras** she went out with her coat over her arm; **la tête baissée, elle pleurait** she hung her head and wept; **assis les jambes pendantes** sitting with one's legs dangling; **j'ai mal à la main droite/au pied** I've got a pain in my right hand/in my foot, my right hand/my foot hurts; **il a la jambe cassée** he's got a broken leg; **croisez les bras** fold your arms; **il a l'air fatigué/le regard malin** he has a tired look/a mischievous look; **il a les cheveux noirs/le cœur brisé** he has black hair/a broken heart; **il a l'air hypocrite** he looks like a hypocrite **g** (*valeur démonstrative*) **il ne faut pas agir de la sorte** you must not do that kind of thing *ou* things like that; **que pensez-vous de la pièce/de l'incident ?** what do you think of the play/of the incident?; **faites attention, les enfants !** be careful children!; **oh le beau chien !** what a lovely dog!, look at that lovely dog!

le[2] [l(ə)], **la** [la] (*pl* **les** [le]) PRON M,F,PL **a** (= *homme*) him; (= *femme, bateau*) her; (= *animal, bébé*) it, him, her; (= *chose*) it; **les** them; **je ne le/la/les connais pas** I don't know him/her/them; **regarde-le/-la/-les** look at him *ou* it/her *ou* it/them; **cette écharpe est à vous, je l'ai trouvée par terre** this scarf is yours, I found it on the floor; **voulez-vous ces fraises ? je les ai apportées pour vous** would you like these strawberries? I brought them for you; **le Canada demande aux USA de le soutenir** Canada is asking the USA for its support **b** (*emphatique*) **il faut le féliciter ce garçon !** this boy deserves congratulations!; **cette femme-là, je la déteste** I can't bear that woman; **cela vous le savez aussi bien que moi** you know that as well as I do; **vous l'êtes, beau** you really do look nice → **copier, voici, voilà c** (*neutre : souvent non traduit*) **vous savez qu'il est malade ? — je l'ai entendu dire** did you know he was ill? — I had heard; **elle n'est pas heureuse, mais elle ne l'a jamais été et elle ne le sera jamais** she is not happy but she never has been and never will be; **pourquoi n'est-il pas venu ? — demande-le-lui/je me le demande** why hasn't he come? — ask him/I wonder; **il était ministre, il ne l'est plus** he used to be a minister but he isn't any longer; **il sera puni comme il le mérite** he'll be punished as he deserves

lé [le] NM [*étoffe*] width; [*papier peint*] length, strip

LEA [elea] NM (ABRÉV = **langues étrangères appliquées**) modern languages

leader [lidœʀ] NM (Pol, Écon, Sport) leader; (*Presse*) leader, leading article; (Comm) **produit ~ leader**, leading product; **~ d'opinion** opinion former, person who shapes public opinion; **cette entreprise est ~ sur son marché** this company is the market leader; **notre société est en position de ~ dans son secteur** our company holds a leading ou lead position in its sector

leadership [lidœʀʃip] NM (Pol) leadership; (Écon) leading position; (= *dirigeants*) leaders; **ils ont perdu leur ~ technologique** they've lost their leading position in the field of technology; **ils ont pris le ~ dans ce secteur** they have taken the lead in this sector

leasing [liziŋ] NM leasing; **acheter qch en ~** to buy sth leasehold

léchage [leʃaʒ] NM (gén) licking; **~ (de bottes)*** bootlicking*, toadying

lèche: [lɛʃ] NF bootlicking*, toadying; **faire de la ~** to be a bootlicker*; **faire de la ~ à qn** to suck up to sb:, lick sb's boots*

lèche-botte* (pl **lèche-bottes**) [lɛʃbɔt] NMF bootlicker*, toady

lèche-cul:: (pl **lèche-culs**) [lɛʃky] NMF arselicker:: (Brit), ass-kisser:: (US), brown nose: (US)

lèchefrite [lɛʃfʀit] NF dripping-pan (Brit), broiler (US)

lécher [leʃe] ▸conjug 6◂ VT **a** (gén) to lick; [+ *assiette*] to lick clean; **se ~ les doigts** to lick one's fingers; **~ la confiture d'une tartine** to lick the jam off a slice of bread → **ours b** [*flammes*] to lick; [*vagues*] to wash against, lap against **c** (* = *fignoler*) to polish up; **article bien léché** polished ou finely honed article; **trop léché** overdone (*attrib*), overpolished **d** (*loc*) **~ les bottes de qn*** to suck up to sb:, lick sb's boots*; **~ le cul à** ou **de qn::** to lick sb's arse:: (Brit), kiss sb's ass:: (US); **~ les vitrines*** to go window-shopping; **s'en ~ les doigts/babines** to lick one's lips/chops

lécheur, -euse [leʃœʀ, øz] NM,F bootlicker*, toady; **il est du genre ~** he's the bootlicking type*, he's always sucking up to someone:

lèche-vitrines* [lɛʃvitʀin] NM INV windowshopping; **faire du ~** to go window-shopping

lécithine [lesitin] NF lecithin

leçon [l(ə)sɔ̃] NF **a** (Scol) (= *cours*) lesson, class; (à *apprendre*) homework (NonC); **~ de danse/de français/de piano** dancing/French/piano lesson; **~s particulières** private lessons ou tuition (Brit); **faire la ~** to teach; **elle a bien appris sa ~** (lit) she's learnt her homework well; (hum) she's learnt her script ou lines well; (fig) **il pourrait vous donner des ~s*** he could teach you a thing or two **b** (= *conseil*) (piece of) advice; **suivre les ~s de qn** to heed sb's advice, take a lesson from

sb; **je n'ai pas de ~ à recevoir de toi** I don't need your advice; **faire la ~ à qn** (= *l'endoctriner*) to tell sb what to do; (= *le réprimander*) to give sb a lecture; **faire des ~s de morale à qn** to sit in judgment on sb; **je n'ai pas besoin de tes ~s de morale** I don't need your moralizing **c** (= *enseignement*) [*fable, parabole*] lesson; **les ~s de l'expérience** the lessons of experience ou that experience teaches; **que cela te serve de ~** let that be a lesson to you; **cela m'a servi de ~** that taught me a lesson; **nous avons tiré la ~ de notre échec** we learnt (a lesson) from our failure; **maintenant que notre plan a échoué, il faut en tirer la ~** now that our plan has failed we should learn from it; **cela lui donnera une ~** that'll teach him a lesson **d** [*manuscrit, texte*] reading

lecteur, -trice [lɛktœʀ, tʀis] **1** NM,F **a** (gén) reader; **c'est un grand ~ de poésie** he reads a lot of poetry; **le nombre de ~s de ce journal a doublé** the readership of this paper has doubled; **~ correcteur** proofreader → **avis b** (*Univ*) (foreign language) assistant, (foreign) teaching assistant (US) **2** NM **a** (Audiov) **~ de cassettes** cassette deck ou player; **~ de disques compacts** ou **~ de CD audio** CD player, compact disc player; **~ de vidéodisque** videodisc player; **~ de son** (reading) head **b** (Ordin) **~ de cartes à puce** smart-card reader; **~ de disquettes/de CD-ROM** disk/CD-ROM drive; **~ optique** optical character reader, optical scanner **c** (Aut) **~ de cartes** map-light

lectorat [lɛktɔʀa] NM **a** (Univ) (teaching) assistantship **b** [*magazine*] readership

lecture [lɛktyʀ] NF **a** [*carte, texte*] reading; (= *interprétation*) reading, interpretation; **la ~ de Proust est difficile** reading Proust is difficult, Proust is difficult to read; **aimer la ~** to like reading; **d'une ~ facile** easy to read, very readable; **ce livre est d'une ~ agréable** this book makes pleasant reading; **la ~ à haute voix** reading aloud; **faire la ~ à qn** to read to sb; (frm) **donner** ou **faire ~ de qch** to read sth out (à qn to sb); **faire une ~ marxiste de Balzac** to read Balzac from a Marxist perspective; (Mus) **~ à vue** sight-reading; **méthode de ~** reading method; **~ rapide** speed reading; **nous n'avons pas la même ~ des événements** we have a different interpretation of the events → **cabinet, livre¹ b** (= *livre*) reading (NonC), book; **c'est une ~ à recommander** it's recommended reading ou it's a book to be recommended (à for); **apportez-moi de la ~** bring me something to read ou some reading matter; **~s pour la jeunesse** books for children; **quelles sont vos ~s favorites ?** what do you like reading best?; **enrichi par ses ~s** enriched by his reading ou by what he has read; **il a de mauvaises ~s** he reads the wrong things **c** [*projet de loi*] reading; **examiner un projet en première ~** to give a bill its first reading; **le projet a été accepté en seconde ~** the bill passed its second reading **d** (Audiov) [CD, *cassette*] (= *bouton*) play; **pendant la ~ de la cassette** while the tape is playing **e** [*disque dur, CD-ROM*] reading; **~ optique** (= *procédé*) optical character recognition; (= *action*) optical scanning; **procédé/tête de ~; écriture** read-write cycle/head; **en ~ seule** read-only → **tête**

Léda [leda] NF (Myth) Leda

ledit [lədi], **ladite** [ladit] (pl **lesdit(e)s** [ledi(t)]) ADJ (frm) the aforementioned (frm), the aforesaid (frm), the said (frm)

légal, e [legal] (mpl **-aux**) [legal, o] ADJ [*âge, dispositions, formalité*] legal; [*armes, moyens*] legal, lawful; [*adresse*] registered, official; **cours ~ d'une monnaie** official rate of exchange of a currency; **monnaie ~e** legal tender, official currency; **la durée ~e du temps de travail** maximum working hours; **recourir aux**

moyens légaux contre qn to take legal action against sb → **fête, heure, médecine**

légalement [legalmɑ̃] ADV legally, lawfully

légalisation [legalizasjɔ̃] NF **a** (= *action*) legalization **b** (= *certification*) authentication

légaliser [legalize] ▸conjug 1◂ VT **a** (= *rendre légal*) to legalize **b** (= *certifier*) to authenticate

légalisme [legalism] NM legalism

légaliste [legalist] **1** ADJ legalist(ic) **2** NMF legalist

légalité [legalite] NF [*régime, acte*] legality, lawfulness; (= *loi*) **rester dans/sortir de la ~** to remain ou keep within/breach the law; **en toute ~** quite legally

légat [lega] NM **~ (du Pape)** (papal) legate

légataire [legatɛʀ] NMF legatee, devisee; **~ universel** sole legatee

légation [legasjɔ̃] NF (Diplomatie) legation

légendaire [leʒɑ̃dɛʀ] ADJ legendary

légende [leʒɑ̃d] NF **a** (= *histoire, mythe*) legend; **entrer dans la ~** to go down in legend, become legendary; **entrer vivant dans la ~** to become a legend in one's own lifetime; **de ~** [*personnage, film, pays*] legendary **b** (= *inscription*) [*médaille*] legend; [*dessin*] caption; [*liste, carte*] key; **« sans ~ »** [*dessin*] "no caption" **c** (péj = *mensonge*) tall story

légender [leʒɑ̃de] ▸conjug 1◂ VT to caption

léger, -ère [leʒe, ɛʀ] **1** ADJ **a** (= *de faible poids*) [*objet, repas, gaz, sauce*] light; (= *délicat*) [*parfum, tissu, style*] light; **arme/industrie légère** light weapon/industry; **construction légère** light ou flimsy (péj) construction; **cuisine légère** low-fat cooking; **~ comme une plume** as light as a feather; **je me sens plus ~** (après un régime, après m'être débarrassé) I feel pounds lighter; (= *soulagé*) that's a weight off my mind; (hum) **je me sens plus ~ de 100 F** I feel 100 francs poorer; **faire qch l'esprit ~** to do sth with a light heart → **poids, sommeil b** (= *agile, souple*) [*personne, geste, allure*] light, nimble; **se sentir ~ (comme un oiseau)** to feel as light as a bird; **il partit d'un pas ~** he walked away with a spring in his step; **avec une grâce légère** with easy grace → **main c** (= *faible*) [*brise*] gentle, slight; [*bruit*] faint; [*couche*] thin, light; [*thé*] weak; [*vin*] light; [*alcool*] not very strong; [*blessure*] slight, minor; [*maladie, châtiment, tabac*] mild; [*coup, maquillage*] light; [*accent*] slight, faint; [*augmentation*] slight; **une légère pointe d'ironie** a touch of irony; **il y a un ~ mieux** there's been a slight improvement; **soprano/ténor ~** light soprano/tenor; **il a été condamné à une peine légère** he was given a light sentence → **blessé d** (= *superficiel*) [*personne*] thoughtless; [*preuve, argument*] lightweight, flimsy; [*jugement, propos*] thoughtless, flippant, careless; **se montrer ~ dans ses actions** to act thoughtlessly; **pour une thèse, c'est un peu ~** it's rather lightweight ou a bit on the flimsy side for a thesis **e** (= *frivole*) [*personne, caractère, humeur*] fickle; [*propos, plaisanterie*] ribald, broad; [*comédie, livre, film*] light; **femme légère** ou **de mœurs légères** loose woman, woman of easy virtue → **cuisse, musique**

2 ADV **voyager ~** to travel light; **manger ~** (non gras) to eat low-fat foods, avoid fatty foods; (peu) to eat lightly; **s'habiller ~** to wear light clothes

3 à la légère LOC ADV [*parler, agir*] rashly, thoughtlessly, without giving the matter proper consideration; **il prend toujours tout à la légère** he never takes anything seriously, he's very casual about everything

légèrement [leʒɛʀmɑ̃] ADV **a** [*habillé, armé, maquillé, poser*] lightly; **il a mangé ~** he ate a light meal; **s'habiller ~** to wear light clothes **b** [*courir*] lightly, nimbly **c** [*blesser, bouger*] slightly; [*parfumé*] lightly; **~ plus grand** slightly bigger; **~ surpris** mildly *ou* slightly surprised; **il boite/louche ~** he has a slight limp/ squint **d** [*agir*] rashly, thoughtlessly, without thinking (properly); **parler ~ de la mort** to speak flippantly *ou* lightly of death, speak of death in an offhand *ou* a flippant way

légèreté [leʒɛʀte] NF **a** [*objet, tissu, style, repas, sauce*] lightness **b** [*démarche*] lightness, nimbleness; **~ de main** lighthandedness; **avec une ~ d'oiseau** with birdlike grace; **marcher/danser avec ~** to walk/ dance lightly *ou* with a light step **c** [*punition, coup*] lightness, mildness; [*tabac*] mildness; [*thé*] weakness; [*vin*] lightness **d** (= *superficialité*) [*conduite, personne, propos*] thoughtlessness; [*preuves, argument*] flimsiness; **faire preuve de ~** to speak (*ou* behave) rashly *ou* thoughtlessly **e** (= *frivolité*) [*personne*] fickleness, flightiness; [*propos*] flippancy; [*plaisanterie*] ribaldry

légiférer [leʒifeʀe] ▶conjug 6◀ VI (*Jur*) to legislate, make legislation

légion [leʒjɔ̃] NF (*Hist, fig*) legion; **~ de gendarmerie** corps of gendarmes; **la Légion (étrangère)** the Foreign Legion; **Légion d'honneur** Legion of Honour; **ils sont ~** they are legion (*frm*), there are any number of them; **les volontaires ne sont pas ~** volunteers are few and far between

---

LÉGION D'HONNEUR

Created by Napoleon Bonaparte in 1802, the **Légion d'honneur** *is a prestigious order awarded for either civil or military merit. The order is divided into five ranks or "classes" : "chevalier", "officier", "commandeur", "grand officier" and "grand-croix" (given here in ascending order). Full regalia worn on official occasions consists of medals and sashes, but on less formal occasions these are replaced by a discreet red ribbon or rosette (according to rank) worn on the lapel.*

---

légionnaire [leʒjɔnɛʀ] **1** NM (*Hist*) legionary; [*Légion étrangère*] legionnaire → **maladie 2** NMF [*Légion d'honneur*] holder of the Legion of Honour

législateur, -trice [leʒislatœʀ, tʀis] NM,F (= *personne*) legislator, lawmaker; (= *la loi*) **le ~ a prévu ce cas** the law makes provision for this case

législatif, -ive [leʒislatif, iv] **1** ADJ legislative; **les (élections) législatives** the legislative elections, ≈ the general election (*Brit*), ≈ the Congressional elections (*US*) → ÉLECTIONS **2** NM legislature

législation [leʒislasjɔ̃] NF legislation; **~ fiscale** fiscal *ou* tax legislation, tax laws; **~ du travail** labour laws, industrial *ou* job legislation

législature [leʒislatyʀ] NF (*Parl*) (= *durée*) term (of office); (= *corps*) legislature

légiste [leʒist] NM jurist → **médecin**

légitimation [leʒitimasjɔ̃] NF [*enfant*] legitimization; [*pouvoir*] recognition, legitimation; (*littér*) [*action, conduite*] legitimation

légitime [leʒitim] **1** ADJ **a** (= *légal*) [*droits, gouvernement*] legitimate, lawful; [*union, femme*] lawful; [*enfant*] legitimate; [*héritier*] legitimate, rightful; **la ~ défense** self-defence; **j'étais en état de ~ défense** I was acting in self-defence **b** (= *juste*) [*excuse, intérêt*] legitimate; [*colère*] justifiable, justified; [*revendication*] legitimate, rightful; [*récompense*] just, legitimate; **rien de plus ~ que ...** nothing could be more justified than ... **2** NF (†,*) **ma ~** the missus*, the wife*

légitimement [leʒitimmɑ̃] ADV (*gén*) rightfully; (*Jur*) legitimately

légitimer [leʒitime] ▶conjug 1◀ VT [+ *enfant*] to legitimate, legitimize; [+ *conduite, action*] to legitimate, legitimize, justify; [+ *titre*] to recognize; [+ *pouvoir*] to recognize, legitimate

légitimisme [leʒitimism] NM (*Hist*) legitimism

légitimiste [leʒitimist] NMF, ADJ (*Hist*) legitimist

légitimité [leʒitimite] NF (*gén*) legitimacy

Lego® [lego] NM Lego®; **en ~** Lego (*épith*)

Le Greco [ləgʀeko] NM El Greco

legs [lɛg] NM (*Jur*) legacy, bequest; (*fig*) legacy; **faire un ~ à qn** to leave sb a legacy; **~ (de biens immobiliers)** devise; **~ (de biens mobiliers)** legacy; **~ (à titre) universel** general legacy

léguer [lege] ▶conjug 6◀ VT (*Jur*) to bequeath; [+ *tradition, vertu, tare*] to hand down *ou* on, pass on; **~ qch à qn par testament** to bequeath sth to sb (in one's will); **la mauvaise gestion qu'on nous a léguée** the bad management that we inherited

légume [legym] **1** NM (*lit, fig*) vegetable; **~s secs** pulses; **~s verts** green vegetables, greens* → **bouillon 2** NF (= *personne importante*) **grosse ~*** bigwig*, big shot*

légumier, -ière [legymje, jɛʀ] **1** ADJ vegetable (*épith*) **2** NM (= *plat*) vegetable dish; (*Belg* = *commerçant*) greengrocer

légumineuse [legyminøz] NF legume, leguminous plant; **les ~s** legumes, Leguminosae (*Spéc*)

leitmotiv [lɛtmotiv, lajtmotif] NM (*lit, fig*) leitmotiv, leitmotif

Léman [lemɑ̃] NM **le (lac) ~** Lake Geneva

lemmatisation [lematizasjɔ̃] NF lemmatization

lemmatiser [lematize] ▶conjug 1◀ VT to lemmatize

lemme [lɛm] NM lemma

lemming [lemiŋ] NM lemming

lémur [lemyʀ] NM lemur

lémure [lemyʀ] NM (*Antiq*) lemur; **~s** lemures

lémurien [lemyʀjɛ̃] NM lemur

lendemain [lɑ̃dmɛ̃] **1** NM **a** (= *jour suivant*) **le ~** the next *ou* following day, the day after; **le ~ de son arrivée/du mariage** the day after he arrived/after the marriage, the day following his arrival/the marriage; **le ~ matin/soir** the next *ou* following morning/evening; **~ de fête** day after a holiday; **au ~ de la guerre/des élections** just after the war/the election; **au ~ de la défaite/de son mariage** soon after *ou* in the days following the defeat/his marriage → **jour, remettre b** (= *avenir*) **le ~** tomorrow, the future; **penser au ~** to think of tomorrow *ou* the future; **bonheur/succès sans ~** short-lived happiness/success **2** **lendemains** NMPL (= *conséquences*) consequences, repercussions; (= *perspectives*) prospects, future; **cette affaire a eu de fâcheux ~s** this business had unfortunate consequences *ou* repercussions; **des ~s qui chantent** a brighter *ou* better future; **ça nous promet de beaux ~s** the future looks very promising for us; **on peut s'attendre à des ~s qui déchantent** we can expect bad days *ou* hard times ahead

lénifiant, e [lenifjɑ̃, jɑ̃t] ADJ **a** (= *apaisant*) [*médicament*] soothing **b** [*propos, discours*] mollifying, soothing; (*péj* = *amollissant*) [*atmosphère*] languid, enervating; [*climat*] enervating, draining (*attrib*)

lénifier [lenifje] ▶conjug 7◀ VT (= *apaiser*) to soothe; (*péj* = *amollir*) to enervate

Lénine [lenin] NM Lenin

léninisme [leninism] NM Leninism

léniniste [leninist] ADJ, NMF Leninist

lénitif, -ive [lenitif, iv] ADJ, NM lenitive

lent, e¹ [lɑ̃, lɑ̃t] ADJ (*gén*) slow, slow; [*poison*] slow, slow-acting; [*mort*] slow, lingering; (*Fin*) [*croissance*] sluggish, slow; **à l'esprit ~** slowwitted, dim-witted; **il est ~ à comprendre** he is slow to understand *ou* slow on the uptake*; **elle est ~e à manger** she's a slow eater, she

eats slowly; **marcher d'un pas ~** to walk at a slow pace *ou* slowly; **« véhicules ~s »** "slow-moving vehicles", "crawler lane" (*Brit*)

lente² [lɑ̃t] NF (*Zool*) nit

lentement [lɑ̃tmɑ̃] ADV slowly; **progresser ~** to make slow progress; **~ mais sûrement** slowly but surely ■(*PROV*) **qui va ~ va sûrement** slow and steady wins the race (*PROV*)

lenteur [lɑ̃tœʀ] NF slowness; **avec ~** slowly; **~ d'esprit** slow-wittedness; **la ~ de la construction** the slow progress of the building work; **des retards dus à des ~s administratives** delays due to slow *ou* cumbersome administrative procedures

lenticulaire [lɑ̃tikylɛʀ] ADJ lenticular, lentoid

lentigo [lɑ̃tigo] NM lentigo

lentille [lɑ̃tij] NF (*Bot, Culin*) lentil; (*Opt*) lens; **gros comme une ~** as big as a small pea; **~s (cornéennes *ou* de contact) dures/souples** hard/soft contact lenses; **~ micro-cornéenne** microcorneal lens; **~s d'eau** duckweed

lentisque [lɑ̃tisk] NM mastic tree

Léonard [leɔnaʀ] NM Leonard; **~ de Vinci** Leonardo da Vinci

léonin, e [leɔnɛ̃, in] ADJ (= *de lion*) leonine; [*rime*] Leonine; (= *injuste*) [*contrat, partage*] one-sided

léopard [leɔpaʀ] NM leopard; **manteau de ~** leopardskin coat; (*Mil*) **tenue ~** camouflage (uniform)

LEP [lɛp] NM (ABRÉV = **lycée d'enseignement professionnel**) → **lycée**

lépidoptère [lepidɔptɛʀ] **1** ADJ lepidopterous **2** NM lepidopteran, lepidopterous insect; **les ~s** Lepidoptera

lépiote [lepjɔt] NF parasol mushroom

lèpre [lɛpʀ] NF (*Méd*) leprosy; (*fig* = *mal*) scourge, plague; **mur rongé de ~** flaking *ou* peeling wall

lépreux, -euse [lepʀø, øz] **1** ADJ (*lit*) leprous, suffering from leprosy; [*mur*] flaking, peeling; [*quartier, maison*] rundown **2** NM,F (*lit, fig*) leper

léproserie [lepʀozʀi] NF leper-house

lequel [ləkɛl], **laquelle** [lakɛl] (*pl* **lesquel(le)s** [lekɛl]) (*contraction avec* **à**, **de** : **auquel**, **auxquels**, **auxquelles**, **duquel**, **desquels**, **desquelles**) **1** PRON **a** (*relatif*) (*personne* : *sujet*) who; (*personne* : *objet*) whom; (*chose*) which; **j'ai écrit au directeur de la banque, ~ n'a jamais répondu** I wrote to the bank manager, who has never answered; **la patience avec laquelle il écoute** the patience with which he listens; **le règlement d'après ~ ...** the ruling whereby ...; **la femme à laquelle j'ai acheté mon chien** the woman from whom I bought my dog, the woman (who *ou* that) I bought my dog from; **c'est un problème auquel je n'avais pas pensé** that's a problem I hadn't thought of *ou* which hadn't occurred to me; **le pont sur ~ vous êtes passé** the bridge you came over *ou* over which you came; **le docteur/le traitement sans ~ elle serait morte** the doctor without whom/the treatment without which she would have died; **cette société sur le compte de laquelle on dit tant de mal** this society about which so much ill is spoken; **la plupart desquels** (*personnes*) most of whom; (*choses*) most of which; **les gens chez lesquels j'ai logé** the people at whose house I stayed, the people I stayed with → **importer² b** (*interrogatif*) which; **~ des deux acteurs préférez-vous ?** which of the two actors do you prefer?; **dans ~ de ces hôtels avez-vous logé ?** in which of these hotels did you stay?; **laquelle des sonates de Mozart avez-vous entendue ?** which of Mozart's sonatas *ou* which Mozart sonata did you hear?; **laquelle des chambres est la sienne ?** which is his room?, which of the rooms is his?; **je ne sais à laquelle des vendeuses m'adresser** I don't know which saleswoman I should speak to; **devinez lesquels de ces tableaux elle aimerait avoir** guess which of these pictures she would like to have; **donnez-moi un melon/deux melons — ~ ?/lesquels ?** give me one melon/two melons — which one?/which ones?; **va voir ma sœur — laquelle ?** go and see my sister — which one?

2 ADJ **son état pourrait empirer, auquel cas je reviendrais** his condition could worsen, in which case I would come back; (*littér, iro*) **il écrivit au ministre, ~ ministre ne répondit jamais** he wrote to the minister but the latter *ou* the said minister never replied

lerch(e)* [lɛʀʃ] ADV **pas ~** not much; **il n'y en a pas ~** there's not much of it

lérot [leʀo] NM lerot, garden dormouse

les [le] → **le¹**, **le²**

lesbianisme [lɛsbjanism] NM lesbianism

lesbien, -ienne [lɛsbjɛ̃, jɛn] 1 ADJ lesbian 2 **lesbienne** NF lesbian

lèse-majesté [lɛzmaʒɛste] NF lese-majesty → **crime**

léser [leze] ▸conjug 6◂ VT a (*Jur = frustrer*) [+ *personne*] to wrong; [+ *intérêts*] to damage; **la partie lésée** the injured party; **~ les droits de qn** to infringe on sb's rights; (*fig*) **je ne voudrais ~ personne** I don't want to cheat anyone b (*Méd = blesser*) [+ *organe*] to injure

lésiner [lezine] ▸conjug 1◂ VI to skimp (**sur qch** on sth); **ne pas ~ sur les moyens** (*gén*) to use all the means at one's disposal; (*pour mariage, repas*) to push the boat out*, pull out all the stops*

lésinerie [lezinʀi] NF stinginess (*NonC*)

lésion [lezjɔ̃] NF (*Jur, Méd*) lesion; **~s internes** internal injuries

lésionnel, -elle [lezjɔnɛl] ADJ [*trouble*] caused by a lesion; [*syndrome*] of a lesion

Lesotho [lezoto] NM Lesotho

lessivable [lesivabl] ADJ [*papier peint*] washable

lessivage [lesivaʒ] NM (*gén*) washing; (*Chim, Géol*) leaching

lessive [lesiv] NF a (*= produit*) (*en poudre*) washing powder (*Brit*), (powdered) laundry detergent (*US*); (*liquide*) liquid detergent; (*Tech = soude*) lye b (*= lavage*) washing (*NonC*); **le jeudi est mon jour de ~** Thursday is washday for me; **faire la ~** to do the washing; **faire quatre ~s par semaine** to do four washes a week; **mettre une chemise à la ~** to put a shirt in the wash *ou* in the laundry; (*fig*) **la grande ~** the big cleanup c (*= linge*) washing (*NonC*); **porter sa ~ à la blanchisserie** to take one's washing to the laundry

lessiver [lesive] ▸conjug 1◂ VT a [+ *mur, plancher, linge*] to wash b (*Chim, Géol*) to leach c (*✶ = battre*) (*au jeu*) to clean out*; [+ *adversaire*] to lick✶ d (*✶ = fatiguer*) to tire out, exhaust; **être lessivé** to be dead-beat* *ou* all-in* *ou* tired out

lessiveuse [lesivøz] NF boiler (*for washing laundry*)

lessiviel [lesivjɛl] ADJ M **produit ~** detergent product

lessivier [lesivje] NM (*= fabricant*) detergent manufacturer

lest [lɛst] NM (*Naut, Aviat*) ballast; **sur son ~** in ballast; **garnir un bateau de ~** to ballast a ship; **jeter** *ou* **lâcher du ~** (*lit*) to dump ballast; (*fig*) to make concessions

lestage [lɛstaʒ] NM ballasting

leste [lɛst] ADJ a [*personne, animal*] nimble, agile; [*démarche*] light, nimble → **main** b (*= grivois*) [*plaisanterie*] risqué c (*= cavalier*) [*ton, réponse*] offhand

lestement [lɛstəmɑ̃] ADV a (*= souplement*) with great agility, nimbly b (*= cavalièrement*) [*traiter*] offhandedly

▸ GRAMMAIRE ACTIVE: **lettre** 48.1

lester [lɛste] ▸conjug 1◂ VT a (*= garnir de lest*) to ballast b (* = *remplir*) [+ *portefeuille, poches*] to fill, cram; **~ son estomac** ◊ **se ~ (l'estomac)** to fill one's stomach; **lesté d'un repas copieux** weighed down with a heavy meal

let [lɛt] NM (*Tennis*) let; **balle ~** let ball; **jouer une balle ~** ◊ **faire un ~** to play a let

létal, e (*mpl* -aux) [letal, o] ADJ [*dose, gène*] lethal

léthargie [letaʀʒi] NF (*= apathie, Méd*) lethargy; **tomber en ~** to fall into a state of lethargy

léthargique [letaʀʒik] ADJ lethargic; **état ~** lethargic state, state of lethargy

lette [lɛt] NM (*Ling*) Latvian, Lett, Lettish

letton, -on(n)e [letɔ̃, ɔn] 1 ADJ Latvian, Lett, Lettish 2 NM (*Ling*) Latvian, Lett, Lettish 3 **Letton(ne)** NM,F Latvian, Lett

Lettonie [letɔni] NF Latvia

lettrage [letʀaʒ] NM lettering

▼ **lettre** [lɛtʀ] 1 NF a (*= caractère*) letter; **mot de six ~s** six-letter word, word of six letters; **écrire un nom en toutes ~s** to write out a name in full; **écrivez la somme en (toutes) ~s** write out the sum in full; **c'est en toutes ~s dans les journaux** it's there in black and white *ou* it's there for all to read in the newspapers; **c'est en grosses ~s dans les journaux** it's made headlines; **c'est écrit en toutes ~s sur sa figure** it's written all over his face; **c'est à écrire en ~s d'or** it's a momentous event, it's something to celebrate; **inscrit** *ou* **gravé en ~s de feu** written in letters of fire; **cette lutte est écrite en ~s de sang** this bloody struggle will remain branded *ou* engraved on people's memories → **cinq, majuscule, minuscule** b (*= missive*) letter; **~s** (*= courrier*) letters, mail, post; **faire une ~** to write a letter (**à** to); **jeter** *ou* **mettre une ~ à la boîte** *ou* **à la poste** to post *ou* mail (*US*) a letter; **y avait-il des ~s aujourd'hui ?** were there any letters today?, was there any mail *ou* post today?; **écris-lui donc une petite ~** write him a note, drop him a line*; **~ d'injures** abusive letter; **~ de condoléances/de félicitations/de réclamation** letter of condolence/of congratulations/of complaint; **~ d'amour/d'affaires** love/business letter; **~ de rupture** letter ending a relationship, Dear John letter; **"« ~ suit »"** "letter follows" c (*= sens strict*) **prendre qch au pied de la ~** to take sth literally; **suivre la ~ de la loi** to follow the letter of the law; **exécuter des ordres à la ~** to carry out orders to the letter d (*loc*) **rester ~ morte** [*remarque, avis, protestation*] to go unheeded; **devenir ~ morte** [*loi, traité*] to become a dead letter; **c'est passé comme une ~ à la poste** it went off smoothly *ou* without a hitch; **Anne Lemoine, ce féministe (bien) avant la ~** Anne Lemoine, a feminist (long) before the term existed *ou* had been coined

2 **lettres** NFPL a (*= littérature*) **les (belles) ~s** literature; **femme/homme/gens de ~s** woman/man/men of letters; **le monde des ~s** the literary world; **avoir des ~s** to be well-read b (*Scol, Univ*) (*gén*) arts (subjects); (*= français*) French literature and language; **il est très fort en ~s** he's very good at arts subjects; **il fait des ~s** he's doing an arts degree; **professeur de ~s** teacher of French, French teacher (*in France*); **~s classiques** classics *sg*; **~s modernes** (*= section*) French department, department of French (language and literature); (*= discipline*) French (language and literature) → **faculté, licence**

3 COMP ▸ **lettre d'accompagnement** covering (*Brit*) *ou* cover (*US*) letter ▸ **lettre de cachet** (*Hist*) lettre de cachet ▸ **lettre de change** bill of exchange ▸ **lettre de château** thank-you letter ▸ **lettre circulaire** circular ▸ **lettres de créance** credentials ▸ **lettre de crédit** letter of credit

▸ **lettre exprès** express letter ▸ **lettre d'intention** letter of intent ▸ **lettres de noblesse** (*lit*) letters patent of nobility; (*fig*) **donner ses ~s de noblesse à** to lend credibility to; **gagner ses ~s de noblesse** to win acclaim, establish one's pedigree ▸ **lettre ouverte** (*Presse*) open letter ▸ **lettres patentes** letters (of) patent, letters patent of nobility ▸ **lettre de rappel** reminder ▸ **lettre de recommandation** letter of recommendation, reference ▸ **lettre recommandée** (*attestant sa remise*) recorded delivery letter; (*assurant sa valeur*) registered letter ▸ **lettre de service** notification of command ▸ **lettres supérieures** (*Scol*) first year of two-year preparatory course for the arts section of the École normale supérieure ▸ **lettre de voiture** consignment note, waybill → **motivation, relance**

lettré, e [letʀe] 1 ADJ well-read 2 NM,F man (*ou* woman) of letters

lettrine [letʀin] NF a [*dictionnaire*] headline b [*chapitre*] dropped initial

leu [lø] NM → **queue**

leucémie [løsemi] NF leukaemia (*Brit*), leukemia (*US*)

leucémique [løsemik] 1 ADJ leukaemic (*Brit*), leukemic (*US*) 2 NMF leukaemia (*Brit*) *ou* leukemia (*US*) sufferer

leucocytaire [løkositɛʀ] ADJ leucocytic, leukocytic (*US*)

leucocyte [løkosit] NM leucocyte, leukocyte (*US*); **~ mononucléaire** monocyte; **~ polynucléaire** polymorphonuclear leucocyte

leucorrhée [løkɔʀe] NF leucorrhoea

leucotomie [løkɔtɔmi] NF leucotomy

leur [lœʀ] 1 PRON PERS them; **je le ~ ai dit** I told them; **il ~ est facile de le faire** it is easy for them to do it; **elle ~ serra la main** she shook their hand, she shook them by the hand; **je ~ en ai donné** I gave them some, I gave some to them

2 ADJ POSS a (*gén*) their; **~ jardin est une vraie forêt vierge** their garden is a real jungle; **~ maladroite de sœur** that clumsy sister of theirs; **ils ont passé tout ~ dimanche à travailler** they spent all Sunday working b (*littér*) theirs, their own; **un ~ cousin** a cousin of theirs; **ils ont fait ~s ces idées** they made these ideas their own; **ces terres qui étaient ~s** these estates of theirs *ou* which were theirs

3 PRON POSS **le ~, la ~, les ~s** theirs; **ces sacs sont les ~s** these bags are theirs, these are their bags; **ils sont partis dans une voiture qui n'était pas la ~** they left in a car which wasn't theirs *ou* their own; **à la (bonne) ~ !** their good health!, here's to them!; *pour autres locutions voir* **sien**

4 NM a (*= énergie, volonté*) **ils y ont mis du ~** they pulled their weight, they did their bit* → **sien** b **les ~s** (*= famille*) their family, their (own) folks*; (*= partisans*) their own people; **nous étions des ~s** we were with them; **l'un des ~s** one of their people

leurre [lœʀ] NM (*= illusion*) delusion, illusion; (*= duperie*) deception; (*= piège*) trap, snare; (*Fauconnerie, Pêche*) lure; (*Chasse, Mil*) decoy

leurrer [lœʀe] ▸conjug 1◂ VT (*gén*) to deceive, delude; (*Fauconnerie, Pêche*) to lure; **ils nous ont leurrés par des promesses fallacieuses** they deluded us with false promises; **ils se sont laissé ~** they let themselves be taken in *ou* deceived; **ne vous leurrez pas** don't delude yourself; **ne nous leurrons pas sur leurs intentions** we should not delude ourselves about their intentions

levage [ləvaʒ] NM (*Tech*) lifting; (*Culin*) rising, raising → **appareil**

levain [ləvɛ̃] NM leaven; **sans ~** unleavened;

pain au ~ leavened bread; **~ de haine/de vengeance** seeds of hate/of vengeance

levant [ləvã] [1] ADJ **soleil ~** rising sun; **au soleil ~** at sunrise [2] NM [a] (= *est*) east; **du ~ au couchant** from east to west; **les chambres sont au ~** the bedrooms face east [b] (= *l'Orient*) **le Levant** the Levant

levantin, -ine† [ləvãtẽ, in] [1] ADJ Levantine [2] NM,F **Levantin(e)** NM,F Levantine

levé[1] [l(ə)ve] NM (= *plan*) survey; **~ de terrain** land survey

levé[2], **e**[1] [l(ə)ve] (*ptp de lever*) [1] ADJ (= *sorti du lit*) **être ~** to be up; **sitôt ~** as soon as he is up; **il n'est pas encore ~** he isn't up yet; **toujours le premier ~** always the first up → **pierre** [2] NM (*Mus*) up-beat

levée[2] [l(ə)ve] [1] NF [a] [*blocus, siège*] raising; [*séance, interdiction, punition*] lifting; **ils ont voté la ~ de son immunité parlementaire** they voted to take away ou to withdraw his parliamentary immunity [b] (*Poste*) collection; **la ~ du matin est faite** the morning collection has been made, the morning post has gone (*Brit*); **dernière ~ à 19 heures** last collection (at) 7 p.m. [c] (*Cartes*) trick; **faire une ~** to take a trick [d] [*impôts*] levying; [*armée*] raising, levying [e] (= *remblai*) levee [2] COMP ► **levée de boucliers** (*fig*) general outcry, hue and cry ► **levée du corps: la ~ du corps aura lieu à 10 heures** the funeral will start from the house at 10 o'clock ► **levée d'écrou** release (from prison) ► **levée de jugement** transcript (of a verdict) ► **levée en masse** mass conscription ► **levée des scellés** removal of the seals ► **levée de terre** levee

lever[1] [l(ə)ve] ▶ conjug 5 ◀ [1] VT [a] (= *soulever, hausser*) [+ *poids, objet*] to lift; [+ *main, bras, vitre*] to raise; (*à la manivelle*) to wind up; [+ *tête*] to raise, lift up; (*en classe*) **levez la main ou le doigt** put your hand up; **lève ton coude, je veux prendre le papier** lift ou raise your elbow, I want to take the paper away; **lève les pieds quand tu marches** pick your feet up when you walk; **~ les yeux** to lift up ou raise one's eyes, look up (*de* from); **~ les yeux sur qn** (= *le regarder*) to look at sb; († = *vouloir l'épouser*) to set one's heart on marrying sb; **~ le visage vers qn** to look up at sb; **~ un regard suppliant/éploré vers qn** to look up imploringly/tearfully at sb [b] (= *faire cesser, supprimer*) [+ *blocus*] to raise; [+ *séance, audience*] to close; [+ *obstacle, difficulté*] to remove; [+ *interdiction, sanction, restriction*] to lift; [+ *ambiguïté*] to clear up; [+ *immunité parlementaire*] to withdraw, take away; **~ les scellés** to remove the seals; **cela a levé tous ses scrupules** that has removed all his scruples; **on lève la séance?*** shall we call it a day?, shall we break up? (*US*) [c] (*Fin, Jur*) [+ *option*] to exercise, take up [d] (= *ramasser*) [+ *impôts*] to levy; [+ *armée*] to raise, levy; [+ *fonds*] to raise; (*Cartes*) [+ *pli*] to take; [*facteur*] [+ *lettres*] to collect [e] (*Chasse*) [+ *lapin*] to start; [+ *perdrix*] to flush; ‡ [+ *femme*] to pick up* → **lièvre** [f] (= *établir*) [+ *plan*] to draw (up); [+ *carte*] to draw [g] (= *sortir du lit*) [+ *enfant, malade*] to get up; **le matin, pour le faire ~, il faut se fâcher** in the morning, you have to get angry before he'll get up ou to get him out of bed [h] (= *prélever*) [+ *morceau de viande*] to take off, remove; **~ les filets d'un poisson** to fillet a fish [i] (*loc*) **~ l'ancre** (*Naut*) to weigh anchor; * (*fig*) to make tracks*; **~ les bras au ciel** to throw one's arms up in the air; **~ les yeux au ciel** to raise one's eyes heavenwards; **~ le camp** (*lit*) to strike ou break camp; (*fig = partir*) to clear off*; **~ le siège** (*lit*) to lift ou raise the siege; (*fig = partir*) to clear off*; **il lève bien le coude*** he enjoys a drink, he drinks a fair bit*; [*chien*] **~ la patte** (*pour uriner*) to cock ou

lift its leg; (*pour dire bonjour*) to give a paw; **le pied** (= *disparaître*) to vanish; (= *ralentir*) to slow down; **entre Paris et Lyon, il n'a pas levé le pied** he didn't take his foot off the accelerator between Paris and Lyons; **~ la main sur qn** to raise one's hand to sb; (*Théât*) **~ le rideau** to raise the curtain; **~ le voile** to reveal the truth (*sur* about); **~ le masque** to unmask o.s.; **~ son verre à la santé de qn** to raise one's glass to sb, drink (to) sb's health → **main, pied**

[2] VI [a] [*plante, blé*] to come up [b] (*Culin*) to rise; **faire ~ la pâte** leave the dough to rise

[3] **se lever** VPR [a] [*rideau, main*] to go up; **toutes les mains se levèrent** every hand went up [b] (= *se mettre debout*) to stand up, get up; **se ~ de table/de sa chaise** to get down from the table/get up from one's chair; **le maître les fit se ~** the teacher made them stand up ou get up; **levez-vous!** stand up! [c] (= *sortir du lit*) to get up; **se ~ tôt** to get up early, rise early; **le convalescent commence à se ~** the convalescent is beginning to walk about; **ce matin, il s'est levé du pied gauche** he got up out of bed on the wrong side this morning; **se ~ sur son séant** to sit up; **il faut se ~ de bonne heure pour le convaincre!*** you've got your work cut out for you if you want to persuade him [d] [*soleil, lune*] to rise; [*jour*] to break; **le soleil n'était pas encore levé** the sun had not yet risen ou was not yet up [e] (*Mét*) [*vent*] to get up, rise; [*brume*] to lift, clear; [*mer*] to swell; **le temps se lève ◊ ça se lève** the weather ou it is clearing [f] (= *se révolter*) to rise up

lever[2] [ləve] NM [a] **~ de soleil** sunrise, sunup* (*US*); **le ~ du jour** daybreak, dawn; **il partit dès le ~ du jour** he left at daybreak ou dawn [b] (*au réveil*) **prenez trois comprimés au ~** take three tablets when you get up; **au ◊ à son ~** (*présent*) when he gets up; (*passé*) when he got up; **le ~ du roi** the levee of the king [c] (*Théât*) **le ~ du rideau** (= *action de monter le rideau*) the raising of the curtain; (= *commencement d'une pièce*) curtain up; (= *pièce, match*) **un ~ de rideau** a curtain-raiser; **en ~ de rideau, nous avons ...** as a curtain-raiser ou to start with, we have ... [d] = **levé**[1]

lève-tard [lɛvtaʀ] NMF INV late riser

lève-tôt [lɛvto] NMF INV early riser

lève-vitre [lɛvvitʀ] (*pl* **lève-vitres**) NM (window) winder; **~ électrique** electric window

Léviathan [levjatã] NM (*Bible*) Leviathan

levier [ləvje] NM lever; **~ de commande** control lever; **~ de changement de vitesse** gear lever (*Brit*), gearshift (*US*), stick shift* (*US*); **~ de frein** handbrake (lever); **faire ~ sur qch** to lever sth up (*ou* off *etc*); (*fig*) **être aux ~s (de commande)** to be in control ou command; **l'argent est un puissant ~** money is a powerful lever

lévitation [levitasjõ] NF levitation; **être en ~** to be levitating

lévite [levit] NM Levite

Lévitique [levitik] NM **le ~** Leviticus

levraut [ləvʀo] NM leveret

lèvre [lɛvʀ] NF [a] [*bouche*] lip; **le sourire aux ~s** with a smile on one's lips; **la cigarette aux ~s** with a cigarette between one's lips; **son nom est sur toutes les ~s** his name is on everyone's lips; (*fig*) **j'ai les ~s scellées** my lips are sealed → **bout, pincer, rouge** *etc* [b] [*plaie*] edge; [*vulve*] lip, labium (*SPÉC*); **petites/grandes ~s** labia minora/majora (*SPÉC*) [c] (*Géog*) [*faille*] side; **~ soulevée/abaissée** upthrow/downthrow side

levrette [ləvʀɛt] NF (= *femelle*) greyhound bitch; (= *variété de lévrier*) Italian greyhound;

(= *position sexuelle*) **en ~** doggie-style, doggie-fashion

lévrier [levʀije] NM greyhound; **courses de ~s** greyhound racing; **~ afghan** Afghan (hound); **~ irlandais** Irish wolfhound; **~ italien** Italian greyhound

levure [l(ə)vyʀ] NF (= *ferment*) yeast; **~ de bière** brewers' yeast; **~ de boulanger** ou **de boulangerie** baker's yeast; **~ chimique** baking powder

lexème [lɛksɛm] NM lexeme

lexical, e (*mpl* **-aux**) [lɛksikal, o] ADJ lexical

lexicalisation [lɛksikalizasjõ] NF lexicalization

lexicalisé, e [lɛksikalize] ADJ lexicalized

lexicographe [lɛksikɔgʀaf] NMF lexicographer

lexicographie [lɛksikɔgʀafi] NF lexicography

lexicographique [lɛksikɔgʀafik] ADJ lexicographical

lexicologie [lɛksikɔlɔʒi] NF lexicology

lexicologique [lɛksikɔlɔʒik] ADJ lexicological

lexicologue [lɛksikɔlɔg] NMF lexicologist

lexie [lɛksi] NF lexical item

lexique [lɛksik] NM [a] (= *glossaire*) glossary; (*d'une langue ancienne*) lexicon [b] (= *mots d'une langue*) lexicon, lexis (*SPÉC*); (= *mots d'une personne*) vocabulary, lexicon

lézard [lezaʀ] NM (= *animal*) lizard; (= *peau*) lizardskin; **~ vert/des murailles** green/wall lizard; **sac/gants en ~** lizardskin bag/gloves; **faire le ~ (au soleil)*** to bask in the sun; **y a pas de ~!*** no problem!*, no prob!*

lézarde [lezaʀd] NF (= *fissure*) crack

lézarder[1]* [lezaʀde] ▶ conjug 1 ◀ VI to bask in the sun

lézarder[2] VT, **se lézarder** VPR [lezaʀde] ▶ conjug 1 ◀ (= *craquer*) to crack

Lhassa [lasa] N Lhasa, Lassa

liaison [ljɛzõ] NF [a] (= *fréquentation*) **~ (amoureuse)** (love) affair, liaison; **avoir/rompre une ~** to have/break off an affair ou a love affair [b] (= *contact*) **assurer la ~ entre les différents services** to liaise between the different departments; (*péj*) **avoir des ~s avec** to have links ou dealings with; **j'espère que nous allons rester en ~** I hope that we shall remain in contact ou in touch; **entrer/être en ~ étroite avec qn** to get/be in close contact with sb; **travailler en ~ étroite avec qn** to work closely with ou in close collaboration with sb; **en ~ (étroite) avec nos partenaires, nous avons décidé de ...** in (close) collaboration with ou after (close) consultation with our partners, we have decided to ...; **se tenir en ~ avec l'état-major** to keep in contact with headquarters, liaise with headquarters; **officier** ou **agent de ~** liaison officer [c] (*Radio, Téléc*) **~ radio** radio contact; **les ~s téléphoniques avec le Japon** telephone links with Japan; **~ par satellite/câble** satellite/cable link; **je suis en ~ avec notre envoyé spécial à Moscou** I have our special correspondent on the line from Moscow; (*Ordin*) **~ de transmission** data link [d] (= *rapport, enchaînement*) connection; **manque de ~ entre deux idées** lack of connection between two ideas; **il n'y a aucune ~ entre les deux idées/événements** the two ideas/events are unconnected [e] (*Gram, Phon*) liaison; **consonne de ~** linking consonant; **mot** ou **terme de ~** link-word; **faire la ~** to make a liaison [f] (*Transport*) link; **~ aérienne/routière/ferroviaire/maritime** air/road/rail/sea link [g] (*Culin*) (= *action*) thickening, liaison; (= *ingrédients*) liaison [h] (*Mus*) (*même hauteur*) tie; (*hauteurs différentes*) slur [i] (*Chim*) bond

⌐ (Constr) (= action) bonding; (= mortier) bond

liane [ljan] NF creeper, liana

liant, liante [ljɑ̃, ljɑ̃t] **1** ADJ sociable **2** NM **a** (littér: en société) sociable disposition; **il a du ~** he has a sociable disposition ou nature, he is sociable **b** (Métal = souplesse) flexibility **c** (= substance) binder

liard [ljaʀ] NM (Hist) farthing; **je n'ai pas un ~ †** I haven't (got) a farthing †

lias [ljɑs] NM (Géol) Lias

liasique [ljazik] ADJ (Géol) Liassic

liasse [ljɑs] NF (billets) wad; (papiers) bundle; **mettre des billets en ~s** to make (up) wads of notes

Liban [libɑ̃] NM **(le) ~** (the) Lebanon

libanais, e [libanɛ, ɛz] **1** ADJ Lebanese **2** **Libanais(e)** NM,F Lebanese

libanisation [libanizasjɔ̃] NF (Pol) **la ~ du pays** the fragmentation of the country

libation [libasjɔ̃] NF (Antiq) libation; (fig) **faire de copieuses ~s** to indulge in great libations (hum)

libelle [libɛl] NM (= satire) lampoon; **faire des ~s contre qn** to lampoon sb

libellé [libele] NM (gén) wording; (Fin) description, particulars

libeller [libele] ▸conjug 1◂ VT (+ acte) to draw up; (+ chèque) to make out (à l'ordre de to); (+ lettre, demande, réclamation) to word; **sa lettre était ainsi libellée** so went his letter, his letter was worded thus

libelliste [libelist] NM (littér) lampoonist

libellule [libelyl] NF dragonfly

liber [libɛʀ] NM (Bot) phloem

libérable [libeʀabl] ADJ (militaire) dischargeable; **permission ~** leave in hand (allowing early discharge)

libéral, e (mpl -aux) [libeʀal, o] **1** ADJ **a** (Pol) Liberal **b** (Écon) (économie, modèle) freemarket (épith); **travailler en ~** (médecin) to have a private practice; (chauffeur de taxi) to work for oneself **c** (= tolérant) liberal, open-minded **2** NM,F (Pol) Liberal

libéralement [libeʀalmɑ̃] ADV liberally

libéralisation [libeʀalizasjɔ̃] NF (gén) liberalization; **la ~ du commerce** trade liberalization, the easing of restrictions on trade; **~ de l'avortement** liberalization of the abortion laws

libéraliser [libeʀalize] ▸conjug 1◂ VT (gén) to liberalize; **~ la vente des seringues** to lift restrictions on the sale of syringes

libéralisme [libeʀalism] NM (gén) liberalism; **être partisan du ~ économique** to be a supporter of economic liberalism ou of free enterprise

libéralité [libeʀalite] NF (littér) (= générosité) liberality; (gén pl = don) generous gift, liberality (frm); **vivre des ~s d'un ami** to live off a friend's generosity

libérateur, -trice [libeʀatœʀ, tʀis] **1** ADJ **guerre/croisade libératrice** war/crusade of liberation; **rire ~** liberating laugh; **expérience libératrice** liberating experience **2** NM,F liberator

libération [libeʀasjɔ̃] NF **a** (prisonnier, otage) release; (soldat) discharge; (pays, peuple, ville) freeing, liberation; **front/mouvement de ~** liberation front/movement; (Hist) **la Libération** the Liberation; **~ anticipée** early release; **~ conditionnelle** release on parole; **la ~ de la femme** Women's Liberation; **~ sexuelle** sexual liberation **b** (Fin) **~ de capital** paying up of capital, payment in full of capital; **~ des prix** price deregulation **c** (Sci) (énergie, électrons) release → **vitesse**

libératoire [libeʀatwaʀ] ADJ (Fin) **paiement ~** payment in full discharge; **prélèvement ~** levy at source (on share dividends)

libéré, e [libeʀe] (ptp de **libérer**) ADJ liberated

libérer [libeʀe] ▸conjug 6◂ **1** VT **a** (+ prisonnier) to discharge, release (de from); (+ otage) to release, set free; (+ soldat) to discharge (de from); (+ élèves, employés) to let go; (+ pays, peuple, ville) to free, liberate; (Jur) **être libéré sur parole** to be released on parole → **caution**

b (+ esprit, personne) (de soucis) to free (de from); (d'inhibition) to liberate (de from); **~ qn de** (+ liens) to release ou free sb from; (+ promesse) to release sb from; (+ dette) to free sb from; **ça m'a libéré de lui dire ce que je pensais** it was a relief to tell him what I was thinking

c (+ appartement) to move out of, vacate; (+ étagère) to clear; (+ tiroir) to empty; **nous libérerons la salle à 11 heures** we'll clear the room at 11 o'clock; **~ le passage** to free ou unblock the way; **ça a libéré trois postes** it made three jobs available

d (Tech) (+ levier, cran d'arrêt) to release; (Écon) (+ échanges commerciaux) to ease restrictions on; (+ prix) to decontrol; (Méd) (+ intestin) to unblock

e (= soulager) **~ son cœur/sa conscience** to unburden one's heart/one's conscience; **~ ses instincts** to give free rein to one's instincts

f (Sci) (+ énergie, électrons, hormones) to release; (+ gaz) to release, give off

2 **se libérer** VPR **a** (personne) (de ses liens) to free o.s. (de from); (d'une promesse) to release o.s. (de from); (d'une dette) to clear o.s. (de of); **se ~ d'un rendez-vous** to get out of a meeting; **désolé, jeudi je ne peux pas me ~** I'm sorry, I'm not free on Thursday; **je n'ai pas pu me ~ plus tôt** I couldn't get away any earlier; (= s'affranchir) **se ~ du joug de l'oppresseur** to free o.s. from the yoke of one's oppressor

b (appartement) to become vacant; (place assise) to become available; (poste) to become vacant ou available

Libéria [libeʀja] NM Liberia

libérien, -ienne [libeʀjɛ̃, jɛn] **1** ADJ Liberian **2** **Libérien(ne)** NM,F Liberian

libériste [libeʀist] **1** NMF (= sportif) hang-glider **2** ADJ hang-gliding

libéro [libeʀo] NM (Ftbl) libero (SPÉC), ≈ sweeper

libertaire [libɛʀtɛʀ] ADJ, NMF libertarian

liberté [libɛʀte] **1** NF **a** (gén, Jur) freedom, liberty; **rendre la ~ à un prisonnier** to free ou release a prisoner, set a prisoner free; **elle a quitté son mari et repris sa ~** she has left her husband and regained her freedom ou her independence; **sans la ~ de critiquer/de choisir aucune opinion n'a de valeur** without the freedom to criticize/to choose any opinion is valueless; **avoir toute ~ pour agir** to have full liberty ou freedom ou scope to act; **donner à qn toute ~ d'action** to give sb complete freedom of action, give sb a free hand; **agir en toute** ou **pleine ~** to act with complete freedom, act quite freely

b (loc) **laisser en ~** to allow to remain at liberty; **mise en ~** (prisonnier) discharge, release; **être en ~** to be free; **animaux en ~** animals in the wild ou natural state; **les animaux sont en ~ dans le parc** the animals roam free in the park; **le voleur est encore en ~** the thief is still at large; **remettre en ~** (+ animal) to set free (again); (+ otage, prisonnier) to release, set free

c (gén, Pol = indépendance) freedom; **~ de la presse/d'opinion/de conscience** freedom of the press/of thought/of conscience; **~ individuelle** personal freedom; **~ d'information/d'expression** freedom of information/of expression; **~ religieuse** ou **de culte** religious freedom, freedom of worship; **vive la ~!** long live freedom!; **~, égalité, fraternité** liberty, equality, fraternity

d (= loisir) **heures/moments de ~** free hours/

moments; **ils ont droit à deux jours de ~ par semaine** they are allowed two free days a week ou two days off each week; **son travail ne lui laisse pas beaucoup de ~** his work doesn't leave him much free time

e (= absence de retenue, de contrainte) **~ d'esprit/de jugement** independence of mind/of judgment; **~ de langage/de mœurs** freedom of language/of morals; **la ~ de ton du ministre a étonné** the fact that the minister expressed himself so openly ou freely surprised people; **la ~ de ton de l'émission a choqué** the frank approach of the programme shocked people; **s'exprimer avec (grande) ~** to express o.s. (very) freely; **prendre la ~ de faire** to take the liberty of doing; **prendre** ou **se permettre des ~s avec** (+ personne, texte, grammaire, règlement) to take liberties with

f (= droit) **la ~ du travail** the right ou freedom to work; **~ d'association/de réunion** right of association/to meet ou hold meetings; **~s individuelles** individual freedoms ou liberties; **~s syndicales** union rights; **~s civiles** civil liberties; (Hist) **~s des villes** borough franchises

2 COMP ► **liberté conditionnelle** parole; **être mis en ~ conditionnelle** to be granted parole, be released on parole; **mise en ~ conditionnelle** release on parole ► **liberté provisoire** temporary release; **être mis en ~ provisoire** to be released temporarily ► **liberté surveillée** release on probation; **être mis en ~ surveillée** to be put on probation

libertin, e [libɛʀtɛ̃, in] **1** ADJ (= dissolu) (personne) libertine, dissolute; (= grivois) (roman) licentious; (Hist = irréligieux) (philosophe) libertine **2** NM,F (littér = dévergondé) libertine **3** NM (Hist = libre-penseur) libertine, freethinker

libertinage [libɛʀtinaʒ] NM (= débauche) (personne) debauchery, dissoluteness; (= grivoiserie) (roman) licentiousness; (Hist = impiété) libertine outlook ou philosophy

liberty® [libɛʀti] NM INV Liberty fabric®

libidinal, e (mpl -aux) [libidinal, o] ADJ libidinal

libidineux, -euse [libidinø, øz] ADJ (littér, hum) libidinous, lustful

libido [libido] NF libido

libraire [libʀɛʀ] NMF bookseller; **~-éditeur** publisher and bookseller; **en vente chez votre ~** available in all good bookshops

librairie [libʀeʀi] NF **a** (= magasin) bookshop (Brit), bookstore (US); **~ d'art/de livres anciens** art/antiquarian bookshop; **~-papeterie** bookseller's and stationer's; **ça ne se vend plus en ~** it's no longer in the bookshops, the bookshops no longer sell it; **ce livre va bientôt paraître en ~** this book will soon be on sale (in the shops) ou will soon be available **b** **la ~** (= activité) bookselling (NonC); (= corporation) the book trade

▼**libre** [libʀ] **1** ADJ **a** (= sans contrainte) (personne, presse, commerce, prix) free; (Sport) (figure, programme) free; **garder l'esprit** ou **la tête ~** to keep a clear mind; **être ~ comme l'air** to be as free as a bird; **être/rester ~** (non marié) to be/remain unattached; **il n'est plus ~ (de lui-même)** he is no longer a free agent; **être ~ de ses mouvements** to be free to do what one pleases; **avoir la ~ disposition de ses biens** to have free disposal of one's property; **la ~ circulation des personnes** the free movement of people; (Pol) **le monde ~** the free world → **vente**

b **~ de** free from; **~ de tout engagement/préjugé** free from any commitment/all prejudice; **~ de faire qch** free to do sth; **à vous de poser vos conditions** you are free to ou it's (entirely) up to you to state your conditions; **vous êtes parfaitement ~ de refuser l'invitation** you're quite free ou at liberty to refuse the invitation

c (= non occupé) (passage, voie) clear; (taxi)

for hire; [*personne, place*] free; [*salle*] free, available; [*toilettes*,] vacant; **poste ~** vacancy, vacant position; **« ~ de suite »** (*appartement à louer*) "available immediately"; (*appartement à vendre*) "with immediate vacant possession"; (*Téléc*) **la ligne n'est pas ~** the line *ou* number is busy *ou* engaged (*Brit*); (*Téléc*) **ça ne sonne pas ~** I'm getting an engaged tone (*Brit*), there's a busy signal (*US*); **est-ce que cette place est ~?** is this seat free *ou* empty?; **heure ~** *ou* **de ~*** free hour; (*Scol*) free period; **avoir du temps ~** *ou* **de ~*** to have some spare *ou* free time; **avoir des journées ~s** to have some free days; **êtes-vous ~ ce soir?** are you free this evening?; **vous ne pouvez pas voir M. Durand, il n'est pas ~ aujourd'hui** you can't see Mr Durand, he's not free *ou* available today; **le jeudi est son jour ~** Thursday is his free day *ou* his day off; **je vais essayer de me rendre ~ pour demain** I'll try to keep tomorrow free → **air¹, champ**

d (*Scol = non étatisé*) [*enseignement*] private and Roman Catholic; **école ~** private *ou* independent Roman Catholic school → EDUCATION NATIONALE

e (= *autorisé, non payant*) [*entrée, accès*] free → **auditeur, entrée**

f (= *non entravé*) [*mouvement, respiration*] free; [*traduction, improvisation, adaptation*] free; [*pignon, engrenage*] disengaged; **robe qui laisse le cou ~** dress which leaves the neck bare *ou* which shows the neck; **robe qui laisse la taille ~** dress which is not tight-fitting round the waist *ou* which fits loosely at the waist; **avoir les cheveux ~** to have one's hair loose; **le sujet de la dissertation est ~** the subject of this essay is left open → **main, roue, vers²**

g (= *sans retenue*) [*personne*] free *ou* open in one's behaviour; [*plaisanteries*] broad; **tenir des propos assez ~s sur la politique du gouvernement** to be fairly plain-spoken *ou* make fairly candid remarks about the policies of the government; **être très ~ avec qn** to be very free with sb; **donner ~ cours à sa colère/son indignation** to give free rein *ou* vent to one's anger/one's indignation

2 COMP ► **libre arbitre** free will; **avoir son ~ arbitre** to have free will ► **libre concurrence, libre entreprise** free enterprise; **un partisan de la ~ entreprise** *ou* **concurrence** a free-marketeer, a supporter of the free-market economy *ou* of free enterprise ► **libre pensée** freethinking ► **libre penseur, -euse** freethinker

libre-échange (*pl* **libres-échanges**) [libʀeʃɑ̃ʒ] NM free trade

libre-échangisme [libʀeʃɑ̃ʒism] NM (doctrine of) free trade

libre-échangiste (*pl* **libres-échangistes**) [libʀeʃɑ̃ʒist] **1** ADJ free-market (*épith*), free-trade (*épith*) **2** NMF free-trader

librement [libʀəmɑ̃] ADV [*agir*] freely; **~ adapté d'une pièce de Molière** freely adapted from a play by Molière

libre-service (*pl* **libres-services**) [libʀəsɛʀvis] NM (= *restaurant*) self-service restaurant; (= *magasin*) self-service store; **ce magasin propose un fax et une photocopieuse en ~** the shop provides self-service fax and photocopying facilities

librettiste [libʀetist] NMF librettist

libretto† [libʀeto] (*pl* **librettos** *ou* **libretti** [libʀeti]) NM libretto

Libreville [libʀəvil] N Libreville

Libye [libi] NF Libya

libyen, -enne [libjɛ̃, ɛn] **1** ADJ Libyan **2** **Libyen(ne)** NM,F Libyan

lice [lis] NF (*Hist*) lists; (*fig*) **entrer en ~** to enter the lists; **les candidats encore en ~** candidates still in contention

licence [lisɑ̃s] NF **a** (*Univ*) ≈ (bachelor's) degree; **~ ès lettres** Arts degree, ≈ B.A.; **~ ès**

sciences Science degree, ≈ B.Sc.; **faire une ~ d'anglais** to do a degree in English → DIPLÔMES **b** (= *autorisation*) permit; (*Comm, Jur*) licence (*Brit*), license (*US*); (*Sport*) membership card; **un produit sous ~** a licensed product; **fabriqué sous ~ française** manufactured under French licence; **~ d'exploitation** [*logiciel, réseau*] licence; [*ligne aérienne*] operating permit; **~ d'exportation** export licence **c** (*littér = liberté*) (**des mœurs**) licentiousness (*NonC*); **avoir toute** *ou* **pleine ~ pour faire qch** to have a free hand to do sth; **prendre des ~s avec qn** to take liberties with sb; (*Littérat*) **~ poétique** poetic licence; **une ~ orthographique** an accepted alternative spelling

licencié, e [lisɑ̃sje] **1** ADJ (*Univ*) **professeur ~** graduate teacher; **elle est ~e** she is a graduate **2** NM,F **a** (*Univ*) **~ ès lettres/ès sciences/en droit** arts/science/law graduate, ≈ Bachelor of Arts/of Science/of Law **b** (*Sport*) member **c** (*Jur*) licensee

licenciement [lisɑ̃simɑ̃] NM (*pour raisons économiques*) redundancy; (*pour faute professionnelle*) dismissal; **il y a eu des centaines de ~s pour raisons économiques** hundreds of people were laid off *ou* made redundant (*Brit*), there were hundreds of redundancies; **~ abusif** unfair dismissal; **~ collectif** mass redundancy *ou* lay-offs *ou* redundancies (*Brit*); **~ sec** compulsory redundancy (*without any compensation*); **lettre de ~** letter of dismissal, pink slip* (*US*) → **indemnité**

licencier [lisɑ̃sje] ▶conjug 7◀ VT (*pour raisons économiques*) to lay off, make redundant (*Brit*); (*pour faute*) to dismiss; **on licencie beaucoup dans ce secteur** there are a lot of redundancies in this sector

licencieusement [lisɑ̃sjøzmɑ̃] ADV licentiously

licencieux, -ieuse [lisɑ̃sjø, jøz] ADJ (*littér*) licentious

lichen [likɛn] NM (*Bot, Méd*) lichen

licher* [liʃe] ▶conjug 1◀ VT (= *boire*) to drink; (= *lécher*) to lick

lichette* [liʃɛt] NF **a** (= *morceau*) **~ de pain/de fromage** tiny piece of bread/of cheese; **tu en veux une ~?** do you want a bit?; **il n'en restait qu'une ~** there was only a (tiny) taste left **b** (*Belg = attache*) loop

licite [lisit] ADJ lawful, licit

licitement [lisitmɑ̃] ADV lawfully, licitly

licol† [likɔl] NM halter

licorne [likɔʀn] NF unicorn; **~ de mer** narwhal, sea unicorn

licou [liku] NM halter

licteur [liktœʀ] NM lictor

lie [li] **1** NF [*vin*] sediment, lees; (*péj*) **la ~ (de la société)** the dregs of society → **boire** **2** COMP ► **lie de vin** ADJ INV wine(-coloured)

lié, e [lje] (*ptp de* **lier**) ADJ **a** [*personne*] **être très ~ à** *ou* **avec qn** to be very close to sb; **ils sont très ~s** they're very close **b** (*Mus*) **note ~e** tied note; (*Ling*) **morphème ~** bound morpheme

Liechtenstein [liʃtɛnʃtajn] NM Liechtenstein

liechtensteinois, e [liʃtɛnʃtajnwa, waz] **1** ADJ of Liechtenstein **2** **Liechtensteinois(e)** NM,F inhabitant *ou* native of Liechtenstein

lied (*pl* **lieder** *ou* **lieds**) [lid, lidœʀ] NM lied

liège [ljɛʒ] NM cork; **de** *ou* **en ~** cork (*épith*) → **bout**

liégeois, e [ljeʒwa, waz] **1** ADJ of *ou* from Liège; **café/chocolat ~** coffee/chocolate sundae **2** **Liégeois(e)** NM,F inhabitant *ou* native of Liège

lien [ljɛ̃] NM **a** (*lit, fig = attache*) bond; **le prisonnier se libéra de ses ~s** the prisoner freed himself from his bonds; **de solides ~s de cuir** strong leather straps; **être lié par les ~s du**

serment to be bound by oath; **un ~ très fort l'attache à son pays** he has a very strong bond with his home country **b** (= *corrélation*) link, connection; **il y a un ~ entre les deux événements** there's a link *ou* connection between the two events; **servir de ~ entre deux personnes** to act as a link between two people; **idées sans ~** unconnected *ou* unrelated ideas **c** (= *relation*) tie; **~s affectifs** emotional ties *ou* bonds; **~s de parenté/de sang** family/blood ties; **avoir un ~ de parenté avec qn** to be related to sb; **~s d'amitié** bonds of friendship; **~ qui unit deux personnes** bond which unites two people; **~s du mariage** marriage bonds *ou* ties; **le ~ social** social cohesion

lier [lje] ▶conjug 7◀ **1** VT **a** (= *attacher*) [+ *mains, pieds*] to bind, tie up; [+ *fleurs, bottes de paille*] to tie up; **elle lui a lié les pieds et les mains** she bound him hand and foot; **~ de la paille en bottes** to bind *ou* tie straw into bales; **~ qn à un arbre/une chaise** to tie sb to a tree/a chair; **~ qch avec une ficelle** to tie sth with a piece of string → **fou, pied** **b** (= *relier*) [+ *mots, phrases*] to link up, join up; **~ la cause à l'effet** to link cause to effect; **tous ces événements sont étroitement liés** all these events are closely linked *ou* connected; **cette maison est liée à tout un passé** there is a whole history attached to this house; **tout est lié** everything links up *ou* ties up; (*Mus*) **~ les notes** to slur the notes; **~ un passage** to play a passage legato **c** (= *unir*) [+ *personnes*] to bind, unite; **l'amitié qui nous lie à elle** the friendship which binds us to her; **l'amitié qui les lie** the friendship which unites them; **un goût/mépris commun pour le théâtre les liait** they were united by a common liking/scorn for the theatre **d** [*contrat*] to bind; **~ qn par un serment/une promesse** to bind sb with an oath/a promise **e** (*Culin*) [+ *sauce*] to thicken; (*Constr*) **~ des pierres avec du mortier** to bind stones with mortar **f** (*loc*) **~ amitié/conversation** to strike up a friendship/conversation; **~ la langue à qn** to make sb tongue-tied **2** **se lier** VPR to make friends (**avec qn** with sb); **se ~ d'amitié avec qn** to strike up a friendship with sb; **il ne se lie pas facilement** he doesn't make friends easily; **se ~ par un serment** to bind o.s. by an oath

lierre [ljɛʀ] NM ivy; **~ terrestre** ground ivy

liesse [ljes] NF (*littér = joie*) jubilation; **en ~** jubilant

▼**lieu¹** (*pl* **lieux**) [ljø] **1** NM **a** (*gén = endroit*) place; [*événement*] scene; **adverbe de ~** adverb of place; **~ de pèlerinage/résidence/retraite** place of pilgrimage/residence/retreat; **sur le ~ de travail** in the workplace; **le club est devenu un ~ de vie important dans le quartier** the club has become a major centre of social activity in the area; **il faut maintenir la personne âgée dans son ~ de vie habituel** old people should be allowed to stay in their usual environment; **en quelque ~ qu'il soit** wherever he may be, wherever he is; **en tous ~x** everywhere; **en aucun ~ du monde** nowhere in the world; **cela varie avec le ~** it varies from place to place; **en ~ sûr** in a safe place → **haut, nom** **b** (*avec notion temporelle*) **en premier/second ~** in the first/second place, firstly/secondly; **en dernier ~** lastly, finally; **ce n'est pas le ~ d'en parler** this isn't the place to speak about it; **en son ~** in due course → **temps¹** **c** (*loc*) **avoir ~** (= *se produire*) to take place, occur; **avoir ~ d'être inquiet/de se plaindre** to have (good) grounds for being worried/for complaining, have (good) reason to be worried/to complain; **il y a ~ d'être inquiet** there is cause for anxiety *ou* good reason to be anxious; **il y a tout ~ de s'étonner** we have every reason to be surprised; **vos craintes/**

► GRAMMAIRE ACTIVE: **lieu** 42.2, 44.2

critiques n'ont pas ~ d'être your fears/criticisms are groundless; **vous appellerez le médecin, s'il y a ~** send for the doctor if necessary *ou* if need be; **donner ~ à des critiques/désagréments** to give rise to criticism/trouble; **ça donne ~ de craindre le pire** it means we should fear the worst; **elle lui a tenu ~ de mère** she took the place of his mother; **ce vieux manteau tient ~ de couverture** this old overcoat serves as a blanket *ou* does instead of a blanket

2 **lieux** NMPL (= *locaux*) premises; **quitter** *ou* **vider les ~x** (= get out, leave; (*Admin*) to vacate the premises; **se rendre sur les ~x du crime** to go to the scene of the crime; **être sur les ~x de l'accident** to be at *ou* on the scene of the accident; **notre envoyé est sur les ~x** our special correspondent is on the spot *ou* at the scene → **état**

3 **au lieu de** LOC PRÉP instead of; **tu devrais téléphoner au ~ d'écrire** you should telephone instead of writing; **il devrait se réjouir, au ~ de cela, il se plaint** he should be glad, instead of which he complains *ou* but instead he complains; **signer en ~ et place de qn** to sign on behalf of sb

4 **au lieu que** LOC CONJ instead of; **au ~ que nous partions** instead of (us) leaving

5 COMP ► **lieux d'aisances** († *ou hum*) lavatory (*Brit*), comfort station (*US*) ► **lieu commun** commonplace ► **lieu de débauche** († *ou hum*) den of iniquity ► **lieu géométrique** (*Math, fig*) locus ► **lieu de naissance** (*gén*) birthplace; (*Admin*) place of birth ► **lieu de passage** (*entre régions*) crossing point; (*entre villes*) stopping-off place; (*dans un bâtiment*) place where people are constantly coming and going ► **lieu de perdition** den of iniquity ► **lieu de promenade** place *ou* spot for walking ► **lieu public** public place ► **lieu de rendez-vous** meeting place ► **les Lieux saints** the Holy Places ► **lieu de vacances** (*gén*) place *ou* spot for one's holidays (*Brit*) *ou* vacation (*US*); (= *ville*) holiday (*Brit*) *ou* vacation (*US*) resort

lieu² [ljø] NM (= *poisson*) ► **jaune** pollack, pollock; ► **noir** saithe, coley, coalfish

lieu-dit (*pl* **lieux-dits**) [ljødi] NM locality; **au ~ le Bouc étourdi** at the place known as the Bouc étourdi

lieue [ljø] NF (*Hist*) league; **j'étais à mille ~s de penser à vous** you were far from my mind; **j'étais à cent** *ou* **mille ~s de penser qu'il viendrait** it never occurred to me *ou* I never dreamt for a moment that he'd come; **il sent son marin d'une ~** you can tell he's a sailor a mile off*, the fact that he's a sailor sticks out a mile; **à vingt ~s à la ronde** for miles around → **botte**

lieuse [ljøz] NF (*Agr*) binder

lieutenant [ljøt(ə)nɑ̃] 1 NM (*armée de terre*) lieutenant (*Brit*), first lieutenant (*US*); (*armée de l'air*) flying officer (*Brit*), first lieutenant (*US*); (*marine marchande*) (first) mate, first officer; (*gén = second*) lieutenant, second in command; **oui mon ~ !** yes sir!; (*fig*) **l'un de ses ~s** one of his right-hand men 2 COMP ► **lieutenant de vaisseau** (*marine nationale*) lieutenant

lieutenant-colonel (*pl* **lieutenants-colonels**) [ljøt(ə)nɑ̃kɔlɔnɛl] NM (*armée de terre*) lieutenant colonel; (*armée de l'air*) wing commander (*Brit*), lieutenant colonel (*US*)

lièvre [ljɛvʀ] NM (*Zool*) hare; (*Sport*) pacemaker; (*fig*) **courir** *ou* **chasser deux ~s à la fois** to try to do *ou* juggle two things at once; (*fig*) **vous avez levé** *ou* **soulevé un ~** you've hit on a problem there

lift [lift] NM topspin

lifter [lifte] ►conjug 1◄ 1 VT **a** (*Sport*) to put topspin on; **balle liftée** ball with topspin; **elle a un jeu très lifté** she uses a lot of topspin

b [+ *personne, bâtiment, image de marque*] to give a face-lift to 2 VI to put topspin on the ball

liftier, -ière [liftje, jɛʀ] NM,F lift (*Brit*) *ou* elevator (*US*) attendant

lifting [liftiŋ] NM (*lit, fig*) face-lift; **se faire faire un ~** to have a face-lift

ligament [ligamɑ̃] NM ligament

ligamentaire [ligamɑ̃tɛʀ] ADJ ligamentary

ligamenteux, -euse [ligamɑ̃tø, øz] ADJ ligamentous, ligamentary

ligature [ligatyʀ] NF **a** (*Méd*) (= *opération*) ligation (*SPÉC*), tying; (= *lien*) ligature; **~ des trompes** tubal ligation (*SPÉC*), tying of the Fallopian tubes **b** (*Agr*) (= *opération*) tying up; (= *lien*) tie **c** (*Typo*) ligature **d** (*Mus*) ligature, tie

ligaturer [ligatyʀe] ►conjug 1◄ VT (*Méd*) to ligature, tie up; (*Agr*) to tie up; **se faire ~ les trompes** to have one's Fallopian tubes tied, have one's tubes tied*

lige [liʒ] ADJ liege; (*Hist*) **homme ~** liegeman; (*fig*) **être l'homme ~ de qn** to be sb's henchman

light [lajt] ADJ INV (*gén*) light; [*boisson, chocolat*] diet (*épith*), low-calorie (*épith*)

lignage [liɲaʒ] NM **a** (= *extraction*) lineage; **de haut ~** of noble lineage **b** (*Typo*) linage, lineage

▼**ligne¹** [liɲ]

1 NOM FÉMININ	2 COMPOSÉS

1 NOM FÉMININ

a = **trait, limite** line; **~ brisée/courbe** broken/curved line; **~ pointillée** dotted line; **~ droite** (*gén*) straight line; (*Aut*) stretch of straight road; (*lit, fig*) **la dernière ~ droite avant l'arrivée** the final *ou* home straight; **courir en ~ droite** to run in a straight line; **la route coupe la forêt en ~ droite** the road cuts right *ou* straight through the forest; **ça fait 4 km en ~ droite** it's 4 km as the crow flies; **il arrive en droite ~ de son Texas natal** he has come straight from his native Texas; **~ de départ/d'arrivée** starting/finishing line; **la ~ de fracture au sein de la majorité** the rift dividing the majority; (*Rugby*) **la ~ des 10/22 mètres** the 10/22 metre line; **les ~s de la main** the lines of the hand; **~ de vie/de cœur** life/love line; **la ~ des collines dans le lointain** the line of hills in the distance; **passer la ~ (de l'équateur)** to cross the line → **juge**

b = **contour, silhouette** [*meuble, voiture*] line(s); [*personne*] figure; **avoir la ~** to have a slim figure; **garder/perdre la ~** to keep/lose one's figure; **elle mange peu pour garder la ~** she doesn't eat much because she's watching her figure; **la ~ lancée par les dernières collections** the look launched by the most recent collections; **voiture aux ~s aérodynamiques** streamlined car, car built on aerodynamic lines

c = **règle, orientation** line; **~ de conduite/d'action** line of conduct/of action; **~ politique** political line; **la ~ du parti** the party line; **les grandes ~s d'un programme** the broad lines *ou* outline of a programme; **l'objectif a été fixé dans ses grandes ~s** the objective has been established in broad outline; **à propos de ce problème, les deux présidents sont sur la même ~ (= ils sont d'accord)** the two presidents are in agreement *ou* are of one mind with regard to this problem; **ce projet s'inscrit dans la droite ~ de la politique européenne** this project is fully *ou* directly in line with European policy; **son livre est dans la droite ~ du roman américain** his book is in the direct tradition of the American novel

d = **suite de personnes, de choses** line; (= *rangée*) row; (*Mil*) line; [*cocaïne*] line; **une ~ d'arbres le long de l'horizon** a line *ou* row of trees on the horizon; (*Ftbl*) **la ~ d'avants** *ou* **des avants/d'arrières** *ou* **des arrières** the forwards/

backs; (*Rugby*) **la première/deuxième/troisième ~ (de mêlée)** the front/second/back row (of the scrum); **un première ~** a man in the front row; (*Mil, fig*) **en première ~** on the front line → **hors**

♦ **en ligne** (= *alignés*) **enfants placés en ~** children in a line *ou* lined up; **coureurs en ~ pour le départ** runners lined up for the start *ou* on the starting line; **mettre des personnes en ~** to line people up, get people lined up; **se mettre en ~** to line up, get lined up, get into line → **cylindre** (*Mil*) **monter en ~** to go off to war *ou* to fight (= *en accord*) **ces résultats sont en ~ avec les prévisions** these results are in line *ou* on target with projections; **pour le chiffre de ventes, nous sommes en ~** our sales figures are on target → **f**

e = **Transport** (*Rail*) line; **~ d'autobus** (= *service*) bus service; (= *parcours*) bus route; **~ aérienne** (= *compagnie*) airline; (= *service*) (air) service, air link; (= *trajet*) (air) route; **~ maritime** shipping line; **~ de chemin de fer/de métro** railway (*Brit*) *ou* railroad (*US*)/underground (*Brit*) *ou* subway (*US*) line; (*Rail*) **les grandes ~s** (= *voies*) main lines; (= *services*) main-line services; (*Aviat*) **~s intérieures/internationales** domestic/international flights; **nous espérons vous revoir prochainement sur nos ~s** we look forward to seeing you on board again soon, we hope that you will fly with us again soon; **la ~ d'autobus passe dans notre rue** the bus (route) goes along our street; **quelle ~ faut-il prendre ?** which train *ou* bus should I take?; **il faut prendre la ~ 12 (en autobus)** you have to take the number 12 bus → **avion, grand, pilote**

f = **Élec, Téléc, Ordin** line; (= *câbles*) wires; (*TV: composant l'image*) line; **la ~ est occupée** the line is engaged (*Brit*) *ou* busy (*US*); **la ~ a été coupée** we've been cut off; **la ~ passe dans notre jardin** the wires go through our garden; (*Élec*) **~ d'alimentation** feeder

♦ **en ligne** (*Téléc*) **être en ~** to be connected; **vous êtes en ~** you're connected *ou* through now, I am connecting you now; **je suis encore en ~** I'm still holding; **M. Lebrun est en ~ (= est occupé)** Mr Lebrun's line is engaged (*Brit*) *ou* busy (*US*); (= *il veut vous parler*) I have Mr Lebrun on the line for you (*Ordin*) on-line; **services/réseaux en ~** on-line services/networks

g = **texte écrit** line; **écrire quelques ~s to** write a few lines; **donner 100 ~s à faire à un élève** to give a pupil 100 lines to do; **je vous envoie ces quelques ~s** I'm sending you these few lines *ou* this short note → **lire¹**

♦ **à la ligne** (*dans une dictée*) **« à la ~ »** "new paragraph", "new line"; **aller à la ~** to start on the next line, begin a new paragraph (*dans l'édition, la presse*) **rédacteur payé à la ~** editor paid by the line; **tirer à la ~** to pad out an article

♦ **en ligne de compte** : **entrer en ~ de compte** to be taken into account *ou* consideration; **prendre** *ou* **faire entrer en ~ de compte** to take into account *ou* consideration; **votre vie privée n'entre pas en ~ de compte** your private life doesn't come *ou* enter into it

♦ **sur toute la ligne** from start to finish; **il m'a menti sur toute la ~** he lied to me from start to finish *ou* from beginning to end; **c'est une réussite sur toute la ~** it's a success throughout

h = **Comm** **~ de produits** (product) line; **notre nouvelle ~ de maquillage** our new range of make-up

i = **Pêche** (fishing) line

j = **série de générations** **~ directe/collatérale** direct/collateral line; **descendre en ~ directe** *ou* **en droite ~ de ...** to be a direct descendant of ...

k = **Belg = raie dans les cheveux** parting

2 COMPOSÉS
▶ **ligne de ballon mort** (*Rugby*) dead-ball line ▶ **ligne blanche** (*Aut*) white line; franchir la ~ blanche (*lit*) to cross the white line; (*fig*) to overstep the mark ▶ **ligne de but** goal line ▶ **ligne continue** (*Aut*) solid line ▶ **ligne de côté** (*Tennis*) sideline, tramline (*Brit*) ▶ **ligne de crédit** credit line, line of credit ▶ **ligne de crête** (*gén*) ridge; (= *ligne de partage des eaux*) watershed ▶ **ligne de défense** (*gén, Mil*) line of defence (*Brit*) ou defense (*US*); (*Sport*) la ~ de défense irlandaise the Irish defenders ou defence (*Brit*) ou defense (*US*) ▶ **ligne de démarcation** (*gén*) boundary; demarcation line ▶ **ligne directrice** (*Géom*) directrix; (*fig*) guiding line ▶ **ligne discontinue** (*Aut*) broken line ▶ **ligne d'eau** (*Natation*) lane ▶ **ligne de faille** fault line ▶ **ligne de faîte** = ligne de crête ▶ **ligne de feu** line of fire ▶ **ligne de flottaison** water line ▶ **ligne de flottaison en charge** load line, Plimsoll line ▶ **ligne de fond** (*Pêche*) ledger line; (*Basket*) end line; (*Tennis*) ~ de fond (de court) baseline ▶ **lignes de force** (*Phys*) lines of force; (*fig*) [*discours, politique*] main themes ▶ **ligne de front** (*Mil*) frontline ▶ **ligne à haute tension** high-voltage line ▶ **ligne d'horizon** skyline ▶ **ligne jaune** (*Aut*) = ligne blanche ▶ **ligne médiane** (*gén, Tennis*) centre line; (*Ftbl, Rugby etc*) halfway line ▶ **ligne de mire** line of sight; (*fig*) avoir qn dans sa ~ de mire to have sb in one's sights; être dans la ~ de mire de qn to be in sb's sights ▶ **ligne de partage des eaux** watershed, height of land (*US*) ▶ **ligne de service** (*Tennis*) service line ▶ **ligne supplémentaire** (*Mus*) ledger line ▶ **ligne de tir** = ligne de mire ▶ **ligne de touche** (*gén*) sideline; (*Ftbl, Rugby*) touchline; (*Basket*) boundary line ▶ **ligne de visée** line of sight

ligne² [liɲ] NF (*Can*) line (*3,175 mm*)

lignée [liɲe] NF (= *postérité*) descendants; (= *race, famille*) line, lineage; **laisser une nombreuse ~** to leave a lot of descendants; **le dernier d'une longue ~** the last of a long line; **de bonne ~ irlandaise** of good Irish stock ou lineage; **dans la ~ des grands romanciers** in the tradition of the great novelists

ligneux, -euse [liɲø, øz] ADJ woody, ligneous (*SPÉC*)

lignifier (se) [liɲifje] ▶conjug 1◀ VPR to lignify

lignite [liɲit] NM lignite, brown coal

ligoter [ligɔte] ▶conjug 1◀ VT [+ *personne*] to bind hand and foot; **~ qn à un arbre** to tie sb to a tree

ligue [lig] NF league; **la Ligue des droits de l'homme** the League of Human Rights; **la Ligue arabe** the Arab League; (*Rel*) **la (Sainte) Ligue** the Catholic Holy League

liguer [lige] ▶conjug 1◀ VT to unite (**contre** against); **être ligué avec** to be in league with **2 se liguer** VPR to league, form a league (**contre** against); **tout se ligue contre moi** everything is in league ou is conspiring against me

ligueur, -euse [ligœʀ, øz] NM,F member of a league

ligure [ligyʀ] (*Hist*) **1** ADJ Ligurian **2** NM (*Ling*) Ligurian **Ligure** NMF Ligurian

Ligurie [ligyʀi] NF Liguria

lilas [lila] NM, ADJ INV lilac

liliacée [liljase] NF liliaceous plant; **les ~s** liliaceous plants, the Liliaceae (*SPÉC*)

lilliputien, -ienne [lilipysjɛ̃, jɛn] **1** ADJ Lilliputian **2 Lilliputien(ne)** NM,F Lilliputian

Lilongwe [lilɔ̃gwe] N Lilongwe

Lima [lima] N Lima

limace [limas] NF (*Zool*) slug; (†,‡ = *chemise*) shirt; **quelle ~!** (= *personne*) what a sluggard! ou slowcoach! (*Brit*)* ou slowpoke (*US*)*; (= *train*) this train is just crawling along!, what a dreadfully slow train!

limaçon [limasɔ̃] NM (†† = *escargot*) snail; (*Anat*) cochlea

limage [limaʒ] NM filing

limaille [limaj] NF filings; **~ de fer** iron filings

limande [limɑ̃d] NF (= *poisson*) dab; **~-sole** lemon sole; **fausse ~** flatfish → plat¹

limbe [lɛ̃b] **1** NM (*Astron, Bot, Math*) limb **2 limbes** NMPL (*Rel*) limbo; (*Rel*) **dans les ~s** in limbo; **c'est encore dans les ~s** [*projet, science*] it's still very much in limbo, it's still up in the air

limbique [lɛ̃bik] ADJ [*système*] limbic

lime [lim] NF **a** (*Tech*) file; **~ douce** smooth file; **~ à ongles** nail file, fingernail file (*US*); **donner un coup de ~ à qch** to run a file over sth, give sth a quick file **b** (*Zool*) lima **c** (*Bot*) (= *fruit*) lime; (= *arbre*) lime (tree)

limer [lime] ▶conjug 1◀ VT [+ *ongles*] to file; [+ *métal*] to file (down); [+ *aspérité*] to file off; **le prisonnier avait limé un barreau pour s'échapper** the prisoner had filed through a bar to escape

limier [limje] NM (*Zool*) bloodhound; (*fig*) sleuth, detective; **c'est un fin ~** he's a really good sleuth

liminaire [liminɛʀ] ADJ [*discours, note*] introductory

limitatif, -ive [limitatif, iv] ADJ restrictive; **liste limitative/non limitative** closed/open list

limitation [limitasjɔ̃] NF limitation, restriction; **~ des prix/des naissances** price/birth control; **un accord sur la ~ des armements** an agreement on arms limitation ou control; **sans ~ de durée** without a ou with no time limit; **une ~ de vitesse (à 60 km/h)** a (60 km/h) speed limit; **l'introduction de ~s de vitesse** the introduction of speed restrictions ou limits; **~ de la circulation automobile** traffic restrictions

limite [limit] **1** NF **a** [*pays, jardin*] boundary; **la rivière marque la ~ du parc** the river marks the boundary of the park **b** [*pouvoir, période*] limit; **~ d'âge/de poids** age/weight limit; **il connaît ses ~s** he knows his limits; **ma patience a des ~s!** there's a limit to my patience!; **la tolérance a des ~s!** tolerance has its limits!; **la bêtise a des ~s!** you can only be so stupid!; **sa joie ne connaissait pas de ~s** his joy knew no bounds; **sa colère ne connaît pas de ~s** his anger knows no limits; **ce crime atteint les ~s de l'horreur** this crime is too horrible to imagine; **il franchit ou dépasse les ~s!** he's going a bit too far!; **sans ~(s)** [*patience*] infinite; [*pouvoir*] limitless; [*joie, confiance*] boundless; **son ambition est sans ~** his ambition knows no bounds ou limits **c** (*Math*) limit **d** (*loc*) **à la ~ on croirait qu'il le fait exprès** you'd almost think he's doing it on purpose; **à la ~, j'accepterais ces conditions, mais pas plus** if pushed ou if absolutely necessary, I'd accept those conditions, but no more; **à la ~ tout roman est réaliste** ultimately ou at a pinch you could say any novel is realistic; **c'est à la ~ de l'insolence** it borders ou verges on insolence; **dans une certaine ~** up to a point, to a certain extent ou degree; **« dans la ~ des stocks disponibles »** "while stocks last"; **dans les ~s du possible/du sujet** within the limits of what is possible/of the subject; **l'entrée est gratuite dans la ~ des places disponibles** admission is free subject to availability; **dans les ~s de mes moyens** (*aptitude*) within my capabilities; (*argent*) within my means; **tu peux t'inscrire jusqu'à demain dernière ~** you have until tomorrow to register; **jusqu'à la**

dernière ~ [*rester, résister*] to the bitter end, till the end; [*se battre*] to the death; **jusqu'à la ~ de ses forces** to the point of exhaustion; (*Boxe*) **avant la ~** inside ou within the distance; (*Boxe*) **aller ou tenir jusqu'à la ~** to go the distance **2** ADJ **a** (= *extrême*) **cas ~** borderline case; **prix ~** upper price limit; (*Bourse*) **cours ~** limit price; **vitesse/âge ~** maximum speed/age; **hauteur/longueur/charge ~** maximum height/length/load; **heure ~** deadline **b** (* = *juste*) **elle a réussi son examen/à attraper la balle, mais c'était ~** she passed her exam/managed to catch the ball — but only just; **ils ne se sont pas injuriés/battus, mais c'était ~** they didn't actually insult each other/come to blows but they came fairly close; **sa remarque était vraiment ~** she was pushing it with that remark*; **l'acoustique était ~*** the acoustics were OK but only just, the acoustics were OK but not brilliant **3** COMP ▶ **limite d'élasticité** elastic limit ▶ **limite de rupture** breaking point

limité, e [limite] (*ptp de limiter*) ADJ [*durée, choix, portée*] limited; [*nombre*] limited, restricted; **je n'ai qu'une confiance ~e en ce remède** I only trust this treatment so far; **il est un peu ~*** (*intellectuellement*) he's not very bright; **comme romancier, il est un peu ~** as a novelist, he's a bit limited → société, tirage

limiter [limite] ▶conjug 1◀ **1** VT **a** (= *restreindre*) [+ *dépenses, pouvoirs, temps*] to limit, restrict (**à** to); **ils ont dû liquider leur affaire pour ~ les dégâts** they had to sell up the business to cut ou minimize their losses; **on a réussi à ~ les dégâts en marquant deux buts** we managed to limit the damage by scoring two goals; **nous limiterons notre étude à quelques cas généraux** we'll limit ou restrict our study to a few general cases; **la vitesse est limitée à 50 km/h** the speed limit is 50 km/h **b** (= *délimiter*) [*frontière, montagnes*] to border; **les collines qui limitent l'horizon** the hills which bound the horizon **2 se limiter** VPR **a** [*personne*] **se ~ à** [+ *remarque*] to confine o.s. to; [+ *consommation*] to limit o.s. to; **je me limite à cinq cigarettes par jour** I only allow myself five cigarettes a day, I limit ou restrict myself to five cigarettes a day; **il faut savoir se ~** you have to know when to stop **b** [*connaissance, sanctions*] **se ~ à** to be limited to

limitrophe [limitʀɔf] ADJ [*département*] bordering, adjoining; [*population*] border (*épith*); **provinces ~s de la France** (*françaises*) border provinces of France; (*étrangères*) provinces bordering on France

limnée [limne] NF great pond snail

limogeage [limɔʒaʒ] NM dismissal

limoger [limɔʒe] ▶conjug 3◀ VT to dismiss (**de** from)

limon [limɔ̃] NM **a** (*Géog*) alluvium; (*gén*) silt **b** [*attelage*] shaft; (*Constr*) string-board

limonade [limɔnad] NF **a** (*gazeuse*) (fizzy) lemonade (*Brit*) **b** († = *citronnade*) (homemade) lemonade ou lemon drink

limonadier, -ière [limɔnadje, jɛʀ] NM,F **a** (= *fabricant*) soft drinks manufacturer **b** † (= *commerçant*) café owner

limoneux, -euse [limɔnø, øz] ADJ silt-laden, silty

limousin, e¹ [limuzɛ̃, in] **1** ADJ of ou from Limousin **2** NM **a** (*Ling*) Limousin dialect **b** (= *région*) Limousin **3 Limousin(e)** NM,F inhabitant ou native of Limousin

limousine² [limuzin] NF (= *voiture*) limousine; († = *pèlerine*) cloak

limpide [lɛ̃pid] ADJ [*eau, air, ciel, regard*] clear, limpid; [*explication*] clear, crystal-clear (*attrib*); [*style*] lucid, limpid; [*affaire*] clear, straightforward; (*iro*) straightforward; (*iro*) **tu as**

compris ? — c'était ~ ! do you get it? — it was crystal-clear! (*iro*) *ou* as clear as mud!

limpidité [lɛ̃pidite] NF [*eau, air, ciel, regard*] clearness, limpidity; [*explication*] clarity, lucidity; [*style*] lucidity, limpidity; [*affaire*] clarity, straightforwardness

lin [lɛ̃] NM (= *plante, fibre*) flax; (= *tissu*) linen → **huile, toile**

linceul [lɛ̃sœl] NM (*lit, fig*) shroud

lindane [lɛ̃dan] NM lindane

linéaire [lineɛʀ] 1 ADJ linear 2 NM (*Comm*) shelf space

linéairement [lineɛʀmɑ̃] ADV linearly

linéaments [lineamɑ̃] NMPL (*littér*) [a] [*visage*] lineaments (*littér*), features; [*forme*] lines, outline [b] (= *ébauche*) outline

linéarité [linearite] NF linearity

linge [lɛ̃ʒ] 1 NM [a] (= *draps, serviettes*) linen; (= *sous-vêtements*) underwear; **le gros** ~ household linen; **le petit** ~ small items of linen; (*fig*) **il y avait du beau** ~ **à leur mariage** all the right people were at their wedding [b] (= *lessive*) **le** ~ the washing; **laver/tendre le** *ou* **son** ~ to wash/hang out the *ou* one's washing → **laver** [c] (= *morceau de tissu*) cloth; **essuyer qch avec un** ~ to wipe sth with a cloth; **blanc** *ou* **pâle comme un** ~ as white as a sheet [d] (*Helv* = *serviette de toilette*) towel 2 COMP ▸ **linges d'autel** altar cloths ▸ **linge de corps** underwear ▸ **linge de maison** household linen ▸ **linge de table** table linen ▸ **linge de toilette** bathroom linen

lingère [lɛ̃ʒɛʀ] NF (= *personne*) linen maid; (= *meuble*) linen cupboard *ou* closet

lingerie [lɛ̃ʒʀi] NF [a] (= *local*) linen room [b] (= *sous-vêtements féminins*) (women's) underwear; ~ **fine** lingerie; **rayon** ~ lingerie department

lingette [lɛ̃ʒɛt] NF towelette

lingot [lɛ̃go] NM [*métal*] ingot; (*Typo*) slug; ~ **d'or** gold ingot

lingua franca [lɛ̃gwafʀɑ̃ka] NF (*Ling*) lingua franca

lingual, e (*pl* -**aux**) [lɛ̃gwal, o] ADJ lingual

lingue [lɛ̃g] NF (= *poisson*) ling

linguiste [lɛ̃gɥist] NMF linguist

linguistique [lɛ̃gɥistik] 1 NF linguistics *sg* 2 ADJ (*gén*) linguistic; [*barrière, politique*] language (*épith*); **communauté** ~ speech community

linguistiquement [lɛ̃gɥistikmɑ̃] ADV linguistically

liniment [linimɑ̃] NM liniment

linnéen, -enne [lineɛ̃, ɛn] ADJ Linn(a)ean

lino* [lino] NM (ABRÉV = **linoléum**) lino

linoléique [linɔleik] ADJ **acide** ~ linoleic acid

linoléum [linɔleɔm] NM linoleum

linon [linɔ̃] NM (= *tissu*) lawn

linotte [linɔt] NF linnet → **tête**

linotype® [linɔtip] NF Linotype®

linteau (*pl* **linteaux**) [lɛ̃to] NM lintel

lion [ljɔ̃] NM [a] (*Zool, fig*) lion; ~ **de mer** sea lion; **tu as mangé** *ou* **bouffé* du** ~ ! you're full of beans!* → **fosse, part** [b] (*Astron*) **le Lion** Leo, the Lion; **il est Lion** ◊ **il est du (signe du) Lion** he's (a) Leo

lionceau (*pl* **lionceaux**) [ljɔ̃so] NM lion cub

lionne [ljɔn] NF lioness

lipase [lipaz] NF lipase

lipide [lipid] NM lipid

lipidique [lipidik] ADJ lipid (*épith*)

liposoluble [lipɔsɔlybl] ADJ fat-soluble

liposome [lipozom] NM liposome

liposuccion [lipɔsy(k)sjɔ̃] NF liposuction

lippe [lip] NF (*littér*) (fleshy) lower lip; **faire la** ~ (= *bouder*) to sulk; (= *faire la moue*) to pout; (= *faire la grimace*) to make *ou* pull a face

lippu, e [lipy] ADJ thick-lipped

liquéfaction [likefaksjɔ̃] NF (*Chim*) liquefaction

liquéfiable [likefjabl] ADJ liquefiable

liquéfiant, e [likefjɑ̃, jɑ̃t] ADJ (*Chim*) liquefying; [*atmosphère, chaleur*] draining (*attrib*), exhausting

liquéfier [likefje] ▸ conjug 7 ◂ 1 VT (*Chim*) to liquefy; (* = *amollir*) to drain, exhaust; **je suis liquéfié*** I'm dead beat* *ou* dog-tired* 2 **se liquéfier** VPR (*lit*) to liquefy; (* = *avoir peur, être ému*) to turn to jelly; (* = *avoir chaud*) to be melting

liquette* [liket] NF (= *chemise d'homme*) shirt; (*chemisier*) ~ (woman's) shirt

liqueur [likœʀ] NF (= *boisson*) liqueur; (†† = *liquide*) liquid; (*Pharm*) ~ **titrée/de Fehling** standard/Fehling's solution

liquidateur, -trice [likidatœʀ, tʀis] NM,F (*Jur*) ≈ liquidator, ≈ receiver; ~ **judiciaire** *ou* **de faillite** ≈ official liquidator; **placer une entreprise entre les mains d'un** ~ to put a company into the hands of a receiver *ou* into receivership (*Brit*)

liquidatif, -ive [likidatif, iv] ADJ **valeur liquidative** market price *ou* value

liquidation [likidasjɔ̃] NF [a] (= *règlement légal*) [*dettes, compte*] settlement, payment; [*société*] liquidation; [*biens, stock*] selling off, liquidation; [*succession*] settlement; [*problème*] elimination; ~ **judiciaire** compulsory liquidation; ~ **(judiciaire) personnelle** personal bankruptcy; **mettre une société en** ~ to put a company into liquidation *ou* receivership, liquidate a company; **afin de procéder à la** ~ **de votre retraite** in order to commence payment of your pension; **« 50% de rabais jusqu'à ~ du stock »** "stock clearance, 50% discount" → **bilan** [b] (= *vente*) selling (off), sale [c] (‡ = *meurtre*) liquidation, elimination [d] (*Bourse*) ~ **de fin de mois** (monthly) settlement

liquide [likid] 1 ADJ [*corps, son*] liquid; **la sauce/peinture est trop** ~ the sauce/paint is too runny *ou* too thin; **argent** ~ cash 2 NM [a] (= *substance*) liquid; ~ **de frein** brake fluid; ~ **de refroidissement** coolant; ~ **vaisselle*** washing-up liquid (*Brit*), (liquid) dish soap (*US*); ~ **amniotique/céphalorachidien** amniotic/cerebrospinal fluid [b] (= *argent*) cash; **je n'ai pas beaucoup de** ~ I haven't much ready money *ou* ready cash; **payer** *ou* **régler en** ~ to pay (in) cash; **être payé en** ~ to be paid cash in hand 3 NF (*Ling*) liquid

liquider [likide] ▸ conjug 1 ◂ VT [a] (*Fin, Jur*) [+ *succession, dettes*] to settle, pay; [+ *compte*] to settle, clear; [+ *société*] to liquidate, wind up; [+ *biens, stock*] to liquidate, sell off [b] (= *vendre*) to sell (off) [c] (‡ = *tuer*) to liquidate, eliminate [d]* (= *régler*) [+ *problème*] to get rid of; (= *finir*) to finish off; **c'est liquidé maintenant** it is all finished *ou* over now

liquidité [likidite] NF (*Chim, Jur*) liquidity; ~**s** liquid assets

liquoreux, -euse [likɔʀø, øz] ADJ [*vin*] syrupy

lire¹ [liʀ] ▸ conjug 43 ◂ VT [a] (= *déchiffrer*) to read; [+ *message enregistré*] listen to; **il sait** ~ **l'heure** he can *ou* knows how to tell the time; **à sept ans, il ne lit pas encore** *ou* **il ne sait pas encore** ~ he's seven and he still can't read; ~ **sur les lèvres** to lip-read; ~ **ses notes avant un cours** to read over *ou* read through *ou* go over one's notes before a lecture; ~ **un discours/un rapport devant une assemblée** to read (out) a speech/a report at a meeting; **il l'a lu dans le journal** he read (about) it in the paper; **chaque soir, elle lit des histoires à ses enfants** every night she reads stories to her children; **à le ~, on croirait que …** from what he writes *ou* from reading what he writes one would think that …; (*erratum*) **là où il y a 634, ~** *ou* **lisez 643** for 634 read 643; **ce roman se lit bien** *ou* **se laisse** ~ the novel is very readable; **ce roman se lit facilement/très vite** the novel

makes easy/quick reading; **ce roman mérite d'être lu** *ou* **est à ~** the novel is worth reading; ~ **entre les lignes** to read between the lines; **je lis en lui à livre ouvert** I can read him like an open book → **lu** [b] (*fig* = *deviner*) to read; ~ **dans le cœur de qn** to see into sb's heart; **la peur se lisait** *ou* **on lisait la peur sur son visage/dans ses yeux** you could see *ou* read fear in his face/in his eyes, fear showed on his face/in his eyes; ~ **l'avenir dans les lignes de la main de qn** to read in sb's palm; **elle m'a lu les lignes de la main** she read my palm, she did a palm-reading for me; ~ **l'avenir dans le marc de café** ≈ to read (the future in) tea leaves; ~ **dans une boule de cristal** to gaze into a crystal ball; ~ **dans le jeu de qn** to see through sb, see what sb is up to [c] (*formule de lettre*) **nous espérons vous ~ bientôt** we hope to hear from you soon; **à bientôt de vous ~** hoping to hear from you soon [d] (= *interpréter*) [+ *statistiques, événement*] to read, interpret

lire² [liʀ] NF lira

lis [lis] NM lily; **blanc comme un** ~ ◊ **d'une blancheur de** ~ lily-white → **fleur**

Lisbonne [lisbɔn] N Lisbon

liseré [liz(ə)ʀe], **liséré** [lizeʀe] NM (= *bordure*) border, edging; **un** ~ **de ciel bleu** a strip of blue sky

liserer [liz(ə)ʀe], **lisérer** [lizeʀe] ▸ conjug 6 ◂ VT to edge with ribbon

liseron [lizʀɔ̃] NM bindweed, convolvulus

liseur, -euse [lizœʀ, øz] 1 NM,F reader 2 **liseuse** NF (= *couvre-livre*) book jacket; (= *vêtement*) bedjacket

lisibilité [lizibilite] NF [*écriture*] legibility; [*livre*] readability; **d'une parfaite** ~ perfectly legible; **le manque de** ~ **des textes officiels** the fact that official documents are so difficult to read; **ils se plaignent d'une mauvaise** ~ **de l'action gouvernementale** they're complaining that the government's policy lacks clarity

lisible [lizibl] ADJ [*écriture*] legible; [*livre*] readable, worth reading; **une carte peu** ~ a map that is difficult to read; **ce livre est** ~ **à plusieurs niveaux** the book can be read on several levels; **leur stratégie est peu** ~ their strategy lacks clarity

lisiblement [liziblǝmɑ̃] ADV legibly

lisier [lizje] NM liquid manure

lisière [lizjɛʀ] NF [a] [*bois, village*] edge; **à la** ~ **de** *ou* **en** ~ **de forêt** on the edge of the forest; **ils sont à la** ~ **de la légalité** they're only just within the law [b] (*Tex*) selvage

lissage [lisaʒ] NM smoothing

lisse¹ [lis] ADJ [*peau, surface*] smooth; [*cheveux*] sleek, smooth; [*pneu*] bald; (*Anat*) [*muscle*] smooth

lisse² [lis] NF (*Naut*) (= *rambarde*) handrail; (*de la coque*) ribband

lisser [lise] ▸ conjug 1 ◂ VT [+ *cheveux*] to smooth (down); [+ *moustache*] to smooth, stroke; [+ *papier, drap froissé*] to smooth out; [+ *vêtement*] to smooth (out); **l'oiseau lisse ses plumes** *ou* **se lisse les plumes** the bird is preening itself *ou* its feathers; **fromage blanc lissé** creamy fromage blanc

listage [listaʒ] NM (= *action*) listing; (= *liste*) list; (*Ordin*) print-out

▼ **liste¹** [list] 1 NF (*gén*) list; **faire** *ou* **dresser une** ~ to make a list, draw up a list; **faire la** ~ **de** to make out *ou* draw up a list of, list; **s'il fallait faire la** ~ **de tous ses défauts !** if you had to list *ou* make out a list of all his faults!; **faites-moi la** ~ **des absents** make me out a list of people who are absent; ~ **des courses** shopping list; ~ **nominative des élèves** class roll *ou* list [b] (*Pol*) [*candidats*] (list of) candidates; **être inscrit sur les ~s électorales** to be on the electoral roll, be registered to vote; **la** ~ **de la gau-**

che the list of left-wing candidates; **~ unique** (*commune*) joint list (of candidates); (*sans choix*) single list (of candidates); **leurs partis présentent une ~ commune** their parties are putting forward a joint list (of candidates) → **scrutin**

2 COMP ► **liste d'attente** waiting list ► **liste civile** civil list ► **liste de contrôle** = **liste de vérification** ► **liste d'envoi** mailing list ► **liste de mariage** wedding list ► **liste noire** blacklist; (*pour élimination*) hit list ► **liste de publipostage** mailing list ► **liste rouge** (*Téléc*) **demander à être sur (la) ~ rouge** (to ask) to go ex-directory (*Brit*) ou unlisted (*US*); **il est sur ~ rouge** he's ex-directory (*Brit*), he's unlisted (*US*) ► **liste de vérification** check list

liste² [list] NF [*cheval*] list

listel (*pl* **listels** ou **-eaux**) [listɛl, o] NM (*Archit*) listel, fillet; [*monnaie*] rim

lister [liste] ►conjug 1◄ VT to list

listeria [listerja] NF INV listeria

listériose [listerjoz] NF listeriosis

listing [listiŋ] NM = **listage**

lit [li] 1 NM a (= *meuble*) bed; (= *structure*) bedstead, bed; **~ d'une personne** ou **à une place** single bed; **~ de deux personnes** ou **à deux places** double bed; **~ de fer/de bois** iron/wooden bedstead; **~ d'hôpital/d'hôtel** hospital/hotel bed; **hôpital de 250 ~s** hospital with 250 beds; **aller** ou **se mettre au ~** to go to bed; **garder le ~** to stay in bed; **mettre un enfant au ~** to put a child to bed; **être/lire au ~** to be/read in bed; **faire le ~** to make the bed; (*fig*) **faire le ~ de** (= *renforcer*) to bolster; (= *préparer le terrain pour*) to pave the way for ■ (*PROV*) **comme on fait son ~, on se couche** you've made your bed, now you must lie on it; **faire ~ à part** to sleep in separate beds; **le ~ n'avait pas été défait** the bed had not been slept in; **au ~ les enfants!** bedtime ou off to bed children!; **arracher** ou **sortir qn du ~** to drag ou haul sb out of bed; **tomber du ~** to be up bright and early → **saut**

b (*Jur = mariage*) **enfants du premier/deuxième ~** children of the first/second marriage; **enfants d'un autre ~** children of a previous marriage

c [*rivière*] bed; **les pluies ont fait sortir le fleuve de son ~** the river has burst ou overflowed its banks because of the rains

d (= *couche, épaisseur*) layer; **~ d'argile** bed ou layer of clay; **~ de cendres** ou **de braises** bed of hot ashes; (*Culin*) **~ de salade** bed of lettuce

e (*Naut*) [*vent, marée, courant*] set

2 COMP ► **lit à baldaquin** canopied fourposter bed ► **lit bateau** cabin bed ► **lit breton** box bed ► **lit de camp** campbed ► **lit clos** box bed ► **lit de coin** bed (standing) against the wall ► **lit à colonnes** fourposter bed ► **lit conjugal** marriage bed ► **lit de douleur** bed of pain ► **lit d'enfant** cot ► **lit gigogne** pullout ou stowaway bed ► **lits jumeaux** twin beds ► **lit de justice** bed of justice ► **lit de mort** deathbed ► **lit nuptial** wedding-bed ► **lit de parade**: **sur un ~ de parade** lying in state ► **lit pliant** folding bed ► **lit en portefeuille** apple-pie bed ► **lit de repos** couch ► **lit de sangle** trestle bed ► **lits superposés** bunk beds

litanie [litani] NF (*Rel, fig péj*) litany

lit-cage (*pl* **lits-cages**) [likaʒ] NM (folding metal) bed

litchi [litʃi] NM lychee, litchi

liteau [lito] NM (*pour toiture*) batten; (*pour tablette*) bracket; (*dans tissu*) stripe

litée [lite] NF (= *jeunes animaux*) litter

literie [litri] NF bedding

lithiase [litjaz] NF lithiasis

lithiné, e [litine] 1 ADJ **eau ~e** lithia water 2 **lithinés** NMPL lithium salts

lithium [litjɔm] NM lithium

litho• [lito] NF (ABRÉV = **lithographie**) litho

lithographe [litɔgraf] NMF lithographer

lithographie [litɔgrafi] NF (= *technique*) lithography; (= *image*) lithograph

lithographier [litɔgrafje] ►conjug 7◄ VT to lithograph

lithographique [litɔgrafik] ADJ lithographic

lithosphère [litɔsfɛr] NF lithosphere

lithotritie [litɔtrisi] NF lithotripsy

lithuanien, -ienne [litɥanjɛ̃, jɛn] ADJ, NM,F = **lituanien, -ienne**

litière [litjɛr] NF (= *couche de paille*) litter (*NonC*); (*pour cheval*) bedding; (*Hist* = *palanquin*) litter; **il s'était fait une ~ avec de la paille** he had made himself a bed of straw; **~ pour chats** cat litter (*Brit*), Kitty Litter® (*US*); (*littér*) **faire ~ de qch** to scorn ou spurn sth

litige [litiʒ] NM (*gén*) dispute; (*Jur*) lawsuit; **être en ~** (*gén*) to be in dispute (*avec* with); (*Jur*) to be at law ou in litigation; **les parties en ~** the litigants, the disputants (*US*); **point/objet de ~** point/object of contention

litigieux, -ieuse [litiʒjø, jøz] ADJ [*point, question*] contentious; [*article, document*] controversial; [*facture, frontière*] disputed; **cas ~** contentious issue

litorne [litɔrn] NF fieldfare

litote [litɔt] NF (*gén*) understatement; (*Littérat*) litotes (*SPÉC*)

litre [litr] NM (= *mesure*) litre (*Brit*), liter (*US*); (= *récipient*) litre (*Brit*) ou liter (*US*) bottle

litron: [litrɔ̃] NM **~ (de vin)** litre (*Brit*) ou liter (*US*) of wine

littéraire [literɛr] 1 ADJ (*gén*) literary; [*souffrance, passion*] affected; **faire des études ~s** to study literature 2 NMF (*par don, goût*) literary person; (= *étudiant*) arts student; (= *enseignant*) arts teacher, teacher of arts subjects

littérairement [literɛrmɑ̃] ADV in literary terms

littéral, e (*mpl* **-aux**) [literal, o] ADJ (*littér, Math*) literal; **arabe ~** written Arabic

littéralement [literalmɑ̃] ADV (*lit, fig*) literally

littéralité [literalite] NF literality, literalness

littérateur [literatœr] NM man of letters; (*péj* = *écrivain*) literary hack

littérature [literatyr] NF a (= *art*) literature; (= *profession*) writing; **faire de la ~** to go in for writing, write; **tout cela, c'est de la ~** it's of trifling importance; **écrire de la ~ alimentaire** to write potboilers; **~ de colportage** chapbooks b (= *manuel*) history of literature; (= *ensemble d'ouvrages*) literature; (= *bibliographie*) literature; **il existe une abondante ~ sur ce sujet** there's a wealth of literature ou studies on this subject

littoral, e (*mpl* **-aux**) [litɔral, o] 1 ADJ coastal, littoral (*SPÉC*) → **cordon** 2 NM coast, littoral (*SPÉC*)

Lituanie [litɥani] NF Lithuania

lituanien, -ienne [litɥanjɛ̃, jɛn] 1 ADJ Lithuanian 2 NM (*Ling*) Lithuanian 3 **Lituanien(ne)** NM,F Lithuanian

liturgie [lityrʒi] NF liturgy

liturgique [lityrʒik] ADJ liturgical

livarde [livard] NF sprit

livarot [livaro] NM Livarot (*creamy Normandy cheese*)

livide [livid] ADJ a (= *pâle*) (*par maladie*) pallid; (*de peur*) white b (*littér* = *bleuâtre*) livid

lividité [lividite] NF lividness

living [liviŋ], **living-room** (*pl* **living-rooms**) [liviŋrum] NM (= *pièce*) living room; (= *meuble*) unit

Livourne [livurn] N Leghorn, Livorno

livrable [livrabl] ADJ which can be delivered; **cet article est ~ dans les 10 jours/à domicile** this article will be delivered within 10 days/can be delivered to your home

▼ **livraison** [livrɛzɔ̃] NF a [*marchandise*] delivery; **«~ à domicile»** "we deliver", "home deliveries"; **«payable à la ~»** "payable on delivery", "cash on delivery", "COD"; **la ~ à domicile est comprise dans le prix** the price includes (the cost of) delivery; **faire une ~** to make a delivery; **faire la ~ de qch** to deliver sth; **prendre ~ de qch** to take ou receive delivery of sth b [*revue*] part, instalment

livre¹ [livr] 1 NM a (= *ouvrage*) book; (= *commerce*) **le ~** the book industry, the book trade (*Brit*); **~ de géographie** geography book; **~ du maître/de l'élève** teacher's/pupil's textbook; **il a toujours le nez dans les ~s** ◊ **il vit dans les ~s** he's always got his nose in a book; **je ne connais l'Australie que par les ~s** I only know Australia through ou from books; **ça n'arrive que dans les ~s** it only happens in books; **écrire/faire un ~ sur** to write/do a book on → **parler**

b (= *volume*) book; **le ~ 2** ou **le second ~ de la Genèse** book 2 of Genesis, the second book of Genesis

2 COMP ► **livre blanc** (*gén*) official report; [*gouvernement*] white paper ► **livre de bord** (*Naut*) logbook ► **livre de caisse** (*Comm*) cashbook ► **livre de chevet** bedside book ► **livre de classe** schoolbook, textbook ► **les livres de commerce** (*Comm*) the books, the accounts ► **livre de comptes** account(s) book ► **livre de cuisine** cookbook, cookery book (*Brit*) ► **livre d'enfant** children's book ► **livre d'heures** book of hours ► **livre d'images** picture book ► **livre journal** (*Comm*) daybook ► **livre de lecture** reader, reading book ► **livre de messe** missal ► **livre d'or** visitors' book ► **livre de poche** paperback ► **livre de prières** prayer book ► **livre scolaire** = **livre de classe**

livre² [livr] NF a (= *poids*) half a kilo, ≈ pound; (*Can*) pound b (= *monnaie*) pound; (*Hist française*) livre; **~ sterling** pound sterling; **~ égyptienne** Egyptian pound; **~ irlandaise** Irish pound, punt; **ce chapeau coûte 6 ~s** this hat costs £6

livre-cassette (*pl* **livres-cassettes**) [livrkasɛt] NM talking book, book on cassette ou on tape

livrée [livre] NF a (= *uniforme*) livery; **en ~** in livery (*attrib*), liveried b [*animal, oiseau*] markings

livre-jeu (*pl* **livres-jeux**) [livrʒø] NM activity book

livrer [livre] ►conjug 1◄ 1 VT a [+ *commande, marchandises*] to deliver; **se faire ~ qch** to have sth delivered; **~ qn** to deliver sb's order; **je serai livré demain** ◊ **ils me livreront demain** they'll do the delivery tomorrow; **nous livrons à domicile** we do home deliveries

b (= *abandonner*: *à la police, à l'ennemi*) to hand over (*à* to); **~ qn à la mort** to send sb to their death; **~ qn au bourreau** to deliver sb up ou hand sb over to the executioner; **le pays a été livré au pillage/à l'anarchie** the country was given over to pillage/to anarchy; **être livré à soi-même** to be left to o.s. ou to one's own devices

c (= *confier*) **~ les secrets de son cœur** to give away the secrets of one's heart; **il m'a livré un peu de lui-même** he opened up to me a little

d (*loc*) **~ bataille** to do ou join battle (*à* with); **~ passage à qn** to let sb pass

2 **se livrer** VPR a (= *se rendre*) to give o.s. up, surrender (*à* to); **se ~ à la police** to give o.s. up to the police

b (= *se confier*) to open up; **se ~ à un ami** to confide in a friend, open up to a friend; **il ne se livre pas facilement** he doesn't open up easily

[c] (= s'abandonner à) **se ~ à** [+ destin] to abandon o.s. to; [+ plaisir, excès, douleur] to give o.s. over to; **elle s'est livrée à son amant** she gave herself to her lover

[d] (= faire, se consacrer à) **se ~ à** [+ exercice, analyse, expérience] to do; [+ jeu] to play; [+ sport] to practise; [+ recherches] to do, engage in, carry out; [+ enquête] to hold, set up; **se ~ à l'étude** to study, devote o.s. to study; **se ~ à des pratiques répréhensibles** to indulge in illegal practices

livresque [livʀɛsk] ADJ [connaissances] acquired from books, academic; **enseignement purement ~** purely theoretical ou academic training

livret [livʀɛ] [1] NM [a] (Mus) **~ (d'opéra)** (opera) libretto [b] († = petit livre) booklet; (= catalogue) catalogue → **compte** [2] COMP ► **livret de caisse d'épargne** (= carnet) (savings) bankbook; (= compte) savings account ► **livret de famille** official family record book (containing registration of births and deaths in a family) ► **livret matricule** (Mil) army file ► **livret militaire** military record ► **livret scolaire** (= carnet) (school) report book; (= appréciation) (school) report

livreur [livʀœʀ] NM delivery man (ou boy)

livreuse [livʀøz] NF delivery woman (ou girl)

Ljubljana [ljubljana] N Ljubljana

lob [lɔb] NM (Tennis) lob; **faire un ~** to hit a lob

lobby (pl **lobbies**) [lɔbi] NM (Pol) lobby

lobbying [lɔbiiŋ], **lobbyisme** [lɔbiism] NM lobbying

lobbyiste [lɔbiist] NMF lobbyist

lobe [lɔb] NM [a] (Anat, Bot) lobe; **~ de l'oreille** earlobe [b] (Archit) foil

lobé, e [lɔbe] (ptp de **lober**) ADJ [a] (Bot) lobed; [b] (Archit) foiled

lobectomie [lɔbɛktɔmi] NF lobectomy

lobélie [lɔbeli] NF lobelia

lober [lɔbe] ▸conjug 1◂ [1] VI (Tennis) to lob [2] VT (Ftbl, Tennis) to lob (over)

lobotomie [lɔbɔtɔmi] NF lobotomy

lobotomiser [lɔbɔtɔmize] ▸conjug 1◂ VT to perform a lobotomy on

lobule [lɔbyl] NM lobule

local, e (mpl **-aux**) [lɔkal, o] [1] ADJ local; **averses ~es** scattered ou local showers, rain in places → **anesthésie**, **couleur**, **impôt** [2] NM (= salle) premises; **~ (à usage) commercial** commercial premises, private (dwelling) house; **~ professionnel** business premises; **le club cherche un ~** the club is looking for premises ou for a place in which to meet; **il a un ~ au fond de la cour qui lui sert d'atelier** he's got a place at the far end of the yard which he uses as a workshop [3] **locaux** NMPL (= bureaux) offices, premises; **dans les locaux de la police** on police premises; **les locaux de la société sont au deuxième étage** the company's offices ou premises are on the second floor

localement [lɔkalmɑ̃] ADV (= ici) locally; (= par endroits) in places

localisable [lɔkalizabl] ADJ localizable; **facilement ~** easy to localize

localisation [lɔkalizasjɔ̃] NF (= repérage) localization; (= emplacement) location; **système de ~ par satellite** satellite locating system; **la ~ des investissements est libre** investors are free to invest wherever they wish

localisé, e [lɔkalize] (ptp de **localiser**) ADJ [conflit, douleur] localized; [gymnastique, musculation] concentrating on one part of the body; **le cancer est resté très ~** the cancer remained very localized; **la production est très ~e** production is highly localized

localiser [lɔkalize] ▸conjug 1◂ VT [a] (= circonscrire: gén) to localize; [+ épidémie, incendie] to confine; **l'épidémie s'est localisée**

dans cette région the epidemic was confined to this area [b] (= repérer) to locate

localité [lɔkalite] NF (= ville) town; (= village) village

locataire [lɔkatɛʀ] NMF (gén) tenant; (habitant avec le propriétaire) lodger, roomer (US); **les ~s de mon terrain** the people who rent land from me, the tenants of my land; **nous sommes ~s de nos bureaux** we rent our office space; **avoir/prendre des ~s** to have/take in tenants; **l'ancien/le nouveau ~ de Matignon** the former/present French Prime Minister

locatif, -ive [lɔkatif, iv] [1] ADJ [a] (valeur, secteur) rental; **local à usage ~** premises for letting (Brit) ou rent (US); **risques ~s** tenant's risks; **réparations locatives** repairs incumbent upon the tenant; **marché ~** rental ou letting market → **charge** [b] (Gram) **préposition locative** preposition of place [2] NM (Gram) locative (case); **au ~** in the locative

location [lɔkasjɔ̃] [1] NF [a] (par le locataire) [maison, terrain] renting; [matériel, voiture] renting, hire (Brit), hiring (Brit); **prendre en ~** [+ maison] to rent; [+ voiture, matériel] to rent, hire (Brit); **c'est pour un achat ou pour une ~?** is it to buy or to rent? [b] (par le propriétaire) [maison, terrain] renting (out), letting (Brit); [matériel, véhicule] renting, hiring (out) (Brit); **mettre en ~** [+ maison] to rent out, let (Brit); [+ véhicule] rent, to hire out (Brit); **"~ de voitures** (écriteau) "car rental", "cars for hire" (Brit), "car-hire" (Brit); (métier) car rental, car hiring (Brit); **« ~ de voitures sans chauffeur »** "self-drive car rental ou hire (Brit)"; **c'est pour une vente ou pour une ~?** is it to sell or to rent? ou to let? (Brit); **nous ne faisons pas de ~ de matériel** we don't rent out ou hire out [material] equipment [c] (= bail) lease; **contrat de ~** lease [d] (= logement) rented accommodation (NonC); **il a trois ~s dans la région** he has got three properties (for letting) in the area; **il a pris une ~ pour un mois** he has taken ou rented a house ou a flat for a month; **être/habiter en ~** to be/live in rented accommodation [e] (= réservation) [spectacle] reservation, booking (Brit); **bureau de ~** (advance) booking office; (Théât) box office, booking office; **la ~ des places se fait quinze jours à l'avance** seats must be reserved ou booked two weeks in advance

[2] COMP ► **location avec option d'achat** leasing, lease-option agreement ► **location saisonnière** holiday let (Brit), vacation ou summer rental (US)

location-gérance (pl **locations-gérances**) [lɔkasjɔ̃ʒeʀɑ̃s] NF ≈ management agreement; **être en ~** [entreprise] to be run by a manager

location-vente (pl **locations-ventes**) [lɔkasjɔ̃vɑ̃t] NF hire purchase (Brit), instalment (Brit) ou installment (US) plan; **acheter un ordinateur en ~** to buy a computer on instalments

loch [lɔk] NM (Naut = appareil) log; (= lac) loch

loche [lɔʃ] NF [a] (= poisson) **~ (de rivière)** loach; **~ de mer** rockling [b] (= limace) grey slug

loci [lɔki] nmpl de **locus**

lockout, lock-out [lɔkaut] NM INV lockout

lockouter, lock-outer [lɔkaute] ▸conjug 1◂ VT to lock out

loco* [lɔko] NF (ABRÉV = **locomotive**) loco*

locomoteur, -trice¹ [lɔkɔmɔtœʀ, tʀis] ADJ locomotive; **ataxie locomotrice** locomotor ataxia

locomotion [lɔkɔmɔsjɔ̃] NF locomotion → **moyen**

locomotive [lɔkɔmɔtiv] NF [a] (Rail) locomotive, engine; **~ haut le pied** light engine (Brit), wildcat (US) [b] (= entreprise, secteur, région) driving force, powerhouse; (= coureur) pacesetter, pacemaker; **les exportations sont les ~s**

de la croissance exports are the driving force behind economic growth; **cet élève est la ~ de la classe** this pupil sets the standard for the rest of the class

locomotrice² [lɔkɔmɔtʀis] NF motive ou motor unit

locus [lɔkys] (pl **locus** ou **loci** [lɔki]) NM (Bio) locus

locuste [lɔkyst] NF locust

locuteur, -trice [lɔkytœʀ, tʀis] NM,F (Ling) speaker; **~ natif** native speaker

locution [lɔkysjɔ̃] NF phrase, locution (SPÉC); **~ figée** set phrase, idiom; **~ verbale/ adverbiale / prépositive** verbal / adverbial / prepositional phrase

loden [lɔdɛn] NM (= tissu) loden; (= manteau) loden coat

lœss [løs] NM loess

lof [lɔf] NM (Naut) windward side; **aller ou venir au ~** to luff; **virer ~ pour ~** to wear (ship)

lofer [lɔfe] ▸conjug 1◂ VI (Naut) to luff

loft [lɔft] NM loft (converted living space)

log [lɔg] NM (ABRÉV = **logarithme**) log

logarithme [lɔgaʀitm] NM logarithm

logarithmique [lɔgaʀitmik] ADJ logarithmic

loge [lɔʒ] NF [a] [concierge, francs-maçons] lodge;† [bûcheron] hut; **la Grande Loge de France** the Grand Lodge of France [b] (Théât) [artiste] dressing room; [spectateur] box; **premières ~s** boxes in the dress ou grand (Brit) circle; (fig) **être aux premières ~s** to have a ringside seat, have a front seat; **secondes ~s** boxes in the upper circle [c] (= salle de préparation) (individual) exam room [d] (Archit) loggia [e] (Bot) loculus; **les ~s** loculi

logé, e [lɔʒe] (ptp de **loger**) ADJ **être ~, nourri, blanchi** to have board and lodging ou room and board and one's laundry done; **être bien ~** to be comfortably housed; **les personnes mal ~es** people in inadequate housing, people who are poorly housed; **je suis mal ~** I'm not really comfortable where I live; **être ~ à la même enseigne** to be in the same boat; **on n'est pas tous ~s à la même enseigne** we don't all get treated in the same way

logeable [lɔʒabl] ADJ (= habitable) habitable, fit to live in (attrib); (= spacieux, bien conçu) roomy

logement [lɔʒmɑ̃] NM [a] (= hébergement) housing; **le ~ était un gros problème en 1950** housing was a big problem in 1950; **trouver un ~ provisoire chez des amis** to find temporary accommodation with friends [b] (= appartement) accommodation (NonC), flat (Brit), apartment (US); **~s collectifs** apartment buildings (US), blocks of flats (Brit); **~s sociaux** ≈ council houses (ou flats) (Brit), ≈ local authority housing (NonC) (Brit), ≈ housing projects (US); **il a réussi à trouver un ~** he managed to find somewhere to live → **fonction** [c] (Mil) [troupes] (à la caserne) quartering; (chez l'habitant) billeting; **~s** (à la caserne) quarters; (chez l'habitant) billet [d] (Tech) housing

loger [lɔʒe] ▸conjug 3◂ [1] VI [a] [personne] to live (dans in, chez with, at); **~ à l'hôtel/rue Lepic** to live in a hotel/in rue Lepic; **~ chez l'habitant** (Mil) to be billeted on the local inhabitants; [touriste] to stay with the local inhabitants [b] [meuble, objet] to belong, go [2] VT [a] [+ amis] to put up; [+ clients, élèves] to accommodate; [+ objet] to put; [+ soldats] (chez l'habitant) to billet; **on va ~ les malles dans le grenier** we're going to put ou store the trunks in the loft [b] (= contenir) to accommodate; **hôtel qui peut ~ 500 personnes** hotel which can accommodate 500 people; **salle qui loge beaucoup de monde** room which can hold ou accommodate a lot of people

c (= *envoyer*) **~ une balle dans** to lodge a bullet in; **il s'est logé une balle dans la tête** he shot himself in the head, he put a bullet through his head

3 **se loger** VPR **a** (= *habiter*: *gén*) to find a house (*ou* flat *etc*), find somewhere to live, find accommodation, [*touristes*] to find accommodation, find somewhere to stay; **il n'a pas trouvé à se ~** he hasn't found anywhere to live *ou* any accommodation; **il a trouvé à se ~ chez un ami** a friend put him up; **la haine se logea dans son cœur** hatred filled his heart **b** (= *tenir*) **crois-tu qu'on va tous pouvoir se ~ dans la voiture?** do you think we'll all be able to fit into the car?

c (= *se ficher ou coincer dans*) [*balle, ballon*] **se ~ dans/entre** to lodge itself in/between; **le ballon alla se ~ entre les barreaux de la fenêtre** the ball lodged itself *ou* got stuck between the bars of the window; **le chat est allé se ~ sur l'armoire** the cat sought refuge on top of the cupboard; [*objet tombé*] **où est-il allé se ~ ?** where has it gone and hidden itself?, where has it got to?

logeur [lɔʒœʀ] NM landlord (*who lets furnished rooms*)

logeuse [lɔʒøz] NF landlady

loggia [lɔdʒja] NF loggia

logiciel, -ielle [lɔʒisjɛl] **1** ADJ software (*NonC*) **2** NM piece of software, software program *ou* package; **~ intégré** integrated software (*NonC*); **~ d'application** application software (*NonC*) *ou* program

logicien, -ienne [lɔʒisjɛ̃, jɛn] NM,F logician

▼ **logique** [lɔʒik] **1** NF **a** (= *rationalité*) logic; **cela manque un peu de ~** that's not very logical; **c'est dans la ~ des choses** it's in the nature of things; **en toute ~** logically **b** (= *façon de raisonner*) logic; **~ déductive** deductive reasoning; **le pays est entré dans une ~ de guerre** the country has embarked on a course that will inevitably lead to war; **cet accord répond à une ~ de marché** this agreement is in keeping with market principles *ou* practice **c** (= *science*) **la ~** logic

2 ADJ logical; **il ne serait pas ~ de refuser** it wouldn't make sense to refuse; **tu n'es pas ~** you're not thinking straight; **sois ~ avec toi-même** don't contradict yourself; **sa candidature s'inscrit dans la suite ~ des choses** it is quite logical that he should become a candidate; **c'est toujours moi qui fais tout, ce n'est pas ~!*** I'm the one who does everything, it's not fair! → **analyse**

3 COMP ► **logique formelle** formal logic ► **logique moderne** (*Math*) modern logic ► **logique pure** = **logique formelle**

▼ **logiquement** [lɔʒikmɑ̃] ADV (= *rationnellement*) logically, (= *normalement*) **~, il devrait faire beau** the weather should be good

logis [lɔʒi] NM (*littér*) dwelling, abode (*littér*); **rentrer au ~** to return to one's abode (*littér*); **le ~ paternel** the paternal home → **corps, fée, fou, maréchal**

logisticien, -ienne [lɔʒistisjɛ̃, jɛn] NM,F logistician

logistique [lɔʒistik] **1** ADJ logistic **2** NF logistics *sg*

logithèque [lɔʒitɛk] NF software library

logo [lɔgo] NM logo

logomachie [lɔgɔmaʃi] NF (= *verbiage*) verbosity

logomachique [lɔgɔmaʃik] ADJ verbose

logorrhée [lɔgɔʀe] NF logorrhoea (*Brit*), logorrhea (*US*)

logotype [lɔgɔtip] NM = **logo**

loi [lwa] **1** NF **a** (= *concept, justice*) **la ~** the law; **la ~ du plus fort** the law of the strongest; **c'est la ~ de la jungle** it's the law of the jungle; **la ~ naturelle** *ou* **de la nature** natural law;

dicter *ou* **imposer sa ~** to lay down the law; (*frm*) **subir la ~ de qn** to be ruled by sb; (*frm*) **se faire une ~ de faire qch** to make a point *ou* rule of doing sth, make it a rule to do sth; **avoir la ~ pour soi** to have the law on one's side; **il n'a pas la ~ chez lui!*** he's not master in his own house!; **tu ne feras pas la ~ ici!*** you're not going to lay down the law here!; **ce qu'il dit fait ~** his word is law, what he says goes; **c'est la ~ et les prophètes** it's taken as gospel; **tomber sous le coup de la ~** [*activité, acte*] to be an offence *ou* a criminal offence; **être hors la ~** [*personne, organisation, pratique*] to be outlawed; **mettre** *ou* **déclarer hors la ~** to outlaw → **force, nom**

b (= *décret*) law, act; **la ~ sur l'égalité des chances** the Equal Opportunities Act; **voter une ~** to pass a law *ou* an act; **les ~s de la République** the laws of the Republic

c (= *vérité d'expérience*) law; **la ~ de la chute des corps** the law of gravity; **la ~ de Faraday** Faraday's law; **la ~ de l'offre et de la demande** the law of supply and demand; **la ~ des grands nombres** the law of large numbers; **trois trains ont déraillé ce mois-ci, c'est la ~ des séries** three trains have been derailed this month — disasters always seem to happen in a row *ou* it's one disaster after another

d (= *code humain*) **les ~s de la mode** the dictates of fashion; **les ~s de l'honneur** the code of honour; **les ~s de l'hospitalité** the laws of hospitality; **la ~ du milieu** the law of the underworld; **la ~ du silence** the law of silence; **les ~s de l'étiquette** the rules of etiquette

2 COMP ► **loi de finances** Finance Act ► **loi informatique et liberté** ≈ data protection act (*Brit*) ► **loi martiale** martial law ► **loi d'orientation** blueprint law ► **loi salique** Salic law ► **loi du talion** (*Hist*) lex talionis; (*fig*) **appliquer la ~ du talion** to demand an eye for an eye

loi-cadre (*pl* **lois-cadres**) [lwakadʀ] NF framework law

loin [lwɛ̃] **1** ADV **a** (*en distance*) far, a long way; **est-ce ~ ?** is it far?; **ce n'est pas très ~** it's not very far; **c'est assez ~ d'ici** it's quite a long way from here; **plus ~** further, farther; **moins ~** not so far; **la gare n'est pas ~ du tout** the station is no distance at all *ou* isn't far at all; **vous nous gênez, mettez-vous plus ~** you're in our way, go and stand (*ou* sit) somewhere else; **il est ~ derrière/devant** he's a long way behind/in front, he's far behind/ahead; **aussi ~ que vous alliez, vous ne trouverez pas d'aussi beaux jardins** however far you go *ou* wherever you go, you won't find such lovely gardens; **nous n'avons pas ~ à aller** we don't have far to go; (*lit*) **aller ~** to go a long way, go far (*afield*) → **d**

b au ~ in the distance, far off; **partir au ~** to go a long way away; **de ~** from a distance; **de très ~** from a great distance, from afar (*littér*); **il voit mal de ~** he can't see distant objects clearly; **d'aussi ~** *ou* **du plus ~ qu'elle le vit, elle courut vers lui** she saw him in the distance and she ran towards him; **de ~ en ~** brillaient quelques lumières a few lights shone here and there → **pousser**

c (*dans le temps*) **le temps est ~ où cette banlieue était un village** it's a long time since this suburb was a village; **c'est ~ tout cela!** ◊ **comme c'est ~ !** (*passé*) that was a long time ago!, what a long time ago that was!; (*futur*) that's a long way in the future!, that's (still) a long way off!; **l'été n'est plus ~ maintenant** summer's not far off now, summer's just around the corner; **Noël est encore ~** Christmas is still a long way off; **~ dans le passé** in the remote past, a long time ago; **voir** *ou* **prévoir ~** to be farsighted, see a long way *ou* far ahead; **ne pas voir plus ~ que le bout de son nez** to see no further than the end of one's nose; **d'aussi ~ que je me**

rappelle for as long as I can remember; **en remontant ~ dans le temps** if you go back a long way in time; **en remontant plus ~ encore dans le passé** by looking even further back into the past; **de ~ en ~** every now and then, every now and again

d (*loc*) **il est doué, il ira ~** he's very gifted, he'll go far (in life); **tu vas trop ~ !** you're going too far!; **on ne va pas ~ avec 100 F** 100 francs doesn't go very far; **j'irais même plus ~** I would go even further; **il faudrait aller** *ou* **chercher (très) ~ pour trouver un si bon médecin** you'd have to look far and wide *ou* far afield to find such a good doctor; **cette affaire peut mener** *ou* **aller (très) ~** this matter could have far-reaching consequences *ou* repercussions; **il est de (très) ~ le meilleur** he is by far the best, he is far and away the best; **le directeur voit ces problèmes de très ~** the manager isn't directly involved in these issues; **suivre de ~ les événements** to follow events from a distance; **d'ici à l'accuser de vol il n'y a pas ~** it's tantamount to an accusation of theft, it's practically an accusation of theft; **il leur doit pas ~ de 1 000 F** he owes them little short of *ou* not far off 1,000 francs ■ (*PROV*) **~ des yeux, ~ du cœur** out of sight, out of mind (*PROV*) ■ (*PROV*) **il y a ~ de la coupe aux lèvres** there's many a slip 'twixt cup and lip (*PROV*)

2 **loin de** LOC PRÉP **a** (*en distance*) far from, a long way from, far away from; (*dans le temps*) a long way off from; **~ de là** (*lieu*) far from there; (*fig*) far from it; **non ~ de là** not far from there; **leur maison est ~ de toute civilisation** their house is a long way from civilization; **on est encore ~ de la vérité/d'un accord** we're still a long way from the truth/from reaching an agreement; (*fig*) **on est ~ du compte** we're far short of the target; **être très ~ du sujet** to be way off the subject; **~ de moi/de lui la pensée de vous blâmer !** far be it from me/from him to blame you!; (*littér, hum*) **~ de moi** *ou* **de nous !** begone! (*littér, aussi hum*) **elle est ~ d'être certaine de réussir** she is far from being certain of success, she is by no means assured of success; **ceci est ~ de lui plaire** he's far from pleased with this; **c'est très ~ de ce que nous attendions de lui** this is not at all what we expected of him

b (*avec nég*) **il ne doit pas y avoir ~ de 5 km d'ici à la gare** it can't be much less than 5 km from here to the station; **il n'est pas ~ de 10 heures** it's getting on for 10 o'clock; **il n'y a pas ~ de 5 ans qu'ils sont partis** it's not far off 5 years since they left; **ils ne sont pas ~ de le croire coupable** they almost believe him to be guilty

lointain, e [lwɛ̃tɛ̃, ɛn] **1** ADJ **a** (*dans l'espace*) [*région*] faraway, distant, remote; [*musique, horizons, exil*] distant; (*littér*) **contrées ~es** far-off lands (*littér*) **b** (*dans le temps*) [*ancêtre, passé*] distant, remote; [*avenir*] distant; **les jours ~s** far-off days **c** (= *vague*) [*parent, rapport*] remote, distant; [*regard*] faraway; [*cause*] indirect, distant; [*ressemblance*] remote **2** NM **a** **au ~** ◊ **dans le ~** in the distance **b** (*Peinture*) background

lointainement [lwɛ̃tɛnmɑ̃] ADV (= *vaguement*) remotely, vaguely

loi-programme (*pl* **lois-programmes**) [lwapʀɔgʀam] NF *act providing framework for government programme*

loir [lwaʀ] NM dormouse → **dormir**

Loire [lwaʀ] NF **la ~** (= *fleuve, département*) the Loire

loisible [lwazibl] ADJ (*frm*) **s'il vous est ~ de vous libérer quelques instants** if you could possibly spare a few moments; **il vous est tout à fait ~ de refuser** you are perfectly at liberty to refuse

loisir [lwaziʀ] NM **a** (*gén pl* = *temps libre*) leisure (*NonC*), spare time (*NonC*); **pendant mes**

► GRAMMAIRE ACTIVE: **logique** 53.4   **logiquement** 53.4

heures de ~ in my spare *ou* free time, in my leisure hours *ou* time; **que faites-vous pendant vos ~s?** what do you do in your spare *ou* free time?
b (= *activités*) **~s** leisure *ou* spare-time activities; **quels sont vos ~s préférés?** what are your favourite leisure activities?, what do you like doing best in your spare *ou* free time?; **équipements de ~s** recreational *ou* leisure facilities; **la société de ~s** the leisure society → **base, parc**
c (*loc frm*) **avoir (tout) le ~ de faire qch** to have leisure (*frm*) *ou* time to do sth; **je n'ai pas eu le ~ de vous écrire** I have not had the leisure *ou* time to write to you; **(tout) à ~** (= *en prenant son temps*) at leisure; (*autant que l'on veut*) at will, at one's pleasure (*frm*), as much as one likes; **donner** *ou* **laisser à qn le ~ de faire** to allow sb (the opportunity) to do

lolita* [lɔlita] NF nymphet

lolo [lolo] NM **a** (*langage enfantin* = *lait*) milk **b** (: = *sein*) tit:, boob:

lombaire [lɔ̃bɛʀ] **1** ADJ lumbar → **ponction 2** NF lumbar vertebra

lombalgie [lɔ̃balʒi] NF lumbago

lombard, e [lɔ̃baʀ, aʀd] **1** ADJ Lombard **2** NM (*Ling*) Lombard dialect **3** **Lombard(e)** NM,F Lombard

Lombardie [lɔ̃baʀdi] NF Lombardy

lombes [lɔ̃b] NMPL loins

lombric [lɔ̃bʀik] NM earthworm

Lomé [lɔme] N Lomé

lompe [lɔ̃p] NM = **lump**

londonien, -ienne [lɔ̃dɔnjɛ̃, jɛn] **1** ADJ London (*épith*), of London **2** **Londonien(ne)** NM,F Londoner

Londres [lɔ̃dʀ] N London

long, longue [lɔ̃, lɔ̃g] **1** ADJ **a** (*dans l'espace*) [*cheveux, liste, robe*] long; **un pont ~ de 30 mètres** a 30-metre bridge, a bridge 30 metres long; **2 cm plus ~/trop ~** 2 cm longer/too long; **plus ~/trop ~ de 2 cm** longer/too long by 2 cm → **chaise, culotte**
b (*dans le temps*) [*carrière, série, tradition, voyage*] long; [*amitié, habitude*] long-standing; **il est mort des suites d'une longue maladie** he died after a long illness; (*Ciné*) **version longue** uncut version; **lait longue conservation** longlife milk; **il écouta (pendant) un ~ moment le bruit** he listened to the noise for a long while; **l'attente fut longue** there was a long *ou* lengthy wait, I (*ou* they *etc*) waited a long time; **les heures lui paraissaient longues** the hours seemed long to him *ou* seemed to drag by; **faire de longues phrases** to produce long-winded sentences; **avoir une longue habitude de qch/de faire qch** to be long accustomed to sth/to doing sth; **cinq heures, c'est ~** five hours is a long time; **je sois pas trop ~** don't be too long; **nous pouvons vous avoir ce livre, mais ce sera ~** we can get you the book, but it will take some time *ou* a long time; **vin ~ en bouche** wine which lingers long on the palate
c (+ *inf*) **ce travail est ~ à faire** this work takes a long time; **il fut ~ à se mettre en route/à s'habiller** he took a long time *ou* it took him a long time to get started/to get dressed; **la réponse était longue à venir** the reply was a long time coming
d (*Culin*) [*sauce*] thin
e (*loc*) **au ~ cours** [*voyage*] ocean (*épith*); [*navigation*] deep-sea (*épith*), ocean (*épith*); [*capitaine*] seagoing (*épith*), ocean-going (*épith*); (*lit, fig*) **faire ~ feu** to fizzle out; **ce pot de confiture n'a pas fait ~ feu** that jar of jam didn't last long; **il n'a pas fait ~ feu à la tête du service** he didn't last long as head of department; **préparé de longue main** prepared well *ou* long beforehand, prepared well in advance; **il est ~ comme un jour sans pain** he's a

real beanpole (*Brit*) *ou* string bean (*US*) → **date, échéance, haleine, terme**
2 ADV **s'habiller ~** to wear long clothes; **s'habiller trop ~** to wear clothes that are too long; **en savoir ~/trop ~/plus ~** to know a lot/too much/more (**sur** about); **en dire ~** [*attitude*] to speak volumes; [*images*] to be eloquent; **regard qui en dit ~** meaningful *ou* eloquent look, look that speaks volumes; **cela en dit ~ sur ses intentions** that tells us a good deal *ou* speaks volumes about his intentions; **son silence en dit ~** his silence speaks for itself *ou* speaks volumes *ou* tells its own story
3 NM **a** **un bateau de 7 mètres de ~** a boat 7 metres long; **en ~** lengthways, lengthwise
b (= *vêtements*) **le ~** long skirts (*ou* dresses); **la mode est au ~ cette année** hemlines are down this year
c (*loc*) **tomber de tout son ~** to fall sprawling (onto the ground), fall headlong; **étendu de tout son ~** spread out at full length; **(tout) le ~ du fleuve/de la route** (all) along the river/the road; **tout le ~ du jour/de la nuit** all *ou* the whole day/night long; **tout au ~ de sa carrière/son récit** throughout his career/his story; **l'eau coule le ~ du caniveau** the water flows down *ou* along the gutter; **grimper le ~ d'un mât** to climb up a mast; **tout du ~** (*dans le temps*) the whole time, all along; **tirer un trait tout du ~** (= *de la page*) to draw a line right down the page; **tout au ~ du parcours** all along the route, the whole way; **de ~ en large** back and forth, to and fro, up and down; **en ~ et en large** in great detail, at great length; **je lui ai expliqué en ~, en large et en travers*** I explained it to him over and over again; **écrire qch au ~** to write sth in full
4 **longue** NF (*Ling* = *voyelle*) long vowel; (*Poésie* = *syllabe*) long syllable; (*Mus* = *note*) long note; (*Cartes*) **avoir une longue à carreaux** to have a long suit of diamonds
5 **à la longue** LOC ADV **à la longue, il s'est calmé** in the end he calmed down; **à la longue, ça a fini par coûter cher** in the long run *ou* in the end it turned out very expensive; **à la longue ça s'arrangera/ça s'usera** it will sort itself out/it will wear out in time *ou* eventually

longanimité [lɔ̃ganimite] NF (*littér*) forbearance

long-courrier (*pl* **long-courriers**) [lɔ̃kuʀje] **1** ADJ (*Naut*) ocean-going (*épith*); (*Aviat*) [*vol, avion*] long-haul (*épith*), long-distance (*épith*) **2** NM (*Naut*) ocean liner, ocean-going ship; (*Aviat*) long-haul *ou* long-distance aircraft

longe [lɔ̃ʒ] NF **a** (*pour attacher*) tether; (*pour mener*) lead **b** (*Boucherie*) loin

longer [lɔ̃ʒe] ◇ conjug 3 ◇ VT **a** [*bois*] to border; [*mur, sentier, voie ferrée*] to border, run along(side); **la voie ferrée longe la nationale** the railway line runs along(side) the main road **b** [*personne*] to go along, walk along *ou* alongside; [*voiture, train*] to go *ou* pass along *ou* alongside; **naviguer en longeant la côte** to sail along *ou* hug the coast; **~ les murs pour ne pas se faire voir** to keep close to the walls to stay out of sight

longeron [lɔ̃ʒʀɔ̃] NM **a** [*pont*] (central) girder **b** [*châssis*] side frame; [*fuselage*] longeron; [*aile*] spar

longévité [lɔ̃ʒevite] NF (= *longue vie*) longevity; (*Sociol* = *durée de vie*) life expectancy; **il attribue sa ~ à la pratique de la bicyclette** he attributes his long life *ou* longevity to cycling; **tables de ~** life-expectancy tables

longiligne [lɔ̃ʒiliɲ] ADJ [*objet, forme*] slender; [*personne*] tall and slender; **sa silhouette ~** her willowy figure

longitude [lɔ̃ʒityd] NF longitude; **à** *ou* **par 50° de ~ ouest/est** at 50° longitude west/east

longitudinal, e (*mpl* **-aux**) [lɔ̃ʒitydinal, o] ADJ [*section, coupe*] longitudinal; [*vallée, poutre,*

rainure] running lengthways; **moteur ~** front-to-back engine

longitudinalement [lɔ̃ʒitydinalmɑ̃] ADV longitudinally, lengthways

longtemps [lɔ̃tɑ̃] ADV **a** [*durer, parler, attendre, rester*] (for) a long time; (*dans phrase nég ou interrog*) (for) long; **pendant ~** (for) a long time, (for) long; **absent pendant ~** absent (for) a long time; **pendant ~ ils ne sont pas sortis** for a long time *ou* a long while they didn't go out; **avant ~** (= *sous peu*) before long; (*dans phrase nég*) **pas avant ~** not for a long time; **~ avant/après** long before/after; **on ne le verra pas de ~** we won't see him for a long time *ou* for ages; **il ne reviendra pas d'ici ~** he won't be back for a long time *ou* for ages* yet; **il vivra encore ~** he'll live (for) a long time yet; **il n'en a plus pour ~** (*pour finir*) it won't be long before he's finished; (*avant de mourir*) he hasn't got long; **y a-t-il ~ à attendre?** is there long to wait?, is there a long wait?, will it take long?; **je n'en ai pas pour ~** I won't be long, it won't take me long; **il a mis ~, été* ◇ ça lui a pris ~** it took him a long time, he was a long time over it *ou* doing it; **il arrivera dans ~?** will it be long before he gets here?; **rester assez ~ quelque part** (*trop*) to stay somewhere (for) quite *ou* rather a long time *ou* (for) quite a while; (*suffisamment*) to stay somewhere long enough; **tu es resté si ~!** you stayed so long! *ou* (for) such a long time!; **tu peux le garder aussi ~ que tu veux** you can keep it as long as you want
b (*avec* **depuis, il y a, cela fait, voilà**) (*indiquant une durée*) (for) a long time, (for) long; (*indiquant une action terminée*) a long time ago, long ago; **il habite ici depuis ~ ◇ il y a** *ou* **cela fait** *ou* **voilà ~ qu'il habite ici** he has been living here (for) a long time; **il n'était pas là depuis ~ quand je suis arrivé** he hadn't been here (for) long when I arrived; **c'était il y a ~/il n'y a pas ~** that was a long time ago/not long ago; **j'ai fini depuis ~** I finished a long time ago *ou* long ago; **il y a** *ou* **cela fait** *ou* **voilà ~ que j'ai fini** I finished a long time ago *ou* ages ago; **ça fait ~ qu'il n'est plus venu** it's (been) a long time now since he came, he hasn't come for a long time; **je n'y mangeais plus depuis ~** I had given up eating there long before then

longue [lɔ̃g] ADJ F, NF → **long**

longuement [lɔ̃gmɑ̃] ADV (= *longtemps*) [*regarder, parler, hésiter*] for a long time; (= *en détail*) [*expliquer, étudier, raconter, interroger*] at length; **plus ~** for longer; (= *en plus grand détail*) at greater length; **le plan avait été ~ médité** the plan had been pondered over at length; **elle a ~ insisté sur le fait que ...** she strongly emphasized the fact that ...; **il m'a remercié ~** he thanked me profusely; **j'ai écrit ~ sur le sujet** I wrote at length on the subject; **je t'écrirai plus ~ plus tard** I'll write to you more fully later

longuet, -ette [lɔ̃gɛ, ɛt] **1** ADJ [*film, discours*] a bit long (*attrib*), a bit on the long side* (*attrib*); **tu as été ~!** you took your time!; **il est ~ à manger** he's a bit of a slow eater **2** NM (= *gressin*) bread stick

longueur [lɔ̃gœʀ] NF **a** (= *espace*) length; **mesures/unités de ~** measures/units of length, linear measures/units; **la pièce fait trois mètres de** *ou* **en ~** the room is three metres in length *ou* three metres long; **la plage s'étend sur une ~ de 7 km** the beach stretches for 7km; **dans le sens de la ~** lengthways, lengthwise; **s'étirer en ~** to stretch out lengthways; **pièce tout en ~** long, narrow room; (*lit, fig*) **~ d'onde** wavelength; (*fig*) **nous ne sommes pas sur la même ~ d'onde** we're not on the same wavelength
b (= *durée*) length; **à ~ de journée/de semaine/d'année** all day/week/year long; **à ~ de temps** all the time; **traîner** *ou* **tirer en ~** to

drag on; **tirer les choses en ~** to drag things out; **attente qui tire** *ou* **traîne en ~** long-drawn-out wait

[c] (*Courses, Natation*) length; **faire des ~s** [*nageur*] to do lengths; **l'emporter de plusieurs ~s** to win by several lengths; **avoir une ~ d'avance (sur qn)** (*lit*) to be one length ahead (of sb); (*fig*) to be ahead (of sb); **prendre deux ~s d'avance** to go into a two-length lead; (*Alpinisme*) **~ de corde** (*passage*) pitch; (*distance*) rope-length

[d] (= *remplissage*) **~s** overlong passages; **ce film/livre a des ~s** parts of this film/book are overlong *ou* seem to drag on

longue-vue (*pl* **longues-vues**) [lɔ̃gvy] NF telescope

loofa(h) [lufa] NM (= *plante*) luffa, dishcloth gourd; (= *éponge*) loofa(h), luffa (*US*)

look[*] [luk] NM (= *style, allure*) [*personne*] look, image; [*chose*] look, style; **soigner son ~** to pay great attention to one's look *ou* one's image; **il a un ~ d'enfer** he looks dead cool[*]

looké, e[*] [luke] ADJ [*produit*] sexy[*], well-packaged; **la pochette de l'album est ~e six-ties** the album cover has got a very sixties look; **je veux pas être ~ impeccable** I don't want to look too well-groomed

looping [lupin] NM (*Aviat*) looping the loop (*NonC*); **faire des ~s** to loop the loop

looser [luzœʀ] NM = **loser**

lope[*] [lɔp], **lopette**[*] [lɔpɛt] NF (*péj*) queer[*] (*péj*), fag[*] (*péj*) (*surtout US*)

lopin [lɔpɛ̃] NM **~ (de terre)** patch of land, plot (of land)

loquace [lɔkas] ADJ talkative, loquacious (*frm*)

loquacité [lɔkasite] NF talkativeness, loquacity (*frm*)

loque [lɔk] NF [a] (= *vêtements*) **~s** rags (and tatters); **être en ~s** to be in rags; **vêtu de ~s** dressed in rags; **tomber en ~s** to be falling to bits [b] (*péj* = *personne*) wreck; **je suis une vraie ~ ce matin** I feel a wreck *ou* like a wet rag this morning

loquet [lɔkɛ] NM latch

loqueteau (*pl* **loqueteaux**) [lɔk(ə)to] NM (small) latch, catch

loqueteux, -euse [lɔk(ə)tø, øz] [1] ADJ [*personne*] ragged, (dressed) in rags *ou* in tatters; [*vêtement, livre*] tattered, ragged [2] NM,F pauper

lordose [lɔʀdoz] NF hollow-back (*NonC*), lordosis (*SPÉC*)

lorgner[*] [lɔʀɲe] ▸ conjug 1 ◂ [1] VT [*+ objet*] to peer at, eye; [*+ personne*] (*gén*) to eye; (*avec concupiscence*) to ogle, eye up[*] (*Brit*); [*+ poste, décoration, héritage, pays*] to have one's eye on; **~ qch du coin de l'œil** to look *ou* peer at sth out of the corner of one's eye, cast side-long glances at sth [2] VI **~ sur** [*+ journal, copie*] to sneak a look at; [*+ entreprise, marché*] to have one's eye on; [*+ personne*] to ogle, eye up[*] (*Brit*); **ils lorgnent vers l'Amérique pour y trouver des modèles économiques** they are looking towards *ou* to America for economic models

lorgnette [lɔʀɲɛt] NF opera glasses; (*fig*) **regarder** *ou* **voir les choses par le petit bout de la ~** to take a very limited *ou* narrow view of things

lorgnon [lɔʀɲɔ̃] NM (= *face-à-main*) lorgnette; (= *pince-nez*) pince-nez

lori [lɔʀi] NM (= *oiseau*) lory

loriot [lɔʀjo] NM **(jaune)** golden oriole

lorrain, e [lɔʀɛ̃, ɛn] [1] ADJ *ou* from Lorraine → **quiche** [2] NM (*Ling*) Lorraine dialect [3] **Lorrain(e)** NM,F inhabitant *ou* native of Lorraine [4] **Lorraine** NF (= *région*) Lorraine

lors [lɔʀ] ADV **~ de** (= *au moment de*) at the time of; (= *durant*) during; **~ de sa mort** at the time of his death; **elle a annoncé sa démission ~ de la réunion** she announced her resigna-

tion during the meeting; **~ même que** even though *ou* if; **pour ~** for the time being, for the moment → **dès**

lorsque [lɔʀsk(ə)] CONJ when; **lorsqu'il entra/entrera** when *ou* as he came/comes in

losange [lɔzɑ̃ʒ] NM diamond, lozenge; **en forme de ~** diamond-shaped; **dallage en ~s** diamond tiling

losangé, e [lɔzɑ̃ʒe] ADJ [*morceau*] diamond-shaped; [*dessin, tissu*] with a diamond pattern

loser[*] [luzœʀ] NM (*péj*) loser[*]

lot [lo] NM [a] (*Loterie*) prize; **le gros ~** the first prize, the jackpot; **~ de consolation** consolation prize [b] (= *portion*) share; **~ (de terre)** plot (of land); **chaque jour apporte son ~ de surprises/mauvaises nouvelles** every day brings its share of surprises/bad news [c] (*Comm*) [*tablettes de chocolat, cassettes*] pack; [*livres, chiffons*] batch; [*draps, vaisselle*] set; (*aux enchères*) lot; (*Ordin*) batch; **vendu par ~s de cinq** sold in packs of five; **dans le ~, il n'y avait que deux candidats valables** in the whole batch there were only two worthwhile applicants; **se détacher du ~** [*personne, produit*] to stand out [d] (*fig, littér = destin*) lot (*littér*), fate; **~ commun** common fate *ou* lot *ou* destiny; **~ quotidien** daily *ou* everyday lot

loterie [lɔtʀi] NF [a] (= *jeu*) lottery; (*dans une kermesse*) raffle; **mettre qch en ~** to put sth up to be raffled; **la Loterie nationale** the French national lottery *ou* sweepstake; **jouer à la ~** to buy tickets for the raffle *ou* lottery; **gagner à la ~** to win on the raffle *ou* lottery [b] (= *hasard*) lottery; **c'est une vraie ~** it's (all) the luck of the draw; **la vie est une ~** life is a game of chance, life is a lottery

Loth [lɔt] NM Lot

loti, e [lɔti] (*ptp de* **lotir**) ADJ **être bien/mal ~** to be well-/badly off; **il n'est guère mieux ~ (que nous)** he's scarcely any better off (than we are); (*iro*) **on est bien ~ avec un chef comme lui !** with a boss like him who could ask for more? (*iro*)

lotion [losjɔ̃] NF lotion; **~ capillaire** hair lotion; **~ après rasage** after-shave lotion; **~ avant rasage** preshave lotion

lotionner [losjɔne] ▸ conjug 1 ◂ VT to apply (a) lotion to

lotir [lɔtiʀ] ▸ conjug 2 ◂ VT [a] (= *diviser*) to divide into plots; (= *vendre*) to sell by lots; **terrains à ~** plots for sale [b] (*Jur*) (= *succession*) to share out, share out; **~ qn de qch** to allot sth to sb, provide sb with sth

lotissement [lɔtismɑ̃] NM [a] (= *terrains à bâtir*) housing estate *ou* site; (= *terrains bâtis*) (housing) development *ou* estate; (= *parcelle*) plot, lot [b] [*terrain*] (= *division*) division; (= *vente*) sale (by lots) [c] (*Jur*) [*succession*] sharing out

loto [lɔto] NM (= *jeu de société*) lotto; (= *matériel*) lotto set; (= *loterie à numéros*) national lottery; **le ~ sportif** ≈ the pools; **gagner au ~** to win the Lottery

lotte [lɔt] NF (*de rivière*) burbot; (*de mer*) angler(fish), devilfish, monkfish; (*Culin*) monkfish

lotus [lɔtys] NM lotus; **être/se mettre en position du ~** to be/sit in the lotus position

louable [lwabl] ADJ [a] [*efforts*] praiseworthy, commendable, laudable [b] [*maison*] rentable; **bureau difficilement ~ à cause de sa situation** office that is hard to let (*Brit*) *ou* rent (*US*) because of its location

louage [lwaʒ] NM hiring; **(contrat de) ~** rental contract; **~ de services** work contract

louange [lwɑ̃ʒ] NF praise; **il méprise les ~s** he despises praise; **chanter les ~s de qn** to sing sb's praises; **faire un discours à la ~ de qn** to make a speech in praise of sb; **je dois dire, à sa ~, que ...** I must say, to his credit *ou* in his praise, that ...

louanger [lwɑ̃ʒe] ▸ conjug 3 ◂ VT (*littér*) to praise, extol, laud (*littér*)

louangeur, -euse [lwɑ̃ʒœʀ, øz] ADJ (*littér*) laudatory, laudative

loubard, e[*] [lubaʀ, aʀd] NM,F hooligan, yob[*] (*Brit*)

louche¹ [luʃ] ADJ [*affaire, manœuvre, milieu, passé*] shady; [*individu*] shifty, shady, dubious; [*histoire*] dubious, fishy[*]; [*bar, hôtel*] seedy; [*conduite, acte*] dubious, suspicious, shady; [*réaction, attitude*] dubious, suspicious; **j'ai entendu du bruit, c'est ~** I heard a noise, that's funny *ou* odd; **il y a du ~ dans cette affaire** this business is a bit shady *ou* fishy[*] it isn't quite above board

louche² [luʃ] NF (= *ustensile*) ladle; (= *quantité*) ladleful; **serrer la ~ à qn**[*] to shake hands with sb, shake sb's hand; **il y en a environ 3 000, à la ~**[*] there are about 3,000 of them, roughly

loucher [luʃe] ▸ conjug 1 ◂ VI (*Méd*) to squint, have a squint; **~ sur** [*+ objet*] to eye; [*+ personne*] to ogle, eye up[*] (*Brit*); [*+ poste, héritage*] to have one's eye on; **ils louchent vers l'Europe pour y trouver des modèles économiques** they are looking towards *ou* to Europe for economic models

louer¹ [lwe] ▸ conjug 1 ◂ [1] VT to praise; **~ qn de** *ou* **pour qch** to praise sb for sth; **on ne peut que le ~ d'avoir agi ainsi** he deserves only praise *ou* one can only praise him for acting in that way; (*Rel*) **louons le Seigneur !** (let us) praise the Lord!; (*fig*) **Dieu soit loué !** thank God!; **loué soit le fax !** thank God for fax machines! [2] **se louer** VPR **se ~ de** [*+ employé, appareil*] to be very happy *ou* pleased with; [*+ action, mesure*] to congratulate o.s. on; **se ~ d'avoir fait qch** to congratulate o.s. on *ou* for having done sth; **n'avoir qu'à se ~ de** [*+ employé, appareil*] to have nothing but praise for; **nous n'avons qu'à nous ~ de ses services** we have nothing but praise for the service he gives, we have every cause for satisfaction with his services

louer² [lwe] ▸ conjug 1 ◂ VT [a] [*propriétaire*] [*+ maison, chambre*] to rent out, let (out) (*Brit*); [*+ voiture, tente, téléviseur*] to rent (out), hire out (*Brit*); **~ ses services** *ou* **se ~ à un fermier** to hire o.s. (out) to a farmer [b] [*locataire*] [*+ maison, chambre*] to rent; [*+ voiture, tente*] to rent, hire (*Brit*); [*+ place*] to reserve, book (*Brit*); **ils ont loué une maison au bord de la mer** they rented a house by the sea; **à ~** [*appartement, bureau*] to let (*Brit*), for rent (*US*); [*véhicule*] for hire (*Brit*), for rent (*US*); **cette maison doit se ~ cher** that house must be expensive to rent

loueur, -euse [lwœʀ, øz] NM,F (= *entreprise*) rental *ou* hire (*Brit*) company; **~ de bateaux/de gîtes** (= *personne*) person who rents *ou* hires (*Brit*) out boats/who rents holiday homes

loufiat[*] [lufja] NM waiter

loufoque[*] [lufɔk] ADJ [*personne, humour, film*] zany[*]; **comédie ~** screwball[*] comedy

loufoquerie[*] [lufɔkʀi] NF zaniness[*]

Louis [lwi] NM Louis

louis [lwi] NM **~ (d'or)** (gold) louis

louise-bonne (*pl* **louises-bonnes**) [lwizbɔn] NF louise-bonne pear

Louisiane [lwizjan] NF Louisiana

louis-philippard, e [lwifilipaʀ, aʀd] ADJ (*péj*) of *ou* relating to the reign of Louis Philippe

loukoum [lukum] NM Turkish delight (*NonC*); **un ~** a piece of Turkish delight

loulou¹ [lulu] NM (= *chien*) spitz; **~ de Poméranie** Pomeranian dog, Pom[*]

loulou²[*], **loulout(t)e**[*] [lulu, lulut] NM,F [a] (*terme affectueux*) darling; (*péj*) fishy customer[*], seedy character [b] = **loubard, e**

loup [lu] NM [a] (= *carnassier*) wolf; **mon (gros ou petit) ~**[*] (my) pet[*] *ou* love; **le grand méchant ~** the big bad wolf ▪ (*PROV*) **les ~s ne**

se mangent pas *ou* **ne se dévorent pas entre eux** there is honour among thieves (PROV); **l'homme est un ~ pour l'homme** brother will turn on brother ■ (PROV) **quand on parle du ~ (on en voit la queue)** talk *ou* speak of the devil; **enfermer** *ou* **mettre le ~ dans la bergerie** to set the fox to mind the geese; **crier au ~** to cry wolf; (hum) **voir le ~** to lose one's virginity → **gueule, hurler, jeune** etc **b** (= *poisson*) bass **c** (= *masque*) (eye) mask **d** (= *malfaçon*) flaw **2** COMP ► **loup de mer*** (= *marin*) old salt*, old seadog*; (= *vêtement*) (short-sleeved) jersey

loupage* [lupaʒ] NM failure; **après plusieurs ~s** after several failures

loup-cervier (*pl* **loups-cerviers**) [lusɛʀvje] NM lynx

loupe [lup] NF **a** (Opt) magnifying glass; **examiner** *ou* **regarder qch à la ~** (lit) to look at sth with *ou* through a magnifying glass; (fig) to go through sth with a fine-tooth comb, look into *ou* examine sth in great detail **b** (Méd) wen **c** [arbre] burr; **table en ~ de noyer** table in burr walnut

loupé* [lupe] (*ptp de* **louper**) NM (= *échec*) failure; (= *défaut*) defect, flaw

louper* [lupe] ► conjug 1 ◄ **1** VT **a** [+ *occasion, train, balle, personne*] to miss; **loupé! missed!**; (*iro*) **il n'en loupe pas une!** he's forever putting his big foot in it!*; **la prochaine fois, je ne te louperai pas!** I'll get you next time! **b** [+ *travail, gâteau*] to mess up*, make a mess of; [+ *examen*] to flunk*; **~ son entrée** to fluff* *ou* bungle one's entrance; **il a loupé son coup/son suicide** he bungled *ou* botched* it/his suicide attempt **2** VI **je t'ai dit qu'il ferait une erreur, ça n'a pas loupé!** I told you that he'd make a mistake and sure enough he did!; **ça va tout faire ~** that'll muck everything up* **3** **se louper*** VPR **a** (= *rater son suicide*) to bungle one's suicide attempt; (*accident*) **tu ne t'es pas loupée!** that's a nasty cut (*ou* bruise etc)! **b** (= *ne pas se rencontrer*) **nous nous sommes loupés de peu** we just missed each other

loup-garou (*pl* **loups-garous**) [lugaʀu] NM werewolf; **le ~ va te manger!** the Bogeyman will get you!

loupiot, -iotte* [lupjo, jɔt] NM,F kid*

loupiote* [lupjɔt] NF (= *lampe*) (small) light

lourd, e¹ [luʀ, luʀd] **1** ADJ **a** (= *de poids élevé*) [objet, vêtement] heavy; [armement, artillerie, industrie, métal] heavy (épith); **terrain ~** heavy *ou* soft ground; **c'est trop ~ à porter** it's too heavy to carry → **eau, franc²** **b** (= *désagréablement pesant*) [silence, sommeil] heavy, deep; [chagrin] deep; [parfum, odeur] heavy, strong; [aliment, vin] heavy; [repas] heavy, big; **yeux ~s de sommeil/fatigue** eyes heavy with sleep/tiredness; **il avait les paupières ~es** his eyelids were *ou* felt heavy; **c'est ~ (à digérer)** it's heavy (on the stomach *ou* the digestion); **se sentir ~** ◊ **avoir l'estomac ~** to feel bloated; **j'ai** *ou* **je me sens les jambes ~es** my legs feel heavy; **j'ai** *ou* **je me sens la tête ~e** my head feels fuzzy, I feel a bit headachy*; **il a un ~ passé** he's a man with a past → **hérédité** **c** (Mét) [ciel, nuage] heavy; [temps, chaleur] sultry, close; **il fait ~** the weather is close, it's sultry **d** (= *massif, gauche*) [construction] ponderous (frm), inelegant, monolithic; [démarche] heavy, cumbersome; [mouvement, style] heavy, ponderous; [plaisanterie] unsubtle; [compliment] clumsy; **marcher d'un pas ~** to tread heavily, walk with a heavy step; **oiseau au vol ~** bird with a heavy *ou* cumbrous flight; **avoir l'esprit ~** to be slow-witted *ou* dull-witted; (à un plaisantin) **tu es un peu ~*** you're just not funny **e** (= *important*) [dettes, impôts, tâche, responsabilité, charge] heavy, weighty; [pertes]

heavy, severe, serious; [faute] serious, grave; [chirurgie] extensive; **les tendances ~es du marché** the broad *ou* main trends in the market; **de ~es présomptions pèsent sur lui** suspicion falls heavily on him; **les cas les plus ~s sont gardés à l'hôpital** the most serious *ou* severe cases are kept in hospital **f** (= *difficile à gérer*) [dispositif] unwieldy; **35 enfants par classe, c'est trop ~** 35 children per class is too much; **trois enfants à élever, c'est ~/trop ~ (pour elle)** bringing up three children is a lot/too much (for her) **g** (= *chargé*) **le silence était ~ de menaces** there was a threatening *ou* an ominous silence; **décision ~e de conséquences** decision fraught with consequences; **cette défaite est ~e de signification** this defeat is extremely *ou* highly significant **2** ADV* **il n'y a pas ~ de pain** there isn't much bread; **du bon sens, il n'en a pas ~!** he hasn't got much common sense; **il n'en sait/n'en fait pas ~** he doesn't know/do much; **il ne gagne pas ~** he doesn't earn much; **ça ne fait pas ~** it doesn't amount to much → **peser**

lourdaud, e* [luʀdo, od] **1** ADJ oafish, clumsy **2** NM,F oaf

lourde²* [luʀd] NF (= *porte*) door

lourdement [luʀdəmɑ̃] ADV (gén) heavily; **marcher ~** to walk with a heavy tread; **se tromper ~** to be sadly mistaken, make a big mistake; **insister ~ sur qch/pour faire qch** to insist strenuously on sth/on doing sth; **s'endetter ~** to get heavily into debt

lourder* [luʀde] ► conjug 1 ◄ VT to kick out*, boot out*; **se faire ~** to get kicked out* *ou* booted out*

lourdeur [luʀdœʀ] NF **a** (= *pesanteur*) [objet, fardeau] heaviness, weight; [bureaucratie, infrastructure] cumbersomeness; [tâche, responsabilité] weight; (Bourse) [marché] slackness, sluggishness; **les ~s administratives/bureaucratiques** administrative/bureaucratic red tape **b** [édifice] heaviness, massiveness; [démarche] heaviness; [style, forme] heaviness, ponderousness; **~ d'esprit** dull-wittedness, slow-wittedness; **s'exprimer avec ~** to express o.s. clumsily *ou* ponderously; **avoir des ~s de tête** to have a fuzzy* head, feel headachy*; **avoir des ~s d'estomac** to have indigestion, feel a bit bloated; **j'ai des ~s dans les jambes** my legs feel heavy; **cette traduction comporte des ~s** this translation is a bit heavy *ou* awkward in places **c** [temps] sultriness, closeness

lourdingue* [luʀdɛ̃g] ADJ [plaisanterie] predictable; [personne] oafish, clumsy; [construction] hefty-looking*; [phrase] laboured (Brit), labored (US), clumsy

loustic* [lustik] NM (= *enfant*) kid*; (= *taquin*) villain* (hum); (= *type*) (funny) guy* *ou* chap* (Brit); **faire le ~** to play the fool, act the goat* (Brit); **un drôle de ~** (= *type*) an oddball*, an oddbod* (Brit); (= *enfant*) a little villain* (hum) *ou* rascal

loutre [lutʀ] NF (= *animal*) otter; (= *fourrure*) otter-skin; **~ de mer** sea otter

louve [luv] NF she-wolf

louveteau (*pl* **louveteaux**) [luv(ə)to] NM (Zool) (wolf) cub; (Scoutisme) cub (scout)

louvoiement [luvwamɑ̃] NM **a** (Naut) tacking (NonC) **b** (= *tergiversations*) hedging (NonC), dithering, shilly-shallying* (Brit); **assez de ~s** stop beating about the bush

louvoyer [luvwaje] ► conjug 8 ◄ VI **a** (Naut) to tack; **~ au plus près** to beat to windward; **il doit ~ entre les tendances différentes de son parti** he has to tread a delicate path *ou* steer a delicate course between the different political currents in his party **b** (= *tergiverser*) to hedge, dither, shilly-shally* (Brit)

Louvre [luvʀ] NM **le (Musée du) ~** the Louvre (museum); **l'École du ~** the Ecole du Louvre

(training college for museum curators and guides based at the Louvre)

Louxor [luksɔʀ] N Luxor

lover [lɔve] **►** conjug 1 ◄ **1** VT to coil **2** **se lover** VPR [serpent] to coil up; [personne] to curl up

loxodromie [lɔksɔdʀɔmi] NF (Naut) loxodromics sg, loxodromy

loyal, e (*mpl* **-aux**) [lwajal, o] ADJ **a** (= *fidèle*) [sujet, ami] loyal, faithful, trusty; **après 50 ans de bons et loyaux services** after 50 years of good and faithful service **b** (= *honnête*) [personne, procédé] fair, honest; [conduite] upright, fair; [jeu] fair, straight*; **se battre à la ~e*** to fight cleanly

loyalement [lwajalmɑ̃] ADV [agir] fairly, honestly; [servir] loyally, faithfully; [se battre] cleanly; **accepter ~ une défaite** to take a defeat sportingly *ou* in good part (Brit)

loyalisme [lwajalism] NM loyalty

loyaliste [lwajalist] **1** ADJ **a** (= *fidèle*) loyal **b** (Pol) loyalist, Loyalist **2** NMF **a** (= *fidèle*) loyal supporter **b** (Pol) loyalist, Loyalist

loyauté [lwajote] NF **a** (= *fidélité*) loyalty, faithfulness **b** (= *honnêteté*) honesty, fairness; [conduite] fairness, uprightness; **avec ~** fairly, honestly

loyer [lwaje] NM rent; **~ commercial** office rent; **~ de l'argent** rate of interest, interest rate

LP [ɛlpe] NM (ABRÉV = **lycée professionnel**) → **lycée**

LSD [ɛlɛsde] NM (ABRÉV = **Lysergsäure Diethylamid**) LSD

lu, e [ly] (*ptp de* **lire**) ADJ **lu et approuvé** read and approved; **elle est très lue en Europe** she is widely read in Europe

Luanda [luɑ̃da] N Luanda

lubie [lybi] NF (= *centre d'intérêt, passe-temps*) fad; (= *idée*) hare-brained idea; (= *mode*) craze, fad; **encore une de ses ~s!** another of his hare-brained *ou* mad ideas!; **il lui a pris la ~ de ne plus manger de pain** he has taken it into his head not to eat bread any more

lubricité [lybʀisite] NF [personne] lustfulness, lechery; [propos, conduite] lewdness

lubrifiant, e [lybʀifjɑ̃, jɑ̃t] **1** ADJ lubricating **2** NM lubricant

lubrification [lybʀifikasjɔ̃] NF lubrication

lubrifier [lybʀifje] ► conjug 7 ◄ VT to lubricate

lubrique [lybʀik] ADJ [personne] lustful, lecherous; [propos] lewd, libidinous; [danse] lewd; [amour] lustful, carnal; **regarder qch d'un œil ~** to gaze at sth with a lustful eye

Luc [lyk] NM Luke

lucarne [lykaʀn] NF [toit] skylight; (en saillie) dormer window; (Ftbl) **envoyer la balle dans la ~** to send the ball into the top corner of the net; **la petite ~** ◊ **les étranges ~s** (= *télévision*) the small screen

lucide [lysid] ADJ **a** (= *conscient*) [malade, vieillard] lucid; [accidenté] conscious **b** (= *perspicace*) [personne] lucid, clear-headed; [esprit, analyse, raisonnement] lucid, clear; **il a une vision plus ~ des choses** he has a clearer view of things; **le témoin le plus ~ de son temps** the most clear-sighted *ou* perceptive observer of the times he lived in; **juger qch d'un œil ~** to judge sth with a lucid *ou* clear eye

lucidement [lysidmɑ̃] ADV lucidly, clearly

lucidité [lysidite] NF **a** [malade, vieillard] lucidity; [accidenté] consciousness; **il a des moments de ~** he has moments of lucidity; **un vieillard qui a gardé sa ~** an old man who still has the use of his faculties **b** (= *perspicacité*) [personne, raisonnement] lucidity, clear-headedness; [esprit, analyse, raisonnement] lucidity, clearness; **il a analysé la situation avec ~** he gave a very clear-headed analysis of the situation

Lucifer [lysifɛʀ] NM Lucifer

luciole [lysjɔl] NF firefly

lucratif, -ive [lykratif, iv] ADJ [entreprise] lucrative, profitable; [emploi] lucrative, well-paid; **association à but ~/non ~** profit-making/non-profit-making ou not-for-profit (US) organization

lucrativement [lykrativmã] ADV lucratively

lucre [lykʀ] NM (péj) lucre (péj)

Lucrèce [lykʀɛs] **1** NM Lucretius **2** NF Lucretia

ludiciel [lydisjɛl] NM computer game; **~s** computer games, game software (NonC)

ludion [lydjɔ̃] NM Cartesian diver

ludique [lydik] ADJ playful, ludic (Spéc); **activité ~** (Scol) play activity; (de loisir) recreational activity; **l'informatique ~** computer games; **il veut une émission plus ~** he wants the programme to be more entertaining

ludo-éducatif, -ive (mpl **ludo-éducatifs**) [lydoedykatif, iv] ADJ [programme, logiciel] edutainment (épith)

ludothèque [lydɔtɛk] NF games library

luette [lɥɛt] NF uvula

lueur [lɥœʀ] NF **a** [flamme] glimmer (NonC); [étoile, lune, lampe] (faint) light; [braises] glow (NonC); **à la ~ d'une bougie** by candlelight; **les ~s de la ville** the city lights; **les premières ~s de l'aube/du jour** the first light of dawn/of day; **les ~s du couchant** the glow of sunset **b** [désir, colère] gleam; [raison, intelligence] glimmer; **il avait une ~ malicieuse dans le regard** he had a mischievous gleam ou glint in his eye; **pas la moindre ~ d'espoir** not the faintest glimmer of hope **c** (gén hum = connaissances) **il a quelques ~s sur le sujet** he knows a bit about the subject; **peux-tu apporter quelques ~s sur le fonctionnement de cette machine?** can you shed some light on the working of this machine?

luge [lyʒ] NF toboggan, sledge (Brit), sled (US); **faire de la ~** to toboggan, sledge (Brit), sled (US)

luger [lyʒe] ▸conjug 3◂ VI to toboggan, sledge (Brit), sled (US)

lugeur, -euse [lyʒœʀ, øz] NM,F tobogganist

lugubre [lygybʀ] ADJ [pensée, ambiance, récit] gloomy, dismal, lugubrious (littér); [paysage] dreary, dismal; [maison] gloomy; [musique, cri] mournful; **d'un ton ~** in a funereal voice

lugubrement [lygybʀəmã] ADV gloomily, dismally, lugubriously

lui [lɥi] **1** PRON PERS (objet indirect) (homme) him; (femme) her; (animal, bébé) it, him, her; (bateau, nation) her, it; (insecte, chose) it; **je le ~ ai dit** (à un homme) I told him; (à une femme) I told her; **tu ~ as donné de l'eau?** (à un animal) have you given it (ou him ou her) some water?; (à une plante) have you watered it?; **je ne le ~ ai jamais caché** I have never kept it from him (ou her); **il ~ est facile de le faire** it's easy for him (ou her) to do it; **je ne ~ connais pas de défauts** he's (ou she's) got no faults that I know of; **je ~ ai entendu dire que** I heard him (ou her) say that; **le bateau est plus propre depuis qu'on ~ a donné un coup de peinture** the boat is cleaner now they've given her (ou it) a coat of paint

2 PRON M (fonction objet) (personne) him; (animal) him, her; (chose) it; (pays, bateau) her, it; **elle n'admire que ~** she only admires him; **à ~, elle n'a pas dit un mot** she never said a word to him; **~, le revoir? jamais!** see him again? never!; **c'est ~, je le reconnais** it's him, I recognize him; **je l'ai bien vu, ~!** I saw him all right!*, I definitely saw him!; **si j'étais ~, j'accepterais** if I were him ou he (frm) I would accept → **même, non, seul**

b (sujet, gén emphatique) (personne) he; (chose) it; (animal) it, he, she; **elle est vendeuse, ~ est maçon** she's a saleswoman and he's a bricklayer; **~, furieux, a refusé** furious, he refused; **le Japon, ~, serait d'accord** Japan, for

its ou her part, would agree; **l'enfant, ~, avait bien vu les bonbons** the child had seen the sweets all right; **qu'est-ce qu'ils ont dit? — ~, rien** what did they say? — he said nothing; **elle est venue mais pas ~** she came but not him ou but he didn't; **mon frère et ~ sont partis ensemble** my brother and he went off together; **~ parti, j'ai pu travailler** with him gone ou after he had gone I was able to work; **~(, il) n'aurait jamais fait ça ◊ il n'aurait jamais fait ça, ~** he would never have done that; **est-ce qu'il le sait, ~?◊ est-ce que ~(, il) le sait?** does he know about it?; **~, se marier? jamais!** him get married? that'll be the day!

c (emphatique avec qui, que) **c'est ~ que nous avions invité** it's ou it was him we had invited; **c'est à ~ que je veux parler** it's him I want to speak to, I want to speak to him; **il y a un hibou dans le bois, c'est ~ que j'ai entendu** there is an owl in the wood — that's what I heard; **c'est ~ qui me l'a dit** he told me himself, it was he who told me; **c'est ~ qui le dit!** that's his story!, that's what he says!; (frm) **ce fut ~ qui le premier découvrit ...** it was he who first discovered ...; **chasse le chien, c'est ~ qui m'a mordu** chase that dog away — it's the one that bit me; **de tous les arbres, c'est ~ le bois le plus dur** of all the trees it's this one that has the hardest wood; **ils ont trois chats, et ~ qui ne voulait pas d'animaux!** they have three cats and to think that he didn't want any animals!

d (dans des comparaisons: sujet) he, him; (objet) him; **elle est plus mince que ~** she is slimmer than he is ou than him; **j'ai mangé plus/moins que ~** I ate more/less than he did ou than him; **ne fais pas comme ~** don't do as he does ou did, don't do the same as he did; **je ne la connais pas aussi bien que ~** (que je la connais) I don't know her as well as (I know) him; (qu'il la connaît) I don't know her as well as he does

lui-même [lɥimɛm] PRON → **même**

luire [lɥiʀ] ▸conjug 38◂ VI [métal] to shine, gleam; [surface mouillée] to glisten; [reflet intermittent] to glint; [étoile] to twinkle; (en scintillant) to glimmer, shimmer; (en rougeoyant) to glow; **l'herbe/l'étang luisait au soleil du matin** the grass/the pond glistened in the morning sunlight; **yeux qui luisent de colère/d'envie** eyes gleaming with anger/with desire; **le lac luisait sous la lune** the lake shimmered ou glimmered in the moonlight; **l'espoir luit encore** there is still a glimmer of hope

luisant, e [lɥizã, ãt] **1** ADJ [métal] gleaming, shining; [surface mouillée] glistening; [reflet intermittent] glinting; (en scintillant) glimmering, shimmering; (en rougeoyant) glowing; **front ~ de sueur** forehead gleaming ou glistening with sweat; **vêtements ~s d'usure** clothes shiny with wear; **yeux ~s de fièvre** eyes bright with fever → **ver 2** NM [étoffe] sheen; [pelage] gloss

lumbago [lɔ̃bago] NM lumbago

lumière [lymjɛʀ] **1** NF **a** (gén, Phys) light; **la ~ du jour** daylight; **la ~ du soleil l'éblouit** he was dazzled by the sunlight; **à la ~ des étoiles** by the light of the stars, by starlight; **à la ~ artificielle/électrique** by artificial/electric light; **la ~ entrait à flots dans la pièce** daylight streamed into the room; **il n'y a pas beaucoup/ça ne donne guère de ~** there isn't/it doesn't give much light; **donne-nous de la ~** switch ou put the light on, will you?; **il y a de la ~ dans sa chambre** there's a light on in his room; (Bible) **il dit « que la ~ soit » et la ~ fut** He said "let there be light" and there was light; **les ~s de la ville** (gén) the lights of the town; (plus grande) the city lights → **effet, habit**

b (= connaissance) light; **avoir/acquérir quelque ~ sur qch** to have/gain some knowledge of sth, have/gain some insight into sth;

avoir des ~s sur une question to have some ideas ou some knowledge on a question, know something about a question; **aidez-nous de vos ~s** give us the benefit of your wisdom ou insight

c (= personne) light; **il fut une des ~s de son siècle** he was one of the (shining) lights of his age; **le pauvre garçon, ce n'est pas une ~** the poor boy, he's no Einstein* ou no genius

d (Tech) [machine à vapeur] port; [canon] sight; (Aut) **~ d'admission/d'échappement** inlet/exhaust port ou valve

e (loc) **mettre qch en ~** to bring sth to light, bring sth out; **jeter une nouvelle ~ sur qch** to throw ou shed new light on sth; **à la ~ des récents événements** in the light of recent events; **faire (toute) la ~ sur qch** to get right to the bottom of sth; **la ~ de la foi/de la raison** the light of faith/of reason; **entrevoir la ~ au bout du tunnel** to see the light at the end of the tunnel → **siècle**

2 COMP ▸ **lumière blanche** white light ▸ **lumière cendrée** (Astron) earth-light, earthshine ▸ **lumière noire** black light ▸ **lumière stroboscopique** strobe lighting ▸ **lumière de Wood** = **lumière noire**

lumignon [lyminɔ̃] NM (= lampe) (small) light; (= bougie) candle-end

luminaire [lyminɛʀ] NM (gén) light, lamp; (= cierge) candle; **magasin de ~s** lighting shop

luminescence [lyminesãs] NF luminescence

luminescent, e [lyminesã, ãt] ADJ luminescent

lumineusement [lyminøzmã] ADV [expliquer] lucidly, clearly; **son explication était ~ claire** his explanation was crystal clear

lumineux, -euse [lyminø, øz] ADJ **a** [corps, intensité, cadran, aiguille] luminous; [fontaine, enseigne] illuminated; [rayon, faisceau] of light; **onde/source lumineuse** light wave/source → **flèche¹, panneau b** [teint, regard] radiant; [ciel, couleur] luminous; [pièce, appartement] bright, light **c** (littér = pur, transparent) luminous (littér), lucid; (iro) [exposé] limpid, brilliant; **j'ai compris, c'est ~** I understand, it's as clear as daylight ou it's crystal clear → **idée**

luminosité [lyminozite] NF **a** [teint, regard] radiance; [ciel, couleur] luminosity; **il y a beaucoup de ~** there's lots of light, it's very bright **b** (Photo, Sci) luminosity

lump [lœp] NM lumpfish, lumpsucker → **œuf**

lunaire¹ [lynɛʀ] ADJ [année, cycle, paysage, sol] lunar; [roche] moon (épith); (fig) [visage] moonlike

lunaire² [lynɛʀ] NF (Bot) honesty

lunaison [lynɛzɔ̃] NF lunar month

lunapark [lynapaʀk] NM (fun)fair

lunatique [lynatik] ADJ moody

lunch (pl **lunch(e)s**) [lœntʃ] NM buffet

lundi [lœdi] NM Monday; **le ~ de Pâques/de Pentecôte** Easter/Whit Monday; **(ça va) comme un ~** how are you? — I've got the Monday blues* ou I'm already longing for the weekend; pour autres locutions voir **samedi**

lune [lyn] NF **a** (Astron) moon; **pleine/nouvelle ~** full/new moon; **nuit sans ~** moonless night; **~ rousse** April moon → **clair¹, croissant b** (* = derrière) bottom*, backside* **c** (loc) **~ de miel** (lit, fig) honeymoon; **être dans la ~** to have one's head in the clouds, be in a dream; **tomber de la ~** to have dropped in from another planet; **demander ou vouloir la ~** to ask ou cry for the moon; **il décrocherait la ~ pour elle** he'd move heaven and earth to please her; **promettre la ~** to promise the moon ou the earth; **elle veut lui faire voir la ~ en plein midi** she's trying to pull the wool over his eyes; **il y a (bien) des ~s**† many moons ago → **face, vieux**

luné, e* [lyne] ADJ **être bien/mal ~** to be in a good/bad mood; **comment est-elle ~e ce matin?** what sort of (a) mood is she in this morning?

lunetier, -ière [lyn(ə)tje, jɛʀ] **1** ADJ [*industrie*] spectacle (*épith*) **2** NM,F (= *vendeur*) optician; (= *fabricant*) spectacle *ou* eyeglasses (*US*) manufacturer

lunette [lynɛt] **1** NF **a** (*Astron* = *télescope*) telescope; [*fusil*] sight(s) **b** (*Archit*) lunette **2** **lunettes** NFPL (*correctives*) glasses, eyeglasses (*US*), spectacles†; (*de protection*) goggles, glasses; **mets tes ~s!** (*lit, fig*) put your glasses *ou* specs* on!; **un intello* à ~s** a bespectacled intellectual **3** COMP ► **lunette d'approche** telescope ► **lunette arrière** (*Aut*) rear window ► **lunette astronomique** astronomical telescope ► **lunette (des cabinets)** (= *cuvette*) toilet bowl; (= *siège*) toilet rim ► **lunettes de glacier** snow goggles ► **lunette méridienne** meridian circle ► **lunettes de natation** swimming goggles ► **lunettes noires** dark glasses ► **lunettes de plongée** swimming *ou* diving goggles ► **lunettes de ski** ski goggles ► **lunettes de soleil** sunglasses ► **lunettes de vue** prescription *ou* corrective glasses

lunetterie [lynɛtʀi] NF spectacle trade

lunule [lynyl] NF [*ongle*] half-moon, lunula (*SPÉC*); (*Math*) lune

lupanar [lypanaʀ] NM (*littér*) brothel

lupin [lypɛ̃] NM lupin

lupus [lypys] NM lupus

lurette [lyʀɛt] NF **il y a belle ~ de cela*** that was ages ago *ou* donkey's years* (*Brit*) ago; **il y a belle ~ que je ne fume plus*** I stopped smoking ages ago, it's ages since I stopped smoking

lurex [lyʀɛks] NM lurex

luron* [lyʀɔ̃] NM **(joyeux** *ou* **gai) ~** likely lad; **c'est un (sacré) ~**† he's a great one for the girls*, he's quite a lad*

luronne* [lyʀɔn] NF **(gaie) ~** (lively) lass; **c'est une (sacrée) ~**† she's a great one for the men*, she's quite a lass*

Lusaka [lusaka] N Lusaka

lusitanien, -ienne [lyzitanjɛ̃, jɛn] **1** ADJ Lusitanian **2** **Lusitanien(ne)** NM,F Lusitanian

lusophone [lyzɔfɔn] **1** ADJ Portuguese-speaking **2** NMF Portuguese speaker

lustrage [lystʀaʒ] NM (*Tech*) [*étoffe, peaux, fourrures*] lustring; [*glace*] shining

lustral, e (*mpl* -**aux**) [lystʀal, o] ADJ (*littér*) lustral (*littér*)

lustre [lystʀ] NM **a** [*objet, peaux, vernis*] shine, lustre (*Brit*), luster (*US*); [*personne, cérémonie*] lustre; **redonner du ~ à une institution** to restore the prestige of an institution **b** (= *luminaire*) centre light (*with several bulbs*); (*très élaboré*) chandelier **c** (*littér* = 5 *ans*) lustrum (*littér*); **depuis des ~s** for ages, for aeons

lustré, e [lystʀe] (*ptp de lustrer*) ADJ [*cheveux, fourrure, poil*] glossy; [*manche usée*] shiny

lustrer [lystʀe] ►conjug 1◄ VT (*Tech*) [+ *étoffe, peaux, fourrures*] to lustre; [+ *glace*] to shine; (*gén* = *faire briller*) to shine, put a shine on; (*par l'usure*) to make shiny; **le chat lustre son poil** the cat is licking its fur; **la pluie lustrait le feuillage** the rain put a sheen on the leaves; **ce tissu se lustre facilement** this fabric gets shiny very quickly

lustrerie [lystʀəʀi] NF lighting (appliance) trade

lustrine [lystʀin] NF (*Tex*) lustre

Lutèce [lytɛs] N Lutetia

lutétium [lytesjɔm] NM lutetium

luth [lyt] NM lute

Luther [lytɛʀ] NM Luther

luthéranisme [lyteʀanism] NM Lutheranism

luthérien, -ienne [lyteʀjɛ̃, jɛn] **1** ADJ Lutheran **2** **Luthérien(ne)** NM,F Lutheran

luthier, -ière [lytje, jɛʀ] NM,F (stringed-) instrument maker

luthiste [lytist] NMF lutenist, lutanist

lutin, e [lytɛ̃, in] **1** ADJ impish, mischievous **2** NM (= *farfadet*) (*gentil*) imp, sprite; (*méchant*) goblin; (*irlandais*) leprechaun; (= *enfant*) **(petit) ~** (little) imp

lutiner [lytine] ►conjug 1◄ VT to fondle, tickle

lutrin [lytʀɛ̃] NM (*sur pied*) lectern; (*sur table*) book-rest

lutte [lyt] **1** NF **a** (*gén* = *combat*) struggle, fight (**contre** against); **~s politiques** political struggles; **~ antipollution/contre l'alcoolisme** fight against pollution/against alcoholism; **~ contre le crime** crime prevention; **~ antidrogue** battle *ou* fight against drugs; (*Bio, fig*) **~ pour la vie** struggle for existence *ou* survival; **~ entre le bien et le mal** conflict *ou* struggle between good and evil; **~ de l'honneur et de l'intérêt** conflict between honour and self-interest; **aimer la ~** to enjoy a struggle; **engager/abandonner la ~** to take up/give up the struggle *ou* fight; **nous sommes engagés dans une ~ inégale** we're fighting an uneven battle, it's an unequal struggle; **après plusieurs années de ~** after several years of struggling; **gagner** *ou* **conquérir qch de haute ~** to win sth after a brave fight *ou* struggle **b** (*loc*) **entrer/être en ~ (contre qn)** to enter into/be in conflict (with sb); **en ~ ouverte contre sa famille** in open conflict with his family; **travailleurs en ~** (*en grève*) striking workers; (*Mil*) **le pays en ~** the country at war; (*Pol*) **les partis en ~** the opposing parties **c** (*Sport*) wrestling; **~ libre/gréco-romaine** all-in/Greco-Roman *ou* Graeco-Roman (*Brit*) wrestling; **faire de la ~** to wrestle **2** COMP ► **lutte armée** armed struggle; **en ~ armée** in armed conflict ► **lutte des classes** class struggle *ou* war ► **lutte d'influence(s)** struggle for influence ► **lutte d'intérêts** conflict *ou* clash of interests

lutter [lyte] ►conjug 1◄ VI **a** (= *se battre*) to struggle, fight; **~ contre un adversaire** to struggle *ou* fight against an opponent; **~ contre le vent** to fight against *ou* battle with the wind; **~ contre l'ignorance/un incendie** to fight ignorance/a fire; **~ contre l'adversité/le sommeil** to fight off adversity/sleep; **~ contre la mort** to fight *ou* struggle for one's life; **~ pour ses droits/la liberté** to fight for one's rights/freedom; **~ avec sa conscience** to struggle *ou* wrestle with one's conscience; **les deux navires luttaient de vitesse** the two ships were racing each other **b** (*Sport*) to wrestle

lutteur, -euse [lytœʀ, øz] NM,F (*Sport*) wrestler; (*fig*) fighter

lux [lyks] NM lux

luxation [lyksasjɔ̃] NF dislocation, luxation (*SPÉC*)

luxe [lyks] NM **a** (= *richesse*) luxury; [*maison, objet*] luxuriousness, sumptuousness; **vivre dans le ~** to live in (the lap of) luxury; **de ~** [*produits*] de luxe (*épith*); [*voiture, appartement*] luxury (*épith*); (*Aut*) **modèle (de) grand ~** de luxe model; **boutique de ~** shop selling luxury goods; **deux salles de bains, c'est le** *ou* **du ~!** two bathrooms, it's the height of luxury! *ou* what luxury!; **je me suis acheté un nouveau manteau, ce n'était pas du ~** I bought myself a new coat, I badly needed one; **j'ai lavé la cuisine, ce n'était pas du ~!** I washed the kitchen floor, it badly needed it **b** (= *plaisir coûteux*) luxury; **son seul ~: sa**

chaîne hi-fi his only luxury *ou* indulgence was his stereo system; **il s'est offert** *ou* **payé le ~ d'aller au casino** he allowed himself the indulgence *ou* luxury of a trip to the casino; **je ne peux pas me payer** *ou* **m'offrir le ~ d'être malade/d'aller au restaurant** I can't afford the luxury of being ill/eating out **c** (= *profusion*) [*détails*] wealth, host; [*précautions*] host; **il nous l'a décrit avec un ~ de précisions** he described it to us in great *ou* lavish detail

Luxembourg [lyksɑ̃buʀ] NM **(le grand-duché de) ~** (the Grand Duchy of) Luxembourg; (*Pol*) **le palais du ~** the seat of the French Senate

luxembourgeois, e [lyksɑ̃buʀʒwa, waz] **1** ADJ of *ou* from Luxembourg **2** **Luxembourgeois(e)** NM,F inhabitant *ou* native of Luxembourg

luxer [lykse] ►conjug 1◄ VT to dislocate, luxate (*SPÉC*); **se ~ un membre** to dislocate a limb; **avoir l'épaule luxée** to have a dislocated shoulder

luxueusement [lyksɥøzmɑ̃] ADV luxuriously

luxueux, -euse [lyksɥø, øz] ADJ luxurious

luxure [lyksyʀ] NF lust

luxuriance [lyksyʀjɑ̃s] NF luxuriance

luxuriant, e [lyksyʀjɑ̃, jɑ̃t] ADJ [*végétation*] luxuriant, lush; [*imagination*] fertile, luxuriant (*littér*)

luxurieux, -ieuse [lyksyʀjø, jøz] ADJ lustful, lascivious

luzerne [lyzɛʀn] NF (*cultivée*) lucerne, alfalfa; (*sauvage*) medick (*Brit*), medic (*US*)

lycanthropie [likɑ̃tʀɔpi] NF lycanthropy

lycée [lise] NM lycée, ≈ secondary school, high school (*US*); **~ (technique et) professionnel** ◊ **~ d'enseignement professionnel**† *secondary school for vocational training*

│ LYCÉE │

Lycées *are state secondary schools where pupils study for their "baccalauréat" after leaving the "collège". The* **lycée** *covers the school years known as "seconde" (15-16 year-olds), "première" (16-17 year-olds) and "terminale" (up to leaving age at 18). The term* **lycée professionnel** *refers to a* **lycée** *which provides vocational training as well as the more traditional core subjects.* → │BAC│; │COLLÈGE│; │ÉDUCATION NATIONALE│

---

lycéen, -éenne [liseɛ̃, eɛn] **1** ADJ [*journal, manifestation*] (secondary school *ou* high school (*US*)) students' (*épith*); **le mouvement ~** the (secondary school) students' protest movement **2** NM secondary school *ou* high-school (*US*) boy *ou* student; **lorsque j'étais ~** when I was at secondary school *ou* in high school (*US*); **quelques ~s étaient attablés à la terrasse** some boys from the secondary school were sitting at a table outside the café; **les ~s sont en grève** secondary school students are on strike **3** **lycéenne** NF secondary school *ou* high-school (*US*) girl *ou* student

lychee [litʃi] NM = **litchi**

Lycra® [likʀa] NM Lycra®; **en ~** Lycra (*épith*)

lymphatique [lɛ̃fatik] ADJ (*Bio*) lymphatic; (*péj*) lethargic, sluggish, lymphatic (*frm*)

lymphe [lɛ̃f] NF lymph

lymphocyte [lɛ̃fɔsit] NM lymphocyte; **~ T4** T4 lymphocyte

lymphoïde [lɛ̃fɔid] ADJ lymphoid

lymphome [lɛ̃fom] NM (*Méd*) lymphoma

lynchage [lɛ̃ʃaʒ] NM (= *exécution, pendaison*) lynching; (= *coups*) beating; **il a fait l'objet d'un ~ médiatique** he was torn to pieces by the media

lyncher [lɛ̃ʃe] ▸conjug 1◂ VT (= *tuer, pendre*) to lynch; (= *malmener*) to beat up; **je vais me faire ~ si je rentre en retard*** they'll lynch *ou* kill me if I come home late

lynx [lɛ̃ks] NM lynx → **œil**

Lyon [ljɔ̃] N Lyon(s)

lyonnais, e [ljɔnɛ, ɛz] **1** ADJ of *ou* from Lyon(s) **2** NM (= *région*) **le Lyonnais** the Lyon(s) region **3** **Lyonnais(e)** NM,F inhabitant *ou* native of Lyon(s)

lyophile [ljɔfil] ADJ lyophilic

lyophilisation [ljɔfilizasjɔ̃] NF lyophilization

lyophiliser [ljɔfilize] ▸conjug 1◂ VT to freeze-dry, lyophilize (SPÉC); **café lyophilisé** freeze-dried coffee

lyre [liʁ] NF lyre

lyrique [liʁik] **1** ADJ **a** (*Poésie*) lyric **b** (*Mus, Théât*) [*ouvrage, représentation, répertoire*] operatic; [*saison*] opera (*épith*); [*ténor, soprano*] lyric, operatic; **l'art ~** opera; **artiste ~** opera singer; **théâtre** *ou* **scène ~** opera house; **comédie/tragédie ~** comic/tragic opera; **spectacle ~** opera → **envolée** **c** (= *exalté*) [*film, style*] lyrical; **il a été ~ sur le sujet** he waxed lyrical on the topic **2** NM **a** (*Mus, Théât*) **le ~** opera **b** (= *poète*) lyric poet

lyriquement [liʁikmɑ̃] ADV lyrically

lyrisme [liʁism] NM (*Littérat, Poésie*) lyricism; (= *exaltation*) **s'exprimer avec ~ sur** to wax lyrical about, enthuse over; **film plein de ~** lyrical film

lys [lis] NM = **lis**

M

M, m¹ [ɛm] NM (= *lettre*) M, m; **M6** *private television channel broadcasting mainly serials and music programmes*

M. (ABRÉV = **Monsieur**) Mr; **M. Dupont** Mr Dupond

m² (ABRÉV = **mètre**) m; **m²** (ABRÉV = **mètre carré**) m², sq. m.; **m³** (ABRÉV = **mètre cube**) m³, cu. m.

m' [m] → **me**

MA [ɛma] NMF (ABRÉV = **maître auxiliaire**) → **maître**

ma [ma] ADJ POSS → **mon**

Maastricht [mastʀiʃt] N **le traité/les accords de ~** the Maastricht Treaty/agreement; **répondre aux critères de ~** to meet the Maastricht criteria (for economic and monetary union)

maastrichtien, -ienne [mastʀiʃtjɛ̃, jɛn] ① ADJ Maastricht (*épith*) ② **Maastrichtien(ne)** NM,F inhabitant *ou* native of Maastricht

maboul, eᵃ⁺† [mabul] ① ADJ crazy* ② NM,F loony*, crackpot*

mac: [mak] NM (= *souteneur*) pimp, ponce* (*Brit*)

macabre [makɑbʀ] ADJ [*histoire, découverte*] macabre, gruesome; [*goûts, humour*] macabre, ghoulish → **danse**

macache:† [makaʃ] ADV nothing doing!*; **~!** **tu ne l'auras pas** nothing doing!* *ou* not bloody likely!* (*Brit*) you're not getting it; **~ (bono)! il n'a pas voulu** nothing doing!* *ou* not a chance!* he wouldn't have it

macadam [makadam] NM [*pierres*] macadam; [*goudron*] tarmac(adam)® (*Brit*), blacktop (*US*); **sur le ~** [*rue*] on the road; [*aéroport*] on the tarmac; **sur le ~ parisien** on the streets of Paris

macadamisage [makadamizaʒ] NM, **macadamisation** [makadamizasjɔ̃] NF (= *empierrement*) macadamization, macadamizing; (= *goudronnage*) tarmacking

macadamiser [makadamize] ▶ conjug 1 ◀ VT (= *empierrer*) to macadamize; (= *goudronner*) to tarmac; **chaussée** *ou* **route macadamisée** macadamized *ou* tarmac road

macaque [makak] NM (*Zool*) macaque; **~ rhésus** rhesus monkey; (*péj*) **qui est ce (vieux) ~?*** who's that ugly (old) ape?:

macareux [makaʀø] NM puffin

macaron [makaʀɔ̃] NM ⓐ (*Culin*) macaroon ⓑ (= *insigne*) (round) badge; (= *autocollant*) (round) sticker; (* = *décoration*) medal, gong*; **~ publicitaire** publicity badge; (*sur voiture*) advertising sticker ⓒ (*Coiffure*) **~s** coils, earphones*

macaroni [makaʀɔni] NM ⓐ (*Culin*) piece of macaroni; **~s** macaroni; **~(s) au gratin** macaroni cheese (*Brit*), macaroni and cheese (*US*) ⓑ (*injurieux = Italien*) **~◊ mangeur de ~s:** Eyeti:‡ (*injurieux*), wop:‡ (*injurieux*)

macaronique [makaʀɔnik] ADJ (*Poésie*) macaronic

maccarthysme [makkaʀtism] NM McCarthyism

maccarthyste [makkaʀtist] ADJ, NMF McCarthyist

macchabée: [makabe] NM stiff:, corpse

macédoine [masedwan] NF ⓐ (*Culin*) **~ de légumes** diced mixed vegetables, macedoine (of vegetables); **~ de fruits** (*gén*) fruit salad; (*en boîte*) fruit cocktail ⓑ (*Géog*) **Macédoine** Macedonia

macédonien, -ienne [masedɔnjɛ̃, jɛn] ① ADJ Macedonian ② **Macédonien(ne)** NM,F Macedonian

macération [maseʀasjɔ̃] NF ⓐ (= *procédé*) maceration, soaking; (= *liquide*) marinade; **pendant leur ~ dans le vinaigre** while they are soaking in vinegar; **arroser la viande avec le cognac de ~** baste the meat with the brandy in which it has been marinated ⓑ (*Rel = mortification*) mortification, scourging (of the flesh); **s'infliger des ~s** to scourge one's body *ou* flesh

macérer [maseʀe] ▶ conjug 6 ◀ ① VT ⓐ (*Culin*) to macerate, soak; **cerises macérées dans l'eau de vie** cherries macerated in brandy ⓑ (*Rel = mortifier*) **~ sa chair** to mortify one's *ou* the flesh ② VI ⓐ (*Culin*) **faire** *ou* **laisser ~** to macerate, soak ⓑ (*péj*) **~ dans son ignorance** to wallow in one's ignorance; **laisser ~ qn (dans son jus)*** (= *le faire attendre*) to let sb stew in his own juice*

macfarlane [makfaʀlan] NM (= *manteau*) Inverness cape

Mach [mak] NM Mach; **voler à ~ 2** to fly at Mach 2; **nombre de ~** Mach (number)

machaon [makaɔ̃] NM swallowtail butterfly

mâche [mɑʃ] NF corn salad, lamb's lettuce

mâchefer [mɑʃfɛʀ] NM clinker (*NonC*), cinders

mâcher [mɑʃe] ▶ conjug 1 ◀ VT [*personne*] to chew; (*avec bruit*) to munch; [*animal*] to chomp; (*Tech*) to chew up; **il faut lui ~ tout le travail** you have to do half his work for him *ou* to spoon-feed him*; **il ne mâche pas ses mots** he doesn't mince his words → **papier**

machette [maʃɛt] NF machete

Machiavel [makjavɛl] NM Machiavelli

machiavélique [makjavelik] ADJ Machiavellian

machiavélisme [makjavelism] NM Machiavell(ian)ism

mâchicoulis [mɑʃikuli] NM machicolation; **à ~** machicolated

machin* [maʃɛ̃] NM ⓐ (= *chose*) (*dont le nom échappe*) what-d'you-call-it*, thingummyjig* (*Brit*), thingamajig* (*US*), whatsit* (*Brit*); (*qu'on n'a jamais vu avant*) thing, contraption; (*qu'on ne prend pas la peine de nommer*) thing; **passe-moi ton ~** give me your thingy*; **les antibiotiques! il faut te méfier de ces ~s-là** antibiotics! you should beware of those things; (*péj*) **espèce de vieux ~!** doddering old fool!* ⓑ (= *personne*) **Machin (chouette)** ◊ **Machin (chose)** what's-his-name*, what-d'you-call-him*, thingumabob*; **hé! Machin!** hey (you), what's-your-name!*; **le père/la mère Machin** Mr/Mrs what's-his-/her-name* → **Machine**

machinal, e (*mpl* **-aux**) [maʃinal, o] ADJ (= *automatique*) mechanical, automatic; (= *instinctif*) automatic, unconscious

machinalement [maʃinalmɑ̃] ADV (= *automatiquement*) mechanically, automatically; (= *instinctivement*) unconsciously; **il regarda ~ sa montre** he looked at his watch without thinking; **j'ai fait ça ~** I did it automatically *ou* without thinking

machination [maʃinasjɔ̃] NF (= *complot*) plot, conspiracy; (= *coup monté*) put-up job*, frame-up*; **je suis victime d'une ~** I've been framed*; **être victime d'une ~ politique** to be a victim of a political conspiracy *ou* of political machinations

Machine* [maʃin] NF (= *personne*) what's-her-name*, what-d'you-call-her*; **hé! ~!** hey! (you) — what's-your-name!* → **machin**

machine [maʃin] ① NF ⓐ (*Tech*) machine; (= *locomotive*) engine, locomotive; (= *avion*) plane, machine; * (= *bicyclette, moto*) bike*, machine; (= *ordinateur*) machine; **il n'est qu'une ~ à penser** he's nothing more than a sort of thinking machine; (* = *corps*) **la ~ est usée/fatiguée** the old body is wearing out/getting tired → **salle** ⓑ (= *lave-linge*) (washing) machine; (= *lessive*) washing; **faire une ~/trois ~s** to do a load of washing/three loads of washing; **ça va en ~** it's machine-washable; **laver/passer qch en** *ou* **à la ~** to wash/put sth in the (washing) machine ⓒ (= *structure*) machine; (= *processus*) machinery; **la ~ politique/parlementaire** the political/parliamentary machine; **la ~ de l'État** the machinery of state; **la ~ humaine** the human body; **la ~ administrative** the bureaucratic machine *ou* machinery; (= *film*) **une grosse ~ hollywoodienne** a Hollywood blockbuster* ⓓ (*Naut*) engine; **faire ~ arrière** (*lit*) to go astern; (*fig*) to back-pedal → **salle** ② **à la machine** LOC ADV **faire qch à la ~** to machine sth, do sth on a machine; **fait à la ~** machine-made, done *ou* made on a machine; **cousu/tricoté à la ~** machine-sewn/-knitted → **taper** ③ COMP ► **machine à adresser** addressing machine ► **machine à affranchir** franking machine ► **machine agricole** agricultural machine ► **machine à café** coffee machine ► **machine à calculer** calculating machine ► **machine à coudre** sewing machine ► **machine à écrire** typewriter ► **machine de guerre** machine of war, instrument of warfare ► **machine infernale**† time bomb, (explosive) device ► **machine à laver** washing machine ► **machine à laver séchante** washer-dryer ► **machine à laver la vaisselle** dishwasher ► **machine simple** simple machine ► **machine à sous** (*de jeu*) slot machine, one-armed bandit (*Brit*), fruit machine (*Brit*); (= *distributeur automatique*) slot *ou* vending machine ► **machine à timbrer** = **machine à affranchir** ► **machine à tisser** power loom ► **machine à** *ou* **de traitement de texte** word processor ► **machine à tricoter** knitting machine ► **machine à vapeur** steam engine ► **machine volante** flying machine

machine-outil (*pl* **machines-outils**) [maʃinuti] NF machine tool

machiner [maʃine] ▸conjug 1 ◀ VT [+ *trahison*] to plot; [+ *complot*] to hatch; **tout était machiné d'avance** the whole thing was fixed beforehand *ou* was prearranged, it was all a put-up job*; **c'est lui qui a tout machiné** he engineered the whole thing; **qu'est-ce qu'il est en train de ~?** what's he cooking up?* *ou* hatching?*

machinerie [maʃinʀi] NF [a] (= *équipement*) machinery, plant (*NonC*) [b] (= *salle*) (*Naut*) engine room; (= *atelier*) machine room

machinisme [maʃinism] NM mechanization

machiniste [maʃinist] NMF (*Théât*) scene shifter, stagehand; (*Ciné*) grip; (*Transport*) driver; **« faire signe au ~ »** ≈ "request stop"

machisme [ma(t)ʃism] NM (= *sexisme*) male chauvinism

machiste [ma(t)ʃist] ADJ (male) chauvinist

macho* [matʃo] [1] ADJ [*comportement*] macho, male chauvinist (*épith*); **il est (un peu) ~** he's a (bit of a) male chauvinist* [2] NM (*d'apparence physique*) macho man; (*sexiste*) male chauvinist; **sale ~!** male chauvinist pig!*

mâchoire [maʃwaʀ] NF (*Anat, Tech, Zool*) jaw; **~s de frein** brake shoes → **bâiller**

mâchonnement [maʃɔnmã] NM chewing; (*Méd*) bruxism (*SPÉC*)

mâchonner [maʃɔne] ▸conjug 1 ◀ VT [*personne*] to chew (at); [*cheval*] to munch; **~ son crayon** to chew *ou* bite one's pencil

mâchouiller* [maʃuje] ▸conjug 1 ◀ VT to chew (away) at *ou* on

mâchurer [maʃyʀe] ▸conjug 1 ◀ VT [a] (= *salir*) [+ *papier, habit*] to stain (black); [+ *visage*] to blacken; (*Typo*) to mackle, blur [b] (*Tech* = *écraser*) to dent [c] (= *mâcher*) to chew

macle¹ [makl] NF (*Bot*) water chestnut

macle² [makl] NF (= *cristal*) twin, macle; (*Hér*) mascle

maclé, e [makle] ADJ [*cristal*] twinned, hemitrope

maçon [masɔ̃] NM [a] (*gén*) builder; (*qui travaille la pierre*) (stone) mason; (*qui pose les briques*) bricklayer; **ouvrier** *ou* **compagnon ~** builder's mate (*Brit*) *ou* helper (*US*) [b] = **franc-maçon**

maçonnage [masɔnaʒ] NM [a] (= *travail*) building; (*en briques*) bricklaying; (*en pierres*) masonry, stonework; (*en briques*) brickwork; (= *revêtement*) facing

maçonne [masɔn] ADJ F → **abeille, fourmi**

maçonner [masɔne] ▸conjug 1 ◀ VT (= *construire*) to build; (= *consolider*) to build up; (= *revêtir*) to face; (= *boucher*) (*avec briques*) to brick up; (*avec pierres*) to block up (with stone)

maçonnerie [masɔnʀi] NF [a] (= *ouvrage*) [*pierres*] masonry, stonework; [*briques*] brickwork; **~ de béton** concrete; **~ en blocage** *ou* **de moellons** rubble work [b] (= *travail*) building; (*avec briques*) bricklaying; **entrepreneur/ entreprise de ~** building contractor/firm; **grosse ~** erection of the superstructure; **petite ~** finishing and interior building [c] = **franc-maçonnerie**

maçonnique [masɔnik] ADJ masonic, Masonic

macoute [makut] ADJ (*terme d'Haïti*) [*groupe, prison*] Macoute; **(tonton) ~** Macoute, member of the Tonton Macoute(s)

macramé [makʀame] NM macramé; **en ~** macramé (*épith*)

macre [makʀ] NF = **macle¹**

macreuse [makʀøz] NF (*Culin*) shoulder of beef; (*Orn*) scoter

macro(-) [makʀo] PRÉF (*dans les composés à trait d'union, le préfixe reste invariable*) macro(-)

macrobiotique [makʀobjɔtik] [1] ADJ macrobiotic [2] NF macrobiotics *sg*

macrocéphale [makʀosefal] ADJ macrocephalic

macrocosme [makʀokɔsm] NM macrocosm

macro-économie [makʀoekɔnɔmi] NF macroeconomics *sg*

macro-économique [makʀoekɔnɔmik] ADJ macroeconomic

macrographie [makʀogʀafi] NF macrography

macro-instruction [makʀoɛ̃stʀyksjɔ̃] NF macro instruction

macromoléculaire [makʀomolekylɛʀ] ADJ macromolecular

macromolécule [makʀomolekyl] NF macromolecule

macrophage [makʀofaʒ] [1] ADJ macrophagic [2] NM macrophage

macrophotographie [makʀofotogʀafi] NF macrophotography

macroscopique [makʀoskopik] ADJ macroscopic

macrostructure [makʀostʀyktyʀ] NF macrostructure

maculage [makylaʒ] NM [a] (*gén*) maculation [b] (*Typo*) (= *action*) offsetting; (= *tache*) offset, set-off

macule [makyl] NF [a] [*encre*] smudge, mackle; (*Typo*) smudge, set-off, blot, mackle [b] (*Astron, Méd*) macula [c] (= *papier*) rough brown (wrapping) paper; (= *feuille intercalaire*) interleaf

maculer [makyle] ▸conjug 1 ◀ VT [a] (= *salir*) to stain (with); **chemise maculée de boue/ sang** shirt spattered *ou* covered with mud/ blood [b] (*Typo*) to mackle, blur

Madagascar [madagaskaʀ] N Madagascar; **République démocratique de ~** Malagasy Republic

Madame [madam] (*pl* **Mesdames** [medam]) NF [a] (*s'adressant à qn*) **bonjour ~** (*gén*) good morning; (*nom connu*) good morning, Mrs X; (*frm*) good morning, Madam; **bonjour Mesdames** good morning; **~, vous avez oublié quelque chose** excuse me *ou* Madam (*frm*) you've forgotten something; (*devant un auditoire*) **Mesdames** ladies; **Mesdames, Mesdemoiselles, Messieurs** ladies and gentlemen; **~ la Présidente** [*société, assemblée*] Madam Chairman; [*gouvernement*] Madam President; **oui, ~ la Générale/la Marquise** yes Mrs X/ Madam; (*Scol*) **~!** please Mrs X!, please Miss!; (*au restaurant*) **et pour (vous) ~?** and for (you) madam?; (*frm*) **~ est servie** dinner is served (Madam); (*iro*) **~ n'est pas contente!** her ladyship *ou* Madam isn't pleased! (*iro*) [b] (*parlant de qn*) **~ X est malade** Mrs X is ill; **~ votre mère**† your dear *ou* good mother; (*frm*) **~ est sortie** Madam *ou* the mistress is not at home; **je vais le dire à ~** (*parlant à un visiteur*) I'll inform Madam (*frm*) *ou* Mrs X; (*parlant à un autre employé de maison*) I'll tell Mrs X *ou* the missus* †; **~ dit que c'est à elle** the lady says it belongs to her; (*en adresse*) **~ la Présidente** Madam Chairman; **veuillez vous occuper de ~** please attend to this lady('s requirements) [c] (*sur une enveloppe*) **~ X** Mrs X; (*Admin*) **~ veuve X** Mrs X, widow of the late John *etc* X; **Mesdames X** the Mrs X; **Mesdames X et Y Mrs** X and Mrs Y; **Monsieur X et ~** Mr and Mrs X; **~ la Maréchale X** Mrs X; **~ la Marquise de X** the Marchioness of X; **Mesdames les employées de la comptabilité** (the ladies on) the

staff of the accounts department [d] (*en-tête de lettre*) Dear Madam; **Chère ~** Dear Mrs X; (*Admin*) **~, Mademoiselle, Monsieur** Dear Sir or Madam; **~ la Maréchale/ Présidente/Duchesse** Dear Madam [e] (*Hist*) Madame (*title given to female members of the French royal family*) [f] (*sans majuscule, pl* **madames** : *souvent péj*) lady; **jouer à la madame** to play the fine lady, put on airs and graces; **toutes ces (belles) madames** all these fine ladies; **c'est une petite madame maintenant** she's quite a (grown-up) young lady now

made in [medin] LOC ADJ (*Comm*) made in; **la machine est ~ Germany** the machine is German-made *ou* made in Germany; **le prestige du ~ France** the prestige of French brand names; (*fig*) **des habitudes ~ USA** typically American habits

Madeleine [madlɛn] NF Magdalen(e), Madel(e)ine → **pleurer**

madeleine [madlɛn] NF (*Culin*) madeleine; (*fig*) **c'est la ~ de Proust** it brings back a flood of memories

Madelon [madlɔ̃] NF **la ~** old French song popular during World War I

Mademoiselle [madmwazɛl] (*pl* **Mesdemoiselles** [medmwazɛl]) NF [a] (*s'adressant à qn*) **bonjour ~** (*gén*) good morning; (*nom connu* : *frm*) good morning, Miss X; **bonjour Mesdemoiselles** good morning ladies; (*jeunes filles*) good morning young ladies; **~, vous avez oublié quelque chose** excuse me miss, you've forgotten something; (*au restaurant*) **et pour vous ~?** and for the young lady?, and for you, miss?; (*devant un auditoire*) **Mesdemoiselles** ladies; **~ n'est pas contente!** her ladyship isn't pleased! [b] (*parlant de qn*) **~ X est malade** Miss X is ill; **~ votre sœur**† your dear sister; (*frm*) **~ est sortie** the young lady (of the house) is out; **je vais le dire à ~** I shall tell Miss X; **~ dit que c'est à elle** the young lady says it's hers [c] (*sur une enveloppe*) **~ X** Miss X; **Mesdemoiselles X** the Misses X; **Mesdemoiselles X et Y** Miss X and Miss Y [d] (*en-tête de lettre*) Dear Madam; **Chère ~** Dear Miss X [e] (*Hist*) Mademoiselle (*title given to the nieces of the French King*)

madère [madɛʀ] [1] NM Madeira (wine) → **sauce** [2] **Madère** NF (*l'île de*) **Madère** Madeira

madériser (se) [maderize] ▸conjug 1 ◀ VPR [*eau-de-vie, vin*] to maderize

Madone [madon] NF [a] (*Art, Rel*) Madonna [b] (= *beauté*) **madone** beautiful woman, Madonna-like woman; **elle a un visage de madone** she has the face of a Madonna

madras [madʀas] [1] NM (= *étoffe*) madras (cotton); (= *foulard*) (madras) scarf [2] **Madras** N Madras

madré, e [madʀe] ADJ [a] (*littér* = *malin*) crafty, wily, sly; (*hum*) **c'est une petite ~e!** she's a crafty *ou* fly* (*Brit*) one! (*hum*) [b] [*bois*] whorled

madrépore [madʀepɔʀ] NM madrepore; **les ~s** madrepores, Madrepora (*SPÉC*)

Madrid [madʀid] N Madrid

madrier [madʀije] NM (*Constr*) beam

madrigal (*pl* **-aux**) [madʀigal, o] NM (*Littérat, Mus*) madrigal; († = *propos galant*) compliment

madrilène [madʀilɛn] [1] ADJ of *ou* from Madrid [2] **Madrilène** NMF inhabitant *ou* native of Madrid

maelström, maelstrom [malstʀɔm] NM (*lit, fig*) maelstrom

maestria [maɛstʀija] NF (masterly) skill, mastery (**à faire qch** in doing sth); **avec ~** brilliantly, in a masterly fashion, with consummate skill

maestro [maɛstʀo] NM (*Mus*) maestro

mafflu, e [mafly] ADJ (*littér*) [*visage, joues*] round, full; [*personne*] chubby(-cheeked *ou* -faced)

maf(f)ia [mafja] NF [a] **la Maf(f)ia** the Maf(f)ia [b] [*bandits, trafiquants*] gang, ring; **c'est une vraie ~!** what a bunch* *ou* shower* (*Brit*) of crooks!; **~ d'anciens élèves** old boy network

maf(f)ieux, -ieuse [mafjø, jøz] ADJ Mafia (*épith*); **pratiques maf(f)ieuses** Mafia-like practices [2] NM,F maf(f)ioso

maf(f)ioso [mafjozo] (*pl* **maf(f)iosi** [mafjozi]) NM maf(f)ioso

magasin [magazɛ̃] [1] NM [a] (= *boutique*) shop, store; (= *entrepôt*) warehouse; **grand ~** department store; **faire** *ou* **courir les ~s** to go shopping, go (a)round *ou* do* the shops; **nous ne l'avons pas en ~** we haven't got it in stock → **chaîne** [b] [*fusil, appareil-photo*] magazine [2] COMP ► **magasin des accessoires** (*Théât*) prop room ► **magasin d'alimentation** grocery store ► **magasin d'armes** armoury ► **magasin (d'articles) de sport** sports shop (*Brit*), sporting goods store (*US*) ► **magasin de confection** (ready-to-wear) dress shop *ou* tailor's, clothing store (*US*) ► **magasin des décors** (*Théât*) scene dock ► **magasins généraux** (*Comm, Jur*) bonded warehouse ► **magasin à grande surface** supermarket, hypermarket (*Brit*) ► **magasin d'habillement** (*Mil*) quartermaster's stores ► **magasin à succursales (multiples)** chain store ► **magasin d'usine** factory shop *ou* outlet ► **magasin de vivres** (*Mil*) quartermaster's stores

magasinage [magazinaʒ] NM [a] (*Comm*) warehousing; **frais de ~** storage costs [b] (*Can*) shopping; **faire son ~** to do one's shopping

magasiner [magazine] ▶ conjug 1 ◀ VI (*Can*) to go shopping

magasinier [magazinje] NM [*usine*] storekeeper, storeman; [*entrepôt*] warehouseman

magazine [magazin] NM [a] (*Presse*) magazine; **~ de luxe** glossy* (magazine) [b] (*TV, Radio*) magazine (programme (*Brit*) *ou* program (*US*)); **~ féminin/pour les jeunes** women's/ children's programme; **~ d'actualités** news magazine; **~ d'information** current affairs programme

magdalénien, -ienne [magdalenjɛ̃, jɛn] [1] ADJ Magdalenian [2] NM **le Magdalénien** the Magdalenian

mage [maʒ] NM (*Antiq, fig*) magus; (= *devin, astrologue*) witch; (*Rel*) **les (trois) Rois ~s** the Magi, the (Three) Wise Men, the Three Kings

Magellan [maʒelɑ̃] NM Magellan; **le détroit de ~** the Strait of Magellan; **les nuages de ~** the Magellanic Clouds

magenta [maʒɛta] ADJ INV, NM magenta

Maghreb [magʀɛb] NM **le ~** the Maghreb, North Africa

maghrébin, e [magʀebɛ̃, in] [1] ADJ of *ou* from the Maghreb *ou* North Africa [2] **Maghrébin(e)** NM,F North African

magicien, -ienne [maʒisjɛ̃, jɛn] NM,F (= *illusionniste*) magician, conjuror; (= *sorcier*) magician; (= *sorcière*) enchantress; (*fig*) wizard, magician; **c'est un ~ du verbe** *ou* **des mots** he's a wizard *ou* magician with words

magie [maʒi] NF magic; **~ blanche/noire** white/black magic; **la ~ du verbe** the magic of words; **comme par ~** like magic, (as if) by magic; **c'est de la ~** it's (like) magic; [*prestidigitateur*] **faire de la ~** to perform *ou* do magic tricks

Maginot [maʒino] NM **la ligne ~** the Maginot Line

magique [maʒik] ADJ [*mot, baguette, pouvoir*] magic; (= *enchanteur*) [*spectacle*] magical → **lanterne**

magiquement [maʒikmɑ̃] ADV magically

magister† [maʒistɛʀ] NM (*village*) schoolmaster; (*péj*) pedant

magistère [maʒistɛʀ] NM [a] (*Univ*) diploma taken over 3 years after completing 2 years at university, usually in vocational subjects, ≈ master's degree [b] (*Rel*) magisterium [c] (*Alchimie*) magistery

magistral, e (*mpl* **-aux**) [maʒistʀal, o] ADJ [a] [*œuvre*] masterly, brilliant; [*réussite, démonstration*] brilliant, magnificent; [*adresse*] masterly; **elle est ~e dans le rôle de Phèdre** she's brilliant as Phèdre; **son interprétation du concerto fut ~e** he gave a brilliant performance of the concerto [b] [*ton*] authoritative, masterful; (*Univ*) **cours ~** lecture; **enseignement ~** lecturing [c] (*intensif*) [*victoire, réussite*] magnificent [d] (*Pharm*) magistral [e] (*Tech*) **ligne ~e** magistral line

magistralement [maʒistʀalmɑ̃] ADV brilliantly, magnificently; **réussir ~ qch** to make a brilliant job of sth

magistrat [maʒistʀa] NM (*Jur*) (*gén*) magistrate; (= *juge*) judge; **~ du parquet** public prosecutor (*Brit*), prosecuting *ou* district attorney (*US*); **~ du siège** judge; **~ municipal** town councillor; **c'est le premier ~ de France/du département** he holds the highest public office in France/the department; **~ militaire** judge advocate

magistrature [maʒistʀatyʀ] NF [a] (*Jur*) magistracy, magistrature; **la ~ assise** *ou* **du siège** the judges, the bench; **la ~ debout** *ou* **du parquet** the state prosecutors; **entrer dans la ~** to be appointed a judge (*ou* a state prosecutor) [b] (*Admin, Pol*) public office; **la ~ suprême** *ou* **highest office** the supreme *ou* highest office

magma [magma] NM (*Chim, Géol*) magma; (= *mélange*) jumble, muddle

magmatique [magmatik] ADJ magmatic

magnanime [maɲanim] ADJ magnanimous; **se montrer ~** to show magnanimity

magnanimement [maɲanimmɑ̃] ADV magnanimously

magnanimité [maɲanimite] NF magnanimity

magnat [maɲa] NM tycoon, magnate; **~ de la presse/de la télévision** press/television baron *ou* lord *ou* tycoon; **~ de l'audiovisuel** broadcasting tycoon; **~ du pétrole** oil tycoon *ou* magnate

magner (se)* [maɲe] ▶ conjug 1 ◀ VPR to get a move on*, hurry up; **on a intérêt à se ~** we'd better get cracking*; **magne-toi (le train** *ou* **le popotin)!** get a move on!*, get moving!*; **magne-toi le cul!**** shift your arse!* (*Brit*) *ou* ass!* (*US*)

magnésie [maɲezi] NF magnesia

magnésien, -ienne [maɲezjɛ̃, jɛn] ADJ [*roche, magma*] magnesian; **déficit ~** magnesium deficiency

magnésium [maɲezjɔm] NM magnesium → **éclair**

magnétique [maɲetik] ADJ (*Phys, fig*) magnetic → **bande¹**

magnétisable [maɲetizabl] ADJ [a] (*Phys*) magnetizable [b] (= *sujet à l'hypnose*) hypnotizable

magnétisation [maɲetizasjɔ̃] NF [a] (*Phys*) magnetization [b] (= *hypnose*) mesmerization, hypnotization

magnétiser [maɲetize] ▶ conjug 1 ◀ VT [a] (*Phys*) to magnetize [b] (= *hypnotiser*) to mesmerize, hypnotize

magnétiseur, -euse [maɲetizœʀ, øz] NM,F (= *hypnotiseur*) hypnotizer; (= *guérisseur*) magnetic healer

magnétisme [maɲetism] NM (= *charme, Phys*) magnetism; (= *hypnotisme*) hypnotism, mesmerism; **~ terrestre** terrestrial magnetism; **le ~ d'un grand homme** the magnetism *ou* charisma of a great man

magnétite [maɲetit] NF lodestone, magnetite

magnéto¹* [maɲeto] NM ABRÉV = **magnétophone**

magnéto² [maɲeto] NF (*Élec*) magneto

magnétocassette [maɲetokasɛt] NM cassette player *ou* recorder

magnétoélectrique [maɲetoelektʀik] ADJ magnetoelectric

magnétophone [maɲetɔfɔn] NM tape recorder; **~ à cassette(s)** cassette recorder; **enregistré au ~** (tape-)recorded, taped

magnétoscope [maɲetɔskɔp] NM (= *appareil*) video (tape *ou* cassette) recorder, VCR; **enregistrer au ~** to video(-tape)

magnétoscoper [maɲetɔskɔpe] ▶ conjug 1 ◀ VT to video(-tape)

magnificence [maɲifisɑ̃s] NF (*littér*) [a] (= *faste*) magnificence, splendour [b] (= *prodigalité*) munificence (*littér*), lavishness

magnifier [maɲifje] ▶ conjug 7 ◀ VT (*littér*) (= *louer*) to magnify (*littér*), glorify; (= *idéaliser*) to idealize

magnifique [maɲifik] ADJ [*appartement, repas*] magnificent, sumptuous; [*cortège*] splendid, magnificent; [*cadeau, réception*] magnificent, lavish; [*femme, fleur*] gorgeous, superb; [*paysage, temps*] magnificent, gorgeous; [*projet, situation*] magnificent, marvellous; **~!** fantastic!, great!*; **il a été ~ hier soir!** he was magnificent *ou* fantastic last night!; **Soliman/Laurent le Magnifique** Suleiman/Lorenzo the Magnificent

magnifiquement [maɲifikmɑ̃] ADV magnificently

magnitude [maɲityd] NF (*Astron, Géol*) magnitude; **séisme de ~ 7 sur l'échelle de Richter** earthquake measuring 7 *ou* of magnitude 7 on the Richter scale

magnolia [maɲɔlja] NM magnolia

magnum [magnɔm] NM magnum

magot [mago] NM [a] (= *singe*) Barbary ape, magot [b] (= *figurine*) magot [c]* (= *somme d'argent*) pile (of money)*, packet*; (= *argent volé*) loot; (= *économies*) savings, nest egg; **ils ont amassé un joli ~** (*gén*) they've made a nice little pile* *ou* packet*; (*économies*) they've got a tidy sum put by *ou* a nice little nest egg; **où ont-ils caché le ~?** where did they stash* the loot?

magouillage* [magujaʒ] NM, **magouille*** [maguj] NF (*péj*) scheming (*péj*); **c'est le roi de la magouille** he's a born schemer; **ça sent la magouille** there's some funny business* going on; **~ électoral** pre-election scheming; **magouilles politiques** political skulduggery; **magouilles financières** financial wheeling and dealing* (*NonC*), sharp practice* (*NonC*) (*Brit*); **sombre magouille** dirty bit of business

magouiller* [maguje] ▶ conjug 1 ◀ [1] VI (*péj*) to wheel and deal*; **il a dû ~ pour avoir le permis de construire** he had to do a bit of wheeling and dealing* to get planning permission [2] VT **qu'est-ce qu'il magouille?** what's he up to?*

magouilleur, -euse* [magujœʀ, øz] [1] ADJ (*péj*) crafty* [2] NM,F (*péj*) schemer (*péj*), crafty operator* (*Brit*)

magret [magʀɛ] NM **~ (de canard)** fillet of duck, duck breast

magyar, e [magjaʀ] [1] ADJ Magyar [2] **Magyar(e)** NM,F Magyar

mahara(d)jah [maaʀa(d)ʒa] NM Maharajah

maharani [ma(a)ʀani] NF, **maharané** [maaʀane] NF Maharanee

mahatma [maatma] NM mahatma

mah-jong (*pl* **mah-jongs**) [maʒɔ̃ɡ] NM mah-jong(g)

Mahomet [maɔmɛt] NM Mahomet, Mohammed

mahométan, -ane† [maɔmetɑ̃, an] ADJ Mahometan, Mohammedan

mahométisme† [maɔmetism] NM Mohammedanism

mahonia [maɔnja] NM mahonia

mahorais, e [maɔʀɛ, ɛz] [1] ADJ of ou from Mayotte [2] **Mahorais(e)** NM,F inhabitant ou native of Mayotte

mahous* [maus] ADJ = **maous**

mai [mɛ] NM May; **le joli mois de ~** the merry month of May; *pour autres locutions voir* **septembre** *et* **premier**

MAI 68

Widespread unrest in 1968, both in French industry and among students, resulted in huge demonstrations in May and culminated in a general strike. The events were perceived both as a challenge to the established order and a utopian cry for freedom, though the government was not in fact overthrown and order soon returned. The term "soixante-huitard(e)" literally means a person who participated in the events, but used as an adjective it also refers to the kind of anarchistic and utopian ideals expressed by many of the demonstrators. These ideals are also effectively summed up in their best-known slogan, "sous les pavés, la plage" (literally, "under the paving stones there's a beach").

---

maie [mɛ] NF (= *huche*) bread box; (*pour pétrir*) dough trough

maïeutique [majøtik] NF maieutics sg

maigre [mɛgʀ] [1] ADJ [a] [*personne*] thin, skinny (*péj*); [*animal*] thin, scraggy; [*visage, joue*] thin, lean; [*membres*] thin, scrawny (*péj*); skinny (*péj*); **~ comme un clou** ou **un coucou*** as thin as a rake ou a lath (*Brit*) ou a rail (*US*) [b] (*Culin*: *après n*) [*bouillon*] clear; [*viande*] lean; [*fromage*] low-fat [c] (*Rel*) **repas ~** meal without meat; **faire ~ (le vendredi)** (*gén*) to abstain from meat (on Fridays); (= *manger du poisson*) to eat fish (on Fridays); **le vendredi est un jour ~** people don't eat meat on Fridays [d] (= *peu important*) [*profit, revenu*] meagre, small, slim; [*ration, salaire*] meagre, poor; [*ressources, moyens, budget*] meagre, scanty; [*résultat*] poor; [*exposé, conclusion*] sketchy, skimpy, slight; [*espoir, chance*] slim, slight; [*public*] sparse; **comme dîner, c'est un peu ~** it's a bit of a skimpy ou meagre dinner, it's not much of a dinner; **c'est une ~ consolation** it's small consolation, it's cold comfort [e] (= *peu épais*) [*végétation*] thin, sparse; [*récolte, terre*] poor; **un ~ filet d'eau** a thin trickle of water; (*hum*) **avoir le cheveu ~** to be a bit thin on top [f] (*Typo*) **caractère ~** light-faced letter [2] NMF **grand/petit ~** tall/small thin person; **les gros et les ~s** fat people and thin people; **c'est une fausse ~** she looks deceptively thin [3] NM [a] (*Culin*) (= *viande*) lean meat; (= *jus*) thin gravy [b] (*Typo*) light face; **en ~** in light face [c] [*poisson*] meagre

maigrelet, -ette [mɛgʀəlɛ, ɛt] [1] ADJ thin, scrawny, skinny; **gamin ~** skinny little kid* [2] NM **un petit ~** a skinny little chap ou fellow ou man

maigrement [mɛgʀəmɑ̃] ADV poorly, meagrely; **être ~ payé** to be badly ou poorly paid

maigreur [mɛgʀœʀ] NF [a] [*personne*] thinness, leanness; [*animal*] thinness, scrawniness, scragginess; [*membre*] thinness, scrawniness, skinniness; **il est d'une ~!** he's so thin! ou skinny!; **d'une ~ excessive** ou **extrême** extremely thin, emaciated [b] [*végétation*] thinness, sparseness; [*sol*] poverty; [*profit*] meagreness, smallness, scantiness; [*salaire*] meagreness, poorness; [*réponse, exposé*] sketchiness, poverty; [*preuve, sujet, auditoire*] thinness

maigrichon, -onne* [mɛgʀiʃɔ̃, ɔn], **maigriot, -iotte*** [mɛgʀijo, ijɔt] ADJ = **maigrelet**

maigrir [megʀiʀ] ▶conjug 2◀ [1] VI to grow ou get thinner, lose weight; **je l'ai trouvé maigri** I thought he had got thinner ou he was thinner ou he had lost weight; **il a maigri de visage** his face has got thinner; **il a maigri de 5 kg** he has lost 5 kg; **régime pour ~** reducing ou slimming (*Brit*) diet; **se faire ~** to diet (to lose weight), slim (*Brit*); **faire ~ qn** to make sb lose weight [2] VT [a] **~ qn** [*vêtement*] to make sb look slim(mer); [*maladie, régime*] to make sb lose weight [b] (*Tech*) to thin

mail [maj] NM [a] (= *promenade*) mall†, tree-lined walk [b]†† (= *jeu, terrain*) (pall-)mall; (= *maillet*) mall

mailing [meliŋ] NM mailing; **faire un ~** to do a mailing ou a mailshot (*Brit*)

maillage [majaʒ] NM [a] (*Pêche*) [*filet*] meshing [b] (= *quadrillage*) **un système ferroviaire au ~ très lâche** a very loose railway network; **le ~ complet du territoire avec des centres de soins** the creation of a network of clinics throughout the country; **le ~ de la région par l'entreprise est insuffisant** the company has not set up enough outlets in the region

maillant [majɑ̃] ADJ M **filet ~** gill net

maille [maj] NF [a] (*Couture*) stitch; [*tissu, tricot*] ~ **qui a filé** stitch which has run; [*bas*] **filée** run, ladder (*Brit*); **~ (à l')endroit** plain (stitch); **~ (à l')envers** purl (stitch); **une ~ à l'endroit, une ~ à l'envers** knit one, purl one; **tissu à fines ~s** fine-knit material; **la ~** (= *tissu*) tricot; (= *secteur économique*) the knitwear industry [b] [*filet*] mesh; (*lit, fig*) **passer entre** ou **à travers les ~s (du filet)** to slip through the net; **à larges/fines ~s** wide/fine mesh (*épith*) [c] [*armure, grillage*] link → **cotte** [d] (*loc*) **avoir ~ à partir avec qn** to get into trouble with sb, have a brush with sb

maillé, e [maje] (*ptp de* **mailler**) ADJ [a] [*organisation*] network-based; **réseau ~** dense ou closely-knit network; **au niveau transports en commun, la région est maintenant ~e** the area now has an integrated public transport network [b] [*oiseau*] speckled; [*poisson*] netted

maillechort [majʃɔʀ] NM nickel silver

mailler [maje] ▶conjug 1◀ VT [a] (*Naut*) [+ *chaîne*] to shackle; [+ *filet*] to mesh [b] [+ *région*] to create a network in [c] (*Helv* = *tordre*) to twist; **se ~ de rire** to be doubled up ou bent double with laughter

maillet [majɛ] NM mallet

mailloche [majɔʃ] NF (*Tech*) beetle, maul; (*Mus*) bass drumstick

maillon [majɔ̃] NM [a] (*lit, fig = anneau*) link; **il n'est qu'un ~ de la chaîne** he's just one link in the chain; **c'est le ~ faible** it's the weak link (in the chain) [b] (= *petite maille*) small stitch

maillot [majo] [1] NM [a] (*gén*) vest; [*danseur*] leotard; [*footballeur*] (football) shirt ou jersey; [*coureur, basketteur*] singlet; **s'épiler le ~** to do one's bikini line; (*Cyclisme*) **~ jaune** yellow jersey (*worn by the leading cyclist in the Tour de France*); **il est ~ jaune** he's the leader in the Tour (de France) [b] [*bébé*] swaddling clothes (*Hist*), baby's wrap; **enfant** ou **bébé au ~**† babe in arms [2] COMP ▶ **maillot de bain** [*homme*] swimming ou bathing (*Brit*) trunks; [*femme*] swimming ou bathing (*Brit*) costume, swimsuit; **~ de bain une pièce/deux pièces** one-piece/two-piece swimsuit ▶ **maillot de corps** vest (*Brit*), undershirt (*US*)

---
main [mɛ̃]

[1] NOM FÉMININ	[3] COMPOSÉS
[2] ADVERBE	

[1] NOM FÉMININ

[a] [Anat] hand; **donner la ~ à qn** ou **tenir la ~ à** ou **de qn** to hold sb's hand; **donne-moi la ~ pour traverser** give me your hand ou let me

hold your hand to cross the street; **ils se tenaient (par) la ~** ou **se donnaient la ~** they were holding hands; (*fig*) **tu es aussi maladroit que moi, on peut se donner la ~** you're as clumsy as me, we're two of a kind; **il entra le chapeau à la ~** he came in with his hat in his hand; **il me salua de la ~** he waved to me; **il me fit adieu de la ~** he waved goodbye to me; **il m'a pris le plateau des ~s** he took the tray from me; **prendre qch des** ou **à deux ~s/de la ~ gauche** to take sth with both hands/with one's left hand; **à ~ droite/gauche** on the right-/left-hand side; **applaudir/signer des deux ~s** (*avec enthousiasme*) to applaud/sign enthusiastically; (*Ftbl*) **il y a ~!** hands!, hand ball!; **regarde, sans les ~s!** look, no hands!; **les ~s en l'air!** ◊ **haut les ~s!** hands up!, stick 'em up!*; **j'en mettrais ma ~ au feu** ou **ma ~ à couper** I'd stake my life on it; (*fig*) **passer la ~ dans le dos à qn** to butter sb up*; **ils se passaient la ~ dans le dos** they were patting one another on the back; (*hum*) **la ~ sur le cœur** [*déclarer, protester*] hand on heart; **il va prendre ma ~ sur la figure!*** he's going to get a smack in the face!; **il lui a mis la ~ aux fesses*** ou **au panier***, ou **au cul**** he groped her behind*; (*lit, fig*) **prendre qn par la ~** to take sb by the hand; **tu n'as qu'à te prendre par la ~ si tu veux que ça soit terminé plus vite** you'll just have to sort things out yourself if you want it finished more quickly; **prends-toi par la ~ si tu n'es pas content** do it yourself if you're not happy ► **lever, serrer, tendre** *etc*

♦ **de la main à la main** [*payer, verser*] directly (*without receipt*)

♦ **de main en main** [*passer, circuler*] from hand to hand; **cette moto a passé de ~ en ~ depuis cinq ans** this motorbike has had a number of owners in the past five years

♦ **en main**: **il se promenait, micro en ~** he walked around holding the microphone ou with the microphone in his hand → **clé, montre**

♦ **(la) main dans la main** (*contact physique, collaboration*) hand in hand; (*complicité*) hand in glove

♦ **les mains dans les poches** (*lit*) with one's hands in one's pockets; (*fig = sans rien préparer*) unprepared

♦ **la main dans le sac**: **on l'a pris la ~ dans le sac** he was caught red-handed ou in the act

♦ **sous la main**: **avoir tout sous la ~** to have everything to hand ou at hand ou handy; **j'ai pris ce qui m'est tombé sous la ~** I took whatever came to hand; **ce papier m'est tombé sous la ~** I came across this paper

[b] = **instrument de l'action, du choix** hand; **être adroit/maladroit de ses ~s** to be clever/clumsy with one's hands; **il ne sait rien faire de ses ~s** he's no good ou he's useless with his hands; **d'une ~ experte** with an expert hand; **dans cette affaire, on a cru voir la ~ de la CIA** the CIA was believed to have had a hand in ou some involvement in this affair; **mettre la dernière ~ à qch** to put the finishing touches to sth; **il a eu la ~ heureuse**: **il a choisi le numéro gagnant** he was lucky — he picked the winning number; **en engageant cet assistant, on a vraiment eu la ~ heureuse** when we took on that assistant we really picked a winner; **avoir la ~ légère** (*pour toucher, masser*) to have a light touch; (*pour diriger*) to be lenient; **tu as eu la ~ légère avec le sel** you didn't put enough salt in; **il a la ~ leste** he's free ou quick with his hands; **laisser les ~s libres à qn** to give sb a free hand ou rein; **avoir les ~s liées** to have one's hands tied; **ce boucher a toujours la ~ lourde** this butcher always gives ou cuts you more than you ask for; **le juge a eu la ~ lourde** the judge gave him (ou her *etc*) a stiff sentence; **j'ai eu la ~ lourde avec le sel** I overdid the salt; **mettre la ~ à la pâte** to lend a hand, muck in*; **il n'y va pas de ~ morte** he doesn't pull his punches;

avoir la **~ verte** to have green fingers (*Brit*), have a green thumb (*US*) → **plein, quatre**

♦ **à la main** : fait à la **~** (*gén*) handmade; [*artisanat*] handmade, handcrafted; écrit à la **~** handwritten; **cousu à la ~** hand-sewn, hand-stitched

♦ **à main armée** : vol/attaque à **~** armée armed robbery/attack

♦ **à main levée** [*vote, voter*] on *ou* by a show of hands; [*dessin, dessiner*] freehand

♦ **à mains nues** [*boxer*] without gloves; [*combattre*] with one's bare fists *ou* hands; [*combat*] bare-knuckle, bare-fisted

♦ **à sa** (*ou* **ma** *etc*) **main** : il faudrait être à sa **~** pour réparer ce robinet you'd have to be able to get at this tap properly to mend it; **je ne suis pas à ma ~** I can't get a proper hold *ou* grip

♦ **de la main de** : dessin de la **~** de Cézanne drawing by Cézanne; **c'était** (écrit) de sa **~** it was in his hand(writing); **une lettre signée de sa ~** a personally signed letter, a letter signed in his own hand

♦ **de main de maître** masterfully, expertly

♦ **en sous main** → **sous-main**

[c] = *symbole d'autorité, d'aide, de possession* hand; la **~** de Dieu/du destin the hand of God/ of fate; **il lui faut une ~ ferme** he needs a firm hand; **une ~ de fer dans un gant de velours** an iron hand in a velvet glove; **avoir la haute ~ sur qch** to have supreme control of sth; **trouver une ~ secourable** to find a helping hand; **donner la ~ à qn** (= *l'aider*) to give sb a hand; **se donner la ~** (= *s'aider*) to give one another a helping hand; **tomber aux** *ou* **dans les ~s de l'ennemi** to fall into the hands of the enemy *ou* into enemy hands; **dans** *ou* **entre des ~s étrangères** in foreign hands; **être en** (de) **bonnes ~s** to be in good hands; **en ~ sûres** in safe hands; (*Fin*) **en ~ tierce** in escrow; **les ~s vides** empty-handed; **faire ~ basse sur qch** (*gén*) to help o.s. to sth; (*et prendre la fuite*) to run off *ou* make off with sth; **ils font ~ basse sur nos plus beaux hôtels** they're buying up all our best hotels; **mettre la ~ sur** [*+ objet, livre*] to lay (one's) hands on; [*+ coupable*] to lay hands on, collar*; **je ne peux pas mettre la ~ sur mon passeport** I can't lay my hands on my passport; **si vous portez la ~ sur elle, je ...** if you lay a hand on her, I'll ... → **opération, prêter, tendre**

♦ **coup de main*** (= *aide*) (helping) hand, help; **donne-moi un coup de ~** give me a hand → **d**

♦ **de première/seconde main** [*information, témoignage*] firsthand/secondhand; (*Comm*) **acheter une voiture de première ~** to buy a car secondhand (*which has only had one previous owner*); **il a obtenu ces renseignements de seconde ~** he got this information second-hand; **travailler sur des ouvrages de seconde ~** [*chercheur*] to work from secondary sources

♦ **en main** (= *non disponible*) : **ce livre est en ~** this book is in use *ou* is out

(= *sous contrôle*) **avoir une voiture bien en ~** to have the feel of a car; **avoir la situation** (bien) **en ~** to have the situation (well) in hand *ou* (well) under control; **prendre qn/qch en ~** to take sb/sth in hand; **il lui a fallu deux heures pour prendre en ~ sa nouvelle voiture** it took him a couple of hours to get used to *ou* to get the feel of his new car; **la prise en ~ de l'organisation par des professionnels** the takeover of the organization by professionals

♦ **en mains propres** : **il me l'a remis en ~s propres** he handed *ou* gave it to me personally

♦ **entre les mains de** : être entre les **~s de qn** to be in sb's hands; **la décision est entre ses ~s** the decision is in his hands *ou* lies with him; **je l'ai mis entre les ~s d'un bon entraîneur** I put him in the hands of a good coach; **ce livre**

n'est pas à mettre entre toutes les **~s** this book is not suitable for the general public

[d] = *manière, habileté* **se faire la ~** to get one's hand in; **garder la ~** to keep one's hand in; **perdre la ~** to lose one's touch; **on reconnaît la ~ de l'artiste/de l'auteur** it is easy to recognize the artist's/the writer's touch

♦ **coup de main** (= *habileté*) knack; **avoir le coup de ~** (pour faire qch) to have the knack (of doing sth); **j'ai dû m'y reprendre à plusieurs fois avant d'avoir le coup de ~** I had to try several times before getting the hang of it *ou* the knack; **pour la mayonnaise, tout est dans le coup de ~** there's a knack to making mayonnaise

(= *attaque*) raid → **homme**

[f] † = *permission d'épouser* **demander/obtenir la ~ d'une jeune fille** to ask for/win a girl's hand (in marriage); **accorder la ~ de sa fille à qn** to give sb one's daughter's hand in marriage

[g] Cartes hand; **avoir la ~** (= *jouer le premier*) to lead; (= *distribuer les cartes*) to deal; **perdre la ~** to lose the lead; **passer la ~ à qn** (*lit*) to lead to sb; (*fig*) **à 65 ans, il est temps qu'il passe la ~** at 65 it's time he made way for someone else *ou* stood down; (*Casino*) **la ~ passe!** next deal!; (*Casino*) **faire la ~** être à la **~** to have the deal

[h] Couture **première ~** head seamstress → **petit**

[i] Comm [*papier*] ≈ quire (*25 sheets*)

[j] Imprim bulk

[k] par analogie de forme [*bananes*] hand, bunch

[2] ADVERBE

entièrement fait ~ (*gén*) entirely handmade; (*artisanat*) entirely handmade *ou* handcrafted; **cousu ~** (*lit*) hand-sewn, hand-stitched; (*fig*) **c'est du cousu ~*** it's first-rate *ou* top-quality stuff

[3] COMPOSÉS

▸ **la main chaude** (*Jeux*) hot cockles
▸ **main courante** (= *câble*) handrail; (*Comm*) rough book, daybook; (*Police*) **faire établir une ~ courante** to notify the police of a complaint
▸ **main de Fatma** hand of Fatima ▸ **main de ressort** (*Aut*) dumb iron

---

mainate [mɛnat] NM myna(h) bird

main-d'œuvre (*pl* **mains-d'œuvre**) [mɛ̃dœvʀ] NF (= *travail*) labour (*Brit*), labor (*US*), man-power; (= *personnes*) workforce, labour (*Brit*) *ou* labor (*US*) force; **embaucher de la ~** to hire workers; **~ qualifiée** skilled labour; **la ~ locale disponible** the local available workforce *ou* labour force; **industries de ~** labour-intensive industries; **il m'a compté deux heures de ~** he charged me two hours' labour

main(-)forte [mɛ̃fɔʀt] NF INV → **prêter**

mainlevée [mɛ̃l(ə)ve] NF (*Jur*) withdrawal; (*Fin*) **~ d'hypothèque** release of mortgage

mainmise [mɛ̃miz] NF (= *prise de contrôle*) take-over; (= *emprise*) grip; (*autoritaire*) strangle-hold; **la ~ de l'Église sur l'éducation** the Church's stranglehold on education; **avoir la ~ sur** to have a grip *ou* a stranglehold on

maint, mainte [mɛ̃, mɛ̃t] ADJ (*frm*) (a great *ou* good) many + *npl*, many a + *nsg*; **~ exemple** many an example; **~s exemples** many *ou* numerous examples; **à ~es reprises** ◊ (**~es et**) **~es fois** time and (time) again, many a time; **en ~ endroit** in many places; **en ~es occasions** on numerous *ou* many occasions

maintenance [mɛ̃t(ə)nɑ̃s] NF maintenance, servicing; **contrat de ~** maintenance *ou* service contract; **assurer la ~ d'une machine** to service a machine

▼ **maintenant** [mɛ̃t(ə)nɑ̃] ADV [a] (= *en ce moment*) now; **que fait-il ~?** what's he doing

now?; **il doit être arrivé ~** he must have arrived by now; **~ qu'il est grand** now that he's bigger; **à toi ~** it's your turn now → **dès, jusque, partir¹**

[b] (= *ce moment*) now, by now; **ils devaient ~ chercher à se nourrir** they now had to try and find something to eat; **ils étaient ~ très fatigués** by now they were very tired; **ils marchaient ~ depuis deux heures** (by) now they had been walking for two hours

[c] (= *actuellement*) today, nowadays; **les jeunes de ~** young people nowadays *ou* today

[d] (= *ceci dit*) now (then); **~ ce que j'en dis, c'est pour ton bien** now (then) what I say is for your own good; **il y a un cadavre, certes, ~, y a-t-il un crime?** we're agreed there's a corpse, now the question is, is there a crime?

[e] (= *à partir de ce moment*) from now on; **il l'ignorait ? ~ il le saura** he didn't know that? he will now *ou* from now on

maintenir [mɛ̃t(ə)niʀ] ▸ conjug 22 ◂ [1] VT [a] (= *soutenir, contenir*) [*+ édifice*] to hold *ou* keep up, support; [*+ cheville, os*] to give support to, support; **~ qch fixe/en équilibre** to keep *ou* hold sth in position/balanced; **les oreillers le maintiennent assis** the pillows keep him in a sitting position *ou* keep him sitting up; **~ la tête hors de l'eau** to keep one's head above water; **~ les prix** to keep prices steady *ou* in check

[b] (= *garder* : *gén*) to keep; [*+ statu quo, tradition*] to maintain, preserve, uphold; [*+ décision*] to maintain, stand by, uphold; [*+ candidature*] to maintain; **~ qn en vie** to keep sb alive; **~ des troupes en Europe** to keep troops in Europe; **~ l'ordre/la paix** to keep *ou* maintain law and order/the peace; **~ qn en poste** to keep sb on, keep sb at *ou* in his job; **pour ~ les personnes âgées à leur domicile** to enable old people to go on living in their own homes

[c] (= *affirmer*) to maintain; **je l'ai dit et je le maintiens!** I've said it and I'm sticking to it! *ou* I'm standing by it!; **~ que ...** to maintain *ou* hold that ...

[2] **se maintenir** VPR [*temps*] to stay fair, hold; [*amélioration*] to persist; [*préjugé*] to live on, persist, remain; [*malade*] to hold one's own; **se ~ en bonne santé** to keep in good health, manage to keep well; **les prix se maintiennent** prices are keeping *ou* holding steady; **cet élève devrait se ~ dans la moyenne** this pupil should be able to keep up with the middle of the class; **comment ça va ? — ça se maintient*** how are you doing? — bearing up* *ou* so-so* *ou* not too badly; **se ~ en équilibre sur un pied/sur une poutre** to balance on one foot/on a beam; **~ au pouvoir** to remain in power; (*Pol*) **le candidat s'est maintenu au deuxième tour** the candidate stayed through to the second round

maintien [mɛ̃tjɛ̃] NM [a] (= *sauvegarde*) [*tradition*] preservation, upholding, maintenance; **assurer le ~ de** [*+ tradition*] to maintain, pre-serve, uphold; **le ~ de troupes/de l'ordre** the maintenance of troops/of law and order; **ils veulent le ~ du pouvoir d'achat** they want to keep *ou* maintain their purchasing power; **qu'est-ce qui a pu justifier le ~ de sa décision/candidature?** what(ever) were his reasons for standing by his decision/for maintaining his candidature?; **ils souhaitent le ~ des personnes âgées à domicile** they want old people to be looked after *ou* cared for in their own homes [b] (= *soutien*) sup-port; **ce soutien-gorge assure un bon ~ de la poitrine** this bra gives firm support [c] (= *posture*) bearing, deportment; **leçon de ~** lesson in deportment; **professeur de ~** teacher of de-portment

maire [mɛʀ] NM mayor; (*hum*) **passer devant**

(monsieur) **le ~** to tie the knot*, get married → **adjoint, écharpe**

MAIRE

Each French "commune" has its **maire**, *elected by the "conseil municipal" (or, in Paris, Lyons and Marseille, by the "conseil d'arrondissement"). The "maire" is responsible for organizing council meetings and ensuring that the decisions of the "conseil municipal" are carried out. He or she has a wide range of administrative duties as the chief civic representative of the "commune", including maintaining public order through the municipal police. As a representative of the State, he or she is empowered to perform marriages (which take place in the "salle des mariages" at the "mairie") and is responsible for keeping the local register of births, marriages and deaths.*

The **maire** *is assisted in his or her functions by one or several "adjoints" (deputies). Note that a "député-maire" is not a deputy mayor but a* **maire** *who is also a member of parliament. →* CONSEIL ; COMMUNE ; DÉPUTÉ

---

mairesse† [mɛʀɛs] NF mayoress

mairie [meʀi] NF (= *bâtiment*) town hall, city hall; (= *administration*) town council, municipal corporation; (= *charge*) mayoralty, office of mayor; **la ~ a décidé que ...** the (town) council has decided that ... → MAIRIE

▼ **mais¹** [mɛ] ① CONJ ⓐ (*objection, restriction, opposition*) but; **ce n'est pas bleu ~ (bien) mauve** it isn't blue, it's (definitely) mauve; **non seulement il boit ~ (encore** *ou* **en outre) il bat sa femme** not only does he drink but on top of that *ou* even worse he beats his wife; **il est peut-être le patron ~ tu as quand même des droits** he may be the boss but you've still got your rights; **il est parti ? ~ tu m'avais promis qu'il m'attendrait !** he has left? but you promised he'd wait for me!

ⓑ (*renforcement*) **je n'ai rien mangé hier, ~ vraiment rien** I ate nothing at all yesterday, absolutely nothing; **tu me crois ? — ~ oui** *ou* **bien sûr** *ou* **certainement** do you believe me? — (but) of course *ou* course I do!; **je te jure que c'est vrai !** but I swear it's true!; **~ si, je veux bien !** but of course I agree!, sure, I agree!; **~ ne te fais pas de soucis !** don't you worry!; **je vous dérange ? — pas du tout** am I disturbing you? — not at all; **je croyais qu'il serait content, ~ pas du tout !** I thought he'd be happy — but no!

ⓒ (*transition, surprise*) **~ qu'arriva-t-il ?** but what happened (then)?; **~ alors qu'est-ce qui est arrivé ?** well then *ou* for goodness' sake what happened?; **~ dites-moi, c'est intéressant tout ça !** well, well *ou* well now that's all very interesting!; **~ j'y pense, vous n'avez pas déjeuné** by the way I've just thought, you haven't had any lunch; **~, vous pleurez** good Lord *ou* good gracious, you're crying; **~ enfin, tant pis !** well, too bad!

ⓓ (*protestation, indignation*) **ah ~ ! il verra de quel bois je me chauffe !** I can tell you he'll soon have to see what I have to say about it!; **non ~ (des fois)!*** *ou* **(alors)!*** hey look here!*, for goodness sake!*; **non ~ (des fois)* tu me prends pour un imbécile ?** I ask you!* *ou* come off it!‡, do you think I'm a complete idiot?; **~ enfin, tu vas te taire ?‡** look here, are you going to *ou* will you shut up?*

② NM (*sg*) objection, snag; (*pl*) buts; **je ne veux pas de ~** I don't want any buts; **il n'y a pas de ~ qui tienne** there's no but about it; **il y a un ~** there's one snag *ou* objection; **il va y avoir des si et des ~** there are sure to be some ifs and buts

mais²† [mɛ] ADV (*littér*) **il n'en pouvait ~** (*impuissant*) he could do nothing about it; (*épuisé*) he was exhausted *ou* worn out

maïs [mais] NM (*gén*) maize (*Brit*), Indian corn (*Brit*), corn (*US*); (*en conserve*) sweet corn; **~ en épi** corn on the cob; **papier ~** corn paper (*used for rolling cigarettes*) → **farine**

maison [mezɔ̃] ① NF ⓐ (= *bâtiment*) house; (= *immeuble*) building; (*locatif*) block of flats (*Brit*), apartment building (*US*); **~ individuelle** house (*as opposed to apartment*); (*secteur*) **la ~ individuelle** private housing

ⓑ (= *logement, foyer*) home; **être/rester à la ~** to be/stay at home *ou* in; **rentrer à la ~** to go (back) home; **quitter la ~** to leave home; **tenir la ~ de qn** to keep house for sb; **les dépenses de la ~** household expenses; **fait à la ~** home-made; **c'est la ~ du bon Dieu** their door is always open → **linge, maître, train**

ⓒ (= *famille, maisonnée*) family; **quelqu'un de la ~ m'a dit ...** someone in the family told me ...; **un ami de la ~** a friend of the family; **il n'est pas heureux à la ~** he doesn't have a happy home life; **nous sommes 7 à la ~** there are 7 of us at home

ⓓ (= *entreprise*) firm, company; (= *magasin de vente*) (*grand*) store; (*petit*) shop; **il est dans la ~ depuis 15 ans** ◊ **il a 15 ans de ~** he's been *ou* he has worked with the firm for 15 years; **la ~ n'est pas responsable de ...** the company *ou* management accepts no responsibility for ...; **c'est offert par la ~** it's on the house; **la ~ ne fait pas crédit** no credit (given); (*arg Police*) **la grande ~** the police force

ⓔ (= *famille royale*) House; **la ~ de Hanovre/de Bourbon** the House of Hanover/of Bourbon

ⓕ (= *place de domestiques, domesticité*) household; **la ~ du Roi/du président de la République** the Royal/Presidential Household; **~ civile/militaire** civil/military household; **gens**† *ou* **employés de ~** servants, domestic staff

② ADJ INV ⓐ [*gâteau, confiture*] home-made; [*personne*] (* = *formé sur place*) trained by the firm; (* = *travaillant exclusivement pour l'entreprise*) in-house (*épith*); (*au restaurant*) **pâté** ~ pâté maison, chef's own pâté; **est-ce que c'est fait ~ ?** do you make it yourself?

ⓑ (*: intensif*) first-rate; **il y a eu une bagarre (quelque chose de) ~** there was an almighty* *ou* a stand-up fight; **il avait une bosse ~ sur la tête** he had one hell of a bump on his head‡; **il s'est fait engueuler‡ quelque chose (de) ~ !** he got one hell of a talking to!*

③ COMP **~ d'arrêt** prison ► **la Maison Blanche** the White House ► **maison bourgeoise** large impressive house ► **maison de campagne** house in the country ► **maison centrale** prison, (*state*) penitentiary (*US*) ► **maison close** brothel ► **maison de commerce** (*commercial*) firm ► **maison de correction** († *Jur*) reformatory† ► **maison de couture** couture house ► **maison de la culture** (*community*) arts centre ► **la Maison de Dieu** *ou* **la Maison du Seigneur** ► **maison de disques** record company ► **maison d'édition** publishing house ► **maison d'éducation surveillée** approved school (*Brit*), reform school (*US*) ► **maison familiale** [*famille*] family home; (= *centre de formation*) training centre for young apprentices; (= *lieu de vacances*) holiday (*Brit*) *ou* vacation (*US*) centre (*for low-income families*) ► **maison de fous*** (*lit, fig*) ≈ madhouse ► **maison de gros** wholesaler's ► **maison de jeu** gambling *ou* gaming club ► **maison des jeunes et de la culture** ≈ community arts centre, ≈ youth club and arts centre ► **maison de maître** mansion ► **maison mère** (*Comm*) parent company; (*Rel*) mother house ► **maison de passe** hotel used as a brothel ► **maison de poupée** doll's house ► **maison de la presse** ≈ newsagent's

(*Brit*), ≈ newsdealer (*US*) ► **maison de rapport** block of flats for letting (*Brit*), rental apartment building (*US*) ► **maison de redressement**† reformatory† ► **maison religieuse** convent ► **maison de rendez-vous**† *house used by lovers as a discreet meeting-place* ► **maison de repos** convalescent home ► **maison de retraite** old people's home ► **maison de santé** (= *clinique*) nursing home; (= *asile*) mental home ► **la Maison du Seigneur** the House of God ► **maison de titres** securities firm *ou* house ► **maison de tolérance** = **maison close**

maisonnée [mezɔne] NF household, family

maisonnette [mezɔnɛt] NF small house

maistrance [mɛstʀɑ̃s] NF petty officers

maître, maîtresse [mɛtʀ, mɛtʀɛs] ① ADJ ⓐ (= *principal*) [*branche*] main; [*qualité*] chief, main, major; [*atout, carte*] master (*épith*); (*Ordin*) [*document, ordinateur*] master (*épith*); **c'est une œuvre maîtresse** it's a major work; **c'est la pièce maîtresse de la collection** it's the major *ou* main *ou* principal piece in the collection; **poutre maîtresse** main beam; **position maîtresse** major *ou* key position; **idée maîtresse** principal *ou* governing idea; **c'est le ~ mot** it's the key word *ou* THE word; (*Ordin*) **en mode ~-esclave** in master-slave mode → **pièce**

ⓑ (*avant n : intensif*) **un ~ filou** *ou* **fripon** an arrant *ou* out-and-out rascal; **c'est une maîtresse femme** she's a very capable woman

② NM ⓐ (*gén*) master; (*Art*) master; (*Pol* = *dirigeant*) ruler; **parler/agir en ~** to speak/act authoritatively; **ils se sont installés en ~s dans ce pays** they have set themselves up as the ruling power in the country, they have taken command of the country; **d'un ton de ~** in an authoritative *ou* a masterful tone; **je vais t'apprendre qui est le ~ ici !** I'll teach you who's the boss* round here! *ou* who's in charge round here!; **la main/l'œil du ~** the hand/the eye of the master; **le ~ de céans** the master of the house; **le ~/la maîtresse des lieux** the master/the mistress *ou* lady of the house; (*Naut*) **seul ~ à bord après Dieu** sole master on board under God; **les ~s du monde** the masters of the world; **grand ~** (*Échecs*) grandmaster; (*Franc-maçonnerie*) Grand Master; (*fig*) **le grand ~ des études celtiques** the greatest authority on Celtic studies → **chauffeur, toile**

ⓑ (*Scol*) **~ (d'école)** teacher, (school)master; **~ de piano/d'anglais** piano/English teacher

ⓒ (= *artisan*) **~ charpentier/maçon** master carpenter/builder

ⓓ (= *titre*) **Maître** *term of address given to lawyers, artists, professors etc*; (*Art*) maestro; (*dans la marine*) petty officer; **mon cher Maître** Dear Mr *ou* Professor *etc* X; (*Jur*) **Maître X** Mr X

ⓔ (*loc*) **coup de ~** masterstroke; (*Cartes*) **être ~ à cœur** to have *ou* hold the master *ou* best heart; **le roi de cœur est ~** the king of hearts is master, the king is the master *ou* best heart; **être ~ chez soi** to be master in one's own home; **être ~ de soi (propre)** ~ to be one's own master; **être ~ de refuser/faire** to be free to refuse/do; **rester ~ de soi** to retain *ou* keep one's self-control; **être ~ de soi** to be in control *ou* have control of o.s.; **être/rester ~ de la situation** to be/remain in control of the situation, have/keep the situation under control; **être/rester ~ de sa voiture** to be/remain in control of one's car; **être ~ de sa destinée** to be the master of one's fate; **être/rester ~ du pays** to be/remain in control *ou* command of the country; **être ~ d'un secret** to be in possession of a secret; **être ~ de son sujet** to have a mastery of one's subject; **se rendre ~ de** [+ *ville, pays*] to gain control *ou* possession of; [+ *personne, animal, incendie, situation*] to bring *ou* get under control; **il est passé ~ dans l'art**

▶ GRAMMAIRE ACTIVE: **mais** 53.3

de mentir he's a past master in the art of lying

3 **maîtresse** NF [a] (= *amante*) mistress [b] (*Scol*) **maîtresse (d'école)** teacher, (school)mistress; **maîtresse !** (please) Miss! [c] (*loc*) **être/rester/se rendre/passer maîtresse (de)** → 2e

4 COMP ▶ **maître d'armes** fencing master ▶ **maître artisan** (*gén*) master craftsman; (= *boulanger*) master baker ▶ **maître assistant†** (*Univ*) ≈ (senior) lecturer (*Brit*), assistant professor (*US*) ▶ **maître auxiliaire** non-certified teacher ▶ **maître/maîtresse de ballet** ballet master/mistress ▶ **maître de cérémonies** master of ceremonies ▶ **maître chanteur** (= *escroc*) blackmailer; (*Mus*) Meistersinger, mastersinger ▶ **maître de chapelle** choirmaster, precentor ▶ **maître de conférences** NMF (*Univ*) ≈ (senior) lecturer (*Brit*), ≈ assistant professor (*US*) ▶ **maître d'équipage** boatswain ▶ **maître/maîtresse d'études** (*Scol*) master/mistress in charge of homework preparation ▶ **maître de forges†** ironmaster ▶ **maître d'hôtel** [*maison*] butler; [*hôtel, restaurant*] head waiter, maître (d'hôtel) (*US*); (*Naut*) chief steward; (*Culin*) **pommes de terre ~ d'hôtel** maître d'hôtel potatoes ▶ **maître/maîtresse d'internat** house master/mistress ▶ **maître Jacques** jack-of-all-trades ▶ **maître de maison** host ▶ **maîtresse de maison** housewife; (= *hôtesse*) hostess ▶ **maître nageur** swimming teacher *ou* instructor ▶ **maître d'œuvre** (*Constr*) project manager; **la mairie est ~ d'œuvre de ce projet** the town council is in charge of the project ▶ **maître d'ouvrage** (*Constr*) ≈ owner ▶ **maître à penser** intellectual guide *ou* leader ▶ **maître queux** (*Culin*) chef ▶ **maître des requêtes** (*Admin*) NMF counsel of the Conseil d'État ▶ **maître titulaire** permanent teacher (*in primary school*)

maître-autel (*pl* **maîtres-autels**) [mɛtʀotɛl] NM (*Rel*) high altar

maître-chien (*pl* **maîtres-chiens**) [mɛtʀəʃjɛ̃] NM dog handler

maîtrisable [metrizabl] ADJ [a] (= *contrôlable*) controllable; **difficilement** *ou* **guère ~** almost uncontrollable, scarcely controllable [b] [*langue, technique*] which can be mastered

maîtrise [metriz] NF [a] (= *sang-froid*) **~ (de soi)** self-control, self-command, self-possession [b] (= *contrôle*) [*domaine*] mastery, command, control; [*budget*] control; **sa ~ du français** his command of the French language; (*Mil*) **avoir la ~ de la mer** to have command *ou* control *ou* mastery of the sea(s), control the sea; (*Comm*) **avoir la ~ d'un marché** to control *ou* have control of a market; **avoir la ~ de l'atome** to have mastered the atom; **pour une plus grande ~ des dépenses de santé** to ensure better control of health expenditure [c] (= *habileté*) skill, mastery, expertise; **faire** *ou* **exécuter qch avec ~** to do sth with skill *ou* skilfully [d] (*Ind*) supervisory staff → **agent** [e] (*Rel*) (= *école*) choir school; (= *groupe*) choir [f] (*Univ*) research degree; ≈ master's degree; **~ de conférences** ≈ senior lectureship → DIPLÔMES

maîtriser [metrize] ▶ conjug 1 ◀ **1** VT [a] (= *soumettre*) [+ *cheval, feu, foule, forcené*] to control, bring under control; [+ *adversaire*] to overcome, overpower; [+ *émeute, révolte*] to suppress, bring under control; [+ *problème, difficulté*] to master, overcome; [+ *inflation*] to curb; **nous maîtrisons la situation** the situation is under control [b] [+ *langue, technique*] to master; **il ne maîtrise pas du tout cette langue** he has no command of the language, he has a very poor grasp of the language [c] (= *contenir*) [+ *émotion, geste, passion*] to control, master, restrain; [+ *larmes, rire*] to force back, restrain, control; **il ne peut plus ~**

ses nerfs he can no longer control *ou* contain his temper **2** **se maîtriser** VPR to control o.s.; **elle ne sait pas se ~** she has no self-control

maïzena® [maizena] NF cornflour (*Brit*), cornstarch (*US*)

majesté [maʒɛste] NF [a] (= *dignité*) majesty; (= *splendeur*) majesty, grandeur; **la ~ divine** divine majesty; (*Art*) **de** *ou* **en ~** in majesty, enthroned → **lèse-majesté, pluriel** [b] **Votre Majesté** Your Majesty; **Sa Majesté** (= *roi*) His Majesty; (= *reine*) Her Majesty

majestueusement [maʒɛstɥøzmã] ADV majestically, in a stately way

majestueux, -euse [maʒɛstɥø, øz] ADJ (= *solennel*) [*personne, démarche*] majestic, stately; (= *imposant*) [*taille*] imposing, impressive; (= *beau*) [*fleuve, paysage*] majestic, magnificent

majeur, e [maʒœʀ] **1** ADJ [a] [*problème, crise*] (= *très important*) major; (= *le plus important*) main, major, greatest; **ils ont rencontré une difficulté ~e** they came up against a major *ou* serious difficulty; **c'est son œuvre ~e** it's his magnum opus *ou* main concern; **c'est une œuvre ~e de la littérature irlandaise** it's one of the major *ou* greatest works of Irish literature; **sa préoccupation ~e** his major *ou* main *ou* prime concern; **pour des raisons ~es** for reasons of the greatest importance; **en ~e partie** for the most part; **la ~e partie de ...** the greater *ou* major part of ..., the bulk of ...; **la ~e partie des gens sont restés** most of *ou* the majority of the people have stayed on → **cas** [b] (*Jur*) of age (*attrib*); **il sera ~ en l'an 2005** he will come of age in the year 2005; **il n'est pas encore ~** he's still under age; (*hum*) **il est ~ et vacciné** he's old enough to look after himself; (*fig*) **les électeurs sont ~s** voters are responsible adults [c] (*Mus*) [*intervalle, mode*] major; **en sol ~** in G major [d] (*Logique*) [*terme, prémisse*] major [e] (*Rel*) **ordres ~s** major orders; **causes ~es** causae majores [f] (*Cartes*) **tierce/quarte ~e** tierce/quart major **2** NM,F person who has come of *ou* who is of age, person who has attained his (*ou* her) majority, major (*SPÉC*) **3** NM middle finger **4** **majeure** NF [a] (*Logique*) major premise [b] (*Univ* = *matière*) main subject (*Brit*), major (*US*) [c] (*Écon*) major company

majolique [maʒɔlik] NF majolica, maiolica

major [maʒɔʀ] **1** NM [a] (*Mil* = *sous-officier*) ≈ warrant officer; (*Helv* = *commandant*) major; (*médecin*) ≈ medical officer, M.O.; **~ général** (*Mil*) ≈ deputy chief of staff (*Brit*), ≈ major general (*US*); (*Naut*) ≈ rear admiral [b] (*Univ*) **être ~ de promotion** ≈ to be *ou* come first in one's year [c] NF (*Écon*) major company **3** ADJ INV → **état-major, infirmier, sergent¹, tambour**

majoration [maʒɔʀasjɔ̃] NF (= *hausse*) rise, increase (de in); (= *supplément*) surcharge, additional charge; (= *surestimation*) overvaluation, overestimation; **~ sur une facture** surcharge on a bill; **~ pour retard de paiement** surcharge *ou* additional charge for late payment → IMPÔTS

majordome [maʒɔʀdɔm] NM butler, majordomo

majorer [maʒɔʀe] ▶ conjug 1 ◀ VT [a] (= *accroître*) [+ *impôt, prix*] to increase, raise, put up (de by); [+ *facture*] to increase, put a surcharge on; [+ *risque*] to increase [b] (= *surestimer*) to overestimate [c] (= *accorder trop d'importance à*) to lend *ou* give too much importance to

majorette [maʒɔʀɛt] NF (drum) majorette

majoritaire [maʒɔʀitɛʀ] **1** ADJ [*actionnaire, groupe, motion*] majority (*épith*); **vote ~** majority vote; **les femmes sont ~s dans cette pro-**

fession women are in the majority in this profession; **les socialistes sont ~s dans le pays** the socialists are the majority *ou* largest party in the country; **ils sont ~s à l'assemblée** they are the majority party *ou* in the majority in Parliament; **dans ce vote, nous serons sûrement ~s** we shall certainly have a majority on this vote → **scrutin 2** NMF (*Pol*) member of the majority party

majoritairement [maʒɔʀitɛʀmã] ADV [*choisir, voter*] by a majority; **le lectorat est ~ féminin** the readership is predominantly female, the majority of the readers are women; **il est celui que, ~, les Français soutiennent** he is the one who most French people support; (*Fin*) **le groupe contrôle ~ notre société** the group has a majority holding in our company

majorité [maʒɔʀite] NF [a] (*électorale*) majority; **~ absolue/relative/simple** absolute/relative/simple majority; **~ qualifiée** *ou* **renforcée** qualified majority; **élu à une ~ de ...** elected by a majority of ...; **avoir la ~** to have the majority [b] (= *parti majoritaire*) government, party in power; **député de la ~** member of the governing party *ou* of the party in power; ≈ government backbencher (*Brit*), ≈ majority party Representative (*US*); **la ~ et l'opposition** the majority party *ou* the government (*Brit*) and the opposition [c] (= *majeure partie*) majority; **ils détiennent la ~ du capital de l'entreprise** they have a majority holding in the company; **il y a des mécontents, mais ce n'est pas la ~** there are some dissatisfied people, but they're not in the majority; **la ~ silencieuse** the silent majority; **être en ~** to be in (the) majority; **la ~ est d'accord** the majority agree; **les hommes dans leur grande ~** the great majority of mankind; **dans la ~ des cas** in the majority of cases, in most cases; **groupe composé en ~ de ...** group mainly *ou* mostly composed of ...; **les enseignants sont en ~ des femmes** teachers are, in the majority, women [d] (*Jur*) **atteindre sa ~** to come of age, reach one's majority; **jusqu'à sa ~** until he comes of age *ou* reaches his majority; **~ pénale** legal majority; **atteindre la ~ civile** to reach voting age

Majorque [maʒɔʀk] NF Majorca

majorquin, e [maʒɔʀkɛ̃, in] **1** ADJ Majorcan **2** **Majorquin(e)** NM,F Majorcan

majuscule [maʒyskyl] **1** ADJ capital; (*Typo*) upper case; **A ~** capital A **2** NF (*lettre*) capital letter; (*Typo*) upper case letter; **en ~s d'imprimerie** in block *ou* capital letters; **écrivez votre nom en ~s (d'imprimerie)** please print your name in block letters; **mettre une ~ à qch** (*gén*) to write sth with a capital; (*Typo*) to capitalize sth

makaire [makɛʀ] NM (= *poisson*) marlin

---

mal¹ [mal]

1 ADVERBE	**2** ADJECTIF INVARIABLE

1 ADVERBE

Lorsque mal est suivi d'un participe passé adjectif (ex: mal logé/loti/connu/aimé/vécu) chercher aussi sous l'adjectif ou le verbe concerné.

[a] = de façon défectueuse [*entretenu, organisé, réparé*] badly, poorly; **ce travail est ~ fait** ◊ **c'est du travail ~ fait** this is poor *ou* shoddy work, this work is badly done; **il se nourrit ~** he doesn't eat properly; **il travaille ~** he doesn't do his work properly, his work isn't good; **cette porte ferme ~** this door doesn't shut properly; **j'ai ~ dormi** I didn't sleep well, I slept badly; **il parle ~ l'anglais** his English isn't good *ou* is poor; **nous sommes ~ nourris/logés à l'hôtel** the food/accommodation is poor *ou* bad at the hotel; **tout va ~** everything's going wrong → **tomber**

♦ **de mal en pis** from bad to worse; **son entreprise va de ~ en pis** things are going from bad to worse in his company

□**b** **= de façon peu judicieuse** *ou* **opportune** **~ choisi/inspiré** ill-chosen/-advised; **cette annonce tombe au plus ~** this announcement couldn't have come at a worse moment

□**c** **= avec difficulté** with difficulty; **il respire ~** he has difficulty in breathing, he can't breathe properly; **ils vivent très ~ avec un seul salaire** they have difficulty living on *ou* off just one income; **on s'explique** *ou* **comprend ~ pourquoi** it is not easy *ou* it is difficult to understand why; **nous voyons très ~ comment ... we fail to see how ...**

□**d** **= de façon répréhensible** [*se conduire*] badly, wrongly; **il ne pensait pas ~ faire** ◊ **il ne pensait pas à ~** he didn't think he was doing the wrong thing *ou* doing wrong; **il ne pense qu'à ~ faire** he's always up to no good, he's always thinking up some nasty trick; **tu trouves ça ~ qu'il y soit allé?** do you think it was wrong of him to go? → **juger, porter, sentir, trouver** *etc*

□**e**
♦ **pas mal** (= *assez bien*) not badly, rather well; **on est pas ~ (assis) dans ces fauteuils** these armchairs are quite comfortable; **il ne s'est pas trop ~ débrouillé** he managed quite well; **vous (ne) vous en êtes pas ~ tirés** you haven't done *ou* come off badly, you've done rather well; **vous (ne) feriez pas ~ de le surveiller** you would be well-advised to keep *ou* it wouldn't be a bad thing if you kept an eye on him; **ça va? — pas ~** how are you? — not (too) bad *ou* pretty good
(= *très, beaucoup*) [*déçu, surpris*] quite, rather; **on a pas ~ travaillé aujourd'hui** we've done quite a lot of work today, we've worked pretty hard today; **il est pas ~ fatigué** he's rather *ou* pretty tired; **il a pas ~ vieilli** he's aged quite a bit *ou* quite a lot; **elle a pas ~ grossi** she's put on quite a bit *ou* quite a lot of weight

□**f**
♦ **pas mal de** (= *beaucoup*) quite a lot of; **il y a pas ~ de temps qu'il est parti** it's quite a time since he left, he's been away for quite a time; **pas ~ de gens pensent que ...** quite a lot of people think that ...

② ADJECTIF INVARIABLE

□**a** **= contraire à la morale** wrong, bad; **c'est ~ de mentir/de voler** it is bad *ou* wrong to lie/to steal; (*iro*) **(pour elle) il ne peut rien faire de ~** (in her eyes) he can do no wrong; **c'est ~ à lui** (*frm*) *ou* **de sa part de dire cela** it's bad *ou* wrong of him to say this

□**b** **= malade** ill; **j'ai été ~ toute la matinée** I felt ill all morning; **il est très ~ ce soir** he's very ill *ou* not at all well tonight; **le malade est au plus ~** the patient's condition couldn't be worse; **je me sens ~ quand il fait trop chaud** the heat doesn't agree with me; **elle s'est sentie ~** she felt faint

♦ **mal en point** [*personne, voiture*] in a bad *ou* sorry state, in a bad way; [*secteur économique, parti*] in a bad way

□**c** **= mal à l'aise** uncomfortable; **vous devez être ~ sur ce banc** you can't be comfortable on that seat, that seat can't be comfortable *ou* must be uncomfortable → **aise, peau**

□**d** **= en mauvais termes** **être ~ avec qn** to be on bad terms with sb, be in sb's bad books*; **les deux cousins sont au plus ~** the two cousins are at daggers drawn; **se mettre ~ avec qn** to get on the wrong side of sb, get into sb's bad books*

□**e**
♦ **pas mal** (= *assez bien*) not bad, quite *ou* fairly good; **il n'est pas ~ dans le rôle** he's not bad *ou* quite good in that role; **c'est pas ~ (du tout)** it's not bad (at all)
(= *assez beau*) [*personne*] quite good-looking, not bad; [*maison*] quite nice, not bad; **tu n'es**

pas ~ sur cette photo that's quite a good picture of you

---

mal² [mal]

pl **maux**	
① NOM MASCULIN	② COMPOSÉS

① NOM MASCULIN

□**a** **Philo : opposé au bien** **le ~** evil; **le conflit entre le bien et le ~** the conflict between good and evil; **distinguer le bien du ~** to tell right from wrong, know the difference between right and wrong; **faire le ~ pour le ~** to commit evil for its own sake *ou* for evil's sake; **rendre le ~ pour le ~** to return evil for evil

□**b** **= souffrance morale, peine** sorrow, pain; **le ~ du siècle** (= *fléau*) the scourge of the age; (*littér* = *mélancolie*) world-weariness; **des paroles qui font du ~** words that hurt, hurtful words

□**c** **= dommage** harm; **excusez-moi — il n'y a pas de ~** I'm sorry — no harm done; **il n'y a pas grand ~** there's no real harm done; **il n'y a pas de ~ à (faire)** ça/à ce qu'il fasse there's no harm in (doing) that/in his *ou* him doing; **~ lui en a pris de sortir** going out was a grave mistake (on my part); **ces médicaments, ça fait plus de ~ que de bien** these medicines do more harm than good; **ça fait du ~ au commerce** it's not good for business; **vouloir du ~ à qn** to wish sb ill *ou* harm, be ill-disposed towards sb; **je ne lui veux pas de** *ou* **aucun ~** I don't wish him any harm → **peur**

♦ **mettre à mal** [+ *personne, relations*] to harm; [+ *principe, politique, processus, système, réputation*] to harm, damage

□**d** **= travail pénible, difficulté** difficulty; **on n'a rien sans ~** you get nothing without (some) effort; **faire qch sans trop de ~/non sans ~** to do sth without undue difficulty/not without difficulty; **j'ai obtenu son accord/le document, mais non sans ~!** I had to agree/I got the document, but it wasn't easy!; **il a dû prendre son ~ en patience** (= *attendre*) he had to put up with the delay; (= *supporter*) he had to grin and bear it

♦ **avoir du mal à faire qch** to have trouble *ou* difficulty doing sth; **je n'ai eu aucun ~ à l'imaginer** I had no difficulty imagining it; (*elliptiquement*) **j'ai du ~** it's hard for me, I find it hard *ou* difficult

♦ **donner du mal à qn** to give sb trouble; **ce travail/cet enfant m'a donné du ~/bien du ~** this work/this child gave me some trouble/a lot of trouble; **se donner du ~** to go to a lot of trouble; **se donner du ~ pour faire qch** to take trouble *ou* pains over sth, go to great pains to do sth; **ne vous donnez pas ce ~** don't bother; **se donner un ~ de chien pour faire qch*** to bend over backwards *ou* go to great lengths to do sth

□**e** **= ce qui est mauvais** evil, ill; **c'est un ~ nécessaire** it's a necessary evil; **accuser qn de tous les maux** to accuse sb of all the evils in the world; **les maux dont souffre notre société** the ills *ou* evils afflicting our society; **penser/dire du ~ de qn/qch** to think/speak ill of sb/sth; **sans penser** *ou* **songer à ~** without meaning any harm ■(*PROV*) **aux grands maux les grands remèdes** desperate times call for desperate measures → **moindre**

□**f** **= douleur physique** pain, ache; (= *maladie*) illness, disease, sickness; **le ~ s'aggrave** (*lit*) the disease is getting worse, he (*ou* she *etc*) is getting worse; (*fig*) the situation is deteriorating, things are getting worse; **faire du ~ à qn** to harm *ou* hurt sb; **ne leur faites pas de ~!** don't harm *ou* hurt them!; **il ne ferait pas de ~ à une mouche** he wouldn't hurt *ou* harm a fly; **prendre ~†** to be taken ill, feel unwell; **~ de tête** headache; **des maux d'estomac** stomach pains

♦ **avoir mal : je me suis cogné — tu as ~ ?/très ~ ?** I bumped myself — does it hurt?/really hurt?; **où avez-vous ~ ?** where does it hurt?, where is the pain?; **avoir ~ partout** to be aching all over; **avoir ~ au cœur** to feel nauseous *ou* sick (*Brit*); **ils ont souvent ~ au cœur en voiture** they often get carsick; **avoir ~ à la gorge** to have a sore throat; **avoir ~ à la tête** to have a headache *ou* a bad head*; **avoir ~ aux dents/aux oreilles** to have toothache/earache; **j'ai ~ au pied/au ventre** my foot hurts; **j'ai ~ au dos/à l'estomac** I've got backache/stomach ache *ou* a pain in my back/stomach, my back/stomach hurts

♦ **faire mal** (*physiquement*) to hurt; (*psychologiquement*) to be hurtful; **des critiques qui font ~** hurtful criticism; (*fig*) **3 000 F de réparations, ça fait ~!*** 3,000 francs in repairs, that hurts!; **ça va faire ~!*** (*confrontation, match*) it's going to be tough!; **le jour où le fisc s'occupera de lui, ça va faire ~!*** the day the taxman catches up with him, he'll be in real trouble!; **ils sortent un nouvel album, ça va faire ~!*** they're bringing out a new album, it's going to be a big hit!

♦ **faire mal à** to hurt; **tu m'as fait ~!** you hurt me!; **mon coude me fait ~** my elbow hurts; **ces chaussures me font ~ (au pied)** these shoes hurt *ou* pinch (my feet); **il s'est fait ~ en tombant** he hurt himself when he fell; **se faire ~ au genou** to hurt one's knee; **ça me fait ~ au cœur** (= *ça me rend malade*) it makes me feel sick; (= *ça me fait pitié* *ou* *de la peine*) it breaks my heart; (= *ça me révolte*) it makes me sick, it's sickening; **ça me ferait ~ (au ventre** *ou* **aux seins)!*** it would make me sick!, it would really piss me off!**

□**g**
♦ **en mal de** (= *en manque de*) [+ *argent, idées*] short of; [+ *tendresse, amour*] yearning for; **journaliste en ~ de copie** journalist short of copy; **être en ~ d'inspiration** to be lacking in inspiration, have no inspiration; **association en ~ de publicité/reconnaissance** organization craving publicity/recognition

② COMPOSÉS

► **mal de l'air** airsickness ► **mal blanc†** whitlow ► **mal de l'espace** space sickness ► **mal des grands ensembles** depression resulting from life in a high-rise block ► **le mal joli†** (*hum*) the pains of (giving) birth ► **mal de mer** seasickness; **avoir le ~ de mer** to be seasick ► **mal des montagnes** mountain sickness; **avoir le ~ des montagnes** to have mountain sickness ► **le mal du pays** homesickness; **avoir le ~ du pays** to feel homesick ► **mal de la route** carsickness ► **mal des transports** travel *ou* motion (*US*) sickness; **pilule contre le ~ des transports** travel-sickness pill, anti-motion-sickness pill (*US*) ► **mal de vivre** profound discontentment

---

Malabar [malabaʀ] NM **le ~** ◊ **la côte de ~** the Malabar (Coast)

malabar* [malabaʀ] NM muscle man*, hefty fellow*

Malabo [malabo] N Malabo

Malachie [malaʃi] NM (*Bible*) Malachi

malachite [malaʃit] NF malachite

malade [malad] ① ADJ □**a** (= *atteint*) [*personne*] ill, unwell (*attrib*), sick (*surtout US*); [*organe, plante*] diseased; [*dent, poitrine*] bad; [*jambe, bras*] bad, gammy* (*Brit*) (*épith*); **être bien/gravement/sérieusement ~** to be really/gravely/seriously ill; **être ~ du cœur** ◊ **avoir le cœur ~** to have heart trouble *ou* a bad heart *ou* a heart condition; **être ~ des reins** to have kidney trouble; **tomber ~** to fall ill *ou* sick; **se faire porter ~** to report *ou* go sick; **faire le ~** to feign *ou* sham illness; **j'ai été ~** (*gén*) I was ill; (= *j'ai vomi*) I was sick; **je me sens (un peu) ~** I feel (a bit) peculiar*, I don't feel very well; **être ~ comme un chien*** *ou* **une bête*** (*gén*) to be dreadfully ill; (*euph = vomir*) to be as sick as a dog*; **être ~ à crever:** to be dreadfully ill, feel like death (warmed up (*Brit*) *ou* warmed over (*US*))*

b (= *fou*) mad; **tu n'es pas (un peu) ~?:** are you out of your mind?; **être ~ d'inquiétude** to be sick *ou* ill with worry; **être ~ de jalousie** to be mad *ou* sick with jealousy; **rien que d'y penser j'en suis ~* ◊ ça me rend ~ rien que d'y penser*** the very thought of it makes me sick *ou* ill

c (= *en mauvais état*) [*objet, pays*] in a sorry state; **l'entreprise étant ~, ils durent licencier** as the business was failing, they had to lay people off; **le gouvernement est trop ~ pour durer jusqu'aux élections** the government is too shaky to last till the elections; **notre économie est bien ~** our economy is in bad shape *ou* a bad way

2 NMF a (*Méd*) (*gén*) invalid, sick person; (*d'un médecin*) patient; **grand ~** seriously ill person; **faux ~** malingerer; **~ imaginaire** hypochondriac; **~ mental** mentally sick *ou* ill person; **les ~s** the sick; **les grands ~s** the seriously *ou* critically ill; **le médecin et ses ~s** the doctor and his patients

b (* = *fanatique*) **un ~ de la moto** a (motor)bike freak: *ou* fanatic; **un ~ de la vitesse** a speed merchant* (*Brit*) *ou* demon* (*US*)

c (* = *fou*) maniac*; **il conduit comme un ~** he drives like a maniac* *ou* madman*; **elle frappait comme une ~** she was knocking like mad* *ou* like a mad woman

maladie [maladi] **1** NF a (*Méd*) illness, disease; [*plante, vin*] disease; **~ bénigne** minor *ou* slight illness, minor complaint; **~ grave** serious illness; **~ de cœur/foie** heart/liver complaint *ou* disease; **ces enfants ont eu une ~ après l'autre** these children have had one sickness *ou* illness after another; **le cancer est la ~ du siècle** cancer is the disease of this century; **il a fait une petite ~*** he's been slightly ill, he's had a minor illness; **elle est en ~*** she's off sick*; **en longue ~** (off) on extended sick leave; (* *fig*) **il en a fait une ~** he got into a terrible state about it, he had a fit*; **tu ne vas pas en faire une ~!** don't you get in (such) a state over it!, don't make a song and dance about it!*; **mes rosiers ont la ~*** my rose bushes are in a bad way*

b **la ~** illness, ill health; **la ~ et la famine dans le monde** disease and famine in the world → **assurance**

c (*Vét*) **la ~** distemper

d (* = *obsession*) mania; **avoir la ~ de la vitesse** to be a speed maniac; **quelle ~ as-tu de toujours intervenir!** what a mania you have for interfering!; **c'est une ~ chez lui** it's a mania with him

2 COMP ► **la maladie bleue** the blue disease, cyanosis ► **maladie honteuse**† = **maladie vénérienne** ► **maladie infantile** childhood *ou* infantile disease *ou* complaint ► **maladie de langueur** wasting disease ► **maladie du légionnaire** legionnaires' disease ► **maladie mentale** mental illness ► **maladie mortelle** fatal illness *ou* disease ► **maladie de peau** skin disease *ou* complaint ► **maladie professionnelle** occupational disease ► **maladie sexuellement transmissible** sexually transmitted disease, STD ► **la maladie du sommeil** sleeping sickness ► **maladie du travail** = **maladie professionnelle** ► **maladie tropicale** tropical disease ► **maladie vénérienne** venereal disease, VD → **Alzheimer, Carré, Hodgkin**

maladif, -ive [maladif, iv] ADJ a [*personne*] sickly, weak; [*air, pâleur*] sickly, unhealthy b [*obsession, peur*] pathological; **il est d'une timidité maladive** he's pathologically shy; **il faut qu'il mente, c'est ~ chez lui** he's a pathological liar

maladivement [maladivmã] ADV [*pâle, maigre*] unhealthily; [*anxieux, timide*] pathologically

maladrerie† [maladʀəʀi] NF lazaret†, lazar house†

maladresse [maladʀɛs] NF a (= *gaucherie*) [*personne, geste, expression*] clumsiness, awkwardness; [*ouvrage, style, intervention*] clumsiness b (= *indélicatesse*) [*personne, remarque*] clumsiness, tactlessness; **quelle ~!** how tactless! c (= *bévue*) blunder, gaffe; **~s de style** awkward *ou* clumsy turns of phrase

maladroit, e [maladʀwa, wat] **1** ADJ a (= *malhabile*) [*personne, geste, expression*] clumsy, awkward; [*ouvrage, style, dessin, intervention, mensonge*] clumsy; **il est vraiment ~ de ses mains** he's really useless with his hands b (= *indélicat*) [*personne, remarque*] clumsy, tactless; **ce serait ~ de lui en parler** it would be tactless *ou* ill-considered to mention it to him **2** NM,F (= *malhabile*) clumsy person *ou* oaf*; (= *qui fait tout tomber*) butterfingers*; (= *indélicat*) tactless person, blunderer*; **quel ~ je fais!** how clumsy of me!

maladroitement [maladʀwatmã] ADV [*marcher, dessiner*] clumsily, awkwardly; [*agir*] clumsily, tactlessly

malaga [malaga] NM (= *vin*) Malaga (wine); (= *raisin*) Malaga grape

mal-aimé, e (*mpl* **mal-aimés**) [maleme] NM,F unpopular figure; **il est devenu le ~ de la presse** he has become the man the press love to hate, he has become an unpopular figure with the press

malais, e¹ [male, ɛz] **1** ADJ Malay(an) **2** NM (*Ling*) Malay **3** **Malais(e)** NM,F Malay(an)

malaise² [malɛz] NM a (*gén*) feeling of general discomfort *ou* ill-being; (*Méd*) feeling of sickness *ou* faintness, malaise (*frm*); **~ cardiaque** mild heart attack; **être pris d'un ~ ◊ avoir un ~** to feel faint *ou* dizzy, come over faint *ou* dizzy b (= *trouble*) uneasiness; **éprouver un ~** to feel uneasy; **le ~ étudiant/politique** student/political unrest; **~ économique/social** economic/social malaise

malaisé, e [maleze] ADJ difficult

malaisément [malezemã] ADV with difficulty

Malaisie [malezi] NF Malaysia

malaisien, -ienne [malezjɛ̃, jɛn] **1** ADJ Malaysian **2** **Malaisien(ne)** NM,F Malaysian

malandrin† [malãdʀɛ̃] NM (*littér*) brigand (*littér*), bandit

malappris, e [malapʀi, iz] **1** ADJ ill-mannered, boorish **2** NM ill-mannered lout, boor, yob* (*Brit*)

malard [malaʀ] NM drake; (*sauvage*) mallard

malaria [malaʀja] NF malaria (*NonC*)

malavisé, e [malavize] ADJ [*personne, remarque*] ill-advised, injudicious, unwise

Malawi [malawi] NM Malawi

malawien, -ienne [malawjɛ̃, jɛn] **1** ADJ Malawian **2** **Malawien(ne)** NM,F Malawian

malaxage [malaksaʒ] NM a [*argile, pâte*] kneading; [*muscle*] massaging; [*beurre*] creaming b (= *mélange*) blending, mixing

malaxer [malakse] ▶ conjug 1 ◀ VT a [+ *argile, pâte*] to knead; [+ *muscle*] to massage; [+ *beurre*] to cream b (= *mélanger*) to blend, mix

malaxeur [malaksœʀ] **1** ADJ M mixing **2** NM mixer

malchance [malʃãs] NF (= *déveine*) bad *ou* ill luck, misfortune; (= *mésaventure*) misfortune, mishap; **il a eu beaucoup de ~** he's had a lot of bad luck; **j'ai eu la ~ de ...** I had the misfortune to ..., I was unlucky enough to ...; **par ~** unfortunately, as ill luck would have it; **il a joué de ~** (*gén*) he was out of luck; (*de manière répétée*) he had one bit of bad luck after another

malchanceux, -euse [malʃãsø, øz] ADJ unlucky

malcommode [malkɔmɔd] ADJ [*objet, vêtement*] impractical, unsuitable; [*horaire*]

awkward, inconvenient; [*outil, meuble*] inconvenient, impractical; **ça m'est vraiment très ~** it's really most inconvenient for me, it really doesn't suit me at all

Maldives [maldiv] NFPL **les ~** the Maldives

maldonne [maldɔn] NF (*Cartes*) misdeal; **faire (une) ~** to misdeal, deal the cards wrongly; **il y a ~** (*lit*) there's been a misdeal, the cards have been dealt wrongly; (*fig*) there's been a mistake somewhere

Malé [male] N Malé

mâle [mal] **1** ADJ a (*Bio, Tech*) male b (= *viril*) [*voix, courage*] manly; [*style, peinture*] virile, strong, forceful **2** NM male; **titre de noblesse transmis par les ~s** noble title handed down through the male line; **c'est un ~ ou une femelle?** is it a he or a she?*, is it a male or a female?; (*hum*) **c'est un beau ~*** he's a real hunk*, he's a fine specimen (of manhood) (*hum*); (**éléphant**) **~** bull (elephant); (**lapin**) **~** buck (rabbit); (**moineau**) **~** cock (sparrow); (**ours**) **~** he-bear; **souris ~** male mouse

malédiction [malediksjɔ̃] **1** NF (*Rel* = *imprécation, adversité*) curse, malediction (*littér*); **la ~ divine** the curse of God; **n'écoute pas les ~s de cette vieille folle** don't listen to the curses of that old fool; **la ~ pèse sur nous** a curse is hanging over us, we're under a curse; **appeler la ~ sur qn** to call down curses upon sb **2** EXCL (*littér*) curse it!*, damn!*; **~! j'ai perdu la clé** curse it!* I've lost the key

maléfice [malefis] NM evil spell

maléfique [malefik] ADJ [*étoile*] malefic (*littér*), unlucky; [*charme, signe, pouvoir*] evil, baleful; **les puissances ~s** the forces of evil

malemort [malmɔʀ] NF (††, *littér*) cruel death; **mourir de ~** to die a cruel *ou* violent death

malencontreusement [malãkɔ̃tʀøzmã] ADV [*arriver*] at the wrong moment, inopportunely, inconveniently; [*faire tomber*] inadvertently; **faire ~ remarquer que ...** to make the unfortunate remark that ...

malencontreux, -euse [malãkɔ̃tʀø, øz] ADJ a (= *malheureux*) [*erreur, incident*] unfortunate; [*geste*] awkward; [*remarque*] awkward, unfortunate; [*décision*] unwise, unfortunate b (= *déplacé*) [*allusion*] inopportune c (= *à contretemps*) [*événement*] untimely

malentendant, e [malãtãdã, ãt] NM,F person who is hard of hearing; **les ~s** hearing-impaired people, people who are hard of hearing

malentendu [malãtãdy] NM misunderstanding

mal-être [malɛtʀ] NM INV [*personne*] malaise, disquiet, ill-being (*US*); [*groupe social*] malaise

malfaçon [malfasɔ̃] NF fault, defect (*due to bad workmanship*)

malfaisant, e [malfəzã, ãt] ADJ [*personne*] evil, wicked, harmful; [*influence*] evil, harmful; [*animal, théories*] harmful

malfaiteur [malfɛtœʀ] NM (*gén*) criminal; (= *gangster*) gangster; (= *voleur*) burglar, thief; **dangereux ~** dangerous criminal

malformation [malfɔʀmasjɔ̃] NF malformation

malfrat [malfʀa] NM (= *escroc*) crook; (= *bandit*) thug, gangster

malgache [malgaʃ] **1** ADJ Malagasy, Madagascan **2** NM (*Ling*) Malagasy **3** **Malgache** NMF Malagasy, Madagascan

malgracieux, -ieuse [malgʀasjø, jøz] ADJ (*littér*) [*silhouette*] ungainly, clumsy; † [*caractère*] loutish, boorish

malgré [malgʀe] **1** PRÉP a (= *en dépit de*) in spite of, despite; **~ son père/l'opposition de son père, il devint avocat** despite his *ou* in spite of his father/his father's objections he became a barrister; **~ son intelligence, il n'a pas réussi** in spite of *ou* for all *ou* notwithstanding (*frm*) his undoubted intelligence he hasn't succeeded; **j'ai signé ce contrat ~ moi** (*en hésitant*) I signed the contract reluctantly *ou* against my better judgment; (*contraint et forcé*) I signed the contract against my will; **j'ai fait cela presque ~ moi** I did it almost in spite of myself; **il est devenu célèbre/un sex-symbol ~ lui** he became a reluctant celebrity/ sex-symbol, he became famous/a sex-symbol in spite of himself

b (*loc*) **~ tout** (= *en dépit de tout*) in spite of everything, despite everything; (*concession = quand même*) all the same, even so, after all; **~ tout, c'est dangereux** all the same *ou* after all it's dangerous; **il a continué ~ tout** he went on in spite of *ou* despite everything; **je le ferai ~ tout** I'll do it all the same *ou* come what may

2 CONJ **~ que*** in spite of the fact that, despite the fact that, although; (*littér*) **~ qu'il en ait** despite his wishes

malhabile [malabil] ADJ clumsy, awkward; **~ à (faire) qch** unskilful *ou* bad at (doing) sth

malhabilement [malabilmã] ADV clumsily, awkwardly, unskilfully

malheur [malœʀ] NM **a** (= *événement pénible*) misfortune; (= *événement très grave*) calamity; (= *épreuve*) ordeal, hardship; (= *accident*) accident, mishap; **il a supporté ses ~s sans se plaindre** he suffered his misfortunes without complaint; **cette famille a eu beaucoup de ~s** this family has had a lot of misfortune; **un ~ est si vite arrivé** accidents *ou* mishaps happen so easily; **en cas de ~** in case anything should go wrong; **cela a été le grand ~ de sa vie** it was the great tragedy of his life; **ce n'est pas un gros ~ !** ◊ **c'est un petit ~ !** it's not such a calamity! *ou* tragedy! *ou* disaster! ▪ (*PROV*) **un ~ n'arrive jamais seul** troubles never come singly, it never rains but it pours (*PROV*) ▪ (*PROV*) **à quelque chose ~ est bon** every cloud has a silver lining (*PROV*), it's an ill wind that blows nobody any good (*PROV*)

b **le ~** (= *l'adversité*) adversity; (= *la malchance*) ill luck, misfortune; **dans son ~** amongst all his misfortune; **ils ont eu le ~ de perdre leur mère** they had the misfortune to lose their mother; **nos voisins sont dans le ~** our neighbours are going through hard times ▪ (*PROV*) **le ~ des uns fait le bonheur des autres** it's an ill wind that blows nobody any good (*PROV*); **le ~ a voulu qu'un policier le voie** as ill luck would have it a policeman saw him ▪ (*PROV*) **c'est dans le ~ qu'on connaît ses amis** a friend in need is a friend indeed (*PROV*), it's in times of trouble that you know who your real friends are

c **de ~*** (= *maudit*) wretched; **cette pluie de ~ a tout gâché** this wretched rain has spoilt everything → **oiseau**

d (*loc*) **~ !** oh, lord!*, hell!*; (*Bible*) **~ à l'homme** *ou* **à celui par qui le scandale arrive** woe to that man by whom the offence cometh; **~ à (celui) qui ...** † woe betide him who ...; **~ à toi si tu y touches!** woe betide you if you touch it!; **par ~** unfortunately, as ill luck would have it; **le ~ c'est que ...** ◊ **il n'y a qu'un ~, c'est que ...** the trouble *ou* snag is that ...; **son ~, c'est qu'il boit** his trouble is that he drinks; **le ~ dans tout cela, c'est qu'elle a perdu tout son argent** the sad thing about it *ou* the tragedy is that she lost all her money; **faire le ~ de ses parents** to bring sorrow to one's parents, cause one's parents nothing but unhappiness; **faire un ~** (= *avoir un gros succès*) [*spectacle*] to be a big hit; [*artiste, joueur*] to make a great hit, be all the rage; **s'il continue à m'ennuyer, je fais un ~*** if he carries on annoying me I'll do something I'll regret; **quel ~ qu'il ne soit pas venu** what a shame *ou* pity he didn't come; **il a eu le ~ de dire que cela ne lui plaisait pas** he made the big mistake of saying he didn't like it; **pour son ~** for his sins; **ne parle pas de ~ !** God forbid! → **comble, jouer**

▼ **malheureusement** [malœʀøzmã] ADV unfortunately

malheureux, -euse [malœʀø, øz] **1** ADJ

a (= *infortuné*) unfortunate; **les malheureuses victimes des bombardements** the unfortunate *ou* hapless (*frm*) victims of the bombings

b (= *regrettable, fâcheux*) [*résultat, jour, geste*] unfortunate; **pour un mot ~** because of an unfortunate remark; **c'est bien ~ qu'il ne puisse pas venir** it's very unfortunate *ou* it's a great shame *ou* it's a great pity that he can't come; **si c'est pas ~ d'entendre ça !*** it makes you sick to hear that!*; **ah te voilà enfin, c'est pas ~ !*** oh, there you are at last and about time too!*

c (= *triste, qui souffre*) [*enfant, vie*] unhappy, miserable; **on a été très ~ pendant la guerre** we had a miserable life during the war; **il était très ~ de ne pouvoir nous aider** he was most distressed *ou* upset at not being able to help us; **prendre un air ~** to look unhappy *ou* distressed; **rendre qn ~** to make sb unhappy; **être ~ comme les pierres** to be wretchedly unhappy *ou* utterly wretched

d (*après n = malchanceux*) [*candidat*] unsuccessful, unlucky; [*tentative*] unsuccessful; **il prit une initiative malheureuse** he took an unfortunate step; **il a été félicité par ses adversaires ~** he was congratulated by his defeated opponents; **être ~ au jeu/en amour** to be unlucky at gambling/in love; **amour ~** unhappy love affair → **heureux, main**

e (*: *avant n = insignifiant*) wretched, miserable; **toute une histoire pour un ~ billet de 100 F/pour une malheureuse erreur** such a to-do for a wretched *ou* measly* *ou* mouldy* 100-franc note/for a miserable mistake; **il y avait deux ou trois ~ spectateurs** there was a miserable handful of spectators; **sans même un ~ coup de fil** without so much as a phone call

2 NM,F (= *infortuné*) poor wretch *ou* soul *ou* devil*; (= *indigent*) needy person; **il a tout perdu? le ~ !** did he lose everything? the poor man!; **un ~ de plus** another poor devil*; **ne fais pas cela, ~ !** don't do that, you fool!; **aider les ~** (= *indigents*) to help the needy *ou* those who are badly off; **la malheureuse a agonisé pendant des heures** the poor woman suffered for hours before she died

malhonnête [malɔnɛt] **1** ADJ **a** (= *déloyal*) dishonest; (= *crapuleux*) crooked **b** († = *indécent*) rude **2** NMF (= *personne déloyale*) dishonest person; (= *escroc*) crook

malhonnêtement [malɔnɛtmã] ADV dishonestly

malhonnêteté [malɔnɛtte] NF **a** (= *improbité*) dishonesty, crookedness; **faire des ~s** to carry on dishonest *ou* crooked dealings **b** († = *manque de politesse*) rudeness; **dire des ~s** to make rude remarks, say rude things

Mali [mali] NM Mali

malice [malis] NF **a** (= *espièglerie*) mischievousness; **réponse pleine de ~** mischievous reply; **... dit-il non sans ~** ... he said somewhat mischievously; **boîte/sac à ~** box/bag of tricks **b** (= *méchanceté*) malice, spite; **par ~** out of malice *ou* spite; **elle a dit ça sans ~** she meant no harm by it; **il est sans ~** he is quite guileless; **il n'y voit** *ou* **entend pas ~** he means no harm by it

malicieusement [malisjøzmã] ADV mischievously, roguishly

malicieux, -ieuse [malisjø, jøz] ADJ [*personne, remarque*] mischievous; [*sourire*] mischievous, impish; **notre oncle est très ~** our uncle is a great tease; **petit ~ !** little imp *ou* monkey!

malien, -enne [maljɛ̃, ɛn] **1** ADJ of *ou* from Mali, Malian **2 Malien(ne)** NM,F Malian, inhabitant *ou* native of Mali

maligne [maliɲ] ADJ F, NF → **malin**

malignité [maliɲite] NF **a** (= *malveillance*) malice, spite **b** (*Méd*) malignancy

malin, maligne, maline* [malɛ̃, maliɲ, malin] **1** ADJ **a** (= *intelligent*) [*personne, air*] smart, shrewd, cunning; **sourire ~** cunning *ou* knowing *ou* crafty smile; **il est ~ comme un singe** [*adulte*] he's a crafty old devil*; [*enfant*] he's a crafty little devil*; **bien ~ qui le dira !** who can tell!; **il n'est pas bien ~** he isn't very bright *ou* clever; (*iro*) **c'est ~ !** oh, very clever! (*iro*) **si tu te crois ~ de faire ça !** I suppose you think that's clever? → **jouer**

b (* = *difficile*) **ce n'est pourtant pas bien ~** but it isn't so difficult *ou* tricky; **ce n'est pas plus ~ que ça** it's as easy *ou* simple as that, that's all there is to it

c (= *mauvais*) [*influence*] malignant, baleful, malicious; **prendre un ~ plaisir à faire qch** to take (a) malicious pleasure in doing sth; **l'esprit ~** the devil

d (*Méd*) malignant

2 NM,F **c'est un (petit) ~** he's a crafty one, he knows a thing or two, there are no flies on him (*Brit*); (*iro*) **gros ~ !** you're a bright one! (*iro*); **ne fais pas ton** *ou* **le ~*** don't try to show off; **à ~, ~ et demi** there's always someone cleverer than you

3 NM **le Malin** the Devil

malingre [malɛ̃gʀ] ADJ [*personne*] sickly, puny; [*corps*] puny

malinois [malinwa] NM police dog, ≈ German Shepherd, ≈ Alsatian (*Brit*)

malintentionné, e [malɛ̃tãsjɔne] ADJ ill-intentioned, malicious, spiteful (**envers** towards)

malle [mal] NF **a** (= *valise*) trunk; **faire sa ~** *ou* **ses ~s** to pack one's trunk; **ils se sont fait la ~:** they've cleared off*, they've done a bunk‡ (*Brit*) *ou* a runner* (*Brit*); **on a intérêt à se faire la ~:** we'd better make ourselves scarce*, we'd better scarper* (*Brit*); **il a quitté sa famille avec sa ~ à quatre nœuds†** he left home with all his worldly possessions tied up in a bundle **b** (*Aut*) (= *arrière*) boot (*Brit*), trunk (*US*) **c** (*Hist*) **la Malle des Indes** the Indian Mail

malléabilité [maleabilite] NF [*métal*] malleability; [*caractère*] malleability, pliability, flexibility

malléable [maleabl] ADJ [*métal*] malleable; [*caractère*] malleable, pliable, flexible

malle-poste (*pl* **malles-poste**) [malpɔst] NF (*Hist* = *diligence*) mail coach

mallette [malɛt] NF **a** (= *valise*) (small) suitcase; (= *porte-documents*) briefcase, attaché case; **~ de voyage** overnight case, grip **b** (*Belg* = *cartable*) schoolbag, satchel

mal-logé, e [malɔʒe] NM,F *person living in substandard housing*

malmener [malməne] ▶conjug 5◀ VT (= *brutaliser*) [+ *personne*] to manhandle, handle roughly; (*Mil, Sport*) [+ *adversaire*] to give a rough time *ou* handling to; (*fig*) **être malmené par la critique** to be given a rough ride by the critics

malnutrition [malnytʀisjɔ̃] NF malnutrition

malodorant, e [malɔdɔʀɑ̃, ɑ̃t] ADJ [*personne, pièce*] foul-smelling, malodorous (*frm*), smelly; [*haleine*] bad, foul (*Brit*)

malotru, e [malɔtʀy] NM,F lout, boor, yob* (*Brit*)

malouin, e [malwɛ̃, in] **1** ADJ of *ou* from Saint-Malo **2 Malouin(e)** NM,F inhabitant *ou* native of Saint-Malo **3 Malouines** NFPL **les (îles) Malouines** the Falkland Islands, the Falklands

mal-pensant, e (*mpl* **mal-pensants**) [malpɑ̃sɑ̃, ɑ̃t] **1** ADJ malicious **2** NM,F malicious person

malpoli, e [malpɔli] ADJ impolite, discourteous

malpropre [malpʀɔpʀ] **1** ADJ **a** (= *sale*) [*personne, objet*] dirty, grubby, grimy; [*travail*]

▶ GRAMMAIRE ACTIVE: **malheureusement** 29.3, 39.2, 47.4, 52.5, 52.6

shoddy, slovenly, sloppy [b] (= *indécent*) [*allusion, histoire*] smutty, dirty, unsavoury [c] (= *indélicat*) [*conduite, personne, action*] unsavoury, dishonest, despicable [2] NMF (*hum*) swine; **se faire chasser comme un ~*** to be thrown *ou* kicked* out

malproprement [malpRɔpRəmã] ADV in a dirty way; **manger ~** to be a messy eater

malpropreté [malpRɔpRəte] NF [a] **la ~** dirtiness, grubbiness, griminess [b] (= *acte*) low *ou* shady *ou* despicable trick; (= *parole*) low *ou* unsavoury remark

malsain, e [malsɛ̃, ɛn] ADJ [a] [*climat, logement*] unhealthy; [*travail*] hazardous to one's health [b] [*influence, littérature, curiosité*] unhealthy, unwholesome; [*esprit, mentalité*] nasty, unhealthy; **il a une relation ~e avec l'argent** he has an unhealthy relationship with money; **c'est un film** ~ it's a pretty sick film; **le climat ~ qui règne dans certaines entreprises** the unsavoury *ou* unwholesome atmosphere in some companies; **l'atmosphère devient ~e au bureau** things are getting a bit unpleasant at work; **tous ces monopoles, c'est ~ pour l'économie** all these monopolies are bad for the economy; **sauvons-nous, ça devient ~** (*dangereux*) let's get out of here, things are looking a bit dangerous *ou* dodgy* (*Brit*); **c'est quelqu'un de ~** he's an unsavoury character

malséant, e [malseã, ãt] ADJ (*littér*) unseemly, unbecoming, improper

malsonnant, e [malsɔnã, ãt] ADJ (*littér*) [*propos*] offensive

malt [malt] NM malt; **whisky pur ~** malt (whisky)

maltage [maltaʒ] NM malting

maltais, e [maltɛ, ɛz] [1] ADJ Maltese; **(orange) ~e** *type of juicy orange* [2] NM (*Ling*) Maltese [3] **Maltais(e)** NM,F Maltese

maltase [maltaz] NF maltase

Malte [malt] NF Malta

malter [malte] ▶ conjug 1 ◀ VT to malt

malthusianisme [maltyzjanism] NM Malthusianism; **~ économique** Malthusian economics *sg*

malthusien, -ienne [maltyzjɛ̃, jɛn] [1] ADJ (*Écon, Sociol*) Malthusian [2] NM,F Malthusian

maltose [maltoz] NM maltose, malt sugar

maltraitance [maltRɛtãs] NF **~ d'enfants** *ou* **à enfants** ill-treatment of children; (*sexuelle*) child abuse

maltraitant, e [maltRɛtã, ãt] ADJ [*famille, parent*] abusive

maltraiter [maltRete] ▶ conjug 1 ◀ VT [a] (= *brutaliser*) to manhandle, handle roughly, ill-treat; [+ *enfant*] to abuse [b] (= *mal user de*) [+ *langue, grammaire*] to misuse [c] (= *critiquer*) [+ *œuvre, auteur*] to give a rough ride to

malus [malys] NM (car insurance) surcharge

malveillance [malvejãs] NF (= *méchanceté*) spite, malevolence; (= *désobligeance*) ill will (**pour, envers** towards); (*Jur*) **avoir agi sans ~** to have acted without malicious intent; **acte de ~** spiteful *ou* malevolent action; **propos dus à la ~ publique** spiteful *ou* malicious public rumour; **regarder qn avec ~** to look at sb malevolently; **je dis cela sans ~ à son égard** I say that without wishing to be spiteful to him; **c'est par pure ~ qu'il a agi ainsi** he did that out of sheer spite *ou* malevolence

malveillant, e [malvejã, ãt] ADJ [*personne, regard, remarque*] malevolent, malicious, spiteful

malvenu, e [malvəny] ADJ (= *déplacé*) out of place (*attrib*), out-of-place (*épith*); (= *mal développé*) malformed → **venu**

malversation [malvɛRsasjɔ̃] NF (*gén pl*) embezzlement (*NonC*), misappropriation of funds

malvoisie [malvwazi] NM (= *vin*) malmsey (wine); (= *cépage*) malvasia

malvoyant, e [malvwajã, ãt] NM,F person who is partially sighted; **les ~s** the partially sighted

maman [mamã] NF mother, mum* (*Brit*), mummy* (*Brit*), mom* (*US*), mommy* (*US*) → **futur**

mambo [mã(m)bo] NM mambo

mamelle [mamɛl] NF [a] (*Zool*) teat; (= *pis*) udder, dug [b]† [*femme*] breast; (*péj*) tit*; [*homme*] breast; **à la ~** at the breast; (*fig*) **dès la ~** from infancy; (*fig*) **les deux ~s de …** the lifeblood of …

mamelon [mam(ə)lɔ̃] NM [a] (*Anat*) nipple [b] (*Géog*) knoll, hillock

mamelonné, e [mam(ə)lɔne] ADJ hillocky

mamelu, e [mam(ə)ly] ADJ (*péj ou hum*) big-breasted, well-endowed (*hum*)

mamel(o)uk [mamluk] NM Mameluke

mamie[1] [mami] NF (*langage enfantin* = *grand-mère*) granny*, gran*

mamie[2]††, **m'amie** [mami] NF = **ma mie** → **mie[2]**

mammaire [mamɛR] ADJ [*glande*] mammary

mammectomie [mamɛktɔmi] NF mastectomy

mammifère [mamifɛR] [1] NM mammal; **les ~s** mammals [2] ADJ mammalian

mammographie [mamɔgrafi] NF mammography

Mammon [mamɔ̃] NM Mammon

mammouth [mamut] NM mammoth

mammy [mami] NF = **mamie[1]**

mamours* [mamuR] NMPL (*hum*) **faire des ~ à qn** to caress *ou* fondle sb; **se faire des ~** to bill and coo

mam'selle*, **mam'zelle*** [mamzɛl] NF ABRÉV = **mademoiselle**

Man [mã] NF **l'île de ~** the Isle of Man

manade [manad] NF (*en Provence*) [*taureaux*] herd of bulls; [*chevaux*] herd of horses

management [manaʒmã, manadʒmɛnt] NM management

manager[1] [manadʒɛR] NM (*Écon, Sport*) manager; (*Théât*) agent

manager[2] [mana(d)ʒe] ▶ conjug 3 ◀ VT to manage

managérial, e [manaʒeRjal, jo] ADJ (*mpl* **-iaux**) [*pratique*] managerial; **équipe ~e** management team

Managua [managwa] N Managua

Manama [manama] N Manama

manant [manã] NM [a] (†, *littér*) churl† [b] (*Hist*) (= *villageois*) yokel; (= *vilain*) villein

Manche [mãʃ] NF **la ~** (= *mer*) the English Channel; (= *département français*) la Manche; (= *région d'Espagne*) la Mancha; **des deux côtés/de l'autre côté de la ~** on both sides of/across the Channel

manche[1] [mãʃ] [1] NF [a] (*Habillement*) sleeve; **à ~s courtes/longues** short-/long-sleeved; **sans ~s** sleeveless; **se mettre en ~s** to roll up one's sleeves; **avoir qn dans sa ~**† to be well in with sb*; (*lit, fig*) **relever** *ou* **retrousser ses ~s** to roll up one's sleeves; **faire la ~*** [*mendiant*] to beg; [*artiste*] to perform in the streets, busk (*Brit*) [b] (= *chemise, effet, paire* [b] = *partie*) (*gén, Pol, Sport*) round; (*Bridge*) game; (*Tennis*) set; **décisive** tiebreak(er); (*fig*) **on a gagné la première ~** we've won the first round in the battle [c] (*Aviat*) sleeve

[2] COMP ▶ **manche à air** (*Aviat*) wind sock; (*Naut*) airshaft ▶ **manche ballon** puff sleeve ▶ **manche à crevés** slashed sleeve ▶ **manche gigot** leg-of-mutton sleeve ▶ **manche kimono** kimono *ou* loose sleeve ▶ **manche montée** set-in sleeve ▶ **manche raglan** raglan sleeve ▶ **manche trois-quarts** three-quarter sleeve ▶ **manche à vent** airshaft

manche[2] [mãʃ] [1] NM [a] (*gén*) handle; (*long*) shaft; (*Mus*) neck; **être du côté du ~*** to be on the winning side; **se mettre du côté du ~*** to side with the winner; **jeter le ~ après la cognée** to throw in one's hand; **il ne faut pas jeter le ~ après la cognée !** don't give up so easily! → **branler** [b] (* = *incapable*) clumsy fool *ou* oaf, clot (*Brit*); **conduire comme un ~** to be a hopeless *ou* rotten* driver; **tu t'y prends comme un ~ !** you're making a real mess* *ou* a hash* of it! [2] COMP ▶ **manche à balai** (*gén*) broomstick, broomshaft (*Brit*); (*Aviat, Ordin*) joystick ▶ **manche à gigot** leg-of-mutton holder ▶ **manche de gigot** knuckle (of a leg-of-mutton)

mancheron[1] [mãʃRɔ̃] NM [*vêtement*] short sleeve

mancheron[2] [mãʃRɔ̃] NM [*charrue*] handle

manchette [mãʃɛt] NF [a] [*chemise*] cuff; (*protectrice*) oversleeve [b] (*Presse* = *titre*) headline; **mettre en ~** to headline, put in headlines [c] (= *note*) marginal note; **en ~** in the margin [d] (= *coup*) forearm blow

manchon [mãʃɔ̃] NM [a] (*Habillement*) (*pour les mains*) muff; (= *guêtre*) snow gaiter → **chien** [b] (*Tech*) **~ à incandescence** incandescent (gas) mantle [c] (*Culin*) conserve of poultry wing [d] (*Tech*) [*tuyau*] coupler

manchot, e [mãʃo, ɔt] [1] ADJ (*d'un bras*) one-armed; (*des deux bras*) armless; (*d'une main*) one-handed; (*des deux mains*) with no hands, handless; **être ~ du bras droit/gauche** to have the use of only one's left/right arm; **il n'est pas ~ !*** (*adroit*) he's clever *ou* he's no fool with his hands!; (*courageux*) he's no lazybones!* [2] NM,F (*d'un bras*) one-armed person; (*des deux bras*) person with no arms [3] NM (*Orn*) penguin; **~ royal/empereur** king/emperor penguin

mandala [mãdala] NM mandala

mandale* [mãdal] NF biff*, cuff, clout (*Brit*)

mandant, e [mãdã, ãt] NM,F (*Jur*) principal; (*frm : Pol*) **je parle au nom de mes ~s** I speak on behalf of my constituents

mandarin [mãdaRɛ̃] NM (*Hist, péj*) mandarin; (*Ling*) Mandarin (Chinese); (*Orn*) mandarin duck

mandarinal, e [mãdaRinal, o] ADJ (*mpl* **-aux**) mandarin

mandarinat [mãdaRina] NM (*Hist*) mandarinate; (*péj*) academic establishment (*péj*)

mandarine [mãdaRin] [1] NF mandarin (orange), tangerine [2] ADJ INV tangerine

mandarinier [mãdaRinje] NM mandarin (orange) tree

mandat [mãda] [1] NM [a] (*gén, Pol*) mandate; **donner à qn ~ de faire** to mandate sb to do, give sb a mandate to do; **obtenir le renouvellement de son ~** to be re-elected, have one's mandate renewed; **la durée du ~ présidentiel** the president's term of office; **territoires sous ~** mandated territories, territories under mandate [b] (*Comm*) **~ (postal)** money order, postal order (*Brit*) [c] (*Jur* = *procuration*) power of attorney, proxy; (*Police*) warrant [2] COMP ▶ **mandat d'amener** ≈ summons ▶ **mandat d'arrêt** ≈ warrant for arrest ▶ **mandat de comparution** ≈ summons (to appear), ≈ subpoena ▶ **mandat de dépôt** ≈ committal order; **placer qn sous ~ de dépôt** ≈ to place sb under a committal order ▶ **mandat d'expulsion** eviction order ▶ **mandat international** (*Fin*) international money order ▶ **mandat de perquisition** search warrant

mandataire [mãdatɛR] NMF (*Jur*) proxy, attorney; (= *représentant*) representative; **je ne suis que son ~** I'm only acting as a proxy for him; **~ aux Halles** (sales) agent (at the Halles)

mandat-carte (*pl* **mandats-cartes**) [mãdakaRt] NM (*Comm*) money *ou* postal (*Brit*) order (*in postcard form*)

mandatement [mãdatmã] NM [a] [*somme*]

payment (by money order) **b** [*personne*] appointment, commissioning

mandater [mɑ̃date] ▸conjug 1◂ VT **a** (= *donner pouvoir à*) [+ *personne*] to appoint, commission; (*Pol*) [+ *député*] to give a mandate to, elect **b** (*Fin*) **~ une somme** (= *écrire*) to write out a money order for a sum; (= *payer*) to pay a sum by money order

mandat-lettre (*pl* **mandats-lettres**) [mɑ̃daletʀ] NM (*Comm*) money *ou* postal (*Brit*) order (*with space for correspondence*)

mandchou, e [mɑ̃tʃu] **1** ADJ Manchu(rian) **2** NM (*Ling*) Manchu **3** **Mandchou(e)** NM,F Manchu

Mandchourie [mɑ̃tʃuʀi] NF Manchuria

mandement [mɑ̃dmɑ̃] NM **a** (*Rel*) pastoral **b** (*Hist = ordre*) mandate, command; (*Jur = convocation*) subpoena

mander [mɑ̃de] ▸conjug 1◂ VT **a** †† (= *ordonner*) to command; (= *convoquer*) to summon **b** (*littér = dire par lettre*) **~ qch à qn** to send *ou* convey the news of sth to sb, inform sb of sth

mandibule [mɑ̃dibyl] NF mandible; **jouer des ~s*** (*Brit*), chow down* (*US*)

mandoline [mɑ̃dɔlin] NF mandolin(e)

mandragore [mɑ̃dʀagɔʀ] NF mandrake

mandrill [mɑ̃dʀil] NM mandrill

mandrin [mɑ̃dʀɛ̃] NM (*pour serrer*) chuck; (*pour percer, emboutir*) punch; (*pour élargir, égaliser des trous*) drift; (*tour*) mandrel

manducation [mɑ̃dykasjɔ̃] NF manducation

manécanterie [manekɑ̃tʀi] NF (parish) choir school

manège [manɛʒ] NM **a** [*fête foraine*] fairground attraction; **~ (de chevaux de bois)** merry-go-round, roundabout (*Brit*), carousel (*US*) → **tour²** **b** (*Équitation = piste, salle*) ring, school; **~ couvert** indoor school; **faire du ~** to do exercises in the indoor school **c** (*fig = agissements*) game, ploy; **j'ai deviné son petit ~** I guessed what he was up to, I saw through his little game

mânes [mɑn] NMPL (*Antiq Rel*) manes; (*littér*) **les ~ de ses ancêtres** the shades of his ancestors (*littér*)

maneton [man(ə)tɔ̃] NM (*Aut*) crankpin

manette [manɛt] NF lever, tap; **~ des gaz** throttle lever; **~ de jeux** joystick; **être aux ~s*** to be in charge → **fond**

manganate [mɑ̃ganat] NM manganate

manganèse [mɑ̃ganɛz] NM manganese

mangeable [mɑ̃ʒabl] ADJ (*lit, fig*) edible, eatable

mangeaille [mɑ̃ʒaj] NF (*péj*) (= *nourriture mauvaise*) pigswill, disgusting food; (= *grande quantité de nourriture*) mounds of food; **il nous venait des odeurs de ~** we were met by an unappetizing smell of food (cooking)

mange-disques [mɑ̃ʒdisk] NM INV slot-in record player (*for singles*)

mangeoire [mɑ̃ʒwaʀ] NF (*gén*) trough, manger; [*oiseaux*] feeding dish

mangeotter* [mɑ̃ʒɔte] ▸conjug 1◂ VT to nibble

manger [mɑ̃ʒe] ▸conjug 3◂ **1** VT **a** (*gén*) to eat; [+ *soupe*] to drink, eat; **~ dans une assiette/dans un bol** to eat off *ou* from a plate/out of a bowl; **il mange peu** he doesn't eat much; **il ne mange pas** *ou* **rien en ce moment** he's off his food at present, he is not eating at all at present; **ils ont mangé tout ce qu'elle avait (à la maison)** they ate her out of house and home; **il a mangé tout ce qui restait** he has eaten (up) all that was left; **cela se mange?** can you eat it?, is it edible?; **ce plat se mange très chaud** this dish should be eaten piping hot; **ils leur ont fait** *ou* **donné à ~ un excellent poisson** they served *ou* gave them some excellent fish (to eat); **faire ~ qn** to feed sb; **faire ~ qch à qn** to give sb sth to

eat, make sb eat sth; **donner à ~ à un bébé/un animal** to feed a baby/an animal; **~ goulûment** to wolf down one's food, eat greedily; **~ salement** to be a messy eater; **~ comme un cochon*** to eat like a pig*; **finis de ~!** ◊ **mange!** eat up!; **on mange bien/mal ici** the food is good/bad here; **les enfants ne mangent pas à leur faim à l'école** the children don't get *ou* are not given enough to eat at school

b (= *faire un repas*) **~ dehors** *ou* **au restaurant** to eat out, have a meal out; **c'est l'heure de ~** (*midi*) it's lunchtime; (*soir*) it's dinnertime; **inviter qn à ~** to invite sb for a meal; **boire en mangeant** to drink with one's meal; **~ sur le pouce** to have a (quick) snack, snatch a bite (to eat) → **carte**

c (*fig: avec avidité*) **~ qn des yeux** to gaze hungrily at sb, devour sb with one's eyes; **~ qn de baisers** to smother sb with kisses; **allez le voir, il ne vous mangera pas** go and see him, he won't eat you; **il va te ~ tout cru** he'll have you for breakfast, he'll swallow you whole; **se faire ~ par les moustiques** to get eaten alive *ou* bitten to death by mosquitoes

d (= *ronger*) to eat (away); **mangé par les mites** *ou* **aux mites** moth-eaten; **la grille (de fer) est mangée par la rouille** the (iron) railing is eaten away with *ou* by rust; **le soleil a mangé la couleur** the sun has taken out *ou* faded the colour

e (= *faire disparaître, consommer*) **toutes ces activités lui mangent son temps** all these activities take up his time; **~ ses mots** to swallow one's words; **les grosses entreprises mangent les petites** the big firms swallow up the smaller ones; **une barbe touffue lui mangeait le visage** his face was half hidden under a bushy beard; **des yeux énormes lui mangeaient le visage** his face seemed to be just two great eyes

f (= *dilapider*) [+ *fortune, capital, économies*] to go through, squander; **l'entreprise mange de l'argent** the business is eating money; **dans cette affaire il mange de l'argent** he's spending more than he earns *ou* his outgoings are more than his income in this business

g (*loc*) **~ la consigne** *ou* **la commission** to forget one's errand; **~ comme un oiseau** to eat like a bird; **~ le morceau*** (= *parler*) to spill the beans*, talk, come clean*; **~ son pain blanc le premier** to have it easy at the start; **je ne mange pas de ce pain-là** I'm having nothing to do with that!, I'm not stooping to anything like that!; **ça ne mange pas de pain!** it doesn't cost much!, you won't have to do much!; **~ son blé en herbe** to spend one's money in advance *ou* before one gets it, eat one's seed corn (*US*); **~ à tous les râteliers** to cash in* on all sides; **~ la soupe sur la tête de qn*** to tower over sb → **laine, sang, vache** *etc*

2 NM food; **préparer le ~ des enfants*** to get the children's food *ou* meal ready; **« ici on peut apporter son ~ »*** "customers may consume their own food on the premises"; **à prendre après ~** to be taken after meals; **je rentrerai avant ~** I'll be back before lunch (*ou* dinner) → **perdre**

mange-tout [mɑ̃ʒtu] NM INV (**pois**) **~** mangetout peas; (**haricots**) **~** string beans

mangeur, -euse [mɑ̃ʒœʀ, øz] NM,F eater; **être gros** *ou* **grand/petit ~** to be a big/small eater; **c'est un gros ~ de pain** he eats a lot of bread, he's a big bread-eater*; **~ d'hommes** man-eater

manglier [mɑ̃glije] NM mangrove tree

mangoustan [mɑ̃gustɑ̃] NM mangosteen

mangouste [mɑ̃gust] NF (= *animal*) mongoose; (= *fruit*) mangosteen

mangrove [mɑ̃gʀɔv] NF mangrove swamp

mangue [mɑ̃g] NF mango

manguier [mɑ̃gje] NM mango(tree)

maniabilité [manjabilite] NF [*objet*] handiness, manageability; [*voiture*] driveability; [*avion, bateau*] manoeuvrability; **appareil d'une grande ~** implement which is very easy to handle, very handy implement; **c'est un véhicule d'une étonnante ~** this vehicle is incredibly easy to handle *ou* drive

maniable [manjabl] ADJ **a** [*objet, taille*] handy, manageable, easy to handle (*attrib*); [*véhicule*] easy to handle *ou* drive (*attrib*); [*avion, bateau*] easy to manoeuvre (*attrib*); **peu ~** [*objet*] awkward, cumbersome; [*véhicule*] difficult to handle **b** (= *influençable*) [*électeur*] easily swayed *ou* influenced (*attrib*) **c** (= *accommodant*) [*personne, caractère*] accommodating, amenable **d** (*Naut*) [*temps*] good; [*vent*] moderate

maniaco-dépressif, -ive (*mpl* **maniaco-dépressifs**) [manjakodepʀesif, iv] ADJ, NM,F manic-depressive

maniaque [manjak] **1** ADJ [*personne*] finicky, fussy, pernickety; **faire qch avec un soin ~** to do sth with almost fanatical *ou* obsessive care **2** NMF **a** (= *fou*) maniac, lunatic; **~ sexuel** sex maniac **b** (= *fanatique*) fanatic, enthusiast; (= *méticuleux*) **quel ~ tu fais!** you're so fussy!; **c'est un ~ de la propreté** he's fanatical about cleanliness, cleanliness is an obsession with him; **c'est un ~ de l'exactitude** he's fanatical about punctuality, he's a stickler for punctuality; **c'est un ~ de la voile** he's sailing mad* *ou* a sailing fanatic

maniaquerie [manjakʀi] NF fussiness; **il est d'une ~!** he's so fussy!

manichéen, -enne [manikeɛ̃, ɛn] ADJ, NM,F Manich(a)ean

manichéisme [manikeism] NM (*Philo*) Manich(a)eism; (*péj*) over-simplification; (*fig*) **il fait du ~** he sees everything in black and white, everything is either good or bad to him

manichéiste [manikeist] ADJ, NM,F = **manichéen, -enne**

manie [mani] NF **a** (= *habitude*) odd habit; **elle est pleine de (petites) ~s** she's got all sorts of funny little ways *ou* habits; **avoir ses petites ~s** to have one's little ways; **mais quelle ~ tu as de te manger les ongles!** you've got a terrible habit of biting your nails!; **elle a la ~ de tout nettoyer** she's a compulsive *ou* obsessive cleaner **b** (= *obsession*) mania; (*Méd*) **~ de la persécution** persecution mania *ou* complex

maniement [manimɑ̃] NM **a** (= *manipulation*) handling; **d'un ~ difficile** difficult to handle; **le ~ de cet objet est pénible** this object is difficult to handle; **il possède à fond le ~ de la langue** he has a thorough understanding of how to use *ou* handle the language **b** (*Mil*) **~ d'armes** arms drill (*Brit*), manual of arms (*US*)

manier [manje] ▸conjug 7◂ **1** VT [+ *objet, langue, foule*] to handle; [+ *épée, outil*] to wield, handle; [+ *pâte*] to knead; [+ *personne*] to handle; (*péj*) to manipulate; **~ l'aviron** to pull *ou* ply (*littér*) the oars; **~ de grosses sommes d'argent** to handle large sums of money; **cheval/voiture facile à ~** horse/car which is easy to handle; **il sait ~ le pinceau** ◊ **il manie le pinceau avec adresse** he knows how to handle a brush, he's a painter of some skill; **savoir ~ la plume** to be a good writer; **savoir ~ l'ironie** to handle irony skilfully **2** **se manier** VPR = **se magner**

maniéré, e [manjeʀe] ADJ **a** (*péj = affecté*) [*personne, style, voix*] affected **b** (*Art*) [*genre*] mannered; **les tableaux très ~s de ce peintre** the mannered style of this painter's work

manière [manjɛʀ] **1** NF **a** (= *façon*) way; **sa ~ d'agir/de parler** the way he behaves/speaks; **il le fera à sa ~** he'll do it (in) his own way; **~ de vivre** way of life; **~ de voir (les choses)** outlook (on things); **c'est sa ~ d'être habituelle** that's just the way he is, that's just how he usually is; **ce n'est pas la bonne ~ de s'y prendre** this is not the right *ou* best way to go about it; **d'une ~ efficace** in an efficient way; **de quelle ~ as-tu fait cela ?** how did you do that?; **à la ~ d'un singe** like a monkey, as a monkey would do

b (= *savoir-faire*) **avec les animaux/les enfants, il a la ~** he's good with animals/children; (*Art* = *style*) **c'est un Matisse dernière ~** it's a late Matisse *ou* an example of Matisse's later work; **dans la ~ classique** in the classical style; **à la ~ de Racine** in the style of Racine; **robe/examen nouvelle ~** new-style *ou* new-look dress/exam; **démocrate/directeur nouvelle ~** new-style democrat/director

c (*Gram*) **adverbe/complément de ~** adverb/adjunct of manner

d (*loc*) **employer la ~ forte** ◊ **user de la ~ forte** to use strong-arm methods *ou* tactics; **il l'a giflé de belle ~ !** he gave him a sound *ou* good slap!; **en ~ d'excuse** by way of (an) excuse; **d'une ~ générale** generally speaking, as a general rule; **de cette ~** (in) this way; **de telle ~ que ...** in such a way that ...; **d'une ~ ou d'une autre** somehow or other; **d'une certaine ~** in a way, in some ways; (*frm*) **en quelque ~** in a certain way; **en aucune ~** ◊ **d'aucune ~** in no way, under no circumstances; **je n'accepterai en aucune ~** I shall not agree on any account; **de ~ à faire** so as to do; **de ~ (à ce) que nous arrivions à l'heure** ◊ **de ~ à arriver à l'heure** so that we get there on time

e († = *genre*) kind; **une ~ de pastiche** a kind of pastiche; **quelle ~ d'homme est-ce ?** what kind *ou* sort of a man is he?, what manner of man is he?†

2 **manières** NFPL manners; **avoir de bonnes/mauvaises ~s** to have good/bad manners; **apprendre les belles ~s** to learn good manners; **il n'a pas de ~s** ◊ **il est sans ~s** he has no manners; **ce ne sont pas des ~s !** that's no way to behave!; **en voilà des ~s !** what a way to behave!; **je n'aime pas ces ~s !** I don't like this kind of behaviour!; **faire des ~s** (*minauderies*) to be affected, put on airs; (*chichis*) to make a fuss; **ne fais pas de ~s avec nous** you needn't stand on ceremony with us

maniérisme [manjeʀism] NM (*Art*) mannerism

maniériste [manjeʀist] 1 ADJ mannerist(ic) 2 NMF mannerist

manieur, -ieuse [manjœʀ, jøz] NM,F **~ d'argent** *ou* **de fonds** big businessman

manif* [manif] NF (ABRÉV = **manifestation**) demo*

manifestant, e [manifestɑ̃, ɑ̃t] NM,F demonstrator, protester

manifestation [manifestasjɔ̃] NF a (*Pol*) demonstration b (= *expression*) (*opinion, sentiment*) expression; (*maladie*) (= *apparition*) appearance; (= *symptômes*) outward sign *ou* symptom; **~ de mauvaise humeur** show of bad temper; **~ de joie** demonstration *ou* expression of joy; **accueillir qn avec de grandes ~s d'amitié** to greet sb with great demonstrations of friendship c [*Dieu*] (= *vérité*) revelation d (= *réunion, fête*) event; **~ artistique/culturelle/sportive** artistic/cultural/sporting event; **le maire assistait à cette sympathique ~** the mayor was present at this happy gathering *ou* on this happy occasion

manifeste [manifest] 1 ADJ [*vérité, injustice*] manifest, obvious, evident; [*sentiment, différence*] obvious, evident; **erreur ~** glaring error; **il est ~ que ...** it is quite obvious *ou* evident that ... 2 NM (*Littérat, Pol*) manifesto; (*Aviat, Naut*) manifest

manifestement [manifestəmɑ̃] ADV manifestly, obviously; **~, ça n'a servi à rien** it was obviously a waste of time; **il est ~ ivre** he's obviously drunk; **c'est fini ? — ~ is it finished? — apparently**

manifester [manifeste] ▸ conjug 1 ◂ 1 VT [+ *opinion, intention, sentiment*] to show, indicate; [+ *courage*] to show, demonstrate; **il m'a manifesté son désir de venir** he indicated to me that he wanted to come; (*frm*) **par ce geste, la France tient à nous ~ son amitié** France intends this gesture as a demonstration *ou* an indication of her friendship towards us

2 VI (*Pol*) to demonstrate, hold a demonstration

3 **se manifester** VPR a (= *se révéler*) [*émotion*] to express itself; [*difficultés*] to emerge, arise; [*phénomène*] to be apparent; **sa frustration se manifeste par des crises de colère** his frustration expresses *ou* manifests itself in angry outbursts; **cette maladie se manifeste par l'apparition de boutons** the appearance of a rash is the first symptom of this disease *ou* indicates the onset of this disease; **la crise se manifeste par l'effondrement des marchés** the crisis is reflected in the collapse of the markets; **la violence se manifeste à différents niveaux de la société** violence occurs at various levels of society; **Dieu s'est manifesté aux hommes** God revealed himself to mankind

b (= *se présenter*) [*personne*] to appear, turn up; (*par écrit, par téléphone*) to get in touch *ou* contact; [*bénévole, candidat, témoin*] to come forward

c (= *intervenir*) [*élève*] to participate (in class); **il n'a pas eu l'occasion de se ~ dans le débat** he didn't get a chance to make himself heard in the discussion; **il s'est manifesté par une déclaration fracassante** he came to public notice *ou* he attracted attention with a sensational statement

manigance [manigɑ̃s] NF (*gén pl*) scheme, trick, ploy; **encore une de ses ~s** another of his little schemes *ou* tricks *ou* ploys

manigancer [manigɑ̃se] ▸ conjug 3 ◂ VT to plot, devise; **qu'est-ce qu'il manigance maintenant ?** what's he up to now?, what's his latest little scheme?; **c'est lui qui a tout manigancé** he set the whole thing up*, he engineered it all

manille¹ [manij] 1 NM Manila cigar 2 **Manille** N Manila

manille² [manij] NF a (*Cartes*) (= *jeu*) manille; (= *dix*) ten b (*Tech*) shackle

manillon [manijɔ̃] NM ace (*in game of manille*)

manioc [manjɔk] NM manioc, cassava

manip* [manip] NF ABRÉV = **manipulation**

manipulateur, -trice [manipylatœʀ, tʀis] 1 ADJ a (*péj*) [*personne*] manipulative b (*Tech*) **bras ~** manipulator arm 2 NM,F a (= *technicien*) technician; **~ de laboratoire** laboratory technician; **~ radio** radiographer b (*péj*) manipulator c (= *prestidigitateur*) conjurer 3 NM (*Téléc*) key

manipulation [manipylasjɔ̃] NF a (= *maniement*) handling; **ces produits chimiques sont d'une ~ délicate** these chemicals should be handled with great care, great care should be taken in handling these chemicals b (*Sci*) experiment; **obtenu par ~ génétique** genetically engineered; **les ~s génétiques posent des problèmes éthiques** genetic engineering poses ethical problems c (*péj*) manipulation (*NonC*); **il y a eu des ~s électorales** there's been some vote-rigging d (= *prestidigitation*) sleight of hand e (*Méd*) [*os*] manipulation

manipule [manipyl] NM (*Antiq, Rel*) maniple

manipuler [manipyle] ▸ conjug 1 ◂ VT a [+ *objet, produit*] to handle b (*péj*) [+ *électeurs, presse, information*] to manipulate; [+ *statistiques*] to massage, doctor; **~ une élection** to rig an election; **~ les écritures** to rig *ou* fiddle* (*Brit*) the accounts, cook the books* (*Brit*)

manique [manik] NF [*ouvrier*] protective glove; [*cuisinier*] oven glove

Manitoba [manitɔba] NM Manitoba

manitou [manitu] NM a **grand ~*** big shot*, big noise* (*Brit*); **le grand ~ de l'entreprise** the big boss* in the company b (*Rel*) manitou

manivelle [manivɛl] NF (*gén*) crank; (*pour changer une roue*) wheel crank; (*pour démarrer*) crank, starting handle; **faire partir à la ~** to crank(-start) → **retour, tour**

manne [man] NF a (*Rel*) **la ~** manna; **recevoir la ~ (céleste)** (*la bonne parole*) to receive the word from on high b (= *aubaine*) godsend, manna; **ça a été pour nous une ~ (providentielle ou céleste)** that was a godsend for us, it was heaven-sent c (*Bot*) manna d (= *panier*) large wicker basket

mannequin [mankɛ̃] NM a (= *personne*) model, mannequin†; **être ~ chez ...** to model for ... → **défilé, taille¹** b (= *objet*) [*couturière*] (tailor's) dummy, mannequin; [*vitrine*] model, dummy; [*peintre*] model; (= *pantin*) stuffed dummy c (= *panier*) small (gardener's) basket

manœuvrabilité [manœvʀabilite] NF (*gén*) manoeuvrability *ou* driveability

manœuvrable [manœvʀabl] ADJ (*gén*) manoeuvrable, easy to handle; [*voiture*] easy to handle *ou* drive

manœuvre [manœvʀ] 1 NF a (= *opération*) manoeuvre (*Brit*), maneuver (*US*), operation; (*Rail*) **~ (d'aiguillage)** shunting (*NonC*) (*Brit*), switching (*NonC*) (*US*); **diriger/surveiller la ~** to control/supervise the operation *ou* manoeuvre; (*Aut, Naut*) **faire une ~** to do a manoeuvre; **je ne sais pas faire les ~s** (*en voiture*) I'm not good at parking (*ou* reversing *etc*); (*Naut*) **les ~s sont difficiles par gros temps** it's difficult to manoeuvre (the boat) in bad weather; **il voulait se garer mais il a manqué sa ~** he tried to park but he got the angle wrong; **fausse ~** (*lit*) mistake; (*fig*) wrong *ou* false move; **une fausse ~ et il perd les élections** if he puts one foot wrong *ou* makes one wrong move he'll lose the election; (*Rail*) **faire la ~** to shunt

b (*Mil*) manoeuvre (*Brit*), maneuver (*US*); **champ ou terrain de ~s** parade ground; **~ d'encerclement** encircling movement; **les grandes ~s de printemps** spring army manoeuvres *ou* exercises; **être en ~s** ◊ **faire des ~s** to be on manoeuvres

c (= *agissement, combinaison*) manoeuvre (*Brit*), maneuver (*US*); (= *machination, intrigue*) manoeuvring, ploy; **il a toute liberté de ~** he has complete freedom of manoeuvre; **~ de diversion** diversionary tactic; **~s électorales** vote-catching ploys; **~s frauduleuses** fraudulent schemes *ou* devices; **~ d'obstruction** obstructive move; **~ boursière** stockmarket manipulation; **il a été victime d'une ~ de l'adversaire** he was caught out by a clever move *ou* trick on the part of his opponents; **les grandes ~s politiques** intense political manoeuvring

d (*Naut* = *cordages*) **~s dormantes/courantes** standing/running rigging

2 NM (*gén*) labourer; (*en usine*) unskilled worker; **c'est un travail de ~** it's unskilled labour *ou* work; **~ agricole** farm labourer *ou* hand

manœuvrer [manœvʀe] ▸ conjug 1 ◂ 1 VT a [+ *véhicule*] to manoeuvre (*Brit*), maneuver (*US*); [+ *machine*] to operate, work b (= *manipuler*) [+ *personne*] to manipulate; **il se laisse ~ par sa femme** he allows himself to be manipulated by his wife 2 VI (*gén*) to manoeuvre; (*fig*) **il a manœuvré habilement** he moved *ou* manoeuvred skilfully

manœuvrier, -ière [manœvʀije, ijɛʀ] 1 ADJ manoeuvring 2 NM,F (*Mil*) tactician; (*Pol*) manoeuvrer

manoir [manwaʀ] NM manor *ou* country house

manomètre [manɔmɛtʀ] NM gauge, manometer

manométrique [manɔmetʀik] ADJ manometric

manouche* [manuʃ] NMF gipsy

manouvrier, -ière† [manuvʀije, ijɛʀ] NM,F (casual) labourer

manquant, e [mɑ̃kɑ̃, ɑ̃t] **1** ADJ missing → **chaînon 2** NM,F missing one

manque [mɑ̃k] **1** NM **a** ~ **de** (= pénurie) [+ nourriture, argent] lack of, shortage of, want of; (= faiblesse) [+ intelligence, goût] lack of, want of; **son ~ de sérieux au travail** his unreliability at work; **par ~ de** through lack ou shortage of, for want of; **quel ~ de chance! ou de pot!* ou de bol!*** what bad ou hard luck!; **~ à gagner** loss of profit ou earnings; **cela représente un sérieux ~ à gagner pour les cultivateurs** that means a serious loss of income ou a serious drop in earnings ou income for the farmers; **c'est un ~ de respect** it shows a lack of respect (**pour, à l'égard de** for), it's disrespectful (**pour, à l'égard de** to) **b** (= vide) gap, emptiness; (Drogue) withdrawal; **je ressens comme un grand ~** it's as if there were a great emptiness inside me; **un ~ que rien ne saurait combler** a gap which nothing could fill; **symptômes de ~** withdrawal symptoms; **être en état de ~** to be experiencing withdrawal symptoms **c** (Tex) flaw; **il faut faire un raccord (de peinture), il y a des ~s** we'll have to touch up the paintwork, there are bare patches **d** (Roulette) manque **2 manques** NMPL (= défauts) [roman] faults, flaws; [personne] failings, shortcomings; [mémoire, connaissances] gaps **3 à la manque:** LOC ADJ (péj) [chanteur] crummy‡, second-rate; **lui et ses idées à la ~** him and his half-baked* ou crummy‡ ideas

manqué, e [mɑ̃ke] (ptp de **manquer**) ADJ **a** [essai] failed, abortive, missed; [photo] spoilt; [vie] wasted; (Tech) [pièce] faulty; **occasion ~e** lost ou wasted opportunity; **roman ~** flawed novel; **c'est un écrivain ~** (vocation ratée) he should have been a writer → **garçon, rendez-vous b** (Culin) (gâteau) ~ ≈ sponge cake

manquement [mɑ̃kmɑ̃] NM (frm) ~ **à** [+ discipline, règle] breach of; ~ **au devoir** dereliction of duty; **au moindre ~** at the slightest lapse; (Jur) ~ **(à des obligations contractuelles)** default

▼ **manquer** [mɑ̃ke] ▸conjug 1◂ **1** VT **a** (= ne pas atteindre, saisir ou rencontrer) [+ but, occasion, personne, train] to miss; **la gare est sur la place, tu ne peux pas la ~** the station's right on the square, you can't miss it; ~ **une marche** to miss a step; **il l'a manqué qn de peu** (en lui tirant dessus) he missed him by a fraction, he just missed him; (à un rendez-vous) he just missed him; **je l'ai manqué de 5 minutes** I missed him by 5 minutes; **c'est un film/une pièce à ne pas ~** this film/play is a must*, it's a film/play that's not to be missed; **il ne faut pas ~ ça!** it's not to be missed!; (iro) **il n'en manque jamais une!*** he puts his foot in it every time!*; **vous n'avez rien manqué (en ne venant pas)** you didn't miss anything (by not coming); **je ne le manquerai pas** (= je vais lui donner une leçon) I won't let him get away with it → **coche b** (= ne pas réussir) [+ photo, gâteau] to spoil, make a mess of*, botch*; [+ examen] to fail; **il a manqué sa vie** he has wasted his life → **coup c** (= être absent de) (involontairement) to be absent from, miss; (volontairement) to miss, skip; ~ **l'école** to be absent from ou miss school; **il a manqué deux réunions** he missed two meetings **2** VI **a** (= faire défaut) to be lacking; **l'argent/la nourriture vint à ~** money/food ran out ou ran short; **les occasions ne manquent pas (de faire)** there is no shortage of ou there are endless opportunities (to do); **ici, les chats c'est pas ça qui manque*** there's no shortage of cats round here; **les mots manquent pour décrire …** no words can describe …; **ce qui lui manque, c'est l'imagination** what he lacks ou what he hasn't got is (the) imagination; **les mots me manquent pour exprimer …** I can't find the words to express …; **le temps me manque pour raconter la suite** I don't have (the) time to tell you the rest of the story; **j'irais bien, ce n'est pas l'envie qui me ou m'en manque** I would like to go, it's not that I don't want to; **le pied lui manqua** his foot slipped, he missed his footing; **la voix lui manqua** words failed him, he stood speechless; **un carreau manquait à la fenêtre** there was a pane missing in ou from the window; (hum) **qu'est-ce qui manque à ton bonheur?** is there something not to your liking?, what are you unhappy about?; (hum) **il lui manque toujours dix-neuf sous pour faire un franc** he doesn't have two pennies to rub together **b** (= être absent) to be absent; (= avoir disparu) to be missing (à from); (Scol) **il a souvent manqué l'an dernier** he was often absent last year, he missed a lot of school last year; ~ **à l'appel** (lit) to be absent from roll call; (fig) to be missing; (fig) **il ne manque pas un bouton de guêtre** everything's in apple-pie order, there's not a thing out of place **c** (= être regretté) **il nous manque ◊ sa présence nous manque** we miss him; **la campagne me manque** I miss the country **d** (= échouer) [expérience] to fail **e** (= être dans le besoin) **il a toujours peur de ~** he's always afraid of being hard up* **f** (= se dérober) **le sol a manqué sous ses pieds** the ground gave (way) beneath his feet **g** (avec infin = faillir) **il a manqué mourir** he nearly ou almost died; **elle a manqué (de) se faire écraser** she nearly ou almost got run over **3 manquer à** VT INDIR (= ne pas respecter) ~ **à ses promesses** to go back on one's promises, fail to keep one's word; ~ **à tous les usages** to flout every convention; **il manque à tous ses devoirs** he neglects all his duties; ~ **à son honneur/devoir** to fail in one's honour/duty; ~ **à qn†** (= être impoli) to be disrespectful to sb **4 manquer de** VT INDIR **a** (= être dépourvu de) [+ intelligence, générosité] to lack; [+ argent, main-d'œuvre] to be short of, lack; **ils ne manquent de rien** they want for nothing, they don't want for anything, they lack nothing; **le pays ne manque pas d'un certain charme** the country is not without a certain charm; **on manque d'air ici** there's no air in here, it's stuffy in here; (fig) **tu ne manques pas d'audace!** ou **d'air!* ou de culot!*** you've got a ou some nerve!*; **nous manquons de personnel** we're short-staffed, we're short of staff **b** (formules négatives) **ne manquez pas de le remercier pour moi** don't forget to thank him for me, be sure to thank him for me; **je ne manquerai pas de le lui dire** I'll be sure to tell him; **nous ne manquerons pas de vous en informer** we shall inform you without fail; **il n'a pas manqué de le lui dire** he made sure he told him; **remerciez-la — je n'y manquerai pas** thank her — I won't forget; **on ne peut ~ d'être frappé par …** one cannot fail to marvel at …, one cannot help but be struck by …; **ça ne va pas ~ (d'arriver)*** it's bound to happen; **j'avais prévu qu'il se fâcherait, et ça n'a pas manqué!** I knew he'd be angry and sure enough he was! **5** VB IMPERS **il manque un pied à la chaise** there's a leg missing from the chair; **il (nous) manque dix personnes/deux chaises** (= elles ont disparu) there are ten people/two chairs missing; (= on en a besoin) we are ten people/two chairs short, we are short of ten people/two chairs; **il ne manquera pas de gens pour dire** … there'll be no shortage of people who say …; **il ne lui manque que de savoir danser** the only thing he can't do is dance; (en parlant d'un animal) **il ne lui manque que la parole** if only he could talk; **il ne manquait plus que ça** that's all we needed, that's the last straw*; **il ne manquerait plus que ça!** that really would be the end!*; **il ne manquerait plus qu'il parte sans elle!** it really would be the end* if he went off without her!

6 se manquer VPR **a** (= rater son suicide) to fail (in one's attempt to commit suicide); **cette fois-ci, il ne s'est pas manqué** he made a good job of it this time **b** (à un rendez-vous) to miss each other; **ils se sont manqués à la gare** they missed each other at the station

mansarde [mɑ̃saʀd] NF (= pièce) attic, garret

mansardé, e [mɑ̃saʀde] ADJ [chambre, étage] attic; (épith) **la chambre est ~e** the room has a sloping ceiling, it's an attic room

mansuétude [mɑ̃sɥetyd] NF leniency, indulgence

mante [mɑ̃t] NF **a** (= insecte) mantis; (= poisson) manta (ray); ~ **religieuse** (lit) praying mantis; (fig) man-eater (hum) **b** († = manteau) (woman's) mantle, cloak

manteau (pl **manteaux**) [mɑ̃to] **1** NM **a** (Habillement) coat; ~ **de pluie** raincoat; ~ **trois-quarts** three-quarter-length coat; (fig) **sous le ~** clandestinely, on the sly **b** (littér) [neige] mantle, blanket; [ombre, hypocrisie] cloak; **sous le ~ de la nuit** under (the) cover of darkness **c** [mollusque] mantle **d** (Hér) mantle, mantling **e** (Géol) mantle **2** COMP ▸ **manteau d'Arlequin** proscenium arch ▸ **manteau de cheminée** mantelpiece

mantelet [mɑ̃t(ə)lɛ] NM (Habillement) short cape, mantelet; (Naut) deadlight

mantille [mɑ̃tij] NF mantilla

mantisse [mɑ̃tis] NF mantissa

Mantoue [mɑ̃tu] N Mantua

mantra [mɑ̃tʀa] NM mantra

manucure [manykyʀ] **1** NMF (= personne) manicurist **2** NM ou F (= soins) manicure

manucurer [manykyʀe] ▸conjug 1◂ VT to manicure; **se faire ~** to have a manicure

manuel, -elle [manɥɛl] **1** ADJ manual; **passer en ~** (Aviat) to switch over to manual (control); (Photo) to switch to manual → **travail, travailleur 2** NM,F (= travailleur) manual worker; (qui a du sens pratique) **c'est/ce n'est pas un ~** he's good/he's not very good with his hands **3** NM (= livre) manual, handbook; ~ **de lecture** reader; ~ **scolaire** textbook; ~ **d'entretien** service manual; ~ **d'utilisation/de l'utilisateur** instruction/user's manual

manuellement [manɥɛlmɑ̃] ADV [fabriquer] by hand, manually; [fonctionner] manually; **être bon ~** to be good with one's hands

manufacture [manyfaktyʀ] NF **a** (= usine) factory; ~ **d'armes/de porcelaine/de tabac** munitions/porcelain/tobacco factory; ~ **de tapisserie** tapestry workshop **b** (= fabrication) manufacture

manufacturer [manyfaktyʀe] ▸conjug 1◂ VT to manufacture → **produit**

manufacturier, -ière [manyfaktyʀje, jɛʀ] **1** ADJ manufacturing (épith) **2** NM† factory owner

manu militari [manymilitaʀi] LOC ADV by (main) force

manuscrit, e [manyskʀi, it] **1** ADJ (= écrit à la main) handwritten; **pages ~es** manuscript pages **2** NM manuscript; (dactylographié) manuscript, typescript; **les ~s de la mer Morte** the Dead Sea Scrolls

manutention [manytɑ̃sjɔ̃] NF (= opération) handling; (= local) storehouse; **frais de ~** handling charges; ~ **portuaire** dock work

▸ GRAMMAIRE ACTIVE: **manquer** 37.1

manutentionnaire [manytɑ̃sjɔnɛʀ] NMF packer

manutentionner [manytɑ̃sjɔne] ▸conjug 1◂ VT to handle, pack

Mao (Tsé-toung) [mao(tsetuŋ)] NM Mao (Tse Tung)

maoïsme [maɔism] NM Maoism

maoïste [maɔist] ADJ, NMF Maoist

maori, e [maɔʀi] [1] ADJ Maori [2] NM (Ling) Maori [3] **Maori(e)** NM,F Maori

maous, -ousse* [maus] ADJ [personne] hefty; [animal, objet] enormous, colossal, whacking great* (Brit) (épith)

Mao Zedong [maɔzedɔ̃ŋ] NM Mao Zedong

mappemonde [mapmɔ̃d] NF (= carte) map of the world (in two hemispheres); (= sphère) globe

Maputo [maputo] N Maputo

maquer: [make] ▸conjug 1◂ [1] VT (= prostituer) to be a pimp for [2] **se maquer** VPR se ~ ou être maqué avec qn to (go and) live with sb, shack up with sb: (péj)

maquereau[1] (pl **maquereaux**) [makʀo] NM (= poisson) mackerel → groseille

maquereau[2]: (pl **maquereaux**) [makʀo] NM (= proxénète) pimp, ponce: (Brit)

maquerelle: [makʀɛl] NF (mère) ~ madam*

maquette [makɛt] NF [a] (à échelle réduite) (Archit, Ind) (scale) model; (Art, Théât) model [b] (grandeur nature) (Ind) mock-up, model; (= livre) dummy [c] (Peinture = carton) sketch [d] (Typo) (= mise en page) layout; (= couverture) artwork

maquettiste [makɛtist] NMF [modèles réduits] model maker; [livre] dummy maker

maquignon [makiɲɔ̃] NM (lit) horse dealer; (péj) shady ou crooked dealer

maquignonnage [makiɲɔnaʒ] NM (lit) horse dealing; (fig, péj) underhand dealings, sharp practice (Brit)

maquignonner [makiɲɔne] ▸conjug 1◂ VT (péj) [+ animal] to sell by shady methods; [+ affaire] to rig, fiddle

maquillage [makijaʒ] NM [a] (= crème, fard) make-up; **passer du temps à son ~** to spend a long time putting on one's make-up ou making up [b] (péj) [voiture] disguising, doing over*; [document, vérité, faits] faking, doctoring; [chiffres, résultats] massaging, fiddling* (Brit)

maquiller [makije] ▸conjug 1◂ [1] VT [a] [+ visage, personne] to make up; **très maquillé** heavily made-up [b] [+ document, vérité, faits] to fake, doctor; [+ résultats, chiffres] to massage, fiddle* (Brit); [+ voiture] to do over*, disguise; **meurtre maquillé en accident** murder made to look like an accident [2] **se maquiller** VPR to make up, put on one's make-up; **elle est trop jeune pour se ~** she is too young to use make-up; **se ~ les yeux** to put eye make-up on

maquilleur [makijœʀ] NM make-up man, make-up artist

maquilleuse [makijøz] NF make-up artist, make-up girl

maquis [maki] NM [a] (Géog) scrub, bush; **le ~ corse** the Corsican scrub; **prendre le ~** to take to the bush [b] (fig = labyrinthe) tangle, maze; **le ~ de la procédure** the jungle of legal procedure [c] (Hist: deuxième Guerre mondiale) maquis; **prendre le ~** to take to the maquis, go underground

maquisard [makizaʀ] NM maquis, member of the Resistance

marabout [maʀabu] NM [a] (Orn) marabou(t) [b] (Rel) marabout; (= envoûteur) witch doctor

maraca [maʀaka] NF maraca

maraîchage [maʀɛʃaʒ] NM market gardening (Brit), truck farming (US); **~ sous verre** glasshouse cultivation

maraîcher, -ère [maʀɛʃe, ɛʀ] [1] NM,F market gardener (Brit), truck farmer (US) [2] ADJ **culture maraîchère** market gardening (NonC) (Brit), truck farming (NonC) (US); **produits ~s** market garden produce (NonC), truck (NonC) (US); **jardin ~** market garden (Brit), truck farm (US)

marais [maʀɛ] NM [a] (= terrain) marsh, swamp; **~ salant** (gén) salt marsh; (exploité) saltern → gaz [b] **le Marais** historic area in the heart of Paris that contains the old Jewish quarter and many fashionable bars and galleries

marasme [maʀasm] NM [a] (Écon, Pol) stagnation, slump; **les affaires sont en plein ~** business is completely stagnant, there is a complete slump in business [b] (= accablement) dejection, depression [c] (Méd) marasmus

marasquin [maʀaskɛ̃] NM maraschino

marathon [maʀatɔ̃] NM [a] (Sport, fig) marathon; **~ de danse** dance marathon; **visite-/négociations-~** marathon visit/talks; **faire/courir un ~** to do/run a marathon [b] (= ville) **Marathon** Marathon

marathonien, -ienne [maʀatɔnjɛ̃, jɛn] NM,F marathon runner

marâtre [maʀatʀ] NF (= mauvaise mère) cruel ou unnatural mother; (†† = belle-mère) stepmother

maraud, e[1]†† [maʀo, od] NM,F rascal, rogue

maraudage [maʀodaʒ] NM pilfering, thieving (of poultry, crops etc)

maraude[2] [maʀod] NF [a] (= vol) thieving, pilfering (of poultry, crops etc), pillaging (from farms, orchards) [b] (loc) **taxi en ~** cruising ou prowling taxi, taxi cruising ou prowling for fares; **vagabond en ~** tramp on the prowl

marauder [maʀode] ▸conjug 1◂ VI [personne] to thieve, pilfer; [taxi] to cruise ou prowl for fares

maraudeur, -euse [maʀodœʀ, øz] [1] NM,F (= voleur) prowler; (= soldat) marauder [2] ADJ **oiseau ~** thieving bird

marbre [maʀbʀ] NM [a] (Géol) marble; **de ou en ~** marble; **~ de Carrare** Carrara marble; **peindre un mur en faux ~** to marble a wall; (fig) **rester de ~** ◊ **garder un visage de ~** to remain stony-faced ou impassive; **ça l'a laissé de ~** it left him cold; **avoir un cœur de ~** to have a heart of stone; **passer une voiture au ~** to check a car for structural damage → froid [b] (= surface) marble top; (= statue) marble (statue) [c] (Typo) stone, bed; **être sur le ~** [journal] to be put to bed, be on the stone; [livre] to be at ou in press; **rester sur le ~** to be excess copy

marbré, e [maʀbʀe] (ptp de **marbrer**) ADJ [papier, cuir] marbled; [peau] mottled, blotchy; [fromage] veined; **(gâteau) ~** marble cake

marbrer [maʀbʀe] ▸conjug 1◂ VT (Tech) [+ papier, cuir] to marble; [+ bois, surface] to vein, mottle

marbrerie [maʀbʀəʀi] NF (= atelier) marble mason's workshop ou yard; (= industrie) marble industry; **travailler dans la ~** to be a marble mason; (funéraire) to be a monumental mason

marbrier, -ière [maʀbʀije, ijɛʀ] [1] ADJ [industrie] marble (épith) [2] NM (funéraire) monumental mason [3] **marbrière** NF marble quarry

marbrure [maʀbʀyʀ] NF [a] (Tech) [papier, cuir] marbling [b] [peau] ~s (par le froid) blotches, mottling; (par un coup) marks; [bois, surface] veins, mottling

Marc [maʀk] NM Mark; **~ Aurèle** Marcus Aurelius; **~-Antoine** Mark Antony

marc[1] [maʀ] NM (= poids, monnaie) mark; (Jur) **au ~ le franc** pro rata, proportionally

marc[2] [maʀ] NM [raisin, pomme] marc; **~ (de café)** (coffee) grounds ou dregs; **(eau de vie de) ~ marc** brandy → lire

marcassin [maʀkasɛ̃] NM young wild boar

marcassite [maʀkasit] NF marcasite

marcel* [maʀsɛl] NM (Habillement) vest

marchand, e [maʀʃɑ̃, ɑ̃d] [1] ADJ [valeur] market (épith); [prix] trade (épith); [rue] shopping (épith); **navire ~** merchant ship; **secteur ~/non ~** market sector/non-market sector → galerie, marine[2]

[2] NM,F (= boutiquier) shopkeeper, tradesman (ou tradeswoman); (sur un marché) stallholder; [vins, fruits, charbon, grains] merchant; [meubles, bestiaux, cycles] dealer; **~ au détail** retailer; **~ en gros** wholesaler; **la ~e de chaussures me l'a dit** the woman in the shoe shop ou the shoe shop owner told me; **jouer au ~** (ou à la ~e) to play shop (Brit) ou store (US) [b] (= boutique) shop, store; **rapporte-le chez le ~** take it back to the shop ou shopkeeper

[3] COMP ▸ **marchand ambulant** hawker, door-to-door salesman, pedlar (Brit), peddler (US) ▸ **marchande d'amour** (hum) lady of pleasure (hum) ▸ **marchand d'art** art dealer ▸ **marchand de biens** property agent ▸ **marchand de canons** (péj) arms dealer ▸ **marchand de couleurs** hardware dealer, ironmonger (Brit) ▸ **marchand de frites** (= boutique) chip shop (Brit), chippy* (Brit) ▸ **marchand de fromages** cheese vendor ou seller, cheesemonger (Brit) ▸ **marchand de fruits** fruit merchant ou vendor ou seller, fruiterer (Brit) ▸ **marchand de glaces** ice cream vendor ▸ **marchand d'illusions** purveyor of illusions, illusionmonger ▸ **marchand de journaux** newsagent (Brit), newsdealer (US) ▸ **marchand de légumes** greengrocer (Brit), produce dealer (US) ▸ **marchand de marrons** chestnut seller ▸ **marchand de meubles** furniture dealer ▸ **marchand de poissons** fish merchant, fishmonger (Brit), fish vendor ou seller (US) ▸ **marchand des quatre saisons** street merchant (selling fresh fruit and vegetables), costermonger (Brit) ▸ **marchand de rêves** dream-merchant ▸ **marchand de sable** (fig) sandman; **le ~ de sable est passé** it's bedtime, the sandman is coming ▸ **marchand de sommeil** (péj) slum landlord, slumlord* (US) ▸ **marchand de soupe** (péj) (= restaurateur) low-grade restaurant owner, profiteering café owner; (Scol) money-grubbing ou profit-minded headmaster (of a private school) ▸ **marchand de tableaux** art dealer ▸ **marchand de tapis** carpet dealer; (péj) **c'est un vrai ~ de tapis** he drives a really hard bargain, he haggles over everything; **des discussions de ~ de tapis** endless haggling ▸ **les marchands du Temple** (Bible) the moneychangers in the Temple ▸ **marchand de vin** wine merchant, vintner ▸ **marchand de voyages** tour operator

marchandage [maʀʃɑ̃daʒ] NM [a] (au marché) bargaining, haggling; (péj: aux élections) bargaining; **je viens si tu promets de m'aider — mais qu'est-ce-que c'est que ce ~?** I'll come if you promise to help me — what's this, blackmail? [b] (Jur) **le ~** subcontracting of labour

marchander [maʀʃɑ̃de] ▸conjug 1◂ VT [a] [+ objet] to haggle over, bargain over; **savoir ~** to know how to haggle; **il a l'habitude de ~** he is used to haggling ou bargaining; **son soutien électoral** to use one's political support as a bargaining chip [b] (fig) **il ne marchande pas sa peine** he spares no pains, he grudges no effort; **il ne m'a pas marchandé ses compliments** he wasn't sparing of his compliments [c] (Jur) to subcontract

marchandeur, -euse [maʀʃɑ̃dœʀ, øz] NM,F [a] [objet, prix] haggler [b] (Jur) subcontractor (of labour)

marchandisage [maʀʃɑ̃dizaʒ] NM merchandizing

▼ **marchandise** [maʁʃɑ̃diz] NF a (= *article, unité*) commodity; **~s** goods, merchandise (*NonC*), wares†; **~s en gros/au détail** wholesale/retail goods; **il a de la bonne ~** he has *ou* sells good stuff b (= *cargaison, stock*) **la ~** the goods, the merchandise; **la ~ est dans l'entrepôt** the goods are *ou* the merchandise is in the warehouse; **faire valoir** *ou* **vanter la ~*** to show o.s. off *ou* to show off one's wares to advantage, make the most of o.s. *ou* one's wares; **elle étale la ~*** she displays her charms (*hum*), she shows you *ou* she flaunts all she's got*

marchante [maʁʃɑ̃t] ADJ F → **aile**

marche¹ [maʁʃ] 1 NF a (= *action, Sport*) walking; **il fait de la ~** he goes in for walking, he does quite a bit of walking; **poursuivre sa ~** to walk on; **chaussures de ~** walking shoes

b (= *démarche*) walk, step, gait; (= *allure, rythme*) pace, step; **une ~ pesante** a heavy step *ou* gait; **régler sa ~ sur celle de qn** to adjust one's pace *ou* step to sb else's

c (= *trajet*) walk; **faire une longue ~** to go for a long walk; (*Hist*) **la Longue Marche** the Long March; **le village est à deux heures/à dix km de ~ d'ici** the village is a two-hour walk/a ten-km walk from here; **une ~ de 10 km** a 10-km walk

d (= *mouvement, Mil, Pol*) march; **air/chanson de ~** marching tune/song; **armée en ~** marching army; **fermer la ~** to bring up the rear; (*lit, fig*) **ouvrir la ~** to lead the way; **faire ~ sur** to march upon; **~ victorieuse sur la ville** victorious march on the town; **en avant, ~!** quick march!, forward march! → **ordre¹**

e (= *fonctionnement*) [*train, voiture*] running; [*machine*] running, working; [*navire*] sailing; [*étoile*] course; [*horloge*] working; [*usine, établissement*] running, working, functioning; **dans le sens de la ~** facing the engine; **dans le sens contraire de la ~** with one's back to the engine; **ne montez pas dans un véhicule en ~** do not board a moving vehicle; **j'ai pris le bus en ~** I jumped onto the bus while it was moving; **en (bon) état de ~** in (good) working order; **régler la ~ d'une horloge** to adjust the workings *ou* movement of a clock; **assurer la bonne ~ d'un service** to ensure the smooth running of a service; (*Tech*) **~ — arrêt** on — off

f (= *développement*) [*maladie*] progress; [*affaire, événements, opérations*] course; [*histoire, temps, progrès*] march; **la ~ de l'intrigue** the unfolding *ou* development of the plot

g (*loc*) **être en ~** [*personnes, armées*] to be on the move; [*moteur*] to be running; [*machine*] to be (turned) on; **se mettre en ~** [*personne*] to make a move, get moving; [*machine*] to start; **mettre en ~** [*+ moteur, voiture*] to start (up); [*+ machine*] to put on, turn on, set going; [*+ pendule*] to start (going); **lire les instructions avant la mise en ~ de l'appareil** read the instructions before starting the machine; **remettre en ~** [*usine, machine*] to restart → **train**

h (*Mus*) march; **~ funèbre/militaire/nuptiale** funeral *ou* dead/military/wedding march

2 COMP ► **marche arrière** (*Aut*) reverse; **entrer/sortir en ~ arrière** to reverse in/out, back in/out; **faire ~ arrière** (*Aut*) to reverse; (*fig*) to back-pedal, backtrack ► **marche avant** forward; **en ~ avant** in forward gear ► **marche forcée** (*Mil*) forced march; **se rendre vers un lieu à ~(s) forcée(s)** to get to a place by forced marches; **la privatisation à ~ forcée des entreprises** the accelerated privatization of companies; **ils avancent à ~ forcée sur la voie de la démocratisation** they're on the fast track to democracy; **l'entreprise se modernise à ~ forcée** the company is undergoing a rapid modernization programme ► **marche à suivre** (= *procédure*) (correct) procedure (**pour** for); (= *mode d'emploi*) directions (for use)

marche² [maʁʃ] NF [*véhicule*] step; [*escalier*] step, stair; **manquer une ~** to miss a step; **attention à la ~** mind (*Brit*) *ou* watch (*US*) the step; **sur les ~s** (*de l'escalier*) on the stairs; (*de l'escalier extérieur, de l'escabeau*) on the steps; **~ palière** last step before the landing, ≈ top step; **~ dansante** winder

marche³ [maʁʃ] NF (*gén pl: Géog, Hist*) march; **les ~s** the Marches

marché [maʁʃe] 1 NM a (= *lieu*) market; (= *ville*) trading centre; **~ aux bestiaux/aux fleurs/aux poissons** cattle/flower/fish market; **~ couvert/en plein air** covered/open-air market; **aller au ~** ◊ **aller faire le ~** to go to (the) market; **aller faire son ~** to go to the market; (*plus gén*) to go shopping; (*fig*) **le choix est vaste, il faut faire son ~** there is a vast choice available, you have to shop around; **faire les ~s** [*marchand, acheteur*] to go round *ou* do the markets; **boucher qui fait les ~s** butcher who has a market stall; **vendre/acheter au ~** *ou* **sur les ~s** to buy/sell at the market; **Lyon, le grand ~ des soieries** Lyons, the great trading centre for silk goods

b (*Comm, Écon = débouchés, opérations*) market; **~ monétaire** money market; **~ libre** open market; (*Pétrole*) **le ~ libre de Rotterdam** the Rotterdam spot market; **le ~ unique européen** the single European market; **~ gris** grey market; **acquérir** *ou* **trouver de nouveaux ~s (pour)** to find new markets (for); **lancer/offrir sur le ~** to launch/put sth on the market; **le ~ de l'immobilier** the real estate market; **le ~ du travail** the labour market; **il n'y a pas de ~ pour ces produits** there is no market for these goods → **analyse, étude**

c (= *transaction, contrat*) bargain, transaction, deal; **faire un ~ avantageux** to make *ou* strike a good bargain; **un ~ de dupes** a fool's bargain *ou* deal; **conclure** *ou* **passer un ~ avec qn** to make a deal with sb; **~ conclu!** it's a deal!; **~ ferme** firm deal; **~ de gré à gré** mutual agreement, private contract; **~ public** procurement contract; **mettre le ~ en main à qn** to give sb an ultimatum

d (*Bourse*) market; **le ~ est animé** the market is lively; **~ des valeurs/des actions** securities/share market; **~ des changes** *ou* **des devises** foreign exchange market; **~ financier** financial market; **~ obligataire** bond market; **~ au comptant/à terme** *ou* **à règlement mensuel** spot *ou* cash/forward market; **~ à terme d'instruments financiers** ◊ **à terme international de France** French financial futures market, ≈ LIFFE (*Brit*); **second ~** ≈ unlisted securities market

e (*loc*) **bon ~** [*acheter*] cheap; [*produit*] cheap, inexpensive; **c'est meilleur ~** it's better value, it's cheaper

2 COMP ► **Marché commun** Common Market ► **marché international du disque et de l'édition musicale** music industry trade fair ► **marché d'intérêt national** wholesale market for perishable food and horticultural products ► **marché noir** black market; **faire du ~ noir** to buy and sell on the black market ► **marché aux puces** flea market

marché-gare (*pl* **marchés-gares**) [maʁʃegaʁ] NM *wholesale market to which goods are transported by rail*

marchepied [maʁʃəpje] NM (*Rail*) step; (*Aut*) running board; (*fig*) stepping stone; **servir de ~ à qn** to be sb's stepping stone

marcher [maʁʃe] ▸ conjug 1 ◂ VI a (*gén*) to walk; [*soldats*] to march; **~ à grandes enjambées** *ou* **à grands pas** to stride (along); **marche en boitant** he walks with a limp; **~ en canard** to walk like a duck; **~ sur les mains/à quatre pattes** to walk on one's hands/on all fours; **on marche sur la tête!*** it's crazy!, there's no rhyme or reason to it!; **venez, on va ~ un peu** come on, let's have a walk *ou* let's go for a walk; **il marchait sans but** he walked *ou* wandered (along) aimlessly; (*fig*) **~ sur des œufs** to act with caution; **faire ~ un bébé** to get a baby to walk, help a baby walk; **c'est marche ou crève !*** it's sink or swim! → **pas¹**

b (= *mettre le pied sur, dans*) **~ dans une flaque d'eau** to step in a puddle; **défense de ~ sur les pelouses** keep off the grass; (*lit*) **~ sur les pieds de qn/sur sa robe** to stand *ou* tread on sb's toes/on one's dress; (*fig*) **ne te laisse pas ~ sur les pieds** don't let anyone tread on your toes *ou* take advantage of you; (*fig*) **~ sur qn** to walk all over sb → **brisée, côté, trace** *etc*

c (= *progresser*) ► **à la conquête de la gloire/vers le succès** to be on the road to fame/to success, step out *ou* stride towards fame/success; **~ au supplice** to walk to one's death *ou* to the stake; **~ au combat** to march into battle; (*Mil*) **~ sur une ville/un adversaire** to advance on *ou* march against a town/an enemy

d (= *obéir*) to toe the line; (* = *consentir*) to agree, play*; (* = *croire naïvement*) **il marche à tous les coups** he is taken in *ou* falls for it* every time; **on lui raconte n'importe quoi et il marche** you can tell him anything and he'll swallow it*; **il n'a pas voulu ~ dans la combine** he didn't want to be involved in the affair; **faire ~ qn** (= *taquiner*) to pull sb's leg; (= *tromper*) to take sb for a ride*, lead sb up the garden path*; **il sait faire ~ sa grand-mère** he knows how to get round his grandmother; **son père saura le faire ~ (droit)** his father will soon have him toeing the line

e (*avec véhicule*) **le train a/nous avons bien marché jusqu'à Lyon** the train/we made good time as far as Lyon; **nous marchions à 100 à l'heure** we were doing a hundred

f (= *fonctionner*) [*appareil*] to work; [*ruse*] to work, come off; [*usine*] to work (well); [*affaires, études*] to go (well); [*train*] to run; **faire ~** [*+ appareil*] to work, operate; [*+ entreprise*] to run; **ça fait ~ les affaires** it's good for business; **ça marche à l'électricité** it works by *ou* on electricity; **est-ce que le métro marche aujourd'hui?** is the underground running today?; **ces deux opérations marchent ensemble** these two procedures go *ou* work together; **les affaires marchent mal** things are going badly, business is bad; **son restaurant marche bien** his restaurant does good business *ou* does a brisk trade; **le film a bien marché en Europe** the film was a big success in Europe; **il marche au whisky*** whisky keeps him going; **les études, ça marche ?*** how's studying going?; **rien ne marche** nothing's going right, nothing's working; **ça marche !** (*dans un restaurant*) coming up!; (= *c'est d'accord*) great!, OK!*; **ça marche pour 8 h/lundi** 8 o'clock/Monday is fine → **roulette**

marcheur, -euse [maʁʃœʁ, øz] 1 ADJ [*oiseau*] flightless 2 NM,F (*gén*) walker; (= *manifestant*) marcher 3 **marcheuse** NF (= *figurante*) walk-on

Marco Polo [maʁkɔpɔlo] NM Marco Polo

marcottage [maʁkɔtaʒ] NM (*Bot*) layering

marcotte [maʁkɔt] NF (*Bot*) layer, runner

marcotter [maʁkɔte] ▸ conjug 1 ◂ VT (*Bot*) to layer

mardi [maʁdi] NM Tuesday; **Mardi gras** Shrove *ou* Pancake* (*Brit*) Tuesday, Mardi Gras; (*hum*) **elle se croit à ~ gras !** she's dressed up like a dog's dinner!; *pour autres locutions voir* **samedi**

mare [maʁ] NF a (= *étang*) pond; **~ aux canards** duck pond; **la ~ aux harengs*** the North Atlantic → **pavé** b (= *flaque*) pool; **~ de sang/d'huile** pool of blood/of oil

marécage [maʁekaʒ] NM (*Géog*) marsh, swamp, bog; (*péj*) quagmire

marécageux, -euse [maʁekaʒø, øz] ADJ [*terrain*] marshy, swampy, boggy; [*plante*] marsh (*épith*)

maréchal (*pl* **-aux**) [maʁeʃal, o] NM (*armée française*) marshal; (*armée britannique*) field marshal; (*Hist*) **~ de camp** brigadier; **Maréchal de**

France Marshal of France; **~ des logis** ≈ sergeant; **~ des logis-chef** ≈ battery *ou* squadron sergeant-major → **bâton**

maréchalat [maʀeʃala] NM rank of marshal, marshalcy

maréchale [maʀeʃal] NF marshal's wife → **Madame**

maréchalerie [maʀeʃalʀi] NF (= *atelier*) smithy, blacksmith's (shop); (= *métier*) blacksmith's trade

maréchal-ferrant [maʀeʃalferɑ̃] (*pl* **maréchaux-ferrants** [maʀeʃoferɑ̃]) NM blacksmith, farrier

maréchaussée [maʀeʃose] NF (*hum*) **la ~** the police (force), the boys in blue* (*hum*); (*Hist*) the mounted constabulary

marée [maʀe] NF [a] (*lit*) tide; **~ montante/descendante** flood *ou* rising/ebb tide; **à (la) ~ montante/descendante** when the tide comes in/goes out, when the tide is rising/ebbing *ou* falling; **(à) ~ haute** (at) high tide *ou* water; **(à) ~ basse** (at) low tide *ou* water; **grande ~** spring tide; **faible** *ou* **petite ~** neap tide; **~ noire** oil slick; **ça sent la ~** it smells of the sea [b] (*fig*) [*produits, nouveaux immeubles*] flood; [*touristes*] flood, influx; **~ humaine** great flood *ou* influx of people [c] (*Comm = poissons de mer*) **la ~** the fresh catch, the fresh (sea) fish

marelle [maʀel] NF (= *jeu*) hopscotch; (= *dessin*) (drawing of a) hopscotch game; **jouer à la ~** to play hopscotch

marémoteur, -trice [maʀemɔtœʀ, tʀis] ADJ (*Élec*) [*énergie*] tidal; **usine marémotrice** tidal power station

marengo [maʀɛ̃go] [1] ADJ INV (*Culin*) **poulet/veau (à la) ~** chicken/veal marengo [2] NM *black flecked cloth*

marennes [maʀɛn] NF Marennes oyster

mareyage [maʀejaʒ] NM fish trade

mareyeur, -euse [maʀejœʀ, øz] NM,F wholesale fish merchant

margarine [maʀgaʀin] NF margarine, marge* (*Brit*), oleo* (*US*)

marge [maʀʒ] [1] NF [a] [*feuille*] margin; **faire des annotations en ~** to make notes in the margin [b] (= *latitude*) **il y a de la ~** (*du temps*) there's time to spare; (*de l'espace*) there's plenty of room; (*de l'argent*) there's enough (money) left over; **c'est une taille 42, j'ai de la ~!** it's size 14, it's easily big enough for me; **donner de la ~ à qn** (*temps*) to give sb a reasonable margin of time; (*latitude*) to give sb some leeway *ou* latitude or scope [2] COMP ► **marge (bénéficiaire)** (profit) margin, mark-up ► **marge brute** gross margin ► **marge brute d'autofinancement** cash flow ► **marge commerciale** gross margin *ou* profit, trading margin ► **marge continentale** (*Géog*) continental terrace ► **marge d'erreur** margin of error ► **marge de garantie** (*Fin*) margin ► **marge de liberté** *ou* **de manœuvre** room for *ou* to manoeuvre, leeway; **ça ne nous laisse pas une grande ~ de manœuvre** it doesn't leave us much room for manoeuvre ► **marge de sécurité** safety margin ► **marge de tolérance** tolerance [3] **en marge de** LOC PRÉP **vivre en ~ de la société** to live on the fringe of society; **vivre en ~ du monde/des affaires** to live cut off from the world/from business; **activités en ~ du festival** fringe activities; **en ~ de cette affaire, on peut aussi signaler que ...** in addition, one might also point out that ...

margelle [maʀʒɛl] NF **~ (de puits)** coping (of a well)

marger [maʀʒe] ► conjug 3 ◄ VT [+ *machine à écrire, feuille*] to set the margins on; (*Typo*) to feed (in)

margeur [maʀʒœʀ] NM [*machine à écrire*] margin stop

marginal, e (*mpl* **-aux**) [maʀʒinal, o] [1] ADJ [a] (= *secondaire*) [*phénomène*] marginal, minor; [*activité, rôle*] marginal, peripheral; **ces réactions/critiques restent ~es** only a minority of people have these reactions/make these criticisms; **l'évasion fiscale reste ~e** tax evasion is still relatively rare *ou* uncommon [b] (*Écon, Fin, Stat*) [*coût, taux*] marginal [c] (= *non conformiste*) unconventional; **groupe ~** fringe *ou* marginal group; **l'accroissement d'une population ~e** the increase in the number of people living on the fringes *ou* margins of society; **les partis politiques plus marginaux** the more marginal political parties [d] (= *sur le bord*) **notes ~es** marginal notes, marginalia *pl*; **récifs marginaux** fringing reefs [2] NMF [a] (= *déshérité*) dropout; (= *non-conformiste*) unconventional figure

marginalement [maʀʒinalmɑ̃] ADV marginally

marginalisation [maʀʒinalizasjɔ̃] NF marginalization; **pour éviter la ~ sociale** to prevent people from being marginalized in society *ou* from becoming marginalized

marginaliser [maʀʒinalize] ► conjug 1 ◄ [1] VT to marginalize, edge out; **il n'a pas l'intention de se laisser ~** he has no intention of being marginalized *ou* of being sidelined *ou* of being left out in the cold; **ils se sentent de plus en plus marginalisés** they feel more and more marginalized [2] **se marginaliser** VPR [*personne, pays, parti*] to become marginalized

marginalité [maʀʒinalite] NF marginality; **vivre/tomber dans la ~** to live as/become a dropout

margis [maʀʒi] NM (ABRÉV = **maréchal des logis**) (*arg Mil*) sarge (*arg*)

margoulette* [maʀgulɛt] NF (= *mâchoires, visage*) face, mug*

margoulin [maʀgulɛ̃] NM (*péj*) swindler, shark (*fig*)

margrave [maʀgʀav] NM (*Hist*) margrave

marguerite [maʀgəʀit] NF [a] (*Bot*) marguerite, (oxeye) daisy → **effeuiller** [b] (*Typo*) daisywheel

marguillier [maʀgije] NM (*Hist*) churchwarden

mari [maʀi] NM husband; **son petit ~** her hubby*

mariable [maʀjabl] ADJ marriageable

▼ **mariage** [maʀjaʒ] [1] NM [a] (= *institution, union*) marriage; (*Rel*) matrimony; **50 ans de ~** 50 years of married life *ou* of marriage; **ils ont fêté leurs 20 ans de ~** they celebrated their 20th (wedding) anniversary; **au début de leur ~** when they were first married, at the beginning of their marriage; **son ~ avec son cousin** her marriage to her cousin; **on parle de ~ entre eux** there is talk of their getting married; **il avait un enfant d'un premier ~** he had a child from his first marriage; **il l'a demandée en ~** he asked if he could marry her; **promettre/donner qn en ~ à** to promise/give sb in marriage to; **elle lui a apporté beaucoup d'argent en ~** she brought him a lot of money when she married him; **faire un riche ~** to marry into money; **hors ~** [*cohabitation*] outside of marriage; [*naissance, né*] out of wedlock; [*relations sexuelles*] extramarital → **acte, demande** [b] (= *cérémonie*) wedding; **grand ~** society wedding; **cadeau/faire-part/messe de ~** wedding present/invitation/service → **corbeille, liste***; → |MAIRE| [c] [*couleurs, parfums, matières*] marriage, blend; [*entreprises*] merger, amalgamation; **c'est le ~ de la carpe et du lapin** (*couple*) they make an odd couple; (*associés*) they are strange *ou* unlikely bedfellows [d] (*Cartes*) **avoir le ~ à cœur** to have *ou* hold

(the) king and queen of hearts; **faire des ~s** to collect kings and queens [2] COMP ► **mariage d'amour** love match; **faire un ~ d'amour** to marry for love, make a love match ► **mariage d'argent** marriage for money, money match ► **mariage blanc** (*non consommé*) unconsummated marriage; (*de convenance*) marriage of convenience ► **mariage en blanc** white wedding ► **mariage civil** civil wedding, registry (office) wedding (*Brit*) ► **mariage de convenance** marriage of convenience ► **mariage à l'essai** trial marriage ► **mariage d'intérêt** money *ou* social match; **faire un ~ d'intérêt** to marry for money ► **mariage mixte** mixed marriage ► **mariage politique** political alliance ► **mariage de raison** marriage of convenience ► **mariage religieux** church wedding

marial, e (*mpl* **marials**) [maʀjal] ADJ (*Rel*) [*culte*] Marian

Marianne [maʀjan] NF (*Pol*) Marianne (*symbol of the French Republic*)

| MARIANNE |

Marianne is an allegorical figure representing a woman wearing a "bonnet phrygien" (a red woollen conical hat worn by commoners under the "Ancien Régime"). The name **Marianne** was used at the end of the 18th century to refer to the French Republic, and statues and busts began to appear around fifty years later. All "mairies" have a bust of **Marianne** on public view, and she also appears on postage stamps. **Marianne**'s face changes from time to time, Brigitte Bardot and Catherine Deneuve both having been used as models in recent years.

Mariannes [maʀjan] NFPL **les (îles) ~** ◊ **l'archipel des ~** the Mariana Islands; **les ~-du-Nord** the Northern Mariana Islands

Marie [maʀi] NF Mary; **~ Stuart** Mary Stuart, Mary Queen of Scots

marié, e [maʀje] (*ptp de* **marier**) [1] ADJ married; **non ~** unmarried, single [2] NM (bride) groom; **les ~s** (*jour du mariage*) the bride and (bride)groom; (*après le mariage*) the newlyweds → **jeune, nouveau** [3] **mariée** NF bride; (*fig*) **trouver** *ou* **se plaindre que la ~e est trop belle** to object that everything's too good to be true; **couronne/robe/voile de ~e** wedding headdress/dress/veil → **jeune**

marie-couche-toi-là †‡ [maʀikuʃtwala] NF INV (*péj*) slut, tart‡ (*Brit*)

Marie-Galante [maʀigalɑ̃t] NF Marie Galante

marie-jeanne [maʀiʒan] NF INV (*arg Drogue*) Mary Jane (*arg*), pot (*arg*)

marie-louise (*pl* **maries-louises**) [maʀilwiz] NF [*assiette*] inner surface; [*encadrement*] inner frame

▼ **marier** [maʀje] ► conjug 7 ◄ [1] VT [a] [*maire, prêtre*] to marry; **il a marié sa fille à un homme d'affaires** he married his daughter to a businessman; **il a fini par ~ sa fille** he finally got his daughter married, he finally married off his daughter; (*hum*) **demain, je marie mon frère** tomorrow I see my brother (get) married; **nous sommes mariés depuis 15 ans** we have been married for 15 years; **il a encore deux filles à ~** he still has two unmarried daughters, he still has two daughters to marry off; **fille (bonne) à ~** daughter of marriageable age, marriageable daughter; (*fig*) **on n'est pas mariés avec lui !*** we don't owe him anything! [b] [+ *couleurs, goûts, parfums, styles*] to blend, harmonize; [+ *entreprises*] to merge, amalgamate [2] **se marier** VPR [a] [*personne*] to get married; **se ~ à** *ou* **avec qn** to marry sb, get married to sb; **se ~ à la mairie/à l'église** to get married at a registry office/in church; **se ~ de**

la main gauche† to live as man and wife
b [*couleurs, goûts, parfums, styles*] to blend, harmonize; **le beige se marie très bien avec le noir** beige goes very well with black

marie-salope (*pl* **maries-salopes**) [marisalɔp] NF **a** (= *péniche*) hopper (barge) **b** (‡ *péj = souillon*) slut

marieur, -ieuse [marjœr, jøz] NM,F matchmaker

marigot [marigo] NM backwater, cutoff, oxbow lake

marihuana, marijuana [mariʀwana] NF marijuana

marimba [marimba] NM marimba

marin, e[1] [marɛ̃, in] **1** ADJ [*air*] sea; [*carte*] maritime, navigational; [*faune, flore*] marine, sea; **bateau (très) ~** seaworthy ship; **missile ~** sea-based missile; **sciences ~es** marine science; **costume ~** sailor suit → **mille**[2], **pied** *etc* **2** NM sailor; (*grade*) **(simple) ~** ordinary seaman; **~ pêcheur** fisherman; **~ d'eau douce** landlubber; **un peuple de ~s** a seafaring nation, a nation of seafarers; **béret/tricot de ~** sailor's hat/jersey → **fusilier**

marina [marina] NF marina

marinade [marinad] NF **a** (*Culin*) marinade; **~ de viande** meat in (a) marinade, marinaded meat **b** (*Can*) **~s** pickles

marine[2] [marin] **1** NF **a** (= *flotte, administration*) navy; **terme de ~** nautical term; **au temps de la ~ à voiles** in the days of sailing ships; **~ (de guerre)** navy; **~ marchande** merchant navy → **lieutenant, officier**[1] **b** (= *tableau*) seascape **2** NM (= *soldat*) (*britannique*) Royal Marine; (*américain*) US Marine; **les ~s** the Marines **3** ADJ INV (*couleur*) navy (blue) → **bleu**

mariner [marine] ▷conjug 1◁ **1** VT (*Culin*) to marinade, marinate; (*dans la saumure*) to pickle; **harengs marinés** pickled herrings **2** VI **a** (*Culin*) **(faire) ~** to marinade, marinate **b** (* = *attendre*) to hang about*; **~ en prison** to stew* in prison; **faire** *ou* **laisser ~ qn** (*à un rendez-vous*) to keep sb waiting *ou* hanging about*; (*pour une décision*) to let sb stew* (for a bit)

maringouin [marɛ̃gwɛ̃] NM (*Can*) mosquito

marinier [marinje] NM bargee (*Brit*), bargeman (*US*) → **officier**[1]

marinière [marinjɛr] NF (*Habillement*) overblouse, smock → **moule**[2]

mariol(le)* [marjɔl] NM **c'est un ~** (*malin*) he's a crafty *ou* sly one; (*qui plaisante*) he's a bit of a joker *ou* a waster*; (*incompétent*) he's a bungling idiot*; **(ne) fais pas le ~** stop trying to be clever *ou* smart*, stop showing off

marionnette [marjɔnɛt] NF (*lit, fig = pantin*) puppet; (= *spectacle*) **~s** puppet show; **~ à doigt/à gaine** finger/glove puppet; **faire les ~s** to move one's hands (*to amuse a baby*) → **montreur, théâtre**

marionnettiste [marjɔnɛtist] NMF puppeteer, puppet-master (*ou -mistress*)

mariste [marist] NMF Marist; **frère/sœur ~** Marist brother/sister

marital, e (*mpl* **-aux**) [marital, o] ADJ (*Jur*) **autorisation ~e** husband's permission *ou* authorization; **la vie ~e** living together, cohabitation

maritalement [maritalmã] ADV **vivre ~** to live as husband and wife, cohabit

maritime [maritim] ADJ **a** [*climat*] maritime; [*ville*] seaboard, coastal, seaside; [*province*] seaboard, coastal, maritime → **gare**[1], **pin, port**[1] **b** [*navigation*] maritime; [*commerce, agence*] shipping; [*droit*] shipping, maritime; [*assurance*] maritime; (*Pol*) **une grande puissance ~** a great sea power; **affecté à la navigation ~** seagoing → **arsenal**

maritorne† [maritɔrn] NF (= *souillon*) slut, slattern

marivaudage [marivodaʒ] NM (*littér = badinage*) light-hearted gallantries; (*Littérat*) sophisticated banter in the style of Marivaux

marivauder [marivode] ▷conjug 1◁ VI (*littér*) to engage in lively sophisticated banter; (†: *Littérat*) to write in the style of Marivaux

marjolaine [marʒɔlɛn] NF marjoram

mark [mark] NM (*Fin*) mark; **le deutsche ~** the Deutsche mark; **le ~ allemand/finlandais** the German/Finnish mark

marketing [marketiŋ] NM marketing; **~ direct** direct marketing; **~ téléphonique** telemarketing, telephone sales; **~ politique** political marketing

marlin [marlɛ̃] NM marlin

marlou‡ [marlu] NM (= *souteneur*) pimp; (= *voyou*) wide boy‡ (*Brit*), punk‡ (*US*)

marmaille* [marmɑj] NF gang *ou* horde of kids* *ou* brats* (*péj*); **toute la ~ était là** the whole brood was there

marmelade [marmǝlad] NF **a** (*Culin*) stewed fruit, compote; **~ de pommes/poires** stewed apples/pears, compote of apples/pears; **~ d'oranges** (orange) marmalade **b**‡ **en ~** [*légumes, fruits*] (*cuits*) cooked to a mush; (*crus*) reduced to a pulp; **avoir le nez en ~** to have one's nose reduced to a pulp; **réduire qn en ~** to smash sb to pulp, reduce sb to a pulp

marmite [marmit] **1** NF (*Culin*) (cooking-)pot; (*arg Mil*) heavy shell; **une ~ de soupe** a pot of soup → **bouillir, nez 2** COMP ▶ **marmite (de géants)** (*Géog*) pothole ▶ **marmite norvégienne** ≈ haybox

marmiton [marmitɔ̃] NM kitchen boy

marmonnement [marmɔnmã] NM mumbling, muttering

marmonner [marmɔne] ▷conjug 1◁ VTI to mumble, mutter; **~ dans sa barbe** to mutter into one's beard, mutter to o.s.

marmoréen, -éenne [marmɔreɛ̃, ɛɛn] ADJ (*littér*) marble (*épith*), marmoreal (*littér*)

marmot* [marmo] NM kid*, brat* (*péj*) → **croquer**

marmotte [marmɔt] NF (*Zool*) marmot; (*fig*) sleepyhead, dormouse; (= *cerise*) type of bigarreau cherry → **dormir**

marmottement [marmɔtmã] NM mumbling, muttering

marmotter [marmɔte] ▷conjug 1◁ VTI to mumble, mutter; **qu'est-ce que tu as à ~?*** what are you mumbling (on) about? *ou* muttering about?

marmouset [marmuze] NM (*Sculp*) quaint *ou* grotesque figure; (*†* = *enfant*) pipsqueak*

marnage[1] [marnaʒ] NM (*Agr*) marling

marnage[2] [marnaʒ] NM (*Naut*) tidal range

marne [marn] NF (*Géol*) marl, calcareous clay

marner [marne] ▷conjug 1◁ **1** VT (*Agr*) to marl **2** VI (* = *travailler dur*) to slog*; **faire ~ qn** to make sb slog*

marneux, -euse [marnø, øz] ADJ marly

marnière [marnjɛr] NF marlpit

Maroc [marɔk] NM Morocco

marocain, e [marɔkɛ̃, ɛn] **1** ADJ Moroccan **2 Marocain(e)** NM,F Moroccan

maronite [marɔnit] ADJ, NMF Maronite

maronner* [marɔne] ▷conjug 1◁ VI **a** (= *grommeler*) to grouse*, moan* **b** **faire ~ qn** (= *faire attendre qn*) keep sb hanging about*

maroquin [marɔkɛ̃] NM **a** (= *cuir*) morocco (leather); **relié en ~** morocco-bound **b** (*Pol*) (minister's) portfolio; **obtenir un ~** to be made a minister

maroquinerie [marɔkinri] NF (= *boutique*) shop selling fancy *ou* fine leather goods; (= *atelier*) tannery; (= *métier*) fine leather craft; (= *préparation*) tanning; **(articles de) ~** fancy *ou* fine leather goods; **il travaille dans la ~** [*artisan*] he does fine leatherwork; [*commerçant*] he's in the (fine) leather trade

maroquinier [marɔkinje] NM (= *marchand*) dealer in fine leather goods; (= *fabricant*) leather worker *ou* craftsman

marotte [marɔt] NF **a** (= *dada*) hobby, craze; **c'est sa ~!** it's his pet craze!; **encore une de ses ~s** another one of his daft ideas*; **le voilà lancé sur sa ~!** there he goes on his pet subject! **b** (*Hist = poupée*) fool's bauble; (*Coiffure, Habillement = tête*) milliner's *ou* hairdresser's dummy head

maroufler [marufle] ▷conjug 1◁ VT [+ *toile*] to mount

marquage [markaʒ] NM **a** [*linge, marchandises*] marking; [*animal*] branding; [*arbre*] blazing **b** (*sur la chaussée*) road-marking **c** (*Sport*) [*joueur*] marking; **~ à la culotte** close marking

marquant, e [markã, ãt] ADJ [*personnage, événement*] outstanding; [*souvenir*] vivid; **je n'ai rien vu de très ~** I didn't see anything very striking *ou* worth talking about; **le fait le plus ~** the most significant *ou* striking fact

marque [mark] NF **a** (= *repère, trace*) mark; (= *signe*) (*lit, fig*) mark, sign; (= *preuve*) token; [*livre*] bookmark; [*linge*] name tab; **~s de doigts** fingermarks, fingerprints; **~s de pas** footmarks, footprints; **~s d'une blessure/de coups/de fatigue** marks of a wound/of blows/of fatigue; **il porte encore les ~s de son accident** he still bears the scars from his accident; **faites une ~ au crayon devant chaque nom** put a pencil mark beside each name, tick each name; **~ de confiance/de respect** sign *ou* token *ou* mark of confidence/of respect; **porter la ~ du pluriel** to be in the plural (form)
b (= *estampille*) [*or, argent*] hallmark; [*meubles, œuvre d'art*] mark; [*viande, œufs*] stamp; **la ~ du génie** the hallmark *ou* stamp of genius
c (*Comm*) [*nourriture, produits chimiques*] brand; [*automobiles, produits manufacturés*] make; **~ de fabrique** *ou* **de fabrication** *ou* **du fabricant** trademark, trade name, brand name; **~ d'origine** maker's mark; **~ déposée** registered trademark *ou* trade name *ou* brand name; **une grande ~ de vin/de voiture** a well-known brand of wine/make of car; **produits de ~** high-class products; **personnage de ~** distinguished person, VIP; **visiteur de ~** important *ou* distinguished visitor → **image**
d (= *insigne*) [*fonction, grade*] badge; (*frm*) **les ~s de sa fonction** the insignia *ou* regalia of his office
e (= *décompte de points*) **la ~** the score; **tenir la ~** to keep (the) score; **mener à la ~** to lead on the scoresheet, be ahead on goals, be in the lead; **ouvrir la ~** to open the scoring
f (*Sport = empreinte*) marker; **à vos ~s! prêts! partez!** (*athlètes*) on your marks! get set! go!; (*enfants*) ready, steady, go! (*Brit*), ready, set, go! (*US*); (*Rugby*) **~!** mark!; **prendre ses ~s** (*lit*) to place one's marker (*for one's run-up*); (*fig*) to get one's bearings; (*fig*) **il cherche encore ses ~s** he's trying to find his bearings

marqué, e [marke] (*ptp de* **marquer**) ADJ **a** (= *accentué*) marked, pronounced; (*Ling*) marked **b** (= *signalé*) **le prix ~** the price on the label; **au prix ~** at the labelled price, at the price shown on the label; (*fig*) **c'est un homme ~** he's a marked man; **il est très ~ politiquement** his political leanings are very obvious

marque-page (*pl* **marque-pages**) [mark(ǝ)paʒ] NM bookmark

marquer [marke] ▷conjug 1◁ **1** VT **a** (*par un signe distinctif*) [+ *objet personnel*] to mark (*au nom de qn* with sb's name); [+ *animal, criminel*] to brand; [+ *arbre*] to blaze; [+ *marchandise*] to label, stamp
b (= *indiquer*) [+ *limite, position*] to mark; (*sur une carte*) [+ *village, accident de terrain*] to mark, show, indicate; [*thermomètre*] to show, register; [*balance*] to register; [*isotope radioactif*] to

trace; **~ sa page (avec un signet)** to mark one's page (with a bookmark); **marquez la longueur voulue d'un trait de crayon** mark off the length required with a pencil; **l'animal marque son territoire** the animal marks its territory; **j'ai marqué ce jour-là d'une pierre blanche/noire** I'll remember it as a red-letter day/black day; **marquez d'une croix l'emplacement du véhicule** mark the position of the vehicle with a cross; **la pendule marque 6 heures** the clock shows *ou* says 6 o'clock; *(Couture)* **des pinces marquent la taille** darts emphasize the waist(line); **robe qui marque la taille** dress which shows off the waistline; **cela marque (bien) que le pays veut la paix** that definitely indicates *ou* shows that the country wants peace, that's a clear sign that the country wants peace

c [+ *événement*] to mark; **un bombardement a marqué la reprise des hostilités** a bomb attack marked the renewal *ou* resumption of hostilities; **des réjouissances populaires ont marqué la prise de pouvoir par la junte** the junta's takeover was marked by public celebrations; **pour ~ cette journée on a distribué ...** to mark *ou* commemorate this day they distributed ...

d (= *écrire*) [+ *nom, rendez-vous, renseignement*] to write down, note down, make a note of; **~ les points** *ou* **les résultats** to keep *ou* note the score; **on l'a marqué absent** he was marked absent; **j'ai marqué 3 heures sur mon agenda** I've got 3 o'clock (noted) down in my diary; **il a marqué qu'il fallait prévenir les élèves** he noted down that the pupils should be told, he made a note to tell the pupils; **qu'y a-t-il de marqué?** what does it say?, what's written (on it)?

e (= *endommager*) [+ *glace, bois*] to mark; (= *affecter*) [+ *personne*] to mark; (*influencer*) **~ son époque** to put one's mark *ou* stamp on one's time; **la souffrance l'a marqué** suffering has left its mark on him; **il est marqué par la vie** life has left its mark on him; **visage marqué par la maladie** face marked by illness; **visage marqué par la petite vérole** face pitted *ou* scarred with smallpox; **la déception se marquait sur son visage** disappointment showed in his face *ou* was written all over his face

f (= *manifester, montrer*) [+ *désapprobation, fidélité, intérêt*] to show

g *(Sport)* [+ *joueur*] to mark; [+ *but, essai*] to score; **~ qn de très près** *ou* **à la culotte** *(Sport)* to mark sb very closely *ou* tightly; *(fig)* to keep close tabs on sb

h *(loc)* **~ le coup*** (= *fêter un événement*) to mark the occasion; (= *accuser le coup*) to react; **j'ai risqué une allusion, mais il n'a pas marqué le coup*** I made an allusion to it but he showed no reaction; **~ un point/des points (sur qn)** to score a point/several points (against sb); **~ la mesure** to keep the beat; **~ le pas** (*lit*) to beat *ou* mark time; *(fig)* to mark time; **~ un temps d'arrêt** to pause momentarily

2 VI a [*événement, personnalité*] to stand out, be outstanding; [*coup*] to reach home, tell; **cet incident a marqué dans sa vie** that particular incident stood out in *ou* had a great impact on his life

b [*crayon*] to write; [*tampon*] to stamp; **ne pose pas le verre sur ce meuble, ça marque** don't put the glass down on that piece of furniture, it will leave a mark

marqueté, e [maʀkəte] ADJ [*bois*] inlaid

marqueterie [maʀkɛtʀi] NF (= *technique*) marquetry; (= *objet*) marquetry, inlaid work; *(fig)* mosaic; **table en ~** inlaid *ou* marquetry table

marqueur, -euse [maʀkœʀ, øz] **1** NM,F [*bétail*] brander; *(Sport, Jeux)* [*points*] scorekeeper, scorer; (= *buteur*) scorer **2** NM **a** (= *stylo*) felt-tip pen; (*indélébile*) marker pen **b** *(Méd = substance radioactive)* tracer; **~ génétique** genetic marker **c** (= *tableau*) score-

board **d** *(Ling)* marker; **~ syntagmatique phrase marker 3 marqueuse** NF *(Comm = appareil)* (price) labeller

marquis [maʀki] NM marquis, marquess; *(péj)* **petit ~** lordling

marquisat [maʀkiza] NM marquisate

marquise [maʀkiz] NF **a** (= *noble*) marchioness → **Madame b** (= *auvent*) glass canopy *ou* awning, (= *tente de jardin*) marquee (*Brit*), garden tent *(US)* **c les (îles) Marquises** the Marquesas Islands **d** *(Culin)* **~ au chocolat** chocolate charlotte **e** (= *siège*) marquise **f** (= *bague*) marquise

marraine [maʀɛn] NF [*enfant*] godmother; [*navire*] christener, namer; [*dans un club*] sponsor, proposer; **~ de guerre** soldier's wartime (woman) penfriend

Marrakech [maʀakɛʃ] N Marrakech, Marrakesh

marrant, e* [maʀɑ̃, ɑ̃t] ADJ **a** (= *amusant*) funny; **c'est un ~** ◊ **il est ~** he's a scream* *ou* a great laugh*; **ce n'est pas ~** it's not funny, it's no joke; **il n'est pas ~** (*ennuyeux, triste*) he's pretty dreary*, he's not much fun; *(sévère)* he's pretty grim*; (*empoisonnant*) he's a pain in the neck*; *(iro)* **tu es ~ toi! comment vais-je faire sans voiture?** don't make me laugh! what am I going to do without a car? **b** (= *étrange*) funny, odd

marre [maʀ] ADV **en avoir ~** to be fed up* *ou* cheesed off* (*Brit*) (**de** with), be sick* (**de** of); **j'en ai ~ de toi** I've just about had enough of you*, I am fed up with you*; **c'est ~!** ◊ **il y en a ~!** that's enough!

marrer (se)* [maʀe] ▸ conjug 1 ◂ VPR to laugh, have a good laugh*; **on s'est (bien) marré!** (= *on a ri*) we had a good laugh!*; (= *on s'est bien amusés*) we had a great time!; *(iro)* that was a barrel of laughs!; **il se marrait comme un fou** he was in fits* (of laughter) *ou* kinks* (*Brit*); **on ne se marre pas tous les jours au boulot!** work isn't always fun and games* *ou* a laugh a minute; **faire marrer qn** to make sb laugh; **tu me fais marrer avec ta démocratie!** you make me laugh with all your talk about democracy!

marri, e [maʀi] ADJ (*littér, †* = *triste*) sad, doleful (**de** about); (= *désolé*) sorry, grieved† (**de** about)

marron¹ [maʀɔ̃] **1** NM **a** *(Bot, Culin)* chestnut; **~ d'Inde** horse chestnut; **~s chauds** roast chestnuts; **~ glacé** marron glacé; **tirer les ~s du feu** (= *en bénéficiant*) to reap the benefits; (= *être la victime*) to be a cat's paw → **purée b** (= *couleur*) brown **c** (* = *coup*) blow, thump, cuff, clout (*Brit*); **tu veux un ~?** do you want a cuff *ou* a thick ear* (*Brit*)? **2** ADJ INV **a** (= *couleur*) brown **b* être ~** (= *être trompé*) to be had*

marron², -onne [maʀɔ̃, ɔn] ADJ (= *sans titres*) **médecin ~** quack, unqualified doctor; (= *sans scrupule*) **notaire/avocat ~** crooked notary/ lawyer; *(Hist)* **esclave ~** runaway *ou* fugitive slave

marronnier [maʀɔnje] NM **a** *(Bot)* chestnut (tree); **~ (d'Inde)** horse chestnut tree **b** *(arg Presse)* chestnut (*arg*)

Mars [maʀs] NM *(Astron, Myth)* Mars → **champ**

mars [maʀs] NM (= *mois*) March; **arriver** *ou* **venir** *ou* **tomber comme ~ en carême** to come *ou* happen as sure as night follows day; *pour autres locutions voir* **septembre**

marseillais, e [maʀseje, ɛz] **1** ADJ of *ou* from Marseilles → **histoire 2 Marseillais(e)** NM,F inhabitant *ou* native of Marseilles **3 Marseillaise** NF **la Marseillaise** the Marseillaise *(French national anthem)*

Marseille [maʀsej] N Marseilles

Marshall [maʀʃal] N **les îles ~** the Marshall Islands

marsouin [maʀswɛ̃] NM *(Zool)* porpoise; (*†: Mil*) marine

marsupial, e (*mpl* **-iaux**) [maʀsypjal, jo] ADJ, NM marsupial; **poche ~e** marsupium

marte [maʀt] NF = **martre**

marteau (*pl* **marteaux**) [maʀto] **1** NM **a** *(Menuiserie, Mus, Sport)* hammer; [*enchères, médecin*] hammer; [*président, juge*] gavel; [*horloge*] striker; [*porte*] knocker; [*forgeron*] (sledge) hammer; **il l'a cassé à coups de ~** he broke it with a hammer; **donner un coup de ~ sur qch** to hit sth with a hammer; **enfoncer qch à coups de ~** to hammer sth in, drive sth in with a hammer; **passer sous le ~ du commissaire-priseur** to be put up for auction, go under the (auctioneer's) hammer; *(fig)* **entre le ~ et l'enclume** between the devil and the deep blue sea; **être ~*** to be nuts* *ou* bats* *ou* cracked* → **faucille, requin b** *(Anat)* hammer, malleus *(SPÉC)* **2** COMP ▸ **marteau pneumatique** pneumatic drill

marteau-perforateur (*pl* **marteaux-perforateurs**) [maʀtopɛʀfɔʀatœʀ] NM hammer drill

marteau-pilon (*pl* **marteaux-pilons**) [maʀtopilɔ̃] NM power hammer

marteau-piolet (*pl* **marteaux-piolets**) [maʀtopjɔlɛ] NM piton hammer

marteau-piqueur (*pl* **marteaux-piqueurs**) [maʀtopikœʀ] NM pneumatic drill

martel [maʀtɛl] NM **se mettre ~ en tête** to worry o.s. sick, get all worked up*

martelage [maʀtəlaʒ] NM *(Métal)* hammering, planishing

martelé, e [maʀtəle] (*ptp de* **marteler**) ADJ **cuivre ~** planished *ou* beaten copper; *(Mus)* **notes ~es** martelé notes

martèlement [maʀtɛlmɑ̃] NM [*bruit, obus*] hammering, pounding; [*pas*] pounding, clanking; [*mots*] hammering out, rapping out

marteler [maʀtəle] ▸ conjug 5 ◂ VT [*marteau, obus, coups de poings*] to hammer, pound; [+ *objet d'art*] to planish, beat; [+ *thème, message*] to drum out; **~ ses mots** to hammer out *ou* rap out one's words; **ce bruit qui me martèle la tête** that noise hammering *ou* pounding through my head; **ses pas martelaient le sol gelé** his footsteps were pounding on the frozen ground

martellement [maʀtɛlmɑ̃] NM = **martèlement**

martial, e (*mpl* **-iaux**) [maʀsjal, jo] ADJ (*hum, littér*) [*peuple, discours*] martial, warlike, soldierlike; [*allure*] soldierly, martial; **arts martiaux** martial arts → **cour, loi**

martialement [maʀsjalmɑ̃] ADV (*hum, littér*) martially, in a soldierly manner

martien, -ienne [maʀsjɛ̃, jɛn] ADJ, NM,F Martian

martinet [maʀtinɛ] NM **a** (= *fouet*) small whip (*used on children*), strap **b** (= *oiseau*) swift **c** (= *marteau*) tilt hammer

martingale [maʀtɛ̃gal] NF *(Habillement)* half belt; *(Équitation)* martingale; *(Roulette)* (= *combinaison*) winning formula; (= *mise double*) doubling-up

martiniquais, e [maʀtinike, ɛz] **1** ADJ of *ou* from Martinique **2 Martiniquais(e)** NM,F inhabitant *ou* native of Martinique

Martinique [maʀtinik] NF Martinique

martin-pêcheur (*pl* **martins-pêcheurs**) [maʀtɛ̃peʃœʀ] NM kingfisher

martre [maʀtʀ] NF marten; **~ zibeline** sable

martyr, e¹ [maʀtiʀ] **1** ADJ [*soldats, peuple*] martyred; **enfant ~** battered child **2** NM,F martyr (**d'une cause** to a cause); **ne prends pas ces airs de ~!** stop acting the martyr!, it's no use putting on that martyred look!; **c'est le ~ de la classe** he's always being bullied by the rest of the class

martyre² [maʀtiʀ] NM *(Rel)* martyrdom; *(fig = souffrance)* martyrdom, agony; **le ~ de ce peuple** the martyrdom *ou* suffering of this people; **sa vie fut un long ~** his life was one long agony; **cette longue attente est un ~** it's agony waiting so long; **mettre au ~** to torture

martyriser [maʀtiʀize] ▸ conjug 1 ◂ VT **a** (= faire souffrir) [+ personne, animal] to torture; [+ élève] to bully; [+ enfant, bébé] to batter **b** (Rel) to martyr

martyrologe [maʀtiʀɔlɔʒ] NM martyrology

marxien, -ienne [maʀksjɛ̃, jɛn] ADJ Marxian

marxisant, e [maʀksizɑ̃, ɑ̃t] ADJ leaning towards Marxism

marxisme [maʀksism] NM Marxism; **~-léninisme** Marxism-Leninism

marxiste [maʀksist] ADJ, NMF Marxist; **~-léniniste** Marxist-Leninist

maryland [maʀilɑ̃(d)] NM **a** (= tabac) type of Virginia tobacco, ≈ virginia **b** (= État) **le Maryland** Maryland

mas [mɑ(s)] NM mas (house or farm in Provence)

mascara [maskaʀa] NM mascara

mascarade [maskaʀad] NF **a** (péj = tromperie) farce, masquerade; **ce procès est une ~** this trial is a farce **b** (= réjouissance, déguisement) masquerade

Mascareignes [maskaʀɛɲ] NFPL **l'archipel des ~** the Mascarene Islands

mascaret [maskaʀɛ] NM (tidal) bore

mascarpone [maskaʀpɔn] NM (Culin) Mascarpone

Mascate [maskat] N Muscat

mascotte [maskɔt] NF mascot

masculin, e [maskylɛ̃, in] **1** ADJ [hormone, population, sexe] male; [mode] men's; (péj = hommasse) [femme, silhouette] mannish, masculine; (Gram) masculine; **voix ~e** [homme] male voice; [femme] masculine voice; (virile) manly voice; (Sport) **l'équipe ~e** the men's team → **rime** **2** NM (Gram) masculine; **« fer » est (du) ~** "fer" is masculine

masculiniser [maskylinize] ▸ conjug 1 ◂ VT **a** **~ qn** to make sb look mannish ou masculine **b** (Bio) to make masculine

masculinité [maskylinite] NF masculinity; (= virilité) manliness; [femme] mannishness; (Démographie) **taux de ~** male population rate

Maseru [mazeʀu] N Maseru

maskinongé [maskinɔ̃ʒe] NM (Can = brochet) muskellunge, muskie* (Can), maskinonge

maso* [mazo] ABRÉV = **masochiste** **1** ADJ masochistic; (fig) **il est complètement ~!** he's a glutton for punishment! **2** NMF masochist

masochisme [mazɔʃism] NM masochism

masochiste [mazɔʃist] **1** ADJ masochistic **2** NMF masochist

masque [mask] **1** NM **a** (= objet, Méd, Ordin) mask; **~ de saisie** data entry form; (Phys) **effet de ~** masking effect → **bas** **b** (= expression du visage) mask-like expression; **dès que je lui ai dit ça, ça été le ~*** when I told him his face froze **c** (= cosmétique) **~ (de beauté)** face pack; **~ nettoyant** cleansing mask; **se faire un ~** to put on a face pack ou mask **d** (= apparence) mask, façade, front; **ce n'est qu'un ~** it's just a mask ou front ou façade; **sous ou derrière le ~ de la respectabilité** beneath the façade of respectability; **lever ou jeter le ~** to unmask o.s., reveal o.s. in one's true colours; **arracher son ~ à qn** to unmask sb **e** (Hist = personne déguisée) mask, masker **2** COMP ▸ **masque anti-pollution** anti-pollution mask ▸ **masque de carnaval** carnival mask ▸ **masque chirurgical** ou **de chirurgien** surgical mask ▸ **masque funéraire** funeral mask ▸ **masque à gaz** gas mask ▸ **masque de grossesse** chloasma ▸ **masque mortuaire** death mask ▸ **masque à oxygène** oxygen mask ▸ **masque de plongée** diving mask

masqué, e [maske] (ptp de **masquer**) ADJ [bandit] masked; [personne déguisée] wearing ou in a mask; (fig) **s'avancer ~** to hide one's hand; (Aut) **virage ~** blind corner ou bend → **bal**

masquer [maske] ▸ conjug 1 ◂ **1** VT (lit, fig = cacher) (gén) to hide, mask, conceal (à qn from sb); [+ lumière] to screen, shade; [+ vue] to block out; (Mil) [+ troupes] to screen, mask; **ça masque le goût** it masks the flavour; **ces questions secondaires ont masqué l'essentiel** these questions of secondary importance masked ou obscured the essential point; **avec un mépris à peine masqué** with barely concealed contempt **2** **se masquer** VPR **a** (= mettre un masque) to put on a mask **b** (= se cacher) [sentiment] to be hidden; [personne] to hide, conceal o.s. (**derrière** behind)

Massachusetts [masaʃysɛts] NM **le ~** Massachusetts

massacrante [masakʀɑ̃t] ADJ F → **humeur**

massacre [masakʀ] NM **a** (= tuerie) [personnes] slaughter (NonC), massacre; [animaux] slaughter (NonC); **ce fut un véritable ~** it was sheer butchery; **échapper au ~** to escape the massacre ou slaughter; **envoyer des soldats au ~** to send soldiers to the slaughter; **le ~ des bébés phoques** seal cull(ing); **~ écologique** ecological disaster; (Bible) **le ~ des innocents** the massacre of the innocents; **le Massacre de la Saint-Barthélemy** the Saint Bartholomew's Day Massacre; **je vais faire un ~!*** I'm going to kill somebody! → **jeu** **b*** **quel ~! ◊ c'est un vrai ~!*** (= sabotage) it's a complete mess!; (= défaite sportive) what a massacre!*; **arrête le ~!** stop before you do any more damage! **c** (* = succès) **faire un ~** [spectacle, chanteur] to be a roaring success* **d** (Chasse) stag's head ou antlers **e** (Hér) attire

massacrer [masakʀe] ▸ conjug 1 ◂ VT **a** (= tuer) [+ personnes] to slaughter, massacre; [+ animaux] to slaughter, butcher; **se ~** to massacre ou slaughter one another **b** (* = saboter) [+ opéra, pièce] to murder, botch up; [+ travail] to make a mess ou hash* of; (= mal découper, scier) [+ viande, planche] to hack to bits, make a mess of **c** (* = vaincre) [+ adversaire] to massacre, slaughter, make mincemeat of*; **il s'est fait ~ par son adversaire** he was massacred by his opponent, his opponent made mincemeat of him* **d** (* = éreinter) [+ œuvre, auteur] to slam*, tear to pieces, slate* (Brit)

massacreur, -euse* [masakʀœʀ, øz] NM,F (= saboteur) bungler, botcher; (= tueur) slaughterer, butcher

massage [masaʒ] NM massage; **~ facial** facial ou face massage; **~ thaïlandais** Thai massage; **faire un ~ à qn** to give sb a massage; **faire un ~ cardiaque à qn** to give sb cardiac ou heart massage

masse [mas] **1** NF **a** (= volume, Phys) mass; (= forme) massive shape ou bulk; **~ d'eau** [lac] body ou expanse of water; [chute] mass of water; **~ de nuages** bank of clouds; (Mét) **~ d'air** air mass; **~ musculaire** muscle mass; **la ~ de l'édifice** the massive structure of the building; **pris ou taillé dans la ~** carved from the block; **la ~ instrumentale/vocale** the massed instruments/voices; (Astron) **la ~ manquante (de l'Univers)** the missing ou hidden mass (of the Universe); **s'écrouler ou tomber comme une ~** to slump down ou fall in a heap **b** (= foule) **les ~s (laborieuses)** the (working) masses, the toiling masses; **les ~s populaires** the masses, **les ~s paysannes** the agricultural work force; † the peasantry; **la (grande) ~ des lecteurs** the (great) majority of readers; **ça plaît à la ~ ou aux ~s** it appeals to the masses; **éducation/psychologie des ~s** mass education/psychology, education/psychology of the masses; **culture/manifestation/tourisme/production de ~** mass culture/demonstration/tourism/production → **fon-**

dre, noyer **c** (* = beaucoup) **une ~ de ◊ des ~s de** masses of, loads of*; **des ~s de touristes** crowds ou masses of tourists; **des gens comme lui, je n'en connais pas des ~** I don't know many people like him, you don't meet his sort every day; **tu as aimé ce film? — pas des ~!** did you like that film? — not all that much!; **il n'y en a pas des ~** [= eau, argent] there isn't much; [chaises, spectateurs] there aren't many **d** (Élec) earth (Brit), ground (US); **mettre à la ~** to earth (Brit), ground (US); **faire ~** to act as an earth (Brit) ou a ground (US); **être à la ~*** (fou) to be nuts* ou crazy*; (fatigué) to be out of it* **e** (= argent) (Mil) fund; (Prison) prisoner's earnings; **~ monétaire** money supply; **~ salariale** wage bill; (Jur) **~ active** assets; **~ passive** liabilities **f** (= maillet) sledgehammer; [huissier] mace; **~ d'armes** mace; (fig) **ça a été le coup de ~!** (choc émotif) it was quite a blow!; (prix excessif) it cost a bomb! **2 en masse** LOC ADJ, LOC ADV [exécutions, production] mass (épith); **arrivée en ~** mass arrival, arrival en masse; **fabriquer ou produire en ~** to mass-produce; **acheter/vendre en ~** to buy/sell in bulk; **manifester/protester en ~** to hold a mass demonstration/protest; **venir en ~** to come en masse; **ils sont venus en ~ à son concert** people flocked to his concert, people came in droves to his concert; **il en a en ~** he has masses ou lots ou loads* (of them)

massé [mase] NM (Billard) massé (shot); **faire un ~** to play a massé shot

masselotte [mas(ə)lɔt] NF (Aut) lead (for wheel balancing); (en fonderie) feeder

massepain [maspɛ̃] NM marzipan

masser¹ [mase] ▸ conjug 1 ◂ **1** VT **a** (= grouper) [+ gens] to assemble, bring ou gather together; [+ choses] to put ou gather together; [+ troupes] to mass; **les cheveux massés en (un) chignon** her hair gathered in a chignon/at the back of the head **b** (Art) to group **2 se masser** VPR [foule] to mass, gather, assemble

masser² [mase] ▸ conjug 1 ◂ VT **a** (= frotter) [+ personne] to massage; **se faire ~** to have a massage, be massaged; **masse-moi le dos!** massage ou rub my back! **b** (Billard) **~ la bille** to play a massé shot

massette [masɛt] NF **a** (Tech) sledgehammer **b** (Bot) bulrush, reed mace

masseur [masœʀ] NM (= personne) masseur; (= machine) massager; **~-kinésithérapeute** physiotherapist

masseuse [masøz] NF masseuse

massicot [masiko] NM (Typo) guillotine; (Chim) massicot

massicoter [masikɔte] ▸ conjug 1 ◂ VT [+ papier] to guillotine

massif, -ive [masif, iv] **1** ADJ **a** (d'aspect) [meuble, bâtiment, porte] massive, solid, heavy; [personne] sturdily built; [visage] large, heavy; **front ~** massive forehead; **homme de carrure massive** big strong man **b** (= pur) or/argent/chêne ~ solid gold/silver/oak **c** (= important) [afflux, bombardement, dose, vote] massive **d** (= de nombreuses personnes) [arrestations, licenciements, exode, manifestation] mass (épith); **armes de destruction massive** weapons of mass destruction; **l'arrivée massive des réfugiés** the mass ou massive influx of refugees **e** (Ling) **terme ~** mass noun **2** NM **a** (Géog) **~ (montagneux)** massif; **le Massif central** the Massif Central **b** (Bot) [fleurs] clump, bank; [arbres] clump **c** (Archit) pillar

massique [masik] ADJ [volume] mass (épith); **puissance ~** power-weight ratio; **activité ~** specific activity

massivement [masivmɑ̃] ADV [démissionner, partir, répondre] en masse; [injecter, administrer]

mass(-)media in massive doses; **investir ~** to invest heavily, make huge investments (**dans** in); **ils ont ~ approuvé le projet** the overwhelming *ou* massive majority was in favour of the project

mass(-)media [masmedja] NMPL mass media

massue [masy] NF club, bludgeon; **~ de gymnastique** (Indian) club; **coup de ~** (*lit*) blow with a club (*ou* bludgeon); **ça a été le coup de ~!*** (*très cher*) it cost a bomb!*; (*choc émotif*) it was quite a blow! → **argument**

mastaba [mastaba] NM mastaba(h)

mastectomie [mastɛktɔmi] NF = **mammectomie**

mastère [mastɛR] NM *diploma awarded by a grande école or university for a year's advanced study or research*

mastic [mastik] [1] NM [a] [*vitrier*] putty; [*menuisier*] filler, mastic [b] (*Bot*) mastic [c] (*Typo*) [*caractères, pages*] (faulty) transposition [2] ADJ INV putty-coloured; **imperméable (couleur) ~** light-coloured *ou* off-white raincoat

masticage [mastikaʒ] NM [*vitre*] puttying; [*fissure*] filling

masticateur, -trice [mastikatœR, tRis] ADJ chewing (*épith*), masticatory

mastication [mastikasjɔ̃] NF chewing, mastication

masticatoire [mastikatwaR] [1] ADJ chewing, masticatory [2] NM masticatory

mastiquer¹ [mastike] ▸conjug 1◂ VT (= *mâcher*) to chew, masticate

mastiquer² [mastike] ▸conjug 1◂ VT (*Tech*) [+ *vitre*] to putty, apply putty to; [+ *fissure*] to fill, apply filler to; **couteau à ~** putty knife

mastoc* [mastɔk] ADJ INV [*personne*] hefty*, strapping (*épith*); [*chose*] large and cumbersome; **c'est un (type) ~** he's a big hefty guy* *ou* bloke* (*Brit*), he's a great strapping fellow*; **une statue ~** a great hulking statue

mastodonte [mastɔdɔ̃t] NM [a] (*Zool*) mastodon [b] (*hum*) (= *personne*) colossus, mountain of a man (*ou* woman); (= *animal*) monster; (= *véhicule*) great bus (*hum*) *ou* tank (*hum*); (= *camion*) huge vehicle, juggernaut (*Brit*); (= *firme*) mammoth company

mastoïde [mastɔid] NF (= *os*) mastoid

mastroquet*† [mastRɔkɛ] NM (= *bar*) pub, bar; (= *tenancier*) publican

masturbation [mastyRbasjɔ̃] NF masturbation; (*péj*) **c'est de la ~ intellectuelle** it's mental masturbation

masturber VT, **se masturber** VPR [mastyRbe] ▸conjug 1◂ to masturbate

m'as-tu-vu, e* [matyvy] [1] NM,F (*pl inv*) show-off*, swank*; **il est du genre ~** he's a real show-off* [2] ADJ INV [*mobilier, style*] showy

masure [mazyR] NF tumbledown *ou* dilapidated house, hovel (*péj*)

mat¹ [mat] NM (*Échecs*) **être ~** to be in checkmate; (**tu es**) **~!** checkmate!; **faire ~** to checkmate; **il a fait ~ en 12 coups** he got checkmate in 12 moves; **tu m'as fait ~ en 10 coups** you've (check)mated me in 10 moves [2] NM checkmate → **échec²**

mat², e [mat] ADJ (= *sans éclat*) [*métal*] mat(t), dull; [*couleur*] mat(t), dull, flat; [*peinture, papier, photo*] mat(t); **bruit ~** dull noise, thud; **avoir la peau ~e** *ou* **le teint ~** to have a dark complexion

mat'* [mat] NM (ABRÉV = **matin**) morning; **à deux/six heures du ~** at two/six in the morning

mât [mɑ] [1] NM [a] (*Naut*) mast; **grand ~** mainmast [b] (= *pylône, poteau*) pole, post; (= *hampe*) flagpole; (*Sport*) climbing pole [2] COMP ▸ **mât d'artimon** mizzenmast ▸ **mât de charge** derrick, cargo boom ▸ **mât de cocagne** greasy pole ▸ **mât de**

hune topmast ▸ **mât de misaine** foremast ▸ **mât de perroquet** topgallant mast

matador [matadɔR] NM matador, bullfighter

mataf [mataf] NM (*arg Marine*) sailor

matage [mataʒ] NM [*dorure, verre*] matting; [*soudure*] caulking

matamore [matamɔR] NM (= *fanfaron*) braggart; **jouer les ~s** to swagger

match [matʃ] NM (*Sport*) match, game (*US*); **~ aller** first-leg match; **~ avancé/en retard** *match that has been brought forward/delayed*; **~ retour** return match, second-leg match; **~ amical** friendly (match); **~ nul** tie, draw; **ils ont fait ~ nul** they tied, they drew; **ils ont fait ~ nul 0 à 0/2 à 2** it was a nil-nil/2-2 (*Brit*) draw, they drew nil-nil/2-all (*Brit*), they tied at zero all/ 2-all (*US*); **~ à l'extérieur** *ou* **sur terrain adverse** away match; **~ à domicile** *ou* **sur son propre terrain** home match; **faire un ~ de tennis/volley-ball** to play a tennis/volleyball match → **disputer**

maté [mate] NM maté

matelas [mat(ə)lɑ] NM [a] [*lit*] mattress; **~ de laine/à ressorts** wool/(interior-)sprung mattress; **~ de** *ou* **en mousse** foam mattress; **~ d'eau** water bed; **~ pneumatique** (= *lit*) air bed; (*de plage*) Lilo® (*Brit*), air mattress (*US*); (*Constr*) **~ d'air** air space *ou* cavity; **dormir sur un ~ de feuilles mortes** to sleep on a carpet of dead leaves → **toile** [b] (= *réserve*) [*devises*] reserve, cushion; (*Pol*) **pour préserver son petit ~ de voix** to preserve his small majority; **j'ai un ~ de sécurité** I have something to fall back on; **~ (de billets)*** wad of notes; **il a un joli petit ~*** he's got a tidy sum put by*

matelassé, e [mat(ə)lase] (*ptp de* **matelasser**) [1] ADJ [*veste, jupe, manteau*] quilted, padded; [*doublure*] padded [2] NM quilting

matelasser [mat(ə)lase] ▸conjug 1◂ VT [+ *meuble, porte*] to pad, upholster; [+ *tissu*] to quilt; [+ *vêtement*] (= *rembourrer*) to pad; (= *doubler*) to line; (*avec tissu matelassé*) to quilt

matelassier, -ière [mat(ə)lasje, jɛR] NM,F mattress maker

matelassure [mat(ə)lasyR] NF (= *rembourrage*) padding; (= *doublure*) quilting, lining

matelot [mat(ə)lo] NM [a] (*gén* = *marin*) sailor, seaman; (*dans la marine de guerre*) ordinary rating (*Brit*), seaman recruit (*US*); **~ de première/deuxième/troisième classe** leading/able/ordinary seaman; **~ breveté** able rating (*Brit*), seaman apprentice (*US*) [b] (= *navire*) **~ d'avant/d'arrière** (next) ship ahead/astern

matelote [mat(ə)lɔt] NF [a] (= *plat*) matelote; (= *sauce*) matelote sauce (*made with wine*); **~ d'anguille** eels stewed in wine sauce [b] (= *danse*) hornpipe

mater¹ [mate] ▸conjug 1◂ VT [a] [+ *rebelles*] to bring to heel, subdue; [+ *terroristes*] to bring *ou* get under control; [+ *enfant*] to take in hand; [+ *révolution*] to put down, quell, suppress; [+ *incendie*] to bring under control, check; **je vais les ~!** I'll show them who's boss! [b] (*Échecs*) to put in checkmate, checkmate, mate

mater²* [mate] ▸conjug 1◂ VT (= *regarder*) to eye up*, ogle; (= *épier*) to spy on; **mate si le prof arrive!** keep an eye out for the teacher coming!

mater³ [mate] ▸conjug 1◂ VT [a] (= *marteler*) [+ *métal*] to caulk [b] = **matir**

mater⁴* [matɛR] NF mum* (*Brit*), mom* (*US*); **ma ~** my old woman* *ou* mum‡ (*Brit*) *ou* mom* (*US*)

mâter [mate] ▸conjug 1◂ VT (*Naut*) to mast

matérialisation [materjalizasjɔ̃] NF [*projet, promesse, doute*] materialization; (*Phys*) mass energy conversion; (*Spiritisme*) materialization

matérialiser [materjalize] ▸conjug 1◂ [1] VT [a] (= *concrétiser*) [+ *projet*] to bring about, carry out; [+ *promesse, doute*] to realize; (=

symboliser) [+ *vertu, vice*] to embody; (*Philo*) to materialize [b] (= *signaliser*) [+ *frontière*] to mark; **~ au sol un passage clouté** to mark a pedestrian crossing; **«chaussée non matérialisée»** "unmarked road" [2] **se matérialiser** VPR to materialize

matérialisme [materjalism] NM materialism

matérialiste [materjalist] [1] ADJ materialistic [2] NMF materialist

matérialité [materjalite] NF materiality

matériau (*pl* **matériaux**) [materjo] NM (*Constr*) material; (= *documents*) material (*NonC*); **~x de récupération** waste material; **~x de construction** building materials → **résistance**

matériel, -elle [materjɛl] [1] ADJ [a] [*monde, preuve, bien-être, confort*] material; **être ~** material *ou* physical being; **dégâts ~s** material damage; **j'ai la preuve matérielle de son crime** I have tangible *ou* material proof of his crime; **je suis dans l'impossibilité matérielle de le faire** it's materially impossible for me to do it; **je n'ai pas le temps ~ de le faire** I simply don't have the time to do it [b] [*plaisirs, biens, préoccupations*] worldly [c] (= *financier*) [*gêne, problèmes*] financial; (= *pratique*) [*organisation, obstacles*] practical; **aide matérielle** material aid; **de nombreux avantages ~s** a large number of material advantages; **sa vie matérielle est assurée** his material needs are provided for, he is provided for materially

[2] NM (*Agr, Mil*) equipment (*NonC*), materials; (*Tech*) equipment (*NonC*), plant (*NonC*); (= *attirail*) gear (*NonC*), kit (*NonC*); (= *données*) material (*NonC*); (*Ordin*) **le ~** the hardware; **tout son ~ d'artiste** all his artist's materials *ou* gear*; **~ de camping/d'enregistrement/de jardinage** camping/recording/gardening equipment; **~ de bureau/d'imprimerie/de laboratoire** office/printing/laboratory equipment; **~ de pêche** fishing tackle; **~ pédagogique** teaching equipment *ou* aids

[3] COMP ▸ **matériel d'exploitation** plant (*NonC*) ▸ **matériel génétique** genetic material ▸ **matériel de guerre** weaponry (*NonC*) ▸ **matériel humain** human material, labour force ▸ **matériel roulant** (*Rail*) rolling stock ▸ **matériel scolaire** (= *livres, cahiers*) school (reading *ou* writing) materials; (= *pupitres, projecteurs*) school equipment

matériellement [materjɛlmɑ̃] ADV [a] (= *physiquement*) [*se concrétiser, exister*] physically; **c'est ~ possible** it can be done, it's feasible; **c'est ~ impossible** it cannot be done, it's physically impossible [b] (= *financièrement*) [*aider*] financially

maternage [maternaʒ] NM (= *dorlotement*) mothering, babying*, cosseting; (*fait de mâcher le travail*) spoonfeeding

maternant, e [maternɑ̃, ɑ̃t] ADJ motherly

maternel, -elle [maternɛl] [1] ADJ [a] (= *d'une mère*) [*instinct, amour*] maternal, motherly; (= *comme d'une mère*) [*geste, soin*] motherly; [*lait*] mother's (*épith*); (= *de la mère*) of the mother, maternal; (*Généalogie*) **du côté ~** on one's mother's side, on the maternal side; **c'est mon grand-père ~** he's my grandfather on my mother's side, he's my maternal grandfather; **écoute les conseils ~s!** listen to your mother's advice!; (*Admin*) **la protection maternelle et infantile** ≈ mother and infant welfare → **allaitement, lait, langue** [2] **maternelle** NF (*école*) **maternelle** nursery school; **il est en** *ou* **à la maternelle** he's at nursery school

maternellement [maternɛlmɑ̃] ADV maternally, like a mother

materner [materne] ▸conjug 1◂ VT (= *dorloter*) to mother, baby*, cosset; (= *mâcher le travail à*) to spoonfeed; **se faire ~** (*gén*) to be babied*; [*employé*] to be spoonfed

maternisé [maternize] ADJ M → **lait**

maternité [maternite] NF [a] (= *bâtiment*) maternity hospital *ou* home [b] (*Bio*) pregnancy; **fatiguée par plusieurs ~s** exhausted by several pregnancies *ou* from having had several babies [c] (= *état de mère*) motherhood, maternity; **la ~ l'a mûrie** motherhood *ou* being a mother has made her more mature → **allocation**, **congé** [d] (*Art*) painting of mother and child (*ou* children)

mateur, -euse‡ [matœr, øz] NM,F ogler

math* [mat] NFPL (ABRÉV = **mathématiques**) maths* (*Brit*), math* (*US*); **être en ~ sup/spé** to be in the first/second year advanced maths class preparing for the Grandes Écoles

mathématicien, -ienne [matematisjɛ̃, jɛn] NM,F mathematician

mathématique [matematik] [1] ADJ [*problème, méthode, précision, rigueur*] mathematical; **c'est ~ !*** (*sûr*) it's bound to happen!, it's a dead cert!* (*Brit*); (*logique*) it's logical! [2] NF ~ mathematics *sg* [3] **mathématiques** NFPL mathematics *sg*; **~s modernes/pures** modern/pure maths (*Brit*) *ou* math (*US*); **~s supérieures/spéciales** first/second year advanced maths class preparing for the Grandes Écoles

mathématiquement [matematikmɑ̃] ADV (*Math, fig*) mathematically; **~, il n'a aucune chance** logically he hasn't a hope

mathématiser [matematize] ▶ conjug 1 ◀ VT to express mathematically

matheux, -euse* [matø, øz] NM,F (= *spécialiste*) mathematician, maths (*Brit*) *ou* math (*US*) specialist; (= *étudiant*) maths (*Brit*) *ou* math (*US*) student; **c'est la matheuse de la famille** she's the mathematician *ou* maths expert in the family

Mathieu [matjø] NM Matthew

maths* [mat] NFPL = **math**

Mathusalem [matyzalɛm] NM Methuselah; **ça date de ~*** [*situation*] it goes back a long way; (*objet*) it's as old as the hills

matière [matjɛʀ] [1] NF [a] (*Philo, Phys*) **la ~** matter; **la ~ vivante** living matter [b] (= *substances*) matter (*NonC*), material; **~ combustible/inflammable** combustible/inflammable material; **~ organique** organic matter; **~ précieuse** precious substance; **~s (fécales)** faeces (*Brit*), feces (*US*); **le transport de ~s dangereuses** the transport of hazardous materials [c] (= *fond, sujet*) material, matter; (*Scol*) subject; **cela lui a fourni la ~ de son dernier livre** that gave him the material for his latest book; (*Scol*) **il est bon dans toutes les ~s** he is good at all subjects; **il est très ignorant en la ~** he is completely ignorant on the subject, it's a matter *ou* subject he knows nothing about; **en la ~, il faudrait demander à un spécialiste** it's better to ask a specialist about that kind of thing; (*Univ*) **~ principale** main subject (*Brit*), major (*US*); **~ secondaire** subsidiary (*Brit*), second subject (*Brit*), minor (*US*); **entrée en ~** introduction → **option, table** [d] (*loc*) **en ~ poétique/commerciale** where *ou* as far as poetry/commerce is concerned; **en ~ d'art/de jardinage** as regards art/gardening; **donner ~ à plaisanter** to give cause for laughter; **il y a là ~ à réflexion** this is a matter for serious thought; **ça lui a donné ~ à réflexion** it gave him food for thought; **il n'y a pas là ~ à rire** this is no laughing matter; **il n'y a pas là ~ à se réjouir** this is no matter for rejoicing [2] COMP ▶ **matière(s) grasse(s)** fat content, fat; **yaourt à 15% de ~ grasse** yoghurt with 15% fat content ▶ **matière grise** (*lit, fig*) grey (*Brit*) *ou* gray (*US*) matter; **faire travailler sa ~ grise** to use one's grey matter ▶ **matière imposable** object of taxation ▶ **matière noire** (*Astron*) dark matter ▶ **matière plastique** plastic; **en ~ plastique** plastic (*épith*) ▶ **matière première** raw material

MATIF [matif] NM (ABRÉV = **marché à terme d'instruments financiers** *ou* **marché à terme international de France**) ≈ LIFFE (*Brit*)

Matignon [matiɲɔ̃] NM (**l'hôtel**) **~** the Hotel Matignon (*the offices of the Prime Minister of the French Republic*); **les accords ~** the Matignon Agreements (*which laid down workers' rights*)

matin [matɛ̃] [1] NM [a] (= *partie de journée*) morning; **par un ~ de juin** on a June morning, one June morning; **le 10 au ~** ◊ **le ~ du 10** on the morning of the 10th; **2h du ~** 2 a.m., 2 in the morning; **je suis du ~** (*actif dès le matin*) I'm a morning person; (*de l'équipe du matin*) I'm on *ou* I work mornings; **du ~ au soir** from morning till night, morning noon and night; **je ne travaille que le ~** I only work mornings* *ou* in the morning; (*Méd*) **à prendre ~ midi et soir** to be taken three times a day; **jusqu'au ~** until morning; **de bon** *ou* **de grand ~** early in the morning; **au petit ~** in the small *ou* early hours; **nous avons parlé jusqu'au petit ~** we talked into the small *ou* early hours → **quatre** [b] (*littér*) **au ~ de sa vie** in the morning of one's life [2] ADV† **partir/se lever ~** to leave/get up very early *ou* at daybreak

mâtin [matɛ̃] [1] NM [a] († = *coquin*) cunning devil*, sly dog* [b] (= *chien*) (*de garde*) (big) watchdog; (*de chasse*) hound [2] EXCL† by Jove!, my word!

matinal, e (*mpl* **-aux**) [matinal, o] ADJ [*tâches, toilette*] morning (*épith*); **gelée ~e** early morning frost; **heure ~e** early hour; **être ~** to be an early riser, get up early; **il est bien ~ aujourd'hui** he's up early today

mâtine, e [matin] NF hussy

mâtiné, e [matine] (*ptp de* **mâtiner**) ADJ [*animal*] crossbred; **chien ~** mongrel (dog); **~ de** (*Zool*) crossed with; (*fig*) mixed with; **il parle un français ~ d'espagnol** he speaks a mixture of French and Spanish; (*péj*) **il est ~ cochon d'Inde*** he's a bit of a half-breed (*péj*)

matinée [matine] NF [a] (= *matin*) morning; **je le verrai demain dans la ~** I'll see him sometime (in the course of) tomorrow morning; **en début/en fin de ~** at the beginning/at the end of the morning; **après une ~ de chasse** after a morning's hunting → **gras** [b] (*Ciné, Théât*) matinée, afternoon performance; **j'irai en ~** I'll go to the matinée (performance); **~ dansante** tea dance; **~ enfantine** children's matinée

mâtiner [matine] ▶ conjug 1 ◀ VT [+ *chien*] to cross

matines [matin] NFPL matins

matir [matiʀ] ▶ conjug 2 ◀ VT [+ *verre, argent*] to mat(t), dull

matité [matite] NF [*peinture, teint*] mat(t) aspect; [*son*] dullness; (*Méd*) **~ pulmonaire** flatness

matois, e [matwa, waz] ADJ (*littér* = *rusé*) wily, sly, crafty; **c'est un(e) ~(e)** he's *ou* (she's) a sly character *ou* a crafty one *ou* a sly one

maton, -onne [matɔ̃, ɔn] NM,F (*arg Prison*) screw (*arg*)

matos* [matos] NM equipment (*NonC*), gear (*NonC*)

matou [matu] NM tomcat, tom

matraquage [matʀakaʒ] NM [a] (*par la police*) beating (up) (*with a truncheon*) [b] (*Presse, Radio*) plugging; **le ~ publicitaire** media hype* *ou* overkill; **le ~ idéologique** ideological brainwashing

matraque [matʀak] NF (*police*) baton, truncheon (*Brit*), billy (club) (*US*); [*malfaiteur*] club, cosh (*Brit*); (*lit*) **coup de ~** blow from *ou* with a baton *ou* club; (*fig*) **ça a été le coup de ~*** (*cher*) it cost a bomb*; (*inattendu*) it was a bolt from the blue

matraquer [matʀake] ▶ conjug 1 ◀ VT [a] (*police*) to beat up (*with a truncheon*); [*malfaiteur*] to club, cosh (*Brit*) [b] (* = *escroquer*) **~ le client** to fleece* *ou* soak‡ (*US*) customers; **se faire ~*** to get ripped off* *ou* fleeced* *ou* done* [c] (*Presse, Radio*) [+ *chanson, produit, publicité*] to plug, hype*; [+ *public*] to bombard (**de** with)

matraqueur [matʀakœʀ] NM (*arg Sport*) dirty player; (= *policier, malfaiteur*) dirty worker

matriarcal, e (*mpl* **-aux**) [matʀijaʀkal, o] ADJ matriarchal

matriarcat [matʀijaʀka] NM matriarchy

matricaire [matʀikɛʀ] NF mayweed

matrice [matʀis] NF [a] (= *utérus*) womb [b] (*Tech*) mould, die; (*Ordin, Typo*) matrix; [*disque*] matrix [c] (*Ling, Math*) matrix; **~ réelle/complexe** matrix of real/complex numbers [d] (*Admin*) register; **~ cadastrale** cadastre; **~ du rôle des contributions** ≈ original of register of taxes

matricide [matʀisid] [1] ADJ matricidal [2] NMF, NM matricide

matriciel, -ielle [matʀisjɛl] ADJ (*Math*) matrix (*épith*), done with a matrix; (*Admin*) pertaining to assessment of rates; **loyer ~** rent assessment (*to serve as basis for calculation of rates or taxes*); **imprimante matricielle** dot-matrix printer

matricule [matʀikyl] [1] NM (*Mil*) regimental number; (*Admin*) administrative *ou* official *ou* reference number; **dépêche-toi, sinon ça va barder** *ou* **mal aller pour ton ~ !*** hurry up *ou* your number'll be up!* *ou* you'll really get yourself bawled out!‡ [2] NF roll, register [3] ADJ **numéro ~** → **1**; **registre ~** → **2**; → **livret**

matrilinéaire [matʀilineɛʀ] ADJ matrilineal

matrimonial, e (*mpl* **-iaux**) [matʀimɔnjal, jo] ADJ matrimonial, marriage (*épith*) → **agence, régime**[1]

matrone [matʀɔn] NF (*péj*) (= *mère de famille*) matronly woman; (= *grosse femme*) stout woman; (*Antiq*) wife of a Roman citizen

Matthieu [matjø] NM Matthew

maturation [matyʀasjɔ̃] NF (*Bot, Méd*) maturation; [*fromage*] maturing, ripening; [*idée, projet*] gestation

mature [matyʀ] ADJ [*personne*] mature

mâture [matyʀ] NF masts; **dans la ~** aloft

maturité [matyʀite] NF [a] (*Bio, Bot, fig*) maturity; **arriver** *ou* **parvenir à ~** [*fruit*] to become ripe; [*plante*] to reach maturity; [*idée*] to come to maturity; [*technique*] to be perfected; [*entreprise, service*] to be fully operational; [*sportif*] to be at one's best; **manquer de ~** to be immature; **il manque de ~ politique** he's politically immature; **un homme en pleine ~** a man in his prime *ou* at the height of his powers; **~ d'esprit** maturity of mind; **il fait preuve d'une grande ~** he's very mature; **cet enfant a gagné en ~** this child has matured [b] (*Helv* = *baccalauréat*) secondary school examination giving university entrance qualification, ≈ A-levels (*Brit*), ≈ high school diploma (*US*)

maudire [modiʀ] ▶ conjug 2 ◀ VT to curse

maudit, e [modi, it] (*ptp de* **maudire**) [1] ADJ [a] (*: *avant n*) blasted*, damned‡; **quel ~ temps !** what lousy* *ou* filthy weather! [b] (*après n*: *littér* = *réprouvé*) (ac)cursed (*by God, society*); (*Littérat*) **poète/écrivain ~** accursed poet/writer [c] (*littér*) **~e soit la guerre !** ◊ **la guerre soit ~e !** cursed be the war!; **~ soit le jour où ...** cursed be the day on which ..., a curse *ou* a plague on the day on which ...; **soyez ~ !** curse you!, a plague on you! [2] NM,F damned soul; **les ~s** the damned [3] NM **le Maudit** the Devil

maugréer [mogʀee] ▶ conjug 1 ◀ VI to grouse, grumble (**contre** about, at)

maul [mol] NM (*Rugby*) maul; **faire un ~** to maul

maure, mauresque [mɔʀ, mɔʀɛsk] [1] ADJ Moorish [2] **Maure** NM Moor [3] **Mauresque** NF Moorish woman

Maurice [mɔʀis] NM Maurice, Morris → **île**

mauricien, -ienne [mɔʀisjɛ̃, jɛn] [1] ADJ Mauritian [2] **Mauricien(ne)** NM,F Mauritian

Mauritanie [mɔʀitani] NF Mauritania

mauritanien, -ienne [mɔʀitanjɛ̃, jɛn] [1] ADJ Mauritanian [2] **Mauritanien(ne)** NM,F Mauritanian

mausolée [mozole] NM mausoleum

maussade [mosad] ADJ [personne] sullen, glum, morose; [ciel, temps, paysage] gloomy, sullen; [conjoncture] bleak; [marché] sluggish; **d'un air ~** sullenly, morosely; **être d'humeur ~** to be sullen

maussaderie [mosadʀi] NF sullenness, glumness, moroseness

mauvais, e [mɔvɛ, ɛz] [1] ADJ [a] (= défectueux) [appareil, instrument] bad, faulty; [marchandise] inferior, shoddy, bad; [route] bad, in bad repair; [santé, vue, digestion, mémoire, roman, film] poor, bad; **elle a de ~ yeux** her eyes are ou her eyesight is bad; **~e excuse** poor ou lame ou feeble excuse; (Élec) **un ~ contact** a faulty connection; (Tennis) **la balle est ~e** the ball is out; **son français est bien ~** his French is very bad ou poor

[b] (= inefficace, incapable) [père, élève, acteur, ouvrier] poor, bad; **il est ~ en géographie** he's bad ou weak at geography ■ (PROV) **les ~ ouvriers ont toujours de ~ outils** a bad workman always blames his tools (PROV)

[c] (= erroné) [méthode, moyens, direction, date] wrong; **tu as fait le ~ choix** you made the wrong choice; **il roulait sur le ~ côté de la route** he was driving on the wrong side of the road; **c'est un (très) ~ calcul de sa part** he's (badly) misjudged it ou things; **il ne serait pas ~ de se renseigner** ou **que nous nous renseignions** it wouldn't be a bad idea ou it would be no bad thing if we found out more about this

[d] (= inapproprié) [jour, heure] awkward, bad, inconvenient; **il a choisi un ~ moment** he picked an awkward ou a bad time; **il a choisi le ~ moment** he picked the wrong time

[e] (= dangereux, nuisible) [maladie, blessure] nasty, bad; **il a fait une ~e grippe/rougeole** he's had a bad ou nasty attack ou bout of flu/measles; **la mer est ~e** the sea is rough; **c'est ~ pour la santé** it's bad for your health; **il est ~ de se baigner en eau froide** it's not good for you ou it's not a good idea to bathe in cold water; **vous jugez ~ qu'il sorte le soir ?** do you think it's a bad thing for him to go out at night?

[f] (= défavorable) [rapport, critique] unfavourable, bad; (Scol) [bulletin, note] bad

[g] (= désagréable) [temps] bad, unpleasant, nasty; [nourriture, repas] bad, poor; [odeur] bad, unpleasant, offensive; (= pénible) [nouvelle, rêve] bad; **ce n'est pas ~ !** it's not bad!, it's quite good!; **la soupe a un ~ goût** the soup has an unpleasant ou a nasty taste, the soup tastes nasty; **ce n'est qu'un ~ moment à passer** it's just a bad spell ou patch you've got to get through → **caractère, gré, volonté**

[h] (= immoral, nuisible) [instincts, action, fréquentations, lectures] bad; **il n'a pas un ~ fond** he's not bad at heart → **génie**

[i] (= méchant) [sourire, regard] nasty, malicious, spiteful; [personne, joie] malicious, spiteful; **être ~ comme la gale*** to be a nasty piece of work (fig); **ce n'est pas un ~ garçon** he's not a bad boy; **ce n'est pas un ~ bougre*** ou **le ~ bougre*** ou **le ~ cheval*** he's not a bad guy*; **il est vraiment ~ aujourd'hui** he's in an evil ou a foul mood today

[j] (loc) **quand on l'a renvoyé, il l'a trouvée** ou **eue ~e*** when he was dismissed he didn't appreciate it one little bit ou he was very put out about it ou he took it very badly; **il fait ~ aujourd'hui** the weather's bad today; **il fait ~ le contredire** it is not advisable to contradict him

[2] NM [a] (= partie) **enlève le ~ et mange le reste** cut out the bad part and eat the rest; **la presse ne montre que le ~** the press only shows the bad side (of things)

[b] (= personnes) **les ~** the wicked → **bon¹**

[3] COMP ► **mauvais coucheur** awkward customer ► **mauvais coup : recevoir un ~ coup** to get a nasty blow; **un ~ coup porté à nos institutions** a blow to ou an attack on our institutions; **faire un ~ coup** to play a mean ou dirty trick (**à qn** on sb) ► **mauvaise graine : c'est de la ~e graine** he's (ou she's ou they're) a bad lot (Brit) ou seed (US) ► **mauvaise herbe** weed; **enlever** ou **arracher les ~es herbes du jardin** to weed the garden; (hum) **la ~e herbe, ça pousse !** kids grow like weeds! (hum) ► **mauvais lieu** place of ill repute ► **mauvais œil : avoir le ~ œil** to have the evil eye ► **mauvais pas : tirer qn/se sortir d'un ~ pas** to get sb out of/get out of a tight spot ou corner ► **mauvais plaisant** hoaxer ► **mauvaise plaisanterie** rotten trick ► **mauvaise saison** rainy season ► **mauvais sort** misfortune, ill fate ► **mauvais sujet** bad lot (Brit) ou seed (US) ► **mauvaise tête : c'est une ~e tête** he's headstrong; **faire la ~e tête** (= bouder) to sulk; (= être difficile) to be awkward ou difficult ► **mauvais traitement** ill treatment; **subir de ~ traitements** to be ill-treated; **~ traitements à enfants** child abuse, child battering; **faire subir des ~ traitements à** to ill-treat → **passe¹**

mauve [mov] [1] ADJ, NM (= couleur) mauve [2] NF (Bot) mallow

mauviette [movjɛt] NF (péj) wimp*, weakling

mauvis [movi] NM redwing

maux [mo] NPL → **mal²**

max* [maks] ABRÉV = **maximum** [1] ADV max*; **à 8 heures ~** at 8 o'clock at the latest [2] NM **il a pris le ~** [condamné] ils lui ont filé le ~ they threw the book at him*; **un ~** [dépenser] a hell of a lot*; **ça coûte un ~** it costs a packet*; **il se fait un ~ de fric** he makes loads* ou pots* (Brit) of money; **il m'agace un ~** he drives me up the wall*

maxi [maksi] [1] PRÉF ► ... **maxi** ...; **~jupe** maxi-skirt; **~-bouteille/-paquet** giant-size bottle/packet [2] ADJ INV [a] (* = maximum) maximum [b] (= long) **manteau/jupe ~** maxicoat/-skirt; **la mode** = the maxi-length fashion [3] NM (= mode) maxi; **elle s'habille en ~** she wears maxis; **la mode est au ~** maxis are in (fashion) [4] ADV (* = maximum) (at the) maximum, at the most

maxillaire [maksilɛʀ] [1] ADJ maxillary; **os ~** jawbone [2] NM jawbone, maxilla (SPÉC); **~ supérieur/inférieur** upper/lower maxilla (SPÉC) ou jawbone

maxima [maksima] → **appel, maximum**

maximal, e (mpl -aux) [maksimal, o] ADJ maximum, maximal; **il a été condamné à la peine ~e** he was given the maximum sentence; **la température ~e a été de 33 degrés** the top ou maximum temperature was 33°C, there was a high of 33°C

maximalisme [maksimalism] NM [personne] extremist attitude, extremism

maximaliste [maksimalist] ADJ, NMF radical, extremist

maxime [maksim] NF maxim

maximisation [maksimizasjɔ̃] NF maximization

maximiser [maksimize] ▶conjug 1 ◀ VT to maximize

maximum, maximum ou **maxima** (pl maximum(s) ou maxima) [maksimɔm, maksima] [1] ADJ maximum; **la température ~** the maximum ou highest temperature; **j'attends de vous une aide ~** I expect a maximum of help ou maximum help from you; **j'en ai pour 2 heures ~** I'll be 2 hours maximum ou at the most; **dans un délai ~ de dix jours** within ten days at the latest

[2] NM [a] (gén, Math) maximum; (Jur) maximum sentence; **faire le** ou **son ~** to do one's level best ou one's utmost (**pour** to); **atteindre son ~** [production] to reach its maximum, reach an all-time high; [valeur] to reach its highest ou maximum point

[b] * **il y a un ~ de frais sur un bateau** boats cost a fortune to run; **il m'a fait payer un ~** he charged me a fortune; **ça consomme un ~, ces voitures** these cars are real gas guzzlers*, these cars are really heavy on petrol (Brit)

[3] ADV at the maximum, at the most; **à six heures ~** at six o'clock at the latest

[4] **au maximum** LOC ADV at the maximum, at the most; **sa radio était au ~** his radio was on full; **au ~ de ses capacités** ou **possibilités** [employé, sportif] stretched to one's limits; [usine, chaîne hi-fi] at maximum ou full capacity

maya [maja] [1] ADJ Mayan [2] NM (Ling) Maya(n) [3] **Maya** NMF Maya(n)

mayday [mɛde] NM (Naut) Mayday

mayonnaise [majɔnɛz] NF mayonnaise; **poisson/œufs (à la) ~** fish/eggs (with ou in) mayonnaise; **la ~ n'a pas pris** (lit) the mayonnaise didn't thicken; (fig) the mix was all wrong; **la ~ prend** (lit) the mayonnaise is thickening; (fig) things are looking good; (fig) **faire monter la ~** to stir things ou it up*

Mayotte [majɔt] NF Mayotte

mazagran [mazagʀɑ̃] NM pottery goblet (for coffee)

mazette† [mazɛt] [1] EXCL (admiration, étonnement) my!, my goodness! [2] NF (= incapable) nonentity

mazout [mazut] NM heating ou domestic oil; **chaudière/poêle à ~** oil-fired boiler/stove; **chauffage central au ~** oil-fired central heating

mazouté, e [mazute] ADJ [mer, plage] oil-polluted (épith), polluted with oil (attrib); [oiseaux] oil-covered (épith), covered in oil (attrib)

mazurka [mazyʀka] NF maz(o)urka

Mbabane [mbaban] N Mbabane

MCJ [ɛmseʒi] NF (ABRÉV = **maladie de Creutzfeldt-Jakob**) CJD

Me (ABRÉV = **Maître**) barrister's title; **Me Marlon** ≈ Mr (ou Mrs) Marlon Q.C. (Brit)

me, m' [m(ə)] PRON PERS [a] (objet direct ou indirect) me; **me voyez-vous ?** can you see me?; **elle m'attend** she is waiting for me; **il me l'a dit** he told me (it), he told me about it; **il m'en a parlé** he spoke to me about it; **il me l'a donné** he gave it to me, he gave it me* (Brit); (intensif) **va me fermer cette porte !** shut the door, would you! [b] (réfléchi) myself; **je ne me vois pas dans ce rôle-là** I can't see myself in that part; **je me regardais dans le miroir** I was looking at myself in the mirror

mea-culpa* [meakylpa] NM INV, EXCL my fault!, my mistake!; **faire son ~** (lit) to say one's mea culpa; (fig) to blame oneself

méandre [meɑ̃dʀ] NM (Art, Géog) meander; [politique] twists and turns; [intrigue] ins and outs; **les ~s de sa pensée** the twists and turns ou ins and outs ou complexities of his thought; **se perdre dans les ~s administratifs/juridiques** to get lost in the maze of the administrative/legal system

méat [mea] NM (Anat) meatus; (Bot) lacuna

mec* [mɛk] NM [a] (= homme) guy*, bloke* (Brit); **ça va les ~s ?** how's it going guys?*; **ça c'est un ~ !** he's a real man!; **c'est des histoires de ~s** it's man talk* [b] (= compagnon) **son ~** her man*

mécanicien, -ienne [mekanisjɛ̃, jɛn] [1] ADJ [civilisation] mechanistic [2] NM,F [a] (Aut) (garage ou motor) mechanic; **ouvrier ~** garage hand; **c'est un bon ~** he's a good mechanic, he's good with cars *ou* with machines; **ingénieur ~** mechanical engineer [b] (*Aviat, Naut*) engineer; (*Aviat*) **~ navigant** ◊ **~ de bord** flight engineer → **officier** [c] (*Rail*) train *ou* engine driver (*Brit*), engineer (*US*) [d] (*Dentisterie*) **~ dentiste** dental technician *ou* mechanic (*Brit*)

mécanique [mekanik] [1] ADJ [a] (*gén, Tech*) mechanical; [*tapis*] machine-made; [*jouet*] clockwork (*épith*), wind-up (*épith*); **les industries ~s** mechanical engineering industries; **avoir des ennuis ~s** (*Aut*) to have engine trouble; (*Aviat*) to have mechanical problems; **sports ~s** motor sports → **escalier, piano, rasoir**
[b] (= *machinal*) [*geste, réflexe*] mechanical
[c] (*Philo, Sci*) mechanical; **énergie ~** mechanical energy; **lois ~s** laws of mechanics
[2] NF [a] (*Sci*) (mechanical) engineering; (*Aut, Tech*) mechanics *sg*; **il fait de la ~ (sur sa voiture)** he's tinkering with his car; **la ~, ça le connaît*** he knows what he's doing in mechanics; **~ céleste/ondulatoire** celestial/wave mechanics; **~ hydraulique** hydraulics *sg*; **~ des fluides/quantique** quantum/fluid mechanics
[b] (= *mécanisme*) **la ~ d'une horloge** the mechanism of a clock; **cette voiture, c'est de la** *ou* **une belle ~** this car is a fine piece of engineering; (*fig* = *personne*) **la ~ est rouillée** *ou* **usée*** the old bones* aren't what they used to be

mécaniquement [mekanikmɑ̃] ADV mechanically; **objet fait ~** machine-made object

mécanisation [mekanizasjɔ̃] NF mechanization

mécaniser [mekanize] ▸conjug 1◂ VT to mechanize

mécanisme [mekanism] NM (*Bio, Philo, Psych, Tech*) mechanism; **les ~s économiques/politiques** economic/political mechanisms; **~s psychologiques/biologiques** psychological/biological workings *ou* mechanisms; **le ~ de change(s)** the exchange rate mechanism; **le ~ d'une action** the mechanics of an action

mécaniste [mekanist] ADJ mechanistic

mécano* [mekano] NM (ABRÉV = **mécanicien**) mechanic, grease monkey* (*US*)

mécanographe [mekanɔgraf] NMF comptometer operator, punch card operator

mécanographie [mekanɔgrafi] NF (= *procédé*) (mechanical) data processing; (= *service*) comptometer department

mécanographique [mekanɔgrafik] ADJ [*classement*] mechanized, automatic; **service ~** comptometer department, (mechanical) data processing department; **machine ~** calculator

Meccano® [mekano] NM Meccano®

mécénat [mesena] NM (*Art*) patronage; **~ d'entreprise** corporate sponsorship

mécène [mesen] NM [a] (*Art*) patron [b] **Mécène** (*Antiq*) Maecenas

méchamment [meʃamɑ̃] ADV [a] (= *cruellement*) [*rire, agir*] spitefully, nastily, wickedly [b] (* = *très*) fantastically*, terrifically*; **bon** fantastically* *ou* bloody** (*Brit*) good; **~ abîmé** really badly damaged; **il a été ~ surpris** he got one hell* *ou* heck* of a surprise; **ils se sont ~ disputés** they had a blazing row (*surtout Brit*) *ou* a terrible argument; **on est ~ en retard** we're terribly late

méchanceté [meʃɑ̃ste] NF [a] (= *caractère*) [*personne, action*] nastiness, spitefulness, wickedness; **faire qch par ~** to do sth out of spite; **soit dit sans ~, il n'est pas à la hauteur** I don't want to be nasty, but he's not up to it [b] (= *action*) mean *ou* nasty action; (= *parole*) mean *ou* nasty remark; **~ gratuite** unwarranted piece of unkindness *ou* spitefulness; **dire des ~s à qn** to say nasty things to sb

méchant, e [meʃɑ̃, ɑ̃t] [1] ADJ [a] (= *malveillant*) [*personne*] nasty, malicious; [*enfant*] naughty; [*intention*] malicious; **devenir ~** to

turn *ou* get nasty; **arrête, tu es ~** stop it, you're being horrid *ou* nasty; **il n'est pas ~** ◊ **ce n'est pas un ~ homme** he's not such a bad fellow → **chien**
[b] (= *dangereux, désagréable*) **ce n'est pas bien ~*** [*blessure, difficulté, dispute*] it's nothing to worry about; [*examen*] it's not too difficult; **impliqué dans une ~e affaire de pots de vin** mixed up in an unsavoury bribery scandal; **de ~e humeur** in a foul *ou* rotten mood
[c] (*avant n* : †)£ (= *médiocre, insignifiant*) miserable, mediocre; **~ vers/poète** poor *ou* second-rate verse/poet; **un ~ morceau de fromage** one miserable *ou* sorry-looking bit of cheese; **que de bruit pour une ~e clé perdue !** what a fuss over one stupid lost key!
[d] (*avant n* :* = *sensationnel*) **il a une ~e moto** he's got a fantastic* *ou* a mean* bike; **un ~ cigare** a hell of a big cigar*, a bloody great cigar* (*Brit*)
[2] NM,F **tais-toi, ~ !** be quiet you naughty boy! **les ~s** (*gén*) the wicked; (*dans un film*) the baddies*, the bad guys*; **faire le ~*** to be difficult, be nasty

mèche [meʃ] NF [a] [*bougie, briquet, lampe*] wick; [*bombe, mine*] fuse; [*canon*] match; **~ fusante** safety fuse [b] [*cheveux*] tuft of hair, lock; (*sur le front*) forelock, lock of hair; **~ postiche** ◊ **fausse ~** hairpiece; **~s folles** straggling locks *ou* wisps of hair; **~ rebelle** stray lock (of hair); **se faire faire des ~s** to have highlights *ou* streaks put in (one's hair), have one's hair streaked [c] (*Méd*) pack, dressing; [*fouet*] lash; [*perceuse*] bit [d] (*Naut*) main piece [e] (*Tex*) rove [f] (*loc*) **il a éventé** *ou* **vendu la ~** he gave the game away*, he let the cat out of the bag*; **allumer la ~** to light the fuse (*fig*); **être de ~ avec qn*** to be in cahoots with sb*; **un employé de la banque devait être de ~** a bank employee must have been in on it*; **y a pas ~ !**†* nothing doing!*

mécher [meʃe] ▸conjug 6◂ VT (*Tech*) to sulphurize; (*Méd*) to pack

méchoui [meʃwi] NM (= *repas*) barbecue of a whole roast sheep

mécompte [mekɔ̃t] NM (*frm*) [a] (= *désillusion : gén pl*) disappointment [b] (= *erreur de calcul*) miscalculation, miscount

méconium [mekɔnjɔm] NM meconium

méconnaissable [mekɔnɛsabl] ADJ (= *impossible à reconnaître*) unrecognizable; (= *difficile à reconnaître*) hardly recognizable

méconnaissance [mekɔnɛsɑ̃s] NF (= *ignorance*) lack of knowledge (**de** about), ignorance (**de** of); (*littér* = *mauvais jugement*) lack of comprehension, misappreciation (**de** of); (= *refus de reconnaître*) refusal to take into consideration; **il fait preuve d'une ~ totale de la situation** he knows absolutely nothing about the situation

méconnaître [mekɔnɛtʀ] ▸conjug 57◂ VT (*frm*) [a] (= *ignorer*) [+ *faits*] to be unaware of, not to know; **je ne méconnais pas que ...** I am fully *ou* quite aware that ..., I am alive to the fact that ... [b] (= *mésestimer*) [+ *situation, problème, personne*] to misjudge; [+ *mérites*] to underrate [c] (= *ne pas tenir compte de*) [+ *lois, devoirs*] to ignore

méconnu, e [mekɔny] (*ptp de* **méconnaître**) ADJ [*talent, génie*] unrecognized; [*musicien, écrivain*] underrated; **il se prend pour un ~** he sees himself as a misunderstood man

mécontent, e [mekɔ̃tɑ̃, ɑ̃t] [1] ADJ (= *insatisfait*) discontented, displeased, dissatisfied (**de** with); (= *contrarié*) annoyed (**de** with, at); **il a l'air très ~** he looks very annoyed *ou* displeased; **il n'est pas ~ de cela** he is not altogether dissatisfied *ou* displeased with it [2] NM,F malcontent, grumbler*; (*Pol*) **les ~s** the malcontents; **cette décision va faire des ~s** this decision is going to make some people very unhappy

mécontentement [mekɔ̃tɑ̃tmɑ̃] NM (*Pol*) discontent; (= *déplaisir*) dissatisfaction, displeasure; (= *irritation*) annoyance; **exprimer** *ou* **manifester son ~** to express one's dissatisfaction; **motif** *ou* **sujet de ~** cause for dissatisfaction; **provoquer un vif ~** to cause considerable discontent (**chez** among)

mécontenter [mekɔ̃tɑ̃te] ▸conjug 1◂ VT [*personne, décision*] to displease, annoy

Mecque [mek] NF **la ~** (*lit*) Mecca; (*fig*) the Mecca

mécréant, e [mekʀeɑ̃, ɑ̃t] NM,F († *ou hum* = *non-croyant*) non-believer; **tu n'es qu'un ~** you're just a heathen [b] († *péj* = *bandit*) scoundrel, miscreant †

médaillable [medajabl] ADJ [*sportif*] likely to win a medal; **les ~s des Jeux Olympiques** the potential medal-winners at the Olympic Games

▼ **médaille** [medaj] NF [a] (= *pièce, décoration*) medal; († * = *tache*) stain, mark; **~ militaire** military decoration; **~ pieuse** medal (*of a saint etc*); **~ du travail** long-service medal (*in industry etc*); **elle est ~ d'argent** she's got a silver medal, she's a silver medallist → **profil, revers**
[b] (= *insigne d'identité*) [*employé*] badge; [*chien*] identification disc, name tag; [*volaille*] guarantee tag

médaillé, e [medaje] (*ptp de* **médailler**) [1] ADJ (*Admin, Mil*) decorated (*with a medal*); (*Sport*) holding a medal [2] NM,F medal-holder; **il est** *ou* **c'est un ~ olympique** he is an Olympic medallist, he is the holder of an Olympic medal

médailler [medaje] ▸conjug 1◂ VT (*Admin, Sport*) to award a medal to; (*Mil*) to decorate, award a medal to; **se ~** †* (= *se tacher*) to get a stain *ou* mark on one's clothing

médaillon [medajɔ̃] NM (*Art*) medallion; (= *bijou*) locket; (*Culin*) medallio

mède [mɛd] [1] ADJ of Media [2] **Mède** NMF Mede

médecin [med(ə)sɛ̃] NM doctor, physician (*frm*); **femme ~** woman doctor; **~ de l'âme** confessor; (*Naut*) **~ de bord** ship's doctor; **~ de campagne** country doctor; **~-chef** head doctor; **~-conseil** *doctor who advises whether certain forms of medical treatment should be reimbursed by the Sécurité sociale*; **~ de famille** family practitioner *ou* doctor; **~ des hôpitaux** ≈ consultant, ≈ physician *ou* doctor (*Brit*) with a hospital appointment; **~ légiste** forensic scientist *ou* pathologist, expert in forensic medicine, medical examiner (*US*); **~ généraliste** *ou* **~e générale** general practitioner, G.P. (*Brit*), family practitioner (*US*); **~ militaire** army medical officer; **~ scolaire** school doctor, schools medical officer (*Brit, Admin*); **~ du sport** sports doctor; **~ traitant** attending physician; **votre ~ traitant** your (usual *ou* family) doctor; **~ du travail** company doctor; **~ de ville** doctor (*working in a town*)

médecine [med(ə)sin] NF [a] (= *science*) medicine; **~ alternative** *ou* **parallèle** alternative *ou* complementary medicine; **~ douce** *ou* **naturelle** natural medicine; **~ générale** general medicine; **~ hospitalière** *medicine practised in hospitals*; **~ infantile** paediatrics *sg* (*Brit*), pediatrics (*US*); **~ légale** forensic medicine *ou* science; **~ libérale** *medicine as practised by doctors in private practice*; **~ opératoire** surgery; **~ préventive** preventive medicine; **~ du travail** occupational *ou* industrial medicine; **~ du sport** sports medicine; **~ spécialisée** specialized branches of medicine; **~ de ville** *medicine as practised in general practices in towns*; **~ d'urgence** emergency medicine; **faire des études de ~** ◊ **faire (sa) ~** to study *ou* do medicine; **pratiquer une ~ révolutionnaire** to practise a revolutionary type of medicine; **il exerçait la ~ dans un petit village** he had a (medical) practice *ou* he was a doctor in a

small village → **docteur, étudiant, faculté**
b († = *médicament*) medicine

medecine-ball (*pl* **medecine-balls**) [medsinbol] NM medicine ball

média [medja] NM medium; **les ~s** the media; **dans les ~s** in the media

médial, e (*mpl* **-aux**) [medjal, o] **1** ADJ medial **2** **médiale** NF median

médian, e [medjã, jan] **1** ADJ (*Math, Stat*) median; (*Ling*) medial **2** **médiane** NF (*Math, Stat*) median; (*Ling*) medial sound, mid vowel → **ligne¹**

médiante [medjãt] NF (*Mus*) mediant

médiat, e [medja, jat] ADJ mediate

médiateur, -trice [medjatœʁ, tʁis] **1** ADJ (*gén, Pol*) mediatory, mediating; (*Ind*) arbitrating **2** NM,F (*gén*) mediator; (*Ind*) arbitrator; (*Pol*) ≈ Ombudsman, ≈ Parliamentary Commissioner (*Brit*); (*Méd*) **~ chimique** transmitter substance; **jouer le rôle de ~ ◊ servir de ~** to act as a mediator **3** **médiatrice** NF (*Géom*) median

médiathèque [medjatɛk] NF multimedia library

médiation [medjasjɔ̃] NF **a** (*gén, Philo, Pol*) mediation; (*Ind*) arbitration; **offrir sa ~ dans un conflit** (*Pol*) to offer to mediate in a conflict; (*Ind*) to offer to arbitrate *ou* intervene in a dispute; **tenter une ~ entre deux parties** to attempt to mediate between two parties **b** (*Logique*) mediate inference

médiatique [medjatik] ADJ [*image, couverture, battage*] media (*épith*); **c'est quelqu'un de très ~** he comes across really well in the media, he's very media-friendly; **sport très ~** sport that lends itself to media coverage; **ce fut une rencontre très ~** this meeting got a lot of media attention

médiatisation [medjatizasjɔ̃] NF **a** (= *diffusion par les médias*) media coverage; **la ~ à outrance de ces jeunes chanteurs** the excessive media coverage given to these young singers **b** (*Hist, Philo*) mediatization

médiatiser [medjatize] ▶ conjug 1 ◀ VT **a** (= *diffuser par les médias*) to give media coverage to; **cet événement a été très médiatisé** the event was given a lot of (media) coverage **b** (*Hist, Philo*) to mediatize

médiator [medjatɔʁ] NM plectrum

médiatrice [medjatʁis] ADJ F, NF → **médiateur**

médical, e (*mpl* **-aux**) [medikal, o] ADJ medical; **délégué** *ou* **visiteur ~** medical representative *ou* rep* → **examen, visite**

médicalement [medikalmã] ADV medically

médicalisation [medikalizasjɔ̃] NF **a** (*région, population*) provision of medical care for **b** [*problème, grossesse*] medicalization

médicaliser [medikalize] ▶ conjug 1 ◀ VT **a** [+ *région, population*] to provide with medical care; **c'est une population peu médicalisée** these people have little access to medical care; **la distribution médicalisée de la drogue** the distribution of drugs under medical supervision; **ils sont traités en milieu médicalisé** they receive treatment in a medical environment; **résidence** *ou* **maison de retraite médicalisée** nursing home; **ils prônent la maîtrise médicalisée des dépenses de santé** they want health expenditure to be supervised by medical professionals; **avion/hélicoptère médicalisé** hospital plane/helicopter **b** [+ *problème, grossesse*] to medicalize

médicament [medikamã] NM medicine, drug; **prendre des ~s** to take medicines *ou* medication; **~ de confort** ≈ pain-relieving medicine

médicamenteux, -euse [medikamãtø, øz] ADJ [*plante, substance*] medicinal; [*traitement, intoxication, prescription*] drug (*épith*)

médicastre† [medikastʁ] NM (*hum*) charlatan, quack

médication [medikasjɔ̃] NF (medical) treatment, medication

médicinal, e (*mpl* **-aux**) [medisinal, o] ADJ [*plante, substance*] medicinal

medicine-ball (*pl* **medicine-balls**) [medisinbol] NM medicine ball

médico- [mediko] PRÉF (*dans les mots composés à trait d'union, le préfixe reste invariable*) **~social** [*mesure, structure*] for health care and social welfare; **centre** *ou* **institut ~éducatif** *ou* **~pédagogique** special school (*for physically or mentally handicapped children*); **examen ~psychologique** medical and psychological examination; **centre ~psychologique** psychiatric clinic mainly dealing with prisoners, people who have attempted suicide and drug addicts

médico-chirurgical, e (*mpl* **-aux**) [medikoʃiʁyʁʒikal, o] ADJ **centre ~** clinic (*with a surgical unit*); **personnel/matériel ~** medical and surgical staff/equipment

médico-légal, e (*mpl* **-aux**) [medikolegal, o] ADJ [*expert*] forensic; **certificat** *ou* **rapport ~** forensic report; **expertise ~e** forensic analysis *ou* examination; **institut ~** mortuary (*where autopsies and forensic examinations are carried out*), medico-legal institute (*US*)

médiéval, e (*mpl* **-aux**) [medjeval, o] ADJ medieval

médiéviste [medjevist] NMF medievalist

médina [medina] NF medina

Médine [medin] N Medina

médiocre [medjɔkʁ] **1** ADJ [*travail, roman, élève*] mediocre, second-rate; (*sur copie d'élève*) poor; [*intelligence, qualité*] poor, mediocre, inferior; [*résultats, situation économique*] poor; [*revenu, salaire*] meagre, poor; [*vie, existence*] mediocre; **il a une situation ~** he holds some second-rate position; **il a montré un intérêt ~ pour ce projet** he showed little or no interest in the project; **génie incompris par les esprits ~s** genius misunderstood by those with small minds **2** NMF nonentity, second-rater*

médiocrement [medjɔkʁəmã] ADV [*intéressé, intelligent*] not very, not particularly; **gagner ~ sa vie** to earn a poor living; **~ satisfait** barely satisfied, not very well satisfied; **il joue ~ du piano** he plays the piano indifferently, he's not very good at (playing) the piano

médiocrité [medjɔkʁite] NF [*travail*] poor quality, mediocrity; [*élève, homme politique*] mediocrity; [*copie d'élève*] poor standard; [*revenu, salaire*] meagreness, poorness; [*intelligence*] mediocrity, inferiority; [*vie*] mediocrity; **étant donné la ~ de ses revenus** given the slimness of his resources, seeing how slight *ou* slim his resources are; **cet homme est une (vraie) ~** this man is a complete mediocrity

médique [medik] ADJ (*Antiq*) Median

médire [mediʁ] ▶ conjug 37 ◀ VI **~ de qn** to speak ill of sb; (*à tort*) to malign sb; **elle est toujours en train de ~** she's always running people down *ou* saying nasty things about people; **je ne voudrais pas ~ mais ...** I don't want to tittle-tattle *ou* to gossip, but ...

médisance [medizãs] NF **a** (= *diffamation*) malicious gossip (*NonC*); **être en butte à la ~** to be made a target of malicious gossip **b** (= *propos*) piece of scandal; **~s** scandal (*NonC*), gossip (*NonC*); **ce sont des ~s!** that's just scandal! *ou* malicious gossip!; **arrête de dire des ~s** stop spreading scandal *ou* gossip

médisant, e [medizã, ãt] **1** ADJ [*paroles*] slanderous; [*personne*] malicious; **les gens sont ~s** people say nasty things; **sans vouloir être ~, il faut reconnaître que ...** I don't want to sound nasty, but we have to admit that ... **2** NM,F scandalmonger, slanderer

méditatif, -ive [meditatif, iv] ADJ [*caractère*] meditative, thoughtful; [*air*] musing, thoughtful

méditation [meditasjɔ̃] NF (= *pensée*) meditation; (= *recueillement*) meditation (*NonC*); **après de longues ~s sur le sujet** after giving the subject much *ou* deep thought, after lengthy meditation on the subject; **il était plongé dans la ~** *ou* **une profonde ~** he was sunk in deep thought, he was deep in thought

méditer [medite] ▶ conjug 1 ◀ **1** VT [+ *pensée*] to meditate on, ponder (over); [+ *livre, projet, vengeance*] to meditate; **~ de faire qch** to contemplate doing sth, plan to do sth **2** VI to meditate; **~ sur qch** to ponder *ou* muse over sth

Méditerranée [mediteʁane] NF **la (mer) ~** the Mediterranean (Sea)

méditerranéen, -enne [mediteʁaneɛ̃, ɛn] **1** ADJ Mediterranean **2** **Méditerranéen(ne)** NM,F (*gén*) inhabitant *ou* native of a Mediterranean country; (*en France*) (French) Southerner

médium [medjɔm] NM (= *spirite, moyen de communication*) medium; (*Mus*) middle register; (*Logique*) middle term

médiumnique [medjɔmnik] ADJ [*dons, pouvoir*] of a medium

médiumnité [medjɔmnite] NF powers of a medium, mediumship

médius [medjys] NM middle finger

médoc [medɔk] NM (= *vin*) Médoc (wine); (= *région*) **le Médoc** the Médoc

médullaire [medylɛʁ] ADJ medullary

méduse [medyz] NF **a** (*Zool*) jellyfish **b** (*Myth*) **Méduse** Medusa

méduser [medyze] ▶ conjug 1 ◀ VT (*gén pass*) to dumbfound, stupefy; **je suis resté médusé par ce spectacle** I was rooted to the spot *ou* dumbfounded by this sight

meeting [mitin] NM (*Pol, Sport*) meeting; **~ aérien** *ou* **d'aviation** air show *ou* display; **~ d'athlétisme** athletics meeting

méfait [mefɛ] NM **a** (= *ravages*) **~s** [*temps*] ravages; [*passion, épidémie*] ravages, damaging effects; **les ~s de l'alcoolisme/de la drogue/du soleil** the damaging *ou* ill effects of alcohol/of drugs/of the sun **b** (= *acte*) wrongdoing; (*hum*) misdeed

méfiance [mefjãs] NF distrust, mistrust, suspicion; **avoir de la ~ envers qn** to mistrust *ou* distrust sb; **apaiser/éveiller la ~ de qn** to allay/arouse sb's suspicion(s); **regarder qn/qch avec ~** to look at sb/sth suspiciously; **être sans ~** (= *avoir confiance*) to be completely trusting; (= *ne rien soupçonner*) to be quite unsuspecting; **ce projet paraît peu sérieux, ~!** this project doesn't seem very worthwhile, we'd better be careful!

méfiant, e [mefjã, jãt] ADJ [*personne*] distrustful, mistrustful, suspicious; **air** *ou* **regard ~** distrustful *ou* mistrustful *ou* suspicious look, look of distrust *ou* mistrust *ou* suspicion

méfier (se) [mefje] ▶ conjug 7 ◀ VPR **a** (= *ne pas avoir confiance*) **se méfier de qn/des conseils de qn** to mistrust *ou* distrust sb/sb's advice; **je me méfie de lui** I mistrust him, I don't trust him, I'm suspicious of him; **méfiez-vous de lui** *ou* **il faut vous méfier de lui** don't trust him, beware of him; **je ne me méfie pas assez de mes réactions** I should be more wary of my reactions; **méfiez-vous des imitations** *ou* **des contrefaçons** beware of imitations; **se méfier de qn/qch comme de la peste** to be highly suspicious of sb/sth **b** (= *faire attention*) **se méfier de qch** to be careful about sth; **il faut vous méfier** you must be careful *ou* watch out; **méfie-toi de cette marche** watch *ou* mind (*Brit*) the step, look out for the step*; **méfie-toi, tu vas tomber** look out* *ou* be careful or you'll fall

méforme [mefɔʁm] NF (*Sport*) lack of fitness; **traverser une période de ~** to be (temporarily) off form; **être en ~** to be off form

méga [mega] 1 PRÉF a (Sci) mega b (*: intensif) ~-concert/événement mega-concert/-event; ~-entreprise huge ou enormous company, mega-company; ~-dissertation essay and a half*; un ~-cigare à la bouche a whopping great* ou humungous* (US) cigar in his mouth 2 NM (ABRÉV = **méga-octet**) (Ordin) megabyte

mégacycle [megasikl] NM megacycle

mégahertz [megaɛʀts] NM megahertz

mégalithe [megalit] NM megalith

mégalithique [megalitik] ADJ megalithic

mégalo* [megalo] ADJ, NMF (ABRÉV = **mégalomaniaque, mégalomane**) [personne] megalomaniac; [projet] self-indulgent; il est complètement ~ c'est un ~ he thinks he's God

mégalomane [megaloman] 1 ADJ [personne] megalomaniac; [projet] self-indulgent 2 NMF megalomaniac

mégalomaniaque [megalomanjak] ADJ (Méd) megalomaniac; [projet] self-indulgent; délire ~ (Méd) megalomaniac delusion

mégalomanie [megalomani] NF megalomania

mégalopole [megalopol] NF megalopolis

méga-octet (pl **méga-octets**) [megaɔkte] NM megabyte

mégaphone† [megafɔn] NM (= porte-voix) megaphone

mégapole [megapol] NF = **mégalopole**

mégarde [megaʀd] ♦ **par mégarde** LOC ADV (= accidentellement) accidentally, by accident; (= par erreur) by mistake, inadvertently; (= par négligence) accidentally; un livre que j'avais emporté par ~ a book that I had accidentally ou inadvertently taken away with me

mégatonne [megatɔn] NF megaton

mégère [meʒɛʀ] NF (péj = femme) shrew; (Théât) « la Mégère apprivoisée » "the Taming of the Shrew"

mégisserie [meʒisʀi] NF (= lieu) tawery

mégissier [meʒisje] NM tawer

mégot* [mego] NM [cigarette] cigarette butt ou end, fag end* (Brit); [cigare] stub, butt

mégotage* [megotaʒ] NM cheeseparing ou miserly attitude

mégoter* [megote] ▶ conjug 1 ◀ VI to skimp; le patron mégote sur des détails et dépense des fortunes en repas d'affaires the boss is cheeseparing ou skimps over small items and spends a fortune on business lunches; pour marier leur fille ils n'ont pas mégoté they really went to town* for ou they spent a small fortune on their daughter's wedding

méhari [meaʀi] NM dromedary, mehari

méhariste [meaʀist] NM camel rider; (Hist) soldier in the French Camel corps

meilleur, e [mɛjœʀ] 1 ADJ a (compar de **bon**) better; il est ~ que moi (plus charitable) he's a better person than I am; (plus doué) he's better than I am (en at); avoir ~ goût [+ aliment] to taste better; ce gâteau est (bien) ~ avec du rhum this cake tastes ou is (much) better with rum; il est ~ chanteur que compositeur he makes a better singer than (a) composer, he is better at singing than (at) composing; de ~e qualité of better ou higher quality; ~ marché cheaper; être en ~e santé to be better, be in better health; (Sport) faire un ~ temps au deuxième tour to put up ou do a better time on the second lap; partir de ~e heure† to leave earlier; prendre (une) ~e tournure to take a turn for the better; ~s vœux best wishes; ce sera pour des jours/des temps ~s that will be for better days/happier times; il n'y a rien de ~ there's nothing better, there's nothing to beat it

b (superl de **bon**) le ~ des deux the better of the two; la ~e de toutes the best of all; c'est le ~ des hommes ◊ c'est le ~ homme du monde he is the best of men, he's the best man in the world; les ~s spécialistes the best ou top specialists; son ~ ami his best ou closest friend; servir les ~s mets/vins to serve the best ou finest dishes/wines; information tirée des ~es sources information from the most reliable sources; tissu de la ~e qualité best quality material; le ~ marché the cheapest; acheter au ~ prix to buy at the lowest price

2 ADV il fait ~ qu'hier it's better ou nicer (weather) than yesterday; sentir ~ to smell better ou nicer

3 NM,F (= personne) le ~/la ~e the best one; ce sont toujours les ~s qui partent les premiers it's always the best people who die first; que le ~ gagne may the best man win → **raison**

4 NM (= partie, chose) le ~ the best; il a choisi le ~ he took the best (one); pour le ~ et pour le pire for better or for worse; donner le ~ de soi-même to give of one's best; passer le ~ de sa vie à faire ... to spend the best days ou years of one's life doing ...; (Sport) prendre le ~ sur qn to get the better of sb; garder ou réserver le ~ pour la fin to keep the best till ou last; et le ~ dans tout ça, c'est qu'il avait raison! and the best bit about it all was that he was right!

5 **meilleure*** NF ça alors, c'est la ~e! that's the best one yet!; j'en passe et des ~es and that's not all; tu connais la ~e? il n'est même pas venu! haven't you heard the best (bit) though? he didn't even come!

méiose [mejoz] NF meiosis

meistre [mɛstʀ] NM = **mestre**

méjuger [meʒyʒe] ▶ conjug 3 ◀ (littér) 1 VT to misjudge 2 **méjuger de** VT INDIR to underrate, underestimate 3 **se méjuger** VPR to underestimate o.s.

Mékong [mekɔ̃g] NM Mekong

mélamine [melamin] NF melamine

mélaminé, e [melamine] ADJ melamine-coated

mélancolie [melɑ̃kɔli] NF melancholy, gloom; (Méd) melancholia; elle avait des accès de ~ she suffered from bouts of melancholy → **engendrer**

mélancolique [melɑ̃kɔlik] ADJ [personne, paysage, musique] melancholy; (Méd) melancholic

mélancoliquement [melɑ̃kɔlikmɑ̃] ADV with a melancholy air, melancholically

Mélanésie [melanezi] NF Melanesia

mélanésien, -ienne [melanezjɛ̃, jɛn] 1 ADJ Melanesian 2 NM (Ling) Melanesian 3 **Mélanésien(ne)** NM,F Melanesian

mélange [melɑ̃ʒ] NM a (= opération) [produits] mixing; [vins, tabacs] blending; faire un ~ de [+ substances] to make a mixture of; [+ idées] to mix up; quand on boit il ne faut pas faire de ~s you shouldn't mix your drinks b (= résultat) (Chim, Culin, fig) mixture; [vins, tabacs, cafés] blend; ~ détonant ou explosif (lit) explosive mixture; (fig) explosive combination ou mixture; ~ réfrigérant freezing mixture; (Aut) ~ pauvre/riche weak/rich mixture; joie sans ~ unalloyed ou unadulterated joy; (littér) sans ~ de ... free from ..., unadulterated by ...; (Littérat) ~s miscellanies, miscellany

mélanger [melɑ̃ʒe] ▶ conjug 3 ◀ 1 VT a (gén, Chim, Culin) to mix; [+ couleurs, vins, parfums, tabacs] to blend; [+ cartes] to shuffle; mélangez le beurre et la farine mix the butter and flour together; un public très mélangé a very varied ou mixed public

b (= confondre) [+ dates, idées] to mix (up), muddle up (surtout Brit), confuse; tu mélanges tout! you're getting it all mixed up! ou muddled up! (surtout Brit); (fig) il ne faut pas ~ les torchons et les serviettes we (ou you etc) must sort out the sheep from the goats

c (= mettre en désordre) [+ documents] to mix up, muddle up

2 **se mélanger** VPR a [produits, personnes] to mix; [vins] to mix, blend

b (en désordre) les dates se mélangent dans ma tête I'm confused about the dates, I've got the dates mixed up ou in a muddle; se ~ les pieds* ou les pédales* ou les pinceaux* ou les crayons* to get mixed up ou into a muddle (surtout Brit)

mélangeur [melɑ̃ʒœʀ] NM (= appareil) mixer; (Plomberie) mixer tap (Brit), mixing faucet (US); (Ciné, Radio) mixer

mélanine [melanin] NF melanin

mélanocyte [melanɔsit] NM melanocyte

mélanome [melanom] NM melanoma

mélasse [melas] NF a (Culin) treacle (Brit), molasses (US) b (*, péj = boue) muck; (= brouillard) murk; (= problèmes, confusion) quelle ~! what a mess!; être dans la ~ (= avoir des ennuis) to be in the soup*, be in a sticky situation*; (= être dans la misère) to be down and out, be on one's beam ends* (Brit)

mélatonine [melatɔnin] NF melatonin

Melba [mɛlba] ADJ INV Melba; pêche/ananas ~ peach/pineapple Melba

mêlé, e¹ [mele] (ptp de **mêler**) ADJ [sentiments] mixed, mingled; [couleurs, tons] mingled; [monde, société] mixed

mêlée² [mele] NF a (= bataille) mêlée; (hum) fray, kerfuffle* (Brit); ~ générale free-for-all; la ~ devint générale it developed into a free-for-all, scuffles broke out all round ou on all sides; (lit, fig) se jeter dans la ~ to plunge into the fray; (fig) rester au-dessus de ou à l'écart de la ~ to stay ou keep aloof, keep out of the fray b (Rugby) scrum, scrummage; faire une ~ to go into a scrum; ~ ordonnée set scrum; ~ ouverte ou spontanée ruck, loose scrum; dans la ~ ouverte in the loose

mêler [mele] ▶ conjug 1 ◀ 1 VT a (= unir, mettre ensemble) [+ substances] to mingle, mix together; [+ races] to mix; (Vét) to cross; (Culin = mélanger) to mix, blend; (= joindre, allier) to combine, mingle; les deux fleuves mêlent leurs eaux the two rivers mingle their waters; elles mêlèrent leurs larmes/leurs soupirs their tears/their sighs mingled; vin mêlé d'eau wine mixed with water

b (= mettre en désordre, embrouiller) [+ papiers, dossiers] to muddle (up), mix up; (= battre) [+ cartes] to shuffle; ~ la réalité et le rêve to confuse reality and dream

c (= associer) ~ à ou avec to mix ou mingle with; ~ la douceur à la fermeté to combine gentleness with firmness; ~ du feuillage à un bouquet to put some greenery in with a bouquet; récit mêlé de détails comiques story interspersed with comic(al) details; joie mêlée de remords pleasure mixed with ou tinged with remorse

d (= impliquer) ~ qn à [+ affaire suspecte] to involve sb in, get sb mixed up ou involved in; [+ action, négociations] to involve sb in; j'y ai été mêlé contre mon gré I was dragged into it against my will, I got mixed up ou involved in it against my will; il a été mêlé au scandale/à une affaire d'espionnage he got mixed up in ou got involved in the scandal/in a spy scandal; ~ qn à la conversation to bring ou draw sb into the conversation

2 **se mêler** VPR a (= se mélanger) [odeurs, voix] to mingle; [cultures, races] to mix

b se ~ à (= se joindre à) to join; (= s'associer à) to mix with; [cris, sentiments] to mingle with; il se mêla à la foule he joined the crowd, he mingled with the crowd; se ~ à une querelle to get mixed up ou involved in a quarrel; il ne se mêle jamais aux autres enfants he never mixes with other children; il se mêlait à toutes les manifestations he got involved in ou took part in all the demonstrations; des rires se mêlaient aux applaudissements there was laughter mingled with the applause; se ~ à la conversation to join in the conversation

c **se ~ de** (= *s'impliquer dans*) to get mixed up *ou* involved in; (= *s'ingérer dans*) to meddle with, interfere with; **je ne veux pas me ~ de politique** I don't want to get mixed up *ou* involved in politics; **se ~ des affaires des autres** to meddle *ou* interfere in other people's business *ou* affairs; **mêle-toi de ce qui te regarde!** *ou* **de tes affaires!** *ou* **de tes oignons!*** mind your own business!; (*iro*) **de quoi je me mêle!*** what business is it of yours?, what's it got to do with you?; **si le mauvais temps s'en mêle, nous n'y arriverons jamais** if the weather turns against us, we'll never make it; **quand la politique/l'amour s'en mêle ...** when politics/love comes into it ...; **se ~ de faire qch** to take it upon o.s. to do sth, make it one's business to do sth; **voilà qu'il se mêle de nous donner des conseils!** who is he to give us advice!, look at him butting in with his advice!; **ne vous mêlez pas d'intervenir!** don't you take it into your head to interfere!, just you keep out of it!

mélèze [melɛz] NM larch

mélilot [melilo] NM melilot, sweet clover

méli-mélo* (*pl* **mélis-mélos**) [melimelo] NM [*situation*] mess, muddle (*surtout Brit*); [*objets*] jumble; **cette affaire est un véritable ~!** what a terrible mess *ou* muddle this business is!; (*Culin*) **~ de poissons/de légumes** assortment of fish/of vegetables

mélioratif, -ive [meljɔʀatif, iv] **1** ADJ meliorative **2** NM meliorative term

mélisse [melis] NF (*Bot*) (lemon) balm

mellifère [melifɛʀ] ADJ melliferous

mélo* [melo] **1** ADJ (ABRÉV = **mélodramatique**) [*film, roman*] soppy*, sentimental; **feuilleton ~** (*Presse*) sentimental serial; (*TV*) soap (opera) **2** NM ABRÉV = **mélodrame**

mélodie [melɔdi] NF **a** (= *motif, chanson*) melody, tune; **les ~s de Debussy** Debussy's melodies *ou* songs; **une petite ~ entendue à la radio** a little tune heard on the radio **b** (= *qualité*) melodiousness

mélodieusement [melɔdjøzmɑ̃] ADV melodiously, tunefully

mélodieux, -ieuse [melɔdjø, jøz] ADJ melodious, tuneful

mélodique [melɔdik] ADJ melodic

mélodiste [melɔdist] NMF melodist; **c'est un excellent ~** he composes fine melodies, he's a very good melodist

mélodramatique [melɔdʀamatik] ADJ (*Littérat, péj*) melodramatic

mélodrame [melɔdʀam] NM (*Littérat, péj*) melodrama

mélomane [melɔman] **1** ADJ music-loving (*épith*), keen on music (*attrib*) **2** NMF music lover

melon [m(ə)lɔ̃] NM **a** (*Bot*) melon; **~ d'Espagne** ≈ honeydew melon; **~ (cantaloup)** cantaloup(e); **~ d'eau** watermelon **b** (*Habillement*) **(chapeau) ~** bowler (hat) (*Brit*), derby (hat) (*US*)

mélopée [melɔpe] NF **a** (*gén = chant monotone*) monotonous chant, threnody (*littér*) **b** (*Hist Mus*) recitative

membrane [mɑ̃bʀan] NF (*gén*) membrane; [*haut-parleur*] diaphragm; (*Bio*) **~ cellulaire** plasma *ou* cell membrane

membraneux, -euse [mɑ̃bʀanø, øz] ADJ membran(e)ous

membre [mɑ̃bʀ] NM **a** (*Anat, Zool*) limb; **~ inférieur/supérieur** lower/upper limb; **~ antérieur/postérieur** fore/hind limb; **~ (viril)** male member *ou* organ **b** [*famille, groupe, société savante*] member; [*académie*] fellow; **~ fondateur** founder member; **~ actif/perpétuel** active/life member; **~ permanent du Conseil de sécurité** permanent member of the Security Council; **un ~ de la société/du public** a member of society/of the

public; **les ~s du gouvernement** the members of the government; **être ~ de** to be a member of; **devenir ~ d'un club** to become a member of a club, join a club; **ce club a 300 ~s** this club has a membership of 300 *ou* has 300 members; **pays/États ~s (de l'Union européenne)** member countries/states (of the European union)
c (*Math*) member; **premier/second ~** left-hand/right-hand member
d (*Ling*) **~ de phrase** (sentence) member
e (*Archit*) member
f (*Naut*) timber, rib

membré, e [mɑ̃bʀe] ADJ limbed; **bien/mal ~** strong-/weak-limbed; **bien ~*** [*homme*] well-hung*

membru, e [mɑ̃bʀy] ADJ (*littér*) strong-limbed

membrure [mɑ̃bʀyʀ] NF (*Anat*) limbs, build; (*Naut*) rib; (*collectif*) frame; **homme à la ~ puissante** strong-limbed *ou* powerfully built man

mémé* [meme] NF (*langage enfantin = grand-mère*) gran(ny)*, grandma; (= *vieille dame*) old lady; (*péj*) old granny* (*péj*); **ça fait ~*** it looks dowdy; **tu fais ~ avec cette robe** that dress makes you look like an old lady *ou* makes you look dowdy

▼ **même** [mɛm] **1** ADJ **a** (*avant n = identique*) same, identical; **des bijoux de ~ valeur** jewels of equal *ou* of the same value; **ils ont la ~ taille/la ~ couleur** ◊ **ils sont de ~ taille/de ~ couleur** they are the same size/the same colour; **j'ai exactement la ~ robe qu'hier** I am wearing the very same dress I wore yesterday *ou* exactly the same dress as yesterday; **nous sommes du ~ avis** we are of the same mind *ou* opinion, we agree; **ils ont la ~ voiture que nous** they have the same car as we have *ou* as us*; **que vous veniez ou non, c'est la ~ chose** it makes no difference *ou* odds (*Brit*) whether you come or not; **c'est toujours la ~ chose!** it's always the same (old story)!; **c'est la ~ chose** (= *c'est équivalent*) it amounts to the same (thing), it's six of one and half a dozen of the other*; **arriver en ~ temps (que)** to arrive at the same time (as); **en ~ temps qu'il le faisait, l'autre s'approchait** as *ou* while he was doing it the other drew nearer
b (*après n ou pron = exact, personnifié*) very, actual; **ce sont ses paroles ~s** those are his very *ou* actual words; **il est la générosité/gentillesse ~** he is generosity/kindness itself, he is the (very) soul of generosity/kindness; **il est la méchanceté/bêtise ~** he's wickedness/stupidity itself; **la grande maison, celle-là ~ que vous avez visitée** the big house, the very one you visited *ou* precisely the one you visited
c **moi-~** myself; **toi-~** yourself; **lui-~** himself; **elle-~** herself; **nous-~s** ourselves; **vous-~** yourself; **vous-~s** yourselves; **eux-** *ou* **elles-~s** themselves; **un autre soi-~** another self; **on est soi-~ conscient de ses propres erreurs** one is aware (oneself) of one's own mistakes; **nous devons y aller nous-~s** we must go ourselves; **s'apitoyer sur soi-~** to feel sorry for oneself; **tu n'as aucune confiance en toi-~** you have no confidence in yourself; **c'est lui-~ qui l'a dit** ◊ **il l'a dit lui-~** he said it himself, he himself said it; **au plus profond d'eux-~s/de nous-~s** in their/our heart of hearts; **elle fait ses habits elle-~** she makes her own clothes, she makes her clothes herself; **c'est ce que je me dis en ~ à moi-~** that's what I tell myself (inwardly), that's what I think to myself; **elle se disait en elle-~ que ...** she thought to herself that ...; **faire qch de soi-~** to do sth on one's own initiative *ou* off one's own bat* (*Brit*); **faire qch (par) soi-~** to do sth (by) oneself

2 PRON INDÉF (*avec le, la, les*) **ce n'est pas le ~** it's not the same (one); **la réaction n'a pas été la ~ qu'à Paris** the reaction was not the same

as in Paris; **elle est bien toujours la ~!** she's just the same as ever!; **ce sont toujours les ~s qui se font prendre** it's always the same ones who catch it*; **c'est le ~ que j'ai revu plus tard** it was the same man that I saw later on; **les ~s, trois heures plus tard** (*aussi hum*) same scene, three hours later → **pareil, revenir**

3 ADV **a** (*gén*) even; **ils sont tous sortis, ~ les enfants** they are all out, even the children; **il n'a ~ pas** *ou* **pas ~ de quoi écrire** he hasn't even got anything to write with; **il est intéressant et ~ amusant** he's interesting and amusing too *ou* besides; **elle ne me parle ~ plus** she no longer even speaks to me, she doesn't even speak to me anymore; **~ lui ne sait pas** even he doesn't know; **personne ne sait, ~ pas lui** nobody knows, not even him; **~ si** even if, even though; **c'est vrai, ~ que je peux le prouver!*** it's true, and what's more I can prove it!
b (= *précisément*) **aujourd'hui ~** this very day; **ici ~** in this very place, on this very spot; **c'est celui-là ~ qui ...** he's the very one who ...; **c'est cela ~** that's just *ou* exactly it
c (*loc*) **boire à ~ la bouteille** to drink (straight) from the bottle; **coucher à ~ le sol** to lie on the bare ground; **à ~ la peau** next to the skin; **être à ~ de faire** to be able *ou* to be in a position to do; **je ne suis pas à ~ de juger** I'm in no position to judge; **il fera de ~** he'll do the same, he'll likewise, he'll follow suit; **vous le détestez? moi de ~** you hate him? so do I *ou* I do too *ou* me too *ou* same here*; **de ~ qu'il nous a dit que ...** just as he told us that ...; **il en est** *ou* **il en va de ~ pour moi** it's the same for me, same here*; **quand ~** ◊ **tout de ~** (= *en dépit de cela*) all the same, even so, for all that; (= *très*) quite, really; (*indignation*) **tout de ~!** *ou* **quand ~!** honestly!, I mean to say!; **quel crétin quand ~!** what an absolute idiot!, really, what an idiot!; (*lit, hum*) **merci quand ~** thanks all the same *ou* just the same; **c'est tout de ~** *ou* **quand ~ agaçant** all the same it is annoying, it's really most annoying; (= *tout à fait*) **il est gentil tout de ~** he's ever so nice; **elle m'agace!** — **elle est gentille tout de ~** she irritates me! — she's quite nice really; **tout de ~** *ou* **quand ~, il aurait pu nous prévenir** all the same *ou* even so he might have warned us; **il exagère tout de ~!** really, he's going too far!; **il a tout de ~ réussi à s'échapper** he managed to escape nevertheless *ou* all the same; **c'est tout de ~ étonnant** it's quite surprising (**que** that)

mêmement [mɛmmɑ̃] ADV (*frm*) likewise

mémento [memɛto] NM (= *agenda*) appointments book *ou* diary (*Brit*), engagement diary (*Brit*) *ou* calendar (*US*); (*Scol* = *aide-mémoire*) summary; (*Rel*) **~ des vivants/des morts** prayers for the living/the dead

mémère* [memɛʀ] NF (*langage enfantin = grand-mère*) granny*, grandma; (*péj = vieille dame*) old dear*; (*hum*) **le petit chien à sa ~** mummy's little doggy (*hum*); **elle fait ~ avec ce chapeau** she looks like an old granny in that hat*

mémo* [memo] NM (ABRÉV = **mémorandum**) memo

mémoire¹ [memwaʀ] NF **a** (*Psych, Sci*) memory; **citer de ~** to quote from memory; **de ~ d'homme** in living memory; **de ~ de Parisien, on n'avait jamais vu ça** no one could remember such a thing happening in Paris before; **pour ~** (*gén*) as a matter of interest; (*Comm*) for the record; **~ associative/collective** associative/collective memory; **~ auditive/visuelle/olfactive** aural/visual/olfactory memory → **effort, rafraîchir, trou**
b (*loc*) **avoir de la ~/une très bonne ~** to have a good memory/a very good memory; **si j'ai bonne ~** if I remember right *ou* rightly, if my memory serves me right; **il n'a pas de ~** ◊ **il n'a aucune ~** he can never remember anything; **avoir la ~ courte** to have a short

memory; **avoir une ~ d'éléphant** to have a memory like an elephant('s); **perdre la ~** to lose one's memory; **avoir la ~ des noms** to have a good memory for names; **je n'ai pas la ~ des dates/visages** I have no memory for dates/faces, I can never remember dates/faces; **garder qch en ~** to remember sth; (*frm*) **j'ai gardé (la) ~ de cette conversation** I remember *ou* recall this conversation; **chercher un nom dans sa ~** to try to recall a name, rack one's brains to remember a name; **ça y est, ça me revient en ~** I remember now, it's coming back to me now; **il me l'a remis en ~** he reminded me of it, he brought it back to me; **son nom restera (gravé) dans notre ~** his name will remain (engraved) in our memories

〔c〕 (= *réputation*) memory, good name; (= *renommée*) memory, fame, renown; **soldat de glorieuse ~** soldier of blessed memory; **de sinistre ~** of evil memory, remembered with fear *ou* horror; (*hum*) fearful, ghastly; **salir la ~ de qn** to sully the memory of sb; **à la ~ de** in memory of, to the memory of

〔d〕 (*Ordin*) memory; **~ cache/externe** cache/external storage; **~ vive** RAM, random access memory; **~ morte** ROM, read-only memory; **~ volatile** volatile memory; **~ de masse** ◊ **~ auxiliaire** mass memory *ou* storage; **~ centrale** *ou* **principale** main memory; **avoir 24 Mo de ~ centrale** to have 24 Mb of main memory; **~ tampon** buffer memory; **capacité de ~** storage capacity, memory size; **mettre qch en ~** to store sth; **mise en ~** storage

mémoire² [memwaʀ] 〔1〕 NM (= *requête*) memorandum; (= *rapport*) report; (= *exposé*) paper, dissertation (*Brit*); (= *facture*) bill; (*Jur*) statement of case; (*Univ*) **~ de maîtrise** dissertation *done for research degree*, ≈ master's thesis → DIPLÔMES 〔2〕 **mémoires** NMPL (= *souvenirs*) memoirs; (*hum*) **tu écris tes ~s?** are you writing your life story? (*hum*)

mémorable [memɔʀabl] ADJ memorable, unforgettable

mémorandum [memɔʀɑ̃dɔm] NM (*Pol*) memorandum; (*Comm*) order sheet, memorandum; (= *carnet*) notebook, memo book

mémorial (*pl* **-iaux**) [memɔʀjal, jo] NM (*Archit*) memorial; (*Littérat*) **Mémorial** Chronicles

mémorialiste [memɔʀjalist] NMF memorialist, writer of memoirs

mémorisation [memɔʀizasjɔ̃] NF memorization, memorizing; (*Ordin*) storage

mémoriser [memɔʀize] ▸ conjug 1 ◂ VT to memorize, commit to memory; (*Ordin*) to store

menaçant, e [mənasɑ̃, ɑ̃t] ADJ [*geste, paroles, foule, orage, regard*] threatening, menacing; [*nuages*] ominous, threatening; [*ciel*] lowering (*épith*), threatening, menacing; **sa voix se fit ~e** his voice took on a threatening *ou* menacing tone; **elle se fit ~e** she started to make *ou* issue threats

menace [mənas] NF 〔a〕 (= *intimidation*) threat; **c'est une ~?** is that a threat?, are you threatening me?; **il eut un geste de ~** he made a threatening gesture; **il eut des paroles de ~** he made some threats; **il y a des ~s de grève** there's a threat of strike action; **signer sous la ~** to sign under duress; **sous la ~ de** under (the) threat of; **sous la ~ d'un couteau/d'un pistolet** at knife-point/gunpoint 〔b〕 (= *danger*) threat; **la ~ nucléaire** the nuclear threat; **~ d'épidémie** threat of an epidemic; **être sous la ~ d'une expulsion/de sanctions** to be threatened with *ou* be under threat of expulsion/of sanctions 〔c〕 (*Jur*) **~s** intimidation, threats; **recevoir des ~s de mort** to receive death threats *ou* threats on one's life

menacer [mənase] ▸ conjug 3 ◂ VT 〔a〕 (= *faire peur à*) to threaten, menace *gén pass*; **~ qn de mort/d'un revolver** to threaten sb with death/ with a gun; **~ qn du poing/de sa canne** to shake one's fist/one's stick at sb; **~ de faire**

qch to threaten to do sth 〔b〕 (= *mettre en danger*) [+ *équilibre, projet*] to jeopardize; **ses jours sont menacés** his life is threatened *ou* in danger; **la guerre menaçait le pays** the country was threatened *ou* menaced by *ou* with war; **espèces menacées** threatened *ou* endangered species; **le processus de paix est menacé** the peace process is in jeopardy 〔c〕 (= *risquer de survenir*) [*chômage, grève, guerre*] to loom large; **la pluie menace** it looks like rain, it's threatening to rain; **le temps menace** the weather looks threatening; **l'orage menace (d'éclater)** the storm is about to break *ou* is threatening to break; **chaise qui menace de se casser** chair which is showing signs of *ou* looks like breaking (*Brit*) *ou* looks like it will break; **pluie/discours qui menace de durer** rain/speech which threatens to last some time; **la maison menace ruine** the house is in danger of falling down

ménage [menaʒ] NM 〔a〕 (= *entretien d'une maison*) housekeeping; (= *nettoyage*) housework; **les soins du ~** the housework, the household duties; **s'occuper de** *ou* **tenir son ~** to look after one's house, keep house; **faire du ~** to do some housework *ou* cleaning; **faire le ~** (= *nettoyer*) to do the housework; (= *licencier*) to get rid of the deadwood; (*Pol*) to get rid of the lame ducks; (*Sport*) to sort out the opposition; **faire le ~ à fond** to clean the house from top to bottom, do the housework thoroughly; **faire le ou du ~ dans ses archives/ses tiroirs** to sort out *ou* tidy one's files/one's drawers; **faire du ~ dans sa vie** to sort one's life out; **faire des ~s** to work as a cleaning woman; (*Can*) **le grand ~** the spring-cleaning → **femme** 〔b〕 (= *couple, communauté familiale*) married couple, household; (*Écon*) household; **~ sans enfant** childless couple; **~ à trois** ménage à trois; **jeune/vieux ~** young/old couple; **cela ne va pas dans le ~** their marriage is a bit shaky *ou* isn't really working; **être heureux/malheureux en ~** to have a happy/an unhappy married life; **se mettre en ~ avec qn** to set up house with sb, move in with sb; **querelles de ~** domestic quarrels *ou* rows; **faire bon/mauvais ~ avec qn** to get on well/badly with sb, hit it off/not hit it off with sb*; **notre chat et la perruche font très bon ~** our cat and the budgie get on (*Brit*) *ou* along (*US*) famously *ou* like a house on fire* → **paix, scène** 〔c〕 († = *ordinaire*) **de ~** [*chocolat*] for ordinary *ou* everyday consumption; [*pain*] homemade

ménagement [menaʒmɑ̃] 〔1〕 NM 〔a〕 (= *douceur*) care; (= *attention*) attention; **traiter qn avec ~** to treat sb considerately *ou* tactfully; **traiter qn sans ~** (*gén*) to show no consideration towards sb; (*avec brutalité*) to manhandle sb; **il les a congédiés sans ~** he dismissed them without further ado *ou* with scant ceremony; **annoncer qch sans ~ à qn** to break the news of sth bluntly to sb, tell sb sth bluntly; **il lui annonça la nouvelle avec ~** he broke the news to her gently *ou* cautiously; **elle a besoin de ~ car elle est encore très faible** she needs care and attention as she's still very weak 〔2〕 **ménagements** NMPL (= *égards*) (respectful) consideration (*NonC*) *ou* attentions

ménager¹, -ère [menaʒe, ɛʀ] 〔1〕 ADJ [*ustensiles, appareils*] household (*épith*), domestic (*épith*); **travaux ~s** ◊ **tâches ménagères** housework, domestic chores; **collège d'enseignement ~** † school of domestic science → **art, eau, ordure** 〔2〕 **ménagère** NF 〔a〕 (= *femme d'intérieur*) housewife 〔b〕 (= *couverts*) canteen (of cutlery)

ménager² [menaʒe] ▸ conjug 3 ◂ 〔1〕 VT 〔a〕 (= *traiter avec prudence*) [+ *personne puissante, adversaire*] to handle carefully, treat tactfully *ou* considerately; [+ *sentiments*] to spare, show consideration for; **elle est très sensible, il faut la ~** she's very sensitive, you must treat her gently; **~ les deux parties** to keep both parties

happy; **afin de ~ les susceptibilités** so as not to offend people's sensibilities; **~ la chèvre et le chou** (= *rester neutre*) to sit on the fence; (= *être conciliant*) to keep both parties sweet* 〔b〕 (= *utiliser avec économie ou modération*) [+ *appareil*] to go easy on; [+ *réserves*] to use carefully *ou* sparingly; [+ *vêtement*] to treat with care; [+ *argent, temps*] to use carefully, economize; [+ *expressions*] to moderate, tone down; **c'est un homme qui ménage ses paroles** he's a man of few words; **~ ses forces** to save *ou* conserve one's strength; **~ sa santé** to take great care of one's health, look after o.s.; **il n'a pas ménagé ses efforts** he spared no effort; **nous n'avons rien ménagé pour vous plaire** we've spared no pains to please you; **il ne lui a pas ménagé les louanges** he heaped praise on him 〔c〕 (= *préparer*) [+ *entretien, rencontre*] to arrange, organize; [+ *transition*] to contrive, bring about; **~ l'avenir** to prepare for the future; **il nous ménage une surprise** he's got a surprise in store for us; **il sait ~ ses effets** [*orateur*] he knows how to make the most of his effects 〔d〕 (= *disposer, pratiquer*) [+ *porte, fenêtre*] to put in; [+ *chemin*] to cut; **~ un espace entre** to make a space between; **~ une place pour** to make room for

〔2〕 **se ménager** VPR 〔a〕 (= *ne pas abuser de ses forces*) to take it easy; **il faut** *ou* **vous devriez vous ~ un peu** you should take things easy, you should try not to overtax yourself; **l'athlète se ménage pour la finale** the athlete is conserving his energy *ou* is saving himself for the final 〔b〕 (= *se réserver*) **se ~ du temps pour se reposer** to set time aside to rest; **se ~ une marge de manœuvre** to leave o.s. room for manoeuvre; **se ~ un passage** to clear a path for o.s.; **se ~ une revanche** to plan one's revenge

ménagerie [menaʒʀi] NF (*lit*) menagerie; (* *fig*) zoo

menchevik [mɛnʃevik] NMF Menshevik (*épith*)

mendélévium [mɛ̃delevjɔm] NM mendelevium

mendiant, e [mɑ̃djɑ̃, jɑ̃t] NM,F beggar, mendicant† (*littér*); (*Culin*) ◊ (**quatre**) **~s** mixed dried fruit(s) and nuts (*raisins, hazelnuts, figs, almonds*) → **frère, ordre¹**

mendicité [mɑ̃disite] NF begging; **arrêter qn pour ~** to arrest sb for begging; **être réduit à la ~** to be reduced to beggary *ou* begging

mendier [mɑ̃dje] ▸ conjug 7 ◂ 〔1〕 VT [+ *argent, nourriture, caresse, emploi*] to beg for; **~ qch à qn** to beg sb for sth; **~ des compliments** to fish for compliments 〔2〕 VI to beg

mendigot* [mɑ̃digo] NM (*péj*) beggar

mendigoter* [mɑ̃digɔte] ▸ conjug 1 ◂ VTI to beg; **toujours à ~ (quelque chose)** always begging (for something)

meneau (*pl* **meneaux**) [məno] NM (*horizontal*) transom; (*vertical*) mullion → **fenêtre**

menée [məne] 〔1〕 NF 〔a〕 (*Vénerie*) stag's track (*in flight*) 〔b〕 (*Helv* = *amas de neige*) snowdrift 〔2〕 **menées** NFPL (= *machinations*) intrigues, manoeuvres, machinations; **déjouer les ~s de qn** to foil sb's manoeuvres *ou* little game*; **~s subversives** subversive activities

mener [m(ə)ne] ▸ conjug 5 ◂ VT 〔a〕 (= *conduire*) [+ *personne*] to take, lead; (*en voiture*) to drive, take (**à** to, **dans** into); **~ un enfant à l'école/chez le médecin** to take a child to school/on to see the doctor; **~ la voiture au garage** to take the car to the garage; **mène ton ami à sa chambre** show *ou* take *ou* see your friend to his room; **~ promener le chien** to take the dog for a walk; **~ qn en bateau*** to take sb for a ride*, lead sb up the garden path*, have sb on*; **il a bien su ~ sa barque** he's managed his career very effectively 〔b〕 [*véhicule, personne*] to take; [*route*] to lead, take; [*profession, action*] to lead, get (**à** to, **dans**

into); **c'est le chemin qui mène à la mer** this is the path (leading) to the sea; **le car vous mène à Chartres en deux heures** the bus will take ou get you to Chartres in two hours; **cette route vous mène à Chartres** this road will take you to Chartres, you'll get to Chartres on this road; **où mène ce chemin?** where does this path go ou lead (to)?; **où tout cela va-t-il nous ~?** where's all this going to get us?, where does all this lead us?; **cela ne (nous) mène à rien** this won't get us anywhere, this will get us nowhere; **le journalisme mène à tout** all roads are open to you in journalism; **de telles infractions pourraient le ~ loin** offences such as these could get him into trouble ou into deep water; **~ qn à faire ...** to lead sb to do ... → **chemin**

c (= commander) [+ personne, cortège] to lead; [+ pays] to run, rule; [+ entreprise] to manage, run; [+ navire] to command); **il sait ~ les hommes** he knows how to lead men, he is a good leader; **~ qn par le bout du nez** to lead sb by the nose; **il est mené par le bout du nez par sa femme** his wife has got him on a string; **elle se laisse ~ par son frère** she lets herself be led by her brother; **l'argent mène le monde** money rules the world, money makes the world go round; **~ le jeu ou la danse** to call the tune, say what goes*; **~ les débats** to chair the discussion

d (gén, Sport = être en tête) to lead; (emploi absolu) to lead, be in the lead; (Tennis) **il mène (par) 3 jeux à 1** he's leading (by) 3 games to 1; **la France mène (l'Écosse par 2 buts à 1)** France is in the lead ou is leading (by 2 goals to 1 against Scotland)

e (= orienter) [+ vie] to lead, live; [+ négociations, lutte, conversation] to carry on; [+ enquête] to carry out, conduct; [+ affaires] to manage, run; [+ carrière] to handle, manage; **~ les choses rondement** to manage things efficiently; **~ qch à bien ou à bonne fin ou à terme** to see sth through, carry sth through to a successful conclusion; **il mène deux affaires de front** he runs ou manages two businesses at once; **~ la vie dure à qn** to rule sb with an iron hand, keep a firm hand on sb; **il n'en menait pas large** his heart was in his boots → **barque, train** etc

f (Math) **~ une parallèle à une droite** to draw a line parallel to a straight line

ménestrel [menɛstʁɛl] NM minstrel

ménétrier [menetʁije] NM fiddler

meneur, -euse [mənœʁ, øz] NM,F (= chef) (ring) leader; (= agitateur) agitator; **~ d'hommes** born leader; **~ de jeu** [spectacles, variétés] master of ceremonies, compere (Brit), emcee (US); [jeux-concours] quizmaster; (Sport) team leader; (Music-hall) **meneuse de revue** captain (of chorus girls)

menhir [meniʁ] NM menhir, standing stone

méninge [menɛ̃ʒ] NF (Méd) meninx; **~s** meninges; **se creuser les ~s*** to rack one's brains; **tu ne t'es pas fatigué les ~s!*** you didn't strain* ou overtax yourself!

méningé, e [menɛ̃ʒe] ADJ meningeal

méningite [menɛ̃ʒit] NF meningitis (NonC); **faire une ~** to have meningitis; **ce n'est pas lui qui attrapera une ~!** he's not one to strain himself!*

ménisque [menisk] NM (Anat, Opt, Phys) meniscus; (Bijouterie) crescent-shaped jewel

ménopause [menopoz] NF menopause; **troubles de la ~** menopausal problems

ménopausée [menopoze] 1 ADJ F postmenopausal 2 NF post-menopausal woman, woman past the menopause

ménopausique [menopozik] ADJ [troubles] menopausal

menotte [mənɔt] 1 NF (langage enfantin) little ou tiny hand, handy (langage enfantin) 2 **menottes** NFPL handcuffs; **il est parti, ~s aux poignets** he left handcuffed ou in handcuffs; **mettre ou passer les ~s à qn** to handcuff sb

mensonge [mɑ̃sɔ̃ʒ] NM a (= contre-vérité) lie; **faire ou dire un ~** to tell a lie; **~ par omission** lie by omission; **pieux ~** white lie; (hum) **c'est vrai, ce ~?** are you sure you're not fibbling?; **tout ça, c'est des ~s*** it's all a pack of lies b le **~** lying, untruthfulness; **je hais le ~** I hate lies ou untruthfulness; **il vit dans le ~** he's living a lie c (littér = illusion) illusion

mensonger, -ère [mɑ̃sɔ̃ʒe, ɛʁ] ADJ (= faux) [rapport, nouvelle] untrue, false; [promesse] deceitful, false; (littér = trompeur) [bonheur] illusory, delusive, deceptive

mensongèrement [mɑ̃sɔ̃ʒɛʁmɑ̃] ADV untruthfully, falsely, deceitfully

menstruation [mɑ̃stʁyasjɔ̃] NF menstruation

menstruel, -elle [mɑ̃stʁyɛl] ADJ menstrual

menstrues [mɑ̃stʁy] NFPL menses

mensualisation [mɑ̃syalizasjɔ̃] NF [salaires, impôts, factures] monthly payment; **effectuer la ~ des salaires** to put workers on monthly salaries, pay salaries monthly; **la ~ de l'impôt** the monthly payment of tax → **IMPÔTS**

mensualiser [mɑ̃syalize] ▸conjug 1◂ VT [+ salaires, employés, impôts, factures] to pay on a monthly basis; **être mensualisé** [salaire] to be paid monthly ou on a monthly basis; [employé] to be on a monthly salary; [contribuable] to pay income tax monthly

mensualité [mɑ̃syalite] NF (= traite) monthly payment ou instalment; (= salaire) monthly salary; **payer par ~s** to pay monthly ou in monthly instalments

mensuel, -elle [mɑ̃syɛl] 1 ADJ monthly 2 NM (Presse) monthly (magazine)

mensuellement [mɑ̃syɛlmɑ̃] ADV [payer] monthly, every month

mensuration [mɑ̃syʁasjɔ̃] NF (= mesure, calcul) mensuration; (= mesures) **~s** measurements; [femme] **quelles sont ses ~s?** what are her measurements ou vital statistics* (hum)?

mental, e (mpl -aux) [mɑ̃tal, o] 1 ADJ [maladie, âge, processus] mental → **calcul, malade** 2 NM (= état d'esprit) **le ~** the mental state

mentalement [mɑ̃talmɑ̃] ADV mentally; **calculer qch ~** to calculate sth ou work sth out in one's head

mentalité [mɑ̃talite] NF mentality; **les ~s ont changé** people think differently now, (people's) attitudes have changed; (iro) **quelle ~! ◊ jolie ~!** what an attitude!; **avoir une sale ~*** to be a nasty piece of work*

menterie [mɑ̃tʁi] NF (= mensonge) untruth, falsehood; (hum) **ce sont des ~s** it's all a pack of lies

menteur, -euse [mɑ̃tœʁ, øz] 1 ADJ [proverbe] fallacious, false; [enfant] untruthful, lying; **il est très ~** he's an awful liar, he's always lying 2 NM,F liar, fibber*; **sale ~!** you dirty liar! 3 [Cartes] cheat

menthe [mɑ̃t] NF a (Bot) mint; **~ poivrée** peppermint; **~ verte** spearmint, garden mint; **à la ou de ~** mint (épith) → **alcool, pastille, thé** b (= boisson fraîche) peppermint cordial; (= infusion) mint tea; **une ~ à l'eau** a glass of peppermint cordial → **diabolo**

menthol [mɑ̃tɔl] NM menthol

mentholé, e [mɑ̃tɔle] ADJ mentholated, menthol (épith)

mention [mɑ̃sjɔ̃] NF a (= note brève) mention; **faire ~ de** to mention, make mention of; **il n'y a pas ~ de son nom dans la liste** there's no reference to his name on the list, he isn't mentioned on the list; **faire l'objet d'une ~** to be mentioned b (= annotation) note, comment; **le paquet est revenu avec la ~ « adresse inconnue »** the parcel was returned marked "address unknown"; (Admin) **« rayer la ~ inutile »** "delete as appropriate"

c (Scol, Univ) grade; **~ très honorable** [doctorat] (with) distinction; **être reçu avec ~** to pass with distinction ou honours; **être reçu sans ~** to get a pass; **~ passable** ≈ pass, ≈ pass mark (Brit), ≈ passing grade (US), ≈ (grade) C; **~ assez bien** (Scol) ≈ (grade) B; (Univ) ≈ lower second class honours (Brit), ≈ (grade) B (US); **~ bien** (Scol) ≈ B+ ou A-; (Univ) ≈ upper second class honours (Brit), ≈ (grade) B (US); **très bien** (Scol) ≈ A ou A+; (Univ) ≈ first class honours (Brit), ≈ magna cum laude (US); **son film a obtenu une ~ spéciale lors du dernier festival** his film received a special award at the last festival

▼ **mentionner** [mɑ̃sjɔne] ▸conjug 1◂ VT to mention; **la personne mentionnée ci-dessus** the above-mentioned person; **l'île n'est pas mentionnée sur la carte** the island doesn't appear on the map

mentir [mɑ̃tiʁ] ▸conjug 16◂ 1 VI a [personne] to lie (à qn to sb, sur about); [photo, apparences] to be deceptive; **tu mens!** you're a liar!, you're lying!; **~ effrontément** to lie boldly, be a barefaced liar; **je t'ai menti** I lied to you, I told you a lie; **sans ~** (quite) honestly; **il ment comme il respire ou comme un arracheur de dents** he's a compulsive liar, he lies in ou through his teeth* ▪ (PROV) **a beau ~ qui vient de loin** long ways long lies (PROV); **ne me fais pas ~!** don't prove me wrong!; **faire ~ le proverbe** to give the lie to the proverb, disprove the proverb

b (littér) **~ à** (= manquer à) to betray; (= démentir) to belie; **il ment à sa réputation** he belies ou does not live up to his reputation; († ou hum) **vous en avez menti** you told an untruth

2 **se mentir** VPR [personnes] to lie to each other; **se ~ à soi-même** to fool o.s.; **il se ment à lui-même** he's not being honest with himself, he's fooling himself

menton [mɑ̃tɔ̃] NM (Anat) chin; (Zool) mentum; **~ en galoche** protruding ou jutting chin; **~ fuyant** receding chin, weak chin; **double/triple ~** double/triple chin

mentonnière [mɑ̃tɔnjɛʁ] NF [coiffure] (chin) strap; (Hist) [casque] chin piece; (Mus) chin rest; (Méd) chin bandage

mentor [mɛ̃tɔʁ] NM (frm) mentor

menu¹ [məny] NM a (= repas) meal; (= carte) menu; **faites votre ~ à l'avance** plan your meal in advance; **quel est le ou qu'y a-t-il au ~?** what's on the menu?; **vous prenez le ~ (à prix fixe) ou la carte?** are you having the set menu or the à la carte (menu)?; **~ du jour** today's menu; **~ dégustation** tasting menu; **~ touristique** set menu; **~ gastronomique** gourmet menu; **~ enfant** children's menu b (= programme) **quel est le ~ de la réunion?*** what's the agenda for the meeting?; **au ~ du festival** in the festival programme (Brit) ou program (US); **au ~ de l'émission, il y a ...** lined up (for you) on the programme (Brit) ou program (US) is ...; **au ~ de son voyage officiel, il ...** during his official visit, he ... c (Ordin) menu; **~ déroulant** pull-down menu

menu², e [məny] 1 ADJ a (= fin) [doigt, tige, taille] slender, slim; [personne] slim, slight; [pied] slender; [herbe] fine; [écriture] small, tiny; [voix] thin; **en ~s morceaux** in tiny pieces

b (= peu important) [difficultés, incidents, préoccupations] minor, petty, trifling; **dire/raconter dans les ~s détails** to tell/relate in minute detail; **~s frais** incidental ou minor expenses; (lit, fig) **~ fretin** small fry; **~s larcins** pilferage, pilfering; **~e monnaie** small ou loose change; **~ peuple** humble folk; (Hist) **Menus Plaisirs** (royal) entertainment (NonC); **se réserver de l'argent pour ses ~s plaisirs** to keep some

➤ GRAMMAIRE ACTIVE: **mentionner** 53.2

money by for (one's) amusements; **~s propos** small talk (*NonC*) [c] (*loc*) **par le ~** in detail; **raconter qch par le ~** to relate sth in great detail; **on fit par le ~ la liste des fournitures** they made a detailed list of the supplies [2] ADV [*couper, hacher, piler*] fine(ly); **écrire ~** to write small

menuet [mənμε] NM minuet

menuiserie [mənμizʀi] NF [a] (= *métier*) joinery; (*pour le bâtiment*) carpentry; **~ d'art** cabinetwork; **spécialiste en ~ métallique** specialist in metal fittings (*for doors, windows etc*); (*passe-temps*) **faire de la ~** to do woodwork *ou* carpentry *ou* joinery [b] (= *atelier*) joiner's workshop [c] (= *ouvrage*) woodwork (*NonC*), joinery (*NonC*), carpentry (*NonC*)

menuisier [mənμizje] NM [*meubles*] joiner; [*bâtiment*] carpenter; **~ d'art** cabinet-maker

Méphistophélès [mefistɔfeles] NM Mephistopheles

méphistophélique [mefistɔfelik] ADJ Mephistophelean

méphitique [mefitik] ADJ noxious, noisome†, mephitic

méphitisme [mefitism] NM sulphurous (air) pollution

méplat [mepla] NM (*Anat, Archit*) plane

méprendre (se) [mepʀɑ̃dʀ] ▶conjug 58◀ VPR (*littér*) to make a mistake, be mistaken (**sur** about); **se méprendre sur qn** to misjudge sb, be mistaken about sb; **se méprendre sur qch** to make a mistake about sth, misunderstand sth; **ils se ressemblent tellement que c'est à s'y méprendre** *ou* **qu'on pourrait s'y méprendre** they are so alike that you can't tell them apart *ou* that it's difficult to tell which is which

mépris [mepʀi] NM [a] (= *mésestime*) contempt, scorn; **avoir** *ou* **éprouver du ~ pour qn** to despise sb, feel contempt for sb; **sourire/regard de ~** scornful *ou* contemptuous smile/look; **avec ~** contemptuously, scornfully, with contempt *ou* scorn [b] (= *indifférence*) **~ de** *ou* **pour** [+ *argent, gens, honneurs, danger*] contempt for, disregard for; **avoir le ~ des convenances/traditions** to have no regard for conventions/traditions; **au ~ du danger/des lois/de l'opinion publique** regardless *ou* in defiance of danger/the law/public opinion; **au ~ de leur (propre) vie** without giving a single thought to *ou* without thought for their own lives

méprisable [mepʀizabl] ADJ contemptible, despicable

méprisant, e [mepʀizɑ̃, ɑ̃t] ADJ contemptuous, scornful; (= *hautain*) disdainful

méprise [mepʀiz] NF (= *erreur*) mistake, error; (= *malentendu*) misunderstanding; **par ~** by mistake

mépriser [mepʀize] ▶conjug 1◀ VT [+ *personne*] to despise, look down on; [+ *danger, conseil, offre*] to scorn, spurn; [+ *vice, faiblesse*] to scorn, despise; **~ les conventions** to scorn *ou* spurn convention

mer [mɛʀ] [1] NF [a] (= *océan*) sea; **~ fermée** *ou* **intérieure** inland *ou* landlocked sea; **~ de glace** glacier; **~ de sable** sea of sand; **naviguer sur une ~ d'huile** to sail on a glassy sea *ou* on a sea as calm as a millpond; **aller à la ~** to go to the seaside; **il a navigué sur toutes les ~s** he has sailed the seven seas; **vent/port de ~** sea breeze/harbour; **gens de ~** sailors, seafarers, seafaring men; **coup de ~** heavy swell → **bras, mal** [b] (= *marée*) tide; **la ~ est haute** *ou* **pleine/basse** the tide is high *ou* in/low *ou* out; **c'est la haute** *ou* **pleine/basse** it is high/low tide [c] (*loc*) **en ~** at sea; **en haute** *ou* **pleine ~** out at sea, on the open sea; **prendre la ~** [*personne, bateau*] to put out to sea; **mettre une embarcation à la ~** to launch a boat; **ba-** teau qui tient bien la **~** good seagoing boat; **aller/voyager par ~** to go/travel by sea; **ce n'est pas la ~ à boire !*** it's no big deal!; **j'avalerais** *ou* **boirais la ~ et les poissons** I could drink gallons (and gallons)

[2] COMP ► **la mer des Antilles** the Caribbean (Sea) ► **la mer d'Aral** the Aral Sea ► **la mer d'Azov** the Sea of Azov ► **la mer des Caraïbes** the Caribbean (Sea) ► **la mer Caspienne** the Caspian Sea ► **la mer de Chine** the China Sea ► **la mer Égée** the Aegean Sea ► **la mer Icarienne** the Icarian Sea ► **la mer Ionienne** the Ionian Sea ► **la mer d'Irlande** the Irish Sea ► **la mer d'Iroise** the Iroise Sea ► **la mer de Marmara** the Sea of Marmara ► **la mer Morte** the Dead Sea ► **la mer Noire** the Black Sea ► **la mer du Nord** the North Sea ► **la mer d'Oman** the sea of Oman ► **la mer Rouge** the Red Sea ► **la mer des Sargasses** the Sargasso Sea ► **les mers du Sud** the South Seas ► **la mer Tyrrhénienne** the Tyrrhenian Sea

mercanti [mɛʀkɑ̃ti] NM (*péj*) profiteer; (= *marchand oriental ou africain*) bazaar merchant

mercantile [mɛʀkɑ̃til] ADJ (*péj*) mercenary, venal

mercantilisme [mɛʀkɑ̃tilism] NM (*péj*) mercenary *ou* venal attitude; (*Écon, Hist*) mercantile system, mercantilism

mercantiliste [mɛʀkɑ̃tilist] ADJ, NM mercantilist

mercatique [mɛʀkatik] NF marketing

mercenaire [mɛʀsənɛʀ] [1] ADJ [*soldat*] mercenary, hired; (*péj*) [*attitude, personne*] mercenary [2] NM (*Mil*) mercenary; (*péj*) **tous ces ~s qui se vendent au plus offrant** all these mercenary individuals who sell themselves to the highest bidder

mercerie [mɛʀsəʀi] NF (= *boutique*) haberdasher's shop (*Brit*), notions store (*US*); (= *articles*) haberdashery (*Brit*), notions (*US*), dry goods (*US*); (= *profession*) haberdashery (*Brit*) *ou* notions (*US*) (trade)

mercerisé [mɛʀsəʀize] ADJ **coton ~** mercerized cotton

merchandising [mɛʀʃɑ̃dajziŋ, mɛʀʃɑ̃diziŋ] NM merchandising

▼**merci** [mɛʀsi] [1] EXCL [a] (*pour remercier*) thank you; **~ bien** thank you, many thanks; **~ beaucoup** thank you very much, thanks a lot*; **~ mille fois** thank you (ever) so much; **~ de** *ou* **pour votre carte** thank you for your card; **~ d'avoir répondu** thank you for replying; **sans même me dire ~** without even thanking me, without even saying thank you; (*iro*) **~ du compliment !** thanks for the compliment!; **~ mon chien !*** thank you too! (*iro*), don't bother saying thank you! (*iro*) → **dieu** [b] (*pour accepter*) **du lait ? — (oui) ~** some milk? — (yes) please [c] (*pour refuser*) **Cognac ? — (non) ~** Cognac? — no thank you; **y retourner ? ~ (bien) !** go back there? no thank you!

[2] NM thank-you; **je n'ai pas eu un ~** I didn't get *ou* hear a word of thanks; **nous vous devons/nous devons vous dire un grand ~ pour ...** we owe you/we must say a big thank-you for ...; **et encore un grand ~ pour votre cadeau** and once again thank you so much *ou* many thanks for your present; **mille ~s** many thanks

[3] NF [a] (= *pitié*) mercy; **crier/implorer ~** to cry/beg for mercy; **sans ~** [*concurrence*] merciless, ruthless; [*guerre, lutte*] ruthless; [*combattre*] ruthlessly [b] (*risque, éventualité, pouvoir*) **à la ~ de qn** at sb's mercy; **tout le monde est à la ~ d'une erreur** anyone can make a mistake; **nous sommes toujours à la ~ d'un accident** accidents can happen at any time; **exploitable à ~** liable to be ruthlessly exploited, open to ruthless exploitation → **taillable**

mercier, -ière [mɛʀsje, jɛʀ] NM,F haberdasher (*Brit*), notions dealer (*US*)

mercredi [mɛʀkʀədi] [1] NM Wednesday; **~ des Cendres** Ash Wednesday; *pour autres locutions voir* **samedi** [2] EXCL* sugar!*, shoot!* (*US*)

mercure [mɛʀkyʀ] NM [a] (*Chim*) mercury [b] (*Astron, Myth*) **Mercure** Mercury

mercuriale [mɛʀkyʀjal] NF [a] (*littér* = *reproche*) reprimand, rebuke [b] (*Bot*) mercury [c] (*Comm*) market price list

mercurochrome® [mɛʀkyʀokʀom] NM Mercurochrome®

merde [mɛʀd] [1] NF‡ [a] (= *excrément*) shit‡; (= *étron*) turd‡; **une ~ de chien** some dog shit‡, a dog turd‡ [b] (= *livre, film*) crap‡; **son dernier bouquin est de la vraie** *ou* **une vraie ~** his latest book is a load of crap‡; **quelle voiture de ~ !** what a fucking awful car!‡, what a shitty car!‡; **quel boulot de ~ !** what a crap‡ *ou* shitty‡ job! [c] (= *ennuis*) **quelle ~ !** shit!‡; **la moto est en panne, quelle ~** *ou* **c'est la ~ !** the bike's broken down, what a bummer!‡; **on est dans la ~** we're really in the shit‡, we're in one hell of a mess‡; **ils sont venus pour foutre‡ la ~** they came to cause trouble; **il a mis** *ou* **foutu‡ la ~ dans mes affaires** he messed up* my things; **mettre** *ou* **foutre‡ qn dans la ~** to land sb in the shit‡; **il ne m'arrive que des ~s** I've had one godamm‡ problem after another [d] (*loc*) **je te dis ~ !** (*insulte*) you can go to hell!‡; (*bonne chance*) good luck!, break a leg!*; **tu le veux, oui ou ~ ?** for Christ's sake *ou* for God's sake, do you want it or not?‡; **tu as de la ~ dans les yeux !** are you blind or what?*; **il ne se prend pas pour de la ~** *ou* **une ~** he thinks the sun shines out of his arse‡ (*Brit*) *ou* ass‡ (*US*), he thinks his shit doesn't stink‡ (*US*) [2] EXCL ‡ (*impatience, contrariété*) hell!‡, shit!‡; (*indignation, surprise*) shit!‡, bloody hell!‡ (*Brit*); **~ alors !** damn‡!; **~ pour lui !** to hell with him!‡

merder‡ [mɛʀde] ▶conjug 1◀ VI [*personne*] to cock up‡, fuck up‡; **t'arrives à le réparer ? — non, ça merde** can you fix it? — no, it's knackered‡; **le projet a merdé du début à la fin** the project was a bloody‡ (*Brit*) *ou* godamm‡ (*US*) mess *ou* shambles from start to finish; **j'ai merdé en anglais/à l'écrit** I fucked up‡ my English exam/the written paper

merdeux, -euse‡ [mɛʀdø, øz] [1] ADJ shitty‡; **il se sent ~** he feels shitty‡ [2] NM,F squirt*, twerp*

merdier‡ [mɛʀdje] NM (= *situation*) fuck-up‡, muck-up*; (= *désordre*) shambles *sg*; **être dans un beau ~** to be really in the shit‡, be up shit creek (without a paddle)‡; **c'est le ~ dans ses dossiers** his files are an absolute shambles

merdique‡ [mɛʀdik] ADJ [*film, discours, idée*] pathetic, moronic, crappy‡; **c'était ~, cette soirée** that party was the pits‡ *ou* was bloody awful‡ (*Brit*)

merdouille‡ [mɛʀduj] NF = **merde**

merdouiller‡ [mɛʀduje] ▶conjug 1◀ VI = **merder**

mère [mɛʀ] [1] NF [a] (= *génitrice*) mother; **elle est ~ de quatre enfants** she is a *ou* the mother of four (children); (*fig hum*) **tu es une ~ pour moi** you are like a mother to me; (*littér*) **la France, ~ des arts** France, mother of the arts; **frères par la ~** half-brothers (on the mother's side); **devenir ~** to become a mother → **Madame, reine** [b] (= *femme*) (*péj*) **la ~ Morand*** old mother Morand, old Ma Morand (*péj*); **allons la petite ~, dépêchez-vous !** come on missis, hurry up!*; (*affectueux: à une enfant, un animal*) **ma petite ~** my little pet *ou* love; (*dial*) **bonjour, ~ Martin** good day to you, Mrs Martin [c] (*Rel*) mother; **(la) Mère Catherine** Mother Catherine; **oui, ma ~** yes, Mother

▶ GRAMMAIRE ACTIVE: **merci** 48.1, 49, 52.4

d (*Tech* = *moule*) mould

e (*apposition: après n*) (= *cellule, compagnie*) parent; (*Ordin*) **fichier ~** mother file; (*Ling*) **langue ~** mother tongue *ou* language → **carte, maison**

2 COMP ► **Mère abbesse** mother abbess ► **mère d'accueil** = **mère porteuse** ► **mère biologique** natural *ou* biological mother ► **mère de famille** mother, housewife ► **mère génétique** = **mère biologique** ► **mère patrie** motherland ► **mère porteuse** surrogate mother ► **mère poule*** mother hen; **c'est une vraie ~ poule* ◊ elle est très ~ poule*** she's a real mother hen ► **mère de substitution** = **mère porteuse** ► **mère supérieure** Mother Superior ► **mère de vinaigre** mother of vinegar

mère-grand† (*pl* **mères-grand**) [mɛʀgʀɑ̃] NF grandma

merguez [mɛʀɡɛz] NF merguez sausage (*type of spicy sausage from North Africa*)

mergule [mɛʀɡyl] NM **~ (nain)** little auk

méridien, -ienne [meʀidjɛ̃, jɛn] **1** ADJ (*Sci*) meridian; (*littér*) meridian (*littér*), midday (*épith*) **2** NM (*Astron, Géog*) **~ d'origine** prime meridian; **le ~ de Greenwich** Greenwich meridian **3** **méridienne** NF **a** (*Astron*) meridian line; (*Géodésie*) line of triangulation points **b** (= *fauteuil*) meridienne **c** (*littér* = *sieste*) siesta

méridional, e (*mpl* **-aux**) [meʀidjɔnal, o] **1** ADJ (= *du Sud*) southern; (= *du sud de la France*) Southern (French) **2** **Méridional(e)** NM,F (= *du Sud*) Southerner; (= *du sud de la France*) Southern Frenchman (*ou* French-woman), Southerner

meringue [mɛʀɛ̃ɡ] NF meringue

meringuer [mɛʀɛ̃ɡe] ▶ conjug 1 ◀ VT (*gén ptp*) to coat *ou* cover with meringue; **tarte au citron meringuée** lemon meringue pie

mérinos [meʀinos] NM merino → **pisser**

merise [məʀiz] NF wild cherry

merisier [məʀizje] NM (= *arbre*) wild cherry (tree); (= *bois*) cherry (wood)

méritant, e [meʀitɑ̃, ɑ̃t] ADJ deserving

mérite [meʀit] NM **a** (= *vertu intrinsèque*) merit; (= *respect accordé*) credit; **le ~ de cet homme est grand** he is a man of great merit; **il n'en a que plus de ~** he deserves all the more credit, it's all the more to his credit; **il n'y a aucun ~ à cela** there's no merit in that; **tout le ~ lui revient** all the credit is due to him, he deserves all the credit; **il a le grand ~ d'avoir réussi** it's greatly to his credit that *ou* his great merit is that he succeeded; **il a au moins le ~ d'être franc** at least he's frank; **cette explication a la ~ de la clarté** this explanation has the virtue of being clear; **elle a bien du ~ de le supporter** she deserves a lot of credit for putting up with him **b** (= *valeur*) merit, worth; (= *qualité*) quality; **salaire au ~** merit pay; **promotion au ~** promotion on merit; **de grand ~** of great worth *ou* merit; **ce n'est pas sans ~** it's not without merit; **si nombreux que soient ses ~s** however many qualities he may have; **son geste n'a eu d'autre ~ que ...** the only good point about *ou* merit in what he did was that ... **c** (= *décoration*) **l'ordre national du Mérite** the national order of merit (*French decoration*) **d** (*Rel*) **~(s) du Christ** merits of Christ

mériter [meʀite] ▶ conjug 1 ◀ VT **a** [+ *louange, châtiment*] to deserve, merit; **tu mériterais qu'on t'en fasse autant** you deserve (to get) the same treatment; **cette action mérite des louanges/une punition** this action deserves *ou* merits *ou* warrants praise/punishment; **~ l'estime de qn** to be worthy of *ou* deserve *ou* merit sb's esteem; **tu n'as que ce que tu mérites** you've got (just) what you deserved, it serves you right; **il mérite la prison/la corde** he deserves to go to prison/to be hanged;

repos/blâme bien mérité well-deserved rest/reprimand; **on a les amis qu'on mérite** you have the friends you deserve; **ça se mérite !** you have to earn it! **b** (= *valoir*) to merit, deserve, be worth; (= *exiger*) to call for, require; **le fait mérite d'être noté** the fact is worth noting, the fact is worthy of note; **ceci mérite réflexion *ou* qu'on y réfléchisse** (*exiger*) this calls for *ou* requires careful thought; (*valoir*) this merits *ou* deserves careful thought; **ça lui a mérité le respect de tous** this earned him everyone's respect **c** **il a bien mérité de la patrie** (*frm*) he deserves well of his country; (*hum*) he deserves a medal for that

méritocratie [meʀitɔkʀasi] NF meritocracy

méritoire [meʀitwaʀ] ADJ meritorious, praise-worthy, commendable

merlan [mɛʀlɑ̃] NM **a** (*Zool*) whiting **b** (†,* = *coiffeur*) barber, hairdresser **c** (*Boucherie*) ≈ topside (*Brit*), ≈ top round (*US*)

merle [mɛʀl] NM **a** (*Orn*) blackbird; **~ à plastron** ring ouzel; **elle cherche le ~ blanc** (*gén*) she's asking for the impossible; (*mari*) she's looking for her Prince Charming; (*péj*) **vilain ~** nasty customer **b** (*Can: Orn*) (American) robin

merlette [mɛʀlɛt] NF female blackbird, she-blackbird

merlin [mɛʀlɛ̃] NM **a** [*bûcheron*] axe; (*Boucherie*) cleaver **b** (*Naut*) marline

merlu [mɛʀly] NM hake

merluche [mɛʀlyʃ] NF **a** (*Culin*) dried cod, stockfish **b** = **merlu**

merluchon [mɛʀlyʃɔ̃] NM small hake

mérou [meʀu] NM grouper

mérovingien, -ienne [meʀɔvɛ̃ʒjɛ̃, jɛn] **1** ADJ Merovingian **2** **Mérovingien(ne)** NM,F Merovingian

merveille [mɛʀvɛj] **1** NF **a** (= *chose exceptionnelle*) marvel, wonder; **les ~s de la technique moderne** the wonders *ou* marvels of modern technology; **cette montre est une ~ de précision** this watch is a marvel of precision; **les ~s de la nature** the wonders of nature; **cette machine est une (petite) ~** this machine is a (little) marvel; **regarde ma bague — quelle ~ !** look at my ring — it's beautiful!; **faire ~ *ou* des ~s** to work wonders; **c'est ~ que vous soyez vivant** it's a wonder *ou* a marvel that you are alive; **on en dit ~ *ou* des ~s** people say it's marvellous → **huitième, sept** **b** (*Culin*) fritter

2 **à merveille** LOC ADV perfectly, wonderfully, marvellously; **cela te va à ~** it suits you perfectly *ou* to perfection; **se porter à ~** to be in excellent health, be in the best of health; **ça s'est passé à ~** it went off like a dream *ou* without a single hitch; **ça tombe à ~** this comes at an ideal moment *ou* just at the right time

merveilleusement [mɛʀvɛjøzmɑ̃] ADV (*propre*) wonderfully, amazingly; [*interpréter*] brilliantly; **elle joue ~ bien au tennis** she's a brilliant tennis player; **la maison est ~ située** the house is in a marvellous position; **l'endroit se prête ~ à ce genre de festival** the place is wonderful for this kind of festival

merveilleux, -euse [mɛʀvɛjø, øz] **1** ADJ **a** (= *magnifique*) [*paysage, bijou*] wonderful **b** (= *sensationnel*) [*nouvelle, événement heureux, personne*] wonderful, fantastic; **il est ~ de dévouement** he's wonderfully devoted **c** (*après n* = *surnaturel*) magic **2** NM **le ~** the supernatural; (*Art, Littérat*) the fantastic element **3** **merveilleuse** NF (*Hist*) fine lady, belle

mes [me] ADJ POSS → **mon**

mésalliance [mezaljɑ̃s] NF misalliance, marriage beneath one's station†; **faire une ~** to marry beneath o.s. *ou* one's station†

mésallier (se) [mezalje] ▶ conjug 7 ◀ VPR to marry beneath o.s. *ou* one's station†

mésange [mezɑ̃ʒ] NF tit(mouse); **~ bleue** blue tit; **~ charbonnière** great tit; **~ huppée** crested tit; **~ à longue queue** long-tailed tit; **~ noire** coal tit

mésaventure [mezavɑ̃tyʀ] NF misadventure; **il a connu bien des ~s** he's had many misadventures; **après la récente ~ survenue à notre navigateur** after our navigator's recent misadventure *ou* accident

mescaline [mɛskalin] NF mescaline

mesclun [mɛsklœ̃] NM mixed green salad

Mesdames [medam] NFPL → **Madame**

Mesdemoiselles [medmwazɛl] NFPL → **Mademoiselle**

mésencéphale [mezɑ̃sefal] NM midbrain, mesencephalon (*SPÉC*)

mésentente [mezɑ̃tɑ̃t] NF (= *désaccord profond*) dissension, disagreement; (= *incompréhension*) misunderstanding; **la ~ règne dans leur famille** there is constant disagreement in their family; (*Sport*) **il y a eu (une) ~ entre les deux joueurs** the two players misread each other; **faire le ménage est une source de ~ conjugale** housework is a source of marital strife; **~ sexuelle** sexual incompatibility

mésentère [mezɑ̃tɛʀ] NM mesentery

mésestime [mezɛstim] NF (*littér*) [*personne*] low regard, low esteem; **tenir qn en ~** to have little regard for sb, hold sb in low esteem

mésestimer [mezɛstime] ▶ conjug 1 ◀ VT (*littér* = *sous-estimer*) [+ *difficulté, adversaire*] to underestimate, underrate; [+ *opinion*] to set little store by, have little regard for; [+ *personne*] to have little regard for, hold in low esteem

mésintelligence [mezɛ̃teliʒɑ̃s] NF disagreement (**entre** between), dissension, discord

mesmérisme [mɛsmeʀism] NM mesmerism

mésoderme [mezɔdɛʀm] NM mesoderm, mesoblast

mésolithique [mezɔlitik] **1** ADJ Mesolithic **2** NM **le ~** the Mesolithic

méson [mezɔ̃] NM meson

Mésopotamie [mezɔpɔtami] NF Mesopotamia

mésopotamien, -ienne [mezɔpɔtamjɛ̃, jɛn] **1** ADJ Mesopotamian **2** **Mésopotamien(ne)** NM,F Mesopotamian

mésothérapie [mezoteʀapi] NF mesotherapy (*method of treatment with injections from several small needles*)

mésozoïque [mezɔzɔik] **1** ADJ Mesozoic **2** NM **le ~** the Mesozoic (era)

mesquin, e [mɛskɛ̃, in] ADJ (= *avare*) stingy, mean (*Brit*); (= *vil*) mean, petty; **c'est un esprit ~** he is a mean-minded *ou* small-minded *ou* petty person; **le repas faisait un peu ~** the meal was a bit stingy

mesquinement [mɛskinmɑ̃] ADV [*agir*] meanly, pettily; [*distribuer*] stingily

mesquinerie [mɛskinʀi] NF (= *bassesse*) meanness, pettiness; (= *avarice*) stinginess, meanness; (= *procédé*) mean *ou* petty trick

mess [mɛs] NM (*Mil*) mess

▼ **message** [mesaʒ] NM (*gén, Jur, Littérat, Tech*) message; **~ chiffré** coded message, message in code *ou* cipher; **~ publicitaire** *ou* **commercial** commercial, advertisement; **~ téléphoné** telegram (*dictated by telephone*); **film/chanson à ~** film/song with a message; **dans ce livre, l'auteur essaie de faire passer un ~** the author tries to put a message across in this book; **j'espère que le ~ est passé** I hope they've (*ou* he's *etc*) got the message; **j'ai compris le ~ !** I got the message!

messager, -ère [mesaʒe, ɛʀ] NM,F messenger; (*littér*) **~ de bonheur/du printemps** harbinger of glad tidings/of spring (*littér*); **~ de malheur** bearer of bad tidings *ou* news

messagerie [mesaʒʀi] NF [a] (*Transport*) **(service de) ~s** parcel service; (= *entreprise*) **~s aériennes/maritimes** air freight/shipping company; **~s de presse** press distribution service; (*Hist*) **les ~s royales** the royal mail-coach service [b] (*Ordin, Téléc*) ► **électronique** electronic mail, e-mail; **~ vocale** voice mail → **rose**

messe [mes] [1] NF (*Mus, Rel*) mass; **aller à la ~** to go to mass; **célébrer la ~** to celebrate mass; **entendre la ~** to hear *ou* attend mass → **livre¹** [2] COMP ► **messe basse** (*Rel*) low mass; (*péj*) **~s basses** muttering, muttered conversation *ou* talk; **finissez vos ~s basses** stop muttering *ou* whispering together ► **messe chantée** sung mass ► **messe de minuit** midnight mass ► **messe des morts** mass for the dead ► **messe noire** black mass

Messeigneurs [mesɛɲœʀ] NMPL → **Monseigneur**

messeoir†† [meswaʀ] ►conjug 26◄ VI (*littér*) (*moralement*) to be unseemly (*littér*) (**à** for), ill befit (*littér*); (*pour l'allure*) to ill become (*littér*), be unbecoming (*littér*) (**à** to); **avec un air qui ne lui messied pas** with a look that is not unbecoming to him; **il vous messiérait de le faire** it would be unseemly for you to do it, it would ill become you to do it

messianique [mesjanik] ADJ messianic

messianisme [mesjanism] NM (*Rel, fig*) messianism; **la tendance au ~ de certains révolutionnaires** the messianic tendencies of certain revolutionaries

messidor [mesidɔʀ] NM Messidor (*tenth month in the French Republican Calendar*)

messie [mesi] NM messiah; **le Messie** the Messiah; **ils l'ont accueilli comme le Messie** they welcomed him like a saviour *ou* the Messiah → **attendre**

Messieurs [mesjø] NMPL → **Monsieur**

messire†† [mesiʀ] NM (= *noble*) my lord; (= *bourgeois*) Master; **oui ~** yes my lord, yes sir; **~ Jean** my lord John, master John

mestrance [mɛstʀɑ̃s] NF = **maistrance**

mestre [mɛstʀ] NM (*Naut*) mainmast

mesurable [məzyʀabl] ADJ [*grandeur, quantité*] measurable; **difficilement ~** hard to measure

▼ **mesure** [m(ə)zyʀ] NF [a] (= *évaluation, dimension*) measurement; **appareil de ~** measuring instrument *ou* device; **système de ~** system of measurement; **prendre les ~s de qch** to take the measurements of sth *ou* **poids** [b] (= *taille*) **la ~ de ses forces/sentiments** the measure of his strength/feelings; **monde/ville à la ~ de l'homme** world/town on a human scale; **il est à ma ~** [*travail*] it's within my capabilities, I am able to do it; [*adversaire*] he's a match for me; **trouver un adversaire à sa ~** to find one's match; **le résultat n'est pas à la ~ de nos espérances** the result is not up to our expectations; **prendre la (juste *ou* pleine) ~ de qn/qch** to size sb/sth up, get the measure of sb/sth; **donner (toute) sa ~ *ou* sa pleine ~** to show one's worth, show what one is capable of *ou* made of; **elle a donné toute la ~ de son talent** she showed the (full) extent of her talent [c] (= *unité, récipient, quantité*) measure; **~ de capacité** (*pour liquides*) liquid measure; (*pour poudre, grains*) dry measure; **~ de superficie/volume** square/cubic measure; **~ de longueur** measure of length; **~ graduée** measuring jug; **donne-lui deux ~s d'avoine** give it two measures of oats; **faire bonne ~** to give good measure; (*fig*) **pour faire bonne ~** for good measure [d] (= *quantité souhaitable*) **la juste *ou* bonne ~** the happy medium; **la ~ est comble** that's the limit; **dépasser *ou* excéder *ou* passer la ~** to overstep the mark, go too far; **boire outre ~** to drink immoderately *ou* to excess; **cela ne me gêne pas outre ~** that doesn't bother me

overmuch, I'm not too bothered [e] (= *modération*) moderation; **il n'a pas le sens de la ~** he has no sense of moderation; **avec ~** with *ou* in moderation; **il a beaucoup de ~** he's very moderate; **se dépenser sans ~** (= *se dévouer*) to give one's all; (= *se fatiguer*) to overtax one's strength *ou* o.s. [f] (= *disposition, moyen*) measure, step; **~s d'hygiène** health *ou* hygiene measures; **par ~ d'hygiène** in the interest of hygiene; **~s sociales** social measures; **~s de soutien à l'économie** measures to bolster the economy; **~s de rétorsion** reprisals, retaliatory measures; **prendre des ~s d'urgence** to take emergency action *ou* measures; **il faut prendre les ~s nécessaires pour …** the necessary measures *ou* steps must be taken to …; **par ~ de restriction** as a restrictive measure [g] (*Mus*) (= *cadence*) time, tempo; (= *division*) bar; (*Poésie*) metre; **en ~** in time *ou* tempo; **~ composée/simple/à deux temps/à quatre temps** compound/simple/duple/common *ou* four-four time; **être/ne pas être en ~** to be in/out of time; **jouer quelques ~s** to play a few bars; **deux ~s pour rien** two bars for nothing → **battre** [h] (*Habillement*) measure, measurement; **prendre les ~s de qn** to take sb's measurements; **ce costume est-il bien à ma ~ *ou* à mes ~s ?** is this suit my size?, will this suit fit me?; **acheter *ou* s'habiller sur ~** to have one's clothes made to measure; **costume fait à la ~ *ou* sur ~** made-to-measure suit; **c'est du sur ~** (*lit*) it's made to measure, it's tailor-made; (*fig*) it's tailor-made; **j'ai un emploi du temps/un patron sur ~** my schedule/boss suits me down to the ground; **c'est un rôle/emploi (fait) sur ~** it's a role/job that was tailor-made for me (*ou* him *etc*) [i] [⎵] (*Escrime*) (fencing) measure [j] (*loc*) **hors de ~** out of proportion (**avec** with); **dans la ~ de mes forces *ou* capacités** as far as *ou* insofar as I am able, to the best of my ability; **dans la ~ de mes moyens** as far as my circumstances permit, as far as I am able; **dans la ~ du possible** as far as possible; **dans la ~ où** inasmuch as, insofar as; **dans une certaine ~** to some *ou* to a certain extent; **dans une large ~** to a large extent, to a great extent; **être en ~ de faire qch** (*gén*) to be able to do sth; (= *avoir le droit*) to be in a position to do sth; **(au fur et) à ~ que** as; **il les pliait et me les passait (au fur et) à ~** he folded them and handed them to me one by one *ou* as he went along → **commun**

mesuré, e [məzyʀe] (*ptp de mesurer*) ADJ [*ton*] steady; [*pas*] measured; [*personne, attitude, propos*] moderate; **il est ~ dans ses paroles/ses actions** he is moderate *ou* temperate in his language/his actions

mesurer [məzyʀe] ►conjug 1◄ [1] VT [a] [+ *chose*] to measure; [+ *personne*] to take the measurements of, measure (up); (*par le calcul*) [+ *distance, pression, volume*] to calculate; [+ *longueur à couper*] to measure off *ou* out; **il a mesuré 3 cl d'acide** he measured out 3 cl of acid; **il m'a mesuré 3 mètres de tissu** he measured me off *ou* out 3 metres of fabric; **~ les autres à son aune** to judge others by one's own standards [b] (= *évaluer, juger*) [+ *risque, efficacité*] to assess, weigh up; [+ *valeur d'une personne*] to assess, rate; **vous n'avez pas mesuré la portée de vos actes !** you did not weigh up *ou* consider the consequences of your actions!; **on n'a pas encore mesuré l'étendue des dégâts** the extent of the damage has not yet been assessed; **~ les efforts aux *ou* d'après les résultats (obtenus)** to gauge *ou* assess the effort expended by *ou* according to the results (obtained); **~ ses forces avec qn** to pit o.s. against sb, measure one's strength with sb; **~ qn du regard** to look sb up and down

[c] (= *avoir pour taille*) to measure; **cette pièce mesure 3 mètres sur 10** this room measures 3 metres by 10; **il mesure 1 mètre 80** [*personne*] he's 1 metre 80 tall; [*objet*] it's 1 metre 80 long *ou* high, it measures 1 metre 80 [d] (*avec parcimonie*) to limit; **elle leur mesure la nourriture** she rations them on food, she limits their food; **le temps nous est mesuré** our time is limited, we have only a limited amount of time [e] (*avec modération*) **~ ses paroles** (= *savoir rester poli*) to moderate one's language; (= *être prudent*) to weigh one's words [f] (= *proportionner*) to match (**à, sur** to), gear (**à, sur** to); **~ le travail aux forces de qn** to match *ou* gear the work to sb's strength; **~ le châtiment à l'offense** to make the punishment fit the crime, match the punishment to the crime → **brebis** [2] **se mesurer** VPR **se ~ à *ou* avec** [+ *personne*] to pit o.s. against; [+ *difficulté*] to confront, tackle; **se ~ des yeux** to weigh *ou* size each other up

mesureur [məzyʀœʀ] [1] NM (= *personne*) measurer; (= *appareil*) gauge, measure [2] ADJ M **verre ~** measuring cup (*ou* glass *ou* jug)

mésuser [mezyze] ►conjug 1◄ ♦ **mésuser de** VT INDIR (*littér : gén*) to misuse; **~ de son pouvoir** to abuse one's power

métabolique [metabɔlik] ADJ metabolic

métaboliser [metabɔlize] ►conjug 1◄ VT (*Physiol*) to metabolize

métabolisme [metabɔlism] NM metabolism

métacarpe [metakaʀp] NM metacarpus

métacarpien, -ienne [metakaʀpjɛ̃, jɛn] [1] ADJ metacarpal [2] **métacarpiens** NMPL metacarpals, metacarpal bones

métairie [meteʀi] NF smallholding, farm (*held on a métayage agreement*)

métal (*pl* -aux) [metal, o] NM [a] (*gén, Chim, Fin, Min*) metal; **~ blanc** white metal; (*Fin*) **le ~ jaune** gold; **les métaux précieux** precious metals; **en ~ argenté/doré** [*couverts*] silver-/gold-plated [b] (*littér = matière*) metal (*littér*), stuff

métalangage [metalɑ̃gaʒ] NM, **métalangue** [metalɑ̃g] NF metalanguage

métalinguistique [metalɛ̃gɥistik] [1] ADJ metalinguistic [2] NF metalinguistics *sg*

métallifère [metalifɛʀ] ADJ metalliferous (*SPÉC*), metal-bearing (*épith*)

métallique [metalik] ADJ [a] (*gén, Chim*) metallic; [*voix, couleur*] metallic; [*objet*] (= *en métal*) metal (*épith*); (= *qui ressemble au métal*) metallic; **bruit *ou* son ~** [*clés*] jangle, clank; [*épée*] clash [b] (*Fin*) → **encaisse, monnaie**

métallisation [metalizasjɔ̃] NF [*métal*] plating; [*miroir*] silvering

métallisé, e [metalize] (*ptp de métalliser*) ADJ [*bleu, gris*] metallic; [*peinture, couleur*] metallic, with a metallic finish; [*miroir*] silvered; [*papier*] metallic, metallized

métalliser [metalize] ►conjug 1◄ VT [a] (= *couvrir*) [+ *surface*] to plate, metallize; [+ *miroir*] to silver [b] (= *donner un aspect métallique à*) to give a metallic finish to

métallo° [metalo] NM (ABRÉV = **métallurgiste**) steelworker, metalworker

métallographie [metalɔgʀafi] NF metallography

métallographique [metalɔgʀafik] ADJ metallographic

métalloïde [metalɔid] NM metalloid

métalloplastique [metaloplastik] ADJ copper asbestos (*épith*)

métallurgie [metalyʀʒi] NF (= *industrie*) metallurgical industry; (= *technique, travail*) metallurgy

métallurgique [metalyʀʒik] ADJ metallurgic

métallurgiste [metalyʀʒist] NM **(ouvrier) ~**

► GRAMMAIRE ACTIVE: **mesure** 43.4, 53.6

steelworker, metalworker; **(industriel)** ~ metallurgist

métamorphique [metamɔrfik] ADJ metamorphic, metamorphous

métamorphiser [metamɔrfize] ▸ conjug 1 ◀ VT (*Géol*) to metamorphose

métamorphisme [metamɔrfism] NM metamorphism

métamorphose [metamɔrfoz] NF (*Bio*, *Myth*) metamorphosis; (*fig*) (complete) transformation, metamorphosis

métamorphoser [metamɔrfoze] ▸ conjug 1 ◀ [1] VT (*Myth*, *fig*) to transform, metamorphose *gén pass* (**en** into); **son succès l'a métamorphosé** his success has (completely) transformed him *ou* has made a new man of him [2] **se métamorphoser** VPR (*Bio*) to be metamorphosed; (*Myth*, *fig*) to be transformed (**en** into)

métaphore [metafɔr] NF metaphor; **par ~** metaphorically

métaphorique [metafɔrik] ADJ metaphorical

métaphoriquement [metafɔrikmɑ̃] ADV metaphorically

métaphysicien, -ienne [metafizisjɛ̃, jɛn] [1] ADJ metaphysical [2] NM,F metaphysician, metaphysicist

métaphysique [metafizik] [1] ADJ (*Philo*) metaphysical; [*amour*] spiritual; (*péj*) [*argument*] abstruse, obscure [2] NF (*Philo*) metaphysics *sg*

métaphysiquement [metafizikmɑ̃] ADV metaphysically

métapsychique [metapsiʃik] ADJ psychic; **recherches ~s** psychic(al) research

métapsychologie [metapsikɔlɔʒi] NF parapsychology, metapsychology

métastase [metastaz] NF metastasis; **former des ~s** to metastasize; **il a des ~s** he's got secondaries *ou* secondary cancer *ou* metastases (*SPÉC*)

métastaser [metastaze] ▸ conjug 1 ◀ VI to metastasize

métatarse [metatars] NM metatarsus

métatarsien, -ienne [metatarsjɛ̃, jɛn] [1] ADJ metatarsal [2] **métatarsiens** NMPL metatarsals, metatarsal bones

métathèse [metatez] NF metathesis

métayage [metejaʒ] NM métayage system (*where farmer pays rent in kind*), sharecropping (*US*)

métayer [meteje] NM (tenant) farmer (*paying rent in kind*), sharecropper (tenant) (*US*)

métayère [metejɛr] NF (= *épouse*) farmer's *ou* sharecropper's wife; (= *paysanne*) (woman) farmer *ou* sharecropper (*US*)

métazoaire [metazɔɛr] NM metazoan; **les ~s** metazoans, Metazoa (*SPÉC*)

méteil [metɛj] NM *mixed crop of wheat and rye*

métempsycose [metɑ̃psikoz] NF metempsychosis, transmigration of the soul

météo [meteo] [1] ADJ ABRÉV = **météorologique** [2] NF [a] (= *science*, *service*) = **météorologie** [b] (= *bulletin*) (weather) forecast, weather report; **la ~ est bonne/mauvaise** the weather forecast is good/bad; **la ~ marine** the shipping forecast; **présentateur (de la) ~** weather forecaster, weatherman*

météore [meteɔr] NM (*lit*) meteor; (*fig*) **passer comme un ~** to have a brief but brilliant career

météorique [meteɔrik] ADJ (*Astron*) meteoric

météorisme [meteɔrism] NM (*Méd*) meteorism

météorite [meteɔrit] NM *ou* F meteorite

météorologie [meteɔrɔlɔʒi] NF (*Sci*) meteorology; (= *services*) **la ~ nationale** the meteorological office, the Met Office* (*Brit*), ≈ the Weather Bureau (*US*)

météorologique [meteɔrɔlɔʒik] ADJ [*phénomène*, *observation*] meteorological; [*conditions*, *carte*, *prévisions*, *station*] weather (*épith*) → **bulletin**

météorologiste [meteɔrɔ̍lɔʒist], **météorologue** [meteɔrɔlɔg] NMF meteorologist

métèque [metɛk] NMF [a] (⁂, *injurieux*) Mediterranean, wop⁂ (*injurieux*) [b] (*Hist*) metic

méthadone [metadɔn] NF methadone

méthane [metan] NM methane

méthanier [metanje] NM (liquefied) gas carrier *ou* tanker

méthanol [metanɔl] NM methanol

méthode [metɔd] NF [a] (= *moyen*) method; **de nouvelles ~s d'enseignement du français** new methods of *ou* for teaching French, new teaching methods for French; **la ~ douce** the softly-softly approach; **avoir une bonne ~ de travail** to have a good way *ou* method of working; **avoir sa ~ pour faire qch** to have one's own way of *ou* method for *ou* of doing sth; **elle n'a pas vraiment la ~ avec les enfants** she doesn't really know how to handle children, she's not very good with children; **service des ~s** process planning department [b] (= *ordre*) **il a beaucoup de ~** he's very methodical, he's a man of method; **il n'a aucune ~** he's not in the least methodical, he has no (idea of) method; **faire qch avec/sans ~** to do sth methodically *ou* in a methodical way/unmethodically [c] (= *livre*) manual, tutor; **~ de piano** piano manual *ou* tutor; **~ de latin** Latin primer

méthodique [metɔdik] ADJ methodical

méthodiquement [metɔdikmɑ̃] ADV methodically

méthodisme [metɔdism] NM Methodism

méthodiste [metɔdist] ADJ, NMF Methodist

méthodologie [metɔdɔlɔʒi] NF methodology

méthodologique [metɔdɔlɔʒik] ADJ methodological

méthyle [metil] NM methyl

méthylène [metilɛn] NM (*Comm*) methyl alcohol; (*Chim*) methylene → **bleu**

méthylique [metilik] ADJ methyl

méticuleusement [metikyløzmɑ̃] ADV meticulously

méticuleux, -euse [metikylø, øz] ADJ [*soin*] meticulous, scrupulous; [*personne*] meticulous; **d'une propreté méticuleuse** [*endroit*, *objets*] spotlessly *ou* scrupulously clean

méticulosité [metikylozite] NF meticulousness

métier [metje] NM [a] (= *travail*) job; (*Admin*) occupation; (*commercial*) trade; (*artisanal*) craft; (*intellectuel*) profession; **~ manuel** manual job; **donner un ~ à son fils** to have one's son learn a job (*ou* trade *ou* craft *ou* profession); **enseigner son ~ à son fils** to teach one's son one's trade; **il a fait tous les ~s** he's tried his hand at everything, he's done all sorts of jobs; **après tout ils font leur ~** they are only doing their job (after all); **les ~s du livre/de la communication** the publishing/communications industry; **prendre le ~ des armes** to become a soldier, join the army → **corps**, **gâcher**

[b] (= *technique*) (acquired) skill; (= *expérience*) experience; **avoir du ~** to have practical experience; **manquer de ~** to be lacking in practical experience; **avoir deux ans de ~** to have two years' experience, have been in the job (*ou* trade *ou* profession) for two years

[c] (*loc*) **homme de ~** expert, professional, specialist; **il est plombier de son ~** he is a plumber by trade; (*euph*) **le plus vieux ~ du monde** the oldest profession (in the world); **il est du ~** he is in the trade; **il connaît son ~** he knows his job, he's good at his job; **je connais mon ~!** I know what I'm doing!; **tu ne vas pas m'apprendre mon ~!** you're not going to teach me my job!; **ce n'est pas mon ~** it's not my job; **quel ~!** what a job!; (*hum*) **c'est le ~ qui rentre*** it's just learning the hard way; **chacun son ~ (et les vaches seront bien gardées)** you should stick to what you know

[d] (*Tech* = *machine*) loom; **~ à tisser** (weaving) loom; **~ à filer** spinning frame; **~ à broder** embroidery frame; (*littér*) **remettre qch sur le ~** to make some improvements to sth; **vingt fois sur le ~ remettez votre ouvrage** you should keep going back to your work and improving it

métis, -isse [metis] [1] ADJ [*personne*] mixed-race (*épith*), of mixed race (*attrib*); [*animal*] crossbred; [*chien*] crossbred, mongrel; [*plante*] hybrid; [*tissu*, *toile*] made of cotton and linen [2] NM,F (= *personne*) person of mixed race; (= *animal*) crossbreed; (= *chien*) crossbreed, mongrel; (= *plante*) hybrid [3] NM (*Tex*) **toile/drap de ~** linen-cotton mix *ou* blend fabric/sheet

métissage [metisaʒ] NM [*gens*] interbreeding; [*animaux*] crossbreeding, crossing; [*plantes*] crossing

métisser [metise] ▸ conjug 1 ◀ VT [+ *plantes*, *animaux*] to crossbreed, cross; **population très métissée** population with a lot of mixed blood

métonymie [metɔnimi] NF metonymy

métonymique [metɔnimik] ADJ metonymical

métrage [metraʒ] NM [a] (*Couture*) length; **grand/petit ~** long/short length; **quel ~ vous faut-il?** how many yards *ou* metres do you need? [b] (= *mesure*) measuring, measuring (in metres); **procéder au ~ de qch** to measure sth out [c] (*Ciné*) footage, length; **court ~** short (film), one-reeler [d]; **(film) long ~** feature(-length) film; **moyen ~** medium-length film

métré [metre] NM (= *métier*) quantity surveying; (= *mesure*) measurement; (= *devis*) bill of quantities

mètre [metr] NM [a] (*Math*) metre (*Brit*), meter (*US*); **~ carré/cube** square/cubic metre; **vendre qch au ~ linéaire** to sell sth by the metre [b] (= *instrument*) (metre (*Brit*) *ou* meter (*US*)) rule; **~ étalon** standard metre; **~ pliant** folding rule; **~ à ruban** tape measure, measuring tape [c] (*Athlétisme*) **le 100/400 ~s** the 100/400 metres (*Brit*) *ou* meters (*US*), the 100-/400-metre (*Brit*) *ou* -meter (*US*) race [d] (*Ftbl*, *Rugby*) **les 22/50 ~s** the 22 metre (*Brit*) *ou* meter (*US*)/halfway line [e] (*Littérat*) metre (*Brit*), meter (*US*)

métrer [metre] ▸ conjug 6 ◀ VT (*Tech*) to measure (in metres); [*vérificateur*] to survey

métreur, -euse [metrœr, øz] [1] NM,F **~ (vérificateur)** quantity surveyor [2] **métreuse** NF (*Ciné*) footage counter

métrique [metrik] [1] ADJ (*Littérat*) metrical, metric; (*Mus*) metrical; (*Math*) [*système*, *tonne*] metric; **géométrie ~** metrical geometry [2] NF (*Littérat*) metrics *sg*; (*Math*) metric theory

métro [metro] [1] NM (= *système*) underground (*Brit*), subway (*US*); (= *station*) (*gén*) underground (*Brit*) *ou* subway (*US*) station; (*à Paris*) metro station; **~ aérien** elevated railway, el* (*US*); **le ~ de Paris** the Paris metro; **le ~ de Londres** the London underground, the tube; **j'irai en ~** I'll go by underground; **le premier ~** the first *ou* milk train; **le dernier ~** the last train; **c'est ~, boulot, dodo*** it's the same old routine day in day out, it's work work work; **il a toujours un ~ de retard*** he's always one step behind [2] NMF (⁂ : *terme des îles*) person from metropolitan France

métrologie [metrɔlɔʒi] NF (*Sci*) metrology

métrologique [metrɔlɔʒik] ADJ metrological

métrologiste [metrɔlɔʒist] NMF metrologist

métronome [metrɔnɔm] NM metronome; **avec la régularité d'un ~** with clockwork regularity, like clockwork

métronomique [metʀɔnɔmik] ADJ [*mouvement*] metronomic; **avec une régularité ~** with clockwork ou metronomic regularity

métropole [metʀɔpɔl] NF a (= *ville*) metropolis; **~ régionale** large regional centre; **la Métropole** (metropolitan) France; **quand est prévu votre retour en ~?** when do you go back home? ou back to the home country?; **en ~ comme à l'étranger** at home and abroad b (*Rel*) metropolis

métropolitain, e [metʀɔpɔlitɛ̃, ɛn] 1 ADJ (*Admin, Rel*) metropolitan; **la France ~e** metropolitan France; **troupes ~es** home troops 2 NM a (*Rel*) metropolitan b († = *métro*) underground (*Brit*), subway (*US*)

mets [mɛ] NM (*Culin*) dish

mettable [metabl] ADJ (*gén nég*) wearable, decent; **ça n'est pas ~** this is not fit to wear ou to be worn; **je n'ai rien de ~** I've got nothing (decent) to wear ou nothing that's wearable; **ce costume est encore ~** you can still wear that suit, that suit is still decent ou wearable

metteur [metœʀ] NM (*Bijouterie*) **~ en œuvre** mounter; (*Radio*) **~ en ondes** producer; (*Typo*) **~ en pages** layout ou make-up artist; (*Tech*) **~ au point** adjuster; (*Théât, Ciné*) **~ en scène** director

mettre [mɛtʀ]

▸ conjug 56 ◂
1 VERBE TRANSITIF   2 VERBE PRONOMINAL

1 VERBE TRANSITIF

Lorsque **mettre** *s'emploie dans des expressions telles que* **mettre qch en place, mettre qn au pas/au régime** *etc, cherchez sous le nom.*

a = **placer** to put (**dans** in, into, **sur** on); (*fig = classer*) to rank, rate; **~ une assiette/carte sur une autre** to put a plate/card on top of another; **où mets-tu tes verres?** where do you keep your glasses?, where are your glasses kept?; **elle lui mit la main sur l'épaule** she put ou laid her hand on his shoulder; **elle met son travail avant sa famille** she puts her work before her family; **je mets Molière parmi les plus grands écrivains** I rank ou rate Molière among the greatest writers; **~ qch debout** to stand sth up; **~ qn sur son séant/sur ses pieds** to sit/stand sb up; **~ qch à ou par terre** to put sth down (on the ground); **~ qch à l'ombre/au frais** to put sth in the shade/in a cool place; **~ qch à plat** to lay sth down (flat); **~ qch droit** to put ou set sth straight up, to put rights, straighten sth out ou up; **~ qn au ou dans le train** to put sb on the train; **mettez-moi à la gare, s'il vous plaît*** take me to ou drop me at the station please; **elle a mis la tête à la fenêtre** she put ou stuck her head out of the window; **mettez les mains en l'air** put your hands up, put your hands in the air; **mets le chat dehors ou à la porte** put the cat out

b = **ajouter** **~ du sucre dans son thé** to put sugar in one's tea; **~ une pièce à un drap** to put a patch in ou on a sheet, patch a sheet; **~ une idée dans la tête de qn** to put an idea into sb's head; **ne mets pas d'encre sur la nappe** don't get ink on the tablecloth

c = **placer dans une situation** **~ un enfant à l'école** to send a child to school; **~ qn au régime** to put sb on a diet; **~ qn dans la nécessité ou l'obligation de faire** to oblige ou compel sb to do; **~ au désespoir** to throw into despair; **cela m'a mis dans une situation difficile** that has put me in ou got me into a difficult position; **on l'a mis* à la manutention/aux réclamations** he was put in the packing/complaints department; **~ qn au pas** to bring sb into line, make sb toe the line

d = **revêtir** [+ *vêtements, lunettes*] to put on; **~ une robe/du maquillage** to put on a dress/some make-up; **depuis qu'il fait chaud je ne mets plus mon gilet** since it has got warmer I've stopped wearing ou I've left off my cardi-

gan; **elle n'a plus rien à ~ sur elle** she's got nothing (left) to wear; **mets-lui son chapeau et on sort** put his hat on (for him) and we'll go; **il avait mis un manteau** he was wearing a coat, he had a coat on; **elle avait mis du bleu** she was wearing blue, she was dressed in blue

e = **consacrer** **j'ai mis 2 heures à le faire** I took 2 hours to do ou 2 hours over it, I spent 2 hours on ou over it ou 2 hours doing it; **le train met 3 heures** it takes 3 hours by train, the train takes 3 hours; **~ toute son énergie à faire** to put all one's effort ou energy into doing; **~ tous ses espoirs dans** to pin all one's hopes on; **~ beaucoup de soin à faire** to take great care in doing, take great pains to do; **~ de l'ardeur à faire qch** to do sth eagerly ou with great eagerness; **il y a mis le temps!** he's taken his time (about it)!, he's taken an age ou long enough! → **cœur**

f = **faire fonctionner** **~ la radio/le chauffage** to put ou switch ou turn the radio/the heating on; **~ les informations** to put ou turn the news on; **~ le réveil (à 7 heures)** to set the alarm (for 7 o'clock); **~ le réveil à l'heure** to put the alarm clock right; **~ le verrou** to bolt ou lock the door; **mets France Inter/la 2ème chaîne** put on France Inter/channel 2; **~ une machine en route** to start up a machine

g = **installer** [+ *eau*] to lay on; [+ *placards*] to put in, build, install; [+ *étagères*] to put up ou in, build; [+ *moquette*] to fit, lay; [+ *rideaux*] to put up; **~ du papier peint** to hang some wallpaper; **~ de la peinture** to put on a coat of paint

h ◆ **mettre qch à** + *infinitif*: **~ qch à cuire/à chauffer** to put sth on to cook/heat; **~ du linge à sécher** (*à l'intérieur*) to put ou hang washing up to dry; (*à l'extérieur*) to put ou hang washing out to dry

i = **écrire** **~ en anglais/au pluriel** to put into English/the plural; **~ à l'infinitif/au futur** to put in(to) the infinitive/the future tense; **~ des vers en musique** to set verse to music; **~ sa signature (à)** to put ou append one's signature (to); **~ un mot à qn*** to drop a line to sb; **mettez bien clairement que ...** put (down) quite clearly that ...; **il met qu'il est bien arrivé** he says in his letter ou writes that he arrived safely

j = **dépenser** **~ de l'argent sur un cheval** to put money on a horse; **~ de l'argent dans une affaire** to put money into a business; **combien avez-vous mis pour cette table?** how much did you pay for that table?; **~ de l'argent sur son compte** to put money into one's account; **je suis prêt à ~ 500F** I'm willing to give ou I don't mind giving 500 francs; **si on veut du beau il faut y ~ le prix** if you want something nice you have to pay the price ou pay for it → **caisse**

k = **lancer** **~ la balle dans le filet** to put the ball into the net; **~ une balle à la peau de qn*** to put a bullet in sb*; **~ son poing dans ou sur la figure de qn** to punch sb in the face, give sb a punch in the face

l = **supposer** **mettons que je me suis ou sois trompé** let's say ou (just) suppose ou assume I've got it wrong; **nous arriverons vers 10 heures, mettons, et après?** say we arrive about 10 o'clock, then what?, we'll arrive about 10 o'clock, say, then what?

m **loc ~ les bouts ou les voiles*** ◊ **les ~** to clear off*, beat it*, scarper* (*Brit*); **qu'est-ce qu'ils nous ont mis!** (*bagarre, match*) they gave us a real hammering!*; **va te faire ~!**** fuck off!**, bugger off!****

2 **se mettre** VERBE PRONOMINAL

a = **se placer** [*objet*] to go; **mets-toi là** (*debout*) (go and) stand there; (*assis*) (go and) sit there; **se ~ au piano/dans un fauteuil** to sit down at the piano/in an armchair; **se ~ au chaud/à l'ombre** to come ou go into the

warmth/into the shade; (*fig*) **elle ne savait plus où se ~** she didn't know where to look, she didn't know where to put herself ou what to do with herself; **il s'est mis dans une situation délicate** he's put himself in ou got himself into an awkward situation; **se ~ autour (de)** to gather round; **ces verres se mettent dans le placard** these glasses go in the cupboard; **l'infection s'y est mise** it has become infected; **les vers s'y sont mis** the maggots have got at it; **il y a un bout de métal qui s'est mis dans l'engrenage** a piece of metal has got caught in the works → **poil, rang, table, vert**

b **météo ~ au froid/au chaud/à la pluie** to turn cold/warm/wet; **on dirait que ça se met à la pluie** it looks like rain, it looks as though it's turning to rain

c = **s'habiller** **se ~ en robe/en short** ◊ **se ~ une robe/un short** to put on a dress/a pair of shorts; **se ~ en bras de chemise** to take off one's jacket; **se ~ nu** to strip (off ou naked), take (all) one's clothes off; **comment je me mets?** what (sort of thing) should I wear?; **elle s'était mise très simplement** she was dressed very simply; **elle s'était mise en robe du soir** she was wearing ou she had on an evening dress; **se ~ une veste/du maquillage** to put on a jacket/some make-up; **elle n'a plus rien à se ~** she's got nothing (left) to wear

d = **s'ajouter** **se ~ une idée dans la tête** to get an idea into one's head; **il s'est mis de l'encre sur les doigts** he's got ink on his fingers; **il s'en est mis partout** he's covered in it, he's got it all over him

e = **commencer**

◆ **se mettre à** + *nom*: **se ~ au régime** to go on a diet; **se ~ au travail** to set to work, get down to work, set about one's work; **se ~ à une traduction** to start ou set about (doing) a translation; **se ~ à la peinture** to take up painting, take to painting; **se ~ au latin** to take up Latin; **il s'est bien mis à l'anglais** he's really taken to English

◆ **se mettre à** + *infinitif*: **se ~ à rire/à manger** to start laughing/eating, start ou begin to laugh/eat; **se ~ à traduire** to start to translate, start translating, start about translating; **se ~ à boire** to take to drink ou the bottle*; **voilà qu'il se met à pleuvoir!** and now it's beginning ou starting to rain!, and now it's coming on to (*Brit*) rain!; **il est temps de s'y ~** it's (high) time we got down to it ou got on with it; **qu'est-ce que tu es énervant quand tu t'y mets!*** you can be a real pain when you get going!* ou once you get started!*

f = **se grouper** **ils se sont mis à plusieurs/deux pour pousser la voiture** several of them/the two of them joined forces to push the car; **se ~ avec qn** (= *faire équipe*) to team up with sb; (= *prendre parti*) to side with sb; (*: en ménage*) to move in with sb*, shack up* (*péj*) with sb; **se ~ bien/mal avec qn** to get on the right/wrong side of sb; **se ~ d'un parti/d'une société** to join a party/a society → **partie²**

g **loc** **on s'en est mis jusque-là ou plein la lampe*** we had a real blow-out*; (*bagarre*) **qu'est-ce qu'ils se sont mis!*** they really laid into each other!* ou had a go at each other!*, they didn't half (*Brit*) lay into each other!* ou have a go at each other!*

meublant, e [mœblɑ̃, ɑ̃t] ADJ [*papier, étoffe*] decorative, effective; **ce papier est très ~** this paper finishes off the room nicely, this paper really makes* the room → **meuble**

meuble [mœbl] 1 NM a (= *objet*) piece of furniture; **les ~s** the furniture (*NonC*); **~ de rangement** cupboard, storage unit; **~ hi-fi** hi-fi unit; **faire la liste des ~s** to make a list ou an inventory of the furniture, list each item of furniture; **nous sommes dans nos ~s** we have our own home; (*péj, hum*) **il fait partie des ~s** he's part of the furniture → **sauver** b (=

ameublement) **le ~** furniture [c] (*Jur*) movable; **~s meublants** furniture, movables; **en fait de ~s possession vaut titre** possession is nine tenths *ou* points of the law [d] (*Hér*) charge [2] ADJ [*terre, sol*] loose, soft; [*roche*] soft, crumbly → **bien**

meublé, e [mœble] (*ptp de* **meubler**) [1] ADJ furnished; **non ~** unfurnished [2] NM (= *pièce*) furnished room; (= *appartement*) furnished apartment *ou* flat (*Brit*); **être** *ou* **habiter en ~** to be *ou* live in furnished accommodation

meubler [mœble] ▸ conjug 1 ◂ [1] VT [+ *pièce, appartement*] to furnish (**de** with); [+ *pensée, mémoire, loisirs*] to fill (**de** with); [+ *dissertation*] to fill out, pad out (**de** with); **~ la conversation** to keep the conversation going; **une table et une chaise meublaient la pièce** the room was furnished with a table and a chair; **étoffe/papier qui meuble bien** decorative *ou* effective material/paper [2] **se meubler** VPR to buy *ou* get (some) furniture, furnish one's home; **ils se sont meublés dans ce magasin/pour pas cher** they got *ou* bought their furniture from this shop/for a very reasonable price

meuf: [mœf] NF (= *femme*) woman, bird*, broad: (*US*)

meuglement [møgləmã] NM mooing (*NonC*), lowing† (*NonC*)

meugler [møgle] ▸ conjug 1 ◂ VI to moo, low†

meuh [mø] EXCL, NM moo; **faire ~** to moo

meulage [mølaʒ] NM grinding

meule¹ [møl] NF [a] (*à moudre*) millstone; (*à polir*) buff wheel; (*Dentisterie*) wheel; ~ (**à aiguiser**) grindstone; **~ courante** *ou* **traînante** upper (mill)stone [b] (*Culin*) ~ (**de gruyère**) round of gruyère [c] (‡ = *motocyclette*) bike, hog‡ (*US*)

meule² [møl] NF (*Agr*) stack, rick; (= *champignonnière*) mushroom bed; **~ de foin** haystack, hayrick; **~ de paille** stack *ou* rick of straw; **mettre en ~s** to stack, rick

meuler [møle] ▸ conjug 1 ◂ VT (*Tech, Dentisterie*) to grind down

meulière [møljɛʀ] NF (**pierre**) ~ millstone, buhrstone

meunerie [mønʀi] NF (= *industrie*) flour trade; (= *métier*) milling

meunier, -ière [mønje, jɛʀ] [1] ADJ milling [2] NM miller [3] **meunière** NF miller's wife; (*Culin*) **sole/truite meunière** sole/trout meunière

meurette [mœʀɛt] NF red wine sauce; **œufs en ~** eggs in red wine sauce

meurtre [mœʀtʀ] NM murder; **au ~ !** murder!; (*fig*) **crier au ~** to scream blue murder

meurtrier, -ière [mœʀtʀije, ijɛʀ] [1] ADJ [*intention, fureur*] murderous; [*arme*] deadly, lethal; [*combat*] deadly; [*épidémie*] fatal; † [*personne*] murderous; **week-end ~** weekend of carnage on the roads; **cette route est meurtrière** this road is lethal *ou* a deathtrap; **le bombardement a été particulièrement ~** the bombing claimed very many lives; **c'est le séisme le plus ~ depuis 1995** the worst *ou* deadliest earthquake since 1995 [2] NM murderer [3] **meurtrière** NF [a] (= *criminelle*) murderess [b] (*Archit*) arrow slit, loophole

meurtrir [mœʀtʀiʀ] ▸ conjug 2 ◂ VT [a] [+ *chair, fruit*] to bruise; **être tout meurtri** to be covered in bruises, be black and blue all over [b] (*littér*) [+ *personne, âme*] to wound, bruise (*littér*)

meurtrissure [mœʀtʀisyʀ] NF [a] [*chair, fruit*] bruise [b] (*littér*) [*âme*] scar, bruise; **les ~s laissées par la vie/le chagrin** the scars *ou* bruises left by life/sorrow

meute [møt] NF (*Chasse, péj*) pack; **lâcher la ~ sur** to set the pack on; **une ~ de journalistes** a pack of journalists

mévente [mevãt] NF (*Écon*) slump *ou* drop in sales; († = *vente à perte*) selling at a loss; **une période de ~** a slump, a period of poor sales

---

mexicain, e [mɛksikɛ̃, ɛn] [1] ADJ Mexican [2] **Mexicain(e)** NM,F Mexican

Mexico [mɛksiko] N Mexico City

Mexique [mɛksik] NM **le ~** Mexico

mézigue: [mezig] PRON PERS me, yours truly*; **c'est pour ~** it's for yours truly*

mezzanine [mɛdzanin] NF (*Archit*) (= *étage*) mezzanine (floor); (= *fenêtre*) mezzanine window; (*Théât*) mezzanine

mezza-voce [mɛdzavɔtʃe] ADV (*Mus*) mezza voce; (*littér*) in an undertone

mezzo [mɛdzo] [1] NM mezzo (voice) [2] NF mezzo

mezzo-soprano (*pl* **mezzo-sopranos**) [mɛdzosɔpʀano] [1] NM mezzo-soprano (voice) [2] NF mezzo-soprano

mezzo-tinto [mɛdzotinto] NM INV mezzotint

MF [a] (ABRÉV = **modulation de fréquence**) FM [b] (ABRÉV = **millions de francs**) → **million**

mg (ABRÉV = **milligramme**) mg

Mgr (ABRÉV = **Monseigneur**) Mgr

mi [mi] NM (*Mus*) E; (*en chantant la gamme*) mi, me

mi- [mi] PRÉF (*le préfixe reste invariable dans les mots composés à trait d'union*) half, mid-; **la ~janvier** the middle of January, mid-January; **à ~cuisson ajoutez le vin** add the wine half way through cooking; **pièce ~salle à manger ~salon** living-dining room, dining-cum-living room (*Brit*); **~riant ~pleurant** half-laughing half-crying, halfway between laughing and crying

MIAGE [mjaʒ] NF (ABRÉV = **maîtrise d'informatique appliquée à la gestion des entreprises**) master's degree in business data processing

miam-miam* [mjammjam] EXCL (*langage enfantin*) yum-yum!*, yummy!*; **faire ~** to eat

miaou [mjau] EXCL, NM miaow; **faire ~** to miaow

miasme [mjasm] NM (*gén pl*) miasma; **~s** putrid fumes, miasmas

miaulement [mjolmã] NM mewing, meowing

miauler [mjole] ▸ conjug 1 ◂ VI to mew, meow

mi-bas [miba] NM INV (*pour homme*) knee-length sock; (*pour femme*) pop sock (*Brit*), knee-high (*US*)

mica [mika] NM (= *roche*) mica; (*pour vitre, isolant*) Muscovy glass, white mica

micacé, e [mikase] ADJ [*couleur*] mica-tinted; [*substance*] mica-bearing, micaceous

mi-carême [mikaʀɛm] NF **la ~** the third Thursday in Lent

micaschiste [mikaʃist] NM mica-schist

miche [miʃ] [1] NF [*pain*] round loaf, cob loaf (*Brit*) [2] **miches** NFPL (= *fesses*) bum* (*Brit*), butt: (*surtout US*)

Michel-Ange [mikelɑ̃ʒ] NM Michelangelo

micheline [miʃlin] NF railcar

mi-chemin [miʃ(ə)mɛ̃] ◆ **à mi-chemin** LOC ADV **je l'ai rencontré à ~** I met him halfway there; **la poste est à ~** the post office is halfway there, the post office is halfway *ou* midway between the two; **à ~ de la gare** halfway *ou* midway to the station; **ces reportages sont à ~ de la fiction et du réel** these reports are a mixture of fiction and truth *ou* are half fiction half truth; (*lit, fig*) **à ~ entre ...** halfway *ou* midway between ...

micheton† [miʃtɔ̃] NM (*arg Crime*) punter* (*Brit*), John: (*US*)

Michigan [miʃigã] NM Michigan; **le lac ~** Lake Michigan

mi-clos, e [miklo, kloz] ADJ half-closed; **les yeux ~** with half-closed eyes, with one's eyes half-closed

micmac* [mikmak] NM (*péj*) (= *intrigue*) funny business*; (= *confusion*) mix-up; **je devine leur petit ~** I can guess their little game* *ou* what they're playing at*; **tu parles d'un ~ pour aller**

---

jusqu'à chez elle ! it's such a hassle getting to her place!

micocoulier [mikɔkulje] NM nettle tree, European hackberry

mi-combat [mikɔ̃ba] ◆ **à mi-combat** LOC ADV halfway through the match

mi-corps [mikɔʀ] ◆ **à mi-corps** LOC ADV up to *ou* down to the waist; **plongé à ~ dans l'eau glacée** waist-deep in the icy water

mi-côte [mikot] ◆ **à mi-côte** LOC ADV halfway up (*ou* down) the hill

mi-course [mikuʀs] ◆ **à mi-course** LOC ADV (*Sport*) halfway through the race, at the halfway mark; **piston bloqué à ~** piston jammed at half-stroke

micro [mikʀo] [1] NM [a] ABRÉV = **microphone** microphone, mike*; (*Radio, TV*) **dites-le au ~** *ou* **devant le ~** say it in front of the mike*; **parlez dans le ~** speak into the microphone; **ils l'ont dit au ~** (*dans un aéroport, une gare*) they announced it over the intercom *ou* PA system; **il était au ~ de France Inter** he was on France Inter [b] (ABRÉV = **micro-ordinateur**) [2] NF ABRÉV = **micro-informatique**

micro... [mikʀo] PRÉF micro...; **~curie** microcurie; **~séisme** microseism

microalgue [mikʀoalg] NF microalga

microampère [mikʀoãpɛʀ] NM microamp

microbalance [mikʀobalãs] NF microbalance

microbe [mikʀɔb] NM [a] (*Méd*) germ, bug*; microbe (*SPÉC*) [b] (* péj) pipsqueak*, little runt: (*péj*)

microbien, -ienne [mikʀɔbjɛ̃, jɛn] ADJ [*culture*] microbial, microbic; [*infection*] bacterial; **maladie microbienne** bacterial disease

microbille, micro-bille (*pl* **micro-billes**) [mikʀobij] NF [*abrasif*] micro-granule, micro-particle

microbiologie [mikʀobjɔlɔʒi] NF microbiology

microbiologique [mikʀobjɔlɔʒik] ADJ microbiological

microbiologiste [mikʀobjɔlɔʒist] NMF microbiologist

microcassette [mikʀokaset] NF microcassette

microcéphale [mikʀosefal] ADJ, NMF microcephalic

microchirurgie [mikʀoʃiʀyʀʒi] NF microsurgery

microcircuit [mikʀosiʀkɥi] NM microcircuit

microclimat [mikʀoklima] NM microclimate

microcoque [mikʀokɔk] NM micrococcus

microcosme [mikʀokɔsm] NM microcosm

microcosmique [mikʀokɔsmik] ADJ microcosmic

microcoupure [mikʀokupyʀ] NF (*Ordin*) power dip

micro-cravate (*pl* **micros-cravates**) [mikʀokʀavat] NM clip-on microphone *ou* mike*

microculture [mikʀokyltyʀ] NF (*Bio*) microculture

microéconomie [mikʀoekɔnɔmi] NF microeconomics sg

microéconomique [mikʀoekɔnɔmik] ADJ microeconomic

microédition [mikʀoedisjɔ̃] NF desktop publishing, DTP

microélectronique [mikʀoelɛktʀɔnik] NF microelectronics sg

micro-entreprise (*pl* **micro-entreprises**) [mikʀoãtʀəpʀiz] NF micro-business

microfibre [mikʀofibʀ] NF microfibre; **tissu/fil ~** microfibre fabric/thread; **en ~s** microfibre (*épith*)

microfiche [mikʀofiʃ] NF microfiche

microfilm [mikʀofilm] NM microfilm

micrographie [mikʀogʀafi] NF micrography

micrographique [mikʀogʀafik] ADJ micrographic

micro-informatique [mikʀoɛ̃fɔʀmatik] NF microcomputing

micromécanique [mikʀomekanik] NF micro-mechanics *sg*

micromètre [mikʀomɛtʀ] NM micrometer

micrométrie [mikʀometʀi] NF micrometry

micrométrique [mikʀometʀik] ADJ micro-metric(al)

micron [mikʀɔ̃] NM micron

Micronésie [mikʀonezi] NF Micronesia

micronésien, -ienne [mikʀonezjɛ̃, jɛn] ① ADJ Micronesian ② **Micronésien(ne)** NM,F Micronesian

micro-onde (*pl* **micro-ondes**) [mikʀoɔ̃d] ① NF microwave ② NM (**four à**) **~s** micro-wave (oven)

micro-ordinateur (*pl* **micro-ordinateurs**) [mikʀoɔʀdinatœʀ] NM microcomputer

micro-organisme (*pl* **micro-organismes**) [mikʀoɔʀganism] NM microorganism

microphone [mikʀofɔn] NM microphone

microphotographie [mikʀofotɔgʀafi] NF (= *procédé*) photomicrography; (= *image*) photo-micrograph

microphysique [mikʀofizik] NF microphys-ics *sg*

microprocesseur [mikʀopʀosesœʀ] NM microprocessor

microscope [mikʀoskɔp] NM microscope; **examiner qch au ~** (*lit*) to examine sth ou look at sth under a microscope; (*fig*) to put sth under the microscope; **~ électronique** electron microscope; **~ (électronique) à balayage (par transmission)** scanning electron microscope

microscopie [mikʀoskɔpi] NF microscopy

microscopique [mikʀoskɔpik] ADJ micro-scopic

microseconde [mikʀos(ə)gɔ̃d] NF microsec-ond

microsillon [mikʀosijɔ̃] NM (= *sillon*) micro-groove; (**disque**) **~** LP, microgroove record

microsonde [mikʀosɔ̃d] NF microprobe

microstructure [mikʀostʀyktyʀ] NF micro-structure

micro-trottoir (*pl* **micros-trottoirs**) [mikʀotʀɔtwaʀ] NM **faire un ~** to interview people in the street, do a vox pop* (*Brit*)

miction [miksjɔ̃] NF micturition

mi-cuisse(s) [mikɥis] ♦ **à mi-cuisses** LOC ADV **ses bottes lui arrivaient à mi-cuisses** his boots came up to his thighs ou over his knees; **l'eau leur arrivait à mi-cuisses** they were thigh-deep in water, they were up to their thighs in wa-ter

MIDEM [midɛm] NM (ABRÉV = **marché interna-tional du disque et de l'édition musicale**) → **marché**

midi [midi] ① NM ⓐ (= *heure*) midday, 12 (o'clock), noon; **~ dix** 10 past 12; **de ~ à 2 heures** from 12 ou (12) noon to 2; **entre ~ et 2 heures** between 12 ou (12) noon and 2; **hier à ~** yesterday at 12 o'clock ou at noon ou at midday; **pour le ravoir, c'est ~ (sonné)**†* there isn't a hope ou you haven't a hope of getting it back → **chacun, chercher, coup**
ⓑ (= *période du déjeuner*) lunchtime, lunch hour; (= *mi-journée*) midday, middle of the day; **à/pendant ~** at/during lunchtime, at/during the lunch hour; **demain ~** tomorrow lunchtime; **tous les ~s** every lunchtime ou lunch hour; **que faire ce ~ ?** what shall we do at lunchtime? ou midday?, what shall we do this lunch hour?; **le repas de ~** the midday meal, lunch; **qu'est-ce que tu as eu à ~ ?** what did you have for lunch?; **à ~ on va au restau-rant** we're going to a restaurant for lunch; **en plein ~** (= *à l'heure du déjeuner*) (right) in the middle of the day, at midday; (= *en plein zé-nith*) at the height of noon, at high noon; **ça s'est passé en plein ~** it happened right in

the middle of the day → **démon**
ⓒ (*Géog* = *sud*) south; **exposé au** ou **en plein ~** facing due south; **le ~ de la France** ◊ **le Midi** the South of France, the Midi → **accent**
② ADJ INV (*chaîne hi-fi, slip, jupe*) midi

midinette [midinɛt] NF (= *jeune fille*) young girl; († = *vendeuse*) shopgirl (*in the dress indus-try*); († = *ouvrière*) dressmaker's apprentice; (*péj*) **elle a des goûts de ~** she has the tastes of a sixteen-year-old schoolgirl

mi-distance [midistɑ̃s] ♦ **à mi-distance (en-tre)** LOC PRÉP halfway ou midway (between); **à ~ de Vienne et de Prague** halfway ou midway between Vienna and Prague

mie[1] [mi] NF soft part (*of bread*); (*Culin*) bread with crusts removed; **il a mangé la croûte et laissé la ~** he's eaten the crust and left the soft part ou the inside (*of the bread*); **faire une farce avec de la ~ de pain** to make stuffing with fresh white breadcrumbs → **pain**

mie[2] †† [mi] NF (*littér* = *bien-aimée*) lady-love†, beloved (*littér*)

mie[3] †† [mi] ADV not; **ne le croyez ~** believe it not †

miel [mjɛl] ① NM honey; **bonbon/boisson au ~** honey sweet (*Brit*) ou candy (*US*)/drink; **être tout ~** [*personne*] to be all sweetness and light; **~ rosat** rose honey; (*fig*) **faire son ~ de qch** to turn sth to one's advantage → **gâteau, lune** ② EXCL (*euph* *) sugar!*

miellat [mjɛla] NM honeydew

miellé, e [mjɛle] ADJ (*littér*) honeyed

mielleusement [mjɛløzmɑ̃] ADV (*péj*) unctu-ously

mielleux, -euse [mjɛlø, øz] ADJ (*péj*) [*personne*] unctuous, syrupy, smooth-tongued; [*paroles*] honeyed, smooth; [*ton*] honeyed, sugary; [*sourire*] sugary, sickly sweet; († ou *littér*) [*saveur*] sickly sweet

mien, mienne [mjɛ̃, mjɛn] ① PRON POSS **le ~** ◊ **la mienne** ◊ **les ~s** ◊ **les miennes** mine; **ce sac n'est pas le ~** this bag is not mine, this is not my bag; **ton prix/ton jour sera le ~** name your price/the day; **vos fils sont sages compa-rés aux ~s** your sons are well-behaved com-pared to mine ou my own ② **miens** NMPL **les ~s** (= *ma famille*) my family, my (own) folks*; (= *mon peuple*) my people ③ ADJ POSS († ou *littér*) **un ~ cousin** a cousin of mine; **je fais miennes vos observations** I agree whole-heartedly (with you) → **sien**

miette [mjɛt] NF [*pain, gâteau*] crumb; (*Culin*) **~s de crabe/de thon** flaked crab/tuna; **en ~s** [*verre*] in bits ou pieces; [*gâteau*] in pieces; [*bonheur*] in pieces ou shreds; **leur voiture est en ~s** there's nothing left of their car, their car was totaled* (*US*); **les ~s de sa fortune** the remnants of his fortune; **je n'en prendrai qu'une ~** I'll just have a tiny bit ou a sliver; **il n'en a pas laissé une ~** (*repas*) he didn't leave a scrap; (*fortune*) he didn't leave a penny (*Brit*) ou one red cent (*US*); **mettre** ou **réduire qch en ~s** to break ou smash sth to bits ou to smith-ereens; **il ne perdait pas une ~ de la conversation/du spectacle** he didn't miss a scrap of the conversation/the show

mieux [mjø] (*compar, superl de* **bien**) ① ADV ⓐ (*gén*) better; **aller** ou **se porter ~** to be bet-ter; **il ne s'est jamais ~ porté** he's never been ou felt better in his life; **plus il s'entraîne, ~ il joue** the more he practises the better he plays; **elle joue ~ que lui** she plays better than he does; **c'est (un peu/beaucoup) ~ expliqué** it's (slightly/much) better explained; **il n'écrit pas ~ qu'il ne parle** he writes no better than he speaks; **s'attendre à ~** to expect better; **espérer ~** to hope for better (things); **il peut faire ~** he can do ou is capable of better; **tu fe-rais ~ de te taire** you'd better shut up* → **reculer, tant, valoir** *etc*
ⓑ **le ~** ◊ **la ~** ◊ **les ~** (*de plusieurs*) (the) best; (*de deux*) (the) better; **je passe par les rues les**

~ éclairées I take the better lit streets; **c'est ici qu'il dort le ~** he sleeps best here, this is where he sleeps best; **tout va le ~ du monde** everything's going beautifully; **tout est pour le ~ dans le meilleur des mondes** everything is for the best in the best of all possible worlds; **une école des ~ conçues/équipées** one of the best planned/best equipped schools; **un dîner des ~ réussis** a most ou highly successful din-ner; **j'ai fait le ~** ou **du ~ que j'ai pu** I did my (level ou very) best, I did the best I could; **des deux, elle est la ~ habillée** she is the better dressed of the two
ⓒ (*loc*) **~ que jamais** better than ever; **~ vaut trop de travail que pas assez** too much work is better than not enough; **il va de ~ en ~** he's getting better and better; (*iro*) **de ~ en ~ !** maintenant il s'est mis à boire** that's great ou terrific (*iro*), now he has taken to the bottle*; **il nous a écrit, ~, il est venu nous voir** he wrote to us, and better still he came to see us; **à qui ~ ~** (*gén*) each one more so than the other; [*crier*] each one louder than the other; [*frapper*] each one harder than the other ■ (*PROV*) **~ vaut tard que jamais** better late than never (*PROV*) ■ (*PROV*) **~ vaut prévenir que gué-rir** prevention is better than cure (*PROV*)
② ADJ INV ⓐ (= *plus satisfaisant*) better; **le ~** ◊ **la ~** ◊ **les ~** (*de plusieurs*) (the) best; (*de deux*) (the) better; **c'est la ~ de nos secré-taires*** she is the best of our secre-taries, she's our best secretary; (*de deux*) she's the better of our secretaries; **il est ~ qu'à son arrivée** he's improved since he (first) came, he's better than when he (first) came; **c'est beaucoup ~ ainsi** it's (much) better this way; **le ~ serait de ...** the best (thing ou plan) would be to ...; **c'est ce qu'il pourrait faire de ~** it's the best thing he could do
ⓑ (= *en meilleure santé*) better; (= *plus à l'aise*) better, more comfortable; **le ~** ◊ **la ~** ◊ **les ~** (the) best, (the) most comfortable; **être ~/le ~ du monde** to be better/in perfect health; **je le trouve ~ aujourd'hui** I think he is looking bet-ter ou he seems better today; **ils seraient ~ à la campagne qu'à la ville** they would be better (off) in the country than in (the) town; **c'est à l'ombre qu'elle sera le ~** she'll be more com-fortable in the shade → **sentir**
ⓒ (= *plus beau*) better looking, more attrac-tive; **le ~** ◊ **la ~** ◊ **les ~** (*de plusieurs*) (the) best looking, (the) most attractive; (*de deux*) (the) better looking, (the) more attractive; **elle est ~ les cheveux longs** she looks better with her hair long ou with long hair, long hair suits her better; **c'est avec les cheveux courts qu'elle est le ~** she looks best with her hair short ou with short hair, short hair suits her best; **il est ~ que son frère** he's better looking than his brother
ⓓ (*loc*) **c'est ce qui se fait de ~** it's the best there is ou one can get; **tu n'as rien de ~ à fai-re que (de) traîner dans les rues ?** haven't you got anything better to do than hang around the streets?; **c'est son frère, en ~** he's (just) like his brother only better looking; **ce n'est pas mal, mais il y a ~** it's not bad, but I've seen better; **qui ~ est** even better, better still → **changer, faute**
③ **au mieux** LOC ADV (*gén*) at best; **en mettant les choses au ~** at (the very) best; **tout se passe au ~ avec nos collègues** we get on extremely well with our colleagues; **utili-ser au ~ les ressources/le temps** to make best use of (one's) resources/time; **pour appréci-er au ~ les charmes de la ville** to best appreciate ou enjoy the charms of the town; **il sera là au ~ à midi** he'll be there by midday at the earli-est; **faites au ~** do what you think best ou whatever is best; **être au ~ avec qn** to be on the best of terms with sb; (*Fin*) **acheter/vendre au ~** to buy/sell at the best price
④ **au mieux de** LOC PRÉP **au ~ de sa forme** in

peak condition; **au ~ de nos intérêts** in our best interests

5 NM **a** (= *ce qui est préférable*) **le ~** best; **le ~ serait d'accepter** the best thing to do would be to accept; **j'ai fait pour le ~** I did what I thought best; **tout allait pour le ~ avant qu'il n'arrive** everything was perfectly fine before he came ■ (*PROV*) **le ~ est l'ennemi du bien** (it's better to) let well alone; **partez tout de suite, c'est le ~** it's best (that) you leave immediately, the best thing would be for you to leave immediately

b (*avec adj poss*) **faire de son ~** to do one's (level *ou* very) best, do the best one can; **aider qn de son ~** to do one's best to help sb, help sb the best one can *ou* to the best of one's ability; **j'ai essayé de répondre de mon ~ aux questions** I tried to answer the questions to the best of my ability

c (= *amélioration, progrès*) improvement; **il y a un ~ ou du ~** there's (been) some improvement

mieux-disant (*pl* **mieux-disants**) [mjødizã] NM (*Fin*) lowest bidder *ou* tenderer; (*fig*) **le ~ culturel** striving for excellence in cultural matters

mieux-être [mjøzɛtʀ] NM INV (*gén*) greater welfare; (*matériel*) improved standard of living; **ils ressentent un ~ psychologique** they feel better in themselves

mieux-vivre [mjøvivʀ] NM INV improved standard of living

mièvre [mjɛvʀ] ADJ [*paroles, musique, roman*] soppy; [*tableau*] pretty-pretty*; [*sourire*] mawkish; [*charme*] vapid; **elle est un peu ~** she's a bit colourless (*Brit*) *ou* colorless (*US*) *ou* insipid

mièvrerie [mjɛvʀəʀi] NF [*paroles, musique*] sentimentality, soppiness; [*tableau*] pretty-prettiness*; [*sourire*] mawkishness; [*charme*] vapidity; [*personne*] colourlessness (*Brit*), colorlessness (*US*), insipidness; (= *propos*) insipid *ou* sentimental talk (*NonC*); **il faut éviter de tomber dans la ~** we must avoid getting all sentimental; **ses chansons sont d'une ~ affligeante** his songs are incredibly soppy

mi-figue mi-raisin [mifigmiʀezɛ̃] ADJ INV [*sourire*] wry; [*remarque*] half-humorous, wry; **on leur fit un accueil ~** they received a mixed reception

mi-fin [mifɛ̃] ADJ M [*petits pois*] medium

mignard, e [miɲaʀ, aʀd] ADJ [*style*] mannered, precious; [*décor*] pretty-pretty*, over-ornate; [*musique*] pretty-pretty*, over-delicate; [*manières*] precious, dainty, simpering (*péj*)

mignardise [miɲaʀdiz] NF **a** [*tableau, poème, style*] preciousness; [*décor*] ornateness; [*manières*] preciousness (*péj*), daintiness, affectation (*péj*) **b** (= *fleur*) **de la ~ ◊ des œillets ~** pinks

mignon, -onne [miɲɔ̃, ɔn] **1** ADJ **a** (= *joli*) [*enfant*] sweet, cute; [*femme*] sweet(-looking), pretty; [*homme*] cute; [*bras, pied, geste*] dainty, cute; (= *gentil, aimable*) nice, sweet; **donne-le-moi, tu seras mignonne*** give it to me, there's a dear* *ou* love* (*Brit*), be a dear* and give it to me; **c'est ~ chez vous** you've got a nice little place → **péché** **2** NM,F (little) darling, poppet* (*Brit*), cutie* (*US*); **mon ~ ◊ ma mignonne** sweetheart, pet* **3** NM **a** (*Hist = favori*) minion **b** (*Boucherie*) **(filet) ~** fillet (*Brit*) *ou* filet (*US*) mignon

mignonnet, -ette [miɲɔnɛ, ɛt] **1** ADJ [*enfant, objet*] sweet, cute*; **c'est ~ chez eux** they've got a cute little place* → **mignonnette** NF **a** (= *bouteille*) miniature **b** (*Bot*) (= *œillet*) wild pink; (= *saxifrage*) Pyrenean saxifrage **c** (= *poivre*) coarse-ground pepper **d** (= *gravier*) fine gravel

migraine [migʀɛn] NF (*gén*) headache; (*Méd*) migraine; **j'ai la ~** I've got a bad headache, my head aches

migraineux, -euse [migʀenø, øz] **1** ADJ migrainous **2** NM,F person suffering from migraine

migrant, e [migʀã, ãt] ADJ, NM,F migrant

migrateur, -trice [migʀatœʀ, tʀis] **1** ADJ migratory **2** NM migrant, migratory bird

migration [migʀasjɔ̃] NF (*gén*) migration; (*Rel*) transmigration; **oiseau en ~** migrating bird

migratoire [migʀatwaʀ] ADJ migratory

migrer [migʀe] ▸ conjug 1 ◂ VI to migrate (**vers** to)

mi-hauteur [miotœʀ] ◆ **à mi-hauteur** LOC ADV halfway up (*ou* down); **des carreaux s'élevaient à ~ du mur** the lower half of the wall was covered with tiles

mi-jambe(s) [miʒãb] ◆ **à mi-jambe(s)** LOC ADV up (*ou* down) to the knees; **l'eau leur arrivait à mi-jambes** they were knee-deep in water, they were up to their knees in water

mijaurée [miʒɔʀe] NF pretentious *ou* affected woman *ou* girl; **faire la ~** to give o.s. airs (and graces); **regarde-moi cette ~ !** just look at her with her airs and graces!; **petite ~ !** little madam!

mijoter [miʒɔte] ▸ conjug 1 ◂ **1** VT **a** (= *cuire*) [+ *plat, soupe*] to simmer; (= *préparer avec soin*) to cook *ou* prepare lovingly; **plat mijoté** dish which has been slow-cooked *ou* simmered; **il lui mijote des petits plats** he cooks (up) *ou* concocts tempting *ou* tasty dishes for her **b** (* = *tramer*) to cook up*; **~ un complot** to hatch a plot; **il mijote un mauvais coup** he's cooking up* *ou* plotting some mischief; **qu'est-ce qu'il peut bien ~ ?** what's he up to?*, what's he cooking up?*; **il se mijote quelque chose** something's brewing *ou* cooking* **2** VI [*plat, soupe*] to simmer; [*complot*] to be brewing; **laissez** *ou* **faites ~ 20 mn** (leave to) simmer for 20 mins; **laisser qn ~ (dans son jus)*** to leave sb to stew*, let sb stew in his own juice*

mijoteuse® [miʒɔtøz] NF slow cooker

mikado [mikado] NM (= *jeu*) jackstraws *sg*, spillikins *sg*; **jouer au ~** to play jackstraws, have a game of jackstraws

mil¹ [mil] NM (*dans une date*) a *ou* one thousand

mil² [mij, mil] NM = **millet**

milady [miledi] NF (titled English) lady; **oui ~** yes my lady

milan [milã] NM (*Orn*) kite

milanais, e [milanɛ, ɛz] **1** ADJ Milanese; **escalope (à la) ~e** escalope milanaise **2** **Milanais(e)** NM,F Milanese

mildiou [mildju] NM (*Agr*) mildew

mildiousé, e [mildjuze] ADJ (*Agr*) mildewed

mile [majl] NM mile (*1 609 m*)

milice [milis] NF **a** (= *corps paramilitaire*) militia; (*Hist de France*) **la Milice** the Milice (*collaborationist militia during the German occupation*) **b** (*Belg*) (= *armée*) army; (= *service militaire*) military service

milicien [milisjɛ̃] NM (*gén*) militiaman; (*Belg*) conscript (*Brit*), draftee (*US*)

milicienne [milisjɛn] NF woman serving in the militia

milieu (*pl* **milieux**) [miljø] **1** NM **a** (= *centre*) middle; **casser/couper/scier qch en son ~** *ou* **par le ~** to break/cut/saw sth down *ou* through the middle; **le bouton/la porte du ~** the middle *ou* centre knob/door; **je prends celui du ~** I'll take the one in the middle *ou* the middle one; **tenir le ~ de la chaussée** to keep to the middle of the road; (*Ftbl*) **~ de terrain** midfield player; (*Ftbl*) **le ~ du terrain** the midfield; **il est venu vers le ~ de l'après-midi/la matinée** he came towards the middle of the afternoon/the morning, he came about mid-afternoon/mid-morning; **vers/depuis le ~ du 15ème siècle** towards/since the mid-15th century, towards/since the

mid-1400s → **empire**
b (= *état intermédiaire*) middle course *ou* way; **il n'y a pas de ~ (entre)** there is no middle course *ou* way (between); **avec lui, il n'y a pas de ~** there's no in-between with him; **le juste ~** the happy medium, the golden mean; **un juste ~** a happy medium; **il est innocent ou coupable, il n'y a pas de ~** he is either innocent or guilty, he can't be both; **tenir le ~** to steer a middle course
c (*Bio, Géog*) environment; (*Chim, Phys*) medium; **~ physique/géographique/humain** physical/geographical/human environment; **~ de culture** culture medium; **les animaux dans leur ~ naturel** animals in their natural surroundings *ou* environment *ou* habitat
d (= *entourage social, moral*) milieu, environment; (= *groupe restreint*) set, circle; (= *provenance*) background; **le ~ familial** (*gén*) the family circle; (*Sociol*) the home *ou* family background, the home environment; **s'adapter à un nouveau ~** to adapt to a different milieu *ou* environment; **il ne se sent pas dans son ~** he feels out of place, he doesn't feel at home; **elle se sent** *ou* **est dans son ~ chez nous** she feels (quite) at home with us; **de quel ~ sort-il ?** what is his (social) background?; **les ~x littéraires/financiers** literary/financial circles; **dans les ~x autorisés/bien informés** in official/well-informed circles; **c'est un ~ très fermé** it is a very closed circle *ou* exclusive set
e (*Crime*) **le ~** the underworld; **les gens du ~** (people of) the underworld; **membre du ~** gangster, mobster
2 **au milieu** LOC ADV in the middle
3 **au milieu de** LOC PRÉP (= *au centre de*) in the middle of; (= *parmi*) amid, among, in the midst of, amidst (*littér*); **il est là au ~ de ce groupe** he's over there in the middle of that group; **au ~ de toutes ces difficultés/aventures** in the middle *ou* midst of *ou* amidst all these difficulties/adventures; **au ~ de son affolement** in the middle *ou* midst of his panic; **elle n'est heureuse qu'au ~ de sa famille/de ses enfants** she's only happy when she's among *ou* surrounded by her family/her children *ou* with her family/her children around her; **au ~ de la journée** in the middle of the day; **au ~ de la nuit** in the middle of the night; **comment travailler au ~ de ce vacarme ?** how can anyone work in this din?; **au ~ de la descente** halfway down (the hill); **au ~ de la page** in the middle of the page, halfway down the page; **au ~/en plein ~ de l'hiver** in mid-winter/the depth of winter; **au ~ de l'été** in mid-summer, at the height of summer; **au beau ~ de ◊ en plein ~ de** right *ou* bang* *ou* slap bang* in the middle of, in the very middle of; **il est parti au beau ~ de la réception** he left right in the middle of the party

militaire [militɛʀ] **1** ADJ military, army (*épith*) → **attaché, service** **2** NM serviceman, soldier; **il est ~** he's in the forces *ou* services, he's a soldier; **~ de carrière** professional *ou* career soldier; **les ~s sont au pouvoir** the army *ou* the military are in power

militairement [militɛʀmã] ADV [*saluer*] in military fashion *ou* style; **la ville a été occupée ~** the town was occupied by the army; **occuper ~ une ville** to (send in the army to) occupy a town

militant, e [militã, ãt] ADJ, NM,F activist, militant; **~ de base** rank and file *ou* grassroots militant; **~ pour les droits de l'homme** human rights activist *ou* campaigner

militantisme [militãtism] NM (political) activism, militancy

militarisation [militaʀizasjɔ̃] NF militarization

militariser [militaʀize] ▸ conjug 1 ◂ **1** VT to militarize **2** **se militariser** VPR to become militarized

militarisme [militaʀism] NM militarism

militariste [militaʀist] ① ADJ militaristic ② NMF militarist

militer [milite] ▸ conjug 1 ◂ VI ⓐ [personne] to be a militant ou an activist; **il milite au parti communiste** he is a communist party militant, he is a militant in the communist party; **~ pour les droits de l'homme** to campaign for human rights ⓑ [arguments, raisons] **~ en faveur de** ou **pour** to militate in favour of, argue for; **~ contre** to militate ou tell against

milk-shake (pl **milk-shakes**) [milkʃɛk] NM milk shake

millage [milaʒ] NM (Can) mileage

mille¹ [mil] ① ADJ INV ⓐ (= nombre) a ou one thousand; **~ un** a ou one thousand and one; **trois ~** three thousand; **deux ~ neuf cents** two thousand nine hundred; **page ~** page one thousand; (dans les dates) **l'an ~** the year one thousand
ⓑ (= nombreux) **~ regrets** I'm terribly sorry; **je lui ai dit ~ fois** I've told him a thousand times; **tu as ~ fois raison** you're absolutely right; **c'est ~ fois trop grand** it's far too big; **~ excuses** ou **pardons** I'm (ou we're) terribly sorry; **le vase s'est cassé/était en ~ morceaux** the vase smashed into smithereens/was in smithereens
ⓒ (loc) **~ et un problèmes/exemples** a thousand and one problems/examples; (Littérat) **« Les contes des Mille et Une Nuits »** "The Thousand and One Nights", "(Tales from) the Arabian Nights"; **dans un décor des Mille et Une Nuits** in a setting like something from the Arabian Nights; **je vous le donne en ~*** you'll never guess; (hum) **~ sabords !*** blistering barnacles!*
② NM INV ⓐ a ou one thousand; **cinq pour ~ d'alcool** five parts of alcohol to a thousand; **cinq enfants sur ~** five children out of ou in every thousand; **vendre qch au ~** to sell sth by the thousand; **deux ~ de boulons** two thousand bolts; **l'ouvrage en est à son centième ~** the book has sold 100,000 copies → **gagner**
ⓑ (Sport) (cible) bull's-eye, bull (Brit); **mettre** ou **taper (en plein) dans le ~** (lit) to hit the bull's-eye ou bull (Brit); (fig) to score a bull's-eye, be bang on target*; **tu as mis dans le ~ en lui faisant ce cadeau** you were bang on target* with the present you gave him

mille² [mil] NM ⓐ **~ (marin)** nautical mile ⓑ (Can) mile (1 609 m)

millefeuille [milfœj] NM (Culin) mille feuilles, ≈ cream ou vanilla slice (Brit), ≈ napoleon (US)

millénaire [milenɛʀ] ① ADJ (lit) thousand-year-old; millenial; (= très vieux) ancient, very old; **monument ~** thousand-year-old monument; **des rites plusieurs fois ~s** rites several thousand years old, age-old rites ② NM (= période) millennium, a thousand years; (= anniversaire) thousandth anniversary, millennium; **nous entrons dans le troisième ~** we're beginning the third millenium

millénarisme [milenaʀism] NM millenarianism

millénariste [milenaʀist] ADJ, NMF millenarian

millénium [milenjɔm] NM millennium

mille-pattes [milpat] NM INV centipede, millipede

millepertuis, mille-pertuis [milpɛʀtɥi] NM St-John's-wort

mille-raies [milʀɛ] NM INV (= tissu) finely-striped material; **velours ~** needlecord

millésime [milezim] NM (= date, Admin, Fin) year, date; (vin) year, vintage; **vin d'un bon ~** vintage wine; **quel est le ~ de ce vin ?** what is the vintage ou year of this wine?

millésimé, e [milezime] ADJ vintage; **bouteille ~e** bottle of vintage wine; **un bordeaux ~** a vintage Bordeaux

millet [mijɛ] NM (Agr) millet; **donner des grains de ~ aux oiseaux** to give the birds some millet ou (bird)seed

milli... [mili] PRÉF milli...; **~rem** millirem

milliaire [miljɛʀ] ADJ (Antiq) milliary; **borne ~** milliary column

milliampère [miljɑ̃pɛʀ] NM milliamp

milliard [miljaʀ] NM billion, thousand million; **un ~ de personnes** a billion ou a thousand million people; **10 ~s de francs** 10 billion francs, 10 thousand million francs; **des ~s de** billions of, thousands of millions of

milliardaire [miljaʀdɛʀ] ① NMF multimillionaire ② ADJ **il est ~** he's worth millions, he's a multimillionaire; **une société plusieurs fois ~ en dollars** a company worth (many) billions of dollars

milliardième [miljaʀdjɛm] ADJ, NM thousand millionth, billionth

millibar [milibaʀ] NM millibar

millième [miljɛm] ADJ, NM thousandth; **c'est la ~ fois que je te le dis !** I've told you a thousand times!; (Théât) **la ~ (représentation)** the thousandth performance

millier [milje] NM (= mille) thousand; (= environ) a thousand or so, about a thousand; **par ~s** in (their) thousands, by the thousand; **il y en a des ~s** there are thousands (of them)

milligramme [miligram] NM milligram(me)

millilitre [mililitʀ] NM millilitre (Brit), milliliter (US)

millimétré, e [milimetre] ADJ [papier] graduated (in millimetres); (= précis) [passe, tir] right on target

millimètre [milimɛtʀ] NM millimetre (Brit), millimeter (US)

millimétrique [milimetʀik] ADJ millimetric

million [miljɔ̃] NM million; **2 ~s de francs** 2 million francs; **être riche à ~s** to be a millionaire, have millions, be worth millions; **ça a coûté des ~s** it cost millions

millionième [miljɔnjɛm] ADJ, NM millionth

millionnaire [miljɔnɛʀ] ① NMF millionaire ② ADJ **la société est ~** the company is worth millions ou worth a fortune; **il est plusieurs fois ~** he's a millionaire several times over; **un ~ en dollars** a dollar millionaire

millivolt [milivɔlt] NM millivolt

mi-long, mi-longue [milɔ̃, milɔ̃g] ADJ [manteau, jupe] calf-length (épith); [manche] elbow-length (épith); [cheveux] shoulder-length (épith)

milord†* [milɔʀ] NM (= noble anglais) lord, nobleman; (= riche étranger) immensely rich foreigner; **oui ~ !** yes my lord!

mi-lourd [miluʀ] NM, ADJ (Boxe) light heavy-weight

mime [mim] NM ⓐ (= personne) (Théât) mime artist, mime; (= imitateur) mimic ⓑ (Théât = art, action) mime, miming; **il fait du ~** he's a mime (artist); **(spectacle de) ~** mime show

mimer [mime] ▸ conjug 1 ◂ VT (Théât) to mime; (= singer) to mimic, imitate; (pour ridiculiser) to take off

mimétique [mimetik] ADJ mimetic

mimétisme [mimetism] NM (Bio) (protective) mimicry; (fig) unconscious imitation, mimetism; **il croisa les bras, par ~ avec son frère** he folded his arms, unconsciously imitating ou in unconscious imitation of his brother

mimi* [mimi] ① NM ⓐ (langage enfantin) (= chat) pussy(cat), puss*; (= baiser) little kiss; (= câlin) cuddle; **faire des ~s à qn** to kiss and cuddle sb ⓑ (terme affectueux) **mon ~** darling, sweetie* ② ADJ INV (= mignon) cute, lovely

mimique [mimik] NF ⓐ (= grimace comique) comical expression, funny face; **ce singe a de drôles de ~s !** this monkey makes such funny faces!; **il eut une ~ de dégoût** he grimaced in disgust ⓑ (= signes, gestes) gesticulations;

[sourds-muets] sign language (NonC); **il eut une ~ expressive pour dire qu'il avait faim** his gestures ou gesticulations made it quite clear that he was hungry

mimodrame [mimɔdʀam] NM (Théât) mime show

mi-mollet [mimɔlɛ] ◆ **à mi-mollet** LOC ADV (arrivant à) ~ [jupe] calf-length, below-the-knee (épith); **j'avais de l'eau jusqu'à ~** the water came up to just below my knees

mimosa [mimoza] NM mimosa → **œuf**

mi-moyen [mimwajɛ̃] NM, ADJ (Boxe) welter-weight

MIN [min] NM (ABRÉV = **marché d'intérêt national**) → **marché**

min. ⓐ (ABRÉV = **minimum**) min ⓑ (ABRÉV = **minute**) min

minable [minabl] ① ADJ ⓐ (= décrépit) [lieu, aspect, personne] shabby(-looking), seedy(-looking); (= médiocre) [devoir, film, personne] hopeless*, useless*, pathetic*; [salaire, vie] miserable, wretched; [voyou] wretched; [complot] shoddy; **habillé de façon ~** shabbily dressed ② NMF (péj) loser*, dead loss*; (espèce de) **~ !** you're so pathetic!*; **une bande de ~s** a pathetic ou useless bunch*

minablement [minabləmɑ̃] ADV ⓐ (= médiocrement) hopelessly*, uselessly*, pathetically* ⓑ [habillé] shabbily

minage [minaʒ] NM [pont, tranchée] mining

minaret [minaʀɛ] NM minaret

minauder [minode] ▸ conjug 1 ◂ VI to simper, put on simpering airs; **oh oui, dit-elle en minaudant** oh yes, she simpered; **je n'aime pas sa façon de ~** I don't like her (silly) simpering ways

minauderie [minodʀi] NF **~s** simpering (airs); **faire des ~s** to put on simpering airs, simper

minaudier, -ière [minodje, jɛʀ] ADJ affected, simpering (épith)

mince [mɛ̃s] ① ADJ ⓐ (= peu épais) thin; (= svelte, élancé) slim, slender; **tranche ~** thin slice; **elle est ~ comme un fil** she's (as) thin as a rake; **~ comme une feuille de papier à cigarette** ou **comme une pelure d'oignon** paper-thin, wafer-thin; **avoir la taille ~** to be slim ou slender
ⓑ (= faible, insignifiant) [profit] slender; [salaire] meagre (Brit), meager (US), small; [prétexte] lame, weak; [preuve, chances] slim, slender; [excuse] lame; [connaissance, rôle, mérite] slight, small; **l'intérêt du film est bien ~** the film is decidedly lacking in interest ou is of very little interest; **ce n'est pas une ~ affaire** it's quite a job ou business, it's no easy task; **c'est un peu ~ comme réponse*** that's a rather lame ou feeble reply, that's not much of an answer
② ADV [couper] thinly, in thin slices
③ EXCL **~ (alors) !** (contrariété) drat (it)!*, blow (it)!* (Brit), darn (it)!* (US); (surprise) you don't say!; (admiration) wow!*

minceur [mɛ̃sœʀ] NF ⓐ (= finesse) thinness; (= gracilité) slimness, slenderness; **cuisine ~** cuisine minceur; **régime ~** slimming diet; **produits ~** slimming products ⓑ (= insignifiance) **la ~ des preuves** the slimness ou the insufficiency of the evidence

mincir [mɛ̃siʀ] ▸ conjug 2 ◂ ① VI to get slimmer, get thinner ② VT [vêtement] **cette robe te mincit** this dress makes you look slimmer

mine¹ [min] ① NF ⓐ (= physionomie) expression, look; **... dit-il, la ~ réjouie ...** he said with a cheerful ou delighted expression on his face; **elle est arrivée, la ~ boudeuse** she arrived, looking sulky ou with a sulky expression on her face; **ne fais pas cette ~-là** stop making ou pulling that face; **faire triste ~ à qn** to give sb a cool reception, greet sb unenthusiastically → **gris**
ⓑ (= allure) exterior, appearance; **tu as la ~**

de quelqu'un qui n'a rien compris you look as if you haven't understood a single thing; **il cachait sous sa ~ modeste un orgueil sans pareil** his modest exterior concealed an overweening pride; **votre rôti a bonne ~** your roast looks good *ou* appetizing; (*iro*) **tu as bonne ~ maintenant!** now you look (like) an utter *ou* a right* idiot! → **payer**

c (= *teint*) **avoir bonne ~** to look well; **il a mauvaise ~** he doesn't look well, he looks unwell *ou* poorly; **avoir une sale ~** to look awful* *ou* dreadful; **avoir une ~ de papier mâché** to look washed out; **il a meilleure ~ qu'hier** he looks better than (he did) yesterday; **tu as une ~ superbe** you look terrific

d (*loc*) **faire ~ de faire qch** to pretend to do sth; **j'ai fait ~ de le croire** I pretended to have believed it; **j'ai fait ~ de lui donner une gifle** I made as if to slap him; **il n'a même pas fait ~ de résister** he didn't even put up a token resistance, he didn't even offer a show of resistance; **il est venu nous demander comment ça marchait, ~ de rien*** he came and asked us with a casual air *ou* all casually* how things were going; **~ de rien, tu sais qu'il n'est pas bête*** though you wouldn't think it to look at him he's no dummy* *ou* he's not daft* (*Brit*) you know; **~ de rien, ça fait deux heures qu'on attend/ça nous a coûté 1 500 F** you wouldn't think it but we've been waiting for two hours/it cost us 1 500 francs

2 mines NFPL [*personne*] simpering airs; [*bébé*] expressions; **faire des ~s** to put on simpering airs, simper; **il fait ses petites ~s** [*bébé*] he makes (funny) little faces

mine² [min] **1** NF **a** (= *gisement*) deposit, mine; (*exploité*) mine; (*lit, fig*) **~ d'or** gold mine; **région de ~s** mining area *ou* district; **~ à ciel ouvert** opencast mine; **la nationalisation des ~s** (*gén*) the nationalization of the mining industry; (*charbon*) the nationalization of coal *ou* of the coalmining industry; **~ de charbon** (*gén*) coalmine; (*puits*) pit, mine; (*entreprise*) colliery; **descendre dans la ~** to go down the mine *ou* pit; **travailler à la ~** to work in the mines, be a miner → **carreau, galerie, puits**

b (= *source*) [*renseignements*] mine; **une ~ inépuisable de documents** an inexhaustible source of documents; **cette bibliothèque est une (vraie) ~** this library is a treasure trove

c ~ (de crayon) (pencil) lead; **crayon à ~ dure/tendre** hard/soft pencil, pencil with a hard/soft lead; **~ de plomb** black lead, graphite

d (*Mil*) (= *galerie*) gallery, sap, mine; (= *explosif*) mine; **~ dormante/flottante** unexploded/floating mine; **~ terrestre** landmine → **champ, détecteur**

2 Mines NFPL **les Mines** (*Admin*) ≈ the (National) Mining and Geological service; **l'École des Mines** ≈ the (National) School of Mining Engineering; **ingénieur des Mines** (state qualified) mining engineer; **le service des Mines** *the French government vehicle testing service*

miner [mine] ▶conjug 1◀ VT **a** (= *garnir d'explosifs*) to mine; **ce pont est miné** this bridge has been mined **b** (= *ronger*) [+ *falaise, fondations*] to undermine, erode, eat away; [+ *société, autorité, santé*] to undermine; [+ *force*] to sap, undermine; **la maladie l'a miné** his illness has left him drained (of energy) *ou* has sapped his strength; **miné par le chagrin/l'inquiétude** worn down by grief/anxiety; **miné par la jalousie** eaten up *ou* consumed with jealousy; **tout ça le mine** all this is eating into him; (*fig*) **c'est un sujet/terrain miné** it's a highly sensitive subject/area

minerai [minʀɛ] NM ore; **~ de fer/cuivre** iron/copper ore

minéral, e (*mpl* **-aux**) [mineʀal, o] ADJ **1** [*huile, sel, règne*] mineral; [*chimie*] inorganic; [*paysage*] stony → **chimie, eau 2** NM mineral

minéralier [mineʀalje] NM ore tanker

minéralisation [mineʀalizasjɔ̃] NF mineralization

minéralisé, e [mineʀalize] (*ptp de* **minéraliser**) ADJ [*eau*] mineralized; **peu/moyennement ~e** with a low/medium mineral content

minéraliser [mineʀalize] ▶conjug 1◀ VT to mineralize

minéralogie [mineʀalɔʒi] NF mineralogy

minéralogique [mineʀalɔʒik] ADJ (*Géol*) mineralogical; (*Aut*) **numéro ~** registration (*Brit*) *ou* license (*US*) number → **plaque**

minéralogiste [mineʀalɔʒist] NMF mineralogist

minerve [minɛʀv] NF **a** (*Méd*) (surgical) collar **b** (*Typo*) platen machine **c** (*Myth*) **Minerve** Minerva

minet, -ette [minɛ, ɛt] **1** NM,F (*langage enfantin* = *chat*) puss*, pussy (cat), kitty (cat) (*surtout US*); (*terme affectif*) **mon ~ ◊ ma minette** (my) pet*, sweetie(-pie)* **2** NM (*péj* = *jeune élégant*) pretty boy*, young trendy* (*Brit*) **3 minette** NF (* = *jeune fille*) (cute) chick*

mineur¹, e [minœʀ] **1** ADJ **a** (*Jur*) minor; **enfant ~** young person who is under age, minor (*Jur*); **être ~** to be under age, be a minor (*Jur*) **b** (= *peu important*) [*soucis, œuvre, artiste*] minor → **Asie c** (*Mus*) [*gamme, intervalle, mode*] minor; **en do ~** in C minor **d** (*Logique*) [*terme, proposition*] minor **2** NM,F (*Jur*) minor, young person under 18 (years of age); **« établissement interdit aux ~s »** "no person under 18 allowed on the premises"; **le film est interdit aux ~s de moins de 12 ans** the film is unsuitable for children under 12 → **détournement 3** NM (*Mus*) minor; **en ~** in a minor key **4 mineure** NF **a** (*Logique*) minor premise **b** (*Univ* = *matière*) subsidiary (*Brit*), second subject (*Brit*), minor (*US*)

mineur² [minœʀ] NM **a** (*Ind*) miner; [*houille*] (coal) miner; **~ de fond** pitface *ou* underground worker, miner at the pitface; **village de ~s** mining village **b** (*Mil*) sapper (*who lays mines*)

mini [mini] **1** ADJ INV **a** (*Mode*) **la mode ~** the fashion for minis **b** (= *très petit*) **c'est ~ chez eux*** they've got a minute *ou* tiny (little) place; **~ budget ◊ budget ~** shoestring budget **2** NM INV (*Mode*) **elle s'habille (en) ~** she wears minis; **la mode est au ~** minis are in (fashion)

mini- [mini] PRÉF mini; **~conférence de presse** mini press-conference

miniature [minjatyʀ] **1** NF **a** (*gén*) miniature; **en ~** in miniature; **cette région, c'est la France en ~** this region is a miniature France *ou* France in miniature **b** (*Art*) miniature **c** (* = *nabot*) (little) shrimp* *ou* tich* (*Brit*), tiddler* (*Brit*); **tu as vu cette ~?** did you see that little shrimp?* **2** ADJ miniature; **train/jeu d'échecs ~** miniature train/chess set

miniaturisation [minjatyʀizasjɔ̃] NF miniaturization

miniaturiser [minjatyʀize] ▶conjug 1◀ VT to miniaturize; **transistor miniaturisé** miniaturized transistor; **les ordinateurs se miniaturisent** computers are becoming smaller and smaller

miniaturiste [minjatyʀist] NMF miniaturist

minibar [minibaʀ] NM (= *réfrigérateur*) minibar; (= *chariot*) refreshments trolley (*Brit*) *ou* cart

minibus [minibys] NM minibus

minicassette [minikasɛt] NF minicassette

minichaîne [miniʃɛn] NF mini (music) system

minidosée [minidoze] ADJ F **pilule ~** mini-pill

minier, -ière [minje, jɛʀ] ADJ mining

minigolf [minigɔlf] NM (= *jeu*) mini-golf, crazy-golf; (= *lieu*) mini-golf *ou* crazy-golf course

minijupe [miniʒyp] NF miniskirt

minima [minima] → **minimum**

minimal, e (*mpl* **-aux**) [minimal, o] ADJ [*température, pension*] minimal, minimum; **art ~** minimal art

minimalisme [minimalism] NM minimalism

minimaliste [minimalist] NMF minimalist

minime [minim] **1** ADJ [*dégât, rôle, différence*] minor (*épith*), minimal; [*salaire, somme*] paltry **2** NMF **a** (*Sport*) junior (*13-15 years*) **b** (*Rel*) Minim

minimisation [minimizasjɔ̃] NF minimization

minimiser [minimize] ▶conjug 1◀ VT [+ *risque, rôle*] to minimize; [+ *incident, importance*] to play down

minimum [minimɔm] (*f* **minimum** *ou* **minima** [minima]) (*pl* **minimum(s)** *ou* **minima**) **1** ADJ minimum; **vitesse/âge ~** minimum speed/age; **la température ~ a été de 6° C** the minimum temperature was 6° C, there was a low of 6° C today; (*Transport*) **assurer un service ~** to run a reduced service; (*TV*) **programme ~** restricted service → **revenu, salaire**

2 NM **a** (*gén, Math*) minimum; (*Jur*) minimum sentence; **dans le ~ de temps** in the shortest time possible; **il faut un ~ de temps/d'intelligence pour le faire** you need a minimum amount of time/a modicum of intelligence to be able to do it; **il faut quand même travailler ~** you still have to do a minimum (amount) of work; **avec un ~ d'efforts il aurait réussi** with a minimum of effort he would have succeeded; **il a pris que le ~ de précautions** he took only minimum *ou* minimal precautions; **c'est vraiment le ~ que tu puisses faire** it's the very least you can do; **la production a atteint son ~** production has sunk to its lowest level (yet) *ou* an all-time low; **dépenses réduites au/à un ~** expenditure cut (down) to the/to a minimum; **avoir tout juste le ~ vital** (*salaire*) to earn barely a living wage; (*subsistance*) to be *ou* live at subsistence level; **il faut rester le ~ (de temps) au soleil** you must stay in the sun as little as possible; (*Admin*) → **vieillesse** basic old age pension

b (*loc*) **au ~** at least, at a minimum; **ça coûte au ~ 100 F** it costs at least 100 francs *ou* a minimum of 100 francs

3 ADV at least, at a minimum; **ça dure quinze jours ~** it lasts at least fifteen days

mini-ordinateur (*pl* **mini-ordinateurs**) [miniɔʀdinatœʀ] NM minicomputer

minipilule [minipilyl] NF minipill

ministère [ministɛʀ] **1** NM **a** (= *département*) ministry, department (*surtout US*); **employé de ~** government employee; **~ de l'Agriculture/de l'Éducation (nationale)** ministry *ou* department (*US*) of Agriculture/of Education → **2**

b (= *cabinet*) government, cabinet; **sous le ~ (de) Pompidou** under the premiership of Pompidou, under Pompidou's government; **le premier ~ Poincaré** Poincaré's first government *ou* cabinet; **former un ~** to form a government *ou* a cabinet; **~ de coalition** coalition government

c (*Jur*) **le ~ public** (= *partie*) the Prosecution; (= *service*) the public prosecutor's office; **par ~ d'huissier** served by a bailiff

d (*Rel*) ministry; **exercer son ~ à la campagne** to have a country parish

e (*littér* = *entremise*) agency; **proposer son ~ à qn** to offer to act for sb

2 COMP ▶ **ministère des Affaires étrangères** Ministry of Foreign Affairs, Foreign Office (*Brit*), Department of State (*US*), State Department (*US*) ▶ **ministère des Affaires européennes** Ministry of European Affairs ▶ **ministère des Affaires sociales** Social Services Ministry ▶ **ministère des Anciens Combattants** *Ministry responsible for ex-servicemen*, ≈ Veterans Administration (*US*) ▶ **ministère du Budget** Ministry of Finance, ≈ Treasury (*Brit*), ≈ Treasury Department (*US*) ▶ **ministère du Commer-**

ce Ministry of Trade, Department of Trade and Industry (*Brit*), Department of Commerce (*US*) ► **ministère du Commerce extérieur** Ministry of Foreign Trade, Board of Trade (*Brit*) ► **ministère de la Culture** Ministry for the Arts ► **ministère de la Défense nationale** Ministry of Defence (*Brit*), Department of Defense (*US*) ► **ministère des Départements et Territoires d'outre-mer** *Ministry for French overseas territories* ► **ministère de l'Économie et des Finances** Ministry of Finance, ≈ Treasury (*Brit*), ≈ Treasury Department (*US*) ► **ministère de l'Environnement** Ministry of the Environment, ≈ Department of the Environment (*Brit*), ≈ Environmental Protection Agency (*US*) ► **ministère de l'Industrie** ≈ Department of Trade and Industry (*Brit*), ≈ Department of Commerce (*US*) ► **ministère de l'Intérieur** Ministry of the Interior, ≈ Home Office (*Brit*) ► **ministère de la Jeunesse et des Sports** Ministry of Sport ► **ministère de la Justice** Ministry of Justice, Lord Chancellor's Office (*Brit*), Department of Justice (*US*) ► **ministère de la Santé** Ministry of Health, ≈ Department of Health and Social Security (*Brit*), ≈ Department of Health and Human Services (*US*) ► **ministère des Transports** Ministry of Transport (*Brit*), Department of Transportation (*US*) ► **ministère du Travail** Ministry of Employment (*Brit*), Department of Labor (*US*)

ministériel, -elle [ministeʀjɛl] ADJ [*document, solidarité*] ministerial; [*crise, remaniement*] cabinet (*épith*); **département ~** ministry, department (*surtout US*); **accéder à une fonction ministérielle** to become a minister → **arrêté, officier¹**

ministrable [ministʀabl] ADJ, NMF **il est ~ ◊ c'est un ~** he's a potential minister *ou* likely to be appointed minister, he's in line for a ministerial post

ministre [ministʀ] **1** NM **a** [*gouvernement*] minister (*Brit*), secretary (*surtout US*); **pourriez-vous nous dire Monsieur le ~ ...** could you tell us Minister (*Brit*), could you tell us Mr (*ou* Madam) Secretary (*US*) ...; **Premier ~** Prime Minister, Premier; **Madame/Monsieur le Premier ~** Prime Minister; **les ~s** the members of the cabinet; **~ de l'Agriculture/de l'Éducation (nationale)** minister (*Brit*) *ou* secretary (*surtout US*) of Agriculture/of Education, Agriculture/Education minister (*Brit*) *ou* secretary (*surtout US*); **~ délégué** minister of state (**à** for, **auprès de** reporting to), ≈ junior minister (*Brit*), ≈ undersecretary (*US*); **~ d'État** (*sans portefeuille*) minister without portfolio; (*de haut rang*) senior minister; **~ sans portefeuille** minister without portfolio → **2**; → **bureau, conseil, papier**
b (= *envoyé, ambassadeur*) envoy; **~ plénipotentiaire** (*minister*) plenipotentiary (*Brit*), ambassador plenipotentiary (*US*)
c (*Rel*) (*protestant*) minister, clergyman; (*catholique*) priest; **~ du culte** minister of religion; **~ de Dieu** minister of God
d (*littér* = *représentant*) agent
2 COMP ► **ministre des Affaires étrangères** Minister of Foreign Affairs, Foreign Secretary (*Brit*), ≈ Secretary of State (*US*) ► **ministre des Affaires européennes** Minister of European Affairs ► **ministre des Affaires sociales** Social Services Minister ► **ministre du Budget** Finance Minister *ou* Secretary, ≈ Chancellor of the Exchequer (*Brit*), ≈ Secretary of the Treasury (*US*) ► **ministre du Commerce** Minister of Trade (*Brit*), Secretary of Commerce (*US*) ► **ministre de la Culture** ≈ Minister for Arts ► **ministre de la Défense nationale** Defence Minister (*Brit*), Defense Secretary (*US*) ► **ministre des Départements et**

Territoires d'outre-mer *Minister for French overseas territories* ► **ministre de l'Économie et des Finances** Finance Minister *ou* Secretary, ≈ Chancellor of the Exchequer (*Brit*), ≈ Secretary of the Treasury (*US*) ► **ministre de l'Environnement** ≈ Minister of the Environment (*Brit*), ≈ Director of the Environmental Protection Agency (*US*) ► **ministre de l'Industrie** Secretary of State for Trade and Industry (*Brit*), Secretary of Commerce (*US*) ► **ministre de l'Intérieur** Minister of the Interior, Home Secretary (*Brit*), Secretary of the Interior (*US*) ► **ministre de la Jeunesse et des Sports** Sports Minister ► **ministre de la Justice** Minister of Justice, ≈ Lord Chancellor (*Brit*), ≈ Attorney General (*US*) ► **ministre de la Santé (et de la Sécurité sociale)** ≈ Minister of Health and Social Security (*Brit*), ≈ Secretary of Health and Human Services (*US*) ► **ministre des Transports** Minister of Transport (*Brit*), Transportation Secretary (*US*) ► **ministre du Travail** Minister of Employment, Labor Secretary (*US*)

Minitel® [minitɛl] NM Minitel®; **obtenir un renseignement par (le) ~** to get information on Minitel® → **rose**

┌── MINITEL ──┐

The Minitel *has been widely used in French businesses and households for many years, and despite the growing importance of the Internet it remains a familiar feature of daily life.* Minitel *is a public-access information system consisting of a small terminal with a built-in modem, screen and keyboard. Users key in the access code for the service they require, and pay for the time spent linked to the server as part of their regular telephone bill. The term "Minitel rose" refers to sex chatlines available on* Minitel.

---

minitéliste [minitelist] NMF Minitel user

minium [minjɔm] NM (*Chim*) red lead, minium; (*Peinture*) red lead paint

minivague [minivag] NF soft perm; **se faire faire une ~** to have a soft perm

Minnesota [minezɔta] NM Minnesota

minoen, -enne [minɔɛ̃, ɛn] ADJ, NM Minoan

minois [minwa] NM (= *visage*) little face; **son joli ~** her pretty little face

minoration [minɔʀasjɔ̃] NF (= *réduction*) cut, reduction (**de** in)

minorer [minɔʀe] ▸ conjug 1 ◂ VT **a** [+ *taux, impôts*] to cut, reduce (**de** by) **b** [+ *incident, importance*] to play down (the importance of)

minoritaire [minɔʀitɛʀ] **1** ADJ minority (*épith*); **groupe ~** minority group; **ils sont ~s** they are a minority, they are in a *ou* in the minority; **ils sont ~s au Parlement** they have a minority in Parliament → **2** NMF member of a minority party (*ou* group *etc*); **les ~s** the minority (party)

minorité [minɔʀite] NF **a** (= *âge*) (*gén*) minority; (*Jur*) minority, (legal) infancy, nonage; **pendant sa ~** while he is (*ou* was) under age, during his minority *ou* infancy (*Jur*); **~ pénale** ≈ legal infancy **b** (= *groupe*) minority (group); **~ ethnique/nationale** racial *ou* ethnic/national minority; **~ agissante/opprimée** active/oppressed minority; (*Écon*) **~ de blocage** blocking minority **c** **~ de** minority of; **dans la ~ des cas** in the minority of cases; **je m'adresse à une ~ d'auditeurs** I'm addressing a minority of listeners; **être en ~** to be in a *ou* in the minority, be a minority; **le gouvernement a été mis en ~ sur la question du budget** the government was defeated on the budget

Minorque [minɔʀk] NF Minorca

minorquin, e [minɔʀkɛ̃, in] **1** ADJ Minorcan **2 Minorquin(e)** NM,F Minorcan

Minos [minɔs] NM Minos

Minotaure [minɔtɔʀ] NM Minotaur

minoterie [minɔtʀi] NF (= *industrie*) flour-milling (industry); (= *usine*) (flour-)mill

minotier [minɔtje] NM miller

minou [minu] NM **a** (*langage enfantin* = *chat*) pussy(cat), puss* **b** (*terme d'affection*) **mon ~** sweetie(-pie)*, (my) pet* **c** (* = *sexe de femme*) pussy**

minuit [minɥi] NM midnight, twelve (o'clock) (at night); **à ~** at (twelve) midnight, at twelve (o'clock) (at night); **~ vingt** twenty past twelve *ou* midnight; (*hum*) **il est ~, l'heure du crime** it's midnight, the witching hour; **de ~** [*soleil, messe*] midnight (*épith*); **bain de ~** midnight *ou* moonlight swim

minus* [minys] NMF (*péj*) dead loss*, washout*; **viens ici, ~!** come over here, you wimp!*; **~ habens** moron

minuscule [minyskyl] **1** ADJ **a** (= *très petit*) minute, tiny, minuscule **b** (*Écriture*) small; (*Typo*) lower case; **h ~** small h **2** NF small letter; (*Typo*) lower case letter

minutage [minytaʒ] NM (strict *ou* precise) timing

minute [minyt] **1** NF **a** (= *division de l'heure, d'un degré*) minute; (= *moment*) minute, moment; **une ~ de silence** a minute's silence, a minute of silence; **la ~ de vérité** the moment of truth; **je n'ai pas une ~ à moi/à perdre** I don't have a minute *ou* moment to myself/to lose; **une ~ d'inattention a suffi** a moment's inattention was enough; **~ (papillon)!*** hey, just a minute!*, hold *ou* hang on (a minute)!*; **une ~, j'arrive!** just a second *ou* a minute, I'm coming!; **attendez une petite ~** can you wait just a *ou* half a minute?; **une (petite) ~! je n'ai jamais dit ça!** hang on a minute! I never said that!; **elle va arriver d'une ~ à l'autre** she'll be here any minute now; **en (l'espace de) cinq ~s, c'était fait** it was done in five minutes
b (*en apposition*) **steak *ou* entrecôte ~** minute steak; **"talons ~"** "shoes repaired while you wait", "heel bar"
c (*Jur*) [*contrat*] original draft; **les ~s de la réunion** the minutes of the meeting; **rédiger les ~s de qch** to minute sth
2 à la minute LOC ADV **on me l'a apporté à la ~** it has just this instant *ou* moment been brought to me; **avec toi, il faut toujours tout faire à la ~** you always have to have things done there and then *ou* on the spot; **réparations à la ~** on-the-spot repairs, repairs while you wait; **elle arrive toujours à la ~ (près)** she's always there on the dot*, she always arrives to the minute *ou* right on time*; **on n'est pas à la ~ près** there's no rush

minuter [minyte] ▸ conjug 1 ◂ VT **a** (= *chronométrer, limiter*) to time; (= *organiser*) to time to time (carefully *ou* to the last minute); **dans son emploi du temps tout est minuté** everything's worked out *ou* timed down to the last second in his timetable; **mon temps est minuté** I've got an extremely tight schedule **b** (*Jur*) to draw up, draft

minuterie [minytʀi] NF [*lumière*] time switch; [*horloge*] regulator; [*four*] timer; [*bombe*] timing device, timer; **allumer la ~** to switch on the (automatic) light (*on stairs, in passage etc*)

minuteur [minytœʀ] NM [*cafetière, four*] timer

minutie [minysi] NF **a** [*personne, travail*] meticulousness; **j'ai été frappé par la ~ de son inspection** I was amazed by the detail of his inspection, I was amazed how detailed his inspection was; **l'horlogerie demande beaucoup de ~** clock-making requires a great deal of precision; **avec ~** (= *avec soin*) meticulously; (= *dans le détail*) in minute detail **b** (= *détails : péj*) **~s** trifles, trifling details, minutiae

minutieusement [minysjøzmɑ̃] ADV (= *avec soin*) meticulously; (= *dans le détail*) in minute detail

minutieux, -ieuse [minysjø, jøz] ADJ [*personne, soin*] meticulous; [*dessin*] minutely detailed; [*description, inspection*] minute; **il s'agit d'un travail ~** it's a job that demands painstaking attention to detail; **c'est une opération minutieuse** it's an operation demanding great care, it's an extremely delicate operation; **il est très ~** he is very meticulous

miocène [mjɔsɛn] **1** ADJ Miocene **2** NM **le Miocène** the Miocene

mioche* [mjɔʃ] NMF (= *gosse*) kid*, nipper* (*Brit*); (*péj*) brat*; **sale ~!** dirty *ou* horrible little brat!*

mi-pente [mipɑ̃t] ◆ **à mi-pente** LOC ADV halfway up *ou* down the hill

mirabelle [miʀabɛl] NF (= *prune*) cherry plum; (= *alcool*) plum brandy

mirabellier [miʀabelje] NM cherry-plum tree

miracle [miʀakl] **1** NM **a** (*lit, fig*) miracle; **~ économique** economic miracle; **son œuvre est un ~ d'équilibre** his work is a miracle *ou* marvel of balance; **cela tient** *ou* **relève du ~** it's a miracle; **faire** *ou* **accomplir des ~s** (*lit*) to work *ou* do *ou* accomplish miracles; (*fig*) to work wonders *ou* miracles; **c'est ~ qu'il résiste dans ces conditions** it's a wonder *ou* a miracle he manages to cope in these conditions; **il faudrait une ~ pour qu'il soit élu** nothing short of a miracle will get him elected, it'll take a miracle for him to get elected; **par ~** miraculously, by a *ou* by some miracle; (*iro*) **comme par ~!** surprise, surprise! → **crier b** (*Hist, Littérat*) miracle (play)

2 ADJ INV **remède/solution ~** miracle cure/solution; **potion ~** magic potion; **il n'y a pas de recette ~** there's no miracle solution; **médicament ~** wonder *ou* miracle drug

miraculé, e [miʀakyle] ADJ, NM,F **(malade) ~** (person) who has been miraculously cured *ou* who has been cured by a miracle; **les trois ~s de la route** the three (people) who miraculously *ou* who by some miracle survived the accident; (*hum*) **voilà le ~!** here comes the miraculous survivor!

miraculeusement [miʀakyløzmɑ̃] ADV miraculously

miraculeux, -euse [miʀakylø, øz] ADJ [*guérison*] miraculous; [*progrès, réussite*] wonderful; **traitement** *ou* **remède ~** miracle cure; **ça n'a rien de ~** there's nothing so miraculous *ou* extraordinary about that

mirador [miʀadɔʀ] NM (*Mil*) watchtower, mirador; (*pour l'observation d'animaux*) raised (observation) hide; (*Archit*) belvedere, mirador

mirage [miʀaʒ] NM **a** (*lit, fig*) mirage; (*hum*) **c'est un ~!** you (*ou* I *etc*) must be seeing things! **b** [*œufs*] candling

miraud, e* [miʀo, od] ADJ (= *myope*) shortsighted; **tu es ~!** you need glasses!; **il est complètement ~** he's as blind as a bat

mire [miʀ] NF (*TV*) test card; (*Arpentage*) surveyor's rod; **prendre sa ~** (= *viser*) to take aim; **point de ~** (*lit*) target; (*fig*) focal point → **cran, ligne**[1]

mire-œufs [miʀø] NM INV light (*for candling eggs*)

mirer [miʀe] ▸ conjug 1 ◂ **1** VT **a** [+ œufs] to candle **b** (*littér*) to mirror **2 se mirer** VPR (*littér*) [*personne*] to gaze at o.s. *ou* at one's reflection (*in the mirror, water etc*); [*chose*] to be mirrored *ou* reflected (*in the water etc*)

mirettes* [miʀɛt] NFPL eyes, peepers* (*hum*); **ils en ont pris plein les ~** they were completely dazzled by it

mirifique [miʀifik] ADJ (*hum*) wonderful, fantastic

mirliflore†† [miʀliflɔʀ] NM fop†, coxcomb†; (*péj*) **faire le ~** to put on foppish airs†, play the fine fellow

---

mirliton [miʀlitɔ̃] NM (*Mus*) reed pipe, mirliton; [*carnaval*] novelty whistle, kazoo → **vers**

mirmidon [miʀmidɔ̃] NM = **myrmidon**

mirobolant, e* [miʀɔbɔlɑ̃, ɑ̃t] ADJ (*hum*) [*contrat, salaire*] fabulous, fantastic; [*résultats*] brilliant

miroir [miʀwaʀ] **1** NM (*lit*) mirror; (*fig*) mirror, reflection; (*littér*) **le ~ des eaux** the glassy waters; **un roman n'est jamais le ~ de la réalité** a novel is never a true reflection of reality *ou* never really mirrors reality; **écriture/image en ~** mirror writing/image **2** COMP ▶ **miroir aux alouettes** (*lit*) decoy; (*fig*) lure ▶ **miroir de courtoisie** (*Aut*) vanity mirror ▶ **miroir déformant** distorting mirror ▶ **miroir d'eau** ornamental pond ▶ **miroir grossissant** magnifying mirror

miroitant, e [miʀwatɑ̃, ɑ̃t] ADJ [*collier, vitres*] sparkling; [*métal*] gleaming; [*eau, lac*] sparkling, shimmering; [*étoffe*] shimmering

miroitement [miʀwatmɑ̃] NM (= *étincellement*) sparkling (*NonC*), gleaming (*NonC*); (= *chatoiement*) shimmering (*NonC*)

miroiter [miʀwate] ▸ conjug 1 ◂ VI **a** (= *étinceler*) to sparkle, gleam; (= *chatoyer*) to shimmer; (= *faire entrevoir*) **il lui fit ~ les avantages qu'elle aurait à accepter ce poste** he painted in glowing colours what she stood to gain from taking the job

miroiterie [miʀwatʀi] NF **a** (*Comm*) mirror trade; (*Ind*) mirror industry **b** (= *usine*) mirror factory

miroitier, -ière [miʀwatje, jɛʀ] NM,F (= *vendeur*) mirror dealer; (= *fabricant*) mirror manufacturer; (= *artisan*) mirror cutter, silverer

mironton* [miʀɔ̃tɔ̃], **miroton** [miʀɔtɔ̃] NM **(bœuf) miroton** boiled beef in onion sauce

mis, e[1]† [mi, miz] (*ptp de* **mettre**) ADJ (= *vêtu*) attired†, clad; **bien ~** nicely turned out

misaine [mizɛn] NF **(voile de) ~** foresail → **mât**

misanthrope [mizɑ̃tʀɔp] **1** ADJ [*attitude*] misanthropic; **il est devenu très ~** he's come to dislike everyone *ou* to hate society, he's turned into a real misanthropist **2** NMF misanthropist, misanthrope

misanthropie [mizɑ̃tʀɔpi] NF misanthropy

misanthropique [mizɑ̃tʀɔpik] ADJ (*frm*) misanthropic, misanthropical

miscellanées [miselane] NFPL miscellanea

miscible [misibl] ADJ miscible (**à** with)

mise² [miz] **1** NF **a** (= *enjeu*) stake, ante; (*Comm*) outlay; **récupérer sa ~** to recoup one's outlay; **gagner 1000 F pour une ~ de 100 F** to make 1 000 francs on an outlay of 100 francs → **sauver b** (= *habillement*) attire, clothing, garb (*hum*); **avoir une ~ débraillée** to be untidily dressed, have an untidy appearance; **juger qn sur** *ou* **à sa ~** to judge sb by his clothes *ou* by what he wears; **soigner sa ~** to take pride in one's appearance **c être de ~** (†† *Fin*) to be in circulation, be legal currency; (*fig*) to be acceptable, be in place *ou* season; **ces propos ne sont pas de ~** those remarks are out of place **2** (= *action de mettre*) putting, setting → **boîte, bouteille** etc **2** COMP ▶ **mise en plis** (*Coiffure*) set; **se faire faire une ~ en plis** to have a set, have one's hair set; (*pour autres expressions voir sous le second terme*)

miser [mize] ▸ conjug 1 ◂ VT **a** (= *parier*) [+ argent] to stake, bet (**sur** on); **~ sur un cheval** to bet on a horse, put money on a horse; **à 8 contre 1** to bet at odds of 8 to 1, take 8 to 1; (*fig*) **il a misé sur le mauvais cheval** he backed the wrong horse → **tableau b** (* = *compter sur*) to bank on, count on **c** (*Helv*) (= *vendre*) to sell by auction; (= *acheter*) to buy by auction; **~ sur qn** to overbid sb

---

misérabilisme [mizeʀabilism] NM misérabilism, tendency to dwell on the sordid side of life

misérabiliste [mizeʀabilist] ADJ [*personne*] miserabilist, who dwells on the sordid side of life; [*livre, film*] which dwells on the sordid side of life

misérable [mizeʀabl] **1** ADJ **a** (= *pauvre*) [*famille, personne*] destitute, poverty-stricken; [*région*] impoverished, poverty-stricken; [*logement*] seedy, mean, dingy; [*vêtements*] shabby; **d'aspect ~** shabby-looking, seedy-looking **b** (= *pitoyable*) [*existence, conditions*] miserable, wretched, pitiful; [*personne, famille*] pitiful, wretched **c** (= *sans valeur, minable*) [*somme d'argent*] paltry, miserable; **un salaire ~** a pittance, a miserable salary; **ne te mets pas en colère pour 20 ~s francs** don't get all worked up about a measly* 20 francs **d** (††, *littér* = *méprisable*) vile†, base†, contemptible **2** NMF (†, *littér*) (= *méchant*) wretch, scoundrel; (= *pauvre*) poor wretch; **petit ~!** you (little) rascal! *ou* wretch!

misérablement [mizeʀabləmɑ̃] ADV (= *pitoyablement*) miserably, wretchedly; (= *pauvrement*) in great *ou* wretched poverty

misère [mizeʀ] NF **a** (= *pauvreté*) (extreme) poverty, destitution (*frm*); **la ~ en gants blancs** *ou* **dorée** genteel poverty; **être dans la ~** to be destitute *ou* poverty-stricken; **vivre dans la ~** to live in poverty; **tomber dans la ~** to fall on hard *ou* bad times, become destitute; **traitement** *ou* **salaire de ~** starvation wage; **~ noire** utter destitution; **réduire qn à la ~** to make sb destitute, reduce sb to a state of (dire) poverty; **crier** *ou* **pleurer ~** (*pour ne pas payer*) to plead poverty; (*pour obtenir de l'argent*) **il est venu chez nous crier** *ou* **pleurer ~** he came to us begging for money, he came to us with a sob story* about having no money **b** (= *carence*) **~ culturelle** lack of culture; **~ sexuelle** sexual deprivation; **~ physiologique** malnutrition **c** (= *malheur*) **~s** woes, miseries, misfortunes; (* = *ennuis*) **petites ~s** little troubles; **faire des ~s à qn*** to be nasty to sb; **les ~s de la guerre** the miseries of war; **c'est une ~ de la voir s'anémier** it's pitiful *ou* wretched to see her growing weaker; **quelle ~!** what a wretched shame!; († *littér*) **~!** ◊ **~ de moi!** woe is me!† (*hum*); (*Rel*) **la ~ de l'homme** man's wretchedness **d** (= *somme négligeable*) **il l'a eu pour une ~** he got it for a song* *ou* for next to nothing; **c'est une ~ pour eux** that's nothing *ou* a trifle to them **e** (= *plante*) tradescantia, wandering Jew

miserere, miséréré [mizeʀeʀe] NM (= *psaume, chant*) Miserere

miséreux, -euse [mizeʀø, øz] **1** ADJ [*existence, ville*] poverty-stricken; [*population, famille*] destitute **2** NM,F destitute person; **les ~** the destitute

miséricorde [mizeʀikɔʀd] **1** NF **a** (= *pitié*) mercy, forgiveness; **la ~ divine** divine mercy → **péché b** (*stalle*) misericord **2** EXCL † mercy me!†, mercy on us!†

miséricordieux, -ieuse [mizeʀikɔʀdjø, jøz] ADJ merciful, forgiving

miso [mizo] NM miso

misogyne [mizɔʒin] **1** ADJ misogynous **2** NMF misogynist, woman-hater

misogynie [mizɔʒini] NF misogyny

miss [mis] NF **a** [*concours de beauté*] beauty queen; **Miss France** Miss France **b** († = *nurse*) (English *ou* American) governess **c** (= *vieille demoiselle*) **~ anglaise** elderly English spinster

missel [misɛl] NM missal

missile [misil] NM (*Aviat*) missile; **~ antichar/antiaérien** antitank/antiaircraft missile; **~ antimissile** antimissile missile; **~ nucléaire/balistique** nuclear/ballistic missile; **~ sol-sol/**

sol-air etc ground-to-ground/ground-(to)-air etc missile; **~ de moyenne portée** ou **de portée intermédiaire** intermediate-range weapon ou missile; **~ tactique/de croisière** tactical/cruise missile; **~ de courte/longue portée** short-/long-range missile; **~ à tête chercheuse** homing missile

mission [misjɔ̃] NF a (= charge, tâche) (gén, Rel) mission; (Pol) mission, assignment; [intérimaire] brief, assignment; **~ lui fut donnée de ...** he was commissioned to ...; **partir/être en ~** (Admin, Mil) to go/be on an assignment; [prêtre] to go/be on a mission; **accomplie** mission accomplished; (Mil) **~ de reconnaissance** reconnaissance mission, recce* (Brit); **~ diplomatique/scientifique/d'information** diplomatic/scientific/fact-finding mission; **~ impossible** (lit) impossible task; (hum) mission impossible **→ chargé, ordre²** b (= but, vocation) task, mission; **la ~ de la littérature** the task of literature; **il s'est donné pour ~ de faire cela** he set himself the task of doing it, he has made it his mission (in life) to do it c (Rel) (= bâtiment) mission (station); (= groupe) mission

missionnaire [misjɔnɛʀ] ADJ, NMF missionary

Mississippi [misisipi] NM Mississippi

missive [misiv] 1 ADJ F (Jur) (lettre) ~ document (in the form of a letter, postcard or telegram) 2 NF (hum = lettre) missive

Missouri [misuʀi] NM Missouri

mistigri [mistigʀi] NM a (†,* = chat) malkin† b (Cartes) jack of clubs; (fig) **repasser** ou **refiler* le ~ à qn** to leave sb holding the baby

mistoufle ††* [mistufl] NF **être dans la ~** to have hit it hard ou bad times, be on one's beam ends* (Brit)

mistral [mistʀal] NM mistral

mitage [mitaʒ] NM **le ~ des campagnes** intensive building of houses in the countryside

mitaine [mitɛn] NF (fingerless) mitten ou mitt

mitan [mitɑ̃] NM (†† ou dial) middle, centre; **dans le ~ de** in the middle of

mitard [mitaʀ] NM (arg Crime) solitary*; **il a fait 15 jours de ~** he did 2 weeks (in) solitary*

mite [mit] NF clothes moth; **mangé aux ~s** moth-eaten; **~ du fromage** cheese mite; **avoir la ~ à l'œil** †* to have sleep in one's eyes

mité, e [mite] (ptp de **se miter**) ADJ moth-eaten

mi-temps [mitɑ̃] 1 NF INV (Sport) (= période) half; (= repos) half-time; **à la ~** at half-time; **première/seconde ~** first/second half; **l'arbitre a sifflé la ~** the referee blew (the whistle) for half-time; (hum) **la troisième ~** the post-match celebrations 2 NM (travail à) part-time work; **~ thérapeutique** part-time working hours granted for medical reasons; **à ~** part-time; **travailler à ~** to work part-time, do part-time work; **elle est serveuse à ~** she's a part-time waitress

miter (se) [mite] ▸conjug 1◂ VPR to be ou become moth-eaten; **pour éviter que les vêtements se mitent** to stop the moths getting at the clothes

miteux, -euse [mitø, øz] 1 ADJ [lieu] seedy, grotty* (Brit); [vêtement] shabby, tatty*, grotty* (Brit); [personne] shabby(-looking), seedy(-looking) 2 NM,F seedy(-looking) character

Mithridate [mitʀidat] NM Mithridates

mithridatisation [mitʀidatizasjɔ̃] NF, **mithridatisme** [mitʀidatism] NM mithridatism

mithridatiser [mitʀidatize] ▸conjug 1◂ VT ~ **qn** to mithridatize sb (SPÉC), to make sb immune to a poison by administering small doses in gradually increasing amounts; **mithridatisé** immunized

mitigation [mitigasjɔ̃] NF (Jur) mitigation

mitigé, e [mitiʒe] (ptp de **mitiger**) ADJ [ardeur] mitigated; [accueil, convictions, enthousiasme] lukewarm, half-hearted; **sentiments ~s** mixed

feelings; **joie ~e de regrets** joy mixed ou mingled with regret

mitiger† [mitiʒe] ▸conjug 3◂ VT to mitigate

mitigeur [mitiʒœʀ] NM mixer tap (Brit) ou faucet (US); **~ thermostatique** temperature control tap (Brit) ou faucet (US)

mitochondrie [mitɔkɔ̃dʀi] NF mitochondrion

mitonner [mitɔne] ▸conjug 1◂ 1 VT a (Culin) (à feu doux) to simmer, cook slowly; (avec soin) to prepare ou cook with loving care; **elle (lui) mitonne des petits plats** she cooks (up) ou concocts tasty dishes (for him) b * [+ affaire] to cook up quietly*; [+ personne] to cosset 2 VI to simmer, cook slowly

mitose [mitoz] NF mitosis; **se reproduire par ~** to replicate; **reproduction par ~** replication

mitoyen, -yenne [mitwajɛ̃, jɛn] ADJ [bâtiments, jardins] adjoining; **mur ~** party wall; **cloison mitoyenne** partition wall; **maisons mitoyennes** (deux) semi-detached houses (Brit), duplex houses (US); (plus de deux) terraced houses (Brit), town houses (US); **notre jardin est ~ avec le leur** our garden adjoins theirs

mitoyenneté [mitwajɛnte] NF [mur] common ownership; **la ~ des maisons** the (existence of a) party wall between the houses

mitraillade [mitʀajad] NF a (= coups de feu) (volley of) shots; (= échauffourée) exchange of shots b = **mitraillage**

mitraillage [mitʀajaʒ] NM machine-gunning; **~ au sol** strafing

mitraille [mitʀaj] NF a († Mil) (= projectiles) grapeshot; (= décharge) volley of shots, hail of bullets; **fuir sous la ~** to flee under a hail of bullets b (* = petite monnaie) loose ou small change

mitrailler [mitʀaje] ▸conjug 1◂ VT a (Mil) to machine-gun; **~ au sol** to strafe; **~ qn de cailloux/grains de riz** to pelt sb with stones/grains of rice b (* = photographier) [+ monument] to take shot after shot of; **les touristes mitraillaient la cathédrale** the tourists' cameras were clicking away madly at the cathedral; **être mitraillé par les photographes** to be mobbed ou besieged by the photographers c **~ qn de questions** to bombard sb with questions, fire questions at sb

mitraillette [mitʀajɛt] NF submachine gun; **tirer à la ~** to shoot ou fire with a submachine gun

mitrailleur [mitʀajœʀ] NM (Mil) machine gunner; (Aviat) air gunner

mitrailleuse [mitʀajøz] NF machine gun

mitral, e (mpl **-aux**) [mitʀal, o] ADJ (Anat) mitral

mitre [mitʀ] NF a (Rel) mitre; **recevoir** ou **coiffer la ~** to be appointed bishop, be mitred b [cheminée] cowl

mitré, e [mitʀe] ADJ mitred **→ abbé**

mitron [mitʀɔ̃] NM a (= boulanger) baker's boy; (= pâtissier) pastrycook's boy b [cheminée] chimney top

mi-vitesse [mivitɛs] ◆à mi-vitesse LOC ADV at half speed

mi-voix [mivwa] ◆à mi-voix LOC ADV [parler] in a low ou hushed voice; [lire] in a low voice; [chantonner] softly

mixage [miksaʒ] NM (Ciné, Radio) (sound) mixing

mixer¹ [mikse] ▸conjug 1◂ VT (Ciné, Radio) to mix; (Culin) to blend

mixer², mixeur [miksœʀ] NM (Culin) blender, liquidizer (Brit)

mixité [miksite] NF (de sexes) (gén) mixing of the sexes; (Scol) coeducation; **il faut une plus grande ~ sociale/de l'habitat dans nos villes** we need a greater social mix/more variety of housing in our towns

mixte [mikst] ADJ a (= des deux sexes) [équipe] mixed; [classe, école, enseignement] mixed, coeducational, coed*; (= de races différentes) [cou-

ple, mariage] mixed **→ double** b (= d'éléments divers) [économie, train] mixed (épith); [équipe] combined (épith); [tribunal, commission] joint; [rôle] dual (épith); (Chim, Géog) [roche, végétation] mixed; **outil à usage ~** dual-purpose tool; **peau ~** combination skin; **navire** ou **cargo ~** cargo-passenger ship ou vessel; **cuisinière ~** combined gas and electric stove ou cooker (Brit); **l'opéra-bouffe est un genre ~** comic opera is a mixture of genres

mixtion [mikstjɔ̃] NF (Chim, Pharm) (= action) blending, compounding; (= médicament) mixture

mixture [mikstyʀ] NF (Chim, Pharm) mixture; (Culin) mixture, concoction; (péj) concoction

MJC [ɛmʒise] NF (ABRÉV = **maison des jeunes et de la culture**) **→ maison**

ml (ABRÉV = **millilitre**) ml

MLF [ɛmɛlɛf] NM (ABRÉV = **Mouvement de libération de la femme**) Women's Liberation Movement, Women's Lib*

Mlle (ABRÉV = **Mademoiselle**) **~ Martin** Miss Martin

Mlles (ABRÉV = **Mesdemoiselles**) **→ Mademoiselle**

MM (ABRÉV = **Messieurs**) Messrs

mm (ABRÉV = **millimètre**) mm

Mme (ABRÉV = **Madame**) Mrs; **~ Martin** Mrs Martin

Mmes (ABRÉV = **Mesdames**) **→ Madame**

mn (ABRÉV = **minute**) min

mnémonique [mnemɔnik] ADJ mnemonic

mnémotechnique [mnemotɛknik] 1 ADJ mnemonic 2 NF mnemonics sg, mnemotechnics sg

Mo (ABRÉV = **mégaoctet**) Mb, MB

mob* [mɔb] NF ABRÉV = **mobylette**

mobile [mɔbil] 1 ADJ a [pièce, objet] (= qui bouge) moving; (= qui peut bouger) movable; [feuillets de cahier, calendrier] loose **→ échelle, fête** b [main-d'œuvre, population] mobile c [reflet] changing; [traits] mobile, animated; [regard, yeux] mobile, darting (épith) d [troupes] mobile; **boxeur très ~** boxer who is very quick on his feet, nimble-footed boxer; **avec la voiture on est très ~** you can really get around ou about with a car, having a car makes you very mobile **→ garde¹, garde²** 2 NM a (= impulsion) motive (de for); **quel était le ~ de son action?** what was the motive for ou what prompted his action?; **chercher le ~ du crime** to look for the motive for the crime b (Art, Jeux) mobile c (Phys) moving object ou body d (téléphone) ~ mobile phone 3 COMP ► **mobile home** mobile home

mobilier, -ière [mɔbilje, jɛʀ] 1 ADJ (Jur) [propriété, bien] movable, personal; [valeurs] transferable; **saisie/vente mobilière** seizure/sale of personal ou movable property; **contribution** ou **cote mobilière**† property tax 2 NM a (= ameublement) furniture; **le ~ du salon** the lounge furniture; **nous avons un ~ Louis XV** our furniture is Louis XV, our house is furnished in Louis XV (style); (hum) **il fait partie du ~** he's part of the furniture (hum); **~ de bureau** office furniture; **~ urbain** street furniture; **le Mobilier national** state-owned furniture (used to furnish buildings of the state) b (Jur) personal ou movable property

mobilisable [mɔbilizabl] ADJ [citoyen] who can be called up ou mobilized; [énergie, ressources] that can be mobilized; [capitaux] mobilizable; (Mil) **il n'est pas ~** he cannot be called up

mobilisateur, -trice [mɔbilizatœʀ, tʀis] ADJ **slogan/projet ~** slogan/plan which will stir people into action; **c'est un thème très ~ chez les étudiants** it's an issue about which students have strong feelings ou that rouses students to action; **il faut définir de nouveaux**

objectifs ~s new objectives capable of attracting people's support *ou* of having direct appeal for people must be defined

mobilisation [mɔbilizasjɔ̃] NF a [*citoyens*] mobilization, calling up; [*troupes, ressources*] mobilization; (*Physiol*) mobilization; ~ **générale/partielle** general/partial mobilization; **il appelle à la ~ de tous contre le racisme** he's calling on everybody to join forces and fight racism b (*Fin*) [*fonds*] mobilization of realty, raising; ~ **d'actif** conversion into movable property, mobilization of realty (*US*)

mobiliser [mɔbilize] ▸ conjug 1 ◂ 1 VT a (= *faire appel à*) [+ *citoyens*] to call up, mobilize; [+ *troupes, ressources, adhérents*] to mobilize; [+ *fonds*] to raise, mobilize; ~ **les enthousiasmes** to summon up *ou* mobilize people's enthusiasm; ~ **les esprits (en faveur d'une cause)** to rally people's interest (in a cause); **les (soldats) mobilisés** the mobilized troops; **tout le monde était mobilisé pour la servir** everyone was put to work attending to her needs, everyone had to jump to (it) and attend to her needs b (*Méd* = *faire bouger*) [+ *articulation, muscle*] to control

2 **se mobiliser** VPR [*personnes*] to join forces (and take action) (**contre** against); **il faut se ~ contre le chômage/pour la sauvegarde de nos droits** we must join forces and fight unemployment/to protect our rights; **ils se sont mobilisés autour du Premier ministre** they rallied around the Prime Minister

mobilité [mɔbilite] NF (*gén*) mobility; ~ **géographique/professionnelle/sociale** geographic/professional/social mobility; ~ **sociale ascendante** upward (social) mobility; (*sur CV*) « **~ géographique totale** » "willing to relocate"; **la ~ de son regard** his darting eyes; **la voiture nous permet une plus grande ~** having the car means we can get around more easily *ou* makes us more mobile

Möbius [møbjys] NM (*Math*) **bande** *ou* **ruban de ~** Möbius strip *ou* band

Mobylette® [mɔbilɛt] NF moped

mocassin [mɔkasɛ̃] NM (*gén*) moccasin, loafer; (*indien*) moccasin

moche* [mɔʃ] ADJ a (= *laid*) ugly; ~ **comme un pou** as ugly as sin b (= *mauvais, méchant*) rotten*, nasty; **tu es ~ avec elle** you're rotten* to her; **c'est ~ ce qu'il a fait** that was a nasty thing he did; **c'est ~ ce qui lui arrive** it's awful what's happening to him

mocheté* [mɔʃte] NF a (= *laideur*) ugliness b (= *personne*) fright; (= *objet, bâtiment*) eyesore; **c'est une vraie ~!** she's an absolute fright! *ou* as ugly as sin!

modal, e (*mpl* **-aux**) [mɔdal, o] 1 ADJ modal 2 NM (= *verbe*) modal (verb)

modalité [mɔdalite] NF a (= *forme*) form, mode; (= *méthode*) method; ~ **d'application de la loi** mode of enforcement of the law; ~**s de remboursement** methods of funding; ~**s de remboursement** terms of repayment; ~**s de paiement** methods *ou* modes of payment; (*Jur*) ~**s de mise en œuvre** details of implementation; (*Scol*) ~**s de contrôle** methods of assessment b (*Ling, Mus, Philo*) modality; **adverbe de ~** modal adverb c (*Jur* = *condition*) clause

mode¹ [mɔd] 1 NF a (= *tendance*) fashion; (*péj*) fad*, craze; **la ~ des années 60** Sixties' fashions; **la ~ automne-hiver de cette année** this year's autumn and winter fashions; **c'est la dernière ~** it's the very latest thing *ou* fashion; **suivre la ~** to follow fashion, keep up with the fashions; (*péj*) **une de ces nouvelles ~s** one of these new fads* *ou* crazes; **passer de ~** [*vêtement*] to go out of fashion; [*pratique*] to become outdated; **c'est passé de ~** [*vêtement*] it's gone out of fashion; [*pratique*] it's outdated; **c'est la ~ des talons hauts** high heels are in fashion *ou* are in*; **marchande de ~s**††

milliner

b **à la ~** fashionable, in fashion; **femme très à la ~** very fashionable woman; **les jupes courtes sont très à la ~** short skirts are very much in fashion *ou* are really in* *ou* are all the rage*; **être habillé très à la ~** (*gén*) to be very fashionably dressed; [*jeunes*] to be very trendily* dressed; **habillé à la dernière ~** dressed in the latest fashion *ou* style; **mettre qch à la ~** to make sth fashionable, bring sth into fashion; **revenir à la ~** to come back into fashion *ou* vogue, to come back (in)*

c (*Comm, Ind*) **la ~** the fashion industry *ou* business; **travailler dans la ~** to work *ou* be in the fashion world *ou* industry *ou* business; **journal/présentation/rédactrice de ~** fashion magazine/show/editor → **gravure**

d † (= *mœurs*) custom; (= *goût, style*) style, fashion; **selon la ~ de l'époque** according to the custom of the day; (*habillé*) **à l'ancienne ~** (dressed) in the old style; (*hum*) **cousin à la ~ de Bretagne** distant cousin, cousin six times removed (*hum*); (*Jur, hum*) **oncle** *ou* **neveu à la ~ de Bretagne** first cousin once removed; **à la ~ du 18e siècle** in the style of *ou* after the fashion of the 18th century, in 18th century style → **bœuf**, **tripe**

2 ADJ INV [*coiffure*] fashionable; **tissu ~** fashion fabric; **coloris ~** fashion *ou* fashionable colours; **c'est très ~** it's very fashionable

mode² [mɔd] NM a (= *méthode*) form, mode, method; (= *genre*) way; **quel est le ~ d'action de ce médicament?** how does this medicine work?; ~ **de gouvernement/de transport** mode of government/of transport; ~ **de scrutin** voting system; ~ **de pensée/de vie** way of thinking/of life; ~ **de paiement** method *ou* mode of payment; ~ **d'emploi** (*gén*) directions for use; (= *document*) instructions leaflet; ~ **de cuisson** (*gén*) cooking method; (*sur boîte, paquet*) cooking instructions; ~ **de calcul/fonctionnement** way of calculating/working; ~ **de production** mode *ou* method of production; ~ **de gestion** management method b (*Gram, Ling*) mood; (*Mus, Philo*) mode; **au ~ subjonctif** in the subjunctive mood c (*Ordin*) mode; ~ **synchrone / asynchrone / interactif / émulation / natif** synchronous/asynchronous/interactive/emulation/native mode; **fonctionner en ~ local** to operate in local mode

modelage [mɔd(ə)laʒ] NM (= *activité*) modelling; (= *ouvrage*) model

modelé [mɔd(ə)le] NM [*sculpture, corps*] contours; (*Géog*) relief

modèle [mɔdɛl] 1 NM a (*Comm*) model; (*Mode*) design, style; **nous avons tous nos ~s en vitrine** our full range is *ou* all our models are in the window; **petit/grand ~** small/large version *ou* model; (*boîte*) **voulez-vous le petit ou le grand ~?** do you want the small or the big size (box)?; (*voiture*) **il a le ~ 5 portes** he has the 5-door hatchback model *ou* version; **Chanel présente ses ~s d'automne** Chanel presents its autumn models *ou* styles b (*à reproduire, à imiter*) pattern, model; (*Scol* = *corrigé*) fair copy; **fabriquer qch d'après le ~** to make sth from the model *ou* pattern; **faire qch sur le ~ de ...** to model sth on ..., make sth on the pattern *ou* model of ...; ~ **de conjugaison/déclinaison** conjugation/declension pattern; **son courage devrait nous servir de ~** his courage should be a model *ou* an example to us; **c'est un ~ du genre** it's a model of the genre c (= *personne exemplaire*) model, example; ~ **de vertu** paragon of virtue; **c'est le ~ du bon élève/ouvrier** he's a model pupil/workman, he's the epitome of the good pupil/workman; **elle est un ~ de loyauté** she is a model *ou* the very model of loyalty; **il restera pour nous un ~** he will remain an example to us; **prendre qn pour ~** to model *ou* pattern o.s. upon sb

d (*Art*) model; **dessiner/peindre d'après ~** to draw/paint from a model *ou* from life

2 ADJ (= *parfait*) [*conduite, ouvrier, mari, usine*] model (*épith*); (= *de référence*) [*appartement*] show (*épith*); **petite fille ~** perfect little girl

3 COMP ▸ **modèle courant** standard *ou* production model ▸ **modèle déposé** registered design ▸ **modèle économique** (*Écon*) economic model ▸ **modèle économique** (= *paquet géant*) economy-size pack; (= *voiture*) economy model ▸ **modèle de fabrique** factory model ▸ **modèle réduit** small-scale model; ~ **réduit au 1/100** model on the scale (of) 1 to 100; ~ **réduit d'avion** ◊ **avion ~ réduit** model plane, scale model of a plane; **monter des ~s réduits d'avions/de bateaux** to build model aircraft/ships ▸ **modèle de série** = **modèle courant**

modeler [mɔd(ə)le] ▸ conjug 5 ◂ VT a (= *façonner*) [+ *statue, poterie, glaise*] to model; [+ *corps*] to shape; [+ *chevelure*] to style; [+ *intelligence, caractère*] to shape, mould (*Brit*), mold (*US*); **le relief a été modelé par la glaciation** the ground *ou* the terrain was moulded *ou* shaped by glaciation; **cuisse bien modelée** shapely thigh → **pâte** b (= *conformer*) ~ **ses attitudes/réactions sur** to model one's attitudes/reactions on; **se ~ sur qn/qch** to model *ou* pattern o.s. (up)on sb/sth

modeleur, -euse [mɔd(ə)lœr, øz] NM,F (*Art*) 'modeller; (*Tech*) pattern maker

modélisation [mɔdelizasjɔ̃] NF modelling; ~ **par** *ou* **sur ordinateur** computer modelling

modéliser [mɔdelize] ▸ conjug 1 ◂ VT to model

modélisme [mɔdelism] NM model building

modéliste [mɔdelist] NMF a [*mode*] (dress) designer b [*maquettes*] model maker

modem [mɔdɛm] NM (ABRÉV = **modulateur-démodulateur**) modem; ~ **courte/longue distance** limited-distance/long-haul modem; **transmettre des données par ~** to transmit data via *ou* by modem

modérantisme [mɔderɑ̃tism] NM (*Hist*) moderantism

modérantiste [mɔderɑ̃tist] ADJ, NMF (*Hist*) moderantist

modérateur, -trice [mɔderatœr, tris] 1 ADJ [*action, influence*] moderating (*épith*), restraining (*épith*) → **ticket** 2 NM (*Tech*) regulator; (*Nucl Phys*) moderator; (*fig*) **jouer le rôle de ~** to have a moderating influence, play a moderating role

modération [mɔderasjɔ̃] NF a (= *retenue*) moderation, restraint; **avec ~** [*réagir*] with restraint; [*utiliser*] sparingly; **faire preuve de ~ dans ses propos** to adopt a moderate tone b (= *diminution*) [*inflation, impôt, vitesse*] reduction (**de** in); (*Jur*) [*peine*] mitigation

modéré, e [mɔdere] (*ptp de* **modérer**) ADJ [*personne*] (*dans ses idées*) moderate; (*dans ses désirs*) moderate, restrained; (*Pol*) moderate (**dans** in); [*prix*] reasonable, moderate; [*hausse, chaleur, vent*] moderate; (*Pol*) **les ~s** the moderates; **il a tenu des propos très ~s** he took a very moderate line in the discussion, he was very restrained in what he said; **d'un optimisme ~** cautiously *ou* guardedly optimistic → **habitation**

modérément [mɔderemɑ̃] ADV [*boire, manger*] in moderation; [*satisfait*] moderately; **je n'apprécie que ~ ses plaisanteries** I find his jokes only half funny; **il se montre ~ optimiste** he's cautiously *ou* guardedly optimistic

modérer [mɔdere] ▸ conjug 6 ◂ 1 VT [+ *colère, passion*] to restrain; [+ *ambitions, exigences*] to moderate; [+ *dépenses, désir, appétit*] to curb; [+ *vitesse*] to reduce; [+ *impact négatif*] to reduce, limit; **modérez vos propos!** tone down your remarks! *ou* language! 2 **se modérer** VPR (= *s'apaiser*) to calm down, control o.s.; (= *montrer de la mesure*) to restrain o.s.

moderne [mɔdɛʀn] **1** ADJ (*gén*) modern; [*cuisine, équipement*] up-to-date, modern; [*opposé à classique*] [*études*] modern; **le héros ~** the modern-day hero; **la femme ~** the woman of today, today's woman; **à l'époque ~** in modern times → **confort, lettre** **2** NM **a** **le ~** (= *style*) modern style; (= *meubles*) modern furniture; **aimer le ~** to like modern (style) furniture *ou* the contemporary style of furniture; **meublé en ~** with modern furniture, furnished in contemporary style **b** (= *personne*) modern painter (*ou* novelist *etc*) → **ancien**

modernisateur, -trice [mɔdɛʀnizatœʀ, tʀis] **1** ADJ modernizing **2** NM,F modernizer

modernisation [mɔdɛʀnizasjɔ̃] NF modernization; **des efforts de ~ ont été faits dans notre entreprise** steps have been taken towards modernizing our company

moderniser [mɔdɛʀnize] ▶ conjug 1 ◀ **1** VT to modernize, bring up to date **2** **se moderniser** VPR to modernize, be modernized

modernisme [mɔdɛʀnism] NM modernism

moderniste [mɔdɛʀnist] **1** NMF modernist **2** ADJ modernistic

modernité [mɔdɛʀnite] NF modernity; **ce texte est d'une ~ surprenante** this text is amazingly modern; **la ~ des pièces de Shakespeare** the modernity of *ou* the contemporary relevance of Shakespeare's plays

modern style [mɔdɛʀnstil] ADJ INV, NM ≈ Art Nouveau

modeste [mɔdɛst] ADJ **a** (*vie, appartement, tenue*) modest; [*revenu*] modest; **c'est un cadeau bien ~** it's a very modest gift, it's not much of a present; **un train de vie ~** an unpretentious *ou* a modest way of life; **je ne suis qu'un ~ employé** I'm only a simple *ou* modest employee; **être d'un milieu *ou* d'origine ~** to have *ou* come from a modest *ou* humble background; **il est ~ dans ses ambitions** his ambitions are modest, he has modest ambitions **b** [*personne, attitude, air*] modest; **faire le ~** to put on *ou* make a show of modesty; **tu fais le ~** you're just being modest; **avoir le triomphe ~** to be a modest winner **c** († *ou littér* = *pudique*) modest

modestement [mɔdɛstəmɑ̃] ADV modestly

modestie [mɔdɛsti] NF (= *absence de vanité*) modesty; (= *réserve, effacement*) self-effacement; (*littér* = *pudeur*) modesty; **en toute ~** with all due modesty; **fausse ~** false modesty

modicité [mɔdisite] NF [*prix*] lowness; [*salaire*] lowness, smallness

modifiable [mɔdifjabl] ADJ modifiable; **les dates du billet ne sont pas ~s** the dates on the ticket cannot be changed

modificateur, -trice [mɔdifikatœʀ, tʀis] **1** ADJ modifying, modificatory **2** NM modifier

modificatif, -ive [mɔdifikatif, iv] ADJ **décision modificative de budget** decision to alter a budget; **permis (de construire) ~** planning permission (*for alterations*)

modification [mɔdifikasjɔ̃] NF [*comportement*] change, alteration; [*règles, statut*] change, alteration; **apporter des ~s à** [+ *statut, règles*] to change, alter; [+ *constitution*] to alter, modify; [+ *texte*] to make alterations to

modifier [mɔdifje] ▶ conjug 7 ◀ **1** VT **a** [+ *statut, règles*] to change, alter; [+ *constitution, comportement*] to alter, modify; (*Gram*) to modify, alter **2** **se modifier** VPR [*comportement, situation*] to change, alter; [*habitudes*] to change

modique [mɔdik] ADJ [*salaire, prix*] modest; **pour la ~ somme de** for the modest sum of; **il ne recevait qu'une pension ~** he received only a modest *ou* meagre pension

modiste [mɔdist] NF milliner

modulable [mɔdylabl] ADJ [*tarif, mesure, siège, espace, salle*] adjustable; [*horaire*] flexible; (*Fin*) [*prêt*] adjustable, flexible

modulaire [mɔdylɛʀ] ADJ modular

modulateur, -trice [mɔdylatœʀ, tʀis] **1** ADJ modulating (*épith*) **2** NM (*Élec, Radio*) modulator; **~ démodulateur** modulator-demodulator

modulation [mɔdylasjɔ̃] NF (*Ling, Mus, Radio*) modulation; [*tarif, mesure*] adjustment; **~ de fréquence** frequency modulation; **poste à ~ de fréquence** VHF *ou* FM radio; **écouter une émission sur *ou* en ~ de fréquence** to listen to a programme on VHF *ou* on FM

module [mɔdyl] NM (= *étalon*, Archit, Espace, Ordin) module; (*Math, Phys*) modulus; (*Univ*) module, unit; (= *éléments d'un ensemble*) unit; **~ lunaire** lunar module, mooncraft; **acheter une cuisine par ~s** to buy a kitchen in separate units

moduler [mɔdyle] ▶ conjug 1 ◀ **1** VT [+ *voix*] to modulate, inflect; [+ *tarif, mesure*] to adjust; (*Mus, Radio*) to modulate; **~ les peines en fonction des délits** to make the punishment fit the crime **2** VI (*Mus*) to modulate

modus operandi [mɔdysɔpeʀɑ̃di] NM modus operandi; **trouver un ~ avec qn** to work out a modus operandi with sb

modus vivendi [mɔdysvivɛ̃di] NM INV modus vivendi, working arrangement; **trouver un ~ avec qn** to reach *ou* find a modus vivendi with sb

moelle [mwal] NF (*Anat*) marrow, medulla (*SPÉC*); (*Bot*) pith; (*fig*) pith, core; **~ osseuse** bone marrow; **~ épinière** spinal cord; (*Culin*) **(de bœuf)** beef marrow; **être transi jusqu'à la ~ (des os)** to be frozen to the marrow; **pourri* *ou* corrompu jusqu'à la ~** rotten to the core, rotten through and through → **os, substantifique**

moelleusement [mwaløzmɑ̃] ADV [*étendu*] luxuriously

moelleux, -euse [mwaløˌ øz] **1** ADJ [*tapis, lit*] soft; [*couleur, son*] mellow; [*viande*] tender; [*gâteau*] moist; **vin ~** sweet wine **2** NM [*tapis, lit, veste*] softness; [*vin*] mellowness

moellon [mwalɔ̃] NM (*Constr*) rubble stone

mœurs [mœʀ(s)] NFPL **a** (= *morale*) morals; (*euph*) **il a des ~ particulières** he has certain tendencies (*euph*); **contraire aux bonnes ~** contrary to accepted standards of (good) behaviour; **femme de ~ légères *ou* faciles** woman of easy virtue; **femme de mauvaises ~** loose woman; (*Jur, Presse*) **affaire *ou* histoire de ~** sex case; **la police des ~ ◊ les Mœurs*** ≈ the vice squad → **attentat, certificat, outrage** **b** (= *coutumes, habitudes*) [*peuple, époque*] customs, habits, mores (*frm*); [*abeilles, fourmis*] habits; **c'est (entré) dans les ~** it's (become) normal practice, it's (become) a standard *ou* an everyday feature of life; **les ~ politiques/littéraires de notre siècle** the political/literary practices *ou* customs of our century; **avoir des simples/aristocratiques ~** to lead a simple/an aristocratic life, have a simple/an aristocratic life style → **autre** **c** (= *manières*) manners, ways; (*Littérat*) manners; **ils ont de drôles de ~** they have some peculiar ways *ou* manners; **quelles ~ ! ◊ drôles de ~ !** what a way to behave! *ou* carry on!, what manners! → **comédie, peinture**

Mogadiscio [mogadiʃjo] N Mogadishu

mohair [mɔɛʀ] NM mohair

Mohammed [mɔamed] NM Mohammed

Mohican [mɔikɑ̃] NM Mohican

moi [mwa] **1** PRON PERS **a** (*objet direct ou indirect*) me; **aide-~** help me; **donne-~ ton livre** give me your book, give your book to me; **donne-le-~** give it to me; **si vous étiez ~, que feriez-vous ?** if you were me *ou* in my shoes what would you do?; **il nous a regardés ma femme et ~** he looked at my wife and me; **écoute-~ ça !*** just listen to that!; **il n'obéit qu'à ~** he only obeys me, I'm the only one he obeys; **~, elle me déteste** she hates me → **même, non**

b (*sujet*) I (*emphatique*), I myself (*emphatique*), me; **qui a fait cela ? — (c'est) ~/(ce n'est) pas ~** who did this? — I did/I didn't *ou* me*/not me*; **~, le saluer ? jamais !** me, say hallo to him? never!; **mon mari et ~ (nous) refusons** my husband and I refuse; **~ malade, que ferez-vous ?** when I'm ill what will you do?, what will you do with me ill?; **et ~ de rire de plus belle !** and so I (just) laughed all the more!; **je ne l'ai pas vu, ~** I didn't see him myself, I myself didn't see him; **~, je ne suis pas d'accord** (for my part) I don't agree

c (*emphatique avec* **qui, que**) **c'est ~ qui vous le dis !** you can take it from me!, I'm telling you!; **merci — c'est ~ (qui vous remercie)** thank you — it's ME; **~ qui vous parle, je l'ai vu** I saw him personally *ou* with my own eyes; **c'est ~ qu'elle veut voir** it's me she wants to see; **~ que le théâtre passionne, je n'ai jamais vu cette pièce** even I, with all my great love for the theatre, have never seen this play; **et ~ qui avais espéré gagner !** and to think that I had hoped to win!; **à ~ !** (= *au secours*) help (me)!; (*dans un jeu*) my turn!; (*passe au rugby etc*) over here!

d (*dans comparaisons*) I, me; **il est plus grand que ~** he is taller than I (am) *ou* than me; **il mange plus/moins que ~** he eats more/less than I (do) *ou* than me; **fais comme ~** do as I do, do like me*, do the same as me; **il l'aime plus que ~** (*plus qu'il ne m'aime*) he loves her more than (he loves) me; (*plus que je ne l'aime*) he loves her more than I do

2 NM **le ~** the self, the ego; **notre vrai ~** our true self

moignon [mwaɲɔ̃] NM stump; **il n'avait plus qu'un ~ de bras** he had just the *ou* a stump of an arm left

moi-même [mwamɛm] PRON → **autre, même**

moindre [mwɛ̃dʀ] ADJ **a** (*compar*) (= *moins grand*) less, lesser; (= *inférieur*) lower, poorer; **les dégâts sont bien *ou* beaucoup ~s** the damage is much less; **à ~ prix** at a lower price; **de ~ qualité *ou* de qualité ~** of lower *ou* poorer quality; **enfant de ~ intelligence** child of lower intelligence; **c'est un inconvénient ~** it's less of a drawback; **c'est un ~ mal** it's the lesser evil **b** (*superl*) **le ◊ la ◊ les ~s** the least, the slightest; (*de deux*) the lesser; **le ~ bruit** the slightest noise; **la ~ chance/idée** the slightest *ou* remotest chance/idea; **jusqu'au ~ détail** down to the smallest detail; **sans se faire le ~ souci** without worrying in the slightest; **c'est la ~ de mes difficultés** that's the least of my difficulties; **merci — c'est la ~ des choses !** thank you — it's a pleasure! *ou* you're welcome! *ou* not at all!; **remerciez-le m'avoir aidé — c'était la ~ des choses** thank him for helping me — it was the least he could do; **la ~ des politesses veut que ...** common politeness *ou* courtesy demands that ...; **il n'a pas fait le ~ commentaire** he didn't make a single comment; **la loi du ~ effort** the line of least resistance *ou* effort; **certains spécialistes et non des ~s disent que ...** some specialists and important ones at that say that ...; **c'est un de nos problèmes et non le ~ *ou* des ~s** it is by no means the least of our problems; **de deux maux il faut choisir le ~** you must choose the lesser of two evils

moindrement [mwɛ̃dʀəmɑ̃] ADV (*littér: avec nég*) **il n'était pas le ~ surpris** he was not in the least surprised, he was not surprised in the slightest; **sans l'avoir le ~ voulu** without having in any way wanted this

moine [mwan] NM **a** (*Rel*) monk, friar; **~ bouddhiste** Buddhist monk → **habit** **b** (= *phoque*) monk seal; (= *macareux*) puffin **c** (*Hist* = *chauffe-lit*) bedwarmer

moineau (*pl* **moineaux**) [mwano] NM (*Orn*) sparrow; ~ **domestique** house sparrow; (*péj*) **sale** *ou* **vilain** ~† dirty dog (*péj*); **manger comme un** ~ ◊ **avoir un appétit de** ~ to eat like a bird

moinillon [mwanijɔ̃] NM young monk; (*hum*) little monk (*hum*)

---

moins [mwɛ̃]

1 ADVERBE (*emploi comparatif*)	3 PRÉPOSITION
2 ADVERBE (*emploi superlatif*)	4 NOM MASCULIN
	5 COMPOSÉS

1 ADVERBE (*emploi comparatif*)

◆ **moins** + *adjectif ou adverbe* **(que)** less ... (than); **beaucoup/un peu** ~ much/a little less; **tellement** ~ so much less; **encore** ~ even less; **trois fois** ~ three times less; **rien n'est** ~ **sûr** ◊ (il n'y a) rien de ~ sûr nothing is less certain; **non** ~ **célèbre/idiot** no less famous/silly; MAIS **c'est tellement** ~ **cher** it's so much cheaper

Notez que l'anglais a souvent recours à d'autres formes, en particulier not as *ou* not so ... as
il est ~ **intelligent qu'elle** he's not as *ou* so intelligent as her *ou* as she is, he's less intelligent than her *ou* than she does; **c'est** ~ **grand que je le croyais** it's not as big as I thought (it was); **il ressemble à son père, en** ~ **grand** he looks like his father only he's not as tall, he's a smaller version of his father; **c'est le même genre de livre, en** ~ **bien** it's the same kind of book, only *ou* but not as *ou* so good; **il est non** ~ **évident que** ... it is equally *ou* just as clear that ...; **c'est deux fois** ~ **grand/large** it's half as big/ wide

b

◆ *verbe* + **moins (que)** less (than); **exiger/ donner** ~ to demand/give less; **je gagne (un peu)** ~ **que lui** I earn (a little) less than him *ou* than he does; **il travaille** ~ **que vous** he works less than you (do); **il a fait** ~ **froid qu'hier** it's been less cold than yesterday; **nous sortons** ~ **(souvent)** we don't go out so often *ou* so much, we go out less often; **il tousse** ~ **qu'avant** he coughs less than he used to

Notez que là encore l'anglais a souvent recours à d'autres formes, en particulier not as *ou* not so ... as
j'aime ~ **la campagne en hiver (qu'en été)** I don't like the countryside as *ou* so much in winter (as in summer), I like the countryside less in winter (than in summer); **cela coûtait deux/ trois fois** ~ it was half/one-third the price

c

◆ **moins de (... que)** + *nom non comptable* less (... than), not so much (... as)

◆ **moins de (... que)** + *nom comptable* fewer (... than), not so many (... as); **je mange** ~ **de pain (qu'avant)** I eat less bread (than I used to), I don't eat so much bread (as I used to); **j'ai perdu** ~ **d'argent/de poids que je ne croyais** I've lost less money/weight that I thought I had, I haven't lost as much money/weight as I thought I had; **mange** ~ **de bonbons** eat fewer sweets, don't eat so many sweets; **il y aura** ~ **de monde demain** there'll be fewer people tomorrow, there won't be so many people tomorrow; **il a eu** ~ **de mal que nous à trouver une place** he had less trouble than we did *ou* than us finding a seat; **ils publient** ~ **d'essais que de romans** they publish fewer essays than novels

◆ **moins de** + *nombre*: **les** ~ **de 25 ans** the under-25s; **les enfants de** ~ **de quatre ans voyagent gratuitement** children under four (years of age) travel free; **nous l'avons fait en** ~ **de cinq minutes** we did it in less than *ou* in under five minutes; **il y a** ~ **de deux ans qu'il vit ici** he's been living here (for) less than two years; **il devrait y avoir** ~ **de 100 personnes** there should be under 100 people *ou* fewer *ou* less than 100 people; **il y avait beaucoup** ~ **de**

100 personnes there were well under 100 people; **il est** ~ **de minuit** it is not yet midnight; **il était un peu** ~ **de 6 heures** it was a little before 6 o'clock; **vous ne pouvez pas lui donner** ~ **de 100 F** you can't give him less than 100 francs; **vous ne trouverez rien à** ~ **de 100 F** you won't find anything under 100 francs *ou* for less than 100 francs; **la frontière est à** ~ **de 3 km** the border is less than 3 km away

◆ **en moins de rien** ◊ **en moins de deux*** in next to no time

◆ **moins ..., moins ...** : ~ **je mange,** ~ **j'ai d'appétit** the less I eat, the less hungry I feel; ~ **il y a de clients,** ~ **j'ai de travail** the fewer customers I have, the less work I have to do

◆ **moins ..., plus .../mieux ...** : ~ **je fume, plus je mange/mieux je me porte** the less I smoke, the more I eat/the better I feel; ~ **j'ai de coups de fil, mieux je travaille** the fewer phone calls I get, the better I work

◆ **moins que rien** : **cela m'a coûté** ~ **que rien** it cost me next to nothing; **je l'ai eu pour** ~ **que rien** I got it for next to nothing; **ne me remerciez pas, c'est** ~ **que rien** don't thank me, it's nothing at all → **5**

◆ **à moins** : **vous ne l'obtiendrez pas à** ~ you won't get it for less; **il est ravi/fatigué — on le serait à** ~ he's delighted/tired — as well he might (be) *ou* that's hardly surprising

◆ **à moins de** + *infinitif* unless; **à** ~ **de faire une bêtise, il devrait gagner** unless he does something silly he should win; **vous ne trouverez plus de billet, à** ~ **de payer 10 fois le prix** you won't get a ticket unless you're prepared to pay 10 times the price; MAIS **à** ~ **d'un accident/d'un désastre, ça devrait marcher** barring accidents/disasters, it should work; **à** ~ **d'une blessure, il jouera dans le prochain match** barring injury, he'll play in the next match

◆ **à moins que** + *subjonctif* unless; **à** ~ **qu'il ne vienne** unless he comes; **l'entreprise devra fermer, à** ~ **qu'on ne trouve un repreneur** the company will have to close unless a buyer is found

◆ **de moins** : **il gagne 500 F de** ~ **qu'elle** he earns 500 francs less than she does; **vous avez cinq ans de** ~ **qu'elle** you're five years younger than her *ou* than she is; **ah, si j'avais 20 ans de** ~ ... ah, if only I were 20 years younger ...

◆ **de moins en moins** less and less; **c'est de** ~ **en** ~ **utile** it's less and less useful; **il entend de** ~ **en** ~ **bien** his hearing is getting worse and worse; **il a de** ~ **en** ~ **de clients** he has fewer and fewer clients; **j'ai de** ~ **en** ~ **de temps libre** I've got less and less free time

◆ **en moins** : **il y a trois verres en** ~ there are three glasses missing; **ça me fera du travail en** ~ ! that'll be less work for me!; **c'est la même voiture, le toit ouvrant en** ~ it's the same car minus the sunroof *ou* except it hasn't got a sunroof

◆ **pas moins (de/que)** : **un crapaud ne mange pas** ~ **de 400 insectes chaque jour** a toad eats no less than 400 insects a day; **pas** ~ **de 40 km les sépare de la ville la plus proche** the nearest town is no less than 40 km away; **gravement malade, il n'en continue pas** ~ **d'écrire** despite being seriously ill, he still continues to write; **la situation n'en comporte pas** ~ **de nombreux risques** the situation is still very risky for all that; **je suis tolérante mais je n'en suis pas** ~ **choquée par leur attitude** I'm tolerant but that doesn't mean I'm not shocked by their behaviour; **le résultat n'en demeure pas** ~ **surprenant** the result is none the less surprising for that; **il n'en reste pas** ~ **que** ... the fact remains that ..., even so ...; **il n'en est pas** ~ **vrai que** ... it is no less true that ... → **penser**

2 ADVERBE (*emploi superlatif*)

a

◆ **le** *ou* **la** *ou* **les moins** + *adjectif ou adverbe* (*de plusieurs*) the least; (*de deux*) the less; **c'est le** ~ **doué de mes élèves** he's the least gifted of my pupils; **c'est le** ~ **doué des deux** he's the less

gifted of the two; **ce sont les fleurs les** ~ **chères** they are the least expensive *ou* the cheapest flowers

b

◆ *verbe* + **le moins** (the) least; **c'est celle que j'aime le** ~ it's the one I like (the) least; **l'émission que je regarde le** ~ (souvent) the programme I watch (the) least often; **de nous tous, c'est lui qui a bu le** ~ (d'alcool) of all of us, he was the one who drank the least (alcohol); **c'est bien le** ~ **qu'on puisse faire** it's the least one can do; **ce qui me dérangerait le** ~ what would be least inconvenient for me; MAIS **c'est le** ~ **qu'on puisse dire !** that's putting it mildly!; **ce qui lui déplairait le** ~ what he would prefer

c

◆ **le moins (...) possible** : **je lui parle le** ~ **possible** I talk to him as little as possible; **je prends le métro/des médicaments le** ~ **souvent possible** I take the underground/medicine as little as possible; **afin de payer le** ~ **d'impôts possible** in order to pay as little tax as possible; **j'y resterai le** ~ **longtemps** *ou* **de temps possible** I won't stay there any longer than I have to; **pour que les choses se passent le** ~ **mal possible** so that things go as smoothly as possible

3 PRÉPOSITION

a soustraction   **6** ~ **2 font 4** 6 minus 2 equals 4, 2 from 6 makes 4; **j'ai retrouvé mon sac,** ~ **le portefeuille** I found my bag, minus the wallet; **nous avons roulé sept heures,** ~ **l'arrêt pour déjeuner** we drove for seven hours not counting the stop for lunch

b heure   to; **il est 4 heures** ~ **5 (minutes)** it's 5 (minutes) to 4; **nous avons le temps, il n'est que** ~ **10*** we've got plenty of time, it's only 10 to*; (*fig*) **il s'en est tiré, mais il était** ~ **cinq*** *ou* ~ **une*** he got out of it but it was a close shave* *ou* a near thing*

c nombre négatif (*température*) below; **il fait** ~ **5°** it's 5° below freezing *ou* minus 5°; (*Math*) **dix puissance** ~ **sept** ten to the power (of) minus seven

4 NOM MASCULIN

a Math (signe) ~ **minus sign**

b

◆ **à tout le moins** (*frm*) to say the least, at the very least

◆ **au moins** at least; **elle a payé cette robe au** ~ **3 000 F** she paid at least 3,000 francs for that dress; **600 au** ~ at least 600, 600 at the least; **la moitié au** ~ at least half; **la moitié au** ~ **du personnel/des candidats** at least half (of) the staff/the candidates; **ça fait au** ~ **dix jours qu'il est parti** it's at least ten days since he left; **vous en avez au** ~ **entendu parler** you must at least have heard about it; **tout au** ~ at (the very) least

◆ **du moins** (*restriction*) at least; **il ne pleuvra pas, du** ~ **c'est ce qu'annonce la radio** it's not going to rain, at least that's what it says on the radio; **laissez-le sortir, du** ~ **s'il** *ou* **si du** ~ **il ne fait pas froid** let him go out, as long as it isn't cold; MAIS **j'arriverai vers 4 heures, du** ~ **si l'avion n'a pas de retard** I'll be there around 4 o'clock — if the plane's on time, that is

◆ **pour le moins** (*avec adjectif ou verbe*) to say the least; **sa décision est pour le** ~ **bizarre** his decision is odd to say the least (*évaluation d'une quantité*) at the very least; **ils étaient 2 000, pour le** ~ there were 2,000 of them at the very least

5 COMPOSÉS

► **moins que rien*** NMF (*péj* = minable) complete loser*, schlemiel‡ (*US*); **on les traite comme des** ~ **que rien** they're treated like scum

---

moins-perçu (*pl* **moins-perçus**) [mwɛ̃pɛʀsy] NM amount not drawn, short payment

moins-value (*pl* **moins-values**) [mwɛ̃valy] NF

(*Comm*) depreciation, capital loss; **~ de re-cettes fiscales** taxation shortfall

moirage [mwaraʒ] NM (= *procédé*) watering; (= *reflet*) watered effect

moire [mwaʀ] NF (= *tissu*) moiré; (= *soie*) watered *ou* moiré silk; (= *procédé*) watering

moiré, e [mwaʀe] (*ptp de* **moirer**) **1** ADJ [*papier peint, tissu*] moiré; [*soie*] watered, moiré; [*papier*] marbled; (*fig*) shimmering **2** NM (*Tech*) moiré, water; (*littér*) [*lac*] shimmering ripples

moirer [mwaʀe] ▸conjug 1 ◂ VT (*Tech*) to water; (*littér*) **la lune moirait l'étang de reflets argentés** the moon cast a shimmering silvery light over the pool

moirure [mwaʀyʀ] NF (*Tech*) moiré; (*littér*) shimmering ripples

mois [mwa] NM **a** (= *période*) month; **le ~ de Marie** the month of Mary; (*Culin*) **les ~ en R** when there is an R in the month; **au ~ de janvier** in (the month of) January; **dans un ~** in a month('s time); (*Comm*) **le 10 de ce ~** the 10th of this month, the 10th inst(ant).; **au ~** [*payer, louer*] monthly, by the month; **300 F par ~** 300 francs a *ou* per month; (*Comm*) **billet à 3 ~** bill at 3 months; **un bébé de 6 ~** a 6-month-old baby; **tous les 4 ~** every 4 months; **devoir 3 ~ de loyer** to owe 3 months' rent → **tout b** (= *salaire*) monthly pay, monthly salary; **toucher son ~*** to draw one's pay *ou* salary for the month *ou* one's month's pay *ou* salary; **~ double** extra month's pay (*as end-of-year bonus*); **treizième/quatorzième ~** one month's/two months' extra pay → **fin²**

Moïse [mɔiz] NM **a** (*Bible*) Moses **b** **moïse** (= *berceau*) Moses basket

moisi, e [mwazi] (*ptp de* **moisir**) **1** ADJ mouldy, moldy (*US*), mildewed **2** NM mould (*NonC*), mold (*US*) (*NonC*), mildew (*NonC*); **odeur de ~** musty *ou* fusty smell; **goût de ~** musty taste; **ça sent le ~** it smells musty *ou* fusty

moisir [mwaziʀ] ▸conjug 2 ◂ **1** VT to make mouldy *ou* moldy (*US*) **2** VI **a** [*mur, papier*] to go mouldy *ou* moldy (*US*), mould, mold (*US*) **b** (*fig*) [*personne*] (*dans une prison, une entreprise*) to rot; (= *attendre*) to hang around; **on ne va pas ~ ici jusqu'à la nuit!*** we're not going to hang around here till night-time!*; **il ne faut pas laisser ~ votre argent** you shouldn't let your money gather dust

moisissure [mwazisyʀ] NF (*gén*) mould (*NonC*), mold (*US*) (*NonC*); (*par l'humidité*) mould (*NonC*), mold (*US*) (*NonC*), mildew (*NonC*); **enlever les ~s sur un fromage** to scrape the mould off a piece of cheese

moisson [mwasɔ̃] NF **a** (*Agr*) (= *saison, travail*) harvest; (= *récolte*) harvest; **à l'époque de la ~** at harvest time; **rentrer la ~** to bring in the harvest; **faire la ~** to harvest, reap **b** [*don-nées*] wealth, crop; **faire une abondante ~ de renseignements/souvenirs** to gather *ou* amass a wealth of information/memories

moissonner [mwasɔne] ▸conjug 1 ◂ VT [+ *céréale*] to harvest, reap; [+ *champ*] to reap; [+ *récompenses*] to carry off, reap; [+ *renseignements*] to gather, garner; **il a commencé à ~** he's started harvesting *ou* the harvest; **notre pays moissonne les médailles** our country is winning one medal after the other

moissonneur, -euse [mwasɔnœʀ, øz] **1** NM,F harvester, reaper† (*littér*) **2 moissonneuse** NF (= *machine*) harvester

moissonneuse-batteuse(-lieuse) (*pl* **moissonneuses-batteuses(-lieuses)**) [mwasɔ-nøzbatøz(ljøz)] NF combine harvester

moissonneuse-lieuse (*pl* **moissonneuses-lieuses**) [mwasɔnøzljøz] NF self-binder

moite [mwat] ADJ [*peau, mains*] sweaty, clam-my; [*atmosphère*] sticky, muggy; [*chaleur*]

sticky; **il a le front ~ de sueur** his forehead is damp with sweat

moiteur [mwatœʀ] NF [*peau, mains*] sweati-ness; [*atmosphère*] stickiness, mugginess

moitié [mwatje] NF **a** (= *partie*) half; **partager qch en deux ~s** to halve sth, divide sth in half *ou* into (two) halves; **quelle est la ~ de 40?** what is half of 40?; **donne-m'en la ~** give me half (of it); **faire la ~ du chemin avec qn** to go halfway *ou* half of the way with sb; (*dans une négociation*) **je veux bien faire la ~ du che-min** I'm prepared to meet you halfway; **la ~ des habitants a été sauvée** *ou* **ont été sauvés** half (of) the inhabitants were rescued; **la ~ du temps** half the time; **il en faut ~ plus/moins** you need half as much again/half (of) that; **~ anglais, ~ français** half-English, half-French **b** (= *milieu*) halfway mark, half; **parvenu à la ~ du trajet** having completed half the jour-ney, having reached halfway *ou* the halfway mark; **parvenu à la ~ de sa vie, il ...** halfway through his life, he ...; **arrivé à la ~ du travail** having done half the work *ou* got halfway through the work **c** (*hum* = *époux, épouse*) **ma ~** my better half* (*hum*); **ma tendre ~** my ever-loving wife (*ou* husband) (*hum*) **d** **à ~** half; **il a fait le travail à ~** he has (only) half done the work; **il a mis la table à ~** he's half set the table; **il ne fait jamais rien à ~** he never does things by halves; **à ~ plein/mûr** half-full/-ripe; **à ~ chemin** (at) halfway, at the halfway mark; **à ~ prix** (at) half-price **e** (*loc*) **de ~** by half; **réduire de ~** [+ *trajet, production, coût*] to cut *ou* reduce by half, halve; **plus grand de ~** half as big again, big-ger by half; **être/se mettre de ~ dans une en-treprise** to have half shares/go halves in a business; **par ~** in two, in half; **diviser qch par ~** to divide sth in two *ou* in half; **il est pour ~ dans cette faillite** he is half responsible *ou* half to blame for this bankruptcy; **on a parta-gé le pain ~ ~** we halved *ou* shared the bread between us; **ils ont partagé au fait ~ ~** they went halves *ou* fifty-fifty* *ou* Dutch*; **ça a marché? — ~ ~*** how did it go? — so-so*

moka [mɔka] NM (= *gâteau à la crème*) cream cake, cream gâteau; (= *gâteau au café*) mocha *ou* coffee cake, mocha *ou* coffee gâteau; (= *café*) mocha coffee

mol [mɔl] ADJ M → **mou¹**

molaire¹ [mɔlɛʀ] NF (= *dent*) molar

molaire² [mɔlɛʀ] ADJ (*Chim*) molar

molasse [mɔlas] NF = **mollasse²**

moldave [mɔldav] **1** ADJ Moldavian **2 Moldave** NMF Moldavian

Moldavie [mɔldavi] NF Moldavia

mole [mɔl] NF (*Chim*) mole, mol

môle [mol] NM (= *digue*) breakwater, mole; (= *quai*) pier, jetty

moléculaire [mɔlekylɛʀ] ADJ molecular

molécule [mɔlekyl] NF molecule

moleskine [mɔleskin] NF imitation leather, leatherette®

molester [mɔleste] ▸conjug 1 ◂ VT to man-handle, rough up; **molesté par la foule** mauled by the crowd

moleté, e [mɔlte] ADJ [*roue, vis*] knurled

molette [mɔlɛt] NF **a** (*Tech*) toothed wheel; (*pour couper*) cutting wheel **b** [*briquet*] striker wheel; [*clé*] adjusting screw; [*éperon*] rowel; **~ de mise au point** [*jumelles*] focussing wheel → **clé**

moliéresque [mɔljeʀɛsk] ADJ Molieresque

mollah [mɔ(l)la] NM mulla(h)

**mollard* ** [mɔlaʀ] NM (= *crachat*) gob of spit*

mollasse¹* ** [mɔlas] ADJ **1 (*péj*) (= *léthargique*) sluggish, lethargic; (= *flasque*) flabby, flaccid; **une grande fille ~** a great lump* of a girl **2** NMF great lump*

mollasse² [mɔlas] NF (*Géol*) molasse

mollasserie [mɔlasʀi] NF sluggishness, lethar-gy

mollasson, -onne* [mɔlasɔ̃, ɔn] (*péj*) **1** ADJ sluggish, lethargic **2** NM,F great lump*

molle [mɔl] ADJ F → **mou¹**

mollement [mɔlmɑ̃] ADV (= *doucement*) [*tomber*] softly; [*couler*] gently, sluggishly; (= *paresseusement*) [*travailler*] half-heartedly, unenthusiastically; (= *faiblement*) [*réagir, pro-tester*] feebly, weakly; **les jours s'écoulaient ~** one day turned into the next, the days drift-ed by

mollesse [mɔlɛs] NF **a** (*au toucher*) [*substance, oreiller*] softness; [*poignée de main*] limpness, flabbiness **b** (*à la vue*) [*contours, lignes*] soft-ness; [*relief*] softness, gentleness; [*traits du vi-sage*] flabbiness, sagginess; [*Peinture*] [*dessin, traits*] lifelessness, weakness **c** (= *manque d'énergie*) [*geste*] lifelessness, feebleness; [*pro-testations, opposition*] weakness, feebleness; † [*vie*] indolence, softness; [*style*] vagueness, woolliness (*Brit*); (*Mus*) [*exécution*] lifelessness, dullness; [*personne*] (= *indolence*) sluggishness, lethargy; (= *manque d'autorité*) spinelessness; (= *grande indulgence*) laxness; **la ~ de la police face aux manifestants** the feebleness of the police's response to the demonstrators

mollet¹, -ette [mɔlɛ, ɛt] ADJ [*lit*] soft → **œuf**

mollet² [mɔlɛ] NM (*Anat*) calf; (*fig*) **~s de coq** wiry legs

molletière [mɔltjɛʀ] ADJ, NF **(bande) ~** puttee

molleton [mɔltɔ̃] NM (= *tissu*) cotton fleece, swansdown; (*pour table*) felting

molletonner [mɔltɔne] ▸conjug 1 ◂ VT to put a warm lining in; **anorak molletonné** quilted anorak, anorak with a warm lining

mollir [mɔliʀ] ▸conjug 2 ◂ VI **a** (= *fléchir*) [*sol*] to give (way), yield; [*ennemi*] to yield, give way, give ground; [*père, créancier*] to come round, relent; [*courage, personne*] to flag; **sa plaidoirie a fait ~ les jurés** his speech for the defence softened the jury's attitude *ou* made the jury relent; **ce n'est pas le moment de ~!*** you (*ou* we etc) mustn't slacken now!; **il a senti ses jambes/genoux ~ sous lui** he felt his legs/knees give way beneath him **b** [*subs-tance*] to soften, go soft **c** [*vent*] to abate, die down

mollo* ** [mɔlo] ADV **(vas-y) ~! take it easy!*, (go) easy!*, easy does it!*

mollusque [mɔlysk] NM (*Zool*) mollusc, mol-lusk (*US*); (* *péj* = *personne*) great lump*

molosse [mɔlɔs] NM (*littér, hum*) big (fero-cious) dog, huge hound

Molotov [mɔlɔtɔf] NM → **cocktail**

Moluques [mɔlyk] NFPL **les ~** the Moluccas, the Molucca Islands

molybdène [mɔlibdɛn] NM molybdenum

môme [mom] NMF (* = *enfant*) kid*; (*péj*) brat*; (‡ = *fille*) bird‡ (*Brit*), chick‡ (*US*); **belle ~‡** nice-looking piece‡ (*Brit*) *ou* chick‡ (*US*); **quels sales ~s!‡** horrible little brats!*

moment [mɔmɑ̃] NM **a** (= *long instant*) while, moment; **je ne l'ai pas vu depuis un (bon) ~** I haven't seen him for a (good) while *ou* for quite a time *ou* while; **j'en ai pour un petit ~** it'll take me some time *ou* quite a while **b** (= *court instant*) moment; **il réfléchit pendant un ~** he thought for a moment; **c'est l'affaire d'un ~** it won't take a minute *ou* mo-ment, it'll only take a minute; **je n'en ai que pour un petit ~** it won't take me long, it'll only take me a moment; **ça ne dure qu'un ~** it doesn't last long, it (only) lasts a minute; **un ~ de silence** a moment of silence, a mo-ment's silence; **j'ai eu un ~ de panique** I had a moment's panic, for a moment I panicked; **dans un ~ de colère** in a moment of anger, in a momentary fit of anger; **dans un ~** in a little while, in a moment; **un ~, il arrive !** just a moment *ou* a minute *ou* a mo'* (*Brit*), he's coming!

[c] (= *période*) time; **à quel ~ est-ce arrivé ?** at what point in time *ou* when exactly did this occur?; **connaître/passer de bons ~s** to have/spend (some) happy times; **les ~s que nous avons passés ensemble** the times we spent together; **il a passé un mauvais** *ou* **sale ~*** he went through *ou* had a difficult time, he had a rough time; **je n'ai pas un ~ à moi** I haven't got a moment to myself; **le ~ présent** the present time; **à ses ~s perdus** in his spare time; **les grands ~s de l'histoire** the great moments of history; **il a ses bons et ses mauvais ~s** he has his good times and his bad times; **il est dans un de ses mauvais ~s** it's one of his off *ou* bad spells, he's having one of his off *ou* bad spells; **la célébrité/le succès du ~** the celebrity/the success of the moment *ou* day; **n'attends pas le dernier ~ pour réviser ta leçon** don't wait till the last minute to do your revision

[d] (= *occasion*) **il faut profiter du ~** you must take advantage of *ou* seize the opportunity; **ce n'est pas le ~** this is not the right moment; **tu arrives au bon ~** you've come just at the right time; **c'était le ~ de réagir** it was time to react; **le ~ psychologique** the psychological moment → **jamais**

[e] (*Tech*) moment; (*Phys*) momentum

[f] (*loc*) **en ce ~** (= *maintenant*) at the moment, at present, just now; (= *ces temps-ci*) currently, presently; **au ~ de l'accident** at the time of the accident, when the accident happened; **au ~ de partir** just as I (*ou he etc*) was about to leave, just as I (*ou he etc*) was on the point of leaving; **au ~ où elle entrait, lui sortait** as she was going in he was coming out; **au ~ où il s'y attendait le moins** (at a time) when he was least expecting it; **à un ~ donné il cesse d'écouter** at a certain point he stops listening; **il se prépare afin de savoir quoi dire le ~ venu** he's getting ready so that he'll know what to say when the time comes; **le ~ venu ils s'élancèrent** when the time came they hurled themselves forward; **des voitures arrivaient à tout ~** *ou* **à tous ~s** cars were constantly *ou* continually arriving, cars kept on arriving; **il peut arriver à tout ~** he may arrive (at) any time (now) *ou* any moment (now); **à ce ~-là** (*temps*) at that point *ou* time; (*circonstance*) in that case, if that's the case, if that's so; **à aucun ~ je n'ai dit que ...** I never at any time said that ..., at no point did I say that ...; **on l'attend d'un ~ à l'autre** he is expected any moment now *ou* (at) any time now; **du ~ où** *ou* **que** since, seeing that; **dès le ~ que** *ou* **où** as soon as, from the moment *ou* time when; **par ~s** now and then, at times, every now and again; **pour le ~** for the time being *ou* the moment, at present; **sur le ~** at the time

momentané, e [mɔmɑ̃tane] ADJ [*absence, gêne, crise, arrêt*] momentary (*épith*); [*espoir, effort*] short-lived, brief

momentanément [mɔmɑ̃tanemɑ̃] ADV (= *en ce moment*) at *ou* for the moment, at present; (= *un court instant*) for a short while, momentarily; **la signature de l'accord est ~ suspendue** the signing of the agreement has been postponed for the moment

mômeries* [momʀi] NFPL childish behaviour; **arrête tes ~!** stop your silly nonsense!*, stop acting like a big baby!*

momie [mɔmi] NF mummy; **ne reste pas là comme une ~*** don't stand there like a stuffed dummy*

momification [mɔmifikasjɔ̃] NF mummification

momifier [mɔmifje] ▸ conjug 7 ◂ [1] VT to mummify [2] **se momifier** VPR [*esprit*] to atrophy, fossilize

mon [mɔ̃], **ma** [ma] (*pl* **mes** [me]) ADJ POSS [a] (*possession, relation*) my, my own (*emphatique*); **~ fils et ma fille** my son and (my) daughter; **j'ai ~ idée là-dessus** I have my own ideas *ou* views about that; *pour autres locutions voir* **son¹** [b] (*valeur affective, ironique, intensive*) **alors voilà ~ type/~ François qui se met à m'injurier*** and then the fellow/our François starts bawling insults at me; **voilà ~ mal de tête qui me reprend** that's my headache back again; **on a changé ~ Paris** they've changed the Paris I knew *ou* what I think of as Paris; **j'ai eu ~ lundi*** I got Monday off → **son¹** [c] (*dans termes d'adresse*) my; **~ cher ami** my dear friend; **~ cher Monsieur** my dear Sir; (*Rel*) **oui ~ père/ma sœur/ma mère** yes Father/Sister/Mother; (*Rel*) **mes (bien chers) frères** my (dear) brethren

monacal, e (*mpl* **-aux**) [mɔnakal, o] ADJ (*lit, fig*) monastic

monachisme [mɔnaʃism] NM monachism

Monaco [mɔnako] NM **(la principauté de) ~** (the principality of) Monaco

monade [mɔnad] NF monad

monarchie [mɔnaʀʃi] NF monarchy; **~ absolue/constitutionnelle/parlementaire** absolute/constitutional/parliamentary monarchy; (*Hist*) **la Monarchie de Juillet** the July Monarchy

monarchique [mɔnaʀʃik] ADJ monarchic, monarchial

monarchisme [mɔnaʀʃism] NM monarchism

monarchiste [mɔnaʀʃist] ADJ, NMF monarchist

monarque [mɔnaʀk] NM monarch; **~ absolu** absolute monarch; **~ de droit divin** monarch *ou* king by divine right

monastère [mɔnastɛʀ] NM monastery

monastique [mɔnastik] ADJ monastic

monceau (*pl* **monceaux**) [mɔ̃so] NM **un ~ de** [+ *objets*] a heap *ou* pile of; [+ *erreurs*] a heap *ou* load* of; **des ~x de** heaps *ou* piles of

mondain, e [mɔ̃dɛ̃, ɛn] [1] ADJ [a] [*réunion, vie*] society (*épith*); [*public*] fashionable; **plaisirs ~s** pleasures of society; **chronique ~e** society gossip column; **alcoolisme ~** *alcoholism brought about by social drinking*; **mener une vie ~e** to be a socialite; **goût pour la vie ~e** taste for society life *ou* the high life; **leurs obligations ~es** their social obligations; **ils sont très ~s** they are great socialites, they like moving in fashionable society *ou* circles → **carnet, soirée** [b] [*politesse, ton*] refined, urbane, sophisticated; **il a été très ~ avec moi** he treated me with studied politeness *ou* courtesy [c] (*Philo*) mundane, (*Rel*) worldly, earthly [d] (*ancienm*) **la police** *ou* **brigade ~e** ◊ **la Mondaine*** (*des mœurs*) ≈ the vice squad; (*des stupéfiants*) ≈ the drugs squad

[2] NM socialite

[3] **mondaine** NF (= *femme*) society woman, socialite

mondanité [mɔ̃danite] [1] NF [a] (= *goût*) taste for *ou* love of society life; (= *habitude, connaissance des usages*) savoir-faire [b] (*Rel*) worldliness [2] **mondanités** NFPL (= *divertissements, soirées*) society life; (= *politesses, propos*) polite small talk; (*Presse = chronique*) society gossip column; **toutes ces ~s me fatiguent** I'm exhausted by this social whirl *ou* round

monde [mɔ̃d] NM [a] (= *univers, terre*) world; **dans le ~ entier** *ou* **de par le ~** all over the world, the world over, throughout the world; **le ~ entier s'indigna** the whole world was outraged; **le ~ des vivants** the land of the living; **il se moque** *ou* **se fiche*** *ou* **se fout* du ~** he's got a nerve* *ou* cheek* (*Brit*), he's got a damn* *ou* bloody* (*Brit*) nerve; **venir au ~** to be born, come into the world; **mettre un enfant au ~** to bring a child into the world; **si je suis encore de ce ~** if I'm still here *ou* in the land of the living; **depuis qu'il est de ce ~** since he was

born; **elle n'est plus de ce ~** she is no longer with us, she has departed this life; **rêver à un ~ meilleur** to dream of a better world; **où va le ~ ?** whatever is the world coming to?; **dans ce (bas) ~** here below, in this world; **l'Ancien/le Nouveau Monde** the Old/the New World; **ce village, c'est le bout du ~** that village is in the middle of nowhere *ou* at the back of beyond*; **il irait au bout du ~ pour elle** he would go to the ends of the earth for her; (*fig*) **ce n'est pas le bout du ~ !** it won't kill you!; **si tu as 10 F à payer, c'est le bout du ~*** at the (very) worst it might cost you 10 francs → **depuis, unique**

[b] (= *ensemble, groupement spécifique*) world; **le ~ végétal/animal** the vegetable/animal world; **le ~ des affaires/du théâtre** the world of business/of (the) theatre, the business/the theatre world; **le ~ chrétien/communiste** the Christian/communist world

[c] (= *domaine*) world, realm; **le ~ de l'illusion/du rêve** the realm of illusion/of dreams; **le ~ de la folie** the world *ou* realm of madness; **elle vit dans son ~** *ou* **dans un ~ à elle** she lives in a world of her own

[d] (*intensif*) **du ~** ◊ **au ~** in the world, on earth; **produit parmi les meilleurs au** *ou* **du ~** product which is among the best in the world *ou* among the world's best; (*littér*) **au demeurant, le meilleur homme du ~** otherwise, the finest man alive; **tout s'est passé le mieux du ~** everything went (off) perfectly *ou* like a dream*; **pas le moins du ~ !** not at all!, not in the least!; **il n'était pas le moins du ~ anxieux** he was not the slightest *ou* least bit worried, he wasn't worried in the slightest *ou* in the least, he wasn't the least bit worried; **sans se préoccuper le moins du ~ de ses adversaires** without giving a single thought *ou* the least thought to his opponents; **je ne m'en séparerais pour rien au ~** ◊ **je ne m'en séparerais pas pour tout l'or du ~** I wouldn't part with it for anything (in the world) *ou* for all the world *ou* for all the tea in China; **nul au ~ ne peut ...** nobody in the world can ...; **j'en pense tout le bien du ~** I have the highest opinion of him (*ou* her *ou* it)

[e] (*loc: Rel*) **l'autre ~** the next world; **envoyer** *ou* **expédier qn dans l'autre ~** to send sb to kingdom come, send sb to meet his (*ou* her) maker; **c'est le ~ à l'envers !** *ou* **renversé !** whatever next!; **comme le ~ est petit !** it's a small world!; **se faire (tout) un ~ de qch** to get worked up about sth; **se faire un ~ de rien** to make a mountain out of a molehill, make a fuss over nothing; **se faire un ~ de tout** to make a fuss over everything, make everything into a great issue; **c'est un ~ !*** it's (just) not right!, it's (just) not on!* (*Brit*); **il y a un ~ entre ces deux personnes/conceptions** these two people/concepts are worlds apart, there's a world of difference between these two people/concepts

[f] (= *gens*) **j'entends du ~ à côté** I can hear people in the next room; **est-ce qu'il y a du ~ ?** (= *qn est-il présent ?*) is there anybody there?; (= *y a-t-il foule ?*) are there many people there?, are there a lot of people there?; **il y a du ~** (= *ce n'est pas vide*) there are some people there; (= *il y a foule*) there's quite a crowd; **il n'y a pas grand ~** there aren't very many (people) here; **il y a beaucoup de ~** there's a real crowd, there are a lot of people; **il y avait un ~!** *ou* **un ~ fou!*** there were crowds!, the place was packed!; **ils voient beaucoup de ~** they have a busy social life; **ils reçoivent beaucoup de ~** they entertain a lot, they do a lot of entertaining; **ce week-end nous avons du ~** we have people coming *ou* visitors this weekend; **il y a du ~ au balcon!**: she's very well-endowed!*; **elle est venue avec tout son petit ~** she came with her entire brood; **tout ce petit ~ s'est bien amusé ?** and did everyone have a nice time?, did we all

enjoy ourselves?; **il connaît son ~** he knows the people he deals with; **je n'ai pas encore tout mon ~** my group *ou* lot* (*Brit*) aren't all here yet → **Monsieur, tout**

g (*Rel*) **le ~** the world; **les plaisirs du ~** worldly pleasures, the pleasures of the world **h** (= *milieu social*) set, circle; (= *la bonne société*) **le** (**grand** *ou* **beau**) **~** (high) society; (*péj*) **embarquez: tout ce beau ~** cart this lot* away; **aller dans le ~** to mix with high society; **appartenir au meilleur ~** to move in the best circles; **il n'est pas de notre ~** he is from a different set, he's not one of our set *ou* crowd*; **nous ne sommes pas du même ~** we don't move in *ou* belong to the same circles (of society); **cela ne se fait pas dans le ~ that** isn't done in the best circles *ou* in polite society; **homme/femme/gens du ~** society man/woman/people; **se conduire en parfait homme du ~** to be a perfect gentleman

monder [mɔ̃de] ▶ conjug 1 ◀ VT [+ *orge*] to hull; [+ *amandes, noisettes*] to blanch

mondial, e (*mpl* **-iaux**) [mɔ̃djal, jo] ADJ [*guerre, population, production*] world (*épith*); [*épidémie, tendance, réseau, crise*] world (*épith*), worldwide; **une célébrité ~e** a world-famous personality *ou* celebrity

mondialement [mɔ̃djalmɑ̃] ADV throughout the world, the (whole) world over; **il est ~ connu** he's known the (whole) world over *ou* throughout the world, he's world-famous

mondialisation [mɔ̃djalizasjɔ̃] NF [*échanges, économie, marchés*] globalization; **pour éviter la ~ du conflit** to prevent the conflict from spreading throughout the world *ou* worldwide

mondialiser [mɔ̃djalize] ▶ conjug 1 ◀ **1** VT [+ *activité, capitaux*] to globalize **2 se mondialiser** VPR [*économie, offre*] to become globalized; **l'entreprise s'est mondialisée** the company has extended its operations worldwide *ou* globalized its operations; **ce phénomène se mondialise** this is becoming a world-wide phenomenon; **dans une économie de plus en plus mondialisée** in an increasingly globalized economy

mondialisme [mɔ̃djalism] NM internationalism

mondialiste [mɔ̃djalist] ADJ, NMF internationalist

mond(i)ovision [mɔ̃d(j)ɔvizjɔ̃] NF worldwide (satellite) television broadcast; **retransmis en ~** broadcast (by satellite) worldwide

monégasque [mɔnegask] **1** ADJ Monegasque, Monacan **2 Monégasque** NMF Monegasque, Monacan

monème [mɔnɛm] NM moneme

MONEP [mɔnɛp] NM (ABRÉV = **Marché des options négociables de Paris**) (*Fin*) **le ~** the traded-options exchange in the Paris stock market

monétaire [mɔnetɛʀ] ADJ [*valeur, unité, système, politique*] monetary; **le marché ~** the money market → **circulation, masse, union**

monétarisme [mɔnetaʀism] NM monetarism

monétariste [mɔnetaʀist] ADJ, NMF monetarist

monétique [mɔnetik] NF electronic banking (services)

monétiser [mɔnetize] ▶ conjug 1 ◀ VT to monetize

mongol, e [mɔ̃gɔl] **1** ADJ Mongol, Mongolian; **République populaire ~** Mongolian People's Republic **2** NM (*Ling*) Mongolian **3 Mongol(e)** NM,F (*gén*) Mongol, Mongoloid; (= *habitant ou originaire de la Mongolie*) Mongolian

Mongolie [mɔ̃gɔli] NF Mongolia; **République populaire de ~** People's Republic of Mongolia; **~-Intérieure** Inner Mongolia, **~-Extérieure** Outer Mongolia

mongolien, -ienne† [mɔ̃gɔljɛ̃, jɛn] (*Méd*) **1** ADJ with Down's syndrome (*attrib*), Down's syndrome (*épith*) **2** NM,F (= *enfant*) Down's syndrome baby (*ou* boy *ou* girl); (= *adulte*) person with Down's syndrome

mongolique [mɔ̃gɔlik] ADJ (*Géog*) Mongol(ic), Mongolian

mongolisme† [mɔ̃gɔlism] NM Down's syndrome, mongolism †

monisme [mɔnism] NM monism

moniste [mɔnist] **1** ADJ monistic **2** NMF monist

moniteur [mɔnitœʀ] NM **a** (*Sport*) instructor, coach; [*colonie de vacances*] supervisor (*Brit*), (camp) counselor (*US*); **~ de ski** skiing instructor; **~ d'auto-école** driving instructor **b** (*Tech, Ordin* = *appareil*) monitor; **~ cardiaque** heart-rate monitor **c** (*Univ*) graduate assistant

monitorage [mɔnitɔʀaʒ] NM = **monitoring**

monitorat [mɔnitɔʀa] NM (= *formation*) training to be an instructor; (= *fonction*) instructorship; **il prépare son ~ de ski** he's training to be a ski instructor

monitoring [mɔnitɔʀiŋ] NM (*gén*) monitoring

monitrice [mɔnitʀis] NF (*Sport*) instructress; [*colonie de vacances*] supervisor (*Brit*), (camp) counselor (*US*); (*Univ*) graduate assistant

monnaie [mɔnɛ] **1** NF **a** (= *espèces, devises*) currency; **~ forte/faible** strong/weak currency; **~ d'or/d'argent** gold/silver currency; **~ décimale** decimal coinage *ou* currency; (*Bourse*) **la ~ américaine** the American dollar; **la ~ allemande** the German mark → **battre, faux²** **b** (= *pièce, médaille*) coin; **une ~ d'or** a gold coin; **émettre/retirer une ~** to issue/withdraw a coin **c** (= *appoint*) change; (= *petites pièces*) (loose) change; **petite** *ou* **menue ~** small change; **vous n'avez pas de ~?** (*pour payer*) don't you have (the) change? *ou* any change?; **auriez-vous de la ~?** ◊ **pourriez-vous me faire de la ~?** could you give me some change?; **faire de la ~** to get (some) change; **faire la ~ de 100 F** to get change for *ou* to change a 100-franc note *ou* 100 francs; **faire** *ou* **donner à qn la ~ de 50F** to change 50 francs for sb, give sb change for 50 francs; **elle m'a rendu la ~ sur 50 F** she gave me the change out of *ou* from 50 francs; **passez** *ou* **envoyez la ~!*** let's have the money!, cough up! everyone! **d** (= *bâtiment*) **la Monnaie** ◊ **l'hôtel des ~s** the Mint **e** (*loc*) **c'est ~ courante** [*faits, événements*] it's common *ou* widespread, it's a common *ou* an everyday occurrence; [*actions, pratiques*] it's common practice; **donner** *ou* **rendre à qn la ~ de sa pièce** to pay sb back in the same *ou* in his own coin, repay sb in kind; **à l'école, les billes servent de ~ d'échange** at school, marbles are used as money *ou* as a currency; **otages qui servent de ~ d'échange** hostages who are used as bargaining chips *ou* counters; **payer qn en ~ de singe** to fob sb off with empty promises

2 COMP ► **monnaie de banque** = **monnaie scripturale** ► **monnaie divisionnaire** fractional currency ► **monnaie électronique** plastic money ► **monnaie fiduciaire** fiduciary currency, paper money ► **monnaie légale** legal tender ► **monnaie métallique** coin (*NonC*) ► **monnaie de papier** paper money ► **monnaie plastique** plastic money ► **monnaie scripturale** representative *ou* bank money ► **monnaie unique** (*Europe*) single currency

monnaie-du-pape (*pl* **monnaies-du-pape**) [mɔnɛdypap] NF (*Bot*) honesty

monnayable [mɔnɛjabl] ADJ [*terres, titres*] convertible into cash; [*diplôme*] marketable; **c'est un diplôme facilement ~** you can easily get a job with that qualification

monnayer [mɔneje] ▶ conjug 8 ◀ VT [+ *terres, titres*] to convert into cash; **~ son talent/ses capacités** to make money from one's talents/one's abilities; **~ son silence/soutien** to sell one's silence/support; **ce genre de service, ça se monnaie** you have to pay to get that kind of help; **dans ce pays, tout se monnaie** in that country, you can get whatever you want as long as you're willing to pay for it

monnayeur [mɔnejœʀ] NM (= *machine*) change machine

mono* [mɔno] **1** NMF (ABRÉV = **moniteur**) [*Sport*] instructor; [*colonie de vacances*] supervisor (*Brit*), (camp) counselor (*US*) **2** NM ABRÉV = **monoski** **3** NF (ABRÉV = **monophonie**) **en ~** in mono **4** ADJ INV (ABRÉV = **monophonique**) [*disque, électrophone*] mono

mono... [mɔno] PRÉF mono...

monoacide [mɔnoasid] ADJ mon(o)acid

monobasique [mɔnobazik] ADJ monobasic

monobloc [mɔnoblɔk] ADJ cast in one piece

monocaméral (*pl* **-aux**) [mɔnokameʀal, o] ADJ M unicameral

monocamérisme [mɔnokameʀism] NM unicameralism

monochromatique [mɔnokʀɔmatik] ADJ monochromatic

monochrome [mɔnokʀom] ADJ monochrome, monochromatic

monocle [mɔnɔkl] NM monocle, eyeglass

monoclonal, e (*mpl* **-aux**) [mɔnoklɔnal, o] ADJ monoclonal

monocoque [mɔnokɔk] **1** ADJ [*voiture, avion*] monocoque; [*yacht*] monohull, single-hull; **voilier ~** monohull **2** NM (= *voilier*) monohull

monocorde [mɔnokɔʀd] **1** ADJ [*instrument*] with a single chord; [*voix, timbre, discours*] monotonous; **sur un ton ~** in a monotonous voice **2** NM monochord

monocorps [mɔnokɔʀ] ADJ [*voiture*] monobox, with a one-box design

monocotylédone [mɔnokɔtiledɔn] **1** ADJ monocotyledonous **2** NF monocotyledon; **les ~s** monocotyledons, the Monocotyledonae (*SPÉC*)

monocratie [mɔnokʀasi] NF monocracy

monoculture [mɔnokyltyʀ] NF single-crop farming, monoculture

monocycle [mɔnosikl] NM monocycle, unicycle

monocylindre [mɔnosilɛ̃dʀ] NM single-cylinder engine

monocyte [mɔnɔsit] NM monocyte

monodie [mɔnɔdi] NF monody

monogame [mɔnɔgam] **1** ADJ monogamous; (*Zool*) **union ~** pair-bonding **2** NMF monogamist

monogamie [mɔnɔgami] NF monogamy

monogamique [mɔnɔgamik] ADJ monogamistic

monogramme [mɔnɔgʀam] NM monogram

monographie [mɔnɔgʀafi] NF monograph

monoï [mɔnɔj] NM INV monoï (*perfumed oil made from coconut and Tahitian flowers*)

monokini [mɔnokini] NM topless swimsuit, monokini; **faire du ~** to go topless

monolingue [mɔnolɛ̃g] ADJ monolingual

monolinguisme [mɔnolɛ̃gɥism] NM monolingualism

monolithe [mɔnolit] **1** NM monolith **2** ADJ monolithic

monolithique [mɔnolitik] ADJ (*lit, fig*) monolithic

monolithisme [mɔnolitism] NM (*Archit, Constr*) monolithism

monologue [mɔnolɔg] NM monologue, soliloquy; (*Littérat*) **~ intérieur** stream of consciousness

monologuer [mɔnɔlɔge] ▶conjug 1◀ VI to soliloquize; (*péj*) **il monologue pendant des heures** he talks away *ou* holds forth for hours

monomane [mɔnɔman], **monomaniaque** [mɔnɔmanjak] ADJ, NMF monomaniac

monomanie [mɔnɔmani] NF monomania

monôme [mɔnom] NM (*Math*) monomial; (*arg Scol*) students' rag procession

monomère [mɔnɔmɛʀ] 1 ADJ monomeric 2 NM monomer

monométallisme [mɔnɔmetalism] NM monometallism

monomoteur, -trice [mɔnɔmɔtœʀ, tʀis] 1 ADJ single-engined 2 NM single-engined aircraft

mononucléaire [mɔnɔnykleɛʀ] 1 ADJ (*Bio*) mononuclear 2 NM mononuclear (cell), mononucleate

mononucléose [mɔnɔnykleoz] NF mononucleosis; **~ infectieuse** infectious mononucleosis (*SPÉC*), glandular fever (*Brit*)

monoparental, e (*mpl* **-aux**) [mɔnɔpaʀɑ̃tal, o] ADJ **famille ~e** single-parent *ou* lone-parent *ou* one-parent family; **foyer ~** single-parent *ou* lone-parent *ou* one-parent household

monophasé, e [mɔnɔfaze] 1 ADJ single-phase (*épith*) 2 NM single-phase current

monophonie [mɔnɔfɔni] NF monaural *ou* monophonic reproduction

monophonique [mɔnɔfɔnik] ADJ monaural, monophonic

monoplace [mɔnɔplas] 1 ADJ single-seater (*épith*), one-seater (*épith*) 2 NMF (*Aut, Aviat*) single-seater, one-seater

monoplan [mɔnɔplɑ̃] NM monoplane

monoplégie [mɔnɔpleʒi] NF monoplegia

monopole [mɔnɔpɔl] NM (*Écon, fig*) monopoly; **avoir le ~ de** (*Écon*) to have the monopoly of; [+ *vérité, savoir*] to have a monopoly on; **avoir un ~ sur** to have a monopoly in; **être en situation de ~** to have a monopoly, be in a monopoly position; **~ d'achat** monopsony, buyer's monopoly; **~ d'État** state *ou* public monopoly; **~ fiscal** tax monopoly

monopolisateur, -trice [mɔnɔpɔlizatœʀ, tʀis] NM,F monopolizer

monopolisation [mɔnɔpɔlizasjɔ̃] NF monopolization

monopoliser [mɔnɔpɔlize] ▶conjug 1◀ VT (*lit, fig*) to monopolize; **il a monopolisé la parole toute la soirée** he monopolized the conversation all evening, he didn't let anybody get a word in all evening

monopoliste [mɔnɔpɔlist], **monopolistique** [mɔnɔpɔlistik] ADJ monopolistic

Monopoly ® [mɔnɔpɔli] NM Monopoly®; **jouer au ~** to play Monopoly; (*fig*) **c'est un vaste jeu de ~** it's one great big Monopoly game

monoprix ® [mɔnɔpʀi] NM *well-known French department store*

monorail [mɔnɔʀaj] NM (= *voie*) monorail; (= *voiture*) monorail coach

monosémique [mɔnɔsemik] ADJ monosemic

monoski [mɔnɔski] NM monoski; **faire du ~** to go monoskiing

monospace [mɔnɔspas] NM people carrier (*Brit*), minivan (*US*)

monosyllabe [mɔnɔsi(l)lab] NM (*lit, fig*) monosyllable; **répondre par ~s** to reply in monosyllables

monosyllabique [mɔnɔsi(l)labik] ADJ monosyllabic

monosyllabisme [mɔnɔsil(l)abism] NM monosyllabism

monothéique [mɔnɔteik] ADJ monotheistic

monothéisme [mɔnɔteism] NM monotheism

monothéiste [mɔnɔteist] 1 ADJ monotheistic 2 NMF monotheist

monothérapie [mɔnɔteʀapi] NF (*Méd*) monotherapy, single-drug treatment

monotone [mɔnɔtɔn] ADJ [*son, voix, paysage, tâche*] monotonous; [*spectacle, style, discours*] monotonous, dull, dreary; [*existence, vie*] monotonous, humdrum, dull; (*Math*) monotone

monotonie [mɔnɔtɔni] NF [*son, voix, paysage, tâche*] monotony; [*discours, spectacle, vie*] monotony, dullness

monotrème [mɔnɔtʀɛm] 1 ADJ monotrematous 2 NM monotreme; **les ~s** monotremes, the Monotremata (*SPÉC*)

monotype [mɔnɔtip] NM (*Art*) monotype; (*Naut*) one-design sailboat

monovalent, e [mɔnɔvalɑ̃, ɑ̃t] ADJ (*Chim*) monovalent, univalent

monoxyde [mɔnɔksid] NM monoxide; **~ de carbone** carbon monoxide; **~ d'azote** nitric oxide

monozygote [mɔnɔzigɔt] ADJ monozygotic

Monrovia [mɔ̃ʀɔvja] N Monrovia

Monseigneur [mɔ̃sɛɲœʀ] (*pl* **Messeigneurs** [mesɛɲœʀ]) NM a (*formule d'adresse*) (*à archevêque, duc*) Your Grace; (*à cardinal*) Your Eminence; (*à évêque*) Your Grace, Your Lordship, My Lord (Bishop); (*à prince*) Your (Royal) Highness b (*à la troisième personne*) (*à archevêque, duc*) His Grace; (*à cardinal*) His Eminence; (*à évêque*) His Lordship; (*à prince*) His (Royal) Highness

Monsieur [məsjø] (*pl* **Messieurs** [mesjø]) NM a (*s'adressant à qn*) **bonjour ~** (*gén*) good morning; (*nom connu*) good morning Mr X; (*nom inconnu*) good morning, good morning, sir (*frm*); **bonjour Messieurs** good morning (gentlemen); **(bonjour) Messieurs Dames*** morning all *ou* everyone*; **~, vous avez oublié quelque chose** excuse me, you've forgotten something; (*au restaurant*) **et pour (vous) ~/ Messieurs?** and for you, sir/gentlemen?; (*devant un auditoire*) **Messieurs** gentlemen; **Messieurs et chers collègues** gentlemen; **~ le Président** [*gouvernement*] Mr President; [*entreprise*] Mr Chairman; **oui, ~ le juge** ≈ yes, Your Honour *ou* My Lord *ou* Your Worship; **~ l'abbé** Father; **~ le curé** Father; **~ le ministre** Minister; **~ le duc** Your Grace; **~ le comte** (*ou* **baron** *etc*) Your Lordship, my Lord; (*frm*) **~ devrait prendre son parapluie** I suggest you take your umbrella, sir (*frm*); (*frm*) **~ est servi** dinner is served, sir (*frm*); (*iro*) **~ n'est pas content?** is something not to Your Honour's (*iro*) *ou* Your Lordship's (*iro*) liking?; **mon bon ou pauvre ~*** my dear sir → **Madame**
b (*parlant de qn*) **~ X est malade** Mr X is ill; († *ou iro*) **~ votre fils** your dear son; (*frm*) **est sorti** Mr X *ou* the Master (of the house) is not at home; **~ dit que c'est à lui** the gentleman says it's his; **~ le Président** the President, the Chairman; **~ le juge X** ≈ (His Honour) Judge X; **~ le duc de X** (His Grace) the Duke of X; **~ l'abbé (X)** Father X; **~ le curé** the parish priest; **~ le curé X** Father X; (*Cirque*) **~ loyal** ringmaster
c (*sur une enveloppe*) **~ John X** Mr John X, John X Esq; (*à un enfant*) Master John X; **Messieurs Dupont** Messrs Dupont and Dupont; **Messieurs J. et P. Dupont** Messrs J and P Dupont; **Messieurs Dupont et fils** Messrs Dupont and Son; **Messieurs X et Y** Messrs X and Y → **Madame**
d (*en-tête de lettre*) **~** (*gén*) Dear Sir; (*personne connue*) Dear Mr X; **cher ~** Dear Mr X; **~ et cher collègue** My dear Sir, Dear Mr X; **~ le Président** [*gouvernement*] Dear Mr President; [*entreprise*] Dear Mr Chairman
e (*Hist = parent du roi*) Monsieur
f (*sans majuscule*) gentleman; (= *personnage important*) great man; **ces messieurs désirent?** what would you like, gentlemen?; **maintenant il se prend pour un monsieur** he thinks he's quite the gentleman now, he fancies himself as a (proper) gentleman now (*Brit*); **les beaux**

messieurs the well-to-do *ou* smart (*Brit*) gentlemen; **c'est un grand monsieur** he's a great man; (*langage enfantin*) **un méchant monsieur** a nasty man
g (= *représentant*) **~ Tout-le-monde** the man in the street, the average man; **~ Muscle** Muscleman; (= *responsable*) **~ Météo** the weatherman

monstre [mɔ̃stʀ] 1 NM a (*Bio, Zool*) (*par la difformité*) freak (of nature), monster; (*par la taille*) monster
b (*Myth*) monster; (*fig*) **~ sacré** giant; **un ~ sacré du théâtre** a legendary figure in the theatre; **un ~ sacré du cinéma** a screen giant *ou* legend
c (*péj = méchant*) monster, brute; **c'est un ~ (de laideur)** he is monstrously *ou* hideously ugly; **c'est un ~ (de méchanceté)** he's a wicked *ou* an absolute monster; **quel ~ d'égoïsme !/d'orgueil !** what fiendish *ou* monstrous egoism!/pride!; **être un ~ froid** to be pitiless
d (* : *affectueux*) **petit ~!** you little monster!* *ou* horror!*
2 ADJ* (*rabais*) gigantic, colossal, mammoth; [*manifestation, foule, embouteillage*] massive; **succès ~** runaway *ou* raving* success; **elle a un culot ~** she's got a hell of a nerve*; **il gagne un argent ~** he earns a vast amount of money; **faire une publicité ~ à qch** to launch a massive publicity campaign for sth; **j'ai un travail ~** I've got loads* of work to do *ou* a horrendous amount of work to do; **un dîner ~** a colossal dinner, a whacking* great dinner (*Brit*)

monstrueusement [mɔ̃stʀyøzmɑ̃] ADV [*laid*] monstrously, hideously; [*intelligent*] prodigiously, stupendously; [*riche*] enormously; **il est ~ gros** he's massively overweight

monstrueux, -euse [mɔ̃stʀyø, øz] ADJ (= *difforme*) [*bête*] monstrous; [*personne*] freakish; [*bâtiment*] hideous; (= *abominable*) [*guerre, massacre*] horrendous; [*crime*] heinous, monstrous; (* = *gigantesque*) [*erreur, bruit*] horrendous; [*appétit*] terrific, huge; **faire du chantage, c'est ~!** blackmail! that's monstrous!

monstruosité [mɔ̃stʀyozite] NF a [*crime*] monstrousness, monstrosity b (= *acte*) monstrous act, monstrosity; (= *propos*) monstrous remark; **dire des ~s** to say monstrous *ou* horrendous things c (= *laideur*) hideousness

mont [mɔ̃] 1 NM a (= *montagne*) (*littér*) mountain; (*avec un nom propre*) **le ~ X** Mount X; (*littér*) **par ~s et par vaux** up hill and down dale; **être toujours par ~s et par vaux*** to be always on the move* → **promettre** b (*Voyance*) [*main*] mount 2 COMP ▸ **les monts d'Auvergne** the mountains of Auvergne, the Auvergne mountains ▸ **le mont Blanc** Mont Blanc ▸ **le mont Carmel** Mount Carmel ▸ **le mont des Oliviers** the Mount of Olives ▸ **le mont Sinaï** Mount Sinaï ▸ **mont de Vénus** (*Anat*) mons veneris

montage [mɔ̃taʒ] NM a (= *assemblage*) [*appareil, montre*] assembly; [*bijou*] mounting, setting; [*manche*] setting in; [*tente*] pitching, putting up; **le ~ d'une opération publicitaire** the mounting *ou* organization of an advertising campaign; **~ financier** financial set-up *ou* arrangement; **il faut décider du ~ financier de l'opération** we must decide how the operation is to be funded; **le ~ juridique adopté pour l'entreprise** the legal arrangements for setting up the company → **chaîne**
b (*Ciné*) (= *opération*) editing; **~ final** final cut *ou* edit; **réalisé par** edited *ou* editing by; **~ photographique** photomontage; **~ audiovisuel** slide show with sound; **~ vidéo** (= *film*) video(-tape); **table/salle de ~** cutting table/ room; **le film est en cours de ~** the film is being cut out *ou* edited; **cette scène a disparu au ~** this scene ended up on the cutting room floor *ou* was edited out

c (*Élec*) wiring (up); [*radio etc*] assembly; ~ **en parallèle/en série** connection in parallel/in series

d (*Typo*) paste-up

montagnard, e [mɔ̃taɲaʀ, aʀd] **1** ADJ mountain (*épith*), highland (*épith*); (*Hist Pol*) Mountain (*épith*) **2** NM,F **a** (*Géog*) mountain dweller; **~s** mountain people *ou* dwellers **b** (*Hist Pol*) **Montagnard(e)** Montagnard

montagne [mɔ̃taɲ] **1** NF **a** (= *sommet*) mountain; (= *région montagneuse*) **la ~** the mountains; **vivre à** *ou* **habiter la ~** to live in the mountains; **faire de la ~** (*en randonnée*) to go mountain-hiking; (*en escalade*) to go mountain-climbing *ou* mountaineering; **haute/moyenne/basse ~** high/medium/low mountains; **plantes des ~s** mountain plants → **chaîne**, **guide**

b (*intensif*) **une ~ de** a mountain of, masses* *ou* mountains of; **une ~ de travail l'attendait** a mountain of work was waiting for him, there was masses* of work waiting for him; **recevoir une ~ de lettres/cadeaux** to receive a whole stack of *ou* a (great) mountain of letters/presents

c (*loc*) **se faire une ~ de** *ou* **d'un rien** to make a mountain out of a molehill; **il se fait une ~ de cet examen** he's getting really worked up about this exam, he's blown this exam out of all proportion ∎ (*PROV*) **il n'y a que les ~s qui ne se rencontrent pas** there are none so distant that fate cannot bring them together; **déplacer** *ou* **soulever des ~s** to move mountains; **c'est la ~ qui accouche d'une souris** after all that it's a bit of an anticlimax; **c'est gros comme une ~*** it's obvious, it's plain for all to see

d (*Hist Pol*) **la Montagne** the Mountain

2 COMP ► **montagnes russes** roller-coaster, big dipper, scenic railway ► **montagne à vaches** low hills; (*hum*) **nous faisons de la ~ à vaches mais pas d'escalade** we only go hill walking, not rock climbing

montagneux, -euse [mɔ̃taɲø, øz] ADJ (*Géog*) mountainous; (= *accidenté*) hilly

Montana [mɔ̃tana] NM Montana

montant, e [mɔ̃tɑ̃, ɑ̃t] **1** ADJ [*mouvement*] upward, rising; [*bateau*] (travelling) upstream; [*col*] high; [*robe, corsage*] high-necked; [*chemin*] uphill; **train ~** up train; **voie ~e** up line → **chaussure**, **colonne**, **garde¹**

2 NM **a** [*échelle*] upright; [*lit*] post; [*porte*] jamb; [*échafaudage*] pole; **les ~s de la fenêtre** the uprights of the window frame; (*Ftbl*) **~ (de but)** (goal) post

b (= *somme*) (sum) total, total amount; **le ~ s'élevait à** the total added up to, the total (amount) came to *ou* was; **chèque d'un ~ de 500 F** cheque for the sum of 500 francs; **emprunt d'un ~ de 2 millions de francs** loan of 2 million francs; (*Europe*) **~s compensatoires en matière agricole** farming subsidies; **~s compensatoires monétaires** monetary compensation amounts; (*Fin, Jur*) **~ dû/forfaitaire** outstanding/flat-rate amount; (*Fin, Jur*) **~ nominal** par value; (*Jur*) **~ net d'une succession** residuary estate

c (*Équitation*) cheek-strap

mont-blanc (*pl* **monts-blancs**) [mɔ̃blɑ̃] NM (*Culin*) chestnut cream dessert (*topped with cream*)

mont-de-piété (*pl* **monts-de-piété**) [mɔ̃d(ə)pjete] NM (state-owned) pawnshop *ou* pawnbroker's; **mettre qch au ~** to pawn sth

monte [mɔ̃t] NF **a** (*Équitation*) horsemanship **b** (*Vét*) **station/service de ~** stud farm/service; **mener une jument à la ~** to take a mare to be covered

monté, e [mɔ̃te] (*ptp de* **monter**) ADJ **a** (= *équipé, pourvu*) equipped; **être bien/mal ~ en qch** to be well/ill equipped with sth **b** (**~**: *physiquement*) **il est bien ~** he's well hung* *ou* well endowed*

monte-charge (*pl* **monte-charges**) [mɔ̃tʃaʀʒ] NM hoist, goods lift (*Brit*), service elevator (*US*)

montée [mɔ̃te] NF **a** (= *escalade*) climb, climbing; **la ~ de la côte** the ascent of the hill, the climb up the hill, climbing *ou* going up the hill; **la ~ de l'escalier** climbing the stairs; **c'est une ~ difficile** it's a hard *ou* difficult climb; **en escalade, la ~ est plus facile que la descente** when you're climbing, going up is easier than coming down; **la côte était si raide qu'on a fait la ~ à pied** the hill was so steep that we walked up *ou* we went up on foot

b (= *ascension*) [*ballon, avion*] ascent; **pendant la ~ de l'ascenseur** while the lift is (*ou* was) going up

c (= *mouvement ascendant*) [*eaux*] rise; [*lait*] inflow; [*sève, homme politique, colère, hostilités*] rise; **la soudaine ~ des prix/de la température** the sudden rise in prices/in (the) temperature; **la ~ du mécontentement populaire** the rise of *ou* growth in popular discontent; **la ~ des périls en Europe** the growing danger of war in Europe

d (= *côte, pente*) hill, uphill slope; **la maison était en haut de la ~** the house stood at the top of the hill *ou* rise; **une petite ~ mène à leur maison** there is a little slope leading up to their house

monte-en-l'air*† [mɔ̃tɑ̃lɛʀ] NM INV (= *voleur*) cat burglar

monténégrin, e [mɔ̃tenegʀɛ̃, in] **1** ADJ Montenegrin, from Montenegro **2 Monténégrin(e)** NM,F Montenegrin

Monténégro [mɔ̃tenegʀo] NM Montenegro

monte-plats [mɔ̃tpla] NM INV service lift (*Brit*), dumbwaiter

monter¹ [mɔ̃te] ► conjug 1 ◄ **1** VI (*avec auxiliaire être*) **a** (*gén*) to go up (**à** to, **dans** into); [*oiseau*] to fly up; [*avion*] to climb; **~ à pied/à bicyclette/en voiture** to walk/cycle/drive up; **~ en courant/en titubant** to run/stagger up; **~ en train/par l'ascenseur** to go up by train/in the lift; **~ dans** *ou* **à sa chambre** to go up(stairs) to one's room; **il est monté en courant jusqu'au grenier** he ran up to the attic; **monte me voir** come up and see me; **monte le prévenir** go up and tell him; (*visiteur*) **faites-le ~** ask him to come up; **~ aux arbres** to climb trees; **~ à Paris** (*en voyage*) to go up to Paris; (*pour travailler*) to go to work in Paris; (*pour s'installer*) to move to Paris

b **~ sur** [+ *table, rocher, toit*] to climb (up) on *ou* onto; **monté sur une chaise, il accrochait un tableau** he was standing on a chair hanging a picture; **~ sur un arbre/une échelle** to climb up a tree/a ladder; **~ sur une colline** to go up *ou* climb up *ou* walk up a hill; **~ sur une bicyclette** to get on a bicycle; **monté sur un cheval gris** riding *ou* on a grey horse; (*fig*) **~ sur le trône** to come to *ou* ascend the throne

c (*Transport*) **~ en voiture** to get into a car; **~ dans un train/un avion** to get on *ou* into a train/an aircraft, board a train/an aircraft; **beaucoup de voyageurs sont montés à Lyon** a lot of people got on at Lyon; **~ à bord (d'un navire)** to go on board *ou* aboard (a ship); **~ à bicyclette** (= *faire du vélo*) to ride a bicycle; **~ à cheval** (= *se mettre en selle*) to get on *ou* mount a horse; (= *faire de l'équitation*) to ride, go riding; **je n'ai jamais monté** I've never been on a horse; **elle monte bien** she's a good horsewoman, she rides well

d (= *progresser: dans une hiérarchie*) to rise, go up; [*vedette*] to be on the way up; **c'est l'artiste qui monte** he's the up-and-coming artist; **c'est l'homme qui monte** he's on the way up → **grade**

e [*eau, vêtements*] **~ à** *ou* **jusqu'à** to come up to; **robe qui monte jusqu'au cou** high-necked dress; **la vase lui montait jusqu'aux genoux** the mud came right up to his knees, he was knee-deep in the mud

f (= *s'élever*) [*colline, route*] to go up, rise; [*soleil, flamme, brouillard*] to rise; **~ en pente douce** to slope gently upwards, rise gently; **le chemin monte en lacets** the path winds *ou* twists upwards; **jusqu'où monte le téléphérique?** where does the cable car go up to?; **notre maison monte très lentement** building is progressing very slowly on our house, our house is going up very slowly; **un bruit/une odeur montait de la cave** there was a noise/a smell coming from the cellar, a noise was drifting up/a smell was wafting up from the cellar

g (= *hausser de niveau*) [*mer, marée*] to come in; [*fleuve*] to rise; [*prix, température, baromètre*] to rise, go up; (*Mus*) [*voix, note*] to go up; **le lait monte** (*sur le feu*) the milk's about to boil over; (*dans le sein*) the milk is coming in; **~ dans l'estime de qn** to go up *ou* rise in sb's estimation; **ça a fait ~ les prix** it sent *ou* put *ou* pushed prices up; **la colère/la tension monte** tempers are/tension is rising; **le ton monte** (*colère*) the discussion is getting heated, voices are being raised; (*animation*) the conversation is getting noisier; **le tricot monte vite avec cette laine*** this wool knits up quickly; **la voiture peut ~ jusqu'à 250 km/h** the car can do up to 250 km/h, the car can reach speeds of up to 250 km/h; **ce tableau peut ~ jusqu'à 30 000 F** this painting could fetch up to 30,000 francs; (*Culin*) **les blancs montent/n'arrivent pas à ~** the egg whites are going stiff/won't whip up *ou* won't go stiff → **flèche, neige**

h (*exprimant des émotions*) **elle sentait la colère/peur ~ en elle** she could feel (the) anger/fear well up inside her; **les larmes lui montaient aux yeux** tears were welling up in her eyes, tears filled her eyes; **ça lui a fait ~ les larmes aux yeux** it brought tears to his eyes; **le vin lui monte à la tête** wine goes to his head; **le succès lui monte à la tête** success is going to his head → **moutarde, rouge**

i (*Agr*) [*plante*] to bolt, go to seed; **la salade est (toute) montée** the lettuce has bolted *ou* has gone to seed → **graine**

j (*Cartes*) to play a higher card; **il est monté à cœur** he played a higher heart

2 VT (*avec auxiliaire avoir*) **a** (= *gravir*) to go up; **~ l'escalier** *ou* **les marches précipitamment** to rush upstairs *ou* up the steps; **~ l'escalier** *ou* **les marches quatre à quatre** to go upstairs *ou* up the steps four at a time; **~ une côte** (*en marchant*) to walk *ou* go *ou* come up a hill; (*en courant*) to run up a hill; (*Mus*) **~ la gamme** to go up the scale

b (= *porter*) [+ *valise, meuble*] to take *ou* carry *ou* bring up; **montez-lui son petit déjeuner** take his breakfast up to him; **faire ~ ses valises** to have one's luggage brought *ou* taken *ou* sent up

c **~ un cheval** to ride a horse; **ce cheval n'a jamais été monté** this horse has never been ridden

d (= *augmenter*) **~ le son** to turn the sound *ou* volume up

e (= *exciter*) **~ qn contre qn** to set sb against sb; **être monté contre qn** to be dead set against sb; **~ la tête** *ou* **le bourrichon* à qn** to get sb worked up; **quelqu'un lui a monté la tête contre moi** someone has set him against me

f (*Vét* = *couvrir*) to cover, serve

g **~ la garde** (*Mil*) to mount guard, go on guard; [*chien*] to be on guard; (*sur un écriteau*) **« je monte la garde ! »** "beware of the dog"

3 **se monter** VPR **a** **se ~ à** [*prix, frais*] to come to, amount to; [*dette*] to amount to

b **se ~ la tête** *ou* **le bourrichon*** to get (all) worked up *ou* het up*; **il se monte la tête pour un rien** he gets het up* *ou* worked up over nothing

monter² [mɔ̃te] ► conjug 1 ◄ VT (*avec auxiliaire avoir*) **a** (= *assembler*) [+ *machine*] to assemble; [+ *tente*] to pitch, put up; [+ *film*] to edit, cut; [+ *robe*] to assemble, sew together; ~ **des mailles** to cast on stitches; (*Élec, Radio*) ~ **en parallèle/en série** to connect in parallel/in series

b (= *organiser*) [+ *pièce de théâtre*] to put on, stage; [+ *opération, campagne publicitaire*] to mount, organize, set up; [+ *affaire*] to set up; [+ *canular*] to play; [+ *complot*] to hatch; ~ **un coup** to plan a job; ~ **le coup à qn** to take sb for a ride♣; ~ **une histoire pour déshonorer qn** to cook up* *ou* invent a scandal to ruin sb's good name; **c'est une histoire montée de toutes pièces** it's a complete fabrication

c (= *pourvoir, équiper*) to equip; ~ **son ménage** *ou* **sa maison** to set up house; **se ~ en linge** to equip o.s. with linen; **se ~** to get o.s. (well) set up

d (= *fixer*) [+ *diamant, perle*] to set, mount; [+ *pneu*] to put on; ~ **qch en épingle** to blow sth up out of all proportion, make a thing of sth*; **faire ~ un diamant en bague** to have a ring made with a diamond

monteur, -euse [mɔ̃tœʀ, øz] NM,F **a** (*Tech*) fitter **b** (*Ciné*) (film) editor **c** (*Typo*) paste-up artist

Montevideo [mɔ̃tevideo] N Montevideo

montgolfière [mɔ̃gɔlfjɛʀ] NF hot-air balloon; **voyage en ~** hot-air balloon trip

monticule [mɔ̃tikyl] NM (= *colline*) hillock, mound; (= *tas*) mound, heap

montmartrois, e [mɔ̃maʀtʀwa, waz] **1** ADJ of *ou* from Montmartre **2** **Montmartrois(e)** NM,F inhabitant *ou* native of Montmartre

montmorency [mɔ̃mɔʀɑ̃si] NF INV morello cherry

montrable [mɔ̃tʀabl] ADJ [*personne*] fit to be seen (*attrib*); [*objet*] which can be shown; **tu es tout à fait ~** you're quite presentable

montre¹ [mɔ̃tʀ] NF **a** (*gén*) watch; ~ **analogique** analogue watch; **~-bracelet** wrist watch; ~ **digitale** *ou* **à affichage numérique** digital watch; ~ **de gousset** fob watch; ~ **de plongée** diver's watch; ~ **de précision** precision watch; ~ **à quartz** quartz watch; ~ **à remontoir** stem-winder, stem-winding watch; ~ **à répétition** repeating *ou* repeater watch **b** (*loc*) **il est 2 heures à ma ~** it is 2 o'clock by my watch; **j'ai mis 2 heures ~ en main** it took me exactly *ou* precisely 2 hours, it took me 2 hours exactly by the clock → **chaîne, course, sens**

montre² [mɔ̃tʀ] NF **a** **faire ~ de** [+ *courage, ingéniosité*] to show, display **b** (*littér = ostentation*) **pour la ~** for show, for the sake of appearances **c** († *Comm = en vitrine*) display, show; **publication interdite à la ~** publication banned from public display; **en ~** on display *ou* show

Montréal [mɔ̃ʀeal] N Montreal

montréalais, e [mɔ̃ʀealɛ, ɛz] **1** ADJ of *ou* from Montreal **2** **Montréalais(e)** NM,F Montrealer

▼ **montrer** [mɔ̃tʀe] ▶ conjug 1 ◀ **1** VT **a** (*gén*) to show (**à** to); (*par un geste*) to point to; (= *faire remarquer*) [+ *détail, personne, faute*] to point out (**à** to); (*avec ostentation*) to show off, display (**à** to); (= *faire visiter*) **je vais vous ~ le jardin** I'll show you (round) the garden; ~ **un enfant au docteur** to let the doctor see a child; **l'aiguille montre le nord** the needle points north; ~ **ses fesses*** *ou* **son cul⁂** (= *se déculotter*) to show one's bare bottom *ou* arse⁂ (*Brit*) *ou* ass⁂ (*US*); (= *se déshabiller*) to bare all, strip naked; **je l'ai ici — montre!** I've got it here — show me!

b (= *laisser voir*) to show; **jupe qui montre le genou** skirt which leaves the knee uncovered *ou* bare; **elle montrait ses jambes en s'asseyant** she showed her legs as she sat down; (*hum*) **elle montre ses charmes** she's showing off *ou* displaying her charms (*hum*)

c (= *mettre en évidence*) to show, prove; **il a montré que l'histoire était fausse** he has

shown *ou* proved the story to be false *ou* that the story was false; **l'avenir montrera qui avait raison** the future will show *ou* prove who was right; ~ **la complexité d'un problème** to show how complex a problem is, demonstrate the complexity of a problem; **l'auteur montre un pays en décadence** the author shows *ou* depicts a country in decline; **ce qui montre bien que j'avais raison** which just goes to show that I was right

d (= *manifester*) [+ *humeur, courage*] to show, display; [+ *surprise*] to show; **son visage montra de l'étonnement** his face registered (his) surprise

e (= *apprendre*) ~ **à qn à faire** *ou* **comment faire qch** to show sb how *ou* the way to do sth

2 **se montrer** VPR **a** [*personne*] to appear, show o.s.; [*chose*] to appear; **elle ne s'est pas montrée au dîner** she didn't appear at dinner; **il n'aime pas se ~ avec elle** he doesn't like to be seen with her; **j'y vais juste pour me ~** I'm going there just to put in an appearance; (*fig*) **ton père devrait se ~ davantage** your father should assert himself more *ou* show his authority more; **sa lâcheté s'est montrée au grand jour** his cowardice was plain for all to see

b (= *s'avérer*) [*personne*] to show o.s. (to be), prove (o.s.) (to be); [*chose*] to prove (to be); **se ~ digne de sa famille** to show o.s. (to be) *ou* prove o.s. worthy of one's family; **il s'est montré très désagréable** he was very unpleasant, he behaved very unpleasantly; **il s'est montré intraitable** he was *ou* he showed himself quite unrelenting; **il faudrait se ~ plus prudent** we should be more careful; **le traitement s'est montré efficace** the treatment proved (to be) effective; **se ~ d'une lâcheté révoltante** to show *ou* display despicable cowardice; **si les circonstances se montrent favorables** if conditions prove (to be) *ou* turn out to be favourable; **il faut se ~ ferme** you must appear firm, you must show firmness

montreur, -euse [mɔ̃tʀœʀ, øz] NM,F **~ de marionnettes** puppet master (*ou* mistress), puppeteer; **~ d'ours** bear leader

montueux, -euse [mɔ̃tɥø, øz] ADJ (*littér*) (very) hilly

monture [mɔ̃tyʀ] NF **a** (= *cheval*) mount → **voyager** **b** (*Tech*) mounting; [*lunettes*] frame; [*bijou, bague*] setting; **lunettes à ~ d'écaille/de métal** horn-/metal-rimmed glasses

monument [mɔnymɑ̃] NM **a** (= *statue, ouvrage commémoratif*) monument, memorial; ~ **(funéraire)** monument; ~ **aux morts** war memorial **b** (= *bâtiment, château*) monument, building; ~ **historique** ancient monument, historic building; **la maison est classée ~ historique** the house is listed (*Brit*) *ou* is a listed building (*Brit*), the house is on the historical register (*US*); ~ **public** public building; **visiter les ~s de Paris** to go sight-seeing in Paris, see the sights of Paris **c** (= *œuvre majeure*) monument; **c'est un ~ de la littérature française** it's one of the monuments *ou* great masterpieces of French literature; **ce buffet est un ~, on ne peut pas le soulever** this sideboard is so huge, we can't shift it*; **c'est un ~ de bêtise!** what colossal *ou* monumental stupidity!

monumental, e [mɔnymɑ̃tal, o] ADJ **a** [*taille, erreur*] monumental, colossal; [*œuvre*] monumental; **d'une bêtise ~e** incredibly *ou* unbelievably stupid **b** (*Archit*) monumental

monumentalité [mɔnymɑ̃talite] NF monumentality

moquer [mɔke] ▶ conjug 1 ◀ **1** VT († *ou littér*) to mock; **j'ai été moqué** I was laughed at *ou* mocked

2 **se moquer** ◊ **se moquer de** VPR **a** (= *ridiculiser*) to make fun of, poke fun at; **on va se ~ de toi** people will laugh at you *ou* make

fun of you, you'll make yourself a laughing stock; († *ou frm*) **tu riais — oui, mais je ne me moquais pas** you were laughing — yes but I wasn't laughing at you *ou* making fun of you (*ou him etc*); **vous vous moquez, j'espère** I trust that you are not in earnest (*frm*)

b (= *tromper*) **vous vous moquez du monde** *ou* **des gens!** you've got a nerve!; **je n'aime pas qu'on se moque de moi!** I don't like being made a fool of; **le réparateur s'est vraiment moqué de nous** the repairman really took us for a ride*; **de qui se moque-t-on?** who are they trying to kid?*; **du champagne? ils ne se sont pas moqués de vous!** champagne? they really treat you right!*

c (= *mépriser*) [+ *conseils, autorité*] to scorn; **il se moque bien de nous maintenant qu'il est riche** he looks down on us *ou* looks down his nose at us now that he's rich

d (= *être indifférent*) **je m'en moque** I don't care; **je m'en moque pas mal*** I couldn't care less*; **je me moque de ne pas être cru** *ou* **qu'on ne me croie pas** I don't care if nobody believes me → **an, chemise, tiers**

moquerie [mɔkʀi] NF **a** (= *caractère*) mockery, mocking **b** (= *quolibet, sarcasme*) mockery (*NonC*), jibe; **en butte aux ~s continuelles de sa sœur** the target of constant mockery from his sister *ou* of his sister's constant mockery

moquette [mɔket] NF (= *tapis*) wall-to-wall carpeting (*NonC*), fitted carpet (*Brit*); (*Tex*) moquette; **faire poser une ~** *ou* **de la ~** to have a wall-to-wall *ou* a fitted (*Brit*) carpet laid; ~ **murale** fabric wall covering

moquetter [mɔkete] ▶ conjug 1 ◀ VT to carpet (wall-to-wall); **chambre moquettée** bedroom with wall-to-wall *ou* (a) fitted (*Brit*) carpet

moqueur, -euse [mɔkœʀ, øz] ADJ **a** (*remarque, sourire*) mocking; **il est très ~** he's always making fun of people **b** (*oiseau*) ~ mocking bird

moqueusement [mɔkøzmɑ̃] ADV mockingly

moraine [mɔʀɛn] NF moraine

morainique [mɔʀenik] ADJ morainic, morainal

moral, e¹ [mɔʀal, o] **1** ADJ **a** (= *éthique*) [*valeurs, problème*] moral; **j'ai pris l'engagement ~ de le faire** I'm morally committed to doing it; **avoir l'obligation ~e de faire** to be under a moral obligation *ou* be morally obliged to do; **conscience ~e** moral conscience; **n'avoir aucun sens ~** to be totally amoral, have no sense of right and wrong

b (= *honnête, vertueux*) [*personne, œuvre*] moral; [*conduite*] ethical, moral; **ce n'est pas très ~ de faire cela** it's not very moral *ou* ethical to do that

c (= *mental, psychologique*) [*courage, soutien, victoire*] moral; [*douleur*] mental; **il a fait preuve d'une grande force ~e** he showed great moral fibre

2 NM **a** (= *état d'esprit*) morale; **les troupes ont bon/mauvais ~** the morale of the troops is high/low; **avoir le ◊ avoir (un) bon ~** *ou* **avoir un ~ d'acier** to be in good spirits; **tu vas garder ses enfants? tu as le ~!*** you're going to babysit for him? that's brave of you!; **il a mauvais ◊ il n'a pas le ~** he is in low *ou* poor spirits; **avoir le ~ à zéro*** to be (feeling) down in the dumps*; **son ~ est (tombé) très bas** his morale is very low *ou* is at a low ebb, he's in very low spirits; **le ~ est atteint** it has shaken *ou* undermined his morale *ou* his confidence; **garder le ~** to keep one's spirits up; **remonter le ~ de qn** to cheer sb up; **il faut remonter le ~ de l'équipe** we need to boost the team's morale

b **au ~ comme au physique** mentally as well as physically; **au ~ il est irréprochable** morally he is beyond reproach

morale² [mɔʀal] NF **a** (= *doctrine*) moral doctrine *ou* code, ethic (*Philo*); (= *mœurs*) morals; (= *valeurs traditionnelles*) morality, moral standards, ethic (*Philo*); (*Philo*) **la ~** moral philosophy, ethics; **action conforme à la ~** act in keeping with morality *ou* moral standards; **c'est contraire à la ~** it's immoral; **faire la ~ à qn** to lecture sb, preach at sb; **avoir une ~ relâchée** to have loose morals; **~ protestante** Protestant ethic [b] [*fable*] moral; **la ~ de cette histoire** the moral of this story

moralement [mɔralmɑ̃] ADV [a] (= *selon l'éthique*) [*agir, se conduire*] morally [b] (= *psychologiquement*) [*responsable*] morally; **soutenir qn ~** to give moral support to sb; **il était ~ vainqueur** he scored a moral victory

moralisant, e [mɔralizɑ̃, ɑ̃t] ADJ moralizing

moralisateur, -trice [mɔralizatœʀ, tʀis] [1] ADJ [*discours, ton*] moralizing, sententious (*frm*); [*histoire*] edifying, elevating [2] NM,F moralizer

moralisation [mɔralizasjɔ̃] NF raising of moral standards (**de** in)

moraliser [mɔralize] ▶conjug 1◀ [1] VI to moralize, sermonize (*péj*) (**sur** about) [2] VT [a] (= *sermonner*) **~ qn** to preach at sb, lecture sb [b] (= *rendre plus moral*) [+ *société*] to moralize, improve the morals of; [+ *vie politique, profession*] to make more ethical

moralisme [mɔralism] NM moralism

moraliste [mɔralist] [1] ADJ moralistic [2] NMF moralist

moralité [mɔralite] NF [a] (= *mœurs*) morals, morality, moral standards; **d'une ~ douteuse** [*personne*] of doubtful morals; [*film*] of dubious morality; **d'une haute ~** [*personne*] of high moral standards; [*discours*] of a high moral tone; **la ~ publique** public morality; **il n'a aucune ~** he has no sense of right or wrong, he's totally amoral → **témoin** [b] (= *valeur*) [*attitude, action*] morality [c] (= *enseignement*) [*fable*] moral; **~ : il ne faut jamais mentir !** the moral is: never tell lies!; **~, j'ai eu une indigestion*** the result was (that) I had indigestion [d] (*Littérat*) morality play

morasse [mɔras] NF (*Typo*) final *ou* foundry proof

moratoire¹ [mɔratwaʀ] ADJ moratory; **intérêts ~s** interest on arrears

moratoire² [mɔratwaʀ], **moratorium†** [mɔratɔʀjɔm] NM (*Jur*) moratorium (**sur** on)

morave [mɔrav] [1] ADJ Moravian [2] **Morave** NMF Moravian

Moravie [mɔravi] NF Moravia

morbide [mɔrbid] ADJ (*gén, Méd*) morbid

morbidité [mɔrbidite] NF morbidity

morbier [mɔrbje] NM (= *fromage*) cow's milk cheese from the Jura; (*Helv* = *comtoise*) grandfather clock

morbleu [mɔrblø] EXCL (††, *hum*) zounds!†, gadzooks!†

morceau (*pl* **morceaux**) [mɔrso] NM [a] (= *comestible*) [*pain*] piece, bit; [*sucre*] lump; [*viande*] (*à table*) piece, bit; (*chez le boucher*) piece, cut; **~ de choix** choice morsel *ou* piece; **c'était un ~ de roi** it was fit for a king; **manger un ~** to have a bite (to eat) *ou* a snack; (*fig*) **manger** *ou* **lâcher** *ou* **cracher le ~*** (= *dénoncer*) to spill the beans*; (= *avouer*) to come clean*; **il a emporté le ~*** (= *il a gagné*) he carried it off → **bas¹, sucre**
[b] (= *fragment*: *gén*) piece; [*bois*] piece, lump; [*fer*] lump; [*ficelle*] bit; [*terre*] piece, patch, plot; [*tissu*] piece; **en ~x** in pieces; **couper en ~x** to cut into pieces; **mettre qch en ~x** to pull sth to bits *ou* pieces; **tomber en ~x** [*empire, relation*] to crumble, fall apart; [*gâteau*] to crumble to bits
[c] (*Littérat, Mus*) (= *œuvre*) piece; (= *extrait*) passage, excerpt; **(recueil de) ~x choisis** (collection of) selected passages *ou* extracts; **un beau ~ d'éloquence** a fine piece of eloquence; **c'est un ~ d'anthologie** it's a classic; **~ de bravoure** (*Littérat*) purple passage; (*Mus*) bravura passage; **~ de concours** competition piece; **~ pour piano/violon** piece for piano/violin
[d] (* = *personne, objet*) **c'est un sacré ~** he (*ou* it *etc*) is a hell of a size*; **beau ~** (= *femme*) nice bit of stuff* (*Brit*), nice-looking woman

morceler [mɔrsəle] ▶conjug 4◀ VT [+ *domaine, terrain*] to parcel out, divide up; [+ *héritage*] to divide up; [+ *troupes, territoire*] to divide up, split up; (*Pol*) **opposition morcelée** divided opposition

morcellement [mɔrsɛlmɑ̃] NM [a] (= *action*) [*domaine, terrain*] parcelling (out), dividing (up); [*héritage*] division, dividing (up); [*troupes, territoire*] division, dividing (up), splitting (up) [b] (= *résultat*) division

mordant, e [mɔrdɑ̃, ɑ̃t] [1] ADJ [a] (= *caustique*) [*ton, réplique*] cutting, scathing, mordant, caustic; [*pamphlet*] scathing, cutting; [*polémiste, critique*] scathing; **avec une ironie ~e** with caustic *ou* biting *ou* mordant irony [b] [*froid*] biting (*épith*) [2] NM [a] (= *dynamisme*) [*personne*] spirit, drive; [*troupe, équipe*] spirit, keenness; [*style, écrit*] bite, punch; **discours plein de ~** speech full of bite *ou* punch [b] [*scie*] bite [c] (*Tech*) mordant [d] (*Mus*) mordent

mordicus* [mɔrdikys] ADV [*défendre, soutenir, affirmer*] obstinately, stubbornly

mordieu†† [mɔrdjø] EXCL 'sdeath!†

mordillage [mɔrdijaʒ], **mordillement** [mɔrdijmɑ̃] NM nibble, nibbling (*NonC*)

mordiller [mɔrdije] ▶conjug 1◀ VT to chew at, nibble at

mordoré, e [mɔrdɔre] ADJ, NM (lustrous) bronze; **les tons ~s de l'automne** the rich bronze tints *ou* the browns and golds of autumn

mordorure [mɔrdɔryr] NF (*littér*) bronze; **les ~s de l'étoffe** the bronze lustre of the cloth

mordre [mɔrdr] ▶conjug 41◀ [1] VT [a] (*animal, personne*) to bite; **~ qn à la main** to bite sb's hand; **un chien l'a mordu à la jambe** ◊ **il s'est fait ~ à la jambe par un chien** a dog bit him on the leg, he was bitten on the leg by a dog; **~ une pomme** to bite into an apple; **~ un petit bout de qch** to bite off a small piece of sth, take a small bite (out) of sth; **le chien l'a mordu jusqu'au sang** the dog bit him and drew blood; **approche, je ne mords pas** come closer, I won't bite you; **~ la poussière** to bite the dust; **faire ~ la poussière à qn** to make sb bite the dust
[b] [*lime, vis*] to bite into; [*acide*] to bite (into), eat into; [*froid*] to bite, nip; **les crampons mordaient la glace** the crampons gripped the ice *ou* bit into the ice; **l'inquiétude/la jalousie lui mordait le cœur** worry/jealousy was eating at *ou* gnawing at his heart
[c] (= *toucher*) **la balle a mordu la ligne** the ball (just) touched the line; **~ la ligne de départ** to be touching the starting line; (*Aut*) **~ la ligne blanche** to go over *ou* cross the white line
[2] **mordre sur** VT INDIR (= *empiéter sur*) [+ *vacances*] to overlap into, eat into; [+ *espace*] to overlap into, encroach onto; (= *corroder*) to bite into; **ça ~ a sur l'autre semaine** that will go over into *ou* overlap into *ou* cut into the following week; **~ sur la marge** to go over into the margin; **ils mordent sur notre clientèle** they're eating into *ou* cutting into our customer base; (*Aut*) **il a mordu sur la ligne blanche** he went over *ou* crossed the white line
[3] VI [a] **~ dans** [+ *fruit*] to bite into; (*Naut*) **~ dans le sable** [*ancre*] to grip *ou* hold the sand [b] (*Pêche, fig*) to bite; **~ (à l'hameçon** *ou* **à l'appât)** (*lit*) to bite, rise (to the bait); (*fig*) to rise to the bait; **ça mord aujourd'hui ?** are the fish biting *ou* rising today?; **il a mordu au latin/aux maths*** he's taken to Latin/to maths [c] (*Gravure*) to bite; [*étoffe*] to take the dye; [*teinture*] to take [d] (*Tech*) **l'engrenage ne mord plus** the gear won't mesh any more
[4] **se mordre** VPR **se ~ la joue** to bite the inside of one's mouth; **se ~ la langue** (*lit*) to bite one's tongue; (*fig*) (= *se retenir*) to hold one's tongue; (= *se repentir*) to bite one's tongue; **maintenant il s'en mord les doigts** he could kick himself now*; **tu t'en mordras les doigts** you'll live to regret it, you'll rue the day; **se ~ la queue** [*chien*] to chase its tail; (* *fig*) to chase one's tail

mordu, e [mɔrdy] (*ptp de* **mordre**) [1] ADJ [a] (* = *amoureux*) smitten; **il est vraiment ~** he's really smitten with her, he's crazy* about her [b] (* = *fanatique*) **~ de football/jazz** crazy* *ou* mad* about *ou* mad keen* on (*Brit*) football/ jazz [2] NM,F (* = *fanatique*) enthusiast, buff*, fan; **~ de la voile/de musique** sailing/music enthusiast *ou* buff*; **~ de l'ordinateur** computer buff* *ou* freak*; **c'est un ~ de football** he's a great football fan *ou* buff*

more [mɔr], **moresque** [mɔresk] ADJ, NMF = **maure, mauresque**

morfal, e (*mpl* **morfals**) ‡ [mɔrfal] NM,F greedy guts‡, pig‡

morfler‡ [mɔrfle] ▶conjug 1◀ VI (= *souffrir*) to have a hard time of it; (= *se faire battre*) to catch it*, cop it‡ (*Brit*); **j'ai une rage de dents, qu'est-ce que je morfle !** I've got a toothache, it's agony!* *ou* it's killing me!*; **ça va ~ !** there's going to be trouble!

morfondre (se) [mɔrfɔ̃dr] ▶conjug 42◀ VPR (*tristement*) to mope; (*nerveusement*) to fret; **il se morfondait en attendant le résultat** he waited fretfully for the result; **les enfants qui se morfondent dans les orphelinats** children languishing in orphanages

morfondu, e [mɔrfɔ̃dy] (*ptp de* **morfondre**) ADJ (*littér*) dejected, crestfallen

morganatique [mɔrganatik] ADJ morganatic

morgue¹ [mɔrg] NF (*littér* = *orgueil*) pride, haughtiness; **il me répondit plein de ~ que ...** he answered me haughtily that ...

morgue² [mɔrg] NF (*Police*) morgue; [*hôpital*] mortuary

moribond, e [mɔribɔ̃, ɔ̃d] [1] ADJ [*personne*] dying; [*économie, marché, institution*] moribund [2] NM,F dying man (*ou* woman); **les ~s** the dying

moricaud, e* [mɔriko, od] (*injurieux*) [1] ADJ dark(-skinned) [2] NM,F darkie‡ (*injurieux*), wog‡ (*injurieux*)

morigéner [mɔriʒene] ▶conjug 6◀ VT (*littér*) to take to task, reprimand; **il faut le ~** he will have to be taken to task (over it) *ou* reprimanded (for it)

morille [mɔrij] NF morel

morillon [mɔrijɔ̃] NM [a] (= *canard*) tufted duck [b] (= *raisin*) kind of black grape [c] (= *pierre*) small rough emerald

mormon, e [mɔrmɔ̃, ɔn] ADJ, NM,F Mormon

mormonisme [mɔrmɔnism] NM Mormonism

morne [mɔrn] ADJ [*personne, visage*] doleful, glum; [*temps*] gloomy, dismal, dull; [*silence*] mournful, gloomy, dismal; [*conversation, vie, paysage, ville*] dismal, dreary, dull; **d'un ton ~** gloomily; **passer un après-midi ~** to spend a dreary *ou* dismal afternoon

mornifle‡ [mɔrnifl] NF slap, clout* (*Brit*); **donner** *ou* **filer** *ou* **flanquer une ~ à qn** to box sb's ears, give sb a clip round the ear (*Brit*)

Moroni [mɔrɔni] N Moroni

morose [mɔroz] ADJ [*humeur, personne, ton*] sullen, morose; [*marché, Bourse, journée*] sluggish, dull → **délectation**

morosité [mɔrozite] NF [*personne*] sullenness, moroseness; [*temps*] dullness; [*marché, économie*] sluggishness; **climat de ~ économique/sociale** gloomy *ou* depressed economic/social climate

morphe [mɔrf] NM morph

Morphée [mɔrfe] NM Morpheus → **bras**

morphème [mɔʀfɛm] NM morpheme; **~ libre/lié** free/bound morpheme

morphine [mɔʀfin] NF morphine; **~-base** morphine base

morphinique [mɔʀfinik] ADJ [médicament, substance] morphinated, containing morphine

morphinisme [mɔʀfinism] NM morphinism

morphinomane [mɔʀfinɔman] **1** ADJ addicted to morphine **2** NMF morphine addict

morphinomanie [mɔʀfinɔmani] NF morphine addiction, morphinomania

morphologie [mɔʀfɔlɔʒi] NF morphology

morphologique [mɔʀfɔlɔʒik] ADJ morphological

morphologiquement [mɔʀfɔlɔʒikmɑ̃] ADV morphologically

morphophonologie [mɔʀfɔfɔnɔlɔʒi] NF morphophonology

morphosyntaxe [mɔʀfosɛ̃taks] NF morphosyntax

morphosyntaxique [mɔʀfosɛ̃taksik] ADJ morphosyntactical

morpion [mɔʀpjɔ̃] NM **a** (Jeux) ≈ noughts and crosses (Brit), ≈ tic tac toe (US) **b** (** = pou du pubis) crab* **c** (*, péj = gamin) brat*

mors [mɔʀ] NM **a** (Équitation) bit; **prendre le ~ aux dents** [cheval] to take the bit between its teeth; (= agir) to take the bit between one's teeth; (= s'emporter) to fly off the handle*, blow one's top* ou stack* (US); (= prendre l'initiative) to take the matter into one's own hands **b** (Tech) jaw; (Reliure) joint

morse¹ [mɔʀs] NM (Zool) walrus

morse² [mɔʀs] NM (= code) Morse (code)

morsure [mɔʀsyʀ] NF bite; **~ de chien** dog bite; **~ de serpent** snakebite; (littér) **les ~s du vent/du froid** the biting wind/cold

▼ **mort¹** [mɔʀ] **1** NF **a** (Physiol) death; **~ clinique/cérébrale** clinical/brain death; **~ naturelle** natural death; **~ subite du nourrisson** cot (Brit) ou crib (US) death, sudden infant death syndrome; **~ volontaire** suicide; (hum) **tu veux ma ~?** do you want to kill me or what?*; **trouver la ~ dans un accident** to die ou be killed in an accident; **souhaiter la ~** to long for death, long to die; **souhaiter la ~ de qn** to wish death upon sb (littér), wish sb (were) dead; **donner la ~ (à qn)** to kill (sb); **se donner la ~** to take one's own life, kill o.s.; **périr** ou **mourir de ~ violente/accidentelle** to die a violent/an accidental death; **mourir dans son sommeil** c'est une belle **~** dying in one's sleep is a good way to go; **à la ~ de sa mère** on the death of his mother, when his mother died; **il a vu la ~ de près** he has come close to death, he has looked death in the face; **il n'y a pas eu ~ d'homme** no one was killed, there was no loss of life; (littér) **la petite ~** orgasm, petite mort (littér); **ça coûte 100 F, ce n'est pas la ~!** it's only 100 francs, it won't kill you (ou me etc)!* → **hurler, pâle**
b (= destruction, fin) death, end; **c'est la ~ de ses espoirs** that puts an end to ou is the end of his hopes, that puts paid to his hopes (Brit); **le supermarché sera la ~ du petit commerce** supermarkets will spell the end ou the death of small businesses; **cet enfant sera ma ~!** this child will be the death of me!*
c (= douleur) **souffrir mille ~s** to suffer agonies, be in agony; **la ~ dans l'âme** with a heavy ou an aching heart, grieving inwardly; **il avait la ~ dans l'âme** his heart ached
d (dans slogan) **~ au tyran!** ◊ **à ~ le tyran!** down with the tyrant!, death to the tyrant!; **~ aux vaches!** down with the cops!* ou pigs!* → **mort²**

2 de mort LOC ADJ **silence de ~** deathly ou deathlike hush; **d'une pâleur de ~** deathly ou deadly pale; **engin de ~** lethal ou deadly weapon

3 à mort LOC ADJ, LOC ADV **lutte à ~** fight to the death; **détester qn à ~** to hate sb to death; **blessé à ~** (dans un combat) mortally wounded; (dans un accident) fatally injured; **frapper qn à ~** to strike sb dead; **mettre à ~** [+ personne] to deliver the death blow to; [+ taureau] to put to death; **mise à ~** [taureau] kill; (fig) **nous sommes fâchés à ~** we're at daggers drawn (with each other); (fig) **en vouloir à qn à ~** to be bitterly resentful of sb; **il m'en veut à ~** he hates me ou my guts‡ (for it); (fig) **défendre qch à ~** to defend sth to the bitter end; **freiner à ~*** to jam on the brakes ou the anchors* (Brit); **s'ennuyer à ~** to be bored to death; **visser qch à ~*** to screw sth right home, screw sth tight

mort², e [mɔʀ, mɔʀt] (ptp de **mourir**) **1** ADJ
a [être animé, arbre, feuille] dead; **il est ~ depuis deux ans** he's been dead (for) two years, he died 2 years ago; **on l'a laissé pour ~** he was left for dead; **il est ~ et bien ~** he's dead and gone; **il est ~ et enterré** he's dead and buried; **ramenez-les ~s ou vifs** bring them back dead or alive; (Mil) **~ au champ d'honneur** killed in action; **il était comme ~** he looked (as though he were) dead; **tu es un homme ~!** you're a dead man!*
b (fig) **je suis ~ (de fatigue)!** I'm dead (tired)! ou dead beat!*, I'm all in!* (Brit); **il était ~ de peur** ou **plus ~ que vif** he was frightened to death ou scared stiff*; **ils étaient ~s de rire** they were doubled up with laughter → **ivre**
c (= inerte, sans vie) [chair, peau, rivière] dead; [pied, doigt] dead, numb; [yeux] lifeless, dull; (Fin) [marché] dead; **la ville est ~e le dimanche** the town is dead on a Sunday; **opération ville ~e** decision to close shops and businesses for a short period in protest, mourning etc → **poids, point¹, temps¹**
d (= qui n'existe plus) [civilisation] extinct, dead; [langue] dead; **leur vieille amitié est ~e** their old friendship is dead; **le passé est bien ~** the past is over and done with ou is dead and gone
e (* = usé, fini) [pile, radio, moteur] dead

2 NM **a** (= personne) dead man; **les ~s** the dead; **les ~s de la guerre** those ou the men killed in the war, the war dead; **il y a eu un ~** one person was killed, there was one death; **il y a eu de nombreux ~s** many (people) were killed, there were many deaths; **l'accident a fait cinq ~s** five (people) were killed in the accident; **jour** ou **fête des ~s** All Souls' Day; **office/messe/prière des ~s** office/mass/prayer for the dead; **c'est un ~ vivant/un ~ en sursis** he's more dead than alive/living on borrowed time; **faire le ~** (lit) to pretend to be dead, sham death; (fig = ne pas se manifester) to lie low; (Aut) **la place du ~** the (front) seat next to the driver ou **monument, tête**
b (Cartes) dummy; **être le ~** to be dummy

3 morte NF dead woman

mortadelle [mɔʀtadɛl] NF mortadella

mortaise [mɔʀtɛz] NF mortise

mortaiser [mɔʀteze] ▶ conjug 1 ◀ VT to mortise

mortalité [mɔʀtalite] NF mortality, death rate; **~ infantile** infant mortality; **régression de la ~** fall in the death rate

mort-aux-rats [mɔʀ(t)oʀa] NF INV rat poison

morte-eau (pl **mortes-eaux**) [mɔʀto] NF neap tide

mortel, -elle [mɔʀtɛl] **1** ADJ **a** (= qui périt) mortal → **dépouille**
b (= entraînant la mort) [chute, maladie] fatal; [blessure, plaie] fatal, lethal; [poison] deadly, lethal; **danger ~** mortal danger; **coup ~** (lit) lethal ou fatal blow; (fig) death-blow; **cela a porté un coup ~ au parti** this dealt the death-blow to the party; **cette révélation lui serait mortelle** such a discovery would kill him ou would be fatal to him
c (= intense) [frayeur] mortal; [pâleur, silence] deadly, deathly; [ennemi] mortal, deadly;

[haine] deadly; **il fait un froid ~** it's deathly cold, it's as cold as death; **cette attente mortelle se prolongeait** this deadly wait dragged on; **allons, ce n'est pas ~!** come on, it's not all that bad! ou it won't kill you!
d (* = ennuyeux) [livre, soirée] deadly*, deadly boring ou dull; **il est ~** he's a deadly* ou crashing* bore

2 NM,F (littér, hum) mortal; **simple ~** mere mortal; **heureux ~!*** lucky fellow!* ou chap!* (Brit); (hum) **nous autres pauvres ~s** we lesser mortals → **commun**

mortellement [mɔʀtɛlmɑ̃] ADV [blesser] (dans un combat) mortally; (dans un accident) fatally; [offenser, vexer] mortally, deeply; **~ pâle** deadly ou deathly pale; **~ ennuyeux** deadly boring ou dull

morte-saison (pl **mortes-saisons**), **morte saison** [mɔʀt(ə)sɛzɔ̃] NF off-season, slack season; **à la ~** in ou during the off-season

mortier [mɔʀtje] NM (Constr, Culin, Mil, Pharm) mortar; (= toque) cap (worn by certain French judges); **attaque au ~** mortar attack

mortifère [mɔʀtifɛʀ] ADJ (hum) [ambiance, discours] deadly*

mortifiant, e [mɔʀtifjɑ̃, jɑ̃t] ADJ [paroles] hurtful; [expérience] mortifying; [échec] humiliating

mortification [mɔʀtifikasjɔ̃] NF mortification

mortifier [mɔʀtifje] ▶ conjug 7 ◀ VT (Rel) to mortify; (= vexer) to mortify

mortinatalité [mɔʀtinatalite] NF incidence of stillbirths

mort-né, mort-née (mpl **mort-nés**, fpl **mort-nées**) [mɔʀne] ADJ [enfant] stillborn; [projet] abortive, stillborn

mortuaire [mɔʀtɥɛʀ] ADJ [chapelle] mortuary (épith); [rites] mortuary (épith), funeral (épith); [cérémonie] funeral (épith); (Can) **salon ~** funeral home ou parlor (US, Can); **la chambre ~** the death chamber; **la maison ~** the house of the departed ou deceased → **couronne, drap, masque**

morue [mɔʀy] NF **a** (Zool) cod; **~ fraîche/séchée/salée** fresh/dried/salted cod; **~ verte** undried salted cod → **brandade, huile b** (* = prostituée) whore, tart‡

morutier, -ière [mɔʀytje, jɛʀ] **1** ADJ cod-fishing (épith) **2** NM (= pêcheur) cod-fisherman; (= bateau) cod-fishing boat

morve [mɔʀv] NF snot‡, (nasal) mucus; (Vét) glanders sg

morveux, -euse [mɔʀvø, øz] **1** ADJ **a** [enfant] snotty(-nosed)‡; ■ (PROV) **qui se sent ~, qu'il se mouche** if the cap ou shoe (US) fits, wear it (PROV) **b** (Zool) glandered **2** NM,F‡ (= enfant) nasty little brat*; (= adulte) jerk*

mosaïque¹ [mɔzaik] NF (Art, Bot) mosaic; [champs] chequered pattern, patchwork; [idées, peuples] medley; **de** ou **en ~** mosaic (épith)

mosaïque² [mɔzaik] ADJ (Bible) Mosaic(al), of Moses

Moscou [mɔsku] N Moscow

moscovite [mɔskɔvit] **1** ADJ of ou from Moscow, Moscow (épith), Muscovite **2 Moscovite** NMF Muscovite

Moselle [mozɛl] NF Moselle

mosquée [mɔske] NF mosque

▼ **mot** [mo] **1** NM **a** (gén) word; **le ~ (d')orange** the word "orange"; **ce ne sont que des ~s** it's just (so many) empty words, it's just talk; **je n'en crois pas un (traître)** I don't believe a (single) word of it; **paresseux, c'est bien le ~!** lazybones is the right word to describe him!; **ça alors, c'est bien le ~!** you've said it!, you never spoke ou said a truer word!; **de grands ~s** high-flown ou fancy words; **tout de suite les grands ~s!** you start straight in with these high-sounding words!; **voilà le grand ~ lâché!** you've come out with it at last!; **génie, c'est** un bien grand ~! genius, that's a big word!; **à ces ~s** at this *ou* that; **sur ces ~s** with this *ou* that, so saying, with these words; **à ~s couverts** in veiled terms; **en d'autres ~s** in other words; **en un ~** in a word; **en un ~ comme en cent** in a nutshell, in brief; **faire du ~ à ~ ◊ traduire ~ à ~** to translate word for word; **c'est du ~ à ~** it's a word for word rendering *ou* translation; **rapporter une conversation ~ pour ~** to give a word for word *ou* a verbatim report of a conversation

[b] (= *message*) word; (= *courte lettre*) note, line; **je vais lui en toucher un ~** I'll have a word with him about it, I'll mention it to him; **glisser un ~ à qn** *ou* **dans l'oreille de qn** to have a word in sb's ear; **se donner** *ou* **se passer le ~** to send *ou* pass the word round, pass the word on; **mettez-lui un petit ~** drop him a line *ou* note, write him a note; **il ne m'a même pas dit un ~ de remerciement** he didn't even thank me

[c] (= *expression frappante*) saying; **~s célèbres/historiques** famous/historic sayings; **bon ~** witticism, witty remark; **il aime faire des bons ~s** he likes to make witty remarks [d] (*Ordin*) word; **~ machine** machine word [e] (*loc*) **avoir des ~s avec qn** to have words with sb; **avoir toujours le ~ pour rire** to be a born joker; **le ~ de l'énigme** the key to the mystery; **avoir le ~ de la fin** *ou* **le dernier ~** to have the last word; **c'est votre dernier ~?** (*gén*) is that your last word in the matter?; (*dans négociations*) is that your final offer?; **je n'ai pas dit mon dernier ~** you (*ou* they *etc*) haven't heard the last of me; **sans ~ dire** without saying a *ou* one word; **vous n'avez qu'un ~ à dire et je le ferai** (you have only to) say the word and I'll do it; **j'estime avoir mon ~ à dire dans cette affaire** I think I'm entitled to have my say in this matter; **je vais lui dire deux ~s** I'll give him a piece of my mind; **prendre qn au ~** to take sb at his word; **il n'en connaît** *ou* **n'en sait pas le premier ~** he doesn't know the first thing about it; **il ne sait pas le premier ~ de sa leçon** he doesn't know a word of his lesson; **il ne sait pas un (traître) ~ d'allemand** he doesn't know a (single) word of German; **je n'ai pas pu lui tirer un ~** I couldn't get a word out of him; **il lui a dit le ~ de Cambronne** ≈ he said a four-letter word to him; **pas un ~ à qui que ce soit** mum's the word, don't breathe a word of this to anyone; **il n'a jamais un ~ plus haut que l'autre** he's very even-tempered; **j'ai dû dire un ~ de travers** I must have said something wrong; **au bas** ~ at the very least, by the lowest estimate ■ (*PROV*) **qui ne dit ~ consent** silence gives consent

[2] COMP ► **mot apparenté** (*Ling*) cognate ► **mot d'auteur** revealing *ou* witty remark from the author ► **mot composé** compound ► **mots croisés** crossword (puzzle); **faire des ~s croisés** to do crosswords; **faire les ~s croisés** (*d'un journal*) to do the crossword (puzzle) ► **mot d'emprunt** loan word ► **mot d'enfant** child's (funny) remark ► **mot d'esprit** witticism, witty remark ► **mot d'excuse** (*gén*) letter of apology; (*Scol*) (*gén*) (absence) note; (*pour maladie*) sick note ► **mots fléchés** crossword (puzzle) (*with clues given inside the boxes*) ► **mot d'ordre** watchword, slogan ► **mot de passe** password ► **mot souche** root-word

motard, -arde [mɔtaʀ, aʀd] [1] NM,F motorcyclist, biker* [2] NM (*Police*) motorcycle policeman *ou* cop*; (*de la gendarmerie, de l'armée*) motorcyclist; **les ~s de l'escorte présidentielle** the president's motorcycle escort, the president's motorcade

mot-clé (*pl* mots-clés), **mot clé** [mokle] NM keyword

motel [mɔtɛl] NM motel

motet [mɔtɛ] NM motet, anthem

---

moteur¹ [mɔtœʀ] NM [a] (*Tech*) engine; (*électrique*) motor; **~ atmosphérique** atmospheric engine; **~ à combustion interne ◊ ~ à explosion** internal combustion engine; **~ à 2/4 temps** 2-/4-stroke engine; **à ~** power-driven, motor (*épith*); (*Ciné*) **~!** action!; (*Ordin*) **~ de recherche** search engine → **frein** [b] (= *force*) mover, mainspring; (*littér*) **le grand ~ de l'univers** the prime mover of the universe; **être le ~ de qch** to be the mainspring of sth, be the driving force behind sth

moteur², -trice [mɔtœʀ, tʀis] [1] ADJ [a] (*Anat*) [*muscle, nerf, troubles*] motor (*épith*) [b] (*Rail*) **engin ~** power unit; (*lit, fig*) **force motrice** driving force → **arbre, roue** [2] **motrice** NF (*Rail*) power unit

motif [mɔtif] NM [a] (= *raison*) motive (**de** for), grounds (**de** for); (= *but*) purpose (**de** of); **quel est le ~ de votre visite?** what is the motive for *ou* the purpose of your visit?; **quel ~ as-tu de te plaindre?** what grounds have you got for complaining?; **il a de bons ~s pour le faire** he has good grounds for doing it; (**†** *ou hum*) **fréquenter une jeune fille pour le bon ~** to court a girl with honourable intentions; **qch sans ~** to have no motive for doing sth; **colère sans ~** groundless *ou* irrational anger; **~ d'inquiétude** cause for concern; **donner des ~s de satisfaction à qn** to give sb grounds *ou* cause for satisfaction [b] (= *ornement*) motif, design, pattern; (*Peinture, Mus*) motif; **tissu à ~s** patterned material; **papier peint à ~ de fleurs** floral wallpaper, wallpaper with a floral design *ou* motif [c] (*Jur*) [*jugement*] grounds (**de** for)

motion [mosjɔ̃] NF (*Jur, Pol*) motion; **déposer une ~ de censure** to raise *ou* table (*Brit*) a censure motion; **voter la ~ de censure** to pass a vote of no confidence *ou* of censure

motivant, e [mɔtivɑ̃, ɑ̃t] ADJ [*travail*] rewarding, satisfying; **rémunération ~e** attractive salary

motivation [mɔtivasjɔ̃] NF [a] (= *justification*) motivation (**de** for); **quelles sont ses ~s?** (*raisons personnelles*) what are his motives? (**pour** for); **lettre de ~** covering letter, letter in support of one's application [b] (= *dynamisme*) motivation

motivé, e [mɔtive] (*ptp de* **motiver**) ADJ [a] [*action*] (= *expliqué*) reasoned, justified; (= *légitime*) well-founded, motivated; **non ~** unexplained, unjustified; (*Scol*) **absence ~e** legitimate *ou* genuine absence; **refus ~** justified refusal [b] [*personne*] motivated; **non ~** unmotivated

motiver [mɔtive] ▸ conjug 1 ◂ VT [a] (= *justifier, expliquer*) [+ *action, attitude, réclamation*] to justify, account for; **il a motivé sa conduite en disant que ...** he justified his behaviour by saying that ...; **rien ne peut ~ une telle conduite** nothing can justify *ou* warrant such behaviour [b] (= *fournir un motif à*) [+ *refus, intervention, jugement*] to motivate, found; (*Psych*) to motivate [c] (= *pousser à agir*) [*personne, salaire*] to motivate

moto [moto] NF ABRÉV = **motocyclette** [a] (= *véhicule*) motorbike, motorcycle, bike*; **je viendrai à** *ou* **en ~** I'll come by bike* *ou* on my bike*; **~ de course** racing motorcycle; **~ de route** (standard) motorbike; **~ de trial** trial bike (*Brit*), dirt bike (*US*) [b] (= *activité*) motorcycling, biking*

motocross, moto-cross [motokʀɔs] NM INV (= *sport*) motocross, scrambling; (= *épreuve*) motocross race, scramble

moto-crottes* (*pl* motos-crottes) [motokʀɔt] NF motorbike pooper scooper

motoculteur [mɔtɔkyltœʀ] NM (motorized) cultivator

motocycle [mɔtɔsikl] NM (*Admin*) motor bicycle

---

motocyclette [mɔtɔsiklɛt] NF motorcycle, motorbike

motocyclisme [mɔtɔsiklism] NM motorcycle racing

motocycliste [mɔtɔsiklist] [1] NMF motorcyclist [2] ADJ [*course*] motorcycle (*épith*); **le sport ~** motorcycle racing

motonautique [motonotik] ADJ **sport ~** speedboat *ou* motorboat racing

motonautisme [motonotism] NM speedboat *ou* motorboat racing

motoneige [motonɛʒ] NF snow-bike, skidoo® (*Can*)

motoneigiste [motonɛʒist] NMF snow-bike *ou* skidoo (*Can*) rider

motopompe [motopɔ̃p] NF motor-pump, power-driven pump

motorisation [mɔtɔʀizasjɔ̃] NF (*Tech*) motorization; (= *type de moteur*) engine type

motorisé, e [mɔtɔʀize] (*ptp de* **motoriser**) ADJ [a] [*mécanisme*] motorized, motor-driven; (*Mil*) [*compagnie, patrouille*] motorized, mechanized; (*Admin*) **la circulation ~e** motor traffic; **sports ~s** motor sports → **deux-roues** [b] [*personne*] **être ~*** (= *posséder un véhicule*) to have a car; (= *être en voiture*) to have transport (*Brit*) *ou* transportation (*US*), be car-borne*; **tu es ~?** sinon je te ramène** have you got wheels?* *ou* any transport? if not I'll drop you home; **les voyageurs non ~s** passengers without cars, foot passengers

motoriser [mɔtɔʀize] ▸ conjug 1 ◂ VT (*Mil, Tech*) to motorize

motoriste [mɔtɔʀist] NM (= *mécanicien*) car *ou* auto (*US*) mechanic; (= *constructeur*) engine manufacturer

mot-outil (*pl* mots-outils) [mouti] NM grammatical word

motrice [mɔtʀis] ADJ, NF → **moteur²**

motricité [mɔtʀisite] NF motivity

motte [mɔt] NF [a] (*Agr*) **~ (de terre)** lump of earth, clod (of earth); **~ de gazon** turf, sod; **en ~** [*plante*] balled [b] (*Culin*) **~ de beurre** lump *ou* block of butter; **acheter du beurre en** *ou* **à la ~** to buy butter loose

motus* [mɔtys] EXCL **~ (et bouche cousue)!** mum's the word!*, keep it under your hat!, don't breathe a word!

mot-valise (*pl* mots-valises) [movaliz] NM portmanteau word

mou¹, molle [mu, mɔl] (*m: devant voyelle ou h muet* **mol** [mɔl]) [1] ADJ [a] (*au toucher*) [*substance, oreiller*] soft; [*tige, tissu*] limp; [*chair, visage*] flabby; **ce melon est tout ~** this melon has gone all soft *ou* mushy → **chapeau** [b] [*traits du visage*] (*Art*) [*trait*] weak, slack [c] (*à l'oreille*) **bruit ~** muffled noise, soft thud; **voix aux inflexions molles** gently lilting voice [d] (= *sans énergie*) [*geste, poignée de main*] limp, lifeless; [*protestations, opposition*] weak, feeble; **†** [*vie*] soft, indolent; (*Littérat*) [*style*] feeble, dull, woolly; (*Mus*) [*exécution*] dull, lifeless; [*reprise économique, marché*] sluggish; **personne molle** (*apathique*) indolent *ou* lethargic *ou* sluggish person; (*sans autorité*) spineless character; (*trop indulgent*) lax *ou* soft person; **j'ai les jambes molles** my legs feel weak *ou* like jelly (*Brit*); **dépêche-toi, c'est ~ tout ça!** you're so slow, hurry up!; **il est ~ comme une chiffe** *ou* **chique** he's spineless [e] [*temps*] muggy; [*tiédeur*] languid

[2] ADV **vas-y ~*** †‡ go easy*, take it easy*

[3] NM [a] [*corde*] **avoir du ~** to be slack *ou* loose; **donner du ~** to give some slack, loosen; (*Aut*) **il y a du ~ dans la pédale de frein** the brakes are soft *ou* spongy; **donne un peu de ~ pour que je puisse faire un nœud** let the rope out a bit *ou* give a bit of play on the rope so that I can make a knot; (*fig*) **donner** *ou* **laisser du ~ à qn** to give sb some leeway [b] (= *personne*) spineless character

mou² [mu]   NM (*Boucherie*) lights, lungs; **bourrer le ~ à qn:** to take sb in, have sb on* (*Brit*)

mouchard, e [muʃaʀ, aʀd] 1 NM,F (*: *Scol*) sneak* 2 NM a (*arg Police*) informer, grass* (*Brit*), fink: (*US*) b (*Tech = enregistreur*) [*avion, train*] black box; [*camion*] tachograph; [*veilleur de nuit*] control clock; (*Mil*) spy plane; [*porte*] spyhole

mouchardage* [muʃaʀdaʒ]   NM (*Scol*) sneaking*; (*arg Police*) informing, grassing* (*Brit*), ratting* (*US*); **il y a eu des ~s auprès de la direction** someone's been sneaking to the management

moucharder* [muʃaʀde] ▸conjug 1◂ VT (*Scol*) to sneak on*, split on* (*Brit*); (*arg Police*) to inform on, grass on* (*Brit*), rat on* (*US*)

mouche [muʃ] 1 NF a (*Zool, Pêche*) fly; **quelle ~ t'a piqué?** what's bitten you?*, what's got into you?*; **il faut toujours qu'il fasse la ~ du coche** he's always fussing around as if he's indispensable; **mourir/tomber comme des ~s** to die (off)/fall like flies; **prendre la ~** to get into ou go into a huff*, get huffy* ▪ (*PROV*) **on ne prend pas les ~s avec du vinaigre** you have to be nice if you want something → **voler, fin¹, mal** b (*Escrime*) button; **faire ~** (*Tir*) to score a ou hit the bull's-eye; (*fig*) to score, hit home → **poids** c (*en taffetas*) patch, beauty spot; (= *touffe de poils sous la lèvre*) short goatee 2 **mouches** NFPL (*Opt*) specks, spots 3 COMP ▸ **mouche bleue** = **mouche de la viande** ▸ **mouche d'escadre** (*Naut*) advice boat ▸ **mouche à feu** (*Can*) firefly ▸ **mouche à merde:** dung fly ▸ **mouche à miel** honey bee ▸ **mouche tsé-tsé** tsetse fly ▸ **mouche à vers** blowfly ▸ **mouche verte** greenbottle ▸ **mouche de la viande** bluebottle ▸ **mouche du vinaigre** fruit fly

moucher [muʃe] ▸conjug 1◂ 1 VT a **~ (le nez de) qn** to blow sb's nose; **moucher ton nez** blow your nose; **il mouche du sang** there are traces of blood (in his handkerchief) when he blows his nose b (* = *remettre à sa place*) **~ qn** to put sb in his place; **se faire ~** to get put in one's place c [+ *chandelle*] to snuff (out) 2 **se moucher** VPR to blow one's nose; **il ne se mouche pas du coude** (= *il est prétentieux*) he thinks he's it* ou the cat's whiskers* (*Brit*) ou meow (*US*); (= *il ne se refuse rien*) he doesn't deny himself anything

moucheron [muʃʀɔ̃] NM (= *insecte*) midge, gnat; (* = *enfant*) kid*, nipper* (*Brit*)

moucheté, e [muʃ(ə)te] (*ptp de* **moucheter**) ADJ [*œuf*] speckled; [*poisson*] spotted; [*laine*] flecked → **fleuret**

moucheter [muʃ(ə)te] ▸conjug 4◂ VT a (= *tacheter*) to fleck (**de** with) b [+ *fleuret*] to put a button on → **fleuret**

mouchetis [muʃ(ə)ti] NM (*Constr*) pebble dash (*Brit*), rock dash (*US*)

mouchette [muʃɛt] 1 NF (*Archit*) [*larmier*] lip; [*fenêtrage*] outer fillet 2 **mouchettes** NFPL (*Hist*) snuffers

moucheture [muʃ(ə)tyʀ] NF (*sur les habits*) speck, spot, fleck; (*sur un animal*) spot, patch; (*Hér*) **~s d'hermine** ermine tips

mouchoir [muʃwaʀ] NM (*de poche, en tissu*) handkerchief, hanky*; (†: *autour du cou*) neckerchief; **~ (en papier)** tissue, paper handkerchief; **jardin grand comme un ~ de poche** garden as big as ou the size of ou no bigger than a pocket handkerchief; **cette pièce est grande comme un ~ de poche** this room's tiny, there isn't room to swing a cat in here (*Brit*); **ils sont arrivés dans un ~** it was a close finish; **les deux candidats se tiennent dans un ~** the two candidates are neck and neck → **nœud**

moudjahiddin [mudʒa(j)idin]   NMPL mujaheddin, mujahedeen

moudre [mudʀ] ▸conjug 47◂ VT [+ *blé*] to mill, grind; [+ *café, poivre*] to grind; (†: *Mus*) [+ *air*] to grind out; **~ qn de coups**† to thrash sb, give sb a drubbing → **grain, moulu**

moue [mu] NF pout; **faire la ~** (*gén*) to pull a face; [*enfant gâté*] to pout; **faire une ~ de dédain/de dégoût** to give a disdainful pout/a pout of disgust; **il eut une ~ dubitative** he looked doubtful

mouette [mwɛt] NF (sea) gull; **~ rieuse** black-headed gull; **~ tridactyle** kittiwake

mou(f)fette [mufɛt] NF skunk

moufle [mufl] 1 NF (= *gant*) mitt, mitten; (*pour plats chauds*) oven glove 2 NM ou F (*Tech = poulie*) pulley block; [*four*] muffle

mouflet, -ette* [muflɛ, ɛt] NM,F brat* (*péj*), kid*

mouflon [muflɔ̃] NM mouf(f)lon

mouf(e)ter: [mufte] ▸conjug 1 ou 4◂ VI to blink; **il n'a pas mouf(e)té** he didn't bat an eyelid

mouillage [mujaʒ] NM a (*Naut* = *action*) [*navire*] anchoring, mooring; [*ancre*] casting; [*mine*] laying; **au ~** (= *lying*) at anchor b (= *abri, rade*) anchorage, moorage c (*Tech*) [*cuir, linge*] moistening, damping; [*vin, lait*] watering(-down)

mouillé, e [muje] (*ptp de* **mouiller**) ADJ a [*herbe, vêtement, personne*] wet; [*regard*] watery, tearful; [*voix*] tearful; **tout ~** all wet; (*hum*) **il pèse 50 kilos tout ~** he weighs 50 kilos soaking wet ou with his socks on (*Brit, hum*); **tu sens le chien ~** you smell like a wet dog; **ne marche pas dans le ~** don't tread in the wet patch → **poule¹** b (*Ling*) **l ~** palatalized l, palatal l

mouillement [mujmɑ̃] NM (*Ling*) palatalization

mouiller [muje] ▸conjug 1◂ 1 VT a (*pour humidifier*) [+ *linge, sol*] to dampen; (*accidentellement*) [+ *vêtement, livre*] to get ou make wet; **~ son doigt pour tourner la page** to moisten one's finger to turn the page; (*fig*) **sa chemise** ou **son maillot*** to put in some hard work ou graft* (*Brit*) b [*pluie*] [+ *route*] to make wet; **se faire ~** to get wet c (*Culin*) [+ *vin, lait*] to water (down); [+ *viande*] to moisten (with stock ou wine etc) d (*Naut*) [+ *mine*] to lay; [+ *sonde*] to heave; **~ l'ancre** to cast ou drop anchor e (* = *compromettre*) [+ *personne*] to drag (**dans** into), mix up (**dans** in); **plusieurs personnes ont été mouillées dans l'histoire** several people were mixed up in the affair f (*Ling*) to palatalize 2 VI a (*Naut*) to lie ou be at anchor; **ils mouillèrent 3 jours à Papeete** they anchored ou they lay at anchor at Papeete for 3 days b (: = *avoir peur*) to be scared out of one's mind, be scared shitless: c : (*sexuellement*) to be wet 3 **se mouiller** VPR a (= *se tremper*) (*accidentellement*) to get o.s. wet; (*pour un bain rapide*) to have a quick dip; **se ~ les pieds** (*sans faire exprès*) to get one's feet wet; (*exprès*) to dabble one's feet in the water, have a little paddle b [*yeux*] to fill ou brim with tears c * (= *prendre des risques*) to get one's feet wet, commit o.s.; (= *se compromettre*) to get mixed up ou involved (**dans** in)

mouillette [mujɛt] NF finger of bread, soldier* (*Brit*)

mouilleur [mujœʀ] NM a [*timbres*] (stamp) sponge b (*Naut*) [*ancre*] tumbler; **~ de mines** minelayer

mouillure [mujyʀ] NF a (= *trace*) wet mark b (*Ling*) palatalization

mouise: [mwiz] NF **être dans la ~** (*misère*) to be flat broke*, be on one's beam-ends* (*Brit*); (*ennuis*) to be up the creek* (*Brit*); **c'est lui qui m'a sorti de la ~** he got me out of a hole*

moujik [muʒik] NM mujik, muzhik

moujingue: [muʒɛ̃g] NMF brat* (*péj*), kid*

moukère†: [mukɛʀ] NF woman, female

moulage¹ [mulaʒ] NM a (= *fabrication*) [*briques, pain*] moulding (*Brit*), molding (*US*); [*caractères d'imprimerie*] casting; [*statue, buste*] casting; **le ~ d'un bas-relief** making ou taking a cast of a bas-relief b (= *reproduction*) cast; **prendre un ~ de** to take a cast of; **sur la cheminée il y avait le ~ en plâtre d'une statue** there was a plaster figure on the mantelpiece; **ce n'est qu'un ~** it's only a copy

moulage² [mulaʒ] NM [*grain*] milling, grinding

moulant, e [mulɑ̃, ɑ̃t] ADJ [*robe*] figure-hugging; [*pantalon, pull*] tight(-fitting)

moule¹ [mul] 1 NM a (*Art, Ind*) mould (*Brit*), mold (*US*); (*Typo*) matrix; (*fig*) **le ~ est cassé** ou **on a cassé le ~** they broke the mould; **il n'a jamais pu sortir du ~ étroit de son éducation** he has never been able to free himself from ou break out of the straitjacket of his strict upbringing; (*lit, fig*) **fait sur** ou **coulé dans le même ~** cast in the same mould; **être fait au ~** (= *être beau*) to be shapely; **se couler** ou **se fondre** ou **entrer dans le ~** ou **un ~** to conform to the ou a norm; **il refuse d'entrer dans le ~ de l'école** he refuses to fit into the school mould b (*Culin*) (*pour gâteaux*) tin (*Brit*), pan (*US*); (*pour aspic*) mould (*Brit*), mold (*US*) 2 COMP ▸ **moule à beurre** butter print ▸ **moule à briques** brick mould ▸ **moule à cake** loaf tin ▸ **moule à gâteaux** cake tin (*Brit*), cake pan (*US*) ▸ **moule à gaufres** waffle-iron ▸ **moule à manqué** (deep) sandwich tin (*Brit*), deep cake pan (*US*) ▸ **moule à pisé** clay mould ▸ **moule à soufflé** soufflé dish ▸ **moule à tarte** pie plate, flan dish

moule² [mul] NF a (*Zool*) mussel; **~s marinières** moules marinières (*mussels cooked in their own juice with white wine and shallots*) b (* = *idiot*) idiot, twit* c (*:* = *sexe féminin*) cunt:

mouler [mule] ▸conjug 1◂ VT a (= *couler*) [+ *briques, pain*] to mould (*Brit*), mold (*US*); [+ *caractères d'imprimerie*] to cast; [+ *statue, buste*] to cast; **~ un buste en plâtre** to cast a bust in plaster; **fromage blanc moulé à la louche** ≈ farmhouse fromage frais; (*Méd*) **selles moulées** solid stools b (= *prendre l'empreinte de*) [+ *bas-relief, buste*] to make ou take a cast of; **en plâtre/en cire** [+ *visage, buste*] to make a plaster/wax cast of c [+ *lettre, mot*] to shape ou form with care d (= *calquer sur*) **~ son style/sa conduite sur** to model one's style/one's conduct on e [+ *cuisses, hanches*] to hug, fit closely round; **une robe qui moule** a figure-hugging dress; **pantalon qui moule** tight(-fitting) trousers; **une robe qui lui moulait les hanches** a dress which clung to ou around her hips; **son corps se moulait au sien** her body pressed closely against his

mouleur [mulœʀ] NM caster, moulder (*Brit*), molder (*US*)

moulin [mulɛ̃] NM a (= *instrument, bâtiment*) mill; **~ à eau** water mill; **~ à vent** windmill; **~ à café/poivre** coffee/pepper mill; **~ à légumes** vegetable mill; **~ à paroles** chatterbox; **~ à prières** prayer wheel; **on y entre comme dans un ~** anyone can just walk right in b (* = *moteur*) engine

mouliner [muline] ▸conjug 1◂ 1 VT a (*Culin*) to put through a vegetable mill; (*Pêche*) to reel in b (*:* *Ordin*) to process, crunch* c [+ *soie*] to throw 2 VI [*cycliste*] to pedal rapidly (*without any effort*)

moulinet [mulinɛ] NM (*Pêche*) reel; (*Tech*) winch; (*Escrime*) flourish; (*Danse*) moulinet; **faire des ~s avec une canne** to twirl *ou* whirl a walking stick; **faire des ~s avec les bras** to whirl one's arms about *ou* round

moulinette® [mulinɛt] NF vegetable mill; **passer qch à la ~** (*Culin*) to put sth through the vegetable mill; (*fig*) to subject sth to close scrutiny; (**: Ordin*) to process *ou* crunch* sth

moult [mult] ADV (†† *ou hum*) (= *beaucoup*) many; (= *très*) very; **~ gens** many people, many a person; **~ fois** oft(en)times (*hum*), many a time

moulu, e [muly] (*ptp de* **moudre**) ADJ [a] [*café, poivre*] ground (*épith*) [b] († = *meurtri*) bruised, black and blue; **~ (de fatigue)*** dead-beat*, worn-out, all-in*

moulure [mulyʀ] NF (*gén*) moulding (*Brit*), molding (*US*); (*sur porte*) beading

moulurer [mulyʀe] ▶conjug 1◀ VT to decorate with mouldings (*Brit*) *ou* moldings (*US*); **machine à ~** moulding (*Brit*) *ou* molding (*US*) machine; **panneau mouluré** moulded (*Brit*) *ou* molded (*US*) panel

moumoute* [mumut] NF [a] (*hum*) (= *perruque*) wig; (= *postiche*) (*pour hommes*) hairpiece, toupee; (*pour femmes*) hairpiece [b] (= *veste*) fleece-lined *ou* fleecy jacket

mouquère†‡ [mukɛʀ] NF = **moukère**

mourant, e [muʀɑ̃, ɑ̃t] [1] ADJ [*personne, feu, jour*] dying; [*voix*] faint; [*regard*] languishing [2] NM,F **un ~** a dying man; **une ~e** a dying woman; **les ~s** the dying

mourir [muʀiʀ] ▶conjug 19◀ [1] VI [a] [*être animé, plante*] to die; **~ dans son lit** to die in one's bed; **~ de sa belle mort** to die a natural death; **~ avant l'âge** to die young *ou* before one's time; **~ à la peine** *ou* **à la tâche** to die in harness (*fig*); **~ assassiné** to be murdered; **~ empoisonné** (*crime*) to be poisoned (and die); (*accident*) to die of poisoning; **~ en héros** to die a hero's death; **il est mort très jeune** he died very young, he was very young when he died; **faire ~ qn** to kill sb; **cet enfant me fera ~** this child will be the death of me; **c'est une simple piqûre, tu n'en mourras pas !** it's only a little injection, it won't kill you!; **je l'aime à (en) ~** I love him more than life itself; **s'ennuyer à ~** to be bored to death *ou* to tears; **ennuyeux à ~** deadly boring; **il attend que le patron meure pour prendre sa place** he's waiting for his boss to die so that he can step into his shoes ▪ (*PROV*) **on ne meurt qu'une fois** you only die once (*PROV*); **plus bête que lui, tu meurs !*** you can't possibly be more stupid than he is!, he's as stupid as they come!* [b] [*civilisation, empire, coutume*] to die out; [*bruit*] to die away; [*jour*] to fade, die; [*feu*] to die out, die down; **la vague vint ~ à ses pieds** the wave died away at his feet; **le ballon vint ~ à ses pieds** the ball came to rest at his feet [c] (*suivi d'un complément*) **~ de vieillesse/chagrin** to die of old age/grief; **~ d'une maladie/d'une blessure** to die of a disease/from a wound; **~ de froid** (*lit*) to die of exposure; (*fig*) **on meurt de froid ici** it's freezing *ou* perishing (*Brit*) cold in here; **je meurs de sommeil** I'm dead on my feet; **~ de faim** (*lit*) to starve to death, die of hunger; (*fig = avoir faim*) to be starving *ou* famished *ou* ravenous; **faire ~ qn de faim** to starve sb to death; **~ de soif** (*lit*) to die of thirst; (*fig = avoir soif*) to be parched; **il me fera ~ d'inquiétude** he'll drive me to my death with worry; **~ de honte** to die of shame; **~** *ou* **être mort de peur** to be frightened *ou* scared to death; **il me fera ~ de peur** he'll frighten the life out of me; **~ d'ennui** to be bored to death *ou* to tears; **il meurt d'envie de le faire** he's dying to do it; **faire ~ qn d'impatience** to keep sb on tenterhooks; **faire ~ qn à petit feu** (*lit*) to kill sb slowly *ou* by inches; (*fig*) to torment the life

out of sb; (*littér*) **(se) ~ d'amour pour qn** to pine for sb

[2] **se mourir** VPR (*littér*) to be dying

mouroir [muʀwaʀ] NM (*péj: pour vieillards*) old people's home; **le camp/l'hôpital est devenu un ~** the camp/the hospital has become a place for people to die

mouron [muʀɔ̃] NM [a] (*Bot*) pimpernel; **~ rouge** scarlet pimpernel; **~ blanc** *ou* **des oiseaux** chickweed [b] (*loc*) **se faire du ~*** to worry o.s. sick*; **arrête de te faire du ~ (pour lui)*** stop worrying *ou* fretting (about him)

mouscaille* [muskaj] NF **être dans la ~** (*misère*) to be down and out, be stony broke*, be on one's beam-ends* (*Brit*); (*ennuis*) to be up the creek*

mousquet [muskɛ] NM musket

mousquetaire [muskətɛʀ] NM musketeer; **col/poignet ~** musketeer collar/cuff

mousqueton [muskətɔ̃] NM (= *boucle*) snap hook, clasp; (= *fusil*) carbine; (*Alpinisme*) crab, karabiner; **coup de ~** musket shot

moussaillon* [musajɔ̃] NM ship's boy; **par ici ~ !** over here, (my) boy!

moussaka [musaka] NF moussaka

moussant, e [musɑ̃, ɑ̃t] ADJ [*savon, crème à raser*] foaming, lathering → **bain**

mousse¹ [mus] [1] NF [a] (*Bot*) moss → **pierre, vert** [b] (= *écume*) [*bière, eau, café, lait*] froth; [*savon*] lather; [*champagne*] bubbles; **la ~ sur le verre de bière** the head on the beer [c] (* = *bière*) pint* [d] (*Culin*) mousse; **~ au chocolat** chocolate mousse; **~ d'avocat** avocado mousse [e] (= *caoutchouc*) foam rubber; **matelas en ~** foam rubber mattress; **balle (en) ~** rubber ball; (= *nylon*) **collant/bas ~** stretch tights (*Brit*) *ou* pantyhose (*US*)/stockings; **~ de caoutchouc** foam rubber [f] † **se faire de la ~*** to worry o.s. sick*, get all het up*; **ne te fais pas de ~*, tout ira bien** don't worry *ou* don't get so het up*, everything'll be alright [2] COMP ▶ **mousse carbonique** (firefighting) foam ▶ **mousse coiffante** styling mousse ▶ **mousse de nylon** (= *tissu*) stretch nylon; (*pour rembourrer*) foam ▶ **mousse de platine** platinum sponge ▶ **mousse à raser** shaving foam → **point²**

mousse² [mus] NM ship's boy

mousseline [muslin] NF [a] (*Tex*) (= *coton*) muslin; (= *soie, tergal*) chiffon; **verre ~** muslin glass [b] (*Culin* = *mousse*) mousseline → **pomme, sauce**

mousser [muse] ▶conjug 1◀ VI [a] [*bière, eau*] to froth; [*champagne*] to bubble, sparkle; [*détergent*] to foam, lather; [*savon, shampooing, crème à raser*] to lather; **faire ~** [+ *savon, détergent*] to lather up [b] **faire ~ qn*** (*vanter*) to boost sb*, puff sb up* (*US*); (*mettre en colère*) to make sb mad* *ou* wild*; **se faire ~*** to blow one's own trumpet, sing one's own praises (*auprès de* to); (*auprès d'un supérieur*) to sell o.s. hard* (*auprès de* to)

mousseron [musʀɔ̃] NM meadow mushroom

mousseux, -euse [musø, øz] [1] ADJ [*vin*] sparkling (*épith*); [*bière, chocolat*] frothy; **eau mousseuse** soapy water [2] NM sparkling wine

mousson [musɔ̃] NF monsoon

moussu, e [musy] ADJ [*sol, arbre*] mossy; [*banc*] moss-covered

moustache [mustaʃ] NF [*homme*] moustache, mustache (*US*); [*animal*] **~s** whiskers; **porter la ~** *ou* **des ~** to have *ou* wear a moustache; [*femme*] **avoir de la ~** to have a moustache, have hair on one's upper lip; **il s'était fait une ~ blanche en buvant le lait** he had a white moustache from drinking the milk; **~ en brosse** toothbrush moustache; **~ en croc** *ou* **en guidon de vélo*** handlebar moustache; **~ (à la) gauloise** walrus moustache

moustachu, e [mustaʃy] ADJ with a moustache, moustached; **c'est un ~** he has a mous-

tache; **elle est un peu ~e** she's got a bit of a moustache

moustérien, -ienne [musteʀjɛ̃, jɛn] [1] ADJ Mousterian [2] NM **le Moustérien** the Mousterian

moustiquaire [mustikɛʀ] NF (= *rideau*) mosquito net; [*fenêtre, porte*] mosquito screen

moustique [mustik] NM (*Zool*) mosquito; (* = *enfant*) (little) kid*, tich* (*Brit*), nipper* (*Brit*)

moût [mu] NM [*raisin*] must; [*bière*] wort

moutard* [mutaʀ] NM brat* (*péj*), kid*

moutarde [mutaʀd] [1] NF mustard; **~ blanche** white mustard; **~ (extra-)forte** English mustard, hot mustard (*US*); **~ à l'estragon** *ou* **aux aromates** French mustard; **~ à l'ancienne** grain mustard; **~ de Dijon** Dijon mustard; **graines de ~** mustard seeds; **la ~ me monta au nez** I flared up, I lost my temper; **il sentit la ~ lui monter au nez** he felt his temper flaring, he felt he was going to flare up [2] ADJ INV (**jaune**) **~** mustard(-yellow) → **gaz, sauce**

moutardier [mutaʀdje] NM (= *pot*) mustard pot; (= *fabricant*) mustard maker *ou* manufacturer; **il se croit le premier ~ du pape**† he thinks he's the bee's knees (*Brit*) *ou* the cat's whiskers (*Brit*) *ou* the cat's meow (*US*)

mouton, -onne [mutɔ̃, ɔn] [1] ADJ sheeplike [2] NM [a] (= *animal*) sheep; (= *peau*) sheepskin; **doublé de ~** lined with sheepskin; **relié en ~** bound in sheepskin, sheepskin-bound; **manteau en ~ doré** Persian lamb coat; (*fig*) **mais revenons** *ou* **retournons à nos ~s** but let's get back to the subject, but to get back to the subject; **compter les ~s** (*pour s'endormir*) to count sheep [b] (= *viande*) mutton; **côte de ~** mutton chop [c] (* = *personne*) (*grégaire, crédule*) sheep; (*doux, passif*) sheep, lamb; **c'est un ~** (*grégaire*) he's easily led, he goes with the crowd; (*doux*) he's as gentle as a lamb; **il m'a suivi comme un ~** he followed me like a lamb; **ils se comportent comme des ~s de Panurge** they behave like sheep [d] (*arg Police: dans une prison*) stool pigeon (*arg*), grass (*Brit, arg*) [e] (*Constr*) ram, monkey [3] **moutons** NMPL (*sur la mer*) white horses (*Brit*), white caps (*US*); (*sur le plancher*) (bits of) fluff; (*dans le ciel*) fluffy *ou* fleecy clouds [4] COMP ▶ **mouton à cinq pattes** rare bird, rara avis (*littér*) ▶ **mouton à laine** sheep reared for wool ▶ **mouton retourné** sheepskin ▶ **mouton à viande** sheep reared for meat

---

MOUTON DE PANURGE

The expression **mouton de Panurge** *is an allusion to a famous scene in Rabelais' "Pantagruel", in which Pantagruel throws a sheep into the sea and the rest of the flock throw themselves in after it. The term* **mouton de Panurge** *is used metaphorically to refer to any person who blindly follows the herd.*

---

moutonnant, e [mutɔnɑ̃, ɑ̃t] ADJ [*mer*] flecked with white horses (*Brit*) *ou* with white caps (*US*); (*littér*) [*collines*] rolling (*épith*)

moutonné, e [mutɔne] (*ptp de* **moutonner**) ADJ [*ciel*] flecked with fleecy *ou* fluffy clouds

moutonnement [mutɔnmɑ̃] NM **contempler le ~ de la mer** to look at the white horses (*Brit*) *ou* white caps (*US*) on the sea; (*littér*) **le ~ des collines** the rolling hills

moutonner [mutɔne] ▶conjug 1◀ VI [*mer*] to be flecked with white horses (*Brit*) *ou* white caps (*US*); (*littér*) [*collines*] to roll; [*ciel*] to be flecked with fleecy *ou* fluffy clouds

moutonneux, -euse [mutɔnø, øz] ADJ [*mer*] flecked with white horses (*Brit*) *ou* with white caps (*US*); [*ciel*] flecked with fleecy *ou* fluffy clouds

moutonnier, -ière [mutɔnje, jɛʀ] ADJ [*réflexe, personne*] sheep-like; **ils ont un comportement ~** they behave like sheep

mouture [mutyʀ] NF [a] (= *action*) [*blé*] milling, grinding; [*café*] grinding [b] (= *résultat*) [*café*] **une ~ fine** finely ground coffee; [*article, rapport*] **c'est la première ~** it's the first draft; (*péj*) **c'est la 3ᵉ ~ du même livre** it's the 3rd rehash of the same book

mouvance [muvɑ̃s] NF [a] (= *domaine d'influence*) sphere of influence; **entraîner qn dans sa ~** to draw sb into one's sphere of influence; (*Pol*) **il n'appartient pas à la ~ présidentielle** he's not at the same end of the political spectrum as the president; **les différents partis de la ~ islamiste** the different Islamic political parties [b] (*gén péj*) [*pensée, situation*] ever-changing nature; **la ~ politique/sociale** the ever-changing political/ social scene; **une culture en perpétuelle ~** an ever-changing culture [c] (*Hist*) subinfeudation; (*Philo*) mobility

mouvant, e [muvɑ̃, ɑ̃t] ADJ [*situation*] unsettled, fluid; [*ombre, flamme*] moving, changing; [*pensée, univers*] changing; [*frontières*] shifting; [*terrain*] unsteady, shifting; (*fig*) **être sur un ~ en terrain ~** to be on shaky *ou* uncertain ground → **sable**¹

mouvement [muvmɑ̃] NM [a] (= *geste*) movement, motion; **~s de gymnastique** (physical) exercises; **il a des ~s très lents** he is very slow in his movements; **il approuva d'un ~ de tête** he nodded his approval, he gave a nod of approval; **elle refusa d'un ~ de tête** she shook her head in refusal, she refused with a shake of her head; **elle eut un ~ de recul** she started back; **le ~ des lèvres** the movement of the lips; **faire un ~** to move, make a move; **elle ne pouvait plus faire le moindre ~** she could no longer move at all; **rester sans ~** to remain motionless → **faux, temps**¹

[b] (= *impulsion, réaction*) impulse, reaction; **dans un ~ de colère/d'indignation** in a fit *ou* a burst of anger/of indignation; **les ~s de l'âme** the impulses of the soul; **des ~s dans l'auditoire** a stir in the audience; **discours accueilli avec des ~s divers** speech which got a mixed reception; **son premier ~ fut de refuser** his first impulse was to refuse; **agir de son propre ~** to act of one's own accord; **avoir un bon ~** to make a nice *ou* kind gesture; **allons, un bon ~!** come on, just a small gesture!; **dans un bon ~** on a kindly impulse

[c] (= *activité*) [*ville, entreprise*] activity, bustle; **une rue pleine de ~** a busy *ou* lively street; **il aime le ~** (= *il est dynamique*) he likes to be on the go; (= *il aime l'animation*) he likes the bustle of the city; **il n'y a pas beaucoup de ~ le dimanche** not much happens on Sundays

[d] (= *déplacement*) movement; **être sans cesse en ~** to be constantly on the move *ou* on the go; **mettre qch en ~** to set sth in motion, set sth going; **se mettre en ~** to set off, get going; **suivre le ~** to follow the crowd; (*lit, fig*) **presser le ~** to step up the pace; (*lit, fig*) **~ de balancier** swing of the pendulum, pendulum swing; **le ~ perpétuel** perpetual motion; **~ de foule** movement in the crowd; (*Sociol*) **~s de population** shifts in population; **d'importants ~s de troupes à la frontière** large-scale troop movements at *ou* along the frontier; (*Mil*) **~ de repli** withdrawal; **~ tournant** (out)flanking movement; **~ de marchandises/de capitaux** *ou* **de fonds** movement of goods/of capital; **les ~s monétaires internationaux** fluctuations on the world money markets; (*Banque*) **~ d'un compte** account activity, turnover in an account; **~ de personnel** changes in staff *ou* personnel → **guerre**

[e] (*Philo, Pol etc* = *évolution*) **le ~ des idées** the evolution of ideas; **le parti du ~** the party in favour of change, the party of progress; **être dans le ~** to keep up-to-date; **un ~ d'opinion**

se dessine en faveur de ... one can detect a trend of opinion in favour of ...; **le ~ des prix** price trends; **~ de baisse/de hausse (sur les ventes)** downward/upward movement *ou* trend (in sales)

[f] (= *rythme*) [*phrase*] rhythm; [*tragédie*] movement, action; [*mélodie*] tempo

[g] (*Pol, Sociol* = *groupe, action*) movement; **~ politique** political movement; **le ~ ouvrier/ étudiant** the labour/student movement; **Mouvement de libération de la femme** Women's Liberation Movement, Women's Lib*; **~(s) de grève** strike *ou* industrial action (*NonC*); **~ de protestation** *ou* **de contestation** protest movement

[h] (*Mus*) movement

[i] (*Tech* = *mécanisme*) movement; **par un ~ d'horlogerie** by clockwork; **fermeture à ~ d'horlogerie** time lock

[j] (= *ligne, courbe*) [*sculpture*] contours; [*draperie, étoffe*] drape; [*collines*] undulations, rise and fall (*NonC*); **~ de terrain** undulation

mouvementé, e [muvmɑ̃te] ADJ [*vie, poursuite, récit*] eventful; [*séance*] turbulent, stormy; [*terrain*] rough; **j'ai eu une journée assez ~** I've had quite a hectic day

mouvoir [muvwaʀ] ▸ conjug 27 ◂ [1] VT (*gén ptp*) [a] (+ *machine*) to drive, power; (+ *bras, levier*) to move; **il se leva comme mû par un ressort** he sprang up as if propelled by a spring *ou* like a Jack-in-the-box [b] (*motif, sentiment*) to drive, prompt [2] **se mouvoir** VPR to move; **faire (se)** (+ *partie du corps*) to move; (+ *robot*) (*gén*) to move; [*source d'énergie*] to drive, power

▼ **moyen¹, -yenne¹** [mwajɛ̃, jɛn] ADJ [a] (= *ni grand ni petit, modéré*) [*taille*] medium, average; [*ville, maison*] medium-sized; [*prix*] moderate; **les moyennes entreprises** medium-sized companies; **un produit de qualité moyenne** a product of average *ou* medium quality → **cours, onde, poids**

[b] (= *intermédiaire*) [*cadre, classe, revenu*] middle; **la solution moyenne** the middle-of-the-road solution; **il doit exister une voie moyenne entre liberté totale et discipline** there must be a middle way between complete freedom and discipline; **une voiture de gamme moyenne** a mid-range *ou* middle-of-the-range car → **cours**

[c] (= *du type courant*) average; **le Français/le lecteur ~** the average Frenchman/reader

[d] (= *ni bon ni mauvais*) [*résultats, intelligence, équipe*] average; (*Scol : sur copie d'élève*) fair, average; **nous avons eu un temps ~** we had mixed weather, the weather was so-so*; **il est ~ en géographie** he is average at geography; **son devoir est très ~** his essay is pretty poor*; **comment as-tu trouvé le spectacle ?** — **très ~** what did you think of the show? — pretty average

[e] (*d'après des calculs*) [*température, âge*] average, mean; [*prix, durée, densité, vitesse*] average; **le revenu ~ par tête d'habitant** the average per capita income; **la consommation moyenne annuelle de chocolat** the average annual consumption of chocolate

[f] (*Géog*) **le cours ~ du fleuve** the middle reaches of the river; **les régions de la Loire moyenne** the middle regions of the Loire

[g] (*Ling*) **voyelle moyenne** mid *ou* central vowel

moyen² [mwajɛ̃] [1] NM [a] (= *procédé, manière*) means, way; **il y a toujours un ~** there's always a way, there are ways and means; **par quel ~ allez-vous le convaincre ?** how will you manage to convince him?; **connaissez-vous un bon ~ pour ...?** do you know a good way to ...?; **c'est le meilleur ~ de rater ton examen** it's the best way to fail your exam; **c'est l'unique ~ de s'en sortir** it's the only way out, it's the only way we can get out of it; (*péj*) **tous les ~s lui sont bons** he'll stop at nothing *ou* he'll do anything to get what he wants;

quand on veut réussir tous les ~s sont bons anything goes when one wants to succeed; **tous les ~s seront mis en œuvre pour réussir** we shall use all possible means to succeed; **par tous les ~s** (*gén*) by all possible means; (*même malhonnêtes*) by fair means or foul, by hook or by crook; **essayer par tous les ~s** to try every possible means; **j'ai essayé par tous les ~s de le convaincre** I've done everything to try and convince him; **au ~ de ◊ par le ~ de** by means of, through; **se débrouiller avec les ~s du bord** to get by as best one can, make do and mend; **employer les grands ~s** to resort to *ou* take drastic *ou* extreme measures; **trouver le ~ de faire qch** (*lit*) to find some means *ou* way of doing sth; (*fig hum*) **il a trouvé (le) ~ de se perdre** he managed *ou* contrived (*frm*) to get lost; **il trouve toujours (un) ~ de me mettre en colère** he always manages to make me angry; **nous avons les ~s de vous faire parler!** we have ways of making you talk!; (*Gram*) **adverbe de ~** = adverb of means → **fin**²

[b] (= *possibilité*) **est-ce qu'il y a ~ de lui parler ?** is it possible to speak to him?; **voyons s'il y a ~ de trouver les fonds** let's see if it's possible to get *ou* if there's some way of getting the funding; **le ~ de faire autre chose!** what else could I say?; **le ~ de lui refuser!** how could I possibly refuse?; **il n'y a pas ~ de sortir par ce temps** there's no way you can go out in this weather; **pas ~ d'avoir une réponse claire!** there's no way you can get a clear answer!; **pas ~ de savoir ce qu'ils se sont dit** there's no (way of) knowing what they said to each other; **non, il n'y a pas ~!** no, nothing doing!*, no, no chance!*; **il n'y a plus ~ de lui parler** you can't talk to him any more; **il n'y a jamais ~ qu'il fasse son lit** you'll never get him to make his bed, he'll never make his bed

[2] **moyens** NMPL [a] (= *capacités intellectuelles, physiques*) **il a de grands ~s (intellectuels)** he has great powers of intellect *ou* intellectual powers; **ça lui a enlevé** *ou* **fait perdre tous ses ~s** it left him completely at a loss, it completely threw him*; **il était en pleine possession de ses ~s** *ou* **en possession de tous ses ~s** (*gén*) his powers were at their peak; [*personne âgée*] he was in full possession of his faculties; **c'est au-dessus de ses ~s** it's beyond him, it's beyond his abilities *ou* capabilities; **par ses propres ~s** [*réussir*] all by oneself, on one's own; **ils ont dû rentrer par leurs propres ~s** they had to make their own way home, they had to go home under their own steam* (*Brit*)

[b] (= *ressources financières*) means; **il a les ~s** he has the means, he can afford it; **avoir de gros/petits ~s** to have a large/small income, be well/badly off; **c'est dans mes ~s** I can afford it; **il vit au-dessus de ses ~s** he lives beyond his means; **il n'a pas les ~s de s'acheter une voiture** he can't afford to buy a car; **c'est au-dessus de ses ~s** he can't afford it, it's beyond his means

[3] COMP ▸ **moyen d'action** means of action ▸ **moyen anglais** Middle English ▸ **moyens audiovisuels** audiovisual aids ▸ **moyen de communication** means of communication ▸ **moyen de défense** means of defence ▸ **moyen d'existence** means of existence ▸ **moyen d'expression** means of expression ▸ **moyen de locomotion** means of transport ▸ **moyen de paiement** method *ou* means of payment ▸ **moyen de pression** means of (applying) pressure; **nous n'avons aucun ~ de pression sur lui** we have no means of putting pressure on him *ou* no hold on him ▸ **moyen de production** means of production ▸ **moyen de transport** means *ou* mode of transport

Moyen Âge, Moyen-Âge [mwajenɑʒ] NM **le ~** the Middle Ages; **le haut ~** the early Middle Ages; **au ~** in the Middle Ages

▸ GRAMMAIRE ACTIVE: moyen 44.1

moyenâgeux, -euse [mwajɛnɑʒø, øz] ADJ [*ville, costumes*] medieval; (*péj*) [*pratiques, théorie*] antiquated, outdated

moyen-courrier (*pl* **moyens-courriers**) [mwajɛ̃kuʀje] [1] ADJ [*vol*] medium-haul [2] NM (*Aviat*) medium-haul aircraft

moyennant [mwajɛnɑ̃] PRÉP [+ *argent*] for; [+ *service*] in return for; [+ *travail, effort*] with; ~ **finance(s)** for a fee *ou* a consideration; ~ **quoi** in return for which, in consideration of which

moyenne² [mwajɛn] [1] NF [a] (*gén*) average; **au-dessus/au-dessous de la ~** above/below average; **faites la ~ de ces chiffres** work out the average of these figures; **la ~ d'âge/des températures** the average *ou* mean age/temperature; **la ~ des gens pense que ...** most people *ou* the broad mass of people think that ...; (*Math*) **~ géométrique/arithmétique** geometric/arithmetic mean; **le taux de natalité y est inférieur à la ~ nationale** the birthrate there is lower than the national average [b] (*Scol*) **avoir la ~** (*à un devoir*) to get fifty per cent, get half marks (*Brit*); (*à un examen*) to get a pass *ou* a pass mark (*Brit*); **~ générale (de l'année)** average (for the year); **améliorer** *ou* **remonter sa ~** to improve one's marks *ou* grades; **la ~ de la classe est de 9 sur 20** the class average is 9 out of 20; **cet élève est dans la ~/la bonne ~** this pupil is about/above average [c] (*Aut, Sport*) average speed; **faire du 100 de ~** to average 100 km/h, drive at an average speed of 100 km/h

[2] **en moyenne** LOC ADV on average; **l'usine produit en ~ 500 voitures par jour** the factory turns out 500 cars a day on average, the factory averages 500 cars a day

moyennement [mwajɛnmɑ̃] ADV [a] (= *médiocrement*) **c'est ~ bon** it's pretty average; **c'est ~ intéressant/drôle** it's not that interesting/funny; **il est ~ apprécié** he's not liked that much; **c'est très ~ payé** it's poorly paid; **j'ai réussi ~ en anglais** I didn't do that well in English; **j'aime ~ ça** I don't like it that much, I'm not that keen on it (*Brit*); **ça va ? — ~*** how are things? — so-so* *ou* could be worse* [b] (= *dans la moyenne*) [*radioactif, sucré*] moderately; **~ intelligent** of average intelligence

Moyen-Orient [mwajɛnɔʀjɑ̃] NM **le ~** the Middle East; **au ~** in the Middle East; **les pays/villes du ~** Middle Eastern countries/cities

moyen-oriental, e (*mpl* **moyen-orientaux**) [mwajɛ̃ɔʀjɑ̃tal, o] ADJ Middle Eastern

moyeu (*pl* **moyeux**) [mwajø] NM [*roue*] hub; [*hélice*] boss

mozambicain, e [mɔzɑ̃bikɛ̃, ɛn] [1] ADJ Mozambican [2] **Mozambicain(e)** NM,F Mozambican

Mozambique [mɔzɑ̃bik] NM Mozambique

Mozart [mɔzaʀ] NM Mozart

mozartien, -ienne [mɔzaʀtjɛ̃, jɛn] ADJ Mozartian, of Mozart

MRAP [mʀap] NM (ABRÉV = **mouvement contre le racisme, l'antisémitisme et pour l'amitié des peuples**) French anti-racist and peace movement

MST [ɛmɛste] NF [a] (ABRÉV = **maladie sexuellement transmissible**) STD [b] (ABRÉV = **maîtrise de sciences et techniques**) master's degree in science and technology

mu [my] NM INV mu

mû, mue¹ [my] ptp de **mouvoir**

mucilage [mysilaʒ] NM mucilage

mucosité [mykozite] NF (*gén pl*) mucus (*NonC*)

mucoviscidose [mykovisidoz] NF cystic fibrosis, mucoviscidosis (*SPÉC*)

mucus [mykys] NM mucus (*NonC*)

---

mue² [my] NF [a] (= *transformation*) [*oiseau*] moulting (*Brit*), molting (*US*); [*serpent*] sloughing; [*mammifère*] shedding, moulting (*Brit*), molting (*US*); [*cerf*] casting; [*voix*] breaking (*Brit*), changing (*US*); **la ~ (de la voix) intervient vers 14 ans** the voice breaks (*Brit*) *ou* changes (*US*) at about 14 years of age [b] (= *époque*) moulting *etc* season [c] (= *peau, plumes*) [*serpent*] slough; [*mammifère*] moulted *ou* shed hair; [*oiseau*] moulted *ou* shed feathers [d] (*Agr* = *cage*) coop

muer [mɥe] ▶conjug 1◀ [1] VI [*oiseau*] to moult (*Brit*), molt (*US*); [*serpent*] to slough (its skin), shed its skin; [*mammifère*] to moult (*Brit*), molt (*US*), shed hair (*ou* skin *etc*); [*cerf*] to cast its antlers; **sa voix mue ◊ il mue** his voice is breaking (*Brit*) *ou* changing (*US*) [2] VT (*littér*) **~ qch en** to transform *ou* change *ou* turn sth into [3] **se muer** VPR (*littér*) **se ~ en** to transform *ou* change *ou* turn into

muesli [myysli] NM muesli

muet, muette [mɥɛ, mɥɛt] [1] ADJ [a] (*Méd*) dumb [b] (= *silencieux*) [*colère, prière, personne*] silent, mute; (*littér*) [*forêt*] silent; **~ de colère/surprise** speechless with anger/surprise; **~ de peur** dumb with fear; **le code est ~ à ce sujet** the law is silent on this matter; **~ comme une tombe** (as) silent as the grave; **rester ~** [*témoin, rapport*] to remain silent (**sur** on); **il est resté ~ comme une carpe** he never opened his mouth; **en rester ~ (d'étonnement)** to stand speechless, be struck dumb (with astonishment) [c] (*Ciné, Théât*) [*film, cinéma*] silent; [*rôle*] non-speaking (*épith*); [*scène*] with no dialogue; (*au restaurant*) **carte muette** menu without prices (*given to guests*) [d] (*Ling*) mute, silent [e] (*Scol, Géog*) [*carte, clavier de machine à écrire*] blank; (*Mus*) **clavier ~** dummy keyboard [2] NM [a] (= *infirme*) mute, dumb man [b] (*Ciné*) **le ~** the silent cinema *ou* screen [3] **muette** NF mute, dumb woman; (*Mil*) **la grande Muette** the army

muezzin [mɥedzin] NM muezzin

mufle [myfl] NM [a] (*Zool* = *museau*) [*bovin*] muffle; [*chien, lion*] muzzle [b] (* = *goujat*) boor, lout; **~ (ou yob*** (*Brit*)!

muflerie [myfləʀi] NF boorishness (*NonC*), loutishness (*NonC*)

muflier [myflije] NM antirrhinum, snapdragon

mufti [myfti] NM (*Rel*) mufti

muge [myʒ] NM grey mullet

mugir [myʒiʀ] ▶conjug 2◀ VI [a] [*vache*] to low, moo; [*bœuf*] to bellow [b] (*littér*) [*vent*] to howl; [*mer*] to roar; [*sirène*] to wail

mugissement [myʒismɑ̃] NM [*vache*] lowing, mooing; [*bœuf*] bellowing [b] (*littér*) [*vent*] howling; [*mer*] roaring; [*sirène*] wailing

muguet [mygɛ] NM [a] (*Bot*) lily of the valley; (*Méd*) thrush; (†† = *élégant*) fop, coxcomb†, popinjay†

mulâtre, mulâtresse [mylatʀ, mylatʀɛs] NM,F, **mulâtre** ADJ INV mulatto

mule [myl] NF [a] (*Zool*) (female) mule → **tête, têtu** [b] (= *pantoufle*) mule; **la ~ du pape** the Pope's slipper [c] (*arg Drogue*) mule (*arg*)

mulet [mylɛ] NM [a] (*Zool*) (male) mule; (= *poisson*) mullet [b] (*arg Aut*) spare *ou* replacement car

muletier, -ière [myl(ə)tje, jɛʀ] [1] ADJ **sentier** *ou* **chemin ~** mule track [2] NM,F mule-driver, muleteer

mullah [myla] NM = **mollah**

mulot [mylo] NM field mouse

multi(-) [mylti] PRÉF (*dans les mots composés à trait d'union, le préfixe reste invariable*) multi(-); **multi-usage** multipurpose

multicarte [myltikaʀt] ADJ → **représentant**

---

multicellulaire [myltiselylɛʀ] ADJ multicellular

multicolore [myltikɔlɔʀ] ADJ multicoloured (*Brit*), many-coloured (*US*)

multiconfessionnel, -elle [myltikɔ̃fesjɔnɛl] ADJ [*association, État*] multi-denominational

multicoque [myltikɔk] ADJ, NM (**voilier**) **~** multihull

multicouche [myltikuʃ] ADJ [*revêtement*] multi-layered; (*Photo*) **objectif ~** lens with multiple coatings

multicritères, multi-critères [myltikʀitɛʀ] ADJ (*Ordin*) [*recherche*] multicriteria (*épith*)

multiculturalisme [myltikyltyʀalism] NM multiculturalism

multiculturel, -elle [myltikyltyʀɛl] ADJ multicultural

multidiffusion [myltidifyzjɔ̃] NF (*Audiov*) repeat broadcasting; **le film passera en ~** the film will be broadcast several times, there will be several repeats *ou* repeat broadcasts of the film

multidimensionnel, -elle [myltidimɑ̃sjɔnɛl] ADJ multidimensional

multidisciplinaire [myltidisiplinɛʀ] ADJ multidisciplinary

multiethnique, multi-ethnique [myltietnik] ADJ multi-ethnic

multifactoriel, -elle [myltifaktɔrjɛl] ADJ multifactorial

multifenêtre [myltifənɛtʀ] ADJ (*Ordin*) multi-window (*épith*)

multiflore [myltiflɔʀ] ADJ multiflora

multifonction [myltifɔ̃ksjɔ̃] ADJ (*gén*) multifunction (*épith*); (*Ordin*) multiprocessing (*épith*), multitask(ing) (*épith*)

multiforme [myltifɔʀm] ADJ [*apparence*] multiform; [*problème*] many-sided

multigrade [myltigʀad] ADJ **huile ~** multigrade oil

multilatéral, e (*mpl* **-aux**) [myltilateʀal, o] ADJ multilateral

multilatéralisme [myltilateʀalism] NM (*Écon*) multilateralism

multilingue [myltilɛ̃g] ADJ multilingual

multilinguisme [myltilɛ̃gɥism] NM multilingualism

multimédia [myltimedja] [1] ADJ multimedia [2] NM **le ~** multimedia

multimédiatique [myltimedjatik] ADJ multimedia (*épith*)

multimilliardaire [myltimiljaʀdɛʀ], **multimillionnaire** [myltimiljɔnɛʀ] ADJ, NMF multimillionaire

multinational, e (*mpl* **-aux**) [myltinasjɔnal, o] [1] ADJ multinational [2] **multinationale** NF multinational (company)

multiniveaux [myltinivo] ADJ multilevel

multipare [myltipaʀ] [1] ADJ multiparous [2] NF (= *femme*) multipara; (= *animal*) multiparous animal

multipartenariat [myltipaʀtənaʀja] NM *having several sexual partners*

multipartisme [myltipaʀtism] NM (*Pol*) multiparty system

multipartite [myltipaʀtit] ADJ (*Pol*) multiparty (*épith*)

multiple [myltipl] [1] ADJ [a] (= *nombreux*) numerous, multiple, many; (*Méd*) [*fracture, blessures, grossesse*] multiple; **dans de ~s cas** in numerous *ou* many instances; **en de ~s occasions** on numerous *ou* many occasions; **pour des raisons ~s** *ou* **de ~s raisons** for multiple reasons; **à de ~s reprises** time and again, repeatedly; **à têtes ~s** [*missile*] multiple-warhead; [*outil*] with (a range of) attachments; **outil à usages ~s** multi-purpose tool; **choix ~** multiple choice *ou* **magasin, prise** [b] (= *variés*) [*activités, aspects*] many, multifarious, manifold [c] (= *complexe*) [*pensée,* *problème, homme*] many-sided, multifaceted; [*monde*] complex, mixed d (*Math*) **100 est ~ de 10** 100 is a multiple of 10 2 NM multiple; **plus petit commun ~** lowest common multiple

multiplex [myltipleks] ADJ, NM (*Téléc*) multiplex; **émission (réalisée) en ~** multiplex programme

multiplexage [myltipleksaʒ] NM (*Téléc*) multiplexing

multiplexe [myltipleks] NM (*Ciné*) multiplex (cinema), multiscreen cinema

multiplexeur [myltipleksœR] NM (*Téléc*) multiplexer

multipliable [myltiplijabl] ADJ multipli(c)able

multiplicande [myltiplikãd] NM multiplicand

multiplicateur, -trice [myltiplikatœR, tRis] 1 ADJ multiplying; **effet ~** multiplier effect 2 NM multiplier

multiplicatif, -ive [myltiplikatif, iv] ADJ (*Math*) multiplying; (*Gram*) multiplicative

multiplication [myltiplikasjɔ̃] NF a (= *prolifération*) increase in the number of; (*Bible*) **la ~ des pains** the miracle of the loaves and fishes b (*Bio, Bot, Math*) multiplication; (*Math*) **faire une ~** to do a multiplication c (*Tech*) gear ratio

multiplicité [myltiplisite] NF multiplicity

multiplier [myltiplije] ▶ conjug 7 ◀ 1 VT (*Math*) to multiply (**par** by); [+ *attaques, difficultés, avertissements*] to multiply, increase; **les prix ont été multipliés par deux/trois** prices have doubled/tripled, prices have increased twofold/threefold; **les autorités multiplient les appels au calme** the authorities are issuing repeated appeals for calm; **je pourrais ~ les exemples** I could give you hundreds of examples; **malgré nos efforts multipliés** in spite of our increased efforts 2 **se multiplier** VPR a [*incidents, attaques, difficultés*] to multiply, increase, grow in number b (= *se reproduire*) [*animaux*] to multiply → **croître** c (*fig* = *se donner à fond*) [*infirmier, soldat*] to do one's utmost, give of one's best (**pour faire** in order to do)

multipoint(s) [myltipwɛ̃] ADJ INV [*serrure*] multipoint; (*Aut*) **injection ~** multipoint fuel injection

multipolaire [myltipɔlɛR] ADJ multipolar

multiposte [myltipɔst] ADJ → **configuration**

multiprise [myltipRiz] NF adaptor

multiprocesseur [myltipRɔsesœR] NM multiprocessor

multiprogrammation [myltipRɔgramasjɔ̃] NF multiprogramming

multipropriété [myltipRɔpRijete] NF timesharing; **acheter un appartement en ~** to buy a timeshare in a flat (*Brit*) ou apartment (*US*)

multiracial, e (*mpl -iaux*) [myltiRasjal, jo] ADJ multiracial

multirécidiviste [myltiResidivist] ADJ (*Jur*) 1 ADJ [*personne*] who has committed several criminal offences 2 NMF persistent offender

multirésistant, e [myltiRezistã, ãt] ADJ (*Bio*) [*microbe, souche*] multi-resistant

multirisque(s) [myltiRisk] ADJ **assurance ~** ≈ comprehensive insurance; **contrat multi-risques habitation** comprehensive home insurance policy

multisalle(s) [myltisal] ADJ (**cinéma** ou **complexe**) ~ multiplex (cinema), multiscreen cinema (complex)

multistandard [myltistãdaR] ADJ [*téléviseur, magnétoscope*] multistandard

multitâche [myltitaʃ] ADJ (*Ordin*) multi-task(ing) (*épith*)

multitraitement [myltitRɛtmã] NM (*Ordin*) multiprocessing

multitude [myltityd] NF a (= *grand nombre*) **(toute) une ~ de** [+ *personnes*] a multitude of, a vast number of; [+ *objets, idées*] a vast number of; **une ~ de gens** a multitude ou a throng of people b (= *ensemble, masse*) mass; **on pouvait voir d'en haut la ~ des champs** from the air you could see the mass of fields c († ou *littér*) **la ~** (= *foule de gens*) the multitude, the throng

mumuse* [mymyz] NF **faire ~** to play (**avec** with); **alors, on fait ~ ?** are you having a nice time then?

Munich [mynik] N Munich

munichois, e [mynikwa, waz] 1 ADJ of ou from Munich, Munich (*épith*); **bière ~e** Munich beer 2 **Munichois(e)** NM,F inhabitant ou native of Munich; (*Pol*) **les Munichois** the men of Munich

municipal, e (*mpl -aux*) [mynisipal, o] 1 ADJ [*élection, taxe, bibliothèque*] municipal; [*employé*] council (*épith*); [*conseil, conseiller*] local, town (*épith*), borough (*épith*) → **arrêté** 2 **municipales** NFPL **les ~es** the local ou council elections

municipalité [mynisipalite] NF a (= *ville*) town b (= *conseil*) town council, municipality (*Admin*)

munificence [mynifisãs] NF (*littér*) munificence

munificent, e [mynifisã, ãt] ADJ (*littér*) munificent

munir [myniR] ▶ conjug 2 ◀ 1 VT **~ un objet de** to provide ou fit an object with; **~ une machine de** to equip ou fit a machine with; **~ un bâtiment de** to equip ou fit out a building with; **~ qn de** to provide ou supply ou equip sb with; **canne munie d'un bout ferré** walking stick with an iron tip; **muni de ces conseils** armed with this advice; **muni d'un bon dictionnaire** equipped with a good dictionary; **muni des sacrements de l'Église** fortified with the rites of the Church 2 **se munir** VPR **se ~ de** [+ *papiers*] to provide o.s. with; [+ *imperméable*] to take; [+ *argent, nourriture*] to take a supply of; **se ~ de courage** to pluck up one's courage; **munissez-vous de votre passeport** take your passport (with you)

munitions [mynisjɔ̃] NFPL a (*Mil, Chasse*) ammunition (*NonC*), munitions b († = *ressources*) supplies

munster [mœstɛR] NM Munster (cheese)

muon [myɔ̃] NM muon

muphti [myfti] NM = **mufti**

muqueux, -euse [mykø, øz] 1 ADJ mucous 2 **muqueuse** NF mucous membrane

mur [myR] 1 NM a (*Constr*) wall; **leur jardin est entouré d'un ~** their garden is walled ou is surrounded by a wall; **une maison aux ~s de brique** a brick house; **~ d'appui** parapet; **mettre/pendre qch au ~** to put/hang sth on the wall; **sauter** ou **faire le ~*** to go over the wall; (*fig*) **on va droit dans le ~** we're heading straight for disaster; **ils n'ont laissé que les (quatre) ~s** they left nothing but the bare walls; **rester entre quatre ~s** [*prisonnier*] to stay within the confines of one's cell; (*chez soi*) to stay indoors ou inside; **l'ennemi est dans nos ~s** the enemy is within our gates; **M. X est dans nos ~s aujourd'hui** we have Mr X with us today; **maintenant que nous sommes dans nos ~s** now (that) we're in our new house (ou flat etc), now we have our own four walls; (*Jur*) **être propriétaire des ~s** to own the premises; **les ~s ont des oreilles!** walls have ears!; (*Sport*) **faire le ~** to make a wall; (*Tennis*) **faire du ~** to practise against a wall b (= *obstacle : Ski*) wall; [*feu, pluie*] wall; [*silence, hostilité*] barrier, wall; **il y a un ~ entre nous** there is a barrier between us; **se heurter à** ou **se trouver devant un ~** to come up against a stone ou a brick wall; **se heurter à un ~ d'incompréhension** to come up against a

wall of incomprehension; **être** ou **avoir le dos au ~** to have one's back to the wall; **on parle à un ~** it's like talking to a brick wall → **pied** c (*Aviat*) **~ du son/de la chaleur** sound/heat barrier; **passer** ou **franchir le ~ du son** to break the sound barrier

2 COMP ▶ **mur artificiel** = mur d'escalade ▶ **le mur de l'Atlantique** (*Mil, Pol*) the Atlantic Wall ▶ **mur d'escalade** climbing wall ▶ **le mur d'Hadrien** Hadrian's Wall ▶ **le Mur des Lamentations** the Wailing Wall

mûr, e[1] [myR] ADJ a [*fruit, projet*] ripe; [*toile, tissu*] worn; **fruit pas ~/trop ~** unripe/overripe fruit b [*personne*] (= *sensé*) mature; (= *âgé*) middle-aged; **une femme assez ~e** a woman of mature years; **il est ~ pour le mariage** he is ready for marriage; **leur pays est-il ~ pour la démocratie ?** is their country ripe for democracy? c (: = *ivre*) tight*, plastered: d **après ~e réflexion** after much thought, on mature reflection

murage [myRaʒ] NM [*ouverture*] walling up, bricking up, blocking up

muraille [myRɑj] NF (high) wall; **la Grande Muraille de Chine** the Great Wall of China; **~ de glace/roche** wall of ice/rock, ice/rock barrier; **couleur (de) ~** (stone) grey

mural, e (*mpl -aux*) [myRal, o] ADJ (*gén*) wall (*épith*); (*Art*) mural; **peinture** ou **fresque ~e** mural (painting)

mûre[2] [myR] NF (*gén*) blackberry; [*mûrier blanc*] mulberry

mûrement [myRmã] ADV **~ réfléchi** [*décision*] carefully thought out; **après avoir ~ réfléchi** ou **délibéré** after much ou considerable thought, after careful consideration

murène [myRɛn] NF moray (eel), muraena (*Brit*), murena (*US*)

murer [myRe] ▶ conjug 1 ◀ 1 VT a [+ *ouverture*] to wall up, brick up, block up; [+ *lieu, ville*] to wall (in) b [+ *personne*] (*lit*) to wall in, wall up; (*fig*) to isolate 2 **se murer** VPR (*chez soi*) to shut o.s. away; **se ~ dans sa douleur/son silence** to immure o.s. in one's grief/in silence; **se ~ dans la solitude** to retreat into solitude; **muré dans son refus du compromis** stubbornly refusing to compromise

muret [myRɛ] NM, **murette** [myRɛt] NF low wall

murex [myRɛks] NM murex

mûrier [myRje] NM (*cultivé*) blackberry bush; (*sauvage*) blackberry bush, bramble (bush); **~ blanc** (white) mulberry tree

mûrir [myRiR] ▶ conjug 2 ◀ 1 VI [*fruit*] to ripen; [*idée*] to mature, develop; [*personne*] to mature; [*abcès, bouton*] to come to a head; **faire ~** [+ *fruit*] to ripen; **il a beaucoup mûri** he has matured a lot, he has become much more mature 2 VT [+ *fruit*] to ripen; [+ *idée, projet*] to nurture; [+ *personne*] to (make) mature

mûrissage [myRisaʒ] NM [*fruits*] ripening

mûrissant, e [myRisã, ãt] ADJ [*fruit*] ripening; [*personne*] of mature years

mûrissement [myRismã] NM [*fruit*] ripening; [*idée*] maturing, development; [*projet*] nurturing

mûrisserie [myRisRi] NF [*bananes*] ripening room

murmure [myRmyR] NM a (= *chuchotement*) [*personne*] murmur; [*ruisseau*] murmur(ing), babble; [*vent*] murmur(ing); [*oiseaux*] twitter(ing); (*Méd*) **~ vésiculaire** vesicular murmur b (= *commentaire*) murmur; **d'approbation/de protestation** murmur of approval/of protest; **obéir sans ~** to obey without a murmur; **~s** (= *protestations*) murmurings, mutterings; (= *objections*) objections; (= *rumeurs*) rumours (*Brit*), rumors (*US*)

murmurer [myRmyRe] ▶ conjug 1 ◀ 1 VT (= *parler bas*) to murmur; **ils se murmuraient des**

mots tendres they were whispering sweet nothings to each other; (*rumeurs*) **on murmure que ... ◊ certains murmurent que ...** it's whispered that ..., rumour has it that ..., it is rumoured that ...; **la situation va s'aggraver, murmurent les spécialistes** there are rumours among the experts that the situation is going to get worse; **de mauvaises langues murmurent que ...** malicious tongues are putting (it) about that ... [2] VI **a** (= *chuchoter*) [*personne, vent*] to murmur; [*ruisseau*] to murmur, babble **b** (= *protester*) to mutter, complain (**contre** about); **il a consenti sans ~** he agreed without a murmur (of protest)

musaraigne [myzaʀɛɲ] NF (*Zool*) shrew

musarder [myzaʀde] ▶ conjug 1 ◀ VI (*littér*) (*en se promenant*) to dawdle (along); (*en perdant son temps*) to idle (about)

musc [mysk] NM musk

muscade [myskad] NF **a** (*Culin*) nutmeg → **noix b** [*prestidigitateur*] (conjurer's) ball; (*lit, fig*) **passez ~ !** hey presto!

muscadet [myskadɛ] NM muscadet (wine)

muscadier [myskadje] NM nutmeg (tree)

muscadin [myskadɛ̃] NM (*Hist* = *élégant*) fop, coxcomb†, popinjay†

muscari [myskaʀi] NM grape hyacinth

muscat [myska] NM (= *raisin*) muscat grape; (= *vin*) muscat(el)

muscle [myskl] NM muscle; **~ cardiaque** heart ou cardiac muscle; **~s lisses/striés** smooth/striated muscles; **il est tout en ~** he's all muscle; **il a des ~s** ou **du ~*** he's muscular ou beefy* ou brawny; **pour gagner** ou **prendre du ~** to build up your muscles

musclé, e [myskle] (*ptp de* **muscler**) ADJ **a** [*corps, membre, personne*] muscular; **elle est très ~ des jambes** she's got very muscular legs, her legs are very muscular **b** [*style*] sinewy; [*pièce de théâtre*] powerful; [*régime, appariteur*] strong-arm (*épith*); [*interrogatoire*] brutal, violent; [*discours*] forceful; **une intervention ~e de la police** a forceful intervention by the police; (*arg Scol*) **un problème ~** a stinker* of a problem, a stiff problem

muscler [myskle] ▶ conjug 1 ◀ [1] VT **a** [+ *corps, membre, personne*] to develop the muscles of **b** [+ *économie, industrie, projet*] to strengthen, beef up* [2] **se muscler** VPR [*personne*] to develop one's muscles; **pour que vos jambes se musclent** to develop your leg muscles

muscu* [mysky] NF (ABRÉV = **musculation**) **faire de la ~** to pump iron*

musculaire [myskylɛʀ] ADJ [*force*] muscular; **fibre ~** muscle fibre

musculation [myskylasjɔ̃] NF body building; **exercices de ~** muscle-development exercises; **salle de ~** weights room; **faire de la ~** to do body building

musculature [myskylatyʀ] NF muscle structure, musculature (*SPÉC*); **il a une ~ imposante** he has an impressive set of muscles

musculeux, -euse [myskylø, øz] ADJ [*corps, membre, femme*] muscular; [*homme*] muscular, brawny

muse [myz] NF (*Littérat, Myth*) Muse; **les (neuf) ~s** the Muses; (*hum*) **cultiver** ou **taquiner la ~** to court the Muse (*hum*)

museau (*pl* **museaux**) [myzo] NM **a** [*chien*] muzzle; [*bovin*] muffle; [*porc*] snout; [*souris*] nose **b** (*Culin*) brawn (*Brit*), headcheese (*US*) **c*** (= *visage*) face, snout*; **elle a un joli petit ~** she's got a pretty little face; (= *bouche*) **essuie ton ~** wipe your mouth

musée [myze] NM (*art, peinture*) art gallery; (*technique, scientifique*) museum; **le ~ des Offices** the Uffizi (gallery); **de cire** waxworks *sg*, wax museum; **Nîmes est une ville-~** Nîmes is a historical town, Nîmes is a town of great historical interest; (*hum*) **~ des horreurs** junkshop (*hum*); **il ferait bien dans un**

~ des horreurs he should be in a chamber of horrors; (*lit, fig*) **objet** ou **pièce de ~** museum piece

museler [myz(ə)le] ▶ conjug 4 ◀ VT [+ *animal*] to muzzle; [+ *personne, liberté, presse*] to muzzle, gag

muselière [myzəljɛʀ] NF muzzle; **mettre une ~ à** to muzzle

musellement [myzɛlmɑ̃] NM [*animal*] muzzling; [*personne, liberté, presse*] muzzling, gagging

muséographie [myzeɔgʀafi] NF museography

muséographique [myzeɔgʀafik] ADJ [*atelier, programme, projet*] museum (*épith*)

muséologie [myzeɔlɔʒi] NF museology

muser [myze] ▶ conjug 1 ◀ VI († ou *littér*) (*en se promenant*) to dawdle (along); (*en perdant son temps*) to idle (about)

musette [myzɛt] [1] NF **a** (= *sac*) [*ouvrier*] lunchbag; †† [*écolier*] satchel; [*soldat*] haversack; [*cheval*] nosebag **b** (*Mus* = instrument, air) musette **c** (*Zool*) common shrew [2] NM (= *bal*) popular dance (to the accordion); (= *genre*) **le ~** accordion music [3] ADJ INV [*bal, style*] musette; [*orchestre*] accordion (*épith*) → **bal**

muséum [myzeɔm] NM **~ (d'histoire naturelle)** (natural history) museum

musical, e (*mpl* -aux) [myzikal, o] ADJ [*chaîne, critique, programmation*] music (*épith*); [*directeur*] musical, music (*épith*); **l'œuvre ~e de Debussy** Debussy's musical works ou compositions; **avoir l'oreille ~e** to have a good ear for music; **spectacle ~** (*gén*) music show; (= *comédie*) musical → **comédie**

musicalement [myzikalmɑ̃] ADV musically

musicalité [myzikalite] NF musicality, musical quality

music-hall (*pl* music-halls) [myzikol] NM (= *spectacle*) music hall; (= *salle*) variety theatre, music hall; **faire du ~** to be in ou do variety; **spectacle/numéro de ~** variety show/turn ou act ou number

musicien, -ienne [myzisjɛ̃, jɛn] [1] ADJ musical [2] NM,F musician

musicographe [myzikɔgʀaf] NMF musicographer

musicographie [myzikɔgʀafi] NF musicography

musicologie [myzikɔlɔʒi] NF musicology

musicologique [myzikɔlɔʒik] ADJ musicological

musicologue [myzikɔlɔg] NMF musicologist

musicothérapie [myzikɔteʀapi] NF music therapy

musique [myzik] [1] NF **a** (= *art, harmonie, notations*) music; [*morceau*] piece of music; **~ folklorique/militaire/sacrée** folk/military/sacred music; **~ pour piano** piano music; **elle fait de la ~** she does music, she plays an instrument; **si on faisait de la ~** let's make some music; **mettre un poème en ~** to set a poem to music; **déjeuner en ~** to lunch against a background of music; **travailler en ~** to work to music; **je n'aime pas travailler en ~** I don't like working with music playing; **elle nous chante maintenant «Manhattan», sur une ~ de Georges Leblanc** she's now going to sing "Manhattan" for us, music by Georges Leblanc; **qui a écrit la ~ du film ?** who wrote the film score? ou the soundtrack?; **il compose beaucoup de ~s de film** he composes a lot of film music; **la ~ adoucit les mœurs** music has a civilizing influence, music soothes the savage breast; **c'est toujours la même ~*** it's always the same old song ou tune; **tu veux toujours aller plus vite que la ~** you always want to do things too quickly → **boîte, connaître, papier b** (= *orchestre, fanfare*) band; **~ militaire** military band; (*Mil*) **marcher** ou **aller ~ en tête** to march with the band leading → **chef[1]** [2] COMP ► **musique d'ambiance** background ou ambient music ► **musique d'ascenseur** (*péj*) Muzak®, elevator ou lift (*Brit*) music ► **musique de ballet** ballet music ► **musique de chambre** chamber music ► **musique classique** classical music ► **musique concrète** concrete music, musique concrète ► **musique de fond** (*gén*) background music; [*film*] incidental music ► **musique légère** light music ► **musique noire** black music ► **musique pop** pop music ► **musique de scène** incidental music ► **musique de supermarché** = **musique d'ascenseur**

musiquette [myziket] NF (*péj*) bland music

musli [mysli] NM = **muesli**

musoir [myzwaʀ] NM (*Naut*) pierhead

musqué, e [myske] ADJ [*odeur, goût*] musky; **bœuf ~** musk ox; **rose ~e** musk rose → **rat**

mussolinien, -ienne [mysɔlinjɛ̃, jɛn] ADJ (*lit*) Mussolini (*épith*); (*péj*) [*architecture*] Mussolini-style; **l'Italie mussolinienne** Italy under the rule of Mussolini

must* [mœst] NM (= *film, livre etc*) **c'est un ~** it's a must*

mustang [mystɑ̃g] NM mustang

musulman, e [myzylmɑ̃, an] ADJ, NM,F Moslem, Muslim

mutabilité [mytabilite] NF (*Bio, Jur*) mutability

mutagène [mytaʒɛn] ADJ mutagenic

mutant, e [mytɑ̃, ɑ̃t] ADJ, NM,F mutant

mutation [mytasjɔ̃] NF **a** (= *transfert*) [*employé*] transfer **b** (= *changement*) (*gén*) transformation; (*Bio*) mutation; **société en ~** changing society; **entreprise en pleine ~** company undergoing massive changes **c** (*Jur*) transfer; (*Mus*) mutation; (*Ling*) **~ consonantique/vocalique/phonétique** consonant/vowel/sound shift

mutatis mutandis [mytatismytɑ̃dis] LOC ADV mutatis mutandis, allowing for a few minor variations

muter [myte] ▶ conjug 1 ◀ VT (*Admin*) to transfer; **il a été muté à Caen/au service informatique** he has been transferred to Caen/to the computer department

mutilant, e [mytilɑ̃, ɑ̃t] ADJ [*opération*] mutilating, mutilative

mutilateur, -trice [mytilatœʀ, tʀis] (*littér*) [1] ADJ mutilating, mutilative [2] NM,F mutilator

mutilation [mytilasjɔ̃] NF [*corps*] mutilation, maiming; [*texte, statue, arbre*] mutilation; **~ volontaire** self-inflicted injury; **~ sexuelle** sexual mutilation

mutilé, e [mytile] (*ptp de* **mutiler**) NM,F (= *infirme*) cripple, disabled person; **les (grands) ~s** the (badly ou severely) disabled; **~ de la face** disfigured person; **~ de guerre** disabled ex-serviceman; **~ du travail** disabled worker

mutiler [mytile] ▶ conjug 1 ◀ VT [+ *personne*] to mutilate, maim; [+ *statue, tableau, arbre, texte*] to mutilate; [+ *paysage*] to disfigure; **être mutilé des deux jambes** to have lost both legs; **se ~ (volontairement)** to mutilate o.s.

mutin, e [mytɛ̃, in] [1] ADJ (= *espiègle*) mischievous, impish [2] NM (= *révolté*) rebel; (*Mil, Naut*) mutineer

mutiné, e [mytine] (*ptp de se mutiner*) [1] ADJ [*marin, soldat*] mutinous [2] NM (*Mil, Naut*) mutineer; (*gén*) rebel

mutiner (se) [mytine] ▶ conjug 1 ◀ VPR (*Mil, Naut*) to mutiny; (*gén*) to rebel, revolt

mutinerie [mytinʀi] NF (*Mil, Naut*) mutiny; (*gén*) rebellion, revolt

mutisme [mytism] NM **a** (= *silence*) silence; **elle s'enferma dans un ~ total** she withdrew into total silence; **la presse observe un ~ total**

the press is maintaining a complete silence *ou* blackout on the subject [b] (*Psych*) mutism

mutité [mytite] NF (*Méd*) muteness

mutualisme [mytɥalism] NM mutual (benefit) insurance system

mutualiste [mytɥalist] [1] ADJ mutualistic; **société (d'assurances) ~** mutual benefit society, mutual (benefit) insurance company, ≈ Friendly Society (*Brit*) [2] NMF mutualist

mutualité [mytɥalite] NF (= *système d'entraide*) mutual (benefit) insurance system; (= *compagnies*) **la ~ française** French mutual insurance companies

mutuel, **-elle** [mytɥɛl] [1] ADJ (= *réciproque*) mutual → **pari** [2] **mutuelle** NF mutual benefit society, mutual (benefit) insurance company, ≈ Friendly Society (*Brit*); **prendre une mutuelle*** to take out (supplementary) private health insurance; **payer sa cotisation à la mutuelle** ≈ to pay one's insurance premium (*for back-up health cover*)

┌─── **MUTUELLE** ───┐

In addition to standard health cover provided by the "Sécurité sociale", many French people contribute to complementary insurance schemes run by mutual benefit organizations known as mutuelles, often linked to specific professions. The mutuelle reimburses some or all of the medical expenses that cannot be met by the "Sécurité sociale". → *SÉCURITÉ SOCIALE*

mutuellement [mytɥɛlmɑ̃] ADV [*s'accuser, se renforcer*] one another, each other; **~ ressenti** mutually felt; **s'aider ~** to give each other mutual help, help one another; **ces options s'excluent ~** these options are mutually exclusive

Myanmar [mijanmaʀ] NM Myanmar

mycélium [miseljɔm] NM mycelium

Mycènes [misen] N Mycenae

mycénien, **-ienne** [misenjɛ̃, jɛn] ADJ Mycenaean

mycologie [mikɔlɔʒi] NF mycology

mycologique [mikɔlɔʒik] ADJ mycologic(al)

mycologue [mikɔlɔg] NMF mycologist

mycorhize [mikɔʀiz] NM myco(r)rhiza

mycose [mikoz] NF mycosis; **la ~ du pied** athlete's foot; **~ vaginale** vaginal thrush

mycosique [mikɔsik] ADJ mycotic

myéline [mjelin] NF myelin

myélinisé, **e** [mjelinize] ADJ (*Bio*) myelinated

myélite [mjelit] NF myelitis

mygale [migal] NF trap-door spider

myocarde [mjɔkaʀd] NM myocardium → **infarctus**

myopathe [mjɔpat] [1] ADJ suffering from myopathy, ≈ suffering from muscular dystrophy [2] NMF person suffering from myopathy, ≈ person suffering from muscular dystrophy

myopathie [mjɔpati] NF myopathy, ≈ muscular dystrophy

myope [mjɔp] [1] ADJ short-sighted, near-sighted (*US*), myopic (*SPÉC*); **tu es ~ ou quoi?*** are you blind?; **~ comme une taupe*** (as) blind as a bat* [2] NMF short-sighted *ou* near-sighted (*US*) person, myope (*SPÉC*)

myopie [mjɔpi] NF short-sightedness, near-sightedness (*US*), myopia (*SPÉC*)

myosotis [mjɔzɔtis] NM forget-me-not

myriade [miʀjad] NF myriad

myriapode [miʀjapɔd] NM myriapods; **les ~s** Myriapoda (*SPÉC*)

myrmidon [miʀmidɔ̃] NM († *péj* = *nabot*) pipsqueak*

myrrhe [miʀ] NF myrrh

myrte [miʀt] NM myrtle

myrtille [miʀtij] NF whortleberry, bilberry (*Brit*), blueberry (*US*)

mystère [misteʀ] NM [a] (= *énigme, dissimulation*) mystery; **pas tant de ~(s)!** don't be so mysterious! *ou* secretive!; **faire (un) ~ de** to make a mystery out of; **elle en fait grand ~** she makes a big mystery of it; **il restera un ~ pour moi** he'll always be a mystery *ou* a closed book to me; **~ et boule de gomme!*** who knows!, search me!*; **ce n'est un ~ pour personne** it's no secret; **il faut travailler beaucoup, il n'y a pas de ~!*** you just have to work hard, there's no two ways about it!*;

(*Rel*) **le ~ de la Trinité/de l'Incarnation** the mystery of the Trinity/of the Incarnation [b] (*Littérat*) mystery (play) [c] ® (= *glace*) ice-cream with a meringue centre, decorated with chopped hazelnuts

mystérieusement [misteʀjøzmɑ̃] ADV mysteriously

mystérieux, **-ieuse** [misteʀjø, jøz] ADJ (= *secret, bizarre*) mysterious; (= *cachottier*) secretive

mysticisme [mistisism] NM mysticism

mystificateur, **-trice** [mistifikatœʀ, tʀis] [1] ADJ **j'ai reçu un coup de fil ~** I had a phone call which was a hoax; **tenir des propos ~s à qn** to say things to trick sb [2] NM,F (= *farceur*) hoaxer, practical joker

mystification [mistifikasjɔ̃] NF (= *farce*) hoax, practical joke; (*péj* = *mythe*) myth

mystifier [mistifje] ▸conjug 7◂ VT to fool, deceive

mystique [mistik] [1] ADJ mystic(al) [2] NMF (= *personne*) mystic [3] NF (= *science, pratiques*) mysticism; (*péj* = *vénération*) blind belief (**de** in); **avoir la ~ du travail** to have a blind belief in work

mystiquement [mistikmɑ̃] ADV mystically

mythe [mit] NM (*gén*) myth

mythifier [mitifje] ▸conjug 7◂ VT (*surtout au ptp*) [+ *passé, personne*] to mythologize, mythicize

mythique [mitik] ADJ mythical

mytho* [mito] ADJ, NMF ABRÉV = **mythomane**

mythologie [mitɔlɔʒi] NF mythology

mythologique [mitɔlɔʒik] ADJ mythological

mythomane [mitɔman] ADJ, NMF mythomaniac; **elle est un peu ~** she has a tendency to embroider the truth; **il est complètement ~** he makes up the most incredible stories

mythomanie [mitɔmani] NF mythomania

mytiliculteur, **-trice** [mitilikyltœʀ, tʀis] NM,F mussel breeder

mytiliculture [mitilikyltyʀ] NF mussel breeding

myxomatose [miksomatoz] NF myxomatosis

N

N¹, n [ɛn] NM (= *lettre*) N, n; (*Math*) n

N² (ABRÉV = **Nord**) N

n' [n] → **ne**

na [na] EXCL (*langage enfantin*) so there!; **je n'en veux pas, ~ !** I don't want any, so there!

nabab [nabab] NM (*Hist*, † *ou littér*) nabob

nabi [nabi] NM (*Art*) Nabi

nabot, e [nabo, ɔt] NM,F (*péj*) dwarf, midget

nabuchodonosor [nabykɔdɔnɔzɔʀ] NM (= *bouteille*) nebuchadnezzar; **Nabuchodonosor** Nebuchadnezzar

nacelle [nasɛl] NF [*ballon, montgolfière, dirigeable*] gondola; [*landau*] carriage; [*engin spatial*] pod; [*ouvrier*] cradle; (*littér = bateau*) skiff

nacre [nakʀ] NF mother-of-pearl

nacré, e [nakʀe] (*ptp de* **nacrer**) ADJ pearly, nacreous (*littér*); [*vernis à ongles*] pearly

nacrer [nakʀe] ▶ conjug 1 ◀ VT (= *iriser*) to cast a pearly sheen over; (*Tech*) to give a pearly gloss to

nadir [nadiʀ] NM nadir

nævus [nevys] (*pl* **nævi** [nevi]) NM naevus

Nagasaki [nagazaki] N Nagasaki

nage [naʒ] NF **a** (= *activité*) swimming; (= *manière*) stroke, style of swimming; **~ sur le dos** backstroke; **~ indienne** sidestroke; **faire un 100 m ~ libre** to swim a 100 m (in) freestyle; **~ sous-marine** underwater swimming, skin diving; **~ de vitesse** speed stroke; **~ synchronisée** synchronized swimming **b** **se sauver à la ~** to swim away *ou* off; **gagner la rive/traverser une rivière à la ~** to swim to the bank/across a river; **faire traverser son chien à la ~** to get one's dog to swim across; (*Culin*) **homard/écrevisses à la ~** lobster/crayfish (cooked) in a court-bouillon **c** **en ~** pouring with sweat, bathed in sweat; **cela m'a mis en ~** it made me sweat, it brought me out in a sweat; **ne te mets pas en ~** don't get yourself in a lather* **d** (*Naut*) **~ à couple/en pointe** rowing two abreast/in staggered pairs → **banc, chef¹**

nageoire [naʒwaʀ] NF [*poisson*] fin; [*phoque, dauphin*] flipper; **~ anale/dorsale/ventrale** anal/dorsal/ventral fin; **~ caudale** [*poisson*] caudal fin; [*baleine*] tail flukes

nager [naʒe] ▶ conjug 3 ◀ **1** VI **a** [*personne, poisson*] to swim; [*objet*] to float; **elle nage bien** she's a good swimmer; **~ comme un fer à repasser*/un poisson*** to swim like a brick/a fish; **la viande nage dans la graisse** the meat is swimming in fat; **tes manches nagent dans la soupe** your sleeves are dipping in the soup; **on nageait dans le sang** the place was swimming in blood, the place was awash with blood → **apprendre, savoir**
b (*fig*) **il nage dans le bonheur** he is overjoyed, his joy knows no bounds; **~ dans l'opulence** to be rolling in money*; **il nage dans ses vêtements** his clothes are miles too big for him; **on nage dans l'absurdité/le grotesque dans ce film** this film is totally absurd/ridiculous; **en allemand, je nage complètement*** I'm completely at sea* *ou* lost

in German
c (*Naut*) to row; **~ à couple/en pointe** to row two abreast/in staggered pairs
2 VT to swim; **~ la brasse/le 100 mètres** to swim breast-stroke/the 100 metres

nageur, -euse [naʒœʀ, øz] NM,F swimmer; (= *rameur*) rower; **~ de combat** naval frogman

Nagorny(ï)-Karabakh [nagɔʀni(i)karabak], **Nagorno-Karabakh** [nagɔʀnokarabak] N Nagorno-Karabakh

naguère [nagɛʀ] ADV (*frm*) (= *il y a peu de temps*) not long ago, a short while ago, of late; (= *autrefois*) formerly

naïade [najad] NF (*Bot, Myth*) naiad; (*hum, littér*) nymph

▼**naïf, naïve** [naif, naiv] **1** ADJ **a** (= *ingénu*) innocent, naïve; **d'un air ~** innocently **b** (= *crédule*) [*personne*] naïve, gullible; [*foi*] naïve **c** (*Art*) [*peintre, art*] naïve **2** NM,F gullible fool, innocent; **vous me prenez pour un ~** you must think I'm a gullible fool *ou* a complete innocent **3** NM (*Art*) naïve painter

nain, e [nɛ̃, nɛn] **1** ADJ dwarfish, dwarf (*épith*); **chêne/haricot ~** dwarf oak/runner bean; **poule ~e** bantam (hen); **rosier ~** miniature rose (bush) **2** NM,F dwarf; (*Cartes*) **le ~ jaune** pope Joan; **~ de jardin** garden gnome **3** **naine** NF (*Astron*) dwarf; **~e blanche/rouge** white/red dwarf

Nairobi [nɛrobi] N Nairobi

naissain [nɛsɛ̃] NM (*Zool*) spat

▼**naissance** [nɛsɑ̃s] NF **a** [*personne, animal*] birth; **à la ~** at birth; **il est aveugle/muet/sourd de ~** he has been blind/dumb/deaf from birth, he was born blind/dumb/deaf; **français de ~** French by birth; **chez lui, c'est de ~*** he was born like that; **nouvelle ~** new arrival *ou* baby; **~ double** birth of twins; **~ multiple** multiple birth → **contrôle, extrait, limitation** etc
b (*frm = origine, famille*) birth; **de ~ obscure/illustre** of obscure/illustrious birth; **de haute** *ou* **bonne ~** of noble *ou* high birth; **peu importe sa ~** no matter what his birth *ou* parentage (is)
c (= *point de départ*) [*rivière*] source; [*langue, ongles*] root; [*cou, colonne*] base; **à la ~ des cheveux** at the roots of the hair; **la ~ des seins** the top of the cleavage
d (*littér = commencement*) [*printemps, monde, idée, amour*] dawn, birth; **la ~ du jour** daybreak; **la ~ du cinéma** the birth *ou* advent of cinema
e (*loc*) **prendre ~** [*projet, idée*] to originate, take form *ou* shape; [*soupçon, sentiment*] to arise (**dans** in); **donner ~ à** [+ *enfant*] to give birth to; [+ *rumeurs, sentiment*] to give rise to

naissant, e [nɛsɑ̃, ɑ̃t] ADJ [*calvitie*] incipient; [*passion*] burgeoning; [*industrie, marché, démocratie, talent*] burgeoning, budding; [*capitalisme*] burgeoning, nascent (*frm*); **une barbe ~e** the beginnings of a beard; (*Chim*) (**à l'état**) **~** nascent

naître [nɛtʀ] ▶ conjug 59 ◀ **1** VI **a** [*personne, animal*] to be born; **quand l'enfant doit-il ~ ?**

when is the baby due?; **il vient tout juste de ~** he has only just been born, he is just newly born; **il est né** *ou* **il naquit** (*frm*) **le 4** he was born on the 4th; **l'homme naît libre** man is born free; **il est né poète** he is a born *ou* natural poet; **l'enfant qui naît aveugle/infirme** the child who is born blind/disabled; **l'enfant qui va ~** ◊ **l'enfant à ~** the unborn child; **l'enfant qui vient de ~** the newborn child; **en naissant** at birth; **prématuré né à 7 mois** baby born prematurely at 7 months, premature baby born at 7 months; **né sous le signe du Verseau** born under (the sign of) Aquarius; **enfant né de père inconnu** child of an unknown father; **être né de parents français** to be of French parentage, be born of French parents; **être né d'une mère anglaise** to be born of an English mother; (*Bible*) **un sauveur nous est né** a saviour is born to us; (*Méd*) **être né coiffé** to be born with a caul; (*fig*) **être né coiffé** *ou* **sous une bonne étoile** to be born lucky *ou* under a lucky star; (*fig*) **il n'est pas né d'hier** *ou* **de la dernière pluie** *ou* **de la dernière couvée** he wasn't born yesterday, he is not as green as he looks; (*fig*) **je l'ai vu ~ !** I've known him since he was born *ou* since he was a baby; **le pays qui l'a vu ~** the land of his birth, his native country → **né**
b (= *apparaître*) [*sentiment, craintes*] to arise, be born; [*idée, projet*] to be born; [*ville, industrie*] to spring up; [*jour*] to break; [*difficultés*] to arise; [*fleur, plante*] to burst forth; **la rivière naît au pied de ces collines** the river has its source *ou* rises at the foot of these hills; **je vis ~ un sourire sur son visage** I saw the beginnings of a smile on his face, I saw a smile creep over his face; **faire ~** [+ *industrie, difficultés*] to create; [+ *soupçons, désir*] to arouse
c (= *résulter de*) **~ de** to spring from, arise from; **la haine née de ces querelles** the hatred arising from *ou* which sprang from these quarrels; **de cette rencontre naquit le mouvement qui ...** from this meeting sprang the movement which ...
d (= *être destiné à*) **il était né pour commander/pour la magistrature** he was born to command/to be a judge; **ils sont nés l'un pour l'autre** they were made for each other
e (*littér = s'éveiller à*) **~ à l'amour/la poésie** to awaken to love/poetry
2 VB IMPERS **il naît plus de garçons que de filles** there are more boys born than girls; (*littér*) **il vous est né un fils** a son has been born to you (*littér*) → **né**

naïvement [naivmɑ̃] ADV (= *ingénument*) innocently, naïvely; (= *crédulement*) naïvely

naïveté [naivte] NF **a** (= *ingénuité*) [*personne*] innocence, naïvety; [*réponse, gaieté*] naïvety **b** (= *crédulité*) [*personne*] naïvety, gullibility; [*foi*] naïvety; **il a eu la ~ de ...** he was naïve enough to ...; **d'une grande ~** very naïve

naja [naʒa] NM cobra

Namibie [namibi] NF Namibia

namibien, -ienne [namibjɛ̃, jɛn] **1** ADJ Namibian **2** **Namibien(ne)** NM,F Namibian

---

nana* [nana] NF (= *femme*) woman; (= *petite amie*) girlfriend

nanan* [nanã] NM **c'est du ~** (*agréable*) it's really nice; (*facile*) it's a walkover* *ou* a doddle* (*Brit*) *ou* a cakewalk* (*US*); (*succulent*) it's scrumptious*

nanar* [nanaʀ] NM (*péj*) (= *objet invendable*) piece of junk; (= *film démodé*) **~ des années 30** second-rate film from the 1930s

nanifier [nanifje] ▸ conjug 7 ◂ VT [+ *arbre*] to dwarf

nanisme [nanism] NM dwarfism, nanism (*SPÉC*)

nankin [nãkɛ̃] NM (= *tissu*) nankeen

nano... [nano] PRÉF nano...

nanomètre [nanɔmɛtʀ] NM nanometre (*Brit*), nanometer (*US*)

nanoseconde [nanos(ə)gɔ̃d] NF nanosecond

nanotechnologie [nanoteknɔlɔʒi] NF nanotechnology

nantais, e [nãtɛ, ɛz] **1** ADJ of *ou* from Nantes **2 Nantais(e)** NM,F inhabitant *ou* native of Nantes

nanti, e [nãti] (*ptp de* **nantir**) ADJ rich, affluent, well-to-do; **les ~s** the rich, the affluent, the well-to-do

nantir [nãtiʀ] ▸ conjug 2 ◂ **1** VT (†, *Jur*) [+ *créancier*] to secure; (*fig, littér = munir*) **~ qn de** to provide *ou* equip sb with; **nanti de** equipped with **2 se nantir** VPR (†, *Jur*) **se ~ de** to provide o.s. with, equip o.s. with

nantissement [nãtismã] NM (*Jur*) security

napalm [napalm] NM napalm

naphtaline [naftalin] NF (= *antimite*) mothballs; **sa théorie sent la ~** his theory is straight out of the ark

naphte [naft] NM naphtha

napoléon [napɔleɔ̃] **1** NM (*Fin*) napoleon; (*Hist*) **Napoléon** Napoleon **2** NF (= *cerise*) type of bigaroon cherry

napoléonien, -ienne [napɔleɔnjɛ̃, jɛn] ADJ Napoleonic

napolitain, e [napɔlitɛ̃, ɛn] **1** ADJ Neapolitan **2 Napolitain(e)** NM,F Neapolitan

nappage [napaʒ] NM (*Culin*) topping

nappe [nap] **1** NF **a** [*table*] tablecloth; **mettre la ~** to put the tablecloth on **b** (= *couche*) layer, sheet; **~ de gaz** layer of gas; **~ d'eau** sheet *ou* expanse of water **c** (*Géom*) nappe **d** (*Tex*) lap **2** COMP ▸ **nappe d'autel** altar cloth ▸ **nappe de brouillard** blanket *ou* layer of fog; **des ~s de brouillard** fog patches ▸ **nappe de charriage** nappe ▸ **nappe de feu** sheet of flame ▸ **nappe de mazout**, **nappe de pétrole** oil slick ▸ **nappe phréatique** ground water

napper [nape] ▸ conjug 1 ◂ VT (*Culin*) to top (**de** with); **nappé de chocolat** topped with chocolate, with a chocolate topping

napperon [napʀɔ̃] NM doily, tablemat; (*pour vase, lampe*) mat

narcisse [naʀsis] NM (*Bot*) narcissus; (*péj = égocentrique*) narcissist; (*Myth*) **Narcisse** Narcissus

narcissique [naʀsisik] **1** ADJ narcissistic **2** NMF narcissist

narcissisme [naʀsisism] NM narcissism

narcodollars [naʀkodɔlaʀ] NMPL drug(s) money (*usually in dollars*); **3 millions de ~** 3 million dollars' worth of drug(s) money

narcose [naʀkoz] NF narcosis

narcotique [naʀkɔtik] ADJ, NM narcotic

narcotrafic [naʀkotʀafik] NM drug trafficking

narcotrafiquant, e [naʀkotʀafikã, ãt] NM,F drug trafficker

narghileh [naʀgile] NM hookah, nargileh, narghile

narguer [naʀge] ▸ conjug 1 ◂ VT [+ *danger, traditions*] to flout, thumb one's nose at; [+ *personne*] to deride, scoff at; **il nous narue avec son argent** we're not good enough for him now he's got all that money

narguilé [naʀgile] NM = **narghileh**

narine [naʀin] NF nostril

narquois, e [naʀkwa, waz] ADJ (= *railleur*) derisive, sardonic, mocking

narquoisement [naʀkwazmã] ADV derisively, sardonically, mockingly

narrateur, -trice [naʀatœʀ, tʀis] NM,F narrator

narratif, -ive [naʀatif, iv] ADJ narrative

narration [naʀasjɔ̃] NF **a** (= *action*) narration → **infinitif, présent** **b** (= *récit*) narration, narrative, account; (*Scol = rédaction*) essay, composition; (*Rhétorique*) narration

narrer [naʀe] ▸ conjug 1 ◂ VT (*frm*) to narrate, relate

narthex [naʀtɛks] NM narthex

narval [naʀval] NM narwhal

NASA, Nasa [naza] NF (ABRÉV = **National Aeronautics and Space Administration**) NASA

nasal, e [mpl **-aux**] [nazal, o] **1** ADJ nasal → **fosse** **2 nasale** NF nasal

nasalisation [nazalizasjɔ̃] NF nasalization

nasaliser [nazalize] ▸ conjug 1 ◂ VT to nasalize

nasalité [nazalite] NF nasality

nase* [naz] **1** ADJ **a** (= *hors d'usage*) bust* (*attrib*), kaput* (*attrib*); **ma télé est ~** my TV's conked out* *ou* is bust*; **je suis ~** (= *exténué*) I'm exhausted *ou* knackered* (*Brit*); (*psychologiquement*) I'm out of it* **b** (= *fou*) cracked* (*attrib*), touched* (*attrib*); (= *nul*) [*projet*] useless; [*personne*] hopeless*; (= *stupide*) stupid, daft* (*Brit*) **2** NMF (= *personne nulle*) moron* **3** NM (= *nez*) conk*, hooter* (*Brit*)

naseau (*pl* **naseaux**) [nazo] NM [*cheval, bœuf*] nostril

nasillard, e [nazijaʀ, aʀd] ADJ [*voix*] nasal; [*gramophone*] whiny, tinny; [*instrument*] tinny

nasillement [nazijmã] NM [*voix*] (nasal) twang; [*microphone, gramophone*] whine; [*instrument*] tinny sound; [*canard*] quack

nasiller [nazije] ▸ conjug 1 ◂ **1** VT to say (*ou* sing *ou* intone) with a (nasal) twang **2** VI [*personne*] to have a (nasal) twang, speak with a nasal voice; [*instrument*] to give a tinny *ou* twangy sound; [*microphone, gramophone*] to whine; [*canard*] to quack

nasique [nazik] NM (= *singe*) proboscis monkey

Nassau [naso] N Nassau

nasse [nas] NF (*pour oiseaux*) hoop net; (*Pêche*) fish trap, creel; (*fig*) **être pris dans la ~** to be caught in the net

Natal [natal] NM (*Géog*) Natal

natal, e (*mpl* **natals**) [natal] ADJ native; **ma maison ~e** the house where I was born; **ma terre ~e** my native soil

nataliste [natalist] ADJ [*politique, argument*] pro-birth, which supports a rising birth rate

natalité [natalite] NF (**taux de**) **~** birth rate

natation [natasjɔ̃] NF swimming; **~ artistique** *ou* **synchronisée** synchronized swimming; **faire la ~** to go swimming, swim

natatoire [natatwaʀ] ADJ swimming (*épith*) → **vessie**

natif, -ive [natif, iv] ADJ, NM,F (*gén*) native; **~ de Nice** native of Nice; **locuteur ~** native speaker; **les ~s du Lion** people born under the sign of Leo

nation [nasjɔ̃] NF (= *pays, peuple*) nation; **les Nations Unies** the United Nations → **société**

national [mpl **-aux**] [nasjɔnal, o] **1** ADJ (*gén*) national; [*économie, monnaie*] domestic; **au plan ~ et international** at home and abroad, at the national and international level; (*Écon*) **entreprise ~e** state-owned company; **grève ~e** nationwide *ou* national strike; **obsèques ~es** state funeral; (**route**) **~e** ≈ A *ou* trunk road (*Brit*), ≈ state highway (*US*) → **assemblée, éducation, fête** **2** **nationaux** NMPL (= *citoyens*) nationals

nationalement [nasjɔnalmã] ADV nationally

nationalisable [nasjɔnalizabl] ADJ targetted for nationalization

nationalisation [nasjɔnalizasjɔ̃] NF nationalization

nationaliser [nasjɔnalize] ▸ conjug 1 ◂ VT to nationalize; (**entreprises**) **nationalisées** nationalized companies

nationalisme [nasjɔnalism] NM nationalism

nationaliste [nasjɔnalist] ADJ, NMF nationalist

nationalité [nasjɔnalite] NF nationality; **les personnes de ~ française** French citizens; **il a la double ~ française et suisse** he has dual French and Swiss *ou* French/Swiss nationality

national-socialisme [nasjɔnalsɔsjalism] NM National Socialism

national-socialiste [nasjɔnalsɔsjalist] (*mpl* **nationaux-socialistes**) ADJ, NMF National Socialist

nativisme [nativism] NM (*Philo*) nativism

nativiste [nativist] ADJ (*Philo*) nativistic

nativité [nativite] NF nativity; (*Art*) (painting of the) nativity, nativity scene

natte [nat] NF (= *tresse*) plait (*Brit*), braid (*US*); (= *paillasse*) mat, matting (*NonC*); **se faire des ~s** to plait (*Brit*) *ou* braid (*US*) one's hair, put one's hair in plaits (*Brit*) *ou* braids (*US*); **~s africaines** corn rows

natter [nate] ▸ conjug 1 ◂ VT [+ *cheveux, laine*] to plait (*Brit*), braid (*US*)

naturalisation [natyʀalizasjɔ̃] NF (*Bot, Ling, Pol*) naturalization; [*animaux morts*] stuffing; [*plantes*] preserving

naturalisé, e [natyʀalize] (*ptp de* **naturaliser**) **1** ADJ naturalized; **Français ~** naturalized Frenchman; **il est ~ français** he's a naturalized Frenchman, he has French citizenship **2** NM,F naturalized citizen

naturaliser [natyʀalize] ▸ conjug 1 ◂ VT (*Bot, Ling, Pol*) to naturalize; [+ *animal*] to stuff; [+ *plante*] to preserve (*with glycerine*); **se faire ~ français** to be granted French citizenship, become a naturalized Frenchman

naturalisme [natyʀalism] NM naturalism

naturaliste [natyʀalist] **1** ADJ naturalistic **2** NMF (*Littérat, Sci*) naturalist; (= *empailleur*) taxidermist; (*pour les plantes*) flower-preserver

nature [natyʀ] **1** NF **a** (= *caractère*) [*personne, substance, sentiment*] nature; **la ~ humaine** human nature; **c'est une** *ou* **il est d'une ~ arrogante** he has an *ou* he is of an arrogant nature; **il est arrogant de** *ou* **par ~** he is naturally arrogant *ou* arrogant by nature; **ce n'est pas dans sa ~** it is not (in) his nature (**d'être** to be); **c'est/ce n'est pas de ~ à arranger les choses** it's liable *ou* it's liable to make things easier; **il n'est pas de ~ à accepter** he's not the sort of person who would agree; **il a une heureuse ~** he has a happy disposition *ou* a sunny temperament; **tu es une petite ~!** you're so delicate!, you've got a delicate constitution!; (*péj*) **quelle petite ~ tu fais!** what a weakling you are!; **c'est dans la ~ des choses** it's in the nature of things → **habitude** **b** (= *monde physique, principe fondamental*) **la ~ nature; vivre (perdu) dans la ~** to live (out) in the country *ou* in the wilds; **en pleine ~** in the middle of nowhere; **la ~ a horreur du vide** nature abhors a vacuum; **laisser agir la ~** to let nature take its course, leave it to nature; **la ~ fait bien les choses** nature is a wonderful thing; **lâcher qn dans la ~*** (*sans indication*) to send sb off without any directions; (*pour commettre un crime*) to let sb loose; **disparaître**

ou **s'évanouir dans la ~*** [*personne*] to vanish into thin air; [*ballon*] to disappear into the undergrowth *ou* bushes; **crimes/goûts contre ~** unnatural crimes/tastes, crimes/tastes which go against nature *ou* which are contrary to nature → **force, retour**

[c] (= *sorte*) nature, kind, sort; **de toute(s) ~(s)** of all kinds, of every kind

[d] (*Art*) **peindre d'après ~** to paint from life; **plus grand que ~** larger than life; **~ morte** still life → **grandeur**

[e] (*Fin*) **en ~** [*payer, don*] in kind

[2] **ADJ INV** [a] (= *sans adjonction*) [*café*] black; [*eau, crêpe, omelette*] plain; [*thé*] without milk; [*yaourt*] natural; [*salade*] without dressing; **riz ~** (plain) boiled rice; **boire le whisky ~** to drink whisky neat *ou* straight; **manger les fraises ~** to eat strawberries without anything on them

[b]* [*personne*] (= *sans artifice*) natural, unaffected; (= *spontané*) **il est très ~!** he's very spontaneous!

naturel, -elle [natyʀɛl] [1] **ADJ** [a] [*caractère, frontière, produit, phénomène*] natural; [*besoins, fonction*] bodily (*épith*); [*soie, laine*] pure; **aliments/produits ~s** natural *ou* organic foods/products

[b] (= *inné*) natural; **son intelligence naturelle** his natural intelligence, his native wit; **elle a un talent ~ pour le piano** playing the piano comes naturally to her, she has a natural talent for the piano

[c] (= *normal, habituel*) natural; **avec sa voix naturelle** in his normal voice; **c'est un geste ~ chez lui** it's a natural thing for him to do; **votre indignation est bien naturelle** your indignation is quite *ou* very natural *ou* quite understandable; **je vous remercie! — c'est (tout) ~** thank you! — don't mention it *ou* you're welcome; **ne me remerciez pas, c'est bien** *ou* **tout ~** don't thank me, anybody would have done the same *ou* it was the obvious thing to do; **il est bien ~ qu'on en vienne à cette décision** it's only natural that this decision should have been reached; **il trouve ça tout ~** he finds it the most natural thing in the world *ou* perfectly normal; **il trouve tout ~ de ...** he thinks nothing of ...

[d] (= *simple, spontané*) [*voix, style, personne*] natural, unaffected; **elle sait rester très naturelle** she manages to stay very natural; **il est très ~ sur les photos** he always looks very natural in photos

[e] (*Mus*) natural

[f] (*Math*) **(nombre entier) ~** natural number

[2] **NM** [a] (= *caractère*) nature, disposition; **être d'un** *ou* **avoir un bon ~** to have a happy *ou* sunny nature *ou* disposition → **chasser**

[b] (= *absence d'affectation*) naturalness; **avec (beaucoup de) ~** (completely) naturally; **il manque de ~** he's not very natural, he has a rather self-conscious manner

[c] (= *indigène*) native

[d] **au ~** (= *sans assaisonnement*) [*thon*] in brine; [*salade, asperges*] without any dressing (*ou* seasoning); **pêches au ~** peaches in natural fruit juice; (= *en réalité*) **elle est mieux en photo qu'au ~** she's better in photos than in real life

naturellement [natyʀɛlmɑ̃] **ADV** [a] (= *sans artifice, avec aisance*) naturally [b] (= *bien sûr*) naturally, of course

naturisme [natyʀism] **NM** (= *nudisme*) naturism; (*Philo*) naturism

naturiste [natyʀist] **ADJ, NMF** (= *nudiste*) naturist; (*Philo*) naturist; (*Méd*) naturopath

naturopathe [natyʀɔpat] **NMF** naturopath

naturopathie [natyʀɔpati] **NF** naturopathy, naturopathic medicine

naufrage [nofʀaʒ] **NM** [a] [*bateau*] wreck, wrecking; **le ~ du Titanic** the sinking of the Titanic; **ils ont trouvé la mort dans un ~** they drowned in a shipwreck; **ces rochers ont cau-**

sé bien des ~s many ships have been wrecked on these rocks; **faire ~** [*bateau*] to be wrecked; [*personne*] to be shipwrecked [b] (= *déchéance*) [*ambitions, réputation*] ruin, ruination; [*projet, pays*] foundering, ruination; [*entreprise*] collapse; **sauver du ~** [+ *personne*] to save from disaster; [+ *argent, biens*] to salvage (from the wreckage); [+ *entreprise*] to save from collapse

naufragé, e [nofʀaʒe] [1] **ADJ** [*marin*] shipwrecked; [*bateau*] wrecked [2] **NM,F** shipwrecked person; (*sur une île*) castaway; **les ~s de la croissance économique** the casualties of economic growth

naufrageur, -euse [nofʀaʒœʀ, øz] **NM,F** (*lit, fig*) wrecker

Nauru [nauʀu] **N** Nauru

nauséabond, e [nozeabɔ̃, ɔ̃d] **ADJ** [*odeur*] putrid, nauseating, foul; [*effluves, fumées*] foulsmelling; [*cloaque*] stinking; (*fig*) nauseating, sickening

nausée [noze] **NF** (= *sensation*) nausea (*NonC*); (= *haut-le-cœur*) bout of nausea; **avoir la ~** to feel sick *ou* nauseous *ou* queasy; **avoir des ~s** to have bouts of nausea; (*lit, fig*) **ça me donne la ~** it makes me (feel) sick, it nauseates me

nauséeux, -euse [nozeø, øz] **ADJ** [*personne*] nauseous, queasy; [*odeur, goût*] nauseating, nauseous; **état ~** nausea

nautile [notil] **NM** (*Zool*) nautilus

nautique [notik] **ADJ** [*science, mille*] nautical; **fête/ballet ~** water festival/ballet; **club ~** watersports centre; **loisirs ~s** water-based recreational activities; **salon ~** boat show → **ski, sport**

nautisme [notism] **NM** water sport(s)

navajo [navaxo] [1] **ADJ** Navajo, Navaho [2] **Navajo NMF** Navajo, Navaho; **les Navajos** the Navajo(s) *ou* Navaho(s), the Navajo *ou* Navaho Indians

naval, e [*mpl* **navals**] [naval] **ADJ** [*combat, base*] naval; [*industrie*] shipbuilding; **école ~e** naval college → **chantier, construction, force**

navarin [navaʀɛ̃] **NM** navarin, ≈ mutton stew

navarrais, e [navaʀɛ, ɛz] [1] **ADJ** Navarrian [2] **Navarrais(e) NM,F** Navarrian

Navarre [navaʀ] **NF** Navarre

navel [navɛl] **NF** navel orange

navet [navɛ] **NM** [a] (= *légume*) turnip; **~ fourrager** fodder beet → **sang** [b] (*péj* = *film*) rubbishy *ou* third-rate film; **quel ~!** what a load of trash *ou* rubbish! (*Brit*)

navette[1] [navɛt] **NF** [a] (*Tex*) shuttle; (= *aiguille*) netting *ou* meshing needle; **~ volante** flying shuttle [b] (= *service de transport*) shuttle (service); **~ diplomatique** diplomatic shuttle; **faire la ~ entre** [*banlieusard, homme d'affaires*] to commute between; [*véhicule*] to operate a shuttle (service) between; [*bateau*] to ply between; [*projet de loi, circulaire*] to be sent backwards and forwards between; **elle fait la ~ entre la cuisine et la chambre** she comes and goes between the kitchen and the bedroom; **faire faire la ~ à qn/qch** to have sb/sth going back and forth (**entre** between) [c] (*Espace*) **~ spatiale** space shuttle [d] (*à encens*) incense holder

navette[2] [navɛt] **NF** (*Bot*) rape

navetteur, -euse [navetœʀ, øz] **NM,F** (*Admin Belg*) commuter

navigabilité [navigabilite] **NF** [*rivière*] navigability; [*bateau*] seaworthiness; [*avion*] airworthiness

navigable [navigabl] **ADJ** [*rivière*] navigable

navigant, e [naviɡɑ̃, ɑ̃t] **ADJ, NM le personnel ~ ◊ les ~s** (*Aviat*) flying personnel; (*Naut*) seagoing personnel

navigateur, -trice [navigatœʀ, tʀis] **NM,F** (= *marin*) sailor; (*chargé de l'itinéraire: Aut, Aviat, Naut*) navigator; **~ solitaire** singlehanded sailor *ou* yachtsman

navigation [navigasjɔ̃] **NF** [a] (*Naut*) (= *trafic*) (sea) traffic (*NonC*); (= *pilotage*) navigation (*NonC*), sailing (*NonC*); **les récifs rendent la ~ dangereuse** the reefs make sailing *ou* navigation dangerous; **canal ouvert/fermé** *ou* **interdit à la ~** canal open/closed to shipping *ou* ships; **~ côtière/intérieure** coastal/inland navigation; **~ de plaisance** (pleasure) sailing; **~ à voiles** sailing, yachting; **compagnie de ~** shipping company; **terme de ~** nautical term [b] (*Aviat*) (= *trafic*) (air) traffic (*NonC*); (= *pilotage*) navigation (*NonC*), flying (*NonC*); **~ aérienne/spatiale** aerial/space navigation [c] (*Ordin*) **~ sur Internet** browsing the Internet; **~ hypertexte** browsing hypertext

naviguer [navige] ▶conjug 1◀ **VI** [a] (= *voyager*) [*bateau, passager, marin*] to sail; [*avion, passager, pilote*] to fly; **~ à la voile** to sail; **ce bateau a beaucoup/n'a jamais navigué** this ship has been to sea a lot *ou* has done a lot of sailing/has never been to sea *ou* has never sailed; **bateau en état de ~** seaworthy ship; **~ à 24 000 pieds** to fly at an altitude of 24,000 feet

[b] (= *piloter*) [*marin*] to navigate, sail; [*aviateur*] to navigate, fly; **~ au compas/aux instruments/à l'estime** to navigate by (the) compass/by instruments/by dead reckoning; **~ à travers Detroit** (*en voiture*) to find one's way through *ou* make one's way across Detroit; **~ entre les obstacles** to negotiate one's way around obstacles

[c] (*Ordin*) **~ sur Internet** to surf *ou* browse the Internet

[d] (*fig*) **pour réussir ici, il faut savoir ~*** to succeed here you need to know how to get around *ou* you need to know the ropes; **c'est un type qui a beaucoup navigué*** he's a man who's been around a lot *ou* who's knocked about quite a bit*; **le gouvernement doit ~ entre les écueils** the government must tread a delicate path; **le dossier a navigué de bureau en bureau** the file found its way from office to office, the file went the rounds of the offices

navire [naviʀ] **NM** (= *bateau*) ship; (*Jur*) vessel; **~ amiral** flagship; **~-citerne** tanker; **~ marchand** *ou* **de commerce** merchant ship, merchantman; **~ jumeau** sister ship; **~ de guerre** warship

navire-école (*pl* **navires-écoles**) [naviʀekɔl] **NM** training ship

navire-hôpital (*pl* **navires-hôpitaux**) [naviʀɔpital, o] **NM** hospital ship

navire-usine (*pl* **navires-usines**) [naviʀyzin] **NM** factory ship

navrant, e [navʀɑ̃, ɑ̃t] **ADJ** (= *attristant*) [+ *spectacle, conduite, nouvelle*] distressing, upsetting; (= *regrettable*) [*contretemps, malentendu*] unfortunate, regrettable; **tu es ~!** you're hopeless!; **un spectacle ~ de bêtise** a depressingly silly show; **ce film est d'une médiocrité ~e** this film is terribly mediocre; **il n'écoute personne, c'est ~** he won't listen to anybody, it's a shame

▼**navré, e** [navʀe] (*ptp de* **navrer**) **ADJ** sorry (**de** to); **je suis (vraiment) ~** I'm (so *ou* terribly) sorry; **~ de vous décevoir mais ...** sorry to disappoint you but ...; **avoir l'air ~** (*pour s'excuser, compatir*) to look sorry; (*d'une nouvelle*) to look distressed *ou* upset; **d'un ton ~** (*exprimant la tristesse*) in a distressed *ou* an upset voice; (*pour s'excuser*) in an apologetic tone, apologetically; (*pour compatir*) in a sympathetic tone

navrer [navʀe] ▶conjug 1◀ **VT** [a] (= *consterner*) [*spectacle, conduite, nouvelle*] to distress, upset [b] (= *contrarier*) [*contretemps, malentendu*] to annoy

nazaréen, -enne [nazaʀeɛ̃, ɛn] [1] **ADJ** Nazarene [2] **Nazaréen(ne) NM,F** Nazarene

Nazareth [nazaʀɛt] **N** Nazareth

naze* [naz] **ADJ** = **nase**

> GRAMMAIRE ACTIVE: navré 45.3

nazi, e [nazi] ADJ, NM,F Nazi

nazisme [nazism] NM Nazism

N.B. [ɛnbe] NM (ABRÉV = **nota bene**) N.B.

N.-D. (ABRÉV = **Notre-Dame**) → **notre**

N'Djamena [nʒamena] N Ndjamena

NDLR (ABRÉV = **note de la rédaction**) → **note**

NdT (ABRÉV = **note du traducteur**) translator's note

ne [nə] ADV NÉG a (*valeur négative, avec négation avant ou après*) **il n'a rien dit** he didn't say anything, he said nothing; **elle ne nous a pas vus** she didn't *ou* did not see us, she hasn't *ou* has not seen us; **personne** *ou* **nul** (*frm*) **n'a compris** nobody *ou* no one understood; **il n'y a aucun mal à ça** there's no harm *ou* there's nothing wrong in that; **il n'est pas du tout** *ou* **nullement idiot** he's no fool, he's by no means stupid; **je ne le ferai jamais** I'll never do it; **je n'ai pas d'argent** I haven't got *ou* I don't have any money, I have no money; **il ne sait plus ce qu'il dit** he no longer knows what he's saying, he doesn't know what he's saying any more; **plus rien ne l'intéresse ◊ rien ne l'intéresse plus** nothing interests him any more, he's not interested in anything any more; **ne me dérangez pas** don't *ou* do not disturb me; **je ne connais ni son fils ni sa fille** I know neither his son nor his daughter, I don't know (either) his son or his daughter; **je n'ai pas du tout** *ou* **aucunement l'intention de refuser** I have not the slightest *ou* least intention of refusing; **je n'ai guère le temps** I scarcely *ou* hardly have the time; **je ne sait pas parler** he can't *ou* cannot speak; **pas un seul ne savait sa leçon** not (a single) one (of them) knew his lesson

b (*valeur négative, sans autre négation: littér*) **il ne cesse de se plaindre** he's always *ou* constantly complaining, he doesn't stop *ou* never stops complaining; **je ne sais qui a eu cette idée** I don't know who had that idea; **elle ne peut jouer du violon sans qu'un voisin (ne) proteste** she can't play her violin without some neighbour objecting; **il n'a que faire de vos conseils** he has no use for your advice, he's not interested in your advice; **que n'a-t-il songé à me prévenir** if only he had thought to warn me; **n'était la situation internationale, il serait parti** had it not been for *ou* were it not for the international situation he would have left; **il n'est de paysage qui ne soit maintenant gâché** not a patch of countryside remains unspoilt, there is no unspoilt countryside left; **il n'est de jour qu'elle ne se plaigne** not a day goes by but she complains (about something) *ou* without her complaining; **cela fait des années que je n'ai été au cinéma** it's years since I (last) went to the cinema, I haven't been to the cinema for years; **il a vieilli depuis que je ne l'ai vu** he has aged since I (last) saw him; **si je ne me trompe** if I'm not mistaken → **cure¹, empêcher, importer²**

c **ne ... que** only; **elle ne a confiance qu'en nous** she trusts only us, she only has confidence in us; **c'est mauvais de ne manger que des conserves** it's bad to eat only canned foods *ou* nothing but canned foods; **il n'a que trop d'assurance** he's only too self-assured; **il n'a d'autre idée en tête que de se lancer dans la politique** his (one and) only thought is to go into politics; **il n'y a que lui pour dire des choses pareilles!** only he *ou* nobody but he would say such things!; **il n'y a pas que vous qui le dites!** you're not the only one who says so!; **et il n'y a pas que ça!** and that's not all! → **demander**

d (*explétif sans valeur nég, gén omis dans la langue parlée*) **je crains** *ou* **j'ai peur qu'il ne vienne** I am afraid *ou* I fear (that) he is coming / that he will come; **je ne doute pas/je ne nie pas qu'il ne soit compétent** I don't doubt/deny that he's competent; **empêche**

que les enfants ne touchent aux animaux stop the children touching *ou* prevent the children from touching the animals; **mangez avant que la viande ne refroidisse** do eat before the meat gets cold; **j'irai la voir avant qu'il/à moins qu'il ne pleuve** I shall go and see her before/unless it rains; **il est parti avant que je ne l'aie remercié** he left before I'd thanked him; **il est parti sans que je ne l'aie remercié** he left without my having thanked him; **peu s'en faut qu'il n'ait oublié la réunion** he all but *ou* he very nearly forgot the meeting; **il est plus/moins malin qu'on ne pense** he's more cunning than/not as cunning as you (might) think

né, e [ne] (*ptp de* **naître**) ADJ **orateur-/acteur-~** born orator/actor; **bien/mal ~** of noble *ou* high/humble *ou* low birth; **Paul est son premier-/dernier-~** Paul is her first-/last-born *ou* her first/last child; **Mme Durand, ~e Dupont** Mme Durand née Dupont → **naître**

néandertalien, -ienne [neɑ̃dɛrtaljɛ̃, jɛn] 1 ADJ Neanderthal (*épith*) 2 NM Neanderthal man

néanmoins [neɑ̃mwɛ̃] ADV (= *pourtant*) nevertheless, yet; **il était malade, il est ~ venu** he was ill, (and) nevertheless *ou* (and) yet he came; **c'est incroyable mais ~ vrai** it's incredible but nonetheless true *ou* but it's true nevertheless; **il est agressif et ~ patient** he is aggressive yet patient, he is aggressive but nevertheless patient

néant [neɑ̃] NM **le ~** nothingness (*NonC*); **le ~ de la vie/de l'homme** the emptiness of life/man; **replonger dans le ~** to sink back into oblivion; **et après c'est le ~** then there's a total blank; **signes particuliers : ~** distinguishing marks: none; **sortir/surgir du ~** to appear/ spring up out of nowhere → **réduire**

Nébraska [nebraska] NM Nebraska

nébuleuse¹ [nebylœz] NF (*Astron*) nebula; (*fig*) loose conglomeration; (*fig*) **c'est encore à l'état de ~** it's still very vague

nébuleusement [nebylœzmɑ̃] ADV nebulously, vaguely

nébuleux, -euse² [nebylø, øz] ADJ [*ciel*] cloudy, overcast; [*écrivain*] nebulous, obscure; [*projet, idée, discours*] nebulous, vague, woolly (*Brit*), wooly (*US*)

nébuliseur [nebylizœr] NM nebulizer

nébulosité [nebylozite] NF [*ciel*] cloud covering, nebulosity (*SPÉC*); [*discours*] obscureness, vagueness, woolliness (*Brit*), wooliness (*US*)

▼ **nécessaire** [neseser] 1 ADJ a (*gén, Math, Philo*) necessary; **il est ~ de le faire** it needs to be done, it has *ou* it's got to be done; **il est ~ qu'on le fasse** we need to do it, we have *ou* we've got to do it, we must do it; **est-ce (bien) ~ ?** have we (really) got to?, do we (really) need *ou* have to?, is it (really) necessary?; **ce n'est pas ~ (de le faire)** there's no need to (do it), you don't need *ou* have to (do it), it's not (really) necessary (for you to do it); **l'eau est ~ à la vie/aux hommes/pour vivre** water is necessary for life/to man/to live; **un bon repos vous est ~** you need a good rest; **cette attitude lui est ~ pour réussir** he has to have *ou* maintain this attitude to succeed; **cette attitude est ~ pour réussir** this is a necessary attitude *ou* this attitude is necessary *ou* needed if one wants to get on; **c'est une condition ~** it's a necessary condition (**pour faire** for doing, **de qch** for sth); **c'est une conséquence ~** it's a necessary consequence (**de qch** of sth); **avoir le talent/le temps/ l'argent ~ (pour qch/pour faire qch)** to have the (necessary *ou* requisite) talent/time/ money (for sth/to do sth), have the talent/ time/money (required) (for sth/to do sth); **a-t-il les moyens ~s ?** does he have the necessary *ou* requisite means?, does he have the means required?; **faire les démarches ~s** to take the necessary *ou* requisite steps; **nous fe-**

rons la grève si ~ we'll go on strike if necessary

b [*personne*] indispensable (**à** to); **se sentir ~** to feel indispensable

2 NM a (= *l'indispensable*) **as-tu emporté le ~ ?** have you got all *ou* everything you need?; **je n'ai pas le ~ pour le faire** I haven't got what's needed *ou* the necessary stuff to do it; **il peut faire froid, prenez le ~** it may be cold so take the right *ou* necessary clothes *ou* take what you need to keep warm; **emporter le strict ~** to take the bare *ou* absolute necessities *ou* essentials; **il faut d'abord penser au ~** one must first consider the essentials; **manquer du ~** to lack the (basic) necessities of life; **faire le ~** to do what is necessary *ou* what has to be done; **j'ai fait le ~** I've settled it *ou* seen to it, I've done what was necessary; **je vais faire le ~ (pour que)** I'll see to it (that), I'll make the necessary arrangements (so that)

b (*Philo*) **le ~** the necessary

3 COMP ▶ **nécessaire à couture** (pocket) sewing kit ▶ **nécessaire à ongles** manicure set ▶ **nécessaire à ouvrage** = **nécessaire à couture** ▶ **nécessaire de toilette** travel pack (of toiletries) ▶ **nécessaire de voyage** overnight bag, grip

nécessairement [nesesermɑ̃] ADV necessarily; **dois-je ~ m'en aller ?** is it (really) necessary for me to go?, do I (really) have to go?; **passeras-tu par Londres ? — oui, ~/non, pas ~** will you go via London? — yes, it's unavoidable *ou* you have to/no, not necessarily; **il devra ~ s'y faire** he will (just) have to get used to it; **il ne m'a pas ~ vu** I can't be sure (that) he saw me; **il y a ~ une raison** there must be a reason; **ce n'est pas ~ faux** it isn't necessarily wrong; (*Philo*) **causes et effets sont liés ~** causes and effects are necessarily linked *ou* are of necessity linked

nécessité [nesesite] 1 NF a (= *obligation*) necessity; **c'est une ~ absolue** it's an absolute necessity; **sévère sans ~** unnecessarily severe; **il souligne la ~ d'un débat** he emphasizes the need *ou* necessity for a debate; **je n'en vois pas la ~** I don't see the need for it; **se trouver** *ou* **être dans la ~ de faire qch** to have no choice *ou* alternative but to do sth; **mettre qn dans la ~ de faire** to make it necessary for sb to do; **la ~ où nous nous trouvons de faire cela** the fact that we have no choice *ou* alternative but to do; (*Jur*) **état de ~** necessity

b (*Philo*) **la ~** necessity; **la ~ de mourir** the inevitability of death

c (†† = *pauvreté*) destitution; **être dans la ~** to be in need, be poverty-stricken

d (*loc*) **je l'ai fait par ~** I did it because I had to *ou* because I had no choice; **de première ~** absolutely essential; **articles de première ~** bare necessities *ou* essentials; **faire de ~ vertu** to make a virtue of necessity ▪ (*PROV*) **~ fait loi** necessity knows no law (*PROV*)

2 **nécessités** NFPL **les ~s de la vie** the necessities *ou* essentials of life; **les ~s du service** the demands *ou* requirements of the job; **~s financières** (financial) liabilities

nécessiter [nesesite] ▶ conjug 1 ◀ VT (= *requérir*) to require, call for, necessitate; **l'intervention nécessite plusieurs jours d'hospitalisation** the operation means *ou* involves a hospital stay of several days; **la maison nécessite de gros travaux** the house needs a lot of work (done on it) *ou* is in need of a lot of renovation

nécessiteux, -euse (*frm*) [nesesitø, øz] 1 ADJ needy, necessitous (*frm*) 2 NM,F needy person; **les ~** the needy, the poor

nec plus ultra [nɛkplysyltra] NM **c'est le ~** it's the last word (**de** in)

nécrologie [nekrɔlɔʒi] NF (= *liste*) obituary column; (= *notice biographique*) obituary

nécrologique [nekrɔlɔʒik] ADJ obituary (*épith*)

nécromancie [nekrɔmɑ̃si] NF necromancy

nécromancien, -ienne [nekʀɔmɑ̃sjɛ̃, jɛn] NM,F necromancer

nécrophage [nekʀɔfaʒ] ADJ necrophagous

nécrophile [nekʀɔfil] 1 ADJ necrophilic 2 NMF necrophiliac

nécrophilie [nekʀɔfili] NF necrophilia

nécropole [nekʀɔpɔl] NF necropolis

nécrose [nekʀoz] NF necrosis

nécroser VT, **se nécroser** VPR [nekʀoze] ▸conjug 1◂ to necrose, necrotize

nectar [nɛktaʀ] NM (= *boisson, Bot, Myth, fig*) nectar

nectarine [nɛktaʀin] NF nectarine

néerlandais, e [neɛʀlɑ̃dɛ, ɛz] 1 ADJ Dutch, of the Netherlands 2 NM a (*Ling*) Dutch b **Néerlandais** Dutchman; **les Néerlandais** the Dutch 3 **Néerlandaise** NF Dutch-woman

nef [nɛf] NF a (*Archit*) nave; ~ **latérale** side aisle b (†† *ou littér* = *bateau*) vessel, ship

néfaste [nefast] ADJ (= *nuisible*) harmful (**à** to); (= *funeste*) ill-fated, unlucky; **cela lui fut** ~ it had disastrous consequences for him

nèfle [nɛfl] NF medlar; **des ~s!**! nothing doing!*, not likely!*

néflier [neflije] NM medlar (tree)

négateur, -trice [negatœʀ, tʀis] (*littér*) 1 ADJ given to denying, contradictory 2 NM,F denier

négatif, -ive [negatif, iv] 1 ADJ [*attitude, réponse*] negative; [*quantité, nombre*] negative, minus (*épith*); **particule négative** negative particle 2 NM (*Photo, Ling*) negative; **au** ~ in the negative 3 ADV **vous êtes prêts ? — ~ !*** are you ready? — negative!* 4 **négative** NF **répondre par la négative** to reply in the negative; **dans la négative** if not

négation [negasjɔ̃] NF (*gén*) negation; (*Ling*) negative; **double** ~ double negative

négationnisme [negasjɔnism] NM revisionism (*denying the existence of the Nazi gas chambers*)

négationniste [negasjɔnist] ADJ, NMF revisionist (*denying the existence of the Nazi gas chambers*)

négativement [negativmɑ̃] ADV [*réagir*] negatively; **répondre** ~ to reply in the negative; **juger qch/qn** ~ to be critical of sth/sb

négativisme [negativism] NM negativism, negativity

négativité [negativite] NF (*Phys*) negativity; [*attitude*] negativeness, negativity

négaton† [negatɔ̃] NM negatron

négligé, e [negliʒe] (*ptp de* **négliger**) 1 ADJ [*épouse, ami*] neglected; [*personne, tenue*] slovenly, sloppy; [*ongles*] uncared-for, neglected; [*travail*] slapdash, careless; [*style*] slipshod; [*occasion*] missed (*épith*) 2 NM (= *laisser-aller*) slovenliness; (= *déshabillé*) négligée; **il était en** ~ he was casually dressed *ou* wearing casual clothes; **le ~ de sa tenue** the slovenliness of his dress

négligeable [negliʒabl] ADJ (*gén*) negligible; [*détail*] unimportant, trivial, trifling; [*adversaire*] insignificant; **qui n'est pas ~ ◊ non ~** [*facteur, élément*] not inconsiderable; [*adversaire, aide, effort*] by no means insignificant; [*détail, rôle, nombre*] not insignificant; **une quantité non ~** an appreciable amount

négligemment [negliʒamɑ̃] ADV (= *sans soin*) carelessly, negligently, in a slovenly way; (= *nonchalamment*) casually

négligence [negliʒɑ̃s] NF (= *manque de soin*) negligence, slovenliness; (= *faute, erreur*) omission, act of negligence; (*Jur*) criminal negligence; **il est d'une (telle) ~ !** he's so careless!; **c'est une ~ de ma part** it's an oversight *ou* a careless mistake on my part; **par** ~ out of carelessness; ~ **(de style)** stylistic blunder,

carelessness (*NonC*) of style; **faire preuve de** ~ to be negligent

négligent, e [negliʒɑ̃, ɑ̃t] ADJ (= *sans soin*) negligent, careless; (= *nonchalant*) casual

négliger [negliʒe] ▸conjug 3◂ 1 VT a (*gén*) to neglect; [+ *style, tenue*] to be careless about; [+ *conseil*] to pay no attention *ou* no heed to, disregard; [+ *occasion*] to miss, pass up*; [+ *rhume, plaie*] to ignore; **il néglige ses amis** he neglects his friends; **un rhume négligé peut dégénérer en bronchite** a cold that's not treated *ou* that's neglected can turn into bronchitis; **ce n'est pas à** ~ (*offre*) it's not to be sneezed at; (*difficulté*) it mustn't be overlooked; **rien n'a été négligé** no stone has been left unturned, nothing has been left to chance; **ne rien** ~ **pour réussir** to leave no stone unturned *ou* leave nothing to chance in an effort to succeed

b (= *ne pas prendre la peine de*) ~ **de** to neglect to; **il a négligé de le faire** he didn't bother *ou* he neglected to do it; **ne négligez pas de prendre vos papiers** be sure to *ou* don't neglect to take your papers

2 **se négliger** VPR (*santé*) to neglect o.s., not to look after o.s.; (*tenue*) to neglect *ou* not to look after one's appearance

négoce [negɔs] NM a (*Écon*) trade; **le ~ international** international trade *ou* trading; **faire du** ~ to be in business; **faire du** ~ **avec un pays** to trade with a country; **il fait le** ~ **de** he trades *ou* deals in b († = *boutique, affaire*) business; **dans mon** ~ in my trade *ou* business; **il tenait un** ~ **de fruits et légumes** he sold fruit and vegetables, he had a greengrocery business (*surtout Brit*)

négociabilité [negɔsjabilite] NF negotiability

négociable [negɔsjabl] ADJ negotiable

négociant, e [negɔsjɑ̃, ɑ̃t] NM,F merchant; ~ **en gros** wholesaler; ~ **en vin(s)** wine merchant

négociateur, -trice [negɔsjatœʀ, tʀis] NM,F (*Comm, Pol*) negotiator

négociation [negɔsjasjɔ̃] NF (*Comm, Pol*) negotiation; **engager** *ou* **entamer des ~s** to enter into negotiations; **~s commerciales** trade talks; **~ salariales/bilatérales** wage/bilateral negotiations *ou* talks; **le contrat est actuellement en** ~ the contract is currently under negotiation

négocier [negɔsje] ▸conjug 7◂ 1 VI (*Pol*) to negotiate; (†† : *Comm*) to trade 2 VT (*gén, Fin, Pol*) to negotiate; ~ **un virage** to negotiate a bend

nègre [nɛgʀ] 1 NM a (†, *injurieux* = *personne*) Negro; **travailler comme un** ~ to work like a slave, slave away b (*péj* = *écrivain*) ghost (writer) c (*Culin*) ~ **en chemise** chocolate and cream dessert 2 ADJ (†, *injurieux*) Negro (*épith*) → **art**

négresse [negʀɛs] NF (†, *injurieux*) Negress

négrier, -ière [negʀije, ijɛʀ] 1 ADJ slave (*épith*); **(bateau)** ~ slave ship; **(capitaine)** ~ slave-ship captain 2 NM (= *marchand d'esclaves*) slave trader; (*fig péj* = *patron*) slave driver*

négrillon** [negʀijɔ̃] NM (*injurieux*) piccaninny** (*injurieux*)

négrillonne** [negʀijɔn] NF (*injurieux*) piccaninny** (*injurieux*)

négritude [negʀityd] NF negritude

négro** [negʀo] NM (*injurieux*) nigger** (*injurieux*)

négro-africain, e (*mpl* **négro-africains**) [negʀoafʀikɛ̃, ɛn] ADJ [*littérature*] of Sub-Saharan Africa and the African diaspora; [*population*] of Sub-Saharan Africa

négroïde [negʀɔid] ADJ Negroid

negro-spiritual (*pl* **negro-spirituals**) [negʀospiʀitɥɔl] NM Negro spiritual

Néguev [negɛv] NM **le désert du** ~ the Negev desert

négus [negys] NM (= *titre*) Negus

neige [nɛʒ] 1 NF a (*Mét*) snow; (*arg Drogue* = *cocaïne*) snow (*arg*); **le temps est à la** ~ it looks like (it's going to) snow; **aller à la ~*** to go to the ski resorts, go on a skiing holiday; **cheveux/teint de** ~ snow-white hair/complexion b (*Culin*) **battre** *ou* **faire monter des blancs en** ~ to whisk *ou* beat (up) egg whites to form stiff peaks; **blancs** *ou* **œufs battus en** ~ stiffly beaten egg whites 2 COMP ▸ **neige artificielle** artificial snow ▸ **neige carbonique** dry ice ▸ **neiges éternelles** eternal *ou* everlasting snow(s) ▸ **neige fondue** (= *pluie*) sleet; (*par terre*) slush ▸ **neige fraîche** fresh snow, newly fallen snow ▸ **neige poudreuse** powder snow ▸ **neige de printemps** spring snow → **bonhomme, boule, train** *etc*

neiger [neʒe] ▸conjug 3◂ VB IMPERS to snow; **il neige** it's snowing

neigeux, -euse [neʒø, øz] ADJ [*sommet*] snow-covered, snow-clad; [*temps, aspect*] snowy

nem [nɛm] NM (Vietnamese) small spring roll

nématode [nematɔd] NM nematode (worm); **les ~s** nematodes, Nematoda (*SPÉC*)

Némésis [nemezis] NF Nemesis

néné** [nene] NM boob**, tit**

nénette* [nenɛt] NF (= *jeune femme*) chick**, bird** (*Brit*) → **casser 3b**

nenni [neni] ADV (†† *ou régional* = *non*) nay

nénuphar [nenyfaʀ] NM water lily

néo- [neo] PRÉF neo-; **~libéral/-gaulliste** neoconservative/-Gaullist

néo-calédonien, -ienne [neokaledɔnjɛ̃, jɛn] 1 ADJ New Caledonian 2 **Néo-Calédonien(ne)** NM,F New Caledonian

néo-canadien, -ienne [neokanadjɛ̃, jɛn] 1 ADJ New Canadian 2 **Néo-Canadien(ne)** NM,F New Canadian

néocapitalisme [neokapitalism] NM neocapitalism

néocapitaliste [neokapitalist] ADJ neocapitalist

néoclassicisme [neoklasisism] NM neoclassicism

néoclassique [neoklasik] ADJ neoclassical

néocolonialisme [neokɔlɔnjalism] NM neocolonialism

néocolonialiste [neokɔlɔnjalist] ADJ neocolonialist

néocortex [neokɔʀtɛks] NM neocortex, isocortex

néodarwinisme [neodaʀwinism] NM neo-Darwinism

néo-écossais, e [neoekɔsɛ, ɛz] ADJ, NM,F Nova Scotian

néofascisme, néo-fascisme (*pl* **néo-fascismes**) [neofaʃism] NM neofascism

néofasciste, néo-fasciste (*pl* **néo-fascistes**) [neofaʃist] ADJ, NMF neofascist

néogothique [neogɔtik] ADJ, NM neogothic

néo-libéralisme [neolibeʀalism] NM neoconservatism

néolithique [neolitik] ADJ, NM neolithic

néologie [neolɔʒi] NF neology

néologique [neolɔʒik] ADJ neological

néologisme [neolɔʒism] NM neologism

néon [neɔ̃] NM (= *gaz*) neon; (= *éclairage*) neon lighting (*NonC*)

néonatal, e (*mpl* **néonatals**) [neonatal] ADJ neonatal

néonatologie [neonatɔlɔʒi], **néonatalogie** [neonatalɔʒi] NF neonatology

néonazi, e [neonazi] ADJ, NM,F neo-Nazi

néonazisme [neonazism] NM neo-Nazism

néophyte [neofit] 1 ADJ neophytic 2 NMF (*Rel*) neophyte; (*fig*) novice, neophyte (*frm*)

néoplasique [neoplazik] ADJ neoplastic

néoplasme [neɔplasm] NM neoplasm

néoplatonicien, -ienne [neoplatɔnisjɛ̃, jɛn] 1 ADJ neoplatonic 2 NM,F neoplatonist

néoplatonisme [neoplatɔnism] NM Neo-Platonism

néopositivisme [neopozitivism] NM logical positivism

néopositiviste [neopozitivist] ADJ, NMF logical positivist

néoprène [neɔpʀɛn] NM **colle au ~** neoprene glue

néoréalisme [neoʀealism] NM neorealism

néoréaliste [neoʀealist] ADJ neorealist

néo-zélandais, e [neozelɑ̃dɛ, ɛz] 1 ADJ New Zealand (épith) 2 **Néo-Zélandais(e)** NM,F New Zealander

Népal [nepal] NM Nepal

népalais, e [nepalɛ, ɛz] 1 ADJ Nepalese, Nepali 2 NM (Ling) Nepalese, Nepali 3 **Népalais(e)** NM,F Nepalese, Nepali

népérien, -ienne [nepeʀjɛ̃, jɛn] ADJ Nap(i)erian; **logarithmes ~s** natural ou Nap(i)erian logarithms

néphrétique [nefʀetik] ADJ, NMF nephritic → **colique**

néphrite [nefʀit] NF a (Méd) nephritis; **avoir une ~** to have nephritis b (= jade) nephrite

néphrologie [nefʀɔlɔʒi] NF nephrology

néphrologue [nefʀɔlɔg] NMF nephrologist, kidney specialist

népotisme [nepɔtism] NM nepotism

Neptune [neptyn] NM, NF (Astron, Myth) Neptune

neptunium [neptynjɔm] NM neptunium

néréide [neʀeid] NF (Myth, Zool) nereid

nerf [nɛʀ] 1 NM a (Anat) nerve
b (loc) **avoir les ~s malades** to suffer from nerves; **avoir les ~s fragiles** to be highly strung; **avoir les ~s à vif** to be very edgy ou nervy (Brit), be on edge; **avoir les ~s en boule*** ou **en pelote*** to be very tensed up ou tense ou edgy; **avoir les ~s à toute épreuve** ou **des ~s d'acier** to have nerves of steel; **avoir ses ~s** to have an attack ou a fit of nerves, have a temperamental outburst; **être sur les ~s** to be all keyed up*; **vivre sur les ~s** to live on one's nerves; **porter** ou **taper* sur les ~s de qn** to get on sb's nerves; **passer ses ~s sur qn** to take it out on sb; **ça me met les ~s à vif** that gets on my nerves; **ça va te calmer les ~s** that will calm ou settle your nerves; **ses ~s ont été ébranlés** that shook him; **ses ~s ont craqué*** ou **lâché*** he went to pieces ou cracked up* → **bout, crise, fleur**
c (= vigueur) **allons du ~!** ou **un peu de ~!** come on, buck up!* ou show some spirit!; **son style a du ~** he has a vigorous style; **c'est une voiture qui a du ~** it's a responsive car; **dépêche-toi, ça manque de ~ tout ça!** come on, get a move on, let's have some life about you!; **l'argent est le ~ de la guerre** money is the sinews of war
d (* = tendon) nerve; [viande] **~s** gristle (NonC)
e (Reliure) cord
2 COMP ► **nerf de bœuf†** cosh (Brit), ≈ blackjack (US) ► **nerf gustatif** gustatory nerve ► **nerf moteur** motor nerve ► **nerf optique** optic nerve ► **nerf pneumogastrique** vagus ► **nerf sensitif** sensory nerve ► **nerf vague** vagus

Néron [neʀɔ̃] NM Nero

nerprun [nɛʀpʀœ̃] NM buckthorn

nerveusement [nɛʀvøzmɑ̃] ADV (= d'une manière excitée) nervously, tensely; (= de façon irritable) irritably, touchily; (= avec vigueur) energetically, vigorously; **ébranlé ~** shaken, with shaken nerves

nerveux, -euse [nɛʀvø, øz] 1 ADJ a (Méd) [tension, dépression, fatigue, système] nervous; (Anat) [cellule, centre, tissu] nerve (épith);

pourquoi pleures-tu? — c'est ~! why are you crying? — it's (my) nerves! → **grossesse, système** b (= agité) [personne, animal, rire] nervous, tense; (= irritable) irritable, touchy; (Écon) [marché] nervous, jumpy, jittery; **ça me rend ~** (= anxieux) it makes me nervous; (= excité, tendu) it puts me on edge c (= vigoureux) [corps] energetic, vigorous; [moteur, voiture] responsive; [style] energetic, vigorous; **il n'est pas très ~ dans ce qu'il fait** he's not very energetic in what he does, he doesn't do anything with very much dash ou spirit d (= sec) [personne, main] wiry; [viande] gristly 2 NM,F **c'est un grand ~** he's very highly strung (Brit) ou high-strung (US)

nervi [nɛʀvi] NM (gén pl) bully boy, hatchet man

nervosité [nɛʀvozite] NF a (= agitation) (permanente) nervousness, excitability; (passagère) nervousness, agitation, tension; (Écon) [marché] nervousness, jumpiness, jitteriness; **dans un état de grande ~** in a highly nervous state, in a state of great agitation b (= irritabilité) (permanente) irritability; (passagère) irritability, touchiness c [moteur] responsiveness; **manque de ~** sluggishness

nervure [nɛʀvyʀ] NF (Bot, Zool) nervure, vein; (Archit, Tech) rib; (Typo) raised band

nervuré, e [nɛʀvyʀe] ADJ [feuille] veined, nervate (SPÉC); [aile] veined; [couvercle, voûte] ribbed

Nescafé® [nɛskafe] NM Nescafé®, instant coffee

n'est-ce pas [nɛspɑ] ADV a (appelant l'acquiescement) isn't it?, doesn't he? etc (selon le verbe qui précède); **il est fort, ~?** he's strong, isn't he?; **c'est bon, ~?** it's nice, isn't it? ou don't you think?; **il n'est pas trop tard, ~?** it's not too late, is it?; **tu iras, ~?** you will go, won't you? b (intensif) **~ que c'est bon/difficile?** it's nice/difficult, isn't it?; (iro) **eux, ~, ils peuvent se le permettre** of course they can afford to do it; **le problème, ~, c'est qu'il s'en fiche** the problem is (that) he doesn't care, you see

Net [nɛt] NM (ABRÉV = **Internet**) **le ~** the Net

net¹, nette [nɛt] 1 ADJ a (= propre: après nom) [surface, ongles, mains] clean; [intérieur, travail, copie] neat, tidy; **elle est toujours très nette (dans sa tenue)** she's always neatly dressed ou turned out, she's always very neat and tidy; **avoir la conscience nette** to have a clear conscience; **mettre au ~** [rapport, devoir] to copy out, make a neat ou fair copy of; [plan, travail] to tidy up; **mise au ~** copying out, tidying up → **cœur, place** b (Comm, Fin: après nom) [bénéfice, prix, poids] net; **~ de** free of; **emprunt ~ de tout impôt** tax-free loan; **revenu ~** disposable income c (= clair, précis: après nom) [idée, explication, esprit] clear; (= sans équivoque) [réponse] straight, clear, plain; [refus] flat (épith); [situation, position] clear-cut; **je serai ~ avec vous** I shall be (quite) candid ou frank with you; **son attitude dans cette affaire n'est pas très nette** his attitude in this matter is a bit dubious; **ce type n'est pas très ~*** (bizarre) that guy's slightly odd ou strange*; (fou) that guy's slightly mad* d (= marqué, évident) [différence, amélioration] marked, distinct, sharp; [distinction] marked, sharp, clear(-cut); [avantage] clear; **il y a une très nette odeur** ou **une odeur très nette de brûlé** there's a distinct ou a very definite smell of burning; **il est très ~ qu'il n'a aucune intention de venir** it's quite clear ou obvious that he doesn't intend to come e (= distinct: après nom) [dessin, écriture] clear; [ligne, contour, image] sharp; [voix, son] clear, distinct; [cassure, coupure] clean; **j'ai un souvenir très ~ de sa visite** I remember his visit

very clearly, I have a very clear ou vivid memory of his visit
2 ADV a (= brusquement) [s'arrêter] dead; **se casser ~** to snap (in two), break clean through; **il a été tué ~** he was killed outright ou instantly
b (= franchement) [refuser] flatly, point-blank; **il (m')a dit tout ~ que ...** he made it quite clear (to me) that ..., he told me frankly ou bluntly that ...; **parlons ~** let's be frank; **je vous le dis tout ~** I'm telling you ou I'm giving it to you straight*, I'm telling you bluntly ou frankly; **pour vous** ou **à parler ~** to be blunt ou frank with you
c (Comm) net; **il reste 200 F ~** there remains 200 francs net; **cela pèse 2 kg ~** it weighs 2 kg net
3 NM (Écon) **le ~** net profit

net² [nɛt] 1 ADJ INV (Tennis) net (épith) 2 NM net shot

nettement [nɛtmɑ̃] ADV a (= sans ambiguïté) [expliquer, répondre] clearly; **il refusa ~** he flatly refused, he refused point-blank; **je lui ai dit ~ ce que j'en pensais** I told him bluntly ou frankly what I thought of it; **il a ~ pris position contre nous** he has clearly ou quite obviously taken up a stance against us
b (= distinctement) [apercevoir, entendre, se souvenir] clearly, distinctly; [se détacher, apparaître] clearly, distinctly, sharply
c (= incontestablement) [s'améliorer, se différencier] markedly, distinctly; [mériter] definitely; **j'aurais ~ préféré ne pas venir** I would have definitely ou distinctly preferred not to come; **ça va ~ mieux** things are decidedly ou distinctly better; **~ meilleur/plus grand** markedly ou distinctly better/bigger; **coûter ~ moins cher** to cost much less ou a great deal less; **ils sont ~ moins nombreux** there are far fewer of them; **arriver ~ en avance** to arrive far too early

netteté [nɛtte] NF a (= propreté) [tenue, travail] neatness b (= clarté) [explication, expression, esprit, idées] clearness, clarity c (= caractère distinct) [dessin, écriture] clearness; [contour, image] sharpness, clarity, clearness; [souvenir, voix, son] clearness, clarity; [cassure] cleanness

nettoiement [nɛtwamɑ̃] NM [rues] cleaning; (Agr) [terre] clearing; **service du ~** refuse disposal ou collection service

nettoyable [nɛtwajabl] ADJ **facilement/difficilement ~** easy/difficult to clean; **~ à sec** dry-cleanable

nettoyage [nɛtwajaʒ] NM (gén) cleaning; [plage, rue, rivière] cleaning (up); [écurie, cage, réfrigérateur] cleaning (out); (Mil, Police) cleaning up ou out; **faire le ~ par le vide*** to throw everything out; **~ de printemps** spring-cleaning; **~ à sec** dry cleaning; **un ~ complet** a thorough cleanup; **~ de peau** skin cleansing; (Mil) **opération de ~** mopping-up operation; **entreprise/produit de ~** cleaning firm/agent; (fig) **ils ont fait du ~ dans cette entreprise** they've got rid of the deadwood in this company → **ethnique**

nettoyant, e [nɛtwajɑ̃, ɑ̃t] 1 ADJ cleaning (épith) 2 NM cleaner

nettoyer [nɛtwaje] ▶conjug 8◀ VT a (gén) [+ objet] to clean; [+ plaie] to cleanse, clean; [+ jardin] to clear; [+ canal, rue, plage] to clean (up); [+ écurie, cage, réfrigérateur] to clean (out); **~ au chiffon** to dust; **~ au chiffon ou avec un chiffon** to dust; **~ au balai** to sweep (out); **~ à l'eau/avec du savon** to wash in water/with soap; **~ à la brosse** to brush (out); **~ à l'éponge** to sponge (down); **~ à sec** to dry-clean; **nettoyez-vous les mains au robinet** wash your hands under the tap, give your hands a rinse under the tap; (hum) **~ son assiette** to clean one's plate; (hum) **le chien avait nettoyé le réfrigérateur*** the dog had cleaned out ou emptied the fridge; **l'orage a nettoyé le ciel** the storm has

cleared away the clouds
b * [+ *personne*] (= *tuer*) to kill, finish off*; (= *ruiner*) to clean out; (= *fatiguer*) to wear out; **il a été nettoyé en une semaine par la grippe** the flu finished him off* *ou* did for him* in a week; **~ son compte en banque** to clear one's bank account; **se faire ~ au jeu** to be cleaned out at gambling
c (*Mil, Police*) to clean out *ou* up

nettoyeur, -euse [netwajœʀ, øz] NM,F cleaner

Neuchâtel [nøʃatɛl] N Neuchâtel; **le lac de ~** Neuchâtel Lake

neuf[1] [nœf] ADJ INV, NM INV (= *chiffre*) nine; *pour autres locutions voir* **preuve, six**

neuf[2], neuve [nœf, nœv] **1** ADJ (*gén*) new; [*vision, esprit, pensée*] fresh, new; [*pays*] young, new; **quelque chose de ~** something new; **regarder qch avec un œil ~** to look at sth with new eyes *ou* a fresh eye; **être ~ dans le métier/en affaires** to be new to the trade/to business; **à l'état ◊ comme ~** as good as new, as new; **c'est tout ~** [*objet*] it's brand new; (*littér*) **son bonheur tout ~** his new-found happiness → **flambant, peau**
2 NM new; **il y a du ~** something new has turned up, there's been a new development; **quoi de/rien de ~?** what's/nothing new?; **faire du ~** (*politique*) to introduce new *ou* fresh ideas; (*artisanat*) to make new things; **être vêtu ou habillé de ~** to be wearing new clothes, have new clothes on; **son appartement est meublé de ~** all the furniture in his flat is new; **remettre ou refaire à ~** to do up like new *ou* as good as new; **remise à ~** restoration; **repeindre un appartement à ~** to redecorate a flat; **on ne peut pas faire du ~ avec du vieux** you can't make new things out of old

neurasthénie [nøʀasteni] NF (*gén*) depression; (*Méd*) neurasthenia (SPÉC); **faire de la ~** to be depressed, be suffering from depression

neurasthénique [nøʀastenik] **1** ADJ depressed, depressive; (*Méd*) neurasthenic (SPÉC) **2** NMF depressed person, depressive; (*Méd*) neurasthenic (SPÉC)

neuro... [nøʀo] PRÉF neuro...

neurobiologie [nøʀobjɔlɔʒi] NF neurobiology

neurobiologiste [nøʀobjɔlɔʒist] NMF neurobiologist

neurochimie [nøʀoʃimi] NF neurochemistry

neurochirurgical, e (*mpl* **-aux**) [nøʀoʃiʀyʀʒikal, o] ADJ neurosurgical

neurochirurgie [nøʀoʃiʀyʀʒi] NF neurosurgery

neurochirurgien, -ienne [nøʀoʃiʀyʀʒjɛ̃, jɛn] NM,F neurosurgeon

neuroendocrinien, -ienne [nøʀoɑ̃dɔkʀinjɛ̃, jɛn] ADJ neuroendocrine

neuroleptique [nøʀolɛptik] ADJ, NM neuroleptic

neurologie [nøʀɔlɔʒi] NF neurology

neurologique [nøʀɔlɔʒik] ADJ neurological

neurologiste [nøʀɔlɔʒist], **neurologue** [nøʀɔlɔg] NMF neurologist

neuromédiateur [nøʀomedjatœʀ] NM neurotransmitter

neuromusculaire [nøʀomyskylɛʀ] ADJ neuromuscular

neuronal, e (*mpl* **-aux**) [nøʀonal, o] ADJ (*Méd*) neuronal; (*Ordin*) neural; **réseau ~** neural network; **ordinateur ~** neurocomputer, neural computer

neurone [nøʀɔn] NM neuron

neuropathie [nøʀopati] NF neuropathy

neuropathologie [nøʀopatɔlɔʒi] NF neuropathology

neurophysiologie [nøʀofizjɔlɔʒi] NF neurophysiology

neurophysiologique [nøʀofizjɔlɔʒik] ADJ neurophysiological

neurophysiologiste [nøʀofizjɔlɔʒist] NMF neurophysiologist

neuropsychiatre [nøʀopsikjatʀ] NMF neuropsychiatrist

neuropsychiatrie [nøʀopsikjatʀi] NF neuropsychiatry

neuropsychiatrique [nøʀopsikjatʀik] ADJ neuropsychiatric

neuropsychologie [nøʀopsikɔlɔʒi] NF neuropsychology

neuropsychologue [nøʀopsikɔlɔg] NMF neuropsychologist

neurosciences [nøʀosjɑ̃s] NFPL neuroscience

neurotoxine [nøʀotɔksin] NF neurotoxin

neurotransmetteur [nøʀotʀɑ̃smetœʀ] NM neurotransmitter

neurovégétatif, -ive, neuro-végétatif, -ive (*mpl* **neuro-végétatifs**) [nøʀovegetatif, iv] ADJ neurovegetative

neutralisation [nøtʀalizasjɔ̃] NF neutralization

neutraliser [nøtʀalize] ▸ conjug 1 ◂ **1** VT (*Mil, Pol, Sci*) to neutralize; [+ *gardien, agresseur*] to overpower; (*sur autoroute*) **la voie de gauche est neutralisée** the left-hand lane is closed to traffic; **les poubelles sont neutralisées** the bins have been sealed **2** **se neutraliser** VPR **les deux influences/produits se neutralisent** the two influences/products cancel each other out

neutralisme [nøtʀalism] NM neutralism

neutraliste [nøtʀalist] ADJ, NMF neutralist

neutralité [nøtʀalite] NF neutrality; **rester dans la ~** to remain neutral; **~ bienveillante** benevolent neutrality

neutre [nøtʀ] **1** ADJ (*gén, Chim, Élec, Pol, Phon*) neutral; (*Ling, Zool*) neuter; [*style*] neutral, colourless (*Brit*), colorless (*US*); (= *sans excès*) [*solution*] middle-of-the-road; (*dans un conflit*) **rester ~** to remain neutral, not to take sides (**dans** in) **2** NM (*Ling*) (= *genre*) neuter; (= *nom*) neuter noun; (*Élec*) neutral; (*Zool*) neuter (animal); **les ~s** the neutral nations

neutrino [nøtʀino] NM neutrino

neutron [nøtʀɔ̃] NM neutron → **bombe**

neutronique [nøtʀɔnik] ADJ neutron (*épith*)

neuvaine [nœvɛn] NF novena; **faire une ~** to make a novena

neuvième [nœvjɛm] ADJ, NMF ninth; *pour locutions voir* **sixième**

neuvièmement [nœvjɛmmɑ̃] ADV ninthly, in the ninth place; *pour locutions voir* **sixièmement**

Nevada [nevada] NM Nevada

ne varietur [nevaʀjetyʀ] **1** LOC ADJ [*édition*] definitive **2** LOC ADV without any variation

névé [neve] NM névé, firn

neveu (*pl* **neveux**) [n(ə)vø] NM nephew; (†† *littér* = *descendant*) descendant; **un peu, mon ~!** * you bet!*, of course!, and how!*

névralgie [nevʀalʒi] NF neuralgia (*NonC*); **~ dentaire** dental neuralgia; **avoir des ~s** to suffer from neuralgia

névralgique [nevʀalʒik] ADJ neuralgic; **centre ou point ~** (*Méd*) nerve centre; (*fig*) (= *point sensible*) sensitive spot; (= *point capital*) nerve centre

névrite [nevʀit] NF neuritis (*NonC*)

névritique [nevʀitik] ADJ neuritic

névropathe [nevʀopat] **1** ADJ neuropathic, neurotic **2** NMF neuropath, neurotic

névropathie [nevʀopati] NF neuropathy

névrose [nevʀoz] NF neurosis; **~ obsessionnelle** obsessional neurosis; **~ phobique** phobia

névrosé, e [nevʀoze] ADJ, NM,F neurotic

névrotique [nevʀotik] ADJ neurotic

New Delhi [njudɛli] N New Delhi

New Hampshire [njuɑ̃pʃəʀ] NM New Hampshire

New Jersey [njuʒɛʀze] NM New Jersey

new-look* [njuluk] ADJ, NM INV new look

Newton [njutɔn] NM (= *savant*) Newton; (= *unité*) **newton** newton

newtonien, -ienne [njutɔnjɛ̃, jɛn] ADJ Newtonian

New York [njujɔʀk] **1** N (= *ville*) New York **2** NM **l'État de ~** New York State

new-yorkais, e [njujɔʀkɛ, ɛz] **1** ADJ New-York (*épith*), of *ou* from New York **2** **New-Yorkais(e)** NM,F New Yorker

nez [ne] NM **a** (= *organe*) nose; **avoir le ~ grec/aquilin** to have a Grecian/an aquiline nose; **~ épaté ou écrasé ou aplati** flat nose; **~ en trompette** turned-up nose; **~ en pied de marmite** bulbous turned-up nose; **ton ~ remue, tu mens** I can tell by looking at you that you're lying; **parler du ~** to talk through one's nose; **cela se voit comme le ~ au milieu de la figure ou du visage** it's as plain as the nose on your face, it sticks out a mile; **cela sent le brûlé à plein ~** there's a strong smell of burning; **le bureau sentait la fumée à plein ~** the office reeked of cigarette smoke
b (= *visage, face*) **le ~ en l'air ou au vent** with one's nose in the air; **où est mon sac ? — tu as le ~ dessus ! ou sous ton ~!** where's my bag? — (right) under your nose!; **baisser/lever le ~** to bow/raise one's head; **le ~ dans son assiette** with his head bent over his plate; **il ne lève jamais le ~ de ses livres** he's always got his nose in a book, he's a real bookworm*; **il ne lève jamais le ~ de son travail** he never looks up from his work; **mettre le ~ ou son ~ à la fenêtre/au bureau** to show one's face at the window/at the office; **je n'ai pas mis le ~ dehors hier** I didn't put my nose outside the door yesterday; **il fait un temps à ne pas mettre le ~ dehors** it's weather you wouldn't put a dog out in; **rire/fermer la porte au ~ de qn** to laugh/shut the door in sb's face; (*au téléphone*) **elle m'a raccroché au ~** (*couper la communication*) she hung up on me; (*avec colère*) she slammed the phone down on me; **faire qch au ~ et à la barbe de qn** to do sth under sb's very nose; **regarder qn sous le ~** to stare sb in the face; **sous son ~** (right) under his nose, under his (very) nose; **se trouver ~ à ~ avec qn** to find o.s. face to face with sb; **faire un (drôle de) ~** to pull a (funny) face
c (= *flair*) **il a du ~** he has good instincts; **en affaires, il a du ~ ou le ~ fin** he has a flair for business; **j'ai eu le ~ creux de m'en aller*** I had a hunch that I should leave → **vue[2]**
d (*Aviat, Naut*) nose; (*Naut*) **sur le ~** down at the bows → **piquer**
e (= *créateur de parfums, Œnol*) nose
f (*loc*) **avoir qn dans le ~** * to have it in for sb*, have something against sb; **il m'a dans le ~*** he's got it in for me*, he's got something against me; **avoir un verre ou un coup dans le ~*** to have had one too many*, have had a drop too much*; **se manger ou se bouffer le ~*** to be at each others' throats; **mettre ou fourrer* le ~ ou son ~ dans qch** to poke *ou* stick* one's nose into sth, nose *ou* pry into sth; **l'affaire lui est passée sous le ~*** the bargain slipped through his fingers; **je vais lui mettre le ~ dans sa crotte* ou son caca* ou sa merde**** I'll rub his (*ou* her) nose in it*; **montrer (le bout de) ou pointer son ~** (= *se manifester*) to make an appearance, show up; **il a montré ou pointé le bout de son ~ à la porte et il a disparu** he popped his head round the door *ou* he just showed his face then disappeared; **aujourd'hui, le soleil montre le bout de son ~** today the sun has peeped through → **casser, doigt, mener**

NF [ɛnɛf] **a** (ABRÉV = **norme française**) avoir le label **NF** to have the mark of the approved French standard of manufacture, ≈ have the Kite mark (*Brit*) **b** (ABRÉV = **nouveau(x) franc(s)**) → **franc²**

ni [ni] CONJ (*après la négation*) nor, or; **ni ... ni ...** neither ... nor ...; **il ne boit ni ne fume** he doesn't drink or smoke, he neither drinks nor smokes; **il ne pouvait (ni) parler ni entendre** he could neither speak nor hear, he couldn't speak or hear; **personne ne l'a (jamais) aidé ni (même) encouragé** nobody (ever) helped or (even) encouraged him; **je ne veux ni ne peux accepter** I neither wish to nor can accept, I don't wish to accept, nor can I; **elle est secrétaire, ni plus ni moins** she's just a secretary, no more no less; **il n'est ni plus bête ni plus paresseux qu'un autre** he is neither more stupid nor any lazier than anyone else, he's no more stupid and no lazier than anyone else; **il ne veut pas, ni moi non plus** he doesn't want to and neither do I *ou* and nor do I; **ni lui ni moi** neither he nor I, neither of us, neither him nor me*; **ni l'un ni l'autre** neither one nor the other, neither of them; **ni d'un côté ni de l'autre** on neither one side nor the other, on neither side; **il n'a dit ni oui ni non** he didn't say either yes or no; **ni vu ni connu (je t'embrouille)*** no one'll be any the wiser* → **chaud**, **feu¹**, **foi**

niable [njabl] ADJ deniable; **cela n'est pas ~** that's undeniable, you can't deny that

Niagara [njagaʀa] NM **le ~** the Niagara (river) → **chute**

niais, niaise [njɛ, njɛz] **1** ADJ [*personne, air*] silly; [*rire, sourire, style, livre, film*] silly, inane **2** NM,F simpleton; **pauvre ~!** poor fool!

niaisement [njɛzmɑ̃] ADV [*rire*] inanely

niaiserie [njɛzʀi] NF **a** (= *bêtise*) silliness **b** (= *action*) foolish *ou* inane behaviour (*NonC*); (= *parole*) foolish *ou* inane talk (*NonC*); **dire des ~s** to talk rubbish *ou* twaddle (*Brit*) *ou* nonsense; **ils regardent des ~s à la télé** they're watching some rubbish on TV

niaiseux, -euse [njɛzø, øz] (*Can*) **1** ADJ stupid, idiotic **2** NM,F idiot

Niamey [njamɛ] N Niamey

Nicaragua [nikaʀagwa] NM Nicaragua

nicaraguayen, -enne [nikaʀagwajɛ̃, jɛn] **1** ADJ Nicaraguan **2** **Nicaraguayen(ne)** NM,F Nicaraguan

niche [niʃ] NF **a** (= *alcôve*) niche, recess **b** [*chien*] kennel; **à la ~!** (*à un chien*) (into your) kennel!; (*hum: à une personne*) scram!*; **make yourself scarce!*** **c** († = *farce*) trick, hoax; **faire des ~s à qn** to play tricks on sb **d** (*Comm, Écol*) niche

nichée [niʃe] NF [*oiseaux*] brood; **~ de chiens** litter of puppies; **~ de pinsons** nest *ou* brood of chaffinches; **l'instituteur et toute sa ~ (d'enfants)*** the teacher and all his charges

nicher [niʃe] ▶conjug 1◀ **1** VI [*oiseau*] to nest; * [*personne*] to hang out* **2** **se nicher** VPR [*oiseau*] to nest; (*littér = se blottir*) [*village, maison*] to nestle (**dans** in); (* = *se cacher*) [*personne*] to stick* *ou* put o.s.; [*objet*] to lodge itself; (*hum*) **où la vertu va-t-elle se ~!** of all the unlikely places to find such virtue!; **les cerises nichées dans les feuilles** the cherries nestling among the leaves

nichon* [niʃɔ̃] NM tit**✶**, boob*

nickel [nikɛl] **1** NM nickel **2** ADJ (* = *impeccable*) spotless; **chez eux, c'est ~** their home is always spick and span

nickelage [niklaʒ] NM nickel-plating

nickelé, e [nikle] ADJ nickelled, nickel-plated; **acier ~** nickel-plated steel

nickeler [nikle] ▶conjug 4◀ VT to nickel-plate

niçois, e [niswa, waz] **1** ADJ *ou* from Nice → **salade** **2** **Niçois(e)** NM,F inhabitant *ou*

native of Nice; (*Culin*) **à la ~e** with tomatoes and garlic (*attrib*)

Nicolas [nikɔla] NM Nicholas

Nicosie [nikɔzi] N Nicosia

nicotine [nikɔtin] NF nicotine

nid [ni] **1** NM **a** (*Zool*) nest; **~ d'oiseau/de guêpes** bird's/wasps' nest **b** (= *abri, foyer*) cosy little nest; (= *repaire*) den; **trouver le ~ vide** to find the bird has *ou* the birds have flown, find the nest empty; **surprendre qn au ~ ◊ trouver l'oiseau au ~** to find *ou* catch sb at home *ou* in **2** COMP ► **nid(s) d'abeilles** (= *point*) honeycomb stitch; (= *tissu*) waffle cloth; **radiateur en ~(s) d'abeilles** cellular radiator ► **nid d'aigle** (*Zool, fig*) eyrie ► **nid d'amoureux** love nest ► **nid d'ange** (baby) nest ► **nid de brigands** robbers' den ► **nids d'hirondelles** (*Culin*) birds' nest; **potage aux ~s d'hirondelles** birds' nest soup ► **nid de mitrailleuses** nest of machine guns ► **nid de pie** (*Naut*) crow's-nest ► **nid de poule** pothole ► **nid à poussière** dust trap ► **nid de résistance** (*Mil*) pocket of resistance ► **nid de vipères** (*lit, fig*) nest of vipers

nidation [nidasjɔ̃] NF nidation, implantation

nidification [nidifikasjɔ̃] NF nesting

nidifier [nidifje] ▶conjug 7◀ VI to nest

nièce [njɛs] NF niece

nielle [njɛl] **1** NF (*Agr*) (= *plante*) corncockle; (= *maladie*) **~ (du blé)** blight **2** NM (= *incrustation*) niello

nieller [njele] ▶conjug 1◀ VT (*Agr*) to blight; (*Tech*) to niello

niellure [njelyʀ] NF (*Agr*) blight; (*Tech*) niello

n-ième, nième [ɛnjɛm] ADJ (*Math*) nth; (**✶**: *fig*) nth, umpteenth; **x à la ~ puissance** x to the power (of) n, x to the nth power; **je te le dis pour la ~ fois** I'm telling you for the nth *ou* umpteenth time

nier [nje] ▶conjug 7◀ VT (*gén*) to deny; (*Jur = désavouer*) [+ *dette, fait*] to repudiate; **il nie l'avoir fait** he denies having done it; **~ l'évidence** to deny the obvious; **je ne (le) nie pas** I'm not denying it, I don't deny it; **on ne peut ~ que** one cannot deny that; **l'accusé nia** the accused denied the charges

niet✶ [njɛt] EXCL no way!, nothing doing!*

nietzschéen, -enne [nitʃeɛ̃, ɛn] ADJ, NM,F Nietzschean

nigaud, e [nigo, od] **1** ADJ silly, simple **2** NM,F simpleton; **grand** *ou* **gros ~!** big silly!, big ninny!*, silly billy!* (*Brit*)

nigauderie [nigodʀi] NF (= *caractère*) silliness, simpleness; (= *action*) silly thing to do

Niger [niʒɛʀ] NM **le ~** (the) Niger

Nigéria, Nigeria [niʒeʀja] NM Nigeria

nigérian, e [niʒeʀjã, an] **1** ADJ Nigerian **2** **Nigérian(e)** NM,F Nigerian

nigérien, -ienne [niʒeʀjɛ̃, jɛn] **1** ADJ *ou* from Niger **2** **Nigérien(ne)** NM,F inhabitant *ou* native of Niger

night-club (*pl* **night-clubs**) [najtklœb] NM nightclub

nihilisme [niilism] NM nihilism

nihiliste [niilist(ə)] **1** ADJ nihilistic **2** NMF nihilist

Nikkei [nikej] NM (*Bourse*) **l'indice ~ ◊ le ~** the Nikkei (index)

Nil [nil] NM **le ~** the Nile; **le ~ Blanc/Bleu** the White/Blue Nile

nilotique [nilɔtik] ADJ of *ou* from the Nile, Nile (*épith*)

nimbe [nɛ̃b] NM (*Rel, fig*) nimbus, halo

nimber [nɛ̃be] ▶conjug 1◀ VT (= *auréoler*) to halo; **nimbé de lumière** radiant *ou* suffused with light

nimbostratus [nɛ̃bostʀatys] NM nimbostratus

nimbus [nɛ̃bys] NM (*Mét*) nimbus

n'importe [nɛ̃pɔʀt(ə)] → **importer²**

ninas [ninas] NM small cigar

niobium [njɔbjɔm] NM niobium

niôle✶ [njol] NF = **gnôle**

nippe✶ [nip] NF (old) thing* *ou* rag*; **~s** togs*, gear*; **de vieilles ~s** old togs*, old clothes

nipper✶ [nipe] ▶conjug 1◀ **1** VT (= *habiller*) to deck out, tog out* (*Brit*); **bien/mal nippé** in a nice/an awful getup* *ou* rig-out* (*Brit*), well/badly got up* (*Brit*) **2** **se nipper** VPR to get decked out, get togged up* (*Brit*)

nippon, e *ou* **-onne** [nipɔ̃, ɔn] **1** ADJ Japanese **2** **Nippon(e) ◊ Nippon(ne)** NM,F Japanese **3** NM (= *pays*) **Nippon** Japan

nique [nik] NF **faire la ~ à qn** to thumb one's nose at sb, cock a snook at sb (*Brit*)

niquedouille✶ [nik(ə)duj] ADJ, NM,F = **nigaud**

niquer✶✶ [nike] VT (*sexuellement*) to fuck✶✶, screw✶✶; (= *abîmer*) [+ *machine, ordinateur*] to fuck up✶✶, bugger up✶ (*Brit*), knacker✶ (*Brit*); (*fig*) **se faire ~** to get screwed✶✶

nirvana [niʀvana] NM nirvana

nitouche [nituʃ] NF → **saint**

nitrate [nitʀat] NM nitrate; **~ d'argent** silver nitrate

nitreux, -euse [nitʀø, øz] ADJ nitrous

nitrifier [nitʀifje] ▶conjug 1◀ VT to nitrify

nitrique [nitʀik] ADJ nitric

nitrite [nitʀit] NM nitrite

nitro... [nitʀo] PRÉF nitro...; **~samine** nitrosamine

nitrobenzène [nitʀobɛzɛn] NM nitrobenzene

nitroglycérine [nitʀogliseʀin] NF nitroglycerine

nival, e (*mpl* **-aux**) [nival, o] ADJ nival

▼ **niveau** (*pl* **niveaux**) [nivo] **1** NM **a** (= *hauteur*) [*huile, eau*] level; [*bâtiment*] level, floor; **le ~ de l'eau** the water level; **au ~ de l'eau/du sol** at water/ground level; **cent mètres au-dessus du ~ de la mer** a hundred metres above sea level; **l'eau est arrivée au ~ du quai** the water has risen to the level of the embankment; **la neige m'arrivait au ~ des genoux** the snow came up to my knees *ou* was knee-deep; **une tache au ~ du coude** a mark at the elbow; **serré au ~ de la taille** tight at the waist; **il avait une cicatrice sur la joue au ~ de la bouche** he had a scar on his cheek about level with his mouth; **il s'arrêta au ~ du village** he stopped once he got to the village; **de ~ avec ◊ au même ~ que** level with; **les deux vases sont au même ~** the two vases are level *ou* at the same height; **de ~** level; **mettre qch de ou à ~** to make sth level; **le plancher n'est pas de ~** the floor isn't level; **les deux pièces ne sont pas de ~** the two rooms are not on a level → **courbe, passage**

b (*Scol*) [*connaissances, études*] standard; **le ~ des études en France** the standard of French education; **le ~ d'instruction baisse** educational standards are falling; **cet élève est d'un bon ~** this pupil keeps up a good level of attainment *ou* a good standard; **son anglais est d'un bon ~** his English is of a good standard; **il est/il n'est pas au ~** he is/he isn't up to standard; **ils ne sont pas du même ~** they're not (of) the same standard, they're not on a par *ou* on the same level; **les cours ne sont pas à son ~** the classes aren't up to his standard; **remettre à ~** to bring up to standard; **cours** *ou* **stage de remise à ~** refresher course

c (= *degré*) level; **le ~ intellectuel de la classe moyenne** the intellectual level of the middle class; **le franc a atteint son ~ le plus haut/bas depuis 3 ans** the franc has reached its highest/lowest point for 3 years; **la production littéraire a atteint son ~ le plus bas** literary production has reached its lowest ebb *ou* level; **il faut se mettre au ~ des enfants** you have to put yourself on the same level as the children; **le directeur envisage une remise à ~**

des salaires the director is considering bringing salaries into line with standard rates *ou* upgrading salaries to standard rates; **au ~ de l'usine/des gouvernements** at factory/government level; **au ~ européen** at the European level; **à tous les ~x** at all levels; **négociations au plus haut ~** top-level negotiations; **cela exige un haut ~ de concentration** it demands a high level *ou* degree of concentration; **athlète/cadre de haut ~** top athlete/executive; **des candidats (ayant le) ~ licence** candidates at degree level ⓓ (*Constr*) (= *instrument*) level; (*Aut* = *jauge*) gauge

② COMP ► **niveau de base** (*Géog*) base level ► **niveau à bulle (d'air)** spirit level ► **niveau d'eau** water level ► **niveau d'énergie** energy level ► **niveau hydrostatique** water table ► **niveau de langue** register ► **niveau à lunette** dumpy level ► **niveau de maçon** plumb level ► **niveau social** social standing *ou* rank ► **niveau de vie** standard of living, living standards

nivelage [niv(ə)laʒ] NM [*surface*] levelling; [*fortunes, conditions sociales*] levelling out, evening out

niveler [niv(ə)le] ▶conjug 4◀ VT ⓐ (= *égaliser*) [+ *surface*] to level; [+ *fortunes, conditions sociales*] to level *ou* even out; **l'érosion nivelle les montagnes** erosion wears down *ou* wears away the mountains; **sommets nivelés** mountain tops worn down *ou* worn away by erosion; **~ par le bas/le haut** to level down/up ⓑ (= *mesurer avec un niveau*) to measure with a spirit level, level

niveleur, -euse [niv(ə)lœr, øz] ① ADJ [*doctrine, morale*] egalitarian ② NM (*Hist*) Leveller ③ **niveleuse** NF (*Constr*) grader

nivellement [nivɛlmɑ̃] NM ⓐ [*surface*] levelling; [*fortunes, conditions sociales*] levelling out, evening out; **~ par le bas/par le haut** levelling down/up ⓑ (= *mesure*) surveying

nivoglaciaire [nivoglasjɛr] ADJ snow and ice (*épith*)

nivopluvial, e (*mpl* -**iaux**) [nivoplyvjal, jo] ADJ snow and rain (*épith*)

nivôse [nivoz] NM Nivôse (*fourth month of French Republican calendar*)

NN (ABRÉV = **nouvelles normes**) *revised standard of hotel classification*

nô [no] NM No(h); **le théâtre nô** the No(h) theatre

Nobel [nɔbɛl] NM **le (prix) ~** the Nobel prize

nobélisable [nɔbelizabl] ① ADJ potential Nobel prize-winning (*épith*) ② NMF potential Nobel prize-winner

nobélium [nɔbeljɔm] NM nobelium

nobiliaire [nɔbiljɛr] ① ADJ nobiliary ② NM (= *livre*) peerage list

noble [nɔbl] ① ADJ ⓐ (= *de haute naissance*) noble ⓑ (= *généreux, digne*) [*ton, attitude*] noble, dignified; [*cause*] noble, worthy; **âme/cœur ~** noble spirit/heart; **le ~ art (de la boxe)** the noble art (of boxing) ⓒ (= *supérieur*) [*matière, métal, vin*] noble ② NM ⓐ (= *personne*) nobleman; **les ~s** the nobility ⓑ (= *monnaie*) noble ③ NF noblewoman

noblement [nɔbləmɑ̃] ADV ⓐ (= *généreusement*) nobly; (= *dignement*) with dignity

noblesse [nɔblɛs] NF ⓐ (= *générosité, dignité*) nobleness, nobility; **~ d'esprit/de cœur** nobleness *ou* nobility of spirit/heart ⓑ (= *caste*) **la (haute) ~** the nobility; **la ~ d'épée** the old nobility *ou* aristocracy; **la ~ de robe** the noblesse de robe; **la ~ de cour** the courtiers, the nobility at court; **la petite ~** the minor nobility, the gentry (*Brit*); **~ terrienne** landed gentry; **~ oblige** noblesse oblige

nobliau (*pl* **nobliaux**) [nɔblijo] NM (*péj*) one of the lesser nobility, petty noble

noce [nɔs] NF ⓐ (= *cérémonie*) wedding; (= *cortège, participants*) wedding party; (*frm*) **~s** wedding, nuptials (*frm*); **être de la ~** to be a member of the wedding party, be among the wedding guests; **être de ~** to be invited to a wedding; **aller à la ~ de qn** to go to sb's wedding; **repas/robe/nuit de ~(s)** wedding banquet/dress/night; **~s d'argent/d'or/de diamant** silver/golden/diamond wedding; (*Bible*) **les ~s de Cana** the wedding *ou* marriage feast at Cana; **il l'avait épousée en premières/secondes ~s** she was his first/second wife → **convoler, voyage** ⓑ (*loc*) **faire la ~*** to live it up*, have a wild time; **je n'étais pas à la ~*** I wasn't exactly enjoying myself, I was having a pretty uncomfortable time

noceur, -euse* [nɔsœr, øz] NM,F fast liver, reveller; **il est assez ~** he likes to live it up*

nocif, -ive [nɔsif, iv] ADJ [*gaz, produit*] noxious; [*effet, influence, idéologie*] harmful; **~ pour la couche d'ozone** harmful *ou* damaging to the ozone layer

nocivité [nɔsivite] NF [*gaz, substance*] noxiousness; [*idéologie, doctrine*] harmfulness

noctambule [nɔktɑ̃byl] ADJ, NMF **il est ~** ◇ **c'est un ~** (= *noceur*) he's a night reveller; (= *qui veille la nuit*) he's a night bird *ou* night owl; (†† = *somnambule*) he's a noctambulist†

noctambulisme [nɔktɑ̃bylism] NM (= *débauche*) night-time revelling, night revels; (= *habitudes nocturnes*) nocturnal habits; (†† = *somnambulisme*) noctambulism†

nocturne [nɔktyrn] ① ADJ [*animal*] nocturnal; [*visite, sortie*] night (*épith*); **la vie ~ à Paris** Parisian nightlife; **équipement de vision ~** night-vision equipment → **tapage** ② NM ⓐ (= *oiseau*) night hunter ⓑ (*Rel*) nocturn ⓒ (*Mus*) nocturne; (*Peinture*) nocturne, night scene ③ NF evening fixture; [*magasin*] late night opening; **réunion en ~** evening meeting; (*Sport*) **la rencontre sera jouée en ~** the game will be played under floodlights; **le magasin est ouvert en ~ le vendredi** the shop is open *ou* opens late on Fridays

nodal, e (*mpl* **-aux**) [nɔdal, o] ADJ (*Phys, Ling*) nodal

nodosité [nɔdozite] NF (= *corps dur*) node, nodule; (= *état*) knottiness, nodosity (*SPÉC*)

nodule [nɔdyl] NM nodule; **~ polymétallique** polymetallic nodule

Noé [nɔe] NM Noah

▼**Noël** [nɔɛl] NM ⓐ (= *fête*) Christmas; (= *chant*) (Christmas) carol; **à la ~** at Christmas (time); **que faites-vous pour (la) ~?** what are you doing for *ou* at Christmas?; **joyeux ~!** merry *ou* happy Christmas!; **~ au balcon, Pâques au tison** a warm Christmas means a cold Easter → **bûche, sapin, veille** ⓑ (= *cadeau*) **noël** Christmas present; **que veux-tu pour ton (petit) noël?** what would you like for Christmas?

nœud [nø] ① NM ⓐ (*gén : pour attacher*) knot; (*ornemental : de ruban*) bow; **faire/défaire un ~** to make *ou* tie/untie *ou* undo a knot *ou* bow; **la fillette avait des ~s dans les cheveux** (*rubans*) the little girl had bows *ou* ribbons in her hair; (*cheveux emmêlés*) the little girl's hair was all tangled; **fais un ~ à ton mouchoir!** *ou* make a knot in your hanky!; **avoir un ~ dans la gorge** to have a lump in one's throat; **il y a un ~!*** there's a hitch! *ou* snag!; **les ~s d'un serpent** the coils of a snake; **~ de perles/de diamants** pearl/diamond knot → **corde** ⓑ (*Naut* = *vitesse*) knot → **filer** ⓒ (= *protubérance*) [*planche, canne*] knot; [*branche, tige*] knot, node ⓓ (*fig*) **le ~ de** [*problème, débat*] the crux *ou* nub of; (*Littérat, Théât*) **le ~ de l'intrigue** the crux of the plot ⓔ (*littér* = *lien*) bond; **le (saint) ~ du mariage** the bonds of (holy) wedlock; **les ~s de l'amitié** the bonds *ou* ties of friendship ⓕ (*Astron, Élec, Géog, Ling, Phys, Tech*) node ⓖ (: = *pénis*) cock:*, dick:*, prick:*

ⓗ (: = *crétin*) ninny:*; **il est ~~*** he's a real ninny*

② COMP ► **nœud autoroutier** interchange ► **nœud de chaise** bowline ► **nœud coulant** slipknot, running knot ► **nœud de cravate** tie knot; **faire son ~ de cravate** to knot one's tie ► **nœud ferroviaire** (= *endroit*) rail junction ► **nœud gordien** Gordian knot; **couper** *ou* **trancher le ~ gordien** to cut the Gordian knot ► **nœud pap***, **nœud papillon** bow tie ► **nœud plat** reef knot ► **nœud routier** (= *endroit*) crossroad(s) ► **nœud de vache** granny knot ► **nœud de vipères** (*lit, fig*) nest of vipers ► **nœud vital** nerve centre

noir, e [nwar] ① ADJ ⓐ (= *couleur : gén*) black; [*yeux*] dark; [*fumée, mer, ciel, nuage*] black, dark; **~ de coups** black and blue; **~ comme du jais/de l'encre** jet/ink(y) black, black as jet/ink; **~ comme du cirage** as black as soot; **~ comme l'ébène** jet-black; **mets-moi ça ~ sur blanc** put it down in black and white for me; **je l'ai vu/c'est écrit ~ sur blanc** I saw it/it is (written down) in black and white; **les murs étaient ~s de crasse/suie** the walls were black with dirt/soot; **avoir les mains ~es/les ongles ~s** to have dirty *ou* grubby hands/dirty *ou* grubby fingernails → **beurre, chemise, marée** ⓑ [*personne, race*] black ⓒ (* = *bronzé*) black ⓓ (= *obscur*) dark; **il faisait ~ comme dans un four*** it was pitch dark; **la rue était ~e de monde** the street was teeming *ou* swarming with people → **boîte, chambre, nuit** ⓔ (*fig*) [*désespoir*] deep; [*humeur, pressentiment, colère*] black; [*idée*] gloomy, sombre (*Brit*), somber (*US*); [*jour, année*] dark; **faire un tableau assez ~ de la situation** to paint a rather black *ou* gloomy picture of the situation; (*Hist*) **le jeudi ~** black Thursday; **plongé dans le plus ~ désespoir** *ou* **le désespoir le plus ~** plunged in the depths of despair; **être dans la misère ~e** to be in utter *ou* abject poverty → **bête, humour, liste** *etc* ⓕ (= *hostile, mauvais*) [*âme, ingratitude, trahison, regard*] black; **regarder qn d'un œil ~** to give sb a black look; **il se trame un ~ complot** some dark plot is being hatched; **nourrir de ~s desseins** to be plotting dark deeds → **magie, messe** ⓖ (= *policier*) **roman ~** thriller; **film ~** film noir ⓗ (* = *ivre*) drunk, sloshed:*, tight*

② NM ⓐ (= *couleur*) black; **photo/télévision en ~ et blanc** black and white photo/television; **film en ~ et blanc** black and white film; (*Photo*) **le ~ et blanc** black and white *ou* monochrome photography; (*Casino*) **le ~** black; **le ~ de ses cheveux accentuait sa pâleur** her dark *ou* black hair accentuated her pallor, the blackness of her hair accentuated her pallor; **la mer était d'un ~ d'encre** the sea was inky black; (*fig*) **peindre les choses en ~** to paint things black, paint a black picture; **voir les choses en ~** to take a black view of things; **il voit tout en ~** he sees the black side of everything → **broyer, pousser** ⓑ (= *matière*) **elle avait du ~ sur le menton** she had a black mark *ou* smudge on her chin; **se mettre du ~ aux yeux** to put black eyeliner on; **~ de fumée** lampblack; **~ animal** bone charcoal ⓒ (*Habillement*) **elle ne porte jamais de ~** ◇ **elle n'est jamais en ~** she never wears black; **elle est en ~** she is in *ou* is wearing black; (*en deuil*) she is in mourning ⓓ (= *obscurité*) dark, darkness; **avoir peur du ~** to be afraid of the dark; **dans le ~** (*lit*) in the dark *ou* darkness; (*fig*) in the dark; **nous sommes dans le ~ le plus complet** we're completely in the dark ⓔ (* = *café*) (**petit) ~** (= cup of) black coffee ③ **Noir(e)** NM,F black (person); **les Noirs d'Amérique** American blacks, African Americans

► GRAMMAIRE ACTIVE: **Noël** 50.2

4 noire NF (*Mus*) crotchet (*Brit*), quarter note (*US*)

5 au noir LOC ADV (= *illégalement*) **acheter/ vendre au ~** to buy/sell on the black market; **travailler au ~** (*gén*) to work on the side; (*deuxième emploi*) to moonlight; [*clandestin*] to work illegally; **le travail au ~** (*gén*) working on the side; (= *deuxième emploi*) moonlighting; **il se fait payer au ~** he gets paid cash in hand; **embaucher qn au ~** to hire sb without declaring him

noirâtre [nwaʀɑtʀ] ADJ blackish

noiraud, e [nwaʀo, od] **1** ADJ dark, swarthy **2** NM,F dark ou swarthy person

noirceur [nwaʀsœʀ] NF (*littér*) **a** (= *couleur noire*: *gén*) blackness; [*fumée, mer, ciel, nuage, temps, nuit*] blackness, darkness **b** (= *perfidie*) [*âme, ingratitude, trahison, dessein, regard*] blackness **c** (= *acte perfide*) black ou evil deed

noircir [nwaʀsiʀ] ▶ conjug 2 ◀ **1** VT **a** (= *salir*) [*fumée*] to blacken; [*encre, charbon*] to dirty; **les murs noircis par la crasse** walls black with dirt; (*fig*) **~ du papier** to write page after page **b** (= *colorer*) to blacken; (*à la cire, à la peinture*) to darken **c** (= *dénigrer*) [+ *réputation*] to blacken; **~ qn** to blacken sb's reputation ou name **d** (= *assombrir*) **~ le tableau ou la réalité** to paint a black picture of the situation **2** VI [*fruit, légume*] to go black, discolour (*Brit*), discolor (*US*); [*ciel*] to darken, grow black ou dark; [*couleur*] to darken **3** **se noircir** VPR **a** [*ciel*] to darken, grow black ou dark; [*temps*] to turn stormy; [*couleur, bois*] to darken **b** (†‡ = *s'enivrer*) to get plastered‡

noircissement [nwaʀsismɑ̃] NM **a** (= *salissure*) (*par la fumée*) blackening; (*par l'encre, le charbon*) dirtying **b** (= *coloration*) blackening; (*à la cire, à la peinture*) darkening; [*fruit, légume*] blackening, discolouring (*Brit*), discoloring (*US*); [*ciel*] darkening; **pour éviter le ~ de l'avocat** to stop the avocado discolouring

noircissure [nwaʀsisyʀ] NF black smudge

noise [nwaz] NF **chercher ~ ou des ~s à qn** to try to pick a quarrel with sb

noisetier [nwaz(ə)tje] NM hazel tree

noisette [nwazɛt] **1** NF (= *fruit*) hazel(nut); (= *café*) espresso coffee with a drop of milk; (= *morceau*) **~ de beurre** knob of butter; (*Culin*) **~ d'agneau** noisette of lamb **2** ADJ INV [*couleur, yeux*] hazel; **beurre ~** browned butter → **pomme**

noix [nwa] **1** NF (= *fruit*) walnut; (‡ = *idiot*) nut‡; (*Culin*) [*côtelette*] eye; **à la ~‡** pathetic‡, crummy‡ ▶ **brou, coquille, gîte1** **2** COMP ▶ **noix de beurre** knob of butter ▶ **noix du Brésil** Brazil nut ▶ **noix de cajou** cashew nut ▶ **noix de coco** coconut ▶ **noix de galle** oak apple, oak-gall ▶ **noix (de) muscade** nutmeg ▶ **noix pâtissière** cushion of veal ▶ **noix de pécan** pecan nut ▶ **noix de veau** cushion of veal ▶ **noix vomique** nux vomica

nolens volens [nɔlɛ̃svɔlɛ̃s] ADV (*frm*) willingly or unwillingly

noliser [nɔlize] ▶ conjug 1 ◀ VT to charter; **avion nolisé** charter plane

nom [nɔ̃] **1** NM **a** (= *nom propre*) name; **~ de fille/de garçon** girl's/boy's name; **vos ~ et prénom ?** your surname and first name, please?; **Henri le troisième du ~** Henry III; **un homme du ~ de Dupont** ou **qui a (pour) ~ Dupont** a man called Dupont, a man by the name of Dupont; **il porte le ~ de sa mère** he has his mother's surname; **il ne connaît pas ses élèves par leur ~** he doesn't know his pupils by name ou by their names; **je le connais de ~** I know him by name; **il écrit sous le ~ de Martin Suard** he writes under the name of Martin Suard; **c'est un ~ ou ce n'est qu'un ~ pour moi** he ou it is just a name to me!; **je n'arrive pas à mettre un ~ sur son visage** I can't put a name to his (ou her) face; (*péj*) **~ à coucher dehors‡** unpronounceable ou impossible-sounding name; (*péj*) **~ à charnière ou à rallonge ou à tiroirs** double-barrelled name → **faux2, petit, répondre**

b (= *désignation*) name; **quel est le ~ de cet arbre ?** what is the name of this tree?, what's this tree called?; **c'est une sorte de fascisme qui n'ose pas dire son ~** it's fascism of a kind hiding under ou behind another name; **c'est du dirigisme qui n'ose pas dire son ~** it's covert ou disguised state control; **comme son ~ l'indique** as is indicated by its name, as the name indicates; **il appelle les choses par leur ~** he's not afraid to call a spade a spade; **les beaux ~s de justice, de liberté** these fine-sounding words of justice and liberty; **il n'est spécialiste que de ~** he is only nominally a specialist, he is a specialist in name only; **crime sans ~** unspeakable crime; **ce qu'il a fait n'a pas de ~** what he did was unspeakable

c (= *célébrité*) name; (= *noblesse*) name; **se faire un ~** to make a name for o.s.; **laisser un ~** to make one's mark; **c'est un (grand) ~ dans l'histoire** he's one of the great names of history

d (*Gram*) noun → **complément**

e (*loc*) **en mon/votre ~** in my/your name; **il a parlé au ~ de tous les employés** he spoke for all ou on behalf of all the employees; **au ~ de la loi, ouvrez** open up in the name of the law; **au ~ de quoi vous permettez-vous ... ?** whatever gives you the right to ...?; **au ~ du Père, du Fils ...** in the name of the Father and of the Son ...; **au ~ du ciel !** in heaven's name!; **au ~ de ce que vous avez de plus cher** in the name of everything you hold most dear; **~ de Dieu !‡** God damn it!‡, bloody hell!‡ (*Brit*); **~ de ~ !** ou **d'un chien !** ou **d'une pipe !** ou **d'un petit bonhomme !*** heck!*, blimey!* (*Brit*); **donner à qn des ~s d'oiseaux** to call sb names; **traiter qn de tous les ~s** to call sb everything under the sun

2 COMP ▶ **nom de baptême** Christian name, given name (*US*) ▶ **nom de chose** concrete noun ▶ **nom commercial** (*company*) name ▶ **nom commun** common noun ▶ **nom composé** compound (*word* ou *noun*) ▶ **nom déposé** (registered) trade name ▶ **nom d'emprunt** (*gén*) alias, assumed name; (*écrivain*) pen name, nom de plume; **se présenter sous un ~ d'emprunt** to use an assumed name ou an alias ▶ **nom de famille** surname ▶ **nom de femme mariée** married name ▶ **nom de guerre** nom de guerre ▶ **nom de jeune fille** maiden name ▶ **nom de lieu** place name ▶ **nom de marque** trade name ▶ **nom de plume** nom de plume, pen name ▶ **nom propre** proper noun ▶ **nom de rue** street name ▶ **nom de scène** ou **de théâtre** stage name

nomade [nɔmad] **1** ADJ [*peuple, vie*] nomadic; (*Zool*) migratory **2** NMF (*Ethnol*) nomad; (= *gitan*) traveller

nomadisme [nɔmadism] NM nomadism

no man's land [nɔmanslɑ̃d] NM no-man's-land

nombrable [nɔ̃bʀabl] ADJ countable, numerable; **difficilement ~** difficult to count

nombre [nɔ̃bʀ] **1** NM **a** (*Ling, Sci*) number; **loi des grands ~s** law of large numbers; (*Bible*) **les Nombres** (the Book of) Numbers; **~s rationnels/réels** rational/real numbers; (*Gram*) **s'accorder en ~** to agree in number

b (= *quantité*) number; **le ~ des victimes** the number of victims; **un certain/grand ~ de** a certain/great number of; **dans (un) bon ~ de pays** in a good ou great many countries; **je lui ai dit ~ de fois que ...** I've told him many ou a number of times that ...; **depuis ~ d'années** for many years, for a number of years; **les gagnants sont au ~ de 3** there are 3 winners, the winners are 3 in number; **être supérieur en ~** to be superior in numbers; **être en ~ suffisant** to be in sufficient number(s) ou sufficient in number; **ils sont en ~ égal** their numbers are equal ou even, they are equal in number; **des ennemis sans ~** innumerable ou countless enemies

c (= *masse*) numbers; **être/venir en ~** to be/come in large numbers; **faire ~** to make up the number(s); **être submergé par le ~** ◊ **succomber sous le ~** to be overcome by sheer weight of ou force of numbers; **il y en avait dans le ~ qui riaient** there were some among them who were laughing; **ça ne se verra pas dans le ~** it won't be seen among all the rest ou when they're all together; **pour le plus grand ~** for the great majority (of people)

d (= *parmi*) **je le compte au ~ de mes amis** I count him as ou consider him one of my friends, I number him among my friends; **il n'est plus du ~ des vivants** he is no longer of this world; **est-il du ~ des reçus ?** is he among those who passed?

2 COMP ▶ **nombre aléatoire** random number ▶ **nombre atomique** atomic number ▶ **nombre complexe** complex number ▶ **nombre entier** whole number, integer ▶ **nombre imaginaire** imaginary number ▶ **nombre d'or** golden section ▶ **nombre parfait** perfect number ▶ **nombre premier** prime number → **Mach**

nombrer [nɔ̃bʀe] ▶ conjug 1 ◀ VT († ou *littér*) to number†, count

nombreux, -euse [nɔ̃bʀø, øz] ADJ **a** (= *en grand nombre*) **être ~** [*exemples, visiteurs*] to be numerous; [*accidents*] to be numerous ou frequent; **les cambriolages sont très ~ dans ce quartier** there are a great many burglaries in that area; **~ furent ceux qui ...** there were many who ...; **les gens étaient venus ~** a great number of people had come, people had come in great numbers; **venez ~ !** all welcome!; **certains, et ils sont ~** certain people, and there are quite a few of them; **peu ~** few; **le public était moins/plus ~ hier** there were fewer/more spectators yesterday; **nous ne sommes pas si ~** there aren't so many of us; **les visiteurs arrivaient sans cesse plus ~/de plus en plus ~** visitors kept on arriving in greater ou increasing numbers/in greater and greater ou in ever-increasing numbers; **ils étaient plus ~ que nous** they outnumbered us, there were more of them than of us

b (= *le grand nombre*) numerous, many; **parmi les nombreuses personnalités** amongst the numerous ou many personalities

c (= *un grand nombre de*) **de ~** [*accidents, exemples*] many, numerous

d (= *important*) [*foule, assistance, collection*] large

nombril [nɔ̃bʀi(l)] NM [*personne*] navel, belly button*; **il se prend pour le ~ du monde*** he thinks he's the cat's whiskers* ou God's gift to mankind; **se regarder le ~*** to contemplate one's navel

nombrilisme* [nɔ̃bʀilism] NM (*péj*) navel-gazing; **faire du ~** to contemplate one's navel

nombriliste* [nɔ̃bʀilist] ADJ, NMF **être ~** to spend one's time contemplating one's navel

nomenclature [nɔmɑ̃klatyʀ] NF (*gén* = *liste*) list; (*Ling, Sci*) nomenclature; [*dictionnaire*] word list

nomenklatura [nɔmɛnklatuʀa] NF (*Pol*) nomenklatura, elite

nominal, e [*mpl* **-aux**] [nɔminal, o] **1** ADJ **a** (*gén*) nominal; (*Ling*) [*groupe, phrase*] nominal, noun (*épith*); **liste ~e** list of names; **procéder à l'appel** to call the register ou the roll, do the roll call; **expression ~e** nominal expression; **syntagme ~** noun phrase **b** (= *sans réalité*) [*autorité, pouvoir*] nominal **c** (*Écon, Fin*) [*salaire*] nominal → **valeur d** (*Tech*) [*puissance, vitesse*] rated **2** NM (*Ling*) pronoun

nominalement [nɔminalmɑ̃] ADV (*gén, Ling*) nominally; **appeler qn ~** to call sb by name

nominalisation [nɔminalizasjɔ̃] NF nominalization

nominaliser [nɔminalize] ▶conjug 1◀ VT to nominalize

nominalisme [nɔminalism] NM nominalism

nominaliste [nɔminalist] ADJ, NMF nominalist

nominatif, -ive [nɔminatif, iv] ① ADJ (Fin) [titre, action] registered; (Comm) **état ~** list of items; **liste nominative** list of names; **carte nominative** nontransferable card; **l'invitation n'est pas nominative** the invitation doesn't specify a name ② NM (Ling) nominative

nomination [nɔminasjɔ̃] NF ⓐ (= promotion) appointment, nomination (**à** to); (= titre, acte) appointment ou nomination papers; **obtenir sa ~** to be nominated ou appointed (**au poste de** to the post of); **le film a reçu 6 ~s aux Oscars** the film has received 6 Oscar nominations ⓑ (Ling, Philo) naming

nominativement [nɔminativmã] ADV by name

nominé, e [nɔmine] ADJ [film, acteur, auteur] nominated; **être ~ à qch** to be nominated ou shortlisted for sth

nommément [nɔmemã] ADV ⓐ (= par son nom) by name ⓑ (= spécialement) notably, especially, particularly

nommer [nɔme] ▶conjug 1◀ ① VT ⓐ (= promouvoir) [+ fonctionnaire] to appoint; [+ candidat] to nominate; **~ qn à un poste** to appoint ou nominate sb to a post; **~ qn son héritier** to name ou appoint sb (as) one's heir; **il a été nommé gérant/ministre** he was appointed ou made manager/minister
ⓑ (= appeler) [+ personne] to call, name; (= dénommer) [+ découverte, produit] to name, give a name to; **ils l'ont nommé Richard** they called ou named him Richard, they gave him the name of Richard; **un homme nommé Martin** a man named ou called ou by the name of Martin; **le nommé Martin** the man named ou called Martin; **ce que nous nommons le bonheur** what we call happiness → **point**¹
ⓒ (= citer) [+ fleuves, batailles, auteurs, complices] to name; (hum) **M. Sartin, pour ne pas le ~,** without mentioning any names, Mr Sartin ...; **quelqu'un que je ne nommerai pas** somebody who shall remain nameless, somebody whose name I shall not mention
② **se nommer** VPR ⓐ (= s'appeler) to be called; **comment se nomme-t-il?** what is he called?, what is his name?; **il se nomme Paul** he's called Paul, his name is Paul
ⓑ (= se présenter) to introduce o.s.; **il entra et se nomma** he came in and gave his name ou introduced himself

---

non [nɔ̃]

| ① ADVERBE | ③ PRÉFIXE |
| ② NOM MASCULIN INV | ④ COMPOSÉS |

① ADVERBE

ⓐ réponse négative no; **le connaissez-vous?** — **~ / je ne le crois ~** do you know him? — no (I don't); **est-elle chez elle?** — **~ /~** is she at home? — no (she isn't ou she's not); **je vais ouvrir la fenêtre** — **~ il y aura des courants d'air** I'll open the window — no (don't), it'll make a draught; **il n'a pas encore dit ~!** he hasn't said no yet!, he hasn't refused yet!; **je ne dis pas ~** (= ce n'est pas de refus) I wouldn't say no; (= je n'en disconviens pas) I don't disagree; **ah ça ~!** certainly ou definitely not!, no way!*; **~ et ~!** no, no, no!, absolutely not!; **que ~!** I should say not!, definitely not!; **~ merci!** no thank you!; **certes ~!** most certainly ou definitely not!; **vous n'y allez pas?** — **mais ~!** ou **bien sûr que ~!** aren't you going? — of course not! ou I should think not!; **répondre (par) ~ à toutes les questions** to answer no ou answer in the negative to all the questions; **faire ~ de la tête** to shake one's head

ⓑ remplaçant une proposition not; **est-ce que c'est nécessaire?** — **je pense ou crois que ~** is that necessary? — I don't think so; **je pense que ~** I think not; **je crains que ~** I'm afraid not, I fear not (frm); **il nous quitte?** — **j'espère que ~** is he leaving us? — I hope not ou I hope he isn't; **je le crois — moi ~** I believe him — well I don't ou not me*; **il l'aime bien, moi ~** he likes him but I don't; **dire/répondre que ~** to say/answer it isn't (ou it won't etc); **j'ai demandé si elle était venue, lui dit que ~** I asked if she had come — he says not ou he says no ou he says she hadn't; **ah ~?** really?, no?; **partez-vous ou ~?** are you going or not?, are you going or aren't you?; **il se mandait s'il irait ou ~** he wondered whether to go or not; **erreur ou ~/qu'il l'ait voulu ou ~ le mal est fait** mistake or no mistake/whether he meant it or not the damage is done → **signe**

ⓒ frm = pas not; **c'est par paresse et ~ par prudence que ...** it is through laziness and not caution that ...; **je veux bien de leur aide mais ~ de leur argent** I'm willing to accept their help but not their money ou but I want none of their money; **c'est votre avis ~ le mien** it's your opinion not mine

ⓓ exprimant l'impatience, l'indignation **tu vas cesser de pleurer ~?** will you stop crying?, just stop that crying(, will you?); **~ par exemple!** for goodness sake!, good gracious!; **~ mais alors!** ◊ **~ mais (des fois)!*** for goodness sake!*, honestly!; **~ mais des fois, tu me prends pour qui?*** look here* ou for God's sake,* what do you take me for?; **~ mais je rêve!*** I don't believe this!

ⓔ exprimant le doute no?; **il me l'a dit lui-même — ~?** he told me so himself — no? ou really?; **c'est bon, ~?** it's good, isn't it?

ⓕ
♦ **non** + adverbe ou conjonction ou préposition not; **~ loin d'ici, il y a ...** not far from here there's ...; **c'est une expérience ~ moins intéressante** it's an experience that is no less interesting; **il est ~ moins vrai/évident que ...** it is nonetheless true/obvious that ...; **un homme ~ pas érudit mais instruit** a man who is not erudite but well-informed; **~ pas que j'aie peur, mais ...** not that I'm afraid, but ...; **il a fait ~ sans raison/~ sans mal** he did it not without reason/difficulty; **il y est allé ~ sans protester** he went, but not without protest ou protesting → **seulement**

♦ **non plus** : **il a continué ~ plus en voiture mais en train** he continued on his way, no longer by car but by train; **il parle ~ plus en médecin mais en ami** he is talking now not as a doctor but as a friend; **ils sont désormais associés, et ~ plus rivaux** they're no longer rivals ou they're not rivals any more but associates; **il n'a pas hésité, ~ plus qu'eux d'ailleurs** he didn't hesitate any more than they did

♦ pronom personnel + **non plus** : **il ne l'a pas vu ni moi ~ plus** he didn't see him and neither did I ou and I didn't either; **nous ne l'avons pas vu — nous ~ plus** we didn't see him — neither did we ou we didn't either; **nous ~ plus nous ne l'avons pas vu** we didn't see him either; **il n'a pas compris lui ~ plus** he didn't understand either

② NOM MASCULIN INV
no; **répondre par un ~ catégorique** to reply with a categorical no; **il y a eu 30 ~** there were 30 votes against ou 30 noes → **oui**

③ PRÉFIXE
Dans les mots composés à trait d'union, le préfixe reste invariable.

ⓐ
♦ **non** + adjectif ou participe
Pour ce type de composés (ex: non coupable, non négligeable, non polluant etc), cherchez ci-dessous ou sous l'adjectif concerné.

---

non-, un-; **~ ferreux/gazeux** non-ferrous/gaseous; **~ vérifié** unverified; **~ spécialisé** un-specialized, non-specialized; **les objets ~ réclamés** unclaimed items; **toutes les places ~ réservées** all the unreserved seats, all seats not reserved; **les travaux ~ terminés** the unfinished work

ⓑ
♦ **non-** + nom: **la ~-reconnaissance de qch** the fact that sth is unrecognized; **en cas de (-)réponse** if there is no reply; **le ~-respect de cette règle entraînerait la rupture du contrat** non-observance of this rule will result in breach of contract

④ COMPOSÉS
▶ **non accompli, e** ADJ (Ling) continuous ▶ **non arrondi, e** ADJ (Phon) spread ▶ **non dénombrable** ADJ (Ling) uncountable ▶ **non directif, -ive** ADJ [entretien, questionnaire] with no leading questions; [thérapie] nondirective ▶ **non existant, e** ADJ nonexistent ▶ **non lucratif, -ive** ADJ à but ~ lucratif non-profit-making ▶ **non marqué, e** ADJ (Ling) unmarked ▶ **non voisé, e** ADJ (Phon) unvoiced, voiceless

---

non-activité [nɔnaktivite] NF inactivity

nonagénaire [nɔnaʒenɛʀ] ADJ, NMF nonagenarian, ninety-year-old

non-agression [nɔnagʀesjɔ̃] NF non-aggression

non-aligné, e [nɔnaliɲe] ADJ nonaligned

non-alignement [nɔnaliɲmã] NM nonalignment

nonante [nɔnãt] ADJ (Belg, Helv) ninety

nonantième [nɔnãtjɛm] ADJ (Belg, Helv) ninetieth

non-appartenance [nɔnapaʀtənãs] NF (à un parti, un organisme) non-membership; **sa ~ à l'ethnie dominante** the fact that he did not belong to the dominant ethnic group

non-assistance [nɔnasistãs] NF (Jur) **~ à personne en danger** failure to assist a person in danger

non-belligérance [nɔbeliʒeʀãs] NF non-belligerence

non-belligérant, e [nɔbeliʒeʀã, ãt] ADJ, NM,F nonbelligerent

nonce [nɔ̃s] NM nuncio; **~ apostolique** apostolic nuncio

nonchalamment [nɔ̃ʃalamã] ADV nonchalantly

nonchalance [nɔ̃ʃalãs] NF nonchalance

nonchalant, e [nɔ̃ʃalã, ãt] ADJ nonchalant

nonciature [nɔ̃sjatyʀ] NF nunciature

non-combattant, e [nɔ̃kɔ̃batã, ãt] ADJ, NM,F noncombatant

non-communication [nɔ̃kɔmynikasjɔ̃] NF ⓐ [document, information] non-disclosure ⓑ (dans une entreprise, un couple) non-communication, lack of communication

non-comparution [nɔ̃kɔ̃paʀysjɔ̃] NF (Jur) nonappearance

non-conciliation [nɔ̃kɔ̃siljasjɔ̃] NF refusal to settle out of court

non-concurrence [nɔ̃kɔ̃kyʀãs] NF lack of competition; **clause de ~** non-competition clause, non-compete clause (surtout US)

non-conformisme [nɔ̃kɔ̃fɔʀmism] NM non-conformism

non-conformiste [nɔ̃kɔ̃fɔʀmist] ADJ, NM,F nonconformist

non-conformité [nɔ̃kɔ̃fɔʀmite] NF nonconformity

non-contradiction [nɔ̃kɔ̃tʀadiksjɔ̃] NF **principe de ~** law of noncontradiction

non-covalent, e [nɔ̃kɔvalã, ãt] ADJ non-covalent

non-croyant, e [nɔ̃kʀwajã, ãt] NM,F unbeliever, non-believer

non-cumul [nɔ̃kymyl] NM (*Jur*) **il y a ~ de peines** sentences run concurrently; **le principe
du ~ des fonctions** the rule prohibiting anyone from holding more than one post at a
time

non-dénonciation [nɔ̃denɔ̃sjasjɔ̃] NF [*crime,
sévices*] failure to report; **il a été poursuivi
pour ~ de malfaiteur** he was prosecuted for
failing to report an offence

non-discrimination [nɔ̃diskriminasjɔ̃] NF
nondiscrimination

non-dit [nɔ̃di] NM what is left unsaid; **cette
dispute a fait ressortir tous les ~s** during the
row everything that had been bottled up and
left unsaid came out into the open

non-droit [nɔ̃drwa] NM **zone de ~** ≈ no-go
area*, *urban area where law and order have broken down*; **État de ~** *state in which human and
civil rights are not respected*

non-engagé, **e** [nɔ̃nɑ̃gaʒe] ADJ [*artiste*] with
no political commitment; [*pays*] neutral,
nonaligned

non-engagement [nɔ̃nɑ̃gaʒmɑ̃] NM noninvolvement

non-être [nɔ̃nɛtr] NM (*Philo*) non-being

non-euclidien, **-ienne** [nɔ̃nøklidjɛ̃, jɛn] ADJ
non-Euclidean

non-événement [nɔ̃nevɛnmɑ̃] NM nonevent

non-exécution [nɔ̃nɛgzekysjɔ̃] NF [*contrat*]
non-completion

non-existence [nɔ̃nɛgzistɑ̃s] NF nonexistence

non-figuratif, **-ive** [nɔ̃figyratif, iv] ADJ non-
representational

non-fumeur, **-euse** [nɔ̃fymœr, øz] [1] ADJ
no-smoking (*épith*) [2] NM,F non-smoker
(**compartiment**) **~s** non-smoking compartment (*Brit*) ou car (*US*), non-smoker; (*en avion*)
place fumeur ou ~? smoking or non-
smoking?

non-ingérence [nɔ̃nɛ̃ʒerɑ̃s] NF noninter-
ference

non-initié, **e** [nɔ̃ninisje] [1] ADJ [*lecteur*] lay;
[*observateur*] uninformed [2] NM,F lay person;
pour les ~s to the uninitiated

non-inscrit, **e** [nɔ̃nɛ̃skri, it] (*Pol*) [1] ADJ independent [2] NM,F independent (member)

non-intervention [nɔ̃nɛ̃tɛrvɑ̃sjɔ̃] NF non-
intervention

non-interventionniste [nɔ̃nɛ̃tɛrvɑ̃sjɔnist]
ADJ, NMF noninterventionist

non-jouissance [nɔ̃ʒwisɑ̃s] NF (*Jur*)
nonenjoyment

non-lieu [*pl* **non-lieux**] [nɔ̃ljø] NM (*Jur*) (**arrêt
ou ordonnance de**) **~** dismissal of a charge;
bénéficier d'un ~ to be discharged ou have
one's case dismissed for lack of evidence; **rendre une ordonnance de ~** to dismiss a case for
lack of evidence, direct a nonsuit

non-moi [nɔ̃mwa] NM INV (*Philo*) nonego

nonne [nɔn] NF (††, *hum*) nun

nonnette [nɔnɛt] NF (*Culin*) spiced bun (*made
of pain d'épice*)

nonobstant [nɔnɔpstɑ̃] [1] PRÉP († *ou Jur* =
malgré) notwithstanding, despite, in spite of
[2] ADV († = *néanmoins*) notwithstanding†,
nevertheless

non-paiement [nɔ̃pɛmɑ̃] NM nonpayment

nonpareil, **-eille**†† [nɔ̃parɛj] ADJ nonpareil,
peerless

non-partant [nɔ̃partɑ̃] NM (*Sport*) non-
runner

non-parution [nɔ̃parysjɔ̃] NF failure to appear ou be published

non-pratiquant, **e** [nɔ̃pratikɑ̃, ɑ̃t] NM,F (*Rel,
gén*) person who does not practise his ou her
religion; (= *chrétien*) non-churchgoer

non-prolifération [nɔ̃proliferasjɔ̃] NF non-
proliferation

non-recevoir [nɔ̃r(ə)səvwar] NM INV (*Jur*) demurrer, objection; (*fig*) blunt refusal; **il m'a
opposé une fin de ~** he turned down my request point-blank

non-résident, **e** [nɔ̃rezidɑ̃, ɑ̃t] NM,F nonresi-
dent

non-respect [nɔ̃rɛspɛ] NM [*droit, engagement,
règle*] failure to respect; **en cas de ~ des délais
...** if the deadlines are not met ou observed ...

non-retour [nɔ̃rətur] NM no return → **point**[1]

non-rétroactivité [nɔ̃rɛtrɔaktivite] NF (*Jur*)
nonretroactivity

non-salarié, **e** [nɔ̃salarje] NM,F self-employed
person

non-sens [nɔ̃sɑ̃s] NM INV (= *absurdité*) (piece
of) nonsense; (= *erreur de traduction*) meaningless word (*ou phrase etc*)

non-signataire [nɔ̃siɲatɛr] NMF non-
signatory

non-spécialiste [nɔ̃spesjalist] NMF nonspecialist

non-stop [nɔ̃stɔp] ADJ INV, ADV non-stop

non-syndiqué, **e** [nɔ̃sɛ̃dike] [1] ADJ
nonunion(ized) [2] NM,F nonunion member,
nonmember (of a ou the union)

non-valeur [nɔ̃valœr] NF [a] (*Jur*) unproductiveness; (*Fin*) bad debt; (*fig*) nonproductive
asset, wasted asset [b] (*péj = personne*) nonentity

non-violence [nɔ̃vjɔlɑ̃s] NF nonviolence

non-violent, **e** [nɔ̃vjɔlɑ̃, ɑ̃t] [1] ADJ nonviolent [2] NM,F advocate ou supporter of non-
violence

non-voyant, **e** [nɔ̃vwajɑ̃, ɑ̃t] [1] NM,F visually
handicapped ou impaired person [2] ADJ visually handicapped ou impaired

noosphère [noosfɛr] NF noosphere

noradrénaline [nɔradrenalin] NF noradrena-
lin(e) (*Brit*), norepinephrine (*US*)

nord [nɔr] [1] NM [a] (= *point cardinal*) north;
~ géographique/magnétique true/magnetic
north; **le vent du ~** the north wind; **un vent
du ~** (*gén*) a north(erly) wind; (*Naut*) a northerly; **le vent tourne/est au ~** the wind is
veering north(wards) ou towards the north/is
blowing from the north; **regarder vers le ~** ou
dans la direction du ~ to look north(wards) ou
towards the north; **au ~** (*situation*) in the
north; (*direction*) to the north, north(wards);
au ~ de north of, to the north of; **la maison
est (exposée) au ~/en plein ~** the house faces
(the) north ou northwards/due north →
perdre
[b] (= *région*) north; **pays/peuples du ~** northern countries/peoples, countries/peoples of
the north; **l'Europe/l'Italie/la Bourgogne du ~**
Northern Europe/Italy/Burgundy; **la mer du
Nord** the North Sea; **le ~ de la France** ◊ **le
Nord** the North (of France); **les gens du Nord**
(*dans un pays*) Northerners; **le Grand Nord** the
far North
[2] ADJ INV [*région, partie*] northern (*épith*); [*entrée, paroi*] north (*épith*); [*versant, côte*]
north(ern) (*épith*); [*côté*] north(ward) (*épith*);
[*direction*] northward (*épith*), northerly (*Mét*)
→ **hémisphère**, **latitude**, **pôle**

nord-africain, **e** [*mpl* **nord-africains**)
[nɔrafrikɛ̃, ɛn] [1] ADJ North African
[2] **Nord-Africain(e)** NM,F North African

nord-américain, **e** [*mpl* **nord-américains**)
[nɔramerikɛ̃, ɛn] [1] ADJ North American
[2] **Nord-Américain(e)** NM,F North American

nord-coréen, **-enne** (*mpl* **nord-coréens**)
[nɔrkɔreɛ̃, ɛn] [1] ADJ North Korean
[2] **Nord-Coréen(ne)** NM,F North Korean

nord-est [nɔrɛst] ADJ INV, NM northeast

nordique [nɔrdik] [1] ADJ [*pays, race*] Nordic;
[*langues*] Scandinavian, Nordic → **ski**
[2] **Nordique** NMF Nordic

nordiste [nɔrdist] (*Hist US*) [1] ADJ Northern,
Yankee [2] **Nordiste** NMF Northerner, Yankee

nord-nord-est [nɔrnɔrɛst] ADJ INV, NM
north-northeast

nord-nord-ouest [nɔrnɔrwɛst] ADJ INV, NM
north-northwest

nord-ouest [nɔrwɛst] ADJ INV, NM northwest

nord-vietnamien, **-ienne** (*mpl* **nord-
vietnamiens**) [nɔrvjetnamjɛ̃, jɛn] [1] ADJ North
Vietnamese [2] **Nord-Vietnamien(ne)** NM,F
North Vietnamese

noria [nɔrja] NF noria, bucket waterwheel; **une
~ d'hélicoptères transportait les blessés vers
les hôpitaux** a fleet of helicopters shuttled ou
ferried the wounded to the hospitals

normal, **e** (*mpl* **-aux**) [nɔrmal, o] [1] ADJ (*gén,
Chim, Math, Méd*) normal; (= *courant, habituel*)
normal, usual; **de dimension ~e** normal-sized,
standard-sized; **c'est une chose très ~e** ◊ **ça
n'a rien que de très ~** that's quite usual ou
normal; **rien à signaler, tout est ~** nothing to
report, everything is the same as usual; **il
n'est pas ~** he's not normal, there's something wrong with him; **c'est ~!** it's (quite)
natural!; **ce n'est pas ~** (*gén*) there must be
something wrong; (= *ce n'est pas juste*) that's
not right → **état**, **temps**[1]
[2] **normale** NF **s'écarter de la ~e** to diverge from the norm; **revenir à la ~e** to return
to normality, get back to normal; **au-dessus
de la ~e** above average; **température voisine
des ~es saisonnières** temperature close to the
seasonal average [b] (*Math*) normal (**à** to)
[c] **Normale (sup)** (ABRÉV = **École normale
supérieure**) → **école**

normalement [nɔrmalmɑ̃] ADV [*se dérouler,
fonctionner*] normally; **~, il devrait être là demain** he should be here tomorrow; **~ il vient
le jeudi** he usually ou generally comes on a
Thursday; **tu pourras venir? — ~, oui** will you
be able to come? — I should be able to, yes

normalien, **-ienne** [nɔrmaljɛ̃, jɛn] NM,F
(= *futur professeur*) student at the École normale
supérieure; (= *diplômé*) graduate of the École
normale supérieure; (*Hist = futur instituteur*) student at teacher training college

normalisateur, **-trice** [nɔrmalizatœr, tris]
ADJ [*effet*] normalizing; **une conception norma-
lisatrice de l'éducation** a rigidly conventional
approach to education

normalisation [nɔrmalizasjɔ̃] NF [a] (= *régularisation*) [*situation, relations*] normalization;
on espère une ~ des relations diplomatiques
we are hoping diplomatic relations will be
back to normal soon [b] (= *standardisation*)
[*produit*] standardization

normaliser [nɔrmalize] ▸conjug 1◂ [1] VT
[a] (= *régulariser*) [+ *situation, relations*] to normalize [b] (= *standardiser*) [+ *produit*] to standardize; **taille normalisée** standard size [2] **se
normaliser** VPR [a] (= *revenir à la normale*) to
get back to normal; (= *devenir normal*) to normalize [b] (= *devenir standard*) to be standardized

normalité [nɔrmalite] NF normality

normand, **e** [nɔrmɑ̃, ɑ̃d] [1] ADJ (= *de Normandie*) Norman; (*Hist = scandinave*) Norse → **armoire**, **trou** [2] NM [a] (*Ling*) Norman (French)
[b] **Normand** (= *de Normandie*) Norman; (*Hist =
Scandinave*) Norseman, Northman → **réponse**
[3] **Normande** NF (= *de Normandie*) Norman;
(*Hist = Scandinave*) Norsewoman

Normandie [nɔrmɑ̃di] NF Normandy

normatif, **-ive** [nɔrmatif, iv] ADJ prescriptive,
normative

norme [nɔrm] NF (*Math, gén*) norm; (*Tech*)
standard; **~s de fabrication** standards of
manufacture, manufacturing standards; **mettre qch aux ~s de sécurité** to bring sth into
compliance with safety standards; **ce produit
n'est pas conforme aux ~s françaises** this

product doesn't conform to French standards; **tant que ça reste dans la ~** as long as it's kept within limits; **pourvu que vous restiez dans la ~** provided you don't overdo it ou you don't overstep the limits, provided you keep within the norm; **hors ~(s)** [*personnage*] unconventional; [*carrière*] unusual; **c'est une voiture hors ~(s)** it's no ordinary car

normé, e [nɔrme] ADJ (*Math*) normed

normographe [nɔrmɔgraf] NM stencil

nor(r)ois, e [nɔrwa, waz] ADJ, NM Old Norse

Norvège [nɔrvɛʒ] NF Norway; **la mer de ~** the Norwegian sea

norvégien, -ienne [nɔrveʒjɛ̃, jɛn] **1** ADJ Norwegian → **marmite, omelette 2** NM (*Ling*) Norwegian **3 Norvégien(ne)** NM,F Norwegian

nos [no] ADJ POSS → **notre**

nosocomial, e (*mpl* **-iaux**) [nozɔkɔmjal, jo] ADJ nosocomial

nostalgie [nɔstalʒi] NF nostalgia; **avoir** ou **garder la ~ de ...** to feel nostalgic for ...; **avoir la ~ du pays natal** to be homesick

nostalgique [nɔstalʒik] **1** ADJ nostalgic **2** NMF **les ~s des années 60** those who feel nostalgic for the 1960s; **les ~s de la monarchie** those who look back nostalgically to the monarchy

nota (bene) [nɔta (bene)] NM INV nota bene

notabilité [nɔtabilite] NF notability

notable [nɔtabl] **1** ADJ [*fait*] notable, noteworthy; [*changement, progrès*] notable **2** NM notable, worthy

notablement [nɔtabləmɑ̃] ADV notably

notaire [nɔtɛʀ] NM notary (public); (*en Grande-Bretagne*) ≈ solicitor (*Brit*)

notamment [nɔtamɑ̃] ADV (= *entre autres*) notably, among others; (= *plus particulièrement*) notably, in particular, particularly

notarial, e (*mpl* **-iaux**) [nɔtarjal, jo] ADJ **étude ~e** office of a notary (public); (*en Grande-Bretagne*) ≈ solicitor's office

notariat [nɔtarja] NM profession of (a) notary (public); (*en Grande-Bretagne*) ≈ profession of a solicitor

notarié, e [nɔtarje] ADJ drawn up by a notary (public), notarized (SPÉC); (*en Grande-Bretagne*) ≈ drawn up by a solicitor

notation [nɔtasjɔ̃] NF **a** (= *symboles, système*) notation **b** (= *touche, note*) [*couleurs*] touch; [*sons*] variation; (*Littérat*) **une ~ intéressante** an interesting touch ou variation **c** (= *transcription*) [*sentiment, geste, son*] expression **d** (= *jugement*) [*devoir*] marking (*Brit*), grading (*US*); [*employé*] assessment; (*Fin*) **agence de ~ (financière)** (credit) rating agency

note [nɔt] **1** NF **a** (= *remarque, communication*) note; **~ diplomatique/officielle** diplomatic/official note; **prendre des ~s** to take notes; **prendre (bonne) ~ de qch** to take (good) note of sth; **prendre qch en ~** to make a note of sth, write sth down; (*hâtivement*) to jot sth down; **relire ses ~s** to read over one's notes ou jottings; **remarque en ~** marginal comment, comment in the margin; **c'est écrit en ~** it's written in the margin **b** (= *appréciation chiffrée*) mark (*Brit*), grade (*US*); **mettre une ~ à** [+ *dissertation*] to mark (*Brit*), grade (*US*); [+ *élève*] to give a mark to (*Brit*), grade (*US*); [+ *employé*] to assess; **avoir de bonnes/mauvaises ~s** to have good/bad marks ou grades; **avoir une bonne/mauvaise à un devoir/en histoire** to have a good/bad mark for a homework exercise/for ou in history; (*fig*) **c'est une mauvaise ~ pour lui** it's a black mark against him **c** (= *compte*) [*gaz, blanchisserie*] bill, account; [*restaurant, hôtel*] bill (*Brit*), check (*US*); (*à l'hôtel*) **demander/présenter/régler la ~** to ask for/present/settle the bill (*Brit*) ou check (*US*); (*au restaurant*) **vous me donnerez la ~, s'il vous**

plaît may I have the bill (*Brit*) ou check (*US*) please?, I'd like my bill (*Brit*) ou check (*US*) please; **je vais vous faire la ~** I'll make out the bill (*Brit*) ou check (*US*) for you; **mettez-le sur ma ~** put it on my bill (*Brit*) ou check (*US*); **~ de frais** (= *bulletin*) claim form (for expenses); (= *argent dépensé*) expenses; **~ d'honoraires** (doctor's ou lawyer's) account **d** (*Mus, fig*) note; **donner la ~** (*Mus*) to give the key; (*fig*) to set the tone; **la ~ juste** the right note; **c'est tout à fait dans la ~** it fits in perfectly with the rest; **ses paroles étaient tout à fait dans la ~/n'étaient pas dans la ~** his words struck exactly the right note/struck the wrong note (altogether); **ce n'est pas dans la ~** it doesn't strike the right note at all → **faux²** **e** (= *trace, touche*) note, touch; **mettre une ~ triste** ou **de tristesse dans qch** to lend a touch ou note of sadness to sth; **une ~ d'anxiété/de fierté perçait sous ses paroles** a note of anxiety/pride was discernible in his words; [*parfum*] **une ~ de santal** a hint of sandalwood **2** COMP ► **note de l'auteur** author's note ► **note en bas de page** footnote ► **note de conjoncture** economic outlook report ► **note d'information** memorandum ► **note marginale** marginal note, note in the margin ► **note de passage** (*Mus*) passing note ► **note de la rédaction** editor's note ► **note de service** memorandum ► **note du traducteur** translator's note

noter [nɔte] ▸ conjug 1 ◂ VT **a** (= *inscrire*) [+ *adresse, rendez-vous*] to write down, note down, make a note of; [+ *idées*] to jot down, write down, note down; (*Mus*) [+ *air*] to write down, take down; **si vous pouviez le ~ quelque part** could you make a note of it ou write it down somewhere; **notez que nous serons absents** note that we'll be away **b** (= *remarquer*) [+ *faute, progrès*] to notice; **notez la précision du bas-relief** note the fine bas relief work; **on note une certaine amélioration** there has been some improvement, some improvement has been noted; **notez (bien) que je n'ai rien dit ◊ je n'ai rien dit, notez-le notez (bien)** note that I didn't say anything, mark you, I didn't say anything; **il faut ~ qu'il a des excuses** admittedly he has an excuse, he has an excuse mind you ou mark you (*Brit*); **ceci est à ~** ou **mérite d'être noté** this is worth noting ou making a note of **c** (= *cocher, souligner*) [+ *citation, passage*] to mark **d** (= *juger*) [+ *devoir*] to mark, grade (*US*); [+ *élève*] to give a mark to, grade (*US*); [+ *employé*] to assess; **~ sur 10/20** to mark out of 10/20; **devoir bien/mal noté** homework with a good/bad mark ou grade; **employé bien/mal noté** highly/poorly rated employee, employee with a good/bad record; **elle note sévèrement/large** she is a strict/lenient marker

notice [nɔtis] NF (= *préface, résumé*) note; (= *mode d'emploi*) instructions; **~ biographique/bibliographique** biographical/bibliographical note; **~ explicative** ou **d'emploi** directions for use, explanatory leaflet; **~ technique** specification sheet, specifications; **~ nécrologique** obituary

notificatif, -ive [nɔtifikatif, iv] ADJ notifying; **lettre notificative** letter of notification

notification [nɔtifikasjɔ̃] NF (*Admin*) notification; **~ vous a été envoyée de vous présenter** notification has been sent to you to present yourself; **recevoir ~ de** to be notified of, receive notification of; (*Jur*) **~ d'actes** service of documents

notifier [nɔtifje] ▸ conjug 7 ◂ VT to notify; **~ qch à qn** to notify sb of sth, notify sth to sb; **on lui a notifié que ...** he was notified that ..., he received notice that ...; **~ une citation à qn** to serve a summons ou a writ on sb; **il s'est vu ~ son licenciement** he received notice of his dismissal

notion [nɔsjɔ̃] NF **a** (= *conscience*) notion; **je n'ai pas la moindre ~ de** I haven't the faintest notion of; **perdre la ~ du temps** ou **de l'heure** to lose track of the time **b** (= *connaissances*) **~s** notion, elementary knowledge; **avoir quelques ~s de grammaire** to have some notion of grammar, have a smattering of grammar; (*titre*) **~s d'algèbre/d'histoire** algebra/history primer

notionnel, -elle [nɔsjɔnɛl] ADJ notional

notoire [nɔtwaR] ADJ [*criminel, méchanceté*] notorious; [*fait, vérité*] well-known, acknowledged (*épith*); **il est ~ que** it is common ou public knowledge that, it's an acknowledged fact that

notoirement [nɔtwaRmɑ̃] ADV [*insuffisant*] manifestly; [*malhonnête*] notoriously; **c'est ~ reconnu** it's generally recognized, it's well known

notoriété [nɔtɔrjete] NF [*fait*] notoriety; (= *renommée*) fame; **c'est de ~ publique** that's common ou public knowledge

notre (*pl* **nos**) [nɔtR, no] ADJ POSS **a** (*possession, relation*) our; (*emphatique*) our own; **~ fils et ~ fille** our son and daughter; **nous avons tous laissé ~ manteau et ~ chapeau au vestiaire** we have all left our coats and hats in the cloakroom; **~ bonne ville de Tours est en fête** our fine city of Tours is celebrating; *pour autres locutions voir* **son¹** **b** (*valeur affective, ironique, intensive*) **et comment va ~ malade aujourd'hui ?** and how's the ou our patient today?; **~ héros décide alors ...** and so our hero decides ...; **~ homme a filé sans demander son reste** the fellow ou chap (*Brit*) has run off without asking for his due; **voilà ~ bon Martin!** here's good old Martin!; (*dial*) **~ maître** the master; *pour autres locutions voir* **son¹** **c** (*représentant la généralité des hommes*) **~ planète** our planet; **~ corps/esprit** our bodies/minds; **~ maître à tous** our master, the master of us all; **Notre Seigneur/Père** Our Lord/Father; **Notre-Dame** Our Lady; (*église*) Notre Dame, Our Lady; **Notre-Dame de Paris** (*cathédrale*) Notre Dame of Paris; **Notre-Dame de Chartres/Lourdes** Our Lady of Chartres/Lourdes; **le Notre Père** the Lord's Prayer, Our Father **d** (*de majesté, dans un discours etc* = *mon, ma, mes*) our; **car tel est ~ bon plaisir** for such is our wish, for so it pleases us; **dans cet exposé ~ intention est de ...** in this essay we intend to ...

nôtre [notR] **1** PRON POSS **le ~ ◊ la ~ ◊ les ~s** ours; **cette voiture n'est pas la ~** this car is not ours, this is not our car; **leurs enfants sont sortis avec les ~s** their children are out with ours; **à la (bonne) ~ !** our good health!, here's to us!; *pour autres locutions voir* **sien 2** NM **a** **nous y mettrons du ~** we'll do our bit* → **sien b les ~s** (= *famille*) our family, our folks*; (= *partisans*) our own people; **j'espère que vous serez des ~s ce soir** I hope you will join our party ou join us tonight; **il est des ~s** he's one of us **3** ADJ POSS (*littér*) ours, our own; **ces idées ne sont plus exclusivement ~s** these ideas are no longer ours alone ou exclusively; **ces principes, nous les avons faits ~s** we have made these principles our own

Nouakchott [nwakʃɔt] N Nouakchott

nouba: [nuba] NF **faire la ~** to live it up*, have a rave-up: (*Brit*)

nouer [nwe] ▸ conjug 1 ◂ VT **a** (= *faire un nœud avec*) [+ *ficelle*] to tie, knot; [+ *lacets, foulard, ceinture*] to tie; [+ *cravate*] to knot, fasten; **~ les bras autour de la taille de qn** to put one's arms round sb's waist; **l'émotion lui nouait la gorge** his throat was tight with emotion; **avoir la gorge nouée (par l'émotion)** to have a lump in one's throat; **j'ai l'estomac noué** my stomach is in knots **b** (= *entourer d'une ficelle*) [+ *bouquet, paquet*] to tie up, do up; [+ *cheveux*] to tie up *ou* back **c** (= *former*) [+ *complot*] to hatch; [+ *alliance*] to make, form; [+ *relations*] to strike up; [+ *amitié*] to form, build up; **~ conversation avec qn** to start (up) *ou* strike up a conversation with sb **d** (*Tex*) **~ la chaîne/la trame** to splice the warp/weft **e** (*Littérat*) [+ *action, intrigue*] to build up **2** VI (*Bot*) to set **3 se nouer** VPR **a** (= *s'unir*) [*mains*] to join together; **sa gorge se noua** a lump came to his throat **b** (= *se former*) [*complot*] to be hatched; [*alliance*] to be made, be formed; [*amitié*] to be formed, build up; [*conversation*] to start, be started **c** (*pièce de théâtre*) **c'est là où l'intrigue se noue** it's at that point that the plot takes shape *ou* develops

noueux, -euse [nwø, øz] ADJ [*branche*] knotty, gnarled; [*main*] gnarled; [*vieillard*] wizened

nougat [nuga] NM (*Culin*) nougat; (= *pieds*) **~s**‡ feet; **c'est du ~*** it's dead easy*, it's a cinch* *ou* a piece of cake*; **c'est pas du ~*** it's not so easy

nougatine [nugatin] NF nougatine

nouille [nuj] NF **a** (*Culin*) piece *ou* bit of pasta; **~s** (*gén*) pasta; (*en rubans*) noodles; **~s chinoises** Chinese noodles; (*Art*) **style ~** Art Nouveau **b*** (= *imbécile*) idiot, noodle* (*Brit*); (= *mollasson*) big lump*; **ce que c'est ~*** how idiotic (it is)

noumène [numɛn] NM noumenon

nounou* [nunu] NF nanny

nounours [nunuʀs] NM teddy (bear)

nourri, e [nuʀi] (*ptp de* **nourrir**) ADJ [*fusillade*] heavy; [*applaudissements*] hearty, prolonged; [*conversation*] lively; [*style*] rich; **tirs ~s** heavy *ou* sustained gunfire

nourrice [nuʀis] NF **a** (= *gardienne*) childminder, nanny; (*qui allaite*) wet nurse; **~ sèche†** dry nurse; **~ agréée** registered childminder; **mettre un enfant en ~** to put a child in the care of a nurse *ou* out to nurse (*Brit*); **prendre un enfant en ~** to act as nurse to a child → **épingle b** (= *bidon*) jerry can (*Brit*), can (*US*) **c** (= *abeille*) nurse bee

nourricier, -ière [nuʀisje, jɛʀ] **1** ADJ (*Anat*) [*canal, artère*] nutrient; (*Bot*) [*suc, sève*] nutritive; († = *adoptif*) [*mère, père*] foster (*épith*); (*littér*) **la terre nourricière** the nourishing earth **2** NM († = *père adoptif*) foster father; **les ~s** the foster parents

nourrir [nuʀiʀ] ▸ conjug 2 ◂ **1** VT **a** (= *alimenter*) [+ *animal, personne*] to feed; [+ *feu*] to stoke; [+ *récit, devoir*] to fill out; [+ *cuir, peau*] to nourish; **~ au biberon** to bottle-feed; **~ au sein** to breast-feed, nurse; **~ à la cuiller** to spoon-feed; **~ un oiseau au grain** to feed a bird (on) seed; **les régions qui nourrissent la capitale** the areas which provide food for the capital *ou* provide the capital with food; **bien/mal nourri** well-/poorly-fed → **logé b** (= *faire vivre*) [+ *famille, pays*] to feed, provide for; **cette entreprise nourrit 10 000 ouvriers** this firm gives work to *ou* provides work for 10,000 workers; **ce métier ne nourrit pas son homme** this job doesn't give a man a living wage **c** (= *caresser*) [+ *désir, espoir, illusion*] to nourish, nurture, foster; [+ *haine*] to feel, harbour (*Brit*) *ou* harbor (*US*) feelings of; [+ *rancune*] to harbour (*Brit*), harbor (*US*); [+ *vengeance*] to nourish, harbour (*Brit*) *ou* harbor (*US*) thoughts of; **~ le projet de faire qch** to plan to do sth **d** (*littér* = *former*) **être nourri dans les bons principes** to be nurtured on good principles; **la lecture nourrit l'esprit** reading improves the mind **2** VI to be nourishing

➤ GRAMMAIRE ACTIVE: **nouveau** 48.1, 48.2

3 se nourrir VPR to eat; **se ~ de** [+ *aliments*] to feed (o.s.) on, eat; [+ *illusions*] to feed on, live on; (*fig*) **il se nourrit de romans** novels are his staple diet

nourrissant, e [nuʀisɑ̃, ɑ̃t] ADJ [*aliment*] nourishing, nutritious; [*crème, cosmétique*] nourishing (*épith*)

nourrisson [nuʀisɔ̃] NM (unweaned) infant, nursling (*littér*)

nourriture [nuʀityʀ] NF **a** (= *aliments, fig*) food; **assurer la ~ de qn** to provide sb's meals *ou* sb with food **b** (= *alimentation*) food; **il lui faut une ~ saine** he needs a healthy diet; **il ne supporte aucune ~ solide** he can't take solids; **~ pour animaux** (*de compagnie*) pet food; (*de ferme*) animal feed; **la lecture est une bonne ~ pour l'esprit** reading is good nourishment for the mind

nous [nu] **1** PRON PERS **a** (*sujet*) we; **~ vous écrirons** we'll write to you; **~ avons ri tous les deux** the two of us had a good laugh, we both had a good laugh; **eux ont accepté, ~ non** *ou* **pas ~** they accepted but we didn't, they accepted but not us; **c'est enfin ~ voilà enfin** here we are at last; **qui l'a vu? — ~/pas ~** who saw him? — we did/we didn't *ou* us/not us*; **~, accepter? jamais!** us, accept that? never!, you expect us to accept that?, never! → **même b** (*objet*) us; **aide-~** help us, give us a hand; **donne-~ ton livre** give us your book, give your book to us; **si vous étiez ~ que feriez-vous?** if you were us *ou* if you were in our shoes what would you do?; **donne-le-~** give it to us, give us it; **écoutez-~** listen to us; **il n'obéit qu'à ~** we are the only ones he obeys, he obeys only us **c** (*insistance*) (*sujet*) we, we ourselves; (*objet*) us; **~, le connaissons bien — mais ~ aussi** we know him well ourselves — but so do we *ou* we do too; **pourquoi ne le ferait-il pas ?, ~ l'avons bien fait, ~** why shouldn't he do it?, we did it (all right); **alors ~, ~ restons pour compte?** and what about us, are we to be left out?; **~, elle ~ déteste** she hates us; **elle ~ connaît bien, ~** she knows us all right **d** (*emphatique avec qui, que*) (*sujet*) we; (*objet*) us; **c'est ~ qui sommes fautifs** we are the culprits, we are the ones to blame; **merci — c'est ~ qui vous remercions** thank you — it's we who should thank you; **et ~ (tous) qui vous parlons l'avons vu** we (all) saw him personally; **est-ce ~ qui devons vous le dire?** do we have to tell you?, are we the ones to have to tell you?; **et ~ qui n'avions pas le sou!** and there were we without a penny!, and to think we didn't have a penny!; **~ que le théâtre passionne, ~ n'avons jamais vu cette pièce** great theatre lovers that we are we've still never seen that play, even we with our great love for the theatre have never seen that play; **il ~ dit cela à ~ qui l'avons tant aidé** and that's what he says to us who have helped him so much; **c'est ~ qu'elle veut voir** it's us she wants to see **e** (*avec prép*) us; **à ~ cinq, ~ devrions pouvoir soulever ça** between the five of us we should be able to lift that; **cette maison est à ~** this house belongs to us *ou* is ours; **~ avons une maison à ~** we have a house of our own, we have our own house; **avec/sans ~** with/without us; **c'est à ~ de décider** it's up to us *ou* for us to decide; **elle l'a appris par ~** she heard about it through *ou* from us; **un élève à ~** one of our pupils; **l'un de ~** *ou* **d'entre ~ doit le savoir** one of us must know (it); **nos enfants à ~** our children; **l'idée vient de ~** the idea comes from us *ou* is ours; **elle veut une photo de ~ tous** she wants a photo of us all *ou* of all of us **f** (*dans comparaisons*) we, us; **il est aussi fort que ~** he is as strong as we are *ou* as us; **il mange plus/moins que ~** he eats more/less than we do *ou* than us; **faites comme ~** do as

we do, do the same as us; **il vous connaît aussi bien que ~** (*aussi bien que nous vous connaissons*) he knows you as well as we do *ou* as us; (*aussi bien qu'il nous connaît*) he knows you as well as (he knows) us **g** (*avec vpr*) **~ ~ sommes bien amusés** we had a good time, we thoroughly enjoyed ourselves; **(lui et moi) ~ ~ connaissons depuis le lycée** we have known each other since we were at school; **~ ~ détestons** we hate (the sight of) each other; **asseyons-~ donc** let's sit down, shall we sit down?; **~ ~ écrirons** we'll write to each other **h** (*pl de majesté, dans discours etc* = *moi*) we; **~, préfet des Yvelines, décidons que** we, (the) prefect of the Yvelines, decide that; **dans cet exposé, ~ essaierons d'expliquer** in this paper, we shall try to explain **2** NM **le ~ de majesté** the royal we

nous-même (*pl* **nous-mêmes**) [numɛm] PRON → **même**

▾**nouveau, nouvelle¹** [nuvo, nuvɛl] (*devant nm commençant par une voyelle ou h muet* **nouvel** [nuvɛl]) (*mpl* **nouveaux** [nuvo]) **1** ADJ **a** (*gén après nom* = *qui apparaît pour la première fois*) new; **pommes de terre nouvelles** new potatoes; **vin ~** new wine; **carottes nouvelles** spring carrots; **la mode nouvelle** the latest fashion; **la mode nouvelle du printemps** the new spring fashions; **un sentiment si ~ pour moi** such a new feeling for me; **montrez-moi le chemin, je suis ~ ici** show me the way, I'm new here; **ce rôle est ~ pour lui** this is a new role for him; **tout ~ tout beau*** (just) wait till the novelty wears off → **art, quoi b** (*après nom* = *original*) [*idée*] novel, new, original; [*style*] new, original; (= *moderne*) [*méthode*] new, up-to-date, new-fangled (*péj*); **le dernier de ses romans, et le plus ~** his latest and most original novel; **présenter qch sous un jour ~** to present sth in a new light; **c'est tout ~, ce projet** this project is brand-new; **il n'y a rien de/ce n'est pas ~!** there's/it's nothing new! **c** (= *inexpérimenté*) new (*en, dans* to); **il est ~ en affaires** he's new to business **d** (*avant nom* = *qui succède*) new; **le ~ président** the new president, the newly-elected president; **le nouvel élu** the newly-elected representative; **nous avons un ~ président/une nouvelle voiture** we have a new president/car; **avez-vous lu son ~ livre?** have you read his new *ou* latest book?; **un ~ Napoléon** a second Napoléon; **les ~x philosophes** the new philosophers; **les ~x pauvres** the new poor; **les ~x parents** today's parents, the parents of today; **il y a eu un ~ tremblement de terre** there has been a further *ou* another earthquake; **je ferai un nouvel essai** I'll make another *ou* a new *ou* a fresh attempt; **il y eut un ~ silence** there was another silence; **c'est la nouvelle mode maintenant** it's the new fashion now → **jusque e** (= *qui s'ajoute*) new, fresh; **c'est là une nouvelle preuve que** it's fresh proof *ou* further proof that; **avec une ardeur/énergie nouvelle** with renewed ardour/energy **2** NM **a** (= *homme*) new man; (*Scol*) new boy **b** (= *nouveauté*) **y a-t-il du ~ à ce sujet?** is there anything new on this?; **il y a du ~ dans cette affaire** there has been a fresh *ou* new *ou* further development in this business; **le public veut sans cesse du ~** the public always wants something new; **il n'y a rien de ~ sous le soleil** there's nothing new under the sun **c** (= *encore*) **de ~** again; **faire qch de ~** to do sth again, repeat sth; **à ~** (= *d'une manière différente*) anew, afresh, again; (= *encore une fois*) again; **nous examinerons la question à ~** we'll examine the question anew *ou* afresh *ou* again **3 nouvelle** NF (= *femme*) new woman *ou* girl; (*Scol*) new girl → **nouvelle²**

4 COMP ► **Nouvel An, Nouvelle Année** New Year; **pour le/au Nouvel An** for/at New Year; **le Nouvel An juif/chinois** the Jewish/Chinese New Year ► **nouvelle cuisine** nouvelle cuisine ► **nouvelle lune** new moon ► **nouveaux mariés** newlyweds, newly married couple ► **Nouveau Monde** New World ► **nouveaux pays industrialisés** newly industrialized countries ► **nouveau riche** nouveau riche ► **le nouveau roman** (*Littérat*) the nouveau roman ► **le Nouveau Testament** the New Testament ► **Nouvelle Vague** (*Ciné*) New Wave, Nouvelle Vague ► **nouveau venu, nouvelle venue** NM,F newcomer (**à, dans** to)

Nouveau-Brunswick [nuvobræsvik] NM New Brunswick

Nouveau-Mexique [nuvomeksik] NM New Mexico

nouveau-né, nouveau-née (*mpl* **nouveau-nés**, *fpl* **nouveau-nées**) [nuvone] **1** ADJ newborn **2** NM,F (= *enfant*) newborn child; (= *dernière création*) newest *ou* latest model; **les ~s de notre gamme de jouets** the newest *ou* latest additions to our range of toys

nouveauté [nuvote] NF **a** (= *actualité*) novelty, newness; (= *originalité*) novelty; (= *chose*) new thing, something new; **il n'aime pas la ~** he hates anything new *ou* new ideas, he hates change; **il travaille? c'est une ~!** he's working? that's new! *ou* that's a novelty!; **il est paresseux — ce n'est pas une ~!** he's lazy — that's nothing new! **b** (*Habillement*) **~s de printemps** new spring fashions; **le commerce de la ~†** the fashion trade; **magasin de ~s†** draper's shop (*Brit*), fabric store (*US*) **c** (= *objet*) new thing *ou* article; **les ~s du mois** (= *disques*) the month's new releases; (= *livres*) the month's new titles; (= *machines, voitures*) **les ~s du salon** the new models of the show; **la grande ~ de cet automne** the latest thing this autumn; **une ~ en matière électronique** a new thing in electronics, a new electronic invention

nouvel [nuvɛl] ADJ M → **nouveau**

nouvelle² [nuvɛl] NF **a** (= *écho*) news (*NonC*); **une ~** a piece of news; **une bonne/mauvaise ~** some good/bad news; **la ~ de cet événement nous a surpris** we were surprised by the news of this event; **ce n'est pas une ~!** that's not news!, that's nothing new!; **vous connaissez la ~?** have you heard the news?; **première ~!** that's the first I've heard about it!, it's news to me! → **faux²** **b** **~s** news (*NonC*); **quelles ~s?** what's new?, what's been happening?; **aller aux ~s** to go and find out what is happening; **voici les dernières ~s concernant l'accident** here is the latest news of the accident, here is an up-to-the-minute report on the accident; **aux dernières ~s, il était à Paris** the last I (*ou we etc*) heard (of him) he was in Paris; **avez-vous de ses ~s?** (*de sa propre main*) have you heard from him?, have you had any news from him?; (= *par un tiers*) have you heard anything about *ou* of him?, have you had any news of him?; **j'irai prendre de ses ~s** I'll go and see how he's doing *ou* how he's getting along *ou* on (*Brit*); **il a fait prendre de mes ~s (par qn)** he asked for news of me (from sb); **il ne donne plus de ses ~s** you never hear from him any more; **je suis sans ~s (de lui) depuis huit jours** I haven't heard anything (of him) for a week, I've had no news (of him) for a week; **pas de ~s, bonnes ~s** no news is good news; **il aura** *ou* **entendra de mes ~s!** I'll give him what for!*; **goûtez mon vin, vous m'en direz des ~s*** taste my wine, I'm sure you'll like it **c** (*Presse, Radio, TV*) **les ~s** the news (*NonC*); **écouter/entendre les ~s** to listen to/hear the news; **voici les ~s** here is the news; **les ~s sont bonnes** the news is good **d** (= *court récit*) short story

Nouvelle-Angleterre [nuvɛlãglətɛʀ] NF New England

Nouvelle-Calédonie [nuvɛlkaledɔni] NF New Caledonia

Nouvelle-Écosse [nuvɛlekɔs] NF Nova Scotia

Nouvelle-Guinée [nuvɛlgine] NF New Guinea

nouvellement [nuvɛlmã] ADV newly

Nouvelle-Orléans [nuvɛlɔʀleã] NF New Orleans

Nouvelles-Galles du Sud [nuvɛlgaldysyd] NF New South Wales

Nouvelles-Hébrides [nuvɛlzebʀid] NFPL **les ~** the New Hebrides

Nouvelle-Zélande [nuvɛlzelãd] NF New Zealand

nouvelliste [nuvelist] NMF short story writer, writer of short stories

nova [nɔva] (*pl* **novæ** [nɔvɛ]) NF nova

novateur, -trice [nɔvatœʀ, tʀis] **1** ADJ innovatory, innovative **2** NM,F innovator

novation [nɔvasjɔ̃] NF **a** (*frm* = *nouveauté*) innovation **b** (*Jur*) novation

novélisation, novellisation [nɔvelizasjɔ̃] NF novelization

novembre [nɔvãbʀ] NM November; *pour locutions voir →* **septembre** *et* **onze**

novice [nɔvis] **1** ADJ inexperienced (**dans** in), green* (**dans** at) **2** NMF (= *débutant*) novice, beginner, greenhorn*; (*Rel*) novice, probationer; **être ~ en affaires** to be a novice in business matters

noviciat [nɔvisja] NM (= *bâtiment, période*) noviciate, novitiate; (*Rel*) **de ~** probationary

Novocaïne® [nɔvɔkain] NF Novocaine®

noyade [nwajad] NF drowning; (= *événement*) drowning accident, death by drowning; **il y a eu de nombreuses ~s à cet endroit** many people have drowned *ou* there have been many deaths by drowning at this spot; **sauver qn de la ~** to save sb from drowning

noyau (*pl* **noyaux**) [nwajo] NM **a** [*fruit*] stone, pit; (*Astron, Bio, Phys*) nucleus; (*Géol*) core; (*Ling*) kernel, nucleus; (*Ordin*) kernel; (*Art*) centre, core; (*Élec*) core (*of induction coil etc*); (*Constr*) newel; **enlevez les ~x** remove the stones (from the fruit), pit the fruit **b** (= *groupe humain*) nucleus; (= *groupe de fidèles*) small circle; (= *groupe de manifestants, d'opposants*) small group; **~ de résistance** hard core *ou* pocket of resistance; **~ dur** (*Écon*) hard core shareholders; [*groupe*] (= *irréductibles*) hard core; (= *éléments essentiels*) kernel; **le ~ familial** the family unit

noyautage [nwajotaʒ] NM (*Pol*) infiltration

noyauter [nwajote] ▸ conjug 1 ◂ VT (*Pol*) to infiltrate

noyé, e [nwaje] (*ptp de* **noyer²**) **1** ADJ (*fig* = *ne pas comprendre*) **être ~** to be out of one's depth, be all at sea (**en** in) **2** NM,F drowned person; **il y a eu beaucoup de ~s ici** a lot of people have drowned here

noyer¹ [nwaje] NM (= *arbre*) walnut (tree); (= *bois*) walnut

noyer² [nwaje] ▸ conjug 8 ◂ **1** VT **a** (*gén*) [+ *personne, animal, flamme*] to drown; (*Aut*) [+ *moteur*] to flood; **la crue a noyé les champs** the high water has flooded *ou* drowned *ou* swamped the fields; **il avait les yeux noyés de larmes** his eyes were brimming *ou* swimming with tears; **ils ont noyé la révolte dans le sang** they quelled the revolt with much bloodshed; (*Mil*) **~ la poudre** to wet the powder; **~ son chagrin dans l'alcool** to drown one's sorrows; (*fig*) **~ le poisson** to evade the issue, duck *ou* sidestep the question ■ (*PROV*) **qui veut ~ son chien l'accuse de la rage** give a dog a bad name and hang him (*PROV*)
b (*gén pass* = *perdre*) **~ qn sous un déluge d'explications** to swamp sb with explanations; **quelques bonnes idées noyées dans**

des détails inutiles a few good ideas lost in *ou* buried in *ou* swamped by a mass of irrelevant detail; **être noyé dans l'obscurité/la brume** to be shrouded in darkness/mist; **être noyé dans la foule** to be lost in the crowd; **noyé dans la masse, cet écrivain n'arrive pas à percer** because he's (just) one amongst (so) many, this writer can't manage to make a name for himself; **cette dépense ne se verra pas, noyée dans la masse** this expense won't be noticed when it's lumped *ou* put together with the rest; **ses paroles furent noyées par** *ou* **dans le vacarme** his words were drowned in the din **c** (*Culin*) [+ *alcool, vin*] to water down; [+ *sauce*] to thin too much, make too thin **d** (*Tech*) [+ *clou*] to drive right in; [+ *pilier*] to embed; **noyé dans la masse** embedded **e** (= *effacer*) [+ *contours, couleur*] to blur

2 **se noyer** VPR **a** (*lit*) (*accidentellement*) to drown; (*volontairement*) to drown o.s.; **une personne qui se noie** a drowning person; **il s'est noyé** (*accidentellement*) he drowned *ou* was drowned; (*volontairement*) he drowned himself **b** (*fig*) **se ~ dans un raisonnement** to become tangled up *ou* bogged down in an argument; **se ~ dans les détails** to get bogged down in details; **se ~ dans la foule/dans la nuit** to disappear into the crowd/the night; **se ~ dans un verre d'eau** to make a mountain out of a molehill, make heavy weather of the simplest thing; **se ~ l'estomac** to overfill one's stomach (*by drinking too much liquid*)

NPI [ɛnpei] NMPL (ABRÉV = **nouveaux pays industrialisés**) NIC

N.-S. J.-C. ABRÉV = **Notre-Seigneur Jésus-Christ**

NU (ABRÉV = **Nations Unies**) UN

nu¹, e¹ [ny] **1** ADJ **a** (= *sans vêtement*) [*personne*] naked, nude; [*torse, membres*] naked; [*crâne*] bald; **~-pieds ◊** (**les**) **pieds ~s** barefoot, with bare feet; **aller pieds ~s** *ou* **~-pieds** to go barefoot(ed); **~-tête ◊** (**la**) **tête ~e** bareheaded; **~-jambes ◊** (**les**) **jambes ~es** barelegged, with bare legs; (**les**) **bras ~s** barearmed, with bare arms; (**le**) **torse ~ ◊** jusqu'à la ceinture stripped to the waist, naked from the waist up; **à moitié** *ou* **à demi ~** half-naked; **il est ~ comme un ver** *ou* **comme la main** he is as naked as the day he was born; **tout ~** stark naked; **ne reste pas tout ~!** I put something on!; **se mettre ~** to strip (off), take one's clothes off; **se montrer ~ à l'écran** to appear in the nude on the screen; **poser ~** to pose nude **b** (= *sans ornement*) [*mur, chambre*] bare; [*arbre, pays, plaine*] bare, naked; [*style*] plain; [*vérité*] plain, naked; (= *non protégé*) [*fil électrique*] bare **c** (*Bot, Zool*) naked **d** (*loc*) **mettre à ~** [+ *fil électrique*] to strip; [+ *erreurs, vices*] to expose, lay bare; **mettre son cœur à ~** to lay bare one's heart *ou* soul; **monter un cheval à ~†** to ride bareback
2 NM (*Peinture, Photo*) nude; **album de ~s** album of nude photographs; **le ~ intégral** full frontal nudity

nu² [ny] NM INV (= *lettre grecque*) nu

nuage [nɥaʒ] NM (*lit, fig*) cloud; **~ de grêle/de pluie** hail/rain cloud; **~ de fumée/de tulle/de poussière/de sauterelles** cloud of smoke/tulle/dust/locusts; **~ radioactif** radioactive cloud; (*Math*) **~ de points** scatter of points; (*lit, fig*) **il y a des ~s noirs à l'horizon** there are dark clouds on the horizon; **le ciel se couvre de ~s/est couvert de ~s** the sky is clouding over/has clouded over; **juste un ~** (**de lait**) just a drop (of milk); **il est (perdu) dans les ~s ◊ il suit sur son petit ~** he's got his head in the clouds; **sans ~s** [*ciel*] cloudless; [*bonheur*] unmarred, unclouded; **une amitié qui n'est pas sans ~s** a friendship which is not entirely untroubled *ou* quarrelfree → **Magellan**

nuageux, -euse [nɥaʒø, øz] ADJ [a] [temps] cloudy; [ciel] cloudy, overcast; [zone, bande] cloud (épith); **système ~** cloud system; **couche nuageuse** layer of cloud [b] (= vague) nebulous, hazy

nuance [nɥɑ̃s] NF [a] [couleur] shade, hue; (Littérat, Mus) nuance; **~ de sens** shade of meaning, nuance; **~ de style** nuance of style; **~ politique** shade of political opinion; **de toutes les ~s politiques** of all shades of political opinion
[b] (= différence) slight difference; **il y a une ~ entre mentir et se taire** there's a slight difference between lying and keeping quiet; **je ne lui ai pas dit non, ~! je lui ai dit peut-être** I didn't say no to him, understand, I said perhaps, I didn't say no to him, I said perhaps and there's a difference between the two; **tu vois** ou **saisis la ~?** do you see the difference?
[c] (= subtilité, variation) **les ~s du cœur/de l'amour** the subtleties of the heart/of love; **apporter des ~s à une affirmation** to qualify a statement; **faire ressortir les ~s** to bring out the finer ou subtler points; **tout en ~s** [esprit, discours, personne] very subtle, full of nuances; **sans ~** [discours] unsubtle, cut and dried; [esprit, personne] unsubtle
[d] (= petit élément) touch, hint; **avec une ~ de tristesse** with a touch ou a hint ou a slight note of sadness

nuancé, e [nɥɑ̃se] (ptp de **nuancer**) ADJ [tableau] finely shaded; [opinion] qualified; [attitude] balanced; (Mus) nuanced; **ironie ~e d'amertume** irony with a tinge ou a note ou a hint of bitterness

nuancer [nɥɑ̃se] ▶ conjug 3 ◀ VT [+ tableau, couleur] to shade; [+ opinion] to qualify; (Mus) to nuance

nuancier [nɥɑ̃sje] NM colour (Brit) ou color (US) chart

Nubie [nybi] NF Nubia

nubien, -ienne [nybjɛ̃, jɛn] [1] ADJ [personne] Nubian; [région] of Nubia [2] **Nubien(ne)** NM,F Nubian

nubile [nybil] ADJ nubile

nubilité [nybilite] NF nubility

nubuck [nybyk] NM nubuck; **en ~** nubuck (épith)

nucléaire [nykleɛʀ] [1] ADJ nuclear [2] NM **le ~** '(= énergie) nuclear energy; (= technologie) nuclear technology

nucléarisation [nyklearizasjɔ̃] NF [pays] nuclearization, equipping with nuclear weapons

nucléariser [nyklearize] ▶ conjug 1 ◀ VT [+ pays] (en armes) to equip with nuclear weapons; (en énergie) to equip with nuclear energy

nucléé, e [nyklee] ADJ nucleate(d)

nucléide [nykleid] NM nuclide

nucléine [nyklein] NF nuclein

nucléique [nykleik] ADJ nucleic

nucléon [nykleɔ̃] NM nucleon

nucléosynthèse [nykleosɛ̃tɛz] NF nucleosynthesis

nucléotide [nykleɔtid] NM nucleotide

nudisme [nydism] NM nudism; **faire du ~** to practise nudism

nudiste [nydist] ADJ, NMF nudist; **plage/camp de ~s** nudist beach/camp

nudité [nydite] NF [personne] nakedness, nudity; [mur] bareness; (Art) nude; **la laideur des gens s'étale dans toute sa ~** people are exposed in all their ugliness, people's ugliness is laid bare for all to see

nue² [ny] NF [a] (†† ou littér) (= nuage) **~s** clouds; (= ciel) **la ~** ◊ **les ~s** the skies [b] **porter** ou **mettre qn aux ~s** to praise sb to the skies; **tomber des ~s** to be completely taken aback ou flabbergasted; **je suis tombé des ~s** you could have knocked me down with a feather, I was completely taken aback

nuée [nɥe] NF [a] (littér = nuage) thick cloud; **~s d'orage** storm clouds; **~ ardente** nuée ardente, glowing cloud [b] (= multitude) [insectes] cloud, horde; [flèches] cloud; [photographes, spectateurs, ennemis] horde, host; (fig) **comme une ~ de sauterelles** like a plague ou swarm of locusts

nue-propriété [nyprɔprijete] NF ownership without usufruct; **avoir un bien en ~** to have property without usufruct

nuer [nɥe] ▶ conjug 1 ◀ VT (littér) [+ couleurs] to blend ou match the different shades of

nuire [nɥiʀ] ▶ conjug 38 ◀ [1] **nuire à** VT INDIR (= desservir) [+ personne] to harm, injure; [+ santé, réputation] to damage, harm; [+ action] to prejudice; **sa laideur lui nuit beaucoup** his ugliness is very much against him ou is a great disadvantage to him; **il a voulu le faire mais ça va lui ~** he wanted to do it, but it will go against him ou it will do him harm; **chercher à ~ à qn** to try to harm sb, try to do ou run sb down; **cela risque de ~ à nos projets** there's a risk that it will spoil our plans; **un petit whisky, ça peut pas ~!** a little glass of whisky won't hurt you! ou won't do you any harm! [2] **se nuire** VPR (à soi-même) to do o.s. a lot of harm; (l'un l'autre) to work against each other's interests, harm each other

nuisance [nɥizɑ̃s] NF (gén pl) (environmental) pollution (NonC) ou nuisance (NonC); **les ~s (sonores)** noise pollution

nuisette [nɥizɛt] NF very short nightdress ou nightie*

nuisible [nɥizibl] ADJ [climat, temps] harmful, injurious (à to); [influence, gaz] harmful, noxious (à to); **animaux ~** vermin, pests; **insectes ~s** pests; **~ à la santé** harmful ou injurious to (the) health

nuit [nɥi] [1] NF [a] (= obscurité) darkness, night; **il fait ~** it's dark; **il fait ~ à 5 heures** it gets dark at 5 o'clock; **il fait ~ noire** it's pitch dark ou black; **une ~ d'encre** a pitch dark ou black night; **la ~ tombe** it's getting dark, night is falling; **à la ~ tombante** at nightfall, at dusk; **pris** ou **surpris par la ~** overtaken by darkness ou night; **rentrer avant la ~/à la ~** to come home before dark/in the dark; **la ~ polaire** the polar night ou darkness ■ (PROV) **la ~ tous les chats sont gris** everyone looks the same ou all cats are grey in the dark
[b] (= espace de temps) night; **cette ~** (passée) last night; (qui vient) tonight; **j'ai passé la ~ chez eux** I spent the night at their house; **dans la ~ de jeudi** during Thursday night; **dans la ~ de jeudi à vendredi** during the night of Thursday to Friday; **souhaiter (une) bonne ~ à qn** to wish sb goodnight; **~ blanche** ou **sans sommeil** sleepless night; **~ d'amour** night of love; **leur bébé fait ses ~s*** their baby sleeps right through the night; **~ et jour** night and day; **au milieu de la ~ ◊ en pleine ~** in the middle of the night, at dead of night; **elle part cette ~** ou **dans la ~** she's leaving tonight; **ouvert la ~** open at night; **conduire la** ou **de ~ ne me gêne pas** I don't mind night-driving ou driving at night; **sortir/travailler la ~** to go out/work at night; **voyager de ~** to travel by night; **de ~** [service, travail, garde, infirmière] night (épith); **elle est de ~ cette semaine** she's on nights ou she's working nights this week ■ (PROV) **la ~ porte conseil** it's best to sleep on it
[c] (littér) darkness; **dans la ~ de ses souvenirs** in the darkness of his memories; **ça se perd dans la ~ des temps** it's lost in the mists of time; **ça remonte à la ~ des temps** that goes back to the dawn of time, that's as old as the hills; **la ~ du tombeau/de la mort** the darkness of the grave/of death
[2] COMP ▶ **nuit américaine** day for night ▶ **nuit bleue** night of bombings ▶ **nuit d'hôtel** night spent in a hotel room, overnight stay in a hotel; **payer sa ~ d'hôtel** to pay one's hotel bill ▶ **la Nuit des longs couteaux** (Hist) the Night of the Long Knives ▶ **nuit de noces** wedding night ▶ **nuit de Noël** Christmas Eve ▶ **la nuit des Rois** Twelfth Night

nuitamment [nɥitamɑ̃] ADV by night

nuitée [nɥite] NF (Tourisme) night; **trois ~s** three nights (in a hotel room)

Nuku'alofa [nukualɔfa] N Nuku'alofa

nul, nulle [nyl] [1] ADJ INDÉF [a] (= aucun: devant nom) no; **il n'avait ~ besoin/nulle envie de sortir** he had no need/no desire to go out at all; **~ doute qu'elle ne l'ait vu** there is no doubt (whatsoever) that she saw him; **~ autre que lui (n'aurait pu le faire)** no one (else) but he (could have done it); **sans ~ doute/nulle exception** without any doubt/any exception
[b] (après nom) (= proche de zéro) [résultat, différence, risque] nil (attrib); (= invalidé) [testament, élection, bulletin de vote] null and void (attrib); (= inexistant) [récolte] non-existent; (gén, Math) **pour toute valeur non nulle de x** where x is not equal to zero; (Jur) **~ et non avenu** invalid, null and void; (Jur, fig) **rendre ~** to annul, nullify; **nombre ~/non-~** zero/non-zero number
[c] (Sport) **le résultat** ou **le score est ~** (pour l'instant) there's no score; (en fin de match) (= 0 à 0) the match has ended in a nil draw; (= 2 à 2 etc) the match has ended in a draw → **match**
[d] (= qui ne vaut rien) [film, livre, personne] useless, hopeless; [intelligence] nil; [travail] worthless, useless; **être ~ en géographie** to be hopeless ou useless at geography; **il est ~ pour** ou **dans tout ce qui est manuel** he's hopeless ou useless at anything manual; **ce devoir est ~** this piece of work is worth nothing ou doesn't deserve any marks; **c'est ~ de lui avoir dit ça*** it was really stupid to tell him that
[2] NM, F * idiot
[3] PRON INDÉF (sujet sg = personne, aucun) no one; **~ n'est censé ignorer la loi** ignorance of the law is no excuse; **~ d'entre vous n'ignore que ...** none of you is ignorant of the fact that ...; (frm) **afin que ~ n'en ignore** so that nobody is left in ignorance; **à ~ autre pareil** peerless, unrivalled ■ (PROV) **~ n'est prophète en son pays** no man is a prophet in his own country (PROV) = **impossible**
[4] **nulle part** LOC ADV nowhere; **il ne l'a trouvé nulle part** he couldn't find it anywhere; **je n'ai nulle part où aller** I've got nowhere to go; **nulle part ailleurs** nowhere else

nullard, e* [nylar, ard] [1] ADJ hopeless, useless (en at) [2] NM,F numskull; **c'est un ~** he's a complete numskull, he's a dead loss*

nullement [nylmɑ̃] ADV not at all, not in the least; **il n'a ~ l'intention de ...** he has no intention whatsoever ou he hasn't got the slightest intention of ...; **cela n'implique ~ que ...** this doesn't in any way ou by any means imply that ...

nullipare [nylipar] [1] ADJ nulliparous [2] NF nullipara

nullité [nylite] NF [a] (Jur) nullity; **frapper de ~** to render void → **entacher** [b] (= médiocrité) [employé] incompetence; [élève] uselessness; **ce film est d'une ~ affligeante** the film is absolutely dreadful [c] (= futilité) [raisonnement, objection] invalidity [d] (= personne) nonentity, wash-out*

nûment [nymɑ̃] ADV (littér) (= sans fard) plainly, frankly; (= crûment) bluntly; **dire (tout) ~ que ...** to say (quite) frankly that ...

numéraire [nymerɛʀ] [1] ADJ **pierres ~s** milestones; **espèces ~s** legal tender ou currency; **valeur ~** face value [2] NM specie (SPÉC), cash; **paiement en ~** cash payment, payment in specie (SPÉC)

numéral, e (mpl -aux) [nymeral, o] ADJ, NM numeral

numérateur [nymeʀatœʀ] NM numerator

numération [nymeʀasjɔ̃] NF (= *comptage*) numeration; (= *code*) notation; **~ globulaire** blood count; (*Math, Ordin*) **~ binaire** binary notation

numérique [nymeʀik] ⚀ ADJ (*gén, Math*) numerical; (*Ordin*) [*affichage, son, télévision*] digital ⚁ **le ~** NM digital technology

numériquement [nymeʀikmɑ̃] ADV numerically

Numéris ® [nymeʀis] NM (**réseau**) **~** Numeris (network) (*France Telecom's digital communications system*); **données ~** data transmitted on the Numeris network

numérisation [nymeʀizasjɔ̃] NF digitization

numériser [nymeʀize] ▸conjug 1◂ VT to digitize

numériseur [nymeʀizœʀ] NM digitizer

▾ **numéro** [nymeʀo] NM ⓐ (*gén, Aut, Phys*) number; **j'habite au ~ 6** I live at number 6; **~ atomique** atomic number; **~ d'ordre** number, queue ticket (*Brit*); **~ minéralogique** *ou* **d'immatriculation** *ou* **de police** registration (*Brit*) *ou* license (*US*) number, car number; **~ d'immatriculation à la Sécurité sociale** National Insurance number (*Brit*), Social Security number (*US*); **~ (de téléphone)** ◊ **~ d'appel** (tele)phone number; **~ vert** *ou* **d'appel gratuit** Freefone® (*Brit*) *ou* toll-free (*US*) number; **~ de fax** fax number; **~ de compte** account number; **~ de série** serial number; (*Helv*) **~ postal** post code (*Brit*), zip code (*US*); **faire** *ou* **composer un ~** to dial a number; **pour eux, je ne suis qu'un ~** I'm just a *ou* another number to them; **notre ennemi/problème ~ un** our number one enemy/problem; **le ~ un/deux du textile** the number one/two textile producer *ou* manufacturer; **le ~ un/deux du parti** the party's leader/deputy leader *ou* number two; (*lit*) **le bon/mauvais ~** the right/wrong number; **tirer le bon ~** (*dans une loterie*) to draw the lucky number; (*fig*) to strike lucky; **tirer le mauvais ~** to draw the short straw; **~ gagnant** winning number

ⓑ (*Presse*) issue, number; **le ~ du jour** the day's issue; **vieux ~** back number, back issue; **~ spécial** special issue; **~ zéro** dummy issue → **suite**

ⓒ (= *spectacle*) [*chant, danse*] number; [*cirque, music-hall*] act, turn, number; (*fig*) **il nous a fait son ~ habituel** *ou* **son petit ~** he gave us *ou* put on his usual (little) act

ⓓ (= *personne*) **quel ~!** ◊ **c'est un drôle de ~!** ◊ **c'est un sacré ~!** what a character!

ⓔ (*Tex*) count of yarn

numérologie [nymeʀɔlɔʒi] NF numerology

numérologue [nymeʀɔlɔɡ] NMF numerologist

numérotage [nymeʀɔtaʒ] NM numbering, numeration

numérotation [nymeʀɔtasjɔ̃] NF numbering, numeration; **~ téléphonique** telephone number system; (*Téléc*) **à 10 chiffres** 10-digit dialling

numéroter [nymeʀɔte] ▸conjug 1◂ VT to number; **si tu continues, tu as intérêt à ~ tes abattis!** if you go on like this you'll get what's coming to you!*

numerus clausus [nymeʀysklozys] NM restricted intake

numide [nymid] ⚀ ADJ Numidian ⚁ **Numide** NMF Numidian

Numidie [nymidi] NF Numidia

numismate [nymismat] NMF numismatist

numismatique [nymismatik] ⚀ ADJ numismatic ⚁ NF numismatics *sg*, numismatology

nunchaku [nunʃaku] NM nunchaku

nunuche* [nynyʃ] ⚀ ADJ (*gén*) silly ⚁ NMF ninny*

nu-pieds [nypje] ⚀ NM (= *sandale*) beach sandal, flip-flop (*Brit*) ⚁ ADV barefoot

nu-propriétaire, nue-propriétaire (*mpl* **nus-propriétaires**) [nypʀɔpʀijetɛʀ] NM,F (*Jur*) owner without usufruct

nuptial, e (*mpl* **-iaux**) [nypsjal, jo] ADJ [*bénédiction, messe*] nuptial (*littér*); [*robe, marche,*

anneau, cérémonie] wedding (*épith*); [*lit, chambre*] bridal, nuptial (*littér*); (*Zool*) [*mœurs, vol*] nuptial

nuptialité [nypsjalite] NF (**taux de**) **~** marriage rate

nuque [nyk] NF nape of the neck, nucha (*SPÉC*); **tué d'une balle dans la ~** killed by a bullet in the back of the neck

Nuremberg [nyʀɛ̃bɛʀ] N Nuremberg; (*Hist*) **le procès de ~** the Nuremberg trials

nurse [nœʀs] NF nanny, (children's) nurse

nursery (*pl* **nurserys** *ou* **nurseries**) [nœʀsəʀi] NF [*maison, maternité*] nursery

nutriment [nytʀimɑ̃] NM nutriment

nutritif, -ive [nytʀitif, iv] ADJ (= *nourrissant*) nourishing, nutritious; (*Méd*) [*besoins, fonction, appareil*] nutritive; (*Bio*) **qualité** *ou* **valeur nutritive** food value, nutritional value

nutrition [nytʀisjɔ̃] NF nutrition

nutritionnel, -elle [nytʀisjɔnɛl] ADJ nutritional

nutritionniste [nytʀisjɔnist] NMF nutritionist

Nyasaland, Nyassaland [njasalɑ̃d] NM Nyasaland

nyctalope [niktalɔp] ⚀ ADJ day-blind, hemeralopic (*SPÉC*); **les chats sont ~s** cats see well in the dark ⚁ NMF day-blind *ou* hemeralopic (*SPÉC*) person

nyctalopie [niktalɔpi] NF day blindness, hemeralopia (*SPÉC*)

nylon ® [nilɔ̃] NM nylon; **bas (de) ~** nylons, nylon stockings

nymphe [nɛ̃f] NF (*Myth, fig*) nymph; (*Zool*) nymph, nympha, pupa; (*Anat*) **~s** nymphae, labia minora

nymphéa [nɛ̃fea] NM white water lily

nymphette [nɛ̃fɛt] NF nymphet

nymphomane [nɛ̃fɔman] ADJ, NF nymphomaniac

nymphomanie [nɛ̃fɔmani] NF nymphomania

O¹, O [o] NM (= *lettre*) O, o
O² (ABRÉV = **Ouest**) W
ô [o] EXCL oh!, O!

OAS [oɑɛs] NF (ABRÉV = **Organisation de l'armée secrète**) OAS (*illegal military organization supporting French rule in Algeria in the 60s*)

oasis [ɔazis] NF (*lit*) oasis; (*fig*) oasis, haven; **~ de paix** haven of peace

obédience [ɔbedjɑ̃s] NF **a** (= *appartenance*) **d'~ communiste** of Communist allegiance; **de même ~ religieuse** of the same religious persuasion; **musulman de stricte ~** strict ou devout Muslim; **socialiste de stricte ~** staunch socialist **b** (*Rel, littér* = *obéissance*) obedience

obéir [ɔbeiʀ] ▸conjug 2◂ ◆**obéir à** VT INDIR **a** [+ *personne*] to obey; [+ *ordre*] to obey, comply with; [+ *loi, principe, règle*] to obey; [+ *critère*] to meet; **il sait se faire ~ de ses élèves** he knows how to command obedience from his pupils ou how to make his pupils obey him; **on lui obéit au doigt et à l'œil** he commands strict obedience; **obéissez!** do as you're told!; **je lui ai dit de le faire mais il n'a pas obéi** I told him to do it but he took no notice ou didn't obey (me); **ici, il faut ~** you have to toe the line ou obey orders here **b** (*fig*) [+ *conscience, mode*] to follow (the dictates of); **~ à une impulsion** to act on an impulse; **obéissant à un sentiment de pitié** prompted ou moved by a feeling of pity; **~ à ses instincts** to submit to ou obey one's instincts; **son comportement n'obéit à aucune logique** his behaviour is completely illogical; **l'orthographe obéit à des règles complexes** spelling is governed by ou follows complex rules **c** [*voilier, moteur, monture*] to respond to; **le cheval obéit au mors** the horse responds to the bit; **le moteur/voilier obéit bien** the engine/boat responds well

obéissance [ɔbeisɑ̃s] NF [*animal, personne*] obedience (**à** to)

obéissant, e [ɔbeisɑ̃, ɑ̃t] ADJ obedient (**à** to, towards)

obélisque [ɔbelisk] NM (= *monument*) obelisk

obérer [ɔbeʀe] ▸conjug 6◂ VT (*frm*) [+ *bilan, budget*] to be a burden on; [+ *avenir, situation*] to compromise, be a threat to

obèse [ɔbɛz] **1** ADJ obese **2** NMF obese person

obésité [ɔbezite] NF obesity

obituaire [ɔbitɥɛʀ] ADJ, NM (**registre**) **~** record of memorial services

objectal, e [ɔbʒɛktal, o] ADJ (*Psych*) object (*épith*); **libido/lien ~** object libido/ relationship

objecter [ɔbʒɛkte] ▸conjug 1◂ VT **a** (*à une idée ou une opinion*) **~ un argument à une théorie** to put forward an argument against a theory; **il m'objecta une très bonne raison, à savoir que ...** against that he argued convincingly that ..., he gave me ou he put forward a very sound reason against (doing) that, namely that ...; **~ que ...** to object that ...; **il m'objecta**

que ... he objected to me that ..., the objection he mentioned ou raised to me was that ...; **que puis-je lui ~?** what can I say to him?; **je n'ai rien à ~** I have no objection (to make); **elle a toujours quelque chose à ~** she always has some objection or other (to make), she always raises some objection or other **b** (*à une demande*) **il objecta le manque de temps/la fatigue pour ne pas y aller** he pleaded lack of time/tiredness to save himself going; **il m'a objecté mon manque d'expérience/le manque de place** he objected on the grounds of my lack of experience/on the grounds that there was not enough space, he objected that I lacked experience/that there was not enough space

objecteur [ɔbʒɛktœʀ] NM **~ de conscience** conscientious objector

objectif, -ive [ɔbʒɛktif, iv] **1** ADJ **a** [*article, jugement, observateur*] objective, unbiased **b** (*Ling, Philo*) objective; (*Méd*) [*symptôme*] objective **2** NM **a** (= *but*) objective, purpose; (*Mil* = *cible*) objective, target; **~ de vente** sales target **b** [*télescope, lunette*] objective, object glass, lens; [*caméra*] lens, objective; **~ traité** coated lens; **braquer son ~ sur** to train one's camera on

▾**objection** [ɔbʒɛksjɔ̃] NF objection; **faire une ~** to raise ou make an objection, object; **si vous n'y voyez pas d'~** if you've no objection (to that); **la proposition n'a soulevé aucune ~** there were no objections to the proposal; (*Jur*) **~! objection!**; **~ de conscience** conscientious objection

objectivement [ɔbʒɛktivmɑ̃] ADV objectively

objectiver [ɔbʒɛktive] ▸conjug 1◂ VT to objectivize

objectivisme [ɔbʒɛktivism] NM objectivism

objectivité [ɔbʒɛktivite] NF objectivity; **juger en toute ~** to judge with complete objectivity

objet [ɔbʒɛ] **1** NM **a** (= *chose*) object, thing; **emporter quelques ~s de première nécessité** to take a few basic essentials ou a few essential items ou things; **femme-/homme-~** woman/man as a sex object; **~ sexuel** sex object **b** (= *sujet*) [*méditation, rêve, désir*] object; [*discussion, recherches, science*] subject; **l'~ de la psychologie est le comportement humain** human behaviour forms the subject matter of psychology, psychology is the study of human behaviour **c** (= *cible*) [*mépris, convoitise*] object; **un ~ de raillerie/d'admiration** an object of fun/of admiration **d** **faire** ou **être l'~ de** [+ *discussion, recherches*] to be ou form the subject of; [+ *surveillance, enquête*] to be subjected to; [+ *pressions*] to be subjected to, be under; [+ *soins, dévouement*] to be given ou shown; **le malade fit** ou **fut l'~ d'un dévouement de tous les instants** the patient was shown ou was given every care and attention; **faire l'~ d'une attention particulière** to receive particular attention; **les marchandises faisant l'~ de cette facture** goods covered

by this invoice **e** (= *but*) [*visite, réunion, démarche*] object, purpose; **cette enquête a rempli son ~** the investigation has achieved its purpose ou object ou objective; **craintes sans ~** unfounded ou groundless fears; **votre plainte est dès lors sans ~** you therefore have no grounds for complaint **f** (*Ling, Philo, Ordin*) object; **~ mathématique** mathematical object → **complément** **g** (*Jur*) **l'~ du litige** the matter at issue, the subject of the case **2** COMP ▸ **l'objet aimé** (†† ou *hum*) the beloved one ▸ **objet d'art** objet d'art ▸ **objet social** (*Comm*) business ▸ **objets de toilette** toilet requisites ou articles ▸ **objets trouvés** lost property (office) (*Brit*), lost and found (*US*) ▸ **objets de valeur** valuables ▸ **objet volant non identifié** unidentified flying object

objurgations [ɔbʒyʀgasjɔ̃] NFPL (*littér*) (= *exhortations*) objurgations (*frm*); (= *prières*) pleas, entreaties

oblat, e [ɔbla, at] NM,F oblate

oblation [ɔblasjɔ̃] NF oblation

obligataire [ɔbligatɛʀ] **1** ADJ [*marché*] bond (*épith*); **emprunt ~** bond issue **2** NMF bond ou debenture holder

obligation [ɔbligasjɔ̃] NF **a** (= *contrainte*) obligation; **il faudrait les inviter — ce n'est pas une ~** we should invite them — we don't have to; **avoir l'~ de faire** to be under an obligation to do, be obliged to do; **il se fait une ~ de cette visite/de lui rendre visite** he feels (himself) obliged ou he feels he is under an obligation to make this visit/to visit him; **être** ou **se trouver dans l'~ de faire** to be obliged to do; **sans ~ d'achat** with no ou without obligation to buy; **c'est sans ~ de votre part** there's no obligation on your part, you're under no obligation → **réserve** **b** **~s** (= *devoirs*) obligations, duties; (= *engagements*) commitments; **~s sociales/ professionnelles** social/professional obligations; **~s de citoyen/de chrétien** one's obligations ou responsibilities ou duties as a citizen/Christian; **être dégagé des ~s militaires** to have completed one's military service; **~s familiales** family commitments ou responsibilities; **avoir des ~s envers une autre entreprise** to have a commitment to another firm; (*Pol*) **remplir ses ~s vis-à-vis d'un autre pays** to discharge one's commitments towards another country **c** (*littér* = *reconnaissance*) **~(s)** obligation; **avoir de l'~ à qn** to be under an obligation to sb **d** (*Jur*) obligation; (= *dette*) obligation; **faire face à ses ~s (financières)** to meet one's liabilities; **~ légale** legal obligation; **~ alimentaire** maintenance obligation; **l'~ scolaire** *legal obligation to provide an education for children*; **contracter une ~ envers qn** to contract an obligation towards sb **e** (*Fin* = *titre*) bond, debenture; **~ d'État** government bond; **~s convertibles/à taux fixe/à**

taux variable convertible/fixed-rate/variable-rate bonds

▼ **obligatoire** [ɔbligatwar] ADJ [a] (= *à caractère d'obligation*) compulsory, obligatory; **la scolarité est ~ jusqu'à 16 ans** schooling is compulsory until 16; (*dans un train, pour un spectacle*) **réservation ~** reservations *ou* bookings (*Brit*) required [b] (= *inévitable*) inevitable; **il est arrivé en retard? — c'était ~!** he arrived late? — he was bound to! *ou* it was inevitable!; **c'était ~ qu'il rate son examen** it was inevitable *ou* a foregone conclusion that he would fail his exam, he was bound to fail his exam

obligatoirement [ɔbligatwarmã] ADV [a] (= *nécessairement*) necessarily, obligatorily (*frm*); **les candidats doivent ~ passer une visite médicale** applicants are required to *ou* must have a medical examination; **la réunion se tiendra ~ ici** the meeting will have to be held here; **pas ~** not necessarily [b] (= *inévitablement*) inevitably; **il aura ~ des ennuis s'il continue comme ça** he's bound to *ou* he'll be bound to make trouble for himself if he carries on like that

▼ **obligé, e** [ɔbliʒe] (*ptp de* **obliger**) [1] ADJ [a] (*frm = redevable*) **être ~ à qn** to be (most) obliged to sb, be indebted to sb **de qch** for sth, **d'avoir fait** for having done, for doing) [b] (= *inévitable*) [*conséquence*] inevitable; **c'est ~!** it's inevitable!; **c'était ~!** it had to happen!, it was sure *ou* bound to happen! [c] (= *indispensable*) necessary, required; **le parcours ~ pour devenir ministre** the track record necessary *ou* required in order to become a (government) minister, the required track record of a (government) minister; **ce port est le point de passage ~ pour les livraisons vers l'Europe** all deliveries to Europe have to go through *ou* via this port; **apprendre la langue d'un pays est un passage ~ pour comprendre sa civilisation** learning the language of a country is a prerequisite to understanding *ou* is essential if you want to understand its civilization

[2] NM,F [a] (*Jur*) obligee, debtor; (*Jur*) **le principal ~** the principal obligee [b] (*frm*) **être l'~ de qn** to be under an obligation to sb

obligeamment [ɔbliʒamã] ADV obligingly

obligeance [ɔbliʒãs] NF **ayez l'~ de vous taire pendant que je parle** have the goodness *ou* be good enough to keep quiet while I'm speaking; **il a eu l'~ de me reconduire en voiture** he was obliging *ou* kind enough to drive me back; **nous connaissons tous son ~** we all know how obliging he is

obligeant, e [ɔbliʒã, ãt] ADJ [*offre*] kind, helpful; [*personne, parole*] kind, obliging, helpful

obliger [ɔbliʒe] ▸ conjug 3 ◂ VT [a] (= *forcer*) **~ qn à faire** [*règlement, autorités*] to require sb to do, make it compulsory for sb to do; [*principes moraux*] to oblige *ou* obligate (*US*) sb to do; [*circonstances, agresseur*] to force *ou* oblige *ou* obligate (*US*) sb to do; **le règlement vous y oblige** you are required to by the regulations; **mes principes m'y obligent** I'm bound by my principles (to do it); **l'honneur m'y oblige** I'm honour bound to do it; **quand le temps l'y oblige, il travaille dans sa chambre** when forced *ou* obliged to by the weather, he works in his room; **ses parents l'obligent à travailler dur** his parents make him work hard; **rien ne l'oblige à partir** nothing's forcing him to leave, he's under no obligation to leave; **le manque d'argent l'a obligé à emprunter** lack of money obliged *ou* compelled *ou* forced him to borrow; **tu vas m'~ à me mettre en colère** you're going to make me lose my temper; **je suis obligé de vous laisser** I have to *ou* I must leave you; **il va accepter? — il est bien obligé!** is he going to accept? — he has to! *ou* he has no choice! *ou* alternative!; **tu n'es pas obligé de me croire** you don't have to believe

me [b] (*loc*) **crise économique/compétitivité oblige** given the constraints of the economic crisis/of competitiveness; **tradition oblige** as tradition has it *ou* would have it; **campagne électorale oblige** because of the electoral campaign; **prudence oblige, les gens mettent de l'argent de côté** people have to be cautious and so put money aside → **noblesse** [c] (*Jur*) to bind [d] (= *rendre service à*) to oblige; **vous m'obligeriez en acceptant** *ou* **si vous acceptiez** you would greatly oblige me by accepting *ou* if you accepted; (*formule de politesse*) **je vous serais très obligé de bien vouloir ...** I should be greatly obliged if you would kindly ...; **nous vous serions obligés de bien vouloir nous répondre dans les plus brefs délais** we should appreciate an early reply, we should be grateful to receive an early reply; **entre voisins, il faut bien s'~** neighbours have to help each other *ou* be of service to each other

oblique [ɔblik] [1] ADJ (*gén, Ling, Math*) oblique; **regard ~** sidelong *ou* side glance; (*muscle*) ~ oblique muscle; **en ~** obliquely; **il a traversé la rue en ~** he crossed the street diagonally [2] NF (*Math*) oblique line

obliquement [ɔblikmã] ADV [*planter, fixer*] at an angle; [*se diriger*] obliquely; **regarder qn ~** to look sideways *ou* sidelong at sb, give sb a sidelong look *ou* glance

obliquer [ɔblike] ▸ conjug 1 ◂ VI **obliquez juste avant l'église** turn off just before the church; **~ à droite** to turn off *ou* bear right; **obliquez en direction de la ferme** (*à travers champs*) cut across towards the farm; (*sur un sentier*) turn off towards the farm

obliquité [ɔblik(ɥ)ite] NF [*rayon*] (*Math*) obliqueness, obliquity; (*Astron*) obliquity

oblitérateur [ɔbliteratœr] NM canceller

oblitération [ɔbliterasjɔ̃] NF [a] [*timbre*] cancelling, cancellation; **cachet d'~** postmark [b] († *ou littér*) [*souvenir*] obliteration [c] (*Méd*) [*artère*] obstruction

oblitérer [ɔblitere] ▸ conjug 6 ◂ VT [a] [+ *timbre*] to cancel [b] († *ou littér = effacer*) [+ *souvenir*] to obliterate [c] (*Méd*) [+ *artère*] to obstruct

oblong, -ongue [ɔblɔ̃, 5g] ADJ oblong

obnubiler [ɔbnybile] ▸ conjug 1 ◂ VT to obsess; **se laisser ~ par** to become obsessed by; **elle est obnubilée par l'idée que ...** she's obsessed with the idea that ...

obole [ɔbɔl] NF [a] (= *contribution*) mite, offering; **verser** *ou* **apporter son ~ à qch** to make one's small (financial) contribution to sth [b] (= *monnaie française*) obole; (= *monnaie grecque*) obol

obscène [ɔpsɛn] ADJ [*film, propos, geste*] obscene, lewd; **il est si riche que c'en est ~!** he's obscenely *ou* disgustingly rich!

obscénité [ɔpsenite] NF [a] (= *caractère*) obscenity, lewdness [b] (= *propos, écrit*) obscenity; **dire des ~s** to make obscene remarks

obscur, e [ɔpskyr] ADJ [a] (= *sombre*) [*nuit, ruelle, pièce*] dark → **salle** [b] (= *incompréhensible*) [*texte, passage*] obscure [c] (= *mystérieux*) obscure; **pour des raisons ~es** for some obscure reason; **forces ~es** dark forces [d] (= *vague*) [*malaise*] vague; [*pressentiment, sentiment*] vague, dim [e] (= *méconnu*) [*œuvre, auteur*] obscure; (= *humble*) [*vie, situation, besogne*] obscure, humble; **des gens ~s** humble folk; **de naissance ~e** of obscure *ou* humble birth

obscurantisme [ɔpskyrãtism] NM obscurantism

obscurantiste [ɔpskyrãtist] ADJ, NMF obscurantist

obscurcir [ɔpskyrsir] ▸ conjug 2 ◂ [1] VT [a] (= *assombrir*) to darken; **ce tapis obscurcit la pièce** this carpet makes the room look dark *ou* darkens the room; **des nuages obscurcissaient**

le ciel the sky was dark with clouds [b] (= *compliquer*) to obscure; **ce critique aime ~ les choses les plus simples** this critic likes to obscure *ou* cloud the simplest issues; **cela obscurcit encore plus l'énigme** that deepens the mystery even further [c] (= *troubler*) **le vin obscurcit les idées** wine makes it difficult to think straight

[2] **s'obscurcir** VPR [a] [*ciel*] to darken, grow dark; [*regard*] to darken; **tout d'un coup le temps s'obscurcit** suddenly the sky grew dark *ou* darkened; **son horizon politique s'obscurcit** his political future is looking less and less bright [b] [*style*] to become obscure; [*esprit*] to become confused; [*vue*] to grow dim

obscurcissement [ɔpskyrsismã] NM [*ciel*] darkening; [*esprit*] confusing; [*vue*] dimming

obscurément [ɔpskyremã] ADV obscurely; **il sentait ~ que ...** he felt in an obscure way *ou* a vague (sort of) way that ..., he felt obscurely that ...

obscurité [ɔpskyrite] NF [a] [*nuit*] darkness; **dans l'~** in the dark, in darkness; **la maison fut soudain plongée dans l'~** the house was suddenly plunged into darkness; **il a laissé cet aspect du problème dans l'~** he cast no light *ou* didn't enlighten us on that aspect of the problem [b] [*texte*] obscurity [c] [*vie, situation, besogne, œuvre, auteur*] obscurity; **vivre/travailler dans l'~** to live/work in obscurity [d] (*littér = passage peu clair*) obscure passage

obsédant, e [ɔpsedã, ãt] ADJ [*musique, souvenir*] haunting, obsessive; [*question, idée*] obsessive

obsédé, e [ɔpsede] (*ptp de* **obséder**) NM,F obsessive; **~ (sexuel)** sex maniac; **c'est un ~ de propreté** he's obsessed with cleanliness; (*hum*) **les ~s du caméscope** camcorder freaks*

obséder [ɔpsede] ▸ conjug 6 ◂ VT [a] (= *obnubiler*) to haunt, obsess; **le remords l'obsédait** he was haunted *ou* obsessed by remorse; **être obsédé par** [+ *souvenir, peur*] to be haunted *ou* obsessed by; [+ *idée, problème*] to be obsessed with *ou* by; (*sexuellement*) **il est obsédé** he's obsessed (with sex), he's got a one-track mind* [b] (*littér = importuner*) to pester; **~ qn de ses assiduités** to pester *ou* importune sb with one's attentions

obsèques [ɔpsɛk] NFPL funeral; **~ civiles/religieuses/nationales** civil/religious/state funeral

obséquieusement [ɔpsekjøzmã] ADV obsequiously

obséquieux, -ieuse [ɔpsekjø, jøz] ADJ obsequious

obséquiosité [ɔpsekjozite] NF obsequiousness

observable [ɔpsɛrvabl] ADJ observable; **ce phénomène est difficilement ~** this phenomenon is not easy to observe

observance [ɔpsɛrvãs] NF observance; **de stricte ~** devout

observateur, -trice [ɔpsɛrvatœr, tris] [1] ADJ [*personne, regard*] observant [2] NM,F observer; **avoir des talents d'~** to have a talent for observation; **~ des Nations Unies** United Nations *ou* UN observer

observation [ɔpsɛrvasjɔ̃] NF [a] (= *obéissance*) [*règle*] observance [b] (= *examen, surveillance*) observation; (*Méd*) **être/mettre en ~** to be/put under observation; (*Mil*) **~ aérienne** aerial observation; **technique/instrument d'~** observation technique/instrument; (*Sport*) **round/set d'~** first round/set (*in which one plays a guarded or a wait-and-see game*) → **poste², satellite** [c] (= *chose observée*) observation; **il consignait ses ~s dans son carnet** he noted down his observations *ou* what he had observed in his notebook [d] (= *remarque*) observation, remark; (= *objection*) remark; (= *reproche*) reproof; (*Scol*) warning; **il fit quelques ~s judicieuses** he made one or two judicious remarks *ou* observations; **je lui en fis l'~** I pointed it out to him; **ce film appelle quelques ~s** this film calls for some comment; **pas d'~s je vous prie** no remarks *ou* comments please; **faire une ~ à qn** to reprove sb; *(Scol)* **~s** teacher's comments

observatoire [ɔpsɛʀvatwaʀ] NM a (*Astron*) observatory b (*Mil = lieu*) observation *ou* look-out post; **~ économique** economic research institute

observer [ɔpsɛʀve] ▸conjug 1◂ 1 VT a (= *regarder*) *(gén)* to observe, watch; [+ *adversaire, proie*] to watch; *(Sci)* [+ *phénomène, réaction*] to observe; *(au microscope)* to examine; **se sentant observée, elle se retourna** feeling she was being watched *ou* observed she turned round; **il ne dit pas grand-chose mais il observe** he doesn't say much but he observes what goes on around him *ou* he watches keenly what goes on around him
b (= *contrôler*) **~ ses manières/ses gestes** to be mindful of *ou* watch one's manners/one's gestures
c (= *remarquer*) to notice, observe; **elle n'observe jamais rien** she never notices anything; **faire ~ que** to point out *ou* remark *ou* observe that; **faire ~ un détail à qn** to point out a detail to sb, bring a detail to sb's attention; **je vous ferai ~ qu'il est interdit de fumer ici** I should like to *ou* I must point out (to you) that you're not allowed to smoke here
d (= *dire*) to observe, remark; **vous êtes en retard, observa-t-il** you're late, he observed *ou* remarked
e (= *respecter*) [+ *règlement*] to observe, abide by; [+ *fête, jeûne*] to keep, observe; [+ *coutume, trêve, neutralité*] to observe; **~ une minute de silence** to observe a minute's silence; **faire ~ un règlement** to enforce a rule
f (*littér*) [+ *attitude, maintien*] to keep (up), maintain
2 **s'observer** VPR a (*réciproque*) to observe *ou* watch each other
b (*réfléchi = surveiller sa tenue, son langage*) to keep a check on o.s., be careful of one's behaviour; **il ne s'observe pas assez en public** he's not careful enough of his behaviour in public
c (*passif = se manifester*) to be observed

obsession [ɔpsesjɔ̃] NF obsession; **il avait l'~ de la mort/l'argent** he had an obsession with death/money, he was obsessed by death/money; **je veux aller à Londres — c'est une ~ !/ça tourne à l'~ !** I want to go to London — you're obsessed!/it's becoming an obsession!

obsessionnel, -elle [ɔpsesjɔnɛl] 1 ADJ obsessional, obsessive → **névrose** 2 NM,F obsessive

obsidienne [ɔpsidjɛn] NF obsidian, volcanic glass

obsolescence [ɔpsɔlesɑ̃s] NF (*Tech, littér*) obsolescence

obsolescent, e [ɔpsɔlesɑ̃, ɑ̃t] ADJ (*Tech, littér*) obsolescent

obsolète [ɔpsɔlɛt] ADJ obsolete

obstacle [ɔpstakl] NM (*gén*) obstacle; (*Hippisme*) fence; (*Équitation*) jump, fence; **~ technique/juridique** technical/legal barrier *ou* obstacle; **faire ~ à la lumière** to block (out) *ou* obstruct the light; **faire ~ à un projet** to hinder a project, put obstacles *ou* an obstacle in the way of a project; **tourner l'~** (*Équitation*) to go round *ou* outside the jump; (*fig*) to get round the obstacle *ou* difficulty; (*lit, fig*) **progresser sans rencontrer d'~s** to make progress without meeting any obstacles; **dans ce métier, son âge n'est pas un ~** his age is no impediment *ou* obstacle in this job; **je ne vois pas d'~ à sa venue** *ou* **à ce qu'il vienne** I don't see any reason why he shouldn't come → **course, refuser**

obstétrical, e (*mpl* **-aux**) [ɔpstetʀikal, o] ADJ obstetric(al)

obstétricien, -ienne [ɔpstetʀisjɛ̃, jɛn] NM,F obstetrician

obstétrique [ɔpstetʀik] 1 ADJ obstetric(al) 2 NF obstetrics *sg*

obstination [ɔpstinasjɔ̃] NF [*personne, caractère*] obstinacy, stubbornness; **~ à faire** obstinate *ou* stubborn determination to do; **son ~ à refuser** his persistency in refusing, his persistent refusal

obstiné, e [ɔpstine] (*ptp de* **s'obstiner**) ADJ [*personne, caractère*] obstinate, stubborn; [*efforts, résistance, travail, demandes*] obstinate, persistent; [*refus, silence*] stubborn; [*brouillard, pluie, malchance*] persistent; [*toux*] persistent, stubborn

obstinément [ɔpstinemɑ̃] ADV stubbornly, obstinately; **le téléphone reste ~ muet** the telephone stubbornly refuses to ring

obstiner (s') [ɔpstine] ▸conjug 1◂ VPR to insist, dig one's heels in (*fig*); **s'~ sur un problème** to keep working *ou* labour away stubbornly at a problem; **s'~ dans une opinion** to cling stubbornly *ou* doggedly to an opinion; **s'~ dans son refus (de faire qch)** to refuse categorically *ou* absolutely (to do sth); **s'~ à faire** to persist in doing; **s'~ au silence** to remain obstinately silent, maintain an obstinate *ou* a stubborn silence; **j'ai dit non mais il s'obstine !** I said no but he insists!

obstruction [ɔpstʀyksjɔ̃] NF a (= *blocage*) obstruction, blockage; (*Méd*) obstruction b (= *tactique*) obstruction; **faire de l'~** (*Pol*) to obstruct (the passage of) legislation; (*gén*) to use obstructive tactics, be obstructive; (*Ftbl*) to obstruct; **faire de l'~ parlementaire** to filibuster

obstructionnisme [ɔpstʀyksjɔnism] NM obstructionism, filibustering

obstructionniste [ɔpstʀyksjɔnist] 1 ADJ obstructionist, filibustering (*épith*) 2 NMF obstructionist, filibuster, filibusterer

obstruer [ɔpstʀye] ▸conjug 1◂ 1 VT [+ *passage, circulation, artère*] to obstruct, block; **~ la vue/le passage** to block *ou* obstruct the view/the way 2 **s'obstruer** VPR [*passage*] to get blocked up; [*artère*] to become blocked

obtempérer [ɔptɑ̃peʀe] ▸conjug 6◂ **obtempérer à** VT INDIR to obey, comply with; **il refusa d'~** he refused to comply *ou* obey; **refus d'~** refusal to comply

obtenir [ɔptəniʀ] ▸conjug 22◂ VT a (= *réussir à avoir*) [+ *permission, explication, augmentation, diplôme, visa*] to obtain, get; [+ *récompense, prix*] to obtain; **~ satisfaction** to obtain satisfaction; **~ la main de qn** to gain *ou* win sb's hand; **je peux vous ~ ce livre rapidement** I can get you this book quite quickly; **il m'a fait ~** *ou* **il m'a obtenu de l'avancement** he got me promotion for me, he got me promoted; **il obtint de lui parler** he was (finally) allowed to speak to him; **elle a obtenu qu'il paie** she got him to pay up, she managed to make him pay up; **j'ai obtenu de lui qu'il ne dise rien** I got him to agree not to say anything
b (= *parvenir à*) [+ *résultat, température*] to achieve, obtain; [+ *total*] to reach, arrive at; **~ un succès aux élections** to have *ou* achieve a success in the elections; **cette couleur s'obtient par un mélange** this colour is obtained through *ou* by mixing; **en additionnant ces quantités, on obtient 2 000** when you add these amounts together you arrive at *ou* get 2,000; **~ un corps à l'état gazeux** to obtain a body in the gaseous state

obtention [ɔptɑ̃sjɔ̃] NF [*permission, explication, diplôme*] obtaining; [*résultat, température*] achieving; **pour l'~ du visa** to obtain the visa; **les délais d'~ de la carte de séjour** the time it takes to obtain a resident's permit; (*Culin*) **mélangez le tout jusqu'à (l')~ d'une pâte**

onctueuse mix everything together until the mixture is smooth

obturateur, -trice [ɔptyʀatœʀ, tʀis] 1 ADJ (*Tech*) [*plaque*] obturating; [*membrane, muscle*] obturator (*épith*) 2 NM a (*Photo*) shutter; **~ à secteur** rotary shutter; **~ à rideau** focal plane shutter; **~ à tambour** *ou* **à boisseaux** drum shutter b (*Tech*) obturator; [*fusil*] gas check

obturation [ɔptyʀasjɔ̃] NF [*conduit, ouverture*] closing (up), sealing; [*fuite*] sealing; [*dent*] filling; **faire une ~ (dentaire)** to fill a tooth, do a filling; (*Photo*) **vitesse d'~** shutter speed

obturer [ɔptyʀe] ▸conjug 1◂ VT [+ *conduit, ouverture*] to close (up), seal; [+ *fuite*] to seal *ou* block off; [+ *dent*] to fill

obtus, e [ɔpty, yz] ADJ (*Math*) [*angle*] obtuse; (*fig = stupide*) dull-witted, obtuse

obus [ɔby] NM shell; **~ explosif** high-explosive shell; **~ fumigène** smoke bomb; **~ incendiaire** incendiary *ou* fire bomb; **~ de mortier** mortar shell; **~ perforant** armour-piercing shell → **éclat, trou**

obusier [ɔbyzje] NM howitzer; **~ de campagne** field howitzer

obvier [ɔbvje] ▸conjug 7◂ **obvier à** VT INDIR (*littér*) [+ *danger, mal*] to take precautions against, obviate (*frm*); [+ *inconvénient*] to overcome, obviate (*frm*)

OC (ABRÉV = **ondes courtes**) SW

oc [ɔk] NM → **langue**

LANGUE D'OC, LANGUE D'OIL

The terms **langue d'oc** *(also called "occitan") and* **langue d'oïl** *broadly refer to the local languages and dialects spoken in the southern and northern half of France respectively. "Oc" and "oïl" mean "yes" in southern and northern dialects respectively.*

---

ocarina [ɔkaʀina] NM ocarina

occase [ɔkaz] NF (ABRÉV = **occasion**) a (= *article usagé*) secondhand buy; (= *achat avantageux*) bargain, snip* (*Brit*); **d'~** [*livres, vêtements*] secondhand, used (*US*), pre-owned (*US*); [*acheter, vendre*] secondhand b (= *conjoncture favorable*) (lucky) chance

occasion [ɔkazjɔ̃] NF a (= *circonstance*) occasion; **cela a été l'~ d'une grande discussion** it gave rise to *ou* occasioned a great discussion; **à cette ~** on that occasion; **à l'~ de son anniversaire** on the occasion of his birthday, for his birthday; **dans/pour les grandes ~s** on/for important *ou* special occasions; **la bouteille/la robe des grandes ~s** the bottle put by/the dress kept for special *ou* great occasions; **pour l'~** for the occasion; **je l'ai rencontré à plusieurs ~s** I've met him on several occasions
b (= *conjoncture favorable*) opportunity, chance; **avoir l'~ de faire** to have the *ou* a chance *ou* the *ou* an opportunity of doing *ou* to do; **profiter de l'~ pour faire qch** to take the opportunity to do sth; **sauter sur*** *ou* **saisir l'~** to jump at *ou* seize *ou* grab* the opportunity *ou* chance; **il a laissé échapper** *ou* **passer l'~** he let the opportunity pass him by *ou* slip; **manquer** *ou* **rater*** *ou* **perdre une ~ de faire** to miss an opportunity to do; (*iro*) **tu as manqué** *ou* **raté* une belle** *ou* **bonne ~ de te taire** you'd have done better to have kept quiet *ou* to have kept your mouth shut; **c'est l'~ rêvée !** it's a heaven-sent opportunity!; **c'est l'~ rêvée de faire** it's an ideal opportunity to do; **c'est l'~ ou jamais !** it's now or never!; **c'est l'~ ou jamais d'observer cette comète** it's a once-in-a-lifetime chance *ou* opportunity to observe this comet; **si l'~ se présente** if the opportunity arises, should the opportunity arise; **à la première ~** at the earliest *ou* first opportunity
c (*Comm*) secondhand buy; **(le marché de) l'~** the secondhand market; **faire le neuf et l'~** to deal in new and secondhand goods; **d'~**

[*voiture*] secondhand, used (*US*), pre-owned (*US*); [*livres*] secondhand, used (*US*); [*acheter, vendre*] secondhand

d (* = *acquisition très avantageuse*) bargain, snip* (*Brit*)

e (*loc*) **à l'~** sometimes, on occasions; **à l'~ venez dîner** come and have dinner some time; **d'~** [*amitié, rencontre*] casual; **par la même ~** at the same time; **j'irai à Paris et, par la même ~, je leur rendrai visite** I'll go to Paris and while I'm at it* I'll go and visit them ■ (*PROV*) **l'~ fait le larron** opportunity makes the thief (*PROV*)

occasionnel, -elle [ɔkazjɔnɛl] ADJ **a** (= *non régulier*) [*rencontres, disputes*] occasional (*épith*); [*client, visiteur*] casual, occasional (*épith*); [*travaux, emploi*] casual **b** (= *fortuit*) [*incident, rencontre*] chance (*épith*) **c** (*Philo*) occasional

occasionnellement [ɔkazjɔnɛlmɑ̃] ADV occasionally, from time to time

occasionner [ɔkazjɔne] ▶conjug 1◀ VT [+ *frais, dérangement*] to cause, occasion (*frm*); [+ *accident*] to cause, bring about; **en espérant ne pas vous ~ trop de dérangement** hoping not to put you to *ou* to cause you too much trouble; **cet accident va m'~ beaucoup de frais** this accident is going to involve me in *ou* to cause me a great deal of expense

occident [ɔksidɑ̃] NM (*littér* = *ouest*) west; **l'Occident** the West, the Occident (*littér*) → **empire**

occidental, e (*mpl -aux*) [ɔksidɑ̃tal, o] **1** ADJ (*littér* = *d'ouest*) western; (*Pol*) [*pays, peuple*] Western, Occidental (*littér*) → **Inde 2** **Occidental(e)** NM,F Westerner, Occidental (*littér*); **les Occidentaux** (*gén*) Westerners; (*Pol*) the West, western countries

occidentalisation [ɔksidɑ̃talizasjɔ̃] NF westernization

occidentaliser [ɔksidɑ̃talize] ▶conjug 1◀ **1** VT to westernize **2** **s'occidentaliser** VPR to become westernized

occipital, e (*mpl -aux*) [ɔksipital, o] **1** ADJ occipital; **trou ~** occipital foramen, foramen magnum **2** NM occipital (bone)

occiput [ɔksipyt] NM back of the head, occiput (*SPÉC*)

occire [ɔksiʀ] VT (†† *ou hum*) to slay

occitan, e [ɔksitɑ̃, an] **1** ADJ, NM Occitan **2** **Occitan(e)** NM,F Occitan

Occitanie [ɔksitani] NF *region in France where Occitan is spoken*

occitaniste [ɔksitanist] NMF specialist in Occitan

occlure [ɔklyʀ] ▶conjug 35◀ VT (*Chim, Méd*) to occlude

occlusif, -ive [ɔklyzif, iv] ADJ (*gén*) occlusive; (*Ling*) occlusive, plosive; **(consonne) occlusive** occlusive, stop (consonant)

occlusion [ɔklyzjɔ̃] NF (*Ling, Méd, Mét, Tech*) occlusion; **~ intestinale** intestinal blockage, obstruction of the bowels *ou* intestines, ileus (*SPÉC*)

occultation [ɔkyltasjɔ̃] NF (*Astron*) occultation; (*fig*) overshadowing, eclipse; **l'~ du problème du chômage pendant la campagne électorale** the temporary eclipse of the issue of unemployment during the election campaign

occulte [ɔkylt] ADJ **a** (= *surnaturel*) supernatural, occult → **science b** (= *secret*) [+ *financement, fonds*] secret, covert; [+ *commission, prime*] hidden; [+ *pouvoir, rôle*] secret, hidden

occulter [ɔkylte] ▶conjug 1◀ VT (*Astron, Tech*) to occult; (*fig*) to overshadow, eclipse; **n'essayez pas d'~ le problème** don't try to hide the problem

occultisme [ɔkyltism] NM occultism

occultiste [ɔkyltist] ADJ, NMF occultist

occupant, e [ɔkypɑ̃, ɑ̃t] **1** ADJ (*Pol*) [*autorité, puissance*] occupying; **l'armée ~e** the army of occupation, the occupying army **2** NM,F [*maison*] occupant, occupier; [*place, compartiment, voiture*] occupant; (*gén, Jur*) **le premier ~** the first occupier **3** NM **l'~** ◊ **les ~s** the occupying forces

occupation [ɔkypasjɔ̃] NF **a** (*Mil, Pol*) occupation; **les forces/l'armée d'~** the forces/the army of occupation, the occupying forces/army; (*Hist*) **pendant l'Occupation** during the Occupation; **grève avec ~ d'usine** sit-in, sit-down strike **b** (*Jur*) [*logement*] occupancy, occupation **c** (= *passe-temps*) occupation; (= *emploi*) occupation, job; **vaquer à ses ~s** to go about one's business, attend to one's affairs; **une ~ fixe/temporaire** a permanent/temporary job *ou* occupation; **les enfants, ça donne de l'~** having children certainly keeps you busy

▼**occupé, e** [ɔkype] (*ptp de* **occuper**) ADJ **a** (= *affairé*) busy; (= *non disponible*) busy, engaged; **je suis très ~ en ce moment** I'm very busy at the moment; **il ne peut pas vous recevoir, il est ~** he can't see you, he's busy **b** [*ligne téléphonique*] engaged (*Brit*) (*attrib*), busy (*US*) (*attrib*); [*toilettes*] occupied, engaged (*Brit*) (*attrib*); [*places, sièges*] taken (*attrib*); **ça sonne ~** * it's engaged (*Brit*) *ou* busy (*US*) **c** (*Mil, Pol*) occupied

occuper [ɔkype] ▶conjug 1◀ **1** VT **a** [+ *endroit, appartement*] to occupy; [+ *place, surface*] to occupy, take up; **le bureau occupait le coin de la pièce** the desk stood in *ou* occupied the corner of the room; **leurs bureaux occupent tout l'étage** their offices take up *ou* occupy the whole floor; **le piano occupe très peu/trop de place** the piano takes up very little/too much room; **l'appartement qu'ils occupent est trop exigu** the flat they are living in *ou* occupying is too small **b** [+ *moment, période*] (= *prendre*) to occupy, fill, take up; (= *faire passer*) to occupy, spend, employ; **cette besogne occupait le reste de la journée** this task took up (*up*) *ou* occupied the rest of the day; **la lecture occupe une trop petite/très grande part de mon temps** reading takes up *ou* occupies far too little/a great deal of my time; **comment ~ ses loisirs ?** how should one spend *ou* occupy *ou* employ one's free time? **c** [+ *poste, fonction*] to hold, occupy; [+ *rang*] to hold, have **d** (= *absorber*) [+ *personne, enfant*] to occupy, keep occupied *ou* busy; (= *employer*) [+ *main d'œuvre*] to employ; **mon travail m'occupe beaucoup** my work keeps me very busy; **laisse-le faire, ça l'occupe !** let him get on with it, it keeps him busy! *ou* occupied!; **la ganterie occupait naguère un millier d'ouvriers dans cette région** the glove industry used to employ *ou* give employment to about a thousand workers in this area; **le sujet qui nous occupe aujourd'hui** the matter which concerns us today, the matter at hand **e** (*Mil, Pol*) (= *envahir*) to take over, occupy; (= *être maître de*) to occupy; **ils ont occupé tout le pays/l'immeuble** they took over *ou* occupied the whole country/the whole building; **les forces qui occupaient le pays** the forces occupying the country; **grâce à son nouveau produit, l'entreprise occupe le terrain** thanks to its new product the company has been able to take a prominent position in the market; **il veut ~ le terrain médiatique** he wants to hog* the media limelight

2 **s'occuper** VPR **a** **s'~ de qch** (= *se charger de*) to deal with sth, take care *ou* charge of sth; (= *être chargé de*) to be in charge of sth, be dealing with *ou* taking care of sth; (= *s'intéresser à*) to take an interest in sth, interest o.s. in sth; **je vais m'~ de ce problème** I'll deal with *ou* take care of this problem; **c'est lui qui s'occupe de cette affaire** he's the one in charge of *ou* who is dealing with this matter; **il s'occupe de vous trouver un emploi** he is undertaking to find you a job, he'll see about finding you a job; **je vais m'~ de rassembler les documents nécessaires** I'll set about *ou* see about gathering (together) the necessary documents, I'll undertake to get the necessary documents together; **il s'occupe un peu de politique** he takes a bit of an interest *ou* he dabbles a bit in politics; **je m'occupe de tout** I'll see to everything, I'll take care of everything; **je m'occuperai des boissons** I'll organize *ou* look after the drinks; **il veut s'~ de trop de choses à la fois** he tries to take on *ou* to do too many things at once; **ne t'occupe pas de ça, c'est leur problème** don't worry about it, that's their problem; **occupe-toi de tes affaires*** *ou* **oignons*** mind your own business; **t'occupe (pas) !‡** none of your business!*, mind your own business!

b **s'~ de qn** (= *se charger de*) [+ *enfants, malades*] to take charge *ou* care of, look after; [+ *client*] to attend to; (= *être responsable de*) [+ *enfants, malades*] to be in charge of, look after; **je vais m'~ des enfants** I'll take charge *ou* care of *ou* I'll look after the children; **qui s'occupe des malades ?** who is in charge of *ou* looks after the patients?; **je m'occupe de vous tout de suite** I'll be with you in a moment; **est-ce qu'on s'occupe de vous Madame ?** is someone serving you?, are you being attended to? *ou* served?

c (= *s'affairer*) to occupy o.s., keep o.s. busy; **s'~ à faire qch/à qch** to busy o.s. doing sth/with sth; **il a trouvé à s'~** he has found something to do *ou* to occupy his time *ou* to fill his time with; **il y a de quoi s'~** there is plenty to do *ou* to keep one busy *ou* occupied; **je ne sais pas à quoi m'~** I don't know what to do with myself *ou* how to keep myself busy *ou* occupied; **s'~ l'esprit** to keep one's mind occupied

occurrence [ɔkyʀɑ̃s] NF **a** (*frm*) instance, case; **en cette/toute autre ~** in this/in any other instance; **en l'~** as it happens; **en pareille ~** in such circumstances, in such a case; (*frm*) **suivant** *ou* **selon l'~** according to the circumstances **b** (*Ling*) occurrence, token

OCDE [ɔsedeə] NF (ABRÉV = **Organisation de coopération et de développement économique**) OECD

océan [ɔseɑ̃] NM **a** (*lit*) ocean; (= *Atlantique*) **l'Océan** the Atlantic (Ocean); **un ~ de verdure/de sable** a sea of greenery/of sand; **l'~ Antarctique** *ou* **Austral** the Antarctic (Ocean); **l'~ Arctique** the Arctic (Ocean); **l'~ Atlantique** the Atlantic (Ocean); **l'~ glacial** the polar sea; **l'~ Indien** the Indian Ocean; **l'~ Pacifique** the Pacific (Ocean) **b** (*Myth*) **Océan** Oceanus

océane [ɔsean] ADJ F **a** (*littér*) [*vague, tempête*] ocean (*épith*); [*fureur, senteur*] of the sea *ou* ocean; **l'(autoroute) ~** *the motorway that links Paris to Brittany* **b** (*Culin*) [*salade, paella*] seafood (*épith*)

Océanie [ɔseani] NF **l'~** Oceania, the South Sea Islands

océanien, -ienne [ɔseanjɛ̃, jɛn] **1** ADJ Oceanian, Oceanic **2** NM,F: **O~(ne)** South Sea Islander, Oceanian

océanique [ɔseanik] ADJ oceanic

océanographe [ɔseanɔgʀaf] NMF oceanographer

océanographie [ɔseanɔgʀafi] NF oceanography

océanographique [ɔseanɔgʀafik] ADJ oceanographical

océanologie [ɔseanɔlɔʒi] NF oceanology

océanologique [ɔseanɔlɔʒik] ADJ oceanological

océanologue [ɔseanɔlɔg] NMF oceanologist

ocelle [ɔsɛl] NM ocellus

ocellé, e [ɔsele, ɔsɛlle] ADJ ocellate(d)

> GRAMMAIRE ACTIVE: **occupé** 27.3

ocelot [ɔs(ə)lo] NM (= *animal*) ocelot; (= *fourrure*) ocelot fur

ocre [ɔkʀ] NMF, ADJ INV ochre

ocré, e [ɔkʀe] ADJ ochred

octaèdre [ɔktaɛdʀ] **1** ADJ octahedral **2** NM octahedron

octaédrique [ɔktaedʀik] ADJ octahedral

octal, e [pl **-aux**] [ɔktal, o] ADJ octal; **système ~** octal notation

octane [ɔktan] NM octane → **indice**

octante [ɔktɑ̃t] ADJ INV (*dial*) eighty

octave [ɔktav] NF **a** (*Mus*) octave; **monter à l'~** to go an octave higher **b** (*Escrime, Rel*) octave

octet [ɔktɛ] NM byte

octobre [ɔktɔbʀ] NM October; *pour autres locutions voir* **septembre**

octogénaire [ɔktɔʒenɛʀ] ADJ, NMF octogenarian

octogonal, e [*mpl* **-aux**] [ɔktɔgɔnal, o] ADJ octagonal, eight-sided

octogone [ɔktɔgɔn] NM octagon

octopode [ɔktɔpɔd] **1** ADJ octopod **2** NM octopod; **les ~s** octopods, Octopoda (*SPÉC*)

octosyllabe [ɔktosi(l)lab] **1** ADJ octosyllabic **2** NM octosyllable

octosyllabique [ɔktosi(l)labik] ADJ octosyllabic

octroi [ɔktʀwa] NM **a** [*charte, permission, délai, augmentation*] granting; [*faveur, pardon*] bestowing, granting; **l'~ d'une bourse n'est pas automatique** grants are not given automatically **b** (*Hist*) octroi, city toll

octroyer [ɔktʀwaje] ▸ conjug 8 ◂ **1** VT (*frm*) [+ *charte, permission, délai, augmentation*] to grant (**à** to); [+ *bourse*] to give (**à** to); [+ *faveur, pardon*] to bestow (**à** on, upon), grant (**à** to) **2** **s'octroyer** VPR [+ *droit, pouvoirs*] to claim; (*Sport*) [+ *médaille, place*] to claim, win; **s'~ une augmentation** to give o.s. a pay rise; **je vais m'~ quelques jours de congé** I'm going to allow myself a few days off

octuor [ɔktɥɔʀ] NM (*Mus*) octet

oculaire [ɔkylɛʀ] **1** ADJ (*Anat*) ocular → **globe, témoin** **2** NM (*Opt*) eyepiece, ocular (*SPÉC*)

oculiste [ɔkylist] NMF eye specialist, oculist, eye doctor (*US*)

odalisque [ɔdalisk] NF odalisque

ode [ɔd] NF ode

odeur [ɔdœʀ] NF **a** (*gén: bonne ou mauvaise*) smell, odour (*Brit*), odor (*US*); (*agréable*) [*fleur, parfum*] fragrance, scent; **sans ~** odourless (*Brit*), odorless (*US*), which has no smell; **mauvaise ~** bad *ou* unpleasant smell; **produit qui combat les (mauvaises) ~s** air freshener; **~ suave/délicieuse** sweet/delicious smell *ou* scent; **à l'~ fétide** evil-smelling, foul-smelling; **~ de brûlé/de gaz** smell of burning/of gas; **~ de renfermé** musty *ou* fusty smell; **avoir une bonne/une mauvaise ~** to smell nice/bad → **argent b** (*loc*) **ne pas être en ~ de sainteté auprès de qn** to be in sb's bad books, be out of favour with sb, be in bad odour with sb; (*Rel*) **mourir en ~ de sainteté** to die in the odour of sanctity

odieusement [ɔdjøzmɑ̃] ADV odiously

odieux, -ieuse [ɔdjø, jøz] ADJ **a** (= *infâme*) [*personne, conduite, caractère, tâche*] obnoxious, odious; [*crime*] heinous, odious; [*chantage, accusation*] odious; **tu as été ~ avec elle** you were obnoxious *ou* horrible to her; **c'est ~ ce que tu viens de dire!** that's a horrible thing to say! **b** (= *insupportable*) [*gamin, élève*] obnoxious, unbearable; **la vie m'est odieuse** life is unbearable to me; **cette femme m'est odieuse** I can't bear that woman, I find that woman (quite) unbearable

odontologie [ɔdɔ̃tɔlɔʒi] NF odontology

---

odontologique [ɔdɔ̃tɔlɔʒik] ADJ odontological

odontologiste [ɔdɔ̃tɔlɔʒist] NMF odontologist

odorant, e [ɔdɔʀɑ̃, ɑ̃t] ADJ (*gén*) scented; (*plus agréable*) fragrant, sweet-smelling; [*herbes, essences*] aromatic; [*substance, molécule*] odorous

odorat [ɔdɔʀa] NM (sense of) smell; **avoir l'~ fin** to have a keen sense of smell

odoriférant, e [ɔdɔʀiferɑ̃, ɑ̃t] ADJ sweet-smelling, fragrant, odoriferous (*littér*)

odyssée [ɔdise] NF odyssey; (*Littérat*) **L'Odyssée** the Odyssey

OEA [ɔəa] NF (ABRÉV = **Organisation des États américains**) OAS

œcuménique [ekymenik] ADJ (o)ecumenical → **concile**

œcuménisme [ekymenism] NM (o)ecumenicalism, (o)ecumenism

œcuméniste [ekymenist] ADJ, NMF (o)ecumenist

œdémateux, -euse [edematø, øz] ADJ oedematous, oedematose

œdème [edɛm] NM oedema; **~ du poumon** pulmonary oedema

œdipien, -ienne [edipjɛ̃, jɛn] ADJ oedipal, oedipean

œil [œj]

pluriel **yeux**
1 NOM MASCULIN   **2** COMPOSÉS

1 NOM MASCULIN

a *Anat* eye; **il a les yeux bleus** he has blue eyes, his eyes are blue; **aux yeux bleus** blue-eyed, with blue eyes; **yeux de biche** doe eyes; **aux yeux de biche** doe-eyed (*épith*); **yeux en boutons de bottines** button eyes; **elle se fait les yeux** she's putting her eye make-up on; **elle a les yeux faits** ◊ **elle s'est fait les yeux** she's wearing eye make-up; **avoir un ~ au beurre noir*** *ou* **un ~ poché*** to have a black eye *ou* a shiner*; **avoir les yeux battus** to have dark *ou* black rings under one's eyes; **avoir un ~ qui dit zut*** *ou* **merde!** à l'autre ◊ **avoir les yeux qui se croisent (les bras)*** ◊ **avoir un ~ à Paris, l'autre à Pontoise*** to be cross-eyed* *ou* boss-eyed*, have a squint; **les yeux lui sortaient de la tête** ◊ **il avait les yeux hors de la tête** his eyes were (nearly) popping out of his head, his eyes were out on stalks* (*Brit*); **je vois mal de cet ~** I don't see well with this eye; **je l'ai vu de mes (propres) yeux** ◊ **je l'ai vu, de mes yeux vu** I saw it with my own eyes; **regarde-moi dans les yeux** look me in the eye; **j'ai le soleil dans les yeux** the sun is in my eyes, I've got the sun in my eyes; **la casquette sur l'~** with his cap cocked over one eye; **faire qch pour les beaux yeux de qn** to do sth just for sb *ou* just to please sb; **il n'a pas les yeux en face des trous*** (= *il est endormi*) he's half asleep; (= *il n'arrive pas à réfléchir*) he's not thinking straight; **il a les yeux plus grands** *ou* **gros que le ventre** (*gloutonnerie*) his eyes are bigger than his belly *ou* stomach; (*ambition*) he has bitten off more than he can chew ■ (*PROV*) **~ pour ~, dent pour dent** an eye for an eye, a tooth for a tooth (*PROV*) → **fermer, gros**

♦ **à l'œil nu** [*visible, identifiable, invisible*] to the naked eye; **on peut observer cette comète à l'~ nu** the comet is visible to the naked eye

♦ **les yeux dans les yeux** : **se regarder les yeux dans les yeux** to gaze into each other's eyes; **je lui ai dit/répliqué les yeux dans les yeux ...** I looked him straight in the eye and said/replied ...; **ils en ont discuté les yeux dans les yeux** (*franchement*) they spoke very frankly with each other

b = **regard** **attirer** *ou* **tirer l'~ de qn** to catch sb's eye; **publicité qui attire l'~** eye-catching advertisement; **être agréable à l'~** to be easy on the eye; **n'avoir d'yeux que pour qn/qch** to have one's attention focussed on sb/sth; **il n'a**

---

d'yeux que pour elle he only has eyes for her; **jeter un ~*** à *ou* **sur qn/qch** to have a look* at sb/sth; **cela s'est passé devant nos yeux** it happened in front of *ou* before *ou* under our very eyes → **chercher, couver, dévorer, suivre**

♦ **aux yeux de** (= *en étant vu de*) : **faire qch aux yeux de tous** to do sth in full view of everyone

♦ **les yeux fermés** (= *sans regarder*) with one's eyes closed *ou* shut; (= *avec confiance*) with complete confidence; **j'irais les yeux fermés** I could get there with my eyes closed

♦ **sous l'œil** *ou* **les yeux de** : **vous avez l'article sous les yeux** you have the article there before you *ou* right in front of you *ou* your eyes; **sous l'~ (vigilant/inquiet) de** under the (watchful/anxious) eye *ou* gaze of; **ils jouaient sous l'~ de leur mère** they played under the watchful eye of their mother *ou* with their mother looking on; **sous l'~ des caméras** in front of the cameras

c = **faculté de voir** **avoir de bons/mauvais yeux** to have good/bad eyes *ou* eyesight; **il n'a plus ses yeux de vingt ans** his eyes aren't what they used to be; **avoir un ~** *ou* **des yeux de lynx** (= *avoir une très bonne vue*) to have eyes like a hawk; (*fig*) to be eagle-eyed; **avoir des yeux de chat** (= *voir dans le noir*) to have good night vision; **il faudrait avoir des yeux derrière la tête** you need eyes in the back of your head

d = **expression** look; **il a l'~ taquin/méchant** he has a twinkle/a malicious look in his eye; **elle a l'~ vif** she has a lively look about her *ou* a lively expression; **il le regardait l'~ mauvais** *ou* **d'un ~ mauvais** he fixed him with a threatening stare *ou* look, he looked *ou* stared at him threateningly; **faire des yeux de velours à qn** ◊ **faire les yeux doux à qn** to make sheep's eyes at sb; **faire de l'~ à qn*** to make eyes at sb, give sb the eye*; **faire** *ou* **ouvrir des yeux ronds** ◊ **ouvrir de grands yeux** to stare wide-eyed; **il me regardait avec des yeux comme des soucoupes** he looked at me with eyes like saucers; **regarder qn avec des yeux de merlan frit*** *ou* **de crapaud mort d'amour*** to look at sb like a lovesick puppy; **faire des yeux de merlan frit*** (*surprise*) to gawp*

e = **attention, observation** **il a l'~*** he has sharp *ou* keen eyes; **avoir l'~ à tout** to keep an eye on everything; **avoir l'~ américain** to have a quick eye; **avoir l'~ du spécialiste/du maître** to have a trained/an expert eye, have the eye of a specialist/of an expert; **cacher qch aux yeux de qn** to hide sth from sb's eyes; **il n'a pas les yeux dans sa poche** he doesn't miss a thing; **garder un ~ sur qn/qch** to keep an eye on sb/sth; **être tout yeux*** to be all eyes* → **compas, ouvrir**

♦ **à l'œil** (= *sous surveillance*) **avoir** *ou* **tenir qn à l'~** to keep an eye on sb; **je vous ai à l'~ !** I've got my eye on you!

f = **jugement** **voir** *ou* **regarder qch d'un bon/d'un mauvais ~** to look on *ou* view sth favourably/unfavourably, view sth in a favourable/in an unfavourable light; **considérer qch d'un ~ critique** to consider sth with a critical eye, look at sth critically; **il ne voit pas cela du même ~ qu'elle** he doesn't take the same view as she does; **il voit cela avec les yeux de la foi** he sees it through the eyes of a believer

♦ **aux yeux de** (= *selon l'opinion de*) **aux yeux de l'opinion publique** in the eyes of the public; **à mes yeux** in my opinion *ou* eyes

g

♦ **coup d'œil** (= *regard rapide*) glance, quick look; (= *vue*) view; **d'ici, le coup d'~ est joli** there's a lovely view from here; **ça vaut le coup d'~** it's worth seeing; **au** *ou* **du premier coup d'~** at first glance; (*fig*) **avoir le coup d'~ pour** to have an eye for; **jeter** *ou* **lancer un coup d'~ à qn** to glance at sb, look quickly at sb; **jeter un coup d'~ à** [+ *texte, objet*] to glance at, take *ou* have (*Brit*) a glance *ou* quick look at;

allons jeter un coup d'~ let's go and take *ou* have (*Brit*) a look

h = **trou, boucle** [*aiguille, marteau*] eye; [*filin*] eye, loop

i **Typo** [*caractère*] (*pl* **œils**) face

j **Bot** = **bourgeon** bud; [*pomme de terre*] eye

k **Culin** **les yeux du bouillon** the globules *ou* droplets of fat in the stock

l **loc** **coûter/payer les yeux de la tête** (= *très cher*) to cost/pay the earth *ou* a (small) fortune; **à l'~*** (= *gratuitement*) for nothing, for free*; **mon ~ !***< (= *je n'y crois pas*) my eye!*, my foot!*; (= *je ne le ferai pas*) nothing doing!*, not likely!*

2 COMPOSÉS

► **l'œil du cyclone** (*Mét*) the eye of the cyclone *ou* hurricane; (*fig*) the eye of the storm ► **œil électronique** electric eye ► **œil de verre** glass eye

œil-de-bœuf (*pl* **œils-de-bœuf**) [œjdəbœf] NM bull's-eye (window), œil-de-bœuf

œil-de-chat (*pl* **œils-de-chat**) [œjdəʃa] NM (*Minér*) cat's eye

œil-de-perdrix (*pl* **œils-de-perdrix**) [œjdəpɛrdri] NM (= *cor au pied*) soft corn

œil-de-pie (*pl* **œils-de-pie**) [œjdəpi] NM (*Naut*) eyelet

œil-de-tigre (*pl* **œils-de-tigre**) [œjdətigr] NM (*Minér*) tiger's-eye, tigereye

œillade [œjad] NF wink; **faire des ~s à qn** to make eyes at sb, give sb the eye*; **jeter** *ou* **décocher une ~ à qn** to wink at sb, give sb a wink

œillère [œjɛr] **1** NF (*Méd*) eyebath, eyecup **2** **œillères** NFPL [*cheval*] blinkers; (*fig péj*) **avoir des ~s** to wear blinkers, be blinkered

œillet [œjɛ] NM **a** (= *fleur*) carnation; **~ d'Inde** French marigold; **~ mignardise** pink; **~ de poète** sweet william **b** (= *petit trou*) eyelet; (= *bordure*) grommet

œilleton [œjtɔ̃] NM [*télescope*] eyepiece; [*porte*] spyhole; (*Bot*) bud

œillette [œjɛt] NF (= *pavot*) oil poppy; (= *huile*) poppy(seed) oil

œnologie [enɔlɔʒi] NF oenology

œnologique [enɔlɔʒik] ADJ oenological

œnologue [enɔlɔg] NMF oenologist

œsophage [ezɔfaʒ] NM oesophagus (*Brit*), esophagus (*US*)

œsophagien, -ienne [ezɔfaʒjɛ̃, jɛn], **œsophagique** [ezɔfaʒik] ADJ oesophageal (*Brit*), esophageal (*US*)

œstradiol [ɛstradjɔl] NM oestradiol (*Brit*), estradiol (*US*)

œstral, e (*mpl* **-aux**) [ɛstral, o] ADJ **cycle ~** oestrous (*Brit*) *ou* estrous (*US*) cycle

œstrogène [ɛstrɔʒɛn] NM oestrogen (*Brit*), estrogen (*US*)

œstrus [ɛstrys] NM oestrus (*Brit*), estrus (*US*)

œuf (*pl* **œufs**) [œf, ø] **1** NM **a** (*Bio, Culin*) egg; **~ du jour/frais** new-laid (*Brit*) *ou* freshly-laid (*US*)/fresh egg; **~ de caille/de poule** quail's/hen's egg; **~s de poisson** (*Zool*) spawn; (*Culin*) fish roe; **en (forme d')~** egg-shaped → **blanc, jaune** **b** (* = *idiot*) **quel ~ ce type !** what a blockhead* this fellow is! **c** (= *télécabine*) (egg-shaped) cablecar **d** (*loc*) **étouffer** *ou* **écraser** *ou* **détruire qch dans l'~** to nip sth in the bud; **mettre tous ses ~s dans le même panier** to put all one's eggs in one basket; **c'est comme l'~ de Colomb (, il fallait y penser)!** it's simple when you know how!, it's easy once you think of it!; **c'est l'~ et la poule** it's a chicken and egg situation; **il est à peine sorti de l'~*** he's still wet behind the ears*; **va te faire cuire un ~ !***< (go and) take a running jump!*, get stuffed!*< → **marcher, omelette**

2 COMP ► **œufs brouillés** scrambled eggs ► **œuf en chocolat** chocolate egg ► **œuf à la coque** (soft-)boiled egg ► **œuf dur** hard-boiled egg ► **œuf en gelée** egg in aspic *ou* jelly ► **œufs au lait** ≈ egg custard ► **œufs de lump** lumpfish roe ► **œufs mimosa** eggs mimosa (*hors d'oeuvre made with chopped egg yolks*) ► **œuf (au) miroir** = **œuf sur le plat** ► **œuf mollet** soft-boiled egg ► **œufs à la neige** œufs à la neige, floating islands ► **œufs montés** *ou* **battus en neige** beaten *ou* stiff egg whites ► **œuf de Pâques** Easter egg ► **œuf de pigeon** (*lit*) pigeon's egg; (* = *bosse*) bump (on the head); **gros comme un ~ de pigeon** the size of a pigeon's egg ► **œuf sur le plat** *ou* **au plat** fried egg ► **œuf poché** poached egg ► **œuf à repriser** darning egg

œuvre [œvr] **1** NF **a** (= *livre, tableau, film*) work; (= *ensemble d'une production artistique*) works; **c'est une ~ de jeunesse** it's an early work; **toute l'~ de Picasso** Picasso's entire works; **les ~s complètes/choisies de Victor Hugo** the complete/selected works of Victor Hugo; **l'~ romanesque de Balzac** the novels of Balzac, Balzac's works of fiction **b** (= *tâche*) undertaking, task; (= *travail achevé*) work (*NonC*); **ce sera une ~ de longue haleine** it will be a long-term task *ou* undertaking; **admirant leur ~** admiring their work; **la satisfaction de l'~ accomplie** the satisfaction of a job well done; **ce beau gâchis, c'est l'~ des enfants** this fine mess is the children's doing *ou* work; **ces formations sont l'~ du vent et de l'eau** these formations are the work of wind and water → **maître, pied** **c** (= *acte*) **~(s)** deed, work; **être jugé selon ses ~s** to be judged by one's works *ou* deeds; (*frm, hum*) **enceinte de ses ~s** with child by him, bearing his child; (**bonnes**) **~s** good *ou* charitable works; (*littér*) **faire ~ pie** to do a pious deed; **aide-le, ce sera une bonne ~** help him, that will be a kind act *ou* an act of kindness → **fils** **d** (= *organisation*) **~ (de bienfaisance** *ou* **de charité)** charitable organization, charity; **les ~s** charity, charities **e** (*loc*) **être/se mettre à l'~** to be at/get down to work; **voir qn à l'~** (*lit*) to see sb at work; (*iro*) to see sb in action; **faire ~ utile** to do something worthwhile *ou* useful; **faire ~ de pionnier/médiateur** to act as a pioneer/mediator; **la mort avait fait son ~** death had (already) claimed its own; **le feu avait fait son ~** the fire had wrought its havoc *ou* had done its work; **faire ~ durable** to create a work of lasting significance *ou* importance; **mettre en ~ [+ *moyens*]** to implement, make use of; **il avait tout mis en ~ pour éviter la dévaluation/pour les aider** he had done everything possible *ou* had taken all possible steps to avoid devaluation/to help them; **la mise en ~ d'importants moyens** the implementation *ou* the bringing into play of considerable resources ■ (*PROV*) **à l'~ on** *ou* **c'est à l'~ qu'on connaît l'ouvrier** a man is judged *ou* known by his works *ou* by the work he does

2 NM **a** (*littér*) **l'~ gravé/sculpté de Picasso** the etchings/sculptures of Picasso **b** (*Constr*) **second ~** finishings → **grand, gros**

3 COMP ► **œuvre d'art** (*lit, fig*) work of art ► **œuvres mortes** (*Naut*) upper works, topsides ► **œuvres sociales** (*Jur*) company benefit scheme (*Brit*) *ou* plan (*US*) ► **œuvres vives** (*Naut*) quickwork; (*fig, littér*) vitals

œuvrer [œvre] ► conjug 1 ◄ VI (*littér ou hum*) to work (**à, pour** for)

off [ɔf] ADJ INV (*Ciné*) [*voix, son*] off; [*concert, festival*] fringe, alternative → **voix**

offensant, e [ɔfɑ̃sɑ̃, ɑ̃t] ADJ insulting, offensive

offense [ɔfɑ̃s] NF **a** (*frm* = *affront*) insult; **faire ~ à** to offend, insult; (*hum*) **il n'y a pas d'~***

no offence taken; (*frm*) **soit dit sans ~** no offence (intended *ou* meant) **b** (*Rel* = *péché*) transgression, trespass, offence; **pardonnez-nous nos ~s** forgive us our trespasses; **~ à** *ou* **envers** [+ *chef d'État*] libel against; [+ *Dieu*] offence against

offensé, e [ɔfɑ̃se] (*ptp de* **offenser**) **1** ADJ offended **2** NM,F offended *ou* injured party

offenser [ɔfɑ̃se] ► conjug 1 ◄ **1** VT **a** [+ *personne*] to offend, give offence to; **je n'ai pas voulu vous ~** I didn't mean to give offence (to you) *ou* to offend you; **~ Dieu** to offend God, trespass against God **b** (*littér*) [+ *sentiments*] to offend, insult; [+ *souvenir*] to insult; [+ *personne, bon goût*] to offend; [+ *règles, principes*] to offend against **2** **s'offenser** VPR to take offence (**de qch** at sth)

offenseur [ɔfɑ̃sœr] NM offender

offensif, -ive [ɔfɑ̃sif, iv] ADJ (*Mil*) offensive; (*Sport*) **ils sont très ~s ◊ ils ont un jeu très ~** they play an attacking game

offensive [ɔfɑ̃siv] NF offensive; **prendre l'~** to take the offensive; **passer à l'~** to go on the offensive; **lancer une ~** to launch an offensive (**contre** against); **l'~ de l'hiver/du froid** the onslaught of winter/of the cold; **~ diplomatique/de paix** diplomatic/peace offensive; **~ commerciale de grande envergure** large-scale commercial offensive

offertoire [ɔfɛrtwar] NM (*Rel*) offertory

office [ɔfis] **1** NM **a** (*littér* = *tâche*) duties, office; (*Hist*) charge, office; (*Admin*) **remplir l'~ de directeur/chauffeur** to hold the office *ou* post of manager/chauffeur; **~ ministériel** ministerial office; **le bourreau a fait** *ou* **rempli son ~** the executioner carried out his duties **b** (= *usage*) **faire ~ de** to act *ou* serve as; **faire ~ de chauffeur** to act as (a) chauffeur; **remplir son ~** [*appareil, loi*] to serve its purpose, fulfil its function, do its job* **c** (= *bureau*) office, bureau; **~ national/départemental** national/regional office; **~ du tourisme** tourist information (centre), tourist office; **Office national des forêts** ≈ Forest Commission (*Brit*), ≈ Forestry Service (*US*) → **musée** **d** (*Rel*) (= *messe*) (church) service; (= *prières*) prayers; **l'~ (divin)** the (divine) office; **l'~ des morts** the office *ou* service for the dead; **aller à/manquer l'~** to go to/miss church *ou* the church service **e** (*loc*) **être nommé/mis à la retraite d'~** to be appointed/retired automatically *ou* as a matter of course; **faire qch d'~** (*Admin*) to do sth automatically; (*gén*) to do sth as a matter of course *ou* automatically; **avocat/expert (commis) d'~** officially appointed lawyer/expert **f** (*littér* = *service*) office; (*Pol*) **bons ~s** good offices; **Monsieur bons ~s*** mediator

2 NMF (= *pièce de rangement*) pantry; (= *lieu de repas des domestiques*) servants' hall

officialisation [ɔfisjalizasjɔ̃] NF officializing, officialization

officialiser [ɔfisjalize] ► conjug 1 ◄ VT to make official, officialize

officiant, e [ɔfisjɑ̃, jɑ̃t] **1** ADJ officiating

② NM (**prêtre**) ~ officiant, officiating priest
③ NF (**sœur**) ~e officiating sister

officiel, -elle [ɔfisjɛl] ① ADJ (*gén*) official; (c'est) ~ !* it's no joke!, it's for sure!*; **rendre** ~ to make official *ou* public; **à titre** ~ officially → **journal** ② NM,F official; **les ~s de la course** the race officials

officiellement [ɔfisjɛlmɑ̃] ADV officially

officier¹ [ɔfisje] NM officer; ~ **subalterne/supérieur/général** junior/field/general officer; ~ **de garde** duty officer; ~ **de marine** naval officer; ~ **marinier** petty officer; ~ **mécanicien** engineer officer; ~ **d'ordonnance** aide-de-camp; ~ **de paix** (police) inspector (*Brit*), (police) lieutenant (*US*); ~ **de police** senior police officer; ~ **de police judiciaire** official empowered to make arrests and act as a policeman; ~ **de semaine** ≈ orderly officer; ~ **de l'état civil** (mayor considered in his capacity as) registrar; ~**/grand** ~ **de la Légion d'honneur** Officer/Grand Officer of the Legion of Honour; ~ **ministériel** member of the legal profession; ~ **technicien** technical officer → **col**

officier² [ɔfisje] ▶ conjug 7 ◀ VI (*Rel, hum*) to officiate

officieusement [ɔfisjøzmɑ̃] ADV unofficially

officieux, -ieuse [ɔfisjø, jøz] ADJ unofficial; **à titre** ~ unofficially, in an unofficial capacity

officinal, e (*mpl* **-aux**) [ɔfisinal, o] ADJ [*plante*] medicinal

officine [ɔfisin] NF [*pharmacie*] dispensary; (*Admin, Jur* = *pharmacie*) pharmacy; (*péj* = *repaire*) headquarters, agency

offrande [ɔfʀɑ̃d] NF (= *don*) offering; (*Rel* = *cérémonie*) l'~ the offertory; **apporter qch en** ~ to bring sth as a gift *ou* an offering

offrant [ɔfʀɑ̃] NM (*Jur, Fin*) **au plus** ~ to the highest bidder; (*petites annonces*) « **au plus** ~ » "highest offer secures sale"

▼ **offre** [ɔfʀ] NF (*gén*) offer; (*aux enchères*) bid; (*Admin* = *soumission*) tender; (*Écon*) l'~ **et la demande** supply and demand; (*Écon*) **théorie de l'~** supply-side economics; (*pour un prix, un emploi*) **il m'a fait une** ~ he made me an offer; **as-tu regardé les ~s d'emploi ?** have you checked the job ads?* *ou* situations vacant column? (*Brit*); **il y avait plusieurs ~s d'emploi pour des ingénieurs** there were several jobs advertised for engineers, there were several advertisements *ou* ads* for engineering jobs; ~ **publique d'achat** takeover bid, tender offer (*US*); ~ **publique d'échange** public offer of exchange; ~ **publique de vente** offer for sale; (*frm*) ~(**s**) **de service** offer of service; (*Comm*) ~ **spéciale** special offer, special (*US*); (*Pol*) ~**s de paix** peace overtures → **appel**

offreur, -euse [ɔfʀœʀ, øz] NM,F offerer, offeror

▼ **offrir** [ɔfʀiʀ] ▶ conjug 18 ◀ ① VT ⓐ (= *donner*) to give (**à** to); (= *acheter*) to buy (**à** for); **c'est pour** ~ ? is it for a present? *ou* a gift?; **la joie d'~** the joy of giving; **il lui a offert un bracelet** he gave her a bracelet, he presented her with a bracelet; **il s'est fait** ~ **une voiture** he was given a car; **il nous a offert à boire** (*chez lui*) he gave us a drink; (*au café*) he bought *ou* stood (*Brit*) us a drink; **c'est moi qui offre !** [+ *tournée*] it's my round!, this is on me!; [+ *repas*] I'm paying!, this is on me! ⓑ (= *proposer*) [+ *aide, marchandise, excuse*] to offer; [+ *sacrifice*] to offer up; [+ *choix, possibilité*] to offer, give; [+ *démission*] to tender, offer; ~ **l'hospitalité à qn** to offer sb hospitality; **il m'offrit un fauteuil** he offered me a chair; ~ **son bras à qn** to offer sb one's arm; ~ **ses services à qn** to offer sb one's services; ~ **de faire** to offer to do; **combien m'en offrez-vous ?** how much will you give me for it? *ou* will you offer for it?; ~ **sa vie pour une cause** to offer up one's life to a cause ⓒ (= *présenter*) [+ *spectacle, image*] to present, offer; [+ *vue*] to offer; ~ **son corps aux regards**

to reveal *ou* expose one's body to the world at large; ~ **sa poitrine aux balles** to proffer (*frm*) *ou* present one's chest to the bullets; **le paysage n'offrait rien de particulier** the countryside had no particular features; **ces ruines n'offrent guère d'intérêt** these ruins are of little interest

ⓓ (= *apporter*) [+ *avantage, inconvénient*] to offer, present; [+ *exemple, explication*] to provide, afford (*frm*); [+ *analogie*] to offer, have; [+ *échappatoire*] to offer; ~ **de la résistance** [*coffre-fort*] to resist, offer resistance; [*personne*] to put up *ou* offer resistance (**à** to)

② **s'offrir** VPR ⓐ (= *se présenter*) **s'~ aux regards** [*personne*] to expose *ou* reveal o.s. to the public gaze; [*spectacle*] to present itself to the gaze, meet *ou* greet our (*ou* your *etc*) eyes; **la première idée qui s'est offerte à mon esprit** the first idea that occurred to me *ou* that came into my mind; **il a saisi l'occasion qui s'offrait à lui** he seized the opportunity presented to him; **il s'est offert aux coups** he let the blows rain down on him, he submitted to the blows

ⓑ (*sexuellement*) to offer o.s.

ⓒ **s'~ à** *ou* **pour faire qch** to offer *ou* volunteer to do sth; **s'~ comme guide** to volunteer to act as a guide

ⓓ (= *se payer*) [+ *repas, vacances*] to treat o.s. to; [+ *disque*] to buy o.s., treat o.s. to → **luxe**

offset [ɔfsɛt] ① NM, ADJ INV (*Typo*) offset; **journal tiré en** ~ offset (litho-)printed newspaper ② NF INV offset (printing) machine

offshore [ɔfʃɔʀ] ① ADJ INV [*plateforme, exploitation, pétrole*] offshore; (*Fin*) [*fonds*] offshore ② NM INV (*Sport*) (= *bateau*) powerboat; (= *activité*) powerboat racing; **faire du** ~ to go powerboat racing

offusquer [ɔfyske] ▶ conjug 1 ◀ ① VT to offend; **ses manières offusquent beaucoup de gens** his manners offend many people ② **s'offusquer** VPR to take offence *ou* umbrage (**de** at), be offended (**de** at, by)

oflag [ɔflag] NM oflag

ogival, e (*mpl* **-aux**) [ɔʒival, o] ADJ [*voûte*] (*épith*), ogival (*SPÉC*); [*arc*] pointed, ogival (*SPÉC*); [*architecture, art*] gothic

ogive [ɔʒiv] NF ⓐ (*Archit*) diagonal rib; **arc d'~s** pointed *ou* equilateral arch; **arc en** ~ lancet arch → **croisée, voûte** ⓑ (*Mil*) [*missile*] nose cone; ~ **nucléaire** nuclear warhead

OGM [ɔʒeɛm] NM (ABRÉV = **organisme génétiquement modifié**) (*Bio*) GMO

ogre [ɔgʀ] NM ogre; **manger comme un** ~ ◊ **être un vrai** ~ to eat like a horse

ogresse [ɔgʀɛs] NF ogress; **elle a un appétit d'~** she's got an appetite like a horse

oh [o] EXCL oh!; **pousser des** ~ to exclaim

ohé [ɔe] EXCL hey (there)!; ~ **du bateau !** ahoy (there)!, hey (there)!, hullo (there)!

Ohio [ɔjo] NM Ohio

ohm [om] NM ohm

ohmmètre [ɔmmɛtʀ] NM ohmmeter

oïdium [ɔidjɔm] NM powdery mildew

oie [wa] NF (*Zool*) goose; (*péj* = *niaise*) silly goose; ~ **cendrée** greylag goose; ~ **sauvage** wild goose; ~ **des neiges** snow goose; (*péj*) ~ **blanche** innocent young thing → **caca, jeu, patte** *etc*

oignon [ɔɲɔ̃] NM (= *légume*) onion; (= *bulbe de fleur*) bulb; (*Méd*) bunion; (= *montre*) turnip watch; **petits** ~**s** pickling onions; (*Culin*) **aux petits** ~**s** with (pickling) onions; (*fig*) **soigner qn aux petits** ~**s*** to treat sb like a king (*ou* queen); (*fig*) **c'était aux petits** ~**s*** it was first-rate; **ce n'est pas** *ou* **ce ne sont pas mes** ~**s*** it's none of my business, it's nothing to do with me; **mêle-toi** *ou* **occupe-toi de tes** ~**s*** mind your own business → **pelure, rang**

oïl [ɔjl] NM → **langue**

oindre [wɛ̃dʀ] ▶ conjug 49 ◀ VT to anoint

oint, ointe [wɛ̃, wɛ̃t] (*ptp de* **oindre**) ADJ, NM,F anointed; **l'~ du Seigneur** the Lord's anointed

oiseau (*pl* **oiseaux**) [wazo] ① NM (*Zool*) bird; (*gén péj* = *personne*) customer*, fellow*; **être comme l'~ sur la branche** to be here today and gone tomorrow; **trouver** *ou* **dénicher l'~ rare** to find the man (*ou* woman) in a million; (*fig*) **les ~x s'étaient envolés** the birds had flown; **drôle d'~** odd customer, oddball*; **un** ~ **de passage** a bird of passage; (*hum*) **le petit va sortir !** watch the birdie! → **appétit, cervelle, vol¹** ② COMP ▶ **oiseaux de basse-cour** poultry ▶ **oiseau chanteur** songbird ▶ **oiseau des îles** exotic bird ▶ **oiseau de malheur, oiseau de mauvais augure** (*fig*) bird of ill omen ▶ **oiseau migrateur** migratory bird, migrant ▶ **oiseau moqueur** mocking bird ▶ **oiseau de nuit** (*lit*) night-bird, bird of the night; (*fig*) night owl, night-bird ▶ **oiseau de paradis** bird of paradise ▶ **oiseau de proie** bird of prey

oiseau-lyre (*pl* **oiseaux-lyres**) [wazoliʀ] NM lyrebird

oiseau-mouche (*pl* **oiseaux-mouches**) [wazomuʃ] NM hummingbird

oiseleur [waz(ə)lœʀ] NM bird-catcher

oiselier, -ière [wazəlje, jɛʀ] NM,F bird-seller

oisellerie [wazɛlʀi] NF (= *magasin*) birdshop; (= *commerce*) bird-selling

oiseux, -euse [wazø, øz] ADJ [*dispute, digression, commentaire*] pointless; [*propos*] idle (*épith*), pointless, trifling

oisif, -ive [wazif, iv] ① ADJ idle; **une vie oisive** a life of leisure, an idle life ② NM,F man (*ou* woman) of leisure; **les ~s** (*gén*) the idle; (*Écon = non-actifs*) those not in active employment

oisillon [wazijɔ̃] NM young bird, fledgling

oisivement [wazivmɑ̃] ADV idly; **vivre** ~ to live a life of leisure *ou* idleness

oisiveté [wazivte] NF idleness; ~ **forcée** forced idleness *ou* inactivity ■ (*PROV*) **l'~ est (la) mère de tous les vices** the devil finds work for idle hands (*PROV*)

oison [wazɔ̃] NM (*Zool*) gosling

OIT [ɔite] NF (ABRÉV = **Organisation internationale du travail**) ILO

OK* [oke] EXCL, ADJ INV OK*, okay*; ~, **d'accord !*** OK, fine!*

okapi [ɔkapi] NM okapi

Oklahoma [ɔklaɔma] NM Oklahoma

okoumé [ɔkume] NM gaboon (mahogany)

olé [ɔle] ① EXCL olé! ② **olé olé*** ADJ INV (= *excentrique*) [*tenue*] crazy, over the top* (*Brit*); (= *osé*) [*film, livre, chanson*] risqué, near the knuckle* (*attrib*); [*tenue*] risqué, daring; **elle est un peu** ~ ~ (*d'allure*) she's a bit over the top* (*Brit*) *ou* outrageous; (*de mœurs*) she leads quite a wild life

oléacée [ɔlease] NF member of the Oleaceae family; ~**s** Oleaceae

oléagineux, -euse [ɔleaʒinø, øz] ① ADJ oil-producing, oleaginous (*SPÉC*); **graines oléagineuses** oilseeds; **fruits** ~ nuts, oleaginous fruits (*SPÉC*) ② NM oil-producing *ou* oleaginous (*SPÉC*) plant

oléfine [ɔlefin] NF olefine, alkene

oléiculteur, -trice [ɔleikyltœʀ, tʀis] NM olive grower

oléiculture [ɔleikyltyʀ] NF olive growing

oléifère [ɔleifɛʀ] ADJ oil-producing, oleiferous (*SPÉC*)

oléine [ɔlein] NF olein, triolein

oléoduc [ɔleɔdyk] NM oil pipeline

oléoprotéagineux [ɔleopʀɔteaʒinø] NM (*Agr*) oilseed

oléum [ɔleɔm] NM oleum

OLF [ɔɛlɛf] NM (ABRÉV = **Office de la Langue Française**) → **office**

olfactif, -ive [ɔlfaktif, iv] ADJ olfactory

olfaction [ɔlfaksjɔ̃] NF olfaction

olibrius [ɔlibʀijys] NM (*péj*) (queer) customer* ou fellow*

olifant [ɔlifɑ̃] NM (ivory) horn

oligarchie [ɔligaʀʃi] NF oligarchy

oligarchique [ɔligaʀʃik] ADJ oligarchic

oligarque [ɔligaʀk] NM oligarch

oligocène [ɔligɔsɛn] ① ADJ oligocene ② NM l'~ the Oligocene

oligoélément [ɔligɔelemɑ̃] NM trace element

oligopole [ɔligɔpɔl] NM oligopoly

olivaie [ɔlivɛ] NF = **oliveraie**

olivâtre [ɔlivɑtʀ] ADJ (*gén*) olive-greenish; [*teint*] sallow

olive [ɔliv] ① NF **a** (= *fruit*) olive; ~ **noire/verte** black/green olive → **huile** **b** (= *ornement*) bead ou pearl moulding; (= *interrupteur*) switch **c** (*Anat*) olivary body **d** (*Zool*) olive(-shell) ② ADJ INV olive(-green)

oliveraie [ɔlivʀɛ] NF olive grove

olivette [ɔlivɛt] NF plum tomato

olivier [ɔlivje] NM (= *arbre*) olive tree; (= *bois*) olive (wood) → **jardin**, **mont**, **rameau**

olivine [ɔlivin] NF olivine

olographe [ɔlɔgʀaf] ADJ → **testament**

OLP [ɔɛlpe] NF (ABRÉV = **Organisation de libération de la Palestine**) PLO

Olympe¹ [ɔlɛ̃p] NM (= *mont*) l'~ Mount Olympus

Olympe² [ɔlɛ̃p] N (*Myth*) Olympia

olympiade [ɔlɛ̃pjad] NF Olympiad

Olympie [ɔlɛ̃pi] N Olympia

olympien, -ienne [ɔlɛ̃pjɛ̃, jɛn] ADJ [*dieux*] Olympic; [*calme*] Olympian; **air ~** air of Olympian aloofness

olympique [ɔlɛ̃pik] ADJ Olympic; **il est dans une forme ~** he's in great shape ou top form (*Brit*) → **jeu**, **piscine**

olympisme [ɔlɛ̃pism] NM (= *organisation*) organization of the Olympic games; (= *principe*) Olympic spirit

OM (ABRÉV = **ondes moyennes**) MW

Oman [ɔman] NM (**le Sultanat d'**)~ (the Sultanate of) Oman

omanais, e [ɔmanɛ, ɛz] ① ADJ Omani ② **Omanais(e)** NM,F Omani

ombelle [ɔbɛl] NF umbel; **en ~** umbellate (*SPÉC*), parasol-shaped

ombellifère [ɔbelifɛʀ] ① ADJ umbelliferous ② NF umbellifer; ~**s** Umbelliferae (*SPÉC*)

ombilic [ɔbilik] NM **a** (= *nombril*) umbilicus, navel **b** (= *plante*) navelwort **c** (*Bot*) hilum; (= *renflement*) [*bouclier*] boss; (*Math*) umbilic

ombilical, e [*mpl* -**aux**] [ɔbilikal, o] ADJ (*Anat*) umbilical; (*Sci, Tech*) navel-like → **cordon**

omble [ɔbl(ə)] NM char(r) fish; ~(-)**chevalier** arctic char(r)

ombrage [ɔbʀaʒ] NM **a** (= *ombre*) shade; (= *feuillage*) **sous les ~s (du parc)** in the shade of the trees (in the park), in the leafy shade (of the park) **b** (*loc: frm*) **prendre ~ de qch** to take umbrage ou offence at sth; **porter ~ à qn**† (*aussi littér*) ◊ **causer** ou **donner de l'~ à qn** to offend sb

ombragé, e [ɔbʀaʒe] (*ptp de* **ombrager**) ADJ shaded, shady

ombrager [ɔbʀaʒe] ▶conjug 3◀ VT [*arbres*] to shade; (*fig littér*) **une mèche ombrageait son front** a lock of hair shaded his brow

ombrageux, -euse [ɔbʀaʒø, øz] ADJ **a** [*personne*] touchy, quick to take offence (*attrib*), easily offended; [*caractère*] touchy, prickly **b** [*âne, cheval*] skittish, nervous

ombre¹ [ɔbʀ] ① NF **a** (*lit*) shade (*NonC*); (= *ombre portée*) shadow; (*littér = obscurité*) darkness; **25° à l'~** 25° in the shade; **dans l'~ de l'arbre/du vestibule** in the shade of the tree/of the hall; **ces arbres font de l'~** these trees give (us) shade; **ôte-toi de là, tu me fais de l'~** get out of my light, move — you're in my light;

places sans ~/pleines d'~ shadeless/shady squares; **tapi dans l'~** crouching in the darkness ou in the shadows → **théâtre**
b (= *forme vague*) shadow, shadowy figure ou shape
c (= *anonymat*) obscurity; (= *secret, incertitude*) dark; **laisser une question dans l'~** to leave a question unresolved, deliberately ignore a question; **tramer quelque chose dans l'~** to plot something in the dark; **travailler dans l'~** to work behind the scenes; **sortir de l'~** [*auteur*] to emerge from one's obscurity; [*terroriste*] to come out into the open; **rester dans l'~** [*artiste*] to remain in obscurity; [*meneur*] to keep in the background; [*détail*] to be still obscure, remain unclear
d (= *soupçon*) **une ~ de moustache** a hint ou suspicion of a moustache; **il n'y a pas** ou **ça ne fait pas l'~ d'un doute** there's not the (slightest) shadow of a doubt; **sans l'~ d'un doute** beyond ou without the shadow of a doubt; **tu n'as pas l'~ d'une chance** you haven't got a ghost of a chance; **sans l'~ d'une hésitation** without a moment's hesitation; **une ~ de tristesse passa sur son visage** a look of sadness darkened his face; **il y avait dans sa voix l'~ d'un reproche** there was a hint of reproach in his voice
e (= *fantôme*) shade → **royaume**
f (*loc*) **à l'~ de** (= *tout près de*) in the shadow of, close beside; (= *à l'abri de*) in the shade of; **vivre dans l'~ de qn** to live in the shadow of sb; **être l'~ de qn** to be sb's (little) shadow; (*fig*) **faire de l'~ à qn** to overshadow sb; **mettre qn à l'~*** to put sb behind bars, lock sb up; **il y a une ~ au tableau** there's a fly in the ointment; **seule ~ au tableau: il ne parle pas grec** the only snag ou problem is that he doesn't speak Greek; **n'être plus que l'~ de soi-même** to be a (mere) shadow of one's former self; **jeter une ~ sur qch** to cast a shadow over sth; (*hum*) **il tire plus vite que son ~** he's the fastest draw in the West → **peur, proie, suivre**
② COMP ► **ombres chinoises** (*improvisées*) shadowgraph; (= *spectacle*) shadow show ou pantomime ► **ombre méridienne** noonday shadow ► **ombre à paupières** eye shadow ► **ombre portée** shadow

ombre² [ɔbʀ] NM (= *poisson*) grayling

ombre³ [ɔbʀ] NF (= *terre, couleur*) umber; **terre d'~** umber

ombrelle [ɔbʀɛl] NF (= *parasol*) parasol, sunshade; [*méduse*] umbrella

ombrer [ɔbʀe] ▶conjug 1◀ VT [+ *dessin*] to shade; ~ **ses paupières** to put on eye shadow

ombreux, -euse [ɔbʀø, øz] ADJ (*littér*) [*pièce, forêt*] shady

Ombrie [ɔbʀi] NF Umbria

ombrien, -ienne [ɔbʀijɛ̃, ijɛn] ADJ Umbrian

ombudsman [ɔbydsman] NM (*Can*) ombudsman

OMC [oɛmse] NF (ABRÉV = **Organisation mondiale du commerce**) WTO

oméga [ɔmega] NM omega → **alpha**

omelette [ɔmlɛt] NF omelette; ~ **aux champignons/au fromage** mushroom/cheese omelette; ~ **baveuse** runny omelette; ~ **norvégienne** baked Alaska ■ (*PROV*) **on ne fait pas d'~ sans casser des œufs** you can't make an omelette without breaking eggs (*PROV*)

omettre [ɔmɛtʀ] ▶conjug 56◀ VT to leave out, omit; ~ **de faire qch** to fail ou omit ou neglect to do sth

OMI [ɔemi] NF (ABRÉV = **Organisation maritime internationale**) IMO

omicron [ɔmikʀɔn] NM omicron

omission [ɔmisjɔ̃] NF (= *action*) omission; (= *chose oubliée*) omission, oversight; **pécher par ~** to sin by omission

OMM [ɔɛmɛm] NF (ABRÉV = **Organisation météorologique mondiale**) WMO

omnibus [ɔmnibys] NM (**train**) ~ slow ou local train; (*Hist* = bus) omnibus; **le train est ~ jusqu'à Paris** the train stops at every station before ou until Paris → **barre**

omnidirectionnel, -elle [ɔmnidiʀɛksjɔnɛl] ADJ omnidirectional

omnipotence [ɔmnipɔtɑ̃s] NF omnipotence

omnipotent, e [ɔmnipɔtɑ̃, ɑ̃t] ADJ omnipotent, all-powerful

omnipraticien, -ienne [ɔmnipʀatisjɛ̃, jɛn] NM,F general practitioner

omniprésence [ɔmnipʀezɑ̃s] NF omnipresence

omniprésent, e [ɔmnipʀezɑ̃, ɑ̃t] ADJ omnipresent; **son influence est ~e** his influence is felt everywhere

omniscience [ɔmnisjɑ̃s] NF omniscience

omniscient, e [ɔmnisjɑ̃, jɑ̃t] ADJ omniscient

omnisports [ɔmnispɔʀ] ADJ INV [*terrain*] general-purpose (*épith*); **association ~** (general) sports club; **salle ~** games hall; **palais ~** sports centre

omnium [ɔmnjɔm] NM **a** (*Cyclisme*) prime; (*Courses*) open handicap **b** (*Comm*) corporation

omnivore [ɔmnivɔʀ] ① ADJ omnivorous ② NM omnivorous creature, omnivore (*SPÉC*)

omoplate [ɔmɔplat] NF shoulder blade, scapula (*SPÉC*)

OMS [ɔɛmɛs] NF (ABRÉV = **Organisation mondiale de la santé**) WHO

OMT [ɔɛmte] NF (ABRÉV = **Organisation mondiale du tourisme**) WTO

on [ɔ̃] PRON **a** (*indétermination : souvent traduit par passif*) **on les interrogea sans témoins** they were questioned without (any) witnesses; **on va encore augmenter l'essence** (the price of) petrol's going up again, they are putting up the price of petrol again; (*annonce*) **on demande jeune fille** young girl wanted ou required; **on ne nous a pas demandé notre avis** nobody asked our opinion, our opinion wasn't asked; **on ne devrait pas poser des questions si ambiguës** you ou one shouldn't ask such ambiguous questions; **dans cet hôtel, on n'accepte pas les chiens** dogs aren't allowed in this hotel; **on prétend que ...** they say that ..., it is said that ...; **on se précipita sur les places vides** there was a rush for the empty seats ■ (*PROV*) **on n'est jamais si bien servi que par soi-même** a job is never so well done as when you do it yourself → **dire**
b (= *quelqu'un*) someone, anyone; **on a déposé ce paquet pendant que vous étiez sorti** someone left this parcel ou this parcel was left while you were out; **qu'est-ce que je dis si on demande à vous parler?** what shall I say if someone ou anyone asks to speak to you?; **on vous demande au téléphone** you're wanted on the phone, there's someone on the phone for you; **on frappa à la porte** there was a knock at the door; **est-ce qu'on est venu réparer la porte?** has anyone ou someone been to repair the door?; **on peut très bien aimer la pluie** some people may well like the rain; **je n'admets pas qu'on** ou **que l'on ne sache pas nager** I can't understand how (some) people can't swim
c (*indéf* = *celui qui parle*) you, one (*frm*), we; **on ne dort pas par cette chaleur** you (ou one (*frm*)) can't sleep in this heat; **est-ce qu'on est censé s'habiller pour le dîner?** is one (*frm*) ou are we expected to dress for dinner?; **on aimerait être sûr que ...** one ou we would like to be sure that ...; **de nos fenêtres, on voit les collines from our windows** you (ou we) can see the hills; **on a trop chaud ici** it's too hot here; **quand on est inquiet rien ne peut vous** ou **nous distraire** when you are (ou one is) worried nothing can take your (ou one's) mind off it; **on comprend difficilement pourquoi il**

is difficult to understand why; **on ne pense jamais à tout** you can't think of everything; **on ne lui donnerait pas 70 ans** you wouldn't think she was 70; **on ne dirait pas que ...** you wouldn't think that ...

d (*éloignement dans temps, espace*) they, people; **autrefois, on se préoccupait peu de l'hygiène** years ago, they (*ou* people) didn't worry about hygiene; **en Chine on mange avec des baguettes** in China they eat with chopsticks; **dans aucun pays on ne semble pouvoir arrêter l'inflation** it doesn't seem as if inflation can be stopped in any country, no country seems (to be) able to stop inflation

e (* = *nous*) we; **on a décidé tous les trois de partir chacun de son côté** the three of us decided to go (each) our separate ways; **chez nous on mange beaucoup de pain** we eat a lot of bread in our family; **lui et moi on n'est pas d'accord** we don't see eye to eye, him and me*; **nous, on a amené notre chien** we've brought along the dog; **nous, on a tous réclamé une augmentation** we all (of us) demanded a rise; **on fait ce qu'on peut** *ou* **de son mieux** you can only do your best; **il faut bien qu'on vive** a guy's (*ou* a girl's) got to eat*; **dans ce chapitre on essaiera de prouver...** in this chapter we (*frm*) shall attempt to prove ...

f (*en langue parlée: familiarité, reproche etc*) **on est bien sage aujourd'hui !** aren't we a good boy (*ou* girl) today!, we are a good boy (*ou* girl) today!; **alors, on ne dit plus bonjour aux amis !** don't we say hello to our friends any more?; **alors, on est content ?** well, are you pleased?; (*iro*) **on n'a pas un sou mais on s'achète une voiture !** he hasn't (*ou* they haven't *etc*) a penny to his (*ou* their *etc*) name but he goes and buys (*ou* they go and buy *etc*) a car!; **on parle, on parle et puis on finit par dire des sottises** talk, talk, talk and it's all nonsense in the end

g (*intensif*) **c'est on ne peut plus beau/ ridicule** it couldn't be lovelier/more ridiculous; **je suis on ne peut plus heureux de vous voir** I couldn't be more delighted to see you, I'm absolutely delighted to see you → **pouvoir**[1]

onagre[1] [ɔnagʀ] NM (*Archéol, Zool*) onager

onagre[2] [ɔnagʀ] NF (*Bot*) oenothera (*SPÉC*), evening primrose

onanisme [ɔnanism] NM onanism

once[1] [ɔ̃s] NF (= *mesure, Can*) ounce; **il n'a pas une ~ de bon sens** he hasn't an ounce of common sense

once[2] [ɔ̃s] NF (*Zool*) ounce, snow leopard

oncial, e (*mpl* **-iaux**) [ɔ̃sjal, jo] [1] ADJ uncial [2] **onciale** NF uncial

oncle [ɔ̃kl] NM uncle; (*fig*) **~ d'Amérique** rich uncle; **l'Oncle Sam** Uncle Sam; **l'Oncle Tom** Uncle Tom

oncogène [ɔ̃kɔʒɛn] [1] ADJ oncogenic, oncogenous [2] NM oncogene

oncologie [ɔ̃kɔlɔʒi] NF oncology

oncologiste [ɔ̃kɔlɔʒist], **oncologue** [ɔ̃kɔlɔg] NMF oncologist

oncques†† [ɔ̃k] ADV never

onction [ɔ̃ksjɔ̃] NF (*Rel, fig*) unction; **~ des malades** anointing of the sick

onctueusement [ɔ̃ktɥøzmɑ̃] ADV [*couler*] unctuously; [*parler*] with unction, suavely

onctueux, -euse [ɔ̃ktɥø, øz] ADJ [*crème*] smooth, creamy, unctuous; [*manières, voix*] unctuous, smooth

onctuosité [ɔ̃ktɥozite] NF unctuousness, smoothness, creaminess

onde [ɔ̃d] NF **a** (*gén, Phys*) wave; **~s hertziennes/radioélectriques/sonores** Hertzian/radio/sound waves; **petites ~s** ◊ **~s moyennes** medium waves; **grandes ~s** long waves; **transmettre sur ~s courtes/petites ~s/grandes ~s** to broadcast on short/medium/long wave; (*lit, fig*) **~ de**

choc shock wave → **longueur** **b** (*loc*) **sur les ~s et dans la presse** on the radio and in the press; **nous espérons vous retrouver sur les ~s demain à 6 heures** we hope to join you again on the air tomorrow at 6 o'clock; **il passe sur les ~s demain** he's going on the air tomorrow; (*Radio*) **mise en ~** production; **mettre en ~s** [+ *pièce, récit*] to produce for the radio; **par ordre d'entrée en ~s** in order of appearance **c** (*littér* = *lac, mer*) **l'~** the waters; **l'~ amère** the briny deep (*littér*)

ondé, e[1] [ɔ̃de] ADJ (*littér*) [*tissu*] watered; [*cheveux*] wavy

ondée[2] [ɔ̃de] NF shower (*of rain*)

ondin, e [ɔ̃dɛ̃, in] NM,F water sprite

on-dit [ɔ̃di] NM INV rumour, hearsay (*NonC*); **ce ne sont que des ~** it's only hearsay

ondoiement [ɔ̃dwamɑ̃] NM **a** (*littér*) [*blés, surface moirée*] undulation **b** (*Rel*) provisional baptism

ondoyant, e [ɔ̃dwajɑ̃, ɑ̃t] ADJ **a** [*eaux, blés*] undulating; [*flamme*] wavering; [*reflet*] shimmering; [*démarche*] swaying, supple **b** († *ou littér*) [*caractère, personne*] unstable, changeable

ondoyer [ɔ̃dwaje] ▶ conjug 8 ◀ [1] VI [*blés*] to undulate, ripple; [*drapeau*] to wave, ripple [2] VT (*Rel*) to baptize (*in an emergency*)

ondulant, e [ɔ̃dylɑ̃, ɑ̃t] ADJ **a** [*démarche*] swaying, supple; [*ligne, profil, surface*] undulating **b** (*Méd*) [*pouls*] uneven

ondulation [ɔ̃dylasjɔ̃] NF [*vagues, blés, terrain*] undulation; **~s** [*sol*] undulations; [*cheveux*] waves

ondulatoire [ɔ̃dylatwaʀ] ADJ (*Phys*) undulatory, wave (*épith*) → **mécanique**

ondulé, e [ɔ̃dyle] (*ptp de* **onduler**) ADJ [*surface*] undulating; [*chevelure*] wavy; [*carton, tôle*] corrugated

onduler [ɔ̃dyle] ▶ conjug 1 ◀ [1] VI (*gén*) to undulate; [*drapeau*] to ripple, wave; [*route*] to snake up and down, undulate; [*cheveux*] to be wavy, wave [2] VT † [+ *cheveux*] to wave

onduleur [ɔ̃dylœʀ] NM (*Élec*) inverter

onduleux, -euse [ɔ̃dylø, øz] ADJ [*courbe, ligne*] wavy; [*plaine*] undulating; [*silhouette, démarche*] sinuous, swaying, supple

onéreux, -euse [ɔneʀø, øz] ADJ expensive, costly → **titre**

ONF [ɔɛnɛf] NM (ABRÉV = **Office national des forêts**) → **office**

ONG [ɔɛnʒe] NF (ABRÉV = **organisation non gouvernementale**) NGO

ongle [ɔ̃gl] NM [*personne*] (finger)nail; [*animal*] claw; **~ de pied** toenail; **porter** *ou* **avoir les ~s longs** to have long nails; **avoir les ~s en deuil*** to have dirty (finger)nails; **se faire les ~s** to do one's nails; **avoir les ~s faits** to be wearing nail varnish (*Brit*) *ou* nail polish, have painted nails → **bout, incarné, payer**

onglée [ɔ̃gle] NF **avoir l'~** to have fingers numb with cold

onglet [ɔ̃glɛ] NM **a** [*tranche de livre*] (*dépassant*) tab; (*en creux*) thumb index; **dictionnaire à ~s** dictionary with a thumb index **b** [*lame de canif*] (thumbnail) groove **c** (*Menuiserie*) mitre (*Brit*), miter (*US*); **boîte à ~s** mitre (*Brit*) *ou* miter (*US*) box **d** (*Math*) ungula; (*Bot*) unguis; (*Reliure*) guard **e** (*Boucherie*) prime cut of beef

onglier [ɔ̃glije] NM manicure set

onguent [ɔ̃gɑ̃] NM **a** (*Pharm*) ointment, salve **b** († = *parfum*) unguent

ongulé, e [ɔ̃gyle] [1] ADJ hoofed, ungulate (*SPÉC*) [2] NM hoofed *ou* ungulate (*SPÉC*) animal; **~s** ungulata

onirique [ɔniʀik] ADJ (*Art, Littérat*) dreamlike, dream (*attrib*), oneiric (*frm*)

onirisme [ɔniʀism] NM (*Psych*) hallucinosis; (*Littérat*) fantasizing

onomasiologie [ɔnɔmazjɔlɔʒi] NF onomasiology

onomastique [ɔnɔmastik] [1] ADJ onomastic [2] NF onomastics *sg*

onomatopée [ɔnɔmatɔpe] NF onomatopoeia

onomatopéique [ɔnɔmatɔpeik] ADJ onomatopoeic

ontarien, -ienne [ɔ̃taʀjɛ̃, jɛn] [1] ADJ Ontarian [2] **Ontarien(ne)** NM,F Ontarian

Ontario [ɔ̃taʀjo] NM Ontario; **le lac ~** Lake Ontario

ontogenèse [ɔ̃tɔʒənɛz] ADJ ontogeny, ontogenesis

ontogénétique [ɔ̃tɔʒenetik] ADJ ontogenetic, ontogenic

ontogénie [ɔ̃tɔʒeni] NF = **ontogenèse**

ontogénique [ɔ̃tɔʒenik] ADJ = **ontogénétique**

ontologie [ɔ̃tɔlɔʒi] NF ontology

ontologique [ɔ̃tɔlɔʒik] ADJ ontological

ONU [ɔny] NF (ABRÉV = **Organisation des Nations Unies**) UNO; **l'~** the UN, (the) UNO

onusien, -ienne [ɔnyzjɛ̃, jɛn] [1] ADJ UN (*épith*) [2] NM,F UN official

onyx [ɔniks] NM onyx

onze ['ɔ̃z] [1] ADJ INV eleven; **le ~ novembre** Armistice Day; *pour autres locutions voir* **six** [2] NM INV (*Ftbl*) **le ~ de France** the French eleven *ou* team; *pour autres locutions voir* **six**

onzième ['ɔ̃zjɛm] ADJ, NMF eleventh; (*péj*) **les ouvriers de la ~ heure** last-minute helpers, people who turn up when the work is practically finished; *pour autres locutions voir* **sixième**

onzièmement ['ɔ̃zjɛmmɑ̃] ADV in the eleventh place; *pour autres locutions voir* **sixièmement**

oocyte [ɔɔsit] NM = **ovocyte**

oolithe [ɔɔlit] NM oolite

oolithique [ɔɔlitik] ADJ oolitic

OPA [ɔpea] NF (ABRÉV = **offre publique d'achat**) (*Fin*) takeover bid (*Brit*), tender offer (*US*); (*lit, fig*) **faire une ~ sur** to take over

opacifiant [ɔpasifjɑ̃] NM (*Méd*) contrast medium

opacification [ɔpasifikasjɔ̃] NF opacification

opacifier [ɔpasifje] ▶ conjug 7 ◀ VT to make opaque

opacité [ɔpasite] NF **a** (*Phys*) [*verre, corps*] opacity **b** [*brouillard, nuit*] impenetrability **c** [*mot, personnage, texte*] opaqueness, lack of clarity

opale [ɔpal] NF opal

opalescence [ɔpalesɑ̃s] NF opalescence

opalescent, e [ɔpalesɑ̃, ɑ̃t] ADJ opalescent

opalin, e[1] [ɔpalɛ̃, in] ADJ opaline

opaline[2] [ɔpalin] NF opaline

opaque [ɔpak] ADJ **a** [*verre, corps*] opaque (**à** to); **collants ~s** opaque tights **b** [*brouillard, nuit, forêt*] impenetrable **c** [*mot, personnage*] opaque

op' art [ɔpaʀt] NM op art

op. cit. (ABRÉV = *opere citato*) op. cit.

OPE [ɔpea] NF (ABRÉV = **offre publique d'échange**) → **offre**

opéable [ɔpeabl] [1] ADJ liable to be taken over (*attrib*) [2] NF firm liable to be taken over

open [ɔpɛn] ADJ INV, NM open; (**tournoi**) **~** open (tournament)

OPEP [ɔpɛp] NF (ABRÉV = **Organisation des pays exportateurs de pétrole**) OPEC

opéra [ɔpeʀa] NM (= *œuvre, genre, spectacle*) opera; (= *édifice*) opera house; **~ bouffe** opéra bouffe, comic opera; **~ rock** rock opera; **~ ballet** opéra ballet

opérable [ɔpeʀabl] ADJ operable; **le malade est-il ~ ?** can the patient be operated on?; **ce cancer n'est plus ~** this cancer is too far advanced for an operation *ou* to be operable

opéra-comique (*pl* **opéras-comiques**) [ɔpeʀa-kɔmik] NM light opera, opéra comique

opérande [ɔpeʀɑ̃d] NM (*Math, Ordin*) operand

opérant, e [ɔpeʀɑ̃, ɑ̃t] ADJ (= *efficace*) effective

opérateur, -trice [ɔpeʀatœʀ, tʀis] 1 NM,F a (*sur machine, téléphone, radio*) operator; ~ **(de prise de vues)** cameraman; ~ **de saisie** keyboard operator, keyboarder b (*Bourse*) dealer, trader, operator 2 NM a (*Math, Ordin*) operator; ~ **booléen** Boolean operator b [*calculateur*] processing unit c (*Bourse, Fin*) operator d (*Téléc*) exploitant

opération [ɔpeʀasjɔ̃] NF a (*Méd*) operation; ~ **à cœur ouvert** open-heart surgery (*NonC*); **salle/table d'**~ operating theatre (*Brit*) *ou* room (*US*)/table; **faire** *ou* **pratiquer une** ~ to operate, perform an operation; **subir une** ~ **(chirurgicale)** to have *ou* undergo surgery, have an operation
b (*Math*) operation; **les** ~**s fondamentales** the fundamental operations; **ça peut se résoudre en 2 ou 3** ~**s** that can be solved in 2 or 3 calculations *ou* operations; (*Scol*) **tu as fini tes** ~**s?** have you done your sums?
c (*Mil, gén*) operation; ~ **de police/de sauvetage** police/rescue operation; (*nom de code*) **«** ~ **Tango »** "operation Tango"; ~ **mains propres** anti-corruption operation → **théâtre**
d (*Comm*) (= *campagne*) campaign, drive; (= *action*) operation; ~ **promotionnelle** promotional campaign; **« ~ baisse des prix »** "cut-price sale"; ~ **escargot** go-slow (*Brit*), slow-down (*US*)
e (= *tractation*) (*Comm*) deal; (*Bourse*) deal, transaction, operation; ~ **bancaire** *ou* **de banque** banking operation *ou* transaction; ~ **financière/commerciale/immobilière** financial/commercial/property deal; ~**s de Bourse** stock-exchange transactions; **notre équipe a réalisé une bonne** ~ (*en affaires*) our team got a good deal; (*en sport*) our team did a really good job
f (*Tech, gén*) process, operation; **les diverses** ~**s de la fabrication du papier** the different operations *ou* processes in the making of paper; **l'**~ **de la digestion** the operation of the digestive system; **les** ~**s de la raison** the processes of thought; **par l'**~ **du Saint-Esprit** (*Rel*) through the workings of the Holy Spirit; (*hum*) by magic

opérationnel, -elle [ɔpeʀasjɔnel] ADJ operational

opératoire [ɔpeʀatwaʀ] ADJ (*Méd*) [*méthodes, techniques*] operating; [*maladie, commotion, dépression*] post-operative → **bloc**

opercule [ɔpeʀkyl] NM (*Bot, Zool*) operculum; (*Tech*) protective cap *ou* cover; [*pot de crème, carton de lait*] seal

opéré, e [ɔpeʀe] (*ptp de* **opérer**) NM,F (*Méd*) patient (*who has undergone an operation*)

opérer [ɔpeʀe] ▸ conjug 6 ◂ 1 VT a (*Méd*) [+ *malade, organe*] to operate on (**de** for); [+ *tumeur*] to remove; **on l'a opéré d'une tumeur** he had an operation for a tumour *ou* to remove a tumour; ~ **qn de l'appendicite** to operate on sb for appendicitis, take sb's appendix out; **se faire** ~ to have an operation, have surgery; **se faire** ~ **des amygdales** to have one's tonsils removed *ou* out*; **il faut** ~ we'll have to operate
b (= *exécuter*) [+ *transformation, réforme*] to carry out, implement; [+ *choix, distinction, transition*] to make; **la Bourse a opéré un redressement spectaculaire** the stock exchange made a spectacular recovery; **cette méthode a opéré des miracles** this method has worked wonders; ~ **un retrait/transfert** to make a withdrawal/transfer; **ce traitement a opéré sur lui un changement remarquable** this treatment has brought about an amazing change in him; **un changement considérable s'était opéré** a major change had taken place *ou* occurred

2 VI (= *agir*) [*remède*] to act, work, take effect; [*charme*] to work; (= *procéder*) [*photographe, technicien*] to proceed; **comment faut-il** ~ **pour nettoyer le moteur ?** how does one go about *ou* what's the procedure for cleaning the engine?; **opérons en douceur** let's go about it gently; **les cambrioleurs qui opèrent dans cette région** the burglars who work this area

opérette [ɔpeʀet] NF operetta, light opera; **paysage/village d'**~ chocolate-box landscape/village; **général/bandit d'**~ caricature of a general/bandit

Ophélie [ɔfeli] NF Ophelia

ophidien [ɔfidjɛ̃] NM ophidian; ~**s** Ophidia

ophrys [ɔfʀis] NM *ou* F ophrys

ophtalmie [ɔftalmi] NF ophthalmia; ~ **des neiges** snow blindness

ophtalmique [ɔftalmik] ADJ ophthalmic

ophtalmo* [ɔftalmo] NMF ABRÉV = **ophtalmologiste**

ophtalmologie [ɔftalmɔlɔʒi] NF ophthalmology

ophtalmologique [ɔftalmɔlɔʒik] ADJ ophthalmological

ophtalmologiste [ɔftalmɔlɔʒist], **ophtalmologue** [ɔftalmɔlɔg] NMF ophthalmologist

ophtalmoscope [ɔftalmɔskɔp] NM ophthalmoscope

ophtalmoscopie [ɔftalmɔskɔpi] NF ophthalmoscopy

opiacé, e [ɔpjase] 1 ADJ [*médicament, substance*] opiate, opium-containing; **odeur** ~**e** smell of *ou* like opium 2 NM opiate

opimes [ɔpim] ADJ PL (*hum, littér*) **dépouilles** ~ rich booty *ou* spoils

opinel® [ɔpinel] NM (wooden-handled) pen-knife

opiner [ɔpine] ▸ conjug 1 ◂ VI (*littér*) (= *se prononcer*) ~ **pour/contre qch** to come out in favour of/against sth, pronounce o.s. in favour of/against sth; (= *acquiescer*) ~ **de la tête** to nod one's agreement, nod assent; (*hum*) ~ **du bonnet** *ou* **du chef** to nod (in agreement); (*Jur*) ~ **à qch** to give one's consent to sth

opiniâtre [ɔpinjɑtʀ] ADJ a (= *entêté*) [*personne, caractère*] stubborn, obstinate b (= *acharné*) [*efforts, haine*] unrelenting, persistent; [*résistance, lutte, toux*] stubborn, persistent; [*fièvre*] persistent

opiniâtrement [ɔpinjɑtʀəmɑ̃] ADV (= *avec entêtement*) stubbornly; (= *avec acharnement*) persistently

opiniâtreté [ɔpinjɑtʀəte] NF (= *entêtement*) stubbornness; (= *acharnement*) persistence

▾ **opinion** [ɔpinjɔ̃] NF a (= *jugement, conviction, idée*) opinion (**sur** on, about); ~**s politiques/religieuses** political/religious beliefs *ou* convictions; **avoir une** ~**/des** ~**s** to have an opinion *ou* a point of view/(definite) opinions *ou* views *ou* points of view; **être sans** ~ to have no opinion; **se faire une** ~ to form an opinion (**sur** on), make up one's mind (**sur** about); **mon** ~ **est faite sur son compte** I've made up my mind about him; **c'est une affaire d'**~ it's a matter of opinion; **j'ai la même** ~ I am of the same opinion, I hold the same view; **être de l'**~ **du dernier qui a parlé** to agree with whoever spoke last; **avoir bonne/mauvaise** ~ **de qn/de soi** to have a good/bad opinion of sb/of o.s.; **j'ai piètre** ~ **de lui** I've a very low *ou* poor opinion of him; ~**s toutes faites** cut-and-dried opinions, uncritical opinions
b (= *manière générale de penser*) **l'**~ **publique** public opinion; **l'**~ **ouvrière** working-class opinion; **l'**~ **française** French public opinion; **informer/alerter l'**~ to inform/alert the public; **braver l'**~ to defy public opinion; **l'**~ **est unanime/divisée** opinion is unanimous/divided; **il se moque de l'**~ **des autres** he doesn't care what (other) people think; **avoir**

l'~ **pour soi** to have public opinion on one's side → **presse**
c (*dans les sondages*) **le nombre d'**~**s favorables** those who agreed *ou* said yes

opiomane [ɔpjɔman] NMF opium addict

opiomanie [ɔpjɔmani] NF opium addiction

opium [ɔpjɔm] NM opium; (*fig*) **l'**~ **du peuple** the opium of the people

opossum [ɔpɔsɔm] NM opossum

opportun, e [ɔpɔʀtœ̃, yn] ADJ [*démarche, visite, remarque*] timely, opportune; **il serait** ~ **de faire** it would be appropriate *ou* advisable to do; **nous le ferons en temps** ~ we shall do it at the appropriate *ou* right time

opportunément [ɔpɔʀtynemɑ̃] ADV opportunely; **il est arrivé** ~ his arrival was timely *ou* opportune, he arrived opportunely *ou* just at the right time

opportunisme [ɔpɔʀtynism] NM opportunism

opportuniste [ɔpɔʀtynist] 1 ADJ [*personne*] opportunist; [*maladie, infection*] opportunistic 2 NMF opportunist

opportunité [ɔpɔʀtynite] NF a [*mesure, démarche*] (*qui vient au bon moment*) timeliness, opportuneness; (*qui est approprié*) appropriateness b (= *occasion*) opportunity

opposabilité [ɔpozabilite] NF (*Jur*) opposability

opposable [ɔpozabl] ADJ (*Jur*) opposable (**à** to)

opposant, e [ɔpozɑ̃, ɑ̃t] 1 NM,F opponent (**à** of) 2 ADJ a [*minorité*] (*Jur*) [*partie*] opposing (*épith*) b (*Anat*) [*muscle*] opponent

opposé, e [ɔpoze] (*ptp de* **opposer**) 1 ADJ a [*rive, direction*] opposite; [*parti, équipe*] opposing (*épith*); **venant en sens** ~ coming in the opposite *ou* other direction; **la maison** ~**e à la nôtre** the house opposite *ou* facing ours; **l'équipe** ~**e à la nôtre** the team playing against ours
b (= *contraire*) [*intérêts, forces*] conflicting, opposing; [*opinions*] conflicting; [*caractères*] opposite; [*couleurs, styles*] contrasting; (*Math*) [*nombres, angles*] opposite; ~ **à** conflicting *ou* contrasting with, opposed to; **opinions totalement** ~**es** totally conflicting *ou* opposed opinions, opinions totally at variance; **ils sont d'un avis** ~ (*au nôtre*) they are of a different *ou* the opposite opinion; (*l'un à l'autre*) they are of conflicting opinions, their opinions are at variance with each other; (*Math*) **angles** ~**s par le sommet** vertically opposite angles → **diamétralement**
c (= *hostile à*) ~ **à** opposed to, against; **je suis** ~ **à la publicité/à ce mariage** I'm opposed to *ou* I'm against advertising/this marriage
2 NM a (= *contraire*) **l'**~ the opposite, the reverse; **il fait tout l'**~ **de ce qu'on lui dit** he does the opposite *ou* the reverse of what he is told; **à l'**~**, il serait faux de dire ...** on the other hand *ou* conversely it would be wrong to say ...; **ils sont vraiment à l'**~ **l'un de l'autre** they are totally unalike; **à l'**~ **de Paul, je pense que ...** contrary to *ou* unlike Paul, I think that ...
b (= *direction*) **à l'**~ (= *dans l'autre direction*) the other *ou* opposite way (**de** from); (= *de l'autre côté*) on the other *ou* opposite side (**de** from)

▾ **opposer** [ɔpoze] ▸ conjug 1 ◂ 1 VT a [+ *équipes, boxeurs*] to bring together; [+ *rivaux, pays*] to bring into conflict (**à** with); [+ *idées, personnages, couleurs*] to contrast (**à** with); [+ *objets, meubles*] to place opposite each other; **le match opposant l'équipe de Lyon et** *ou* **à celle de Caen** the match bringing together the team from Lyon and the team from Caen; **on m'a opposé à un finaliste olympique** they pitted me *ou* put me against an Olympic finalist; **des questions d'intérêts les ont opposés/les opposent** matters of personal interest have brought them into conflict/divide them; **quel orateur peut-on ~ à Cicéron ?** what orator could be put *ou* set beside Cicero?; **~ un vase à une statue** to place *ou* set a vase opposite a statue

b (= *utiliser comme défense contre*) **~ à qn/qch** [+ *armée, tactique*] to set against sb/sth; **~ son refus le plus net** to give an absolute refusal (à to); **~ de véhémentes protestations à une accusation** to protest vehemently at an accusation; **opposant son calme à leurs insultes** setting his calmness against their insults; **il nous opposa une résistance farouche** he put up a fierce resistance to us; **il n'y a rien à ~ à cela** there's nothing you can say (*ou* do) against that, there's no answer to that; **~ la force à la force** to match strength with strength

c (= *objecter*) [+ *raisons*] to put forward (à to); **que va-t-il ~ à notre proposition/nous ~ ?** what objections will he make *ou* raise to our proposal/to us?; **il nous opposa que cela coûtait cher** he objected that it was expensive

2 **s'opposer** VPR a [*équipes, boxeurs*] to confront each other, meet; [*rivaux, partis*] to clash (à with); [*opinions, théories*] to conflict; [*couleurs, styles*] to contrast (à with); [*immeubles*] to face each other; **haut s'oppose à bas** high is the opposite of low; (*dans un combat*) **il s'est opposé à plus fort que lui** he took on *ou* he pitted himself against someone *ou* an opponent who was stronger than him

b (= *se dresser contre*) **s'~ à** [+ *parents*] to rebel against; [+ *mesure, mariage, progrès*] to oppose; **je m'oppose à lui en tout** I am opposed to him in everything; **rien ne s'oppose à leur bonheur** nothing stands in the way of their happiness; **je m'oppose formellement à ce que vous y alliez** I am strongly opposed to *ou* I am strongly against your going there; **ma conscience s'y oppose** it goes against my conscience; **sa religion s'y oppose** it is against his religion, his religion doesn't allow it; **votre état de santé s'oppose à tout excès** your state of health makes any excess extremely inadvisable

opposite [ɔpɔzit] NM (*frm*) **à l'~** on the other *ou* opposite side (**de** from)

▼ **opposition** [ɔpozisjɔ̃] 1 NF a (= *résistance*) opposition à qn; **faire de l'~ systématique (à tout ce qu'on propose)** to oppose systematically (everything that is put forward); (*Jur, Pol*) **loi passée sans ~** law passed unopposed

b (= *conflit, contraste*) (*gén*) opposition; [*idées, intérêts*] conflict; [*couleurs, styles, caractères*] contrast; **l'~ des deux partis en cette circonstance ...** (*divergence de vue*) the opposition between the two parties on that occasion ...; (*affrontement*) the clash *ou* confrontation between the two parties on that occasion ...; **l'~ du gris et du noir a permis de ...** contrasting grey with *ou* and black has made it possible to ...; **mettre deux styles/théories en ~** to oppose *ou* contrast two styles/theories

c (*Pol*) **l'~** the opposition; **les partis de l'~** the opposition parties; **les élus de l'~** the members of the opposition parties, opposition MPs (*Brit*); **l'~ parlementaire** the parliamentary opposition, the opposition in parliament

d (*loc*) **en ~ avec** (*contraste, divergence*) in opposition to, at variance with; (*résistance, rébellion*) in conflict with; (*situation dans l'espace*) in opposition to; **agir en ~ avec ses principes** to act contrary to one's principles; **nous sommes en ~ sur ce point** we differ on this point; **ceci est en ~ avec les faits** this conflicts with the facts; (*Astron*) **les deux planètes sont en ~** the two planets are in opposition; **faire** *ou* **mettre ~ à** [+ *loi, décision*] to oppose; [+ *chèque*] to stop; **par ~** in contrast; **par ~ à** as opposed to, in contrast with

2 COMP ► **opposition à mariage** (*Jur*) objection to a marriage ► **opposition à paie-**

ment (*Jur*) objection by unpaid creditor to payment being made to debtor

oppositionnel, -elle [ɔpozisjɔnɛl] 1 ADJ oppositional 2 NM,F oppositionist

oppressant, e [ɔpresɑ̃, ɑ̃t] ADJ [*temps, souvenirs, ambiance, chaleur*] oppressive

oppresser [ɔprese] ▸ conjug 1 ◂ VT [*chaleur, ambiance, souvenirs*] to oppress; [*poids, vêtement serré*] to suffocate; [*remords, angoisse*] to oppress, weigh heavily on, weigh down; **avoir une respiration oppressée** to have difficulty with one's breathing; **se sentir oppressé** to feel suffocated

oppresseur [ɔpresœr] 1 NM oppressor 2 ADJ M oppressive

oppressif, -ive [ɔpresif, iv] ADJ oppressive

oppression [ɔpresjɔ̃] NF (= *asservissement*) oppression; (= *gêne, malaise*) feeling of suffocation *ou* oppression

opprimé, e [ɔprime] (*ptp de* **opprimer**) 1 ADJ oppressed 2 NM,F **les ~s** the oppressed

opprimer [ɔprime] ▸ conjug 1 ◂ VT a [+ *peuple*] to oppress; [+ *opinion, liberté*] to suppress, stifle b (= *oppresser*) [*chaleur*] to suffocate, oppress

opprobre [ɔprɔbr] NM (*littér* = *honte*) opprobrium (*littér*), obloquy (*littér*), disgrace; **accabler** *ou* **couvrir qn d'~** to cover sb with opprobrium; **jeter l'~ sur** to heap opprobrium on; **être l'~ de la famille** to be a source of shame to the family; **vivre dans l'~** to live in infamy

optatif, -ive [ɔptatif, iv] ADJ, NM optative

opter [ɔpte] ▸ conjug 1 ◂ VI (= *choisir*) **~ pour** [+ *carrière, solution, nationalité*] to opt for, choose; **~ entre** to choose *ou* decide between

opticien, -ienne [ɔptisjɛ̃, jɛn] NM,F (*dispensing*) optician

optimal, e (*mpl* -aux) [ɔptimal, o] ADJ optimal, optimum (*épith*)

optimalisation [ɔptimalizasjɔ̃] NF = **optimisation**

optimisation [ɔptimizasjɔ̃] NF optimization

optimiser [ɔptimize] ▸ conjug 1 ◂ VT to optimize

optimisme [ɔptimism] NM optimism; **pêcher par excès d'~** to be overoptimistic; **faire preuve d'~** to be optimistic

optimiste [ɔptimist] 1 ADJ optimistic; **il est ~ de nature** he's a born optimist, he always looks on the bright side 2 NMF optimist

optimum (*pl* **optimums** *ou* **optima**) [ɔptimɔm, a] 1 NM optimum 2 ADJ optimum (*épith*), optimal

option [ɔpsjɔ̃] 1 NF (= *choix*) option, choice; (*Comm, Jur*) option; (= *accessoire auto*) optional extra; (*Scol*) (**matière à**) **~** optional subject (*Brit*), option (*Brit*), elective; **texte à ~** optional text; (*Scol*) **avec ~ mathématique(s)** with a mathematical option, with optional mathematics; **prendre une ~ sur** (*Fin*) to take (out) an option on; **grâce à cette victoire, il a pris une ~ sur le championnat** with this victory he now has a chance of winning the championship; (*Pol*) **l'~ zéro** the zero option; (*Aut*) **climatisation en ~** optional air-conditioning, air-conditioning available as an optional extra 2 COMP ► **option d'achat** (*Fin*) option to buy, call ► **option de vente** (*Fin*) option to sell, put

optionnel, -elle [ɔpsjɔnɛl] ADJ optional; **matière ~le** optional subject (*Brit*), option (*Brit*), elective (*US*)

optique [ɔptik] 1 ADJ [*verre, disque*] optical; [*nerf*] optic → **angle, fibre, télégraphie** 2 NF a (= *science, technique, commerce*) optics *sg*; **~ médicale/photographique** medical/photographic optics; **instrument d'~** optical instrument → **illusion** b (= *lentilles, miroirs*) [*caméra, microscope*] optics *sg* c (= *manière de voir*) perspective; **il faut situer ses arguments dans une ~ sociologique** we must place his arguments

in a sociological perspective; **voir qch avec** *ou* **dans une certaine ~** to look at sth from a certain angle *ou* viewpoint; **j'ai une tout autre ~ que la sienne** my way of looking at things is quite different from his, I have a completely different perspective from his

optoélectronique [ɔptoelɛktrɔnik] 1 ADJ optoelectronic 2 NF optoelectronics *sg*

opulence [ɔpylɑ̃s] NF a (= *richesse*) [*province, région, pays*] wealthiness, richness; [*prairie*] richness; [*personne*] wealth; [*luxe, vie*] opulence; **vivre dans l'~** to live an opulent life; **nager dans l'~** to live in the lap of luxury; **il est né dans l'~** he was born into a life of opulence b (= *ampleur*) **~ des formes** richness *ou* fullness of form; **l'~ de sa poitrine** the ampleness of her bosom

opulent, e [ɔpylɑ̃, ɑ̃t] ADJ a (= *riche*) [*province, pays, personne*] wealthy, rich; [*prairie*] rich; [*luxe, vie*] opulent b (= *abondant*) [*formes*] full; [*poitrine*] ample, generous; (= *abondant*) **une chevelure ~e** a mane of hair

opus [ɔpys] NM opus

opuscule [ɔpyskyl] NM (= *brochure*) opuscule

OPV [ɔpeve] NF (ABRÉV = **offre publique de vente**) → **offre**

or¹ [ɔr] NM a (= *métal*) gold; (= *dorure*) gilt, gilding, gold; **~ blanc** *ou* **gris/jaune/rouge** white/yellow/red gold; **~ fin/massif** fine/solid gold; **bijoux en ~ massif** solid gold jewellery, jewellery in solid gold; (= *pétrole*) **~ noir** oil, black gold; (= *agriculture*) **~ vert** agricultural wealth; **en lettres d'~** in gilt *ou* gold lettering; **ses cheveux d'~** his golden hair; **les blés d'~** the golden cornfields; **les ~s des coupoles/de l'automne** the golden tints of the cupolas/of autumn; **peinture/franc ~** gold paint/franc → **cœur, cousu, étalon, lingot** *etc*

b (*loc*) **en ~** [*objet*] gold; [*occasion*] golden (*épith*); [*mari, enfant, sujet*] marvellous, wonderful; **c'est une affaire en ~** (*achat*) it's a real bargain; (*commerce, magasin*) it's a gold mine; **ils font des affaires en ~** (*ponctuellement*) they're making money hand over fist, they're raking it in*; **c'est de l'~ en barre** (*commerce, investissement*) it's a rock-solid investment, it's as safe as houses (*Brit*); **pour (tout) l'~ du monde** for all the money in the world, for all the tea in China → **pesant, pont, rouler** *etc*

or² [ɔr] CONJ a (*mise en relief*) or, ce jour-là, le soleil brillait now, on that particular day, the sun was shining; **il m'a téléphoné hier, or j'avais pensé à lui le matin même** he phoned me yesterday, and it just so happened that I'd been thinking about him that very morning b (*opposition*) and yet, but; **nous l'attendions, or il n'est pas venu** we waited for him and yet *ou* but he didn't come c (*dans un syllogisme: non traduit*) **tous les chats ont quatre pattes; or mon chien a quatre pattes; donc mon chien est un chat** all cats have four legs; my dog has four legs; therefore my dog is a cat d († *ou frm*) **or donc** thus, therefore

oracle [ɔrakl] NM (*gén*) oracle; **rendre un ~** to pronounce an oracle; (*hum*) **l'~ de la famille** the oracle of the family; **il parlait en ~** *ou* **comme un ~** he talked like an oracle

orage [ɔraʒ] 1 NM a (= *tempête*) thunderstorm, (electric) storm; **pluie/temps d'~** thundery *ou* stormy shower/weather; **vent d'~** stormy wind; **il va y avoir de l'~** *ou* **un ~** there's going to be a (thunder)storm b (= *dispute*) upset; **laisser passer l'~** to let the storm blow over; **elle sentait venir l'~** she could sense the storm brewing c (*littér* = *tumulte*) **les ~s de la vie** the turmoils of life; **les ~s des passions** the tumult *ou* storm of the passions d (*loc*) **il y a de l'~ dans l'air** (*lit*) there is a (thunder)storm brewing; (*fig*) there is trouble *ou* a storm brewing; **le temps est à l'~** there's thunder in the air, the weather is thundery 2 COMP ► **orage de chaleur**

summer storm ▶ **orage magnétique** magnetic storm

orageusement [ɔraʒøzmɑ̃] ADV (fig) tempestuously

orageux, -euse [ɔraʒø, øz] ADJ [a] (lit) [ciel] stormy, lowering (épith); [région, saison] stormy; [pluie, chaleur, atmosphère] thundery; **temps ~** thundery weather [b] (fig = mouvementé) [époque, vie, adolescence, discussion] turbulent, stormy

oraison [ɔrezɔ̃] NF orison (frm), prayer; **~ funèbre** funeral oration

oral, e (mpl **-aux**) [ɔral, o] [1] ADJ [tradition, littérature, épreuve] oral; [confession, déposition] verbal, oral; (Ling, Méd, Psych) oral → **stade, voie** [2] NM (Scol) oral (examination); **il est meilleur à l'~ qu'à l'écrit** his oral work is better than his written work

oralement [ɔralmɑ̃] ADV [transmettre] orally, by word of mouth; [conclure un accord, confesser] verbally, orally; (Méd, Scol) orally

oralité [ɔralite] NF oral character

orange [ɔrɑ̃ʒ] [1] NF (= fruit) orange; (hum) **je t'apporterai des ~s** I'll come and visit you in prison (ou in hospital) [2] NM (= couleur) orange; (= feu de signalisation) **l'~** amber (Brit), yellow (US); **le feu était à l'~** the lights were on amber (Brit), the light was yellow (US); **passer à l'~** to go through on amber (Brit) ou when the lights are (on) amber (Brit), go through a yellow light (US) ou when the light is yellow (US) [3] ADJ INV orange; [feu de signalisation] amber (Brit), yellow (US) [4] COMP ▶ **orange amère** bitter orange ▶ **orange douce** sweet orange ▶ **orange sanguine** blood orange

orangé, e [ɔrɑ̃ʒe] [1] ADJ orangey, orange-coloured [2] NM orangey colour; **l'~ de ces rideaux** the orangey shade of these curtains

orangeade [ɔrɑ̃ʒad] NF orangeade

oranger [ɔrɑ̃ʒe] NM orange tree → **fleur**

orangeraie [ɔrɑ̃ʒrɛ] NF orange grove

orangerie [ɔrɑ̃ʒri] NF (= serre) orangery

orangette [ɔrɑ̃ʒɛt] NF (= fruit) Seville orange, bitter orange; (= friandise) strip of orange covered with chocolate

orangiste [ɔrɑ̃ʒist] (Hist, Pol) [1] ADJ défilé ~ Orange parade ou march [2] NM Orangeman [3] NF Orangewoman

orang-outan(g) (pl **orangs-outan(g)s**) [ɔrɑ̃utɑ̃] NM orang-outang

orateur, -trice [ɔratœr, tris] NM,F (gén) speaker; (= homme politique, tribun) orator, speaker; (Can) Speaker (of House of Commons)

oratoire [ɔratwar] [1] ADJ [art, morceau] oratorical, of oratory; [ton, style] oratorical → **joute, précaution** [2] NM (= chapelle) oratory, small chapel; (au bord du chemin) (wayside) shrine

oratorio [ɔratɔrjo] NM oratorio

orbe[1] [ɔrb] NM (littér = globe) orb; (Astron) (= surface) plane of orbit; (= orbite) orbit

orbe[2] [ɔrb] ADJ (Constr) **mur ~** blind wall

orbital, e (mpl **-aux**) [ɔrbital, o] ADJ orbital

orbite [ɔrbit] NF [a] (Anat) (eye-)socket, orbit (SPÉC); **aux yeux enfoncés dans les ~s** with sunken eyes [b] (Astron, Phys) orbit; **mettre** ou **placer ou en ~** to put ou place in(to) orbit; **la mise en** ou **sur ~ d'un satellite** putting a satellite into orbit; **être sur** ou **en ~** [satellite] to be in orbit; **satellite en ~ à 900 km de la Terre** satellite orbiting 900 km above the earth [c] (fig = sphère d'influence) sphere of influence, orbit; **être/entrer dans l'~ de** to be in/ enter the sphere of influence of; **vivre dans l'~ de** to live in the sphere of influence of; **attirer qn dans son ~** to draw sb into one's orbit [d] (loc) **mettre** ou **placer sur ~** [+ auteur, projet, produit] to launch; **être sur ~** [auteur,

produit, méthode, projet] to be successfully launched

orbiter [ɔrbite] ▶ conjug 1 ◀ VI [satellite] to orbit; **~ autour de la terre** to orbit (around) the earth

orbiteur [ɔrbitœr] NM orbiter

Orcades [ɔrkad] NFPL **les ~** Orkney, the Orkneys, the Orkney Islands

orchestral, e (mpl **-aux**) [ɔrkɛstral, o] ADJ orchestral

orchestrateur, -trice [ɔrkɛstratœr, tris] NM,F orchestrator

orchestration [ɔrkɛstrasjɔ̃] NF [a] (Mus) (= composition) orchestration; (= adaptation) orchestration, scoring [b] (= organisation) [manifestation, propagande, campagne de presse] organization, orchestration

orchestre [ɔrkɛstr] [1] NM [a] (= musiciens) [grande musique, bal] orchestra; [jazz, danse] band; **grand ~** full orchestra → **chef**[1] [b] (Ciné, Théât) (= emplacement) stalls (Brit), orchestra (section) (US); (= fauteuil) seat in the (orchestra) stalls (Brit), seat in the orchestra (section) (US); **l'~ applaudissait** applause came from the stalls (Brit) ou orchestra (section) (US) → **fauteuil, fosse** [2] COMP ▶ **orchestre de chambre** chamber orchestra ▶ **orchestre à cordes** string orchestra ▶ **orchestre de cuivres** brass band ▶ **orchestre de danse** dance band ▶ **orchestre de jazz** jazz band ▶ **orchestre symphonique** symphony orchestra

orchestrer [ɔrkɛstre] ▶ conjug 1 ◀ VT [a] (Mus) (= composer) to orchestrate; (= adapter) to orchestrate, score [b] (= organiser) [+ campagne, manifestation, propagande] to organize, orchestrate; **une campagne savamment orchestrée** a well-orchestrated ou well-organized campaign

orchidée [ɔrkide] NF orchid

orchite [ɔrkit] NF orchitis

ordalie [ɔrdali] NF (Hist) ordeal

ordinaire [ɔrdinɛr] [1] ADJ [a] (= habituel) ordinary, normal; (Jur) [session] ordinary; **avec sa maladresse ~** with his customary ou usual clumsiness; **personnage/fait peu ~** unusual character/fact; **avec un courage pas~** ou **peu ~** with incredible ou extraordinary courage; **ça alors, c'est pas ~!** that's (really) unusual! ou out of the ordinary! [b] (= courant) [vin] ordinary; [vêtement] ordinary, everyday (épith); [service de table] everyday (épith); [qualité] standard; [essence] two-star (Brit), 2-star (US), regular (US); **croissant ~** croissant made with margarine instead of butter [c] (péj = commun) [personne, manières] common; [conversation] ordinary, run-of-the-mill; **un vin très ~** a very indifferent wine; **mener une existence très ~** to lead a humdrum existence [2] NM [a] (= la banalité) **l'~** the ordinary; **ça sort de l'~** that's out of the ordinary; **cet homme-là sort de l'~** he's one of a kind [b] (= nourriture) **l'~** ordinary ou everyday fare [c] (loc: littér) **à l'~** usually, ordinarily; **comme à l'~** as usual; **d'~** ordinarily, usually; **il fait plus chaud que d'~** ou **qu'à l'~** it's warmer than usual; (comme) **à son/mon ~** in his/my usual way, as was his/my wont (littér, aussi hum) [3] COMP ▶ **l'ordinaire de la messe** the ordinary of the Mass

ordinairement [ɔrdinɛrmɑ̃] ADV ordinarily, usually

ordinal, e (mpl **-aux**) [ɔrdinal, o] [1] ADJ ordinal [2] NM ordinal number

ordinateur [ɔrdinatœr] NM computer; **~ individuel** ou **personnel** personal computer; **~ familial** home computer; **~ de bureau** desktop (computer); **~ de bord** (Aviat) onboard computer; (Aut) onboard ou trip computer; **~ central** mainframe computer; **mettre sur ~** [+ don-

nées] to enter into a computer; [+ système] to computerize, put onto a computer; **l'ensemble du système est géré par ~** the entire system is managed by computer ou is computerized; **simulation sur** ou **par ~** computer simulation

ordination [ɔrdinasjɔ̃] NF (Rel) ordination

ordinogramme [ɔrdinɔgram] NM flow chart ou sheet

ordonnance [ɔrdɔnɑ̃s] [1] NF [a] (Méd) prescription; **préparer une ~** to make up a prescription; **ce médicament n'est délivré** ou **vendu que sur ~** this medicine is only available on prescription; **médicament vendu** ou **délivré sans ~** over-the-counter medicine [b] (Jur = arrêté) [gouvernement] order, edict; [juge] (judge's) order, ruling; **par ~ du 2-2-92** in the edict of 2/2/92; **rendre une ~** to give a ruling [c] (= disposition) [poème, phrase, tableau] organization, layout; [bâtiment] plan, layout; [cérémonie] organization; [repas] order [2] NM ou NF (Mil) (= subalterne) orderly, batman (Brit) [b] **d'~** (revolver, tunique) regulation (épith) → **officier**[1] [3] COMP ▶ **ordonnance de paiement** authorization of payment ▶ **ordonnance de police** police regulation ▶ **ordonnance royale** royal decree ou edict

ordonnancement [ɔrdɔnɑ̃smɑ̃] NM [a] (Fin) order to pay [b] (= disposition) [phrase, tableau] organization, layout; [cérémonie] organization

ordonnancer [ɔrdɔnɑ̃se] ▶ conjug 3 ◀ VT [a] (Fin) [+ dépense] to authorize [b] (= agencer) [+ phrase, tableau] to put together; [+ cérémonie] to organize

ordonnancier [ɔrdɔnɑ̃sje] NM (= liasse d'ordonnances) book of prescription forms; (= registre) register of prescriptions

ordonnateur, -trice [ɔrdɔnatœr, tris] NM,F [a] (fête, cérémonie) organizer, arranger; **~ des pompes funèbres** funeral director (in charge of events at the funeral itself) [b] (Fin) official with power to authorize expenditure

ordonné, e [ɔrdɔne] (ptp de **ordonner**) [1] ADJ [a] (= méthodique) [vie] tidy; [employé] methodical [b] (= bien arrangé) [maison] orderly, tidy; [vie] (well-)ordered, orderly; [idées, discours] well-ordered → **charité** [c] (Math) ordered; **couple ~** ordered pair [2] **ordonnée** NF (Math) ordinate, Y-coordinate; **axe des ~es** Y-axis

ordonner [ɔrdɔne] ▶ conjug 1 ◀ [1] VT [a] (= arranger) [+ espace, idées, éléments] to arrange, organize; [+ discours, texte] to organize; (Math) [+ polynôme] to arrange in order; **il avait ordonné sa vie de telle façon que ...** he had arranged ou organized his life in such a way that ... [b] (= commander) (Méd) [+ traitement, médicament] to prescribe; (Jur) [+ huis-clos, enquête] to order; **~ à qn de faire qch** to order sb to do sth, give sb orders to do sth; **il nous ordonna le silence** he ordered us to be quiet; **ils ordonnèrent la fermeture des cafés** they ordered the closure of the cafés; **ce qui m'a été ordonné** what I've been ordered to do; **je vais ~ que cela soit fait immédiatement** I'm going to order that it be done immediately [c] (Rel) [+ prêtre] to ordain; **être ordonné prêtre** to be ordained priest [2] **s'ordonner** VPR [idées, faits] to organize themselves; **les idées s'ordonnaient dans sa tête** the ideas began to organize themselves ou sort themselves out in his head

ordre[1] [ɔrdr] NM [a] (= succession régulière) order; (Ling) **l'~ des mots** word order; **par ~ alphabétique** in alphabetical order; **par ~ d'ancienneté/de mérite** in order of seniority/ of merit; **alignez-vous par ~ de grandeur** line up in order of height ou size; **par ~ d'importance** in order of importance; **dans l'~** in order; **dans le bon ~** in the right order; **par ~** ou **dans l'~ d'entrée en scène** in order of ap-

pearance; (*Sport*) ~ **de départ/d'arrivée** order (of competitors) at the starting/finishing line *ou* post; (*Mil*) **en ~ de bataille/de marche** in battle/marching order; **se replier en bon ~** to retreat in good order; **en ~ dispersé** (*Mil*) in extended order; (*fig*) without a common line *ou* plan of action; (*Jur*) **des descendants en héritiers** order of descent → **numéro, procéder**
b (= *catégorie: Archit , Bio*) order; **l'~ ionique/ dorique** the Ionic/Doric order
c (= *nature, catégorie*) **dans le même ~ d'idées** similarly; **dans un autre ~ d'idées** in a different *ou* another connection; **pour des motifs d'~ personnel/différent** for reasons of a personal/different nature; **c'est dans l'~ des choses** it's in the nature *ou* order of things; **une affaire/un chiffre du même ~** a matter/a figure of the same nature *ou* order; **un chiffre de l'~ de 2 millions** a figure in the region of *ou* of the order of 2 million; **avec une somme de cet ~** with a sum of this order; (*prix*) **donnez-nous un ~ de grandeur** give us a rough estimate *ou* a rough idea; **un chiffre de ou dans cet ~ de grandeur** a figure in that region; **de premier/deuxième/troisième ~** first-/ second-/third-rate; **de dernier ~** third-rate, very inferior; **considérations d'~ pratique/ général** considerations of a practical/general nature
d (= *légalité*) **l'~** order; **l'~ établi** the established order; **l'~ public** law and order; **le maintien de l'~ (public)** the maintenance of law and order *ou* of public order; **quand tout fut rentré dans l'~** when order had been restored, when all was back to order; **le parti de l'~** the party of law and order; **un partisan de l'~** a supporter of law and order; **la remise en ~ du pays** restoring the country to order → **force, rappeler, service**
e (= *méthode, bonne organisation*) [*personne, chambre*] tidiness, neatness, orderliness; **avoir de l'~** (*rangements*) to be tidy *ou* orderly; (*travail*) to have method, be systematic *ou* methodical; **manquer d'~** ◊ **n'avoir pas d'~** to be untidy *ou* disorderly, have no method, be unsystematic *ou* unmethodical; **en ~** [*tiroir, maison, bureau*] tidy, orderly; [*comptes*] in order; **tenir en ~** [+ *chambre*] to keep tidy; [+ *comptes*] to keep in order; **(re)mettre en ~** ◊ **(re)mettre de l'~ dans** [+ *affaires*] to set *ou* put in order, tidy up; [+ *papiers, bureau*] to tidy (up), clear up; **ils travaillent à une remise en ~ de l'économie** they are trying to sort out the economy; **mettre bon ~ à qch** to put sth to rights, sort out sth; **défiler en ~** to go past in an orderly manner; **travailler avec ~ et méthode** to work in an orderly *ou* a methodical *ou* systematic way; **un homme d'~** a man of order → **rentrer**
f (= *condition, état*) **en ~ de marche** [*machine*] in (full) working order
g (= *association, congrégation*) order; [*profession libérale*] ≈ professional association; **~ de chevalerie** order of knighthood; **~ monastique** monastic order; **~ mendiant** mendicant order; **l'~ de la jarretière/du mérite** the Order of the Garter/of Merit; (*Rel*) **les ~s** (holy) orders; (*Rel*) **les ~s majeurs/mineurs** major/minor orders; (*Rel*) **entrer dans les ~s** to take (holy) orders, go into the Church; **l'~ des architectes** the association of architects; **l'~ des avocats** ≈ the Bar, ≈ the Bar Association (*US*); **l'~ des médecins** the medical association, ≈ the British Medical Association (*Brit*), ≈ the American Medical Association (*US*); **l'~ des pharmaciens** the pharmaceutical association → **radier**
h **~ du jour** [*conférence, réunion*] agenda; (*en fin de programme*) « **autres questions à l'~ du jour** » "any other business"; (*Admin*) **l'~ du jour de l'assemblée** the business before the meeting; **passons à l'~ du jour** let's turn to the business of the day; **inscrit à l'~ du jour** on the agenda; **être à l'~ du jour** (*lit*) to be on the agenda; (*fig = être d'actualité*) to be (very) topi-

cal; (*fig*) **ce n'est pas à l'~ du jour** it's not on the agenda → **ordre²**

ordre² [ɔʀdʀ] 1 NM a (= *commandement, directive*) (*gén*) order; (*Mil*) order, command; **donner (l')~ de** to give an order *ou* the order to, to give orders to; **par ~** *ou* **sur les ~s du ministre** by order of the minister, on the orders of the minister; **j'ai reçu des ~s formels** I have formal instructions; **j'ai reçu l'~ de ...** I've been given orders to ...; **je n'ai d'~ à recevoir de personne** I don't take orders from anyone; **être aux ~s de qn** to be at sb's disposal; (*formule de politesse*) **je suis à vos ~s** I am at your service; **dis donc, je ne suis pas à tes ~s !** you can't give me orders!, I don't take orders from you!, I'm not at your beck and call!; (*Mil*) **à vos ~s !** yes sir!; **être/combattre sous les ~s de qn** to be/fight under sb's command; **j'ai agi par ~** I was (just) following orders → **désir, jusque, mot**
b (*Comm, Fin*) order; **à l'~ de** payable to, to the order of; **chèque à mon ~** cheque made out to me; **passer un ~** (*de Bourse*) to put in an order → **billet, chèque, citer**
2 COMP ► **ordre d'achat** buying order ► **ordre d'appel** (*Mil*) call-up papers (*Brit*), draft notice (*US*) ► **ordre de Bourse** stock exchange order ► **ordre de grève** strike call ► **ordre du jour** (*Mil*) order of the day; **citer qn à l'~ du jour** to mention sb in dispatches ► **ordre au mieux** (*Fin*) order at best ► **ordre de mission** (*Mil*) orders (*for a mission*) ► **ordre de prélèvement automatique** direct debit instruction ► **ordre de route** (*Mil*) marching orders ► **ordre de vente** sale order ► **ordre de virement** transfer order

ordure [ɔʀdyʀ] 1 NF a (= *saleté*) dirt (*NonC*), filth (*NonC*); **les chiens qui font leurs ~s sur le trottoir** dogs that foul the pavement
b (*péj* = *chose, personne abjecte*) **ce film est une ~** this film is pure filth; **ce type est une belle** ~‡ that guy's a real bastard‡ c (*littér* = *abjection*) mire (*littér*); **il aime à se vautrer dans l'~** he likes to wallow in filth 2 **ordures** NFPL a (= *détritus*) refuse (*NonC*), rubbish (*NonC*) (*Brit*), garbage (*NonC*) (*US*); **~s ménagères** household refuse; **l'enlèvement** *ou* **le ramassage des ~s** refuse *ou* rubbish (*Brit*) *ou* garbage (*US*) collection; **jeter** *ou* **mettre qch aux ~s** to throw *ou* put sth into the dustbin (*Brit*) *ou* rubbish bin (*Brit*) *ou* garbage can (*US*); **c'est juste bon à mettre aux ~s** it's fit for the dustbin *ou* rubbish bin (*Brit*), it belongs in the garbage can (*US*) → **boîte** b (= *grossièretés*) obscenities, filth; **dire des ~s** to utter obscenities, talk filth; **écrire des ~s** to write filth

ordurier, -ière [ɔʀdyʀje, jɛʀ] ADJ filthy

orée [ɔʀe] NF (*littér*) [*bois*] edge; **à l'~ de l'an 2000** at the beginning of the year 2000

Oregon [ɔʀegɔ̃] NM Oregon

oreillard [ɔʀejaʀ] NM (*gén*) long-eared animal; (= *chauve-souris*) long-eared bat

oreille [ɔʀɛj] NF a (*Anat*) ear; **l'~ moyenne/ interne** the middle/inner ear; **l'~ externe** the outer *ou* external ear, the auricle (*SPÉC*); **~s décollées** protruding *ou* sticking-out ears; **~s en feuille de chou** big flappy ears; **~s en chou-fleur** cauliflower ears; **le béret sur l'~** his beret cocked over one ear *ou* tilted to one side; (*fig*) **animal aux longues ~s** long-eared animal; **aux ~s pointues** with pointed ears; (*fig*) **l'~ basse** crestfallen, (with) one's tail between one's legs; (*fig*) **c'est l'avocat/ l'instituteur qui montre le bout de l'~** it's the lawyer/the schoolteacher coming out in him, it's the lawyer/the schoolteacher in him showing through; **tirer les ~s à qn** (*lit*) to pull *ou* tweak sb's ears; (*fig*) to give sb a (good) telling off*, tell sb off*; (*fig*) **se faire tirer l'~** to take *ou* need a lot of persuading → **boucher¹, boucle, dresser, puce** etc

b (= *ouïe*) hearing, ear; **avoir l'~ fine** to have keen *ou* acute hearing, have a sharp ear; **avoir de l'~** to have a good ear (for music); **il n'a pas d'~** he has no ear for music → **casser, écorcher, écouter**
c (*comme organe de communication*) ear; **écouter de toutes ses ~s** ◊ **être tout ~s** to be all ears; **n'écouter que d'une ~** ◊ **écouter d'une ~ distraite** to only half listen, listen with (only) one ear; **ouvre bien tes ~s** listen carefully; **dire qch à l'~ de qn** ◊ **dire qch à qn dans le creux** *ou* **tuyau de l'~** to have a word in sb's ear about sth; **il pédalait, casque sur les ~s** he was pedalling along with his headphones on; (*hum*) **les ~s ont dû lui tinter** *ou* **siffler** his ears must have been burning; **ce n'est pas tombé dans l'~ d'un sourd** it didn't fall on deaf ears; **ça entre par une ~ et ça (res)sort par l'autre*** it goes in one ear and out the other; **il y a toujours des ~s qui traînent** there's always someone listening; **avoir l'~ de qn** to have sb's ear; **porter qch/venir aux ~s de qn** to let sth be/come to be known to sb, bring sth/ come to sb's attention → **bouche, prêter, rebattre**
d [*écrou, fauteuil*] wing; [*soupière*] handle; [*casquette*] earflap

oreille-de-mer (*pl* **oreilles-de-mer**) [ɔʀɛj- dəmɛʀ] NF (= *coquillage*) ear shell, abalone

oreiller [ɔʀeje] NM pillow; **se réconcilier sur l'~** to make it up in bed → **confidence, taie**

oreillette [ɔʀejɛt] NF a [*cœur*] auricle; **orifice de l'~** atrium b [*casquette*] earflap c (= *écouteur*) earphone → **fauteuil**

oreillon [ɔʀejɔ̃] 1 NM [*abricot*] (apricot) half 2 **oreillons** NMPL (*Méd*) **les ~s** (the) mumps

Orénoque [ɔʀenɔk] NM Orinoco

ores [ɔʀ] ♦ **d'ores et déjà** LOC ADV already

Oreste [ɔʀɛst] NM Orestes

orfèvre [ɔʀfɛvʀ] NM silversmith, goldsmith; (*fig*) **il est ~ en la matière** he's an expert (on the subject)

orfèvrerie [ɔʀfɛvʀəʀi] NF (= *art, commerce*) silversmith's (*ou* goldsmith's) trade; (= *magasin*) silversmith's (*ou* goldsmith's) shop; (= *ouvrage*) (silver) plate, (gold) plate

orfraie [ɔʀfʀɛ] NF white-tailed eagle

organdi [ɔʀgɑ̃di] NM organdie

organe [ɔʀgan] 1 NM a (*Anat, Physiol*) organ; **~s des sens/sexuels** sense/sex(ual) organs; **~s génitaux** genitals → **fonction, greffe¹** b (*fig*) (= *véhicule, instrument*) instrument, organ; (= *institution, organisme*) organ; **le juge est l'~ de la loi** the judge is the instrument of the law; **la parole est l'~ de la pensée** speech is the medium *ou* vehicle of thought; **un des ~s du gouvernement** one of the organs of government c (= *porte-parole*) representative, spokesman; (= *journal*) mouthpiece, organ d († *ou littér* = *voix*) voice; **avoir un bel ~** to have a beautiful voice 2 COMP ► **organes de commande** controls ► **organe de presse** newspaper ► **organes de transmission** transmission system

organigramme [ɔʀganigʀam] NM (= *tableau hiérarchique, structurel*) organization chart; (= *tableau des opérations de synchronisation, Ordin*) flow chart *ou* diagram

organique [ɔʀganik] ADJ (*Chim, Jur, Méd*) organic → **chimie**

organiquement [ɔʀganikmɑ̃] ADV organically

organisateur, -trice [ɔʀganizatœʀ, tʀis] 1 ADJ [*faculté, puissance*] organizing (*épith*) 2 NM,F organizer; **~-conseil** management consultant; **~ de voyages** tour operator

organisation [ɔʀganizasjɔ̃] 1 NF a (= *préparation*) [*voyage, fête, réunion*] organization, arranging; [*campagne*] organization; [*pétition*] organization, getting up; [*service, coopérative*] organization, setting up; (= *agencement*) [*emploi du temps, travail*] organization, setting out; [*journée*] organization; **~ scientifique du**

travail scientific management; **il a l'esprit d'~** he's good at organizing things; **il manque d'~** he's not very organized

[b] (= *structure*) [*service, armée, parti*] organization; [*texte*] organization, layout; **une ~ sociale encore primitive** a still rather basic social structure; **l'~ infiniment complexe du corps humain** the infinitely complex organization of the human body

[c] (= *association, organisme*) organization; **~ non gouvernementale** non-governmental organization; **~ humanitaire** humanitarian organization; **~ syndicale** trade(s) union (*Brit*), labor union (*US*)

[2] COMP ► **Organisation de coopération et de développement économique** Organization for Economic Cooperation and Development ► **Organisation des États américains** Organization of American States ► **Organisation internationale du travail** International Labour Organization ► **Organisation de libération de la Palestine** Palestine Liberation Organization ► **Organisation maritime internationale** International Maritime Organization ► **Organisation météorologique mondiale** World Meteorological Organization ► **Organisation mondiale du commerce** World Trade Organization ► **Organisation mondiale de la santé** World Health Organization ► **Organisation mondiale du tourisme** World Tourism Organization ► **Organisation des Nations Unies** United Nations Organization ► **Organisation des pays exportateurs de pétrole** Organization of Petroleum Exporting Countries ► **Organisation du Traité de l'Atlantique Nord** North Atlantic Treaty Organization ► **Organisation des territoires de l'Asie du Sud-Est** South-East Asia Treaty Organization ► **Organisation de l'unité africaine** Organization of African Unity

organisationnel, -elle [ɔʀganizasjɔnɛl] ADJ [*problème, moyens*] organizational

organisé, e [ɔʀganize] (*ptp de* **organiser**) ADJ organized; **personne bien ~e** well-organized person → **voyage**

▼ **organiser** [ɔʀganize] ▸ conjug 1 ◂ [1] VT [a] (= *mettre sur pied*) [+ *voyage, réunion*] to organize, arrange; [+ *campagne*] to organize; [+ *pétition*] to organize, get up; [+ *service, coopérative*] to organize, set up; **j'organise une petite fête** I'm having a little party [+ *structurer*] [+ *travail, opérations, armée, parti, journée*] to organize; [+ *emploi du temps*] to organize, set out

[2] **s'organiser** VPR [a] (= *se regrouper*) [*personne, entreprise*] to organize o.s. (*ou* itself), get (o.s. *ou* itself) organized [b] (= *agencer son temps*) to organize o.s.; **il ne sait pas s'~** he doesn't know how to organize himself, he can't get (himself) organized; **je m'organiserai en fonction de toi** I'll just fit in with you, I'll fit *ou* arrange my plans round yours [c] (= *s'articuler*) [*ouvrage, histoire*] **s'~ autour d'un thème** to be organized around a theme

organiseur [ɔʀganizœʀ] NM (personal) organizer; **~ électronique** electronic organizer

organisme [ɔʀganism] NM [a] (= *organes, corps*) body, organism (SPÉC); **les besoins/fonctions de l'~** the needs/functions of the body *ou* organism, bodily needs/functions; **~ génétiquement modifié** genetically modified organism [b] (= *individu*) organism; **une nation est un ~ vivant** a nation is a living organism [c] (= *institution, bureau*) body, organization; **~ de crédit** credit company *ou* institution; **~ de recherche** research body *ou* organization; **~ de formation** training institution *ou* body; **les ~s sociaux** social welfare bodies

organiste [ɔʀganist] NMF organist

orgasme [ɔʀgasm] NM orgasm, climax

orgasmique [ɔʀgasmik], **orgastique** [ɔʀgastik] ADJ orgasmic, climactic(al)

orge [ɔʀʒ] NF, NM barley; **~ perlé** pearl barley → **sucre**

orgeat [ɔʀʒa] NM orgeat → **sirop**

orgelet [ɔʀʒəlɛ] NM (*Méd*) sty(e)

orgiaque [ɔʀʒjak] ADJ orgiastic

orgie [ɔʀʒi] NF [a] (*Hist*) (= *repas*) orgy; (= *beuverie*) drinking orgy; **faire une ~** to have an orgy; **faire des ~s de gâteaux** to gorge o.s. on cakes [b] (*fig*) **~ de** profusion of; **~ de fleurs** profusion of flowers; **~ de couleurs** riot of colour

orgue [ɔʀg] [1] NM organ; **tenir l'~** to play the organ; **~ de chœur/de cinéma/électrique/portatif** choir/theatre/electric/portable organ; **~ de Barbarie** barrel organ, hurdy-gurdy → **point**[1] [2] **orgues** NFPL [a] (*Mus*) organ; **les grandes ~s** the great organ; **les petites ~s** the small pipe organ [b] (*Géol*) **~s basaltiques** basalt columns [c] (*Mil*) **~s de Staline** rocket launcher (*mounted on a truck*)

orgueil [ɔʀgœj] NM [a] (= *arrogance*) pride, arrogance; (= *amour-propre*) pride; **gonflé d'~** puffed up *ou* bursting with pride; **~ démesuré** overweening pride *ou* arrogance; **il a l'~ de son rang** he has all the arrogance associated with his rank; **avec l'~ légitime du vainqueur** with the victor's legitimate pride; **par ~ il ne l'a pas fait** he was too proud to do it, it was his pride that stopped him doing it; **le péché d'~** the sin of pride [b] (*loc*) **ce tableau, ~ de la collection** this picture, pride of the collection; **l'~ de se voir confier les clés lui fit oublier sa colère** his pride at being entrusted with the keys made him forget his anger; **avoir l'~ de qch** ◊ **tirer ~ de qch** to take pride in sth, pride o.s. on sth; **mettre son ~ à faire qch** to take pride in doing sth

orgueilleusement [ɔʀgœjøzmɑ̃] ADV proudly, arrogantly

orgueilleux, -euse [ɔʀgœjø, øz] [1] ADJ (*défaut*) proud, arrogant; (*qualité*) proud; **~ comme un paon** as proud as a peacock [2] NM,F (very) proud person

oriel [ɔʀjɛl] NM oriel window

orient [ɔʀjɑ̃] NM [a] (*littér* = *est*) orient (*littér*), east; **l'Orient** the Orient (*littér*), the East; **les pays d'Orient** the countries of the Orient (*littér*), the oriental countries [b] [*perle*] orient [c] → **grand**

orientable [ɔʀjɑ̃tabl] ADJ [*bras d'une machine*] swivelling, rotating; [*lampe, antenne, lamelles de store*] adjustable

oriental, e (*mpl* **-aux**) [ɔʀjɑ̃tal, o] [1] ADJ [*côte, frontière, région*] eastern; [*langue, produits*] oriental; [*musique, arts*] oriental, eastern → **Inde** [2] **Oriental** NM Oriental [3] **Orientale** NF Oriental woman

orientaliser(s') [ɔʀjɑ̃talize] ▸ conjug 1 ◂ VPR [*quartier*] to take on an oriental character; [*personne*] to become orientalized

orientalisme [ɔʀjɑ̃talism] NM orientalism

orientaliste [ɔʀjɑ̃talist] NMF, ADJ orientalist

orientation [ɔʀjɑ̃tasjɔ̃] NF [a] (= *ajustement*) [*lampe, phare, rétroviseur*] adjusting; [*miroir, bras de machine*] positioning, adjusting; [*antenne*] directing, adjusting [b] [*touristes, voyageurs, recherches, enquête*] directing; **en ville, j'ai des problèmes d'~** I have problems finding my way around town → **course, sens, table** [c] (*Scol*) **l'~ professionnelle** careers advising *ou* guidance (*Brit*); **l'~ scolaire** advice *ou* guidance (*Brit*) on courses to be followed; **ils lui suggèrent une ~ vers un lycée professionnel/vers les sciences** they're suggesting he should go to a technical college/he should specialize in science; **il veut changer d'~** he wants to change courses → **centre, conseiller**[2], **cycle**[1] [d] [*carte*] orientating, orientation; (*Math*) [*droite*] orientating, orientation

[e] (= *position*) [*maison*] aspect; [*phare, antenne*] direction; **l'~ du jardin au sud** the garden's southern aspect *ou* the fact that the garden faces south [f] (= *tendance, Bourse*) trend; [*magazine*] leanings, (political) tendencies; **l'~ générale de notre enquête/de ses recherches** the general direction *ou* orientation of our inquiry/of his research; **~ à la hausse** upward trend, upturn; **~ à la baisse** downward trend, downturn

orienté, e [ɔʀjɑ̃te] (*ptp de* **orienter**) ADJ [a] (= *disposé*) **~ à l'est/au sud** [*maison*] facing east/south, with an eastern/a southern aspect; [*antenne*] directed *ou* turned towards the east/the south; **bien/mal ~** [*maison*] well/badly positioned; [*antenne*] properly/badly directed [b] (= *tendancieux*) [*article*] biased; **question ~e** leading question [c] (= *marqué*) [*plan, carte*] orientated; (*Math*) [*droite, vecteur*] oriented [d] (*Bourse*) **bien/mal ~** [*marché*] on a rising/falling trend; **valeurs bien ~es** shares which are on the up [e] (*Ordin*) **~ objet** [*langage, méthode*] object-oriented

orienter [ɔʀjɑ̃te] ▸ conjug 1 ◂ [1] VT [a] (= *disposer*) [+ *maison*] to position; [+ *lampe, phare, rétroviseur*] to adjust; [+ *miroir, bras de machine*] to position, adjust; [+ *antenne*] to direct, adjust; **~ un poste de radio pour améliorer la réception** to turn a radio round to get better reception; **~ qch vers qch** to turn sth towards sth; **~ une maison vers le** *ou* **au sud** to build a house facing south; **~ une antenne vers le** *ou* **au nord** to turn *ou* direct an aerial towards the north; **oriente la lumière vers** *ou* **sur mon livre** turn *ou* direct the light onto my book; **la lampe peut s'~ dans toutes les positions** the lamp is fully adjustable [b] (= *guider*) [+ *touristes, voyageurs*] to direct (**vers** to); [+ *enquête, recherches*] to direct (**vers** towards); **~ un élève** to advise a pupil on what courses to follow *ou* on what subjects to specialize in; **elle a été mal orientée** she was put on the wrong courses; **il a été orienté vers les sciences/vers un lycée professionnel** he was steered towards science subjects/towards technical college; **le patient a été orienté vers un service de cardiologie** the patient was referred to a cardiology unit; **~ la conversation vers un sujet** to turn the conversation onto a subject [c] (= *marquer*) [+ *carte*] to orientate; (*Math*) [+ *droite*] to orient [d] (*Naut*) [+ *voiles*] to trim

[2] **s'orienter** VPR [a] (= *se repérer*) to find one's bearings [b] (= *se diriger vers*) **s'~ vers** (*lit*) to turn towards; [*goûts*] to turn towards; [*chercheur, parti, société*] to move towards; [*étudiant*] **s'~ vers les sciences** to specialize in science; **il s'est orienté vers un lycée professionnel** he decided to go to a technical college [c] (*Bourse*) **le marché s'oriente à la hausse/à la baisse** the market is on a rising/a falling trend, the market is trending upward/downward (*US*)

orienteur, -euse [ɔʀjɑ̃tœʀ, øz] [1] NM,F (*Scol*) careers adviser [2] NM (*Tech*) orientator

orifice [ɔʀifis] NM [*caverne, digue*] opening, orifice, aperture; [*puits, gouffre, four, tuyau*] opening, mouth; (*Anat*) orifice; (*Phon*) cavity; **~ d'admission/d'échappement (des gaz)** intake/exhaust port

oriflamme [ɔʀiflam] NF (= *bannière*) banner, standard; (*Hist*) oriflamme

origami [ɔʀigami] NM origami, (Japanese) paper-folding

origan [ɔʀigɑ̃] NM oregano

originaire [ɔʀiʒinɛʀ] ADJ [a] **~ de** (= *natif de*) [*famille, personne*] originating from; (= *provenant de*) [*plante, coutume, mets*] native to; **il est ~ de** he is a native of, he was born in [b] (= *originel*) [*titulaire, propriétaire*] original, first; [*vice, défaut*] innate, inherent

---

► GRAMMAIRE ACTIVE: **organiser** 52.2

originairement [ɔʀiʒinɛʀmɑ̃] ADV originally, at first

original, e (mpl -aux) [ɔʀiʒinal, o] **1** ADJ **a** (= premier, originel) original; **édition ~e** original ou first edition → **bande¹, version** **b** (= neuf, personnel) [idée, décor] original, novel; [artiste, talent, style, œuvre] original; **cela n'a rien d'~** there's nothing original about that **c** (péj = bizarre) eccentric, odd **2** NM,F (péj) (= excentrique) eccentric; (= fantaisiste) clown*, joker*; **c'est un ~** he's a (real) character ou a bit of an eccentric **3** NM [ouvrage, tableau] original; [document] original (copy); [texte dactylographié] top copy, original (US); **l'~ de ce personnage** the model for ou the original of this character

originalement [ɔʀiʒinalmɑ̃] ADV (= de façon personnelle) originally, in an original way; (= originellement) originally

originalité [ɔʀiʒinalite] NF **a** (= nouveauté) [idée, décor] originality, novelty; [artiste, talent, œuvre] originality; **d'une grande ~** very original **b** (= caractéristique originale) original aspect ou feature **c** (= excentricité) eccentricity

▼ **origine** [ɔʀiʒin] NF **a** (gén) origin; (= commencement) origin, beginning; **les ~s de la vie** the origins of life; **tirer son ~ de ◊ avoir son ~ dans** to have one's (ou its) origins in, originate in; **avoir pour ~** to be caused by; **quelle est l'~ de sa fortune?** where did his fortune come from?, how did he make his fortune?; (titre d'ouvrage) **« l'Automobile, des ~s à nos jours »** "the Motor Car, from its Origins to the Present Day"; **elle a de lointaines ~s bretonnes** she has distant Breton roots **b** d'~ [nationalité, région de production] of origin; [langue, pays d'une personne] native; **d'~ française/noble** of French/noble origin ou extraction; **être d'~ paysanne/ouvrière** to come from peasant stock/a working-class background; **produit d'~ animale** product of animal origin; **mot d'~ française** word of French origin; **coutume d'~ ancienne** long-standing custom, custom of long standing; **les pneus sont d'~** it still has its original tyres, the tyres are the original ones → **méridien** **c** (loc) **à l'~** originally, to begin with; **être à l'~ de** (gén) to be the cause of; [+ proposition, initiative, projet, attentat] to be behind; **dès l'~** at ou from the outset, at ou from the very beginning

originel, -elle [ɔʀiʒinɛl] ADJ [innocence, pureté, beauté] original, primeval; [état, sens] original → **péché**

originellement [ɔʀiʒinɛlmɑ̃] ADV (= primitivement) originally; (= dès le début) from the (very) beginning, from the outset

orignal (pl -aux) [ɔʀiɲal, o] NM moose, Canadian elk

Orion [ɔʀjɔ̃] NM Orion; **le Baudrier d'~** Orion's Belt; **la constellation d'~** the constellation (of) Orion

oripeaux [ɔʀipo] NMPL (= haillons) rags; (= guenilles clinquantes) showy ou flashy rags

ORL [ɔɛʀɛl] **1** NF (ABRÉV = oto-rhino-laryngologie) ENT **2** NMF (ABRÉV = oto-rhino-laryngologie) ENT doctor ou specialist

orléaniste [ɔʀleanist] ADJ, NMF Orleanist

Orlon® [ɔʀlɔ̃] NM Orlon®

orme [ɔʀm] NM elm

ormeau (pl ormeaux) [ɔʀmo] NM (Bot) (young) elm; (Zool) ormer, abalone, ear shell

Ormuz [ɔʀmuz] N Hormuz, Ormuz; **le détroit d'~** the Strait of Hormuz ou Ormuz

orné, e [ɔʀne] (ptp de orner) ADJ [style] ornate, florid; **lettres ~es** illuminated letters

ornement [ɔʀnəmɑ̃] NM (gén) ornament; (Archit, Art) embellishment, adornment; (Mus) grace note(s), ornament; **sans ~(s)** [élégance, toilette, style] plain, unadorned; **d'~** [arbre, jardin] ornamental; **~s de style** ornaments of style; **~s sacerdotaux** vestments

ornemental, e (mpl -aux) [ɔʀnəmɑ̃tal, o] ADJ [style, plante] ornamental; [motif] decorative

ornementation [ɔʀnəmɑ̃tasjɔ̃] NF ornamentation

ornementer [ɔʀnəmɑ̃te] ▸conjug 1◂ VT to ornament

orner [ɔʀne] ▸conjug 1◂ VT **a** (= décorer) [+ chambre, vêtement] to decorate (de with); (= embellir) [+ discours, récit] to embellish (de with); **~ une rue de drapeaux** to deck out a street with flags; **sa robe était ornée d'un galon** her dress was trimmed with braid; **livre orné de dessins** book illustrated with drawings; (littér) **~ la vérité** to adorn ou embellish the truth; (littér) **~ son esprit** to enrich one's mind **b** (= servir d'ornement à) to adorn, decorate, embellish; **la fleur qui ornait sa boutonnière** the flower which adorned ou decorated his buttonhole; **les sculptures qui ornaient la façade** the sculptures which adorned ou decorated ou embellished the façade

ornière [ɔʀnjɛʀ] NF (lit) rut; (fig) **il est sorti de l'~ maintenant** he's out of the wood(s) now; **retomber dans l'~** to go back to one's old ways

ornithologie [ɔʀnitɔlɔʒi] NF ornithology

ornithologique [ɔʀnitɔlɔʒik] ADJ ornithological

ornithologiste [ɔʀnitɔlɔʒist], **ornithologue** [ɔʀnitɔlɔg] NMF ornithologist

ornithorynque [ɔʀnitɔʀɛ̃k] NM duck-billed platypus, ornithorhynchus (SPÉC)

orogenèse [ɔʀɔʒənɛz] NF (= processus) orogenesis; (= période) orogeny

orogénie [ɔʀɔʒeni] NF orogeny

orogénique [ɔʀɔʒenik] ADJ orogenic, orogenetic

orographie [ɔʀɔgʀafi] NF or(e)ography

orographique [ɔʀɔgʀafik] ADJ or(e)ographic(al)

oronge [ɔʀɔ̃ʒ] NF agaric; **~ vraie** imperial mushroom; **fausse ~** fly agaric

orpaillage [ɔʀpajaʒ] NM gold washing

orpailleur [ɔʀpajœʀ] NM gold washer

Orphée [ɔʀfe] NM Orpheus

orphelin, e [ɔʀfəlɛ̃, in] **1** ADJ orphan(ed); **être ~ de père/de mère** to be fatherless/motherless, have lost one's father/mother **2** NM,F orphan → **veuf**

orphelinat [ɔʀfəlina] NM (= lieu) orphanage; (= orphelins) children of the orphanage

orphéon [ɔʀfeɔ̃] NM (= fanfare) (village ou town) band

orphie [ɔʀfi] NF garfish

orphique [ɔʀfik] ADJ Orphic

orphisme [ɔʀfism] NM Orphism

orpiment [ɔʀpimɑ̃] NM orpiment

orpin [ɔʀpɛ̃] NM stonecrop

orque [ɔʀk] NF killer whale

ORSEC [ɔʀsɛk] NF (ABRÉV = Organisation des secours) → **plan¹**

orteil [ɔʀtɛj] NM toe; **gros/petit ~** big/little toe

ORTF† [ɔɛʀteɛf] NF (ABRÉV = Office de radiodiffusion-télévision française) former French broadcasting service

orthocentre [ɔʀtɔsɑ̃tʀ] NM orthocentre

orthodontie [ɔʀtɔdɔ̃ti] NF orthodontics sg, dental orthopaedics sg (Brit) ou orthopedics sg (US)

orthodontique [ɔʀtɔdɔ̃tik] ADJ orthodontic

orthodontiste [ɔʀtɔdɔ̃tist] NMF orthodontist

orthodoxe [ɔʀtɔdɔks] **1** ADJ **a** (Rel, gén) Orthodox → **église** **b** (en emploi négatif) **peu ~ ◊ pas très ~** [méthode, pratiques] rather unorthodox, not very orthodox **2** NMF (Rel) Orthodox; (Pol) one who follows the orthodox (party) line; **les ~s grecs/russes** the Greek/Russian Orthodox

orthodoxie [ɔʀtɔdɔksi] NF orthodoxy

orthodromie [ɔʀtɔdʀomi] NF orthodromy

orthogenèse [ɔʀtɔʒenɛz] NF orthogenesis

orthogénie [ɔʀtɔʒeni] NF family planning; **centre d'~** family planning ou birth control centre

orthogonal, e (mpl -aux) [ɔʀtɔgɔnal, o] ADJ orthogonal

orthographe [ɔʀtɔgʀaf] NF (gén) spelling, orthography (SPÉC); (= forme écrite correcte) spelling; (= système) spelling (system); **réforme de l'~** spelling ou orthographical reform, reform of the spelling system; **quelle est l'~ de votre nom?** how do you spell your name?, how is your name spelt?; **ce mot a deux ~s** this word has two different spellings ou can be spelt in two (different) ways; **il a une bonne ~** he's good at spelling, he's a good speller; **~ d'usage** spelling; **~ d'accord** spelling of grammatical agreements → **faute**

orthographier [ɔʀtɔgʀafje] ▸conjug 7◂ VT to spell (in writing); **mal orthographié** incorrectly ou wrongly spelt

orthographique [ɔʀtɔgʀafik] ADJ spelling (épith), orthographical; **signe ~** orthographical sign

orthonormé, e [ɔʀtɔnɔʀme] ADJ orthonormal

orthopédie [ɔʀtɔpedi] NF orthopaedics sg (Brit), orthopedics sg (US)

orthopédique [ɔʀtɔpedik] ADJ orthopaedic (Brit), orthopedic (US); **chaussures ~s** orthopaedic shoes

orthopédiste [ɔʀtɔpedist] NMF (= médecin) orthopaedic (Brit) ou orthopedic (US) specialist, orthopaedist (Brit), orthopedist (US); (= fabricant) maker of orthopaedic (Brit) ou orthopedic (US) devices; **chirurgien ~** orthopaedic (Brit) ou orthopedic (US) surgeon

orthophonie [ɔʀtɔfɔni] NF (Ling = prononciation correcte) correct pronunciation; (Méd = traitement) speech therapy

orthophoniste [ɔʀtɔfɔnist] NMF speech therapist

orthoptère [ɔʀtɔptɛʀ] **1** ADJ orthopterous, orthopteran **2** NM orthopteran, orthopteron

orthoptiste [ɔʀtɔptist] NMF orthoptist

ortie [ɔʀti] NF (stinging) nettle; **~ blanche** white dead-nettle; **jeter qch aux ~s** to throw sth out of the window; **jeter la soutane** ou le **froc aux ~s** to leave the priesthood → **piqûre**

ortolan [ɔʀtɔlɑ̃] NM ortolan (bunting); (hum) **à l'époque, je ne me nourrissais pas d'~s** those were lean days for me

orvet [ɔʀvɛ] NM slow worm

oryx [ɔʀiks] NM oryx

OS [oɛs] NM (ABRÉV = ouvrier spécialisé) → **ouvrier**

os (pl os) [ɔs, o] **1** NM **a** (Anat) bone; **avoir de petits/gros ~** to be small-boned/big-boned; **viande avec ~** meat on the bone; **viande sans ~** boned ou boneless meat, meat off the bone; **fait en ~** made of bone; **jetons/manche en ~** bone counters/handle; **à manche en ~** bone-handled **b** (loc) **c'est un paquet** ou **sac d'~** he's a bag of bones, he's (all) skin and bone(s); **mouillé** ou **trempé jusqu'aux ~** soaked to the skin, wet through; **donner** ou **jeter un ~ à ronger à qn** to give sb something to keep him occupied ou quiet; **il ne fera pas de vieux ~** (= il ne vivra pas longtemps) he won't last ou live long; **il n'a pas fait de vieux ~ dans cette entreprise** he didn't last long in that firm; **il est pourri jusqu'à l'~** he's rotten to the core; **ils t'ont eu** ou **possédé jusqu'à l'~** they had you good and proper*; **l'avoir dans l'~** (= être roulé) to be had*; **il y a un ~** there's a snag ou hitch; **tomber sur un ~** (obstacle temporaire) to come across ou hit* a snag; (impasse) to be stymied; (échec) to come unstuck → **chair, rompre**

2 COMP ➤ **os à moelle** marrowbone ➤ **os de seiche** cuttlebone

oscar [ɔskaʀ] NM (*Ciné*) Oscar; (*autres domaines*) prize, award (**de** for); **l'~ du meilleur film/scénario** the Oscar for best film/screenplay

oscillateur [ɔsilatœʀ] NM (*Phys*) oscillator

oscillation [ɔsilasjɔ̃] NF (*Élec, Phys*) oscillation; [*pendule*] swinging (*NonC*), oscillation; [*navire*] rocking (*NonC*); [*température, cours, taux, opinion*] fluctuation, variation (**de** in); **les ~s de son esprit** his (mental) fluctuations

oscillatoire [ɔsilatwaʀ] ADJ (*Sci*) oscillatory; [*mouvement*] swinging, oscillatory (*SPÉC*)

osciller [ɔsile] ▸ conjug 1 ◂ VI (*Sci*) to oscillate; [*pendule*] to swing, oscillate; [*navire*] to rock; **le vent fit ~ la flamme/la statue** the wind made the flame flicker/made the statue rock; **sa tête oscillait de droite à gauche** his head rocked from side to side; **il oscillait sur ses pieds** he rocked on his feet; (*fig*) **~ entre** [*personne*] to waver *ou* oscillate between; [*prix, température*] to fluctuate *ou* vary between

oscillogramme [ɔsilɔgʀam] NM oscillogram

oscillographe [ɔsilɔgʀaf] NM oscillograph

oscilloscope [ɔsilɔskɔp] NM oscilloscope

osé, e [oze] (*ptp de* **oser**) ADJ [*tentative, démarche, toilette*] bold, daring; [*sujet, plaisanterie*] risqué, daring

Osée [oze] NM Hosea

oseille [ozɛj] NF **a** (*Bot*) sorrel **b** (‡ = *argent*) dough‡, bread‡, dosh‡ (*surtout Brit*); **avoir de l'~** to be in the money*, have plenty of dough‡ *ou* dosh‡ (*surtout Brit*)

oser [oze] ▸ conjug 1 ◂ VT **a** (*gén*) to dare; **il faut ~ !** one must take risks!; **~ faire qch** to dare (to) do sth; (*littér*) **~ qch** to dare sth; **il n'osait (pas) bouger** he did not dare (to) move; **je voudrais bien mais je n'ose pas** I'd like to but I don't dare *ou* I daren't; **ose le répéter !** I dare you to repeat it!; **approche si tu l'oses !** come over here if you dare!; **il a osé m'insulter** he dared *ou* presumed to insult me; **comment osez-vous !** how dare you! **b** (*loc*) **si j'ose dire** if I may say so, if I may make (*Brit*) *ou* be (*US*) so bold † (*aussi hum*); **si j'ose m'exprimer ainsi** if I can put it that way, if you'll pardon the expression; **j'ose espérer** *ou* **croire que ...** I hope that ...; **j'ose l'espérer** I should hope so; **je n'ose y croire** I daren't believe it; **j'oserais même dire que ...** I'd even venture to *ou* go as far as to say that ...

oseraie [ozʀɛ] NF osier plantation

osier [ozje] NM (*Bot*) willow, osier; (= *fibres*) wicker (*NonC*); **corbeille en ~** wicker(work) basket; **fauteuil en ~** wicker(work) chair, basket chair → **brin**

Osiris [oziʀis] NM Osiris

Oslo [oslo] N Oslo

osmium [ɔsmjɔm] NM osmium

osmonde [ɔsmɔ̃d] NF osmund

osmose [ɔsmoz] NF (*lit, fig*) osmosis; **vivre en ~ avec** to live in harmony with; **~ inverse** reverse osmosis

osmotique [ɔsmɔtik] ADJ osmotic

ossature [ɔsatyʀ] NF [*corps*] frame, skeletal structure (*SPÉC*); [*tête, visage*] bone structure; [*appareil, immeuble*] framework; [*voûte*] frame(work); [*société, discours*] framework, structure; **à ~ grêle/robuste** slender-/heavy-framed

osselet [ɔslɛ] NM **a** (= *jeu*) **~s** knucklebones, jacks **b** (*Anat*) [*oreille*] ossicle **c** (*Vét*) osselet

ossements [ɔsmɑ̃] NMPL (= *squelettes*) bones

osseux, -euse [ɔsø, øz] ADJ **a** [*tissu*] bone (*épith*), osseous (*SPÉC*); [*charpente, carapace*] bony; (*Bio*) [*poisson*] bony; [*Méd*] [*greffe*] bone (*épith*); [*maladie*] bone (*épith*), of the bones **b** (= *maigre*) [*main, visage*] bony

ossification [ɔsifikasjɔ̃] NF (*Méd*) ossification

ossifier VT, **s'ossifier** VPR [ɔsifje] ▸ conjug 7 ◂ (*lit, fig*) to ossify

ossu, e [ɔsy] ADJ (*littér*) large-boned

ossuaire [ɔsɥɛʀ] NM (= *lieu*) ossuary

ostéite [ɔsteit] NF osteitis

ostensible [ɔstɑ̃sibl] ADJ [*mépris, indifférence*] conspicuous, patent; [*charité, compassion, attitude, geste*] conspicuous; **de façon ~** conspicuously

ostensiblement [ɔstɑ̃sibləmɑ̃] ADV conspicuously

ostensoir [ɔstɑ̃swaʀ] NM monstrance

ostentation [ɔstɑ̃tasjɔ̃] NF ostentation; **il détestait toute ~** he hated all ostentation *ou* show, he hated all manner of ostentation *ou* display; **agir avec ~** to act with ostentation *ou* ostentatiously; **courage/élégance sans ~** unostentatious courage/elegance; **faire qch sans ~** to do sth without ostentation *ou* unostentatiously; (*littér*) **faire ~ de qch** to make a display *ou* show of sth, parade sth

ostentatoire [ɔstɑ̃tatwaʀ] ADJ (*littér*) ostentatious

ostéoblaste [ɔsteɔblast] NM osteoblast

ostéogenèse [ɔsteɔʒənɛz], **ostéogénie** [ɔsteɔʒeni] NF osteogenesis

ostéologie [ɔsteɔlɔʒi] NF osteology

ostéomalacie [ɔsteɔmalasi] NF osteomalacia

ostéomyélite [ɔsteɔmjelit] NF osteomyelitis

ostéopathe [ɔsteɔpat] NMF osteopath

ostéopathie [ɔsteɔpati] NF **a** (= *maladie*) bone disease; (= *pratique*) osteopathy

ostéophyte [ɔsteɔfit] NM osteophyte

ostéoplastie [ɔsteɔplasti] NF osteoplasty

ostéoporose [ɔsteɔpɔʀoz] NF osteoporosis

ostéosarcome [ɔsteɔsaʀkom] NM osteosarcoma

ostéotomie [ɔsteɔtɔmi] NF osteotomy

ostraciser [ɔstʀasize] ▸ conjug 1 ◂ VT to ostracize

ostracisme [ɔstʀasism] NM ostracism; **être frappé d'~** to be ostracized; **leur ~ m'était indifférent** being ostracized by them didn't bother me

ostréicole [ɔstʀeikɔl] ADJ [*production*] oyster (*épith*); [*techniques*] oyster-farming (*épith*)

ostréiculteur, -trice [ɔstʀeikyltœʀ, tʀis] NM,F oyster-farmer, ostreiculturist (*SPÉC*)

ostréiculture [ɔstʀeikyltyʀ] NF oyster-farming, ostreiculture (*SPÉC*)

ostrogot(h), e [ɔstʀɔgo, gɔt] **1** ADJ Ostrogothic **2** **Ostrogot(h)(e)** NM,F Ostrogoth **3** NM († *ou hum*) (= *mal élevé*) barbarian; (= *original, olibrius*) odd fish* *ou* fellow

otage [ɔtaʒ] NM hostage; **prendre qn en** *ou* **comme ~** to take sb hostage; **être pris** *ou* **retenu en ~** to be held hostage; **la prise d'~s** hostage-taking incident; **le gouvernement s'élève contre les prises d'~s** the government condemns hostage-taking *ou* the taking *ou* seizure of hostages

OTAN [ɔtɑ̃] NF (ABRÉV = **Organisation du Traité de l'Atlantique Nord**) NATO

otarie [ɔtaʀi] NF sea-lion, otary (*SPÉC*), eared seal (*SPÉC*)

OTASE [ɔtaz] NF (ABRÉV = **Organisation des territoires de l'Asie du Sud-Est**) SEATO

ôter [ote] ▸ conjug 1 ◂ **1** VT **a** (= *enlever*) [+ *ornement*] to take away, remove (**de** from); [+ *lunettes, vêtement*] to take off, remove; [+ *arêtes, épine*] to take out (**de** of), remove (**de** from); [+ *tache*] to take out (**de** of), remove (**de** from), lift (**de** from); [+ *hésitation, scrupule*] to remove, take away; [+ *remords*] to relieve; **ôte les assiettes (de la table)** clear the table, clear the dishes off the table; **un produit qui ôte l'acidité (à une** *ou* **d'une substance)** a product which removes the acidity (from a substance); **ôte tes mains de la porte !** take your hands off the door!; **ôte tes pieds de là !** get your feet off there!; **cela lui a ôté un gros poids** that took a great weight off his chest *ou* lifted a great weight from his chest; **on lui ôta ses menottes** they took his handcuffs off, they unhandcuffed him

b (= *retrancher*) [+ *somme*] to take away; [+ *paragraphe*] to remove, cut out (**de** from); **~ un nom d'une liste** to remove a name from a list, take a name off a list; **5 ôté de 8 égale 3** 5 (taken away) from 8 equals *ou* leaves 3

c (= *prendre*) **~ qch à qn** to take sth (away) from sb; **~ un enfant à sa mère** to take a child (away) from its mother; **~ à qn ses illusions** to rid *ou* deprive sb of his illusions; **~ à qn ses forces/son courage** to deprive sb of his strength/his courage; **ça lui ôtera toute envie de recommencer** that will stop him wanting to do it again, that will rid him of any desire to do it again; **ôte-lui le couteau (des mains)** take the knife (away) from him, take the knife out of *ou* from his hands; **on ne m'ôtera pas de l'idée que ...** I can't get it out of my mind *ou* head that ...; **il faut absolument lui ~ cette idée de la tête** we must get this idea out of his head → **pain**

2 **s'ôter** VPR **ôtez-vous de là** move yourself!, get out of there!; **ôtez-vous de la lumière** ◊ **ôte-toi de mon soleil** (*hum*) get out of my light; (*hum*) **ôte-toi de là (que je m'y mette)!*** (get) out of the way (and give me some room)!, move *ou* shift* out of the way (and give me some room)!; **je ne peux pas m'~ ça de l'idée** I can't get it out of my mind *ou* head; **comment est-ce que ça s'ôte ?** how do you remove it? *ou* take it off?; **s'~ la vie** to take one's (own) life

otite [ɔtit] NF ear infection, otitis (*SPÉC*); **~ moyenne/interne** otitis media/interna

oto-rhino (*pl* **oto-rhinos**) [ɔtɔʀino] NMF = **oto-rhino-laryngologiste**

oto-rhino-laryngologie [ɔtɔʀinolaʀɛ̃gɔlɔʒi] NF oto(rhino)laryngology

oto-rhino-laryngologiste (*pl* **oto-rhino-laryngologistes**) [ɔtɔʀinolaʀɛ̃gɔlɔʒist] NMF ear, nose and throat specialist, oto(rhino)laryngologist

otoscope [ɔtɔskɔp] NM otoscope

Ottawa [ɔtawa] N Ottawa

ottoman, e [ɔtɔmɑ̃, an] **1** ADJ Ottoman **2** NM **a** (= *personne*) **Ottoman** Ottoman **b** (= *tissu*) ottoman **3** **ottomane** NF **a** (= *personne*) **Ottomane** Ottoman woman **b** (= *canapé*) ottoman

ou [u] CONJ **a** (*alternative*) or; **est-ce qu'il doit venir aujourd'hui ou demain ?** is he coming today or tomorrow?; **il faut qu'il vienne aujourd'hui ou demain** he must come (either) today or tomorrow; **avec ou sans sucre ?** with or without sugar?; **que vous alliez chez cet épicier ou chez l'autre, c'est le même prix** it's the same price whether you go to this grocer or (to) the other one; **un kilo de plus ou de moins, cela ne se sent pas** one kilo more or less doesn't show up; **que vous le vouliez ou non** whether you like it or not; **jolie ou non, elle plaît** (whether she's) pretty or not, she's attractive; **est-ce qu'elle veut se lever ou préfère-t-elle attendre demain ?** does she want to get up or does she prefer to wait until tomorrow?; **il nous faut 3 pièces, ou plutôt/ou même 4** we need 3 rooms, or preferably/or even 4; **apportez-moi une bière, ou plutôt non, un café** bring me a beer, or rather a coffee; **ou pour mieux dire** or rather, or I should say

b (*approximation*) or; **à 5 ou 6 km d'ici** 5 or 6 km from here; **ils étaient 10 ou 12** there were (some) 10 or 12 of them

c (*avec exclusion*) **ou ... ou** either ... or; **ou il est malade ou (bien) il est fou** he's either sick or mad, either he's sick or (else) he's mad; **ou (bien) tu m'attends ou (bien) alors tu pars à pied** either you wait for me or (else) you'll have to walk, you (can) either wait for me or (else) go on foot; **il faut qu'il travaille ou (bien) il échouera à son examen** he'll have to work or (else) ou otherwise he'll fail his exam; **donne-moi ça ou je me fâche** give me that or I'll get cross → **tôt**

où [u] **1** PRON **a** (situation, direction) where; **l'endroit où je vais/je suis** the place where I'm going/I am, the place I'm going to/I'm in; **l'endroit idéal où s'établir** the ideal place to settle; **je cherche un endroit où m'asseoir** I'm looking for a place to sit down ou for somewhere to sit; **la ville où j'habite** the town I live in; **le mur où il est accoudé** the wall he's leaning against; **le tiroir où tu as rangé le livre** the drawer you put the book in ou where you put the book; **le tiroir où tu a pris le livre** the drawer you took the book from; **le livre où il a trouvé ce renseignement** the book where ou in which he found this piece of information; **le livre où il a copié ceci** the book he copied this from ou from which he copied this; **le chemin par où il est passé** the road he went along ou he took; **le village par où il est passé** the village he went through; **l'endroit d'où je viens** the place I've come from; **la pièce d'où il sort** the room he's come out of; **la crevasse d'où on l'a retiré** the crevasse they pulled him out of; **une chambre d'où s'échappent des gémissements** a room from which moans are coming; **l'endroit jusqu'où ils ont grimpé** the place (where) they have climbed to ou to which they've climbed → **là, partout**

b (antécédent abstrait : institution, groupe, état, condition) **la famille où il est entré** the family he has become part of, the family he has joined; **la famille/la firme d'où il sort** the family/firm he comes ou has come from; **la ville d'où il vient** (origine) the town he comes from; **l'école où il est inscrit** the school where ou in which he is enrolled; **les mathématiques, domaine où je ne suis guère compétent** mathematics, an area in which I have little skill; **dans l'état où il est** in the state he's in ou in which he is; **l'obligation où il se trouve de partir** the fact that he finds himself obliged to leave; **dans l'embarras où j'étais** in my embarrassment; **les conditions où ils travaillent** the conditions they work in ou in which they work; **la rêverie où il est plongé/ d'où je l'ai tiré** the daydream he's in/from which I roused him; **les extrêmes où il s'égare** the extremes into which he is straying; **le but où tout homme tend** the goal towards which all men strive; **la mélancolie où il se complaît** the melancholy in which he wallows; **au rythme/train où ça va** at the speed/rate it's going; **au prix où c'est** at the price it is; **au tarif où ils font payer ça** at the rate they charge for it; **à l'allure où ils vont** at the rate they're going; **voilà où nous en sommes** that's the position to date ou so far, that's where we're at* → **prix, train**; (et pour autres constructions voir verbes appropriés)

c (temporel) **le siècle où se passe cette histoire** the century in which this story takes place; **le jour où je l'ai rencontré** the day (when ou on which) I met him; **l'époque où on n'avait rien à manger** the time when we had nothing to eat; **à l'instant où il est arrivé** the moment he arrived; **mais là où je me suis fâché, c'est quand il a recommencé** but what (finally) made me explode was when he started doing it again → **moment**

2 ADV REL **a** (situation, direction) where; **j'irai où il veut** I'll go where ou wherever he wants; **s'établir où l'on veut** to settle where one likes; **je ne sais pas d'où il vient** I don't know where he comes from; **on ne peut pas passer par où on veut** you can't just go where you like; **d'où je vois on voit la mer** you can see the sea from where I am; **où que l'on aille/soit** wherever one goes/is; **d'où que l'on vienne** wherever

one comes from; **par où que l'on passe** wherever one goes

b (abstrait) **où cela devient grave, c'est lorsqu'il prétend que ...** where it gets serious is when he claims that ...; **savoir où s'arrêter** to know where ou when to stop; **d'où l'on peut conclure que ...** from which one may conclude that ...; **d'où son silence/ma méfiance** hence his silence/my wariness; (titre de chapitre) « **où l'on voit que ...** » "in which the reader sees ou learns that ..." ■ (PROV) **où il y a de la gêne, il n'y a pas de plaisir** comfort comes first, there's no sense in being uncomfortable; (reproche) talk about making yourself at home!, some people think only of their own comfort

3 ADV INTERROG **a** (situation, direction) where; **où vas-tu/es-tu/l'as-tu mis ?** where are you going/are you/did you put it?; **d'où viens-tu ?** where have you come from?; **par où y aller ?** which way should we (ou I etc) go?; **où aller ?** where should I (ou he etc) go?; **où ça ?*** where's that?

b (abstrait) **où en étais-je ?** where was I?, where had I got to?; **où en êtes-vous ?** where are you up to?; **où allons-nous ?** where are we going?; **d'où vient cette attitude ?** what's the reason for this attitude?; **d'où vient qu'il n'a pas répondu ?** how come he hasn't replied?*, what's the reason for his not having replied?; **d'où le tenez-vous ?** where did you hear that?; **où voulez-vous en venir ?** what are you leading up to? ou getting at?

OUA [oya] NF (ABRÉV = **Organisation de l'unité africaine**) OAU

Ouagadougou [wagadugu] N Ouagadougou

ouah* ['wa] EXCL (joie) wow!*, ooh!*; (aboiement) ~ ! ~ ! woof! woof!

ouailles [waj] NFPL (Rel, hum) flock; **l'une de ses ~** one of his flock

ouais* ['wɛ] EXCL (= oui) yeah*, yep*; (sceptique) oh yeah?*

ouananiche [wananiʃ] NM (Can) fresh water salmon

ouaouaron* ['wawarɔ̃] NM (Can) bullfrog

ouate ['wat] **1** NF **a** (pour pansement) cotton wool (Brit), cotton (US) **b** (pour rembourrage) padding, wadding; **doublé d'~** quilted **2** COMP ► **ouate hydrophile** cotton wool (Brit), absorbent cotton (US) ► **ouate thermogène** Thermogene®

ouaté, e ['wate] (ptp de **ouater**) ADJ **a** [pansement] cotton-wool (épith) (Brit), cotton (épith) (US);† [vêtement] quilted **b** [pas, bruit] muffled; [ambiance] cocoon-like

ouater ['wate] ►conjug 1◄ VT [+ manteau, couverture] to quilt; **les collines ouatées de neige** the hills covered ou blanketed in snow

ouatine [watin] NF wadding, padding

ouatiner [watine] ►conjug 1◄ VT to quilt; **veste ouatinée** quilted jacket

oubli [ubli] NM **a** (= omission) oversight; **il s'agit d'un simple ~** it was just an oversight; **il y a des ~s dans ce récit** there are gaps ou things missed out in this account; **l'~ de cette date a eu des conséquences graves** the fact the date was forgotten has had serious repercussions; **j'ai réparé mon ~** I made up for having forgotten **b** (= trou de mémoire) **ses ~s répétés m'inquiètent** his constant lapses of memory worry me, his constant forgetfulness worries me **c** **l'~** oblivion, forgetfulness; **l'~ de soi(-même)** self-effacement, selflessness; **tirer qch de l'~** to bring sth out of oblivion; **tomber dans l'~** to sink into oblivion; **le temps apporte l'~** memories fade with the passage of time

oublié, e [ublije] NM,F (ptp de **oublier**) forgotten person; **c'est un peu l'~ parmi les grands chanteurs** among the great singers he tends to be overlooked; **les ~s de l'Histoire** those

who have been left out of the history books, those who have been forgotten by history

▼ **oublier** [ublije] ►conjug 7◄ **1** VT **a** (= ne pas se souvenir de) to forget; (= ne plus penser à) [+ soucis, chagrin, client, visiteur] to forget (about); **~ de faire qch** to forget to do sth; **~ pourquoi** to forget why; **ça s'oublie facilement** it's easily forgotten; **j'ai oublié qui je dois prévenir** I can't remember who (it is) ou I've forgotten who (it is) I should warn; **j'ai complètement oublié l'heure** I completely forgot about the time; **j'ai oublié si j'ai bien éteint le gaz** I forget ou I can't remember if I turned off the gas; **n'oublie pas que nous sortons ce soir** remember ou don't forget we're going out tonight; **boire pour ~** to drink to forget; **ah oui, j'oubliais, il faut que tu rappelles ton frère** oh, yes, I almost forgot, you should phone your brother; **il oubliera avec le temps** he'll forget in time, time will help him forget; **oublions le passé** let's forget about the past, let's let bygones be bygones; **c'est oublié, n'y pensons plus** it's all forgotten now, let's not think about it any more; **j'avais complètement oublié sa présence** I had completely forgotten that he was there; **sa gentillesse fait ~ sa laideur** the fact he's so nice makes you forget how ugly he is; **il essaie de se faire ~** he's trying to keep out of the limelight; **mourir oublié** to die forgotten

b (= laisser) [+ chose] to forget, leave behind; [+ fautes d'orthographe] to miss; (= omettre) [+ virgule, phrase] to leave out; **j'ai oublié mon parapluie dans le train** I left my umbrella on the train; **j'ai oublié mon parapluie** I forgot my umbrella, I left my umbrella behind; **tu as oublié (de laver) une vitre** you've missed a pane; (hum) **un jour tu oublieras ta tête !** you'll forget your head one of these days!

c (= négliger) [+ famille, devoir, travail, promesse] to forget, neglect; **~ les règles de la politesse** to forget ou neglect the rules of etiquette; **n'oubliez pas le guide !** don't forget (to tip) the guide!; **il ne faut pas ~ que c'est un pays pauvre** we must not lose sight of the fact ou forget that it's a poor country; **~ qn dans son testament** to forget (to include) sb in one's will; **il ne vous oublie pas** he hasn't forgotten (about) you; **on l'a oublié sur la liste** he's been left off the list

2 **s'oublier** VPR **a** (= ne pas être retenu) to be forgotten; **quelqu'un comme ça ne s'oublie pas facilement** someone like that is not easily forgotten; (iro) **il ne s'est pas oublié (dans le partage)** he didn't forget himself (in the share-out)

b (littér = manquer d'égards) **vous vous oubliez !** you're forgetting yourself!

c (euph = faire ses besoins) **le chat s'est oublié sur la moquette** the cat had an accident on the carpet

oubliettes [ublijɛt] NFPL oubliettes; **jeter ou mettre aux ~** [+ projet] to shelve; **tomber dans les ~ (de l'histoire)** [déclaration, procès] to sink into oblivion; **j'ai oublié/projet est tombé aux ~** this book/plan has been forgotten

oublieux, -ieuse [ublijø, ijøz] ADJ (frm) deliberately forgetful; **~ de** [+ bienfaits] quick to forget; [+ obligations, devoirs] neglectful of

oued [wɛd] NM wadi

ouest [wɛst] **1** NM **a** (= point cardinal) west; **le vent d'~** the west wind; **un vent d'~** a west(erly) wind, a westerly (SPÉC); **le vent tourne/est à l'~** the wind is veering west(wards) ou towards the west/is blowing from the west; **regarder vers l'~** ou **dans la direction de l'~** to look west(wards) ou towards the west; **à l'~** (situation) in the west; (direction) to the west, west(wards); **le soleil se couche à l'~** the sun sets in the west; **à l'~ de** west of, to the west of; **la maison est (exposée) à l'~/ exposée plein ~** the house faces (the) west ou westwards/due west, the house looks west(wards)/due west; **l'Europe/la France/la**

Bourgogne de l'~ Western Europe/France/ Burgundy → **Allemagne**
[b] (= *régions occidentales*) west; (*Pol*) **l'Ouest** the West; **l'~ de la France** ◊ **l'Ouest** the West of France; **les rapports entre l'Est et l'Ouest** East-West relations, relations between the East and the West

[2] ADJ INV [*région, partie*] western; [*entrée, paroi*] west; [*versant, côte*] west(ern); [*côté*] west(ward); [*direction*] westward, westerly → **longitude**

ouest-allemand, e [westalmã, ãd] (*Hist*) [1] ADJ West German [2] **Ouest-Alle- mand(e)** NM,F West German

ouest-nord-ouest [westnɔʀwest] ADJ INV, NM west-northwest

ouest-sud-ouest [westsydwest] ADJ INV, NM west-southwest

ouf [uf] EXCL, NM phew, whew; **pousser un ~ de soulagement** to breathe *ou* give a sigh of relief; **ils ont dû repartir sans avoir le temps de dire ~*** they had to leave again before they had time to catch their breath *ou* before they knew where they were

Ouganda [ugãda] NM Uganda

ougandais, e [ugãdɛ, ɛz] [1] ADJ Ugandan [2] **Ougandais(e)** NM,F Ugandan

ougrien, -ienne [ugʀijɛ̃, ijɛn] ADJ, NM,F → **finno-ougrien**

oui [wi] [1] ADV (*réponse affirmative*) yes; **le connaissez-vous? — ~** do you know him? — yes (I do); **est-elle chez elle? — ~** is she at home? — yes (she is); **vous avez aimé le film? — ~ et non** did you like the film? — yes and no *ou* I did and I didn't; **je vais ouvrir la fenê- tre — ~, cela fera un peu d'air** I'll open the window — yes (do), we could do with some fresh air; **il n'a pas encore dit ~** he hasn't said yes yet, he hasn't agreed *ou* accepted (as) yet; (*pendant le mariage*) **dire ~** to say "I do"; **il ne dit ni ~ ni non** he's not saying either yes or no; **ah, ça ~!** you can say that again!*, and how!*; **que ~!** I should say so!, rather! (*Brit*); **certes ~!** (yes) most definitely *ou* certainly!, yes indeed!; **vous en voulez? — mais ~** *ou* **bien sûr que ~** *ou* **~, bien sûr** do you want some? — of course (I do) *ou* I most certainly do; **~, mais il y a un obstacle** yes but there is a diffi- culty; **eh bien ~, j'avoue** all right (then), I confess; (*slogan*) **contraception ~, avortement non** yes to contraception, no to abortion, contraception — yes, abortion — no; **répon- dre (par) ~ à toutes les questions** to answer yes *ou* answer in the affirmative to all the questions; **répondez par ~ ou par non** answer yes or no; **faire ~ de la tête** ◊ **faire signe que ~** to nod (one's head); **ah ~?** really?, yes?; (†, *hum*) **~-da** yes indeed, absolutely; (*Naut*) **~, capitaine** aye aye sir
[b] (*remplaçant une proposition*) **est-il chez lui?/est-ce qu'il travaille? — je pense** *ou* **je crois que ~** is he at home?/is he working? — (yes) I think so *ou* I believe he is; **il nous quitte? — je crains bien/j'espère que ~** is he leaving us? — I am afraid so *ou* I am afraid he is/I hope so *ou* I hope he is; **est-ce qu'elle sort souvent? — j'ai l'impression que ~** does she often go out? — I have an idea *ou* the impres- sion that she does; **tu as aimé ce film? — moi ~** did you like the film? — I did; **j'ai demandé si elle était venue, lui dit que ~** I asked if she had been and he says she has
[c] (*intensif*) **je suis surprise, ~ très surprise** I'm surprised — indeed very surprised; **c'est un escroc, ~, un escroc** he's a rogue, an abso- lute rogue; **~ vraiment, il a répondu ça?** did he really answer that?; **tu vas cesser de pleurer, ~?** have you quite finished crying?, will you stop crying?; **~ (évidemment), c'est toujours facile de critiquer** of course it's always easy to criticize; **c'est bon, ~?** isn't that good?; **il va accepter, ~ ou non?** is he or is he not going to accept?; **tu te presses, ~ ou non?** will you

please hurry up?, will you hurry up?; **tu te décides ~ ou merde!‡** make up your mind for Christ's sake!‡
[2] NM INV yes, aye; **il y a eu 30 ~** there were 30 votes for, there were 30 ayes; **j'aimerais un ~ plus ferme** I should prefer a more definite yes; **pleurer/réclamer/se disputer pour un ~ (ou) pour un non** to cry/complain/quarrel over the slightest thing

ouï-dire ['widiʀ] NM INV hearsay (*NonC*); **par ~** by hearsay

ouïe¹ ['uj] EXCL = **ouille**

ouïe² [wi] NF hearing (*NonC*); **avoir l'~ fine** to have sharp hearing, have a keen sense of hearing; **être tout ~** to be all ears

ouïes [wi] NFPL (*Zool*) gills; (*Mus*) sound holes

ouille ['uj] EXCL ouch!

ouïr [wiʀ] ▶ conjug 10◀ VT (††, *littér, hum*) to hear; (*Jur*) [+ *témoins*] to hear; **j'ai ouï dire à mon père que ...** I've heard my father say that ...; **j'ai ouï dire que ...** it has come to my ears that ..., I've heard it said that ...; (*hum*) **oyez!** hark!† *ou* hum, hear ye!† *ou* hum; **oyez, oyez, braves** *ou* **bonnes gens!** oyez! oyez! oyez!

ouistiti ['wistiti] NM (*Zool*) marmoset; (= *type*) **un drôle de ~*** an oddball*

oukase [ukaz] NM (*Hist, fig*) ukase

Oulan-Bator [ulanbatɔʀ] N Ulan Bator

ouléma [ulema] NM = **uléma**

ouragan [uʀagã] NM [a] (*Mét*) hurricane [b] (*fig*) storm; **cet homme est un véritable ~** he's like a whirlwind, he's a human tornado; **ce livre va déchaîner un ~** this book is going to create an uproar; **arriver comme un ~** to ar- rive like a whirlwind

Oural [uʀal] NM (= *fleuve*) **l'~** the Ural; **l'~** ◊ **les monts ~** the Urals, the Ural Mountains

ouralo-altaïque [uʀalɔaltaik] ADJ, NM Ural- Altaic

ourdir [uʀdiʀ] ▶ conjug 2◀ VT [a] (*Tex*) to warp [b] (*littér*) [+ *complot*] to hatch; [+ *intrigue*] to weave

ourdou [uʀdu] ADJ INV, NM (*Ling*) Urdu

ourlé, e [uʀle] (*ptp de* **ourler**) ADJ hemmed; **oreilles délicatement ~es** delicately rimmed ears; **lèvres bien ~es** well-defined lips

ourler [uʀle] ▶ conjug 1◀ VT (*Couture*) to hem; (*fig littér*) **~ de** to fringe with

ourlet [uʀlɛ] NM [a] (*Couture*) hem; **faux ~** false hem; **faire un ~ à** to hem [b] (*Tech*) hem [c] (*Anat*) [*oreille*] rim, helix (*SPEC*)

ours [uʀs] [1] NM [a] (*Zool*) bear; **être** *ou* **tourner comme un ~ en cage** to pace up and down like a caged animal → **fosse, montreur, vendre** [b] (= *jouet*) **(en peluche)** teddy bear [c] (*péj = misanthrope*) (old) bear; **vivre comme un ~** to be at odds with the world; **elle est un peu ~** she's a bit of a bear *ou* a gruff individ- ual [d] (*arg Presse*) ≈ credits (*for written publica- tion*) [e] (‡ = *règles*) **avoir ses ~** to have one's period [2] COMP ► **ours blanc** polar bear ► **ours brun** brown bear ► **ours mal léché** (*péj*) uncouth fellow ► **ours marin** furseal ► **ours polaire** = **ours blanc** ► **ours savant** trained *ou* performing bear

ourse [uʀs] NF [a] (*Zool*) she-bear [b] (*Astron*) **la Petite Ourse** the Little Bear, Ursa Minor, the Little Dipper (*US*); **la Grande Ourse** the Great Bear, Ursa Major, the Plough (*Brit*), the Big Dipper (*US*)

oursin [uʀsɛ̃] NM sea urchin, sea hedgehog

ourson [uʀsɔ̃] NM bear cub

oust(e)* ['ust] EXCL buzz off!*, hop it!* (*Brit*); **allez, ouste! dehors!** go on, out with you! *ou* out you go!

out ['awt] ADJ INV [*personne*] out of touch* (*attrib*); (*Tennis*) out

outarde [utaʀd] NF bustard; (*Can = bernache*) Canada goose

outil [uti] NM (*lit, fig*) tool; (*agricole, de jardin*) implement, tool; **~ de travail** tool; **~ pédago- gique** teaching aid; **~ de programmation** pro- gramming tool; **~ de production/gestion** production/management tool; **il maîtrise bien l'~ informatique** he's good with computers → **mauvais**

outillage [utijaʒ] NM [*mécanicien, bricoleur*] (set of) tools; [*fermier, jardinier*] implements, equipment (*NonC*); [*atelier, usine*] equipment (*NonC*)

outiller [utije] ▶ conjug 1◀ VT [+ *ouvrier*] to sup- ply *ou* provide with tools, equip, kit out (*Brit*), outfit (*US*); [+ *atelier*] to fit out, equip; **je suis bien/mal outillé pour ce genre de travail** I'm well-/badly-equipped for this kind of work; **pour ce travail, il faudra qu'on s'outille** to do this job, we'll have to equip ourselves *ou* kit ourselves out (*Brit*) properly; **les ouvriers s'ou- tillent à leurs frais** the workers buy their own tools

outilleur [utijœʀ] NM tool-maker

outplacement [awtplɛsmɛnt] NM outplace- ment; **cabinet d'~** outplacement consultancy firm

outrage [utʀaʒ] [1] NM insult; **accabler qn d'~s** to heap insults on sb; **faire ~ à** [+ *réputa- tion, mémoire*] to dishonour (*Brit*), dishonor (*US*); [+ *pudeur, honneur*] to outrage, be an outrage to; † **faire subir les derniers ~s à une femme** to ravish *ou* violate a woman; **~ au bon sens/à la raison** insult to common sense/ to reason; (*littér*) **les ~s du temps** the ravages of time [2] COMP ► **outrage à agent** (*Jur*) insulting behaviour (*to police officer*) ► **outrage aux bonnes mœurs** (*Jur*) out- rage *ou* affront to public decency ► **outrage à magistrat** (*Jur*) contempt of court ► **outrage public à la pudeur** (*Jur*) inde- cent exposure (*NonC*)

outragé, e [utʀaʒe] ADJ [*air, personne*] gravely offended

outrageant, e [utʀaʒã, ãt] ADJ offensive

outrager [utʀaʒe] ▶ conjug 3◀ VT (*littér*) [+ *personne*] to offend gravely; [+ *mœurs, morale*] to outrage; [+ *bon sens, raison*] to insult

outrageusement [utʀaʒøzmã] ADV (= *ex- cessivement*) outrageously, excessively

outrageux, -euse [utʀaʒø, øz] ADJ (= *excessif*) outrageous, excessive; **de manière outrageuse** outrageously, excessively

outrance [utʀãs] NF [a] (= *caractère*) extrava- gance; **pousser le raffinement jusqu'à l'~** to take refinement to extremes *ou* to excess; **choqué par l'~ de ses propos** shocked by the outrageousness of his remarks [b] (= *excès*) excess; **il y a des ~s dans ce roman** there are some extravagant passages in this novel; **ses ~s de langage** his outrageous language [c] **à ~** [*urbanisation, automatisation*] excessive; [*raffiné*] excessively, to excess; **spécialisé à ~** over- specialized; **cette affaire a été médiatisée à ~** this affair has been hyped up* by the media *ou* has been the subject of intense media hype* → **guerre**

outrancier, -ière [utʀãsje, jɛʀ] ADJ [*personne, propos*] extreme; **son caractère ~** the extreme nature of his character, the extremeness of his character

outre¹ [utʀ] NF goatskin, wine *ou* water skin; **gonflé** *ou* **plein comme une ~** full to bursting

▼**outre²** [utʀ] PRÉP [a] (= *en plus de*) as well as, besides; **~ sa cargaison, le bateau transportait des passagers** besides *ou* as well as its cargo the boat was carrying passengers; **~ son salai- re, il a des pourboires** on top of *ou* in addi- tion to his salary, he gets tips; **~ le fait que** as well as *ou* besides the fact that
[b] (*loc*) **en ~** moreover, besides, further(more); **~ mesure** to excess, overmuch, inordinately; **manger/boire ~ mesure** to eat/ drink to excess *ou* immoderately; **cela ne lui**

► GRAMMAIRE ACTIVE: **outre** 53.5

plaît pas ~ mesure he doesn't like that over-much, he's not overkeen on that (*Brit*), he's not a hundred per cent crazy about that (*US*); **ma décision ne l'a pas étonné/inquiété ~ mesure** he wasn't unduly *ou* overly surprised at/worried by my decision; **passer ~** to carry on regardless; **passer ~ à un ordre** to disregard an order, carry on regardless of an order; **~ qu'il a le temps, il a les capacités pour le faire** not only does he have the time but he also has the ability to do it, apart from having the time *ou* besides having the time he also has the ability to do it; **d'~ en ~** † through and through → **outrecuidance, outremer, outrepasser**

outré, e [utre] (*ptp de* **outrer**) ADJ a (*littér = exagéré*) [*éloges, flatterie*] excessive, exaggerated, overdone (*attrib*); [*description*] exaggerated, extravagant, overdone (*attrib*) b (*= indigné*) outraged (**de, par** at, by)

outre-Atlantique [utratlɑ̃tik] ADV across the Atlantic, in the United States; **les films d'~** American films

outrecuidance [utrəkɥidɑ̃s] NF a (*littér = présomption*) presumptuousness; **parler avec ~** to speak presumptuously b (*= effronterie*) impertinence; **répondre à qn avec ~** to answer sb impertinently; **~s** impudence (*NonC*), impertinences

outrecuidant, e [utrəkɥidɑ̃, ɑ̃t] ADJ a (*= présomptueux*) presumptuous b (*= effronté*) [*attitude, réponse*] impertinent

outre-Manche [utrəmɑ̃ʃ] ADV across the Channel, in Britain; **nos voisins d'~** our British neighbours

outre-mer [utrəmɛr] 1 ADV overseas 2 NM overseas territories; **l'~ français** France's overseas departments and territories

outremer [utrəmɛr] 1 NM (*= pierre*) lapis lazuli; (*= couleur*) ultramarine 2 ADJ INV ultramarine

outrepassé [utrəpase] (*ptp de* **outrepasser**) ADJ → **arc**

outrepasser [utrəpase] ▸ conjug 1 ◂ VT [+ *droits*] to go beyond; [+ *pouvoir, ordres*] to exceed; [+ *limites*] to go beyond, overstep

outre-Pyrénées [utrəpirene] ADV in Spain; **d'~** Spanish

outrer [utre] ▸ conjug 1 ◂ VT a (*littér = exagérer*) to exaggerate; **cet acteur outre son jeu** this actor overacts b (*= indigner*) to outrage; **votre ingratitude m'a outré** your ingratitude has outraged me, I am outraged at *ou* by your ingratitude

outre-Rhin [utrərɛ̃] ADV across the Rhine; **d'~** (*= allemand*) German

outre-tombe [utrətɔ̃b] ADV beyond the grave; **d'une voix d'~** in a lugubrious voice

outsider [autsajdœr] NM (*Sport, fig*) outsider

ouvert, e [uvɛr, ɛrt] (*ptp de* **ouvrir**) ADJ a [*porte, magasin, valise, lieu, espace*] open; [*voiture*] unlocked; [*voyelle, syllabe*] open; [*angle*] wide; [*série, ensemble*] open-ended; [*robinet*] on, running; [*col, chemise*] open, undone (*attrib*); **la bouche ~e** [*dormir*] with one's mouth open; [*rester*] open-mouthed; **entrez, c'est ~!** come in, the door isn't locked! *ou* the door's open!; **~ au public** open to the public; **bibliothèque ~e à tous** library open to all members of the public; **le magasin restera ~ pendant les travaux** the shop will remain open (for business) during the alterations; (*Comm*) **nous sommes ~s jusqu'à Noël** we're open till Christmas; **~ à la circulation** open to traffic; **le col du Simplon est ~** the Simplon pass is open (to traffic); **~ à la navigation** open to ships *ou* for sailing; **une rose trop ~e** a rose which is too (far) open; **elle est partie en laissant le robinet/le gaz ~** she went away leaving the tap *ou* the water on *ou* running/the gas on → **bras, ciel** etc b (*= commencé*) open; **la chasse/pêche est ~e**

the shooting season/fishing season is open → **pari** c (*= percé, incisé*) [*plaie*] open; **il a le crâne/le bras ~** he has a gaping wound in his head/in his arm → **cœur, fracture** d [*débat, compétition sportive*] open; **la question reste ~e** the question remains open; **une partie très ~e** an open-ended game; **pratiquer un jeu ~** to play an open game e (*= déclaré, non dissimulé*) [*guerre, conflit, crise, haine*] open; **de façon ~e** openly, overtly f (*= communicatif, franc*) [*personne, caractère*] open, frank; [*visage, physionomie*] open; (*= éveillé, accessible*) [*intelligence, milieu, marché*] open; **à l'esprit ~** open-minded; **je suis ~ à toute discussion/négociation** I'm open to discussion/negotiation

ouvertement [uvɛrtəmɑ̃] ADV [*dire, avouer*] openly; [*agir*] openly, overtly

ouverture [uvɛrtyr] NF a (*= action*) [*porte, fenêtre, bouteille, parapluie, huîtres, compte bancaire*] opening; [*porte fermée à clé, verrou*] unlocking; [*frontière, passage, chaussée*] opening up; [*robinet*] turning on; **à ~ facile** easy to open; **l'~ de la porte est automatique** the door opens *ou* is operated automatically; **les documents nécessaires à l'~ d'un compte bancaire** the papers required to open a bank account b (*Écon*) [*marché*] opening; **pour obtenir l'~ des marchés nippons** to open up Japanese markets; **ils ont mis en place une politique d'~ économique** they have established a policy of economic openness; (*Fin*) **procéder à une ~ de capital** to float shares c (*Comm*) opening; **jours d'~** days of opening; **heures d'~** [*magasin*] opening hours, hours of business *ou* of opening; [*musée*] opening hours, hours of opening; **le client était là dès l'~** the customer was there as soon as the shop opened; **« ~ de 10 h à 15 h »** "open from 10 till 3"; **à l'heure d'~** ◇ **à l'~** at opening time d (*= commencement*) [*colloque*] opening; **cérémonie/discours/match d'~** opening ceremony/speech/match; **en ~ du festival** to open the festival; **avant l'~ officielle de la campagne électorale** before the official opening of the electoral campaign; (*Bourse*) **après une ~ en hausse** after a strong opening; **ils réclament l'~ immédiate de négociations** they want to open talks immediately; **il a demandé l'~ d'une enquête** he has requested an enquiry; (*Chasse*) **faire l'~** to go on *ou* be at the first shoot; **c'est demain l'~ de la chasse** tomorrow sees the opening of *ou* is the first day of the shooting season e (*= trou, passage, issue*) opening; [*puits*] mouth, opening; **toutes les ~s sont gardées** all the openings *ou* all means of access (*ou* exit) are guarded, all the access points (*ou* exit points) are guarded; **il y a de petites ~s sur le couvercle** there are little holes in the lid f (*= opportunité*) opening; **il y a peut-être une ~ dans notre filiale suisse** there may be an opening in our Swiss subsidiary; (*pour relation amoureuse*) **je crois que j'ai une ~ avec lui** I think I'm in with a chance with him g (*= proposition*) overture; **faire des ~s à qn** to make overtures to sb; **faire des ~s de paix/conciliation** to make peace/conciliatory overtures h (*= tolérance*) **~ d'esprit** ◇ **esprit d'~** open-mindedness; **il a une grande ~ d'esprit** he is extremely open-minded i (*= rapprochement, relation*) **l'absence d'~ sur le monde de certaines universités** the inward-looking attitude of some universities; **leur manque d'~ sur le monde menace leur communauté** their reluctance to embrace other cultures poses a threat to their community; (*Pol*) **l'~ (politique)** the opening up of the political spectrum; (*Pol*) **être partisan de l'~ au centre** to be in favour of an alliance

with the centre; **ils multiplient les signes d'~ en direction des Verts** they are showing more and more signs of being open to an alliance with the Green party; **adopter une politique de plus grande ~ avec l'Est** to develop a more open relationship with the East j (*Mus*) overture; **l'Ouverture solennelle** the 1812 Overture k (*Math*) [*angle*] magnitude; [*compas*] degree of opening; (*Photo*) aperture l (*Cartes*) opening; (*Échecs*) **avoir l'~** to have the first *ou* opening move m (*Ftbl*) through-ball; (*Rugby*) pass (*by the stand-off half to the three-quarter backs*); **faire une ~** (*Ftbl*) to hit *ou* play a through-ball; (*Rugby*) to pass the ball to the three-quarter backs → **demi²**

ouvrable [uvrabl] ADJ **jour ~** weekday, working day; **heures ~s** business hours

ouvrage [uvraʒ] 1 NM a (*= travail*) work (*NonC*); **se mettre à l'~** to set to *ou* get (down) to *ou* start work; (*littér*) **l'~ du temps/du hasard** the work of time/of chance → **cœur** b (*= objet produit*) piece of work; (*Couture*) work (*NonC*); **~ d'orfèvrerie** piece of goldwork; **~ à l'aiguille** (piece of) needlework → **boîte, corbeille, panier** c (*= œuvre*) work; (*= volume*) book; **~ collectif** book to which several authors have contributed; **ce dictionnaire est un ~ collectif** this dictionary was written by a team of editors → **référence** d (*Constr*) work 2 NF († *ou hum = travail*) **de la belle ~** a nice piece of work 3 COMP ▸ **ouvrage d'art** (*Génie Civil*) structure (*bridge or tunnel etc*) ▸ **ouvrage avancé** (*Mil*) outwork ▸ **ouvrage de dames** († *ou hum*) fancy work (*NonC*) ▸ **ouvrage défensif** (*Mil*) defences, defence work(s) ▸ **ouvrage de maçonnerie** masonry work ▸ **ouvrage militaire** fortification

ouvragé, e [uvraʒe] ADJ [*meuble, bois*] (finely) carved; [*napperon*] (finely) embroidered; [*signature*] elaborate; [*métal, bijou*] finely worked

ouvrant, e [uvrɑ̃, ɑ̃t] ADJ [*panneau*] which opens (*attrib*) → **toit**

ouvré, e [uvre] ADJ a (*Tech, littér*) [*meuble, bois*] (finely) carved; [*napperon*] (finely) embroidered; [*métal, bijou*] finely worked b (*Admin*) **jour ~** working day

ouvre-boîte [uvrəbwat] NM can-opener, tin-opener (*Brit*)

ouvre-bouteille (*pl* ouvre-bouteilles) [uvrəbutɛj] NM bottle opener

ouvre-huître (*pl* ouvre-huîtres) [uvr(ə)ɥitr] NM oyster knife

ouvreur, -euse [uvrœr, øz] 1 NM,F (*Cartes*) opener; (*Ski*) forerunner 2 NM [*cinéma, théâtre*] usher 3 **ouvreuse** NF [*cinéma, théâtre*] usherette

ouvrier, -ière [uvrije, ijɛr] 1 ADJ [*enfance, éducation, quartier*] working-class (*épith*); [*conflit, agitation, législation*] industrial (*épith*), labour (*épith*); [*questions, mouvement*] labour (*épith*); **association ouvrière** workers' *ou* working men's association → **cité, classe, syndicat** 2 NM (*gén, Pol, Sociol*) worker; (*= membre du personnel*) workman; **les revendications des ~s** the workers' claims; **il a 15 ~s** he has 15 workmen, he has 15 men working for him; **des mains d'~** workman's hands; **150 ~s ont été mis en chômage technique** 150 men *ou* workers have been laid off; (*fig*) **l'~ de cette réforme** the author of this reform → **mauvais, œuvre** 3 **ouvrière** NF a (*gén, Admin*) female worker; **ouvrière (d'usine)** female factory worker *ou* factory hand; (*jeune*) factory girl, young factory hand; **les ouvrières sortaient de l'usine** the women *ou* girls were coming out of the factory b (*Zool*) **(abeille) ouvrière** worker (bee)

4 COMP ▸ **ouvrier agricole** agricultural labourer, farm worker, farmhand ▸ **ouvrier de chantier** labourer ▸ **ouvrier à façon** pieceworker, jobber ▸ **ouvrier hautement qualifié** highly-skilled worker ▸ **ouvrier à la journée** day labourer ▸ **ouvrier qualifié** skilled workman ▸ **ouvrier spécialisé** unskilled *ou* semiskilled worker ▸ **ouvrier d'usine** factory worker *ou* hand

ouvriérisme [uvʀijeʀism] NM worker control, worker power

ouvriériste [uvʀijeʀist] **1** ADJ [*doctrine, attitude*] in favour of giving power to the workers **2** NMF supporter of control by the workers

ouvrir [uvʀiʀ] ▸ conjug 18 ◂ **1** VT **a** [+ *porte, fenêtre, bouteille, huître*] to open; [+ *verrou, porte fermée à clé*] to unlock; (*par effraction*) [+ *porte, coffre*] to break open; **~ la porte toute grande/le portail tout grand** to open the door/the gate wide; **il a ouvert brusquement la porte** he opened the door abruptly, he threw *ou* flung the door open; **~ sa porte** *ou* **sa maison à qn** to throw open one's doors *ou* one's house to sb; **ils ouvrent leur maison au public tous les étés** they open up their house to the public every summer, they throw their house open to the public every summer; → **parenthèse** ; → **porte**

b [+ *bouche, yeux, paupières*] to open; (*fig*) **~ le bec**◊ **l'~**∵◊ **~ la** *ou* **sa gueule**∴* to open one's mouth *ou* trap∴; (*fig*) **~ l'œil** to keep one's eyes open (*fig*); (*lit*) **~ les yeux** to open one's eyes; (*fig*) **ce voyage en Asie m'a ouvert les yeux** that trip through Asia opened my eyes *ou* was an eye-opener (to me); **ouvre l'œil, et le bon !*** keep your eyes peeled!*; **~ les oreilles** to pin back one's ears*; **elle m'a ouvert son cœur** she opened her heart to me; **ça m'a ouvert l'appétit** that whetted my appetite; **ce séjour à l'étranger lui a ouvert l'esprit** that time he spent abroad has widened his horizons → **œil**

c (= *déplier, déployer*) [+ *journal, couteau, livre*] to open; [+ *parapluie*] to open, put up; [+ *éventail, bras, ailes, main*] to open (out); [+ *manteau, veste*] to undo, unfasten, open; [+ *lit, drap*] to turn down; [+ *couture*] to iron flat; (*Mil*) **ouvrez les rangs !** dress!; (*fig*) **~ ses rangs à qn** to welcome sb among one's ranks

d (= *faire un trou dans*) [+ *chaussée, mur*] to open up; [+ *membre, ventre*] to open up, cut open; **les rochers lui ont ouvert la jambe** he cut his leg open on the rocks; **le médecin pense qu'il faudra ~*** the doctor thinks that they will have to open him (*ou* her *etc*) up*

e (= *faire, construire*) [+ *porte, passage*] to open up, make; [+ *autoroute*] to build; (*fig*) [+ *horizons, perspectives*] to open up; **il a fallu ~ une porte dans ce mur** a doorway had to be made in this wall; **~ un passage dans le roc à la dynamite** to open up *ou* blast a passage in the rock with dynamite; **ils lui ont ouvert un passage** *ou* **le passage dans la foule** they made way for him through the crowd; **s'~ un passage à travers la forêt** to open up *ou* cut a path for o.s. through the forest; **cette autoroute a été ouverte pour desservir la nouvelle banlieue** this motorway has been built to serve the new suburb

f (= *rendre accessible*) [+ *chemin, passage*] to open; **le chasse-neige a ouvert la route** the snowplough opened up the road; (*Sport*) **~ le jeu** to open up the game; (*fig*) **~ la voie (à qn)** to lead the way (for sb); [+ *route, col, frontière*] to open (up); (*Écon*) **le pays a ouvert son marché aux produits étrangers** the country has opened up its market to foreign products; (*Fin*) **l'entreprise a ouvert son capital à de nouveaux actionnaires** the country has opened up its capital to new shareholders; **l'ordinateur à l'école ouvre de nouvelles perspectives**

aux enseignants having computers in the classroom opens up new possibilities for teachers → **horizon**

g (= *créer, commencer à exploiter*) [+ *restaurant, théâtre, magasin, usine*] to open; [+ *école, succursale*] to open (up)

h (= *commencer, mettre en train*) [+ *période, négociations*] to begin; [+ *débat, dialogue, enquête*] to begin, open; **~ le feu** to open fire

i (*Ordin*) [+ *fichier, boîte de dialogue*] to open

j (*Ski*) **~ la piste** to open the piste *ou* run; (*Ftbl*) **~ la marque à la 16ème minute du jeu** to open the scoring after 16 minutes of play; (*Ftbl, Rugby*) **il ouvre toujours sur un joueur faible** he always passes to a weak player; (*Cartes*) **~ le jeu** to open play; (*Cartes*) **il a ouvert à pique** he opened on *ou* with spades → **bal, hostilité**

k (*Fin*) [+ *compte bancaire*] to open; [+ *emprunt*] to take out

l (= *être au début de*) [+ *liste, œuvre*] to head; [+ *procession*] to lead → **marche**[1]

m (= *faire fonctionner*) [+ *électricité, gaz, radio, télévision*] to turn on, switch on, put on; [+ *eau, robinet*] to turn on; [+ *vanne*] to open

2 VI **a** (= *ouvrir la porte*) **on a frappé, va ~ !** there's someone at the door, go and open it!; **ouvrez, au nom de la loi !** open up, in the name of the law!; **n'ouvre à personne !** don't open the door to anybody!; **fais-toi ~ par le gardien** ask *ou* get the caretaker to let you in

b [*fenêtre, porte*] to open; **cette fenêtre ouvre sur la cour** this window opens (out) onto the yard; **la porte de derrière n'ouvre pas** the back door doesn't open

c [*magasin*] to open; **le boulanger ouvre de 7 heures à 19 heures** the baker is open *ou* opens from 7 am till 7 pm

d (= *commencer*) to open

3 **s'ouvrir** VPR **a** (*gén*) to open; [*fleur*] to open (out); [*esprit*] to open out; **robe qui s'ouvre par devant** dress that undoes *ou* unfastens at the front; **sa robe s'est ouverte** her dress came undone *ou* unfastened; **la fenêtre s'ouvre sur une cour** the window opens (out) onto a courtyard; **la foule s'ouvrit pour le laisser passer** the crowd parted to let him through; **la porte s'ouvrit violemment** the door flew open *ou* was flung open *ou* was thrown open; **la porte/boîte a dû s'~** the door/box must have come open

b (= *commencer*) [*récit, séance, exposition*] to open (**par** with); **la séance s'ouvrit par un chahut** the meeting opened in uproar

c (= *se présenter*) **un chemin poussiéreux s'ouvrit devant eux** a dusty path opened in front of *ou* before them; **la vie qui s'ouvre devant elle est pleine d'embûches** the life which is opening in front of *ou* before her is full of pitfalls

d (= *béer*) to open (up); **la terre s'ouvrit devant eux** the ground opened up before them; **le gouffre s'ouvrait à leurs pieds** the chasm lay open *ou* gaped at their feet

e (= *se blesser*) to cut open; **elle s'est ouvert les veines** she slashed *ou* cut her wrists; **il s'ouvrit la jambe en tombant sur une faux** he cut his leg open when he fell onto a scythe

f (= *devenir accessible, communiquer*) **s'~ à** [+ *amour, art, problèmes économiques*] to open one's mind to, become aware of; **son esprit s'est ouvert aux souffrances d'autrui** he became aware of the suffering of others; **pays qui s'ouvre au monde extérieur** country which is opening up to the outside world

g (= *se confier*) **s'~ à qn de** to open one's heart to sb about; **il s'en est ouvert à son confesseur** he opened his heart to his confessor about it

ouvroir [uvʀwaʀ] NM [*couvent*] workroom; [*paroisse*] sewing room

ouzbek [uzbɛk] **1** ADJ Uzbek **2** NM (*Ling*) Uzbek **3** **Ouzbek** NMF Uzbek

Ouzbékistan [uzbekistɑ̃] NM Uzbekistan

ovaire [ɔvɛʀ] NM ovary

ovale [ɔval] **1** ADJ [*table, surface*] oval; [*volume*] egg-shaped → **ballon 2** NM oval; **l'~ du visage** the oval of the face; **en ~** oval(-shaped)

ovalie [ɔvali] NF (*journalistique*) **l'~** the world of rugby *ou* rugger* (*Brit*)

ovariectomie [ɔvaʀjɛktɔmi] NF ovariectomy, oophorectomy

ovarien, -ienne [ɔvaʀjɛ̃, jɛn] ADJ ovarian

ovariotomie [ɔvaʀjɔtɔmi] NF ovariotomy

ovarite [ɔvaʀit] NF ovaritis, oophoritis

ovation [ɔvasjɔ̃] NF ovation; **faire une ~ à qn** to give sb an ovation; **ils se levèrent pour lui faire une ~** they gave him a standing ovation; **sous les ~s du public** to the rapturous applause of the audience (*ou* crowd *etc*)

ovationner [ɔvasjɔne] ▸ conjug 1 ◂ VT **~ qn** to give sb an ovation

ove [ɔv] NM (*Archit*) ovum

ové, e [ɔve] ADJ egg-shaped

overdose [ɔvœʀdoz] NF (*Méd*) (drug) overdose; * [*musique, informations*] overdose; **c'est l'~ !*** I've had enough!

overdrive [ɔvœʀdʀajv] NM overdrive

Ovide [ɔvid] NM Ovid

oviducte [ɔvidykt] NM oviduct

ovin, e [ɔvɛ̃, in] **1** ADJ ovine **2** NMPL **les ~s** the ovine race

ovipare [ɔvipaʀ] **1** ADJ oviparous **2** NM oviparous animal; **~s** ovipara

ovni [ɔvni] NM (ABRÉV = **objet volant non identifié**) UFO

ovocyte [ɔvɔsit] NM oocyte

ovoïde [ɔvɔid] ADJ egg-shaped, ovoid (*SPÉC*)

ovovivipare [ovovivipaʀ] ADJ ovoviviparous

ovulaire [ɔvylɛʀ] ADJ ovular

ovulation [ɔvylasjɔ̃] NF ovulation

ovulatoire [ɔvylatwaʀ] ADJ ovulatory

ovule [ɔvyl] NM (*Physiol*) ovum; (*Bot*) ovule; (*Pharm*) pessary

ovuler [ɔvyle] ▸ conjug 1 ◂ VI to ovulate

oxacide [ɔksasid] NM oxyacid, oxygen acid

oxalique [ɔksalik] ADJ **acide ~** oxalic acid

Oxford [ɔksfɔʀd] N Oxford

oxford [ɔksfɔʀ(d)] NM (*Tex*) oxford

oxfordien, -ienne [ɔksfɔʀdjɛ̃, jɛn] **1** ADJ Oxonian **2** **Oxfordien(ne)** NM,F Oxonian

oxhydrique [ɔksidʀik] ADJ oxyhydrogen (*épith*)

oxonien, -ienne [ɔksɔnjɛ̃, jɛn] **1** ADJ Oxonian **2** **Oxonien(ne)** NM,F Oxonian

oxyacétylénique [ɔksiasetilenik] ADJ oxyacetylene (*épith*)

oxydable [ɔksidabl] ADJ liable to rust, oxidizable (*SPÉC*)

oxydant, e [ɔksidɑ̃, ɑ̃t] **1** ADJ oxidizing **2** NM oxidizer, oxidizing agent

oxydase [ɔksidaz] NF oxidase

oxydation [ɔksidasjɔ̃] NF oxid(iz)ation

oxyde [ɔksid] NM oxide; **~ de carbone** carbon monoxide; **~ de plomb** lead oxide *ou* monoxide; **~ de cuivre/de fer** copper/iron oxide

oxyder [ɔkside] ▸ conjug 1 ◂ **1** VT to oxidize **2** **s'oxyder** VPR to become oxidized

oxydoréduction [ɔksidoʀedyksjɔ̃] NF oxidation-reduction

oxygénation [ɔksiʒenasjɔ̃] NF oxygenation

oxygène [ɔksiʒɛn] NM (*lit*) oxygen; (*fig*) **il est allé chercher un bol d'~ à la campagne** he's gone off to the countryside to get some clean *ou* fresh air into his lungs; **ce week-end fut pour moi une bouffée d'~** that weekend did me a power of good* *ou* really lifted my spirits; **apporter un peu** *ou* **une bouffée d'~ à l'économie** to give the economy a shot in the arm → **ballon**

oxygéner [ɔksiʒene] ▶ conjug 6 ◀ VT (*Chim*) to oxygenate; [+ *cheveux*] to peroxide, bleach; **s'~ (les poumons)*** to get some fresh air (into one's lungs); **elle est allée au concert**

pour s'~ la tête* *ou* **l'esprit** she went to the concert to take her mind off things → **blond, eau**

oxyhémoglobine [ɔksiemɔglɔbin] NF oxyhaemoglobin

oxymore [ɔksimɔʀ], **oxymoron** [ɔksimɔʀɔ̃] NM oxymoron

oxyure [ɔksjyʀ] NM pinworm, threadworm

oyat [ɔja] NM beachgrass

oyez [ɔje] → **ouïr**

ozone [ozon] NM ozone; **la couche d'~** the ozone layer; (*sur emballage*) **« préserve la couche d'~ »** "ozone-friendly"

ozonisation [ozonizasjɔ̃] NF ozonization

ozoniser [ozonize] ▶ conjug 1 ◀ VT to ozonize

P

P, p¹ [pe] NM (= *lettre*) P, p

p² (ABRÉV = **page**) p

PAC [pak] NF (ABRÉV = **politique agricole commune**) CAP

PACA [paka] NF (ABRÉV = **Provence-Alpes-Côte d'Azur**) *region in southern France*

pacage [pakaʒ] NM pasture, grazing (land) (*NonC*)

pacager [pakaʒe] ▶conjug 3◀ 1 VT to pasture, graze 2 VI to graze

pacane [pakan] NF (**noix de**) **~** pecan (nut)

pacemaker [pɛsmekœʀ] NM pacemaker

pacha [paʃa] NM pasha; **mener une vie de ~** ◊ **faire le ~** (= *vivre richement*) to live like a lord; (= *se prélasser*) to live a life of ease

pachyderme [paʃidɛʀm] NM a (*SPÉC*) pachyderm (*SPÉC*); (= *éléphant*) elephant b (*péj, hum* = *personne*) elephant; **de ~** [*allure, démarche*] elephantine, heavy

pacificateur, -trice [pasifikatœʀ, tʀis] 1 ADJ [*action, discours*] placatory, pacifying; **les vertus pacificatrices de la musique** the soothing qualities of music 2 NM,F (= *personne*) peacemaker

pacification [pasifikasjɔ̃] NF pacification

pacifier [pasifje] ▶conjug 7◀ VT [+ *pays*] to pacify, bring peace to; [+ *esprits*] to pacify; **il rêve d'un monde pacifié** he dreams of a world at peace

pacifique [pasifik] 1 ADJ a [*coexistence, manifestation, règlement, intention, solution*] peaceful; [*humeur*] peaceable; [*personne, peuple*] peace-loving, peaceable; **utilisé à des fins ~s** used for peaceful purposes b (*Géog*) Pacific 2 (*Géog*) **le Pacifique** the Pacific; **les îles du Pacifique** the Pacific Islands

pacifiquement [pasifikmɑ̃] ADV peacefully

pacifisme [pasifism] NM pacifism

pacifiste [pasifist] 1 NMF pacifist 2 ADJ [*doctrine*] pacifistic, pacifist; **manifestation ~** peace march *ou* demonstration

pack [pak] NM a (*Rugby*) pack b (*Comm*) pack; **~ de bière/yaourts** pack of beer/ yoghurts c (= *banquise*) pack ice

package [paka(d)ʒ, pakɛdʒ] NM (*Écon, Ordin*) package; (*Tourisme*) **~ (tour)** package holiday

packaging [paka(d)ʒiŋ] NM (*Comm*) packaging

pacotille [pakɔtij] NF a (*de mauvaise qualité*) cheap junk* *ou* trash*; (*clinquant*) showy stuff; **c'est de la ~** it's junk*, it's cheap rubbish (*Brit*); **meubles/bijoux de ~** cheap furniture/ jewellery b (*Hist*) *goods carried free of freightage*

pacson [paksɔ̃] NM packet

pacte [pakt] NM pact, treaty; **~ d'alliance** treaty of alliance; **~ de non-agression** non-aggression pact; **le ~ de Varsovie** the Warsaw Pact; **faire** *ou* **conclure** *ou* **signer un ~ avec qn** to sign a pact *ou* treaty with sb; **il a signé un ~ avec le diable** he made a pact with the devil

pactiser [paktize] ▶conjug 1◀ VI (*péj* = *se liguer*) to make a deal (**avec** with); **~ avec l'ennemi** to collude with the enemy; **~ avec le diable** to make a pact with the devil; **~ avec le racisme/ le nazisme** to condone racism/nazism

pactole [paktɔl] NM (*fig* = *source de richesse*) gold mine; (* = *argent*) fortune; **un bon ~** a tidy sum* *ou* packet*; **un petit ~** a tidy little sum*, a small fortune; (*Géog*) **le Pactole** the Pactolus

paddock [padɔk] NM a [*champ de courses*] paddock b (* = *lit*) bed; **aller au ~** to hit the sack* *ou* the hay*, turn in*

Padoue [padu] N Padua

paella [paela] NF paella

PAF [paf] 1 NM (ABRÉV = **paysage audiovisuel français**) → **paysage** 2 NF (ABRÉV = **police de l'air et des frontières**) → **police¹**

paf [paf] 1 EXCL (*chute*) bam!; (*gifle*) slap!, wham! 2 ADJ INV (‡ = *ivre*) drunk, tight* (*Brit*); **complètement ~** plastered‡

pagaie [pagɛ] NF paddle

pagaille, pagaïe [pagaj] NF a (= *objets en désordre*) mess, shambles (*NonC*); (= *cohue, manque d'organisation*) chaos (*NonC*); **quelle ~ dans cette pièce!** what a mess this room is in!; **c'est la ~ sur les routes/dans le gouvernement** there is (complete) chaos on the roads/ in the government; **il a mis** *ou* **semé la ~ dans mes affaires/dans la réunion** he has messed up all my things/the meeting b (= *beaucoup*) **il y en a en ~*** there are loads* *ou* masses of them

paganiser [paganize] ▶conjug 1◀ VT to paganize, heathenize

paganisme [paganism] NM paganism, heathenism

pagaye [pagaj] NF = **pagaille**

pagayer [pageje] ▶conjug 8◀ VI to paddle

pagayeur, -euse [pagejœʀ, øz] NM,F paddler

page¹ [paʒ] 1 NF a (= *feuillet*) page; (*fig* = *passage*) passage, page; (= *événement*) page, chapter, episode; (**à la**) **~ 35** (on) page 35; **une pleine ~ de publicité** a full-page ad; (*Typo*) **belle/fausse ~** right-hand/left-hand page; (*Ordin*) **~ suivante/précédente** page down/up; **une ~ d'écriture** a page of writing; **les plus belles ~s de Corneille** the finest passages of Corneille; **une ~ glorieuse/nouvelle de l'histoire de France** a glorious chapter/new page in the history of France; **tourner la ~** (*lit, fig*) to turn the page; **une ~ est tournée** a page has been turned; (*Typo*) **mettre en ~** to lay out, make up (into pages); **mise en ~** (*Typo*) layout, make-up; (*Ordin*) layout → **garde¹** b * (*loc*) **être à la ~** to be with it*; **ne plus être à la ~** to be out of touch; **se mettre à la ~** [*institution*] to bring itself up to date; **j'essaie de me mettre à la ~** I try to keep in touch with what's going on

2 COMP ▶ **page blanche** blank page; **l'angoisse de l'écrivain devant la ~ blanche** writer's block ▶ **pages jaunes (de l'annuaire)** yellow pages ▶ **page de publi-** cité (*Radio, TV*) commercial break, commercials ▶ **page de titre** title page

page² [paʒ] NM (*Hist*) page (boy)

page³ [paʒ] NM bed; **se mettre au ~** to turn in*, hit the sack* *ou* the hay*

page-écran (*pl* **pages-écrans**) [paʒekʀɑ̃] NF (*Ordin*) screenful

pageot‡ [paʒo] NM = **page³**

pageoter (se)‡ [paʒɔte] ▶conjug 1◀ VPR to turn in*, hit the sack* *ou* the hay*

pagination [paʒinasjɔ̃] NF (*gén* = *numérotation*) pagination; (*Ordin*) paging; (*Presse* = *nombre de pages*) pagination, page count; **erreur de ~** pagination error

paginer [paʒine] ▶conjug 1◀ VT (*gén*) to paginate; (*Ordin*) to page; **livre non paginé** book without page numbers

pagne [paɲ] NM (*en tissu*) loincloth; (*en paille*) grass skirt

pagode [pagɔd] NF pagoda; **manche ~** pagoda sleeve

paie [pɛ] NF [*militaire*] pay; [*ouvrier*] pay, wages; **jour de ~** payday; **bulletin** *ou* **feuille de ~** payslip; **toucher sa ~** to be paid, get one's wages; **il y a** *ou* **ça fait une ~ que nous ne nous sommes pas vus*** it's been ages since we last saw each other, we haven't seen each other for ages *ou* yonks‡ (*Brit*)

paiement [pɛmɑ̃] NM payment (**de** for); **faire un ~** to make a payment; **~ à la commande** payment *ou* cash with order; **~ à la livraison** cash on delivery; **~ comptant** payment in full; **~ échelonné** payment by *ou* in instalments; **~ en liquide** cash payment; **~ par chèque/d'avance** payment by cheque/in advance; **~ électronique** electronic payment → **facilité**

païen, païenne [pajɛ̃, pajɛn] ADJ, NM,F pagan, heathen

paierie [peʀi] NF **~ (générale)** local office of the treasury (*paying salaries, state bills etc*)

paillage [pajaʒ] NM (*Agr*) mulching

paillard, e* [pajaʀ, aʀd] ADJ [*personne*] bawdy, coarse; [*histoire*] bawdy, lewd, dirty; **chanson ~e** bawdy song

paillardise [pajaʀdiz] NF (= *débauche*) bawdiness; (= *plaisanterie*) dirty *ou* lewd joke (*ou* story *ou* remark *etc*)

paillasse¹ [pajas] NF a (= *matelas*) straw mattress b [*évier*] draining board, drainboard (*US*); [*laboratoire*] (tiled) work surface c († = *prostituée*) trollop† d (* : *loc*) **crever la ~ à qn** to do sb in*; **se crever la ~** to slog one's guts out doing sth

paillasse² [pajas] NM (= *clown*) clown

paillasson [pajasɔ̃] NM [*porte*] doormat; (*péj* = *personne*) doormat (*fig*); (*Agr*) matting → **clé**

paille [paj] 1 NF a (= *tige coupée*) straw; (*pour boire*) (drinking) straw; **chapeau/panier de ~** straw hat/basket; **botte de ~** bale of straw; **boire avec une ~** to drink through a straw b (*loc*) **être sur la ~** to be penniless; **mettre qn sur la ~** to reduce sb to poverty;

mourir sur la ~ to die penniless *ou* in poverty; **voir la ~ dans l'œil du prochain (mais pas la poutre dans le sien)** to see the mote in one's neighbour's *ou* one's brother's eye (but not the beam in one's own); **c'est la ~ et la poutre** it's the pot calling the kettle black; **deux millions de francs ? une ~!** two million francs? that's peanuts!* → **court**[1], **feu**[1], **homme** c (*Tech* = *défaut*) flaw [2] ADJ INV **jaune** ~ straw-coloured (*Brit*) *ou* -colored (*US*) [3] COMP ► **paille de fer** steel wool ► **paille de riz** rice straw; **balai en ~ de riz** straw broom

pailler [paje] ▶conjug 1◀ VT [+ *chaise*] to put a straw bottom in; [+ *arbre, fraisier*] to mulch; **chaise paillée** straw-bottomed chair

pailleté, e [paj(ə)te] (*ptp de* **pailleter**) ADJ [*robe*] sequined; **yeux noisette ~s d'or** hazel eyes speckled with gold

pailleter [paj(ə)te] ▶conjug 4◀ VT (*gén*) to spangle; [+ *robe*] to sew sequins on

paillette [pajɛt] NF a (*Habillement*) sequin, spangle; **corsage à ~s** sequined blouse, blouse with sequins *ou* spangles on it b [*or*] speck; [*mica, lessive*] flake; **savon en ~s** soapflakes c (*Méd*) ~ **sperme** sperm straw d [*maquillage*] ~s glitter (*NonC*)

paillis [paji] NM mulch

paillon [pajɔ̃] NM [*bouteille*] straw case *ou* wrapping; [*métal*] small strip

paillote [pajɔt] NF straw hut

pain [pɛ̃] [1] NM a (= *substance*) bread (*NonC*); **du gros ~** bread sold by weight; **du ~ frais/dur/rassis** fresh/dry/stale bread; **~ de ménage/de boulanger** home-made/baker's bread; (*Rel*) **le ~ et le vin** the bread and the wine; **notre ~ quotidien** our daily bread; **mettre qn au ~ sec** to put sb on dry bread; **je vais au ~*** I'm going to get the bread
b (= *miche*) loaf; **un ~ (de 2 livres)** a (2-lb) loaf; **un ~ long/rond** a long/round loaf; **deux ~s** two loaves (of bread); **gros ~** large (crusty) loaf
c (*en forme de pain*) [*cire*] bar; [*savon*] bar, cake; (*Culin*) **~ de poisson/de légumes** *etc* fish/vegetable loaf; **~ de glace** block of ice; **le liquide s'est pris en ~ (dans le congélateur)** the liquid has frozen into a block of ice (in the deep-freeze); **~ dermatologique** hypoallergenic cleansing bar
d (* = *coup*) punch, sock*; **se prendre un ~** to get punched *ou* socked one*; **mettre un ~ à qn** to punch *ou* sock sb one*
e (*loc*) **on a du ~ sur la planche*** (*beaucoup à faire*) we've got a lot to do, we've got a lot on our plate (*Brit*); (*travail difficile*) we have our work cut out (for us); **il reste du ~ sur la planche** there's still a lot to do *ou* to be done; **ôter *ou* retirer le ~ de la bouche de qn** to take the bread out of sb's mouth; **ôter *ou* faire passer le goût du ~ à qn*** to do sb in* → **bouchée**[2], **manger, petit** *etc*
[2] COMP ► **pain azyme** unleavened bread ► **pain bénit** consecrated bread; (*fig*) **c'est ~ bénit** it's a godsend ► **pain bis** brown bread ► **pain brioché** brioche bread; (= *miche*) brioche loaf ► **pain brûlé** ADJ INV deep golden brown ► **pain à cacheter** bar of sealing wax, sealing wafer ► **pain de campagne** farmhouse bread; (= *miche*) farmhouse loaf ► **pain au chocolat** pain au chocolat, chocolate croissant ► **pain complet** wholewheat *ou* wholemeal (*Brit*) bread; (= *miche*) wholewheat *ou* wholemeal (*Brit*) loaf ► **pain d'épice(s)** cake made with honey, rye, aniseed, etc, ≈ gingerbread ► **pain de Gênes** sponge cake ► **pain grillé** toast ► **pain de gruau** = pain viennois ► **pain au lait** *kind of sweet bun* ► **pain au levain** leavened bread ► **pain de mie** sandwich bread; (= *miche*) sandwich loaf ► **pain parisien** *long loaf of bread* ► **pain perdu** French toast ► **pain de plastic** stick of gelignite ► **pain**

pita pitta *ou* pita bread ► **pain aux raisins** ≈ Danish pastry (*with raisins*) ► **pain de seigle** rye bread; (= *miche*) rye loaf ► **pain de son** bran bread; (= *miche*) bran loaf ► **pain de sucre** sugar loaf; **montagne en ~ de sucre** sugar-loaf mountain; **tête en ~ de sucre** egg-shaped head ► **pain viennois** Vienna bread; (= *miche*) Vienna loaf

pair[1] [pɛʀ] NM a (= *dignitaire*) peer b (= *égaux*) ~s peers → **hors** c (*Fin*) par; **valeur remboursée au ~** stock repayable at par; **cours au ~** par rate d (*loc*) **travailler/être au ~** to work as/be an au pair; **jeune fille au ~** au pair (girl); **jeune homme au ~** (male) au pair; **aller *ou* marcher de ~** to go hand in hand; **aller de ~ avec** to go hand in hand with

pair[2], **e**[1] [pɛʀ] ADJ [*nombre*] even; **le côté ~ de la rue** the side of the street with even numbers; **jours ~s** even dates; **jouer ~** to bet on the even numbers

paire[2] [pɛʀ] NF a [*ciseaux, lunettes, tenailles, chaussures*] pair; [*bœufs*] yoke; [*pistolets, pigeons*] brace; (*Cartes*) pair; **ils forment une ~ d'amis** the two of them are great friends; **une belle ~ d'escrocs** a real pair of crooks; **avoir une bonne ~ de joues** to be chubby-cheeked b (*loc*) **les deux font la ~** they're two of a kind; **ils font la ~ ces deux-là !*** they're a right pair!*; **c'est une autre ~ de manches*** that's another kettle of fish, that's another story; **se faire la ~*** to clear off*, beat it*

pairesse [pɛʀɛs] NF peeress

pairie [pɛʀi] NF peerage

paisible [pezibl] ADJ a [*personne, caractère*] quiet; [*vie, quartier, village, retraite*] peaceful, quiet; **dormir d'un sommeil ~** to be sleeping peacefully b (*Jur*) quiet, peaceable

paisiblement [peziblǝmã] ADV peacefully

paître [pɛtʀ] ▶conjug 57◀ [1] VI to graze; **le pâturage où ils font ~ leur troupeau** the pasture where they graze their herd; **envoyer ~ qn*** to send sb packing* [2] VT [+ *herbe*] to graze on; [+ *feuilles, fruits*] to feed on; **~ l'herbe d'un pré** to graze in a meadow

paix [pɛ] NF a (*Mil, Pol*) peace; **~ armée** armed peace; **~ séparée** separate peace agreement; **demander la ~** to sue for peace; **signer la ~** to sign a peace treaty; **en temps de ~** in peacetime; **traité/pourparlers de ~** peace treaty/talks; **soldats de la ~** peacekeeping force; **Mouvement pour la ~** Peace Movement ■ (*PROV*) **si tu veux la ~, prépare la guerre** if you wish to have peace, prepare for war b (= *état d'accord*) peace; **ramener la ~ entre ...** to make peace between ...; **il a fait la ~ avec son frère** he has made his peace with his brother, he and his brother have made up *ou* made it up (*Brit*); (*hum*) **être pour la ~ des ménages** to believe in domestic harmony → **baiser, gardien, juge** c (= *tranquillité*) peace, quiet; (= *silence*) stillness, peacefulness; **tout le monde est sorti, quelle ~ dans la maison !** how peaceful the quiet it is in the house now everyone has gone out!; **est-ce qu'on pourrait avoir la ~ ?** could we have a bit of peace and quiet? d (= *calme intérieur*) peace; **la ~ de l'âme** inner peace; (*Rel*) **allez *ou* partez en ~** go in peace; (*hum*) **~ à sa mémoire *ou* à son âme *ou* à ses cendres** God rest his soul; (*Bible*) **~ sur la terre aux hommes de bonne volonté** peace on Earth and good will to all men; **avoir la conscience en ~** ◊ **être en ~ avec sa conscience** to have a clear *ou* an easy conscience, be at peace with one's conscience; **qu'il repose en ~** may he rest in peace; **laisser qn en ~** ◊ **laisser la ~ à qn** to leave sb alone *ou* in peace; **fous-moi* *ou* fiche-moi* la ~ !** stop pestering me!, clear off!*; **la ~ !** shut up!*, quiet!

Pakistan [pakistã] NM Pakistan

pakistanais, e [pakistanɛ, ɛz] [1] ADJ Pakistani [2] **Pakistanais(e)** NM,F Pakistani

PAL [pal] NM (ABRÉV = **Phase Alternative Line**) PAL

pal (*pl* **pals**) [pal] NM (*Hér*) pale; (= *pieu*) stake; **le (supplice du) ~** torture by impalement

palabrer [palabʀe] ▶conjug 1◀ VI (= *bavarder*) to talk *ou* chat away; (= *parlementer*) to argue endlessly; **je n'ai pas envie de l'entendre ~ pendant des heures** I don't want to listen to him going on *ou* waffling on* (*Brit*) for hours; **assez palabré, il faut agir** that's enough talk, let's have some action

palabres [palabʀ] NFPL never-ending discussions

palace [palas] NM luxury hotel

paladin [paladɛ̃] NM paladin

palais [palɛ] [1] NM a (= *édifice*) palace → **révolution** b (*Jur*) **le Palais** the law courts; **en argot du Palais** ◊ **en termes de Palais** in legal parlance; **les gens du Palais** lawyers c (*Anat*) palate; **~ dur/mou** hard/soft palate; **avoir le ~ desséché** to be parched, be dying of thirst; (*fig*) **avoir le ~ fin** to have a discerning palate; (*Méd*) **~ fendu** cleft palate → **flatter, voile**[2] [2] COMP ► **le palais Brongniart** the Paris Stock Exchange ► **le palais de Buckingham** Buckingham Palace ► **palais des congrès** convention centre ► **le palais de l'Élysée** the Élysée Palace ► **palais des expositions** exhibition centre ► **Palais de justice** law courts ► **le palais du Luxembourg** *the seat of the French Senate* ► **le palais des Nations** the Palais des Nations ► **Palais des sports** sports stadium

Palais-Bourbon [palɛbuʀbɔ̃] NM **le ~** (the seat of) the French National Assembly

palan [palã] NM hoist

palangre [palãgʀ] NF (*Pêche*) long-line; **la pêche à la ~** long-lining

palanque [palãk] NF stockade

palanquin [palãkɛ̃] NM palanquin, palankeen

palatal, e (*mpl* **-aux**) [palatal, o] [1] ADJ (*Ling*) [*consonne*] palatal (*épith*); [*voyelle*] front (*épith*); (*Anat*) palatal [2] **palatale** NF (= *consonne*) palatal consonant; (= *voyelle*) front vowel

palatalisation [palatalizasjɔ̃] NF palatalization

palataliser [palatalize] ▶conjug 1◀ VT to palatalize

palatin, e [palatɛ̃, in] [1] ADJ a (*Hist*) Palatine; **le comte/l'électeur ~** the count/the elector Palatine; **princesse Palatine** Princess Palatine b (*Géog*) **le (mont) Palatin** the Palatine Hill c (*Anat*) palatine [2] NM (*Hist*) Palatine; (*Anat*) palatine

Palatinat [palatina] NM **le ~** the Palatinate

pale [pal] NF [*hélice, rame*] blade; [*roue, écluse*] paddle

pâle [pal] [1] ADJ a [*teint, personne*] pale; (= *maladif*) pallid, pale; **~ comme un linge** as white as a sheet; **~ comme la mort** deathly pale *ou* white; **~ de peur** white with fear; **~ de colère** pale *ou* white *ou* livid with anger; **se faire porter ~*** to report *ou* go* sick → **visage** b [*lueur*] pale, weak; [*couleur, soleil, ciel*] pale c [*style*] weak; [*imitation*] pale, poor; [*sourire*] faint, wan; (*péj*) **un ~ crétin** a downright *ou* an utter fool

palefrenier, -ière [palfʀǝnje, jɛʀ] NM,F groom; (*Hist*) [*auberge*] ostler

palefroi [palfʀwa] NM (*Hist*) palfrey

paléochrétien, -ienne [paleokʀetjɛ̃, jɛn] ADJ early Christian

paléographe [paleogʀaf] NMF palaeographer (*Brit*), paleographer (*US*)

paléographie [paleogʀafi] NF palaeography (*Brit*), paleography (*US*)

paléographique [paleogʀafik] ADJ palaeographic(al) (*Brit*), paleographic(al) (*US*)

paléolithique [paleɔlitik] [1] ADJ Palaeolithic (*Brit*), Paleolithic (*US*) [2] NM **le ~** the Palaeolithic (*Brit*) *ou* Paleolithic (*US*) (age)

paléomagnétisme [paleomaɲetism]   NM palaeomagnetism (*Brit*), paleomagnetism (*US*)

paléontologie [paleɔ̃tɔlɔʒi] NF palaeontology (*Brit*), paleontology (*US*)

paléontologique [paleɔ̃tɔlɔʒik] ADJ palaeontologic(al) (*Brit*), paleontologic(al) (*US*)

paléontologiste [paleɔ̃tɔlɔʒist], **paléontologue** [paleɔ̃tɔlɔg] NMF palaeontologist (*Brit*), paleontologist (*US*)

paléozoïque [paleozik] [1] ADJ Palaeozoic (*Brit*), Paleozoic (*US*) [2] NM **le ~** the Palaeozoic (*Brit*) ou Paleozoic (*US*) (age)

Palerme [palɛrm] N Palermo

paleron [palrɔ̃] NM (*Boucherie*) chuck (steak)

Palestine [palɛstin] NF Palestine

palestinien, -ienne [palɛstinjɛ̃, jɛn] [1] ADJ Palestinian [2] **Palestinien(ne)** NM,F Palestinian

palet [palɛ] NM (*gén*) (metal ou stone) disc; [*hockey*] puck

paletot [palto] NM (thick) cardigan; **il m'est tombé** ou **m'a sauté sur le ~**∗ he jumped on me

palette [palɛt] NF [a] (*Peinture: lit, fig*) palette [b] [*produits, services*] range [c] (*Boucherie*) shoulder [d] (= *aube de roue*) paddle; (= *battoir à linge*) beetle; (*Manutention, Constr*) pallet

palétuvier [paletyvje] NM mangrove

pâleur [palœr] NF [*teint*] paleness; (*maladive*) pallor, paleness; [*couleur, ciel*] paleness

pâlichon, -onne∗ [paliʃɔ̃, ɔn] ADJ [*personne*] (a bit) pale ou peaky∗ (*Brit*) ou peaked∗ (*US*); [*soleil*] watery

palier [palje] NM [a] [*escalier*] landing; **être voisins de ◊ habiter sur le même ~** to live on the same landing; **~ de repos** half landing [b] (*fig = étape*) stage; [*graphique*] plateau; **les prix ont atteint un nouveau ~** prices have found a ou risen to a new level; **procéder par ~s** to proceed in stages [c] [*route, voie*] level, flat; (*Aviat*) **voler en ~** to fly level [d] (*Tech*) bearing; **~ de butée** thrust bearing

palière [paljɛr] ADJ F → **marche²**, **porte**

palimpseste [palɛ̃psɛst] NM palimpsest

palindrome [palɛ̃drom] NM palindrome

palinodie [palinɔdi] NF (*Littérat*) palinode; (*fig*) **~s** recantations

pâlir [palir] ▶ conjug 2 ◀ [1] VI [*personne*] to turn ou go pale; [*lumière, étoiles*] to grow dim; [*ciel*] to grow pale; [*couleur, encre*] to fade; (*fig*) [*souvenir*] to fade (away), dim; [*gloire*] to dim, fade; **~ de colère** to go ou turn pale ou white with anger; **~ de crainte** to turn pale ou white with fear, blench (with fear); **faire ~ qn d'envie** ou **de jalousie** to make sb green with envy [2] VT (*littér*) [+ *ciel*] to turn pale; **encre pâlie par le soleil** ink faded by the sun

palissade [palisad] NF [*pieux*] fence; [*planches*] boarding; (*Mil*) stockade

palissandre [palisɑ̃dr] NM rosewood

pâlissant, e [palisɑ̃, ɑ̃t] ADJ [*teinte, lumière*] wan, fading

palladium [paladjɔm] NM (*Chim, fig*) palladium

Pallas Athena [palasatena] NF Pallas Athena

palliatif, -ive [paljatif, iv] [1] ADJ (*Méd*) palliative [2] NM (*Méd*) palliative (**à** to, for); (= *mesure*) palliative, stopgap measure; (= *réparation sommaire*) makeshift repair

pallier [palje] ▶ conjug 7 ◀ [1] VT [+ *difficulté*] to overcome, get round; [+ *manque*] to offset, compensate for, make up for; (*littér*) [+ *défaut*] to disguise, palliate (*littér*) [2] **pallier à** VT INDIR (*usage critiqué*) [+ *difficulté, manque*] = **pallier**

palmarès [palmarɛs] NM [a] (= *classement*) [*lauréats, cinéastes*] (list of) prizewinners ou award winners; [*sportifs*] (list of) medal winners; [*chansons*] charts, hit parade; **le ~ des**

universités françaises (the list of) the top French universities; **le ~ des émissions les plus écoutées** (the list of) the most popular programmes; **cette voiture est** ou **figure au ~ des meilleures ventes** this car is among the best-selling models ou is a best-seller; **la Grèce figure au ~ des pays les plus visités** Greece is one of the most visited countries in the world [b] (= *liste de victoires, de titres etc*) record ou list of achievements; **il a de nombreuses victoires à son ~** he has a number of victories to his credit ou under his belt; **c'est un titre qu'il n'a pas encore à son ~** this is a title that he can't yet call his own

palme [palm] NF [a] (*Archit, Bot*) palm leaf; (= *symbole*) palm; **vin/huile de ~** palm wine/oil [b] (= *distinction*) prize; **la ~ revient à ...** the prize goes to ...; **disputer la ~ à qn** to compete with sb; **remporter la ~** to win, be the winner; **pour ce qui est des bêtises, il remporte la ~** when it comes to being silly he wins hands down; (*Ciné*) **la Palme d'or** the Palme d'or; **la ~ du martyre** the crown of martyrdom; (*Mil*) **décoration avec ~** ≈ decoration with a bar; **~s académiques** *decoration for services to education in France* [c] [*nageur*] flipper

palmé, e [palme] ADJ [*feuille*] palmate (*SPÉC*); [*patte*] webbed; [*oiseau*] webfooted, palmate (*SPÉC*); **avoir les pieds ~s** to have webbed feet; (*hum*) **il a la ~es∗** he's bone-idle∗

palmer [palmɛr] NM (*Tech*) micrometer

palmeraie [palmərɛ] NF palm grove

palmier [palmje] NM [a] (*Bot*) palm tree; **~-dattier** date palm [b] (= *gâteau*) heart-shaped biscuit made of flaky pastry

palmipède [palmiped] [1] NM palmiped (*SPÉC*) [2] ADJ webfooted

palmiste [palmist] ADJ M → **chou¹**

palombe [palɔ̃b] NF woodpigeon, ringdove

palonnier [palɔnje] NM (*Aviat*) rudder bar; (*Aut*) compensator; [*cheval*] swingletree; (*en ski nautique*) handle; [*appareil de levage*] crosspiece

palot [palo] NM (= *baiser*) kiss

pâlot, -otte∗ [palo, ɔt] ADJ [*personne*] (a bit) pale ou peaky∗ (*Brit*) ou peaked∗ (*US*)

palourde [palurd] NF clam

palpable [palpabl] ADJ (*lit, fig*) palpable

palpation [palpasjɔ̃] NF palpation

palper [palpe] ▶ conjug 1 ◀ VT [a] [+ *objet*] to feel, finger; (*Méd*) to palpate [b]∗ [+ *argent*] (= *recevoir*) to get; (= *gagner*) to make; **qu'est-ce qu'il a dû ~ (comme argent)!** he must have made a fortune ou a mint!∗

palpeur [palpœr] NM [*chaleur, lumière*] sensor

palpitant, e [palpitɑ̃, ɑ̃t] [1] ADJ [a] (= *passionnant*) [*livre, moment*] thrilling, exciting; [*vie*] exciting; **d'un intérêt ~** ◊ **~ d'intérêt** terribly exciting, thrilling; **être ~ d'émotion** to be quivering with emotion [b] [*chair*] quivering (*épith*), wobbly; [*blessure*] throbbing (*épith*) [2] NM (∗ = *cœur*) ticker∗

palpitation [palpitasjɔ̃] NF [*cœur*] racing (*NonC*); [*paupières*] fluttering (*NonC*); [*lumière, flamme*] quivering (*NonC*); (*Méd*) **avoir des ~s** to have palpitations; (*fig*) **ça m'a donné des ~s** it gave me quite a turn

palpiter [palpite] ▶ conjug 1 ◀ VI [*cœur*] (= *battre*) to beat; (= *battre rapidement*) to race; [*paupières*] to flutter; [*chair*] to quiver; [*blessure*] to throb; [*narines, lumière, flamme*] to quiver

paltoquet [paltɔkɛ] NM (*littér: péj*) (= *rustre*) boor; (= *freluquet*) pompous fool

palu∗ [paly] NM ABRÉV = **paludisme**

paluche∗ [palyʃ] NF (= *main*) hand, paw∗; **serrer la ~ à qn** to shake hands with sb, shake sb's hand

paludéen, -enne [palydeɛ̃, ɛn] ADJ (*Méd*) malarial

paludisme [palydism] NM paludism (*SPÉC*), malaria

palustre [palystr] ADJ (*Bot*) paludal

pâmer (se) [pame] ▶ conjug 1 ◀ VPR (*littér*) to swoon†; (*fig*) **se pâmer** ou **être pâmé devant qch** to swoon ou be in raptures ou be ecstatic over sth; **se pâmer d'admiration/d'amour** to be overcome with admiration/with love; **se pâmer de rire** to be convulsed with laughter

pâmoison [pamwazɔ̃] NF (*littér, hum*) swoon†; (*lit*) **tomber en ~** to swoon†; (*fig*) **tomber en ~ devant un tableau** to swoon over ou go into raptures over a painting

pampa [pɑ̃pa] NF pampas *pl*

pamphlet [pɑ̃flɛ] NM satirical tract, lampoon

pamphlétaire [pɑ̃fletɛr] NMF lampoonist

pampille [pɑ̃pij] NF [*lustre*] pendant

pamplemousse [pɑ̃pləmus] NM grapefruit

pamplemoussier [pɑ̃pləmusje] NM grapefruit tree

pampre [pɑ̃pr] NM (*littér*) vine branch

Pan [pɑ̃] NM Pan → **flûte**

pan¹ [pɑ̃] [1] NM [a] (= *morceau*) piece; [*habit*] tail; (= *face, côté*) side, face; [*toit*] side; [*nappe*] overhanging part; [*lumière*] patch [b] [*économie, industrie*] area; [*société*] section; **un ~ de ma vie/de l'histoire de France** a chapter in ou of my life/in the history of France [2] COMP ▶ **pan de chemise** shirt-tail; **se promener en ~s de chemise** to wander about in (one's) shirt-tails ou with just one's shirt on ▶ **pan de ciel** patch of sky ▶ **pan coupé** cut-off corner (of room); **maison en ~ coupé** house with a slanting ou cut-off corner; **mur en ~ coupé** wall with a cut-off corner ▶ **pan de mur** (section of) wall ▶ **pan de rideau** curtain

pan² [pɑ̃] EXCL [*coup de feu*] bang!; [*gifle*] slap!, whack!; (*langage enfantin*) **je vais te faire ~ ~ (les fesses)** you'll get your bottom smacked

panacée [panase] NF panacea, cure-all

panachage [panaʃaʒ] NM [a] (*Pol*) voting for candidates from different parties instead of for the set list of one party [b] (= *mélange*) [*couleurs*] combination; [*programmes, plats*] selection

panache [panaʃ] NM [a] (= *plumet*) plume, panache; **~ de fumée** plume of smoke [b] (= *brio*) [*personne*] panache; **avoir du ~** to have panache; **personnage sans ~** lacklustre individual; **victoire sans ~** unimpressive victory

panaché, e [panaʃe] (*ptp de* **panacher**) [1] ADJ [a] [*fleur, feuilles*] variegated, many-coloured (*Brit*) ou -colored (*US*); **pétunias blancs ~s de rouge** white petunias with splashes of red ou with red stripes [b] [*foule, assortiment*] motley; [*glace*] two- ou mixed-flavour (*Brit*) ou -flavor (*US*) (*épith*); [*salade*] mixed; **bière ~e** shandy [2] NM (= *boisson*) shandy

panacher [panaʃe] ▶ conjug 1 ◀ VT (= *mélanger*) [+ *couleurs, fleurs*] to put together; [+ *genres*] to mix, combine; [+ *plantes*] to cross; [+ *biscuits, bonbons*] to make an assortment ou a selection of; (= *varier*) [+ *programmes, exercices*] to vary; **dois-je prendre l'un des menus ou puis-je ~ (les plats)?** do I have to take a set menu or can I make my own selection (of courses)?; **~ une liste électorale** to vote for candidates from different parties instead of for the set list of one party

panachure [panaʃyr] NF (*gén pl*) motley colours (*Brit*) ou colors (*US*)

panade [panad] NF bread soup; (*fig*) **être dans la ~**∗ (= *avoir des ennuis*) to be in the soup∗, be in a sticky situation; (= *avoir des ennuis d'argent*) to be strapped for cash∗ (*Brit*), be down to one's last dollar (*US*)

panafricain, e [panafrikɛ̃, ɛn] ADJ Pan-African

panafricanisme [panafrikanism] NM Pan-Africanism

panais [panɛ] NM parsnip

panama [panama] NM [a] (*Géog*) **le Panama** Panama [b] (= *chapeau*) Panama hat

Paname* [panam] N Paris

panaméen, -enne [panameɛ̃, ɛn] [1] ADJ Panamanian [2] **Panaméen(ne)** NM,F Panamanian

panaméricain, e [panamerikɛ̃, ɛn] ADJ Pan-American; **route ~e** Pan-American Highway

panaméricanisme [panamerikanism] NM Pan-Americanism

panamien, -ienne [panamjɛ̃, jɛn] ADJ = **panaméen, -enne**

panarabe [panaʀab] ADJ Pan-Arab(ic)

panarabisme [panaʀabism] NM Pan-Arabism

panard* [panaʀ] NM foot; **c'est le ~!** it's magic!* *ou* ace* (*Brit*)!

panaris [panaʀi] NM whitlow

pan-bagnat (*pl* **pans-bagnats**) [pɑ̃baɲa] NM sandwich (*with tomatoes, lettuce, hard-boiled eggs, tuna and anchovies, seasoned with olive oil*)

pancarte [pɑ̃kaʀt] NF (*gén*) sign, notice; (*Aut*) (road)sign; [*manifestant*] placard

pancréas [pɑ̃kʀeas] NM pancreas

pancréatique [pɑ̃kʀeatik] ADJ pancreatic

panda [pɑ̃da] NM panda; **grand ~** giant panda

pandémie [pɑ̃demi] NF pandemic (disease); **la ~ de sida** the Aids pandemic

pandémonium [pɑ̃demɔnjɔm] NM (*littér*) pandemonium; **le Pandémonium** Pandemonium

pandit [pɑ̃di(t)] NM pandit, pundit

Pandore [pɑ̃dɔʀ] NF (*Myth*) Pandora

pandore*† [pɑ̃dɔʀ] NM (= *gendarme*) cop*, gendarme

panégyrique [paneʒiʀik] NM (*frm*) panegyric; **faire le ~ de** *qn* to extol sb's merits; (*hum*) **quel ~ de son chef il a fait!** what a tribute to pay to his boss!

panégyriste [paneʒiʀist] NMF panegyrist

panel [panɛl] NM (= *jury*) panel; (= *échantillon*) sample group

paner [pane] ▸conjug 1◂ VT to coat with breadcrumbs; **pané** [*escalope*] coated with breadcrumbs, breaded

panetière [pan(ə)tjɛʀ] NF breadbin (*Brit*), breadbox (*US*)

paneuropéen, -enne [panøʀɔpeɛ̃, ɛn] ADJ Pan-European

pangermanisme [pɑ̃ʒɛʀmanism] NM Pan-Germanism

pangermaniste [pɑ̃ʒɛʀmanist] [1] ADJ Pan-German(ic) [2] NMF Pan-German

panhellénique [panelenik] ADJ Panhellenic

panhellénisme [panelenism] NM Panhellenism

panier [panje] [1] NM [a] (*gén, Sport*) basket; (= *contenu*) basket(ful); (*fig*) **ils sont tous à mettre dans le même ~** there's not much to choose between them, they are all much of a muchness (*Brit*); (*fig*) **ne les mets pas tous dans le même ~** don't lump them all together; **mettre** *ou* **jeter** *qch* **au ~** to throw sth out; (*Sport*) **réussir** *ou* **marquer un ~** to score *ou* make a basket → **anse, dessus, œuf** [b] (*Photo: pour diapositives*) magazine; **~ circulaire** rotary magazine [c] (= *vêtement*) pannier; **robe à ~s** dress with panniers [2] COMP ▸ **panier à bouteilles** bottle-carrier ▸ **panier de crabes** (*fig*) **c'est un ~ de crabes** they're always fighting among themselves, they're always at each other's throats ▸ **panier à frites** chip basket (*Brit*), fry basket (*US*) ▸ **panier à linge** linen basket ▸ **le panier de la ménagère** (*Écon*) the housewife's shopping basket ▸ **panier de monnaies** (*Fin*) basket of currencies ▸ **panier à ouvrage** workbasket ▸ **panier percé** (*fig*) spendthrift ▸ **panier à provisions** shopping basket ▸ **panier à salade**

(*Culin*) salad shaker *ou* basket; (* = *camion*) police van, Black Maria* (*Brit*), paddy waggon‡ (*US*)

panière [panjɛʀ] NF large basket

panier-repas (*pl* **paniers-repas**) [panjeʀəpa] NM lunch *ou* dinner *ou* picnic basket, packed lunch

panifiable [panifjabl] ADJ (suitable for) bread-making (*épith*)

panification [panifikasjɔ̃] NF bread-making

panifier [panifje] ▸conjug 7◂ VT to make bread from

paniquant, e* [panikɑ̃, ɑ̃t] ADJ scary*

paniquard* [panikaʀ] NM (*péj*) coward, yellow belly*

panique [panik] [1] NF panic; **pris de ~** panic-stricken; **un mouvement de ~ a saisi** *ou* **s'est emparé de la foule** a wave of panic swept through the crowd; **cela a provoqué un mouvement de ~ parmi la population** it caused panic among *ou* sent a wave of panic through the population; **il y a eu un début de ~ chez les investisseurs** investors were beginning to panic *ou* were showing signs of panic; **pas de ~!*** don't panic!, there's no need to panic!; **c'était la ~ (générale)*** it was panic all round *ou* panic stations* (*Brit*) → **semer, vent** [2] ADJ **terreur** *ou* **peur ~** panic

paniquer* [panike] ▸conjug 1◂ [1] VT **~** *qn* to put the wind up sb*, give sb a scare; **il a essayé de me ~** he tried to put the wind up me* [2] VI, **se paniquer** VPR to panic, get the wind up*; **commencer à ~** *ou* **à se ~** to get panicky; **il n'a pas paniqué** ◊ **il ne s'est pas paniqué** he didn't panic, he kept his head; **être paniqué** to be in a panic; **être paniqué à l'idée de faire** *qch* to be scared stiff at the idea of doing sth

panislamique [panislamik] ADJ Panislamic

panislamisme [panislamism] NM Panislamism

panne[1] [pan] NF [a] (= *incident*) breakdown; **être** *ou* **tomber en ~** [*machine*] to break down; **je suis tombé en ~ (de voiture)** my car has broken down; **je suis tombé en ~ sèche** *ou* **en ~ d'essence** I have run out of petrol (*Brit*) *ou* gas (*US*); **je suis en ~ de réfrigérateur/radio** my refrigerator/radio is broken; **«en ~»** [*machine*] "out of order"; [*voiture*] "broken-down"; **~ de courant** *ou* **d'électricité** power *ou* electrical failure; **~ de secteur** local mains failure; **de moteur** [*avion, voiture*] engine failure; **il n'a pas trouvé la ~** he couldn't find the fault *ou* problem; (*hum*) **il m'a fait le coup de la ~** he tried on the old trick about the car breaking down [b] (*fig*) **le candidat est resté en ~** the candidate was at a loss for words; **les travaux sont en ~** work has come to a halt; **ce projet est en ~** work is at a standstill *ou* has come to a halt on this project; **laisser** *qn* **en ~** to leave sb in the lurch, let sb down; **je suis en ~ de cigarettes/d'idées/d'inspiration** I've run out of *ou* I'm out of cigarettes/of ideas/of inspiration; **rester en ~ devant une difficulté** to be stumped* (by a problem); (*hum*) **avoir une ~ d'oreiller** to oversleep; **il a eu une ~** (*sexuellement*) he couldn't rise to the occasion (*hum*) [c] (*Naut*) **mettre en ~** to bring to, heave to [d] (*Théât* = *rôle mineur*) bit part

panne[2] [pan] NF [a] (= *graisse*) fat [b] (= *étoffe*) panne [c] (= *poutre*) purlin [d] [*marteau*] peen; [*piolet*] adz(e)

panneau (*pl* **panneaux**) [pano] [1] NM (*Art, Couture, Menuiserie*) panel; (= *écriteau*) sign, notice; (*Constr*) prefabricated section; (*Basket*) backboard; **les ~x qui ornent la salle** the panelling round the room; **à ~x** panelled; (*fig*) **tomber** *ou* **donner dans le ~*** to fall *ou* walk (right) into the trap, fall for it* [2] COMP ▸ **panneau d'affichage** (*pour résultats etc*)

notice board (*Brit*), bulletin board (*US*); (*pour publicité*) billboard, hoarding (*Brit*) ▸ **panneau d'écoutille** (*Naut*) hatch cover ▸ **panneaux électoraux** *notice boards for election posters* ▸ **panneau indicateur** signpost ▸ **panneau lumineux** electronic display (sign)board; [*stade*] electronic scoreboard ▸ **panneau de particules** chipboard (*NonC*) ▸ **panneau publicitaire** billboard, hoarding (*Brit*) ▸ **panneau de signalisation** roadsign, traffic sign ▸ **panneau solaire** solar panel ▸ **panneau de stop** stop sign ▸ **panneau vitré** glass panel

panonceau (*pl* **panonceaux**) [panɔ̃so] NM (= *plaque de médecin*) plaque; (= *écriteau publicitaire*) sign

panoplie [panɔpli] NF [a] (= *jouet*) outfit; **~ d'Indien** Red Indian outfit; **~ d'armes** (*sur un mur*) display of weapons; [*gangster, policier*] armoury (*Brit*), armory (*US*); (*hum* = *instruments*) **il a sorti toute sa ~** he brought out all his equipment [b] (*fig* = *gamme*) [*arguments, médicaments, sanctions*] range; [*mesures*] package, range

panorama [panɔʀama] NM (*lit, fig*) panorama

panoramique [panɔʀamik] [1] ADJ [*vue, appareil-photo, photo*] panoramic; [*restaurant*] with a panoramic view; [*carrosserie*] with panoramic *ou* wraparound windows; [*car, voiture*] with wraparound windscreen; **ascenseur ~** glass lift (*Brit*) *ou* elevator (*US*); (*Ciné*) **écran ~** wide *ou* panoramic screen; **wagon ~** observation car [2] NM (*Ciné, TV*) panoramic shot

panosse [panɔs] NF (*Helv*) floorcloth; **passer la ~** to mop the floor

panse [pɑ̃s] NF [*ruminant*] paunch; * [*personne*] paunch, belly*; (*fig*) [*bouteille*] belly; **s'en mettre plein la ~** to stuff o.s.* *ou* one's face*; **j'ai la ~ bien remplie*** I'm full to bursting; **manger à s'en faire crever** *ou* **éclater la ~*** to eat until one's fit to burst, stuff o.s.* *ou* one's face‡; **je pourrais manger des cerises à m'en faire crever la ~*** I could eat cherries till they come out of my ears*

pansement [pɑ̃smɑ̃] NM (*Méd*) [*plaie, membre*] dressing; (= *bandage*) bandage; (= *sparadrap*) plaster (*Brit*), Band Aid®; **faire un ~** (*gén*) to dress a wound; (*sur une dent*) to put in a temporary filling; **refaire un ~** to put a clean dressing on a wound; **(tout) couvert de ~s** (all) bandaged up; **~ adhésif** sticking plaster (*Brit*), Band Aid®

panser [pɑ̃se] ▸conjug 1◂ VT [a] (*Méd*) [+ *plaie*] to dress; [+ *bras, jambe*] to put a dressing on; (*avec un bandage*) to bandage; (*avec du sparadrap*) to put a plaster (*Brit*) *ou* a Band Aid® on; [+ *blessé*] to dress the wounds of; (*fig*) **le temps panse les blessures (du cœur)** time heals (the wounds of the heart), time is a great healer; (*fig*) **~ ses blessures** to lick one's wounds [b] [+ *cheval*] to groom

panseur, -euse [pɑ̃sœʀ, øz] NM,F *nurse who applies bandages etc*

panslavisme [pɑ̃slavism] NM Pan-Slavism

panslaviste [pɑ̃slavist] [1] ADJ Pan-Slav(onic) [2] NMF Pan-Slavist

pansu, e [pɑ̃sy] ADJ [*personne*] potbellied, paunchy; [*vase*] potbellied

pantagruélique [pɑ̃taɡʀyelik] ADJ pantagruelian

pantalon [pɑ̃talɔ̃] NM [a] (*Habillement*) (pair of) trousers, (pair of) pants (*US*); († = *sous-vêtement*) knickers; **un ~ neuf** a new pair of trousers *ou* pants (*US*), new trousers *ou* pants (*US*); **10 ~s** 10 pairs of trousers *ou* pants (*US*); **~ cigarette** straight(-leg) *ou* cigarette trousers *ou* pants (*US*); **~ en flanelle** flannels; **~ de golf** plus fours; **~ de pyjama** pyjama *ou* pajama (*US*) bottoms; **~ de ski** ski pants → **corsaire, porter** [b] (*Théât*) **Pantalon** Pantaloon

pantalonnade [pɑ̃talɔnad] NF (*Théât*) slapstick comedy, knockabout farce (*Brit*); (*péj*) tomfoolery (*NonC*)

pantelant, e [pɑ̃t(ə)lɑ̃, ɑ̃t] ADJ [*personne*] gasping for breath (*attrib*), panting; [*gorge*] heaving; [*cadavre, animal*] twitching

panthéisme [pɑ̃teism] NM pantheism

panthéiste [pɑ̃teist] [1] ADJ pantheistic [2] NMF pantheist

panthéon [pɑ̃teɔ̃] NM [a] (= *bâtiment*) pantheon; **le Panthéon** the Pantheon [b] (= *divinités, personnages célèbres*) pantheon; **le ~ grec/romain** the Greek/Roman pantheon; **le ~ littéraire** the literary pantheon, the great names of literature; **ce film est entré au ~ du cinéma** this film has become a classic

panthère [pɑ̃tɛʀ] NF [a] (= *félin*) panther; **~ noire** black panther; **sa femme est une vraie ~** his wife is a real hellcat* [b] (*Hist US*) **Panthères noires** Black Panthers

pantin [pɑ̃tɛ̃] NM (= *jouet*) jumping jack; (*péj* = *personne*) puppet

pantographe [pɑ̃tɔgʀaf] NM pantograph

pantois [pɑ̃twa] ADJ M stunned; **j'en suis resté ~** I was stunned

pantomime [pɑ̃tɔmim] NF (= *art*) mime (*NonC*); (= *spectacle*) mime show; (*fig*) pantomime, scene, fuss (*NonC*); **il nous a fait la ~ pour avoir un vélo** he made a great pantomime *ou* fuss about having a bike

pantouflage [pɑ̃tuflaʒ] NM (*arg*: *Admin*) [*fonctionnaire*] leaving the civil service to work in the private sector

pantouflard, e* [pɑ̃tuflaʀ, aʀd] [1] ADJ [*personne, caractère*] stay-at-home (*épith*); [*vie*] quiet, uneventful, humdrum [2] NM,F stay-at-home

pantoufle [pɑ̃tufl] NF slipper; **il était en ~s** he was in his slippers

pantoufler [pɑ̃tufle] ▸ conjug 1 ◂ VI [a] (*arg*: *Admin*) [*fonctionnaire*] to leave the civil service to work in the private sector [b] (* = *paresser*) to laze *ou* lounge around (at home)

panty (*pl* **panties**) [pɑ̃ti] NM (= *gaine*) panty girdle

panure [panyʀ] NF breadcrumbs

Panurge [panyʀʒ] NM → **mouton**

PAO [peao] NF (ABRÉV = **publication assistée par ordinateur**) DTP

paon [pɑ̃] NM peacock; **faire le ~** to strut about (like a peacock); **fier *ou* vaniteux comme un ~** proud as a peacock → **parer**[1]

paonne [pan] NF peahen

PAP [pap] NM (ABRÉV = **prêt aidé d'accession à la propriété**) → **prêt**[2]

papa [papa] NM (*gén*) dad; (*langage enfantin*) daddy; (*langage de bébé*) dada; **~-poule** doting father; **la musique/les voitures de ~*** old-fashioned music/cars; **c'est vraiment l'usine de ~!*** this factory is really antiquated! *ou* behind the times!; **conduire à la ~*** to potter along (*Brit*), drive at a snail's pace; **alors ~, tu avances?*** come on grandad, get a move on!*; (*péj*) **fils** (*ou* **fille**) **à ~** rich kid*; **jouer au ~ et à la maman** to play mummies (*Brit*) *ou* mommies (*US*) and daddies, play house → **gâteau**

papal, e (*mpl* **-aux**) [papal, o] ADJ papal

paparazzi [papaʀadzi] NMPL (*péj*) paparazzi

papauté [papote] NF papacy

papavérine [papaveʀin] NF papaverine

papaye [papaj] NF pawpaw, papaya

papayer [papaje] NM pawpaw *ou* papaya (tree)

pape [pap] NM pope; (*fig*) (*école littéraire etc*) leading light; **le ~ Jean XXIII** Pope John XXIII; **du ~** papal

papé [pape] NM = **papet**

Papeete [papet] N Papeete

papelard[1]* [paplaʀ] NM (= *feuille*) (bit of) paper; (= *article de journal*) article; (= *journal*) paper; (= *papiers d'identité*) **~s** papers

papelard[2]**, e** [paplaʀ, aʀd] ADJ (*littér*) suave

papelardise [paplaʀdiz] NF (*littér*) suavity, suaveness, smoothness

paperasse [papʀas] NF (*péj*) **~(s)** (= *documents*) papers, bumf* (*Brit*); (*à remplir*) forms; **j'ai des ~s ou de la ~ à faire** I've got some paperwork to do

paperasserie [papʀasʀi] NF (*péj*: = *travail*) paperwork; **~ administrative** red tape

paperassier, -ière [papʀasje, jɛʀ] (*péj*) [1] ADJ [*personne*] fond of paperwork; [*administration*] cluttered with red tape, obsessed with form filling [2] NM,F (= *bureaucrate*) penpusher (*Brit*), pencilpusher (*US*); **quel ~!** he's forever poring over his papers!

papesse [papɛs] NF female pope; (*fig*) [*école littéraire etc*] leading light; **la ~ Jeanne** Pope Joan

papet [pape] NM (*terme du Sud*) (= *grand-père*) grandpa*; (= *vieil homme*) old man

papeterie [papetʀi] NF (= *magasin*) stationer's (shop); (= *fourniture*) stationery; (= *fabrique*) paper mill; (= *fabrication*) paper-making industry; (= *commerce*) stationery trade

papetier, -ière [pap(ə)tje, jɛʀ] NM,F (= *vendeur*) stationer; (= *fabricant*) paper-maker; **~-libraire** stationer and bookseller

papi [papi] NM (*langage enfantin*) grandad*, grandpa*; (* = *vieil homme*) old man

papier [papje] [1] NM [a] (= *matière*) morceau/bout de ~ piece/bit *ou* slip of paper; **de *ou* en ~** paper (*épith*); **mets-moi cela sur ~** (*pour ne pas oublier*) write that down for me; (*pour confirmation écrite*) let me have that in writing; **sur le ~** (= *en projet, théoriquement*) on paper; **jeter une idée sur le ~** to jot down an idea → **noircir, pâte**
[b] (= *feuille écrite*) paper; (= *feuille blanche*) sheet *ou* piece of paper; (*Presse* = *article*) article; **~s personnels** personal papers; **être/ne pas être dans les petits ~s de qn** to be in sb's good/bad books; **un ~ à signer/à remplir** a form to be signed/filled in; (*Presse*) **faire un ~ sur qn** to do an article *ou* a story on sb; (*fig*) **rayez cela de vos ~s!** you can forget about that!
[c] (= *emballage*) paper; [*bonbon*] paper, wrapper
[d] **~s (d'identité)** (identity) papers; **vos ~s, s'il vous plaît!** could I see your identity papers, please?; (*Aut*) may I see your driving licence (*Brit*) *ou* driver's license (*US*), please?; **ses ~s ne sont pas en règle** his papers are not in order

[2] COMP ▸ **papier alu***, **papier aluminium** aluminium (*Brit*) *ou* aluminum (*US*) foil, tinfoil ▸ **papier d'argent** silver foil *ou* paper, tinfoil ▸ **papier d'Arménie** incense paper ▸ **papier bible** bible paper, India paper ▸ **papier (de) brouillon** rough paper ▸ **papier buvard** blotting paper ▸ **papier cadeau** gift wrap, wrapping paper ▸ **papier calque** tracing paper ▸ **papier carbone** carbon paper ▸ **papier chiffon** rag paper ▸ **papier à cigarettes** cigarette paper ▸ **papier collant**† sticky tape ▸ **papier collé** (*Art*) (paper) collage ▸ **papier en continu** (*Ordin*) continuous stationery ▸ **papier couché** art paper ▸ **papier crépon** crêpe paper ▸ **papier cul***: bogpaper*: (*Brit*), TP* (*US*) ▸ **papier à dessin** drawing paper ▸ **papier doré** gold paper ▸ **papier d'emballage** (*gén*) wrapping paper; [*brun, kraft*] brown paper ▸ **papier à en-tête** headed notepaper ▸ **papier d'étain** tinfoil, silver paper ▸ **papier glacé** glazed paper ▸ **papiers gras** (= *ordures*) litter, rubbish ▸ **papier hygiénique** toilet paper ▸ **papier journal** newspaper ▸ **papier kraft**® brown wrapping paper ▸ **papier à lettres** writing paper, notepaper ▸ **papier libre** plain unheaded paper; **envoyez votre réponse sur ~ libre à ...** send your answer on a sheet of paper to ... ▸ **papier mâché** papier-mâché; (*fig*) **mine de ~ mâché** pasty complexion ▸ **papier machine** typing paper ▸ **papiers militaires** army papers ▸ **papier millimétré** graph paper ▸ **papier ministre** official paper (*approximately quarto size*); **écrit sur ~ ministre** written on official paper ▸ **papier à musique** manuscript (*Brit*) *ou* music (*US*) paper ▸ **papier paraffiné** (*gén*) wax paper; (*Tech* = *enduit*) greaseproof (*Brit*) *ou* wax (*US*) paper ▸ **papier peint** wallpaper ▸ **papier pelure** India paper ▸ **papier sensible** (*Photo*) bromide paper ▸ **papier de soie** tissue paper ▸ **papier sulfurisé** = **papier paraffiné** ▸ **papier timbré** stamped paper ▸ **papier toilette** toilet paper ▸ **papier de tournesol** litmus paper ▸ **papier de verre** glasspaper, sandpaper

papier-émeri (*pl* **papiers-émeri**) [papjem(ə)ʀi] NM emery paper

papier-filtre (*pl* **papiers-filtres**) [papjefiltʀ] NM filter paper

papier-monnaie (*pl* **papiers-monnaies**) [papjemɔnɛ] NM paper money

papille [papij] NF papilla; **~s gustatives** taste buds

papillon [papijɔ̃] NM (= *insecte*) butterfly; (*fig* = *personne*) fickle person; (= *écrou*) wing *ou* butterfly nut; (* = *contravention*) (parking) ticket; (= *autocollant*) sticker; (= *nage*) (**brasse**) **~** butterfly (stroke); **~ de nuit** moth; (*Aut*) **~ des gaz** throttle valve → **minute, nœud**

papillonnant, e [papijɔnɑ̃, ɑ̃t] ADJ [*personne*] fickle; **esprit ~** butterfly mind

papillonner [papijɔne] ▸ conjug 1 ◂ VI [a] (= *voltiger*) to flit about *ou* around (**entre** between) [b] (*entre activités diverses*) to switch back and forth, chop and change (*Brit*) (**entre** between); **~ d'un sujet/d'un homme à l'autre** to flit from one subject/one man to another; **~ autour d'une femme** to hover round a woman

papillote [papijɔt] NF (= *bigoudi*) curlpaper; [*bonbon*] (sweet (*Brit*) *ou* candy (*US*)) wrapper, (sweet (*Brit*) *ou* candy (*US*)) paper; [*gigot*] frill; (= *papier beurré*) buttered paper; (= *papier aluminium*) tinfoil; **poisson en ~** fish cooked in a parcel *ou* en papillotte; (*fig*) **tu peux en faire des ~s*** you can just chuck it in the bin

papillotement [papijɔtmɑ̃] NM [a] [*lumière, étoiles*] twinkling (*NonC*); [*reflets*] sparkling (*NonC*) [b] [*paupières*] fluttering (*NonC*); [*yeux*] blinking (*NonC*)

papilloter [papijɔte] ▸ conjug 1 ◂ VI [a] [*lumière, étoiles*] to twinkle; [*reflets*] to sparkle [b] [*paupières*] to flutter; [*yeux*] to blink

papisme [papism] NM papism, popery

papiste [papist] NMF papist

papivore [papivɔʀ] NMF avid reader

papotage [papɔtaʒ] NM (= *action*) chattering (*NonC*); (= *propos*) (idle) chatter (*NonC*)

papoter [papɔte] ▸ conjug 1 ◂ VI to chatter, have a natter* (*Brit*)

papou, e [papu] [1] ADJ Papuan [2] NM (*Ling*) Papuan [3] **Papou(e)** NM,F Papuan

papouan-néo-guinéen, -enne [papwɑ̃neɔginee, ɛn] [1] ADJ Papua-New-Guinean, (of) Papua New Guinea [2] **Papouan-Néo-Guinéen(ne)** NM,F Papua-New-Guinean

Papouasie-Nouvelle-Guinée [papwazinuvɛlgine] NF Papua New Guinea

papouille* [papuj] NF tickling (*NonC*); **faire des ~s à qn** to tickle sb

paprika [papʀika] NM paprika (pepper)

papule [papyl] NF papule, papula

papy [papi] NM = **papi**

papyrus [papiʀys] NM papyrus

paqson*: [paksɔ̃] NM = **pacson**

pâque [pɑk] NF **la ~** Passover → **Pâques**

paquebot [pak(ə)bo] NM liner, (steam)ship

pâquerette [pɑkʀɛt] NF daisy

Pâques [pak] [1] NM Easter; **le lundi/la semaine de ~** Easter Monday/week; (fig) **à ~ ou à la Trinité** some fine day (iro); **faire ~ avant les Rameaux†** to become pregnant before marriage; **l'île de ~** Easter Island → **dimanche**; **œuf** [2] NFPL **bonnes** ou **joyeuses ~!** Happy Easter!; **faire ses ~** to go to Easter mass (and take communion)

paquet [pakɛ] NM [a] (pour emballer etc) [bonbons, sucre] bag, packet; [café, biscuits, pâtes, riz, farine, lessive] packet (Brit), package (US); [cigarettes] packet, pack (US); [cartes à jouer] pack (Brit), deck (surtout US); [linge] bundle; **il fume deux ~s par jour** he smokes forty a day, he smokes two packs a day (US); **porter qn comme un ~ de linge sale** to carry sb like a sack of potatoes; (fig) **c'est un vrai ~ de nerfs** he's a bag ou bundle of nerves; **c'est un vrai ~ d'os** he's a bag of bones
[b] (= colis) parcel, package; **mettre en ~** to parcel up, package up; **faire un ~** to make up a parcel ou package
[c] (= tas) **~ de** [+ neige] pile ou mass of; [+ boue] lump of; [+ billets] wad of
[d] (Rugby) **~ (d'avants)** pack (of forwards)
[e] (Naut) **~ de mer** big wave
[f] (* = argent) **ça coûte un ~** it costs a small fortune ou a packet* (Brit); **il a touché un bon ~** he got a tidy sum*; **ils lui ont donné un bon petit ~ pour qu'il se taise** they gave him a tidy little sum* to keep him quiet
[g] (loc) **faire son ~ ou ses ~s** to pack one's bags; **lâcher son ~ à qn†** to tell sb a few home truths; **mettre le ~** (= argent) to spare no expense; (efforts, moyens) to pull out all the stops → **risquer**

paquetage [pak(ə)taʒ] NM (Mil) pack, kit; **faire son ~** to get one's pack ou kit ready

paquet-cadeau (pl **paquets-cadeaux**) [pakɛkado] NM giftwrapped parcel; **pouvez-vous me faire un ~?** could you giftwrap it for me?

paquet-poste (pl **paquets-poste**) [pakɛpɔst] NM mailing box

▼ **par¹** [paʀ]
PRÉPOSITION

Lorsque par s'emploie dans des expressions telles que par cœur, par terre, par principe, passer par, un par un etc, cherchez sous l'autre mot.

[a] agent, cause **le carreau a été cassé ~ l'orage/~ un enfant** the pane was broken by the storm/by a child; **accablé ~ le désespoir** overwhelmed with despair; **elle nous a fait porter des fraises ~ son fils** she got her son to bring us some strawberries, she had her son bring us some strawberries; **il a appris la nouvelle ~ le journal/~ un ami** he learned the news from the paper/from ou through a friend; **elle veut tout faire ~ elle-même** she wants to do everything (for) herself; **la découverte de la pénicilline ~** Fleming Fleming's discovery of penicillin, the discovery of penicillin by Fleming

[b] manière, moyen **~ le train** by rail ou train; **~ route** by road; **~ la poste** by post ou mail, through the post; **communiquer ~ fax/Internet** to communicate by ou via fax/the Internet; **la porte ferme ~ un verrou** the gate is locked with a bolt ou by means of a bolt; **obtenir qch ~ la force/la persuasion/la ruse** to obtain sth by force/with persuasion/by ou through cunning; **arriver ~ l'intelligence/le travail** to succeed through intelligence/hard work; **ils se ressemblent ~ leur sens de l'humour** they are alike in their sense of humour; **ils diffèrent ~ bien des côtés** they are different ou they differ in many ways ou aspects; **il descend des Bourbons ~ sa mère** he is descended from the Bourbons through his mother ou on his mother's side

➤ GRAMMAIRE ACTIVE: **par** 44.1

[c] raison, motif (généralement sans article) **~ pure bêtise** through ou out of sheer stupidity; **~ habitude** by ou out of ou from (sheer) habit; **faire qch ~ plaisir/pitié** to do sth for pleasure/out of pity; **~ souci d'exactitude** for the sake of accuracy, out of a concern for accuracy; **~ manque de temps** owing to lack of time; **la ville est célèbre ~ ses musées** the city is famous for its museums

[d] lieu, direction (= en empruntant ce chemin) by (way of); (= en traversant) through, across; (suivi d'un nom propre) via; (= en longeant) along; **il est sorti ~ la fenêtre** he went out by ou through the window; **il est venu ~ le chemin le plus court** he took the shortest route; **nous sommes venus ~ la côte/~ Lyon/~ l'Espagne** we came along the coast/via Lyons/via ou through Spain; **se promener ~ les rues/les champs** to walk through the streets/through ou across the fields; **~ tout le pays** throughout ou all over the country; **sortez ~ ici/là** go out this/that way; **~ où sont-ils entrés?** which way ou how did they get in?; **~ où est-il venu?** which way did he come?; **la rumeur s'était répandue ~ la ville** the rumour had spread through the town; **l'épave repose ~ 20 mètres de fond** the wreck is lying 20 metres down; **~ 10° de latitude sud** at a latitude of 10° south; **arriver ~ le nord/la gauche/le haut ou en haut** to arrive from the north/the left/the top

[e] distribution, mesure **gagner tant ~ semaine/mois** to earn so much a ou per week/month; **~ an** a ou per year; **rendement de 10% ~ an** yield of 10% per annum; **trois fois ~ jour/semaine/mois** three times a day/a week/a month; **marcher deux ~ deux/trois ~ trois** to walk two by two ou in twos/three by three ou in threes; **six étudiants ~ appartement** six students to a flat ou per flat; **ils déduisent 20 F ~ enfant** they take off 20 francs for each child ou per child; **~ poignées/charretées** in handfuls/cartloads, by the handful/cartload

[f] = pendant **~ une belle nuit d'été** on a beautiful summer('s) night; **il partit ~ une pluvieuse journée de mars** he left on a rainy March day; (en parlant du climat, de la température) **ne restez pas dehors ~ ce froid/cette chaleur** don't stay out in this cold/this heat; **évitez cette route ~ temps de pluie/de brouillard** avoid that road in wet weather ou when it's wet/in fog ou when it's foggy; **sortir ~ moins 10°** to go out when it's minus 10°

[g]
✦ **commencer, finir** etc **par** to start/end with; **on a commencé ~ des huîtres** we started with oysters, we had oysters to start; **la fête se termina ~ un feu d'artifice** the party ended with a fireworks display; **on a clôturé la séance ~ des élections** elections brought the meeting to a close, the meeting closed with elections; **il a fini ~ tout avouer** he finally confessed everything, he ended up confessing everything; **il finit ~ m'agacer avec ses plaisanteries!** his jokes are starting to get on my nerves!

[h] dans des exclamations, des serments by; **~ tous les dieux du ciel** in heaven's name, by heaven; **~ tout ce que j'ai de plus cher, je vous promets que ...** I promise you by all that I hold most dear that ...

[i]
✦ **de par** (frm) (= à travers) **il voyageait de ~ le monde** he travelled throughout ou all over the world; **il y a de ~ le monde des milliers de gens qui pensent que ...** thousands of people the world over ou throughout the world think that ...
(= à cause de) because of; **de ~ son milieu et son éducation, il ...** because of ou by virtue of his background and upbringing, he ...; **de ~ la nature même de ses activités** by the very nature of his activities
(= par l'autorité de, au nom de) **de ~ le roi** by order of the king, in the name of the king; **de ~ la loi** by law, legally

par² [paʀ] NM (Golf) par

para* [paʀa] NM (ABRÉV = **parachutiste**) para*

parabellum [paʀabɛlɔm] NM parabellum, big automatic pistol

parabole [paʀabɔl] NF (Math) parabola; (Rel) parable; (TV) dish aerial, satellite dish, dish antenna (US)

parabolique [paʀabɔlik] [1] ADJ parabolic; **antenne ~** satellite dish, dish aerial, dish antenna (US) [2] NM (= radiateur) electric fire

paracentèse [paʀasɛtɛz] NF paracentesis

paracétamol [paʀasetamɔl] NM paracetamol

parachèvement [paʀaʃɛvmɑ̃] NM perfection, perfecting

parachever [paʀaʃ(ə)ve] ▶conjug 5◀ VT to perfect, put the finishing touches to

parachutage [paʀaʃytaʒ] NM [soldats, vivres] parachuting, dropping ou landing by parachute; **ils n'ont pas apprécié le ~ d'un ministre dans leur département** they didn't like the way a minister was suddenly landed on them; **tout le monde parle de son ~ à la tête du service** everybody is talking about the way he's suddenly been appointed head of department

parachute [paʀaʃyt] NM parachute; **~ ventral/dorsal/de secours** lap-pack/back(-pack)/reserve parachute; **descendre en ~** to parachute down; **faire du ~ ascensionnel** (tiré par une voiture) to go parascending; (tiré par un bateau) to go parasailing

parachuter [paʀaʃyte] ▶conjug 1◀ VT [a] (Mil, Sport) to parachute, drop by parachute [b] (* = désigner) **~ qn à un poste** to pitchfork sb into a job; (Pol) **~ un candidat dans une circonscription** to bring in ou field a candidate from outside a constituency; **ils nous ont parachuté un nouveau directeur de Paris** a new manager from Paris has suddenly been landed on us*

parachutisme [paʀaʃytism] NM parachuting; **~ ascensionnel** (par voiture) parascending; (par bateau) parasailing; **faire du ~** to go parachuting; **faire du ~ en chute libre** to skydive, go skydiving

parachutiste [paʀaʃytist] [1] NMF (Sport) parachutist; (Mil) paratrooper; **nos unités de ~s** our paratroops [2] ADJ [unité] paratrooper (épith)

parade [paʀad] NF [a] (= ostentation) show, ostentation; **faire ~ de** [+ érudition] to parade, display, show off; [+ relations] to boast about, brag about; (péj) **afficher une générosité de ~** to make an outward show ou display of generosity; **ce n'est que de la ~** it's just done for show
[b] (= spectacle) parade; **~ militaire/foraine** military/circus parade; **les troupes s'avancèrent comme à la ~** the troops moved forward as if they were (still) on the parade ground ou on parade; (Zool) **~ nuptiale** mating ou courtship display
[c] (Équitation) pulling up
[d] (Escrime) parry, parade; (Boxe) parry; (Ftbl) dummy; (fig) answer; (orale) riposte, rejoinder; **il faut trouver la (bonne) ~** we must find the (right) answer; **nous n'avons pas encore trouvé la ~ contre cette maladie** we still haven't found a way to counter this disease

parader [paʀade] ▶conjug 1◀ VI (péj) to strut about, show off; (Mil) to parade

paradigmatique [paʀadigmatik] [1] ADJ paradigmatic [2] NF study of paradigmatic relationships

paradigme [paʀadigm] NM paradigm

paradis [paʀadi] NM [a] (lit, fig) paradise, heaven; **le Paradis terrestre** (Bible) the Garden of Eden; (fig) heaven on earth; **aller au ou en ~** to go to heaven; **c'est le ~ des enfants/**

chasseurs ici it's a children's/hunters' paradise here; (fig) **il s'est cru au ~** he was over the moon, he was in (seventh) heaven; **~ fiscal** tax haven → **emporter, oiseau** [b] (†: Théât) **le ~** the gallery, the gods* (Brit)

paradisiaque [paʀadizjak] ADJ heavenly, paradisiacal

paradisier [paʀadizje] NM bird of paradise

▼ **paradoxal, e** (mpl -aux) [paʀadɔksal, o] ADJ paradoxical; **il est assez ~ de …** it doesn't make sense to …, it's somewhat illogical to … → **sommeil**

paradoxalement [paʀadɔksalmɑ̃] ADV paradoxically

paradoxe [paʀadɔks] NM paradox

parafe [paʀaf] NM = **paraphe**

parafer [paʀafe] ▸ conjug 1 ◂ VT = **parapher**

parafeur [paʀafœʀ] NM = **parapheur**

paraffinage [paʀafinaʒ] NM paraffining

paraffine [paʀafin] NF (gén: solide) paraffin wax; (Chim) paraffin

paraffiner [paʀafine] ▸ conjug 1 ◂ VT to paraffin(e) → **papier**

parafiscal, e (mpl -aux) [paʀafiskal, o] ADJ **taxe ~e** special tax (road-fund-tax, stamp duty etc)

parages [paʀaʒ] NMPL ▪ **dans les ~** (= dans la région) in the area, in the vicinity; (* = pas très loin) round about; **est-ce que Sylvie est dans les ~?*** is Sylvie about?; **dans ces ~** in these parts; **dans les ~ de** near, round about, in the vicinity of ▪ [b] (Naut) waters, region

paragraphe [paʀagʀaf] NM paragraph; (Typo) section (mark)

paragrêle [paʀagʀɛl] ADJ anti-hail (épith)

Paraguay [paʀagwɛ] NM Paraguay

paraguayen, -enne [paʀagwajɛ̃, ɛn] [1] ADJ Paraguayan [2] **Paraguayen(ne)** NM,F Paraguayan

paraître [paʀɛtʀ] ▸ conjug 57 ◂ [1] VI [a] (= se montrer: gén) to appear; [personne] to appear, make one's appearance; **~ en scène/à ou sur l'écran/au balcon** to appear on stage/on the screen/on the balcony; **il n'a pas paru de la journée** he hasn't appeared all day; **il n'a pas paru à la réunion** he didn't appear ou turn up at the meeting; **~ en public** to appear in public, make a public appearance; **un sourire parut sur ses lèvres** a smile appeared on his lips ▪ [b] (Presse) to appear, be published, come out; **faire ~ qch** [éditeur] to bring sth out, publish sth; [auteur] to have sth published; **« vient de ~ »** "just out", "just published"; **« à ~ »** "forthcoming"

[c] (= briller) to be noticed; **chercher à ~** to show off; **le désir de ~** the desire to be noticed ou to show off

[d] (= être visible) to show (through); **laisser ~ ses sentiments/son irritation** to let one's feelings/one's annoyance show

[e] (= sembler) to look, seem, appear; **elle paraît heureuse** she seems (to be) happy; **cela me paraît être une erreur** it looks like a mistake to me; **elle paraissait l'aimer** she seemed ou appeared to love him; **il paraît 20 ans** (= il est plus jeune) he looks (at least) 20; (= il est plus âgé) he only looks 20; **le voyage a paru long** the journey seemed long; **cette robe la fait ~ plus grande** that dress makes her look taller

[2] VB IMPERS [a] (= il semble) **il me paraît difficile qu'elle puisse venir** it seems to me that it will be difficult for her to come; **il ne lui paraît pas essentiel qu'elle sache** he doesn't think it essential for her to know; **il lui paraissait impossible de refuser** he didn't see how he could refuse; **il paraîtrait ridicule de s'offenser** it would seem stupid to take offence

[b] (= le bruit court) **il va se marier, paraît-il** ou **à ce qu'il paraît** apparently he's getting married, he's getting married apparently; **il paraît**

qu'on va construire une autoroute apparently ou it seems they're going to build a motorway; **il paraît que oui** so it seems ou appears, apparently; **il paraît que non** apparently not

[c] (avec nég) **il n'y paraîtra bientôt plus** (tache, cicatrice) there will soon be no trace of it left; (maladie) soon no one will ever know you've had it; **sans qu'il n'y paraisse rien** without anything being obvious, without letting anything show; **sans qu'il y paraisse, elle a obtenu ce qu'elle voulait** she got what she wanted without appearing to

[3] NM **le ~** appearance(s)

paralangage [paʀalɑ̃gaʒ] NM paralanguage

paralinguistique [paʀalɛ̃gɥistik] ADJ paralinguistic

paralittérature [paʀaliteʀatyʀ] NF marginal literature

parallactique [paʀalaktik] ADJ parallactic

parallaxe [paʀalaks] NF parallax

parallèle [paʀalɛl] [1] ADJ [a] (Géom, Math) parallel (à to) → **barre** [b] (= comparable) parallel, similar; [enquêtes] parallel; **mener une action ~** to take similar action, act on ou along the same lines; **les deux institutions ont suivi une évolution ~** the two institutions have developed in parallel [c] (= non officiel) [marché, cours, police, économie] unofficial; [énergie, société, médecine] alternative; [diplomatie] parallel, unofficial [d] (= indépendant) [univers] parallel; (Ordin) [machine, traitement] parallel; (Comm) **circuits ~s de distribution** parallel distribution circuits; (dans un couple) **nous menons des vies ~s** we lead (two) separate lives; **nous avons développé des activités ~s** we've developed some activities in parallel

[2] NF (Math) parallel (line); (Élec) **monté en ~** wired (up) in parallel

[3] NM (Géog, fig) parallel; **~ de latitude** parallel of latitude; **établir un ~ entre deux textes** to draw a parallel between two texts; **faire ou mettre en ~** [+ choses opposées] to compare; [+ choses semblables] to draw a parallel between; **avancer en ~** [projets] to move along at the same pace; **une exposition était organisée en ~ (à sa visite)** an exhibition was set up to run in parallel (with his visit) ou concurrently (with his visit); **elle suit des cours en ~ à son travail** she's doing a course at the same time as working

parallèlement [paʀalɛlmɑ̃] ADV (lit) parallel (à to); (fig) (= ensemble) in parallel; (= en même temps) at the same time; (= similairement) in the same way

parallélépipède [paʀalelepipɛd] NM parallelepiped

parallélépipédique [paʀalelepipedik] ADJ parallelepipedal, parallelepipedic

parallélisme [paʀalelism] NM (lit, fig) parallelism; (Aut) wheel alignment; **faire vérifier le ~ de ses roues** to have one's wheels aligned

parallélogramme [paʀalelɔgʀam] NM parallelogram

paralympiques [paʀalɛ̃pik] ADJ, NMPL **les Jeux ~ les Paralympiques** the Paralympics

paralysant, e [paʀalizɑ̃, ɑ̃t] ADJ paralyzing

paralysé, e [paʀalize] (ptp de **paralyser**) [1] ADJ paralyzed; **rester ~** to be left paralyzed; **il est ~ des jambes** his legs are paralyzed; [aéroport] **~ par le brouillard** fogbound; **~ par la neige** snowbound; **~ par la grève** [gare] strikebound; [hôpital] crippled by a strike [2] NM,F paralytic

paralyser [paʀalize] ▸ conjug 1 ◂ VT (Méd, fig) to paralyze

paralysie [paʀalizi] NF (Méd, fig) paralysis; (Bible) palsy; **~ infantile** infantile paralysis; **~ générale (progressive)** general paralysis of the

insane; **être frappé de ~** to be struck down with paralysis

paralytique [paʀalitik] ADJ, NMF paralytic

paramécie [paʀamesi] NF paramecium

paramédical, e (mpl -aux) [paʀamedikal, o] ADJ paramedical

paramètre [paʀamɛtʀ] NM parameter

paramétrer [paʀametʀe] ▸ conjug 1 ◂ VT to define, parametrize

paramilitaire [paʀamilitɛʀ] ADJ paramilitary

parangon [paʀɑ̃gɔ̃] NM paragon; **~ de vertu** paragon of virtue

parano* [paʀano] [1] ADJ, NMF ABRÉV = **paranoïaque** [2] NF ABRÉV = **paranoïa**

paranoïa [paʀanɔja] NF paranoia

paranoïaque [paʀanɔjak] ADJ, NMF paranoiac, paranoid

paranoïde [paʀanɔid] ADJ paranoid

paranormal, e (mpl -aux) [paʀanɔʀmal, o] ADJ paranormal; **le ~** the paranormal

parapente [paʀapɑ̃t] NM (= engin) paraglider; (= sport) **le ~** paragliding; **faire du ~** to go paragliding; **~ à ski** paraskiing, parapenting

parapentiste [paʀapɑ̃tist] NMF paraglider; **~ à ski** paraskier

parapet [paʀapɛ] NM parapet

parapharmacie [paʀafaʀmasi] NF personal hygiene products (sold in pharmacies)

paraphe [paʀaf] NM (= trait) paraph, flourish; (= initiales) initials; (littér = signature) signature

parapher [paʀafe] ▸ conjug 1 ◂ VT (Admin) to initial; (littér = signer) to sign

parapheur [paʀafœʀ] NM signature book

paraphrase [paʀafʀaz] NF paraphrase; **faire de la ~** to paraphrase

paraphraser [paʀafʀaze] ▸ conjug 1 ◂ VT to paraphrase

paraphrastique [paʀafʀastik] ADJ paraphrastic

paraplégie [paʀapleʒi] NF paraplegia

paraplégique [paʀapleʒik] ADJ, NMF paraplegic

parapluie [paʀaplɥi] NM umbrella; **~ atomique ou nucléaire** nuclear shield ou umbrella; (fig) **ouvrir le ~** to take cover (from criticism)

parapsychique [paʀapsiʃik] ADJ parapsychological

parapsychologie [paʀapsikɔlɔʒi] NF parapsychology

parapsychologue [paʀapsikɔlɔg] NMF parapsychologist

parapublic, -ique [paʀapyblik] ADJ (= semi-public) semi-public

parascolaire [paʀaskɔlɛʀ] ADJ extracurricular; **l'édition ~** ◊ **le ~** educational publishing (excluding textbooks)

parasismique [paʀasismik] ADJ earthquake-resistant

parasitage [paʀazitaʒ] NM [discussion, situation] interference (de in, with)

parasitaire [paʀazitɛʀ] ADJ [activités] parasitic(al)

parasite [paʀazit] [1] NM (Bot, Vét) parasite; (péj = personne) parasite, sponger*, scrounger* [2] **parasites** NMPL (= électricité statique) atmospherics, static; (Radio, TV) interference [3] ADJ parasitic(al); (Radio, TV) **bruits ~s** interference; (électricité statique) atmospherics, static

parasiter [paʀazite] ▸ conjug 1 ◂ VT (Bot, Vét) to live as a parasite on; (Radio, TV) to cause interference on; (fig) to interfere with, get in the way of

parasitique [paʀazitik] ADJ parasitic(al)

parasitisme [paʀazitism] NM parasitism

parasitose [paʀazitoz] NF parasitosis

parasol [paʀasɔl] NM [plage] beach umbrella,

parasol; [*café, terrasse*] sunshade, parasol; (†
= *ombrelle*) parasol, sunshade → **pin**

parasympathique [paʀasɛ̃patik] ADJ parasympathetic

parataxe [paʀataks] NF parataxis

parathyroïde [paʀatiʀɔid] NF parathyroid
(gland)

paratonnerre [paʀatɔnɛʀ] NM lightning conductor

paratyphique [paʀatifik] ADJ paratyphoid

paratyphoïde [paʀatifɔid] NF paratyphoid fever

paravent [paʀavɑ̃] NM folding screen *ou* partition; (*fig*) screen

parbleu †† [paʀblø] EXCL by Jove!* †

parc [paʀk] **1** NM **a** (= *jardin public*) park;
[*château*] grounds; (*Mil* = *entrepôt*) depot
b (*Écon* = *ensemble*) stock; **~ automobile**
[*pays*] number of vehicles on the road;
[*entreprise*] fleet; **~ immobilier/locatif** housing/
rental stock; **~ ferroviaire** rolling stock; **~ nucléaire** nuclear installations; **le ~ français des
ordinateurs individuels** the total number of
personal computers owned in France; **la ville
dispose d'un ~ hôtelier de 7 000 chambres** the
town has a total of 7,000 hotel rooms
2 COMP ► **parc à l'anglaise** landscaped
garden ► **parc animalier** safari park ► **parc
d'attractions** amusement park ► **parc à
bébé** playpen ► **parc à bestiaux** cattle pen
ou enclosure ► **parc des expositions** exhibition centre ► **parc à la française** formal
(French) garden ► **parc à huîtres** oyster bed
► **parc industriel** industrial estate (*Brit*) *ou*
park ► **parc de loisirs** leisure park ► **parc
à moules** mussel bed ► **parc à moutons**
sheep pen, sheepfold ► **parc national** national park ► **parc naturel** nature reserve
► **parc récréatif** amusement park ► **parc
régional** country park ► **parc scientifique**
science park ► **parc de stationnement** car
park (*Brit*), parking lot (*US*) ► **parc à thème**
theme park ► **parc zoologique** zoological
gardens

parcage [paʀkaʒ] NM [*moutons*] penning;
[*voitures*] parking

parcellaire [paʀselɛʀ] ADJ (*fig* = *fragmentaire*)
[*plan, travail*] fragmented

parcelle [paʀsɛl] NF fragment, particle, bit;
(*sur un cadastre*) parcel (of land); **~ de terre**
plot of land; **~ de vérité/bon sens** grain of
truth/commonsense; **il n'y a pas la moindre ~
de vérité dans ce que tu dis** there's not a
grain *ou* scrap of truth in what you say; **une ~
de bonheur/gloire** a bit of happiness/fame

parcellisation [paʀselizasjɔ̃] NF [*tâche*] breakdown into individual operations; [*terrain*] dividing up, division

parcelliser [paʀselize] ▶ conjug 1 ◀ VT [+ *tâche*]
to break down into individual operations; [+
terrain] to divide up

parce que [paʀs(ə)kə] CONJ because; **Robert,
de mauvaise humeur ~ fatigué, répondit ...**
Robert, who was in a bad mood because he
was tired, replied ...; **pourquoi n'y vas-tu pas ?
— ~ !** why aren't you going? — because!

parchemin [paʀʃəmɛ̃] NM parchment; (*hum*;
Univ) diploma, degree

parcheminé, e [paʀʃəmine] ADJ (*ptp de* **parcheminer**) [*peau*] wrinkled; [*visage*] wizened

parcheminer [paʀʃəmine] ▶ conjug 1 ◀ VT to
give a parchment finish to **2 se parcheminer** VPR to wrinkle up

parcimonieusement [paʀsimɔnjøzmɑ̃] ADV
parsimoniously, sparingly

parcimonieux, -ieuse [paʀsimɔnjø, jøz] ADJ
[*personne*] parsimonious; [*distribution*] miserly,
ungenerous

par-ci par-là [paʀsipaʀla] ADV (*espace*) here
and there; (*temps*) now and then, from time
to time; **elle mangeait un yaourt par-ci, une**

---

pomme par-là she'd eat the odd yoghurt or
apple; **avec lui, c'est toujours ma maison par-
ci, ma voiture par-là** with him it's always my
house this, my car that; **il m'agace avec ses
bien sûr par-ci, bien sûr par-là** he gets on my
nerves saying "of course" all the time

parcmètre [paʀkmɛtʀ], **parcomètre** [paʀkɔ-
mɛtʀ] NM (parking) meter

parcotrain [paʀkotʀɛ̃] NM train users' car
park (*Brit*) *ou* parking lot (*US*)

parcourir [paʀkuʀiʀ] ▶ conjug 11 ◀ VT **a** [+
trajet, distance] to cover, travel; [+ *lieu*] to go
all over; [+ *pays*] to travel up and down; **ils
ont parcouru toute la région en un mois** they
travelled the length and breadth of the region *ou* they covered the whole region in a
month; **~ la ville à la recherche de qch** to
search for sth all over (the) town, scour the
town for sth; **leurs navires parcourent les mers**
their ships sail all over; **un frisson parcourut
tout son corps** a shiver ran through his body;
le ruisseau parcourt toute la vallée the stream
runs along *ou* through the whole valley *ou*
right along the valley; **l'obus parcourut le ciel**
the shell flew through *ou* across the sky **b** (=
regarder rapidement) [+ *lettre, livre*] to glance *ou*
skim through; **il parcourut la foule des yeux**
he cast *ou* ran his eye over the crowd

parcours [paʀkuʀ] **1** NM **a** (= *distance*) distance; (= *trajet*) journey; (= *itinéraire*) route;
[*fleuve*] course; **le prix du ~** the fare
b (*Sport*) course; **sur un ~ difficile** over a difficult course; **~ de golf** (= *terrain*) golf course;
(= *partie, trajet*) round of golf; **faire *ou*
accomplir un ~ sans faute** (*Équitation*) to have
a clear round; (*dans un jeu télévisé*) to get all
the answers right; **jusqu'à présent, il a réussi
un ~ sans faute** (*dans sa carrière etc*) up to
now, he hasn't put a foot wrong → **accident,
incident**
c (= *activités, progression*) **son ~ politique/
scolaire** his political/school career; **son ~ professionnel** his career path; **son ~ d'écrivain n'a
pas toujours été facile** making a career as a
writer has not always been easy for him
2 COMP ► **parcours du combattant** (*Mil*)
assault course; (*fig*) obstacle course; (*Mil*) **faire
le ~ du combattant** to go round an assault
course ► **parcours de santé** fitness trail

par-delà [paʀdəla] PRÉP [+ *dans l'espace*] beyond; [+ *dans le temps*] across; **~ les
montagnes/les mers** beyond the mountains/
the seas; **~ le temps/les années** across time/
the years; **~ les querelles, la solidarité demeure**
there is a feeling of solidarity which goes
beyond the quarrels

par-derrière [paʀdɛʀjɛʀ] **1** PRÉP (round) behind, round the back of **2** ADV [*passer*]
round the back; [*attaquer, emboutir*] from behind, from the rear; [*être endommagé*] at the
back *ou* rear; [*se boutonner*] at the back; **dire
du mal de qn ~** to speak ill of sb behind their
back

par-dessous [paʀd(ə)su] PRÉP, ADV under-
(neath) → **jambe**

par-dessus [paʀd(ə)sy] **1** PRÉP (over the top
of); **il a mis un pullover ~ sa chemise** he has
put a pullover over *ou* on top of his shirt;
sauter ~ une barrière/un mur to jump over a
barrier/a wall; **~ tout** above all; **en avoir ~ la
tête*** to be fed up to the back teeth*; **j'en ai ~
la tête de toutes ces histoires** I'm sick and
tired* of *ou* I'm fed up to the back teeth* with
all this; **~ le marché** on top of all that; **~ bord**
overboard → **jambe 2** ADV over (the top)

pardessus [paʀdəsy] NM overcoat

par-devant [paʀd(ə)vɑ̃] **1** PRÉP (*Jur*) **~ notaire**
in the presence of *ou* before a lawyer **2** ADV
[*passer*] round the front; [*attaquer, emboutir*]
from the front; [*être abîmé, se boutonner*] at
the front; **il te fait des compliments ~ puis dit
du mal de toi par-derrière** he pays you com-

---

pliments to your face but says nasty things
about you behind your back

par-devers [paʀdəvɛʀ] PRÉP (*Jur*) before; (*frm*)
~ soi (= *en sa possession*) in one's possession

pardi † [paʀdi] EXCL by Jove!* †

pardieu †† [paʀdjø] EXCL by Jove!* ††

pardon [paʀdɔ̃] NM **a** (= *grâce*) forgiveness,
pardon (*frm, Jur*)
b (*Rel*) (*en Bretagne*) pardon (*religious festival*); (= *fête juive*) **le Grand ~ ◊ le jour du
Pardon** the Day of Atonement
c (*: *intensif*) **et puis ~!** **il travaille dur** he
works hard, I'm telling you *ou* I can tell you!;
je suis peut-être un imbécile mais alors lui, ~!
maybe I'm stupid but he's even worse! *ou* he
takes the biscuit!* (*Brit*) *ou* cake!* (*US*); **j'ai une
belle voiture mais alors celle de mon frère, ~!**
I've got a nice car but wow*, you should see
my brother's!; **elle a un œil au beurre noir, ~!**
she's got one hell of a black eye!*, she's got a
real shiner!*
d (*loc*) **demander ~ à qn d'avoir fait qch** to
apologize to sb for doing *ou* having done sth;
demande ~! say you're sorry!; (**je vous demande**) **~** (I'm) sorry, excuse me; **c'est Maud
— ~?** it's Maud — (I beg your) pardon? *ou*
(I'm) sorry?; **t'es débile* — ~?** you're a mor-
on* — I beg your pardon?; **~ Monsieur, avez-
vous l'heure?** excuse me, have you got the
time?; **tu n'y es pas allé — (je te demande
bien)~ j'y suis allé ce matin** you didn't go —
oh yes I did, I went this morning

pardonnable [paʀdɔnabl] ADJ pardonable,
forgivable, excusable; **il l'a oublié mais c'est ~**
he can be forgiven *ou* excused for forgetting
it, he has forgotten it but you have to forgive
ou excuse him

▼ **pardonner** [paʀdɔne] ▶ conjug 1 ◀ **1** VT [+
péché] to forgive, pardon; [+ *indiscrétion*] to
forgive, excuse; **~ (à) qn** to forgive sb; **~ qch à
qn/à qn d'avoir fait qch** to forgive sb for sth/
for doing sth; **pour se faire ~ son erreur** so as
to be forgiven for his mistake; **pardonnez-moi
de vous avoir dérangé** I'm sorry to have disturbed you, excuse me for disturbing you;
vous êtes tout pardonné I'll let you off,
you're forgiven; **on lui pardonne tout** he gets
away with everything; **je ne me le pardonne-
rai jamais** I'll never forgive myself; **ce genre
d'erreur ne se pardonne pas** this is an unforgivable *ou* inexcusable mistake; **pardonnez-
moi, mais je crois que ...** excuse me but I
think that ...; (*Bible*) **pardonnez-leur car ils ne
savent pas ce qu'ils font** forgive them, for
they know not what they do → **faute**
2 VI to forgive; **il faut savoir ~** you have to
forgive and forget; (*fig*) **c'est une maladie/une
erreur qui ne pardonne pas** it's a fatal illness/
mistake

paré, e [paʀe] (*ptp de* **parer²**) ADJ (= *prêt*) ready,
all set; (= *préparé*) prepared; **être ~ contre le
froid** to be prepared for the cold weather

pare-avalanches [paʀavalɑ̃ʃ] NM INV avalanche barrier

pare-balles [paʀbal] **1** ADJ INV bulletproof
2 NM INV bullet shield

pare-boue [paʀbu] NM INV mud flap

pare-brise NM INV, **parebrise** NM [paʀbʀiz]
windscreen (*Brit*), windshield (*US*)

pare-chocs [paʀʃɔk] NM INV (*Aut*) bumper
(*Brit*), fender (*US*); **avancer ~ contre ~** to be
bumper to bumper

pare-éclats [paʀekla] **1** ADJ INV **gilet ~** flak
jacket **2** NM INV (*Mil*) traverse

pare-étincelles [paʀetɛ̃sɛl] NM INV fireguard

pare-feu [paʀfø] NM INV [*forêt*] firebreak, fire
line; [*foyer*] fireguard

parégorique [paʀegɔʀik] ADJ, NM paregoric
→ **élixir**

▼ **pareil, -eille** [paʀej] **1** ADJ **a** (= *identique*)
the same, similar, alike (*attrib*); **il n'y en a pas
deux ~s** no two are the same *ou* alike; **~**

que ◊ **~ à** the same as, similar to, just like; **comment va-t-elle? — c'est toujours ~** how is she? — (she's) just the same (as ever) *ou* there's no change (in her); **c'est toujours ~, il ne peut pas être à l'heure** it's always the same, he's never on time; **il est ~ à lui-même** he doesn't change, he's the same as ever; **tu as vu son sac? j'en ai un ~/presque ~** have you seen her bag? I've got one the same *ou* one just like it/one very similar *ou* almost identical; (*littér*) **à nul autre ~** peerless (*littér*), unrivalled, unmatched; **l'an dernier à pareille époque** this time last year

2 (= *tel*) such (a); **je n'ai jamais entendu ~ discours** *ou* **un discours ~** I've never heard such a speech *ou* a speech like it; **en ~ cas** in such a case; **en pareille occasion** on such an occasion; **à pareille heure, il devrait être debout** he ought to be up at this hour; **se coucher à une heure pareille!** what a time to be going to bed!

2 NM,F **nos ~s** (= *nos semblables*) our fellow men; (= *nos égaux*) our equals *ou* peers; **je ne retrouverai jamais son ~** (*chose*) I'll never find another one like it; (*employé*) I'll never find another one like him *ou* to match him; **ne pas avoir son ~** (*ou* **sa pareille**) to be second to none; **il n'a pas son ~ pour faire la mayonnaise** no-one makes mayonnaise as well as he does; **vous et vos ~s** you and your kind, people like you; **sans ~** unparalleled, unequalled; **c'est du ~ au même*** it doesn't make the slightest difference, it comes to the same thing, it makes no odds → **rendre**

3 ADV* [*s'habiller*] the same, in the same way, alike; **faire ~** to do the same thing (**que** as)

▼ **pareillement** [paʀɛjmɑ̃] ADV (= *de la même manière*) [*s'habiller*] in the same way (**à** as); (= *également*) likewise, also, equally; **cela m'a surpris** it surprised me also *ou* too; **~ heureux** equally happy; **mon père va bien et ma mère ~** my father is well and so is my mother *ou* and my mother too; **à vous ~!** the same to you!

parement [paʀmɑ̃] NM (*Constr, Couture*) facing

parenchyme [paʀɑ̃ʃim] NM parenchyma

parent, e [paʀɑ̃, ɑ̃t] **1** ADJ related **2** NM,F **a** (= *personne apparentée*) relative, relation; **être ~ de qn** to be related to *ou* a relative of sb; **nous sommes ~s par alliance/par ma mère** we are related by marriage/on my mother's side; **~s en ligne directe** blood relations; **~s proches** close relations *ou* relatives; **~s et amis** friends and relations *ou* relatives; **nous ne sommes pas ~s** we aren't related; (*fig*) **~ pauvre** poor relation (**de** to) **b** (*Bio*) parent; **~ isolé** *ou* **unique** single *ou* lone parent **3 parents** NMPL (= *père et mère*) parents; (*littér* = *ancêtres*) ancestors, forefathers; **les devoirs des ~s** parental duties; **accompagné de l'un de ses ~s** accompanied by one parent *ou* one of his parents; **nos premiers ~s** our first parents, Adam and Eve

parental, e (*mpl* **-aux**) [paʀɑ̃tal, o] ADJ parental; **retrait d'autorité ~e** loss of parental rights; **participation ~e** parental involvement

parenté [paʀɑ̃te] NF (= *rapport*) relationship, kinship; (= *ensemble des parents*) relations, relatives; **degré de ~** degree of relationship; **ils se sont découvert une lointaine ~** they found out they were distantly related; **ces deux langues n'ont aucune ~** these two languages are not in any way related *ou* have no common roots → **lien**

parenthèse [paʀɑ̃tɛz] NF (= *digression*) parenthesis, digression; (= *signe*) parenthesis, bracket (*Brit*); (*lit*) **ouvrir/fermer la ~** to open/close the parentheses *ou* brackets (*Brit*); (*fig*) **ouvrir une ~** to digress, make a digression; **je me permets d'ouvrir une ~ pour dire ...** may I interrupt *ou* digress for a moment to say ...; (*fig*) **je ferme la ~ ...** (but) to get back to the subject ...; **mettre qch entre ~s** to put sth in *ou* between parentheses *ou* brackets (*Brit*); **en-**

tre ~s (*lit*) in parentheses *ou* brackets (*Brit*); (*fig*) incidentally, in parenthesis; **il vaut mieux mettre cet aspect entre ~s** it would be better to leave that aspect aside; **entre ~s, ce qu'il dit est faux** by the way, what he says is wrong; **par ~** incidentally, in passing; **soit dit par ~, elle aurait mieux fait de rester** it could *ou* let it be said incidentally *ou* in passing that she would have done better to stay

parenthétisation [paʀɑ̃tetizasjɔ̃] NF parenthesizing, bracketing (*Brit*)

paréo [paʀeo] NM pareo

parer¹ [paʀe] ▶conjug 1 ◀ **1** VT **a** (= *orner*) [+ *chose*] to adorn, bedeck; [+ *personne*] to adorn, deck out (**de** with); **robe richement parée** richly trimmed *ou* ornamented dress; (*fig*) **~ qn de toutes les vertus** to attribute every virtue to sb **b** (= *préparer*) [+ *viande*] to dress, trim; [+ *cuir*] to dress **2 se parer** VPR (*littér* = *se faire beau*) to put on all one's finery; **se ~ de** [+ *bijoux*] to adorn o.s. with; [+ *robe*] to attire o.s. in; (*péj*) [+ *faux titre*] to assume, invest o.s. with; (*fig*) **se ~ des plumes du paon** to take all the credit (for o.s.)

parer² [paʀe] ▶conjug 1 ◀ **1** VT (= *se protéger de*) [+ *coup*] to stave off, fend off; (*Boxe, Escrime*) to parry; (*Ftbl*) [+ *tir*] to deflect; (*fig*) [+ *attaque*] to stave off, parry **2 parer à** VT INDIR **a** (= *remédier*) [+ *inconvénient*] to deal with, remedy, overcome; [+ *danger*] to ward off **b** (= *pourvoir à*) [+ *éventualité*] to prepare for, be prepared for; **~ au plus pressé** to attend to the most urgent things first; **il faut ~ au plus pressé** first things first; (*Naut*) **paré à virer!** about ship!; **paré? alors on s'en va!** ready? off we go!

pare-soleil [paʀsɔlɛj] NM INV [*voiture*] sun visor; (*Archit*) sun screen

paresse [paʀɛs] NF [*personne*] laziness, idleness; (= *péché*) sloth; **~ intellectuelle** *ou* **d'esprit** intellectual *ou* mental laziness; **il est enclin à la ~** he tends to be lazy; **c'est une solution de ~** it's the lazy way out; (*Méd*) **~ intestinale** sluggishness of the digestive system

paresser [paʀese] ▶conjug 1 ◀ VI to laze about *ou* around; **~ au lit** to laze in bed

paresseusement [paʀesøzmɑ̃] ADV (= *avec indolence*) lazily; (= *avec lenteur*) sluggishly, slowly

paresseux, -euse [paʀesø, øz] **1** ADJ [*personne*] lazy, idle; [*allure, pose*] lazy; [*esprit*] slow; [*fleuve*] lazy, sluggish; **~ comme une couleuvre*** *ou* **un loir*** *ou* **un lézard*** thoroughly lazy, bone-idle* (*Brit*); **il est ~ pour se lever** he's not very good at getting up **2** NM,F lazy *ou* idle person, lazybones* **3** NM (*Zool*) sloth

parfaire [paʀfɛʀ] ▶conjug 60 ◀ VT [+ *travail*] to perfect, bring to perfection; [+ *connaissances*] to perfect, round off; [+ *décor, impression*] to complete, put the finishing touches to; [+ *somme*] to make up

parfait, e [paʀfɛ, ɛt] (*ptp de* **parfaire**) **1** ADJ **a** (= *impeccable*) [*travail, condition, exemple, crime*] perfect; [*exécution, raisonnement*] perfect, flawless; [*manières*] perfect, faultless → **filer**

b (= *absolu*) [*bonne foi, tranquillité*] complete, total, perfect; [*ressemblance*] perfect; **il a été d'une discrétion ~e** *ou* **~ de discrétion** (*frm*) he has shown absolute discretion, he has been the soul of discretion; **dans la plus ~e ignorance** in total *ou* utter *ou* complete ignorance; **en ~ accord avec** in perfect *ou* total agreement with; **en ~e harmonie** in perfect harmony

c (= *accompli, achevé*) [*élève, employé*] perfect; (*péj*) [*crétin, crapule*] utter, perfect; **le type même du ~ mari** the epitome of the perfect husband; **~ homme du monde** perfect gentleman **d** (= *à son plein développement*) [*fleur, insecte*] perfect → **accord, gaz, nombre**

e (= *très bon*) **(c'est) ~!** (that's) perfect! *ou* excellent! *ou* great!*; (*iro*) (that's) marvellous!

ou great!*; **vous refusez? (voilà qui est) ~, vous l'aurez voulu!** you won't? (that's) fine — it's up to you!; **vous avez été ~!** you were fantastic!

2 NM **a** (*Culin*) parfait; **~ au café** coffee parfait **b** (*Ling*) perfect

parfaitement [paʀfɛtmɑ̃] ADV **a** (= *très bien*) [*connaître*] perfectly; **je comprends ~** I quite understand, I understand perfectly **b** (= *tout à fait*) [*heureux, clair, exact*] perfectly, quite; [*hermétique, étanche*] completely; [*idiot*] utterly, absolutely, perfectly; **cela m'est ~ égal** it makes absolutely no difference to me, it's all the same to me; **vous avez ~ le droit de le garder** you have a perfect right to keep it, you're perfectly entitled to keep it **c** (= *certainement*) (most) certainly; **tu as fait ce tableau tout seul? — ~!** you did this picture all on your own? — I (most) certainly did! *ou* I did indeed!; **tu ne vas pas partir sans moi! — ~!** you're not going to leave without me! — oh yes you indeed I am!; **je refuse d'obéir, ~, et j'en suis fier** yes, I'm refusing to obey, and I'm proud of it

parfois [paʀfwa] ADV (= *dans certains cas*) sometimes; (= *de temps en temps*) sometimes, occasionally, at times; **~ je lis, ~ je sors** sometimes I (may) read *ou* I'll read, other times I (may) go out *ou* I'll go out; **il y a ~ du brouillard en hiver** occasionally *ou* sometimes there's fog in winter

parfum [paʀfœ̃] NM **a** (= *substance*) perfume, scent, fragrance **b** (= *odeur*) [*fleur, herbe*] scent; [*tabac, vin, café*] aroma; [*glace*] flavour (*Brit*), flavor (*US*); [*savon*] scent, fragrance; [*fruit*] smell; (*fig: littér*) [*louanges, vertu*] odour (*Brit*), odor (*US*); (*fig*) **ceci a un ~ de scandale/d'hérésie** that has a whiff of scandal/of heresy about it **c** (*loc*) **être au ~*** to be in the know*; **mettre qn au ~*** to put sb in the picture*, give sb the lowdown*

parfumé, e [paʀfyme] (*ptp de* **parfumer**) ADJ [*papier à lettres, savon*] scented; [*air, fleur*] fragrant, sweet-smelling; [*vin, fruit*] fragrant; [*huile*] aromatic; [*bougie*] perfumed, scented; **elle est trop ~e** she's wearing too much scent; **~ au citron** [*glace*] lemon-flavour(ed) (*Brit*), lemon-flavor(ed) (*US*); [*savon*] lemon-scented

parfumer [paʀfyme] ▶conjug 1 ◀ **1** VT [+ *pièce, air*] [*fleurs*] to perfume, scent; [*café, tabac*] to fill with its aroma; [+ *mouchoir*] to put scent *ou* perfume on; (*Culin*) to flavour (*Brit*), flavor (*US*) (**à** with); **pour ~ votre linge** to make your linen smell nice; **vous voulez que je vous parfume?** would you like to try some perfume? **2 se parfumer** VPR to use *ou* wear perfume *ou* scent; **elle se parfuma rapidement** she quickly put *ou* dabbed some perfume *ou* scent on

parfumerie [paʀfymʀi] NF (= *usine, industrie*) perfumery; (= *boutique*) perfume shop; (= *rayon*) perfumery (department); (= *produits*) perfumery, perfumes, fragrances

parfumeur, -euse [paʀfymœʀ, øz] NM,F perfumer

pari [paʀi] NM bet, wager; (*Sport*) bet; (= *activité*) betting; **faire/tenir un ~** to make *ou* lay/take up a bet; **~ mutuel (urbain)** ≈ tote, ≈ parimutuel; (*fig*) **les ~s sont ouverts** there's no knowing, it's anyone's guess*; (*fig*) **c'est un ~ sur l'avenir** it's a gamble on the future; **je tiens le ~!** you're on!; **il avait dit qu'il arriverait premier — tenu!** he said he would come first and so he did! *ou* and he managed it! *ou* and he pulled it off!

> **PMU**

The **PMU** *("pari mutuel urbain") is a government-regulated network of horse-racing betting counters run from bars displaying the* **PMU** *sign. Punters buy fixed-price tickets predicting winners*

> ► GRAMMAIRE ACTIVE: **pareillement** 53.5

or finishing positions. The traditional bet is a triple forecast ("tiercé"), although other multiple forecasts ("quarté", "quarté +", "quinté" etc) are also popular.

paria [parja] NM (social) outcast, pariah; (en Inde) Pariah

parier [parje] ▸conjug 7◂ VT [a] (= gager) to bet, wager; **je (te) parie que c'est lui/tout ce que tu veux** I bet you it's him/anything you like; **tu ne le feras pas — qu'est-ce que tu paries?** you won't do it — what do you bet? ou do you want to bet?; **il y a gros à ~ qu'elle ...** the odds are (that) she ..., ten to one she ...; **je l'aurais parié** I might have known; **tu as faim, je parie** I bet you're hungry [b] (Courses) [+ argent] to bet, lay, stake; **~ 100 F sur le favori** to bet ou lay 100 francs on the favourite; **~ sur un cheval** to bet on a horse, back a horse; **~ gros sur un cheval** to bet heavily on ou lay a big bet on a horse; **~ aux courses** to bet on the races

pariétal, e (mpl **-aux**) [parjetal, o] [1] ADJ (Anat) parietal; (Art) wall (épith) [2] NM parietal bone

parieur, -ieuse [parjœr, jøz] NM,F punter, better

parigot, e* [parigo, ɔt] [1] ADJ Parisian [2] **Parigot(e)** NM,F Parisian

Paris [pari] N Paris

Pâris [paris] NM (Myth) Paris

paris-brest (pl **paris-brests**) [paribrɛst] NM choux pastry ring filled with praline-flavoured cream

parisianisme [parizjanism] NM (= habitude) Parisian habit; (= façon de parler) Parisian way of speaking; (= importance donnée à Paris) Paris bias; **faire du ~** to focus excessively on Paris

parisien, -ienne [parizjɛ̃, jɛn] [1] ADJ (gén) Paris (épith), of Paris; [société, goûts, ambiance] Parisian; **le Bassin ~** the Paris basin; **la région parisienne** the Paris region ou area, the region ou area around Paris; **la vie parisienne** Paris ou Parisian life, life in Paris ⇒ **pain** [2] **Parisien(ne)** NM,F Parisian [3] NM (= pain) long loaf of bread

paritaire [pariter] ADJ [commission] joint (épith), with equal representation of both sides; [représentation] equal

paritarisme [paritarism] NM (Écon) (theory of) co-management

parité [parite] NF parity; **la ~ des changes** exchange parity; **réclamer la ~ ou entre les salaires** to demand equal pay

parjure [parʒyr] [1] ADJ [personne] disloyal; [serment] false [2] NM (= violation de serment) betrayal [3] NMF traitor

parjurer (se) [parʒyre] ▸conjug 1◂ VPR to betray one's oath ou promise

parka [parka] NF parka

parking [parkiŋ] [1] NM car park (Brit), parking lot (US); **~ souterrain/à étages** underground/multistorey car park (Brit) ou parking lot (US); **« ~ gratuit »** "free parking", "free car park" (Brit); **~ payant** ≈ pay and display car park (Brit) ou parking lot (US); **~ sauvage** area used illegally for parking [2] ADJ (péj) dead-end (épith), which leads nowhere (attrib); **section-~** dead-end department; **stage-~** dead-end training course, training course which leads nowhere

Parkinson [parkinsɔn] NM **la maladie de ~** Parkinson's disease

parkinsonien, -ienne [parkinsɔnjɛ̃, jɛn] [1] ADJ associated with Parkinson's disease [2] NM,F patient suffering from Parkinson's disease

parlant, e [parlɑ̃, ɑ̃t] [1] ADJ [a] (= doué de parole) speaking (épith), talking (épith); **il n'est pas très ~** he's not very talkative → **cinéma** [b] (fig) [portrait] lifelike; [comparaison, descrip-

---

tion] graphic, vivid; [exemple] eloquent; [geste, regard] eloquent, meaningful; **les chiffres sont ~s** the figures speak for themselves [2] ADV **scientifiquement/économiquement** etc ~ scientifically/economically etc speaking

parlé, e [parle] (ptp de **parler**) [1] ADJ [langue] spoken → **chaîne, journal** [2] NM (Théât) spoken part

parlement [parləmɑ̃] NM parliament; **le Parlement européen** the European Parliament

parlementaire [parləmɑ̃ter] [1] ADJ (Pol) parliamentary [2] NMF [a] (Pol) member of Parliament; (aux USA) member of Congress; (Hist Brit = partisan) Parliamentarian [b] (= négociateur) negotiator, mediator

parlementairement [parləmɑ̃termɑ̃] ADV parliamentarily

parlementarisme [parləmɑ̃tarism] NM parliamentarism

parlementer [parləmɑ̃te] ▸conjug 1◂ VI (= négocier) to negotiate, parley†; (* = discuter) to argue things over; (hum = palabrer) **~ avec qn** to argue endlessly with sb

▾ **parler** [parle]

▸conjug 1◂
[1] VERBE INTRANSITIF | [2] VERBE TRANSITIF
[3] VERBE TRANSITIF INDIR | INDIR
[5] VERBE PRONOMINAL | [4] VERBE TRANSITIF
 | [6] NOM MASCULIN

[1] VERBE INTRANSITIF
[a] |faculté physique| to talk, speak; **il a commencé à ~ à 2 ans** he started talking when he was 2; **votre perroquet parle?** can your parrot talk?; **~ du nez** to talk through one's nose; **~ distinctement** to speak distinctly; **je n'aime pas sa façon de ~** I don't like the way he talks ou speaks; **parlez plus fort!** speak up!, speak louder! → **dent, façon**
[b] (= exprimer sa pensée) to speak; (= bavarder) to talk; **franc/crûment** to speak frankly/bluntly; **~ bien/mal** to be a good/not to be a (very) good speaker; **~ d'or** to speak words of wisdom; **~ avec les mains** to speak with one's hands; (péj) **~ comme un livre** to talk like a book; **~ par paraboles ou par énigmes** to talk ou speak in riddles; **il aime s'écouter ~** he likes the sound of his own voice; **parlons peu mais parlons bien** let's get straight to the point; **~ pour qn** to speak for sb; (iro) **parle pour toi!** speak for yourself!; (Cartes) **c'est à vous de ~** it's your bid; **au lieu de ~ en l'air, renseigne-toi/agis** don't just talk about it, find out/do something; **plutôt que de ~ en l'air, allons lui demander** instead of talking (wildly) let's go and ask him; **~ à tort et à travers** to blether, talk drivel*, talk through one's hat; **~ pour ne rien dire** to talk for the sake of talking; **voilà qui est (bien) parlé!** hear hear!, well said!; **mais je parle, je parle, et toi, comment vas-tu?** but that's enough about me — how are you (doing)?
[c] fig **~ par gestes** to use sign language; **les faits parlent (d'eux-mêmes)** the facts speak for themselves; **faire ~ la poudre** (= se battre) to start a gunfight; (= faire la guerre) to resort to war; **le devoir a parlé** I (ou he etc) heard the call of duty, duty called; **son cœur a parlé** he heeded the call of his heart
[d] |= révéler les faits| to talk; **faire ~** [+ suspect] to make talk, loosen the tongue of; [+ introverti, timide] to draw out
[e] loc **vous n'avez qu'à ~** just say the word, you've only to say the word; **ne m'en parlez pas!** you're telling me!*, I don't need telling!*; **n'en parlons plus!** let's forget (about) it, let's not mention it again; **sans ~ de ...** not to mention ..., to say nothing of ..., let alone ...; **tu as été dédommagé, non? — parlons-en!** (= ça ne change rien) you've been compensated, haven't you? — some good ou a lot of use that is (to me)!*; (= pas du tout) you've been

---

compensated, haven't you? — not likely!* ou **you must be joking!*; tu parles (Charles)!* ◊ vous parlez!*** (= bien sûr) you're telling me!*, you bet!*; (iro) no chance!*, you must be joking!*; **tu parles ou vous parlez d'une brute!** talk about a brute!; **leur proposition, tu parles si on s'en fiche!*** a fat lot we think of their idea!*; (iro) **tu parles si ça nous aide/si c'est pratique!*** a fat lot of help/use that is!*; **tu peux ~!*** you can talk!*

[2] **parler à** VERBE TRANSITIF INDIR
[a] = converser **~ à qn** to talk ou speak to sb; **il faut que je lui parle** I must talk to him ou have a word with him; **nous ne nous parlons pas** we're not on speaking terms; **moi qui vous parle** I myself; (fig) **trouver à qui ~** to meet one's match; (fig) **c'est ~ à un mur** it's like talking to a (brick) wall
[b] fig **~ aux yeux/à l'imagination** to appeal to the eye/the imagination; **~ au cœur** to speak to the heart; **ce tableau/cette œuvre me parle** this painting/this work really speaks to me

[3] **parler de** VERBE TRANSITIF INDIR
[a] = s'entretenir **~ de qch/qn** to talk about sth/sb; (fig) **~ de la pluie et du beau temps** ◊ **~ de choses et d'autres** to talk about the weather (fig), talk of this and that; **faire ~ de soi** to get o.s. talked about; **~ mal de qn** to speak ill of sb; **on parle beaucoup de lui comme ministre** he's being talked about ou spoken of as a possible ou future minister, he's tipped as a likely minister; **on ne parle que de ça** it's the only topic of conversation, it's the only thing ou that's all people are talking about; **tout le monde en parle** everybody's talking about it; **toute la ville en parle** it's the talk of the town; **il n'en parle jamais** he never mentions it ou refers to it ou talks about it; **nous recevons un immense acteur, je veux ~ bien sûr de Jean Lattu** we'll be welcoming a great actor, I am, of course, referring to Jean Lattu; **et je ne parle pas de ...** not to mention ..., to say nothing of ...; (fig) **de quoi ça parle, ton livre?** — **ça parle de bateaux** what is your book about? — it's about ships ou boats
[b] **~ de qch à qn** to tell sb about sth; **parlez-nous de vos vacances/projets** tell us about your holidays/plans; **on m'avait parlé d'une vieille maison** I had been told about an old house; **je lui parlerai de cette affaire** I'll speak to him ou I'll have a word with him about this business; (= soutenir) **il a parlé de moi au patron** he put in a word for me with the boss; **on m'a beaucoup parlé de vous** I've heard a lot about you
[c] |= annoncer une intention| **~ de faire qch** to talk of doing sth; **elle a parlé d'aller voir un docteur** she has talked of going to see a doctor; **on parle de construire une route** they're talking of building a road, there's talk of a road being built ou of building a road
[d] = évoquer **le jardin lui parlait de son enfance** the garden brought back memories of his childhood (to him); **tout ici me parle de toi** everything here reminds me of you

[4] VERBE TRANSITIF
[a] + langue to speak; **~ (l')anglais** to speak English
[b] **~ politique/affaires** to talk politics/business; **~ boutique*** to talk shop; (hum) **si nous parlions finances?** how about talking cash?*

[5] **se parler** VERBE PRONOMINAL
[a] à soi-même to talk to o.s.; (les uns aux autres) to talk to each other ou one another; **depuis cette querelle, ils ne se parlent plus** they haven't been on speaking terms since that argument
[b] = être parlé **ce dialecte ne se parle plus** this dialect is no longer spoken, nobody speaks this dialect any more

[6] NOM MASCULIN
[a] = manière de parler speech; **le ~ vrai** straight talking; **le ~ de tous les jours** everyday

➤ GRAMMAIRE ACTIVE: parler 46.2, 53.2

speech, common parlance; **il a un ~ vulgaire** he has a coarse way of speaking → **franc[1]**

  [b] = **langue régionale** dialect

parleur [parlœr] NM **beau ~** smooth *ou* glib talker

parloir [parlwar] NM [*école, prison*] visiting room; [*couvent*] parlour (*Brit*), parlor (*US*)

parlot(t)e* [parlɔt] NF chitchat* (*NonC*); **toutes ces ~s ne mènent à rien** all this chitchat* is a waste of time; **c'est de la ~ tout ça** it's all *ou* just talk

Parme [parm] [1] N (= *ville*) Parma [2] NM (**jambon de**) **~** Parma ham [3] ADJ (= *couleur*) **parme** violet

Parmentier [parmãtje] N → **hachis**

parmesan, e [parməzã, an] [1] ADJ Parmesan, of *ou* from Parma [2] **Parmesan(e)** NM,F inhabitant *ou* native of Parma [3] NM (*Culin*) Parmesan (cheese)

parmi [parmi] PRÉP among(st); **~ la foule** among *ou* in the crowd; **venez ici ~ nous** come over here with us; **je passerai ~ vous distribuer les questionnaires** I'll come round and give you each a questionnaire; **c'est un cas ~ d'autres** it's one case among many, it's one of many cases; **qui ~ vous en a entendu parler?** have any of you heard of it?; **personne ~ nous/eux/les victimes** none of us/ them/the victims

Parnasse [parnas] NM Parnassus; **le Mont ~** (Mount) Parnassus

parnassien, -ienne [parnasjɛ̃, jɛn] [1] ADJ, NM,F Parnassian [2] NM (= *papillon*) apollo

parodie [parɔdi] NF parody; (*fig*) **une ~ de procès/de démocratie/d'élection** a travesty of a trial/of democracy/of an election

parodier [parɔdje] ▸ conjug 7 ◂ VT to parody

parodique [parɔdik] ADJ [*style*] parodic(al)

parodiste [parɔdist] NMF parodist

paroi [parwa] NF (*gén, Anat, Bot*) wall; [*récipient*] (inside) surface, (inner) wall; [*véhicule, baignoire*] side; (= *cloison*) partition; **~ rocheuse** rock face

paroisse [parwas] NF parish

paroissial, e [parwasjal, jo] ADJ (*mpl* -**iaux**) parish (*épith*); **église ~e** parish church; **salle ~e** church hall; **à l'échelon ~** at the parochial *ou* parish level

paroissien, -ienne [parwasjɛ̃, jɛn] [1] NM,F parishioner; (*fig*) **un drôle de ~*** a funny customer* [2] NM (= *missel*) prayer book, missal

parole [parɔl] NF [a] (= *mot*) word; **comprenez-vous le sens de ses ~s?** can you understand (the meaning of) what he says?; **assez de ~s, des actes!** that's enough talking, now it's time to act!; **il n'a pas dit une ~ de la soirée** he didn't say a word *ou* open his mouth all evening ▪ (*PROV*) **les ~s s'envolent, les écrits restent** verba volant, scripta manent (*PROV*); (*hum*) **voilà une bonne ~!** that's what I like to hear!; **la ~ de Dieu** ◊ **la bonne ~** the word of God; **porter** *ou* **prêcher la bonne ~** (*lit*) to preach *ou* spread the word of God; (*fig*) to spread the (good) word; **toutes ces belles ~s n'ont convaincu personne** all these fine(-sounding) words failed to convince anybody; **~ célèbre** famous words *ou* saying; **prononcer une ~ historique** to make a historic remark; **ce sont des ~s en l'air** it's just idle talk; **il est surtout courageux en ~s** he's brave enough when it's just a matter of words *ou* talking about it; **tout cela est bien joli en ~s mais ...** it sounds fair enough but ... → **boire, moulin, payer**

  [b] (= *texte*) **~s** [*chanson*] words, lyrics; **histoire sans ~s** wordless cartoon; (*légende*) « **sans ~s** » "no caption"

  [c] (= *promesse*) word; **tenir ~** to keep one's word; **il a tenu ~** he kept his word, he was as good as his word; **c'est un homme de ~** ◊ **il est**

de ~ ◊ **il n'a qu'une ~** he's a man of his word, his word is his bond; **il n'a aucune ~** you (just) can't trust a word he says; **je l'ai cru sur ~** I took his word for it; (**je vous donne** *ou* **vous avez ma**) **~ d'honneur!** I give you *ou* you have my word (of honour)!; **~ de scout/marin** *etc* scout's/sailor's *etc* honour; **manquer à sa ~** to fail to keep one's word, go back on one's word; (*fig*) **ma ~!** (upon) my word!; **tu es fou ma ~!*** heavens - you're mad!; **prisonnier sur ~** prisoner on parole

  [d] (= *faculté d'expression*) speech; **doué de ~** capable of speech; **avoir la ~ facile** to find it easy to talk, have the gift of the gab*; **avoir le don de la ~** to be a gifted speaker ▪ (*PROV*) **la ~ est d'argent, le silence est d'or** speech is silver, silence is golden (*PROV*); **perdre/retrouver la ~** to lose/recover one's speech; (*fig*) to lose/find one's tongue*; **il n'a jamais droit à la ~** he's never allowed to get a word in edgeways → **manquer**

  [e] (*Ling*) speech, parole (*SPÉC*); **acte de ~** speech act

  [f] (*Cartes*) **~!** (I) pass!

  [g] (*dans un débat, une discussion*) **droit de ~** right to speak; **temps de ~** speaking time; **puis-je avoir la ~?** may I say something?; **vous avez la ~** (*gén*) it's your turn to speak; (*au parlement etc*) you have the floor; **je vous rends la ~** back *ou* over to you; **qui veut la ~?** who wants to speak?; **laissez-moi la ~** let me speak; **la ~ est à M. Duval** it's Mr Duval's turn to speak; **passer** *ou* **céder la ~ à qn** to hand over to sb; **demander la ~** to ask to be allowed to speak; **prendre la ~** to speak; **je voudrais prendre la ~ pour dire ...** (*gén*) I'd like to say ...; (*au parlement etc*) I'd like to take the floor to say ...; **pour empêcher la prise de ~ des extrémistes** to prevent extremists from voicing their opinions

parolier, -ière [parɔlje, jɛr] NM,F lyric writer

paronyme [parɔnim] NM paronym

paronymie [parɔnimi] NF paronymy

paronymique [parɔnimik] ADJ paronymic

parotide [parɔtid] NF (**glande**) **~** parotid gland

paroxysme [parɔksism] NM [*maladie*] crisis (point), paroxysm (*SPÉC*); [*crise, sensation, sentiment*] paroxysm, height; **être au ~ de la joie/colère** to be beside o.s. with joy/anger; **le bruit était à son ~** the noise was at its loudest *ou* height; **son désespoir était à son ~** he was in the depths of despair; **l'incendie/la douleur avait atteint son ~** the fire/the pain was at its height *ou* at its fiercest; **la crise avait atteint son ~** the crisis had reached a head *ou* climax

paroxystique [parɔksistik] ADJ (*Méd*) paroxysmal; (= *extrême*) [*émotion, pression*] intense; [*situation, état*] extreme; **au moment le plus ~ de la pièce** at the very climax *ou* climactic moment of the play

parpaillot, e [parpajo, ɔt] NM,F (*Hist, péj*) Protestant

parpaing [parpɛ̃] NM (= *pierre pleine*) perpend, parpen (*US*); (*aggloméré*) breeze-block

Parque [park] NF (*Myth*) **la ~** Fate; **les ~s** the Fates, the Parcae

parquer [parke] ▸ conjug 1 ◂ [1] VT [+ *voiture, artillerie*] to park; [+ *moutons, bétail*] to pen (in *ou* up); [+ *huîtres, moules*] to put in a bed (*ou* beds); (*péj*) [+ *personnes*] to pack in; **on les parquait dans des réserves** they were herded into reservations; **les réfugiés étaient parqués comme des bestiaux** the refugees were cooped up *ou* penned in like animals [2] **se parquer*** VPR (*Aut*) to park

parquet [parke] NM [a] (= *plancher*) (*gén*) wooden floor; (*à chevrons etc*) parquet (floor); **les lattes du ~** the floorboards [b] (*Jur*) **le ~** public prosecutor's department *ou* office [c] (*Bourse*) **le ~** (= *enceinte*) the (dealing) floor; (= *agents*) the stock exchange *ou* market

parqueter [parkəte] ▸ conjug 4 ◂ VT to lay a wooden *ou* parquet floor in; **pièce parquetée** room with a wooden *ou* parquet floor

parrain [parɛ̃] NM [a] (*Rel*) godfather; **accepter d'être le ~ d'un enfant** to agree to be a child's godfather *ou* to stand godfather to a child [b] [*navire*] namer, christener [c] (*qui introduit dans un cercle, un club*) proposer; (*qui aide financièrement*) sponsor; [*entreprise, initiative*] promoter; [*œuvre, fondation*] patron; **un ~ de la Mafia** a godfather in the Mafia

parrainage [parɛnaʒ] NM [a] (= *introduction dans un cercle, un club*) proposing (for membership) [b] (= *aide financière*) sponsorship; [*entreprise, initiative*] promoting; (= *appui moral*) [*œuvre, fondation*] patronage; (= *publicité*) advertising sponsorship [c] [*navire*] naming, christening

parrainer [parɛne] ▸ conjug 1 ◂ VT [a] (= *introduire : dans un cercle, un club*) to propose (for membership); **se faire ~ par qn** to be proposed by sb [b] (= *aider financièrement*) to sponsor; [+ *entreprise, initiative*] to promote; (= *patronner*) [+ *œuvre, fondation, association*] to be the patron of

parricide [parisid] [1] ADJ parricidal [2] NMF parricide [3] NM (= *crime*) parricide

parsec [parsɛk] NM parsec

parsemer [parsəme] ▸ conjug 5 ◂ VT [a] (= *répandre*) **~ de** to sprinkle with, strew with (*littér*); **~ le sol de fleurs** to scatter flowers over the ground, strew the ground with flowers (*littér*); **~ un tissu de paillettes d'or** to sew gold sequins all over a piece of material; **~ un texte de citations** to scatter quotations through a text [b] (= *être répandu sur*) to be scattered *ou* sprinkled over; **les feuilles qui parsèment le gazon** the leaves which are scattered *ou* which lie scattered over the lawn; **ciel parsemé d'étoiles** star-studded sky, sky sprinkled *ou* strewn *ou* studded with stars; **champ parsemé de fleurs** field dotted with flowers; **parsemé de difficultés/fautes** riddled with difficulties/mistakes

parsi, e [parsi] [1] ADJ Parsee [2] NM (*Ling*) Parsee [3] **Parsi(e)** NM,F Parsee

▾**part** [par]
NOM FÉMININ

  [a] dans un partage share; (= *portion*) portion; (= *tranche*) slice; **~ d'héritage/de soucis** his share of the inheritance/of worries; **faire huit ~s dans un gâteau** to cut a cake into eight (slices); **c'est 12 F la ~** it's 12 francs a slice; (*fig*) **vouloir sa ~ du gâteau** to want one's slice *ou* share of the cake; **la ~ du lion** the lion's share; **la ~ du pauvre** (*repas*) portion kept for a poor visitor; (*fig*) the crumbs; **~ à deux!** share and share alike!; **chacun paie sa ~** everyone pays his share, everyone chips in*

  ◆ **faire la part belle à qn** to give sb more than his (*ou* her) due

  ◆ **faire la part de qch** : **faire la ~ de la fatigue/ du hasard** to take tiredness/chance into account, allow for *ou* make allowances for tiredness/chance; **il faut faire la ~ du vrai et du faux dans ce qu'elle dit** you can't believe everything she says; **faire la ~ des choses** to make allowances; (*fig*) **faire la ~ du feu** to cut one's losses

  [b] = **participation** part; (*Sécurité sociale*) **~ patronale/salariale** employer's/worker's contribution; **le hasard n'a eu aucune ~ dans leur rencontre** chance had nothing to do with *ou* played no part in their meeting; **il a pris une ~ importante dans l'élaboration du projet** he played an important part in the development of the project

  ◆ **à part entière** : **membre/citoyen à ~ entière** full member/citizen; **Français à ~ entière** person with full French citizenship, fully-fledged French citizen; **artiste à ~ entière** artist in his (*ou* her) own right; **l'Europe sera le**

▸ **GRAMMAIRE ACTIVE:** **part** 53.5

partenaire à ~ entière des USA Europe will be a fully-committed partner for the USA

♦ **avoir part à** *(littér)* to have a share in

♦ **faire part de qch à qn** to announce sth to sb, inform sb of sth, let sb know *ou* tell sb about sth; **il m'a fait ~ de son inquiétude** he told me how worried he was

♦ **prendre part à** [+ *travail*] to take part in, join in, collaborate in; [+ *frais*] to share in, contribute to; [+ *manifestation*] to join in, take part in; **prendre ~ à un débat** to participate in *ou* take part in a debate; **« prenez ~ au développement de votre ville ! »** "help to develop your town!"; **je prends ~ à vos soucis** I share (in) your worries

    c = *partie* part; **c'est une toute petite ~ de sa fortune** it's only a tiny fraction *ou* part of his fortune; *(Écon)* **~ de marché** market share

♦ **pour une part** partly; **cela explique pour une ~ l'ambiance qui règne ici** this partly explains the atmosphere here; **pour une ~, son attitude s'explique par sa timidité** to some extent, one can put his attitude down to shyness; **pour une bonne** *ou* **large ~** largely, to a great extent; **pour une petite ~** in a small way

    d *Fin* ≈ share *(giving right to participate in profits but not running of firm)*; *(Impôts)* ≈ tax unit; **~ de fondateur** founder's share; **~ d'intérêt** *ou* **sociale** partner's *ou* partnership share

    e expressions figées

♦ **à part** *(= de côté)* aside, on one side; *(= séparément)* separately, on its *(ou* their) own; *(= excepté)* except for, apart from, aside from *(surtout US)*; *(Théât = en aparté)* aside; **nous mettrons ces livres à ~ pour vous** we'll put these books aside *ou* on one side for you; **prendre qn à ~** to take sb aside; **étudier chaque problème à ~** to study each problem separately *ou* on its own; **à ~ vous, je ne connais personne ici** apart from *ou* aside from *ou* except for you I don't know anyone here; **à ~ cela** apart *ou* aside from that, otherwise; **plaisanterie à ~** joking apart *ou* aside *(= exceptionnel)* special, extraordinary; **un cas/une place à ~** a special case/place; **c'est un homme à ~** he's in a class of his own; **il est vraiment à ~** there aren't many like him around → **bande²**, **chambre**

♦ **à part soi** *(ou moi etc) (littér)* garder qch à ~ soi to keep sth to o.s.; **je pensais à ~ moi que ...** I thought to myself that ...

♦ **autre part** somewhere else, elsewhere; **il ne veut plus habiter autre ~** he doesn't want to live anywhere else

♦ **d'autre part** *(= de plus)* moreover; *(= par ailleurs)* on the other hand; **il est beau, et d'autre ~ il est riche** he's handsome, and what's more he's rich; *(= en revanche)* **il n'est pas très doué, d'autre ~ il est travailleur** he's not very talented, but on the other hand he's very hard-working; **d'une ~ ..., d'autre ~ ...** on the one hand ..., on the other hand ...

♦ **de la part de** *(provenance)* from; *(= au nom de)* on behalf of; **je viens de la ~ de Guy** *(il m'a envoyé)* I've been sent by Guy; *(comme porteparole)* I've come *ou* I'm here on behalf of Guy; **de la ~ de qui venez-vous ?** who sent you?; **ça demande un peu de bon sens de la ~ de l'utilisateur** it requires a little commonsense on the part of the user *ou* from the user; **cela m'étonne de sa ~** I'm surprised at that *(coming)* from him; **dites-lui bonjour de ma ~** give him my regards; **c'est gentil de sa ~** that's nice of him; *(Téléc)* **c'est de la ~ de qui ?** who's calling? *ou* speaking?

♦ **de part en part** right through

♦ **de part et d'autre** on both sides, on either side

♦ **de toute(s) part(s)** from all sides *ou* quarters

♦ **en bonne/mauvaise part** : **prendre qch en bonne ~** to take sth in good part; **prendre qch en mauvaise ~** to take sth amiss, take offence at sth

♦ **pour ma** *(ou* **ta** *etc)* **part** as for me *(ou* you *etc)*, for my *(ou* your *etc)* part; **pour ma ~ je pense que ...** I for one think that ... → **nul**, **quelque**

partage [paʀtaʒ] NM **a** *(= fractionnement, division)* [*terrain, surface*] dividing up, division; [*gâteau*] cutting; *(Math)* [*nombre*] factorizing; **faire le ~ de qch** to divide sth up; **le ~ du pays en deux camps** the division of the country into two camps; *(Ordin)* **~ de temps** time sharing; **~ du travail** job sharing → **ligne¹** **b** *(= distribution)* [*butin, héritage*] sharing out; **procéder au ~ de qch** to share sth out; **le ~ n'est pas juste** the way it's shared out isn't fair, it isn't fairly shared out; **j'ai été oublié dans le ~** I've been left out (in the share-out); **quel a été le ~ des voix entre les candidats ?** how were the votes divided between the candidates?; *(Pol)* **en cas de ~ des voix** in the event of a tie in the voting **c** *(= participation)* sharing; **l'enquête a conclu au ~ des responsabilités** the inquiry came to the conclusion that the responsibility was shared; **le ~ du pouvoir avec nos adversaires** the sharing of power with our opponents; *(fig)* **fidélité sans ~** undivided loyalty; **un pouvoir sans ~** absolute power; **régner sans ~** to rule supreme **d** *(= part)* share; *(fig = sort)* portion, lot; **donner/recevoir qch en ~** to give/receive sth in a will; **la maison lui échut en ~** the house came to him in the will; *(fig)* **le bon sens qu'il a reçu en ~** the common sense with which he has been endowed

partagé, e [paʀtaʒe] *(ptp de* **partager***)* ADJ **a** *(= divisé)* [*avis, opinion*] divided; **les experts sont très ~s sur la question** the experts are divided on the question; **~ entre l'amour et la haine** torn between love and hatred **b** *(littér = doté)* endowed; **il est bien/mal ~ par le sort** fate has been/has not been kind to him **c** *(Ordin)* **logiciel ~** shareware → **temps¹**

partageable [paʀtaʒabl] ADJ divisible, which can be shared out *ou* divided up; **frais ~s entre tous** costs that are shared by all; **votre gaieté est difficilement ~** it is difficult to share (in) your happiness

▼ **partager** [paʀtaʒe] ► conjug 3 ◄ **1** VT **a** *(= fractionner)* [+ *terrain, feuille, gâteau*] to divide up; **~ en deux/en deux bouts/par moitié** to divide sth in two/into two pieces *ou* bits/in half **b** *(= distribuer, répartir)* [+ *butin, gâteau*] to share (out); [+ *frais*] to share; **il partage son temps entre son travail et sa famille** he divides his time between his work and his family; **il partage son affection entre plusieurs personnes** several people have to share his affections **c** *(= avoir une part de, avoir en commun)* [+ *héritage, gâteau, appartement, sort*] to share (**avec** with); **voulez-vous ~ notre repas ?** will you share our meal?; **~ le lit de qn** to share sb's bed; **il n'aime pas ~** he doesn't like sharing; **les torts sont partagés** there is fault on both (*ou* all) sides **d** *(= s'associer à)* [+ *sentiments, bonheur, goûts*] to share (in); [+ *opinion, idée*] to share, agree with; **je partage votre douleur/surprise** I share your sorrow/surprise; **amour partagé** mutual love; **c'est une opinion largement partagée** it is an opinion that is widely shared **e** *(= diviser)* to divide; **ce débat partage le monde scientifique** th scientific community is divided over this issue **f** *(frm = douer)* to endow; **la nature l'a bien partagé** nature has been generous to him

    2 se partager VPR **a** *(= se fractionner)* to be divided; **ça peut facilement se ~ en trois/en trois morceaux** it can easily be divided (up) *ou* cut in three/into three pieces *ou* bits; [*vote*] **se ~ entre diverses tendances** to be divided between different groups; **pour lui, le monde se partage en deux** for him, there are two kinds

of people; **à l'endroit où les branches se partagent** where the branches fork *ou* divide; **le reste des voix s'est partagé entre les autres candidats** the remaining votes are distributed *ou* shared among the other candidates; **le pouvoir ne se partage pas** power is not something which can be shared; **il se partage entre son travail et son jardin** he divides his time between his work and his garden **b** *(= se distribuer)* **ils se sont partagé le gâteau** *(lit)* they shared the cake between them *ou* among themselves; *(fig)* they shared it out; **ils se sont partagé le butin** they shared the booty between them; **nous nous sommes partagé le travail** we shared the work between us; **les trois candidats se sont partagé les suffrages** the votes were divided among the three candidates; **se ~ les faveurs du public** to be equally popular

partageur, -euse¹ [paʀtaʒœʀ, øz] ADJ ready *ou* willing to share; **il n'est pas ~** he doesn't like sharing

partageux, -euse²† [paʀtaʒø, øz] NM,F distributionist

partance [paʀtɑ̃s] ♦ **en partance** LOC ADV [*train*] due to leave; [*avion*] outward bound; [*bateau*] sailing *(attrib)*, outward bound; **en ~ pour Londres** [*train, avion*] for London, London *(épith)*; [*bateau*] bound *ou* sailing for London *(attrib)*; [*passager*] (bound) for London *(attrib)*

▼ **partant¹, e** [paʀtɑ̃, ɑ̃t] **1** NM,F **a** *(= coureur)* starter; *(= cheval)* runner; **tous ~s** all horses running; **non-~** non-runner **b** *(= personne)* person leaving, departing traveller *(ou* visitor *etc)*; **les ~s et les arrivants** the departures and arrivals **2** ADJ **je suis ~** count me in; **il est toujours ~ pour un bon repas*** he's always ready for a good meal; **si c'est comme ça, je ne suis plus ~** if that's how it is (you can) count me out

partant² [paʀtɑ̃] CONJ *(littér)* hence, therefore, consequently

partenaire [paʀtənɛʀ] NMF partner; **les ~s sociaux** ≈ unions and management, ≈ management and labour; **il était son ~ dans le film** he played opposite her in the film; **~ sexuel** sexual partner

partenarial, e *(pl* **-iaux)* [paʀtənaʀjal, jo] ADJ [*accord*] partnership, joint; [*négociations*] joint

partenariat [paʀtənaʀja] NM partnership

parterre [paʀtɛʀ] NM **a** *(= plate-bande)* border, (flower)bed; (* = *plancher*) floor **b** *(Théât)* *(= emplacement)* stalls *(Brit)*, orchestra *(US)*; *(= public)* (audience in the) stalls *(Brit)* *ou* orchestra *(US)*

Parthe [paʀt] NM Parthian → **flèche¹**

parthénogenèse [paʀtenoʒenɛz] NF parthenogenesis

parthénogénétique [paʀtenoʒenetik] ADJ parthenogenetic

parthénogénétiquement [paʀtenoʒenetikmɑ̃] ADV parthenogenetically

Parthénon [paʀtenɔ̃] NM **le ~** the Parthenon

parti¹ [paʀti] **1** NM **a** *(= groupe : gén, Pol)* party; **le ~ des mécontents** the malcontents; **le ~ de la défaite** the defeatists; **le ~ (communiste)** the Communist party **b** *(= solution)* option, course of action; **hésiter entre deux ~s** to wonder which of two courses *ou* which course to follow; **prendre un ~** to come to *ou* make a decision, make up one's mind; **prendre le ~ de faire qch** to make up one's mind to do sth, decide *ou* resolve to do sth; **mon ~ est pris** my mind is made up; **crois-tu que c'est le meilleur ~ (à prendre) ?** do you think that's the best course (to take)? *ou* the best idea?; **prendre le ~ de qn** ◊ **prendre ~ pour qn** *(= se mettre du côté de qn)* to side with sb, take sb's side; *(= donner raison à qn)* to stand up for sb; **prendre ~ (dans une affaire)** *(= se rallier)* to take sides (on an issue); *(= dire* *ce qu'on pense*) to take a stand (on an issue); **prendre son ~ de qch** to come to terms with sth, reconcile o.s. to sth; **il faut bien en prendre son ~** you just have to come to terms with it *ou* put up with it

c (= *personne à marier*) match; **beau** *ou* **bon** *ou* **riche ~** good match

d (*loc*) **tirer ~ de** [+ *situation, occasion, information*] to take advantage of, turn to (good) account; [+ *outil, ressources*] to put to (good) use; [+ *victoire*] to take advantage of; **tirer le meilleur ~ possible d'une situation** to turn a situation to best account, get the most one can out of a situation; **il sait tirer ~ de tout** (*situation*) he can turn anything to his advantage, he can make capital out of anything; (*objets*) he can put everything to good use; **faire un mauvais ~ à qn** to beat sb up

2 COMP ► **parti pris** (= *préjugé*) prejudice, bias; **je crois, sans ~ pris ...** I think without bias (on my part) ... *ou* being quite objective about it ...; **juger sans ~ pris** to take an unbiased *ou* objective view; **il est de ~ pris** he's prejudiced *ou* biased; **éviter le ~ pris** to avoid being prejudiced *ou* biased; (= *choix*) **~ pris théorique** theoretical perspective *ou* standpoint; **~ pris artistique/esthétique** artistic/aesthetic choice

---
PARTIS POLITIQUES FRANÇAIS

Among the many active right-wing political parties in France, the most prominent include the Gaullist RPR ("le Rassemblement pour la République"), the UDF ("l'Union pour la démocratie française", a more recent movement founded by Valéry Giscard d'Estaing), and the extreme rightwing Front national (FN). On the left, the Parti socialiste (PS) is the most influential party, though the Parti communiste français (PCF) continues to draw a significant number of votes. Of the numerous ecological parties, Les Verts is the most prominent. → COMMUNISTE ; ÉLECTIONS

parti², e¹ [parti] (*ptp de partir*) ADJ a (* = *ivre*) tipsy, tight*; **il est bien ~** he's had a few*, he's well away* (*Brit*) b (*Hér*) party

partial, e (*mpl* **-iaux**) [parsjal, jo] ADJ biased, prejudiced, partial; **être ~ envers qn** to be biased *ou* prejudiced against sb

partialement [parsjalmɑ̃] ADV in a biased way; **juger qch ~** to take a biased view of sth

partialité [parsjalite] NF (**envers** *ou* **contre qn**) bias (against sb); **faire preuve de ~ envers** *ou* **contre qn** to be unfair to sb, be biased against sb, show bias against sb; **se montrer d'une regrettable ~** to be dreadfully biased

participant, e [partisipɑ̃, ɑ̃t] 1 ADJ participating 2 NM,F (*à un concours, une course*) entrant (**à** in); (*à un débat, un projet*) participant, person taking part (**à** in); (*à une association*) member (**à** of); (*à une cérémonie, un complot*) person taking part (**à** in); **les ~s aux bénéfices** those sharing in the profits; **les ~s à la manifestation/au concours** those taking part in the demonstration/in the competition

participatif, -ive [partisipatif, iv] ADJ **gestion participative** participative management; **prêt ~** participating capital loan; **titre ~** nonvoting share (*in a public sector company*)

participation [partisipasjɔ̃] NF a (= *action*) **~ à** [+ *concours, colloque, cérémonie, entreprise*] taking part in, participation in; [+ *spectacle*] appearance in; [+ *aventure, complot, escroquerie*] involvement in; **la réunion aura lieu sans leur ~** the meeting will take place without their taking part *ou* without them; **peu importe l'habileté: c'est la ~ qui compte** skill doesn't really matter: what counts is taking part *ou* joining in; **il s'est assuré la ~ de deux équilibristes** he has arranged for two tightrope walkers to appear; **c'est la ~ de Marie Vincent qui va attirer les spectateurs** it's Marie Vincent who'll draw the crowds, it's

the fact that Marie Vincent is appearing *ou* performing that will draw the crowds; **ce soir, grand gala avec la ~ de plusieurs vedettes** tonight, grand gala with several star appearances; (*Ciné*) **avec la ~ de Deneuve** with guest appearance by Deneuve, with (special) guest star Deneuve; **~ électorale** turnout at the polls (*Brit*), voter turnout (*US*); **fort/faible taux de ~ électorale** high/low turnout at the polls → **participer**

b (*Écon* = *détention d'actions*) interest; **prise de ~s** acquisition of holdings; **prendre une ~ majoritaire dans une entreprise** to acquire a majority interest in a firm; **la ~ (ouvrière)** worker participation; **~ aux bénéfices** profit-sharing; **~s croisées** cross (share-)holdings; **~ du personnel à la marche d'une entreprise** staff participation *ou* involvement in the running of a firm

c (*financière*) contribution; **~ aux frais: 50 F** contribution towards costs: 50 francs; **nous demandons une petite ~ (de 15 F)** we request a small donation (of 15 francs)

participe [partisip] NM participle; **~ passé/présent** past/present participle

participer [partisipe] ▸conjug 1◂ 1 **participer à** VT INDIR a (= *prendre part à*) [+ *concours, colloque, cérémonie*] to take part in; **je compte ~ au concours/à l'épreuve de fond** I intend to take part in *ou* enter the competition/the long-distance event; **peu d'électeurs ont participé au scrutin** there was a low turnout at the polls, there was a low voter turnout (*US*)

b (= *prendre une part active à*) [+ *entreprise, discussion, jeu*] to participate in, take part in, join in; [+ *spectacle*] [*artiste*] to appear in; [+ *aventure, complot, escroquerie*] to take part in, be involved in; **l'important n'est pas de gagner mais de ~** the important thing is not winning but taking part; **à la joie/au chagrin de qn** to share sb's joy/sorrow; **ils ont participé à l'allégresse générale** they joined in the general happy mood; **on demande aux élèves de ~ davantage pendant le cours** pupils are asked to participate more *ou* take a more active part in class

c (= *payer sa part de*) [+ *frais, dépenses*] to share in, contribute to; **~ (financièrement) à** [+ *entreprise, projet*] to make a (financial) contribution to

d (= *avoir part à*) [+ *profits, pertes, succès*] to share in

2 **participer de** VT INDIR (*littér* = *tenir de*) to partake of (*frm*), have something of the nature of

participial, e (*mpl* **-iaux**) [partisipjal, jo] 1 ADJ participial 2 **participiale** NF participial phrase *ou* clause

particularisation [partikylarizasjɔ̃] NF particularization

particulariser [partikylarize] ▸conjug 1◂ 1 VT to particularize 2 **se particulariser** VPR to be distinguished *ou* characterized (**par** by)

particularisme [partikylarism] NM a (*Pol* = *attitude*) sense of identity; (= *particularité*) **~(s)** specific (local) character (*NonC*), specific characteristic(s); (*Pol, Sociol*) **~s régionaux** regional idiosyncrasies b (*Rel*) particularism

particularité [partikylarite] NF a (= *caractéristique*) [*individu, caractère, religion*] particularity, (distinctive) characteristic; [*texte, paysage*] (distinctive) characteristic *ou* feature; [*appareil, modèle*] (distinctive) feature; **ces modèles ont en commun la ~ d'être ...** these models all have the distinctive feature of being ..., these models are all distinguished by being ...; **cet animal présente la ~ d'être herbivore** a distinctive feature *ou* characteristic of this animal is that it is herbivorous b (†, *littér* = *détail*) particular c (*littér* = *unicité*) particularity

particule [partikyl] NF (*Ling, Phys*) particle; **~ (nobiliaire)** nobiliary particle; **nom à ~** = *name with a "de" usually belonging to a noble family*, ≈ name with a handle; **il a un nom à ~** he has a handle to his name

▼**particulier, -ière** [partikylje, jɛʀ] 1 ADJ a (= *spécifique*) [*aspect, point, exemple*] particular, specific; [*trait, style, manière de parler*] characteristic, distinctive; **dans ce cas ~** in this particular case; **il n'avait pas d'aptitudes particulières** he had no particular *ou* special aptitudes; **cette habitude lui est particulière** this habit is peculiar to him; **signes ~s** (*gén*) distinctive signs; (*sur un passeport*) distinguishing marks

b (= *spécial*) exceptional, special, particular; **la situation est un peu particulière** the situation is rather exceptional; **ce que j'ai à dire est un peu ~** what I have to say is slightly unusual; **cela constitue un cas ~** this is a special *ou* an unusual *ou* an exceptional case; **rien de ~ à signaler** nothing unusual to report; **je l'ai préparé avec un soin tout ~** I prepared it with very special care *ou* with particular care

c (= *étrange*) [*mœurs*] peculiar, odd; [*goût, odeur*] strange, odd; **il a toujours été un peu ~** he has always been a bit peculiar *ou* odd

d (= *privé*) [*voiture, secrétaire, conversation, intérêt*] private; **l'entreprise a son service ~ de livraison** the company has its own delivery service; **intervenir à titre ~** to intervene in a private capacity → **hôtel, leçon**

e **en ~** (= *en privé*) [*parler*] in private; (= *séparément*) [*examiner*] separately; (= *surtout*) in particular, particularly, especially; (= *entre autres choses*) in particular

2 NM a (= *personne*) person; (*Admin, Comm*) private individual; **comme un simple ~** like any ordinary person; (*petites annonces*) **vente/location de ~ à ~** private sale/let (*Brit*) *ou* rental (*US*); (*petite annonce*) **« ~ vend »** "for sale privately", "for private sale"

b (* = *individu*) individual, character; **un drôle de ~** an odd individual *ou* character

c (= *chose*) **le ~** the particular; **du général au ~** from the general to the particular

particulièrement [partikyljɛʀmɑ̃] ADV particularly, especially, specially; **~ bon/évolué** particularly *ou* especially good/well-developed; **je ne le connais pas ~** I don't know him very *ou* particularly well; **il aime tous les arts et tout ~ la peinture** he enjoys all the arts, especially *ou* specially painting; **~ difficile** particularly difficult; **~ drôle** exceptionally funny; **je voudrais plus ~ vous faire remarquer ce détail** I'd particularly like to draw your attention to this detail; **voulez-vous du café? — je n'y tiens pas ~** would you like a coffee? — not particularly *ou* specially

partie² [parti] 1 NF a (= *portion, fraction*) part; (= *quantité*) part, amount; **diviser qch en trois ~s** to divide sth into three parts; **il y a des ~s amusantes dans le film** the film is funny in parts, the film has its funny moments; **il ne possède qu'une ~ du terrain** he only owns part of the land; (*Constr*) **~s communes/privatives** common/privately-owned parts; **une petite ~ de l'argent** a small part *ou* amount of the money; **une grande** *ou* **bonne ~ du travail** a large *ou* good part of *ou* a good deal of the work; **la majeure** *ou* **plus grande ~ du temps/du pays** most of *ou* the greater *ou* the best part of the time/of the country; **la majeure ~ des gens** the majority of people, most people; **la plus grande ~ de ce que l'on vous a dit** most of what you were told; **tout ou ~ de** all or part of; (*TV*) **le film sera diffusé en première ~ de soirée** the film will be shown early on in the evening → **iceberg**

b **faire ~ de** [+ *ensemble, obligations, risques*] to be part of; [+ *club, association*] to belong to, be a member of; [+ *catégorie, famille*] to belong to; [+ *élus, gagnants*] to be among, be one of; **la rivière fait ~ du domaine** the river is part of

---
► GRAMMAIRE ACTIVE: **particulier** 53.1
---

the estate; **les villes faisant ~ de ma circonscription** the towns that make up my constituency; **elle fait ~ de notre groupe** she belongs to our group, she's one of our group; **faire ~ intégrante de** to be an integral part of, be part and parcel of

[c] (= *spécialité*) field, subject; **moi qui suis de la ~** knowing the field *ou* subject as I do; **il n'est pas dans** *ou* **de la ~** it's not his line *ou* field; **quand on lui parle électricité, il est dans sa ~** when it comes to electricity, he knows what he's talking about; **demande à ton frère, c'est sa ~** *ou* **il est de la ~** ask your brother — it's his field *ou* his line

[d] (*Cartes, Sport*) game; (*Golf*) round; (= *lutte*) struggle, fight; **faisons une ~ de ...** let's have a game of ...; **on a fait une bonne ~** we had a good game; (*fig*) **abandonner la ~** to give up the fight; **la ~ est délicate** it's a tricky situation *ou* business; (*lit, fig*) **la ~ n'est pas égale** it's an uneven contest

[e] (*Jur*) [*contrat*] party; [*procès*] litigant; (*Mil* = *adversaire*) opponent; **la ~ adverse** the opposing party; **les ~s en présence** the parties; **les ~s belligérantes** the warring factions; **avoir affaire à forte ~** to have a strong *ou* tough opponent to contend with; **être ~ prenante dans une négociation** to be a party to a negotiation; (*Jur*) **prise à ~** *action against a judge →* **juge**

[f] (*Mus*) part

[g] († *euph*) **~s sexuelles** *ou* **génitales** private parts; **~s viriles** male organs; **les ~s*** the privates*

[h] (*loc*) **avoir la ~ belle** to be sitting pretty*; **se mettre de la ~** to join in; **je veux être de la ~** I don't want to miss this, I want to be in on this*; (*littér*) **avoir ~ liée (avec qn)** to be hand in glove (with sb); **ce n'est que ~ remise** it will be for another time, we'll take a raincheck* (*US*); **prendre qn à ~** (= *apostropher*) to take sb to task; (= *malmener*) to set on sb; (*Comm*) **comptabilité en ~ simple/double** single-/double-entry book-keeping

[i] **en ~** partly, in part; **en grande** *ou* **majeure ~** largely, mainly; **cela s'explique, en grande ~, par ...** this can be explained, for the most part, by ..., this can largely be explained by ...

[2] COMP ▶ **partie de campagne** day *ou* outing in the country ▶ **partie carrée** wife-swapping party ▶ **partie de chasse** shooting party *ou* expedition ▶ **partie civile** (*Jur*) private party associating in a court action with public prosecutor; **se porter** *ou* **se constituer ~ civile** to associate in a court action with the public prosecutor; **constitution de ~ civile** independent brand of action for damages ▶ **partie du discours** (*Ling*) part of speech ▶ **partie fine** orgy ▶ **partie de jambes en l'air*** tout ce qui l'intéresse, c'est une ~ de jambes en l'air all he's interested in is getting his leg over* ▶ **partie de pêche** fishing party *ou* trip ▶ **partie de plaisir** (*fig*) **ce n'est pas une ~ de plaisir!** it's no picnic!*, it's not my idea of fun!

partiel, -elle [paʀsjɛl] [1] ADJ (*gén*) partial; **paiement ~** part payment; **les (élections) partielles** by(e)-elections ▶ **temps ~** [2] NM (*Univ*) class (*Brit*) *ou* mid-term (*US*) exam

partiellement [paʀsjɛlmã] ADV partially, partly

partir¹ [paʀtiʀ] ▶ conjug 16 ◀ [1] VI [a] (= *quitter un lieu*) to go, leave; (= *se mettre en route*) to leave, set off, set out; (= *s'éloigner*) to go away *ou* off; **pars, tu vas être en retard** go *ou* off you go, you're going to be late; **pars, tu m'embêtes** go away, you're annoying me; **es-tu prêt à ~?** are you ready to go?; **allez, je pars** I'm off now; **il est parti sans laisser d'adresse** he left without leaving an address; **nos voisins sont partis il y a six mois** our neighbours left six months ago; (*euph* = *mourir*) **depuis que mon pauvre mari est parti** since my poor husband passed on *ou* away;

ma lettre ne partira pas ce soir my letter won't go this evening; **quand partez-vous (pour Paris)?** when are you going (to Paris)? *ou* leaving (for Paris)?, when are you off (to Paris)?*; **~ pour le bureau** to leave *ou* set off for the office; **elle est partie de Nice à 9 heures** she left Nice *ou* set off from Nice at 9 o'clock; **sa femme est partie de la maison** his wife has left home; **sa femme est partie avec un autre** his wife has gone off with another man; **le mauvais temps a fait ~ les touristes** the bad weather has driven the tourists away; **j'espère que je ne vous fais pas ~** I hope I'm not chasing you away; **fais ~ le chat de ma chaise** get the cat off my chair; **ceux-là, quand ils viennent bavarder, c'est dur de les faire ~** when that lot come round for a chat, it's hard to get rid of them*; **~, c'est mourir un peu** to leave is to die a little

[b] (= *aller*) to go; **il est parti en Irlande** (*il y est encore*) he has gone to Ireland; (*il en est revenu*) he went to Ireland; **il est parti dans sa chambre/acheter du pain** he has gone to his room/to buy some bread; **~ faire des courses/se promener** to go (out) shopping/for a walk; **pars devant acheter les billets** go on ahead and buy the tickets; **~ à la chasse/à la pêche** to go shooting/fishing; **~ en vacances/en voyage** to go on holiday/on a trip; **~ à pied** to set off on foot; **tu pars en avion ou en voiture?** are you flying or driving?, are you going by plane or (by) car?; **~ à la guerre/au front** to go (off) to the war/to the front

[c] (= *démarrer*) [*moteur*] to start; [*avion*] to take off; [*train*] to leave; [*coureur*] to start off; [*plante*] to take; **la voiture partit sous son nez** the car started up *ou* drove off and left him standing; **il partit en courant** he ran *ou* dashed off; **il partit en trombe** *ou* **comme une flèche** he was off *ou* set off like a shot; **attention, le train va ~** look out, the train's leaving; **l'avion va ~ dans quelques minutes** the plane is taking off in a few minutes; **ce cheval est bien/mal parti** that horse got off to a good/bad start; **~ gagnant** to begin as if one is sure of success; **les voilà partis!** they're off!; **c'est parti (mon kiki)!*** here we go!*; **faire ~ une voiture/un moteur** to start (up) a car/an engine → **marque**

[d] (= *être lancé*) [*fusée*] to go off *ou* up; [*coup de feu*] to go off; [*bouchon*] to pop *ou* shoot out; **le coup est parti tout seul** the gun went off on its own; **le coup ne partit pas** the gun didn't go off, the gun misfired; **le bouchon est parti au plafond** the cork shot up to *ou* hit the ceiling; **les cris qui partaient de la foule** the shouts *ou* cries (coming *ou* that came) from the crowd; **le pétard n'a pas voulu ~** the banger wouldn't go off; **le mot partit malgré lui** the word came out *ou* slipped out before he could stop it; **le ballon partit comme un boulet de canon** the ball shot off like a bullet; **faire ~** [+ *fusée*] to launch; [+ *pétard*] to set off, light

[e] (= *être engagé*) **~ sur une idée fausse/une mauvaise piste** to start off with the wrong idea/on the wrong track; **~ bien/mal** to get off to a good/bad start, start (off) well/badly; **le pays est mal parti** the country is in a bad way *ou* in a mess *ou* in a sorry state; **nous sommes mal partis pour arriver à l'heure** it seems unlikely we'll arrive on time now; **son affaire est bien partie** his business has got off to a good start; **il est bien parti pour gagner** he seems all set to win; **~ dans des digressions sans fin** to wander off *ou* launch into endless digressions; **quand ils sont partis à discuter, il y en a pour des heures*** once they're off* *ou* launched into one of their discussions, they'll be at it for hours*; **~ à rire*** *ou* **d'un éclat de rire** to burst out laughing; **il est (bien) parti pour parler deux heures** the way he's going, he'll be talking for *ou* he looks all set to talk for two hours; **la pluie est partie pour (durer) toute la journée** the rain has set in for the

day; **on est parti pour ne pas déjeuner** at this rate *ou* the way things are going, we won't get any lunch

[f] (= *commencer*) **~ de** [*contrat, vacances*] to begin on, run from; [*course, excursion*] to start *ou* leave from; **l'autoroute part de Lille** the motorway starts at Lille; **un chemin qui part de l'église** a path going from *ou* leaving the church; **les branches qui partent du tronc** the branches going out from the trunk; **c'est le troisième en partant de la droite** it's (the) third from the right; **cet industriel est parti de rien** *ou* **de zéro** this industrialist started from scratch *ou* from *ou* with nothing; **cette rumeur est partie de rien** this rumour grew up out of nothing; **notre analyse part de cette constatation** our analysis is based on this observation *ou* takes this observation as its starting point; **partons de l'hypothèse que ...** let's assume that ...; **si tu pars du principe que tu as toujours raison/qu'ils ne peuvent pas gagner** if you start off by assuming that you're always right/that they can't win; **en partant de ce principe, rien n'est digne d'intérêt** on that basis, nothing's worthy of interest; **en partant de là, on peut faire n'importe quoi** looking at things that way, one can do anything

[g] (= *provenir*) **~ de** to come from; **ces mots partent/ça part du cœur** these words come/it comes (straight) from the heart; **cela part d'un bon sentiment/d'un bon naturel** that comes from his (*ou* her *etc*) kindness/good nature

[h] (= *disparaître*) [*tache*] to go, come out; [*crochet, bouton*] to come off; [*douleur*] to go; [*rougeurs, boutons*] to go, clear up; [*odeur*] to go, clear; **la tache est partie au lavage** the stain has come out in the wash *ou* has washed out; **toute la couleur est partie** all the colour has gone *ou* faded; **faire ~** [+ *tache*] to remove; [+ *odeur*] to clear, get rid of

[2] **à partir de** LOC PRÉP from; **à ~ d'aujourd'hui** (as) from today, from today onwards; **à ~ de 4 heures** from 4 o'clock on(wards); **à ~ de maintenant** from now on; **à ~ de ce moment-là** from then on; **à ~ du moment où ...** (= *dès que*) as soon as ...; (= *pourvu que*) so *ou* as long as ...; **à ~ d'ici le pays est plat** from here on(wards) the land is flat; **c'est le troisième à ~ de la gauche** it's the third (along) from the left; **lire à ~ de la page 5** to start reading at page 5; **allez jusqu'à la poste et, à ~ de là, c'est tout droit** go as far as the post office and after that it's straight ahead; **pantalons à ~ de 300 F** trousers from 300 francs (upwards); **à ~ de ces 3 couleurs vous pouvez obtenir toutes les nuances** with *ou* from these 3 colours you can get any shade; **c'est fait à ~ de produits chimiques** it's made from chemicals

partir² [paʀtiʀ] VT → **maille**

partisan, e [paʀtizã, an] [1] ADJ [a] (= *partial*) partisan [b] **être ~ de qch/de faire qch** to be in favour (*Brit*) *ou* favor (*US*) of sth/of doing sth; **être ~ du moindre effort** to be a believer in (taking) the line of least resistance [2] NM,F [*personne, thèse, régime*] supporter; [*action*] supporter, advocate, proponent; [*doctrine, réforme*] partisan, supporter, advocate; (*Mil*) partisan; **c'est un ~ de la fermeté** he's an advocate of *ou* a believer in firm measures, he supports *ou* advocates firm measures

partita [paʀtita] NF (*Mus*) partita

partitif, -ive [paʀtitif, iv] [1] ADJ partitive [2] NM partitive (article)

partition [paʀtisjɔ̃] NF [a] (*Mus*) score; **grande ~** full score [b] (*frm, gén Pol* = *division*) partition

partouse* [paʀtuz] NF orgy

partouser* [paʀtuze] ▶ conjug 1 ◀ VI to have an orgy

partout [paʀtu] ADV everywhere, everyplace (US); ~ **où** everywhere (that), wherever; **avoir mal** ~ to ache all over; **tu as mis des papiers** ~ you've put papers all over the place; (Sport) **2/15** ~ 2/15 all; (Tennis) **40** ~ deuce

partouze: [paʀtuz] NF = **partouse**

parturiente [paʀtyʀjɑ̃t] ADJ F, NF parturient

parturition [paʀtyʀisjɔ̃] NF parturition

parure [paʀyʀ] NF **a** (= toilette) costume, finery (NonC), (= bijoux) jewels; (= sous-vêtements) set of lingerie; (fig, littér) finery, livery (littér); ~ **de table/de lit** set of table/bed linen; ~ **de berceau** cot (Brit) ou crib (US) set; ~ **de diamants** set of diamond jewellery; (littér) **les arbres ont revêtu leur** ~ **de feuilles** the trees have put on their leafy finery (littér) **b** (= déchet) trimming

parution [paʀysjɔ̃] NF publication; **dès sa** ~, **ce roman a eu beaucoup de succès** this novel was a huge success as soon as it came out

parvenir [paʀvəniʀ] ▶ conjug 22 ◀ **1** **parvenir à** VT INDIR **a** (= arriver) [+ sommet] to get to, reach; [+ honneurs] to achieve; [+ état, âge] to reach; ~ **aux oreilles de qn** to reach sb's ears; **ma lettre lui est parvenue** my letter reached him, he got my letter; **ses ordres nous sont parvenus** his orders reached us; **faire** ~ **qch à qn** to send sth to sb; ~ **à ses fins** to achieve one's ends, get what one wants; **sa renommée est parvenue jusqu'à notre époque** ou **nous** his renown survives to this day **b** (= réussir) ~ **à faire qch** to manage to do sth, succeed in doing sth; **il y est parvenu** he managed it; **il n'y parvient pas tout seul** he can't manage on his own **2** VI (péj = faire fortune) to succeed ou get on in life, arrive

parvenu, e [paʀvəny] (ptp de **parvenir**) **1** ADJ upstart **2** ADJ, NM,F (péj) parvenu, upstart

parvis [paʀvi] NM square (in front of church or public building)

pas¹ [pɑ] **1** NM **a** (gén) step; (= bruit) footstep; (= trace) footprint; **faire un** ~ **en arrière/en avant** ◊ **reculer/avancer d'un** ~ to step back/forward, take a step ou a pace back/forward; (fig) **(il fait) un** ~ **en avant et deux en arrière** (he takes) one step forward and two steps back; **il reconnut son** ~ **dans le couloir** he recognized the sound of her footsteps in the corridor; **revenir** ou **retourner sur ses** ~ to retrace one's steps; **je vais là où me conduisent mes** ~ I am going where my steps take me; (lit, fig) **avancer à petits** ~ to inch forward, inch one's way along; **faire de grands** ~/**de petits** ~ to take long strides/short steps; **la politique des petits** ~ the policy of taking things one step at a time; **marcher à grands** ~ to stride along; **à** ~ **mesurés** ou **comptés** with measured steps; (lit, fig) **à** ~ **de loup** step by step; (lit, fig) **à chaque** ~ at every step; **il ne peut pas faire un** ~ **sans elle/sans la rencontrer** he can't go anywhere without her/without meeting her; **ne le quittez pas d'un** ~ follow him wherever he goes; **arriver sur les** ~ **de qn** to arrive just after sb, follow close on sb's heels; **marcher sur les** ~ **de qn** to follow in sb's footsteps; **faire ses premiers** ~ to start walking ou to walk **b** (= distance) pace; **à 20** ~ at 20 paces; **c'est à deux** ~ **d'ici** it's only a minute away, it's just a stone's throw from here **c** (= vitesse) pace; (Mil) step; [cheval] walk; **aller** ou **marcher d'un bon** ~ to walk at a good ou brisk pace; **marcher d'un** ~ **lent** to walk slowly; **changer de** ~ to change step; **allonger** ou **hâter** ou **presser le** ~ to hurry on, quicken one's step ou pace; **ralentir le** ~ to slow down; **marcher au** ~ to march; **se mettre au** ~ to get in step; **marcher son cheval au** ~ to walk one's horse; (Aut) **rouler** ou **aller au** ~ to crawl along, go at a walking pace; **« roulez au ~ »** "dead slow"; **au** ~ **cadencé** in quick time; **au** ~ **de charge** at the double; **au** ~ **de course** at a run;

au ~ **de gymnastique** at a jog trot; **au** ~ **redoublé** in double time, double-quick **d** (= démarche) tread; **d'un** ~ **lourd** ou **pesant** with a heavy tread; ~ **d'éléphant** heavy tread **e** (Danse) step; ~ **de danse/valse** dance/waltz step → **esquisser** **f** (Géog = passage) [montagne] pass; [mer] strait **g** (Tech) [vis, écrou] thread; [hélice] pitch **h** (loc) **faire un grand** ~ **en avant** to take a big step ou a great leap forward; **la science avance à grands** ~/**à** ~ **de géant** science is taking great/gigantic steps forward; **il progresse à** ~ **de géant** he's coming on in leaps and bounds; **faire le(s) premier(s)** ~ to take the initiative, make the first move; **il n'y a que le premier** ~ **qui coûte** the first step is the hardest; **à** ~ **de loup** ◊ **à** ~ **feutrés** stealthily; **d'un** ~ **léger** (= avec insouciance) airily, blithely; (= joyeusement) with a spring in one's step; (= agilement) **entrer/sortir d'un** ~ **léger** to pad in/out; **j'y vais de ce** ~ I'll go straightaway (Brit) ou at once; **mettre qn au** ~ to bring sb to heel, make sb toe the line; **avoir le** ~ **sur qn** to rank before ou above sb; **prendre le** ~ **sur** [+ considérations, préoccupations] to override; [+ théorie, méthode] to supplant; [+ personne] to steal a lead over; **franchir** ou **sauter le** ~ to take the plunge; **du mensonge à la calomnie il n'y a qu'un** ~ it's a short ou small step from lies to slander → **céder, cent¹, faux²**

2 COMP ▶ **pas battu** (Danse) pas battu ▶ **le pas de Calais** (= détroit) the Straits of Dover ▶ **pas de clerc** (littér) blunder ▶ **pas de deux** (Danse) pas de deux ▶ **pas de l'oie** (Mil) goose-step; **faire le** ~ **de l'oie** to goose-step ▶ **le pas de la porte** the doorstep; **sur le** ~ **de la porte** on the doorstep, in the doorway ▶ **pas de tir** (champ de tir) shooting range; (Espace) launching pad ▶ **pas de vis** thread

pas² [pɑ] **1** ADV NÉG (avec ne : formant nég verbale) not; **je ne vais** ~ **à l'école** (aujourd'hui) I'm not ou I am not going to school; (habituellement) I don't ou I do not go to school; **ce n'est** ~ **vrai** ◊ **c'est** ~ **vrai*** it isn't ou it's not ou it is not true; **je ne suis** ~/**il n'est** ~ **allé à l'école** I/he didn't ou did not go to school; **je ne trouve** ~ **mon sac** I can't ou cannot find my bag; **je ne la vois** ~ I can't ou cannot see her; **je ne prends** ~/**je ne veux** ~ **de pain** I won't have/I don't want any bread; **ils n'ont** ~ **de voiture/d'enfants** they don't have ou haven't got a car/any children, they have no car/children; **il m'a dit de (ne)** ~ **le faire** he told me not to do it; **ça me serait insupportable de ne** ~ **le voir** ◊ **ne** ~ **le voir me serait insupportable** it would be unbearable not to see him, not to see him would be unbearable; **je pense qu'il ne viendra** ~ I don't think he'll come; **ce n'est** ~ **sans peine que je l'ai convaincu** it was not without (some) difficulty that I convinced him; **non** ~ ou **ce n'est** ~ **qu'il soit bête** (it's) not that he's a fool; **ce n'est** ~ **que ça** it's not just that; **il n'y a** ~ **que lui** he's not the only one; **je n'en sais** ~ **plus que vous** I don't know any more about it than you (do); **il n'y avait** ~ **plus de 20 personnes** there were no more than 20 people there; **il n'est** ~ **plus/moins intelligent que vous** he is no more/no less intelligent than you; **ne me parle** ~ **sur ce ton** don't speak to me like that, do NOT speak to me like that **b** (indiquant un renforcement opposition) **elle travaille, (mais) lui** ~ she works, but he doesn't; **il aime ça,** ~ **toi?** he likes it, don't you?; **ils sont quatre et non** ~ **trois** there are four of them, not three; **vient-il ou (ne vient-il)** ~ **?** is he coming or not?, is he coming or isn't he?; **leur maison est chauffée, la nôtre** ~ their house is heated but ours isn't ou is not **c** (dans réponses négatives) not; ~ **de sucre, merci !** no sugar, thanks!; ~ **du tout** not at all,

not a bit; **il t'a remercié, au moins ?** — ~ **du tout** ou **absolument** ~ he did at least thank you? — he certainly didn't ou did not; ~ **encore** not yet; **tu as aimé le film ?** — ~ **plus que ça** ou so-so*; — it was so-so*; ~ **tellement*** ◊ — **tant que ça** not (all) that much, not so very much; ~ **des masses*** not a lot*, not an awful lot*; **qui l'a prévenu ?** — **moi/elle** etc who told him? — not me/her etc ou I didn't/she didn't etc **d** (devant adj, n, dans excl: *) **ce sont des gens** ~ **fiers** they're not proud people; **il est dans une situation** ~ **banale** ou ~ **ordinaire** he's in an unusual situation; **un** ~ **est venu** not one ou none (of them) came; ~ **possible !** no!, you don't say!*; ~ **de chance*** hard ou bad luck*!, too bad*; ~ **vrai ?*** isn't that so?, (isn't that) right?; **tu es content ? eh bien** ~ **moi !** are you satisfied? well I'm not!; **tu es content,** ~ **vrai ?!*** you're pleased, aren't you? ou admit it; **t'es** ~ **un peu fou ?*** you must be ou you're crazy!*; ~ **d'histoires** ou **de blagues, il faut absolument que j'arrive à l'heure** no nonsense now, I absolutely must be on time; **(c'est)** ~ **bête, cette idée !** that's not a bad idea (at all)!; **si c'est** ~ **malheureux !*** ou **honteux !*** isn't it disgraceful!; **tu viendras,** ~ **?*** you're coming, aren't you?, you'll come, won't you?; ~ **de ça!** we'll have none of that!; **ah non,** ~ **ça!** oh no, anything but that!; **ah non,** ~ **lui !** oh no, not him! → **falloir, fou**

2 COMP ▶ **pas grand-chose** (péj) NMF INV good-for-nothing

Pascal [paskal] NM (Ordin) Pascal

pascal¹, e (mpl **-aux**) [paskal, o] ADJ [agneau] paschal; [messe] Easter

pascal² (pl **pascals**) [paskal] NM (Phys) pascal; (*† = billet) 500 franc note

pascalien, -ienne [paskaljɛ̃, jɛn] ADJ of Pascal

pas-de-porte [pɑdpɔʀt] NM INV (= argent) ≈ key money (for shop, flat etc)

pasionaria [pasjɔnaʀja] NF passionate (female) militant; **Marie Dupont, la** ~ **de la libération des femmes** Marie Dupont, the ardent champion of women's liberation

paso doble [pasodɔbl] NM paso doble

passable [pasabl] ADJ passable, tolerable; (sur copie d'élève) fair; (Univ) **mention** ~ ≈ pass(-mark); **à peine** ~ barely passable, not so good

passablement [pasabləmɑ̃] ADV (jouer, travailler) tolerably ou moyennement) tolerably well; (= assez) [irritant, long] rather, fairly, pretty*; (= beaucoup) quite a lot ou a bit*; **il faut** ~ **de courage pour ...** it requires a fair amount of courage to ...

passade [pasad] NF passing fancy, whim, fad; (amoureuse) brief affair

passage [pasaʒ] **1** NM **a** (= venue) **guetter le** ~ **du facteur** to watch for the postman to come by, be on the look-out for the postman; **attendre le** ~ **de l'autobus** to wait for the bus to come; **agrandir une voie pour permettre le** ~ **de gros camions** to widen a road to allow heavy vehicles to use it ou to allow heavy vehicles through; **observer le** ~ **des oiseaux dans le ciel** to watch the birds fly by ou over; **pour empêcher le** ~ **de l'air sous la porte** to stop draughts (coming in) under the door; **lors de votre** ~ **à la douane** when you go ou pass through customs; **lors d'un récent** ~ **à Paris** when I (ou he etc) was in ou visiting Paris recently, on a recent trip to Paris; **la navette d'autobus fait quatre** ~**s par jour** the shuttle bus runs four times a day; **prochain** ~ **de notre représentant le 8 mai** our representative will be in the area again on May 8th; **« ~ interdit »** "no entry", "no thoroughfare"; **« ~ de troupeaux »** "cattle crossing"; **livrer** ~ to make way; **il y a beaucoup de** ~ **l'été** a lot of people come through here in the summer; **commerçant qui travaille avec le** ~ ou **les clients de** ~ shopkeeper catering for passing trade; **il est de** ~ **à Paris** he is in ou visiting ou passing through Paris at the moment; **amours/amants de ~** casual *ou* passing affairs/ lovers; **je l'ai saisi au ~** (*je passais devant*) I grabbed him as I went by *ou* past; (*il passait devant*) I grabbed him as he went by *ou* past → **lieu¹**

[b] (= *transfert*) **le ~ de l'état solide à l'état gazeux** the change from the solid to the gaseous state; **le ~ de l'enfance à l'adolescence** the transition *ou* passage from childhood to adolescence; **le ~ du jour à la nuit** the change from day to night; **le ~ du grade de capitaine à celui de commandant** promotion from captain to major; **le ~ de l'alcool dans le sang** the entry of alcohol into the bloodstream; **son ~ en classe supérieure est problématique** there are problems about his moving up *ou* promotion (*US*) to the next class (*Brit*) *ou* grade (*US*); **~ à l'acte** taking action, acting → **examen**

[c] (= *lieu*) passage; (= *chemin*) way, passage; (= *itinéraire*) route; (= *rue*) passage(way), alley(way); **un ~ dangereux sur la falaise** a dangerous section of the cliff; **il faut trouver un ~ dans ces broussailles** we must find a way through this undergrowth; **on a mis des barrières sur le ~ de la procession** barriers have been put up along the route of the procession; **on se retourne sur son ~** people turn round and look when he goes past; **l'ouragan dévasta tout sur son ~** the hurricane demolished everything in its path; **barrer le ~ à qn** to block sb's way; **laisser le ~ à qn** to let sb pass *ou* past; **va plus loin, tu gènes le ~** move along, you're in the way; **ne laissez pas vos valises dans le ~** don't leave your cases in the way; **le ~ du Nord-Ouest** the North-West Passage → **frayer**

[d] (*Naut*) **payer son ~** to pay for one's passage, pay one's fare

[e] (= *fragment*) [*livre, symphonie*] passage

[f] (= *traversée*) [*rivière, limite, montagnes*] crossing; (*Naut*) **le ~ de la ligne** crossing the Line

[g] (*loc*) **il a eu un ~ à vide** (*syncope*) he felt a bit faint; (*baisse de forme*) he went through a bad patch; **j'ai toujours un petit ~ à vide vers 16 h** I always start to flag around 4 o'clock

[2] COMP ► **passage clouté** pedestrian crossing, ≈ zebra crossing (*Brit*), ≈ crosswalk (*US*) ► **passage à niveau** level crossing (*Brit*), grade crossing (*US*) ► **passage (pour) piétons** pedestrian walkway ► **passage protégé** (*Aut*) priority *ou* right of way (*over secondary road*) ► **passage souterrain** (*gén*) underground *ou* subterranean passage; (*pour piétons*) underpass, subway (*Brit*) ► **passage à tabac** beating up

passager, -ère [pasaʒe, ɛʀ] [1] ADJ [a] (= *de courte durée*) [*malaise*] passing (*épith*), brief; [*inconvénient*] temporary; [*bonheur, beauté*] passing (*épith*), transient, ephemeral; **j'ai eu un malaise ~** I felt faint for a few minutes; **pluies passagères** intermittent *ou* occasional showers *ou* rain [b] [*rue*] busy [2] NM,F passenger; **~ clandestin** stowaway

passagèrement [pasaʒɛʀmɑ̃] ADV for a short while, temporarily

passant, e [pasɑ̃, ɑ̃t] [1] ADJ [*rue*] busy [2] NM,F passer-by [3] NM [*ceinture*] loop

passation [pasasjɔ̃] NF [*contrat*] signing; (*Comm*) [*écriture*] entry; **~ de pouvoirs** handing over of office *ou* power, transfer of power

passavant [pasavɑ̃] NM [a] (*Comm, Jur*) transire, carnet [b] (*Naut*) catwalk

passe¹ [pas] [1] NF [a] (*Escrime, Ftbl, Tauromachie*) pass; **faire une ~** to pass (à to); **~ en retrait/en avant** back/forward pass; (*Ftbl*) **~ croisée** cross; **faire une ~ croisée à qn** to cross to sb [b] [*magnétiseur*] pass [c] [*Roulette*] passe [d] (*Naut = chenal*) pass, channel [e] [*prostituée*] **c'est 200 F la ~** it is 200 francs a time; **faire 20 ~s par jour** to have 20 clients *ou*

customers a day → **hôtel, maison**

[f] (*Imprim*) (**main de**) **~** surplus paper; **exemplaire de ~** over, surplus copy

[g] (*loc*) **être en ~ de faire qch** to be on one's *ou* the way to doing; **il est en ~ de réussir** he is poised to succeed; **cette espèce est en ~ de disparaître** this species is on the way to extinction *ou* looks likely to die out; **être dans une bonne ~** to be in a healthy situation; **être dans** *ou* **traverser une mauvaise ~** (*gén*) to be having a rough time, be going through a bad patch; (*santé*) to be in a poor state; **est-ce qu'il va sortir de cette mauvaise ~?** will he manage to pull through (this time)? → **mot**

[2] COMP ► **passe d'armes** (*fig*) heated exchange ► **passe de caisse** (*Comm*) sum allowed for cashier's errors ► **passes magnétiques** hypnotic passes

passe² [pas] NM ABRÉV = **passe-partout**

passé, e [pase] [1] (*ptp de* **passer**) [2] ADJ [a] (= *dernier*) last; **c'est arrivé le mois ~/l'année ~** it happened last month/last year; **au cours des semaines/années ~es** over these last *ou* the past (few) weeks/years [b] (= *révolu*) [*action, conduite*] past; **songeant à sa gloire ~e/ses angoisses ~es** thinking of his past *ou* former glory/distress; **regrettant sa jeunesse/sa beauté ~e** yearning for her vanished youth/beauty; **si l'on se penche sur les événements ~s** if one looks back over past events; **cette époque est ~e maintenant** that era is now over; **ce qui est ~ est ~** what's done is done, that's all in the past (now); **j'ai 60 ans ~s** he's over 60; **où sont mes années ~es?** where has my life gone?; **il se rappelait le temps ~** he was thinking back to days *ou* times gone by [c] (= *fané*) [*couleur, fleur*] faded; **tissu ~** material that has lost its colour, faded material [d] (= *plus de*) **il est 8 heures ~es** it's past *ou* gone (*Brit*) 8 o'clock; **il est rentré à 9 heures ~es** it was past *ou* gone (*Brit*) 9 o'clock when he got back; **ça fait une heure ~e que je t'attends** I've been waiting for you for more than *ou* over an hour

[2] NM [a] **le ~** the past; **il faut oublier le ~** we should forget the past; **c'est du ~, n'en parlons plus** it's (all) in the past now, let's not say any more about it; **il est revenu nous voir comme par le ~** he came back to see us as he used to in the past; **il a eu plusieurs condamnations dans le ~** he had several previous convictions [b] (= *vie écoulée*) past; **pays fier de son ~** country proud of its past; **bandit au ~ chargé** gangster with a past; **son ~ m'est inconnu** I know nothing of his past [c] (*Gram*) past tense; **les temps du ~** the past tenses; **mettez cette phrase au ~** put this sentence into the past (tense); **~ antérieur** past anterior; **~ composé** perfect; **~ simple** past historic, preterite

[3] PRÉP after; **~ 6 heures on ne sert plus les clients** after 6 o'clock we stop serving; **~ cette maison, on quitte le village** after this house, you are out of the village

passe-crassane (*pl* **passe-crassanes**) [paskʀasan] NF *type of winter pear*

passe-droit (*pl* **passe-droits**) [pasdʀwa] NM (*undeserved*) privilege, favour (*Brit*), favor (*US*); **il a obtenu un ~** he got preferential treatment

passéisme [paseism] NM (*péj*) attachment to the past

passéiste [paseist] [1] ADJ (*péj*) backward-looking [2] NMF (*péj*) devotee of the past

passe-lacet (*pl* **passe-lacets**) [paslasɛ] NM bodkin → **raide**

passement [pasmɑ̃] NM braid (*NonC*)

passementer [pasmɑ̃te] ▸ conjug 1 ◂ VT to braid

passementerie [pasmɑ̃tʀi] NF (= *objets*) soft furnishings; (= *commerce*) soft furnishings, sale of soft furnishings; **rayon de ~** department selling soft furnishings

passementier, -ière [pasmɑ̃tje, jɛʀ] [1] ADJ **industrie passementière** soft furnishings industry [2] NM,F (= *fabricant*) manufacturer of soft furnishings; (= *vendeur*) salesman (*ou* -woman) specializing in soft furnishings

passe-montagne (*pl* **passe-montagnes**) [pasmɔ̃taɲ] NM balaclava

passe-muraille [pasmyʀaj] NM INV (*hum*) chameleon*

passe-partout [paspaʀtu] [1] ADJ INV [*tenue*] for all occasions, all-purpose (*épith*); [*formule*] all-purpose (*épith*), catch-all (*épith*) [2] NM INV [a] (= *clé*) master *ou* skeleton key [b] (= *encadrement*) passe-partout [c] (= *scie*) cross-cut saw

passe-passe [paspas] NM INV **tour de ~** [*magicien*] conjuring trick; (*fig*) trick, piece of trickery; **faire des tours de ~** to perform conjuring tricks; **par un simple tour de ~ financier** by a bit of financial sleight of hand

passe-plat (*pl* **passe-plats**) [paspla] NM serving hatch

passepoil [paspwal] NM piping (*NonC*)

passepoilé, e [paspwale] ADJ piped

passeport [paspɔʀ] NM (*Admin*) passport; **demander ses ~s** [*ambassadeur*] to withdraw one's credentials; **ce diplôme est un ~ pour l'emploi** this degree is a passport to a job

▼ **passer** [pase]

┌─────────────────────────────────────┐
│ ▸ conjug 1 ◂   │
│ [1] VERBE INTRANSITIF [3] VERBE PRONOMINAL │
│ [2] VERBE TRANSITIF   │
└─────────────────────────────────────┘

[1] VERBE INTRANSITIF
avec aux être

Lorsque **passer** *s'emploie dans des locutions figurées telles que* **passer** *sous le nez de qn,* **passer** *sur le ventre/le corps à qn etc, cherchez sous le nom.*

[a] **gén** to pass, go *ou* come past; **~ en courant** to run past; **~ à pas lents** to go slowly past; **le train va bientôt ~** the train will be coming past *ou* by soon; **où passe la route?** where does the road go?; **laisse ~ les piétons** to let the pedestrians cross → **bouche, main**

◆ **passer** + *préposition ou adverbe* (*lit*) **~ sous/ sur/devant/derrière** etc to go under/over/in front of/behind *etc*; **la route passe à Vierzon** the road goes through Vierzon; **la Seine passe à Paris** the Seine flows through Paris; **les poissons sont passés au travers du filet** the fish slipped through the net; **les camions ne passent pas dans notre rue** lorries don't come along *ou* down our street; **il passait dans la rue avec son chien/en voiture** he was walking down the street with his dog/driving down the street; **le fil passe dans ce tuyau** the wire goes down *ou* through this pipe; **une lueur cruelle passa dans son regard** a cruel gleam came into his eyes; **il est passé sous l'autobus** he was run over by the bus; **~ devant la maison de qn** to go past *ou* to pass sb's house; **je passe devant vous pour vous montrer le chemin** I'll go in front to show you the way; **passez donc devant** you go first; **la voie ferrée passe le long du fleuve** the railway line runs alongside the river; **la balle/flèche n'est pas passée loin** the bullet/arrow didn't miss by much; **pour y aller, je passe par Amiens** I go *ou* pass through Amiens to get there, I go there via Amiens; **je passe par la gare, je peux vous déposer** I'm going by the station, I can drop you off; **par où êtes-vous passé?** which way did you go? *ou* come?; **le chien est trop gros pour ~ par le trou** the dog is too big to get through the hole; **ça fait du bien par où ça passe!*** that's just what the doctor ordered!*; **l'air passe sous la porte** there's a draught from under the door; ~ sous les fenêtres de qn to go past *ou* to pass sb's window

(*fig*) le confort, ça passe après comfort is less important *ou* comes second; le travail passe avant tout/avant les loisirs work comes first/before leisure; ~ devant Monsieur le maire to get married *ou* hitched*; ~ devant un jury to go before a jury; ma famille passe en premier my family comes first; une idée m'est passée par la tête an idea occurred to me; elle dit tout ce qui lui passe par la tête she says whatever comes into her head; ~ sur [+ *faute*] to pass over, overlook; [+ *détail inutile ou scabreux*] to pass over; je veux bien ~ sur cette erreur I'm willing to pass over *ou* overlook this mistake; je passe sur les détails I shall pass over *ou* leave out *ou* skip the details

◆ **en passant** (= *sur le chemin*) j'irai le voir en passant I'll call in to see him *ou* I'll call in and see him on my way

(*dans la conversation*) il m'a glissé quelques remarques en passant he said a few words to me in passing → **dire**

(*dans une énumération*) il aime tous les sports, du football à la boxe en passant par le golf he likes all sports, from football to golf to boxing

[b] = **faire une halte rapide** ~ au *ou* par le bureau/chez un ami to call in at *ou* drop in at *ou* drop by the office/a friend's; je ne fais que ~ (*chez qn*) I'm not stopping*, I can't stay long; (*dans une ville*) I'm just passing through; ~ à la visite médicale to go for a medical; ~ à la douane to go through customs, clear customs; le facteur est passé the postman has been; à quelle heure passe le laitier? what time does the milkman come?; le releveur du gaz passera demain the gasman will call tomorrow

◆ **passer** + *infinitif* : ~ chercher *ou* prendre qn to call for sb, go *ou* come and pick sb up; je passerai prendre ce colis demain I'll come and pick the parcel up tomorrow; ~ voir qn *ou* rendre visite à qn to call (in) on sb; le médecin passera te voir ce soir the doctor will come and see you this evening; puis-je ~ te voir en vitesse ? can I pop round (to see you)?

[c] = **changer de lieu, d'attitude, d'état** to go; ~ d'une pièce dans une autre to go from one room to another; si nous passions au salon ? shall we go into *ou* through to the sitting room?; ~ à table to sit down to eat; il est passé en Belgique he went over to Belgium; ~ à l'ennemi/l'opposition to go over *ou* defect to the enemy/the opposition; la photo passa de main en main the photo was passed *ou* handed round; ~ d'un extrême à l'autre to go from one extreme to the other; ~ de l'état solide à l'état liquide to go *ou* change from the solid to the liquid state; ~ du rire aux larmes to switch from laughter to tears; ~ à un ton plus sévère to take a harsher tone; ~ dans les mœurs/les habitudes to become the custom/the habit; ~ dans la langue to pass *ou* come into the language; ~ en proverbe to become proverbial; son argent de poche passe en bonbons *ou* dans les bonbons all his pocket money goes on sweets; l'alcool passe dans le sang alcohol enters the bloodstream; le reste des légumes est passé dans le potage the left-over vegetables went into the soup

[d] Aut ~ en première/marche arrière to go into first/reverse; ~ en seconde/quatrième to go *ou* change into second/fourth; les vitesses passent mal the gears are stiff

[e] = **franchir un obstacle** [*véhicule*] to get through; [*cheval, sauteur*] to get over; (*Alpinisme*) to get up; (*Aut : en manœuvrant*) ça passe? can I make it?, have I got enough room?

[f] = **s'écouler : temps** to go by, pass; comme le temps passe (vite) ! how time flies!; ça fait ~ le temps it passes the time

[g] = **s'écouler : liquide** to go *ou* come through, seep through; [*café*] to go through; (= *circuler*) [*courant électrique*] to get through

[h] = **être digéré, avalé** to go down; mon déjeuner ne passe pas my lunch won't go down; prendre un cachet pour faire ~ le déjeuner to take a tablet to help one's lunch down; prends de l'eau pour faire ~ le gâteau have some water to wash down the cake

[i] = **être accepté** [*demande, proposition*] to pass; je ne pense pas que ce projet de loi passera I don't think this bill will be passed *ou* will go through; cette plaisanterie ne passe pas dans certains milieux that joke doesn't go down well *ou* isn't appreciated in some circles; il y a des plaisanteries/erreurs qui passent dans certaines circonstances mais pas dans d'autres there are certain jokes/mistakes which are all right in some circumstances but not in others; le gouvernement se demande comment faire ~ les hausses de prix the government is wondering how to get the price increases through; il est passé de justesse à l'examen he only just scraped through *ou* passed the exam; il est passé dans la classe supérieure he's moved up to the next class (*Brit*), he's passed *ou* been promoted to the next grade (*US*); l'équipe est passée en 2ᵉ division (*progrès*) the team were promoted to *ou* have moved up to the second division; (*recul*) the team have been relegated to *ou* have moved down to the second division; ça passe ou ça casse it's make or break (time)

[j] = **devenir** to become; ~ directeur/président to become *ou* be appointed director/chairman

[k] = **être montré** (*Ciné*) [*film*] to be showing, be on; (*TV*) [*émission*] to be on; [*personne*] to be on, appear; ~ à la radio/à la télé* to be on the radio/on TV

[l] = **être présenté** (*Jur, Parl*) to come up; le projet de loi va ~ devant la Chambre the bill will come *ou* be put before Parliament; il est passé devant le conseil de discipline de l'école he came up *ou* was brought up before the school disciplinary committee

[m] = **dépasser** le panier est trop petit, la queue du chat passe the basket is too small — the cat's tail is sticking out; son manteau est trop court, la robe passe her coat is too short — her dress shows underneath; ne laisse pas ~ ton bras par la portière don't put your arm out of the window

[n] = **disparaître** [*douleur*] to pass, wear off; (*lit, fig*) [*orage*] to blow over, die down; [*beauté, couleur*] to fade; [*colère*] to die down; [*mode*] to die out; (= *mourir*) [*personne*] to pass on *ou* away; la jeunesse passe (vite) you're old before you know it; faire ~ à qn le goût *ou* l'envie de faire to cure sb of doing; cela fera ~ votre rhume that will get you over your cold *ou* get rid of your cold for you; le plus dur est passé the worst is over now; il était très amoureux, mais ça lui a passé he was very much in love but he got over it; il voulait être pompier mais ça lui a passé he wanted to be a fireman but he grew out of it; ça lui passera (avant que ça me reprenne) !* [*sentiment*] he'll get over it!; [*habitude*] he'll grow out of it!

[o] Cartes to pass

[p] ~ par [+ *intermédiaire*] to go through; [+ *expérience*] to go through, undergo; pour lui parler, j'ai dû ~ par sa secrétaire I had to go through *ou* via his secretary *ou* I had to see his secretary before I could speak to him; pour téléphoner, il faut ~ par le standard you have to go through the switchboard to make a call; ~ par de dures épreuves to go through some very trying times; il est passé par des moments difficiles he's been through some hard times; ~ par l'université/un lycée technique to go through university/technical college; elle est passée par toutes les couleurs de l'arc-

en-ciel (*gêne*) she blushed to the roots of her hair; (*peur*) she turned pale; nous sommes tous passés par là we've all been through that, that's happened to all of us

◆ **en passer par** : il faudra bien en ~ par là there's no way round it; il a bien fallu en ~ par là it had to come to that (in the end); il faudra bien en ~ par ce qu'il demande we'll have to give him what he wants, we'll have to comply with *ou* give in to his request

[q]

◆ **passer pour** : je ne voudrais pas ~ pour un imbécile I wouldn't like to be taken for a fool; il pourrait ~ pour un Allemand you could take him for a German, he could pass for *ou* as a German; auprès de ses amis, il passait pour un séducteur he was regarded by his friends as (being) a ladies' man; il passe pour un intellectuel he passes for an intellectual; il passe pour intelligent he's thought of as intelligent, he's supposed to be intelligent; il passe pour beau auprès de certaines femmes some women think *ou* find him good-looking, he's considered good-looking by some women; il passe pour un escroc people say he's a crook; cela passe pour vrai it's thought to be true; se faire ~ pour to pass o.s. off as; il s'est fait ~ pour son patron he passed himself off as his boss; il s'est fait ~ pour fou pour se faire réformer he pretended to be mad so he could be declared unfit for service; faire ~ qn pour to make sb out to be; tu veux me faire ~ pour un idiot ! do you want to make me look stupid?

[r]

◆ **y passer*** : on a eu la grippe, tout le monde y est passé we've had the flu — everybody got it *ou* nobody escaped it; si tu conduis comme ça, on va tous y ~ if you go on driving like that, we've all had it*; toute sa fortune y est passée he spent all his fortune on it, his whole fortune went on it; (*sexuellement*) si elle veut une promotion, il faudra bien qu'elle y passe if she wants to be promoted, she'll have to sleep with the boss

[s]

◆ **laisser passer** [+ *air, lumière*] to let in; [+ *personne, procession*] to let through *ou* past; [+ *erreur*] to overlook, miss; [+ *occasion*] to let slip, miss; il faut laisser ~ le temps give it time; s'écarter pour laisser ~ qn to move back to let sb (get) through *ou* past; nous ne pouvons pas laisser ~ cette affaire sans protester we cannot let this matter pass without a protest, we can't let this matter rest there — we must protest

[t] loc qu'il soit menteur, passe (encore), mais voleur c'est plus grave he may be a liar, that's one thing, but a thief, that's more serious; passe pour cette erreur, mais si tu recommences ... we'll forget about it this time, but if you make the same mistake again ...; passons let's say no more (about it)

[2] VERBE TRANSITIF

avec aux avoir

[a] = **franchir** [+ *rivière, frontière, seuil*] to cross; [+ *porte*] to go through; [+ *haie*] to jump *ou* get over; ~ une rivière à la nage/en bac to swim across/take the ferry across a river

[b] = **se soumettre à** [+ *examen*] to sit, take; ~ son permis (de conduire) to take one's driving test; ~ une visite médicale to have a medical (examination); ~ un examen avec succès to pass an exam

[c] = **utiliser** [+ *temps, vacances*] to spend; ~ sa vie à faire to spend one's life doing; (faire qch) pour ~ le temps (to do sth) to while away *ou* pass the time; j'ai passé la soirée chez Luc I spent the evening at Luc's (place) → **mauvais**

[d] = **assouvir** ~ sa colère/sa mauvaise humeur sur qn to take one's anger/one's bad mood out on sb; ~ son envie de chocolat to satisfy one's craving for chocolate

[e] = **omettre** [+ *mot, ligne*] to leave out, miss out (*Brit*); ~ **son tour** to miss one's turn; **et j'en passe!** and that's not all!; **j'en passe, et des meilleures!** and that's not all — I could go on!, and that's the least of them! → **silence**

[f] = **permettre**   ~ **une faute à qn** to overlook sb's mistake; ~ **un caprice à qn** to humour sb, indulge sb's whim; **on lui passe tout** [+ *bêtises*] he gets away with anything; [+ *désirs*] he gets everything he wants; **passez-moi l'expression** (if you'll) pardon the expression

[g] = **transmettre** [+ *consigne, message, maladie*] to pass on; (*Sport*) [+ *ballon*] to pass; ~ **qch à qn** to give ou hand sth to sb; **tu (le) fais ~** pass ou hand it round; ~ **une affaire/un travail à qn** to hand a matter/a job over to sb; **passe-moi une cigarette** pass ou give me a cigarette; **passez-moi du feu** give me a light; **il m'a passé un livre** he's lent me a book; **je suis fatigué, je vous passe le volant** I'm tired, you take the wheel ou you drive; (*au téléphone*) **je vous passe M. Duroy** [*standard*] I'm putting you through to Mr Duroy; (= *je lui passe l'appareil*) here's Mr Duroy; **passe-lui un coup de fil** phone ou call ou ring (*Brit*) him, give him a ring (*Brit*); **passez-moi tous vos paquets** give me ou let me have all your parcels

[h] Douane   ~ **la douane** to go through customs; **après avoir passé la douane, je** ... once I'd been through ou cleared Customs, I ...; ~ **des marchandises en transit** to carry goods in transit; ~ **qch en fraude** to smuggle sth (in ou out ou through etc); ~ **des faux billets** to pass forged notes

[i] = **enfiler** [+ *pull*] to slip on; [+ *robe*] to slip into; ~ **une bague au doigt de qn** to slip a ring on sb's finger; ~ **un lacet dans qch** to thread a lace through sth; ~ **la corde au cou de qn** to put the rope round sb's neck

[j] = **mettre** ~ **la tête à la porte** to poke one's head round the door; ~ **la main/tête à travers les barreaux** to stick one's hand/head through the bars

[k] = **dépasser** [+ *gare, maison*] to pass, go past; ~ **le poteau** to pass the post, cross the finishing line; ~ **les limites** ou **les bornes** to go too far; **tu as passé l'âge (de ces jeux)** you're too old (for these games); **il ne passera pas la nuit/la semaine** he won't last the night/the week, he won't see the night/the week out → **cap**

[l] Culin [+ *thé, lait*] to strain;† [+ *café*] to pour the water on; ~ **la soupe** (à la passoire) to strain the soup; (*au mixer*) to blend the soup, put the soup through the blender

[m] Aut   ~ **la seconde/la troisième** to go ou change (up ou down) into second/third (gear)

[n] = **montrer, faire écouter** [+ *film, diapositives*] to show; [+ *disque*] to put on, play; **qu'est-ce qu'ils passent au cinéma?** what's on ou showing at the cinema?

[o] Comm [+ *écriture*] to enter; [+ *commande*] to place; [+ *accord*] to reach, come to; [+ *contrat*] to sign; ~ **un marché** to do a deal → **profit**

[p] = **faire subir une action** ~ **une pièce à l'aspirateur** to vacuum ou hoover® (*Brit*) a room, go over a room with the vacuum cleaner; ~ **la cuisine à la serpillière** ◊ ~ **la serpillière dans la cuisine** to wash (down) the kitchen floor; ~ **le balai/l'aspirateur/le chiffon dans une pièce** to sweep/vacuum ou hoover® (*Brit*)/dust a room; **passe le chiffon dans le salon** dust the sitting room, give the sitting room a dust; ~ **une couche de peinture sur qch** to give sth a coat of paint; ~ **un mur à la chaux** to whitewash a wall; ~ **qch sous le robinet** to rinse ou run sth under the tap; **elle lui passa la main dans les cheveux** she ran her hand through his hair; **passe-toi de l'eau sur le visage** give your face a (quick) wash; **qu'est-ce qu'il lui a passé (comme savon)!*** he gave him a really

rough time!*, he really laid into him!* → **arme, éponge, menotte, revue, tabac**

3 **se passer** VERBE PRONOMINAL

[a] = **avoir lieu** to take place; (= *arriver*) to happen; (*Théât*) **la scène se passe à Paris** the scene takes place in Paris; **qu'est-ce qui s'est passé?** what happened?; **que se passe-t-il?** what's happening?; ◊ **qu'est-ce qu'il se passe?** what's going on?, what's happening?; **ça ne s'est pas passé comme je l'espérais** it didn't work out as I'd hoped; **tout s'est bien passé** everything went off smoothly; **ça s'est mal passé** it turned out badly, it went off badly; **je ne sais pas ce qui se passe en lui** I don't know what's the matter with him ou what's come over him ou what's got into him; **ça ne se passera pas comme ça!** I won't stand for that!, I won't let it rest at that!

[b] = **s'écouler** to pass; (= *finir*) to pass, be over; **il ne se passe pas un seul jour sans qu'il ne pleuve** not a day goes by ou passes without it raining; **il faut attendre que ça se passe** you'll have to wait till it's over ou it passes

[c] = **s'appliquer, se mettre à soi-même** [+ *produit*] **elle s'est passé de la crème solaire sur les épaules** she put some sun cream on her shoulders; **il se passa un mouchoir sur le front** he wiped his forehead with a handkerchief; **se ~ les mains à l'eau** to rinse one's hands

[d] = **s'accorder** **il faut bien se ~ quelques fantaisies** you've got to allow yourself a few ou indulge in a few extravagances

[e] **se transmettre** [+ *ballon, plat*] to pass to each other; [+ *notes de cours, livre*] to give to each other

♦ **se passer de** [+ *chose*] to do without; [+ *personne*] to manage without; **s'il n'y en a plus, je m'en passerai** if there isn't any more, I'll do without; **je peux me ~ de ta présence** I can manage without you around; **nous nous voyons dans l'obligation de nous ~ de vos services** we find ourselves obliged to dispense with your services; **je me passe de tes conseils!** I can do without your advice!; **la citation se passe de commentaires** the quotation needs no comment ou speaks for itself

♦ **se passer de** + *infinitif*: **on peut se ~ d'aller au théâtre** we can do without going to the theatre; **je me passerais bien d'y aller!** I could do without having to go!; **il se passerait de manger plutôt que de faire la cuisine** he'd go without eating ou without food rather than cook; (*iro*) **tu pourrais te ~ de fumer** you could refrain from smoking

passereau (*pl* **passereaux**) [pasʀo]   NM (*Orn*) passerine; († = *moineau*) sparrow

passerelle [pasʀɛl]   NF (= *pont*) footbridge; (*Naut* = *pont supérieur*) bridge; (*Aviat, Naut* = *voie d'accès*) gangway; (*fig*) bridge; (*Ordin*) gateway; (*Scol*) **(classe)** ~ reorientation class (*facilitating change of course at school*); **jeter** ou **lancer des ~s entre** to build bridges between

passerose, passe-rose (*pl* **passe(-)roses**) [pasʀoz]   NF hollyhock

passe-temps [pastɑ̃] NM INV pastime, hobby; **c'est un ~ national** it's a national pastime

passe-thé [paste] NM INV tea strainer

passette [pasɛt] NF tea strainer

passeur [pasœʀ] NM [*rivière*] ferryman, boatman; [*frontière*] smuggler (*of drugs, refugees etc*)

passe-vue (*pl* **passe-vues**) [pasvy] NM slide changer

passible [pasibl] ADJ ~ **d'une amende/peine** [*personne*] liable to a fine/penalty; [*délit*] punishable by a fine/penalty; ~ **d'un impôt** liable for tax; (*Comm*) ~ **de droits** liable to duty

passif, -ive [pasif, iv]   **1** ADJ (*gén*) passive; **rester ~ devant une situation** to remain passive in the face of a situation → **défense¹**
2 NM [a] (*Ling*) passive; **au ~** in the passive

(*voice*) [b] (*Fin*) liabilities; **le ~ d'une succession** the liabilities on an estate; (*fig*) **mettre qch au ~ de qn** to add sth to sb's list of weak points

passiflore [pasiflɔʀ]   NF passionflower, passiflora (*SPÉC*)

passing-shot (*pl* **passing-shots**) [pasiŋʃɔt] NM passing shot; **faire un ~** to play a passing shot

passion [pasjɔ̃] NF [a] (= *goût*) passion; **avoir la ~ du jeu/des voitures** to have a passion for gambling/for cars; **le tennis est sa ~** ou **est une ~ chez lui** he is mad* ou crazy* about tennis, his one passion is tennis [b] (= *amour*) passion; **déclarer sa ~** to declare one's love; **aimer à la** ou **avec ~** to love passionately [c] (= *émotion, colère*) passion; **emporté par la ~** carried away by passion; **discuter avec ~/sans ~** to argue passionately ou heatedly/dispassionately ou coolly; **débat sans ~** lifeless debate; **œuvre pleine de ~** work full of passion [d] (*Mus, Rel*) **Passion** Passion; **le dimanche de la Passion** Passion Sunday; **le jour de la Passion** the day of the Passion; **la semaine de la Passion** Passion week; **la Passion selon saint Matthieu** (*Rel*) the Passion according to St Matthew; (*Mus*) the St Matthew Passion → **fruit¹**

passionaria [pasjɔnaʀja] NF = **pasionaria**

passionnant, e [pasjɔnɑ̃, ɑ̃t] ADJ [*personne*] fascinating; [*livre, film*] gripping, fascinating; [*métier, match*] exciting

passionné, e [pasjɔne] (*ptp de* **passionner**) **1** ADJ [*personne, tempérament, haine*] passionate; [*description, orateur, jugement*] impassioned; **être ~ de** ou **pour qch** to have a passion for sth; **un photographe ~** a keen photographer; **débat ~** heated ou impassioned debate **2** NM,F [a] (= *personne exaltée*) passionate person [b] (= *amateur*) enthusiast; **c'est un ~ de jazz** he's a jazz enthusiast; **c'est un ~ de voyages** he loves travelling

passionnel, -elle [pasjɔnɛl] ADJ [*débat, relation, sentiment*] passionate; **les négociations se sont déroulées dans un climat ~** the atmosphere at the talks was heated → **crime**

passionnément [pasjɔnemɑ̃] ADV passionately, with passion; ~ **amoureux de** madly ou passionately in love with; **s'intéresser ~ à qch** to have a passionate interest in sth

passionner [pasjɔne] ▸ conjug 1 ◂ **1** VT [+ *personne*] [*mystère, match*] to fascinate, grip; [*livre, sujet*] to fascinate; [*sport, science*] to be a passion with; [+ *débat*] to inflame; **ce film/roman m'a passionné** I found that film/novel fascinating; **la musique le passionne** music is his passion, he has a passion for music; **j'ai un métier qui me passionne** I have a fascinating job **2** **se passionner** VPR **se ~ pour** [+ *livre, mystère*] to be fascinated by; [+ *sport, science*] to have a passion for, be mad keen on*; [+ *métier*] to be fascinated by

passivation [pasivasjɔ̃]   NF (*Ling*) putting in the passive (*voice*); (*Tech*) passivation; (*Chim*) making passive

passivement [pasivmɑ̃] ADV passively

passivité [pasivite] NF passivity, passiveness

passoire [paswaʀ] NF (*gén*) sieve; [*thé*] strainer; [*légumes*] colander; (*fig*) **être une (vraie) ~** to be like a sieve; **quelle ~ ce gardien de but!** what a useless goalkeeper — he lets everything in!; **avoir la tête** ou **la mémoire comme une ~** to have a memory like a sieve; **troué comme une ~** riddled with ou full of holes

pastel [pastɛl] **1** NM (*Bot*) woad, pastel; (= *teinture pastel*) pastel; (= *bâtonnet de couleur*) pastel (crayon); (= *œuvre*) pastel; **au ~** in pastels **2** ADJ INV [*tons*] pastel; **un bleu/vert ~** a pastel blue/green

pastelliste [pastelist] NMF pastellist

pastenague [pastənag] NF stingray

pastèque [pastɛk] NF watermelon

pasteur [pastœʀ] NM [a] (*Rel* = *prêtre*) minister, pastor, preacher (*US*) [b] (*littér, Rel* = *berger*) shepherd; **le Bon Pasteur** the Good Shepherd

pasteurien, -ienne [pastœʀjɛ̃, jɛn] [1] ADJ of Pasteur; **la méthode pasteurienne** Pasteur's method [2] NM,F scientist of the Pasteur Institute

pasteurisation [pastœʀizasjɔ̃] NF pasteurization

pasteuriser [pastœʀize] ▸conjug 1◂ VT to pasteurize

pastiche [pastiʃ] NM (= *imitation*) pastiche

pasticher [pastiʃe] ▸conjug 1◂ VT to do (*ou* write *etc*) a pastiche of

pasticheur, -euse [pastiʃœʀ, øz] NM,F (*gén*) imitator; (= *auteur*) author of pastiches

pastille [pastij] NF [*médicament, sucre*] pastille, lozenge; [*encens, couleur*] block; [*papier, tissu*] disc; **~s de menthe** mints; **~s pour la toux** cough drops *ou* lozenges *ou* pastilles (*Brit*); **~s pour la gorge** throat lozenges *ou* pastilles (*Brit*); **~ de silicium** silicon chip

pastis [pastis] NM (= *boisson*) pastis; (‡ *dial = ennui*) fix*; **être dans le ~** to be in a fix* *ou* a jam*

pastoral, e (*mpl* **-aux**) [pastɔʀal, o] [1] ADJ (*gén*) pastoral [2] **pastorale** NF (*Littérat, Peinture, Rel*) pastoral; (*Mus*) pastorale

pastorat [pastɔʀa] NM pastorate

pastorien, -ienne [pastɔʀjɛ̃, jɛn] ADJ, NM,F = **pasteurien**

pastoureau (*pl* **pastoureaux**) [pastuʀo] NM (*littér*) shepherd boy

pastourelle [pastuʀɛl] NF (*littér*) shepherd girl; (*Mus*) pastourelle

pat [pat] [1] ADJ INV stalemate(d) [2] NM **le ~** stalemate; **faire ~** to end in (a) stalemate; **faire qn ~** to stalemate sb

patachon [pataʃɔ̃] NM → **vie**

patagon, -onne [patagɔ̃, ɔn] [1] ADJ Patagonian [2] **Patagon(ne)** NM,F Patagonian

Patagonie [patagɔni] NF Patagonia

patagonien, -ienne [patagɔnjɛ̃, jɛn] [1] ADJ Patagonian [2] **Patagonien(ne)** NM,F Patagonian

pataphysique [patafizik] NF pataphysics *sg*

patapouf [patapuf] [1] EXCL (*langage enfantin*) whoops!; **faire ~** to tumble (down) [2] NMF* fatty*; **un gros ~** a big fat lump*

pataquès [patakɛs] NM [a] (= *faute de liaison*) mistaken elision; (= *faute de langage*) malapropism [b] (*péj*) (= *discours*) incoherent jumble; (= *confusion*) muddle; **il a fait un ~** (*discours*) his speech was an incoherent jumble; (*confusion*) he got things really confused, he muddled things up (*surtout Brit*)

patata* [patata] EXCL → **patati**

patate [patat] NF [a] (*Bot, Culin*) **~ (douce)** sweet potato [b] (* = *pomme de terre*) potato, spud* (*surtout Brit*) [c] (‡ = *imbécile*) chump*, clot* [d] (‡ = *coup de poing*) punch; **il s'est reçu une ~ en pleine figure** he got smacked in the mouth*, he got punched in the face → **gros**

patati [patati] EXCL **et ~ et patata*** and so on and so forth

patatras [patatʀa] EXCL crash!

pataud, e [pato, od] [1] ADJ clumsy, lumpish (*Brit*) [2] NM,F lump [3] NM (= *chien*) pup(py) (*with large paws*)

pataugas® [patogas] NM hiking boot

pataugeoire [patoʒwaʀ] NF paddling pool

patauger [patoʒe] ▸conjug 3◂ VI [a] (= *marcher*) (*avec effort*) to wade about; (*avec plaisir*) to paddle, splash about; **on a dû ~ dans la boue pour y aller** we had to squelch through the mud to get there [b] (*dans un discours*) to get bogged down; (*dans une matière*) to flounder; **le projet patauge** the project is getting nowhere

patch [patʃ] NM (*Méd* = *timbre*) (skin) patch

patchouli [patʃuli] NM patchouli

patchwork [patʃwœʀk] NM patchwork; **en ~** patchwork (*épith*)

pâte [pat] [1] NF [a] (*Culin*) (*à tarte*) pastry; (*à gâteaux*) mixture; (*à pain*) dough; (*à frire*) batter; **il est de la ~ dont sont faits les héros** he's the stuff heroes are made of → **bon¹, coq¹, main**
[b] [*fromage*] cheese; **(fromage à) ~ dure/molle/cuite/fermentée** hard/soft/cooked/fermented cheese
[c] **~s (alimentaires)** pasta; (*dans la soupe*) noodles
[d] (*gén*) (= *substance*) paste; (= *crème*) cream
[e] (*Art*) paste
[2] COMP ► **pâte d'amandes** almond paste, marzipan ► **pâte brisée** shortcrust (*Brit*) *ou* pie crust (*US*) pastry ► **pâte à choux** choux pastry ► **pâte à crêpes** pancake (*Brit*) *ou* crepe batter ► **pâte dentifrice** toothpaste ► **pâte feuilletée** puff *ou* flaky (*Brit*) pastry ► **pâte à frire** batter ► **pâte de fruits** fruit jelly; **une framboise en ~ de fruit** a raspberry fruit jelly ► **pâte à modeler** modelling clay, Plasticine® ► **pâte molle** (*péj*) milksop, spineless individual ► **pâte à pain** (bread) dough ► **pâte à papier** wood pulp ► **pâtes pectorales** cough drops *ou* pastilles (*Brit*) ► **pâte sablée** sablé (*Brit*) *ou* sugar crust (*US*) pastry ► **pâte à sel** *modelling dough used in arts and crafts made from a mixture of flour, water and salt* ► **pâte de verre** *molten glass*; **bijoux en ~ de verre** paste jewellery

pâté [pate] NM [a] (*Culin*) pâté; **~ en croûte** ≈ pork pie; **petit ~** meat patty, small pork pie; **~ de campagne** pâté de campagne, farmhouse pâté; **~ de foie** liver pâté; **~ impérial** spring roll (*Brit*), egg roll (*US*) [b] (= *tache d'encre*) (ink) blot [c] **~ de maisons** block (of houses) [d] **~ (de sable)** sandpie, sandcastle

pâtée [pate] NF [a] [*volaille*] mash (*NonC*), feed (*NonC*); [*porcs*] swill (*NonC*); **~ pour chiens** dog food [b] (* = *punition, défaite*) hiding*; **recevoir la *ou* une ~** to get a hiding*; **donner la *ou* une ~ à qn** to give sb a hiding*

patelin¹* [patlɛ̃] NM village; (*péj*) **~ paumé** godforsaken place*

patelin², e [patlɛ̃, in] ADJ (*littér péj*) bland, smooth, ingratiating

patelinerie [patlinʀi] NF (*littér péj*) blandness (*NonC*), smoothness (*NonC*)

patelle [patɛl] NF (*Zool*) limpet; (= *vase*) patera

patène [patɛn] NF(*F*) paten

patenôtre [pat(ə)notʀ(ə)] NF (†, *péj*) (= *prière*) paternoster, orison† (*littér*); (= *marmonnement*) gibberish (*NonC*)

patent, e¹ [patɑ̃, ɑ̃t] ADJ obvious, manifest, patent (*frm*); **il est ~ que ...** it is patently obvious that ... → **lettre**

patentable [patɑ̃tabl] ADJ (*Comm*) liable to trading dues, subject to a (trading) licence

patente² [patɑ̃t] NF (*Comm*) trading dues *ou* licence; (*Naut*) bill of health

patenté, e [patɑ̃te] ADJ (*Comm*) licensed; (*hum* = *attitré*) established, officially recognized; **c'est un menteur ~** he's a thoroughgoing liar

pater [patɛʀ] NM INV [a] (‡ = *père*) old man*, pater* † (*Brit*) [b] (*Rel*) **Pater** pater, paternoster [c] (*Antiq, fig*) **familias** paterfamilias

patère [patɛʀ] NF (= *portemanteau*) (hat- *ou* coat-)peg; [*rideau*] curtain hook; (= *vase, rosace*) patera

paternalisme [patɛʀnalism] NM paternalism

paternaliste [patɛʀnalist] ADJ paternalistic

paterne [patɛʀn] ADJ (*littér*) bland

paternel, -elle [patɛʀnɛl] [1] ADJ [a] [*autorité, descendance*] paternal; **du côté ~** on one's father's side; **ma grand-mère paternelle** my grandmother on my father's side, my pater-

nal grandmother; **quitter le domicile ~** to leave one's father's house; **demander l'autorisation paternelle** to ask for one's father's permission; **elle a repris l'entreprise paternelle** she took over her father's company; **sa fibre paternelle n'est pas très développée** he's not really cut out to be a father [b] (= *bienveillant*) [*personne, regard, conseil*] fatherly [2] NM (‡ = *père*) old man*

paternellement [patɛʀnɛlmɑ̃] ADV [*agir, sourire*] paternally, in a fatherly way

paternité [patɛʀnite] NF [a] (*Jur*) paternity, fatherhood; **attribution de ~** paternity; **action en recherche de ~** paternity suit; **jugement en constatation de ~** paternity order [b] [*roman*] paternity, authorship; [*invention, théorie*] paternity

pâteux, -euse [patø, øz] ADJ (*gén*) pasty; [*pain*] doughy; [*encre*] thick; [*langue*] coated, furred (*Brit*); [*voix*] thick; [*style*] woolly (*Brit*); **avoir la bouche pâteuse** to have a coated tongue

pathétique [patetik] [1] ADJ moving, full of pathos (*attrib*); (*Anat*) pathetic [2] NM **le ~** pathos

pathétiquement [patetikmɑ̃] ADV movingly

pathétisme [patetism] NM (*littér*) pathos

pathogène [patoʒɛn] ADJ pathogenic

pathologie [patɔlɔʒi] NF pathology

pathologique [patɔlɔʒik] ADJ pathological; **c'est un cas ~*** he's (*ou* she's) sick*

pathologiquement [patɔlɔʒikmɑ̃] ADV pathologically

pathologiste [patɔlɔʒist] NMF pathologist

pathos [patos] NM (overdone) pathos, emotionalism

patibulaire [patibylɛʀ] ADJ [*personnage*] sinister-looking; **avoir une mine *ou* un air ~** to look sinister, be sinister-looking

patiemment [pasjamɑ̃] ADV patiently

patience¹ [pasjɑ̃s] NF [a] (*gén*) patience; **souffrir avec ~** to bear one's sufferings with patience *ou* patiently; **perdre ~** to lose (one's) patience; **prendre *ou* s'armer de ~** to be patient, have patience; **il faut avoir une ~ d'ange pour le supporter** it takes the patience of a saint *ou* of Job to put up with him; **je suis à bout de ~** I'm at the end of my patience, my patience is exhausted; **ma ~ a des limites !** there are limits to my patience! → **mal** [b] (*Cartes*) (= *jeu*) patience (*Brit*) (*NonC*), solitaire (*US*) (*NonC*); (= *partie*) game of patience (*Brit*) *ou* solitaire (*US*); **faire des ~s** to play patience (*Brit*) *ou* solitaire (*US*) [c] (*loc*) **~, j'arrive !** wait a minute! *ou* hang on!*, I'm coming; **~, il est bientôt l'heure** it's almost time; **encore un peu de ~** not long now — hold on; **~, j'aurai ma revanche** I'll get even in the end

patience² [pasjɑ̃s] NF (*Bot*) (patience) dock

patient, e [pasjɑ̃, jɑ̃t] [1] ADJ patient [2] NM,F (*Méd*) patient

patienter [pasjɑ̃te] ▸conjug 1◂ VI to wait; **faites-le ~** (*pour un rendez-vous*) ask him to wait, have him wait; (*au téléphone*) ask him to hold; **si vous voulez ~ un instant** could you wait *ou* bear with me a moment?; **lisez ce journal, ça vous fera ~** read this paper to fill in *ou* pass the time; **pour ~, il regardait les tableaux** to fill in *ou* pass the time, he looked at the paintings; **patientez encore un peu** not long now — hold on

patin [patɛ̃] NM [a] [*patineur*] skate; [*luge*] runner; [*rail*] base; (*pour le parquet*) cloth pad (*used as slippers on polished wood floors*); **~ (de frein)** brake block; **~s à glace** ice-skates; **~s à roulettes** roller skates; **~s en ligne** rollerblades, in-line skates; **faire du ~ à glace** to go ice-skating; **faire du ~ à roulettes** to go roller-skating; **faire du ~ en ligne** to go rollerblading [b] (‡ = *baiser*) French kiss; **rouler un ~ à qn** to give sb a French kiss

patinage¹ [patinaʒ] NM (*Sport*) skating; (*Aut*) [*roue*] spinning; [*embrayage*] slipping; **~ artistique** figure skating; **~ à roulettes** roller-skating; **~ de vitesse** speed skating

patinage² [patinaʒ] NM (*Tech*) patination

patine [patin] NF (= *dépôt naturel, vert-de-gris*) patina; (= *coloration, vernis*) sheen; **la ~ du temps** the patina of age; **la table a pris une certaine ~ avec le temps** the table has acquired a patina with age

patiner¹ [patine] ▶conjug 1◀ VI [a] (*Sport*) to skate [b] [*roue*] to spin; [*embrayage*] to slip; **la voiture patina sur la chaussée verglacée** the car skidded on the icy road; **faire ~ l'embrayage** to slip the clutch; **ça patine sur la route** the roads are very slippery [c] [*négociations*] to be at a virtual standstill, be making no headway; [*projet*] to be making no headway

patiner² [patine] ▶conjug 1◀ VT (*Tech*) [+ *bois, bronze, meuble*] to patinate, give a patina to; **des meubles patinés (par les siècles)** furniture that has acquired a patina (over the centuries)

patinette [patinɛt] NF scooter; **~ à pédale** pedal scooter; **faire de la ~** to ride a scooter

patineur, -euse [patinœʀ, øz] NM,F skater

patinoire [patinwaʀ] NF skating rink, ice rink; **cette route est une vraie ~** this road is like an ice rink

patio [pasjo] NM patio

pâtir [pɑtiʀ] ▶conjug 2◀ VI (*littér*) to suffer (**de** because of, on account of)

pâtisserie [pɑtisʀi] NF [a] (= *magasin*) cake shop, patisserie; (= *gâteau*) cake; (*avec pâte à tarte*) pastry; **~ industrielle** (= *gâteaux*) factory-baked cakes; (= *usine*) bakery, cake factory [b] **la ~** (= *art ménager*) cake-making, pastry-making, baking; (= *métier, commerce*) ≈ confectionery; **apprendre la ~** (*comme métier*) to learn to be a pastrycook; ≈ learn confectionery; **faire de la ~** (*en amateur*) to make cakes; **moule/ustensiles à ~** pastry dish/utensils → **rouleau** [c] (= *stuc*) fancy (plaster) moulding

pâtissier, -ière [pɑtisje, jɛʀ] NM,F (*de métier*) pastrycook, ≈ confectioner; **~glacier** confectioner and ice-cream maker; **~chocolatier** confectioner and chocolate maker; **il est bon ~** he makes good cakes → **crème**

pâtisson [pɑtisɔ̃] NM custard marrow (*Brit*) ou squash (*US*)

patois, e [patwa, waz] [1] ADJ patois (*épith*), dialectal, dialect (*épith*) [2] NM patois, (provincial) dialect; **parler (en) ~** to speak (in) patois

patoisant, e [patwazɑ̃, ɑ̃t] [1] ADJ patois-speaking, dialect-speaking [2] NM,F patois ou dialect speaker

patoiser [patwaze] ▶conjug 1◀ VI to speak (in) dialect ou patois

patraque* [patrak] ADJ peaky* (*Brit*), off-colour (*Brit*) (*attrib*), peaked* (*US*); **être/se sentir ~** to be/feel off-colour* (*Brit*) ou peaked* (*US*)

pâtre [pɑtʀ] NM (*littér*) shepherd

patriarcal, e (*mpl* **-aux**) [patʀijaʀkal, o] ADJ patriarchal

patriarcat [patʀijaʀka] NM (*Rel*) patriarchate; (*Sociol*) patriarchy, patriarchate

patriarche [patʀijaʀʃ] NM patriarch

patricien, -ienne [patʀisjɛ̃, jɛn] ADJ, NM,F patrician

Patrick [patʀik] NM Patrick

patrie [patʀi] NF [*personne*] (= *pays*) homeland, native country ou land; (= *région*) native region; (= *ville*) native town; **mourir pour la ~** to die for one's country; **c'est ma seconde ~** it's my adoptive country; **Florence, la ~ de l'art** Florence, cradle of the arts; **la France, ~ des**

---

droits de l'homme France, the birthplace of human rights → **mère**

patrimoine [patʀimwan] NM (*gén*) inheritance, patrimony (*frm*); (*Jur*) patrimony (*Fin = biens*) property; (*fig = bien commun*) heritage, patrimony (*frm*); (*Bio*) **~ héréditaire** ou **génétique** genetic inheritance; **~ culturel/national/naturel** cultural/national/natural heritage; **site inscrit au ~ mondial de l'Unesco** Unesco World Heritage Site; **~ immobilier** [*ville*] public buildings; [*personne*] residential property; **~ social** (= *logements*) public housing

┌─────────────────────────┐
│ **JOURNÉES DU PATRIMOINE** │
└─────────────────────────┘
The term **les Journées du patrimoine** *refers to an annual cultural event held throughout France, during which state properties are opened to the public for the weekend. The rare opportunity to visit the inside of such prestigious institutions as ministries and the Élysée Palace has made the* **Journées du patrimoine** *extremely popular.*

patrimonial, e (*mpl* **-iaux**) [patʀimɔnjal, jo] ADJ (*d'un pays*) relating to its national (ou cultural) heritage; (*d'un particulier*) relating to personal assets; **déclaration de situation ~e** statement of net personal assets (*made by a politician when taking up office*); **le droit ~** inheritance law, law of succession; **intérêts patrimoniaux** proprietary interests

patriotard [patʀijɔtaʀ, aʀd] (*péj*) [1] ADJ jingoistic [2] NM,F jingoist

patriote [patʀijɔt] [1] ADJ patriotic [2] NMF (*gén*) patriot; (*Hist*) **les ~s** the Patriots

patriotique [patʀijɔtik] ADJ patriotic

patriotiquement [patʀijɔtikmɑ̃] ADV patriotically

patriotisme [patʀijɔtism] NM patriotism

patron¹ [patʀɔ̃] [1] NM [a] (= *propriétaire*) owner, boss; (= *gérant*) manager, boss; (= *employeur*) employer; **le ~ est là?** is the boss in?; **le ~ de l'usine** the factory owner ou manager; **le ~ du restaurant** the proprietor of the restaurant, the restaurant owner; **il est ~ d'hôtel** he's a hotel proprietor; **c'est le grand ~*** he's (ou she's) the big boss*; **un petit ~** a boss of a small (ou medium-sized) company; **~ boulanger/boucher** master baker/butcher [b] (*Hist, Rel = protecteur*) patron; **saint ~** patron saint [c] (‡ = *mari*) **le ~** her (ou my ou your) old man* [d] (*Hôpital*) ≈ senior consultant (*of teaching hospital*) [2] COMP ▶ **patron (pêcheur)** (*Naut*) skipper ▶ **patron d'industrie** captain of industry ▶ **patron de presse** press baron ou tycoon ou magnate ▶ **patron de thèse** (*Univ*) supervisor (*of a doctoral thesis*)

patron² [patʀɔ̃] NM (*Couture*) pattern; (= *pochoir*) stencil; **~ de robe** dress pattern; **(taille) demi-~/~/grand ~** small/medium/large (size)

patronage [patʀɔnaʒ] NM [a] (= *protection*) patronage; **sous le (haut) ~ de** under the patronage of [b] (= *organisation*) youth club; (*Rel*) youth fellowship; (*fig*) **spectacle de ~** middle-brow show

patronal, e (*mpl* **-aux**) [patʀɔnal, o] ADJ (*Ind*) [*responsabilité, cotisation*] employer's, employers'; (*Rel*) [*fête*] patronal

patronat [patʀɔna] NM (*Ind*) **le ~** the employers

patronne [patʀɔn] NF [a] (= *propriétaire*) owner, boss; (= *gérante*) manager, boss; (= *employeur*) employer [b] (* = *épouse*) **la ~** the ou his (ou my ou your) missus* (*Brit*), his (ou my ou your) old lady* [c] (= *sainte*) patron saint

patronner [patʀɔne] ▶conjug 1◀ VT [+ *association, personne, projet, candidature*] to support; (*financièrement*) to sponsor; **négociations de paix patronnées par l'ONU** peace talks sponsored by the UN

---

patronnesse [patʀɔnɛs] NF → **dame**

patronyme [patʀɔnim] NM patronymic

patronymique [patʀɔnimik] ADJ patronymic

patrouille [patʀuj] NF patrol; **partir** ou **aller en/être de ~** to go/be on patrol; **~ de reconnaissance/de chasse** reconnaissance/fighter patrol

patrouiller [patʀuje] ▶conjug 1◀ VI to patrol, be on patrol; **~ dans les rues** to patrol the streets

patrouilleur [patʀujœʀ] NM (= *soldat*) soldier on patrol (duty), patroller; (*Naut*) patrol boat; (*Aviat*) patrol ou scout plane

patte¹ [pat] [1] NF [a] (= *jambe d'animal*) leg; (= *pied*) [*chat, chien*] paw; [*oiseau*] foot; **~s de devant** forelegs, forefeet; **~s de derrière** hindlegs, hind feet; (*fig*) **coup de ~** cutting remark; **donner un coup de ~ à qch** [*animal*] to hit sth with its paw; **le chien tendit la ~** the dog put its paw out ou gave a paw; **faire ~ de velours** [*chat*] to draw in ou sheathe its claws; [*personne*] to be all sweetness and light; **ça ne va** ou **ne marche que sur trois ~s** [*affaire, projet*] it limps along; [*relation amoureuse*] it struggles along → **bas¹, mouton** [b] (= *jambe*) leg; **nous avons 50 km dans les ~s** we've walked 50 km; **à ~s** on foot; **nous y sommes allés à ~s** we walked ou hoofed‡ it; **bas** ou **court sur ~s** [*personne*] short-legged; [*table, véhicule*] low; **il est toujours dans mes ~s** he's always under my feet; **tirer** ou **traîner la ~** to hobble along; **avoir une ~ folle** to have a gammy* (*Brit*) ou a game* (*US*) leg [c] (‡ = *main*) hand, paw*; **s'il me tombe sous la ~, gare à lui!** if I get my hands on him he'd better look out!; **tomber dans les/se tirer des ~s de qn** to fall into/get out of sb's clutches; **montrer ~ blanche** to show one's credentials [d] (= *style*) [*auteur, peintre*] style, touch; **elle a un bon coup de ~** ≈ she has a nice style ou touch [e] [*ancre*] palm, fluke; (= *languette*) [*poche*] flap; [*vêtement*] strap; (*sur l'épaule*) epaulette; [*portefeuille*] tongue; [*chaussure*] tongue [f] (= *favoris*) **~s (de lapin)** sideburns → **fil, graisser, quatre** *etc* [2] COMP ▶ **pantalon (à) pattes d'éléphant** ou **pattes d'ef*** bell-bottom ou flared trousers, bell-bottoms, flares ▶ **patte à glace** mirror clamp ▶ **patte(s) de mouche** spidery scrawl; **faire des ~s de mouche** to write (in) a spidery scrawl

patte² [pat] NF (*Helv* = *chiffon*) rag; **~ à poussière** duster (*Brit*), dustcloth (*US*); **~ à relaver** tea ou dish towel

patte-d'oie (*pl* **pattes-d'oie**) [patdwa] NF (= *rides*) crow's-foot; (= *carrefour*) branching crossroads ou junction

pattemouille [patmuj] NF damp cloth (for ironing)

pâturage [pɑtyʀaʒ] NM (= *lieu*) pasture; (= *action*) grazing, pasturage; (= *droits*) grazing rights

pâture [pɑtyʀ] NF [a] (= *nourriture*) food; (*lit, fig*) **donner qn en ~ aux fauves** to throw sb to the lions; **il fait sa ~ de romans noirs** he is an avid reader of detective stories, detective stories form his usual reading matter; **les dessins animés qu'on donne en ~ à nos enfants** the cartoons served up to our children; **donner une nouvelle en ~ aux journalistes** to feed a story to journalists [b] (= *pâturage*) pasture

pâturer [pɑtyʀe] ▶conjug 1◀ [1] VI to graze [2] VT **~ l'herbe** to graze

paturon [patyʀɔ̃] NM pastern

Paul [pɔl] NM Paul

paulinien, -ienne [polinjɛ̃, jɛn] ADJ of Saint Paul, Pauline

paulownia [polɔnja] NM paulownia

paume [pom] NF [*main*] palm; **jeu de ~** (= *sport*) real ou royal tennis; (= *lieu*) real-tennis ou royal-tennis court; **jouer à la ~** to play real ou royal tennis

paumé, e⁑ [pome]   (ptp de **paumer**) 1 ADJ a (dans un lieu) lost; (dans un milieu inconnu) bewildered; (dans une explication) lost, at sea*; **habiter un bled ou trou ~** (isolé) to live in a godforsaken place ou hole⁑, live in the middle of nowhere; (sans attrait) to live in a real dump ou godforsaken hole⁑; b (= socialement inadapté) **la jeunesse ~e d'aujourd'hui** the young drop-outs* of today; **il est complètement ~** he's totally lost, he hasn't got a clue where he's going in life 2 NM,F (= marginal) misfit; **un pauvre ~** a poor bum⁑

paumelle [pomɛl]   NF (= gond) split hinge; (Naut) palm

paumer⁑ [pome]   ▷conjug 1◁ 1 VT a (= perdre) to lose b (= prendre) **se faire ~** [criminel] to get nabbed* 2 **se paumer** VPR to get lost

paupérisation [poperizasjɔ̃]   NF pauperization, impoverishment

paupériser [poperize]   ▷conjug 1◁ VT to pauperize, impoverish

paupérisme [poperism]   NM pauperism

paupière [popjɛr]   NF eyelid; **il écoutait, les ~s closes** he was listening with his eyes closed; **battre ou cligner des ~s** to flutter one's eyelashes

paupiette [popjɛt]   NF **~ de veau** veal olive

pause [poz]   NF (= arrêt) break; (en parlant) pause; (Mus) pause; (Sport) half-time; **faire une ~** to have a break, break off; **marquer une ~** [orateur] to pause; [négociations] to break off momentarily; **ils ont marqué une ~ dans la diversification** they have stopped diversifying for the time being, they have put their diversification programme on hold; **ça fait sept ans que je fais ce métier, j'ai besoin de marquer une ~** I've been doing this job for seven years now, I need (to take) a break; **~ café-/thé-/déjeuner** coffee/tea/lunch break; **la ~ de midi** the midday break; **~ publicitaire** commercial break; **faire une ~-cigarette** to stop for a cigarette

pauser [poze]   ▷conjug 1◁ VI **laissez ~ la permanente/le masque 20 minutes** leave the perm in/the face-pack on for 20 minutes; **faire ~ qn**† to keep sb waiting

pauvre [povr]   1 ADJ a [personne, pays, sol, minerai, gisement] poor; [végétation] sparse, poor; [style] weak; (Aut) [mélange] weak; [mobilier, vêtements] cheap-looking; [nourriture, salaire] meagre (Brit), meager (US), poor; **minerai ~ en cuivre** ore with a low copper content, ore poor in copper; **air ~ en oxygène** air low in oxygen; **pays ~ en ressources/hommes** country short of ou lacking resources/men; **nourriture ~ en calcium** (par manque) diet lacking in calcium; (par ordonnance) low-calcium diet; **un village ~ en distractions** a village which is lacking in ou short of amusements; **~ comme Job** as poor as a church mouse; **les couches ~s de la population** the poorer ou deprived sections of the population; **je suis ~ en vaisselle** I don't have much crockery → **rime** b (avant n = piètre) [excuse, argument] weak, pathetic; [devoir] poor; [orateur] weak, bad; **de ~s chances de succès** only a slim ou slender chance of success; **il esquissa un ~ sourire** he smiled weakly ou gave a weak smile c (avant n) poor; **~ type !*** (= malheureux) poor guy!* ou chap!* (Brit); (= crétin) stupid bastard!⁑; **c'est un ~ type** (mal adapté) he's a sad case; (minable) he's a dead loss*; (salaud) he's a swine⁑; **pourquoi une fille comme elle épouserait-elle un ~ type comme moi ?** why would a girl like that marry a nobody* like me?; **~ con !⁑** you stupid bastard!⁑ ou sod!⁑ (Brit); **tu es bien naïve ma ~ fille !** poor dear, you're so naïve!; **c'est une ~ fille** she's a sad case; (littér, hum) **~ hère** down-and-out*; (Rel) **les ~s d'esprit** (= simple d'esprit) half-wit; (Rel) **les ~s**

d'esprit the poor in spirit; **comme disait mon ~ mari** as my poor (dear) husband used to say; (hum) **~ de moi !** poor (little) me!; **~ petit !** poor (little) thing!; **mon ~ ami** my dear friend; **tu es complètement fou, mon ~ vieux !** you must be crazy, mate!* (Brit) ou man!* ; **elle me faisait pitié avec son ~ petit air** I felt sorry for her, she looked so wretched ou miserable 2 NM,F (= personne pauvre) poor man ou woman, pauper†; **les ~s** the poor; **ce pays compte encore beaucoup de ~s** there's still a lot of poverty ou there are still many poor people in this country; **le caviar du ~** the poor man's caviar b (*: marquant dédain ou commisération) **mon** (ou **ma**) **~, si tu voyais comment ça se passe ...** but my dear fellow (ou girl etc) ou friend, if you saw what goes on ...; **le ~, il a dû en voir !** the poor guy* ou chap* (Brit), he must have had a hard time of it!; **les ~s !** the poor things!

pauvrement [povrəmɑ̃]   ADV [meublé, éclairé, vivre] poorly; [vêtu] poorly, shabbily

pauvresse† [povrɛs]   NF poor woman ou wretch

pauvret, -ette [povrɛ, ɛt]   NM,F poor (little) thing

pauvreté [povrəte]   NF [personne] poverty; [mobilier] cheapness; [langage] weakness, poorness; [sol] poverty, poorness; **la ~ des moyens disponibles** the dearth of available resources, the inadequacy of the available resources; **la ~ de leur vocabulaire** the poverty of their vocabulary ■ (PROV) **~ n'est pas vice** poverty is not a vice, there is no shame in being poor → **vœu**

pavage [pavaʒ]   NM (avec des pavés) cobbling; (avec des dalles) paving; **refaire le ~ d'une rue** to recobble (ou repave) a street

pavane [pavan]   NF pavane

pavaner (se) [pavane]   ▷conjug 1◁ VPR to strut about; **se pavaner comme un dindon** to strut about like a turkey-cock

pavé [pave]   NM a [chaussée, cour] cobblestone; **déraper sur le ~ ou les ~s** to skid on the cobbles; **être sur le ~** (sans domicile) to be on the streets, be homeless; (sans emploi) to be out of a job; **mettre ou jeter qn sur le ~** (domicile) to turn ou throw sb out (onto the streets); (emploi) to give sb the sack*, throw sb out; **j'ai l'impression d'avoir un ~ sur l'estomac*** I feel as if I've got a lead weight in my stomach; **c'est l'histoire du ~ de l'ours** it's another example of misguided zeal; (fig) **jeter un ~ dans la mare** to set the cat among the pigeons → **battre, brûler, haut** b (* = livre épais) massive ou hefty* tome c (Culin) (= viande) thickly-cut steak; (= gâteau) **~ au chocolat** chocolate slab cake d (Presse) **~ publicitaire** (large) display advertisement e (Ordin) **~ numérique** numeric keypad

pavement [pavmɑ̃]   NM ornamental tiling

paver [pave]   ▷conjug 1◁ VT (avec des pavés) to cobble; (avec des dalles) to pave; **cour pavée** cobbled (ou paved) yard → **enfer**

paveur [pavœr]   NM paver

pavillon [pavijɔ̃]   1 NM a (= villa) house; (= loge de gardien) lodge; (= section d'hôpital) ward, pavilion; (= corps de bâtiment) wing, pavilion; [jardin] pavilion; [club de golf] clubhouse b (Naut) flag; **sous ~ panaméen** under the Panamanian flag → **baisser, battre** c (Mus) [instrument] bell; [phonographe] horn d [oreille] pavilion, pinna 2 COMP ▶ **pavillon de banlieue** suburban house, house in the suburbs ▶ **pavillon de chasse** hunting lodge ▶ **pavillon de complaisance** flag of convenience ▶ **pavillon de détresse** distress flag ▶ **pavillon de guerre** war flag ▶ **pavillon noir** Jolly Roger ▶ **pavillon de quarantaine** yellow flag ▶ **pavillon à tête de mort** skull and cross-

bones ▶ **pavillon de verdure** leafy arbour ou bower

pavillonnaire [pavijɔnɛr]   ADJ **lotissement ~** private housing estate; **banlieue ~** residential suburb (consisting of houses rather than apartment blocks)

Pavlov [pavlɔv]   N Pavlov; **le chien de ~** Pavlov's dog; **réflexe de ~** Pavlovian response ou reaction

pavlovien, -ienne [pavlɔvjɛ̃, jɛn]   ADJ Pavlovian

pavois [pavwa]   NM (Naut = bordage) bulwark; (Hist = bouclier) shield; **hisser le grand ~** to dress over all ou full; **hisser le petit ~** to dress with masthead flags; **hisser qn sur le ~** to carry sb shoulder-high

pavoiser [pavwaze]   ▷conjug 1◁ 1 VT [+ navire] to dress; [+ monument] to deck with flags 2 VI to put out flags; (fig, Sport) [supporters] to rejoice, wave the banners, exult; **toute la ville a pavoisé** there were flags out all over the town; **il pavoise maintenant qu'on lui a donné raison publiquement** he's rejoicing openly now that he has been publicly acknowledged to be in the right; **il n'y a pas de quoi ~ !** it's nothing to write home about! ou to get excited about!

pavot [pavo]   NM poppy

payable [pejabl]   ADJ payable; **~ en 3 fois** [somme] payable in 3 instalments; [objet] that can be paid for in 3 instalments; **l'impôt est ~ par tous** taxes must be paid by everyone; (Fin) **billet ~ à vue** bill payable at sight; **chèque ~ à** cheque payable to; **appareil ~ à crédit** piece of equipment which can be paid for on credit

payant, e [pejɑ̃, ɑ̃t]   ADJ [spectateur] paying; [billet, place] which one must pay for, not free (attrib); [spectacle] with an admission charge; (= rentable) [affaire] profitable; [politique, conduite, effort] which pays off; **« entrée ~e »** "admission fee payable"; **c'est ~ ?** do you have to pay (to get in)?

paye [pej]   NF = **paie**

payement [pejmɑ̃]   NM = **paiement**

payer [peje]   ▷conjug 8◁ 1 VT a [+ somme, cotisation, intérêt] to pay; [+ facture, dette] to pay, settle; **~ comptant** to pay cash; **~ rubis sur l'ongle**† to pay cash on the nail; **c'est lui qui paie** he's paying ■ (PROV) **qui paie ses dettes s'enrichit** the rich man is the one who pays his debts b [+ employé] to pay; [+ tueur] to hire; [+ entrepreneur] to pay, settle up with; **être payé par chèque/en espèces/en nature/à l'heure** to be paid by cheque/in cash/in kind/by the hour; **être payé à la pièce** to be on piecework; **~ qn de ou en paroles/promesses** to fob sb off with (empty) words/promises; **je ne suis pas payé pour ça*** that's not what I'm paid for; (fig) **il est payé pour le savoir !** he should know! c [+ travail, service, maison, marchandise] to pay for; **je l'ai payé de ma poche** I paid for it out of my own pocket; **les réparations ne sont pas encore payées** the repairs haven't been paid for yet; **il m'a fait ~ 50 F** he charged me 50 francs (**pour** for); **~ le déplacement de qn** to pay sb's travelling expenses; **~ la casse** to pay for the damage; (fig) **~ les pots cassés** to pick up the pieces; **travail bien/mal payé** well-paid/badly-paid work → **addition, congé** d (* = offrir) **~ qch à qn** to buy sth for sb; **c'est moi qui paie (à boire)** the drinks are on me*, have this one on me*; **~ des vacances/un voyage à qn** to pay for sb to go on holiday/on a trip; **~ à boire à qn** to stand ou buy sb a drink; **sa mère lui a payé une voiture** his mother bought him a car e (= récompenser) to reward; **le succès le paie de tous ses efforts** his success makes all his efforts worthwhile ou rewards him for all his efforts; **il l'aimait et elle le payait de retour** he

f (= *expier*) [+ *faute, crime*] to pay for; **~ qch de cinq ans de prison** to get five years in jail for sth; **il l'a payé de sa vie/santé** it cost him his life/health; **il a payé cher son imprudence** he paid dearly for his rashness, his rashness cost him dear(ly); (*en menace*) **il me le paiera!** he'll pay for this!, I'll make him pay for this!

2 VI **a** [*effort, tactique*] to pay off; [*métier*] to be well-paid; **le crime ne paie pas** crime doesn't pay; **~ pour qn** (*lit*) to pay for sb; (*fig*) to take the blame instead of sb, carry the can for sb*

b (*loc*) **~ d'audace** to take a gamble *ou* a risk; **~ de sa personne** to make sacrifices; **pour que notre association fonctionne, il faut que chacun paie de sa personne** in order for our association to work, everyone must pull their weight *ou* make a real effort; **ce poisson ne paie pas de mine** this fish doesn't look very appetizing; **l'hôtel ne paie pas de mine** the hotel isn't much to look at

3 se payer VPR **a** **tout se paie** (*lit*) everything must be paid for; (*fig*) everything has its price; **payez-vous et rendez-moi la monnaie** take what I owe you and give me the change **b** (* = *s'offrir*) [+ *objet*] to buy o.s., treat o.s. to; **on va se ~ un bon dîner/le restaurant** we're going to treat ourselves to a slap-up* meal/to a meal out; **se ~ une pinte de bon sang†** to have a good laugh*; **se ~ la tête de qn** (= *ridiculiser*) to make fun of sb, take the mickey out of sb* (*Brit*); (= *tromper*) to take sb for a ride*, have sb on* (*Brit*); **se ~ une bonne grippe** to get a bad dose of the flu; **il s'est payé un arbre/le trottoir/un piéton** he wrapped his car round a tree/ran into the kerb/mowed a pedestrian down; **j'ai glissé et je me suis payé la chaise** I slipped and banged *ou* crashed into the chair; **ils s'en sont drôlement payé ◊ ils s'en sont payé une bonne tranche** they had (themselves) a good time *ou* a whale of a time*; **se ~ qn!** (*physiquement*) to knock the living daylights out of sb*; (*verbalement*) to give sb what for* → **luxe** **c** (= *se contenter*) **on ne peut plus se ~ de mots** it's time we stopped all the talking and took some action; **dans la lutte contre le chômage, il ne s'agit pas de se ~ de mots** fine words are not enough in the battle against unemployment

payeur, -euse [pɛjœʀ, øz] **1** ADJ **organisme/service ~** claims department/office; **établissement ~** [*chèque*] paying bank **2** NM,F payer; (*Mil, Naut*) paymaster; **mauvais ~** bad debtor → **conseilleur**

pays¹ [pei] **1** NM **a** (= *contrée, habitants*) country; **des ~ lointains** far-off countries *ou* lands; **les ~ membres de l'Union européenne** the countries which are members of *ou* the member countries of the European Union; **la France est le ~ du vin** France is the land of wine → **mal**
b (= *région*) region; **un ~ de légumes, d'élevage et de lait** a vegetable-growing, cattle-breeding and dairy region; **c'est le ~ de la tomate** it's tomato-growing country; **le ~ de Balzac/Yeats** Balzac/Yeats country; **nous sommes en plein ~ du vin** we're in the heart of the wine country; **revenir au ~** to go back home; **il est du ~** he's from these parts *ou* this area; **les gens du ~** the local people, the locals; **vin de** *ou* **du ~** locally-produced *ou* local wine, vin de pays (*Brit*); **melons/pêches de** *ou* **du ~** local(ly)-grown melons/peaches → **jambon**
c († = *village*) village
d (*loc*) **le ~ des fées** fairyland; **le ~ des rêves** *ou* **des songes** the land of dreams, dreamland; **je veux voir du ~** I want to travel around; **il a vu du ~** he's been round a bit *ou* seen the world; **se comporter comme en ~ conquis** to lord it over everyone, act all high and mighty; **être en ~ de connaissance** (*dans*

une réunion) to be among friends *ou* familiar faces; (*sur un sujet, dans un lieu*) to be on home ground *ou* on familiar territory

2 COMP ► **pays d'accueil** [*conférences, jeux*] host country; [*réfugiés*] country of refuge ► **le Pays basque** the Basque Country ► **pays de cocagne** land of plenty, land of milk and honey ► **pays développé** developed country *ou* nation ► **le pays de Galles** Wales ► **pays industrialisé** industrialized country *ou* nation; **nouveaux ~ industrialisés** newly industrialized countries ► **les pays les moins avancés** the less developed countries ► **pays en voie de développement** developing country ► **pays en voie d'industrialisation** industrializing country

pays², e [pei, peiz] NM,F (*dial* = *compatriote*) **nous sommes ~** we come from the same village *ou* region *ou* part of the country; **elle est ma ~e** she comes from the same village *ou* region *ou* part of the country as me

paysage [peizaʒ] NM **a** (*gén*) landscape, scenery (*NonC*); (*Peinture*) landscape (painting); **on découvrait un ~ magnifique/un ~ de montagne** a magnificent/a mountainous landscape lay before us; **nous avons traversé des ~s magnifiques** we drove through (some) magnificent scenery; **les ~s orientaux** the landscape *ou* the scenery of the East; **ce bâtiment nous gâche le ~** that building spoils our view; **le ~ urbain** the urban landscape; (*iro*) **ça fait bien dans le ~!** it's all part of the image!, it fits the image!; (*Ordin*) **mode ~** landscape mode **b** (= *situation*) scene; **le ~ politique/cinématographique** the political/film scene; **dans le ~ audiovisuel français** on the French broadcasting scene

paysagé, e [peizaʒe], **paysager, -ère** [peizaʒe, ɛʀ] ADJ **parc paysager** landscaped garden; **bureau ~** open-plan office

paysagiste [peizaʒist] NMF (*Peinture*) landscape painter; **architecte/jardinier ~** landscape architect/gardener

paysan, -anne [peizɑ̃, an] **1** ADJ **a** (= *agricole*) [*monde, problème*] farming (*épith*); [*agitation, revendications*] farmers', of the farmers; (= *rural*) [*vie, coutumes*] country (*épith*); (*péj*) [*air, manières*] peasant (*épith*), rustic **b** (*Culin*) **salade paysanne** salad with onions and chopped bacon; **à la paysanne** with onions and chopped bacon **2** NM **a** (*gén*) (small) farmer; (*péj*) peasant **b** (*Hist*) peasant **3 paysanne** NF (*gén*) (small) farmer; (*Hist*) peasant (woman); (*péj*) peasant

paysannerie [peizanʀi] NF (*Hist ou péj*) peasantry

paysannat [peizana] NM (small) farmers

Pays-Bas [peiba] NMPL **les ~** the Netherlands

PC [pese] NM **a** (ABRÉV = **parti communiste**) → **parti¹** **b** (ABRÉV = **poste de commandement**) → **poste²** **c** (*Ordin*) (ABRÉV = **personal computer**) PC

PCB [pesebe] NM (ABRÉV = **polychlorobiphényle**) PCB

Pcc (ABRÉV = **pour copie conforme**) → **copie**

PCF [peseef] NM (ABRÉV = **parti communiste français**) French political party

▼ **PCV** [peseve] NM (ABRÉV = **percevoir**) (*Téléc*) **(appel en) ~** reverse-charge call (*Brit*), collect call (*US*); **appeler en ~** to make a reverse-charge call (*Brit*), call collect (*US*)

PDG [pedeʒe] NM INV (ABRÉV = **président-directeur général**) → **président**

PE [peə] NM (ABRÉV = **Parlement européen**) EP

PEA [peəa] NM (ABRÉV = **plan d'épargne en actions**) → **plan¹**

péage [peaʒ] NM (= *droit*) toll; (= *barrière*) tollgate; **autoroute à ~** toll motorway (*Brit*), turnpike (*US*); **pont à ~** toll bridge; **poste de ~** tollbooth; (*TV*) **chaîne/télévision à ~** pay channel/TV

péagiste [peaʒist] NMF tollbooth attendant

peau (*pl* **peaux**) [po] **1** NF **a** [*personne*] skin; **avoir une ~ de pêche** to have a peach-like complexion; **soins de la/maladie de ~** skin care/disease; **~x mortes** dead skin; **n'avoir que la ~ et les os** to be all skin and bones; **attraper qn par la ~ du cou** *ou* **du dos** *ou* **des fesses** (= *empoigner rudement*) to grab sb by the scruff of the neck; (= *s'en saisir à temps*) to grab hold of sb in the nick of time; **faire ~ neuve** [*parti politique, administration*] to adopt *ou* find a new image; [*personne*] (*en changeant d'habit*) to change (one's clothes); (*en changeant de conduite*) to turn over a new leaf → **coûter, fleur**
b (* = *corps, vie*) **jouer** *ou* **risquer sa ~** to risk one's neck* *ou* hide*; **il y a laissé sa ~** it cost him his life; **sauver sa ~** to save one's skin *ou* hide*; **tenir à sa ~** to value one's life*; **sa ~ ne vaut pas cher ◊ je ne donnerai pas cher de sa ~** he's dead meat*; **se faire crever** *ou* **trouer la ~** to get killed, get a bullet in one's hide*; **recevoir douze balles dans la ~** to be gunned down by a firing squad *ou* an execution squad; **on lui fera la ~!** we'll bump him off*; **je veux** *ou* **j'aurai sa ~!** I'll have his hide for this!*; **être bien/mal dans sa ~** (*physiquement*) to feel great*/awful*; (*mentalement*) **être bien dans sa ~** to be happy in o.s.; **il est mal dans sa ~** he's not a happy person; **avoir qn dans la ~*** to be crazy about sb*; **avoir le jeu** *etc* **dans la ~** to have gambling *etc* in one's blood; **se mettre dans la ~ de qn** to put o.s. in sb's place *ou* shoes; **entrer dans la ~ du personnage** to get (right) into the part; **je ne voudrais pas être dans sa ~** I wouldn't like to be in his shoes *ou* place*; **avoir la ~ dure*** (= *être solide*) to be hardy; (= *résister à la critique*) [*personne*] to be thick-skinned, have a thick skin; [*idées, préjugés*] to be difficult to get rid of *ou* to overcome
c [*animal*] (*gén*) skin; (= *cuir*) hide; (= *fourrure*) pelt; [*éléphant, buffle*] hide; **gants/vêtements de ~** leather gloves/clothes; **cuir pleine ~** full leather → **vendre**
d [*fruit, lait, peinture*] skin; [*fromage*] rind; (= *épluchure*) peel; (*lit, fig*) **glisser sur une ~ de banane** to slip on a banana skin; **enlever la ~ de** [+ *fruit*] to peel; [+ *fromage*] to take the rind off
e **~ de balle!** nothing doing!*, not a chance!*, no way!*

2 COMP ► **peau d'âne†** (= *diplôme*) diploma, sheepskin* (*US*) ► **peau de chagrin** (*lit*) shagreen; **diminuer** *ou* **rétrécir** *ou* **se réduire comme une ~ de chagrin** to shrink away ► **peau de chamois** chamois leather, shammy ► **peau d'hareng*:** **quelle ~ d'hareng tu fais!** you naughty thing!* ► **peau lainée** treated sheepskin ► **peau de mouton** sheepskin; **en ~ de mouton** sheepskin (*épith*) ► **peau de porc** pigskin ► **peau d'orange** (*Physiol*) orange peel effect ► **peau de serpent** snakeskin ► **peau de tambour** drumskin ► **peau de vache*** (= *homme*) bastard**; (= *femme*) bitch** ► **peau de zénana** *ou* **de zébi: c'est en ~ de zénana** *ou* **de zébi** it's made of some sort of cheap stuff

peaucier [posje] ADJ M, NM **(muscle) ~** platysma

peaufiner [pofine] ▶ conjug 1 ◀ VT [+ *travail*] to polish up, put the finishing touches to; [+ *style*] to polish

Peau-Rouge (*pl* **Peaux-Rouges**) [poʀuʒ] NMF Red Indian, Redskin

peausserie [posʀi] NF (= *articles*) leatherwear (*NonC*); (= *commerce*) skin trade; (= *boutique*) suede and leatherware shop

peaussier [posje] **1** ADJ M leather (*épith*) **2** NM (= *ouvrier*) leatherworker; (= *commerçant*) leather dealer

pébroc*, **pébroque*** [pebʀɔk] NM umbrella, brolly* (Brit)

pécan, **pecan** [pekã] NM (**noix de**) ~ pecan (nut)

pécari [pekaʀi] NM peccary

peccadille [pekadij] NF (= vétille) trifle; (= faute) peccadillo

pechblende [pɛʃblɛ̃d] NF pitchblende

péché [peʃe] [1] NM sin; **pour mes ~s** for my sins; **à tout ~ miséricorde** every sin can be forgiven ou pardoned; **vivre dans le ~** (gén) to lead a sinful life; (sans être marié) to live in sin; **mourir en état de ~** to die a sinner; **commettre un ~** to sin, commit a sin [2] COMP ► **péché capital** deadly sin; **les sept ~s capitaux** the seven deadly sins ► **péché de chair**† sin of the flesh ► **péché de jeunesse** youthful indiscretion ► **péché mignon**: **le whisky, c'est son ~ mignon** he's rather partial to whisky ► **péché mortel** mortal sin ► **le péché d'orgueil** the sin of pride ► **le péché originel** original sin ► **péché véniel** venial sin

pêche¹ [pɛʃ] [1] NF [a] (= fruit) peach; **~-abricot** ◊ **~ jaune** ou **abricotée** yellow peach; **~ blanche** white peach; **~ de vigne** bush peach; **avoir un teint de ~** to have a peaches and cream complexion → **fendre**, **peau** [b] (* = vitalité) **avoir la ~** to be on form; **avoir une ~ d'enfer** to be on top form, be full of beans* (Brit); **ça donne la ~** it gets you going; **il n'a pas la ~** he's feeling a bit low (‡ = coup) punch, clout* (Brit); **donner une ~ à qn** to punch sb, give sb a clout* (Brit) [2] ADJ peach-coloured (Brit) ou -colored (US)

pêche² [pɛʃ] NF [a] (= activité) fishing; (= saison) fishing season; **la ~ à la ligne** (en mer) line fishing; (en rivière) angling; **la ~ à la baleine** whaling; **la ~ au gros** big-game fishing; **grande ~ au large** deep-sea fishing; **la ~ au harpon** harpoon fishing; **la ~ à la crevette** shrimp fishing; **la ~ à la truite** trout fishing; **la ~ aux moules** mussel gathering; **aller à la ~** (lit) to go fishing; **aller à la ~ aux informations** to go fishing for information; **aller à la ~ aux voix** to canvass, go vote-catching*; **filet/barque de ~** fishing net/boat → **canne** [b] (= poissons) catch; **faire une belle ~** to have ou make a good catch; **la ~ miraculeuse** (Bible) the miraculous draught of fishes; (fête foraine) the bran tub (Brit), the lucky dip (Brit), the go-fish tub (US)

▼ pêcher [peʃe] ▸conjug 6◂ VI [a] (Rel) to sin; **~ par orgueil** to commit the sin of pride [b] **~ contre la politesse/l'hospitalité** to break the rules of courtesy/of hospitality; **~ par négligence/imprudence** to be too careless/reckless; **~ par ignorance** to err through ignorance; **~ par excès de prudence/d'optimisme** to be over-careful/over-optimistic, err on the side of caution/of optimism; **ça pèche par bien des points** ou **sur bien des côtés** it has a lot of weaknesses ou shortcomings

pêcher¹ [peʃe] ▸conjug 1◂ [1] VT (= être pêcheur de) to fish for; (= attraper) to catch, land; **~ des coquillages** to gather shellfish; **~ la baleine/la crevette** to go whaling/shrimping; **~ la truite/la morue** to fish for trout/cod, go trout-/cod-fishing; **~ qch à la ligne/à l'asticot** to fish for sth with rod and line/with maggots; **~ qch au chalut** to trawl for sth; **où as-tu été ~ cette idée/cette boîte ?*** where did you dig that idea/that box up from?*; **où a-t-il été ~ que ...?*** wherever did he get the idea that ...? [2] VI to fish, go fishing; (avec un chalut) to trawl, go trawling; **~ à la ligne** to go angling; **~ à l'asticot** to fish with maggots; **~ à la mouche** to fly-fish; (fig) **~ en eau trouble** to fish in troubled waters

pêcher² [peʃe] NM (= arbre) peach tree

pêcherie [peʃʀi] NF fishery, fishing ground

pêcheur, **pêcheresse** [peʃœʀ, peʃʀɛs] [1] ADJ sinful [2] NM,F sinner

pêcheur* [peʃœʀ] [1] NM fisherman; (à la ligne) angler; **~ de crevettes** shrimper; **~ de baleines** whaler; **~ de palourdes** clamdigger; **~ de perles** pearl diver; **~ de corail** coral fisherman [2] ADJ [bateau] fishing

pêcheuse [peʃøz] NF fisherwoman; (à la ligne) (woman) angler

pecnot [pɛkno] NM = **péquenaud**

PECO [peko] NMPL (ABRÉV = **pays d'Europe centrale et orientale**) **les ~** the CEEC

pécore* [pekɔʀ] NF (péj = imbécile) silly goose; [2] NMF (péj = paysan) country bumpkin, yokel, hick* (US)

pectine [pɛktin] NF pectin

pectique [pɛktik] ADJ pectic

pectoral, e (mpl -aux) [pɛktɔʀal, o] [1] ADJ [a] (Anat, Zool) pectoral [b] (Méd) [sirop, pastille] throat (épith), cough (épith), expectorant (SPÉC) (épith) [2] NM (Anat) pectoral muscle

pécule [pekyl] NM (= économies) savings, nest egg; [détenu, soldat] earnings, wages (paid on release or discharge); **se faire** ou **se constituer un petit ~** to build up a little nest egg

pécuniaire [pekynjɛʀ] ADJ [embarras] financial, pecuniary (frm); [aide, avantage, situation] financial

pécuniairement [pekynjɛʀmã] ADV financially

pédagogie [pedagɔʒi] NF (= éducation) education; (= art d'enseigner) teaching skills; (= méthodes d'enseignement) educational methods; **avoir beaucoup de ~** to have excellent teaching skills, be a skilled teacher

pédagogique [pedagɔʒik] ADJ [intérêt, contenu, théorie, moyens, méthode, projet] educational, pedagogic(al); **outils ~s** teaching aids; **stage (de formation)** ~ teacher-training course; **il a fait un exposé très** ~ he gave a very clear lecture; **ouvrage/musée à vocation** ~ educational work/museum → **conseiller**

pédagogiquement [pedagɔʒikmã] ADV (= sur le plan de la pédagogie) from an educational standpoint, pedagogically (SPÉC); (= avec pédagogie) clearly

pédagogue [pedagɔg] NMF (= professeur) teacher; (= spécialiste) teaching specialist, educationalist; **c'est un bon ~** ◊ **il est bon** ~ he's a good teacher

pédale [pedal] NF [a] [bicyclette, piano, voiture] pedal; [machine à coudre ancienne, tour] treadle [b] (Mus) **douce/forte** soft/sustaining pedal; **(note de)** ~ pedal (point); **~ wah-wah** wah-wah pedal; (fig) **mettre la ~ douce*** to soft-pedal*, go easy* → **emmêler**, **perdre** [c] (‡ péj = homosexuel) queer‡, poof‡ (Brit), fag‡ (US); **être de la ~**† to be (a) queer‡ ou a poof‡ (Brit) ou a fag‡ (US)

pédaler [pedale] ▸conjug 1◂ VI to pedal; (* = se dépêcher) to hurry; **~ dans la choucroute**‡ ou **la semoule**‡ ou **le yaourt**‡ (= ne rien comprendre) to be all at sea, be at a complete loss; (= ne pas progresser) to get nowhere (fast)*

pédaleur, -euse [pedalœʀ, øz] NM,F (Cyclisme) pedaler

pédalier [pedalje] NM [bicyclette] pedal and gear mechanism; [orgue] pedal-board, pedals

pédalo® [pedalo] NM pedalo, pedal boat; **faire du ~** to go for a ride on a pedal boat

pédant, e [pedã, ãt] [1] ADJ pedantic [2] NM,F pedant

pédanterie [pedãtʀi] NF (littér) pedantry

pédantesque [pedãtɛsk] ADJ pedantic

pédantisme [pedãtism] NM pedantry

pédé‡ [pede] NM (ABRÉV = **pédéraste**) (péj) queer‡, poof‡ (Brit), fag‡ (US); **être** ~ to be (a) queer‡ ou a poof‡ (Brit) ou a fag‡ (US); **il est comme un phoque**‡ he's as queer as a coot‡ ou as a three-dollar bill‡ (US)

pédéraste [pedeʀast] NM pederast; (par extension) homosexual

pédérastie [pedeʀasti] NF pederasty; (par extension) homosexuality

pédérastique [pedeʀastik] ADJ pederast; (par extension) homosexual

pédestre [pedɛstʀ] ADJ (littér, hum) **promenade** ou **circuit** ~ walk, ramble, hike; **sentier** ~ pedestrian footpath

pédestrement [pedɛstʀəmã] ADV (littér, hum) on foot

pédiatre [pedjatʀ] NMF paediatrician (Brit), pediatrician (US)

pédiatrie [pedjatʀi] NF paediatrics sg (Brit), pediatrics sg (US)

pédiatrique [pedjatʀik] ADJ paediatric (Brit), pediatric (US)

pedibus (cum jambis) [pedibys(kumʒãbis)] ADV on foot, on Shanks' pony* (Brit) ou mare* (US)

pédicule [pedikyl] NM (Anat) pedicle; (Bot, Zool) peduncle

pédicure [pedikyʀ] NMF chiropodist, podiatrist (US)

pédicurie [pedikyʀi] NF (= soins médicaux) chiropody, podiatry (US); (= soins de beauté) pedicure

pedigree [pedigʀe] NM pedigree

pédologie [pedɔlɔʒi] NF [a] (Géol) pedology [b] (Méd) paedology (Brit), pedology (US)

pédologique [pedɔlɔʒik] ADJ (Géol) pedological

pédologue [pedɔlɔg] NMF (Géol) pedologist

pédoncule [pedɔ̃kyl] NM (Anat, Bot, Zool) peduncle

pédonculé, e [pedɔ̃kyle] ADJ pedunculate(d); **chêne** ~ pedunculate oak

pédophile [pedɔfil] [1] NM pedophile, paedophile (Brit) [2] ADJ pedophile (épith), paedophile (épith) (Brit)

pédophilie [pedɔfili] NF pedophilia, paedophilia (Brit)

pédopsychiatre [pedopsikjatʀ] NMF child psychiatrist

pedzouille‡ [pɛdzuj] NM (péj) peasant, country bumpkin, hick* (US)

peeling [piliŋ] NM (= gommage) facial scrub; (Méd) peel, dermabrasion; **se faire un** ~ to use a facial scrub; (Méd) to have dermabrasion

Pégase [pegaz] NM Pegasus

PEGC [peəʒeəse] NM (ABRÉV = **professeur d'enseignement général des collèges**) → **professeur**

pègre [pɛgʀ] NF **la** ~ the underworld; **membre de la** ~ gangster, mobster

peignage [pɛɲaʒ] NM [laine] carding; [lin, chanvre] carding, hackling

peigne [pɛɲ] NM [a] [cheveux] comb; (Tex) [laine] card; [lin, chanvre] card, hackle; [métier] reed; **~ de poche** pocket comb; (fig) **passer qch au ~ fin** to go through sth with a fine-tooth comb; **se donner un coup de ~** to run a comb through one's hair [b] (Zool) [scorpion] comb; [oiseau] pecten; (= mollusque) pecten

peigne-cul‡ (pl **peigne-culs**) [pɛɲky] NM (péj) (= mesquin) creep*; (= inculte) lout, yob* (Brit)

peignée* [pɛɲe] NF (= raclée) thrashing, hiding*; **donner/recevoir une** ou **la** ~ to give/get a thrashing ou hiding*

peigner [pɛɲe] ▸conjug 1◂ [1] VT [+ cheveux] to comb; (Tex) [+ laine] to card; [+ lin, chanvre] to card, hackle; **~ qn** to comb sb's hair; **être bien peigné** [+ personne] to have well-combed hair; **des cheveux bien peignés** well-combed hair; **mal peigné** dishevelled, tousled; (hum) **faire ça** ou **la girafe** it's either that or some other pointless task [2] **se peigner** VPR to comb one's hair, give one's hair a comb

peignoir [pɛɲwaʀ] NM dressing gown; **~ (de bain)** bathrobe

peinard, e* [penaʀ, aʀd] ADJ [a] (= sans tracas) [travail, vie] cushy*, easy; **on est ~s dans ce service** we have a cushy* time of it in this department; **il fait ses 35 heures, ~** he does his 35 hours and that's it; **rester** ou **se tenir ~** to keep out of trouble, keep one's nose clean*; **b** (= *au calme*) [*coin*] quiet, peaceful; **on va être ~s** (*pour se reposer*) we'll have a bit of peace, we can take it easy; (*pour agir*) we'll be left in peace; **il vit ~ sur une île** he leads a nice quiet life on an island

peindre [pɛ̃dR] ▸ conjug 52 ◂ **1** VT (*gén*) to paint; [+ *mœurs*] to paint, depict; **~ en jaune** to paint sth yellow; **~ à la chaux** to whitewash; **tableau peint à l'huile** picture painted in oils; **~ au pinceau/au rouleau** to paint with a brush/a roller; **se faire ~ par qn** to have one's portrait painted by sb; **romancier qui sait bien ~ ses personnages** novelist who portrays his characters well; **il l'avait peint sous les traits d'un vieillard dans son livre** he had depicted him as an old man in his book; (*fig*) **la cruauté était peinte sur ses traits** his face was a mask of cruelty

2 se peindre VPR (= *se décrire*) to portray o.s.; **Montaigne s'est peint dans « Les Essais »** "Les Essais" are a self-portrayal of Montaigne; **la consternation/le désespoir se peignait sur leur visage** dismay/despair was written on their faces

peine [pɛn] NF **a** (= *chagrin*) sorrow, sadness (*NonC*) **~** to be sad ou upset; **être dans la ~** to be grief-stricken; **faire de la ~ à qn** to upset sb, make sb sad, distress sb; **elle m'a fait de la ~ et je lui ai donné de l'argent** I felt sorry for her and gave her some money; **je ne voudrais pas te faire de (la) ~, mais ...** I don't want to disappoint you but ...; **avoir des ~s de cœur** to have an unhappy love life; **cela fait ~ à voir** it hurts to see it; **il faisait ~ à voir** he looked a sorry ou pitiful sight → **âme** **b** (= *effort*) effort, trouble (*NonC*); **il faut se donner de la ◊ cela demande de la ◊** it requires an effort, you have to make an effort; **se donner de la ~ pour faire qch** to go to a lot of trouble to do sth; **si tu te mettais seulement en ~ d'essayer ◊ si tu te donnais seulement la ~ d'essayer** if you would only bother to try ou take the trouble to try; **il ne se donne aucune ~** he just doesn't try ou bother; (*formule de politesse*) **donnez-vous** ou **prenez donc la ~ d'entrer/de vous asseoir** please ou do come in/sit down; **ne vous donnez pas la ~ de venir me chercher** please don't bother to come and get me; **est-ce que c'est la ~ d'y aller?** is it worth going?; **ce n'est pas la ~ de me le répéter** there's no point in repeating that, you've no need to repeat that; **ce n'est pas la ~** don't bother; (*iro*) **c'était bien la ~!** after all that trouble!; (*iro*) **c'était bien la ~ de l'inviter!** ou **qu'on l'invite!** it was a waste of time inviting him!; **cela vaut la ~** it's worth it, it's worth the trouble; **cela valait la ~ d'essayer** it was worth trying ou a try ou a go; **ça vaut la ~ qu'il y aille** it's worth it for him to go, it's worth his while going; **cela ne vaut pas la ~ d'en parler** (*c'est trop mauvais*) it's not worth wasting one's breath over, it's not worth talking about; (= *c'est insignifiant*) it's hardly ou not worth mentioning; **c'est ~ perdue** it's a waste of time and effort; **on lui a donné 500 F pour sa ~** he was given 500 francs for his trouble; **en être pour sa ~** to get nothing for one's pains ou trouble; **tu as été sage, pour la ~, tu auras un bonbon** here's a sweet for being good; **ne vous mettez pas en ~ pour moi** don't go to put yourself to any trouble for me; **toute ~ mérite salaire** the labourer is worthy of his hire (*PROV*), any effort should be rewarded ▪ (*PROV*) **à chaque jour suffit sa ~** sufficient unto the day is the evil thereof (*PROV*) → **bout, mourir** **c** (= *difficulté*) difficulty; **il a eu de la ~ à finir son repas/la course** he had difficulty finishing his meal/the race; **il a eu de la ~ mais il y est arrivé** it wasn't easy (for him) but he man-

aged it; **avoir de la ~ à faire** to have difficulty in doing, find it difficult ou hard to do; **j'ai (de la) ~ à croire que ...** I find it hard to believe that ..., I can hardly believe that ...; **avec ~** with difficulty; **sans ~** without (any) difficulty, easily; **il n'est pas en ~ pour trouver des secrétaires** he has no difficulty ou trouble finding secretaries; **j'ai eu toutes les ~s du monde à le convaincre/à démarrer** I had a real job convincing him/getting the car started; **je serais bien en ~ de vous le dire/d'en trouver** I'd be hard pushed* ou hard pressed to tell you/to find any **d** (= *punition*) punishment, penalty; (*Jur*) sentence; **~ capitale** ou **de mort** capital punishment, death sentence ou penalty; **~ de prison** prison sentence; **~ alternative** ou **de substitution** alternative sentence; **sous ~ de mort** on pain of death; **« défense d'afficher sous ~ d'amende »** "billposters will be fined"; **« défense d'entrer sous ~ de poursuites »** "trespassers will be prosecuted"; **la ~ n'est pas toujours proportionnée au délit** the punishment does not always fit the crime; **on ne peut rien lui dire, sous ~ d'être renvoyé** you daren't ou can't say anything to him for fear of being fired; **pour la** ou **ta ~ tu mettras la table** for that you can set the table **e** **à ~** hardly, scarcely, barely; **il est à ~ 2 heures** it's only just 2 o'clock, it's only just turned 2; **il leur reste à ~ de quoi manger** they hardly have any food left; **il gagne à ~ de quoi vivre** he hardly earns enough to keep body and soul together; **il parle à ~** [*personne silencieuse*] he hardly says anything; [*enfant*] he can hardly ou barely talk; **il était à ~ rentré qu'il a dû ressortir** he had only just got in when he had to go out again; **à ~ dans la voiture, il s'est endormi** no sooner had he got in the car than he fell asleep; **c'est à ~ si on l'entend** you can hardly hear him; **il était à ~ aimable** he was barely civil; **celui-ci est à ~ plus cher que les autres** this one is hardly any more expensive than the others

peiner [pene] ▸ conjug 1 ◂ **1** VI [*personne*] to work hard, toil; [*moteur*] to labour (*Brit*), labor (*US*); [*voiture, plante*] to struggle; **~ sur un problème** to struggle with a problem; **le coureur peinait dans les derniers mètres** the runner was struggling over the last few metres; **le chien peine quand il fait chaud** the dog suffers when it's hot **2** VT to grieve, sadden; **j'ai été peiné de l'apprendre** I was sad to hear it; **... dit-il d'un ton peiné** (*gén*) ... he said in a sad voice; (*vexé*) ... he said in a hurt ou an aggrieved tone; **il avait un air peiné** he looked upset

peintre [pɛ̃tR] NMF (*lit*) painter; **~ en bâtiment** house painter, painter and decorator; **~-décorateur** painter and decorator; **c'est un merveilleux ~ de notre société** (*écrivain*) he paints a marvellous picture of the society we live in

peinture [pɛ̃tyR] **1** NF **a** (= *action, art*) painting; **faire de la ~ (à l'huile/à l'eau)** to paint (in oils/in watercolours) **b** (= *ouvrage*) painting, picture; **vendre sa ~** to sell one's paintings → **voir** **c** (= *surface peinte*) paintwork (*NonC*); **toutes les ~s sont à refaire** all the paintwork needs re-doing **d** (= *matière*) paint; **« attention à la ~ »** ◊ **« ~ fraîche »** "wet paint"; **donner un coup de ~ à un mur** to give a wall a coat of paint **e** (*fig*) (= *action*) portrayal; (= *résultat*) portrait; **c'est une ~ des mœurs de l'époque** it portrays ou depicts the social customs of the period **2** COMP ▸ **peinture abstraite** (*NonC*) abstract art; (= *tableau*) abstract (painting) ▸ **peinture acrylique** acrylic paint ▸ **peinture en bâtiment** house painting, painting and decorating ▸ **peinture brillante** gloss paint ▸ **peinture au doigt**

fingerpainting ▸ **peinture à l'eau** (= *tableau, matière*) watercolour (*Brit*), watercolor (*US*); (*pour le bâtiment*) water(-based) paint ▸ **peinture à l'huile** (= *tableau*) oil painting; (= *matière*) oil paint; (*pour le bâtiment*) oil-based paint ▸ **peinture laquée** gloss paint ▸ **peinture mate** matt emulsion (paint) ▸ **peinture métallisée** metallic paint ▸ **peinture murale** mural ▸ **peinture au pinceau** painting with a brush ▸ **peinture au pistolet** spray painting ▸ **peinture au rouleau** roller painting ▸ **peinture satinée** satin-finish paint ▸ **peinture sur soie** silk painting

peinturer [pɛ̃tyRe] ▸ conjug 1 ◂ VT **a** (* = *mal peindre*) to slap paint on **b** (*Can*) to paint

peinturlurer* [pɛ̃tyRlyRe] ▸ conjug 1 ◂ VT **a** (*péj*) to daub (with paint); **~ qch de bleu** to daub sth with blue paint; **visage peinturluré** painted face; **lèvres peinturlurées en rouge** lips with a slash of red across them; **se ~ le visage** to slap make-up on one's face

péjoratif, -ive [peʒɔRatif, iv] **1** ADJ derogatory, pejorative **2** NM (*Ling*) pejorative word

péjoration [peʒɔRasjɔ̃] NF pejoration

péjorativement [peʒɔRativmɑ̃] ADV in a derogatory fashion, pejoratively

Pékin [pekɛ̃] N Beijing, Peking

pékin [pekɛ̃] NM (*arg Mil*) civvy (*arg*); **s'habiller en ~** to dress in civvies ou mufti

pékinois, e [pekinwa, waz] **1** ADJ Pekinese **2** NM **a** (= *chien*) pekinese, peke* **b** (*Ling*) Mandarin (Chinese), Pekinese **3** **Pékinois(e)** NM,F Pekinese

PEL [peœɛl] NM (ABRÉV = **plan d'épargne logement**) → **plan¹**

pelade [pəlad] NF alopecia

pelage [pəlaʒ] NM coat, fur

pélagique [pelaʒik] ADJ pelagic

pélargonium [pelaRgɔnjɔm] NM pelargonium

pelé, e [pəle] (*ptp de* **peler**) **1** ADJ [*personne*] bald(-headed); [*animal*] hairless; [*vêtement*] threadbare; [*terrain, montagne*] bare **2** NM (* = *personne*) bald-headed man, baldie*; (*fig*) **il n'y avait que trois** ou **quatre ~s et un tondu** there was hardly anyone there

pêle-mêle [pɛlmɛl] **1** ADV any old how; **ils s'entassaient ~ dans l'autobus** they piled into the bus any old how; **on y trouvait ~ des chapeaux, des rubans, des colliers** there were hats, ribbons and necklaces all mixed ou jumbled up together; **un roman où l'on trouve ~ une rencontre avec Charlemagne, un voyage sur Mars ...** a novel containing a hotchpotch of meetings with Charlemagne, trips to Mars ... **2** NM INV (= *cadre*) multiple photo frame

peler [pəle] ▸ conjug 5 ◂ VTI (*gén*) to peel; **ce fruit se pèle bien** this fruit peels easily ou is easy to peel; **on pèle (de froid) ici!‡** it's damn cold here!‡, it's bloody freezing here!‡ (*Brit*)

pèlerin [pɛlRɛ̃] NM pilgrim; (*faucon*) **~** peregrine falcon; (*requin*) **~** basking shark; **criquet ~** migratory locust; (= *individu*) **qui c'est ce ~?*** who's that guy?* ou bloke* (*Brit*)?

pèlerinage [pɛlRinaʒ] NM (= *voyage*) pilgrimage; (*lieu de*) **~** place of pilgrimage, shrine; **aller en** ou **faire un ~ à** to go on a pilgrimage to

pèlerine [pɛlRin] NF cape

pélican [pelikɑ̃] NM pelican

pelisse [pəlis] NF pelisse

pellagre [pelagR] NF pellagra

pelle [pɛl] **1** NF **a** (*gén*) shovel; [*enfant*] spade; **ramasser qch à la ~** to shovel sth up; **on en ramasse** ou **il y en a à la ~** there are loads of them*; **avoir de l'argent** ou **remuer l'argent à la ~** to have loads* ou pots* of money; **(se) ramasser** ou **se prendre une ~‡** (= *tomber, échouer*) to fall flat on one's face, come a cropper* (*Brit*); (*après avoir demandé qch*) to be sent packing* → **rond** **b** (‡ =

baiser) **rouler une ~ à qn** to give sb a French kiss [2] COMP ► **pelle à charbon** coal shovel ► **pelle mécanique** mechanical shovel *ou* digger ► **pelle à ordures** dustpan ► **pelle à poisson** fish slice ► **pelle à tarte** cake *ou* pie server

pelletée [pɛlte] NF shovelful, spadeful; **des ~s de** masses of

pelleter [pɛlte] ▸conjug 4◂ VT to shovel (up)

pelleterie [pɛltri] NF (= *commerce*) fur trade, furriery; (= *préparation*) fur dressing; (= *peau*) pelt

pelleteur [pɛltœr] NM workman (*who does the digging*)

pelleteuse [pɛltøz] NF mechanical shovel *ou* digger, excavator

pelletier, -ière [pɛltje, jɛr] NM,F furrier

pellicule [pelikyl] NF [a] (= *couche fine*) film, thin layer; (*Photo*) film; ~ **couleur/noir et blanc** colour/black and white film; **ne gâche pas de la ~** don't waste film; (**rouleau de) ~** (roll of) film [b] (*Méd*) **~s** dandruff (*NonC*); **lotion contre les ~s** dandruff lotion

pelliculé, e [pelikyle] ADJ [*pochette, couverture de livre*] plastic-coated

péloche* [pelɔʃ] NF (= *film*) film; (= *rouleau*) roll of film

Péloponnèse [pelɔpɔnɛz] NM **le ~** the Peloponnese; **la guerre du ~** the Peloponnesian War

pelotage* [p(ə)lɔtaʒ] NM petting* (*NonC*)

pelotari [p(ə)lɔtari] NM pelota player

pelote [p(ə)lɔt] NF [a] [*laine*] ball; **mettre de la laine en ~** to wind wool into a ball; **faire sa ~†** to feather one's nest, make one's pile*; ~ **d'épingles** pin cushion; (*fig*) **c'est une vraie ~ d'épingles** he (*ou* she) is really prickly → **nerf** [b] (*Sport*) ~ (**basque**) pelota [c] (*Zool*) ~ (**plantaire**) pad

peloter* [p(ə)lɔte] ▸conjug 1◂ VT to feel up*, touch up*; **elle se faisait ~ par Paul** Paul was feeling* *ou* touching* her up; **arrêtez de me ~!** stop pawing me!*, keep your hands to yourself!; **ils se pelotaient** they were petting*

peloteur, -euse* [p(ə)lɔtœr, øz] [1] ADJ **il a des gestes** *ou* **des mains peloteuses** he can't keep his hands to himself [2] NM,F groper*; **c'est un ~** he can't keep his hands to himself

peloton [p(ə)lɔtɔ̃] [1] NM [a] [*laine*] small ball [b] (= *groupe*) cluster, group; [*pompiers, gendarmes*] squad; (*Mil*) platoon; (*Sport*) pack, bunch [2] COMP ► **peloton d'exécution** firing squad ► **peloton de tête** (*Sport*) leaders, leading runners (*ou* riders *etc*); **être dans le ~ de tête** (*Sport*) to be up with the leaders; (*en classe*) to be among the top few; [*pays, entreprise*] to be one of the front runners

pelotonner [p(ə)lɔtɔne] ▸conjug 1◂ [1] VT [+ *laine*] to wind into a ball [2] **se pelotonner** VPR to curl (o.s.) up; **se ~ contre qn** to snuggle up to sb, nestle close to sb; **il s'est pelotonné entre mes bras** he snuggled up in my arms

pelouse [p(ə)luz] NF lawn; (*Courses*) public enclosure; (*Ftbl, Rugby*) field, ground; **« ~ interdite »** "keep off the grass"

peluche [p(ə)lyʃ] NF [a] (*Tex*) plush; (= *poil*) fluff (*NonC*), bit of fluff; **ce pull fait des ~s** this jumper pills [b] (**jouet en) ~** soft *ou* cuddly toy; **chien/lapin en ~** stuffed *ou* fluffy (*Brit*) dog/rabbit → **ours**

pelucher [p(ə)lyʃe] ▸conjug 1◂ VI (*par l'aspect*) to pill, go fluffy; (= *perdre des poils*) to leave fluff

pelucheux, -euse [p(ə)lyʃø, øz] ADJ fluffy

pelure [p(ə)lyr] NF [a] (= *épluchure*) peel (*NonC*), peeling, piece of peel; (* *hum* = *manteau*) overcoat; ~ **d'oignon** (*Bot*) onion skin; (= *vin*) (pale) rosé wine; (= *couleur*) pinkish or-

ange [b] (*papier*) ~ flimsy (paper), copy *ou* bank paper; (= *feuille*) flimsy (copy)

pelvien, -ienne [pɛlvjɛ̃, jɛn] ADJ pelvic → **ceinture**

pelvis [pɛlvis] NM pelvis

pénal, e (*mpl* **-aux**) [penal, o] ADJ [*responsabilité, enquête, justice, loi*] criminal; **le droit ~** criminal law; **poursuivre qn au ~** to sue sb, take legal action against sb → **clause**, **code**

pénalement [penalmɑ̃] ADV **être ~ responsable** to be criminally responsible; **acte ~ répréhensible** act for which one is liable to prosecution

pénalisant, e [penalizɑ̃, ɑ̃t] ADJ [*mesure, réforme*] disadvantageous; **cette réglementation est très ~e pour notre industrie** this regulation puts our industry at a serious disadvantage *ou* severely penalizes our industry

pénalisation [penalizasjɔ̃] NF [a] (*Sport*) (= *action*) penalization; (= *sanction*) penalty; **points de ~** penalty points; **cette mesure prévoit la ~ financière de certains produits polluants** this measure makes provision for imposing financial penalties *ou* sanctions against certain products that cause pollution [b] (*Jur*) [*usage, pratique*] criminalization

pénaliser [penalize] ▸conjug 1◂ VT [+ *contrevenant, faute, joueur*] to penalize; (= *défavoriser*) to penalize, put at a disadvantage; **ils ont été lourdement pénalisés par cette mesure** they were severely penalized by this measure

pénalité [penalite] NF (*Fin, Sport* = *sanction*) penalty; (*Fin*) ~ **de retard** late payment penalty; (*pour retard de livraison*) late delivery penalty; (*Ftbl, Rugby*) **coup de pied de ~** penalty (kick); **il a marqué sur un coup de ~** he scored from a penalty

penalty [penalti] (*pl* **penalties** [penaltiz]) NM (*Ftbl*) (= *coup de pied*) penalty (kick); (= *sanction*) penalty; **marquer sur ~** to score a penalty goal *ou* from a penalty; **tirer un ~** to take a penalty (kick); **siffler un ~** to award a penalty; **point de ~** (= *endroit*) penalty spot

pénard, e* [penar, ard] ADJ = **peinard, e**

pénates [penat] NMPL (*Myth*) Penates; (*fig hum*) home; **regagner ses ~** to go back home; **installer ses ~ quelque part** to settle down somewhere

penaud, e [pəno, od] ADJ sheepish, contrite; **d'un air ~** sheepishly, contritely; **il en est resté tout ~** he became quite sheepish *ou* contrite

pence [pɛns] NMPL pence

penchant [pɑ̃ʃɑ̃] NM (= *tendance*) tendency, propensity (**à faire** to do); (= *faible*) liking, fondness (**pour qch** for sth); **avoir un ~ à faire qch** to be inclined *ou* have a tendency to do sth; **avoir un ~ pour qch** to be fond of *ou* have a liking *ou* fondness for sth; **avoir un ~ pour la boisson** to be partial to a drink; (*littér*) **avoir du ~ pour qn** to be in love with sb; **le ~ qu'ils ont l'un pour l'autre** the fondness they have for each other; **mauvais ~s** baser instincts

penché, e [pɑ̃ʃe] (*ptp de* **pencher**) ADJ [*tableau*] lop-sided; [*mur*] sloping; [*poteau, arbre, colonne*] leaning; [*écriture*] sloping, slanting; [*tête*] tilted (to one side); **le corps ~ en avant/en arrière** leaning forward/back(ward); **être ~ sur ses livres** [*personne*] to be bent over one's books → **tour¹**

pencher [pɑ̃ʃe] ▸conjug 1◂ [1] VT [+ *meuble, bouteille*] to tip up, tilt; ~ **son assiette** to tip one's plate up; ~ **la tête** (*en avant*) to bend one's head forward; (*sur le côté*) to tilt one's head [2] VI [a] (= *être incliné*) [*mur, arbre*] to lean; [*navire*] to list; [*objet en déséquilibre*] to tilt, tip (to one side); **le tableau penche un peu de ce côté** the picture is leaning to this side, this side of the picture is lower than the other;

(*fig*) **faire ~ la balance** to tip the scales (**en faveur de** in favour of)

[b] (= *être porté à*) **je penche pour la première hypothèse** I'm inclined to favour the first hypothesis; **je penche à croire qu'il est sincère** I'm inclined to believe he's sincere

[3] **se pencher** VPR [a] (= *s'incliner*) to lean over; (= *se baisser*) to bend down; **se ~ en avant** to lean forward; **se ~ par-dessus bord** to lean overboard; **se ~ sur un livre** to bend over a book; **« défense de se ~ au dehors** *ou* **par la fenêtre »** "do not lean out of the window" [b] (= *examiner*) **se ~ sur un problème/cas** to look into *ou* study a problem/case; **se ~ sur les malheurs de qn** to turn one's attention to sb's misfortunes

pendable [pɑ̃dabl] ADJ → **cas**, **tour²**

pendaison [pɑ̃dɛzɔ̃] NF hanging; ~ **de crémaillère** house warming, house-warming party

pendant¹, e [pɑ̃dɑ̃, ɑ̃t] ADJ [a] (= *qui pend*) [*bras, jambes*] hanging, dangling; [*langue*] hanging out (*attrib*); [*joue*] sagging; [*oreilles*] drooping; (*Jur*) [*fruits*] on the tree (*attrib*); **ne reste pas là les bras ~s** don't just stand there (doing nothing); **assis sur le mur les jambes ~es** sitting on the wall with his legs hanging down; **le chien haletait la langue ~e** the dog was panting with its tongue hanging out; **chien aux oreilles ~es** dog with drooping ears, lop-eared dog; **les branches ~es du saule** the hanging *ou* drooping branches of the willow [b] (*Admin* = *en instance*) [*question*] outstanding, in abeyance (*attrib*); [*affaire*] pending (*attrib*); (*Jur*) [*procès*] pending (*attrib*)

pendant² [pɑ̃dɑ̃] NM [a] (= *objet*) ~ (**d'oreille**) drop earring, pendant earring; ~ **d'épée** frog [b] (= *contrepartie*) **le ~ de** (*+ œuvre d'art, meuble*) the matching piece to; [*+ personne, institution*] the counterpart of; **faire ~ à** to match, be the counterpart of; **se faire ~** to match; **j'ai un chandelier et je cherche le ~** I've got a candlestick and I'm looking for one to match it *ou* and I'm trying to make up a pair

pendant³ [pɑ̃dɑ̃] [1] PRÉP (= *au cours de*) during; (*indique la durée*) for; ~ **la journée/son séjour** during the day/his stay; ~ **ce temps Paul attendait** during this time *ou* meanwhile Paul was waiting; **qu'est-ce qu'il faisait ~ ce temps-là?** what was he doing during that time? *ou* in the meantime?; **à prendre ~ le repas** [*médicament*] to be taken at mealtimes *ou* with meals; **on a marché ~ des kilomètres** we walked for miles; **il a vécu en France ~ plusieurs années** he lived in France for several years; ~ **quelques mois, il n'a pas pu travailler** for several months he was unable to work; **on est resté sans nouvelles de lui ~ longtemps** we had no news from him for a long time; ~ **un moment on a cru qu'il ne reviendrait pas** for a while we thought he would not return; **avant la guerre et ~** before and during the war

[2] **pendant que** LOC CONJ while, whilst (*frm*); ~ **qu'elle se reposait, il écoutait la radio** while she was resting he would listen to the radio; ~ **que vous serez à Paris, pourriez-vous aller le voir?** while you're in Paris could you go and see him?; ~ **que j'y pense, n'oubliez pas de fermer la porte à clé** while I think of it, don't forget to lock the door; **arrosez le jardin et, ~ que vous y êtes, arrachez les mauvaises herbes** water the garden and do some weeding while you're at *ou* about it; (*iro*) **finissez le plat ~ que vous y êtes!** why don't you eat it all (up) while you're at it! (*iro*); **dire que des gens doivent suivre un régime ~ que des enfants meurent de faim** to think that some people have to go on a diet while there are children dying of hunger

pendard, e†† [pɑ̃dar, ard] NM,F (*hum*) scoundrel

pendeloque [pɑ̃d(ə)lɔk] NF [*boucles d'oreilles*] pendant; [*lustre*] lustre, pendant

pendentif [pɑ̃dɑ̃tif] NM (= *bijou*) pendant; (*Archit*) pendentive

penderie [pɑ̃dʀi] NF (= *meuble*) wardrobe (*with hanging space only*); (= *barre*) clothes rail; **le placard du couloir nous sert de ~** we hang our clothes in the hall cupboard (*Brit*) *ou* closet (*US*); **le côté ~ de l'armoire** the part of the wardrobe you hang things in

pendiller [pɑ̃dije] ▶conjug 1◀ VI [*clés, boucles d'oreilles, corde*] to dangle; [*linge*] to flap gently

Pendjab [pɛ̃dʒab] NM **le ~** the Punjab

pendouiller* [pɑ̃duje] ▶conjug 1◀ VI to dangle, hang down

pendre [pɑ̃dʀ] ▶conjug 41◀ **1** VT **a** [+ *rideau*] to hang, put up (*à* at); [+ *tableau, manteau*] to hang (up) (*à* on); [+ *lustre*] to hang (up) (*à* from); **~ le linge pour le faire sécher** (*dans la maison*) to hang up the washing to dry; (*dehors*) to hang out the washing to dry; **~ la crémaillère** to have a house-warming party *ou* a house warming
b [+ *criminel*] to hang; (*Hist*) **~ qn haut et court** to hang sb; **qu'il aille se faire ~ ailleurs!*** he can go hang!*, he can take a running jump!*; **je veux être pendu si ...** I'll be damned* *ou* hanged if ...; **dussé-je être pendu, je ne dirais jamais cela!** I wouldn't say that even if my life depended on it! → **pis***
2 VI **a** (= *être suspendu*) to hang (down); **des fruits pendaient aux branches** there was fruit hanging from the branches; **cela lui pend au nez*** he's got it coming to him*
b [*bras, jambes*] to dangle; [*joue*] to sag; [*langue*] to hang out; [*robe*] to dip, hang down; [*cheveux*] to hang down; **un lambeau de papier pendait** a strip of wallpaper was hanging off; **laisser ~ ses jambes** to dangle one's legs
3 **se pendre** VPR **a** (= *se tuer*) to hang o.s.
b (= *se suspendre*) **se ~ à une branche** to hang from a branch; **se ~ au cou de qn** to throw one's arms round sb *ou* sb's neck

pendu, e [pɑ̃dy] (*ptp de* **pendre**) **1** ADJ **a** (= *accroché*) hung up, hanging up; **~ à** (*lit*) hanging from; (*fig*) **être toujours ~ aux basques de qn** to keep pestering sb; **il est toujours ~ aux jupes** *ou* **jupons de sa mère** he's always clinging to his mother's skirts, he's still tied to his mother's apron strings; **~ au bras de qn** holding on to sb's arm; **elle est toujours ~e au téléphone** she spends all her time on the phone; **ça fait deux heures qu'il est ~ au téléphone** he's been on the phone for two hours → **langue 2** (= *mort*) hanged **2** NM,F hanged man (*ou* woman); **le (jeu du) ~** hangman; **jouer au ~** to play hangman

pendulaire [pɑ̃dylɛʀ] ADJ pendular; **train ~** tilting train

pendule [pɑ̃dyl] **1** NF clock; **~ à coucou** cuckoo clock; (*fig*) **remettre les ~s à l'heure*** to set the record straight; **tu ne vas pas nous en chier** une ~ (à treize coups)!** you're not going to make a fucking** song and dance about it, are you? **2** NM pendulum; **~ astronomique** pendulum clock; **faire un ~** [*alpiniste*] to do a pendule *ou* a pendulum

pendulette [pɑ̃dylɛt] NF small clock; **~ de voyage** travelling clock

pêne [pɛn] NM [*serrure*] bolt; **~ dormant** dead bolt; **~ demi-tour** latch *ou* spring bolt

Pénélope [penelɔp] NF Penelope; **c'est un travail de ~** it's a never-ending task

pénéplaine [peneplɛn] NF peneplain, peneplane

pénétrabilité [penetʀabilite] NF penetrability

pénétrable [penetʀabl] ADJ [*endroit*] penetrable; **difficilement ~** barely *ou* scarcely penetrable

pénétrant, e [penetʀɑ̃, ɑ̃t] **1** ADJ **a** [*pluie*] drenching; [*froid*] biting, bitter; [*odeur*] penetrating, pervasive; [*crème*] penetrating; (*Phys Nucl*) [*radiations, rayons*] penetrating **b** [*regard*] penetrating, searching, piercing; [*esprit*] penetrating, keen, shrewd; [*analyse, remarque*] penetrating, shrewd; [*charme*] irresistible **2** **pénétrante** NF urban motorway (*Brit*) *ou* freeway (*US*) (*linking centre of town to inter-city routes*)

pénétration [penetʀasjɔ̃] NF **a** (= *action*) penetration; (*Mil*) force of penetration; **la ~ des idées nouvelles** the establishment *ou* penetration of new ideas **b** (= *sagacité*) penetration, perception **c** (*Comm*) penetration; **taux de ~** penetration rate **d** (*sexuelle*) penetration

pénétré, e [penetʀe] (*ptp de* **pénétrer**) ADJ **être ~ de son importance** *ou* **de soi-même** to be full of self-importance, be imbued (*frm*) with a sense of one's own importance; **~ de l'importance de son rôle** imbued (*frm*) with a sense of the importance of his role; **orateur ~ de son sujet** speaker totally engrossed in his subject; **il est ~ de l'idée que ...** he is deeply convinced that ...; **~ de reconnaissance** full of gratitude; **écouter qch d'un air ~** to listen to sth with solemn intensity

pénétrer [penetʀe] ▶conjug 6◀ **1** VI **a** [*personne, véhicule*] **~ dans** [+ *lieu*] to enter; [+ *groupe, milieu*] to penetrate; **personne ne doit ~ ici** nobody must be allowed to enter; **chez qn par la force** to force an entry *ou* one's way into sb's home; **les envahisseurs/les troupes ont pénétré dans le pays** the invaders/the troops have entered the country; **il est difficile de ~ dans les milieux de la finance** it is hard to penetrate financial circles; **faire ~ qn dans une pièce** to show sb into a room; **des voleurs ont pénétré dans la maison en son absence** thieves broke into his house while he was away; **l'habitude n'a pas encore pénétré dans les mœurs** the habit hasn't established itself yet; **faire ~ une idée dans la tête de qn** to instil an idea in sb, get an idea into sb's head
b [*soleil*] to shine *ou* come in; [*vent*] to blow *ou* come in; [*air, liquide, insecte*] to come *ou* get in; **~ dans** to shine *ou* come *ou* blow into, to get into; **la lumière pénétrait dans la cellule (par une lucarne)** light came into *ou* entered the cell (through a skylight); **le liquide pénètre à travers une membrane** the liquid comes *ou* penetrates through a membrane; **la fumée/l'odeur pénètre par tous les interstices** the smoke/the smell comes *ou* gets in through all the cracks; **faire ~ de l'air (dans)** to let fresh air in(to)
c (*en s'enfonçant*) **~ dans** [*crème, balle, verre*] to penetrate; [*aiguille*] to go in, penetrate; [*habitude*] to make its way into; [*huile, encre*] to soak into; **ce vernis pénètre dans le bois** this varnish soaks into the wood; **faire ~ une crème (dans la peau)** to rub a cream in(to the skin)
2 VT **a** (= *percer*) [*froid, air*] to penetrate; [*odeur*] to spread through, fill; [*liquide*] to penetrate, soak through; [*regard*] to penetrate, go through; **le froid les pénétrait jusqu'aux os** the cold cut *ou* went right through them
b (= *découvrir*) [+ *mystère, secret*] to penetrate, fathom; [+ *intentions, idées, plans*] to penetrate, fathom, perceive; **il est difficile à ~** it is difficult to fathom him
c (= *remplir*) **son sang-froid me pénètre d'admiration** his composure fills me with admiration; **le remords pénétra sa conscience** he was filled with remorse, he was conscience-stricken; **il se sentait pénétré de pitié/d'effroi** he was filled with pity/with fright
d (*Comm*) [+ *marché*] to penetrate, break into
e (*sexuellement*) to penetrate
3 **se pénétrer** VPR **a** **se ~ d'une idée** to get an idea firmly fixed *ou* set in one's mind; **s'étant pénétré de l'importance de sa mission** firmly convinced of the importance of his mission; **il faut bien vous ~ du fait que ...** you must be absolutely clear in your mind that *ou* have it firmly in your mind that ...; **j'ai du mal à me ~ de l'utilité de tout cela** I find it difficult to convince myself of the usefulness of all this
b (= *s'imbiber*) **se ~ d'eau/de gaz** to become permeated with water/with gas

pénibilité [penibilite] NF hardness

pénible [penibl] ADJ **a** (= *fatigant, difficile*) [*travail, voyage, ascension*] hard; [*personne*] tiresome; **~ à lire** hard *ou* difficult to read; **les derniers kilomètres ont été ~s (à parcourir)** the last few kilometres were heavy going *ou* hard going; **l'hiver a été ~** it's been a hard winter, the winter has been unpleasant; **tout effort lui est ~** any effort is difficult for him, he finds it hard to make the slightest effort; **il est vraiment ~** [*enfant*] he's a real nuisance; [*adulte*] he's a real pain in the neck*; **sa façon de parler est vraiment ~!** he's got a really irritating way of speaking!
b (= *douloureux*) [*sujet, séparation, moment, maladie*] painful (*à* to); [*nouvelle, spectacle*] sad, painful; [*respiration*] laboured (*Brit*), labored (*US*); **la lumière violente lui est ~** bright light hurts his eyes; **ce bruit est ~ à supporter** this noise is unpleasant *ou* painful to listen to; **il m'est ~ de constater/d'avoir à vous dire que ...** I'm sorry to find/to have to tell you that ...

péniblement [peniblmɑ̃] ADV (= *difficilement*) with difficulty; (= *tristement*) painfully; (= *tout juste*) only just

péniche [peniʃ] NF (= *bateau*) barge; (*Mil*) **~ de débarquement** landing craft; (* = *grosse voiture*) **j'ai une vraie ~** I've got a great tank of a car; (* = *grands pieds*) **tu as vu ~s!** did you see the size of his feet!

pénicilline [penisilin] NF penicillin

pénil [penil] NM mons veneris

péninsulaire [penɛ̃sylɛʀ] ADJ peninsular

péninsule [penɛ̃syl] NF peninsula; **la ~ Ibérique** the Iberian Peninsula; **la ~ Balkanique** the Balkan Peninsula

pénis [penis] NM penis

pénitence [penitɑ̃s] NF **a** (*Rel*) (= *repentir*) penitence; (= *peine, sacrement*) penance; **faire ~ (de)** to repent (of); **pour votre ~** as a penance
b (*gén, Scol* = *châtiment*) punishment; **infliger une ~ à qn** to punish sb; **mettre un enfant en ~** to make a child stand in the corner; **pour ta ~** as a punishment (to you) **c** [*jeux*] forfeit

pénitencier [penitɑ̃sje] NM **a** (= *prison*) prison, penitentiary (*US*) **b** (*Rel*) penitentiary

pénitent, e [penitɑ̃, ɑ̃t] ADJ, NM,F penitent

pénitentiaire [penitɑ̃sjɛʀ] ADJ penitentiary, prison (*épith*); **établissement ~** penal establishment, prison → **colonie**

penne [pɛn] NF (*Zool*) large feather, penna (*SPÉC*); [*flèche*] flight

Pennine [penin] **1** ADJ F **la chaîne ~** the Pennine Chain *ou* Range **2** **Pennines** NFPL **les ~s** the Pennines

Pennsylvanie [pɛnsilvani] NF Pennsylvania

penny (*pl* **pennies**) [peni] NM penny

pénombre [penɔ̃bʀ] NF (= *faible clarté*) half-light, shadowy light; (= *obscurité*) darkness; (*Astron*) penumbra; **ses yeux s'étaient habitués à la ~** his eyes had got accustomed to the dark; (*fig*) **demeurer dans la ~** to stay in the background

pensable [pɑ̃sabl] ADJ thinkable; **ce n'est pas ~** it's unthinkable

pensant, e [pɑ̃sɑ̃, ɑ̃t] ADJ thinking

pense-bête (*pl* **pense-bêtes**) [pɑ̃sbɛt] NM (*gén*) reminder; (= *objet*) note *ou* memo board

pensée¹ [pɑ̃se] NF **a** (= *ce que l'on pense*) thought; **sans déguiser sa ~** without hiding one's thoughts *ou* feelings; **je l'ai fait dans la seule ~ de vous être utile** I only did it thinking it would help you, my only thought in doing it was to help you; **recevez mes plus affectueuses ~s** with fondest love; **saisir/ deviner les ~s de qn** to grasp/guess sb's thoughts *ou* what sb is thinking (about); **plongé dans ses ~s** deep in thought; **avoir une ~ pour qn** to think of sb; (*hum*) **j'ai eu une ~ émue pour toi** I spared a thought for you (*hum*); **si vous voulez connaître le fond de ma ~** if you want to know what I really think (about it) *ou* how I really feel about it; **aller jusqu'au bout de sa ~** (= *raisonner*) to carry one's line of thought through to its conclusion; (= *dire ce qu'on pense*) to say what's on one's mind; **à la ~ de faire qch** at the thought of doing sth; **à la ~ que ...** to think that ..., when one thinks that ...

b (= *faculté, fait de penser*) thought; **la dignité de l'homme est dans la ~** human dignity lies in man's capacity for thought; (*littér*) **arrêter sa ~ sur qch** to pause to think about sth

c (= *manière de penser*) thinking; **~ claire/ obscure** clear/muddled thinking

d (= *esprit*) thought, mind; **venir à la ~ de qn** to occur to sb; **se représenter qch par la ~** *ou* **en ~** to imagine sth in one's mind, conjure up a mental picture of sth; **transportons-nous par la ~ au XVIᵉ siècle** let's imagine ourselves back in the 16th century; **j'ai essayé de chasser ce souvenir de ma ~** I tried to banish this memory from my mind

e (= *doctrine*) thought, thinking; (*péj Pol*) **la ~ unique** doctrinaire approach to government exclusively based on market forces and liberalism; **la ~ marxiste** Marxist thinking *ou* thought; **la ~ de cet auteur est difficile à comprendre** it is difficult to understand what this author is trying to say

f (= *maxime*) thought; **les ~s de Pascal** the thoughts of Pascal

pensée² [pɑ̃se] NF (*Bot*) pansy; **~ sauvage** wild pansy

▼ **penser** [pɑ̃se] ▶ conjug 1 ◀ **1** VI **a** (= *réfléchir*) to think; **façon de ~** way of thinking; **une nouvelle qui donne** *ou* **laisse à ~** a piece of news which makes you (stop and) think *ou* which gives (you) food for thought; **~ tout haut** to think aloud *ou* out loud

b ~ à [+ *ami*] to think of *ou* about; [+ *problème, offre*] to think about *ou* over, turn over in one's mind; **pensez donc à ce que vous dites** just think about what you're saying; **~ aux autres/aux malheureux** to think of others *ou* those who are unhappy; **vous pensez à quelqu'un de précis pour ce travail ?** do you have anyone in particular in mind for this job?; **tu vois à qui/à quoi je pense ?** you see who/what I'm thinking of?; **faire ~ à** to make one think of, remind one of; **cette mélodie fait ~ à Debussy** this tune reminds you of Debussy *ou* is reminiscent of Debussy; **il ne pense qu'à jouer** playing is all he ever thinks about; **pensez-y avant d'accepter** think it over *ou* give it some thought before you accept; **j'ai bien autre chose à ~*** I've got other things on my mind; (*hum*) **il ne pense qu'à ça*** he's got a one-track mind*; **il lui a donné un coup de pied où je pense*** he kicked him you know where*; **faire/dire qch sans y ~** to do/ say sth without thinking (about it); **n'y pensons plus !** let's forget it!; **c'est simple mais il fallait y ~** it's simple when you know how; **mais j'y pense, c'est aujourd'hui, l'anniversaire de Lisa !** I've just remembered, it's Lisa's birthday today!; **ça me fait ~ qu'il ne m'a toujours pas répondu** that reminds me that he still hasn't replied

c ~ à (= *prévoir*) to think of; (= *se souvenir de*) to remember; **il pense à tout** he thinks of everything; **~ à l'avenir/aux conséquences** to think of the future/of the consequences; **a-t-il pensé à rapporter du pain ?** did he think of bringing *ou* did he remember to bring some bread?; **pense à l'anniversaire de ta mère** re-

member *ou* don't forget your mother's birthday; **fais m'y ~** remind me (about that), don't let me forget; **il suffisait d'y ~** it was just a matter of thinking of it; **voyons, pense un peu au danger !** just think of *ou* consider the danger!

d (*loc excl*) **il vient ? — penses-tu !** *ou* **pensez-vous !** is he coming? — is he heck! (*Brit*)* *ou* you must be joking!*; **tu penses !** *ou* **vous pensez !** je le connais trop bien pour le croire** not likely!* I know him too well to believe him; **il va accepter ? — je pense bien !** will he accept? — of course he will! *ou* I should think so! *ou* I should think he will!; **mais vous n'y pensez pas, c'est bien trop dangereux !** don't even think about it, it's much too dangerous!; **tu penses que je vais lui dire !*** you bet I'll tell him!*

2 VT **a** (= *avoir une opinion*) to think (**de** of, about); **~ du bien/du mal de qch/qn** to have a high/poor opinion of sth/sb; **que pense-t-il du film ?** what does he think of the film?; **que pensez-vous de ce projet ?** what do you think *ou* how do you feel about this plan?; **il est difficile de savoir ce qu'il pense** it's difficult to know what he's thinking; **je pense comme toi** I agree with you; **je ne dis rien mais je n'en pense pas moins** I am not saying anything but that doesn't mean that I don't have an opinion; **que penseriez-vous d'un voyage à Rome ?** what would you say to *ou* how would you fancy *ou* how about a trip to Rome?

b (= *supposer*) to think, suppose, believe; (= *imaginer*) to think, expect, imagine; **il n'aurait jamais pensé qu'elle ferait cela** he would never have thought *ou* imagined *ou* dreamt she would do that, he would never have expected her to do that; **quand on lui dit musique, il pense ennui** when you mention the word music to him, his only thought is that it's boring; **je pense que non** I don't think so, I think not (*frm*); **je pense que oui** I think so; **ce n'est pas si bête qu'on le pense** it's not such a silly idea as you might think *ou* suppose; **pensez-vous qu'il vienne ?** *ou* **viendra ?** do you think he'll come?, are you expecting him to come?; **je vous laisse à ~ s'il était content** you can imagine how pleased he was; **pensez (qu')il est encore si jeune !** to think that he's still so young!; **ils pensent avoir trouvé une maison** they think they've found a house; **c'est bien ce que je pensais !** I thought as much!, just as *ou* what I thought!; **vous pensez bien qu'elle a refusé** you can well imagine (that) she refused, as you may well expect, she refused; **j'ai pensé mourir/ m'évanouir** I thought I was going to die/faint; **tout laisse à ~ qu'elle l'a quitté** there is every indication that she has left him

c ~ faire (= *avoir l'intention de*) to be thinking of doing, consider doing; (= *espérer*) to hope to do; **il pense partir jeudi** he's thinking of going on Thursday; **elle pense arriver demain** she's hoping *ou* expecting to arrive tomorrow

d (= *concevoir*) [+ *problème, projet, machine*] to think out; **c'est bien/fortement pensé** it's well/very well thought out

3 NM (*littér*) thought

penseur [pɑ̃sœʀ] **1** NM thinker → **libre 2** ADJ M† thoughtful

pensif, -ive [pɑ̃sif, iv] ADJ thoughtful, pensive; **il était tout ~** he was lost in thought; **d'un air ~** pensively, thoughtfully

pension [pɑ̃sjɔ̃] **1** NF **a** (= *allocation*) pension, **~ de guerre** war pension; **~ d'invalidité** disablement pension; **~ de retraite** old age pension, retirement pension; **~ réversible** *ou* **de réversion** survivor's *ou* reversion pension, reversionary annuity; **toucher sa ~** to draw one's pension

b (= *hôtel*) boarding house; [*chats*] cattery; [*chiens*] (boarding) kennels; [*chevaux*] livery (stables); **mettre en ~** [+ *chien*] to put in kennels; [+ *cheval*] to put in livery (stables); **son**

poney est en ~ her pony's at livery

c (*Scol*) (boarding) school; **mettre qn/être en ~** to send sb to/be at boarding school

d (= *hébergement*) [*personne*] board and lodging, bed and board; **la ~ coûte 380 F par jour** board and lodging is 380 francs a day; **être en ~ chez qn** to board with sb *ou* at sb's; **prendre ~ chez qn** (*lit*) to take board and lodging at sb's; (*hum*) to take up residence at sb's; **prendre qn en ~** to take sb (in) as a lodger, board sb; **chambre sans ~** room (*with no meals provided*); **chambre avec ~ complète** full board; (*hum*) **avoir en ~** [+ *chat, chien*] to look after

e (*Fin*) **taux de prise en ~** repurchase rate

2 COMP ▶ **pension alimentaire** [*étudiant*] living allowance; [*divorcée*] alimony, maintenance allowance ▶ **pension de famille** ≈ boarding house

pensionnaire [pɑ̃sjɔnɛʀ] NMF (*Scol*) boarder; [*famille*] lodger; [*hôtel*] resident; [*sanatorium*] patient; [*Comédie-Française*] salaried actor having no share in the profits

pensionnat [pɑ̃sjɔna] NM (boarding) school

pensionné, e [pɑ̃sjɔne] (*ptp de* **pensionner**) **1** ADJ who gets *ou* draws a pension **2** NM,F pensioner

pensionner [pɑ̃sjɔne] ▶ conjug 1 ◀ VT to give a pension to

pensivement [pɑ̃sivmɑ̃] ADV pensively, thoughtfully

pensum† [pɛ̃sɔm] NM (*Scol*) punishment, lines (*Brit*); (*fig*) chore

pentaèdre [pɛ̃taɛdʀ] **1** ADJ pentahedral **2** NM pentahedron

pentagonal, e (*mpl* -**aux**) [pɛ̃tagɔnal, o] ADJ pentagonal

pentagone [pɛ̃tagɔn] NM pentagon; (*Mil*) **le Pentagone** the Pentagon

pentamètre [pɛ̃tametʀ] ADJ, NM pentameter

Pentateuque [pɛ̃tatøk] NM Pentateuch

pentathlon [pɛ̃tatlɔ̃] NM pentathlon

pentatonique [pɛ̃tatɔnik] ADJ pentatonic

pente [pɑ̃t] NF **a** (*gén*) slope; **être en ~ douce/raide** to slope (down) gently/steeply; **la ~ d'un toit** the pitch *ou* slope of a roof; **en ~** [*toit*] sloping; [*allée, pelouse*] on a slope (*attrib*); **de petites rues en ~ raide** steep little streets; **garé dans une rue en ~** parked on a slope; [*route*] **~ à 4%** gradient of 1 in 25, 4% gradient *ou* incline (*US*) **b** (*loc*) **être sur une** *ou* **la mauvaise ~** to be going downhill, to be on a downward path; (*fig*) **remonter la ~** to get back on one's feet again, fight one's way back again; (*fig*) **être sur une ~ glissante** *ou* **dangereuse** *ou* **savonneuse** to be on a slippery slope (*fig*); **suivre sa ~ naturelle** to follow one's natural bent *ou* inclination → **dalle, rupture**

Pentecôte [pɑ̃tkot] NF **a** (*Rel* = *dimanche*) Whit Sunday, Pentecost, Whitsun; (= *période*) Whit(suntide); **lundi de ~** Whit Monday; **de la ~** Pentecostal, Whit (*épith*) **b** (= *fête juive*) Pentecost

pentecôtiste [pɑ̃tkotist] **1** ADJ [*personne*] Pentecostalist; [*église*] Pentecostal **2** NMF Pentecostalist

penthotal® [pɛ̃tɔtal] NM Pentothal®

pentu, e [pɑ̃ty] ADJ sloping

penture [pɑ̃tyʀ] NF [*volet, porte*] strap hinge

pénultième [penyltjɛm] **1** ADJ penultimate **2** NF penultimate (syllable)

pénurie [penyʀi] NF shortage; **~ de** shortage *ou* lack of; **~ de main-d'œuvre/sucre** labour/ sugar shortage; **on ne peut guère qu'organiser la ~** we must just make the best of a bad job* *ou* the best of what we've got

PEP [pɛp] NM (ABRÉV = **plan d'épargne populaire**) → **plan¹**

pep* [pɛp] NM (= *dynamisme*) pep*, liveliness; **elle a du peps** she's full of pep* *ou*

▶ GRAMMAIRE ACTIVE: **penser** 28.1, 33.1, 35.1, 35.2, 53.2

beans* (Brit); **ça m'a donné un coup de pep!** that pepped* me up! ou gave me a boost!

pépé [pepe] NM grandad*, grandpa*

pépée: [pepe] NF (= fille) girl, chick‡ (US)

pépère* [pepɛʀ] **1** NM **a** (= pépé) grandad*, grandpa*; **un petit ~** a little old man **b un gros ~** (enfant) a bonny (Brit) ou cute (US) child; (homme) an old fatty* **2** ADJ [vie] quiet, uneventful; [travail] cushy*, easy; **un petit coin ~** a nice quiet spot; (en voiture) **avoir une conduite ~** to potter (Brit) ou putter (US) along

pépettes, pépètes† [pepɛt] NFPL dough‡, lolly‡ (Brit); **avoir les ~** (= avoir peur) to have the heebie-jeebies*

pépie [pepi] NF (Orn) pip; (fig) **avoir la ~** to have a terrible thirst, be parched*

pépiement [pepimã] NM chirping (NonC), chirruping (NonC)

pépier [pepje] ▶conjug 7◀ VI to chirp, chirrup

Pépin [pepẽ] NM **~ le Bref** Pepin the Short

pépin [pepẽ] NM **a** (Bot) pip; **sans ~** seedless **b** (* = ennui) snag, hitch; **avoir un ~** to hit a snag*, have a spot of bother (Brit); **j'ai eu un ~ avec ma voiture** I had a problem with my car; **gros/petit ~ de santé** major/slight health problem; **c'est un gros ~ pour l'entreprise** it's a major setback for the company **c** (* = parapluie) umbrella, brolly* (Brit)

pépinière [pepinjɛʀ] NF (lit) tree nursery; (fig) breeding-ground, nursery (**de** for)

pépiniériste [pepinjɛʀist] **1** NM nurseryman **2** NF nurserywoman

pépite [pepit] NF (or) nugget; **~s de chocolat** chocolate chips

péplum [peplɔm] NM (Antiq) peplos, peplum; (= film) epic (set in antiquity)

peps* [pɛps] NM = **pep**

pepsine [pɛpsin] NF pepsin

peptide [pɛptid] NM peptide

peptique [pɛptik] ADJ peptic

péquenaud, e* [pɛkno, od] **1** ADJ peasant (épith) **2** NM,F country bumpkin

péquenot [pɛkno] ADJ, NM = **péquenaud**

péquin [pekẽ] NM (arg Mil) = **pékin**

péquiste [pekist] **1** ADJ of the Parti québécois **2** NMF member of the Parti québécois

PER [pɛɛʀ] NM (ABRÉV = **plan d'épargne retraite**) → **plan¹**

perborate [pɛʀbɔʀat] NM perborate

perçage [pɛʀsaʒ] NM (trou) boring, drilling; [matériau] boring through

percale [pɛʀkal] NF percale

percaline [pɛʀkalin] NF percaline

perçant, e [pɛʀsã, ãt] ADJ [cri, voix] piercing, shrill; [froid] biting, bitter; [vue] sharp, keen; [regard] piercing; [esprit] penetrating

perce [pɛʀs] NF **mettre en ~** [+ tonneau] to broach, tap

percée [pɛʀse] NF (dans une forêt) opening, clearing; (dans un mur) breach, gap; (Mil, Sci, Écon) breakthrough; (Rugby) break; **~ technologique** technological breakthrough; **faire ou réaliser une ~ sur un marché/dans une élection** to achieve a breakthrough in a market/in an election

percement [pɛʀsəmã] NM (trou) piercing; (avec perceuse) drilling, boring; (rue) building; (tunnel) cutting, driving, boring; (fenêtre) making

perce-neige (pl **perce-neige(s)**) [pɛʀsənɛʒ] NM ou F snowdrop

perce-oreille (pl **perce-oreilles**) [pɛʀsɔʀɛj] NM earwig

percepteur, -trice [pɛʀsɛptœʀ, tʀis] **1** ADJ perceptive, of perception **2** NM tax collector, tax man*

perceptibilité [pɛʀsɛptibilite] NF perceptibility

perceptible [pɛʀsɛptibl] ADJ **a** [son, ironie] perceptible (**à** to); **elle fit un mouvement à peine ~** she moved almost imperceptibly; **sa voix était à peine ~** his voice was barely audible; **une amélioration nettement ~** a marked improvement **b** [impôt] collectable, payable

perceptiblement [pɛʀsɛptibləmã] ADV perceptibly

perceptif, -ive [pɛʀsɛptif, iv] ADJ perceptive

perception [pɛʀsɛpsjɔ̃] NF **a** [objet, douleur, son] perception; **~ visuelle** visual perception; **~ extra-sensorielle** extrasensory perception **b** (= compréhension, appréhension) perception; **nous n'avons pas la même ~ de la situation** we don't perceive the situation in quite the same way; **la ~ que nous avons de l'artiste/de la vie** our view of ou the way we perceive the artist/life **c** [impôt, amende, péage] collection; [avantages financiers, allocation] receipt; (= bureau) tax (collector's) office

percer [pɛʀse] ▶conjug 3◀ **1** VT **a** (gén = perforer) to pierce, make a hole in; (avec perceuse) to drill ou bore through, drill ou bore a hole in; [+ lobe d'oreille] to pierce; [+ chaussette, chaussure] to wear a hole in; [+ coffre-fort] to break open, crack*; [+ tonneau] to broach, tap; (Méd) [+ abcès] to lance; [+ tympan] to burst; **avoir une poche/une chaussure percée** to have a hole in one's pocket/shoe; **percé de trous** full of holes, riddled with holes; **la rouille avait percé le métal** rust had eaten into the metal; **on a retrouvé son corps percé de coups de couteau** his body was found full of stab wounds; **se faire ~ les oreilles** to have one's ears pierced → **chaise, panier**
b [+ fenêtre, ouverture] to pierce, make; [+ canal] to build; [+ tunnel] to cut, drive, bore (dans through); **~ un trou dans** to pierce ou make a hole in; (avec perceuse) to drill ou bore a hole through ou in; **ils ont percé une nouvelle route à travers la forêt** they have built a new road through the forest; **~ une porte dans un mur** to make ou open a doorway in a wall; **mur percé de petites fenêtres** wall with small windows set in it
c (= traverser) **~ l'air/le silence** to pierce the air/the silence; **~ les nuages/le front ennemi** to pierce ou break through the clouds/the enemy lines; **~ la foule** to force ou elbow one's way through the crowd; **bruit qui perce les oreilles** ear-splitting noise; **~ qn du regard** to give sb a piercing look; **ses yeux essayaient de ~ l'obscurité** he tried to peer through the darkness; **cela m'a percé le cœur**† it cut me to the heart
d (= découvrir) [+ mystère] to penetrate; [+ complot] to uncover; **~ qch à jour** to see (right) through sth
e [bébé] **~ des ou ses dents** to be teething, cut one's teeth; **il a percé deux dents** he has cut two teeth

2 VI **a** [abcès] to burst; [plante] to come up; [soleil] to come out, break through; (Mil) to break through; (Sport) to make a break; **il a une dent qui perce** he's cutting a tooth; (Comm) **~ sur un nouveau marché** to break into a new market
b [sentiment, émotion] to show; [nouvelle] to filter through ou out; **rien n'a percé des négociations** no news of the negotiations has filtered through; **il ne laisse jamais ~ ses sentiments** he never lets his feelings show; **un ton où perçait l'ironie** a tone tinged with irony
c (= réussir, acquérir la notoriété) to make a name for o.s.

perceur [pɛʀsœʀ] NM driller; **~ de muraille*** burglar; **~ de coffre-fort*** safe-breaker, safe-cracker

perceuse [pɛʀsøz] NF drill; **~ à percussion** hammer drill

percevable [pɛʀsəvabl] ADJ [impôt] collectable, payable

▼ **percevoir** [pɛʀsəvwaʀ] ▶conjug 28◀ VT **a** (= ressentir) [+ objet, son, couleur] to perceive; [+ odeur, nuance, changement] to detect; [+ douleur, émotion] to feel; **j'ai cru ~ une légère hésitation dans sa voix** I thought I detected a slight note of hesitation in his voice **b** (= comprendre) [+ situation] to perceive; **son action a été bien/mal perçue** what he did was well/badly received ou was perceived as something positive/negative; **je le perçois comme quelqu'un de sensible** I see him as a sensitive person; **il perçoit mal les problèmes** he hasn't got a clear grasp of the problems; **c'est quelqu'un que je perçois mal** I can't make him out, I find it hard to get a sense of him; **il perçoit bien les enfants** he understands children **c** (= faire payer) [+ taxe, loyer] to collect; (= recevoir) [+ indemnité, revenu] to receive, be paid

perche¹ [pɛʀʃ] NF (= poisson) perch; **~ de mer** sea perch

perche² [pɛʀʃ] NF **a** (gén) pole; [tuteur] stick; [téléski] ski tow; (Ciné, Radio, TV) boom **saut, tendre¹ b** (* = personne) (grande) **~** beanpole* (Brit), stringbean* (US)

perché, e [pɛʀʃe] (ptp de **percher**) ADJ **voix haut ~e** high-pitched voice; **~e sur des talons aiguille** perched on stilettos; **village ~ sur la montagne** village set high up ou perched in the mountains

percher [pɛʀʃe] ▶conjug 1◀ **1** VI [oiseau] to perch; [volailles] to roost; ‡ [personne] to live, hang out*; (pour la nuit) to stay, crash‡ → **chat 2** VT to stick; **~ qch sur une armoire** to stick sth up on top of a cupboard; **la valise est perchée sur l'armoire** the case is perched up on top of the wardrobe **3** **se percher** VPR [oiseau] to perch; (* = se jucher) to perch

percheron, -onne [pɛʀʃəʀɔ̃, ɔn] **1** ADJ of ou from the Perche **2** **Percheron(ne)** NM,F inhabitant ou native of the Perche **3** NM (= cheval) Percheron

percheur, -euse [pɛʀʃœʀ, øz] ADJ **oiseau ~** perching bird

perchiste [pɛʀʃist] NMF (Sport) pole vaulter; (Ciné, Radio, TV) boom operator; [téléski] ski lift ou ski tow attendant

perchoir [pɛʀʃwaʀ] NM (lit, fig) perch; [volailles] roost; (Pol) seat of the president of the French National Assembly

perclus, e [pɛʀkly, yz] ADJ (= paralysé) crippled, paralyzed (**de** with); (= ankylosé) stiff; (fig) paralyzed

percolateur [pɛʀkɔlatœʀ] NM coffee machine (for making expresso, cappuccino etc)

percussion [pɛʀkysjɔ̃] NF (Méd, Mus, Phys) percussion; **instrument à ou de ~** percussion instrument; **les ~s** [orchestre] the percussion (section)

percussionniste [pɛʀkysjɔnist] NMF percussionist

percutané, e [pɛʀkytane] ADJ percutaneous

percutant, e [pɛʀkytã, ãt] ADJ **a** (Mil) percussion (épith); (Phys) percussive **b** [slogan, titre] snappy, punchy; [réponse] trenchant; [analyse] incisive; [argument, discours, pensée] forceful, powerful; [images] powerful; **il n'a pas été très ~ pendant le débat** he didn't express himself very forcefully in the debate

percuter [pɛʀkyte] ▶conjug 1◀ **1** VT (Mil, Phys) to strike; (Méd) to percuss; [conducteur, véhicule] to smash into ou crash into **2** VI **a** (= heurter) [conducteur, véhicule] to smash ou crash into; [obus] to strike **b** (‡ = comprendre) **il percute vite** he catches on* quickly, he's quick on the uptake*; **je n'ai pas percuté** I didn't twig* ou catch on*

percuteur [pɛʀkytœʀ] NM firing pin, striker

perdant, e [pɛʀdã, ãt] **1** ADJ [numéro, cheval] losing (épith); **je suis ~** (gén) I lose out*; (financièrement) I'm out of pocket, I've lost out; **tu es loin d'être ~** (gén) you're certainly not losing out; (*financièrement*) you're certainly not out of pocket *ou* not losing out [2] NM,F loser; **partir ~** to have lost before one starts; **être bon/mauvais ~** to be a good/a bad loser

perdition [pɛʀdisjɔ̃] NF [a] (*Rel*) perdition; **lieu de ~** den of iniquity [b] (*Naut*) **en ~** in distress; [*jeunesse*] on the wrong path; [*entreprise*] on the road to ruin

perdre [pɛʀdʀ(ə)] ▸conjug 41◂ [1] VT [a] [+ *match, guerre, procès, travail, avantage*] to lose; [+ *habitude*] to lose, get out of; (*volontairement*) to break, get out of; **il a perdu son père à la guerre** he lost his father in the war; **ce quartier est en train de ~ son cachet** this district is losing its distinctive charm; **j'ai perdu le goût de manger** I've lost all interest in food; **j'ai perdu le goût de rire** I don't feel like laughing any more; (*fig*) **n'avoir rien à ~** to have nothing to lose; (*Tennis*) **~ un set/son service** to lose *ou* drop a set/one's serve; **le Président perd 3 points dans le dernier sondage** the President is down 3 points in the latest poll; **l'agriculture a perdu des milliers d'emplois** thousands of jobs have been lost in farming [b] [+ *objet*] (= *ne plus trouver*) to lose; (= *égarer*) to mislay; **~ (le souvenir de)** [+ *nom, date*] to forget; **~ sa page** (*en lisant*) to lose one's place; **~ son chemin** to lose one's way [c] [+ *membre, cheveux, dent*] to lose; **~ du poids** to lose weight; **~ l'appétit/la mémoire/la vie** to lose one's appetite/one's memory/one's life; **il perd la vue** his sight is failing; **il a perdu le souffle** he's out of breath; **~ la parole** to lose the power of speech; **ce tableau a perdu beaucoup de valeur** this painting has lost a lot of its value; **~ l'équilibre** to lose one's balance; **~ espoir/patience** to lose hope/(one's) patience; **~ l'esprit** *ou* **la raison** to go out of one's mind, take leave of one's senses; **~ courage** to lose heart, be downhearted; **~ confiance** to lose one's confidence; (*Méd*) **elle a perdu les eaux** her waters have broken; **la voiture perd de la vitesse** the car is losing speed → **langue** [d] [+ *feuille, pétale, pelage, corne*] to lose, shed; **il perd son pantalon** his trousers are falling *ou* coming down; **tu perds ton collier!** your necklace is coming off!; **ce réservoir perd beaucoup d'eau** this tank leaks badly *ou* loses a lot of water [e] (= *gaspiller*) [+ *temps, peine, souffle, argent*] to waste (**à qch** on sth); (= *abîmer*) [+ *aliments*] to spoil; **tu as du temps/de l'argent à ~!** you've got time to waste/money to burn!; **il a perdu une heure à la chercher** he wasted an hour looking for her; **vous n'avez pas une minute à ~** you haven't (got) a minute to lose; **sans ~ une minute** without wasting a minute [f] (= *manquer*) [+ *occasion*] to lose, miss; **tu ne l'as jamais vu? tu n'y perds rien!** you've never seen him? you haven't missed anything!; **il n'a pas perdu un mot/une miette de la conversation** he didn't miss a single word/a single syllable of the conversation; **il ne perd rien pour attendre!** he's got it coming to him!*; **rien n'est perdu!** nothing is lost! [g] (= *porter préjudice à*) to ruin, be the ruin of; **~ qn dans l'esprit de qn** to lower sb's opinion of sb, send sb down in sb's esteem; **son ambition l'a perdu** ambition was his downfall *ou* the ruin of him, ambition proved his undoing; **c'est le témoignage de son cousin qui l'a perdu** it was his cousin's evidence which was his undoing; (*iro*) **ta bonté te perdra!** you're too kind! (*iro*) [h] (*loc fig*) **~ le nord*** to lose one's way; **il ne perd pas le nord*** he keeps his wits about him; **tu ne perds pas le nord, toi!*** you don't miss a trick!; **~ les pédales*** (*dans une explication*) to get all mixed up; (= *s'affoler*) to lose one's head *ou* one's grip; [*vieillard*] to lose one's marbles*; **~ ses moyens** to crack up*; **~**

la tête (= *s'affoler*) to lose one's head; (= *devenir fou*) to go mad *ou* crazy*; [*vieillard*] to lose one's marbles* → **boule, face, illusion, pied** etc
[2] VI [a] (*gén*) to lose; (*Comm*) **~ sur un article** to lose on an article, sell an article at a loss; **vous y perdez** (*dans une transaction*) you lose by it, you lose out on it; (= *vous ratez quelque chose*) it's your loss → **change** [b] [*citerne, réservoir*] to leak
[3] **se perdre** VPR [a] (= *s'égarer*) to get lost, lose one's way [b] (*fig*) **se ~ dans les détails/dans ses explications** to get bogged down *ou* get lost in details/in one's explanations; **se ~ en conjectures** to become lost in conjecture; **se ~ dans ses pensées** to be lost in thought; **il y a trop de chiffres, je m'y perds** there are too many figures, I'm all confused *ou* all at sea* [c] (= *disparaître*) to disappear, vanish; [*coutume*] to be dying out; (*Naut*) to sink, be wrecked; **c'est un métier qui se perd** it's a dying trade; **se ~ dans la foule** to disappear *ou* vanish into the crowd; **son cri se perdit dans le vacarme** his shout was lost in the din *ou* was drowned (out) by the din; **leurs silhouettes se perdirent dans la nuit** their figures vanished into the night *ou* were swallowed up by the darkness; **ce sens s'est perdu** this meaning has died out *ou* has been lost; **rien ne se perd, rien ne se crée(, tout se transforme)** matter can neither be created nor destroyed(, only transformed) [d] (= *devenir inutilisable*) to be wasted, go to waste; [*denrées*] to go bad; (*fig*) **il y a des gifles/des coups de pied qui se perdent*** he (*ou* she *etc*) deserves to be slapped *ou* a good slap/deserves a kick in the pants*

perdreau (*pl* **perdreaux**) [pɛʀdʀo] NM (young) partridge

perdrix [pɛʀdʀi] NF partridge; **~ blanche** *ou* **des neiges** ptarmigan; **~ de mer** pratincole

perdu, e [pɛʀdy] (*ptp de* **perdre**) [1] ADJ [a] [*bataille, cause, réputation, aventurier*] lost; **il est ~** [*malade*] there's no hope for him; **je suis ~!** I'm done for!, it's all up with me!* (*Brit*); **quand il se vit ~** when he saw he was lost *ou* done for*; **tout est ~** all is lost; **rien n'est ~** nothing's lost, there's no harm done → **corps** [b] (= *égaré*) [*personne, objet*] lost; [*balle, chien*] stray; **ce n'est pas ~ pour tout le monde** somebody's made good use of it; **un(e) de ~(e), dix de retrouvé(e)s** there are plenty more fish in the sea → **salle** [c] (= *gaspillé*) [*occasion*] lost, wasted, missed; [*temps*] wasted; **c'était une soirée de ~e** it was a wasted evening *ou* a waste of an evening; **c'est de l'argent ~** it's money down the drain; **il y a trop de place ~e** there's too much space wasted; **à ses moments ~s ◊ à temps ~** in his spare time → **pain, peine** [d] (= *abîmé*) [*aliment*] spoilt, wasted; [*récolte*] ruined [e] (= *écarté*) [*pays, endroit*] out-of-the-way, isolated [f] (= *non consigné*) [*emballage, verre*] non-returnable, no-deposit (*épith*) [g] [*personne*] (= *embrouillé*) lost, all at sea* (*attrib*); (= *absorbé*) **~ dans ses pensées** lost in thought
[2] NM†† madman; **crier/rire comme un ~** to shout/laugh like a madman

perdurer [pɛʀdyʀe] ▸conjug 1◂ VI (*littér*) [*tradition*] to endure

père [pɛʀ] [1] NM [a] (*gén*) father; **marié et ~ de trois enfants** married with three children *ou* and father of three children; **il est ~ depuis hier** he became a father yesterday; **Martin (le) ~** Martin senior; **de ~ en fils** from father to son, from one generation to the next; **ils sont bouchers de ~ en fils** they've been butchers for generations; **né de ~ inconnu** of an unknown father ■ (*PROV*) **à ~ avare, enfant**

ou fils prodigue a miser will father a spendthrift son; **le coup du ~ François*** a stab in the back; **il m'a fait le coup du ~ François** he stabbed me in the back → **tel** [b] (*pl* = *ancêtres*) **~s** forefathers, ancestors [c] (= *fondateur*) father; **le ~ de la bombe H** the father of the H-bomb [d] (*Zool*) [*animal*] sire [e] (*Rel*) father; **le Père René** Father René; **mon Père** Father → **dieu** [f] (***: = *monsieur*) **le ~ Benoit** old (man) Benoit*; **un gros ~** (= *homme*) a big fat guy*; **dis-donc, petit ~** tell me old man *ou* buddy* [g] (** = enfant*) **un brave petit ~** a fine little fellow*; **un (bon) gros ~** a chubby chap*
[2] COMP **▸ père abbé** (*Rel*) abbot **▸ les Pères blancs** the White Fathers **▸ les Pères de l'Église** (*Rel*) the Church Fathers **▸ le Père éternel** (*Rel*) our Heavenly Father **▸ père de famille** (*Jur*) father; **tu es ~ de famille, ne prends pas de risques** you have a wife and family to think about *ou* you're a family man, don't take risks; **en bon ~ de famille, il ...** as a good father should, he ...; (*hum*) **maintenant, c'est le vrai ~ de famille** now he's the serious family man **▸ le père Fouettard** the Bogeyman **▸ le père Noël** Father Christmas, Santa Claus **▸ père peinard, père tranquille** genial fellow **▸ père spirituel** [*groupe*] spiritual leader; [*personne*] spiritual father → **croire, placement, valeur**

pérégrination [peʀegʀinɑsjɔ̃] NF (*surtout pl*) peregrination

péremption [peʀɑ̃psjɔ̃] NF (*Jur*) limitation period; **il y a ~ au bout de trois ans** there is a three-year limitation period (after which claims are time-barred) → **date**

péremptoire [peʀɑ̃ptwaʀ] ADJ [*argument, ton*] peremptory

péremptoirement [peʀɑ̃ptwaʀmɑ̃] ADV peremptorily

pérennisation [peʀenizɑsjɔ̃] NF perpetuation

pérenniser [peʀenize] ▸conjug 1◂ VT to perpetuate

pérennité [peʀenite] NF [*institution, goûts*] durability; [*tradition*] continuity, perpetuity; [*lignée*] continuity

péréquation [peʀekwɑsjɔ̃] NF [*prix, impôts*] balancing out, evening out; [*notes*] coordination, adjustment; [*salaires*] adjustment, realignment

perestroïka [peʀestʀɔika] NF perestroïka

perfectibilité [pɛʀfɛktibilite] NF perfectibility

perfectible [pɛʀfɛktibl] ADJ perfectible

perfectif, -ive [pɛʀfɛktif, iv] ADJ, NM perfective

perfection [pɛʀfɛksjɔ̃] NF perfection; **la ~ n'est pas de ce monde** there's no such thing as perfection, nothing's perfect; **parvenir à** *ou* **atteindre la ~** to attain perfection; **à la ~** [*jouer, fonctionner*] to perfection; [*connaître*] perfectly; **cela illustre à la ~ ce que je disais** that's a perfect illustration of *ou* that perfectly illustrates what I was saying; **c'est une ~†** he's (*ou* she's *ou* it's) a gem

perfectionné, e [pɛʀfɛksjɔne] (*ptp de* **perfectionner**) ADJ [*dispositif, machine*] sophisticated

perfectionnement [pɛʀfɛksjɔnmɑ̃] NM [a] (*NonC*) (= *amélioration*) improving; (*pour parfaire*) perfecting; **les ordinateurs ont atteint un tel degré de ~ que ...** computers have become so sophisticated that ...; **des cours de ~ en danse/en anglais** advanced dance classes/ English course [b] (= *raffinement*) improvement; **ce logiciel nécessite encore quelques ~s** this software still needs a few improvements; **les derniers ~s techniques** the latest technical developments *ou* improvements

perfectionner [pɛʀfɛksjɔne] ▸conjug 1◂ [1] VT (= *améliorer*) to improve; (= *parfaire*) to perfect

[2] **se perfectionner** VPR [*technique*] to improve; [*personne*] to improve o.s.; **se ~ en anglais** to improve one's English

perfectionnisme [pɛʀfɛksjɔnism] NM perfectionism

perfectionniste [pɛʀfɛksjɔnist] NMF perfectionist

perfide [pɛʀfid] [1] ADJ (*littér*) [*personne, manœuvre, promesse*] perfidious, treacherous, deceitful, false; [*chose*] treacherous [2] NMF (*littér*) traitor; (*en amour*) perfidious *ou* false-hearted person

perfidement [pɛʀfidmɑ̃] ADV (*littér*) perfidiously, treacherously

perfidie [pɛʀfidi] NF (= *caractère*) perfidy, treachery; (= *acte*) act of perfidy *ou* treachery

perforage [pɛʀfɔʀaʒ] NM (= *poinçonnage*) punching; (*Tech*) boring, drilling

perforant, e [pɛʀfɔʀɑ̃, ɑ̃t] ADJ [*instrument*] perforating; [*balle, obus*] armour-piercing (*Brit*), armor-piercing (*US*)

perforateur, -trice [pɛʀfɔʀatœʀ, tʀis] [1] ADJ perforating [2] NM,F (= *ouvrier*) punch-card operator [3] NM (*Méd*) perforator [4] **perforatrice** NF (= *personne*) drilling *ou* boring machine; (*Ordin*) card punch; **perforatrice à clavier** key punch; **perforatrice à air comprimé** compressed-air drill

perforation [pɛʀfɔʀasjɔ̃] NF (*gén, Méd*) perforation; (*Ordin*) (= *action*) punching; (= *trou*) punched hole

perforer [pɛʀfɔʀe] ▸conjug 1◂ VT (= *percer*) to pierce; (*Méd*) to perforate; (= *poinçonner*) to punch; (*Ordin*) **carte perforée** punch card; **bande/feuille perforée** punched tape/sheet

perforeuse [pɛʀfɔʀøz] NF card punch

performance [pɛʀfɔʀmɑ̃s] NF [a] (= *résultat*) result, performance (*NonC*); (= *exploit*) feat, achievement; **ses ~s en anglais** his results *ou* performance in English; **s'il y parvient, ce sera une ~ remarquable** if he succeeds, it'll be an outstanding feat *ou* achievement; **réussir une bonne ~** to achieve a good result [b] [*voiture, machine, économie, industrie*] performance (*NonC*) [c] (*Ling*) **la ~** performance

performant, e [pɛʀfɔʀmɑ̃, ɑ̃t] ADJ [*machine, voiture*] high-performance (*épith*); [*résultat*] outstanding, impressive; [*entreprise, économie*] successful; [*investissement*] high-return (*épith*); [*administrateur, procédé*] effective

performatif, -ive [pɛʀfɔʀmatif, iv] ADJ, NM performative

perfuser [pɛʀfyze] ▸conjug 1◂ VT [+ *patient*] to put on a drip

perfusion [pɛʀfyzjɔ̃] NF (*Méd*) drip (*Brit*), IV (*US*), perfusion; **mettre qn/être sous ~** to put sb/be on a drip (*Brit*) *ou* an IV (*US*); **l'économie de ce pays est encore sous ~** this country's economy is still heavily subsidized *ou* still propped up by subsidies

pergola [pɛʀgɔla] NF pergola

péri [peʀi] ADJ M, NM (*marin*) **~ en mer** sailor lost at sea; **au profit des ~s en mer** in aid of those lost at sea

périanthe [peʀjɑ̃t] NM (*Bot*) perianth

péricarde [peʀikaʀd] NM pericardium

péricarpe [peʀikaʀp] NM (*Bot*) pericarp

péricliter [peʀiklite] ▸conjug 1◂ VI [*affaire, économie*] to be in a state of collapse, collapse

péridot [peʀidɔ] NM peridot

péridural, e [peʀidyʀal, o] [1] ADJ epidural [2] **péridurale** NF epidural; **faire une ~e à qn** to give sb an epidural

périf* [peʀif] NM (ABRÉV = **(boulevard) périphérique**) → **périphérique**

périgée [peʀiʒe] NM perigee

périglaciaire [peʀiglasjɛʀ] ADJ periglacial

péri-informatique [peʀiɛ̃fɔʀmatik] [1] ADJ peripheral [2] NF computer peripherals

péril [peʀil] NM (*littér*) peril, danger; **en ~** [*monument, institution*] in peril; **mettre en ~** to imperil, endanger, jeopardize; **au ~ de sa vie** at the risk of one's life; (*fig*) **il n'y a pas ~ en la demeure** there's no need to hurry; **il y a ~ à faire** it is perilous to do; **le ~ rouge/jaune** the red/yellow peril → **risque**

périlleusement [peʀijøzmɑ̃] ADV (*littér*) perilously

périlleux, -euse [peʀijø, øz] ADJ perilous → **saut**

périmé, e [peʀime] (*ptp de* **périmer**) ADJ [*billet, bon*] out-of-date (*épith*), no longer valid (*attrib*); [*idée*] dated, outdated; * [*nourriture*] past its use-by date; **ce passeport est ~** this passport has expired

périmer [peʀime] ▸conjug 1◂ [1] VI **laisser ~ un passeport/billet** to let a passport/ticket expire [2] **se périmer** VPR (*Jur*) to lapse; [*passeport, billet*] to expire; [*idée*] to date, become outdated

périmètre [peʀimɛtʀ] NM (*Math*) perimeter; (= *zone*) area; **dans un ~ de 3 km** within a 3 km radius; **~ de sécurité** safety zone

périnatal, e (*mpl* **périnatals**) [peʀinatal] ADJ perinatal

périnéal, e (*mpl* **-aux**) [peʀineal, o] ADJ perineal

périnée [peʀine] NM perineum

période [peʀjɔd] NF [a] (*gén*) period; **par ~s** from time to time; **pendant la ~ des vacances** during the holiday period; **en ~ scolaire** during termtime (*Brit*), while school is in session (*US*); **pendant la ~ électorale** at election time; (*Mil*) **~ (d'instruction)** training (*NonC*); **~ d'essai** trial period; **~ ensoleillée/de chaleur** sunny/warm spell *ou* period; **c'est la bonne ~ pour les champignons** it's the right time for mushrooms; **j'ai eu une ~ concert/théâtre*** I went through a period *ou* phase of going to concerts/the theatre a lot; **elle a traversé une ~ difficile** she has been through a difficult period *ou* patch; **la ~ bleue de Picasso** Picasso's blue period; (*Transport*) **~ bleue/blanche** slack/relatively slack period during which discounts are available on tickets; **~ rouge** peak period during which tickets are at their most expensive [b] (*Math*) [*fonction*] period; [*fraction*] repetend [c] (*Phys*) **~ radioactive** half-life

périodicité [peʀjɔdisite] NF periodicity

périodique [peʀjɔdik] [1] ADJ (*gén, Chim, Phys*) periodic; (*Presse*) periodical; (*Méd*) [*fièvre*] recurring; (*Math*) **fraction ~** recurring decimal; (*Math*) **fonction ~** periodic function → **garniture** [2] NM (*Presse*) periodical

périodiquement [peʀjɔdikmɑ̃] ADV periodically

périoste [peʀjɔst] NM periosteum

péripatéticien, -ienne [peʀipatetisjɛ̃, jɛn] [1] ADJ, NM,F (*Philo*) peripatetic [2] **péripatéticienne** NF (*hum* = *prostituée*) streetwalker

péripétie [peʀipesi] NF [a] (= *épisode*) event, episode; **les ~s d'une révolution/d'une exploration** the various episodes in a revolution/an exploration; **après bien des ~s** after all sorts of incidents; **voyage plein de ~s** eventful journey [b] (*Littérat*) peripeteia

périph* [peʀif] NM (ABRÉV = **(boulevard) périphérique**) → **périphérique**

périphérie [peʀifeʀi] NF (= *limite*) periphery; (= *banlieue*) outskirts; **la proche ~** the inner suburbs

périphérique [peʀifeʀik] [1] ADJ (*Anat, Math*) peripheral; [*quartier*] outlying (*épith*); [*activités*] associated; **poste ou radio ou station ~** private radio station (*broadcasting from a neighbouring country*) [2] NM [a] (*Ordin*) peripheral; **~ entrée-sortie** input-output device [b] **(boulevard) ~** ring road, beltway (*US*); **(boulevard) ~ intérieur/extérieur** inner/outer ring road (*Brit*) *ou* beltway (*US*)

périphrase [peʀifʀɑz] NF circumlocution, periphrasis (*SPEC*), periphrase (*SPEC*)

périphrastique [peʀifʀastik] ADJ circumlocutory, periphrastic

périple [peʀipl] NM (*par mer*) voyage; (*par terre*) tour, journey; **au cours de son ~ américain** during his tour of the USA

périr [peʀiʀ] ▸conjug 2◂ VI (*littér*) to perish (*littér*), die; [*navire*] to go down, sink; [*empire*] to perish, fall; **~ noyé** to drown, be drowned; **faire ~** [+ *personne, plante*] to kill; **son souvenir ne périra jamais** his memory will never die *ou* perish (*littér*); (*fig*) **~ d'ennui** to die of boredom

périscolaire [peʀiskɔlɛʀ] ADJ extracurricular

périscope [peʀiskɔp] NM periscope

périscopique [peʀiskɔpik] ADJ periscopic

périssable [peʀisabl] ADJ perishable; **denrées ~s** perishable goods, perishables

périssoire [peʀiswaʀ] NF canoe

péristaltisme [peʀistaltism] NM peristalsis

péristyle [peʀistil] NM peristyle

péritel® [peʀitɛl] ADJ F, NF (**prise**) **~** SCART (socket)

péritoine [peʀitwan] NM peritoneum

péritonite [peʀitɔnit] NF peritonitis

périurbain, e [peʀiyʀbɛ̃, ɛn] ADJ outlying; **zone ~e** outlying suburbs, peri-urban area

perle [pɛʀl] [1] NF [a] (= *bijou*) pearl; (= *boule*) bead; **des dents de ~** pearly teeth; (*fig*) **jeter ou donner des ~s aux pourceaux** to cast pearls before swine → **enfiler** [b] (*littér* = *goutte*) [*eau, sang*] drop(let); [*sueur*] bead [c] (= *personne, chose de valeur*) gem; **la cuisinière est une ~** the cook is an absolute gem *ou* a perfect treasure; **c'est la ~ des maris** he's the best of husbands, you couldn't hope for a better husband; **vous êtes une ~ rare** you're a (real) gem; **la ~ d'une collection** the highlight of a collection [d] (= *erreur*) gem, howler [2] COMP ▸ **perle de culture** cultured pearl ▸ **perle fine, perle naturelle** natural pearl ▸ **perle de rosée** dewdrop

perlé, e [pɛʀle] (*ptp de* **perler**) ADJ [*orge*] pearl (*épith*); [*riz*] polished; [*coton, laine*] pearlized; [*tissu*] beaded; [*travail*] perfect, exquisite; [*rire*] rippling → **grève**

perler [pɛʀle] ▸conjug 1◂ [1] VI [*sueur*] to form; **la sueur perlait sur son front** beads of sweat stood out *ou* formed on his forehead [2] VT† [+ *travail*] to take great pains over

perlier, -ière [pɛʀlje, jɛʀ] ADJ pearl (*épith*)

perlimpinpin [pɛʀlɛ̃pɛ̃pɛ̃] NM → **poudre**

perlouse‡, perlouze‡ [pɛʀluz] NF (= *perle*) pearl; (= *pet*) smelly fart‡

perm* [pɛʀm] NF [a] ABRÉV = **permanence** c [b] (*arg Mil*) ABRÉV = **permission** b

permafrost [pɛʀmafʀɔst] NM permafrost

permanence [pɛʀmanɑ̃s] NF [a] (= *durée*) permanence, permanency; **en ~** [*siéger*] permanently; [*crier*] continuously; **dans ce pays ce sont des émeutes/c'est la guerre en ~** in that country there are constant *ou* continuous riots/there is a permanent state of war [b] (= *service*) **être de ~** to be on duty *ou* on call; **une ~ est assurée le dimanche** there is someone on duty on Sundays, the office is manned on Sundays [c] (= *bureau*) (duty) office; (*Pol*) committee room; (*Scol*) study room *ou* hall (*US*); (*Scol*) **heure de ~** private study period

permanent, e [pɛʀmanɑ̃, ɑ̃t] [1] ADJ (*gén*) permanent; [*armée, comité*] standing (*épith*); [*spectacle*] continuous; [*angoisse*] continuous; [*danger*] permanent; [*conflit, effort*] ongoing; (*Presse*) [*envoyé, correspondant*] permanent; (*Phys*) [*aimantation, gaz*] permanent; (*Ciné*) **~ de 14 heures à minuit** continuous showings from 2 o'clock to midnight; **cinéma ~** cinema showing a continuous programme; **il sont en contact ~** they are in constant *ou* regular contact; **elle s'est installée en France de façon ~e**

she has settled in France permanently [2] NM (*Pol*) (paid) official (*of union, political party*); (*dans une entreprise*) permanent employee; **un ~ du parti** a party worker [3] **permanente** NF (*Coiffure*) perm; **se faire faire une ~e** to have one's hair permed, get a perm

permanenter [pɛʀmanɑ̃te] ▸conjug 1◂ VT to perm; **se faire ~** to have one's hair permed, get a perm; **cheveux permanentés** permed hair

permanganate [pɛʀmɑ̃ganat] NM permanganate

perméabilité [pɛʀmeabilite] NF [a] (*Phys*) permeability (**à** to); ~ **à l'air** air permeability [b] [*frontière*] openness

perméable [pɛʀmeabl] ADJ [a] (*Phys*) permeable (**à** to); ~ **à l'air** permeable to air [b] (= *ouvert*) [*frontière*] open (**à** to); ~ **à** [*personne*] receptive to, open to; **la frontière est trop ~** the border is too open *ou* too easily crossed; **trop ~ aux idées extrémistes** too easily influenced by extremist ideas

▾ **permettre** [pɛʀmɛtʀ] ▸conjug 56◂ [1] VT [a] (= *tolérer*) to allow, permit; ~ **à qn de faire qch** *◇* = **que qn fasse qch** to allow *ou* permit sb to do sth, let sb do sth; **la loi le permet** it is allowed *ou* permitted by law, the law allows *ou* permits it; **le docteur me permet l'alcool** the doctor allows *ou* permits me to drink *ou* lets me drink; **il se croit tout permis** he thinks he can do what he likes *ou* as he pleases; **est-il permis d'être aussi bête !** how can anyone be so stupid!; **il est permis à tout le monde de se tromper!** anyone can make mistakes *ou* a mistake!; **le professeur lui a permis de ne pas aller à l'école aujourd'hui** the teacher has given him permission to stay off school *ou* not to go to school today; **il hurlait comme ce n'est pas permis*** he was screaming like mad* [b] (= *rendre possible*) to allow, permit; **ce diplôme va lui ~ de trouver du travail** this qualification will allow *ou* enable *ou* permit him to find a job; **mes moyens ne me le permettent pas** I can't afford it; **mes occupations ne me le permettent pas** I'm too busy to do that; **sa santé ne le lui permet pas** his health doesn't allow *ou* permit him to do that; **son attitude permet tous les soupçons** his attitude gives cause for suspicion; **si le temps le permet** weather permitting; **autant qu'il est permis d'en juger** as far as one can tell [c] (= *donner le droit*) to entitle; **cette carte lui permet d'obtenir des réductions** this card entitles him to reductions; **être majeur permet de voter** being over 18 entitles one *ou* makes one eligible to vote; **qu'est-ce qui te permet de me juger?** what gives you the right to judge me? [d] (*idée de sollicitation*) **vous permettez?** may I?; **permettez-moi de vous présenter ma sœur/de vous interrompre** may I introduce my sister/interrupt (you)?; **s'il m'est permis de faire une objection** if I may *ou* might (be allowed) raise an objection; **vous permettez que je fume?** do you mind if I smoke?; (*ton irrité*) **vous permettez que je passe!** if you don't mind I'd like to come past!; **permettez! je ne suis pas d'accord** I'm very sorry but I disagree!; **permets-moi de te le dire** let me tell you [2] **se permettre** VPR [a] (= *s'offrir*) to allow o.s.; **je me permets une petite fantaisie de temps en temps** I indulge myself from time to time; **je ne peux pas me ~ d'acheter ce manteau** I can't afford to buy this coat [b] (= *risquer*) [+ *grossièreté, plaisanterie*] to allow o.s. to make, dare to make; **ce sont des plaisanteries qu'on ne peut se ~ qu'entre amis** these jokes are only acceptable among friends; **je me suis permis de sourire** *ou* **un sourire** I allowed myself *ou* gave a smile; **il s'est permis de partir sans permission** he took the liberty of going without permission; **il se permet bien des choses** he takes a lot of liber-

ties; **je me permettrai de vous faire remarquer que ...** I'd like to point out (to you) that ...; **puis-je me ~ de vous offrir un verre?** will you let me buy you a drink?; (*formule épistolaire*) **je me permets de vous écrire au sujet de ...** I am writing to you in connection with ...

permien, -ienne [pɛʀmjɛ̃, jɛn] [1] ADJ permian [2] NM **le ~** the Permian era

▾ **permis, e** [pɛʀmi, iz] (*ptp de* **permettre**) [1] ADJ [*limites*] permitted; (*frm*) **il est ~ de s'interroger sur la nécessité de ...** one might *ou* may well question the necessity of ... [2] NM permit, licence; ~ **de chasse** hunting licence; ~ (**de conduire**) (= *carte*) driving licence (*Brit*), driver's license (*US*); (= *épreuve*) driving test; ~ **à points** driving licence with a penalty point system; ~ **de construire** planning permission (*NonC*); ~ **d'inhumer** burial certificate; ~ **bateau** boating licence; ~ **moto** motorbike licence; ~ **de pêche** fishing permit; ~ **poids lourd** heavy-goods vehicle licence; ~ **de port d'armes** gun licence; ~ **de séjour** residence permit; ~ **de travail** work permit

permissif, -ive [pɛʀmisif, iv] ADJ permissive

permission [pɛʀmisjɔ̃] NF [a] (= *autorisation*) permission; **avec votre ~** with your permission; **accorder à qn la ~ de faire qch** to give sb permission to do sth; **demander la ~** to ask permission (**de** to); **je lui ai demandé la ~** I asked his permission (**de** to); **demander à qn la ~** to ask sb his permission (**de** to); **est-ce qu'il t'a donné la ~ (de le faire)?** did he give you permission (to do it)? [b] (*Mil*) (= *congé*) leave, furlough; (= *certificat*) pass; **en ~** on leave *ou* furlough; ~ **de minuit** late pass

permissionnaire [pɛʀmisjɔnɛʀ] NM soldier on leave

permissivité [pɛʀmisivite] NF permissiveness

permutabilité [pɛʀmytabilite] NF permutability

permutable [pɛʀmytabl] ADJ which can be changed *ou* swapped *ou* switched round; (*Math*) permutable

permutation [pɛʀmytasjɔ̃] NF permutation

permuter [pɛʀmyte] ▸conjug 1◂ [1] VT (*gén*) to change *ou* swap *ou* switch round, permute; (*Math*) to permutate, permute [2] VI to change, swap, switch (seats *ou* positions *ou* jobs etc)

pernicieusement [pɛʀnisjøzmɑ̃] ADV (*littér*) perniciously

pernicieux, -ieuse [pɛʀnisjø, jøz] ADJ (*gén, Méd*) pernicious; ~ **pour** injurious *ou* harmful to

péroné [peʀɔne] NM fibula

péroniste [peʀɔnist] [1] ADJ Peronist [2] **Péroniste** NMF Peronist

péronnelle [peʀɔnɛl] NF (*péj*) silly goose* (*péj*)

péroraison [peʀɔʀɛzɔ̃] NF (*Littérat = conclusion*) peroration, summing up; (*péj = discours*) windy discourse (*péj*)

pérorer [peʀɔʀe] ▸conjug 1◂ VI to hold forth (*péj*), declaim (*péj*)

Pérou [peʀu] NM (*Géog*) Peru; (*loc*) **ce qu'il gagne, ce n'est pas le ~** he doesn't exactly earn a fortune; (*iro*) **on a 300 F? c'est le ~!** we've got 300 francs? we're loaded!* *ou* we're rolling in it* (*iro*)!

Pérouse [peʀuz] N Perugia

peroxyde [pɛʀɔksid] NM peroxide; ~ **d'hydrogène** hydrogen peroxide

peroxydé, e [pɛʀɔkside] ADJ [*cheveux*] peroxide (*épith*)

perpendiculaire [pɛʀpɑ̃dikylɛʀ] ADJ, NF perpendicular (**à** to)

perpendiculairement [pɛʀpɑ̃dikylɛʀmɑ̃] ADV perpendicularly; ~ **à** at right angles to, perpendicular to

perpète* [pɛʀpɛt] NF [a] (*arg Prison = perpétuité*) **il a eu la ~** he got life* [b] (= *loin*) **à ~*** miles

away*; (= *longtemps*) **jusqu'à ~*** forever and a day*

perpétration [pɛʀpetʀasjɔ̃] NF perpetration

perpétrer [pɛʀpetʀe] ▸conjug 6◂ VT to perpetrate

perpette* [pɛʀpɛt] NF = **perpète**

perpétuation [pɛʀpetɥasjɔ̃] NF (*littér*) perpetuation

perpétuel, -elle [pɛʀpetɥɛl] ADJ (= *pour toujours*) perpetual, everlasting; (= *incessant*) perpetual, never-ending; [*fonction, secrétaire*] permanent

perpétuellement [pɛʀpetɥɛlmɑ̃] ADV (= *constamment*) constantly; (*littér = toujours*) perpetually

perpétuer [pɛʀpetɥe] ▸conjug 1◂ [1] VT (= *immortaliser*) to perpetuate; (= *maintenir*) to perpetuate, carry on [2] **se perpétuer** VPR [*usage, abus*] to be perpetuated, be carried on; [*espèce*] to survive; **se ~ dans son œuvre/dans ses enfants** to live on in one's work/in one's children

perpétuité [pɛʀpetɥite] NF perpetuity, perpetuation; **à ~** [*condamnation*] for life; [*concession*] in perpetuity → **réclusion**

perplexe [pɛʀplɛks] ADJ perplexed, puzzled; **rendre** *ou* **laisser ~** to perplex, puzzle

perplexité [pɛʀplɛksite] NF perplexity; **je suis dans une grande ~** I just don't know what to think; **être dans la plus complète ~** to be completely baffled *ou* utterly perplexed

perquisition [pɛʀkizisjɔ̃] NF (*Police*) search; **ils ont fait une ~** they carried out *ou* made a search, they searched the premises → **mandat**

perquisitionner [pɛʀkizisjɔne] ▸conjug 1◂ [1] VI to carry out a search, make a search; ~ **au domicile de qn** to search sb's house, carry out *ou* make a search of sb's house [2] VT * to search

perron [pɛʀɔ̃] NM steps (*leading to entrance*), perron (*SPÉC*); **sur le ~ de l'Élysée** on the steps of the Élysée Palace

perroquet [pɛʀɔkɛ] NM [a] (*Orn, fig*) parrot; ~ **de mer** puffin; **répéter qch comme un ~** to repeat sth parrot fashion [b] (*Naut*) topgallant (sail) [c] (= *boisson*) *apéritif made of pastis and mint syrup*

perruche [pɛʀyʃ] NF [a] (*Orn*) budgerigar, budgie*; (= *femelle du perroquet*) female parrot; (*fig* = *femme bavarde*) chatterbox*, gasbag* (*péj*), windbag* (*péj*) [b] (*Naut*) mizzen topgallant (sail)

perruque [pɛʀyk] NF [a] (= *coiffure*) wig; (*Hist*) wig, periwig, peruke [b] (*Pêche* = *enchevêtrement*) tangle [c]* (= *travail clandestin*) **faire des ~s** to work on the side (*during office hours*); (= *détournement de matériel*) **faire de la ~** to pilfer office equipment for personal use

perruquier, -ière [pɛʀykje, jɛʀ] NM,F wigmaker

pers [pɛʀ] ADJ M [*yeux*] greenish-blue, blue-green

persan, e [pɛʀsɑ̃, an] [1] ADJ Persian; (**chat**) ~ Persian (cat) → **tapis** [2] NM (*Ling*) Persian [3] **Persan(e)** NM,F Persian

perse [pɛʀs] [1] ADJ Persian [2] NM (*Ling*) Persian [3] **Perse** NMF Persian [4] NF (*Géog*) **Perse** Persia

persécuté, e [pɛʀsekyte] NM,F (*gén*) persecuted person; (*Psych*) person suffering from a persecution mania *ou* complex

persécuter [pɛʀsekyte] ▸conjug 1◂ VT (= *opprimer*) to persecute; (= *harceler*) to harass, plague

persécuteur, -trice [pɛʀsekytœʀ, tʀis] [1] ADJ persecuting [2] NM,F persecutor

persécution [pɛʀsekysjɔ̃] NF persecution; **délire de ~** persecution mania *ou* complex

Persée [pɛʀse] NM Perseus

Perséphone [pɛʀsefɔn] NF Persephone

➤ **GRAMMAIRE ACTIVE:**   **permettre** 28.1, 30, 36.1, 37.4   **permis** 36.1, 37.4

persévérance [pɛʀseveʀɑ̃s] NF perseverance

persévérant, e [pɛʀseveʀɑ̃, ɑ̃t] ADJ persevering; **être** ~ to persevere, be persevering

persévérer [pɛʀseveʀe] ▸conjug 6◂ VI to persevere; ~ **dans** [+ effort, entreprise, recherches] to persevere with ou in, persist in; [+ erreur, voie] to persevere in; **je persévère à le croire coupable** I continue to believe he's guilty

persienne [pɛʀsjɛn] NF (louvred) shutter

persiflage [pɛʀsiflaʒ] NM mockery (NonC)

persifler [pɛʀsifle] ▸conjug 1◂ VT to mock, make fun of

persifleur, -euse [pɛʀsiflœʀ, øz] **1** ADJ mocking **2** NM,F mocker

persil [pɛʀsi] NM parsley; ~ **plat/frisé** flat-leaved/curly parsley; **faux** ~ fool's parsley

persillade [pɛʀsijad] NF (= sauce) parsley vinaigrette; (= viande) cold beef served with parsley vinaigrette

persillé, e [pɛʀsije] ADJ [plat] sprinkled with chopped parsley; [viande] marbled; [fromage] veined

persique [pɛʀsik] ADJ Persian → **golfe**

persistance [pɛʀsistɑ̃s] NF [pluie, fièvre, douleur, odeur] persistence; [personne] persistence, persistency (à faire in doing); **cette** ~ **dans le mensonge** this persistent lying; **avec** ~ (= tout le temps) persistently; (= avec obstination) persistently, doggedly, stubbornly

persistant, e [pɛʀsistɑ̃, ɑ̃t] ADJ (gén) persistent; [feuilles] evergreen, persistent (SPEC); **arbre à feuillage** ~ evergreen (tree)

persister [pɛʀsiste] ▸conjug 1◂ VI [pluie] to persist, keep up; [fièvre, douleur, odeur] to persist, linger; [symptôme, personne] to persist; **la pluie/la douleur n'a pas persisté** the rain/the pain didn't last ou persist; ~ **dans qch/à faire qch** to persist in sth/in doing sth; **il persiste dans son refus** he won't go back on his refusal; ~ **dans son opinion/ses projets** to stick to one's opinion/one's plans; **il persiste dans son silence** he persists in keeping quiet; **il persiste à faire cela** he persists in doing ou keeps (on) doing that; **je persiste à croire que ...** I still believe that ...; (fig) **c'est non, je persiste et signe !** the answer is no, and that's final!; **il persistait une odeur de moisi** a musty smell lingered ou persisted; **il persiste un doute** some doubt remains

perso* [pɛʀso] ADJ (ABRÉV = **personnel**) = privé) personal; (= égoïste) selfish; **jouer** ~ (gén) to go one's own way, go solo; (Sport) **il joue trop** ~ he tends to keep the ball to himself

persona [pɛʀsona] NF ► **grata/non grata** persona grata/non grata

personnage [pɛʀsɔnaʒ] NM **a** (= individu) character, individual; **c'est un** ~ ! he's (ou she's) quite a character! **b** (= célébrité) (very) important person; ~ **influent/haut placé** influential/highly placed person; ~ **connu** celebrity, well-known person; ~ **officiel** VIP; **un grand** ~ a great figure; **grands** ~**s de l'État** State dignitaries; ~**s de l'Antiquité/historiques** great names of Antiquity/in history; **il est devenu un** ~ he's become a very important person ou a big name*; **il se prend pour un grand** ~ he really thinks he's someone important, he really thinks he's somebody* **c** (Littérat) character; **liste des** ~**s** dramatis personae, list of characters; (lit, fig) **jouer un** ~ to play a part, act a part ou role → **peau d** (Art) [tableau] figure

personnalisation [pɛʀsɔnalizasjɔ̃] NF personalization

personnaliser [pɛʀsɔnalize] ▸conjug 1◂ VT (gén) to personalize; [+ voiture, appartement] to give a personal touch to, personalize; **crédit/service personnalisé** personalized loan/service

personnalité [pɛʀsɔnalite] NF **a** (Psych) personality; **avoir une forte** ~**/de la** ~ to have a strong personality/lots of personality; **sans** ~

lacking in personality **b** (= personne importante) personality; **il y aura de nombreuses** ~**s pour l'inauguration** there will be a number of key figures ou personalities at the opening **c** (Jur) **acquérir une** ~ **juridique** to acquire legal status

personne [pɛʀsɔn] **1** NF **a** (= être humain) person; **deux** ~**s** two people; **grande** ~ adult, grown-up; **le respect de la** ~ **humaine** respect for human dignity; **les** ~**s qui ...** those who ..., the people who ...; **c'est une** ~ **sympathique** he (ou she) is a very nice ou pleasant person; **une** ~ **de connaissance m'a dit ...** someone ou a person I know told me ...; **il n'y a pas** ~ **plus discrète que lui** there's no one more discreet than he is ou than him; **c'est une drôle de petite/une jolie** ~† she's a funny little/a pretty little thing; **trois gâteaux par** ~ three cakes per person, three cakes each; **100 F par** ~ = 100 francs each ou a head ou per person; **par** ~ **interposée** through an intermediary, through a third party ou person; **querelles/rivalités de** ~**s** personal quarrels/rivalries; (Jur) **les droits de la** ~ the rights of the individual → **tiers**

b (= personnalité) **toute sa** ~ **inspire confiance** everything about him inspires confidence; **j'admire son œuvre mais je le méprise en tant que** ~ I admire his works but I have no time for him as a person; **la** ~ **et l'œuvre de Balzac** Balzac, the man and his work

c (= corps) **être bien (fait) de sa** ~ to be good-looking; **exposer** ou **risquer sa** ~ to risk one's life ou one's neck; **sur ma** ~ on my person; **il semble toujours très content de sa petite** ~ he always seems very pleased with himself; **il prend soin de sa petite** ~ he looks after himself; **je l'ai vu en** ~ I saw him in person; **je m'en occupe en** ~ I'll see to it personally; **c'est la paresse/la bonté en** ~ he's ou she's laziness/kindness itself ou personified → **payer**

d (Gram) person; **à la première/troisième** ~ in the first/third person

2 PRON **a** (= quelqu'un) anyone, anybody; **elle le sait mieux que** ~ **(au monde)** she knows that better than anyone ou anybody (else); **il est entré sans que** ~ **le voie** he came in without anyone ou anybody seeing him; ~ **de blessé ?** is anyone ou anybody injured?, no one hurt?; **elle sait faire le café comme** ~ she makes better coffee than anyone (else)

b (avec ne = aucun) no one, nobody; **presque** ~ hardly anyone ou anybody, practically no one ou nobody; ~ **(d'autre) ne l'a vu** no one ou nobody (else) saw him; **il n'a vu** ~ **(d'autre)** he didn't see anyone ou anybody (else), he saw no one ou nobody (else); ~ **d'autre que lui** no one ou nobody but him ou he; **il n'y a** ~ there's no one ou nobody in, there isn't anyone ou anybody in; **il n'y a eu** ~ **de blessé** no one ou nobody was injured, there wasn't anyone ou anybody injured; **à qui as-tu demandé ? — à** ~ who did you ask? — no one ou nobody ou I didn't ask anyone ou anybody; **ce n'est la faute de** ~ it's no one's ou nobody's fault; **il n'y avait** ~ **d'intéressant à qui parler** there was no one ou nobody interesting to talk to; **il n'y est pour** ~ he doesn't want to see anyone ou anybody; (iro) **pour le travail, il n'y a plus** ~* as soon as there's a bit of work to be done, everyone disappears ou clears off* ou there's suddenly no one ou nobody around; **n'y a-t-il** ~ **qui sache où il est ?** doesn't anyone ou anybody know where he is?

3 COMP ► **personne âgée** elderly person; **mesure en faveur des** ~**s âgées** measure benefiting the elderly ► **personne à charge** dependent ► **personne civile** (Jur) legal entity ► **personnes déplacées** (Pol) displaced persons ► **personne morale** (Jur) = **personne civile** ► **personne physique** (Jur) natural person

personnel, -elle [pɛʀsɔnɛl] **1** ADJ **a** (= particulier, privé) personal; [appel téléphonique] private; **fortune personnelle** personal ou private fortune; **strictement** ~ [lettre] highly confidential, private and personal; [billet] not transferable (attrib); **il a des idées/des opinions très personnelles sur la question** he has ideas/opinions of his own ou he has his own ideas/opinions on the subject; **critiques personnelles** personal criticism **b** (= égoïste) selfish, self-centred; (Sport) [joueur] selfish **c** (Gram) [pronom, nom, verbe] personal; [mode] finite

2 NM [école] staff; [château, hôtel] staff, employees; [usine] workforce, employees, personnel; [service public] personnel, employees; **manquer de** ~ to be shortstaffed ou understaffed; **il y a trop de** ~ **dans ce service** this department is overstaffed; **faire partie du** ~ to be on the staff; **l'usine a 60 membres de** ~ ou **un** ~ **de 60** the factory has 60 people on the payroll, the factory has a workforce ou payroll of 60; ~ **de maison** domestic staff; (Aviat, Mil) ~ **à terre/navigant** ground/flight personnel ou staff; ~ **en civil/en tenue** plain-clothes/uniformed staff; **bureau/chef du** ~ personnel office/officer

▾**personnellement** [pɛʀsɔnɛlmɑ̃] ADV personally; **je lui dirai** ~ I'll tell him myself ou personally; ~ **je veux bien** personally I don't mind, I for one don't mind

personnification [pɛʀsɔnifikasjɔ̃] NF personification; **c'est la** ~ **de la cruauté** he's the personification ou the embodiment of cruelty

personnifier [pɛʀsɔnifje] ▸conjug 7◂ VT to personify; **cet homme personnifie le mal** this man is the embodiment of evil ou is evil itself ou is evil personified; **être la bêtise personnifiée** to be stupidity itself ou personified; **il personnifie son époque** he personifies ou typifies his age, he's the embodiment of his age

perspectif, -ive¹ [pɛʀspɛktif, iv] ADJ perspective

perspective² [pɛʀspɛktiv] NF **a** (Art) perspective; **effet de** ~ 3-D ou 3 dimensional effect **b** (= point de vue) (lit) view; (fig) angle, viewpoint; **dans une** ~ **historique** from a historical angle ou viewpoint, in a historical perspective; **examiner une question sous des** ~**s différentes** to examine a question from different angles ou viewpoints; **il faut mettre les choses en** ~ you have to put things in perspective **c** (= événement en puissance) prospect; (= idée) prospect, thought; **il y a du travail en** ~ there's a lot of work ahead; **des** ~**s d'avenir** future prospects; **quelle** ~ ! what a thought! ou prospect!; **à la** ~ **de** at the prospect ou thought ou idea of

perspicace [pɛʀspikas] ADJ clear-sighted, perspicacious

perspicacité [pɛʀspikasite] NF clear-sightedness, insight, perspicacity

persuader [pɛʀsɥade] ▸conjug 1◂ **1** VT (= convaincre) to persuade, convince (qn de qch sb of sth); ~ **qn (de faire qch)** to persuade sb (to do sth); **il les a persuadés que tout irait bien** he persuaded ou convinced them that all would be well; **on l'a persuadé de partir** he was persuaded to leave; **j'en suis persuadé** I'm quite sure ou convinced (of it); **il sait** ~ he's very persuasive, he knows how to convince people **2** VI (littér) ~ **à qn (de faire)** to persuade sb (to do); **on lui a persuadé de rester** he was persuaded to stay **3** **se persuader** VPR **se** ~ **de qch** to convince ou persuade o.s. of sth; **se** ~ **que ...** to convince ou persuade o.s. that ...

persuasif, -ive [pɛʀsɥazif, iv] ADJ [ton, éloquence] persuasive; [argument, orateur] persuasive, convincing

persuasion [pɛrsɥazjɔ̃] NF (= action, art) persuasion; (= croyance) conviction, belief

▼ **perte** [pɛrt] **1** NF **a** (gén) loss, losing (NonC); (Comm) loss; **vendre à ~** to sell at a loss; **la ~ d'une bataille/d'un procès** the loss of a battle/of a court case, losing a battle/a court case; **essuyer une ~ importante** to suffer heavy losses; (Mil) **de lourdes ~s (en hommes)** heavy losses (in men); **ce n'est pas une grosse ~** it's not a serious loss; **la ~ cruelle d'un être cher** the cruel ou grievous loss of a loved one → **profit**

b (= ruine) ruin; **il a juré sa ~** he has sworn to ruin him; **il court à sa ~** he is on the road to ruin

c (= déperdition) loss; (= gaspillage) waste; **~ de chaleur/d'énergie** loss of heat/of energy, heat/energy loss; **~ de lumière** loss of light; **c'est une ~ de temps/d'énergie** it's a waste of time/of energy

d (loc) **à ~ de vue** (lit) as far as the eye can see; (fig) interminably; **mis à la porte avec ~ et fracas** thrown out

2 COMP ► **pertes blanches** (Méd) vaginal discharge, leucorrhoea (SPÉC) ► **perte de charge** pressure drop, drop in ou loss of pressure ► **perte de connaissance** ou **de conscience** loss of consciousness; **avoir une ~ de connaissance** ou **de conscience** to lose consciousness ► **perte de mémoire** loss of memory, memory loss ► **perte de poids** weight loss ► **pertes de sang** heavy bleeding ► **perte sèche** (Fin) dead loss (Fin), absolute loss ► **perte à la terre** (Élec) earth (Brit) ou ground (US) leakage ► **perte de vitesse**: **être en ~ de vitesse** (Aviat) to lose lift; (fig) [mouvement] to be losing momentum; [entreprise, vedette] to be going downhill

pertinemment [pɛrtinamɑ̃] ADV [parler] pertinently; **il a répondu ~** his reply was to the point; **savoir ~ que ...** to know full well that ..., know for a fact that ...

pertinence [pɛrtinɑ̃s] NF **a** (= à-propos) [remarque, question, idée, analyse] pertinence, relevance; **il remarqua avec ~ que ...** he aptly pointed out that ... **b** (Ling) significance, distinctive nature

pertinent, e [pɛrtinɑ̃, ɑ̃t] ADJ **a** [remarque, question, idée, analyse] pertinent, relevant **b** (Ling) significant, distinctive

pertuis [pɛrtɥi] NM (= détroit) strait(s), channel; [fleuve] narrows

pertuisane [pɛrtɥizan] NF partisan (weapon)

perturbant, e [pɛrtyrbɑ̃, ɑ̃t] ADJ disturbing, perturbing; **le divorce a été très ~ pour l'enfant** the divorce was a very disturbing ou unsettling experience for the child

perturbateur, -trice [pɛrtyrbatœr, tris] **1** ADJ disruptive **2** NM,F (gén) troublemaker; (dans un débat) heckler

perturbation [pɛrtyrbasjɔ̃] NF [services publics, travaux, cérémonie, réunion] disruption; (Radio, TV) [transmission] disruption; (Astron) perturbation; **jeter ou semer la ~ dans** to disrupt; **facteur de ~** disruptive factor; **~s dans l'acheminement du courrier** disruption(s) in the mail service; **les ~s ont surtout affecté les lignes de banlieue** it was mainly the suburban lines that were disrupted; (Météo) **~ (atmosphérique)** (atmospheric) disturbance

perturber [pɛrtyrbe] ▶conjug 1◀ VT **a** [+ services publics, travaux, cérémonie, réunion] to disrupt; (Radio, TV) [+ transmission] to disrupt; (Astron) to perturb; (Mét) to disturb **b** (= déstabiliser) [+ personne] to perturb, disturb; **elle est très perturbée en ce moment** she's very perturbed at the moment; **son divorce l'a profondément perturbé** he was deeply upset by his divorce

péruvien, -ienne [peryvjɛ̃, jɛn] **1** ADJ Peruvian **2** **Péruvien(ne)** NM,F Peruvian

pervenche [pɛrvɑ̃ʃ] **1** NF (Bot) periwinkle; (* = contractuelle) female traffic warden (Brit), meter maid (US) **2** ADJ INV periwinkle blue

pervers, e [pɛrvɛr, ɛrs] **1** ADJ (littér) (= diabolique) perverse; (= vicieux) perverted, depraved; **les effets ~ de la publicité** the pernicious effects of advertising **2** NM,F pervert; **~ sexuel** (sexual) pervert

perversion [pɛrvɛrsjɔ̃] NF perversion, corruption; (Méd, Psych) perversion

perversité [pɛrvɛrsite] NF perversity, depravity

pervertir [pɛrvɛrtir] ▶conjug 2◀ **1** VT (= dépraver) to corrupt, pervert, deprave; (= altérer) to pervert **2** **se pervertir** VPR to become corrupt(ed) ou perverted ou depraved

pesage [pəzaʒ] NM weighing; [jockey] weighing; (= salle) weighing room; (= enceinte) enclosure

pesamment [pəzamɑ̃] ADV [chargé, tomber] heavily; [marcher] with a heavy step ou tread, heavily

pesant, e [pəzɑ̃, ɑ̃t] **1** ADJ **a** (= lourd) [paquet] heavy, weighty; [sommeil] deep; [démarche, pas, architecture] heavy; [esprit] slow, sluggish; [style, ton] heavy, weighty, ponderous **b** (= pénible) [charge, silence] heavy; [présence] burdensome; **il devient ~ avec ses questions** he's becoming a nuisance with all those questions **2** NM **valoir son ~ d'or** [personne] to be worth one's weight in gold; [diplôme] to be worth its weight in gold; (hum) **il faut le voir faire un discours, ça vaut son ~ d'or ou de cacahuètes*** you should hear him make a speech, it's priceless*

pesanteur [pəzɑ̃tœr] NF **a** (Phys) gravity; **défier les lois de la ~** to defy (the laws of) gravity **b** (= lourdeur) [paquet] heaviness, weightiness; [démarche] heaviness; [esprit] slowness, sluggishness; [architecture] heaviness; [style] heaviness, weightiness, ponderousness; **avoir des ~s d'estomac** to have problems with one's digestion; **les ~s administratives** cumbersome administrative procedures

pèse-acide (pl **pèse-acides**) [pɛzasid] NM acidimeter

pèse-alcool (pl **pèse-alcools**) [pɛzalkɔl] NM alcoholometer

pèse-bébé (pl **pèse-bébés**) [pɛzbebe] NM (baby) scales

pesée [pəze] NF **a** (= action) weighing; **effectuer une ~** to find out the weight **b** (= pression, poussée) push, thrust **c** (Sport) **aller à la ~** to weigh in

pèse-lait (pl **pèse-laits**) [pɛzlɛ] NM lactometer

pèse-lettre (pl **pèse-lettres**) [pɛzlɛtr] NM letter scales

pèse-personne (pl **pèse-personnes**) [pɛzpɛrsɔn] NM scales; (dans une salle de bains) (bathroom) scales

▼ **peser** [pəze] ▶conjug 5◀ **1** VT **a** [+ objet, personne] to weigh; **~ qch dans sa main** to feel the weight of sth (in one's hand); **se ~** to weigh o.s.; [sportif] **se faire ~** to get weighed in; (fig) **il pèse 3 millions** he is worth 3 million **b** (= évaluer) to weigh (up); **~ le pour et le contre** to weigh (up) the pros and cons; **~ ses mots/chances** to weigh one's words/ chances; **tout bien pesé** all things considered; **ce qu'il dit est toujours pesé** what he says is always carefully thought out

2 VI **a** (gén) to weigh; [sportif] to weigh in; **cela pèse beaucoup** it weighs a lot; **cela pèse peu** it doesn't weigh much; **~ 60 kg** to weigh 60 kg; **~ lourd** to be heavy; **ce ministre ne pèse pas lourd*** this minister doesn't carry much weight ou doesn't count for much; **il n'a pas pesé lourd (devant son adversaire)** he was no match for his opponent

b (= appuyer) to press, push; **~ sur/contre qch**

(de tout son poids) to press ou push down on/against sth (with all one's weight); **~ sur l'estomac** [aliment, repas] to lie (heavy) on the stomach; **cela lui pèse sur le cœur** that makes him heavy-hearted; **les remords lui pèsent sur la conscience** remorse lies heavy on his conscience, he is weighed down with remorse; **le soupçon/l'accusation qui pèse sur lui** the suspicion/the accusation hanging ou which hangs over him; **la menace/sentence qui pèse sur sa tête** the threat/sentence which hangs over his head; **toute la responsabilité pèse sur lui ou sur ses épaules** all the responsibility is on him ou on his shoulders, he has to shoulder all the responsibility

c (= accabler) **~ à qn** to weigh sb down, weigh heavy on sb; **le silence/la solitude lui pèse** the silence/solitude is getting him down* ou weighs heavy on him; **le temps lui pèse** time hangs heavy on his hands; **ses responsabilités de maire lui pèsent** his responsibilities as mayor weigh heavy on him

d (= avoir de l'importance) to carry weight; **cela va ~ (dans la balance)** that will carry some weight; **sa timidité a pesé dans leur décision** his shyness influenced their decision

peseta [pezeta] NF peseta

peso [pezo, peso] NM peso

pessaire [pesɛr] NM pessary

pessimisme [pesimism] NM pessimism

pessimiste [pesimist] **1** ADJ pessimistic (**sur** about) **2** NMF pessimist

peste [pɛst] **1** NF (Méd) plague; (péj = personne) pest, nuisance, menace; **la ~ bubonique** the bubonic plague; **la ~ noire** the black plague, the Black Death; (Vét) **~ bovine** rinderpest, cattle plague; **fuir qch/qn comme la ~** to avoid sth/sb like the plague **2** EXCL (littér) good gracious!; **~ soit de ...** a plague on ...

pester [pɛste] ▶conjug 1◀ VI to curse; **~ contre qn/qch** to curse sb/sth

pesticide [pɛstisid] **1** ADJ pesticidal **2** NM pesticide

pestiféré, e [pɛstifere] **1** ADJ plague-stricken **2** NM,F plague victim; **fuir qn comme un ~** to avoid sb like the plague

pestilence [pɛstilɑ̃s] NF stench

pestilentiel, -elle [pɛstilɑ̃sjɛl] ADJ (gén) stinking, foul(-smelling); (Méd) pestilent

pet¹: [pɛ] NM **a** (= gaz) fart‡; **faire ou lâcher un ~** to break wind, fart‡; **il a toujours un ~ de travers** he's always got something wrong with him; **partir comme un ~ (sur une toile cirée)** to scarper‡ (Brit), split* → **valoir** **b** (= guet) **faire le ~*** to be on (the) watch ou on (the) look-out

pet²: [pɛ] NM (= coup) thump, bash; (= marque) dent; **la table a pris un ~** the table has taken a bash; **il y a plein de ~s sur l'étagère** the shelf is all dented

pétainiste [petenist] **1** ADJ Pétain (épith) **2** **Pétainiste** NMF Pétain supporter

pétale [petal] NM petal

pétanque [petɑ̃k] NF petanque (type of bowls played in the South of France) → BOULES

pétant, e* [petɑ̃, ɑ̃t] ADJ **à 2 heures ~(es)** at 2 on the dot*

pétaradant, e [petaradɑ̃, ɑ̃t] ADJ [moto] noisy, spluttering, back-firing

pétarade [petarad] NF [moteur, véhicule] backfiring (NonC); [feu d'artifice, fusillade] crackling (NonC)

pétarader [petarade] ▶conjug 1◀ VI [moteur, véhicule] to backfire; [feu d'artifice] to go off; **il les entendait ~ dans la cour** he could hear them revving up their engines in the backyard

---

➤ GRAMMAIRE ACTIVE: **perte** 51.4   **peser** 53.4

pétard [petaʀ] NM [a] (= feu d'artifice) fire-cracker, banger (Brit); (= accessoire de cotillon) cracker; (Rail) detonator (Brit), torpedo (US); (Mil) petard, explosive charge; **tirer** ou **faire partir un ~** to let off a firecracker ou banger (Brit); (fig) **lancer un ~** to drop a bombshell; (fig) **c'était un ~ mouillé** it was a damp squib [b] (‡ = tapage) din*, racket*, row*; **il va y avoir du ~** sparks will fly, there's going to be a hell of a row*; **faire du ~** [nouvelle] to cause a stir, raise a stink*; [personne] to kick up a row* ou fuss* ou stink*; **être en ~** to be raging mad*, be in a flaming temper (**contre** at) [c] (‡ = revolver) gun [d] (‡ = derrière) bottom*, bum* (Brit) [e] (Drogue) joint*, reefer*

pétasse‡ [petas] NF slut*

pétaudière [petodjɛʀ] NF bedlam, bear garden

pet-de-nonne (pl **pets-de-nonne**) [pɛd(ə)nɔn] NM fritter (made with choux pastry)

pété, e‡ [pete] (ptp de **péter**) ADJ (= ivre) plastered‡, pissed‡ (Brit); (= drogué) stoned‡; (= fou) crazy, bonkers‡

pet-en-l'air† [petɑlɛʀ] NM INV bumfreezer*

péter [pete] ▶ conjug 6 ◀ [1] VI [a] [personne] to break wind, fart‡; **il veut ~ plus haut que son derrière** ou **son cul‡** he thinks he's it*, he's a cocky bugger‡ (Brit); **il m'a envoyé ~** he told me to go to hell‡; **~ dans la soie** to live in the lap of luxury [b] * [détonation] to go off; [tuyau] to burst; [ballon] to pop, burst; [ficelle] to snap; **la bombe lui a pété à la figure** the bomb went off ou blew up in his face; **l'affaire lui a pété dans la main** the deal fell through; **la crise est si grave qu'un jour ça va ~** the crisis is so serious that one day all hell's going to break loose* [2] VT [a] [+ ficelle] to snap; [+ transistor, vase] to bust*; **je me suis pété une cheville** I did my ankle in*; **~ la gueule à qn‡** to smash sb's face in*; **se ~ la gueule** (= tomber) to fall flat on one's face; (= s'enivrer) to get plastered‡ ou pissed‡* **c'est un coup à se ~ la gueule‡** you'll (ou he'll etc) break your (ou his etc) neck doing that; **il s'est pété la gueule en vélo‡** he smashed himself up when he came off his bike‡ [b] (loc) **~ le feu** ou **les flammes** [personne] to be full of go* ou beans* (Brit); **~ la** ou **de santé** to be bursting with health; **il pète la forme** he's on top form; **ça va ~ des flammes** there's going to be a heck of a row*; **~ les plombs** to go off the rails*

pète-sec* [pɛtsɛk] NMF INV, ADJ INV **c'est un ~ ◊ il est très ~** he has a very curt ou abrupt manner

péteux, -euse* [petø, øz] [1] ADJ (= peureux) cowardly, yellow, yellow-bellied*; (= honteux) ashamed (attrib) [2] NM,F (= peureux) coward, yellowbelly*; (= prétentieux) pretentious twit*

pétillant, e [petijã, ãt] ADJ [eau, vin] sparkling; [yeux] sparkling, twinkling; **discours ~ d'esprit** speech sparkling with wit

pétillement [petijmã] NM [feu] crackling (NonC); [champagne, vin, eau] bubbling (NonC); [yeux] sparkling (NonC), twinkling (NonC); **entendre des ~s** to hear crackling ou crackles; **ce ~ de malice dans son regard** the mischievous twinkle in his eye

pétiller [petije] ▶ conjug 1 ◀ VI [feu] to crackle; [champagne, vin, eau] to bubble; [joie] to sparkle (**dans** in); [yeux] to sparkle, twinkle (**de** with); **ses yeux pétillaient de malice** his eyes were sparkling ou twinkling mischievously; **il pétillait de bonne humeur** he was bubbling (over) with good humour; **~ d'intelligence** to sparkle with intelligence

pétiole [pesjɔl] NM leafstalk, petiole (SPÉC)

petiot, e* [pətjo, jɔt] [1] ADJ teenyweeny*,

tiny (little) [2] NM little boy ou lad* (Brit) [3] **petiote** NF little girl ou lass* (US)

petit, e [p(ə)ti, it]

[1] ADJECTIF	[4] NOM FÉMININ
[2] LOC ADVERBIALE	[5] COMPOSÉS
[3] NOM MASCULIN	

[1] ADJECTIF

Lorsque **petit** *s'emploie dans des expressions telles que* **les petites gens, entrer par la petite porte, ce n'est pas une petite affaire** *etc, cherchez au mot principal*

[a] **gén, en dimension** [main, personne, objet, colline] small, little (épith); [pointure] small; **mince** short and thin; **~ et carré** squat; **~ et rond** dumpy; **il est tout ~** he's very small ou a very small man; (nuance affective) he's a little ou a tiny (little) man; (fig) **se faire tout ~** to keep a low profile, make o.s. as inconspicuous as possible; **depuis, il se fait tout ~ devant moi** ever since then, he's been acting like he's afraid of me; **un ~ vieux** a little old man; **ces chaussures sont un peu ~es/trop ~es pour moi** these shoes are a bit small ou rather a small fit/too small for me ■ (PROV) **~ poisson deviendra grand** (PROV) **les ~s ruisseaux font les grandes rivières** great ou mighty oaks from little acorns grow (PROV)

♦ **en petit** : **c'est écrit en ~** it's written in small letters; **une cour d'école, c'est le monde en ~** a school playground is the world in miniature; **le dessin est répété en ~ sur les fauteuils** there's a smaller version of the pattern on the armchairs, the pattern is the same on the armchairs but smaller

[b] **= mince** [tranche] thin; **avoir de ~s os** to be small-boned ou slight-boned; **avoir de ~s bras** to have slender ou thin arms; **une ~e pluie (fine) tombait** a (fine) drizzle was falling

[c] **= miniature, jouet** [épith] **~e voiture** toy ou miniature car; **~ train** (= jouet) toy train; (dans un parc) miniature train; (= jeu) **faire le ~ train** to play trains

[d] **= maladif** **avoir une ~e santé** to be in poor health, be frail; **avoir une ~e figure** ou **mine** to look pale ou wan; **tu as de ~s yeux ce matin** you're a bit bleary-eyed this morning

[e] **= jeune** small, young; (avec nuance affective) little; **quand il était ~** when he was small ou little; **un ~ Anglais** an English boy; **les ~s Anglais** English children; **tu es encore trop ~ pour comprendre** you're still too young to understand; **chat/chien** (little) kitten/puppy; **~ lion/tigre/ours** lion/tiger/bear cub; **dans sa ~e enfance** when he was very small, in his early childhood; **quand j'étais ~ garçon** little boy; **je ne suis plus un ~ garçon !** I'm not a child anymore!; **il fait très ~ garçon** he's very boyish; (fig) **à côté de lui, Marc est un ~ garçon** compared to him, Marc is a babe in arms

[f] **= cadet** **son ~ frère** his younger ou little brother; (très petit) his baby ou little brother; **tu vas bientôt avoir une ~e sœur** you'll soon have a baby ou little sister

[g] **= court** [promenade, voyage] short, little; **sur une ~e distance** over a short distance; **par ~es étapes** in short ou easy stages; **une ~e semaine/un ~ mois** (écourtés par congé) it's a short week/a short month; **il est resté deux (pauvres) ~es heures** he stayed for a mere two hours; **il en a pour une ~e heure** it will take him an hour at the most, it won't take him more than an hour; **c'est à un ~ kilomètre d'ici** it's no more than ou just under a kilometre from here

[h] **= faible** [bruit] faint, slight; [cri] little, faint; [coup, tape] light, gentle; [pente] gentle, slight; [somme d'argent, budget] small; [loyer] low; **on entendit deux ~s coups à la porte** we heard two light ou gentle knocks on the door; **il a un ~ appétit** he has a small appetite, he hasn't much of an appetite; **une toute ~e**

voix a tiny voice; **film à ~ budget** low-budget film; (Comm) **c'est un ~ mardi** (= la recette est faible) it's a poor showing for a Tuesday; (Sport) **ils ont gagné par un ~ 1 à 0** they won by a very slim 1-0 → **salaire**

[i] **= peu important** [commerçant, pays, entreprise, groupe] small; [opération, détail] small, minor; [amélioration, changement, inconvénient] slight, minor; [espoir, chance] faint, slight; [odeur, rhume] slight; [fonctionnaire, employé, romancier] minor; [cadeau, bibelot, soirée, réception] little; **le ~ commerce** small businesses; **les ~es et moyennes entreprises/industries** small and medium-sized businesses/industries; **chez le ~ épicier du coin** at the little grocer's down the street; **avec un ~ effort** with a bit of an ou with a little effort; **ce fait n'est connu que d'un ~ nombre** only a small number of people ou a few people are aware of this fact

[j] **péj = mesquin** [attitude, action] mean, petty, low; [personne] petty; **c'est ~ ce qu'il a fait là** that was a mean thing to do, that was mean of him

[k] **avec nuance affective ou euph** little; **vous prendrez bien un ~ dessert/verre ?** you'll have a little dessert/drink, won't you?; **faire une ~e partie de cartes** to play a little game of cards; **juste une ~e signature** can I just have your signature; **un ~ coup de rouge*** a (little) glass of red wine; **une ~e robe d'été** a light summer dress; **ma ~e maman** my mummy; **mon ~ papa** my daddy; **mon ~ chou** ou **rat** etc (my little) darling; **un ~ coin tranquille** a nice quiet spot; **on va se faire un bon ~ souper** we'll make ourselves a nice little (bit of) supper; **cela coûte une ~e fortune** it costs a small fortune; **ce n'est pas grand-chose, mais c'est tout de même une ~e victoire** it's not much but it's a small victory nonetheless; **il y a un ~ vent (agréable)** there's a bit of a breeze; (désagréable) it's a bit windy

[l] **pour déprécier** **espèce de ~ impertinent** you cheeky little so-and-so*; **je vous préviens, mon ~ ami** ou **monsieur** I warn you my good man ou dear fellow; **~ con !‡** stupid jerk!‡

[m] **loc** **c'est de la ~e bière** it's small beer (Brit), it's small potatoes (US); **ce n'est pas de la ~e bière** it's no small matter, it's not without importance; **être aux ~s soins pour qn** to wait on sb hand and foot → **semaine, soulier** etc

[2] **petit à petit** LOC ADV little by little, gradually ■ (PROV) **~ à ~, l'oiseau fait son nid** with time and perseverance one accomplishes one's goals

[3] NOM MASCULIN

[a] **= enfant** (little) boy; **les ~s** the children; **viens ici, ~** come here, son; **pauvre ~** poor little thing; **le ~ Durand** the Durands' son, the Durand boy; **les ~s Durand** the Durand children; **jeu pour ~s et grands** game for old and young (alike) → **tout-petit**

[b] **Scol** junior (boy)

[c] **= jeune animal** **les ~s** the young; **la chatte et ses ~s** the cat and her kittens; **la lionne et ses ~s** the lioness and her young ou cubs; **faire des ~s** to have kittens (ou puppies ou lambs etc); (fig) **son argent a fait des ~s** his money has made more money

[d] **= personne de petite taille** small man; (= personne sans pouvoir) little man; **les ~s** small people; **c'est toujours le ~ qui a tort** it's always the little man who's in the wrong

[4] **petite** NF **= enfant** (little) girl; (= femme) small woman; **la ~e Durand** the Durands' daughter, the Durand girl; **pauvre ~e** poor little thing; **viens ici, ~e** come here, little one

[5] COMPOSÉS

► **petit ami** boyfriend ► **petite amie** girlfriend ► **petit banc** low bench ► **les petits blancs** poor white settlers ► **petit bleu**† wire (telegram) ► **« le Petit Chape-**

ron rouge » "Little Red Riding Hood" ► **petits chevaux** : jouer aux ~s chevaux ≈ to play ludo (*Brit*) ► **le petit coin** (*euph*) the smallest room (*euph*), the bathroom (*euph*), the toilet ► **petit cousin, petite cousine** (= *enfant, jeune*) little *ou* young cousin; (= *enfant du cousin germain*) second cousin; (= *parent éloigné*) distant cousin ► **le petit endroit** (*euph*) = le petit coin ► **petit four** petit four ► **petit gâteau (sec)** biscuit ► **le Petit Livre rouge** the Little Red Book ► **petite main** (*Couture*) apprentice seamstress; (*fig*) minion ► **petit nom*** (= *prénom*) Christian name, first name; (= *surnom*) nickname; (*entre amoureux*) pet name ► **petit pain** ≈ bread roll; ça part *ou* se vend comme des ~s pains* they're selling like hot cakes* ► **petit point** (*Couture*) petit point ► **« le Petit Poucet »** "Tom Thumb" ► **la petite reine** (*fig*) the bicycle ► **petit salé** (*Culin*) salt pork ► **la petite vérole** smallpox ► **petite voiture (d'infirme)** (*gén*) wheelchair; (*à moteur*) invalid carriage

petit-beurre (*pl* **petits-beurre**) [p(ə)tibœr] NM petit beurre biscuit (*Brit*), butter cookie (*US*)

petit-bourgeois, petite-bourgeoise (*pl* **petits-bourgeois**) [p(ə)tiburʒwa, p(ə)titburʒwaz] **1** ADJ (*gén*) lower middle-class; (*péj*) petit-bourgeois, middle-class **2** NM,F (*gén*) lower middle-class person; (*péj*) petit-bourgeois

petit-déjeuner, petit déjeuner (*pl* **petits(-)déjeuners**) [p(ə)tideʒœne] **1** NM breakfast; ~ **anglais/continental** English/continental breakfast **2 petit-déjeuner*** ◂ conjug 1 ◂ VI to have breakfast

petite-fille (*pl* **petites-filles**) [p(ə)titfij] NF granddaughter

petite-maîtresse†† (*pl* **petites-maîtresses**) [p(ə)titmetres] NF lady of fashion

petitement [pətitmɑ̃] ADV (= *chichement*) poorly; (= *mesquinement*) meanly, pettily; **nous sommes ~ logés** our accommodation is cramped

petit-enfant (*pl* **petits-enfants**) [pətitɑ̃fɑ̃, pətizɑ̃fɑ̃] NM grandchild

petite-nièce (*pl* **petites-nièces**) [p(ə)titnjɛs] NF great-niece, grand-niece

petitesse [p(ə)titɛs] NF [*taille, endroit*] smallness, small size; [*somme*] smallness, modesty; [*esprit, acte*] meanness (*NonC*), pettiness (*NonC*)

petit-fils (*pl* **petits-fils**) [p(ə)tifis] NM grandson

petit-gris (*pl* **petits-gris**) [p(ə)tigri] NM **a** (= *escargot*) garden snail **b** (= *écureuil*) Siberian squirrel; (= *fourrure*) grey squirrel fur

pétition [petisjɔ̃] NF **a** (= *demande, requête*) petition; **faire une ~ auprès de qn** to petition sb; **faire signer une ~** to set up a petition **b** (*Philo*) **~ de principe** petitio principii (*SPÉC*), begging the question (*NonC*); **c'est une ~ de principe** it's begging the question

pétitionnaire [petisjɔner] NMF petitioner

petit-lait (*pl* **petits-laits**) [p(ə)tilɛ] NM whey → **lait**

petit-maître†† (*mpl* **petits-maîtres**) [p(ə)timetr] NM coxcomb††, fop†

petit-nègre [pətinegr] NM (*péj*) pidgin French; (= *galimatias*) gibberish, gobbledygook*

petit-neveu (*pl* **petits-neveux**) [p(ə)tin(ə)vø] NM great-nephew, grand-nephew

petit-pois (*pl* **petits-pois**) [pətipwa] NM (*garden*) pea; **il a dans la tête** *ou* **à la place de la cervelle*** he's a bit feather-brained

petit-suisse (*pl* **petits-suisses**) [p(ə)tisɥis] NM petit-suisse (*kind of cream cheese eaten as a dessert*)

---

pétochard, e‡ [petɔʃar, ard] **1** ADJ cowardly, yellow-bellied* **2** NM,F coward, yellow-belly*

pétoche‡ [petɔʃ] NF **avoir la ~** to be scared silly* *ou* stiff*; **flanquer la ~ à qn** to scare the living daylights out of sb*, put the wind up sb‡ (*Brit*)

pétoire* [petwar] NF (= *sarbacane*) peashooter; (= *vieux fusil*) old gun; (= *cyclomoteur*) (motor) scooter

peton* [pətɔ̃] NM (= *pied*) foot, tootsy*

pétoncle [petɔ̃kl] NM queen scallop

Pétrarque [petrark] NM Petrarch

pétrarquisme [petrarkism] NM Petrarchism

pétrel [petrɛl] NM (stormy) petrel

pétri, e [petri] (*ptp de* **pétrir**) ADJ **~ d'orgueil** filled with pride; **~ d'ignorance** steeped in ignorance; **~ de contradictions** full of contradictions; **~ de culture orientale/littérature slave** steeped in Eastern culture/Slavic literature

pétrifiant, e [petrifjɑ̃, jɑ̃t] ADJ [*spectacle*] petrifying; [*nouvelle*] horrifying

pétrification [petrifikasjɔ̃] NF **a** (*Géol*) petrifaction, petrification **b** [*cœur*] hardening; [*idées*] fossilization

pétrifier [petrifje] ◂ conjug 7 ◂ **1** VT **a** (*Géol*) to petrify **b** [+ *personne*] to paralyze, transfix; [+ *cœur*] to freeze; [+ *idées*] to fossilize, ossify; **être pétrifié de terreur** to be petrified **2 se pétrifier** VPR **a** (*Géol*) to petrify, become petrified **b** [*sourire*] to freeze; [*personne*] to be petrified; [*cœur*] to freeze; [*idées*] to become fossilized *ou* ossified

pétrin [petrɛ̃] NM **a** (* = *ennui*) mess*, jam*, fix*; **tirer qn du ~** to get sb out of a mess* *ou* fix* *ou* tight spot*; **être dans le ~** to be in a mess* *ou* jam* *ou* fix*; **laisser qn dans le ~** to leave sb in a mess* *ou* jam* *ou* fix*; **être/se mettre dans un beau ~** to be in/get (o.s.) into a fine mess* **b** (*Boulangerie*) kneading trough; (*mécanique*) kneading machine

pétrir [petrir] ◂ conjug 2 ◂ VT [+ *pâte, argile, muscle, main*] to knead; [+ *personne, esprit*] to mould, shape

pétrissage [petrisaʒ] NM [*pâte*] kneading

pétrochimie [petrɔʃimi] NF petrochemistry

pétrochimique [petrɔʃimik] ADJ petrochemical

pétrochimiste [petrɔʃimist] NMF petrochemist

pétrodollar [petrɔdɔlar] NM petrodollar

pétrographie [petrɔgrafi] NF petrography

pétrographique [petrɔgrafik] ADJ petrographic(al)

pétrole [petrɔl] NM (*brut*) oil, petroleum; **~ (lampant)** paraffin (oil) (*Brit*), kerosene (*US*); **~ brut** crude (oil), petroleum; **lampe/réchaud à ~** paraffin (*Brit*) *ou* kerosene (*US*) *ou* oil lamp/heater; **le ~ vert** agricultural produce *ou* resources

pétrolette† [petrɔlɛt] NF moped

pétroleuse [petrɔløz] NF (*Hist*) pétroleuse (*female fire-raiser during the Commune*); (*fig*) agitator

pétrolier, -ière [petrɔlje, jɛr] **1** ADJ [*industrie, produits*] petroleum (*épith*), oil (*épith*); [*port, société*] oil (*épith*); [*pays*] oil-producing (*épith*) **2** NM (= *navire*) (oil) tanker; (= *personne, financier*) oil magnate, oilman; (= *technicien*) petroleum engineer

pétrolifère [petrɔlifɛr] ADJ [*roches, couches*] oil-bearing; **gisement ~** oilfield

pétromonarchie [petrɔmɔnarʃi] NF oil kingdom, oil-rich nation; **les ~s du Golfe** the oil-kingdoms of the Gulf

P. et T. [peete] NFPL (ABRÉV = **Postes et Télécommunications**) → **poste**⁹

pétulance [petylɑ̃s] NF exuberance, vivacity

pétulant, e [petylɑ̃, ɑ̃t] ADJ exuberant, vivacious

---

pétunia [petynja] NM petunia

peu [pø]

1 ADVERBE	**3** NOM MASCULIN
2 PRONOM INDÉFINI	

1 ADVERBE

Lorsque **peu** *suit un autre mot dans une locution figée telle que* avant peu, sous peu, quelque peu, si peu que ... *etc, cherchez sous l'autre mot.*

a (= *pas beaucoup*) little, not much; **il gagne/mange/lit ~** he doesn't earn/eat/read much; **il s'intéresse ~ à la peinture** he isn't very *ou* greatly interested in painting, he takes little interest in painting; **il se contente de ~** it doesn't take much to satisfy him; **il a donné 50 F, c'est ~** he gave 50 francs, which isn't (very) much → **dire**

◆ *adverbe* + **peu** : **il gagne/mange/lit assez ~** he doesn't earn/eat/read very much; **il gagne/mange/lit très ~** he earns/eats/reads very little; **il y a bien ~ à faire/à voir ici** there's very little *ou* precious little* to do/see here, there's not much at all to do/see here; **il boit trop ~** he doesn't drink enough; **je le connais bien trop ~ pour le juger** I don't know him (nearly) well enough to judge him

◆ **à peu près** about; **il pèse à ~ près 50 kilos** he weighs about 50 kilos; **il sait à ~ près tout ce qui se passe** he knows just about everything that goes on; **à ~ près terminé/cuit** almost finished/cooked, more or less finished/cooked → **à-peu-près**

◆ **de peu** : **il est le plus âgé de ~** he's slightly *ou* a little older; **il l'a battu de ~** he just beat him; **il a manqué le train de ~** he just missed the train → **falloir**

◆ **peu de** (*quantité*) little, not much; **nous avons eu (très) ~ de soleil** we had (very) little sunshine, we didn't have (very) much sunshine; **il me reste très ~ de pain ◊ du pain, il m'en reste très ~** I haven't very much bread left; **il est ici depuis ~ de temps** he hasn't been here long, he's been here (only) for a short while *ou* time; **il est ici pour ~ de temps** he isn't here for long, he's here for (only) a short time *ou* while; **cela a ~ d'importance** that's not important, that's of little importance; **il suffit de ~ de chose pour le choquer** it doesn't take much to shock him; **ne me remerciez pas, c'est ~ de chose** there's no need to thank me, it's nothing

(*nombre*) few, not (very) many; **nous avons eu ~ d'orages** we had few storms, we didn't have many storms; **on attendait beaucoup de touristes, mais il en est venu (très) ~** we were expecting a lot of tourists but not (very) many came *ou* but (very) few came; **~ de monde** *ou* **de gens** few people, not many people; **en ~ de mots** briefly, in a few words; **~ de choses ont changé** not much has changed

◆ **peu ou prou** (*littér*) to a greater or lesser degree, more or less; **ils pensent tous ~ ou prou la même chose** they are all more or less of one mind

◆ **pour ~ que** + *subjonctif* if; **pour ~ qu'il soit sorti sans sa clé ...** if he should have come out without his key ...; **je saurai le convaincre, pour ~ qu'il veuille bien m'écouter** I'll be able to persuade him if *ou* as long as he's willing to listen to me

b (= *pas très*) **◆ peu** + *adjectif* (a) little, not very; **il est ~ sociable** he's not very sociable, he's unsociable; **c'est ~ probable** it's unlikely *ou* not very likely **◆ adverbe** + **peu** + *adjectif* : **il est très ~ sociable** he is not very sociable at all, he is very unsociable; **ils sont (bien) trop ~ nombreux** there are (far) too few of them; **fort ~ intéressant** decidedly uninteresting, of very little interest; **un auteur assez ~ connu** a relatively little-known *ou* relatively unknown author; **il n'est pas ~ fier d'avoir réussi** he's as pleased as Punch about his success; **elle n'est pas ~ soulagée**

d'être reçue she's more than a little relieved at passing her exam

c = pas longtemps il était tombé malade ~ avant he had been taken ill shortly before(hand); je l'ai rencontré ~ avant Noël/midi I met him shortly *ou* just before Christmas/midday; elle est arrivée ~ après she arrived shortly *ou* soon after(wards); ~ après 11 heures/son arrivée shortly after 11 o'clock/his arrival

d = rarement ils se voient ~ they don't see much of each other, they don't see each other very often; elle sort ~ she doesn't go out much

e

♦ **peu à peu** gradually, little by little; ~ à ~, l'idée a gagné du terrain little by little *ou* gradually *ou* bit by bit the idea has gained ground

2 PRONOM INDÉFINI

= personnes ou choses en petit nombre ils sont ~ à croire que ... few believe that ..., there are few people *ou* there aren't many people who believe that ...; bien ~/trop ~ le savent very few/too few people know; ~ d'entre eux sont restés few (of them) stayed, not many (of them) stayed

3 NOM MASCULIN

a = petite quantité little; j'ai oublié le ~ (de français) que j'avais appris I've forgotten the little (French) I'd learnt; elle se contente du ~ (d'argent) qu'elle a she is satisfied with what little (money) she has; son ~ de compréhension/patience lui a nui his lack of understanding/patience hasn't helped him; elle s'est aliéné le ~ d'amis qu'elle avait she alienated the few friends she had; le ~ de cheveux qu'il lui reste what little hair he has left

♦ **un peu de** a little, a bit of; un ~ d'eau a little water, a drop of water; un ~ de patience a little patience, a bit of patience; un ~ de silence/de calme, s'il vous plaît! can we have some quiet *ou* a bit of quiet/some peace *ou* a bit of peace please!; il a un ~ de sinusite/bronchite he has a touch of sinusitis/bronchitis; tu refuses parce que tu as peur? — il y a un ~ de ça* you're refusing because you're afraid? — that's partly it

b

♦ *verbe* + **un peu** a little, slightly, a bit; essaie de manger un ~ try to eat a little *ou* a bit; il boite un ~ he limps slightly *ou* a little *ou* a bit, he is slightly *ou* a bit lame; il te ressemble un ~ he looks rather *ou* a bit like you; restez encore un ~ stay a little longer; tu en veux encore? — un petit ~ would you like some more? — a little bit *ou* just a little; (*en effeuillant la marguerite*) un ~, beaucoup, passionnément, à la folie, pas du tout he loves me, he loves me not

c

♦ **un peu** + *adverbe*: elle va un tout petit ~ mieux she's slightly *ou* a little better; il y a un ~ moins de bruit it is slightly *ou* a little less noisy, there's slightly *ou* a little less noise; nous avons un ~ moins de clients aujourd'hui we don't have quite so many customers today; on trouve ce produit un ~ partout you can get this product just about anywhere; j'aimerais avoir un ~ plus d'argent/d'amis I'd like to have a bit *ou* a little more money/a few more friends; il y a un ~ plus d'un an an a little more than *ou* just over a year ago; un ~ plus et il écrasait le chien/oubliait son rendez-vous he very nearly ran over the dog/forgot his appointment; un ~ plus et j'étais parti I'd very nearly left; il travaille un ~ trop/un ~ trop lentement he works a bit too much/a little *ou* a bit too slowly

d

♦ **un peu** + *adjectif*: c'est un ~ grand/petit it's a little *ou* a bit (too) big/small; elle était un ~ perturbée she was a bit *ou* rather upset; il est un ~ artiste he's a bit of an artist, he's something of an artist

e

♦ **pour un peu**: pour un ~, il m'aurait accusé d'avoir volé *ou* just about* accused me of stealing; pour un ~, je l'aurais giflé! I could have slapped him!

f intensif montre-moi donc un ~ comment tu fais just (you) show me how you do it then; je me demande un ~ où sont les enfants I just wonder where the children are *ou* can be; c'est un ~ fort! that's a bit much!*; un ~! and how!*; tu as vraiment vu l'accident? — un ~ (mon neveu)!* did you really see the accident? — you bet!* *ou* and how!* *ou* I sure did!* (*US*); un ~, qu'il nous a menti!* I'll say he lied to us!*; il nous a menti, et pas qu'un ~!* he lied to us bigtime!*; comme menteur/comique il est un ~ là!* as liars/comedians go, he must be hard to beat!* → poser

peuchère [pøʃɛʀ] EXCL (*dial Midi*) well! well!

peuh [pø] EXCL pooh!, bah!, phooey* (*US*)

peu(h)l, e [pøl] **1** ADJ Fulani **2** NM (*Ling*) Fula(h), Fulani **3** Peu(h)l(e) NM,F Fula(h), Fulani

peuplade [pœplad] NF (small) tribe, people

peuple [pœpl] NM **a** (*Pol = communauté*) people, nation; les ~s d'Europe the peoples *ou* nations of Europe; (*Rel*) le ~ élu the chosen people **b** (= prolétariat) le ~ the people; les gens du ~ the common people, ordinary people; homme du ~ man of the people; (†† : péj) le bas *ou* petit ~ the lower classes (*péj*); (*fig*) il se moque *ou* se fiche du ~ who does he think he is?; (*péj*) faire ~ (= ne pas être distingué) to be common (*péj*); (= vouloir paraître simple) to try to appear working-class; (*hum*) que demande le ~! what more could anyone want! **c** (= foule) crowd (of people); (*littér*) un ~ de badauds/d'admirateurs a crowd of onlookers/of admirers; il y a du ~!* there's a big crowd!

peuplé, e [pœple] (*ptp de* peupler) ADJ [ville, région] populated, inhabited; très/peu ~ densely/sparsely populated

peuplement [pœpləmã] NM **a** (= action) [colonie] populating; [étang] stocking; [forêt] planting (*with trees*) **b** (= population) population

peupler [pœple] ▸conjug 1◂ **1** VT **a** (= pourvoir d'une population) [+ colonie] to populate; [+ étang] to stock; [+ forêt] to plant out, plant with trees; (*littér*) to fill (de with); les rêves/souvenirs qui peuplent mon esprit the dreams/memories that fill my mind; les cauchemars/monstres qui peuplent ses nuits the nightmares/monsters which haunt his nights **b** (= habiter) [+ terre] to inhabit, populate; [+ maison] to live in, inhabit; maison peuplée de souvenirs house filled with *ou* full of memories **2** se peupler VPR [ville, région] to become populated; (= s'animer) to fill (up), be filled (de with); la rue se peuplait de cris the street filled with cries

peupleraie [pøpləʀɛ] NF poplar grove

peuplier [pøplije] NM poplar (tree)

peur [pœʀ] NF **a** la ~ fear; inspirer de la ~ to cause *ou* inspire fear; ressentir de la ~ to feel fear; la ~ lui donnait des ailes fear lent him wings; être vert *ou* mort de ~ to be frightened *ou* scared out of one's wits, be petrified (with fear); la ~ de la punition/de mourir/du qu'en-dira-t-on (the) fear of punishment/of death *ou* dying/of what people might say; prendre ~ to take fright; la ~ du gendarme* the fear of being caught; cacher sa ~ to hide one's fear; être sans ~ to be fearless (de of); faire qch sans ~ to do sth fearlessly

b une ~ a fear; une ~ irraisonnée de se blesser s'empara de lui he was seized by *ou* with an irrational fear of injuring himself; des ~s enfantines childish fears; je n'ai qu'une ~, c'est qu'il ne revienne pas my only fear is that he won't come back, I have only one fear, that he won't come back; il a eu une ~ bleue he had a bad fright *ou* scare; il a eu une ~ bleue de sa femme he's scared stiff* of his wife; il m'a fait une de ces ~s! he gave me a horrible fright! *ou* scare!, he didn't half* give me a fright! *ou* scare! (*Brit*)

c avoir ~ to be frightened *ou* afraid *ou* scared (de of); avoir ~ pour qn to be afraid for sb *ou* on sb's behalf, fear for sb; avoir grand ~ que ... to be very much afraid that ...; n'ayez pas ~ (*craindre*) don't be afraid *ou* frightened *ou* scared; (s'inquiéter) don't worry; il sera puni, n'aie pas ~! he will be punished — don't worry!; il veut faire ce voyage en deux jours, il n'a pas ~, lui au moins!* he wants to do the trip in two days — well, he's a braver man than I!; il prétend qu'il a téléphoné, il n'a pas ~, lui au moins!* he says he phoned — he's got a nerve!; n'ayez pas ~ de dire la vérité don't be afraid *ou* scared to tell *ou* of telling the truth; il n'a ~ de rien he's afraid of nothing, he's not afraid of anything; avoir ~ d'un rien to frighten easily; avoir ~ de son ombre to be frightened *ou* scared of one's own shadow; je n'ai pas ~ des mots I'm not afraid of using plain language; j'ai bien ~/très ~ qu'il ne pleuve I'm afraid/very much afraid it's going to rain *ou* it might rain; il va échouer? — j'en ai (bien) ~ is he going to fail? — I'm (very much) afraid so *ou* I'm afraid he is; j'ai ~ qu'il ne vous ait menti/que cela ne vous gêne I'm afraid *ou* worried *ou* I fear that he might have lied to you/that it might inconvenience you; je n'ai pas ~ qu'il dise la vérité I'm not afraid *ou* frightened he'll tell the truth; il a eu plus de ~ que de mal he was more frightened than hurt, he wasn't hurt so much as frightened; il y a eu *ou* ça a fait plus de ~ que de mal it was more frightening than anything else

d faire ~ à qn (= intimider) to frighten *ou* scare sb; (= causer une frayeur à) to give sb a fright, frighten *ou* scare sb; pour faire ~ aux oiseaux to frighten *ou* scare the birds away *ou* off; l'idée de l'examen lui fait ~ the idea of sitting the exam frightens *ou* scares him, he's frightened *ou* scared at the idea of sitting the exam; cette pensée fait ~ it's a frightening *ou* scary* thought; tout lui fait ~ he's afraid *ou* frightened *ou* scared of everything; le travail ne lui fait pas ~ he's not afraid of hard work; laid *ou* hideux à faire ~ frighteningly ugly; (*iro*) il fait chaud, ça fait ~! it's not exactly roasting!* (*iro*)

e (*loc*) de ~ de for fear of; il a couru de ~ de manquer le train he ran because he was afraid he might miss the train *ou* so as not to miss the train; il a accepté de ~ de les vexer he accepted for fear of annoying them *ou* lest he (should) annoy them; il renonça, de ~ du ridicule he gave up for fear of ridicule; j'ai fermé la porte, de ~ qu'elle ne prenne froid I closed the door so that she didn't catch cold *ou* lest she (should) catch cold

peureusement [pøʀøzmã] ADV fearfully, timorously (*frm*)

peureux, -euse [pøʀø, øz] **1** ADJ fearful, timorous (*frm*) **2** NM,F fearful *ou* timorous (*frm*) person

▼ **peut-être** [pøtɛtʀ] ADV perhaps, maybe; il est ~ intelligent ◊ ~ est-il intelligent perhaps *ou* maybe he's clever, he may *ou* might (well) be clever; il n'est ~ pas beau mais il est intelligent he may *ou* might not be handsome but he is clever, maybe *ou* perhaps he's not handsome but he is clever; ~ bien perhaps (so), it could well be; ~ pas maybe *ou* perhaps not; ~ bien mais ... that's as may be but ..., perhaps so but ...; ~ que ... perhaps ...; ~ bien qu'il pleuvra it may well rain; ~ que oui perhaps so, perhaps he will (*ou* they are *etc*); tu vas y aller? — ~ bien que oui, ~ bien que non will you go? — maybe, maybe not *ou* maybe I will, maybe I won't; je ne sais pas conduire ~? who's (doing the) driving? (*iro*), I do know how to drive, you know!; tu le sais mieux que moi ~? so (you think) you know more about it than I do, do you?, I do know more about it than you, you know!

p.ex. (ABRÉV = par exemple) e.g.

pèze: [pɛz] NM (= argent) dough‡, bread‡

pff(t) [pf(t)], **pfut** [pfyt] EXCL pooh!, bah!

pgcd [peʒesede] NM (ABRÉV = **plus grand commun diviseur**) (*Math*) HCF

pH [peaʃ] NM (ABRÉV = **potentiel d'hydrogène**) pH

phacochère [fakɔʃɛʀ] NM wart hog

Phaéton [faetɔ̃] NM (*Myth*) Phaëthon

phaéton [faetɔ̃] NM (= *calèche*) phaeton; (= *oiseau*) tropicbird

phagocyte [fagɔsit] NM phagocyte

phagocyter [fagɔsite] ▶ conjug 1 ◀ VT (*Bio*) to phagocytose; (*fig*) to absorb, engulf

phagocytose [fagɔsitoz] NF phagocytosis

phalange [falɑ̃ʒ] NF (*Anat*) phalanx; (*Antiq, littér* = *armée*) phalanx; (*Pol*: *espagnole*) **la ~** the Falange

phalangien, -ienne [falɑ̃ʒjɛ̃, jɛn] ADJ (*Anat*) phalangeal

phalangiste [falɑ̃ʒist] ADJ, NMF Falangist

phalanstère [falɑ̃stɛʀ] NM phalanstery

phalène [falɛn] NF *ou* M emerald, geometrid (*SPÉC*)

phallique [falik] ADJ phallic

phallocrate [falɔkʀat] 1 ADJ chauvinist 2 NM (male) chauvinist

phallocratie [falɔkʀasi] NF male chauvinism

phallocratique [falɔkʀatik] ADJ (male) chauvinist

phalloïde [falɔid] ADJ phalloid → **amanite**

phallus [falys] NM (*Anat*) phallus; (*Bot*) stinkhorn

phantasme [fɑ̃tasm] NM = **fantasme**

pharamineux, -euse [faʀaminø, øz] ADJ = **faramineux**

pharaon [faʀaɔ̃] NM Pharaoh

pharaonien, -ienne [faʀaɔnjɛ̃, jɛn], **pharaonique** [faʀaɔnik] ADJ Pharaonic

phare [faʀ] 1 NM a (= *tour*) lighthouse; (*Aviat, fig*) beacon; (*Naut*) **~ à feu fixe/tournant** fixed/revolving light *ou* beacon b (*Aut*) headlight, headlamp; **~ antibrouillard** fog lamp; **~s longue portée** high intensity headlamps; **~ à iode** quartz halogen lamp; **rouler pleins ~s** *ou* **en ~s** to drive with one's headlights full on *ou* on full beam (*Brit*) *ou* with high beams on (*US*) → **appel, code** 2 ADJ INV [*entreprise, produit, secteur, pays, titre boursier*] leading; **l'émission ~ de notre chaîne** our channel's flagship programme; **c'est un film ~** it's a seminal *ou* highly influential film; **personnalité ~** leading light; **c'est l'épreuve ~ de cette compétition** it's the main event *ou* it's the highlight of the competition

pharisaïque [faʀizaik] ADJ (*Hist*) Pharisaic; (*fig*) pharisaic(al)

pharisaïsme [faʀizaism] NM (*Hist*) Pharisaism, Phariseeism; (*fig*) pharisaism, phariseeism

pharisien, -ienne [faʀizjɛ̃, jɛn] NM,F (*Hist*) Pharisee; (*fig*) pharisee

pharmaceutique [faʀmasøtik] ADJ pharmaceutical, pharmaceutic

pharmacie [faʀmasi] NF a (= *magasin*) pharmacy, chemist's (shop) (*Brit*), drugstore (*Can, US*); (= *officine*) dispensary; [*hôpital*] dispensary, pharmacy; **ce produit est vendu en ~** this product is available in pharmacies *ou* from chemists (*Brit*) b (= *science*) pharmacy; **laboratoire de ~** pharmaceutical laboratory c (= *produits*) medicines; (**armoire à**) **~** medicine chest *ou* cabinet *ou* cupboard

pharmacien, -ienne [faʀmasjɛ̃, jɛn] NM,F (= *qui tient une pharmacie*) pharmacist, (dispensing) chemist (*Brit*), druggist (*US*); (= *préparateur*) pharmacist, chemist (*Brit*)

pharmacodépendance [faʀmakodepɑ̃dɑ̃s] NF drug dependency

pharmacologie [faʀmakɔlɔʒi] NF pharmacology

pharmacologique [faʀmakɔlɔʒik] ADJ pharmacological

pharmacopée [faʀmakɔpe] NF pharmacopoeia

pharyngal, e (*mpl* -**aux**) [faʀɛ̃gal, o] 1 ADJ pharyngeal 2 **pharyngale** NF (*Ling*) pharyngeal

pharyngé, e [faʀɛ̃ʒe], **pharyngien, -ienne** [faʀɛ̃ʒjɛ̃, jɛn] ADJ pharyngeal, pharyngal

pharyngite [faʀɛ̃ʒit] NF pharyngitis (*NonC*); **il a fait trois ~s** he had three bouts of pharyngitis

pharynx [faʀɛ̃ks] NM pharynx

phase [faz] NF (*gén, Méd*) phase, stage; (*Astron, Chim, Phys*) phase; (*Élec*) **la ~** the live wire; (*Sport*) **~ de jeu** passage of play; (*Méd*) **~ terminale** terminal stage *ou* phase; **l'économie a connu une longue ~ de croissance** the economy went through a long period of growth; **être en ~** (*Phys*) to be in phase; [*personnes*] to be on the same wavelength; [*projets*] to be in line (**avec** with)

Phébus [febys] NM Phoebus

Phèdre [fɛdʀ] NF Phaedra

Phénicie [fenisi] NF Phoenicia

phénicien, -ienne [fenisjɛ̃, jɛn] 1 ADJ Phoenician 2 NM (*Ling*) Phoenician 3 **Phénicien(ne)** NM,F Phoenician

phénix [feniks] NM a (*Myth*) phoenix b († : *littér*) **ce n'est pas un ~** he (*ou* she) is no genius c (*Bot*) = **phœnix**

phénobarbital (*pl* **phénobarbitals**) [fenɔbaʀbital] NM phenobarbital, phenobarbitone

phénol [fenɔl] NM carbolic acid, phenol

phénoménal, e (*mpl* -**aux**) [fenɔmenal, o] ADJ (*gén*) phenomenal

phénoménalement [fenɔmenalmɑ̃] ADV phenomenally

phénomène [fenɔmɛn] NM a (*gén, Philo*) phenomenon; **~s phénomena; ~ de société/ de mode** social/fashion phenomenon; **les ~s de violence dans les écoles** incidents of violence *ou* violent incidents in schools b (= *monstre de foire*) freak (of nature); (* = *personne*) (*génial*) phenomenon; (*excentrique*) character*; (*anormal*) freak*; **son petit dernier est un sacré ~!** his youngest is a real devil!*

phénoménologie [fenɔmenɔlɔʒi] NF phenomenology

phénoménologique [fenɔmenɔlɔʒik] ADJ phenomenological

phénoménologue [fenɔmenɔlɔg] NMF phenomenologist

phénotype [fenɔtip] NM phenotype

phéromone [feʀɔmɔn] NF pheromone

phi [fi] NM phi

Philadelphie [filadɛlfi] N Philadelphia

philanthrope [filɑ̃tʀɔp] NMF philanthropist

philanthropie [filɑ̃tʀɔpi] NF philanthropy

philanthropique [filɑ̃tʀɔpik] ADJ philanthropic(al)

philatélie [filateli] NF philately, stamp collecting

philatélique [filatelik] ADJ philatelic

philatéliste [filatelist] NMF philatelist, stamp collector

philharmonie [filaʀmɔni] NF philharmonic society

philharmonique [filaʀmɔnik] ADJ philharmonic

philhellène [filelɛn] 1 ADJ philhellenic 2 NMF philhellene, philhellenist

philhellénique [filelenik] ADJ philhellenic

philhellénisme [filelenism] NM philhellenism

philippin, e [filipɛ̃, in] 1 ADJ Philippine 2 **Philippin(e)** NM,F Filipino

Philippines [filipin] NFPL **les ~** the Philippines

philippique [filipik] NF (*littér*) diatribe, philippic (*littér*)

philistin [filistɛ̃] ADJ M, NM (*Hist*) Philistine; (*fig*) philistine

philistinisme [filistinism] NM philistinism

philo [filo] NF (*arg Scol*) ABRÉV = **philosophie**

philodendron [filɔdɛ̃dʀɔ̃] NM philodendron

philologie [filɔlɔʒi] NF philology

philologique [filɔlɔʒik] ADJ philological

philologiquement [filɔlɔʒikmɑ̃] ADV philologically

philologue [filɔlɔg] NMF philologist

philosophale [filɔzɔfal] ADJ F → **pierre**

philosophe [filɔzɔf] 1 NMF philosopher 2 ADJ philosophical

philosopher [filɔzɔfe] ▶ conjug 1 ◀ VI to philosophize (**sur** about)

philosophie [filɔzɔfi] NF philosophy; **il l'a accepté avec ~** he was philosophical about it; **c'est ma ~ (de la vie)** it's my philosophy (of life)

philosophique [filɔzɔfik] ADJ philosophical

philosophiquement [filɔzɔfikmɑ̃] ADV philosophically

philtre [filtʀ] NM philtre; **~ d'amour** love potion

phlébite [flebit] NF phlebitis

phlébologie [flebɔlɔʒi] NF phlebology

phlébologue [flebɔlɔg] NMF vein specialist

phlébotomie [flebɔtɔmi] NF phlebotomy

phlegmon [flɛgmɔ̃] NM abscess, phlegmon (*SPÉC*)

phlox [flɔks] NM INV phlox

Phnom Penh [pnɔ̃mpɛn] N Phnom Penh

phobie [fɔbi] NF phobia; **avoir la ~ de** to have a phobia about

phobique [fɔbik] ADJ, NMF phobic

phocéen, -enne [fɔseɛ̃, ɛn] 1 ADJ Phocaean; **la cité phocéenne** Marseilles 2 **Phocéen(ne)** NM,F Phocaean

phœnix [feniks] NM (*Bot*) phoenix

phonateur, -trice [fɔnatœʀ, tʀis] ADJ phonatory

phonation [fɔnasjɔ̃] NF phonation

phonatoire [fɔnatwaʀ] ADJ = **phonateur**

phone [fɔn] NM phon

phonématique [fɔnematik] NF phonology, phonemics *sg*

phonème [fɔnɛm] NM phoneme

phonémique [fɔnemik] 1 ADJ phonemic 2 NF = **phonématique**

phonéticien, -ienne [fɔnetisjɛ̃, jɛn] NM,F phonetician

phonétique [fɔnetik] 1 NF phonetics *sg*; **~ articulatoire/acoustique/auditoire** articulatory/acoustic/auditory phonetics 2 ADJ phonetic; **loi/système ~** phonetic law/system

phonétiquement [fɔnetikmɑ̃] ADV phonetically

phoniatre [fɔnjatʀ] NMF speech therapist

phoniatrie [fɔnjatʀi] NF speech therapy

phonie [fɔni] NF (*Téléc*) radiotelegraphy, wireless telegraphy (*Brit*)

phonique [fɔnik] ADJ phonic

phono [fono] NM ABRÉV = **phonographe**

phonogramme [fɔnɔgʀam] NM (= *signe*) phonogram

phonographe [fɔnɔgʀaf] NM (*à rouleau*) phonograph; (*à disque*) (wind-up) gramophone, phonograph (*US*); (= *électrophone*) record player, phonograph (*US*)

phonographique [fɔnɔgʀafik] ADJ phonographic

phonologie [fɔnɔlɔʒi] NF phonology

phonologique [fɔnɔlɔʒik] ADJ phonological

phonologue [fɔnɔlɔg] NMF phonologist

phonothèque [fɔnɔtɛk] NF sound archives

phoque [fɔk] NM (= animal) seal; (= fourrure) sealskin → **souffler**

phosphatage [fɔsfataʒ] NM treating with phosphates

phosphate [fɔsfat] NM phosphate

phosphaté, e [fɔsfate] (ptp de **phosphater**) ADJ phosphatic, phosphated; **engrais ~s** phosphate-enriched fertilizers

phosphater [fɔsfate] ▶ conjug 1 ◀ VT to phosphatize, phosphate, treat with phosphates

phosphène [fɔsfɛn] NM phosphene

phosphine [fɔsfin] NF phosphine

phosphore [fɔsfɔʀ] NM phosphorus

phosphoré, e [fɔsfɔʀe] ADJ phosphorous

phosphorer* [fɔsfɔʀe] ▶ conjug 1 ◀ VI to think hard

phosphorescence [fɔsfɔʀesɑ̃s] NF luminosity, phosphorescence (SPÉC)

phosphorescent, e [fɔsfɔʀesɑ̃, ɑ̃t] ADJ luminous, phosphorescent (SPÉC)

phosphoreux, -euse [fɔsfɔʀø, øz] ADJ [acide] phosphorous; [bronze] phosphor (épith)

phosphorique [fɔsfɔʀik] ADJ phosphoric

phosphure [fɔsfyʀ] NM phosphide

phot [fɔt] NM (Phys) phot

photo [fɔto] NF ABRÉV = **photographie** [a] (= image) photo, picture; (instantané, d'amateur) snap(shot); [film] still; **faire une ~ de** ◊ **prendre en ~** to take a photo ou picture of; **ça rend bien en ~** it looks good in a photo; **j'ai mon fils en ~** I've got a photo ou picture of my son; **elle est bien en ~** she takes a good photo, she's photogenic; **qui est sur cette ~?** who is in this photo? ou picture?; **~ de famille** (gén) family photo; (= portrait) family portrait; [collègues etc] group photo; **~ d'identité** passport photo; **~ de mode** fashion photo ou shot; **~s de vacances** holiday (Brit) ou vacation (US) photos ou snaps; **tu veux ma ~?*** what are you staring at?; **il n'y a pas ~*** there's no question about it; **entre les deux candidats il n'y a pas ~** there's no competition between the two candidates → **appareil**
[b] (= art) photography; **faire de la ~** (en amateur) to be an amateur photographer; (en professionnel) to be a (professional) photographer; **je fais de la ~ à mes heures perdues** I take photo(graph)s in my spare time, I do photography in my spare time

photochimie [fɔtoʃimi] NF photochemistry

photochimique [fɔtoʃimik] ADJ photochemical

photocomposer [fɔtokɔ̃poze] ▶ conjug 1 ◀ VT to photocompose, filmset

photocomposeur [fɔtokɔ̃pozœʀ] NM = **photocompositeur**

photocomposeuse [fɔtokɔ̃pozøz] NF (= machine) photocomposer, filmsetter

photocompositeur [fɔtokɔ̃pozitœʀ] NM (photo)typesetter

photocomposition [fɔtokɔ̃pozisjɔ̃] NF filmsetting (Brit), photocomposition (US)

photoconducteur, -trice [fɔtokɔ̃dyktœʀ, tʀis] ADJ photoconductive

photocopie [fɔtokɔpi] NF (= action) photocopying; (= copie) photocopy

photocopier [fɔtokɔpje] ▶ conjug 7 ◀ VT to photocopy; **~ qch en trois exemplaires** to make three photocopies of sth

photocopieur [fɔtokɔpjœʀ] NM, **photocopieuse** [fɔtokɔpjøz] NF photocopier

photocopillage [fɔtokɔpijaʒ] NM illegal photocopying of copyright material

photodissociation [fɔtodisɔsjasjɔ̃] NF photodisintegration

photoélasticimétrie [fɔtoelastisimetʀi] NF photoelasticity

photoélectricité [fɔtoelɛktʀisite] NF photoelectricity

photoélectrique [fɔtoelɛktʀik] ADJ photoelectric; **cellule ~** photoelectric cell, photocell

photo-finish (pl **photos-finish**) [fɔtofiniʃ] NM **l'arrivée de la deuxième course a dû être contrôlée au ~** the second race was a photo finish

photogénique [fɔtoʒenik] ADJ photogenic

photographe [fɔtɔgʀaf] NMF (= artiste) photographer; (= commerçant) camera dealer; **~ de mode/de presse** fashion/press photographer; **vous trouverez cet article chez un ~** you will find this item at a camera shop ou store (US)

photographie [fɔtɔgʀafi] NF [a] (= art) photography; **faire de la ~** (comme passe-temps) to be an amateur photographer, take photographs; (en professionnel) to be a (professional) photographer [b] (= image) photograph, picture; **ce sondage est une ~ de l'opinion publique** this survey is a reflection of public opinion ou offers a clear picture of public opinion; **pour autres locutions voir photo**

photographier [fɔtɔgʀafje] ▶ conjug 7 ◀ VT to photograph, take a photo(graph) of, take a picture of; **se faire ~** to have one's photo(graph) ou picture taken; (= mémoriser) **il avait photographié l'endroit** he had got the place firmly fixed in his mind ou in his mind's eye

photographique [fɔtɔgʀafik] ADJ photographic → **appareil**

photograveur [fɔtɔgʀavœʀ] NM photoengraver

photogravure [fɔtɔgʀavyʀ] NF photoengraving

photojournalisme [fɔtoʒuʀnalism] NM photojournalism

photojournaliste [fɔtoʒuʀnalist] NMF photojournalist

photolithographie [fɔtolitɔgʀafi] NF photolithography

photoluminescence [fɔtolyminesɑ̃s] NF photoluminescence

photolyse [fɔtoliz] NF photolysis

Photomaton® [fɔtomatɔ̃] [1] NM automatic photo booth [2] NM (photo booth) photo; **se faire faire des ~s** to get one's pictures taken (in a photo booth)

photomètre [fɔtɔmɛtʀ] NM photometer

photométrie [fɔtɔmetʀi] NF photometry

photométrique [fɔtɔmetʀik] ADJ photometric(al)

photomontage [fɔtomɔ̃taʒ] NM photomontage

photomultiplicateur [fɔtomyltiplikatœʀ] NM photomultiplier

photon [fɔtɔ̃] NM photon

photopériode [fɔtoperjɔd] NF photoperiod

photopériodique [fɔtoperjɔdik] ADJ photoperiodic

photopériodisme [fɔtoperjɔdism] NM photoperiodism

photophobie [fɔtofɔbi] NF photophobia

photophore [fɔtofɔʀ] NM [mineur] (miner's) cap lamp; (Anat) photophore; (= coupe décorative) globe

photopile [fɔtopil] NF solar cell

photoréalisme [fɔtorealizm] NM photorealism

photoreportage [fɔtoʀəpɔʀtaʒ] NM photo story

photoroman [fɔtoʀɔmɑ̃] NM photo story

photosensibilisant, e [fɔtosɑ̃sibilizɑ̃, ɑ̃t] ADJ [médicament] photosensitive

photosensible [fɔtosɑ̃sibl] ADJ photosensitive; **dispositif ~** photosensor

photosphère [fɔtosfɛʀ] NF (Astron) photosphere

photostat [fɔtosta] NM photostat

photostoppeur, -euse [fɔtostɔpœʀ, øz] NM,F street photographer

photostyle [fɔtostil] NM light pen

photosynthèse [fɔtosɛ̃tɛz] NF photosynthesis

photothèque [fɔtotɛk] NF photographic library, picture library

phrase [fʀɑz] NF [a] (Ling) sentence; (= propos) words; **faire des ~s** [enfant] to make sentences; (péj) to talk in flowery language; **assez de grandes ~s!** enough of the rhetoric ou fine words!; **il termina son discours sur cette ~** he closed his speech with these words; **~ toute faite** stock phrase; **citer une ~ célèbre** to quote a famous phrase ou saying; (Pol) **petite ~** soundbite → **membre** [b] (Mus) phrase

phrasé [fʀɑze] NM (Mus) phrasing

phraséologie [fʀazeɔlɔʒi] NF (gén) phraseology; (péj) **la ~ marxiste/capitaliste** marxist/capitalist jargon

phraser [fʀɑze] ▶ conjug 1 ◀ [1] VT (Mus) to phrase [2] VI (péj) to use fine words (péj) ou high-flown language (péj)

phraseur, -euse [fʀɑzœʀ, øz] NM,F man (ou woman) of fine words (péj)

phrastique [fʀastik] ADJ phrasal

phréatique [fʀeatik] ADJ → **nappe**

phrénique [fʀenik] ADJ phrenic

phrénologie [fʀenɔlɔʒi] NF phrenology

phrénologue [fʀenɔlɔg], **phrénologiste** [fʀenɔlɔʒist] NMF phrenologist

Phrygie [fʀiʒi] NF Phrygia

phrygien, -ienne [fʀiʒjɛ̃, jɛn] [1] ADJ Phrygian → **bonnet** [2] **Phrygien(ne)** NM,F Phrygian

phtaléine [ftalein] NF phthalein

phtisie [ftizi] NF consumption, phthisis (SPÉC); **~ galopante** galloping consumption

phtisiologie [ftizjɔlɔʒi] NF phthisiology

phtisiologue [ftizjɔlɔg] NMF phthisiologist

phtisique [ftizik] ADJ consumptive, phthisical (SPÉC)

phycologie [fikɔlɔʒi] NF phycology

phylactère [filaktɛʀ] NM phylactery

phylloxéra [filɔksera] NM phylloxera

phylogenèse [filoʒənɛz] NF phylogenesis

phylogénétique [filoʒenetik] ADJ phylogenetic, phyletic

physicien, -ienne [fizisjɛ̃, jɛn] NM,F physicist; **~ atomiste ou nucléaire** atomic ou nuclear physicist

physicochimie [fizikoʃimi] NF physical chemistry

physicochimique [fizikoʃimik] ADJ physicochemical

physicomathématique [fizikomatematik] ADJ of mathematical physics

physiocrate [fizjɔkʀat] [1] NMF physiocrat [2] ADJ physiocratic

physiocratie [fizjɔkʀasi] NF physiocracy

physiologie [fizjɔlɔʒi] NF physiology

physiologique [fizjɔlɔʒik] ADJ physiological

physiologiquement [fizjɔlɔʒikmɑ̃] ADV physiologically

physiologiste [fizjɔlɔʒist] [1] NMF physiologist [2] ADJ physiological

physionomie [fizjɔnɔmi] NF (= traits du visage) facial appearance (NonC), physiognomy (frm); (= expression) countenance (frm), face; (= aspect) appearance; (Bourse) **en fonction de la ~ du marché** depending on how the market looks; **la ~ de l'Europe a changé** the face of Europe has changed

physionomiste [fizjɔnɔmist] ADJ **il est (très) ~** he has a (very) good memory for faces

physiopathologie [fizjopatɔlɔʒi] NF physio-pathology

physiothérapeute [fizjoterapøt] NMF *person practising natural medicine*

physiothérapie [fizjoterapi] NF natural medicine

physique [fizik] **1** ADJ **a** (*gén*) physical; **je ne peux pas le supporter, c'est ~** I can't stand him, the very sight of him makes me sick → **amour, culture, personne** *etc* **b** (= *athlétique*) [*joueur, match, jeu*] physical **2** NM (= *aspect*) physical appearance; (= *stature, corps*) physique; **elle sait se servir de son ~** she knows how to use her looks; **avoir un ~ agréable** to be good-looking; **avoir le ~ de l'emploi** to look the part; **au ~** physically **3** NF physics *sg*; **~ nucléaire/des particules** nuclear/particle physics

physiquement [fizikmɑ̃] ADV physically; **il est plutôt bien ~** physically he's quite attractive

phytobiologie [fitobjɔlɔʒi] NF phytology

phytogéographie [fitoʒeɔgʀafi] NF phyto-geography

phytopathologie [fitopatɔlɔʒi] NF phytopathology

phytoplancton [fitoplɑ̃ktɔ̃] NM phytoplankton

phytosanitaire [fitosanitɛʀ] ADJ **produit ~** (*de soins*) plant-care product; (= *pesticide*) pesticide; (= *herbicide*) weedkiller; **contrôles ~s** phytosanitary regulations

phytothérapeute [fitoterapøt] NMF (medical) herbalist, phytotherapist (SPÉC)

phytothérapie [fitoterapi] NF herbal medicine

pi [pi] NM (= *lettre, Math*) pi

p.i. (ABRÉV = **par intérim**) acting, actg

piaf [pjaf] NM sparrow

piaffement [pjafmɑ̃] NM [*cheval*] stamping, pawing

piaffer [pjafe] ▸conjug 1◂ VI [*cheval*] to stamp, paw the ground; [*personne*] **~ d'impatience** to be champing at the bit

piaillement [pjajmɑ̃] NM [*oiseau*] cheeping (NonC), peeping (NonC); (péj) **~s** [*enfant*] whining (NonC)

piailler [pjaje] ▸conjug 1◂ VI [*oiseau*] to cheep, peep; [*enfant*] to whine

piaillerie [pjajʀi] NF = **piaillement**

piailleur, -euse [pjajœʀ, øz] **1** ADJ [*oiseau*] cheeping, peeping; [*enfant*] whining **2** NM,F whiner

piane-piane [pjanpjan] ADV gently; **allez-y ~** go gently *ou* easy*, easy *ou* gently does it*; **le projet avance ~** the project is coming along slowly but surely

pianissimo [pjanisimo] **1** ADV (*Mus*) pianissimo; (*: fig*) very gently **2** NM (*Mus*) pianissimo

pianiste [pjanist] NMF pianist, piano player

pianistique [pjanistik] ADJ pianistic

piano¹ [pjano] NM piano; **~ acoustique/électronique** acoustic/electric piano; **~ de concert/crapaud** concert grand/boudoir grand (piano); **~ droit/à queue** upright/grand piano; **~ demi-queue/quart de queue** baby grand/miniature grand (piano); **~ mécanique** player piano, piano organ, Pianola®; **~ préparé** prepared piano; (*hum*) **~ à bretelles** accordion; **faire** *ou* **jouer du ~** to play the piano; **se mettre au ~** (= *apprendre*) to take up *ou* start the piano; (= *s'asseoir*) to sit down at the piano; **accompagné au ~ par ...** accompanied on the piano by ...

piano² [pjano] ADV (*Mus*) piano; (* *fig*) gently); **allez-y ~** easy *ou* gently does it*, go easy* *ou* gently

piano-bar (*pl* **pianos-bars**) [pjanobaʀ] NM piano bar

piano(-)forte [pjanofɔʀte] NM pianoforte

pianotage [pjanotaʒ] NM (*sur un piano*) tinkling; (*sur un clavier*) tapping; (*sur une table*) drumming

pianoter [pjanɔte] ▸conjug 1◂ **1** VI **a** (= *jouer du piano*) to tinkle away (at the piano) **b** (= *tapoter*) to drum one's fingers; (*sur un clavier*) to tap away; **il pianotait sur son ordinateur** he was tapping away at his computer **2** VT [+ *signal, code*] to tap out; **~ un air** to tinkle out a tune on the piano

piastre [pjastʀ] NF piastre (*Brit*), piaster (*US*); (*Can* = *dollar*) (Canadian) dollar

piaule [pjol] NF (= *chambre louée*) room; **ma ~** my (bed)room

piaulement [pjolmɑ̃] NM [*oiseau*] cheeping (NonC), peeping (NonC); (*: péj*) [*enfant*] whining (NonC), whimpering (NonC)

piauler [pjole] ▸conjug 1◂ VI [*oiseau*] to cheep, peep; (*: péj*) [*enfant*] to whine, whimper

PIB [peibe] NM (ABRÉV = **produit intérieur brut**) GDP

pic [pik] **1** NM **a** [*montagne, courbe*] peak; **à chaque ~ de pollution** whenever pollution levels peak *ou* reach a peak; **atteindre un ~** to reach *ou* hit a peak, peak **b** (= *pioche*) pick(axe); **~ à glace** ice pick **c** (= *oiseau*) **~(-)vert** (green) woodpecker; **~ épeiche** great-spotted woodpecker, pied woodpecker **2** **à pic** LOC ADJ, LOC ADV [*rochers*] sheer, precipitous (*frm*); [*mont, chemin*] steep, precipitous (*frm*); **le chemin s'élève** *ou* **monte à ~** the path rises steeply; **la falaise plonge à ~ dans la mer** the cliff falls *ou* drops sheer (in)to the sea; **arriver** *ou* **tomber à ~*** to come just at the right time *ou* moment; **vous arrivez à ~*** you couldn't have come at a better time *ou* moment, you've come just at the right time *ou* moment → **couler**

pica [pika] NM (*Typo*) pica

picaillons [pikajɔ̃] NMPL cash* (NonC)

picaresque [pikaʀɛsk] ADJ picaresque

piccolo [pikɔlo] NM piccolo

pichenette [piʃnɛt] NF flick; **faire tomber qch d'une ~** to flick sth off *ou* away

pichet [piʃɛ] NM pitcher, jug; (*dans un restaurant*) **un ~ de vin** ≈ a carafe of wine

pickpocket [pikpɔkɛt] NM pickpocket

pick-up †* [pikœp] NM INV (= *bras*) pickup; (= *électrophone*) record player

pico- [piko] PRÉF pico-; **~seconde** picosecond

picoler [pikɔle] ▸conjug 1◂ VI to booze*; **qu'est-ce qu'il peut ~!** he sure can knock it back!*; **~ dur** (*habituellement*) to be a real boozer*; (*à l'occasion*) to hit the bottle* *ou* sauce* (*US*)

picoleur, -euse [pikɔlœʀ, øz] NM,F tippler*, boozer*

picorer [pikɔʀe] ▸conjug 1◂ **1** VI to peck (about); (= *manger très peu*) to nibble **2** VT to peck, peck (away) at

picot [piko] NM [*dentelle*] picot; [*planche*] burr; (= *petite pointe*) spike; (*Ordin*) **dispositif d'entraînement à ~s** tractor drive

picotement [pikotmɑ̃] NM [*peau, membres*] tingling (NonC); **j'ai des ~s dans les yeux** my eyes are smarting *ou* stinging; **j'ai des ~s dans la gorge** I've got a tickle in my throat; **la décharge électrique provoque de légers ~s** the electrical discharge creates a slight tingling sensation

picoter [pikote] ▸conjug 1◂ **1** VT **a** (= *provoquer des picotements*) **~ la gorge** to tickle the throat; **~ la peau** to make the skin tingle; **~ les yeux** to make the eyes smart, sting the eyes; **j'ai les yeux qui me picotent** my eyes are stinging *ou* smarting **b** (*avec une épingle*) to prick **c** (= *picorer*) to peck, peck (away) at **2** VI [*gorge*] to tickle; [*peau*] to tingle; [*yeux*] to smart, sting

picotin [pikotɛ̃] NM (= *ration d'avoine*) oats, ration of oats; (= *mesure*) peck

picouse [pikuz] NF → **piquouse**

picrate [pikʀat] NM (*Chim*) picrate; (* : *péj*) cheap wine, plonk* (*Brit*)

picrique [pikʀik] ADJ **acide ~** picric acid

picrocholin, e [pikʀɔkɔlɛ̃, in] ADJ (*frm*) **guerre** *ou* **dispute ~e** petty wrangling (NonC)

Pictes [pikt] NMPL Picts

pictogramme [piktogram] NM pictogram

pictographie [piktogʀafi] NF pictography

pictographique [piktogʀafik] ADJ pictographic

pictural, e (*mpl* **-aux**) [piktyʀal, o] ADJ pictorial

pidgin [pidʒin] NM pidgin; **~-english** pidgin English

Pie [pi] NM Pius

pie¹ [pi] **1** NF (= *oiseau*) magpie; (* *péj* = *personne*) chatterbox* → **bavard, voleur 2** ADJ INV [*cheval*] piebald; [*vache*] black and white → **voiture**

pie² [pi] ADJ F → **œuvre**

pièce [pjɛs] **1** NF **a** (= *fragment*) piece; **en ~s** in pieces; **mettre en ~s** (*lit*) (= *casser*) to smash to pieces; (= *déchirer*) to pull *ou* tear to pieces; (*fig*) to tear *ou* pull to pieces; **c'est inventé** *ou* **forgé de toutes ~** it's made up from start to finish, it's a complete fabrication; **fait d'une seule ~** made in one piece; **fait de ~s et de morceaux** (*lit*) made with *ou* of bits and pieces; (*fig péj*) cobbled together; **il est tout d'une ~** he's very cut and dried about things → **tailler**

b (*gén* = *unité, objet*) piece; [*jeu d'échecs, de dames*] piece; [*tissu, drap*] length, piece; (*Mil*) gun; (*Chasse, Pêche* = *prise*) specimen; (*Comm*) **se vendre à la ~** to be sold separately *ou* individually; **2 F (la)** = 2 francs each *ou* apiece; **travail à la ~** *ou* **aux ~s** piecework; **payé à la ~** *ou* **aux ~s** on piece(work) rate, on piecework; **on n'est pas aux ~s!** there's no rush!; (*Habillement*) **un deux-~s** (= *costume, tailleur*) a two-piece suit; (= *maillot de bain*) a two-piece (swimsuit); (*Hér*) **~s honorables** honourable ordinaries → **chef¹**

c [*machine, voiture*] part, component; **~s (de rechange)** spares, (spare) parts; **~ d'origine** guaranteed genuine spare part

d (= *document*) paper, document; **avez-vous toutes les ~s nécessaires?** have you got all the necessary papers? *ou* documents?; **juger/décider sur ~s** to judge/decide on actual evidence; **avec ~s à l'appui** with supporting documents; (*Admin, Jur*) **les plaintes doivent être accompagnées de ~s justificatives** complaints must be documented *ou* accompanied by written proof *ou* evidence

e (*Couture, Chir*) patch; **mettre une ~ à qch** to put a patch on sth

f [*maison*] room; **appartement de cinq ~s** five-room(ed) apartment *ou* flat (*Brit*); **un deux ~s (cuisine)** a two-room(ed) apartment *ou* flat (*Brit*) (with kitchen)

g (*Théât*) play; (*Littérat, Mus*) piece; **jouer** *ou* **monter une ~ de Racine** to put on a play by Racine; **une ~ pour hautbois** a piece for oboe

h ~ (de monnaie) coin; **~ d'argent/d'or** silver/gold coin; **une ~ de 5 francs/de 50 centimes** a 5-franc/50-centime coin; **~s jaunes** centime coins, ≈ coppers* (*Brit*); **donner la ~ à qn*** to give sb a tip, tip sb → **rendre**

i (*littér*) **faire ~ à qn/à un projet** to thwart sb *ou* sb's plans/a project

2 COMP ▸ **pièce d'artifice** firework ▸ **pièce d'artillerie** piece of ordnance, gun ▸ **pièce de bétail** head of cattle; **50 ~s de bétail** 50 head of cattle ▸ **pièce de blé** wheat field, cornfield (*Brit*) ▸ **pièce de bois** piece of wood *ou* timber (*for joinery etc*) ▸ **pièce de charpente** member ▸ **pièce de collection** collector's item *ou* piece

► **pièce comptable** accounting record ► **pièce à conviction** (*Jur*) exhibit ► **pièce détachée** spare, (spare) part; **livré en ~s détachées** (delivered) in kit form ► **pièce d'eau** ornamental lake; (*plus petit*) ornamental pond ► **pièce d'identité** identity paper; **avez-vous une ~ d'identité?** have you (got) any identification? ► **pièce maîtresse** [*collection, musée*] (*gén*) showpiece; (*en exposition*) showpiece, prize *ou* main exhibit; [*politique, stratégie*] cornerstone ► **pièce montée** (*Culin*) pyramid-shaped cake made out of choux puffs, eaten on special occasions; (*à un mariage*) ≈ wedding cake ► **pièce de musée** museum piece ► **pièce rapportée** (*Couture*) patch; [*marqueterie, mosaïque*] insert, piece; (*hum = belle-sœur, beau-frère etc*) in-law*; (*dans un groupe*) late addition ► **pièce de résistance** main dish, pièce de résistance ► **pièce de terre** piece *ou* patch of land ► **pièce de théâtre** play ► **pièce de vers** piece of poetry, short poem ► **pièce de viande** side of meat ► **pièce de vin** cask of wine

piécette [pjesεt] NF small coin

---

pied [pje]

| 1 NOM MASCULIN | 2 COMPOSÉS |

1 NOM MASCULIN

a Anat [*personne, animal*] foot; (= *sabot*) [*cheval, bœuf*] hoof; [*mollusque*] foot; **avoir les ~s plats** to have flat feet, be flatfooted; **sauter d'un ~ sur l'autre** to hop from one foot to the other; **avoir ~** [*nageur*] to be able to touch the bottom; **je n'ai plus ~** I'm out of my depth; **avoir bon ~ bon œil** to be as fit as a fiddle, be fighting fit, be hale and hearty; **avoir le ~ léger** to be light of step; **avoir le ~ marin** to be a good sailor; **avoir les (deux) ~s sur terre** to have one's feet firmly (planted) on the ground; **avoir un ~ dans la tombe** to have one foot in the grave; **avoir/garder un ~ dans l'entreprise** to have a foot/keep one's foot in the door, have/maintain a foothold *ou* a toehold in the firm; **conduire** *ou* **foncer (le) ~ au plancher** to drive with one's foot to the floor; **faire du ~ à qn** (= *prévenir qn*) to give sb a warning kick; (*galamment*) to play footsie with sb*; **faire le ~ de grue*** to stand about (waiting), kick one's heels (*Brit*); **faire des ~s et des mains pour obtenir qch** to move heaven and earth to get sth; **cela lui fera les ~s*** that'll teach him (a thing or two)*; **le ~ lui a manqué** he lost his footing, his foot slipped; **mettre ~ à terre** to dismount; **mettre les ~s chez qn** to set foot in sb's house; **je n'y remettrai jamais les ~s** I'll never set foot (in) there again; **je n'ai pas mis les ~s dehors aujourd'hui** I haven't been outside all day; **mettre les ~s dans le plat*** (= *gaffer*) to put one's foot in it; (= *se fâcher*) to put one's foot down; **il est incapable de mettre un ~ devant l'autre** he can't walk straight; **partir du bon ~** to get off to a good start; **partir** *ou* **sortir les ~s devant*** (= *mourir*) to go out feet first; **perdre ~** (*lit, fig*) to be *ou* get out of one's depth; (*en montagne*) to lose one's footing; **prendre ~ sur un marché** to gain *ou* get a foothold in a market; (*fig*) **se prendre les ~s dans le tapis*** to slip up; **il va prendre mon ~ au derrière!*** I'll give him a kick up the backside!*; **repartir du bon ~** to make a clean *ou* fresh start; **sans remuer** *ou* **bouger ni ~ ni patte*** without moving a muscle; **avec lui, on ne sait jamais sur quel ~ danser** you never know where you stand with him; **je ne sais pas sur quel ~ danser** I don't know what to do; **il ne tient pas sur ses ~s** (*ivre*) he can hardly stand up; (*faible*) he's dead on his feet; (*sur une annonce*) « **les ~s dans l'eau** » "on the waterfront"; (*sur un chien*) « **au ~!** » "heel!" → **casser, deux, lâcher, retomber**

♦ **à pied** (*en marchant*) on foot; **aller à ~** to go on foot, walk; **nous avons fait tout le chemin à ~** we walked all the way, we came all the way on foot; **faire de la marche/course à ~** to go walking/running; (*fig*) **ce type, on l'emmerde**: **à ~, à cheval et en voiture!** he can go to hell!:; **mettre qn à ~** to suspend sb; **mise à ~** suspension

♦ **à pied sec** without getting one's feet wet

♦ **à pieds joints** with one's feet together → **sauter**

♦ **au pied levé**: **remplacer qn au ~ levé** to stand in for sb at a moment's notice

♦ **aux pieds de**: **le chien est couché aux ~s de son maître** the dog is lying at its master's feet; **tomber aux ~s de qn** to fall at sb's feet

♦ **de pied en cap** from head to foot, from top to toe

♦ **de pied ferme** resolutely; **s'il veut me créer des ennuis, je l'attends de ~ ferme** if he wants to create trouble for me, I'm ready and waiting for him

♦ **des pieds à la tête** from head to foot

♦ **en pied** [*portrait*] full-length; [*statue*] full-scale, full-size

♦ **le pied à l'étrier**: **avoir le ~ à l'étrier** to be well on the way; **mettre le ~ à l'étrier à qn** to give sb a boost *ou* a leg up (*Brit*)

♦ **pieds et poings liés** (*fig*) tied *ou* bound hand and foot

♦ **pied à pied** [*se défendre, lutter*] every inch of the way

♦ **sur pied** (= *levé, guéri*) **être sur ~** [*personne, malade*] to be up and about; **remettre qn sur ~** to set sb back on his feet again (= *constitué*) **maintenant que l'équipe est sur ~ ...** now that the team has been set up ...; **l'organisation sera sur ~ en mai** the organization will be operational in May; **mettre qch sur ~** to set sth up; **la mise sur ~ de qch** the setting up of sth (= *vivant, non coupé*) **bétail sur ~** beef (*ou* mutton *etc*) on the hoof; **blé sur ~** standing *ou* uncut corn (*Brit*) *ou* wheat (*US*)

b

♦ **coup de pied** (*gén, Sport*) kick; **un coup de ~ au derrière*** *ou* **aux fesses*** a kick in the pants* *ou* up the backside*; **coup de ~ au cul**: kick up the arse** (*Brit*) *ou* in the ass** (*US*); **donner un coup de ~ à** *ou* **dans** to kick; (*fig*) **donner un coup de ~ dans la fourmilière** to stir things up; **il a reçu un coup de ~** he was kicked; (*fig*) **le coup de ~ de l'âne** delayed revenge → **pénalité, touche**

c = partie inférieure, base, support [*arbre, colline, échelle, lit, mur*] foot, bottom; [*table*] leg; [*champignon*] stalk; [*appareil-photo*] stand, tripod; [*lampe*] base; [*lampadaire*] stand; [*verre*] stem; [*colonne*] base, foot; (*Math*) [*perpendiculaire*] foot; [*chaussette*] foot; (= *chaussure*) **le ~ droit me va, mais le gauche est un peu grand** the right shoe fits me, but the left one is a bit too big

♦ **au pied du mur** (*fig*) **être au ~ du mur** to have one's back to the wall; **mettre qn au ~ du mur** to call sb's bluff

♦ **à pied d'œuvre** ready to get down to the job

d Agr [*salade, tomate*] plant; **~ de laitue** lettuce (plant); **~ de céleri** head of celery; **~ de vigne** vine

e Culin [*porc, mouton, veau*] trotter; **~s paquets** *dish made of mutton tripe and pig's trotters*

f = mesure foot; **un poteau de six ~s** a six-foot pole; **j'aurais voulu être à 100 ~s sous terre** I wished the ground would open up (and swallow me), I could have died*

g Poésie foot

h = idiot twit*, idiot; **quel ~, celui-là!** what an idiot!, what a (useless) twit!*

♦ **comme un pied**: **jouer comme un ~** to be a useless* *ou* lousy: player; **il s'y prend comme un ~** he hasn't a clue how to go about it*; **il conduit/chante comme un ~** he's a hopeless *ou* lousy: driver/singer

---

i = plaisir **c'est le ~!** ◊ **quel ~!** it's brilliant!* *ou* great!*; **ce n'est pas le ~** it's no picnic* *ou* fun; **c'est une solution, mais c'est pas le ~** it's a solution but it's not brilliant* *ou* great*; **prendre son ~** (= *s'amuser*) to get one's kicks: (**avec** with); (*sexuellement*) to have it away *ou* off: (**avec** with)

j locutions

♦ **au petit pied** (*littér*) **un Balzac/un Versailles au petit ~** a poor man's Balzac/Versailles; **un don Juan** *ou* **un séducteur au petit ~** a small-time Casanova

♦ **au pied de la lettre** literally; **ne prends pas tout au ~ de la lettre!** don't take everything so literally!; **il a suivi vos conseils au ~ de la lettre** he followed your advice to the letter

♦ **sur le pied de guerre** (all) ready to go, ready for action

♦ **sur un grand pied**: **vivre sur un grand ~** to live in (great *ou* grand) style

♦ **sur un pied d'égalité** ◊ **sur le même pied** [*être, mettre*] on an equal footing; [*traiter*] as equals

2 COMPOSÉS

► **pied d'athlète** (*Méd*) athlete's foot ► **pied autoréglable** = pied de nivellement ► **pied de col** NM (*Couture*) collarstand ► **pied à coulisse** calliper rule ► **pied de fer** (cobbler's) last ► **pied de lit** footboard ► **pied de nez** NM **faire un ~ de nez à qn** to thumb one's nose at sb, cock a snook at sb (*Brit*) ► **les Pieds Nickelés** *early 20th century French cartoon characters*; (*: fig*) **la bande de ~s nickelés qui traîne dans ce café** the gang of good-for-nothings *ou* layabouts* who hang out* in this café ► **pied de nivellement** (*sur un meuble*) self-levelling foot

---

pied-à-terre [pjetatεR] NM INV pied-à-terre

pied-bot (*pl* **pieds-bots**) [pjebo] NM person with a club-foot

pied-d'alouette (*pl* **pieds-d'alouette**) [pjedalwεt] NM larkspur

pied-de-biche (*pl* **pieds-de-biche**) [pjed(ə)biʃ] [*machine à coudre*] presser foot; [*meuble*] cabriole leg; (= *levier*) wrecking bar; (= *arrache-clous*) nail puller *ou* extractor

pied-de-cheval (*pl* **pieds-de-cheval**) [pjed(ə)ʃəval] NM *large specially cultivated oyster*

pied-de-loup (*pl* **pieds-de-loup**) [pjed(ə)lu] NM club moss

pied-de-poule (*pl* **pieds-de-poule**) [pjed(ə)pul] **1** ADJ INV hound's-tooth, dog's-tooth **2** NM hound's-tooth check (*NonC*), dog's-tooth check (*NonC*)

pied-de-roi (*pl* **pieds-de-roi**) [pjed(ə)Rwa] NM (*Can*) folding foot-rule

pied-de-veau (*pl* **pieds-de-veau**) [pjed(ə)vo] NM (*Bot*) lords and ladies, cuckoopint

pied-d'oiseau (*pl* **pieds-d'oiseau**) [pjedwazo] NM (*Bot*) bird's-foot

piédestal (*pl* **-aux**) [pjedεstal, o] NM (*lit, fig*) pedestal; (*fig*) **mettre** *ou* **placer qn sur un ~** to put sb on a pedestal; (*fig*) **descendre/tomber de son ~** to come down from/fall off one's pedestal

pied-noir (*pl* **pieds-noirs**) [pjenwaR] NMF pied-noir (*French colonial born in Algeria*)

pied-plat †† (*pl* **pieds-plats**) [pjepla] NM lout

piégé, e [pjeʒe] (*ptp de* **piéger**) ADJ **engin ~** booby trap; **lettre ~e** letter bomb; **colis** *ou* **paquet ~** parcel *ou* mail bomb; **voiture ~e** car bomb

piège [pjεʒ] NM (*lit, fig*) trap; (= *fosse*) pit; (= *collet*) snare; **~ à rats/à moineaux** rat-/sparrow-trap; **~ à loups** mantrap; **~ à touristes** tourist trap; **c'est un ~ à cons**: it's a con* *ou* a gyp: (*US*); **prendre au ~** (= catch in a) trap; **être pris à son propre ~** to be caught in *ou* fall into one's own trap; **tendre un ~ (à qn)** to set a trap (for sb); **traduction/dictée pleine de ~s**

translation/dictation full of pitfalls; **donner** *ou* **tomber dans le ~** to fall into the trap, be trapped; **c'était un ~ et tu es tombé dedans!** [*question*] it was a trick question and you got caught out!

piégeage [pjeʒaʒ] NM **a** [*animal*] trapping **b** [*bois, arbre*] setting of traps (**de** in); (*avec des explosifs*) [*colis, voiture*] setting of booby traps (**de** in)

piéger [pjeʒe] ◀ conjug 3 ▶ VT **a** [+ *animal, substance*] to trap; [+ *personne*] (*gén*) to trap; (*par une question*) to trick; **se faire ~ par un radar** to get caught in a radar trap; **il s'est laissé ~ par un journaliste** he got caught out by a journalist; **je me suis laissé ~ par son charme** I was completely taken in by his charm; **l'eau se retrouve piégée dans la roche** the water gets trapped in the rock; **la question était piégée** it was a trick question **b** [+ *bois, arbre*] to set a trap *ou* traps in; (*avec des explosifs*) [+ *engin, colis, voiture*] to booby-trap

pie-grièche (*pl* **pies-grièches**) [piɡʀijɛʃ] NF shrike, butcherbird

pie-mère (*pl* **pies-mères**) [pimɛʀ] NF pia mater

Piémont [pjemɔ̃] NM Piedmont

piémontais, e [pjemɔ̃tɛ, ɛz] **1** ADJ Piedmontese **2** NM (*Ling*) Piedmontese **3 Piémontais(e)** NM,F Piedmontese

piéride [pjeʀid] NF pierid, pieridine butterfly; **~ du chou** cabbage white (butterfly)

pierraille [pjeʀaj] NF [*route, sentier*] loose stones, chippings; [*pente, montagne*] scree (*NonC*), loose stones

Pierre [pjɛʀ] NM Peter; (*Hist*) **~ le Grand** Peter the Great

pierre [pjɛʀ] **1** NF **a** (*gén, Méd*) stone; **maison de** *ou* **en ~** stone(-built) house, house built of stone; **mur en ~s sèches** dry-stone wall; **attaquer qn à coups de ~s** to throw stones at sb; **il resta** *ou* **son visage resta de ~** he remained stony-faced; **jeter la première ~** to cast the first stone; **je ne veux pas lui jeter la ~** I don't want to be too hard on him → **âge, casseur** **b** (= *immobilier*) **la ~** bricks and mortar; **investir dans la ~** to invest in bricks and mortar **c** (*loc*) **faire d'une ~ deux coups** to kill two birds with one stone; **il s'est mis une ~ au cou** he's taken on a heavy burden ■ (*PROV*) **~ qui roule n'amasse pas mousse** a rolling stone gathers no moss (*PROV*); **c'est une ~ dans son jardin** it is a black mark against him; **jour à marquer d'une ~ blanche** red-letter day; **jour à marquer d'une ~ noire** black day; **bâtir qch à ~ à ~** to build sth up piece *ou* stone by stone; **ils n'ont pas laissé ~ sur ~** they didn't leave a stone standing; **apporter sa ~ à qch** to add one's contribution to sth; **aimer les vieilles ~s** to like old buildings **2** COMP ▶ **pierre à aiguiser** whetstone ▶ **pierre angulaire** (*lit, fig*) cornerstone ▶ **pierre à bâtir** building stone ▶ **pierre à briquet** flint ▶ **pierre à chaux** limestone ▶ **pierre à feu** flint ▶ **pierre fine** semi-precious stone ▶ **pierre funéraire** tombstone, gravestone ▶ **pierre à fusil** gunflint ▶ **pierre de lard** French chalk, tailor's chalk ▶ **pierre levée** standing stone ▶ **pierre de lune** moonstone ▶ **pierre ollaire** soapstone, steatite (*SPÉC*) ▶ **pierre philosophale** philosopher's stone ▶ **pierre ponce** pumice stone, pumice (*NonC*) ▶ **pierre précieuse** precious stone, gem ▶ **la pierre de Rosette** the Rosetta stone ▶ **pierre de taille** freestone ▶ **pierre tombale** tombstone, gravestone ▶ **pierre de touche** (*lit, fig*) touchstone

pierreries [pjɛʀʀi] NFPL gems, precious stones

pierreux, -euse [pjɛʀø, øz] ADJ [*terrain*] stony; [*fruit*] gritty; (*Méd*) calculous (*SPÉC*)

Pierrot [pjeʀo] NM (*Théât*) Pierrot

pierrot [pjeʀo] NM (= *oiseau*) sparrow

pietà [pjeta] NF pietà

piétaille [pjetaj] NF (*péj*) (*Mil*) rank and file; (= *subalternes*) rank and file, menials; (= *piétons*) foot-sloggers*, pedestrians

piété [pjete] NF (*Rel*) piety; (= *attachement*) devotion, reverence; **~ filiale** filial devotion *ou* respect; **articles/livre de ~** devotional articles/book; **images de ~** pious images

piétement [pjetmɑ̃] NM [*meuble*] base

piétinement [pjetinmɑ̃] NM **a** (= *stagnation*) **le ~ de la discussion** the fact that the discussion is not (*ou* was not) making (any) progress; **vu le ~ de l'enquête** given that the investigation is (*ou* was) at a virtual standstill **b** (= *marche sur place*) standing about; **ce fut moins un défilé qu'un gigantesque ~** it was more of a slow shuffle than a march **c** (= *bruit*) stamping

piétiner [pjetine] ◀ conjug 1 ▶ **1** VI **a** (= *trépigner*) to stamp (one's foot *ou* feet); **~ de colère/d'impatience** to stamp (one's feet) angrily/impatiently **b** (= *ne pas avancer*) [*personne*] to stand about; [*cortège*] to mark time; [*discussion*] to make no progress; [*affaire, enquête*] to be at a virtual standstill, be making no headway; [*économie, science*] to stagnate, be at a standstill; **~ dans la boue** to trudge through the mud **2** VT [+ *sol*] to trample on; [+ *victime*] (*fig*) [+ *adversaire*] to trample underfoot; [+ *parterres, fleurs*] to trample on, trample underfoot, tread on; **plusieurs personnes furent piétinées** several people were trampled on *ou* trampled underfoot; **~ les principes de qn** to trample sb's principles underfoot, ride roughshod over sb's principles → **plat¹**

piétisme [pjetism] NM pietism

piétiste [pjetist] **1** ADJ pietistic **2** NMF pietist

piéton¹ [pjetɔ̃] NM pedestrian

piéton², -onne [pjetɔ̃, ɔn], **piétonnier, -ière** [pjetɔnje, jɛʀ] ADJ pedestrian (*épith*); **rue piétonne** *ou* **piétonnière** (*gén*) pedestrianized street; (*commerciale*) pedestrian shopping street; **zone piétonne** *ou* **piétonnière** (*gén*) pedestrian precinct; (*commerciale*) shopping precinct

piètre [pjɛtʀ] ADJ (*frm*) [*adversaire, écrivain, roman*] very poor, mediocre; [*excuse*] paltry, lame; **c'est une ~ consolation** it's small *ou* little comfort; **dans un ~ état** in a very poor state; **faire ~ figure** to cut a sorry figure; **avoir ~ allure** to be a sorry *ou* wretched sight

piètrement [pjɛtʀəmɑ̃] ADV very poorly

pieu (*pl* **pieux**) [pjø] NM **a** (= *poteau*) post; (*pointu*) stake, pale; (*Constr*) pile **b** (‡ = *lit*) bed; **se mettre au ~** to hit the hay* *ou* sack*, turn in*

pieusement [pjøzmɑ̃] ADV (*Rel*) piously; (= *respectueusement*) reverently; (*hum*) **un vieux tricot qu'il avait ~ conservé** an old sweater which he had lovingly kept

pieuter‡ [pjøte] ◀ conjug 1 ▶ **1** VI (*aller*) **~ chez qn** to crash *ou* kip (*Brit*) at sb's place‡ **2 se pieuter** VPR to hit the hay* *ou* sack*, turn in*

pieuvre [pjœvʀ] NF **a** (= *animal*) octopus; **cette entreprise est une ~** this is a very tentacular company; **cette ville est une ~** this is a huge, sprawling city **b** (= *sandow*) spider

pieux, pieuse [pjø, pjøz] ADJ [*personne*] (= *religieux*) pious, devout; (= *dévoué*) devoted, dutiful; [*pensée, souvenir, lecture, image*] pious; [*silence*] reverent, respectful; **~ mensonge** white lie (*told out of pity etc*)

piézoélectricité [pjezoelɛktʀisite] NF piezoelectricity

piézoélectrique [pjezoelɛktʀik] ADJ piezoelectric

piézomètre [pjezɔmɛtʀ] NM piezometer

pif¹‡ [pif] NM (= *nez*) nose, conk‡ (*Brit*), schnozzle‡ (*US*); **au ~** (= *approximativement*) at a rough guess; (= *au hasard*) [*répondre, choisir*] at random; [+ *plan, exercice, recette*] **faire qch au ~** to do sth by guesswork; **j'ai failli y aller, j'ai eu du ~** I nearly went but I had a funny feeling about it; **je l'ai dans le ~** I can't stand *ou* stick* (*Brit*) him

pif² [pif] EXCL **~! paf!** (*explosion*) bang! bang!; (*gifle*) smack! smack!, slap! slap!

pif(f)er [pife] ◀ conjug 1 ▶ VT **je ne peux pas le ~** I can't stand *ou* stick* (*Brit*) him

pifomètre‡ [pifɔmɛtʀ] NM intuition, instinct; **au ~** at a rough guess; **faire qch au ~** to do sth by guesswork; **j'y suis allé au ~** I followed my nose*

pifrer‡ [pifʀe] ◀ conjug 1 ▶ VT = **pif(f)er**

pige [piʒ] NF **a** (‡ = *année*) **il a 50 ~s** he's 50; **à 60 ~s** at 60 **b** (*Presse, Typo*) **être payé à la ~** [*typographe*] to be paid at piecework rates; [*journaliste*] to be paid by the line; [*artiste*] to be paid per commission; **faire des ~s pour un journal** to do freelance work for a newspaper **c** (‡ = *surpasser*) **faire la ~ à qn** to leave sb standing*, put sb in the shade

pigeon [piʒɔ̃] **1** NM (= *oiseau*) pigeon; (* = *dupe*) mug‡, sucker* **2** COMP ▶ **pigeon d'argile** clay pigeon ▶ **pigeon ramier** woodpigeon, ring dove ▶ **pigeon vole** (= *jeu*) game of forfeits; ≈ Simon says ▶ **pigeon voyageur** carrier *ou* homing pigeon; **par ~ voyageur** by pigeon post

pigeonnant, e [piʒɔnɑ̃, ɑ̃t] ADJ **soutien-gorge ~** uplift bra; **avoir une poitrine ~e** to have a lot of cleavage

pigeonne [piʒɔn] NF hen-pigeon

pigeonneau (*pl* **pigeonneaux**) [piʒɔno] NM young pigeon, squab

pigeonner‡ [piʒɔne] ◀ conjug 1 ▶ VT **~ qn** to do sb‡, take sb for a ride‡; **se laisser** *ou* **se faire ~** to be done‡, be taken for a ride‡, be had*

pigeonnier [piʒɔnje] NM pigeon house *ou* loft; (* = *logement*) garret, attic room

piger‡ [piʒe] ◀ conjug 3 ▶ VI (= *comprendre*) to get it*; **il a pigé** he's got it*, he's twigged* (*Brit*), the penny has dropped* (*Brit*); **tu piges?** (do you) get it?*; **je ne pige rien à la chimie** chemistry's all Greek* *ou* double Dutch* (*Brit*) to me; **je n'y pige rien** I just don't get it (at all)*, I can't make head (n)or tail of it; **tu y piges quelque chose, toi?** can you make anything of it?

pigiste [piʒist] NMF (= *typographe*) (piecework) typesetter; (= *journaliste*) freelance journalist (*paid by the line*); (= *artiste*) freelance artist

pigment [pigmɑ̃] NM pigment

pigmentaire [pigmɑ̃tɛʀ] ADJ pigmentary, pigmental

pigmentation [pigmɑ̃tasjɔ̃] NF pigmentation

pigmenter [pigmɑ̃te] ◀ conjug 1 ▶ VT to pigment

pigne [piɲ] NF (= *pomme de pin*) pine cone; (= *graine*) pine kernel *ou* nut

pignocher [piɲɔʃe] ◀ conjug 1 ▶ VI to pick *ou* nibble at one's food

pignon [piɲɔ̃] NM **a** (*Archit*) gable; **à ~** gabled; (*fig*) **avoir ~ sur rue** to be well-established **b** (= *roue dentée*) cog(wheel), gearwheel; (*petite roue*) pinion **c** (*Bot*) **~ (de pin)** pine kernel *ou* nut

pignouf‡ [piɲuf] NM peasant*, boor

pilaf [pilaf] NM pilaf(f), pilau; **riz ~** pilau rice

pilage [pilaʒ] NM crushing, pounding

pilastre [pilastʀ] NM pilaster

Pilate [pilat] NM Pilate

pilchard [pilʃaʀ] NM pilchard

pile [pil] **1** NF **a** (= *tas*) pile, stack; (*Ordin*) stack **b** [*pont*] support, pile, pier **c** (*Élec*) battery; **à ~(s)** battery (*épith*), battery-operated; **~ sèche** dry cell *ou* battery; **~ bâton** pencil battery; **~ rechargeable** rechargeable battery; **~ plate/ronde** flat/round battery; **~ bouton** watch battery; **~ atomique** nuclear reactor, (atomic) pile; **~ solaire** solar cell; **appareil à ~s** *ou* **fonctionnant sur ~s** battery-operated *ou* battery-driven appliance ⓓ ✦ (*coups*) belting, thrashing; (= *défaite*) hammering*, thrashing*; **donner une ~ à qn** (*rosser*) to give sb a belting *ou* thrashing, lay into sb*; (*vaincre*) to lick sb*, beat sb hollow* (*Brit*); **prendre** *ou* **recevoir une ~** (*coups*) to get a belting; (*défaite*) to be licked*, be beaten hollow* (*Brit*)

ⓔ [*pièce*] pile ✦ **c'est tombé sur (le côté) ~** it came down tails; **~ ou face?** heads or tails?; **~ c'est moi, face c'est toi** tails it's me, heads it's you; **sur le côté ~ il y a ...** on the reverse side there's ...; **on va jouer** *ou* **tirer ça à ~ ou face** we'll toss (up) for it; **tirer à ~ ou face pour savoir si ...** to toss up to find out if ...

ⓕ (*Hér*) pile

② ADV (* = *net*) **s'arrêter ~** to stop dead*; **ça l'a arrêté ~** it stopped him dead* *ou* in his tracks, it brought him up short*; [*personne*] **vous êtes tombé ~ en m'offrant ce cadeau** you've chosen exactly the right present for me; **j'ai ouvert l'annuaire et je suis tombé ~ sur le numéro** I opened the directory and came up with the number right *ou* straight (*Brit*) away; [*chose*] **il lâcha sa gomme qui tomba ~ dans la corbeille à papier** he let go of his eraser and it fell right *ou* straight into the wastepaper basket; **ça tombe ~!** that's just *ou* exactly what I (*ou we etc*) need(ed)!; **on est six et il y en a douze — ça tombe ~** there are six of us and twelve of them — that works out exactly *ou* evenly; **son mariage tombe ~ le jour de son anniversaire** her wedding is on the same day as her birthday; (*survenir*) **tomber** *ou* **arriver ~** [*personne*] to turn up* just at the right moment *ou* time; [*chose*] to come just at the right moment *ou* time; **à 2 heures ~** (at) dead on 2*, at dead on the dot*; **il est 11 heures ~** it's dead on 11*, it's 11 o'clock exactly

piler [pile] ▶ conjug 1 ◀ ① VT ⓐ (*lit*) to crush, pound ⓑ **~ qn** * (= *rosser*) to lay into sb*, give sb a hammering* *ou* belting*; (= *vaincre*) to lick sb*, beat sb hollow* (*Brit*) ② VI (* = *freiner*) to jam on the brakes

pileux, -euse [pilø, øz] ADJ [*follicule*] hair (*épith*) → **système**

pilier [pilje] NM ⓐ (*Anat, Constr*) pillar; [*dispositif, institution, politique*] mainstay, linchpin; (= *personne*) [*organisation, parti*] mainstay; **la famille, ~ de la société** the family, the bedrock of society; **c'est un ~ de bar** *ou* **de bistro** he spends his life propping up the bar, he's a barfly* (*US*) ⓑ (*Rugby*) prop (forward)

pillage [pijaʒ] NM ⓐ [*ville*] pillage, plundering; [*magasin, maison*] looting; [*église, tombe*] looting, plundering; (*Zool*) [*ruche*] robbing; **mettre au ~** to pillage, plunder, loot; **le ~ des caisses de l'État** plundering the state coffers ⓑ (= *plagiat*) [*ouvrage, auteur*] plagiarism

pillard, e [pijar, ard] ① ADJ [*soldats, bande*] pillaging (*épith*), looting (*épith*); [*oiseau*] thieving (*épith*) ② NM,F pillager, plunderer, looter

piller [pije] ▶ conjug 1 ◀ VT ⓐ [+ *ville*] to pillage, plunder; [+ *magasin, maison*] to loot; [+ *église, tombe*] to loot, plunder; [+ *verger*] to raid; **~ les caisses de l'État/les richesses minières d'un pays** to plunder the state coffers/the mineral resources of a country ⓑ (= *plagier*) [+ *ouvrage, auteur*] to plagiarize, borrow wholesale from

pilleur, -euse [pijœr, øz] NM,F pillager, plunderer, looter; († = *plagiaire*) literary pirate, plagiarist; **~ d'épaves** looter (*of wrecked ships*); **~ de tombes** tomb robber

pilon [pilɔ̃] NM (= *instrument*) pestle; (= *jambe*) wooden leg; [*poulet*] drumstick; (*Typo*) **mettre un livre au ~** to pulp a book

pilonnage [pilɔnaʒ] NM ⓐ (*Mil*) shelling, bombardment; **il y a eu des ~s intensifs** there has been intense *ou* heavy shelling ⓑ (*Typo*) pulping ⓒ (*Culin, Pharm*) pounding, crushing

pilonner [pilɔne] ▶ conjug 1 ◀ VT ⓐ (*Mil*) to shell, bombard; **l'artillerie a pilonné la capitale** artillery pounded the capital ⓑ (*Typo*) to pulp ⓒ (*Culin, Pharm*) to pound, crush

pilori [pilɔri] NM pillory, stocks; **mettre** *ou* **clouer au ~** (*lit*) to put in the stocks; (*fig*) to pillory; **être condamné au ~** to be put in the stocks

pilosité [pilozite] NF pilosity; **avoir une ~ très développée** to be very hairy

pilotage [pilɔtaʒ] NM ⓐ (*Aviat*) piloting, flying; (*Naut*) piloting; **école de ~** (*Aviat*) flying school; (*Aut*) driving school (*specializing in advanced driving skills*); **~ automatique** automatic piloting; **l'accident a été attribué à une erreur de ~** the accident was put down to pilot error → **poste** ⓑ [*entreprise, économie, projet*] running, management → **comité**

pilote [pilɔt] ① NM ⓐ (*Aviat, Naut*) pilot; (*Aut*) driver; (= *guide*) guide; **servir de ~ à qn** to show sb round, be sb's guide ⓑ (*Ordin*) driver ⓒ (= *poisson*) pilotfish ⓓ (*en apposition* = *expérimental*) [*école, ferme*] experimental; [*projet, entreprise, usine*] pilot (*épith*); (*Comm*) [*produit*] low-priced ② COMP ▶ **pilote automatique** automatic pilot, autopilot; **être/passer en ~ automatique** to be on/switch to automatic pilot *ou* autopilot ▶ **pilote automobile** racing driver ▶ **pilote de chasse** fighter pilot ▶ **pilote de course** = **pilote automobile** ▶ **pilote d'essai** test pilot ▶ **pilote de guerre** fighter pilot ▶ **pilote de ligne** airline pilot

piloter [pilɔte] ▶ conjug 1 ◀ VT [+ *avion*] to pilot, fly; [+ *navire*] to pilot; [+ *voiture*] to drive; [+ *entreprise, projet*] to run, manage; (*fig*) **~ qn** to show sb round

pilotis [pilɔti] NM pile, pilotis (*SPÉC*); **sur ~** on piles

pilou [pilu] NM flannelette

pilule [pilyl] NF ⓐ (*Pharm*) pill; **prendre la ~** ◊ **être sous ~*** (= *contraceptive*) to be on *ou* be taking the pill; **~ abortive/du lendemain** abortion/morning-after pill; (*fig*) **il a eu du mal à avaler la ~** ◊ **il a trouvé la ~ un peu amère** *ou* **un peu dure à avaler** he found it a bitter pill to swallow, he found it hard to take; **faire qch pour faire passer la ~** to do sth to sweeten *ou* sugar the pill → **dorer** ⓑ (* = *défaite*) thrashing*, hammering*; **on a pris la ~** we were thrashed* *ou* hammered*

pimbêche [pɛ̃bɛʃ] ① ADJ F stuck-up*, full of herself (*attrib*) ② NF stuck-up thing*; **c'est une horrible ~** she's so full of herself, she's horribly stuck-up*

pimbina [pɛ̃bina] NM (*Can*) pembina (*Can*) (*type of cranberry*)

piment [pimã] NM ⓐ (= *plante*) pepper, capsicum; (*Culin*) **~ rouge** chilli; **~ doux** (= *fruit*) pepper, capsicum; (= *poudre*) paprika; **~ vert** green chilli ⓑ (*fig*) spice, piquancy; **avoir du ~** to be spicy *ou* piquant; **donner du ~ à une situation** to add *ou* give spice to a situation; **ça donne du ~ à la vie** it adds a bit of spice to life, it makes life more exciting; **trouver du ~ à qch** to find sth spicy *ou* piquant

pimenté, e [pimãte] (*ptp de* **pimenter**) ADJ [*plat*] hot, spicy; (*fig*) [*récit*] spicy

pimenter [pimãte] ▶ conjug 1 ◀ VT (*Culin*) to put chilli in; (*fig*) to add *ou* give spice to

pimpant, e [pɛ̃pã, ãt] ADJ [*robe, personne*] spruce

pimprenelle [pɛ̃prənɛl] NF (*à fleurs verdâtres*) (salad) burnet; (*à fleurs rouges*) great burnet

pin [pɛ̃] NM (= *arbre*) pine (tree); (= *bois*) pine(wood); **~ maritime/parasol** *ou* **pignon** maritime/umbrella pine; **~ d'Oregon** Oregon

pine; **~ sylvestre** Scotch fir, Scots pine → **aiguille, pomme**

pinacle [pinakl] NM (*Archit*) pinnacle; (*fig*) **être au ~** to be at the top; (*fig*) **porter** *ou* **mettre qn au ~** to praise sb to the skies

pinacothèque [pinakɔtɛk] NF art gallery

pinaillage* [pinajaʒ] NM hair-splitting, quibbling

pinailler* [pinaje] ▶ conjug 1 ◀ VI to quibble, split hairs; **il pinaille sur tout** he's forever splitting hairs

pinailleur, -euse* [pinajœr, øz] ① ADJ pernickety, nitpicking* (*épith*), hair-splitting (*épith*) ② NM,F nitpicker*, quibbler

pinard* [pinar] NM (*gén*) wine; (*péj*) cheap wine, plonk* (*Brit*)

pinardier* [pinardje] NM wine tanker

pince [pɛ̃s] ① NF ⓐ (= *outil*) **~(s)** (*gén*) pair of pliers, pliers; (*à charbon*) pair of tongs, tongs ⓑ (= *levier*) crowbar ⓒ (*Zool*) [*crabe, homard*] pincer, claw ⓓ (*Couture*) dart; **faire des ~s à** to put darts in; **~ de poitrine** bust darts; **pantalon à ~s** front-pleated trousers ⓔ (* = *main*) hand, mitt*, paw*; **je lui ai serré la ~*** I shook hands with him ⓕ (* = *jambe*) leg; **aller à ~s** to foot* *ou* hoof* it; **j'ai fait 15 km à ~s** I footed it for 15 km* ② COMP ▶ **pince à billets** note (*Brit*) *ou* bill (*US*) clip ▶ **pince à cheveux** hair clip ▶ **pince coupante** wire cutters ▶ **pince crocodile** crocodile clip ▶ **pince de cycliste** bicycle clip ▶ **pince à dénuder** wire strippers, wire stripping pliers ▶ **pince à épiler** (eyebrow) tweezers ▶ **pince à escargots** special tongs used for eating snails ▶ **pince à glace** ice tongs ▶ **pince à linge** clothes peg (*Brit*), clothespin (*US, Scot*) ▶ **pince multiprise** = **pince crocodile** ▶ **pince à ongles** nail clippers ▶ **pince plate** flat-nose pliers ▶ **pince à sucre** sugar tongs ▶ **pince universelle** (universal) pliers ▶ **pince à vélo** bicycle clip

pincé, e¹ [pɛ̃se] (*ptp de* **pincer**) ADJ [*personne, air*] stiff, starchy; [*sourire*] stiff, tight-lipped; [*ton*] stiff; **d'un air ~** stiffly; **les lèvres ~es** with pursed lips; **aux lèvres ~es** thin-lipped; (*Mus*) **instrument à cordes ~es** plucked stringed instrument

pinceau (*pl* **pinceaux**) [pɛ̃so] NM (*gén*) brush; (*Peinture*) (paint)brush; (= *manière de peindre*) brushwork; (* = *pied*) foot; **~ à colle** paste brush; **~ lumineux** pencil of light; **coup de ~** brushstroke, stroke of the brush; **donner un coup de ~ à un mur** to give a wall a lick of paint; **avoir un bon coup de ~** to paint well, be a good painter

pincée² [pɛ̃se] NF [*sel, poivre*] pinch

pince-fesses*‡ [pɛ̃sfɛs] NM INV dance, hop*

pincement [pɛ̃smã] NM (*Mus*) plucking; (*Agr*) pinching out; (*Aut*) **~ des roues** toe-in; **elle a eu un ~ de cœur** she felt a twinge of sorrow

pince-monseigneur (*pl* **pinces-monseigneur**) [pɛ̃smɔ̃seɲœr] NF jemmy (*Brit*), crowbar

pince-nez [pɛ̃sne] NM INV pince-nez

pince-oreille (*pl* **pince-oreilles**) [pɛ̃sɔrɛj] NM earwig

pincer [pɛ̃se] ▶ conjug 3 ◀ ① VT ⓐ (*accidentellement, pour faire mal*) to pinch; [*froid*] to nip; **je me suis pincé dans la porte/avec l'ouvre-boîte** I caught myself in the door/with the can opener; **se (faire) ~ le doigt** to catch one's finger; **se (faire) ~ le doigt dans une porte** to trap one's finger in a door; **il s'est fait ~ par un crabe** he was nipped by a crab; **pince-moi, je rêve!** pinch me, I'm dreaming! ⓑ (= *tenir, serrer*) to grip; **~ les lèvres** to purse (up) one's lips; **se ~ le nez** to hold one's nose; **une robe qui pince la taille** a dress which is tight at the waist ⓒ (*Mus*) to pluck ⓓ (*Couture*) [+ *veste*] to put darts in [e] (* = *arrêter, prendre*) to catch, cop*; [*police*] to cop*, catch, nick* (*Brit*); **se faire ~** to get caught [f] (*Agr*) to pinch out, nip out [g] **en ~ pour qn** to be stuck on sb*, be mad about sb*; **il est pincé** he's hooked*

  [2] VI **ça pince (dur)** it's freezing (cold), it's bitterly cold

pince-sans-rire [pɛ̃ssɑ̃RiR] [1] ADJ INV deadpan [2] NMF INV **c'est un ~** he's got a deadpan sense of humour

pincette [pɛ̃sɛt] NF (*gén pl*) (*pour le feu*) pair of (fire) tongs, (fire) tongs; [*horloger*] pair of tweezers, tweezers; **il n'est pas à toucher** *ou* **prendre avec des ~s** (*sale*) he's filthy dirty; (*mécontent*) he's like a bear with a sore head

pinçon [pɛ̃sɔ̃] NM pinch-mark

Pindare [pɛ̃daR] NM Pindar

pindarique [pɛ̃daRik] ADJ Pindaric

pine [pin] NF cock**, prick**

pinéal, e (*mpl* **-aux**) [pineal, o] ADJ pineal; **glande ~e** pineal gland *ou* body

pinède [pinɛd], **pineraie** [pinRɛ] NF pinewood, pine forest

pingouin [pɛ̃gwɛ̃] NM auk; (= *manchot*) penguin; (*petit*) ~ razorbill; (*hum*) **habillé en ~*** in tails; (= *individu*) **qui c'est ce ~ ?*** who's that guy?* *ou* bloke* (*Brit*)?

ping-pong [piŋpɔ̃g] NM INV table tennis, Ping-Pong®

pingre [pɛ̃gR] (*péj*) [1] ADJ stingy, niggardly [2] NMF skinflint, niggard

pingrerie [pɛ̃gRəRi] NF (*péj*) stinginess, niggardliness

Pinocchio [pinɔkjo] NM Pinocchio

pin-pon [pɛ̃pɔ̃] EXCL *sound made by two-tone siren*

pin's [pins] NM INV lapel badge, pin

pinson [pɛ̃sɔ̃] NM chaffinch; **~ du nord** brambling → **gai**

pintade [pɛ̃tad] NF guinea-fowl

pintadeau (*pl* **pintadeaux**) [pɛ̃tado] NM young guinea-fowl, guinea-poult (*SPÉC*)

pinte [pɛ̃t] NF [a] (= *ancienne mesure*) ≈ quart (0.93 *litre*); (= *mesure anglo-saxonne*) pint; (*Can*) quart (1.136 *litre*) → **payer** [b] (*Helv* = *débit de boissons*) bar

pinté, e [pɛ̃te] (*ptp de* **pinter**) ADJ smashed*, plastered*

pinter [pɛ̃te] VI, **se pinter** VPR ▶ conjug 1 ◀ to booze*, liquor up* (*US*); **on s'est pintés au whisky** we got smashed* *ou* plastered* on whisky

pin up [pinœp] NF INV (= *personne*) sexy(-looking) girl; (= *photo*) pinup

pioche [pjɔʃ] NF [a] (*à deux pointes*) pick, pickaxe, pickax (*US*); (*à pointe et à houe*) mattock, pickaxe, pickax (*US*) → **tête** [b] (= *tas de dominos, cartes*) stock, pile

piocher [pjɔʃe] ▶ conjug 1 ◀ [1] VT [+ *terre*] to pickaxe, pickax (*US*); (* = *étudier*) to swot up* (*Brit*), slave *ou* slog (*Brit*) away at*; [+ *examen*] to cram *ou* swot* (*Brit*) for; (*Jeux*) [+ *carte, domino*] to take (from the stock *ou* pile); [+ *numéro*] to take [2] VI (= *creuser*) to dig (with a pick); (*: Jeux*) to pick up *ou* take a card (*ou* domino) (from the stock *ou* pile); **~ dans le tas** (*nourriture*) to dig in; (*objets*) to dig into the pile; **~ dans ses économies** to dip into one's savings

piocheur, -euse* [pjɔʃœR, øz] [1] ADJ hard-working [2] NM,F swot* (*Brit*), grind* (*US*)

piolet [pjɔlɛ] NM ice axe

pion[1] [pjɔ̃] NM (*Échecs*) pawn; (*Dames*) piece, draught (*Brit*), checker (*US*); **n'être qu'un ~ (sur l'échiquier)** to be just a pawn *ou* be nothing but a pawn (in the game) → **damer**

pion[2], pionne [pjɔ̃, pjɔn] NM,F (*arg Scol* = *surveillant*) supervisor (*student paid to supervise schoolchildren*)

---

pioncer* [pjɔ̃se] ▶ conjug 3 ◀ VI to sleep, get some shut-eye*; **j'ai pas pioncé de la nuit** I didn't get a wink of sleep (all night); **il a pioncé deux heures** he got two hours' sleep *ou* kip* (*Brit*)

pionnier, -ière [pjɔnje, jɛR] NM,F (*lit, fig*) pioneer

pioupiou* † [pjupju] NM young soldier, tommy* † (*Brit*)

pipe [pip] NF [a] (*à fumer*) (= *contenant*) pipe; (= *contenu*) pipeful, pipe; **fumer la ~** (*gén*) to smoke a pipe; (*habituellement*) to be a pipe-smoker; **~ de bruyère/de terre** briar/clay pipe → **casser, fendre, tête** [b] (* = *cigarette*) cig *, fag* (*Brit*) [c] (= *futaille*) pipe [d] (** = *acte sexuel*) blow job**; **tailler une ~ à qn** to give sb a blow job**

pipeau (*pl* **pipeaux**) [pipo] NM (*Mus*) (reed-)pipe; [*oiseleur*] bird call; (*gluaux*) **~x** limed twigs; **c'est du ~*** that's a load of rubbish*

pipelet* [piplɛ] NM (*péj*) chatterbox

pipeline [piplin] NM pipeline; (*Ordin*) **traitement en ~** pipelining

piper [pipe] ▶ conjug 1 ◀ VT [+ *cartes*] to mark; [+ *dés*] to load; (*fig*) **les dés sont pipés** the dice are loaded; **ne pas ~ (mot)*** not to breathe a word, keep mum*

piperade [piperad] NF piperade (*kind of omelette with tomatoes and peppers*)

pipette [pipɛt] NF pipette

pipi* [pipi] NM pee*, wee*, wee-wee (*langage enfantin*); **faire ~** to have a pee* *ou* a wee*, have a wee-wee (*langage enfantin*); **faire ~ au lit** to wet the bed; **le chien a fait ~ sur le tapis** the dog has made a puddle* on *ou* has done a wee* on the carpet; **c'est du ~ de chat** [*boisson*] it's dishwater*, it's like cat's piss**; [*livre, film, théorie*] it's pathetic*, it's a waste of time → **dame**

pipi-room* (*pl* **pipi-rooms**) [pipiRum] NM loo* (*Brit*), bathroom (*US*); **aller au ~** to go and spend a penny* (*Brit*), go to the bathroom (*US*)

pipit [pipit] NM pipit; **~ des arbres** tree pipit

piquage [pikaʒ] NM (*Couture*) sewing up, stitching, machining

piquant, e [pikɑ̃, ɑ̃t] [1] ADJ [a] [*barbe*] prickly; (*Bot*) [*tige*] thorny, prickly [b] [*goût, radis, sauce, moutarde*] hot; [*odeur*] pungent; [*fromage*] sharp; [*vin*] sour, tart; **eau ~e** fizzy water; (*Culin*) **sauce ~e** sauce piquante, piquant sauce [c] [*air, froid*] biting [d] [*détail*] (= *paradoxal*) surprising; (= *grivois*) spicy; [*description, style*] racy, piquant; [*conversation, charme, beauté*] piquant [e] (= *mordant*) [*mot, réplique*] biting, cutting [2] NM [a] [*hérisson, oursin*] spine; [*porc-épic*] quill; [*rosier*] thorn, prickle; [*chardon*] prickle; [*barbelé*] barb [b] [*style, description*] raciness; [*conversation*] piquancy; [*aventure*] spice; **~ de l'histoire, c'est que ... ◊ et, détail qui ne manque pas de ~, ...** the most entertaining thing (about it) is that ...

pique [pik] [1] NF (= *arme*) pike; [*picador*] lance; (= *parole blessante*) dig, cutting remark; **il n'a pas arrêté de me lancer des ~s** he kept making cutting remarks [2] NM (= *carte*) spade; (= *couleur*) spades; **le trois de ~** the three of spades

piqué, e [pike] (*ptp de* **piquer**) [1] ADJ [a] (*Couture* = *cousu*) (machine-)stitched; [*couvre-lit*] quilted [b] (= *marqué*) [*linge*] mildewed, mildewy; [*miroir*] speckled; [*livre*] foxed; [*meuble*] worm-eaten; (= *aigre*) [*vin*] sour; **visage ~ de taches de rousseur** freckled face; **~ de rouille** [*métal*] pitted with rust; [*linge*] covered in rust spots; **~ par l'acide** pitted with acid marks; **pas ~ des hannetons*** *ou* **des vers*** brilliant*, great*; (= *excentrique*) wild*; **son article n'est pas ~ des hannetons*** *ou* **des vers*** his article is spot on*; **ce problème n'était pas ~ des hannetons !*** *ou* **des vers !*** it was a tough problem!* [c] (* = *fou*) nuts*, barmy*

---

[d] (*Mus*) [*note*] staccato [2] NM [a] (*Aviat*) dive; **attaque en ~** (*bombardement*) dive bombing run; (*à la mi-trailleuse*) strafing run; **bombardement en ~** dive bombing run; **faire un ~** to (go into a) dive [b] (= *tissu*) piqué

pique-assiette* (*pl* **pique-assiettes**) [pikasjɛt] NMF scrounger*, sponger* (*for a free meal*)

pique-feu (*pl* **pique-feu(x)**) [pikfø] NM poker

pique-fleurs [pikflœR] NM INV flower-holder

pique-nique (*pl* **pique-niques**) [piknik] NM picnic; **faire un ~** to picnic, have a picnic; **demain nous allons faire un ~** tomorrow we're going for *ou* on a picnic

pique-niquer [piknike] ▶ conjug 1 ◀ VI to have a picnic, picnic

pique-niqueur, -euse (*mpl* **pique-niqueurs**) [piknikœR, øz] NM,F picnicker

piquer [pike] ▶ conjug 1 ◀ [1] VT [a] [*guêpe*] to sting; [*moustique, serpent*] to bite; (*avec une épingle, une pointe*) to prick; (*Méd*) to give an injection to, give a shot* *ou* jab* (*Brit*) to; **se faire ~ contre la variole** to have a smallpox injection *ou* shot* *ou* jab* (*Brit*); **faire ~ qn contre qch** to have sb vaccinated *ou* inoculated against sth; (*euph*) **faire ~ un chat/chien** to have a cat/dog put down *ou* put to sleep; **se ~ le doigt** to prick one's finger; **les ronces, ça pique** brambles are prickly → **mouche** [b] [+ *aiguille, fourche, fléchette*] to stick, stab, jab (*dans* into); **rôti piqué d'ail** joint stuck with cloves of garlic; **piqué de lardons** larded; **~ la viande avec une fourchette** to prick the meat with a fork; **~ des petits pois avec une fourchette** to stab peas with a fork; **~ qch au mur** to put *ou* stick sth up on the wall; **~ une fleur sur un corsage** to pin a flower on(to) a blouse; **~ une fleur dans ses cheveux** to stick a flower in one's hair; **des papillons piqués sur une planche** butterflies pinned on a board; **~ (une frite/un haricot) dans le plat*** to help o.s. (to a chip/a bean or two); **~ au hasard*** *ou* **dans le tas*** to choose *ou* pick at random [c] (*Couture*) **~ qch (à la machine)** to machine sth, (*machine*) stitch sth, sew sth up; **ta mère sait-elle ~ ?** can your mother use a sewing machine? [d] [*barbe*] to prick, prickle; [*ortie*] to sting; **tissu qui pique (la peau)** prickly material, material that prickles the skin; **liqueur qui pique la gorge** liqueur which burns the throat; **la fumée me pique les yeux** the smoke is stinging my eyes *ou* is making my eyes sting *ou* smart; **le froid/le vent nous piquait le** *ou* **au visage** the cold/the wind stung our faces; [*démangeaison*] **ça (me) pique** it's itching *ou* itchy, it's making me itch; **les yeux me piquent ◊ j'ai les yeux qui piquent** my eyes are smarting *ou* stinging; **ma gorge me pique** my throat's burning; **tu piques avec ta barbe** you're all prickly with that beard of yours, your beard's prickly; **attention, ça pique** [*alcool sur une plaie*] careful, it's going to sting; [*liquide dans la bouche*] careful, it burns your throat → **frotter** [e] (= *exciter*) [+ *bœufs*] to goad; [+ *curiosité*] to arouse, excite; [+ *intérêt*] to arouse, provoke; († = *vexer*) [+ *personne*] to pique, nettle; [+ *amour-propre*] to pique, hurt; **~ qn au vif** to cut sb to the quick [f] (* = *faire brusquement*) **~ un cent mètres** *ou* **un sprint** to (put on a) sprint, put on a burst of speed; **~ un roupillon*** *ou* **un somme** to have forty winks* *ou* a nap, get a bit of shut-eye*; **~ un galop** to break into a gallop; **~ une** *ou* **sa crise** to throw a fit; **~ une crise de larmes** to have a crying fit; **~ une colère** to fly into a rage, have a fit*; **~ un fard** to go (bright) red; **~ une suée** to break out in a sweat; **~ un plongeon** to dive; **~ une tête dans une piscine** to dive (headfirst) into a pool [g] (* = *attraper*) [+ *manie, maladie*] to pick up, catch, get

h (* = *voler*) [+ *portefeuille*] to pinch*, swipe*, nick* (*Brit*); [+ *idée*] to pinch*, steal (**à qn** from sb)

i (* = *arrêter*) [+ *voleur*] to cop*, nab*, nick* (*Brit*)

j (*Mus*) **~ les notes** to play staccato

2 VI **a** [*avion*] to go into a dive; [*oiseau*] to swoop down; **le cavalier piqua droit sur nous** the horseman came straight at us; **il faudrait ~ vers le village** we'll head towards the village; **~ du nez** [*avion*] to go into a nose-dive; [*bateau*] to dip its head; [*fleurs*] to droop; [*personne*] to fall headfirst; **~ du nez dans son sommeil** (*de sommeil*) to nod off* ou doze off* (*during a meal*); (*de honte*) to hang one's head in shame; **~ des deux** to go full tilt

b [*moutarde, radis*] to be hot; [*vin*] to be sour, have a sour taste; [*fromage*] to be sharp; **eau qui pique** fizzy water

3 se piquer VPR **a** (= *se blesser*) (*avec une aiguille*) to prick o.s.; (*dans les orties*) to get stung, sting o.s.

b [*morphinomane*] to shoot up; [*diabétique*] to give o.s. an injection, inject o.s.; **il se pique à l'héroïne** he uses heroin

c [*bois, linge*] to go mildewed ou mildewy; [*livre*] to become foxed; [*miroir*] to become speckled; [*métal*] to be pitted; [*vin, cidre*] to go ou turn sour

d (= *prétendre connaître ou pouvoir*) **se ~ de littérature/psychologie** to like to think one knows a lot about literature/psychology, pride o.s. on one's knowledge of literature/psychology; **se ~ de faire qch** to pride o.s. on one's ability to do sth

e (= *se vexer*) to take offence; **il s'est piqué au jeu** he became quite taken with it

piquet [pikɛ] NM **a** (= *pieu*) post, stake, picket; [*tente*] peg; (*Ski*) (marker) pole → **raide b** (*Ind*) **~ (de grève)** (strike-)picket, picket line; **organiser un ~ de grève** to organize a picket line; **il y a un ~ de grève à l'usine** there's a picket line at the factory; (*Mil*) **~ d'incendie** fire-fighting squad **c** (*Scol*) **mettre qn au ~** to make sb stand ou put sb in the corner **d** (*Cartes*) piquet

piquetage [pik(ə)taʒ] NM staking (out)

piqueter [pik(ə)te] ▶ conjug 4 ◀ VT **a** [+ *allée*] to stake out, put stakes along **b** (= *moucheter*) to dot (**de** with); **ciel piqueté d'étoiles** star-studded ou star-spangled sky, sky studded with stars

piquette [pikɛt] NF **a** (= *cru local*) local wine; (= *mauvais vin*) cheap wine, plonk* (*Brit*) **b** (* = *défaite*) hammering*, thrashing*; **prendre une ~** to be hammered* ou thrashed*

piqueur, -euse [pikœʀ, øz] **1** ADJ [*insecte*] stinging (*épith*) **2** NM **a** [*écurie*] groom; (*Chasse*) whip **b** (= *mineur*) hewer **c** (* = *surveillant*) foreman **d** (* = *voleur*) thief **3** NM,F (*Couture*) machinist

piquier [pikje] NM pikeman

piquouse* [pikuz] NF shot*, jab*; **il m'a fait une ~** he gave me a jab* ou an injection

piqûre [pikyʀ] NF **a** [*insecte, moustique*] bite; [*guêpe, ortie*] sting; **~ d'épingle** pinprick; (= *plaie*) **la ~ faite par l'aiguille** the hole made by the needle **b** (*Méd*) injection, shot*, jab* (*Brit*); **faire une ~ à qn** to give sb an injection ou a shot* ou a jab* (*Brit*); **se faire faire une ~** to have an injection ou a shot* ou a jab* (*Brit*); **~ de rappel** booster injection ou shot*, booster (*Brit*) **c** [*petit trou*] hole; [*moisi, rouille*] speck, spot; **~ de ver** wormhole **d** (*Couture*) (= *point*) stitch; (= *rang*) stitching (*NonC*); **rang de ~s** row ou line of stitches ou stitching; **jupe à ~s apparentes** skirt with overstitched seams

piranha [piʀana] NM piranha

piratage [piʀataʒ] NM [*cassette, vidéo*] pirating;

[*ligne téléphonique*] hacking (**de** into); **~ (informatique)** (computer) hacking

pirate [piʀat] **1** ADJ [*bateau, émission, radio, télévision*] pirate (*épith*) **2** NM pirate; († = *escroc*) swindler, shark*; **~ de l'air** hijacker, skyjacker*; **~ (informatique)** (computer) hacker; **c'est un vrai ~, cet enfant !** that child's a little rascal!; **~ de la route** carjacker

pirater [piʀate] ▶ conjug 1 ◀ VT [+ *cassette, film, logiciel*] to pirate; [+ *ligne téléphonique*] to hack into

piraterie [piʀatʀi] NF (*NonC*) piracy; (= *acte*) act of piracy; (*fig*) swindle, swindling (*NonC*); **~ commerciale** illegal copying, forgery (*of famous brand name goods*); **acte de ~** act of piracy; **~ aérienne** hijacking, skyjacking*; **c'est de la ~ !** it's daylight robbery!

piraya [piʀaja] NM = **piranha**

pire [piʀ] **1** ADJ **a** (*compar*) worse; **c'est bien ~** it's much worse; **c'est ~ que jamais** it's worse than ever; **c'est ~ que tout** it's the worst thing you can imagine; **c'est de ~ en ~** it's getting worse and worse; **il y a ~ comme chef** you could do worse for a boss; **j'ai déjà entendu ~ !** I've heard worse! ■ (*PROV*) **il n'est ~ eau que l'eau qui dort** still waters run deep (*PROV*); (*PROV*) **il n'est ~ sourd que celui qui ne veut pas entendre** there are none so deaf as those who will not hear (*PROV*) **b** (*superl*) **le ~ ◊ la ~** the worst; **les ~s rumeurs/difficultés** the most terrible rumours/severe difficulties

2 NM **le ~** the worst; **le ~ de tout c'est de ...** the worst thing of all is to ...; **le ~ c'est que ...** the worst of it (all) is that ...; (**en mettant les choses) au ~** at (the very) worst, if the worst comes to the worst; **je m'attends au ~** I expect the worst → **politique**

Pirée [piʀe] NM **le ~** Piraeus

piriforme [piʀifɔʀm] ADJ (*gén*) pear-shaped; [*organe*] pyriform organ

pirogue [piʀɔg] NF dugout, canoe, pirogue; **~ à balancier** outrigger

piroguier [piʀɔgje] NM boatman (*in a pirogue*)

pirouette [piʀwɛt] NF [*danseuse, cheval*] pirouette; (*fig*) (= *volte-face*) about-turn (*fig*); (= *faux-fuyant*) evasive reply; **répondre par une ~** to cleverly side-step ou evade the question

pirouetter [piʀwete] ▶ conjug 1 ◀ VI to pirouette

pis¹ [pi] NM [*vache*] udder

pis² [pi] (*littér*) **1** ADJ worse; **qui ~ est** what is worse **2** ADV worse; **aller de ~ en ~** to get worse and worse; **dire ~ que pendre de qn** to badmouth* sb → **mal, tant 3** NM **le ~** the worst (thing); **au ~** at (the very) worst; **au ~ aller** if the worst comes to the worst

pis-aller [pizale] NM INV stopgap; **cette solution n'est qu'un ~** it's only a stopgap solution; **nous verrons ce film en vidéo, c'est un ~** we'll have to make do with second best and watch the film on video; **au ~** if the worst comes to the worst

piscicole [pisikɔl] ADJ fish-breeding (*épith*), piscicultural (*SPÉC*)

pisciculteur, -trice [pisikyltœʀ, tʀis] NM,F fish breeder ou farmer, pisciculturist (*SPÉC*)

pisciculture [pisikyltyʀ] NF fish breeding ou farming, pisciculture (*SPÉC*)

pisciforme [pisifɔʀm] ADJ pisciform

piscine [pisin] NF **a** (= *bassin*) swimming pool; [*réacteur nucléaire*] cooling pond; **~ municipale** public (swimming) pool, public baths (*Brit*); **~ olympique** Olympic-size(d) (swimming) pool; **faire de la gymnastique en ~** to do water gymnastics **b** (*arg Police*) **la ~** the French secret service

piscivore [pisivɔʀ] **1** ADJ fish-eating (*épith*), piscivorous (*SPÉC*) **2** NM fish eater

Pise [piz] N Pisa → **tour¹**

pisé [pize] NM adobe, pisé

pissaladière [pisaladjɛʀ] NF (*Culin*) Provençal pizza with onions, anchovy fillets and olives

pisse [pis] NF pee*, piss*; (*fig*) **de la ~ d'âne** cat's piss*

pisse-froid [pisfʀwa] NM INV wet blanket*

pissement [pismɑ̃] NM **~ de sang** passing of blood (*with the urine*)

pissenlit [pisɑ̃li] NM dandelion; **manger les ~s par la racine** to be pushing up the daisies*, be dead and buried

pisser [pise] ▶ conjug 1 ◀ **1** VI (= *uriner*) [*personne*] to (have a) pee* ou piss*; [*animal*] to pee*, piss*; (= *couler*) to gush; (= *fuir*) to gush out; **je vais ~ un coup** I'm going for a pee* ou a piss*; **il a pissé dans sa culotte** he wet his trousers, he peed in his pants*; **~ au lit** to wet the ou one's bed, pee in the bed*; (*péj*) **il ne se sent plus ~** he thinks the sun shines out of his arse* (*Brit*) ou ass* (*US*), he thinks his shit doesn't stink* (*US*); **ça pisse** (= *il pleut*) it's coming down in buckets*, it's pissing down* (*Brit*); **ça l'a pris comme une envie de ~** he suddenly got an urge to do it*; **les principes, je leur pisse dessus !** I couldn't give a shit* about principles!; **c'est comme si on pissait dans un violon** it's like pissing in the wind*; **laisse ~ (le mérinos) !** forget it!*, let him (ou them etc) get on with it!; **ça ne pisse pas loin** it's nothing to shout about ou to write home about*

2 VT **~ du sang** to pass blood (*with the urine*); **son nez pissait le sang** blood was gushing ou pouring from his nose; **il pissait le sang** the blood was gushing out of him; **le réservoir pissait l'eau** water was gushing ou pouring out of the tank; (*péj*) **~ de la copie*** to churn out garbage ou rubbish (*Brit*)

pissette [pisɛt] NF (= *filet de liquide*) trickle

pisseur, -euse¹ [pisœʀ, øz] **1** NM,F * weak-bladdered individual, person who is always going for a pee* ou a piss* **2** [pisøz] NF **pisseuse** female (*péj*) **3** COMP **► pisseur de copie** writer (*or journalist etc*) who churns out rubbish

pisseux, -euse² [pisø, øz] ADJ [*couleur*] wishy-washy*, insipid; [*aspect*] tatty*, scruffy; **odeur pisseuse** smell of pee* ou piss*

pisse-vinaigre [pisvinɛgʀ] NM INV (= *rabat-joie*) wet blanket*; (= *avare*) skinflint

pissoir [piswaʀ] NM (*dial*) urinal

pissotière [pisɔtjɛʀ] NF (*street*) urinal

pistache [pistaʃ] **1** NF pistachio (nut) **2** ADJ INV pistachio (green)

pistachier [pistaʃje] NM pistachio (tree)

pistage [pistaʒ] NM [*gibier*] tracking, trailing; [*personne*] tailing

pistard [pistaʀ] NM track cyclist, track racer ou specialist

piste [pist] **1** NF **a** (= *traces*) [*animal, suspect*] track, tracks, trail; **suivre/perdre la ~** to follow/lose the trail; **être/mettre qn sur la (bonne) ~** to be/put sb on the right track; **être sur/perdre la ~ d'un meurtrier** to be on/lose a murderer's trail; **se lancer sur la ~ de qn** to follow sb's trail, set out to track sb down → **brouiller, faux², jeu**

b (*Police* = *indice*) lead

c [*hippodrome*] course; [*vélodrome, autodrome, stade*] track; [*patinage*] rink; [*danse*] (dance) floor; [*cirque*] ring; **en ~ !** (*lit*) into the ring!; (*fig*) off you go!; **être en ~** (*lit*) to be in the ring; (*dans un concours, une élection etc*) to be in the running; **entrer en ~** (*lit*) to enter the ring; (*fig*) to enter the arena, come on(to) the scene; **dès leur entrée en ~** (*lit*) as soon as they entered the ring; (*fig*) as soon as they entered the arena ou came on(to) the scene

d (*Ski*) (ski) run, piste; [*ski de fond*] trail; **il y a 30 km de ~ dans cette station** there are 30 km of pistes ou ski runs at this resort; **~ artificielle** dry ou artificial ski slope; **~ pour débutants** nursery slope; **~ rouge/noire** red/black piste ou ski run; **ski hors ~** off-piste ski-

ing; **faire du hors ~** to go off-piste skiing
[e] (*Aviat*) runway; [*petit aéroport*] airstrip; **~ d'atterrissage/d'envol** landing/takeoff runway
[f] (= *sentier*) track; [*désert*] trail
[g] [*magnétophone*] track; **à 2/4 ~s** 2/4 track; (*Ciné*) **~ sonore** sound track; **~ magnétique** [*carte*] magnetic strip
[2] COMP ► **piste cavalière** bridle path ► **piste cyclable** (*sur route*) (bi)cycle lane; (= *voie séparée*) (bi)cycle path *ou* track

pister [piste] ▸conjug 1◂ VT [+ *gibier*] to track, trail; [*police*] [+ *personne*] to tail

pisteur [pistœʀ] NM (member of the) ski patrol; **les ~s** the ski patrol

pistil [pistil] NM pistil

pistole [pistɔl] NF pistole

pistolet [pistɔlɛ] [1] NM (= *arme*) pistol, gun; (= *jouet*) (toy) pistol, (toy) gun; [*peintre*] spray gun; (* = *urinal*) bed-bottle; **peindre au ~** to spray-paint; (*†) **un drôle de ~** an odd customer*, a weird duck* (*US*) [2] COMP ► **pistolet agrafeur** staple gun ► **pistolet à air comprimé** airgun ► **pistolet d'alarme** alarm gun ► **pistolet d'arçon** horse pistol ► **pistolet à bouchon** popgun ► **pistolet à capsules** cap gun ► **pistolet à eau** water pistol

pistolet-mitrailleur (*pl* **pistolets-mitrailleurs**) [pistɔlɛmitʀajœʀ] NM submachine gun, tommy gun®, Sten gun® (*Brit*)

piston [pistɔ̃] NM [a] (*Tech*) piston [b]* string-pulling*, wire-pulling (*US*); **avoir du ~** to have friends in the right places*; **il a eu le poste par ~** he got the job thanks to a bit of string-pulling* [c] (*Mus*) (= *valve*) valve; (= *instrument*) cornet

pistonner* [pistɔne] ▸conjug 1◂ VT to pull strings *ou* wires (*US*) for* (**auprès de** with); **il s'est fait ~** he got sb to pull some strings for him*

pistou [pistu] NM **soupe au ~** *vegetable soup with basil and garlic*

pita [pita] NM pitta (bread)

pitance† [pitɑ̃s] NF (*péj*) (means of) sustenance† (*frm*)

pit-bull (*pl* **pit-bulls**) [pitbyl] NM pit bull (terrier)

pitchpin [pitʃpɛ̃] NM pitch pine

piteusement [pitøzmɑ̃] ADV pathetically; **échouer ~** to fail miserably

piteux, -euse [pitø, øz] ADJ (= *minable*) [*apparence*] sorry (*épith*), pitiful, pathetic; [*résultats*] pitiful, pathetic; (= *honteux*) [*personne, air*] ashamed, shamefaced; **en ~ état** in a sorry *ou* pitiful state; **faire piteuse figure** to cut a sorry figure, be a sorry *ou* pitiful sight; **avoir piteuse mine** to be shabby-looking

pithécanthrope [pitekɑ̃tʀɔp] NM pithecanthrope

pithiviers [pitivje] NM *pastry with an almond paste filling*

pitié [pitje] NF [a] (= *compassion*) pity; **avoir ~ de qn** to pity sb, feel pity for sb; **prendre qn en ~** to take pity on sb; **il me fait ~** I feel sorry for him, I pity him; **cela me faisait ~ de le voir si malheureux** it was pitiful to see him so unhappy; **son sort me fit ~** I took pity on him; **il est si maigre que c'est à faire ~** he is pitifully *ou* painfully thin; **il ne fait pas ~ !** (= *il est gros, riche*) it's hard to feel sorry for him!; **quelle ~ !** ◊ **c'est une ~ !** what a pity!, it's such a pity!; **c'est (une vraie) ~ ou quelle ~ de voir ça** it's pitiful to see (that)
[b] (= *miséricorde*) pity, mercy; **avoir ~ d'un ennemi** to take pity on an enemy, have pity *ou* mercy on an enemy; **~ !** (*lit* = *grâce*) (have) mercy!; (* = *assez*) for goodness' *ou* pity's *ou* Pete's sake!*; **par ~ !** for pity's sake!; **sans ~** [*agir*] pitilessly, mercilessly; [*regarder*] pitilessly; **il est sans ~** he's pitiless *ou*

merciless *ou* ruthless; **un monde sans ~** a cruel world

piton [pitɔ̃] NM [a] (*à anneau*) eye; (*à crochet*) hook; (*Alpinisme*) piton, peg [b] (*Géog*) peak

pitonner [pitɔne] ▸conjug 1◂ [1] VI [a] (*Alpinisme*) to drive pitons *ou* pegs into the rock [b] (*Can*) (= *zapper*) to channel-hop, zap from channel to channel; (= *saisir sur ordinateur*) to keyboard [2] VT (*Can*) [+ *numéro de téléphone*] to dial; [+ *code*] to enter [3] **pitonner sur** VT INDIR (*Can*) [+ *clavier*] to tap away on

pitonneuse [pitɔnøz] NF (*Can* = *télécommande*) channel-hopper, zapper

pitoyable [pitwajabl] ADJ (*gén*) pitiful, pitiable

pitoyablement [pitwajabləmɑ̃] ADV pitifully; **échouer ~** to fail miserably

pitre [pitʀ] NM (*lit, fig*) clown; **faire le ~** to clown *ou* fool about *ou* around, act the fool

pitrerie [pitʀəʀi] NF tomfoolery (*NonC*); **il n'arrête pas de faire des ~s** he's always *ou* he never stops clowning around *ou* acting the fool; **arrête de faire des ~s!** stop fooling around!

pittoresque [pitɔʀɛsk] [1] ADJ [*site*] picturesque; [*personnage*] picturesque, colourful (*Brit*), colorful (*US*); [*récit, style, détail*] colourful (*Brit*), colorful (*US*), picturesque, vivid [2] NM **le ~** the picturesque; **le ~ de qch** the picturesque quality of sth, the colourfulness *ou* vividness of sth; (*fig*) **le ~ dans tout cela c'est que ...** the amusing *ou* ironic thing about it all is that ...

pittoresquement [pitɔʀɛskəmɑ̃] ADV picturesquely

pivert [pivɛʀ] NM green woodpecker

pivoine [pivwan] NF peony → **rouge**

pivot [pivo] NM (*gén, Sport, Mil*) pivot; (= *chose essentielle*) mainspring, linchpin; (= *personne essentielle*) linchpin; [*dent*] post; (*Bot*) taproot; (*Écon*) **cours ~** central rate; **il a eu un rôle ~** he played a pivotal role

pivotant, e [pivotɑ̃, ɑ̃t] ADJ [*bras, panneau*] pivoting (*épith*), revolving (*épith*); [*fauteuil*] swivel (*épith*) → **racine**

pivoter [pivote] ▸conjug 1◂ VI [*porte*] to revolve, pivot; (*Mil*) to wheel round; [*personne*] **~ (sur ses talons)** to turn *ou* swivel round, turn on one's heels; **faire ~ qch** to pivot *ou* swivel sth round

pixel [piksɛl] NM pixel

pizza [pidza] NF pizza

pizzeria [pidzeʀja] NF pizzeria

pizzicato [pidzikato] (*pl* **pizzicatos** *ou* **pizzicati** [pidzikati]) NM pizzicato

PJ¹ (ABRÉV = **pièce(s) jointe(s)**) enc, encl

PJ² [peʒi] NF (ABRÉV = **police judiciaire**) ≈ CID (*Brit*), ≈ FBI (*US*)

PL (ABRÉV = **poids lourd**) HGV (*Brit*), heavy truck (*US*)

Pl (ABRÉV = **place**) Pl

placage [plakaʒ] NM [a] (*en bois*) veneering (*NonC*), veneer; (*en marbre, pierre*) facing; **~ en acajou** mahogany veneer [b] (*Rugby*) = **plaquage**

placard [plakaʀ] NM [a] (= *armoire*) cupboard; **~ à balai/de cuisine** broom/kitchen cupboard [b] (= *affiche*) poster, notice; [*journal*] **~ publicitaire** display advertisement [c] (*Typo*) galley (proof) [d] (* = *couche*) thick layer, thick coating (*NonC*) [e] (*arg Police* = *casier judiciaire*) (police) record [f] (*loc*) **mettre qn au ~*** (*en prison*) to put sb away*, send sb down*; (*renvoyer*) to fire sb, give sb the push*; (*mettre à l'écart*) to push sb to one side; **mettre qch au ~** to shelve sth

placarder [plakaʀde] ▸conjug 1◂ VT [+ *affiche*] to stick up, put up; [+ *mur*] to stick posters

on; **mur placardé d'affiches** wall covered with posters

▼**place** [plas]
NOM FÉMININ

[a] = **esplanade** square; **la ~ Rouge** Red Square; **la ~ du marché** the market square, the marketplace; **ils ont porté le débat sur la ~ publique** they've brought the discussion into the public arena; **étaler ses divergences sur la ~ publique** to air one's differences in public; **clamer qch sur la ~ publique** to proclaim sth from the rooftops
[b] **objet** place; **changer la ~ de qch** to change the place of sth; **changer qch de ~** to move *ou* shift sth, put sth in a different place; **la ~ des mots dans la phrase** word order in sentences ■ (*PROV*) **une ~ pour chaque chose et chaque chose à sa ~** a place for everything and everything in its place (*PROV*)
[c] **personne** place; (*assise*) seat; **~ d'honneur** place *ou* seat of honour; **à vos ~s!** to your places!; **~s assises 20, ~s debout 40** seating capacity 20, standing passengers 40; **il n'y a que des ~s debout** it's standing room only; **une (voiture de) 4 ~s** a 4-seater (car); (*Aut*) **la ~ du mort** the (front) passenger seat; **tente à 4 ~s** 4-man tent; **j'ai trois ~s dans ma voiture** I've room for three in my car; **avoir sa ~ dans le cœur de qn/l'histoire** to have a place in sb's heart/in history; **il ne donnerait pas sa ~ pour un empire** he wouldn't change places with anyone for all the tea in China* *ou* for the world; **sa ~ n'est pas ici** he doesn't belong here; **se faire une ~ dans la société/dans la littérature** to carve out a place *ou* niche for o.s. in society/in literature; **se faire une ~ au soleil** to find o.s. a place in the sun (*fig*); **laisser sa ~ à qn** (*lit*) to give (up) one's seat to sb; (*fig*) to hand over to sb; **prenez ~** take a seat; **prendre la ~ de qn** to take sb's place; (= *remplacer qn*) to take over from sb, take sb's place; **la religion tient une ~ importante dans cette société** religion holds *ou* has an important place in this society; **elle tient une grande ~ dans ma vie** she means a great deal *ou* a lot to me; **tenir sa ~** (= *bonne figure*) to put up a good show, hold one's own; **trouver *ou* prendre ~ parmi/dans** to find a place (for o.s.) among/in → **chasse**
[d] = **espace libre** room, space; **tenir *ou* prendre de la ~** to take up a lot of room *ou* space; **faire/gagner de la ~** to make/save room *ou* space; **j'ai trouvé une ~ *ou* de la ~ pour me garer** I've found a parking space *ou* place; **pouvez-vous me faire une petite ~ ?** can you make a bit of room for me?; **il y a juste la ~ de mettre un lave-vaisselle** there's just enough room *ou* space for a dishwasher; **on n'a pas la ~ de se retourner** there's no room *ou* space to move *ou* not enough room to swing a cat* (*Brit*); **ne mange pas trop, garde une ~ pour le gâteau** don't eat too much, leave some room for the cake; **ce journal accorde *ou* consacre une ~ importante au sport** this newspaper gives a lot of coverage to sport; **dans notre société, il y a ~ pour de nouvelles initiatives** our company provides scope for new initiatives; (*fig*) **faire ~ à qch** to give way to sth; **faire ~ à qn** (*lit*) to let sb pass; (*fig*) to give way to sb; **~ aux jeunes !** make way for the young!; **faire ~ nette** to make a clean sweep
[e] = **billet** seat; (= *prix, trajet*) fare; (= *emplacement réservé*) space; **louer *ou* réserver sa ~** to book one's seat; **il n'a pas payé sa ~** he hasn't paid for his seat, he hasn't paid his fare; **payer ~ entière** (*au cinéma etc*) to pay full price; (*dans le bus etc*) to pay full fare; **~ de parking** parking space; **parking de 500 ~s** parking (space) for 500 cars; **cinéma de 400 ~s** cinema seating 400 (people) *ou* with a seating capacity of 400
[f] = **rang** (*Scol*) place (in class); (*Sport*) place, placing; **il a eu une bonne ~** he got a good place *ou* a good placing; **être reçu dans les premières ~s** to get one of the top places, be amongst the top; **il a eu une première ~ *ou* une**

> ► GRAMMAIRE ACTIVE: **place** 28, 29

~ **de premier en histoire** he was ou came (Brit) first in history; **ce champion a reconquis la première ~ mondiale** the champion has won back the number one world ranking ou title; **l'entreprise occupe la seconde ~ sur le marché des ordinateurs** the company ranks second in the computer market; **figurer en bonne ~** [personne] to be prominent; **son nom figure en bonne ~ dans la liste** his name is high on the list; **la question figure en bonne ~ dans l'ordre du jour** the matter is ou features high on the agenda; **ses livres trônent en bonne ~ dans la vitrine** his books have pride of place in the shop window

g = **emploi** job; [domestique] position, situation; **une ~ de serveuse/coursier** a job as a waitress/courier; **dans les médias, les ~s sont chères** there's a lot of competition for jobs in the media, jobs in the media are hard to come by

h Mil ~ **(forte ou de guerre)** fortified town; **le commandant de la ~** the fortress commander; **s'introduire/avoir des contacts dans la ~** to get/ have contacts on the inside; (fig) **maintenant il est dans la ~** now he's on the inside; **~ d'armes** parade ground

i Comm, Fin market; **vous ne trouverez pas moins cher sur la ~ de Paris** you won't find cheaper on the Paris market; **dans toutes les ~s financières du monde** in all the money markets of the world; **~ bancaire/commerciale** banking/trade centre; **~ boursière** stock market

j **expressions figées**

♦ **à la place** (= en échange) instead; **si tu n'en veux pas, prends autre chose à la ~** if you don't want any, take something else instead; **ils ont démoli la maison et construit un immeuble à la ~** they've demolished the house and built an apartment building in its place

♦ **à la place de** (= au lieu de) instead of; **elle a emporté ma veste à la ~ de la sienne** she went off with my jacket instead of her own; **ils ont construit un parking à la ~ de la maison** they've built a car park where the house used to be (= en remplaçant qn) **faire une démarche à la ~ de qn** to take steps on sb's behalf; **répondre à la ~ de qn** to reply in sb's place ou on sb's behalf; **se mettre à la ~ de qn** to put o.s. in sb's place ou in sb's shoes; **à votre/sa ~** if I were you/him, in your/his place; **je n'aimerais pas être à sa ~** I wouldn't like to be in his shoes; **à ma ~, tu aurais accepté ?** in my place ou position would you have accepted?, would you have accepted if you were in my shoes?

♦ **à sa (ou ma etc) place** (= à l'endroit habituel ou convenable) **cette lampe n'est pas à sa ~** this lamp isn't in the right place ou in its proper place ou is in the wrong place; **il n'est pas à sa ~ dans ce milieu** he feels out of place in this setting; **remettre qch à sa ~** to put sth back where it belongs ou in its proper place; **remettre qn à sa ~** to take sb down a peg or two*, put sb in his place; **savoir rester à sa ~** to know one's place

♦ **de place en place** here and there, in places

♦ **en place** (adjectival) **les gens en ~** influential people, people with influence; **le pouvoir/ régime en ~** (maintenant) the current government/regime; (à l'époque) the government/regime at the time (adverbial) **être en ~** [plan] to be ready; [forces de l'ordre] to be in place ou stationed; † [domestique] to be in service (chez with); **tout le monde est en ~** everyone is in place ou is seated; **le gouvernement est en ~ depuis trois mois** the government has been in power ou office for three months; **tout est en ~ pour le drame** the scene is set for the tragedy; **en ~ pour la photo !** everybody take up your positions for the photograph!; **mettre en ~** [+ plan] to set up, organize; [+ marchandises] to put on the shelves; [+ service d'ordre] to deploy; [+

mécanisme, dispositif] to install; **le dispositif d'évacuation s'est mis en ~** evacuation procedures have been set up; **mise en ~** [plan] setting up; [service d'ordre] deployment; [marchandises] **il a terminé la mise en ~ au rayon confiserie** he finished stocking the shelves in the confectionery department; **remettre qch en ~** to put sth back where it belongs ou in its proper place; **il ne tient pas en ~** he can't keep ou stay still, he's always fidgeting

♦ **par places** = de place en place

♦ **sur place** on the spot; **être/rester/se rendre sur ~** to be/stay/go there; **les sauveteurs sont déjà sur ~** rescuers are already on the spot ou at the scene; **on annonce l'envoi sur ~ d'observateurs internationaux** it has been announced that international observers are being sent out there; **la situation sur ~ est catastrophique** the situation on the ground is disastrous; **on peut faire la réparation sur ~** we can repair it right here ou on the spot; **sa présence sur ~ est indispensable** his presence on the spot ou on site is essential; **vous trouverez des vélos/des brochures sur ~** bicycles/leaflets are available on site; (Comm) (à consommer) sur ~ **ou à emporter ?** eat in or take away?; **les produits fabriqués sur ~** (dans la région) locally-manufactured products; (dans le magasin) goods made on the premises; **il s'est enfui, abandonnant sur ~ la moto volée** he abandoned the stolen motorbike and fled → **clouer, surplace**

placé, e [plase] (ptp de **placer**) ADJ a (gén) **la fenêtre/leur maison est ~e à gauche** the window/their house is (situated) on the left; **je suis ou je me trouve ~ dans une position délicate** I am (placed) in ou I find myself (placed) in a tricky position; **être bien/mal ~** [terrain] to be well/badly situated, be favourably/unfavourably situated; [objet] to be well/badly placed; [spectateur] to have a good/a poor seat; [concurrent] to be in a good/bad position, be well/badly placed; **leur confiance a été bien/mal ~e** their trust was justified/misplaced; **sa fierté est mal ~e** his pride is misplaced ou out of place; **il est bien ~ pour gagner** he is in a good position ou well placed to win; **il est bien ~ pour le savoir** he should know; **je suis bien/mal ~ pour vous répondre** I'm in a/in no position to answer; **tu es mal ~ pour te plaindre !*** you've got nothing to complain about! → **haut**

b (Courses) **arriver ~** to be placed; **jouer (un cheval) ~** to back a horse each way (Brit), put an each-way (Brit) bet on (a horse), back a horse across the board (US)

placebo [plasebo] NM placebo; **effet ~** placebo effect

placement [plasmã] NM a (Fin) investment; **faire un ~ d'argent** to invest (some) money; **~ de père de famille** gilt-edged investment, safe investment b [employés] placing; **l'école assure le ~ des élèves** the school ensures that the pupils find employment → **bureau** c (Psych) **~ d'office** compulsory admission; **~ volontaire** voluntary admission

placenta [plasɛ̃ta] NM (Anat) placenta; (= arrière-faix) afterbirth, placenta

placentaire [plasɛ̃tɛʀ] 1 ADJ placental 2 NM placental mammal, eutherian; **les ~s** eutherians, Eutheria (SPÉC)

placer [plase] ▶conjug 3 ◀ 1 VT a (= assigner une place à) [+ objet, personne] to place, put; [+ invité] to seat, put; [+ spectateur] to seat, give a seat to, put; (Ftbl) [+ balle] to place; (Boxe) [+ coup] to land, place; (Tech = installer) to put in, fit; **vous me placez dans une situation délicate** you're placing ou putting me in a tricky position; **~ sa voix** to pitch one's voice; **~ ses affaires bien en ordre** to tidy up one's things

b (= situer) to place, set, put; **il a placé l'action de son roman en Provence** he has set

ou situated the action of his novel in Provence; **où placez-vous Lyon ?** whereabouts do you think Lyons is?, where would you put Lyons?; **~ l'honnêteté avant l'intelligence** to set ou put ou place honesty above intelligence; **~ le bonheur dans la vie familiale** to consider that happiness is found in family life; **~ un nom sur un visage** to put a name to a face; **je ne peux pas ~ de nom sur son visage** I can't place him, I can't put a name to his face; **~ ses espérances en qn/qch** to set ou pin one's hopes on sb/sth

c (= introduire) [+ remarque, anecdote, plaisanterie] to put in, get in; **il n'a pas pu ~ un mot** he couldn't get a word in (edgeways)

d (+ ouvrier, malade, écolier) to place (dans in); **~ qn comme vendeur** to get ou find sb a job as a salesman; **~ qn comme apprenti (chez qn)** to apprentice sb (to sb); **~ qn à la comptabilité** to give sb a job ou place sb in the accounts department; **~ qn à la tête d'une entreprise** to put sb at the head of a business, put sb in charge of a business; (hum) **ils n'ont pas encore pu ~ leur fille** they've still not been able to marry off their daughter ou to get their daughter off their hands; **~ qn/qch sous l'autorité/les ordres de** to place ou put sb/sth under the authority/orders of

e (Comm = vendre) [+ marchandise] to place, sell; (fig hum) **elle a réussi à ~ sa vieille machine à laver** she managed to find a home (hum) ou a buyer for her old washing machine

f [+ argent] (à la Bourse) to invest; (à la caisse d'épargne, sur un compte) to deposit; **~ une somme sur son compte** to put ou pay a sum into one's account

2 **se placer** VPR a [personne] to take up a position; (debout) to stand; (assis) to sit (down); [événement, action] to take place; **se ~ de face/contre le mur/en cercle** to stand face on/against the wall/in a circle; **se ~ sur le chemin de qn** to stand in sb's path; **cette démarche se place dans le cadre de nos revendications** these steps should be seen in the context of our claims; (fig) **si nous nous plaçons à ce point de vue ou dans cette perspective** if we look at things from this point of view, if we view the situation in this way; **plaçons-nous dans le cas où cela arriverait** let us suppose that this happens, let us put ourselves in the situation where this actually happens

b [cheval] (Scol, Sport) **se ~ 2ème** to be ou come 2nd, be in 2nd place; **il s'est bien placé dans la course** he was well placed in the race; **se ~ parmi les premiers** to be in the first few

c (= prendre une place) to get ou find a job (comme as); **retraité qui voudrait bien se ~ (dans une institution)** pensioner who would like to find a place in a home

placet [plasɛ] NM (Hist, Jur) petition

placeur [plasœʀ] NM [spectateurs, invités] usher

placeuse [plasøz] NF [spectateurs] usherette

placide [plasid] ADJ placid, calm

placidement [plasidmã] ADV placidly, calmly

placidité [plasidite] NF placidity, placidness, calmness

placier [plasje] NM travelling salesman, traveller; **~ en assurances** insurance broker

Placoplâtre® [plakoplɑtʀ] NM plasterboard

plafond [plafɔ̃] NM a (lit) [salle] ceiling; [voiture, caverne] roof; (Art) ceiling painting; **~ à caissons** coffered ceiling; **pièce haute/basse de ~** high-ceilinged/low-ceilinged room, room with a high/low ceiling; **il est bas de ~*** he hasn't got much up top* → **araignée** b (= limite) [prix, loyer] ceiling; (Mét = nuages) ceiling, cloud cover; (Aviat) ceiling, maximum height; (Aut) top ou maximum speed; **niveau/ prix-~** ceiling, ceiling ou maximum limit/ price; **âge(-)~** maximum age; **~ de crédit** lending ou credit limit; **~ de la Sécurité sociale** upper limit on salary deductions for social security contributions; (*Mét*) **le ~ est bas** the cloud cover is low

plafonnement [plafɔnmɑ̃] NM **il y a un ~ des salaires/cotisations** there is an upper limit on salaries/contributions

plafonner [plafɔne] ▸conjug 1◂ 1 VI (*prix, écolier, salaire*) to reach a ceiling *ou* maximum; (*Aviat*) to reach one's ceiling; (*Aut*) to reach one's top speed *ou* maximum speed; **les ventes plafonnent** sales have reached their *ou* a ceiling (limit); **la voiture plafonne à 100 km/h** the car can't do more than 100 km/h 2 VT a (*Constr*) to put a ceiling in; **grenier plafonné** loft which has had a ceiling put in b [+ *salaires*] to put an upper limit on; **cotisations plafonnées à 1 500 F** contributions which have had their ceiling *ou* upper limit fixed at 1,500 francs

plafonnier [plafɔnje] NM [*voiture*] courtesy *ou* interior light; [*chambre*] ceiling light *ou* lamp

plagal, e (*mpl* -**aux**) [plagal, o] ADJ plagal

plage [plaʒ] 1 NF a [*mer, rivière, lac*] beach; **~ de sable/de galets** sandy/pebble beach; **sac/serviette/robe de ~** beach bag/towel/robe b (= *ville*) (seaside) resort c (= *zone*) (*dans un barème, une progression*) range, bracket; (*dans un horaire etc*) (time) slot; **~ d'ombre** band of shadow, shadowy area; **temps d'écoute divisé en ~s (horaires)** listening time divided into slots; (*Scol*) **~ horaire** slot (in timetable); **~ musicale** intermission; **~ publicitaire** commercial break, commercials; **~ de prix** price range *ou* bracket d [*disque*] track 2 COMP ▸ **plage arrière** (*Naut*) quarterdeck; (*Aut*) parcel shelf, back shelf ▸ **plage avant** (*Naut*) forecastle (head *ou* deck), fo'c'sle

plagiaire [plaʒjɛʀ] NMF plagiarist, plagiarizer

plagiat [plaʒja] NM plagiarism, plagiary; **c'est un véritable ~** it's absolute plagiarism; **faire du ~** to plagiarize

plagier [plaʒje] ▸conjug 7◂ VT to plagiarize

plagiste [plaʒist] NM beach manager *ou* attendant

plaid [plɛd] NM (= *couverture*) car rug, lap robe (*US*)

plaidant, e [plɛdɑ̃, ɑ̃t] ADJ [*partie*] litigant; [*avocat*] pleading

plaider [plede] ▸conjug 1◂ 1 VT to plead; **~ coupable/non coupable/la légitime défense** to plead guilty/not guilty/self-defence; **~ la cause de qn** (*fig*) to plead sb's cause, argue *ou* speak in favour of sb; (*Jur*) to plead for sb, plead sb's case, defend sb; **~ sa propre cause** to speak in one's own defence; **l'affaire s'est plaidée à Paris/à huis clos** the case was heard in Paris/in closed court *ou* in camera 2 VI a [*avocat*] to plead (**pour** for, on behalf of, **contre** against); (*fig*) **~ pour** *ou* **en faveur de qn/qch** to speak in favour of sb/sth b (= *intenter un procès*) to go to court, litigate; **~ contre qn** to take sb to court, take proceedings against sb; **ils ont plaidé pendant des années** their case has dragged on for years

plaideur, -euse [plɛdœʀ, øz] NM,F litigant

plaidoirie [plɛdwaʀi] NF (*Jur*) speech for the defence, defence speech; (*fig*) plea, appeal (**en faveur de** on behalf of)

plaidoyer [plɛdwaje] NM (*Jur*) speech for the defence; (*fig*) defence, plea; (*fig*) **~ en faveur de/contre qch** plea for/against sth

plaie [plɛ] NF (*physique, morale*) wound; (= *coupure*) cut; (*fig*) (*fléau*) scourge; (*fig*) **rouvrir une ~** to open an old wound; **~ ouverte/béante/profonde/vive** open/gaping/deep/raw wound; **quelle ~ !*** (*personne*) he's such a nuisance! *ou* pest*!; (*chose*) what a nuisance! *ou* bind* (*Brit*)!; **remuer** *ou* **tourner le couteau dans la ~** to twist *ou* turn the knife in the wound, rub salt in the wound ■ (*PROV*) **d'argent n'est pas mortelle** money isn't every-

thing; (*Bible*) **les ~s d'Égypte** the plagues of Egypt → **rêver**

plaignant, e [plɛɲɑ̃, ɑ̃t] 1 ADJ **la partie ~e** the plaintiff, the complainant 2 NM,F plaintiff, complainant

plain [plɛ̃] NM (*Naut*) **le ~** high tide

plain-chant (*pl* **plains-chants**) [plɛ̃ʃɑ̃] NM plainchant (*NonC*), plainsong (*NonC*)

plaindre [plɛ̃dʀ] ▸conjug 52◂ 1 VT a [+ *personne*] to pity, feel sorry for; **aimer se faire ~** to like to be pitied; **il est bien à ~** he is to be pitied; **elle n'est pas à ~** (= *c'est bien fait*) she doesn't deserve (any) sympathy, she doesn't deserve to be pitied; (= *elle a de la chance*) she's got nothing to complain about; **je vous plains de vivre avec lui** I pity you *ou* I sympathize with you (for) having to live with him b (* = *donner chichement*) to begrudge, grudge; **donne-moi plus de papier, on dirait que tu le plains** give me some more paper — anybody would think you begrudged it (me); **il ne plaint pas son temps/sa peine** he doesn't grudge his time/his efforts

2 **se plaindre** VPR (= *gémir*) to moan; (= *protester*) to complain, grumble, moan* (**de** about); (*frm, Jur* = *réclamer*) to make a complaint (**de** about, **auprès de** to); (*souffrir*) **se ~ de** [+ *maux de tête etc*] to complain of; **se ~ de qn/qch à qn** to complain to sb about sb/sth; **de quoi te plains-tu ?** (*lit*) what are you complaining *ou* grumbling *ou* moaning* about?; (*iro*) what have you got to complain *ou* grumble *ou* moan* about?; **il se plaint que les prix montent** he's complaining about rising prices *ou* that prices are going up; **ne viens pas te ~ si tu es puni** don't come and complain *ou* moan* (to me) if you're punished; **je vais me ~ à qui de droit** I'm going to make a formal complaint

plaine [plɛn] NF plain; **c'est de la ~** it is flat open country; **en ~** in the plains; **haute ~** high plain; **les Grandes Plaines** the Great Plains

plain-pied [plɛ̃pje] ♦ **de plain-pied** LOC ADV [*pièce*] on the same level (**avec** as); [*maison*] (built) at street-level; **entrer de ~ dans le sujet** to come straight to the point

plainte [plɛ̃t] NF a (= *gémissement*) moan, groan; (*littér*) [*vent*] moaning b (= *doléance*) complaint, moaning* (*NonC*) (*péj*) c (*Jur*) complaint; **porter ~** *ou* **déposer une ~ contre qn** to lodge *ou* register a complaint against sb; **je vais porter ~ !** I'm going to make a formal complaint!; **désirez-vous porter ~ ?** do you wish to press charges?; **~ contre X** complaint against person or persons unknown

plaintif, -ive [plɛ̃tif, iv] ADJ plaintive, doleful

plaintivement [plɛ̃tivmɑ̃] ADV plaintively, dolefully

plaire [plɛʀ] ▸conjug 54◂ 1 VI a (= *être apprécié*) **ce garçon me plaît** I like that boy; **ce garçon ne me plaît pas** I don't like that boy, I don't care for that boy; **ce spectacle/dîner/livre m'a plu** I liked *ou* enjoyed that show/dinner/book; **ce genre de musique ne me plaît pas beaucoup** I don't really care for *ou* I'm not very keen on* (*Brit*) that kind of music, that kind of music doesn't appeal to me very much; **ton nouveau travail te plaît ?** (how) do you like your new job?, how are you enjoying your new job?; **les brunes me plaisent** I like *ou* go for* dark-haired girls, dark-haired girls appeal to me; **tu ne me plais pas avec cette coiffure** I don't like you with your hair like that; **c'est une chose qui me plairait beaucoup à faire** it's something I'd very much like to do *ou* I'd love to do; **on ne peut pas ~ à tout le monde** you can't be liked by everyone; **c'est le genre d'homme qui plaît aux femmes** he's the sort of man that women like *ou* who appeals to women; **le désir de ~** the desire to please; **c'est le genre de personne qui plaît en société** he's the type of person

that people like to have around; (*iro*) **tu commences à me ~ (avec tes questions) !*** you're starting to get on my nerves (with your questions)!

b (= *convenir à*) **ce plan me plaît** this plan suits me; **ça te plairait d'aller au théâtre ?** would you like to go to the theatre?, do you feel like *ou* do you fancy (*Brit*) going to the theatre?; **j'irai si ça me plaît** I'll go if I feel like it *ou* if I want (to); **je travaille quand ça me plaît** I work when I feel like it *ou* when it suits me; **je fais ce qui me plaît** I do what I like *ou* as I please; **si ça ne te plaît pas c'est le même prix !*** if you don't like it (that's just) too bad!* *ou* that's tough!*

c (= *avoir du succès*) **achète des fleurs, cela plaît toujours** buy some flowers, they're always appreciated *ou* welcome; **la pièce/cette réponse a plu** the play/this reply went down well

2 VB IMPERS a **ici, je fais ce qu'il me plaît** I do as I please *ou* like here; **et s'il me plaît d'y aller ?** and what if I want to go?; **vous plairait-il de venir dîner ce soir ?** would you care *ou* like to come for dinner this evening?; (*littér*) **il lui plaît de croire que ...** he likes to think that ...; **comme il vous plaira** just as you like *ou* please *ou* choose *ou* wish

b (*loc*) **s'il te plaît** ◊ **s'il vous plaît** please; **et elle a un manteau de vison, s'il vous plaît !*** and she's got a mink coat if you please! *ou* no less!; (*littér*) **plaise** *ou* **plût à Dieu** *ou* **au ciel qu'il réussisse !** please God that he succeed! (*littér*); (*frm*) **plaît-il ?** I beg your pardon? → **dieu**

3 **se plaire** VPR a (= *se sentir bien, à l'aise*) **il se plaît à Londres** he likes *ou* enjoys being in London, he likes it in London; **j'espère qu'il s'y plaira** I hope he'll like it there; **se ~ avec qn** to enjoy being with sb, enjoy sb's company; **te plais-tu avec tes nouveaux amis ?** do you like being with your new friends?; **les fougères se plaisent à l'ombre** ferns like shade b (= *s'apprécier*) **je ne me plais pas en robe** I don't like myself in a dress; **tu te plais avec ce chapeau ?** do you like yourself in that hat?; **ces deux-là se plaisent** those two get on *ou* along (*Brit*) well together, those two have really hit it off*

c (*littér* = *prendre plaisir à*) **se ~ à lire** to take pleasure in reading, like *ou* be fond of reading; **se ~ à tout critiquer** to delight in criticizing everything; **je me plais à penser que ...** I like to think that ...

plaisamment [plɛzamɑ̃] ADV a (= *agréablement*) pleasantly, agreeably b (= *de façon amusante*) amusingly

plaisance [plɛzɑ̃s] NF **la (navigation de) ~** boating; (*à voile*) sailing, yachting → **bateau, port**

plaisancier [plɛzɑ̃sje] NM (amateur) sailor *ou* yachtsman

plaisant, e [plɛzɑ̃, ɑ̃t] ADJ a (= *agréable*) [*personne, séjour, souvenir*] pleasant, agreeable; [*maison*] pleasant, nice; **~ à l'œil** pleasing to the eye, nice *ou* attractive to look at; **ce n'est guère ~** it's not exactly pleasant, it's not very nice; **c'est une ville très ~e à vivre** it's a very pleasant *ou* nice town to live in; **il n'est pas très ~ à vivre** he's not that easy to get along with → **mauvais** b (= *amusant*) [*histoire, aventure*] amusing, funny; **le ~ de la chose** the funny side *ou* part of it, the funny thing about it c (= *ridicule*) laughable, ridiculous d († = *bizarre*) bizarre, singular; **voilà qui est ~ !** it's quite bizarre!; **je vous trouve bien ~ de parler de la sorte** I consider it most bizarre *ou* singular of you to speak in that way

plaisanter [plɛzɑ̃te] ▸conjug 1◂ 1 VI to joke, have a joke (**sur** about); **je ne suis pas d'humeur à ~** I'm in no mood for jokes *ou* joking, I'm not in a joking mood; **et je ne plaisante pas !** and I mean it!, and I'm not joking!; **c'est quelqu'un qui ne plaisante pas** he's not

▸ GRAMMAIRE ACTIVE: **plaire** 39.2, 41

the sort you can have a joke with; **vous plaisantez** you must be joking *ou* kidding*, you're joking *ou* kidding*; **c'était juste pour ~** it was just a joke; **dit-il pour ~** he said jokingly *ou* in jest; **on ne plaisante pas avec cela** this is no joking *ou* laughing matter; **il ne faut pas ~ avec les médicaments** you shouldn't mess around* with medicines; **il ne plaisante pas sur la discipline/cette question** there's no joking with him over matters of discipline/this subject; **on ne plaisante pas avec la police** the police are not to be trifled with

② VT to make fun of, tease; **~ qn sur qch** to tease sb about sth

plaisanterie [plɛzɑ̃tʀi] NF ⓐ (= *blague*) joke (sur about); **aimer la ~** to be fond of a joke; **~ de corps de garde** barrack-room joke; **par ~** for fun *ou* a joke *ou* a laugh*; **faire une ~** to tell *ou* crack a joke; **tourner qch en ~** to make a joke of sth, laugh sth off; **les ~s les plus courtes sont (toujours) les meilleures** brevity is the soul of wit

ⓑ (= *raillerie*) joke; **il est en butte aux ~s de ses amis** his friends are always making fun of him *ou* poking fun at him; **faire des ~s sur** to joke *ou* make jokes about *ou* at the expense of; **il comprend** *ou* **prend bien la ~** he knows how to *ou* he can take a joke; **il ne faudrait pas pousser la ~ trop loin** we mustn't take the joke too far

ⓒ (= *farce*) (practical) joke, prank → **mauvais**
ⓓ (*loc*) **résoudre ce problème/gagner la course est une ~ pour lui** he could solve this problem/win the race with his eyes shut *ou* standing on his head*; **la ~ a assez duré!** this has gone far enough!, this has gone beyond a joke!; **lui, se lever tôt? c'est une ~!** him, get up early? what a joke! *ou* you must be joking! *ou* you must be kidding!*

plaisantin [plɛzɑ̃tɛ̃] NM ⓐ (= *blagueur*) joker; **c'est un petit ~** he's quite a joker ⓑ (= *fumiste*) phoney*

▼ **plaisir** [plɛziʀ] NM ⓐ (= *joie*) pleasure; **avoir du ~** *ou* **prendre ~ à faire qch** to find *ou* take pleasure in doing sth, delight in doing sth; **prendre (un malin) ~ à faire qch** to take a (mischievous) delight in doing sth; **j'ai le ~ de vous annoncer que ...** I am pleased to inform you that ..., I have great pleasure to inform you that ...; **M. et Mme Lebrun ont le ~ de vous faire part de ...** Mr and Mrs Lebrun are pleased to announce ...; **c'est un ~ de le voir** it's a pleasure to see him; **c'est un ~ chaque fois renouvelé de te voir** it's always a pleasure to see you; **par ~** ◊ **pour le ~** (*gén*) for pleasure; [*bricoler, peindre*] as a hobby; **ranger pour le ~ de ranger** to tidy up just for the sake of it; (*iro*) **je vous souhaite bien du ~!** good luck to you! (*iro*), I wish you (the best of) luck! (*iro*); (*iro*) **ça nous promet du ~ (en perspective)** I can hardly wait! (*iro*); **avec (le plus grand) ~** with (the greatest of) pleasure; **au ~ de vous revoir** ◊ **au ~** (I'll) see you again sometime, (I'll) be seeing you*; **les ~s de la table** good food → **durer, gêne**

ⓑ (*sexuel*) pleasure; **avoir du ~** to experience pleasure; **le ~ solitaire** self-abuse; **les ~s de la chair** the pleasures of the flesh

ⓒ (= *distraction*) pleasure; **les ~s de la vie** life's (little) pleasures; **courir après les ~s** to be a pleasure-seeker; **le golf est un ~ coûteux** golf is an expensive hobby *ou* pleasure; **lieu de ~** house of pleasure

ⓓ (*littér* = *volonté*) pleasure (*littér*), wish; **si c'est votre (bon) ~** if such is your will *ou* wish, if you so desire; **les faits ont été grossis à ~** the facts have been wildly exaggerated; **il s'inquiète/ment à ~** he worries/lies for the sake of it

ⓔ (*loc*) **faire ~ à qn** to please sb; **ce cadeau m'a fait ~** I was very pleased with this gift, this gift gave me great pleasure; **ça me fait ~ de vous entendre dire cela** I'm pleased *ou* de-

lighted to hear you say that; **cela fait ~ à voir** it is a pleasure to see *ou* to behold; **ça t'a agacé? — au contraire, ça m'a fait ~** did it annoy you? — no, I was pleased; **pour me faire ~** (just) to please me; **fais-moi ~: mange ta soupe/arrête la radio** do me a favour, eat your soup/turn off the radio, be a dear and eat your soup/turn off the radio; (*frm*) **voulez-vous me faire le ~ de venir dîner?** I should be most pleased if you would come to dinner, would you do me the pleasure of dining with me (*ou* us)? (*frm*); **fais-moi le ~ de te taire!** would you mind being quiet!, do me a favour and shut up!*; **il se fera un ~ de vous reconduire** he'll be (only too) pleased *ou* glad to drive you back, it will be a pleasure for him to drive you back; **bon, c'est bien pour vous faire ~** *ou* **si cela peut vous faire ~** all right, if it will make you happy; **j'irai, mais c'est bien pour vous faire ~** I'll go (just) to keep you happy; **se faire ~** (= *s'amuser*) to enjoy o.s., have fun; **faites-vous ~, allez dîner au «Gourmet»** treat *ou* spoil yourself, go and have dinner at the "Gourmet"

plan¹ [plɑ̃] ① NM ⓐ [*maison*] plan, blueprint; [*machine*] plan, scale drawing; [*ville, métro*] map, plan; [*région*] map; **acheter une maison sur ~** to buy a house while it's still only a plan on paper; **faire** *ou* **tracer** *ou* **tirer un ~** to draw a plan; **tirer des ~s sur la comète*** to build castles in the air

ⓑ (*Math, Phys* = *surface*) plane
ⓒ (*Ciné, Photo*) shot; (*Peinture, Photo*) **premier ~** foreground; **dernier ~** background; **au second ~** in the background; (*Peinture*) **au deuxième ~** in the middle distance; (*Ciné*) **~ américain** medium close shot → **gros**
ⓓ (*fig*) **mettre qch au deuxième ~** to consider sth of secondary importance; **ce problème est au premier ~ de nos préoccupations** this problem is uppermost in our minds *ou* is one of our foremost preoccupations; **parmi toutes ces questions, l'inflation vient au premier ~** *ou* **nous mettons l'inflation au premier ~** of all these questions, inflation is the key *ou* priority issue *ou* we consider inflation to be the most important; **personnalité de premier ~** key figure; **personnalité de second ~** minor figure; **un savant de tout premier ~** a scientist of the first rank, one of our foremost scientists; **au premier ~ de l'actualité** at the forefront of the news, very much in the news
ⓔ (= *niveau*) level; **mettre sur le même ~** to put on the same plane *ou* level; **au ~ national/international** at the national/international level; **sur le ~ du confort** as far as comfort is concerned, as regards comfort; **sur le ~ moral/intellectuel** morally/intellectually speaking, on the moral/intellectual plane; **sur tous les ~s** in every way, on all fronts
ⓕ (= *projet*) plan, project; (*Écon*) plan, programme; **avoir/exécuter un ~** to have/carry out a plan; **~ de carrière** career path; **~ de cinq ans** five-year plan; **~ de relance** *ou* **de redressement de l'économie** economic recovery plan; **~ d'action/d'attaque** plan of action/of attack; **~ de paix** peace plan; **~ de modernisation/de restructuration** modernization/restructuring plan; **~ de développement économique et social** economic and social development plan; **~ social** *ou* **de licenciements** redundancy scheme *ou* plan
ⓖ (* = *idée*) idea; **tu as un ~ pour les vacances?** have you any ideas for the holidays? *ou* about where to go on holiday?; **c'est un super ~!** *ou* **un ~ d'enfer!** it's a great idea!; **il a toujours des ~s foireux*** he's full of madcap* ideas *ou* schemes; **on s'est fait un ~ restau/ciné hier soir** we ate out/we went to the cinema last night
ⓗ [*livre, dissertation, devoir*] plan, outline; **faire un ~ de qch** to make a plan for sth, plan sth out

ⓘ (*: loc*) **rester en ~** [*personne*] to be left stranded, be left high and dry; [*voiture*] to be abandoned *ou* ditched*; [*projets*] to be abandoned in midstream, be left (hanging) in mid air; **laisser en ~** [+ *personne*] to leave in the lurch *ou* stranded; [+ *voiture*] to abandon, ditch*; [+ *affaires*] to abandon; [+ *projet, travail*] to drop, abandon; **il a tout laissé en ~ pour venir me voir** he dropped everything to come and see me

② COMP ▶ **plan d'aménagement rural** rural development plan ▶ **plan d'amortissement** (*pour un bien, un investissement*) depreciation schedule; (*pour un emprunt*) redemption plan ▶ **plan comptable** French accounting standards ▶ **plan de cuisson** hob (*Brit*), stovetop (*US*) ▶ **plan directeur** (*Mil*) map of the combat area; (*Écon*) blueprint, master plan ▶ **plan d'eau** (*lac*) lake; (*sur un cours d'eau*) stretch of smooth water ▶ **plan d'épargne en actions** stock portfolio (*with tax advantages*) ▶ **plan d'épargne-logement** savings plan for property purchase ▶ **plan d'épargne populaire** individual savings plan ▶ **plan d'épargne-retraite** personal pension plan *ou* scheme ▶ **plan d'équipement** industrial development programme ▶ **plan d'études** study plan *ou* programme ▶ **plan de faille** fault plane ▶ **plan de financement** financing plan ▶ **plan fixe** (*Ciné*) static shot ▶ **plan incliné** inclined plane; **en ~ incliné** sloping ▶ **plan de niveau** floor plan ▶ **plan d'occupation des sols** land use plan (*Brit*), zoning regulations *ou* ordinances (*US*) ▶ **plan ORSEC** scheme set up to deal with major civil emergencies ▶ **plan rapproché** *ou* **serré** (*Ciné*) close-up (shot) ▶ **plan séquence** (*Ciné*) sequence shot ▶ **plan de travail** (*dans une cuisine*) work-top, work(ing) surface (*Brit*), counter (top) (*US*); (*planning*) work plan *ou* programme *ou* schedule ▶ **plan de vol** flight plan → **plan-concave, plan-convexe**

plan², e [plɑ̃, plan] ADJ ⓐ [*miroir*] flat; [*surface*] flat, level ⓑ (*Math*) plane

planant, e* [planɑ̃, ɑ̃t] ADJ [*musique*] mind-blowing*

planche [plɑ̃ʃ] ① NF ⓐ (*en bois*) plank; (*plus large*) board; (= *rayon*) shelf; (*Naut* = *passerelle*) gangplank; (= *plongeoir*) diving board; (* = *ski*) ski; **cabine/sol en ~s** wooden hut/floor; **dormir sur une ~** to sleep on a wooden board; **quand il sera entre quatre ~s*** when he's six foot under* → **pain**

ⓑ (*Typo* = *illustration*) plate
ⓒ (*Hort*) bed
ⓓ (*Natation*) **faire la ~** to float on one's back

② **planches** NFPL (*Théât*) **les ~s** the boards, the stage (*NonC*); **monter sur les ~s** (= *faire du théâtre*) to go on the stage, tread the boards → **brûler**

③ COMP ▶ **planche anatomique** anatomical chart ▶ **planche à billets** banknote plate; **faire marcher la ~ à billets*** to print money ▶ **planche à découper** (*cuisinière*) chopping board; [*boucher*] chopping block ▶ **planche à dessin** *ou* **à dessiner** drawing board ▶ **planche à laver** washboard ▶ **planche à pain** (*lit*) breadboard; (*péj*) **c'est une ~ à pain** she's as flat as a board* *ou* pancake* ▶ **planche à pâtisserie** pastry board ▶ **planche à repasser** ironing board ▶ **planche à roulettes** (*objet*) skateboard; (= *sport*) skateboarding; **faire de la ~ à roulettes** to skateboard, go skateboarding ▶ **planche de salut** (= *appui*) mainstay; (= *dernier espoir*) last hope ▶ **planche de surf** surfboard ▶ **planche à voile** (= *objet*) windsurfing board, sailboard; (= *sport*) windsurfing; **faire de la ~ à voile** to windsurf, go windsurfing

planche-contact (*pl* **planches-contacts**) [plɑ̃ʃkɔ̃takt] NF (*Photo*) contact sheet

planchéié, e [plɑ̃ʃeje] ADJ floored (*lit*)

plancher¹ [plɑ̃ʃe] NM **a** (*Constr*) floor; **faux ~** false floor; **le ~ des vaches*** dry land → **débarrasser**, **pied** **b** (= *limite*) lower limit; **des cotisations** lower limit on contributions; **prix ~** minimum *ou* floor *ou* bottom price **c** (*Anat*) floor; **~ pelvien** pelvic floor

plancher²* [plɑ̃ʃe] ▸ conjug 1 ◂ VI (= *parler*) to talk; **sur quoi as-tu planché?** what did they get you to talk on?; (= *travailler*) **~ sur un rapport** to work on a report

planchette [plɑ̃ʃet] NF (*gén*) (small) board; (= *rayon*) (small) shelf

planchiste [plɑ̃ʃist] NMF windsurfer

plan-concave (*pl* **plan-concaves**) [plɑ̃kɔ̃kav] ADJ plano-concave

plan-convexe (*pl* **plan-convexes**) [plɑ̃kɔ̃veks] ADJ plano-convex

plancton [plɑ̃ktɔ̃] NM plankton

planctonique [plɑ̃ktɔnik] ADJ [*algue, larve*] planktonic

planéité [planeite] NF **a** [*miroir*] flatness; [*surface*] flatness, levelness **b** (*Math*) planeness

planer [plane] ▸ conjug 1 ◂ VI **a** [*oiseau, avion*] to glide; [*brume, fumée*] to hang; **l'oiseau planait au-dessus de sa tête** the bird was hovering above his head *ou* overhead; **il laissa son regard ~ sur la foule** his gaze swept over the crowd → **vol¹** **b** [*danger, soupçons*] **~ sur** to hang over; **laisser ~ une incertitude (sur)** to allow some doubt/some uncertainty to remain (about); **il faisait ~ la menace d'un licenciement** he was using the threat of redundancy; **il a laissé ~ le mystère sur ses intentions** he remained mysterious about his intentions **c** (= *se détacher*) [*arg Drogue*] to have one's head in the clouds **d** (*arg Drogue*) to be high* *ou* spaced out*; **ça fait ~** [*musique, spectacle*] it's really trippy*

planétaire [planetɛʀ] ADJ (*Astron, Tech*) planetary; (= *mondial*) global, worldwide; **à l'échelle ~** on a global *ou* worldwide scale

planétarium [planetaʀjɔm] NM planetarium

planète [planet] NF planet; **la ~ bleue/rouge** the blue/red planet; **sur toute la ~** all over the world; **l'épidémie s'est étendue à la ~ entière** the epidemic has spread throughout the world

planétologie [planetɔlɔʒi] NF planetology

planeur [plɑnœʀ] NM (*Aviat*) glider; **faire du ~** to go gliding

planificateur, -trice [planifikatœʀ, tʀis] (*Écon*) **1** ADJ planning (*épith*) **2** NM,F planner

planification [planifikasjɔ̃] NF **~ (économique)** (economic) planning; **~ familiale** family planning

planifier [planifje] ▸ conjug 7 ◂ VT to plan; **économie planifiée** planned *ou* controlled economy

planimétrie [planimetʀi] NF planimetry

planimétrique [planimetʀik] ADJ planimetric(al)

planisphère [planisfɛʀ] NM planisphere

planning [planiŋ] NM (*Écon, Ind*) programme, schedule; **je vais regarder mon ~** I'll just take a look at my schedule; **avoir un ~ très serré** to have a very tight schedule; **~ familial** family planning

plan-plan* [plɑ̃plɑ̃] ADJ INV [*allure*] laid-back*; **ils mènent une vie ~** they lead a humdrum life; **c'était ~** it was easy going

planque: [plɑ̃k] NF (= *cachette*) hideaway, hideout, hidey-hole*; (*Police*) hideout; (= *travail tranquille*) cushy job *ou* number*; **c'est la ~!** it's a real cushy number!*

planqué, e [plɑ̃ke] (*péj*) **1** NM,F (*: *au travail*) **c'est un ~** he's got a cushy job* **2** NM (*arg*

Mil) (= *non mobilisé*) draft dodger; (*qui évite l'action*) soldier with a desk job

planquer: [plɑ̃ke] ▸ conjug 1 ◂ **1** VT to hide (away), stash away* **2** **se planquer** VPR to hide

plan-relief (*pl* **plans-reliefs**) [plɑ̃ʀəljef] NM (= *maquette*) architectural model, scale model (*of a building*)

plant [plɑ̃] NM (= *plante*) [*légume*] seedling, young plant; [*fleur*] bedding plant; (= *plantation*) [*légumes*] bed, (vegetable) patch; [*fleurs*] (flower) bed; [*arbres*] plantation; **un ~ de salade** a lettuce seedling, a young lettuce (plant); **un ~ de vigne/de bégonia** a young vine/begonia

plantage* [plɑ̃taʒ] NM (*Ordin*) crash; **il y a eu un ~ dans la comptabilité** there was a mess-up* in the books

Plantagenêt [plɑ̃taʒnɛ] NMF Plantagenet

plantain [plɑ̃tɛ̃] NM (= *herbacée*) plantain; **(banane) ~** plantain

plantaire [plɑ̃tɛʀ] ADJ plantar; **verrue ~** verruca (*Brit*), plantar wart (*US*) → **voûte**

plantation [plɑ̃tasjɔ̃] NF **a** (*Hort*) (= *action*) planting; (= *culture*) plant; (= *terrain*) [*légumes*] bed, (vegetable) patch; [*fleurs*] (flower) bed; [*arbres, café, coton*] plantation; **faire des ~s de fleurs** to plant flowers (out); **comment vont tes ~s?** how's your garden doing? **b** (= *exploitation agricole*) plantation

plante¹ [plɑ̃t] NF (*Bot*) plant; **~ annuelle** annual (plant); **~ d'appartement** *ou* **d'agrément** house *ou* pot plant; **~ à fleurs** flowering plant; **~ fourragère** fodder plant; **~ grasse** succulent (plant); **~ grimpante** creeper; **~s médicinales** medicinal plants; **~ de serre** (*lit*) greenhouse *ou* hothouse plant; (*fig*) hothouse plant, delicate flower; **~ textile** fibre (*Brit*) *ou* fiber (*US*) plant; **~ verte** house plant, green (foliage) plant; (*fig*) **c'est une belle ~** she's a lovely *ou* fine specimen

plante² [plɑ̃t] NF (*Anat*) **~ (des pieds)** sole (of the foot)

planté, e [plɑ̃te] (*ptp de* **planter**) ADJ **avoir les dents bien/mal ~es** to have straight/uneven teeth; **ses cheveux sont ~s très bas** he has a very low hairline; **être bien ~ (sur ses jambes)** to be sturdily built; **il est resté ~ au milieu de la rue** he stood stock-still in the middle of the road; **ne restez pas ~ (debout** *ou* **comme un piquet) à ne rien faire!** don't just stand there doing nothing!; **rester ~ devant une vitrine** to stand looking in a shop window

planter [plɑ̃te] ▸ conjug 1 ◂ **1** VT **a** [+ *plante, graine*] to plant, put in; [+ *jardin*] to put plants in; (= *repiquer*) to plant out; **on a planté la région en vignes** the region was planted with vines; **~ un terrain en gazon** to grass over a piece of ground; **avenue plantée d'arbres** tree-lined avenue; (*fig*) **aller ~ ses choux** to retire to the country

b (= *enfoncer*) [+ *clou*] to hammer in, knock in; [+ *pieu*] to drive in; **~ un poignard dans le dos de qn** to stick a knife into sb's back, knife *ou* stab sb in the back; **l'ours planta ses griffes dans son bras** the bear stuck its claws into his arm; **se ~ une épine dans le doigt** to get a thorn stuck in one's finger; **la flèche se planta dans la cible** the arrow hit the target

c (= *mettre*) to stick, put; **il planta son chapeau sur sa tête** he stuck his hat on his head; **il a planté sa voiture au milieu de la rue et il est parti** he stuck his car in the middle of the road and went off; **il nous a plantés sur le trottoir pour aller chercher un journal** he left us hanging about* *ou* standing on the pavement while he went to get a paper; **~ un baiser sur la joue de qn** to plant a kiss on sb's cheek; **~ son regard** *ou* **ses yeux sur qn** to fix one's eyes on sb; **il se planta devant moi** he planted *ou* plonked* himself in front of me; **~ là** (= *laisser sur place*) [+ *personne*] to dump*, leave behind; [+ *voiture*] to dump*, ditch*;

[+ *travail, outils*] to dump*, drop; (= *délaisser*) [+ *épouse*] to walk out on*, ditch*; [+ *travail*] to pack in

d (= *installer*) [+ *échelle, drapeau*] to put up; [+ *tente*] to put up, pitch; **~ une échelle contre un mur** to put a ladder (up) *ou* stand a ladder (up) against a wall; **~ le décor** (*Théât*) to put up *ou* set up the scenery; **cet auteur sait ~ ses personnages** this author is good at characterization

2 **se planter*** VPR **a** (= *se tromper*) to mess up*; **il s'est planté dans ses calculs** he got his calculations wrong; **se ~ à un examen** to fail *ou* flunk* an exam, blow it* in an exam (*US*); **je me suis planté en histoire** I flunked* history, I really blew it* in history; **l'ordinateur s'est planté** the computer crashed

b (= *avoir un accident*) to crash; **il s'est planté en moto** he had a motorbike crash, he crashed his motorbike

3 VI (= *tomber en panne*) **l'ordinateur a planté** ◊ **on a planté** the computer crashed

planteur [plɑ̃tœʀ] NM **a** (= *colon*) planter **b** (*cocktail*) planter's punch

planteuse [plɑ̃tøz] NF (*Agr*) (potato) planter

plantigrade [plɑ̃tigʀad] ADJ, NM plantigrade

plantoir [plɑ̃twaʀ] NM dibble, dibber

planton [plɑ̃tɔ̃] NM (*Mil*) orderly; **être de ~** to be on orderly duty; **faire le ~*** to hang about*, stand around *ou* about (waiting)

plantureusement [plɑ̃tyʀøzmɑ̃] ADV [*manger, boire*] copiously

plantureux, -euse [plɑ̃tyʀø, øz] ADJ **a** [*repas*] copious, lavish; [*femme*] buxom; [*poitrine*] ample **b** [*région, terre*] fertile; **récolte/année plantureuse** bumper crop/year

plaquage [plakaʒ] NM **a** (*Tech*) (*de bois*) veneering; (*de métal*) plating **b** (*Rugby*) tackling (*NonC*), tackle; **~ à retardement** late tackle **c** (‡ = *abandon*) [*fiancé*] jilting*, ditching*, chucking‡; [*épouse*] ditching*; [*emploi*] chucking (in *ou* up)*, packing in* (*Brit*)

plaque [plak] **1** NF **a** [*métal, verre*] sheet, plate; [*marbre*] slab; [*chocolat*] block, slab; [*beurre*] pack; (= *revêtement*) plate, cover(ing) **b** [*verglas*] sheet, patch **c** (= *tache sur la peau*) patch, blotch, plaque (*SPÉC*); [*eczéma*] patch → **sclérose** **d** (*portant une inscription*) plaque; (= *insigne*) badge; (*au casino*) chip; **poser** *ou* **visser sa ~** [*médecin, avocat*] to set up in practice **e** (*Élec, Photo*) plate **f** (*Géol*) plate; **~ continentale/océanique** continental/oceanic plate **g** (‡ = 10 000 F) ten thousand francs **h** (*loc*) **il est à côté de la ~*** he hasn't got a clue*; **j'ai mis à côté de la ~*** I got it completely wrong

2 COMP ▸ **plaque de blindage** armour-plate (*NonC*), armour-plating (*NonC*) ▸ **plaque chauffante** [*cuisinière*] hotplate ▸ **plaque de cuisson** [*four*] baking tray; (= *table de cuisson*) hob, hotplate (*Brit*), burner (*US*) ▸ **plaque de cheminée** fireback ▸ **plaque commémorative** commemorative plaque *ou* plate ▸ **plaque dentaire** dental plaque ▸ **plaque d'égout** manhole cover ▸ **plaque de four** baking tray ▸ **plaque d'identité** [*soldat*] identity disc; [*chien*] name tag, identity disc; [*bracelet*] nameplate ▸ **plaque d'immatriculation** *ou* **minéralogique** *ou* **de police** (*Aut*) number plate, registration plate (*Brit*), license plate (*US*) ▸ **plaque de propreté** fingerplate ▸ **plaque sensible** (*Photo*) sensitive plate ▸ **plaque tournante** (*Rail*) turntable; (*fig*) (= *lien*) hub; (= *personne*) linchpin

plaqué, e [plake] (*ptp de* **plaquer**) **1** ADJ [*bracelet*] plated; [*poches*] patch (*épith*); [*accord*] non-arpeggiated; **~ or/argent** gold-/silver-plated; **~ chêne** oak-veneered **2** NM

a (Orfèvrerie) plate; **en ~** plated; **c'est du ~** it's plated **b** (Menuiserie) veneer

plaquer [plake] ▶conjug 1◀ VT **a** (Tech) [+ bois] to veneer; [+ bijoux] to plate; **~ du métal sur du bois** to plate wood with metal; **~ des bijoux d'or/d'argent** to plate jewellery with gold/silver, gold-plate/silver-plate jewellery **b** (= surajouter) to tack on; **ce passage semble plaqué sur le reste du texte** this passage looks like it has just been stuck onto ou tacked onto the rest of the text **c** (‡ = abandonner) [+ fiancé] to jilt*, ditch*; [+ époux] to ditch*, walk out on; [+ emploi] to chuck (in ou up)‡, pack in* (Brit); **elle a tout plaqué pour le suivre** she chucked up* ou packed in* (Brit) everything to follow him **d** (= aplatir) [+ cheveux] to plaster down; **la sueur plaquait sa chemise contre son corps** the sweat made his shirt cling ou stick to his body; **le vent plaquait la neige contre le mur** the wind was flattening ou plastering the snow up against the wall; **~ une personne contre un mur/au sol** to pin a person to a wall/to the ground; **se ~ les cheveux** to plaster one's hair down (**sur**, on, over); **se ~ au sol/contre un mur** to flatten o.s. on the ground/against a wall **e** (= appliquer) **elle lui plaqua un baiser sur la joue** she planted a kiss on his cheek; **~ sa main sur la bouche de qn** to slap one's hand over sb's mouth **f** (Rugby) to tackle, bring down **g** (Mus) [+ accord] to strike, play

plaquette [plakɛt] NF **a** (= petite plaque) [métal] plaque; [marbre] tablet; [chocolat] block, bar; [sang] platelet; [pilules] blister ou bubble pack ou package; [beurre] pack (Brit), ≈ stick (US); (Aut) **~ de frein** brake pad **b** (= livre) small volume; **~ (publicitaire ou promotionnelle)** (promotional) leaflet

plasma [plasma] NM (Anat, Phys) plasma; **~ sanguin** blood plasma

plastic [plastik] NM plastic explosive

plasticage [plastikaʒ] NM bombing (**de** of), bomb attack (**de** on)

plasticien, -ienne [plastisjɛ̃, jɛn] NM,F (Tech) plastics specialist; (Art) visual artist; (= chirurgien) plastic surgeon

plasticité [plastisite] NF (lit) plasticity; (fig) malleability, plasticity

plastie [plasti] NF plastic surgery; **elle a subi une ~ des doigts** she had plastic surgery on her fingers

plastifiant, e [plastifjɑ̃, jɑ̃t] **1** ADJ plasticizing **2** NM plasticizer

plastification [plastifikasjɔ̃] NF **~ de documents** plastic coating of documents

plastifier [plastifje] ▶conjug 7◀ VT to coat with plastic; **plastifié** plastic-coated

plastiquage [plastikaʒ] NM = **plasticage**

plastique [plastik] **1** ADJ **a** (Art) plastic; **chirurgie ~** plastic surgery **b** (= malléable) malleable, plastic; **en matière ~** plastic **2** NM plastic; **en ~** plastic **3** NF [sculpteur] modelling, plastic art; [statue] modelling; (= arts) plastic arts; [personne] physique

plastiquement [plastikmɑ̃] ADV from the point of view of form, plastically (SPÉC)

plastiquer [plastike] ▶conjug 1◀ VT to blow up, carry out a bomb attack on

plastiqueur [plastikœr] NM terrorist (planting a plastic bomb)

plastoc* [plastɔk] NM plastic; **en ~** plastic (épith)

plastron [plastrɔ̃] NM (Habillement) [corsage] front; [chemise] shirt front; [amovible] false shirt front, dicky*; [escrimeur] plastron; [armure] plastron, breastplate

plastronner [plastrɔne] ▶conjug 1◀ **1** VI to swagger **2** VT to put a plastron on

---

plat¹, plate [pla, plat] **1** ADJ **a** [surface, pays, couture, pli] flat; [mer] smooth, still; [eau] plain, still; (Géom) [angle] straight; [encéphalogramme, ventre, poitrine] flat; [cheveux] straight; **bateau à fond ~** flat-bottomed boat; **chaussure ~e** ou **à talon ~** flat(-heeled) ou low(-heeled) shoe; **elle est ~e de poitrine** ◊ **elle a la poitrine ~e** she is flat-chested; **elle est ~e comme une galette*** ou **une limande*** ou **une planche à pain*** she's as flat as a board* → **assiette, battre b** (= fade) [style] flat, dull, unimaginative; [dissertation, livre] dull, unremarkable, unimaginative; [adaptation] unimaginative, unremarkable; [voix] flat, dull; [vin] insipid; [personne, vie] dull, uninteresting; **ce qu'il écrit est très ~** what he writes is very dull ou flat **c** (= obséquieux) [personne] obsequious, ingratiating (épith); **il nous a fait ses plus ~es excuses** he made the humblest of apologies to us **d** **à ~** : **mettre** ou **poser qch à ~** to lay sth (down) flat; **posez le ruban bien à ~** lay the ribbon down nice and flat; (fig) **mettre qch à ~** to have a close look at things; (fig) **remettre qch à ~** to reexamine sth from every angle; **remise à ~** [dossier, problème, situation] complete ou thorough review; **poser la main à ~ sur qch** to lay one's hand flat on sth; **être à ~** [pneu, batterie] to be flat; * [personne] to be washed out* ou run down; **la grippe l'a mis à ~*** he was laid low by (the) flu; (Aut) **être/rouler à ~** to have/drive on a flat (tyre); **tomber à ~** [remarque, plaisanterie] to fall flat; **tomber à ~ ventre** to fall flat on one's face, fall full-length; **se mettre à ~ ventre** to lie face down; (fig) **se mettre à ~ ventre devant qn** to crawl ou grovel ou toady to sb

2 NM (= partie plate) flat (part); [main] flat; **il y a 15 km de ~ avant la montagne** there is a 15 km flat stretch before the mountain; **course de ~** flat race; (Natation) **faire un ~** to (do a) belly flop; **faire du ~ à qn*** [+ supérieur] to crawl ou grovel ou toady to; [+ femme] to try to pick up, chat up* (Brit)

3 plate NF (= bateau) punt, flat-bottomed boat

4 COMP ▶ **plat de côtes, plates côtes** middle ou best ou short (US) rib

plat² [pla] **1** NM (= récipient, mets) dish; (= partie du repas) course; (= contenu) dish, plate(ful); **~ à gratin** gratin dish; **on en était au ~ de viande** we had reached the meat course; **deux ~s de viande au choix** a choice of two meat dishes ou courses; (fig) **il en a fait tout un ~*** he made a song and dance* ou a great fuss* about it; **il voudrait qu'on lui apporte tout sur un ~ (d'argent)** he wants everything handed to him on a plate (Brit) ou a silver platter (US); **mettre les petits ~s dans les grands** to lay on a first-rate meal, go to town on the meal*; **il lui prépare de bons petits ~s** he makes tasty little dishes for her; (Bible, fig) **pour un ~ de lentilles** for a mess of pottage; (péj) **quel ~ de nouilles !*** he's (ou she's) such an idiot ! → **œuf, pied**

2 COMP ▶ **plat à barbe** shaving mug ▶ **plat à four** oven dish ▶ **plat cuisiné** (chez un traiteur) ready-made meal ▶ **plat garni** main course (served with vegetables) ▶ **plat du jour** dish of the day, plat du jour; **quel est le ~ du jour ?** what's today's special? ▶ **plat de résistance** main course; (fig) pièce de résistance ▶ **plat de service** serving dish

platane [platan] NM plane tree; **faux ~** sycamore; **rentrer dans un ~*** to crash into a tree

plat-bord (pl **plats-bords**) [plabɔr] NM gunwale

plateau (pl **plateaux**) [plato] **1** NM **a** (gén) tray; (de ball-trap) clay pigeon; **~ à fromages** cheeseboard; **~ de fromages** cheeseboard,

---

choice of cheeses (on a menu); **~ d'huîtres** plate of oysters; **~ de fruits de mer** seafood platter; (fig) **il faut tout lui apporter sur un ~ (d'argent)** he wants everything to be handed to him on a plate (Brit) ou a silver platter (US); **la victoire leur a été offerte sur un ~ (d'argent)** victory was handed to them on a plate **b** [balance] pan; [électrophone] turntable, deck; [table] top; [graphique] plateau; **la courbe fait un ~ avant de redescendre** the curve levels off ou reaches a plateau before falling again; **arriver à un ~** (dans une activité, une progression) to reach a plateau; (fig) **mettre qch dans** ou **sur les ~x de la balance** to weigh sth up (fig) **c** (Géog) plateau; **haut ~** high plateau **d** (Théât) stage; (Ciné, TV) set; (= invités) **nous avons un ~ exceptionnel ce soir** we have an exceptional line-up this evening; **sur le ~ de l'émission** on the set **e** (Rail) (= wagon) flat wagon (Brit) ou car (US); (= plate-forme roulante) trailer **f** [pédalier] chain wheel

2 COMP ▶ **plateau continental** continental shelf ▶ **plateau d'embrayage** (Aut) pressure plate ▶ **plateau sous-marin** submarine plateau ▶ **plateau technique** [hôpital etc] technical wherewithal ou capacity ▶ **plateau télé** TV dinner ▶ **plateau de tournage** (Ciné) film set

plateau-repas (pl **plateaux-repas**) [platoRəpa] NM (en avion, en train) tray meal; (devant la télévision) TV dinner

plate-bande (pl **plates-bandes**), **platebande** [platbɑ̃d] NF (de fleurs) flower bed; (Archit) platband; (fig) **marcher sur** ou **piétiner les plates-bandes de qn*** to trespass on sb's preserve, tread on sb's patch, poach on sb's territory

platée [plate] NF (Culin) dish(ful), plate(ful)

plate-forme (pl **plates-formes**), **plateforme** [platfɔrm] NF **a** (gén = terrasse, estrade) platform; [autobus] platform; (Rail = wagon) flat wagon (Brit) ou car (US); (Géog) **~ continentale** continental shelf; **~ (de forage en mer)** (off-shore) oil rig; **~ flottante** floating rig **b** (Ordin) platform; **~ logiciel/matériel** software/hardware platform **c** (Pol) platform; **~ électorale** election platform

platement [platmɑ̃] ADV [écrire, s'exprimer] dully, unimaginatively; [s'excuser] humbly

platine¹ [platin] **1** NM platinum; **~ iridié** platinum-iridium alloy **2** ADJ INV (= couleur) platinum (épith); **blond ~** platinum blond

platine² [platin] NF [électrophone] deck, turntable; [microscope] stage; [presse] platen; [montre, serrure] plate; [machine à coudre] throat plate; **~ laser** laser disk player; **~ cassette** cassette deck

platiné, e [platine] ADJ [cheveux] platinum (épith); **une blonde ~e** a platinum blonde → **vis**

platitude [platityd] NF **a** [style] flatness, dullness; [livre, film, discours, remarque] dullness, lack of imagination (**de** in, of); [vie, personnage] dullness **b** (= propos) platitude; **dire des ~s** to make trite remarks, utter platitudes **c**† (= servilité) [personne] obsequiousness; [excuse] humility; (= acte) obsequiousness (NonC)

Platon [platɔ̃] NM Plato

platonicien, -ienne [platɔnisjɛ̃, jɛn] **1** ADJ Platonic **2** NM,F Platonist

platonique [platɔnik] ADJ [amour] platonic; (hum = de pure forme) **avoir un intérêt ~ pour qch** to have a casual ou passing interest in sth; **les déclarations de l'ONU paraissent plutôt ~s** the statements issued by the UN seem to be nothing more than talk ou a matter of pure form

platoniquement [platɔnikmɑ̃] ADV platonically

platonisme [platɔnism] NM Platonism

plâtrage [platʀaʒ] NM [a] [mur] plastering [b] (Méd) [membre] setting ou putting in plaster; [estomac] lining [c] (Agr) [prairie] liming

plâtras [platʀa] NM (= débris) rubble; (= morceau de plâtre) chunk ou lump of plaster

plâtre [platʀ] NM [a] (= matière) (gén) plaster; (Agr) lime; **mettre une jambe dans le ~** to put ou set a leg in plaster; **j'avais une jambe dans le ~** I had my leg in plaster; [fromage] **c'est du ~!** it's like chalk! → **battre** [b] (= objet : Art, Chir) plaster cast; (Constr) **les ~s** the plasterwork (NonC); (Chir) **porter un ~ au bras** to have one's arm in plaster; **~ de marche** walking plaster (Brit) ou cast (US) → **essuyer**

plâtrer [platʀe] ▸conjug 1◂ VT [a] [+ mur] to plaster [b] (Méd) [+ membre] to set ou put in plaster; [+ estomac] to line; **il a la jambe plâtrée** his leg is in plaster; **elle est plâtrée du genou à la cheville** her leg is in plaster from her knee down to her ankle [c] (Agr) [+ prairie] to lime

plâtrerie [platʀəʀi] NF (= usine) plaster works

plâtreux, -euse [platʀø, øz] ADJ [sol] limey, chalky; [surface] plastered, coated with plaster; [fromage] chalky

plâtrier [platʀije] NM plasterer

plâtrière [platʀijɛʀ] NF (= carrière) gypsum ou lime quarry; (= four) gypsum kiln

plausibilité [plozibilite] NF plausibility, plausibleness

plausible [plozibl] ADJ plausible

plausiblement [ploziblǝmã] ADV plausibly

Plaute [plot] NM Plautus

play-back [plɛbak] NM INV lip-synching; **c'est du ~** they're (ou he is etc) just miming to a prerecorded tape ou lip-synching; **chanter en ~** to mime to a prerecorded tape, lip-synch

play-boy (pl **play-boys**) [plɛbɔj] NM playboy

plèbe [plɛb] NF **la ~** (péj) the plebs, the proles; (Hist) the plebeians

plébéien, -ienne [plebejɛ̃, jɛn] [1] ADJ (Hist) plebeian; [goûts] plebeian, common [2] NM,F plebeian

plébiscitaire [plebisitɛʀ] ADJ of a plebiscite

plébiscite [plebisit] NM plebiscite; **faire** ou **organiser un ~** to hold a referendum

plébisciter [plebisite] ▸conjug 1◂ VT (Pol) (lit) to elect by plebiscite; (= élire à la majorité) to elect by an overwhelming majority; **se faire ~** [candidat] to be elected by an overwhelming majority; **le public a plébiscité ce nouveau magazine** this new magazine has proved a tremendous success with the public

plectre [plɛktʀ] NM plectrum

pléiade [plejad] [1] NF (= groupe) group; (Littérat) **la Pléiade** the Pléiade; **une ~ d'artistes** a whole host of stars [2] **Pléiades** NFPL (Astron) **les Pléiades** the Pleiades

---

┌───┐
│ **plein, pleine** [plɛ̃, plɛn]   │
│   │
│ [1] ADJECTIF   [3] NOM MASCULIN │
│ [2] ADVERBE   │
│   │
│ Lorsque **plein** s'emploie dans des locutions telles │
│ que **à plein droit**, **à plein régime**, **en plein air**, │
│ **en mettre plein la vue** etc, cherchez au nom. │
└───┘

[1] ADJECTIF

[a] **= rempli** [boîte] full; [bus, salle] full (up); [crustacé, coquillage] full; [vie, journée] full, busy; **à craquer** [valise] full to bursting, crammed full; [salle, bus, train] packed (out), crammed full, full to bursting; **un ~ verre de vin** a full glass of wine; **un ~ panier de pommes** a whole basketful of apples, a full basket of apples; **j'ai les mains ~es** my hands are full, I've got my hands full; **~ comme un œuf*** [tiroir] chock-a-block* (Brit), chock-full*; [nez] stuffed up; **être ~ aux as*** to be rolling in money* ou **un ~ in it***, be filthy rich*; (péj) **un gros ~ de soupe*** a big fat slob* (péj)

♦ **plein de** [bonne volonté, admiration, fautes,

vie] full of; [taches, graisse] covered in ou with; **salle ~e de monde** room full of people, crowded room; **j'ai la tête ~e de projets** I'm full of ideas; **son film est ~ de sensualité** his film is very sensual; **leur maison est ~e d'enfants/de fleurs** their house is full of children/of flowers; **voilà une remarque ~e de finesse** that's a very shrewd remark; **il est ~ de santé/d'idées** he's bursting with health/with ideas; **il est ~ de son sujet/de sa nouvelle voiture** he's full of his subject/of his new car; **mets ~ de saveur** dish full of flavour, tasty dish; **être ~ de soi-même** to be full of o.s. ou of one's own importance

[b] **= complet** [succès] complete; [confiance] complete, total; [satisfaction] full, complete, total; **vous avez mon ~ accord** you have my wholehearted consent ou approval; **au ~ sens du terme** in the full ou fullest sense of the word; **absent un jour ~** absent for a whole day; **il a ~ pouvoir pour agir** he has full power ou authority to act; **avoir les ~s pouvoirs** to have full powers → **arc, temps**

[c] **= à son maximum** (Astron) **~e lune** full moon; (Naut) **la mer est ~e** ◊ **c'est la ~e mer** the tide is in, it's high tide

[d] **= entier** **deux volumes, reliure ~ cuir** two volumes fully bound in leather; **manteau de fourrure ~e peau** fur coat made of solid ou full skins

[e] **= non creux** [paroi, porte, pneu, roue] solid; [trait] unbroken, continuous; [son] solid; [voix] rich, sonorous; (= rond) [visage] full; [joues] chubby

[f] *** = ivre** plastered*, stoned* (US); **~ comme une barrique** as drunk as a lord*

[g] **Vét** pregnant, in calf (ou foal ou lamb etc)

[h] **indiquant l'intensité** **la ~e lumière le fatiguait** he found the bright light tiring; **avoir ~e conscience de qch** to be fully aware of sth; **heurter qch de ~ fouet** to crash headlong into sth; **rincer le sol à ~s seaux** to rinse the floor with bucketfuls of water; **ramasser qch à ~s bras/à ~es mains** to pick up armfuls/handfuls of sth; **prendre qch à ~es mains** to lay a firm hold on sth, grasp sth firmly

[i]

♦ **en plein** + nom (= au milieu de, au plus fort de) **en ~e poitrine** full ou right in the chest; **en ~e tête** right in the head; **arriver en ~ (milieu du) cours/en ~e répétition** to arrive (right) in the middle of the class/rehearsal; **en ~ cœur de la ville** right in the centre of the town; **c'est arrivé en ~ Paris/en ~e rue** it happened in the middle of Paris/in the middle of the street; **restaurant en ~ ciel** restaurant up in the sky; **en ~ jour** in broad daylight; **en ~e nuit** in the middle of the night, at dead of night; **en ~ hiver** in the depths ou middle of winter; **son visage était en ~e lumière** the light was shining straight into his face ou at him; **en ~e obscurité** in complete ou utter darkness; **oiseau en ~ vol** bird in full flight; **je suis en ~ travail** I'm in the middle of (my) work, I'm hard at work; **arriver en ~ drame** to arrive in the middle of a crisis; **enfant en ~e croissance** child who is growing fast ou shooting up; **affaire en ~ essor** rapidly expanding ou growing business

[2] ADVERBE

[a] **= en grande quantité dans, partout sur** **il a des bonbons ~ les poches** his pockets are full of ou stuffed with sweets; **j'ai de l'encre ~ les mains** I've got ink all over my hands, my hands are covered in ink; **il a des jouets ~ son placard** he's got a cupboardful ou a cupboard full of toys; **en avoir ~ le dos*** ou **le cul**** de qch to be fed up with sth*, be sick and tired of sth*, be pissed off** with sth; **en avoir ~ les jambes*** ou **les bottes*** ou **les pattes*** to be all-in*

[b] *** = beaucoup**

♦ **plein de** lots of, loads of*; **il y a ~ de bouteilles dans la cave/de gens dans la rue** the

cellar/street is full of bottles/people, there are lots ou loads of bottles in the cellar/people in the street; **un gâteau avec ~ de crème** a cake with lots of ou plenty of cream; **il a mis ~ de chocolat sur sa veste** he's got chocolate all over his jacket; **tu as des romans ? — j'en ai ~** have you any novels? — I've got loads → **tout**

[c] **= exactement vers** **se diriger/donner ~ ouest** to head/face due west

[d] **expressions figées**

♦ **à plein** [fonctionner, tourner] at full capacity; [exploiter] to the full ou maximum; **utiliser à ~ son potentiel/une machine/ses connaissances** to use one's potential/a machine/one's knowledge to the full, make full use of one's potential/a machine/one's knowledge; **il faut profiter à ~ de ces jours de congé** you should make the very most of your time off; **le partenariat joue à ~ dans notre entreprise** partnership plays a full role in our company

♦ **en plein** : **la lumière frappait son visage en ~** the light was shining straight ou right into his face

♦ **en plein dans/sur/dedans** : **en ~ dans l'eau/l'œil** right ou straight in the water/the eye; **la branche est tombée en ~ sur la voiture** the branch fell right on top of the car; **j'ai marché en ~ dedans** I stepped right in it

[3] NOM MASCULIN

[a] **Aut** full tank, tankful; **faire le ~ (d'essence)** to fill up; (faites) **le ~, s'il vous plaît** fill it ou her* up please; **on a fait deux ~s pour descendre jusqu'à Nice** we had to fill up twice to get down to Nice; **faire le ~ d'eau/d'huile** to top up the water/the oil; **le théâtre fait le ~ tous les soirs** the theatre has a full house every night; **faire le ~ de soleil** to get a good dose of the sun; **mangez des fruits, faites le ~ de vitamines** eat fruit and get a full dose of vitamins; **la gauche a fait le ~ des voix aux élections** the left got their maximum possible vote in the elections; **la coalition n'a pas fait le ~ de ses voix** the coalition didn't pick up its full quota of votes; **j'ai fait le ~ de sensations fortes au cours de ce voyage** I had lots of exciting experiences during the trip; **j'ai fait le ~ de souvenirs** I came back with lots of memories; **tu as acheté beaucoup de conserves/livres — oui, j'ai fait le ~*** you bought lots of tins/books — yes I stocked up → **battre**

[b] **Archit** solid

[c] **Calligraphie** downstroke

---

pleinement [plɛnmã] ADV [approuver] wholeheartedly, fully; **utiliser qch ~** to make full use of sth, use sth to the full ou fully; **jouir ~ de qch** to enjoy full use of sth; **vivre ~ sa vie** to live life to the full; **~ responsable/satisfait de** wholly ou entirely ou fully responsible for/satisfied with; **~ rassuré** completely ou totally reassured

plein-emploi, plein emploi [plɛnãplwa] NM full employment

plein-temps (pl **pleins-temps**) [plɛ̃tã] NM (= emploi) full-time job; **je fais un ~** I work full time

pléistocène [plɛistɔsɛn] [1] ADJ Pleistocene [2] NM **le ~** the Pleistocene (period)

plénier, -ière [plenje, jɛʀ] ADJ plenary

plénipotentiaire [plenipɔtãsjɛʀ] ADJ, NM plenipotentiary → **ministre**

plénitude [plenityd] NF [forme] plenitude (littér), fullness; [son] fullness, richness; [droit] completeness; **réaliser ses désirs dans leur ~** to realize one's desires in their entirety; **vivre la vie avec ~** to live one's life to the full; **dans la ~ de sa jeunesse/beauté** in the fullness of his youth/beauty (littér)

plenum [plenɔm] NM plenary session ou meeting

pléonasme [pleɔnasm] NM pleonasm

pléonastique [pleɔnastik] ADJ pleonastic

plésiosaure [plezjozɔr] NM plesiosaurus

pléthore [pletɔr] NF overabundance, plethora

pléthorique [pletɔrik] ADJ [nombre] excessive; [effectifs, documentation] overabundant; [classe] overcrowded; (Méd) obese

pleur [plœr] NM `a` (littér) (= larme) tear; (= sanglot) sob; (hum) **verser un ~** to shed a tear `b` (loc) **en ~s** in tears; **il y aura des ~s et des grincements de dents quand ...** there'll be much wailing and gnashing of teeth when ...; **essuyer ou sécher les ~s de qn** to wipe away ou dry sb's tears `c` (Bot) bleeding

pleurage [plœraʒ] NM (Élec) wow

pleural, e [mpl -aux] [plœral, o] ADJ pleural

pleurant [plœrɑ̃] NM (Art) weeping figure

pleurard, e [plœrar, ard] (péj) `1` ADJ [enfant] whining (épith), who never stops crying; [ton] whimpering (épith), whining (épith) `2` NM,F crybaby*, whiner

pleurer [plœre] ▸ conjug 1 ◂ `1` VI `a` (= larmoyer) [personne] to cry, weep; [yeux] to water, run; **s'endormir en pleurant** to cry oneself to sleep; **~ de rire** to shed tears of laughter, laugh until one cries; **~ de rage** to weep ou cry with rage, shed tears of rage; **~ de joie** to cry ou weep for joy, shed tears of joy; **~ d'avoir fait qch** to cry ou weep at ou over having done sth; **j'ai perdu mon sac, j'en aurais pleuré** I lost my bag — I could have cried ou wept; **il vaut mieux en rire que d'en ~** it's better to laugh (about it) than cry about ou over it; **faire ~ qn** to make sb cry, bring tears to sb's eyes; **les oignons me font ~** onions make my eyes water ou make me cry; **~ comme un veau** (péj) **ou une Madeleine ou à chaudes larmes** to cry one's eyes ou one's heart out; **être sur le point de ~** to be almost in tears, be on the point ou verge of tears; **aller ~ dans le gilet de qn*** to run crying to sb; **triste à (faire) ~** dreadfully ou terribly sad; **bête à (faire) ~** pitifully stupid; **c'est bête à (faire) ~** it's enough to make you weep `b` **~ sur** to lament (over); **~ sur son propre sort** to bemoan one's lot `c` (péj = réclamer) **elle est tout le temps à ~** she's always whining ou begging for something; **~ après qch** to shout for sth; **il a été ~ à la direction pour obtenir une augmentation** he's been whingeing to the management about getting a rise `d` (littér) [sirène, violon] to wail

`2` VT `a` [+ personne] to mourn (for); [+ chose] to bemoan; [+ faute] to bewail, bemoan, lament; **mourir sans être pleuré** to die unlamented ou unmourned; **~ des larmes de joie** to weep ou shed tears of joy, weep for joy; **~ des larmes de sang** to shed tears of blood; **tout son soûl ou toutes les larmes de son corps** to cry one's eyes out; **~ misère** to cry poverty; **~ sa jeunesse** to mourn for one's lost youth

`b` (péj) (= quémander) [+ augmentation, objet] to beg for; (= lésiner sur) [+ nourriture, fournitures] to begrudge, stint; **il ne pleure pas sa peine** he spares no effort; **il ne pleure pas son argent*** he's very free with his money

pleurésie [plœrezi] NF pleurisy; **avoir une ~** to have pleurisy

pleurétique [plœretik] ADJ pleuritic

pleureur, -euse [plœrœr, øz] `1` ADJ `a` [enfant] whining (épith), always crying (attrib); [ton] tearful, whimpering (épith); **c'est un ~/une pleureuse** he/she is always crying; (péj: quémandeur) he/she is always begging for something `b` (Bot) [frêne, mûrier etc] weeping → **saule** `2` **pleureuse** NF (hired) mourner

pleurnichard, e [plœrniʃar, ard] ADJ, NM,F = **pleurnicheur**

pleurnichement [plœrniʃmɑ̃] NM = **pleurnicherie**

pleurnicher [plœrniʃe] ▸ conjug 1 ◂ VI to snivel*, whine

pleurnicherie [plœrniʃri] NF snivelling* (NonC), whining (NonC), grizzling* (Brit) (NonC)

pleurnicheur, -euse [plœrniʃœr, øz] `1` ADJ [enfant] snivelling* (épith), whining (épith), grizzling* (Brit) (épith); [ton] whining (épith) `2` NM,F crybaby*, whiner, grizzler* (Brit)

pleuropneumonie [plœrɔpnømɔni] NF pleuropneumonia

pleurote [plœrɔt] NF oyster mushroom, pleurotus (SPÉC)

pleurotomie [plœrɔtɔmi] NF pleurotomy

pleutre [pløtr] (littér) `1` ADJ cowardly `2` NM coward

pleutrerie [pløtrəri] NF (littér) (= caractère) cowardice; (= acte) act of cowardice

pleuvasser [pløvase], **pleuviner** [pløvine], **pleuvioter** [pløvjɔte] VB IMPERS ▸ conjug 1 ◂ (= crachiner) to drizzle, spit (with rain); (par averses) to be showery

pleuvoir [pløvwar] ▸ conjug 23 ◂ `1` VB IMPERS to rain; **il pleut** it's raining; **les jours où il pleut** on rainy days; **on dirait qu'il va ~** it looks like rain; **il pleut à grosses gouttes** it's raining heavily; **il pleut à flots ou à torrents ou à seaux ou à verse ◊ il pleut des cordes ou des hallebardes** it's pouring (with rain); **il pleut comme vache qui pisse‡** it's pouring down, it's pissing it down‡ (Brit); **qu'il pleuve ou qu'il vente** (come) rain or shine; **il a reçu des cadeaux comme s'il en pleuvait** he was showered with presents; **il ramasse de l'argent comme s'il en pleuvait*** he's raking it in*, he's raking in the money*; (hum) **tu vas faire ~ !** (à une personne qui chante mal) you'll shatter the (glass in the) windows! (hum)

`2` VI [coups, projectiles] to rain down; [critiques, invitations] to shower down; **faire ~ des coups sur qn** to rain blows on sb; **faire ~ des injures sur qn** to shower insults on sb, subject sb to a torrent of insults ou abuse; **les invitations pleuvaient sur lui** he was showered with invitations, invitations were showered on him

pleuvoter [pløvɔte] ▸ conjug 1 ◂ VB IMPERS = **pleuvasser**

plèvre [plɛvr] NF pleura

Plexiglas® [pleksiglas] NM Perspex®, Plexiglass® (US)

plexus [pleksys] NM plexus; **~ solaire** solar plexus

pli [pli] `1` NM `a` [tissu, rideau, ourlet, accordéon] fold; (Couture) pleat; **(faux) ~** crease; **faire un ~ à un pantalon** (au fer) to put a crease in a pair of trousers; (par négligence) to crease a pair of trousers; **jupe/robe à ~s** pleated skirt/dress; **son manteau est plein de ~s** his coat is all creased; **ton manteau fait un ~ dans le dos** your coat has a crease at the back, your coat creases (up) at the back; **son corsage est trop étroit, il fait des ~s** her blouse is too tight — it's all puckered (up); **les ~s et les replis de sa cape** the many folds of her cloak; **il va refuser, cela ne fait pas un ~*** he'll refuse, no doubt about it; **j'avais dit qu'elle oublierait, ça n'a pas fait de ~** I'd said she'd forget and sure enough she did!

`b` (= jointure) [genou, bras] bend; (= bourrelet) [menton, ventre] (skin-)fold; (= ligne) [bouche, yeux] crease; (= ride) [front] crease, furrow, line; **sa peau faisait des ~s au coin des yeux/sur son ventre** his skin was creased round his eyes/made folds on his stomach; **le ~ de l'aine** (the fold of the) groin; **les ~s et les replis de son menton** the many folds under his chin, his quadruple chin (hum)

`c` (= forme) [vêtement] shape; **garder un beau ou bon ~** to keep its shape; **prendre un mauvais ~** [vêtement] to get crushed; [cheveux] to curl the wrong way → **mise²**

`d` (= habitude) habit; **prendre le ~ de faire qch** to get into the habit of doing sth; **il a pris un mauvais ~** he's got into a bad habit; **c'est un ~ à prendre !** you get used to it!

`e` (= enveloppe) envelope; (Admin = lettre) letter; **sous ce ~** enclosed, herewith; **sous ~ cacheté** in a sealed envelope

`f` (Cartes) trick; **faire un ~** to win ou take a trick

`g` (Géol) fold

`2` COMP ▸ **pli d'aisance** (Couture) inverted pleat ▸ **pli creux** (Couture) box pleat ▸ **pli de pantalon** trouser crease ▸ **pli plat** (Couture) flat pleat ▸ **pli de terrain** fold in the ground, undulation

pliable [plijabl] ADJ pliable, flexible

pliage [plijaʒ] NM (= action) folding; (= feuille) folded piece of paper; **l'art du ~** origami

pliant, e [plijɑ̃, ɑ̃t] `1` ADJ [lit, table, vélo] collapsible, folding (épith); [mètre] folding (épith); [canot] collapsible `2` NM folding ou collapsible (canvas) stool, campstool

plie [pli] NF plaice

plier [plije] ▸ conjug 7 ◂ `1` VT `a` [+ papier, tissu] (gén) to fold; (= ranger) to fold up; **~ le coin d'une page** to fold over ou fold down ou turn down the corner of a page

`b` (= rabattre) [+ lit, table, tente] to fold up; [+ éventail] to fold; [+ livre, cahier] to close (up); [+ volets] to fold back; (fig) **~ bagage** to pack up (and go); **on leur fit rapidement ~ bagage** they were sent packing*

`c` (= ployer) [+ branche] to bend; [+ genou, bras] to bend, flex; **~ le genou devant qn** (lit) to go down on one knee before sb; (fig) to bow before sb; **être plié par l'âge** to be bent (double) with age; **être plié (en deux) ◊ être plié de rire** to be doubled up with laughter; **être plié de douleur** to be doubled up with pain

`d` [+ personne] **~ qn à une discipline** to force a discipline upon sb; **~ qn à sa volonté** to bend sb to one's will; **~ qn à sa loi** to lay down the law to sb

`e` (* = endommager) [+ voiture] to wreck

`2` VI `a` [arbre, branche] to bend (over); [plancher, paroi] to sag, bend over; **les branches plient sous le poids des pêches** the branches bending ou sagging under the weight of the peaches; **faire ~ le plancher sous son poids** to make the floor sag beneath one's weight; **~ sous le poids des soucis/des ans** to be weighed down by worry/the years

`b` (= céder) [personne] to yield, give in, knuckle under; [armée] to give way, lose ground; [résistance] to give way; **~ devant l'autorité** to give in ou yield ou bow to authority; **faire ~ qn** to make sb give in ou knuckle under; (Sport) **notre défense plie mais ne rompt pas** our defence is weakening but isn't breaking down completely

`3` **se plier** VPR `a` [meuble, objet] to fold (up) `b` **se ~ à** [+ règle] to submit to, abide by; [+ discipline] to submit o.s. to; [+ circonstances] to bow to, submit to, yield to; [+ désirs, caprices de qn] to give in to, submit to

Pline [plin] NM Pliny

plinthe [plɛ̃t] NF (gén) skirting board; (Archit) plinth

pliocène [plijɔsɛn] `1` ADJ Pliocene `2` NM **le ~** the Pliocene

plissage [plisaʒ] NM pleating

plissé, e [plise] (ptp de **plisser**) `1` ADJ [jupe] pleated; [terrain] folded; [peau] creased, wrinkled `2` NM pleats; **~ soleil** sunray pleats

plissement [plismɑ̃] NM `a` [lèvres] puckering (up); [yeux] screwing up; [front] creasing; [nez] wrinkling `b` [papier] folding; (Géol) folding; **le ~ alpin** the folding of the Alps; **~ de terrain** fold

plisser [plise] ▸ conjug 1 ◂ `1` VT `a` [+ jupe] to pleat, put pleats in; [+ papier] to fold (over) `b` [+ lèvres, bouche] to pucker (up); [+ yeux] to screw up; [+ *nez*] to wrinkle; **un sourire plissa son visage** his face creased into a smile; **il plissa le front** he knitted his brow; **une ride lui plissa le front** a wrinkle furrowed his brow **c** (= *froisser*) [+ *vêtement*] to crease **d** (*Géol*) to fold **2** VI [*vêtement*] to be creased; **elle a les bas qui plissent** her stockings are wrinkled **3 se plisser** VPR **a** [*front*] to crease, furrow; [*lèvres, bouche*] to pucker (up); [*nez*] to wrinkle **b** (= *se froisser*) to become creased; **le lin se plisse très facilement** linen creases easily *ou* is easily creased

plissure [plisyʀ] NF pleats

pliure [plijyʀ] NF fold; [*bras, genou*] bend; (*Typo*) folding

ploc [plɔk] EXCL plop!

ploiement [plwamɑ̃] NM bending

plomb [plɔ̃] NM **a** (= *métal*) lead; **de ~** [*tuyau*] lead; [*soldat*] tin; [*ciel*] leaden; [*soleil*] blazing; [*sommeil*] deep, heavy; **j'ai des jambes de ~** my legs are *ou* feel like lead; **sans ~** [*essence*] unleaded, lead-free; **il n'a pas de ~ dans la tête** *ou* **la cervelle** he's featherbrained; **ça lui mettra du ~ dans la tête** *ou* **la cervelle** that will knock some sense into him **b** (*Chasse*) (lead) shot (*NonC*); **j'ai trouvé trois ~s dans le lièvre en le mangeant** I found three pieces of (lead) shot in the hare when I was eating it; **du gros ~** buckshot; **du petit ~** small shot; (*fig*) **avoir du ~ dans l'aile** to be in a bad way **c** (*Pêche*) sinker; (*Typo*) type; [*vitrail*] lead; (= *sceau*) (lead) seal; (*Élec* = *fusible*) fuse; (*Couture*) lead weight; (*Naut*) **~ (de sonde)** sounding lead; **les ~s ont sauté** the fuses have blown *ou* gone → **péter b** **d** (*loc*) **mettre un mur à ~** to plumb a wall; **le soleil tombe à ~** the sun is blazing straight down

plombage [plɔ̃baʒ] NM **a** [*dent*] filling; **j'ai perdu mon ~** my filling has come out **b** [*canne, ligne, rideaux*] weighting (with lead) **c** [*colis, wagon*] sealing (with lead)

plombe: [plɔ̃b] NF hour; **ça fait deux ~s que j'attends** I've been waiting two hours now; **à trois ~s du matin** at three o'clock in the morning

plombé, e [plɔ̃be] (*ptp de* **plomber**) **1** ADJ [*teint, couleur, ciel*] leaden; [*essence*] leaded; [*dent*] filled; **canne ~e** *ou* **à bout ~** walking stick with a lead(en) tip **2 plombée** NF (= *arme*) bludgeon; (*Pêche*) sinkers, weights

plomber [plɔ̃be] ▸ conjug 1 ◂ **1** VT **a** (= *Méd*) [+ *dent*] to fill, put a filling in **b** (= *garnir de plomb*) [+ *canne, ligne, rideaux*] to weight (with lead) **c** (= *sceller*) [+ *colis, wagon*] to seal (with lead), put a lead seal on **d** (*Constr*) [+ *mur*] to plumb **e** (*Agr*) to tamp (down) **f** (= *colorer en gris*) to turn leaden **g** (*Fin*) **les nouveaux investissements ont plombé les comptes de l'entreprise** the new investments have been a drain on the company accounts **h**: (= *contaminer*) to infect **2 se plomber** VPR [*ciel*] to turn leaden; [*visage*] to become livid

plomberie [plɔ̃bʀi] NF **a** (= *métier, installations*) plumbing; (= *atelier*) plumber's (work)shop; (= *industrie*) lead industry; **faire de la ~** to do some plumbing

plombier [plɔ̃bje] NM **a** (= *ouvrier*) plumber **b** (* = *agent secret*) mole*, spy (*who plants bugs*)

plombières [plɔ̃bjɛʀ] NF INV tutti-frutti (ice cream)

plombifère [plɔ̃bifɛʀ] ADJ plumbiferous

plonge: [plɔ̃ʒ] NF dishwashing, washing-up (*in restaurant*); **faire la ~** to do the washing-up

plongé, e¹ [plɔ̃ʒe] (*ptp de* **plonger**) ADJ **~ dans** [+ *obscurité, désespoir, misère*] plunged in; [+ *vice*] steeped in; [+ *méditation, pensées*] immersed in, deep in; **~ dans la lecture d'un livre** buried *ou* immersed in a book; **~ dans le sommeil** sound asleep, in a deep sleep

plongeant, e [plɔ̃ʒɑ̃, ɑ̃t] ADJ [*décolleté, tir*] plunging; **vue ~e** view from above

plongée² [plɔ̃ʒe] NF **a** [*nageur, sous-marin, gardien de but*] dive; **faire de la ~** to go diving; **effectuer plusieurs ~s** to make several dives; **en ~, le sous-marin ...** when diving, the submarine ...; **~ sous-marine** (*gén*) diving; (*avec scaphandre autonome*) skin *ou* scuba diving; **~ avec tuba** snorkelling; **~ avec bouteille(s)** diving with breathing apparatus; **l'avion a fait une ~ sur la ville** the plane swooped down over the town; (*fig*) **cette ~ dans la préhistoire/le passé** this journey deep into prehistory/the past **b** [*cours, monnaie*] (nose-)dive **c** (*Ciné* = *prise de vue*) high angle shot; **faire une ~ sur qch** to take a high angle shot of sth; **en ~ verticale** from above

plongeoir [plɔ̃ʒwaʀ] NM diving board

plongeon¹ [plɔ̃ʒɔ̃] NM (*Ftbl, Natation*) dive; **faire un ~** [*nageur*] to dive; [*gardien de but*] to make a dive, dive; (= *tomber*) to go head over heels; **faire le ~** [*société*] to go under suddenly; [*prix, valeurs*] to nose-dive, take a nose dive

plongeon² [plɔ̃ʒɔ̃] NM (= *oiseau*) diver (*Brit*), loon (*US*)

plonger [plɔ̃ʒe] ▸ conjug 3 ◂ **1** VI **a** [*personne, sous-marin*] to dive (**dans** into, **sur** on, onto); [*avion, oiseau*] to dive, make a dive; [*gardien de but*] to dive, make a dive; **l'avion a plongé sur son objectif** the plane dived (down) *ou* swooped down towards its target; **l'oiseau plongea sur sa proie** the bird swooped (down) onto its prey **b** [*route, terrain*] to plunge (down), dip (sharply *ou* steeply); [*racines*] to go down; **~ dans le sommeil** to fall (straight) into a deep sleep; **mon regard plongeait sur la vallée** I gazed down on the valley; **il a plongé dans l'alcool/la drogue** he turned to drink/to drugs; **il a plongé dans la dépression** he sank into a deep depression **c** [*société*] to go under; [*prix, valeurs*] to nose-dive, take a nose-dive, plummet; [*notes scolaires*] to plummet **d** (*arg Crime*) [*truand*] to get busted* *ou* done* (*Brit*) (**pour** for) **2** VT **~ qch dans** [+ *sac*] to plunge *ou* thrust sth into; [+ *eau*] to plunge sth into; **~ qn dans** [+ *obscurité, misère, sommeil, méditation, vice*] to plunge sb into; [+ *désespoir*] to throw *ou* plunge sb into; **il plongea sa main dans sa poche pour prendre son mouchoir** he plunged his hand into his pocket to get his handkerchief out; **~ qn dans la surprise** to surprise sb greatly; **vous me plongez dans l'embarras** you've put me in a difficult position; **il lui plongea un poignard dans le cœur** he plunged a dagger into his heart; **plante qui plonge ses racines dans le sol** plant that thrusts its roots deep into the ground; **~ son regard sur/vers** to cast one's eyes at/towards; **il plongea son regard dans mes yeux** he looked deeply into my eyes **3 se plonger** VPR **se ~ dans** [+ *études, lecture*] to bury *ou* immerse o.s. in, throw o.s. into; [+ *dossier, eau, bain*] to plunge into, immerse o.s. in; **se ~ dans le vice** to throw o.s. into a life of vice

plongeur, -euse [plɔ̃ʒœʀ, øz] **1** ADJ diving **2** NM,F **a** (*Sport*) diver; **~ sous-marin** (*gén*) diver; (*sans scaphandre*) skin diver → **plonge b** [*restaurant*] dishwasher, washer-up (*Brit*) **3** NM (= *oiseau*) diver (*Brit*), loon (*US*)

plosive [ploziv] NF plosive

plot [plo] NM (*Élec*) contact; [*billard électrique*] pin; [*piscine*] **~ (de départ)** (starting) block

plouc: [pluk] **1** NM (*péj*) (= *paysan*) country bumpkin; (= *crétin*) ninny* **2** ADJ **il est ~** he's a ninny*; **sa robe fait ~** her dress looks dowdy

plouf [pluf] EXCL splash!; **il est tombé dans l'eau avec un gros ~** he fell into the water with a splash; **la pierre a fait ~ en tombant**

dans l'eau the stone made a splash as it fell into the water

ploutocrate [plutɔkʀat] NM plutocrat

ploutocratie [plutɔkʀasi] NF plutocracy

ploutocratique [plutɔkʀatik] ADJ plutocratic

ployer [plwaje] ▸ conjug 8 ◂ (*littér*) **1** VI [*branche, dos*] to bend; [*poutre, plancher*] to sag; [*genoux, jambes*] to give way, bend; [*armée*] to yield, give way; [*résistance*] to give way; **faire ~ le plancher sous son poids** to make the floor sag beneath one's weight; **~ sous l'impôt** to be weighed down by taxes; (*Sport*) **notre défense ploie mais ne rompt pas** our defence is weakening but not breaking down completely; (*fig*) **~ sous le joug** to bend beneath the yoke **2** VT to bend; **~ un pays sous son autorité** to make a country bow down *ou* submit to one's authority

pluches [plyʃ] NFPL **a** (*arg Mil*) **être de (corvée de) ~** to be on potato-peeling *ou* spud-bashing* (*Brit*) duty **b** (*Culin*) **~ de cerfeuil** chervil sprigs

pluie [plɥi] NF **a** (*gén*) rain; (= *averse*) shower (of rain); **les ~s** the rains; **la saison des ~s** the rainy season; **le temps est à la ~** we're in for some rain, it looks like rain; **jour/temps de ~** wet *ou* rainy day/weather; **sous la ~** in the rain; **~ battante** driving *ou* lashing rain; **~ diluvienne** pouring rain (*NonC*), downpour; **~ fine** drizzle; **une ~ fine tombait** it was drizzling; **~ jaune/acide** yellow/acid rain **b** [*cadeaux, cendres*] shower; [*balles, pierres, coups*] hail, shower; **en ~** in a shower; **tomber en ~** to shower down; (*Culin*) **versez le riz en ~** add the rice gradually **c** (*loc*) **après la ~ (vient) le beau temps** (*lit*) the sun is shining again after the rain; (*fig*) everything's fine again; (*fig*) **faire la ~ et le beau temps** to call the shots*; **il n'est pas né** *ou* **tombé de la dernière ~** he wasn't born yesterday ◼ (*PROV*) **petite ~ abat grand vent** a small effort can go a long way → **ennuyeux, parler**

plumage [plymaʒ] NM plumage (*NonC*), feathers

plumard: [plymaʀ] NM bed; **aller au ~** to turn in*, hit the hay* *ou* the sack*

plume [plym] **1** NF **a** [*oiseau*] feather; **chapeau à ~s** feathered hat, hat with feathers; **oreiller/lit de ~s** feather pillow/bed; **être aussi léger qu'une ~** *ou* **ne pas peser plus lourd qu'une ~** to be as light as a feather; **soulever qch comme une ~** to lift sth up as if it weighed practically nothing; **se mettre dans les ~s** to hit the sack* *ou* the hay*, turn in*; **il y a laissé des ~s** (*gén*) he came off badly; (*financièrement*) he got his fingers burnt; (*hum*) **il perd ses ~s** his hair is falling out, he's going bald → **gibier, poids, voler¹** **b** (*pour écrire*) (*d'oiseau*) quill (pen); (*en acier*) (pen) nib; (= *stylo*) **écrire à la ~** to write with a fountain pen; **~ d'oie** goose quill; **dessin à la ~** pen-and-ink drawing; **écrire au fil** *ou* **courant de la ~** to write just as the ideas come to one *ou* come into one's head; **il a la ~ facile** writing comes easy to him; **vivre de sa ~** to live by writing *ou* by one's pen; **prendre la ~ pour ...** to take up one's pen to ..., put pen to paper to ...; (*hum*) **il a pris sa plus belle ~ pour écrire au percepteur** he wrote the tax inspector a very elaborate letter; (*dans une lettre*) **je lui passe la ~** I'll hand over to him, I'll let him carry on; (*fig*) **tremper sa ~ dans le poison** to steep one's pen in venom → **homme c** (*Pêche*) quill **d** [*coquille*] pen **2** NM = **plumard 3** COMP ► **plume à vaccin** vaccine point

plumeau (*pl* **plumeaux**) [plymo] NM feather duster

plumer [plyme] ▸ conjug 1 ◂ VT **a** [+ *volaille*] to

pluck [b]* [+ *personne*] to fleece*; **se faire ~** to be *ou* get fleeced*

plumet [plymɛ] NM plume

plumetis [plym(ə)ti] NM (= *tissu*) Swiss muslin; (= *broderie*) raised satin stitch

plumeux, -euse [plymø, øz] ADJ feathery

plumier [plymje] NM pencil box

plumitif [plymitif] NM (*péj*) (= *employé*) pen-pusher (*péj*); (= *écrivain*) scribbler (*péj*)

▼ **plupart** [plypaʀ] NF **la ~ des gens** most people, the majority of people; **la ~ des gens qui se trouvaient là** most of the people there; **la ~ (d'entre eux) pensent que ...** most (of them) *ou* the majority (of them) think that ...; **dans la ~ des cas** in most cases, in the majority of cases; **pour la ~** mostly, for the most part; **ces gens qui, pour la ~, avaient tout perdu** these people who, for the most part, had lost everything, these people, most of whom had lost everything; **la ~ du temps** most of the time; **la ~ de mon temps** most of my time, the greater part of my time

plural, e (*mpl* **-aux**) [plyʀal, o] ADJ [*vote*] plural

pluralisme [plyʀalism] NM pluralism

pluraliste [plyʀalist] [1] ADJ pluralistic [2] NMF pluralist

pluralité [plyʀalite] NF multiplicity, plurality

pluriannuel, -elle [plyʀianɥɛl] ADJ [*contrat*] long-term; (*Bot*) perennial

pluriculturel, -elle [plyʀikyltyʀɛl] ADJ multicultural

pluridisciplinaire [plyʀidisiplinɛʀ] ADJ (*Scol*) pluridisciplinary, multidisciplinary

pluridisciplinarité [plyʀidisiplinaʀite] NF pluridisciplinary, multidisciplinary nature

pluriel, -elle [plyʀjɛl] [1] ADJ plural; [*livre, pièce de théâtre*] **c'est une œuvre plurielle** it is a work which can be read (*ou* understood *etc*) on many different levels [2] NM plural; **au ~** in the plural; **la première personne du ~** the first person plural; **le ~ de majesté** the royal "we"; **le ~ de « cheval » est « chevaux »** the plural of "cheval" is "chevaux"

pluriethnique [plyʀiɛtnik] ADJ multiethnic

plurifonctionnalité [plyʀifɔ̃ksjɔnalite] NF [*appareil, salle*] versatility

plurilatéral, e (*mpl* **-aux**) [plyʀilateʀal, o] ADJ multilateral

plurilingue [plyʀilɛ̃g] ADJ multilingual

plurilinguisme [plyʀilɛ̃gɥism] NM multilingualism

pluripartisme [plyʀipaʀtism] NM (*Pol*) multi-party system

plurivalent, e [plyʀivalɑ̃, ɑ̃t] ADJ multivalent, polyvalent

▼ **plus**

[1] ADVERBE DE NÉGATION	[3] ADVERBE (*emploi superlatif*)
[2] ADVERBE (*emploi comparatif*)	[4] CONJONCTION
	[5] NOM MASCULIN

Lorsque **plus** *s'emploie dans des locutions telles que* d'autant plus, raison de plus, tant et plus, à plus forte raison, non ... plus *etc, cherchez à l'autre mot.*

[1] ADVERBE DE NÉGATION

[ply] *devant consonne et en fin de phrase,* [plyz] *devant voyelle.*

◆ **(ne +)** *verbe* **+ plus** (*temps*) not any longer *ou* any more, no longer; (*quantité*) no more, not any more; **il ne la voit ~** he no longer sees her, he doesn't see her any more; **il n'a ~ besoin de son parapluie** he doesn't need his umbrella any longer *ou* any more; **il n'a ~ à s'inquiéter/travailler maintenant** he doesn't need to worry/work any more now; **il ne reviendrai ~/~ jamais** I won't/I'll never come back again; **il n'a ~ dit un mot** he didn't say another word (after that); **il n'est ~ là ◊ il est ~ là*** he isn't here anymore; (*euph*) **son père n'est ~** his fa-

ther has passed away (*euph*); **elle n'est ~ très jeune** she's not as young as she used to be; **~ besoin de rester !** there's no need to stay now; **t'as ~ faim ?*** aren't you hungry any more?

◆ **plus de** + *nom* : **elle n'a ~ de pain/d'argent** she's got no more *ou* she hasn't got any more bread/money, she's got no (more) bread/money left; **elle ne veut ~ de pain** she doesn't want any more bread; **il n'y a ~ guère** *ou* **beaucoup de pain** there's hardly any bread left; (*hum*) **il n'y a ~ d'enfants/de jeunesse !** children/young people aren't what they used to be!; **~ de doute !** there's no longer any doubt about it; **~ de vin, merci** no more wine, thank you; **des fruits ? y en a ~*** fruit? there's none left *ou* there's no more left *ou* there isn't any (more) left

◆ **plus que** (= *seulement*) **il n'y a ~ que des miettes** there are only crumbs left, there's nothing left but crumbs; **ça ne tient ~ qu'à elle** it's up to her now; **il n'y a (guère) ~ que huit jours avant les vacances** there's only (about) a week to go before the holidays; **il ne nous reste ~ qu'à attendre** all we've got to do now is wait; **il ne me reste ~ qu'à vous dire au revoir** it only remains for me to say goodbye; **~ que 5 km à faire** only another 5 km to go

◆ **plus rien/personne/aucun** : **il n'y a ~ rien** there's nothing left; **il n'y a ~ rien d'autre à faire** there's nothing else to do; **on n'y voit presque ~ rien** you can hardly see anything now; **(il n'y a) ~ personne à la maison** there's no one left in the house; **il n'y a ~ aucun espoir** there's no hope left

[2] ADVERBE (*emploi comparatif*)

[ply] *devant consonne,* [plyz] *devant voyelle,* [plys] *en fin de phrase,* [ply(s)] *devant* **que**.

[a]

◆ *verbe* **+ plus** (**que**) : **il devrait sortir/lire ~** he should go out/read more; **vous travaillez ~ (que nous)** you work more (than us); **il ne gagne pas ~ (que vous)** he doesn't earn any more (than you); **j'aime la poésie ~ que tout au monde** I like poetry more than anything (else) in the world ▪ (*PROV*) **~ fait douceur que violence** kindness succeeds where force will fail

[b]

◆ **plus** + *adjectif ou adverbe court* (**+ que**)

Lorsque l'adjectif ou l'adverbe est court, c'est-à-dire qu'il n'a qu'une ou deux syllabes, son comparatif se forme généralement avec **-er**.

il est ~ foncé/large (que l'autre) it's darker/wider (than the other one); **elle n'est pas ~ grande (que sa sœur)** she isn't any taller *ou* she is no taller (than her sister); **il est ~ vieux qu'elle de 10 ans** he's 10 years older than her *ou* than she is than she (*frm*); **il court ~ vite (qu'elle)** he runs faster (than her *ou* than she does); **une heure ~ tôt/tard** an hour earlier/later; **ne venez pas ~ tard que 6 heures** don't come any later than 6 o'clock

Lorsque l'adjectif se termine par **y**, *son comparatif est formé avec* **-ier**.

elle est ~ jolie/bête she's prettier/sillier; **c'était ~ drôle** it was funnier

Lorsque l'adjectif n'a qu'une syllabe avec une voyelle brève et se termine par une consonne, il y a doublement de cette consonne finale.

il est ~ gros/mince he's bigger/slimmer

Certains mots de deux syllabes admettent les deux types de comparatifs mais l'usage privilégie une forme plutôt que l'autre.

c'est ~ simple it's simpler, it's more simple; **cette méthode est ~ courante que l'autre** this method is more common *ou* is commoner than the other one; **~ souvent que tu ne le penses** more often than you think, oftener than you think

Certaines terminaisons telles que -ing, -ed, -s, -ly *interdisent l'ajout du suffixe de comparaison sur des mots de deux syllabes.*

il est ~ malin he's more cunning; **c'est encore ~ pompeux** it's even more pompous; **pour y arriver ~ rapidement** to get there more quickly; **prends-le ~ doucement** take hold of it more gently

Attention aux comparatifs irréguliers.
c'est ~ loin it's further, it's farther

Notez les autres traductions possibles lorsque la comparaison porte sur une même personne ou un même objet.
il est ~ bête que méchant he's stupid rather than malicious, he's more stupid than malicious; **c'est ~ agaçant que douloureux** it's not so much painful as annoying, it's more annoying than painful

[c]

◆ **plus** + *adjectif ou adverbe long*

Lorsque l'adjectif ou l'adverbe est long, c'est-à-dire qu'il a au moins trois syllabes, son comparatif se forme généralement avec **more**.

il est ~ compétent (que vous/moi) he is more competent (than you (are)/than me *ou* than I am *ou* than I (*frm*)); **beaucoup ~ facilement** much more *ou* a lot more easily; [*MAIS*] **il est ~ malheureux que jamais** he's unhappier than ever

Notez l'emploi possible de **as** *pour traduire les expressions avec* **fois**.
deux fois ~ souvent que ... twice as often as ...; **deux ou trois fois ~ cher que ...** two or three times more expensive than ..., two or three times as expensive as ...; **il est deux fois ~ âgé qu'elle** he's twice as old as her, he's twice her age

◆ **à plus tard !** ◊ **à plus !*** see you later!

[d]

◆ **plus que** + *adjectif ou adverbe* : **il est ~ qu'intelligent** he's clever to say the least; **un résultat ~ qu'honorable** a more than honourable result, an honourable result to say the least; **~ que jamais** more than ever; **je lui ai parlé ~ que gentiment** I spoke to him most kindly; **j'en ai ~ qu'assez !** I've had more than enough of this!

[e]

◆ **de plus** (*comparaison*) **elle a 10 ans de ~ (que lui)** she's 10 years older (than him); **il y a dix personnes de ~ (qu'hier)** there are ten more people (than yesterday); **ça leur a pris dix minutes de ~ (que la veille)** it took them ten minutes longer (than the day before)
(= *en outre*) furthermore, what is more, moreover
(= *encore*) **une fois de ~** once more, once again; **il me faut une heure de ~** I need one more *ou* another hour

◆ **de plus en plus** more and more; **il fait de ~ en ~ beau** the weather's getting better and better; **aller de ~ en ~ vite** to go faster and faster; **de ~ en ~ drôle** funnier and funnier, more and more funny

◆ **en plus** (= *en supplément*) **les frais d'envoi sont en ~** postal charges are extra *ou* are not included; **on nous a donné deux verres en ~** we were given two more *ou* extra glasses; (= *de trop*) we were given two glasses too many; (= *en prime*) we were given two glasses free; **vous n'avez pas une chaise en ~ ?** you wouldn't have a spare chair?; **elle a choisi le même chapeau avec les fleurs en ~** she chose the same hat but with flowers on it; **il est doué, rapide, et en ~ il travaille !** he's talented, quick and on top of that *ou* and what's more he's a good worker!

◆ **en plus** + *adjectif* : **il ressemble à sa mère, mais en ~ blond** he's like his mother only fairer; **je cherche le même genre de maison en ~ grand** I'm looking for the same kind of house only bigger

◆ **en plus de** : **en ~ de son travail, il prend des cours du soir** on top of his work, he's taking evening classes; **en ~ de cela** on top of (all) that, in addition to that

- **... et plus** : les enfants de six ans et ~ children aged six and over; **les familles de trois enfants et ~** families with three or more children; **100 000 F et ~** 100,000 francs and more *ou* and over
- **ni plus ni moins** : **il est compétent, mais ni ~ ni moins que sa sœur** he's competent, but neither more (so) nor less so than his sister; **elle est secrétaire, ni ~ ni moins** she's just a secretary, no more no less; **c'est du vol, ni ~ ni moins** it's sheer *ou* daylight robbery; (*iro*) **il envisage, ni ~ ni moins, de licencier la moitié du personnel** he's considering sacking half of the staff, no less
- **plus de** (= *davantage de*) **(un peu) ~ de pain** (a little *ou* a bit) more bread; **j'ai ~ de pain que vous** I've got more bread than you (have); **il y aura (beaucoup) ~ de monde demain** there will be (a lot *ou* many) more people tomorrow; **il n'y aura pas ~ de monde demain** there won't be any more people tomorrow
  (= *au-delà de*) **il y aura ~ de 100 personnes** there will be more than *ou* over 100 people; **à ~ de 100 mètres d'ici** more than *ou* over 100 metres from here; **il roulait à ~ de 100 km/h** he was driving at over 100 km per hour; **les enfants de ~ de 4 ans** children over 4; **les ~ de 30/40 ans** the over 30s/40s; **il n'y avait pas ~ de 10 personnes** there were no more than 10 people; **il est ~ de 9 heures** it's after *ou* past *ou* gone* 9 o'clock; **~ d'un** more than one; **~ d'un aurait refusé** many would have refused
- **plus ..., moins ...**, **~ on le connaît, moins on l'apprécie** the more you get to know him, the less you like him
- **plus ..., plus ...** the more ..., the more ...; **~ il en a, ~ il en veut** the more he has, the more he wants; **~ on boit, ~ on a soif** the more you drink, the thirstier you get; **~ ça change, ~ c'est la même chose** plus ça change... ■ (*PROV*) **~ on est de fous, ~ on rit** *ou* **s'amuse** the more the merrier
- **plus ou moins** (= *à peu près, presque*) more or less; **ils sont ~ ou moins fiancés** they're more or less engaged; **des pratiques ~ ou moins douteuses** more or less shady practices; **à ~ ou moins long terme** sooner or later; (= *pas très*) **je l'ai trouvé ~ ou moins sympathique** I didn't find him very friendly; **est-elle efficace ? — ~ ou moins** is she efficient? — not particularly; **les gens sont ~ ou moins réceptifs à la publicité** (*variant avec les individus*) some people are more receptive to advertising than others; (*selon leur humeur etc*) people can be more or less receptive to advertising; **il supporte ~ ou moins bien cette situation** he just about puts up with the situation; **je le connais ~ ou moins** I know him vaguely; **ils utilisent cette méthode avec ~ ou moins de succès/d'enthousiasme** they use this method with varying degrees of success/of enthusiasm
- **qui plus est** furthermore, what's more, moreover

3 ADVERBE (*emploi superlatif*)

> [ply(s)] *devant consonne*, [plyz] *devant voyelle*, [plys] *en fin de phrase*.

a

- *verbe* + **le plus** : **ce qui m'a frappé le ~** what struck me most; **ce qui les a le ~ étonnés** what surprised them (the) most; **ce que j'aime le ~** what I most like, what I like (the) most *ou* (the) best

b

- **le plus** + *adjectif ou adverbe court*

> *Lorsque l'adjectif ou l'adverbe est court, c'est-à-dire qu'il n'a qu'une ou deux syllabes, son superlatif se forme avec -est.*

c'est le ~ grand peintre qui ait jamais vécu he is the greatest painter that ever lived; **il a couru le ~ vite** he ran the fastest

> *Lorsque l'adjectif se termine par y son superlatif se forme avec -iest.*

c'est la ~ jolie/bête she's the prettiest/silliest;

c'était le moment le ~ drôle du film that was the funniest part of the film

> *Lorsque l'adjectif n'a qu'une syllabe avec une voyelle brève et se termine par une consonne, il y a doublement de cette consonne finale.*

c'est le ~ gros/mince he's the biggest/slimmest

> *Certains mots de deux syllabes admettent les deux types de superlatifs mais l'usage privilégie une forme plutôt que l'autre.*

c'est le ~ simple it's the simplest, it's the most simple; **c'est la méthode la ~ courante** it's the commonest *ou* the most common method

> *Certaines terminaisons telles que -ing, -ed, -s, -ly interdisent l'ajout du suffixe sur des mots de deux syllabes.*

l'enfant le ~ doué que je connaisse/de la classe the most gifted child I've (ever) met/in the class; **c'est la partie la ~ ennuyeuse** it's the most boring part; **c'est ce que j'ai de ~ précieux** it's the most precious thing I possess; **c'est le livre que je lis le ~ souvent** it's the book I read most often

> *Attention aux superlatifs irréguliers.*

c'est le ~ loin it's the furthest, it's the farthest

> *Lorsque la comparaison se fait entre deux personnes ou deux choses, on utilise la forme du comparatif.*

le ~ petit (des deux) the smaller (of the two); *MAIS* **le ~ petit (de tous)** the smallest (of all)

c

- **le plus** + *adjectif ou adverbe long*

> *Lorsque l'adjectif ou l'adverbe est long, c'est-à-dire qu'il a au moins trois syllabes, son superlatif se forme généralement avec the most.*

c'est le ~ intéressant it's the most interesting; **le ~ beau de tous mes livres** the most beautiful of all my books; *MAIS* **c'est la personne la ~ désordonnée que je connaisse** she's the untidiest person I know

> *Attention : lorsque la comparaison se fait entre deux personnes ou deux choses, on utilise la forme du comparatif.*

le ~ beau (des deux) the more beautiful (of the two)

d

- **le plus de** + *nom* : **c'est nous qui avons cueilli le ~ de fleurs** we've picked the most flowers; **c'est le samedi qu'il y a le ~ de monde** it's on Saturdays that there are the most people; **les films qui rapportent le ~ d'argent** the films that make the most money; **ce qui m'a donné le ~ de mal** the thing I found (the) most difficult; **celui qui a le ~ de chances de gagner** the one who has the most chances of winning
- **le plus (...) possible** : **pour y arriver le ~ rapidement possible** to get there as quickly as possible; **il a couru le ~ vite possible** he ran as fast as possible *ou* as fast as he could; **prends-en le ~ possible** take as much (*ou* as many) as possible *ou* as you can; **prends le ~ possible de livres/de beurre** take as many books/as much butter as possible
- **au plus** at the most; **il y a au ~ un quart d'heure qu'il est parti** he left a quarter of an hour ago at the most; **ça vaut 100 F au ~** its worth 100 francs maximum *ou* at (the) most; **ils étaient une vingtaine au ~** there were twenty of them at (the) most *ou* at the outside
- **au plus** + *adverbe* : **rappelle-moi au ~ vite** call me back as soon as you can *ou* as soon as possible; **~ tard, tôt**
- **des plus** + *adjectif* : **une situation des ~ embarrassantes** a most embarrassing situation; **l'entreprise est des ~ rentables** the company is highly profitable; **ses craintes sont des ~ justifiées** he has every reason to be afraid
- **tout au plus** at the very most; **il a trente ans, tout au ~** he's thirty at (the) most *ou* at the outside; **tout au ~ peut-on** *ou* **on peut tout au ~ affirmer que ...** all we can say is that ..., the best we can say is that ...

4 CONJONCTION [plys] plus, and; **deux ~ deux font quatre** two and two are four, two plus two make four; **tous les voisins, ~ leurs enfants** all the neighbours, plus their children *ou* and their children (as well); **il paie sa chambre, ~ le téléphone et l'électricité** he pays for his room, plus the telephone and electricity bills; **il fait ~ deux aujourd'hui** it's plus two (degrees) today, it's two above freezing today

5 NOM MASCULIN [plys]
a Math (*signe*) ~ plus (sign)
b = *avantage* plus; **ici, parler breton est un ~ indéniable** being able to speak Breton is definitely a plus *ou* is quite an asset here; **les ~ de ce nouveau modèle: ABS, airbag etc** the new model's plus points: ABS, airbag etc; **quels sont les ~ de ce produit par rapport aux autres ?** what does this product have that the others don't?

---

plusieurs [plyzjœʀ] 1 ADJ INDÉF PL several; **on ne peut pas être en ~ endroits à la fois** you can't be in more than one place at once; **ils sont ~** there are several (of them), there are a number of them; **ils sont ~ à vouloir venir** several of them want to come; **un ou ~** one or more; **~ fois** ◊ **à ~ reprises** several times, on several occasions; **payer en ~ fois** to pay in instalments 2 PRON INDÉF PL several (people); **~ (d'entre eux)** several (of them); **ils se sont mis à ~ pour ...** several people got together to ...; **nous nous sommes mis à ~ pour ...** several of us got together to ...

plus-que-parfait [plyskəpaʀfɛ] NM (*Gram*) pluperfect (tense), past perfect

plus-value (*pl* **plus-values**) [plyvaly] NF a (= *accroissement de valeur*) appreciation (*NonC*), increase in value; (= *bénéfice réalisé*) capital gain; (= *excédent*) surplus, profit; **réaliser** *ou* **faire** *ou* **dégager une ~** [*personne*] to make a profit; **ces actions ont enregistré une ~ importante** the shares have yielded a substantial capital gain → **impôt** b (*dans la pensée marxiste*) surplus value

Plutarque [plytaʀk] NM Plutarch

Pluton [plytɔ̃] NM (*Astron, Myth*) Pluto

plutonium [plytɔnjɔm] NM plutonium

plutôt [plyto] ADV a (= *de préférence*) rather; (= *à la place*) instead; **ne lis pas ce livre, prends ~ celui-ci** don't read that book, take this one instead; **prends ce livre ~ que celui-là** take this book rather than *ou* instead of that one; **cette maladie affecte ~ les enfants** this illness affects children for the most part *ou* tends to affect children; **je préfère ~ celui-ci** (= *je voudrais celui-ci de préférence*) I'd rather *ou* sooner have this one; (= *j'aime mieux celui-ci*) I prefer this one, I like this one better; **~ mourir que souffrir** it is better to die than to suffer; **~ que de me regarder, viens m'aider** instead of (just) watching me, come and help; **n'importe quoi ~ que cela !** anything but that!, anything rather than that!; **~ mourir (que de ...) !** I'd sooner die (than ...)!
b (= *plus exactement*) rather; **il n'est pas paresseux mais ~ apathique** he's not so much lazy as apathetic; **il est ignorant ~ que sot** he's more ignorant than stupid, he's not so much stupid as ignorant; **ou ~, c'est ce qu'il pense** or rather that's what he thinks; **c'est un journaliste ~ qu'un romancier** he's more of a journalist than a novelist, he's a journalist more *ou* rather than a novelist; **il s'y habitue ~ qu'il n'oublie** he's getting used to it rather than *ou* more than forgetting about it
c (= *assez*) [*chaud, bon*] rather, quite, fairly; **il remange, c'est ~ bon signe** he's eating again — that's quite a good sign; **nos vacances sont ~ compromises avec cet événement** our holidays are somewhat in the balance because of this incident; **un homme brun, ~ petit** a dark-haired man, rather *ou* somewhat on the short side *ou* rather short; **il est ~ pénible, celui-là !**

he's a bit of a pain in the neck!*; **il faisait beau ? — non, il faisait ~ frais** was the weather good? — no, if anything it was cool; **qu'est-ce qu'il est pénible, celui-là ! — ah oui, ~ !*** what a pain in the neck he is!* — you said it!* ou you're telling me!*

pluvial, e (*mpl* -**iaux**) [plyvjal, jo] ADJ [*régime, écoulement*] pluvial; **eau ~e** rainwater

pluvier [plyvje] NM plover; **~ guignard** dotterel

pluvieux, -ieuse [plyvjø, jøz] ADJ rainy, wet

pluviner [plyvine] ▸ conjug 1 ◂ VB IMPERS = **pleuvasser**

pluviomètre [plyvjɔmɛtʀ] NM pluviometer (*SPÉC*), rain gauge

pluviométrie [plyvjɔmetʀi] NF pluviometry

pluviométrique [plyvjɔmetʀik] ADJ pluviometric(al); **carte ~** isopluvial map; **courbe ~** rainfall graph

pluviôse [plyvjoz] NM Pluviôse (*fifth month in the French Republican calendar*)

pluviosité [plyvjozite] NF [*temps, saison*] raininess, wetness; (= *pluie tombée*) (average) rainfall

PLV [peelve] NF (ABRÉV = **publicité sur le lieu de vente**) → **publicité**

PM [peɛm] ① NF ⓐ (ABRÉV = **préparation militaire**) → **préparation** ⓑ (ABRÉV = **police militaire**) MP ② NM ⓐ (ABRÉV = **pistolet-mitrailleur** ⓑ (ABRÉV = **poids moléculaire**) → **poids**

PMA [peɛma] ① NF (ABRÉV = **procréation médicale(ment) assistée**) → **procréation** ② NMPL (ABRÉV = **pays les moins avancés**) LDCs

PME [peɛmə] NF INV (ABRÉV = **petite et moyenne entreprise**) small (ou medium-sized) business; **les ~** small (and medium-sized) businesses

PMI [peɛmi] NF ⓐ (ABRÉV = **petite et moyenne industrie**) small (ou medium-sized) industry; **les ~** small and medium-sized industries ⓑ (ABRÉV = **protection maternelle et infantile**) → **protection**

PMU [peɛmy] NM (ABRÉV = **Pari mutuel urbain**) pari-mutuel, ≈ tote* (*Brit*); **jouer au ~** to bet on the horses, ≈ bet on the tote* (*Brit*); **le bureau du ~** the betting office → *PMU*

PNB [peɛnbe] NM (ABRÉV = **Produit national brut**) GNP

pneu [pnø] NM ABRÉV = **pneumatique** ⓐ [*véhicule*] tyre (*Brit*), tire (*US*); **~ clouté** studded tyre; **~ sans chambre** ou **tubeless** tubeless tyre; **~-neige** snow tyre; **~ plein** solid tyre; **~ radial** ou **à carcasse radiale** radial(ply) tyre ⓑ (= *message*) letter sent by pneumatic dispatch ou tube; **par ~** by pneumatic dispatch ou tube

pneumatique [pnømatik] ① ADJ (*Sci*) pneumatic; (= *gonflable*) inflatable → **canot, marteau, matelas** ② NF pneumatics *sg* ③ NM = **pneu**

pneumectomie [pnømɛktɔmi] NF pneumectomy

pneumoconiose [pnømokɔnjoz] NF pneumoconiosis

pneumocoque [pnømɔkɔk] NM pneumococcus

pneumocystose [pnømosistoz] NF pneumocystis carinii pneumonia, PCP

pneumogastrique [pnømogastʀik] ① ADJ pneumogastric ② NM vagus nerve

pneumologie [pnømɔlɔʒi] NF pneumology

pneumologue [pnømɔlɔg] NMF lung specialist

pneumonectomie [pnømɔnɛktɔmi] NF pneumonectomy

pneumonie [pnømɔni] NF pneumonia (*NonC*); **faire** ou **avoir une ~** to have pneumonia

pneumonique [pnømɔnik] ① ADJ pneumonic ② NMF pneumonia patient

pneumothorax [pnømotɔʀaks] NM pneumothorax

Pnom-Penh [pnɔmpɛn] N Phnom Penh

PO (ABRÉV = **petites ondes**) MW

Pô [po] NM **le Pô** the Po

pochade [pɔʃad] NF (= *dessin*) quick sketch (*in colour*); (= *histoire*) humorous piece

pochard, e: [pɔʃaʀ, aʀd] NM,F drunk, lush*

poche¹ [pɔʃ] NF ⓐ [*vêtement, sac*] pocket; **~ revolver/intérieur** hip/inside pocket; **~ de pantalon** trouser pocket; **~ appliquée** ou **plaquée** patch pocket; **~ coupée** inset pocket; **fausse ~** false pocket ⓑ (*loc*) **de ~** [*collection, livre*] paperback (*épith*); [*sous-marin, couteau, mouchoir*] pocket (*épith*); [*jeu, ordinateur*] pocket-size (*épith*); **j'avais 10 F/ je n'avais pas un sou en ~** I had 10 francs/I didn't have a penny on me; **(son) diplôme en ~, il a cherché du travail** armed with his diploma ou with his diploma under his belt, he started looking for a job; **il a sa nomination en ~** his appointment is in the bag*; **sans diplôme en ~, on ne peut rien faire** you can't do anything without qualifications; **s'en mettre plein les ~s*** ◊ **se remplir les ~s*** to line one's pockets; **en être de sa ~*** to be out of pocket, lose out* (financially); **il a payé de sa ~** it came ou he paid for it out of his (own) pocket; **il a mis le maire dans sa ~** he's got the mayor in his pocket; **c'est dans la ~ !*** it's in the bag!*; **ce n'est pas dans la ~ !*** it's not in the bag yet!*; **faire les ~s à qn*** to go through sb's pockets; **connaître un endroit comme sa ~** to know a place like the back of one's hand ou inside out; **mets ça dans ta ~ (et ton mouchoir par-dessus)** [+ *somme d'argent*] put that in your pocket (and forget about it); [+ *renseignement*] keep it under your hat* → **argent, langue, œil** *etc* ⓒ (= *déformation*) **faire des ~s** [*veste*] to lose its shape; [*pantalon*] to go baggy; **avoir des ~s sous les yeux** to have bags under one's eyes ⓓ (*Comm*) (carrier) bag ⓔ [*kangourou*] pouch ⓕ (= *cavité*) pocket; **~ d'air** air pocket; **~ d'eau** pocket of water; **~ de pus** pus sac; **~ de sang** haematoma (*Brit*), hematoma (*US*); **~ des eaux** amniotic sac ⓖ (*Culin*) **~ à douille** piping bag ⓗ (= *secteur*) **~ de résistance** pocket of resistance; **~ de chômage/pauvreté** pocket of unemployment/poverty ⓘ (*Méd*) colostomy bag

poche² [pɔʃ] NM (= *livre*) paperback; **ce roman est paru en ~** this novel has come out in paperback

pocher [pɔʃe] ▸ conjug 1 ◂ ① VT (*Culin*) to poach; (*Art*) to sketch; **~ un œil à qn** to give sb a black eye ② VI [*pantalon*] **~ aux genoux** to go baggy at the knees; **~ derrière** to go baggy in the bottom ou seat (*Brit*)

pochetée: [pɔʃte] NF oaf, twit*

pochetron, -onne: [pɔʃtʀɔ̃, ɔn] NM,F = **pochard, e**

pochette [pɔʃɛt] NF (= *mouchoir*) pocket handkerchief; (= *petite poche*) breast pocket; (= *sac*) clutch ou envelope bag; [*timbres, photos*] wallet, envelope; [*serviette, aiguilles*] case; [*disque*] sleeve, jacket (*US*); **~ d'allumettes** book of matches

pochette-surprise (*pl* **pochettes-surprises**) [pɔʃɛtsyʀpʀiz] NF lucky bag, Cracker Jack® (*US*); (*hum*) **il a eu son permis dans une ~ !** God knows where he got his driving licence from!; (*hum*) **elle a eu son diplôme dans une ~** she's got a Mickey Mouse* degree

pocheuse [pɔʃøz] NF (egg)poacher

pochoir [pɔʃwaʀ] NM (= *cache*) stencil; (= *tampon*) transfer; **dessin au ~** stencil drawing; **faire** ou **peindre qch au ~** to stencil sth

podagre [pɔdagʀ] ① NF †† gout ② ADJ † suffering from gout

podium [pɔdjɔm] NM (= *estrade*) podium; [*défilé de mode*] catwalk; **il peut espérer une place sur le ~ (du 400 m haies)** [*sportif*] he can hope to come away with a medal (in the 400 metre hurdles); **pour assurer notre présence sur les ~s olympiques** to ensure that we are among the Olympic medal winners; **monter sur le ~** to mount the podium; **monter sur la plus haute marche du ~** [*sportif, équipe*] (*gén*) to be the winner; (*aux Jeux Olympiques*) to get the gold medal

podologie [pɔdɔlɔʒi] NF chiropody, podiatry (*US*)

podologue [pɔdɔlɔg] NMF chiropodist, podiatrist (*US*)

podomètre [pɔdɔmɛtʀ] NM pedometer

poêle¹ [pwal] NF **~ (à frire)** frying pan; (* = *détecteur de métaux*) metal detector; **passer qch à la ~** to fry sth; **~ à crêpes** pancake (*Brit*) ou crêpe pan; **~ à marrons** chestnut-roasting pan

poêle² [pwal] NM stove; **~ à mazout/à pétrole** oil/paraffin (*Brit*) ou kerosene (*US*) stove; **~ à bois** wood(-burning) stove

poêle³ [pwal] NM [*cercueil*] pall

poêlée [pwale] NF **une ~ de** a frying pan full of; (= *plat*) **~ de champignons/de légumes** mixed fried mushrooms/vegetables

poêler [pwale] ▸ conjug 1 ◂ VT to fry

poêlon [pwalɔ̃] NM casserole

poème [pɔɛm] NM poem; **~ en prose/ symphonique** prose/symphonic poem; **c'est tout un ~*** (= *c'est compliqué*) it's a whole lot of hassle*, it's a real palaver* (*Brit*)

poésie [pɔezi] NF (= *art, qualité*) poetry; (= *poème*) poem, piece of poetry; **faire de la ~** to write poetry; **roman/film plein de ~** poetic novel/film

poète [pɔɛt] ① NM poet; (= *rêveur*) poet, dreamer → **œillet** ② ADJ [*tempérament*] poetic; **être ~** to be a poet; **femme ~** poetess

poétesse [pɔetɛs] NF poetess

poétique [pɔetik] ① ADJ poetic, poetical (*frm*) ② NF poetics *sg*

poétiquement [pɔetikmã] ADV poetically

poétisation [pɔetizasjɔ̃] NF (= *action*) poetizing; (= *résultat*) poetic depiction

poétiser [pɔetize] ▸ conjug 1 ◂ VT to poetize

pogne: [pɔɲ] NF mitt:, paw*; **être à la ~ de qn** to be under sb's thumb; **avoir qn à sa ~** to have sb under one's thumb

pognon: [pɔɲɔ̃] NM cash, dough:; **ils sont pleins de ~:** they're loaded*

pogrom(e) [pɔgʀɔm] NM pogrom

poids [pwa] NM ⓐ (*gén*) weight; **prendre du ~** [*adulte*] to put on ou gain weight; [*bébé*] to gain weight; **perdre du ~** to lose weight; **ce genre d'alimentation favorise la prise de ~** this kind of food makes you put on weight; **quel ~ fait-il ?** how much does he weigh?, what's his weight?; **vendu au ~** sold by weight; **ces bijoux d'argent seront vendus au ~ du métal** this silver jewellery will be sold by the weight of the metal; **la branche pliait sous le ~ des fruits** the branch was weighed down with (the) fruit ou was bending beneath the weight of the fruit; **elle s'appuyait contre lui de tout son ~** she leaned against him with all her weight; **elle a ajouté une pomme pour faire le ~** she put in an extra apple to make up the weight; **faire bon ~** to give good weight; (*fig*) **il ne fait vraiment pas le ~** he really doesn't measure up; **il ne fait pas le ~ face à son adversaire** he's no match for his opponent ⓑ (= *objet*) [*balance, horloge*] weight; (*Sport*) shot; (*Sport*) **lancer le ~** to put(t) the shot → **deux** ⓒ (= *charge*) weight; **tout le ~ de l'entreprise repose sur lui** he carries the weight of the whole business on his shoulders; **syndicat qui**

a beaucoup de ~ union which carries a lot of weight; **plier sous le ~ des soucis/des impôts** to be weighed down by worries/taxes; **être courbé sous le ~ des ans** to be bent by (the weight of) years; (hum) **c'est le ~ des ans** old age never comes alone (hum); **enlever un ~ (de la conscience) à qn** to take a weight ou a load off sb's mind; **c'est un ~ sur sa conscience** it lies ou weighs heavy on his conscience, it's a weight on his conscience; **avoir** ou **se sentir un ~ sur l'estomac** to have something lying heavy on one's stomach; **j'ai un ~ sur la poitrine** my chest feels tight

$\boxed{d}$ (= force, influence) weight; **argument de ~** weighty ou forceful argument, argument of great weight; **homme de ~** man who carries weight ou influence; **cela donne du ~ à son hypothèse** that gives ou lends weight to his hypothesis; **ses arguments ont eu beaucoup de ~ dans les négociations** his arguments carried a lot of weight in the negotiations

$\boxed{e}$ (Boxe) **~ coq** bantamweight; **~ léger** lightweight; **~ mi-lourd** light heavyweight; **~ mi-mouche** light flyweight; **~ mi-moyen** ou **welter** welterweight; **~ mouche** flyweight; **~ moyen** middleweight; **~ plume** featherweight; **c'est un ~ plume*** he's (ou she's) as light as a feather; [objet] it's as light as a feather; **c'est un tissu ~ plume** it's an ultra-light fabric; **~ super-léger** light welterweight; **~ super-mi-moyen** light middle-weight → **2**

$\boxed{2}$ COMP ► **poids atomique**† atomic weight ► **poids brut** gross weight ► **poids et haltères** (Sport) NMPL weightlifting; **faire des ~ et haltères** (spécialité) to be a weight-lifter; (pour s'entraîner) to do weight training ou weightlifting ► **poids lourd** (= boxeur) heavyweight; (= camion) heavy goods vehicle, heavy truck (US); (= entreprise) big name*; (= personne) heavyweight, big name*; **c'est un ~ lourd de la finance/de l'industrie** he's a financial/industrial heavyweight, he's a big name in finance/in industry; (Boxe) **le championnat du monde (des) ~ lourds** the world heavyweight championship ► **poids et mesures** NMPL weights and measures ► **poids moléculaire** molecular weight ► **poids mort** (Tech, péj) dead weight ► **poids net** net weight ► **poids net égoutté** drained weight ► **poids spécifique** specific gravity ► **poids total autorisé en charge** gross weight ► **poids utile** net weight ► **poids à vide** [véhicule] tare

poignant, e [pwaɲɑ̃, ɑ̃t] ADJ [spectacle] heartrending, harrowing; [musique, atmosphère] poignant

poignard [pwaɲaʀ] NM dagger; **coup de ~** (lit) stab; **frappé d'un coup de ~ en plein cœur** stabbed in ou through the heart; **on l'a tué à coups de ~** he was stabbed to death; **cette décision est un coup de ~ au processus de paix** this decision is a serious blow for the peace process; **c'est un coup de ~ dans le dos** it's a stab in the back

poignarder [pwaɲaʀde] ▶ conjug 1 ◀ VT to stab, knife; **mortellement poignardé** stabbed to death; (lit, fig) **~ qn dans le dos** to stab sb in the back

poigne [pwaɲ] NF (= étreinte) grip; (= main) hand; (= autorité) firm-handedness; **avoir de la ~** (lit) to have a strong grip; (fig) to rule with a firm hand; **à ~** [personne, gouvernement] firm-handed

poignée [pwaɲe] NF $\boxed{a}$ (lit = quantité) handful; [billets de banque] fistful; (= petit nombre) handful; **ajoutez une ~ de sel** add a handful of salt; **à** ou **par ~s** in handfuls; **je perds mes cheveux par ~s** my hair is coming out in handfuls $\boxed{b}$ [porte, tiroir, valise] handle; [épée] handle, hilt; **~ de frein** brake handle; (hum) **~s d'amour** love handles $\boxed{c}$ **~ de main** handshake; **donner une ~ de main à qn** to shake

hands with sb, shake sb's hand ou sb by the hand

poignet [pwaɲɛ] NM (Anat) wrist; (Habillement) cuff; **~ de force** wrist band → **force**

poil [pwal] $\boxed{1}$ NM $\boxed{a}$ (Anat) hair; **avoir du ~** ou **des ~s sur la poitrine** to have a hairy chest; **avoir du ~ aux pattes**‡ to have hairy legs; **les ~s de sa barbe** (entretenue) the bristles ou hairs of his beard; (mal rasée) the stubble on his face; **sans ~s** [poitrine, bras] hairless; **il n'a pas un ~ sur le caillou*** he's as bald as a coot* ou an egg*; **il n'a pas un ~ de sec*** (pluie) he's drenched, he's soaked to the skin; (sueur) he's drenched with sweat

$\boxed{b}$ [animal] hair; (= pelage) coat; **animal à ~ ras/court/long** smooth-/short-/long-haired animal; **animal au ~ soyeux/roux** animal with a silky/ginger coat; **en ~ de chèvre** goathair (épith); **en ~ de chameau** camelhair (épith); **ca-resser dans le sens du ~** [+ chat] to stroke the right way; [+ personne] to butter up → **gibier**

$\boxed{c}$ [brosse à dents, pinceau] bristle; [tapis, étoffe] strand; (Bot) [plante] down (NonC); [artichaut] choke (NonC); **les ~s d'un tapis** the pile of a carpet; **les ~s d'un tissu** the pile ou nap of a fabric

$\boxed{d}$ (* = un petit peu) **s'il avait un ~ de bon sens** if he had an iota ou an ounce of good sense; **à un ~ près, l'armoire ne passait pas dans la porte** a fraction more and the cupboard wouldn't have gone through the doorway; **ça mesure environ un mètre, à un ~ près** it measures one metre as near as makes no difference; **il n'y a pas un ~ de différence entre les deux** there isn't the slightest difference between the two; **pousser qch d'un ~** to shift sth a fraction; **il s'en est fallu d'un ~** it was a near ou close thing ou a close shave* → **quart**

$\boxed{e}$ **à ~**‡ (= nu) stark naked, starkers‡ (Brit); **des mecs**‡**/des filles à ~** naked guys*/girls; **à ~ !** (à chanteur, orateur) off! off!‡; (déshabillez-vous) get your clothes off!, get 'em off!‡ (Brit); **se mettre à ~** to strip off; **se baigner à ~** to go skinny-dipping*

$\boxed{f}$ **au (quart de) ~*** (= magnifique) great*, fantastic*; (= précisément) [réglé, convenir] perfectly; **tu arrives au ~, j'allais partir** you've come just at the right moment — I was just about to leave; **ça me va au ~*** it suits me fine* ou to a T*

$\boxed{g}$ (loc) **de tout ~** ◊ **de tous ~s** of all sorts ou kinds; **des artistes de tout ~** all sorts ou kinds of artists; **avoir un ~ dans la main*** to be bone-idle*; **ce n'est plus un ~ qu'il a dans la main, c'est une canne !** ou **un bambou !*** he's as lazy as they come; (péj) **un jeune blanc-bec qui n'a même pas de ~ au menton*** a young guy who's still wet behind the ears* (péj), a babe in arms (péj); **tu parleras quand tu auras du ~ au menton** you can have your say when you're out of short pants*; **être de bon/de mauvais ~*** to be in a good/bad mood; **avoir qn sur le ~*** to be breathing down one's neck; **tomber sur le ~ à qn*** (agresser) to go for* ou lay into* sb; [police] to pounce on sb*; [fisc] to come down on sb; **reprendre du ~ de la bête*** [malade] to pick up (again), regain strength; [plante] to pick up (again); [rebelles, mouvement] to regain strength; [parti] to be on the way up again

$\boxed{2}$ COMP ► **poil de carotte** [personne] red-haired, red-headed; [cheveux] red, carroty ► **poils follets** down (NonC) ► **poil à gratter** itching powder

poilant, e‡ [pwalɑ̃, ɑ̃t] ADJ hilarious

poiler (se)‡ [pwale] ▶ conjug 1 ◀ VPR to kill o.s. (laughing)‡

poilu, e [pwaly] $\boxed{1}$ ADJ hairy $\boxed{2}$ NM poilu (French soldier in First World War)

poinçon [pwɛ̃sɔ̃] NM $\boxed{a}$ (= outil) [cordonnier] awl; [menuisier] awl, bradawl; [brodeuse] bod-kin; [graveur] style; [bijou, or] die, stamp $\boxed{b}$ (= estampille) hallmark $\boxed{c}$ (= matrice) pattern

poinçonnage [pwɛ̃sɔnaʒ], **poinçonne-ment** [pwɛ̃sɔnmɑ̃] NM $\boxed{a}$ [marchandise] stamping; [pièce d'orfèvrerie] hallmarking $\boxed{b}$ [billet] punching, clipping $\boxed{c}$ [tôle] punching

poinçonner [pwɛ̃sɔne] ▶ conjug 1 ◀ VT $\boxed{a}$ (= estampiller) [+ marchandise] to stamp; [+ pièce d'orfèvrerie] to hallmark $\boxed{b}$ (= perforer) [+ billet] to punch (a hole in), clip $\boxed{c}$ (= découper) [+ tôle] to punch

poinçonneur, -euse [pwɛ̃sɔnœʀ, øz] $\boxed{1}$ NM,F (Hist = personne) ticket-puncher $\boxed{2}$ **poinçonneuse** NF (= machine) punching machine, punch press

poindre [pwɛ̃dʀ] ▶ conjug 49 ◀ $\boxed{1}$ VI (littér) [jour] to break, dawn; [aube] to break; [plante] to come up, peep through; **un sentiment de jalousie/haine commençait à ~** he (ou she) began to feel the first stirrings of jealousy/hatred $\boxed{2}$ VT (littér) [tristesse] to afflict; [douleur, amour] to sting (littér)

poing [pwɛ̃] $\boxed{1}$ NM $\boxed{a}$ (gén) fist; **les ~s sur les hanches** with (one's) hands on (one's) hips, with (one's) arms akimbo; **lever le ~** (gén) to raise one's fist; (salut) to give the clenched fist salute; **ils défilaient le ~ levé** they marched with clenched fists raised; **montrer le ~** to shake one's fist; **menacer qn du ~** to shake one's fist at sb; **taper** ou **frapper du ~ sur la table** (lit) to thump the table (with one's fist), bang ou thump one's fist on the table; (fig) to put one's foot down; **revolver au ~** revolver in hand; **je vais t'envoyer** ou **te coller* mon ~ dans la figure** you'll get my fist in your face*; **tu veux mon ~ dans** ou **sur la gueule ?**‡ do you want my fist in your face?, do you want a knuckle sandwich? → **dormir, pied, serrer** etc $\boxed{b}$ **coup de ~** punch; **donner un coup de ~ ou des coups de ~ à qn** to punch sb; **donner des coups de ~ dans une porte** to bang on a door; **il a reçu** ou **pris un coup de ~ dans la figure** he was punched in the face; **faire le coup de ~ avec qn/contre qn** to fight alongside sb/ against sb; **opération coup de ~** (= raid) lightning raid; (= action d'envergure) blitz; **opéra-tion coup de ~ contre le chômage/les fraudeurs** assault on unemployment/blitz ou crackdown on tax dodgers; **« opération coup de ~ sur les prix »** "prices slashed"

$\boxed{2}$ COMP ► **poing américain** (= arme) knuckleduster

---

▼**point¹** [pwɛ̃]

$\boxed{1}$ NOM MASCULIN	$\boxed{2}$ COMPOSÉS

$\boxed{1}$ NOM MASCULIN

$\boxed{a}$ **= endroit** point, place; (Astron, Géom) point; **pour aller d'un ~ à un autre** to go from one point ou place to another; **fixer un ~ pré-cis dans l'espace** to stare at a fixed point in space; **le fleuve déborde en plusieurs ~s** the riv-er overflows at several points ou in several places; **ils étaient venus de tous les ~s de l'hori-zon** they had come from the four corners of the earth; **je reprends mon discours au ~ où je l'ai laissé** I take up my speech where I left off

$\boxed{b}$ **= situation** point, stage; **avoir atteint le ~ où ...** ◊ **en être arrivé au ~ où ...** to have reached the point ou stage where ...; **nous en sommes toujours au même ~** we haven't got any fur-ther, we're no further forward; **c'est bête d'en être (arrivé) à ce ~-là et de ne pas finir** it's silly to have got so far ou to have reached this point ou stage and not to finish; **au ~ où en sont les choses** as matters ou things stand; **au ~ où nous en sommes, cela ne changera pas grand-chose** considering the situation we're in, it won't make much difference; **on conti-nue ? — au ~ où on en est...** shall we go on? — we've got this far so we might as well

$\boxed{c}$

◆ **au point** [image, photo] in focus; [affaire] completely finalized ou settled; [procédé, tech-nique, machine] perfected; [discours, ouvrage]

▶ GRAMMAIRE ACTIVE: **point** 33.3, 53.3, 53.4

finalized, up to scratch (*attrib*); **ce n'est pas encore au ~** [*machine, spectacle, organisation*] it isn't quite up to scratch yet; [*discours, devoir*] it's not quite finalized yet, it still needs some working on; **ce n'est pas au ~** [*appareil photo, caméra*] it's out of focus

◆ **mettre au point** [+ *photo, caméra*] to (bring into) focus; [+ *stratégie, technique*] to perfect; [+ *médicament, invention, système*] to develop; [+ *moteur*] to tune; [+ *mécanisme*] to tune, adjust; [+ *projet*] to finalize; **mettre une affaire au ~ avec qn** to finalize *ou* settle all the details of a matter with sb

◆ **mise au point** [*appareil photo, caméra*] focusing; [*stratégie, technique*] perfecting; [*médicament, invention, système*] development; [*moteur*] tuning; [*mécanisme*] tuning, adjustment; (*Ordin*) debugging; [*affaire, projet*] finalizing; (*fig* = *explication, correction*) clarification; **publier une mise au ~** to issue a statement (*setting the record straight or clarifying a point*)

boxed(d) **= degré, niveau** (*gén*) point, stage; (*Sci*) point; **~ d'ébullition/de congélation** boiling/freezing point; **est-il possible d'être bête à ce ~(-là)!** how stupid can you get?*; **il n'est pas inquiet à ce ~-là** he's not that worried; (*littér*) **il s'est montré grossier au dernier ~** he was extremely rude; **vous voyez à quel ~ il est généreux** you see how (very) generous he is *ou* the extent of his generosity; **sa colère avait atteint un ~ tel** *ou* **un tel ~** he was so (very) angry that ..., his anger was such that ...; **il en était arrivé à un tel ~ d'avarice que ...** he had become so miserly that ..., his miserliness had reached such proportions that ...

◆ **à ce** *ou* **tel point que ...**: **c'était à ce ~ absurde que ...** it was so (very) absurd that ...; **elles se ressemblent à ce** *ou* **tel ~ qu'on pourrait les confondre** they look so alike that you could easily mistake one for the other; **son invention a eu du succès, à tel ~ qu'il est devenu célèbre** his invention was a success, so much so that *ou* to such an extent *ou* degree that he became famous

◆ **à point** (*Culin* = *bon à consommer*) [*fruit*] just ripe (*attrib*), nicely ripe; [*fromage*] just right for eating (*attrib*); [*viande*] medium; **quelle cuisson ? — à ~** how would you like it cooked? — medium rare; **le rôti est cuit à ~** the roast is cooked *ou* done to a turn

◆ **au plus haut point** [*détester, admirer*] intensely; **se méfier au plus haut ~ de qch** to be extremely mistrustful *ou* highly sceptical about sth; **être au plus haut ~ de la gloire** to be at the peak *ou* summit of glory

◆ **au point de** + *infinitif* so much that; **il ne pleut pas au ~ de mettre des bottes** it isn't raining enough for you to put boots on, it isn't raining so much that you need boots; **tirer sur une corde au ~ de la casser** to pull on a rope so hard that it breaks, pull a rope to the point where it breaks

◆ **au point que** = à ce *ou* tel point que

boxed(e) **= aspect, détail, subdivision** point; **exposé en trois ~s** three-point presentation; **~ de théologie/de philosophie** point of theology/of philosophy; **passons au ~ suivant de l'ordre du jour** let us move on to the next item on the agenda; **~ d'accord/de désaccord** point of agreement/of disagreement; **~ mineur** *ou* **de détail** minor point, point of detail; **nous abordons maintenant un ~ capital** we now come to a crucial point *ou* issue; **voilà déjà un ~ acquis** *ou* **réglé** that's one thing *ou* point settled; **avoir des ~s communs** to have things in common; **je n'ai aucun ~ commun avec elle** I have nothing in common with her; **ils sont d'accord sur ce ~/sur tous les ~s** they agree on this point *ou* score/on all points *ou* scores *ou* counts; **exécutez ces instructions de ~ en ~** (*frm*) carry these instructions out point by point *ou* in every detail

◆ **en tout point** ◊ **en tous points** in every respect; **ils se ressemblent en tout ~** they re-

semble each other in every respect; **ce fut en tous ~s réussi** it was an all-round *ou* unqualified success

◆ **jusqu'à un certain point** up to a point, to a certain extent

◆ **point par point** point by point; **nous avons repris la question ~ par ~** we went over the question point by point; **il répondit ~ par ~ aux accusations** he answered the charges point by point *ou* taking each point in turn

boxed(f) **temps**

◆ **à point (nommé)** [*arriver, venir*] just at the right moment, just when needed; **cela tombe à ~ (nommé)** that comes just at the right moment, that's just *ou* exactly what I (*ou* we *etc*) need

◆ **sur le point de** + *infinitif*: **être sur le ~ de faire qch** to be (just) about to do sth, be just going to do sth, be on the point of doing sth; **j'étais sur le ~ de faire du café** I was just going to *ou* (just) about to make some coffee; **une bombe sur le ~ d'exploser** a bomb about to go off; **elle est sur le ~ de quitter son mari** she is about to leave *ou* is on the verge of leaving her husband

boxed(g) **= position** (*Aviat, Naut*) position; **recevoir le ~ par radio** to be given one's position by radio; (*Naut*) **faire le ~** to take a bearing, plot one's position; (*Mil*) **faire le ~ cartographique** *ou* **géographique** to take a bearing; **faire le ~ horaire** to give regular bulletins, have regular updates; **faire le ~ de la situation** (= *examiner*) to take stock of the situation, review the situation; (= *faire un compte rendu*) to sum up the situation; **nous allons faire le ~ sur les derniers événements** let's have an update on the latest events; (*Journalisme*) **et maintenant, le ~ sur la grève des transports** and now, the latest (update) on the transport strike; (*Aviat*) **~ fixe** (engine) run-up

boxed(h) **= marque** (*gén, Mus, en morse, sur i*) dot; (= *ponctuation*) full stop (*Brit*), period (*US*); (= *petite tache*) spot, speck; [*dé*] pip; (*fig*) **mettre les ~s sur les i** to dot one's i's and cross one's t's), spell it out; **~, à la ligne** (*lit*) new paragraph; (*fig*) full stop (*Brit*), period (*US*); **tu n'iras pas, un ~ c'est tout** you're not going and that's all there is to it *ou* and that's that, you're not going — full stop (*Brit*) *ou* period (*US*); **le bateau n'était plus qu'un ~ à l'horizon** the ship was now nothing but a dot *ou* speck *ou* spot on the horizon

boxed(i) **d'un score** (*Cartes, Sport*) point; (*Scol, Univ*) mark, point; (*Cartes*) **~s d'honneurs/de distribution** points for honours/for distribution; (*Cartes*) **je n'ai pas les ~s d'annonce** I haven't got enough points to open the bidding; (*Boxe*) **gagner aux ~s** to win on points; **il a échoué d'un ~** he failed by one mark *ou* point; **la partie se joue en 15 ~s** the winner is the first person to get to *ou* to score 15 (points); (*Tennis*) **faire** *ou* **marquer le ~** to win the point; (*fig*) **rendre des ~s à qn** to give sb points, give sb a (head) start; (*Scol*) **enlever un ~ par faute** to take a mark *ou* point off for every mistake; **bon/mauvais ~** good/bad mark (*for conduct etc*); (*fig*) plus/minus (mark); **la maîtresse m'a donné deux bons ~s †** ≈ the teacher gave me two stars; (*fig*) **un bon ~ pour vous !** that's a point in your favour! → compter, marquer

boxed(j) **Écon, Bourse, sondages** point; **sa cote de popularité a baissé de 3 ~s** his popularity rating has fallen (by) 3 points *ou* is down 3 points; **~ de base** basis point

boxed(k) **Méd** **avoir un ~ dans le dos** to have a twinge (of pain) in one's back; **vous avez un ~ de congestion là** you have a spot of congestion there

boxed(l) **TV, Typo** point; **caractère de 8/10 ~s** 8-/10-point type

boxed[2] **COMPOSÉS**

▶ **point d'appui** (*Mil*) base of operations; [*levier*] fulcrum; [*personne*] (*lit, fig*) support; **chercher un ~ d'appui** to look for something to

lean on; **l'échelle a glissé de son ~ d'appui** the ladder slipped from where it was leaning ▶ **points cardinaux** points of the compass, cardinal points ▶ **point chaud** (*Mil*) trouble spot, hot spot; (*fig*) (= *endroit*) trouble spot; (= *fait*) **c'est un des ~s chauds de l'actualité** it's one of the burning *ou* most topical issues of the moment ▶ **point de chute** (*lit*) landing place; (*fig*) **vous avez un ~ de chute à Rome ?** do you have somewhere to stay in Rome? ▶ **points de conduite** (*Typo*) dot leaders ▶ **point de contrôle** checkpoint ▶ **point de côté** stitch, pain in the side ▶ **point critique** (*Phys, fig*) critical point ▶ **point culminant** [*gloire, réussite, panique, épidémie*] height; [*affaire, scandale*] climax, culmination; [*montagne*] peak, summit; [*carrière*] height, zenith ▶ **point de départ** [*train, autobus*] point of departure; [*science, réussite, aventure*] starting point; [*enquête*] point of departure, starting point; (*Sport*) start; **revenir à son ~ de départ** to come back to where it (*ou* one) started; (*fig*) **nous voilà revenus au ~ de départ** (so) we're back to square one*, we're back where we started ▶ **point de distribution** [*eau*] supply point; (*Comm*) distribution outlet ▶ **point de droit** point of law ▶ **point d'eau** (= *source*) watering place; [*camping*] water (supply) point ▶ **point d'équilibre** (*Phys*) equilibrium point; (*Fin*) break-even point; (*fig*) **le gouvernement doit trouver le ~ d'équilibre** the government needs to find the right balance *ou* the happy medium ▶ **point d'exclamation** exclamation mark (*Brit*) *ou* point (*US*) ▶ **point faible** weak point ▶ **point final** (*lit*) full stop (*Brit*), period (*US*); (*fig*) **je refuse, ~ final** I refuse, full stop (*Brit*) *ou* period (*US*), I refuse and that's final; (*fig*) **mettre un ~ final à qch** to put an end to sth, bring sth to an end ▶ **point fort** strong point ▶ **point géométrique** (geometrical) point ▶ **point d'honneur** point of honour; **mettre un ~ d'honneur à** *ou* **se faire un ~ d'honneur de faire qch** to make it a point of honour to do sth ▶ **point d'impact** point of impact ▶ **point d'incidence** point of incidence ▶ **point d'information** point of information ▶ **point d'interrogation** question mark; **qui sera élu, c'est là le ~ d'interrogation** who will be elected — that's the big question (mark) *ou* that's the 64,000-dollar question* ▶ **point d'intersection** point of intersection ▶ **point du jour** daybreak, break of day ▶ **point lumineux** dot *ou* spot of light ▶ **point mort** (*Tech*) dead centre; (*Aut*) neutral; (*Fin*) break-even point; **au ~ mort** (*Aut*) in neutral; [*négociations, affaires*] at a standstill ▶ **point névralgique** (*Méd*) nerve centre; (*fig*) sensitive spot ▶ **point noir** (= *comédon*) blackhead; (= *problème*) problem, difficulty; (*Aut = lieu d'accidents*) blackspot ▶ **point de non-retour** point of no return ▶ **point d'ordre** point of order ▶ **point d'orgue** (*Mus*) pause; (*fig*) [*festival, conférence*] break ▶ **point de passage** (*lit*) crossing point; (*fig*) **ce café est le ~ de passage obligé du tout-Paris médiatique** this café is the place to be seen in Parisian media circles ▶ **point de presse** press briefing ▶ **point de ralliement** rallying point ▶ **point de rassemblement** (à *l'aéroport etc*) meeting point; (*Naut*) muster station ▶ **point de ravitaillement** (*en nourriture*) refreshment point, staging point; (*en essence*) refuelling point ▶ **points de reprise** (*Mus*) repeat marks ▶ **points de retraite** *points calculated on the basis of social security contributions that count towards retirement pensions* ▶ **point de rouille** spot *ou* speck of rust ▶ **point de saturation** (*Sci, fig*) saturation point ▶ **point sensible** (*sur la peau*) tender spot; (*Mil*) trouble spot; (*fig*) sensitive area, sore point ▶ **point de soudure** spot *ou* blob of solder ▶ **point stratégique** key point ▶ **points de suspension** (*gén*) suspension points; (*en* *dictant*) dot, dot, dot ► **point de tangence** tangential point ► **point de vente** (*Comm*) point of sale, sales outlet; « ~s de vente dans toute la France » "on sale throughout France"; **liste des ~s de vente** list of stockists *ou* retailers ► **point de vue** (*lit*) view(point); (*fig*) point of view, standpoint; **du** *ou* **au ~ de vue moral** from a moral point of view, from a moral standpoint; **au ~ de vue argent** as regards money, moneywise*; **nous aimerions connaître votre ~ de vue sur ce sujet** we should like to know your point of view *ou* standpoint *ou* where you stand in this matter

point² [pwɛ̃] **1** NM (*Couture, Tricot*) stitch; **bâtir à grands ~s** to tack; **coudre à grands ~s** to sew using a long stitch; **faire un (petit) ~ à qch** to put a stitch in sth

2 COMP ► **point d'Alençon** Alençon lace ► **point d'arrêt** finishing-off stitch ► **point arrière** backstitch ► **point de chaînette** chain stitch ► **point de chausson** (*Couture*) blind hem stitch; (*Broderie*) closed herringbone stitch ► **point de couture** stitch ► **point de croix** cross-stitch ► **point devant** running stitch ► **point d'épine** feather stitch ► **point de feston** blanket stitch ► **point de jersey** stocking stitch ► **point mousse** garter stitch ► **point d'ourlet** hem-stitch ► **point de riz** moss stitch ► **point de suture** (*Méd*) stitch; **faire des ~s de suture à qch** to put stitches in sth, stitch sth up ► **point de tapisserie** canvas stitch ► **point de tige** stem stitch ► **point de torsade** cable stitch ► **point de tricot** (*gén*) knitting stitch; (*maille à l'endroit*) knit stitch ► **point de Venise** rose point

point³ [pwɛ̃] ADV (*littér, hum*) = **pas²**

pointage [pwɛ̃taʒ] NM **a** (= *fait de cocher*) ticking *ou* checking *ou* marking off; (*Ind*) [*personnel*] (*à l'arrivée*) clocking in *ou* on; (*au départ*) clocking out; **procéder au ~ des voix** to count the votes **b** [*fusil*] pointing, aiming, levelling (**vers, sur** at); [*jumelles, lunette, télescope*] training (**vers, sur** on); [*lampe*] directing (**vers, sur** towards) **c** (*Mus*) [*note*] dotting **d** (*Tech*) [*trou de vis*] starting off **e** (= *contrôle*) check

pointe [pwɛ̃t] **1** NF **a** (= *extrémité*) [*aiguille, épée*] point; [*flèche, lance*] head, point; [*couteau, crayon, clocher, clou*] point, tip; [*canne*] (*pointed*) end, tip, point; [*montagne*] peak, top; [*menton, nez, langue, sein, ski*] tip; [*moustache, col*] point; [*chaussure*] toe, tip; **à la ~ de l'île** at the tip of the island; **chasser l'ennemi à la ~ de l'épée/de la baïonnette** to chase away the enemy with swords drawn/at bayonet point

b (= *partie saillante*) [*grillage*] spike; [*côte*] headland; **la côte forme une ~** *ou* **s'avance en ~ à cet endroit** the coast juts out (into the sea) *ou* forms a headland at that point; **objet qui forme une ~** object that tapers (in)to a point

c **en ~** [*barbe, clou*] pointed; **décolleté en ~** V-neckline; **tailler en ~** [+ *arbre, barbe*] to cut *ou* trim into a point; [+ *crayon*] to sharpen (in)to a point; **canne qui se termine en ~** pointed stick

d (= *clou*) tack; (*Sport*) [*chaussure de football, d'alpiniste*] spike; (= *outil pointu*) point; **tu cours avec des tennis ou avec des ~s?** do you run in trainers or spikes?

e (*Danse*) (**chaussons à**) **~s** points, point shoes; **faire des ~s** to dance on points

f (= *foulard*) triangular (neck)scarf; († = *couche de bébé*) (triangular-shaped) nappy (*Brit*) *ou* diaper (*US*)

g (= *allusion ironique*) pointed remark; (= *trait d'esprit*) witticism

h (= *petite quantité*) **une ~ d'ail/d'ironie/de jalousie** a touch *ou* hint of garlic/of irony/of jealousy; **il a une ~ d'accent** he has the merest

hint of an accent *ou* a very slight accent

i (= *maximum*) peak; (*Aut*) **faire** *ou* **pousser une ~ jusqu'à Paris** to push *ou* press on as far as Paris; **faire** *ou* **pousser une ~ de vitesse** [*athlète, cycliste, automobiliste*] to put on a burst of speed, put on a spurt; **j'ai fait une ~ (de vitesse) de 180 (km/h)** I hit 180 km/h; **faire du 200 km/h en ~** to have a top *ou* maximum speed of 200 km/h; **à la ~ du combat** in the forefront of (the) battle; **à la ~ de l'actualité** in the forefront of current affairs *ou* of the news; **à la ~ du progrès** in the forefront *ou* front line *ou* at the leading edge of progress

j **de ~** [*industrie*] leading, high-tech; [*technique*] latest, ultramodern, advanced; [*vitesse*] top, maximum; **heure** *ou* **période de ~** (*gaz, électricité, téléphone*) peak period; (*circulation*) rush *ou* peak hour; (*magasin*) peak shopping period, busy period

k (*Naut*) [*compas*] point

2 COMP ► **pointe d'asperge** asparagus tip *ou* spear ► **pointe Bic**® Biro® (*Brit*), Bic (pen)® (*US*) ► **pointe fibre** (*stylo*) fibre-tip (pen) (*Brit*), fiber-tip (pen) (*US*) ► **pointe du jour** (*littér*) **à la ~ du jour** at daybreak, at the crack of dawn ► **la pointe des pieds** the toes; (**se mettre**) **sur la ~ des pieds** (to stand) on tiptoe *ou* on one's toes; **marcher/entrer sur la ~ des pieds** to walk/come in on tiptoe *ou* on one's toes, tiptoe in/out; (*fig*) **il faut y aller sur la ~ des pieds (avec lui)** you have to tread very carefully (when dealing with him) ► **pointe sèche** (*Art*) dry-point; **gravure à la ~ sèche** dry-point engraving ► **pointe du sein** nipple ► **pointe de terre** spit *ou* tongue of land, headland

pointeau (*pl* **pointeaux**) [pwɛ̃to] NM **a** [*carburateur, graveur*] needle **b** (*Ind* = *surveillant*) timekeeper

pointer¹ [pwɛ̃te] ▸conjug 1◂ **1** VT **a** (= *cocher*) to tick off, check off, mark off; (*Naut*) **~ (sa position sur) la carte** to prick off *ou* plot one's position → **zéro 2** (*Ind*) [*personnel*] (*à l'arrivée*) to clock in *ou* on; (*au départ*) to clock out **c** (= *braquer*) [+ *fusil*] to point, aim, level (**vers, sur** at); [+ *jumelles*] to train (**vers, sur** on); [+ *lampe*] to direct (**vers, sur** towards); [+ *boule de pétanque*] to roll (*as opposed to throw*); **il pointa vers elle un index accusateur** he pointed an accusing finger at her **d** (*Mus*) [+ *note*] to dot; **notes pointées** dotted rhythm **e** (*Tech*) [+ *trou de vis*] to start off **2** VI [*employé*] (*à l'arrivée*) to clock in *ou* on; (*au départ*) to clock out; **~ à l'ANPE** to sign on (*at the national employment agency*); **il pointe au chômage depuis trois mois** he's been on the dole* (*Brit*) *ou* on welfare (*US*) for three months **3** **se pointer*** VPR (= *arriver*) to turn up*, show up*

pointer² [pwɛ̃te] ▸conjug 1◂ **1** VT **a** (= *piquer*) to stick (**dans** into); **il lui pointa sa lance dans le dos** he stuck his lance into his back **b** (= *dresser*) **église qui pointe ses tours vers le ciel** church whose towers soar (up) into the sky; **le chien pointa les oreilles** the dog pricked up its ears **2** VI (*littér*) **a** (= *s'élever*) [*tour*] to soar up **b** (= *apparaître*) [*plante*] to peep out; (*ironie*) to pierce through; **ses seins pointaient sous la robe** her nipples showed beneath her dress; **le jour pointait** day was breaking *ou* dawning

pointer³ [pwɛ̃tɛʀ] NM (= *chien*) pointer

pointeur [pwɛ̃tœʀ] NM (*Ind, Sport*) timekeeper; (*Ordin*) pointer; [*boules*] player who aims at the jack; [*canon*] gun-layer

pointeuse [pwɛ̃tøz] NF (= *personne*) timekeeper; (= *machine-outil*) jig borer; (**horloge**) **~** time clock

pointillage [pwɛ̃tijaʒ] NM stipple, stippling

pointillé, e [pwɛ̃tije] (*ptp de* **pointiller**) **1** ADJ dotted **2** NM **a** (*Art*) (= *procédé*) stipple, stippling; (= *gravure*) stipple **b** (= *trait*) dotted line; (= *perforations*) perforation(s); **en ~** (*lit*)

dotted; [*sous-entendu*] hinted at; (= *discontinu*) [*carrière, vie*] marked by stops and starts; « **détacher** *ou* **découper suivant le ~** » "tear *ou* cut along the dotted line"; **un nouvel accord se dessine en ~** the first signs of a new agreement are emerging

pointillement [pwɛ̃tijmɑ̃] NM = **pointillage**

pointiller [pwɛ̃tije] ▸conjug 1◂ (*Art*) **1** VI to draw (*ou* engrave) in stipple **2** VT to stipple

pointilleux, -euse [pwɛ̃tijø, øz] ADJ particular, pernickety (*péj*), fussy (*péj*) (**sur** about)

pointillisme [pwɛ̃tijism] NM pointillism

pointilliste [pwɛ̃tijist] ADJ, NMF pointillist

pointu, e [pwɛ̃ty] **1** ADJ **a** (= *en forme de pointe*) pointed; (= *aiguisé*) sharp **b** (*péj*) [*air*] peeved; [*caractère*] touchy, peevish; [*voix, ton*] shrill; **accent ~** northern French accent **c** [*analyse*] in-depth; [*sujet*] specialized; [*connaissances*] thorough; [*diagnostic*] precise; **des normes d'hygiène de plus en plus ~es** increasingly stringent *ou* rigorous standards of hygiene **2** ADV **parler ~** to speak with *ou* have a northern French accent

pointure [pwɛ̃tyʀ] NF [*gant, chaussure*] size; **quelle est votre ~?** ◊ **quelle ~ faites-vous?** what size do you take? *ou* are you?; **c'est une (grande** *ou* **grosse) ~ dans la chanson/ce domaine*** he's a big name* in songwriting/this field

point-virgule (*pl* **points-virgules**) [pwɛ̃viʀgyl] NM semi-colon

poire [pwaʀ] **1** NF **a** (= *fruit*) pear; **il m'a dit cela entre la ~ et le fromage** he told me that quite casually over lunch (*ou* dinner) → **couper, garder b** (* = *tête*) mug*, face; **il a une bonne ~** he's got a nice enough face; **se ficher de** *ou* **se payer la ~ de qn** (*ridiculiser*) to have a good laugh at sb's expense, take the mickey out of sb* (*Brit*); (*tromper*) to take sb for a ride*; **en pleine ~** right in the face **c** (* = *dupe*) sucker*, mug* (*Brit*); **c'est une bonne ~** he's a real sucker* *ou* mug* (*Brit*); **et moi, bonne ~, j'ai dit oui** and like a sucker* *ou* mug* (*Brit*) I said yes **d** (*vaporisateur*) squeezer **2** ADJ **être ~** to be a sucker* *ou* mug* (*Brit*) **3** COMP ► **poire Belle-Hélène** stewed pear with chocolate sauce and cream ► **poire électrique** (pear-shaped) switch ► **poire à injections** douche, syringe ► **poire à lavement** enema syringe ► **poire à poudre** powder horn

poiré [pwaʀe] NM perry

poireau (*pl* **poireaux**) [pwaʀo] NM leek; **faire le ~*** to hang about*

poireauter* [pwaʀote] ▸conjug 1◂ VI to hang about*; **faire ~ qn** to leave sb hanging about*

poirée [pwaʀe] NF (= *bette*) Swiss chard

poirier [pwaʀje] NM (= *arbre*) pear tree; (= *acrobatie*) **faire le ~** to do a headstand

poiroter* [pwaʀote] ▸conjug 1◂ VI = **poireauter**

pois [pwa] **1** NM **a** (= *légume*) pea; **petits ~** (garden) peas **b** (*Habillement*) (polka) dot, spot; **robe à ~** spotted *ou* polka dot dress → **purée 2** COMP ► **pois cassés** split peas ► **pois chiche** chickpea, garbanzo (bean); **il a un ~ chiche dans la tête*** he's a pea-brain*, he's short on grey matter* ► **pois gourmands** mangetout peas ► **pois de senteur** sweet pea → **mange-tout**

poiscaille* [pwaskaj] NM *ou* M (*souvent péj*) fish

poison [pwazɔ̃] **1** NM (*lit, fig*) poison; **on a mis du ~ dans sa soupe** there was poison in his soup, his soup was poisoned **2** NMF* (= *personne*) nuisance; (= *enfant*) little horror*; (= *chose*) drag*, bind* (*Brit*)

poissard, e [pwasaʀ, aʀd] **1** ADJ [*accent, langage*] vulgar, coarse **2** **poissarde** NF **parler comme une ~e** to talk like a fishwife

poisse* [pwas] NF rotten luck*, bad luck; **avoir la ~** to have rotten* *ou* bad luck; **quelle ~!** ◊ **c'est la ~!** just my (*ou* our) (rotten)

luck!*; **ne le fais pas, ça porte la ~** don't do that — it's bad luck *ou* it's unlucky; **ça leur a porté la ~** it brought them bad luck

poisser [pwase] ▶conjug 1◀ VT a (: = *attraper*) to nab*, cop: b (= *salir*) to make sticky; (= *engluer*) [+ *cordage*] to pitch; **ça poisse** it's all sticky

poisseux, -euse [pwasø, øz] ADJ [*mains, surface*] sticky

poisson [pwasɔ̃] 1 NM a (*gén*) fish; **pêcher du ~** to fish; **deux ~s** two fish *ou* fishes; **fourchette/couteau à ~** fish fork/knife; **être (heureux) comme un ~ dans l'eau** to be in one's element; **être comme un ~ hors de l'eau** to be like a fish out of water; **engueuler qn comme du ~ pourri:** to call sb all the names under the sun, bawl sb out; **un gros ~***, a big fish* ▶ **petit, queue** b (*Astron*) **les Poissons** Pisces, the Fishes; **c'est un Poissons** ◊ **il est (du signe du) Poissons** he's a Pisces 2 COMP ▶ **poisson d'argent** silverfish ▶ **poisson d'avril!** April fool!; **c'est un ~ d'avril** it's an April fool's trick ▶ **poisson d'eau douce** freshwater fish ▶ **poisson lune** sunfish ▶ **poisson de mer** saltwater fish ▶ **poisson pilote** pilotfish ▶ **poisson plat** flatfish ▶ **poisson rouge** goldfish ▶ **poisson volant** flying fish

┌─────────────────────┐
│ **POISSON D'AVRIL** │
└─────────────────────┘

In France, as in Britain, April 1st is a day for playing practical jokes. The expression **poisson d'avril** *comes from the tradition of pinning or sticking a paper fish on the back of an unsuspecting person, though by extension it can also refer to any form of practical joke played on April 1st.*

poisson-chat (*pl* **poissons-chats**) [pwasɔ̃ʃa] NM catfish

poisson-épée (*pl* **poissons-épées**) [pwasɔ̃epe] NM swordfish

poissonnerie [pwasɔnri] NF (= *boutique*) fish shop, fishmonger's (shop) (*surtout Brit*); (= *métier*) fish trade

poissonneux, -euse [pwasɔnø, øz] ADJ full of fish (*attrib*), well-stocked with fish

poissonnier [pwasɔnje] NM fishmonger (*surtout Brit*), fish merchant (*US*)

poissonnière [pwasɔnjɛʀ] NF a (= *personne*) (woman) fishmonger (*surtout Brit*), fish merchant (*US*) b (= *ustensile*) fish kettle

poisson-perroquet (*pl* **poissons-perroquets**) [pwasɔ̃pɛʀɔke] NM parrotfish

poisson-scie (*pl* **poissons-scies**) [pwasɔ̃si] NM sawfish

poitrail [pwatʀaj] NM (*Zool*) breast; (*hum* = *poitrine*) chest; (*Constr*) lintel

poitrinaire† [pwatʀinɛʀ] 1 ADJ **être ~** to have TB, be tuberculous (*SPÉC*) 2 NMF tuberculosis sufferer

poitrine [pwatʀin] NF (*gén*) chest, breast (*littér*); (= *seins*) bust, bosom; (*Culin*) [*veau, mouton*] breast; [*porc*] belly; **~ salée** (*ou* **fumée**) streaky bacon; **~ de bœuf** brisket (of beef); **maladie de ~**† chest complaint; **elle a beaucoup de ~** she's got a big bust *ou* bosom, she's big-busted; **elle n'a pas de ~** she's flat-chested; **un cri jaillit de sa ~** he uttered a cry → **fluxion, tour², voix**

poivrade [pwavʀad] NF (*Culin*) vinaigrette (sauce) with pepper; **(à la) ~** with salt and pepper

poivre [pwavʀ] 1 NM pepper ▶ **moulin, steak** 2 COMP ▶ **poivre blanc** white pepper ▶ **poivre de Cayenne** Cayenne pepper ▶ **poivre en grains** whole pepper, peppercorns ▶ **poivre gris** black pepper ▶ **poivre moulu** ground pepper ▶ **poivre noir** black pepper ▶ **poivre en poudre** = **poivre moulu** ▶ **poivre rouge** red pepper ▶ **poivre et**

sel ADJ INV [*cheveux*] pepper-and-salt ▶ **poivre vert** green pepper (*spice*)

poivré, e [pwavʀe] (*ptp de* **poivrer**) ADJ a [*plat, goût, odeur*] peppery; [*histoire*] spicy, juicy*, saucy* b (: = *soûl*) pickled:, plastered:

poivrer [pwavʀe] ▶conjug 1◀ 1 VT to pepper, put pepper in *ou* on 2 **se poivrer** VPR (= *se soûler*) to get pickled: *ou* plastered:

poivrier [pwavʀije] NM a (*Bot*) pepper plant b (*Culin*) pepperpot, pepper shaker (*US*)

poivrière [pwavʀijɛʀ] NF a (*Culin*) pepperpot, pepper shaker (*US*) b (= *plantation*) pepper plantation c (*Archit*) pepper-box

poivron [pwavʀɔ̃] NM (sweet) pepper, capsicum; **~ (vert)** green pepper; **~ rouge** red pepper

poivrot, e* [pwavʀo, ɔt] NM,F drunkard, wino:

poix [pwa] NF pitch (*tar*)

poker [pɔkɛʀ] NM (*Cartes*) (= *jeu*) poker; (= *partie*) game of poker; **faire un ~** to have a game of poker; **~ d'as/de dames** four aces/ queens; **~ d'as** (= *jeu*) poker dice; **~ menteur** bluff; **coup de ~** gamble; **tenter un coup de ~** to take a gamble; **tout s'est joué sur un coup de ~** it was all a big gamble; **on ne joue pas sa carrière sur un coup de ~** you don't gamble *ou* risk your entire career on a throw of the dice

polaire [pɔlɛʀ] 1 ADJ a (*Chim, Géog, Math*) polar; **froid ~** arctic cold; **laine ~** (= *tissu*) fleece; **(sweat en) laine ~** fleece (sweatshirt) → **cercle, étoile** 2 NF a (*Math*) polar b (= *vêtement*) fleece jacket (*ou* sweatshirt *etc*)

polaque [pɔlak] NM (*injurieux*) Polack** (*injurieux*)

polar¹* [pɔlaʀ] NM (= *roman*) detective novel

polar² [pɔlaʀ] NM (*arg Scol*) swot* (*Brit*), grind* (*US*)

polarisant, e [pɔlaʀizɑ̃, ɑ̃t] ADJ (*Élec, Phys*) polarizing

polarisation [pɔlaʀizasjɔ̃] NF (*Élec, Phys*) polarization; (*fig*) focusing

polariser [pɔlaʀize] ▶conjug 1◀ 1 VT a (*Élec, Phys*) to polarize; **lumière polarisée** polarized light b (= *faire converger sur soi*) [+ *attention, regards*] to attract; **ce problème polarise tout le mécontentement** this problem is the focus of all the discontent c (= *concentrer*) **~ son attention/ses efforts sur qch** to focus *ou* centre one's attention/one's efforts on sth; **~ son énergie sur qch** to bring all one's energies to bear on sth 2 **se polariser** VPR (*Phys*) to polarize; **se ~** *ou* **être polarisé sur qch** [*débat, mécontentement, critiques*] to be centred around *ou* upon sth, be focused upon sth; [*personne*] to focus *ou* centre one's attention on sth; **elle est trop polarisée sur sa réussite professionnelle** she's too bound up *ou* wrapped up in her career

polariseur [pɔlaʀizœʀ] ADJ, NM **(prisme) ~** polarizer

polarité [pɔlaʀite] NF (*Bio, Ling, Math, Phys*) polarity

Polaroïd® [pɔlaʀɔid] N Polaroid®; **(appareil-photo) ~** Polaroid® (camera)

polder [pɔldɛʀ] NM polder

poldérisation [pɔldeʀizasjɔ̃] NF converting into a polder

pôle [pol] NM a (*Sci*) pole; **le ~ Nord/Sud** the North/South Pole; **~ magnétique** magnetic pole b (= *centre*) **d'activité** [*entreprise*] area of activity; **~ de conversion** relocation area; **~ de développement** pole of development; **~ universitaire** university centre; **la ville est devenue un ~ d'attraction pour les artistes/les investisseurs** the town has become a magnet for artists/investors, the town is drawing artists/investors like a magnet; **Montpellier est le ~ économique de la région** Montpellier is the economic hub of the region

polémique [pɔlemik] 1 ADJ [*sujet*] controversial, contentious; [*écrit, article*] polemical; **j'ai pris part à la discussion sans aucun esprit ~** I took part in the discussion without wanting to be contentious 2 NF (= *controverse*) controversy, argument (**sur** about, over); **chercher à faire de la ~** to try to stir up controversy; **engager une ~ avec qn** to enter into an argument with sb; **une violente ~ s'est engagée sur ...** a fierce controversy has flared up about ...; **relancer une ~** to rekindle a controversy

polémiquer [pɔlemike] ▶conjug 1◀ VI to argue (**sur** about, over); **sans vouloir ~, j'ai toujours pensé que ...** I don't want to be controversial, but I've always thought that ...; **je ne veux pas ~ sur ce point** I don't want to be drawn into an argument on this issue

polémiste [pɔlemist] NMF polemist, polemicist

polémologie [pɔlemɔlɔʒi] NF study of war

polenta [pɔlenta] NF polenta

pole position [pɔlpozisjɔ̃] NF (*Aut, fig*) pole position; **être en ~** to be in pole position

poli¹, e [pɔli] ADJ [*personne, refus, silence*] polite; **ce n'est pas ~ de parler la bouche pleine** it's bad manners *ou* it's rude *ou* it's not nice to talk with your mouth full; **ce n'est pas très ~ de dire ça** that's a rather rude thing to say, it's rather rude to say that; **soyez ~ !** don't be rude!; **elle a été tout juste ~e avec moi** she was barely civil to me

poli², e [pɔli] (*ptp de* **polir**) 1 ADJ [*bois, ivoire*] polished; [*métal*] burnished, polished; [*caillou*] smooth 2 NM shine; **donner du ~ à** to put a shine on, polish (up)

police¹ [pɔlis] 1 NF a (= *corps*) police (*NonC*), police force; **voiture de ~** police car; **être dans** *ou* **de la ~** to be in the police (force); **la ~ est à ses trousses** the police are after him *ou* are on his tail; **la guerre des ~s** the rivalry between different branches of the police; **toutes les ~s de France** the police throughout France; **après avoir passé la douane et les formalités de ~** once you've gone through customs and immigration → **plaque, salle** b (= *maintien de l'ordre*) policing, enforcement of (law and) order; **les pouvoirs de ~ dans la société** powers to enforce *ou* maintain law and order in society; **exercer** *ou* **faire la ~** to keep (law and) order; **faire la ~ dans une classe** to keep order in a class, keep a class in order; **faire sa propre ~** to do one's own policing, keep (law and) order for o.s. c (= *règlements*) regulations; **~ intérieure d'une école** internal regulations of a school d (= *tribunal*) **passer en simple ~** to be tried in a police *ou* magistrates' court → **tribunal** 2 COMP ▶ **police de l'air et des frontières** border police ▶ **police à cheval** (*Can*) mounted police, mounties* ▶ **police de la circulation** traffic police ▶ **police judiciaire** ≈ Criminal Investigation Department ▶ **police des mœurs, police mondaine** ≈ vice squad ▶ **police montée** (*Can*) mounted police, mounties* ▶ **police municipale** ≈ local police ▶ **police nationale** national police force ▶ **police parallèle** ≈ secret police ▶ **police des polices** Complaints and Discipline Branch (*Brit*), Internal Affairs (*US*) ▶ **police privée** private police force ▶ **police de la route** traffic police (*Brit*), state highway patrol (*US*) ▶ **police secours** ≈ emergency services; **appeler ~ secours** ≈ to dial 999 (*Brit*) *ou* 911 (*US*), ≈ call the emergency services ▶ **police secrète** secret police

police² [pɔlis] NF a (*Assurances*) (insurance) policy; **~ d'assurance vie** life insurance *ou* assurance policy; **~ d'assurance contre l'incendie** fire insurance policy b (*Typo, Ordin*) **~ (de caractères)** font

policé, e [pɔlise] (*ptp de* **policer**) ADJ (*frm*) [*mu-*

sique, société] refined; [langue, manières] refined, polished

policer [pɔlise] ▶ conjug 3 ◀ VT †† to civilize

polichinelle [pɔliʃinɛl] NM [a] (Théât) **Polichinelle** Punchinello → **secret** [b] (= marionnette) Punch; **avoir un ~ dans le tiroir*** to have a bun in the oven* [c] (péj = personne) buffoon; **faire le ~** to act the buffoon

policier, -ière [pɔlisje, jɛʀ] [1] ADJ [chien, enquête, régime] police (épith); [film, roman] detective (épith) [2] NM [a] (= agent) policeman, police officer; **femme ~** policewoman, woman police officer [b] (= roman) detective novel; (= film) detective film

policlinique [pɔliklinik] NF out-patients' clinic

poliment [pɔlimɑ̃] ADV politely

polio [pɔljo] [1] NF (ABRÉV = **poliomyélite**) polio [2] NMF* (ABRÉV = **poliomyélitique**) polio victim

poliomyélite [pɔljɔmjelit] NF poliomyelitis, polio

poliomyélitique [pɔljɔmjelitik] [1] ADJ suffering from polio [2] NMF polio victim

polir [pɔliʀ] ▶ conjug 2 ◀ VT [a] [+ meuble, chaussures, pierre, verre] to polish; [+ métal] to polish, burnish, buff; **se ~ les ongles** to buff one's nails [b] (= parfaire) [+ discours, style, phrase] to polish; [+ manières] to polish, refine

polissage [pɔlisaʒ] NM [meuble, chaussures, pierre, verre] polishing; [métal] polishing, burnishing, buffing; [ongles] buffing

polisseur, -euse [pɔlisœʀ, øz] [1] NM,F polisher [2] **polisseuse** NF (= machine) polisher, polishing machine

polissoir [pɔliswaʀ] NM polisher, polishing machine; **~ à ongles** nail buffer

polisson, -onne [pɔlisɔ̃, ɔn] [1] ADJ [a] (= espiègle) [enfant, air] naughty, mischievous [b] (= grivois) [chanson] naughty, saucy; [regard] saucy, randy* [2] NM,F (= enfant) (little) rascal, (little) devil*, mischief*; (= personne égrillarde) saucy devil*; (†† = petit vagabond) street urchin

polissonner † [pɔlisɔne] ▶ conjug 1 ◀ VI to be naughty

polissonnerie [pɔlisɔnʀi] NF [a] (= espièglerie) naughty trick [b] (= grivoiserie) (= parole) naughty ou saucy remark; (= action) naughty thing

politesse [pɔlitɛs] NF [a] (= savoir-vivre) politeness, courtesy; **par ~** out of politeness, to be polite; **je vais t'apprendre la ~ !** I'll teach you some manners!; **tu aurais pu avoir la ~ de lui répondre** you could at least have had the courtesy to reply to him; **il a eu la ~ de ne rien dire** he was polite enough to say nothing, he politely said nothing → **brûler, formule, visite** [b] (= parole) polite remark; (= action) polite gesture; **rendre une ~** to return a favour; **se faire des ~s** (paroles) to exchange polite remarks; (actions) to make polite gestures to one another; **ce serait la moindre des ~s** it's the least you (ou he etc) can do, it would only be polite

politicaillerie* [pɔlitikajʀi] NF (péj) politicking (péj)

politicard, e [pɔlitikaʀ, aʀd] (péj) [1] ADJ [ambitions] petty political [2] NM,F politician, political schemer (péj)

politicien, -ienne [pɔlitisjɛ̃, jɛn] [1] ADJ (péj) [manœuvre, querelle] (petty) political; **la politique politicienne** politicking [2] NM,F politician, political schemer (péj)

politico- [pɔlitiko] PRÉF politico-

politique [pɔlitik] [1] ADJ [a] [institutions, économie, parti, prisonnier, pouvoir, réfugié] political; [carrière] political, in politics; **compte rendu de la semaine ~** report on the week in politics → **homme, science**

[b] (littér = habile) [personne] diplomatic; [acte, invitation] diplomatic, politic [2] NF [a] (= science, carrière) politics sg; **parler ~** to talk politics; **faire de la ~** (militantisme) to be a political activist; (métier) to be in politics [b] (Pol) (= ligne de conduite) policy; (= manière de gouverner) policies; **~ intérieure/industrielle/sociale** domestic/industrial/social policy; **il critique la ~ du gouvernement** he criticizes the government's policies; **avoir une ~ de gauche/droite** to follow left-/right-wing policies; **discours ou déclaration de ~ générale** policy speech; (Europe) **~ agricole commune** Common Agricultural Policy [c] (= manière d'agir) policy; **il est de bonne ~ de ...** it is good policy to ...; **la ~ du moindre effort** the principle of least effort; **la ~ du pire** making things worse in order to further one's own ends; **faire ou pratiquer la ~ de la chaise vide** to make a show of non-attendance; **pratiquer la ~ de l'autruche** to bury one's head in the sand; **c'est la ~ de l'autruche** it's like burying one's head in the sand [3] NM (= politicien) politician; (= aspects politiques) **le ~** politics sg

politique-fiction [pɔlitikfiksjɔ̃] NF political fantasy ou fiction; **film de ~** political thriller; **ce n'est pas de la ~, ces lois existent** this does not belong to the realms of political fantasy, these laws exist

politiquement [pɔlitikmɑ̃] ADV (lit) politically; (littér) diplomatically; **~ correct** politically correct, PC; **~ incorrect** politically incorrect, non-PC

politiquer* † [pɔlitike] ▶ conjug 1 ◀ VI to talk (about) politics

politisation [pɔlitizasjɔ̃] NF politicization

politiser [pɔlitize] ▶ conjug 1 ◀ [1] VT [+ débat] to politicize, bring politics into; [+ événement] to make a political issue of; [+ personne, mouvement, action] to politicize; **être très politisé** [personne] to be highly politicized, be politically aware [2] **se politiser** VPR [action, mouvement, débat] to become politicized; [personne] to become politicized ou politically aware

politologie [pɔlitɔlɔʒi] NF political science

politologue [pɔlitɔlɔg] NMF political pundit ou analyst ou expert

polka [pɔlka] NF polka

pollen [pɔlɛn] NM pollen

pollinisateur, -trice [pɔlinizatœʀ, tʀis] ADJ **insecte ~** insect pollinator, pollinating insect

pollinisation [pɔlinizasjɔ̃] NF pollination

polluant, e [pɔlɥɑ̃, ɑ̃t] ADJ polluting; **produit ~** pollutant, polluting agent; **non ~** non-polluting, environment-friendly; **c'est très/peu ~** it produces a lot of/little pollution; **industrie très ~e** highly polluting industry

polluer [pɔlɥe] ▶ conjug 1 ◀ VT to pollute

pollueur, -euse [pɔlɥœʀ, øz] [1] ADJ polluting [2] NM,F (= substance) pollutant, polluting agent; (= industrie, personne) polluter; **le principe ~-payeur** the polluter-pays principle

pollution [pɔlysjɔ̃] NF pollution; **~ atmosphérique/acoustique/radioactive** atmospheric/noise/radioactive pollution; **~ de l'air/des eaux/de l'environnement** air/water/environmental pollution; **~ par les nitrates** nitrate pollution; (Méd) **~s nocturnes** nocturnal emissions (SPÉC), wet dreams

polo [pɔlo] NM [a] (Sport) polo [b] (= chemise) polo shirt

polochon* [pɔlɔʃɔ̃] NM bolster; **sac ~** duffel bag

Pologne [pɔlɔɲ] NF Poland

polonais, e [pɔlɔnɛ, ɛz] [1] ADJ Polish [2] NM [a] (Ling) Polish [b] **Polonais** Pole [3] **polonaise** NF [a] **Polonaise** Pole [b] (= danse, Mus) polonaise [c] (= gâteau) polonaise

(meringue-covered sponge cake containing preserved fruit and Kirsch)

polonium [pɔlɔnjɔm] NM polonium

poltron, -onne [pɔltʀɔ̃, ɔn] [1] ADJ cowardly, craven (littér) [2] NM,F coward

poltronnerie [pɔltʀɔnʀi] NF cowardice

poly... [pɔli] PRÉF poly...

polyacide [pɔliasid] ADJ, NM polyacid

polyamide [pɔliamid] NM polyamide

polyandre [pɔliɑ̃dʀ] ADJ polyandrous

polyandrie [pɔliɑ̃dʀi] NF polyandry

polyarchie [pɔliaʀʃi] NF polyarchy

polyarthrite [pɔliaʀtʀit] NF polyarthritis

polycarburant [pɔlikaʀbyʀɑ̃] ADJ M [moteur] multifuel (épith)

polychlorure [pɔliklɔʀyʀ] NM **~ de vinyle** polyvinyl chloride

polychrome [pɔlikʀom] ADJ polychrome, polychromatic

polyclinique [pɔliklinik] NF private general hospital

polycopie [pɔlikɔpi] NF duplication, stencilling; **tiré à la ~** duplicated, stencilled

polycopié [pɔlikɔpje] NM (Univ) duplicated lecture notes

polycopier [pɔlikɔpje] ▶ conjug 7 ◀ VT to duplicate, stencil; **cours polycopiés** duplicated lecture notes; **machine à ~** duplicator

polyculture [pɔlikyltyʀ] NF mixed farming

polyèdre [pɔljɛdʀ] [1] ADJ [angle, solide] polyhedral [2] NM polyhedron

polyédrique [pɔljedʀik] ADJ polyhedral

polyester [pɔliɛstɛʀ] NM polyester

polyéthylène [pɔlietilɛn] NM polyethylene

polygame [pɔligam] [1] ADJ polygamous [2] NM polygamist

polygamie [pɔligami] NF polygamy

polyglotte [pɔliglɔt] ADJ, NMF polyglot

polygonal, e (mpl -aux) [pɔligɔnal, o] ADJ polygonal, many-sided

polygone [pɔligɔn] NM (Math) polygon; (Mil) **~ de tir** rifle range

polygraphe [pɔligʀaf] NMF polygraph

poly-insaturé, e [pɔliɛ̃satyʀe] ADJ polyunsaturated

polymère [pɔlimɛʀ] [1] ADJ polymeric [2] NM polymer

polymérisation [pɔlimeʀizasjɔ̃] NF polymerization

polymériser VT, **se polymériser** VPR [pɔlimeʀize] ▶ conjug 1 ◀ to polymerize

polymorphe [pɔlimɔʀf] ADJ polymorphous, polymorphic

polymorphie [pɔlimɔʀfi] NF, **polymorphisme** [pɔlimɔʀfism] NM polymorphism

Polynésie [pɔlinezi] NF Polynesia; **~ française** French Polynesia

polynésien, -ienne [pɔlinezjɛ̃, jɛn] [1] ADJ Polynesian [2] NM (Ling) Polynesian [3] **Polynésien(ne)** NM,F Polynesian

polynévrite [pɔlinevʀit] NF polyneuritis

Polynice [pɔlinis] NM Polynices

polynôme [pɔlinom] NM polynomial (Math)

polynucléaire [pɔlinykleɛʀ] [1] ADJ polynuclear, multinuclear [2] NM polymorphonuclear leucocyte

polype [pɔlip] N (Zool) polyp; (Méd) polyp, polypus (Spéc)

polyphasé, e [pɔlifaze] ADJ polyphase

Polyphème [pɔlifɛm] NM Polyphemus

polyphonie [pɔlifɔni] NF polyphony (Mus)

polyphonique [pɔlifɔnik] ADJ polyphonic (Mus)

polyphosphate [pɔlifɔsfat] NM polyphosphate

polypier [pɔlipje] NM polypary

polypore [pɔlipɔʀ] NM polyporus

polypropylène [pɔlipʀɔpilɛn] NM (Chim) polypropylene, polypropene

polysémie [pɔlisemi] NF polysemy

polysémique [pɔlisemik] ADJ polysemous, polysemic

polystyrène [pɔlistiʀɛn] NM polystyrene; ~ **expansé** expanded polystyrene

polysyllabe [pɔlisi(l)lab] ① ADJ polysyllabic ② NM polysyllable

polysyllabique [pɔlisi(l)labik] ADJ polysyllabic; **mot** ~ polysyllable

polytechnicien, -ienne [pɔliteknisjɛ̃, jɛn] NM,F student or ex-student of the École polytechnique

polytechnique [pɔliteknik] ADJ, NF **l'École** ~ ◊ **Polytechnique** the École polytechnique

┌─────────────────────────────┐
│ **POLYTECHNIQUE** │
└─────────────────────────────┘

The term **Polytechnique** is not to be confused with the English word "polytechnic" which used to refer to a particular kind of higher education establishment in Britain. In France, **Polytechnique** is the name of one of the most prestigious engineering schools, also known as "l'X".
→ GRANDES ÉCOLES

polythéisme [pɔliteism] NM polytheism

polythéiste [pɔliteist] ① ADJ polytheistic ② NMF polytheist

polythérapie [pɔliteʀapi] NF combination therapy

polytoxicomanie [pɔlitɔksikɔmani] NF multiple (drug) addiction

polytransfusé, e [pɔlitʀɑ̃sfyze] NM,F person who has been given multiple blood transfusions

polyuréthan(n)e [pɔliyʀetan] NM polyurethan(e); **mousse de** ~ polyurethan(e) foam

polyvalence [pɔlivalɑ̃s] NF (Chim, Méd) polyvalency; [personne, mot] versatility

polyvalent, e [pɔlivalɑ̃, ɑ̃t] ① ADJ [sérum, vaccin] polyvalent; [salle] multi-purpose (épith); [personne] versatile; **formation ~e** comprehensive training; **professeur** ~ teacher who teaches a variety of subjects; **nous recherchons une personne ~e** we're looking for a good all-rounder (Brit) ou for someone who's good all-around (US) ② NM tax inspector (sent to examine company's books) ③ **polyvalente** NF (Can) secondary school teaching academic and vocational subjects

polyvinylique [pɔlivinilik] ADJ polyvinyl (épith)

poméló [pɔmelo] NM grapefruit, pomelo (US)

Poméranie [pɔmeʀani] NF Pomerania → **loulou¹**

pommade [pɔmad] NF (pour la peau) ointment; (pour les cheveux) cream, pomade; ~ **pour les lèvres** lip salve ou balm; (Culin) **beurre en** ~ softened butter; **passer de la** ~ **à qn*** to butter sb up*, soft-soap sb* (Brit)

pommader [pɔmade] ▸conjug 1 ◂ VT [+ cheveux] to pomade

pomme [pɔm] ① NF ⓐ (= fruit) apple; (= pomme de terre) potato; **tomber dans les ~s*** to faint, pass out; **elle est restée longtemps dans les ~s*** she was out (cold)* for some time; **c'est aux ~s !*** it's ace!* → **haut** ⓑ [chou, laitue] heart; [canne, lit] knob; [arrosoir] rose; [mât] truck; ~ **de douche** showerhead ⓒ (* = tête) head, nut*; (= visage) face, mug*; **c'est pour ma** ~ (* = gén) it's for me ou for yours truly*; (qch de désagréable) it's for yours truly* ou for muggins here‡ (Brit); **je m'occupe d'abord de ma** ~ I'm looking after number one*; **c'est pour ta** ~ it's for you ⓓ (* = naïf, indulgent) sucker*, mug* (Brit); **et moi, bonne ~, j'ai dit oui** and like a sucker* ou mug* (Brit) I said yes

② COMP ► **pomme d'Adam** Adam's apple ► **pommes allumettes** matchstick potatoes ► **pomme d'amour** (= sucrerie) toffee apple; (= tomate) love apple ► **pomme d'api** type of small apple ► **pommes boulangère** (Culin) fried potatoes with onions ► **pomme cannelle** custard apple, sweetsop (Brit) ► **pomme à cidre** cider apple ► **pomme à couteau** eating apple ► **pomme à cuire** cooking apple, cooker* ► **pommes dauphine** pommes dauphine, ≈ potato croquettes (without breadcrumbs) ► **pomme de discorde** (fig) bone of contention ► **pomme fruit** apple ► **pommes mousseline** mashed potatoes ► **pommes noisettes** ≈ mini potato croquettes (without breadcrumbs) ► **pommes paille** straw potatoes, ≈ shoestring potatoes (US) ► **pomme de pin** pine ou fir cone ► **pomme sauvage** crab apple ► **pomme de terre** potato ► **pommes vapeur** boiled potatoes → **frite**

pommé, e [pɔme] (ptp de pommer) ADJ [chou] firm and round; [laitue] with a good heart

pommeau (pl **pommeaux**) [pɔmo] NM [épée, selle] pommel; [canne] knob

pommelé, e [pɔm(ə)le] (ptp de pommeler) ADJ [cheval] dappled; [ciel] full of fluffy ou fleecy clouds; **gris** ~ dapple-grey

pommeler (se) [pɔm(ə)le] ▸conjug 4 ◂ VPR [ciel] to become full of fluffy ou fleecy clouds; [chou, laitue] to form a head ou heart

pommelle [pɔmɛl] NF filter (over a pipe)

pommer [pɔme] ▸conjug 1 ◂ VI (Bot) to form a head ou heart

pommeraie [pɔm(ə)ʀɛ] NF apple orchard

pommette [pɔmɛt] NF cheekbone; **le rouge lui monta aux ~s** his cheeks reddened; **~s saillantes** high cheekbones

pommier [pɔmje] NM apple tree; ~ **sauvage** crab-apple tree; ~ **du Japon** Japan (flowering) quince (tree)

Pomone [pɔmɔn] NF Pomona

pompage [pɔ̃paʒ] NM pumping; ~ **optique** optical pumping

pompe¹ [pɔ̃p] ① NF ⓐ (= machine) pump; ~ **à air/à vide/de bicyclette** air/vacuum/bicycle pump ⓑ (* = chaussure) shoe; (fig) **être à l'aise ou bien dans ses ~s** to feel good; **je suis à côté de mes ~s en ce moment** I'm not quite with it* at the moment; **ce type est vraiment à côté de ses ~s** that guy's really out of it* ⓒ (* : loc) **à toute** ~ at top speed, flat out*; (Mil) (**soldat de**) **deuxième** ~ private; (Sport) **faire des ~s** to do press-ups (Brit) ou push-ups (US); **c'est juste un petit coup de ~** I'm (ou we're) just feeling a bit drained; **j'ai eu un** ou **le coup de** ~ I felt drained, I was shattered* ② COMP ► **pompe aspirante** suction ou lift pump; ~ **aspirante et foulante** suction and force pump ► **pompe à chaleur** heat pump ► **pompe à essence** (= distributeur) petrol (Brit) ou gas(oline) (US) pump; (= station) petrol (Brit) ou gas (US) station ► **pompe foulante** force pump ► **pompe à incendie** fire engine (apparatus)

pompe² [pɔ̃p] NF ⓐ (littér = solennité) pomp; **en grande** ~ with great pomp ⓑ (Rel = vanités) **~s** pomps and vanities; **renoncer au monde et à ses ~s** to renounce the world and all its pomps and vanities ⓒ **~s funèbres** undertaker's, funeral director's (Brit), mortician's (US); **entreprise de ~s funèbres** funeral home, funeral director's (Brit), funeral parlor (US); **employé de ~s funèbres** undertaker's ou mortician's (US) assistant

pompé, e* [pɔ̃pe] (ptp de pomper) ADJ (= fatigué) dead-beat*, knackered‡ (Brit), pooped* (US)

Pompée [pɔ̃pe] NM Pompey

Pompéi [pɔ̃pei] N Pompeii

pompéien, -ienne [pɔ̃pejɛ̃, jɛn] ① ADJ Pompeiian ② **Pompéien(ne)** NM,F Pompeiian

pomper [pɔ̃pe] ▸conjug 1 ◂ VT ⓐ [+ air, liquide] to pump; [moustique] to suck; (= évacuer) to pump out; (= faire monter) to pump up; ~ **de l'eau** to get water from the pump, pump water out; **tu me pompes (l'air)‡** you're getting on my nerves, I'm fed up with you*; **il m'a pompé pas mal d'argent*** he sponged* quite a lot of money off me; **les impôts nous pompent tout notre argent*** all our money gets eaten up in tax ⓑ [éponge, buvard] to soak up ⓒ (arg Scol = copier) to crib* (**sur** from); **il m'a pompé toutes mes idées** he copied* ou lifted* all my ideas; **elle a pompé mon style** she has copied ou imitated my style ⓓ (* = boire) to knock back*; **qu'est-ce qu'il pompe!** he can't half (Brit) ou he sure can (US) knock it back!* ⓔ (* = épuiser) to wear out, tire out; **tout ce travail m'a pompé** I'm worn out* ou knackered‡ (Brit) ou pooped* (US) after all that work

pompette* [pɔ̃pɛt] ADJ tipsy*, tiddly* (Brit); **être/se sentir** ~ to be/feel a bit tipsy* ou tiddly* (Brit)

pompeusement [pɔ̃pøzmɑ̃] ADV pompously, pretentiously

pompeux, -euse [pɔ̃pø, øz] ADJ (= ampoulé) pompous, pretentious; (= imposant) solemn

pompier, -ière [pɔ̃pje, jɛʀ] ① ADJ (péj) [style, écrivain] pompous, pretentious; [morceau de musique] slushy*; (Art) **art** ~ official art ② NM ⓐ (= personne) fireman, firefighter; **appeler les ~s** to call the fire brigade (Brit) ou department (US) ou **fumer** ⓑ (‡ = acte sexuel) blow job‡; **faire un** ~ **à qn** to give sb a blow job‡

pompiste [pɔ̃pist] NMF petrol pump (Brit) ou gas station (US) attendant

pompon [pɔ̃pɔ̃] NM [chapeau, coussin] pompom; [frange, instrument] bobble; **c'est le** ~ ! it's the last straw!, that beats everything!*, that's the limit!*; **avoir son** ~†* to be tipsy* ou tiddly* (Brit); (fig, aussi iro) **décrocher le** ~ to hit the jackpot; **décerner le** ~ **à qn** to give first prize to sb → **rose**

pomponner [pɔ̃pɔne] ▸conjug 1 ◂ ① VT to titivate, doll up*; [+ bébé] to dress up; **bien pomponné** all dolled up* ou dressed up ② **se pomponner** VPR to doll o.s. up*, get dolled up* ou dressed up

ponant [pɔnɑ̃] NM (littér) west

ponçage [pɔ̃saʒ] NM ⓐ (avec du papier de verre) sanding (down), sandpapering; (avec une ponceuse) sanding (down) ⓑ (avec une pierre ponce) pumicing

ponce [pɔ̃s] NF ⓐ (**pierre**) ~ pumice (stone) ⓑ (Art) pounce box

ponceau (pl **ponceaux**) [pɔ̃so] ① NM (= fleur) corn ou Flanders ou field poppy, coquelicot; (= colorant) ponceau ② ADJ ponceau, dark red

Ponce Pilate [pɔ̃spilat] NM Pontius Pilate

poncer [pɔ̃se] ▸conjug 3 ◂ VT ⓐ (= décaper) (avec du papier de verre) to sand (down), sandpaper; (avec une ponceuse) to sand (down); **il faut commencer par** ~ it needs sanding down first ⓑ (= polir : avec une pierre ponce) to pumice ⓒ (Art) [+ dessin] to pounce

ponceuse [pɔ̃søz] NF sander

poncho [pɔ̃(t)ʃo] NM (= cape) poncho

poncif [pɔ̃sif] NM (= cliché) commonplace, cliché; (Art) stencil (for pouncing)

ponction [pɔ̃ksjɔ̃] NF ⓐ (Méd) (lombaire) puncture; (pulmonaire) tapping; **faire une ~ lombaire à qn** to perform a lumbar puncture on sb; **faire une ~ pulmonaire à qn** to drain fluid from sb's lungs ⓑ [argent] draining; ~ **fiscale** (tax) levy (**sur** on); **les ~s opérées sur nos bénéfices** the levies on our profits; **les ~s massives opérées sur notre pouvoir d'achat** the huge drain on our spending power; **par de fréquentes ~s il a épuisé son capital** he has dipped into ou drawn on his capital so often he has used it all up; **faire une sérieuse ~ dans ses économies** [impôt] to make a large hole in *ou* make serious inroads into one's savings; [*personne*] to draw heavily on one's savings

ponctionner [pɔ̃ksjɔne] ▶conjug 1◀ VT [+ *région lombaire*] to puncture; [+ *poumon*] to tap; [+ *réserves*] to tap; [+ *contribuable, entreprise*] to tax

ponctualité [pɔ̃ktɥalite] NF (= *exactitude*) punctuality; (= *assiduité*) punctiliousness (*frm*), meticulousness

ponctuation [pɔ̃ktɥasjɔ̃] NF punctuation

ponctuel, -elle [pɔ̃ktɥɛl] ADJ a (= *à l'heure*) punctual; (= *scrupuleux*) punctilious (*frm*), meticulous b (*Phys*) punctual c [*intervention, contrôles, aide*] (= *limité*) limited; (= *ciblé*) selective; [*problème*] localized, isolated; **ces terroristes se livrent à des actions ponctuelles** the terrorists make sporadic attacks; **je n'ai fait que quelques modifications ponctuelles** I've only changed a few things here and there d (*Ling*) [*aspect*] punctual

ponctuellement [pɔ̃ktɥɛlmɑ̃] ADV a (= *avec exactitude*) [*arriver*] punctually b (= *de temps en temps*) from time to time; (= *ici et là*) here and there

ponctuer [pɔ̃ktɥe] ▶conjug 1◀ VT (*lit, fig*) to punctuate (**de** with); (*Mus*) to phrase

pondéral, e (*mpl* **-aux**) [pɔ̃deral, o] ADJ weight (*épith*)

pondérateur, -trice [pɔ̃deratœr, tris] ADJ [*influence*] stabilizing, steadying

pondération [pɔ̃derasjɔ̃] NF a [*personne*] level-headedness b (= *équilibrage*) balancing; (*Écon, Math*) weighting; **~ des pouvoirs** balance of powers; **le coefficient de ~ est 3** it's weighted by a factor of 3

pondéré, e [pɔ̃dere] (*ptp de* **pondérer**) ADJ a [*personne, attitude*] level-headed b (*Écon*) **indice ~** weighted index

pondérer [pɔ̃dere] ▶conjug 6◀ VT (= *équilibrer*) to balance; (= *compenser*) to counterbalance (**par** by); (*Écon*) [+ *indice*] to weight

pondéreux, -euse [pɔ̃derø, øz] 1 ADJ [*marchandises, produits*] heavy 2 NMPL heavy goods

pondeur [pɔ̃dœr] NM (*péj*) **~ de romans** writer who churns out books

pondeuse [pɔ̃døz] NF (**poule**) **~** good layer; (**: péj ou hum*) prolific child-bearer (*hum*)

pondre [pɔ̃dr] ▶conjug 41◀ 1 VT [+ *œuf*] to lay; *** [+ *enfant*] to produce; [+ *devoir, texte*] to produce, turn out***; **œuf frais pondu** new-laid egg 2 VI [*poule*] to lay; [*poisson, insecte*] to lay its eggs

poney [pɔnɛ] NM pony

pongé(e) [pɔ̃ʒe] NM (*Tex*) pongee

pongiste [pɔ̃ʒist] NMF table tennis player

pont [pɔ̃] 1 NM a (*Constr*) bridge; (= *lien*) bridge, link (**entre** between); **passer un ~** to go over *ou* cross a bridge; **vivre** *ou* **coucher sous les ~s** to sleep rough, live on the streets; **solide comme le Pont-Neuf** (as) strong as an ox; **se porter comme le Pont-Neuf*** to be hale and hearty; **faire un ~ d'or à qn** (*pour l'employer*) to offer sb a fortune (*to take on a job*); **couper les ~s avec qn** to sever all links with sb; **jeter un ~ sur une rivière** to bridge a river, throw a bridge over a river; **jeter un ~ entre les générations/deux cultures** to build bridges between generations/two cultures → **eau**
b (= *acrobatie*) crab; **faire le ~** to do a crab
c (*Naut*) deck; **~ avant/arrière** fore/rear deck; **~ principal/supérieur** main/upper *ou* top deck; **navire à deux/trois ~s** two/three decker; **tout le monde sur le ~!** all hands on deck!
d (*Aut*) axle; **~ avant/arrière** front/rear axle
e (*Mécanique*) (= *élévateur*) (hydraulic) ramp; **mettre une voiture sur le ~** to put a car on the ramp
f (= *vacances*) extra day(s) off (*taken between two public holidays or a public holiday and*

a weekend); **on a un ~ de trois jours pour Noël** we have three extra days (off) for *ou* at Christmas; **faire le ~** to take the extra day (off), make a long weekend of it → FÊTES LÉGALES
g (*Antiq*) **(royaume du) Pont** Pontus
h (*Ftbl*) **petit ~** nutmeg (*Brit*), between-the-leg pass (*US*); **faire un grand ~ à qn** to send the ball round sb's legs; **faire un petit ~ à qn** to send the ball between sb's legs, nutmeg sb (*Brit*)
i (*Élec*) bridge (circuit); **~ de Wheatstone** Wheatstone bridge
2 COMP ▶ **pont aérien** airlift ▶ **pont aux ânes** pons asinorum; (*fig*) **c'est le ~ aux ânes** any fool knows that ▶ **pont basculant** bascule bridge ▶ **les Ponts et Chaussées** (= *service*) the highways department, the department of civil engineering; (= *école*) school of civil engineering; **ingénieur des ~s et chaussées** civil engineer ▶ **pont d'envol** (*Naut*) flight deck ▶ **pont flottant** pontoon bridge ▶ **pont garage** car deck, vehicle deck ▶ **pont de glace** (*Can*) ice bridge *ou* road ▶ **pont de graissage** (*Aut*) ramp (*in a garage*) ▶ **pont mobile** movable bridge ▶ **pont à péage** tollbridge ▶ **pont promenade** (*Naut*) promenade deck ▶ **pont roulant** (*Rail*) travelling crane ▶ **pont suspendu** suspension bridge ▶ **pont tournant** swing bridge ▶ **pont transbordeur** transporter bridge → **hauban**

pontage [pɔ̃taʒ] NM (*Naut*) decking; (*Méd*) **~ (cardiaque)** (heart) bypass operation *ou* surgery (*NonC*); **~ coronarien** coronary bypass operation *ou* surgery (*NonC*); **faire un ~ à qn** to carry out a (heart) bypass operation on sb; **on lui a fait un triple ~** he had triple bypass surgery *ou* a triple bypass operation

pont-canal (*pl* **ponts-canaux**) [pɔ̃kanal, o] NM canal bridge

ponte[1] [pɔ̃t] NF (= *action*) laying (of eggs); (= *œufs*) eggs, clutch; (= *saison*) (egg-)laying season; **~ ovulaire** ovulation

ponte[2] [pɔ̃t] NM a (** = pontife*) bigwig***; **les grands ~s de l'université/du parti** the academic/party bigwigs; **un ~ de la médecine** a leading light in the medical world; **un ~ de la banque** a bigshot* in the banking world b (*Jeux*) punter

ponter[1] [pɔ̃te] ▶conjug 1◀ VT (*Naut*) to deck, lay the deck of

ponter[2] [pɔ̃te] ▶conjug 1◀ (*Jeux*) 1 VI to punt 2 VT to bet

Pont-Euxin [pɔ̃tøksɛ̃] NM **le ~** the Euxine Sea

pontife [pɔ̃tif] NM a (*Rel*) pontiff → **souverain** b (** = personne importante*) big shot***, pundit***

pontifiant, e* [pɔ̃tifjɑ̃, jɑ̃t] ADJ [*personne, ton*] pontificating

pontifical, e (*mpl* **-aux**) [pɔ̃tifikal, o] ADJ (*Antiq*) pontifical; (*Rel*) [*messe*] pontifical; [*siège, gardes, États*] papal

pontificat [pɔ̃tifika] NM pontificate

pontifier* [pɔ̃tifje] ▶conjug 7◀ VI to pontificate

pont-levis (*pl* **ponts-levis**) [pɔ̃l(ə)vi] NM drawbridge

ponton [pɔ̃tɔ̃] NM (= *plate-forme*) pontoon, (floating) landing stage; (= *chaland*) lighter; (= *navire*) hulk

ponton-grue (*pl* **pontons-grues**) [pɔ̃tɔ̃gry] NM floating crane

pontonnier [pɔ̃tɔnje] NM (*Mil*) pontoneer, pontonier

pool [pul] NM [*producteurs, dactylos*] pool; **~ bancaire** banking pool

pop [pɔp] 1 ADJ INV [*musique, art*] pop 2 NM **le ~** (= *musique*) pop (music); (= *art*) pop art

pop art, pop'art [pɔpart] NM pop art

pop-corn [pɔpkɔrn] NM INV popcorn

pope [pɔp] NM (Orthodox) priest

popeline [pɔplin] NF poplin

popote [pɔpɔt] 1 NF a (** = cuisine*) cooking; **faire la ~** to cook b (*Mil*) mess, canteen 2 ADJ INV *** stay-at-home (*épith*), home-loving; **il est très ~** he likes his home comforts

popotin* [pɔpɔtɛ̃] NM bottom*** → **magner**

populace [pɔpylas] NF (*péj*) rabble, mob

populaire [pɔpylɛr] ADJ a (= *du peuple*) [*gouvernement, front, croyance, tradition*] popular; [*démocratie*] popular, people's; [*république*] people's; [*mouvement, manifestation*] mass; **la République ~ de ...** the People's Republic of ... b (= *pour la masse*) [*roman, art, chanson*] popular; [*édition*] cheap → **bal, soupe** c (= *plébéien*) [*goût*] common; (= *ouvrier*) [*milieu, quartier, origines*] working-class; **les classes ~s** the working classes d (= *qui plaît*) popular, well-liked; **très ~ auprès des jeunes** very popular with young people e (*Ling*) [*mot, expression*] vernacular; [*étymologie*] popular; [*latin*] popular

populairement [pɔpylɛrmɑ̃] ADV (*gén*) popularly; [*parler*] in the vernacular

popularisation [pɔpylarizasjɔ̃] NF (= *vulgarisation*) popularization; (= *propagation*) **avec la ~ des concepts freudiens** with Freudian theories becoming more widely known; **la télévision a joué un rôle important dans la ~ de l'art lyrique** television played an important role in making opera accessible to *ou* in bringing opera to the general public

populariser [pɔpylarize] ▶conjug 1◀ 1 VT to popularize 2 **se populariser** VPR to become more (and more) popular

popularité [pɔpylarite] NF popularity

population [pɔpylasjɔ̃] NF population; **région à ~ musulmane/mixte** area with a large Muslim population/with a mixed population; **~ active/agricole** working/farming population; **~ carcérale/civile/scolaire** prison/civilian/school population; **mouvement de ~** population movement; **l'attentat a fait quatre victimes parmi la ~** the bomb attack claimed four civilian casualties

populeux, -euse [pɔpylø, øz] ADJ [*pays, ville*] densely populated, populous; [*rue*] crowded

populisme [pɔpylism] NM a (*Pol*) populism b (*Littérat*) populisme (*a literary movement of the 1920s and 1930s which sets out to describe the lives of ordinary people*)

populiste [pɔpylist] ADJ, NMF populist

populo* [pɔpylo] NM (*péj = peuple*) ordinary people *ou* folks***; (= *foule*) crowd (of people)

porc [pɔr] NM a (= *animal*) pig, hog (*US*); (= *viande*) pork; (= *peau*) pigskin b (** péj*) pig, swine***

porcelaine [pɔrsəlɛn] NF a (= *matière*) porcelain, china; (= *objet*) piece of porcelain; **~ dure/tendre** soft-paste/hard-paste porcelain; **~ tendre naturelle** bone china, **~ vitreuse** vitreous china; **~ de Saxe/de Sèvres** Dresden/Sèvres china; **~ de Chine** China china; **~ de Limoges** Limoges porcelain; **de** *ou* **en ~** china, porcelain b (*Zool*) cowrie

porcelainier, -ière [pɔrsəlenje, jɛr] 1 ADJ china (*épith*), porcelain (*épith*) 2 NM (= *fabricant*) porcelain *ou* china manufacturer

porcelet [pɔrsəlɛ] NM (*Zool*) piglet; (*Culin*) sucking pig

porc-épic (*pl* **porcs-épics**) [pɔrkepik] NM porcupine; (= *personne irritable*) prickly customer***; (= *homme mal rasé*) **tu es un vrai ~!** you're all bristly!

porche [pɔrʃ] NM porch; **sous le ~ de l'immeuble** in the entrance to the building

porcher, -ère [pɔrʃe, ɛr] NM,F pig-keeper, swineherd†

porcherie [pɔrʃəri] NF (*lit, fig*) pigsty, pigpen (*US*)

porcin, e [pɔrsɛ̃, in] [1] ADJ (*lit*) porcine; (*fig*) piglike [2] NM pig; **les ~s** pigs

pore [pɔr] NM pore; **il sue l'arrogance par tous les ~s** he exudes arrogance from every pore

poreux, -euse [pɔrø, øz] ADJ porous

porno* [pɔrno] [1] ADJ (ABRÉV = **pornographique**) porn*, porno*; **film/revue/cinéma ~** porn(o)* film/magazine/cinema [2] NM (ABRÉV = **pornographie**) porn*

pornographe [pɔrnɔgraf] [1] NMF pornographer [2] ADJ of pornography (*attrib*), pornographic

pornographie [pɔrnɔgrafi] NF pornography

pornographique [pɔrnɔgrafik] ADJ pornographic

porosité [pɔrozite] NF porosity

porphyre [pɔrfir] NM porphyry

porphyrique [pɔrfirik] ADJ porphyritic

port¹ [pɔr] [1] NM [a] (= *bassin*) harbour (*Brit*), harbor (*US*); (*commercial*) port; (= *ville*) port; (*littér* = *abri*) port, haven; **se promener sur le ~** to walk around the harbour *ou* along the quayside; **sortir du ~** to leave port *ou* harbour; **arriver au ~** (*Naut*) to dock; (*fig*) to reach one's destination; **arriver à bon ~** to arrive intact, arrive safe and sound; (*fig*) **un ~ dans la tempête** a port in a storm [b] (*dans les Pyrénées*) pass [c] (*Ordin*) port; **~ parallèle/série** parallel/serial port

[2] COMP ► **port artificiel** artificial harbour (*Brit*) *ou* harbor (*US*) ► **port d'attache** (*Naut*) port of registry; (*fig*) home base ► **port autonome** (= *gestion*) port authority; (= *lieu*) port (*publicly managed*) ► **port de commerce** commercial port ► **port fluvial** river port ► **port franc** free port ► **port de guerre** naval base ► **port maritime**, **port de mer** sea port ► **port militaire** military port ► **port de pêche** fishing port ► **port de plaisance** (= *bassin*) marina; (= *ville*) sailing *ou* yachting resort

port² [pɔr] NM [a] (= *fait de porter*) [*objet*] carrying; [*habit, barbe, décoration*] wearing; **le ~ du casque est obligatoire sur le chantier** hard hats must be worn on the building site; **~ d'armes prohibé** illegal carrying of firearms; (*Mil*) **se mettre au ~ d'armes** to shoulder arms [b] (= *prix*) postage; (= *transport*) carriage; **franco** *ou* **franc de ~** carriage paid; **(en) ~ dû/payé** postage due/paid [c] (= *comportement*) bearing, carriage; **elle a un ~ majestueux** *ou* **de reine** she has a noble *ou* majestic *ou* queenly bearing; **elle a un joli ~ de tête** she holds her head very nicely [d] (*Mus*) **~ de voix** portamento

portabilité [pɔrtabilite] NF (*gén, Ordin*) portability

portable [pɔrtabl] [1] ADJ [*vêtement*] wearable; (= *portatif*: *gén*) portable; [*téléphone*] mobile; **logiciels ~s** portable software [2] NM (*Ordin*, *gén*) portable; (= *qui tient sur les genoux*) laptop; (= *téléphone*) mobile phone, mobile*

portage [pɔrtaʒ] NM [a] [*marchandise*] porterage; (*Naut, Can*) portage; (*Presse*) **~ à domicile** home delivery

portager [pɔrtaʒe] ▸conjug 3 ◂ VI (*Can*) to portage

portail [pɔrtaj] NM gate

portance [pɔrtɑ̃s] NF (*Aviat*) lift; (*Constr*) load-bearing capacity

portant, e [pɔrtɑ̃, ɑ̃t] [1] ADJ [a] [*mur*] structural, supporting; [*roue*] running; (*Aviat*) **surface ~e** aerofoil (*Brit*), airfoil (*US*); (*Naut*) **vent ~** fair wind [b] **être bien/mal ~** to be healthy *ou* in good health/in poor health → **bout** [2] NM (= *anse*) handle; (*Théât*) upright; (= *présentoir*) rack

portatif, -ive [pɔrtatif, iv] ADJ portable

Port-au-Prince [pɔropʀɛ̃s] N Port-au-Prince

porte [pɔrt] [1] NF [a] [*maison, voiture, meuble*] door; [*forteresse, jardin, stade, ville*] gate; (= *seuil*) doorstep; (= *embrasure*) doorway; **~ pliante/coulissante** folding/sliding door; **franchir** *ou* **passer la ~** to go through *ou* come through the door(way); **sonner à la ~** to ring the (door)bell; **c'est à ma ~** it's close by, it's on the doorstep; **le bus me descend** *ou* **met à ma ~** the bus takes me right to my door; **j'ai trouvé ce colis à ma ~** I found this parcel on my doorstep; **ils se réfugièrent sous la ~** they took shelter in the doorway; **une (voiture) 3/5 ~s** a 3-door/5-door (car); **il y a 100 km/j'ai mis deux heures (de) ~ à ~** it's 100 km/it took me two hours (from) door to door; **de ~ en ~** from house to house; **faire du ~ à ~** (= *vendre*) to sell from door to door, be a door-to-door salesman; **do** doorstep selling (*Brit*); (= *chercher du travail*) to go around knocking on doors; **l'ennemi est à nos ~s** the enemy is at our gate(s); **Dijon, ~ de la Bourgogne** Dijon, the gateway to Burgundy → **casser, clé** etc [b] [*aéroport*] gate [c] (*écluse*) (lock) gate; (*Ski*) gate [d] (*loc*) **c'est/ce n'est pas la ~ à côté*** it's practically/it's not exactly on our (*ou* my *etc*) doorstep; **la ~!*** (shut the) door!; **(à) la ~!** (get out!); **être à la ~** to be locked out; **mettre** *ou* **flanquer qn à la ~*** (*licencier*) to fire sb*, sack sb* (*Brit*), give sb the sack* (*Brit*); (*Scol*) to expel sb; (*Univ*) to send sb down (*Brit*), flunk sb out* (*US*); (*éjecter*) to throw *ou* boot* sb out; **montrer la ~ à qn** to show sb the door; **claquer/fermer la ~ au nez de qn** to slam/shut the door in sb's face; (*fig*) **entrer** *ou* **passer par la petite/la grande ~** to start at the bottom (rung of the ladder)/at the top; **le ministre est sorti** *ou* **s'est en allé par la petite ~** the minister left quietly *ou* made a discreet exit; **ça lui a permis de sortir par la grande ~** this allowed him to leave with dignity *ou* without losing face; **fermer** *ou* **refuser sa ~ à qn** to close the door to sb, bar sb from one's house; (*fig*) **fermer la ~ à** to close the door on sth; **j'ai trouvé ~ close** *ou* **de bois** (*Belg*) (*maison*) no one answered the door; (*magasin, bâtiment public*) it was closed; (*fig*) **vous avez frappé** *ou* **sonné à la bonne/mauvaise ~** you've come to the right/wrong person *ou* place; (*fig*) **c'est la ~ ouverte** *ou* **c'est ouvrir la ~ à tous les abus** it means leaving the door wide open *ou* the way open to all sorts of abuses; **toutes les ~s lui sont ouvertes** every door is open to him; **laisser la ~ ouverte à un compromis** to leave the way open for compromise; **journée ~(s) ouverte(s)** open day (*Brit*), open house (*US*); **opération ~(s) ouverte(s)** open day event; **il faut qu'une ~ soit ouverte ou fermée** you can't have it both ways; **aux ~s de la mort** at death's door; **parler à qn entre deux ~s** to have a quick word with sb, speak to sb very briefly *ou* in passing; **recevoir qn entre deux ~s** to meet sb very briefly; **prendre la ~** to go away, leave; **aimable** *ou* **souriant comme une ~ de prison** like a bear with a sore head

[2] ADJ **veine ~** portal vein

[3] COMP ► **porte accordéon** folding door ► **porte à deux battants** double door *ou* gate ► **les portes du Ciel** the gates of Heaven ► **porte cochère** carriage entrance, porte-cochère ► **porte d'embarquement** (*Aviat*) departure gate ► **les portes de l'Enfer** the gates of Hell ► **porte d'entrée** front door ► **les Portes de Fer** (*Géog*) the Iron Gate(s) ► **porte palière** front door (*of an apartment*) ► **porte de secours** emergency exit *ou* door ► **porte de service** rear *ou* tradesman's (*surtout Brit*) entrance ► **porte de sortie** (*lit*) exit, way out (*surtout Brit*); (*fig*) way out, let-out* (*Brit*); **se ménager une ~ de sortie** to leave o.s. a way out *ou* loophole

porté, e¹ [pɔrte] (*ptp de* **porter**) ADJ **être ~ à faire qch** to be apt *ou* inclined to do sth, tend

to do sth; **nous sommes ~s à croire que ...** we are inclined to believe that ...; **être ~ à la colère/à l'exagération** to be prone to anger/to exaggeration; **être ~ sur qch** to be fond of *ou* keen on (*Brit*) sth, be partial to sth; **être ~ sur la chose*** to have a one-track mind*

porte-aéronefs [pɔrtaerɔnɛf] NM INV aircraft carrier

porte-à-faux [pɔrtafo] NM INV [*mur*] slant; [*rocher*] precarious balance, overhang; (*Archit*) cantilever; **en ~** [*mur, construction*] slanting, out of plumb; [*rocher*] precariously balanced; (*fig*) [*personne*] (= *dans une situation délicate*) in an awkward position; (= *en décalage, isolé*) out on a limb; **être** *ou* **se trouver en ~ par rapport à** *ou* **avec qch** to be at odds *ou* out of step with sth; **mettre qn en ~** to put sb in an awkward position

porte-aiguilles [pɔrteguij] NM INV (= *boîte*) needle case; (*en tissu*) needle book

porte-avions [pɔrtavjɔ̃] NM INV aircraft carrier

porte-bagages [pɔrt(ə)bagaʒ] NM INV [*vélo*] rack; [*train*] (luggage) rack

porte-bébé (*pl* **porte-bébés**) [pɔrt(ə)bebe] NM (= *nacelle*) carrycot (*Brit*); (= *à bretelles*) baby sling, baby carrier

porte-billet [pɔrt(ə)bijɛ] NM INV wallet, notecase, billfold (*US*)

porte-bonheur [pɔrt(ə)bɔnœr] NM INV lucky charm; **acheter du muguet ~** to buy lily of the valley for good luck

porte-bouquet (*pl* **porte-bouquets**) [pɔrt(ə)bukɛ] NM flower holder

porte-bouteille(s) (*pl* **porte-bouteilles**) [pɔrt(ə)butɛj] NM (= *à anse*) bottle-carrier; (= *à casiers*) wine rack; (= *hérisson*) bottle-drainer

porte-cartes [pɔrt(ə)kart] NM INV [*papiers d'identité*] card wallet *ou* holder; [*cartes géographiques*] map wallet

porte-chéquier (*pl* **porte-chéquier**) [pɔrt(ə)ʃekje] NM chequebook (*Brit*) *ou* checkbook (*US*) holder

porte-cigares [pɔrt(ə)sigar] NM INV cigar case

porte-cigarettes [pɔrt(ə)sigarɛt] NM INV cigarette case

porte-clés [pɔrt(ə)kle] NM INV [a] (= *anneau*) key ring; (= *étui*) key case [b] (†† = *geôlier*) turnkey††

porte-conteneurs [pɔrt(ə)kɔ̃t(ə)nœr] NM INV container ship

porte-copie (*pl* **porte-copies**) [pɔrt(ə)kɔpi] NM copy holder

porte-couteau (*pl* **porte-couteaux**) [pɔrt(ə)kuto] NM knife rest

porte-crayon (*pl* **porte-crayons**) [pɔrt(ə)krɛjɔ̃] NM pencil holder

porte-croix [pɔrt(ə)krwa] NM INV cross bearer

porte-documents [pɔrt(ə)dɔkymɑ̃] NM INV briefcase, attaché case, document case

porte-drapeau (*pl* **porte-drapeaux**) [pɔrt(ə)drapo] NM (*lit, fig*) standard bearer

portée² [pɔrte] NF [a] (= *distance*) range, reach; [*fusil, radar*] range; [*cri, voix*] carrying-distance, reach; **canon à faible/longue ~** short-/long-range gun; **missile de moyenne ~** intermediate-range weapon; **à ~ de la main** within (arm's) reach, at *ou* on hand; **restez à ~ de voix** stay within earshot; **restez à ~ de vue** don't go out of sight; **cet hôtel est/n'est pas à la ~ de toutes les bourses** this hotel is/is not within everyone's means, this hotel suits/does not suit everyone's purse; **ne laissez pas les médicaments à ~ de main** *ou* **à la ~ des enfants** keep medicines out of the reach of children; **hors de ~** (*lit*) out of reach *ou* range; (*fig*) beyond reach; **hors de ~ de fusil/de voix** out of rifle range/earshot [b] (= *capacité*) [*intelligence*] reach, scope, capacity; (= *niveau*) level; **ce concept dépasse la**

~ de l'intelligence ordinaire this concept is beyond the reach *ou* scope *ou* capacity of the average mind; **être à la ~ de qn** to be understandable to sb; **il faut savoir se mettre à la ~ des enfants** you have to be able to come down to a child's level; **mettre la science à la ~ de tous** to bring science within everyone's reach

[c] (= *effet*) [*parole, écrit*] impact, import; [*acte*] significance, consequences; **il ne mesure pas la ~ de ses paroles/ses actes** he doesn't think about the import of what he's saying/the consequences of his actions; **la ~ de cet événement est incalculable** it is impossible to foresee the consequences of this event; **sans ~ pratique** of no practical consequence *ou* importance *ou* significance

[d] (*Archit*) (= *poussée*) loading; (= *distance*) span

[e] (*Mus*) stave, staff

[f] (*Vét*) litter

porte-étendard (*pl* **porte-étendards**) [pɔʀtetɑ̃daʀ] NM (*lit fig*) standard bearer

porte-étrivière (*pl* **porte-étrivières**) [pɔʀtetʀivjɛʀ] NM stirrup leather holder

portefaix†† [pɔʀtəfɛ] NM INV porter

porte-fenêtre (*pl* **portes-fenêtres**) [pɔʀt(ə)fənɛtʀ] NF French window (*Brit*) *ou* door (*US*)

portefeuille [pɔʀtəfœj] NM [*argent*] wallet, billfold (*US*); (*Assurances, Bourse, Pol*) portfolio; **société de ~** holding *ou* investment company; **avoir un ~ bien garni** to be well-off → **lit, ministre**

porte-fusibles [pɔʀtəfyzibl] NM INV fuse box

porte-greffe (*pl* **porte-greffes**) [pɔʀtəgʀɛf] NM (*Agr*) stock (*for graft*)

porte-hélicoptères [pɔʀtelikɔptɛʀ] NM INV helicopter carrier

porte-jarretelles [pɔʀt(ə)ʒaʀtɛl] NM INV suspender belt (*Brit*), garter belt (*US*)

porte-jupe (*pl* **porte-jupes**) [pɔʀtəʒyp] NM skirt hanger

porte-malheur [pɔʀt(ə)maloeʀ] NM INV (= *chose*) jinx; (= *personne*) jinx, Jonah

portemanteau (*pl* **portemanteaux**) [pɔʀt(ə)mɑ̃to] NM [a] (= *cintre*) coat hanger; (*accroché au mur*) coat rack; (*sur pied*) hat stand; **accrocher une veste au ~** to hang up a jacket [b] (†† = *malle*) portmanteau

porte-menu (*pl* **porte-menus**) [pɔʀt(ə)məny] NM menu holder

portemine [pɔʀtəmin] NM propelling pencil

porte-monnaie [pɔʀt(ə)mɔnɛ] NM INV (*gén*) purse (*Brit*), coin purse (*US*); (*pour homme*) wallet; **~ électronique** electronic purse; **on fait souvent appel au ~ du contribuable** the taxpayer is often asked to dip into his pocket; **avoir le ~ bien garni** to be well-off

porte-musique [pɔʀt(ə)myzik] NM INV music case

porte-objet (*pl* **porte-objets**) [pɔʀt(ə)ɔbʒɛ] NM (= *lamelle*) slide; (= *platine*) stage

porte-outil (*pl* **porte-outils**) [pɔʀtuti] NM (*Tech*) chuck

porte-parapluies [pɔʀt(ə)paʀaplɥi] NM INV umbrella stand

porte-parole [pɔʀt(ə)paʀɔl] NM INV (*gén*) spokesperson; (= *homme*) spokesman; (= *femme*) spokeswoman; **le ~ du gouvernement** the government spokesperson, ≈ the press secretary (*US*); **se faire le ~ de qn** to act as spokesman for sb, speak on sb's behalf; **leur journal est le ~ du parti** their newspaper is the mouthpiece *ou* organ of the party

porte-plume (*pl* **porte-plumes**) [pɔʀtəplym] NM penholder; (*Ping-Pong*) **prise ~** penholder grip

porter [pɔʀte] ▸ conjug 1 ◂ [1] VT [a] [+ *parapluie, paquet, valise*] to carry; (*fig*) [+ *responsabilité*] to bear, carry; **~ un enfant dans ses bras/sur son dos** to carry a child in one's arms/on one's back; **pouvez-vous me ~ ma valise?** can you carry my case for me?; **laisse-toi ~ par la vague** let yourself be carried by the waves; **ses jambes ne le portent plus** his legs can no longer carry him; **ce pont n'est pas fait pour ~ des camions** this bridge isn't meant to carry lorries *ou* meant for lorries *ou* can't take the weight of a lorry; (*Mil*) **portez ... arme!** present ... arms!; **la tige qui porte la fleur** the stem which bears the flower, the stem with the flower on; **cette poutre porte tout le poids du plafond** this beam bears *ou* carries *ou* takes the whole weight of the ceiling; (*fig*) **~ sa croix** to carry *ou* bear one's cross; (*fig*) **~ le poids de ses fautes** to bear the weight of one's mistakes

[b] (= *apporter*) to take; **~ qch à qn** to take sth to sb; **porte-lui ce livre** take this book to him, take him this book; **le facteur porte les lettres et les colis** the postman delivers letters and parcels; **je vais ~ la lettre à la boîte** I'm going to take the letter to the postbox, I'm going to put this letter in the postbox; **~ les plats sur la table** to take the dishes (out *ou* over) to the table; **porte-la sur le lit** put *ou* lay her on the bed; **~ la main à son front** to put one's hand to one's brow; **~ la main à son chapeau** to lift one's hand to one's hat; **~ la main sur qn** to raise one's hand to sb; **~ qch à sa bouche** to lift *ou* put sth to one's lips; **~ de l'argent à la banque** to take some money to the bank; **se faire ~ à manger** to have food brought (to one); **~ l'affaire sur la place publique/devant les tribunaux** to take *ou* carry the matter into the public arena/before the courts; **~ la nouvelle à qn** to take *ou* bring the news to sb; (*Ciné, Théât*) **~ une œuvre à l'écran/à la scène** to transfer a work to the screen/to the stage; **~ chance** *ou* **bonheur/malheur (à qn)** to be lucky/unlucky (for sb), bring (sb) (good) luck/bad luck; **ça porte bonheur!** it brings good luck!, it's lucky!

■ (*PROV*) **~ de l'eau à la rivière** to carry coals to Newcastle; (*littér*) **portant partout la terreur et la mort** carrying fear and death everywhere

[c] [+ *vêtement, bague, laine, lunettes*] to wear; [+ *armes héraldiques*] to bear; [+ *barbe*] to have, wear; [+ *nom*] to have, bear; **~ les cheveux longs** to wear one's hair long, have long hair; **~ le nom d'une fleur** to be called after a flower; **~ le nom de Jérôme** to be called Jerome; **il porte bien son nom** his name suits him; **elle porte bien son âge** she looks good for her age; **elle porte bien le pantalon** trousers suit her; (*fig*) **c'est elle qui porte le pantalon** *ou* **la culotte** she's the one that wears the trousers (*Brit*) *ou* pants (*US*); (*fig*) **je ne veux pas ~ le chapeau*** I don't want to carry the can* *ou* take the rap* (**pour** for); **on lui a fait ~ le chapeau*** he carried the can* *ou* took the rap*

[d] (= *tenir*) to hold, keep; **~ la tête haute** (*lit*) to hold *ou* keep one's head up; (*fig*) to hold one's head high; **~ le corps en avant** to lean *ou* stoop forward

[e] (= *montrer*) [+ *signe, trace*] to show, bear; [+ *blessure, cicatrice*] to have, bear; [+ *inscription, date*] to bear; **il porte la bonté sur son visage** he has a very kind(-looking) face, his face is a picture of kindness; **ce livre porte un beau titre** this book has a good title; **la lettre porte la date du 12 mai** the letter is dated *ou* bears the date of May 12th; (*Ling*) **~ la marque de** to be marked for

[f] (= *inscrire*) [+ *nom*] to write down, put down (**sur** on, in); (*Comm*) [+ *somme*] to enter (**sur** in); **~ de l'argent au crédit d'un compte** to credit an account with some money; **nous portons cette somme à votre débit** we are debiting this sum from your account; **se faire ~ absent** to go absent; **se faire ~ malade** to report *ou* go sick; **~ qn absent** (*Mil*) to report sb absent; (*Scol*) to mark sb absent; **porté disparu/au nombre des morts** reported missing/dead; **porté manquant** unaccounted for

[g] (= *diriger*) [+ *regard*] to direct, turn (**sur, vers** towards); [+ *attention*] to turn, give (**sur** to), focus (**sur** on); [+ *effort*] to direct (**sur** towards); [+ *pas*] to turn (**vers** towards); [+ *coup*] to deal (**à** to); [+ *accusation*] to make (**contre** against); [+ *attaque*] to make (**contre** on); **il fit ~ son attention sur ce détail** he turned his attention to *ou* focused his attention on this detail; **il fit ~ son choix sur ce livre** he chose this book, his choice fell on this book

[h] (= *ressentir*) [+ *amour, haine*] to feel (**à** for); [+ *reconnaissance*] to feel (**à** to, towards); **~ de l'amitié à qn** to feel friendship towards sb

[i] (*Méd*) [+ *enfant*] to carry; (*Vét*) [+ *petits*] to carry; (*Fin*) [+ *intérêts*] to yield; (*Bot*) [+ *graines, fruit*] to bear; [+ *récolte, moisson*] to yield; **cette ardeur/haine qu'il portait en lui** the passion/hatred which he carried with him; **idée qui porte en soi les germes de sa propre destruction** idea which carries (within itself) *ou* bears the seeds of its own destruction; (*fig*) **~ ses fruits** to bear fruit

[j] (= *conduire, amener*) to carry; (= *entraîner*) [*foi*] to carry along; [*vent*] to carry away; **se laisser ~ par la foule** to let o.s. be carried away by the crowd; **~ qn au pouvoir** to bring *ou* carry sb to power; **~ qch à sa perfection/à son paroxysme/à l'apogée** to bring sth to perfection/to a peak/to a climax; **~ la température à 800°/le salaire à 16 000 F/la vitesse à 30 nœuds** to bring the temperature up to 800°/the salary up to 16,000 francs/the speed up to 30 knots; **cela porte le nombre de blessés à 20** that brings the number of casualties (up) to 20

[k] (= *inciter*) **~ qn à faire qch** to prompt *ou* induce *ou* lead sb to do sth; **ça le portera à l'indulgence** that will prompt him to be indulgent, that will make him indulgent; **tout (nous) porte à croire que ...** everything leads us to believe that ... → **porté**

[l] (*Ordin*) [+ *logiciel*] to port (**sous** to)

[2] VI [a] [*bruit, voix, canon*] to carry; **le son/le coup a porté à 500 mètres** the sound/the shot carried 500 metres; **le fusil porte à 300 mètres** the rifle has a range of 300 metres

[b] [*reproche, coup*] **~ (juste)** to hit *ou* strike home; **tous les coups portaient** every blow told; **un coup qui porte** a telling blow; **ses conseils ont porté** his advice had some effect *ou* was of some use

[c] (*Méd*) [*femme*] to carry her child *ou* baby; (*Vét*) [*animal*] to carry its young

[d] (= *frapper*) **sa tête a porté sur le bord du trottoir** his head struck the edge of the pavement; **c'est la tête qui a porté** his head took the blow

[e] (= *reposer*) [*édifice, pilier*] to be supported by *ou* on; **tout le poids du plafond porte sur cette poutre** the whole weight of the ceiling is supported by this beam, this beam bears the whole weight of the ceiling; **~ à faux** [*mur*] to be out of plumb *ou* true; [*rocher*] to be precariously balanced; (*fig*) [*remarque*] to be out of place

[f] **~ sur** (= *concerner*) [*débat, cours*] to turn on, revolve around, be about; [*revendications, objection*] to concern; [*étude, effort, action*] to be concerned with, focus on; [*accent*] to fall on; **la question portait sur des auteurs au programme** the question was on some of the authors on the syllabus; **il a fait ~ son exposé sur la situation économique** in his talk he concentrated *ou* focused on the economic situation

[3] **se porter** VPR [a] [*personne*] **se ~ bien/mal** to be well/unwell *ou* in poor health; **comment vous portez-vous?** — **je me porte bien** how are you? — I'm fine *ou* I'm very well; **se ~ comme un charme** to be fighting fit, be as fit as a fiddle*; **buvez moins, vous ne vous en porterez que mieux** drink less and you'll feel

(all the) better for it; **et je ne m'en suis pas plus mal porté** and I didn't come off any worse for it, and I was no worse off for it → **pont**

b (= se présenter comme) **se ~ candidat** to put o.s. up ou stand (Brit) ou run as a candidate; **se ~ acquéreur (de)** to put in a bid (for); **se ~ fort pour qn** to answer for sb → **caution** etc

c (= aller) to go; **se ~ à la rencontre** ou **au-devant de qn** to go to meet sb; **se ~ à** (= se laisser aller à) [+ voies de fait, violences] to commit; **se ~ à des extrémités** to go to extremes; **se ~ sur** (= se diriger vers) [soupçon, choix] to fall on; **son regard se porta sur moi** his eyes ou gaze fell on me, he looked towards me; **son attention se porta sur ce point** he focused ou concentrated his attention on this point

d (= être porté) [vêtement] **les jupes se portent très courtes** the fashion's for very short skirts, skirts are being worn very short; **ça ne se porte plus** that's out of fashion, nobody wears that any more

porte-revues [pɔrt(ə)rəvy] NM INV magazine rack

porte-savon (pl **porte-savons**) [pɔrt(ə)sav5] NM soapdish

porte-serviette [pɔrt(ə)sɛrvjɛt] NM INV (= pochette) napkin-holder; (péj Pol) sidekick*, flunkey

porte-serviettes [pɔrt(ə)sɛrvjɛt] NM INV towel rail; **~ chauffant** heated towel rail

porte-skis [pɔrtəski] NM INV ski rack

porteur, -euse [pɔrtœr, øz] **1** ADJ [fusée] booster (épith); [courant] carrier (épith); [mur] load-bearing; **thème ~** key theme; (Écon) **marché/créneau ~** growth market/area; (Phys) **onde porteuse** carrier (wave) → **mère**

2 NM,F **a** [valise, colis] porter; [message] messenger; [chèque] bearer; [titre, actions] holder; **~ d'eau** water carrier; **~ de journaux** newsboy, paper boy; **le ~ du message** the bearer of the message; **il arriva ~ d'une lettre/d'une nouvelle alarmante** he came bearing ou with a letter/an alarming piece of news; **il était ~ de faux papiers** he was carrying forged papers; **être ~ d'espoir** to bring hope; **le ~ du ballon** the person with the ball ou who has (possession of) the ball; **payable au ~** payable to bearer; (Fin) **les petits/gros ~s** small/big shareholders **b** (Méd) carrier; **~ de germes** germ carrier; **~ sain** carrier; **il est ~ du virus** he is carrying the virus

porte-vélos [pɔrtəvelo] NM INV bicycle rack

porte-voix [pɔrtəvwa] NM INV megaphone; (électrique) loudhailer; **mettre ses mains en ~** to cup one's hands round one's mouth; **il était le ~ des SDF** he spoke out on behalf of the homeless

portfolio [pɔrtfɔljo] NM [gravures, photographies] portfolio

portier [pɔrtje] NM porter, commissionaire (Brit, Can); (Rel) (frère) ~ porter; **~ de nuit** night porter; **~ électronique** entrance intercom, entry phone

portière [pɔrtjɛr] NF **a** (Aut, Rail) door **b** (= rideau) portiere **c** (Rel) (sœur) ~ portress

portillon [pɔrtij5] NM gate; [métro] gate, barrier; **~ automatique** (automatic) ticket barrier → **bousculer**

portion [pɔrsj5] NF [héritage] portion, share; (Culin) portion, helping; (= partie) portion, section, part; **fromage en ~s** cheese portions; (fig) **être réduit à la ~ congrue** to get the smallest ou meanest share; **bonne/mauvaise ~ de route** good/bad stretch of road

portique [pɔrtik] NM (Archit) portico; (Sport) crossbar and stands (for holding gymnastic apparatus); (à l'aéroport) **~ électronique** ou **de sécurité** ou **de détection** metal detector, diver's gate (SPÉC); (Rail) **~ à signaux** signal gantry

Port-Louis [pɔrlui] N Port-Louis

Port Moresby [pɔrmɔrɛsbi] N Port Moresby

Porto [pɔrto] N Oporto, Porto

porto [pɔrto] NM port (wine); **verre à ~** sherry ou Madeira ou port glass

Port of Spain [pɔrɔfspejn] N Port of Spain

Porto-Novo [pɔrtonovo] N Porto Novo

portoricain, e [pɔrtɔrikɛ̃, ɛn] **1** ADJ Puerto Rican **2 Portoricain(e)** NM,F Puerto Rican

Porto Rico [pɔrtoriko] NF Puerto Rico

portrait [pɔrtrɛ] NM **a** (= peinture) portrait; (= photo) photograph; (* = visage) face, mug*; **~ fidèle** good likeness; **~ de famille** family portrait; **~ en pied/en buste** full-length/head-and-shoulders portrait; **c'est tout le ~ de son père** he's the spitting image of his father; **faire le ~ de qn** (lit) to paint sb's portrait; **se faire tirer le ~*** to have one's photograph taken; **se faire abîmer** ou **esquinter le ~*** to get one's face ou head bashed in* ou smashed in*; **il t'a bien abîmé le ~!** he made a real mess of your face! **b** (= description) [personne] portrait, description; [situation] picture; **faire** ou **brosser** ou **dresser le ~ de qn** to draw ou paint a portrait of sb, paint a picture of sb; **elle en a fait un ~ flatteur** she painted a flattering picture ou portrait of him; **~-charge** caricature; **jouer au ~** to play twenty questions **c** (= genre) **le ~** portraiture

portraitiste [pɔrtrɛtist] NMF portrait painter, portraitist

portrait-robot (pl **portraits-robots**) [pɔrtrɛrɔbo] NM Identikit® picture, Photofit® (picture); **la police a diffusé** ou **donné le ~ du suspect** the police issued a Photofit ou Identikit (picture) of the suspect; **faire le ~ de** [+ criminel] to make up a Photofit ou Identikit (picture) of; **faire le ~ du Français moyen** to draw the profile of the average Frenchman

portraiturer [pɔrtrɛtyre] ▶ conjug 1 ◀ VT (lit, fig) to portray

portuaire [pɔrtɥɛr] ADJ port (épith), harbour (épith) (Brit), harbour (épith) (US)

portugais, e [pɔrtygɛ, ɛz] **1** ADJ Portuguese **2** NM (Ling) Portuguese **3 portugaise** NF **a Portugaise** Portuguese **b** (= huître) Portuguese oyster; (* = oreille) **il a les ~es ensablées** he's as deaf as a post

Portugal [pɔrtygal] NM Portugal

Port-Villa [pɔrvila] N Port Vila

POS [peɔɛs] NM (ABRÉV = **plan d'occupation des sols**) → **plan¹**

pose [poz] NF **a** (= installation) [tableau, rideaux] hanging, putting up; [tapis] laying, putting down; [moquette] fitting, laying; [vitre] putting in, fixing; [serrure] fitting; [chauffage] installation, putting in; [gaz, électricité] laying on, installation; [canalisations] laying, putting in; [fondations, mines, voie ferrée] laying **b** (= attitude) pose, posture; (Art) pose; **garder la ~** to hold the pose; **prendre une ~** to strike a pose; **prendre des ~s (devant le miroir)** to pose (in front of the mirror); **faire prendre une ~ à qn** to pose sb **c** (Photo = vue) exposure; **un film (de) 36 ~s** a 36-exposure film; **déterminer le temps de ~** to decide on the exposure (time); **indice de ~** exposure index; **mettre le bouton sur ~** to set the button to time exposure; **prendre une photo en ~** ou **à la ~** to take a photo in time exposure **d** (= affectation) posing, pretention

posé, e [poze] (ptp de **poser**) ADJ **a** (= pondéré) [personne] level-headed; **d'un ton ~ mais ferme** calmly but firmly **b** (Mus) **bien/mal ~** [voix] steady/unsteady

Poséidon [poseid5] NM Poseidon

posément [pozemã] ADV [parler] calmly, deliberately; [agir] calmly, unhurriedly

posemètre [pozmɛtr] NM exposure meter

---

poser [poze] ▶ conjug 1 ◀ **1** VT **a** (= placer) [+ objet] to put down, lay down, set down; (debout) to stand (up), put (up); (= ôter) **~ son manteau/chapeau** to take off one's coat/hat; **~ qch sur une table/par terre** to put sth (down) on the table/on the floor; **~ sa main/tête sur l'épaule de qn** to put ou lay one's hand/head on sb's shoulder; **~ sa tête sur l'oreiller** to lay one's head on the pillow; **~ une échelle contre un mur** to lean ou stand ou put (up) a ladder against a wall; **où ai-je posé mes lunettes?** where have I put my glasses?; **pose ton journal et viens à table** put your paper down and come and have your dinner; **il a posé son regard** ou **les yeux sur elle** he looked at her, his gaze came to rest on her; **le pilote posa son avion en douceur** the pilot brought his plane down ou his plane gently; (Mus) **~ la voix de qn** to train sb's voice

b (= installer) [+ tableau, rideaux] to hang, put up; [+ antenne] to put up; [+ tapis, carrelage] to lay, put down; [+ moquette] to fit, lay; [+ vitre] to put in; [+ serrure] to fit; [+ chauffage] to put in, install (Brit), instal (US); [+ gaz, électricité] to lay on, install (Brit), instal (US); [+ canalisations] to lay, put in; [+ fondations, mines, voie ferrée] to lay; [+ bombe] to plant; (lit, fig) **~ la première pierre** to lay the foundation stone; **~ des étagères au mur** to put up some shelves → **jalon**

c (Math) [+ opération, chiffres] to write, set down; **je pose 4 et je retiens 3** (I) put down 4 and carry 3, 4 and 3 to carry

d (fig = énoncer) [+ principe, condition] to lay ou set down, set out; [+ question] to ask; (à un examen) to set; [+ devinette] to set, ask; **~ sa candidature à un poste** to apply for a post, put in ou submit an application for a post; (Pol) **~ sa candidature** to put o.s. up ou run (US) for election; **dire cela, c'est ~ que ...** in saying that, one is supposing that ou taking it for granted that ...; **ceci posé** supposing that this is (ou was etc) the case, assuming this to be the case; **posons que ...** let us suppose ou assume ou take it that ... → **problème**, **question**

e (= demander) **~ des jours de congé** to put in a request for leave

f **~ qn** (= lui donner de l'importance) to give standing to sb; (professionnellement) to establish sb's reputation; **voilà ce qui pose un homme** that's what sets a man up; **avoir un frère ministre, ça vous pose!** having a brother who's a cabinet minister really makes people look up to you! ou gives you real status!; **une maison comme ça, ça (vous) pose*** with a house like that people really think you're somebody

2 VI **a** (Art, Photo) to pose, sit (**pour** for); (= chercher à se faire remarquer) to swank (Brit), show off, put on airs; (hum) **~ pour la postérité** to pose for posterity; (fig) **~ pour la galerie** to play to the gallery; (= faire attendre) **faire ~ qn*** to keep sb hanging about* ou around* **b** **~ à** (= jouer à) **~ au grand patron/à l'artiste** to play ou act ou come* the big businessman/the artist, pretend to be a big businessman/an artist; **~ au martyr** to play the martyr **c** (Constr) **~ sur** [poutre] to bear ou rest on, be supported by

3 **se poser** VPR **a** [insecte, oiseau] to land, settle (**sur** on); [avion] to land; [regard] to (come to) rest, settle, fix (**sur** on); (Aviat) **se ~ en catastrophe/sur le ventre** to make an emergency landing/a belly-landing; **son regard se posa sur la pendule** he turned his eyes to the clock, his glance fell on the clock; **une main se posa soudain sur son épaule** he suddenly felt a hand on his shoulder; **pose-toi là*** sit down here **b** [question, problème] to come up, crop up, arise → **problème**, **question** **c** (= se présenter) **se ~ en chef/en expert** to pass o.s. off as *ou* pose as a leader/an expert; **se ~ comme victime** to pretend *ou* claim to be a victim; **se ~ en défenseur des droits de l'homme** to claim to be a defender of human rights

[d] (*: *loc*) **comme menteur, vous vous posez (un peu) là!** you're a terrible *ou* an awful liar!; **comme erreur, ça se posait (un peu) là!** that was some mistake! *ou* some blunder!*; **tu as vu leur chien/père?** — **il se pose là!** have you seen their dog/father? — it's/he's enormous! *ou* huge! *ou* massive!

poseur, -euse [pozœʀ, øz] [1] ADJ affected [2] NM,F [a] (*péj*) show-off, poseur [b] (= *ouvrier*) **~ de carrelage/de tuyaux** tile/pipe layer; **~ d'affiches** billposter, billsticker (*Brit*); **~ de bombes** terrorist (*who plants bombs*)

posidonie [pozidɔni] NF Posidonia (oceanica)

positif, -ive [pozitif, iv] [1] ADJ (*gén, Ling, Sci*) positive; [*cuti*] positive; [*fait, preuve*] positive, definite; [*personne, esprit*] pragmatic, down-to-earth; [*action, idée*] positive, constructive; [*avantage*] positive, real; (*sang*) **Rhésus ~** Rhesus positive [2] NM [a] (= *réel*) positive, concrete; **je veux du ~!** I want something positive! [b] (*Mus*) (= *clavier d'un orgue*) choir organ (*division of organ*); (= *instrument*) positive organ [c] (*Photo*) positive [d] (*Ling*) positive (degree); **au ~** in the positive (form)

position [pozisjɔ̃] NF [a] (*gén, Ling, Mil* = *emplacement*) position; [*navire*] bearings, position; (*Comm*) [*produit*] position; **~ de défense/fortifiée** defensive/fortified position; (*lit*) **rester sur ses ~s** to stand one's ground; (*fig*) **rester** *ou* **camper sur ses ~s** to stand one's ground, stick to one's guns *ou* line; **abandonner ses ~s** to retreat, abandon one's position, withdraw; (*Mil, fig*) **avoir une ~ de repli** to have a fallback position; **la ville jouit d'une ~ idéale** the town is ideally situated; **les joueurs ont changé de ~** the players have changed position(s); **être en première/seconde ~** (*dans une course*) to be in the lead/in second place; (*sur une liste*) to be at the top of/second on the list; **être en dernière ~** (*dans une course*) to be last, bring up the rear; (*sur une liste*) to be at the bottom *ou* end of the list; **arriver en première/deuxième/dernière ~** to come first/second/last; **en première ~, Banjo** (*dans une course*) (and it's) Banjo leading *ou* in the lead; (*Ling*) **syllabe en ~ forte/faible** stressed/unstressed syllable, syllable in (a) stressed/(an) unstressed position; (*Ling*) **voyelle en ~ forte/faible** stressed *ou* strong/unstressed *ou* weak vowel → **feu¹, guerre**

[b] (= *posture*) position; **dormir dans une mauvaise ~** to sleep in the wrong position *ou* in an awkward position; **être assis/couché dans une mauvaise ~** to be sitting/lying in an awkward position; (*Mil, gén*) **se mettre en ~** to take up (one's) position(s), get into position; **en ~!** (get to your) positions!; **en ~ de combat** in a fighting position; **en ~ allongée/assise/verticale** in a reclining/sitting/vertical *ou* upright position; **la ~ du missionnaire** the missionary position

[c] (= *situation*) position, situation; (*dans la société*) position; **être dans une ~ délicate/fausse** to be in a difficult *ou* an awkward/in a false position; **être en ~ de force pour négocier** to be bargaining from a position of strength; **être en ~ de faire qch** to be in a position to do sth; **dans sa ~ il ne peut se permettre une incartade** a man in his position dare not commit an indiscretion; **il occupe une ~ importante** he holds an important position

[d] (= *attitude*) position, stance; **le gouvernement doit définir sa ~ sur cette question** the government must make its position *ou* stance on this question clear; **prendre ~** to take a stand, declare o.s.; **prendre (fermement) ~ en faveur de qch** to come down (strongly) in favour of sth; **prise de ~** stand; **sa politique est en contradiction avec ses prises de ~** his poli-

cy is at odds with the stands that he takes [e] (*Fin*) [*compte bancaire*] position, balance; **demander sa ~** to ask for the balance of one's account [f] (*Bourse*) position; **~ acheteur/vendeur** bull *ou* long/bear *ou* short position

positionnement [pozisjɔnmɑ̃] NM [*objet, produit, entreprise*] positioning; (*Aviat*) **~ avant/arrière** nose out/in positioning

positionner [pozisjɔne] ▸conjug 1◂ [1] VT [a] (= *placer*) (*gén, Mil*) to position; (*Comm*) [+ *produit*] to position [b] (= *repérer*) [+ *navire, troupes*] to locate [c] [+ *compte bancaire*] to establish the position *ou* balance of [2] **se positionner** VPR (*gén*) to position o.s.; [*troupe*] to take up (one's) position, get into position; (*dans un débat*) to take a stand; **comment se positionne ce produit sur le marché?** what slot does this product fill in the market?; **comment vous positionnez-vous dans ce débat?** what's your position *ou* stand in this debate?

positivement [pozitivmɑ̃] ADV (*gén, Sci*) positively; **je ne le sais pas ~** I'm not positive about it

positiver [pozitive] ▸conjug 1◂ [1] VT **~ son angoisse/son stress** to channel one's anxiety/one's stress; **essayez de ~ votre choix** try to concentrate on the positive aspects *ou* the plus side of your decision; **ils essaient de ~ l'opinion des employés envers les cadres** they're trying to get the workers to have a more positive attitude towards *ou* to be more favourably disposed towards management [2] VI to think positive, look on the bright side (of things)

positivisme [pozitivism] NM positivism

positiviste [pozitivist] ADJ, NMF positivist

positivité [pozitivite] NF positivity

positon [pozitɔ̃], **positron** [pozitʀɔ̃] NM (*Phys*) positron

posologie [pozɔlɔʒi] NF (= *étude*) posology; (= *indications*) directions for use, dosage

possédant, e [pɔsedɑ̃, ɑ̃t] [1] ADJ propertied, wealthy [2] NM **les ~s** the wealthy, the rich

possédé, e [pɔsede] (*ptp de* **posséder**) [1] ADJ possessed (**de** by); **~ du démon** possessed by the devil [2] NM,F person possessed; **crier comme un ~** to cry like one possessed

posséder [pɔsede] ▸conjug 6◂ [1] VT [a] [+ *bien, maison, fortune*] to possess, own, have; **c'est tout ce que je possède** it's all I possess *ou* all I've got; † **~ une femme** to possess a woman; **pour ~ le cœur d'une femme** to capture a woman's heart [b] [+ *caractéristique, qualité, territoire*] to have, possess; [+ *expérience*] to have (had); [+ *diplôme, titre*] to have, hold; **cette maison possède une vue magnifique/deux entrées** this house has a magnificent view/two entrances; **il croit ~ la vérité** he believes that he possesses the truth [c] (= *bien connaître*) [+ *métier*] to have a thorough knowledge of, know inside out; [+ *technique*] to have mastered; [+ *langue*] to have a good command of; **elle possède parfaitement l'anglais** she has a perfect command of English; **~ la clé de l'énigme** to possess *ou* have the key to the mystery; **bien ~ son rôle** to be really on top of *ou* into* one's role *ou* part [d] (= *égarer*) [*démon*] to possess; **la fureur/jalousie le possède** he is beside himself with *ou* he is overcome *ou* consumed with rage/jealousy; **quel démon** *ou* **quelle rage te possède?** what's got into you?*, what's come over you? → **possédé** [e] (* = *duper*) **~ qn** to take sb in*; **se faire ~** to be taken in*, be had*

[2] **se posséder** VPR **elle ne se possédait plus de joie** she was beside herself *ou* was overcome with joy; **lorsqu'il est en colère, il ne se**

possède pas when he's angry he loses all self-control *ou* all control of himself

possesseur [pɔsesœʀ] NM [*bien*] possessor, owner; [*diplôme, titre, secret*] holder, possessor; [*billet de loterie*] holder; **être ~ de** [+ *objet*] to have; [+ *diplôme*] to hold; [+ *secret*] to possess, have

possessif, -ive [pɔsesif, iv] [1] ADJ (*gén, Ling*) possessive [2] NM (*Ling*) possessive

possession [pɔsesjɔ̃] NF [a] (= *fait de posséder*) [*bien*] possession, ownership; [*diplôme, titre*] holding, possession; [*billet de loterie*] holding; **la ~ d'une arme/de cet avantage le rendait confiant** having a weapon/this advantage made him feel confident; **~ vaut titre** possession amounts to title; **avoir qch en sa ~** to have sth in one's possession; **être en ~ de qch** to be in possession of sth; **tomber en la ~ de qn** to come into sb's possession; **prendre ~ de ◊ entrer en ~ de** [+ *fonction*] to take up; [+ *bien, héritage*] to take possession of, enter into possession of; [+ *appartement*] to take possession of; [+ *voiture*] to take delivery of; **à la prise de ~ des terres** when he (*ou* they *etc*) took possession of the land; **être en ~ de toutes ses facultés** to be in possession of all one's faculties; **il était en pleine ~ de ses moyens** he was in full possession of his faculties [b] (= *chose possédée*) possession; **nos ~s à l'étranger** our overseas possessions [c] (= *maîtrise*) **~ de soi** self-control; **reprendre ~ de soi-même** to regain one's self-control *ou* one's composure [d] (= *connaissance*) [*langue*] command, mastery [e] (*Rel* = *envoûtement*) possession

possessivité [pɔsesivite] NF possessiveness

▼**possibilité** [pɔsibilite] NF (*gén*) possibility; (*Stat*) **~ non nulle** non-zero probability; **il y a plusieurs ~s** there are several possibilities; **je ne vois pas d'autre ~ (que de ...)** I don't see any other possibility (than to ...); **ai-je la ~ de faire du feu/de parler librement?** is it possible for me to light a fire/to speak freely?; **~s** (= *moyens*) means; (= *potentiel*) possibilities, potential; **quelles sont vos ~s financières?** how much money can you put up?, what is your financial situation?; **quelles sont vos ~s de logement?** how many people can you accommodate? *ou* put up?; **les ~s d'une découverte/d'un pays neuf** the possibilities *ou* potential of a discovery/of a new country; **~ (de réalisation)** [*entreprise, projet*] feasibility

▼**possible** [pɔsibl] [1] ADJ [a] (= *faisable*) [*solution*] possible; [*projet, entreprise*] feasible; **il est ~/il n'est pas ~ de ...** it is possible/impossible to ...; **nous avons fait tout ce qu'il était humainement ~ de faire** we've done everything that was humanly possible; **lui serait-il ~ d'arriver plus tôt?** could he possibly *ou* would it be possible for him to come earlier?; **arrivez tôt si (c'est)** arrive early if possible *ou* if you can; **c'est parfaitement ~** it's perfectly possible *ou* feasible; **ce n'est pas ~ autrement** there's no other way, otherwise it's impossible; **il n'est pas ~ qu'il soit aussi bête qu'il en a l'air** he can't possibly be as stupid as he looks; **c'est dans les choses ~s** it's a possibility; **la paix a rendu ~ leur rencontre** peace has made a meeting between them possible *ou* has made it possible for them to meet [b] (= *éventuel*: *gén*) [*danger*] possible, potential; **une erreur est toujours ~** a mistake is always possible; **il est ~ qu'il vienne/qu'il ne vienne pas** he may *ou* might come/not come, it's possible (that) he'll come/he won't come; **il est bien ~ qu'il se soit perdu en route** he may very well have *ou* it could well be *ou* it's quite possible that he has lost his way; **c'est (bien) ~/très ~** possibly/very possibly; **son ~ retour sur la scène politique** his possible return to the political stage [c] (= *indiquant une limite*) possible; **dans le**

meilleur des mondes ~s in the best of all possible worlds; **il a essayé tous les moyens ~s** he tried every possible means *ou* every means possible; **il a eu toutes les difficultés ~s et imaginables à obtenir un visa** he had all kinds of problems getting a visa, he had every possible *ou* conceivable difficulty getting a visa; **venez aussi vite/aussitôt que ~** come as quickly as possible *ou* as you (possibly) can/as soon as possible *ou* as you (possibly) can; **venez le plus longtemps ~** come for as long as you (possibly) can; **venez le plus vite/tôt ~** come as quickly/as soon as you (possibly) can; **il sort le plus (souvent)/le moins (souvent) ~** he goes out as often/as little as possible *ou* as he can; **il a acheté la valise la plus légère ~** he bought the lightest possible suitcase *ou* the lightest suitcase possible; **le plus grand nombre ~ de personnes** as many people as possible, the greatest possible number of people → **autant**

d (*: *nég* = *acceptable*) **cette situation n'est plus ~** the situation has become impossible; **il n'est pas ~ de travailler dans ce bruit** it just isn't possible *ou* it's (quite) impossible to work in this noise; **un bruit/une puanteur pas ~*** an incredible racket*/stink*; **il est d'une méchanceté pas ~*** he's incredibly *ou* unbelievably nasty

e (*loc*) **est-ce ~!** I don't believe it!; **c'est pas ~!** (*faux*) that can't be true! *ou* right!; (*étonnant*) well I never!*; (*irréalisable*) it's out of the question!, it's impossible!; **ce n'est pas ~ d'être aussi bête!** how can anyone be so stupid!, how stupid can you get!*; **elle voudrait vous parler — c'est (bien) ~, mais il faut que je parte** she'd like a word with you — that's as may be, but I've got to go; **il devrait se reposer! — c'est (bien) ~, mais il n'a pas le temps** he ought to take a rest! — maybe (he should), but he's too busy

2 NM (*gén*) **faire reculer les limites du ~** to push back the frontiers of what is possible *ou* of the possible; **essayons, dans les limites du ~, de ...** let's try, as far as possible, to...; **c'est dans le domaine *ou* dans les limites du ~** it's within the realms of possibility; **faire (tout) son ~** to do one's utmost *ou* one's best, do all one can (**pour** to, **pour que** to make sure that); **il a été grossier/aimable au ~** he couldn't have been ruder/nicer (if he'd tried), he was as rude/nice as it's possible to be; **c'est énervant au ~** it's extremely annoying → **mesure**

possiblement [pɔsibləmã] ADV possibly

post- [pɔst] PRÉF (*dans les mots composés à trait d'union, le préfixe reste invariable*) post-; **~électoral-surréaliste** post-election (*épith*)/-surrealist; **grossesse ~ménopausique** post-menopausal pregnancy; **~baccalauréat** [*formation, classe, enseignement*] post-baccalauréat

postal, e (*mpl* **-aux**) [pɔstal, o] ADJ [*service, taxe, voiture*] postal, mail; [*train, avion*] mail; [*colis*] sent by post *ou* mail; **code ~** postcode (*Brit*), zip code (*US*); **sac ~** postbag, mailbag → **carte, chèque, franchise**

postcolonial, e (*pl* **-iaux**) [pɔstkɔlɔnjal, jo] ADJ postcolonial

postcommunisme [pɔstkɔmynism] NM postcommunism

postcommuniste [pɔstkɔmynist] ADJ [*ère*] postcommunist

postcure [pɔstkyr] NF aftercare

postdater [pɔstdate] ▶conjug 1◀ VT to post-date

▼ **poste¹** [pɔst] 1 NF a (= *administration, bureau*) post office; **employé/ingénieur des ~s** post office worker/engineer; **les Postes et Télécommunications** ◊ **les Postes, Télécommunications et Télédiffusion**† *French post office and telecommunications service*; **la grande ~** ◊ **la ~ principale** ◊ **le bureau de ~** principal the main *ou* head post office b (= *service postal*)

mail, post (*surtout Brit*), postal *ou* mail service; **envoyer qch par la ~** to send sth by post *ou* mail; **mettre une lettre à la ~** to post *ou* mail a letter → **cachet** c (*Hist*) post; **maître de ~** postmaster; **cheval de ~** post horse; **courir la ~** to go posthaste → **chaise, voiture** 2 COMP ► **poste aérienne** airmail ► **poste auxiliaire** sub post office ► **poste restante** poste restante (*Brit*), general delivery (*US*)

poste² [pɔst] 1 NM a (= *emplacement*) post; **~ de douane** customs post; **être/rester à son ~** to be/stay at one's post; **mourir à son ~** to die at one's post; **à vos ~s!** to your stations! *ou* posts!; **à vos ~s de combat!** action stations!; (*fig hum*) **toujours fidèle au ~?** still manning the fort? b (*Police*) **~ (de police)** (police) station; **conduire** *ou* **emmener qn au ~** to take sb to the police station; **il a passé la nuit au ~** he spent the night in the cells c (= *emploi*) (*gén*) job, [*fonctionnaire*] post, appointment (*frm*); (*dans une hiérarchie*) position; (= *nomination*) appointment; **être en ~ à Paris/à l'étranger** to hold an appointment *ou* a post in Paris/abroad; **il a trouvé un ~ de bibliothécaire** he has found a post *ou* job as a librarian; **il a un ~ de professeur/en fac** he is a teacher/a university lecturer; **la liste des ~s vacants** the list of positions available *ou* of unfilled appointments; **~ d'enseignant** teaching position *ou* post *ou* job d (*Radio, TV*) set; **~ émetteur/récepteur** transmitting/receiving set, transmitter/receiver; **~ de radio/de télévision** radio/television (set); **ils l'ont dit au ~*** (*à la radio*) they said so on the radio; (*à la télévision*) they said so on the TV *ou* the box* (*Brit*) e (*Téléc* = *ligne*) extension f (*Fin* = *opération*) item, entry; [*budget*] item, element g (*Ind*) shift; **~ de huit heures** eight-hour shift

2 COMP ► **poste d'aiguillage** (*Rail*) signal box ► **poste avancé** (*Mil*) advanced post ► **poste budgétaire** budget item ► **poste de commande** position of responsibility; **ceux qui sont aux ~s de commande du pays** those who are at the helm of the country, the country's leaders ► **poste de commandement** headquarters ► **poste de contrôle** checkpoint ► **poste d'équipage** (*Naut*) crew's quarters ► **poste d'essence** filling station, petrol (*Brit*) *ou* gas (*US*) station ► **poste frontière** border *ou* frontier post ► **poste de garde** (*Mil*) guardroom ► **poste d'incendie** fire point ► **poste de lavage** (*Aut*) car wash ► **poste d'observation** observation post ► **poste de pilotage** (*Aviat*) cockpit ► **poste de police** (*Police*) police station; (*Mil*) guard-room, guardhouse ► **poste de secours** first-aid post ► **poste téléphonique** telephone ► **poste de travail** (*Ordin*) work station; (= *emplacement*) post; (= *emploi*) job, post

posté, e [pɔste] (*ptp de* **poster**) ADJ **travail/travailleur ~** shift work/worker

poster¹ [pɔste] ▶conjug 1◀ 1 VT a [+ *lettre*] to post (*surtout Brit*), mail (*surtout US*) b [+ *sentinelle*] to post, station 2 **se poster** VPR to take up (a) position, position o.s., station o.s.

poster² [pɔstɛr] NM poster

postérieur, e [pɔsterjœr] 1 ADJ (*dans le temps*) [*date, document*] later; [*événement*] subsequent, later; (*dans l'espace*) [*partie*] back, posterior (*frm*); [*membre*] hind, rear, back; [*voyelle*] back; **ce document est légèrement/très ~ à cette date** this document dates from slightly later/much later; **l'événement est ~ à 1850** the event took place later than *ou* after 1850; **~ à 1800** after 1800 2 NM* **behind***, rear, posterior (*hum*)

postérieurement [pɔsterjœrmã] ADV later, subsequently; **~ à** after

posteriori [pɔsterjɔri] → **a posteriori**

postériorité [pɔsterjɔrite] NF posteriority

postérité [pɔsterite] NF (= *descendants*) descendants; (= *avenir*) posterity; (*frm*) **mourir sans ~** to die without issue; **être jugé par la ~** to be judged by posterity; **entrer dans la ~** ◊ **passer à la ~** to go down in history

postface [pɔstfas] NF postscript, postface

postglaciaire [pɔstglasjɛr] ADJ postglacial

posthume [pɔstym] ADJ posthumous; **à titre ~** posthumously

postiche [pɔstiʃ] 1 ADJ [*cheveux, moustache*] false; [*ornement, fioriture*] postiche, superadded; [*sentiment*] fake; (*Ling*) [*élément, symbole*] dummy 2 NM (*pour homme*) toupee; (*pour femme*) hairpiece, postiche

postier, -ière [pɔstje, jɛr] NM,F post office worker; **grève des ~s** postal strike

postillon [pɔstijɔ̃] NM (*Hist* = *cocher*) postilion; (* = *salive*) sputter; **envoyer des ~s** to sputter, splutter

postillonner* [pɔstijɔne] ▶conjug 1◀ VI to sputter, splutter

postimpressionnisme [pɔstɛ̃presjɔnism] NM postimpressionism

postimpressionniste [pɔstɛ̃presjɔnist] ADJ, NMF postimpressionist

post(-)industriel, -elle [pɔstɛ̃dystrijɛl] ADJ post-industrial

Post-it® [pɔstit] NM INV Post-it®

postmoderne [pɔstmɔdɛrn] ADJ postmodern

postmodernisme [pɔstmɔdɛrnism] NM postmodernism

postnatal, e (*mpl* **postnatals**) [pɔstnatal] ADJ postnatal

postopératoire [pɔstɔperatwar] ADJ postoperative

postposer [pɔstpoze] ▶conjug 1◀ VT to place after the verb (*ou* noun *etc*); **sujet postposé** postpositive subject, subject placed after the verb

postposition [pɔstpozisjɔ̃] NF postposition; **verbe à ~** phrasal verb

postprandial, e (*mpl* **-iaux**) [pɔstprãdjal, jo] ADJ postprandial

post-production, postproduction [pɔstprɔdyksjɔ̃] NF (*Ciné*) postproduction

postscolaire [pɔstskɔlɛr] ADJ [*enseignement*] further (*épith*), continuing (*épith*)

post-scriptum [pɔstskriptɔm] NM INV postscript

postsonorisation [pɔstsɔnɔrizasjɔ̃] NF dubbing

postsonoriser [pɔstsɔnɔrize] ▶conjug 1◀ VT to dub

postsynchronisation [pɔstsɛ̃krɔnizasjɔ̃] NF (*Ciné*) dubbing

postsynchroniser [pɔstsɛ̃krɔnize] ▶conjug 1◀ VT (*Ciné*) to dub

postulant, e [pɔstylã, ãt] NM,F applicant; (*Rel*) postulant

postulat [pɔstyla] NM premise; (*Philo*) postulate; **~ de base** *ou* **de départ** basic premise; **partant du ~ que ...** starting from the premise that ...

postuler [pɔstyle] ▶conjug 1◀ 1 VT a [+ *emploi*] to apply for, put in for b [+ *principe*] to postulate 2 VI a **~ à** *ou* **pour un emploi** to apply for a job b (*Jur*) **~ pour** to represent

posture [pɔstyr] NF posture, position; **être en bonne ~** to be in a good position; **être en très mauvaise ~** to be in a really bad position *ou* a tight corner; (†, *littér*) **en ~ de faire qch** in a position to do sth

pot [po] 1 NM a (= *récipient*) (*en verre*) jar; (*en terre*) pot; (*en métal*) can, tin (*Brit*); (*en carton*) carton; **petit ~ (pour bébé)** jar of baby food; **il ne mange encore que des petits ~s** all he eats at the moment is baby food; **~ à**

confiture jamjar, jampot (*Brit*); **~ de confiture** jar *ou* pot (*Brit*) of jam; **mettre en ~** [+ *fleur*] to pot; [+ *confiture*] to put in jars, pot (*Brit*); **plantes en ~** pot plants; **mettre un enfant sur le ~** to put a child on the potty; (*fig*) **tourner autour du ~** to beat about *ou* around the bush → **cuiller, découvrir, fortune** etc

[b] * (= *boisson*) drink; (= *réunion*) drinks party; **~ d'adieu** farewell party; **~ de départ** (*à la retraite* etc) leaving party *ou* do* (*Brit*); **tu viens prendre** *ou* **boire un ~?*** are you coming for a drink?

[c] * (* = *chance*) luck; **avoir du ~** to be lucky; **tu as du ~!** some people have all the luck!, you're a lucky beggar!*; **t'as du ~, il est encore là** you're lucky *ou* in luck, he's still here; **je n'ai jamais eu de ~ dans la vie/avec les hommes** I've always been unlucky *ou* I've never had any luck in life/with men; **manquer de ~** to be unlucky *ou* out of luck; **pas de** *ou* **manque de ~!** just his (*ou* your etc) luck!; **c'est un vrai coup de ~!** what a stroke of luck!

[d] (*Cartes*) (= *enjeu*) kitty; (= *restant*) pile [e] **plein ~*** **rouler plein ~** to drive flat out*; **payer plein ~** to pay the full whack*

[2] COMP ► **pot à bière** (*en verre*) beer mug; (*en terre ou en métal*) tankard ► **pot catalytique** catalytic converter ► **pot de chambre** chamberpot ► **pot de colle** (*lit*) pot of glue; (*péj* = *crampon*) leech; **il est du genre ~ de colle!** you just can't shake him off!, he sticks like a leech! ► **pot à eau** (*pour se laver*) water jug, pitcher; (*pour boire*) water jug ► **pot d'échappement** exhaust pipe; (*silencieux*) silencer (*Brit*), muffler (*US*) ► **pot de fleurs** (= *récipient*) plant pot, flowerpot; (= *fleurs*) pot plant; (*péj ou hum*) **elle fait un peu ~ de fleurs** she just sits there and looks pretty ► **pot à lait** (*pour transporter*) milk can; (*sur la table*) milk jug ► **pot au noir** (*Naut*) doldrums ► **pot de peinture** can *ou* pot *ou* tin (*Brit*) of paint; (*péj*) **c'est un vrai ~ de peinture*** she wears far too much make-up, she plasters herself with make-up* ► **pot à tabac** (*lit*) tobacco jar; († *fig*) dumpy little person ► **pot de terre** earthenware pot; **un particulier qui se bat contre l'administration, c'est le ~ de terre contre le ~ de fer** one individual struggling against the authorities can't hope to win ► **pot de yaourt** (*en verre*) pot of yoghurt; (*en carton*) carton *ou* pot of yoghurt

potable [pɔtabl] ADJ (*lit*) drinkable, potable (*frm*); (* = *acceptable*) passable, decent; **eau ~** drinking water; **eau non ~** water which is not for drinking, non-drinking water; **il ne peut pas faire un travail ~** he can't do a decent piece of work; **le film est ~** the film isn't bad; **ce travail est tout juste ~** this piece of work is barely passable *ou* acceptable

potache* [pɔtaʃ] NM schoolboy, schoolkid*; **plaisanteries (de) ~** schoolboy pranks

potage [pɔtaʒ] NM soup; **être dans le ~*** (*mal réveillé*) to be in a daze; (*désorienté*) to be in a muddle; (*en mauvaise posture*) to be in the soup*

potager, -ère [pɔtaʒe, ɛʀ] [1] ADJ [*plante*] edible; **jardin ~** kitchen *ou* vegetable garden [2] NM kitchen *ou* vegetable garden

potasse [pɔtas] NF (= *hydroxide*) potassium hydroxide, caustic potash; (= *carbonate*) potash (*impure potassium carbonate*)

potasser* [pɔtase] ▸conjug 1◂ [1] VT [+ *livre, discours, examen*] to cram *ou* bone up* *ou* swot up* (*Brit*) for; [+ *sujet*] to bone up (on)*, swot up (on)* (*Brit*) [2] VI to cram, swot* (*Brit*)

potassique [pɔtasik] ADJ potassic

potassium [pɔtasjɔm] NM potassium

pot-au-feu [pɔtofø] [1] ADJ INV† stay-at-home* (*épith*), home-loving [2] NM INV (= *plat*) (beef) stew; (= *viande*) stewing beef

pot-de-vin (*pl* **pots-de-vin**) [pod(ə)vɛ̃] NM bribe, backhander* (*Brit*), payola* (*US*); **donner**

---

un ~ à qn to bribe sb, grease sb's palm, give sb a backhander* (*Brit*)

pote* [pɔt] NM pal*, mate* (*Brit*), buddy* (*US*); **salut, mon ~!** hi there!*

poteau (*pl* **poteaux**) [pɔto] [1] NM [a] (= *pilier*) post; (*Courses*) **rester au ~** to be left at the (starting) post; **elle a les jambes comme des ~x*** she's got legs like tree trunks* [b] **~ (d'exécution)** execution post, stake (*for execution by shooting*); **envoyer au ~** to sentence to execution by firing squad; **au ~!** lynch him!, string him up!*; **le directeur au ~!** down with the boss! [c] (*† = *ami*) pal*, buddy* (*US*) [2] COMP ► **poteau d'arrivée** winning *ou* finishing post ► **poteau de but** goal-post ► **poteau de départ** starting post ► **poteau électrique** electricity pole ► **poteau indicateur** signpost ► **poteau télégraphique** telegraph post *ou* pole ► **poteau de torture** torture post

potée [pɔte] NF [a] (*Culin*) ≈ hotpot (*of pork and cabbage*) [b] (*Tech*) **~ d'étain** tin putty, putty powder

potelé, e [pɔt(ə)le] ADJ [*enfant*] chubby; [*bras*] plump

potence [pɔtɑ̃s] NF [a] (= *gibet*) gallows *sg* → **gibier** [b] (= *support*) bracket; **en ~** (= *en équerre*) L-shaped; (= *en T*) T-shaped

potentat [pɔtɑ̃ta] NM (*lit*) potentate; (*péj*) despot

potentialiser [pɔtɑ̃sjalize] ▸conjug 1◂ VT (*Pharm*) to potentiate; [+ *mécanisme*] to maximize the potential of, potentiate

potentialité [pɔtɑ̃sjalite] NF potentiality

potentiel, -ielle [pɔtɑ̃sjɛl] [1] ADJ [*marché, risque, client*] potential [2] NM [a] (*Sci*) potential; **~ électrique** electric potential [b] (= *capacité*) potential; **industriel/militaire/nucléaire** industrial/military/nuclear potential; **ce candidat a un bon ~** this applicant has good potential; **ce pays a un énorme ~ économique/de croissance** this country has huge economic/growth potential

potentiellement [pɔtɑ̃sjɛlmɑ̃] ADV potentially

potentille [pɔtɑ̃tij] NF potentilla

potentiomètre [pɔtɑ̃sjɔmɛtʀ] NM potentiometer

poterie [pɔtʀi] NF (= *atelier, art*) pottery; (= *objet*) piece of pottery; **~s** earthenware, pieces of pottery

poterne [pɔtɛʀn] NF postern

potiche [pɔtiʃ] NF (large) oriental vase; (*péj* = *prête-nom*) figurehead; **il ne veut pas être un juge/président ~** he doesn't want to be a mere figurehead judge/president; **elle ne veut pas jouer les ~s** she doesn't want to just sit there and look pretty

potier, -ière [pɔtje, jɛʀ] NM,F potter

potimarron [pɔtimaʀɔ̃] NM variety of gourd

potin* [pɔtɛ̃] NM [a] (= *vacarme*) din*, racket*; **faire du ~** (*lit*) to make a noise; (*fig*) to kick up a fuss*; **ça va faire du ~** (*lit*) there'll be a lot of noise, it'll be noisy; (*fig*) this is going to stir things up*, there'll be quite a rumpus (over this) [b] (= *commérage*) **~s** gossip, tittle-tattle

potiner [pɔtine] ▸conjug 1◂ VI to gossip

potion [posjɔ̃] NF (*lit*) potion; (*lit, fig*) **~ magique** magic potion; (*fig*) **~ amère** bitter pill; **la ~ sera amère** it will be a bitter pill to swallow

potiron [pɔtiʀɔ̃] NM pumpkin

pot-pourri (*pl* **pots-pourris**) [popuʀi] NM (= *fleurs*) pot-pourri; (*Mus*) potpourri, medley; (*fig*) mixture, medley

potron-minet* [pɔtʀɔ̃minɛ] **♦dès potron-minet** LOC ADV at the crack of dawn, at daybreak

pou (*pl* **poux**) [pu] NM louse; **~ du pubis** pubic louse, crab (*louse*)*; **couvert de ~x** covered in lice, lice-ridden → **chercher, laid**

pouah [pwa] EXCL ugh!, yuk!

---

poubelle [pubɛl] [1] NF [a] [*ordures*] (dust)bin (*Brit*), trash *ou* garbage can (*US*); **descendre/sortir la ~** to take down/put out the bin (*Brit*) *ou* the garbage (*US*) *ou* trash (*US*); **les ~s sont passées?*** have the binmen (*Brit*) *ou* the garbage men (*US*) been?; **allez, hop! à la ~!** right! (let's) throw it out!; **jeter/mettre qch à la ~** to throw/put sth in the (dust)bin (*Brit*) *ou* trash can (*US*) *ou* garbage can (*US*); **c'est bon à mettre à la ~** it's only fit for the (dust)bin (*Brit*), you can put it right into the trash *ou* garbage can (*US*); **faire les ~s** to rummage through bins (*Brit*) *ou* garbage cans (*US*); **il roule dans une ~*** his car is a real tip* (*Brit*), his car is a garbage can on wheels (*US*); **ça appartient aux ~s de l'histoire** that has been consigned to the scrap heap of history [b] (*en apposition*) **camion(-)poubelle** bin lorry (*Brit*), garbage truck (*US*), **classe(-)poubelle** class of rejects; **chaîne(-)poubelle** trashy* television channel; **navire(-)poubelle** coffin ship (*often transporting dangerous nuclear waste etc*); **la presse(-)poubelle** the gutter press [2] COMP ► **poubelle de table** container placed on a table for bones, wrappers etc

pouce [pus] NM [a] (*Anat*) [*main*] thumb; [*pied*] big toe; **se tourner** *ou* **se rouler les ~s** to twiddle one's thumbs; **mettre les ~s*** to give in *ou* up; (*au jeu*) **~!** truce!, pax! (*Brit*); **on a déjeuné** *ou* **on a pris un morceau sur le ~*** we had a quick snack *ou* a bite to eat*; (*Can*) **faire du ~ ◊ voyager sur le ~** to thumb* a lift, hitch*, hitch-hike; **coup de ~** (*pour aider qn*) nudge in the right direction; **donner un coup de ~ aux ventes** to give sales a bit of a boost; **donner un coup de ~ à un projet** to help a project along [b] (= *mesure*) inch; (*fig*) **ils n'ont pas cédé un ~ de terrain** (*armée*) they haven't yielded an inch of land; **son travail n'a pas avancé d'un ~** he hasn't made the least *ou* the slightest bit of progress in his work; **il n'a pas bougé d'un ~** (*dans sa prise de position*) he refused to budge, he wouldn't budge an inch; **la situation/ville n'a pas changé d'un ~** the situation/town hasn't changed in the slightest *ou* hasn't changed the least little bit; **il n'a pas varié ou dévié d'un ~ dans sa politique** he hasn't altered his policy in the slightest; **et le ~!*** and the rest!

Poucet [pusɛ] NM **« le Petit ~ »** "Tom Thumb"

Pouchkine [puʃkin] NM Pushkin

pouding [pudiŋ] NM = **pudding**

poudingue [pudɛ̃g] NM (*Géol*) pudding stone

poudre [pudʀ] [1] NF [a] (*gén*) powder; (= *poussière*) dust; (= *fard*) (face) powder; (= *explosif*) (gun) powder; (*Méd*) powder; (*arg Drogue* = *héroïne*) smack*; **~ d'or/de diamant** gold/diamond dust; **réduire qch en ~** to reduce *ou* grind sth to powder, powder sth; **en ~** [*lait, œufs*] dried, powdered; **chocolat en ~** cocoa powder; **se mettre de la ~** to powder one's face *ou* nose; **se mettre de la ~ sur** to powder; **~ libre/compacte** loose/pressed powder; **prendre la ~ d'escampette*** to take to one's heels, skedaddle*; **de la ~ de perlimpinpin** magical cure; **jeter de la ~ aux yeux de qn** to impress sb; **c'est de la ~ aux yeux** it's all just for show → **feu**; **inventer** [2] COMP ► **poudre à canon** gunpowder ► **poudre dentifrice** tooth powder ► **poudre à éternuer** sneezing powder ► **poudre à laver** washing powder (*Brit*), soap powder (*Brit*), (powdered) laundry detergent (*US*) ► **poudre à récurer** scouring powder ► **poudre de riz** face powder

poudrer [pudʀe] ▸conjug 1◂ [1] VT to powder [2] VI (*Can*) [*neige*] to drift [3] **se poudrer** VPR to powder one's face *ou* nose

poudrerie¹ [pudʀəʀi] NF (= *fabrique*) gunpowder *ou* explosives factory

poudrerie² [pudʀəʀi] NF (*Can*) blizzard, drifting snow

poudreux, -euse [pudʁø, øz] 1 ADJ (= *poussiéreux*) dusty; **neige poudreuse** powder snow 2 **poudreuse** NF a (= *neige*) powder snow b (= *meuble*) dressing table c (*Agr*) duster

poudrier [pudʁije] NM (powder) compact

poudrière [pudʁijɛʁ] NF powder magazine; (*fig*) powder keg (*fig*)

poudroiement [pudʁwamɑ̃] NM dust haze

poudroyer [pudʁwaje] ▶conjug 8◀ VI [*poussière*] to rise in clouds; [*neige*] to rise in a flurry; **la route poudroyait** clouds of dust rose up from the road

pouf [puf] 1 NM pouffe 2 EXCL thud!; **faire ~** to tumble (over); **~ par terre!** whoops-a-daisy!

pouffer [pufe] ▶conjug 1◀ VI **~ (de rire)** to burst out laughing

pouf(f)iasse: [pufjas] NF (*péj*) tart:, slag: (*Brit*); (= *prostituée*) whore, tart:

pouh [pu] EXCL pooh!

pouillerie [pujʁi] NF squalor

pouilleux, -euse [pujø, øz] 1 ADJ a (*lit*) lousy, flea-ridden, verminous b (= *sordide*) [*quartier, endroit*] squalid, seedy; [*personne*] dirty, filthy 2 NM,F (= *pauvre*) down-and-out; (= *couvert de poux*) flea-ridden *ou* lice-ridden *ou* verminous person

pouillot [pujo] NM warbler; **~ fitis** willow warbler; **~ véloce** chiffchaff

poujadisme [puʒadism] NM Poujadism

poujadiste [puʒadist] ADJ, NMF Poujadist

poulailler [pulaje] NM henhouse; (*Théât*) **le ~**: the gallery, the gods* (*Brit*)

poulain [pulɛ̃] NM a (*Zool*) foal, colt; (*fig*) promising youngster; (= *protégé*) protégé b (*Tech*) **~ (de chargement)** skid

poulaine [pulɛn] NF (*Hist* = *soulier*) poulaine, long pointed shoe

poularde [pulaʁd] NF fattened chicken

poulbot [pulbo] NM street urchin (*in Montmartre*)

poule¹ [pul] 1 NF a (*Zool*) hen; (*Culin*) (boiling) fowl; **se lever avec les ~s** to be an early riser, get up with the lark (*Brit*) *ou* birds (*US*); **se coucher avec les ~s** to go to bed early; **quand les ~s auront des dents** never in a month of Sundays; **être comme une ~ qui a trouvé un couteau** to be at a complete loss → **chair, lait** b (= *maîtresse*) mistress; (= *fille*) bird* (*Brit*), broad* (*US*), chick* (*US*); (*prostituée*) whore, tart:, hooker* (*US*); **~ de luxe** high-class prostitute c (= *terme affectueux*) **ma ~** (my) pet 2 COMP ▶ **poule d'eau** moorhen ▶ **poule faisane** hen pheasant ▶ **poule mouillée** (= *lâche*) softy*, coward* ▶ **la poule aux œufs d'or** the goose that lays the golden eggs; **tuer la ~ aux œufs d'or** to kill the goose that lays the golden eggs ▶ **poule pondeuse** laying hen, layer ▶ **poule au pot** (*Culin*) boiled chicken; (*Hist*) **la ~ au pot tous les dimanches** a chicken in the pot every Sunday ▶ **poule au riz** chicken and rice

poule² [pul] NF a (= *enjeu*) pool, kitty b (= *tournoi*) (*gén*) tournament; (*Escrime*) pool; (*Rugby*) group c (*Courses*) **~ d'essai** maiden race

poulet [pulɛ] NM a (*Culin, Zool*) chicken; **~ de grain/fermier** corn-fed/free-range (*Brit*) chicken; **mon (petit) ~!** (my) love! *ou* pet! (*Brit*) b (: = *policier*) cop: c (†† = *billet doux*) love letter

poulette [pulɛt] NF a (*Zool*) pullet; **ma ~!** (my) love *ou* pet (*Brit*)! b (* = *fille*) girl, lass*, bird* (*Brit*), chick* (*US*) c (*Culin*) **sauce ~** sauce poulette (*made with eggs and lemon juice*)

pouliche [puliʃ] NF filly

poulie [puli] NF pulley; (*avec sa caisse*) block; **~ simple/double/fixe** single/double/fixed block; **~ folle** loose pulley

▶ GRAMMAIRE ACTIVE: **pour** 53.4

pouliner [puline] ▶conjug 1◀ VI to foal

poulinière [pulinjɛʁ] ADJ F, NF (**jument**) **~** brood mare

poulot, -otte †: [pulo, ɔt] NM,F **mon ~!** *◊* **ma poulotte!** poppet!*, (my) pet! (*Brit*) *ou* love!

poulpe [pulp] NM octopus

pouls [pu] NM pulse; **prendre** *ou* **tâter le ~ de qn** (*lit*) to feel *ou* take sb's pulse; (*fig*) to sound sb out; (*fig*) **prendre** *ou* **tâter le ~ de [**+ *opinion publique*] to test, sound out; [+ *économie*] to feel the pulse of

poumon [pumɔ̃] NM (*Anat*) lung; **respirer à pleins ~s** to breathe deeply; **chanter/crier à pleins ~s** to sing/shout at the top of one's voice; **~ artificiel/d'acier** artificial/iron lung; **cette région est le ~ économique du pays** this region is the hub of the country's economy; **la forêt amazonienne, ~ de la terre** the Amazon rainforest, the lungs of the earth; **Hyde Park, le ~ de Londres** Hyde Park, London's green lung

poupard [pupaʁ] 1 ADJ† chubby(-cheeked) 2 NM bouncing *ou* bonny (*Brit*) baby

poupe [pup] NF (*Naut*) stern → **vent**

poupée [pupe] NF a (= *jouet*) doll; **~(s) gigogne(s)** *ou* **russe(s)** nest of dolls, Russian dolls; **~ gonflable** inflatable *ou* blow-up doll; **~ de son** rag doll (*stuffed with bran*); **elle joue à la ~** she's playing with her doll(s) → **maison** b (* = *jolie femme*) doll*; **bonjour, ~!** hullo, doll! c (= *pansement*) finger bandage; **faire une ~ à qn** to bandage sb's finger d (*Tech*) **~ fixe** headstock; **~ mobile** tailstock

poupin, e [pupɛ̃, in] ADJ chubby

poupon [pupɔ̃] NM little baby, babe-in-arms

pouponner [pupɔne] ▶conjug 1◀ VI to play mother; **tu vas bientôt (pouvoir) ~** soon you'll be fussing around like a fond mother (*ou* father *etc*)

pouponnière [pupɔnjɛʁ] NF day nursery, crèche

▼**pour** [puʁ]

1 PRÉPOSITION	2 NOM MASCULIN

1 PRÉPOSITION

a direction for, to; **partir ~ l'Espagne** to leave for Spain; **il part ~ l'Espagne demain** he leaves for Spain *ou* he is off to Spain tomorrow; **partir ~ l'étranger** to go abroad; **un billet ~ Caen** a ticket to *ou* for Caen; **le train ~ Londres** the London train, the train for London

b temps for; **tu restes à Paris ~ Noël?** are you staying in Paris for Christmas?; **il est absent ~ deux jours** he's away for two days; **promettre qch ~ le mois prochain/~ dans huit jours/~ après les vacances** to promise sth for next month/ for next week/for after the holidays; **ce sera ~ l'an prochain** we'll have to wait for *ou* until next year; **il lui faut sa voiture ~ demain** he must have her car for *ou* by tomorrow; **~ le moment** *ou* **l'instant** for the moment; **~ toujours** for ever

◆ **en avoir pour** [+ *durée*] **tu en as ~ combien de temps?** how long are you going to be?, how long will it take you?; **ne m'attendez pas, j'en ai encore ~ une heure** don't wait for me, I'll be another hour (yet); **elle en a bien ~ trois semaines** it'll take her at least three weeks; **quand il se met à pleuvoir, on en a ~ trois jours** once it starts raining, it goes on *ou* sets in for three days

(*distance*) **on en a encore ~ 20 km de cette mauvaise route** there's another 20 km of this awful road

c intention, destination for; **faire qch ~ qn** to do sth for sb; **il ferait tout ~ elle/sa mère** he would do anything for her *ou* for her sake/his mother *ou* his mother's sake; **faire qch ~ le plaisir** to do sth for pleasure; **il n'est pas fait ~ le travail de bureau** he's not made for office work; **c'est fait** *ou* **étudié ~!** that's what it's meant *ou* made for!; **il travaille ~ un cabinet**

d'architectes he works for a firm of architects; **ce n'est pas un livre ~ (les) enfants** it's not a book for children, it's not a children's book; **c'est mauvais/bon ~ vous/~ la santé** it's bad/good for you/for the health; **c'est trop compliqué ~ elle** it's too complicated for her; **son amour ~ elle/les bêtes** his love for her/of animals; **il a été très gentil ~ ma mère** he was very kind to my mother; **~ la plus grande joie des spectateurs** to the delight of the onlookers; **coiffeur ~ dames** ladies' hairdresser; **sirop ~ la toux** cough mixture (*Brit*) *ou* syrup (*US*); **pastilles ~ la gorge** throat tablets

◆ **pour** + *infinitif* (= *afin de*) to; **trouvez un argument ~ le convaincre** find an argument to convince him *ou* that will convince him; **il sera d'accord ~ nous aider** he'll agree to help us; **~ mûrir, les tomates ont besoin de soleil** tomatoes need sunshine to ripen; **je ne l'ai pas dit ~ le vexer** I didn't say that to annoy him; **je n'ai rien dit ~ ne pas le blesser** I didn't say anything so as not to hurt him; **elle se pencha ~ ramasser son gant** she bent down to pick up her glove; **il tendit le bras ~ prendre la boîte** he reached for the box; **creuser ~ trouver de l'eau/du pétrole** to dig for water/oil; **il y a des gens assez innocents ~ le croire** some people are naive enough to believe him; **il finissait le soir tard ~ reprendre le travail tôt le lendemain** he used to finish work late at night only to start again early the next morning; **il est parti ~ ne plus revenir** he left never to return, he left and never came back again

◆ **pour que** + *subjonctif* (= *afin que*) so that, in order that (*frm*); **écris vite ta lettre ~ qu'elle parte ce soir** write your letter quickly so (that) it will go *ou* it goes this evening; **il a mis une barrière ~ que les enfants ne sortent pas** he has put up a fence so that the children won't get out; (*iro*) **c'est ça, laisse ton sac là ~ qu'on te le vole!** that's right, leave your bag there for someone to steal it! *ou* so that someone steals it!

(*introduisant une conséquence*) **il est trop tard ~ qu'on le prévienne** it's too late to warn him *ou* for him to be warned; (*iro*) **elle est assez grande ~ qu'on puisse la laisser seule** she's old enough to be left on her own

d cause **~ quelle raison?** for what reason?, why?; **être condamné ~ vol** to be convicted for theft; **« fermé ~ réparations »** "closed for repairs"; **il n'en est pas plus heureux ~ ça!** he's none the happier for all that!, he's no happier for all that!; **on l'a félicité ~ son audace/~ son élection** he was congratulated on his daring/ on his election; **il est connu ~ sa générosité** he is known for his generosity; **quelle histoire ~ si peu** what a fuss *ou* to-do* over *ou* about such a little thing; **pourquoi se faire du souci ~ ça?** why worry about that?; **il est ~ quelque chose/~ beaucoup dans le succès de la pièce** he is partly/largely responsible for the success of the play, he had something/a lot to do with the play's success

◆ **pour** + *infinitif* (*introduisant une cause*) **elle a été punie ~ avoir menti** she was punished for lying *ou* having lied; **on l'a félicité ~ avoir sauvé l'enfant** he was congratulated for having saved the child

(= *susceptible de*) **le travail n'est pas ~ l'effrayer** *ou* **~ lui faire peur** he's not afraid of hard work; **ce n'est pas ~ arranger les choses** this isn't going to help matters, this will only make things worse

e approbation for, in favour (*Brit*) *ou* favor (*US*) of; **manifester ~ la paix** to demonstrate *ou* march for peace; **je suis ~ les réformes/~ réduire** *ou* **qu'on réduise les dépenses** I'm in favour of the reforms/of reducing expenditure; **je suis ~ !*** I'm all for it!*, I'm all in favour (of it)!

f = du point de vue de qn **~ lui, le projet n'est pas réalisable** as he sees it *ou* in his opinion *ou* in his view the plan isn't feasible; **~ moi, elle était déjà au courant** if you ask me, she already knew; **~ moi, je suis d'accord** personally *ou* for my part I agree; **sa fille est tout ~ lui** his daughter is everything to him

g = en ce qui concerne **~ (ce qui est de) notre voyage, il faut y renoncer** as for our trip *ou* as far as our trip goes, we'll have to forget it; **et ~ les billets, c'est toi qui t'en charges ?** so, are you going to take care of the tickets?; **ça ne change rien – nous** that makes no difference as far as we're concerned; **le plombier est venu/a téléphoné ~ la chaudière** the plumber came/phoned about the boiler

h = à la place de, en échange de **payer ~ qn** to pay for sb; **signez ~ moi** sign in my place *ou* for me; (*Comm*) **~ le directeur** p.p. Manager; **il a parlé ~ nous** he spoke on behalf of all of us *ou* on our behalf, he spoke for all of us; **donnez-moi ~ 200 F d'essence** give me 200 francs' worth of petrol; **il l'a eu ~ 10 F** he got it for 10 francs

♦ **en avoir pour** + *prix* : **j'en ai eu ~ 50 F de photocopies** it cost me 50 francs to do the photocopies

i rapport, comparaison for; **il est petit ~ son âge** he is small for his age; **il fait chaud ~ la saison** it's warm for the time of year; **c'est bien trop cher ~ ce que c'est !** it's far too expensive for what it is!; **~ un Anglais, il parle bien le français** he speaks French well for an Englishman; **~ cent/mille** per cent/thousand; **~ 500 g de farine, il te faut six œufs** for 500 grams of flour you need six eggs; **~ un qui s'intéresse, il y en a dix qui bâillent** for every one that takes an interest there are ten who just sit there yawning; **mourir ~ mourir, je préfère que ce soit ici** if I have to die I should prefer it to be here

j = comme for, as; **prendre qn ~ femme** to take sb as one's wife; **il a ~ adjoint son cousin** he has his cousin as his deputy; **il a ~ principe/méthode de faire ...** it is his principle /method to do ...; **ça a eu ~ effet de changer son comportement** this had the effect of changing his behaviour

k emphatique **~ un sale coup, c'est un sale coup !*** of all the unfortunate things (to happen)!; **~ une vedette, c'en est une !** that's what I call a star!; **~ être furieux, je suis furieux !** I am so angry!

l indiquant une restriction **~ avoir réussi, il n'en est pas plus heureux** he's no happier *ou* none the happier for having succeeded *ou* for his success; **~ être petite, elle n'en est pas moins solide** she may be small but that doesn't mean she's not strong; **~ riche qu'il soit, il n'est pas généreux** (as) rich as he is *ou* rich though he is, he's not generous

m

♦ **pour peu que** + *subjonctif*: **~ peu qu'il soit sorti sans sa clé ...** if he's left without his key ...; **il la convaincra, ~ peu qu'il sache s'y prendre** he'll convince her if he goes about it (in) the right way

n

♦ **être pour** + *infinitif* (* = être sur le point de) **j'étais ~ partir** I was just going, I was just about to go, I was on the point of leaving

2 NOM MASCULIN

a = arguments **le ~ et le contre** the arguments for and against, the pros and cons; **il y a du ~ et du contre** there are arguments on both sides *ou* arguments for and against → **peser**

b = personne **les ~ ont la majorité** those in favour are in the majority; **devant ses tableaux, il y a le ~ et le contre** people either like or dislike his paintings

pourboire [puʀbwaʀ] NM tip; **~ interdit** no gratuities, our staff do not accept gratuities; **donner un ~ de 10 F à qn** ◊ **donner 10 F de ~ à qn** to tip sb 10 francs, give sb a 10 franc tip

---

pourceau (pl **pourceaux**) [puʀso] NM (*littér, péj*) pig, swine *inv* → **perle**

pour-cent [puʀsɑ̃] NM INV (= commission) percentage, cut*

pourcentage [puʀsɑ̃taʒ] NM percentage; **résultat exprimé en ~** result expressed in percentages; **fort ~ d'abstentions** high abstention rate; **travailler au ~** to work on commission; **toucher un ~ sur les bénéfices** to get a share *ou* a cut* of the profits; **côte à fort ~** hill with a steep gradient, steep slope

pourchasser [puʀʃase] ▸ conjug 1 ◂ VT [*police, chasseur, ennemi*] to pursue, hunt down; [*créancier, importun*] to hound; **~ la misère/le crime** to hunt out *ou* seek out poverty/crime; **~ les fautes d'orthographe** to hunt out spelling mistakes

pourfendeur [puʀfɑ̃dœʀ] NM (*hum*) destroyer

pourfendre [puʀfɑ̃dʀ] ▸ conjug 41 ◂ VT (*littér*) [+ *adversaire*] to set about, assail; [+ *abus*] to fight against, combat

pourlécher (se) [puʀleʃe] ▸ conjug 6 ◂ VPR (*lit, fig*) to lick one's lips; **je m'en pourlèche déjà** (*lit*) my mouth is watering already; (*fig*) I can hardly wait; **se pourlécher les babines*** (*lit*) to lick one's chops*; (*fig*) to lick *ou* smack one's lips

pourparlers [puʀpaʀle] NMPL talks, negotiations, discussions; **entrer en ~ avec qn** to start negotiations *ou* discussions with sb, enter into talks with sb; **être en ~ avec qn** to be negotiating with sb, be having talks *ou* discussions with sb

pourpier [puʀpje] NM portulaca; (*comestible*) purslane

pourpoint [puʀpwɛ̃] NM doublet, pourpoint

pourpre [puʀpʀ] **1** ADJ (*gén*) crimson; (*Hér*) purpure; **il devint ~** (*furieux*) he went purple (in the face); (*gêné*) he turned crimson *ou* scarlet **2** NM **a** (= couleur) crimson; (*Hér*) purpure; **~ rétinien** visual purple **b** (*Zool*) murex **3** NF (= matière colorante, étoffe, symbole) purple; (= couleur) scarlet; **~ royale** royal purple; **accéder à la ~ cardinalice** *ou* **romaine** to be given the red hat; **né dans la ~** born in the purple

pourpré, e [puʀpʀe] ADJ (*littér*) crimson

▼ **pourquoi** [puʀkwa] **1** CONJ why; **~ est-il venu ?** why did he come?, what did he come for?; **~ les avoir oubliés ?** why did he (*ou* they *etc*) forget them?; **c'est ou voilà ~ il n'est pas venu** that's (the reason) why he didn't come **2** ADV why; **tu me le prêtes ? — ~ (donc) ?** can you lend me it? — why? *ou* what for?; **tu viens ? — ~ pas ?** are you coming? — why not?; **il a réussi, ~ pas vous ?** (*dans le futur*) he succeeded so why shouldn't you?; (*dans le passé*) he succeeded so why didn't you? *ou* so how come you didn't?*; **je vais vous dire ~** I'll tell you why; **il faut que ça marche, ou que ça dise ~*** it had better work or else*, it had better work, or I'll want to know why (not); **allez savoir ou comprendre ~ !** ◊ **je vous demande bien ~** I just can't imagine why! **3** NM INV (= raison) reason (**de** for); (= question) question; **le ~ de son attitude** the reason for his attitude; **il veut toujours savoir le ~ et le comment** he always wants to know the whys and wherefores; **il est difficile de répondre à tous les ~ des enfants** it isn't easy to find an answer for everything children ask you

pourri, e [puʀi] (*ptp de* **pourrir**) **1** ADJ **a** [*fruit*] rotten, bad; [*bois*] rotten; [*feuille*] decayed, rotting; [*viande*] bad; [*œuf*] rotten, bad, addled; [*enfant*] spoilt rotten (*attrib*); [*cadavre*] decomposed, putrefied; **être ~** [*pomme*] to have gone rotten *ou* bad; [*œuf*] to have gone bad → **poisson b** [*roche*] crumbling, rotten; [*neige*] melting, half-melted **c** (= mauvais) [*temps, été*] rotten; [*personne, société*] rotten, corrupt; **flic ~*** bent copper* (*Brit*), dirty *ou*

---

bad cop* (*US*); **~ de fric*** stinking* *ou* filthy* rich; **~ de défauts** full of *ou* riddled with faults; **~ de talent*** oozing with talent **2** NM **a** = partie gâtée] rotten *ou* bad part; **sentir le ~** to smell rotten *ou* bad **b** (* = crapule) swine*; **bande de ~s !** (you) bastards!** **c** (* = policier corrompu) bent copper* (*Brit*), dirty *ou* bad cop* (*US*)

pourrir [puʀiʀ] ▸ conjug 2 ◂ **1** VI [*fruit*] to go rotten *ou* bad, spoil; [*bois*] to rot (away); [*œuf*] to go bad; [*cadavre*] to rot (away); [*corps, membre*] to be eaten away; [*relations*] to deteriorate; **récolte qui pourrit sur pied** harvest rotting on the stalk; **~ dans la misère** to languish in poverty; **~ en prison** to rot (away) in prison; **laisser ~ la situation** to let the situation deteriorate *ou* get worse; **laisser ~ une grève** to let a strike peter out **2** VT **a** [+ *fruit*] to rot, spoil; [+ *bois*] to rot; (= infecter) [+ *corps*] to eat away (at) **b** (= gâter) [+ *enfant*] to spoil rotten; (= corrompre) [+ *personne*] to corrupt, spoil; **les ennuis qui pourrissent notre vie** the worries which spoil our lives **3** **se pourrir** VPR [*fruit*] to go rotten *ou* bad, spoil; [*bois*] to rot (away); [*relations, situation*] to deteriorate, get worse

pourrissement [puʀismɑ̃] NM [*situation*] deterioration, worsening (**de** in, of)

pourriture [puʀityʀ] NF **a** (*lit, Agr*) rot; [*société*] rottenness; **odeur de ~** putrid smell; **~ noble** noble rot, botrytis (*SPÉC*) **b** (* péj) (= homme) louse*, swine*; (= femme) bitch**

pour-soi [puʀswa] NM (*Philo*) pour-soi

poursuite [puʀsyit] NF **a** [*voleur, animal*] chase (**de** after), pursuit (**de** of); [*bonheur, gloire*] pursuit (**de** of); **se mettre** *ou* **se lancer à la ~ de qn** to chase *ou* run after sb, go in pursuit of sb **b** (*Jur*) **~s (judiciaires)** legal proceedings; **engager des ~s contre qn** to start legal proceedings against sb, take legal action against sb; **s'exposer à des ~s** to lay o.s. open to *ou* run the risk of prosecution **c** (= continuation) continuation; **ils ont voté/décidé la ~ de la grève** they voted/decided to continue the strike **d** (**course**) **~** (*Sport*) track race; (*Police*) chase, pursuit; **~ individuelle** individual pursuit; **~ en voiture** car chase

poursuiteur, -euse [puʀsyitœʀ, øz] NM,F track rider *ou* cyclist

poursuivant, e [puʀsyivɑ̃, ɑ̃t] **1** ADJ (*Jur*) **partie ~e** plaintiff **2** NM,F (= ennemi) pursuer; (*Jur*) plaintiff

poursuivre [puʀsyivʀ] ▸ conjug 40 ◂ **1** VT **a** (= courir après) [+ *fugitif, ennemi*] to pursue; [+ *animal*] to chase (after), hunt down, pursue; [+ *malfaiteur*] to chase (after), pursue; **un enfant poursuivi par un chien** a child (being) chased *ou* pursued by a dog; **les motards poursuivaient la voiture** the police motorcyclists were chasing the car *ou* were in pursuit of the car **b** (= harceler) [*importun, souvenir*] to hound; **être poursuivi par ses créanciers** to be hounded by one's creditors; **~ qn de sa colère/de sa haine** to be bitterly angry with sb/hate sb bitterly; **~ une femme de ses assiduités** to force one's attentions on a woman; **cette idée le poursuit** he can't get the idea out of his mind, he's haunted by the idea; **les photographes ont poursuivi l'actrice jusque chez elle** the photographers followed the actress all the way home **c** (= chercher à atteindre) [+ *fortune, gloire*] to seek (after); [+ *vérité*] to pursue, seek (after); [+ *rêve*] to pursue, follow; [+ *but, idéal*] to strive towards, pursue **d** (= continuer: *gén*) to continue, go *ou* carry on with; [+ *avantage*] to follow up, pursue; **~ sa marche** to carry on walking **e** (*Jur*) **~ qn (en justice)** (au criminel) to prosecute sb, bring proceedings against sb; (au civil) to sue sb, bring proceedings against sb;

➤ **GRAMMAIRE ACTIVE:**   **pourquoi** 28.1

être poursuivi pour vol to be prosecuted for theft

2 VI **a** (= *continuer*) to carry on, go on, continue; **poursuivez, cela m'intéresse** go on *ou* tell me more, I'm interested; **puis il poursuivit: voici pourquoi ...** then he went on *ou* continued: that's why ...
b (= *persévérer*) to keep at it, keep it up

3 **se poursuivre** VPR [*négociations, débats*] to go on, continue; [*enquête, recherches, travail*] to be going on; **les débats se sont poursuivis jusqu'au matin** discussions went on *ou* continued until morning

pourtant [puʀtɑ̃] ADV (= *néanmoins, en dépit de cela*) yet, nevertheless, all the same, even so; (= *cependant*) (and) yet; **et ~** and yet, but nevertheless; **frêle mais ~ résistant** frail but (nevertheless) resilient, frail (and) yet resilient; **il faut ~ le faire** it's got to be done nevertheless *ou* all the same *ou* even so; **il n'est ~ pas très intelligent** (and) yet he's not very clever, he's not very clever though; (*intensif*) **c'est ~ facile !** but it's easy!, but it's not difficult!; **on lui a ~ dit de faire attention** and yet we told him *ou* did tell him to be careful

pourtour [puʀtuʀ] NM [*cercle*] circumference; [*rectangle*] perimeter; (= *bord*) surround; **le ~ méditerranéen** the Mediterranean region; **sur le ~ de** around

pourvoi [puʀvwa] NM (*Jur*) appeal; **~ en grâce** appeal for clemency; **former un ~ en cassation** to (lodge an) appeal

pourvoir [puʀvwaʀ] ▸ conjug 25 ◂ **1** VT **a** **~ qn de qch** to provide *ou* equip *ou* supply sb with sth; **~ un enfant de vêtements chauds** to provide a child with warm clothes; **la nature l'a pourvu d'une grande intelligence** nature has endowed him with great intelligence; **la nature l'a pourvue d'une grande beauté** she is graced with great natural beauty; **~ sa maison de tout le confort moderne** to fit one's house out *ou* equip one's house with all modern conveniences; **~ sa cave de vin** to stock one's cellar with wine → **pourvu¹**
b [+ *poste*] to fill; **il y a deux postes à ~** there are two posts to fill

2 **pourvoir à** VT INDIR [+ *éventualité*] to provide for, cater for; [+ *emploi*] to fill; **~ aux besoins de qn** to provide for *ou* cater for *ou* supply sb's needs; **~ à l'entretien du ménage** to provide for the upkeep of the household; **j'y pourvoirai** I'll see to it *ou* deal with it

3 **se pourvoir** VPR **a** **se ~ de** [+ *argent, vêtements*] to provide o.s. with; [+ *provisions, munitions*] to provide o.s. with, equip o.s. with, supply o.s. with
b (*Jur*) to appeal, lodge an appeal; **se ~ en appel** to take one's case to the Court of Appeal; **se ~ en cassation** to (lodge an) appeal

pourvoyeur, -euse [puʀvwajœʀ, øz] **1** NM,F supplier, purveyor; [*drogue*] supplier, pusher* **2** NM (*Mil* = *servant de pièce*) artilleryman

pourvu¹, e [puʀvy] (*ptp de* **pourvoir**) ADJ **a** [*personne*] **être ~ de** [+ *intelligence, imagination*] to be endowed with, be endowed with; [+ *grâce*] to be endowed with; **avec ces provisions nous voilà ~s pour l'hiver** with these provisions we're stocked up for the winter; **nous sommes très bien/très mal ~s en commerçants** we're very well-off/very badly off for shops; **après l'héritage qu'il a fait c'est quelqu'un de bien ~** with the inheritance he's received, he's very well-off *ou* very well provided for
b [*chose*] **être ~ de** to be equipped *ou* fitted with; **feuille de papier ~e d'une marge** sheet of paper with a margin; **animal (qui est) ~ d'écailles** animal which has scales *ou* which is equipped with scales

pourvu² [puʀvy] ♦ **pourvu que** LOC CONJ (*souhait*) let's hope; (*condition*) provided (that), so long as; **~ que ça dure !** let's hope it lasts!

poussa(h) [pusa] NM (= *jouet*) wobbly toy, Weeble®; (*péj* = *homme*) potbellied man

pousse [pus] NF **a** (= *bourgeon*) shoot; **~s de bambou** bamboo shoots; **~s de soja** beansprouts; **la plante fait des ~s** the plant is putting out shoots **b** (= *action*) [*feuilles*] sprouting; [*dents, cheveux*] growth

poussé, e¹ [puse] (*ptp de* **pousser**) **1** ADJ [*études*] advanced; [*enquête*] extensive, exhaustive; [*interrogatoire*] intensive; [*moteur*] souped-up*; **très ~** [*organisation, technique, dessin*] elaborate, sophisticated; [*précision*] high-level (*épith*), extreme; **il n'a pas eu une formation/éducation très ~e** he hasn't had much training/education; **une plaisanterie un peu ~e** a joke which goes a bit too far **2** NM (*Mus*) up-bow

pousse-au-crime* [pusokrim] NM INV (= *boisson*) firewater*; (*fig*) **c'est du ~ !** [*décolleté, tenue*] it's an open invitation!; **c'est une société ~** it's a society that drives people to crime

pousse-café* [puskafe] NM INV liqueur

poussée² [puse] NF **a** (= *pression*) [*foule*] pressure, pushing; (*Archit, Aviat, Géol, Phys*) thrust (*NonC*); **sous la ~** under the pressure; **la ~ d'Archimède** Archimedes' principle; (*Bot*) **~ radiculaire** root pressure **b** (= *coup*) push, shove; [*ennemi*] thrust; **écarter qn d'une ~** to thrust *ou* push *ou* shove sb aside; **enfoncer une porte d'une ~ violente** to break a door down with a violent heave *ou* shove **c** (= *éruption*) [*acné*] attack, eruption; [*prix*] rise, upsurge, increase; **~ de fièvre** (sudden) high temperature; **la ~ de la gauche/droite aux élections** the upsurge of the left/right in the elections; **la ~ révolutionnaire de 1789** the revolutionary upsurge of 1789

pousse-pousse [puspus] NM INV rickshaw

pousser [puse] ▸ conjug 1 ◂ **1** VT **a** (*gén*) [+ *voiture, meuble, personne*] to push; [+ *brouette, landau*] to push, wheel; [+ *verrou*] (= *ouvrir*) to slide, push back; (= *fermer*) to slide, push to *ou* home; [+ *objet gênant*] to move, shift, push aside; [+ *pion*] to move; **~ une chaise contre le mur/près de la fenêtre/dehors** to push a chair (up) against the wall/over to the window/outside; **~ les gens vers la porte** to push the people towards *ou* to the door; **il me poussa du genou/du coude** he nudged me with his knee/(with his elbow); **~ un animal devant soi** to drive an animal in front of one; **~ la porte/la fenêtre** (*fermer*) to push the door/window to *ou* shut; (*ouvrir*) to push the door/window open; **~ un caillou du pied** to kick a stone (along); **le vent nous poussait vers la côte** the wind was blowing *ou* pushing *ou* driving us towards the shore; **le courant poussait le bateau vers les rochers** the current was carrying the boat towards the rocks; (*balançoire, voiture en panne*) **peux-tu me ~ ?** can you give me a push?; **peux-tu ~ ta voiture ?** can you move your car (out of the way)?; **pousse tes fesses !**⁎ shift your backside!⁎, shove over!⁎; **(ne) poussez pas, il y a des enfants !** don't push *ou* stop pushing, there are children here!; **il m'a poussé** he pushed me; **il y a une voiture qui me pousse au derrière*** *ou* **au cul***⁎ the car behind me is right up my backside* (*Brit*), there's a car riding my ass*⁎ (*US*); (*fig*) **faut pas ~ (grand-mère dans les orties) !**⁎ that's going a bit far!, you (*ou* he) must be kidding!⁎; (*fig*) **~ un peu loin le bouchon** to push it*, go a bit far; **ne pousse pas le bouchon trop loin** don't push it*, don't push your luck → **pointe**
b (= *stimuler*) [+ *élève, ouvrier*] to urge on, egg on, push; [+ *cheval*] to ride hard; [+ *moteur*] (*techniquement*) to soup up, hot up, hop up (*US*); (*en accélérant*) to flog* (*surtout Brit*), drive hard; [+ *voiture*] to drive hard *ou* fast; [+ *machine*] to work hard; [+ *feu*] to stoke up; [+ *chauffage*] to turn up; (= *mettre en*

valeur) [+ *candidat, protégé*] to push; [+ *dossier*] to help along; **c'est l'ambition qui le pousse** he is driven by ambition, it's ambition which drives him on; **dans ce lycée on pousse trop les élèves** the pupils are worked *ou* driven *ou* pushed too hard in this school; **ce prof l'a beaucoup poussé en maths** this teacher has really pushed him *ou* made him get on in maths; **pousse le son, on n'entend rien !** turn it up a bit, we can't hear a thing!

c **~ qn à faire qch** [*faim, curiosité*] to drive sb to do sth; [*personne*] (= *inciter*) to urge *ou* press sb to do sth; (= *persuader*) to persuade sb to do sth, talk sb into doing sth; **ses parents le poussent à entrer à l'université/vers une carrière médicale** his parents are urging *ou* encouraging *ou* pushing him to go to university/to take up a career in medicine; **c'est elle qui l'a poussé à acheter cette maison** she talked him into *ou* pushed him into buying this house; **son échec nous pousse à croire que ...** his failure leads us to think that ..., because of his failure we're tempted to think that ...; **~ qn au crime/au désespoir** to drive sb to crime/to despair; **~ qn à la consommation** to encourage sb to buy (*ou* eat *ou* drink *etc*); **~ qn à la dépense** to encourage sb to spend money; **le sentiment qui le poussait vers sa bien-aimée** the feeling which drove him to his beloved; **~ qn sur un sujet** to get sb onto a subject

d (= *poursuivre*) [+ *études, discussion*] to continue, carry on (with), go on with; [+ *avantage*] to press (home), follow up; [+ *affaire*] to follow up, pursue; [+ *marche, progression*] to continue, carry on with; **~ l'enquête/les recherches plus loin** to carry on *ou* press on with the inquiry/the research; **~ la curiosité/la plaisanterie un peu (trop) loin** to take curiosity/the joke a bit (too) far; **~ qch à la perfection** to carry *ou* bring sth to perfection; **il pousse les choses au noir** he always looks on the black side (of things) *ou* takes a black view of things; **il a poussé le dévouement/la gentillesse/la malhonnêteté jusqu'à faire ...** he was devoted/kind/dishonest enough to do ..., his devotion/kindness/dishonesty was such that he did ...; **~ l'indulgence jusqu'à la faiblesse** to carry indulgence to the point of weakness; **~ qn à bout** to push sb to breaking point, drive sb to his wits' end *ou* the limit

e [+ *cri, hurlement*] to let out, utter, give; [+ *soupir*] to heave, give; **~ des cris** to shout, scream; **~ des rugissements** to roar; **les enfants poussaient des cris perçants** the children were shrieking; **le chien poussait de petits jappements plaintifs** the dog was yelping pitifully; (*hum*) **~ la chansonnette** *ou* **la romance** ◊ **une** *ou* **une*** to sing a (little) song

2 VI **a** [*plante*] (= *sortir de terre*) to sprout; (= *se développer*) to grow; [*barbe, enfant*] to grow; [*dent*] to come through; [*ville*] to grow, expand; **alors, les enfants, ça pousse ?*** and how are the kids doing?*; **son bébé pousse bien*** her baby's growing well; **mes choux poussent bien** my cabbages are coming on *ou* doing nicely *ou* well; **tout pousse bien dans cette région** everything grows well in this region; **ils font ~ des tomates par ici** they grow tomatoes in these parts, this is a tomato-growing area; **la pluie fait ~ les mauvaises herbes** the rain makes the weeds grow; **ça pousse comme du chiendent** they grow like weeds; **il se fait** *ou* **se laisse ~ la barbe** he's growing a beard; **il se fait** *ou* **se laisse ~ les cheveux** he's growing his hair, he's letting his hair grow; **il a une dent qui pousse** he's cutting a tooth, he's got a tooth coming through; **~ comme un champignon** to be shooting up; **de nouvelles villes poussaient comme des champignons** new towns were springing up *ou* sprouting like mushrooms, new towns were mushrooming
b (= *faire un effort*) (*pour accoucher, aller à la*

selle) to push; (fig) **~ à la roue** to do a bit of pushing, push a bit; **~ (à la roue) pour que qn fasse qch** to keep nudging *ou* pushing sb to get him to do sth; (Fin) **~ à la hausse** to push prices up; (Fin) **~ à la baisse** to force prices down

[c] (= aller) **nous allons ~ un peu plus avant** we're going to go on *ou* push on a bit further; **~ jusqu'à Lyon** to go on *ou* push on as far as *ou* carry on to Lyons

[d] (* = exagérer) to go too far, overdo it; **tu pousses!** that's going a bit far!; **faut pas ~!** that's going a bit far!, that's overdoing it a bit!

[e] [vin] to referment in spring

[3] **se pousser** VPR [a] (= se déplacer) to move, shift; (= faire de la place) to move *ou* shift over (*ou* up *ou* along *ou* down); (en voiture) to move; **pousse-toi de là que je m'y mette*** move over and make room for me

[b] (= essayer de s'élever) **se ~ (dans la société)** to make one's way *ou* push o.s. up in society *ou* in the world

poussette [pusɛt] NF (pour enfant) pushchair (Brit), stroller (US); (à provisions) shopping trolley (Brit), shopping cart (US); (arg Cyclisme) push (given to a cyclist to spur him on in a race)

poussette-canne (pl **poussettes-cannes**) [pusɛtkan] NF baby buggy, (folding) stroller (US)

poussier [pusje] NM coaldust, screenings (SPÉC)

poussière [pusjɛʀ] [1] NF [a] (= particules) dust; **faire** *ou* **soulever de la ~** to raise a lot of dust; **prendre la ~** to collect *ou* gather dust; **faire la ~*** to do the dusting; **couvert de ~** dusty, covered in dust; **avoir une ~ dans l'œil** to have a speck of dust in one's eye; (frm) **leur ~ repose dans ces tombes** their ashes *ou* mortal remains lie in these tombs; (fig) **une ~ de** a myriad of; **réduire/tomber en ~** to reduce to/ crumble into dust

[b] (loc) **30 F et des ~s** just over 30 francs; **il a 50 ans et des ~s** he's just over 50; **il était 22 heures et des ~s** it was just gone *ou* a little after 10 o'clock

[2] COMP ► **poussière d'ange** (= drogue) angel dust ► **poussière de charbon** coaldust ► **poussière cosmique** cosmic dust ► **poussière d'étoiles** stardust ► **poussière d'or** gold dust ► **poussière radioactive** radioactive particles *ou* dust (NonC) ► **poussière volcanique** volcanic ash *ou* dust

poussiéreux, -euse [pusjeʀø, øz] ADJ (lit) dusty, covered in dust; (fig) fusty

poussif, -ive [pusif, iv] ADJ [personne] wheezy, short-winded; [cheval] broken-winded; [moteur] puffing, wheezing; [style] laboured (Brit), labored (US)

poussin [pusɛ̃] NM [a] (Zool) chick; (terme affectueux) **mon ~!** pet!, poppet!* [b] (Sport) under eleven, junior [c] (arg Mil) first-year cadet in the air force

poussivement [pusivmɑ̃] ADV **il monta ~ la côte/l'escalier** he wheezed up *ou* puffed up the hill/the stairs

poussoir [puswaʀ] NM [sonnette] button; (Aut) **~ (de soupape)** tappet

poutre [putʀ] NF (en bois) beam; (en métal) girder; (Gym) beam; **~s apparentes** exposed beams → **maître, paille**

poutrelle [putʀɛl] NF (en bois) beam; (en métal) girder

poutser [putse] ▶ conjug 1 ◀ VT (Helv) to clean

▼**pouvoir¹** [puvwaʀ]

▶ conjug 33 ◀
| [1] VERBE AUXILIAIRE | [3] VERBE TRANSITIF |
| [2] VERBE IMPERSONNEL | [4] VERBE PRONOMINAL |

[1] VERBE AUXILIAIRE
[a] permission

Lorsque **pouvoir** *exprime la permission donnée par le locuteur à quelqu'un, il peut se traduire par* can *ou* may ; can *est le plus courant et couvre la majorité des cas ;* may *appartient à une langue plus soutenue et indique nettement un ton de supériorité.*

tu peux le garder si tu veux you can keep it if you want; **maintenant, tu peux aller jouer** now you can *ou* may go and play; **vous pouvez desservir** you can *ou* may (frm) clear the table

On emploie can *ou* be allowed to *lorsque la permission dépend d'une tierce personne ou d'une autorité.*

vous ne pouvez pas avoir accès à ces documents you are not allowed access to these documents; **crois-tu qu'il pourra venir?** do you think he'll be allowed to come?; **sa mère a dit qu'il ne pouvait pas rester** his mother said he couldn't stay *ou* wasn't (allowed) to stay; **on ne peut pas marcher sur les pelouses** you can't walk *ou* you aren't allowed to walk on the grass; **elle ne pourra lui rendre visite qu'une fois par semaine** she'll only be allowed to visit him once a week; **arrêtez de la taquiner! — si on ne peut plus s'amuser maintenant!** stop teasing her! — we can have a bit of fun, can't we?

Notez l'usage de have to, be obliged to *lorsque la proposition infinitive est une négative.*

il peut ne pas venir he doesn't have to come, he's not obliged to come; **tu peux très bien ne pas accepter** you don't have to accept

[b] demande

Lorsque l'on demande à quelqu'un la permission de faire quelque chose, on utilise can *ou la forme plus polie* could ; may *appartient à un registre plus soutenu et* might *appartient à une langue très recherchée.*

est-ce que je peux fermer la fenêtre? ◊ **puis-je** (frm) **fermer la fenêtre?** can I *ou* may I (frm) shut the window?; **puis-je emprunter votre stylo?** can *ou* could *ou* may I borrow your pen?; **pourrais-je vous parler?** ◊ **puis-je** (frm) **vous parler?** can *ou* could *ou* may I (frm) I have a word with you?; **puis-je vous être utile?** can I be of any help (to you)?, can *ou* may I be of assistance?

Lorsque l'on demande un service à quelqu'un ou qu'on lui donne un ordre poli, on utilise can *ou la forme plus courtoise* could.

tu peux m'ouvrir la porte, s'il te plaît? can you *ou* could you open the door for me, please?; **pourriez-vous nous apporter du thé?** could you bring us some tea?

[c] = avoir de bonnes raisons pour should; **je suis désolé — tu peux (l'être)!** I'm sorry — so you should be!; **ils se sont excusés — ils peuvent!** they said they were sorry — I should think they did!; **elle s'est plainte/a demandé une indemnité — elle peut!** she complained/demanded compensation — I should think she did!

[d] possibilité

Lorsque **pouvoir** *exprime une possibilité ou une capacité physique, intellectuelle ou psychologique, il se traduit généralement par* can *ou par* be able to ; can *étant un verbe défectif,* be able to *le remplace aux temps où il ne peut être conjugué.*

peut-il venir? can he come?; **ne peut-il pas venir?** can't he come?, isn't he able to come?; **il ne peut pas ne pas venir** he can't not come; **il ne peut pas venir** he can't come, he isn't able to *ou* is unable to come; **peut-il marcher sans canne?** can he walk *ou* is he able to walk without a stick?; **il ne pourra plus jamais marcher** he will never be able to walk again; **je ne peux que vous féliciter** I can only congratulate you; **je voudrais ~ vous aider** I would like to be able to help you, I wish I could help you; **il pourrait venir demain si vous aviez besoin de lui** he could come tomorrow if you needed him; **il aurait pu venir s'il avait été prévenu plus tôt** he

could have come *ou* he would have been able to come if he had been told earlier; **il n'a (pas) pu** *ou* **ne put** (littér) **venir** he couldn't come, he wasn't able to *ou* was unable to come; **comment as-tu pu (faire ça)!** how could you (do such a thing)!; **la salle peut contenir 100 personnes** the auditorium can seat 100 people; **la nouvelle moto pourra faire du 300 km/h** the new motorcycle will be able to do 300 km/h; **c'est fait de telle manière qu'on ne puisse pas l'ouvrir** it's made so that it's impossible to open *ou* so that you can't open it; **j'ai essayé de le joindre, mais je n'ai pas pu** I tried to get in touch with him but I couldn't *ou* but I wasn't able to; **à l'époque, je pouvais soulever 100 kg** in those days, I could lift *ou* I was able to lift 100 kilos; **on peut dire ce qu'on veut, les diplômes c'est utile** whatever anyone says *ou* you can say what you like, a degree is useful

Lorsque **pouvoir** *implique la notion de réussite, on peut également employer* to manage ; *dans ces exemples,* can, could *ne peuvent pas être utilisés.*

il a pu réparer la machine à laver he was able to *ou* he managed to fix the washing machine; **tu as pu lui téléphoner?** did you manage to phone him?

[e] probabilité, hypothèse

Lorsque **pouvoir** *exprime une probabilité, une éventualité, une hypothèse ou un risque, il se traduit par* may *ou* could ; might *implique une plus grande incertitude.*

il peut être italien he may *ou* could *ou* might be Italian; **peut-il être italien?** could *ou* might he be Italian?; **il peut ne pas être italien** he may *ou* might not be Italian; **il pourrait être italien** he might *ou* could be Italian; **ça peut laisser une cicatrice** it might leave a scar; **ça aurait pu être un voleur!** it might *ou* could have been a burglar!; **vous pourriez en avoir besoin** you may *ou* might need it; **les cambrioleurs ont pu entrer par la fenêtre** the burglars could *ou* may *ou* might have got in through the window; **il pouvait être 2 heures du matin** it could *ou* may *ou* might have been 2 o'clock in the morning; **cela pourrait arriver** that might *ou* could happen; MAIS **il ne peut pas être italien** he can't be Italian; **une lettre peut toujours se perdre** letters can *ou* do get lost

♦ **bien + pouvoir** : **il pourrait bien avoir raison** he could *ou* may *ou* might well be right; **où ai-je bien pu mettre mon stylo?** where on earth can I have put my pen?; **qu'est-ce qu'elle a bien pu lui raconter?** what on earth can she have told him?; **qu'est-ce qu'il peut bien faire?** what on earth is he doing?, what CAN he be doing?; **tu pourrais bien le regretter** you may *ou* might well regret it; **il a très bien pu entrer sans qu'on le voie** he could very well have come in without anyone seeing him; MAIS **qu'est-ce que cela peut bien lui faire?*** what's it to him?*

[f] suggestion could, can; **je pourrais venir te chercher** I could come and pick you up; **tu peux bien lui prêter ton livre!** you can lend him your book, can't you?, surely you can lend him your book; **il peut bien faire cela** that's the least he can do

might *peut être utilisé pour exprimer l'agacement.* **elle pourrait arriver à l'heure!** she might *ou* could at least be on time!; **tu aurais pu me dire ça plus tôt!** you might *ou* could have told me sooner!

[g] souhaits

Dans une langue soutenue, **pouvoir** *s'utilise au subjonctif pour exprimer les souhaits ; il se traduit alors différemment selon les contextes.*

puisse Dieu/le ciel les aider! (may) God/Heaven help them!; **puisse-t-il guérir rapidement!** let's hope he makes a speedy recovery!; **puissiez-vous dire vrai!** let's pray *ou* hope you're right!; **puissé-je le revoir un jour!** I only hope I see him again one day!

> GRAMMAIRE ACTIVE : **pouvoir** 28.1, 30, 31, 36, 42, 43

pouvoir (cont.)

2 VERBE IMPERSONNEL

La probabilité, l'éventualité, l'hypothèse ou le risque sont rendues par may *ou* could *;* might *implique une plus grande incertitude.*

il peut *ou* pourrait pleuvoir it may *ou* could *ou* might rain; il pourrait y avoir du monde there may *ou* could *ou* might be a lot of people there; il aurait pu y avoir un accident! there could have been an accident!; il pourrait s'agir d'un assassinat it could be murder; il pourrait se faire qu'elle ne soit pas chez elle she may *ou* might well not be at home

3 VERBE TRANSITIF

a = être capable ou avoir la possibilité de faire
est-ce qu'on peut quelque chose pour lui? is there anything we can do for him?; il partira dès qu'il (le) pourra he will leave as soon as he can; il fait ce qu'il peut he does what he can; il a fait tout ce qu'il a pu he did all he could *ou* everything in his power; il peut beaucoup he can do a lot; *(frm)* que puis-je pour vous? what can I do for you?; can I do anything to help you? ■ *(PROV)* qui peut le plus peut le moins he who can do more can do less

♦ **n'y pouvoir rien** : on n'y peut rien it can't be helped, nothing can be done about it; désolé, mais je n'y peux rien I'm sorry, but I can't do anything *ou* there's nothing I can do about it; la justice ne peut rien contre eux the law is powerless *ou* can do nothing against them; je ne peux rien faire pour vous I can't do anything for you

b

♦ **on ne peut plus/mieux** : il a été on ne peut plus aimable/prudent he couldn't have been kinder/more careful; il a été on ne peut plus clair he couldn't have made it clearer; c'est on ne peut mieux it couldn't be better; elle le connaît on ne peut mieux no one knows him better than she does; ils sont on ne peut plus mal avec leurs voisins they couldn't be on worse terms with their neighbours, they're on the worst possible terms with their neighbours

c

♦ **n'en pouvoir plus** : je n'en peux plus *(fatigue)* I'm worn out *ou* exhausted, I've had it*; *(énervement)* I've had it (up to here)*; *(désespoir)* I can't go on, I can't take it any longer, I can't take any more; *(impatience)* I can't stand it any longer; je n'en pouvais plus dans la montée I tired myself out on the way up; ma voiture n'en peut plus *(usée)* my car's had it*; regarde-le sur sa moto, il n'en peut plus!* *(de fierté)* look at him on that motorbike, he's as proud as punch!

d

♦ **n'en pouvoir plus de** + *nom* : elle n'en pouvait plus de joie she was beside herself with joy; je n'en pouvais plus de honte I was absolutely mortified; ils n'en peuvent plus des humiliations they can't take any more humiliation, they've had enough of being humiliated; elle n'en peut plus de leur machisme she's had enough of their macho attitude

♦ **n'en pouvoir plus de** + *infinitif* : il n'en peut plus d'attendre he's fed up with waiting*, he can't bear to wait any longer; je n'en pouvais plus de rire I laughed so much it hurt

d

♦ **n'en pouvoir mais** *(littér)* il n'en pouvait mais he could do nothing about it

4 **se pouvoir** VERBE PRONOMINAL

L'éventualité, l'hypothèse ou le risque sont rendus par may, might, could, be possible *ou un adverbe.*

ça se peut* possibly, perhaps, maybe, it's possible; tu crois qu'il va pleuvoir? — ça se pourrait bien do you think it's going to rain? — it might; ça ne se peut pas* that's impossible, that's not possible; essayez, s'il se peut, de la convaincre *(frm)* try to convince her, if at all possible

♦ **il se peut/se pourrait que** + *subjonctif* : il se

peut/se pourrait qu'elle vienne she may/might come; il se pourrait bien qu'il pleuve it might *ou* could well rain; se peut-il que ...? is it possible that ...?, could *ou* might it be that ...?; comment se peut-il que le dossier soit perdu? how can the file possibly be lost?; il se peut, éventuellement, que ... it may possibly be that ...

pouvoir² [puvwaʀ] 1 NM a (= faculté) power; (= capacité) ability, capacity; (Phys) power; **avoir le ~ de faire qch** to have the power *ou* ability to do sth; **il a le ~ de se faire des amis partout** he has the ability *ou* he is able to make friends everywhere; **il a un extraordinaire ~ d'éloquence/de conviction** he has remarkable *ou* exceptional powers of oratory/of persuasion; **ce n'est pas en mon ~** it's not within *ou* in my power, it's beyond my power; **il n'est pas en son ~ de vous aider** it's beyond *ou* it doesn't lie within his power to help you; **il fera tout ce qui est en son ~** he will do everything (that is) in his power *ou* all that he possibly can; **~ absorbant** absorption power, absorption factor *(SPÉC)*; **~ d'attraction** [ville, idée] appeal, attractiveness; **~ couvrant/éclairant** covering/lighting power
b (= autorité) power; (= influence) influence; **avoir beaucoup de ~** to have a lot of power *ou* influence, be very powerful *ou* influential; **avoir du ~ sur** to have influence *ou* power over sb; **n'avoir aucun ~ sur qn** to have no influence *ou* authority over sb; **le père a ~ sur ses enfants** a father has power over his children; **tenir qn en son ~** to hold sb in one's power; **le pays entier est en son ~** the whole country is in his power, he has the whole country in his power; **avoir du ~ sur soi-même** to have self-control; **le troisième ~** (= magistrature) the magistracy; **le quatrième ~** (= presse) the press, the fourth estate
c (= droit, attribution) power; **dépasser ses ~s** to exceed one's powers; **en vertu des ~s qui me sont conférés** by virtue of the power which has been vested in me; **séparation des ~s** separation *ou* division of powers; **avoir ~ de faire qch** (autorisation) to have authority to do sth; (droit) to have the right to do sth; **je n'ai pas ~ pour vous répondre** I have no authority to reply to you → **plein**
d (Pol) **le ~** (= direction des pays) power; (= dirigeants) the government; **~ absolu** absolute power; **~ central** central government; **le parti (politique) au ~** the (political) party in power *ou* in office, the ruling party; **avoir le ~** to have *ou* hold power; **exercer le ~** to exercise power, rule, govern; **prendre le ~** ◊ **arriver au ~** (légalement) to come to power *ou* into office; (illégalement) to seize power; **prise de** *ou* **du ~** (légal) coming to power; (illégal, par la force) seizure of power; **des milieux proches du ~** sources close to the government; **le ~ actuel dans ce pays** the present régime in this country; **l'opinion et le ~** public opinion and the authorities, us and them*
e (Jur = procuration) proxy; **~ par-devant notaire** power of attorney; **donner ~ à qn de faire qch** to give sb proxy to do sth (Jur), empower sb to do, give sb authority to do → **fondé**

2 COMP ► **pouvoir d'achat** purchasing *ou* buying power ► **pouvoir de concentration** powers of concentration ► **les pouvoirs constitués** the powers that be ► **pouvoir de décision** decision-making power(s) ► **pouvoir disciplinaire** disciplinary power(s) ► **pouvoirs exceptionnels** emergency powers ► **le pouvoir exécutif** executive power ► **le pouvoir judiciaire** judicial power ► **le pouvoir législatif** legislative power ► **pouvoirs publics** authorities ► **pouvoir spirituel** spiritual power ► **pouvoir temporel** temporal power

p.p. (ABRÉV = per procurationem) p.p.

pp (ABRÉV = **pages**) pp

ppcm [pepeseem] NM (ABRÉV = **plus petit commun multiple**) LCM

PQ [peky] 1 NM ABRÉV = **Parti québécois** et de **Province de Québec** 2 NM (* = papier hygiénique) bog paper* (Brit), loo paper* (Brit), TP* (US)

PR [peɛʀ] 1 NM (ABRÉV = **parti républicain**) French political party 2 NF (ABRÉV = **poste restante**) → **poste¹**

Pr (ABRÉV = **professeur**) Prof

practice [pʀaktis] NM [golf] driving range

præsidium [pʀezidjɔm] NM praesidium; **le ~ suprême** the praesidium of the Supreme Soviet

pragmatique [pʀagmatik] 1 ADJ pragmatic 2 NF **la ~** pragmatics sg

pragmatisme [pʀagmatism] NM pragmatism

pragmatiste [pʀagmatist] 1 ADJ pragmatic, pragmatist 2 NMF pragmatist

Prague [pʀag] N Prague

Praia [pʀaja] N Praia

praire [pʀɛʀ] NF clam

prairial [pʀeʀjal] NM Prairial (ninth month of French Republican calendar)

prairie [pʀeʀi] NF meadow; (aux USA) **la ~** the prairie; **des hectares de ~** acres of grassland

pralin [pʀalɛ̃] NM (Culin) praline (filling for chocolates)

praline [pʀalin] NF a (Culin) (à l'amande) praline, sugared almond; (à la cacahuète) caramelized peanut; (Belg = chocolat) chocolate b (* = balle) bullet

praliné, e [pʀaline] 1 ADJ [amande] sugared; [glace, crème] praline-flavoured 2 NM praline-flavoured ice cream

prame [pʀam] NF (Naut) pram, praam

praséodyme [pʀazeodim] NM praseodymium

praticable [pʀatikabl] 1 ADJ a [projet, moyen, opération] practicable, feasible; [chemin] passable, negotiable, practicable; **route difficilement ~ en hiver** road which is almost impassable in winter b (Théât) [porte, décor] working 2 NM (Théât = décor) piece of working scenery; (Ciné = plate-forme) gantry; (Sport) floor mat

praticien, -ienne [pʀatisjɛ̃, jɛn] NM,F (gén, Méd) practitioner; **~ hospitalier** hospital doctor

pratiquant, e [pʀatikɑ̃, ɑ̃t] 1 ADJ practising (épith), practicing (épith) (US); **catholique/juif/musulman ~** (allant à l'église) he's/he isn't a regular churchgoer, he goes to *ou* attends/he doesn't go to church regularly; **c'est un catholique non ~** he's a non-practising Catholic; **elle n'est pas ~e** she isn't a practising Christian (*ou* Catholic etc) 2 NM,F practising Christian (*ou* Catholic etc); (qui va à l'église) (regular) churchgoer; (= adepte) follower; **cette religion compte 30 millions de ~s** the religion has 30 million followers *ou* 30 million faithful

pratique [pʀatik] 1 ADJ a (= non théorique) [jugement, connaissance] practical; (Scol) [exercice, cours] practical; **considération d'ordre ~** practical consideration → **travail¹**
b (= réaliste) [personne] practical(-minded); **il faut être ~ dans la vie** you have to be practical in life; **avoir le sens** *ou* **l'esprit ~** to be practical-minded
c (= commode) [livre, moyen, vêtement, solution] practical; [instrument] practical, handy; [emploi du temps] convenient; **c'est très ~, j'habite à côté du bureau** it's very convenient *ou* handy, I live next door to the office

2 NF a (= application) practice; **dans la ~** in practice; **dans la ~ de tous les jours** in the ordinary run of things, in the normal course of events; **en ~** in practice; **mettre qch en ~** to put sth into practice; **la mise en ~ ne sera pas**

aisée putting it into practice won't be easy, it won't be easy to put it into practice *ou* to carry it out in practice

b (= *expérience*) practical experience; **il a une longue ~ des élèves** he has a lot of practical teaching experience; **il a perdu la ~** he is out of practice, he's lost the knack; **avoir la ~ du monde††** to be well-versed in *ou* be familiar with the ways of society

c (= *coutume, procédé*) practice; **c'est une ~ générale** it is widespread practice; **des ~s malhonnêtes** dishonest practices, sharp practice; **~s religieuses/sexuelles** religious/sexual practices

d (= *exercice, observance*) [*règle*] observance; [*médecine*] practising, exercise; [*sport*] practising; [*vertu*] exercise, practice; **la ~ de l'escrime/du cheval/du golf développe les réflexes** fencing/horse-riding/golfing *ou* (playing) golf develops the reflexes; **la ~ du yoga** the practice of yoga, doing yoga; **~ (religieuse)** religious practice *ou* observance; **condamné pour ~ illégale de la médecine** convicted of practising medicine illegally

e (†† = *clientèle*) [*commerçant*] custom (*NonC*), clientele (*NonC*); [*avocat*] practice, clientele (*NonC*); **donner sa ~ à un commerçant** to give a tradesman one's custom

f (†† = *client*) [*commerçant*] customer; [*avocat*] client

g (†† = *fréquentation*) [*personne, société*] frequenting, frequentation [*auteur*] close study

pratiquement [pratikmɑ̃] ADV (= *en pratique, en réalité*) in practice; (= *presque*) practically, virtually; **c'est la même chose ◊ ça revient au même** it's practically *ou* basically the same (thing); **il n'y en a ~ plus** there are virtually *ou* practically none left, there are hardly any left; **je ne l'ai ~ jamais utilisé** I've hardly ever used it; **je ne les ai ~ pas vus** I hardly saw them; **~, la méthode consiste à ...** in practical terms, the method involves ...

▼ **pratiquer** [pratike] ▶ conjug 1 ◀ **1** VT **a** (= *mettre en pratique*) [+ *philosophie, politique*] to put into practice, practise (*Brit*), practice (*US*); [+ *règle*] to observe; [+ *vertu, charité*] to practise (*Brit*), practice (*US*), exercise; [+ *religion*] to practise (*Brit*), practice (*US*)

b (= *exercer*) [+ *profession, art*] to practise (*Brit*), practice (*US*); [+ *football, golf*] to play; **~ l'escrime/le cheval/la pêche** to go fencing/horse-riding/fishing; **~ la photo** to go in for photography; **il est recommandé de ~ un sport** it is considered advisable to play *ou* practise *ou* do a sport; **ils pratiquent l'exploitation systématique du touriste** they systematically exploit tourists

c (= *faire*) [+ *ouverture, trou*] to make; [+ *route*] to make, build; [*Méd*] [+ *intervention*] to carry out (**sur** on)

d (= *utiliser*) [+ *méthode*] to practise (*Brit*), practice (*US*), use; [+ *système*] to use; **~ le chantage** to use blackmail; **~ le bluff** to bluff

e (*Comm*) [+ *rabais*] go give; **ils pratiquent des prix élevés** they keep their prices high

f (†† = *fréquenter*) [+ *auteur*] to study closely; [+ *personne, haute société*] to frequent

2 VI **a** (*Rel*) to practise (*Brit*) *ou* practice (*US*) one's religion *ou* faith, be a practising (*Brit*) *ou* practicing (*US*) Christian (*ou* Muslim *etc*); (= *aller à l'église*) to go to church, be a churchgoer

b (*Méd*) to be in practice, have a practice

3 se pratiquer VPR [*méthode*] to be used; [*religion*] to be practised (*Brit*) *ou* practiced (*US*); [*sport*] to be played; **cela se pratique encore dans les villages** it is still the practice in the villages; **comme cela se pratique en général** as is the usual practice; **les prix qui se pratiquent à Paris** Paris prices; **le vaudou se pratique encore dans cette région** voodoo is still practised in this region

praxis [praksis] NF praxis

Praxitèle [praksitɛl] NM Praxiteles

pré [pre] **1** NM meadow; (*Hist*) **aller sur le ~** to fight a duel; **mettre un cheval au ~** to put a horse out to pasture **2** COMP ▶ **pré carré** private preserve *ou* domain *ou* territory

pré... [pre] PRÉF pre...

préachat, pré-achat (*pl* pré-achats) [preaʃa] NM [*billet*] buying in advance, advance purchasing; [*film, droits de diffusion*] buying up

pré-acheter [preaʃ(ə)te] ▶ conjug 1 ◀ VT [+ *billet*] to buy *ou* purchase in advance; [+ *film, scénario*] to buy up

préadolescent, e [preadɔlesɑ̃, ɑ̃t] **1** ADJ preadolescent, pre-teenage (*épith*) **2** NM,F preadolescent, pre-teenager

préalable [prealabl] **1** ADJ [*entretien, condition, étude*] preliminary; [*accord, avis*] prior, previous; **faites un essai ~ sur une petite zone** test first on a small area; **~ à** preceding; **lors des entretiens ~s aux négociations** during the discussions (which took place) prior to the negotiations; **vous ne pouvez pas partir sans l'accord ~ du directeur** you cannot leave without first obtaining the director's permission *ou* without the prior agreement of the director; **sans avis** *ou* **avertissement ~** without prior *ou* previous notice **2** NM (= *condition*) precondition, prerequisite; († = *préparation*) preliminary; **poser qch comme ~ à** to lay sth down as a preliminary condition for; **au ~** first, beforehand

préalablement [prealabləmɑ̃] ADV first, beforehand; **~ à** prior to; **~ à toute négociation** before any negotiation can take place, prior to any negotiation

Préalpes [prealp] NFPL **les ~** the Pre-Alps

préalpin, e [prealpɛ̃, in] ADJ of the Pre-Alps

préambule [preɑ̃byl] NM [*discours, loi*] preamble (**de** to); [*contrat*] recitals; (= *prélude*) prelude (**de** to); **sans ~** without any preliminaries, straight off

préau (*pl* préaux) [preo] NM [*école*] covered playground; [*prison*] (exercise) yard; [*couvent*] inner courtyard; **sous le ~ de l'école** in the covered part of the school playground

préavis [preavi] NM (advance) notice; **un ~ d'un mois** a month's notice *ou* warning; **~ de licenciement** notice (of termination); **~ de grève** strike notice; **déposer un ~ de grève** to give notice *ou* warning of strike action; **sans ~** [*faire grève, partir*] without (previous) notice, without advance warning; [*retirer de l'argent*] on demand, without advance *ou* previous notice

prébende [prebɑ̃d] NF (*Rel*) prebend; (*péj*) emoluments, payment (*NonC*)

prébendé, e [prebɑ̃de] ADJ prebendal

prébendier [prebɑ̃dje] NM prebendary

précaire [prekɛr] ADJ [*position, situation, bonheur, équilibre, paix*] precarious; [*emploi*] insecure; [*santé*] shaky, precarious; [*abri*] makeshift; (*Jur*) **possesseur/possession (à titre) ~** precarious holder/tenure

précairement [prekɛrmɑ̃] ADV precariously

précambrien, -ienne [prekɑ̃brijɛ̃, ijɛn] ADJ, NM Precambrian

précancéreux, -euse [prekɑ̃serø, øz] ADJ [*état, lésion*] precancerous

précarisation [prekarizasjɔ̃] NF [*situation*] jeopardizing; [*emploi*] casualization

précariser [prekarize] ▶ conjug 1 ◀ VT [+ *situation, statut*] to jeopardize; [+ *emploi*] to make insecure; **un tel taux de chômage précarise la société** such a high unemployment rate is a threat to *ou* undermines social stability

précarité [prekarite] NF (*gén, Jur*) precariousness; **~ de l'emploi** lack of job security; **prime/indemnité de ~** bonus/allowance paid to an employee to compensate for lack of job security; **la ~ des installations nucléaires** the haz-

ards of *ou* the potential dangers of nuclear plants

précaution [prekosjɔ̃] NF **a** (= *disposition*) precaution; **prendre la ~ de faire qch** to take the precaution of doing sth; **prendre des** *ou* **ses ~s** to take precautions; **s'entourer de ~s** to take a lot of precautions; **prendre** *ou* **s'entourer de ~s oratoires** to choose one's words with great care; **il ne s'est pas embarrassé de ~s oratoires** he didn't beat about the bush; **faire qch avec les plus grandes ~s** to do sth with the utmost care *ou* with the greatest precaution; **~s d'emploi** (*pour appareil*) safety instructions; (*pour médicament*) precautions before use → **deux b** (= *prudence*) caution, care; **avec ~** cautiously; **« à manipuler avec ~ »** "handle with care"; **par ~** as a precaution (**contre** against); **par mesure de ~** as a precautionary measure; **pour plus de ~** to be on the safe side; **sans ~** carelessly

précautionner (se) [prekosjɔne] ▶ conjug 1 ◀ VPR to take precautions (**contre** against)

précautionneusement [prekosjɔnøzmɑ̃] ADV (= *par précaution*) cautiously; (= *avec soin*) carefully

précautionneux, -euse [prekosjɔnø, øz] ADJ (= *prudent*) cautious; (= *soigneux*) careful

précédemment [presedamɑ̃] ADV before, previously

précédent, e [presedɑ̃, ɑ̃t] **1** ADJ previous; **un discours/article ~** a previous *ou* an earlier speech/article; **le discours/film ~** the preceding *ou* previous speech/film; **le jour/mois ~** the previous day/month, the day/month before **2** NM (= *fait, décision*) precedent; **sans ~** unprecedented, without precedent; **créer un ~** to create *ou* set a precedent

précéder [presede] ▶ conjug 6 ◀ **1** VT **a** (= *venir avant*) (*dans le temps, dans une hiérarchie*) to precede, come before; (*dans l'espace*) to precede, be in front of, come before; (*dans une file de véhicules*) to be in front *ou* ahead of, precede; **les jours qui ont précédé le coup d'État** the days preceding *ou* leading up to the coup d'état; **être précédé de** to be preceded by; **faire ~ son discours d'un préambule** to precede one's speech by *ou* preface one's speech with an introduction, give a short introduction to one's speech

b (= *devancer*) (*dans le temps, l'espace*) to precede, go in front *ou* ahead of; (*dans une carrière etc*) to precede, get ahead of; **quand j'y suis arrivé, j'ai vu que quelqu'un m'avait précédé** when I got there I saw that someone had got there before me *ou* ahead of me *ou* had preceded me; **il la précéda dans la chambre** he went into the room in front of him, he entered the room ahead of *ou* in front of him; **il m'a précédé de cinq minutes** he got there five minutes before me *ou* ahead of me; **sa mauvaise réputation l'avait précédé** his bad reputation had gone before *ou* preceded him

2 VI to precede, go before; **les jours qui ont précédé** the preceding days; **dans tout ce qui a précédé** in all that has been said (*ou* written *etc*) before *ou* so far; **dans le chapitre/la semaine qui précède** in the preceding chapter/week

précepte [presept] NM precept

précepteur [preseptœr] NM private tutor

préceptorat [preseptɔra] NM tutorship, tutorage (*frm*)

préceptrice [preseptris] NF governess

préchauffage [preʃofaʒ] NM preheating

préchauffer [preʃofe] ▶ conjug 1 ◀ VT to preheat

prêche [prɛʃ] NM (*lit, fig*) sermon

prêcher [preʃe] ▶ conjug 1 ◀ **1** VT **a** (*Rel, fig*) to preach; [+ *personne*] to preach to; **~ un converti** to preach to the converted → **parole** **b** (= *recommander*) [+ *modération, non-violence, tolérance*] to advocate; **~ le faux pour**

▶ GRAMMAIRE ACTIVE: **pratiquer** 46.2

savoir le vrai to make false statements in order to discover the truth [2] VI (*Rel*) to preach; (*fig*) to preach, preachify, sermonize; (*fig*) **dans le désert** to preach in the wilderness; **~ d'exemple** *ou* **par l'exemple** to practise what one preaches, preach by example; **~ pour son saint** *ou* **sa paroisse** to look after one's own interests, look after *ou* take care of number one*

prêcheur, -euse [pʀeʃœʀ, øz] [1] ADJ [*personne, ton*] moralizing; (*Rel*) **frères ~s** preaching friars [2] NM,F (*Rel*) preacher; (*fig*) moralizer

prêchi-prêcha [pʀeʃipʀeʃa] NM INV (*péj*) preachifying (*NonC*), continuous moralizing (*NonC*) *ou* sermonizing (*NonC*)

précieusement [pʀesjøzmɑ̃] ADV [a] (= *soigneusement*) [*conserver*] carefully; **garde ces lettres** ~ take great care of these letters [b] (= *de manière affectée*) [*parler*] in an affected manner

précieux, -ieuse [pʀesjø, jøz] [1] ADJ [a] (= *de valeur*) [*pierre, métal, bois, bijou*] precious [b] (= *très utile*) [*collaborateur, aide, conseil*] invaluable (à to); **votre aide m'est précieuse** your help is invaluable to me [c] (= *cher*) [*ami*] valued, precious [d] (= *affecté*) precious, affected [e] (*Littérat*) [*écrivain, salon*] précieux, precious [2] **précieuse** NF précieuse

préciosité [pʀesjozite] NF [a] **la ~** (*Littérat*) preciosity; (= *affectation*) preciosity, affectation [b] (= *formule, trait*) stylistic affectation, euphuism (*frm*)

précipice [pʀesipis] NM [a] (= *gouffre*) chasm; (= *paroi abrupte*) precipice; **un ~ de plusieurs centaines de mètres** a drop of several hundred metres; **la voiture s'immobilisa au bord du ~/tomba dans le ~** the car stopped at the very edge *ou* brink of the precipice/went over the precipice; **ne t'aventure pas près du ~** you mustn't go too near the edge [b] (*fig*) abyss; **être au bord du ~** to be at the edge of the abyss

précipitamment [pʀesipitamɑ̃] ADV hurriedly, hastily, precipitately (*frm*); **sortir ~** to rush *ou* dash out

précipitation [pʀesipitasjɔ̃] [1] NF [a] (= *hâte*) haste; (= *hâte excessive*) great haste, violent hurry; **dans ma ~, je l'ai oublié chez moi** in my haste, I left it at home; **avec ~** in great haste, in a great rush *ou* hurry [2] (*Chim*) precipitation [2] **précipitations** NFPL (*Mét*) rainfall, precipitation; **de fortes ~s** heavy rainfall; **de nouvelles ~s sont prévues** more rain is forecast

précipité, e [pʀesipite] (*ptp de* **précipiter**) [1] ADJ [*départ, décision*] hurried, hasty, precipitate (*frm*); [*fuite*] headlong; [*pas*] hurried; [*pouls, respiration, rythme*] fast, rapid; **tout cela est trop ~** it's all happening too fast [2] NM (*Chim*) precipitate

précipiter [pʀesipite] ▸ conjug 1 ◂ [1] VT [a] (= *jeter*) [+ *personne*] to throw, push; [+ *objet*] to throw, hurl (**contre** against, at, **vers** towards, at); **~ qn du haut d'une falaise** to push sb off a cliff; **~ qn dans un escalier** to push sb downstairs; **le choc l'a précipité contre le pare-brise** the shock threw *ou* hurled him against the windscreen; **~ qn dans le malheur** to plunge sb into misfortune [b] (= *hâter*) [+ *pas*] to quicken, speed up; [+ *événement*] to hasten, precipitate; [+ *départ*] to hasten; **il ne faut rien ~** we mustn't be too hasty, we mustn't rush things [c] (*Chim*) to precipitate [2] VI (*Chim*) to precipitate [3] **se précipiter** VPR [a] (= *se jeter*) [*personne*] **se ~ dans le vide** to hurl o.s. into empty space; **se ~ du haut d'une falaise** to jump off *ou* throw o.s. off a cliff [b] (= *se ruer*) **se ~ vers** to rush *ou* race towards; **se ~ sur** to rush at; **se ~ contre** [*personne*] to rush at, throw o.s. against;

[*voiture*] to smash into; **se ~ au devant de qn/aux pieds de qn** to throw o.s. in front of sb/at sb's feet; **se ~ sur l'ennemi** to rush at *ou* hurl o.s. on *ou* at the enemy; **elle se précipita dans ses bras** she rushed into *ou* threw herself into *ou* flew into his arms; **il se précipita à la porte pour ouvrir** he rushed to open the door; **il se précipita sur le balcon** he raced *ou* dashed *ou* rushed out onto the balcony [c] (= *s'accélérer*) [*rythme*] to speed up; [*pouls*] to quicken, speed up; **les choses** *ou* **événements se précipitaient** everything was happening at once [d] (= *se dépêcher*) to hurry, rush; **ne nous précipitons pas** let's not rush things

précis, e [pʀesi, iz] [1] ADJ [a] (= *exact*) [*style, vocabulaire, terme, indication, témoignage*] precise; [*sens*] precise, exact; [*description*] accurate, precise; [*chiffre, calcul*] accurate, precise; [*instrument, tir, montre*] accurate; **sois plus ~ dans le choix de tes mots** be more precise in your choice of words, choose your words more carefully [b] (= *bien défini, particulier*) [*idée, donnée, règle*] precise, definite; [*heure, date*] precise, exact; [*ordre, demande*] precise; [*fait, raison*] precise, particular, specific; [*souvenir*] clear; **sans raison ~e** for no particular *ou* precise reason; **sans but ~** with no clear aim, with no particular aim in mind; **je ne pense à rien de ~** I'm not thinking of anything in particular; **à cet instant ~** at that precise *ou* very moment; **au moment ~ où ...** at the precise *ou* exact *ou* very moment when ...; **à 4 heures ~es** at 4 o'clock sharp *ou* on the dot*, at 4 o'clock precisely; **à l'endroit ~ où...** at the exact place where...; **sans que l'on puisse dire de façon ~e ...** although we can't say precisely *ou* with any precision ...; **se référer à un texte de façon ~e** to make precise reference to a text [c] (= *net*) [*point*] precise, exact; [*contours*] precise, distinct; [*geste, esprit*] precise; [*trait*] distinct [2] NM (= *résumé*) précis, summary; (= *manuel*) handbook

▼ **précisément** [pʀesizemɑ̃] ADV [a] (= *avec précision*) [*décrire, chiffrer*] accurately, precisely; [*définir, déterminer, expliquer*] clearly; **ou plus ~** or more precisely *ou* exactly, or to be more precise [b] (= *justement*) **je venais ~ de sortir** I had in fact just gone out, as it happened I'd just gone out; **c'est lui ~ qui m'avait conseillé de le faire** as a matter of fact it was he *ou* it so happens that it was he who advised me to do it; **c'est ~ la raison pour laquelle** *ou* **c'est ~ pour cela que je viens vous voir** that's precisely *ou* just why I've come to see you, it's for that very *ou* precise reason that I've come to see you; **mais je ne l'ai pas vu ! — ~ !** but I didn't see him! — precisely! *ou* exactly! *ou* that's just it! *ou* that's just the point! [c] (= *exactement*) exactly, precisely; **c'est ~ ce que je cherchais** that's exactly *ou* precisely *ou* just what I was looking for; **il est arrivé ~ à ce moment-là** he arrived right *ou* just at that moment *ou* at that exact *ou* precise *ou* very moment; **ce n'est pas ~ un chef-d'œuvre** it's not exactly what I'd call a masterpiece

préciser [pʀesize] ▸ conjug 1 ◂ [1] VT [+ *idée, intention*] to specify, make clear, clarify; [+ *fait, point*] to be more specific about, clarify; [+ *destination*] to name, specify; **je vous préciserai la date de la réunion plus tard** I'll let you know the exact date of the meeting *ou* precisely when the meeting is later; **il a précisé que ...** he explained that ..., he made it clear that ...; **je dois ~ que ...** I must point out *ou* add that ...; **pourriez-vous ~ quand cela est arrivé ?** could you say exactly when it happened?; **pourriez-vous ~ ?** could you be more precise? *ou* specific? [2] **se préciser** VPR [*idée*] to take shape; [*danger, intention*] to become clear *ou* clearer; **la situation commence à se ~**

we are beginning to see the situation more clearly

précision [pʀesizjɔ̃] NF [a] (*gén*) precision, preciseness; [*description, instrument*] precision, preciseness, accuracy; [*contours*] precision, preciseness, distinctness; [*trait*] distinctness; **avec ~** precisely, with precision; **de ~** precision (*épith*); **de haute ~** high-precision (*épith*) [b] (= *détail*) point, piece of information; **j'aimerais vous demander une ~/des ~s** I'd like to ask you to explain one thing/for further information; **il a apporté des ~s intéressantes** he revealed some interesting points *ou* facts *ou* information; **il n'a donné aucune ~ sur ce point** he didn't go into any detail on this point; **encore une ~** one more point *ou* thing; **sans autre ~** without any further information *ou* details; **il m'a dit cela sans autre ~** he told me no more than that

précité, e [pʀesite] ADJ aforesaid, aforementioned; (*par écrit*) aforesaid, above(-mentioned)

précoce [pʀekɔs] ADJ [*fruit, saison, gelée*] early; [*plante*] early-flowering, early-fruiting, precocious (*SPÉC*); [*calvitie, sénilité*] premature; [*mariage*] young (*épith*), early (*épith*); [*diagnostic*] early; [*enfant*] (*intellectuellement*) precocious, advanced for his (*ou* her) age (*attrib*); (*sexuellement*) sexually precocious

précocement [pʀekɔsmɑ̃] ADV precociously

précocité [pʀekɔsite] NF [*fruit, saison*] earliness; [*enfant*] (*intellectuelle*) precocity, precociousness; (*sexuelle*) sexual precocity *ou* precociousness

précolombien, -ienne [pʀekɔlɔ̃bjɛ̃, jɛn] ADJ pre-Colombian

précombustion [pʀekɔ̃bystjɔ̃] NF precombustion

précompte [pʀekɔ̃t] NM (= *évaluation*) estimate; (= *déduction*) ~ (**fiscal**) tax withholding

précompter [pʀekɔ̃te] ▸ conjug 1 ◂ VT (= *évaluer*) to estimate; (= *déduire*) to deduct (**sur** from)

préconception [pʀekɔ̃sepsjɔ̃] NF preconception

préconçu, e [pʀekɔ̃sy] ADJ preconceived; **idée ~e** preconceived idea

préconisation [pʀekɔnizasjɔ̃] NF recommendation

préconiser [pʀekɔnize] ▸ conjug 1 ◂ VT [+ *remède*] to recommend; [+ *méthode, mode de vie, plan, solution*] to advocate

précontraint, e [pʀekɔ̃tʀɛ̃, ɛ̃t] [1] ADJ, NM (**béton**) ~ prestressed concrete [2] **précontrainte** NF (*Tech*) prestressing

précuit, e [pʀekɥi, it] ADJ precooked

précurseur [pʀekyʀsœʀ] [1] ADJ M precursory; **~ de** preceding → **signe** [2] NM (= *personne*) forerunner, precursor; (*Bio*) precursor; **il fait figure de ~ dans ce domaine** he's something of a trail-blazer in this field

prédateur, -trice [pʀedatœʀ, tʀis] [1] ADJ predatory [2] NM (*gén*) predator; (*Écon*) raider

prédation [pʀedasjɔ̃] NF predation

prédécesseur [pʀedesesœʀ] NM predecessor

prédécoupé, e [pʀedekupe] ADJ precut

prédestination [pʀedɛstinasjɔ̃] NF predestination

prédestiné, e [pʀedɛstine] (*ptp de* **prédestiner**) ADJ predestined (**à qch** for sth, **à faire** to do), fated (**à faire** to do); **elle portait un nom ~** she bore a prophetic name

prédestiner [pʀedɛstine] ▸ conjug 1 ◂ VT to predestine (**à qch** for sth, **à faire** to do); **rien ne le prédestinait à devenir président** nothing about him suggested that he might one day become president

prédétermination [pʀedetɛʀminasjɔ̃] NF predetermination

prédéterminer [pʀedetɛʀmine] ▸ conjug 1 ◂ VT to predetermine

➤ GRAMMAIRE ACTIVE: **précisément** 40.2, 53.1

prédicant [pʀedikɑ̃] NM preacher

prédicat [pʀedika] NM predicate

prédicateur [pʀedikatœʀ] NM preacher

prédicatif, -ive [pʀedikatif, iv] ADJ predicative

prédication¹ [pʀedikasjɔ̃] NF (= activité) preaching; (= sermon) sermon

prédication² [pʀekikasjɔ̃] NF (Ling) predication

prédiction [pʀediksjɔ̃] NF prediction

prédigéré, e [pʀediʒeʀe] ADJ predigested

prédilection [pʀedilɛksjɔ̃] NF (pour qn, qch) predilection, partiality (**pour** for); **avoir une ~ pour qch** to be partial to sth; **de ~** favourite

prédire [pʀediʀ] ▶conjug 37◀ VT (prophète) to foretell; (gén) to predict; **~ l'avenir** to tell ou predict the future; **~ qch à qn** to predict sth for sb; **il m'a prédit que je ...** he predicted (that) I ..., he told me (that) I ...

prédisposer [pʀedispoze] ▶conjug 1◀ VT to predispose (**à qch** to sth, **à faire qch** to do sth); **être prédisposé à une maladie** to be predisposed ou prone to an illness; **être prédisposé en faveur de qn** to be predisposed in sb's favour; **cela peut entraîner une prise de poids chez les sujets prédisposés** this may cause people to put on weight if they are prone to it

prédisposition [pʀedispozisjɔ̃] NF predisposition (**à qch** to sth, **à faire qch** to do sth); **~ génétique** genetic (pre)disposition; **avoir une ~ à l'obésité/à l'hypertension** to have a tendency to put on weight/to high blood pressure; **elle avait des ~s pour la peinture** she showed a talent for painting

prédominance [pʀedɔminɑ̃s] NF (gén) predominance, predominancy (**sur** over); [couleur] predominance, prominence; **population à ~ protestante** predominantly Protestant population; **œuvres à ~ littéraire** mainly literary works

prédominant, e [pʀedɔminɑ̃, ɑ̃t] ADJ (gén) predominant; [avis, impression] prevailing; [couleur] predominant, most prominent; **ce pays occupe une place ~e sur le marché européen** this country occupies a dominant position in the European market

prédominer [pʀedɔmine] ▶conjug 1◀ VI (gén) to predominate; [avis, impression] to prevail; [couleur] to predominate, be most prominent; **le souci qui prédomine dans mon esprit** the worry which is uppermost in my mind

pré-électoral, e (mpl **-aux**) [pʀeelɛktɔʀal, o] ADJ pre-election (épith)

pré-emballé, e [pʀeɑ̃bale] ADJ prepacked, prepackaged

prééminence [pʀeeminɑ̃s] NF pre-eminence; **donner la ~ à qch** to give pre-eminence to sth

prééminent, e [pʀeeminɑ̃, ɑ̃t] ADJ pre-eminent

préempter [pʀeɑ̃pte] ▶conjug 1◀ VT (Jur) to pre-empt

préemption [pʀeɑ̃psjɔ̃] NF pre-emption; **droit de ~** pre-emptive right

préencollé, e [pʀeɑ̃kɔle] ADJ **papier peint ~** pre-pasted ou ready-pasted wallpaper; **enveloppe ~e** gummed envelope

préenregistré, e [pʀeɑ̃ʀ(ə)ʒistʀe] (ptp de **préenregistrer**) ADJ [émission] prerecorded; **rires ~s** canned laughter

préétabli, e [pʀeetabli] (ptp de **préétablir**) ADJ [schéma, plan] preestablished; (Philo) **harmonie ~e** preestablished harmony

préétablir [pʀeetabliʀ] ▶conjug 2◀ VT to pre-establish

préexistant, e [pʀeɛgzistɑ̃, ɑ̃t] ADJ pre-existent, pre-existing

préexistence [pʀeɛgzistɑ̃s] NF pre-existence

préexister [pʀeɛgziste] ▶conjug 1◀ VI to pre-exist; **~ à** to exist before

---

préfabrication [pʀefabʀikasjɔ̃] NF prefabrication

préfabriqué, e [pʀefabʀike] **1** ADJ prefabricated **2** NM (= maison) prefabricated house, prefab*; (= matériau) prefabricated material; **en ~** prefabricated

préface [pʀefas] NF preface; (fig = prélude) preface, prelude (**à** to)

préfacer [pʀefase] ▶conjug 3◀ VT [+ livre] to write a preface for, preface

préfacier [pʀefasje] NM preface writer

préfectoral, e (mpl **-aux**) [pʀefɛktɔʀal, o] ADJ (Admin française, Antiq) prefectorial, prefectural → **arrêté**

préfecture [pʀefɛktyʀ] NF (Admin française, Antiq) prefecture; **~ de police** police headquarters; **~ maritime** police port authority

┌─────────────────────────┐
│ **PRÉFECTURE, PRÉFET** │
└─────────────────────────┘

In France, a préfet is a high-ranking civil servant who represents the State at the level of the "département" or the "région". Besides a range of important administrative duties, the role of the préfet is to ensure that government decisions are carried out properly at local level. The term préfecture refers to the area over which the préfet has authority (in effect, the "département"), to the town where the administrative offices of the préfet are situated, and to these offices themselves. Official documents such as driving licences are issued by the préfecture. → DÉPARTEMENT ; RÉGION

préférable [pʀefeʀabl] ADJ preferable (**à qch** to sth); **il est ~ que je parte** it is preferable ou better that I should leave ou for me to leave; **il serait ~ d'y aller** ou **que vous y alliez** it would be better if you went ou for you to go; **il est ~ de ...** it is preferable ou better to ...

préférablement [pʀefeʀabləmɑ̃] ADV preferably; **~ à** in preference to

▼ **préféré, e** [pʀefeʀe] (ptp de **préférer**) ADJ, NM,F favourite (Brit), favorite (US)

▼ **préférence** [pʀefeʀɑ̃s] NF preference; **de ~** preferably; **de ~ à** in preference to, rather than; **donner la ~ à** to give preference to; **avoir une ~ marquée pour ...** to have a marked preference for ...; **avoir la ~ sur** to have preference over; **je n'ai pas de ~** I have no preference, I don't mind; **par ordre de ~** in order of preference; (Europe) **la ~ communautaire** Community preference; (Pol) **la ~ nationale** discrimination in favour of a country's own nationals

préférentiel, -ielle [pʀefeʀɑ̃sjɛl] ADJ preferential; **tarif ~** (gén) preferential ou special rate; (Douane) preferential tariff; (Bourse) **action préférentielle** preferred ou preference share

préférentiellement [pʀefeʀɑ̃sjɛlmɑ̃] ADV preferentially

▼ **préférer** [pʀefeʀe] ▶conjug 6◀ VT to prefer (**à** to); **je préfère ce manteau à l'autre** I prefer this coat to the other one, I like this coat better than the other one; **je te préfère avec les cheveux courts** I like you better ou prefer you with short hair; **je préfère aller au cinéma** I prefer to go ou I would rather go to the cinema; **il préfère que ce soit vous qui le fassiez** he would rather you did it; **nous avons préféré attendre avant de vous le dire** we preferred to wait ou we thought it better to wait before telling you; **nous avons préféré attendre que d'y aller tout de suite** we preferred to wait ou thought it better to wait rather than go straight away; **que préférez-vous, du thé ou du café ?** what would you rather have ou what would you prefer — tea or coffee?; **si tu préfères** if you prefer, if you like, if you'd rather; **comme vous préférez** as you prefer ou like ou wish ou please; **j'aurais préféré ne jamais l'avoir rencontré** I wish I'd never met him

---

préfet [pʀefe] NM (Admin française, Antiq) prefect; (Belg = directeur) headmaster, principal (of a college), head (Brit); **~ de police** prefect of police, chief of police

préfète [pʀefɛt] NF **a** (= femme préfet) (female ou woman) prefect; (= femme du préfet) prefect's wife **b** (Belg = directrice) headmistress, principal (of a college), head (Brit)

préfiguration [pʀefigyʀasjɔ̃] NF prefiguration, foreshadowing

préfigurer [pʀefigyʀe] ▶conjug 1◀ VT to prefigure, foreshadow

préfixal, e (mpl **-aux**) [pʀefiksal, o] ADJ prefixal

préfixation [pʀefiksasjɔ̃] NF prefixation

préfixe [pʀefiks] NM prefix

préfixer [pʀefikse] ▶conjug 1◀ VT to prefix

préglaciaire [pʀeglasjeʀ] ADJ preglacial

prégnance [pʀegnɑ̃s] NF (littér) [souvenir] vividness; [tradition] resonance; (Psych) pregnance (SPÉC), Prägnanz (SPÉC)

prégnant, e [pʀegnɑ̃, ɑ̃t] ADJ (littér) [souvenir] vivid; [débat] meaningful; **cette tradition est encore très ~e** this tradition still has great resonance

préhenseur [pʀeɑ̃sœʀ] ADJ M prehensile

préhensile [pʀeɑ̃sil] ADJ prehensile

préhension [pʀeɑ̃sjɔ̃] NF prehension

préhispanique [pʀeispanik] ADJ [civilisation, culture] pre-Hispanic

préhistoire [pʀeistwaʀ] NF prehistory; **les animaux/les hommes de la ~** prehistoric animals/men; **depuis la ~** since prehistoric times

préhistorien, -ienne [pʀeistɔʀjɛ̃, jɛn] NM,F prehistorian

préhistorique [pʀeistɔʀik] ADJ prehistoric; (= suranné) antediluvian, ancient

préimplantatoire [pʀeɛ̃plɑ̃tatwaʀ] ADJ **diagnostic ~** pre-implantation screening

préindustriel, -ielle [pʀeɛ̃dystʀijɛl] ADJ preindustrial; **la Grande-Bretagne préindustrielle** preindustrial Britain, Great Britain before the industrial revolution

préinscription [pʀeɛ̃skʀipsjɔ̃] NF (à l'université) preregistration (**à** at); (à un concours) preregistration (**à** for)

préjudice [pʀeʒydis] NM (matériel, financier) loss; (moral) harm (NonC), damage (NonC), wrong; **subir un ~** (matériel) to sustain a loss; (moral) to be wronged; **le ~ subi par la victime** (financier, matériel) the loss sustained by the victim; (moral) the moral wrong ou damage suffered by the victim; **causer un ~** ou **porter ~ à qn** (gén) to do sb harm, harm sb; [décision] to be detrimental to sb ou to sb's interests; **ce supermarché a porté ~ aux petits commerçants** this supermarket was detrimental to (the interests of) small tradesmen; **je ne voudrais pas vous porter ~ en leur racontant cela** I wouldn't like to harm you ou your case ou make difficulties for you by telling them about this; **au ~ de sa santé/de la vérité** to the prejudice (frm) ou at the expense ou at the cost of his health/of the truth; **au ~ de M. Dufeu** to the prejudice (frm) ou at the expense of Mr Dufeu; **sans ~** without prejudice to; **~ commercial/financier** commercial/financial loss; **~ matériel** material loss ou damage; **~ moral** moral wrong

préjudiciable [pʀeʒydisjabl] ADJ prejudicial, detrimental, harmful (**à** to)

préjugé [pʀeʒyʒe] NM prejudice; **avoir un ~ contre** to be prejudiced ou biased against; **sans ~** unprejudiced, unbiased; **bénéficier d'un ~ favorable** to be favourably considered; **~s de classe** class bias; **~ de race** racial prejudice

préjuger [pʀeʒyʒe] ◆ **préjuger de** ▶conjug 3◀ VT INDIR to prejudge; **~ d'une réaction** to foresee a reaction, judge what a reaction might be; **autant qu'on peut le ◊ à ce qu'on en**

➤ GRAMMAIRE ACTIVE: **préféré** 34.1 **préférence** 34.5 **préférer** 31, 34.1, 34.4, 35.5

peut ~ as far as it is possible to judge in advance

prélasser (se) [pʀelase] ▸conjug 1◂ VPR (*dans un fauteuil*) to sprawl, lounge; (*au soleil*) to bask

prélat [pʀela] NM prelate

prélature [pʀelatyʀ] NF prelacy

prélavage [pʀelavaʒ] NM prewash

prélaver [pʀelave] ▸conjug 1◂ VT to prewash

prélèvement [pʀelɛvmɑ̃] NM **a** (*Méd, Sci*) [*échantillon*] taking (NonC); [*organe*] removal; **faire un ~ de sang** ou **sanguin/de moelle** to take a blood/bone-marrow sample **b** (*Fin*) [*montant, pourcentage*] deduction; (*sur un compte*) (*par le titulaire*) withdrawal, drawing out (NonC); (*par un créancier*) debit; **~ automatique** [*somme fixe*] standing order; [*somme variable*] direct debit; **~ bancaire** standing ou banker's order (*Brit*), automatic deduction (*US*) **c** [*impôt*] levying (NonC), levy, imposition; **~ fiscal/compensatoire/sur le capital/à l'importation** tax/compensatory/capital/import levy; **~s obligatoires** tax and social security deductions

prélever [pʀel(ə)ve] ▸conjug 5◂ VT **a** (*Méd, Sci*) [+ *échantillon*] to take (**sur** from); [+ *sang*] to take (a sample of); [+ *organe*] to remove **b** (*Fin*) [+ *montant, pourcentage*] to deduct (**sur** from); [+ *somme*] (*sur un compte*) [*titulaire*] to withdraw (**sur** from); [*créancier*] to debit (**sur** from); **ses factures d'électricité sont automatiquement prélevées sur son compte** his electricity bills are debited ou automatically deducted from his account **c** [+ *impôt*] to levy, impose (**sur** on)

préliminaire [pʀeliminɛʀ] **1** ADJ (*gén*) preliminary; [*discours*] introductory **2 préliminaires** NMPL preliminaries; [*négociations*] preliminary talks

prélude [pʀelyd] NM (*Mus = morceau*) prelude; (*pour se préparer*) warm-up; (*fig*) prelude (**à** to)

préluder [pʀelyde] ▸conjug 1◂ **1** VI (*Mus*) to warm up; **~ par qch** to begin with sth **2 préluder à** VT INDIR to be a prelude to, lead up to

prématuré, e [pʀematyʀe] **1** ADJ [*bébé, nouvelle*] premature; [*mort*] untimely, premature; **il est ~ de ...** it is premature to ..., it's too early to ...; **~ de 3 semaines** 3 weeks premature ou early **2** NM,F premature baby

prématurément [pʀematyʀemɑ̃] ADV prematurely; **une cruelle maladie l'a enlevé ~ à notre affection** a grievous illness brought his untimely departure from our midst

prémédication [pʀemedikasjɔ̃] NF premedication, premed*

préméditation [pʀemeditasjɔ̃] NF premeditation; **avec ~** [*crime*] premeditated; [*tuer*] with intent, with malice aforethought; **meurtre sans ~** unpremeditated murder

préméditer [pʀemedite] ▸conjug 1◂ VT to premeditate; **~ de faire qch** to plan to do sth; **meurtre prémédité** premeditated ou wilful murder

prémenstruel, -elle [pʀemɑ̃stʀyɛl] ADJ premenstrual; **syndrome ~** premenstrual tension ou syndrome

prémices [pʀemis] NFPL (*littér*) beginnings; [*récolte*] first fruits; [*animaux*] first-born (animals); [*guerre, crise*] first ou warning signs; [*évolution*] beginnings

▼**premier, -ière**¹ [pʀəmje, jɛʀ] **1** ADJ **a** (*dans le temps*) first; [*impression*] first, initial; **les premières heures du jour** the early hours (of the morning), the small hours; **dès les ~s jours** from the very first days; **ses ~s poèmes** his first ou early poems; **les ~s habitants de la Terre** the earliest ou first inhabitants of the Earth; **les premières années de sa vie** the first few ou the early years of his life; **c'est la première et la dernière fois que je suis tes conseils** it's the first and last time I follow

your advice; **au ~ signe de résistance** at the first ou slightest sign of resistance; **à mon ~ signal** at the first signal from me, as soon as you see my signal → lit, main *etc* **b** (*dans un ordre*) first; (*à un examen*) first, top; (*en importance*) leading, foremost, top; **~ commis/clerc** chief clerk (*Brit*) ou store (*US*) assistant/clerk; **le ~ constructeur automobile européen** the leading European car manufacturer; **le ~ personnage de l'État** the country's leading ou most senior statesman; **arriver/être ~** to arrive/be first; **il est toujours ~ en classe** he's always top of the class ou first in the class; **être reçu ~** to come first **c** (*dans l'espace*) [*branche*] lower, bottom; [*rangée*] front; **la première marche de l'escalier** (*en bas*) the bottom step; (*en haut*) the top step; **le ~ barreau de l'échelle** the bottom ou first ou lowest rung of the ladder; **le ~ mouchoir de la pile** the first handkerchief in the pile, the top handkerchief in the pile; **les 100 premières pages** the first 100 pages; (*Presse*) **en première page** on the front page; **lire un livre de la première à la dernière ligne** to read a book from beginning to end ou from cover to cover **d** (= *de base*) [*échelon, grade*] bottom; [*ébauche, projet*] first, rough; **quel est votre ~ prix pour ce type de voyage?** what do your prices start at for this kind of trip?; **apprendre les ~s rudiments d'une science** to learn the first ou basic rudiments of a science **e** (*après n = originel, fondamental*) [*cause, donnée*] basic; [*principe*] first, basic; [*objectif*] basic, primary, prime; [*état*] initial, original; **c'est la qualité première d'un chef d'État** it's the prime ou essential quality for a head of state; **retrouver sa vivacité première/son éclat ~** to regain one's former ou initial liveliness/sparkle

2 NM,F **a** (*dans le temps, l'espace*) first (one); **parler/passer/sortir le ~** to speak/go/go out first; **arriver les ~s** to arrive (the) first; **arriver dans les ~s** to be one of ou be among the first to arrive; **les ~s arrivés seront les ~s servis** first come, first served; **elle sera servie la première** she will be served first; **au ~ de ces messieurs** next gentleman please; **il a été le ~ à reconnaître ses torts** he was the first to admit that he was in the wrong; **elle fut l'une des premières à ...** she was one of the first to ... → né **b** (*dans une hiérarchie, un ordre*) (*Scol, Univ*) **il a été reçu dans** ou **parmi les ~s** he was in the top ou first few; **il est le ~ de sa classe** he is top of his class; (*péj*) **il a une tête de ~ de la classe** he looks like a real egghead* ou swot* (*Brit*); (*Sport*) **il s'est classé dans les dix ~s** he was ranked in ou among the top ou first ten; (*Bible*) **les ~s seront les derniers (, et les derniers seront les ~s)** the last shall be first (, and the first last) → jeune **c** (*dans une série, une comparaison*) **Pierre et Paul sont cousins, le ~ est médecin** Peter and Paul are cousins, the former is a doctor; **le ~ semble mieux** (*entre deux*) the first one seems better; (*dans une série*) the first one seems best

3 NM (*gén*) first; (= *étage*) first floor (*Brit*), second floor (*US*); (= *enfant*) **c'est leur ~** it's their first child; (*charade*) **mon ~ est ...** my first is in ...

4 en premier LOC ADV [*arriver, parler*] (the) first; **je l'ai servi en ~** I served him first; **en ~ je dirai que ...** firstly ou first ou to start with I'd like to say that ...; **cela vient en ~ dans ma liste de priorités** that's first on ou top of my list of priorities; **pour lui, la famille vient toujours en ~** his family always comes first

5 COMP ▸ **le premier de l'an** New Year's Day ▸ **le premier avril** the first of April, April Fool's Day, All Fools' Day ▸ **le Premier Mai** the first of May, May Day

première² [pʀəmjɛʀ] **1** NF **a** (*gén*) first; (*Aut*) first (gear); (*Hippisme*) first (race); (*Aut*)

être en/passer la ~ to be in/go into first (gear) **b** (*Théât*) first night; (*Ciné*) première; (= *exploit*) (*gén*) first; (*Alpinisme*) first ascent; (*Ciné*) **le soir de la ~, il ...** on the opening night, he ...; **le public des grandes ~s** firstnighters; **c'est une ~ mondiale** (*gén*) it's a world first; (*Ciné*) it's a world première; **c'est une grande ~ pour notre équipe** it's a big first for our team **c** (*Aviat, Rail*) first class; **voyager en ~** to travel first-class; **billet de ~** first-class ticket **d** (*Scol*) (*classe de*) ≈ lower sixth (form) (*Brit*), ≈ eleventh grade (*US*); **élève de ~** lower sixth former (*Brit*), eleventh grader (*US*), junior (in high school) (*US*) **e** (*Couture*) head seamstress **f** (= *semelle*) insole

2 de première* LOC ADJ **c'est de ~!** it's first-class!; **il a fait un boulot de ~** he's done a first-class ou a first-rate job; **c'est un salaud* de ~!** he's an out-and-out ou a right (*Brit*) bastard!*; **il est de ~ pour trouver les bons restaurants/pour les gaffes!** he's got a real knack* for ou he's great* at finding good restaurants/making blunders!

▼**premièrement** [pʀəmjɛʀmɑ̃] ADV (= *d'abord*) first(ly); (= *en premier lieu*) in the first place; (*introduisant une objection*) for a start; **~ il ne m'a rien dit, et en plus ...** for a start, he didn't say anything to me, and what's more ...

premier-maître (*pl* **premiers-maîtres**) [pʀəmjemɛtʀ] NM chief petty officer

premier-né [pʀəmjene] **première-née** [pʀəmjene] (*mpl* **premiers-nés**) ADJ, NM,F first-born

prémisse [pʀemis] NF premise, premiss

prémix [pʀemiks] NM alcopop

prémolaire [pʀemɔlɛʀ] NF premolar (tooth)

prémonition [pʀemɔnisjɔ̃] NF premonition

prémonitoire [pʀemɔnitwaʀ] ADJ premonitory

prémunir [pʀemyniʀ] ▸conjug 2◂ **1** VT (*littér*) (= *mettre en garde*) to warn; (= *protéger*) to protect (**contre** against) **2 se prémunir** VPR to protect o.s. (**contre** from), guard (**contre** against)

prenant, e [pʀənɑ̃, ɑ̃t] ADJ **a** (= *captivant*) [*film, livre*] absorbing, engrossing, compelling; [*voix*] fascinating, captivating **b** (= *qui prend du temps*) [*activité*] time-consuming; **ce travail est trop ~** this job is too time-consuming ou takes up too much of my (ou our etc) time **c** (*Zool*) [*queue*] prehensile

prénatal, e (*mpl* **prénatals**) [pʀenatal] ADJ [*diagnostic, dépistage, examen, visite*] antenatal, prenatal; [*allocation*] maternity (*épith*); **clinique ~e** antenatal clinic

prendre [pʀɑ̃dʀ]

▸conjug 58◂
1 VERBE TRANSITIF   **3** VERBE PRONOMINAL
2 VERBE INTRANSITIF
Lorsque **prendre** *s'emploie dans des locutions telles que* **prendre** *une photo/du poids/son temps,* **prendre en charge** *etc, cherchez aussi au nom.*

1 VERBE TRANSITIF

a (= *saisir*) [+ *objet*] to take; **prends-le dans le placard/sur l'étagère** take it out of the cupboard/off ou (down) from the shelf; **il l'a pris dans le tiroir** he took ou got it out of the drawer; **il prit un journal/son crayon sur la table** he picked up ou took a newspaper/his pencil from the table; **il la prit par le cou/par la taille** he put his arms round her neck/round her waist; **~ qn par le bras/la taille** to take sb by the arm/the waist; **~ qch des mains de qn** (= *débarrasser*) to take sth out of sb's hands; (= *enlever*) to take sth off sb ou away from sb; **c'est toujours ça de pris** that's something at least; **c'est à ~ ou à laisser** [*offre*] (you can) take it or leave it; **je vous le fais à 500 F, c'est à ~ ou à laisser** I'll let you have it for 500 francs, that's my final offer; **avec lui, il faut en ~ et en laisser** you can only believe half of what he says, you must take what he tells you with a pinch of salt; **je prends** (*dans un jeu de questions-réponses*) I'll answer; (*appel téléphonique*) I'll take it

b = **choisir** to take; **il y a plusieurs livres, lequel prends-tu?** there are several books — which one are you going to take? *ou* which one do you want?; **il a pris le bleu** he took the blue one

c = **se munir de** [+ *instrument*] **tiens, prends ce marteau** here, use this hammer; **il faut ~ un tournevis pour faire ça** you need a screwdriver for that; **si tu sors, prends ton parapluie** if you go out, take your umbrella (with you); **prends ta chaise et viens t'asseoir ici** bring your chair and come and sit over here; **as-tu pris les valises?** have you brought the suitcases?; **prends tes lunettes pour lire** put your glasses on to read

d = **aller chercher** [+ *chose*] to pick up, get, fetch (*Brit*); [+ *personne*] to pick up; (= *emmener*) to take; **passer ~ qn à son bureau** to pick sb up *ou* call for sb at his office; **je passerai les ~ chez toi** I'll come and collect *ou* get them *ou* I'll call in for them at your place; **pouvez-vous me ~ (dans votre voiture)?** can you give me a lift?; **je ne veux plus de ce manteau, tu peux le ~** I don't want this coat any more — you can take *ou* have it; **prends du beurre dans le réfrigérateur** get some butter out of the fridge

e = **s'emparer de force** [+ *poisson, voleur*] to catch; [+ *argent, place, otage*] to take; (*Mil*) [+ *ville*] to take, capture; (*Cartes, Échecs*) to take; **un voleur lui a pris son portefeuille** a thief has taken *ou* stolen his wallet *ou* has robbed him of his wallet; **il m'a pris mon idée** he has taken *ou* used *ou* pinched* (*Brit*) my idea; **il prend tout ce qui lui tombe sous la main** he takes *ou* grabs everything he can lay his hands on; (*Tennis*) **~ le service de qn** to break sb's service; **se faire ~** [*voleur*] to be *ou* get caught; **le voleur s'est fait ~** the robber was *ou* got caught → **tel**

f *** : **sexuellement** [+ *personne*] to take; **il l'a prise par devant/derrière** he took her from the front/from behind

g = **assaillir** [*colère*] to come over; [*fièvre, douleur*] to strike; **la colère le prit soudain** he was suddenly overcome with anger, anger suddenly overcame him; **il fut pris d'un doute** he suddenly had a doubt, he felt doubtful all of a sudden; **la douleur m'a pris au genou** I suddenly got a pain in my knee; **les douleurs la prirent** her labour pains started; **ça me prend dans le bas du dos et ça remonte*** it starts in my lower back and works its way up; **qu'est-ce qui te prend?*** what's the matter *ou* what's up* with you?, what's come over you?*; **ça te prend souvent?*** are you often like that? (*iro*); **quand ça me prend*, je peux rêvasser pendant des heures** I can daydream for hours when I feel like it *ou* when the mood takes me → **tête**

h = **surprendre** to catch; **~ qn à faire qch** to catch sb doing sth; **je vous y prends!** caught you!; (*menace*) **si je t'y prends (encore)** ◊ **que je t'y prenne** just *ou* don't let me catch you doing that (again) *ou* at it (again); **~ qn sur le fait** to catch sb in the act *ou* red-handed; **il s'est fait ~ en train de copier sur son voisin** he got caught copying from his neighbour

i = **duper** to take in; **on ne m'y prendra plus** I won't be taken in again, I won't be had a second time*; **se laisser ~ à des paroles aimables** to let o.s. be sweet-talked *ou* taken in by sweet talk

j = **manger, boire** [+ *aliment, boisson*] to have; [+ *médicament*] to take; **prenez-vous du sucre?** do you take sugar?; **est-ce que vous prendrez du café?** will you have *ou* would you like some coffee?; **à ~ avant les repas** to be taken before meals; **fais-lui ~ son médicament** give him his medicine; **ce médicament se prend dans de l'eau** this medicine must be taken in water; **as-tu pris de ce bon gâteau?** have you had some of this nice cake?; **il n'a rien pris depuis hier** he hasn't eaten anything since yesterday; **le docteur m'interdit de ~ de l'alcool** the doctor won't allow me *ou* has forbidden me (to drink) alcohol

k = **voyager par** [+ *métro, taxi*] to take, travel *ou* go *ou* come by; [+ *voiture*] to take; (= *s'engager dans*) [+ *direction, rue*] to take; **il prit le train puis l'avion de Paris à Londres** he took the train *ou* went by train then flew from Paris to London; **j'ai pris l'avion/le train de 4 heures** I caught the 4 o'clock plane/train; **je préfère ~ ma voiture** I'd rather take the car *ou* go in the car; **ils ont pris la rue Blanche** they went down (*ou* up) the rue Blanche

l = **acheter** [+ *billet, essence*] to get; [+ *voiture*] to buy; (= *réserver*) [+ *couchette, place*] to book; **il prend toujours son pain à côté** he always gets *ou* buys his bread from the shop next door; **peux-tu me ~ du pain?** can you get me some bread?; **nous avons pris une maison** (*loué*) we've taken *ou* rented a house; (*acheté*) we've bought a house; **je prends du 38 (en chaussures/en robe)** I take a size 38 (shoe/dress)

m = **accepter** [+ *client*] to take; [+ *passager*] to pick up; [+ *locataire*] to take (in); [+ *personnel*] to take on; [+ *domestique*] to engage, take on; **l'école ne prend plus de pensionnaires** the school no longer takes boarders; **ce train ne prend pas de voyageurs** this train doesn't pick up passengers; **il l'a prise comme interprète** he took her on as an interpreter

n = **noter** [+ *renseignement, adresse, nom, rendez-vous*] to write down, take down; [+ *mesures, température, empreintes*] to take; (*sous la dictée*) [+ *lettre*] to take (down); **~ des notes** to take notes

o = **adopter** [+ *air, ton*] to put on, assume; [+ *décision*] to take, make, come to; [+ *risque, mesure*] to take; [+ *attitude*] to strike, take up; **il prit un ton menaçant** a threatening note crept into his voice, his voice took on a threatening tone

p = **acquérir** **~ de l'autorité** to gain authority; **cela prend un sens particulier** it takes on a particular meaning

q = **s'accorder** [+ *congé*] to take; [+ *vacances*] to take, have, go on; [+ *repos*] to have, take; **je prends quelques jours à Noël** I'm having a few days off at Christmas → **temps**

r = **coûter** [+ *temps, place, argent*] to take; **cela me prend tout mon temps** it takes up all my time; **la réparation a pris des heures** the repair took hours *ou* ages; **attendez ici, ça ne prendra pas longtemps** wait here, it won't take long

s = **faire payer** to charge; **ils (m')ont pris 100 F pour une petite réparation** they charged (me) 100 francs for a minor repair; **ce spécialiste prend très cher** this specialist charges very high fees, this specialist's charges *ou* fees are very high; **ce plombier prend cher de l'heure** this plumber's hourly rate is high

t = **prélever** [+ *pourcentage*] to take; **ils prennent un pourcentage sur la vente** they charge a commission on the sale, they take a percentage on the sale; **il prend sa commission sur la vente** he takes his commission on the sale; **~ de l'argent à la banque/sur son compte** to draw (out) *ou* withdraw money from the bank/from one's account; **la cotisation à la retraite est prise sur le salaire** the pension contribution is taken off one's salary *ou* deducted from one's salary; **il a dû ~ sur ses économies pour payer les dégâts** he had to dip into *ou* go into his savings to pay for the damage; **il a pris sur son temps pour venir m'aider** he gave up some of his time to help me

u * = **recevoir, subir** [+ *coup, choc*] to get, receive; **il a pris la porte en pleine figure** the door hit *ou* got* him right in the face; **qu'est-ce qu'on a pris!*** ◊ **on en a pris plein la tronche!** (*reproches*) we really got it in the neck!*, we really got what for!*; (*défaite*) we got hammered!*; (*averse*) we got drenched!; (*emploi absolu*) **il a pris pour les autres** he took the rap*; **c'est toujours moi qui prend pour ma sœur!** I always get the blame for what my sister does!; **le seau d'eau s'est renversé et c'est moi qui ai tout pris** the bucket of water tipped over and I got it all over me

v = **réagir à** [+ *nouvelle*] to take; **si vous le prenez ainsi ...** if that's how you want it ...; **il a bien/mal pris la chose** ◊ **il l'a bien/mal pris** he took it well/badly; **il a bien pris ce que je lui ai dit** he took what I said in good part *ou* quite well; **il a mal pris ce que je lui ai dit** he took exception *ou* didn't take kindly to what I said to him; **~ qch avec bonne humeur** to take sth good-humouredly *ou* in good part; **~ les choses comme elles sont/la vie comme elle vient** to take things as they come/life as it comes

w = **manier** [+ *personne*] to handle; [+ *problème*] to handle, tackle, deal with, cope with; **elle sait le ~** she knows how to handle *ou* approach *ou* get round him; **c'est quelqu'un de gentil mais il faut savoir le ~** he's nice but you have to keep on the right side of him; **il y a plusieurs façons de ~ le problème** there are several ways of going about *ou* tackling the problem → **bout**

x

♦ **prendre qn/qch pour** (= *considérer comme*) to take sb/sth for; **pour qui me prenez-vous?** what *ou* who do you take me for?, what *ou* who do you think I am?; **~ qn pour un autre** to take sb for *ou* think sb is somebody else, mistake sb for somebody else; **je n'aime pas qu'on me prenne pour un imbécile** I don't like being taken for a fool

(= *utiliser comme*) to take sb/sth as; **~ qch pour prétexte/cible** to take sth as a pretext/target

y

♦ **prendre sur soi** (= *se maîtriser*) to grin and bear it; **savoir ~ sur soi** to keep a grip on o.s. (= *assumer*) **j'ai dû ~ tout cela sur moi** I had to cope on my own; **~ sur soi de faire qch** to take it upon o.s. to do sth

z

♦ **à tout prendre** on the whole, all in all

2 VERBE INTRANSITIF

a = **durcir** [*ciment, pâte, crème*] to set

b = **réussir** [*plante*] to take (root); [*vaccin*] to take; [*mouvement, mode*] to catch on; [*livre, spectacle*] to be a success; **le lilas a bien pris** the lilac's doing really well; **la teinture prend mal avec ce tissu** this material is difficult to dye; **la plaisanterie a pris** the joke was a great success; **avec moi, ça ne prend pas*** it doesn't work with me*, it won't wash with me* (*Brit*)

c = **commencer à brûler** [*feu*] (*gén*) to go; (*accidentellement*) to start; [*allumette*] to light; [*bois*] to catch fire; **le feu ne veut pas ~** the fire won't go; **le feu a pris sur le toit** the fire took hold in the roof

d = **se diriger** to go; **~ à gauche** to go *ou* turn *ou* bear left; **~ par les petites rues** to take to *ou* go along *ou* keep to the side streets

3 **se prendre** VERBE PRONOMINAL

a = **se considérer** **il se prend pour un intellectuel** he thinks *ou* likes to think he's an intellectual; **pour qui se prend-il?** (just) who does he think he is?; **se ~ au sérieux** to take o.s. seriously

b = **accrocher, coincer** to catch, trap; **le chat s'est pris la patte dans un piège** the cat got its paw trapped, the cat caught its paw in a trap; **le rideau se prend dans la fenêtre** the curtain gets caught (up) *ou* stuck in the window; **mon manteau s'est pris dans la porte** I caught *ou* trapped my coat in the door, my coat got trapped *ou* caught in the door; **se ~ les pieds dans le tapis** (*lit*) to catch one's foot in the rug, trip on the rug; (*fig*) to trip oneself up

c

♦ **se prendre à** + *infinitif* (*littér* = *commencer*) **se ~ à faire qch** to begin to do *ou* begin doing sth, start to do *ou* start doing sth

d

♦ **s'en prendre à** [+ *personne*] (= *agresser*) to lay into*, set about; (= *passer sa colère sur*) to take it out on; (= *blâmer*) to lay *ou* put the blame on, attack; **tu ne peux t'en ~ qu'à toi** you've only got yourself to blame [+ *chose*] **il s'en est pris à son ordinateur** he took it out on his computer*; (= *remettre en question*) [+ *tradition, préjugé*] to challenge; (= *critiquer*) [+ *autorité, organisation*] to attack, take on

e

♦ **s'y prendre** to set about (doing) it; **il ne sait pas s'y ~** he doesn't know how to go *ou* set about it; **je ne sais pas comment tu t'y prends** I don't know how you manage it; **il ne s'y serait pas pris autrement s'il avait voulu tout faire échouer** he couldn't have done better if he had actually set out to ruin the whole thing; **il fallait s'y ~ à temps** you should have done something about it *ou* started before it was too late; **il faut s'y ~ à l'avance** you have to do it in advance; **il s'y est bien/mal pris (pour le faire)** he went about it the right/wrong way; **il s'y est pris drôlement pour le faire** he chose the oddest way of doing it, he went about it in the strangest way; **s'y ~ à deux fois/plusieurs fois pour faire qch** to try twice/several times to do sth, make two/several attempts to do sth; **il faut s'y ~ à deux** it needs two of us (to do it); **s'y ~ bien** *ou* **savoir s'y ~ avec qn** to handle sb the right way; **il sait s'y ~ avec les enfants** he really knows how to deal with children

preneur, -euse [prənœr, øz] NM,F (= *acheteur*) buyer; (= *locataire*) lessee (*Jur*), tenant; (*Ciné*) **~ de son** sound engineer; **~ d'otages** hostage taker; **trouver ~** to find a buyer; **ces restes de gâteau vont vite trouver ~** there'll be no problem finding a taker for the rest of this cake; **cet objet n'avait pas trouvé ~** there were no takers for this object; **je suis ~ à 100 F** I'll buy *ou* take it for 100 francs; **je ne suis pas ~** I'm not interested

prénom [prenɔ̃] NM (*gén*) Christian name, first name; (*Admin*) forename, given name (*US*); **~ usuel** name by which one is known; **il a dû se faire un ~** he had to make a name for himself in his own right

prénommé, e [prenɔme] (*ptp de* **prénommer**) 1 ADJ **le ~ Paul** the said Paul 2 NM,F (*Jur*) above-named

prénommer [prenɔme] ▸conjug 1◂ 1 VT to call, name, give a name to; **on l'a prénommé comme son oncle** he was called *ou* named after his uncle, he was given the same name as his uncle 2 **se prénommer** VPR to be called *ou* named

prénuptial, e [prenypsjal, o] ADJ (*mpl* -aux) premarital

préoccupant, e [preɔkypɑ̃, ɑ̃t] ADJ worrying

préoccupation [preɔkypasjɔ̃] NF a (= *souci*) worry, anxiety; **sa mauvaise santé était une ~ supplémentaire pour ses parents** his ill health was a further worry to *ou* cause for concern to his parents b (= *priorité*) preoccupation, concern; **sa seule ~ était de ...** his one concern *ou* preoccupation was to ...

préoccupé, e [preɔkype] (*ptp de* **préoccuper**) ADJ (= *absorbé*) preoccupied (**de qch** with sth, **de faire qch** with doing sth); (= *soucieux*) concerned (**de qch** about sth, **de faire qch** to do sth), worried (**de qch** about sth, **de faire qch** about doing sth); **tu as l'air ~** you look worried

▼ **préoccuper** [preɔkype] ▸conjug 1◂ 1 VT

a (= *inquiéter*) to worry; **il y a quelque chose qui le préoccupe** something is worrying *ou* bothering him, he's got *ou* there's something on his mind; **l'avenir de son fils le préoccupe** he's concerned *ou* anxious about his son's future

b (= *absorber*) to preoccupy; **cette idée lui préoccupe l'esprit** *ou* **le préoccupe** he is preoccupied with the idea; **il est uniquement préoccupé de sa petite personne** all he ever thinks about is himself, he's totally wrapped up in himself

2 **se préoccuper** VPR to concern o.s. (**de** with), be concerned (**de** with), to worry (**de** about); **se ~ de la santé de qn** to show (great) concern about sb's health; **il ne se préoccupe pas beaucoup de notre sort** he isn't very worried *ou* he doesn't care very much about what happens to us; **il ne s'en préoccupe guère** he hardly gives it a thought

préopératoire [preɔperatwar] ADJ preoperative

prépa [prepa] NF (*arg Scol*) (ABRÉV = **classe préparatoire**) → **préparatoire**

préparateur, -trice [preparatœr, tris] NM,F (*gén*) assistant; (*Univ*) demonstrator; **~ en pharmacie** pharmaceutical *ou* chemist's (*Brit*) assistant

préparatifs [preparatif] NMPL preparations (**de** for); **nous en sommes aux ~ de départ** we're getting ready *ou* we're preparing to leave

préparation [preparasjɔ̃] NF a (= *confection*: *gén*) preparation; [*repas*] preparation, making; [*médicament*] preparation, making up; [*complot*] laying, hatching; [*plan*] preparation, working out, drawing up; **la ~ de ce plat demande des soins minutieux** this dish requires very careful preparation b (= *apprêt*: *gén*) preparation; [*table*] laying, getting ready; [*peaux, poisson, volaille*] dressing; [*attaque, départ, voyage*] preparation (**de** for); **la ~ de l'avenir** preparing *ou* preparation for the future; **attaque après ~ d'artillerie** attack following initial assault by the artillery; **elle a plusieurs livres en ~** she has several books in the pipeline c (= *étude*) [*examen*] preparation, getting ready (**de** for) d (= *entraînement*) [*personne*] (*à un examen*) preparation (**à** for); (*à une épreuve sportive*) preparation, training (**à** for); **annoncer quelque chose sans ~** to announce something abruptly *ou* without preparation e (*Chim, Pharm*) preparation f (*Scol*) (= *classe préparatoire*) **faire une ~ à Polytechnique** to prepare for entrance to the École polytechnique (*in one of the classes préparatoires*); (= *devoir*) **une ~ française** a French exercise, a piece of French homework; (*Mil*) **faire sa ~ militaire** to do a training course in preparation for one's military service

préparatoire [preparatwar] ADJ [*travail, démarche, conversation*] preparatory, preliminary; **classe ~ (aux Grandes Écoles)** class which prepares students for the entry exams to the Grandes Écoles → **cours**

┌─────────────────────────────┐
│ **CLASSES PRÉPARATOIRES** │
└─────────────────────────────┘

Classes préparatoires *is the term given to the two years of intensive study required to sit the competitive entrance examinations to the "grandes écoles". They are extremely demanding post- "baccalauréat" courses, usually taken in a "lycée". Schools which provide such classes are more highly regarded than those which do not.* → BACCALAURÉAT ; CONCOURS ; GRANDES ÉCOLES ; LYCÉE

préparer [prepare] ▸conjug 1◂ 1 VT a (= *confectionner*: *gén*) to prepare; [+ *repas*] to pre-

pare, make; [+ *médicament*] to prepare, make up; [+ *piège, complot*] to lay, hatch; [+ *plan*] to draw up, work out, prepare; [+ *cours, discours*] to prepare; [+ *thèse*] to be doing, be working on, prepare; **elle nous prépare une tasse de thé** she's making a cup of tea for us, she's getting us a cup of tea; **il lui prépare de bons petits plats** he makes *ou* cooks tasty dishes for her; **plat préparé** ready(-made) meal

b (= *apprêter*) (*gén*) to prepare; [+ *table*] to lay, get ready; [+ *affaires, bagages, chambre*] to prepare, get ready; [+ *peaux, poisson, volaille*] to dress; (*Agr*) [+ *terre*] to prepare; [+ *attaque, rentrée, voyage*] to prepare (for), get ready for; [+ *transition*] to prepare for; **~ le départ** to get ready *ou* prepare to leave, make ready for one's departure (*frm*); **~ l'avenir** to prepare for the future; **~ ses effets** to time one's effects carefully, prepare one's effects; **il a préparé la rencontre des deux ministres** he made the preparations for *ou* he organized *ou* he set up the meeting between the two ministers; **l'attaque avait été soigneusement préparée** the attack had been carefully prepared *ou* organized; **le coup avait été préparé de longue main** they (*ou* he *etc*) had been preparing for it for a long time; (*Mil, fig*) **~ le terrain** to prepare the ground

c (*Scol*) [+ *examen*] to prepare for, study for; **~ Normale Sup** to study for entrance to the École normale supérieure

d (= *habituer, entraîner*) **~ qn à qch/à faire qch** to prepare sb for sth/to do sth; **~ les esprits** to prepare people('s minds) (**à qch** for sth); **~ qn à un examen** to prepare *ou* coach sb for an exam; **il a essayé de la ~ à la triste nouvelle** he tried to prepare her for the sad news; **je n'y étais pas préparé** I wasn't prepared for it, I wasn't expecting it

e (= *réserver*) **~ qch à qn** to have sth in store for sb; **je me demande ce qu'elle nous prépare** I wonder what she's got in store *ou* she's cooking up for us*; **on ne sait pas ce que l'avenir nous prépare** we don't know what the future holds (in store) for us *ou* has in store for us; **il nous prépare une surprise** he has a surprise in store for us, he's got a surprise up his sleeve; (*iro*) **le temps nous prépare de joyeuses vacances !** if this weather continues the holidays will be just great!* (*iro*); **il nous prépare un bon rhume** he's getting a cold

2 **se préparer** VPR a (= *s'apprêter*) to prepare (o.s.), get ready (**à qch** for sth, **à faire** to do); **attendez, elle se prépare** wait a minute, she's getting ready; **se ~ à une mauvaise nouvelle** to prepare o.s. for some bad news; **se ~ au combat** *ou* **à combattre** to prepare to fight *ou* to do battle; **se ~ pour les Jeux olympiques** to prepare *ou* train for the Olympics; **préparez-vous au pire** prepare for the worst; **je ne m'y étais pas préparé** I hadn't prepared myself for it, I wasn't expecting it; **se ~ pour un bal/pour sortir dîner en ville** to get ready *ou* dressed for a dance/to go out to dinner; **préparez-vous à être appelé d'urgence** be prepared to be called out urgently; **vous vous préparez des ennuis** you're making trouble *ou* storing up trouble for yourself

b (= *approcher*) [*orage*] to be brewing; **il se prépare une bagarre** there's going to be a fight; **il se prépare quelque chose de louche** there's something fishy going on*

prépayé, e [prepeje] ADJ [*billet*] prepaid, paid in advance

prépondérance [prepɔ̃derɑ̃s] NF [*nation, groupe*] ascendancy, preponderance, supremacy (**sur** over); [*idée, croyance, théorie*] supremacy (**sur** over); [*trait de caractère*] domination (**sur** over)

prépondérant, e [prepɔ̃derɑ̃, ɑ̃t] ADJ [*rôle*] dominating, preponderant; (*Pol*) **voix ~e** casting vote

préposé [prepoze] NM (*gén*) employee; (= *facteur*) postman (*Brit*), mailman (*US*); [*douane*] official, officer; [*vestiaire*] attendant

préposée [prepoze] NF (*gén*) employee; (= *factrice*) postwoman (*Brit*), mailwoman (*US*); [*vestiaire*] attendant

préposer [prepoze] ▸conjug 1◂ VT to appoint (à to); **préposé à** in charge of

prépositif, -ive [prepozitif, iv] ADJ prepositional

préposition [prepozisjɔ̃] NF preposition

prépositionnel, -elle [prepozisjɔnɛl] ADJ prepositional

prépositivement [prepozitivmɑ̃] ADV prepositionally, as a preposition

préprogrammé, e [preprɔgrame] ADJ (*Ordin*) preprogrammed

prépuce [prepys] NM foreskin, prepuce (*SPÉC*)

préraphaélisme [prerafaelism] NM Pre-Raphaelitism

préraphaélite [prerafaelit] ADJ, NM Pre-Raphaelite

prérégler [preregle] ▸conjug 6◂ VT to preset

prérentrée [prerɑ̃tre] NF (*Scol*) preparatory day for teachers before school term starts

préretraite [prerǝtrɛt] NF (= *état*) early retirement; (= *pension*) early retirement pension; **partir en ~** to take early retirement; **être mis en ~** to be given early retirement, be retired early

préretraité, e [prerɑ̃trete] NM,F *person who has taken early retirement*

prérogative [prerɔgativ] NF prerogative

préroman, e [prerɔmɑ̃, an] ADJ [*art*] pre-Romanesque

préromantique [prerɔmɑ̃tik] ADJ pre-Romantic; **les ~s** the pre-Romantics, the pre-Romantic poets (*ou* musicians *etc*)

préromantisme [prerɔmɑ̃tism] NM pre-Romanticism

près [prɛ] **1** ADV **a** (*dans l'espace*) near(by), close (by); (*dans le temps*) near, close; **la gare est tout ~** we're very close to the station, the station is very nearby; **il habite assez/tout ~** he lives quite/very near(by) *ou* close (by); **ne te mets pas trop ~** don't get too close *ou* near; **c'est plus/moins ~ que je ne croyais** (*espace*) it's nearer *ou* closer than/further than I thought; (*temps*) it's nearer *ou* sooner *ou* closer than/not as near as I thought *ou* further off than I thought; **Noël est très ~ maintenant** Christmas is (getting) very near *ou* close now, it'll very soon be Christmas now

b (*loc*) **c'est terminé à peu de chose ~** it's more or less *ou* pretty well* finished; **ce n'est pas aussi bon, à beaucoup ~** it's nothing like *ou* nowhere near as good; **ils sont identiques, à la couleur ~** they are identical apart from *ou* except for the colour; **à cela ~ que ...** if it weren't for *ou* apart from the fact that ...; **je vais vous donner le chiffre à un franc/à un centimètre ~** I'll give you the figure to within about a franc/a centimetre; **cela fait 100 F à quelque chose ~ ou à peu de chose(s) ~** that comes to 100 francs, or as near as makes no difference; **il a raté le bus à une minute ~** he missed the bus by a minute or so; **il n'est pas à 10 minutes/à un kilo de sucre/à 100 F ~** he can spare 10 minutes/a kilo of sugar/100 francs; **il n'est pas à un crime ~** he won't let a crime stop him; **il n'est plus à 10 minutes ~** he can wait another 10 minutes → **peu**

2 PRÉP (*littér ou Admin*) (*lieu*) near; **ambassadeur ~ le roi de ...** ambassador to the king of ...

3 **près de** LOC PRÉP **a** (*dans l'espace*) close to, near (to); **leur maison est ~ de l'église** their house is close to *ou* near the church; **le plus/moins ~ possible de la porte/de Noël** as

close *ou* near to/as far away as possible from the door/Christmas; **une robe ~ du corps** a close-fitting dress; **ils étaient très ~ l'un de l'autre** they were very close to each other; **elle est ~ de sa mère** she's with her mother; **être très ~ du but** to be very close *ou* near to one's goal; (*fig*) **être ~ de son argent** *ou* **de ses sous*** to be close- *ou* tight-fisted

b (*dans le temps*) close to; **il est ~ de minuit** it's close to midnight, it's nearly midnight; **il est ~ de la retraite** he's close to *ou* nearing retirement; **arriver ~ de la fin d'un voyage** to be nearing the end *ou* coming near *ou* close to the end of a journey; **il est ~ de la cinquantaine** he's nearly *ou* almost fifty, he's going on fifty, he's coming up to fifty (*Brit*)

c (*approximativement*) nearly, almost; **il a dépensé ~ de la moitié de son salaire** he has spent nearly *ou* almost half his salary; **il y a ~ de 5 ans qu'ils sont partis** they left nearly *ou* close on 5 years ago, it's nearly 5 years since they left

d (*avec verbe à l'infinitif* = *sur le point de*) **être très ~ d'avoir trouvé la solution** to have almost *ou* nearly found the solution; **elle a été très ~ de refuser** she was on the point of refusing, she was about to refuse, she came close to refusing; **je suis très ~ de croire que ...** I'm (almost) beginning to think that ...; **je ne suis pas ~ de partir/de réussir** at this rate, I'm not likely to be going (yet)/to succeed; **je ne suis pas ~ d'y retourner/de recommencer** I won't go back there/do that again in a hurry, you won't catch me going back there/doing that again in a hurry

4 **de près** LOC ADV **le coup a été tiré de ~** the shot was fired at close range; **il voit mal/bien de ~** he can't see very well/he can see all right close to; **surveiller qn de ~** to keep a close watch on sb, watch sb closely; **il a vu la mort de ~** he has stared *ou* looked death in the face; **il faudra examiner cette affaire de plus ~** we must have *ou* take a closer look at *ou* look more closely into this business; **on a frôlé de très ~ la catastrophe** we came within an inch of disaster, we had a close shave *ou* a narrow escape; **de ~ ou de loin** [*ressembler*] more or less; **tout ce qui touche de ~ ou de loin au cinéma** everything remotely connected with cinema → **rasé, regarder**

présage [prezaʒ] NM omen, presage (*littér*); **bon/mauvais/heureux ~** good/ill/happy omen; **ces bons résultats sont le ~ de jours meilleurs** these good results are the sign of better days to come

présager [prezaʒe] ▸conjug 3◂ VT (= *annoncer*) to be a sign *ou* an omen of, presage (*littér*); (= *prévoir*) to predict, foresee; **cela ne présage rien de bon** nothing good will come of it, that's an ominous sign; **cela nous laisse ~ que ...** it leads us to predict *ou* expect that ...; **rien ne laissait ~ la catastrophe** there was nothing to suggest that such a disaster might happen; **rien ne laissait ~ que ...** there was nothing to suggest that ...

pré-salé (*pl* **prés-salés**) [presale] NM (**agneau/mouton de**) **~** salt meadow lamb/sheep; (= *viande*) salt meadow lamb/mutton

presbyte [prɛsbit] ADJ long-sighted, far-sighted (*US*), presbyopic (*SPÉC*)

presbytère [prɛsbiter] NM presbytery

presbytérianisme [prɛsbiterjanism] NM Presbyterianism

presbytérien, -ienne [prɛsbiterjɛ̃, jɛn] ADJ, NM,F Presbyterian

presbytie [prɛsbisi] NF long-sightedness, far-sightedness (*US*), presbyopia (*SPÉC*)

prescience [presjɑ̃s] NF prescience, foresight

prescient, e [presjɑ̃, jɑ̃t] ADJ prescient, far-sighted

préscolaire [preskɔler] ADJ preschool (*épith*); **enfant d'âge ~** preschool child, child of preschool age

prescripteur, -trice [prɛskriptœr, tris] NM,F (*Comm*) prescriber; (*Scol*) teacher (*who recommends schoolbooks*); (**médecin**) **~** consultant

prescriptible [prɛskriptibl] ADJ prescriptible

prescription [prɛskripsjɔ̃] NF **a** (*Méd*) prescription, directions; **« se conformer aux ~s du médecin »** "to be taken in accordance with the doctor's instructions"; **obtenu sur ~ médicale** obtained on prescription **b** (= *ordre*) (*gén*) order, instruction; [*morale, règlement*] dictate; (= *recommandation*) [*ouvrage, méthode*] recommendation; **~s techniques** technical requirements **c** (*Jur*) (*droit civil*) prescription; (*droit pénal*) statute of limitations; **au bout de sept ans il y a ~** the statute of limitations is seven years; (*hum*) **il y a ~ maintenant, on peut en parler** it's ancient history now so it's all right to talk about it

prescrire [prɛskrir] ▸conjug 39◂ VT (*Méd, Jur*) to prescribe; [+ *objet, méthode, livre*] to recommend; [*morale, honneur, loi*] to stipulate, lay down; (= *ordonner*) to order, command; **à la date prescrite** on the prescribed date, on the date stipulated; (*Méd*) **« ne pas dépasser la dose prescrite »** "do not exceed the prescribed dose"; [*peine, dette*] **être prescrit ◊ se ~** to lapse

préséance [preseɑ̃s] NF precedence (*NonC*); **par ordre de ~** in order of precedence

présélecteur [preselɛktœr] NM preselector

présélection [preselɛksjɔ̃] NF (*gén*) preselection; [*candidats*] preselection, shortlisting (*Brit*); (*Radio*) **bouton** *ou* **touche de ~** preset button; **programme de ~** preset programme; **effectuer une ~ des demandeurs d'emploi** to shortlist *ou* preselect job applicants; (*Aut*) **boîte de vitesses à ~** pre-selector gearbox

présélectionner [preselɛksjɔne] ▸conjug 1◂ VT [+ *chaîne de radio*] to preset, preselect; [+ *candidats*] to preselect, short-list (*Brit*)

présence [prezɑ̃s] **1** NF **a** [*personne, chose, pays*] presence; (*au bureau, à l'école*) attendance; (*Rel*) presence; **la ~ aux cours est obligatoire** attendance at classes is compulsory; **fuir la ~ de qn** to avoid sb, keep well away from sb; (*frm*) **Monsieur le maire nous a honoré de sa ~** the Mayor honoured us with his presence; **j'ai juste à faire de la ~** I just have to be there *ou* present; **~ assidue au bureau** regular attendance at the office; **~ policière** police presence → **acte, feuille, jeton**

b (= *personnalité*) presence; **avoir de la ~** to have (a) great presence; **elle a beaucoup de ~ à l'écran/sur scène** she has great screen/stage presence

c (= *être*) **j'ai senti une ~** I felt a presence, I suddenly felt that I was not alone

d (*loc*) **les forces en ~** the opposing armies; **mettre deux personnes en ~** to bring two people together *ou* face to face; (*Jur*) **les parties en ~** the litigants, the opposing parties; **en ~ de** in the presence of; **cela s'est produit en ma/hors de ma ~** it happened while I was there *ou* in my presence/while I was not there *ou* in my absence; **en ~ de tels incidents** faced with *ou* in the face of such incidents; **mettre qn en ~ de qn/qch** to bring sb face to face with sb/sth

2 COMP ► **présence d'esprit** presence of mind

présent¹, e [prezɑ̃, ɑ̃t] **1** ADJ **a** [*personne*] present; (*Rel*) present; (*frm*) **les personnes ici ~es** those present, the persons here present (*frm*); **les personnes (qui étaient) ~es au moment de l'incident** the people who were present *ou* there when the incident occurred; **être ~ à une cérémonie** to be present at *ou* attend a ceremony; **être ~ à l'appel** to be present at roll call; **~!** present!; **répondre ~** (*lit*) to answer "present"; (*fig*) **il a toujours répondu ~ quand j'ai eu besoin de lui** he always came through *ou* he was always there when I needed him; **cette année au festival, beaucoup de jeunes musiciens ont répondu ~(s)** many young musicians attended this year's festival; (*hum*) **pour un bon repas, il est toujours ~!** you can always count on him to be there when there's good food around!; **je suis ~ en pensée** my thoughts are with you (*ou* him *etc*), I'm thinking of you (*ou* him *etc*)

b [*chose*] present; **métal ~ dans un minerai** metal present *ou* found in an ore; **son pessimisme est partout ~ dans son dernier roman** his pessimism runs right through *ou* is evident throughout his latest novel; **sa gentillesse est ~e dans chacun de ses actes** his kindness is evident in everything he does; **avoir qch à l'esprit** to have sth fresh in one's mind; **je n'ai pas les chiffres ~s à l'esprit** I can't bring the figures to mind, I can't remember the figures offhand; **j'aurai toujours ce souvenir ~ à l'esprit** this memory will be ever-present in my mind *ou* will always be fresh in my mind; **gardez ceci ~ à l'esprit** keep *ou* bear this in mind

c (= *actuel*) [*circonstances, état, heure, époque*] present; **le 15 du mois ~** on the 15th inst. (*Admin*) *ou* of this month

d (*Gram*) [*temps, participe*] present

e (= *dont il est question*) present; **le ~ récit** the present account, this account; (*Admin*) **nous vous signalons par la ~e lettre que ...** we hereby inform you that ...

f (= *actif*) **ils sont très ~s dans le secteur informatique** they have a strong foothold in the computer sector; (*Sport*) **il est très ~ sur le terrain** he covers the field really well; (*Tennis*) **elle est très ~e au filet** she covers the net really well

2 NM **a** (= *époque*) **le ~** the present

b (*Gram*) present (tense); **au ~** in the present (tense); **~ de l'indicatif** present indicative; **~ historique** *ou* **de narration** historic(al) *ou* narrative present

c (= *personne*) **les ~s et les absents** those present and those absent; **il n'y avait que cinq ~s** there were only five people present *ou* there

d (*loc*) **à ~** (= *en ce moment*) at present, presently (*US*); (= *maintenant*) now; (= *de nos jours*) now, nowadays; **à ~ que nous savons** now that we know; **la jeunesse/les gens d'à ~** young people/people of today, young people/people nowadays → **dès, jusque**

3 **présente** NF (*Admin* = *lettre*) **veuillez recevoir par la ~e ...** please find enclosed ...; **nous vous signalons par la ~e que ...** we hereby inform you that ...; **le contrat annexé à la ~e** the contract enclosed herewith

présent² [pʀezɑ̃] NM (*littér*) gift, present; **faire ~ de qch à qn** to present sb with sth

présentable [pʀezɑ̃tabl] ADJ presentable; **avec cet œil au beurre noir, je ne suis pas ~** with this black eye, I'm not fit to be seen

présentateur, -trice [pʀezɑ̃tatœʀ, tʀis] NM,F (*Radio, TV*) [*jeu, causerie, variétés*] host, compere (*Brit*), emcee (*US*); [*débat*] presenter; [*nouvelles*] newscaster, newsreader

présentation [pʀezɑ̃tasjɔ̃] NF **a** (*gén*) presentation; **sur ~ d'une pièce d'identité** on presentation of proof of identity

b [*nouveau venu, conférencier*] introduction; (*frm : à la cour*) presentation; **faire les ~s** to make the introductions, introduce people to one another

c (*au public*) [*tableaux, pièce*] presentation; [*marchandises*] presentation, display; [*film*] presentation, showing; (*Radio, TV*) [*émission*] presentation, introduction; **~ de mode** fashion show

d (= *manière de présenter*) [*idée, produit, travail*] presentation; [*personne*] **avoir une bonne/mauvaise ~** to have a good *ou* pleasant/an unattractive *ou* off-putting appearance

e (*Rel*) **la Présentation** the Presentation

f (*Méd*) [*fœtus*] presentation; **~ par la tête/le siège** head/breech presentation

g (*Fin*) presentation; **payable sur ~** payable on presentation *ou* at call *ou* at sight *ou* over the counter

présentement [pʀezɑ̃tmɑ̃] ADV (= *en ce moment*) at present, presently (*US*); (= *maintenant*) now

présenter [pʀezɑ̃te] ▸ conjug 1 ◂ **1** VT **a** [+ *personne*] (*à qn d'autre, à un groupe*) to introduce (**à** to, **dans** into); (*au roi, à la cour*) to present (**à** to); **je vous présente ma femme** this is my wife, have you met my wife?, may I introduce my wife (to you)?

b (= *montrer*) [+ *billet, passeport*] to present, show, produce; **il présentait une apparence de calme** he appeared calm; **la ville présente un aspect inhabituel** the town looks different from usual *ou* doesn't look the same as it usually does

c (= *proposer au public*) [+ *marchandises*] to present, display (**à** to), set out (**à** before); (*Théât*) [+ *acteur, pièce*] to present; (*Radio, TV*) [+ *émission*] to present, introduce; [+ *jeux*] to present, compere (*Brit*); [+ *mode, tableaux*] to present; (*TV*) **c'est lui qui présente les nouvelles** he presents *ou* reports the news

d (= *offrir*) [+ *plat*] to present, hold out; [+ *rafraîchissements*] to offer, hand round; [+ *bouquet*] to present; **~ son bras à qn** to offer one's arm to sb

e (= *exposer*) [+ *problème*] to set out, explain; [+ *idées*] to present, set *ou* lay out; [+ *théorie*] to expound, set out; **un travail bien/mal présenté** a well-/badly presented *ou* laid-out piece of work; **les plats sont bien/mal présentés** the food is/isn't nicely *ou* attractively presented; **présentez-lui cela avec tact** explain it to him *ou* put it to him tactfully; **il nous a présenté son ami comme un héros** he spoke of his friend as a hero → **jour**

f (= *exprimer*) [+ *excuses*] to present, offer, make; [+ *condoléances, félicitations*] to present, offer; [+ *respects*] to present, pay; [+ *objection*] to raise

g (= *comporter*) [+ *avantage, intérêt*] to present, afford; [+ *différences*] to reveal, present; [+ *risque, difficulté, obstacle*] to present; **ce malade présente des symptômes de tuberculose** this patient presents *ou* shows symptoms of tuberculosis; **ce tissu présente de nombreux défauts** this material has a number of flaws; **le budget présente un déficit important** there is a big deficit in the budget; **la situation présente un caractère d'urgence** the situation is *ou* appears urgent

h (= *soumettre*) [+ *note, facture, devis, bilan*] to present, submit; [+ *thèse*] to submit; [+ *motion*] to move; [+ *projet de loi*] to present, introduce; [+ *rapport, requête*] to present, put in, submit; **~ sa candidature à un poste** to apply for *ou* put in for a job; **il a présenté sa démission** he has handed in his resignation; **~ un candidat à un concours** to put a candidate in *ou* enter a candidate for a competitive examination; (*Scol*) **à l'examen, il a présenté un texte de Camus** he chose *ou* did a text by Camus for the exam

i (= *tourner dans la direction de*) to turn; **~ le flanc à l'ennemi** to turn one's flank towards the enemy; **bateau qui présente le travers au vent** ship turning *ou* sailing broadside on to the wind

j (*Mil*) [+ *armes*] to present; [+ *troupes*] to present (*for inspection*) → **arme**

k (*Tech* = *placer*) to position, line up

2 VI [*personne*] **~ bien/mal** to have a good *ou* pleasant/an unattractive *ou* off-putting (*Brit*) appearance

3 **se présenter** VPR **a** (= *se rendre*) to go, come, appear; **se ~ chez qn** to go to sb's house; **il ose encore se ~ chez toi!** does he still dare to show himself *ou* to appear at your house!; **il ne s'est présenté personne** no

one turned up *ou* came *ou* appeared; **je ne peux pas me ~ dans cette tenue** I can't appear dressed like this; (*dans une annonce*) **« ne pas écrire, se ~ »** "(interested) applicants should apply in person"; (*Jur*) **se ~ à l'audience** to appear in court, make a court appearance

b (= *être candidat*) to come forward; **se ~ pour un emploi** to put in *ou* apply for a job; **se ~ à** [+ *examen*] to sit (*Brit*), take; [+ *concours*] to go in for, enter; **se ~ aux élections** to stand (*Brit*) *ou* run (*surtout US*) for election, stand (*Brit*) *ou* run (*surtout US*) in the elections; **se ~ aux élections présidentielles** to stand for president *ou* in the presidential elections (*Brit*), run for president (*surtout US*); **se ~ comme candidat** (*aux élections*) to be a candidate, stand (*Brit*) *ou* run (*surtout US*) as a candidate (**à** in); (*à un poste*) to apply (**à** for)

c (= *se faire connaître : gén*) to introduce o.s. (**à** to)

d (= *surgir*) [*occasion*] to arise, present itself; [*difficulté*] to crop *ou* come up, arise, present itself; [*solution*] to come to mind, present itself; **un problème se présente à nous** we are faced *ou* confronted with a problem; **il lit tout ce qui se présente** he reads everything he can get his hands on, he reads anything that's going*; **il faut attendre que quelque chose se présente** we must wait until something turns up; **deux noms se présentent à l'esprit** two names come *ou* spring to mind; **un spectacle magnifique se présenta à ses yeux** a magnificent sight met his eyes

e (= *apparaître*) **cela se présente sous forme de cachets** it's presented *ou* it comes in tablet form; **l'affaire se présente bien/mal** things are looking good/aren't looking too good; **les choses se présentent sous un nouveau jour** things appear in a new light; **comment se présente le problème ?** what exactly is the problem?, what is the nature of the problem?; (*Méd*) **comment l'enfant se présente-t-il ?** how is the baby presenting?

présentoir [pʀezɑ̃twaʀ] NM (= *étagère*) display

présérie [pʀeseʀi] NF pilot production

préservateur, -trice [pʀezɛʀvatœʀ, tʀis] **1** ADJ preventive, protective **2** NM (*Chim*) preservative

préservatif, -ive [pʀezɛʀvatif, iv] **1** ADJ preventive, protective **2** NM (= *masculin*) condom; **~ féminin** female condom; **refuser le ~** to refuse to wear a condom

préservation [pʀezɛʀvasjɔ̃] NF [*environnement, espèce, patrimoine*] preservation, protection; [*identité culturelle*] preservation; [*emploi*] protection; **les gens sont obnubilés par la ~ de leur emploi** people are obsessed with holding on to their jobs

préserver [pʀezɛʀve] ▸ conjug 1 ◂ VT [+ *emploi, droits*] to safeguard, preserve; [+ *identité culturelle, paix, liberté, valeurs, équilibre, indépendance*] to preserve; [+ *environnement, patrimoine, intérêts*] to preserve, protect (**de** from, against); [+ *vie*] (= *protéger*) to protect; (= *sauver*) to save; **se ~ du soleil** to protect o.s. from the sun; **le ciel** *ou* **Dieu m'en préserve !** Heaven preserve me!, Heaven forbid!

présidence [pʀezidɑ̃s] NF [*État, tribunal*] presidency; [*comité, réunion*] chairmanship; [*firme*] chairmanship, directorship; [*université*] vice-chancellorship (*Brit*), presidency (*US*); (*Pol*) **candidat à la ~** presidential candidate **b** (= *résidence*) presidential residence *ou* palace

président [pʀezidɑ̃] **1** NM **a** (*Pol*) president; **Monsieur/Madame le ~** Mr/Madam President; **~ de la République française/des États-Unis** President of the French Republic/of the United States **b** [*comité, réunion, conseil d'administration, commission*] chairman; [*club, société savante*] president; [*firme*] chairman, president; [*jury d'examen*] chairman, chief examiner; [*université*] vice-chancellor (*Brit*), president (*US*), chancellor (*US*) **c** (*Jur*) [*tribunal*] presiding judge *ou* magistrate; [*jury*] foreman; **Monsieur (*ou* Madame) le ~** Your Honour

2 COMP ► **président de l'Assemblée nationale** President of the National Assembly ► **président du Conseil** (*Hist*) Prime Minister ► **président-directeur général** chairman and managing director (*Brit*), chief executive officer (*US*) ► **le président Mao** Chairman Mao ► **président du Parlement européen** President of the European Parliament ► **président du Sénat** President of the Senate ► **président à vie** life president

présidente [pʀezidɑ̃t] NF **a** (*en titre : Pol*) president; [*comité, réunion, conseil d'administration, commission*] chairwoman; [*club, société savante*] president; [*firme*] chairwoman, president; [*jury d'examen*] chairwoman; [*université*] vice-chancellor (*Brit*), president (*US*), chancellor (*US*); (*Jur*) [*tribunal*] presiding judge *ou* magistrate; [*jury*] forewoman **b** († = *épouse*) (*gén*) president's *ou* chairman's wife; (*Pol*) president's wife, first lady

présidentiable [pʀezidɑ̃sjabl] ADJ **être ~** to be a possible *ou* potential presidential candidate

présidentialisme [pʀezidɑ̃sjalism] NM presidentialism

présidentiel, -ielle [pʀezidɑ̃sjɛl] ADJ presidential; **les (élections) présidentielles** the presidential elections → *ÉLECTIONS*

présider [pʀezide] ▸ conjug 1 ◂ **1** VT [+ *tribunal, conseil, assemblée*] to preside over; [+ *comité, débat, séance*] to chair; **~ un dîner** to be the guest of honour at a dinner; **c'est M. Leblanc qui préside** [+ *séance*] Mr Leblanc is in *ou* taking the chair; [+ *club*] Mr Leblanc is president **2 présider à** VT INDIR [+ *préparatifs, décisions, exécution*] to direct, be in charge *ou* command of; [+ *destinées*] to rule over; [+ *cérémonie*] to preside over; **règles qui président à qch** rules which govern sth; **la volonté de conciliation a présidé aux discussions** a conciliatory spirit prevailed throughout the talks

présidium [pʀezidjɔm] NM presidium

présocratique [pʀesɔkʀatik] ADJ, NM pre-Socratic

présomptif, -ive [pʀezɔ̃ptif, iv] ADJ **héritier ~** heir apparent

présomption [pʀezɔ̃psjɔ̃] NF **a** (= *supposition*) presumption, assumption; (*Jur*) presumption; **de lourdes ~s pèsent sur lui** he is under grave suspicion; **il a été condamné sur de simples ~s** he was convicted on suspicion alone; **~ de paternité** presumption of paternity; **~ d'innocence** presumption of innocence; **faire respecter la ~ d'innocence** to respect the principle that the defendant is innocent until proven guilty **b** (= *prétention*) presumptuousness, presumption

présomptueusement [pʀezɔ̃ptɥøzmɑ̃] ADV presumptuously

présomptueux, -euse [pʀezɔ̃ptɥø, øz] ADJ presumptuous, self-assured; **d'un ton *ou* d'un air ~** presumptuously

presque [pʀɛsk] ADV **a** (*contexte positif*) almost, nearly, virtually; **j'ai ~ terminé** I've almost *ou* nearly *ou* as good as finished; **~ à chaque pas** at almost every step; **une espèce d'inquiétude, ~ d'angoisse** a kind of anxiety — almost anguish; **c'est ~ de la folie** it's little short of madness; **c'est ~ impossible** it's almost *ou* virtually *ou* well-nigh impossible; **c'est sûr ou ~** it's almost *ou* practically *ou* virtually certain **b** (*contexte négatif*) hardly, scarcely, almost, virtually; **personne/rien ou ~ ◊ ~ personne/rien** hardly *ou* scarcely anyone/anything, almost

nobody/nothing, next to nobody/nothing; **as-tu trouvé des fautes ? — ~ pas** did you find any mistakes? — hardly any; **a-t-il dormi ? — ~ pas** did he sleep? — hardly at all *ou* no, not really; **je ne l'ai ~ pas entendu** I hardly *ou* scarcely heard him; **il n'y a ~ plus de vin** there's hardly any wine left, the wine has nearly all gone; **ça n'arrive ~ jamais** it hardly *ou* scarcely ever happens, it almost *ou* practically never happens

c (*avant n*) **dans la ~ obscurité** in the near darkness; **la ~ totalité des lecteurs** almost *ou* nearly all the readers; **j'en ai la ~ certitude** I'm almost *ou* virtually certain

presqu'île [pʀeskil] NF peninsula

pressage [pʀesaʒ] NM [*disque, raisin*] pressing

pressant, e [pʀesɑ̃, ɑ̃t] ADJ [*besoin, danger, invitation*] urgent, pressing (*épith*); [*situation, travail, désir, demande*] urgent; [*personne*] insistent; **demander qch de façon ~e** to ask for sth urgently; **le créancier a été/s'est fait ~** the creditor was insistent/started to insist *ou* started to press him (*ou me etc*); (*euph*) **avoir un besoin ~ ou une envie ~e** to need to answer an urgent call of nature, need to spend a penny (*euph, Brit*) *ou* to go to the restroom (*US*)

press-book (*pl* **press-books**) [pʀesbuk] NM [*mannequin*] portfolio

presse [pʀɛs] NF **a** (= *institution*) press; (= *journaux*) (news)papers; **la grande ~** the popular press; **la ~ écrite** the press; **c'est dans toute la ~** it's in all the papers; **la ~ périodique** periodicals, journals; **~ régionale/mensuelle** regional/monthly press *ou* papers; **~ féminine/automobile** women's/car magazines; **~ d'opinion** papers specializing in analysis and commentary; **~ d'information** newspapers; **~ à scandale *ou* à sensation** gutter press; **~ du cœur** romance magazines; **avoir bonne/mauvaise ~** (*lit*) to get *ou* have a good/bad press; (*fig*) to be well/badly thought of; **agence/attaché/conférence de ~** press agency/attaché/conference → **délit, liberté, service**

b (= *appareil*) (*gén*) press; (*Typo*) (printing) press; **~ à cylindres/à bras** cylinder/hand press; **mettre sous ~** [+ *livre*] to send to press; [+ *journal*] to put to bed; **le livre a été mis sous ~** the book has gone to press; **le journal a été mis sous ~** the (news)paper has gone to bed; **livre sous ~** book in press; **correct au moment de la mise sous ~** correct at the time of going to press

c (*littér* = *foule*) throng (*littér*), press (*littér*)

d (= *urgence*) **pendant les moments de ~** when things get busy; **il n'y a pas de ~*** there's no rush *ou* hurry

pressé, e [pʀese] (*ptp de presser*) ADJ **a** [*pas*] hurried; **avoir un air ~** to look as though one is in a hurry; **marcher d'un pas ~** to hurry along; **je suis (très) ~** I'm in a (great) hurry *ou* (very) pressed for time; **je ne suis pas ~** I'm in no hurry *ou* not in any hurry; **être ~ de partir** to be in a hurry to leave **b** (= *urgent*) [*travail, lettre*] urgent; **c'est ~ ?** is it urgent?; **il n'a eu rien de plus ~ que de faire ...** he wasted no time doing ..., he just couldn't wait to do ...; **si tu n'as rien de plus ~ à faire que de ...** if you have nothing more urgent to do than ...; **il faut parer au plus ~** we must do the most urgent thing(s) first, first things first

presse-agrumes [pʀesagʀym] NM INV (*électrique*) (electric) juice extractor (*Brit*), (electric) juicer (*US*); (*manuel*) orange (*ou* lemon *etc*) squeezer

presse-ail [pʀesaj] NM INV garlic press *ou* crusher

presse-bouton [pʀesbutɔ̃] ADJ INV push-button

presse-citron (*pl* **presse-citrons**) [pʀesitʀɔ̃] NM lemon squeezer

pressentiment [pʀesɑ̃timɑ̃] NM (= *intuition*) foreboding, presentiment, premonition; (= *idée*) feeling; **j'ai comme un ~ qu'il ne viendra pas** I've got a feeling he won't come; **avoir le ~ de qch/que ...** to have a premonition of sth/that ...

pressentir [pʀesɑ̃tiʀ] ▸ conjug 16 ◂ VT **a** [+ *danger*] to sense, have a foreboding *ou* a premonition of; **~ que ...** to have a feeling *ou* a premonition that ...; **j'avais pressenti quelque chose** I had sensed something; **il n'a rien laissé ~ de ses projets** he gave no hint of his plans; **rien ne laissait ~ cette catastrophe** there was nothing to suggest that such a disaster might happen **b** [+ *personne*] to sound out, approach; **il a été pressenti pour le poste** he has been sounded out *ou* approached about taking the job; **ministre pressenti** prospective minister

presse-papiers [pʀespapje] NM INV paperweight

presse-purée [pʀespyʀe] NM INV potato-masher

presser [pʀese] ▸ conjug 1 ◂ **1** VT **a** [+ *éponge, fruit*] to squeeze; [+ *raisin*] to press; **un citron pressé** a glass of freshly-squeezed lemon juice; **~ qn comme un citron** to squeeze sb dry; (*fig*) **on presse l'orange *ou* le citron et on jette l'écorce** you use people as long as they can be of service to you and then you cast them aside; (*hum*) **si on lui pressait le nez, il en sortirait du lait** he's barely out of nappies (*Brit*) *ou* diapers (*US*)

b (= *serrer*) [+ *objet*] to squeeze; **les gens étaient pressés les uns contre les autres** people were squashed up *ou* crushed up against one another; **~ qn dans ses bras** to hug sb; **~ qn contre sa poitrine** to clasp sb to one's chest; **~ la main de *ou* à qn** to squeeze sb's hand, give sb's hand a squeeze

c (= *appuyer sur*) [+ *bouton, sonnette*] to press, push; **~ une matrice dans la cire** to press a mould into the wax

d (= *façonner*) [+ *disque, pli de pantalon*] to press

e (= *inciter à*) **~ qn de faire qch** to urge *ou* press sb to do sth

f (= *hâter*) [+ *affaire*] to speed up; [+ *départ*] to hasten, speed up; **(faire) ~ qn** to hurry sb (up); **(faire) ~ les choses** to speed things up; **~ le pas *ou* l'allure** to speed up, hurry on; **il fit ~ l'allure** he speeded up *ou* quickened the pace; **~ le mouvement** to hurry up, pick up the pace; **qu'est-ce qui vous presse ?** what's the hurry?; **rien ne vous presse** there's no hurry

g (= *harceler*) [+ *débiteur*] to press, put pressure on; (*littér, Mil*) [+ *ennemi*] to press; **être pressé par le besoin** to be driven *ou* pressed by need; (*littér*) **le désir qui le presse** the desire which drives him; **~ qn de questions** to ply sb with questions

2 VI (= *être urgent*) to be urgent; **l'affaire presse** it's urgent; **le temps presse** time is short; **cela ne presse pas ◊ rien ne presse** there's no hurry *ou* rush *ou* urgency, there's no need to rush *ou* hurry

3 se presser VPR **a** (= *se serrer*) **se ~ contre qn** to squeeze up against sb; **les gens se pressaient pour entrer** people were pushing to get in, there was a crush to get in; **les gens se pressaient autour de la vedette** people were pressing *ou* crowding round the star **b** (= *se hâter*) to hurry (up); **ils allaient/travaillaient sans se ~** they went/were working at a leisurely pace; **pressez-vous, il est tard** hurry up *ou* get a move on*, it's getting late; **il faut se ~** we must hurry *ou* get cracking* *ou* get a move on*; **presse-toi de partir** hurry up and go; **allons, pressons(-nous)!** come on, come on!, come on, we must hurry!

presse-raquette (*pl* **presse-raquettes**) [pʀesʀakɛt] NM racket press

pressing [pʀesiŋ] NM **a** (= *établissement*) dry-cleaner's **b** (*Sport*) pressure; **faire le ~ sur qn** to put the pressure on sb

pression [pʀesjɔ̃] NF **a** (= *action*) pressure; **je sentais la ~ de sa main sur la mienne** I could feel the pressure of his hand on mine ou his hand pressing on mine; **une simple ~ du doigt suffit pour l'ouvrir** to open it, just press; **faire ~ sur le couvercle d'une boîte** (*pour fermer*) to press (down) on the lid of a box; (*pour ouvrir*) to push up the lid of a box **b** (*Méd, Phys*) pressure; **~ artérielle/atmosphérique** blood/atmospheric pressure; **à haute/basse ~** high/low pressure (*épith*); **être sous ~** [*machine*] to be under pressure; [*cabine*] to be pressurized; [*personne*] to be keyed up, be tense; **mettre sous ~** to pressurize; (*excès de travail*) **je suis sous ~ en ce moment** I am under pressure just now; (*fig*) **faire monter/baisser la ~** to increase/reduce the pressure **c** (= *contrainte*) pressure; **~ sociale/fiscale** social/tax pressure; **sous la ~ des événements** under the pressure of events; **faire ~ ou exercer une ~ sur qn (pour qu'il fasse qch)** to put pressure on sb (to do sth), bring pressure to bear on sb (to do sth), pressurize sb (into doing sth); **être soumis à des ~s** to be under pressure → **groupe** **d** **bière à la ~** draught (*Brit*) ou draft (*US*) beer, beer on draught (*Brit*) ou draft (*US*); **deux ~(s)*, s'il vous plaît** two (draught) beers, please **e** (= *bouton*) press stud (*Brit*), snap (fastener) (*US*), popper* (*Brit*)

pressoir [pʀeswaʀ] NM **a** (= *appareil*) [*vin*] wine press; [*cidre*] cider press; [*huile*] oil press **b** (= *local*) press-house

pressurage [pʀesyʀaʒ] NM [*fruit*] pressing

pressurer [pʀesyʀe] ▸ conjug 1 ◂ VT [+ *fruit*] to press; [+ *personne*] to pressurize, put under pressure; **se ~ le cerveau** to rack one's brains

pressurisation [pʀesyʀizasjɔ̃] NF pressurization

pressuriser [pʀesyʀize] ▸ conjug 1 ◂ VT to pressurize; **cabine pressurisée** pressurized cabin

prestance [pʀestɑ̃s] NF presence; **avoir de la ~** to have great presence

prestataire [pʀestatɛʀ] NM person receiving benefits ou allowances; **~ de service** service provider

prestation [pʀestasjɔ̃] **1** NF **a** (= *allocation*) [*assurance*] benefit **b** (*gén pl* = *services*) [*hôtel, restaurant*] service; **« ~s luxueuses »** "luxuriously appointed" **c** (= *performance*) [*artiste, sportif*] performance; **faire une bonne ~** to put up a good performance, perform well **2** COMP ▸ **prestations familiales** State benefits paid to the family (*maternity benefit, family income supplement, rent rebate etc*) ▸ **prestation d'invalidité** disablement benefit ou allowance ▸ **prestation en nature** payment in kind ▸ **prestation de serment** taking the oath; **la ~ de serment du président a eu lieu hier** the president was sworn in yesterday ▸ **prestations sociales** social security benefits, welfare payments ▸ **prestation de service** provision of a service ▸ **prestation de vieillesse** old age pension

preste [pʀest] ADJ (*littér*) nimble

prestement [pʀestəmɑ̃] ADV (*littér*) nimbly

prestesse [pʀestes] NF (*littér*) nimbleness

prestidigitateur, -trice [pʀestidiʒitatœʀ, tʀis] NM,F conjurer, magician

prestidigitation [pʀestidiʒitasjɔ̃] NF conjuring; **faire de la ~** to do conjuring tricks; **tour de ~** conjuring trick; (*hum*) **ça relève de la ~!** it's pure wizardry!

prestige [pʀestiʒ] NM (*gén*) prestige; **le ~ de l'uniforme** the glamour of uniforms; **de ~** [*politique, opération, voiture*] prestige (*épith*); **fai-**

re qch pour le ~ to do sth for the glory of it ou for (the) prestige

prestigieux, -ieuse [pʀestiʒjø, jøz] ADJ prestigious; (*Comm*) renowned, prestigious; **une marque prestigieuse de voiture** a famous ou prestigious make of car

presto [pʀesto] ADV (*Mus*) presto; (* *fig*) double-quick*

présumable [pʀezymabl] ADJ presumable; **il est ~ que ...** it may be presumed that ...

présumer [pʀezyme] ▸ conjug 1 ◂ **1** VT to presume, assume; **présumé innocent** presumed innocent; **l'auteur présumé du livre** the presumed author of the book; **le meurtrier présumé** the alleged killer; **affaire de corruption présumée** alleged corruption affair; (*Jur*) **le père présumé** the putative father **2** **présumer de** VT INDIR **trop ~ de qch/qn** to overestimate ou overrate sth/sb; **(trop) ~ de ses forces** to overestimate one's strength

présupposé [pʀesypoze] NM presupposition

présupposer [pʀesypoze] ▸ conjug 1 ◂ VT to presuppose

présupposition [pʀesypozisjɔ̃] NF presupposition

présure [pʀezyʀ] NF rennet

prêt¹, prête [pʀɛ, pʀɛt] **1** ADJ **a** (= *préparé*) ready; **~ à** ou **pour qch/à** ou **pour faire qch** ready for sth/to do sth; **~ à fonctionner** ou **à l'emploi** ready for use; **poulet ~ à cuire** ou **rôtir** oven-ready chicken; **~ au départ** ou **à partir** ready to go ou leave, ready for the off* (*Brit*); **être fin ~ (au départ)** to be all set, be raring* to go; **tout est (fin) ~** everything is (quite) ready; **se tenir ~ à qch/à faire qch** to hold o.s. ou be ready for sth/to do sth; **tiens ta monnaie ~e pour payer** have your money ready to pay; **il est ~ à tout** (*criminel*) he'll do anything, he'll stop at nothing; **on m'a averti : je suis ~ à tout** they've warned me and I'm ready for anything; (*devise scoute*) **toujours ~!** be prepared! → **marque** **b** (= *disposé*) **~ à** ready ou prepared ou willing to do; **être tout ~ à faire qch** to be quite ready ou prepared ou willing to do sth

prêt² [pʀɛ] **1** NM **a** (= *action*) loaning, lending; (= *somme*) loan; **le service de ~ d'une bibliothèque** the lending department of a library; **~ inter-bibliothèques** inter-library loan; **~ sur gages** (= *service*) pawnbroking; (= *somme*) loan against security → **bibliothèque** **b** (*Mil*) pay **c** (= *avance*) advance **2** COMP ▸ **prêt aidé d'accession à la propriété** *loan for first-time home buyers* ▸ **prêt bancaire** bank loan; **~ (à taux) bonifié** subsidized ou guaranteed loan ▸ **prêt à la construction** building loan ▸ **prêt conventionné** regulated mortgage loan ▸ **prêt d'honneur** (*government*) *loan made with no guarantee of repayment* ▸ **prêt immobilier** ≈ mortgage (loan), ≈ real-estate loan (*US*) ▸ **prêt locatif aidé (d'insertion)** *low-cost subsidized housing loan* ▸ **prêt personnel** personal loan ▸ **prêt privilégié** guaranteed loan ▸ **prêt relais** bridging loan

prêt-à-coudre (*pl* **prêts-à-coudre**) [pʀɛtakudʀ] NM ready-to-sew garment

prêt-à-manger (*pl* **prêts-à-manger**) [pʀɛtamɑ̃ʒe] NM ready-made meals

prêt-à-monter (*pl* **prêts-à-monter**) [pʀɛtamɔ̃te] NM kit

prêt-à-porter (*pl* **prêts-à-porter**) [pʀɛtapɔʀte] NM ready-to-wear (clothes); **acheter qch en ~** to buy sth ready to wear ou off the peg (*Brit*) ou off the rack (*US*); **je n'achète que du ~** I only buy ready-to-wear ou off-the-peg (*Brit*) ou off-the-rack (*US*) clothes

prêt-bail (*pl* **prêts-bails**) [pʀɛbaj] NM leasing

prêté [pʀɛte] NM **c'est un ~ pour un rendu** it's tit for tat

prétendant, e [pʀetɑ̃dɑ̃, ɑ̃t] **1** NM (= *prince*)

pretender; (*littér* = *galant*) suitor **2** NM,F (= *candidat*) candidate (à for)

prétendre [pʀetɑ̃dʀ] ▸ conjug 41 ◂ **1** VT **a** (= *affirmer*) to claim, maintain, assert, say; **il prétend être** ou **qu'il est le premier à avoir trouvé la réponse** he claims to be the first to have found the answer, he claims ou maintains (that) he's the first to have found the answer; **il se prétend insulté/médecin** he makes out ou claims he's been insulted/he's a doctor; **je ne prétends pas qu'il l'ait fait** I don't say ou I'm not saying he did it; **on le prétend très riche** he is said ou alleged to be very rich; **en prétendant qu'il venait chercher un livre** on the pretence of coming to get a book, making out ou claiming that he had come to get a book; **à ce qu'il prétend** according to him ou to what he says, if what he says is true; **à ce qu'on prétend** allegedly, according to what people say **b** (= *avoir la prétention de*) to pretend; **tu ne prétends pas le faire tout seul ?** you don't pretend ou expect to do it on your own?; **je ne prétends pas me défendre** I don't pretend ou I'm not trying to justify myself **c** (*littér* = *vouloir*) to want; (= *avoir l'intention de*) to mean, intend; **que prétendez-vous de moi ?** what do you want of me? (*littér*); **que prétend-il faire ?** what does he mean ou intend to do?; **je prétends être obéi** ou **qu'on m'obéisse** I mean to be obeyed **2** **prétendre à** VT INDIR [+ *honneurs, emploi*] to lay claim to, aspire to; [+ *femme*] to aspire to; **~ à faire qch** to aspire to do sth

prétendu, e [pʀetɑ̃dy] (*ptp de* **prétendre**) **1** ADJ [*ami, expert*] so-called, supposed; [*alibi, preuves, déclaration*] alleged **2** NM,F († = *fiancé*) intended†

prétendument [pʀetɑ̃dymɑ̃] ADV supposedly, allegedly

prête-nom (*pl* **prête-noms**) [pʀɛtnɔ̃] NM frontman

prétentaine† [pʀetɑ̃tɛn] NF **courir la ~** to go gallivanting

prétentieusement [pʀetɑ̃sjøzmɑ̃] ADV pretentiously

prétentieux, -ieuse [pʀetɑ̃sjø, jøz] **1** ADJ [*personne, manières, ton*] pretentious, conceited; [*appellation*] pretentious, fancy; [*maison*] pretentious, showy **2** NM,F conceited person; **c'est un petit ~ !** he's so conceited!

prétention [pʀetɑ̃sjɔ̃] NF **a** (= *exigence*) claim; **avoir des ~s à** ou **sur** to lay claim to; (= *salaire*) **quelles sont vos ~s ?** what sort of salary do you expect? ou are you looking for?*; **écrire avec CV et ~s** write enclosing CV and stating expected salary **b** (= *ambition*) pretension, claim (à to); **avoir la ~ de faire qch** to claim to be able to do sth, like to think one can do sth; **je n'ai pas la ~ de rivaliser avec lui** I don't claim ou expect ou pretend (to be able) to compete with him; **il n'a pas la ~ de tout savoir** he makes no pretence of knowing everything, he doesn't pretend ou claim to know everything; **sa ~ à l'élégance** her claims ou pretensions to elegance; **sans ~** [*maison, repas*] unpretentious; [*robe*] simple **c** (= *vanité*) pretentiousness, pretension, conceitedness; **avec ~** pretentiously, conceitedly

prêter [pʀete] ▸ conjug 1 ◂ **1** VT **a** [+ *objet, argent*] to lend; **~ qch à qn** to lend sth to sb, lend sb sth; **peux-tu me ~ ton stylo ?** can you lend me your pen, can I borrow your pen?; **ils prêtent à 10%** they lend (money) at 10%, they give loans at 10%; **ils m'ont prêté 100 F** they lent me 100 francs; **~ sur gages** to lend against security ■ (*PROV*) **on ne prête qu'aux riches** unto those that have shall more be given (*PROV*) **b** (= *attribuer*) [+ *sentiment, facultés*] to attribute, ascribe; **on lui prête l'intention de démissionner** he is alleged ou said to be intending to resign; **on me prête des paroles que je**

n'ai pas dites people are claiming I said things that I didn't; **nous prêtons une grande importance à ces problèmes** we consider these problems of great importance, we accord a great deal of importance to these problems
c (= *apporter, offrir*) [+ *aide, appui*] to give, lend; **~ assistance/secours à qn** to go to sb's assistance/aid; **~ main forte à qn** to lend sb a hand, come to sb's assistance, come to help sb; **~ son concours à** to give one's assistance to; **~ sa voix à une cause** to speak on behalf of *ou* in support of a cause; **~ sa voix pour un gala** to sing at a gala performance; **dans cette émission il prêtait sa voix à Napoléon** in this broadcast he played *ou* spoke the part of Napoleon; **~ son nom à** to lend one's name to; **~ la main à une entreprise/un complot** to be *ou* get involved in *ou* take part in an undertaking/a plot; **~ attention à** to pay attention to, take notice of; **il faut ~ la plus grande attention à mes paroles** you must listen very closely *ou* you must pay very close attention to what I have to say; **~ le flanc à la critique** to lay o.s. open to criticism, invite criticism; **~ l'oreille** to listen, lend an ear (**à** to); **~ serment** to take an *ou* the oath; **faire ~ serment à qn** to administer the oath to sb; (*hum*) **si Dieu me prête vie** if God grants me life, if I am spared (*hum*)

2 **prêter à** VT INDIR **son attitude prête à équivoque/à la critique/aux commentaires** his attitude is ambiguous/is open to criticism/is likely to make people talk; **cette décision prête à (la) discussion** the decision is open to debate; **sa conduite prête à rire** his behaviour makes you want to laugh *ou* is laughable

3 VI [*tissu, cuir*] to give, stretch

4 **se prêter** VPR a (= *consentir*) **se ~ à** [+ *expérience*] to participate in; [+ *projet, jeu*] to fall in with, go along with; **il n'a pas voulu se ~ à leurs manœuvres** he didn't want any part in *ou* refused to have anything to do with their schemes
b (= *s'adapter*) **se ~ (bien) à qch** to lend itself (well) to sth; **la salle se prête mal à une réunion intime** the room doesn't lend itself to informal meetings
c [*chaussures, cuir*] to give, stretch

prétérit [preterit] NM preterite (tense); **au ~** in the preterite (tense)

prétérition [preterisjɔ̃] NF paralipsis, paraleipsis

préteur [pretœr] NM (*Antiq*) praetor

prêteur, -euse [pretœr, øz] 1 ADJ unselfish; **il n'est pas ~** [*enfant*] he's possessive about his toys *ou* belongings, he doesn't like lending his things; [*adulte*] he isn't willing to lend things, he doesn't believe in lending (things) 2 NM,F (money) lender; **~ sur gages** pawnbroker

▼ **prétexte** [pretɛkst] NM pretext, excuse; **mauvais ~** poor *ou* lame excuse; **sous ~ d'aider son frère** on the pretext *ou* pretence of helping his brother; **sous (le) ~ que ...** on *ou* under the pretext that ..., on the pretence that ...; **sous ~ qu'elle est jeune on lui passe tout** just because she's young she gets away with everything; **sous aucun ~** on no account; **il a pris ~ du froid** *ou* **il a donné le froid comme ~ pour rester chez lui** he used the cold weather as a pretext *ou* an excuse for staying at home; **tous les ~s sont bons pour ne pas aller chez le dentiste** any excuse will do not to go to the dentist; **servir de ~ à qch/à faire qch** to be a pretext *ou* an excuse for sth/ to do sth; **ça lui a servi de ~** *ou* **ça lui a donné un ~ pour refuser** it provided him with an excuse to refuse *ou* with a pretext for refusing; **il saisit le premier ~ venu pour partir** he made the first excuse he could think of for leaving; **ce n'est qu'un ~** it's just an excuse; **pour elle**

tout est ~ à se plaindre she'll complain about anything and everything

prétexter [pretɛkste] ▶ conjug 1 ◀ VT to give as a pretext *ou* an excuse; **il a prétexté qu'il était trop fatigué** he said he was too tired; **en prétextant que ...** on the pretext that ...; **~ une angine pour refuser une invitation** to say one has a sore throat to get out of an invitation

prétoire [pretwar] NM (*Antiq*) praetorium; (*Jur : frm*) court

Pretoria [pretɔrja] N Pretoria

prétorien, -ienne [pretɔrjɛ̃, jɛn] ADJ, NM (*Antiq*) praetorian

prêtraille [pretraj] NF (*péj*) **la ~** priests, the clergy

prêtre [pretr] NM priest; **se faire ~** to become a priest; (*lit*) **grand ~** high priest; **les grands ~s du monétarisme** the high priests of monetarism

prêt-relais (*pl* **prêts-relais**) [prerəlɛ] NM bridging loan

prêtre-ouvrier (*pl* **prêtres-ouvriers**) [pretruvrije] NM worker priest

prêtresse [pretrɛs] NF priestess

prêtrise [pretriz] NF priesthood; **recevoir la ~** to be ordained

preuve [prœv] 1 NF a (= *démonstration*) proof, evidence; **faire la ~ de qch/que** to prove sth/that; **avoir la ~ de/que** to have proof *ou* evidence of/that; **pouvez-vous apporter la ~ de ce que vous dites?** can you prove *ou* can you produce proof *ou* evidence of what you're saying?; **c'est la ~ que ...** that proves that ...; **j'avais prévu cela, la ~, j'ai déjà mon billet*** I'd thought of that, and to prove it I've already got my ticket; **jusqu'à ~ (du) contraire** until we find proof *ou* evidence to the contrary, until there's proof *ou* evidence that it's not the case; **n'importe qui peut conduire, à ~ mon fils*** anyone can drive, just look at *ou* take my son (for instance); **il a réussi, à ~ qu'il ne faut jamais désespérer*** he succeeded, which just goes to show *ou* prove you should never give up hope
b (= *indice*) proof (*NonC*), evidence (*NonC*), piece of evidence; **je n'ai pas de ~s** I have no proof *ou* evidence; **c'est une ~ supplémentaire de sa culpabilité** it's further proof *ou* it's further evidence of his guilt; **il y a trois ~s irréfutables qu'il ment** there are three definite pieces of evidence which prove quite clearly that he's lying; **affirmer qch ~s en mains** to back sth up with concrete proof *ou* evidence
c (= *marque*) proof (*NonC*); **c'est une ~ de bonne volonté/d'amour** it's proof of his good intentions/of his love
d (*Math*) [*opération*] proof; **faire la ~ par neuf** to cast out the nines
e (*loc*) **faire ~ de** to show; **faire ses ~s** [*personne*] to prove o.s., show one's ability; [*voiture*] to prove itself; **cette nouvelle technique n'a pas encore fait ses ~s** this new technique hasn't yet proved its worth
2 COMP ▶ **preuve par l'absurde** reductio ad absurdum ▶ **preuve concluante** conclusive *ou* positive proof ▶ **preuve a contrario** a contrario proof ▶ **preuve matérielle** material evidence (*NonC*)

preux †† [prø] 1 ADJ valiant†, gallant† 2 NM valiant knight†

prévaloir [prevalwar] ▶ conjug 29 ◀ 1 VI (*littér*) to prevail (**sur** over, **contre** against); **faire ~ ses droits** to insist upon one's rights; **faire ~ son opinion** to win agreement *ou* acceptance for one's opinion; **son opinion a prévalu sur celle de ses collègues** his opinion prevailed over *ou* overrode that of his colleagues; **rien ne peut ~ contre ses préjugés** nothing can overcome his prejudices 2 **se prévaloir** VPR a (= *se flatter*) **se ~ de** to pride o.s. on b (= *profiter*) **se ~ de** to take advantage of

prévaricateur, -trice [prevarikatœr, tris] 1 ADJ corrupt 2 NM,F corrupt official

prévarication [prevarikasjɔ̃] NF corrupt practices

prévariquer [prevarike] ▶ conjug 1 ◀ VI to be guilty of corrupt practices

prévenance [prev(ə)nɑ̃s] NF thoughtfulness (*NonC*), consideration (*NonC*), kindness (*NonC*); **toutes les ~s que vous avez eues pour moi** all the consideration *ou* kindness you've shown me; **entourer qn de ~s** to be very considerate to *ou* towards sb; **il n'a aucune ~ pour les autres** he shows *ou* has no consideration for others, he's very thoughtless

prévenant, e [prev(ə)nɑ̃, ɑ̃t] ADJ [*personne*] considerate, kind (**envers** to), thoughtful (**envers** of); [*manières*] kind, attentive

prévendre [prevɑ̃dr] ▶ conjug 41 ◀ VT [+ *billets, marchandises*] to pre-sell

▼ **prévenir** [prev(ə)nir] ▶ conjug 22 ◀ VT a (= *avertir*) to warn (**de qch** about *ou* against *ou* of sth); (= *aviser*) to inform, tell (**de qch** about sth); **qui faut-il ~ en cas d'accident?** who should be informed *ou* told if there's an accident?; **~ le médecin/la police** to call the doctor/the police; **tu es prévenu!** you've been warned!; **partir sans ~** to leave without warning, leave without telling anyone; **il aurait pu ~** he could have let us know
b (= *empêcher*) [+ *accident, catastrophe*] to prevent, avert, avoid; [+ *maladie*] to prevent, guard against; [+ *danger*] to avert, avoid; [+ *malheur*] to ward off, avoid, provide against → **mieux**
c (= *devancer*) [+ *besoin, désir*] to anticipate; [+ *question, objection*] to forestall; (*littér*) **voulait arriver le premier mais son frère l'avait prévenu** he wanted to be the first to arrive but his brother had anticipated him *ou* had got there before him
d (*frm* = *influencer*) **~ qn contre qn** to prejudice *ou* bias sb against sb; **~ qn en faveur de qn** to prejudice *ou* predispose sb in sb's favour

prévente [prevɑ̃t] NF pre-selling

préventif, -ive [prevɑ̃tif, iv] 1 ADJ [*mesure, médecine*] preventive; **à titre ~** as a precaution *ou* preventive measure; **la lutte préventive contre le sida** AIDS prevention 2 NF (*Jur*) **être en préventive** to be on remand, be remanded in custody; **mettre qn en préventive** to remand sb in custody, hold sb on remand; **il a fait 6 mois de (prison) préventive** he was remanded in custody for 6 months

prévention [prevɑ̃sjɔ̃] NF a [*accident, crime, corruption, maladie, délinquance*] prevention; **~ routière** road safety; **faire de la ~** to take preventive action; **campagne/politique de ~** prevention campaign/policy; **mesures de ~** preventive measures b (*Jur*) custody, detention; **mettre en ~** to detain, remand in *ou* take into custody c (= *préjugé*) prejudice (**contre** against); **considérer qch sans ~** to take an unprejudiced *ou* unbiased view of sth

préventivement [prevɑ̃tivmɑ̃] ADV [*agir*] preventively, as a precaution *ou* preventive measure; (*Jur*) **être incarcéré ~** to be remanded *ou* held in custody *ou* detention (awaiting trial)

prévenu, e [prev(ə)ny] (*ptp de* **prévenir**) 1 ADJ (*Jur*) charged; **être ~ d'un délit** to be charged with *ou* accused of a crime 2 NM,F (*Jur*) defendant, accused (person)

préverbe [prevɛrb] NM verbal prefix, preverb

prévisibilité [previzibilite] NF foreseeable nature

prévisible [previzibl] ADJ [*réaction, résultat, personne*] predictable; [*événement, évolution*] foreseeable, predictable; **difficilement ~** difficult to foresee; **dans un avenir ~** in the foreseeable future; **une amélioration est ~ dans les prochains mois** an improvement can be expected *ou* is foreseeable within the next few months; **il était ~ que ...** it was to be expected that ..., it was predictable that ...

prévision [pʀevizjɔ̃] NF [a] (*gén pl = prédiction*) prediction, expectation; (*Fin*) forecast, estimate, prediction; **~s budgétaires** budget estimates; **~s météorologiques** weather forecast; **~ à court/long terme** short-term/long-term forecast; **il a réussi au-delà de toute ~** he has succeeded beyond all expectations [b] (*= action*) **la ~ du temps** weather forecasting; **la ~ de ses réactions est impossible** it's impossible to predict his reactions *ou* to foresee what his reactions will be; **en ~ de son arrivée/d'une augmentation du trafic** in anticipation *ou* expectation of his arrival/of an increase in the traffic

prévisionnel, -elle [pʀevizjɔnɛl] ADJ [*mesure, plan*] forward-looking; [*budget*] projected

prévisionniste [pʀevizjɔnist] NMF (economic) forecaster

prévoir [pʀevwaʀ] ▸ conjug 24 ◂ VT [a] (*= anticiper*) [+ *événement, conséquence*] to foresee, anticipate; [+ *temps*] to forecast; [+ *réaction, contretemps*] to expect, reckon on, anticipate; **~ le pire** to expect the worst; **il faut ~ les erreurs éventuelles** we must allow for *ou* make provision for possible errors; **nous n'avions pas prévu qu'il refuserait** we hadn't reckoned on his refusing, we hadn't anticipated *ou* foreseen that he'd refuse; **cela fait ou laisse ~ un malheur** it bodes ill; **rien ne laisse ~ une amélioration rapide** there's no prospect *ou* suggestion of a quick improvement; **tout laisse ~ une issue rapide/qu'il refusera** everything points *ou* all the signs point to a rapid solution/to his refusing; **rien ne faisait ou ne laissait ~ que ...** there was nothing to suggest *ou* to make us think that ...; **on ne peut pas tout ~** you can't think of everything; **plus tôt que prévu** earlier than expected *ou* anticipated → **programme**
[b] (*= projeter*) [+ *voyage, construction*] to plan; **~ de faire qch** to plan to do *ou* on doing sth; **pour quand prévoyez-vous votre arrivée ?** when do you plan to arrive?; **au moment prévu** at the appointed *ou* scheduled *ou* prescribed time; **comme prévu** as planned, according to plan; [*autoroute*] **« ouverture prévue pour la fin de l'année »** "scheduled to open at the end of the year"
[c] (*= préparer, envisager*) to allow; **il faudra ~ des trous pour l'écoulement des eaux** you must leave *ou* provide some holes for drainage; **prévoyez de l'argent en plus pour les faux frais** allow some extra money for incidental expenses; **il vaut mieux ~ quelques couvertures en plus** you'd better allow a few extra blankets *ou* bring (along) a few extra blankets; **il faudrait ~ un repas** you ought to make plans for *ou* to organize a meal; **tout est prévu pour l'arrivée de nos hôtes** everything is in hand *ou* organized for the arrival of our guests; **cette voiture est prévue pour quatre personnes** this car is designed for four people; **vous avez prévu grand** you've planned things on a grand scale; **déposez vos lettres dans la boîte prévue à cet effet** put your letters in the box provided; **on a prévu des douches** (*à installer*) they have made provision for showers to be built; (*déjà installées*) they have laid on *ou* provided showers
[d] (*Jur*) [*loi, règlement*] to provide for, make provision for; **c'est prévu à l'article 8** article 8 makes provision for that, it's provided for in article 8; **le code pénal prévoit que ...** the penal code holds that ...; **la loi prévoit une peine de prison** the law makes provision for a prison sentence; **ce n'est pas prévu dans le contrat** it is not provided for in the contract, the contract makes no provision for it

prévôt [pʀevo] NM (*Hist, Rel*) provost; (*Mil*) provost marshal

prévôtal, e [pʀevotal, o] ADJ of a provost

prévôté [pʀevote] NF (*Hist*) provostship; (*Mil*) military police

prévoyance [pʀevwajɑ̃s] NF foresight, forethought; **caisse de ~** contingency fund; **société de ~** provident society

prévoyant, e [pʀevwajɑ̃, ɑ̃t] ADJ provident

Priam [pʀijam] NM Priam

priapisme [pʀijapism] NM priapism

prie-Dieu [pʀidjø] NM INV prie-dieu

▾ **prier** [pʀije] ▸ conjug 7 ◂ [1] VT [a] [+ *Dieu, saint*] to pray to; **~ Dieu de faire un miracle** to pray for a miracle; **je prie Dieu que cela soit vrai** pray God that it is true
[b] (*= implorer*) to beg, beseech (*littér*); **elle le pria de rester** she begged *ou* urged *ou* pressed him to stay; **je vous prie de me pardonner** please forgive me; **dites oui, je vous en prie !** please say yes!; **Pierre, je t'en prie, calme-toi !** Pierre, for heaven's sake, calm down!; **je t'en prie, ça suffit !** please, that's quite enough!
[c] (*= inviter*) to invite, ask; (*frm*) to request (*frm*); **il m'a prié à déjeuner ou de venir déjeuner** he has invited *ou* asked me to lunch; **vous êtes prié de vous présenter à 9 heures** you are requested to present yourself at 9 o'clock; **on l'a prié d'assister à la cérémonie** he was invited to be present *ou* his presence was requested at the ceremony; **nous vous prions d'honorer de votre présence la cérémonie** we request the honour *ou* pleasure of your company at the ceremony
[d] (*= ordonner*) **je vous prie de sortir** will you please leave the room; **vous êtes prié de répondre quand on vous parle/de rester assis** please reply when spoken to/remain seated; **taisez-vous, je vous prie** would you please be quiet
[e] (*formules de politesse*) **je vous en prie** (*faites donc*) please do, of course; (*= après vous*) after you; (*idée d'irritation*) do you mind!; **excusez-moi — je vous en prie** I'm sorry — not at all; **merci beaucoup — je vous en prie** thank you — don't mention it *ou* you're welcome; **voulez-vous ouvrir la fenêtre je vous prie ?** would you mind opening the window please?, would you be so kind as to open the window please? → **agréer**
[f] (*loc*) **il s'est fait ~** he needed coaxing *ou* persuading; **il ne s'est pas fait ~** he didn't need persuading, he didn't wait to be asked twice, he was only too willing (to do it); **il a accepté l'offre sans se faire ~** he accepted the offer without hesitation; **allez, viens, ne te fais pas ~ !** come on! don't be such a bore!
[2] VI to pray (**pour** for); **prions, mes frères** brothers, let us pray

prière [pʀijɛʀ] NF [a] (*Rel = oraison, office*) prayer; **être en ~** to be praying *ou* at prayer; **dire ou faire ses ~s** to say one's prayers; **se rendre à la ~** to go to prayer; (*hum*) **ne m'oubliez pas dans vos ~s** remember me in your prayers, pray for me → **livre[1], moulin**
[b] (*= demande*) plea, entreaty; **céder aux ~s de qn** to give in to sb's requests; **à la ~ de qn** at sb's request *ou* behest (*littér*); **j'ai une ~ à vous adresser** I have a request to make to you; **il est resté sourd à mes ~s** he turned a deaf ear to my pleas *ou* entreaties
[c] (*loc*) **~ de ...** please ...; **~ de répondre par retour du courrier** please reply by return of post; **~ de vous présenter à 9 heures** you are requested to present yourself *ou* please present yourself at 9 o'clock; **« ~ de ne pas fumer »** "no smoking (please)"; **« ~ de ne pas se pencher à la fenêtre »** "(please) do not lean out of the window"; (*Édition*) **~ d'insérer** please insert

prieur [pʀijœʀ] NM (*père*) **~** prior

prieure [pʀijœʀ] NF (*mère*) **~** prioress

prieuré [pʀijœʀe] NM (*= couvent*) priory; (*= église*) priory (church)

prima donna [pʀimadɔna] (*pl inv ou* **prime donne** [pʀimedɔne]) NF prima donna

primaire [pʀimɛʀ] [1] ADJ [a] (*Écon, Élec, Méd, Pol*) (*Géol*) [*ère*] primary, palaeozoic; (*Psych*) [*personne, caractère, fonction*] primary (*SPEC*); [*élection*] primary; **délinquant ~** first offender; **école ~** primary *ou* elementary school, grade school (*US*) [b] (*péj = simpliste*) [*personne*] simple-minded, limited*; [*raisonnement*] simplistic; [*plaisanterie*] obvious (*Scol*) [2] NM (*Scol*) primary school *ou* education; (*Élec*) primary; (*Géol*) Primary, Palaeozoic; (*Scol*) **être en ~** to be in primary school [3] NF (*Pol*) primary (election)

primal, e [pʀimal, o] ADJ (*mpl* **-aux**) **cri ~** primal scream; **thérapie ~e** primal (scream) therapy, scream therapy

primarité [pʀimaʀite] NF primarity

primat [pʀima] NM [a] (*Rel*) primate [b] (*littér = primauté*) primacy

primate [pʀimat] NM [a] (*Zool*) primate [b] (* *péj = personne*) ape*

primauté [pʀimote] NF (*Rel*) primacy; (*fig*) primacy, pre-eminence (**sur** over); **donner la ~ à qch** to prioritize sth

prime[1] [pʀim] NF [a] (*= cadeau*) free gift; **donné en ~ avec qch** given away *ou* given as a free gift with sth; (*iro*) **cette année il a eu la rougeole, la varicelle et les oreillons en ~ !** this year he had the measles, chickenpox and the mumps to boot! *ou* on top of that!
[b] (*= bonus*) bonus; (*= subvention*) premium, subsidy; (*= indemnité*) allowance; **~ d'allaitement** nursing mother's allowance; **~ d'ancienneté** seniority bonus *ou* pay; **~ de déménagement** relocation allowance; **~ de départ** *bonus paid to an employee when leaving a job*; (*importante*) golden handshake; **~ à l'exportation** export premium *ou* subsidy; **~ de fin d'année/de rendement** Christmas/productivity bonus; **~ d'intéressement** performance(-related) bonus; **~ de licenciement** severance pay, redundancy payment; **~ de risque** danger money (*NonC*); **~ de transport** transport allowance; **c'est donner une ~ à la paresse !** it's just paying people to sit around doing nothing! → **précarité**
[c] (*Assurances, Bourse*) premium; **~ d'assurances** insurance premium; **~ d'émission** issuing share *ou* premium; **~ de remboursement** redemption premium; **faire ~** to be at a premium

prime[2] [pʀim] ADJ [a] **de ~ abord** at first glance; **dès sa ~ jeunesse** from his earliest youth; **il n'est plus de ~ jeunesse** he's no longer in the prime of youth *ou* the first flush of youth [b] (*Math*) prime; **n ~** n prime

primé, e [pʀime] (*ptp de* **primer**) ADJ [*film, reportage*] award-winning (*épith*); [*animal*] prize(-winning); [*invention, produit*] prize-winning; **ce film a été plusieurs fois ~** this film has won several awards

primer [pʀime] ▸ conjug 1 ◂ [1] VT [a] (*= surpasser*) to prevail over, take precedence over; **chez elle, l'intelligence prime la générosité** in her case, intelligence is more in evidence *ou* to the fore than generosity [b] (*= récompenser*) to award a prize to; (*= subventionner*) to subsidize [2] VI (*= dominer*) to be the prime *ou* dominant feature, dominate; (*= compter, valoir*) to be of prime importance, take first place; **c'est le bleu qui prime dans ce tableau** blue is the dominant colour in this picture; **pour moi ce sont les qualités de cœur qui priment** the qualities of the heart are what count the most for me

primerose [pʀimʀoz] NF hollyhock

primesautier, -ière [pʀimsotje, jɛʀ] ADJ impulsive; **être d'humeur primesautière** to have an impulsive temperament *ou* nature

prime time [pʀajmtajm] NM INV (*TV*) prime

time; **diffusé en ~** broadcast on prime-time television *ou* in prime time

primeur [primœr] [1] NFPL (*Comm*) **~s** early fruit and vegetables; **marchand de ~s** greengrocer (*Brit*) *ou* grocer (*US*) (*specializing in early produce*) [2] NF [a] (*Presse = nouvelle*) scoop; **avoir la ~ d'une nouvelle** to be the first to hear a piece of news; **je vous réserve la ~ de mon manuscrit** I'll let you be the first to read my manuscript [b] **vin (de) ~** nouveau wine, wine of the latest vintage

primevère [primver] NF (*sauvage*) primrose; (*cultivée*) primula; (*jaune*) primrose

primigeste [primiʒɛst] NF primigravida

primipare [primipar] [1] ADJ primiparous [2] NF primipara

primitif, -ive [primitif, iv] [1] ADJ [a] (*= originel*) [*forme, état*] original, primitive; [*projet, question, préoccupation*] original, first; [*église*] primitive, early; [*peintre*] primitive; (*Logique*) [*proposition, concept*] basic; (*Art*) [*couleurs*] primary; (*Géol*) [*terrain*] primitive, primeval; **ville construite sur le site ~ d'une cité romaine** town built on the original site of a Roman city; **je préfère revenir à mon projet ~/à mon idée primitive** I'd rather revert to my original *ou* initial *ou* first plan/idea [b] (*Sociol*) [*peuple, art, mœurs*] primitive [c] (*= sommaire*) [*installation*] primitive, crude [d] (*Ling*) [*temps, langue*] basic; [*mot*] primitive; [*sens*] original [e] (*Math*) **fonction primitive** primitive [2] NM,F (*Art, Sociol*) primitive [3] **primitive** NF (*Math*) primitive

primitivement [primitivmɑ̃] ADV originally

primitivisme [primitivism] NM (*Art*) primitivism

primo [primo] ADV first (of all), firstly

primo-accédant, e (*pl* **primo-accédants**) [primoaksedɑ̃, ɑ̃t] NM,F ► (à la propriété) first-time (home-)buyer

primogéniture [primoʒenityr] NF primogeniture

primo-infection (*pl* **primo-infections**) [primoɛ̃fɛksjɔ̃] NF primary infection

primordial, e (*mpl* **-iaux**) [primɔrdjal, jo] ADJ [a] (*= vital*) [*élément, question*] essential, vital; [*objectif, préoccupation*] chief, main; [*rôle*] crucial, key (*épith*); **d'une importance ~e** of the utmost *ou* of paramount *ou* primordial importance [b] (*littér = originel*) primordial

primordialement [primɔrdjalmɑ̃] ADV essentially

prince [prɛ̃s] [1] NM [a] (*lit*) prince; (*fig*) **le ~ des chanteurs** *etc* the prince *ou* king of singers *etc*; **Robin des bois, le ~ des voleurs** Robin Hood, Prince of Thieves → **fait¹** [b] (*loc*) **être** *ou* **se montrer bon ~** to be magnanimous *ou* generous, behave generously; **être habillé/vivre comme un ~** to be dressed/live like a prince [2] COMP ► **prince des apôtres** Prince of the apostles ► **le Prince charmant** Prince Charming; **elle attend le** *ou* **son ~ charmant** she's waiting for her Prince Charming *ou* for Mr. Right* to come along, she's waiting for her knight in shining armour ► **prince consort** Prince Consort ► **le Prince des ténèbres** *ou* **des démons** the prince of darkness ► **prince de l'Église** prince of the Church ► **prince de Galles** Prince of Wales; (*= tissu*) Prince of Wales check ► **prince héritier** crown prince ► **prince du sang** prince of royal blood

princeps [prɛ̃sɛps] ADJ [*édition*] first

princesse [prɛ̃sɛs] NF princess; **faire la** *ou* **sa ~** ◊ **prendre des airs de ~** to put on airs; **robe ~** princess dress → **frais²**

princier, -ière [prɛ̃sje, jɛr] ADJ (*lit, fig*) princely

princièrement [prɛ̃sjɛrmɑ̃] ADV in (a) princely fashion

▼ **principal, e** (*mpl* **-aux**) [prɛ̃sipal, o] [1] ADJ [a] [*entrée, bâtiment, résidence*] main; [*clerc, employé*] chief, head; [*question, raison, but*] principal, main; [*personnage, rôle*] leading, main, principal; **elle a eu l'un des rôles principaux dans l'affaire** she played a major role *ou* she was one of the leading *ou* main figures in the business [b] (*Gram*) [*proposition*] main [2] NM [a] (*Fin*) principal [b] (*Scol*) headmaster, principal, head (*Brit*); (*Admin*) chief clerk [c] (*= chose importante*) **le ~** the most important thing, the main point; **c'est le ~** that's the main thing [d] (*Mus*) principal [3] **principale** NF [a] (*Gram*) main clause [b] (*Scol*) headmistress, principal, head (*Brit*)

principalement [prɛ̃sipalmɑ̃] ADV principally, mainly, chiefly

principat [prɛ̃sipa] NM princedom

principauté [prɛ̃sipote] NF principality; **la Principauté (de Monaco)** Monaco

principe [prɛ̃sip] NM [a] (*= règle*) [*science, géométrie*] principle; **il nous a expliqué le ~ de la machine** he explained the principle on which the machine worked; **le ~ d'Archimède** Archimedes' principle → **pétition** [b] (*= hypothèse*) principle, assumption; **partir du ~ que ...** ◊ **poser comme ~ que ...** to work on the principle *ou* assumption that ... → **accord** [c] (*= règle morale*) principle; **il a des ~s** he's a man of principle, he's got principles; **il n'a pas de ~s** he's unprincipled, he has no principles; **avoir pour ~ de faire qch** to make it a principle to do sth, make a point of doing sth; **je ne mens pas, c'est un ~ chez moi** I make a point of not telling lies, it's a rule with me that I don't tell lies; **il n'est pas dans mes ~s de ...** I make it a principle not to ...; **il a manqué à ses ~s** he has failed to stick to his principles [d] (*= origine*) principle; **remonter jusqu'au ~ des choses** to go back to first principles [e] (*= élément*) principle, element, constituent; **~ nécessaire à la nutrition** necessary principle of nutrition [f] (*= rudiment*) **~s** rudiments, principles [g] (*loc*) **par ~** on principle; **en ~** (*= d'habitude, en général*) as a rule; (*= théoriquement*) in principle, theoretically; **de ~** [*hostilité, objection, opposition, soutien*] systematic, automatic; **décision de ~** decision in principle; **c'est une question de ~** it's a matter of principle; **faire qch pour le ~** to do sth on principle *ou* for the sake of it → **accord, déclaration**

printanier, -ière [prɛ̃tanje, jɛr] ADJ [*soleil, couleur, temps, vêtement*] spring (*épith*); [*atmosphère*] spring-like; (*Culin*) **navarin (d'agneau) ~** navarin of lamb with spring vegetables

printemps [prɛ̃tɑ̃] NM spring; **au ~** in (the) spring(time); (*littér*) **au ~ de la vie** in the springtime of life; (*hum*) **mes 40 ~** my 40 summers (*hum*)

prion [prijɔ̃] NM prion

priorat [prijɔra] NM priorate

priori [prijɔri] → **a priori**

prioritaire [prijɔritɛr] [1] ADJ [a] [*projet, opération*] priority (*épith*); **être ~** [*personne, projet*] to take *ou* have priority [b] (*Aut*) [*véhicule, personne*] **être ~** to have priority *ou* right of way; **il était sur une route ~** he had priority *ou* right of way, he was on the main road [2] NMF (*Aut*) person who has right of way *ou* priority

prioritairement [prijɔritɛrmɑ̃] ADV (*gén*) first and foremost; [*traiter*] as a (matter of) priority; **ces places sont ~ réservées aux handicapés** the disabled have priority for these seats, these seats are reserved first and foremost for the disabled

priorité [prijɔrite] NF [a] (*gén*) priority; **donner la ~ absolue à qch** to give top priority to sth; **discuter qch en ~** to discuss sth as a (matter of) priority; **venir en ~** to come first; **l'une des choses à faire en grande ~** ◊ **l'une**

des ~s essentielles one of the first *ou* top priorities; **il nous faudrait en ~ des vivres** first and foremost we need supplies, we need supplies as a matter of urgency [b] (*Aut*) priority, right of way; **avoir la ~** to have right of way (**sur** over); **~ à droite** (*principe*) system of giving way to traffic coming from the right; (*panneau*) give way to the vehicles on your right; **laisser** *ou* **céder la ~ à qn** to give way to sb (*Brit*), yield to sb (*US*) → **refus**

pris, prise¹ [pri, priz] (*ptp de prendre*) ADJ [a] [*place*] taken; **avoir les mains ~es** to have one's hands full; **tous les billets sont ~** the tickets are sold out, all the tickets have been sold; **toutes les places sont ~es** all the seats are taken *ou* have gone; **toute ma journée est ~e** I'm busy all day; **ça me fera 250 F, c'est toujours ça de ~*** I'll get 250 francs, that's better than nothing [b] [*personne*] busy; **le directeur est très ~ cette semaine** the manager is very busy this week; **si vous n'êtes pas ~ ce soir ...** if you're free *ou* if you've got nothing on *ou* if you're not doing anything this evening ...; **désolé, je suis ~** sorry, I'm busy [c] (*Méd*) [*nez*] stuffy, stuffed-up; [*gorge*] hoarse; **j'ai le nez ~** my nose is stuffed up; **j'ai la gorge ~e** my throat is hoarse; **les poumons sont ~** the lungs are (now) affected [d] (*Culin*) [*crème, mayonnaise*] set; **mer ~e par les glaces** frozen sea [e] † **avoir la taille bien ~e** to have a neat waist; **la taille ~e dans un manteau de bonne coupe** wearing a well-cut coat to show off a neat waist [f] (*= envahi par*) **~ de peur/remords** stricken with *ou* by fear/remorse; **~ d'une inquiétude soudaine** seized by a sudden anxiety; **j'ai été ~ d'une envie soudaine de chocolat** I had a sudden urge to eat some chocolate; **~ de boisson** (*frm*) under the influence*, the worse for drink

prise² [priz] [1] NF [a] (*= moyen d'empoigner, de prendre*) hold (*NonC*), grip (*NonC*); (*pour soulever, faire levier*) purchase (*NonC*); (*Catch, Judo*) hold; (*Alpinisme*) hold; (*Sport : sur raquette, club, batte*) grip; **faire une ~ à qn** to get sb in a judo hold; **on n'a pas de ~ pour soulever la caisse** there's no purchase to lift the chest, you can't get a hold on the chest to lift it; **cette construction offre trop de ~ au vent** this building catches the wind very badly; **avoir ~ sur** to have a hold on *ou* over; **on n'a aucune ~ sur lui** no one has any hold *ou* influence over him; **ces théories n'ont que trop de ~ sur elle** these theories have all too great a hold *ou* over her; **donner ~ à** to give rise to; **son attitude donne ~ aux soupçons** his attitude gives rise to *ou* lays him open to suspicion → **lâcher** [b] (*Chasse, Pêche = butin*) catch; (*= saisie*) [*contrebande, drogue*] capture, seizure; (*Mil*) [*ville, navire*] capture; [*Échecs, Dames*] capture [c] (*Élec*) **~ (de courant)** (*mâle*) plug; (*femelle*) socket, point, power point (*SPÉC*); (*au mur*) socket; **~ multiple** adaptor; (*avec rallonge*) trailing socket; **triple ~** three-way adaptor; **~ pour rasoir électrique** razor point → **2** [d] [*tabac*] pinch of snuff; [*cocaïne*] snort* [e] (*Méd*) **à administrer en plusieurs ~s par jour** to be given *ou* administered at intervals throughout the day; **arrêter la ~ de la pilule** to stop taking the pill; **la ~ de ce médicament est déconseillée pendant la grossesse** it is not recommended that this medicine be taken during pregnancy [f] (*= durcissement*) [*ciment, enduit*] setting; **à ~ rapide** quick-setting

[2] **aux prises avec** LOC PRÉP **être** *ou* **se trouver aux ~s avec des difficultés** to be battling *ou* wrestling with difficulties; **être aux ~s avec un créancier** to be battling against *ou* doing battle with a creditor; **cette campagne met aux ~s deux hommes bien**

► GRAMMAIRE ACTIVE : **principal 53.2**

différents this campaign pits two extremely different men against each other; (*hum*) **je l'ai trouvé aux ~s avec son ordinateur** I found him battling with *ou* trying to get to grips with his computer

③ **en prise** LOC ADV (*Aut*) **être/mettre en ~** to be in/put the car into gear; **en ~ (directe)** in direct drive; (*fig*) **en ~ (directe) avec** *ou* **sur** tuned into; **un gouvernement en ~ avec les réalités du pays** a government in tune with *ou* that is tuned into the realities of the country; **littérature en ~ directe avec les mutations de la société** writing that has its finger on the pulse of a changing society

④ COMP ► **prise d'air** air inlet *ou* intake ► **prise d'armes** military review *ou* parade ► **la prise de la Bastille** the storming of the Bastille ► **prise de bec*** row*, set-to*; **avoir une ~ de bec avec qn** to have a row* *ou* a set-to* with sb, fall out with sb ► **prise de corps** (*Jur*) arrest ► **prise d'eau** water (supply) point; (= *robinet*) tap (*Brit*), faucet (*US*) ► **prise de guerre** spoils of war ► **prise péritel** → **péritel** ► **prise de sang** blood test; **faire une ~ de sang à qn** to take a blood sample from sb ► **prise de son** (*Ciné, Radio, TV*) sound recording; **~ de son: J. Dupont** sound (engineer): J. Dupont ► **prise de téléphone** phone socket ► **prise de terre** (*Élec, Radio*) earth (*Brit*), ground (*US*); **la machine à laver n'a pas de ~ de terre** the washing machine isn't earthed (*Brit*) *ou* grounded (*US*) ► **prise de vue(s)** (*Ciné, TV*) filming, shooting; **~ de vue** (= *photographie*) shot; **~ de vue(s): J. Dupont** camera(work): J. Dupont → **charge, conscience, contact** etc

priser¹ [pʀize] ▸ conjug 1 ◂ VT (*littér*) to prize, value; **très bien prisé** highly prized; **je prise fort peu ce genre de plaisanterie** I don't appreciate this sort of joke at all

priser² [pʀize] ▸ conjug 1 ◂ ① VT [+ *tabac*] to take; [+ *drogue*] to take, snort: → **tabac** ② VI to take snuff

priseur, -euse [pʀizœʀ, øz] NM,F snuff taker

prismatique [pʀismatik] ADJ prismatic

prisme [pʀism] NM prism

prison [pʀizɔ̃] NF ① (= *lieu*) prison, jail, penitentiary (*US*); (= *demeure sombre*) prison; (*Hist*) ► **pour dettes** debtors' prison; **mettre qn en ~** to send sb to prison *ou* jail, imprison sb; **~ ouverte** open prison; (*fig*) **elle vit dans une ~ dorée** she's like a bird in a gilded cage → **porte** ⓑ (= *emprisonnement*) prison, jail; **peine de ~** prison sentence; **faire de la ~** to go to *ou* be in prison; **faire 6 mois de ~** to spend 6 months in jail *ou* prison; **condamné à 3 mois de ~ ferme/à la ~ à vie** sentenced to 3 months' imprisonment/to life imprisonment

prisonnier, -ière [pʀizɔnje, jɛʀ] ① ADJ [*soldat*] captive; **être ~** (= *enfermé*) to be trapped, be a prisoner; (*en prison*) to be imprisoned, be a prisoner; **être ~ de ses vêtements** to be hampered by one's clothes; **être ~ de ses préjugés/de l'ennemi** to be a prisoner of one's prejudices/of the enemy ② NM,F prisoner; **~ d'opinion** prisoner of conscience; **~ politique** political prisoner; **faire/retenir qn ~** to take/hold sb prisoner; **~ de guerre** prisoner of war → **camp, constituer**

Prisunic® [pʀizynik] NM department store (*for inexpensive goods*), ≈ Woolworth's®, ≈ five and dime (*US*); (*péj*) **de ~** cheap

privatif, -ive [pʀivatif, iv] ① ADJ ⓐ (*Gram*) privative ⓑ (*Jur* = *qui prive*) which deprives of rights (*ou* liberties *etc*) ⓒ (*Jur* = *privé*) private; **avec jardin ~** with private garden; (*sur annonce*) «**jardin ~**» "own garden" → **carte** ② NM (*Gram*) privative (prefix *ou* element)

privation [pʀivasjɔ̃] NF ⓐ (= *suppression*) deprivation; (*Jur*) **la ~ des droits civiques** the forfeiture *ou* deprivation of civil rights; **la ~ de liberté** the loss of liberty; **la ~ de la vue/d'un membre** the loss of one's sight/of a limb; **la ~**

de nourriture/sommeil food/sleep deprivation ⓑ (*gén pl = sacrifice*) privation, hardship; **~s que je me suis imposées** the things I went *ou* did *ou* managed without, the hardships I bore; **souffrir de ~s** to endure hardship

privatisation [pʀivatizasjɔ̃] NF privatization; **~ partielle/totale** partial/wholesale privatization; **entreprise en cours de ~** company undergoing privatization

privatiser [pʀivatize] ▸ conjug 1 ◂ VT [+ *entreprise*] to privatize; **entreprise privatisée** privatized company

privautés [pʀivote] NFPL liberties; **prendre des ~ avec** to take liberties with; **~ de langage** familiar *ou* coarse language

privé, e [pʀive] ① ADJ (*gén*) private; (*Presse*) [*source*] unofficial; (*Jur*) [*droit*] civil; [*télévision, radio*] independent; **personne ~e** private person; **en séjour (à titre) ~** on a private visit ② NM ⓐ **le ~** (= *vie*) private life; (*Comm* = *secteur*) the private sector; **dans le ~** (*gén*) in one's private life; (*Comm*) in the private sector; **en ~** [*conversation, réunion*] private, in private (*attrib*); [*parler*] privately, in private ⓑ (* = *détective*) private eye*, private detective

privément [pʀivemɑ̃] ADV (*littér*) privately

priver [pʀive] ▸ conjug 1 ◂ ① VT ⓐ (*délibérément, pour punir*) **~ qn de qch** to deprive sb of sth; **il a été privé de dessert** he was deprived of dessert, he had to go without his dessert; **il a été privé de récréation** he was kept in at playtime; **on l'a privé de sa liberté/ses droits** he was deprived of his freedom/his rights ⓑ (= *faire perdre*) **~ qn de ses moyens** to deprive sb of *ou* strip sb of his means; **cette perte m'a privé de ma seule joie** this loss has deprived me of my only joy *ou* has taken my only joy from me; **l'accident l'a privé d'un bras** he lost an arm in the accident; **privé de connaissance** unconscious; **privé de voix** speechless, unable to speak; **un discours privé de l'essentiel** a speech from which the main content had been removed *ou* which was stripped of its essential content ⓒ (= *démunir*) **nous avons été privés d'électricité pendant 3 jours** we were without *ou* we had no *ou* we were deprived of electricity for 3 days; **il a été privé de sommeil** he didn't get any sleep; **on m'interdit le sel, ça me prive beaucoup** I'm not allowed salt and I must say I miss it *ou* and I don't like having to go *ou* do without it; **cela ne me prive pas du tout** (*de vous le donner*) I can spare it (quite easily); (*de ne plus en manger*) I don't miss it at all; (*de ne pas y aller*) I don't mind at all

② **se priver** VPR ⓐ (*par économie*) to go without, do without; **se ~ de qch** to go *ou* do *ou* manage without sth; **ils ont dû se ~ pour leurs enfants** they had to go *ou* do without for the sake of their children; **je n'ai pas l'intention de me ~** I've no intention of going *ou* doing without, I don't intend to go short (*Brit*) ⓑ (= *se passer de*) **se ~ de** to manage without, do without, deny o.s., forego; **il se prive de dessert par crainte de grossir** he does without dessert for fear of putting on weight; **se ~ de cigarettes** to deny o.s. cigarettes; **ils ont dû se ~ d'une partie de leur personnel** they had to manage without *ou* do without some of their staff; **tu te prives d'un beau spectacle en refusant d'y aller** you'll miss out on* *ou* you'll deprive yourself of a fine show by not going ⓒ (*gén nég = se retenir*) **il ne s'est pas privé de le dire/le critiquer** he made no bones about *ou* he had no hesitation in saying it/criticizing him; **j'aime bien manger et quand j'en ai l'occasion je ne m'en prive pas** I love eating and whenever I get the chance I don't hold back; **si tu veux y aller, ne t'en prive pas**

pour moi if you want to go don't stop yourself because of me

privilège [pʀivilɛʒ] NM (*gén*) privilege; **j'ai eu le ~ d'assister à la cérémonie** I had the privilege of attending *ou* I was privileged to attend the ceremony; **avoir le triste ~ de faire qch** to have the unhappy privilege of doing sth; **ce pays a le triste ~ d'être le pays le plus pollué** this country has the dubious distinction *ou* privilege of being the most polluted country

privilégié, e [pʀivileʒje] (*ptp de* **privilégier**) ① ADJ [*personne, site, climat*] privileged; (*Fin*) [*action*] preference (*épith*) (*Brit*), preferred (*US*); [*créancier*] preferential; **les classes ~es** the privileged classes ② NM,F privileged person; **c'est un ~** he is fortunate *ou* lucky; **quelques ~s** a privileged *ou* lucky few

privilégier [pʀivileʒje] ▸ conjug 7 ◂ VT to favour (*Brit*), favor (*US*); **privilégié par le sort** fortunate, lucky; **la police semble ~ la thèse de l'attentat** the police appear to favour the theory that it was a terrorist attack; **il a été privilégié par la nature** nature has been kind to him

prix [pʀi] ① NM ⓐ (= *coût*) [*objet, produit*] price; [*location, transport*] cost; **le ~ d'un billet Paris-Lyon** the fare between Paris and Lyons, the price of a ticket between Paris and Lyons; **à quel ~ vend-il/sont ses tapis?** what price is he asking for/are his carpets?, how much is he charging *ou* asking for/are his carpets?; **quel ~ veut-elle de sa maison?** what (price) is she asking *ou* how much does she want for her house?; **quels sont vos ~?** (*pour service*) what are your rates?; (*pour objet*) what sort of prices do you charge?; **je l'ai payé 600 F! — c'est le ~** I paid 600 francs for it! — that's the going rate; **10 000 F, ~ à débattre** 10,000 francs *ou* nearest offer, 10,000 francs o.n.o. (*Brit*); **au ~ que ça coûte, il ne faut pas le gaspiller** at that price we'd better not waste any; **au ~ où sont les choses** *ou* **où est le beurre!*** with prices what they are!; **votre ~ sera le mien** name *ou* state your price; **c'était le premier ~** it was the cheapest; **quel est votre dernier ~?** (*pour vendre*) what's the lowest you'll go?; (*pour acheter*) what's your final offer?; **acheter qch à ~ d'or** to pay a (small) fortune for sth; **payer le ~ fort** (*lit*) to pay the full price; (*fig*) to pay a heavy price; **faire payer le ~ fort** to charge the full price; **au ~ fort** at the highest possible price; **à bas ~** [*produit, terrain*] cheap; [*acheter, vendre*] cheaply; **je l'ai eu à bas ~** I got it cheap; **ça n'a pas de ~** it's priceless; **je vous fais un ~ (d'ami)** I'll let you have it cheap *ou* at a reduced price, I'll knock a bit off for you*; **j'y ai mis le ~ (qu'il fallait)** I had to pay a lot *ou* quite a price for it, it cost me a lot; **il faut y mettre le ~** you have to be prepared to pay for it; **il n'a pas voulu y mettre le ~** he didn't want to pay that much; **je cherche une robe — dans quels ~?** I'm looking for a dress — in what price range?; **c'est dans mes ~** that's affordable *ou* within my price range; **c'est hors de ~** it's outrageously expensive; **cette table est hors de ~** the price of this table is exorbitant *ou* outrageous; **ce magasin est hors de ~** the prices in this shop are exorbitant *ou* outrageous; **c'est un objet qui n'a pas de ~** it's a priceless object; (*enchères*) **mettre qch à ~** to set a reserve price (*Brit*) *ou* an upset price (*US*) on sth; **mettre à ~ la tête de qn** to put a price on sb's head, offer a reward for sb's capture; (*enchères*) **mise à ~: 1 000 F** reserve (*Brit*) *ou* upset (*US*) price: 1,000 francs; **objet de ~** expensive item → **bas¹** ⓑ (*fig*) price; **le ~ du succès/de la gloire** the price of success/of glory; **j'apprécie votre geste à son juste ~** I appreciate the true worth of what you did; **son amitié n'a pas de ~ pour moi** I cannot put a price on his friendship; **donner du ~ à** [+ *exploit, aide*] to make (even) more worthwhile; **leur pauvreté donne**

encore plus de ~ à leur cadeau their poverty makes their present even more precious *ou* impressive, their poverty increases the value *ou* worth of their gift even more

c (= récompense, Scol) prize; (Scol) **(livre de) ~** prize(-book); **le ~ Nobel de la paix** the Nobel Peace Prize

d (= vainqueur) (= personne) prizewinner; (= livre) prizewinning book; **premier ~ du Conservatoire** first prizewinner at the Conservatoire; **as-tu lu le dernier ~ Goncourt ?** have you read the book that won the last *ou* latest Prix Goncourt?

e (Courses) race; (Aut) **Grand Prix (automobile)** Grand Prix

f (loc) **à tout ~** at all costs, at any price; **à aucun ~** on no account, not at any price; **au ~ de grands efforts/sacrifices** after much effort/many sacrifices

2 COMP ► **prix d'achat** purchase price ► **prix actuel** going price (de for) ► **prix agricoles** (Europe) agricultural prices ► **prix d'appel** introductory price ► **prix conseillé** manufacturer's recommended price, recommended retail price ► **prix coûtant** cost price ► **prix de départ** asking price ► **prix de détail** retail price ► **prix d'encouragement** special prize (for promising entrant) ► **prix d'excellence** (Scol) prize for coming first in the class *ou* for being top of the form ► **prix de fabrique** factory price ► **prix fixe** (gén) set price; (menu) set (price) menu; **(repas à) ~ fixe** set (price) meal ► **prix forfaitaire** contract price ► **prix de gros** wholesale price ► **prix imposé** (Comm) regulation price ► **prix d'interprétation féminine/masculine** (Ciné, Théât) prize for best actress/actor ► **prix d'intervention** intervention price ► **prix de lancement** introductory price ► **prix littéraire** literary prize ► **prix marqué** marked price ► **prix à la production** *ou* **au producteur** farm gate price ► **prix public** retail *ou* list *ou* base price ► **prix de revient** cost price ► **prix sortie d'usine** factory price ► **prix de vente** selling price, sale price ► **prix de vertu** paragon of virtue

┌─────────────────────┐
│ **PRIX LITTÉRAIRES** │
└─────────────────────┘

The prix Goncourt, France's best-known annual literary prize, is awarded for the year's finest prose work (usually a novel). The winner is chosen by a jury made up of members of the Académie Goncourt, who make their final decision over lunch at Drouant, a famous Paris restaurant.

There are over 100 other important literary prizes in France, the most coveted of which include the Prix Fémina, the Prix Interallié, the Prix Renaudot and the Prix Médicis.

pro* [pʀo] NMF (ABRÉV = **professionnel**) pro*; **c'est un travail de ~** it's a professional job; **il est très ~** he's very professional, he's a real pro*

pro- [pʀo] PRÉF pro-; **~américain/chinois** pro-American/-Chinese; **~Maastricht** pro-Maastricht

probabilisme [pʀobabilism] NM probabilism
probabiliste [pʀobabilist] ADJ (Stat) probability (épith)

▼ **probabilité** [pʀobabilite] NF a (= vraisemblance) [événement, hypothèse] probability, likelihood; **selon toute ~** in all probability *ou* likelihood b (Math, Stat) probability; **calcul/théorie des ~s** probability calculus/theory

▼ **probable** [pʀobabl] 1 ADJ a (= vraisemblable) [événement, hypothèse, évolution] probable, likely; **il est ~ qu'il gagnera** it's likely that he will win, he's likely to win, he'll probably win, the chances are (that) he'll win; **il est peu ~ qu'il vienne** he's unlikely to come, there's little chance of his coming, the chances are (that) he won't come; **il est fort ~**

qu'il ait raison in all likelihood he's right, it's highly likely that he's right; **c'est (très) ~** it's (very *ou* highly) probable, (most *ou* very) probably, it's (highly) likely; **c'est son successeur ~** he's likely to succeed him b (Math, Stat) probable 2 ADV (* = sûrement) **j'ai dû l'oublier dans le bus — ~** I must have left it on the bus — most likely

▼ **probablement** [pʀobabləmã] ADV probably; **il viendra ~** he's likely to come, he'll probably come; **~ pas** probably not

probant, e [pʀobã, ãt] ADJ [argument, expérience] convincing; (Jur) probative

probation [pʀobasjɔ̃] NF (Jur, Rel) probation; **stage de ~** trial *ou* probationary period

probatoire [pʀobatwaʀ] ADJ [examen, test] grading, preliminary; **stage ~** trial *ou* probationary period

probe [pʀob] ADJ (littér) upright, honest
probité [pʀobite] NF probity, integrity

problématique [pʀoblematik] 1 ADJ problematic(al) 2 NF (= problème) problem, issue; (= science) problematics sg

▼ **problème** [pʀoblɛm] NM a (= difficulté) problem; (= question débattue) problem, issue; **le ~ du logement** the housing problem, the problem of housing; **~ de santé** health problem; **j'ai eu quelques ~s de santé dernièrement** I've had some problems with my health *ou* health problems recently, my health hasn't been too good recently; **c'est tout un ~** it's a real problem; **elle risque d'avoir de sérieux ~s avec la police** she could run into serious trouble with the police; **soulever un ~** to raise a problem; **faire ~** to pose problems; **(il n'y a) pas de ~** no problem!, no sweat!*; **ça lui pose un ~ de conscience** this is troubling his conscience; **il a bien su poser le ~** he put *ou* formulated the problem well; **ce retard pose un ~** this delay poses a problem *ou* confronts us with a problem; **son admission au club pose des ~s** his joining the club is problematic *ou* is not straightforward; **son cas nous pose un sérieux ~** his case poses a difficult problem for us, his case presents us with a difficult problem; **le ~ qui se pose** the problem we are faced with *ou* we must face; **si tu viens en voiture, le ~ ne se pose pas** if you come by car the problem doesn't arise; **le ~ ne se pose pas dans ces termes** that isn't the problem, the problem shouldn't be stated in these terms → **faux²** b **à ~s** [peau, cheveux, enfant] problem (épith); **famille à ~s** problem *ou* dysfunctional family; **quartier/banlieue à ~s** problem area/suburb (in which there is a lot of crime) c (Math) problem; (Scol) **~s de robinets** sums about the volume of water in containers; **le prof nous a posé un ~ difficile** the teacher set us a difficult problem

procédé [pʀosede] NM a (= méthode) process; ► **de fabrication** manufacturing process b (= conduite) behaviour (Brit) (NonC), behavior (US) (NonC), conduct (NonC); **avoir recours à un ~ malhonnête** to do something in a dishonest way, resort to dishonest behaviour; **ce sont là des ~s peu recommandables** that's pretty disreputable behaviour → **échange** c (Billard) tip

procéder [pʀosede] ▶ conjug 6 ◀ 1 VI (= agir) to proceed; (moralement) to behave; **~ par ordre** to take things one by one, do one thing at a time; **~ avec prudence** to proceed with caution; **~ par élimination** to use a process of elimination; **je n'aime pas sa façon de ~ (envers les gens)** I don't like the way he behaves (towards people)

2 **procéder à** VT INDIR (= opérer) [+ enquête, expérience] to conduct, carry out; [+ dépouillement] to start; **ils ont procédé à l'ouverture du coffre** they proceeded to open the chest, they set about opening the chest; **nous avons fait ~ à une étude sur ...** we have initiat-

ed *ou* set up a study on ...; **~ au vote** to take a vote (sur on); **~ à une élection** to hold an election; **~ à l'élection du nouveau président** to hold an election for the new president, elect the new president

3 **procéder de** VT INDIR (frm = provenir de) to come from, proceed from, originate in; (Rel) to proceed from; **cette philosophie procède de celle de Platon** this philosophy originates in *ou* is a development from that of Plato; **cela procède d'une mauvaise organisation** it comes from *ou* is due to bad organization

procédural, e (mpl -aux) [pʀosedyʀal, o] ADJ procedural

procédure [pʀosedyʀ] NF a (= marche à suivre) procedure; **quelle ~ doit-on suivre pour obtenir ... ?** what procedure must one follow to obtain ...?, what's the (usual) procedure for obtaining ...? b (Jur) (= règles) procedure; (= procès) proceedings; **~ accélérée** expeditious procedure; **~ de conciliation** conciliation procedure; **~ civile** civil (law) procedure; **~ pénale** criminal (law) procedure; **problème de ~** procedural problem

procédurier, -ière [pʀosedyʀje, jɛʀ] ADJ (péj) [tempérament, attitude] quibbling (épith), pettifogging (épith); **il est très ~** he's a real stickler for the regulations

procès [pʀosɛ] 1 NM a (Jur = poursuite) (legal) proceedings, (court) action, lawsuit; [cour d'assises] trial; **faire/intenter un ~ à qn** to take/start *ou* institute (frm) (legal) proceedings against sb; **engager un ~ contre qn** to take (court) action against sb, bring an action against sb, take sb to court, sue sb; **intenter un ~ en divorce** to institute divorce proceedings; **être en ~ avec qn** to be involved in a lawsuit with sb; **gagner/perdre son ~** to win/lose one's case; **réviser un ~** to review a case *ou* judgment

b (fig) **faire le ~ de qn/la société capitaliste** to put sb/capitalism on trial *ou* in the dock; **faire le ~ de qch** to pick holes in sth, criticize sth; **là tu me fais un ~ d'intention** you're putting words into my mouth; **vous me faites un mauvais ~** you're making unfounded *ou* groundless accusations against me → **forme** c (Anat, Ling) process

2 COMP ► **procès civil** civil proceedings *ou* action ► **procès criminel** criminal proceedings *ou* trial

processeur [pʀosɛsœʀ] NM processor

procession [pʀosesjɔ̃] NF (gén) procession; **marcher en ~** to walk in procession

processionnaire [pʀosesjɔnɛʀ] 1 ADJ processionary 2 NF processionary caterpillar

processionnel, -elle [pʀosesjɔnɛl] ADJ processional

processionnellement [pʀosesjɔnɛlmã] ADV in procession

processus [pʀosesys] NM a (= procédure) process; **~ de paix** peace process; **le ~ d'intégration européenne** the European integration process b [maladie] progress; **l'apparition d'un ~ cancéreux** the appearance of a cancerous growth c (Anat) process

procès-verbal (pl **procès-verbaux**) [pʀosɛvɛʀbal, o] NM a (= compte rendu) minutes; (Jur = constat) report, statement; (de contravention) statement; **dresser (un) ~ à un automobiliste** to give a ticket to *ou* book (Brit) a motorist

prochain, e [pʀoʃɛ̃, ɛn] 1 ADJ a (= suivant) [réunion, numéro, semaine] next; **lundi/le mois ~** next Monday/month; **le 8 septembre ~** on the 8th September (of this year); **la ~e rencontre aura lieu à Paris** the next meeting will take place in Paris; **la ~e fois que tu viendras** (the) next time you come; **la ~e fois** *ou* **la fois ~e, je le saurai** I'll know next time; **à la ~e occasion** at the next *ou* first opportunity; **à la ~e !*** see you!*, be seeing you!*; **au revoir,**

▶ GRAMMAIRE ACTIVE: probabilité 42.2 probable 42.2, 43.2 probablement 42.2, 43.2, 53.6 problème 53.1, 53.2, 53.3

à une **~e fois !** goodbye, see you again!*; **je ne peux pas rester dîner aujourd'hui, ce sera pour une ~e fois** I can't stay for dinner today — it'll have to be *ou* I'll have to come some other time; **je descends à la ~e*** I'm getting off at the next stop (*ou* station *etc*); **au ~ (client) !** next please!

b (= *proche*) [*arrivée, départ*] impending, imminent; [*mort*] imminent; [*avenir*] near, immediate; **un jour ~** soon, in the near future; **un de ces ~s jours** one of these days, before long

c [*village*] (= *suivant*) next; (= *voisin*) neighbouring (*Brit*), neighboring (*US*), nearby; (= *plus près*) nearest

d (*littér*) [*cause*] immediate

2 NM fellow man; (*Rel*) neighbour (*Brit*), neighbor (*US*)

prochainement [prɔʃɛnmɑ̃] ADV soon, shortly; (*Ciné*) **~ (sur vos écrans) ...** coming soon ... *ou* shortly ...

proche [prɔʃ] **1** ADJ **a** (*dans l'espace*) [*village*] neighbouring (*Brit*) (*épith*), neighboring (*US*) (*épith*), nearby (*épith*); [*rue*] nearby (*épith*); **être (tout) ~** to be (very) near *ou* close, be (quite) close by; **~ de la ville** near the town, close to the town; **le magasin le plus ~** the nearest shop; **les maisons sont très ~s les unes des autres** the houses are very close together; **de ~ en ~** step by step, gradually; **la nouvelle se répandit de ~ en ~** the news gradually spread

b (= *imminent*) [*mort*] close (*attrib*), at hand (*attrib*); [*départ*] imminent, at hand (*attrib*); **dans un ~ avenir** in the near *ou* immediate future; **être ~** [*fin, but*] to be drawing near, near at hand; **être ~ de** [+ *fin, victoire*] to be nearing, be close to; [+ *dénouement*] to be reaching, be drawing close to; **être ~ de la mort** to be near death *ou* close to death; **la nuit est ~** it's nearly nightfall; **l'heure est ~ où ... the time is at hand when ... → futur**

c (= *récent*) [*événement*] close (*attrib*), recent

d [*parent*] close, near; **mes plus ~s parents** my nearest *ou* closest relatives, my next of kin (*Admin*)

e [*ami*] close; **je me sens très ~ d'elle** I feel very close to her; **les ~s conseillers/collaborateurs du président** the president's closest *ou* immediate advisers/associates

f **~ de** (= *avoisinant*) close to; (= *parent de*) closely related to; **l'italien est ~ du latin** Italian is closely related to Latin; **une désinvolture ~ de l'insolence** offhandedness verging on insolence; **nos positions sont très ~s** we take a very similar position *ou* line; **selon des sources ~s de l'ONU** according to sources close to the UN

2 NM (*surtout pl*) close relation; **les ~s** close relations, next of kin (*Admin*)

Proche-Orient [prɔʃɔrjɑ̃] NM **le ~** the Near East; **du ~** Near Eastern, in *ou* from the Near East

proche-oriental, e (*mpl* **proche-orientaux**) [prɔʃɔrjɑ̃tal, o] ADJ Near Eastern

proclamateur, -trice [prɔklamatœr, tris] NM,F proclaimer

proclamation [prɔklamasjɔ̃] NF **a** (= *reconnaissance officielle*) [*république, juge d'urgence*] proclamation, declaration; [*verdict, résultats d'élection, résultats d'examen*] announcement; **~ d'indépendance** declaration of independence **b** (= *texte*) proclamation

proclamer [prɔklame] ▸ conjug 1 ◂ VT **a** (= *affirmer*) [+ *conviction, vérité*] to proclaim; **~ son innocence** to proclaim *ou* declare one's innocence; **~ que ...** to proclaim *ou* declare *ou* assert that ...; **il se proclamait le sauveur du pays** he proclaimed *ou* declared himself (to be) the saviour of the country; (*littér*) **chez eux, tout proclamait la pauvreté** everything in their house proclaimed their poverty **b** (= *reconnaître officiellement*) [+ *république, état d'urgence, état de siège, indépendance*] to pro-

claim, declare; [+ *décret*] to publish; [+ *verdict, résultats*] to announce; **~ qn roi** to proclaim sb king

proclitique [prɔklitik] ADJ, NM proclitic

proconsul [prɔkɔ̃syl] NM proconsul

procrastination [prɔkrastinasjɔ̃] NF (*littér*) procrastination

procréateur, -trice [prɔkreatœr, tris] (*littér*) **1** ADJ procreative **2** NM,F procreator

procréation [prɔkreasjɔ̃] NF (*littér*) procreation (*littér*), reproduction; **~ artificielle** *ou* **médicale(ment) assistée** artificial *ou* assisted reproduction

procréer [prɔkree] ▸ conjug 1 ◂ VT (*littér*) to procreate

procuration [prɔkyrasjɔ̃] NF (*Jur*) (*pour voter, représenter qn*) proxy; (*pour toucher de l'argent*) power of attorney; **avoir (une) ~** to have power of attorney *ou* an authorization; **avoir ~ sur un compte en banque** to have power of attorney over a bank account; **donner (une) ~ à qn** to give sb power of attorney, authorize sb; **par ~** (*lit*) by proxy; (*fig*) [*vivre, voyager*] vicariously

procurer [prɔkyre] ▸ conjug 1 ◂ **1** VT **a** (= *faire obtenir*) **~ qch à qn** to get *ou* obtain sth for sb, find sth for sb, provide sb with sth **b** (= *apporter*) [+ *joie, ennuis*] to bring; [+ *avantage*] to bring, give, procure; **le plaisir que procure le jardinage** the pleasure that gardening brings *ou* that one gets from gardening **2** **se procurer** VPR (= *obtenir*) to get, procure, obtain (for o.s.); (= *trouver*) to find, come by (= *acheter*) to get, buy (o.s.)

procureur [prɔkyrœr] NM **a** (*Jur*) **~ (de la République)** public *ou* state prosecutor; **~ général** public prosecutor (*in appeal courts*); (*Can*) **~ de la Couronne** Crown prosecutor (*Can*) **b** (*Rel*) procurator

prodigalité [prɔdigalite] NF **a** (= *caractère*) prodigality, extravagance **b** (= *dépenses*) **~s** extravagance, extravagant expenditure (*NonC*) **c** (*littér* = *profusion*) [*détails*] abundance, profusion, wealth

prodige [prɔdiʒ] **1** NM (= *événement*) marvel, wonder; (= *personne*) prodigy; **un ~ de la nature/science** a wonder of nature/science; **tenir du ~** to be astounding *ou* extraordinary; **faire des ~s** to work wonders; **grâce à des ~s de courage/patience** thanks to his (*ou* her *etc*) prodigious *ou* extraordinary courage/patience **2** ADJ **enfant ~** child prodigy

prodigieusement [prɔdiʒjøzmɑ̃] ADV [*ennuyeux, long, compliqué, cher*] incredibly; **~ doué** prodigiously talented; **cela nous a agacé ~** we found it intensely irritating

prodigieux, -ieuse [prɔdiʒjø, jøz] ADJ [*foule, force, bêtise*] prodigious, incredible, phenomenal; [*personne, génie*] prodigious, phenomenal; [*effort*] prodigious, tremendous, fantastic

prodigue [prɔdig] **1** ADJ (= *dépensier*) extravagant, wasteful, prodigal; (= *généreux*) generous; **être ~ de ses compliments** to be lavish with one's praise; **être ~ de conseils** to be full of advice *ou* free with one's advice; **lui, en général si peu ~ de compliments/conseils** he who is usually so sparing of compliments/advice; **être ~ de son temps** to be unsparing *ou* unstinting of one's time; **être ~ de son bien** to be lavish with one's money; (*Rel*) **l'enfant** *ou* **le fils ~** the prodigal son **2** NMF spendthrift

prodiguer [prɔdige] ▸ conjug 1 ◂ VT [+ *compliments, conseils*] to be full of, pour out; [+ *argent*] to be lavish with; **~ des compliments/conseils à qn** to lavish compliments/advice on sb, pour out compliments/advice to sb; **elle me prodigua ses soins** she lavished care on me; **malgré les soins que le médecin lui a prodigués** in spite of the care *ou* treatment the doctor gave him; **se ~ sans compter** to

spare no effort, give unsparingly *ou* unstintingly of o.s.

pro domo [prɔdomo] LOC ADJ **faire un plaidoyer ~** (*Jur*) to defend o.s., plead one's own case; (*fig*) to justify o.s.; **le discours du ministre était un véritable plaidoyer ~** the minister's speech was a real exercise in self-justification

prodrome [prɔdrom] NM (*littér*) forerunner; (*Méd*) prodrome

producteur, -trice [prɔdyktœr, tris] **1** ADJ **pays ~ de pétrole** oil-producing country, oil producer; **pays ~ de blé** wheat-growing country, wheat producer; (*Ciné*) **société productrice** film company **2** NM,F **a** (*Comm*) producer; (*Agr*) [*œufs*] producer; [*blé, tomates*] grower, producer; **du ~ au consommateur** from the producer to the consumer **b** (*Ciné, TV*) producer; (*TV*) **~-réalisateur** producer and director

productible [prɔdyktibl] ADJ producible

productif, -ive [prɔdyktif, iv] ADJ productive; (*Fin*) **~ d'intérêts** that bears interest, interest-bearing

production [prɔdyksjɔ̃] NF **a** (*NonC*) (*Ind*) production; (*Agr*) production, growing; [*rouille, humidité, son*] production **b** (= *ensemble de produits, rendement*) (*Ind*) production, output; (*Agr*) production, yield; **~ annuelle de blé** annual wheat production *ou* yield; **notre ~ est inférieure à nos besoins** our output is lower than our needs; **~ brute** gross output; **capacité/coûts de ~** production capacity/costs; **directeur de la ~** production manager → **moyen** **c** (= *produit*) product; **~s** (*Agr*) produce; (*Comm, Ind*) products, goods **d** (= *œuvre*) work; (= *ensemble de l'œuvre*) works; **la ~ cinématographique/dramatique du XXᵉ siècle** 20th-century cinema/plays; **les ~s de l'esprit** creations of the mind **e** (*Jur*) [*document*] presentation **f** (*Ciné, Radio, TV*) production; **assistant/directeur de ~** production assistant/manager → **société**

productique [prɔdyktik] NF factory *ou* industrial automation

productivisme [prɔdyktivism] NM emphasis on high productivity, productivism (*SPEC*)

productiviste [prɔdyktivist] **1** ADJ [*société*] that puts strong emphasis on high productivity, productivist (*SPEC*); **pour rompre avec la logique ~** to break away from the over-emphasis on high productivity **2** NMF advocate of high productivity, productivist (*SPEC*)

productivité [prɔdyktivite] NF productivity, productiveness; (*Écon, Ind* = *rendement*) productivity

produire [prɔdɥir] ▸ conjug 38 ◂ **1** VT **a** (*Ind*) to produce; (*Agr*) to produce, grow; **pays qui produit du pétrole** country which produces oil, oil-producing country; **cette école a produit plusieurs savants** this school has produced several scientists

b (= *créer*) [+ *roman*] to produce, write; [+ *tableau*] to produce, paint; **un poète qui ne produit pas beaucoup** a poet who doesn't write much

c (*Fin*) [+ *intérêt*] to yield, return; **arbre/terre qui produit de bons fruits** tree/soil which yields *ou* produces good fruit; **certains sols produisent plus que d'autres** some soils are more productive *ou* give a better yield than others

d (= *causer*) [+ *rouille, humidité, son*] to produce, make; [+ *effet*] to produce, have; [+ *changement*] to produce, bring about; [+ *résultat*] to produce, give; [+ *sensation*] to cause, create; **~ une bonne/mauvaise impression sur qn** to make a good/bad impression on sb; **il a produit une forte impression sur les examinateurs** he made a great impression on the examiners, the examiners were highly impressed by him

e (*Jur*) [+ *document*] to present, produce; [+

témoin] to produce
[f] (*Ciné, Radio, TV*) [+ *film, émission*] to produce

[2] **se produire** VPR [a] (= *survenir*) to happen, occur, take place; **cela peut se ~** it can happen; **ce cas ne s'était jamais produit** this kind of case had never come up before; **il s'est produit un revirement dans l'opinion** there has been a complete change in public opinion; **le changement qui s'est produit en lui** the change that has come over him *ou* taken place in him
[b] [*acteur, chanteur*] to perform, give a performance, appear; **se ~ sur scène** to appear live *ou* on stage; **se ~ en public** to appear in public, give a public performance

produit [pʀɔdɥi] [1] NM [a] (= *denrée, article*) product; **~s** (*Agr*) produce (*Comm, Ind*) goods, products; **il faudrait acheter un ~ pour nettoyer les carreaux** we'll have to buy something to clean the windows (with); **chef** *ou* **responsable** (**de**) ~ product manager, brand manager; (*fig*) **un ~ typique de notre université** a typical product of our university; **c'est le** (**pur**) ~ **de ton imagination** it's a (pure) figment of your imagination
[b] (= *rapport*) product, yield; (= *bénéfice*) profit; (= *revenu*) income; **le ~ de la collecte sera donné à une bonne œuvre** the proceeds from the collection will be given to charity; **vivre du ~ de sa terre** to live off the land
[c] (*Math*) product
[d] (*Chim*) product, chemical
[e] (*Zool = petit*) offspring *inv*

[2] COMP ▶ **produits agricoles** agricultural *ou* farm produce ▶ **produits alimentaires** foodstuffs ▶ **produit d'appel** loss leader ▶ **produit bancaire** banking product ▶ **produits de beauté** cosmetics, beauty products ▶ **produits blancs** white goods ▶ **produits bruns** brown goods ▶ **produit brut** (= *bénéfice*) gross profit; (= *objet*) unfinished product ▶ **produit chimique** chemical ▶ **produit de consommation** consumable; **~ de consommation courante** basic consumable; **~s de grande consommation** consumer goods ▶ **produits dérivés** (*Comm, Fin*) derivatives ▶ **produit d'entretien** clean(s)ing product ▶ **produit d'épargne** savings product ▶ **produit financier** financial product ▶ **produit de l'impôt** tax yield ▶ **produits industriels** industrial goods *ou* products ▶ **produit intérieur brut** gross domestic product ▶ **produits manufacturés** manufactured goods ▶ **produit national brut** gross national product ▶ **produit net** net profit ▶ **produit pétrolier** oil product ▶ **produit pharmaceutique** pharmaceutical (product) ▶ **produits de première nécessité** vital commodities ▶ **produits de toilette** toiletries ▶ **produit pour la vaisselle** washing-up liquid (*Brit*), dish soap (*US*) ▶ **produit des ventes** income *ou* proceeds from sales → **substitution**

proéminence [pʀɔeminɑ̃s] NF prominence, protuberance

proéminent, e [pʀɔeminɑ̃, ɑ̃t] ADJ prominent, protuberant

prof* [pʀɔf] NMF (ABRÉV = **professeur**) (*Scol*) teacher; (*Univ*) ≈ lecturer (*Brit*), ≈ instructor (*US*), ≈ prof* (*US*); (*avec chaire*) prof*

profanateur, -trice [pʀɔfanatœʀ, tʀis] [1] ADJ profaning (*épith*), profane [2] NM,F profaner

profanation [pʀɔfanasjɔ̃] NF [a] [*église, autel, hostie, sépulture*] desecration, profanation [b] [*sentiment, souvenir, nom*] defilement, profanation; [*institution*] debasement; [*talent*] prostitution, debasement

profane [pʀɔfan] [1] ADJ [a] (= *non spécialiste*) **je suis ~ en la matière** I'm a layman in the field, I don't know (very) much about the subject [b] [*fête*] secular; [*auteur, littérature,*

musique] secular, profane (*littér*) [2] NMF [a] (*gén*) layman, lay person; **aux yeux du ~** to the layman *ou* the uninitiated; **un ~ en art** a person who is uninitiated in the field of art, a person who knows nothing about art [b] (*Rel*) non-believer [3] NM (*Rel*) **le ~** the secular, the profane (*littér*); **le ~ et le sacré** the sacred and the profane

profaner [pʀɔfane] ▶conjug 1◀ VT [a] [+ *église, autel, hostie, sépulture*] to desecrate, profane [b] [+ *sentiments, souvenir, nom*] to defile, profane; [+ *institution*] to debase; [+ *talent*] to prostitute, debase

proférer [pʀɔfeʀe] ▶conjug 6◀ VT [+ *parole*] to utter; [+ *injures*] to utter, pour out

professer [pʀɔfese] ▶conjug 1◀ VT [a] [+ *opinion*] to profess, declare, state; [+ *théorie*] to profess; [+ *sentiment*] to profess, declare; **~ que ...** to profess *ou* declare *ou* claim that ... [b] (*Scol*) to teach

professeur [pʀɔfesœʀ] [1] NM (*gén*) teacher; [*lycée, collège*] (school) teacher; (*Univ*) ≈ lecturer (*Brit*), ≈ instructor (*US*); (*avec chaire*) professor; **elle est ~** she's a (school)teacher; (*Univ*) (**Monsieur**) **le ~ Durand** Professor Durand; **~ de piano/de chant** piano/singing teacher *ou* master (*Brit*) *ou* mistress (*Brit*); **~ de droit** lecturer in law, professor of law; **l'ensemble des ~s** the teaching staff [2] COMP ▶ **professeur agrégé** (*gén*) qualified schoolteacher (*who has passed the agrégation*); (*en médecine*) professor of medicine (*holder of the agrégation*); (*Can Univ*) associate professor ▶ **professeur certifié** qualified schoolteacher (*who has passed the CAPES*) ▶ **professeur des écoles** primary school teacher ▶ **professeur d'enseignement général des collèges** basic-grade schoolteacher (*in a collège*) ▶ **professeur principal** ≈ class teacher (*Brit*), ≈ form tutor (*Brit*), ≈ homeroom teacher (*US*) → **associé**

profession [pʀɔfesjɔ̃] [1] NF [a] (*gén*) occupation; (*manuelle*) trade; (*libérale*) profession; **exercer la ~ de médecin** to be a doctor by profession, practise as a doctor (*Brit*), practice medicine (*US*); **menuisier de ~** carpenter by trade; (*hum*) **menteur de ~** professional liar; (*Admin*) « **sans ~** » (*gén*) "unemployed"; (*femme mariée*) "housewife" [b] (= *personnes*) (**les gens de**) **la ~** (*gén*) the people in the profession; (= *artisans*) the people in the trade [c] (*loc*) **faire ~ de non-conformisme** to profess nonconformism; **ceux qui font ~ de démocratiser l'information** those who proclaim that they want to make information available to all [2] COMP ▶ **profession de foi** (*Rel, fig*) profession of faith ▶ **profession libérale** (liberal) profession; **les membres des ~s libérales** professional people, the members of the (liberal) professions

professionnalisation [pʀɔfesjɔnalizasjɔ̃] NF [*armée, recherche*] professionalization; **la ~ des études est renforcée par les stages en entreprise** work experience schemes in companies help to give a vocational focus to studies

professionnaliser [pʀɔfesjɔnalize] ▶conjug 1◀ [1] VT [+ *armée, métier*] to professionalize; [+ *sportif*] to make professional; **filière/ formation professionnalisée** vocational course/training [2] **se professionnaliser** VPR [*sport, activité*] to become professionalized, professionalize; [*sportif*] to turn professional

professionnalisme [pʀɔfesjɔnalism] NM professionalism

professionnel, -elle [pʀɔfesjɔnel] [1] ADJ [a] [*activité, maladie*] occupational (*épith*); [*école*] technical (*épith*); **faute professionnelle** (professional) negligence (*NonC*); (*Méd*) malpractice; **formation/orientation professionnelle** vocational training/guidance; **cours ~** vocational training course; **frais ~s** business expenses; (**être tenu par**) **le secret ~** (to be bound by) professional secrecy →

certificat, conscience, déformation
[b] [*écrivain, sportif*] professional; (*hum*) [*menteur*] professional, adept; **il est très ~** (**dans ce qu'il fait**) he's very professional, he has a very professional attitude

[2] NM,F [a] (*gén, Sport*) professional; **c'est un travail de ~** (*pour un professionnel*) it's a job for a professional; (*bien fait*) it's a professional job; **passer ~** to turn professional; **les ~s du tourisme** people working in the tourist industry
[b] (*Ind*) skilled worker

professionnellement [pʀɔfesjɔnelmɑ̃] ADV professionally

professoral, e (*mpl* **-aux**) [pʀɔfesɔʀal, o] ADJ [*ton, attitude*] professorial; **le corps ~** (*gén*) (the) teachers, the teaching profession; [*école*] the teaching staff

professorat [pʀɔfesɔʀa] NM **le ~** the teaching profession; **le ~ de français** French teaching, the teaching of French

profil [pʀɔfil] NM [a] (= *silhouette*) [*personne*] profile; [*édifice*] outline, profile, contour; [*voiture*] line, contour; **de ~** [*dessiner*] in profile; [*regarder*] sideways on, in profile; (*fig*) **un ~ de médaille** a finely chiselled profile; **garder** (**le**) ~ **bas** ◊ **prendre** *ou* **adopter un ~ bas** to keep a low profile [b] (= *coupe*) [*bâtiment, route*] (*Géol*) [*sol*] section [c] (*Psych*) profile; **~ de carrière** career profile; **le ~ d'un étudiant** the profile of a student's performance; **il a le bon ~ pour le métier** his previous experience *ou* his career to date *ou* his career profile seems right for the job

profilé, e [pʀɔfile] (*ptp de* **profiler**) [1] ADJ (*gén*) shaped; (= *aérodynamique*) streamlined [2] NM (*Tech*) **~** (**métallique**) metal section

profiler [pʀɔfile] ▶conjug 1◀ [1] VT [a] (*Tech*) (= *dessiner*) to profile, represent in profile; (= *fabriquer*) to shape; (= *rendre aérodynamique*) to streamline [b] (= *faire ressortir*) **la cathédrale profile ses tours contre le ciel** the cathedral towers stand out *ou* stand outlined *ou* are silhouetted against the sky [2] **se profiler** VPR [*objet*] to stand out (in profile), be outlined (**sur, contre** against); [*ennuis, solution*] to emerge; **les obstacles qui se profilent à l'horizon** the obstacles looming on the horizon

profit [pʀɔfi] [1] NM [a] (*Comm, Fin* = *gain*) profit; (**faire**) **passer qch par** *ou* **aux ~s et pertes** (*lit, fig*) to write sth off (as a loss); **il n'y a pas de petit(s) ~(s)** great oaks from little acorns grow (*PROV*), look after the pennies and the pounds will look after themselves (*Brit*) → **compte**
[b] (= *avantage*) benefit, advantage, profit; **être d'un grand ~ à qn** to be of great benefit *ou* most useful to sb; **faire du ~** (*gén*) to be economical, be good value (for money); * [*vêtement*] to wear well; [*rôti*] to go a long way; **ce rôti n'a pas fait de ~** that roast didn't go very far; **ses vacances lui ont fait beaucoup de ~** *ou* **lui ont été d'un grand ~** his holiday did him a lot of good, he greatly benefited from his holiday; **il fait** (**son**) **~ de tout** he turns everything to (his) advantage; **vous avez ~ à faire cela** it's in your interest *ou* to your advantage to do that; **s'il le fait, c'est qu'il y trouve son ~** if he does it, it's because it's to his advantage *ou* in his interest *ou* because he's getting something out of it*; **il a suivi les cours sans (en tirer) aucun ~** he attended the classes without deriving any benefit from them; **il a suivi les cours avec ~** he attended the classes and got a lot out of them *ou* and gained a lot from them; **tirer ~ de** [+ *leçon, affaire*] to profit *ou* benefit from; **tirer ~ du malheur des autres** to profit from *ou* take advantage of other people's misfortune

[2] **à profit** LOC ADV **mettre à ~** [+ *idée, invention*] to turn to (good) account; [+ *jeunesse, temps libre, sa beauté*] to make the most of, take advantage of; **tourner qch à ~** to turn sth

to good account; **il a mis à ~ le mauvais temps pour ranger le grenier** he made the most of *ou* took advantage of the bad weather to tidy the attic, he turned the bad weather to (good) account by tidying up the attic

3 **au profit de** LOC PRÉP *(gén)* for; (= *pour aider)* in aid of; **il est soupçonné d'espionnage au ~ d'un pays étranger** he's suspected of spying for a foreign country; **collecte au ~ des aveugles** collection in aid of the blind; **ils ont perdu du terrain/la ville au ~ des socialistes** they've lost ground/the town to the socialists; **il sacrifie sa vie de famille au ~ de son travail** he sacrifices his family life to his work; **le dessin a disparu au ~ de la photo** drawing has been replaced *ou* supplanted by photography; **le fioul a été abandonné au ~ du gaz** oil has been dropped in favour of gas

profitabilité [pʀɔfitabilite] NF profitability

profitable [pʀɔfitabl] ADJ (= *utile)* beneficial, of benefit *(attrib)*; (= *lucratif)* profitable (à to); **le stage lui a été très ~** he got a lot out of the training course, the training course was of great benefit to him

profiter [pʀɔfite] ▶conjug 1◀ **1** **profiter de** VT INDIR (= *tirer avantage de)* [+ *situation, privilège, occasion, crédulité]* to take advantage of; (= *jouir de)* [+ *jeunesse, vacances]* to make the most of, take advantage of; **ils ont profité de ce que le professeur était sorti pour se battre** they took advantage of the fact that the teacher had gone out to have a fight; **elle en a profité pour se sauver** she took advantage of the opportunity to slip away; **profitez de la vie !** make the most of life!; **je n'ai pas assez profité de mes enfants (quand ils étaient petits)** I wasn't able to enjoy being with my children as much as I would have liked (when they were small)

2 **profiter à** VT INDIR (= *rapporter à)* **~ à qn** [*affaire, circonstances]* to be profitable *ou* of benefit to sb, to be to sb's advantage; [*repos]* to benefit sb, be beneficial to sb; [*conseil]* to benefit *ou* profit sb, be of benefit to sb; **à qui cela profite-t-il ?** who stands to gain by it?, who will that help?; **à qui profite le crime ?** who would benefit from the crime? → **bien**

3 VI* (= *se développer)* [*enfant]* to thrive, grow; (= *être économique)* [*plat]* to go a long way, be economical; [*vêtement]* to wear well

profiterole [pʀɔfitʀɔl] NF profiterole

profiteur, -euse [pʀɔfitœʀ, øz] NM,F profiteer; **~ de guerre** war profiteer

profond, e [pʀɔfɔ̃, ɔ̃d] **1** ADJ **a** *(lit)* deep; **décolleté ~** plunging neckline; **peu ~** [*eau, vallée, puits]* shallow; [*coupure]* superficial; **de 3 mètres** 3 metres deep; **forage ~** deep-sea drilling → **eau**

b (= *grand, extrême)* [*soupir, silence]* deep, heavy; [*sommeil]* deep, sound; [*coma, respect]* deep; [*mystère, malaise]* deep, profound; *(littér)* [*nuit]* deep *(littér)*, dark; [*changement, joie, foi, différence, influence]* profound; [*erreur]* serious; [*ignorance]* profound, extreme; [*intérêt, sentiment]* profound, keen; [*ennui]* profound, acute; [*révérence]* low, deep; **les couches ~es** [*peau]* the deeper *ou* lower layers; [*sol]* the (earth's) substrata

c (= *caché, secret)* [*cause, signification]* underlying, deeper; *(Ling)* [*structure]* deep; [*tendance]* deep-seated, underlying; **son comportement traduit sa nature ~e** his true nature is reflected in his behaviour; **la France ~e** *(gén)* the broad mass of French people; *(des campagnes)* rural France; **l'Amérique ~e** middle America

d (= *pénétrant)* [*penseur, réflexion]* profound, deep; [*esprit, remarque]* profound

e [*couleur, regard, voix]* deep

2 ADV [*creuser]* deep; [*planter]* deep (down)

3 **au plus profond de** LOC PRÉP [+ *désespoir, forêt]* in the depths of; **au plus ~ de la mer** at the (very) bottom of the sea, in the depths of the sea; **au plus ~ de la nuit** at dead of night;

au plus ~ de mon être in the depths of my being, in my deepest being

profondément [pʀɔfɔ̃demɑ̃] ADV [*choqué, ému]* deeply, profoundly; [*préoccupé]* deeply, intensely; [*attristé, bouleversé]* deeply; [*convaincu]* deeply, utterly; [*différent]* profoundly, vastly; [*influencer, se tromper]* profoundly; [*réfléchir]* deeply, profoundly; [*aimer, ressentir, regretter]* deeply; [*respirer]* deep(ly); [*creuser, pénétrer]* deep; [*s'incliner]* low; **il dort ~** *(en général)* he sleeps soundly, he's a sound sleeper; *(en ce moment)* he's sound *ou* fast asleep; **s'ennuyer ~** to be utterly *ou* acutely *ou* profoundly bored; **idée ~ ancrée dans les esprits** idea deeply rooted in people's minds; **une tradition ~ enracinée** a deeply-rooted tradition; **ça m'est ~ égal** I really couldn't care less

profondeur [pʀɔfɔ̃dœʀ] **1** NF **a** [*boîte, mer, trou]* depth; [*plaie]* deepness, depth; **à cause du peu de ~ de la rivière** because of the shallowness of the river; **cela manque de ~** it's not deep enough; **creuser en ~** to dig deep; **creuser jusqu'à 3 mètres de ~** to dig down to a depth of 3 metres; **avoir 10 mètres de ~** to be 10 metres deep *ou* in depth; **à 10 mètres de ~** 10 metres down, at a depth of 10 metres; *(Photo)* **~ de champ** depth of field

b (= *fond)* [*métro, mine, poche]* **~s** depths; **les ~s de l'être** the depths of the human psyche; *(Sport)* **se retrouver dans les ~s du classement** to be at the bottom of the table(s)

c [*personne]* profoundness, profundity, depth; [*esprit, remarque]* profoundness, profundity; [*sentiment]* depth, keenness; [*sommeil]* soundness, depth; [*regard]* depth; [*couleur, voix]* deepness

2 **en profondeur** LOC ADV, LOC ADJ [*agir, exprimer]* in depth; [*réformer]* radically, completely; [*nettoyage]* thorough; [*réforme]* radical, thorough(going); **cette pommade agit en ~** this cream works deep into the skin

pro forma [pʀɔfɔʀma] ADJ INV **facture ~** pro forma invoice

profus, e [pʀɔfy, yz] ADJ *(littér)* profuse

profusément [pʀɔfyzemɑ̃] ADV *(littér)* profusely, abundantly

profusion [pʀɔfyzjɔ̃] **1** NF [*fleurs, lumière]* profusion; [*idées, conseils]* wealth, abundance, profusion; **il nous a décrit la scène avec une incroyable ~ de détails** he described the scene to us in the most elaborate detail; **nous ne nous attendions pas à une telle ~ de candidatures** we didn't expect such a flood of applicants *ou* such a large number of applications

2 **à profusion** LOC ADV **il y a des fruits à ~ sur le marché** there is fruit galore* *ou* in plenty *ou* there is plenty of fruit on the market; **nous en avons à ~** we've got plenty *ou* masses*

progéniture [pʀɔʒenityʀ] NF [*homme, animal]* offspring, progeny *(littér)*; *(hum = famille)* offspring *(hum)*

progestatif [pʀɔʒestatif] NM progestogen, progestin

progestérone [pʀɔʒesteʀɔn] NF progesterone

progiciel [pʀɔʒisjel] NM software package

programmable [pʀɔgʀamabl] ADJ programmable; **touche ~** user-definable key; *(Hi-fi)* **l'enchaînement des titres est ~** (à l'avance) the sequence of tracks can be preset

programmateur, -trice [pʀɔgʀamatœʀ, tʀis] **1** NM,F *(Radio, TV)* programme *(Brit)* *ou* program *(US)* planner **2** NM (= *appareil*: *gén)* time switch; *(four)* autotimer

programmation [pʀɔgʀamasjɔ̃] NF *(Radio, TV)* programming, programme *(Brit)* *ou* program *(US)* planning; *(Ordin)* programming

programmatique [pʀɔgʀamatik] ADJ *(Pol)* programmatic; **document ~** policy document

programme [pʀɔgʀam] NM **a** (= *éléments prévus)* [*cinéma, concert, radio, télévision]* pro-

gramme *(Brit)*, program *(US)*; **au ~** on the programme; *(Radio, TV)* **voici le ~ de la matinée** here is a rundown of the morning's programmes; *(Radio, TV)* **fin de nos ~s à minuit** our programmes will end at midnight, closedown will be at midnight *(Brit)*, we will be closing down at midnight *(Brit)*; **changement de ~** change in (the) *ou* of programme

b (= *brochure)* [*cinéma, théâtre, concert]* programme *(Brit)*, program *(US)*; [*radio, télévision]* *(gén)* guide, listings magazine; (= *section de journal)* listings

c *(Scol)* [*matière]* syllabus; [*classe, école]* curriculum; **le ~ de français** the French syllabus; **quel est le ~ cette année ?** what's (on) the curriculum this year?; **les œuvres du** *ou* **au ~** the set *(Brit)* *ou* assigned *(US)* books *ou* works, the books on the syllabus

d (= *projet, Pol)* programme *(Brit)*, program *(US)*; **~ d'action/de travail** programme of action/of work; **~ commun** joint programme; **~ économique/nucléaire/de recherches** economic/nuclear/research programme; **~ électoral** election programme *ou* platform; **le ~ européen Erasmus** the European Erasmus programme; **c'est tout un ~ !*** ◊ **vaste ~ !*** that'll take some doing!

e (= *calendrier)* programme *(Brit)*, program *(US)*; **quel est le ~ de la journée ?** *ou* **des réjouissances ?*** what's the programme for the day?, what's on the agenda?*; **j'ai un ~ très chargé** I have a very busy timetable; **il y a un changement de ~** there's been a change of plan; **ce n'était pas prévu au ~** it wasn't expected, that wasn't on the agenda; **son frère n'était pas prévu au ~** his brother wasn't supposed to come along

f [*machine à laver]* programme *(Brit)*, program *(US)*; *(Ordin)* (computer) program; **~ source/objet** source/object program

g *(Sport)* programme *(Brit)*, program *(US)*; [*patinage artistique]* **~ libre** free skating

programmer [pʀɔgʀame] ▶conjug 1◀ **1** VT **a** [+ *émission]* to schedule; [+ *machine]* to programme *(Brit)*, program *(US)*; [+ *magnétoscope]* to set, programme *(Brit)*, program *(US)*; [+ *ordinateur]* to program; *(Typo)* **composition programmée** computer(ized) *ou* electronic typesetting; **~ à l'avance** [+ *magnétoscope]* to preset **b** (= *prévoir, organiser)* [+ *opération, naissance, vacances]* to plan; **son dernier concert est programmé à Paris** his last concert is scheduled to take place in Paris; **ce bébé n'était pas vraiment programmé*** this baby wasn't really planned **2** VI *(Ordin)* to (write a) program

programmeur, -euse [pʀɔgʀamœʀ, øz] NM,F (computer) programmer

progrès [pʀɔgʀɛ] **1** NM **a** (= *amélioration)* progress *(NonC)*; **faire des ~/de petits ~** to make progress/a little progress; **il y a du ~ !** *(gén)* there is some progress *ou* improvement; *(iro)* you're *(ou* he's *etc)* improving! *ou* getting better! *(iro)*; **c'est un grand ~** it's a great advance, it's a great step forward; **il a fait de grands ~** he has made great progress *ou* shown (a) great improvement; **nos ventes ont enregistré un léger/net ~** our sales have increased slightly/sharply; **les ~ de la médecine** advances in medicine; **les grands ~ technologiques de ces dix dernières années** the great strides forward *ou* the great advances made in technology in the last ten years

b **le ~** (= *évolution)* progress *(NonC)*; **le ~ économique** economic progress *ou* development; **le ~ social** social progress; **c'est le ~ !** that's progress!; **on n'arrête pas le ~ !** you can't stop progress!; *(iro)* that's progress for you!; *(Pol)* **les forces de ~** the forces of progress; **les hommes et les femmes de ~** progressives, progressive people

c (= *progression)* [*incendie, inondation]* spread, progress; [*maladie]* progression, progress; [*armée]* progress, advance; [*criminalité,* *délinquance*] rise (**de** in); **suivre les ~ de** [+ *incendie, maladie*] to monitor the progress of

2 **en progrès** LOC ADV **être en ~** [*élève*] to be making progress; [*résultats d'un élève*] to be improving; [*résultats économiques*] to be improving, show an increase; [*productivité, rentabilité*] to be increasing *ou* improving; [*monnaie*] to gain ground; **le franc est en léger ~** the franc is up slightly; **hier, le dollar était en net ~** yesterday the dollar rose sharply; **avec le PIB en ~ de 2%** with GDP up by 2%; **leur parti est en ~ par rapport aux dernières élections** their party has gained ground since the last elections; **il est en net ~ dans les sondages** he's gaining a lot of ground in the polls

progresser [pʀɔgʀese] ▸conjug 1◂ VI **a** (= *s'améliorer*) [*élève*] to progress, make progress; **il a beaucoup progressé cette année** he has made a lot of progress *ou* has come on well this year **b** (= *augmenter*) [*prix, ventes, production, chômage*] to rise, increase, go up; [*monnaie*] to rise; [*criminalité, délinquance*] to be on the increase; **le mark a progressé de 3% face au franc** the mark rose 3% against the franc; **la criminalité a encore progressé** crime is on the rise again; **il a progressé dans les sondages** he has gained ground in the polls; **elle a progressé de 3 points dans les sondages** she has gained 3 points in the polls **c** (= *avancer*) [*ennemi, explorateurs, sauveteurs*] to advance, make headway *ou* progress; [*maladie*] to progress; [*recherches, science*] to advance, progress; [*projet*] to progress; [*idée, théorie*] to gain ground, make headway; **afin que notre monde/la science progresse** so that our world/science goes forward *ou* progresses *ou* makes progress

progressif, -ive [pʀɔgʀesif, iv] ADJ [*détérioration, réduction, développement*] progressive, gradual; [*impôt, taux*] progressive; (*Ling*) progressive; **de manière progressive** gradually

progression [pʀɔgʀesjɔ̃] **1** NF **a** [*élève, explorateurs*] progress; [*ennemi*] advance; [*maladie*] progression, spread; [*science*] progress, advance; [*idées*] spread, advance; **il faut stopper la ~ du racisme** we must stop the spread of racism, we must stop racism from spreading **b** (*Math, Mus*) progression; **~ arithmétique/géométrique** arithmetic/geometric progression; **~ économique** economic advance; **ventes en ~** rising *ou* increasing sales **2** **en progression** LOC ADV **être en ~** [*chiffre d'affaires, ventes*] to be increasing, be up; [*monnaie*] to be gaining ground; **le PIB est en ~ de 3%** GDP is up *ou* has risen by 3%; **le chômage est en ~ constante/de 5%** unemployment is steadily increasing/has increased by 5%; **le chiffre d'affaires est en ~ par rapport à l'année dernière** turnover is up on last year

progressisme [pʀɔgʀesism] NM progressivism

progressiste [pʀɔgʀesist] ADJ, NMF progressive

progressivement [pʀɔgʀesivmɑ̃] ADV gradually, progressively

progressivité [pʀɔgʀesivite] NF progressiveness

prohibé, e [pʀɔibe] (*ptp de* **prohiber**) ADJ [*marchandise, action*] prohibited, forbidden; [*arme*] illegal

prohiber [pʀɔibe] ▸conjug 1◂ VT to prohibit, ban, forbid

prohibitif, -ive [pʀɔibitif, iv] ADJ [*prix*] prohibitive; [*mesure*] prohibitory, prohibitive

prohibition [pʀɔibisjɔ̃] NF (*gén*) prohibition (**de** of, on); (*Hist US*) **la Prohibition** Prohibition; **~ du port d'armes** ban on the carrying of weapons; **ils veulent imposer la ~ de l'alcool** they want a ban on alcohol to be introduced

prohibitionnisme [pʀɔibisjɔnism] NM prohibitionism

prohibitionniste [pʀɔibisjɔnist] ADJ, NMF prohibitionist

proie [pʀwɑ] **1** NF (*lit, fig*) prey (*NonC*); **c'est une ~ facile pour des escrocs** he's easy prey *ou* game* for swindlers; **être la ~ de** to fall prey *ou* victim to, be the prey of; **le pays fut la ~ des envahisseurs** the country fell prey to invaders; **la maison était la ~ des flammes** the house was engulfed in flames; (*fig*) **lâcher** *ou* **laisser la ~ pour l'ombre** to give up what one has (already) for some uncertain *ou* fanciful alternative → **oiseau**

2 **en proie à** LOC PRÉP **être en ~ à** [+ *guerre, crise, violence, récession*] to be plagued by, be in the grip of; [+ *difficultés financières*] to be plagued *ou* beset by; [+ *doute, émotion*] to be prey to; [+ *colère*] to be seething with; [+ *douleur*] to be racked *ou* tortured by; **il était en ~ au remords** he was stricken with *ou* racked by remorse; **en ~ au désespoir** racked by despair; **en ~ à la panique** panic-stricken

projecteur [pʀɔʒɛktœʀ] NM **a** [*diapositives, film*] projector; **~ sonore** sound projector **b** (= *lumière*) [*théâtre*] spotlight; [*prison, bateau*] searchlight; [*monument public, stade*] floodlight; (*Aut*) headlamp unit *ou* assembly, headlight; [*fig*] **être (placé) sous les ~s (de l'actualité)** to be in the spotlight *ou* limelight; **braquer les ~s de l'actualité sur qch** to turn the spotlight on sth; (*fig*) **jeter un coup de ~ sur qch** to put sth under the spotlight

projectif, -ive [pʀɔʒɛktif, iv] ADJ projective

projectile [pʀɔʒɛktil] NM (*gén*) missile; (*Mil, Tech*) projectile

projection [pʀɔʒɛksjɔ̃] NF **a** [*ombre*] casting, projection, throwing; [*film*] (= *action*) projection, screening, showing; (= *séance*) screening, showing; **~ privée/publique** private/public screening *ou* showing; **~ vidéo** video screening; **appareil de ~** projector; **conférence avec des ~s (de diapositives)** lecture (illustrated) with slides, slide lecture → **cabine, salle** **b** (= *lancement*) [*liquide, vapeur*] discharge, ejection; [*pierre*] throwing (*NonC*); (*Géol*) **~s volcaniques** volcanic ejections *ou* ejecta; **~ de cendres** emission of ash **c** (= *prévision*) forecast; **selon les ~s officielles, le déficit public devrait augmenter** according to official forecasts *ou* predictions, the public deficit is going to rise; **faire des ~s** to make forecasts; **si nous faisons des ~s sur sept ans** if we forecast seven years ahead *ou* make forecasts for the next seven years **d** (*Math, Psych*) projection (**sur** onto); **~ de Mercator** Mercator's projection

projectionniste [pʀɔʒɛksjɔnist] NMF projectionist

projet [pʀɔʒɛ] NM **a** (= *dessein, intention*) plan; **~s criminels/de vacances** criminal/holiday plans; **faire des ~s d'avenir** to make plans for the future, make future plans; **faire** *ou* **former le ~ de faire qch** to plan to do sth; **ce ~ de livre/d'agrandissement** this plan for a book/for an extension; **quels sont vos ~s pour le mois prochain?** what are your plans *ou* what plans have you got for next month?; **ce n'est encore qu'un ~** ◊ **c'est encore à l'état de ~ ou en ~** it's still only at the planning stage; **c'est resté à l'état de ~** (*gén*) it never came to anything; [*réforme, mesure*] it never got off the drawing-board **b** (= *ébauche*) [*roman*] (preliminary) draft; [*maison, ville*] plan; **~ de budget** budget proposal; **~ de loi** bill; **~ de réforme** reform bill; **~ de réforme constitutionnelle** constitutional amendment bill; **~ de résolution de l'ONU** UN draft resolution; **établir un ~ d'accord/de contrat** to draft an agreement/a contract, produce a draft agreement/contract; **~ de société** vision of society; **~ de vie** life plan **c** (= *travail en cours*) project; **~ de**

construction de logements house-building scheme *ou* project

▼**projeter** [pʀɔʒ(ə)te] ▸conjug 4◂ **1** VT **a** (= *envisager*) to plan (**de faire** to do); **as-tu projeté quelque chose pour les vacances?** have you made any plans *ou* have you planned anything for your holidays? **b** (= *jeter*) [+ *gravillons*] to throw up; [+ *étincelles*] to throw off; [+ *fumée*] to send out, discharge; [+ *lave*] to eject, throw out; **attention! la poêle projette de la graisse** careful! the frying pan is spitting (out) fat; **être projeté hors de** to be thrown *ou* hurled *ou* flung out of; **on lui a projeté de l'eau dans les yeux** someone threw water into his eyes **c** (= *envoyer*) [+ *ombre, reflet*] to cast, project, throw; [+ *film, diapositive*] to project; (= *montrer*) to show; **on peut ~ ce film sur un petit écran** this film may be projected onto *ou* shown on a small screen; **on nous a projeté des diapositives** we were shown some slides **d** (*Math, Psych*) to project (**sur** onto) **2** **se projeter** VPR [*ombre*] to be cast, fall (**sur** on)

projeteur, -euse [pʀɔʒ(ə)tœʀ, øz] NM,F project designer

projo* [pʀɔʒo] NM ABRÉV = **projecteur**

prolapsus [pʀɔlapsys] NM prolapse

prolégomènes [pʀɔlegɔmɛn] NMPL prolegomena

prolepse [pʀɔlɛps] NF (*Littérat*) prolepsis

prolétaire [pʀɔlɛtɛʀ] **1** ADJ proletarian **2** NMF proletarian; **les enfants de ~s** children of working-class people; **~s de tous les pays, unissez-vous!** workers of the world, unite!

prolétariat [pʀɔlɛtaʀja] NM proletariat

prolétarien, -ienne [pʀɔlɛtaʀjɛ̃, jɛn] ADJ proletarian

prolétarisation [pʀɔlɛtaʀizasjɔ̃] NF proletarianization

prolétariser [pʀɔlɛtaʀize] ▸conjug 1◂ VT to proletarianize

prolifération [pʀɔliferasjɔ̃] NF proliferation

proliférer [pʀɔlifere] ▸conjug 6◂ VI to proliferate; **les guerres civiles prolifèrent** civil wars are breaking out all over the world

prolifique [pʀɔlifik] ADJ prolific

prolixe [pʀɔliks] ADJ [*orateur, discours*] verbose, wordy, prolix (*frm*)

prolixement [pʀɔliksəmɑ̃] ADV verbosely, wordily

prolixité [pʀɔliksite] NF verbosity, wordiness, prolixity (*frm*)

prolo* [pʀɔlo] ABRÉV = **prolétaire 1** NMF working-class person, prole* (*péj*) **2** ADJ [*quartier, personne*] working-class; **ça fait ~** it's common

prologue [pʀɔlɔg] NM prologue (**à** to)

prolongateur [pʀɔlɔ̃gatœʀ] NM extension cable *ou* lead

prolongation [pʀɔlɔ̃gasjɔ̃] NF **a** (*dans le temps*) [*séjour, trêve, séance, visa, délai, contrat*] extension; [*vie, maladie*] prolongation; (*Mus*) [*note*] prolongation; (*Ftbl*) **~s** extra time (*NonC*) (*Brit*), overtime (*NonC*) (*US*); **obtenir une ~** to get an extension; **ils ont joué les ~s** (*Ftbl*) they played extra time (*Brit*) *ou* overtime (*US*), the game *ou* they went into extra time (*Brit*) *ou* overtime (*US*); (*hum: en vacances, pour un travail*) they stayed on **b** (*dans l'espace*) [*rue*] extension; (*Math*) [*ligne*] prolongation

prolonge [pʀɔlɔ̃ʒ] NF ammunition wagon; **~ d'artillerie** gun carriage

prolongé, e [pʀɔlɔ̃ʒe] (*ptp de* **prolonger**) ADJ [*débat, séjour, absence*] prolonged, lengthy; [*rire, cri, sécheresse*] prolonged; [*effort*] prolonged, sustained; **exposition ~e au soleil** prolonged exposure to the sun; (*hum ou †*) **jeune fille ~e** old maid; **c'est un adolescent ~**

▶ GRAMMAIRE ACTIVE: **projeter** 35.2

he's an overgrown teenager; **rue de la Paix ~e** continuation of Rue de la Paix; **en cas d'arrêt ~ in case of prolonged stoppage; week-end ~** long weekend; **la station assise/debout ~e peut provoquer des douleurs** sitting/standing in the same position for an extended period of time can cause aches and pains; **ce déodorant a une action ~e** this deodorant has a long-lasting effect; **«pas d'utilisation ~e sans avis médical»** "not to be taken for long periods without medical advice"

prolongement [prɔlɔ̃ʒmɑ̃] NM [a] [*bâtiment, voie ferrée, ligne de métro, route, délai, période*] extension; **l'outil doit être un ~ du bras** the tool should be like an extension of one's arm; **décider le ~ d'une route** to decide to extend *ou* continue a road; **cette rue se trouve dans le ~ de l'autre** this street runs on from the other *ou* is the continuation of the other [b] (= *suite*) [*affaire, politique, rapport*] repercussion, consequence; **c'est le ~ logique de la politique entreprise** it's the logical extension *ou* consequence of the policy that has been undertaken; **ce rapport est dans le ~ du précédent** this report follows on from the previous one; **dans le ~ de ce que je disais ce matin** following on from *ou* to continue with what I was saying this morning; **dans le ~ de la réflexion amorcée en 1998, il a déclaré que...** expanding on *ou* developing the line of thought first outlined in 1998, he declared that ...

prolonger [prɔlɔ̃ʒe] ▶conjug 3◀ [1] VT [a] (*dans le temps*) [+ *séjour, trêve, séance, délai, contrat*] to extend, prolong; [+ *visa*] to extend; [+ *vie, maladie*] to prolong; (*Mus*) [+ *note*] to prolong; **nous ne pouvons ~ notre séjour** we can't stay any longer, we can't prolong our stay [b] (*dans l'espace*) [+ *rue*] to extend, continue; (*Math*) [+ *ligne*] to prolong, produce; **on a prolongé le mur jusqu'au garage** we extended *ou* continued the wall as far as *ou* up to the garage; **ce bâtiment prolonge l'aile principale** this building is an extension *ou* a continuation of the main wing [2] **se prolonger** VPR [a] (= *continuer*) [*attente*] to go on; [*situation*] to go on, last, persist; [*effet*] to last, persist; [*débat*] to last, go on, carry on; [*maladie*] to continue, persist; (= *se perpétuer*) **il voudrait se ~ dans ses enfants** he would like to live on in his children [b] (= *s'étendre*) [*rue, chemin*] to go on, carry on (*Brit*), continue

promenade [prɔm(ə)nad] NF [a] (*à pied*) walk, stroll; (*en voiture*) drive, ride; (*en bateau*) sail; (*en vélo, à cheval*) ride; **partir en ~ faire une ~** to go for a walk *ou* stroll (*ou* drive *etc*); **être en ~** to be out walking *ou* out for a walk; **faire faire une ~ à qn** to take sb (out) for a walk; **cette course a été une vraie ~ pour lui** the race was a walkover for him; **ça n'a pas été une ~ de santé** it was no picnic* [b] (= *avenue*) walk, esplanade; (= *front de mer*) promenade

promener [prɔm(ə)ne] ▶conjug 5◀ [1] VT [a] (*emmener*) ~ qn to take sb (out) for a walk *ou* stroll; **~ le chien** to walk the dog, take the dog out (for a walk); **~ des amis à travers une ville** to show *ou* take friends round a town; **cela te promènera** it will get you out for a while; **il promène son nounours partout*** he trails his teddy bear around everywhere with him; **est-ce qu'il va nous ~ encore longtemps à travers ces bureaux?*** is he going to trail us round these offices much longer? → **envoyer** [b] (*fig*) **~ son regard sur qch** to run *ou* cast one's eyes over sth; **~ ses doigts sur qch** to run *ou* pass one's fingers over sth; **il promène sa tristesse/son ennui** he goes around looking sad/bored all the time; **il promenait sa caméra/son micro dans les rues de New York** he roved the streets of New York with his camera/his microphone

[2] **se promener** VPR [a] (= *aller en promenade*) to go for a walk *ou* stroll (*ou* drive *etc*); **aller se ~** to go (out) for a walk *ou* stroll (*ou* drive *etc*); **viens te ~ avec maman** come for a walk with mummy; **se ~ dans sa chambre** to walk *ou* pace up and down in one's room; **allez vous ~!*** go and take a running jump!*, get lost!‡; **je ne vais pas laisser tes chiens se ~ dans mon jardin** I'm not going to let your dogs wander round my garden; (*Sport*) **il s'est vraiment promené dans cette course** the race was a walkover for him [b] [*pensées, regard, doigts*] to wander; **son crayon se promenait sur le papier** he let his pencil wander over the paper, his pencil wandered over the paper; **ses affaires se promènent toujours partout*** he always leaves his things lying around

promeneur, -euse [prɔm(ə)nœr, øz] NM,F walker, stroller; **les ~s du dimanche** people out for a Sunday walk *ou* stroll

promenoir [prɔm(ə)nwar] NM (†: *Théât*) promenade (gallery), standing gallery; [*école, prison*] (covered) walk

promesse [prɔmɛs] NF (= *assurance*) promise; (= *parole*) promise, word; (*Comm*) commitment, undertaking; **~ de mariage** promise of marriage; **~ en l'air** *ou* **d'ivrogne** *ou* **de Gascon** empty *ou* vain promise; **~ d'achat/de vente** agreement to buy/to sell, purchase/sales agreement; **fausses ~s** empty *ou* false promises; **méfiez-vous des belles ~s des politiques** beware of politicians and their big promises; **faire une ~** to make a promise, give one's word; **il m'en a fait la ~** he gave me his word; **manquer à/tenir sa ~** to break/keep one's promise *ou* word; **honorer/respecter ses ~s** to honour/keep one's promises; **j'ai sa ~** I have his word for it, he has promised me; **auteur plein de ~s** writer showing much promise *ou* full of promise, very promising writer; **sourire plein de ~s** smile that promised (*ou* promises) much

Prométhée [prɔmete] NM Prometheus

prométhéen, -enne [prɔmeteɛ̃, ɛn] ADJ Promethean; **le rêve ~** man's dream of becoming master of his own destiny

prométhium [prɔmetjɔm] NM promethium

prometteur, -euse [prɔmetœr, øz] ADJ [*début, signe*] promising; [*acteur, politicien*] up-and-coming, promising

promettre [prɔmɛtr] ▶conjug 56◀ [1] VT [a] [+ *chose, aide*] to promise; **je lui ai promis un cadeau** I promised him a present; **je te le promets** I promise (you); **il n'a rien osé ~** he couldn't promise anything, he didn't dare commit himself; **il a promis de venir** he promised to come; **il m'a promis de venir** *ou* **qu'il viendrait** he promised me (that) he would *ou* he'd come; **~ la lune** ◊ **~ monts et merveilles** to promise the moon *ou* the earth; **tu as promis, il faut y aller** you've promised *ou* you've given your word so you have to go; **il ne faut pas ~ quand on ne peut pas tenir** one mustn't make promises that one cannot keep; **~ le secret** to promise to keep a secret; **~ son cœur/sa main/son amour** to pledge one's heart/one's hand/one's love [b] (= *prédire*) to promise; **je vous promets qu'il ne recommencera pas** I (can) promise you he won't do that again; **il sera furieux, je te le promets** he'll be furious, I can promise you that; **on nous promet du beau temps/un été pluvieux** we are promised *ou* we are in for* some fine weather/a rainy summer; **ces nuages nous promettent de la pluie** these clouds mean *ou* promise rain; **cela ne nous promet rien de bon** this doesn't look at all hopeful *ou* good (for us) [c] (= *faire espérer*) to promise; **le spectacle/dîner promet d'être réussi** the show/dinner promises to be a success; **cet enfant promet** this child shows promise *ou* is promising,

he's (*ou* she's) a promising child; (*iro*) **ça promet!** that's a good start! (*iro*), that's promising! (*iro*); (*iro*) **ça promet pour l'avenir/pour l'hiver!** that bodes well for the future/(the) winter! (*iro*)

[2] **se promettre** VPR **se ~ du bon temps** *ou* **du plaisir** to promise o.s. a good time; **je me suis promis un petit voyage** I've promised myself a little trip; **se ~ de faire qch** to mean *ou* resolve to do sth; **je me suis bien promis de ne jamais plus l'inviter** I vowed never to invite him again; **elles se sont promis de garder le secret** they promised each other they'd keep it a secret

promis, e [prɔmi, iz] (*ptp de* **promettre**) [1] ADJ [a] (= *assuré*) promised; **comme ~, il est venu** as promised, he came; **voilà la photo ~e** here's the photograph I promised you; **tu le feras? — ~(, juré)! ou c'est ~!** you'll do it? — yes, cross my heart! *ou* I promise! [b] (= *destiné*) **être ~ à un bel avenir** [*personne*] to be destined for great things, have a bright future ahead of one; [*invention*] to have a bright future; **quartier ~ à la démolition** area earmarked *ou* scheduled for demolition → **chose, terre** [2] NM,F (††, *dial*) betrothed†

promiscuité [prɔmiskyite] NF [a] [*lieu public*] crowding (*NonC*) (de in); [*chambre*] lack of privacy (*NonC*) (de in); **vivre dans la ~** to live in very close quarters, live on top of one another [b] **~ sexuelle** (sexual) promiscuity

promo* [prɔmo] NF ABRÉV = **promotion**

promontoire [prɔmɔ̃twar] NM (*Géog*) headland, promontory

promoteur, -trice [prɔmɔtœr, tris] [1] NM,F (= *instigateur*) promoter; **~ (immobilier)** property developer; **~ de ventes** sales promoter [2] NM (*Chim*) promoter

promotion [prɔmosjɔ̃] NF [a] (= *avancement*) promotion (**à un poste** to a job); **~ sociale** social advancement [b] (*Scol*) year, class (*US*); **être le premier de sa ~** to be first in one's year *ou* class (*US*) [c] (*Comm* = *réclame*) special offer; **notre ~ de la semaine** this week's special offer; **article en ~** item on special offer; **il y a une ~ sur les chemises** shirts are on special offer, there's a special on shirts (*US*); **~ des ventes** sales promotion [d] (= *encouragement*) promotion; **faire la ~ de** [+ *politique, idée, technique*] to promote

promotionnel, -elle [prɔmosjɔnɛl] ADJ [*article*] on (special) offer; [*vente, campagne*] promotional; **tarif ~** special offer; **offre promotionnelle** special offer, special (*US*); **matériel ~** publicity material

promouvoir [prɔmuvwar] ▶conjug 27◀ VT [+ *personne*] to promote, upgrade (**à** to); [+ *politique, recherche, idée, technique*] to promote; (*Comm*) [+ *produit*] to promote; **il a été promu directeur** he was promoted *ou* upgraded to (the rank of) manager

prompt, prompte [prɔ̃(pt), prɔ̃(p)t] ADJ [*réaction, départ*] prompt, swift; [*changement*] quick, swift; **je vous souhaite un ~ rétablissement** get well soon, I wish you a speedy recovery; **~ à l'injure/aux excuses/à réagir/à critiquer** quick to insult/to apologize/to react/to criticize; **avoir le geste ~** to be quick to act; **il a l'esprit ~** he has a quick *ou* ready wit; **~ comme l'éclair** *ou* **la foudre** as quick as lightning; (*Comm*) **dans l'espoir d'une ~e réponse** hoping for an early reply

promptement [prɔ̃ptəmɑ̃] ADV [*agir, réagir*] quickly, swiftly; [*finir*] quickly; [*répondre, riposter*] promptly

prompteur [prɔ̃ptœr] NM Autocue® (*Brit*), teleprompter® (*US*)

promptitude [prɔ̃(p)tityd] NF [*répartie, riposte*] quickness; [*réaction*] promptness, swiftness; [*départ, changement*] suddenness; [*guérison*] speed; **il a réagi avec ~** he was quick to react

promulgation [prɔmylgasjɔ̃] NF promulgation

promulguer [prɔmylge] ▸conjug 1◂ VT to promulgate

pronateur [prɔnatœr] ADJ M, NM (muscle) ~ pronator

pronation [prɔnasjɔ̃] NF pronation

prône [pron] NM sermon

prôner [prone] ▸conjug 1◂ VT (= vanter) to laud, extol; (= préconiser) to advocate, recommend

pronom [prɔnɔ̃] NM pronoun

pronominal, e [mpl **-aux**] [prɔnɔminal, o] ADJ pronominal; (**verbe**) ~ pronominal ou reflexive (verb); **mettre un verbe à la forme ~e** to put a verb in its pronominal ou reflexive form

pronominalement [prɔnɔminalmɑ̃] ADV pronominally, reflexively

prononçable [prɔnɔ̃sabl] ADJ pronounceable; **son nom est difficilement ~** his name is hard to pronounce; **ce mot n'est pas ~** that word is unpronounceable

prononcé, e [prɔnɔ̃se] (ptp de **prononcer**) [1] ADJ [accent, goût, trait] marked, pronounced, strong [2] NM (Jur) pronouncement

▼ **prononcer** [prɔnɔ̃se] ▸conjug 3◂ [1] VT [a] (= articuler) [+ mot, son] to pronounce; **son nom est impossible à ~** his name is impossible to pronounce ou is unpronounceable; **comment est-ce que ça se prononce ?** how is it pronounced?, how do you pronounce it?; **cette lettre ne se prononce pas** that letter is silent ou is not pronounced; **tu prononces mal** your pronunciation is poor; **mal ~ un mot** to mispronounce a word, pronounce a word badly; **~ distinctement** to speak clearly, pronounce one's words clearly

[b] (= dire) [+ parole, nom] to utter; [+ souhait] to utter, make; [+ discours] to make, deliver; **sortir sans ~ un mot** to go out without uttering a word; **ne prononcez plus jamais ce nom !** don't you ever mention ou utter that name again!; (Rel) **~ ses vœux** to take one's vows

[c] [+ sentence] to pronounce, pass; [+ dissolution, excommunication] to pronounce; **~ le huis clos** to order that a case (should) be heard in camera

[2] VI (Jur) to deliver ou give a verdict; (littér) **~ en faveur de/contre** to come down ou pronounce in favour of/against

[3] **se prononcer** VPR (= se décider) (gén) to reach ou come to a decision (**sur** on, about); (Jur) to reach a verdict (**sur** on); (= s'exprimer) (avis) to give ou express an opinion (**sur** on); (décision) to give a decision (**sur** on); (Jur) to give a verdict (**sur** on); **le médecin ne s'est toujours pas prononcé** the doctor still hasn't given a verdict ou a firm opinion; **se ~ en faveur de qn/pour qch** to come down ou pronounce o.s. in favour of sb/in favour of sth; **se ~ contre une décision** to declare one's opposition to ou pronounce o.s. against a decision; (sondage) **«ne se prononcent pas»** "don't know"

prononciation [prɔnɔ̃sjasjɔ̃] NF [a] (Ling) pronunciation; **la ~ de ce mot est difficile** this word is hard to pronounce; **il a une bonne/mauvaise ~** he speaks/doesn't speak clearly, he pronounces/doesn't pronounce his words clearly; (dans une langue étrangère) his pronunciation is good/poor; **faute ou erreur de ~** pronunciation error, error of pronunciation; **faire une faute de ~** to mispronounce a word; **défaut ou vice de ~** speech impediment ou defect [b] (Jur) pronouncement

pronostic [prɔnɔstik] NM (gén) forecast, prognostication (frm); (Méd) prognosis; (Courses) tip; (Sport) forecast; **quels sont vos ~s ?** what's your forecast?; **au ~ infaillible** unerring in his (ou her etc) forecasts; **elle a fait le bon ~** (gén)

her prediction proved correct; (Méd) she made the right prognosis; (gén) **se tromper dans ses ~s** to get one's forecasts wrong; (Courses) **mes ~s donnaient le 11 gagnant** I tipped number 11 to win; **faire des ~s sur les matchs de football** to forecast the football results

pronostiquer [prɔnɔstike] ▸conjug 1◂ VT (= prédire) to forecast, prognosticate (frm); (= être le signe de) to foretell, be a sign of; (Courses) to tip

pronostiqueur, -euse [prɔnɔstikœr, øz] NM,F (gén) forecaster, prognosticator (frm); (Courses) tipster

pronunciamiento [prɔnunsjamjento] NM pronunciamiento

pro-occidental, e (mpl **pro-occidentaux**) [prɔɔksidɑ̃tal, o] ADJ pro-Western

propagande [prɔpagɑ̃d] NF propaganda; **~ électorale/de guerre** electioneering/war propaganda; **faire de la ~ pour qch/qn** to push ou plug* sth/sb; **je ne ferai pas de ~ pour ce commerçant/ce produit** I certainly won't be doing any advertising for ou plugging* this trader/this product; **journal de ~** propaganda sheet ou newspaper; **film/discours de ~** propaganda film/speech; **discours de ~ électorale** electioneering speech

propagandiste [prɔpagɑ̃dist] NMF propagandist

propagateur, -trice [prɔpagatœr, tris] NM,F [méthode, religion, théorie] propagator; [nouvelle] spreader

propagation [prɔpagasjɔ̃] NF [a] [foi, idée] propagation; [nouvelle] spreading; [maladie, épidémie] spread; [rumeur] spreading, putting about (Brit); **pour arrêter la ~ de l'incendie** to stop the fire spreading [b] (Phys) [son, onde, lumière, chaleur] propagation; **vitesse de ~** velocity of propagation [c] (Bio) propagation

propager [prɔpaʒe] ▸conjug 3◂ [1] VT [a] (= diffuser) [+ foi, idée] to propagate; [+ nouvelle, maladie] to spread; [+ rumeur] to spread, put about (Brit) [b] (Phys) [+ son, lumière, onde] to propagate [c] (Bio) [+ espèce] to propagate [2] **se propager** VPR [a] (= se répandre) [incendie, idée, nouvelle, maladie] to spread [b] (Phys) [onde] to be propagated [c] (Bio) [espèce] to propagate

propane [prɔpan] NM propane

propédeutique† [prɔpedøtik] NF (Univ) foundation course for first-year university students

propène [prɔpɛn] NM propene

propension [prɔpɑ̃sjɔ̃] NF proclivity (frm) (à qch to ou towards sth, à faire to do), propensity (à qch for sth, à faire to do); (Écon) **~ à consommer/économiser** propensity to spend/save

propergol [prɔpɛrgɔl] NM [fusée] propellant, propellent

prophète [prɔfɛt] NM (gén) prophet, seer; (Rel) prophet; **faux ~** false prophet; **~ de malheur** prophet of doom, doomsayer; (Bible) **les (livres des) Prophètes** the Books of (the) Prophets → **nul**

prophétesse [prɔfetɛs] NF (gén) prophetess, seer; (Rel) prophetess

prophétie [prɔfesi] NF (Rel, gén) prophecy

prophétique [prɔfetik] ADJ prophetic

prophétiquement [prɔfetikmɑ̃] ADV prophetically

prophétiser [prɔfetize] ▸conjug 1◂ VT to prophesy; **il est facile de ~** it's easy to make predictions ou prophesies

prophylactique [prɔfilaktik] ADJ prophylactic

prophylaxie [prɔfilaksi] NF disease prevention, prophylaxis (SPÉC)

propice [prɔpis] ADJ [circonstance, occasion] favourable (Brit), favorable (US), auspicious,

propitious; [milieu, terrain] favourable (Brit), favorable (US); **attendre le moment ~** to wait for the right moment ou an opportune (frm) moment; **cherchons un endroit plus ~ pour discuter** let's look for a more suitable place to talk; **être ~ à qch** to favour sth, be favourable to sth; **un climat ~ à la négociation** an atmosphere favourable ou conducive to negotiation; (littér, hum) **que les dieux vous soient ~s !** may the gods look kindly ou smile upon you! (littér, hum)

propitiation [prɔpisjasjɔ̃] NF propitiation; **victime de ~** propitiatory victim

propitiatoire [prɔpisjatwar] ADJ propitiatory

propolis [prɔpɔlis] NF propolis, bee glue, hive dross

proportion [prɔpɔrsjɔ̃] [1] NF (Art, Math) proportion; **la ~ hommes/femmes** the proportion ou ratio of men to women; **hors de (toute)** out of (all) proportion (**avec** with); **sans ~ avec** out of proportion to; **toute(s) ~(s) gardée(s)** relatively speaking, making due allowance(s)

[2] **proportions** NFPL (= taille, importance) proportions; **édifice de belles ~s** well-proportioned building; **cela a pris des ~s considérables** it reached considerable proportions; **il faut ramener l'affaire à de justes ~s** this matter must be put into perspective; **augmenter/réduire qch dans des ~s considérables** to increase/reduce sth considerably

[3] **à proportion de** LOC PRÉP in proportion to, proportionally to

[4] **en proportion** LOC ADV proportionately, in proportion; **si le chiffre d'affaires augmente, les salaires seront augmentés en ~** if turnover increases, salaries will be raised proportionately ou commensurately; **il a un poste élevé et un salaire en ~** he has a top position and a correspondingly high salary; **pour maintenir un tel train de vie, il faut avoir des revenus en ~** to maintain such a lavish lifestyle, you must have an income to match

[5] **en proportion de** LOC PRÉP (= relatif à) proportional ou proportionate to, in proportion to, relative to; (= relativement à) proportionally to; **l'entreprise investira en ~ de son chiffre d'affaires** the amount of money the company invests will be relative ou proportional to its turnover; **c'est bien peu, en ~ du service qu'il m'a rendu** it's nothing, compared to all the favours he has done me

proportionnalité [prɔpɔrsjɔnalite] NF proportionality; (Pol) proportional representation; **~ de l'impôt** proportional taxation (system)

proportionné, e [prɔpɔrsjɔne] (ptp de **proportionner**) ADJ **~ à** proportional ou proportionate to; **bien ~** well-proportioned; **admirablement ~** admirably well-proportioned

proportionnel, -elle [prɔpɔrsjɔnɛl] [1] ADJ (gén, Math, Pol) proportional; **~ à** proportional ou proportionate to, in proportion to ou with; **directement/inversement ~ à** directly/inversely proportional to, in direct/inverse proportion to [2] **proportionnelle** NF (Math) proportional; (Pol) **la proportionnelle (intégrale)** (pure) proportional representation; **élu à la proportionnelle** elected by proportional representation

proportionnellement [prɔpɔrsjɔnɛlmɑ̃] ADV proportionally, proportionately; **~ plus grand** proportionally ou proportionately bigger; **~ à** in proportion to, proportionally to

proportionner [prɔpɔrsjɔne] ▸conjug 1◂ VT to proportion, make proportional, adjust (à to)

propos [prɔpo] NM [a] (gén pl) words; **ses ~ ont irrité tout le monde** what he said annoyed everyone; **ce sont des ~ en l'air** it's just empty ou idle talk ou hot air*; **tenir des ~**

blessants to say hurtful things, make hurtful remarks; **tenir des ~ désobligeants à l'égard de qn** to make offensive remarks about sb, say offensive things about sb; (*péj*) **des ~ de personne soûle** drunken ramblings

b (*littér* = *intention*) intention, aim; **mon ~ est de vous expliquer ...** my intention *ou* aim is to explain to you ...; **il n'entre pas dans mon ~ de ...** it is not my intention to ...; **tel n'était pas mon ~** that was not my intention; **avoir le ferme ~ de faire qch** to have the firm intention of doing sth; **faire qch de ~ délibéré** to do sth deliberately *ou* on purpose

c (= *sujet*) **à quel ~ voulait-il me voir?** what did he want to see me about?; **à quel ~ est-il venu?** what was his reason for coming?, what brought him?*; **c'est à quel ~?** what is it about?, what is it in connection with?; **à ~ de ta voiture** about your car, on the subject of your car; **je vous écris à ~ de l'annonce** I am writing regarding *ou* concerning the advertisement *ou* in connection with the advertisement; **à tout ~** (= *sans arrêt*) every other minute; **il se plaint à tout ~** he complains at the slightest (little) thing; **il se met en colère à ~ de tout et de rien** *ou* **à tout ~** he loses his temper at the slightest (little) thing *ou* for no reason at all; **à ce ~** in this connection, (while) on this subject; **hors de ~** irrelevant

d **à ~** [*décision*] well-timed, opportune, timely; [*remarque*] apt, pertinent, apposite; [*arriver*] at the right moment *ou* time; **tomber** *ou* **arriver mal à ~** to happen (just) at the wrong moment *ou* time; **voilà qui tombe à ~/mal à ~!** it couldn't have come at a better/worse time! *ou* moment!; **il a jugé à ~ de nous prévenir** he thought it right to let us know, he saw fit to let us know; **à ~, dis-moi ...** incidentally *ou* by the way, tell me ...

▶ **proposer** [pʀɔpoze] ▸ conjug 1 ◀ **1** VT **a** (= *suggérer*) [+ *arrangement, interprétation, projet, appellation*] to suggest, propose; [+ *solution, interprétation*] to suggest, put forward, propose; [+ *candidat*] to propose, nominate, put forward; (*Scol, Univ*) [+ *sujet, texte*] to set (*Brit*), assign (*US*); (*Pol*) [+ *loi*] to move, propose; **on a proposé mon nom pour ce poste** my name has been put forward for this post; **~ qch à qn** to suggest *ou* put sth to sb; **~ de faire qch** to suggest *ou* propose doing sth; (*TV*) **le film que nous vous proposons (de voir) ce soir** the film we are showing this evening, our film this evening ■ (*PROV*) **l'homme propose, Dieu dispose** man proposes, God disposes (*PROV*); **je vous propose de passer me voir** I suggest that you come round and see me; **~ qu'une motion soit mise aux voix** to move that a motion be put to the vote; **~ qu'un comité soit établi** to move *ou* propose that a committee be set up

b (= *offrir*) [+ *aide, prix, situation*] to offer; **~ qch à qn** to offer sth to sb, offer sb sth; **~ de faire qch** to offer to do sth; **on me propose une nouvelle voiture** I am being offered *ou* I have the offer of a new car; **je lui ai proposé de la raccompagner** I offered to see her home

2 **se proposer** VPR **a** (= *offrir ses services*) to offer one's services; **elle s'est proposée pour garder les enfants** she offered to look after the children

b (= *envisager*) [+ *but, tâche*] to set o.s.; **se ~ de faire qch** to intend *ou* mean *ou* propose to do sth; **il se proposait de prouver que ...** he set out to prove that ...

proposition [pʀɔpozisjɔ̃] NF **a** (= *suggestion*) proposal, suggestion; (*Comm*) proposition; (*Pol* = *recommandation*) proposal; **~s de paix** peace proposals; **~ de réforme** reform proposal; (*Jur*) **~ de résolution** proposal *ou* motion for a resolution; (*Pol*) **~ de loi** private bill, private member's bill (*Brit*); **sur (la) ~ de** at the suggestion of, on the proposal of; **sur sa ~, il a été décidé d'attendre** at his suggestion it was decided to wait; **la ~ de qn à un grade su-**

périeur the nomination of sb to a higher position; **faire une ~ (à qn)** to make (sb) a proposition; **faire des ~s (malhonnêtes) à une femme** to proposition a woman; **il a eu plusieurs ~s de films** he's been approached by several film directors

b (*Math, Philo*) (= *postulat*) proposition; (= *déclaration*) proposition, assertion

c (*Gram*) clause; **~ principale/subordonnée/indépendante** main/subordinate/independent clause; **~ consécutive** *ou* **de conséquence** consecutive *ou* result clause

propositionnel, -elle [pʀɔpozisjɔnɛl] ADJ propositional

propre¹ [pʀɔpʀ] **1** ADJ **a** (= *pas sali, nettoyé*) [*linge, mains, maison, personne*] clean; **des draps bien ~s** nice clean sheets; **~ comme un sou neuf** as clean as a new pin; **leurs enfants sont toujours (tenus) très ~s** their children are always very neat and tidy *ou* very neatly turned out; **ce n'est pas ~ de manger avec les doigts** it's messy *ou* dirty to eat with your fingers; **nous voilà ~s!*** now we're in a fine *ou* proper mess!*; **c'est quelqu'un de très ~ sur lui*** he's very clean-cut

b (= *soigné*) [*travail, exécution*] (*d'un morceau de musique*) neat, neatly done; (*Scol*) [*cahier, copie*] neat; (= *soigneux*) [*personne*] tidy, neat

c (= *qui ne salit pas*) [*chien, chat*] house-trained; [*enfant*] toilet-trained, potty-trained*; (= *non polluant*) [*moteur, voiture, produit*] clean; **il n'est pas encore ~** he still isn't toilet-trained *ou* potty-trained*

d (= *honnête*) [*personne*] honest, decent; [*affaire, argent*] honest; [*mœurs*] decent; **il n'a jamais rien fait de ~** he's never done a decent *ou* an honest thing in his life; **une affaire pas très ~** a slightly suspect *ou* shady piece of business; **ce garçon-là, ce n'est pas grand-chose de ~*** that young man hasn't got much to recommend him *ou* isn't up to much*

2 NM **sentir le ~*** to smell clean; **mettre** *ou* **recopier qch au ~** to make a fair copy of sth, copy sth out neatly; **c'est du ~!*** (*gâchis*) what a mess!, what a shambles!*; (*comportement*) what a way to behave!, it's an absolute disgrace!

propre² [pʀɔpʀ] **1** ADJ **a** (*intensif possessif*) own; **il a sa ~ voiture** he's got his own car *ou* a car of his own; **ce sont ses ~s mots** those are his own *ou* his very *ou* his actual words; **de mes ~s yeux** with my own eyes; **ils ont leurs caractères/qualités ~s** they have their own (specific) *ou* their particular characters/qualities → **chef, initiative, main, moyen**

b (= *particulier, spécifique*) **c'est un trait qui lui est ~** it's a trait which is peculiar to him, it's a distinctive *ou* special characteristic of his; **les coutumes ~s à certaines régions** the customs peculiar to *ou* characteristic of *ou* proper to *ou* (*frm*) certain regions; (*Jur*) **biens ~s** personal property → **fonds, nom, sens**

c (= *qui convient*) suitable, appropriate (**à** for); **le mot ~** the right *ou* proper word; **ce n'est pas un lieu ~ à la conversation** it isn't a suitable *ou* an appropriate place for talking; **sol ~ à la culture du blé** soil suitable for *ou* suited to wheat-growing; **on l'a jugé ~ à s'occuper de l'affaire** he was considered the right man for *ou* suitable for the job

d (= *de nature à*) **un poste ~ à lui apporter des satisfactions** a job likely to bring him satisfaction; **exercice ~ à développer les muscles des épaules** exercise that will develop the shoulder muscles; **un lieu/une musique ~ au recueillement** a place/a type of music favourable *ou* conducive to meditation; **c'est bien ~ à vous dégoûter de la politique** it's (exactly) the sort of thing that turns you *ou* to turn you right off politics, it's guaranteed to put you off politics

2 NM **a** (= *qualité distinctive*) peculiarity, (exclusive *ou* distinctive) feature; **la raison est le ~ de l'homme** reason is a (distinctive) feature

of man, reason is peculiar to man; **la parole est le ~ de l'homme** speech is man's special gift *ou* attribute; **c'est le ~ de ce système d'éducation de fabriquer des paresseux** it's a peculiarity *ou* feature of this educational system that it turns out idlers; **avoir un domaine en ~** to be the sole owner of an estate, have exclusive possession of an estate; **cette caractéristique que la France possède en ~** this feature which is peculiar *ou* exclusive to France

b (*Ling*) **au ~** in the literal sense *ou* meaning, literally

propre-à-rien (*pl* **propres-à-rien**) [pʀɔpʀaʀjɛ̃] NMF good-for-nothing, ne'er-do-well, waster

proprement [pʀɔpʀəmɑ̃] ADV **a** (= *avec propreté*) cleanly; (= *avec netteté*) neatly, tidily; (= *comme il faut*) properly; (= *décemment*) decently; **tenir une maison très ~** to keep a house very clean; **mange ~!** don't make such a mess (when you're eating)!, eat properly!; **se conduire ~** to behave properly *ou* correctly

b (= *exactement*) exactly, literally; (= *exclusivement*) specifically, strictly; (= *vraiment*) absolutely; **à ~ parler** strictly speaking; **le village ~ dit** the actual village, the village itself; **la linguistique ~ dite** linguistics proper; **c'est un problème ~ français** it's a specifically French problem; **c'est ~ scandaleux** it's absolutely disgraceful; **il m'a ~ fermé la porte au nez** he simply shut the door in my face; **on l'a ~ rossé** he was well and truly beaten up

propret, -ette [pʀɔpʀɛ, ɛt] ADJ [*personne*] neat (and tidy); [*chose*] neat (and tidy), spick-and-span (*attrib*)

propreté [pʀɔpʀəte] NF **a** [*linge, mains, maison, personne*] cleanliness, cleanness; **ils n'ont aucune notion de ~** they have no notion of hygiene; **l'apprentissage de la ~ chez l'enfant** toilet-training in the child; **apprendre la ~ à un chiot** to house-train a puppy; **d'une ~ méticuleuse** scrupulously clean; **d'une ~ douteuse** not very clean; **des meubles luisants de ~** sparkling clean furniture → **plaque**

b [*travail, exécution d'un morceau de musique*] neatness; (*Scol*) [*cahier, copie*] neatness

propriétaire [pʀɔpʀijetɛʀ] **1** NM **a** (*gén*) [*voiture, chien, maison*] owner; [*hôtel, entreprise*] proprietor, owner; **il est ~ (de sa maison)** he owns his (own) house; **quand on est ~, il faut ...** when one is a home-owner *ou* house-owner *ou* householder one has to ... → **tour²**

b [*location*] landlord, owner; **mis à la porte par son ~** thrown out by his landlord

c [*terres, immeubles etc*] landowner, owner; **~ éleveur** breeder; **~ récoltant** grower; **achat direct au ~** direct purchase from the grower; **~ terrien** landowner; **~ foncier** property owner; **les petits ~s** smallholders **2** NF (*gén*) owner; [*hôtel, entreprise*] proprietress, owner; [*location*] landlady, owner

propriété [pʀɔpʀijete] **1** NF **a** (= *droit*) ownership, property (*frm, Jur*); (= *possession*) property; **~ de l'État/collective** state/collective ownership; **la petite ~** (*gén*) small estates; (*Agr*) smallholdings; **la grande ~** large estates; (*Agr*) large farms; **posséder qch en toute ~** to be the sole owner of sth, have sole ownership of sth; **recevoir qch en pleine ~** to acquire the freehold of sth → **accession, titre**

b (= *immeuble, maison*) property; (= *terres*) property (*NonC*), land (*NonC*), estate; **revenu d'une ~** revenue from a property *ou* a piece of land

c (= *qualité*) property; **~s chimiques/physiques/thérapeutiques** chemical/physical/therapeutic properties

d (= *correction*) [*mot*] appropriateness, suitability, correctness

2 COMP ▶ **propriété artistique** artistic copyright ▶ **propriété bâtie** developed property ▶ **propriété commerciale** security of tenure (*of industrial or commercial ten-*

▶ **GRAMMAIRE ACTIVE:** proposer 28.1

ant) ► **propriété foncière** property ownership ► **propriétés immobilières** real estate (*NonC*), realty (*NonC*) (*Jur*) ► **propriété industrielle** patent rights ► **propriété intellectuelle** intellectual property ► **propriété littéraire** author's copyright ► **propriété non bâtie** undeveloped property ► **propriété privée** private property ► **propriété publique** public property

proprio* [prɔprijo] NMF (ABRÉV = **propriétaire**) (= *homme*) landlord; (= *femme*) landlady

propulser [prɔpylse] ▸ conjug 1 ◂ [1] VT [a] [+ *voiture*] to propel, drive (along *ou* forward); [+ *missile*] to propel, power [b] (= *projeter*) to hurl, fling; **il a été propulsé contre le mur** he was hurled *ou* flung against the wall [c] (= *promouvoir*) **on l'a propulsé à la direction du service** he suddenly found himself at the head of the department; **avant de se retrouver propulsé au sommet de la hiérarchie** before suddenly finding himself at the top of *ou* thrust to the top of the hierarchy; **le voilà propulsé au rang de star/à la tête de l'entreprise** and now he's suddenly become a star/the head of the company; **on se retrouve propulsés dans un monde féerique** we suddenly find ourselves transported to a magical world [2] **se propulser** VPR (= *avancer*) to propel o.s.; **l'entreprise s'est propulsée à la première place du marché** the company has shot into the lead

propulseur [prɔpylsœr] [1] ADJ M propulsive, driving (*épith*) [2] NM [a] [*fusée*] thruster; ~ **d'appoint** booster [b] (*Ethnol*) throwing stick

propulsif, -ive [prɔpylsif, iv] ADJ propelling, propellent

propulsion [prɔpylsjɔ̃] NF propulsion; **moteur à** ~ propulsion engine; **système de** ~ propulsion system; **à** ~ **atomique/nucléaire** atomic-/nuclear-powered; **sous-marin à** ~ **classique** conventionally-powered submarine

propylène [prɔpilɛn] NM propylene

prorata [prɔrata] NM INV proportional share, proportion; **au** ~ **de** in proportion to, proportionally to, on the basis of; **paiement au** ~ payment on a pro rata basis

prorogation [prɔrɔgasjɔ̃] NF [a] [*délai, durée*] extension; [*échéance*] putting back, deferment [b] [*séance*] adjournment, (*Parl*) prorogation

proroger [prɔrɔʒe] ▸ conjug 3 ◂ VT [a] (= *prolonger*) [+ *délai, durée*] to extend; (= *reporter*) [+ *échéance*] to put back, defer [b] (= *ajourner*) [+ *séance*] to adjourn; (*Parl*) to prorogue; **le parlement s'est prorogé jusqu'en octobre** the parliament has adjourned *ou* prorogued until October

prosaïque [prɔzaik] ADJ [*esprit, personne, vie, style, remarque, détail*] mundane, prosaic; [*goûts*] mundane, commonplace

prosaïquement [prɔzaikmɑ̃] ADV prosaically; **vivre** ~ to lead a mundane life *ou* a prosaic existence; **plus** ~, **je dirais ...** more prosaically, I would say ...

prosaïsme [prɔzaism] NM mundanity, mundaneness

prosateur [prɔzatœr] NM prose-writer, writer of prose

proscription [prɔskripsjɔ̃] NF [a] [*idéologie, activité, drogue, mot*] banning, prohibition, proscription [b] [*personne*] (= *mise hors la loi*) outlawing (*NonC*); (= *exil*) banishment, exiling (*NonC*)

proscrire [prɔskrir] ▸ conjug 39 ◂ VT [a] [+ *idéologie, activité*] to ban, prohibit, proscribe; [+ *drogue, mot*] to ban, prohibit the use of, proscribe; ~ **une expression de son vocabulaire** to banish an expression from one's vocabulary [b] [+ *personne*] (= *mettre hors la loi*) to outlaw; (= *exiler*) to banish, exile

proscrit, e [prɔskri, it] (*ptp de* **proscrire**) NM,F (= *hors-la-loi*) outlaw; (= *exilé*) exile

prose [prɔz] NF (*gén*) prose; (= *style*) prose (style); **poème/tragédie en** ~ prose poem/tragedy; **écrire en** ~ to write in prose; **faire de la** ~ to write prose; (*péj*) **la** ~ **administrative** officialese; (*péj*) **je viens de lire sa** ~ (*lettre*) I've just read his epistle (*hum*); (*devoir, roman*) I've just read his great work (*iro, hum*)

prosélyte [prɔzelit] NMF proselyte (*frm*), convert; **les** ~**s des médecines douces** converts to alternative medicine

prosélytisme [prɔzelitism] NM proselytism; **faire du** ~ to proselytize, preach

prosodie [prɔzɔdi] NF prosody

prosodique [prɔzɔdik] ADJ prosodic; **trait** ~ prosodic feature

prosopopée [prɔzɔpɔpe] NF prosopopoeia, prosopopeia

prospect [prɔspe(kt)] NM (*Écon*) prospect, prospective customer

prospecter [prɔspɛkte] ▸ conjug 1 ◂ VT [a] (*Min*) to prospect [b] (*Comm*) [+ *marché*] to explore; [+ *région, clientèle*] to canvass; **j'ai prospecté le quartier pour trouver une maison** I scoured *ou* searched the area to find a house

prospecteur, -trice [prɔspɛktœr, tris] NM,F prospector

prospecteur-placier (*pl* **prospecteurs-placiers**) [prɔspɛktœrplasje] NM employment officer, job placement officer (*Brit*)

prospectif, -ive [prɔspɛktif, iv] [1] ADJ prospective [2] **prospective** NF (*gén*) futurology; (*Écon*) economic forecasting

prospection [prɔspɛksjɔ̃] NF [a] (*Min*) prospecting; **ils font de la** ~ **pétrolière** they are prospecting for oil [b] (*Comm*) [*marché*] exploring; [*région, clientèle*] canvassing; **faire de la** ~ to canvass for business; ~ **téléphonique** telephone canvassing

prospectiviste [prɔspɛktivist] NMF (*gén*) futurologist; (*Écon*) (economic) forecaster

prospectus [prɔspɛktys] NM leaflet; ~ **publicitaire** publicity *ou* advertising leaflet

prospère [prɔspɛr] ADJ [a] [*commerce, pays, collectivité*] prosperous, thriving, flourishing; [*période*] prosperous [b] [*personne*] blooming with health (*attrib*); **avoir une mine** ~ to look healthy; **être d'une santé** ~ to be blooming with health

prospérer [prɔspere] ▸ conjug 6 ◂ VI [*commerce*] to prosper, thrive, flourish; [*personne*] to prosper, do well; [*animal, activité, plante*] to thrive, flourish

prospérité [prɔsperite] NF [a] (*matérielle*) prosperity; (*économique*) prosperity, affluence [b] (= *santé*) (flourishing) health

prostaglandine [prɔstaglɑ̃din] NF prostaglandin

prostate [prɔstat] NF prostate (gland)

prostatectomie [prɔstatɛktɔmi] NF prostatectomy

prostatique [prɔstatik] [1] ADJ prostatic [2] NM prostate sufferer

prosternation [prɔstɛrnasjɔ̃] NF prostration

prosterné, e [prɔstɛrne] (*ptp de* **prosterner**) ADJ prostrate

prosternement [prɔstɛrnəmɑ̃] NM (= *action*) prostration; (= *attitude*) prostrate attitude; (*fig*) grovelling

prosterner (se) [prɔstɛrne] ▸ conjug 1 ◂ [1] VT (*littér*) to bow low; **il prosterna le corps** he prostrated himself [2] **se prosterner** VPR (= *s'incliner*) to bow low, bow down, prostrate o.s. (**devant** before); (= *s'humilier*) to grovel (**devant** before), kowtow (**devant** to)

prostituté* [prɔstitɥe] NM male prostitute, rent boy* (*Brit*)

prostituée [prɔstitɥe] NF prostitute

prostituer [prɔstitɥe] ▸ conjug 1 ◂ [1] VT (*lit*) ~ **qn** to make a prostitute of sb [2] **se prostituer** VPR (*lit, fig*) to prostitute o.s.

prostitution [prɔstitysjɔ̃] NF (*lit, fig*) prostitution

prostration [prɔstrasjɔ̃] NF (*Méd, Rel*) prostration

prostré, e [prɔstre] ADJ (*fig*) prostrate, prostrated; (*Méd*) prostrate

protactinium [prɔtaktinjɔm] NM protactinium

protagoniste [prɔtagɔnist] NMF protagonist; **les principaux** ~**s de l'affaire/du conflit** the main players *ou* protagonists in the affair/the conflict

protecteur, -trice [prɔtɛktœr, tris] [1] ADJ [a] (*gén, Chim, Écon*) protective (**de** of); (*Cosmétique*) [*film*] protective; **crème protectrice** protective *ou* barrier cream → **société** [b] [*ton, air*] patronizing [2] NM,F (= *défenseur*) protector, guardian; [*arts*] patron; ~ **de la nature/l'environnement** protector of nature/the environment [3] NM (= *souteneur*) pimp (*péj*); († = *galant*) fancy man †

protection [prɔtɛksjɔ̃] [1] NF [a] (= *défense*) protection (**contre** against, from); ~ **contre les rayonnements** radiation protection; **assurer la** ~ **de** to protect; (= *protéger*) **assurer la** ~ **rapprochée du chef de l'État** in charge of the close protection *ou* personal safety of the head of state; **zone sous** ~ **policière/militaire** area under police/military protection; **région sous** ~ **de l'ONU** UN protection zone, area under UN protection; **sous la** ~ **de** under the protection of; **elle a été placée sous la** ~ **de la police** she was given police protection; **prendre qn sous sa** ~ to give sb one's protection, take sb under one's wing; **l'ambassade est sous haute** ~ **policière** the embassy is under heavy police guard; **crème solaire/indice haute** ~ high-protection sun cream/factor; **rapports sexuels sans** ~ unprotected sex [b] **de** ~ [*équipement, grille, lunettes, mesures*] protective; **zone de** ~ [*population*] safe haven; **système de** ~ security system [c] (= *patronage*: *gén*) protection; [*personne puissante, mécène*] patronage; **placer un enfant sous la** ~ **de qn** to place a child in sb's care; **prendre qn sous sa** ~ to give sb one's patronage, take sb under one's wing; **obtenir une place par** ~ to get a post by pulling strings [d] (= *dispositif*) (*pour une partie du corps*) item of protective clothing (*ou* gear); (= *blindage*) [*navire*] armour(-plating) (*Brit*), armor(-plating) (*US*) [e] (*Ordin*) protection; ~ **contre l'écriture** write protection [2] COMP ► **protection aérienne** air *ou* aerial protection ► **protection civile** (*lors de catastrophes*) disaster and emergency services; (*en temps de guerre*) civil defence ► **protection du consommateur** consumer protection ► **protection de l'emploi** job protection ► **protection de l'enfance** child welfare ► **protection de l'environnement** environmental protection ► **protection maternelle et infantile** mother and child care ► **protection de la nature** nature conservation ► **protection périodique** sanitary towel (*Brit*) *ou* napkin (*US*) ► **protection des sites** preservation *ou* protection of beauty spots ► **protection sociale** social welfare; **personnes sans** ~ **sociale** people not covered by social security *ou* with no social welfare cover ► **protection solaire** (= *produit*) sun cream (*ou* lotion)

protectionnisme [prɔtɛksjɔnism] NM protectionism

protectionniste [prɔtɛksjɔnist] ADJ, NMF protectionist

protectorat [prɔtɛktɔra] NM protectorate

protégé, e [prɔteʒe] (*ptp de* **protéger**) [1] ADJ [a] [*espèce, site, zone*] protected; (*Écon*) [*secteur, marché*] protected; (*Ordin*) [*disquette*] write-protected; [*logiciel*] copy-protected; ~ **en écriture** write-protected; **la reproduction d'œu-**

vres ~es the reproduction of works under copyright protection *ou* of copyright works; **rapports sexuels ~s/non ~s** safe/unprotected sex → **passage** [b] (*pour handicapé*) **atelier** ~ sheltered workshop; **emploi** ~ job in a sheltered workshop [2] NM protégé; (* = *chouchou*) favourite, pet* [3] **protégée** NF protégée; (* = *favorite*) favourite, pet*

protège-bas [prɔtɛʒba] NM INV sockette

protège-cahier (*pl* **protège-cahiers**) [prɔtɛʒkaje] NM exercise-book cover

protège-dents [prɔtɛʒdã] NM INV gumshield

protéger [prɔteʒe] ▸conjug 6et3 [1] VT [a] [+ *personne*] (= *veiller à la sécurité de*) to protect, guard; (= *abriter*) to protect, shield; (*moralement*) to protect, guard, shield; [+ *plantes, lieu*] (*des éléments*) to protect, shelter; [+ *équipement, matériel, membres*] (*des chocs etc*) to protect; [+ *institution, tradition*] to protect (**de, contre** from); **~ les intérêts de qn** to protect sb's interests; **crème qui protège contre le soleil** cream that gives (good) protection against the sun

[b] (= *patronner*) [+ *personne*] to be a patron of; [+ *carrière*] to further; [+ *arts, sports, artisanat*] to patronize

[c] (*Comm*) [+ *produits locaux*] to protect

[d] (*Ordin*) to protect

[2] **se protéger** VPR to protect o.s. (**de** from, **contre** against); **se ~ contre le** *ou* **du sida/contre le** *ou* **du soleil** to protect o.s. against AIDS/against the sun; **se ~ du froid/contre les piqûres d'insectes** to protect o.s. from the cold/against insect bites

protège-slip (*pl* **protège-slips**) [prɔtɛʒslip] NM panty liner

protège-tibia (*pl* **protège-tibias**) [prɔtɛʒtibja] NM shin guard

protéiforme [prɔteifɔrm] ADJ protean

protéine [prɔtein] NF protein

protéique [prɔteik] ADJ protein (*épith*), proteinic

protestable [prɔtɛstabl] ADJ protestable, which may be protested

protestant, e [prɔtɛstã, ãt] ADJ, NM,F Protestant

protestantisme [prɔtɛstãtism] NM Protestantism

protestataire [prɔtɛstatɛr] [1] ADJ [*personne*] protesting (*épith*); [*marche, mesure*] protest (*épith*) [2] NMF protestor, protester

protestation [prɔtɛstasjɔ̃] NF [a] (= *plainte*) protest (**contre** against); (*Jur*) protesting, protestation; **en signe de ~** as a (sign of) protest; **lettre/marche/mouvement de ~** protest letter/march/movement [b] (*souvent pl* = *déclaration*) protestation, profession; **faire des ~s d'amitié à qn** to profess one's friendship to sb

▼ **protester** [prɔtɛste] ▸conjug 1◂ [1] VI to protest (**contre** against, about); **~ de son innocence/de sa loyauté** to protest one's innocence/one's loyalty; **« mais non », protesta-t-il** "no", he protested [2] VT (*Jur*) to protest; (*frm* = *déclarer*) to declare, affirm, profess; (*frm*) **il protesta la plus vive admiration pour elle** he declared that he had the keenest admiration for her

protêt [prɔtɛ] NM (*Comm, Jur*) protest

prothèse [prɔtɛz] NF [a] (= *appareil*) prosthesis (*SPÉC*); (= *membre artificiel*) artificial limb (*ou* hand *ou* arm etc), prosthesis (*SPÉC*); **~ dentaire** dentures, false teeth, dental prosthesis (*SPÉC*); **~ auditive** hearing aid; **~ mammaire** breast prosthesis; **pose d'une ~ de hanche** hip replacement (operation) [b] (= *science, technique*) prosthetics *sg*; **la ~ dentaire** prosthodontics *sg*

prothésiste [prɔtezist] NMF prosthetist, prosthetic technician; **~ (dentaire)** dental technician, prosthodontist

protide [prɔtid] NM protein

proto... [prɔto] PRÉF proto...

protocolaire [prɔtɔkɔlɛr] ADJ [*invitation, cérémonie*] formal; **question ~** question of protocol; **ce n'est pas très ~!** it doesn't show much regard for protocol!

protocole [prɔtɔkɔl] NM [a] (= *étiquette*) etiquette; (*Pol*) protocol; **il est très attaché au ~** he's a stickler for form; **chef du ~** chief *ou* head of protocol [b] (= *procès-verbal*) protocol; (= *résolutions*) agreement; **~ d'accord/de coopération/financier** draft/cooperation/financial agreement [c] (*Ordin, Sci*) protocol; (*rédaction d'ouvrage*) style guide; **~ thérapeutique** medical protocol

proton [prɔtɔ̃] NM proton

protoplasma [prɔtɔplasma], **protoplasme** [prɔtɔplasm] NM protoplasm

protoplasmique [prɔtɔplasmik] ADJ protoplasmic

prototype [prɔtɔtip] NM prototype; **~ d'avion** prototype aircraft

protoxyde [prɔtɔksid] NM protoxide

protozoaire [prɔtɔzɔɛr] NM protozoon; **~s** protozoa

protubérance [prɔtyberãs] NF bulge, protuberance; (*Astron*) **~ solaire** (solar) prominence

protubérant, e [prɔtyberã, ãt] ADJ [*ventre, yeux*] bulging, protuberant, protruding; [*nez, menton*] protuberant, protruding

prou [pru] ADV → **peu**

proue [pru] NF bow, bows, prow → **figure**

prouesse [prues] NF (*frm*) feat; **faire des ~s** to work miracles, perform amazing feats; **il a fallu faire des ~s pour le convaincre** it was quite a feat to convince him, we had our work cut out for us trying to convince him; **il nous racontait ses ~s (sexuelles)** he regaled us with tales of his sexual exploits; **cela n'a pu être réalisé qu'au prix de ~s techniques** this could not have been achieved without technical wizardry; **ses ~s d'haltérophile** his prowess as a weightlifter

proustien, -ienne [prustjɛ̃, jɛn] ADJ Proustian

prout* [prut] NM **faire (un) ~** to fart⁑

prouvable [pruvabl] ADJ provable; **allégations difficilement ~s** allegations which are difficult to prove

▼ **prouver** [pruve] ▸conjug 1◂ VT (*gén*) to prove; **les faits ont prouvé qu'il avait raison/qu'il était innocent** the facts proved him (to be) right/innocent *ou* proved that he was right/innocent; **il est prouvé que ...** it has been proved that ...; **cela prouve que ...** it proves *ou* shows that ...; **il n'est pas prouvé qu'il soit coupable** there is no proof that he is guilty *ou* of his guilt; **cela n'est pas prouvé** there's no proof of it, that hasn't been proved, that remains to be proved; **sa culpabilité reste à ~** it has yet to be proved that he is guilty; **cette réponse prouve de l'esprit** that answer gives proof of his (*ou* her etc) wit *ou* shows wit; **comment vous ~ ma reconnaissance ?** how can I show *ou* demonstrate my gratitude to you?; **il a voulu se ~ (à lui-même) qu'il en était capable** he wanted to prove to himself that he was capable of it; **son efficacité n'est plus à ~** its effectiveness is no longer in doubt *ou* in question; **j'ai 25 ans d'expérience, je n'ai plus rien à ~** I have 25 years' experience, I have nothing to prove → **A¹, absurde**

provenance [prɔv(ə)nãs] NF origin, provenance (*frm*); **j'ignore la ~ de cette lettre** I don't know where this letter comes *ou* came *ou* was sent from; **pays de ~** country of origin; **des objets de toutes ~s** articles of every possible origin; **de ~ étrangère** of foreign origin; **le train en ~ de Cherbourg** the train from Cherbourg

provençal, e (*mpl* **-aux**) [prɔvãsal, o] [1] ADJ Provençal; (*Culin*) **(à la) ~e** (à la) Provençale [2] NM (*Ling*) Provençal [3] **Provençal(e)** NM,F Provençal

Provence [prɔvãs] NF Provence

provenir [prɔv(ə)nir] ▸conjug 22◂ ♦ **provenir de** VT INDIR (= *venir de*) [+ *pays*] to come from, be from; (= *résulter de*) [+ *cause*] to be due to, be the result of; **son genre de vie provient de son éducation** his life style is the result of his upbringing; **mot qui provient d'une racine grecque** word which comes *ou* derives from a Greek root; **cette fortune provient d'une lointaine cousine** this fortune comes from a distant cousin; **vase provenant de Chine** vase (that comes) from China; **je me demande d'où provient sa fortune** I wonder where he got his money from, I wonder how he came by so much money

proverbe [prɔvɛrb] NM proverb; **comme dit le ~** as the saying goes; **passer en ~** to become proverbial; (*Bible*) **le livre des Proverbes** the (Book of) Proverbs

proverbial, e (*mpl* **-iaux**) [prɔvɛrbjal, jo] ADJ proverbial

proverbialement [prɔvɛrbjalmã] ADV proverbially

providence [prɔvidãs] NF (*Rel*) providence; (= *sauveur*) guardian angel; (*fig*) **cette bouteille d'eau a été notre ~** that bottle of water was our salvation *ou* was a lifesaver; **vous êtes ma ~ !** you're my salvation! → **état**

providentiel, -ielle [prɔvidãsjɛl] ADJ providential; **voici l'homme ~** here's the man we need

providentiellement [prɔvidãsjɛlmã] ADV providentially

province [prɔvẽs] NF [a] (= *région*) province; **Paris et la ~** Paris and the provinces; **vivre en ~** to live in the provinces; **ville de ~** provincial town; (*péj*) **il arrive de sa ~** where has he been?; (*péj*) **elle fait très ~** she's very provincial; (*Hist*) **les Provinces Unies** the United Provinces [b] (*au Canada*) province; **les Provinces maritimes** the Maritime Provinces, the Maritimes (*Can*); **habitant des Provinces maritimes** Maritimer; **les Provinces des prairies** the Prairie Provinces (*Can*); **la Belle Province** Quebec

provincial, e (*mpl* **-iaux**) [prɔvẽsjal, jo] [1] ADJ [a] (*gén, Rel*) provincial [b] (*au Canada*) **gouvernement ~** Provincial government [2] NM,F provincial; **les provinciaux** people who live in the provinces, provincials [3] NM [a] (*Rel*) Provincial [b] (*au Canada*) **le ~** the Provincial Government

provincialisme [prɔvẽsjalism] NM provincialism

proviseur [prɔvizœr] NM [*lycée*] headmaster, principal, head (*Brit*); **~-adjoint** ≈ deputy *ou* assistant head (*Brit*), ≈ assistant *ou* vice-principal (*US*)

provision [prɔvizjɔ̃] NF [a] (= *réserve*) [*vivres, cartouches*] stock, supply; [*eau*] supply; **faire (une) ~ de** [+ *nourriture, papier*] to stock up with, lay *ou* get in a stock of; [+ *énergie, courage*] to build up a stock of; **j'ai acheté toute une ~ de bonbons** I've bought a good supply *ou* stock of sweets; **j'ai une bonne ~ de conserves** I have a good stock of canned food, I've got plenty of canned food in; **avoir une bonne ~ de courage** to have considerable reserves of courage

[b] (= *vivres*) **~s** provisions, food (*NonC*); **faire ses ~s** ◊ **aller aux ~s*** to go shopping (for groceries *ou* food); **elle posa ses ~s sur la table** she put her groceries on the table; **faire des ~s pour l'hiver** (*lit*) to buy in food *ou* provisions for the winter, stock up (with food *ou* provisions) for the winter; (*hum: financièrement*) to put something away for a rainy day; (*hum: trop manger*) **tu fais des ~s pour**

---

l'hiver ? are you fattening yourself up for the winter?; **~s de guerre** war supplies; **~s de bouche** provisions; **filet/panier à ~s** shopping bag/basket; **armoire** ou **placard à ~s** food cupboard
[c] (= *arrhes*) (*chez un avocat*) retainer, retaining fee; (*pour un achat*) deposit; (*Banque*) **y a-t-il ~ au compte ?** are there sufficient funds in the account?; (*immeuble d'habitation*) **~s sur charges** interim payment for maintenance ou service charges; **~s pour créances douteuses** provision for bad debts; **~s pour risques contingency** reserve → **chèque**

provisionnel, -elle [pRɔvizjɔnEl] ADJ (*Jur*) provisional; **acompte** ou **tiers ~** provisional payment (*towards one's income tax*) → IMPÔTS

provisionner [pRɔvizjɔne] ▸ conjug 1 ◂ VT (*Banque*) [+ *compte*] to pay money ou funds into; **la banque a provisionné à 20% ses risques sur l'immobilier** the bank has set aside 20% of its capital in provision against ou to cover real estate losses

provisoire [pRɔvizwaR] [1] ADJ [*arrêt, jugement*] provisional; [*mesure, solution*] provisional, temporary; [*bonheur, liaison, installation*] temporary; [*adjoint*] temporary, acting (*épith*); [*gouvernement*] provisional, interim (*épith*); **à titre ~** temporarily, provisionally → **liberté** [2] NM **c'est du ~** it's a temporary ou provisional arrangement

provisoirement [pRɔvizwaRmɑ̃] ADV (= *momentanément*) temporarily; (= *pour l'instant*) for the time being

provitamine [pRɔvitamin] NF provitamin

provoc* [pRɔvɔk] NF ABRÉV = **provocation**

provocant, e [pRɔvɔkɑ̃, ɑ̃t] ADJ provocative

provocateur, -trice [pRɔvɔkatœR, tRis] [1] ADJ provocative → **agent** [2] NM agitator

provocation [pRɔvɔkasjɔ̃] NF [a] (= *défi*) provocation; **~ en duel** challenge to a duel; **ils ont accusé les manifestants de faire de la ~** they accused the demonstrators of being provocative ou of trying to provoke trouble; **il l'a fait par pure ~** he did it just to be provocative ou to get a reaction; **leur façon de s'habiller, c'est de la ~** (*gén*) they're out to shock people by the way they dress; (*pour exciter*) they dress to be provocative; **il a multiplié les ~s à l'égard des autorités** he has increasingly tried to provoke the authorities [b] (= *incitation*) **~ à (faire) qch** incitement to (do) sth; **~ à la haine raciale/au crime** incitement to racial hatred/to commit a crime; **~ au suicide** ≈ assisted suicide

▼ **provoquer** [pRɔvɔke] ▸ conjug 1 ◂ VT [a] (= *défier*) to provoke; **~ qn en duel** to challenge sb to a duel; **elle aime ~ les hommes** she likes to provoke men; **~ qn du regard** to give sb a defiant look; (*pour exciter*) to give sb a provocative look; **les deux adversaires s'étaient provoqués** the two opponents had provoked each other
[b] (= *causer*) [+ *accident, incendie, explosion, dégâts*] to cause; [+ *réaction, changement d'attitude*] to provoke, prompt, produce; [+ *courant d'air*] to create, cause; [+ *crise, révolte*] to cause, bring about, provoke; [+ *commentaires*] to give rise to, provoke, prompt; [+ *colère*] to arouse, spark off; [+ *curiosité*] to arouse, excite; [+ *gaieté*] to cause, provoke; [+ *aveux, explications*] to prompt; [+ *accouchement*] to induce; **l'accident a provoqué la mort de six personnes** six people were killed in the accident; **médicament qui provoque le sommeil** sleep-inducing drug; **le malade est sous sommeil provoqué** the patient is in an induced sleep; (*Chim*) **l'élévation de température a provoqué cette réaction** the rise in temperature brought about ou triggered off ou started up this reaction; **les émeutes ont provoqué la chute du régime** rioting brought about ou led to the fall of the regime; **~ des élections anticipées** to force an

early election
[c] (= *inciter*) **~ qn à** to incite sb to

proxénète [pRɔksenet] NMF procurer

proxénétisme [pRɔksenetism] NM procuring; **il a été condamné pour ~** he was convicted of living off immoral earnings

proximité [pRɔksimite] NF [a] (*dans l'espace*) nearness, closeness, proximity; **à ~** nearby, close by; **à ~ de** near (to), close to, in the vicinity of; **commerce de ~** local shop (*Brit*) ou store (*US*), neighborhood store (*US*); **emploi de ~** job created at local community level, typically involving childminding, domestic work, caring for old people etc; **la police de ~** community policing; **il faut développer les services de ~** we need to develop local community-based services [b] (*dans le temps*) closeness; **c'est lié à la ~ de l'élection** it's connected to the fact that the elections are so close

pruche [pRyʃ] NF (*Can*) hemlock spruce

prude [pRyd] [1] ADJ prudish [2] NF prude; **faire la ~** ◊ **jouer les ~s** to behave prudishly

prudemment [pRydamɑ̃] ADV [*conduire*] carefully; [*avancer, répondre*] cautiously; **garder le silence** to keep a cautious silence

prudence [pRydɑ̃s] NF [a] (= *circonspection*) care, caution, cautiousness, prudence; (= *réserve*) caution, cautiousness, caginess; **~! ça glisse** careful! it's slippery; **faire preuve de ~** to be cautious ou careful; **il a manqué de ~** he wasn't cautious ou careful enough; **par (mesure de) ~** as a precaution; **avec la plus grande ~** with the greatest caution, extremely carefully ou cautiously; **il faudra lui annoncer la nouvelle avec beaucoup de ~** the news must be broken to him very carefully ◼ (*PROV*) **~ est mère de sûreté** discretion is the better part of valour (*PROV*) [b] (= *sagesse*) wisdom; **il a eu la ~ de partir** he had the good sense ou he was wise ou sensible enough to leave

▼ **prudent, e** [pRydɑ̃, ɑ̃t] ADJ [a] (= *circonspect*) careful, cautious, prudent; (= *réservé*) cautious, cagey; **soyez ~!** (*gén*) be careful!, take care!; (*sur la route*) drive carefully!; **il s'est montré très ~ au sujet du résultat** he was very cautious ou cagey about the result; **c'est un ~** he's a careful ou cautious man; **avancer à pas ~s** to move forward cautiously ou with cautious steps; **soyez plus ~ à l'avenir** be more careful in future; **il n'est pas très ~ en voiture** he's not a careful driver
[b] (= *sage*) wise, sensible; **il est ~ de faire** it is wise ou advisable to do; **il serait ~ de vous munir d'un parapluie** it would be wise ou sensible to take an umbrella, you would be well-advised to take an umbrella; **ce n'est pas ~** it's not advisable, it's not a good idea; **ce n'est pas ~ de boire avant de conduire** it's not sensible ou wise ou advisable to drink before driving; **c'est plus ~** it's wiser ou safer ou more sensible; **il jugea plus ~ de se taire** he thought it prudent ou wiser ou more sensible to keep quiet

pruderie [pRydRi] NF (*littér*) prudishness (*NonC*), prudery

prud'homal, e (*mpl* -aux) [pRydɔmal, o] ADJ of an industrial tribunal (*Brit*) ou labor relations board (*US*)

prud'homie [pRydɔmi] NF jurisdiction of an industrial tribunal (*Brit*) ou labor relations board (*US*) → **prud'homme**

prud'homme [pRydɔm] NM ≈ member of an industrial tribunal (*Brit*) ou labor relations board (*US*); **conseil des ~s** ◊ **les ~s** ≈ industrial tribunal (*Brit*), ≈ labor relations board (*US*) (*with wide administrative and advisory powers*); **aller aux** ou **devant les ~s** to go before an industrial tribunal (*Brit*) ou the labor relations board (*US*)

prudhommerie [pRydɔmRi] NF sententiousness, pomposity

prudhommesque [pRydɔmɛsk] ADJ sententious, pompous

prune [pRyn] [1] NF [a] (= *fruit*) plum; (= *alcool*) plum brandy; **pour des ~s*** for nothing; **des ~s!*** not likely!*, not on your life!*, no way!* [b] (‡ = *contravention*) ticket (*for speeding, illegal parking etc*) **~** he gave me a ticket, he booked me (*Brit*) [c] (‡† = *coup*) clout*; **filer une ~ à qn‡** to give sb a clout*, clout* sb [2] ADJ INV plum-coloured (*Brit*) ou -colored (*US*)

pruneau (*pl* pruneaux) [pRyno] NM [a] (= *fruit sec*) prune; (*Helv* = *quetsche*) kind of dark-red plum [b] (‡ = *balle*) slug*

prunelle [pRynɛl] NF [a] (*Bot*) sloe; (= *eau-de-vie*) sloe gin [b] (*Anat* = *pupille*) pupil; (= *œil*) eye; **il y tient comme à la ~ de ses yeux** he treasures ou cherishes it; (*personne*) she (ou he) is the apple of his eye, she (ou he) is very precious to him; **il/elle jouait de la ~*** he/she was giving her/him the eye*

prunellier [pRynɔlje] NM sloe, blackthorn

prunier [pRynje] NM plum tree → **secouer**

prunus [pRynys] NM prunus, Japanese flowering cherry

prurigineux, -euse [pRyRiʒinø, øz] ADJ pruriginous

prurigo [pRyRigo] NM prurigo

prurit [pRyRit] NM (*Méd*) pruritus; (*hum*) **leur ~ réformateur/égalitaire** their zeal for reform/egalitarianism; **le ~ de l'écriture le démange** he's got the writing bug

Prusse [pRys] NF Prussia → **bleu**

prussien, -ienne [pRysjɛ̃, jɛn] [1] ADJ Prussian [2] **Prussien(ne)** NM,F Prussian

prytanée [pRitane] NM (*Antiq*) prytaneum; **~ militaire** military academy

P.-S. [peɛs] NM (ABRÉV = **post-scriptum**) ps

PS [peɛs] NM (ABRÉV = **parti socialiste**) French political party

psallette [psalet] NF choir

psalmiste [psalmist] NM psalmist

psalmodie [psalmɔdi] NF (*Rel*) psalmody, chant; (*littér*) drone (*NonC*)

psalmodier [psalmɔdje] ▸ conjug 7 ◂ [1] VT (*Rel*) to chant; (*littér*) to drone out [2] VI to chant; (*littér*) to drone (on ou away)

psaume [psom] NM psalm; (*Bible*) **le livre des Psaumes** the Book of Psalms

psautier [psotje] NM psalter

pschitt [pʃit] [1] EXCL hiss [2] NM (*= *atomiseur*) spray; **vaporisez deux coups de ~ sur un chiffon** spray twice onto a cloth

pseudo* [psodo] NM ABRÉV = **pseudonyme**

pseudo- [psødo] PRÉF (*gén*) pseudo-; **~historien** pseudo-historian; **~science/-réalité** pseudo-science/-reality; **les ~révélations parues dans leur journal** the pseudo-revelations ou so-called revelations published in their newspaper

pseudonyme [psødɔnim] NM (*gén*) assumed ou fictitious name; [*écrivain*] pen name, pseudonym; [*comédien*] stage name; (*Jur, hum*) alias

psitt [psit] EXCL ps(s)t!

psittacisme [psitasism] NM (= *répétition mécanique*) parrotry; (*Psych*) psittacism

psittacose [psitakoz] NF psittacosis

psoriasis [psɔRjazis] NM psoriasis

psy* [psi] [1] ADJ INV ABRÉV = **psychologique, psychique, psychosomatique** [2] NMF (ABRÉV = **psychiatre, psychologue, psychothérapeute, psychanalyste**) **il va chez son ~ toutes les semaines** he goes to see his analyst ou shrink* every week [3] NF ABRÉV = **psychiatrie, psychologie**

psychanalyse [psikanaliz] NF [*personne*] psychoanalysis, analysis; [*texte*] psychoanalytical study; **entreprendre/faire/suivre une ~** to start/do/undergo analysis

---

▶ GRAMMAIRE ACTIVE: provoquer 44.2 prudent 29.2

psychanalyser [psikanalize] ▸ conjug 1 ◂ VT [+ *personne*] to psychoanalyze; [+ *texte*] to study from a psychoanalytical viewpoint; **se faire ~** to have o.s. psychoanalyzed

psychanalyste [psikanalist] NMF psychoanalyst, analyst

psychanalytique [psikanalitik] ADJ psychoanalytic(al)

psyché [psiʃe] NF **a** (*Psych*) psyche **b** (= *miroir*) cheval glass, swing mirror **c** (*Myth*) **Psyché** Psyche

psychédélique [psikedelik] ADJ psychedelic

psychédélisme [psikedelism] NM psychedelic state

psychiatre [psikjatʀ] NMF psychiatrist

psychiatrie [psikjatʀi] NF psychiatry

psychiatrique [psikjatʀik] ADJ [*troubles*] psychiatric; [*hôpital*] psychiatric, mental (*épith*)

psychique [psiʃik] ADJ psychological, psychic(al)

psychiquement [psiʃikmɑ̃] ADV psychologically

psychisme [psiʃism] NM psyche, mind

psycho⁎ [psiko] NF ABRÉV = **psychologie**

psychodrame [psikɔdʀam] NM (*Psych*) psychodrama; (= *drame*) drama

psychogène [psikɔʒɛn] ADJ psychogenic

psychokinésie [psikokinezi] NF psychokinesis

psycholinguistique [psikolɛ̃ɡɥistik] **1** ADJ psycholinguistic **2** NF psycholinguistics *sg*

psychologie [psikɔlɔʒi] NF psychology; **la ~ de l'enfant/des foules/du comportement** child/crowd/behavioural psychology; **il faut faire preuve de ~** you have to be perceptive about people, you have to have good insight into people; **il manque complètement de ~** he's completely unperceptive about people, he's got absolutely no insight into people

psychologique [psikɔlɔʒik] ADJ psychological; **tu sais, mon vieux, c'est ~!** it's psychological *ou* it's all in the mind, my friend! → **moment**

psychologiquement [psikɔlɔʒikmɑ̃] ADV psychologically

psychologue [psikɔlɔɡ] **1** ADJ (= *intuitif*) **il est/il n'est pas très ~** he's very/he's not very perceptive about people **2** NMF psychologist; **~ d'entreprise** industrial psychologist; **~ scolaire** educational psychologist

psychométrie [psikɔmetʀi] NF psychometry, psychometrics *sg*

psychométrique [psikɔmetʀik] ADJ psychometric

psychomoteur, -trice [psikɔmɔtœʀ, tʀis] ADJ psychomotor

psychopathe [psikɔpat] NMF psychopath; **tueur ~** psychopathic killer

psychopathie [psikɔpati] NF psychopathy

psychopathologie [psikopatɔlɔʒi] NF psychopathology

psychopédagogie [psikopedagɔʒi] NF educational psychology

psychopédagogique [psikopedagɔʒik] ADJ [*études, formation*] in educational psychology

psychophysiologie [psikofizjɔlɔʒi] NF psychophysiology

psychophysiologique [psikofizjɔlɔʒik] ADJ psychophysiological

psychose [psikoz] NF (*Psych*) psychosis; (= *obsession*) obsessive fear; **~ maniacodépressive** manic depressive psychosis; **~ collective** collective hysteria; **~ de guerre** war psychosis *ou* hysteria

psychosensoriel, -ielle [psikosɑ̃sɔʀjɛl] ADJ psychosensory

psychosocial, e (*mpl* -**iaux**) [psikosɔsjal, jo] ADJ psychosocial

psychosociologie [psikosɔsjɔlɔʒi] NF psychosociology

psychosomatique [psikosɔmatik] **1** ADJ psychosomatic **2** NF psychosomatics *sg*

psychotechnicien, -ienne [psikoteknisjɛ̃, jɛn] NM,F psychotechnician, psychotechnologist

psychotechnique [psikoteknik] **1** ADJ psychotechnical, psychotechnological **2** NF psychotechnics *sg*, psychotechnology

psychothérapeute [psikoteʀapøt] NMF psychotherapist

psychothérapie [psikoteʀapi] NF psychotherapy; **~ de soutien** supportive therapy; **entreprendre/faire/suivre une ~** to start/do/undergo (a course of) psychotherapy

psychothérapique [psikoteʀapik] ADJ psychotherapeutic

psychotique [psikɔtik] ADJ, NMF psychotic

Pte ABRÉV = **porte**

ptérodactyle [pteʀɔdaktil] NM pterodactyl

Ptolémée [ptɔleme] NM Ptolemy

ptose [ptoz] NF ptosis

P.T.T. [petete] NFPL (ABRÉV = **Postes, Télécommunications et Télédiffusion**) → **poste¹**

ptyaline [ptjalin] NF ptyalin

puant, puante [pɥɑ̃, pɥɑ̃t] ADJ **a** (*lit*) stinking, foul-smelling **b** (⁎: *péj*) [*personne, attitude*] arrogant; **il est ~ ◊ c'est un type ~** he's an arrogant creep⁎; **~ d'orgueil** bloated with pride

puanteur [pɥɑ̃tœʀ] NF stink, stench

pub¹ [pœb] NM (= *bar*) pub

pub²⁎ [pyb] NF (= *annonce*) ad⁎, advert⁎ (*Brit*); (*Ciné, TV*) commercial, ad⁎, advert⁎ (*Brit*); (*métier*) **la ~** advertising; **faire de la ~ pour qch** (*Comm*) to advertise sth; (= *inciter à acheter qch*) to plug sth⁎, give sth a plug⁎; **ça lui a fait de la ~** it was a plug⁎ for him; **coup de ~** publicity stunt; **ses disques ne se vendent qu'à coups de ~** his records are selling only as a result of heavy advertising

pubère [pybɛʀ] ADJ pubescent

puberté [pybɛʀte] NF puberty

pubien, -ienne [pybjɛ̃, jɛn] ADJ pubic; **région pubienne** pubic region, pubes

pubis [pybis] NM (= *os*) pubis; (= *bas-ventre*) pubes; **os ~** pubic bone

publiable [pyblijabl] ADJ publishable; **ce n'est pas ~** it's not fit for publication

public, -ique [pyblik] **1** ADJ **a** (= *non privé*) [*intérêt, lieu, opinion, vie*] public; [*vente, réunion*] public, open to the public (*attrib*); **danger/ennemi/homme ~** public danger/enemy/figure; **la nouvelle est maintenant publique** the news is now common *ou* public knowledge; **la nouvelle a été rendue publique hier** the news was made public *ou* was released yesterday → **domaine, droit³, notoriété** **b** (= *de l'État*) [*services, secteur, finances*] public; [*école, instruction*] State (*épith*), public (*US*) → **charge, chose, dette** etc **2** NM **a** (= *population*) **le ~** the (general) public; **« interdit au ~ »** "no admittance to the public" **b** (= *audience, assistance*) audience; **œuvre conçue pour un jeune ~** work written for a young audience; **le ~ parisien est très exigeant** Paris audiences are very demanding; **des huées s'élevèrent du ~** the audience started booing; **cet écrivain s'adresse à un vaste ~** this author writes for a wide readership; **cet acteur a son ~** this actor has his fans *ou* followers; **cet ouvrage plaira à tous les ~s** this work will be appreciated by all kinds of readers; **un ~ clairsemé assistait au match** the match was attended by very few spectators; **le ~ est informé que ...** the public is advised that ...; **en ~** in public; **le grand ~** the general public; **roman destiné au grand ~** novel written for the general reader *ou* public; **appareils**

électroniques grand ~ consumer electronics; **film grand ~** film with mass appeal; (*fig*) **il lui faut toujours un ~** he always needs an audience; **être bon/mauvais ~** to be easy/hard to please **c** (= *secteur*) **le ~** the public sector

publicain [pyblikɛ̃] NM (*Hist romaine*) publican, tax-gatherer

publication [pyblikasjɔ̃] NF (= *action*) publication, publishing; (= *écrit publié*) publication; **après sa ~ aux États-Unis** after being published *ou* after its publication in the United States; **ce livre a été interdit de ~** this book has been banned; **~ des bans (de mariage)** publication *ou* reading of the banns; **assistée par ordinateur** desktop publishing

publiciste [pyblisist] NMF **a** (⁎ = *publicitaire*) advertising executive **b** (*Jur*) public law specialist

publicitaire [pyblisitɛʀ] **1** ADJ [*budget, affiche, agence, campagne*] advertising (*épith*); [*film*] promotional; **annonce ~** advertisement; **échantillon ~** give-away, free sample; **grande vente ~** big promotional sale; **matériel ~** publicity material; **rédacteur ~** copywriter **2** NMF advertising executive

publicité [pyblisite] NF **a** (*Comm* = *méthode, profession*) advertising; **il travaille dans la ~** he's in advertising, he's an adman; **faire de la ~ pour qch** (*Comm*) to advertise sth; (= *inciter à acheter qch*) to plug sth⁎; **il sait bien faire sa propre ~** he's good at selling himself; **cette marque fait beaucoup de ~** this make does a lot of advertising; **son livre a été lancé à grand renfort de ~** his book was launched amid a blaze of publicity *ou* amid much media hype⁎; **coup de ~** publicity stunt; **~ par affichage** poster advertising; **~ collective/comparative** collective/comparative advertising; **~ directe** direct advertising; **~ de rappel** reminder advertising; **~ mensongère** misleading advertising; **~ sur les lieux de vente** point-of-sale advertising; (*Comm*) **matériel de ~** publicity material; **dépenses de ~** advertising costs; **campagne de ~** publicity *ou* advertising campaign → **agence** etc **b** (= *annonce*) advertisement, ad⁎, advert⁎ (*Brit*); (*Ciné, TV*) commercial, advertisement; **~ rédactionnelle** special advertising feature, advertorial (*US*) **c** (= *révélations*) publicity; **on a fait trop de ~ autour de cette affaire** this affair has had *ou* has been given too much publicity **d** (*Jur*) **la ~ des débats** the public nature of the proceedings

publier [pyblije] ▸ conjug 7 ◂ VT **a** [+ *livre*] [*auteur*] to publish; [*éditeur*] to publish, bring out **b** [+ *bans, décret*] to publish; (*littér*) [+ *nouvelle*] to publish (abroad) (*littér*), make public; **ça vient d'être publié** it's just out, it has just come out *ou* been published; **~ un communiqué** to release a statement (**au sujet de** about)

publiphone® [pyblifɔn] NM public telephone, payphone; **~ à carte** card phone

publipostage [pyblipɔstaʒ] NM mailshot, mass mailing

publiquement [pyblikmɑ̃] ADV publicly; **le ministre a exprimé ~ son désaccord** the minister went on the record to express his disagreement, the minister publicly expressed his disagreement; **le président a dû intervenir ~** the president had to issue a public statement

publireportage [pybliʀ(ə)pɔʀtaʒ] NM special advertising feature, advertorial (*US*)

puce [pys] **1** NF **a** (*Zool*) flea; **~ de mer** *ou* **de sable** sand flea; **~ d'eau** water flea; **ça m'a mis la ~ à l'oreille** that started *ou* got me thinking; **le marché aux ~s ◊ les ~s** the flea market; **oui, ma ~⁎** yes, pet⁎; (*fig*) **c'est une petite ~** she's a tiny little thing; **être agité** *ou* **excité comme une ~** to be all excited → **sac¹,**

secouer [b] **jeu de ~s** tiddlywinks; **jouer aux ~s** to play tiddlywinks [c] (*Ordin*) (silicon) chip; **~ électronique** microchip; **~ mémoire** memory chip [2] ADJ INV (= *couleur*) puce

puceau* (*pl* puceaux) [pyso] [1] ADJ M **être ~** to be a virgin [2] NM virgin

pucelage* [pys(ə)laʒ] NM virginity

pucelle††* [pysɛl] (*hum*) [1] ADJ F **être ~** to be a virgin; **elle n'est plus ~** she has lost her virginity, she's not a virgin [2] NF virgin, maid(en) (*littér*); (*Hist*) **la Pucelle d'Orléans** the Maid of Orleans

puceron [pys(ə)ʀɔ̃] NM aphid, greenfly; **~ cendré** blackfly

pucier* [pysje] NM bed

pudding [pudiŋ] NM *close-textured fruit sponge*

puddlage [pydlaʒ] NM puddling

pudeur [pydœʀ] NF [a] (*concernant le corps*) modesty; **elle a beaucoup de ~** she has a keen sense of modesty; **elle est sans ~** ◊ **elle n'a aucune ~** she has no modesty, she's quite shameless; **expliquer qch sans fausse ~** to explain sth without undue prudery *ou* quite openly; **il parle de sa maladie sans fausse ~** he talks about his illness quite openly → **attentat, outrage** [b] (= *délicatesse*) sense of propriety *ou* decency; **agir sans ~** to act with no regard to propriety; **il aurait pu avoir la ~ de ne pas en parler** he could have had the decency not to talk about it

pudibond, e [pydibɔ̃, ɔ̃d] ADJ (excessively) prudish, prim and proper

pudibonderie [pydibɔ̃dʀi] NF (excessive) prudishness, (excessive) primness

pudicité [pydisite] NF (*littér*) (= *chasteté*) modesty; (= *discrétion*) discretion

pudique [pydik] ADJ [a] (= *chaste*) [*personne, geste*] modest [b] (= *discret*) [*allusion*] discreet; **un terme ~ pour désigner ...** a nice way of saying ..., a euphemism for ...

pudiquement [pydikmɑ̃] ADV [a] (= *chastement*) modestly [b] (= *avec tact*) discreetly; **ils détournaient les yeux ~** they looked away discreetly *ou* out of a sense of decency [c] (= *par euphémisme*) discreetly; **cela désigne ~ ...** it's a nice way of saying ..., it's a euphemism for ...

puer [pɥe] ▸ conjug 1 ◂ [1] VI to stink; **il pue des pieds** his feet stink, he has smelly feet; **il pue de la gueule** his breath stinks; **ça pue !** it stinks! [2] VT to stink *ou* reek of; **ça pue l'argent** it reeks ou stinks of money

puériculteur, -trice [pɥeʀikyltœʀ, tʀis] NM,F (*dans un hôpital*) paediatric (*Brit*) *ou* pediatric (*US*) nurse; (*dans une crèche*) nursery nurse

puériculture [pɥeʀikyltyʀ] NF (*gén*) infant care; (*dans une crèche*) nursery nursing; (*en pédiatrie*) paediatric (*Brit*) *ou* pediatric (*US*) nursing; **donner des cours de ~ aux mamans** to give courses on infant care to mothers

puéril, e [pɥeʀil] ADJ puerile, childish

puérilement [pɥeʀilmɑ̃] ADV childishly

puérilité [pɥeʀilite] NF (= *caractère*) puerility, childishness; (= *acte*) childish behaviour (*Brit*) *ou* behavior (*US*) (*NonC*)

puerpéral, e (*mpl* **-aux**) [pɥeʀpeʀal, o] ADJ puerperal

pugilat [pyʒila] NM (fist) fight

pugiliste [pyʒilist] NM (*littér*) pugilist (*littér*)

pugilistique [pyʒilistik] ADJ (*littér*) pugilistic (*littér, frm*)

pugnace [pygnas] ADJ pugnacious

pugnacité [pygnasite] NF (*littér*) pugnacity

puîné, e† [pɥine] [1] ADJ (= *de deux*) younger; (= *de plusieurs*) youngest [2] NM,F (*de deux*) younger brother (*ou* sister); (*de plusieurs*) youngest brother (*ou* sister)

puis [pɥi] ADV (= *ensuite*) then; (*dans une énumération*) then, next; (= *en outre*) **et ~** and besides; **et ~ ensuite** *ou* **après** and then, and af-

ter that; **et ~ c'est tout** and that's all *ou* that's it *ou* that's all there is to it; **il est parti, et ~ voilà !** off he went, and that was that!; **et ~ après tout** and after all; **et ~ après ?** (= *ensuite*) and what next?, and then (what)?; (= *et alors ?*) so what?*, what of it?; **et ~ quoi ?** (= *quoi d'autre*) well, what?, and then what?; (= *et alors ?*) so what?*, what of it?; **et ~ quoi encore ?** (= *tu exagères*) whatever next?

puisage [pɥizaʒ] NM drawing (of water)

puisard [pɥizaʀ] NM (*gén*) cesspool, sink; (*Naut*) well; (*Min*) sump

puisatier [pɥizatje] NM well-digger

puiser [pɥize] ▸ conjug 1 ◂ VT [+ *eau*] to draw (**dans** from); [+ *exemple, renseignement, inspiration*] to draw, take (**dans** from); **les deux auteurs ont puisé aux mêmes sources** the two authors drew on the same sources; **~ dans son sac/ses économies** to dip into one's bag/one's savings; **j'ai dû ~ dans mes réserves pour finir la course** I had to draw on my reserves to finish the race

▼ **puisque** [pɥisk(ə)] CONJ [a] (= *du moment que*) since, seeing that; **ces animaux sont donc des mammifères, puisqu'ils allaitent leurs petits** these animals are therefore mammals, seeing that *ou* since they suckle their young; **ça doit être vrai, puisqu'il le dit** it must be true since he says so [b] (= *comme*) as, since, seeing that; **~ vous êtes là, venez m'aider** as *ou* since *ou* seeing that you're here come and help me; **ces escrocs, puisqu'il faut les appeler ainsi ...** these crooks — as *ou* since one must call them that ...; **son échec, ~ échec il y a ...** his failure, given that he has indeed failed..., his failure, seeing as that is what it amounts to...; **~ c'est comme ça, je ne viendrai plus !** if that's how it is, I won't come anymore! [c] (*valeur intensive*) **~ je te le dis !** I'm telling you (so)!; **~ je te dis que c'est vrai !** I'm telling you it's true!

puissamment [pɥisamɑ̃] ADV (= *fortement*) powerfully; (= *beaucoup*) greatly; (*iro*) **~ raisonné !** what brilliant reasoning! (*iro*)

puissance [pɥisɑ̃s] [1] NF [a] (= *force*) [*armée, muscle, impulsion*] power, strength; [*vent*] strength, force [b] (*Élec, Phys*) power; [*microscope*] (magnifying) power; [*moteur, voiture, haut-parleur*] power; **~ en watts** wattage; **~ de sortie** [*chaîne hifi*] output; (*Ordin*) **~ de calcul/de traitement** computing/processing power *ou* capacity; **modifier la ~ de l'éclairage** to adjust the lighting; (*Aut*) **~ effective** *ou* **au frein d'un moteur** engine power output; **bombe de forte ~** powerful *ou* high-powered bomb; **bombe de faible ~** low-power bomb; **la ~ de destruction de ce missile** this missile's destructive potential [c] (= *capacité*) power; **la ~ d'évocation de la musique** the evocative power of music; **une grande ~ de séduction/suggestion** great seductive/suggestive power(s), great powers of seduction/suggestion; **la ~ d'attraction de la capitale** the pull of the capital; **grâce à la ~ de sa volonté** thanks to his willpower *ou* his strength of will; **avoir une grande ~ de travail** to have a great capacity for work; **avoir une grande ~ d'imagination** to have a very powerful imagination *ou* great powers of imagination [d] (= *pouvoir*) [*classe sociale, pays, argent*] power; **l'or/le pétrole est une ~** gold/oil confers power; **les ~s qui agissent sur le monde** the powers that influence the world [e] (*Pol*) power; **grande ~** major *ou* great power, superpower; **la première ~ économique/nucléaire mondiale** the world's leading economic/nuclear power [f] (*Math*) power; **élever un nombre à la ~ 10** to raise a number to the power of 10; **10 ~ 4** 10 to the power of 4, 10 to the 4th

[g] (*Jur, hum*) **être en ~ de mari** to be under a husband's authority [2] **en puissance** LOC ADJ, LOC ADV [a] (*délinquant, dictateur*) potential; **l'homme est en ~ dans l'enfant** the man is latent in the child; **exister en ~** to have a potential existence; **c'est là en ~** it is potentially present [b] **monter en ~** [*idée, théorie*] to gain ground; **montée en ~** [*pays, mouvement, personne*] increase in power; [*secteur*] increase in importance [3] COMP ▸ **puissance administrative** (*Aut*) engine rating ▸ **les puissances d'argent** the forces of money ▸ **puissance de feu** (*Mil*) fire power ▸ **puissance fiscale** = **puissance administrative** ▸ **puissance au frein** (*Aut*) brake horsepower ▸ **puissance maritale** (*Jur*) marital rights ▸ **les puissances occultes** unseen *ou* hidden powers ▸ **puissance paternelle** (*Jur*) parental rights *ou* authority; **exercer/être déchu de sa ~ paternelle** to exercise/have lost one's parental rights ▸ **la puissance publique** the public authorities ▸ **les puissances des ténèbres** the powers of darkness

puissant, e [pɥisɑ̃, ɑ̃t] [1] ADJ (*gén*) powerful; [*drogue, remède*] potent, powerful [2] NM **les ~s** the mighty *ou* powerful

puits [pɥi] [1] NM [*eau, pétrole*] well; (*Min*) shaft; (*Constr*) well, shaft; (*fig*) **c'est un ~ sans fond** it's a bottomless pit [2] COMP ▸ **puits d'aérage** *ou* **d'aération** ventilation shaft ▸ **puits d'amour** ≈ cream puff ▸ **puits artésien** artesian well ▸ **puits à ciel ouvert** (*Min*) opencast mine ▸ **puits d'érudition** (*fig*) = **puits de science** ▸ **puits d'extraction** winding shaft ▸ **puits de jour** *ou* **de lumière** (*Constr*) light shaft ▸ **puits de mine** mine shaft ▸ **puits perdu** cesspool, sink ▸ **puits de pétrole** oil well ▸ **puits de science** (*fig*) fount of knowledge

pull [pyl] NM pullover, sweater, jumper (*Brit*); **~ chaussette** skinnyrib sweater

pullman [pulman] NM Pullman (car)

pull-over (*pl* **pull-overs**) [pylɔvɛʀ] NM pullover, sweater, jumper (*Brit*)

pullulation [pylylasjɔ̃] NF, **pullulement** [pylylmɑ̃] NM (= *action*) proliferation; (= *profusion*) [*insectes*] multitude; [*insectes volants*] swarm, multitude

pulluler [pylyle] ▸ conjug 1 ◂ VI (= *se reproduire*) to proliferate, multiply, pullulate (*frm*); (= *grouiller*) to swarm, pullulate (*frm*); [*erreurs, contrefaçons*] to abound, pullulate (*frm*); **la ville pullule de touristes** the town is swarming with tourists; **la rivière pullule de truites** the river is teeming with trout

pulmonaire [pylmɔnɛʀ] ADJ [*maladie*] pulmonary, lung (*épith*); [*artère*] pulmonary; **congestion ~** congestion of the lungs

pulpe [pylp] NF [*fruit, dent, bois*] pulp; [*doigt*] pad; **boisson/yaourt à la ~ de fruits** real fruit drink/yoghurt

pulpeux, -euse [pylpø, øz] ADJ [*fruit*] pulpy; [*lèvres*] full, fleshy; [*femme*] curvaceous

pulsar [pylsaʀ] NM pulsar

pulsation [pylsasjɔ̃] NF (*Méd*) [*cœur, pouls*] beating (*NonC*), beat, pulsation (*SPÉC*); (*Phys*) pulsation; (*Élec*) pulsatance; **~s (du cœur)** (= *rythme cardiaque*) heartbeat; (= *battements*) heartbeats

pulsé [pylse] ADJ M **chauffage à air ~** forced air heating

pulsion [pylsjɔ̃] NF (*Psych*) drive, urge; **la ~ sexuelle** the sex drive; **~s sexuelles** sexual urges; **~ de mort** death wish; **~ meurtrière/suicidaire** murderous/suicidal impulse; **~ de vie** life instinct

pulsionnel, -elle [pylsjɔnɛl] ADJ [*comportement*] instinctual; **réaction pulsionnelle** impulsive reaction

▸ GRAMMAIRE ACTIVE: **puisque**   44.1

pulvérisable [pylvɛʀizabl] ADJ [+ *liquide, médicament*] in spray form

pulvérisateur [pylvɛʀizatœʀ] NM (*à parfum*) spray, atomizer; (*à peinture*) spray; (*pour médicament*) spray, vaporizer; (*Agr*) **~ d'insecticide** (crop) duster

pulvérisation [pylvɛʀizasjɔ̃] NF [a] (= *broyage*) pulverizing, pulverization [b] (= *vaporisation*) spraying; (*Méd*) **« trois ~s dans chaque narine »** "spray three times into each nostril"; **le médecin a ordonné des ~s (nasales)** the doctor prescribed a nasal spray [c] (= *anéantissement*) [*adversaire*] pulverizing, demolishing; * [*record*] smashing*, shattering*; [*argument*] demolition, demolishing

pulvériser [pylvɛʀize] ▶conjug 1◀ VT [a] (= *broyer*) to pulverize, reduce to powder [b] [+ *liquide, insecticide*] to spray; **~ des insecticides sur un champ** to spray a field with insecticides [c] (= *anéantir*) [+ *adversaire*] to pulverize, demolish; * [+ *record*] to smash*, shatter*; [+ *argument*] to demolish, pull to pieces; **bâtiment pulvérisé par l'explosion** building reduced to rubble by the explosion

pulvériseur [pylvɛʀizœʀ] NM disc harrow

pulvérulence [pylvɛʀylɑ̃s] NF pulverulence

pulvérulent, e [pylvɛʀylɑ̃, ɑ̃t] ADJ pulverulent

puma [pyma] NM puma, cougar, mountain lion

punaise [pynɛz] NF [a] (*Zool*) bug; **~ d'eau** water stick insect; (*péj*) **c'est une vraie ~** he's a real mischief-maker; **~ !*** well!, blimey!* (*Brit*), gee!* (*US*); (*péj*) **~ de sacristie*** churchy woman [b] (= *clou*) drawing pin (*Brit*), thumbtack (*US*)

punaiser [pyneze] ▶conjug 1◀ VT to pin up (*ou* down *ou* on *etc*); **~ une affiche au mur** to pin up a poster, pin a poster up on the wall

punch¹ [pɔ̃ʃ] NM (= *boisson*) punch

punch² [pœnʃ] NM [a] (= *énergie*) punch; **avoir du ~** [*personne*] to have lots of drive, have a lot of get up and go; [*slogan*] to be catchy* *ou* punchy*; [*cheveux*] to have lots of bounce; **pour donner du ~ à vos cheveux** to give new life to your hair; **manquer de ~** [*personne*] to lack dynamism *ou* drive; [*entreprise, économie*] to lack dynamism; **cette mise en scène manque de ~** the production isn't punchy* enough [b] (*Boxe*) punching ability; **avoir du ~** to pack *ou* have a good punch

puncheur [pœnʃœʀ] NM good puncher, hard hitter

punching-ball (*pl* **punching-balls**) [pœnʃiŋbol] NM punching bag, punchbag (*Brit*), punchball; (*fig*) **je lui sers de ~** he uses me as a punching bag

punique [pynik] ADJ Punic

punir [pyniʀ] ▶conjug 2◀ VT [a] [+ *criminel, enfant*] to punish (**pour** for); **être puni de prison/de mort** to be sentenced to prison/to death [b] (= *faire souffrir*) to punish; **il a été puni de son imprudence** he was punished for his recklessness, he suffered for his recklessness; **tu as été malade, ça te punira de ta gourmandise** you've been ill — that'll teach you not to be greedy; **il est orgueilleux, et l'en voilà bien puni** he's paying the penalty for *ou* being made to suffer for his pride; **il est puni par où il a péché** he has got his (just) deserts, he's paying for his sins [c] (= *sanctionner*) [+ *faute, infraction, crime*] to punish; **tout abus sera puni (de prison)** all abuses are punishable *ou* will be punished (by prison); **ce crime est puni par la loi/puni de mort** this crime is punishable by law/punishable by death

punissable [pynisabl] ADJ punishable (**de** by)

punitif, -ive [pynitif, iv] ADJ **action punitive** punitive action (*NonC*); **expédition punitive** [*armée, rebelles*] punitive expedition *ou* raid; [*criminels, gang*] revenge killing

punition [pynisjɔ̃] NF punishment (**de qch** for sth); (*Scol*) **avoir une ~** to be given a punish-

ment; **~ corporelle** corporal punishment (*NonC*); **en ~ de ses fautes** as a punishment for his mistakes; **pour ta ~** as a punishment

punk [pœ̃k] ADJ INV, NMF punk

pupille¹ [pypij] NF (*Anat*) pupil

pupille² [pypij] NMF (= *enfant*) ward; **~ de l'État** child in (local authority) care; **~ de la Nation** war orphan

pupitre [pypitʀ] NM (*Scol*) desk; (*Rel*) lectern; (*Mus*) [*musicien*] music stand; [*piano*] music rest; [*chef d'orchestre*] rostrum; (*Ordin*) console; (*Mus*) **au ~, Henri Dupont** at the rostrum — Henri Dupont, conducting — Henri Dupont; (*Mus*) **chef de ~** head of section

pupitreur, -euse [pypitʀœʀ, øz] NM,F (*Ordin*) system operator

pur, e [pyʀ] [1] ADJ [a] (= *sans mélange*) [*alcool, eau, race, métal*] pure; [*vin*] undiluted; [*whisky, gin*] neat, straight; [*ciel*] clear; [*voyelle*] pure; [*diamant*] flawless; **~ fruit** [*confiture*] real fruit (*épith*); **~ beurre** [*sablé*] all butter; **~ porc** [*saucisson*] pure pork; **~e laine** pure wool; **c'est un communiste/capitaliste ~ jus** *ou* **sucre** he's a dyed-in-the-wool communist/capitalist; **c'est un Parisien ~ jus** *ou* **sucre** he's a Parisian through and through *ou* to the core; **c'est du Woody Allen ~ jus** it's stock Woody Allen; **un ~ produit de la bourgeoisie** a pure product of the middle class; **un Australien de ~e souche** an Australian born and bred; **boire son vin ~** to drink one's wine without water *ou* undiluted; (*Chim*) **à l'état ~** in the pure state; **l'air ~ de la campagne** the pure *ou* fresh country air → **esprit, pur-sang** [b] (= *théorique*) [*science, mathématiques*] pure [c] (= *innocent*) [*âme, cœur, intentions, pensées*] pure; [*personne*] pure, pure-hearted; [*conscience*] clear; [*regard*] frank [d] (= *parfait*) [*style*] pure; (= *limpide*) [*voix*] pure, clear; **un visage d'un ovale très ~** a perfectly oval face; **elle parle un français très ~** she speaks very pure French [e] (= *exact, strict*) pure, sheer; **c'est de la folie ~e** it's pure *ou* sheer *ou* utter madness; **c'est de la poésie/de l'imagination toute ~e** it's pure *ou* sheer poetry/imagination; **c'est de l'insubordination ~e et simple** it's insubordination pure and simple; **c'était du racisme ~ et simple** *ou* **à l'état ~** it was straight *ou* plain racism; **ils réclament la suppression ~e et simple de la loi** they're quite simply asking for the law to be withdrawn; **il ne s'agit pas d'une ~e et simple déclaration publique** it's not just *ou* it's not purely and simply a public statement; **cela relève de la ~e fiction** it's pure fiction; **il a dit cela par ~e méchanceté** he said that out of pure spite; **œuvre de ~e imagination** work of pure imagination; **c'est une question de ~e forme** it's merely *ou* purely a question of form; **c'est par ~ hasard que je l'ai vu** I saw it by sheer chance *ou* purely by chance; **c'est la ~e vérité** it's the plain *ou* simple (unadulterated) truth; **en ~e perte** for absolutely nothing, fruitlessly; **il a travaillé en ~e perte** absolutely nothing came of his work, his work was fruitless; **par ~e ignorance** out of sheer ignorance; (*Pol*) **~ et dur** hard-line

[2] NM,F (*Pol*) **~ (et dur)** hard-liner

purée [pyʀe] NF **~ (de pommes de terre)** mashed potato(es); **~ de marrons/de tomates** chestnut/tomato purée; (*fig*) **c'est de la ~ de pois** it's murky fog *ou* a peasouper* (*Brit*); **être dans la ~*** to be in a real mess*; **~, je l'ai oublié !*** darn (it)* *ou* sugar*, I forgot!

purement [pyʀmɑ̃] ADV purely; **~ et simplement** purely and simply

pureté [pyʀte] NF [a] (*Chim*) [*métal, substance*] purity [b] (= *perfection*) [*traits*] perfection; [*style*] purity; [*air, eau, son*] purity, pureness; [*voix*] purity, clarity; [*diamant*] flawlessness [c] (= *innocence*) [*âme, cœur, personne, inten-*

tions, pensées] purity; [*conscience*] clearness; [*regard*] frankness

purgatif, -ive [pyʀɡatif, iv] [1] ADJ purgative [2] NM purgative, purge

purgation [pyʀɡasjɔ̃] NF (*Méd*) (= *action*) purgation; (= *remède*) purgative, purge

purgatoire [pyʀɡatwaʀ] NM (*Rel, fig*) purgatory; **elle a déjà fait son ~** she's already done her penance

purge [pyʀʒ] NF (*Méd*) purge, purgative; (*Pol*) purge; (*Tech*) [*conduite*] flushing out, draining; [*freins, radiateur*] bleeding

purger [pyʀʒe] ▶conjug 3◀ [1] VT [a] (= *vidanger*) [+ *conduite, radiateur*] to bleed, flush (out), drain; [+ *circuit hydraulique, freins*] to bleed [b] (*Méd*) to purge, give a purgative to [c] (*Jur*) [+ *peine*] to serve [d] (= *débarrasser*) to purge, cleanse, rid (**de** of) [2] **se purger** VPR to take a purgative *ou* purge

purgeur [pyʀʒœʀ] NM [*tuyauterie*] drain-cock, tap (*Brit*); [*radiateur*] bleed-tap

purifiant, e [pyʀifjɑ̃, jɑ̃t] ADJ purifying, cleansing

purificateur, -trice [pyʀifikatœʀ, tʀis] [1] ADJ purifying, cleansing, purificatory [2] NM (= *appareil*) (air) purifier

purification [pyʀifikasjɔ̃] NF [*air, liquide, langue*] purification, purifying; [*métal*] refinement; [*âme*] cleansing, purging; **~ ethnique** ethnic cleansing; (*Rel*) **la Purification** the Purification

purificatoire [pyʀifikatwaʀ] ADJ (*littér*) purificatory, purifying, cleansing

purifier [pyʀifje] ▶conjug 7◀ [1] VT (*gén*) to purify, cleanse; [+ *air, langue, liquide*] to purify; [+ *métal*] to refine; (*littér*) [+ *âme*] to cleanse, purge; **~ l'atmosphère** (*lit*) to purify the atmosphere *ou* air; (*fig*) to clear the air [2] **se purifier** VPR to cleanse o.s.

purin [pyʀɛ̃] NM slurry

purisme [pyʀism] NM purism

puriste [pyʀist] ADJ, NMF purist

puritain, e [pyʀitɛ̃, ɛn] [1] ADJ puritan(ical); (*Hist*) Puritan [2] NM,F puritan; (*Hist*) Puritan

puritanisme [pyʀitanism] NM puritanism; (*Hist*) Puritanism

purpurin, e [pyʀpyʀɛ̃, in] ADJ (*littér*) crimson

pur-sang [pyʀsɑ̃] NM INV thoroughbred, purebred

purulence [pyʀylɑ̃s] NF purulence, purulency

purulent, e [pyʀylɑ̃, ɑ̃t] ADJ purulent

pus [py] NM pus

pusillanime [pyzi(l)lanim] ADJ (*littér*) pusillanimous (*littér*), fainthearted

pusillanimité [pyzi(l)lanimite] NF (*littér*) pusillanimity (*littér*), faintheartedness

pustule [pystyl] NF pustule

pustuleux, -euse [pystylø, øz] ADJ pustular

putain [pytɛ̃] NF [a] (= *prostituée*) whore, hooker*, hustler* (*US*); (= *fille facile*) slut*, slag* (*Brit*); **faire la ~*** (*lit*) to be a whore *ou* hooker* *ou* hustler* (*US*), turn tricks* (*US*); (*fig*) to sell one's soul, sell out* [b] (*en exclamation*) **~ !** bloody hell!* (*Brit*), goddammit!* (*US*); (*intensif*) **cette ~ de guerre** this bloody* (*Brit*) awful *ou* goddamn* (*US*) war; **ce ~ de réveil !** that bloody* (*Brit*) *ou* goddamn* (*US*) alarm clock!; **quel ~ de vent !** this fucking** wind!, this bloody* (*Brit*) awful wind!

putassier, -ière* [pytasje, jɛʀ] ADJ [a] [*personne, mœurs*] sluttish; [*maquillage, tenue*] sluttish, tarty*; **avoir un langage ~** to swear like a trooper, be foul-mouthed [b] (= *servile*) **comportement ~** bootlicking, arse-licking** (*Brit*), ass-licking** (*US*)

putatif, -ive [pytatif, iv] ADJ putative, presumed; **père ~** putative father

pute* [pyt] NF whore, hooker*, hustler* (*US*)

putois [pytwa] NM (= *animal*) polecat; (= *fourrure*) fitch; **crier comme un ~** to shout *ou* scream one's head off (in protest), scream *ou* yell blue murder* (*Brit*)

putréfaction [pytʀefaksjɔ̃] NF putrefaction; **cadavre en ~** body in a state of putrefaction, putrefying *ou* rotting body

putréfiable [pytʀefjabl] ADJ putrefiable

putréfier [pytʀefje] ▸conjug 7◂ ① VT to putrefy, rot ② **se putréfier** VPR to putrefy, rot, go rotten

putrescence [pytʀesɑ̃s] NF putrescence

putrescent, e [pytʀesɑ̃, ɑ̃t] ADJ putrescent

putrescible [pytʀesibl] ADJ putrescible

putride [pytʀid] ADJ putrid

putridité [pytʀidite] NF putridity, putridness

putsch [putʃ] NM putsch

putschiste [putʃist] NM putschist

puvathérapie [pyvateʀapi] NF PUVA treatment *ou* therapy

puzzle [pœzl] NM (*lit*) jigsaw (puzzle); (*fig*) jigsaw; **faire un ~** to do a jigsaw; (*fig*) **reconstituer le ~** ◊ **rassembler toutes les pièces du ~** to fit *ou* put the pieces of the jigsaw together again

p.-v.* [peve] NM (ABRÉV = **procès-verbal**) (*Aut*) (*gén*) fine; (*pour stationnement interdit*) (parking) ticket; (*pour excès de vitesse*) speeding ticket; **je me suis pris un ~** I got a ticket, I got booked (*Brit*)

PVC [pevese] NM INV (ABRÉV = **polyvinyl chloride**) PVC; **en (plastique) ~** PVC (*épith*)

pygargue [pigaʀg] NM white-tailed eagle

Pygmalion [pigmaljɔ̃] NM Pygmalion; **il a voulu jouer les ~s avec elle** he wanted to be her Pygmalion

pygmée [pigme] ADJ, NMF pygmy, pigmy; (*péj*) **c'est un vrai ~** he's a dwarf

pyjama [piʒama] NM pyjamas, pajamas (*US*); **il était en ~(s)** he was in his pyjamas; **acheter un ~** to buy a pair of pyjamas, buy some pyjamas; **deux ~s** two pairs of pyjamas → **veste**

pylône [pilon] NM pylon; **~ électrique** electricity pylon

pylore [pilɔʀ] NM pylorus

pylorique [pilɔʀik] ADJ pyloric

Pyongyang [pjɔ̃ŋjɑ̃] N Pyongyang

pyorrhée [pjɔʀe] NF pyorrhoea, pyorrhea

pyralène® [piʀalen] NM Pyralene®

pyramidal, e (*mpl* **-aux**) [piʀamidal, o] ADJ pyramid-shaped, pyramid-like, pyramidal (*SPÉC*)

pyramide [piʀamid] NF (*Anat, Archit, Géom, fig*) pyramid; **~ inversée** inverted pyramid; **~ humaine** human pyramid; **~ des âges** population pyramid; (*Anat*) **~s rénales** *ou* **de Malpighi** Malpighian pyramids; **structure/organisation en ~** pyramidal structure/organization

Pyrénées [piʀene] NFPL **les ~** the Pyrenees

pyrex® [piʀɛks] NM Pyrex®; **assiette en ~** Pyrex dish

pyrite [piʀit] NF pyrites

pyrograver [piʀogʀave] ▸conjug 1◂ VT to do pyrography *ou* poker-work

pyrograveur, -euse [piʀogʀavœʀ, øz] NM,F pyrographer

pyrogravure [piʀogʀavyʀ] NF (*Art*) pyrography, poker-work; (= *objet*) pyrograph

pyrolyse [piʀɔliz] NF pyrolysis

pyromane [piʀoman] NMF (*Méd*) pyromaniac; (*gén, Jur*) arsonist, fire raiser

pyromanie [piʀomani] NF pyromania

pyromètre [piʀomɛtʀ] NM pyrometer

pyrométrie [piʀometʀi] NF pyrometry

pyrométrique [piʀometʀik] ADJ pyrometric

pyrotechnie [piʀotɛkni] NF pyrotechnics *sg*, pyrotechny

pyrotechnique [piʀotɛknik] ADJ pyrotechnic

Pyrrhon [piʀɔ̃] NM Pyrrho

pyrrhonien, -ienne [piʀɔnjɛ̃, jɛn] ① ADJ Pyrrhonic, Pyrrhonian ② NM,F Pyrrhonist, Pyrrhonian

pyrrhonisme [piʀɔnism] NM Pyrrhonism

Pyrrhus [piʀys] NM Pyrrhus → **victoire**

Pythagore [pitagɔʀ] NM Pythagoras

pythagoricien, -ienne [pitagɔʀisjɛ̃, jɛn] ADJ, NM,F Pythagorean

pythagorique [pitagɔʀik] ADJ Pythagorean

Pythie [piti] NF ⓐ (*Antiq*) **la ~** (*de Delphes*) the Pythia ⓑ **pythie** (= *devineresse*) prophetess; **jouer la pythie** to be a seer *ou* soothsayer

python [pitɔ̃] NM python

pythonisse [pitɔnis] NF prophetess

Q

Q, q [ky] NM (= *lettre*) Q, q; **fièvre Q** Q fever

qat [kat] NM = **khat**

Qatar [katar] NM Qatar

qatari, e [katari] 1 ADJ Qatari 2 **Qatari(e)** NM,F Qatari; **les Qatari** Qataris

qch (ABRÉV = **quelque chose**) sth

QCM [kyseem] NM (ABRÉV = **questionnaire à choix multiple**) → **questionnaire**

QF [kyɛf] NM (ABRÉV = **quotient familial**) → **quotient**

QG [kyʒe] NM (ABRÉV = **quartier général**) HQ

QHS † [kyaʃes] NM (ABRÉV = **quartier de haute sécurité**) → **quartier**

QI [kyi] NM (ABRÉV = **quotient intellectuel**) IQ

qn (ABRÉV = **quelqu'un**) sb

qq ABRÉV = **quelque**

qu' [k] → **que**

quadra* [k(w)adra] NMF (ABRÉV = **quadragénaire**) (*Pol*) up-and-coming politician (*in his or her early forties*)

quadragénaire [k(w)adraʒenɛr] 1 ADJ = (*de quarante ans*) forty-year-old (*épith*); (= *de quarante à cinquante ans*) **il est** ~ he's in his forties; (*hum*) **maintenant que tu es** ~ now that you're forty (years old), now that you've reached forty 2 NMF forty-year-old man (*ou* woman)

Quadragésime [kwadraʒezim] NF Quadragesima

quadrangle [k(w)adrɑ̃gl] NM (*Géom*) quadrangle

quadrangulaire [k(w)adrɑ̃gylɛr] ADJ quadrangular

quadrant [kadrɑ̃] NM quadrant

quadrature [k(w)adratyr] NF (*gén*) quadrature; (*Math*) ~ **du cercle** quadrature *ou* squaring of the circle; (*fig*) **c'est la** ~ **du cercle** it's like trying to square the circle, it's attempting the impossible

quadriceps [k(w)adrisɛps] NM quadriceps

quadrichromie [k(w)adrikrɔmi] NF four-colour (printing) process

quadriennal, e (*mpl* **-aux**) [k(w)adrijenal, o] ADJ four-year (*épith*), quadrennial; **assolement** ~ four-year rotation

quadrige [k(w)adriʒ] NM quadriga

quadrijumeaux [k(w)adriʒymo] ADJ MPL → **tubercule**

quadrilatéral, e (*mpl* **-aux**) [k(w)adrilateral, o] ADJ quadrilateral

quadrilatère [k(w)adrilatɛr] NM (*Géom, Mil*) quadrilateral

quadrilingue [k(w)adrilɛ̃g] ADJ quadrilingual

quadrillage [kadrijaʒ] NM a [= *dessin*) [*papier*] square pattern; [*tissu*] check pattern; [*rues*] criss-cross *ou* grid pattern *ou* layout b [*ville, pays*] (*gén*) covering; (*Mil, Police*) covering, control(ling); **la police a établi un** ~ **serré du quartier** the area is under close *ou* tight police control

quadrille [kadrij] NM (= *danse, danseurs*) quadrille; ~ **des lanciers** lancers

quadrillé, e [kadrije] (*ptp de* **quadriller**) ADJ [*papier, feuille*] squared

quadriller [kadrije] ▸ conjug 1 ◂ VT [+ *papier*] to mark out in squares; [+ *ville, pays*] (*gén*) to cover; (*Mil, Police*) to cover, control; **la ville est étroitement quadrillée par la police** the town is under close *ou* tight police control; **la ville est quadrillée par un réseau de rues** the town is criss-crossed by a network of streets

quadrillion [k(w)adriljɔ̃] NM quadrillion (*Brit*), septillion (*US*)

quadrimoteur [kadrimɔtœr] 1 ADJ M four-engined 2 NM four-engined plane

quadriparti, e [k(w)adriparti], **quadripartite** [k(w)adripartit] ADJ (*Bot*) quadripartite; (*Pol*) **conférence quadripartite** (*entre pays*) four-power conference; (*entre partis*) four-party conference

quadriphonie [k(w)adrifɔni] NF quadraphony

quadriphonique [k(w)adrifɔnik] ADJ quadraphonic

quadriréacteur [k(w)adrireaktœr] 1 ADJ M four-engined 2 NM four-engined jet *ou* plane

quadrisyllabe [k(w)adrisi(l)lab] NM quadrisyllable

quadrisyllabique [k(w)adrisi(l)labik] ADJ quadrisyllabic

quadrumane [k(w)adryman] 1 ADJ quadrumanous 2 NM quadrumane

quadrupède [k(w)adrypɛd] 1 ADJ fourfooted, quadruped 2 NM quadruped

quadruple [k(w)adrypl] 1 ADJ [*nombre, quantité, rangée*] quadruple; **une quantité ~ de l'autre** a quantity four times (as great as) the other; **en ~ exemplaire** in four copies; **la ~ championne d'Europe** the European champion four times over → **croche** 2 NM (*Math, gén*) quadruple; **je l'ai payé le ~/le ~ de l'autre** I paid four times as much for it/four times as much as the other for it; **augmenter qch au ~** to increase sth fourfold

quadrupler [k(w)adryple] ▸ conjug 1 ◂ VTI to quadruple, increase fourfold *ou* four times

quadruplés, -ées [k(w)adryple] (*ptp de* **quadrupler**) NM,F PL quadruplets, quads*

quadruplex [k(w)adryplɛks] NM (*Téléc*) quadruplex system

quai [ke] 1 NM (*port*) (*gén*) quay; (*pour marchandises*) wharf, quay; [*gare*] platform; [*rivière*] bank, embankment; (= *route*) riverside road; **droits de** ~ dockage, wharfage; **être à** ~ [*bateau*] to be alongside (the quay); [*train*] to be in (the station); **venir à** ~ [*bateau*] to berth; **sur les ~s de la Seine** on the banks *ou* embankments of the Seine → **accès, billet** 2 COMP ▸ **le Quai des Orfèvres** police headquarters (*in Paris*), ≈ (New) Scotland Yard (*Brit*), ≈ the FBI (*US*) ▸ **le Quai (d'Orsay)** *the French Foreign Office*

quaker, quakeresse [kwɛkœr, kwɛkrɛs] NM,F Quaker

quakerisme [kwɛkœrism] NM Quakerism

qualifiable [kalifjabl] ADJ a (*Sport*) [*équipe, joueur*] able to qualify b (*Jur*) **cet acte n'est pas juridiquement** ~ this act cannot be legally defined; (*fig*) **une telle conduite n'est pas** ~ such behaviour is beyond description *ou* defies description

qualifiant, e [kalifjɑ̃, jɑ̃t] ADJ [*formation*] leading to a qualification

qualificateur [kalifikatœr] NM (*Ling*) qualifier

qualificatif, -ive [kalifikatif, iv] 1 ADJ [*adjectif*] qualifying; (*Sport*) **épreuves qualificatives** qualifying heats *ou* rounds 2 NM (*Ling*) qualifier; (= *mot*) term; **ce produit mérite le ~ de révolutionnaire** this product deserves to be described as revolutionary

▼ **qualification** [kalifikasjɔ̃] NF a (*Sport*) **obtenir sa** ~ to qualify (**en, pour** for); **la ~ de notre équipe demeure incertaine** it's still not certain whether our team will qualify; **épreuves de** ~ qualifying heats *ou* rounds, qualifiers; **c'est le but de la** ~ this goal secures the team's qualification b (= *aptitude*) skill; (= *diplôme*) qualification; ~ **professionnelle** professional qualification; [*personne*] **sans** ~ (= *sans compétence*) unskilled; (= *sans diplômes*) unqualified; **ce travail demande un haut niveau de** ~ this is highly skilled work c (*Jur*) **la ~ d'homicide involontaire a été retenue contre lui** he was charged with manslaughter d (*Ling*) qualification e (= *nom*) label, description

qualifié, e [kalifje] (*ptp de* **qualifier**) ADJ a (= *compétent*) (*gén*) qualified; (*Ind*) [*emploi, main-d'œuvre, ouvrier*] skilled; **non** ~ [*emploi, main-d'œuvre, ouvrier*] unskilled; **emploi/ouvrier très** ~ highly skilled job/worker; **il n'est pas ~ pour ce poste/gérer le service** he isn't qualified for this post/to manage the department; **je ne suis pas ~ pour en parler** I'm not qualified to talk about it b (*Sport*) **les joueurs ~s pour la finale** the players who have qualified for the final, the qualifiers for the final c (*Jur*) [*vol, délit*] aggravated; (*fig*) **c'est du vol** ~ it's daylight robbery; **c'est de l'hypocrisie ~e** it's blatant hypocrisy

qualifier [kalifje] ▸ conjug 7 ◂ 1 VT a [+ *conduite, projet*] to describe (**de** as); **cet accord a été qualifié d'historique** this agreement has been described as historic; **sa maison qu'il qualifiait pompeusement (de) manoir** his house which he described pompously as a

manor; **~ qn de menteur** to call sb a liar
b (*Sport*) **~ une équipe** to ensure a team
qualifies **c** (*Ling*) to qualify **2 se qualifier**
VPR (*Sport*) to qualify (**pour** for); (*hum*) **il se
qualifie d'artiste** he describes himself as an
artist, he calls himself an artist

qualitatif, -ive [kalitatif, iv] ADJ qualitative

qualitativement [kalitativmã] ADV qualitatively

qualité [kalite] NF **a** [*marchandise*] quality; **la
~ de (la) vie** the quality of life; **de ~** [*article,
ouvrage, spectacle*] quality (*épith*); **de bonne/
mauvaise ~** of good *ou* high/bad *ou* poor quality; **produits de haute ~** high-quality products; **article de première ~** top-quality article,
article of the highest quality; **fruits de ~ supérieure** fruit of superior quality, superior-
quality fruit; (*Ordin*) **~ courrier** near letter
quality
b (*Ind: pour homologation*) quality; **service ~**
quality (control) department
c [*personne*] (= *vertu*) quality; (= *don*) skill; **~s
humaines/personnelles** human/personal qual-
ities; **ses ~s de cœur** his noble-heartedness;
~s professionnelles professional skills; **~s de
gestionnaire** management *ou* managerial
skills; **cette œuvre a de grandes ~s littéraires**
this work has great literary qualities
d (= *fonction*) position; **sa ~ de directeur** his
position as manager; **en sa ~ de maire** in his
capacity as mayor; **en (ma) ~ d'auteur/de
femme mariée** as an author/a married woman; **sa ~ d'étranger** his alien status; **la ~ de
Français** status as a French citizen; (*Admin*) **vos
nom, prénom et ~** surname, forename (*Brit*) *ou*
given name (*US*) and occupation; (*Jur*) **avoir ~
pour** to have authority to
e († = *noblesse*) quality; **les gens/un homme
de ~** people/a man of quality

qualiticien, -ienne [kalitisjɛ̃, jɛn] NM,F quality controller (*Brit*) *ou* controler (*US*)

quand [kã] **1** CONJ **a** (= *lorsque*) when; **~ ce
sera fini, nous irons prendre un café** when it's
finished we'll go and have a coffee; **sais-tu de
~ était sa dernière lettre ?** do you know when
his last letter was written? *ou* what was the
date of his last letter?; **~ je te le disais !** I told
you so!; **~ je pense que ...!** when I think that
...!, to think that ...!
b (= *alors que*) when; **pourquoi ne pas acheter une voiture ~ nous pouvons nous le
permettre ?** why not buy a car when we can
afford it?; **pourquoi vivre ici ~ tu pourrais avoir
une belle maison ?** why live here when you
could have a beautiful house?
c **~ bien même** even though *ou* if; **~ bien
même tu aurais raison, je n'irais pas** even
though *ou* even if you were right, I wouldn't
go → **même**
2 ADV when; **~ pars-tu ? ◊ ~ est-ce que tu
pars ? ◊ tu pars ~ ?*** when are you leaving?;
dis-moi ~ tu pars tell me when you're leaving
ou when you'll be leaving; **à ~ le voyage ?**
when are you going?; **c'est pour ~ ?** (*devoir*)
when is it due? *ou* for?; (*rendez-vous*) when is
it?; (*naissance*) when is it to be?; **ça date de
~ ?** (*événement*) when did it take place?; (*lettre*)
what's the date on it?, when was it written?
→ **depuis, importer², jusque**

quant [kã] ADV **~ à** (= *pour ce qui est de*) as for,
as to; (= *au sujet de*) as regards, regarding; **~ à
moi, je pense qu'il est fou** as far as I'm concerned, he's mad; **~ à moi, je pars** as for me,
I'm leaving; **à affirmer cela ...** as for stating
that ...; **je n'ai rien su ~ à ce qui s'est passé** I
knew nothing about *ou* of what happened; **~
à cela, tu peux en être sûr** you can be quite
sure about that; **~ à cela, je n'en sais rien** as to
that *ou* as regards that *ou* as far as that goes, I
know nothing about it

quanta [k(w)ãta] *pl de* **quantum**

quant-à-soi [kãtaswa] NM INV reserve; **il est**

---

resté sur *ou* **a gardé son ~** he kept his own
counsel

quantième [kãtjɛm] NM (*Admin*) day (*of the
month*)

quantifiable [kãtifjabl] ADJ quantifiable;
facteurs non ~s factors which cannot be
quantified, unquantifiable factors

quantificateur [kãtifikatœr] NM quantifier

quantification [kãtifikasjɔ̃] NF (*gén, Philo*)
quantification; (*Phys*) quantization

quantifier [kãtifje] ▸conjug 7◂ VT (*gén, Philo*)
to quantify; (*Phys*) to quantize

quantique [k(w)ãtik] **1** ADJ quantum (*épith*)
2 NF quantum physics

quantitatif, -ive [kãtitatif, iv] ADJ quantitative

quantitativement [kãtitativmã] ADV quantitatively

quantité [kãtite] NF **a** (= *nombre, somme*)
quantity, amount; **la ~ d'eau nécessaire à
l'organisme** the amount *ou* quantity of water
necessary for the body; **la ~ de gens qui ne
paient pas leurs impôts** the number of people
who don't pay their taxes; **quelle ~ de pétrole s'est déversée dans la mer ?** how much oil
was spilled into the sea?; **en ~s industrielles**
in vast quantities *ou* amounts; **en grande/
petite ~** in large/small quantities *ou*
amounts; **en ~ suffisante** in sufficient quantities
b (= *grand nombre*) **(une) ~ de** [+ *raisons,
personnes*] a great many, a lot of; **des ~s** *ou*
(une) ~ de gens croient que ... a great many
people *ou* a lot of people believe that ...; **~
d'indices révèlent que ...** many signs *ou* a
(great) number of signs indicate that ...; **il y a
des fruits en (grande) ~** fruit is in plentiful
supply; **il y a eu des accidents en ~** there have
been a great number of *ou* a lot of *ou* a great
many accidents; **du travail en ~** a great deal of
work
c (*Ling, Sci*) quantity; (*Sci*) **~ négligeable**
negligible quantity *ou* amount; (*fig*) **considérer qn comme ~ négligeable** to consider sb as
totally insignificant, consider sb of minimal
importance

quantum [k(w)ãtɔm] (*pl* **quanta** [k(w)ãta]) NM
(*Jur, Phys*) quantum; **la théorie des quanta**
quantum theory

quarantaine [karãtɛn] NF **a** (= *âge, nombre*)
about forty; *pour locutions voir* **soixantaine**
b (*Méd, Naut*) quarantine; **mettre en ~** (*lit*) [+
animal, malade, navire] to quarantine, put in
quarantine; (*fig = ostraciser*) [+ *personne*] to
blacklist, send to Coventry (*Brit*); [+ *pays*] to
blacklist → **pavillon**

quarante [karãt] ADJ INV, NM INV forty; **les
Quarante** the members of the French Academy;
un ~-cinq tours (= *disque*) a single, a forty-five;
pour autres locutions voir **soixante, an** ; →
ACADÉMIE

quarantenaire [karãtnɛr] **1** ADJ **a** (*période*)
forty-year (*épith*) **b** (*Méd, Naut*) quarantine
(*épith*) **2** NM (= *anniversaire*) fortieth anniversary

quarantième [karãtjɛm] ADJ, NMF fortieth;
(*Naut*) **les ~s rugissants** the Roaring Forties

quark [kwark] NM quark

quart [kar] **1** NM **a** (= *fraction*) quarter; (=
250 g) 250 g, ≈ half a pound; (= *250 ml*)
quarter litre; **un ~ de poulet** a quarter chick-
en; **un ~ de beurre** 250 g of butter; **un ~ de vin**
a quarter-litre carafe of wine; **un kilo/une livre
un ~** *ou* **et ~** a kilo/a pound and a quarter; **on
n'a pas fait le ~ du travail** we haven't done a
quarter of the work; **c'est réglé au ~ de poil***
it's finely *ou* perfectly tuned → **tiers, trois**
b (*Mil* = *gobelet*) beaker (*of 1/4 litre capacity*)
c (*dans le temps*) **~ d'heure** quarter of an
hour, quarter-hour (*surtout US*); **3 heures
moins le ~** (a) quarter to *ou* of (*US*) 3; **3 heures
et ~ ◊ 3 heures un ~** (a) quarter past *ou* after

(*US*) 3; **il est le ~/moins le ~** it's (a) quarter
past/(a) quarter to; **de ~ d'heure en ~ d'heure**
every quarter of an hour; **passer un mauvais
ou sale ~ d'heure** to have a bad *ou* hard time
of it; **il lui a fait passer un mauvais ~ d'heure**
he gave him a bad *ou* hard time; **~ d'heure
américain** lady's choice; **~ de seconde** (*lit*)
a quarter of a second; (*fig*) a split second; **en
un ~ de seconde** (*lit*) in a quarter of a second;
(*fig*) in no time at all; **un ~ de siècle** a quarter
of a century
d (*Naut*) watch; **être de ~** to keep the watch;
prendre le ~ to take the watch; **de ~** [*homme,
matelot*] on watch; **officier de ~** officer of the
watch; **petit ~** dogwatch; **grand ~** six-hour
watch
2 COMP ▸ **quart de cercle** quarter-circle
▸ **quarts de finale** quarter finals; **être en ~s
de finale** to be in the quarter finals ▸ **quart
de soupir** semiquaver rest (*Brit*), sixteenth
rest (*US*) ▸ **quart de ton** quarter tone
▸ **quart de tour** quarter turn; **donner un ~
de tour à un bouton de porte** to turn a knob
round a quarter of the way, give a knob a
quarter turn; **démarrer** *ou* **partir au ~ de tour**
[*engin*] to start (up) first time; * [*personne*] to
have a short fuse; **comprendre au ~ de tour***
to understand straight off*, be quick on the
uptake

quart-de-rond (*pl* **quarts-de-rond**) [kardərɔ̃]
NM ovolo, quarter round

quarte [k(w)art] **1** NF (*Escrime*) quarte;
(*Cartes*) quart; (*Mus*) fourth; (*Hist* = *deux pintes*)
quart **2** ADJ F → **fièvre**

quarté [k(w)arte] NM *French system of forecast
betting on four horses in a race*

quarteron, -onne [kartərɔ̃, ɔn] **1** NM,F (=
métis) quadroon **2** NM (*péj* = *groupe*) small *ou*
insignificant band, minor group

quartette [k(w)artet] NM (*Mus*) jazz
quartet(te)

quartier [kartje] **1** NM **a** [*ville*] (*Admin* = *division*) district, area; (*gén* = *partie*) neighbourhood (*Brit*), neighborhood (*US*), area; **le ~ chinois** Chinatown, the Chinese quarter *ou* area;
le ~ juif the Jewish quarter *ou* area; **les vieux
~s de la ville** the old part of the town; **les
gens du ~** local people, the people in the
neighbourhood; **vous êtes du ~ ?** do you live
around here?; **le ~ est/ouest de la ville** the
east/west end *ou* side of (the) town; **~
commerçant** shopping area *ou* district; **le ~
des affaires** the business district *ou* area; **le
Quartier latin** the Latin Quarter; **de ~** [*cinéma,
épicier*] local (*épith*); **association/maison de ~**
community association/centre; **la vie de ~**
community life → **bas¹, beau**
b (= *portion*) [*bœuf*] large piece, chunk; [*viande*] large
piece, chunk; [*fruit*] piece, segment; (*lit, fig*)
mettre en ~s to tear to pieces
c (*Astron, Hér*) quarter
d († = *grâce, pitié*) quarter †; **demander/faire
~** to ask for/give quarter; **ne pas faire de ~** to
give no quarter; **pas de ~ !** show no mercy!
e (*Mil*) **~(s)** quarters; **rentrer au(x) ~(s)** to return to quarters; **avoir ~(s) libre(s)** (*Mil*) to
have leave from barracks; [*élèves, touristes*] to
be free (for a few hours); (*lit, fig*) **prendre ses
~s d'hiver** to go into winter quarters; (*fig*)
c'est là que nous tenons nos ~s this is where
we have our headquarters
2 COMP ▸ **quartier général** (*Mil, fig*) headquarters; (*Mil*) **grand ~ général** general headquarters ▸ **quartier de haute sécurité,
quartier de sécurité renforcée** [*prison*]
high *ou* maximum *ou* top security wing
▸ **quartier de noblesse** (*lit*) degree of noble lineage (*representing one generation*); (*fig*)
avoir ses ~s de noblesse to be well established and respected, have earned one's colours ▸ **quartier réservé** red-light district

quartier-maître (*pl* **quartiers-maîtres**)
[kartjemɛtr] NM (*Naut*) ≈ leading seaman; **~**

de 1ère classe leading rating (*Brit*), petty officer third class (*US*)

quartile [kwaʀtil] NM quartile

quart-monde (*pl* **quarts-mondes**) [kaʀmɔ̃d] NM **le ~** the Fourth World

quarto [kwaʀto] ADV fourthly

quartz [kwaʀts] NM quartz

quartzite [kwaʀtsit] NM quartzite

quasar [kazaʀ] NM quasar

quasi¹ [kazi] NM (*Culin*) cut of meat from upper part of leg of veal

quasi² [kazi] ① ADV almost, nearly ② PRÉF near, quasi- (*surtout US*); **~-certitude/obscurité** near certainty/darkness; **~-monnaie** near money; **~-contrat** quasi-contract; (*Aviat*) **~-collision** near miss; **la ~-totalité des dépenses** almost all (of) the expenditure

quasi-délit (*pl* **quasi-délits**) [kazideli] NM (*Jur*) technical offence (*Brit*) *ou* offense (*US*)

quasiment [kazimɑ̃] ADV (*dans une affirmation*) practically; **c'est ~ fait** it's as good as done; **~ jamais** hardly ever; **il n'a ~ pas parlé/dormi** he hardly said a word/slept; **je n'y vais ~ plus** I hardly ever *ou* almost never go there anymore

Quasimodo [kazimɔdo] NF **la ~** ◊ **le dimanche de ~** Low Sunday

quaternaire [kwateʀnɛʀ] ① ADJ (*gén, Chim*) quaternary; (*Géol*) Quaternary ② NM (*Géol*) **le ~** the Quaternary (period)

quatorze [katɔʀz] ADJ INV, NM INV fourteen; **avant/après (la guerre de) ~** before/after the First World War; **le ~ juillet** the Fourteenth of July, Bastille Day (*French national holiday*) → **chercher, repartir**; *pour autres locutions voir* **six**; → *LE QUATORZE JUILLET*

quatorzième [katɔʀzjɛm] ADJ INV, NMF fourteenth; *pour locutions voir* **sixième**

quatrain [katʀɛ̃] NM quatrain

quatre [katʀ] ① ADJ INV, NM INV four; (*lit, fig*) **aux ~ coins de** in the four corners of; (*Mus*) **à ~ mains** [*morceau*] for four hands, four-handed; [*jouer*] four-handed; **marcher à ~ pattes** to walk on all fours; **nos amis à ~ pattes** our four-legged friends; (*Pol*) **les ~ grands** the Big Four; **monter/descendre (l'escalier) ~ à ~** to rush up/down the stairs four at a time; **manger comme ~** to eat like a horse; **une robe de ~ sous** a cheap dress; **il avait ~ sous d'économies** he had a modest amount of savings; **s'il avait ~ sous de bon sens** if he had a scrap *ou* modicum of common sense; **être tiré à ~ épingles** to be dressed up to the nines; **un de ces ~ (matins)*** one of these (fine) days; **faire les ~ cents coups** to lead a wild life; **tomber les ~ fers en l'air** to fall flat on one's back; **faire ses ~ volontés** to do exactly as one pleases; **faire les ~ volontés de qn** to satisfy sb's every whim; **dire à qn ses ~ vérités** to tell sb a few plain *ou* home truths, eat enough for four (people); **se mettre** *ou* **se couper en ~ pour (aider) qn** to bend over backwards to help sb*; **elle se tenait à ~ pour ne pas rire/pour ne pas le gifler** she was doing all she could to keep from laughing/to keep from smacking him; **je n'irai pas par ~ chemins** I'm not going to beat about the bush; **entre ~ murs** within *ou* between four walls; **je n'ai pas ~ bras!*** I've only got one pair of hands!; **quand il sera entre ~ planches*** when he's six foot under*; **entre ~'z'yeux** ◊ **entre quat-z-yeux*** (= *directement*) face to face; (= *en privé*) in private → **trèfle, vent** *etc*; *pour autres locutions voir* **six** ② NM (*Naut*) **~ barré** coxed four; **~ sans barreur** coxless four

quatre-cent-vingt-et-un [katʀəsɑ̃vɛ̃teœ̃] NM INV dice game

quatre-épices [katʀepis] NM INV allspice

quatre-heures* [katʀœʀ] NM INV (*langage enfantin*) afternoon tea (*Brit*) *ou* snack

quatre-huit [kat(ʀə)ɥit] NM INV (*Mus*) common time

quatre-mâts [kat(ʀə)mɑ] NM INV four-master

quatre-quarts [kat(ʀə)kaʀ] NM INV (*Culin*) pound cake

quatre-quatre [kat(ʀə)katʀ] ADJ INV, NM INV four-wheel drive

quatre-vingt-dix [katʀəvɛ̃dis] ADJ INV, NM INV ninety

quatre-vingt-dixième [katʀəvɛ̃dizjɛm] ADJ INV, NMF ninetieth

quatre-vingt-et-un [katvɛ̃teœ̃] NM INV = **quatre-cent-vingt-et-un**

quatre-vingtième [katʀəvɛ̃tjɛm] ADJ INV, NMF eightieth

quatre-vingt-onze [katʀəvɛ̃ɔ̃z] ADJ INV, NM INV ninety-one

quatre-vingt-onzième [katʀəvɛ̃ɔ̃zjɛm] ADJ INV, NMF ninety-first

quatre-vingts [katʀəvɛ̃] ADJ INV, NM INV eighty

quatre-vingt-un [katʀəvɛ̃ɛ̃] ADJ INV, NM INV eighty-one

quatre-vingt-unième [katʀəvɛ̃ynjɛm] ADJ INV, NMF eighty-first

quatrième [katʀijɛm] ① ADJ fourth; **le ~ pouvoir** the fourth estate; **le ~ âge** (= *personnes*) the over 75s; (= *état*) the fourth age (*75 onwards*); **faire qch en ~ vitesse** to do sth at top speed; *pour autres locutions voir* **sixième** ② NMF (= *joueur de cartes*) fourth player ③ NF (*Aut* = *vitesse*) fourth gear; (*Cartes* = *quarte*) quart; (*Scol* = *classe*) ≈ third form *ou* year (*Brit*), ≈ third year (in junior high school) (*US*); **~ de couverture** [*livre*] back cover

quatrièmement [katʀijɛmmɑ̃] ADV fourthly, in the fourth place

quatrillion [k(w)atʀiljɔ̃] NM quadrillion (*Brit*), septillion (*US*)

quattrocento [kwatʀotʃɛnto] NM **le ~** the quattrocento

quatuor [kwatɥɔʀ] NM (= *œuvre, musiciens*) quartet(te); (*fig*) quartet(te), foursome; **~ à cordes** string quartet(te)

que [kə]

Devant voyelle *ou* h *muet* = **qu'**.

①	CONJONCTION	③	PRONOM REL
②	ADVERBE	④	PRONOM INTERROG

---

① CONJONCTION

Lorsque **que** *sert à former des locutions conjonctives* (**afin que, à mesure que, dès que, tant que, tel que, plus/moins ... que** *etc*), *reportez-vous à l'autre mot.*

☐ a

Lorsque **que** *introduit une subordonnée complétive, il se traduit généralement par* that *mais est souvent omis.*

elle sait ~ tu es prêt she knows (that) you're ready; **tu crois qu'il réussira?** do you think he'll succeed?; **c'est agréable qu'il fasse beau** it's nice that the weather's fine; **c'est dommage qu'il pleuve** it's a pity (that) it's raining; **l'idée qu'il pourrait échouer** the idea of him *ou* his failing, the idea that he might fail

---

Avec un verbe de volonté, l'anglais emploie une proposition infinitive.

je veux/j'aimerais qu'il vienne I want him/would like him to come; **je ne veux pas qu'il vienne** I don't want him to come; MAIS **j'aimerais qu'il ne vienne pas** I'd rather he didn't come

---

Avec les verbes d'opinion tels que **penser, croire** *suivis de* **oui, si, non, que** *n'est pas traduit.*

je pense ~ oui/non I think/don't think so; **mais il n'a pas de voiture! — il dit ~ si** but he has no

---

car! — **he says he has** → **craindre, douter, peur** *etc*

☐ b

Lorsque **que** *est précédé d'une préposition introduite par* **si, quand, comme, que** *etc, il ne se traduit pas.*

si vous êtes sages et qu'il fait beau, nous sortirons if you are good and the weather is fine, we'll go out; **il vous recevra quand il rentrera et qu'il aura déjeuné** he'll see you when he comes home and he's had a meal; **comme la maison est petite et qu'il n'y a pas de jardin ...** as the house is small and there's no garden ...; **bien qu'il soit en retard et ~ nous soyons pressés** although he's late and we're in a hurry

☐ c ☐ hypothèse (= *si*) whether; **il ira, qu'il veuille** *ou* **non** he'll go whether he wants to or not *ou* whether he likes it or not; **qu'il parte** *ou* **qu'il reste, ça m'est égal** whether he leaves or stays, it's all the same to me, he can leave or he can stay, it's all the same to me

☐ d ☐ but **tenez-le, qu'il ne tombe pas** hold him in case he falls *ou* so that he won't fall; **venez ~ nous causions** come along and we'll have *ou* so that we can have a chat

☐ e ☐ temps **elle venait à peine de sortir qu'il se mit à pleuvoir** she had no sooner gone out than it started raining, she had hardly *ou* just gone out when it started raining; **ils ne se connaissaient pas depuis 10 minutes qu'ils étaient déjà amis** they had only known each other for 10 minutes and already they were friends → **faire, ne, si²**

☐ f ☐ ordre, souhait, résignation

Lorsque **que** *suivi d'une* 3e *personne exprime l'ordre, le souhait, la résignation ou la menace, il se traduit par un verbe, un adverbe ou une conjonction.*

qu'il se taise! I wish he would be quiet!; **~ la lumière soit** let there be light; **~ la guerre finisse!** if only the war would end!; **qu'ils me laissent en paix!** I wish they'd leave me in peace!; **eh bien, qu'il vienne!** all right, he can come *ou* let him come!; **~ le Seigneur ait pitié de lui!** (may) (the) Lord have mercy upon him!; **qu'elle vienne me reprocher quelque chose(, je saurai la recevoir)!** she'd better not start criticizing!; **qu'il essaie seulement!** just let him try!

☐ g

Notez l'emploi d'adverbes ou de l'auxiliaire en anglais lorsque **que** *renforce une affirmation ou une négation.*

~ oui! yes indeed!; **il était fâché? — ~ oui!** was he angry? — was he ever!; **~ non!** certainly not!, not at all!; **tu viens? — ~ non/oui!** are you coming? — no I am not!/you bet I am!*; **mais il n'en veut pas! — ~ si/non** but he doesn't want any! — yes he does/no he doesn't

☐ h ☐ pour reprendre ce qui vient d'être dit **~ tu crois!*** that's what YOU think!; **~ je l'aide? tu plaisantes!** me, help him? you must be joking!; **~ tu y ailles seul? c'est trop dangereux!** go on your own? that's far too dangerous!

☐ i ☐ après un discours rapporté « **viens ici!** », **qu'il me crie*** "come here", he shouted; « **et pourquoi?** » **~ je lui fais*** "why's that?", I go to him*

☐ j

♦ **que ... ne ...** (*littér*) (= *sans que*) **il ne se passe pas une minute ~ je ne pense à lui** not a minute goes by when I don't think about him *ou* without me thinking about him (*introduisant une opposition*) **ils pourraient me supplier ~ je n'accepterais pas** even if they begged me I wouldn't accept; **j'avais déjà fini de déjeuner qu'elle n'avait pas commencé** I'd already finished my lunch and she hadn't even started

② ADVERBE

☐ a ☐ valeur intensive

♦ **que** ◊ **qu'est-ce que** (*devant adjectif, ad-*

verbe) how; (*devant nom singulier*) what a; (*devant nom pluriel*) what a lot of; (**qu'est-ce**) ~ **tu es lent!** you're so slow!, how slow you are!; **qu'est-ce qu'il est bête!** he's such an idiot!; ~ **de monde!** ◊ **qu'est-ce qu'il y a comme monde!** what a crowd (there is)!, what a lot of people!; ~ **de voitures!** ◊ **qu'est-ce qu'il y a comme circulation!** there's so much traffic!; ~ **de mal vous vous donnez!** what a lot of trouble you're taking!; (**qu'est-ce**) **qu'il joue bien!** doesn't he play well!, what a good player he is!

b | dans des interrogatives | (= *pourquoi*) why; **qu'avais-tu besoin de lui en parler?** why did you have to go and talk to him about it?; (*littér*) ~ **n'es-tu venu me voir?** why didn't you come to see me?

3 PRONOM REL

a | antécédent personne |

que *se traduit par* **who** *ou par* **that**, *ce dernier étant souvent omis; dans une langue plus soutenue, on peut employer* **whom**.

la fille qu'il a rencontrée là-bas et qu'il a épousée par la suite the girl (that) he met there and later married; **les enfants ~ tu vois jouer dans la rue** the children (that) you see playing in the street; **la femme qu'il aime toujours** the woman (whom (*frm*)) he still loves

Quand l'antécédent est un nom propre, on traduit obligatoirement par **who** *ou* **whom**.

il y avait David Legrand, ~ je n'avais pas vu depuis des années David Legrand, who *ou* whom (*frm*) I hadn't seen for years, was there

b | antécédent animal ou chose |

que *se traduit par* **which** *ou* **that**, *ce dernier étant souvent omis.*

le chaton qu'il a trouvé dans la cave the kitten (that) he found in the cellar; **j'ai déjà les livres qu'il m'a offerts** I've already got the books he gave me; **la raison qu'il a donnée** the reason (that *ou* which) he gave

c | en incise |

Notez que lorsque la relative est en incise, on n'emploie jamais **that**.

un certain M. Leduc, ~ je ne connais même pas, m'a appelé a certain Mr Leduc, who *ou* whom (*frm*) I don't even know, called me; **l'étiquette, ~ j'avais pourtant bien collée, est tombée** the label, which I'd stuck on properly, fell off all the same

d | temps | when; **un jour/un été ~ ...** * one day/one summer when ...; **tu te souviens de l'hiver qu'il a fait si froid?** * do you remember the winter (when) it was so cold? → **temps**

e | dans des formes attributives | **quel homme charmant ~ votre voisin!** what a charming man your neighbour is!; **tout distrait qu'il est, il s'en est aperçu** absent-minded though he is, he still noticed it; **et moi, aveugle ~ j'étais, je ne m'en suis pas aperçu** and blind as I was, I didn't see it; **pour ignorante qu'elle soit** ignorant though she may be, however ignorant she is *ou* may be; **c'est un inconvénient ~ de ne pas avoir de voiture** it's inconvenient not having a car; **de brune qu'elle était, elle est devenue blonde** once a brunette, she has now turned blonde; **en bon fils qu'il est** being the good son (that) he is; **plein d'attentions qu'il était** *, ce jeune homme!** he was so considerate that young man was!*

4 PRONOM INTERROG

what; ~ **fais-tu?** ◊ **qu'est-ce ~ tu fais?** what are you doing?; **qu'est-ce qu'il voulait?** what did he want?; **qu'en sais-tu?** what do you know about it?

Notez que dans les cas où il y a discrimination ou choix, on emploie **which**.

qu'est-ce ~ tu préfères, le rouge ou le noir? which (one) do you prefer, the red or the black?

♦ **qu'est-ce qui** what; **qu'est-ce qui l'a mis en**

colère? what made him so angry?; **qu'est-ce qui t'empêchait de le faire?** what stopped you from doing it?

Québec [kebɛk] **1** N (= *ville*) Quebec (City) **2** NM (= *province*) **le** ~ Quebec

| **QUÉBEC** |

Quebec's history as a French-speaking province of Canada has meant that the French spoken there has developed many distinctive characteristics. Since the 1970s, the government of Quebec has been actively promoting the use of French terms instead of Anglicisms in everyday life in order to preserve the Francophone identity of the province, over 80% of whose inhabitants have French as their mother tongue. → | OFFICE DE LA LANGUE FRANÇAISE | ; | RÉVOLUTION TRANQUILLE |

québécisme [kebesism] NM *expression (ou word etc) used in Quebec*

québécois, e [kebekwa, waz] **1** ADJ Quebec (*épith*); **le Parti ~** the Parti Québécois **2** NM (*Ling*) Quebec French **3** **Québécois(e)** NM,F Quebecker, Quebecer, Québécois (*Can*)

quechua [ketʃwa] ADJ, NM Quechua, Kechua

Queensland [kwinzlãd] NM Queensland

quel, quelle [kɛl] **1** ADJ **a** (*interrog : dir, indir*) (*être animé : attrib*) who; (*être animé : épith*) what; (*chose*) what; ~ **est cet auteur?** who is that author?; **sur ~ auteur va-t-il parler?** what author is he going to talk about?; **quelles ont été les raisons de son départ?** what were the reasons for his leaving? *ou* departure?; **dans ~s pays êtes-vous allé?** what countries have you been to?; **lui avez-vous dit à quelle adresse (il faut) envoyer la lettre?** have you told him the *ou* what address to send the letter to?; **j'ignore ~ est l'auteur de ces poèmes** I don't know who wrote these poems *ou* who the author of these poems is

b (*interrog discriminatif*) which; ~ **acteur préférez-vous?** which actor do you prefer?; ~ **est le vin le moins cher des trois?** which wine is the cheapest of the three?

c (*excl*) what; **quelle surprise/coïncidence!** what a surprise/coincidence!; ~ **courage!** what courage!; ~**s charmants enfants!** what charming children!; ~ **imbécile je suis!** what a fool I am!; ~ **(sale) temps!** what rotten weather!; **il a vu ~s amis fidèles il avait** he saw what faithful friends he had; **j'ai remarqué avec quelle attention ils écoutaient** I noticed how attentively they were listening

d (*relatif*) (*être animé*) whoever; (*chose*) whatever; (*discriminatif*) whichever, whatever; **quelle que soit ou quelle que puisse être votre décision, écrivez-nous** write to us whatever your decision may be *ou* whatever you decide; ~ **que soit le train que vous preniez, vous arriverez trop tard** whichever *ou* whatever train you take, you will be too late; **quelles que soient les conséquences** whatever the consequences (may be); **quelle que soit la personne qui vous répondra** whoever answers you; ~ **qu'il soit, le prix sera toujours trop élevé** whatever the price (is), it will still be too high; **les hommes, ~s qu'ils soient** all men, irrespective of who they are

2 PRON INTERROG which; **de tous ces enfants, ~ est le plus intelligent?** of all these children, which (one) is the most intelligent?; **des deux solutions quelle est celle que vous préférez?** of the two solutions, which (one) do you prefer?

quelconque [kɛlkɔ̃k] ADJ **a** (= *n'importe quel*) some (or other), any; **une lettre envoyée par un ami ~ ou par un ~ de ses amis** a letter sent by some friend of his *ou* by some friend or other (of his); **choisis un stylo ~ parmi ceux-là** choose any one of those pens; **sous un prétexte ~** on some pretext or other; **pour une raison ~** for some reason (or other); **à partir d'un point ~ du cercle** from any point on the

circle → **triangle**

b (= *moindre*) **un** *ou* **une ~** any, the least *ou* slightest; **il n'a pas manifesté un désir ~ d'y aller** he didn't show the slightest *ou* least desire *ou* any desire to go; **avez-vous une ~ idée de l'endroit où ça se trouve?** have you any idea where it might be?

c (= *médiocre*) [*repas*] poor, indifferent; [*élève, devoir*] poor; [*acteur*] poor, second-rate; **c'est un repas/devoir ~** this is a poor meal/ essay, this meal/essay isn't up to much* (*Brit*); **c'est quelqu'un de très ~** (*laid*) he's not very good-looking at all; (*ordinaire*) he's a very ordinary *ou* nondescript sort of person

quelque [kɛlk(ə)]

| **1** ADJECTIF INDÉFINI | **2** ADVERBE |

1 | ADJECTIF INDÉFINI |

a | au singulier | some; **il habite à ~ distance d'ici** he lives some distance *ou* way from here; **dans ~ temps** before long, in a (little) while; **attendre ~ temps** to wait a while; **je ne le vois plus depuis ~ temps** I haven't seen him for some time *ou* for a while, it's some time *ou* a while since I've seen him; **il faut trouver ~ autre solution** we'll have to find some other solution; **j'ai ~ peine à croire cela** I find that rather *ou* somewhat difficult to believe, I have some difficulty in believing that; **avec ~ impatience/inquiétude** with some impatience/ anxiety; **désirez-vous ~ autre chose?** would you like something or anything else?

♦ **en quelque sorte** (= *pour ainsi dire*) as it were, so to speak; (= *bref*) in a word; (= *d'une certaine manière*) in a way; **le liquide s'était en ~ sorte solidifié** the liquid had solidified as it were *ou* so to speak; **en ~ sorte, tu refuses** in a word, you refuse; **on pourrait dire en ~ sorte que ...** you could say in a way that ...

♦ **quelque chose** (*gén*) something; (*avec interrog*) anything, something; ~ **chose d'extraordinaire** something extraordinary; ~ **chose d'autre** something else; **puis-je faire ~ chose pour vous?** is there anything *ou* something I can do for you?; **il a ~ chose (qui ne va pas)** (*maladie*) there's something wrong *ou* the matter with him; (*ennuis*) there's something the matter with him; **vous prendrez bien ~ chose (à boire)** do have something to drink; **il/ça y est pour ~ chose** he/it has got something to do with it; **il y a ~ chose comme une semaine** something like a week ago, a week or so ago; **je t'ai apporté un petit ~ chose** I've brought you a little something → **déjà, dire, malheur**

faire ~ chose à qn to have an effect on sb; **ça m'a fait ~ chose d'apprendre sa mort** I was upset when I heard he had died; **quand il me prend dans ses bras, ça me fait ~ chose** it does something to me when he takes me in his arms

(* : *intensif*) **il a plu ~ chose (de bien)!** it rained like anything!*, it didn't half rain!* (*Brit*); **je tiens ~ chose comme rhume!** I've got a terrible *ou* a dreadful cold!; **il se prend pour ~ chose** he thinks he's quite something; **ce film/être pilote, c'est ~ chose!** that film/being a pilot is quite something!; (*ton irrité*) **ça alors, c'est ~ chose!** that's (a bit) too much!, that's a bit stiff!* (*Brit*)

♦ **quelque part** somewhere; **posez votre paquet ~ part dans un coin** put your parcel down in a corner somewhere; (*euph* = *toilettes*) **je vais ~ part** I'm going to wash my hands (*euph*); (*euph*) **tu veux mon pied ~ part?** * do you want a kick up the backside?*

b | au pluriel | ~**s** a few, some; **M. Dupont va vous dire ~s mots** Mr Dupont is going to say a few words (to you); ~**s milliers (de)** a few thousand; **il ne peut rester que ~s instants** he can only stay (for) a few moments; ~**s autres** some *ou* a few others; **avez-vous ~s feuilles de papier à me passer?** could you let me have a few sheets of paper?

◆ **et quelques** : 20 kg et **~s*** a bit over 20 kg*; **il doit être trois heures et ~s*** it must be a bit* *ou* a little after three

[c]

◆ **les** *ou* **ces** *ou* **ses** *etc* **quelques ...**: **les ~s enfants qui étaient venus** the few children who had come; **ces ~s poèmes** these few poems; **les ~s centaines/milliers de personnes qui ...** the few hundred/thousand people who ...

[d]

◆ **quelque ... que** whatever; *(discriminatif)* whichever, whatever; **de ~ façon que l'on envisage le problème** whatever *ou* whichever way you look at the problem; **par ~ temps qu'il fasse** whatever the weather (may be *ou* is like); **il veut l'acheter, à ~ prix que ce soit, par ~ moyen que ce soit** he wants to buy it no matter what the cost and no matter how

2 **ADVERBE**

[a] **(= environ, à peu près)** some, about; **il y a ~ 20 ans qu'il enseigne ici** he has been teaching here for some *ou* about 20 years *ou* for 20 years or so; **ça a augmenté de ~ 50 F** it's gone up by about 50 francs *ou* by 50 francs or so *ou* by some 50 francs

[b]

◆ **quelque peu** rather, somewhat; **~ peu déçu** rather *ou* somewhat disappointed; **~ peu grivois** a touch *ou* somewhat risqué; **il est ~ peu menteur** he is something of *ou* a bit of a liar

[c]

◆ **quelque ... que** *(littér)* however; **~ pénible que soit la tâche** however laborious the task may be

quelquefois [kɛlkəfwa] ADV sometimes, occasionally, at times

quelques-uns, -unes [kɛlkəzœ̃, yn] PRON INDÉF PL some, a few; **~ de nos lecteurs/ses amis** some *ou* a few of our readers/his friends; **privilège réservé à ~** privilege reserved for a very few

quelqu'un [kɛlkœ̃] PRON INDÉF [a] *(gén)* somebody, someone; *(avec interrog)* anybody, anyone; **~ d'autre** somebody *ou* someone else; **c'est ~ de sûr/d'important** he's a reliable/an important person, he's someone reliable/important; **Claire, c'est ~ de bien** Claire is a nice person; **il faudrait ~ de plus** we need one more person; **~ pourrait-il répondre ?** could somebody answer?; **il y a ~ ?** is there anybody there? [b] *(intensif)* **c'est vraiment ~ cette fille** that girl's really something else*; **c'est ~ (d'important) dans le monde du cinéma** she's really somebody in cinema; **dans ce métier, c'est difficile de devenir ~*** it's not easy to make a name for yourself in this profession; **ça alors, c'est ~ ! †*** that's (a bit) too much!, that's a bit stiff!* (Brit)

quémander [kemɑ̃de] ▶conjug 1◀ VT [+ argent, faveur] to beg for; [+ louanges] to beg *ou* fish *ou* angle for

quémandeur, -euse [kemɑ̃dœʀ, øz] NM,F *(littér)* beggar

qu'en-dira-t-on [kɑ̃diratɔ̃] NM INV *(commérage)* **le ~** gossip; **il se moque du ~** he doesn't care what people say, he doesn't care about gossip

quenelle [kənɛl] NF *(Culin)* quenelle

quenotte [kənɔt] NF *(langage enfantin)* tooth, toothy-peg *(Brit, langage enfantin)*

quenouille [kənuj] NF distaff; **tomber en ~** *(Hist)* to pass into female hands; **(= échouer)** to fall through; **(= être abandonné)** [pouvoir, privilège] to be forsaken

quéquette* [keket] NF *(langage enfantin)* willy* (Brit), peter* (US)

querelle [kəʀɛl] NF [a] **(= dispute)** quarrel; **~ d'amoureux** lovers' tiff; **~ d'ivrognes** drunken row; **~ d'Allemand** ◊ **mauvaise ~** quarrel over nothing; **chercher une ~ d'Allemand** *ou* **une mauvaise ~ à qn** to pick a quarrel with sb for

nothing *ou* for no reason at all; **~ de famille** *ou* **familiale** family quarrel *ou* squabble; *(grave)* family feud; **~ de chapelle** *ou* **de clocher** petty squabbling (NonC) *ou* in-fighting (NonC) [b] **(= polémique)** dispute (sur over, about); **la ~ sur l'enseignement privé** the dispute over private education [c] *(††, littér = cause, parti)* cause, quarrel†; **épouser** *ou* **embrasser la ~ de qn** to take up *ou* fight sb's cause → **chercher, vider**

quereller [kəʀele] ▶conjug 1◀ [1] VT *(† = gronder)* to scold [2] **se quereller** VPR to quarrel (with one another); **se ~ au sujet** *ou* **à propos de qch** to quarrel *ou* squabble over *ou* about sth

querelleur, -euse [kəʀelœʀ, øz] ADJ quarrelsome

quérir [keʀiʀ] ▶conjug 21◀ VT *(littér = chercher)* **envoyer** *ou* **faire ~ qn** to summon sb, bid sb (to) come†; **aller ~ qn** to go seek sb†, go in quest of sb†

questeur [kɛstœʀ] NM *(Antiq)* quaestor *(Brit)*, questor *(US)*; *(Pol française)* questeur *(administrative and financial officer elected to the French Parliament)*

▼ **question** [kɛstjɔ̃] NF [a] **(= demande)** *(gén)* question; *(pour lever un doute)* query, question; **~ piège** *(d'apparence facile)* trick question; *(pour nuire à qn)* loaded question; **~ subsidiaire** tiebreaker; **évidemment ! cette ~ !** *ou* **quelle ~ !** obviously! what a question!; **c'est la grande ~** *(problème)* it's the main *ou* major issue *ou* question; **c'est la grande ~** ◊ **c'est la ~ à mille francs*** *(interrogation)* it's the big question *ou* the sixty-four thousand dollar question* [b] *(Pol)* **~ écrite/orale** written/oral question; **séance de ~s au gouvernement** question and answer session *(at the French National Assembly)*, ≈ question time *(Brit)* [c] **(= problème)** question, matter, issue; **~s économiques/sociales** economic/social questions *ou* matters *ou* issues; **pour des ~s de sécurité/d'hygiène** for reasons of security/of hygiene; *(Presse)* **d'actualité** topical question; **la ~ est délicate** it's a delicate question *ou* matter; **la ~ est de savoir si ...** the question is whether ...; **la ~ sociale** the social question *ou* issue; **sortir de la ~** to stray *ou* wander from the point; **la ~ n'est pas là** ◊ **là n'est pas la ~** that's not the point; **c'est toute la ~** ◊ **c'est la grosse** *ou* **grande ~** that's the big question, that's the crux of the matter, that's the whole point; **il n'y a pas de ~, c'est lui le meilleur** he is indisputably *ou* unquestionably the best, there's no question about it — he's the best; **cela ne fait pas ~** there's no question about it; **c'est une ~ de temps** it's a question *ou* matter of time; **c'est une ~ d'heures/de vie ou de mort/d'habitude** it's a matter *ou* question of time/of life or death/of habit; **je ne céderai pas, c'est une ~ de principe** I won't give in, it's a matter of principle; *(ordre du jour)* **« autres ~s »** "any other business" → **autre**

[d] *(* = en ce qui concerne)* **~ argent** as far as money goes, money-wise*; **~ bêtise, il se pose là !** he's an idiot!; **~ cuisine, elle est nulle** when it comes to cooking, she's useless*

[e] *(avec poser, se poser)* **poser une ~ à qn** to ask sb a question, put a question to sb; **l'ambiguïté de son attitude pose la ~ de son honnêteté** his ambivalent attitude makes you wonder how honest he is *ou* makes you question his honesty; **sans poser de ~s** without asking any questions, without raising any queries; **la ~ me semble mal posée** I think the question is badly put; *(Pol)* **poser la ~ de confiance** to ask for a vote of confidence; **la ~ qui se pose** the question which must be asked *ou* considered; **il y a une ~ que je me pose** there's one thing I'd like to know, I wonder about one thing; **je me pose la ~**

that's the question, that's what I'm wondering; **il commence à se poser des ~s** he's beginning to wonder *ou* to have doubts; **il l'a fait sans se poser de ~s** he did it without a second thought

[f] *(loc)* **de quoi est-il ~ ?** what is it about?; **il fut d'abord ~ du budget** first they spoke about *ou* discussed the budget; **il est ~ de lui comme ministre** *ou* **qu'il soit ministre** there's some question *ou* talk of his being a minister; **il n'est plus ~ de ce fait dans la suite** no further mention of this fact is made subsequently, there is no further reference to this fact thereafter; **il n'est pas ~ que nous y renoncions/d'y renoncer** there's no question of our *ou* us giving it up/of giving it up; **il n'en est pas ~ !** that's out of the question!; **moi y aller ? pas ~ !*** me go? nothing doing!* *ou* no way!*; **c'est hors de ~** it is out of the question

[g] *(loc)* **en ~** **(= dont on parle)** in question; **(= en jeu)** **c'est votre vie qui est en ~** it's your life which is at stake; **mettre** *ou* **remettre en ~** [+ autorité, théorie] to question, challenge; [+ compétence, honnêteté, pratique] to question, call *ou* bring into question; **la remise en ~ de nos accords** the fact that our agreements are being called into question; **cela remet sa compétence en ~** this puts a question mark over his competence; **le projet est sans cesse remis en ~** the project is continually being called into question; **il faut se remettre en ~ de temps en temps** it's important to do some soul-searching *ou* to take a good look at oneself from time to time; **elle ne se remet jamais en ~** she never questions herself

[h] *(Hist = torture)* question; **soumettre qn à la ~** ◊ **infliger la ~ à qn** to put sb to the question

questionnaire [kɛstjɔnɛʀ] NM questionnaire; **~ à choix multiple** multiple choice question paper

questionnement [kɛstjɔnmɑ̃] NM [a] **(= remise en cause)** questioning; **le ~ des valeurs de notre temps** the questioning *ou* the calling into question of contemporary values [b] [personne] questioning (sur about); **(= questions)** **le ~ des philosophes** the questions philosophers are asking themselves

questionner [kɛstjɔne] ▶conjug 1◀ VT **(= interroger)** to question (sur about); **arrête de ~ toujours comme ça** stop pestering me with questions all the time, stop questioning me all the time

questionneur, -euse [kɛstjɔnœʀ, øz] NM,F questioner

questure [kɛstyʀ] NF *(Antiq)* quaestorship *(Brit)*, questorship *(US)*; *(Pol française)* administrative and financial commission at the French Parliament

quête [kɛt] NF [a] **(= collecte)** collection; **faire la ~** *(à l'église)* to take (the) collection; [artiste de rue] to go round with the hat; [association caritative] to collect for charity [b] *(littér)* **âme en ~ d'absolu** soul in pursuit *ou* quest *ou* search of the absolute → **Graal** [c] **se mettre en ~ de** [+ pain] to set out to look for *ou* to find, go in search of; [+ appartement] to (go on the) hunt for; **être en ~ de travail** to be looking for *ou* seeking work

quêter [kete] ▶conjug 1◀ [1] VI *(à l'église)* to take (the) collection; *(dans la rue)* to collect money; **~ pour les aveugles** to collect for the blind [2] VT [+ louanges] to seek (after), fish *ou* angle for; [+ suffrages] to seek; [+ sourire, regard] to seek, try to win

quêteur, -euse [ketœʀ, øz] NM,F *(dans la rue, à l'église)* collector

quetsche [kwɛtʃ] NF kind of dark-red plum

quetzal [kɛtzal] NM **(= oiseau)** que(t)zal; **(= monnaie)** que(t)zal

queue [kø] [1] NF [a] [animal, avion, comète, lettre, note] tail; [orage] tail end; [classement] bottom; [casserole, poêle] handle; [feuille, fruit] stalk; [*fleur*] stem, stalk; [*colonne, train*] rear; **en ~ de phrase** at the end of the sentence; **en ~ de liste/classe** at the bottom of the list/class; **être en ~ de peloton** (*lit*) to be at the back of the pack; (*fig*) to be lagging behind; **en ~ (de train)** at the rear of the train; **compartiments de ~** rear compartments → **diable**

b (= *file de personnes*) queue (*Brit*), line (*US*); **faire la ~** to queue (up) (*Brit*), stand in line (*US*); **il y a trois heures de ~** there's a three-hour queue (*Brit*) *ou* line (*US*); **mettez-vous à la ~** join the queue (*Brit*) *ou* line (*US*)

c (‼ = *pénis*) cock‼, prick‼

d (*loc*) **la ~ basse*** *ou* **entre les jambes*** with one's tail between one's legs; **à la ~ leu leu** [*arriver, marcher*] in single file; [*venir se plaindre*] one after the other; **il n'y en avait pas la ~ d'un*** there wasn't a single one; (*Aut*) **faire une ~ de poisson à qn** to cut in front of sb; **finir en ~ de poisson** to come to an abrupt end; **histoire sans ~ ni tête*** cock-and-bull story; **mettre des ~s aux zéros** [*marchand*] to overcharge; (*Billard*) **faire une fausse ~** to miscue

2 COMP ► **queue d'aronde** dovetail; **assemblage en ~ d'aronde** dovetail joint ► **queue de billard** (billiard) cue ► **queue de cheval** ponytail; **se faire une ~ de cheval** to put one's hair in a ponytail ► **queue de vache** ADJ INV [*couleur, cheveux*] reddish-brown

queue-de-morue (*pl* **queues-de-morue**) [kød(ə)mɔʀy] NF **a** (= *pinceau*) (medium) paintbrush **b** †† (= *basques*) tails; (= *habit*) tail coat

queue-de-pie (*pl* **queues-de-pie**) [kød(ə)pi] NF (*habit*) tails, tail coat

queue-de-rat (*pl* **queues-de-rat**) [kød(ə)ʀa] NF (= *lime*) round file

queue-de-renard (*pl* **queues-de-renard**) [kød(ə)ʀənaʀ] NF (*Bot*) **à épi vert clair** green amaranth; **~ des jardins** love-lies-bleeding

queuter* [køte] ► conjug 1 ◄ VI to go wrong, backfire; **~ à un examen** to fail *ou* flunk* an exam

queux [kø] NM → **maître**

qui [ki]
1 PRONOM INTERROG **2** PRONOM REL
Pour les proverbes commençant par **qui**, *cherchez sous le verbe, le nom ou l'adjectif.*

1 PRONOM INTERROG

a sujet
Lorsque **qui** *ou* **qui est-ce qui** *sont sujets, ils se traduisent par* **who**.
~ l'a vu ? ◊ **~ est-ce ~ l'a vu ?** who saw him?; **vous devinez ~ me l'a dit** you can guess who told me!; **on m'a raconté ... — ~ ça ?** somebody told me ... — who was that?; **~ va là ?** who goes there?; **je me demande ~ est là** I wonder who's there

Notez l'emploi de **which** *lorsqu'il y a discrimination entre plusieurs personnes.*
~ d'entre eux *ou* **parmi eux saurait ?** which of them would know?; **~, parmi les candidats, pourrait répondre ?** which (one) of the candidates could reply?

b objet
Lorsque **qui** *est objet, il se traduit par* **who** *dans la langue courante et par* **whom** *dans une langue plus soutenue.*
~ a-t-elle vu ? who *ou* whom (*frm*) did she see?; **elle a vu ~ ?*** ◊ **~ est-ce qu'elle a vu ?** who did she see?; (*surprise*) **elle a vu ~ ?** she saw who?, who did she see?; **je me demande ~ il a invité** I wonder who *ou* whom (*frm*) he has invited

c
♦ *préposition +* **qui**
Notez la place de la préposition en anglais : avec **who** *et* **whose**, *elle est rejetée en fin de proposition, alors qu'elle précède toujours* **whom**.
à *ou* **avec ~ voulez-vous parler ?** who would you

like to speak to?; **à ~ donc parlais-tu ?** who were you talking to?, who was it you were talking to?; **elle ne sait pas à ~ parler** she doesn't know who to talk to; (*sens possessif*) **à ~ est ce sac ?** whose bag is this?, who does this bag belong to?, whose is this bag?; **chez ~ allez-vous ?** whose house are you going to?; **de ~ parles-tu ?** who are you talking about?; **de ~ est la pièce ?** who is the play by?; **pour ~ ont-ils voté ?** who did they vote for?, for whom (*frm*) did they vote?

2 PRONOM REL

a sujet
Lorsque **qui** *est sujet, il se traduit par* **who** *ou* **that** *quand l'antécédent est une personne ; si c'est un nom propre, on traduit obligatoirement par* **who**.
je connais des gens ~ se plaindraient I know some people who *ou* that would complain; **j'ai rencontré Luc ~ m'a raconté que ...** I met Luc, who told me that ...

qui *sujet se traduit par* **that** *ou* **which** *quand l'antécédent est un animal ou une chose.*
il a un perroquet ~ parle he's got a parrot that *ou* which talks

Notez que lorsque la relative est en incise, on n'emploie jamais **that**.
Tom, ~ travaille à la poste, m'a dit ... Tom, who works at the post office, told me ...; **la table, ~ était en acajou, était très lourde** the table, which was made of mahogany, was very heavy

Lorsque la proposition définit ou qualifie l'antécédent, le pronom peut être omis.
les amis ~ viennent ce soir sont américains the friends (who *ou* that are) coming tonight are American; **prends le plat ~ est sur la table** take the dish which *ou* that is on the table; **Paul, ~ traversait la rue, trébucha** Paul tripped (as he was) crossing the street; **je la vis ~ nageait vers le pont** I saw her swimming towards the bridge; **moi ~ espérais rentrer tôt !** and there I was thinking I was going to get home early tonight! → **ce, moi, toi**

♦ *préposition +* **qui**
Le pronom relatif est parfois omis en anglais ; notez la place de la préposition (voir aussi **1c**).
la personne à ~ j'ai parlé the person (who *ou* that) I spoke to; **l'élève de ~ il attendait de meilleurs résultats** the pupil (who *ou* that) he was expecting better results from, the pupil from whom (*frm*) he was expecting better results; **le patron pour ~ il travaille** the employer (that *ou* who) he works for, the employer for whom (*frm*) he works; **la femme sans ~ il ne pouvait vivre** the woman (who *ou* that) he couldn't live without

c sans antécédent
Lorsque **qui** *n'a pas d'antécédent, il représente toujours un être animé au pluriel, et se traduit par* **whoever, anyone who, anyone that**.
ira ~ voudra whoever wants *ou* anyone who wants to go can go; **il a dit à ~ voulait l'entendre que ...** he told anyone who *ou* that would listen that ..., he told whoever would listen that ...; **amenez ~ vous voulez** bring along whoever you like *ou* anyone (that) you like; **les verrait ensemble ne devinerait jamais ça** anyone seeing them together would never guess, anyone who *ou* that saw them together would never guess; **pour ~ s'intéresse à la physique, ce livre est indispensable** for anyone (who *ou* that is) interested in physics this book is indispensable; *MAIS* **ils ont pris tout ce qu'ils ont pu : ~ une chaise, ~ une table, ~ un livre** they took whatever they could: one took a chair, one a table, another a book

Notez les traductions possibles dans les structures comparatives.
c'est à ~ des deux mangera le plus vite each tries to eat faster than the other; **c'est à ~ criera le plus fort** each tries to shout louder than

the other
♦ **à ~ mieux mieux** (*gén*) each one more so than the other; (*crier*) each one louder than the other; (*frapper*) each one harder than the other

♦ **qui de droit** (*Admin*) « **à ~ de droit** » "to whom it may concern"; **je le dirai à ~ de droit** I will tell whoever is concerned *ou* is the proper authority; **le tableau a été restitué à ~ de droit** the painting was returned to its rightful owner; **je remercierai ~ de droit** I'll thank whoever I have to thank

♦ **qui que ce soit** anybody, anyone; **j'interdis à ~ que ce soit d'entrer ici** I forbid anybody *ou* anyone to come in here

♦ **qui tu sais** ◊ **qui vous savez** : **cela m'a été dit par ~ vous savez** I was told that by you-know-who*

quia [kɥija] ADV **mettre à ~** to confound sb†, nonplus sb; **être à ~** to be at a loss for an answer

quiche [kiʃ] NF **~ (lorraine)** quiche (Lorraine); **~ au crabe** crab quiche

quick [kwik] NM **court** *ou* **terrain (de tennis) en ~** all-weather court, hard court

quiconque [kikɔ̃k] **1** PRON REL (= *celui qui*) whoever, anyone who, whosoever†; **~ a tué sera jugé** whoever has killed will be judged; **la loi punit ~ est coupable** the law punishes anyone who is guilty **2** PRON INDÉF (= *n'importe qui, personne*) anyone, anybody; **je le sais mieux que ~** I know better than anyone (else); **il ne veut recevoir d'ordres de ~** he won't take orders from anyone *ou* anybody

quid [kwid] PRON INTERROG **~ de la démocratie ?** (= *et au sujet de la démocratie ?*) and what about democracy?; (= *que va-t-il advenir de la démocratie ?*) whither democracy?

quidam† [k(ɥ)idam] NM (*hum = individu*) fellow, chap (*Brit*), cove† (*Brit*)

quiet, quiète†† [kjɛ, kjɛt] ADJ (*littér*) calm, tranquil

quiétisme [kjetism] NM quietism

quiétiste [kjetist] ADJ, NMF quietist

quiétude [kjetyd] NF (*littér*) [*lieu*] quiet, tranquility; [*personne*] peace (of mind); **en toute ~** (= *sans soucis*) with complete peace of mind; (= *sans obstacle*) in (complete) peace; **les voleurs ont pu opérer en toute ~** the thieves were able to go about their business undisturbed

quignon [kiɲɔ̃] NM **~ (de pain)** (= *croûton*) crust (of bread), heel of the loaf; (= *morceau*) hunk *ou* chunk of bread

quille [kij] NF **a** (*Jeux*) skittle; **(jeu de) ~s** ninepins, skittles → **chien b** (* = *jambe*) pin* **c** (*arg Mil*) **la ~** demob (*arg, Mil*) (*Brit*) **d** (*Naut*) keel; **la ~ en l'air** bottom up(wards), keel up

quincaillerie [kɛ̃kajʀi] NF (= *métier, ustensiles*) hardware, ironmongery (*Brit*); (= *magasin*) hardware shop *ou* store, ironmonger's (shop) (*Brit*); (*fig péj = bijoux*) cheap(-looking) jewellery (*Brit*) *ou* jewelry (*US*); **elle a sorti toute sa ~** she's put on all her trinkets

quincaillier, -ière [kɛ̃kaje, jɛʀ] NM,F hardware dealer, ironmonger (*Brit*)

quinconce [kɛ̃kɔ̃s] ♦ **en quinconce** LOC ADV in staggered rows

quinine [kinin] NF quinine

quinquagénaire [kɛ̃kaʒenɛʀ] **1** ADJ (= *de cinquante ans*) fifty-year-old (*épith*); (= *de cinquante à soixante ans*) **il est ~** he is in his fifties; (*hum*) **maintenant que tu es ~** now that you're fifty (years old), now that you've reached fifty **2** NMF fifty-year-old man (*ou* woman)

Quinquagésime [kɥɛ̃kwaʒezim] NF Quinquagesima

quinquennal, e (*mpl* **-aux**) [kɛ̃kenal, o] ADJ

five-year (*épith*), quinquennial; **assolement ~** five-year rotation

quinquennat [kɛ̃kena] NM (*Pol*) five year term (of office)

quinquet [kɛ̃kɛ] NM (*Hist*) oil lamp; († = *yeux*) **~s*** peepers* (*hum*)

quinquina [kɛ̃kina] NM (*Bot*, *Pharm*) cinchona; **(apéritif au) ~** quinine tonic wine

quint [kɛ̃] ADJ → **Charles**

quintal (*pl* -**aux**) [kɛ̃tal, o] NM quintal (*100 kg*); (*Can*) hundredweight

quinte [kɛ̃t] NF [a] (*Méd*) **~ (de toux)** coughing fit [b] (*Mus*) fifth; (*Escrime*) quinte; (*Cartes*) quint

quinté [kɛ̃te] NM *French forecast system involving betting on five horses*

quintessence [kɛ̃tesɑ̃s] NF (*Chim*, *Philo*, *fig*) quintessence; (*hum*) **abstracteur de ~** hairsplitter

quintet [k(ɥ)ɛ̃tɛ] NM (*Jazz*) jazz quintet

quintette [k(ɥ)ɛ̃tɛt] NM (= *morceau*, *musiciens*) quintet(te); **~ à cordes/à vent** string/wind quintet

quinteux, -euse †† [kɛ̃tø, øz] ADJ (*littér*) [*vieillard*] crotchety, crabbed †

quintillion [kɛ̃tiljɔ̃] NM quintillion (*Brit*), nonillion (*US*)

quintuple [kɛ̃typl] [1] ADJ [*quantité*, *rangée*, *nombre*] quintuple; **une quantité ~ de l'autre** a quantity five times (as great as) the other; **en ~ exemplaire/partie** in five copies/parts; **le ~ champion du monde** the world champion five times over [2] NM (*Math*, *gén*) quintuple (**de** of); **je l'ai payé le ~/le ~ de l'autre** I paid five times as much for it/five times as much as the other for it; **je vous le rendrai au ~** I'll repay you five times over; **augmenter au ~** to increase fivefold

quintupler [kɛ̃typle] ▸conjug 1◂ VTI to quintuple, increase fivefold *ou* five times

quintuplés, -ées [kɛ̃typle] (*ptp de* **quintupler**) NM,F PL quintuplets, quins* (*Brit*), quints* (*US*)

quinzaine [kɛ̃zɛn] NF (= *nombre*) about fifteen, fifteen or so; (= *salaire*) two weeks' *ou* fortnightly (*Brit*) *ou* fortnight's (*Brit*) pay; (= *deux semaines*) **une ~ (de jours)** two weeks, a fortnight (*Brit*); **~ publicitaire** *ou* **commerciale** (two-week) sale; **~ du blanc** (two-week) linen sale; **« ~ des soldes »** "two-week sale", "sales fortnight" (*Brit*)

quinze [kɛ̃z] [1] NM INV fifteen; (*Rugby*) **le ~ de France** the French fifteen; *pour autres locutions voir* **six** [2] ADJ INV fifteen; **le ~ août** the 15th August, Assumption; **demain en ~** a fortnight tomorrow (*Brit*), two weeks from tomorrow (*US*); **lundi en ~** a fortnight on Monday (*Brit*), two weeks from Monday (*US*); **dans ~ jours** in two weeks, in a fortnight (*Brit*), in a fortnight's time (*Brit*), in two weeks' time (*Brit*); **tous les ~ jours** every two weeks, every fortnight (*Brit*) → ˹FÊTES LÉGALES˺

quinzième [kɛ̃zjɛm] ADJ, NMF fifteenth; *pour locutions voir* **sixième**

quinzièmement [kɛ̃zjɛmmɑ̃] ADV in the fifteenth place, fifteenthly

quiproquo [kiprɔkɔ] NM [a] (= *méprise sur une personne*) mistake; (= *malentendu sur un sujet*) misunderstanding; **le ~ durait depuis un quart d'heure, sans qu'ils s'en rendent compte** they had been talking at cross-purposes for a quarter of an hour without realizing it [b] (*Théât*) (case of) mistaken identity

Quito [kito] N Quito

quittance [kitɑ̃s] NF (= *reçu*) receipt; (= *facture*) bill; **~ d'électricité** receipt (*to show one has paid one's electricity bill*); **~ de loyer** rent receipt; (*frm*) **donner ~ à qn de qch** to acquit sb of sth (*frm*)

quitte [kit] ADJ [a] **être ~ envers qn** to be quits* *ou* all square with sb, be no longer in sb's debt; **être ~ envers sa patrie** to have served one's country; **être ~ envers la société** to have paid one's debt to society; **nous sommes ~s** (*dette*) we're quits* *ou* all square; (*méchanceté*) we're even *ou* quits* *ou* all square; **tu es ~ pour cette fois** I'll let you off this time, I'll let you get away with it this time; **je ne vous tiens pas ~** you still owe me [b] **être/tenir qn ~ d'une dette/obligation** to be/consider sb rid *ou* clear of a debt/an obligation; **je suis ~ des mes dettes envers vous** all my debts to you are clear *ou* are paid off; **nous en sommes ~s pour la peur** we got off with a fright [c] **~ à** (*idée de risque*) even if it means; **~ à s'ennuyer, ils préfèrent rester chez eux** they prefer to stay at home even if it means getting bored; (*idée de nécessité*) **~ à aller au restaurant, autant en choisir un bon** if we're going to a restaurant, we might as well go to a good one [d] **~ ou double** (= *jeu*) double or quits; (*fig*) **c'est (du) ~ ou double ◊ c'est jouer à ~ ou double** it's a big gamble, it's risking a lot

▼ **quitter** [kite] ▸conjug 1◂ [1] VT [a] [+ *école*, *pays*, *personne*] to leave; [+ *métier*] to leave, quit, give up; **il n'a pas quitté la maison depuis trois jours** he hasn't been outside *ou* he hasn't set foot outside the house for three days, he hasn't left the house for three days; **je suis pressé, il faut que je vous quitte** I'm in a hurry so I must leave you *ou* I must be off*; **il a quitté sa femme** he's left his wife; **ne pas ~ la chambre** to be confined to one's room; **« les clients sont priés de ~ la chambre avant 11 heures »** "guests are requested to vacate their rooms before 11 o'clock"; **~ l'autoroute à Lyon** to turn off *ou* leave the motorway at Lyon; **le camion a quitté la route** the lorry ran off *ou* left the road; **le train a quitté la voie** *ou* **les rails** the train derailed *ou* jumped the rails; (*euph*) **il a quitté ce monde** he has departed this world; (*fig*) **~ la place** to withdraw, retire; **si je le quitte des yeux une seconde** if I take my eyes off him for a second, if I let him out of my sight for a second; (*Téléc*) **ne quittez pas** hold the line, hold on a moment → **lieu¹**, **semelle** [b] (= *renoncer à*) [+ *espoir*, *illusion*] to give up, forsake; (= *abandonner*) [*crainte*, *énergie*] to leave, desert; **tout son courage l'a quitté** all his courage left *ou* deserted him [c] († = *enlever*) [+ *vêtement*] to take off; **~ le deuil** to come out of mourning; (*fig*) **~ l'habit** *ou* **la robe** to leave the priesthood; (*Mil*) **~ l'uniforme** to leave the army (*ou* navy *etc*) [d] (*Ordin*) to quit, exit

[2] **se quitter** VPR [*couple*] to split up, part; **nous nous sommes quittés bons amis** we parted good friends; **ils ne se quittent pas** they are always together, you never see them apart; **nous nous sommes quittés à 11 heures** we left each other at 11

quitus [kitys] NM (*Comm*) full discharge, quietus

qui-vive [kiviv] NM INV **être sur le ~** to be on the alert

quiz(z) [kwiz] NM INV quiz; **quizz télévisé** TV quiz show

quoi [kwa] PRON [a] (*interrog*) what; **de ~ parles-tu ? ◊ tu parles de ~ ?*** what are you talking about?, what are you on about?* (*Brit*); **on joue ~ au cinéma ?*** what's on at the cinema?; **en ~ puis-je vous aider ?** how can I help you?; **en ~ est cette statue ?** what is this statue made of?; **vers ~ allons-nous ?** what are we heading for?; **à ~ reconnaissez-vous le cristal ?** how can you tell that something is crystal?; **~ faire/lui dire ?** what are we (going) to do/to say to him?; **~ encore ?** (*gén*) what else?; (*exaspération*) what is it now?; **~ de plus beau que ...?** what can be more beautiful than ...?; **~ de neuf ?** *ou* **de nouveau ?** what's new?; **à ~ bon ?** what's the use? (**faire** of doing) [b] (*interrog indir*) what; **dites-nous à ~ cela sert** tell us what that's for; **il voudrait savoir de ~ il est question/en ~ cela le concerne** he would like to know what it's about/what that's got to do with him; **je ne vois pas avec ~/sur ~ vous allez écrire** I don't see what you are going to write with/on; **devinez ~ j'ai mangé*** guess what I've eaten; **je ne sais ~ lui donner** I don't know what to give him [c] (*relatif*) **je sais à ~ tu fais allusion** I know what (it is) you're referring to; **c'est en ~ tu te trompes** that's where you're wrong; **as-tu de ~ écrire ?** have you got a pen?; **ils n'ont même pas de ~ vivre** they haven't even got enough to live on; **il n'y a pas de ~ rire** it's no laughing matter, there's nothing to laugh about; **il n'y a pas de ~ pleurer** it's not worth crying over *ou* about, there's nothing to cry about; **il n'y a pas de ~ s'étonner** there's nothing surprising about *ou* in that; **ils ont de ~ occuper leurs vacances** they've got enough *ou* plenty to occupy them on their holiday; **avoir/emporter de ~ manger** to have/take something to eat → **comme**, **sans** [d] (*loc*) **~ qu'il arrive** whatever happens; **~ qu'il en soit** be that as it may, however that may be; **~ qu'on en dise/qu'elle fasse** whatever *ou* no matter what people say/she does; **si vous avez besoin de ~ que ce soit** if there's anything (at all) you need [e] (*loc*) (*excl*) **~ ! tu oses l'accuser ?** what! you dare to accuse him!; (*pour faire répéter*) **~ ?** **qu'est-ce qu'il a dit ?** what was it *ou* what was that he said?; (*iro*) **et puis ~ encore !** what next!; **puisque je te le dis, ~ !*** I'm telling you it's true!**:**; **de ~ (de ~)!:** what's all this nonsense!; **merci beaucoup ! — il n'y a pas de ~** many thanks! — don't mention it *ou* (it's) a pleasure *ou* not at all *ou* you're welcome; **ils n'ont pas de ~ s'acheter une voiture** they can't afford to buy a car; **avoir de ~** to have means; **des gens qui ont de ~** people of means → **chat**

quoique [kwak(ə)] CONJ (= *bien que*) although, though; **quoiqu'il soit malade et qu'il n'ait pas d'argent** although *ou* though he is ill and has no money; **je ne pense pas qu'il faisait semblant, ~ ...** I don't think he was pretending, but then *ou* there again...

quolibet † [kɔlibɛ] NM (= *raillerie*) gibe, jeer; **couvrir qn de ~s** to gibe *ou* jeer at sb

quorum [kɔrɔm] NM quorum; **le ~ a/n'a pas été atteint** the quorum was/was not a quorum, we (*ou* they *etc*) had/did not have a quorum

quota [k(w)ɔta] NM (*Admin*) quota; **~s d'importation** import quotas; **1 000 personnes sélectionnées selon la méthode des ~s** a quota sample of 1,000 people

quote-part (*pl* quotes-parts) [kɔtpaʀ] NF (*lit*, *fig*) share

quotidien, -ienne [kɔtidjɛ̃, jɛn] [1] ADJ (= *journalier*) [*nourriture*, *trajet*, *travail*] daily (*épith*); (= *banal*) [*incident*] everyday (*épith*), daily (*épith*); [*existence*] everyday (*épith*), humdrum; **dans la vie quotidienne** in everyday *ou* daily life → **pain** [2] NM [a] (= *journal*) daily (paper), (news)paper; **les grands ~s** the big national dailies [b] (= *routine*) **le ~** everyday life; **la pratique médicale/l'enseignement au ~** day-to-day medical practice/teaching

quotidiennement [kɔtidjɛnmɑ̃] ADV daily, every day

quotidienneté [kɔtidjɛnte] NF everyday nature

quotient [kɔsjɑ̃] NM (*Math*) quotient; **~ intellectuel** intelligence quotient, IQ; (*Impôts*) **~ familial** dependents' allowance set against tax

quotité [kɔtite] NF (*Fin*) quota; (*Jur*) **~ disponible** *portion of estate of which testator may dispose at his discretion*

QWERTY [kwɛʀti] ADV INV **clavier ~** QWERTY keyboard

➤ GRAMMAIRE ACTIVE: **quitter** 27.3, 27.4, 27.5

R

R, r [ɛR] NM (= *lettre*) R, r → **mois**

rab* [Rab] NM a [*nourriture*] extra; **est-ce qu'il y a du ~ ?** is there any extra (left)?, is there any extra food (left)?; **qui veut du ~ ?** anyone for seconds?; **il reste un ~ de viande** ◊ **il reste de la viande en ~** there is still (some) extra meat left (over) b [*temps*] (*gén, Mil*) extra time; **un ~ de 5 minutes** *ou* **5 minutes de ~ pour finir le devoir** 5 minutes' extra time *ou* 5 minutes extra to finish off the exercise; **faire du ~** (*travail*) to do *ou* work extra time; (*Mil*) to do *ou* serve extra time

rabâchage [Rabaʃaʒ] NM (= *répétition*) [*histoire*] harping on about*; (= *révision*) [*leçon*] going over and over; (= *radotage*) constant harping on*; **ses conférences, c'est du ~** he always says the same old thing in his lectures

rabâcher [Rabaʃe] ▶conjug 1◀ 1 VT (= *ressasser*) [+ *histoire*] to harp on about*, keep (on) repeating; (= *réviser*) [+ *leçon*] to go over and over, keep going back over (**à qn** for sb); **il rabâche toujours la même chose** he keeps rambling *ou* harping on about the same (old) thing 2 VI (= *radoter*) to keep repeating o.s.

rabâcheur, -euse [RabaʃœR, øz] NM,F repetitive *ou* repetitious bore; **il est du genre ~** he's the type who never stops repeating himself *ou* harping on*

rabais [Rabɛ] NM reduction, discount; **10 F de ~** ◊ **~ de 10 F** reduction *ou* discount of 10 francs, 10 francs off; **faire un ~ de 20 F sur qch** to give a reduction *ou* discount of 20 francs on sth, knock 20 francs off (the price of) sth; **au ~** [*acheter, vendre*] at a reduced price, (on the) cheap; (*péj*) [*acteur, journaliste*] third-rate; (*péj*) [*enseignement, médecine*] cheap-rate, on the cheap (*attrib*); (*péj*) **je ne veux pas travailler au ~** I won't work for a pittance

rabaissant, e [Rabɛsɑ̃, ɑ̃t] ADJ [*remarque*] disparaging, derogatory; [*métier*] degrading

rabaisser [Rabese] ▶conjug 1◀ 1 VT a (= *dénigrer*) [+ *personne*] to disparage; [+ *efforts, talent, travail*] to belittle, disparage b (= *réduire*) [+ *pouvoirs*] to reduce, decrease; [+ *orgueil*] to humble; [+ *exigences*] to moderate, reduce; [+ *qualité*] to impair; **il voulait 50 000 F par mois, mais il a dû ~ ses prétentions** he wanted 50,000 francs a month but he had to lower his sights → **caquet** c (= *diminuer*) [+ *prix*] to reduce, knock down, bring down d (= *baisser*) [+ *robe, store*] to pull (back) down 2 **se rabaisser** VPR to belittle o.s.; **elle se rabaisse toujours** she never gives herself enough credit, she's always belittling herself *ou* running herself down; **se ~ devant qn** to humble o.s. *ou* bow before sb

rabane [Raban] NF raffia fabric

Rabat [Raba] N Rabat

rabat [Raba] NM a [*table*] flap, leaf; [*poche, enveloppe*] flap; [*drap*] fold (*over the covers*); [*avocat, prêtre*] bands; **poche à ~** flapped pocket b = **rabattage**

rabat-joie [Rabaʒwa] NM INV killjoy, spoilsport, wet blanket*; **faire le ~** to spoil the fun, act like *ou* be a spoilsport, be a wet blanket*;

---

il est drôlement ~ he's an awful killjoy *ou* spoilsport *ou* wet blanket*

rabattable [Rabatabl] ADJ [*siège*] folding (*épith*)

rabattage [Rabataʒ] NM (*Chasse*) beating

rabatteur, -euse [RabatœR, øz] 1 NM,F (*Chasse*) beater; (*fig : péj*) tout; [*prostituée*] procurer, pimp; **le ~ de l'hôtel** the hotel tout 2 NM [*moissonneuse*] reel

rabattre [RabatR] ▶conjug 41◀ 1 VT a [+ *capot, clapet*] to close *ou* shut down; [+ *couvercle*] to close; [+ *drap*] to fold over *ou* back; [+ *col*] to turn down; [+ *bord de chapeau*] to turn *ou* pull down; [+ *strapontin*] (= *ouvrir*) to pull down; (= *fermer*) to put up; [+ *jupe*] to pull down; **le vent rabat la fumée** the wind blows the smoke back down; **il rabattit ses cheveux sur son front** he brushed his hair down over his forehead; **le chapeau rabattu sur les yeux** his hat pulled down over his eyes; **~ les couvertures** (*pour couvrir*) to pull the blankets up; (*pour découvrir*) to push *ou* throw back the blankets

b (= *diminuer*) to reduce; (= *déduire*) to deduct, take off; **il n'a pas voulu ~ un centime (du prix)** he wouldn't take *ou* knock a halfpenny (*Brit*) *ou* cent (*US*) off (the price), he wouldn't come down (by) one centime (on the price); **~ l'orgueil de qn** to humble sb's pride; **en ~** (= *de ses prétentions*) to climb down; (*de ses ambitions*) to lower one's sights; (*de ses illusions*) to lose one's illusions → **caquet**

c (*Chasse*) [+ *gibier*] to drive; [+ *terrain*] to beat; [*prostituée*] **~ des clients*** to tout for customers

d (*Tricot*) **~ des mailles** to cast off; (*Couture*) **~ une couture** to stitch down a seam

e (*Arboriculture*) [+ *arbre*] to cut back

2 **se rabattre** VPR a [*voiture*] to cut in; [*coureur*] to cut in, cut across; **se ~ devant qn** [*voiture*] to cut in front of sb; [*coureur*] to cut *ou* swing in front of *ou* across sb; **le coureur s'est rabattu à la corde** the runner cut *ou* swung across to the inside lane

b (= *prendre faute de mieux*) **se ~ sur** [+ *marchandise, personne*] to fall back on, make do with

c (= *se refermer*) [*porte*] to fall *ou* slam shut; [*couvercle*] [*boîte*] to fold down, fold away; **la porte se rabattit sur lui** the door closed *ou* shut on *ou* behind him

rabattu, e [Rabaty] (*ptp de* **rabattre**) ADJ [*col, bords*] turned down; [*poche*] flapped

rabbin [Rabɛ̃] NM rabbi; **grand ~** chief rabbi

rabbinat [Rabina] NM rabbinate

rabbinique [Rabinik] ADJ rabbinic(al)

rabbinisme [Rabinism] NM rabbinism

rabelaisien, -ienne [Rablɛzjɛ̃, jɛn] ADJ Rabelaisian

rabibochage* [Rabibɔʃaʒ] NM (= *réconciliation*) reconciliation

rabibocher* [Rabibɔʃe] ▶conjug 1◀ 1 VT (= *réconcilier*) [+ *amis, époux*] to bring together (again), reconcile, patch things up between

---

2 **se rabibocher** VPR to make it up, patch things up (**avec** with)

rabiot* [Rabjo] NM = **rab**

rabioter* [Rabjɔte] ▶conjug 1◀ VT a (= *obtenir*) to wangle*; **j'ai rabioté cinq minutes de sommeil** I managed to snatch another five minutes' sleep b (= *voler*) [+ *temps, argent*] to fiddle* (*Brit*); **qch à qn** sth from sb); **le plombier m'a rabioté 100 F/un quart d'heure** the plumber swindled *ou* did* me out of 100 francs/a quarter of an hour; **un commerçant qui rabiote** a shopkeeper who makes a bit on the side; **~ sur la quantité** to give short measure

rabioteur, -euse* [RabjɔtœR, øz] NM,F (= *qui vole*) **c'est un vrai ~** he's always trying to make a bit on the side, he's always on the fiddle* (*Brit*)

rabique [Rabik] ADJ rabies (*épith*)

râble [Rabl] NM (*Zool*) back; (* = *dos*) small of the back; **tomber** *ou* **sauter sur le ~ de qn*** to set on sb*, go for sb*; **le pauvre, il ne sait pas ce qui va lui tomber sur le ~ !** the poor guy doesn't know what he's in for!; (*Culin*) **~ de lièvre** saddle of hare

râblé, e [Rable] ADJ [*homme*] stocky, well-set (*Brit*), heavy-set (*US*); [*cheval*] broad-backed

rabot [Rabo] NM plane; **passer qch au ~** to plane sth (down)

rabotage [Rabɔtaʒ] NM planing (down)

raboter [Rabɔte] ▶conjug 1◀ VT a (*Menuiserie*) to plane (down) b (* = *racler*) [+ *objet*] to scrape; [+ *partie du corps*] to graze, scrape; **mon pare-chocs a raboté le mur** my bumper scraped the wall; **baisse-toi si tu ne veux pas te ~ la tête contre le plafond** bend down if you don't want to scrape your head on the ceiling c (*fig = diminuer*) to reduce; **crédits/salaires rabotés** reduced credits/wages

raboteur [RabɔtœR] NM (= *ouvrier*) planer

raboteuse¹ [Rabɔtøz] NF (= *machine*) planing machine

raboteux, -euse² [Rabɔtø, øz] ADJ (= *rugueux*) [*surface, arête*] uneven, rough; [*chemin*] rugged, uneven, bumpy; (*littér*) [*style*] rough, rugged; [*voix*] rough

rabougri, e [Rabugri] (*ptp de* **rabougrir**) ADJ (= *chétif*) [*plante*] stunted, scraggy; [*personne*] stunted, puny; (= *desséché*) [*plante*] shrivelled; [*vieillard*] wizened, shrivelled

rabougrir [RabugriR] ▶conjug 2◀ 1 VT [+ *personne*] to (cause to) shrivel up; [+ *plante*] (= *dessécher*) to shrivel (up); (= *étioler*) to stunt 2 **se rabougrir** VPR [*personne*] to become shrivelled (with age), become wizened; [*plante*] to shrivel (up), become stunted

rabougrissement [Rabugrismɑ̃] NM (= *action*) [*plante*] stunting, shrivelling (up); [*personne*] shrivelling up; (= *résultat*) [*plante*] scragginess; [*personne*] stunted appearance; [*vieillard*] wizened appearance

rabouter [Rabute] ▶conjug 1◀ VT [+ *tubes, planches*] to join (together) (end to end); [+ *étoffes*] to seam *ou* sew together

rabrouer [ʀabʀue] ▸conjug 1◀ VT to snub, rebuff; **elle me rabroue tout le temps** she rebuffs me all the time; **se faire ~** to be rebuffed

racaille [ʀakɑj] NF rabble, riffraff

raccommodable [ʀakɔmɔdabl] ADJ [*vêtement*] repairable, mendable

raccommodage [ʀakɔmɔdaʒ] NM [a] (= *action*) [*vêtement, accroc, filet*] mending, repairing; [*chaussettes*] darning, mending; **faire du ~ ou des ~s** (*pour soi*) to do some mending; (*comme métier*) to take in mending [b] (= *endroit réparé: gén*) mend, repair; [*chaussette*] darn

raccommodement* [ʀakɔmɔdmɑ̃] NM (= *réconciliation*) reconciliation

raccommoder [ʀakɔmɔde] ▸conjug 1◀ [1] VT [a] [+ *vêtements, accroc*] to mend, repair; [+ *chaussette*] to darn, mend [b]* [+ *ennemis*] to bring together again, patch things up between [2] **se raccommoder*** VPR to make it up, be reconciled

raccommodeur, -euse [ʀakɔmɔdœʀ, øz] NM,F [*linge, filets*] mender; **~ de porcelaines**†† china restorer

raccompagner [ʀakɔ̃paɲe] ▸conjug 1◀ VT to take *ou* see back (**à** to); **~ qn (chez lui)** to take *ou* see *ou* accompany sb home; **~ qn au bureau en voiture/à pied** to drive sb back/walk back with to the office; **~ qn à la gare** to see sb off at *ou* take sb to the station; **~ qn (jusqu')à la porte** to see sb to the door; **il l'a raccompagnée jusqu'à sa voiture** he walked *ou* saw her to her car

raccord [ʀakɔʀ] NM [a] [*papier peint*] join; **~ (de maçonnerie)** pointing (*NonC*); **faire un ~** (*de papier peint*) to line up the pattern; **faire un ~ de peinture/de maquillage** to touch up the paintwork/one's makeup; **on ne voit pas les ~s (de peinture)** you can't see where the paint has been touched up; (*papier peint*) **les ~s sont mal faits** the pattern isn't matched properly; **papier peint sans ~s** random match wallpaper [b] [*texte, discours*] link, join; (*Ciné*) [*séquence*] continuity; [*scène*] link shot; (= *collage*) [*film, bande magnétique*] splice; (*Ciné*) **à cause des coupures, nous avons dû faire des ~s** because of the cuts, we had to do some link shots; **ce plan n'est pas ~** this shot doesn't follow on from the preceding one [c] (= *pièce, joint*) link; [*pompe à vélo*] nozzle

raccordement [ʀakɔʀdəmɑ̃] NM [a] (*NonC*) [*routes, bâtiments, voies ferrées*] linking, joining, connecting; [*fils électriques*] joining; [*tuyaux*] joining, connecting; (*Ciné*) linking; **~ (au réseau)** (*Téléc*) connection (to the phone network); (*à l'électricité*) connection (to the mains); **ils sont venus faire le ~** (*Téléc*) they've come to connect the phone; (*à l'électricité*) they've come to connect the electricity → **bretelle, taxe, voie** [b] (= *soudure, épissure*) join; (= *tunnel, passage*) connecting passage; (= *carrefour, voie ferrée*) junction

raccorder [ʀakɔʀde] ▸conjug 1◀ [1] VT [a] [+ *routes, bâtiments, voies ferrées*] to link up, join (up), connect (**à** with, to); [+ *fils électriques*] to join; [+ *tuyaux*] to join, connect (**à** to); **les motifs du papier peint sont parfaitement raccordés** the wallpaper is perfectly lined up [b] (*Ciné*) [+ *plans, scènes*] to link up [c] **~ qn au réseau** (*Téléc*) to connect sb's phone; (*à l'électricité*) to connect sb to the mains; **quand les deux tuyaux seront raccordés** when the two pipes are joined together *ou* connected [d] (= *établir une relation entre*) to connect [2] **se raccorder** VPR [*routes*] to link *ou* join up (**à** with); [*faits*] **se ~ à** to tie up *ou* in with

raccourci [ʀakuʀsi] NM [a] (= *chemin*) short cut; **prendre un ~ par la forêt** to take a short cut through the forest [b] (= *formule frappante*) pithy turn of phrase; (= *résumé*) summary; **en ~** (= *en miniature*) in miniature; (= *dans les grandes lignes*) in (broad) outline; (= *en bref*)

in a nutshell, in brief [c] (*Art*) foreshortening; **figure en ~** foreshortened figure → **bras**

raccourcir [ʀakuʀsiʀ] ▸conjug 2◀ [1] VT [a] [+ *distance, temps*] to shorten; [+ *vêtement*] to shorten, take up; [+ *vacances*] to shorten, cut short; [+ *texte*] to cut; **j'ai raccourci le chapitre de trois pages** *ou* shortened the chapter by three pages; **ça raccourcit le trajet de 5 km** it cuts *ou* knocks 5 km off the journey; **passons par là, ça (nous) raccourcit** let's go this way, it's shorter *ou* quicker; **les vêtements amples raccourcissent la silhouette** baggy clothes make people look shorter [b] (* *hum = décapiter*) **~ qn** to chop sb's head off [2] VI [*jours*] to grow shorter, draw in; [*vêtement*] (*au lavage*) to shrink; (*Mode*) **les jupes ont raccourci cette année** skirts are shorter this year, hemlines have gone up this year

raccourcissement [ʀakuʀsismɑ̃] NM [*distance, temps, jour, vacances, texte*] shortening; [*vêtement*] (*en cousant*) shortening; (*au lavage*) shrinking

raccoutumer [ʀakutyme] ▸conjug 1◀ VT = **réaccoutumer**

raccroc [ʀakʀo] NM (*frm*) **par ~** (= *par hasard*) by chance; (= *par un heureux hasard*) by a stroke of good fortune

▾**raccrocher** [ʀakʀɔʃe] ▸conjug 1◀ [1] VI [a] (*Téléc*) to hang up, ring off (*surtout Brit*); **ne raccroche pas** hold on, don't hang up *ou* ring off (*surtout Brit*); **~ au nez de qn*** to put the phone down on sb, hang up on sb [b] (*arg Sport*) to retire [2] VT [a] [+ *vêtement, tableau*] to hang back up; [+ *combiné*] to put down; **j'avais mal raccroché** I hadn't put the receiver down properly; (*Sport*) **~ les gants/chaussures** to hang up one's gloves/boots [b] (= *racoler*) [*vendeur, portier*] to tout for; [*prostituée*] **~ le client** to solicit, accost customers [c] (= *attraper*) [+ *personne, bonne affaire*] to grab *ou* get hold of; **il m'a raccroché dans la rue** he stopped *ou* waylaid *ou* buttonholed me in the street [d] (= *relier*) [+ *wagons, faits*] to link, connect (**à** to, with) [e] (* = *rattraper*) [+ *affaire, contrat*] to save, rescue [3] **se raccrocher** VPR **se ~ à** [+ *branche, rampe*] to catch *ou* grab (hold of); [+ *espoir, personne*] to cling to, hang on to; **cette idée se raccroche à la précédente** this idea ties in with the previous one → **branche**

race [ʀas] NF [a] (= *ethnie*) race; **la ~ humaine** the human race; **être de ~ indienne** to be of Indian stock *ou* blood; **un individu de ~ blanche/noire** a white/black person; (*péj*) **c'est de la sale ~ !*** they're just scum!* [b] (*Zool*) breed; **la ~ chevaline** horses, equines; **la ~ bovine normande** Normandy cattle; **de ~** (*gén*) pedigree (*épith*), purebred (*épith*); [*cheval*] thoroughbred; **avoir de la ~** to be of good stock → **chien** [c] (= *ancêtres*) stock, race; **être de ~ noble** to be of noble stock *ou* blood *ou* race; **avoir de la ~** to have breeding [d] (= *catégorie*) breed; **lui et les gens de sa ~** him and others like him; **les cordonniers, c'est une ~ qui disparaît** cobblers are a dying breed *ou* race; **il est de la ~ des héros** he's the stuff heroes are made of

racé, e [ʀase] ADJ [*animal*] purebred (*épith*), pedigree (*épith*); [*cheval*] thoroughbred; [*personne*] distinguished; [*voiture, voilier, ligne*] sleek

rachat [ʀaʃa] NM [a] [*objet que l'on possédait avant*] buying back, repurchase; [*objet d'occasion*] buying, purchase; [*usine en faillite*] buying up *ou* out *ou* over; [*dette, rente*] redemption; **~ d'entreprise par l'encadrement/par les salariés** management/employee buyout; **option** *ou* **possibilité de ~** buy-back option; **après le ~ du journal par le groupe** af-

ter the group bought the paper back [b] [*esclave, otage*] ransom, ransoming [c] (= *réparation*) redemption, atonement; (*Rel*) redemption

rachetable [ʀaʃ(ə)tabl] ADJ [*dette, rente*] redeemable; [*péché*] expiable; [*pécheur*] redeemable; **cette faute n'est pas ~** you can't make up for this mistake

racheter [ʀaʃ(ə)te] ▸conjug 5◀ [1] VT [a] [+ *objet que l'on possédait avant*] to buy back, repurchase; [+ *nouvel objet*] to buy *ou* purchase another; [+ *pain, lait*] to buy some more; [+ *objet d'occasion*] to buy, purchase; [+ *entreprise*] to buy out, take over; [+ *usine en faillite*] to buy up *ou* out *ou* over; **je lui ai racheté son vieux vélo** I bought his old bike from *ou* off him; **il a racheté toutes les parts de son associé** he bought his partner out, he bought up all his partner's shares; **j'ai dû ~ du tissu/des verres** I had to buy some more material/some more glasses [b] [+ *dette, rente*] to redeem [c] [+ *esclave, otage*] to ransom, pay a ransom for [d] (= *réparer*) [+ *péché, crime*] to atone for, expiate; [+ *mauvaise conduite, faute*] to make amends for, make up for; [+ *imperfection*] to make up *ou* compensate for; [+ *pécheur*] to redeem; **il n'y en a pas un pour ~ l'autre*** they're both (just) as bad as each other [e] (*Scol*) [+ *candidat*] to mark up [f] (*Archit*) to modify [2] **se racheter** VPR [*pécheur*] to redeem o.s.; [*criminel*] to make amends; **se ~ aux yeux de qn** to redeem o.s. in sb's eyes; **essaie de te ~ en t'excusant** try and make up for it *ou* try to make amends by apologizing

rachidien, -ienne [ʀaʃidjɛ̃, jɛn] ADJ of the spinal column, rachidian (*SPÉC*)

rachis [ʀaʃis] NM (*Anat*) vertebral *ou* spinal column, r(h)ac (*SPÉC*)

rachitique [ʀaʃitik] ADJ [*personne*] (*Méd*) suffering from rickets, rachitic (*SPÉC*); (= *maigre*) puny; [*arbre, poulet*] scraggy, scrawny; **c'est un ~** ◊ **il est ~** he suffers from rickets

rachitisme [ʀaʃitism] NM rickets *sg*, rachitis (*SPÉC*); **faire du ~** to have rickets

racial, e (*mpl* **-iaux**) [ʀasjal, jo] ADJ [*haine, tensions, injure, intégration*] racial; [*discrimination, lois*] racial, race (*épith*); [*émeutes, relations*] race (*épith*)

racine [ʀasin] [1] NF [a] (*gén*) root; (*Bot*) **la carotte est une ~** the carrot is a root (vegetable), carrots are a root crop; **prendre ~** (*lit*) to take *ou* strike root(s), put out roots; (*fig* = *s'établir*) to put down (one's) roots; (*: *chez qn, à attendre*) to take root*; **prendre le mal à la ~** ◊ **s'attaquer aux ~s du mal** to get to the root of the problem → **rougir** [b] (*Math*) [*équation*] root; [*nombre*] **~ carrée/cubique/dixième** square/cube/tenth root [c] (*Ling*) [*mot*] root [2] **racines** NFPL (= *attaches, origines*) roots; **il est sans ~s** he's rootless, he belongs nowhere; **cette idée a des ~s profondes dans notre société** this idea is deeply rooted in our society [3] COMP ▸ **racine adventive** adventitious root ▸ **racine aérienne** aerial root ▸ **racine fasciculée** fascicled root ▸ **racine pivotante** taproot

racinien, -ienne [ʀasinjɛ̃, jɛn] ADJ Racinian

racisme [ʀasism] NM racism; **~ antijeunes** anti-youth prejudice

raciste [ʀasist] ADJ, NMF racist

racket [ʀaket] NM (= *activité*) racketeering (*NonC*); (= *vol*) (extortion) racket; **~ scolaire** school children bullying other children for money etc; **faire du ~** ◊ **se livrer au ~** (= *contre protection*) to run a protection racket; **c'est du ~ !** it's daylight robbery!

racketter [ʀakete] ▸conjug 1◀ VT **~ qn** to extort money from sb; **il se fait ~ à l'école** children bully him into giving them money (*ou* his personal belongings *etc*) at school

racketteur [rakɛtœr] NM racketeer

raclage [rɑklaʒ] NM (*Tech*) scraping

raclée* [rɑkle] NF (= *coups*) hiding, thrashing; (= *défaite*) thrashing*; **flanquer une bonne ~ à qn** to give sb a good hiding; **il a pris une bonne ~ aux élections** he got thrashed* *ou* hammered* in the elections

raclement [rɑkləmã] NM (= *bruit*) scraping (noise); **on entendit un ~ de gorge** someone could be heard clearing their throat

racler [rɑkle] ▶ conjug 1 ◀ VT [a] (*gén, Méd, Tech*) to scrape; [+ *fond de casserole*] to scrape out; [+ *parquet*] to scrape (down); **ce vin racle le gosier** this wine is really rough; **se ~ la gorge** to clear one's throat → **fond** [b] (= *ratisser*) [+ *allée, gravier, sable*] to rake [c] (= *enlever*) [+ *tache, croûte*] to scrape away *ou* off; [+ *peinture, écailles*] to scrape off; **~ la boue de ses semelles** to scrape the mud off one's shoes [d] (*péj*) [+ *violon*] to scrape *ou* saw (a tune) on; [+ *guitare*] to strum (a tune) on

raclette [rɑklɛt] NF [a] (= *outil*) scraper [b] (*Culin*) raclette (*melted cheese served with boiled potatoes and cold meats*)

racloir [rɑklwar] NM scraper

raclure [rɑklyr] NF [a] (*gén pl = déchet*) scraping [b]* (*péj*) louse*

racolage [rɑkɔlaʒ] NM [a] (*par une prostituée*) soliciting [b] (*péj: par un agent électoral, un portier, un vendeur*) soliciting, touting; **faire du ~** to solicit, tout; **cette émission fait du ~ émotionnel** this programme deliberately plays on people's emotions

racoler [rɑkɔle] ▶ conjug 1 ◀ VT [a] [*prostituée*] **~ des clients** to solicit for clients; **~ en voiture** to solicit in a car [b] (*péj*) [*agent électoral, portier, vendeur*] to solicit, tout for [c] (*Hist*) [*soldats*] to pressgang

racoleur, -euse [rɑkɔlœr, øz] [1] NM (*pour spectacle*) tout; († *Mil*) crimp; (*péj Pol*) canvasser [2] **racoleuse** NF (= *prostituée*) streetwalker, whore [3] ADJ [*slogan, publicité*] (*gén*) eye-catching, enticing; (*Pol*) vote-catching

racontable [rɑkɔ̃tabl] ADJ repeatable; **cette histoire n'est pas ~ devant des enfants** this story is not fit to be told in front of children

racontar [rɑkɔ̃tar] NM story, bit of gossip; **ce ne sont que des ~s !** it's just gossip!

raconter [rɑkɔ̃te] ▶ conjug 1 ◀ [1] VT [a] (= *relater*) [+ *histoire, légende*] to tell; **~ qch à qn** to tell sb sth; **~ sa vie** to tell one's life story; **il nous a raconté ses malheurs** he told us about his misfortunes; **il raconte qu'il a vu la reine** he says that he's seen the queen; **elle m'a raconté qu'elle t'avait rencontré** she told me that she had met you; **on raconte que ...** people say that ...; **à ce qu'on raconte** from what people say; **il est un peu radin à ce qu'on raconte** he's a bit mean by all accounts *ou* from what people say; **le témoin a raconté ce qui s'était passé** the witness described *ou* recounted what had happened; **il raconte bien** he tells a good story, he's a good storyteller; **alors, raconte !** come on, tell me! (*ou* us!); **alors, qu'est-ce que tu racontes ?*** so, what's new?*, so, how are things with you?*; **je te raconte pas !*** you can imagine!
[b] (= *dire de mauvaise foi*) **qu'est-ce que tu racontes ?** what on earth are you talking about?, what are you (going) on about?*; **il raconte n'importe quoi** he's talking nonsense *ou* rubbish* (*Brit*); **~ des histoires ◊ en ~** to tell stories, spin yarns; **il a été ~ qu'on allait divorcer** he's been (going around) telling people we're getting divorced

[2] **se raconter** VPR [*écrivain*] to talk about o.s.; (= *se leurrer*) **se ~ des histoires** to lie to o.s.

raconteur, -euse [rɑkɔ̃tœr, øz] NM,F storyteller; **~ de** narrator of

---

racornir [rɑkɔrnir] ▶ conjug 2 ◀ [1] VT [a] (= *durcir*) [+ *peau, cuir*] to toughen, harden; [+ *cœur, personne*] to harden; **cuir racorni** hardened *ou* dried-up leather; **dans son cœur racorni** in his hard heart [b] (= *ratatiner*) [+ *personne, plante*] to shrivel (up); **un vieillard racorni** a shrivelled(-up) *ou* wizened old man [2] **se racornir** VPR [a] (= *se durcir*) [*peau, cuir, cœur, personne*] to become tough *ou* hard [b] (= *se ratatiner*) [*personne, plante*] to shrivel (up), become shrivelled (up)

racornissement [rɑkɔrnismã] NM [*peau, cuir*] toughening, hardening; [*plante*] shrivelling (up)

rad [rad] NM rad

radar [radar] NM radar; **système/écran ~** radar system/screen; (*Aut*) **contrôle ~** speed check; **il s'est fait prendre au ~*** he was caught by a speed trap*; (*fig*) **marcher** *ou* **fonctionner au ~*** to be on automatic pilot*

radariste [radarist] NMF radar operator

rade [rad] NF [a] (= *port*) (natural) harbour (*Brit*) *ou* harbor (*US*), roads (*SPÉC*), roadstead (*SPÉC*); **en ~** in harbour, in the roads (*SPÉC*); **en ~ de Brest** in Brest harbour [b] (* *loc*) **laisser en ~** [+ *personne*] to leave in the lurch, leave high and dry; [+ *projet*] to forget about, drop, shelve; [+ *voiture*] to leave behind; **elle/sa voiture est restée en ~** she/her car was left stranded; **tomber en ~** (*panne d'essence*) to run out of petrol (*Brit*) *ou* gas (*US*); (*ennuis mécaniques*) to break down

radeau (*pl* **radeaux**) [rado] NM raft; (= *train de bois*) timber float *ou* raft; **~ de sauvetage/pneumatique** rescue/inflatable raft; (*Art*) **« le Radeau de la Méduse »** "the Raft of the Medusa"

radial, e (*mpl* **-iaux**) [radjal, jo] [1] ADJ (*gén*) radial [2] **radiale** NF (= *route*) urban motorway (*Brit*) *ou* highway (*US*)

radian [radjã] NM radian

radiant, e [radjã, jãt] ADJ [*énergie*] radiant; (*Astron*) (**point**) **~** radiant

radiateur [radjatœr] NM (*à eau, à huile*) radiator; (*à gaz, à barres chauffantes*) heater; [*voiture*] radiator; **~ à accumulation** storage radiator *ou* heater; **~ électrique** electric heater; **~ soufflant** fan heater; **~ parabolique** electric fire

radiation [radjasjɔ̃] NF [a] (*Phys*) radiation [b] [*nom, mention*] crossing *ou* striking off; **on a demandé sa ~ du club** they've asked that he should be struck off the club register

radical, e (*mpl* **-aux**) [radikal, o] [1] ADJ [*changement, mesure, solution*] radical, drastic; (*Bot, Math, Hist, Pol*) radical; **une rupture ~e avec les pratiques passées** a complete break with past practices; **essayez ce remède, c'est ~*** try this remedy, it works like a charm *ou* it really does the trick*; **un mois de ce régime et tu maigris, c'est ~ !*** one month on this diet and you lose weight, it never fails! [2] NM [*mot*] stem, radical, root; (*Chim, Pol*) radical; (*Math*) radical sign; (*Chim*) **radicaux libres** (free) radicals

radicalement [radikalmã] ADV [*changer, différer*] radically; [*faux, nouveau*] completely; **~ opposé à/différent** radically opposed to/different; **rompre ~ avec** to make a complete break with

radicalisation [radikalizasjɔ̃] NF [*position, revendications*] toughening; [*conflit*] intensification; [*régime, parti*] radicalization; **certains élus préconisent une ~ du texte** some representatives would like the text to be made even more radical

radicaliser [radikalize] ▶ conjug 1 ◀ [1] VT [+ *position*] to toughen, harden; [+ *politique*] to toughen [2] **se radicaliser** VPR [*personne, parti, position, régime*] to become more radical; [*conflit*] to intensify

radicalisme [radikalism] NM (*Pol*) radicalism

---

radical-socialisme [radikalsɔsjalism] NM radical socialism

radical-socialiste, radicale-socialiste [radikalsɔsjalist] (*mpl* **radicaux-socialistes** [radikosɔsjalist]) ADJ, NMF radical socialist

radicelle [radisɛl] NF rootlet, radicle (*SPÉC*)

radiculaire [radikyler] ADJ radicular

radicule [radikyl] NF radicule

radié, e [radje] (*ptp de radier*) ADJ (= *rayonné*) rayed, radiate

radier [radje] ▶ conjug 7 ◀ VT [+ *mention, nom*] to cross off, strike off; **il a été radié de l'Ordre des médecins** he has been struck off the medical register

radiesthésie [radjɛstezi] NF (power of) divination, dowsing (*based on the detection of radiation emitted by various bodies*)

radiesthésiste [radjɛstezist] NMF diviner, dowser

radieusement [radjøzmã] ADV radiantly; **~ beau** [*personne*] radiantly *ou* dazzlingly beautiful; [*temps*] absolutely glorious

radieux, -ieuse [radjø, jøz] ADJ [*personne*] (*de joie*) radiant with happiness *ou* joy; (*de beauté*) radiantly *ou* dazzlingly beautiful; [*air, sourire*] radiant, beaming (*épith*); [*soleil, beauté*] radiant, dazzling; [*journée, temps*] brilliant, glorious

radin, e* [radɛ̃, in] [1] ADJ stingy, tight-fisted [2] NM,F skinflint

radiner* VI, **se radiner*** VPR [radine] ▶ conjug 1 ◀ (= *arriver*) to turn up, show up*, roll up*; (= *accourir*) to rush over, dash over; **allez, radine(-toi)!** come on, step on it!* *ou* get your skates on!* (*Brit*)

radinerie* [radinri] NF stinginess (*NonC*), tight-fistedness (*NonC*)

radio [radjo] [1] NF [a] (= *poste*) radio; **mets la ~** turn on *ou* put on the radio → **poste²** [b] (= *radiodiffusion*) **la ~** (the) radio; **avoir la ~** to have a radio; **parler à la ~** to speak on the radio; **passer à la ~** to be on the radio; **travailler à la ~** to work in broadcasting *ou* on the radio; **antenne/fréquence ~** radio aerial/frequency (= *station*) radio station; **~ pirate** pirate radio station; **la ~ du Caire** Cairo radio; **~ libre** *ou* **locale privée** independent local radio station [d] (= *radiotéléphonie*) radio; **message ~** radio message; **la ~ de bord du navire** the ship's radio [e] (= *radiographie*) X-ray (photograph); **passer une ~** to have an X-ray (taken); **on lui a fait passer une ~** he was X-rayed [2] NM (= *opérateur*) radio operator; † (= *message*) radiogram, radiotelegram

radioactif, -ive [radjoaktif, iv] ADJ radioactive; **déchets faiblement/hautement ~s** low-level/highly *ou* high-level radioactive waste

radioactivité [radjoaktivite] NF radioactivity; **~ naturelle** natural *ou* naturally-occurring radioactivity

radioalignement [radjoalin(ə)mã] NM radio navigation system

radioamateur [radjoamatœr] NM radio ham*

radioastronome [radjoastrɔnɔm] NMF radio astronomer

radioastronomie [radjoastrɔnɔmi] NF radio astronomy

radiobalisage [radjobalizaʒ] NM radio beacon signalling

radiobalise [radjobaliz] NF radio beacon

radiobaliser [radjobalize] ▶ conjug 1 ◀ VT to equip with a radio beacon system

radiobiologie [radjobjɔlɔʒi] NF radiobiology

radiocarbone [radjokarbɔn] NM radiocarbon, radioactive carbon

radiocassette [radjokasɛt] NM cassette radio, radio cassette player

radiocobalt [radjokɔbalt] NM radio cobalt, radioactive cobalt

radiocommande [Radjokɔmɑ̃d] NF radio control

radiocommunication [Radjokɔmynikasjɔ̃] NF radio communication

radiocompas [Radjokɔpα] NM radio compass

radioconducteur [Radjokɔ̃dyktœR] NM detector

radiodiagnostic [Radjodjagnɔstik] NM radiodiagnosis

radiodiffuser [Radjodifyze] ▸ conjug 1 ◂ VT to broadcast (by radio); **interview radiodiffusée** broadcast ou radio interview

radiodiffuseur [RadjodifyzœR] NM (radio) broadcaster

radiodiffusion [Radjodifyzjɔ̃] NF broadcasting (by radio)

radioélectricien, -ienne [RadjoelɛktRisjɛ̃, jɛn] NM,F radio-engineer

radioélectricité [RadjoelɛktRisite] NF radio-engineering

radioélectrique [RadjoelɛktRik] ADJ radio (épith)

radioélément [Radjoelemɑ̃] NM radio-element

radiofréquence [Radjofrekɑ̃s] NF radio frequency

radiogénique [Radjoʒenik] ADJ radiogenic

radiogoniomètre [RadjogɔnjɔmɛtR] NM direction finder, radiogoniometer

radiogoniométrie [RadjogɔnjɔmetRi] NF radio direction finding, radiogoniometry

radiogramme [RadjogRam] NM (= télégramme) radiogram, radiotelegram; (= film) radiograph, radiogram

radiographie [Radjografi] NF a (= technique) radiography, X-ray photography; **passer une ~** to have an X-ray (taken), be X-rayed b (= photographie) X-ray (photograph), radiograph

radiographier [Radjogrfje] ▸ conjug 7 ◂ VT to X-ray

radiographique [Radjogrfik] ADJ X-ray (épith)

radioguidage [Radjogidaʒ] NM (Aviat) radio control, radiodirection; (Radio) **le ~ des automobilistes** broadcasting traffic reports to motorists

radioguidé, e [Radjogide] ADJ radio-controlled

radioguider [Radjogide] ▸ conjug 1 ◂ VT to radio-control

radio-isotope (pl **radio-isotopes**) [Radjoizɔtɔp] NM radio-isotope

radiologie [Radjolɔʒi] NF radiology

radiologique [Radjolɔʒik] ADJ radiological

radiologiste [Radjolɔʒist], **radiologue** [Radjolɔg] NMF radiologist

radiomessagerie [RadjomesaʒRi] NF radio-paging

radiomètre [RadjɔmɛtR] NM radiometer

radionavigant [Radjonavigɑ̃] NM radio officer

radionavigation [Radjonavigasjɔ̃] NF radio navigation

radiophare [Radjofar] NM radio beacon

radiophonie [Radjɔfɔni] NF radiotelephony

radiophonique [Radjɔfɔnik] ADJ radio (épith)

radioprotection [Radjoprɔtɛksjɔ̃] NF radiation protection

radioreportage [RadjoR(ə)pɔRtaʒ] NM radio report

radioreporter [RadjoR(ə)pɔRtɛR] NM radio reporter

radio-réveil (pl **radio-réveils**) [Radjorevɛj] NM radio-alarm, clock-radio

radioscopie [Radjɔskɔpi] NF radioscopy

radioscopique [Radjɔskɔpik] ADJ radioscopic

radiosondage [Radjosɔ̃daʒ] NM (Mét) radio-sonde exploration; (Géol) seismic prospecting

radiosonde [Radjosɔ̃d] NF radiosonde

radiosource [Radjosurs] NF radio source, star source

radio-taxi (pl **radio-taxis**) [Radjotaksi] NM radio taxi, radio cab

radiotechnique [Radjotɛknik] 1 NF radio technology 2 ADJ radiotechnological

radiotélégraphie [Radjotelegrafi] NF radio-telegraphy, wireless telegraphy

radiotélégraphique [RadjotelegRafik] ADJ radiotelegraphic

radiotélégraphiste [Radjotelegrafist] NMF radiotelegrapher

radiotéléphone [Radjotelefɔn] NM radiotelephone

radiotéléphonie [Radjotelefɔni] NF radio-telephony, wireless telephony

radiotélescope [Radjotelɛskɔp] NM radio telescope

radiotélévisé, e [Radjotelevize] ADJ broadcast on both radio and television, broadcast and televised

radiotélévision [Radjotelevizjɔ̃] NF radio and television

radiothérapeute [Radjoterapøt] NMF radio-therapist

radiothérapie [Radjoterapi] NF radiotherapy

radis [Radi] NM a (Bot) radish; **~ noir** black winter radish b (‡ = sou) penny, cent (US); **je n'ai pas un ~** I haven't got a penny (to my name) (Brit) ou a cent* ou a bean (US)*; **ça ne vaut pas un ~** it's not worth a penny ou a bean (Brit)*

radium [Radjɔm] NM radium

radius [Radjys] NM (Anat) radius

radjah [Radʒa] NM = rajah

radome [Radom] NM radome

radon [Radɔ̃] NM radon

radotage [Radɔtaʒ] NM (péj) drivel (NonC), rambling

radoter [Radɔte] ▸ conjug 1 ◂ 1 VI (péj) to ramble on ou drivel (on); **tu radotes*** you're talking a load of drivel* 2 VT (péj) **il radote toujours les mêmes histoires*** he's always going on ou wittering on* about the same old things

radoteur, -euse [RadɔtœR, øz] NM,F (péj) drivelling (old) fool, (old) driveller

radoub [Radu] NM (Naut) refitting; **navire au ~** ship under repair ou undergoing a refit → **bassin**

radouber [Radube] ▸ conjug 1 ◂ VT [+ navire] to repair, refit; [+ filet de pêche] to repair, mend

radoucir [RadusiR] ▸ conjug 2 ◂ 1 VT [+ ton, attitude] to soften; [+ temps] to make milder 2 **se radoucir** VPR [personne] (après une colère) to calm down, be mollified; (avec l'âge) to mellow; [voix] to soften, become milder; [temps] to become milder

radoucissement [Radusismɑ̃] NM a (Mét) (de la température) rise in (the) temperature; **on prévoit un léger/net ~** the forecast is for slightly/much milder weather b [ton, attitude] softening; [personne] calming down

rafale [Rafal] NF [vent] gust; [pluie] sudden shower; [mitrailleuse] burst; [neige] flurry; **une soudaine ~ (de vent)** a sudden gust of wind; **~ de mitrailleuse** burst of machine gun fire; **en ou par ~s** [souffler] in gusts; [tirer] in bursts; **tir en ~s** firing ou shooting in bursts; **une ~ ou des ~s de balles** a hail of bullets; **le gouvernement publiait des communiqués en ~s** the government issued statements in rapid-fire succession

raffermir [RafɛRmiR] ▸ conjug 2 ◂ 1 VT a [+ muscle] to harden, tone up; [+ chair] to firm up, make firm(er); [+ peau] to tone up b [+ gouvernement, popularité] to strengthen, reinforce; [+ prix, marché, cours] to steady; [+ courage, résolution] to strengthen 2 **se raffermir** VPR a [muscle] to harden;

[chair] to firm up, become firm(er) b [autorité] to strengthen, become strengthened ou reinforced; [prix, marché, cours, voix] to become steadier; **son visage se raffermit** his face became more composed; **ma résolution se raffermit** I grew stronger in my resolve; **se ~ dans ses intentions** to strengthen one's resolve; **le cours du dollar s'est légèrement raffermi** the dollar is slightly steadier

raffermissant, e [Rafɛrmisɑ̃, ɑ̃t] ADJ (Cosmétique) toning

raffermissement [Rafɛrmismɑ̃] NM a [muscle] strengthening; [chair] firming; [peau] firming up; [voix] steadying b [gouvernement, popularité] reinforcement; [cours, monnaie] steadying; [courage, résolution] strengthening; **la nouvelle a provoqué un ~ du dollar** the news steadied the dollar

raffinage [Rafinaʒ] NM refining

raffiné, e [Rafine] (ptp de **raffiner**) ADJ a [pétrole, sucre] refined b [personne, mœurs, style] refined, polished, sophisticated; [esprit, gourmet, goûts] discriminating, refined; [confort, décor] elegant; [cuisine, élégance] refined; **peu ~** unrefined, unsophisticated; **supplice ~** slow torture

raffinement [Rafinmɑ̃] NM a (= caractère) [personne, civilisation] refinement, sophistication b (gén pl = détail raffiné) nicety, refinement c (= excès) **c'est du ~** that's being oversubtle; **avec un ~ de luxe/de cruauté** with refinements of luxury/of cruelty

raffiner [Rafine] ▸ conjug 1 ◂ 1 VT a [+ pétrole, sucre, papier] to refine b [+ langage, manières] to refine, polish 2 VI (dans le raisonnement) to be oversubtle; (sur les détails) to be (over)meticulous

raffinerie [RafinRi] NF refinery; **~ de pétrole/ de sucre** oil/sugar refinery

raffineur, -euse [RafinœR, øz] NM,F refiner

raffoler [Rafɔle] ▸ conjug 1 ◂ ♦ **raffoler de** VT INDIR to be mad ou crazy* ou wild* about; **le chocolat, j'en raffole !** I'm mad* about chocolate!

raffut* [Rafy] NM (= vacarme) row, racket; **faire du ~** (= être bruyant) to make a row ou racket; (= protester) to kick up a fuss ou stink*; **ils ont fait un ~ de tous les diables** they made a hell* of a racket; **sa démission va faire du ~** his resignation will cause a row ou a stink*

rafiot [Rafjo] NM (péj = bateau) (old) tub (péj)

rafistolage* [Rafistɔlaʒ] NM (= action : lit, fig) patching up; (= résultat qu'un ou que du ~ (lit) it's only a patched-up ou makeshift repair; (fig) it's just a stopgap (solution)

rafistoler* [Rafistɔle] ▸ conjug 1 ◂ VT (= réparer) to patch up

rafle [Rafl] NF (police) roundup ou raid, swoop; **la police a fait une ~** the police rounded up some suspects; **être pris dans une ~** to be caught in a roundup ou a raid; (Hist) **la ~ du Vél' d'Hiv** the roundup of Jews in the Paris Vélodrome d'Hiver during the Second World War

rafler* [Rafle] ▸ conjug 1 ◂ VT (= prendre) [+ récompenses] to run off with; [+ place] to bag*, grab; (= voler) [+ bijoux] to swipe‡; **les clients avaient tout raflé** the customers had swept up ou snaffled* everything; **elle a raflé tous les prix** she ran away ou off with all the prizes, she made a clean sweep of the prizes; **le film a raflé sept Oscars** the film scooped seven Oscars

rafraîchir [RafRefiR] ▸ conjug 2 ◂ 1 VT a (= refroidir) [+ air] to cool (down), freshen; [+ vin] to chill; [+ boisson] to cool, make cooler; [+ haleine] to freshen → **fruit** b (= redonner du tonus à) [+ visage, corps] to freshen (up) c (= désaltérer) [boisson] to refresh d (= rénover) [+ vêtement] to smarten up, brighten up; [+ tableau, couleur] to brighten up, freshen up; [+ appartement] to do up, brighten up; [+ connaissances] to brush up; [+ appartement] « à ~ » "needs some work"; **se faire ~ les cheveux** to have a trim, have one's hair trimmed; **~ la mémoire ou les idées de qn** to jog ou refresh sb's memory

[e] (Ordin) [+ écran] to refresh

[2] VI [vin etc] to cool (down); **mettre à ~** [+ vin, dessert] to chill

[3] **se rafraîchir** VPR [a] (Mét) **le temps/ça se rafraîchit** the weather/it's getting cooler ou colder

[b] (en se lavant) to freshen (o.s.) up; (en buvant) to refresh o.s.; **on se rafraîchirait volontiers** a cool drink would be very welcome

rafraîchissant, e [RafRefisɑ̃, ɑ̃t] ADJ [vent] refreshing, cooling; [boisson] refreshing; (fig) [idée, œuvre] refreshing

rafraîchissement [RafRefismɑ̃] NM [a] [température] cooling; **dû au ~ de la température** due to the cooler weather ou the cooling of the weather; **on s'attend à un ~ rapide de la température** we expect temperatures to drop sharply, we expect the weather to get rapidly cooler [b] (= boisson) cool ou cold drink; (= glaces, fruits) **~s** refreshments [c] (Ordin) refresh; **fréquence de ~** refresh rate

raft [Raft] NM raft

rafting [Raftiŋ] NM rafting; **faire du ~** to raft, go rafting

ragaillardir [Ragajaʀdiʀ] ▸conjug 2◂ VT to perk up, buck up*; **tout ragaillardi par cette nouvelle** bucked up by this news*

rage [Raʒ] NF [a] (= colère) rage, fury; **la ~ au cœur** (inwardly) seething with rage ou anger; **mettre qn en ~** to infuriate ou enrage sb, make sb's blood boil; **être dans une ~ folle** ◊ **être ivre ou fou de ~** to be mad with rage, be in a raging temper; **être en ~** ◊ **avoir la ~**: to be absolutely furious, be fuming*; **suffoquer ou étouffer de ~** to choke with anger ou rage; **dans sa ~ de ne pouvoir l'obtenir, il …** in his rage ou fury at not being able to obtain it, he …; **être pris d'une ~ aveugle/destructrice** to fly into a blind/destructive rage → **amour**

[b] (= envie violente) **avoir la ~ de (faire) qch** to have a passion for (doing) sth; **sa ~ de vaincre** his dogged determination to win; **sa ~ de vivre** his voracious appetite ou his incredible lust for life

[c] **faire ~** [guerre, incendie, tempête, polémique] to rage; [concurrence] to be fierce

[d] (Méd) **la ~** rabies sg → **noyer**

[e] **~ de dents** raging toothache

rageant, e* [Raʒɑ̃, ɑ̃t] ADJ infuriating, maddening; **ce qui est ~ avec lui, c'est que …** the infuriating ou maddening thing about him is that …

rager [Raʒe] ▸conjug 3◂ VI to fume; **ça (me) fait ~!** it makes me fume! ou furious! ou mad!; **rageant de voir que les autres n'étaient pas punis** furious that the others weren't punished

rageur, -euse [Raʒœʀ, øz] ADJ [enfant] hot-tempered, quick-tempered; [voix, geste] bad-tempered, angry; **il était ~** he was furious ou livid

rageusement [Raʒøzmɑ̃] ADV angrily

ragga [Raga] NM (Mus) ragga (music)

raglan [Raglɑ̃] NM, ADJ INV raglan

ragondin [Ragɔ̃dɛ̃] NM (= animal) coypu; (= fourrure) nutria

ragot* [Rago] NM piece of (malicious) gossip ou tittle-tattle; **~s** gossip, tittle-tattle

ragougnasse* [Raguɲas] NF (péj = nourriture) pigswill (NonC)

ragoût [Ragu] NM stew, ragout; **~ de mouton** lamb stew; **en ~** stewed

ragoûtant, e [Ragutɑ̃, ɑ̃t] ADJ **peu ~** [mets] unappetizing; [individu] unsavoury; [travail] un-

---

wholesome, unpalatable; **ce n'est guère ~** that's not very inviting ou tempting

ragtime [Ragtajm] NM ragtime

rahat-loukoum (pl **rahat-loukoums**) [Raatlukum] NM = loukoum

rai [Re] NM (littér = rayon) ray; (Tech) spoke (of wooden wheel)

rai [Raj] [1] ADJ INV rai (épith) [2] NM INV rai

raid [Red] NM (Mil) raid, hit-and-run attack; **~ aérien** air raid; (Sport) **~ automobile/à skis** long-distance car/ski trek; **~ boursier** raid; (Fin, Mil) **faire un ~ sur** to raid

raide [Red] [1] ADJ [a] [corps, membre, geste, étoffe] stiff; [cheveux] straight; [câble] taut, tight; **être ou se tenir ~ comme un échalas ou un piquet ou un manche à balai ou la justice** to be (as) stiff as a poker; **assis ~ sur sa chaise** sitting bolt upright on his chair; **avoir une jambe ~** to have a stiff leg; **ses cheveux sont ~s comme des baguettes de tambour** her hair is dead straight → **corde**

[b] [pente, escalier] steep, abrupt

[c] (= inflexible) [attitude, morale, personne] rigid, inflexible; [manières] stiff, starchy; [démarche] stiff

[d] (= fort, âpre) [alcool] rough

[e] (* = difficile à croire) **c'est un peu ~** that's a bit hard to swallow ou a bit far-fetched; **elle est ~ celle-là!** that's a bit much!*; **il en a vu de ~s** he's seen a thing or two*

[f] (* = osé) **assez ou un peu ~** [propos, passage, scène] daring; **il s'en passe de ~s, chez eux** all sorts of things go on at their place; **il en raconte de ~s** he tells some pretty daring stories

[g] (: = sans argent) broke*; **être ~ comme un passe-lacet** to be flat ou stony (Brit) broke*

[h] (: = ivre) drunk, sloshed*; (= drogué) stoned*, high*; **être complètement ~** (sous l'effet d'une drogue) to be completely stoned‡, be as high as a kite*; (sous l'effet de l'alcool) to be blind drunk*

[2] ADV [a] (= en pente) **ça montait/descendait ~** (ascension, descente) it was a steep climb/climb down; (pente) it climbed/fell steeply

[b] (= net) **tomber ~** to drop to the ground ou floor; **quand elle m'a dit ça, j'en suis tombé ~*** I was thunderstruck when she told me; **tomber ~ mort** to drop ou fall down dead; **tuer qn ~*** to kill sb outright ou stone dead (Brit); **il l'a étendu ~ (mort)*** he laid him out cold*; **être ~ fou ou dingue*** to be completely crazy ou nuts*

raider [Redœʀ] NM (Bourse) raider

raideur [Redœʀ] NF [a] [corps, membre, geste, étoffe] stiffness; [cheveux] straightness; [câble] tautness, tightness; **j'ai une ~ dans la nuque** I've got a stiff neck [b] [pente, escalier] steepness, abruptness [c] [attitude, morale, personne] rigidity, inflexibility; [manières] stiffness, starchiness; [démarche] stiffness; **avec ~** [répondre, saluer, marcher] stiffly [d] (= âpreté) [alcool] roughness

raidillon [Redijɔ̃] NM steep path

raidir [Redir] ▸conjug 2◂ [1] VT [+ drap, tissu] to stiffen; [+ corde, fil de fer] to pull taut ou tight, tighten; **~ ses muscles** to tense ou stiffen one's muscles; **des corps raidis par la mort** stiff corpses; (fig) **~ sa position** to harden ou toughen one's position, take a hard(er) ou tough(er) line [2] **se raidir** VPR [a] [toile, tissu] to stiffen, become stiff(er); [corde] to grow taut; (fig) [position] to harden [b] [personne] (= bander ses muscles) to stiffen; (= se préparer moralement) to brace ou steel o.s.; (= s'entêter) to take a hard(er) ou tough(er) line

raidissement [Redismɑ̃] NM (= perte de souplesse) stiffening; (fig = intransigeance) **ce ~ soudain du parti adverse** this sudden tough(er) line taken by the opposing party

raidisseur [Redisœʀ] NM (= tendeur) tightener

---

raie¹ [Re] NF [a] (= trait) line; (Agr = sillon) furrow; (= éraflure) mark, scratch; **faire une ~** to draw a line; **attention, tu vas faire des ~s** careful, you'll scratch it; **la ~ des fesses** the cleft between the buttocks [b] (= bande) stripe; **chemise avec des ~s** striped ou stripy (Brit) shirt; **les ~s de son pelage** the stripes on its fur; (Phys) **~ d'absorption/d'émission** absorption/emission line [c] (Coiffure) parting (Brit), part (US); **avoir la ~ au milieu/sur le côté** to have a centre/side parting (Brit) ou part (US), have one's hair parted in the middle/to the side

raie² [Re] NF (= poisson) skate, ray; (Culin) skate; **~ bouclée** thornback ray; **~ manta** manta ray; **~ électrique** electric ray → **gueule**

raifort [Refɔʀ] NM (= aromate) horseradish; (= radis noir) black winter radish

rail [Raj] NM [a] (= barre) rail; (= voie) **les ~s** the rails, the track; **~ conducteur** live rail; **~ de sécurité** guardrail, crash barrier (Brit); **le ~ est plus pratique que la route** it's more practical to travel by train than by road; (fig) **être sur les ~s** to be under way; (lit, fig) **remettre sur les ~s** to put back on the rails; **quitter les ~s** ◊ **sortir des ~s** to jump the rails, go off the rails; **transport ~-route** road-rail transport; (Ciné) **~ de travelling** dolly [b] (Naut) lane

railler [Raje] ▸conjug 1◂ [1] VT (frm = se moquer de) [+ personne, chose] to scoff at, jeer at, mock at [2] VI (†† = plaisanter) to jest; **vous raillez?** you jest?; **…, dit-il en raillant** …, he quipped [3] **se railler††** VPR to scoff, jeer, mock (**de** at)

raillerie [Rajri] NF (frm) (= ironie) mockery, scoffing; (= remarque) gibe; **il sortit de scène sous les ~s du public** he left the stage to the booing ou catcalls of the audience

railleur, -euse [Rajœʀ, øz] [1] ADJ mocking, derisive, scoffing [2] NM scoffer, mocker

railleusement [Rajøzmɑ̃] ADV mockingly, derisively, scoffingly

rainer [Rene] ▸conjug 1◂ VT to groove

rainette [Renet] NF [a] (= grenouille) tree frog [b] = reinette

rainurage [RenyRaʒ] NM grooved surface

rainure [RenyR] NF (longue, formant glissière) groove; (courte, pour emboîtage) slot; **les ~s du parquet** the gaps between the floorboards

rainurer [RenyRe] ▸conjug 1◂ VT to groove

rais [Re] NM = rai

raïs [Rais] NM head of state (of an Arab country)

raisin [Rezɛ̃] [1] NM [a] (= espèce) grape; (= fruit) **du ~** ◊ **des ~s** grapes; **~ noir/blanc** black/white grape; **c'est un ~ qui donne du bon vin** it's a grape that yields a good wine → **grain, grappe, jus** [b] (= papier) ≈ royal [c] (= œufs) **~s de mer** [seiche] cuttlefish eggs; [poulpe] octopus eggs [2] COMP ▸ **raisins de Corinthe** currants ▸ **raisins secs** raisins ▸ **raisins de Smyrne** sultanas ▸ **raisin de table** dessert ou eating grapes

raisiné [Rezine] NM (= jus) grape jelly; (= confiture) pear ou quince jam made with grape jelly; (: † = sang) blood

▾ **raison** [Rezɔ̃] [1] NF [a] (gén, Philo = faculté de discernement) reason; **seul l'homme est doué de ~** man alone is endowed with reason; **conforme/contraire à la ~** reasonable/unreasonable; **il n'a plus sa ~** ◊ **il a perdu la ~** he has lost his reason, he has taken leave of his senses, he is not in his right mind; **si tu avais toute ta ~ tu verrais que …** if you were in your right mind, you would see that …; **manger/boire plus que de ~** to eat/drink more than is sensible ou more than one should → **âge, mariage, rime**

[b] (= motif) reason; **la ~ pour laquelle je suis venu** the reason (why ou that) I came; **pour quelles ~s l'avez-vous renvoyé?** why ou on what grounds did you fire him?, what were your reasons for firing him?; **la ~ de cette**

---

réaction the reason for this reaction; **il n'y a pas de ~ de s'arrêter** there's no reason to stop; **j'ai mes ~s** I have my reasons; **pour (des) ~s politiques/familiales** for political/family reasons; **pour ~s de santé** for health reasons, on grounds of (ill) health; **~s cachées** hidden motives *ou* reasons; **il a refusé pour la simple ~ que ...** he refused simply on the grounds that ..., he refused simply because ...; **j'ai de bonnes ~s de penser que ...** I have good *ou* every reason to think that ...; **la ~ en est que ...** the reason is that ...

[c] (= *argument, explication, excuse*) reason; **sans ~** without reason; **sans ~ valable** for no valid reason; (*iro*) **il a toujours de bonnes ~s!** he's always got a good excuse! *ou* reason! ■ (*PROV*) **la ~ du plus fort est toujours la meilleure** might is right (*PROV*); **ce n'est pas une ~!** that's no excuse! *ou* reason! → **comparaison, rendre**

[d] **avoir ~** to be right (**de faire** in doing, to do); **tu as bien ~!** you're absolutely *ou* dead* right!; **avoir ~ de qn/qch** to get the better of sb/sth; **donner ~ à qn** [*événement*] to prove sb right; **tu donnes toujours ~ à ta fille** you're always siding with your daughter, you're always on your daughter's side; **la justice a fini par lui donner ~** the court eventually decided in his favour

[e] (*Math*) ratio; **~ directe/inverse** direct/inverse ratio *ou* proportion

[f] (*loc*) **avec (juste) ~** ◊ **à juste ~** rightly, justifiably, with good reason; **~ de plus** all the more reason (**pour faire** for doing); **à plus forte ~, je n'irai pas** all the more reason for me not to go; **à plus forte ~ si/quand ...** all the more so if/when ...; **comme de ~** as one might expect; **pour une ~ ou pour une autre** for some reason or other, for one reason or another; **rire sans ~** to laugh for no reason; **non sans ~** not without reason; **se faire une ~** to accept it; **entendre ~** ◊ **se rendre à la ~** to listen to *ou* see reason; **faire entendre ~ à qn** ◊ **ramener qn à la ~** to make sb see sense *ou* reason; **mettre qn à la ~†** to bring sb to their senses, make sb see sense *ou* reason, talk (some) sense into sb; (†, *littér*) **demander ~ à qn de** [+ *offense*] to demand satisfaction from sb for (*frm*); **en ~ du froid** because of *ou* owing to the cold weather; **en ~ de son jeune âge** because of *ou* on the grounds of his youth; **on est payé en ~ du travail fourni** we are paid according to *ou* in proportion to the work produced; **à ~ de 100 F par caisse** at the rate of 100 francs per crate; **payé à ~ de 40 lignes par page** paid on the basis of 40 lines a page; **à ~ de 3 fois par semaine** 3 times a week

[2] COMP ► **raison d'État** reasons of state ► **raison d'être** raison d'être; **cet enfant est toute sa ~ d'être** this child is her whole life *ou* her entire reason for living *ou* her entire raison d'être; **cette association n'a aucune ~ d'être** this association has no reason to exist *ou* no raison d'être ► **raison sociale** (*Comm*) corporate name ► **raison de vivre** reason for living

raisonnable [ʀɛzɔnabl] ADJ [a] (= *sensé*) [*personne, solution, conduite*] sensible, reasonable; [*conseil, opinion, propos*] sensible; **soyez ~** be reasonable; **elle devrait être plus ~ à son âge** she should know better *ou* she should have more sense at her age; **réaction bien peu ~** very unreasonable reaction; **boire trop avant un match, ce n'est pas ~** it isn't sensible *ou* it's silly to drink too much before a match; **1 000 F pour cette vieillerie, ce n'est pas ~!** 1,000 francs for this old thing, that's crazy! *ou* ridiculous!; (*hum*) **est-ce bien ~?** is it wise? [b] (= *décent*) [*prix, demande, salaire, quantité*] reasonable, fair; [*heure, limite, délai*] reasonable; **le déficit budgétaire reste ~** the budget deficit is still at a reasonable level [c] (*littér* = *doué de raison*) rational, reasoning

raisonnablement [ʀɛzɔnabləmɑ̃] ADV [*conseiller*] sensibly, soundly; [*agir*] sensibly, reasonably; [*boire*] in moderation; [*dépenser*] moderately; [*travailler, rétribuer*] reasonably *ou* fairly well; **on peut ~ espérer que ...** one can reasonably hope that ...

raisonné, e [ʀɛzɔne] (*ptp de raisonner*) ADJ [a] (= *mûri, réfléchi*) [*attitude, projet*] well thought-out, reasoned; (= *mesuré*) [*confiance, optimisme*] cautious; **il a pris une décision ~e** he made a reasoned decision; **c'est bien ~** it's well reasoned *ou* argued [b] (= *systématique*) **grammaire/méthode ~e de français** reasoned grammar/primer of French; **catalogue ~** catalogue raisonné

raisonnement [ʀɛzɔnmɑ̃] NM [a] (= *activité de la raison*) reasoning (*NonC*); (= *faculté de penser*) power of reasoning; (= *façon de réfléchir*) way of thinking; (= *cheminement de la pensée*) thought process; **~ analogique/par déduction/par induction** analogical/deductive/inductive reasoning; **~ économique/politique** economic/political thinking; **prouver qch par le ~** to prove sth by one's reasoning *ou* by the use of reason → **absurde** [b] (= *argumentation*) argument; **il tient le ~ suivant** his argument *ou* reasoning is as follows; **il m'a tenu ce ~** he gave me this explanation; **si l'on tient le même ~ que lui** if you take the same line as he does; **si tu tiens ce ~** if this is the view you hold *ou* take, if this is how you think; **j'ai du mal à suivre son ~** I'm having trouble following his argument *ou* his line of thought; **un ~ logique** a logical argument, a logical line *ou* chain of reasoning; **ses ~s m'étonnent** his reasoning surprises me; **ce n'est pas un ~!*** that's not a valid argument! [c] (*péj* = *ergotages*) **~s** arguing, argument; **tous les ~s ne changeront pas ma décision** no amount of arguing *ou* argument will alter my decision

raisonner [ʀɛzɔne] ▶ conjug 1 ◀ [1] VI [a] (= *penser, réfléchir*) to reason (**sur** about); **~ par induction/déduction** to reason by induction/deduction; **il raisonne juste/mal** his reasoning is/isn't very sound; **il raisonne comme une pantoufle*** he can't follow his own argument [b] (= *discourir, argumenter*) to argue (**sur** about); **on ne peut pas ~ avec lui** you (just) can't argue *ou* reason with him [c] (*péj* = *ergoter*) to argue, quibble (**avec** with) [2] VT [a] (= *sermonner*) to reason with; **inutile d'essayer de le ~** it's useless to try and reason with him [b] (= *justifier par la raison*) [+ *croyance, conduite, démarche*] to reason out [3] **se raisonner** VPR to reason with o.s., make o.s. see reason; **raisonne-toi** try to be reasonable *ou* to make yourself see reason; **l'amour ne se raisonne pas** love cannot be reasoned *ou* knows no reason

raisonneur, -euse [ʀɛzɔnœʀ, øz] [1] ADJ [a] (*péj*) quibbling (*épith*), argumentative [b] (= *réfléchi*) reasoning (*épith*) [2] NM,F [a] (*péj* = *ergoteur*) arguer, quibbler; **ne fais pas le ~** stop arguing *ou* quibbling [b] (= *penseur*) reasoner

rajah [ʀa(d)ʒa] NM rajah

rajeunir [ʀaʒœniʀ] ▶ conjug 2 ◀ [1] VT [a] **~ qn** [*cure*] to rejuvenate sb; [*repos, expérience*] to make sb feel younger; [*soins de beauté, vêtement*] to make sb look younger; **l'amour/ce chapeau la rajeunit de 10 ans** being in love/that hat takes 10 years off her* *ou* makes her look 10 years younger; **tu le rajeunis (de 5 ans), il est né en 1950** you're making him out to be (5 years) younger than he is — he was born in 1950; (*hum*) **ça ne nous rajeunit pas!** that makes you realize we're not getting any younger! [b] [+ *institution*] to modernize; [+ *installation, mobilier*] to modernize, give a new look to; [+ *manuel, image de marque*] to update, bring up to date; [+ *vieux habits*] to give a new look to,

brighten up; [+ *personnel, entreprise*] to bring new *ou* young blood into, recruit younger people into; [+ *thème, théorie*] to inject new life into; **ils cherchent à ~ leur clientèle/public** they're trying to attract younger customers/a younger audience

[2] VI [*personne*] (= *se sentir plus jeune*) to feel younger; (= *paraître plus jeune*) to look younger; [*institution, quartier*] (= *se moderniser*) to be modernized; (= *avoir un personnel, des habitants plus jeunes*) to have a younger feel; **notre public rajeunit** our audience is getting younger; **avec les enfants, la vieille demeure rajeunissait** with the children around, the old house had a younger feel to it

[3] **se rajeunir** VPR (= *se prétendre moins âgé*) to make o.s. younger than one is; (= *se faire paraître moins âgé*) to make o.s. look younger

rajeunissant, e [ʀaʒœnisɑ̃, ɑ̃t] ADJ [*traitement, crème*] rejuvenating

rajeunissement [ʀaʒœnismɑ̃] NM [*personne*] rejuvenation; [*manuel*] updating; [*installation, mobilier*] modernization; [*vieux habits*] brightening up; **~ du personnel** injection of new *ou* young blood into the staff; **nous assistons à un ~ de la population/clientèle** the population is/the customers are getting younger; (*fig*) **la cathédrale a subi une cure de ~** the cathedral has been given a face-lift

rajout [ʀaʒu] NM addition (**sur** to)

rajouter [ʀaʒute] ▶ conjug 1 ◀ VT [+ *du sucre*] to put on *ou* put in *ou* add (some) more; [+ *un sucre*] to add another; **après avoir donné 50 F, il en rajouta 10** having already given 50 francs he added another 10; **il rajouta que ...** he added that ...; (*fig*) **en ~*** to lay it on (thick)*, exaggerate; **il ne faut pas croire tout ce qu'il dit, il en rajoute* toujours** you mustn't believe everything he says, he always exaggerates

rajustement [ʀaʒystəmɑ̃] NM = **réajustement**

rajuster [ʀaʒyste] ▶ conjug 1 ◀ VT = **réajuster**

raki [ʀaki] NM raki

râlant, e* [ʀɑlɑ̃, ɑ̃t] ADJ infuriating; **attendre pour rien, c'est ~!** it's infuriating, all this waiting around for nothing!

râle¹ [ʀɑl] NM [a] [*blessé*] groan; [*mourant*] **~ (d'agonie** *ou* **de la mort)** death rattle [b] (*Méd*) rale

râle² [ʀɑl] NM (*Orn*) rail; **~ des genêts** corn-crake; **~ d'eau** *ou* **~ noir** water rail

ralenti, e [ʀalɑ̃ti] (*ptp de ralentir*) [1] ADJ [*vie*] slow-moving, slow; [*mouvement*] slow [2] NM [a] (*Ciné*) slow motion; **en ~** *ou* **au ~** [*filmer, projeter*] in slow motion [b] (*Aut*) **régler le ~** to adjust the idle *ou* the tick-over (*Brit*); **le moteur est un peu faible au ~** the engine doesn't idle too well *ou* doesn't tick over (*Brit*); **tourner au ~** to idle, tick over (*Brit*) [c] (*loc*) **vivre au ~** to live at a slower pace; **cette existence paisible, au ~** this peaceful, slow existence; **usine qui tourne au ~** factory which is just idling *ou* ticking over (*Brit*); (*péj*) **ça tourne au ~ chez lui!** he's a bit slow!*

ralentir [ʀalɑ̃tiʀ] ▶ conjug 2 ◀ [1] VT [+ *processus, véhicule*] to slow down; [+ *mouvement, expansion*] to slow down *ou* up; (*Mil*) [+ *avance*] to check, hold up; [+ *effort, zèle*] to slacken; **~ l'allure** to slow down *ou* up, reduce speed; **~ le pas** to slacken one's *ou* the pace, slow down [2] VI [*marcheur*] to slow down, slacken one's pace; [*véhicule, automobiliste*] to slow down, reduce speed; (*Aut*) **« ralentir »** "slow", "reduce speed now" [3] **se ralentir** VPR [*production*] to slow down *ou* up, slacken (up); (*Mil*) [*offensive*] to let up, ease off; [*ardeur, zèle*] to flag; (*Physiol*) [*fonctions*] to slow down; [*rythme*] to slow down (*ou* up); **sa respiration s'est ralentie** he is breathing more slowly; **l'inflation s'est ralentie** inflation has slowed down

ralentissement [ʀalɑ̃tismɑ̃] NM [a] [*processus, véhicule, automobiliste, marcheur*] slowing down; [*mouvement, expansion*] slowing down *ou* up; (*Mil*) [*avance*] checking, holding up; [*effort, zèle*] slackening; **un ~ de l'activité économique** a slowdown in economic activity; **un ~ sur 3 km** a 3 km tailback (*Brit*) *ou* hold-up (*US*) **b** [*production*] falloff; (*Mil*) [*offensive*] letting up, easing; [*ardeur, zèle*] flagging; (*Physiol*) [*fonctions*] slowing down; **provoquer le ~ de qch** to slow sth down

ralentisseur [ʀalɑ̃tisœʀ] NM **a** (*Tech*) [*camion*] speed reducer **b** (*sur route*) speed bump, sleeping policeman (*Brit*) **c** (*Phys*) moderator

râler [ʀɑle] ▸ conjug 1 ◂ VI **a** [*blessé*] to groan, moan; [*mourant*] to give the death rattle **b** (* = *protester*) to moan (and groan)*, grouse*; **il est allé ~ chez le prof** he went to moan* to the teacher; **il râlait contre** *ou* **après moi** he was moaning* about me; **faire ~ qn** to infuriate sb; **ça (vous) fait ~** it's infuriating

râleur, -euse* [ʀɑlœʀ, øz] **1** ADJ **des gens ~s** moaners*; **il est ~** he never stops moaning **2** NM,F moaner*; **quel ~, celui-là!** he never stops moaning!

ralingue [ʀalɛ̃g] NF boltrope

ralliement [ʀalimɑ̃] NM **a** (*Chasse, Mil, Naut*) rallying; (= *union*) [*groupe, parti*] rallying, uniting; **le ~ des troupes** the rallying of troops **b** (= *adhésion*) [*personne, groupe*] winning over, rallying; **~ à** joining, going over to; **je suis étonné de son ~** (à notre cause) I am surprised by the fact that he joined (our cause); **signe/cri de ~** rallying sign/cry; **point de ~** rallying point

rallier [ʀalje] ▸ conjug 7 ◂ **1** VT **a** (*Chasse, Mil, Naut* = *regrouper*) to rally **b** (= *gagner*) [*personne, groupe*] to win over, rally (**à** to); [*suffrages*] to bring in, win; **~ qn à son avis/sa cause** to bring sb round (*Brit*) *ou* win sb over to one's way of thinking/one's cause **c** (= *unir*) [*groupe, parti*] to rally, unite; **groupe rallié autour d'un idéal** group united by an ideal **d** (= *rejoindre*) (*Mil, Naut*) to rejoin; (*Pol*) **~ la majorité** to rejoin the majority; (*Naut*) **~ le bord** to rejoin ship; **~ la côte** *ou* **la terre** to make landfall **2** **se rallier** VPR **a** (= *suivre*) **se ~ à** [*parti*] to join; [*ennemi*] to go over to; [+ *cause*] to rally round *ou* to; [+ *doctrine, cause*] to be won over to **b** (*Mil, Naut* = *se regrouper*) to rally

rallonge [ʀalɔ̃ʒ] NF **a** [*table*] (extra) leaf; [*fil électrique*] extension lead *ou* cord *ou* cable (*Brit*); [*vêtement*] piece (*used to lengthen an item of clothing*); [*compas*] extension arm; [*perche*] extension piece; **table à ~(s)** extendable table **b** (* = *supplément*) **une ~ d'argent** a bit of extra *ou* some extra money; **une ~ de vacances** a few extra days holiday; **obtenir une ~ de crédit** to get an extension of credit; **une ~ de deux jours** an extra two days, a two-day extension **c** (*péj*) **histoire à ~** never-ending story; **nom à ~** (*gén*) long, complicated surname; (*en deux mots*) double-barrelled name

rallongement [ʀalɔ̃ʒmɑ̃] NM [*vêtement*] (*en ajoutant du tissu*) lengthening; (*en défaisant l'ourlet*) letting down; [*vacances, fil, table, bâtiment*] extension

rallonger [ʀalɔ̃ʒe] ▸ conjug 3 ◂ **1** VT [*vêtement*] (*en ajoutant*) to lengthen, make longer; (*en défaisant l'ourlet*) to let down; [+ *texte, service militaire, piste*] to lengthen, extend, make longer; [+ *vacances, fil, table, bâtiment*] to extend; **~ une robe de 2 cm** to let down a dress by 2 cm; **j'ai rallongé le texte de trois pages** I added three pages to the text; **par ce chemin/en bus, ça me rallonge de 10 minutes*** this way/by bus, it takes me 10 minutes longer **2** VI ***les jours rallongent** the days are getting longer; **les jupes rallongent** hemlines are going down **3** **se rallonger** VPR [*personne*] to lie down again; (= *devenir plus long*) to get longer

rallumer [ʀalyme] ▸ conjug 1 ◂ **1** VT **a** (*lit*) [+ *feu*] to light again, relight; [+ *cigarette*] to re-light, light up again; [+ *lampe*] to switch *ou* turn *ou* put on again; **~ (l'électricité** *ou* **la lumière)** to switch *ou* turn *ou* put the light(s) on again; **~ (dans) le bureau** to switch *ou* turn *ou* put the light(s) on again in the office **b** (*fig*) [+ *courage, haine, querelle*] to revive, rekindle; [+ *conflit, guerre*] to stir up again, revive, re-kindle **2** **se rallumer** VPR **a** [*incendie*] to flare up again; [*lampe*] to come on again; **le bureau se ralluma** the light(s) in the office went *ou* came on again **b** [*guerre, querelle*] to flare up again; [*haine, courage*] to revive, be revived

rallye [ʀali] NM (*Aut*) (car) rally; (*mondain*) series of society parties (*organized to enable young people to meet suitable friends*)

RAM [ʀam] NF (ABRÉV = **Random Access Memory**) (*Ordin*) RAM

Ramadan, ramadan [ʀamadɑ̃] NM Ramadan; **faire** *ou* **observer le ~** to observe Ramadan

ramage [ʀamaʒ] NM **a** (*littér* = *chant*) song, warbling (*NonC*) **b** (= *branchages, dessin*) **~(s)** foliage; **tissu à ~s** fabric with a leafy design *ou* pattern

ramassage [ʀamasaʒ] NM **a** (*gén*) collection; [*cahiers, copies*] taking in, collection; **~ scolaire** (= *service*) school bus service; (= *action*) picking up of pupils; **point de ~** pick-up point; **quels sont les horaires de ~ des poubelles?** what time is the waste collected? **b** (= *cueillette*) [*bois mort, coquillages, foin*] gathering; [*épis, fruits tombés*] gathering (up); [*champignons*] picking, gathering; [*pommes de terre*] digging up, lifting; [*balles de tennis*] picking up; **faire l'objet d'un ~** [*valeur boursière*] to be snapped up

ramassé, e [ʀamase] (*ptp de ramasser*) ADJ (*pour se protéger*) huddled (up); (*pour bondir*) crouched; (= *trapu*) squat, stocky; (= *concis*) compact, condensed; **le petit village ~ dans le fond de la vallée** the little village nestling in the heart of the valley

ramasse-miettes [ʀamasmjɛt] NM INV table tidy (*Brit*), silent butler (*US*)

ramasse-monnaie [ʀamasmɔnɛ] NM INV (change-)tray

ramasser [ʀamase] ▸ conjug 1 ◂ **1** VT **a** (*lit, fig* = *prendre*) [+ *objet, personne*] to pick up; **il était à ~ à la petite cuiller*** (*blessé*) they had to scrape him off the ground; (*fatigué*) he was completely shattered*; **~ une bûche*** *ou* **un gadin*** *ou* **une gamelle*** *ou* **une pelle*** to fall flat on one's face, come a cropper* (*Brit*) **b** (= *collecter*) [+ *objets épars*] to pick up, gather up; [+ *cartes, idées, informations*] to pick up; [+ *élèves*] to pick up, collect; [+ *copies, cahiers*] to collect, take in; [+ *cotisations, ordures*] to collect; * [+ *argent*] to pick up, pocket* **c** (= *récolter*) [+ *bois, feuilles, coquillages*] to gather, collect; [+ *fruits tombés*] to gather (up); [+ *foin*] to gather; [+ *pommes de terre*] to lift, dig up; [+ *champignons*] to pick, gather; (*Bourse*) [+ *titres*] to snap up; **~ qch à la pelle** (*lit*) to shovel sth up; (*fig: en abondance*) to get loads* *ou* stacks* of sth **d** (= *resserrer*) [+ *jupons, draps, cheveux*] to gather (up); (*fig*) [+ *style*] to condense **e** (* = *attraper*) [+ *rhume, maladie*] to catch, get; [+ *réprimande, coups*] to collect, get; [+ *amende*] to pick up, collect, get; [+ *mauvaise note*] to get; **il a ramassé 100 F (d'amende)** he picked up *ou* collected a 100-franc fine, he was done for 100 francs* (*Brit*); **où as-tu ramassé ce mec?*** where the hell did you find that guy?* **f** *** se faire ~** (= *échouer*) [*candidat*] to fail; [*dragueur*] to get the cold shoulder*; (= *se faire réprimander*) **il va se faire ~ par sa mère** he'll get told off *ou* ticked off (*Brit*) by his mother*; **il s'est fait ~ en anglais** he failed his English;

se faire ~ dans une manif* to get picked up at a demo* **2** **se ramasser** VPR **a** (= *se pelotonner*) to curl up; (*pour bondir*) to crouch **b** (= *se relever*) to pick o.s. up **c** (* = *tomber*) to fall over *ou* down, come a cropper* (*Brit*); (* = *échouer*) [*candidat*] to come a cropper* (*Brit*), take a flat beating (*US*)

ramasseur, -euse [ʀamasœʀ, øz] **1** NM,F (= *personne*) collector; **~ de lait** milk collector; (*Tennis*) **~/ramasseuse de balles** ballboy/ballgirl; **~ de pommes de terre/champignons** potato/mushroom picker **2** NM (= *outil, machine*) pickup **3** **ramasseuse** NF (= *machine*) **ramasseuse-presse** baler

ramassis [ʀamasi] NM (*péj*) **~ de** [+ *voyous*] pack *ou* bunch of; [+ *doctrines, objets*] jumble of

rambarde [ʀɑ̃baʀd] NF guardrail

ramdam* [ʀamdam] NM (= *tapage*) racket, row (*surtout Brit*); (= *protestation*) row; **faire du ~** (*bruit*) to kick up* *ou* make a racket *ou* row; (*protestation*) to kick up* a fuss *ou* a row*; (*scandale*) to cause a stir

rame [ʀam] NF **a** (= *aviron*) oar; **aller à la ~** to row; (*littér*) **faire force de ~s** to ply the oars (*littér*), row hard; **il n'en fiche pas une ~*** he doesn't do a damned* thing, he doesn't do a stroke (of work) **b** (*Rail*) train; **~ (de métro)** (underground (*Brit*) *ou* subway (*US*)) train **c** (*Typo*) ream; (*Tex*) tenter; (*Agr*) stake, stick → **haricot**

rameau (*pl* **rameaux**) [ʀamo] NM (*lit*) (small) branch; (*fig*) branch; (*Anat*) ramification; (*lit, fig*) **~ d'olivier** olive branch; (*Rel*) **(dimanche des) Rameaux** Palm Sunday

ramée [ʀame] NF (*littér* = *feuillage*) leafy boughs (*littér*); (*coupé*) leafy *ou* green branches; **il n'en fiche pas une ~*** he doesn't do a damned* thing, he doesn't do a stroke (of work)

ramener [ʀam(ə)ne] ▸ conjug 5 ◂ **1** VT **a** [+ *personne, objet*] to bring back, take back; [+ *paix, ordre*] to bring back, restore; **je vais te ~ en voiture** I'll drive you back (home), I'll take you back (home) in the car; **ramène du pain/les enfants** bring *ou* fetch (*Brit*) some bread/the children back (**de** from); **ça l'a ramené en prison** it put *ou* landed* him back in prison; **l'été a ramené les accidents/la mode des chapeaux** summer has seen a resurgence of accidents/has brought hats back into fashion **b** (= *tirer*) [+ *voile*] to draw; [+ *couverture*] to pull, draw; **~ ses cheveux sur son front/en arrière** to brush one's hair forward/back; **~ les épaules en arrière** to pull one's shoulders back **c** (= *faire revenir à*) **~ à** to bring back to; **~ à la vie** [+ *personne*] to revive, bring back to life; [+ *région*] to revitalize, bring back to life; **~ le compteur à zéro** to put the meter back to zero, reset the meter at zero; **~ les prix à un juste niveau** to bring prices back (down) *ou* restore prices to a reasonable level; **il ramène toujours tout à lui** he always brings everything back to himself; **~ un incident à de plus justes proportions** to get *ou* bring an incident into proportion; **ils ont ramené ces bagarres au rang de simple incident** they played down the fighting, passing it off as a mere incident; **~ la conversation sur un sujet** to bring *ou* steer *ou* lead the conversation back (on)to a subject; **cela nous ramène 20 ans en arrière** it takes us back 20 years → **raison** **d** (= *réduire à*) **~ à** to reduce to; **~ l'inflation à moins de 3%** to reduce inflation to less than 3%, bring inflation back down to below 3% **e** (*loc*) **la ~* ◊ ~ sa fraise*** *ou* **sa gueule*** (= *protester*) to kick up a fuss* *ou* a row (*surtout Brit*); (= *intervenir*) to interfere, put *ou* shove one's oar in* (*Brit*) **2** **se ramener** VPR **a** (= *se réduire à*) **se ~ à** [*problèmes*] to come down to, boil down to;

(*Math*) [*fraction*] to reduce to, be reduced to ⓑ (: = *arriver*) to roll up*, turn up*

ramequin [Ramkɛ̃] NM ramekin, ramequin

ramer¹ [Rame] ▸ conjug 1 ◂ VI ⓐ (*Sport*) to row; **~ en couple** to scull ⓑ (* = *travailler dur*) to work hard, slog one's guts out* (*Brit*); (= *avoir des difficultés*) **elle a ramé six mois avant de trouver du travail** she struggled for six long hard months before she found a job; (= *être perdu*) **je rame complètement** I haven't got a clue what I'm doing

ramer² [Rame] ▸ conjug 1 ◂ VT (*Agr*) to stake

ramette [Ramɛt] NF [*papier à lettres*] ream

rameur [RamœR] NM (= *sportif*) oarsman, rower; (= *galérien*) rower; **~ en couple** sculler

rameuse [Ramøz] NF (= *sportive*) oarswoman, rower

rameuter [Ramøte] ▸ conjug 1 ◂ VT [+ *foule, partisans*] to gather together, round up; [+ *chiens*] to round up, form into a pack again; **les gens s'étaient rameutés** people had formed a crowd

rami [Rami] NM rummy; **faire ~** to get rummy

ramier [Ramje] NM (**pigeon**) **~** woodpigeon, ringdove

ramification [Ramifikasjɔ̃] NF (*Bot, Anat*) ramification, branching; [*réseau routier*] branch; [*voie ferrée*] branch line; [*organisation, maffia*] branch; **les ~s du complot/scandale** the ramifications of the plot/scandal

ramifié, e [Ramifje] (*ptp de* **se ramifier**) ADJ (*lit, fig*) ramified

ramifier (se) [Ramifje] ▸ conjug 7 ◂ VPR [*veines*] to ramify; [*routes, branches, famille*] to branch out (**en** into); **cette science s'est ramifiée en plusieurs disciplines** this science has branched out into several different disciplines

ramille [Ramij] NF (= *brindille*) twig

ramolli, e [Ramɔli] (*ptp de* **ramollir**) ADJ [*biscuit, beurre*] soft; [*personne* = *avachi*] soft; (= *stupide*) soft (in the head), soft-headed; (*péj*) **il a le cerveau ~** he is *ou* has gone soft in the head*

ramollir [RamɔliR] ▸ conjug 2 ◂ ① VT [+ *matière*] to soften; [+ *courage, résolution*] to weaken; **~ qn** [*plaisir*] to soften sb; [*climat*] to enervate sb ② VI, **se ramollir** VPR [*beurre, argile*] to soften (up), go soft; [*personne*] to go to seed; **depuis que j'ai arrêté le tennis, je me suis ramolli** I've been out of condition since I've stopped playing tennis; (*hum*) **son cerveau se ramollit** he's going soft in the head*

ramollissement [Ramɔlismɑ̃] NM softening; **~ cérébral** softening of the brain

ramollo* [Ramɔlo] ADJ (= *avachi*) droopy; (= *gâteux*) soft (in the head)

ramonage [Ramɔnaʒ] NM chimney-sweeping; (*Alpinisme*) chimney-climbing

ramoner [Ramɔne] ▸ conjug 1 ◂ ① VT [+ *cheminée*] to sweep; [+ *pipe*] to clean out ② VI (*Alpinisme*) to climb a chimney

ramoneur [RamɔnœR] NM (chimney) sweep

rampant, e [Rɑ̃pɑ̃, ɑ̃t] ① ADJ ⓐ [*animal*] crawling, creeping; [*plante, inflation*] creeping; [*caractère, employé*] grovelling, cringing; (*arg Aviat*) **personnel ~** ground crew *ou* staff ⓑ (*Hér*) rampant; **lion ~** lion rampant ② NM ⓐ (*arg Aviat*) member of the ground crew *ou* staff; **les ~s** the ground crew *ou* staff ⓑ (*Archit*) pitch

rampe [Rɑ̃p] ① NF ⓐ (= *voie d'accès*) ramp, slope; (= *côte*) slope, incline, gradient ⓑ [*escalier*] banister(s); [*chemin*] handrail ⓒ (*Théât* = *projecteurs*) **la ~** the footlights, the floats (*Brit*); **passer la ~** to get across to the audience ⓓ (*loc*) **tenez bon la ~*** hold on to your hat*; **elle tient bon la ~*** she's still going strong; (= *mourir*) **lâcher la ~*** to kick the bucket: ② COMP ▸ **rampe d'accès** approach ramp ▸ **rampe de balisage** runway

lights ▸ **rampe de débarquement** disembarkation ramp ▸ **rampe de graissage** oil gallery ▸ **rampe de lancement** launching pad

ramper [Rɑ̃pe] ▸ conjug 1 ◂ VI ⓐ [*serpent*] to crawl, slither; [*quadrupède, homme*] to crawl; [*plante, ombre, feu*] to creep; [*sentiment, brouillard, mal, maladie*] to lurk; **entrer/sortir en rampant** to crawl in/out; **le lierre rampe contre le mur** the ivy creeps up the wall ⓑ (*fig péj* = *s'abaisser*) to grovel (**devant** before), crawl, cringe (**devant** to)

ramponneau: (*pl* **ramponneaux**) [Rɑ̃pɔno] NM bump, knock; **donner un ~ à qn** to bump *ou* knock sb

Ramsès [Ramses] NM Rameses, Ramses

ramure [RamyR] NF [*cerf*] antlers; [*arbre*] boughs, foliage

rancard: [RɑkaR] NM ⓐ (= *renseignement*) tip ⓑ (= *rendez-vous*: *gén*) meeting, date; [*amoureux*] date; **donner (un) ~ à qn** to arrange to meet sb, make a date with sb; **avoir (un) ~ avec qn** to have a meeting with sb, have a date with sb; **j'ai ~ avec lui dans une heure** I'm meeting him in an hour

rancarder: [RɑkaRde] ▸ conjug 1 ◂ ① VT (= *renseigner*) to tip off; **il m'a rancardé sur le voyage** he told me about *ou* genned me up on* (*Brit*) the trip ② **se rancarder** VPR (= *s'informer*) **se ~ sur qch** to get information on sth, find out about sth

rancart [RɑkaR] ▸ **au rancart:** LOC ADV **mettre au ~** [+ *objet, idée, projet*] to chuck out:, scrap; [+ *personne*] to throw on the scrap heap*; **bon à mettre au ~** fit for the scrap heap

rance [Rɑ̃s] ADJ [*beurre*] rancid; [*odeur*] rank, rancid; (*fig*) stale; **sentir le ~** to smell rancid *ou* rank; **odeur de ~** rank *ou* rancid smell

ranch (*pl* **ranchs** *ou* **ranches**) [Rɑ̃tʃ] NM ranch

ranci, e [Rɑ̃si] (*ptp de* **rancir**) ① ADJ [*beurre*] rancid; (*péj*) [*personne*] stale ② NM **sentir le ~** to smell rank *ou* rancid

rancir [Rɑ̃siR] ▸ conjug 2 ◂ VI [*lard, beurre*] to go rancid *ou* off* (*Brit*); (*fig*) to grow stale

rancœur [RɑkœR] NF (*frm*) resentment (*NonC*), rancour (*Brit*) (*NonC*), rancor (*US*) (*NonC*); **avoir de la ~ contre qn** to be full of rancour against sb, feel resentment against sb; **les ~s s'étaient accumulées depuis des années** the resentment had been building up for years

rançon [Rɑ̃sɔ̃] NF (*lit*) ransom; (*fig*) **c'est la ~ de la gloire/du progrès** that's the price you have to pay for being famous/for progress, that's the price of fame/of progress; (*littér*) **mettre à ~** to hold to ransom

rançonneur, -euse [RɑsɔnœR, øz] NM,F (*lit*) person demanding a ransom, ransomer; (*fig*) extortioner, extortionist

rancune [Rɑ̃kyn] NF grudge, rancour (*Brit*) (*NonC*) (*frm*), rancor (*US*) (*NonC*); **avoir de la ~ à l'égard de** *ou* **contre qn** ◊ **garder ~ à qn** to hold *ou* harbour a grudge against sb, bear sb a grudge (**de qch** for sth); **oubliez vos vieilles ~s** put aside your old grudges; **sans ~ !** no hard *ou* ill feelings!

rancunier, -ière [Rɑ̃kynje, jɛR] ADJ **être ~** to bear grudges

rand [Rɑ̃d] NM rand

randomiser [Rɑ̃dɔmize] ▸ conjug 1 ◂ VT to randomize

randonnée [Rɑ̃dɔne] NF ⓐ (= *promenade*) (*en voiture*) drive, ride; (**à bicyclette**) (bike) ride; **~ pédestre** *ou* **à pied** (*courte, à la campagne*) walk, ramble; (*longue, en montagne*) hike; **faire une ~ à ski** to go cross-country skiing; **~ équestre** *ou* **à cheval** pony trek; **partir en ~** (*courte*) to go for a walk, go (off) for a ramble; (*longue*) to go hiking; **faire une ~ en voiture** to go for a drive; **cette ~ nocturne se termina mal** this night escapade ended badly ⓑ (=

activité) **la ~** (*à pied*) rambling, hiking; **la ~ équestre** pony trekking; **chaussures de ~** hiking boots; **ski de ~** cross-country skiing; **sentier de grande ~** (*registered*) hiking trail

randonner [Rɑ̃dɔne] ▸ conjug 1 ◂ VI (*gén*) to go walking *ou* rambling; (*en terrain accidenté*) to hike, go hiking; **ils ont découvert les Pyrénées en randonnant** they went on a hike through the Pyrenees

randonneur, -euse [RɑdɔnœR, øz] NM,F hiker, rambler

rang [Rɑ̃] NM ⓐ (= *rangée*) [*maisons, personnes, objets, tricot*] row; (= *file*) line; (*Mil*) rank; **collier à trois ~s (de perles)** necklace with three rows of pearls; **porter un ~ de perles** to wear a string *ou* row of pearls; **assis au troisième ~** sitting in the third row; (= *d'affilée*) **deux jours de ~** two days running *ou* in succession; **en ~s serrés** in close order, in serried ranks; **en ~ d'oignons** in a row *ou* line; **en ~ par deux/quatre** two/four abreast; **sur deux/quatre ~s** two/four deep; **se mettre sur un ~** to get into *ou* form a line; **se mettre en ~s par quatre** (*Scol*) to line up in fours; (*Mil*) to form fours; **plusieurs personnes sont sur** *ou* **se sont mises sur les ~s pour l'acheter** several people are in the running *ou* have got themselves lined up to buy it, several people have indicated an interest in buying it; (*Mil*) **servir dans les ~s de** to serve in the ranks of; (*fig*) **grossir les ~s de** to swell the ranks of; (*fig*) **nous l'avons admis dans nos ~s** we allowed him to enter our ranks; (*Mil*) **à vos ~s, fixe !** fall in!; **officier sorti du ~** officer who has risen through *ou* from the ranks → **rentrer, rompre, serrer**

ⓑ (*Can*) country road (*bordered by farms at right angles*), concession road (*in Quebec*); **les ~s** the country

ⓒ (= *condition*) station; **de haut ~** (= *noble*) noble; [*officier*] high-ranking (*épith*); **du plus haut ~** of the highest standing; **tenir** *ou* **garder son ~** to maintain one's rank

ⓓ (*hiérarchique* = *grade, place*) rank; **avoir ~ de** to hold the rank of; **avoir ~ parmi** to rank among; **par ~ d'âge/de taille** in order of age/ of size *ou* height; **être reçu dans un bon ~** to be in the top few; **13ᵉ, c'est un bon ~** 13th place isn't bad; **être placé au deuxième ~** to be ranked *ou* placed second; **ce pays se situe au troisième ~ mondial des exportateurs de pétrole** this country is the third largest oil exporter in the world; **mettre un écrivain au ~ des plus grands** to rank a writer among the greatest; **c'est au premier/dernier ~ de mes préoccupations** that's the first/last thing on my mind; **il est au premier ~ des artistes contemporains** he is one of the highest ranking of *ou* he ranks among the best of contemporary artists; **écrivain/journaliste de second ~** second-rate writer/journalist

┌─ **LES RANGS** ─┐

In Quebec, rural areas are divided into districts known as **rangs**. *The word* **rang** *refers to a series of rectangular fields (each known as a "lot"), usually laid out between a river and a road (the road itself also being called a* **rang**). *The* **rangs** *are numbered or given names so that they can be easily identified and used in addresses (e.g. "le deuxième rang", "le rang Saint-Claude"). In Quebec, the expression "dans les rangs" means "in the countryside".*

rangé, e¹ [Rɑ̃ʒe] (*ptp de* **ranger**) ADJ (= *ordonné*) orderly; (= *sans excès*) settled, steady; **il est ~ (des voitures:)** **maintenant** [*escroc*] he's going straight now; [*séducteur*] he's settled down now; **petite vie bien ~e** well-ordered existence; **jeune fille ~e** well-behaved young lady → **bataille**

range-CD [Rɑ̃ʒ(ə)sede] NM INV CD rack

rangée² [Rɑ̃ʒe] NF [maisons, arbres] row, line; [objets, spectateurs, perles] row

rangement [Rɑ̃ʒmɑ̃] NM a (= action) [objets, linge] putting away; [pièce, meuble] tidying (up); **faire du ~** to do some tidying up b (= espace) [appartement] cupboard space; [remise] storage space; **capacité de ~ d'une bibliothèque** shelf space of a bookcase; **la maison manque d'espaces de ~** the house lacks storage ou cupboard space → **meuble** c (= arrangement) arrangement

ranger¹ [Rɑ̃ʒe] ▸conjug 3◂ 1 VT a (= mettre en ordre) [+ tiroir, maison] to tidy (up); [+ dossiers, papiers] to tidy (up), arrange; [+ mots, chiffres] to arrange, order; **tout est toujours bien rangé chez elle** it's always (nice and) tidy at her place; **rangé par ordre alphabétique** listed ou arranged alphabetically ou in alphabetical order
b (= mettre à sa place) [+ papiers, vêtements] to put away; [+ bateau] to moor, berth; [+ voiture, vélo] (au garage) to put away; (dans la rue) to park; **où se rangent les tasses ?** where do the cups go? ou belong?; **je le range parmi les meilleurs** I rank ou put it among the best; **ce roman est à ~ parmi les meilleurs** this novel ranks ou is to be ranked among the best
c (= disposer) [+ écoliers] to line up, put ou form into rows; [+ soldats] to draw up; [+ invités] to place; (fig) **~ qn sous son autorité** to bring sb under one's authority
d (Naut) **~ la côte** to sail along the coast
2 **se ranger** VPR a [automobiliste] (= stationner) to park; (= venir s'arrêter) to pull in ou up, draw up; **la voiture se rangea contre le trottoir** the car pulled in ou up ou drew up at the kerb; **le navire se rangea contre le quai** the ship moored ou berthed ou came alongside the quay
b (= s'écarter) [piéton] to step ou stand aside, make way; [véhicule] to pull over; **il se rangea pour la laisser passer** he stepped ou stood aside to let her go by, he made way for her
c (= se mettre en rang) to line up, get into line ou rows; **se ~ par deux/quatre** to line up in twos/fours, get into rows of two/four
d (= se rallier à) **se ~ à** [+ décision] to go along with, abide by; [+ avis] to come round ou over to, fall in with; **se ~ du côté de qn** to side with sb
e (* = cesser son activité) **se ~ (des voitures)**‡ [escroc] to go straight; [séducteur] to settle down

ranger² [Rɑ̃dʒœR] NM (= soldat) ranger; (= scout) rover; (= chaussure) canvas walking boot

Rangoon [Rɑ̃gun] N Rangoon

rani [Rani] NF rani, ranee

ranimer [Ranime] ▸conjug 1◂ 1 VT [+ blessé] to revive, bring to, bring round (Brit); [+ feu, braises] to rekindle; [+ région, souvenir, époque, conversation] to revive, bring back to life; [+ rancune, querelle] to rake up, revive; [+ forces, ardeur] to renew, restore; [+ amour, haine, espoir] to rekindle, renew; [+ douleur] to revive, renew; [+ couleurs] to brighten up, revive 2 **se ranimer** VPR [personne] to revive, come to, come round (Brit); [feu, braises] to rekindle, be rekindled; [haine, passion] to be rekindled; [conversation, débat] to pick up (again); [souvenirs, espoirs] to be revived

raout† [Raut] NM (= réception) rout†

rap [Rap] NM (= musique) rap (music); (= technique) rapping

rapace [Rapas] 1 NM (Orn) bird of prey, raptor (SPÉC); (fig) vulture 2 ADJ predatory, raptorial (SPÉC); (fig) rapacious, grasping

rapacité [Rapasite] NF (lit, fig) rapaciousness, rapacity

râpage [Rɑpaʒ] NM [carottes, fromage] grating; [bois] rasping; [tabac] grinding

rapatrié, e [Rapatrije] (ptp de **rapatrier**) 1 ADJ repatriated 2 NM,F repatriate; **les ~s d'Algé-**

rie French settlers repatriated after Algerian independence

rapatriement [Rapatrimɑ̃] NM repatriation; **~ sanitaire** repatriation on medical grounds; **~ volontaire** voluntary repatriation

rapatrier [Rapatrije] ▸conjug 7◂ VT [+ personne, capitaux] to repatriate; [+ objet] to send ou bring back (home); **il a fait ~ le corps de son fils** he had his son's body sent back home

râpe [Rɑp] NF (= ustensile de cuisine) grater; (pour le bois) rasp; (pour le tabac) grinder; **~ à fromage** cheese grater

râpé, e [Rɑpe] (ptp de **râper**) 1 ADJ (= usé) [veste] threadbare; [coude] through, worn (attrib); [carottes, fromage] grated; (* = raté) **c'est ~ pour ce soir** we've had it for tonight* 2 NM (= fromage) grated cheese

râper [Rɑpe] ▸conjug 1◂ VT [+ carottes, fromage] to grate; [+ bois] to rasp; [+ tabac] to grind; **vin qui râpe la gorge** ou **le gosier** rough wine; **tissu qui râpe la peau** scratchy material

rapetassage* [Rap(ə)tasaʒ] NM patching up

rapetasser* [Rap(ə)tase] ▸conjug 1◂ VT to patch up

rapetissement [Rap(ə)tismɑ̃] NM a [manteau] taking up, shortening; [taille, encolure] taking in; [objet] shortening, shrinking b (= rabaissement) belittling c (= action de faire paraître plus petit) dwarfing; **le ~ des objets dû à la distance** the fact that objects look smaller when seen from a distance

rapetisser [Rap(ə)tise] ▸conjug 1◂ 1 VT a (= raccourcir) [+ manteau] to take up, shorten; [+ taille, encolure] to take in; [+ objet] to shorten; **l'âge l'avait rapetissé** he had shrunk with age b (= rabaisser) to belittle c (= faire paraître plus petit) **~ qch** to make sth seem ou look small(er); **le château rapetissait toutes les maisons alentour** the castle dwarfed all the surrounding houses, the castle made all the surrounding houses look ou seem small 2 VI* [jours] to get shorter; **les objets rapetissent à distance** objects look smaller from a distance 3 **se rapetisser** VPR a [vieillard] to shrink, grow shorter ou smaller b (= se rabaisser) **se ~ aux yeux de qn** to belittle o.s. in sb's eyes

râpeux, -euse [Rɑpø, øz] ADJ rough

Raphaël [Rafaɛl] NM Raphael

raphaélique [Rafaelik] ADJ Raphaelesque

raphia [Rafja] NM raffia

rapiat, e [Rapja, jat] (péj) 1 ADJ niggardly, stingy, tight-fisted 2 NM,F niggard, skinflint

rapide [Rapid] 1 ADJ a (en déplacement) [coureur, marche, pas] fast, quick; [véhicule, route] fast; [animal] fast(-moving); [fleuve] fast(-flowing), swift-flowing; **~ comme une flèche** ou **l'éclair** incredibly fast; **il est ~ à la course** he's a fast runner; **elle marchait d'un pas ~** she was walking quickly → **voie**
b (dans le temps) [travail, guérison, progrès, remède, réponse] quick, fast; [intervention, visite, fortune, recette] quick; [poison] quick-acting, fast-acting; [accord] speedy, swift; **examen (trop) ~ de qch** cursory examination of sth; **décision trop ~** hasty decision; **faire un calcul ~** to do a quick calculation; **c'est ~ à faire** (plat) it's very quick to make
c [pente, descente] steep
d [mouvement, coup d'œil] rapid, quick; [esprit, intelligence] quick; [travailleur] quick, fast; **d'une main ~** (= vite) quickly, rapidly; (= adroitement) deftly; **avoir des réflexes ~s** to have good reflexes; **tu n'es pas très ~ ce matin** you're a bit slow ou you're not on the ball* this morning; **c'est une ~** (qui agit vite) she's a fast worker; (qui comprend vite) she's quick on the uptake; **ce n'est pas un ~** he's a bit slow
e (en fréquence) [pouls, rythme, respiration] fast, rapid
f [style, récit] lively
g (Tech) [pellicule] fast; [ciment] quick-setting

2 NM a (= train) express (train), fast train; **le ~ Paris-Nice** the Paris-Nice express
b [cours d'eau] rapids; **descendre des ~s en kayak** to canoe down some rapids, shoot ou ride some rapids in a canoe

rapidement [Rapidmɑ̃] ADV quickly, rapidly; **la situation se dégrade ~** the situation is rapidly degenerating; **les pompiers sont intervenus ~** the fire brigade arrived very quickly; **il faut mettre ~ un terme à ce conflit** we must put a swift end to the conflict; **j'ai parcouru ~ le journal** I quickly skimmed through the paper

rapidité [Rapidite] NF (gén) speed; [réponse, geste] swiftness, quickness; [style] briskness, liveliness; [pouls] quickness; **~ d'esprit** quickness of mind; **~ de décision** quick ou speedy decision-making; **la ~ de sa réaction m'a étonné** the speed with which he reacted surprised me, I was surprised at how quickly he reacted; **la ~ d'adaptation est essentielle dans ce métier** the ability to adapt quickly is essential in this profession; **avec ~** quickly; **avec la ~ de l'éclair** ou **de la foudre** ou **d'une flèche** with lightning speed

rapido* [Rapido], **rapidos*** [Rapidos] ADV pronto*

rapiéçage [Rapjesaʒ], **rapiècement** [Rapjɛsmɑ̃] NM a [vêtement, pneu] patching (up); [chaussure] mending, repairing b (= pièce) patch

rapiécer [Rapjese] ▸conjug 3 et 6◂ VT [+ vêtement, pneu] to patch (up), put a patch in; [+ chaussure] to mend, repair; **il portait une veste toute rapiécée** he was wearing a patched-up old jacket

rapière [Rapjɛʀ] NF rapier

rapin [Rapɛ̃] NM († ou péj = artiste peintre) painter, dauber

rapine [Rapin] NF (littér) plundering, plunder; **vivre de ~(s)** to live by plunder

rapiner [Rapine] ▸conjug 1◂ VTI (littér) to plunder

raplapla* [Raplapla] ADJ INV (= fatigué) done in*; (= plat) flat

raplatir [RaplatiR] ▸conjug 2◂ VT to flatten out

rappareiller [Rapaʀeje] ▸conjug 1◂ VT to match up

rapparier [Rapaʀje] ▸conjug 7◂ VT to pair up, match up

rappel [Rapɛl] NM a [ambassadeur] recall, recalling; (Mil) [réservistes] recall; [marchandises défectueuses] callback; **il y a eu trois ~s** (Théât) there were three curtain calls; (à un concert) they (ou he etc) came back on stage for three encores → **battre**
b [événement] reminder; (Comm) [référence] quote; (Admin = deuxième avis) reminder; (Admin = somme due) back pay (NonC); (Méd = vaccination) booster; **au ~ de cette bévue, il rougit** he blushed at being reminded of this blunder; **toucher un ~ (de salaire)** to get some back pay; (Aut) **~ de limitation de vitesse** speed limit sign, reminder of the speed limit; (Radio, TV) **~ des titres de l'actualité** summary of the day's headlines; **~ à l'ordre** call to order; **~ de couleur** colour repeat
c (Tech) [pièce, levier] return; (Alpinisme) **~ (de corde)** (= technique) abseiling, roping down; (= opération) abseil; **faire un ~** ◊ **descendre en ~** to abseil, rope down; (Naut) **faire du ~** to sit out; (Tech) **ressort de ~** return spring → **descente**

rappelé [Rap(ə)le] NM recalled soldier

▾**rappeler** [Rap(ə)le] ▸conjug 4◂ 1 VT a (= faire revenir) [+ personne, acteur, chien] to call back; (Mil) [+ réservistes, classe] to recall, call up (again); [+ diplomate] to recall; **~ qn au chevet d'un malade** ou **auprès d'un malade** to call ou summon sb back to a sick person's bedside; **ses affaires l'ont rappelé à Paris** he was called back to Paris on business; (frm) **Dieu l'a**

➤ GRAMMAIRE ACTIVE: **rappeler** 27.2, 27.3, 27.5, 28.1

rappelé à lui he (has) departed this world *ou* life; (*Mil*) **~ des réservistes au front** to recall reservists to the front; (*Ordin*) **~ un fichier (à l'écran)** to call up a file (onto the screen)

b **~ qch à qn** (= *évoquer, remettre en mémoire*) to remind sb of sth; **il rappela les qualités du défunt** he evoked *ou* mentioned the qualities of the deceased, he reminded the audience of the qualities of the deceased; **faut-il ~ que ...** must I remind you that ...?, must it be repeated that ...?; **ces dessins rappellent l'art arabe** those drawings are reminiscent of *ou* remind one of Arabian art; **le motif des poches rappelle celui du bas de la robe** the design on the pockets is repeated round the hem of the dress; **cela ne te rappelle rien?** doesn't that remind you of anything?; **tu me rappelles ma tante** you remind me of my aunt; **rappelle-moi mon rendez-vous** remind me about my appointment; **rappelez-moi votre nom** sorry — could you tell me your name again?; **attends, ça me rappelle quelque chose** wait, it rings a bell; (*frm*) **rappelez-moi à son bon souvenir** please remember me to him, please give him my kind regards

c **~ qn à la vie** *ou* **à lui** to bring sb back to life, revive sb; **~ qn à l'ordre** to call sb to order; **~ qn à son devoir** to remind sb of their duty; **~ qn à de meilleurs sentiments** to put sb in a better frame of mind

d (= *retéléphoner à*) to call *ou* phone *ou* ring back (*Brit*); **il vient de ~** he's just called *ou* phoned back *ou* rung (*Brit*)

e (*Comm*) [+ *référence*] to quote

f (= *tirer*) (*Tech*) [+ *pièce, levier*] to return; (*Alpinisme*) [+ *corde*] to pull to *ou* through

2 se rappeler VPR (*gén*) to remember, recollect, recall; **se ~ que ...** to remember *ou* recall *ou* recollect that ...; **autant que je me rappelle** as far as I can remember *ou* recollect *ou* recall; (*frm*) **je me permets de me ~ à votre bon souvenir** I am sending you my kindest regards (*frm*); **rappelle-toi que ton honneur est en jeu** remember (that) your honour is at stake; **il ne se rappelle plus** (rien) he doesn't *ou* can't remember a thing

rapper [Rape] ▸ conjug 1 ◂ VI to rap, play rap music

rappeur, -euse [Rapœr, øz] NM,F (*Mus*) rapper

rappliquer: [Raplike] ▸ conjug 1 ◂ VI (= *revenir*) to come back; (= *arriver*) to turn up, show up*; **rapplique tout de suite à la maison!** come home right away!, get yourself back here right away!*

▼ **rapport** [RapɔR] NM **a** (= *lien, corrélation*) connection, relationship, link; **établir un ~/des ~s entre deux incidents** to establish a link *ou* connection/links *ou* connections between two incidents; **avoir un certain ~/beaucoup de ~ avec qch** to have something/a lot to do with sth, have some/a definite connection with sth; **avoir ~ à qch** to bear some relation to sth, have something to do *ou* some connection with sth; **n'avoir aucun ~ avec** *ou* **sans ~ avec qch** to bear no relation to sth, have nothing to do *ou* no connection with sth; **les deux incidents n'ont aucun ~** the two incidents have nothing to do with each other *ou* are unconnected; **je ne vois pas le ~** I don't see the connection; **être en ~ avec qch** to be in keeping with sth; **une situation en ~ avec ses goûts** a job in keeping *ou* in harmony *ou* in line with his tastes; **son train de vie n'est pas en ~ avec son salaire** his lifestyle doesn't match *ou* isn't in keeping with his salary

b (= *relation personnelle*) relationship (**à, avec** with); **~s** relations; **~s sociaux/humains** social/human relations; **les ~s d'amitié entre les deux peuples** the friendly relations *ou* the ties of friendship between the two nations; **les ~s entre (les) professeurs et (les) étudiants** relations between teachers and students,

student-teacher *ou* student-staff relations; **son ~ à l'argent est bizarre** he has a strange relationship with money; **ses ~s avec les autres sont difficiles** he has problems dealing with *ou* getting along *ou* on (*Brit*) with people; **avoir** *ou* **entretenir de bons/mauvais ~s avec qn** to be on good/bad terms with sb; **être en ~ avec qn** to be in touch *ou* contact with sb; **nous n'avons jamais été en ~ avec cette société** we have never had any dealings *ou* anything to do with that company; **se mettre en ~ avec qn** to get in touch *ou* contact with sb; **mettre qn en ~ avec qn d'autre** to put sb in touch *ou* contact with sb else

c **~ (sexuel)** sexual intercourse (*NonC*); **avoir des ~s (sexuels)** to have (sexual) intercourse *ou* sexual relations *ou* sex; **~s protégés** safe sex; **~s non protégés** unprotected sex

d (= *exposé, compte rendu*) report; (*Mil* = *réunion*) (post-exercise) conference; **au ~!** (*Mil*) read!; (*hum*) let's hear what you've got to say!; (*Écon*) **~ (annuel) d'activité** annual report; (*Scol*) **~ d'inspection** evaluation (report); **~ de police** police report

e (= *revenu, profit*) yield, return, revenue; [*tiercé*] **~s** winnings; **être d'un bon ~** to give a good profit, have a good yield, give a good return; **ces champs sont en plein ~** these fields are bringing in a full yield → **immeuble, maison**

f (*Math, Tech*) ratio; (*Aut*) **~ de transmission** gear ratio; **dans le ~ de 1 à 100/de 100 contre 1** in a ratio of 1 to 100/of 100 to 1; **le ~ qualité-prix** the quality-price ratio; **il y a un bon ~ qualité-prix** it's really good value for money; **ce n'est pas d'un bon ~ qualité-prix** it's not good value for money

g (*loc*) **par ~ à** (= *comparé à*) in comparison with, in relation to; (= *en fonction de*) in relation to; (= *envers*) with respect *ou* regard to, towards; **le cours de la livre par ~ au dollar** the price of the pound against the dollar; **le ~ de** *ou* **des forces entre les deux blocs** the balance of power between the two blocs; **envisager des relations sous l'angle d'un ~ de forces** to see relationships in terms of a power struggle; **~ à** about, in connection with, concerning; **je viens vous voir ~ à votre annonce:** I've come (to see you) about your advertisement; **il n'y a aucune inquiétude à avoir sous le ~ de l'honnêteté** from the point of view of honesty *ou* as far as honesty is concerned there's nothing to worry about; **sous tous les ~s** in every respect; (*hum*) **jeune homme bien sous tous ~s** clean-living young man

rapportage [RapɔRtaʒ] NM (*arg Scol* = *mouchardage*) tale-telling (*NonC*), tattling (*NonC*) (*US*)

rapporté, e [RapɔRte] (*ptp de* **rapporter**) ADJ (*gén*) added; (*Couture*) sewn-on; [*terre*] piled-up; **poche ~e** patch pocket → **pièce**

rapporter [RapɔRte] ▸ conjug 1 ◂ **1** VT **a** (= *apporter*) [+ *objet, souvenir, réponse*] to bring back; [*chien*] [+ *gibier*] to retrieve; (*à un chien*) **Toby, rapporte!** fetch, Toby!; **~ qch à qn** to bring *ou* take sth back to sb; **n'oublie pas de lui ~ son parapluie** don't forget to return his umbrella to him; **il rapportera du pain en rentrant** he'll bring some bread when he gets back; **~ une bonne impression de qch** to come back *ou* come away with a good impression of sth; **quand doit-il ~ la réponse?** when does he have to come *ou* be back with the answer?

b (*Fin fig* = *produire un gain*) [*actions, terre*] to yield (a return of), bring in (a yield *ou* revenue of); [*métier*] to bring in; [*vente*] to bring in (a profit *ou* revenue of); **placement qui rapporte du 5%** investment that yields (a return of) 5%; **ça rapporte beaucoup d'argent** it's extremely profitable, it brings in a lot of money, it gives a high return; **ça ne lui rapportera rien** [*mauvaise action*] it won't do him any good; **ça leur a rapporté 100F net** they netted 100 francs, it brought them in

100 francs net

c (= *faire un compte rendu de*) [+ *fait*] to report; (= *mentionner*) to mention; (= *citer*) [+ *mot célèbre*] to quote; (= *répéter pour dénoncer*) to report; **on nous a rapporté que son projet n'avait pas été bien accueilli** we were told that his project hadn't been well received; **~ à qn les actions de qn** to report sb's actions to sb; **il a rapporté à la maîtresse ce qu'avaient dit ses camarades** he told the teacher what his classmates had said, he reported what his classmates had said to the teacher

d (= *ajouter*: *gén*) to add; [+ *bande de tissu, poche*] to sew on; **~ une aile à une maison** to build an extra wing onto a house; **~ un peu de terre pour surélever le sol** to pile up some earth to raise the level of the ground; **c'est un élément rapporté** it's been added on

e (= *rattacher à*) **~ à** to relate to; **il faut tout ~ à la même échelle de valeurs** everything has to be related *ou* referred to the same scale of values; **il rapporte tout à lui** he brings everything back to himself

f (= *annuler*) [+ *décret, décision, mesure*] to revoke

g (*Math*) **~ un angle** to plot an angle

2 VI **a** (*Chasse*) [*chien*] to retrieve

b (*Fin*) [*investissement*] to give a good return *ou* yield; **ça rapporte bien** *ou* **gros** [*domaine d'activité*] it's very profitable, it brings in a lot of money; [*travail*] it pays very well

c (*arg Scol* = *moucharder*) **~ (sur ses camarades)** to tell tales *ou* sneak* (on one's friends), to tell on (*Brit*)* *ou* tattle on* (*US*) one's friends

3 se rapporter VPR **a** **se ~ à qch** to relate to sth; (*Gram*) **se ~ à** (= *antécédent*) to relate *ou* refer to; **ce paragraphe ne se rapporte pas du tout au sujet** this paragraph bears no relation at all to the subject, this paragraph is totally irrelevant to *ou* unconnected with the subject; **ça se rapporte à ce que je disais tout à l'heure** that ties *ou* links up with *ou* relates to what I was saying just now

b **s'en ~ à qn** to rely on sb; **s'en ~ au jugement/témoignage de qn** to rely on sb's judgment/account

rapporteur, -euse [RapɔRtœR, øz] **1** NM,F (= *mouchard*) telltale, sneak*, tattler* (*US*); **elle est rapporteuse** she's a telltale *ou* sneak* *ou* tattler (*US*) **2** NM **a** (*Jur*) [*tribunal*] (court) reporter; [*commission*] rapporteur, reporter (*member acting as spokesman*) **b** (*Géom*) protractor

rapprendre [RapRɑ̃dR] ▸ conjug 58 ◂ VT = **réapprendre**

rapproché, e [RapRɔʃe] (*ptp de* **rapprocher**) ADJ **a** (= *proche*) [*échéance, objet, bruit*] close; **l'objet le plus ~ de toi** the object closest *ou* nearest to you; **à une date ~e** *ou* ◊ **dans un avenir ~** in the near *ou* not too distant future; **elle a des yeux très ~s** she's got close-set eyes, her eyes are very close together; **surveillance ~e** close surveillance → **combat, garde, protection b** (= *répété*) [*incidents*] frequent; **des crises de plus en plus ~es** increasingly frequent crises, crises which have become more and more frequent; **trois explosions très ~es** trois explosions in quick succession *ou* very close together; **à intervalles ~s** in quick succession, at short *ou* close intervals; **des grossesses ~es** (a series of) pregnancies at short *ou* close intervals

rapprochement [RapRɔʃmɑ̃] NM **a** (= *action de rapprocher*) [*objet, meuble*] bringing closer *ou* nearer; [*objets, meubles*] bringing closer *ou* nearer to each other; [*ennemis*] bringing together, reconciliation; [*partis, factions*] bringing together; [*points de vue, textes*] comparison, bringing together, comparing; (*Méd*) **le ~ des lèvres d'une plaie** joining the edges of a wound, closing (the lips of) a wound

b (= *action de se rapprocher*) [*bruit*] coming closer; [*ennemis, famille*] coming together, reconciliation; [*partis, factions*] coming together, rapprochement; (*Pol*) **ce ~ avec la droite nous inquiète** their moving closer to the right worries us; **le ~ des bruits de pas** the noise of footsteps drawing *ou* coming closer

[c] (= *lien, rapport*) parallel; **je n'avais pas fait le ~ (entre ces deux incidents)** I hadn't made *ou* established the connection *ou* link (between the two incidents); **il y a de nombreux ~s intéressants/troublants** there are many interesting/disturbing parallels *ou* comparisons to be made

rapprocher [ʀapʀɔʃe] ▸ conjug 1 ◂ [1] VT [a] (= *approcher*) to bring closer *ou* nearer (**de** to); **~ sa chaise (de la table)** to pull *ou* draw one's chair up (to the table); **~ deux objets l'un de l'autre** to move two objects (closer) together; **~ les lèvres d'une plaie** to join the edges of a wound, close (the lips of) a wound; **il a changé d'emploi : ça le rapproche de chez lui** he has changed jobs — that brings him closer *ou* nearer to home

[b] (= *réconcilier, réunir*) [+ *ennemis*] to bring together; **nous nous sentions rapprochés par un malheur commun** we felt drawn together by a common misfortune, we felt that a common misfortune had brought *ou* drawn us together; **leur amour de la chasse les rapproche** their love of hunting brings them together *ou* draws them to *ou* towards each other

[c] (= *mettre en parallèle, confronter*) [+ *indices, textes*] to put together *ou* side by side, compare, bring together; (= *établir un lien entre, assimiler*) [+ *indices, textes*] to establish a connection *ou* link *ou* parallel between; **essayons de ~ ces indices de ceux-là** let's try and put *ou* bring these two sets of clues together, let's try and compare these two sets of clues; **on peut ~ cela du poème de Villon** we can relate *ou* connect that to Villon's poem, we can establish a connection *ou* link *ou* parallel between that and Villon's poem; **ce qu'on disait tout à l'heure** that ties up *ou* connects with *ou* relates to what we were saying earlier

[2] **se rapprocher** VPR [a] (= *approcher*) [*échéance, personne, véhicule, orage*] to get closer *ou* nearer, approach; **rapproche-toi (de moi)** come closer *ou* nearer (to me); **il se rapprocha d'elle sur la banquette** he edged his way towards her *ou* drew closer to her on the bench; **pour se ~ de chez lui, il a changé d'emploi** to get closer *ou* nearer to home he changed jobs; **plus on se rapprochait de l'examen ...** the closer *ou* nearer we came *ou* got to the exam ...; **se ~ de la vérité** to come close *ou* get near *ou* close to the truth; **les bruits se rapprochèrent** the noises got closer *ou* nearer

[b] (*dans le temps*) [*crises, bruits*] to become more frequent

[c] (= *se réconcilier*) [*ennemis*] to come together, be reconciled; (= *trouver un terrain d'entente*) [*points de vue*] to draw closer together; [*société*] to form links; **il s'est rapproché de ses parents** he became *ou* drew closer to his parents; (*Pol*) **il a essayé de se ~ de la droite** he tried to move *ou* draw closer to the right; **leur position s'est rapprochée de la nôtre** their position has drawn closer to ours; **se ~ des autres actionnaires** to join forces with the other shareholders

[d] (= *s'apparenter à*) to be close to; **ça se rapproche de ce qu'on disait tout à l'heure** that's close to *ou* ties up *ou* connects with what we were saying earlier; **ses opinions se rapprochent beaucoup des miennes** his opinions are very close *ou* similar to mine

rapsode [ʀapsɔd] NM = **rhapsode**

rapsodie [ʀapsɔdi] NF = **rhapsodie**

rapt [ʀapt] NM (= *enlèvement*) abduction

raquer⁑ [ʀake] ▸ conjug 1 ◂ VTI (= *payer*) to fork out⁎; **d'accord, mais il va falloir ~ !** OK, but it'll cost you!⁎

raquette [ʀakɛt] NF [a] (*Tennis, Squash*) racket; (*Ping-Pong*) bat; (= *joueur*) **c'est une bonne ~** he's a good tennis (*ou* squash) player [b] (*à neige*) snowshoe [c] (*Basket*) free-throw area [d] (*Bot*) nopal, prickly pear

raquetteur, -euse [ʀakɛtœʀ, øz] NM,F (*Can*) snowshoer

rare [ʀaʀ] ADJ [a] (= *peu commun*) [*objet, mot, édition*] rare; **ça n'a rien de ~** there's nothing uncommon *ou* unusual about it, it's not a rare occurrence; **il était ~ qu'il ne sache pas** he rarely *ou* seldom did not know; **il n'était pas ~ de le rencontrer** it was not unusual *ou* uncommon to meet him; **c'est ~ de le voir fatigué** it's rare *ou* unusual to see him tired, you rarely *ou* seldom see him tired; **c'est bien ~ s'il ne vient pas**⁎ I'd be surprised *ou* it would be unusual if he didn't come → **oiseau, perle**

[b] (= *peu nombreux*) [*cas, exemples*] rare, few; [*visites*] rare; [*passants, voitures*] few; **les ~s voitures qui passaient** the few *ou* odd cars that went by; **les ~s amis qui lui restent** the few friends still left to him; **à de ~s intervalles** at rare intervals; **les ~s fois où ...** on the rare occasions (when) ...; **il est l'un des ~s qui ...** he's one of the few (people) who ...; **à cette heure les clients sont ~s** at this time of day customers are scarce *ou* are few and far between; **à de ~s exceptions près** with very few exceptions

[c] (= *peu abondant*) [*nourriture, main d'œuvre*] scarce; [*barbe, cheveux*] thin, sparse; [*végétation*] sparse; **il a le cheveu ~** he's rather thin on top; **se faire ~** [*argent*] to become scarce, be tight; [*légumes*] to become scarce, be in short supply; (*hum*) **vous vous faites ~** we haven't seen much of you recently, we rarely see you these days

[d] (= *exceptionnel*) [*talent, qualité, sentiment, beauté*] rare; [*homme, énergie*] exceptional, singular; [*saveur, moment*] exquisite; (*hum*) [*imbécile, imprudence*] utter; **avec un ~ courage** with rare *ou* singular *ou* exceptional courage; **une attaque d'une ~ violence** an exceptionally *ou* extremely violent attack; **d'une ~ beauté** exceptionally *ou* extremely beautiful; **il est d'une ~ stupidité** he's utterly stupid

[e] (*Chim*) [*gaz*] rare

raréfaction [ʀaʀefaksjɔ̃] NF [*oxygène*] rarefaction; [*nourriture*] (= *action*) increased scarcity; (= *résultat*) scarcity, short supply

raréfiable [ʀaʀefjabl] ADJ rarefiable

raréfier [ʀaʀefje] ▸ conjug 7 ◂ [1] VT [+ *air*] to rarefy; **gaz raréfié** rarefied gas [2] **se raréfier** VPR [*oxygène*] to rarefy; [*argent, nourriture*] to grow *ou* become scarce, be in short supply

rarement [ʀaʀmɑ̃] ADV rarely, seldom; **le règlement est ~ respecté** the rule is rarely *ou* seldom observed; **il ne rate que ~ sa cible** he only rarely misses his target; **cela arrive plus ~** it happens less often *ou* frequently

rareté [ʀaʀte] NF [a] [*édition, objet*] rarity; [*mot, cas*] rareness, rarity; [*vivres, argent*] scarcity; **la ~ des touristes/visiteurs** the small numbers of tourists/visitors; **se plaindre de la ~ des lettres/visites de qn** to complain of the infrequency of sb's letters/visits [b] (= *objet précieux*) rarity, rare object; **une telle erreur de sa part, c'est une ~** it's a rare *ou* an unusual occurrence for him to make a mistake like that

rarissime [ʀaʀisim] ADJ extremely rare; **fait ~, la pièce est restée six mois à l'affiche** the play ran for six months, which is very rare

R.A.S. [ɛʀɑɛs] (ABRÉV = **rien à signaler**) → **rien**

ras¹ [ʀɑs] NM (= *titre éthiopien*) ras

ras², e [ʀɑ, ʀɑz] ADJ [a] [*poil, herbe*] short; [*cheveux*] close-cropped; [*étoffe*] with a short pile; [*mesure, tasse*] full; **il avait la tête ~e** he had close-cropped hair; **à poil ~** [*chien*] short-haired; [*étoffe*] with a short pile; **ongles/cheveux coupés ~** *ou* **à ~** nails/hair cut short [b] **à** *ou* **au ~ de** (= *au niveau de*) **au ~ de la**

terre *ou* **du sol/de l'eau** level with the ground/the water; **arbre coupé à ~ de terre** tree cut down to the ground; **ses cheveux lui arrivent au ~ des fesses** she can almost sit on her hair; **ça lui arrive au ~ des chevilles** it comes down to her ankles; (= *tout près de*) **voler au ~ du sol/au ~ de l'eau** to fly close to *ou* just above the ground/the water, skim the ground/the water; **le projectile lui est passé au ~ de la tête/du visage** the projectile skimmed his head/his face; **la discussion est au ~ des pâquerettes**⁎ the discussion is pretty lowbrow; **soyons pragmatiques, restons au ~ des pâquerettes**⁎ let's be pragmatic and keep our feet on the ground

[c] (*loc*) **à ~ bord(s)** to the brim; **remplir un verre à ~ bord** to fill a glass to the brim *ou* top; **plein à ~ bord** [*verre*] full to the brim, brimful; [*baignoire*] full to overflowing *ou* to the brim; **en ~e campagne** in open country; **pull** *ou* **du cou** crew-neck *ou* round-neck sweater; **j'en ai ~ le bol**⁎ *ou* **le pompon**⁎ *ou* **la casquette**⁎ (**de tout ça**) I'm sick to death of it⁎, I'm fed up to the back teeth (with it all) (*Brit*) → **ras-le-bol**

rasade [ʀɑzad] NF glassful

rasage [ʀɑzaʒ] NM [a] [*barbe*] shaving → **lotion** [b] (*Tex*) shearing

rasant, e [ʀɑzɑ̃, ɑ̃t] ADJ [a] (⁎ = *ennuyeux*) boring; **qu'il est ~!** he's a (real) bore! *ou* drag!⁎ [b] [*lumière*] low-angled; [*fortification*] low-built; **tir ~** grazing fire

rascasse [ʀaskas] NF scorpion fish

rasé, e [ʀɑze] (*ptp de* **raser**) ADJ [*menton*] (clean-)shaven; [*tête*] shaven; **être bien/mal ~** to be shaven/unshaven; **~ de près** close-shaven; **~ de frais** freshly shaven; **avoir les cheveux ~s** to have a shaven head

rase-mottes [ʀɑzmɔt] NM INV hedgehopping; **faire du ~** ◊ **voler en ~** to hedgehop; **vol en ~** hedgehopping flight

raser [ʀɑze] ▸ conjug 1 ◂ [1] VT [a] (= *tondre*) [+ *barbe, cheveux*] to shave off; [+ *menton, tête*] to shave; [+ *malade*] to shave; **~ un prêtre/condamné** to shave a priest's/convict's head; **se faire ~ la tête** to have one's head shaved; **à ~ crème, gel, mousse** shaving (épith) [b] (= *effleurer*) [*projectile, véhicule*] to graze, scrape; [*oiseau, balle de tennis*] to skim (over); **~ les murs** to hug the walls [c] (= *abattre*) [+ *maison*] to raze (to the ground); **~ un navire** to bring a ship's masts down [d] (⁎ = *ennuyer*) to bore; **ça me rase!** it bores me stiff!⁎ *ou* to tears!⁎ [e] (*Tech*) (= *mesure à grains*) to strike; [+ *velours*] to shear [2] **se raser** VPR [a] (*toilette*) to shave, have a shave; **se ~ la tête/les jambes** to shave one's head/one's legs [b] (⁎ = *s'ennuyer*) to be bored stiff⁎ *ou* to tears⁎

raseur, -euse⁎ [ʀɑzœʀ, øz] [1] ADJ boring; **qu'il est ~!** he's a (real) bore! *ou* drag!⁎ [2] NM,F bore

rasibus⁎ [ʀɑzibys] ADV [*couper*] very close *ou* fine; **passer ~** [*projectile*] to whizz past very close

ras-le-bol⁎ [ʀɑl(ə)bɔl] [1] EXCL enough is enough! [2] NM INV (= *mécontentement*) discontent; **provoquer le ~ général** to cause widespread discontent; **le ~ étudiant** the students' discontent *ou* dissatisfaction, student unrest → **table**

rasoir [ʀɑzwaʀ] [1] NM razor; **~ électrique** (electric) shaver, electric razor; **~ mécanique** *ou* **de sûreté** safety razor; **~ à main** *ou* **de coiffeur** cut-throat *ou* straight razor; **~ jetable** *ou* throwaway razor; **se donner un coup de ~** to have a quick shave → **feu**⁎, **fil** etc [2] ADJ (⁎ = *ennuyeux*) [*film, livre*] dead boring⁎; **qu'il est ~!** what a bore *ou* drag⁎ he is!

Raspoutine [ʀasputin] NM Rasputin

rassasier [ʀasazje] ▸ conjug 7 ◂ (*frm*) [1] VT [a] (= *assouvir*) [+ *faim, curiosité, désirs*] to satisfy

b (= *nourrir*) ~ **qn** [*aliment*] to satisfy sb *ou* sb's appetite; ~ **qn de qch** (= *lui en donner suffisamment*) to satisfy sb with sth *ou* sb's appetite *ou* hunger with sth; (= *lui en donner trop*) to give sb too much of sth; **être rassasié** (= *n'avoir plus faim*) to be satisfied, have eaten one's fill; (= *en être dégoûté*) to be satiated *ou* sated, have had more than enough; **on ne peut pas le ~ de chocolats** you can't give him too many chocolates; ~ **ses yeux de qch** to feast one's eyes on sth; **je suis rassasié de toutes ces histoires** I've had quite enough of all this!

2 se rassasier VPR (= *se nourrir*) to satisfy one's hunger, eat one's fill; **se ~ d'un spectacle** to feast one's eyes on a sight; **je ne me rassasierai jamais de ...** I'll never tire *ou* have enough of ...

rassemblement [rasɑ̃bləmɑ̃] NM **a** (= *action de regrouper*) [*troupeau*] rounding up; [*objets, documents*] gathering, collecting **b** [*pièces, mécanisme*] reassembly **c** (*Équitation*) [*cheval*] collecting **d** (= *réunion, attroupement*) (*gén*) assembly, gathering; [*manifestants*] rally; (*Mil*) ~ ! fall in!; **à 9 heures sur le quai** we'll meet at 9 o'clock on the platform; (*Pol*) ~ **pour la paix** peace rally → **point**

rassembler [rasɑ̃ble] ▶ conjug 1 ◀ **1** VT **a** (= *regrouper*) [+ *personnes*] to gather, assemble; [+ *troupes*] to muster; [+ *troupeau*] to round up; [+ *sympathisants*] to round up, rally; [+ *objets épars*] to gather together, collect; **il rassembla les élèves dans la cour** he gathered *ou* assembled the pupils in the playground; **le festival rassemble les meilleurs musiciens** the festival brings together the best musicians **b** (= *rallier*) to rally; **cette cause a rassemblé des gens de tous horizons** people from all walks of life have rallied to this cause **c** [+ *documents, manuscrits, notes*] to gather together, collect, assemble **d** [+ *idées, souvenirs*] to collect; [+ *courage, forces*] to summon up, muster; ~ **ses esprits** to collect one's thoughts **e** (= *remonter*) [+ *pièces, mécanisme*] to put back together, reassemble **f** (*Équitation*) [+ *cheval*] to collect

2 se rassembler VPR **a** [*se regrouper*] to gather; [*soldats, participants*] to assemble, gather; **nous nous rassemblons deux fois par semaine** we get together twice a week; (*Naut*) **en cas d'urgence, rassemblez-vous sur le pont** in an emergency, assemble on deck; **rassemblés autour du père** gathered round the fire; **toute la famille était rassemblée** the whole family was gathered together **b** (= *s'unir*) **nous devons nous ~ autour du président/pour lutter contre ...** we must unite behind the president/to fight against ... **c** (*Sport*) to bend (*to gather one's strength*)

rassembleur, -euse [rasɑ̃blœʀ, øz] **1** ADJ [*discours*] rallying; [*thème, projet*] unifying **2** NM,F unifier; **il fut le ~ d'une nation divisée** he was the unifier of *ou* he unified a divided nation

rasseoir [raswaʀ] ▶ conjug 26 ◀ **1** VT [+ *bébé*] to sit back up (straight); [+ *objet*] to put back up straight **2 se rasseoir** VPR to sit down again; **faire (se) ~ qn** to make sb sit down again; **rassieds-toi !** sit down!

rasséréné, e [raseʀene] (*ptp de* **rasséréner**) ADJ [*ciel, personne, visage*] serene

rasséréner [raseʀene] ▶ conjug 6 ◀ **1** VT to make serene again **2 se rasséréner** VPR [*personne, ciel, visage*] to become serene again, recover one's (*ou* its) serenity

rassir VI, **se rassir** VPR [rasiʀ] ▶ conjug 2 ◀ to go stale

rassis, e [rasi, iz] (*ptp de* **rassir, rasseoir**) ADJ **a** [*pain*] stale; [*viande*] hung **b** [*personne*] (= *pondéré*) composed, calm; (*péj*) stale

rassortiment [rasɔʀtimɑ̃] NM = **réassortiment**

rassortir [rasɔʀtiʀ] ▶ conjug 2 ◀ VT = **réassortir**

---

rassurant, e [rasyʀɑ̃, ɑ̃t] ADJ [*nouvelle, voix*] reassuring, comforting; [*discours, présence, visage*] reassuring; [*indice*] encouraging; **« ne vous inquiétez pas », dit-il d'un ton ~** "don't worry", he said reassuringly; **il a tenu des propos peu ~s** he said some rather worrying things; (*iro*) **c'est ~ !** that's very reassuring! (*iro*), that's a great comfort!* (*iro*)

rassurer [rasyʀe] ▶ conjug 1 ◀ **1** VT ~ **qn** to put sb's mind at ease *ou* rest, reassure sb; **le médecin m'a rassuré sur son état de santé** the doctor reassured me about the state of his health; **je ne me sentais pas rassuré dans sa voiture** I didn't feel at ease in his car; **je ne suis pas très rassuré** (*danger, situation inattendue*) I feel a bit uneasy; (*examen, entretien*) I feel a bit nervous; **me voilà rassuré maintenant** I've got nothing to worry about now, that's put my mind at rest **2 se rassurer** VPR **à cette nouvelle, il se rassura** the news put his mind at ease *ou* rest, he was relieved *ou* reassured when he heard the news; **il essayait de se ~ en se disant que c'était impossible** he tried to reassure himself by saying it was impossible; **rassure-toi** don't worry

rasta [rasta] ADJ, NMF (ABRÉV = **rastafari**) Rasta

rastafari [rastafaʀi] ADJ, NM Rastafarian

rastaquouère [rastakweʀ] NM (*péj*) flashy foreigner (*péj*)

rat [ra] **1** NM (*Zool*) rat; (*péj* = *avare*) miser; **c'est un vrai ~, ce type** that guy's really stingy* *ou* a real skinflint*; (*fig*) **les ~s quittent le navire** the rats are leaving the sinking ship; **s'ennuyer** *ou* **s'emmerder‡ comme un ~ mort** to be bored stiff* *ou* to death*; (*terme d'affection*) **mon (petit) ~** (my) pet, darling; **petit ~ de l'Opéra** pupil of the Opéra de Paris ballet class (*working as an extra*) → **chat, fait² 2** COMP ▶ **rat d'Amérique** muskrat, musquash (*Brit*) ▶ **rat de bibliothèque** bookworm (*who spends all his time in libraries*) ▶ **rat de cave** wax taper (*used for lighting one's way in a cellar or on a staircase*) ▶ **rat des champs** fieldmouse ▶ **rat d'eau** water vole ▶ **rat d'égout** sewer rat ▶ **rat d'hôtel** hotel thief ▶ **rat musqué** muskrat, musquash (*Brit*) ▶ **rat palmiste** ground squirrel

rata† [rata] NM (*arg Mil*) (= *nourriture*) grub*; (= *ragoût*) stew

ratafia [ratafja] NM (= *liqueur*) ratafia

ratage* [rataʒ] NM **a** (= *échec*) failure; **des ~s successifs** successive failures; **son film est un ~** his film is a complete failure *ou* flop **b** (= *action*) [*travail, affaire*] messing up, spoiling; [*mayonnaise, sauce*] spoiling; [*examen*] failing, flunking*

rataplan [rataplɑ̃] EXCL, NM rat-a-tat-tat

ratatiné, e [ratatine] (*ptp de* **ratatiner**) ADJ **a** [*pomme*] dried-up, shrivelled; [*visage, personne*] wrinkled, wizened **b**‡ [*voiture*] smashed-up*, banjaxed‡ (*US*); [*personne*] exhausted, knackered‡ (*Brit*)

ratatiner [ratatine] ▶ conjug 1 ◀ **1** VT **a** [+ *pomme*] to dry up, shrivel; **ratatiné par l'âge** [*visage, personne*] wrinkled *ou* wizened with age **b** (‡ = *détruire*) [+ *maison*] to wreck; [+ *machine, voiture*] to smash to bits *ou* pieces; **se faire ~** (*battre*) to get thrashed *ou* a thrashing; (*tuer*) to get done in‡ *ou* bumped off‡; **sa voiture a été complètement ratatinée** his car was a complete write-off (*Brit*), his car was totaled* (*US*) **2 se ratatiner** VPR [*pomme*] to shrivel *ou* dry up; [*visage*] to become wrinkled *ou* wizened; [*personne*] (*par l'âge*) to become wrinkled *ou* wizened; (*pour tenir moins de place*) to curl up

ratatouille [ratatuj] NF (*Culin*) ~ **(niçoise)** ratatouille; (*péj* = *ragoût*) bad stew; (= *cuisine*) lousy* food

rate¹ [rat] NF (= *organe*) spleen → **dilater, fouler**

---

rate² [rat] NF (= *animal*) she-rat

raté, e [rate] (*ptp de* **rater**) **1** ADJ [*tentative, mariage, artiste*] failed; [*vie*] wasted; [*départ*] bad, poor; **un film ~** a flop; **ma mayonnaise/la dernière scène est complètement ~e** my mayonnaise/the last scene is a complete disaster; **encore une occasion ~e !** another missed opportunity! **2** NM,F (* = *personne*) failure **3** NM **a** (*Aut: gén pl*) misfiring (*NonC*); **avoir des ~s** to misfire; (*fig*) **il y a eu des ~s dans les négociations** there were some hiccups in the negotiations **b** [*arme à feu*] misfire

râteau (*pl* **râteaux**) [ratо] NM (*Agr, Roulette*) rake; [*métier à tisser*] comb

râtelier [ratəlje] NM [*bétail, armes, outils*] rack; (* = *dentier*) (set of) false teeth; ~ **à pipes** pipe rack → **manger**

rater [rate] ▶ conjug 1 ◀ **1** VI **a** [*projet, affaire*] to fail, fall through; **ce contretemps/cette erreur risque de tout faire ~** this hitch/this mistake could well ruin everything; **je t'avais dit qu'elle y allait : ça n'a pas raté*** I told you she'd go and I was dead right* (*Brit*) *ou* and (*so*) she did; **ça ne rate jamais !** it never fails! **b** [*arme*] to fail to go off, misfire

2 VT **a** (= *manquer*) [+ *balle, cible, occasion, train, rendez-vous, spectacle, personne*] to miss; **c'est une occasion à ne pas ~** it's an opportunity not to be missed; **raté !** missed!; **ils se sont ratés de peu** they just missed each other; **si tu croyais m'impressionner, c'est raté** if you were trying to impress me, it hasn't worked!; (*iro*) **il n'en rate pas une !** he's always putting his foot in it!*; **je ne te raterai pas !** I'll get you!*, I'll show you!; **il voulait faire le malin mais je ne l'ai pas raté** he tried to be smart but I soon sorted him out I didn't let him get away with it; **il ne t'a pas raté !** he really got you there!* **b** (= *ne pas réussir*) [+ *travail, affaire*] to mess up, spoil; [+ *mayonnaise, sauce, plat*] to make a mess of; [+ *examen*] to fail, flunk*; **ces photos sont complètement ratées** these photos are a complete disaster; **un écrivain raté** a failed writer; ~ **son entrée** to miss one's entrance; **j'ai raté mon effet** I didn't achieve the effect I was hoping for; ~ **sa vie** to make a mess of one's life; **il a raté son coup** he didn't pull it off; **il a raté son suicide ◊ il s'est raté** he bungled his suicide attempt; **le coiffeur m'a raté** the hairdresser made a mess of my hair

ratiboiser* [ratibwaze] ▶ conjug 1 ◀ VT **a** (= *rafler*) ~ **qch à qn** (*au jeu*) to clean sb out of sth*; (*en le volant*) to pinch* *ou* nick‡ (*Brit*) sth from sb; **on lui a ratiboisé son portefeuille ◊ il s'est fait ~ son portefeuille** he got his wallet pinched* *ou* nicked‡ (*Brit*) **b** (= *dépouiller*) ~ **qn** to skin sb (*alive*)*, clean sb out* **c** (= *abattre*) [+ *maison*] to wreck; **il a été ratiboisé en moins de deux** [*personne*] in next to no time he was dead **d** (= *couper les cheveux à*) [+ *personne*] to scalp* (*fig*); **se faire ~** to be scalped*

raticide [ratisid] NM rat poison

ratier [ratje] NM (**chien**) ~ ratter

ratière [ratjɛʀ] NF rattrap

ratification [ratifikasjɔ̃] NF (*Admin, Jur*) ratification; ~ **de vente** sales confirmation

ratifier [ratifje] ▶ conjug 7 ◀ VT (*Admin, Jur*) to ratify; (*littér* = *confirmer*) to confirm, ratify

ratine [ratin] NF (*Tex*) ratine

rating [ratiŋ, retiŋ] NM (*Écon, Naut*) rating

ratio [rasjo] NM ratio

ratiocination [rasjosinasjɔ̃] NF (*littér péj*) (= *action*) hair-splitting, quibbling; (= *raisonnement*) hair-splitting argument, quibbling (*NonC*)

ratiociner [rasjosine] ▶ conjug 1 ◀ VI (*littér péj*) to split hairs, quibble (**sur** over)

ratiocineur, -euse [rasjosinœʀ, øz] NM,F (*littér péj*) hair-splitter, quibbler

ration [Rasjɔ̃] NF (= *portion limitée*) ration; [*soldat*] rations; [*animal*] (feed) intake; [*organisme*] (food) intake; **~ de viande/fourrage** meat/fodder ration; **~ alimentaire** food intake; **~ d'entretien** minimum daily requirement; **~ de survie** survival rations; **il a eu sa ~ d'épreuves/de soucis** he had his share of trials/of worries

rationalisation [Rasjɔnalizasjɔ̃] NF rationalization

rationaliser [Rasjɔnalize] ▶ conjug 1 ◀ VT to rationalize

rationalisme [Rasjɔnalism] NM rationalism

rationaliste [Rasjɔnalist] ADJ, NMF rationalist

rationalité [Rasjɔnalite] NF rationality

rationnel, -elle [Rasjɔnɛl] ADJ rational

rationnellement [Rasjɔnɛlmɑ̃] ADV rationally

rationnement [Rasjɔnmɑ̃] NM rationing → **carte**

rationner [Rasjɔne] ▶ conjug 1 ◀ 1 VT [+ *pain, eau*] to ration; [+ *personne*] (*lit*) to put on rations; (*fig hum* = *ne pas donner assez à*) to give short rations to 2 **se rationner** VPR to ration o.s.

ratissage [Ratisaʒ] NM (*Agr*) raking; (*Mil, Police*) combing

ratisser [Ratise] ▶ conjug 1 ◀ VT [+ *gravier*] to rake; [+ *feuilles*] to rake up; (*Mil, Police*) to comb; (*Rugby*) [+ *ballon*] to heel; (* = *dépouiller au jeu*) to clean out*; **~ large** to cast the net wide; **il s'est fait ~ (au jeu)*** he was cleaned out* *ou* he lost everything at the gambling table

raton [Ratɔ̃] NM [a] (*Zool*) young rat; **~ laveur** racoon [b] (**‡**, *raciste*) *racist term applied to North Africans in France* [c] (= *terme d'affection*) **mon ~!** (my) pet!

raton(n)ade [Ratɔnad] NF *racist attack (mainly on North African Arabs)*

RATP [ɛRatepe] NF (ABRÉV = **Régie autonome des transports parisiens**) → **régie**

rattachement [Rataʃmɑ̃] NM (*Admin, Pol*) uniting (**à** with), joining (**à** to); **le ~ de la Savoie à la France** the incorporation of Savoy into France; **demander son ~ à** to ask to be united with *ou* joined to; **quel est votre service de ~?** which service are you attached to?

rattacher [Rataʃe] ▶ conjug 1 ◀ VT [a] (= *attacher de nouveau*) [+ *animal, prisonnier, colis*] to tie up again; [+ *ceinture, lacets, jupe*] to do up *ou* fasten again [b] (= *annexer, incorporer*) [+ *territoire*] to incorporate (**à** into); [+ *commune, service*] to join (**à** to), unite (**à** with); [+ *employé, fonctionnaire*] to attach (**à** to) [c] (= *comparer, rapprocher*) [+ *problème, question*] to link, connect, tie up (**à** with); [+ *fait*] to relate (**à** to); **cela peut se ~ au premier problème** that can be related to *ou* tied up with the first problem; **on peut ~ cette langue au groupe slave** this language can be related to *ou* linked with the Slavonic group [d] (= *relier*) [+ *personne*] to bind, tie (**à** to); **rien ne le rattache plus à sa famille** he has no more ties with his family, nothing binds *ou* ties him to his family any more

rattrapable [Ratrapabl] ADJ [*erreur, gaffe*] which can be put right; [*heure, journée*] which can be made up

rattrapage [Ratrapaʒ] NM [*maille*] picking up; [*erreur*] making good; [*candidat d'examen*] passing; **le ~ d'une bêtise/d'un oubli** making up for something silly/for an omission; **le ~ du retard** [*élève*] catching up, making up for lost time; [*conducteur*] making up for lost time; **~ scolaire** remedial teaching *ou* classes; **cours de ~** remedial class *ou* course; **suivre des cours de ~** to go to remedial classes; (*Scol*) **épreuve de ~** additional exam for borderline cases; **session de ~** retakes, resits (*Brit*); **pour permettre le ~ économique de certains pays européens** to allow certain European economies to catch up; **le ~ des salaires sur les prix** an increase in salaries to keep up with *ou* keep pace with prices

rattraper [Ratrape] ▶ conjug 1 ◀ 1 VT [a] (= *reprendre*) [+ *animal échappé, prisonnier*] to recapture [b] (= *retenir*) [+ *objet, personne qui tombe*] to catch (hold of) [c] (= *réparer*) [+ *maille*] to pick up; [+ *mayonnaise*] to salvage; [+ *erreur*] to make good, make up for; [+ *bêtise, parole malheureuse, oubli*] to make up for [d] (= *regagner*) [+ *argent perdu*] to recover, get back, recoup; [+ *sommeil*] to catch up on; [+ *temps perdu*] to make up for; **le conducteur a rattrapé son retard** the driver made up for lost time; **cet élève ne pourra jamais ~ son retard** this pupil will never be able to catch up *ou* make up for the time he has lost; **ce qu'il perd d'un côté, il le rattrape de l'autre** what he loses in one way he gains in another, what he loses on the swings he gains on the roundabouts (*Brit*) [e] (= *rejoindre : lit, fig*) **~ qn** to catch sb up, catch up with sb; **le coût de la vie a rattrapé l'augmentation de salaire** the cost of living has caught up with the increase in salaries [f] (*Scol* = *repêcher*) **~ qn** to give sb a pass, let sb get through

2 **se rattraper** VPR [a] (= *reprendre son équilibre*) to stop o.s. falling, catch o.s. (just) in time; **se ~ à la rampe/à qn** to catch hold of the banister/of sb to stop o.s. falling; **j'ai failli gaffer, mais je me suis rattrapé in extremis** I nearly put my foot in it but stopped myself just in time → **branche** [b] (= *compenser*) to make up for it; **j'ai passé trois nuits sans dormir, mais hier je me suis rattrapé** I had three sleepless nights, but I made up for it yesterday; **les plats ne sont pas chers mais ils se rattrapent sur les vins** the food isn't expensive but they make up for it on the wine; **les fabricants comptent sur les marchés extérieurs pour se ~** manufacturers are looking to foreign markets to make up their losses; **le joueur avait perdu les deux premiers sets, mais il s'est rattrapé au troisième** the player had lost the first two sets but he pulled back in the third

rature [RatyR] NF deletion, erasure, crossing out; **faire une ~** to make a deletion *ou* an erasure; (*Admin*) **sans ~s ni surcharges** without deletions or alterations

raturer [RatyRe] ▶ conjug 1 ◀ VT (= *corriger*) [+ *mot, phrase, texte*] to make an alteration *ou* alterations to; (= *barrer*) [+ *lettre, mot*] to cross out, erase, delete

RAU† [ɛRay] NF (ABRÉV = **République arabe unie**) UAR†

rauque [Rok] ADJ [*voix*] (*gén*) hoarse; (*chanteuse de blues*) husky, throaty; [*cri*] raucous

ravage [Ravaʒ] NM [a] (*littér* = *action*) [*pays, ville*] laying waste, ravaging, devastation [b] (*gén pl* = *dégâts*) [*guerre, maladie*] ravages, devastation (*NonC*); [*temps*] ravages; [*chômage, crise, alcool, drogue*] devastating effects, ravages; **la grêle a fait des ~s dans les vignes** the hailstorm wrought havoc in the vineyards *ou* played havoc with the vines; **l'épidémie a fait de terribles ~s parmi les jeunes** the epidemic has caused terrible losses among young people; (*fig hum*) **faire des ~s** [*séducteur*] to be a real heartbreaker; [*doctrine*] to gain a lot of ground

ravagé, e [Ravaʒe] (*ptp de* **ravager**) ADJ [a] (= *tourmenté*) [*visage*] harrowed, haggard; **avoir les traits ~s** to have harrowed *ou* ravaged *ou* haggard features; **visage ~ par la maladie** face ravaged by illness [b] (**‡** = *fou*) **il est complètement ~** he's completely nuts* *ou* bonkers‡ (*Brit*), he's off his head‡

ravager [Ravaʒe] ▶ conjug 3 ◀ VT [+ *pays*] to lay waste, ravage, devastate; [+ *maison, ville*] to ravage, devastate; [+ *visage*] [*maladie*] to rav-

age; [*chagrin, soucis*] to harrow; [+ *personne, vie*] to wreak havoc upon

ravageur, -euse [RavaʒœR, øz] 1 ADJ [*passion, sourire*] devastating; [*humour*] scathing; **insectes ~s** pests; **les effets ~s de la drogue** the devastating effects of drugs 2 NM,F (= *pillard*) ravager, devastator

ravalement [Ravalmɑ̃] NM [a] (*Constr*) (= *nettoyage*) cleaning; (= *remise en état*) [*façade, mur*] restoration; [*immeuble*] renovation, facelift*; **faire le ~ de** to clean, restore, give a facelift to*; **faire un ~*** (= *retoucher son maquillage*) to fix one's warpaint* [b] (*littér* = *avilissement*) [*dignité, personne, mérite*] lowering

ravaler [Ravale] ▶ conjug 1 ◀ 1 VT [a] (*Constr* = *nettoyer*) to clean; (= *remettre en état*) [+ *façade, mur*] to clean; [+ *immeuble*] to renovate, give a facelift to* [b] (= *avaler*) [+ *salive, dégoût*] to swallow; [+ *sanglots*] to swallow, choke back; [+ *colère*] to stifle; [+ *larmes*] to hold *ou* choke back; [+ *sourire*] to suppress; **faire ~ ses paroles à qn** to make sb take back *ou* swallow their words [c] (*littér*) [+ *dignité, personne, mérite*] to lower; **ce genre d'acte ravale l'homme au rang de la bête** this kind of behaviour brings man down *ou* reduces man to the level of animals 2 **se ravaler** VPR [a] (= *s'abaisser*) to lower o.s.; **se ~ au rang de ...** to reduce o.s. to the level of ...; [b]* **se ~ la façade** to slap on* some make-up

ravaleur [RavalœR] NM (= *maçon*) stone restorer

ravaudage [Ravodaʒ] NM [*vêtement*] mending, repairing; [*chaussette*] darning; [*objet*] makeshift repair; **faire du ~** to mend, darn

ravauder [Ravode] ▶ conjug 1 ◀ VT (*littér* = *repriser*) [+ *vêtement*] to repair, mend; [+ *chaussette*] to darn

rave [Rav] NF (= *navet*) turnip; (= *radis*) radish → **céleri**

ravenelle [Ravnɛl] NF (= *giroflée*) wallflower; (= *radis*) wild radish

Ravenne [Ravɛn] N Ravenna

ravi, e [Ravi] (*ptp de* **ravir**) ADJ (= *enchanté*) delighted; **je n'étais pas franchement ~ de sa décision** I wasn't exactly overjoyed about his decision; **~ de vous connaître** delighted *ou* pleased to meet you

ravier [Ravje] NM *hors d'oeuvres dish*

ravigotant, e* [Ravigɔtɑ̃, ɑ̃t] ADJ [*air*] bracing; **ce vin est ~** this wine bucks you up* *ou* puts new life into you

ravigote [Ravigɔt] NF (= *vinaigrette*) (oil and vinegar) dressing (*with hard-boiled eggs, shallot and herbs*)

ravigoter* [Ravigɔte] ▶ conjug 1 ◀ VT [*alcool*] to buck up*, pick up; [*repas, douche, nouvelle, chaleur*] to buck up*, put new life into; **(tout) ravigoté par une bonne nuit** feeling refreshed after a good night's sleep

ravin [Ravɛ̃] NM (*gén*) gully; (*encaissé*) ravine

ravine [Ravin] NF (small) ravine, gully

ravinement [Ravinmɑ̃] NM (= *action*) gullying (*Géog*); (= *rigoles, ravins*) **~s** gullies; (= *aspect*) **le ~ de ces pentes** the (numerous) gullies furrowing these slopes; **le ~ affecte particulièrement ces sols** gully erosion *ou* gullying affects these kinds of soil in particular

raviner [Ravine] ▶ conjug 1 ◀ VT [+ *visage, chemin*] to furrow; [+ *versant*] to gully (*Géog*); **visage raviné par les larmes** tear-streaked face, face streaked with tears; **les bords ravinés de la rivière** the gullied (*Géog*) *ou* furrowed banks of the river

ravioli [Ravjɔli] NM **~s** ravioli (*NonC*)

ravir [RaviR] ▶ conjug 2 ◀ VT (*littér*) [a] (= *charmer*) to delight; **cela lui va à ~** that suits her beautifully, she looks delighted in it; **il danse à ~** he's a beautiful dancer; **elle est jolie à ~** she's as pretty as a picture [b] (= *enlever*) **~ à qn** [+

trésor, être aimé, honneur] to rob sb of, take (away) from sb; **elle lui a ravi son titre de championne d'Europe** she took the European championship title off her → **vedette** [c] († = *kidnapper*) to ravish†, abduct

raviser (se) [Raviʒe] ▸conjug 1◂ VPR to change one's mind, decide otherwise; **après avoir dit oui, il s'est ravisé** after saying yes he changed his mind *ou* decided otherwise *ou* decided against it; **il s'est ravisé** he decided against it, he thought better of it

ravissant, e [Ravisɑ̃, ɑ̃t] ADJ [*beauté*] ravishing; [*femme, robe*] ravishing, beautiful; [*maison, tableau*] delightful, beautiful

ravissement [Ravismɑ̃] NM [a] (*gén, Rel*) rapture; **plonger qn dans le ~** to send sb into raptures; **plongé dans le ~** in raptures; **regarder qn avec ~** to look at sb rapturously [b] († *ou littér* = *enlèvement*) ravishing†, abduction

ravisseur, -euse [Ravisœr, øz] NM,F kidnapper, abductor

ravitaillement [Ravitajmɑ̃] NM [a] (*NonC*) (*en vivres, munitions*) [*armée, ville, navire*] resupplying; [*coureurs, skieurs*] getting fresh supplies to; (*en carburant*) [*véhicule, avion, embarcation*] refuelling; **~ en vol** in-flight refuelling; **le ~ des troupes (en vivres/munitions)** supplying the troops (with food/ammunition), the provision *ou* providing of the troops with fresh supplies (of food/ammunition); **aller au ~** to go for fresh supplies; **les voies de ~ sont bloquées** supply routes are blocked; **convoi de ~** supply convoy [b] (= *provisions*) supplies

ravitailler [Ravitaje] ▸conjug 1◂ [1] VT (*en vivres, munitions*) [+ *armée, ville, navire*] to provide with fresh supplies, resupply; [+ *coureurs, skieurs*] to give fresh supplies to; (*en carburant*) [+ *véhicule, avion, embarcation*] to refuel; **~ une ville en combustible** to provide a town with fresh supplies of fuel; **~ un avion en vol** to refuel an aircraft in flight [2] **se ravitailler** VPR [*ville, armée, coureurs, skieurs*] to get fresh supplies; [*véhicule, avion*] to refuel; (= *faire des courses*) to stock up

ravitailleur [Ravitajœr] [1] NM (*Mil*) (= *navire*) supply ship; (= *avion*) supply plane; (= *véhicule*) supply vehicle; **~ en vol** aerial tanker [2] ADJ [*navire, avion, véhicule*] supply (*épith*)

raviver [Ravive] ▸conjug 1◂ VT [+ *feu, sentiment, douleur*] to revive, rekindle; [+ *couleur*] to brighten up; [+ *souvenir*] to revive, bring back to life; (*Tech*) [+ *métal*] to clean; (*Méd*) [+ *plaie*] to reopen; **sa douleur/sa jalousie s'est ravivée** his grief/his jealousy was revived *ou* rekindled

ravoir [Ravwar] ▸conjug 34◂ VT [a] (= *recouvrer*) to have *ou* get back [b] (* = *nettoyer*: *gén nég*) [+ *tissu, métal*] to get clean; **cette casserole est difficile à ~** this saucepan is hard to clean, it's hard to get this saucepan clean

rayage [Rejaʒ] NM [a] [*nom*] crossing *ou* scoring out [b] [*canon*] rifling

rayé, e [Reje] (*ptp de* **rayer**) ADJ [a] [*tissu, pelage*] striped; [*papier à lettres*] ruled, lined [b] [*surface*] scratched; [*disque*] scratched, scratchy [c] (*Tech*) [*canon*] rifled

rayer [Reje] ▸conjug 8◂ VT [a] (= *marquer de raies*) [+ *papier à lettres*] to rule, line; **des cicatrices lui rayaient le visage** scars lined his face [b] (= *érafler*) to scratch [c] (= *biffer*) to cross *ou* score out [d] (= *exclure*) **~ qn de** to cross sb *ou* sb's name off; **il a été rayé de la liste** his name has been crossed *ou* struck off the list; **«~ la mention inutile»** "cross out where not applicable", "delete where inapplicable"; **~ qch de sa mémoire** to blot out *ou* erase sth from one's memory; (*fig*) **~ un pays/une ville de la carte** to wipe a country/a town off the map; (*fig*) **je l'ai rayé de mes tablettes** I want nothing to do with him ever again [e] (*Tech*) [+ *canon*] to rifle

ray-grass [Regras] NM INV rye-grass, English meadow grass

rayon [Rejɔ̃] [1] NM [a] (*gén* = *trait, faisceau, Opt, Phys*) ray; [*astre*] ray; [*lumière, jour*] ray, beam; [*phare*] beam [b] (= *radiations*) **~s** rays; **~s infrarouges/ultraviolets** infrared/ultraviolet rays; **~s alpha/bêta** alpha/beta rays; **~s X** X-rays; **traitement par les ~s** radiation treatment; **on lui fait des ~s** he's having radiation treatment [c] (*fig* = *lueur*) ray; **~ d'espoir** ray *ou* gleam of hope [d] (*Math*) radius [e] [*roue*] spoke [f] (= *planche*) shelf; [*bibliothèque*] (book)shelf; **le livre n'est pas en ~** the book is not on display *ou* on the shelves [g] (*Comm*) department; (*petit*) counter; **le ~ (de l')alimentation/(de la) parfumerie** (= *comptoir*) the food/perfume counter; (= *section*) the food/perfume department; **le ~ frais** the fresh food department; **le ~ enfants** the children's department; **c'est/ce n'est pas son ~** (*spécialité*) that's/that isn't his line; (*responsabilité*) that's/that's not his concern *ou* responsibility *ou* department*; **il en connaît un ~*** he knows masses about it*, he's really clued up about it* (*Brit*) [h] [*ruche*] (honey)comb [i] (= *périmètre*) radius; **dans un ~ de 10 km** within a radius of 10 km *ou* a 10-km radius [j] (*Agr* = *sillon*) drill
[2] COMP ▸ **rayon d'action** (*lit*) range; (*fig*) field of action, scope, range; **engin à grand ~ d'action** long-range missile ▸ **rayon de braquage** (*Aut*) turning circle, (steering) lock (*Brit*) ▸ **rayon cathodique** cathode ray ▸ **rayons cosmiques** cosmic rays ▸ **rayon de courbure** radius of curvature ▸ **rayons gamma** gamma rays *ou* radiation ▸ **rayon ionisant** ionizing radiation ▸ **rayon laser** laser beam ▸ **rayon de lune** moonbeam ▸ **le rayon de la mort** the death ray ▸ **rayon de soleil** (*lit*) ray of sunlight *ou* sunshine, sunbeam; (*fig*) ray of sunshine ▸ **rayon vert** green flash (*Opt*) ▸ **rayon visuel** line of vision *ou* sight

rayonnage [Rejɔnaʒ] NM [a] (= *planches*) set of shelves, shelving (*NonC*); **~s** (sets of) shelves, shelving [b] (*Agr*) drilling

rayonnant, e [Rejɔnɑ̃, ɑ̃t] ADJ [a] (= *radieux*) [*beauté, air, personne*] radiant; [*sourire*] radiant, beaming (*épith*); [*visage*] wreathed in smiles, beaming; **visage ~ de joie/santé** face radiant with joy/glowing *ou* radiant with health [b] (= *en étoile*) [*motif, fleur*] radiating; **le style (gothique) ~** High Gothic; **chapelles ~es** radiating chapels [c] (*Phys*) [*énergie, chaleur*] radiant; (*Méd*) [*douleur*] spreading

rayonne [Rejɔn] NF rayon; **en ~** rayon (*épith*)

rayonnement [Rejɔnmɑ̃] NM [a] (= *influence bénéfique*) [*culture, civilisation*] influence; (= *magnétisme*) [*personnalité*] radiance [b] (= *éclat*) [*jeunesse, beauté*] radiance; **dans tout le ~ de sa jeunesse** in the full radiance of his youth; **le ~ de son bonheur** his radiant happiness [c] (= *lumière*) [*astre, soleil*] radiance [d] (= *radiations*) [*chaleur, lumière, astre*] radiation; **~ ionisant** ionizing radiation; **chauffage par ~** radiant heating; **~ fossile** background radiation

rayonner [Rejɔne] ▸conjug 1◂ VI [a] (= *étinceler*) [*influence, culture, personnalité*] to shine forth; (= *se répandre*) **~ sur/dans** [*influence, prestige*] to extend over/in, make itself felt over/in; [*culture*] to extend over/in, be influential over/in; [*personnalité*] to be influential over/in [b] (= *être éclatant*) [*joie, bonheur*] to shine *ou* beam forth; [*beauté*] to shine forth, be radiant; [*visage, personne*] (*de joie, de beauté*) to be radiant (**de** with); **le bonheur faisait ~ son visage** his face glowed with happiness; **l'amour rayonne dans ses yeux** love shines *ou* sparkles

in his eyes; **~ de bonheur** to be radiant *ou* glowing *ou* beaming with happiness; **~ de beauté** to be radiantly *ou* dazzlingly beautiful [c] (*littér = briller*) [*lumière, astre*] to shine (forth), be radiant [d] (*Phys = émettre un rayonnement*) [*chaleur, énergie, lumière*] to radiate [e] (= *faire un circuit*) **~ autour d'une ville** [*touristes*] to use a town as a base for touring (around a region); [*cars*] to service the area around a town; **~ dans une région** [*touristes*] to tour around a region (from a base); [*cars*] to service a region [f] (= *aller en rayons*) [*avenues, lignes*] to radiate (**autour de** from, out from) [2] VT (= *garnir ou rayonnages*) to shelve

rayure [Rejyr] NF [a] (= *dessin*) stripe; (= *éraflure*) scratch; [*fusil*] groove; **papier/tissu à ~s** striped paper/material; **à ~s noires** with black stripes, black-striped; **costume à ~s fines** pinstriped suit

raz-de-marée, raz de marée [Radmare] NM INV (*Géog, fig*) tidal wave; **~ électoral** (*victoire*) landslide (election) victory; (*changement*) big swing (*to a party in an election*)

razzia [Ra(d)zja] NF raid, foray, razzia; (*fig*) **faire une ~ dans une maison/le frigo*** to raid a house/the fridge

razzier [Ra(d)zje] ▸conjug 7◂ VT (*lit, fig = piller*) to raid, plunder

RDA† [ɛrdea] NF (ABRÉV = **République démocratique allemande**) GDR†

rdc ABRÉV = **rez-de-chaussée**

RDS [ɛrdeɛs] NM (ABRÉV = **remboursement de la dette sociale**) → **remboursement**

ré [Re] NM (*Mus*) D; (*en chantant la gamme*) re, ray; **en ré mineur** in D minor

réabonnement [Reabɔnmɑ̃] NM renewal of subscription; **le ~ doit se faire dans les huit jours** renewal of subscription must be made within a week, subscriptions must be renewed within a week

réabonner [Reabɔne] ▸conjug 1◂ [1] VT **~ qn** to renew sb's subscription (**à** to) [2] **se réabonner** VPR to renew one's subscription, take out a new subscription (**à** to)

réabsorber [Reapsɔrbe] ▸conjug 1◂ VT to reabsorb

réabsorption [Reapsɔrpsjɔ̃] NF reabsorption

réac* [Reak] ADJ, NMF ABRÉV = **réactionnaire**

réaccoutumer [Reakutyme] ▸conjug 1◂ [1] VT to reaccustom [2] **se réaccoutumer** VPR to reaccustom o.s., become reaccustomed (**à** to)

réacteur [Reaktœr] NM (*Aviat*) jet engine; (*Chim, Phys*) reactor; **~ nucléaire** nuclear reactor; **~ thermique** thermal reactor; **~ à neutrons rapides** fast-breeder reactor; **~ à eau pressurisée** pressurised water reactor

réactif, -ive [Reaktif, iv] [1] ADJ [a] (= *qui réagit*) reactive; **papier ~** reagent *ou* test paper; **peau réactive** sensitive skin [b] [*employé, entreprise*] resourceful, adaptable [2] NM (*Chim, fig*) reagent

▾**réaction** [Reaksjɔ̃] NF [a] (*gén, Sci*) reaction; **être *ou* rester sans ~** to show no reaction; **être en ~ contre** to be in reaction against; **en ~ contre les abus, ils ...** as a reaction against the abuses, they ...; **en ~ à** [*propos, décision*] in reaction *ou* response to; **~ de défense/en chaîne** defence/chain reaction; **une ~ de rejet à l'égard de ce parti** a rejection of this party; **cette décision a provoqué *ou* suscité de violentes ~s dans l'opinion publique** there was strong public reaction to this decision; **la ~ des marchés boursiers a été immédiate** the stock markets reacted immediately; **sa ~ a été excessive** he overreacted; **cette voiture a de bonnes ~s** this car responds well → **cutiréaction** [b] (*Pol*) **la ~** reaction [c] (*Aviat*) **moteur à ~** jet engine; **propulsion par ~** jet propulsion → **avion**

réactionnaire [ʀeaksjɔnɛʀ] ADJ, NMF reactionary

réactionnel, -elle [ʀeaksjɔnɛl] ADJ (Chim, Physiol) reactional; (Psych) reactive; **psychose réactionnelle** reactive psychosis

réactivation [ʀeaktivasjɔ̃] NF reactivation

réactiver [ʀeaktive] ▸conjug 1◂ VT [+ négociations, processus de paix, programme] to revive, restart; [+ croissance, économie, mesures, projet] to revive; [+ machine, système] to reactivate

réactivité [ʀeaktivite] NF [a] (Phys, Méd) reactivity [b] [employé] adaptability, resourcefulness

réactualisation [ʀeaktɥalizasjɔ̃] NF updating, bringing up to date

réactualiser [ʀeaktɥalize] ▸conjug 1◂ VT to update, bring up to date

réadaptation [ʀeadaptasjɔ̃] NF [personne] readjustment; (Méd) rehabilitation; [muscle] re-education; **centre de ~ à la vie sauvage** animal sanctuary (where animals are prepared for release into the wild); (Méd) **~ fonctionnelle** rehabilitation

réadapter [ʀeadapte] ▸conjug 1◂ [1] VT [+ personne] to readjust (à to) [2] **se réadapter** VPR to readjust, become readjusted (à to)

réadmettre [ʀeadmɛtʀ] ▸conjug 56◂ VT to re-admit

réadmission [ʀeadmisjɔ̃] NF readmission, re-admittance

ready-made [ʀedimɛd] NM INV (Art) ready-made

réaffectation [ʀeafɛktasjɔ̃] NF [crédits, terrain, personne] reallocation

réaffecter [ʀeafɛkte] ▸conjug 1◂ VT (surtout passif) [+ crédits, terrain, personne] to reallocate (à to)

réaffirmer [ʀeafiʀme] ▸conjug 1◂ VT to reaffirm, reassert

réagir [ʀeaʒiʀ] ▸conjug 2◂ VI [a] (gén, Chim) to react (à to, **contre** against); (= répondre) to respond (à to); **il a réagi positivement à ma proposition** he reacted positively to my proposal; **tu réagis trop violemment** you're over-reacting; **ils ont assisté à la scène sans ~** they witnessed the scene and did nothing; **il faut ~!** you have to do something!; **souhaitez-vous ~ à cette déclaration?** would you like to respond to that statement?; **il réagit bien au traitement** he's responding well to treatment; **sa voiture réagit mal au freinage** the brakes on his car don't respond well; **les organes des sens réagissent aux excitations** sense organs respond to stimuli [b] **~ sur** to have an effect on, affect; **cet événement a réagi sur les sondages** this event affected the polls

réajustement [ʀeaʒystəmɑ̃] NM [prix, loyer, salaires, taux] adjustment

réajuster [ʀeaʒyste] ▸conjug 1◂ [1] VT [a] (= remettre en place) [+ mécanisme] to readjust; [+ vêtement] to straighten (out), tidy; [+ cravate, lunettes] to straighten, adjust; [+ coiffure] to rearrange, tidy; **elle réajusta sa toilette** she straightened her clothes [b] (= recentrer) [+ tir] to (re)adjust; [+ loyers, prix, salaires, taux] to adjust [2] **se réajuster** VPR [personne] to tidy ou straighten o.s. up

réalignement [ʀealiɲ(ə)mɑ̃] NM (Écon) [monnaie, taux] realignment

réalisable [ʀealizabl] ADJ [rêve] attainable; (Fin) [capital] realizable; [projet] workable, feasible

réalisateur, -trice [ʀealizatœʀ, tʀis] NM,F (Ciné) (film) director, film-maker; (Radio, TV) director

réalisation [ʀealizasjɔ̃] NF [a] [ambition, rêve] realization, fulfilment; [projet] realization, carrying out; [exploit] achievement; **plusieurs projets sont en cours de ~** several projects are in the pipeline ou are under way

[b] [meuble, bijou] making; [étude, sondage] carrying out; **une sauce dont la ~ est très délicate** a sauce that is very tricky to make; **de ~ facile** easy to make; **j'étais chargé de la ~ de cette étude** I was asked to carry out this study [c] (Fin) [capital, valeurs, patrimoine] realization [d] (Comm) realization; [vente, contrat] conclusion [e] (= création) achievement, creation; **c'est la plus belle ~ de l'architecte** it is the architect's finest achievement [f] (Ciné) direction; (Radio, TV) production; **« ~ (de) John Huston »** "directed by John Huston"; **la ~ du film a duré six mois** the film took six months to make; **assistant à la ~** production assistant [g] (Mus) realization

réaliser [ʀealize] ▸conjug 1◂ [1] VT [a] [+ ambition, désir] to realize, fulfil; [+ effort] to make; [+ exploit] to achieve, carry off; [+ projet] to carry out, carry through; **~ un rêve** to make a dream come true, realize a dream; (Sport) **il a réalisé le meilleur temps aux essais** he got the best time in the trials [b] (= effectuer) [+ meuble, bijou] to make; [+ étude, sondage] to carry out; **c'est lui qui a réalisé tous les maquillages** he did all the makeup [c] (* = saisir) to realize; **~ l'importance de qch** to realize the importance of sth; **je n'ai pas encore réalisé** it hasn't sunk in yet [d] (Ciné) to direct; (Radio, TV) to produce; **il vient de ~ son premier film** he's just made his first film; **émission conçue et réalisée par...** programme devised and produced by ... [e] (Comm) to realize; [+ achat, vente, bénéfice, économie] to make; [+ contrat] to conclude; **l'entreprise réalise un chiffre d'affaires de 100 000 F par semaine** the firm has a turnover of ou turns over 100,000 francs a week [f] (Fin) [+ capital, biens] to realize; **la banque a réalisé une partie de son portefeuille** part of the bank's portfolio was liquidated [g] (Mus) realize

[2] **se réaliser** VPR [a] [rêve, vœu] to come true; [prédiction] to be fulfilled; [projet] to be carried out, be achieved [b] [caractère, personnalité] to be fulfilled; **il s'est complètement réalisé dans son métier** he's completely fulfilled in his job

réalisme [ʀealism] NM realism; **le ~ socialiste** socialist realism

réaliste [ʀealist] [1] ADJ [description, négociateur] realistic; (Art, Littérat) realist [2] NMF realist

▾**réalité** [ʀealite] NF [a] (= existence effective) reality (NonC); **différentes ~s** different types of reality; **en ~** in (actual) fact, in reality; **~ virtuelle** virtual reality [b] (= chose réelle) reality; **c'est une ~ incontournable** it's an inescapable fact; **parfois la ~ dépasse la fiction** (sometimes) truth can be stranger than fiction; **oublieux des ~s de la vie en communauté** neglecting the realities ou facts of communal life; **détaché des ~s de ce monde** divorced from the realities of this world; **ce sont les dures ~s de la vie** those are the harsh realities of life; **son rêve est devenu (une) ~** his dream became (a) reality ou came true → **désir, sens**

reality show, reality-show (pl reality(-)shows) [ʀealitiʃo] NM (TV) studio discussion programme (focusing on real-life dramas)

realpolitik [ʀealpɔlitik] NF realpolitik

réaménagement [ʀeamenaʒmɑ̃] NM [site, espace] redevelopment; [pièce] refitting; [calendrier, horaires, structure, service] reorganization; **~ monétaire** currency readjustment

réaménager [ʀeamenaʒe] ▸conjug 3◂ VT [+ site] to redevelop; [+ appartement, bâtiment] to refit, refurbish; [+ horaires, structure, service] to reorganize; [+ taux d'intérêt] to adjust

réamorcer [ʀeamɔʀse] ▸conjug 3◂ VT [a] (lit) [+ pompe] to prime again; (fig) **~ la pompe** to get things going again, set things in motion again; **ces investissements permettront de ~ la pompe de l'économie** these investments will give the economy a kickstart [b] [+ dialogue, négociations, processus] to start again, reinitiate

réanimateur, -trice [ʀeanimatœʀ, tʀis] [1] NM,F (= personne) resuscitator [2] NM (= respirateur) ventilator, respirator

réanimation [ʀeanimasjɔ̃] NF resuscitation; **être en (service de) ~** to be in the intensive care unit, be in intensive care

réanimer [ʀeanime] ▸conjug 1◂ VT [a] [+ personne] to resuscitate, revive [b] (= faire revivre) [+ quartier, région] to revive

réapparaître [ʀeapaʀɛtʀ] ▸conjug 57◂ VI [soleil] to come out again, reappear; [maladie, symptôme] to recur; [personne] to reappear, come back

réapparition [ʀeapaʀisjɔ̃] NF [soleil] reappearance; [maladie, symptôme] recurrence; [artiste] comeback; **la mode des chapeaux a fait sa ~** hats are back in ou have come back into fashion

réapprendre [ʀeapʀɑ̃dʀ] ▸conjug 58◂ VT (gén) to relearn, learn again; (littér) [+ solitude, liberté] to get to know again, relearn (littér), learn again (littér); **~ qch à qn** to teach sth to sb again, teach sb sth again; **~ à faire qch** to learn to do sth again

réapprentissage [ʀeapʀɑ̃tisaʒ] NM **le ~ de qch** relearning sth, learning sth again; **cela va demander un long ~** that will take a long time to relearn ou to learn again

réapprovisionnement [ʀeapʀɔvizjɔnmɑ̃] NM [a] (Fin) **le ~ d'un compte en banque** putting (more) money into a bank account [b] (= ravitaillement) resupplying [c] [magasin] restocking, stocking up again

réapprovisionner [ʀeapʀɔvizjɔne] ▸conjug 1◂ [1] VT [a] [+ compte en banque] to put (more) money into [b] (= ravitailler) to resupply [c] (Comm) [+ magasin] to restock (en with) [2] **se réapprovisionner** VPR to stock up again (en with)

réargenter [ʀeaʀʒɑ̃te] ▸conjug 1◂ [1] VT to resilver [2] **se réargenter*** VPR (= se renflouer) to get back on a sound financial footing

réarmement [ʀeaʀməmɑ̃] NM [a] [fusil] reloading; [appareil-photo] winding on [b] (Naut) [navire] refitting [c] [pays] rearmament; **politique de ~** policy of rearmament

réarmer [ʀeaʀme] ▸conjug 1◂ [1] VT [a] [+ fusil] to reload; [+ appareil-photo] to wind on [b] (Naut) [+ bateau] to refit [c] [+ pays] to rearm [2] VI, **se réarmer** VPR [pays] to rearm

réarrangement [ʀeaʀɑ̃ʒmɑ̃] NM rearrangement; (Phys) **~ moléculaire** molecular rearrangement

réarranger [ʀeaʀɑ̃ʒe] ▸conjug 3◂ VT [+ coiffure, fleurs, chambre] to rearrange; [+ cravate, jupe] to straighten (up) again; [+ entrevue] to rearrange

réassignation [ʀeasiɲasjɔ̃] NF (Jur) resummons sg; (Fin) reallocation

réassigner [ʀeasiɲe] ▸conjug 1◂ VT (gén) to reassign; (Jur) to resummon; (Fin) to reallocate

réassort [ʀeasɔʀ] NM (= action) restocking; (= marchandises) fresh stock ou supply

réassortiment [ʀeasɔʀtimɑ̃] NM (= action) [stock] replenishment; [verres] replacement, matching (up); [service de table, tissu] matching (up); (= marchandises) new ou fresh stock

réassortir [ʀeasɔʀtiʀ] ▸conjug 2◂ [1] VT [+ magasin] to restock (en with); [+ stock] to replenish; [+ service de table] to match (up); [+ verres] to replace, match (up) [2] **se réassortir** VPR (Comm) to stock up again (de with), replenish one's stock(s) (de of)

▸ GRAMMAIRE ACTIVE: **réalité** 53.3, 53.4, 53.6

réassurance [ʀeasyʀɑ̃s] NF reinsurance

réassurer VT, **se réassurer** VPR [ʀeasyʀe] ▶ conjug 1 ◀ to reinsure

réassureur [ʀeasyʀœʀ] NM reinsurer, reinsurance underwriter

rebaisser [ʀ(ə)bese] ▶ conjug 1 ◀ **1** VI [prix] to go down again; [température, niveau d'eau] to fall again **2** VT [+ prix] to bring back down, bring down again, lower again; [+ radio, son, chauffage] to turn down again; [+ store, levier] to pull down again, lower again

rebaptiser [ʀ(ə)batize] ▶ conjug 1 ◀ VT [+ enfant] to rebaptize; [+ rue] to rename; [+ navire] to rechristen

rébarbatif, -ive [ʀebaʀbatif, iv] ADJ (= rebutant) [mine] forbidding, unprepossessing; [sujet, tâche] daunting, forbidding; [style] off-putting

rebâtir [ʀ(ə)batiʀ] ▶ conjug 2 ◀ VT to rebuild

rebattre [ʀ(ə)batʀ] ▶ conjug 41 ◀ VT **a** (Cartes) to reshuffle **b** il m'a rebattu les oreilles de son succès he kept harping on about his success; il en parlait toute la journée, j'en avais les oreilles rebattues he talked of it all day long until I was sick and tired of hearing about it*

rebattu, e [ʀ(ə)baty] (ptp de **rebattre**) ADJ [sujet, citation] hackneyed

rebec [ʀabɛk] NM rebec(k)

rebelle [ʀəbɛl] **1** ADJ **a** [troupes, soldat] rebel (épith), [enfant, cheval] rebellious, refractory; [esprit] intractable, rebellious; [fièvre, maladie] stubborn; [mèche, cheveux] unruly; (hum) [cœur] rebellious; (fig) [matière] unworkable, refractory, stubborn **b** ~ à [+ patrie, souverain] unwilling to serve; [+ discipline] unamenable to; il est ~ à la géographie (= il n'y comprend rien) geography is a closed book to him; (= il ne veut pas apprendre) he doesn't want to know about geography; virus ~ à certains remèdes virus resistant to certain medicines; cheveux ~s à la brosse unruly hair **2** NMF rebel

rebeller (se) [ʀ(ə)bele] ▶ conjug 1 ◀ VPR to rebel (contre against)

rébellion [ʀebeljɔ̃] NF (= révolte) rebellion; (= rebelles) la ~ the rebels

rebelote [ʀəbəlɔt] EXCL (Cartes) rebelote! (said when the king of trumps is played after the queen or the queen of trumps is played after the king); (* : fig) here we go again!

rebiffer (se)* [ʀ(ə)bife] ▶ conjug 1 ◀ VPR (= résister) [personne] to hit ou strike back (contre at); (fig) [corps, conscience] to rebel (contre against)

rebiquer* [ʀ(ə)bike] ▶ conjug 1 ◀ VI (= se redresser) [mèche de cheveux] to stick up; [col] to curl up at the ends

reblanchir [ʀ(ə)blɑ̃ʃiʀ] ▶ conjug 2 ◀ VT (gén) to rewhiten; [+ mur] to rewhitewash

reblochon [ʀəblɔʃɔ̃] NM kind of cheese from Savoie

reboisement [ʀ(ə)bwazmɑ̃] NM reforestation, reafforestation

reboiser [ʀ(ə)bwaze] ▶ conjug 1 ◀ VT to reforest, reafforest

rebond [ʀ(ə)bɔ̃] NM **a** [balle] (sur le sol) bounce; (contre un mur) rebound; **rattraper une balle au ~** to catch a ball on the bounce **b** [histoire] development **c** (= amélioration) [activité économique, marché] recovery; **on note un léger ~ de la consommation** consumption has picked up slightly

rebondi, e [ʀ(ə)bɔ̃di] (ptp de **rebondir**) ADJ [objet, bouteille, forme] rounded; [croupe] rounded; [poitrine] well-developed; [ventre] fat; [joues, visage] chubby; [femme] curvaceous, amply proportioned; [homme] portly, corpulent; [porte-monnaie] well-lined; **elle avait des formes ~es** she was amply proportioned; **il a**

un ventre ~ he has a paunch, he has a fat stomach

rebondir [ʀ(ə)bɔ̃diʀ] ▶ conjug 2 ◀ VI **a** [balle] (sur le sol) to bounce; (contre un mur) to rebound; **faire ~ une balle par terre/contre un mur** to bounce a ball on the ground/against a wall **b** [conversation] to get going ou moving again; [scandale, affaire, procès] to be revived; (Théât) [action, intrigue] to get moving again, take off again; **l'affaire n'en finit pas de ~** there are new developments in the affair all the time; **faire ~** [+ conversation] to give new impetus to, set ou get going again; [+ action d'une pièce] to get ou set moving again; [+ scandale, procès] to revive **c** [économie, marché, actions] to pick up again; **ça l'a aidé à ~ après son licenciement/son divorce** it helped him get back on his feet again after his dismissal/his divorce

rebondissement [ʀ(ə)bɔ̃dismɑ̃] NM (= développement) (sudden new) development (de in); (= réapparition) sudden revival (NonC) (de of); [feuilleton/récit à ~s] action-packed serial/story; **l'affaire vient de connaître un nouveau ~** there has been a new development in the affair; **le ~ de la controverse sur la peine de mort** the sudden revival of the controversy about the death penalty

rebord [ʀ(ə)bɔʀ] NM **a** [assiette, tuyau, plat, pot] rim; [puits, falaise] edge; [corniche, table, buffet] (projecting) edge; **le ~ de la cheminée** the mantelpiece ou mantelshelf; **le ~ de la fenêtre** the windowsill, the window ledge **b** [vêtement] hem

reborder [ʀ(ə)bɔʀde] ▶ conjug 1 ◀ VT [+ vêtement] to put a new edging on; [+ enfant] to tuck in again

reboucher [ʀ(ə)buʃe] ▶ conjug 1 ◀ **1** VT [+ trou] to fill in again; [+ bouteille] to recork; [+ carafe] to put the stopper back in; [+ tube] to put the cap back on **2** se reboucher VPR [tuyau] to get blocked again

rebours [ʀ(ə)buʀ] ◆ **à rebours** LOC ADV **a** (= à rebrousse-poil) **caresser un chat à ~** to stroke a cat the wrong way; **lisser un tissu à ~** to smooth out a fabric against the nap ou pile; (fig) **prendre qn à ~** to rub sb up the wrong way **b** (= à l'envers) **faire un trajet à ~** to make a trip the other way round; **prendre une rue en sens unique à ~** to go the wrong way up a one-way street; **feuilleter un magazine à ~** to flip through a magazine from back to front; **compter à ~** to count backwards; (Mil) **prendre l'ennemi à ~** to surprise the enemy from behind → compte **c** (= de travers) **comprendre à ~** to misunderstand, get the wrong idea, get the wrong end of the stick*; **faire tout à ~** to do everything the wrong way round ou back to front (Brit) **d** (= à l'opposé de) **à ~ de** against; **aller à ~ de la tendance générale** to go against ou run counter to the general trend; **c'est à ~ du bon sens!** it goes against ou flies in the face of common sense!

rebouteur, -euse [ʀ(ə)butœʀ, øz], **rebouteux, -euse** [ʀ(ə)butø, øz] NM,F bonesetter

reboutonner [ʀ(ə)butɔne] ▶ conjug 1 ◀ **1** VT to button up again, rebutton **2** se reboutonner VPR to do o.s. up again, do up one's buttons again

rebrousse-poil [ʀəbʀuspwal] ◆ **à rebrousse-poil** LOC ADV [caresser] the wrong way; **lisser un tissu à ~** to smooth out a fabric against the pile ou nap; (fig) **prendre qn à ~** to rub sb up the wrong way; **cette évolution prend toutes les habitudes à ~** this development goes right against the grain of established habits

rebrousser [ʀ(ə)bʀuse] ▶ conjug 1 ◀ VT **a** ~ **chemin** to turn back, turn round and go back **b** [+ poil] to brush up; [+ cheveux] to brush back; (Tech) [+ cuir] to strike; (fig) ~ **le poil de qn** to rub sb up the wrong way

rebuffade [ʀ(ə)byfad] NF rebuff; **essuyer une ~** to be rebuffed, suffer a rebuff

rébus [ʀebys] NM (= jeu) rebus; (fig = énigme) puzzle

rebut [ʀəby] NM **a** (= déchets) scrap; **c'est du ~** (objets) it's scrap; (vêtements) they're just cast-offs; **c'est le ~ de la cave** it's all the unwanted stuff from the cellar; **mettre** ou **jeter au ~** to scrap, throw out, discard; [+ vêtements] to discard, throw out; **ces vieux journaux vont aller au ~** these old papers are going to be thrown out ou discarded; **marchandises de ~** trash goods; **bois de ~** old wood **b** (péj = racaille) **le ~ de la société** the scum ou dregs of society **c** (Poste) **~s** dead letters

rebutant, e [ʀ(ə)bytɑ̃, ɑ̃t] ADJ (= dégoûtant) repellent; (= décourageant) disheartening, off-putting

rebuter [ʀ(ə)byte] ▶ conjug 1 ◀ VT (= décourager) to dishearten, discourage, put off; (= répugner) to repel; (littér = repousser durement) to repulse; **il ne faut pas te ~ tout de suite** don't be deterred ou put off straight away

recacheter [ʀ(ə)kaʃ(ə)te] ▶ conjug 4 ◀ VT to reseal

recadrage [ʀ(ə)kadʀaʒ] NM **a** (Ciné, Photo) cropping, reframing **b** [politique] refocusing; **le projet a subi de nombreux ~s** the project has been altered and redefined on numerous occasions

recadrer [ʀ(ə)kadʀe] ▶ conjug 1 ◀ VT **a** (Ciné, Photo) to crop, reframe **b** [+ politique] to refocus; [+ action, projet] to redefine the terms of; **il faut ~ nos priorités** we need to redefine our priorities; **le gouvernement a recadré sa réflexion sur l'éducation** the government has redefined ou rethought its position on education

récalcitrant, e [ʀekalsitʀɑ̃, ɑ̃t] **1** ADJ (= indocile) [animal] refractory, stubborn; [personne] recalcitrant, refractory; [appareil, pièce] unmanageable **2** NM,F recalcitrant

recalculer [ʀ(ə)kalkyle] ▶ conjug 1 ◀ VT [+ budget] to recalculate

recalé, e [ʀ(ə)kale] (ptp de **recaler**) ADJ (Scol, Univ) [étudiant] failed, who has been failed; **les (candidats) ~s à la session de juin** the exam candidates who were failed in June

recaler [ʀ(ə)kale] ▶ conjug 1 ◀ VT (Scol = refuser) to fail; **se faire ~** ou **être recalé en histoire** to fail (in) ou flunk* history; **il a été recalé trois fois au permis de conduire** he failed his driving test three times

recapitalisation [ʀ(ə)kapitalizasjɔ̃] NF (Écon) recapitalization

récapitulatif, -ive [ʀekapitylatif, iv] **1** ADJ [chapitre] recapitulative, recapitulatory; [état, tableau] summary (épith); **dresser un état ~ d'un compte** to draw up a summary statement of an account **2** NM summary, recapitulation

récapitulation [ʀekapitylasjɔ̃] NF recapitulation, summing up, recap; **faire la ~ de** to recapitulate, sum up, recap

récapituler [ʀekapityle] ▶ conjug 1 ◀ VT to recapitulate, sum up, recap

recarreler [ʀ(ə)kaʀle] ▶ conjug 4 ◀ VT to retile

recaser* [ʀ(ə)kaze] ▶ conjug 1 ◀ VT [+ chômeur] to find a new job for; [+ réfugié] to rehouse; **il a pu se ~** [veuf, divorcé] he managed to get hitched* again ou to find himself someone new; [chômeur] he managed to find a new job

recauser* [ʀ(ə)koze] ▶ conjug 1 ◀ VI ~ **de qch** to talk about sth again; **je vous en recauserai** we'll talk about it again

recéder [ʀ(ə)sede] ▶ conjug 6 ◀ VT (= rétrocéder) to give ou sell back; (= vendre) to resell

recel [ʀəsɛl] NM ~ **(d'objets volés)** (= action) receiving (stolen goods); (= résultat) possession of ou possessing stolen goods; ~ **de malfaiteur**

harbouring a criminal; **condamné pour ~** sentenced for possession of stolen goods *ou* for receiving (stolen goods)

receler [R(ə)sale] ▸conjug 5◂ VT [a] (*Jur*) [+ *objet volé*] to receive, fence*; [+ *malfaiteur*] to harbour [b] (= *contenir*) [+ *secret, erreur, trésor*] to conceal

receleur, -euse [R(ə)səlœR, øz] NM,F (*Jur*) receiver of stolen goods, fence*

récemment [Resamã] ADV [a] (= *depuis peu*) recently; **la pluie ~ tombée rendait la route glissante** the rain which had fallen recently *ou* had just fallen made the road slippery; **~ publié** recently published [b] (= *dernièrement*) recently, lately (*gén dans phrases nég ou interrog*); **l'as-tu vu ~ ?** have you seen him lately? *ou* recently?; **encore (tout) ~ il était très en forme** just recently *ou* even quite recently he was still in tiptop form

recensement [R(ə)sãsmã] NM [*population*] census; [*objets*] inventory; [*Mil*] registration (*of young men eligible for military service*); **faire le ~ de la population** to take a *ou* the census of the population, make *ou* take a population census; **faire le ~ des besoins en matériel** to take *ou* make an inventory of equipment requirements

recenser [R(ə)sãse] ▸conjug 1◂ VT [+ *population*] to take a *ou* the census of, make a census of; [+ *objets*] to make *ou* take an inventory of; [+ *futurs conscrits*] to compile a register of; [+ *malades, victimes*] to make a list of; **le pays compte trois millions de chômeurs recensés** the country has three million people registered as unemployed *ou* officially unemployed

recenseur, -euse [R(ə)sãsœR, øz] ADJ M, NM,F **(agent) ~** census taker

recension [R(ə)sãsjɔ̃] NF (*littér*) (= *collationnement*) recension, critical revision (*of a text*); (= *inventaire*) [*documents, faits*] inventory; (= *analyse*) [*œuvre littéraire*] review

récent, e [Resã, ãt] ADJ (= *survenu récemment*) [*événement, traces*] recent; (= *nouveau, de fraîche date*) [*propriétaire, bourgeois*] new; **les chiffres les plus ~s montrent que ...** the latest figures show that ...; **jusqu'à une période ~e** up until recently; **ce phénomène est relativement ~** this phenomenon is relatively recent *ou* new; **ce bâtiment est tout ~** this building is quite new

recentrage [R(ə)sãtRaʒ] NM [*parti*] movement towards the centre; [*politique*] redefinition, reorientation; (*Écon*) [*activités*] refocusing

recentrer [R(ə)sãtRe] ▸conjug 1◂ [1] VT (*Ftbl*) to centre again; [+ *politique*] to redefine, reorient; [+ *débat*] to bring back to the main point; (*Écon*) [+ *activités*] to refocus [2] **se recentrer** VPR **se ~ sur une activité** to refocus on an activity

récépissé [Resepise] NM (= *reçu*) (acknowledgement of) receipt

réceptacle [Reseptakl] NM (= *déversoir*) (*gén, Bot*) receptacle; (*Géog*) catchment basin

récepteur, -trice [ReseptœR, tRis] [1] ADJ receiving; **poste ~** receiving set, receiver [2] NM (*gén, Téléc*) receiver; (*Radio, TV*) (receiving) set, receiver; (*Bio, Physiol*) receptor; **~ (de télévision)** television set; **~ téléphonique** (telephone) receiver

réceptif, -ive [Reseptif, iv] ADJ receptive (**à** to); (*Méd*) susceptible (**à** to)

▾**réception** [Resepsjɔ̃] NF [a] (= *réunion, gala*) reception → **jour** [b] (= *accueil*) reception, welcome; **faire bonne/mauvaise ~ à qn** to give a good/bad reception *ou* welcome to sb; **discours de ~ (à un nouveau sociétaire)** welcoming speech *ou* address of welcome (given to a new member of a society); (*Admin*) **heures de ~ de 14 à 16 heures** consultations between 2 and 4 p.m.; **quelles sont vos heures de ~ ?** (*Scol*) when are

you available to see parents?; (*Univ*) when are you available to see students? [c] (= *entrée, salon*) [*appartement, villa*] reception room; [*hôtel*] entrance hall; (= *bureau*) [*hôtel*] reception desk, reception; **salle de ~** function room, stateroom; **salons de ~** reception rooms; **adressez-vous à la ~** ask at the reception desk *ou* at reception [d] (= *action de recevoir*) [*paquet, lettre*] receipt; (*Bio, Radio, TV*) reception; **à la ~ de sa lettre** on receipt of *ou* on receiving his letter; **c'est lui qui s'occupe de la ~ des marchandises** he is the one who takes delivery of the goods; (*Radio*) **la ~ est mauvaise aujourd'hui** reception is bad *ou* poor today → **accusé, accuser** [e] (*Sport*) (= *prise, blocage*) [*ballon*] trapping, catching; (= *atterrissage*) [*sauteur, parachutiste*] landing; **le footballeur a manqué sa ~** the footballer failed to trap *ou* catch the ball; **après une bonne ~ du ballon** after trapping *ou* catching the ball well; **le sauteur a manqué sa ~** the jumper made a bad landing *ou* landed badly [f] (*Constr*) **~ des travaux** acceptance of work done (*after verification*)

réceptionnaire [ResepsjɔnɛR] NMF [*hôtel*] head of reception; (*Comm*) [*marchandises*] receiving clerk; (*Jur*) receiving agent

réceptionner [Resepsjɔne] ▸conjug 1◂ [1] VT [+ *marchandises*] to receive, take delivery of, check and sign for; [+ *client*] to receive, welcome; (*Sport*) [+ *balle*] to receive [2] **se réceptionner** VPR (*Sport*) to land

réceptionniste [Resepsjɔnist] NMF receptionist; **~-standardiste** receptionist and telephonist

réceptivité [Reseptivite] NF (*gén*) receptivity, receptiveness; (*Méd*) susceptibility (**à** to)

récessif, -ive [Resesif, iv] ADJ (*Bio*) recessive

récession [Resesjɔ̃] NF recession; **de ~** recessionary; **~ avec inflation** slumpflation

récessionniste [Resesjɔnist] ADJ recessionary; **tendance ~** recessionary trend

récessivité [Resesivite] NF recessiveness

recette [R(ə)sɛt] NF [a] (*Culin*) recipe; (*Chim*) [*teinture, produit*] formula; (*fig* = *truc, secret*) formula, recipe (**de** for) [b] (= *encaisse*) takings; **aujourd'hui, j'ai fait une bonne ~** I've made a good day's takings, the takings were good today; (*fig* = *avoir du succès*) **faire ~** to be a big success, be a winner [c] (= *rentrées d'argent*) **~s** receipts; **l'excédent des ~s sur les dépenses** the excess of receipts *ou* revenue over expenses *ou* outlay; **~s fiscales** tax revenue(s), revenue from taxation [d] (*Impôts*) (= *recouvrement*) collection; (= *bureau*) tax (collector's) office, revenue office; **~ municipale** local tax office; **~(-perception)** tax office; **~ principale** main tax office → **garçon**

recevabilité [R(ə)səvabilite] NF (*Jur*) [*pourvoi, témoignage*] admissibility

recevable [R(ə)səvabl] ADJ (*Jur*) [*demande, appel, pourvoi*] admissible, allowable; [*personne*] competent; **témoignage non ~** inadmissible evidence

receveur [R(ə)səvœR] NM [a] (*Méd*) recipient; **~ universel** universal recipient [b] **~ (d'autobus)** conductor; **~ (des contributions)** tax collector *ou* officer; **~ (des postes)** postmaster; **~ municipal** local tax officer

receveuse [R(ə)səvøz] NF [a] (*Méd*) recipient; **~ universelle** universal recipient [b] **~ (d'autobus)** conductress; **~ (des contributions)** tax collector *ou* officer; **~ (des postes)** postmistress

recevoir [R(ə)səvwaR] ▸conjug 28◂ [1] VT [a] (*gén*) [+ *lettre, ordre, argent, blessure, ovation*] to receive, get; [+ *secours*] to receive; [+ *approbation, refus*] to meet with, receive, get; [+ *modifications*] to undergo, receive; [+ *émission, station de radio*] to get, receive; [+ *confession*] to hear; (*Rel*) [+ *vœux, sacrement*] to

receive; (*Rel*) **~ les ordres** to take holy orders; **nous avons bien reçu votre lettre du 15 juillet** we acknowledge *ou* confirm receipt of your letter of July 15th; (*Radio, fig*) **je vous reçois cinq sur cinq** I'm reading *ou* receiving you loud and clear; **procédé qui a reçu le nom de son inventeur** process which has taken *ou* got its name from the inventor; **l'affaire recevra toute notre attention** the matter will receive our full attention; **nous avons reçu la pluie** we got *ou* had rain; **j'ai reçu le caillou sur la tête** the stone hit me on the head, I got hit on the head by the stone; **il a reçu un coup de pied/un coup de poing dans la figure** he got kicked/punched in the face, he got a kick/a punch in the face; **c'est lui qui a tout reçu** (*blâme, coups*) he got the worst of it, he bore the brunt of it; (*sauce, éclaboussures*) he got the worst of it; (*formule épistolaire*) **recevez, cher Monsieur** (*ou* **chère Madame**), **l'expression de mes sentiments distingués** yours faithfully (*Brit*) *ou* truly (*US*) → **leçon, ordre**[2]

[b] [+ *invité*] (= *accueillir*) to receive, welcome, greet; (= *traiter*) to entertain; (= *loger*) to take in, receive; [+ *jeux olympiques, championnat*] to host; (*Admin*) [+ *employé, demandeur*] to see; [+ *demande, déposition, plainte*] to receive, admit; **~ qn à dîner** to have sb to dinner; **ils ont reçu le roi** they entertained the king; **être bien/mal reçu** [*proposition, nouvelles*] to be well/badly received; [*personne*] to receive a good/bad welcome, get a good/bad reception; **on est toujours bien/mal reçu chez eux** they always/ never make you feel welcome; **~ qn à bras ouverts** to welcome sb with open arms; **il est reçu partout dans la haute société** all doors are open to him in society; **les Dupont reçoivent beaucoup** the Duponts entertain a lot; **la baronne reçoit le jeudi** the baroness is at home (to visitors) on Thursdays; **le directeur reçoit le jeudi** the principal receives visitors on Thursdays; **le docteur reçoit de 10 h à 12 h** the doctor is in his office from ten till noon, the doctor's surgery is from ten a.m. till noon; **~ la visite de qn/d'un cambrioleur** to receive *ou* have a visit from sb/from a burglar; **se faire ~*** to get shouted at → **chien**

[c] (*Scol, Univ*) [+ *candidat*] to pass; **être reçu à un examen** to pass an exam, be successful in an exam; **il a été reçu dans les premiers/dans les derniers** he was near the top/bottom in the exam; **il a été reçu premier/deuxième/dernier** he came first/second/last *ou* bottom in the exam → **reçu**

[d] (= *contenir*) [*hôtel, lycée*] to take, hold, accommodate; (= *récolter*) [*gouttière*] to collect; **par manque de locaux on n'a pas pu ~ plus d'élèves cette année** lack of space prevented us from taking *ou* admitting more pupils this year; **~ un affluent** [*rivière*] to be joined by a tributary; **leur chambre ne reçoit jamais le soleil** their room never gets any sun

[e] (*Tech*) [+ *pièce mobile*] to take, receive; **cette encoche reçoit le crochet qui assure la fermeture de la porte** this notch receives *ou* takes the hook which keeps the door shut

[2] **se recevoir** VPR [a] (= *tomber*) to land; **se ~ sur une jambe/sur les mains** to land on one leg/on one's hands; **il s'est mal reçu** he landed badly

[b] (= *se fréquenter*) **elles se connaissent mais ne se reçoivent pas** they know each other but they are not on visiting terms

rechange [R(ə)ʃãʒ] NM [a] **~ (de vêtements)** change of clothes; **as-tu ton ~ ?** have you got a change of clothes? [b] **de ~** (= *de remplacement*) [*solution, politique*] alternative; (= *de secours*) [*outil*] spare; **avoir du linge de ~** to have a change of clothes; **j'ai apporté des chaussures de ~** I brought a spare *ou* an extra pair of shoes → **pièce**

rechanger [R(ə)ʃãʒe] ▸conjug 3◂ VT to change again

▸ GRAMMAIRE ACTIVE: **réception** 47.2, 52.1

rechanter [R(ə)ʃɑ̃te] ▸conjug 1◂ VT to sing again

rechapage [R(ə)ʃapaʒ] NM (= *opération*) retreading, remoulding (*Brit*); (= *résultat*) **le ~ n'a pas duré** the retread *ou* remould (*Brit*) didn't last long

rechaper [R(ə)ʃape] ▸conjug 1◂ VT [+ *pneu*] to retread, remould (*Brit*); **pneus rechapés** retreads, remoulds (*Brit*)

réchappé, e [Reʃape] (*ptp de* **réchapper**) NM,F survivor (**de** of); **les ~s du naufrage** the survivors of the shipwreck

réchapper [Reʃape] ▸conjug 1◂ VI **~ de** *ou* **à** [+ *accident, maladie*] to come through; **tu as eu de la chance d'en ~** you were lucky to escape with your life; **si jamais j'en réchappe** if ever I come through this

recharge [R(ə)ʃaRʒ] NF **a** (= *action*) (*Élec*) recharging; (*Mil*) reloading **b** (= *cartouche*) [*arme*] reload; [*stylo, agenda*] refill

rechargeable [R(ə)ʃaRʒabl] ADJ [*stylo, vaporisateur, aérosol*] refillable; [*briquet*] refillable, rechargeable; [*batterie, pile, appareil électrique, carte à puce*] rechargeable

rechargement [R(ə)ʃaRʒəmɑ̃] NM **a** [*stylo*] refilling; [*briquet*] refilling, recharging; [*batterie, pile*] recharging; **~ en combustible d'un réacteur nucléaire** refuelling a nuclear reactor **b** (*Tech*) [*route*] remetalling; [*voie, rails*] relaying

recharger [R(ə)ʃaRʒe] ▸conjug 3◂ **1** VT **a** [+ *arme, appareil-photo*] to reload; [+ *stylo*] to refill; [+ *briquet*] to refill, recharge; [+ *batterie, pile*] to recharge; (*fig*) **~ ses batteries** *ou* **ses accus*** to recharge one's batteries **b** [+ *véhicule*] to load up again **c** (*Tech*) [+ *route*] to remetal; [+ *voie, rails*] to relay **2** **se recharger** VPR (= *être rechargeable*) [*stylo*] to be refillable; [*briquet, batterie, pile*] to be rechargeable; (= *se charger à nouveau*) [*batterie, pile*] to recharge

réchaud [Reʃo] NM **a** (= *appareil de cuisson*) (portable) stove; **~ à gaz** gas stove *ou* ring (*Brit*); **~ à alcool** spirit stove **b** (= *chauffe-plat*) plate-warmer **c** (= *cassolette*) burner (*for incense etc*)

réchauffage [Reʃofaʒ] NM [*aliment*] reheating

réchauffé, e [Reʃofe] (*ptp de* **réchauffer**) **1** ADJ [*nourriture*] reheated, warmed-up; (*péj*) [*plaisanterie*] stale, old hat (*attrib*); [*théories*] rehashed, old hat (*attrib*); **des manches courtes en décembre? eh bien! tu es ~!** you're wearing short sleeves in December? you don't feel the cold, do you! **2** NM **c'est du ~** (*ragoût*) it's reheated *ou* warmed-up; (*vieille affaire*) it's old hat

réchauffement [Reʃofmɑ̃] NM [*eau, membres, personne*] warming (up); **le ~ de la planète** global warming; **on constate un ~ de la température** the temperature is rising; **on espère un ~ de la température** we're hoping for warmer weather; **ceci a favorisé le ~ des relations entre les deux pays** this has made for warmer relations between the two countries

réchauffer [Reʃofe] ▸conjug 1◂ **1** VT **a** [+ *aliment*] to reheat, heat *ou* warm up again; **réchauffe** *ou* **fais ~ la soupe** ◊ **mets la soupe à ~** reheat the soup, heat *ou* warm the soup up again **b** [+ *personne*] to warm up; **une bonne soupe, ça réchauffe** a nice bowl of soup warms you up; (*littér, hum*) **~ un serpent dans son sein** to nurse a viper in one's bosom **c** (= *réconforter*) [+ *cœur*] to warm; (= *ranimer*) [+ *courage*] to stir up, rekindle; **cela m'a réchauffé le cœur de les voir** it did my heart good *ou* it was heartwarming to see them **d** [*soleil*] to heat up, warm up; **le soleil réchauffe la terre** the sun warms the earth; **ce rayon de soleil va ~ l'atmosphère** this ray of sunshine will warm up the air; **les tons bruns**

réchauffent la pièce the browns make the room seem warmer

2 **se réchauffer** VPR **a** [*temps, température*] to get warmer, warm up; **on dirait que ça se réchauffe** it feels as if it's getting warmer *ou* warming up **b** [*personne*] to warm o.s. (up); **alors tu te réchauffes un peu?** are you warming up now? *ou* feeling a bit warmer now?; **se ~ les doigts** ◊ **~ ses doigts** to warm one's fingers (up)

réchauffeur [ReʃofœR] NM heater

rechausser [R(ə)ʃose] ▸conjug 1◂ **1** VT **a** (*Agr*) [+ *arbre*] to earth up; (*Constr*) [+ *mur*] to consolidate **b** **~ un enfant** (*chaussures enlevées*) to put a child's shoes back on; (*chaussures neuves*) to buy a child new shoes; **~ une voiture** to put new tyres (*Brit*) *ou* tires (*US*) on a car **c** **~ ses skis** to put one's skis back on **2** **se rechausser** VPR to put one's shoes back on; (= *acheter de nouvelles chaussures*) to buy (o.s.) new shoes

rêche [Reʃ] ADJ (*au toucher*) [*tissu, peau*] rough, harsh; (*au goût*) [*vin*] rough; [*fruit vert*] harsh; (*péj*) [*personne*] abrasive

recherche [R(ə)ʃɛRʃ] NF **a** (= *action de rechercher*) search (**de** for); **la ~ de ce papier m'a pris plusieurs heures** it took me several hours to search for the paper; **la ~ de l'albumine dans le sang est faite en laboratoire** tests to detect albumin in the blood are performed in a laboratory; **à la ~ de** in search of; (*Littérat*) **« À la ~ du temps perdu »** "In Search of Lost Time", "Remembrance of Things Past"; **être/se mettre à la ~ de qch/qn** to be/go in search of sth/sb, search for sth/sb; **je suis à la ~ de mes lunettes** I'm searching *ou* hunting *ou* looking for my glasses; **ils sont à la ~ d'un appartement/d'une maison** they are flat-hunting (*Brit*) *ou* apartment-hunting (*US*)/house-hunting, they're looking for a flat (*Brit*) *ou* an apartment (*US*)/a house; **nous avons fait toute la ville à la ~ d'un livre sur la Norvège** we looked all over town for a book on Norway; **il a dû se mettre à la ~ d'une nouvelle situation** he had to start looking *ou* hunting for a new job; **il est toujours à la ~ d'une bonne excuse** he's always on the look-out for a good excuse, he's always trying to come up with *ou* find a good excuse **b** (= *enquête*) **~s** investigations; **faire des ~s** to make *ou* pursue investigations; **malgré toutes leurs ~s, ils n'ont pas trouvé le document nécessaire** in spite of all their searching *ou* hunting they haven't found the necessary document; **toutes nos ~s pour retrouver l'enfant sont demeurées sans résultat** all our attempts to find the child remained fruitless; **jusqu'ici il a échappé aux ~s de la police** until now he has escaped the police hunt *ou* search **c** (*fig = poursuite*) pursuit (**de** of), search (**de** for); **la ~ des plaisirs** the pursuit of pleasure, pleasure-seeking; **la ~ de la gloire** the pursuit of glory; **la ~ de la perfection** the search *ou* quest for perfection **d** (*Scol, Univ*) (= *métier, spécialité*) **la ~** research; (= *études, enquêtes*) **~s** research; **faire des ~s sur un sujet** to do *ou* carry out research into a subject; **que fait-il comme ~s?** what (kind of) research does he do?, what is he doing research on? *ou* in?; **être dans la ~** ◊ **faire de la ~** to be (engaged) in research, do research; **il fait de la ~ en chimie** he's doing research in chemistry; **bourse/étudiant de ~** research grant/student; **travail de ~** research work; **~ appliquée/fondamentale** applied/basic research; **~ clinique** clinical research; **~ et développement** research and development, R & D; **~ opérationnelle** operational research **e** (= *raffinement*) [*tenue, ameublement*] studied elegance; (*péj = affectation*) affectation; **être habillé avec ~/sans ~** to be dressed with stud-

ied elegance/carelessly **f** (*Ordin*) search

recherché, e [R(ə)ʃɛRʃe] (*ptp de* **rechercher**) ADJ **a** [*tableau, livre*] much sought-after; [*produits, acteur, conférencier*] in great demand (*attrib*), much sought-after; (= *apprécié des connaisseurs*) [*morceau délicat, plaisir*] choice (*épith*), exquisite **b** (= *étudié, soigné*) [*style*] mannered; [*expression*] studied; [*vocabulaire*] recherché, carefully chosen; [*tenue*] meticulous; (*péj*) affected

recherche-développement [R(ə)ʃɛRʃdev(ə)lɔpmɑ̃] NF research and development, R and D

rechercher [R(ə)ʃɛRʃe] ▸conjug 1◂ VT **a** (= *chercher à trouver*) [+ *objet égaré ou désiré, enfant perdu*] to search for, hunt for; [+ *coupable, témoin*] to try to trace *ou* find, look for; [+ *cause d'accident*] to try to determine *ou* find out *ou* ascertain, inquire into; **~ l'albumine dans le sang** to look for (evidence of *ou* the presence of) albumin in the blood; **~ comment/pourquoi** to try to find out how/why; **~ qch dans sa mémoire** to search one's memory for sth; **il faudra ~ ce document dans tous les vieux dossiers** we'll have to search through all the old files to find this document; (*Ordin*) **~ un mot dans un fichier** to search a file for a word; (*dans une annonce*) **« on recherche femme de ménage »** "cleaning lady required"; **recherché pour meurtre** wanted for murder; **les policiers le recherchent depuis deux ans** the police have been looking for him *ou* have been after him for two years; **la police recherche ...** the police want to interview ... **b** (= *viser à*) [+ *honneurs, compliment*] to seek; [+ *danger*] to court, seek; [+ *succès, plaisir*] to pursue; **~ la perfection** to strive for *ou* seek perfection; **~ l'amitié/la compagnie de qn** to seek sb's friendship/company; **un écrivain qui recherche l'insolite** a writer who strives to capture the unusual **c** (= *chercher à nouveau*) to search for *ou* look for again; **il faudra que je recherche dans mon sac** I must have another look (for it) in my bag, I must look in *ou* search my bag again; **recherche donc cette lettre** search *ou* look for that letter again, have another look *ou* search for that letter **d** (= *reprendre*) [+ *personne*] to collect, fetch

rechigner [R(ə)ʃiɲe] ▸conjug 1◂ VI (= *renâcler*) to balk, jib (**à, devant qch** at sth, **à faire** at doing); **quand je lui ai dit de m'aider, il a rechigné** when I told him to help me he balked *ou* he made a sour face; **faire qch en rechignant** to do sth with bad grace *ou* reluctantly; **il m'a obéi sans trop ~** he obeyed me without making too much fuss

rechute [R(ə)ʃyt] NF (*Méd*) relapse; (*fig: dans l'erreur, le vice*) lapse (**dans** into); (*Méd*) **faire** *ou* **avoir une ~** to have a relapse

rechuter [R(ə)ʃyte] ▸conjug 1◂ VI (*Méd*) to relapse, have a relapse

récidivant, e [Residivɑ̃, ɑ̃t] ADJ (*Méd*) recurring

récidive [Residiv] NF **a** (*Jur*) second *ou* subsequent offence (*Brit*) *ou* offense (*US*); **en cas de ~** in the event of a second *ou* subsequent offence, in the event of a repetition of the offence; **escroquerie avec ~** second offence of fraud; **être en ~** to reoffend, be a recidivist (*SPÉC*); **les cas de ~ se multiplient chez les jeunes délinquants** reoffending *ou* recidivism (*SPÉC*) is on the increase among juvenile delinquents; **à la première ~, je le fiche à la porte** if he does that once again, I'll throw him out **b** (*Méd*) recurrence; (*fig = nouvelle incartade*) repetition (*of one's bad ways*)

récidiver [Residive] ▸conjug 1◂ VI (*Jur*) to reoffend; [*enfant, élève*] to do it again; (*Méd*) to recur; **il a récidivé 15 minutes plus tard avec**

un second but he did it again* 15 minutes later with a second goal

récidivisme [residivism] NM reoffending, recidivism (*SPÉC*)

récidiviste [residivist] NMF second offender, recidivist (*SPÉC*); (*plusieurs répétitions*) habitual offender, recidivist (*SPÉC*); **condamné ~** recidivist

récidivité [residivite] NF (*Méd*) recurring nature

récif [resif] NM reef; **~ corallien** *ou* **de corail** coral reef; **~ frangeant** fringing reef; **~-barrière** barrier reef

récipiendaire [resipjɑ̃dɛr] NM (*Univ*) recipient (*of a diploma*); [*société*] newly elected member, member elect

récipient [resipjɑ̃] NM container

réciprocité [resiprɔsite] NF reciprocity

réciproque [resiprɔk] **1** ADJ [*sentiments, confiance, tolérance, concessions*] reciprocal, mutual; (*Math*) [*figure, transformation*] reciprocal; [*adjectif, verbe, pronom*] reciprocal; (*Logique*) **propositions ~s** converse propositions; **je lui fais confiance et c'est ~** I trust him and he trusts me; **il la détestait et c'était ~** he hated her and the feeling was mutual **2** NF **la ~** (= *l'inverse*) (*gén*) the opposite, the reverse; (*Logique*) the converse; (= *la pareille*) the same (treatment); **il me déteste mais la ~ n'est pas vraie** he hates me but the opposite *ou* reverse isn't true; **s'attendre à la ~** to expect the same (treatment) *ou* to be paid back

réciproquement [resiprɔkmɑ̃] ADV [a] (= *l'un l'autre*) each other, one another; **ils se félicitaient ~** they congratulated each other *ou* one another [b] (= *vice versa*) vice versa; **il me déteste et ~** he hates me and vice versa *ou* and the feeling is mutual; **un employé doit avoir de l'estime pour son chef et ~** an employee must have regard for his boss and vice versa

réciproquer [resiprɔke] ▸conjug 1◂ VT (*Belg*) [+ *vœux, aide*] to reciprocate

récit [resi] NM [a] (= *action de raconter*) account, story; (= *histoire*) story; (= *genre*) narrative; **~ autobiographique** autobiographical account; **~ de voyage** travel story; **faire le ~ de** to give an account of, tell the story of; **au ~ de ces exploits** on hearing the story of these exploits [b] (*Théât* = *monologue*) (narrative) monologue

récital (*pl* **récitals**) [resital] NM recital; **donner un ~ de piano** to give a piano recital

récitant, e [resitɑ̃, ɑ̃t] **1** ADJ (*Mus*) solo **2** NM,F (*Mus, Radio, Théât, TV*) narrator

récitatif [resitatif] NM recitative

récitation [resitasjɔ̃] NF [a] (= *matière, classe*) recitation; **composition de ~** recitation test; **leçon de ~** verse to be recited by heart [b] [*texte, poème*] recitation, piece (to be recited) [c] (= *action*) recital, reciting

réciter [resite] ▸conjug 1◂ VT [a] [+ *leçon, chapelet, prière*] to recite [b] (*péj*) [+ *profession de foi, témoignage*] to trot out, recite

réclamation [reklamasjɔ̃] NF [a] (= *plainte*) complaint; (*Sport*) objection; **faire/déposer une ~** to make/lodge a complaint; **adressez vos ~s à ... ◊** pour toute ~ **s'adresser à ...** all complaints should be referred to ...; « **(bureau** *ou* **service des) ~s** » "complaints department *ou* office"; (*Téléc*) **téléphonez aux ~s** ring the engineers [b] (= *récrimination*) protest, complaint

réclame† [reklam] NF (= *annonce publicitaire*) advertisement, ad*, advert (*Brit*); (= *publicité*) **la ~** advertising, publicity; **faire de la ~ pour un produit** to advertise *ou* publicize a product; **ça ne leur fait pas de ~** that's not very good publicity for them; (*fig*) **je ne vais pas lui faire de la ~** I'm not going to give him free publicity; **en ~** on (special) offer; **article ~** special offer

réclamer [reklame] ▸conjug 1◂ **1** VT [a] (= *demander*) [+ *silence, paix, aide*] to ask *ou* call for; [+ *argent, augmentation*] to ask for; [+ *pain*] to ask *ou* beg for; **je lui ai réclamé mon stylo** I asked him for my pen back; **~ qch avec insistance** *ou* **haut et fort** to clamour for sth; **~ l'indulgence de qn** to beg *ou* crave sb's indulgence; **je réclame la parole !** I want to say something!; **il m'a réclamé à boire/un jouet** he asked me for a drink/a toy; **je n'aime pas les enfants qui réclament** I don't like children who are always asking for things; **l'enfant malade réclame sa mère** the sick child is calling *ou* asking for his mother, the sick child wants his mother

[b] (= *exiger*) [+ *droit, dû*] to claim; (*plus énergique*) [+ *rançon*] to demand; [+ *part*] to claim, lay claim to; **~ justice** to demand justice; **les policiers lui ont réclamé ses papiers d'identité** the police officers demanded (to see) his identity papers; **certains réclament que cette question soit inscrite à l'ordre du jour** some people are insisting that this issue be put on the agenda; **~ la démission du ministre** to call for the minister to resign *ou* for the minister's resignation

[c] (= *nécessiter*) [+ *patience, soin*] to call for, demand, require

2 VI (= *protester*) to complain; **si vous n'êtes pas content, allez ~ ailleurs** if you're not happy, go and complain *ou* make your complaints elsewhere; **~ contre qch** to cry out against sth

3 **se réclamer** VPR **se ~ de** [+ *parti, organisation*] to claim to represent; [+ *théorie, principe*] to claim to adhere to; [+ *personne*] to claim to be a follower of; **doctrine politique qui se réclame de la Révolution française** political doctrine that claims to go back to the spirit of *ou* that claims to have its roots in the French Revolution; **il se réclame de l'école romantique** he claims to draw *ou* take his inspiration from the romantic school; **il s'est réclamé du ministre pour obtenir ce poste** he used the minister's name (as a reference) to obtain this position

reclassement [rəklasmɑ̃] NM [a] [*salarié*] redeployment; [*chômeur*] placement; [*ex-prisonnier*] rehabilitation; **~ externe** outplacement [b] [*objet, dossier*] reclassifying [c] [*salaires, fonctionnaire*] regrading; **~ de la fonction publique** establishing a new wage scale for the public sector

reclasser [rəklase] ▸conjug 1◂ **1** VT [a] (= *réinsérer*) [+ *salarié*] to redeploy; [+ *chômeur*] to place; [+ *ex-prisonnier*] to rehabilitate [b] [+ *objet, dossier*] to reclassify [c] (= *ajuster le salaire de*) to regrade **2** **se reclasser** VPR (= *se réinsérer*) to find a placement; **elle s'est reclassée dans la restauration** she changed direction and went into catering

reclouer [rəklue] ▸conjug 1◂ VT to nail back on, nail back together

reclus, e [rəkly, yz] **1** ADJ cloistered; **il vit ~ ◊ il a** *ou* **mène une vie ~e** he leads the life of a recluse, he leads a cloistered life; **une vieille dame ~ dans sa chambre** an old lady shut up in her room **2** NM,F recluse

réclusion [reklyzjɔ̃] NF (*littér*) reclusion (*littér*); **~ (criminelle)** imprisonment; **~ criminelle à perpétuité** life imprisonment; **condamné à dix ans de ~ (criminelle)** sentenced to ten years' imprisonment

réclusionnaire [reklyzjɔnɛr] NMF (*Jur*) convict

recoiffer [rəkwafe] ▸conjug 1◂ **1** VT **~ ses cheveux** to do one's hair; **~ qn** to do sb's hair **2** **se recoiffer** VPR (= *se peigner*) to do one's hair; (= *remettre son chapeau*) to put one's hat back on

recoin [rəkwɛ̃] NM (*lit*) nook; (*fig*) hidden *ou* innermost recess; **les ~s du grenier** the nooks and crannies of the attic; **dans les ~s de sa**

mémoire in the recesses of his mind; **il connaît les moindres ~s des Pyrénées** he knows the Pyrenees like the back of his hand, he knows every nook and cranny of the Pyrenees → **coin**

recollage [rəkɔlaʒ] NM [*étiquette*] resticking; [*morceau, vase*] sticking back together again; [*enveloppe*] resticking

recoller [rəkɔle] ▸conjug 1◂ **1** VT [a] [+ *étiquette*] to stick back on *ou* down, restick; [+ *morceaux, vase*] to stick back together; [+ *enveloppe*] to stick back down, restick; (*fig* = *réconcilier*) **~ les morceaux** to patch things up [b] (= *remettre*) **~ son oreille à la porte** to stick one's ear against the door again; **~ qn en prison*** to stick sb back in prison*; **ne recolle pas tes affaires dans ce coin !*** don't just stick your things back down in that corner!* [c] (* = *redonner*) **~ une amende à qn** to give another fine to sb; **on nous a recollé le même moniteur que l'année dernière** we got stuck with the same group leader as last year; **arrête ou je t'en recolle une*** stop it or you'll get another slap

2 **recoller à** VT INDIR (*Sport*) **le coureur a recollé au peloton** the runner caught up with *ou* closed the gap with the rest of the pack

3 **se recoller** VPR [a] [*os*] to mend, knit (together) [b] (* = *subir*) **il a fallu se ~ la vaisselle** we got stuck with the washing-up again [c] (* = *se remettre*) **on va se ~ au boulot** let's get back down to work; **allez, on s'y recolle !** come on, let's get back to it! [d] (* = *se remettre en ménage*) to get back together

récoltant, e [rekɔltɑ̃, ɑ̃t] ADJ, NM,F **(propriétaire) ~** farmer (*who harvests his own crop*), grower

récolte [rekɔlt] NF [a] (= *activité*: *gén*) harvesting; [*perles*] gathering; **il y a deux ~s par an** there are two harvests a year; **faire la ~ des pommes de terre** to harvest potatoes [b] [*souvenirs, documents, signatures*] collecting, gathering; [*argent*] collecting [c] (= *produit*) [*blé, maïs, etc*] harvest, crop; [*pommes de terre, fraises, raisin, miel*] crop; **cette année, on a fait une excellente ~ (de fruits)** this year we had an excellent crop (of fruit); **~ sur pied** standing crop; **la saison des ~s** harvest time [d] [*documents, souvenirs*] collection; (= *argent récolté*) takings; (= *documents*) **la ~ est maigre** I didn't get much information

récolter [rekɔlte] ▸conjug 1◂ VT [a] (*gén*) to harvest; [+ *perles*] to gather; (*fig*) **~ ce qu'on a semé** to reap what one has sown → **semer** [b] (= *recueillir*) [+ *souvenirs, documents, signatures*] to collect, gather; [+ *argent*] to collect; [+ *renseignements*] to gather; * [+ *contravention, coups, mauvaise note*] to get; (*Pol*) [+ *suffrages, points, voix*] to gain; **je n'ai récolté que des ennuis** all I got was a lot of trouble

recombinant, e [rəkɔ̃binɑ̃, ɑ̃t] ADJ (*Méd*) [*produit, virus*] recombinant

recommandable [rəkɔmɑ̃dabl] ADJ (= *estimable*) commendable; **peu ~** [*personne*] disreputable; [*comportement, moyen*] not very commendable

recommandation [rəkɔmɑ̃dasjɔ̃] NF [a] (= *conseil*) (*gén, Pol*) recommendation; **faire des ~s à qn** to make recommendations to sb; **~s de l'ONU** UN recommendations; (*Ling*) **c'est la ~ officielle pour « jet-stream »** it's the recommended official French word for "jet-stream" [b] (= *avis favorable*) [*hôtel, livre, guide*] recommendation; **je l'ai acheté sur sa ~** I bought it on his recommendation [c] (= *appui*) recommendation; **sur la ~ de qn** on sb's recommendation; **donner une ~ à qn pour un employeur** to give sb a reference (for an employer) → **lettre** [d] (*Poste*) [*lettre, paquet*] recording; (*avec valeur assurée*) registration [e] (*Rel*) commandation

recommandé, e [R(ə)kɔmɑ̃de] (ptp de **recommander**) ADJ a (Poste) [lettre, paquet] recorded; (avec valeur assurée) registered; «envoi (en) ~» "recorded delivery" (Brit), "certified mail" (US); (avec valeur assurée) "registered mail", "registered post" (Brit); **envoyer qch en ~** to send sth recorded delivery (Brit) ou by certified mail (US); (avec valeur assurée) to send sth by registered mail ou post (Brit) → **lettre** b (= conseillé) [produit, hôtel] recommended; [mesure, initiative] advisable, recommended; **est-ce bien ~?** is it advisable? (**de faire qch** to do sth); **il est ~ de ...** it's advisable ou recommended to ...; **ce n'est pas très ~*** it's not very ou really advisable, it's not really recommended

▼ **recommander** [R(ə)kɔmɑ̃de] ▶ conjug 1 ◀ 1 VT a (= appuyer) [+ candidat] to recommend (à to); **est-il recommandé?** has he been recommended?; **sa probité intellectuelle le recommande autant que ses découvertes** his intellectual honesty commends him as much as his discoveries
b (= conseiller) [+ hôtel, livre, film, produit] to recommend (à to); **~ à qn de faire qch** to recommend ou advise sb to do sth; **le médecin lui a recommandé le repos** the doctor advised him to rest; **je te recommande la modération/ la discrétion** I advise you to be moderate/discreet, I recommend that you be moderate/discreet; **je te recommande (de lire) ce livre** I recommend (that you read) this book; (ton menaçant) **je te recommande de partir** I strongly advise you to leave; **je ne saurais trop vous ~ de faire cette démarche** I strongly urge you to do this; **est-ce bien à ~?** is it advisable?
c (Rel) **~ son âme à Dieu** to commend one's soul to God
d (Poste) to record; (avec valeur assurée) to register
2 **se recommander** VPR a (= se réclamer de) **se ~ de qn** to give sb's name as a reference
b (= s'en remettre à) **se ~ à qn/Dieu** to commend o.s. to sb/God
c (= montrer sa valeur) **il se recommande par son talent/son expérience** his talent/his experience commends him

recommencement [R(ə)kɔmɑ̃smɑ̃] NM **l'histoire/la vie est un éternel ~** history/life is a process of constant renewal; **les ~s sont toujours difficiles** beginning again ou making a fresh start is always difficult

recommencer [R(ə)kɔmɑ̃se] ▶ conjug 3 ◀ 1 VT a (= continuer) [+ récit, lecture] to begin ou start again, resume; [+ lutte, combat] to resume; **faites attention, ça fait la troisième fois que je recommence** pay attention, that's the third time I've told you; **~ à ou de** (littér) **faire qch** to begin ou start to do sth again, begin ou start doing sth again; **il recommence à neiger** it's beginning ou starting to snow again
b (= refaire) [+ travail, expérience] to start (over) again, start afresh; (= répéter) [+ erreur] to make again; **laisser bouillir 5 mn, ~ l'opération trois fois** leave to boil for 5 minutes, repeat three times; **~ sa vie** to make a fresh start (in life), start one's life (over) again; **si c'était à ~** if I could start ou have it over again; **tout est à ~** we (ou I etc) will have to start all over again; **on prend les mêmes et on recommence!*** it's always the same old people! → **zéro**
2 VI [pluie, orage] to begin ou start again; [combat] to start up again, start afresh, resume; **la pluie recommence** it's beginning ou starting to rain again, the rain is beginning ou starting again; **en septembre, l'école recommence** school begins ou starts again ou resumes in September; **je leur ai dit de se taire, et voilà que ça recommence!** I told them to be quiet and now they're at it again!; **ça y est, ça recommence!*** here we go again!; **on**

lui dit de ne pas le faire, mais deux minutes plus tard, **il recommence** he is told not to do it but two minutes later he does it again ou he's at it again; **il m'a promis qu'il ne recommencerait plus** he promised he wouldn't do it again

recomparaître [R(ə)kɔ̃paRetR] ▶ conjug 57 ◀ VI (Jur) to appear (in court) again

récompense [Rekɔ̃pɑ̃s] NF (= action, chose) reward; (= prix) award; **obtenir la plus haute ~ pour qch** to receive the highest accolade for sth; **en ~ de** in return for, as a reward for; **en ~ de vos services** in return for your services; **je me sacrifie et voilà ma ~** I make sacrifices and that's all the reward I get; **sa réussite est la ~ de son travail** his success is just reward for his work; (dans une annonce) «**forte ~**» "generous reward"

récompenser [Rekɔ̃pɑ̃se] ▶ conjug 1 ◀ VT to reward; **être récompensé d'avoir fait qch** to be rewarded for having done sth; **j'ai été largement récompensé de mes efforts** I have been amply rewarded for my efforts; **le biologiste a été récompensé pour sa découverte** the biologist received an award for his discovery; **ce prix récompense le premier roman d'un auteur** this prize is awarded for an author's first novel

recomposer [R(ə)kɔ̃poze] ▶ conjug 1 ◀ VT a [+ puzzle] to put together (again); **il parvint à ~ la scène** he succeeded in reconstructing the scene; **l'œil recompose l'image** the eye reconstitutes the image b (Chim) to recompose c (Téléc) [+ numéro] to dial again, redial d (Typo) [+ ligne, texte] to reset

recomposition [R(ə)kɔ̃pozisjɔ̃] NF a (de mémoire) reconstitution b (Chim) recomposition c (Téléc) [numéro] redialling d (Typo) resetting

recompter [R(ə)kɔ̃te] ▶ conjug 1 ◀ VT to count again, recount

réconciliateur, -trice [Rekɔ̃siljatœR, tRis] NM,F reconciler

réconciliation [Rekɔ̃siljasjɔ̃] NF reconciliation

▼ **réconcilier** [Rekɔ̃silje] ▶ conjug 7 ◀ 1 VT (Rel) to reconcile; [+ personnes, théories] to reconcile (avec with); **~ qn avec une idée** to reconcile sb to an idea; **cette émission m'a réconcilié avec la télévision** this programme restored my faith in television 2 **se réconcilier** VPR to be ou become reconciled (avec with); **ils se sont réconciliés** they have made their peace with one another, they've patched things up; **se ~ avec soi-même** to feel ou be at peace with o.s.

reconductible [R(ə)kɔ̃dyktibl] ADJ renewable

reconduction [R(ə)kɔ̃dyksjɔ̃] NF renewal; **tacite ~** renewal by tacit agreement

reconduire [R(ə)kɔ̃dɥiR] ▶ conjug 38 ◀ VT a (= continuer) [+ politique, budget, bail] to renew; **commande tacitement reconduite** order renewed by tacit agreement b (= raccompagner) **~ qn chez lui/à la gare** to see ou take sb (back) home/to the station; **il a été reconduit à la frontière par les policiers** he was escorted (back) to the frontier by the police; **~ qn à pied/en voiture chez lui** to walk/drive sb (back) home; **il m'a reconduit à la porte** he showed me to the door

reconduite [R(ə)kɔ̃dɥit] NF [personne en situation irrégulière] **~ (à la frontière)** escorting (back) to the border; **le nombre de ~s exécutées** the number of people who were escorted back to the border

reconfiguration [R(ə)kɔ̃figyRasjɔ̃] NF a (Ordin) reconfiguration b (Écon) [entreprise] re-engineering

reconfigurer [R(ə)kɔ̃figyRe] ▶ conjug 1 ◀ VT a (Ordin) to reconfigurate b (Écon) [+ entreprise] to re-engineer

réconfort [Rekɔ̃fɔR] NM comfort; **avoir besoin de ~** to need comforting; **sa présence m'a apporté un grand ~** his presence was a great comfort to me; **~ moral** solace; **elle a trouvé un ~ dans la lecture** she found some consolation in reading

réconfortant, e [Rekɔ̃fɔRtɑ̃, ɑ̃t] ADJ (= rassurant) [parole, idée] comforting; (= stimulant) [remède] tonic (épith), fortifying; [aliment] fortifying

réconforter [Rekɔ̃fɔRte] ▶ conjug 1 ◀ 1 VT [paroles, présence] to comfort; [alcool, aliment, remède] to fortify 2 **se réconforter** VPR (moralement) to comfort o.s., cheer o.s. up, make o.s. feel better; (physiquement) to fortify o.s.

reconnaissable [R(ə)kɔnesabl] ADJ recognizable (à by, from); **il n'était pas ~** he was unrecognizable, you wouldn't have recognized him; **son style est ~ entre mille** his style is unmistakable; **difficilement ~** hard to recognize

▼ **reconnaissance** [R(ə)kɔnesɑ̃s] 1 NF a (= gratitude) gratitude, gratefulness (à qn to ou towards sb); **avoir/éprouver de la ~ pour qn** to be/feel grateful to sb; **en ~ de ses services/de son aide** in recognition of ou acknowledgement of ou gratitude for his services/his help; **être pénétré de ~ pour la générosité de qn** to be filled with gratitude to sb for his generosity; **je lui voue une ~ éternelle** I am eternally grateful to him; (hum) **il n'a même pas la ~ du ventre** he's not even grateful for what he's been given
b (Pol) [État, indépendance] recognition; (Jur) [droit] recognition, acknowledgement; [diplôme, rôle, statut] recognition; **il a soif de ~ sociale** he craves social recognition
c (= exploration) reconnaissance, survey; (Mil) reconnaissance, recce*; (lit, fig) **envoyer en ~** to send (out) on reconnaissance ou on a recce*; (lit, fig) **partir en ~** to go and reconnoitre (the ground); (Mil) **faire ou pousser une ~** to make a reconnaissance, go on reconnaissance; **mission/patrouille de ~** reconnaissance mission/patrol
d (= identification) recognition; **il lui fit un petit signe de ~** he gave her a little sign of recognition; **il tenait un journal en signe de ~** he was carrying a newspaper so that he could be recognized ou identified
e (littér = aveu) acknowledgement, admission
f (Ordin) recognition; **~ vocale** ou **de la parole** speech recognition; **~ de formes** pattern recognition; **~ optique de caractères** optical character recognition, OCR
2 COMP ► **reconnaissance de dette** acknowledgement of a debt, IOU ► **reconnaissance d'enfant** legal recognition of a child ► **reconnaissance du mont-de-piété** pawn ticket ► **reconnaissance d'utilité publique** official approval

▼ **reconnaissant, e** [R(ə)kɔnesɑ̃, ɑ̃t] ADJ grateful (à qn de qch to sb for sth); **se montrer ~ envers qn** to show one's gratitude to sb; **je vous serais ~ de me répondre rapidement** I would be grateful if you would reply quickly ou for a speedy reply

▼ **reconnaître** [R(ə)kɔnetR] ▶ conjug 57 ◀ 1 VT a (gén = identifier) to recognize; **je l'ai reconnu à sa voix** I recognized him ou I knew it was him ou I could tell it was him from ou by (the sound of) his voice; **je le reconnaîtrais entre mille** I'd recognize him anywhere; **elle reconnut l'enfant à son foulard rouge** she recognized the child by his red scarf; **~ la voix/le pas de qn** to recognize sb's voice/walk; **~ le corps** (d'un mort) to identify the body; **ces jumeaux sont impossibles à ~** these twins are impossible to tell apart, it's impossible to tell which of these twins is which; **on reconnaît un gros fumeur à ses doigts jaunis** you can tell

➤ GRAMMAIRE ACTIVE: **recommander** 28.1, 46.4 **réconcilier** 53.4 **reconnaissance** 49 *ou* recognize a heavy smoker by his stained fingers; **on reconnaît bien là sa paresse** that's just typical of his laziness; **je le reconnais bien là!** that's just like him!, that's him all over!; **méfiez-vous, il sait ~ un mensonge** be careful — he knows *ou* recognizes *ou* he can spot a lie when he hears one; **on ne le reconnaît plus** you wouldn't know *ou* recognize him now

b (= *convenir de*) [+ *innocence, supériorité, valeur*] to recognize, acknowledge; (= *avouer*) [+ *torts*] to recognize, acknowledge, admit; **il reconnut peu à peu la difficulté de la tâche** he gradually came to recognize the difficulty of the task; **il faut ~ les faits** we must face *ou* recognize the facts; **il a reconnu s'être trompé/qu'il s'était trompé** he admitted to *ou* acknowledged making a mistake/that he had made a mistake; **je reconnais que j'avais tout à fait oublié ce rendez-vous** I must confess *ou* admit (that) I had completely forgotten this appointment

c (= *admettre*) [+ *maître, chef*] to recognize; (*Pol*) [+ *État, gouvernement*] to recognize; (*Jur*) [+ *enfant*] to recognize legally, acknowledge; [+ *dette*] to acknowledge; [+ *diplôme*] to recognize; **~ qn pour** *ou* **comme chef** to acknowledge *ou* recognize sb as (one's) leader; **~ la compétence d'un tribunal** to acknowledge *ou* recognize the competence of a court; **~ qn coupable** to find sb guilty; **~ sa signature** to acknowledge one's signature; **il ne reconnaît à personne le droit d'intervenir** he doesn't acknowledge that anyone has the right to intervene

d (*Mil*) [+ *côte, île, terrain*] to reconnoitre; **on va aller ~ les lieux** *ou* **le terrain** we're going to see how the land lies, we're going to reconnoitre (the ground); **les gangsters étaient certainement venus ~ les lieux auparavant** the gangsters had probably been to look over the place beforehand

e (*littér* = *montrer de la gratitude pour*) to recognize, acknowledge

2 se reconnaître VPR **a** (*dans la glace*) to recognize o.s.; (*entre personnes*) to recognize each other; **elle ne se reconnaît pas du tout dans ses filles** she (just) can't see any likeness between herself and her daughters

b (*lit, fig* = *se retrouver*) to find one's way about *ou* around; **je ne m'y reconnais plus** I'm completely lost; **je commence à me ~** I'm beginning to find my bearings

c (= *être reconnaissable*) to be recognizable (**à** by); **le pêcher se reconnaît à ses fleurs roses** the peach tree is recognizable by its pink flowers, you can tell a peach tree by its pink flowers

d (= *s'avouer*) **se ~ vaincu** to admit *ou* acknowledge defeat; **se ~ coupable** to admit *ou* acknowledge one's guilt

reconnecter VT, **se reconnecter** VPR [R(ə)kɔnɛkte] ▸conjug 1◂ (*gén*) to reconnect (**à** to)

reconnu, e [R(ə)kɔny] (*ptp de* **reconnaître**) ADJ [*fait*] recognized, accepted; [*auteur, chef, diplôme*] recognized; **c'est un fait ~ que ...** it's a recognized *ou* an accepted fact that ...; **il est ~ que ...** it is recognized *ou* accepted *ou* acknowledged that ...

reconquérir [R(ə)kɔ̃keRiR] ▸conjug 21◂ VT (*Mil*) to reconquer, recapture, capture back; [+ *personne, titre, siège de député*] to win back; [+ *dignité, liberté*] to recover, win back

reconquête [R(ə)kɔ̃kɛt] NF (*Mil*) reconquest, recapture; [*droit, liberté*] recovery

reconsidérer [R(ə)kɔ̃sidere] ▸conjug 6◂ VT to reconsider

reconstituant, e [R(ə)kɔ̃stitɥɑ̃, ɑ̃t] **1** ADJ [*ali-*

---

ment, régime] energy-giving **2** NM energy-giving food, energizer

reconstituer [R(ə)kɔ̃stitɥe] ▸conjug 1◂ **1** VT **a** [+ *parti, armée, association*] to re-form; [+ *fortune, capital, réserves*] to build up again; **bifteck haché reconstitué** mincemeat (*Brit*) *ou* hamburger (*US*) patty **b** [+ *crime, faits, histoire*] to reconstruct, piece together; [+ *décor*] to recreate; [+ *puzzle*] to put together (again); [+ *fichier*] to rebuild; [+ *texte*] to restore, reconstitute; [+ *édifice, vieux quartier*] to restore, reconstruct **c** [+ *objet brisé*] to put *ou* piece together again **d** (*Bio*) [+ *organisme*] to regenerate **2** **se reconstituer** VPR [*équipe, parti*] to re-form; [+ *réserves*] to be built up again

reconstitution [R(ə)kɔ̃stitysjɔ̃] NF **a** [*parti, armée, association*] re-forming; [*fortune, capital, réserves*] rebuilding **b** [*crime, faits, puzzle, histoire*] reconstruction, piecing together; [*fichier*] rebuilding; [*texte*] restoration, reconstitution; **la ~ du crime** the reconstruction of the crime (*in the presence of the examining magistrate and the accused*) **c** [*objet brisé*] repairing **d** (*Bio*) [*organisme*] regeneration

reconstructeur, -trice [R(ə)kɔ̃stryktœR, tRis] ADJ [*chirurgie*] reconstructive

reconstruction [R(ə)kɔ̃stryksjɔ̃] NF [*maison, ville, pays*] rebuilding, reconstruction; [*fortune*] rebuilding

reconstruire [R(ə)kɔ̃stryiR] ▸conjug 38◂ VT [+ *maison, ville, pays*] to rebuild, reconstruct; [+ *fortune*] to build up again, rebuild; **il a dû ~ sa vie** he had to rebuild his life

reconversion [R(ə)kɔ̃vɛRsjɔ̃] NF [*usine*] reconversion; [*personnel*] redeployment, retraining; [*région*] redevelopment; [*économie*] restructuring; **stage/plan de ~** retraining course/scheme

reconvertir [R(ə)kɔ̃vɛRtiR] ▸conjug 2◂ **1** VT [+ *personnel*] to retrain; [+ *région*] to redevelop; [+ *économie, entreprise*] to restructure; **l'ancienne fabrique a été reconvertie en école** the old factory has been converted into a school **2** **se reconvertir** VPR [*personne*] to move into *ou* turn to a new type of employment; [*entreprise*] to change activity; **il s'est reconverti dans la publicité** he has changed direction and gone into advertising; **nous nous sommes reconvertis dans le textile** we have moved over *ou* gone over into textiles

recopier [R(ə)kɔpje] ▸conjug 7◂ VT (= *transcrire*) to copy out, write out; (= *recommencer*) to copy out *ou* write out again; **~ ses notes au propre** to write up one's notes, make a clean *ou* fair (*Brit*) copy of one's notes

record [R(ə)kɔR] **1** NM (*Sport*) record; **~ masculin/féminin** men's/women's record; **~ de vitesse/d'altitude** speed/altitude record; **~ du monde/d'Europe** world/European record; **le yen a battu son ~ historique** the yen has hit *ou* reached a record high *ou* an all-time high; **le ministre bat tous les ~s d'impopularité** the minister breaks *ou* beats all the records for unpopularity; **ça bat (tous) les ~s!*** that beats everything!; **le film a connu des ~s d'affluence** the film broke box-office records; **un ~ d'abstentions** a record number of abstentions; **j'ai lu deux livres en une semaine, c'est mon ~** I read two books within a week, it's a personal record

2 ADJ INV [*chiffre, niveau, production, taux*] record (*épith*); **les bénéfices ont atteint un montant ~ de 5 milliards** profits reached a record total of 5 billion; **en un temps ~** in record time

recorder [R(ə)kɔRde] ▸conjug 1◂ VT [+ *raquette*] to restring

recordman [R(ə)kɔRdman] (*pl* **recordmen** [R(ə)kɔRdmɛn]) NM (men's) record holder

recordwoman [R(ə)kɔRdwuman] (*pl* **recordwomen** [R(ə)kɔRdwumɛn]) NF (women's) record holder

---

recorriger [RəkɔRiʒe] ▸conjug 3◂ VT to re-correct, correct again; (*Scol*) to mark *ou* grade again

recoucher [R(ə)kuʃe] ▸conjug 1◂ **1** VT [+ *enfant*] to put back to bed; [+ *objet*] to lay *ou* put down again **2** **se recoucher** VPR to go back to bed

recoudre [R(ə)kudR] ▸conjug 48◂ VT [+ *ourlet*] to sew up again; [+ *bouton*] to sew back on, sew on again; [+ *plaie*] to stitch up (again), put stitches (back) in; [+ *opéré*] to stitch (back) up

recoupement [R(ə)kupmɑ̃] NM cross-check, cross-checking (*NonC*); **par ~** by cross-checking; **faire des ~s** to cross-check

recouper [R(ə)kupe] ▸conjug 1◂ **1** VT **a** (*gén*) to cut again; [+ *vêtement*] to recut; [+ *route*] to intersect; **~ du pain** to cut (some) more bread; **elle m'a recoupé une tranche de viande** she cut me another slice of meat **b** [+ *vin*] to blend **c** [*témoignage*] to tie up *ou* match up with, confirm, support **2** VI (*Cartes*) to cut again **3** **se recouper** VPR [*faits*] to tie *ou* match up, confirm *ou* support one another; [*droites, cercles*] to intersect; [*chiffres, résultats*] to add up

recourbé, e [R(ə)kuRbe] (*ptp de* **recourber**) ADJ (*gén*) curved; (*accidentellement*) bent; [*bec*] curved, hooked; **nez ~** hooknose

recourber [R(ə)kuRbe] ▸conjug 1◂ **1** VT [+ *bois*] to bend (over); [+ *métal*] to bend, curve **2** **se recourber** VPR to curve (up), bend (up)

recourir [R(ə)kuRiR] ▸conjug 11◂ **1** VT (*Sport*) to run again **2** **recourir à** VT INDIR [+ *opération, emprunt*] to resort to, have recourse to; [+ *force*] to resort to; [+ *personne*] to turn to, appeal to; **j'ai recouru à son aide** I turned *ou* appealed to him for help **3** VI **a** (*Sport*) to race again, run again; **j'ai recouru le chercher** I ran back *ou* raced back *ou* nipped back* (*Brit*) to get it **b** (*Jur*) **~ contre qn** to (lodge an) appeal against sb

recours [R(ə)kuR] **1** NM resort, recourse; (*Jur*) appeal; **le ~ à la violence ne sert à rien** resorting to violence doesn't do any good; **en dernier ~** as a last resort, in the last resort; **nous n'avons plus qu'un ~** there's only one course (of action) left open to us; **il n'y a aucun ~ contre cette décision** there is no way of changing this decision, there is no appeal possible *ou* no recourse against this decision; **il n'y a aucun ~ contre cette maladie** there is no cure *ou* remedy for this disease; **la situation est sans ~** there's nothing we can do about the situation, there's no way out of the situation; **avoir ~ à** [+ *mesure, solution*] to resort to, have recourse to; [+ *force*] to resort to; [+ *personne*] to turn to, appeal to

2 COMP ▸ **recours en cassation** appeal to the supreme court ▸ **recours contentieux** *submission for a legal settlement* ▸ **recours en grâce** (= *remise de peine*) plea for pardon; (= *commutation de peine*) plea for clemency ▸ **recours gracieux** *submission for an out-of-court settlement* ▸ **recours hiérarchique** *disciplinary complaint*

recouvrable [R(ə)kuvRabl] ADJ **a** [*impôt*] collectable, which can be collected; [*créance*] recoverable, reclaimable, retrievable **b** [*peinture*] recoatable

recouvrement [R(ə)kuvRəmɑ̃] NM **a** (= *action*) covering (up); (= *résultat*) cover; (*Constr*) **assemblage à ~** lap joint **b** (*Fin*) [*cotisations*] collection, payment; [*impôt*] collection, levying; (*littér*) [*créance*] recovery **c** (*littér*) [*forces, santé*] recovery

recouvrer [R(ə)kuvRe] ▸conjug 1◂ VT **a** [+ *santé, vue*] to recover, regain; [+ *liberté*] to regain; [+ *amitié*] to win back; **~ la raison** to recover one's senses, come back to one's senses **b** (*Fin*) [+ *cotisation*] to collect; [+ *impôt*] to collect, levy; (*littér*) [+ *créance*] to recover

---

smaller; **prendre du ~** (*lit*) to step back, stand back; (*fig*) to stand back (**par rapport à** from); **après cette dispute, j'ai besoin de prendre un peu de ~** after that quarrel I need to take stock; **avec du** *ou* **le ~** with (the benefit of) hindsight; **il manque de ~** (*pour faire demi-tour*) he hasn't got enough room; (*pour prendre une photo*) he's too close; (*pour juger objectivement*) he's not objective enough; **nous manquons de ~** *ou* **nous n'avons pas assez de ~ pour mesurer les effets à long terme** not enough time has passed *ou* it is still too soon for us to assess the long-term effects; **cette salle n'a pas assez de ~** you can't get back far enough in this room
 [d] [*arme à feu*] recoil, kick
 [e] (= *report*) [*échéance*] postponement
 [f] (= *déplacement*) [*véhicule*] backward movement → **phare**

reculade [R(ə)kylad] NF (*Mil*) retreat, withdrawal; (*fig péj*) retreat, climb-down*; **c'est la ~ générale** they're all backing down

reculé, e [R(ə)kyle] (*ptp de* **reculer**) ADJ [*époque*] remote, distant; [*région, village*] remote, out-of-the-way (*épith*), out of the way (*attrib*); **en ces temps ~s** in those far-off times

reculer [R(ə)kyle] ▶ conjug 1 ◀ [1] VI [a] [*personne*] to move *ou* step back; (*par peur*) to draw back, back away; [*automobiliste, automobile*] to reverse, back (up), move back; [*cheval*] to back; [*mer*] to recede; (*Mil*) to retreat; **~ de deux pas** to go back *ou* move back two paces, take two paces back; **~ devant l'ennemi** to retreat from *ou* draw back from the enemy; **~ d'horreur** to draw back *ou* shrink back in horror, recoil (in horror); **c'est ~ pour mieux sauter** it's just putting off the evil day; **faire ~** [+ *foule*] to move back, force back; [+ *cheval*] to move back; [+ *ennemi*] to push *ou* force back; [+ *désert*] to drive back; **ce spectacle le fit ~** he recoiled at the sight
 [b] (= *hésiter*) to shrink back; (= *changer d'avis*) to back down, back out; **tu ne peux plus ~ maintenant** you can't back out *ou* back down now; **~ devant la dépense/difficulté** to shrink from the expense/difficulty; **je ne reculerai devant rien** ◊ **rien ne me fera ~** I'll stop *ou* stick (*Brit*) at nothing, nothing will stop me; **il ne faut pas ~ devant ses obligations** you mustn't shrink from your obligations; **il ne recule pas devant la dénonciation** he doesn't flinch at *ou* shrink from informing on people; **cette condition ferait ~ de plus braves** this condition would make braver men (than I *ou* you *etc*) draw back *ou* hesitate
 [c] (= *diminuer*) (*gén*) to be on the decline; [*patois*] to be on the decline, lose ground; [*chômage*] to decline, subside, go down; [*eaux*] to subside, recede, go down; [*incendie*] to subside, lose ground; [*civilisation, science*] to be on the decline; [*élève*] **il a reculé en français** he's gone down in French; **faire ~ l'épidémie** to get the epidemic under control; **faire ~ le chômage** to reduce the number of unemployed; **faire ~ l'inflation** to curb inflation; (*Bourse*) **les mines d'or ont reculé d'un point** gold shares fell back a point
 [d] [*arme à feu*] to recoil

 [2] VT [+ *chaise, meuble*] to move back, push back; [+ *véhicule*] to reverse, back (up); [+ *frontières*] to extend, push *ou* move back; [+ *livraison, date*] to put back, postpone; [+ *décision*] to put off, defer, postpone; [+ *échéance*] to defer, postpone

 [3] **se reculer** VPR to stand *ou* step *ou* move back, take a step back

reculons [R(ə)kylɔ̃] ◆ **à reculons** LOC ADV [*aller, marcher*] backwards; [*accepter*] reluctantly, unwillingly; **sortir à ~ d'une pièce/d'un garage** to back out of a room/a garage; **ce pays entre à ~ dans l'Europe** this country is reluctant about going into Europe; (*fig*) **ils y vont à ~** they're dragging their feet

récup* [Rekyp] NF ABRÉV = **récupération**

récupérable [RekypeRabl] ADJ [*créance*] recoverable; [*heures*] which can be made up; [*ferraille*] which can be salvaged; [*vieux habits*] worth rescuing; **délinquant qui n'est plus ~** irredeemable delinquent, delinquent who is beyond redemption

récupérateur, -trice [RekypeRatœR, tRis]
 [1] ADJ (*péj*) [*discours, procédé*] designed to win over dissenting opinion (*ou* groups *etc*)
 [2] NM, F (= *personne*) [*carton, plastique, papier*] salvage dealer; [*métal*] scrap metal dealer, scrap merchant [3] NM (*Tech*) [*chaleur*] recuperator, regenerator; [*arme*] recuperator

récupération [RekypeRasjɔ̃] NF [a] [*argent, biens, forces*] recovery; (*Ordin*) [+ *données, fichier*] retrieval, recovery; **la capacité de ~ de l'organisme** the body's powers of recuperation *ou* recovery [b] [*ferraille, chiffons, emballages*] salvage, reclamation; [*déchets*] retrieval; [*chaleur, énergie*] recovery; [*délinquant*] rehabilitation; **matériaux de ~** salvaged materials [c] [*journées de travail*] making up; **deux jours de ~** two days to make up [d] (*Pol: péj*) [*mouvement, personnes*] takeover, hijacking

récupérer [RekypeRe] ▶ conjug 6 ◀ [1] VT [a] [+ *argent, biens, territoire*] to get back, recover; [+ *objet prêté*] to get back; [+ *forces*] to recover, get back, regain; (*Ordin*) [+ *enfant, bagages*] to pick up, collect; [+ *sièges, voix*] (= *reprendre à un autre*) to take; (= *s'approprier*) to win, take; (*Pol*) **il a récupéré son siège** he won back his seat; **ils sont allés ~ les pilotes abattus en territoire ennemi** they went to rescue the pilots that had been shot down in enemy territory
 [b] (= *réhabiliter*) [+ *délinquant*] to rehabilitate
 [c] [+ *ferraille, chiffons, emballages*] to salvage, reclaim; [+ *chaleur, énergie*] to recover; [+ *déchets*] to retrieve; [+ *délinquant*] to rehabilitate; **toutes les pêches étaient pourries, je n'ai rien pu** all the peaches were rotten and I wasn't able to save *ou* rescue a single one; **regarde si tu peux ~ quelque chose dans ces vieux habits** have a look and see if there's anything you can rescue *ou* retrieve from among these old clothes; **où es-tu allé ~ ce chat ?*** wherever did you pick up *ou* get that cat?
 [d] [+ *journées de travail*] to make up; **on récupérera samedi** we'll make it up *ou* we'll make the time up on Saturday
 [e] (*Pol: péj*) [+ *personne, mouvement*] to take over, hijack; **se faire ~ par la gauche/la droite** to find o.s. taken over *ou* hijacked by the left/the right; **~ une situation/un événement à son profit** to cash in on a situation/an event
 [2] VI (*après des efforts, une maladie*) to recover, recuperate

récurage [RekyRaʒ] NM scouring

récurer [RekyRe] ▶ conjug 1 ◀ VT to scour → **poudre**

récurrence [RekyRɑ̃s] NF (*Math, Méd, littér* = *répétition*) recurrence

récurrent, e [RekyRɑ̃, ɑ̃t] ADJ [*cauchemar, phénomène, problème, thème*] recurring, recurrent; (*Anat, Ling, Méd*) recurrent; (*Math*) **série ~e** recursion series; **fièvre ~e** recurrent *ou* relapsing fever; **ces rumeurs apparaissent de façon ~e** these rumours keep popping up *ou* pop up again and again

récursif, -ive [RekyRsif, iv] ADJ recursive
récursivité [RekyRsivite] NF recursiveness

récusable [Rekyzabl] ADJ [*témoin*] challengeable; [*témoignage*] impugnable

récusation [Rekyzasjɔ̃] NF [*témoin, juge, juré*] challenging (*NonC*), objection; [*témoignage*] impugnment, challenging (*NonC*), challenge; **droit de ~** right to challenge

récuser [Rekyze] ▶ conjug 1 ◀ [1] VT [+ *témoin, juge, juré*] to challenge, object to; [+ *témoignage*] to impugn, challenge; [+ *accusa-*

tion] to deny, refute; (*Jur*) **~ un argument** to make objection to an argument; **~ la compétence d'un tribunal** to challenge the competence of a court [2] **se récuser** VPR to decline to give an opinion *ou* accept responsibility; (*Jur*) [*juge*] to decline to act

recyclable [R(ə)siklabl] ADJ recyclable

recyclage [R(ə)siklaʒ] NM [a] [*élève*] reorientation; [*employé*] retraining; **stage de ~** retraining *ou* refresher course [b] (*Tech*) recycling [c] (*Fin*) reinvestment; [*argent sale*] money-laundering

recycler [R(ə)sikle] ▶ conjug 1 ◀ [1] VT [a] [+ *élève*] to reorientate; [+ *employé*] (*dans son domaine*) to send on a refresher course; (*pour un nouveau métier*) to retrain [b] (*Tech*) [+ *déchets, eaux usées*] to recycle; **papier recyclé** recycled paper [c] (*Fin*) (= *réinvestir*) to reinvest; (= *blanchir*) to launder [2] **se recycler** VPR [*personne*] (*dans son domaine*) to go on a refresher course; (*pour un nouveau métier*) to retrain; **elle s'est recyclée dans la restauration** she changed direction and went into catering; **je ne peux pas me ~ à mon âge** I can't learn a new job *ou* trade at my age; **se ~ en permanence** to be constantly updating one's skills; **il a besoin de se ~ !*** he needs to get with it!*

rédacteur, -trice [RedaktœR, tRis] [1] NM,F (*Presse*) sub-editor; [*article*] writer; [*loi*] drafter; [*encyclopédie, dictionnaire*] compiler, editor; **~ politique/économique** political/economics editor; **~ sportif** sports editor, sportswriter [2] COMP ▸ **rédacteur en chef** editor ▸ **rédacteur publicitaire** copywriter ▸ **rédacteur technique** technical writer

rédaction [Redaksjɔ̃] NF [a] [*contrat, projet*] drafting, drawing up; [*thèse, article*] writing; [*encyclopédie, dictionnaire*] compiling, compilation; (*Admin, Jur*) wording; **ce n'est que la première ~** it's only the first draft; **~ technique** technical writing [b] (*Presse*) (= *personnel*) editorial staff; (= *bureaux*) editorial offices → **salle, secrétaire** [c] (*Scol*) essay, composition

rédactionnel, -elle [Redaksjɔnɛl] ADJ editorial

reddition [Redisjɔ̃] NF (*Mil*) surrender; [*comptes*] rendering; **~ sans conditions** unconditional surrender

redécoupage [Rədekupaʒ] NM **effectuer un ~ électoral** to make boundary changes

redécouverte [R(ə)dekuvɛRt] NF rediscovery

redécouvrir [R(ə)dekuvRiR] ▶ conjug 18 ◀ VT to rediscover

redéfaire [R(ə)defɛR] ▶ conjug 60 ◀ VT [+ *paquet, lacet*] to undo again; [+ *manteau*] to take off again; [+ *couture*] to unpick again; **le nœud s'est redéfait** the knot has come undone *ou* come untied again

redéfinir [R(ə)definiR] ▶ conjug 2 ◀ VT to redefine

redéfinition [R(ə)definisjɔ̃] NF redefinition

redemander [Rəd(ə)mɑ̃de, R(ə)dəmɑ̃de] ▶ conjug 1 ◀ VT [+ *adresse*] to ask again for; [+ *aliment*] to ask for more; [+ *bouteille*] to ask for another; **redemande-le-lui** (*une nouvelle fois*) ask him for it again; (*récupère-le*) ask him to give it back to you, ask him for it back; **~ du poulet** to ask for more chicken *ou* another helping of chicken; (*iro*) **en ~*** to ask for more*

redémarrage [R(ə)demaRaʒ] NM [a] [*moteur, réacteur, usine*] starting up again [b] (= *reprise*) [*économie, activité, ventes*] resurgence, upturn; [*inflation*] resurgence; [*croissance*] pickup (**de** in)

redémarrer [R(ə)demaRe] ▶ conjug 1 ◀ VI [a] [*moteur*] to start up again; [*véhicule*] to move off again; [*réacteur*] to be started up again; **le chauffeur a redémarré au feu vert** the driver moved *ou* drove off again when the light turned green [b] [*processus*] to start again;

[*économie*] to get going again, take off again; [*croissance*] to pick up again; [*inflation*] to rise again; **il tente de faire ~ son entreprise** he's trying to get his company started again

rédempteur, -trice [ʀedɑ̃ptœʀ, tʀis] **1** ADJ redemptive, redeeming **2** NM,F redeemer

rédemption [ʀedɑ̃psjɔ̃] NF **a** (*Rel*) redemption **b** (*Jur*) [*rente*] redemption; [*droit*] recovery

redéploiement [ʀ(ə)deplwamɑ̃] NM [*armée, effectifs*] redeployment; [*groupe industriel, activités, crédits*] restructuring

redéployer [ʀ(ə)deplwaje] ▸ conjug 8 ◂ **1** VT [+ *efforts, ressources, troupes*] to redeploy; [+ *crédits, effectifs*] to redeploy, reassign; **l'entreprise a redéployé ses activités autour de trois pôles** the company has reorganized its operations around three core areas; **un nouveau musée a été construit pour ~ l'ensemble des collections** a new museum has been built so that the collection can be displayed in a new way **2** **se redéployer** VPR [*armée, effectifs*] to redeploy; [*entreprise*] to reorganize its operations

redescendre [ʀ(ə)desɑ̃dʀ] ▸ conjug 41 ◂ **1** VT (*avec aux avoir*) **a** [+ *escalier*] to go ou come (back) down again; **la balle a redescendu la pente** the ball rolled down the slope again ou rolled back down the slope **b** [+ *objet*] (*à la cave*) to take downstairs again; (*du grenier*) to bring downstairs again; (*d'un rayon*) to get ou lift (back) down again; (*d'un crochet*) to take (back) down again; **~ qch d'un cran** to put sth one notch lower down **2** VI (*avec aux être*) **a** (*dans l'escalier*) to go ou come (back) downstairs again; (*d'une colline*) to go ou come (back) down again; **l'alpiniste redescend** (*à pied*) the mountaineer climbs down again; (*avec une corde*) the mountaineer ropes down again; **~ de voiture** to get ou climb out of the car again **b** [*ascenseur, avion*] to go down again; [*marée*] to go out again, go back out; [*chemin*] to go ou slope down again; [*baromètre, fièvre*] to fall again

redevable [ʀ(ə)dəvabl] ADJ **a** (*Fin*) **être ~ de 100 F à qn** to owe sb 100 francs; **~ de l'impôt** liable for tax **b** (*fig*) **être ~ à qn de** [+ *aide, service*] to be indebted to sb for; **je vous suis ~ de la vie** I owe you my life

redevance [ʀ(ə)dəvɑ̃s] NF **a** (= *impôt*) tax; (*Radio, TV*) annual fee paid to the government to cover the costs of public television, licence fee (*Brit*); (*Téléc*) rental charge **b** = *bail, rente*] dues, fees; (*touchée par l'inventeur*) royalties

redevenir [ʀ(ə)dəvniʀ] ▸ conjug 22 ◂ VI to become again; **le temps est redevenu glacial** the weather has become ou gone very cold again; **il est redevenu lui-même** he is his old self again

redevoir [ʀ(ə)dəvwaʀ] ▸ conjug 28 ◂ VT **il me redoit 10 000 F** he still owes me 10,000 francs

rédhibitoire [ʀediƀitwaʀ] ADJ [*défaut*] crippling, damning; [*conditions*] totally unacceptable; **un échec n'est pas forcément ~** one failure does not necessarily spell the end of everything; **sa mauvaise foi est vraiment ~** his insincerity puts him quite beyond the pale; **il est un peu menteur, mais ce n'est pas ~** he's a bit of a liar but that doesn't rule him out altogether; (*Jur*) **vice ~** latent defect

rediffuser [ʀ(ə)difyze] ▸ conjug 1 ◂ VT [+ *émission*] to repeat, rerun

rediffusion [ʀ(ə)difyzjɔ̃] NF [*émission*] repeat, rerun

rédiger [ʀediʒe] ▸ conjug 3 ◂ VT [+ *article, lettre*] to write, compose; (*à partir de notes*) to write up; [+ *encyclopédie, dictionnaire*] to compile, write; [+ *contrat*] to draw up, draft; **bien rédigé** well-written

redingote [ʀ(ə)dɛ̃gɔt] NF (*Hist*) frock coat; [*femme*] **manteau ~** fitted coat

redire [ʀ(ə)diʀ] ▸ conjug 37 ◂ VT **a** [+ *affirmation*] to say again, repeat; [+ *histoire*] to tell again, repeat; [+ *médisance*] to (go and) tell, repeat; **~ qch à qn** to say sth to sb again, tell sb sth again, repeat sth to sb; **il redit toujours la même chose** he's always saying ou he keeps saying the same thing; **je te l'ai dit et redit** I've told you that over and over again ou time and time again; **je lui ai redit cent fois que ...** I've told him countless times that ...; **redis-le après moi** repeat after me; **ne le lui redites pas** don't go and tell him ou don't go and repeat (to him) what I've said; **il ne se le fait pas ~ deux fois** he doesn't need telling ou to be told twice

b **avoir** ou **trouver à ~ à qch** to find fault with sth; **il trouve à ~ à tout** he finds fault with everything, he's always ready to criticize; **on ne peut rien trouver à ~ là-dessus** there's nothing to say ou you can say to that; **je ne vois rien à ~ (à cela)** I don't have any complaint(s) about that, I can't see anything wrong with that

rediscuter [ʀ(ə)diskyte] ▸ conjug 1 ◂ VT to discuss again, have further discussion on

redistribuer [ʀ(ə)distʀibɥe] ▸ conjug 1 ◂ VT [+ *biens*] to redistribute; [+ *emplois, rôles, tâches*] to reallocate; [+ *cartes*] to deal again; **cet événement va ~ les cartes dans la bataille électorale** this event will change the face of the electoral battle

redistributif, -ive [ʀ(ə)distʀibytif, iv] ADJ (*Écon*) [*effet, fiscalité*] redistributive

redistribution [ʀ(ə)distʀibysjɔ̃] NF [*richesses, revenus, pouvoirs*] redistribution; [*cartes*] redeal; **la ~ des cartes dans le secteur des télécommunications** the reorganization of the telecommunications sector

redite [ʀ(ə)dit] NF (needless) repetition

redondance [ʀ(ə)dɔ̃dɑ̃s] NF **a** [*style*] redundancy (*NonC*), diffuseness (*NonC*); (*Ling, Ordin*) redundancy (*NonC*) **b** (= *expression*) unnecessary ou superfluous expression

redondant, e [ʀ(ə)dɔ̃dɑ̃, ɑ̃t] ADJ [*mot*] superfluous, redundant; [*style*] redundant, diffuse; (*Ling, Ordin*) redundant

redonner [ʀ(ə)dɔne] ▸ conjug 1 ◂ VT **a** (= *rendre*) [+ *objet, bien*] to give back, return; [+ *forme, idéal*] to give back, give again; [+ *espoir, énergie*] to restore, give back; **l'air frais te redonnera des couleurs** the fresh air will put some colour back in your cheeks ou bring some colour back to your cheeks; **cela te redonnera des forces** that will build your strength back up ou put new strength into you ou restore your strength; **cette crème ~a du tonus à votre peau** this cream will revitalize your skin; **~ de la confiance/du courage à qn** to give sb new ou fresh confidence/courage, restore sb's confidence/courage; **ce voyage m'a redonné goût à la vie** this trip restored my appetite for life; **~ la parole à qn** to let sb speak again; **~ vie à un quartier/un village** to give an area/a village a new lease of life; **ça a redonné le même résultat** it produced the same result as before

b (= *donner de nouveau*) [+ *adresse*] to give again; [+ *pain, eau*] to give some more; **~ une couche de peinture** to give another coat of paint; **redonne-toi un coup de peigne** give your hair another quick comb; **tu peux me ~ de la viande/des carottes ?** can you give me some more meat/some more carrots? ou another helping of meat/of carrots?; **redonne-lui une bière/à boire** give him another beer/another drink

c (*Théât*) to put on again

redorer [ʀ(ə)dɔʀe] ▸ conjug 1 ◂ VT to regild; **~ son blason** [*famille*] to boost the family fortunes by marrying into money; [*entreprise, émission*] to regain prestige

redormir [ʀ(ə)dɔʀmiʀ] ▸ conjug 16 ◂ VI to sleep some more

redoublant, e [ʀ(ə)dublɑ̃, ɑ̃t] NM,F (*Scol*) pupil who is repeating (ou has repeated) a year at school, repeater (*US*)

redoublement [ʀ(ə)dubləmɑ̃] NM (*Ling*) reduplication; (= *accroissement*) increase (**de** in), intensification (**de** of); **je vous demande un ~ d'attention** I need you to pay even closer attention, I need your increased attention; **avec un ~ de larmes** with a fresh flood of tears; (*Scol*) **le ~ permet aux élèves faibles de rattraper** repeating a year ou a grade (*US*) ou being kept down (*Brit*) helps the weaker pupils to catch up

redoubler [ʀ(ə)duble] ▸ conjug 1 ◂ **1** VT **a** (= *accroître*) [+ *joie, douleur, craintes*] to increase, intensify; [+ *efforts*] to step up, redouble; **frapper à coups redoublés** to bang twice as hard, bang even harder; **hurler à cris redoublés** to yell twice as loud

b (*Ling*) [+ *syllabe*] to reduplicate; (*Couture*) [+ *vêtement*] to reline; (*Scol*) **~ (une classe)** to repeat a year ou a grade (*US*), be held back ou kept down (*Brit*) a year

2 **redoubler de** VT INDIR **~ d'efforts** to step up ou redouble one's efforts, try extra hard; **~ de prudence/de vigilance** to be extra careful/vigilant, be doubly careful/vigilant; **le vent redouble de violence** the wind is getting even stronger ou is blowing even more strongly

3 VI (*gén*) to increase, intensify; [*froid, douleur*] to become twice as bad, get even worse; [*vent*] to become twice as strong; [*joie*] to become even more intense; [*larmes*] to flow ou fall even faster; [*cris*] to get even louder ou twice as loud

redoutable [ʀ(ə)dutabl] ADJ [*arme, adversaire, concurrence*] formidable, fearsome; [*maladie*] dreadful; [*problème*] formidable, dreadful; [*question*] tough, difficult; **son charme ~** his devastating charm; **elle est d'une efficacité ~** she's frighteningly efficient

redoutablement [ʀ(ə)dutabləmɑ̃] ADV [*agile, efficace*] formidably; [*dangereux*] extremely; **un couteau ~ effilé** a dangerously sharp knife

redoute [ʀədut] NF (*Mil*) redoubt

redouter [ʀ(ə)dute] ▸ conjug 1 ◂ VT [+ *ennemi, avenir, conséquence*] to dread, fear; **je redoute de l'apprendre** I dread finding out about it; **je redoute qu'il ne l'apprenne** I dread his finding out about it

redoux [ʀədu] NM (= *temps plus chaud*) spell of milder weather; (= *dégel*) thaw

redresse [ʀ(ə)dʀɛs] **◆ à la redresse:**† LOC ADJ [*personne*] tough

redressement [ʀ(ə)dʀɛsmɑ̃] NM **a** [*poteau*] setting upright, righting; [*tige*] straightening (up); [*tôle*] straightening out, knocking out; [*courant*] rectification; [*buste, corps*] straightening up **b** [*bateau*] righting; [*roue, voiture, avion*] straightening up **c** [*situation*] (= *action*) putting right; (= *résultat*) recovery **d** [*économie*] recovery, upturn; [*entreprise*] recovery, turnaround; **plan de ~** recovery package; **~ économique/financier** economic/financial recovery; (*Jur*) **être mis ou placé en ~ judiciaire** to be put into receivership ou administration **e** [*erreur*] righting, putting right; [*abus, torts*] righting, redress; [*jugement*] correcting; (*Fin*) **~ fiscal** tax adjustment → **maison**

redresser [ʀ(ə)dʀɛse] ▸ conjug 1 ◂ **1** VT **a** (= *relever*) [+ *arbre, statue, poteau*] to right, set upright; [+ *tige, poutre*] to straighten (up); [+ *tôle cabossée*] to straighten out, knock out; [+ *courant*] to rectify; (*Opt*) [+ *image*] to straighten; **~ un malade sur son oreiller** to sit ou prop a patient up against his pillow; **~ les épaules** to straighten one's shoulders, throw one's shoulders back; **~ le corps (en arrière)** to stand up straight, straighten up; **~ la tête** (*lit*) to hold up *ou* lift (up) one's head; (*fig* = *être fier*) to hold one's head up high; (*fig* = *se révolter*) to show signs of rebellion; **se faire ~ les dents** to have one's teeth straightened

[b] (= *rediriger*) [+ *roue, voiture*] to straighten up; [+ *bateau*] to right; [+ *avion*] to lift the nose of, straighten up; **redresse !** straighten up! → **barre**

[c] (= *rétablir*) [+ *économie*] to redress, put *ou* set right; [+ *entreprise déficitaire*] to turn round; [+ *situation*] to put right, straighten out; **~ le pays** to get *ou* put the country on its feet again

[d] (*littér* = *corriger*) [+ *erreur*] to rectify, put right, redress; [+ *torts, abus*] to right, redress; **~ le jugement de qn** to correct sb's opinion

[2] **se redresser** VPR [a] (= *se mettre assis*) to sit up; (= *se mettre debout*) to stand up; (= *se mettre droit*) to stand up straight; (*après s'être courbé*) to straighten up; (*fig* = *être fier*) to hold one's head up high; **redresse-toi !** sit *ou* stand up straight!

[b] [*bateau*] to right itself; [*avion*] to flatten out, straighten up; [*voiture*] to straighten up; [*pays, économie*] to recover; [*situation*] to correct itself, put itself to rights

[c] [*coin replié, cheveux*] to stick up; **les blés, couchés par le vent, se redressèrent** the corn which had been blown flat by the wind straightened up again *ou* stood up straight again

redresseur [ʀ(ə)dʀɛsœʀ] [1] NM [a] (*Hist, iro*) **~ de torts** righter of wrongs; **~ d'entreprises** corporate rescuer [b] (*Élec*) rectifier [2] ADJ M [*muscle*] erector; [*prisme*] erecting

réduc* [ʀedyk] NF ABRÉV = **réduction b**

réducteur, -trice [ʀedyktœʀ, tʀis] [1] ADJ [a] (*Chim*) reducing; [*engrenage*] reduction [b] (*péj* = *simplificateur*) [*analyse, concept*] simplistic [2] NM (*Chim*) reducing agent; (*Photo*) reducer; **~ (de vitesse)** speed reducer; **~ de tête** head shrinker

réductibilité [ʀedyktibilite] NF reducibility

réductible [ʀedyktibl] ADJ (*Chim, Math*) reducible (**en, à** to); (*Méd*) [*fracture*] which can be reduced (*SPÉC*) *ou* set; [*quantité*] which can be reduced

réduction [ʀedyksjɔ̃] NF [a] (= *diminution*) [*dépenses, personnel, production, déficit*] reduction, cut (**de** in); **~ de salaire/d'impôts** wage/tax cut, reduction *ou* cut in wages/in taxes; **~ du temps de travail** reduction in working time *ou* hours; **obtenir une ~ de peine** to get a reduction in one's sentence, get one's sentence cut [b] (= *rabais*) discount, reduction; **faire/obtenir une ~** to give/get a discount *ou* a reduction; **une ~ de 10%** a 10% discount *ou* reduction; **~ (pour les) étudiants/chômeurs** concessions for students/the unemployed; (*Comm*) **carte de ~** discount card; **bénéficier d'une carte de ~ dans les transports** to have a concessionary fare *ou* a discount travel card [c] (= *reproduction*) [*plan, photo*] reduction; (*fig*) **en ~** in miniature [d] (*Méd*) [*fracture*] reduction (*SPÉC*), setting; (*Bio, Chim, Math*) reduction [e] (*Culin*) reduction (by boiling) [f] (*Mil*) [*ville*] capture; [*rebelles*] quelling

réductionnisme [ʀedyksjɔnism] NM reductionism

réductionniste [ʀedyksjɔnist] ADJ, NMF reductionist

réduire [ʀedɥiʀ] ▸ conjug 38◂ [1] VT [a] (= *diminuer*) [+ *hauteur, vitesse, temps de travail, inégalités*] to reduce; [+ *peine, impôt, consommation*] to reduce, cut; [+ *prix*] to reduce, cut, bring down; [+ *pression*] to reduce, lessen; [+ *texte*] to shorten, cut; [+ *production*] to reduce, cut (back), lower; [+ *dépenses*] to reduce, cut, cut down *ou* back (on); [+ *risques*] to reduce, lower; [+ *voilure*] to shorten; [+ *tête coupée*] to

shrink; **il va falloir ~ notre train de vie** we'll have to cut down on *ou* curb our spending; **~ petit à petit l'autorité de qn/la portée d'une loi** to chip away at sb's authority/a law

[b] (= *reproduire*) [+ *dessin, plan*] to reduce, scale down; [+ *photographie*] to reduce, make smaller; [+ *figure géométrique*] to scale down

[c] (= *contraindre*) **~ à** [+ *soumission, désespoir*] to reduce to; **~ qn à l'obéissance/en esclavage** to reduce sb to obedience/to slavery; **après son accident, il a été réduit à l'inaction** since his accident he's been unable to get about; **il en est réduit à mendier** he has been reduced to begging

[d] **~ à** (= *ramener à*) to reduce to, bring down to; (= *limiter à*) to limit to, confine to; **~ des fractions à un dénominateur commun** to reduce *ou* bring down fractions to a common denominator; **~ des éléments différents à un type commun** to reduce different elements to one general type; **je réduirai mon étude à quelques aspects** I shall limit *ou* confine my study to a few aspects; **~ à sa plus simple expression** (*Math*) [+ *polynôme*] to reduce to its simplest expression; (*fig*) [+ *mobilier, repas*] to reduce to the absolute *ou* bare minimum; **~ qch à néant** *ou* **à rien** *ou* **à zéro** to reduce sth to nothing

[e] (= *transformer*) **~ en** to reduce to; **réduisez les grammes en milligrammes** convert the grammes to milligrammes; **~ qch en miettes/en morceaux** to smash sth to tiny pieces/to pieces; **~ qch en bouillie** to crush *ou* reduce sth to a pulp; **~ qch en poudre** to grind *ou* reduce sth to a powder; **sa maison était réduite en cendres** his house was reduced to ashes *ou* burnt to the ground; **les cadavres étaient réduits en charpie** the bodies were torn to shreds

[f] (*Méd*) [+ *fracture*] to set, reduce (*SPÉC*); (*Chim*) [+ *minerai, oxyde*] to reduce; (*Culin*) [+ *sauce*] to reduce (by boiling)

[g] (*Mil*) [+ *place forte*] to capture; [+ *rebelles*] to quell; **~ l'opposition** to silence the opposition

[2] VI (*Culin*) [*sauce*] to reduce; **faire** *ou* **laisser ~ la sauce** to cook *ou* simmer the sauce to reduce it; **les épinards réduisent à la cuisson** spinach shrinks when you cook it

[3] **se réduire** VPR [a] **se ~** [*affaire, incident*] to boil down to, amount to; [*somme, quantité*] to amount to; **mon profit se réduit à bien peu de chose** the profit I've made amounts to very little; **notre action ne se réduit pas à quelques discours** the action we are taking involves more than *ou* isn't just a matter of a few speeches; **je me réduirai à quelques exemples** I'll limit *ou* confine myself to a few examples, I'll just select *ou* quote a few examples

[b] **se ~ en** to be reduced to; **se ~ en cendres** to be burnt *ou* reduced to ashes; **se ~ en poussière** to be reduced *ou* crumble away *ou* turn to dust; **se ~ en bouillie** to be crushed to a pulp

[c] (= *dépenser moins*) to cut down on one's spending *ou* expenditure

réduit, e [ʀedɥi, it] (*ptp de* **réduire**) [1] ADJ [a] (= *petit*) small; **de taille** *ou* **dimension ~e** small-scale; **reproduction à échelle ~e** small-scale reproduction; **un nombre ~ de ...** a small number of ...; **métal à teneur en plomb ~e** metal with a low lead content → **modèle** [b] (= *diminué*) [*tarif, prix, taux*] reduced; [*délai*] shorter; [*moyens, débouchés*] limited; **livres à prix ~s** cut-price books, books at a reduced price *ou* at reduced prices; **avancer à vitesse ~e** to move forward at low speed *ou* at a reduced speed; **maintenant ils produisent ces voitures en nombre ~** they're now producing a smaller number of these cars *ou* fewer of these cars; **travail à temps ~** short-time work; **chômeur ayant exercé une activité ~e** unemployed person who has worked a limited

number of hours; **« service ~ le dimanche »** "reduced service on Sundays"; **tête ~e** shrunken head

[2] NM (= *pièce*) tiny room; (*péj*) cubbyhole, poky little hole; (= *recoin*) recess; (*Mil*) enclave; [*maquisards*] hideout

rééchelonnement [ʀeeʃ(ə)lɔnmɑ̃] NM [*dettes*] rescheduling

rééchelonner [ʀeeʃ(ə)lɔne] ▸ conjug 1◂ VT [+ *dettes*] to reschedule

réécrire [ʀeekʀiʀ] ▸ conjug 39◂ VT [+ *roman, inscription*] to rewrite; [+ *lettre*] to write again; (*fig*) **~ l'histoire** to rewrite history; **il m'a réécrit** he has written to me again, he has written me another letter

réécriture [ʀeekʀityʀ] NF rewriting; (*Ling*) **règle de ~** rewrite *ou* rewriting rule

réédification [ʀeedifikasjɔ̃] NF rebuilding, reconstruction

réédifier [ʀeedifje] ▸ conjug 7◂ VT to rebuild, reconstruct; (*fig*) to rebuild

rééditer [ʀeedite] ▸ conjug 1◂ VT (*Typo*) to republish; (* *fig*) to repeat

réédition [ʀeedisjɔ̃] NF (*Typo*) new edition; (* *fig*) repetition, repeat

rééducation [ʀeedykasjɔ̃] NF [a] (*Méd*) [*malade*] rehabilitation; [*membre*] re-education; (= *spécialité médicale*) physiotherapy, physical therapy (*US*); **faire de la ~** to undergo *ou* have physiotherapy, have physical therapy (*US*); **exercice de ~** physiotherapy exercise; **~ de la parole** speech therapy; **centre de ~** rehabilitation centre [b] (*gén, lit, Pol*) re-education; [*délinquant*] rehabilitation

rééduquer [ʀeedyke] ▸ conjug 1◂ VT [a] (*Méd*) [+ *malade*] to rehabilitate; [+ *membre*] to re-educate [b] (*gén, Pol, lit*) to re-educate; [+ *délinquant*] to rehabilitate

réel, -elle [ʀeel] [1] ADJ [a] [*fait, chef, existence, avantage*] real; [*besoin, cause*] real, true; [*danger, plaisir, amélioration, douleur*] real, genuine; **faire de réelles économies** to make significant *ou* real savings; **son héros est très ~** his hero is very lifelike *ou* realistic [b] (*Math, Opt, Philo, Phys*) real; (*Fin*) [*valeur, salaire*] real, actual; **taux d'intérêt ~** effective interest rate [2] NM **le ~** reality, the real

réélection [ʀeelɛksjɔ̃] NF re-election

rééligibilité [ʀeeliʒibilite] NF re-eligibility

rééligible [ʀeeliʒibl] ADJ re-eligible

réélire [ʀeeliʀ] ▸ conjug 43◂ VT to re-elect; **ne pas ~ qn** to vote sb out

réellement [ʀeelmɑ̃] ADV really, truly; **je suis ~ désolé** I'm really *ou* truly sorry; **ça m'a ~ consterné/aidé** that really worried/helped me, that was a genuine worry/help to me; **~, tu exagères !** really *ou* honestly, you're going too far!

réembarquer [ʀeɑ̃baʀke] ▸ conjug 1◂ VTI = **rembarquer**

réembaucher [ʀeɑ̃boʃe] ▸ conjug 1◂ VT to take on again, re-employ; **l'entreprise réembauchera à l'automne prochain** the company will start hiring again next autumn

réembobiner [ʀeɑ̃bɔbine] ▸ conjug 1◂ VT = **rembobiner**

réemploi [ʀeɑ̃plwa] NM [a] [*méthode, produit*] re-use [b] (= *réinvestissement*) reinvestment [c] (= *nouvelle embauche*) re-employment

réemployer [ʀeɑ̃plwaje] ▸ conjug 8◂ VT [a] [+ *méthode, produit*] to re-use [b] (= *réinvestir*) to reinvest [c] (= *réembaucher*) to re-employ, take back on

réemprunter [ʀeɑ̃pʀœ̃te] ▸ conjug 1◂ VT [a] [+ *argent, objet*] (*une nouvelle fois*) to borrow again; (*davantage*) to borrow more [b] **~ le même chemin** to take the same road again, go the same way again

réengagement [ʀeɑ̃gaʒmɑ̃] NM = **rengagement**

réengager [ʀeɑ̃gaʒe] ▸ conjug 3◂ VT = **rengager**

réenregistrable [ReāR(ə)ʒistrabl] ADJ [CD] re-recordable

réenregistrer [ReāR(ə)ʒistre] ▶conjug 1◀ VT [+ musique, titre] to re-record; **j'ai réenregistré un documentaire par-dessus le film** I recorded a documentary over the film

réentendre [ReātādR] ▶conjug 41◀ VT to hear again

rééquilibrage [Reekilibraʒ] NM [chargement] readjustment; [budget, finances, comptes] rebalancing; [pouvoirs] restoring the balance; (Aut) **le ~ des roues** balancing the wheels; **le ~ des forces au sein du gouvernement** the redistribution of power within the government

rééquilibrer [Reekilibre] ▶conjug 1◀ VT [+ chargement] to readjust; (Aut) [+ roues] to balance; [+ économie] to restabilize, find a new equilibrium for; [+ budget, comptes, finances] to rebalance; **~ les pouvoirs/la balance commerciale** to restore the balance of power/ the balance of trade

réescompte [Reeskɔ̃t] NM rediscount

réescompter [Reeskɔ̃te] ▶conjug 1◀ VT to rediscount

réessayer [Reeseje] ▶conjug 8◀ VT [+ robe] to try on again; [+ recette] to try again; **je réessaierai plus tard** I'll try again later

réétudier [Reetydje] ▶conjug 7◀ VT [+ dossier, question] to reexamine

réévaluation [Reevalɥasjɔ̃] NF [a] [monnaie] revaluation; [salaire] (à la hausse) upgrading; (à la baisse) downgrading [b] [situation, place, méthode] reappraisal, reassessment

réévaluer [Reevalɥe] ▶conjug 1◀ VT [a] [+ monnaie] to revalue (par rapport à against); [+ salaire] (à la hausse) to upgrade; (à la baisse) to downgrade [b] [+ situation, place, méthode] to reappraise, reassess

réexamen [Reegzamē] NM [malade] re-examination; [problème, situation, dossier, candidature, décision] reconsideration; **demander un ~ de la situation** to ask for the situation to be reconsidered

réexaminer [Reegzamine] ▶conjug 1◀ VT [+ malade] to re-examine; [+ problème, situation, candidature, décision] to examine again, reconsider

réexpédier [Reekspedje] ▶conjug 7◀ VT [a] (= retourner, renvoyer) to return, send back; **on l'a réexpédié dans son pays** he was sent back to his country [b] (= faire suivre) to send on, forward

réexpédition [Reekspedisjɔ̃] NF [a] (= retour) returning [b] (= fait de faire suivre) forwarding; **enveloppe/frais de ~** forwarding envelope/ charges

réexportation [Reekspɔrtasjɔ̃] NF re-export

réexporter [Reekspɔrte] ▶conjug 1◀ VT to re-export

réf. (ABRÉV = **référence**) ref.

refaçonner [Rəfasɔne] ▶conjug 1◀ VT [+ sculpture] to remodel; [+ émission] to redesign; [+ phrase, texte] to rework

réfaction [Refaksjɔ̃] NF (Comm) allowance, rebate

refaire [Rəfɛr] ▶conjug 60◀ [1] VT [a] (= recommencer) (gén) [+ travail, dessin, maquillage] to redo, do again; [+ voyage] to make ou do again; [+ pansement] to put on ou do up again, renew; [+ article, devoir] to rewrite; [+ nœud, paquet] to do up again, tie again, retie; **elle a refait sa vie avec lui** she started a new life ou she made a fresh start (in life) with him; **il m'a refait une visite** he paid me another call, he called on me again ou on another occasion; **il refait (du) soleil** the sun has come out again; **tu refais toujours la même faute** you always make ou you keep on making ou repeating the same mistake; **il a refait de la fièvre/de l'asthme** he has had another bout of fever/of asthma; **il refait du vélo** he has taken

up cycling again; **il va falloir tout ~ depuis le début** it will have to be done all over again, we'll have to start again from scratch; **si vous refaites du bruit** if you start making a noise again, if there's any further noise from you; **il va falloir ~ de la soupe** we'll have to make some more soup; **je vais me ~ une tasse de café** I'm going to make myself another cup of coffee; **son éducation est à ~** he'll have to be re-educated; (en parlant) **~ le monde** to try to solve the world's problems; **si c'était à ~!** if I had to do it again! ou begin again!; (Cartes) **à ~** re-deal

[b] (= retaper) [+ toit] to redo, renew; [+ route] to repair; [+ mur] to rebuild, repair; [+ meuble] to do up, renovate, restore; [+ chambre] (gén) to do up, redecorate; (en peinture) to repaint; (en papier) to repaper; **on refera les peintures/ les papiers au printemps** we'll repaint/repaper in the spring, we'll redo the paintwork/the wallpaper in the spring; **nous allons faire ~ le carrelage du salon** we're going to have the tiles in the lounge done again; **se faire ~ le nez** to have one's nose remodeled, have a nose job*; **~ qch à neuf** to do sth up like new; **~ ses forces/sa santé** to recover one's strength/one's health; **à son âge, tu ne referas pas** at her age, you won't change her

[c] (* = duper) to take in; **il a été refait** ◊ **il s'est fait ~** he has been taken in ou had*; **il m'a refait de 50 F** he did* ou diddled* (Brit) me out of 50 francs

[2] **se refaire** VPR (= retrouver la santé) to recuperate, recover; (= regagner son argent) to make up one's losses; **se ~ une santé dans le Midi** to (go and) recuperate in the south of France, recover ou regain one's health in the south of France; **se ~ une beauté** to freshen up; **que voulez-vous, on ne se refait pas!** what can you expect — you can't change how you're made!* ou you can't change your own character! → **virginité**

réfection [Refɛksjɔ̃] NF [route] repairing; [mur, maison] rebuilding, repairing; **la ~ de la route va durer trois semaines** the road repairs ou the repairs to the road will take three weeks

réfectoire [Refɛktwar] NM (Scol) dining hall, canteen; (Rel) refectory; [usine] canteen

refend [Rəfā] NM **mur de ~** supporting (partition) wall; **bois de ~** wood in planks

référé [Refere] NM (Jur) (procédure en) ~ summary proceedings; (arrêt ou jugement en) ~ interim ruling; **assigner qn en ~** to apply for summary judgment against sb; **juge des ~s** judge in chambers

référence [Referās] NF [a] (= renvoi) reference; (en bas de page) reference, footnote; **par ~ à** in reference to; **en ~ à votre courrier du 2 juin** with reference to your letter of June 2nd; **l'auteur cité en ~** (plus haut) the abovementioned author; **ouvrage/numéro de ~** reference book/number; **période/prix de ~** base ou reference period/price; (Fin) **taux de ~** benchmark ou reference rate; **prendre qch comme point de ~** to use sth as a point of reference; **faire ~ à** to refer to, make (a) reference to; **servir de ~** [chiffres, indice, taux] to be used as a benchmark; [personne] to be a role model → **année**

[b] (= recommandation) (gén) reference; **cet employé a-t-il des ~s?** (d'un employeur) has this employee got a reference? ou a testimonial? (Brit); (de plusieurs employeurs) has this employee got references? ou testimonials? (Brit); **lettre de ~** letter of reference, testimonial (Brit); **il a un doctorat, c'est quand même une ~** he has a doctorate which is not a bad recommendation ou which is something to go by; (iro) **ce n'est pas une ~** that's no recommendation

[c] (Ling) reference

référencer [Referāse] ▶conjug 3◀ VT to reference

référendaire [Referādɛr] [1] ADJ (pour un référendum) referendum (épith) [2] NM (conseiller) ~ public auditor

référendum [Referēdɔm] NM referendum; **faire ou organiser un ~** to hold a referendum

référent [Referā] NM referent

référentiel, -elle [Referāsjɛl] [1] ADJ referential [2] NM system of reference

référer [Refere] ▶conjug 6◀ [1] **en référer à** VT INDIR **en ~ à qn** to refer ou submit a matter ou question to sb [2] **se référer** VPR **se ~ à** (= consulter) to consult; (= faire référence à) to refer to; (= s'en remettre à) to refer to; **si l'on s'en réfère à son dernier article** if we refer to his most recent article

refermer [Rəfɛrme] ▶conjug 1◀ [1] VT to close ou shut again; **peux-tu ~ la porte?** can you close ou shut the door?; (fig) **~ un dossier** to close a file [2] **se refermer** VPR [plaie] to close up, heal up; [fleur] to close up (again); [fenêtre, porte] to close ou shut (again); **le piège se referma sur lui** the trap closed ou shut on him

refiler: [Rəfile] ▶conjug 1◀ VT to give (à qn to sb); **refile-moi ton livre** let me have your book, give me your book; **il m'a refilé la rougeole** I've caught measles off him, he has passed his measles on to me; **il s'est fait ~ une fausse pièce** someone has palmed ou fobbed a forged coin off on him* → **bébé**

refinancement [Rəfināsmā] NM refinancing; **plan de ~** refinancing plan

réfléchi, e [Refleʃi] (ptp de **réfléchir**) [1] ADJ [a] (= pondéré) [action] well-thought-out (épith), well thought out (attrib), well-considered; [personne, air] thoughtful; **tout bien ~** after careful consideration ou thought, having weighed up all the pros and cons; **c'est tout ~** my mind is made up, I've made my mind up [b] (Gram) reflexive [c] (Opt) reflected [2] NM (Gram) reflexive

réfléchir [Refleʃir] ▶conjug 2◀ [1] VI to think, reflect; **prends le temps de ~** take time to reflect ou to think about it ou to consider it; **cela donne à ~** it's food for thought, it makes you think; **cet accident, ça fait ~** an accident like that makes you think; **il faut ~ avant d'agir** you must think before you act; **je demande à ~** I'd like time to consider it ou to think things over; **elle a accepté sans ~** she accepted without thinking; **la prochaine fois, tâche de ~** next time just try and think a bit ou try and use your brains a bit; **j'ai longuement réfléchi et je suis arrivé à cette conclusion** I have given it a lot of thought and have come to this conclusion

[2] **réfléchir à** ou **sur qch** VT INDIR to think about sth, turn sth over in one's mind; **réfléchissez-y** think about it, think it over; **réfléchis à ce que tu vas faire** think about what you're going to do; **à bien y ~ ...** when you really think about it ...

[3] VT [a] **~ que** to realize that; **il n'avait pas réfléchi qu'il ne pourrait pas venir** he hadn't thought ou realized that ou it hadn't occurred to him that he wouldn't be able to come [b] [+ lumière, son] to reflect; **les arbres se réfléchissent dans le lac** the trees are reflected in the lake, you can see the reflection of the trees in the lake

réfléchissant, e [Refleʃisā, āt] ADJ reflective

réflecteur, -trice [Reflɛktœr, tris] [1] ADJ reflecting [2] NM (gén) reflector

reflet [Rəfle] NM [a] (= éclat) (gén) reflection; [cheveux] (naturel) glint, light; (artificiel) highlight; **les ~s moirés de la soie** the shimmering play of light on silk; **les ~s du soleil sur la mer** the reflection ou glint ou flash of the sun on the sea; **la lame projetait des ~s sur le mur** the reflection of the blade shone on the wall, the blade threw a reflection onto the wall; **se faire faire des ~s (dans les cheveux)** to have one's hair highlighted

➤ GRAMMAIRE ACTIVE: **référer** 46.1 **réfléchir** 29.3

b (lit = image) reflection; **le ~ de son visage dans le lac** the reflection of his face in the lake **c** (fig = représentation) reflection; **les habits sont le ~ d'une époque/d'une personnalité** clothes reflect ou are the reflection of an era/ of one's personality; **c'est le pâle ~ de son prédécesseur** he's a pale reflection of his predecessor; **c'est le ~ de son père** he's the image of his father

refléter [ʀ(ə)flete] ▶ conjug 6 ◀ **1** VT (lit, fig) to reflect, mirror; **son visage reflète la bonté** his kindness shows in his face **2 se refléter** VPR to be reflected, be mirrored (**dans** in, **sur** on); **son trouble se reflétait sur son visage** his agitation showed on his face

refleurir [ʀ(ə)flœʀiʀ] ▶ conjug 2 ◀ **1** VI (Bot) to flower ou blossom again; (= renaître) to flourish ou blossom again **2** VT [+ tombe] to put fresh flowers on

reflex [ʀefleks] **1** ADJ reflex **2** NM reflex camera; **à un objectif/deux objectifs** single-lens/twin-lens reflex (camera)

réflexe [ʀefleks] **1** ADJ reflex **2** NM (Physiol) reflex; (= réaction) reaction; **~ rotulien** knee jerk; **~ conditionné** ou **conditionnel** conditioned reflex ou response; **~ de défense** (Physiol) defence reflex; (gén) defensive reaction; **~ de survie** instinct for survival; **~ de solidarité** instinctive feeling of solidarity; **avoir de bons/mauvais ~s** to have quick ou good/ slow ou poor reflexes; **il eut le ~ de couper l'électricité** his immediate ou instant reaction was to switch off the electricity, he instinctively switched off the electricity; **manquer de ~** to be slow to react; **son premier ~ a été d'appeler la police** his first reaction was to call the police; **par ~, j'ai regardé derrière moi** I instinctively looked behind me; **il a freiné par ~** he braked instinctively

réflexibilité [ʀefleksibilite] NF reflexibility

réflexible [ʀefleksibl] ADJ reflexible

réflexif, -ive [ʀefleksif, iv] ADJ (Math) reflexive; (Psych) introspective

réflexion [ʀefleksjɔ̃] NF **a** (= méditation) thought, reflection (NonC); **plongé** ou **absorbé dans ses ~s** deep ou lost in thought; **ceci donne matière à ~** this is food for thought, this gives you something to think about; **ceci mérite ~** (offre) this is worth thinking about ou considering; [problème] this needs thinking about ou over; **ceci nécessite une ~ plus approfondie sur les problèmes** further thought needs to be given to the problems; **avec ~** thoughtfully; **elle a fait son choix au terme d'une longue ~ personnelle** she made her choice after much heart-searching; **~ faite** ou **à la ~, je reste** on reflection ou on second thoughts, I'll stay; **à la ~, on s'aperçoit que c'est faux** when you think about it you can see that it's wrong; (Pol) **groupe** ou **cellule** ou **cercle de ~** think tank; **laissez-moi un délai** ou **un temps de ~** give me (some) time to think (about it); **après un temps de ~, il ajouta ...** after a moment's thought, he added ...; **nous organiserons une journée de ~ sur ce thème** we will organise a one-day conference on this topic → **mûr b** (= remarque) remark, reflection; (= idée) thought, reflection; **consigner ses ~s dans un cahier** to write down one's thoughts ou reflections in a notebook; **je m'en suis moi-même fait la ~** I noticed that myself; **je ne me suis pas fait cette ~** I didn't think of that; **garde tes ~s pour toi** keep your remarks ou comments to yourself; **les clients commencent à faire des ~s** the customers are beginning to make comments; **on m'a fait des ~s sur son travail** people have complained to me ou made complaints to me about his work **c** (Phys) reflection

réflexivité [ʀefleksivite] NF reflexiveness; (Math) reflexivity

réflexologie [ʀefleksɔlɔʒi] NF reflexology

refluer [ʀ(ə)flye] ▶ conjug 1 ◀ VI [liquide] to flow back; [marée] to go back, ebb; [foule] to pour ou surge back; [sang] to rush back; [fumée] to blow back down; [souvenirs] to rush ou flood back; **faire ~ la foule** to push ou force the crowd back

reflux [ʀəfly] NM [foule] backward surge; [marée] ebb; (Méd) reflux → **flux**

refondateur, -trice [ʀ(ə)fɔ̃datœʀ, tʀis] **1** ADJ [courant] radically reformist **2** NM,F radical reformer

refondation [ʀ(ə)fɔ̃dasjɔ̃] NF [parti politique] radical reform

refonder [ʀ(ə)fɔ̃de] ▶ conjug 1 ◀ VT [+ alliance] to reforge; [+ parti politique] to radically reform; [+ système, modèle] to build on new foundations; **elle voudrait ~ son foyer sur des bases plus saines** she'd like to start her family life over again on a sounder basis

refondre [ʀ(ə)fɔ̃dʀ] ▶ conjug 41 ◀ **1** VT **a** [+ métal] to remelt, melt down again; [+ cloche] to recast **b** (= réviser) [+ texte, dictionnaire] to revise; [+ système, programme] to overhaul; **édition entièrement refondue et mise à jour** completely revised and updated edition **2** VI to melt again

refonte [ʀ(ə)fɔ̃t] NF **a** [métal] remelting; [cloche] recasting **b** [texte, dictionnaire] revision; [système, programme] overhaul; **l'opposition exige une ~ radicale de la politique économique** the opposition is demanding a radical rethink of economic policy

reforestation [ʀ(ə)fɔʀestasjɔ̃] NF re(af)forestation

réformable [ʀefɔʀmabl] ADJ (gén) reformable; [jugement] which may be reversed; [loi] which may be amended ou reformed

reformatage [ʀ(ə)fɔʀmataʒ] NM (Ordin, TV) reformatting

reformater [ʀ(ə)fɔʀmate] ▶ conjug 1 ◀ VT [+ disquette, grille de programmes] to reformat

réformateur, -trice [ʀefɔʀmatœʀ, tʀis] **1** ADJ reforming **2** NM,F reformer

réformation [ʀefɔʀmasjɔ̃] NF reformation, reform; (Rel) **la Réformation** the Reformation

réforme [ʀefɔʀm] NF **a** (= changement) reform; **~ agraire/de l'orthographe** land/spelling reform **b** (Mil) [appelé] declaration of unfitness for service; [soldat] discharge; **mettre à la ~** [+ objets] to scrap; [+ cheval] to put out to grass; **mise à la ~** [soldat] discharge; [objets] scrapping **c** (Rel) reformation

réformé, e [ʀefɔʀme] (ptp de **réformer**) **1** ADJ **a** (Rel) Reformed; **la religion ~e** the Protestant Reformed religion **b** (Mil) [appelé] declared unfit for service; [soldat] discharged, invalided out (Brit) **2** NM,F (Rel) Protestant

reformer [ʀ(ə)fɔʀme] ▶ conjug 1 ◀ **1** VT to reform; (Mil) **~ les rangs** to fall in again, fall into line again **2 se reformer** VPR [armée, nuage] to re-form; [parti] to re-form, be reformed; [groupe, rangs] to form up again

réformer [ʀefɔʀme] ▶ conjug 1 ◀ **1** VT **a** (= améliorer) [+ loi, mœurs, religion] to reform; [+ abus] to correct, (put) right, reform; [+ méthode] to improve, reform; [+ administration] to reform, overhaul **b** (Jur) [+ jugement] to reverse, quash (Brit) **c** (Mil) [+ appelé] to declare unfit for service; [+ soldat] to discharge, invalid out (Brit); [+ matériel] to scrap; **il s'est fait ~** he got himself declared unfit for service, he got himself discharged on health grounds ou invalided out (Brit) **2 se réformer** VPR to change one's ways, turn over a new leaf

réformette* [ʀefɔʀmet] NF so-called reform

réformisme [ʀefɔʀmism] NM reformism

réformiste [ʀefɔʀmist] ADJ, NMF reformist

reformuler [ʀ(ə)fɔʀmyle] ▶ conjug 1 ◀ VT [+ proposition, théorie] to reformulate; [+ de-

mande, plainte] to change the wording of; [+ question] to rephrase; (Chim) to reformulate

refoulé, e [ʀ(ə)fule] (ptp de **refouler**) **1** ADJ [personne] repressed, inhibited; [conflits, sentiments, sexualité] repressed **2** NM,F (= personne) repressed ou inhibited person **3** NM (Psych) **le ~** the repressed

refoulement [ʀ(ə)fulmɑ̃] NM **a** [envahisseur, attaque] driving back, repulsing; [manifestant] driving back; [immigré, étranger] turning back **b** [désir, instinct, souvenir] repression, suppression; [colère] repression; (Psych) repression **c** [liquide] **le ~ de l'eau** the reversal of the flow of the water **d** (Rail) backing, reversing

refouler [ʀ(ə)fule] ▶ conjug 1 ◀ **1** VT **a** [+ envahisseur, attaque] to drive back, repulse; [+ manifestant] to drive back; [+ immigré, étranger] to turn back; **les clandestins ont été refoulés à la frontière** the illegal immigrants were turned back at the border **b** [+ larmes] to force ou hold back, repress; [+ désir, instinct, souvenir] to repress, suppress; [+ colère] to repress, hold in check; [+ sanglots] to choke back, force back; (Psych) to repress **c** (= faire refluer) [+ liquide] to force back, reverse ou invert the flow of **d** (Rail) to back, reverse **e** (Naut) [+ courant, marée] to stem **2** VI [siphon, tuyauterie] to flow back; [cheminée] to smoke

refourguer* [ʀ(ə)fuʀge] ▶ conjug 1 ◀ VT (= vendre) to flog* (à to), unload* (à onto); (= donner, se débarrasser de) **~ à qn** [+ problème] to unload onto sb, palm off onto sb*; [+ responsabilités] to unload onto sb; **elle m'a refourgué un dossier gênant** she offloaded a difficult case onto me; **il m'a refourgué un faux billet** he palmed a forged banknote off onto me

refoutre: [ʀ(ə)futʀ] VT **refous-le là** shove* it back in there; **refous un peu de colle dessus** stick some more glue back on it; **ne refous plus jamais les pieds ici!** don't you dare show your face in here again!

réfractaire [ʀefʀaktɛʀ] **1** ADJ **a** **~ à** [+ autorité, virus, influence] resistant to; [+ musique] impervious to; **maladie ~** stubborn illness; **je suis ~ à la poésie** poetry is a closed book to me; **être ~ à la discipline** to resist discipline; (Hist) **prêtre ~** non-juring priest **b** [métal] refractory; [brique, argile] fire (épith); [plat] ovenproof, heat-resistant **2** NM (Hist, Mil) draft dodger, draft evader; **les ~s au STO** French civilians who refused to work in Germany during the Second World War

réfracter [ʀefʀakte] ▶ conjug 1 ◀ **1** VT to refract **2 se réfracter** VPR to be refracted

réfracteur, -trice [ʀefʀaktœʀ, tʀis] ADJ refractive, refracting (épith)

réfraction [ʀefʀaksjɔ̃] NF refraction; **indice de ~** refractive index

réfractomètre [ʀefʀaktɔmetʀ] NM refractometer

refrain [ʀ(ə)fʀɛ̃] NM (Mus: en fin de couplet) refrain, chorus; (= chanson) tune; **c'est toujours le même ~*** it's always the same old story; **change de ~!** change the record!*, give it a rest!*

refréner [ʀ(ə)fʀene] ▶ conjug 6 ◀ VT [+ désir, impatience] to curb, hold in check, check

réfrigérant, e [ʀefʀiʒeʀɑ̃, ɑ̃t] **1** ADJ [fluide] refrigerant, refrigerating; [accueil, personne] icy, frosty → **mélange 2** NM (Tech) cooler

réfrigérateur [ʀefʀiʒeʀatœʀ] NM refrigerator, fridge; (fig) **mettre un projet au ~** to put a plan on ice

réfrigération [ʀefʀiʒeʀasjɔ̃] NF refrigeration; (Tech) cooling

réfrigérer [ʀefʀiʒeʀe] ▶ conjug 6 ◀ VT **a** (gén) to refrigerate; (Tech) to cool; [+ local] to cool; **véhicule réfrigéré** refrigerated vehicle; **vitrine réfrigérée** refrigerated display; **je suis réfrigéré*** I'm frozen stiff* **b** (fig) [+

enthousiasme] to put a damper on, cool; [+ _personne_] to have a cooling _ou_ dampening effect on

réfringence [ʀefʀɛ̃ʒɑ̃s] NF refringence

réfringent, e [ʀefʀɛ̃ʒɑ̃, ɑ̃t] ADJ refringent

refroidir [ʀ(ə)fʀwadiʀ] ▶ conjug 2 ◀ **1** VT **a** [+ _nourriture_] to cool (down) **b** (_fig_) [+ _personne_] to put off, have a cooling effect on; [+ _zèle_] to cool, put a damper on, dampen **c** (‡ = _tuer_) to do in‡, bump off‡ **2** VI (= _cesser d'être trop chaud_) to cool (down); (= _devenir trop froid_) to get cold; **laisser** _ou_ **faire ~** [+ _mets trop chaud_] to leave to cool, let cool (down); (_involontairement_) to let get cold; [+ _moteur_] to let cool; (_péj_) [+ _projet_] to let slide _ou_ slip; **mettre qch à ~** to put sth to cool (down); (_jeu_) **tu refroidis!** you're getting cold! **3** **se refroidir** VPR [_ardeur_] to cool (off); [_mets_] to get cold; [_temps_] to get cooler _ou_ colder; [_personne_] (= _avoir froid_) to get cold; (= _attraper un rhume_) to catch a chill

refroidissement [ʀ(ə)fʀwadismɑ̃] NM **a** [_air, liquide_] cooling; **~ par air/eau** air-/water-cooling; **~ de la température** drop in temperature; **on observe un ~ du temps** the weather is getting cooler _ou_ colder **b** (_Méd_) chill; **prendre un ~** to catch a chill **c** (_fig_) [_passion_] cooling (off); **on note un ~ des relations entre les deux pays** relations between the two countries are cooling

refroidisseur, -euse [ʀ(ə)fʀwadisœʀ, øz] **1** ADJ cooling **2** NM cooler (_en industrie_) cooling tower

refuge [ʀ(ə)fyʒ] NM (_gén_) refuge; (_pour piétons_) refuge, (traffic) island; (_en montagne_) refuge, (mountain) hut; **lieu de ~** place of refuge _ou_ safety; (_Bourse_) **valeur ~** safe investment; **chercher/trouver ~** to seek/find refuge (**dans** in, **auprès de** with); **il a cherché ~ dans une église** he sought refuge _ou_ sanctuary in a church; **la forêt lui a servi de ~** he found refuge in the forest

réfugié, e [ʀefyʒje] (_ptp de_ **se réfugier**) ADJ, NM,F refugee; **~ politique** political refugee

réfugier (se) [ʀefyʒje] ▶ conjug 7 ◀ VPR (_lit, fig_) to take refuge

refus [ʀ(ə)fy] NM (_gén, Équitation_) refusal; (_Jur_) **~ de comparaître** refusal to appear (in court); (_Aut_) **~ de priorité** refusal to give way (_Brit_) _ou_ to yield (_US_); **~ d'obéissance** (_gén_) refusal to obey; (_Mil_) insubordination; **ce n'est pas de ~*** I wouldn't say no; **en cas de ~ de paiement ou de payer, il peut être poursuivi** if he refuses to pay, he may be taken to court; **ils persistent dans leur ~ de négocier/de signer** they are still refusing to negotiate/to sign

▼ **refuser** [ʀ(ə)fyze] ▶ conjug 1 ◀ **1** VT **a** (= _ne pas accepter_) [+ _cadeau_] to refuse; [+ _offre, invitation_] to refuse, decline, turn down; [+ _manuscrit_] to reject, turn down, refuse; [+ _marchandise, racisme, inégalité_] to reject, refuse to accept; [+ _politique, méthodes_] to refuse, reject; **~ la lutte** _ou_ **le combat** to refuse to fight; **le cheval a refusé (l'obstacle)** the horse refused (the fence); **~ le risque** to refuse to take risks; **il a toujours refusé la vie routinière** he has always refused to accept a routine life **b** (= _ne pas accorder_) [+ _permission, entrée, consentement_] to refuse; [+ _demande_] to refuse, turn down; [+ _compétence, qualité_] to deny; **~ l'entrée à qn** to refuse admittance _ou_ entry to sb, turn sb away; **~ sa porte à qn** to bar one's door to sb; **je me suis vu ~ un verre d'eau** I was refused a glass of water; **on lui a refusé l'accès aux archives** he was refused _ou_ denied access to the records; (_Aut_) **il m'a refusé la priorité** he didn't give me right of way (_Brit_), he didn't yield to me (_US_); **elle est si gentille, on ne peut rien lui ~** she's so nice, you just can't say no to her; **je lui refuse toute générosité** I refuse to accept _ou_ admit that he has any generosity **c** [+ _client_] to turn away; [+ _candidat_] (_à un_

examen) to fail; (_à un poste_) to turn down, reject; **il s'est fait ~ au permis de conduire** he failed his driving test; **on a dû ~ du monde** they had to turn people away **d** **~ de faire qch** to refuse to do sth; **il a refusé net (de le faire)** he refused point-blank (to do it); **la voiture refuse de démarrer** the car won't start

2 VI [_pieu_] to resist; [_vent_] to haul

3 **se refuser** VPR **a** (= _se priver de_) to refuse o.s., deny o.s.; (_iro_) **tu ne te refuses rien!** you certainly spoil yourself! **b** **ça ne se refuse pas** [_offre_] it is not to be turned down _ou_ refused; **un apéritif, ça ne se refuse pas** I wouldn't say no to an apéritif **c** **se ~ à** [+ _méthode, solution_] to refuse (to accept), reject; **se ~ à tout commentaire** to refuse to (make any) comment; (_frm_) **elle s'est refusée à lui** she refused to give herself to him; **se ~ à faire qch** to refuse to do sth

réfutable [ʀefytabl] ADJ refutable, which can be disproved _ou_ refuted; **facilement ~** easily refuted _ou_ disproved

réfutation [ʀefytasjɔ̃] NF refutation; **fait qui apporte la ~ d'une allégation** fact which refutes _ou_ disproves an allegation

réfuter [ʀefyte] ▶ conjug 1 ◀ VT to refute, disprove

regagner [ʀ(ə)gaɲe] ▶ conjug 1 ◀ VT **a** (= _récupérer_) [+ _amitié, faveur_] to regain, win _ou_ gain back; [+ _argent perdu au jeu_] to win back; [+ _confiance, parts de marché_] to regain, win back; (_Mil, fig_) **~ du terrain** to regain ground, win _ou_ gain ground again; **~ le terrain perdu** to win back lost ground; **il a regagné sa place en tête du classement** he regained his place _ou_ position at the top of the league **b** [+ _lieu_] to get _ou_ go back to; [+ _pays_] to arrive back in, get back to; **les sinistrés ont pu ~ leur domicile** the disaster victims were allowed to return to their homes; **il regagna enfin sa maison** he finally arrived back home _ou_ got back home; **~ sa place** to return to one's place _ou_ seat; **les spationautes ont regagné la Terre** the astronauts returned to earth

regain [ʀəgɛ̃] NM **a** **~ de** [+ _jeunesse_] renewal of; [+ _popularité_] revival of; [+ _activité, influence_] renewal _ou_ revival of; **un ~ d'intérêt/d'optimisme/d'énergie** renewed interest/optimism/energy; **~ de violence** new _ou_ fresh outbreak of violence, renewed (outbreak of) violence; (_Pol_) **~ de tension** rise in tension **b** (_Agr_) second crop of hay, aftermath †

régal (_pl_ **régals**) [ʀegal] NM delight, treat; **ce gâteau est un ~!** ◊ **ce gâteau, quel ~!** this cake is absolutely delicious!; **c'est un ~ pour les yeux** it is a sight for sore eyes, it is a delight _ou_ treat to look at; **quel ~ de manger des cerises** what a treat to have cherries

régalade [ʀegalad] **à la régalade** LOC ADV [_boire_] without letting one's lips touch the bottle (_ou_ glass _etc_)

régaler [ʀegale] ▶ conjug 1 ◀ **1** VT **~ qn** to treat sb to a delicious meal; **c'est moi qui régale** I'm treating everyone, it's my treat; **c'est le patron qui régale** it's on the house; **chaque soir, il nous régalait de ses histoires** in the evenings he would regale us with his stories

2 **se régaler** VPR (= _bien manger_) to have a delicious meal; (= _éprouver du plaisir_) to have a wonderful time*; **~ de gâteaux** to treat o.s. to some delicious cakes; **on s'est (bien) régalé** (_au repas_) it was delicious, (_au cinéma, théâtre_) we had a great time*, we really enjoyed ourselves; (_fig péj_) **il y en a qui se sont régalés dans cette vente** some people did really well out of that sale; (_hum péj_) **les cafetiers se régalent avec cette vague de chaleur** the café owners are making a mint* _ou_ doing really well in this heatwave; **se ~ de romans** (_habituellement_) to be a keen reader of _ou_ very keen on (_Brit_) novels; (_en vacances etc_) to

gorge o.s. on novels, have a feast of novel-reading

régalien, -ienne [ʀegaljɛ̃, jɛn] ADJ [_droits_] kingly

regard [ʀ(ə)gaʀ] NM **a** (= _yeux_) eyes; **son ~ bleu/noir** his blue/black eyes; **son ~ se posa sur moi** his gaze _ou_ eyes came to rest on me; **soustraire qch aux ~s** to hide sth from sight _ou_ from view, put sth out of sight; **cela attire tous les ~s** it catches everyone's eye _ou_ attention; **tous les ~s étaient fixés sur elle** all eyes were on her _ou_ were turned towards her; **il restait assis, le ~ perdu (dans le vide)** he was sitting there, staring into space; **son ~ était dur/tendre** he had a hard/tender look in his eye; **il avançait, le ~ fixe** he was walking along with a fixed stare; **dévorer/menacer qn du ~** to look hungrily/threateningly at sb, fix sb with a hungry/threatening look _ou_ stare; **sous le ~ attentif de sa mère** under his mother's watchful eye; **sous le ~ des caméras** in front of the cameras → **chercher, croiser, détourner** **b** (= _coup d'œil_) look, glance; **échanger des ~s avec qn** to exchange looks _ou_ glances with sb; **échanger des ~s d'intelligence** to exchange knowing looks; **lancer un ~ de colère à qn** to glare at sb, cast an angry look _ou_ glare at sb; **au premier ~** at first glance _ou_ sight; **~ en coin** _ou_ **en coulisse** sideways _ou_ sidelong glance; **il lui lança un ~ noir** he shot him a black _ou_ dark look; **il jeta un dernier ~ en arrière** he took one last look behind him, he looked back one last time **c** (= _point de vue, opinion_) **porter** _ou_ **jeter un ~ critique sur qch** to take a critical look at sth, look critically at sth; **porter un ~ extérieur sur qch** to look at sth from the outside; **il mène sa vie sans se soucier du ~ des autres** he lives his own life and isn't concerned about what other people think **d** [_égout_] manhole; [_baignoire_] inspection hole **e** (_loc_) **au ~ de la loi** in the eyes of the law, from the legal viewpoint; **texte avec photos en ~** text with photos on the opposite facing _ou_ page; **en ~ de ce qu'il gagne** compared with _ou_ in comparison with what he earns → **droit³**

regardant, e [ʀ(ə)gaʀdɑ̃, ɑ̃t] ADJ careful with money; **il n'est pas ~** he's quite free with his money; **ils sont/ne sont pas ~s sur l'argent de poche** they are not very/they are quite generous with pocket money; **il n'est pas très ~ sur la propreté/les manières** he's not very particular about cleanliness/manners

regarder [ʀ(ə)gaʀde] ▶ conjug 1 ◀ **1** VT **a** (= _diriger son regard vers_) [+ _paysage, scène_] to look at; [+ _action en déroulant, film, match_] to watch; **elle regardait les voitures sur le parking** she was looking at the cars in the car park; **elle regardait les voitures défiler** _ou_ **qui défilaient** she was watching the cars driving past _ou_ the cars as they drove past; **~ tomber la pluie** _ou_ **la pluie tomber** to watch the rain falling; **il regarda sa montre** he looked at _ou_ had a look at his watch; **regarde, il pleut** look, it's raining; **regarde bien, il va sauter** watch _ou_ look, he's going to jump; **~ la télévision/une émission à la télévision** to watch television/a programme on television; **~ le journal** to look at _ou_ have a look at the paper; **~ sur le livre de qn** (= _partager_) to share sb's book; (= _tricher_) to look at sb's book; **~ par la fenêtre** (_du dedans_) to look out of the window; (_du dehors_) to look in through the window; **regarde les oiseaux par la fenêtre** look through _ou_ out of the window at the birds, watch the birds through _ou_ out of the window; **regarde devant toi/derrière toi** look in front of you/behind you; **regarde où tu marches** watch _ou_ look where you're going _ou_ putting your feet; **regarde voir* dans l'armoire** take _ou_ have a look in the wardrobe; **regarde voir* s'il arrive** look _ou_ have a look and see if

---

➤ GRAMMAIRE ACTIVE: **refuser** 35.5, 39.3, 46.5, 52.5

he's coming; **attends, je vais ~** hang on, I'll go and look *ou* I'll take a look; **regardez-moi ça/son écriture*** just (take) a look at that/at his writing; **tu ne m'as pas regardé !*** what do you take me for!*, who do you think I am!*; **j'ai regardé partout, je n'ai rien trouvé** I looked everywhere but I couldn't find anything; **regarde à la pendule quelle heure il est** look at the clock to see what time it is, look and see what time it is by the clock; **regardez-le faire** (*gén*) watch him *ou* look at him do it; (*pour apprendre*) watch *ou* look how he does it; **elles sont allées ~ les vitrines/les magasins** they've gone to do some window-shopping/to have a look around the shops; **sans ~** [*traverser*] without looking; [*payer*] regardless of cost *ou* the expense → **chien**

b (*rapidement*) to glance at, have a glance *ou* a (quick) look at; (*furtivement*) to steal a glance at, glance sidelong at; (*longuement*) to gaze at; (*fixement*) to stare at; **~ un texte rapidement** to glance at *ou* through a text, have a quick look *ou* glance at *ou* through a text; **~ (qch) par le trou de la serrure** to peep *ou* look (at sth) through the keyhole; **~ qch de près/de plus près** to have a close/closer look at sth, look closely/more closely at sth; **~ sans voir** to look with unseeing eyes; **~ qn avec colère** to glare angrily at sb; **~ qn avec méfiance** to look at *ou* eye sb suspiciously; **~ qn de haut** to give sb a scornful look, look scornfully at sb; (*lit, fig*) **~ qn droit dans les yeux/bien en face** to look sb straight in the eye/straight in the face; **~ qn dans le blanc des yeux** to look sb straight in the face *ou* eye

c (= *vérifier*) [+ *appareil, malade*] to look at; [+ *huile, essence*] to look at, to check; **peux-tu ~ la lampe? elle ne marche pas** can you have *ou* take a look at the lamp? it doesn't work; **regarde dans l'annuaire** look in the phone book; **~ un mot dans le dictionnaire** to look up *ou* check a word in the dictionary

d (= *considérer*) [+ *situation, problème*] to view; **~ l'avenir avec appréhension** to view the future with trepidation; **il ne regarde que son propre intérêt** he is only concerned with *ou* he only thinks about his own interests; **nous le regardons comme un ami** we look upon *ou* we regard him as a friend

e (= *concerner*) to concern; **cette affaire me regarde quand même un peu** this business does concern me a little; **en quoi cela te regarde-t-il ?** (= *de quoi te mêles-tu ?*) what business is it of yours?, what has it to do with you?; (= *en quoi es-tu touché ?*) how does it affect *ou* concern you?; **fais ce que je te dis, la suite me regarde** do what I tell you, what happens next is my concern *ou* business; **que vas-tu faire ? — ça me regarde** what will you do? — that's my business *ou* my concern; **non mais, ça vous regarde !*** what business is it of yours?; **cela ne le regarde pas** that's none of his business, that's no concern of his; **mêlez-vous de ce qui vous regarde** mind your own business

f (= *être orienté vers*) [*maison*] **~ (vers)** to face

2 VT INDIR to think of *ou* about; **y ~ à deux fois avant de faire qch** to think twice before doing sth; **il n'y regarde pas de si près** he's not that fussy *ou* particular; **à y bien ~** on thinking it over; **c'est quelqu'un qui va ~ à deux francs** he's the sort of person who will niggle over *ou* worry about two francs; **il regarde à s'acheter un costume neuf** he always thinks twice before laying out money for a new suit; **quand il fait un cadeau, il ne regarde pas à la dépense** when he gives somebody a present he doesn't worry how much he spends; **acheter qch sans ~ à la dépense** to buy sth without bothering about the expense

3 **se regarder** VPR a (*soi-même*) **~ dans une glace** to look at o.s. in a mirror; (*fig*) **elle ne peut plus se ~ dans une glace** she's ashamed of herself; (*iro*) **il ne s'est pas re-**

---

gardé ! he should take a look at himself!

b (*mutuellement*) [*personnes*] to look at each other *ou* one another; [*maisons*] to face each other *ou* one another

regarnir [ʀ(ə)gaʀniʀ] ▶conjug 2◀ VT [+ *magasin, rayon*] to stock up again, restock; [+ *trousse*] to refill, replenish; [+ *réfrigérateur*] to fill (up) again; [+ *coussin*] to refill

régate [ʀegat] NF **~(s)** regatta

régater [ʀegate] ▶conjug 1◀ VI to sail in a regatta

régatier, -ière [ʀegatje, jɛʀ] NM,F regatta competitor

regeler [ʀəʒ(ə)le, ʀ(ə)ʒəle] ▶conjug 5◀ VT, VB IMPERS to freeze again

régence [ʀeʒɑ̃s] 1 NF (*Pol*) regency; (*Hist*) **la Régence** the Regency 2 ADJ INV [*meuble*] (*en France*) (French) Regency; (*en Grande-Bretagne*) Regency; (*fig*) [*personne, mœurs*] overrefined

régénérateur, -trice [ʀeʒeneʀatœʀ, tʀis] 1 ADJ regenerative 2 NM regenerator

régénération [ʀeʒeneʀasjɔ̃] NF regeneration

régénérer [ʀeʒeneʀe] ▶conjug 6◀ VT (*Bio, Rel*) to regenerate; [+ *personne, forces*] to revive, restore

régent, e [ʀeʒɑ̃, ɑ̃t] 1 ADJ regent; **prince ~** prince regent 2 NM,F (*Pol*) regent; (*Admin* = *directeur*) manager

régenter [ʀeʒɑ̃te] ▶conjug 1◀ VT (*gén*) to rule over; [+ *personne*] to dictate to; **il veut tout ~** he wants to run the whole show*

reggae [ʀege] NM reggae

régicide [ʀeʒisid] 1 ADJ regicidal 2 NMF (= *personne*) regicide 3 NM (= *crime*) regicide

régie [ʀeʒi] NF a (= *gestion*) [*État*] state control; [*commune*] local government control (**de** over); **en ~** under state (*ou* local government) control; **~ directe ou simple** direct state control; **~ intéressée** public service concession; **travaux en ~** public work contracting (*by the government*) b (= *société*) **~ (d'État)** state-owned company, government corporation; **la Régie française des tabacs** *the French national tobacco company*; **la Régie autonome des transports parisiens** *the Paris city transport authority*; **~ publicitaire** advertising sales division c (*Ciné, Théât, TV*) production department; (*Radio, TV* = *salle de contrôle*) control room

regimber [ʀ(ə)ʒɛ̃be] ▶conjug 1◀ VI [*personne*] to rebel (**contre** against); [*cheval*] to jib; **fais-le sans ~** do it without grumbling; **quand je lui ai demandé de le faire, il a regimbé** when I asked him to do it he jibbed at the idea

régime[1] [ʀeʒim] NM a (*Pol*) (= *mode*) system (of government); (= *gouvernement*) government; (*péj*) régime; **~ monarchique/républicain** monarchical/republican system (of government) → **ancien**

b (*Admin*) (= *système*) scheme, system; (= *règlements*) regulations; **~ douanier/des hôpitaux** (= *système*) customs/hospital system; (= *règle*) customs/hospital regulations; **~ de la Sécurité sociale** Social Security system; **~ maladie** health insurance scheme (*Brit*) *ou* plan (*US*); **~ vieillesse** pension scheme

c (*Jur*) **~ (matrimonial)** marriage settlement; **se marier sous le ~ de la communauté/de la séparation de biens** to opt for a marriage settlement based on joint ownership of property/on separate ownership of property

d (*Méd*) diet; **être/mettre qn au ~** to be/put sb on a diet; **suivre un ~ (alimentaire)** (*gén*) to be on a diet; (*scrupuleusement*) to follow *ou* keep to a diet; **~ sec/sans sel/lacté/basses calories/amaigrissant** alcohol-free/salt-free/milk/low-calorie/slimming (*Brit*) *ou* reducing (*US*) diet; **chocolat/produit de ~** diet chocolate/product; (*hum*) **être/se mettre au ~ jockey*** to be/go on a starvation *ou* crash diet

e [*moteur*] (engine *ou* running) speed; **ce moteur est bruyant à haut ~** this engine is

---

noisy when it's revving hard; **~ de croisière** cruising speed; **à ce ~, nous n'aurons bientôt plus d'argent** (if we go on) at this rate *ou* at the rate we're going we'll soon have no money left; **fonctionner ou marcher ou tourner à plein ~** [*moteur*] to run at top speed, be on *ou* at full throttle; [*usine*] to run at full capacity; **baisse de ~** (= *ralentissement*) slowdown; **il a disputé trois sets sans la moindre baisse de ~** he played three sets without once slackening his *ou* the pace; **montée en ~** [*moteur*] revving (up); **la montée en ~ de l'entreprise** the increased activity in the company

f (*Mét*) [*pluies, fleuve*] régime

g (*Gram*) object; **~ direct/indirect** direct/indirect object; **cas ~** objective case

h (*Phys*) [*écoulement*] rate of flow

régime[2] [ʀeʒim] NM [*dattes*] cluster, bunch; [*bananes*] bunch

régiment [ʀeʒimɑ̃] NM a (*Mil*) (= *corps*) regiment; * (= *service militaire*) military *ou* national service; **être au ~*** to be doing (one's) national *ou* military service; **aller au ~*** to go into the army, be called up b (* = *masse*) [*personnes*] regiment, army; [*choses*] mass(es), loads; **il y en a pour tout un ~** there's enough for a whole army

régimentaire [ʀeʒimɑ̃tɛʀ] ADJ regimental

région [ʀeʒjɔ̃] NF (*Admin, Géog*) (*étendue*) region; (*limitée*) area; (*Anat*) region, area; (= *conseil régional*) regional council; (*fig* = *domaine*) region; **~s polaires/équatoriales** polar/equatorial regions; **la ~ parisienne/londonienne** the Paris/London area *ou* region; **Toulouse et sa ~** Toulouse and the surrounding area; **ça se trouve dans la ~ de Lyon** it's in the Lyons area *ou* around Lyons *ou* in the region of Lyons; **si vous passez dans la ~, allez les voir** if you are in the area *ou* if you go that way, go and see them; **les habitants de la ~** the local inhabitants; **je ne suis pas de la ~** I'm not from around here; **dans nos ~s** (= *où nous sommes*) in these parts, in our part of the world; (= *d'où nous venons*) where we come from; **en ~** in the provinces

┌─────────────┐
│ **RÉGION** │
└─────────────┘

*The 22 **régions** are the largest administrative divisions in France, each being made up of several "départements". Each **région** is administered by a "conseil régional", whose members ("les conseillers régionaux") are elected for a six-year term in the "élections régionales". The expression "la **région**" is also used by extension to refer to the regional council itself.* → `DÉPARTEMENT` ; `ÉLECTIONS`

régional, e (*mpl* **-aux**) [ʀeʒjɔnal, o] 1 ADJ [*presse, élections*] regional 2 NM (*Cyclisme*) **le ~ de l'étape** *cyclist from the particular region through which the Tour de France is passing* 3 **régionales** NFPL (= *élections*) regional elections; (= *nouvelles*) regional news (*NonC*)

régionalisation [ʀeʒjɔnalizasjɔ̃] NF regionalization

régionaliser [ʀeʒjɔnalize] ▶conjug 1◀ VT to regionalize

régionalisme [ʀeʒjɔnalism] NM a (*Pol*) regionalism b (*Ling*) regionalism, regional expression

régionaliste [ʀeʒjɔnalist] 1 ADJ regionalist(ic) 2 NMF regionalist

régir [ʀeʒiʀ] ▶conjug 2◀ VT (*gén, Ling*) to govern

régisseur, -euse [ʀeʒisœʀ, øz] NM,F [*propriété*] steward; (*Théât*) stage manager; (*Ciné, TV*) assistant director; **~ de plateau** studio director

registre [ʀəʒistʀ] 1 NM a (= *livre*) register; **~ maritime/d'hôtel/du commerce** shipping/hotel/trade register; (*Scol*) **~ de notes** mark book (*Brit*), grade book *ou* register (*US*); (*Scol*) **~ d'absences** attendance register b (*Mus*) [*orgue*] stop; [*voix*] (= *étage*) register; (=

étendue) register, range [c] (Ling) (= niveau) register, level (of language); (= style) register, style [d] (Tech) [fourneau] damper, register; (Ordin, Typo) register [e] (fig = genre, ton) mood, vein; **il a complètement changé de ~** [écrivain] he's completely changed his style; **cet auteur joue sur tous les ~s** this author has a very varied style [2] COMP ► **registre de comptabilité** ledger ► **registre de l'état civil** register of births, marriages and deaths ► **registre mortuaire** register of deaths ► **registre de vapeur** throttle valve

réglable [Reglabl] ADJ [a] [mécanisme, débit] adjustable; **siège à dossier ~** reclining seat [b] (= payable) payable

réglage [Regla3] NM [a] [mécanisme, débit] regulation, adjustment; [moteur] tuning; [allumage, thermostat] setting, adjustment; [dossier de chaise, tir] adjustment [b] [papier] ruling

réglé, e [Regle] (ptp de **régler**) ADJ [a] (= régulier) [vie] (well-)ordered, regular; [personne] steady, stable; **c'est ~ comme du papier à musique*, il arrive tous les jours à 8 heures** he arrives at 8 o'clock every day, as regular as clockwork; **être ~ comme une horloge** to be as regular as clockwork [b] [adolescente] **elle n'est pas encore ~e** she hasn't started having periods yet; **elle est bien ~e** her periods are regular [c] [papier] ruled, lined

règle [Regl] NF [a] (= loi, principe) rule; **~ de conduite** rule of conduct; **~ de 3** rule of 3; **les ~s de la bienséance/de l'honneur** the rules of propriety/of honour; **~ d'or** golden rule; **~s de sécurité** safety regulations; **respecter les ~s élémentaires d'hygiène** to observe the basic hygiene rules, observe basic hygiene; **me lever à 7 heures, j'en ai fait une ~ de vie** I've made it a rule to get up at 7 in the morning; **ils ont pour ~ de se réunir chaque jour** they make it a rule to meet every day; (lit, fig) **c'est la ~ du jeu** those are the rules of the game; (lit, fig) **se plier aux ~s du jeu** to play the game according to the rules; **c'est la ~ (de la maison)** that's the rule (of the house); **cela n'échappe pas à la ~** that's no exception to the rule; (Sport) **laisser jouer la ~ de l'avantage** to play the advantage rule [b] (= instrument) ruler; **trait tiré à la ~** line drawn with a ruler; **~ à calcul** ou **à calculer** slide rule [c] (= menstruation) **~s** period(s); **avoir ses ~s** to have one's period(s); **pendant la période des ~s** during menstruation; **avoir des ~s douloureuses** to suffer from ou get period pains, have painful periods [d] (Rel) rule [e] (loc) **il est de ~ qu'on fasse** ou **de faire un cadeau** it's usual ou it's standard practice ou the done thing to give a present; **dans ce métier, la prudence est de ~** in this profession, caution is the rule; **en ~** [comptabilité, papiers] in order; [avertissement] given according to the rules; [réclamation] made according to the rules; [attaque, critique] all-out (épith); **il lui a fait une cour en ~** he did all the right things to win her hand; **être en ~ avec les autorités** to be straight with ou in order with the authorities; **se mettre en ~ avec les autorités** to sort out ou straighten out one's position with the authorities; **je ne suis pas en ~** my papers are not in order; **se mettre en ~ avec Dieu** to make things right with God; **en ~ générale** as a (general) rule; **il faut faire la demande dans** ou **selon les ~s** you must make the request through the proper channels ou according to the rules ou the proper procedures; **effectué dans les ~s de l'art** (lit) carried out professionally; (hum) **dans les ~s de l'art** according to the rule book

▼ **règlement** [Reglamã] NM [a] (Admin, Police, Univ) (= règle) regulation; (= réglementation) rules, regulations; **c'est contraire au ~** it's against the rules ou against regulations; **~ de**

service administrative rule ou regulation; **~ intérieur** (Scol) school rules; [entreprise] policies and procedures (manual); (Europe) **d'après le ~ communautaire** ou **européen du 2 mars** under the community ou European regulation of 2nd March [b] [affaire, conflit] settlement, settling; [facture, dette] settlement, payment; **~ en espèces** cash settlement ou payment; **faire un ~ par chèque** to pay ou make a payment by cheque; **la date de ~ est inscrite sur la facture** the due date ou the date when payment is due appears on the bill; (Bourse) **marché à ~ mensuel** forward market; (Jur) **~ judiciaire** (compulsory) liquidation; **être mis en ~ judiciaire** to be put into receivership, be put into the hands of the receiver; (Jur) **~ (à l')amiable** amicable settlement, out-of-court settlement; (fig) **~ de compte(s)** settling of scores; (de gangsters) gangland killing; **le ~ de votre dossier interviendra sous un mois** your request will be dealt with within a month

réglementaire [Reglamãter] ADJ [uniforme, taille] regulation (épith); [procédure] statutory, laid down in the regulations; **ça n'est pas très ~** that isn't really allowed, that's really against the rules; **dans le temps ~** in the prescribed time; **ce certificat n'est pas ~** this certificate doesn't conform to the regulations; **dispositions ~s** regulations; **pouvoir ~** power to make regulations

réglementairement [Reglamãtermã] ADV in accordance with ou according to the regulations, statutorily

réglementation [Reglamãtasjõ] NF (= règles) regulations; (= contrôle) [prix, loyers] control, regulation; **~ des changes** exchange control regulations

réglementer [Reglamãte] ▶ conjug 1 ◀ VT to regulate, control; **la vente des médicaments est très réglementée** the sale of medicines is strictly controlled → **stationnement**

▼ **régler** [Regle] ▶ conjug 6 ◀ VT [a] (= conclure) [+ affaire, conflit] to settle; [+ problème] to settle, sort out; [+ dossier] to deal with; **~ qch à l'amiable** (gén) to settle sth amicably; (Jur) to settle sth out of court; **alors, c'est une affaire réglée** ou **c'est réglé, vous acceptez?** that's settled then — you accept?; **on va ~ ça tout de suite** we'll get that settled ou sorted out straightaway [b] (= payer) [+ note, dette] to settle (up), pay (up); [+ compte] to settle; [+ commerçant, créancier] to settle up with, pay; [+ travaux] to settle up for, pay for; **est-ce que je peux ~?** can I settle up (with you)? ou settle ou pay the bill?; **je viens ~ mes dettes** I've come to settle my debts ou to square up with you; **~ qch en espèces** to pay for sth in cash; **est-ce que je peux (vous) ~ par chèque?** can I give you a cheque?, can I pay (you) by cheque?; **~ son compte à un employé** (lit) to settle up with an employee; (fig = renvoyer) to give an employee his cards ou books* (Brit) ou pink slip* (US); **j'ai un compte à ~ avec lui** I've got a score to settle with him, I've got a bone to pick with him; **on lui a réglé son compte!** (vengeance) they've settled his hash*; (assassinat) they've taken care of him (euph); **les deux bandes veulent ~ leurs comptes** the two gangs want to settle the score* [c] [+ mécanisme, débit, machine] to regulate, adjust; [+ dossier de chaise, tir] to adjust; [+ moteur] to tune; [+ allumage, ralenti] to set, adjust; [+ réveil] to set; **~ le thermostat à 18°** to set the thermostat to ou at 18°; **~ une montre** (mettre à l'heure) to put a watch right (sur by); (réparer) to regulate a watch; **le carburateur est mal réglé** the carburettor is badly tuned [d] (= fixer) [+ modalités, date, programme] to settle (on), fix (up), decide on; [+ conduite, réactions] to determine; **~ l'ordre d'une cérémonie** to settle ou fix (up) the order of (a) ceremony; **il ne sait pas ~ l'emploi de ses**

journées he is incapable of planning out ou organizing his daily routine; **~ le sort de qn** to decide ou determine sb's fate [e] (= prendre comme modèle) **~ qch sur** to model sth on, adjust sth to; **~ sa vie sur (celle de) son père** to model one's life on that of one's father; **~ sa conduite sur les circonstances** to adjust one's conduct ou behaviour to the circumstances; **se ~ sur qn d'autre** to model o.s. on sb else; **il essaya de ~ son pas sur celui de son père** he tried to walk in step with his father; **~ sa vitesse sur celle de l'autre voiture** to adjust ou match one's speed to that of the other car [f] [+ papier] to rule (lines on)

réglette [Reglet] NF (Typo) setting stick; (= petite règle) small ruler

régleur, -euse [Reglœr, øz] [1] NM,F (= ouvrier) setter, adjuster [2] **régleuse** NF ruling machine

réglisse [Reglis] NF ou NM liquorice; **bâton/ rouleau de ~** liquorice stick/roll

réglo* [Reglo] ADJ INV [personne] straight*, honest, dependable; **c'est ~** it's O.K.*, it's in order; **ce n'est pas très ~** it's not really right, it's not really on* (Brit)

régnant, e [Reɲã, ãt] ADJ [famille, prince] reigning (épith); [théorie, idée] reigning (épith), prevailing (épith)

règne [Reɲ] NM [a] [roi, tyran] (= période) reign; (= domination) rule, reign; **sous le ~ de Louis XIV** (période) in the reign of Louis XIV; (domination) under the reign ou rule of Louis XIV [b] [mode, banquiers] reign; [justice, liberté] reign, rule [c] (Bot, Zool) kingdom; **~ animal/ végétal/minéral** animal/vegetable ou plant/ mineral kingdom

régner [Reɲe] ▶ conjug 6 ◀ VI [a] (= être sur le trône) to reign; (= exercer sa domination) to rule (sur over); (fig) **il règne (en maître) sur le village** he reigns ou rules (supreme) over the village; **elle règne dans la cuisine** she reigns over ou rules in the kitchen; (littér) **~ sur nos passions** to rule over ou govern our passions → **diviser** [b] (= prédominer) [paix, silence] to reign, prevail (sur over); [accord, confiance, opinion] to prevail; [peur] to reign, hold sway (sur over); **la confusion la plus totale régnait dans la chambre** utter confusion prevailed in the room, the room was in utter confusion; **maison où l'ordre règne** house where order reigns; **faire ~ l'ordre** to maintain law and order; **faire ~ la terreur/le silence** to make terror/silence reign; (iro) **la confiance règne!** that's ou there's trust for you! (iro)

regonflage [R(ə)gõflaʒ], **regonflement** [R(ə)gõfləmã] NM blowing up (again), reinflating; (avec une pompe à main) pumping up (again)

regonfler [R(ə)gõfle] ▶ conjug 1 ◀ [1] VT [a] (= gonfler à nouveau) to blow up again, reinflate; (avec une pompe à main) to pump up again [b] (= gonfler davantage) to blow up harder, pump up further [c]* [+ personne] to cheer up; [+ ventes, bénéfices] to boost; **il est regonflé (à bloc)** he's back on top of things*; **~ le moral de qn** to bolster sb up [2] VI [rivière] to swell ou rise again; (Méd) to swell up again

regorgement [R(ə)gɔRʒəmã] NM overflow

regorger [R(ə)gɔRʒe] ▶ conjug 3 ◀ VI [a] **~ de** [région, pays] to abound in; [maison, magasin] to be packed ou crammed with; **la région regorge d'ananas** pineapples are plentiful in the region, the region abounds in pineapples; **cette année le marché regorge de fruits** this year there is a glut ou an abundance of fruit on the market; **le pays regorge d'argent** the country has enormous financial assets; **il regorge d'argent** he is rolling in money*, he has got plenty of money; **sa maison regorgeait de livres/d'invités** his house was packed with ou crammed with ou cram-full of books/guests; **la rue regorge de petits étals**

► GRAMMAIRE ACTIVE: **règlement** 47.5 **régler** 47.5

the street is packed with little market stalls; **la ville regorge de festivaliers** the town is swarming with festival-goers; **son livre regorge de bonnes idées/de fautes** his book is (jam-)packed *ou* crammed with good ideas/is riddled with mistakes
b [*liquide*] to overflow

régresser [ʀegʀese] ▸conjug 1◂ VI [*science, enfant*] to regress; [*douleur, épidémie*] to recede, diminish; [*chiffre d'affaires, ventes*] to drop, fall; **le taux de chômage a nettement régressé** the rate of unemployment has dropped sharply

régressif, -ive [ʀegʀesif, iv] ADJ [*évolution, raisonnement*] regressive; [*marche*] backward (*épith*); (*Phon*) anticipatory; (*Géol*) **érosion régressive** headward erosion; **forme régressive** regressive *ou* recessive form; (*Ling*) **dérivation régressive** back formation; (*Fin*) **impôt ~** regressive tax

régression [ʀegʀesjɔ̃] NF (*gén*) regression, decline; (*Bio, Math, Psych*) regression; **être en (voie de) ~** to be on the decline *ou* decrease, be declining *ou* decreasing; (*Géol*) **~ marine** marine regression

▼**regret** [ʀ(ə)gʀɛ] NM a [*décision, faute*] regret (**de** for); [*passé*] regret (**de** about); **le ~ d'une occasion manquée la faisait pleurer** she wept with regret at the lost opportunity, she wept in regret at losing the opportunity; **les ~s causés par une occasion manquée** the regrets felt at *ou* for a missed opportunity; **le ~ du pays natal** homesickness; **le ~ d'avoir échoué** the regret that he had failed *ou* at having failed; **vivre dans le ~ d'une faute** to spend one's life regretting a mistake; **c'est avec ~ que je vous le dis** I am sorry *ou* I regret to have to tell you this; **sans ~** with no regrets; **je te le donne — sans ~s ?** take this — are you (really) sure?; (*sur une tombe*) **~s éternels** sorely missed
b (*loc*) **à ~** [*partir*] with regret, regretfully; [*accepter, donner*] with regret, reluctantly; **je suis au ~ de ne pouvoir ...** I'm sorry *ou* I regret that I am unable to ...; **j'ai le ~ de vous informer que ...** I regret to inform you that ..., I must regretfully inform you that ... (*frm*); **à mon grand ~** to my great regret

▼**regrettable** [ʀ(ə)gʀetabl] ADJ [*incident, conséquence*] regrettable, unfortunate; **il est ~ que ...** it's unfortunate *ou* regrettable that ...

regrettablement [ʀ(ə)gʀetabləmɑ̃] ADV (*littér*) regrettably

▼**regretter** [ʀ(ə)gʀete] ▸conjug 1◂ VT a [+ *personne, pays natal*] to miss; [+ *jeunesse*] to miss, regret; [+ *occasion manquée, temps perdu*] to regret; **nous avons beaucoup regretté votre absence** we were very sorry *ou* we greatly regretted that you weren't able to join us; **il regrette son argent** he regrets spending the money; **c'était cher, mais je ne regrette pas mon argent** it was expensive but I don't regret buying it *ou* spending the money; **notre regretté président** our late lamented president; **on le regrette beaucoup dans le village** he is greatly *ou* sadly missed in the village
b (= *se repentir de*) [+ *décision, imprudence, péché*] to regret; **tu le regretteras** you'll regret it, you'll be sorry for it; **tu ne le regretteras pas** you won't regret it; **je ne regrette rien** I have no regrets; **je regrette mon geste** I'm sorry I did that, I regret doing that
c (= *désapprouver*) [+ *mesure, décision hostile*] to regret, deplore
d (= *être désolé*) to be sorry, regret; **je regrette, mais il est trop tard** I'm sorry, but it's too late, I'm afraid it's too late; **ah non! je regrette, il était avec moi** no! I'm sorry (to contradict you) but he was with me; **nous regrettons qu'il soit malade** we regret *ou* are sorry that he is ill; **je regrette de ne pas lui avoir écrit** I'm sorry *ou* I regret that I didn't write to him, I regret not writing *ou* not having written to him; **je regrette de vous avoir fait attendre** I'm sorry to have kept you waiting; **je ne regrette pas d'être venu** I'm not sorry *ou* I'm glad I came

regrimper [ʀ(ə)gʀɛ̃pe] ▸conjug 1◂ 1 VT [+ *pente, escalier*] to climb (up) again 2 VI [*route*] to climb (up) again; [*fièvre*] to go up *ou* rise again; [*prix*] to go up *ou* climb again; **~ dans le train** to climb back into the train; **ça va faire ~ les prix/la fièvre** it'll put up prices/his temperature again

regrossir [ʀ(ə)gʀosiʀ] ▸conjug 2◂ VI to put on weight again

regroupement [ʀ(ə)gʀupmɑ̃] NM a [*objets, pièces de collection*] bringing together; [*industries, partis, parcelles*] grouping together; (*Fin, Jur*) **~s de sociétés** groupings of companies
b (= *fait de réunir de nouveau*) [*armée, personnes*] reassembling; [*bétail*] rounding up again; (*Jur*) **~ familial** family reunification
c (*Sport*) [*coureurs*] bunching together; [*rugbymen*] loose scrum

regrouper [ʀ(ə)gʀupe] ▸conjug 1◂ 1 VT a (= *réunir*) [+ *objets*] to put *ou* group together; [+ *pièces de collection*] to bring together; [+ *industries, partis, parcelles*] to group together; [+ *territoires*] to consolidate; (= *fusionner*) [+ *services, classes*] to merge b (= *réunir de nouveau*) [+ *armée, personnes*] to reassemble; [+ *parti*] to regroup; [+ *bétail*] to round up, herd together
2 **se regrouper** VPR a (= *se réunir*) [*personnes*] to gather (together), assemble; [*entreprises*] to group together; **se ~ autour d'une cause** to unite behind a cause
b (*Sport*) [*coureurs*] to bunch together again; [*rugbymen*] to form a loose scrum

régularisation [ʀegylaʀizasjɔ̃] NF a [*situation*] regularization; [*passeport, papiers*] sorting out b [*mécanisme, débit*] regulation c (*Fin*) equalization; **~ des cours** price stabilization

régulariser [ʀegylaʀize] ▸conjug 1◂ 1 VT a [+ *passeport, papiers*] to sort out; **~ sa situation** (*gén*) to get one's situation sorted out; [*immigré*] to get one's papers in order, have one's (immigration) status regularized; **ils ont fini par ~*** (= *ils se sont mariés*) they ended up making it official; **faire ~ ses papiers** to have one's papers put in order *ou* sorted out b (= *régler*) [+ *mécanisme, débit*] to regulate; **~ le cours d'un fleuve** to regulate the flow of a river c (*Méd*) [+ *pouls, respiration, rythme cardiaque, circulation*] to regulate d (*Fin*) [+ *monnaie*] to equalize 2 **se régulariser** VPR [*pouls, respiration, rythme cardiaque, circulation*] to return to normal

régularité [ʀegylaʀite] NF a [*pouls, travail, effort, respiration, rythme*] regularity, steadiness; [*qualité, résultats*] consistency, evenness; [*vitesse, vent*] steadiness; [*habitudes, progrès, paiement, visites, service de transport*] regularity; **avec ~** [*se produire*] regularly; [*progresser*] steadily b (= *uniformité*) [*répartition, couche, ligne*] evenness; (= *symétrie*) symmetry; (= *harmonie*) [*traits, paysage*] regularity, evenness; [*écriture*] regularity; (= *égalité*) [*humeur*] steadiness, evenness; (*Math*) [*polygone*] regularity c (= *légalité*) [*élection, procédure*] legality, lawfulness

régulateur, -trice [ʀegylatœʀ, tʀis] 1 ADJ regulating 2 NM (*Tech, fig*) regulator; **~ de vitesse/de température** speed/temperature control *ou* regulator

régulation [ʀegylasjɔ̃] NF [*économie, trafic*] regulation; [*mécanisme*] regulation, adjustment; **~ des naissances** birth control; (*Physiol*) **~ thermique** regulation of body temperature, thermotaxis (*SPÉC*); **~ de la circulation** traffic control, regulation of traffic flow

réguler [ʀegyle] ▸conjug 1◂ VT [+ *flux, marché, taux*] to regulate; **~ la circulation routière** to regulate the flow of traffic, control traffic

régulier, -ière [ʀegylje, jɛʀ] 1 ADJ a (*en fréquence, en force*) [*pouls, rythme, respiration, travail, effort*] regular, steady; [*qualité, résultats*] even, consistent; [*progrès, vitesse, vent*] steady; [*habitudes, paiement, revenus, visites*] regular; (*Transport*) [*ligne, vol*] scheduled; [*service de train, bus*] regular; **rivière régulière** river which has a regular *ou* steady flow; **frapper qch à coups ~s** to strike sth with regular *ou* steady blows; **à intervalles ~s** at regular intervals; **prendre ses repas à (des) heures régulières** to eat at regular intervals; **exercer une pression régulière sur qch** to exert steady pressure on sth; **être en correspondance régulière avec qn** to be in regular correspondence with sb
b (= *uniforme*) [*répartition, couche, ligne*] even; [*façade*] regular; [*traits, paysage*] regular, even; [*écriture*] regular, neat; (*Math*) [*polygone*] regular; [*humeur*] steady, even; [*vie*] ordered; **avoir un visage ~** to have regular features; **il faut que la pression soit bien régulière partout** the pressure must be evenly distributed over the whole area; **il est ~ dans son travail** he's steady in his work, he's a regular *ou* steady worker
c (= *légal*) [*gouvernement*] legitimate; [*élection, procédure*] in order (*attrib*); [*jugement*] regular, in order (*attrib*); [*tribunal*] legal, official; **être en situation régulière** to have one's papers in order
d (= *honnête*) [*opération, coup*] aboveboard (*attrib*); [*homme d'affaires*] on the level (*attrib*), straightforward, straight (*attrib*); (= *correct*) **vous me faites faire quelque chose qui n'est pas très ~** you're getting me into something that is not quite on the level *ou* aboveboard; **être ~ en affaires** to be straight *ou* honest in business; **coup ~** (*Boxe*) fair blow; (*Échecs*) correct move
e (*Mil*) [*troupes*] regular; [*armée*] regular, standing; (*Rel*) [*clergé, ordre*] regular
f [*vers, verbe, pluriel*] regular
g (*Can* = *normal*) normal, regular (*US*)
2 NM (= *client, Mil, Rel*) regular
3 **régulière** NF a (*, †) (= *femme*) missus*, old woman*; (= *maîtresse*) lady-love (*hum*)
4 **à la régulière*** LOC ADV [*battre*] fair and square

régulièrement [ʀegyljɛʀmɑ̃] ADV a [*rencontrer, se réunir, organiser, réviser*] regularly; **il est ~ en retard** he's habitually late b [*répartir, disposer*] evenly c [*progresser*] steadily d (= *selon les règles*) properly; **élu ~** properly elected, elected in accordance with the rules; **opération effectuée ~** operation carried out in the correct *ou* proper fashion; **coup porté ~** fairly dealt blow e* (= *en principe*) normally, in principle; (= *d'habitude*) normally, usually

régurgitation [ʀegyʀʒitasjɔ̃] NF regurgitation

régurgiter [ʀegyʀʒite] ▸conjug 1◂ VT to regurgitate

réhabilitation [ʀeabilitasjɔ̃] NF a (*Jur*) [*condamné*] clearing (the name of), rehabilitation; [*failli*] discharge; **obtenir la ~ de qn** to get sb's name cleared, get sb rehabilitated
b (= *revalorisation*) [*profession, art, idéologie*] restoring to favour c (= *rénovation*) [*quartier, immeuble*] restoration, rehabilitation; (*Écol*) **~ des sites** site remediation

réhabiliter [ʀeabilite] ▸conjug 1◂ 1 VT a [+ *condamné*] to clear (the name of), rehabilitate; [+ *failli*] to discharge; **~ la mémoire de qn** to restore sb's good name b (= *revaloriser*) [+ *profession, art, idéologie*] to bring back into favour, restore to favour c (= *rénover*) [+ *quartier, immeuble*] to restore, rehabilitate; (*Écol*) [+ *sites*] to remediate d (= *rétablir*) **~ qn dans ses fonctions** to reinstate sb (in their job); **~ qn dans ses droits** to restore sb's rights (to them) 2 **se réhabiliter** VPR [*condamné, criminel*] to rehabilitate o.s.; [*candidat*] to redeem o.s.

réhabituer [ʀeabitɥe] ▸conjug 1◂ 1 VT **~ qn à (faire) qch** to get sb used to (doing) sth again,

➤ GRAMMAIRE ACTIVE: **regret** 36.3, 45.3, 46.5, 52.5 **regrettable** 45.3 **regretter** 45.3, 47.2

reaccustom sb to (doing) sth **2 se réhabi-tuer** VPR se ~ à (faire) qch to get used to (doing) sth again, reaccustom o.s. to (doing) sth; **ça va être dur de se ~** it will be difficult to get used to it again

rehaussement [ʀəosmɑ̃] NM **a** [mur, clôture] heightening; [plafond, chaise] raising, heightening **b** (Fin) [plafond] raising

rehausser [ʀəose] ▶conjug 1◀ VT **a** [+ mur, clôture] to heighten, make higher; [+ plafond, chaise] to raise, heighten; **on va le ~ avec un coussin** [+ enfant] we'll put a cushion under him so he's sitting up a bit higher **b** (= augmenter, souligner) [+ beauté, couleur, image de marque] to enhance; [+ goût] to bring out; [+ mérite, prestige] to enhance, increase; [+ popularité] to increase; [+ détail] to bring out, accentuate, underline; **les épices rehaussent la saveur d'un plat** spices bring out the flavour of a dish **c** (= orner) [+ tableau, robe] to brighten, liven up; **rehaussé de** embellished with

rehausseur [ʀəosœʀ] ADJ M, NM [siège d'enfant] **de siège** ◊ **siège ~** booster seat

réhydratation [ʀeidʀatasjɔ̃] NF (gén) rehydration; [peau] moisturizing

réhydrater [ʀeidʀate] ▶conjug 1◀ VT (gén) to rehydrate; [+ peau] to moisturize

réification [ʀeifikasjɔ̃] NF reification

réifier [ʀeifje] ▶conjug 7◀ VT to reify

réimperméabilisation [ʀeɛ̃pɛʀmeabilizasjɔ̃] NF reproofing

réimperméabiliser [ʀeɛ̃pɛʀmeabilize] ▶conjug 1◀ VT to reproof

réimplantation [ʀeɛ̃plɑ̃tasjɔ̃] NF [embryon, organe] reimplantation

réimplanter [ʀeɛ̃plɑ̃te] ▶conjug 1◀ **1** VT [+ entreprise existante] to relocate; [+ nouvelle entreprise] to set up; [+ embryon, organe] to reimplant **2 se réimplanter** VPR [entreprise] to relocate; [personne] to reestablish oneself

réimportation [ʀeɛ̃pɔʀtasjɔ̃] NF reimportation

réimporter [ʀeɛ̃pɔʀte] ▶conjug 1◀ VT to reimport

réimposer [ʀeɛ̃poze] ▶conjug 1◀ VT **a** (Fin) to impose a new ou further tax on **b** (Typo) to reimpose

réimposition [ʀeɛ̃pozisjɔ̃] NF **a** (Fin) further taxation **b** (Typo) reimposition

réimpression [ʀeɛ̃pʀesjɔ̃] NF (= action) reprinting; (= livre) reprint; **l'ouvrage est en cours de ~** the book is being reprinted

réimprimer [ʀeɛ̃pʀime] ▶conjug 1◀ VT to reprint

Reims [ʀɛ̃s] N Rheims

rein [ʀɛ̃] **1** NM (= organe) kidney; **être sous ~ artificiel** to be on a kidney machine; **~ flottant** renal ptosis **2 reins** NMPL (= région) small of the back; (= taille) waist; **avoir mal aux ~s** to have backache (in the lower back), have an ache in the small of one's back; **ses cheveux tombent sur ses ~s** her hair comes down to her waist; **il donna un coup de ~s pour se relever** he heaved himself up; **donner un coup de ~s pour soulever qch** to heave sth up; **avoir les ~s solides** (lit) to have a strong ou sturdy back; (fig) **ils ont/n'ont pas les ~s assez solides** they are/aren't in a strong enough financial position; (fig) **casser** ou **briser les ~s à qn** to ruin ou break sb; (fig) **il m'a mis l'épée dans les ~s** he really turned on the pressure → **creux**

réincarcération [ʀeɛ̃kaʀseʀasjɔ̃] NF reimprisonment, reincarceration

réincarcérer [ʀeɛ̃kaʀseʀe] ▶conjug 6◀ VT to reimprison, reincarcerate

réincarnation [ʀeɛ̃kaʀnasjɔ̃] NF reincarnation

réincarner (se) [ʀeɛ̃kaʀne] ▶conjug 1◀ VPR to be reincarnated (en as)

réincorporer [ʀeɛ̃kɔʀpɔʀe] ▶conjug 1◀ VT [+

soldat] to re-enlist; **~ son régiment** to re-enlist in one's regiment

reine [ʀɛn] **1** NF (Échecs, Pol, Zool, fig) queen; **la ~ de Saba** the Queen of Sheba; **la ~ d'Angleterre** the Queen of England; **la ~ Élisabeth** Queen Elizabeth; **la ~ mère** (lit) the Queen mother; (* fig) her ladyship*; **la ~ du bal** the queen ou la belle of the ball; **la ~ de beauté** beauty queen; **la ~ des abeilles/des fourmis** the queen bee/ant; **comme une ~** [vivre] in the lap of luxury; [traiter] like a queen; **être vêtue comme une ~** to look like a queen; (Cartes) **la ~ de cœur/pique** the queen of hearts/spades; **c'est la ~ des idiotes*** she's a prize idiot* → **bouchée², petit, port² 2** COMP ▶ **reine des reinettes** rennet

reine-claude (pl **reines-claudes**) [ʀɛnklod] NF greengage

reine-des-prés (pl **reines-des-prés**) [ʀɛndepʀe] NF meadowsweet

reine-marguerite (pl **reines-marguerites**) [ʀɛnmaʀɡəʀit] NF (China) aster

reinette [ʀɛnɛt] NF ≈ (Cox's orange) pippin; **~ grise** russet

réinfecter [ʀeɛ̃fɛkte] ▶conjug 1◀ VT to reinfect; **la plaie s'est réinfectée** the wound has become infected again

réinfection [ʀeɛ̃fɛksjɔ̃] NF reinfection

réinitialiser [ʀeinisjalize] ▶conjug 1◀ VT (Ordin) to reboot

réinjecter [ʀeɛ̃ʒɛkte] ▶conjug 1◀ VT (Méd) to re-inject; **~ des fonds dans une entreprise** to pump more money into a company; **ils ont réinjecté une partie des bénéfices dans la recherche** they put some of the profits back into research

réinscriptible [ʀeɛ̃skʀiptibl] ADJ (Ordin) [disque] rewriteable

réinscription [ʀeɛ̃skʀipsjɔ̃] NF reregistration, re-enrolment (Brit), re-enrollment (US)

réinscrire [ʀeɛ̃skʀiʀ] ▶conjug 39◀ **1** VT [+ épitaphe] to reinscribe; [+ date, nom] to put down again; [+ élève] to re-enrol, reregister; **je n'ai pas réinscrit mon fils à la cantine cette année** I haven't put my son's name down for school meals this year **2 se réinscrire** VPR to re-enrol, reregister (à for)

réinsérer [ʀeɛ̃seʀe] ▶conjug 6◀ VT **a** [+ publicité, feuillet] to reinsert **b** [+ délinquant, handicapé] to reintegrate, rehabilitate; **se ~ dans la société** to rehabilitate o.s. ou become reintegrated in society

réinsertion [ʀeɛ̃sɛʀsjɔ̃] NF **a** [publicité, feuillet] reinsertion **b** [délinquant, handicapé] reintegration, rehabilitation; **la ~ sociale des anciens détenus** the (social) rehabilitation of ex-prisoners

réinstallation [ʀeɛ̃stalasjɔ̃] NF **a** (= remise en place) [cuisinière] putting back, reinstallation; [étagère] putting up again; [téléphone] reinstallation **b** (= réaménagement) **notre ~ à Paris/dans l'appartement va poser des problèmes** settling back in Paris/into the flat is going to create problems for us

réinstaller [ʀeɛ̃stale] ▶conjug 1◀ **1** VT **a** (= remettre en place) [+ cuisinière] to put back, reinstall; [+ étagère] to put back up, put up again; [+ téléphone] to reconnect, reinstall **b** (= réaménager) [+ pièce, appartement] to refurnish; **les bureaux ont été réinstallés à Paris** the offices were moved back to Paris **c** (= rétablir) **~ qn chez lui** to move sb back into their own home; **~ qn dans ses fonctions** to reinstate sb in their job, give sb their job back **2 se réinstaller** VPR (dans un fauteuil) to settle down again (dans in); (dans une maison) to settle back (dans into); **il s'est réinstallé à Paris** (gén) he's gone back to live in Paris; [commerçant] he's set up in business again in Paris; **se ~ au pouvoir** to come back to power

réintégration [ʀeɛ̃teɡʀasjɔ̃] NF **a** [employé] reinstatement (dans in) **b** (= retour) return (de to); **~ du domicile conjugal** returning to the marital home

réintégrer [ʀeɛ̃teɡʀe] ▶conjug 6◀ VT **a** (= rétablir) **~ qn (dans ses fonctions)** to reinstate sb (in their job), restore sb to their (former) position; **~ qn dans ses droits** to restore sb's rights **b** (= regagner) to return to, go back to; **~ le domicile conjugal** to return to the marital home

réinterpréter [ʀeɛ̃tɛʀpʀete] ▶conjug 6◀ VT to reinterpret

réintroduction [ʀeɛ̃tʀɔdyksjɔ̃] NF [personne, mode, projet de loi] reintroduction; **la ~ d'espèces en voie de disparition** reintroducing endangered species

réintroduire [ʀeɛ̃tʀɔdɥiʀ] ▶conjug 38◀ **1** VT **a** (= réinsérer) [+ objet] to reinsert; **~ une clé dans une serrure** to put a key back into a lock; **~ des erreurs dans un texte** to reintroduce errors ou put errors back into a text **b** (= présenter de nouveau) [+ personne] to introduce again; [+ projet de loi] to reintroduce **c** (= relancer) [+ mode] to reintroduce, introduce again **2 se réintroduire** VPR se ~ dans [+ lieu, milieu] to get back into

réinventer [ʀeɛ̃vɑ̃te] ▶conjug 1◀ VT to reinvent

réinvestir [ʀeɛ̃vɛstiʀ] ▶conjug 2◀ VT (Fin) [+ capital] to reinvest (dans in); **une partie des bénéfices a été réinvestie dans l'entreprise** some of the profits have been reinvested in ou have gone straight back into the company

réinviter [ʀeɛ̃vite] ▶conjug 1◀ VT to invite back, ask back again, reinvite

réislamisation [ʀeislamizasjɔ̃] NF revival of Islam; **cela a conduit à une ~ du pays/des mœurs** this has led to a revival of Islam in the country/in people's lives

réitératif, -ive [ʀeiteʀatif, iv] ADJ reiterative

réitération [ʀeiteʀasjɔ̃] NF reiteration, repetition

réitérer [ʀeiteʀe] ▶conjug 6◀ VT [+ promesse, ordre, question] to reiterate, repeat; [+ demande, exploit] to repeat; **attaques réitérées** repeated attacks; **le criminel a réitéré** the criminal has repeated his crime ou has done it again

reître [ʀɛtʀ] NM (littér) ruffianly ou roughneck soldier

rejaillir [ʀ(ə)ʒajiʀ] ▶conjug 2◀ VI **a** (= éclabousser) [liquide] to splash back ou up (sur onto, at); (avec force) to spurt back ou up (sur onto, at); [boue] to splash up (sur onto, at); **l'huile m'a rejailli à la figure** the oil splashed up in my face **b** (= retomber) **~ sur qn** [scandale, honte] to rebound on sb; [gloire] to be reflected on sb; **les bienfaits de cette invention rejailliront sur tous** everyone stands to benefit from this invention; **sa renommée a rejailli sur ses collègues** his fame brought his colleagues some reflected glory

rejaillissement [ʀ(ə)ʒajismɑ̃] NM **a** [liquide, boue] splashing up; (avec force) spurting up **b** [scandale, honte] rebounding; [gloire] reflection

rejet [ʀəʒɛ] NM **a** [épave, corps] casting up, washing up **b** [fumée, gaz, déchets] discharge; [lave] throwing out, spewing out **c** (= refus) [candidat, candidature, manuscrit, projet de loi, offre, demande, conseil] rejection; [recours en grâce, hypothèse] rejection, dismissal **d** (Littérat) enjamb(e)ment, rejet **e** (Ling) **le ~ de la préposition à la fin de la phrase** putting the preposition at the end of the sentence **f** (Bot) shoot **g** (Géol) throw **h** (Méd) [greffe] rejection; (lit, fig) **phénomène de ~** rejection; **faire un ~** (Méd) to reject a transplant; **la musique baroque, moi je fais un ~*** I can't bear baroque music **i** (Ordin) reject

▼ **rejeter** [ʀəʒ(ə)te, ʀ(ə)ʒəte] ▸ conjug 4◂ ① VT
⎿a⏌ (= *relancer*) [+ *objet*] to throw back (**à** to); ~ **un poisson à l'eau** to throw a fish back (into the water)

⎿b⏌ [+ *fumée, gaz, déchets*] to discharge; **il ou son estomac rejette toute nourriture** his stomach rejects everything, he can't keep anything down; **le volcan rejette de la lave** the volcano is spewing *ou* throwing out lava; **le cadavre a été rejeté par la mer** the corpse was washed up on the shore

⎿c⏌ (= *refuser*) [+ *domination, amant, candidat, candidature, manuscrit*] to reject; [+ *projet de loi*] to reject, throw out; [+ *accusation*] to refute, deny; [+ *offre, demande, conseil*] to reject, turn down; [+ *recours en grâce, hypothèse*] to reject, dismiss; [+ *indésirable*] to cast out, expel; [+ *envahisseur*] to push back, drive back; **la machine rejette les mauvaises pièces de monnaie** the machine rejects *ou* refuses invalid coins; **la proposition de paix a été rejetée** the peace proposal has been rejected; **le village l'a rejeté après ce dernier scandale** the village has cast him out after this latest scandal; ~ **qn d'un parti** to expel sb from *ou* throw sb out of a party

⎿d⏌ (= *faire porter*) ~ **une faute sur qn/qch** to put the blame on sb/sth, blame sb/sth; **il rejette la responsabilité sur moi** he blames me, he lays the responsibility at my door

⎿e⏌ (= *placer*) **la préposition est rejetée à la fin** the preposition is put at the end; ~ **la tête en arrière** to throw *ou* toss one's head back; ~ **ses cheveux en arrière** (*avec la main*) to push one's hair back; (*en se coiffant*) to comb *ou* brush one's hair back; (*d'un mouvement de la tête*) to toss one's hair back; ~ **les épaules en arrière** to pull one's shoulders back; **le chapeau rejeté en arrière** with his hat tilted back; ~ **la terre hors d'une tranchée** to throw the earth out of a trench

⎿f⏌ (*Méd*) [+ *greffon*] to reject

⎿g⏌ (*Ordin*) to reject

② **se rejeter** VPR ⎿a⏌ (= *se reculer*) **se ~ en arrière** to jump *ou* leap back(wards)

⎿b⏌ (= *se jeter de nouveau*) **il s'est rejeté dans l'eau** he jumped back *ou* threw himself back into the water

⎿c⏌ (= *se renvoyer*) **ils se rejettent (mutuellement) la responsabilité de la rupture** they lay the responsibility for the break-up at each other's door, each wants the other to take responsibility for the break-up

▸ **rejeton** [ʀəʒ(ə)tɔ̃, ʀ(ə)ʒ(ə)tɔ̃] NM ⎿a⏌ (* = *enfant*) kid*; **ils sont venus avec leurs ~s** they brought their kids* *ou* offspring (*hum*) with them

⎿b⏌ (*Bot*) shoot; (*fig*) offshoot

▸ **rejoindre** [ʀ(ə)ʒwɛ̃dʀ] ▸ conjug 49◂ ① VT ⎿a⏌ (= *regagner, retrouver*) [+ *lieu*] to get (back) to; [+ *route*] to (re)join, get (back) (on)to; [+ *personne*] to (re)join, meet (again); [+ *poste, régiment*] to rejoin, return to; **la route rejoint la voie ferrée à ...** the road meets (up with) *ou* (re)joins the railway line at ...

⎿b⏌ (= *rattraper*) to catch up (with); **je n'arrive pas à le ~** I can't manage to catch up with him *ou* to catch him up (*Brit*)

⎿c⏌ (= *se rallier à*) [+ *parti*] to join; [+ *point de vue*] to agree with; **je vous rejoins sur ce point** I agree with you on that point; **mon idée rejoint la vôtre** my idea is closely akin to yours *ou* is very much like yours; **c'est ici que la prudence rejoint la lâcheté** this is where prudence comes close to *ou* is closely akin to cowardice

⎿d⏌ (= *réunir*) [+ *personnes*] to reunite, bring back together (again); [+ *choses*] to bring together (again); [+ *lèvres d'une plaie*] to close

② **se rejoindre** VPR [*routes*] to join, meet; [*idées*] to concur, be closely akin to each other; [*personnes*] (*pour rendez-vous*) to meet (up) (again); (*sur point de vue*) to agree

▸ **rejointoyer** [ʀ(ə)ʒwɛ̃twaje] ▸ conjug 8◂ VT to repoint, regrout

▸ **rejouer** [ʀ(ə)ʒwe] ▸ conjug 1◂ ① VT (*gén*) to play again; [+ *match*] to replay; (*Cartes*) ~ **cœur** to lead hearts again; **on rejoue une partie ?** shall we have *ou* play another game?; ~ **une pièce** [*acteurs*] to perform a play again, give another performance of a play; [*théâtre*] to put on a play again; **nous rejouons demain à Marseille** [*acteurs*] we're performing again tomorrow in Marseilles; [*joueurs*] we're playing again tomorrow in Marseilles ② VI [*enfants, joueurs*] to play again; [*musicien*] to play *ou* perform again; **acteur qui ne pourra plus jamais ~** actor who will never be able to act *ou* perform again

▸ **réjoui, e** [ʀeʒwi] (*ptp de* **réjouir**) ADJ [*air, mine*] joyful, joyous

▼ **réjouir** [ʀeʒwiʀ] ▸ conjug 2◂ ① VT [+ *personne, regard*] to delight; [+ *cœur*] to gladden; **cette perspective le réjouit** this prospect delights *ou* thrills him, he is delighted *ou* thrilled at this prospect; **cette idée ne me réjouit pas beaucoup** I don't find the thought of it particularly appealing

② **se réjouir** VPR to be delighted *ou* thrilled (**de faire** to do); **se ~ de** [+ *nouvelle, événement*] to be delighted *ou* thrilled about *ou* at; [+ *malheur*] to take delight in, rejoice over; **vous avez gagné et je m'en réjouis pour vous** you've won and I'm delighted for you; **se ~ (à la pensée) que ...** to be delighted *ou* thrilled (at the thought) that ...; **je me réjouis à l'avance de les voir** I am greatly looking forward to seeing them; **réjouissez-vous !** rejoice!; **je me réjouis que tu aies réussi** I'm delighted *ou* thrilled that you've succeeded

▸ **réjouissance** [ʀeʒwisɑ̃s] NF rejoicing; **~s** festivities, merrymaking (*NonC*); (*fig hum*) **quel est le programme des ~s pour la journée ?** what delights are in store (for us) today? (*hum*), what's on the agenda for today?*

▸ **réjouissant, e** [ʀeʒwisɑ̃, ɑ̃t] ADJ [*histoire*] amusing, entertaining; [*nouvelle*] cheering; (*iro*) **quelle perspective ~e !** what a delightful prospect! (*iro*); **les prévisions ne sont guère ~es** the forecasts aren't very encouraging *ou* heartening; **ce n'est pas ~ !** it's no joke!

▸ **rejuger** [ʀ(ə)ʒyʒe] ▸ conjug 3◂ VT (*Jur*) [+ *affaire, accusé*] to retry

▸ **relâche** [ʀəlɑʃ] ① NM *ou* NF ⎿a⏌ (*littér = répit*) respite, rest; **prendre un peu de ~** to take a short rest *ou* break; **se donner ~** to give o.s. a rest *ou* a break; **sans ~** relentlessly ⎿b⏌ (*Théât*) closure; **faire ~** to be closed, close; « **relâche** » "no performance(s) (today *ou* this week *etc*)"; **le lundi est le jour de ~ du cinéma local** the local cinema is closed on Monday(s) ② NF (*Naut*) port of call; **faire ~ dans un port** to put in at *ou* call at a port

▸ **relâché, e** [ʀəlɑʃe] (*ptp de* **relâcher**) ADJ [*style*] loose, limp; [*conduite, mœurs*] lax; [*discipline, autorité*] lax, slack; [*prononciation*] lax

▸ **relâchement** [ʀəlɑʃmɑ̃] NM ⎿a⏌ [*étreinte*] relaxation, loosening; [*lien*] loosening, slackening; [*muscle*] relaxation; [*ressort*] release ⎿b⏌ [*attention, discipline, effort, zèle*] relaxation, slackening; [*surveillance*] relaxation; [*courage, attention*] flagging; **il y a du ~ dans la discipline** discipline is getting lax *ou* slack; **~ des mœurs** loosening *ou* slackening of moral standards

▸ **relâcher** [ʀ(ə)lɑʃe] ▸ conjug 1◂ ① VT ⎿a⏌ [+ *étreinte*] to relax, loosen; [+ *lien*] to loosen, slacken (off); [+ *muscle*] to relax; [+ *ressort*] to release; **il a relâché le poisson dans l'eau** he threw the fish back (into the water); ~ **les intestins** to loosen the bowels

⎿b⏌ [+ *discipline, surveillance*] to relax; [+ *effort*] to relax, let up; **ils relâchent leur attention** their attention is wandering

⎿c⏌ [+ *prisonnier, otage, gibier*] to release, let go, set free

⎿d⏌ (= *refaire tomber*) [+ *objet*] to drop (again),

let go of (again); **ne relâche pas la corde** don't let go of the rope (again)

② VI (*Naut*) ~ **(dans un port)** to put into port

③ **se relâcher** VPR ⎿a⏌ [*courroie*] to loosen, go ou get loose *ou* slack; [*muscle*] to relax

⎿b⏌ [*surveillance, discipline*] to become *ou* get lax *ou* slack; [*mœurs*] to become *ou* get lax; [*style*] to become sloppy; [*courage, attention*] to flag; [*zèle*] to slacken, flag; [*effort*] to let up; **il se relâche** he's letting up; **ne te relâche pas maintenant !** don't let up *ou* slack(en) off now!; **il se relâche dans son travail** he's growing slack in his work, his work is getting slack

▸ **relais** [ʀ(ə)lɛ] NM ⎿a⏌ (*Sport*) relay (race); (*Alpinisme*) stance; ~ **4 fois 100 mètres** 4 by 100 metres (relay); **passer le ~ à son coéquipier** to hand over to one's team-mate; **à cause du mauvais passage du ~** because one of the runners fumbled the baton *ou* pass ⎿b⏌ (*Ind*) **ouvriers/équipe de** ~ shift workers/team; **travail par** ~ shift work; **passer le ~ à qn** to hand over to sb; **le passage de ~ entre l'ancien et le nouveau directeur** the handover from the old manager to the new one; **prendre le ~ (de qn)** to take over (from sb); (*dans une transaction*) **servir de ~** to act as an intermediary *ou* a go-between; **la pluie ayant cessé, c'est la neige qui a pris le ~** once the rain had stopped the snow took over *ou* set in → **crédit-relais**, **prêt**

⎿c⏌ (= *chevaux, chiens*) relay; ~ **(de poste)** (*Hist* = *auberge*) post house, coaching inn; (*Mil*) staging post; ~ **routier** transport café (*Brit*), truck stop (*US*); **ville** ~ stopover → **cheval** ⎿d⏌ (*Elec, Radio, Téléc*) (= *action*) relaying; (= *dispositif*) relay; ~ **de télévision** television relay station; ~ **hertzien** radio relay; **avion/satellite de** ~ relay plane/satellite

▸ **relance** [ʀəlɑ̃s] NF ⎿a⏌ (= *reprise*) [*économie, industrie, emploi*] boosting, stimulation; [*idée, projet*] revival, relaunching; [*négociations*] reopening; (*Écon*) reflation; **pour permettre la ~ du processus de paix** in order to restart the peace process; **la ~ de l'économie n'a pas duré** the boost (given) to the economy did not last; **la ~ du terrorisme est due à ...** the fresh outburst of *ou* upsurge in terrorism is due to ...; **provoquer la ~ de** [+ *économie*] to give a boost to, boost, stimulate; [+ *projet*] to revive, relaunch; **mesures/politique de ~** reflationary measures/policy ⎿b⏌ (*Poker*) **faire une ~** to raise the stakes, make a higher bid; **limiter la ~** to limit the stakes ⎿c⏌ [*débiteur*] chasing up; [*client*] following up; **lettre de** ~ reminder

▸ **relancer** [ʀ(ə)lɑ̃se] ▸ conjug 3◂ VT ⎿a⏌ (= *renvoyer*) [+ *objet, ballon*] to throw back (again) ⎿b⏌ (= *faire repartir*) [+ *gibier*] to start (again); [+ *moteur*] to restart; [+ *idée, projet*] to revive, relaunch; [+ *polémique, dialogue, négociations*] to reopen; [+ *économie, industrie, emploi, inflation*] to boost, give a boost to, stimulate; ~ **la machine économique** to kick-start the economy ⎿c⏌ (= *harceler*) [+ *débiteur*] to chase up; (*sexuellement*) [+ *personne*] to harass, pester, chase after; ~ **un client par téléphone** to make a follow-up call to a customer ⎿d⏌ (*Cartes*) [+ *enjeu*] to raise ⎿e⏌ (*Ordin*) to restart

▸ **relaps, e** [ʀəlaps] ① ADJ relapsed ② NM,F relapsed heretic

▸ **relater** [ʀ(ə)late] ▸ conjug 1◂ VT (*littér*) [+ *événement, aventure*] to relate, recount; (*Jur*) [+ *pièce, fait*] to record; **le journaliste relate que ...** the journalist says that ... *ou* tells us that ...; **pourriez-vous ~ les faits tels que vous les avez observés ?** could you state the facts exactly as you observed them?

▸ **relatif, -ive** [ʀ(ə)latif, iv] ① ADJ (*gén, Gram, Mus*) relative; [*silence, luxe*] relative, comparative; **tout est ~** everything is relative; **discussions relatives à un sujet** discussions relative to *ou* relating to *ou* connected with a subject; **faire preuve d'un enthousiasme tout ~**

➤ GRAMMAIRE ACTIVE: **rejeter** 39.1   **réjouir** 38.2

to be less than enthusiastic; **faire preuve d'un optimisme ~** to be guardedly optimistic; (Mus) **(ton) majeur/mineur ~** relative major/minor (key) **2** NM **a** (Gram) relative pronoun **b avoir le sens du ~** to have a sense of proportion **3 relative** NF (Gram) relative clause

relation [R(ə)lasjɔ̃] **1** NF **a** (gén, Math, Philo) relation(ship); **~ de cause à effet** relation(ship) of cause and effect; **la ~ entre l'homme et l'environnement** the relation(ship) between man and the environment; **il y a une ~ évidente entre ...** there is an obvious connection ou relation(ship) between ...; **c'est sans ~** ou **cela n'a aucune ~ avec ...** it has no connection with ..., it bears no relation to ...; **faire la ~ entre deux événements** to make the connection between two events
b (= personne) acquaintance; **une de mes ~s** an acquaintance of mine, someone I know; **trouver un poste par ~s** to find a job through one's connections, find a job by knowing somebody ou by knowing the right people; **avoir des ~s** to have (influential) connections, know (all) the right people
c (= récit) account, report; **~ orale/écrite** oral/written account ou report; **d'après la ~ d'un témoin** according to a witness's account; **faire la ~ des événements/de son voyage** to give an account of ou relate the events/one's journey
2 relations NF PL relations; (= rapports) (gén) relations; (sur le plan personnel) relationship, relations; **~s diplomatiques/culturelles/publiques/internationales** diplomatic/ cultural/public/international relations; **~s patrons-ouvriers/patronat-syndicats** labour-management/union-management relations; **~s humaines** human relationships; **les ~s sont tendues/cordiales entre nous** relations between us are strained/cordial, the relationship between us ou our relationship is strained/cordial; **avoir des ~s (sexuelles) avec qn** to have sexual relations ou (sexual) intercourse with sb; **avoir des ~s amoureuses avec qn** to have an affair ou a love affair with sb; **avoir de bonnes ~s/des ~s amicales avec qn** to be on good/friendly terms with sb, have a good/friendly relationship with sb; **être en ~s d'affaires avec qn** to have business relations ou business dealings ou a business relationship with sb; **être/rester en ~(s) avec qn** to be/keep in touch ou contact with sb; **entrer** ou **se mettre en ~(s) avec qn** to get in touch ou make contact with sb; **nous sommes en ~s suivies** we are in constant ou close contact

relationnel, -elle [R(ə)lasjɔnɛl] ADJ (Psych) [problèmes] relationship (épith); [grammaire] relational; **base de données relationnelle** relational data base

relativement [R(ə)lativmɑ̃] ADV **a** [facile, honnête, rare] relatively, comparatively **b ~ à** (= par comparaison à) in relation to, compared to; (= concernant) with regard to, concerning

relativisation [Rəlativizasjɔ̃] NF relativization
relativiser [R(ə)lativize] ▶ conjug 1 ◀ VT to relativize
relativisme [R(ə)lativism] NM relativism
relativiste [R(ə)lativist] **1** ADJ relativistic **2** NMF relativist
relativité [R(ə)lativite] NF relativity; **découvrir la ~ des choses/des valeurs** to realize that things/values are relative; **(théorie de la) ~ générale/restreinte** general/special (theory of) relativity
relaver [R(ə)lave] ▶ conjug 1 ◀ VT to wash again, rewash
relax* [Rəlaks] ADJ = **relaxe²**
relaxant, e [R(ə)laksɑ̃, ɑ̃t] ADJ relaxing
relaxation [R(ə)laksasjɔ̃] NF relaxation; **j'ai besoin de ~** I need to relax, I need a bit of relaxation; **faire de la ~** to do relaxation exercises

relaxe¹ [Rəlaks] NF (= acquittement) acquittal, discharge; (= libération) release
relaxe²* [Rəlaks] ADJ [ambiance] relaxed, informal, laid back*; [tenue] informal, casual; [personne] relaxed, easy-going, laid-back*; [vacances] relaxing; **siège** ou **fauteuil ~** reclining chair, recliner
relaxer¹ [R(ə)lakse] ▶ conjug 1 ◀ VT (= acquitter) to acquit, discharge; (= libérer) to release
relaxer² [R(ə)lakse] ▶ conjug 1 ◀ **1** VT [+ muscles] to relax **2 se relaxer** VPR to relax
relayer [R(ə)leje] ▶ conjug 8 ◀ **1** VT **a** [+ personne] to relieve, take over from; [+ appareil] to replace; [+ initiative] to take over; **~ l'information** to pass the message on; **se faire ~** to get somebody to take over, hand over to somebody else **b** (Radio, TV) to relay **2 se relayer** VPR (pour faire to do, at doing), take it in turns (pour faire to do); (dans un relais) to take over from one another
relayeur, -euse [R(ə)lejœR, øz] NM,F relay runner
relecture [R(ə)lɛktyR] NF rereading; **~ d'épreuves** proofreading; **cet auteur nous propose une ~ de l'histoire contemporaine** this author offers us a rereading of contemporary history
relégation [R(ə)legasjɔ̃] NF **a** [personne, problème, objet] relegation **b** (Sport) relegation (en to) **c** (Jur = exil) relegation, banishment
reléguer [R(ə)lege] ▶ conjug 6 ◀ VT **a** (= confiner) [+ personne, problème] to relegate (à to); [+ objet] to consign, relegate (à, dans to); **~ qch/qn au second plan** to relegate sth/sb to a position of secondary importance **b** (Sport) to relegate (en to); **ils se trouvent relégués à la dixième place/en deuxième division** they have been relegated to tenth place/to the second division **c** (Jur = exiler) to relegate, banish
relent [Rəlɑ̃] NM foul smell, stench (NonC); **un ~** ou **des ~s de poisson pourri** a stench ou foul smell of rotten fish, the reek of rotten fish; **des ~s de vengeance** a whiff of revenge; **ça a des ~s de racisme** it smacks of racism
relevable [Rəl(ə)vabl, R(ə)ləvabl] ADJ [siège] tip-up (épith), fold-away (épith)
relevage [Rəl(ə)vaʒ] NM **station de ~** sewage treatment plant, sewage pumping station
relevé, e [Rəl(ə)ve] (ptp de **relever**) **1** ADJ **a** [col] turned-up; [virage] banked; [manches] rolled-up; [tête] (lit) held up; (fig) held high; **chapeau à bords ~s** hat with a turned-up brim; **porter les cheveux ~s** to wear one's hair up; (Équitation) **pas ~** high-step
b (= noble) [style, langue, sentiments] elevated, lofty; [conversation] refined, sophisticated; **cette expression n'est pas très ~e** it's not a very choice ou refined expression; **plaisanterie peu ~e** rather crude joke
c (Culin) [sauce, mets] highly-seasoned, spicy, hot
2 NM **a** [dépenses] summary, statement; [cote] plotting; [citations, adresses] list; (= facture) bill; [construction, plan] layout; **faire un ~ de** [+ citations, erreurs] to list, note down; [+ notes] to take down; [+ compteur] to read; **prochain ~ du compteur dans deux mois** next meter reading in two months; **~ de gaz/de téléphone** gas/telephone bill; **~ bancaire** ◊ ou **de compte** bank statement; **~ de condamnations** police record; **~ d'identité bancaire** particulars of one's bank account; **~ d'identité postal** particulars of one's post-office bank account; **~ de notes** marks sheet (Brit), grade sheet (US) **b** (Danse) relevé
relève [R(ə)lɛv] NF **a** (= personne) relief; (= travailleurs) relief (team); (= troupe) relief **b** (= sentinelles) relief (guard) **b** (= action) relief; **la ~ de la garde** the changing of the guard; **assurer** ou **prendre la ~ de qn** (lit) to relieve sb, take over from sb; (fig) to take over (from sb)

relèvement [R(ə)lɛvmɑ̃] NM **a** (= redressement) recovery; **on assiste à un ~ spectaculaire du pays/de l'économie** the country/the economy is making a spectacular recovery **b** (= rehaussement) [niveau] raising; [cours, salaires, impôts, taux] raising; **le ~ du plancher** raising the level of the floor; **un ~ de 5%** a 5% rise; **le ~ du salaire minimum** (action) the raising of the minimum wage; (résultat) the rise in the minimum wage **b** (Naut) **faire un ~ de sa position** to plot one's position

relever [Rəl(ə)ve, R(ə)ləve] ▶ conjug 5 ◀ **1** VT **a** (= redresser) [+ statue, meuble] to stand up (again); [+ chaise] to stand up (again), pick up; [+ véhicule, bateau] to right; [+ personne] to help (back) up, help (back) to his feet; [+ blessé] to pick up; **~ une vieille dame tombée dans la rue** to help up an old lady who has fallen in the street; **l'arbitre a fait ~ les joueurs** the referee made the players get up; **~ la tête** (lit) to lift ou hold up one's head; (fig) (= se rebeller) to raise one's head, show signs of rebelling; (fig = être fier) to hold one's head up ou high
b (= remonter) [+ col] to turn up; [+ chaussettes] to pull up; [+ jupe] to raise, lift; [+ manche, pantalon] to roll up; [+ voile] to lift, raise; [+ cheveux] to put up; [+ vitre] (en poussant) to push up; (avec bouton ou manivelle) to wind up; [+ store] to roll up, raise; [+ siège] to tip up; [+ manette] to push up; [+ couvercle] to lift (up); **lorsqu'il releva les yeux** when he lifted (up) ou raised his eyes, when he looked up; **elle avait les cheveux relevés** she had ou was wearing her hair up
c (= mettre plus haut) [+ mur, étagère, plafond] to raise, heighten; [+ niveau] to raise, bring up
d (= remettre en état) [+ ruines] to rebuild; [+ économie] to rebuild, restore; [+ pays, entreprise] to put back on its feet
e (= augmenter, faire monter) [+ salaire, impôts] to raise, increase, put up; [+ niveau de vie] to raise; [+ chiffre d'affaires] to increase; **j'ai dû ~ toutes les notes de deux points** I had to raise ou increase all the marks by two points; **cela ne l'a pas relevé dans mon estime** that didn't raise him in my esteem, that didn't improve my opinion of him; (péj) **il n'y en a pas un pour ~ l'autre*** they're both (just) as bad as one another; **pour ~ le moral des troupes** to boost the morale of the troops
f [+ sauce, plat] to season; **~ le goût d'un mets avec des épices** to bring out the flavour of a dish with spices; **ce plat aurait pu être un peu plus relevé** this dish could have been done with a bit more seasoning; (fig) **mettre des touches de couleurs claires pour ~ un tableau un peu terne** to add dabs of light colour to brighten ou liven up a rather dull picture; **bijoux qui relèvent la beauté d'une femme** jewellery that enhances a woman's beauty
g (= relayer) [+ sentinelle] to relieve, take over from; **à quelle heure viendra-t-on me ~ ?** when will I be relieved?, when is someone coming to take over from me?; **~ la garde** to change the guard
h (= remarquer) [+ faute, fait] to pick out, find; [+ contradiction] to find; [+ traces, empreintes] to find, discover; (Jur) **les charges relevées contre l'accusé** the charges laid ou brought against the accused
i (= enregistrer) [+ adresse, renseignement] to take down, note (down); [+ notes] to take down; [+ plan] to copy out, sketch; (Naut) [+ point] to plot; [+ compteur, électricité, gaz] to read; **j'ai fait ~ le nom des témoins** I had the name of the witnesses noted (down) ou taken down; **~ une cote** to plot an altitude; **les températures relevées sous abri** temperatures recorded in the shade; **~ des empreintes digitales** to take fingerprints; **~ les compteurs:** [proxénète] to collect the takings

1 (= *réagir à*) [+ *injure, calomnie*] to react to, reply to; [+ *défi*] to accept, take up, answer; **je n'ai pas relevé cette insinuation** I ignored this insinuation, I did not react *ou* reply to this insinuation; **il a dit un gros mot mais je n'ai pas relevé** he said a rude word but I didn't react *ou* I ignored it

k (= *ramasser*) [+ *copies, cahiers*] to collect (in), take in; (*Tricot*) **relevez 40 mailles autour de l'encolure** pick up 40 stitches around the neck → **gant**

l **~ qn de qch** to release sb from sth; **je te relève de ta promesse** I release you from your promise; **~ un fonctionnaire de ses fonctions** to relieve an official of his duties

2 relever de VT INDIR **a** (= *se rétablir*) **~ de maladie** to recover from *ou* get over an illness, get back on one's feet (after an illness); **~ de couches** to recover from *ou* get over one's confinement

b (= *être du ressort de*) to be a matter for, be the concern of; (= *être sous la tutelle de*) to come under; **cela relève de la Sécurité sociale** that is a matter for the Social Security; **cela relève de la théologie** that comes *ou* falls within the province of theology; **son cas relève de la psychanalyse** he needs to see a psychoanalyst; **ce service relève du ministère de l'Intérieur** this department comes under the authority of the Home Office; **cette affaire ne relève pas de ma compétence** this matter does not come within my remit; **ça relève de l'imagination la plus fantaisiste** that is a product of pure fancy → **miracle**

3 VI (= *remonter*) [*vêtement*] to pull up, go up; **cette jupe relève par devant** this skirt rides up at the front

4 se relever VPR **a** (= *se remettre debout*) to stand *ou* get up (again), get back (on)to one's feet (again); **le boxeur se releva** the boxer got up again *ou* got back to his feet *ou* picked himself up; **il l'a aidée à se ~** he helped her up

b (= *sortir du lit*) to get up; (= *ressortir du lit*) to get up again; **se ~ la nuit** to get up in the night; **il m'a fait (me) ~ pour que je lui apporte à boire** he made me get up to fetch him a drink

c (= *remonter*) [*strapontin*] to tip up; [*couvercle, tête de lit*] to lift up; **ses lèvres se relevaient dans un sourire** his mouth curled into a smile; **est-ce que cette fenêtre se relève ?** does this window go up?; **à l'heure où tous les stores de magasins se relèvent** when the shopkeepers roll up their shutters

d (= *se remettre*) **se ~ de** [+ *deuil, chagrin, honte*] to recover from, get over; **se ~ de ses ruines/cendres** to rise from its ruins/ashes; **il ne s'en est jamais relevé** he never got over it

releveur, -euse [Rəl(ə)vœR, øz] **1** ADJ **muscle ~** levator (muscle) **2** NM (*Anat*) levator **3** NM, F [*compteur*] meter reader; **~ du gaz/de l'électricité** gasman/electricity man

relief [Rəljɛf] **1** NM **a** (*Géog*) relief; **avoir un ~ accidenté** to be hilly; **région de peu de ~** fairly flat region; **le ~ sous-marin** the relief of the sea bed

b (= *saillies*) [*visage*] contours; [*médaille*] relief, embossed *ou* raised design; (*Art*) relief; **la pierre ne présentait aucun ~** the stone was quite smooth

c (= *profondeur, contraste*) [*dessin*] relief, depth; [*style*] relief; **portrait/photographie qui a beaucoup de ~** portrait/photograph which has plenty of relief *ou* depth; **~ acoustique ou sonore** depth of sound; **personnage qui manque de ~** rather flat *ou* uninteresting character; **votre dissertation manque de ~** your essay is rather flat

d **en ~** [*motif*] in relief, raised; [*caractères*] raised, embossed; [*carte de visite*] embossed; [*photographie, cinéma*] three-dimensional, 3-D, stereoscopic; **l'impression est en ~** the printing stands out in relief; **carte en ~** relief map

mettre en ~ [+ *intelligence*] to bring out; [+ *beauté, qualités*] to set *ou* show off, enhance, accentuate; [+ *idée*] to bring out, accentuate; **l'éclairage mettait en ~ les imperfections de son visage** the lighting brought out *ou* accentuated the imperfections of her face; **je tiens à mettre ce point en ~** I wish to underline *ou* stress *ou* emphasize this point; **il essayait de se mettre en ~ en monopolisant la conversation** he was trying to draw attention to himself *ou* to get himself noticed by monopolizing the conversation

2 reliefs NMPL (*littér: d'un repas*) remains, left-overs; (*littér*) **les ~s de sa gloire** the remnants of his glory

relier [Rəlje] ▶ conjug 7 ◀ VT **a** [+ *points, mots*] to join *ou* link up *ou* together; (*Elec*) to connect (up); [+ *villes*] to link (up); [+ *idées*] to link (up *ou* together); [+ *faits*] to connect (together), link (up *ou* together); **~ deux choses entre elles** to link *ou* join up two things, link *ou* join two things together; **des vols fréquents relient Paris à New York** frequent flights link *ou* connect Paris and *ou* with New York; **nous sommes reliés au studio par voiture-radio** we have a radio-car link to the studio; **ce verbe est relié à son complément par une préposition** this verb is linked to its complement by a preposition; **~ le passé au présent** to link the past to the present, link the past and the present (together)

b [+ *livre*] to bind; [+ *tonneau*] to hoop; **livre relié** bound volume, hardback (book); **livre relié (en) cuir** leather-bound book, book bound in leather

relieur, -ieuse [Rəljœʀ, jøz] NM,F (book-) binder

religieusement [R(ə)liʒøzmã] ADV (*Rel, fig*) religiously; [*écouter*] religiously, reverently; [*tenir sa parole*] scrupulously, religiously; **conserver ou garder ~** [+ *objet*] to keep lovingly; [+ *secret*] to keep scrupulously; **se marier ~** to have a church wedding, get married in church; **il a été élevé ~** he had a religious upbringing

religieux, -ieuse [R(ə)liʒjø, jøz] **1** ADJ **a** (*Rel*) [*édifice, secte, cérémonie, opinion*] religious; [*art*] sacred; [*école, mariage, musique*] church (*épith*); [*vie, ordres, personne*] religious; **l'habit ~** the monk's (*ou* nun's) habit **b** (*fig*) [*respect, soin*] religious; [*silence*] religious, reverent → **mante 2** NM (*gén*) religious figure; (= *moine*) monk, friar **3 religieuse** NF **a** (= *nonne*) nun **b** (*Culin*) iced *ou* frosted (*US*) cream puff (made with choux pastry)

religion [R(ə)liʒjɔ̃] NF **a** (= *culte*) religion, (religious) faith; (= *ensemble de croyances*) **la ~** religion; **la ~ chrétienne/musulmane** the Christian/Muslim religion *ou* faith; **avoir de la ~** to be religious; **les gens sans ~** people who have no religion *ou* without religion; (*hum*) **c'est contraire à ma ~** ◇ **ma ~ me l'interdit** it's against my religion (*hum*) **b** (= *vie monastique*) monastic life; **entrer en ~** to take one's vows; **Anne Dupuis, en ~ sœur Claire** Anne Dupuis, whose religious name is Sister Claire **c** (*fig*) **se faire une ~ de qch** to make a religion of sth; **il a la ~ de la nature** he's a nature lover; (= *conviction*) **sur ce point, sa ~ était faite** he was absolutely convinced of this; **je n'ai pas encore fait ma ~ là-dessus** I haven't made up my mind yet

religiosité [R(ə)liʒjozite] NF religiosity

reliquaire [Rəlikɛʀ] NM reliquary

reliquat [Rəlika] NM [*dette*] remainder, outstanding amount *ou* balance; [*compte*] balance; [*somme*] remainder; **il subsiste un ~ très important/un petit ~** there's a very large/a small amount left (over) *ou* remaining; **arrangez-vous pour qu'il n'y ait pas de ~** work it so that there is nothing left over

relique [Rəlik] NF (*Rel, fig*) relic; (*Bio*) relict;

garder ou conserver qch comme une ~ to treasure sth

relire [R(ə)liR] ▶ conjug 43 ◀ VT [+ *roman*] to read again, reread; [+ *manuscrit*] to read through again, read over (again), reread; **je n'arrive pas à me ~** I can't read what I've written

reliure [RəljyR] NF (= *couverture*) binding; (= *art, action*) (book)binding; **~ pleine** full binding; **donner un livre à la ~** to send a book for binding *ou* to the binder('s)

relocalisation [R(ə)lɔkalizasjɔ̃] NF [*entreprise, production*] relocation, transfer

relogement [R(ə)lɔʒmã] NM rehousing

reloger [R(ə)lɔʒe] ▶ conjug 3 ◀ VT to rehouse

relooker [R(ə)luke] ▶ conjug 1 ◀ VT [+ *produit*] to give a new look to; [+ *personne*] (*physiquement*) to give a new look to; (*changer son image de marque*) to revamp the image of; **relooké pour l'occasion, il ...** specially groomed for the occasion, he ...

relouer [Rəlwe] ▶ conjug 1 ◀ VT [*locataire*] to rent again; [*propriétaire*] to rent out again, relet (*Brit*); **cette année je reloue dans le Midi** I'm renting a place in the South of France again this year

reluire [R(ə)lqiR] ▶ conjug 38 ◀ VI [*meuble, chaussures*] to shine, gleam; [*métal, carrosserie*] (*au soleil*) to gleam, shine; (*sous la pluie*) to glisten; **faire ~ qch** to polish *ou* shine sth up, make sth shine → **brosse**

reluisant, e [R(ə)lqizã, ãt] ADJ **a** [*meubles, parquet, cuivres*] shining, shiny, gleaming; **~ de graisse** shiny with grease; **~ de pluie** glistening in the rain; **~ de propreté** spotless **b** (*fig iro*) **peu ou pas très ~** [*avenir, résultat, situation*] far from brilliant (*attrib*); [*personne*] despicable

reluquer* [R(ə)lyke] ▶ conjug 1 ◀ VT [+ *personne*] to eye (up)*, ogle*; [+ *passant*] to eye, squint at*; [+ *objet, poste*] to have one's eye on

rem [Rɛm] NM rem

remâcher [R(ə)maʃe] ▶ conjug 1 ◀ VT [*ruminant*] to ruminate; [*personne*] [+ *passé, soucis, échec*] to ruminate over *ou* on, chew over, brood on *ou* over; [+ *colère*] to nurse

remailler [R(ə)maje] ▶ conjug 1 ◀ VT = **remmailler**

remake [Rimɛk] NM (*Ciné*) remake; [*livre, spectacle*] new version

rémanence [Remanãs] NF (*Phys*) remanence; **~ des images visuelles** persistence of vision

rémanent, e [Remanã, ãt] ADJ [*magnétisme*] residual; [*pesticide*] persistent; **image ~e** after-image

remanger [R(ə)mãʒe] ▶ conjug 3 ◀ **1** VT (= *manger de nouveau*) to have again; (= *reprendre*) to have *ou* eat some more; **on a remangé du poulet aujourd'hui** we had chicken again today; **j'en remangerais bien** I'd like to have that again, I could eat that again **2** VI to eat again, have something to eat again

remaniement [R(ə)manimã] NM **a** [*roman, discours*] reworking; [*programme*] modification, reorganization; [*plan, constitution*] revision, amendment; **apporter un ~ à qch** to revise *ou* reshape *ou* modify *etc* sth **b** [*équipe*] reorganization; (*Pol*) [*cabinet, ministère*] reshuffle; **~ ministériel** cabinet reshuffle

remanier [R(ə)manje] ▶ conjug 7 ◀ VT **a** [+ *roman, discours*] to rework; [+ *encyclopédie*] to revise; [+ *programme*] to modify, reorganize; [+ *plan, constitution*] to revise, amend **b** [+ *équipe*] to reorganize; (*Pol*) [+ *cabinet, ministère*] to reshuffle

remaquiller [R(ə)makije] ▶ conjug 1 ◀ **1** VT **~ qn** to make sb up again **2 se remaquiller** VPR (*complètement*) to make o.s. up again, redo one's face; (*rapidement*) to touch up one's make-up

remarcher [R(ə)maʀʃe] ▶ conjug 1 ◀ VI [*personne*] to walk again; [*appareil*] to work again

remariage [ʀ(ə)maʀjaʒ] NM second marriage, remarriage

remarier [ʀ(ə)maʀje] ▸conjug 7◂ **1** VT **il aimerait ~ son fils** he'd like to see his son remarried *ou* married again **2** **se remarier** VPR to remarry, marry again

remarquable [ʀ(ə)maʀkabl] ADJ [*personne, exploit, réussite*] remarkable, outstanding; [*événement, fait*] noteworthy, remarkable; **il est ~ par sa taille** he is notable for *ou* he stands out because of his height; **elle est ~ par son intelligence** she is outstandingly intelligent

remarquablement [ʀ(ə)maʀkabləmã] ADV [*beau, doué*] remarkably, outstandingly; [*réussir, jouer*] remarkably *ou* outstandingly well

remarque [ʀ(ə)maʀk] NF (= *observation*) remark, comment; (= *critique*) critical remark; (= *annotation*) note; **faire une ~ désobligeante/pertinente** to make an unpleasant/a pertinent remark; **il m'en a fait la ~** he remarked *ou* commented on it to me; **je m'en suis moi-même fait la ~** that occurred to me as well, I thought that myself; **faire une ~ à qn** to make a critical remark to sb, criticize sb; **il m'a fait des ~s sur ma tenue** he passed comment *ou* he remarked on the way I was dressed; **elle a écrit des ~s sur mon devoir** she wrote some comments on my essay

remarqué, e [ʀ(ə)maʀke] (*ptp de* **remarquer**) ADJ [*entrée, absence*] conspicuous; **il a fait une intervention très ~e** his speech attracted a lot of attention

▼ **remarquer** [ʀ(ə)maʀke] ▸conjug 1◂ **1** VT **a** (= *apercevoir*) to notice; **je l'ai remarqué dans la foule** I caught sight of *ou* noticed him in the crowd; **avec ce chapeau, comment ne pas le ~!** with that hat on, how can you fail to notice her?; **il entra sans qu'on le remarque** *ou* **sans se faire ~** he came in unnoticed *ou* without being noticed; **il aime se faire ~** he likes to be noticed *ou* to draw attention to himself; **je remarque que vous avez une cravate** I notice *ou* see that you are wearing a tie; **je remarque que vous ne vous êtes pas excusé** I note that you did not apologize
b (= *faire une remarque*) to remark, observe; **tu es sot, remarqua son frère** you're stupid, his brother remarked *ou* observed; **il remarqua qu'il faisait froid** he remarked *ou* commented that it was cold; **remarquez (bien) que je n'en sais rien** I don't really know though, mind you I don't know (*Brit*); **ça m'est tout à fait égal, remarque!** I couldn't care less, I can tell you! *ou* mark you! (*Brit*) *ou* mind you!* (*Brit*)
c **faire ~** [+ *détail, erreur*] to point out, draw attention to; **il me fit ~ qu'il faisait nuit/qu'il était tard** he drew my attention to the fact that *ou* he pointed out to me that it was dark/that it was late; **il me fit ~ qu'il était d'accord avec moi** he pointed out (to me) that he agreed with me; **je te ferai seulement ~ que tu n'as pas de preuves** I'd just like to point out (to you) that you have no proof
d (= *marquer de nouveau*) to remark, mark again

2 **se remarquer** VPR [*défaut, gêne, jalousie*] to be obvious, be noticeable; **cette tache se remarque beaucoup/à peine** this stain is quite/hardly noticeable, this stain really/hardly shows; **ça ne se remarquera pas** no one will notice it; **ça finirait par se ~** people would start to notice *ou* start noticing

remballer [ʀãbale] ▸conjug 1◂ VT **a** (= *ranger*) to pack (up) again; (*dans du papier*) to rewrap; **remballe ta marchandise!**: you can clear off and take that stuff with you!:; **tu peux ~ tes commentaires!*** you know what you can do with your remarks!* **b** (: = *rabrouer*) **on s'est fait ~** we were sent packing*, they told us to get lost*

rembarquement [ʀãbaʀkəmã] NM [*passagers*] re-embarkation; [*marchandises*] reloading

rembarquer [ʀãbaʀke] ▸conjug 1◂ **1** VT **a** [+ *passagers*] to re-embark; [+ *marchandises*] to reload **2** VI to re-embark, go back on board (ship); **faire ~ les passagers** to re-embark the passengers **3** **se rembarquer** VPR **a** (*sur un bateau*) to re-embark, go back on board (ship) **b** (= *s'engager*) **elle s'est rembarquée dans une drôle d'affaire** she's got herself involved in something really weird again

rembarrer* [ʀãbaʀe] ▸conjug 1◂ VT **~ qn** (= *recevoir avec froideur*) to brush sb aside, rebuff sb; (= *remettre à sa place*) to put sb in their place, take sb down a peg or two; **on s'est fait ~** we were sent packing*, they told us to get lost*

remblai [ʀãblε] NM (*Rail, pour route*) embankment; (*Constr*) cut; **(terre de) ~** (*Rail*) ballast, remblai; (*pour route*) hard core; (*Constr*) backfill; **travaux de ~** (*Rail, pour route*) embankment work; (*Constr*) cutting work; (*Aut*) **~s récents** soft verges

remblayage [ʀãblεjaʒ] NM [*route, voie ferrée*] banking up; [*fossé*] filling in *ou* up

remblayer [ʀãbleje] ▸conjug 8◂ VT [+ *route, voie ferrée*] to bank up; [+ *fossé*] to fill in *ou* up

rembobiner [ʀãbɔbine] ▸conjug 1◂ VT [+ *film, bande magnétique*] to rewind, wind back; [+ *fil*] to rewind, wind up again

remboîtage [ʀãbwataʒ] NM, **remboîtement** [ʀãbwatmã] NM **a** [*tuyaux*] fitting together, reassembly; (*Méd*) [*os*] putting back (into place) **b** (*Tech*) [*livre*] recasing

remboîter [ʀãbwate] ▸conjug 1◂ VT **a** [+ *tuyaux*] to fit together again, reassemble; (*Méd*) [+ *os*] to put back (into place) **b** (*Tech*) [+ *livre*] to recase

rembourrage [ʀãbuʀaʒ] NM [*fauteuil, matelas*] stuffing; [*vêtement*] padding

rembourrer [ʀãbuʀe] ▸conjug 1◂ VT [+ *fauteuil, matelas*] to stuff; [+ *vêtement*] to pad; **veste rembourrée de plume d'oie** goosedown jacket; **bien rembourré** [+ *coussin*] well-filled, well-padded; * [+ *personne*] well-padded; (*hum*) **rembourré avec des noyaux de pêches*** rock hard

remboursable [ʀãbuʀsabl] ADJ [*billet, médicament*] refundable; [*emprunt*] repayable

remboursement [ʀãbuʀsəmã] NM [*dette*] repayment, settlement; [*emprunt*] repayment; [*somme*] reimbursement, repayment; [*créancier*] repayment, reimbursement; [*frais médicaux*] reimbursement; **obtenir le ~ de son repas** to get one's money back for one's meal, get a refund on one's meal; **envoi contre ~** cash with order; **(contribution au) ~ de la dette sociale** tax introduced in 1996 in order to help pay off the deficit in the French social security budget

rembourser [ʀãbuʀse] ▸conjug 1◂ VT **a** [+ *dette*] to pay back *ou* off, repay, settle (up); [+ *emprunt*] to pay back *ou* off, repay; [+ *somme*] to reimburse, repay, pay back; [+ *créancier*] to pay back *ou* off, repay, reimburse; **~ qn de qch** to reimburse sth to sb, reimburse sb for sth, repay sb sth; **je te rembourserai demain** I'll pay you back *ou* repay you tomorrow, I'll settle *ou* square up with you tomorrow
b [+ *dépenses professionnelles*] to refund, reimburse; [+ *article acheté*] to refund the price of; [+ *billet*] to reimburse; **~ la différence** to refund the difference; **je me suis fait ~ mon repas/voyage** I got back the cost of my meal/journey, I got the cost of my meal/journey refunded; **est-ce remboursé par la Sécurité sociale?** ≈ can we get our (*ou* can I get my *etc*) money back from the NHS (*Brit*) *ou* from Medicaid (*US*)?; **c'est remboursé à 75%** [*médicament, lunettes, etc*] you can get 75% back; **« satisfait ou remboursé »** "satisfaction or

your money back"; (*Théât*) **remboursez!** we want our money back! *ou* a refund!

rembrunir (se) [ʀãbʀyniʀ] ▸conjug 2◂ VPR [*visage, traits*] to darken, cloud (over); [*personne*] to bristle, stiffen; [*ciel*] to become overcast, darken, cloud over; **le temps se rembrunit** it's clouding over, it's getting cloudy

rembrunissement [ʀãbʀynismã] NM (*littér*) [*visage, front*] darkening

remède [ʀ(ə)mεd] NM **a** (*Méd*) (= *traitement*) remedy, cure; (= *médicament*) medicine; **prescrire/prendre un ~ pour un lumbago** to give/take something *ou* some medicine for lumbago; **~ de bonne femme** folk cure *ou* remedy; **~ souverain/de cheval*** sovereign/drastic remedy; **~ universel** cure-all, universal cure *ou* remedy **b** (*fig*) remedy, cure; **porter ~ à qch** to remedy sth; **la situation est sans ~** there is no remedy for the situation, the situation cannot be remedied *ou* is beyond remedy; **le ~ est pire que le mal** the cure is worse than the disease; **c'est un ~ à *ou* contre l'amour!*** it's (*ou* he's *ou* she's *etc*) a real turn-off!* → **mal**

remédiable [ʀ(ə)medjabl] ADJ [*mal*] that can be remedied *ou* cured, remediable

remédier [ʀ(ə)medje] ▸conjug 7◂ • **remédier à** VT INDIR (*lit*) [+ *maladie*] to cure; (*fig*) [+ *mal, situation*] to remedy, put right; [+ *abus*] to remedy, right; [+ *perte*] to remedy, make good; [+ *besoin*] to remedy; [+ *inconvénient*] to remedy, find a remedy for; [+ *difficulté*] to find a solution for, solve

remembrement [ʀ(ə)mãbʀəmã] NM land consolidation

remembrer [ʀ(ə)mãbʀe] ▸conjug 1◂ VT [+ *terres, exploitation*] to consolidate

remémoration [ʀ(ə)memɔʀasjɔ̃] NF recall, recollection

remémorer (se) [ʀ(ə)memɔʀe] ▸conjug 1◂ VPR to recall, recollect

▼ **remerciement** [ʀ(ə)mεʀsimã] **1** NM (= *action*) thanks *pl*, thanking; **~s** (*dans un livre, film*) acknowledgements; **exprimer ses profonds/sincères ~s à qn** to express one's deep/sincere gratitude to sb; **il lui bredouilla un ~** he mumbled his thanks to her; **lettre de ~** thank-you letter, letter of thanks; **elle adressa quelques mots de ~ à ses électeurs** she made a brief thank-you speech to the people who voted for her; **il a reçu une récompense en ~ de ses services** he received an award in recognition of his services; **en ~, il m'a envoyé des fleurs** he sent me some flowers by way of thanks *ou* to thank me **2** **remerciements** NMPL **avec tous mes ~s** with many thanks; **adresser ses ~s à qn** to express one's thanks to sb

▼ **remercier** [ʀ(ə)mεʀsje] ▸conjug 7◂ VT **a** (= *dire merci*) to thank (**qn de** *ou* **pour qch** sb for sth, **qn d'avoir fait qch** sb for doing sth); **~ le ciel** *ou* **Dieu** to thank God; **~ qn par un cadeau/d'un pourboire** to thank sb with a present/with a tip, give sb a present/a tip by way of thanks; **je ne sais comment vous ~** I can't thank you enough, I don't know how to thank you; **il me remercia d'un sourire** he thanked me with a smile, he smiled his thanks; **je vous remercie** thank you; **tu peux me ~!** you've got me to thank for that!; (*iro*) **je te remercie de tes conseils** thanks for the advice (*iro*), I can do without your advice (thank you) **b** (= *refuser poliment*) **vous voulez boire? — je vous remercie** would you like a drink? — no thank you; (*iro*) **sortir avec lui? je te remercie!** go out with him? no thanks! **c** (*euph* = *renvoyer*) [+ *employé*] to dismiss (*from his job*)

réméré [ʀemeʀe] NM (*Fin*) **faculté de ~** option of repurchase, repurchase agreement; **vente à ~** sale with option of purchase; **clause de ~** repurchase clause

remettant [ʀ(ə)mɛtɑ̃] NM (Fin) remitter

remettre [ʀ(ə)mɛtʀ] ▸ conjug 56 ◂ 1 VT a (= replacer) [+ objet] to put back, replace (**dans** in(to), **sur** on); [+ os luxé] to put back in place; ~ **un enfant au lit** to put a child back (in)to bed; ~ **un enfant à l'école** to send a child back to school; ~ **qch à cuire** to put sth on to cook again; ~ **debout** [+ enfant] to stand back on his feet; [+ objet] to stand up again; ~ **qch droit** to put ou set sth straight again; ~ **un bouton à une veste** to sew ou put a button back on a jacket; **il a remis l'étagère/la porte qu'il avait enlevée** he put the shelf back up/ rehung the door he had taken down; **je ne veux plus ~ les pieds ici !** I never want to set foot in here again!; ~ **qn sur la bonne voie** to put sb back on the right track; (fig = recommencer) ~ **le couvert*** (gén) to go at it* again; (sexuellement) to be at it again*

b (= porter de nouveau) [+ vêtement, chapeau] to put back on, put on again; **j'ai remis mon manteau d'hiver** I'm wearing my winter coat again

c (= replacer dans une situation) ~ **un appareil en marche** to restart a machine, start a machine (up) again, set a machine going again; ~ **un moteur en marche** to start up an engine again; ~ **une coutume en usage** to revive a custom; ~ **en question** [+ institution, autorité] to (call into) question, challenge; [+ projet, accord] to cast doubt over; **tout est remis en question à cause du mauvais temps** everything's in the balance again because of the bad weather, the bad weather throws the whole thing back into question; ~ **une pendule à l'heure** to set ou put (Brit) a clock right; (fig) **les pendules à l'heure*** to set the record straight; ~ **qch à neuf** to make sth as good as new again; ~ **qch en état** to repair ou mend sth; **le repos l'a remise (sur pied)** the rest has set her back on her feet; ~ **qn en confiance** to restore sb's confidence; ~ **de l'ordre dans qch** (= ranger) to tidy sth up; (= classer) to sort sth out → **cause, jour, place** etc

d (= donner) [+ lettre, paquet] to hand over, deliver; [+ clés] to hand in ou over, give in, return; [+ récompense] to present; [+ devoir] to hand in, give in; [+ rançon] to hand over; [+ démission] to hand in, give in, tender (**à** to); **il s'est fait ~ les clés par la concierge** he got the keys from the concierge; ~ **un enfant à ses parents** to return a child to his parents; ~ **un criminel à la justice** to hand a criminal over to the law; ~ **à qn un porte-monnaie volé** to hand ou give back ou return a stolen purse to sb

e (= ajourner) [+ réunion] to put off, postpone (**à** until); [+ décision] to put back (Brit) (**à** to); (Jur) to adjourn (**à** until); [+ décision] to put off, postpone, defer (**à** until); [+ date] to postpone, put back (Brit) (**à** to); **une visite qui ne peut se ~ (à plus tard)** a visit that can't be postponed ou put off; ~ **un rendez-vous à jeudi/au 8** to put off ou postpone an appointment till Thursday/the 8th ■ (PROV) **il ne faut jamais ~ à demain** ou **au lendemain ce qu'on peut faire le jour même** never put off till tomorrow what you can do today (PROV)

f (= se rappeler) to remember; **je vous remets très bien** I remember you very well; **je ne le remets pas** I can't place him, I don't remember him; ~ **qch en esprit** ou **en mémoire à qn** (= rappeler) to remind sb of sth, recall sth to sb; **ce livre m'a remis ces événements en mémoire** this book reminded me of these events ou brought these events to mind

g (= rajouter) [+ vinaigre, sel] to add more, put in (some) more; [+ verre, coussin] to add; [+ maquillage] to put on (some) more; **j'ai froid, je vais ~ un tricot** I'm cold — I'll go and put another jersey on; ~ **de l'huile dans un moteur** to top up an engine with oil; **en remettant un peu d'argent, vous pourriez avoir le grand modèle** if you paid a bit more you

could have the large size; **il faut ~ de l'argent sur le compte, nous sommes débiteurs** we'll have to put some money into the account as we're overdrawn; **en ~*** to overdo it, lay it on a bit thick*

h (= rallumer, rétablir) [+ radio, chauffage] to put ou turn ou switch on again; **il y a eu une coupure mais le courant a été remis à midi** there was a power cut but the electricity came back on again ou was put back on again at midday; ~ **le contact** to turn the ignition on again

i (= faire grâce de) [+ dette, peine] to remit; [+ péché] to forgive, pardon, remit; ~ **une dette à qn** to remit sb's debt, let sb off a debt; ~ **une peine à un condamné** to remit a prisoner's sentence

j (= confier) ~ **son sort/sa vie entre les mains de qn** to put one's fate/one's life into sb's hands; ~ **son âme à Dieu** to commit one's soul to God ou into God's keeping

k ~ **ça*** (= recommencer) **dire qu'il va falloir ~ ça !** to think that we'll have to go through all that again!; **quand est-ce qu'on remet ça ?** when can we do it again?; **on remet ça ?** [+ partie de cartes] shall we have another game?; (au café) shall we have another drink? ou round?; [+ travail] let's get back to it*, let's get down to it again, let's get going again*; **garçon, remettez-nous ça !** (the) same again please!*; **les voilà qui remettent ça !** [+ bruit, commentaires] here ou there they go again!*, they're at it again!*; **tu ne vas pas ~ ça avec tes critiques** you're not criticizing again, are you?; **le gouvernement va ~ ça avec les économies d'énergie** the government is going to start trying to save energy again

2 **se remettre** VPR a (= recouvrer la santé) to recover, get better; (psychologiquement) to cheer up; **se ~ d'une maladie/d'un accident** to recover from ou get over an illness/an accident; **remettez-vous !** pull yourself together!; **elle ne s'en remettra pas** she won't get over it

b (= recommencer) **se ~ à (faire) qch** to start (doing) sth again; **se ~ à fumer** to take up ou start smoking again; **il s'est remis au tennis/au latin** he has taken up tennis/Latin again; **après son départ il se remit à travailler** ou **au travail** after she had gone he started working again ou went back ou got back to work; **il se remet à faire froid** the weather ou it is getting ou turning cold again; **le temps s'est remis au beau** the weather has turned fine again, the weather has picked up again; **se ~ en selle** to remount, get back on one's horse; **se ~ debout** to get back to one's feet, get (back) up again, stand up again

c (= se confier) **se ~ entre les mains de qn** to put o.s. in sb's hands; **je m'en remets à vous** I'll leave it (up) to you, I'll leave the matter in your hands; **s'en ~ à la décision de qn** to leave it to sb to decide; **s'en ~ à la discrétion de qn** to leave it to sb's discretion

d (= se réconcilier) **se ~ avec qn** to make it up with sb, make ou patch up one's differences with sb; **ils se sont remis ensemble** they're back together again

remeubler [ʀ(ə)mœble] ▸ conjug 1 ◂ 1 VT to refurnish 2 **se remeubler** VPR to refurnish one's house, get new furniture

rémige [ʀemiʒ] NF remex

remilitarisation [ʀ(ə)militaʀizasjɔ̃] NF remilitarization

remilitariser [ʀ(ə)militaʀize] ▸ conjug 1 ◂ VT to remilitarize

reminéralisant, e [ʀ(ə)mineʀalizɑ̃, ɑ̃t] ADJ [produit, substance] remineralizing

réminiscence [ʀeminisɑ̃s] NF (= faculté mentale) (Philo, Psych) reminiscence; (= souvenir) reminiscence, vague recollection; **sa conversation était truffée de ~s littéraires** literary influences were constantly in evidence in his conversation; **mon latin est bien rouillé,**

mais j'ai encore quelques ~s my Latin is very rusty but I can still remember some; **on trouve des ~s de Rabelais dans l'œuvre de cet auteur** there are echoes of Rabelais in this author's work, parts of this author's work are reminiscent of Rabelais

remisage [ʀ(ə)mizaʒ] NM [outil, voiture] putting away

remise [ʀ(ə)miz] 1 NF a (= livraison) [lettre, paquet] delivery; [clés] handing over; [récompense] presentation; [devoir, rapport] handing in; [rançon] handing over, handover; [armes] surrender, handover; (Jur) ~ **de parts** transfer ou conveyance of legacy; **la ~ des prix/ médailles/diplômes** the prize-giving/medal/ graduation ceremony → **cause, touche**

b (= réduction) [peine] remission, reduction (**de** of, in); **le condamné a bénéficié d'une importante ~ de peine** the prisoner was granted a large reduction in his sentence

c (Comm = rabais) discount, reduction; **ils font une ~ de 5% sur les livres scolaires** they're giving ou allowing (a) 5% discount ou reduction on school books; (Fin) ~ **de dette** condonation, remission of a debt

d (= local : pour outils, véhicules) shed

e (= ajournement) [réunion] postponement, deferment, putting off ou back (Brit); [décision] putting off; ~ **à huitaine d'un débat** postponement of a debate for a week

remiser [ʀ(ə)mize] ▸ conjug 1 ◂ 1 VT [+ voiture, outil, valise] to put away 2 VI (Jeux) to make another bet, bet again 3 **se remiser** VPR [gibier] to take cover

remisier [ʀ(ə)mizje] NM (Bourse) intermediate broker

rémissible [ʀemisibl] ADJ remissible

rémission [ʀemisjɔ̃] NF a [péchés] remission, forgiveness; (Jur) remission b (Méd) [maladie] remission; [douleur, fièvre] subsidence, abatement; (fig littér : dans la tempête, le travail) lull c **sans ~** [travailler, torturer, poursuivre] unremittingly, relentlessly; [payer] without fail; [mal, maladie] irremediable; **si tu recommences, tu seras puni sans ~** if you do it again you'll be punished without fail

remix [ʀamiks] NM (Mus) remix

remixer [ʀ(ə)mikse] ▸ conjug 1 ◂ VT [+ chanson] to remix; **version remixée** remix version

remmailler [ʀɑ̃maje] ▸ conjug 1 ◂ VT [+ tricot, bas] to darn; [+ filet] to mend

remmailleuse [ʀɑ̃majøz] NF darner

remmailloter [ʀɑ̃majɔte] ▸ conjug 1 ◂ VT [+ bébé] to change

remmancher [ʀɑ̃mɑ̃ʃe] ▸ conjug 1 ◂ VT [+ couteau, balai] (= remettre le manche) to put the handle back on; (= remplacer le manche) to put a new handle on

remmener [ʀɑ̃m(ə)ne] ▸ conjug 5 ◂ VT to take back, bring back; ~ **qn chez lui** to take sb back home; ~ **qn à pied** to walk sb back; ~ **qn en voiture** to give sb a lift back, drive sb back

remodelage [ʀ(ə)mɔd(ə)laʒ] NM a [visage, silhouette] remodelling; [nez, joues] reshaping; [ville] remodelling, replanning b [profession, organisation] reorganization, restructuring

remodeler [ʀ(ə)mɔd(ə)le] ▸ conjug 5 ◂ VT a [+ visage, silhouette] to remodel; [+ nez, joues] to reshape; [+ ville] to remodel, replan b [+ profession, organisation] to reorganize, restructure

remontage [ʀ(ə)mɔ̃taʒ] NM [montre] rewinding, winding up; [machine, meuble] reassembly, putting back together; [tuyau] putting back

remontant, e [ʀ(ə)mɔ̃tɑ̃, ɑ̃t] 1 ADJ a [boisson] invigorating, fortifying b [rosier] reflowering, remontant (SPÉC); [fraisier, framboisier] double-cropping, double-fruiting 2 NM tonic, pick-me-up*

remonte [ʀ(ə)mɔ̃t] NF a [bateau] sailing upstream, ascent; [poissons] run b (Équitation) (= *fourniture de chevaux*) remount; (= *service*) remount department

remonté, e¹* [ʀ(ə)mɔ̃te] (*ptp de* **remonter**) ADJ
a (= *en colère*) furious (**contre qn** with sb), mad* (**contre qn** at sb); **être ~ contre qch** to be wound up* about sth; **être ~ contre qn** to be livid* *ou* mad* *ou* furious with sb; **il est ~ aujourd'hui** he's in a foul mood *ou* temper today **b** (= *dynamique*) **il est ~** he's full of energy; **je suis ~ à bloc** (*gén*) I'm on top form; (*avant un examen, un entretien*) I'm all keyed up *ou* psyched up*

remontée² [ʀ(ə)mɔ̃te] NF [*côte*] ascent, climbing; [*rivière*] ascent; [*eaux*] rising; [*prix, taux d'intérêt*] rise; **la ~ des mineurs par l'ascenseur** bringing miners up by lift; **il ne faut pas que la ~ du plongeur soit trop rapide** the diver must not come back up too quickly; **la ~ de l'or à la Bourse** the rise in the price *ou* value of gold on the stock exchange; **faire une (belle) ~** to make a (good) recovery; **faire une ~ spectaculaire (de la 30ᵉ à la 2ᵉᵐᵉ place)** to make a spectacular recovery (from 30th to 2nd place); **le président effectue une ~ spectaculaire dans les sondages** the president is rising swiftly in the opinion polls; (*Sport*) **~s mécaniques** ski-lifts

remonte-pente (*pl* **remonte-pentes**) [ʀ(ə)mɔ̃tpɑ̃t] NM ski tow

▼ **remonter** [ʀ(ə)mɔ̃te] ▶ conjug 1 ◀ **1** VI (*surtout avec aux être*) **a** (= *monter à nouveau*) to go up *ou* come back up; **il remonta à pied** he walked back up; **remonte me voir** come back up and see me; **je remonte demain à Paris (en voiture)** I'm driving back up to Paris tomorrow; **il remonta sur la table** he climbed back (up) onto the table; **~ sur le trône** to come back *ou* return to the throne; (*Théât*) **~ sur les planches** to go back on the stage **b** (*dans un moyen de transport*) **~ en voiture** to get back into one's car, get into one's car again; **~ à cheval** (= *se remettre en selle*) to remount (one's horse), get back on(to) one's horse; (= *se remettre à faire du cheval*) to take up riding again; (*Naut*) **~ à bord** to go back on board (ship) **c** (= *s'élever de nouveau*) [*marée*] to come in again; [*prix, température, baromètre*] to rise again, go up again; [*colline, route*] to go up again, rise again; **la mer remonte** the tide is coming in again; **la fièvre remonte** his temperature is rising *ou* going up again, the fever is getting worse again; **les bénéfices ont remonté au dernier trimestre** profits were up again in the last quarter; **les prix ont remonté en flèche** prices shot up *ou* rocketed again; (*fig*) **ses actions remontent** things are looking up for him (again), his fortunes are picking up (again); **il remonte dans mon estime** my opinion of him is improving again; **il est remonté de la 7ᵉᵐᵉ à la 3ᵉᵐᵉ place** he has come up from 7th to 3rd place **d** [*vêtement*] to go up, pull up; **sa robe remonte sur le côté** her dress goes *ou* pulls up at the side *ou* is higher on one side; **sa jupe remonte quand elle s'assied** her skirt rides up *ou* pulls up *ou* goes up when she sits down **e** (= *réapparaître*) to come back; **les souvenirs qui remontent à ma mémoire** memories which come back to me *ou* to my mind; **~ à la surface** to come back up to the surface, resurface; **sous-marin qui remonte en surface** submarine which is coming back up to the surface *ou* which is resurfacing; **une mauvaise odeur remontait de l'égout** a bad smell was coming *ou* wafting up out of the drain **f** (= *retourner*) to return, go back; **~ à la source/cause** to go back *ou* return to the source/cause; **~ de l'effet à la cause** to go back from the effect to the cause; (*Naut*) **~ au vent** *ou* **dans le vent** to tack close to the wind; **il faut ~ plus haut** *ou* **plus loin pour comprendre l'affaire** you must go *ou* look further back to understand this business; **~ jusqu'au cou-**

pable to trace the guilty person; **aussi loin que remontent ses souvenirs** as far back as he can remember; **~ dans le temps** to go back in time

g **~ à** (= *dater de*) **cette histoire remonte à une époque reculée/à plusieurs années** all this dates back a very long time/several years; (*hum*) **tout cela remonte au déluge!** (= *c'est très ancien*) all that's as old as the hills!; (= *c'est passé depuis longtemps*) all that was ages ago!; **on ne va pas ~ au déluge !** we're not going back over ancient history again!; **la famille remonte aux croisades** the family goes *ou* dates back to the time of the Crusades

2 VT (*avec aux avoir*) **a** [+ *étage, côte, marche*] to go *ou* climb back up; [+ *rue*] to go *ou* come back up; **~ l'escalier en courant** to rush *ou* run back upstairs; **~ la rue à pas lents** to walk slowly (back) up the street; **~ le courant** *ou* **rivière** (*à la nage*) to swim (back) upstream/up a river; (*en barque*) to sail *ou* row (back) upstream/up a river; (*fig*) **~ le courant** *ou* **la pente** to begin to get back on one's feet again **b** (= *rattraper*) [+ *adversaire*] to catch up with; **~ le cortège** to move up towards *ou* work one's way towards the front of the queue; **se faire ~ par un adversaire** to let o.s. be caught up by an opponent; **il a 15 points/places à ~** he has 15 marks/places to catch up in order to be 2nd **c** (= *relever*) [+ *mur*] to raise, heighten; [+ *tableau, étagère*] to raise, put higher up; [+ *vitre*] (*en poussant*) to push up; (*avec bouton ou manivelle*) to wind up; [+ *store*] to roll up, raise; [+ *pantalon, manche*] to pull up; (*en roulant*) to roll up; (*d'une saccade*) to hitch up; [+ *chaussettes*] to pull up; [+ *col*] to turn up; [+ *jupe*] to pick up, raise; (*fig*) [+ *mauvaise note*] to put up, raise; (*fig*) **~ les bretelles à qn*** to give sb a piece of one's mind*; **il s'est fait ~ les bretelles par le patron*** the boss gave him a real tongue-lashing* *ou* dressing-down **d** (= *remporter*) to take *ou* bring back up; **~ une malle au grenier** to take *ou* carry a trunk back up to the attic **e** [+ *montre, mécanisme*] to wind up **f** (= *réinstaller*) [+ *machine, moteur, meuble*] to put together again, put back together (again), reassemble; [+ *robinet, tuyau*] to put back; **ils ont remonté une usine à Lyon** they have set up *ou* built another factory in Lyon; **il a eu du mal à ~ les roues de sa bicyclette** he had a job putting *ou* getting the wheels back on his bicycle **g** (= *réassortir*) [+ *garde-robe*] to renew, replenish; [+ *magasin*] to restock; **mon père nous a remontés en vaisselle** my father has given us a whole new set of crockery; **~ son ménage** (*en meubles*) to buy new furniture; (*en linge*) to buy new linen **h** (= *remettre en état*) [+ *personne*] (*physiquement*) to set *ou* buck* up (again); (*moralement*) to cheer *ou* buck* up (again); [+ *entreprise*] to put *ou* set back on its feet; [+ *mur en ruines*] to rebuild; **le nouveau directeur a bien remonté cette entreprise** the new manager has really got this firm back on its feet; **ce contrat ~ait bien mes affaires** this contract would really give business a boost for me → **moral** **i** (*Théât*) [+ *pièce*] to restage, put on again

3 **se remonter** VPR **a** (= *refaire des provisions*) **se ~ en boîtes de conserves** to get in (further) stocks of canned food, replenish one's stocks of canned food; **se ~ en chaussures** to get some new shoes **b** (= *récupérer*) (*physiquement*) to buck* *ou* set o.s. up (again); (*moralement*) **se ~ (le moral)** to raise (one's spirits), cheer *ou* buck* o.s. up

remontoir [ʀ(ə)mɔ̃twaʀ] NM [*montre*] winder; [*jouet, horloge*] winding mechanism

remontrance [ʀ(ə)mɔ̃tʀɑ̃s] NF **a** (= *reproche*) remonstrance, reproof, reprimand, admonition (*frm*); **faire des ~s à qn (au sujet de qch)**

to remonstrate with sb (about sth), reprove *ou* reprimand *ou* admonish (*frm*) sb (for sth) **b** (*Hist*) remonstrance

remontrer [ʀ(ə)mɔ̃tʀe] ▶ conjug 1 ◀ VT **a** (= *montrer de nouveau*) to show again; **remontrez-moi la bleue** show me the blue one again, let me have another look at the blue one; **ne te remontre plus ici** don't show your face *ou* yourself here again **b** (= *donner des leçons*) **en ~ à qn** to teach sb a thing or two; **dans ce domaine, il pourrait t'en ~** he could teach you a thing or two about this; (= *montrer sa supériorité*) **n'essaie pas de m'en ~** don't bother trying to teach me anything **c** (†, *littér*) **~ à qn que** to point out to sb that

remords [ʀ(ə)mɔʀ] NM remorse (*NonC*); **j'éprouve quelques ~ à l'avoir laissé seul** I feel some remorse at having left him alone; **j'ai eu un ~ de conscience, je suis allé vérifier** I had second thoughts *ou* I thought better of it and went to check; **~ cuisants** agonies of remorse; **avoir des ~** to feel remorse; **être pris de ~** to be stricken *ou* smitten with remorse; **n'avoir aucun ~** to have no (feeling of) remorse, feel no remorse; **je le tuerais sans (le moindre) ~** I'd kill him without (the slightest) compunction *ou* remorse; **je te le donne — (c'est) sans ~ ?** here you are — are you sure?

remorquage [ʀ(ə)mɔʀkaʒ] NM [*voiture, caravane*] towing; [*train*] pulling, hauling; [*bateau, navire*] towing, tugging

remorque [ʀ(ə)mɔʀk] NF **a** (= *véhicule*) trailer; (= *câble*) towrope, towline → **camion** **b** (*loc*) **prendre une voiture en ~** to tow a car; **« en ~ »** "on tow"; **quand ils vont se promener ils ont toujours la belle-sœur en ~** whenever they go for a walk they always have the sister-in-law in tow *ou* they always drag along their sister-in-law; (*péj*) **être à la ~** to trail behind; (*péj*) **être à la ~ de** to tag along behind; [*pays*] **être à la ~ d'une grande puissance** to tag along *ou* to trail behind a great power

remorquer [ʀ(ə)mɔʀke] ▶ conjug 1 ◀ VT **a** [+ *voiture, caravane*] to tow; [+ *train*] to pull, haul; [+ *bateau, navire*] to tow, tug; **je suis tombé en panne et j'ai dû me faire ~ jusqu'au village** I had a breakdown and had to get a tow *ou* get myself towed as far as the village **b** [+ *personne*] to drag along; **~ toute la famille derrière soi** to have the whole family in tow, drag the whole family along

remorqueur [ʀ(ə)mɔʀkœʀ] NM (= *bateau*) tug(boat)

remouiller [ʀ(ə)muje] ▶ conjug 1 ◀ VT **a** (= *mouiller de nouveau*) to wet again; **~ du linge à repasser** to dampen washing ready for ironing; **se faire ~ (par la pluie)** to get wet (in the rain) again; **je viens de m'essuyer les mains, je ne veux pas me les ~** I've just dried my hands and I don't want to get them wet again **b** (*Naut*) **~ (l'ancre)** to drop anchor again

rémoulade [Remulad] NF remoulade, rémoulade (*dressing containing mustard and herbs*) → **céleri**

remoulage [ʀ(ə)mulaʒ] NM **a** (*Art*) recasting **b** (*Tech*) [*café*] regrinding; [*farine*] (= *action*) remilling; (= *résultat*) middlings

remouler [ʀ(ə)mule] ▶ conjug 1 ◀ VT [+ *statue*] to recast

rémouleur [Remulœʀ] NM (knife- *ou* scissor-) grinder

remous [Ramu] NM **a** [*bateau*] (back)wash (*NonC*); [*eau*] swirl, eddy; [*air*] eddy; **emporté par les ~ de la foule** swept along by the bustling *ou* milling crowd **b** (= *agitation*) stir (*NonC*); **~ d'idées** whirl *ou* swirl of ideas; **l'affaire a provoqué de vifs ~ politiques** the affair caused a stir in political circles; **cette décision n'a suscité aucun ~** this decision didn't raise any eyebrows

rempaillage [ʀɑ̃pajaʒ] NM [*chaise*] reseating, rebottoming (*with straw*)

rempailler [ʀɑ̃paje] ▶ conjug 1 ◀ VT [+ *chaise*] to reseat, rebottom (*with straw*)

rempailleur, -euse [ʀɑ̃pajœʀ, øz] NM,F [*chaise*] chair-bottomer

rempaqueter [ʀɑ̃pak(ə)te] ▶ conjug 4 ◀ VT to wrap up again, rewrap

rempart [ʀɑ̃paʀ] NM [a] (*Mil*) rampart; **~s** [*ville*] city walls, ramparts; [*château fort*] battlements, ramparts [b] (*fig*) bastion, rampart (*littér*); **le dernier ~ contre** the last bastion against; **il lui fit un ~ de son corps** he shielded him with his body

rempiler [ʀɑ̃pile] ▶ conjug 1 ◀ [1] VT [+ *objets*] to pile *ou* stack up again [2] VI (*arg Mil*) to join up again, re-enlist

remplaçable [ʀɑ̃plasabl] ADJ replaceable; **difficilement ~** hard to replace

remplaçant, e [ʀɑ̃plasɑ̃, ɑ̃t] NM,F (*gén*) replacement, substitute; [*médecin*] replacement, locum (*Brit*); (*Sport*) reserve; (*pendant un match*) substitute; (*Théât*) understudy; (*Scol*) supply (*Brit*) *ou* substitute (*US*) teacher; **être le ~ de qn** to stand in for sb; **trouver un ~ à un professeur malade** to get sb to stand in *ou* substitute for a sick teacher; **il faut lui trouver un ~** we must find a replacement *ou* a substitute for him

remplacement [ʀɑ̃plasmɑ̃] NM [a] (= *intérim*) [*acteur malade, médecin en vacances*] standing in (**de** for); [*joueur, professeur malade*] standing in (**de** for), substitution (**de** for), deputizing (**de** for); **assurer le ~ d'un collègue pendant sa maladie** to stand in for a colleague during his illness; **faire des ~s** [*secrétaire*] to temp*, do temporary work; [*professeur*] to do supply teaching (*Brit*), work as a supply (*Brit*) *ou* substitute (*US*) teacher; **j'ai fait trois ~s cette semaine** I've had three temporary replacement jobs this week [b] (= *substitution*) replacement (**de** of), taking over (**de** from); [*employé, objet usagé*] replacement; **effectuer le ~ d'une pièce défectueuse** to replace a faulty part; **film présenté en ~ d'une émission annulée** film shown in place of a cancelled programme; **je n'ai plus de stylos, en ~ je vous donne un crayon** I have no more pens so I'll give you a pencil instead; **le ~ du nom par le pronom** the replacement of the noun by the pronoun; **il va falloir trouver une solution de ~** we'll have to find an alternative (solution); **produit/matériel de ~** substitute (product/material)

remplacer [ʀɑ̃plase] ▶ conjug 3 ◀ VT [a] (= *assurer l'intérim de*) [+ *acteur*] to stand in for; [+ *joueur, professeur*] to stand in for, substitute for; [+ *médecin*] to stand in for, do a locum for (*Brit*); **je me suis fait ~** I got someone to stand in for me *ou* to cover for me [b] (= *succéder à*) to replace, take over from, take the place of; **le train a remplacé la diligence** the train replaced *ou* took the place of the stagecoach; **son fils l'a remplacé comme directeur** his son has taken over from him *ou* has replaced him as director; **~ une sentinelle** to take over from *ou* relieve a sentry [c] (= *tenir lieu de*) to take the place of, replace; **le miel peut ~ le sucre** honey can be used in place of *ou* used as a substitute for sugar; **le pronom remplace le nom dans la phrase** the pronoun takes the place of *ou* replaces the noun in the sentence; **on peut ~ le beurre par de l'huile d'olive** you can use olive oil instead of butter; **rien ne remplace le vrai beurre** there's nothing like *ou* you can't beat real butter; **une autre femme l'a vite remplacée (dans son cœur)** she was soon replaced (in his affections) by another woman [d] (= *changer*) [+ *employé*] to replace; [+ *objet usagé*] to replace, change; **un vieux lit par un neuf** to replace an old bed with a new one, change an old bed for a new one; **les pièces défectueuses seront remplacées gratuitement** faulty parts will be replaced free of charge; **~**

un carreau cassé to replace a broken windowpane; **remplacez les pointillés par des pronoms** put pronouns in place of the dotted lines; **un homme comme lui ne se remplace pas aisément** a man like that isn't easy to replace

rempli¹, e [ʀɑ̃pli] (*ptp de* **remplir**) ADJ [*récipient, théâtre*] full (**de** of), filled (**de** with); [*joue, visage*] full, plump; [*journée, vie*] full, busy; **il avait les yeux ~s de larmes** his eyes were brimming with *ou* full of tears; **avoir l'estomac bien ~** to have a full stomach, have eaten one's fill; **texte ~ de fautes** text riddled *ou* packed with mistakes; **sa tête était ~e de souvenirs** his mind was filled with *ou* full of memories; **notre carnet de commandes est bien ~** our order book is full; **il est ~ de son importance/de lui-même** he's full of his own importance/of himself

rempli² [ʀɑ̃pli] NM (*Couture*) tuck

remplir [ʀɑ̃pliʀ] ▶ conjug 2 ◀ [1] VT [a] (= *emplir*) (*gén*) to fill (**de** with); [+ *récipient*] to fill (up); (*à nouveau*) to refill; [+ *questionnaire*] to fill in *ou* out; **~ qch à moitié** to half fill, fill sth half full; **il en a rempli 15 pages** he filled 15 pages with it, he wrote 15 pages on it; **ce chanteur ne remplira pas la salle** this singer won't fill the hall *ou* won't get a full house; **ces tâches routinières ont rempli sa vie** these routine tasks have filled his life, his life has been filled with these routine tasks; **ça remplit la première page des journaux** it fills *ou* covers the front page of the newspapers; **ce résultat me remplit d'admiration** this result fills me with admiration, I am filled with admiration at this result; **~ son temps** to fill one's time; **il remplit bien ses journées** he gets a lot done in (the course of) a day, he packs a lot into his days [b] (= *s'acquitter de*) [+ *contrat, mission, obligation*] to fulfil, carry out; [+ *devoir*] to carry out, do; [+ *rôle*] to fill, play; [+ *besoin*] to fulfil, answer, meet; **~ ses engagements** to meet one's commitments; **~ ses fonctions** to do *ou* carry out one's job, carry out *ou* perform one's functions; **objet qui remplit une fonction précise** object that fulfils a precise purpose; **vous ne remplissez pas les conditions** you do not fulfil *ou* satisfy *ou* meet the conditions [2] **se remplir** VPR [*récipient, salle*] to fill (up) (**de** with); **se ~ les poches*** to line one's pockets; **on s'est bien rempli la panse*** we stuffed ourselves*, we pigged out*

remplissage [ʀɑ̃plisaʒ] NM [*tonneau, bassin*] filling (up); (*péj: dans un livre*) padding; **faire du ~** to pad out one's work (*ou* speech *etc*); **taux de ~ des avions/hôtels** air passenger/hotel occupancy rate

remploi [ʀɑ̃plwa] NM = **réemploi**

remployer [ʀɑ̃plwaje] ▶ conjug 8 ◀ VT = **réemployer**

remplumer (se)* [ʀɑ̃plyme] ▶ conjug 1 ◀ VPR (*physiquement*) to fill out again, get a bit of flesh on one's bones again; (*financièrement*) to get back on one's feet, have some money in one's pocket again

rempocher [ʀɑ̃pɔʃe] ▶ conjug 1 ◀ VT to put back in one's pocket; **le ministre a dû ~ son projet de réforme** the minister had to shelve his reform plan

rempoissonnement [ʀɑ̃pwasɔnmɑ̃] NM restocking (with fish)

rempoissonner [ʀɑ̃pwasɔne] ▶ conjug 1 ◀ VT to restock (with fish)

remporter [ʀɑ̃pɔʀte] ▶ conjug 1 ◀ VT [a] (= *reprendre*) to take away (again), take back [b] [+ *championnat, élections, contrat*] to win; [+ *prix*] to win, carry off; **~ la victoire** to win; **~ un (vif) succès** to achieve (a great) success

rempotage [ʀɑ̃pɔtaʒ] NM repotting

rempoter [ʀɑ̃pɔte] ▶ conjug 1 ◀ VT to repot

remuant, e [ʀəmɥɑ̃, ɑ̃t] ADJ [*enfant*] (= *agité*) fidgety; (= *turbulent*) boisterous; [*public*] rowdy; [*opposition*] active

remue-ménage [ʀ(ə)mymenaʒ] NM INV (= *bruit*) commotion (*NonC*); (= *activité*) hurly-burly (*NonC*), hustle and bustle (*NonC*); **il y a du ~ chez les voisins** the neighbours are making a great commotion; **faire du ~** to make a commotion; **le ~ électoral** the electoral hurly-burly

remue-méninges [ʀ(ə)mymenɛ̃ʒ] NM INV brainstorming

remuement [ʀ(ə)mymɑ̃] NM (*littér*) moving, movement

remuer [ʀəmɥe] ▶ conjug 1 ◀ [1] VT [a] (= *bouger*) [+ *tête, bras, lèvres*] to move; [+ *oreille*] to twitch; **~ la queue** [*vache, écureuil*] to flick its tail; [*chien*] to wag its tail; **~ les bras** *ou* **les mains en parlant** to wave one's arms about *ou* gesticulate as one speaks; **~ les épaules/les hanches en marchant** to swing *ou* sway one's shoulders/one's hips as one walks → **doigt** [b] [+ *objet*] (= *déplacer*) to move, shift; (= *secouer*) to shake; **il essaya de ~ la pierre** he tried to move *ou* shift the stone; **sa valise est si lourde que je ne peux même pas la ~** his suitcase is so heavy that I can't even shift *ou* move *ou* budge it; **arrête de ~ ta chaise** stop moving your chair about; **ne remue pas** *ou* **ne fais pas ~ la table, je suis en train d'écrire** don't shake *ou* move *ou* wobble the table — I'm trying to write [c] (= *brasser*) [+ *café*] to stir; [+ *sable*] to stir up; [+ *salade*] to toss; [+ *terre*] to dig *ou* turn over; **il a remué la sauce/les braises** he gave the sauce a stir/the fire a poke, he stirred the sauce/poked the fire; **il a tout remué dans le tiroir** he turned the whole drawer *ou* everything in the drawer upside down; **la brise remuait les feuilles** the breeze stirred the leaves; **une odeur de terre remuée** a smell of fresh earth *ou* of freshly turned *ou* dug earth; **~ de l'argent (à la pelle)** to deal with *ou* handle vast amounts of money; (*fig*) **~ ciel et terre pour** to move heaven and earth (in order) to; **~ des souvenirs** [*personne nostalgique*] to turn *ou* go over old memories in one's mind; [*évocation*] to stir up *ou* arouse old memories [d] [+ *personne*] (= *émouvoir*) to move; (= *bouleverser*) to upset; **ça vous remue les tripes*** it really tugs at your heartstrings; **elle était toute remuée par cette nouvelle** she was very upset when she heard the news [2] VI [a] (= *bouger*) [*personne*] to move; [*dent, tuile*] to be loose; **cesse de ~!** keep still!, stop fidgeting!; **le vent faisait ~ les branchages** the wind was stirring the branches, the branches were stirring *ou* swaying in the wind; **ça a remué pendant la traversée*** the crossing was pretty rough*; **il a remué toute la nuit** he tossed and turned all night; **j'ai entendu ~ dans la cuisine** I heard someone moving about in the kitchen → **nez** [b] (*fig* = *se rebeller*) to show signs of unrest [3] **se remuer** VPR [a] (= *bouger*) to move; (= *se déplacer*) to move about [b] * (= *se mettre en route*) to get going; (= *s'activer*) to get a move on*, shift *ou* stir o.s.*; **remue-toi un peu!** get a move on!*; **il s'est beaucoup remué pour leur trouver une maison** he's gone to a lot of trouble to find them a house; **il ne s'est pas beaucoup remué** he didn't exactly strain himself *ou* put himself out

remugle [ʀəmygl] NM (*littér*) mustiness, fustiness

rémunérateur, -trice [ʀemyneʀatœʀ, tʀis] ADJ [*emploi*] remunerative, lucrative

rémunération [ʀemyneʀasjɔ̃] NF [*personne*] payment, remuneration (**de** of); [*investissement, capital*] return (**de** on); **la ~ moyenne des cadres** average executive pay; **en ~ de vos services** in payment for your services; **mode de ~** [*salarié*] method of payment; [*investissement*] form of return; **emploi à faible/forte ~** low-paid/highly-paid job; **toucher une ~ de 10 000 F** to be paid 10,000 francs; **placement à faible/forte ~** low-return *ou* low-yield/high-return *ou* high-yield investment

rémunérer [ʀemyneʀe] ▸conjug 6◂ VT [+ *personne*] to pay, remunerate; **~ le travail de qn** to pay *ou* remunerate sb for their work; **travail bien/mal rémunéré** well-paid/badly-paid job; **avoir une activité rémunérée** to be in salaried employment; **emploi rémunéré à 10 000 F** job that pays 10,000 francs; **placement rémunéré à 4,5%** investment that pays 4.5% → **compte**

renâcler [ʀ(ə)nakle] ▸conjug 1◂ VI [*animal*] to snort; (*fig*) [*personne*] to grumble, complain, show (one's) reluctance; **~ à la besogne** *ou* **à la tâche** to grumble, complain (*about having to do a job*); **~ à faire qch** to do sth reluctantly *ou* grudgingly; **sans ~** uncomplainingly, without grumbling; **faire qch en renâclant** to do sth grudgingly *ou* reluctantly *ou* with (a) bad grace

renaissance [ʀ(ə)nɛsɑ̃s] **1** NF (*Rel, fig*) rebirth; (*Hist*) **la Renaissance** the Renaissance **2** ADJ INV [*mobilier, style*] Renaissance

renaissant, e [ʀ(ə)nɛsɑ̃, ɑ̃t] ADJ **a** [*forces*] returning; [*économie*] reviving, recovering; [*espoir, intérêt*] renewed; **toujours** *ou* **sans cesse ~** [*difficultés*] constantly recurring, that keep cropping up; [*obstacles*] that keep cropping up; [*doutes, hésitations, intérêt*] constantly renewed **b** (*Hist*) Renaissance (*épith*)

renaître [ʀ(ə)nɛtʀ] ▸conjug 59◂ VI **a** [*joie*] to spring up again, be revived (*dans* in); [*espoir, doute*] to be revived (*dans* in), be reborn (*littér*); [*conflit*] to spring up again, break out again; [*difficulté*] to recur, crop up again; [*économie*] to revive, recover; [*sourire*] to return (*sur* to), reappear (*sur* on); [*plante*] to come *ou* spring up again; [*jour*] to dawn, break; **le printemps renaît** spring is reawakening; **la nature renaît au printemps** nature comes back to life in spring; **faire ~** [+ *sentiment, passé*] to bring back, revive; [+ *problème, sourire*] to bring back; [+ *espoir, conflit*] to revive
b (= *revivre*) (*gén*) to come to life again; (*Rel*) to be born again (**en** in); (*Myth, fig*) **~ de ses cendres** to rise from one's ashes; **je me sens ~** I feel as if I've been given a new lease of life
c (*littér*) **~ au bonheur** to find happiness again; **~ à l'espérance** to find fresh hope; **~ à la vie** to take on a new lease of life

rénal, e (*mpl* **-aux**) [ʀenal, o] ADJ renal (*SPÉC*), kidney (*épith*)

renard [ʀ(ə)naʀ] NM (= *animal*) fox; (= *fourrure*) fox(-fur); **~ argenté/bleu** silver/blue fox; **~ des sables** fennec; (*fig*) **c'est un vieux ~** he's a sly old fox *ou* dog

renarde [ʀ(ə)naʀd] NF vixen

renardeau (*pl* **renardeaux**) [ʀ(ə)naʀdo] NM fox cub

renardière [ʀ(ə)naʀdjɛʀ] NF (= *terrier*) fox's den; (*Can*) fox farm

renauder*† [ʀənode] ▸conjug 1◂ VI to grouse*, grouch*

rencaisser [ʀɑ̃kese] ▸conjug 1◂ VT **a** [+ *argent*] to put back in the till **b** (*Hort*) to rebox

rencard: [ʀɑ̃kaʀ] NM = **rancard**

rencarder: [ʀɑ̃kaʀde] ▸conjug 1◂ VT = **rancarder**

renchérir [ʀɑ̃ʃeʀiʀ] ▸conjug 2◂ VI **a** (*en paroles, en actes*) to go further, go one better (*péj*); **~ sur ce que qn dit** to add something to what sb says, go further *ou* one better (*péj*) than sb; **~ sur ce que qn fait** to go further than sb; **« et je n'en ai nul besoin » renchérit-il** "and I don't need it in the least", he added; **il faut toujours qu'il renchérisse (sur ce qu'on**

---

dit) he always has to go one better **b** [*prix*] to get dearer *ou* more expensive; **la vie renchérit** the cost of living is going up *ou* rising **c** (*dans une vente : sur l'offre de qn*) to make a higher bid, bid higher (**sur** than); (*sur son offre*) to raise one's bid **2** VT [+ *coût*] to put up, increase; [+ *produit*] to make more expensive, put up the price of

renchérissement [ʀɑ̃ʃeʀismɑ̃] NM [*marchandises*] rise *ou* increase in (the) price (**de** of); [*loyers*] rise, increase (**de** in); **le ~ de la vie** the rise *ou* increase in the cost of living

rencogner (se)* [ʀɑ̃kɔɲe] ▸conjug 1◂ VPR to huddle up, curl up (in a corner)

rencontre [ʀɑ̃kɔ̃tʀ] NF **a** [*amis, diplomates, étrangers*] meeting; (*imprévue*) encounter, meeting; **faire la ~ de qn** to meet sb; (*imprévue*) to meet sb, run into sb; **j'ai peur que dans ces milieux il ne fasse de mauvaises ~s** I am afraid that in these circles he might meet (up with) *ou* fall in with the wrong sort of people; **faire une ~ inattendue/une mauvaise ~** to have an unexpected/an unpleasant encounter; **le hasard d'une ~ a changé ma vie** a chance encounter *ou* meeting changed my life; **~ au sommet** summit meeting; (= *événement culturel*) **~s musicales/théâtrales** music/theatre festival; **~ du premier/ deuxième/troisième type** close encounter of the first/second/third kind
b [*éléments*] conjunction; [*rivières*] confluence; [*routes*] junction; [*voitures*] collision; [*voyelles*] juxtaposition; **la ~ des deux lignes/ routes/rivières se fait ici** the two lines/roads/ rivers meet *ou* join here; **point de ~** meeting point
c (*Athlétisme*) meeting; (*Ftbl etc*) fixture, game; **la ~ (des deux équipes) aura lieu le 15** the two teams will meet on the 15th; **~ de boxe** boxing match
d (*Mil*) skirmish, encounter, engagement; (= *duel*) encounter, meeting
e (*loc*) **aller à la ~ de qn** to go and meet sb, go to meet sb; (*partir*) **à la ~ des Incas** (to go) in search of the Incas; **amours/amis de ~** casual love affairs/friends; **compagnons de ~** chance companions

rencontrer [ʀɑ̃kɔ̃tʀe] ▸conjug 1◂ **1** VT
a (*gén*) to meet; (*par hasard*) to meet, run *ou* bump into*; **j'ai rencontré Paul en ville** I met *ou* ran into* *ou* bumped into* Paul in town; **le Premier ministre a rencontré son homologue allemand** the Prime Minister has had a meeting with *ou* has met his German counterpart; **mon regard rencontra le sien** our eyes met, my eyes met his
b (= *trouver*) [+ *expression*] to find, come across; [+ *occasion*] to meet with; **des gens/ sites comme on n'en rencontre plus** the sort of people/places you don't find any more; **arrête-toi au premier garage que nous rencontrerons** stop at the first garage you come across *ou* find; **avec lui, j'ai rencontré le bonheur** I have found happiness with him
c (= *heurter*) to strike; (= *toucher*) to meet (with); **la lame rencontra un os** the blade struck a bone; **sa main ne rencontra que le vide** his hand met with nothing but empty space
d [+ *obstacle, difficulté, opposition*] to meet with, encounter, come up against; [+ *résistance*] to meet with, come up against
e (*Sport*) [+ *équipe*] to meet, play (against); [+ *boxeur*] to meet, fight (against)
2 **se rencontrer** VPR **a** [*personnes, regards*] to meet; [*rivières, routes*] to meet, join; [*équipes*] to meet, play (each other); [*boxeurs*] to meet, fight (each other); [*véhicules*] to collide (with each other); **faire se ~ deux personnes** to arrange for two people to meet, arrange a meeting between two people; (*frm*) **je me suis déjà rencontré avec lui** I have already met him; **nous nous sommes déjà rencontrés** we have already met

---

b (= *avoir les mêmes idées*) **se ~ (avec qn)** to be of the same opinion *ou* mind (as sb) → **esprit**
c (= *exister*) [*coïncidence, curiosité*] to be found; **cela ne se rencontre plus de nos jours** that isn't found *ou* one doesn't come across that any more nowadays; **il se rencontre des gens qui ...** you do find people who ..., there are people who ...

rendement [ʀɑ̃dmɑ̃] NM [*champ*] yield; [*machine*] output; [*entreprise*] (= *productivité*) productivity; (= *production*) output; [*personne*] output; (*Phys*) efficiency; (*Fin*) [*investissement*] return (**de** on), yield (**de** of); **taux de ~** [*investissement*] (rate of) return, yield; **l'entreprise marche à plein** = the business is working at full capacity; **placement d'un ~ médiocre** low-yielding investment; **il travaille beaucoup, mais il n'a pas de ~*** he works hard but he isn't very productive

rendez-vous [ʀɑ̃devu] NM INV **a** (*gén*) appointment; (*d'amoureux*) date; **donner** *ou* **fixer un ~ à qn** ◊ **prendre ~ avec qn** (*pour affaires, consultation*) to make an appointment with sb; (*entre amis*) to arrange to see *ou* meet sb; **j'ai (un) ~ à 10 heures** I have an appointment *ou* I have to meet someone at 10 o'clock; **nous nous étions donné ~ à l'aéroport** we had arranged to meet at the airport; **ma parole, vous vous êtes donné ~!** my goodness, you must have seen each other coming!; **le soleil était au ~ pour le mariage** it was a sunny day for the wedding; **la croissance espérée n'est pas au ~** the expected growth has not materialized; (*littér*) **avoir ~ avec la mort** to have an appointment with death; **~ d'affaires** business appointment; **~ spatial** docking (in space); **prendre (un) ~ chez le dentiste/ coiffeur** to make a dental/hair appointment; **j'ai ~ chez le médecin** I've got a doctor's appointment *ou* an appointment at the doctor's; **le médecin ne reçoit que sur ~** the doctor only sees patients by appointment; **ce match sera le grand ~ sportif de l'année** this match will be the big sporting event of the year; **le festival est le ~ annuel des cinéphiles** the festival brings cinema lovers together once a year; (*fig*) **~ manqué** missed *ou* wasted opportunity → **galant**
b (= *lieu*) meeting place; **~ de chasse** meet → **maison**
c (* = *personne*) **votre ~ est arrivé** the person you're waiting for has arrived

rendormir [ʀɑ̃dɔʀmiʀ] ▸conjug 16◂ **1** VT to put to sleep again, put back to sleep **2** **se rendormir** VPR to go back to sleep, fall asleep again

rendosser [ʀɑ̃dose] ▸conjug 1◂ VT to put on again

rendre [ʀɑ̃dʀ] ▸conjug 41◂ **1** VT **a** (= *restituer*) (*gén*) to give back, return, take *ou* bring back; [+ *marchandises défectueuses, bouteille vide*] to return, take back; [+ *argent*] to pay *ou* give back, return; [+ *objet volé*] to give back, return; [+ *otage*] to return; [+ *cadeau, bague*] to return, give back; (*Scol*) [+ *copie*] to hand in; **quand pourriez-vous me ~ votre réponse ?** when will you be able to give me *ou* let me have your reply?; **~ son devoir en retard** to hand *ou* give in one's essay late; **~ sa parole à qn** to release sb from a promise, let sb off (his promise); **~ la liberté à qn** to set sb free, give sb his freedom; **~ la santé à qn** to restore sb to health; **~ la vue à qn** to restore sb's sight, give sb back his sight; **cela lui a rendu toutes ses forces/son courage** that gave him back *ou* restored all his strength/his courage; **~ la vie à qn** to save sb's life (*fig*); **rendu à la vie civile** back in civilian life; **cette lessive rend à votre linge l'éclat du neuf** this powder makes your washing as good as new
b (*Jur*) [+ *jugement, arrêt*] to pronounce, render; [+ *verdict*] to return
c (= *donner en retour*) [+ *hospitalité, invitation*]

to return, repay; [+ *salut, coup, baiser*] to return; **je lui ai rendu sa visite** I returned *ou* repaid his visit; **~ coup pour coup** to return blow for blow; **il m'a joué un sale tour, mais je le lui rendrai** he played a dirty trick on me, but I'll get even with him *ou* I'll get my own back on him*; **je lui ai rendu injure pour injure** I gave him as good as I got; **Dieu vous le rendra au centuple** God will return it to you a hundredfold; **~ la politesse à qn** to return sb's kindness; **il la déteste, et elle le lui rend bien** he hates her and she feels exactly the same (way) about him; **~ la monnaie à qn** to give sb his change; **il m'a donné 10 F et je lui en ai rendu 5** he gave me 10 francs and I gave him 5 francs back *ou* 5 francs change; **~ la pareille à qn** to pay sb back in his own coin → **monnaie**

[d] (*avec adj*) to make; **~ qn heureux** to make sb happy; **~ qch public** to make sth public; **~ qn responsable de qch** to make sb responsible for sth; **son discours l'a rendu célèbre** his speech has made him famous; **c'est à vous ~ fou!** it's enough to drive you mad!

[e] (= *exprimer par un autre moyen*) [+ *mot, expression, atmosphère*] to render; **cela ne rend pas sa pensée** that doesn't render *ou* convey his thoughts very well; **le portrait ne rend pas son expression** this portrait has not caught *ou* captured his expression

[f] (= *produire*) [+ *liquide*] to give out; [+ *son*] to produce, make; **le concombre rend beaucoup d'eau** cucumbers give out a lot of water; **l'enquête n'a rien rendu** the inquiry drew a blank *ou* didn't come to anything *ou* produced nothing; **ça ne rend pas grand-chose** [*photo, décor, musique*] it's a bit disappointing

[g] (= *vomir*) [+ *bile*] to vomit, bring up; [+ *déjeuner*] to vomit, bring back *ou* up; **~ tripes et boyaux*** to be as sick as a dog*; **~ du sang (par la bouche)** to cough up *ou* vomit blood

[h] (*Sport*) **~ du poids** [*cheval*] to have a weight handicap; **~ 3 kg** to give *ou* carry 3 kg; **~ de la distance** [*coureur*] to have a handicap; **~ 100 mètres** to have a 100-metre handicap; (*fig*) **~ des points à qn** to give sb points *ou* a head start

[i] (*Mil*) [+ *place forte*] to surrender; **~ les armes** to lay down one's arms

[j] (*loc*) **~ l'âme** *ou* **le dernier soupir** [*personne*] to breathe one's last, give up the ghost; **ma voiture/mon frigo a rendu l'âme*** my car/my fridge has given up the ghost*; **~ gloire à** [+ *Dieu*] to glorify; [+ *hommes*] to pay homage to; **~ grâce(s) à qn** to give *ou* render (*frm*) thanks to sb → **compte, service, visite** etc

[2] VI [a] [*arbres, terre*] to yield, be productive; **les pommiers ont bien rendu** the apple trees have given a good yield *ou* crop; **la pêche a bien rendu** we have got a good catch (of fish); (*fig*) **ma petite expérience n'a pas rendu** my little experiment didn't pay off *ou* didn't come to anything

[b] (= *vomir*) to be sick, vomit; **avoir envie de ~** to feel sick

[c] (= *produire un effet*) **la pendule rendrait mieux dans l'entrée** the clock would look better in the hall; **ça rend mal en photo** a photograph doesn't do it justice

[3] **se rendre** VPR [a] (= *céder*) [*soldat, criminel*] to give o.s. up, surrender; [*troupe*] to surrender; **se ~ à l'avis de qn** to bow to sb's opinion; **se ~ à l'évidence** (= *regarder les choses en face*) to face facts; (= *admettre son tort*) to bow before the evidence; **se ~ aux prières de qn** to give way *ou* give in *ou* yield to sb's pleas; **se ~ aux raisons de qn** to bow to *ou* accept sb's reasons

[b] (= *aller*) **se ~ à** to go to; **il se rend à son travail à pied/en voiture** he walks/drives to work, he goes to work on foot/by car; **alors qu'il se rendait à ...** as he was on his way to ... *ou* going to ...; **la police s'est rendue sur les lieux** the police went to *ou* arrived on the scene; **se**

~ à l'appel de qn to respond to sb's appeal → **lieu¹**

[c] (*avec adj*) **se ~ utile/indispensable** to make o.s. useful/indispensable; **il se rend ridicule** he's making a fool of himself, he's making himself look foolish; **vous allez vous ~ malade** you're going to make yourself ill

rendu, e [ʀɑ̃dy] (*ptp de* **rendre**) [1] ADJ [a] (= *arrivé*) **être ~** to have arrived; **nous voilà ~s!** here we are then!; **on est plus vite ~ par le train** you get there quicker by train [b] (= *remis*) **~ à domicile** delivered to the house [c] (= *fatigué*) exhausted, tired out, worn out [2] NM [a] (*Comm*) return → **prêté** [b] (*Art*) rendering

rêne [ʀɛn] NF rein; (*fig*) **prendre les ~s d'une affaire** to take over a business, assume control *ou* take control of a business; **lâcher les ~s** (*lit*) to loosen *ou* slacken the reins; (*fig*) to let go; (*fig*) **c'est lui qui tient les ~s du gouvernement** it's he who holds the reins of government *ou* who is in the saddle

renégat, e [ʀənega, at] NM,F (*Rel*) renegade; (*gén, Pol*) renegade, turncoat

renégociation [ʀ(ə)negɔsjasjɔ̃] NF renegotiation

renégocier [ʀ(ə)negɔsje] ▸ conjug 7 ◂ VT, VI to renegotiate

reneiger [ʀ(ə)neʒe] ▸ conjug 3 ◂ VB IMPERS to snow again

renfermé, e [ʀɑ̃fɛʀme] (*ptp de* **renfermer**) [1] ADJ [*personne*] withdrawn, uncommunicative [2] NM **ça sent le ~** it smells musty *ou* stuffy (in here) → **odeur**

renfermer [ʀɑ̃fɛʀme] ▸ conjug 1 ◂ [1] VT [a] (= *contenir*) [+ *trésors*] to contain, hold; [+ *erreurs, vérités*] to contain; **phrase qui renferme plusieurs idées** sentence that encompasses *ou* contains several ideas [b] († : *à clé*) to lock again, lock back up [2] **se renfermer** VPR **se ~ (en soi-même)** to withdraw into o.s.; **se ~ dans sa coquille** to withdraw into one's shell

renfiler [ʀɑ̃file] ▸ conjug 1 ◂ VT [+ *perles*] to restring; [+ *aiguille*] to thread again, rethread; [+ *bas, manteau*] to slip back into

renflé, e [ʀɑ̃fle] (*ptp de* **renfler**) ADJ bulging (*épith*), bulbous

renflement [ʀɑ̃fləmɑ̃] NM bulge

renfler [ʀɑ̃fle] ▸ conjug 1 ◂ [1] VT to make a bulge in; [+ *joues*] to blow out [2] **se renfler** VPR to bulge (out)

renflouage [ʀɑ̃flua3], **renflouement** [ʀɑ̃flumɑ̃] NM [a] [*navire*] refloating [b] [*entreprise*] refloating, bailing out; [*personne*] bailing out

renflouer [ʀɑ̃flue] ▸ conjug 1 ◂ [1] VT [a] [+ *navire*] to refloat [b] [+ *entreprise*] to refloat, bail out; [+ *personne*] to set back on their feet again, bail out [2] **se renflouer** VPR [*personne*] to get back on one's feet again (financially)

renfoncement [ʀɑ̃fɔ̃smɑ̃] NM recess; **caché dans le ~ d'une porte** hidden in a doorway

renfoncer [ʀɑ̃fɔ̃se] ▸ conjug 3 ◂ VT [a] [+ *clou*] to knock further in; [+ *bouchon*] to push further in; **il renfonça son chapeau (sur sa tête)** he pulled his hat down (further) [b] (*Typo*) to indent

renforçateur [ʀɑ̃fɔʀsatœʀ] NM (*Photo*) intensifier; (*Psych*) reinforcer; **~ de goût** flavour enhancer

renforcement [ʀɑ̃fɔʀsəmɑ̃] NM [a] [*vêtement, mur*] reinforcement; [*poutre*] reinforcement, trussing; [*régime, position, monnaie, amitié*] strengthening; [*paix, pouvoir*] consolidating [b] [*équipe, armée*] reinforcement; **~ des effectifs de la police** increasing the number of police officers [c] [*crainte, soupçon*] reinforcement, increase; [*argument*] reinforcement, strengthening [d] [*pression, effort, surveillance, contrôle*] intensification, stepping up; [*couleur, ton, expression*] intensification; **un ~**

des sanctions économiques toughening *ou* stepping up economic sanctions; **un ~ du dialogue Nord-Sud** stepping up dialogue between North and South

renforcer [ʀɑ̃fɔʀse] ▸ conjug 3 ◂ [1] VT [a] [+ *vêtement, mur*] to reinforce; [+ *poutre*] to reinforce, truss; [+ *régime, position, monnaie, amitié*] to strengthen; [+ *paix, pouvoir*] to consolidate; **bas à talon renforcé** stocking with reinforced heel [b] [+ *équipe, armée, effectifs*] to reinforce; **ils sont venus ~ nos effectifs** they came to strengthen *ou* swell our numbers [c] [+ *crainte, soupçon*] to reinforce, increase; [+ *argument*] to reinforce, strengthen; **~ qn dans une opinion** to confirm sb's opinion, confirm sb in an opinion; **ça renforce ce que je dis** that backs up *ou* reinforces what I'm saying [d] [+ *pression, effort, surveillance, contrôle*] to intensify, step up; [+ *couleur, son, expression*] to intensify; (*Scol*) **(cours d')anglais renforcé** remedial English (class) [2] **se renforcer** VPR [*craintes, amitié*] to strengthen; [*pression*] to intensify; **notre équipe s'est renforcée de deux nouveaux joueurs** our team has been strengthened by two new players

renfort [ʀɑ̃fɔʀ] NM [a] (*gén*) help, helpers; (*Mil*) **~s** (*en hommes*) reinforcements; (*en matériel*) (further) supplies; **recevoir un ~ de troupes/d'artillerie** to receive more troops/guns, receive reinforcements/a further supply of guns [b] (*Tech*) reinforcement, strengthening piece [c] (*Couture*) patch; **collants avec ~s aux talons** tights with reinforced heels [d] (*loc*) **de ~** [*barre, toile*] strengthening; [*troupe*] back-up, supporting; [*personnel*] extra, additional; **envoyer qn en ~** to send sb as an extra *ou* sb to augment the numbers; **les 500 soldats appelés en ~** the 500 soldiers called in as reinforcements; **embaucher du personnel de** *ou* **en ~** to employ extra *ou* additional staff; **parfum lancé à grand ~ de publicité** perfume launched amid much publicity *ou* a blaze of publicity; **à grand ~ de gestes/d'explications** with a great many gestures/explanations; **à grand ~ de citations/d'arguments** with the help *ou* support of a great many quotations/arguments

renfrogné, e [ʀɑ̃fʀɔɲe] (*ptp de se* **renfrogner**) ADJ [*visage*] sullen, scowling (*épith*), sulky; [*air, personne*] sullen, sulky

renfrognement [ʀɑ̃fʀɔɲmɑ̃] NM scowling, sullenness

renfrogner (se) [ʀɑ̃fʀɔɲe] ▸ conjug 1 ◂ VPR [*personne*] to scowl, pull a sour face

rengagé [ʀɑ̃gaʒe] [1] ADJ M [*soldat*] re-enlisted [2] NM re-enlisted soldier

rengagement [ʀɑ̃gaʒmɑ̃] NM [a] [*discussion*] starting up again; [*combat*] re-engagement [b] (= *réinvestissement*) reinvestment [c] (= *nouveau recrutement*) [*soldat*] re-enlistment; [*ouvrier*] taking back

rengager [ʀɑ̃gaʒe] ▸ conjug 3 ◂ [1] VT [a] [+ *discussion*] to start up again; [+ *combat*] to re-engage [b] (= *réinvestir*) to reinvest [c] (= *recruter de nouveau*) [+ *soldat*] to re-enlist; [+ *ouvrier*] to take back [d] (= *réintroduire*) **~ une clé dans une serrure** to put a key back into a lock; **~ sa voiture dans une rue** to drive (back) into a street again [2] VI (*Mil*) to join up again, re-enlist [3] **se rengager** VPR [a] (*Mil*) to join up again, re-enlist [b] [*discussion*] to start up again [c] (= *entrer à nouveau*) **se ~ dans une rue** to enter a street again

rengaine [ʀɑ̃gɛn] NF (= *formule*) hackneyed expression; (= *chanson*) old (repetitive) song *ou* melody; **c'est toujours la même ~*** it's always the same old refrain (*Brit*) *ou* song* (*US*)

rengainer [ʀɑ̃gene] ▸ conjug 1 ◂ VT [a]* [+ *compliment*] to save, withhold; [+ *sentiments*] to contain, hold back; **rengaine tes beaux discours !** (you can) save *ou* keep your fine speeches! [b] [+ *épée*] to sheathe, put up; [+ *revolver*] to put back in its holster

rengorger (se) [ʀɑ̃gɔʀʒe] ►conjug 3◄ VPR [*oiseau*] to puff out its throat; [*personne*] to puff o.s. up; **se rengorger d'avoir fait qch** to be full of o.s. for having done sth

reniement [ʀənimɑ̃] NM [*foi, opinion*] renunciation; [*frère, patrie, signature, passé, cause, parti*] disowning, repudiation; [*promesse, engagement*] breaking; (Rel) denial; **le ~ de Jésus par saint Pierre** St Peter's denial of Christ

renier [ʀənje] ►conjug 7◄ [1] VT [+ *foi, opinion*] to renounce; [+ *personne, patrie, signature, passé, cause, parti*] to disown; [+ *promesse, engagement*] to go back on, break; (Rel) **il renia Jésus Christ** he denied Christ; **~ Dieu** to renounce God [2] **se renier** VPR to go back on what one has said *ou* done

reniflement [ʀ(ə)nifləmɑ̃] NM [a] (= *action*) [*fleur, objet*] sniffing (*NonC*); [*cheval*] snorting (*NonC*); (*à cause d'un rhume, en pleurant*) sniffing (*NonC*), snuffling (*NonC*), sniffling (*NonC*) [b] (= *bruit*) sniff, sniffle, snuffle; (*plus fort*) snort

renifler [ʀ(ə)nifle] ►conjug 1◄ [1] VT [a] [+ *cocaine*] to snort, take a snort of; [+ *colle*] to sniff [b] [+ *fleur, objet, odeur*] to sniff [c] (* = *pressentir*) [+ *bonne affaire, arnaque*] to sniff out*; **~ quelque chose de louche** to smell a rat [2] VI [*personne*] to sniff; (*en pleurant*) to sniff, snuffle, sniffle; [*cheval*] to snort; **arrête de ~, mouche-toi !** stop sniffing and blow your nose!

renifleur, -euse [ʀ(ə)niflœʀ, øz] [1] ADJ sniffling, snuffling [2] NM,F* sniffler, snuffler → **avion**

renne [ʀɛn] NM reindeer

renom [ʀɑ̃nɔ̃] NM [a] (= *notoriété*) renown, repute, fame; **vin de grand ~** famous wine; **restaurant en ~** celebrated *ou* renowned *ou* famous restaurant; **acquérir du ~** to win renown, become famous; **avoir du ~** to be famous *ou* renowned [b] (*frm* = *réputation*) reputation; **son ~ de sévérité** his reputation for severity; **bon/mauvais ~** good/bad reputation *ou* name

renommé, e[1] [ʀ(ə)nɔme] (*ptp de* **renommer**) ADJ celebrated, renowned, famous; **~ pour** renowned *ou* famed for

renommée[2] [ʀ(ə)nɔme] NF [a] (= *célébrité*) fame, renown; **marque/savant de ~ mondiale** world-famous make/scholar; **de grande ~** of great renown [b] (*littér* = *opinion publique*) public report [c] (*littér* = *réputation*) reputation; **bonne/mauvaise ~** good/bad reputation *ou* name

renommer [ʀ(ə)nɔme] ►conjug 1◄ VT [a] [+ *personne*] to reappoint [b] (Ordin) [+ *fichier, répertoire*] to rename

renonce [ʀ(ə)nɔ̃s] NF (Cartes) **faire une ~** to revoke, renege, fail to follow suit

renoncement [ʀ(ə)nɔ̃smɑ̃] NM (= *action*) renouncement (**à** of); (= *sacrifice*) renunciation; **~ à soi-même** self-abnegation, self-renunciation; **mener une vie de ~** to live a life of renunciation *ou* abnegation

renoncer [ʀ(ə)nɔ̃se] ►conjug 3◄ [1] **renoncer à** VT INDIR [+ *projet, lutte*] to give up, renounce; [+ *fonction, héritage, titre, pouvoir, trône*] to renounce, relinquish; [+ *habitude*] to give up; [+ *métier*] to abandon, give up; **~ à un voyage/au mariage** to give up *ou* abandon the idea of a journey/of marriage; **~ à qn** to give sb up; **au tabac** to give up smoking; **~ à lutter/à comprendre** to give up struggling/trying to understand; **~ à se marier** to give up *ou* abandon the idea of getting married; **~ aux plaisirs/au monde** to renounce pleasures/the world; **je** *ou* **j'y renonce** I give up; (Cartes) **~ à cœur** to fail to follow (in) hearts; (Jur) **~ à tou-**

te prétention to abandon any claim [2] VT (*littér*) [+ *ami*] to give up

renonciation [ʀənɔ̃sjasjɔ̃] NF [*fonction, héritage, titre, pouvoir, trône*] renunciation, relinquishment (**à** of); [*opinion, croyance, idée, projet, lutte*] giving up

renoncule [ʀənɔ̃kyl] NF (*sauvage*) buttercup; (*cultivée*) globeflower, ranunculus (*SPÉC*)

renouer [ʀənwe] ►conjug 1◄ [1] VT [+ *lacet, nœud*] to tie (up) again, re-tie; [+ *cravate*] to reknot, knot again; [+ *conversation, liaison*] to renew, resume [2] VI **~ avec qn** to take up with sb again, become friends with sb again; **~ avec une habitude** to take up a habit again; **~ avec une tradition** to revive a tradition

renouveau (*pl* **renouveaux**) [ʀ(ə)nuvo] NM [a] (= *transformation*) revival; **le ~ des sciences et des arts à la Renaissance** the revival of the sciences and the arts *ou* the renewed interest in *ou* the renewal of interest in the sciences and arts during the Renaissance [b] (= *regain*) **~ de succès/faveur** renewed success/favour; **connaître un ~ de faveur** to enjoy renewed favour, come back into favour [c] (*littér* = *printemps*) **le ~** springtide (*littér*)

renouvelable [ʀ(ə)nuv(ə)labl] ADJ [*bail, contrat, énergie, passeport*] renewable; [*expérience*] which can be tried again *ou* repeated; [*congé*] which can be re-granted; [*assemblée*] that must be re-elected; **le mandat présidentiel est ~ tous les 7 ans** the president must run *ou* stand (Brit) for re-election every 7 years; **ressources naturelles non ~s** non-renewable natural resources; **crédit ~** revolving credit

renouveler [ʀ(ə)nuv(ə)le] ►conjug 4◄ [1] VT [a] [+ *matériel, personnel, équipe*] to renew, replace; [+ *stock*] to renew, replenish; [+ *pansement*] to renew, change; [+ *conseil d'administration*] to re-elect; **~ l'air d'une pièce** to air a room; **~ l'eau d'une piscine** to renew the water in a swimming pool; **~ sa garde-robe** to renew one's wardrobe, buy some new clothes; (Pol) **la chambre doit être renouvelée tous les cinq ans** the house must be re-elected every five years [b] [+ *mode, théorie*] to renew, revive; **cette découverte a complètement renouvelé notre vision des choses** this discovery has given us a whole new insight into things *ou* has cast a whole new light on things for us; **les poètes de la Pléiade renouvelèrent la langue française** the poets of the Pléiade gave new *ou* renewed life to the French language [c] [+ *passeport, abonnement, bail, prêt, mandat*] to renew; (Méd) **à ~** to be renewed [d] [+ *douleur*] to revive [e] [+ *candidature*] to renew; [+ *demande, offre, promesse, erreur*] to renew, repeat; [+ *expérience, exploit*] to repeat, do again; (Rel) [+ *vœux*] to renew; **l'énergie sans cesse renouvelée que requiert ce métier** the constantly renewed energy which this job requires; (*dans une lettre*) **avec mes remerciements renouvelés** with renewed thanks, thanking you once more *ou* once again; **la chambre a renouvelé sa confiance au gouvernement** the house reaffirmed *ou* reasserted its confidence in the government [f] (*littér* = *emprunter*) **épisode renouvelé de l'Antiquité** episode taken *ou* borrowed from Antiquity

[2] **se renouveler** VPR [a] (= *se répéter*) [*incident*] to recur, be repeated; **cette petite scène se renouvelle tous les jours** this little scene recurs *ou* is repeated every day; **et que ça ne se renouvelle plus !** and don't let it happen again! [b] (= *être remplacé*) to be renewed *ou* replaced; **les cellules de notre corps se renouvellent constamment** the cells of our body are constantly being renewed *ou* replaced; **les hommes au pouvoir ne se renouvellent pas**

assez men in power aren't replaced often enough [c] (= *innover*) [*auteur, peintre*] to change one's style, try something new; **il ne se renouvelle pas** [*comique*] he always tells the same old jokes *ou* stories

renouvellement [ʀ(ə)nuvɛlmɑ̃] NM [a] [*matériel, personnel, équipe*] renewal, replacement; [*stock*] renewal, replenishment; [*pansement*] renewal, changing; [*garde-robe*] changing; [*cellules*] renewal [b] [*mode, théorie, art, langue*] renewal, revival; [*genre littéraire*] revival; **elle éprouve un besoin de ~** she feels she needs to start afresh [c] [*passeport, contrat, abonnement, bail, prêt*] renewal; (Pol) **solliciter le ~ de son mandat** to run *ou* stand (Brit) for re-election [d] [*candidature*] renewal; [*demande, offre, promesse, erreur*] renewal, repetition; [*expérience, exploit*] repetition; [*incident*] recurrence; [*douleur*] revival; (Rel) [*vœux*] renewal; **faire son ~** to renew one's first communion promises

rénovateur, -trice [ʀenɔvatœʀ, tʀis] [1] ADJ [*doctrine*] which seeks a renewal, reformist; [*influence*] renewing (*épith*), reforming (*épith*) [2] NM,F (*de la morale, Pol*) reformer; **il est considéré comme le ~ de cette science/de cet art** he's considered as having been the one who injected new life into this science/into this art form [3] NM (= *produit d'entretien*) restorer

rénovation [ʀenɔvasjɔ̃] NF [a] [*maison*] renovation; (= *nouvelle décoration*) refurbishment; [*quartier, monument*] renovation; [*meuble*] restoration; **en (cours de) ~** under renovation; **travaux de ~** renovations, renovation work [b] [*enseignement, institution*] reform; [*science*] renewal, bringing up to date; [*méthode*] reform

rénover [ʀenɔve] ►conjug 1◄ VT [a] [+ *maison*] to renovate; (*nouvelle décoration*) to refurbish; [+ *quartier*] to renovate; [+ *meuble*] to restore [b] [+ *enseignement, institution*] to reform; [+ *science*] to renew, bring up to date; [+ *méthode, parti*] to reform

▼**renseignement** [ʀɑ̃sɛɲmɑ̃] NM [a] (*gén*) information (*NonC*), piece of information; **un ~ intéressant** an interesting piece of information, some interesting information; **demander un ~** *ou* **des ~s à qn** to ask sb for (some) information; **il est allé aux ~s** he has gone to make inquiries *ou* to see what he can find out (about it); **prendre ses ~s** *ou* **demander des ~s sur qn** to make inquiries *ou* ask for information about sb; **~s pris** upon inquiry; **avoir de bons ~s sur le compte de qn** to have good *ou* favourable reports about *ou* on sb; **pourriez-vous me donner un ~ ?** I'd like some information, could you give me some information?; **veuillez m'envoyer de plus amples ~s ...** please send me further details of ... *ou* further information about ...; **je peux te demander un ~ ?** can you give me some information?, can I ask you something?, could you tell me something?; **merci pour le ~** thanks for the information, thanks for telling me *ou* letting me know; **guichet/bureau des ~s** information *ou* inquiry (Brit) desk/office; (*panneau*) **« renseignements »** "information", "inquiries" (Brit); (Téléc) (**service des**) **~s** directory inquiries (Brit), information (US) [b] (Mil) intelligence (*NonC*), piece of intelligence; **agent/service de ~s** intelligence agent/service; **travailler dans le ~** to work in intelligence; **les ~s généraux** *the security branch of the police force*

renseigner [ʀɑ̃sɛɲe] ►conjug 1◄ [1] VT [a] **~ un client/un touriste** to give some information to a customer/a tourist; **~ la police/l'ennemi** to give information to the police/the enemy (*sur about*); **~ un passant/un automobiliste** (*sur le chemin à prendre*) to give directions to a passer-by/a driver, tell a passer-by/a driver the way; **qui pourrait me ~ sur le prix de la voiture/sur lui ?** who could tell me the price of

---

the car/something about him?, who could give me some information *ou* particulars about the price of the car/about him?; **puis-je vous ~ ?** can I help you?; **il pourra peut-être te ~** perhaps he'll be able to give you some information (about it), perhaps he'll be able to tell you *ou* to help you; **document qui renseigne utilement** document which gives useful information; **ça ne nous renseigne pas beaucoup !** that doesn't get us very far!, that doesn't tell us very much! *ou* give us much to go on!; **il a l'air bien renseigné** he seems to be well informed *ou* to know a lot about it; **il est mal renseigné** he doesn't know much about it, he isn't very well informed; **j'ai été mal renseigné** I was misinformed *ou* given the wrong information

b (= *remplir*) [+ *case, champ de données*] to fill in

2 **se renseigner** VPR (= *demander des renseignements*) to make enquiries, ask for information (**sur** about); (= *obtenir des renseignements*) to find out (**sur** about); **je vais me ~ auprès de lui** I'll ask him for information *ou* for particulars, I'll ask him about it; **renseignez-vous auprès de l'office du tourisme/à l'accueil** enquire at *ou* ask at the tourist office/at reception (for details); **j'essaierai de me ~** I'll try to find out, I'll try and get some information; **je vais me ~ sur son compte** I'll make enquiries about him, I'll find out about him; **je voudrais me ~ sur les caméscopes** I'd like some information *ou* particulars about camcorders

rentabilisation [Rɑ̃tabilizasjɔ̃] NF [*produit, entreprise*] making profitable; [*invention*] marketing, commercializing; **la ~ des investissements** securing a return on investments, making investments pay

rentabiliser [Rɑ̃tabilize] ▸conjug 1◂ VT [+ *entreprise, activité*] to make profitable, make pay; [+ *investissements*] to secure a return on, make pay; [+ *équipements*] to make cost-effective, make pay; **notre investissement a été très vite rentabilisé** we got a quick return on our investment; **~ son temps** to make the best use of one's time

rentabilité [Rɑ̃tabilite] NF profitability; **~ des investissements** return on investments; **ce placement a une faible/forte ~** this is a low-return *ou* low-yield/high-return *ou* high-yield investment

rentable [Rɑ̃tabl] ADJ [*entreprise, activité*] profitable; **c'est une affaire très ~** this is a very profitable business, this business really pays; **au prix où est l'essence, les transports privés ne sont pas ~s** with fuel the price it is, private transport isn't a paying *ou* viable proposition *ou* private transport doesn't pay; **il travaille beaucoup mais il n'est pas ~** he works a lot but he isn't very productive; **ce n'est plus du tout ~** (*lit*) it's no longer financially viable; (*fig*) it just isn't worth it any more; **cette prise de position s'est avérée politiquement ~** taking this stand paid off *ou* was a good move politically

rentamer [Rɑ̃tame] ▸conjug 1◂ VT [+ *discours*] to begin *ou* start again

rente [Rɑ̃t] NF a (= *pension*) annuity, pension; (*fournie par la famille*) allowance; **~ de situation** secure *ou* guaranteed income; **~ viagère** life annuity; **faire une ~ à qn** to give an allowance to sb b (= *emprunt d'État*) government stock *ou* loan *ou* bond; **~s perpétuelles** perpetual loans, irredeemable securities c (*loc*) **avoir des ~s** to have a private *ou* an unearned income, have private *ou* independent means; **vivre de ses ~s** to live on *ou* off one's private income

rentier, -ière [Rɑ̃tje, jɛR] NM,F person of independent *ou* private means; **c'est un petit ~** he has a small private income; **mener une vie de ~** to live a life of ease *ou* leisure

---

rentrant, e [Rɑ̃tRɑ̃, ɑ̃t] ADJ [*train d'atterrissage*] retractable; (*Math*) [*angle*] reflex

rentré, e¹ [Rɑ̃tRe] (*ptp de rentrer*) 1 ADJ [*colère*] suppressed; [*yeux*] sunken; [*joues*] sunken, hollow 2 NM (*Couture*) hem

rentre-dedans: [Rɑ̃tR(ə)dədɑ̃] NM INV **il m'a fait du ~** [*dragueur*] he came on really strong to me*; [*vendeur*] he was really pushy*

rentrée² [Rɑ̃tRe] NF a **~** (= *scolaire ou des classes*) start of the new school year, time when the schools go back; **~ universitaire** start of the new academic year; (*du trimestre*) start of the new (school *ou* university) term; **acheter des cahiers pour la ~ (des classes)** to buy exercise books for the new school year; **la ~ aura lieu lundi** the new term begins on Monday, school starts again on Monday; **la ~ s'est bien passée** the term began well; (*Comm*) « **les affaires de la ~** » "back-to-school bargains"; **à la ~ de Noël** at the start of (the) term after the Christmas holidays; **cette langue sera enseignée à partir de la ~ 2004** this language will be part of the syllabus as from autumn 2004 *ou* as from the start of the 2004-5 school year

b [*tribunaux*] reopening; [*parlement*] reopening, reassembly; **la ~ parlementaire aura lieu cette semaine** parliament reassembles *ou* reopens this week, the new session of parliament starts this week; **les députés font leur ~ aujourd'hui** the deputies are returning *ou* reassembling today (for the start of the new session); **faire sa ~ politique** (*après les vacances d'été*) to start the new political season, begin one's autumn campaign; (*après avoir fait autre chose*) to make a *ou* one's political comeback; **c'est la ~ des théâtres parisiens** it's the start of the theatrical season in Paris; **la ~ littéraire** the start of the literary season *ou* calendar; **on craint une ~ sociale agitée** it is feared that there will be some social unrest this autumn; **la réforme entrera en vigueur à la ~ prochaine** the reform will come into effect next autumn; **leur album sortira à la ~ de septembre** their album will come out in September; **la mode de la ~** the autumn fashions; **on verra ça à la ~** we'll see about that after the holidays *ou* when we come back from holiday

c [*acteur, sportif*] comeback

d (= *retour*) return; **pour faciliter la ~ dans la capitale** to make getting back into *ou* the return into the capital easier; **la ~ des ouvriers à l'usine le lundi matin** the workers' return to work on a Monday morning; **à l'heure des ~s dans Paris** when everyone is coming back into Paris; **il m'a reproché mes ~s tardives** he told me off for coming in late; (*Espace*) **~ dans l'atmosphère** re-entry into the atmosphere; **effectuer sa ~ dans l'atmosphère** to re-enter the atmosphere; (*Sport*) **~ en touche** throw-in

e [*récolte*] bringing in; **faire la ~ du blé** to bring in the wheat

f (*Cartes*) cards picked up

g (*Comm, Fin*) **~s** income; **~ d'argent** sum of money (coming in); **je compte sur une ~ d'argent très prochaine** I'm expecting a sum of money *ou* some money very soon; **les ~s de l'impôt** tax revenue

---

RENTRÉE

La rentrée (des classes) *in September each year is not only the time when French children and teachers go back to school; it is also the time when political and social life begins again after the long summer break. The expression "à la rentrée" is thus not restricted to an educational context, but can refer in general to the renewed activity that takes place throughout the country in the autumn.*

---

rentrer [Rɑ̃tRe] ▸conjug 1◂ 1 VI (*avec aux être*) a (= *entrer à nouveau*) (*vu de l'extérieur*) to go back in; (*vu de l'intérieur*) to come back in; **il**

---

pleut trop, rentrez un instant it's raining too hard so come back in for a while; **il est rentré dans la maison/la pièce** he went back (*ou* came back) into the house/the room; **la navette est rentrée dans l'atmosphère** the shuttle re-entered the atmosphere; **il était sorti sans ses clés, il a dû ~ par la fenêtre** he'd gone out without his keys and he had to get back in through the window; **l'acteur est rentré en scène** the actor came on again

b (= *revenir chez soi*) to come back, come (back) home, return (home); (= *s'en aller chez soi*) to go (back) home, return home; (= *arriver chez soi*) to get (back) home, return home; **~ déjeuner/dîner** to go (back) home for lunch/dinner; **est-ce qu'il est rentré ?** is he back?; **elle est rentrée très tard hier soir** she came *ou* got in *ou* back very late last night; **je l'ai rencontré en rentrant** I met him on my way home; **~ de l'école/du bureau** to come back from school/from the office, come (*ou* go) home from school/from the office; **il a dû ~ de voyage d'urgence** he had to come back *ou* come home from his trip urgently, he had to return home urgently; **~ à Paris/de Paris** to go back *ou* come back *ou* return to Paris/from Paris; **je rentre en voiture** I'm driving back, I'm going back by car; **dépêche-toi de ~, ta mère a besoin de toi** hurry home *ou* back, your mother needs you; (*Aviat*) **~ à sa base** to return *ou* go back to base; **le navire rentre au port** the ship is coming back in

c (= *reprendre ses activités*) [*élèves*] to go back to school, start school again; [*université*] to start again; [*tribunaux*] to reopen; [*parlement*] to reassemble; [*députés*] to reassemble, reassemble; **les enfants rentrent en classe ou à l'école lundi** the children go back to school *ou* start school again on Monday; **le trimestre prochain, on ~a un lundi** next term starts *ou* next term we start on a Monday; **elle rentre au lycée l'année prochaine** she's starting secondary school next year

d (= *entrer*) [*personne*] to go in, come in; [*chose*] to go in; **il pleuvait, nous sommes rentrés dans un café** it was raining so we went into a cafe; **les voleurs sont rentrés par la fenêtre** the thieves got in by the window; **cette clé ne rentre pas (dans la serrure)** this key doesn't fit (into the lock), I can't get this key in (the lock); **j'ai grossi, je ne rentre plus dans cette jupe** I've put on weight, I can't get into this skirt any more; **faire ~ qch dans la tête de qn** to get sth into sb's head; **il a le cou qui lui rentre dans les épaules** he has a very short neck; **il était exténué, les jambes lui rentraient dans le corps** he was so exhausted his legs were giving way under him; **tout cela ne ~a pas dans ta valise** that won't all go *ou* fit into your suitcase, you won't get all that into your suitcase; **cubes qui rentrent les uns dans les autres** cubes that fit into one another → **entrer**

e (= *devenir membre de*) **~ dans** [+ *police, entreprise, fonction publique*] to join, go into; [+ *industrie, banque*] to go into; **c'est son père qui l'a fait ~ dans l'usine** his father helped him (to) get a job in the factory *ou* (to) get into the factory

f (= *se heurter à*) **~ dans** to crash into, collide with; **sa voiture a dérapé, il est rentré dans un arbre** his car skidded and he crashed into a tree; (= *agresser*) **furieux, il voulait lui ~ dedans** *ou* **dans le chou*** he was so furious he felt like smashing his head in*; **rentrez-leur dedans !:** get them!*; **il lui est rentré dans le lard:** *ou* **le mou:** *ou* **le buffet:** he beat him up*

g (= *être compris dans*) **~ dans** to be included in, be part of; **cela ne rentre pas dans ses attributions** that is not included in *ou* part of his duties; **les frais de déplacement ne devraient pas ~ dans la note** travelling expenses should not be included in the bill *ou* should not be put on the bill; **~ dans une catégorie** to fall *ou* come into a category

h [argent] to come in; **l'argent ne rentre pas en ce moment** the money isn't coming in at the moment; **l'argent rentre difficilement/bien en ce moment** there isn't much money/there's plenty of money coming in at the moment; **faire ~ les impôts/les fonds** to collect the taxes/the funds; **faire ~ l'argent** to get the money in

i * [connaissances] **la grammaire/les maths, ça ne rentre pas** he can't take grammar/maths in, he can't get the hang of grammar/maths*; **l'anglais, ça commence à ~** English is beginning to sink in

j (loc) **~ dans ses droits** to recover one's rights; **~ dans son argent/dans ses frais** to recover ou get back one's money/one's expenses; **~ dans ses fonds** to recoup one's costs; **tout est rentré dans l'ordre** (dans son état normal) everything is back to normal again; (dans le calme) order has returned, order has been restored; (= tout a été clarifié) everything is sorted out now; **~ dans le rang** to come ou fall back into line → **coquille, grâce, terre** etc

2 VT (avec aux avoir) **a** [+ foins, moisson] to bring in, get in; [+ marchandises, animaux] (en venant) to bring in; (en allant) to take in; **~ sa voiture (au garage)** to put the car away (in the garage); **ne laisse pas ton vélo sous la pluie, rentre-le** don't leave your bicycle out in the rain, put it away ou bring it in; **~ les bêtes à l'étable** to bring the cattle into the cowshed

b [+ train d'atterrissage] to raise; (lit, fig) [+ griffes] to draw in; **~ sa chemise (dans son pantalon)** to tuck one's shirt in (one's trousers); **~ le cou dans les épaules** to hunch up one's shoulders; **ne me rentre pas ton coude dans le ventre** don't jab ou stick your elbow in(to) my stomach; **~ le ou son ventre** to pull one's stomach in; **~ ses larmes** to hold back ou choke back the tears; **~ sa rage** to hold back ou suppress one's anger; (Sport) **~ un but** to score a goal

c (Ordin) [+ données] to enter

3 **se rentrer** VPR **a** (= pouvoir être rentré) **ce lit se rentre sous l'autre** this bed fits under the other one

b (mutuellement) **ils se sont rentrés dedans** (= heurtés) they crashed into each other; * (= battus) they laid into each other

renversant, e• [ʀɑ̃vɛʀsɑ̃, ɑ̃t] ADJ [nouvelle] staggering*, astounding; [personne] amazing, incredible

renverse [ʀɑ̃vɛʀs] NF **a** (Naut) [vent] change; [courant] turn **b** **tomber à la ~** to fall backwards, fall flat on one's back; (fig) **il y a de quoi tomber à la ~!** it's astounding! ou staggering!*

renversé, e [ʀɑ̃vɛʀse] (ptp de **renverser**) ADJ **a** (= à l'envers) [objet] upside down (attrib); [fraction] inverted; [image] inverted, reversed → **crème** **b** (= stupéfait) **être ~** to be bowled over, be staggered* **c** (= penché) [écriture] backhand (épith)

renversement [ʀɑ̃vɛʀsəmɑ̃] NM **a** [image, fraction] inversion; [ordre des mots] inversion, reversal; [vapeur] reversing; [situation] reversal; (Mus) [intervalles, accord] inversion **b** [alliances, valeurs, rôles] reversal; [ministre] removal from office; [gouvernement] (par un coup d'État) overthrow; (par un vote) defeat, voting ou turning out of office; **un ~ de tendance de l'opinion publique** a shift ou swing in public opinion **c** [buste, tête] tilting ou tipping back **d** [courant] changing of direction; [marée, vent] turning, changing of direction

renverser [ʀɑ̃vɛʀse] ▶conjug 1◀ **1** VT **a** (= faire tomber) [+ personne] to knock over; [+ chaise] to knock over, overturn; [+ vase, bouteille] to knock over, upset; [+ piéton] to knock down, run over; **elle l'a renversé d'un coup de poing** she knocked him to the ground; **un camion a renversé son chargement**

sur la route a lorry has shed its load

b (= répandre) [+ liquide] to spill, upset; **~ du vin sur la nappe** to spill ou upset some wine on the tablecloth

c (= mettre à l'envers) to turn upside down; **~ un seau (pour monter dessus)** to turn a bucket upside down (so as to stand on it)

d (= abattre) [+ obstacles] (lit) to knock down; (fig) to overcome; [+ ordre établi, tradition, royauté] to overthrow; [+ ministre] to put ou throw out of office, remove from office; **~ le gouvernement** (par un coup d'État) to overthrow ou overturn ou topple the government; (par un vote) to defeat the government, vote ou throw the government out of office

e (= pencher) **~ la tête en arrière** to tip ou tilt one's head back; **~ le corps en arrière** to lean back; **elle lui renversa la tête en arrière** she tipped ou put his head back

f (= inverser) [+ ordre des mots, courant] to reverse; [+ fraction] to invert; (Opt) [+ image] to invert, reverse; **~ la situation** to reverse the situation, turn things (a)round; **il ne faudrait pas ~ les rôles** don't try to turn the situation round; **~ la vapeur** (lit) [bateau] to go astern; (fig) to change tack

g (* = étonner) to bowl over, stagger; **la nouvelle l'a renversé** the news bowled him over ou staggered him

2 VI (Naut) [marée] to turn

3 **se renverser** VPR **a** **se ~ en arrière** to lean back; **se ~ sur le dos** to lie down (on one's back); **se ~ sur sa chaise** to lean back on one's chair, tip one's chair back

b [voiture, camion] to overturn; [bateau] to overturn, capsize; [verre, vase] to fall over, be overturned

renvoi [ʀɑ̃vwa] NM **a** [employé] dismissal, sacking (Brit); [élève, étudiant] (définitif) expulsion; (temporaire) suspension; **menacer de ~** [+ employé] to threaten with dismissal; (Scol) to threaten to expel ou with expulsion; **j'ai demandé son ~ du club** I asked for him to be expelled from the club

b [accusé, troupes] discharge

c [lettre, colis, cadeau] sending back, return

d (Sport) [balle] sending back; (au pied) kicking back; (à la main) throwing back; (Tennis) return; (Rugby) **~ aux 22 mètres** drop-out; **à la suite d'un mauvais ~ du gardien, la balle a été interceptée** as a result of a poor return ou throw by the goalkeeper the ball was intercepted

e (Téléc) [appel] transfer; **~ temporaire de ligne** call diversion

f [lecteur] referral (à to)

g [rendez-vous] postponement; **~ à date ultérieure** postponement to a later date; (Jur) **~ à huitaine** adjournment for a week

h (= envoi, Jur) **le ~ d'un projet de loi en commission** referral of a bill to a committee; **demande de ~ devant une autre juridiction** application for transfer of proceedings

i (= référence) cross-reference; (en bas de page) footnote; **faire un ~ aux notes de l'appendice** to cross-refer to the notes in the appendix

j (= rot) belch, burp; **avoir un ~** (gén) to belch, burp; [bébé] to burp; **avoir des ~s** to have wind (Brit) ou gas (US); **ça me donne des ~s** it makes me belch, it gives me wind (Brit)

k (Tech) **levier de ~** reversing lever; **poulie de ~** return pulley

l (Mus) repeat mark ou sign

renvoyer [ʀɑ̃vwaje] ▶conjug 8◀ VT **a** [+ employé] to dismiss, fire*, sack (Brit); [+ membre d'un club] to expel; [+ élève, étudiant] (définitivement) to expel; (temporairement) to suspend; **il s'est fait ~ de son travail** he was dismissed ou fired* ou sacked (Brit) from his job

b (= faire retourner) to send back; (= faire repartir) to send away; (= libérer) [+ accusé, troupes] to discharge; [+ importun, créancier] to

send away; **je l'ai renvoyé chez lui** I sent him back home; **~ dans leurs foyers** [+ soldats] to discharge, send (back) home; [+ femmes, enfants] to send (back) home; **les électeurs ont renvoyé les démocrates dans leurs foyers** the voters sent the democrats packing*; **~ un projet de loi en commission** to refer a bill back ou send a bill for further discussion

c (= réexpédier) [+ lettre, colis] to send back, return; [+ cadeau non voulu, bague de fiançailles] to return, give back; **je te renvoie le compliment!** and the same to you!

d (= relancer) [+ balle] to send back; (au pied) to kick back; (à la main) to throw back; (Tennis) to return (à to); (fig) **il m'a renvoyé la balle** (argument) he threw the ou my argument back at me, he came back at me with the same argument; (responsabilité) he handed the responsibility over to me, he left it up to me; **ils se renvoient la balle** (argument) they come back at each other with the same argument; (responsabilité) they each refuse to take responsibility, they both keep trying to pass the buck*; (fig) **~ l'ascenseur** to return the favour

e (= référer) [+ lecteur] to refer (à to); **~ aux notes de l'appendice** to (cross-)refer to notes in the appendix; **~ un procès en Haute Cour** to refer a case to the high court; **~ le prévenu en cour d'assises** to send the accused for trial by the Crown Court; **~ qn de service en service** to send sb from one department to another; **cela (nous) renvoie à l'Antiquité/à la notion d'éthique** this takes us back to ancient times/to the notion of ethics

f (Téléc) [+ appel] to transfer

g (= différer) [+ rendez-vous] to postpone, put off; (Jur) **l'affaire a été renvoyée à huitaine** the case was postponed ou put off for a week; **~ qch aux calendes grecques** to postpone sth ou put sth off indefinitely

h (= réfléchir) [+ lumière, chaleur, image] to reflect; [+ son] to echo

i (Cartes) **~ carreau/pique** to play diamonds/spades again, lead diamonds/spades again

réoccupation [ʀeɔkypasjɔ̃] NF (Mil) reoccupation; **depuis la ~ du village sinistré par les habitants** since the inhabitants of the stricken village moved back in ou came back

réoccuper [ʀeɔkype] ▶conjug 1◀ VT [+ territoire] to reoccupy; [+ fonction] to take up again; **les grévistes ont réoccupé les locaux** the strikers have staged another sit-in; **~ une maison** to move back into a house

réopérer [ʀeɔpeʀe] ▶conjug 1◀ VT to operate again; **elle s'est fait ~** she had another operation, she was operated on again

réorchestration [ʀeɔʀkɛstʀasjɔ̃] NF reorchestration

réorchestrer [ʀeɔʀkɛstʀe] ▶conjug 1◀ VT to reorchestrate

réorganisateur, -trice [ʀeɔʀganizatœʀ, tʀis] NM,F reorganizer

réorganisation [ʀeɔʀganizasjɔ̃] NF reorganization

réorganiser [ʀeɔʀganize] ▶conjug 1◀ **1** VT to reorganize **2** **se réorganiser** VPR [pays, parti] to get reorganized, reorganize itself

réorientation [ʀeɔʀjɑ̃tasjɔ̃] NF [politique] redirecting, reorientation; **~ scolaire** streaming

réorienter [ʀeɔʀjɑ̃te] ▶conjug 1◀ VT [+ politique] to redirect, reorient(ate); [+ élève] to put into a new stream

réouverture [ʀeuvɛʀtyʀ] NF [magasin, théâtre] reopening; [débat] resumption, reopening

repaire [ʀ(ə)pɛʀ] NM (Zool) den, lair; (fig) den, hideout; **cette taverne est un ~ de brigands** this inn is a thieves' den ou a haunt of robbers

repaître [ʀəpɛtʀ] ▶conjug 57◀ **1** VT (littér) **~ ses yeux de qch** to feast one's eyes on sth; **~ son esprit de lectures** to feed one's mind on books [2] **se repaître** VPR [a] **se ~ de** [+ *crimes*] to wallow in; [+ *lectures, films*] to revel in; [+ *illusions*] to revel in, feed on [b] (= *manger*) [*animal*] to eat its fill; [*personne*] to eat one's fill; **se ~ de qch** to gorge o.s. on sth

répandre [Repɑ̃dR] ▸conjug 41◂ [1] VT [a] (= *renverser*) [+ *soupe, vin*] to spill; [+ *grains*] to scatter; (*volontairement*) [+ *sciure, produit*] to spread; **le camion a répandu son chargement sur la chaussée** the truck shed its load; **~ du sable sur le sol** to spread *ou* sprinkle sand on the ground; **la rivière répand ses eaux dans la vallée** the waters of the river spread over *ou* out across the valley [b] (*littér*) [+ *larmes*] to shed; **~ son sang** to shed one's blood; **~ le sang** to spill *ou* shed blood; **beaucoup de sang a été répandu** a lot of blood was shed *ou* spilled there, there was a lot of bloodshed [c] (= *être source de*) [+ *lumière*] to shed, give out; [+ *odeur*] to give off; [+ *chaleur*] to give out *ou* off; **~ de la fumée** [*cheminée*] to give out smoke; [*feu*] to give off *ou* out smoke [d] (= *propager*) [+ *nouvelle, mode, joie, terreur*] to spread; [+ *chaleur*] to lavish, pour out [2] **se répandre** VPR [a] (= *couler*) [*liquide*] to spill, be spilled; [*grains*] to scatter, be scattered; (*sur* over); **le verre a débordé, et le vin s'est répandu par terre** the glass overflowed and the wine spilled onto the floor; **le sang se répand dans les tissus** blood spreads through the tissues; **la foule se répand dans les rues** the crowd spills out *ou* pours out into the streets [b] (= *se dégager*) [*chaleur, odeur, lumière*] to spread (**dans** through); [*son*] to carry (**dans** through); **il se répandit une forte odeur de caoutchouc brûlé** a strong smell of burning rubber was given off [c] (= *se propager*) [*doctrine, mode, nouvelle*] to spread (**dans, à travers** through); [*méthode, opinion*] to become widespread (**dans, parmi** among); [*coutume, pratique*] to take hold, become widespread; **la peur se répandit sur son visage** a look of fear spread over his face → **traînée** [d] **se ~ en calomnies/condoléances/excuses/menaces** to pour out *ou* pour forth slanderous remarks/condolences/excuses/threats; **se ~ en invectives** to let out a torrent of abuse, pour out a stream of abuse

répandu, e [Repɑ̃dy] (*ptp de* **répandre**) ADJ [*opinion, préjugé*] widespread; [*méthode*] widespread, widely used; **idée très ~e** widely *ou* commonly held idea; **une pratique largement ~e dans le monde** a practice that is very common throughout the world; **profession peu ~e** rather unusual profession; **les ordinateurs individuels étaient encore peu ~s** personal computers were still not very widespread *ou* common

réparable [Reparabl] ADJ [*objet*] repairable, which can be repaired *ou* mended; [*erreur*] which can be put right *ou* corrected; [*perte, faute*] which can be made up for; **ce n'est pas ~** [*objet*] it is beyond repair; [*faute*] there's no way of making up for it; [*erreur*] it can't be put right; **les dégâts sont facilement ~s** the damage can easily be repaired; **cette maladresse sera difficilement ~** it will be hard to put such a blunder right *ou* to make up for such a blunder

reparaître [R(ə)paRetR] ▸conjug 57◂ VI [*personne, trait héréditaire*] to reappear; [*lune*] to reappear, come out again; [*roman, texte*] to be republished; [*journal, magazine*] to be back in print

réparateur, -trice [ReparatœR, tRis] [1] ADJ [*sommeil*] refreshing; (*Cosmétique*) **crème réparatrice** conditioning cream → **chirurgie** [2] NM,F repairer; **~ d'objets d'art** restorer of works of art; **~ de porcelaine** porcelain restorer; **le ~ de télévision** the television *ou* TV repairman *ou* engineer

réparation [Reparasjɔ̃] NF [a] [*machine, montre, chaussures, voiture*] mending, repairing, fixing; [*accroc, fuite*] mending; [*maison*] repairing; [*objet d'art*] repairing, restoring; (= *résultat*) repair; **la voiture est en ~** the car is being repaired; **on va faire des ~s dans la maison** we're going to have some repairs done in the house; **pendant les ~s** during the repairs, while the repairs are (*ou* were) being carried out; **atelier de ~** repair shop [b] [*erreur*] correction; [*oubli, négligence*] putting right, rectification [c] [*faute, offense*] atonement (**de** for); [*tort*] redress (**de** for); [*perte*] compensation (**de** for); **en ~ du dommage causé** to make up for the harm that has been done; **obtenir ~ (d'un affront)** to obtain redress (for an insult); **demander ~ par les armes** to demand a duel [d] (*Ftbl*) **coup de pied/points/surface de ~** penalty kick/points/area [e] (= *recouvrement*) [*forces*] restoring, restoration, recovery; **la ~ des tissus sera longue** the tissues will take a long time to heal; **~ cellulaire** cell repair [f] (= *dommages-intérêts*) damages, compensation; (*Hist*) **~s** reparations

réparer [Repare] ▸conjug 1◂ VT [a] [+ *chaussures, montre, machine, voiture*] to mend, repair, fix; [+ *accroc, fuite*] to mend; [+ *maison*] to repair; [+ *route*] to mend, repair; [+ *objet d'art*] to restore, repair; **donner qch à ~** to take sth to be mended *ou* repaired; **faire ~ qch** to get *ou* have sth mended *ou* repaired; **~ sommairement qch** to patch sth up; **j'ai emmené la voiture à ~*** I took the car in (to be repaired) [b] (= *corriger*) [+ *erreur*] to correct, put right; [+ *oubli, négligence*] to put right, rectify [c] (= *compenser*) [+ *faute*] to make up for, make amends for; [+ *tort*] to put right, redress; [+ *offense*] to atone for, make up for; [+ *perte*] to make good, make up for, compensate for; **tu ne pourras jamais ~ le mal que tu m'as fait** you'll never put right *ou* never undo the harm you've done me; **comment pourrais-je ~ ?** what could I do to make up for it? *ou* to make amends?; **comment pourrais-je ~ ma bêtise ?** how could I make amends for *ou* make up for my stupidity?; **cela ne pourra jamais ~ le dommage que j'ai subi** that'll never make up for *ou* compensate for the harm I've suffered; **vous devez ~ en l'épousant†** you'll have to make amends by marrying her, you'll have to make an honest woman of her [d] (= *recouvrer*) [+ *forces, santé*] to restore [e] (*loc*) **il va falloir ~ les dégâts** (*lit*) we'll have to repair the damage; (* *fig*) we'll have to repair the damage *ou* pick up the pieces; (*littér*) **~ le désordre de sa toilette** to straighten *ou* tidy one's dress

reparler [R(ə)paRle] ▸conjug 1◂ [1] VI **~ de qch** to talk about sth again; **~ à qn** to speak to sb again; **nous en reparlerons** (*lit*) we'll talk about it again *ou* discuss it again later; (*dit avec scepticisme*) we'll see about that; **c'est un romancier dont on reparlera** he's a very promising novelist, we'll be hearing more of this novelist; **il commence à ~** [*accidenté, malade*] he's starting to speak again [2] **se reparler** VPR to speak to each other again, be on speaking terms again, be back on speaking terms

repartie, répartie [Reparti] NF retort, rejoinder (*frm*); **avoir de la ~ ◊ avoir la ~** to be good *ou* quick at repartee; **avoir l'esprit de ~** to have a talent *ou* gift for repartee

repartir¹ [Repartir, R(ə)partir], **répartir¹** [Repartir] ▸conjug 16◂ VT (*littér* = *répliquer*) to retort, reply

repartir² [R(ə)partir] ▸conjug 16◂ VI [*voyageur*] to set *ou* start off again; [*machine*] to start (up) again, restart; [*affaire, discussion*] to get going again; **~ chez soi** to go back *ou* return home; **il est reparti hier** he left again yesterday; **il est reparti comme il était venu** he left as he came;

(*Pol*) **~ en campagne** to go back on the campaign trail, start campaigning again; **~ à l'assaut** to launch another attack (**de** on); **~ sur des bases nouvelles** to make a fresh start; **les achats de véhicules neufs sont repartis à la hausse** sales of new cars have taken off *ou* picked up again; **la croissance repart** growth is picking up again; **heureusement, c'est bien reparti** fortunately, things have got off to a good start this time; (*dans une discussion*) **ça y est, les voilà repartis sur la politique !** that's it, they're off again *ou* there they go again, talking politics!; **c'est reparti pour un tour !*** *ou* **comme en 14 !*** *ou* **comme en 40 !*** here we go again!; **faire ~** [+ *entreprise, économie*] to get going again; [+ *moteur*] to start up again → **zéro**

répartir² [Repartir] ▸conjug 2◂ [1] VT [a] (= *diviser*) [+ *ressources, travail*] to share out, distribute (**entre** among); [+ *impôts, charges*] to share out (**en** into, **entre** among), apportion; [+ *butin, récompenses*] to share out, divide up (**entre** among); [+ *rôles*] to distribute (**entre** among); [+ *poids, volume, chaleur*] to distribute; **on avait réparti les joueurs en deux groupes** the players had been divided *ou* split (up) into two groups; (*Culin*) **répartissez le mélange dans les coupelles** divide the mixture equally into small bowls [b] (= *étaler*) [+ *paiement, cours, horaire*] to spread (**sur** over); **on a mal réparti les bagages dans le coffre** the luggage hasn't been evenly distributed in the boot; **les troupes sont réparties le long de la frontière** troops are spread out along the border; **le programme est réparti sur deux ans** the programme is spread (out) over a two-year period [2] **se répartir** VPR [a] (= *se décomposer*) **les charges se répartissent comme suit** the expenses are divided up as follows; **ils se répartissent en deux ensembles** they can be divided into two sets; **ils se sont répartis en deux groupes** they divided themselves *ou* they split into two groups [b] (= *se partager*) **ils se sont réparti le travail** they shared the work out *ou* divided the work up among themselves

répartiteur, -trice [RepartitœR, tRis] [1] NM,F (*gén, littér*) distributor, apportioner; [*impôt*] assessor; **~ d'avaries** averager, average adjuster [2] NM (*Tech*) [*électricité*] divider; [*fluides*] regulator

répartition [Repartisjɔ̃] NF [a] [*ressources, travail*] sharing out (*NonC*), distribution; [*impôts, charges*] sharing out (*NonC*); [*butin, récompenses*] sharing out (*NonC*), dividing up (*NonC*); [*poids, volume, chaleur*] dividing up (*NonC*), distribution; [*population, faune, flore, richesses, rôles*] distribution; (= *agencement*) [*pièces, salles*] layout, distribution; **~ par âge/sexe** distribution by age/sex; **~ géographique** geographical distribution; **la ~ des pouvoirs entre le Président et le Premier ministre** the distribution of power between the President and the Prime Minister [b] [*paiement, cours, horaires*] spreading (*NonC*); (*Comm*) dispatching

reparution [R(ə)parysjɔ̃] NF [*journal*] reappearance; **depuis la ~ du magazine en 1989** since the magazine resumed publication in 1989, since the magazine's reappearance in 1989; **la ~ de l'album en disque compact** the release of the CD version of the album

repas [R(ə)pɑ] NM meal; **~ d'affaires** (= *déjeuner*) business lunch; (= *dîner*) business dinner; **~ à la carte** à la carte meal; **~ léger** light meal; **~ de midi** midday *ou* noon (*US*) meal, lunch; **~ de noces** reception; **~ de Noël** Christmas dinner; **~ scolaire** school lunch; **~ du soir** evening meal, dinner; **il prend tous ses ~ au restaurant** he always eats out; **faire 3 ~ par jour** to have 3 meals a day; **~ complet** three-course meal; **médicament à prendre avant/à chaque ~** medicine to be taken before/with meals; **assister au ~ des fauves** to watch the big cats being fed; **à l'heure du ~ ◊ aux heures des ~** at mealtimes; **manger en dehors des ~ ou entre les ~** to eat between meals

repassage [ʀ(ə)pasaʒ] NM [*linge*] ironing; [*couteau*] sharpening; **faire le ~** to do the ironing; **« ~ superflu »** "wash-and-wear", "non-iron"

repasser [ʀ(ə)pase] ▸conjug 1◂ **1** VT **a** [+ *rivière, montagne, frontière*] to cross again, go ou come back across

b [+ *examen*] to take again, resit (*Brit*); [+ *permis de conduire*] to take again; **~ une visite médicale** to have another medical

c [+ *plat*] to hand round again; [+ *film*] to show again; [+ *émission*] to repeat; [+ *disque, chanson*] to play again; **~ un plat au four** to put a dish in the oven again ou back in the oven

d (*au fer à repasser*) to iron; (*à la pattemouille*) to press; **le nylon ne se repasse pas** nylon doesn't need ironing → **fer, planche, table**

e [+ *couteau, lame*] to sharpen (up)

f [+ *souvenir, leçon, rôle*] to go (back) over, go over again; **~ qch dans son esprit** to go over sth again ou go back over sth in one's mind

g (* = *transmettre*) [+ *affaire, travail*] to hand over ou on; [+ *maladie*] to pass on (**à qn** to sb); **il m'a repassé le tuyau** he passed the tip on to me; (*au téléphone*) **je te repasse ta mère** I'll hand you back to your mother; **je vous repasse le standard** I'll put you back through to the operator

2 VI **a** (= *retourner*) to come back, go back; **je repasserai** I'll come back, I'll call (in) again; **si vous repassez par Paris** (*au retour*) if you come back through Paris; (*une autre fois*) if you're passing through Paris again; **ils sont repassés en Belgique** they crossed back ou went back over into Belgium; **il va falloir je repasse sur le billard*** I've got to have another operation; **tu peux toujours ~ !:** you don't have a prayer!, you've got a hope!* (*Brit*)

b (*devant un même lieu*) to go ou come past again; (*sur un même trait*) to go over again, go back over; **je passai et repassai devant la vitrine** I kept walking backwards and forwards in front of the shop window; **souvenirs qui repassent dans la mémoire** memories that are running through one's mind; **quand il fait un travail, il faut toujours ~ derrière lui** when he does some work you always have to go over it again

repasseur [ʀ(ə)pasœʀ] NM (= *rémouleur*) knife-grinder ou -sharpener

repasseuse [ʀ(ə)pasøz] NF (= *femme*) ironer; (= *machine*) ironer, ironing machine

repavage [ʀ(ə)pavaʒ] NM repaving

repaver [ʀ(ə)pave] ▸conjug 1◂ VT to repave

repayer [ʀ(ə)peje] ▸conjug 8◂ VT to pay again

repêchage [ʀ(ə)pɛʃaʒ] NM **a** [*objet, noyé*] recovery **b** (*Scol*) [*candidat*] letting through, passing; **épreuve/question de ~** exam/question to give candidates a second chance

repêcher [ʀ(ə)pɛʃe] ▸conjug 1◂ VT **a** [+ *objet, noyé*] to recover, fish out; **je suis allé ~ la lettre dans la poubelle** I went and fished the letter out of the bin **b** (*Scol*) [+ *candidat*] to let through, pass (*with less than the official pass mark*); [+ *athlète*] to give a second chance to; **il a été repêché à l'oral** he scraped through ou just got a pass thanks to the oral

repeindre [ʀ(ə)pɛ̃dʀ] ▸conjug 52◂ VT to repaint

rependre [ʀ(ə)pɑ̃dʀ] ▸conjug 41◂ VT to rehang, hang again

repenser [ʀ(ə)pɑ̃se] ▸conjug 1◂ **1** **repenser à** VT INDIR **~ à qch** to think about sth again; **plus j'y repense** the more I think of it; **je n'y ai plus repensé** (*plus avant*) I haven't thought

about it again (*since*), I haven't given it any further thought (*since*); (= *j'ai oublié*) it completely slipped my mind; **j'y repenserai** I'll think about it again, I'll have another think about it **2** VT [+ *concept*] to rethink; **il faut ~ tout l'enseignement** the whole issue of education will have to be rethought; **~ la question** to rethink the question

repentant, e [ʀ(ə)pɑ̃tɑ̃, ɑ̃t] ADJ repentant, penitent

repenti, e [ʀ(ə)pɑ̃ti] (*ptp de* **se repentir**) **1** ADJ repentant, penitent; **buveur/joueur ~** reformed drinker/gambler **2** NM,F (*gén*) reformed man (*ou* woman); (= *ancien malfaiteur*) criminal turned informer; **un ~ de la Mafia** Mafia turncoat

repentir (se)[1] [ʀ(ə)pɑ̃tiʀ] ▸conjug 16◂ VPR **a** (*Rel*) to repent; **se repentir d'une faute/d'avoir commis une faute** to repent of a fault/of having committed a fault **b** (= *regretter*) **se repentir de qch/d'avoir fait qch** to regret sth/having done sth, be sorry for sth/for having done sth; **tu t'en repentiras!** you'll be sorry!

repentir[2] [ʀ(ə)pɑ̃tiʀ] NM (*Rel*) repentance (*NonC*); (= *regret*) regret

repérable [ʀ(ə)peʀabl] ADJ which can be spotted; **~ de loin** easily spotted from a distance; **difficilement ~** (*gén*) difficult to spot; (*Mil*) difficult to locate

repérage [ʀ(ə)peʀaʒ] NM (*Aviat, Mil*) location; **le ~ d'un point sur la carte** locating a point on the map, pinpointing a spot on the map; (*Ciné*) **faire des ~s** to research locations; (*Ciné*) **partir en ~** to go looking for locations

répercussion [ʀepɛʀkysjɔ̃] NF (*gén*) repercussion (**sur, dans** on); **la hausse des taux d'intérêt a eu des ~s sur l'économie** the rise in interest rates has had a knock-on effect on the economy; (*Fin*) **la ~ d'une taxe sur le client** passing a tax on ou along (*US*) to the customer

répercuter [ʀepɛʀkyte] ▸conjug 1◂ **1** VT **a** [+ *son*] to echo; [+ *écho*] to send back, throw back; [+ *lumière*] to reflect **b** (= *transmettre*) **~ une augmentation sur le client** to pass an increase in cost on to the customer; **~ un impôt sur le consommateur** to pass on ou along (*US*) a tax to the consumer **2** **se répercuter** VPR **a** [*son*] to reverberate, echo; [*lumière*] to be reflected, reflect **b** **se ~ sur** to have repercussions on, affect

reperdre [ʀ(ə)pɛʀdʀ] ▸conjug 41◂ VT to lose again

repère [ʀ(ə)pɛʀ] NM (= *marque, trait*) line, mark; (= *jalon, balise*) marker; (= *monument, accident de terrain*) landmark; (= *événement*) landmark; (= *date*) reference point; **~ de niveau** bench mark; **j'ai laissé des branches comme ~s pour retrouver notre chemin** I've left branches as markers so that we can find the way back again; **perdre ses ~s** [*personne*] to lose one's bearings, become disorientated; [*société*] to lose its points of reference; **dans un monde sans ~s** in a world that has lost its way; **la disparition des ~s traditionnels** the loss of traditional points of reference; **point de ~** (*dans l'espace*) landmark; (*dans le temps, fig*) point of reference

repérer [ʀ(ə)peʀe] ▸conjug 6◂ **1** VT **a** (* = *localiser*) [+ *erreur, personne*] to spot; [+ *endroit, chemin*] to locate, find; **se faire ~** (*lit*) to be spotted; (*fig*) to be found out, get caught; **il avait repéré un petit restaurant** he had discovered a little restaurant; **tu vas nous faire ~** we'll be spotted because of you, you'll get us caught **b** (*Mil*) to locate, pinpoint **c** (*Tech* = *jalonner*) [+ *niveau, alignement*] to mark out ou off, stake out **2** **se repérer** VPR (*gén* = *se diriger*) to find one's way about ou around; (= *établir sa position*) to find ou get one's bearings; **j'ai du mal à me ~ dans cette intrigue** I

have difficulty getting my bearings in this plot

répertoire [ʀepɛʀtwaʀ] **1** NM **a** (= *carnet*) index notebook, notebook with alphabetical thumb index; (= *liste*) (alphabetical) list; (= *catalogue*) catalogue; **noter un mot dans un ~** to write a word down in an alphabetical index, index a word

b (*Théât*) repertoire, repertory; [*chanteur, musicien*] repertoire; **les plus grandes œuvres du ~ classique/contemporain/lyrique/symphonique** the greatest classical works/contemporary works/operas/symphonies; **jouer une pièce du ~** to put on a stock play; **elle n'a que deux chansons à son ~** she's only got two songs in her repertoire; (*fig*) **elle a tout un ~ de jurons/d'histoires drôles** she has quite a repertoire of swearwords/of jokes **c** (*Ordin*) directory

2 COMP ▸ **répertoire d'adresses** address book ▸ **répertoire alphabétique** alphabetical index ou list ▸ **répertoire des rues** (*sur un plan*) street index

répertorier [ʀepɛʀtɔʀje] ▸conjug 7◂ VT [+ *information*] to list; [+ *cas, maladie*] to record; [+ *œuvre*] to index; **non répertorié** unlisted; **les restaurants sont répertoriés par quartiers** the restaurants are listed by area; **90 espèces de coccinelles ont été répertoriées** 90 species of ladybird have been listed ou recorded

repeser [ʀ(ə)pəze] ▸conjug 5◂ VT to reweigh, weigh again

répète* [ʀepɛt] NF ABRÉV = **répétition**

▼**répéter** [ʀepete] ▸conjug 6◂ **1** VT **a** (= *redire*) [+ *explication, question*] to repeat, say again; [+ *mot*] to repeat, say again; [+ *histoire*] to repeat, tell again; **~ à qn que ...** to say again that ...; **pourriez-vous me ~ cette phrase ?** could you repeat that sentence?, could you say that sentence (to me) again?; **répète-moi le numéro du code** tell me ou give me the code number again, tell me what the code number is again; **je l'ai répété/je te l'ai répété dix fois** I've said that/I've told you that a dozen times; **il répète toujours la même chose** he keeps saying ou repeating the same thing; (*ton de menace*) **répète !** say that again!; **il ne se l'est pas fait ~** he didn't have to be told ou asked twice, he didn't need asking ou telling twice

b (= *rapporter*) [+ *calomnie*] to repeat, spread about; [+ *histoire*] to repeat; **elle est allée tout ~ à son père** she went and repeated everything to her father, she went and told her father everything; **je vais vous ~ exactement ce qu'il m'a dit** I'll repeat exactly what he said; **c'est un secret, ne le répétez pas !** it's a secret, don't repeat it! ou don't tell anyone!; **il m'a répété tous les détails de l'événement** he went over all the details of the event for me, he related all the details of the event to me

c (= *refaire*) [+ *expérience, exploit*] to repeat, do again; [+ *proposition*] to repeat, renew; [+ *essai*] to repeat; **nous répéterons une nouvelle fois la tentative** we'll repeat the attempt one more time, we'll have another try; **tentatives répétées de suicide/d'évasion** repeated suicide/escape attempts

d [+ *pièce, symphonie, émission*] to rehearse; [+ *rôle, leçon*] to learn, go over; [+ *morceau de piano*] to practise; **nous répétons à 4 heures** we rehearse at 4 o'clock, the rehearsal is at 4 o'clock; **ma mère m'a fait ~ ma leçon/mon rôle** I went over my homework/my part with my mother

e (= *reproduire*) [+ *motif*] to repeat; (*Mus*) [+ *thème*] to repeat, restate; **les miroirs répétaient son image** his image was reflected again and again in the mirrors

2 **se répéter** VPR **a** (= *redire, radoter*) to repeat o.s.; **se ~ qch à soi-même** to repeat sth to o.s.; **la nouvelle que toute la ville se répète** the news which is being repeated all round

the town; **je ne voudrais pas me ~, mais ...** I don't want to repeat myself *ou* say the same thing twice, but ...
[b] (*= se reproduire*) to be repeated, reoccur, recur; **ces incidents se répétèrent fréquemment** these incidents were frequently repeated, these incidents kept recurring *ou* occurred repeatedly; **que cela ne se répète pas!** (just) don't let that happen again!; **l'histoire ne se répète jamais** history never repeats itself

répétiteur, -trice [Repetitœʀ, tʀis] [1] NM,F (*Scol*) tutor, coach [2] NM (*Tech*) **~ de signaux** repeater

répétitif, -ive [Repetitif, iv] ADJ repetitive

répétition [Repetisjɔ̃] NF [a] (*= redite*) repetition; **il y a beaucoup de ~s** there is a lot of repetition, there are numerous repetitions [b] (*Théât = représentation, fig*) rehearsal; **~ générale** (final) dress rehearsal [c] (*= action*: *gén*) repetition; [*pièce, symphonie*] rehearsal; [*rôle*] learning; [*morceau de piano*] practising; **pour éviter la ~ d'une telle mésaventure** to prevent such a mishap happening again; **la ~ d'un tel exploit est difficile** repeating a feat like that *ou* doing a feat like that again is difficult; **la chorale est en ~** the choir is rehearsing *ou* practising [d] († = *leçon particulière*) private lesson, private coaching (*NonC*) [e] (*loc*) **faire des rhumes/des angines à ~** to have one cold/one sore throat after another; **scandales/grèves à ~** one scandal/strike after another, endless scandals/strikes; **fusil/montre à ~** repeater rifle/watch

répétitivité [Repetitivite] NF repetitiveness

repeuplement [Rə(ə)pœplamɑ̃] NM [*région*] repopulation; [*étang, chasse*] restocking; [*forêt*] replanting

repeupler [Rə(ə)pœple] ▸conjug 1◂ [1] VT [+ *région*] to repopulate; [+ *étang, chasse*] to restock (**de** with); [+ *forêt*] to replant (**de** with) [2] **se repeupler** VPR [*région*] to be *ou* become repopulated; **le village commence à se ~** people have started moving back into the village

repincer [Rə(ə)pɛ̃se] ▸conjug 3◂ VT (*lit*) to pinch *ou* nip again; (* *fig*) to catch again, nab* again; **se faire ~** to get caught *ou* nabbed* again

repiquage [Rə(ə)pikaʒ] NM [a] (*Bot*) pricking out; [*riz*] transplanting [b] (*Bio*) subculturing [c] (*Photo*) touching up, retouching [d] (*= réenregistrement*) rerecording; (*= copie*) recording, tape

repiquer [Rə(ə)pike] ▸conjug 1◂ [1] VT [a] (*Bot*) to prick out; [+ *riz*] to transplant; **plantes à ~** bedding plants [b] (*Bio*) to subculture [c] (*Photo*) to touch up, retouch [d] (*= réenregistrer*) to rerecord; (*= faire une copie de*) [+ *disque*] to record, tape [e] (* *= reprendre*) to catch again; **il s'est fait ~ à la frontière** the police caught up with him again at the border [f] [*moustique*] to bite again; [*épine*] to prick again; (*Couture*) **~ un vêtement à la machine** to restitch a garment [2] **repiquer à*** VT INDIR **~ au plat** to take a second helping; **~ au truc** to go back to one's old ways, be at it again*; **elle a repiqué aux somnifères** she's back on sleeping tablets again

répit [Repi] NM (*= rémission*) respite (*frm*); (*= repos*) respite (*frm*), rest; **la douleur ne lui laisse pas de ~** the pain never gives him any respite; **s'accorder un peu de ~** to have a bit of a rest; **accordez-nous 5 minutes de ~** give us 5 minutes' rest *ou* respite; **travailler sans ~** to work continuously *ou* without respite; **harceler qn sans ~** to harass sb relentlessly; **donnez-moi un petit ~ pour vous payer** give me a bit more time to pay you

replacement [Rə(ə)plasmɑ̃] NM [*objet*] replacing, putting back; [*employé*] redeployment

replacer [Rə(ə)plase] ▸conjug 3◂ [1] VT [a] (*= remettre*) [+ *objet*] to replace, put back (in its

place); **~ une vertèbre** to put *ou* ease a vertebra back into place [b] (*= resituer*) **il faut ~ les choses dans leur contexte** we must put things back in their context [c] [+ *employé*] to find a new job for, redeploy [d]* [+ *plaisanterie, expression*] **il faudra que je la replace, celle-là!** I must remember to use that one again! [2] **se replacer** VPR [a] [*employé*] to find a new job [b] (*= s'imaginer*) **~ dans les mêmes conditions** to put o.s. in the same situation; **replaçons-nous au 16e siècle** let's go *ou* look back to the 16th century

replantation [Rə(ə)plɑ̃tasjɔ̃] NF [*forêt*] replanting

replanter [Rə(ə)plɑ̃te] ▸conjug 1◂ VT [+ *plante*] to replant, plant out; [+ *forêt, arbre*] to replant; **~ un bois en conifères** to replant a wood with conifers

replat [Rəpla] NM projecting ledge *ou* shelf

replâtrage [Rə(ə)plɑtʀaʒ] NM [a] [*mur*] replastering [b]* [*amitié, gouvernement*] patching up; (*Pol*) **~ ministériel** patching together *ou* patch-up of the cabinet

replâtrer [Rə(ə)plɑtʀe] ▸conjug 1◂ VT [a] [+ *mur*] to replaster; [+ *membre*] to put another cast on [b]* [+ *amitié, gouvernement*] to patch up

replet, -ète [Rəplɛ, ɛt] ADJ [*personne*] podgy, fat; [*visage*] chubby

repleuvoir [Rə(ə)pløvwaʀ] ▸conjug 23◂ VB IMPERS to rain again, start raining again; **il repleut** it is raining again, it has started raining again

repli [Rəpli] NM [a] [*terrain, papier*] fold; [*intestin, serpent*] coil; [*rivière*] bend, twist; [*peau*] (*dû à l'âge*) wrinkle; (*d'embonpoint*) fold (**de** in) [b] (*Couture*) [*ourlet, étoffe*] fold, turn (**de** in) [c] (*Mil*) withdrawal, falling back; (*Mil, fig*) **position de ~** fallback position; (*Mil, fig*) **~ stratégique** strategic withdrawal [d] (*Bourse*) fall, drop; **le cours de l'étain a accentué son ~** the price of tin has weakened further; **le dollar est en ~ à 5 F** the dollar has fallen back to 5 francs; **mouvement de ~ des taux d'intérêt** downward trend in interest rates [e] (*= réserve*) withdrawal; **~ sur soi-même** withdrawal (into oneself), turning in on oneself [f] (*= recoin*) [*cœur, conscience*] hidden *ou* innermost recess, innermost reaches

repliable [Rə(ə)plijabl] ADJ folding (*épith*)

réplication [Replikasjɔ̃] NF (*Bio*) replication

repliement [Rə(ə)plimɑ̃] NM **~ (sur soi-même)** withdrawal (into oneself), turning in on oneself

replier [Rə(ə)plije] ▸conjug 7◂ [1] VT [a] [+ *carte, journal, robe*] to fold up (again), fold back up; [+ *manche, bas de pantalon*] to roll up, fold up; [+ *coin de feuille*] to fold over; [+ *ailes*] to fold (back); [+ *jambes*] to tuck up; [+ *couteau*] to close; **les jambes repliées sous lui** sitting back with his legs tucked under him; **~ le drap sur la couverture** to fold the sheet back over *ou* down over the blanket [b] (*Mil*) [+ *troupes*] to withdraw; [+ *civils*] to move back *ou* away [2] **se replier** VPR [*serpent*] to curl up, coil up; [*chat*] to curl up; [*lame de couteau*] to fold back; (*Mil*) to fall back, withdraw (**sur** to); (*Bourse*) [*valeurs*] to fall (back), drop; **se ~ (sur soi-même)** to withdraw into oneself, turn in on oneself; **communauté repliée sur elle-même** inward-looking community

réplique [Replik] NF [a] (*= réponse*) retort, rejoinder (*frm*); **il a la ~ facile** he's always ready with a quick answer, he's never at a loss for an answer *ou* a reply; **et pas de ~!** and don't answer back!, and let's not have any backchat!* (*Brit*); **« non »**, **dit-il d'un ton sans ~** "no", he said in a tone that brooked no reply; **argument sans ~** unanswerable *ou* irrefutable argument [b] (*= contre-attaque*) counter-attack; **la ~ ne se fit pas attendre** they weren't slow to retaliate

[c] (*Théât*) line; **dialogue aux ~s spirituelles** dialogue with some witty lines; **oublier sa ~** to forget one's lines *ou* words; **l'acteur a manqué sa ~** the actor missed his cue; **c'est Belon qui vous donnera la ~** (*pour répéter*) Belon will give you your cue; (*dans une scène*) Belon will play opposite you; (*fig*) **je saurai lui donner la ~** I can match him (in an argument), I can give as good as I get [d] (*Art*) replica; (*fig*) **il est la ~ de son jumeau** he's the (spitting) image of his twin brother [e] [*tremblement de terre*] after-shock

répliquer [Replike] ▸conjug 1◂ [1] VT to reply; **il (lui) répliqua que ...** he replied *ou* retorted that ...; **il n'y a rien à ~ à cela** there's no answer to that; **il trouve toujours quelque chose à ~** he's always got an answer for everything [2] VI [a] (*= répondre*) to reply; **~ à la critique** to reply to criticism; **et ne réplique pas!** (*insolence*) and don't answer back!; (*protestation*) and no protests! [b] (*= contre-attaquer*) to retaliate; **il répliqua par des coups de poing/des injures** he retaliated with his fists/with foul language

replonger [Rə(ə)plɔ̃ʒe] ▸conjug 3◂ [1] VT [+ *rame, cuiller*] to dip back (**dans** into); **replongé dans la pauvreté/la guerre/l'obscurité** plunged into poverty/war/darkness again, plunged back into poverty/war/darkness; **replongeant sa main dans l'eau** dipping his hand into the water again; **ce film nous replonge dans l'univers des années 30** this film takes us right back to the 1930s; **elle replongea son nez dans ses dossiers** she buried herself in her files again [2] VI [a] (*dans une piscine*) to dive back, dive again (**dans** into) [b]* [*drogué*] to become hooked* again; [*délinquant*] to go back to one's old ways; [*alcoolique*] to go back to drinking [3] **se replonger** VPR to dive back *ou* again (**dans** into); **il se replongea dans sa lecture** he immersed himself in his book again, he went back to his reading; **se ~ dans les études** to throw oneself into one's studies again

repolir [Rə(ə)pɔliʀ] ▸conjug 2◂ VT [+ *objet*] to repolish; (*fig*) [+ *discours*] to polish up again, touch up again

répondant, e [Repɔ̃dɑ̃, ɑ̃t] [1] NM,F guarantor, surety; **servir de ~ à qn** (*Fin*) to stand surety for sb, be sb's guarantor; (*fig*) to vouch for sb [2] NM [a] (*Fin*) **il a du ~** (*compte approvisionné*) he has money behind him; (* : *beaucoup d'argent*) he has something to fall back on; (* : *le sens de la répartie*) he has a talent for repartee [b] (*Rel*) server

répondeur, -euse [Repɔ̃dœʀ, øz] [1] ADJ* impertinent, cheeky* (*Brit*), sassy* (*US*); **je n'aime pas les enfants ~s** I don't like children who answer back [2] NM **~ (téléphonique)** (telephone) answering machine (*simply giving a recorded message*); **~ (enregistreur)** (telephone) answering machine, answerphone (*on which you can leave a message*); **je suis tombé sur un ~** I got a recorded message → **interrogeable**

▼ **répondre** [Repɔ̃dʀ] ▸conjug 41◂ [1] VT [a] (*gén*) to answer, reply; **il a répondu une grossièreté** he replied with a rude remark, he made a rude remark in reply; **il m'a répondu oui/non** he said *ou* answered yes/no; **il m'a répondu (par) une lettre** he sent me a written reply; **il a répondu qu'il le savait** he answered *ou* replied that he knew; **il m'a répondu qu'il viendrait** he told me (in reply) that he would come; **je lui ai répondu de se taire *ou* qu'il se taise** I told him to be quiet; **vous me demandez si j'accepte, je (vous) réponds que non** you're asking me if I accept and I'm telling you I don't *ou* and my answer is no; **je me suis vu ~ que ...** ◊ **il me fut répondu que ...** I was told that ...; **~ présent à l'appel** (*lit*) to answer present at roll call; (*fig*) to come forward, make oneself known; **réponds quelque** chose, même si c'est faux give an answer, even if it's wrong; (c'est) bien répondu ! well said!; qu'avez-vous à ~ ? what have you got to say in reply?; il n'y a rien à ~ there's no answer to that; qu'est-ce que vous voulez ~ à cela ? what can you say to that?

[b] (Rel) ~ la messe to serve (at) mass

[2] VI [a] (gén) to answer, reply; réponds donc !, well answer (then)!; ~ en claquant la porte to slam the door by way of reply ou by way of an answer; ~ à qn/à une question/à une convocation to reply to ou answer sb/a question/a summons; seul l'écho lui répondit only the echo answered him; je ne lui ai pas encore répondu I haven't yet replied to his letter ou answered his letter ou written back to him; je lui répondrai par écrit I'll reply ou answer in writing, I'll let him have a written reply ou answer; avez-vous répondu à son invitation ? did you reply to his invitation?; il répond au nom de Louis he answers to the name of Louis; ~ par oui ou par non to reply ou answer ou say yes or no; ~ par monosyllabes to reply in words of one syllable; instruments de musique qui se répondent musical instruments that answer each other; ~ par un sourire/en hochant la tête to smile/nod in reply; elle répondit à son salut par un sourire she replied to ou answered his greeting with a smile; il a répondu par des injures he replied with a string of insults, he replied by insulting us (ou them etc)

[b] (= aller ouvrir ou décrocher) ~ (à la porte ou à la sonnette) to answer the door; ~ (au téléphone) to answer the telephone; personne ne répond ◊ ça ne répond pas there's no answer ou reply, no one's answering; on a sonné, va ~ there's the doorbell — go and see who it is; personne n'a répondu à mon coup de sonnette no one answered the door ou the bell when I rang, I got no answer when I rang the bell

[c] (= être impertinent) to answer back; il a répondu à la maîtresse he answered the teacher back

[d] (= réagir) [voiture, commandes, membres] to respond (à to); son cerveau ne répond plus aux excitations his brain no longer responds to stimuli; les freins ne répondaient plus the brakes were no longer responding

[3] répondre à VT INDIR [a] (= correspondre à) [+ besoin] to answer, meet; [+ signalement] to answer, fit; [+ norme, condition] to meet; ça répond tout à fait à l'idée que je m'en faisais that corresponds exactly to what I imagined it to be like; cela répond/ne répond pas à ce que nous cherchons this meets/doesn't meet ou falls short of our requirements; ça répond/ne répond pas à mon attente ou à mes espérances it comes up to/falls short of my expectations

[b] (= payer de retour) [+ attaque, avances] to respond to; [+ amour, affection, salut] to return; [+ politesse, gentillesse, invitation] to repay, pay back; peu de gens ont répondu à cet appel few people responded to this appeal, there was little response to this appeal; ~ à la force par la force to answer ou meet force with force; s'ils lancent une attaque, nous saurons y ~ if they launch an attack we'll fight back ou retaliate

[c] (= être identique à) [+ dessin, façade] to match; les deux ailes du bâtiment se répondent the two wings of the building match (each other)

[4] répondre de VT INDIR [a] (= être garant de) [+ personne] to answer for; ~ de l'innocence/l'honnêteté de qn to answer ou vouch for sb's innocence/honesty; ~ des dettes de qn to answer for sb's debts, be answerable for sb's debts; si vous agissez ainsi, je ne réponds plus de rien if you behave like that, I'll accept no further responsibility; il viendra, je vous en réponds ! he'll come all right, you can take my

word for it!; ça ne se passera pas comme ça, je t'en réponds ! you can take it from me that it won't happen like that!, it won't happen like that, you take it from me!

[b] (= rendre compte de) [+ actes, décision] to be accountable for; (Jur) ~ de ses crimes to answer for one's crimes

répons [repɔ̃] NM (Rel) response

▼**réponse** [repɔ̃s] NF [a] (à demande, lettre, objection) reply, response; (à coup de sonnette, prière, question,) answer, reply; (à énigme, examen, problème) answer (à to); (Mus) answer; en ~ à votre question in answer ou reply ou response to your question; en ~ aux accusations portées contre lui in response ou reply to the accusations brought against him; pour toute ~, il grogna he just grunted in reply; pour toute ~, il me raccrocha au nez he just hung up on me; ma ~ est non my answer is no; télégramme avec ~ payée reply-paid telegram; ma lettre est restée sans ~ my letter remained unanswered; sa demande est restée sans ~ there has been no reply ou response to his request; apporter une ~ au problème de la délinquance to find an answer to the problem of delinquency; (Mil, fig) la ~ ne s'est pas fait attendre they were (ou he was etc) quick to retaliate

[b] (Physiol, Tech = réaction) response; (= écho : à un appel, un sentiment) response; ~ immunitaire immune response

[c] (loc) avoir ~ à tout to have an answer for everything; c'est la ~ du berger à la bergère it's tit for tat; il me fit une ~ de Normand he wouldn't say yes or no, he wouldn't give me a straight answer; il fait les demandes et les ~s he doesn't let anyone get a word in edgeways* (Brit) ou edgewise (US)

repopulation [rəpɔpylasjɔ̃] NF [ville] repopulation; [étang] restocking

report [rəpɔr] NM [a] [match] postponement, putting off; [procès] postponement; [décision] putting off, deferment; [date] putting off, putting back, deferment; (Fin) ~ d'échéance extension of due date; « report » (en bas de page) "carried forward"; (en haut de page) "brought forward" [b] [chiffres, indications] transfer, writing out, copying out; (Comm) [écritures] posting; [somme] carrying forward ou over; (Photo) transfer; faire le ~ de [+ somme] to carry forward ou over; [+ écritures] to post; (Pol) les ~s de voix entre les deux partis se sont bien effectués au deuxième tour the votes were satisfactorily transferred to the party with more votes after the first round of the election

reportage [rəpɔrtaʒ] NM [a] (Presse, Radio, TV) report (sur on); (sur le vif) [match, événement] commentary; ~ photographique/télévisé illustrated/television report; ~ en direct live commentary; faire un ~ sur (Presse) to write a report on; (Radio, TV) to report on; faire ou assurer le ~ d'une cérémonie to cover a ceremony, do the coverage of a ceremony; être en ~ (Presse) to be out on a story, be covering a story; (Radio, TV) to be (out) reporting; c'était un ~ de Julie Durand that report was from Julie Durand, that was Julie Durand reporting [b] (= métier) (news) reporting; il fait du ~ he's a (news) reporter; le grand ~ the coverage of major international events; il a fait plusieurs grands ~s pour ... he has covered several big stories for ...

▼**reporter¹** [rəpɔrte] ▶ conjug 1 ◀ [1] VT [a] (= ramener) [+ objet] to take back; (par la pensée) to take back (à to); cette chanson nous reporte aux années trente this song takes us back to the thirties

[b] (= différer) [+ match] to postpone, put off; [+ décision] to put off, defer; [+ date] to put off ou back (Brit), defer; la réunion est reportée à demain/d'une semaine the meeting has been postponed until tomorrow/until next week ou for a week; (Jur) le jugement est reporté à

huitaine (the) sentence has been deferred for a week

[c] [+ chiffres, indications] to transfer (sur to), write out, copy out (sur on); (Comm) [+ écritures] to post; (Photo) to transfer (sur to); ~ une somme sur la page suivante to carry an amount forward ou over to the next page

[d] (= transférer) ~ son affection/son vote sur to transfer one's affection/one's vote to; ~ son gain sur un autre cheval/numéro to put ou place one's winnings on ou transfer one's bet to another horse/number

[2] reporter à VT INDIR (= en référer à) to report to

[3] se reporter VPR [a] (= se référer à) se ~ à to refer to; reportez-vous à la page 5 turn to ou refer to ou see page 5

[b] (par la pensée) se ~ à to think back to, cast one's mind back to; reportez-vous (par l'esprit) aux années 50 cast your mind back to the fifties; si l'on se reporte à l'Angleterre de cette époque if one thinks back to the England of that period

[c] (= se transférer) son affection s'est reportée sur ses chats he transferred his affection to his cats

reporter² [rəpɔrter] NM reporter; grand ~ special correspondent; ~(-)photographe reporter and photographer; ~-cameraman news reporter and cameraman → radioreporter

reporteur [rəpɔrtœr] NM [a] (Bourse) taker (of stock) [b] (Typo) transfer [c] (TV) reporter; ~ d'images reporter-cameraman

repos [rəpo] NM [a] (= détente) rest; prendre du ~/un peu de ~ to take ou have a rest/a bit of a rest; il ne peut pas rester ou demeurer en ~ 5 minutes he can't rest ou relax for (even) 5 minutes; le médecin lui a ordonné le ~ complet the doctor has ordered him to rest ou ordered complete rest; après une matinée/journée de ~, il allait mieux after a morning's/day's rest he felt better; respecter le ~ dominical to observe Sunday as a day of rest; (hum) le ~ du guerrier a well-earned rest → lit, maison

[b] (= congé) avoir droit à deux jours de ~ hebdomadaire to be entitled to two days off a week; le médecin lui a donné du ~/huit jours de ~ the doctor has given him some time off/a week off

[c] (= tranquillité) peace and quiet; (= quiétude morale) peace of mind; (littér = sommeil, mort) rest, sleep; il n'y aura pas de ~ pour lui tant que ... he'll have no peace of mind until ..., he won't get any rest until ...; le ~ de la tombe the sleep of the dead; le ~ éternel eternal rest

[d] (= pause) [discours] pause; [vers] rest; (Mus) cadence

[e] (= petit palier) half landing

[f] (loc) au ~ [soldat] standing at ease; [masse, machine, animal] at rest; (Mil) ~ ! (stand) at ease!; muscle au ~ ou à l'état de ~ relaxed muscle; sans ~ [travailler] without stopping, relentlessly; [marcher] without a break ou a rest, without stopping; [quête] uninterrupted, relentless; être de ~ to be off; de tout ~ [situation, entreprise] secure, safe; [placement] gilt-edged, safe; [travail] easy; ce n'est pas de tout ~ ! it's not exactly restful!, it's no picnic!*; être en ~ to be resting; avoir la conscience en ~ to have an easy ou a clear conscience; pour avoir l'esprit en ~ to put my (ou your etc) mind at rest; (frm) laisser qn en ~ to leave sb in peace ou alone

reposant, e [rəpozɑ̃, ɑ̃t] ADJ [sommeil] refreshing; [couleur, lieu] restful; [musique, vacances] restful, relaxing; c'est ~ pour la vue it's (very) restful on ou to the eyes

repose [rəpoz] NF [appareil] refitting, re-installation; [tapis] relaying, putting (back) down again

reposé, e [rəpoze] ADJ (ptp de reposer) [air, teint, cheval] fresh, rested (attrib); elle avait le

visage ~ she looked rested; **j'ai l'esprit** ~ my mind is fresh; **maintenant que vous êtes bien** ~ ... now (that) you've had a good rest ... → **tête**

repose-bras [R(ə)pozbRɑ] NM INV armrest

repose-pied (pl **repose-pieds**) [R(ə)pozpje] NM footrest

reposer [R(ə)poze] ▸conjug 1 ◂ **1** VT **a** (= poser à nouveau) [+ verre, livre] to put back down, put down again; [+ tapis] to relay, put back down; [+ objet démonté] to put back together; ~ **ses yeux sur qch** to look at sth again; **va** ~ **ce livre où tu l'as trouvé** go and put that book back where you found it; (Mil) **reposez armes!** order arms!

b (= soulager, délasser) [+ yeux, corps, membres] to rest; [+ esprit] to rest, relax; **se** ~ **l'esprit** to rest one's mind, give one's mind ou brain a rest; **les lunettes de soleil reposent les yeux** ou **la vue** sunglasses rest the eyes, sunglasses are restful to the eyes; ~ **sa tête/jambe sur un coussin** to rest one's head/leg on a cushion; **cela repose de ne voir personne (pendant une journée)** it makes a restful change not to see anyone (for a whole day) → **tête**

c (= répéter) [+ question] to repeat, ask again; [+ problème] to bring up again, raise again; **cela va** ~ **le problème** that will raise the (whole) problem again ou bring the (whole) problem up again; **cet incident va (nous)** ~ **un problème** this incident is going to pose us a new problem ou bring up a new problem for us

2 reposer sur VT INDIR [bâtiment] to be built on; [route] to rest on, be supported by; [supposition] to rest on, be based on; [résultat] to depend on; **sa jambe reposait sur un coussin** his leg was resting on a cushion; **sa théorie ne repose sur rien de précis** his theory doesn't rest on ou isn't based on anything specific; **tout repose sur son témoignage** everything hinges on ou rests on his evidence

3 VI **a** (littér) (= être étendu) to rest, lie (down); (= dormir) to sleep, rest; (= être enterré) to rest; **faire** ~ **son cheval** to rest one's horse; **tout reposait dans la campagne** everything was sleeping ou resting in the countryside; **ici repose ...** here lies ...; **qu'il repose en paix** may he rest in peace; **l'épave repose par 20 mètres de fond** the wreck is lying 20 metres down

b laisser ~ [+ liquide] to leave to settle, let settle ou stand; [+ pâte à pain] to leave to rise, let rise; [+ pâte feuilletée] to (allow to) rest; [+ pâte à crêpes] to leave (to stand); **laisser** ~ **la terre** to let the earth lie fallow

4 se reposer VPR **a** (= se délasser) to rest; **se** ~ **sur ses lauriers** to rest on one's laurels

b se ~ **sur qn** to rely on sb; **je me repose sur vous pour régler cette affaire** I'll leave it to you ou I'm relying on you to sort this business out; **elle se repose sur lui pour tout** she relies on him for everything

c (= se poser à nouveau) [oiseau, poussière] to settle again; [problème] to crop up again

repose-tête (pl **repose-têtes**) [R(ə)poztɛt] NM headrest

repositionner [R(ə)pozisjɔne] ▸conjug 1 ◂ VT to reposition; **nous cherchons à nous** ~ **dans le haut de gamme** we are seeking to position ourselves at the higher end of the market

reposoir [R(ə)pozwaR] NM [église, procession] altar of repose; [maison privée] household altar

repoussage [R(ə)pusaʒ] NM [cuir, métal] repoussé work, embossing

repoussant, e [R(ə)pusɑ̃, ɑ̃t] ADJ [odeur, saleté, visage] repulsive, repugnant; **d'une laideur ~e** repulsive

repousse [R(ə)pus] NF [cheveux, gazon] regrowth; **pour accélérer la** ~ **des cheveux** to help the hair grow again ou grow back in

repousse-peaux [R(ə)puspo] NM INV orange stick

repousser [R(ə)puse] ▸conjug 1 ◂ **1** VT **a** (= écarter, refouler) [+ objet encombrant] to push out of the way, push away; [+ ennemi, attaque] to repel, repulse, drive back; [+ coups] to ward off; [+ soupirant, quémandeur, malheureux] to turn away; ~ **qch du pied** to kick sth out of the way, kick sth away; **il me repoussa avec brusquerie** he pushed me away ou out of the way roughly; **elle parvint à** ~ **son agresseur** she managed to drive off ou beat off her attacker; **les électrons se repoussent** electrons repel each other

b (= refuser) [+ demande, conseil, aide] to turn down, reject; [+ hypothèse] to dismiss, rule out; [+ tentation] to reject, resist, repel; [+ projet de loi] to reject; [+ objections, arguments] to brush aside, dismiss; **la police ne repousse pas l'hypothèse du suicide** the police do not rule out the possibility of suicide

c (= remettre en place) [+ meuble] to push back; [+ tiroir] to push back in; [+ porte] to push to; **repousse la table contre le mur** push the table back ou up against the wall

d (= différer) [+ date, réunion] to put off ou back (Brit), postpone, defer; **la date de l'examen a été repoussée (à huitaine/à lundi)** the exam has been put off ou postponed (for a week/till Monday), the date of the exam has been put back (Brit) (a week/till Monday)

e (= dégoûter) to repel, repulse; **tout en lui me repousse** everything about him repels ou repulses me

f (Tech) [+ cuir, métal] to emboss (by hand), work in repoussé; **en cuir/métal repoussé** in repoussé leather/metal

2 VI [feuilles, cheveux] to grow again; **laisser** ~ **sa barbe** to let one's beard grow again

repoussoir [R(ə)puswaR] NM **a** (à cuir, métal) snarling iron; (à ongles) orange stick **b** (Art) repoussoir, high-toned foreground; (fig = faire-valoir) foil; **servir de** ~ **à qn** to act as a foil to sb **c** (péj,* = personne laide) ugly so-and-so*; **c'est un** ~**!** he's (ou she's) ugly as sin!*

répréhensible [RepReɑ̃sibl] ADJ [acte, personne] reprehensible; **je ne vois pas ce qu'il y a de** ~ **à ça!** I don't see what's wrong with (doing) that!

reprendre [R(ə)pRɑ̃dR] ▸conjug 58 ◂ **1** VT **a** (= récupérer) [+ ville] to recapture; [+ prisonnier] to recapture, catch again; [+ employé] to take back; [+ objet prêté] to take back, get back; ~ **sa place** (sur un siège) to go back to one's seat, resume one's seat; (dans un emploi) to go back to work; **la photo avait repris sa place sur la cheminée** the photo was back in its (usual) place on the mantelpiece; **passer** ~ **qn** to go back ou come back for sb; **il a repris sa parole** he went back on his word; **j'irai** ~ **mon manteau chez le teinturier** I'll go and get my coat (back) from the cleaner's; ~ **son nom de jeune fille** to take one's maiden name again, go back to ou revert to one's maiden name

b (= se resservir de) [+ plat] to have ou take (some) more; **voulez-vous** ~ **des légumes?** would you like a second helping of ou some more vegetables?

c (= retrouver) [+ espoir, droits, forces] to regain, recover; ~ **des couleurs** to get some colour back in one's cheeks; ~ **confiance/courage** to regain ou recover one's confidence/ courage; ~ **ses droits** to reassert itself; ~ **ses habitudes** to get back into one's old habits, take up one's old habits again; ~ **contact avec qn** to get in touch with sb again; ~ **ses esprits** ou **ses sens** to come to, regain consciousness, come round (Brit); ~ **sa liberté** to regain one's freedom; ~ **haleine** ou **son souffle** to get one's breath back → **connaissance, conscience, dessus** etc

d (Comm) [+ marchandises] to take back; (contre un nouvel achat) to take in part exchange; [+ fonds de commerce, usine] to take over; **les articles en solde ne sont pas repris** sale goods cannot be returned ou exchanged; **ils m'ont repris ma vieille télé** they bought my old TV set off me (in part exchange); **j'ai acheté une voiture neuve et ils ont repris la vieille** I bought a new car and traded in the old one ou and they took the old one in part exchange; **il a repris l'affaire de son père** he has taken on ou over his father's business

e (= recommencer, poursuivre) [+ travaux] to resume; [+ études, fonctions, lutte] to take up again, resume; [+ livre] to pick up again, go back to; [+ lecture] to go back to, resume; [+ conversation, récit] to resume, carry on (with); [+ promenade] to resume, continue; [+ hostilités] to reopen, start again; [+ pièce de théâtre] to put on again; ~ **la route** ou **son chemin** [voyageur] to set off again; ~ **la route** [routier] to go back on the road again; ~ **la mer** [marin] to go back to sea; **après déjeuner ils reprirent la route** after lunch they continued their journey ou they set off again; ~ **la plume** to take up the pen again; **reprenez votre histoire au début** start your story from the beginning again, go back to the beginning of your story again; **reprenons les faits un par un** let's go over the facts again one by one; **il reprendra la parole après vous** he will speak again after you; ~ **le travail** (après maladie, grève) to go back to work, start work again; (après le repas) to get back to work, start work again; **la vie reprend son cours** life is back to normal again; (Théât) **il a repris le rôle de Hamlet** he has taken on the role of Hamlet → **collier**

f (= saisir à nouveau) **son mal de gorge l'a repris** his sore throat is troubling ou bothering him again; **ses douleurs l'ont repris** he is in pain again; (iro) **voilà que ça le reprend!** there he goes again!, he's off again!*; **ses doutes reprirent** he started feeling doubtful again

g (= attraper à nouveau) to catch again; (fig) **on ne m'y reprendra plus** I won't let myself be caught (out) again; (menace) **que je ne t'y reprenne pas!** don't let me catch you doing that again!

h (Sport = rattraper) [+ balle] to catch; (Tennis) **revers bien repris par Legrand** backhand well returned by Legrand

i (= retoucher, corriger) [+ tableau] to touch up; [+ article, chapitre] to go over again; [+ manteau] (gén) to alter; (trop grand) to take in; (trop petit) to let out; (trop long) to take up; (trop court) to let down; **il n'y a rien à** ~ there's not a single correction ou alteration to be made; **il y a beaucoup de choses à** ~ **dans ce travail** there are lots of improvements to be made to this work, there are a lot of things that need improving in this work; (Couture) **il faut** ~ **un centimètre à droite** we'll have to take it in half an inch on the right

j (= réprimander) [+ personne] to reprimand, tell off*; (pour faute de langue) to pull up; ~ **un élève qui se trompe** to correct a pupil

k (= répéter) [+ refrain] to take up; [+ critique] to repeat; **il reprend toujours les mêmes arguments** he always repeats the same arguments, he always comes out with the same old arguments; (Mus) **reprenez les 5 dernières mesures** let's have ou take the last 5 bars again; **ils reprirent la chanson en chœur** they all joined in ou took up the song

l (= réutiliser) [+ idée, suggestion] to take up (again), use (again); **l'incident a été repris par les journaux** the incident was taken up by the newspapers

2 VI **a** (= retrouver de la vigueur) [plante] to recover; [affaires] to pick up; **la vie reprenait peu à peu** life gradually returned to normal; **il a bien repris depuis son opération** he has made a good recovery since his operation; **pour faire** ~ **le feu** to get the fire going (again) → **affaire**

b (= *recommencer*) [*bruit, pluie, incendie, grève*] to start again; [*fièvre, douleur*] to come back again; (*Scol, Univ*) to start again, go back; **le froid a repris depuis hier** it has turned cold again since yesterday

c (= *dire*) **« ce n'est pas moi », reprit-il** "it's not me", he went on

3 se reprendre VPR **a** (= *se corriger*) to correct o.s.; (= *s'interrompre*) to stop o.s.; **il allait plaisanter, il s'est repris à temps** he was going to make a joke but he stopped himself *ou* pulled himself up in time

b (= *recommencer*) **se ~ à plusieurs fois pour faire qch** to make several attempts to do sth *ou* at doing sth; **il a dû s'y ~ à deux fois pour ouvrir la porte** he had to make two attempts before he could open the door; **il se reprit à penser à elle** he went back to thinking about her, his thoughts went back to her; **il se reprit à craindre que ...** once more he began to be afraid that ...; **chacun se reprit à espérer** everyone began to hope again, everyone's hopes began to revive again

c (= *se ressaisir*) **après une période de découragement, il s'est repris** after feeling quite despondent for a while he's got a grip on himself *ou* pulled himself together (again); **le coureur s'est bien repris sur la fin** the runner made a good recovery *ou* caught up well towards the end

repreneur [R(ə)pʀənœʀ] NM (*Ind*) (corporate) rescuer; (*péj*) raider; **trouver ~** to find a buyer

représailles [R(ə)pʀezaj] NFPL (*Pol, fig*) reprisals, retaliation (*NonC*); **user de ~** ◊ **exercer des ~** to take reprisals, retaliate (**envers, contre, sur** against); **par ~** in retaliation, as a reprisal; **en ~ de** as a reprisal for, in retaliation for; **menacer un pays de ~ commerciales** to threaten a country with trade reprisals; **mesures de ~** retaliatory measures; **attends-toi à des ~!** you can expect reprisals!

représentable [R(ə)pʀezɑ̃tabl] ADJ [*phénomène*] representable, that can be represented; **c'est difficilement ~** it is difficult to represent it

représentant, e [R(ə)pʀezɑ̃tɑ̃, ɑ̃t] NM,F (*gén*) representative; **~ syndical** union representative, shop steward (*Brit*); **~ de commerce** sales representative, rep*; **~ des forces de l'ordre** police officer; **~ en justice** legal representative; **il est ~ en cosmétiques** he's a representative *ou* a rep* for a cosmetics firm; **~ multicarte** sales representative acting for several firms

représentatif, -ive [R(ə)pʀezɑ̃tatif, iv] ADJ (*gén*) representative; **~ de** (= *typique de*) representative of; **signes ~s d'une fonction** signs representing *ou* which represent a function; **échantillon ~ de la population** representative sample of the population

représentation [R(ə)pʀezɑ̃tasjɔ̃] NF **a** (= *notation, transcription*) [*objet, phénomène, son*] representation; [*paysage, société*] portrayal; [*faits*] representation, description; **~ graphique** graphic(al) representation; **c'est une ~ erronée de la réalité** it's a misrepresentation of reality; (*Ling*) **~ en arbre** tree diagram

b (= *évocation, perception*) representation; **~s visuelles/auditives** visual/auditory representations

c (*Théât* = *action, séance*) performance; **troupe en ~** company on tour; (*fig*) **on a toujours l'impression qu'il est en ~** he always seems to be playing a role

d [*pays, citoyens, mandant*] representation; (= *mandataires, délégation*) representatives; **il assure la ~ de son gouvernement auprès de notre pays** he represents his government in our country; **~ diplomatique/proportionnelle/en justice** diplomatic/proportional/legal representation

e (*Comm*) sales representation; **faire de la ~** to be a (sales) representative *ou* a rep*; **la ~**

entre pour beaucoup dans les frais sales representation is a major factor in costs

f (= *réception*) entertainment

g (*frm = reproches*) **faire des ~s à** to make representations to

représentativité [R(ə)pʀezɑ̃tativite] NF representativeness; **reconnaître la ~ d'une organisation** to recognize an organization as a representative body

représenter [R(ə)pʀezɑ̃te] ▸ conjug 1 ◂ **1** VT **a** (= *décrire*) [*peintre, romancier*] to depict, portray, show; [*photographie*] to represent, show; (*Théât*) **la scène représente une rue** the scene represents a street; **~ fidèlement les faits** to describe *ou* set out the facts faithfully; **on le représente comme un escroc** he's represented as a crook, he's made out to be a crook; **il a voulu ~ un paysage sous la neige/la société du 19e siècle** he wanted to show *ou* depict a snowy landscape/to depict *ou* portray 19th-century society

b (= *symboliser*) to represent; (= *signifier*) to represent, mean; **les parents représentent l'autorité** parents represent *ou* embody authority; **ce poste représente beaucoup pour moi** this job means a lot to me; **ce trait représente un arbre** this line represents a tree; **ça va ~ beaucoup de travail** that will mean *ou* represent *ou* involve a lot of work; **ça représente une part importante des dépenses** it accounts for *ou* represents a large part of the costs; **ils représentent 12% de la population** they make up *ou* represent 12% of the population

c (*Théât*) (= *jouer*) to perform, play; (= *mettre à l'affiche*) to perform, put on, stage; **on va ~ quatre pièces cette année** we (*ou* they *etc*) will perform *ou* put on four plays this year; **« Hamlet » fut représenté pour la première fois en 1603** "Hamlet" was first performed *ou* staged in 1603

d (= *agir au nom de*) [+ *ministre, pays*] to represent; **il s'est fait ~ par son notaire** he was represented by his lawyer; **les personnes qui ne peuvent pas assister à la réunion doivent se faire ~ (par un tiers)** those who are unable to attend the meeting should send someone to replace them

e **~ une maison de commerce** to represent a firm, be a representative for a firm

f (*littér*) **~ qch à qn** to point sth out to sb, (try to) impress sth on sb; **il lui représenta les inconvénients de la situation** he pointed out the drawbacks to him

2 VI († *= en imposer*) **il représente bien/ne représente pas bien** he cuts a fine/a poor *ou* sorry figure

3 se représenter VPR **a** (= *s'imaginer*) to imagine; **je ne pouvais plus me ~ son visage** I could no longer bring his face to mind *ou* visualize his face; **on se le représente bien en Hamlet** you can well imagine him as Hamlet; **tu te représentes la scène quand il a annoncé sa démission !** you can just imagine the scene when he announced his resignation!

b (= *survenir à nouveau*) **l'idée se représenta à lui** the idea occurred to him again; **si l'occasion se représente** if the occasion presents itself *ou* arises again; **le même problème va se ~** the same problem will crop up again

c (= *se présenter à nouveau*) (*Scol, Univ*) to retake, resit (*Brit*); (*Pol*) to run again, stand again (*Brit*); **se ~ à un examen** to retake *ou* resit (*Brit*) an exam; **se ~ à une élection** to run *ou* stand (*Brit*) for re-election

répressif, -ive [Repʀesif, iv] ADJ repressive

répression [Repʀesjɔ̃] NF **a** [*crime, abus*] curbing; [*révolte*] suppression, quelling, repression; (*Pol*) **la ~** repression; **la ~ qui a suivi le coup d'État** the repression *ou* crackdown which followed the coup; **prendre des mesures de ~ contre le crime** to crack down on crime; **le service de la ~ des fraudes** the Fraud Squad **b** (*Bio, Psych*) repression

réprimande [Repʀimɑ̃d] NF reprimand, rebuke; **adresser une sévère ~ à un enfant** to scold *ou* rebuke a child severely; **son attitude mérite une ~** he deserves a reprimand for his attitude; **faire des ~s à qn** to reprimand *ou* rebuke sb

réprimander [Repʀimɑ̃de] ▸ conjug 1 ◂ VT to reprimand, rebuke; **se faire ~ par** to be reprimanded *ou* rebuked by

réprimer [Repʀime] ▸ conjug 1 ◂ VT [+ *insurrection*] to quell, repress, put down; [+ *crimes, abus*] to curb, crack down on; [+ *sentiment, désir*] to repress, suppress; [+ *rire, bâillement*] to suppress, stifle; [+ *larmes, colère*] to hold back, swallow

repris [R(ə)pʀi] NM INV **il s'agit d'un ~ de justice** the man has previous convictions, the man is an ex-prisoner *ou* an ex-convict; **un dangereux ~ de justice** a dangerous known criminal

reprisage [R(ə)pʀizaʒ] NM [*chaussette, lainage*] darning; [*collant, drap, accroc*] mending

reprise [R(ə)pʀiz] NF **a** (= *recommencement*) [*activité, cours, travaux*] resumption; [*hostilités*] resumption, re-opening, renewal; [*froid*] return; (*Théât*) revival; (*Ciné*) rerun, reshowing (*NonC*); (*Mus = passage répété*) repeat; (*Radio, TV = rediffusion*) repeat; (*Mus*) **la ~ des violons** the re-entry of the violins; **la ~ des combats est imminente** fighting will begin again *ou* will be resumed again very soon; **pour éviter la ~ de l'inflation** to stop inflation taking off again; **avec la ~ du mauvais temps** with the return of the bad weather; **les ouvriers ont décidé la ~ du travail** the men have decided to go back to *ou* to return to work; **on espère une ~ des affaires** we're hoping that business will pick up again; **la ~ (économique) est assez forte dans certains secteurs** the (economic) revival *ou* recovery is quite marked in certain sectors

b (*Aut*) **avoir de bonnes ~s** *ou* **de la ~** to have good acceleration, accelerate well; **sa voiture n'a pas de ~s** his car has no acceleration

c (*Boxe*) round; (*Escrime*) reprise; (*Équitation*) (*pour le cavalier*) riding lesson; (*pour le cheval*) dressage lesson; (*Ftbl*) **à la ~** at the start of the second half; (*Tennis*) **~ de volée** volleyed return; (*après arrêt*) **~ !** time!

d (*Comm*) [*marchandise*] taking back; (*pour nouvel achat*) trade-in, part exchange (*Brit*); (*pour occuper des locaux*) key money; **valeur de ~ d'une voiture** trade-in value *ou* part-exchange value (*Brit*) of a car; (*Aut*) **nous vous offrons une ~ de 5 000 F pour l'achat d'un nouveau modèle** we'll give you 5,000 francs when you trade your old car in; **~ des bouteilles vides** return of empties; **la maison ne fait pas de ~** goods cannot be returned *ou* exchanged; **payer une ~ de 5 000 F à l'ancien locataire** to pay the outgoing tenant 5,000 francs for improvements made to the property

e (= *réutilisation*) [*idée, suggestion*] re-using, taking up again

f [*chaussette*] darn; [*drap, chemise*] mend; **faire une ~ perdue** to darn (*ou* mend) invisibly; **faire une ~ ou des ~s à un drap** to mend a sheet

g (*Constr*) **~ en sous-œuvre** underpinning

h (*loc*) **à deux ou trois ~s** on two or three occasions, two or three times; **à maintes/plusieurs ~s** on many/several occasions, many/several times

repriser [R(ə)pʀize] ▸ conjug 1 ◂ VT [+ *chaussette, lainage*] to darn; [+ *collant, drap*] to mend; [+ *accroc*] to mend, stitch up → **aiguille, coton, œuf**

réprobateur, -trice [Repʀobatœʀ, tʀis] ADJ reproachful, reproving; **elle me lança un regard ~** she gave me a reproachful *ou* reproving look, she looked at me reproachfully; **d'un ton ~** reproachfully

réprobation [ʀepʀɔbasjɔ̃] NF [a] (= *blâme*) disapproval, reprobation (*frm*); **air/ton de ~** reproachful *ou* reproving look/tone [b] (*Rel*) reprobation

reproche [ʀ(ə)pʀɔʃ] NM reproach; **faire** *ou* **adresser des ~s à qn** to criticize *ou* reproach sb; **conduite qui mérite des ~s** blameworthy *ou* reprehensible behaviour; (*frm*) **faire ~ à qn d'avoir menti** to reproach *ou* upbraid (*frm*) sb for having lied; **je me fais de grands ~s** I blame myself entirely; **avec ~** reproachfully; **ton/regard de ~** reproachful tone/look; **il est sans ~** he's beyond *ou* above reproach; **sans ~, permettez-moi de vous dire que ...** ◊ **je ne vous fais pas de ~ mais permettez-moi de vous dire que ...** I'm not blaming *ou* criticizing *ou* reproaching you but let me say that ...; **ce n'est pas un ~!** I'm not criticizing!, it's not a criticism! *ou* a reproach!; **soit dit sans ~, tu devrais maigrir un peu** no offence meant but you should lose a bit of weight; **le seul ~ que je ferais à cette cuisine ...** the only criticism I have to make about the kitchen ...

reprocher [ʀ(ə)pʀɔʃe] ▸ conjug 1 ◂ VT [a] **~ qch à qn** to criticize *ou* reproach sb for sth; **~ à qn de faire qch** to criticize *ou* reproach sb for doing sth; (*Jur*) **les faits qui lui sont reprochés** the charges against him; **on lui a reproché sa maladresse** they criticized him for being clumsy; **on lui reproche de nombreuses malhonnêtetés** he is accused of several instances of dishonesty; **il me reproche mon succès/ma fortune** he resents my success/my wealth, he holds my success/my wealth against me; **je ne te reproche rien** I'm not blaming you for anything; **je me reproche de ne pas l'avoir fait** I regret not doing it; **je n'ai rien à me ~** I've nothing to reproach myself with, I've nothing to be ashamed of; **qu'est-ce qu'elle lui reproche?** what has she got against him?; **qu'est-ce que tu me reproches?** what have I done wrong?; **il est très minutieux mais on ne peut pas le lui ~** he's very meticulous but there's nothing wrong with that *ou* but that's no bad thing [b] (= *critiquer*) **qu'as-tu à ~ à mon plan/ce tableau?** what have you got against my plan/this picture?, what don't you like about my plan/this picture?; **je reproche à ce tissu d'être trop salissant** my main criticism of this material is that it gets dirty too easily; **je ne vois rien à ~ à son travail** I can't find any faults *ou* I can't find anything to criticize in his work

reproducteur, -trice [ʀ(ə)pʀɔdyktœʀ, tʀis] [1] ADJ (*Bio*) reproductive; **cheval ~** studhorse, stallion [2] NM [a] (= *animal*) breeder; **~s** breeding stock (*NonC*) [b] (*Tech* = *gabarit*) template

reproductible [ʀ(ə)pʀɔdyktibl] ADJ which can be reproduced, reproducible

reproductif, -ive [ʀ(ə)pʀɔdyktif, iv] ADJ reproductive

reproduction [ʀ(ə)pʀɔdyksjɔ̃] NF [a] [*son, mouvement*] reproduction; [*modèle, tableau*] reproduction, copying; (*par photographie*) reproduction, duplication; [*texte*] reprinting; [*clé*] copying; **« ~ interdite »** "all rights (of reproduction) reserved" [b] (= *copie*) reproduction; **livre contenant de nombreuses ~s** book containing many reproductions; **ce n'est qu'une ~** it's only a copy [c] (*Bio, Bot*) reproduction, breeding; **~ artificielle** artificial reproduction; **organes de ~** reproductive organs; **~ par mitose** *ou* **par division cellulaire** replication

reproduire [ʀ(ə)pʀɔdɥiʀ] ▸ conjug 38 ◂ [1] VT [a] (= *restituer*) [+ *son, mouvement*] to reproduce [b] (= *copier*) [+ *modèle, tableau*] to reproduce, copy; (*par photographie*) to reproduce, duplicate; (*par moulage*) to reproduce; [+ *clé*] to make a copy of; **la photo est reproduite en page 3** the picture is shown *ou* reproduced

on page 3; **le texte de la conférence sera reproduit dans notre magazine** the text of the lecture will be printed in our magazine [c] (= *répéter*) [+ *erreur, expérience*] to repeat [d] (= *imiter*) to copy; **essayant de ~ les gestes de son professeur** trying to copy his teacher's gestures [2] **se reproduire** VPR [a] (*Bio, Bot*) to reproduce, breed; (*Bio*) **se ~ par mitose** *ou* **par division cellulaire** to replicate [b] (= *se répéter*) [*phénomène*] to recur, happen again; [*erreur*] to reappear, recur; **et que cela ne se reproduise plus!** and don't let it happen again!; **ce genre d'incident se reproduit régulièrement** this kind of thing happens quite regularly

reprogrammer [ʀ(ə)pʀɔgʀame] ▸ conjug 1 ◂ VT [a] [+ *ordinateur, magnétoscope*] to reprogram [b] (*Ciné, TV*) to reschedule

reprographie [ʀ(ə)pʀɔgʀafi] NF reprography (*SPÉC*), reprographics (*SPÉC*), repro (*SPÉC*); **le service de ~** the photocopying department

reprographier [ʀ(ə)pʀɔgʀafje] ▸ conjug 7 ◂ VT to (photo)copy, duplicate

réprouvé, e [ʀepʀuve] (*ptp de* **réprouver**) NM,F (*Rel*) reprobate; (*fig*) outcast, reprobate

▼ **réprouver** [ʀepʀuve] ▸ conjug 1 ◂ VT [a] [+ *personne*] to reprove; [+ *attitude, comportement*] to reprove, condemn; [+ *projet*] to condemn, disapprove of; **des actes que la morale réprouve** immoral acts [b] (*Rel*) to damn, reprobate

reps [ʀɛps] NM rep(p)

reptation [ʀɛptasjɔ̃] NF crawling

reptile [ʀɛptil] NM (*Zool*) reptile; (= *serpent*) snake; (*péj* = *personne*) reptile

reptilien, -ienne [ʀɛptiljɛ̃, jɛn] ADJ reptilian

repu, e [ʀəpy] (*ptp de* **repaître**) ADJ [*animal*] sated; [*personne*] full up* (*attrib*); **je suis ~** I'm full, I've eaten my fill; **il est ~ de cinéma** he has had his fill of the cinema

républicain, e [ʀepyblikɛ̃, ɛn] ADJ, NM,F republican; (*Pol US*) Republican; **le calendrier ~** the French Revolutionary calendar → **garde²**

republier [ʀəpyblije] ▸ conjug 7 ◂ VT to republish

république [ʀepyblik] NF republic; **on est en ~!** it's a free country!; (*fig*) **la ~ des Lettres** the republic of letters; **la République française** the French Republic; **la Cinquième République** the Fifth Republic; **la République arabe unie** the United Arab Republic; **la République d'Irlande** the Irish Republic; (*Hist*) **la République démocratique allemande** the German Democratic Republic; **la République fédérale d'Allemagne** the Federal Republic of Germany; **la République islamique d'Iran** the Islamic Republic of Iran; **la République populaire de Chine** the Chinese People's Republic, the People's Republic of China; **la République tchèque** the Czech Republic; (*Hist*) **sous la République de Weimar** in the Weimar Republic; **~ bananière** banana republic

---

LA CINQUIÈME RÉPUBLIQUE

The term "the Fifth Republic" refers to the French Republic since the presidency of General de Gaulle (1959-1969), during which a new Constitution was established.

---

répudiation [ʀepydjasjɔ̃] NF [a] [*épouse*] repudiation [b] [*opinion, foi, engagement*] renouncement [c] [*nationalité, succession*] renouncement, relinquishment

répudier [ʀepydje] ▸ conjug 7 ◂ VT [a] [+ *épouse*] to repudiate [b] [+ *opinion, foi*] to renounce; [+ *engagement*] to renounce, go back on [c] (*Jur*) [+ *nationalité, succession*] to renounce, relinquish

répugnance [ʀepyɲɑ̃s] NF [a] (= *répulsion*) (*pour personnes*) repugnance (**pour** for), dis-

gust (**pour** for), loathing (**pour** of); (*pour nourriture, mensonge*) disgust (**pour** for), loathing (**pour** of); **avoir de la ~ pour** to loathe, have a loathing of; **j'éprouve de la ~ à la vue de ce spectacle** this sight fills me with disgust, I find this sight quite repugnant *ou* disgusting [b] (= *hésitation*) reluctance (**à faire qch** to do sth); **il éprouvait une certaine ~ à nous le dire** he was rather loath *ou* reluctant to tell us; **faire qch avec ~** to do sth reluctantly *ou* unwillingly

répugnant, e [ʀepyɲɑ̃, ɑ̃t] ADJ [*individu*] repugnant; [*laideur*] revolting; [*action*] disgusting, loathsome; [*travail, odeur, nourriture*] disgusting, revolting

répugner [ʀepyɲe] ▸ conjug 1 ◂ [1] **répugner à** VT INDIR [a] (= *dégoûter*) to repel, disgust, be repugnant to; **cet individu me répugne profondément** I find that man quite repugnant; **manger du poisson lui répugnait** it was (quite) repugnant to him to eat fish; **cette odeur lui répugnait** the smell was repugnant to him, he was repelled by the smell; **cette idée ne lui répugnait pas du tout** he didn't find this idea off-putting in the least [b] (= *hésiter*) **~ à faire qch** to be loath *ou* reluctant to do sth; **il répugnait à parler en public/à accepter cette aide** he was loath *ou* reluctant to speak in public/to accept this help; **il ne répugnait pas à mentir quand cela lui semblait nécessaire** he had no qualms about lying if he thought he needed to [2] VB IMPERS (*frm*) **il me répugne de devoir vous le dire** it's very distasteful to me to have to tell you this [3] VT (*littér*) → **1a**

répulsif, -ive [ʀepylsif, iv] [1] ADJ (*gén, Phys*) repulsive [2] NM repellent, repellant

répulsion [ʀepylsjɔ̃] NF (*gén*) repulsion, disgust; (*Phys*) repulsion; **éprouver** *ou* **avoir de la ~ pour** to feel repulsion for, be absolutely repelled by

réputation [ʀepytasjɔ̃] NF [a] (= *honneur*) reputation, good name; **préserver sa ~** to keep up *ou* protect one's reputation *ou* good name [b] (= *renommée*) reputation; **avoir bonne/mauvaise ~** to have a good/bad reputation; **se faire une ~** to make a name *ou* a reputation for o.s.; **sa ~ n'est plus à faire** his reputation is firmly established; **ce film a fait sa ~** this film made his reputation *ou* name; **produit de ~ mondiale** product which has a world-wide reputation; **connaître qn/qch de ~ (seulement)** to know sb/sth (only) by repute; **sa ~ de gynécologue** his reputation as a gynaecologist; **il a une ~ d'avarice** he has a reputation for miserliness; **il a la ~ d'être avare** he has a reputation for *ou* of being miserly, he is reputed to be miserly

réputé, e [ʀepyte] ADJ [a] (= *célèbre*) [*vin, artiste*] reputable, renowned, of repute; **l'un des médecins les plus ~s de la ville** one of the town's most reputable doctors, one of the best-known doctors in town; **c'est un fromage/vin hautement ~** it's a cheese/wine of great repute *ou* renown; **orateur ~ pour ses bons mots** speaker renowned for his witticisms; **ville ~e pour sa cuisine/ses monuments** town which is renowned for *ou* which has a great reputation for its food/its monuments; **il n'est pas ~ pour son honnêteté!** he's not exactly renowned *ou* famous for his honesty! [b] (= *considéré comme*) reputed; **remède ~ infaillible** cure which is reputed *ou* supposed *ou* said to be infallible; **professeur ~ pour être très sévère** teacher who has the reputation of being *ou* who is reputed to be *ou* said to be very strict

requalification [ʀ(ə)kalifikasjɔ̃] NF [a] (= *recyclage*) retraining [b] (*Jur*) **la ~ des faits** amendment of the charges

requalifier [ʀ(ə)kalifje] ▸ conjug 7 ◂ VT [a] [+

requérant, e [ʀəkeʀɑ̃, ɑ̃t] NM,F (*Jur*) applicant

personne] to retrain [b] (*Jur*) [+ *faits, délit*] to amend

requérir [ʀəkeʀiʀ] ▸ conjug 21 ◂ VT [a] (= *nécessiter*) [+ *soins, prudence*] to call for, require; **ceci requiert toute notre attention** this calls for *ou* requires *ou* demands our full attention [b] (= *solliciter*) [+ *aide, service*] to request; (= *exiger*) [+ *justification*] to require; (= *réquisitionner*) [+ *personne*] to call upon; **l'intervention de la police** to require *ou* necessitate police intervention; (*frm*) **je vous requiers de me suivre** I call on you to follow me [c] (*Jur*) [+ *peine*] to call for, demand; **le procureur était en train de ~** the prosecutor was summing up

requête [ʀəkɛt] NF [a] (*Jur*) petition; **adresser une ~ à un juge** to petition a judge; **~ en cassation** appeal; **~ civile** *appeal to a court against its judgment* [b] (= *supplique*) request, petition; **à** *ou* **sur la ~ de qn** at sb's request, at the request of sb

requiem [ʀekɥijɛm] NM INV requiem

requin [ʀəkɛ̃] NM (*Zool, fig*) shark; **~ marteau** hammerhead (shark); **~ blanc/bleu/pèlerin** white/blue/basking shark; **~-baleine/-tigre** whale/tiger shark; **les ~s de la finance** the sharks of the financial world

requinquer* [ʀ(ə)kɛ̃ke] ▸ conjug 1 ◂ [1] VT to pep up*, buck up*; **un whisky vous requinquera** a whisky will pep you up* *ou* buck you up*; **avec un peu de repos, dans trois jours vous serez requinqué** with a bit of a rest in three days you'll be your old (perky) self again* *ou* you'll be back on form again (*Brit*) [2] **se requinquer** VPR to perk up*

requis, e [ʀəki, iz] (*ptp de* **requérir**) ADJ [a] (= *nécessaire*) [*majorité, niveau*] required, necessary; [*qualités, compétence, diplômes*] necessary, required, requisite; **avoir les qualifications ~es pour un poste** to have the necessary *ou* requisite qualifications for a job; **dans les temps** *ou* **délais ~** in the required time; **satisfaire aux conditions ~es** to meet the requirements *ou* the necessary conditions; **avoir l'âge ~** to meet the age requirements; **il a la voix ~e pour ce rôle** he's got the right (kind of) voice for this part [b] (= *réquisitionné*) conscripted

réquisition [ʀekizisjɔ̃] NF [a] [*biens*] requisitioning, commandeering; [*hommes*] conscription, requisitioning; **~ de la force armée** requisitioning of *ou* calling out of the army [b] (*Jur* = *plaidoirie*) **~s** summing-up for the prosecution

réquisitionner [ʀekizisjɔne] ▸ conjug 1 ◂ VT [+ *biens*] to requisition, commandeer; [+ *hommes*] to conscript, requisition; (*hum*) **j'ai été réquisitionné pour faire la vaisselle** I have been drafted in *ou* requisitioned to do the dishes (*hum*)

réquisitoire [ʀekizitwaʀ] NM [a] (*Jur*) (= *plaidoirie*) summing-up for the prosecution (*specifying appropriate sentence*); (= *acte écrit*) instruction, brief (*to examining magistrate*) [b] (*fig*) indictment (**contre** of); **son discours fut un ~ contre le capitalisme** his speech was an indictment of capitalism

RER [ɛʀøɛʀ] NM (ABRÉV = **réseau express régional**) → **réseau**

RES [ʀɛs, ɛʀøɛs] NM (ABRÉV = **rachat d'entreprise par ses salariés**) → **rachat**

resaler [ʀ(ə)sale] ▸ conjug 1 ◂ VT to add more salt to, put more salt in

resalir [ʀ(ə)saliʀ] ▸ conjug 2 ◂ VT [+ *tapis, mur, sol, vêtement*] to get dirty again; **ne va pas te ~** don't go and get yourself dirty *ou* in a mess again; **se ~ les mains** to get one's hands dirty again, dirty one's hands again

rescapé, e [ʀɛskape] [1] ADJ [*personne*] surviving [2] NM,F (*lit, fig*) survivor (**de** of, from)

rescousse [ʀɛskus] NF **venir** *ou* **aller à la ~ de qn** to go to sb's rescue *ou* aid; **appeler qn à la**

~ to call to sb for help; **ils arrivèrent à la ~** they came to the rescue

rescrit [ʀɛskʀi] NM rescript

réseau (*pl* **réseaux**) [ʀezo] NM [a] (*gén*) network; **~ routier/ferroviaire/téléphonique** road/rail/telephone network; **~ bancaire** banking network; **~ de communication/d'information/de distribution** communications/information/distribution network; **~ commercial** *ou* **de vente** sales network; **~ électrique** electricity network *ou* grid (*Brit*); **~ express régional** *rapid-transit train service between Paris and the suburbs*; **~ d'assainissement** sewer *ou* sewerage system; **~ fluvial** river system, network of rivers; **~ de transports en commun** public transport system *ou* network; (*Téléc*) **les abonnés du ~ sont avisés que ...** telephone subscribers are advised that ...; **sur l'ensemble du ~** over the whole network → **câblé, hertzien**
[b] [*amis, relations*] network; [*prostitution, trafiquants, terroristes*] ring; **~ d'espionnage** spy network *ou* ring; **~ de résistants** resistance network; **~ d'intrigues** web of intrigue; **~ d'influence** network of influence
[c] (*Ordin, Sci*) network; **~ étendu** wide-area network, WAN; **~ local** local area network, LAN; **~ neuronal** neural net(work); **sur le ~ Internet** on the Internet; **être en ~** [*personnes, entreprises*] to be on the network; **mettre des ordinateurs en ~** to network computers; **entreprise en ~** networked company, company on the network; **travailler en ~** to work on a network; **la mise en ~ de l'information** information networking
[d] (*Zool*) reticulum
[e] (*Phys*) **~ de diffraction** diffraction pattern; **~ cristallin** crystal lattice

réséda [ʀezeda] NM reseda, mignonette

réservataire [ʀezɛʀvatɛʀ] ADJ, NM (**héritier**) **~** *rightful heir to the* réserve légale

▾ **réservation** [ʀezɛʀvasjɔ̃] NF (*à l'hôtel*) reservation; (*des places*) reservation, booking; (*Jur*) reservation; (*Tourisme*) **~ de groupes** group booking; **bureau de ~** booking office; **faire une ~ dans un hôtel/restaurant** to make a booking *ou* a reservation in a hotel/restaurant, book *ou* reserve a room (in a hotel)/a table (in a restaurant); (*Rail*) **« ~ obligatoire »** "passengers with reservations only"

▾ **réserve** [ʀezɛʀv] NF [a] (= *provision*) reserve; [*marchandises*] reserve, stock; **les enfants ont une ~ énorme d'énergie** children have an enormous reserve *ou* have enormous reserves of energy; **faire des ~s de sucre** to get in *ou* lay in a stock of *ou* reserves of sugar; **heureusement, ils avaient une petite ~ (d'argent)** fortunately they had a little money put by *ou* a little money in reserve; (*Fin*) **monnaie de ~** reserve currency; **les ~s mondiales de pétrole** the world's oil reserves; **les ~s (nutritives) de l'organisme** the organism's food reserves; (*hum*) **il peut jeûner, il a des ~s !** he can afford to do without food — he's quite fat enough as it is!; **avoir des provisions de** *ou* **en ~** to have provisions in reserve *ou* put by; **mettre qch en ~** to put sth by, put sth in reserve; **avoir/tenir qch en ~** (*gén*) to have/keep sth in reserve; (*Comm*) to have/keep sth in stock
[b] (= *restriction*) reservation, reserve; **faire** *ou* **émettre des ~s sur qch** to have reservations *ou* reserves about sth; **sans ~** [*soutien*] unreserved; [*admiration, consentement*] unreserved, unqualified; [*approuver, accepter*] unreservedly, without reservation, unhesitatingly; **sous ~ de** subject to; **le projet est accepté sous ~ que les délais soient respectés** the project has been approved on condition that the deadlines are met; **sous toutes ~s** [*publier*] with all reserve, with all proper reserves; **je vous le dis sous toutes ~s** I can't vouch for *ou* guarantee the truth of what I'm telling you; **tarif/horaire publié sous toutes ~s** prices/timetable correct at time of going to press

[c] (= *prudence, discrétion*) reserve; **être/demeurer** *ou* **se tenir sur la ~** to be/remain very reserved; **il m'a parlé sans ~** he talked to me quite unreservedly *ou* openly; **elle est d'une grande ~** she's very reserved, she keeps herself to herself; **devoir** *ou* **obligation de ~** duty to preserve secrecy
[d] (*Mil*) **la ~** the reserve; **les ~s** the reserves; **officiers/armée de ~** reserve officers/army
[e] (*Sport*) **équipe/joueur de ~** reserve *ou* second string (*US*) team/player
[f] (= *territoire*) [*nature, animaux*] reserve; [*Indiens*] reservation; **~ de pêche/chasse** fishing/hunting preserve; **~ naturelle** nature reserve; **~ ornithologique** *ou* **d'oiseaux** bird sanctuary
[g] [*bibliothèque, musée*] reserve collection; **le livre est à la ~** the book is in reserve
[h] (= *entrepôt*) storehouse; (= *pièce*) storeroom; (*d'un magasin*) stockroom
[i] (*Jur*) **~ (héréditaire** *ou* **légale)** part of the legacy which cannot be withheld from the rightful heirs

réservé, e [ʀezɛʀve] (*ptp de* **réserver**) ADJ [a] [*place, salle*] reserved (**à qn/qch** for sb/sth); **chasse/pêche ~e** private hunting/fishing; **cuvée ~e** vintage cuvée; **j'ai une table ~e** I've got a table reserved *ou* booked; **tous droits ~s** all rights reserved; **voie ~e aux autobus** bus lane → **quartier** [b] (= *discret*) [*caractère, personne*] reserved [c] (= *dubitatif*) **il s'est montré très ~ sur la faisabilité du projet** he sounded very doubtful as to the feasibility of the project; **je suis très ~ quant à sa réussite** I'm not too optimistic about his chances of success

▾ **réserver** [ʀezɛʀve] ▸ conjug 1 ◂ [1] VT [a] (= *mettre à part*) [+ *objets*] to keep, save, reserve (**à, pour** for); [+ *marchandises*] to keep, put aside *ou* on one side (**à** for); **il nous a réservé deux places à côté de lui** he's kept *ou* saved us two seats beside him; **on vous a réservé ce bureau** we've reserved you this office, we've set this office aside for you; **~ le meilleur pour la fin** to keep *ou* save the best till last; **ils réservent ces fauteuils pour les cérémonies** they reserve *ou* keep these armchairs for (special) ceremonies; **pouvez-vous me ~ 5 mètres de ce tissu ?** could you put 5 metres of that material aside *ou* on one side for me?; **ces emplacements sont strictement réservés aux voitures du personnel** these parking places are strictly reserved for staff cars; **nous réservons toujours un peu d'argent pour les dépenses imprévues** we always keep *ou* put a bit of money on one side for unexpected expenses
[b] (= *louer*) [+ *place, chambre, table*] [*voyageur*] to book, reserve; [*agence*] to reserve
[c] (= *destiner*) [+ *dangers, désagréments, joies*] to have in store (**à** for); [+ *accueil, châtiment*] to have in store, reserve (**à** for); **cette expédition devait leur ~ bien des surprises** there were many surprises in store for them on that expedition; **nous ne savons pas ce que l'avenir nous réserve** we don't know what the future has in store for us *ou* holds for us; **le sort qui lui est réservé est peu enviable** he has an unenviable fate in store for him *ou* reserved for him; **c'est à lui qu'il était réservé de marcher le premier sur la Lune** he was to be the first man to walk on the Moon; **c'est à lui que fut réservé l'honneur de porter le drapeau** the honour of carrying the flag fell to him; **tu me réserves ta soirée ?** are you free tonight? *ou* this evening?, could we do something this evening?
[d] (= *remettre à plus tard*) [+ *réponse, opinion*] to reserve; **le médecin préfère ~ son diagnostic** the doctor would rather reserve his diagnosis
[2] **se réserver** VPR [a] (= *prélever*) to keep *ou* reserve for o.s.; **il s'est réservé le meilleur morceau** he kept *ou* saved the best bit for himself

---

➤ GRAMMAIRE ACTIVE: **réservation** 48.3 **réserve** 53.6 **réserver** 48.3

[b] (= *se ménager*) to save o.s.; **se ~ pour une autre occasion** to save o.s. for another opportunity, save o.s. until another opportunity crops up; **il ne mange pas maintenant, il se réserve pour le banquet/pour plus tard** he isn't eating now — he's saving himself for the banquet/for later; (*Sport*) **il faut savoir se ~** one must learn to conserve *ou* save one's strength

[c] **il se réserve d'intervenir plus tard** he's waiting to see whether he'll need to intervene later; **se ~ le droit de faire qch** to reserve the right to do sth

réserviste [Rezervist] NM reservist

réservoir [Rezervwar] NM — (= *cuve*) tank; (= *plan d'eau*) reservoir; [*poissons*] fishpond; [*usine à gaz*] gasometer, gasholder; (*Bio*) [*infection*] reservoir; (*fig*) **ce pays est un ~ de talents/de main-d'œuvre** this country has a wealth of talent/a huge pool of labour to draw on; **~ d'eau** (*gén, Aut*) water tank; (*pour une maison*) water cistern; (*pour eau de pluie*) (*en bois*) water butt; (*en ciment*) water tank; **~ d'essence** petrol (*Brit*) *ou* gas (*US*) tank

résidant, e [Rezidã, ãt] ADJ résidant

résidence [Rezidãs] [1] NF (*gén*) residence; (= *immeuble*) (block of) residential flats (*Brit*), residential apartment building (*US*); **établir sa ~ à** to take up residence in; **changer de ~** to move (house); (*Admin*) **en ~ à** in residence at; **en ~ surveillée** *ou* **forcée** under house arrest; (*Diplomatie*) **la ~** the residency → **assigner**, **certificat** [2] COMP ► **résidence hôtelière** residential *ou* apartment (*US*) hotel ► **résidence principale** main home ► **résidence secondaire** second home ► **résidence universitaire** (university) hall(s) of residence, residence hall (*US*), dormitory (*US*)

résident, e [Rezidã, ãt] [1] NM,F (= *étranger*) foreign national *ou* résident; (= *diplomate*) résident; **ministre ~** résident minister; **avoir le statut de ~ permanent en France** to have permanent résident status in France [2] ADJ (*Ordin*) résident

résidentiel, -ielle [Rezidãsjɛl] ADJ (= *riche*) [*banlieue, quartier*] affluent, plush

résider [Rezide] ▸ conjug 1 ◂ VI (*lit, fig*) to reside; [*difficulté*] to lie (**en, dans** in); **il réside à cet hôtel/à Dijon** he resides (*frm*) at this hotel/in Dijon; **après avoir résidé quelques temps en France** after living *ou* residing (*frm*) in France for some time, after having been resident in France for some time; **le problème réside en ceci que ...** the problem lies in the fact that ...

résidu [Rezidy] NM [a] (= *reste, Chim, fig*) résidue (*NonC*); (*Math*) remainder [b] (= *déchets*) **~s** remnants, résidue (*NonC*); **~s industriels** industrial waste

résiduel, -elle [Reziduɛl] ADJ residual

résignation [Rezipasjõ] NF resignation (**à** to); **avec ~** with resignation, resignedly

résigné, e [Rezipe] (*ptp de* **résigner**) ADJ [*air, geste, ton*] resigned; **~ à son sort** resigned to his fate; **il est ~** he is resigned to it; **dire qch d'un air ~** to say sth resignedly

résigner [Rezipe] ▸ conjug 1 ◂ [1] **se résigner** VPR to resign o.s. (**à** to); **il faudra s'y ~** we'll have to resign ourselves to it *ou* put up with it [2] VT (*littér*) [+ *charge, fonction*] to relinquish, resign

résiliable [Rezjljabl] ADJ [*contrat*] (*à terme*) which can be terminated, terminable; (*en cours*) which can be cancelled, cancellable, which can be rescinded

résiliation [Rezjljasjõ] NF [*contrat, bail, marché, abonnement*] (*à terme*) termination; (*en cours*) cancellation, rescinding; [*engagement*] cancellation

résilience [Reziljãs] NF (*Tech*) ductility

résilient, e [Reziljã, jãt] ADJ (*Tech*) ductile

résilier [Rezilje] ▸ conjug 7 ◂ VT [+ *contrat, bail, marché, abonnement*] (*à terme*) to terminate; (*en cours*) to cancel, rescind; [+ *engagement*] to cancel

résille [Rezij] NF (*gén* = *filet*) net, netting (*NonC*); (*pour les cheveux*) hairnet; [*vitrail*] cames (*SPÉC*), lead(s), leading (*NonC*) → **bas²**

résine [Rezin] NF resin; **~ époxy** epoxy (resin); **~ de synthèse** synthetic resin

résiné, e [Rezine] ADJ, NM (**vin**) **~** retsina

résineux, -euse [Rezinø, øz] [1] ADJ resinous [2] NM coniferous tree; **forêt de ~** coniferous forest

résistance [Rezistãs] NF [a] (= *opposition*) resistance (*NonC*) (**à, contre** to); (*Hist*) **la Résistance** the (French) Resistance; **~ active/passive/armée** active/passive/armed resistance; **l'armée dut se rendre après une ~ héroïque** the army was forced to surrender after putting up a heroic resistance *ou* a heroic fight; **opposer une ~ farouche à un projet** to put up a fierce resistance to a project, make a very determined stand against a project; **malgré les ~s des syndicats** in spite of resistance from the trade unions; **cela ne se fera pas sans ~** that won't be done without some opposition *ou* resistance → **noyau**

[b] (= *endurance*) resistance, stamina; **à la fatigue** resistance to fatigue; **il a une grande ~** *ou* **beaucoup de ~** he has great *ou* a lot of resistance *ou* stamina; **coureur qui a de la ~/qui n'a pas de ~** runner who has lots of/who has no staying power; **ce matériau offre une grande ~ au feu/aux chocs** this material is very heat-/shock-resistant; **acier/béton à haute ~** high-tensile *ou* high-strength steel/concrete → **pièce, plat²**

[c] (*Élec*) [*réchaud, radiateur*] element; (= *mesure*) resistance; **unité de ~** unit of (electrical) resistance

[d] (*Phys* = *force*) resistance; **~ d'un corps/de l'air** resistance of a body/of the air; **~ mécanique** mechanical resistance; **~ des matériaux** strength of materials; **quand il voulut ouvrir la porte, il sentit une ~** when he tried to open the door he felt some resistance

résistant, e [Rezistã, ãt] [1] ADJ [*personne*] robust, tough; [*plante*] hardy; [*tissu, vêtements*] strong, hard-wearing; [*couleur*] fast; [*acier*] resistant; [*métal*] resistant, strong; [*bois*] resistant, hard; **il est très ~** (*gén*) he has a lot of resistance *ou* stamina; (*athlète*) he has a lot of staying power; **~ à la chaleur** heatproof, heat-resistant; **~ aux chocs** shockproof, shock-resistant; **bactéries ~es aux antibiotiques** bacteria that are resistant to antibiotics, antibiotic-resistant bacteria [2] NM,F (*Hist*) (French) Resistance fighter; **il a été ~** he was in the Resistance

▾ **résister** [Reziste] ▸ conjug 1 ◂ ♦ **résister à** VT INDIR [a] (= *s'opposer à*) [+ *ennemi, agresseur, police, passion, tentation, argument*] to resist; [+ *attaque*] to hold out against, withstand, resist; **inutile de ~** it's useless to resist, it's *ou* there's no use resisting; **~ au courant d'une rivière** to fight against the current of a river; **~ à la volonté de qn** to hold out against *ou* resist sb's will; **il n'ose pas ~ à sa fille** he doesn't dare (to) stand up to his daughter; **je n'aime pas que mes enfants me résistent** I don't like my children opposing me; **je n'ai pas résisté à cette petite robe** I couldn't resist (buying) this dress

[b] (= *surmonter*) [+ *fatigue, émotion, privations*] to stand up to, withstand; [+ *chagrin, adversité*] to withstand; [+ *douleur*] to stand, withstand; **leur amour ne résista pas à cette infidélité** their love could not stand up to *ou* could not withstand this infidelity

[c] (= *supporter*) [+ *sécheresse, gelée, vent*] to withstand, stand up to, resist; **ça a bien résisté à l'épreuve du temps** it has really stood the test of time; **le plancher ne pourra pas ~**

au poids the floor won't support *ou* withstand *ou* take the weight; **la porte a résisté** the door held *ou* didn't give; **ça n'a pas résisté longtemps** it didn't resist *ou* hold out for long; **couleur qui résiste au lavage** colour which is fast in the wash, fast colour; **tissu qui résiste au lavage en machine** machine-washable material, material which can be machine-washed; **cette vaisselle résiste au feu** this crockery is heat-resistant *ou* heatproof; **ce raisonnement ne résiste pas à l'analyse** this reasoning does not stand up to analysis

résistivité [Rezistivite] NF (*Élec*) resistivity; **la ~ du cuivre est très faible** copper has a very low resistance

resituer [R(ə)situe] ▸ conjug 1 ◂ VT [+ *action, événement*] to put back in its context; **resituons cet événement dans son contexte économique** let's place this event in its economic context

▾ **résolu, e** [Rezoly] (*ptp de* **résoudre**) ADJ [*personne, ton, air*] resolute; **il est bien ~ à partir** he is firmly resolved *ou* he is determined to leave, he is set on leaving

résoluble [Rezolybl] ADJ [*problème*] soluble; (*Chim*) resolvable; (*Jur*) [*contrat*] annullable, cancellable

résolument [Rezolymã] ADV (= *totalement*) resolutely; (= *courageusement*) resolutely, steadfastly; **je suis ~ contre** I'm firmly against it, I'm resolutely opposed to it

résolutif, -ive [Rezolytif, iv] ADJ, NM resolvent

résolution [Rezolysjõ] NF [a] (*gén, Pol* = *décision*) resolution; **prendre la ~ de faire qch** to make a resolution to do sth, resolve to do sth; **ma ~ est prise** I've made my resolution; **bonnes ~s** good resolutions; **prendre de bonnes ~s pour le nouvel an** to make New Year's resolutions; **adopter une ~** to adopt a resolution; **la ~ 240 du Conseil de sécurité** Security Council resolution 240; **projet/proposition de ~** draft/proposed resolution

[b] (= *énergie*) resolve, resolution; **la ~ se lisait sur son visage** he had a determined *ou* resolute expression on his face

[c] (= *solution*) solution; **il attendait de moi la ~ de son problème** he expected me to give him a solution to his problem *ou* to solve his problem for him; **la ~ du conflit** the resolution of the conflict; (*Math*) **~ d'une équation** (re)solution of an equation; **~ d'un triangle** resolution of a triangle

[d] (*Jur* = *annulation*) [*contrat, vente*] cancellation, annulment

[e] (*Méd, Mus, Phys*) resolution; **~ de l'eau en vapeur** resolution of water into steam

[f] [*image*] resolution; **image de haute ~** high-resolution image; **écran (à) haute ~** high-resolution screen

résolutoire [Rezolytwar] ADJ (*Jur*) resolutive

résonance [Rezonãs] NF (*gén, Élec, Phon, Phys*) resonance (*NonC*); (*fig*) echo; **être/entrer en ~** to be/start resonating; **~ magnétique nucléaire** nuclear magnetic resonance; (*littér*) **ce poème éveille en moi des ~s** this poem strikes a chord with me; **le peintre a su rester en ~ avec son époque** the painter managed to stay in tune with his times → **caisse**

résonateur [Rezonatœr] NM resonator; **~ nucléaire** nuclear resonator

résonnant, e [Rezonã, ãt] ADJ [*voix*] resonant

résonner [Rezone] ▸ conjug 1 ◂ VI [*son*] to resonate, reverberate, resound; [*pas*] to resound; [*salle*] to be resonant; **cloche qui résonne bien/faiblement** bell which resounds well/rings feebly; **ne parle pas trop fort, ça résonne** don't speak too loudly because it echoes; **~ de** to resound *ou* ring *ou* resonate with

résorber [Rezorbe] ▸ conjug 1 ◂ [1] VT [a] (*Méd*) [+ *tumeur, épanchement*] to resorb; **les cicatrices sont résorbées** the scar tissue has healed

b (= éliminer) [+ chômage, inflation] to bring down, reduce (gradually); [+ déficit, surplus] to absorb; [+ stocks] to reduce; **trouver un moyen pour ~ la crise économique** to find some way of resolving the economic crisis **2 se résorber** VPR **a** (Méd) to be resorbed **b** [chômage] to be brought down ou reduced; [déficit] to be absorbed; **l'embouteillage se résorbe peu à peu** the traffic jam is gradually breaking up

résorption [RezɔRpsjɔ̃] NF **a** (Méd) [tumeur, épanchement] resorption **b** [chômage, inflation] bringing down, gradual reduction (de in); [déficit, surplus] absorption

résoudre [RezudR] ▸ conjug 51 ◂ **1** VT **a** [+ mystère, équation, problème de maths] to solve; [+ dilemme, crise] to solve, resolve; [+ difficultés] to solve, resolve, settle; [+ conflit] to settle, resolve; **j'ignore comment ce problème va se ~ ou va être résolu** I can't see how this problem will be solved ou resolved
b (= décider) [+ exécution, mort] to decide on, determine on; **~ de faire qch** to decide ou resolve to do sth, make up one's mind to do sth; **~ qn à faire qch** to prevail upon sb ou induce sb to do sth
c (Méd) [+ tumeur] to resolve
d (Jur = annuler) [+ contrat, vente] to cancel, annul
e (Mus) [+ dissonance] to resolve
f (= transformer) **~ qch en cendres** to reduce sth to ashes; **les nuages se résolvent en pluie/grêle** the clouds turn into rain/hail
2 se résoudre VPR **se ~ à faire qch** (= se décider) to resolve ou decide to do sth, make up one's mind to do sth; (= se résigner) to resign ou reconcile o.s. to doing sth; **il n'a pas pu se ~ à la quitter** he couldn't bring himself to leave her

respect [Respɛ] NM **a** (= considération) respect (de, pour for); **le ~ des principes démocratiques** respect for democratic principles; **le ~ humain†** fear of the judgment of others; **~ de soi** self-respect; **avoir du ~ pour qn** to respect sb, have respect for sb; **il n'a aucun ~ pour le bien d'autrui** he has no respect ou consideration ou regard for other people's property; **manquer de ~ à ou envers qn** to be disrespectful to(wards) sb; **agir dans le ~ des règles/des droits de l'homme** to act in accordance with the rules/with human rights; **par ~ pour sa mémoire** out of respect ou consideration for his memory; **malgré ou sauf le ~ que je vous dois ◊ sauf votre ~†** ou hum with (all) respect, with all due respect
b (formule de politesse) **présenter ses ~s à qn** to pay one's respects to sb; **présentez mes ~s à votre femme** give my regards ou pay my respects to your wife; **mes ~s, mon colonel** good day to you, sir
c (loc) **tenir qn en ~** (avec une arme) to keep sb at a respectful distance ou at bay; (fig) to keep sb at bay

respectabilité [Respɛktabilite] NF respectability

respectable [Respɛktabl] ADJ (= honorable) respectable; (= important) respectable, sizeable; (hum) **il avait un ventre ~*** he had quite a paunch

▼ **respecter** [Respɛkte] ▸ conjug 1 ◂ **1** VT **a** [+ personne] to respect, have respect for; † **~ une femme** to respect a woman's honour; **se faire ~** to be respected (**par** by), command respect (**par** from); **notre très respecté confrère** our highly respected colleague
b [+ formes, loi, droits, environnement] to respect; [+ traditions] to respect, have respect for, honour (Brit), honor (US); [+ calendrier, délais] to keep to, respect; [+ cahier des charges, clause contractuelle] to respect, abide by; [+ cessez-le-feu] to observe, respect; [+ interdiction] to observe, obey; [+ parole donnée, promesse] to keep; **~ ses engagements** to honour one's

commitments; **~ les opinions/sentiments de qn** to respect ou show consideration for sb's opinions/feelings; **respectez son sommeil** let him sleep, don't disturb him while he's asleep; **respectez le matériel !** treat the equipment with respect!, show some respect for the equipment!; **lessive qui respecte les couleurs** washing powder that is kind on colours; **« respectez les pelouses »** "keep off the grass"; **~ une minute de silence** to observe a minute's silence; **ces voyous ne respectent rien** those louts show no respect for anything ou don't respect anything; **classer des livres en respectant l'ordre alphabétique** to classify books in alphabetical order; **faire ~ la loi** to enforce the law; **le programme a été scrupuleusement respecté** the programme was strictly adhered to
2 se respecter VPR to respect o.s.; (hum) **tout professeur/juge/plombier qui se respecte** any self-respecting teacher/judge/plumber; **il se respecte trop pour faire cela** he has too much self-respect to do that sort of thing

respectif, -ive [Respɛktif, iv] ADJ respective

respectivement [Respɛktivmã] ADV respectively; **ils ont ~ 9 et 12 ans** they are 9 and 12 years old respectively

respectueusement [Respɛktɥøzmã] ADV respectfully, with respect

respectueux, -euse [Respɛktɥø, øz] **1** ADJ [langage, personne, silence] respectful (envers, pour to); **se montrer ~ du bien d'autrui** to show respect ou consideration for other people's property; **~ des traditions** respectful of traditions; **~ de la loi** respectful of the law, law-abiding; **projet ~ de l'environnement** environment-friendly ou environmentally sound project; **pays ~ des droits de l'homme** country that respects human rights; **être peu ~ des autres** to show little respect for others; **veuillez agréer, Monsieur (ou Madame), mes salutations respectueuses** yours sincerely ou faithfully (Brit); **voulez-vous transmettre à votre mère mes hommages ~** please give my best regards ou my respects to your mother → **distance 2 respectueuse*** NF (= prostituée) whore, prostitute, tart*

respirable [Respirabl] ADJ breathable; **l'air n'y est pas ~** the air there is unbreathable; (fig) **l'atmosphère n'est pas ~ dans cette famille** the atmosphere in this family is suffocating

respirateur [RespiratœR] NM **~ (artificiel)** (gén) respirator; (pour malade dans le coma) ventilator

respiration [Respirasjɔ̃] NF **a** (= fonction, action naturelle) breathing, respiration (SPÉC); (= souffle) breath; **~ pulmonaire/cutanée/artificielle ou assistée** pulmonary/cutaneous/artificial respiration; **~ entrecoupée** irregular breathing; **~ courte** shortness of breath; **avoir la ~ difficile** to have difficulty (in) ou trouble breathing; **~ bruyante** to breathe heavily ou noisily; **faites trois ~s complètes** breathe in and out three times → **couper, retenir** **b** (Mus) phrasing; **respecter les ~s d'un poème** to respect the phrasing of a poem

respiratoire [RespiratwaR] ADJ [système, voies] respiratory; [troubles] breathing (épith), respiratory

respirer [Respire] ▸ conjug 1 ◂ **1** VI **a** (lit, Bio) to breathe, respire (SPÉC); (chez le médecin) **« respirez ! »** "breathe in!", "take a deep breath!"; **~ par la bouche/le nez** to breathe through one's mouth/one's nose; **est-ce qu'il respire (encore)?** is he (still) breathing?; **~ avec difficulté** to have difficulty (in) ou trouble breathing, breathe with difficulty; **~ profondément** to breathe deeply, take a deep breath; **~ à pleins poumons** to breathe deeply → **mentir**
b (fig) (= se détendre) to get one's breath; (= se rassurer) to breathe again ou easy; **ouf, on respire !** phew, we can breathe again!

2 VT **a** (= inhaler) to breathe (in), inhale; **~ un air vicié/le grand air** to breathe in foul air/the fresh air; **faire ~ des sels à qn** to make sb inhale smelling salts
b (= exprimer) [+ calme, bonheur, santé] to radiate; [+ honnêteté, franchise, orgueil, ennui] to exude, emanate; **son attitude respirait la méfiance** his whole attitude was mistrustful, his attitude was clearly one of mistrust

resplendir [ResplãdiR] ▸ conjug 2 ◂ VI [soleil, lune] to shine; [surface métallique] to gleam, shine; **le lac/la neige resplendissait sous le soleil** the lake/the snow glistened ou glittered in the sun; **le ciel resplendit au coucher du soleil** the sky is radiant ou ablaze at sunset; **toute la cuisine resplendissait** the whole kitchen shone ou gleamed; **il resplendissait de joie/de bonheur** he was aglow ou radiant with joy/with happiness

resplendissant, e [Resplãdisã, ãt] ADJ **a** (lit = brillant) [soleil] radiant, dazzling; [lune] shining, beaming; [surface métallique] gleaming, shining; [lac, neige] glistening, glittering; [ciel] radiant **b** (fig = éclatant) [beauté, santé] radiant; [visage, yeux] shining; **avoir une mine ~e** to look radiant; **être ~ de santé/de joie** to be glowing ou radiant with health/with joy

resplendissement [Resplãdismã] NM [beauté, soleil] brilliance

responsabilisation [Respɔ̃sabilizasjɔ̃] NF **pour encourager la ~ des employés/des parents** to encourage employees/parents to assume more responsibility

responsabiliser [Respɔ̃sabilize] ▸ conjug 1 ◂ VT **~ qn** (= le rendre conscient de ses responsabilités) to make sb aware of their responsibilities, give sb a sense of responsibility; (= lui donner des responsabilités) to give sb responsibilities

▼ **responsabilité** [Respɔ̃sabilite] **1** NF **a** (légale) liability (de for); (morale) responsibility (de for); (ministérielle) responsibility; (financière) (financial) accountability; **emmener ces enfants en montagne, c'est une ~** it's a responsibility taking these children to the mountains; **le Premier ministre a engagé la ~ de son gouvernement** ≈ the prime minister has sought a vote of confidence in his government; **porter la ~ de qch** to take responsibility for sth; **faire porter la ~ de qch à ou sur qn** to hold sb responsible for sth, blame sb for sth; **les bagages sont sous ta ~** you're responsible for ou in charge of the luggage, the luggage is your responsibility; **ces pupils sont sous ma ~** I'm responsible for these pupils, these pupils are my responsibility ou are in my charge → **assurance, société**
b (= charge) responsibility; **de lourdes ~s** heavy responsibilities; **assumer la ~ d'une affaire** to take on the responsibility for a matter; **avoir la ~ de qn** to take ou have responsibility for sb; **avoir la ~ de la gestion/de la sécurité** to be responsible for management/for security; **il fuit les ~s** he shuns (any) responsibility; **il serait temps qu'il prenne ses ~s** it's (high) time he faced up to his responsibilities; **ce poste comporte d'importantes ~s** this post involves ou carries considerable responsibilities; **il a un poste de ~** he's in a position of responsibility; **accéder à de hautes ~s** to reach a position of great responsibility
2 COMP ▸ **responsabilité atténuée** diminished responsibility ▸ **responsabilité civile** civil liability ▸ **responsabilité collective** collective responsibility ▸ **responsabilité contractuelle** contractual liability ▸ **responsabilité pénale** criminal responsibility ▸ **responsabilité pleine et entière** full and entire responsibility

responsable [Respɔ̃sabl] **1** ADJ **a** (= comptable) (légalement) (de dégâts) liable, responsible (de for); (de délits) responsible (de for); (moralement) responsible, accountable (de for, **devant qn** to sb); **reconnu ~ de ses actes** recognized as responsible *ou* accountable for his actions; **il n'est pas ~ des délits/ dégâts commis par ses enfants** he is not responsible for the misdemeanours of/liable *ou* responsible for damage caused by his children; **je le tiens pour ~ de l'accident** I hold him responsible *ou* I blame him for the accident; **civilement/pénalement ~** liable in civil/ criminal law; **le ministre est ~ de ses décisions (devant le parlement)** the minister is responsible *ou* accountable (to Parliament) for his decisions

[b] (= *chargé de*) **~ de** responsible for, in charge of

[c] (= *coupable*) responsible, to blame; **Dupont, ~ de l'échec, a été renvoyé** Dupont, who was responsible *ou* to blame for the failure, has been dismissed; **ils considèrent l'état défectueux des freins comme ~ (de l'accident)** they consider that defective brakes were to blame *ou* were responsible for the accident

[d] (= *sérieux*) [*attitude, employé, étudiant*] responsible; **agir de manière ~** to behave responsibly

2 NMF [a] (= *coupable*) person responsible *ou* who is to blame; **il faut trouver les ~s (de cette erreur)** we must find those responsible *ou* those who are to blame (for this error); **le seul ~ est l'alcool** alcohol alone is to blame *ou* is the culprit

[b] (= *personne compétente*) person in charge; **adressez-vous au ~** see the person in charge

[c] (= *dirigeant*) official; **les ~s du parti** the party officials; **des ~s de l'industrie** heads *ou* leaders of industry; **~ syndical** trade union official; **~ politique** politician

resquillage* [ʀɛskijaʒ] NM, **resquille*** [ʀɛskij] NF (*dans l'autobus, le métro*) fare-dodging*, grabbing a free ride; (*au match, cinéma*) sneaking in, getting in on the sly

resquiller* [ʀɛskije] ▶conjug 1◀ **1** VI (= *ne pas payer*) (*dans l'autobus, le métro*) to sneak a free ride, dodge the fare; (*au match, cinéma*) to get in on the sly, sneak in; (= *ne pas faire la queue*) to jump the queue (*Brit*), cut in (at the beginning of) the line (*US*) **2** VT [+ *place*] to wangle*, fiddle*

resquilleur, -euse* [ʀɛskijœʀ, øz] NM,F (= *qui n'attend pas son tour*) person who doesn't wait his or her turn, queue-jumper (*Brit*); (= *qui ne paie pas*) (*dans l'autobus*) fare-dodger*; (*au stade*) **expulser les ~s** to throw out the people who have wangled their way in without paying

ressac [ʀəsak] NM **le ~** (= *mouvement*) the backwash, the undertow; (= *vague*) the surf

ressaisir [ʀ(ə)seziʀ] ▶conjug 2◀ **1** VT [a] [+ *branche, bouée*] to catch hold of again; [+ *pouvoir, occasion, prétexte*] to seize again; (*Jur*) [+ *biens*] to recover possession of [b] [*peur*] to grip (once) again; [*délire, désir*] to take hold of again [c] (*Jur*) **~ un tribunal d'une affaire** to lay a matter before a court again **2** **se ressaisir** VPR [a] (= *reprendre son sang-froid*) to regain one's self-control; (*Sport : après avoir flanché*) to rally, recover; **ressaisissez-vous !** pull yourself together!, get a grip on yourself!; **le coureur s'est bien ressaisi sur la fin** the runner rallied *ou* recovered well towards the end [b] **se ~ de** [+ *objet*] to recover; [+ *pouvoir*] to seize again

ressaisissement [ʀ(ə)sezismɑ̃] NM recovery

ressassé, e [ʀ(ə)sase] (*ptp de* **ressasser**) ADJ [*plaisanterie, thème*] worn out, hackneyed

ressasser [ʀ(ə)sase] ▶conjug 1◀ VT [+ *pensées, regrets*] to keep turning over; [+ *plaisanteries, conseil*] to keep trotting out

ressaut [ʀəso] NM (*Géog*) (= *plan vertical*) rise; (= *plan horizontal*) shelf; (*Archit*) projection

ressauter [ʀ(ə)sote] ▶conjug 1◀ **1** VI to jump again **2** VT [+ *obstacle*] to jump (over) again

ressayer [ʀeseje] ▶conjug 8◀ VT, VI (*gén*) to try again; (*Couture*) = **réessayer**

ressemblance [ʀ(ə)sɑ̃blɑ̃s] NF [a] (= *similitude visuelle*) resemblance, likeness; (= *analogie de composition*) similarity; **~ presque parfaite entre deux substances** near perfect similarity of two substances; **avoir** *ou* **offrir une ~ avec qch** to bear a resemblance *ou* likeness to sth; **la ~ entre père et fils/ces montagnes est frappante** the resemblance between father and son/ these mountains is striking; **ce peintre s'inquiète peu de la ~** this painter cares very little about getting a good likeness; **toute ~ avec des personnes existant ou ayant existé est purement fortuite** any resemblance to any person living or dead is purely accidental [b] (= *trait*) resemblance; (= *analogie*) similarity

ressemblant, e [ʀ(ə)sɑ̃blɑ̃, ɑ̃t] ADJ [*photo, portrait*] lifelike, true to life; **vous êtes très ~ sur cette photo** this is a very good photo of you; **il a fait d'elle un portrait très ~** he painted a very good likeness of her

▼ **ressembler** [ʀ(ə)sɑ̃ble] ▶conjug 1◀ **1** **ressembler à** VT INDIR [a] (= *être semblable à*) [*personne*] (*physiquement*) to resemble, be *ou* look like; (*moralement, psychologiquement*) to resemble, be, like; [*choses*] (*visuellement*) to resemble, look like; (*par la composition*) to resemble, be like; [*faits, événements*] to resemble, be like; **il me ressemble beaucoup physiquement/moralement** he is very like me *ou* he resembles me closely in looks/in character; **juste quelques accrochages, rien qui ressemble à une offensive** just a few skirmishes — nothing that would pass as *ou* that you could call a real offensive; **il ne ressemble en rien à l'image que je me faisais de lui** he's nothing like how I imagined him; **à quoi ressemble-t-il ?*** what does he look like?, what's he like?; **ton fils s'est roulé dans la boue, regarde à quoi il ressemble !*** your son has been rolling in the mud — just look at the state of him!; **ça ne ressemble à rien !*** [*attitude*] it makes no sense at all!; [*peinture, objet*] it's like nothing on earth!; **à quoi ça ressemble de crier comme ça !*** what's the idea of *ou* what do you mean by shouting like that!

[b] (= *être digne de*) **cela lui ressemble bien de dire ça** it's just like him *ou* it's typical of him to say that; **cela ne te ressemble pas** that's (most) unlike you *ou* not like you

2 **se ressembler** VPR (*physiquement, visuellement*) to look *ou* be alike, resemble each other; (*moralement, par ses éléments*) to be alike, resemble each other; **ils se ressemblent comme deux gouttes d'eau** they're as like as two peas (in a pod); **tu ne te ressembles plus depuis ton accident** you're not yourself since your accident; **aucune ville ne se ressemble** no town is like another, no two towns are alike; **dans cette rue, il n'y a pas deux maisons qui se ressemblent** no two houses look alike in this street; **toutes les grandes villes se ressemblent** all big towns are alike *ou* the same ▪ (*PROV*) **qui se ressemble s'assemble** birds of a feather flock together (*PROV*) → **jour**

ressemelage [ʀ(ə)səm(ə)laʒ] NM soling, resoling

ressemeler [ʀ(ə)səm(ə)le] ▶conjug 4◀ VT to sole, resole

ressemer [ʀəs(ə)me, ʀ(ə)səme] ▶conjug 5◀ **1** VT to resow, sow again **2** **se ressemer** VPR **ça s'est ressemé tout seul** it (re)seeded itself

ressentiment [ʀ(ə)sɑ̃timɑ̃] NM resentment (**contre** against, **de** at); **éprouver du ~** to feel resentful (**à l'égard de** towards); **il en a gardé du ~** it has remained a sore point with him; **avec ~** resentfully, with resentment

ressentir [ʀ(ə)sɑ̃tiʀ] ▶conjug 16◀ **1** VT [+ *douleur, sentiment, coup*] to feel; [+ *sensation*] to feel, experience; [+ *perte, insulte, privation*] to feel, be affected by; **il ressentit les effets de cette nuit de beuverie** he felt the effects of that night's drinking; **il ressent toute chose profondément** he feels everything deeply, he is deeply affected by everything **2** **se ressentir** VPR [a] **se ~ de** [*travail, qualité*] to show the effects of; [*personne, communauté*] to feel the effects of; **la qualité/son travail s'en ressent** the quality/his work is affected, it is telling on the quality/his work; **l'athlète se ressentait du manque de préparation** the athlete's lack of preparation told on his performance [b]* **s'en ~ pour** to feel up to; **il ne s'en ressent pas pour faire ça** he doesn't feel up to doing that

resserre [ʀəsɛʀ] NF (= *cabane*) shed; (= *réduit*) store, storeroom

resserré, e [ʀ(ə)seʀe] (*ptp de* **resserrer**) ADJ [*chemin, vallée*] narrow; **maison ~e entre des immeubles** house squeezed between high buildings; **veste ~e à la taille** jacket fitted at the waist

resserrement [ʀ(ə)seʀmɑ̃] NM [a] (= *action*) [*nœud, étreinte*] tightening; [*pores*] closing; [*liens, amitié*] strengthening; [*vallée*] narrowing; [*crédits*] tightening, squeezing [b] (= *goulet*) [*route, vallée*] narrow part

resserrer [ʀ(ə)seʀe] ▶conjug 1◀ **1** VT [a] [+ *vis*] to tighten (up); [+ *nœud, ceinture, étreinte*] to tighten; **produit qui resserre les pores** product which helps (to) close the pores → **boulon** [b] [+ *discipline*] to tighten up; [+ *cercle, filets*] to draw tighter, tighten; [+ *liens, amitié*] to strengthen; [+ *récit*] to tighten up, compress; [+ *crédits*] to tighten, squeeze; **l'armée resserre son étau autour de la capitale** the army is tightening its grip *ou* the noose around the capital **2** **se resserrer** VPR [a] [*nœud, étreinte*] to tighten; [*pores, mâchoire*] to close; [*chemin, vallée*] to narrow; (*fig*) **l'étau se resserre** the noose is tightening [b] [*liens affectifs*] to grow stronger; [*cercle, groupe*] to draw in; **le filet/l'enquête se resserrait autour de lui** the net/the inquiry was closing in on him

resservir [ʀ(ə)seʀviʀ] ▶conjug 14◀ **1** VT [a] (= *servir à nouveau*) [+ *plat*] to serve (up) again (**à** to), dish up again* (*péj*) (**à** for) [b] (= *servir davantage*) [+ *dîneur*] to give another *ou* a second helping to; **~ de la soupe/ viande** to give another *ou* a second helping of soup/meat [c] [+ *thème, histoire*] to trot out again; **les thèmes qu'ils nous resservent depuis des années** the themes that they have been feeding us with *ou* trotting out to us for years **2** VI [*vêtement usagé, outil*] to serve again, do again; **ça peut toujours ~** it may come in handy *ou* be useful again; **cet emballage peut ~** this packaging can be used again; **ce manteau pourra te ~** you may find this coat useful again (some time) [b] (*Tennis*) to serve again **3** **se resservir** VPR [a] [*dîneur*] to help o.s. again, take another helping; **se ~ de fromage/viande** to help o.s. to some more cheese/meat, take another helping of cheese/meat [b] (= *réutiliser*) **se ~ de** [+ *outil*] to use again; [+ *vêtement*] to wear again

ressort¹ [ʀ(ə)sɔʀ] NM [a] (= *pièce de métal*) spring; **faire ~** to spring back; **à ~** [*mécanisme, pièce*] spring-loaded → **matelas, mouvoir** [b] (= *énergie*) spirit; **avoir du/manquer de ~** to have/lack spirit; **un être sans ~** a spiritless individual [c] (*littér = motivation*) **les ~s psychologiques de qn** sb's psychological motives; **les ~s qui le font agir** what motivates him, what makes him tick*; **les ~s secrets de l'esprit humain/de l'organisation** the inner *ou* se-

➤ GRAMMAIRE ACTIVE: **ressembler** 32.4, 32.5

cret workings of the human mind/the organization; **les ~s secrets de cette affaire** the hidden undercurrents of this affair **d** († = *élasticité*) resilience **2** COMP ► **ressort à boudin** spiral spring ► **ressort hélicoïdal** helical *ou* coil spring ► **ressort à lames** leafspring ► **ressort de montre** hairspring ► **ressort de suspension** suspension spring ► **ressort de traction** drawspring

ressort² [R(ə)sɔr] NM **a** (*Admin, Jur* = *compétence*) **être du ~ de** to be *ou* fall within the competence of; **c'est du ~ de la justice/du chef de service** that is for the law/the head of department to deal with, that is the law's/the head of department's responsibility; (*fig*) **ce n'est pas de mon ~** this is not my responsibility, this is outside my remit **b** (*Jur* = *circonscription*) jurisdiction; **dans le ~ du tribunal de Paris** in the jurisdiction of the courts of Paris **c** (*Jur*) **en dernier ~** without appeal; (*fig = en dernier recours*) as a last resort; (= *finalement*) in the last resort *ou* instance

ressortir¹ [R(ə)sɔrtir] ▶conjug 16◀ **1** VI (*avec aux être*) **a** [*personne*] to go *ou* come out; [*objet*] to come out; (*une nouvelle fois*) to go (*ou* come) out again; **je suis ressorti faire des courses** I went out shopping again; **il a jeté un coup d'œil aux journaux et il est ressorti** he glanced at the newspapers and went (back) out again; **des désirs refoulés/des souvenirs qui ressortent** repressed desires/memories which resurface *ou* come back up to the surface; **le rouge/7 est ressorti** the red/ 7 came out *ou* up again; **ce film ressort sur nos écrans** this film is showing again *ou* has been re-released **b** (= *contraster*) [*détail, couleur, qualité*] to stand out; **faire ~ qch** to make sth stand out, bring out sth

2 **ressortir de** VT INDIR (= *résulter*) to emerge from, be the result of; **il ressort de tout cela que personne ne savait** what emerges from all that is that no one knew

3 VT (*avec aux avoir : à nouveau*) [+ *vêtements d'hiver, outil*] to take out again; [+ *film*] to re-release, bring out again; (*Comm*) [+ *modèle*] to bring out again; **le soleil revenant, ils ont ressorti les chaises sur la terrasse** when the sun came out again, they took *ou* brought the chairs back onto the terrace; **j'ai encore besoin du registre, ressors-le** I still need the register so take *ou* get it (back) out again; **il (nous) ressort toujours les mêmes blagues** he always trots out the same old jokes; **~ un vieux projet d'un tiroir** to dust off an old project

ressortir² [R(ə)sɔrtir] ▶conjug 2◀ ► **ressortir à** VT INDIR [+ *tribunal*] to come under the jurisdiction of; (*frm*) [+ *domaine*] to be the concern *ou* province of, pertain to; **ceci ressort à une autre juridiction** this comes under *ou* belongs to a separate jurisdiction

ressortissant, e [R(ə)sɔrtisã, ãt] NM,F national; **~ français** French national *ou* citizen

ressouder [R(ə)sude] ▶conjug 1◀ **1** VT [+ *objet brisé*] to solder together again; (= *souder à nouveau*) [+ *petite pièce*] to resolder; [+ *grosse pièce*] to reweld; [+ *amitié*] to patch up, renew the bonds of; [+ *équipe, parti*] to reunite **2** **se ressouder** VPR [*os, fracture*] to knit, mend; [*amitié*] to mend; **l'opposition s'est ressoudée autour de son chef** the opposition has reunited around its leader

ressource [R(ə)surs] NF **a** (= *moyens matériels, financiers*) **~s** [*pays*] resources; [*famille, personne*] resources, means; **~s personnelles** personal resources; **avoir de maigres ~s** to have limited *ou* slender resources *ou* means; **une famille sans ~s** a family with no means of support *ou* no resources; **~s naturelles/pétrolières** natural/petroleum resources; **les ~s en hommes d'un pays** the manpower resources of a country; **les ~s de l'État**

ou **du Trésor** the financial resources of the state; **directeur/responsable des ~s humaines** director/head of human resources **b** (= *possibilités*) **~s** [*artiste, aventurier, sportif*] resources; [*art, technique, système*] possibilities; **les ~s de son talent/imagination** the resources of one's talent/imagination; **ce système a des ~s variées** this system has a wide range of possible applications; **les ~s de la langue française** the resources of the French language; **les ~s de la photographie** the various possibilities of photography; **être à bout de ~s** to have exhausted all the possibilities, be at the end of one's resources; **homme/femme de ~(s)** man/woman of resource, resourceful man/woman

c (= *recours*) **n'ayant pas la ~ de lui parler** having no means *ou* possibility of speaking to him; **je n'ai d'autre ~ que de lui téléphoner** the only course open to me is to phone him, I have no other option but to phone him; **sa seule ~ était de …** the only way *ou* course open to him was to …; **vous êtes ma dernière ~** you are my last resort; **en dernière ~** as a last resort

d (*Ordin*) resource

e **avoir de la ~** [*cheval, sportif*] to have strength in reserve; **il y a de la ~*** there's plenty more where that came from

ressourcer (se) [R(ə)surse] ▶conjug 3◀ VPR (= *retrouver ses racines*) to go back to one's roots; (= *recouvrer ses forces*) to recharge one's batteries

ressouvenir (se) [R(ə)suv(ə)nir] ▶conjug 22◀ VPR (*littér*) **se ressouvenir de** to remember, recall; **faire (se) ressouvenir qn de qch** to remind sb of sth; **ce bruit le fit se ressouvenir** *ou* (*littér*) **lui fit ressouvenir de son accident** when he heard the noise he was reminded of his accident

ressurgir [R(ə)syrʒir] ▶conjug 2◀ VI = **resurgir**

ressusciter [Resysite] ▶conjug 1◀ **1** VI **a** (*Rel*) to rise (from the dead); **Christ est ressuscité !** Christ is risen!; **le Christ ressuscité** the risen Christ; **ressuscité d'entre les morts** risen from the dead **b** (*fig = renaître*) [*malade*] to come back to life, revive; [*sentiment, souvenir*] to revive, reawaken; [*pays*] to come back to life, get back on its feet again

2 VT **a** (*lit*) [+ *mourant*] to resuscitate, restore *ou* bring back to life; (*Rel*) to raise (from the dead); **buvez ça, ça ressusciterait un mort*** drink that — it'll put new life into you; **bruit à ~ les morts** noise that would wake *ou* awaken the dead **b** (= *régénérer*) [+ *malade, projet, entreprise*] to bring back to life, inject new life into, revive **c** (= *faire revivre*) [+ *sentiment*] to revive, reawaken, bring back to life; [+ *héros, mode*] to bring back, resurrect (*péj*); [+ *passé, coutume, loi*] to revive, resurrect (*péj*)

restant, e [Rɛstã, ãt] **1** ADJ remaining; **le seul cousin ~** the sole *ou* one remaining cousin, the only *ou* one cousin left *ou* remaining → **poste¹** **2** NM **a** (= *l'autre partie*) **le ~** the rest, the remainder; **tout le ~ des provisions était perdu** all the rest *ou* remainder of the supplies were lost; **pour le ~ de mes jours** *ou* **de ma vie** for the rest of my life **b** (= *ce qui est en trop*) **accommoder un ~ de poulet** to make a dish with some left-over chicken; **faire une écharpe dans un ~ de tissu** to make a scarf out of some left-over material

restau* [Rɛsto] NM = **resto**

restaurant [Rɛstorã] **1** NM restaurant; **on va au ~?** shall we go to a restaurant?, shall we eat out? **2** COMP ► **restaurant d'entreprise** staff canteen, staff dining room ► **restaurant gastronomique** gourmet restaurant ► **restaurant libre-service** self-service restaurant, cafeteria ► **restaurant rapide** fast-food restaurant ► **restaurant sco-**

laire (*Admin*) school canteen ► **restaurant self-service** = **restaurant libre-service** ► **restaurant universitaire** university refectory *ou* canteen *ou* cafeteria

restaurateur, -trice [Rɛstoratœr, tris] NM,F **a** [*tableau, dynastie*] restorer **b** (= *aubergiste*) restaurant owner, restaurateur

restauration [Rɛstorasjɔ̃] NF **a** [*dynastie, tableau, tapisserie*] restoration; [*bâtiment, ville*] restoration, rehabilitation; (*Hist*) **la Restauration** the Restoration (*of the Bourbons in 1830*); **la ~ de la démocratie est en bonne voie dans ce pays** democracy is well on the way to being restored in this country **b** (= *hôtellerie*) catering; **il travaille dans la ~** he works in catering; **la ~ rapide** the fast-food industry *ou* trade; **la ~ collective/scolaire** institutional/ school catering **c** (*Ordin*) [*fichier*] restore

restaurer [Rɛstore] ▶conjug 1◀ **1** VT **a** [+ *dynastie, paix, tableau*] to restore **b** (= *nourrir*) to feed **c** (*Ordin*) to restore **2** **se restaurer** VPR to have something to eat

restauroute [Rɛstorut] NM = **restoroute**

reste [Rɛst] NM **a** **le ~** (*l'autre partie*) the rest; **le ~ de sa vie/du temps/des hommes** the rest of his life/of the time/of humanity; **j'ai lu trois chapitres, je lirai le ~ (du livre) demain** I've read three chapters and I'll read the rest (of the book) tomorrow; **le ~ du lait** the rest of the milk, what is left of the milk; **préparez les bagages, je m'occupe du ~** get the luggage ready and I'll see to the rest *ou* to everything else

b (= *ce qui est en trop*) **il y a un ~ de fromage/ de tissu** there's some *ou* a piece of cheese/ material left over; **s'il y a un ~, je fais une omelette/une écharpe** if there's some *ou* any left *ou* left over I'll make an omelette/a scarf; **ce ~ de poulet ne suffira pas** this left-over chicken won't be enough; **s'il y a un ~ (de laine), j'aimerais faire une écharpe** if there's some spare (wool) *ou* some (wool) to spare, I'd like to make a scarf; **un ~ de tendresse/de pitié la poussa à rester** a last trace *ou* a remnant of tenderness/of pity moved her to stay **c** **les ~s** (= *nourriture*) the left-overs; (*frm* = *dépouille mortelle*) the (mortal) remains; **les ~s de** [+ *repas*] the remains of, the leftovers from; [+ *fortune, bâtiment*] the remains of, what is (*ou* was) left of; **donner les ~s au chien** to give the scraps *ou* leftovers to the dog; (*hum*) **elle a de beaux ~s** she's still a fine(-looking) woman **d** (*Math* = *différence*) remainder **e** (*loc*) **avoir de l'argent/du temps de ~** to have money/time left over *ou* in hand *ou* to spare; **il ne voulait pas être** *ou* **demeurer en ~ avec eux** he didn't want to be outdone by them *ou* one down on them* (*Brit*); (*littér*) **au ~** ◇ **du ~** (and) besides, (and) what's more; **nous la connaissons, du ~, très peu** besides *ou* moreover, we hardly know her at all; **sans demander son ~** (= *sans plus de cérémonie*) without further ado; (= *sans protester*) without a murmur; **il a empoché l'argent sans demander son ~** he pocketed the money without asking any questions; **il est menteur, paresseux et (tout) le ~** he's untruthful, lazy and everything else as well; **avec la grève, la neige et (tout) le ~, ils ne peuvent pas venir** what with the strike, the snow and everything else *ou* all the rest, they can't come; **pour le ~** *ou* **quant au ~** (= *nous verrons bien*) (as) for the rest (we'll have to see); **il a été opéré, le temps fera le ~** he's had an operation, time will do the rest

rester [Rɛste] ▶conjug 1◀ VI **a** (*dans un lieu*) to stay, remain; (* = *habiter*) to live; **~ au lit** [*paresseux*] to stay *ou* lie in bed; [*malade*] to stay in bed; **~ à la maison** to stay *ou* remain in the house *ou* indoors; **~ chez soi** to stay at home *ou* in; **~ au** *ou* **dans le jardin/à la campagne/à l'étranger** to stay *ou* remain in the garden/in the country/abroad; **~ (à)**

dîner/déjeuner to stay for *ou* to dinner/lunch; **je ne peux ~ que 10 minutes** I can only stay *ou* stop* 10 minutes; **la voiture est restée dehors/au garage** the car stayed *ou* remained outside/in the garage; **la lettre va certainement – dans sa poche** the letter is sure to stay in his pocket; **un os lui est resté dans la gorge** a bone got stuck in his throat; *(lit, fig)* **ça m'est resté là*** *ou* **en travers de la gorge** it stuck in my throat; **restez où vous êtes** stay *ou* remain where you are; **~ à regarder la télévision** to stay watching television; **nous sommes restés deux heures à l'attendre** we stayed there waiting for him for two hours; **naturellement, ça reste entre nous** of course we shall keep this to ourselves *ou* this is strictly between ourselves; **il ne peut pas ~ en place** he can't keep still

[b] *(dans un état)* to stay, remain; **~ éveillé/immobile** to keep *ou* stay awake/still; **~ sans bouger/sans rien dire** to stay *ou* remain motionless/silent; **~ indifférent devant qch/insensible à qch** to remain indifferent to sth/impervious to sth; **~ maître de soi** to maintain one's composure; **~ célibataire** to stay single, remain unmarried; **~ handicapé à vie** to be handicapped for life; **~ dans l'ignorance** to remain in ignorance; **~ en fonction** to remain in office; **~ debout** *(lit)* to stand, remain standing; *(ne pas se coucher)* to stay up; **je suis resté assis/debout toute la journée** I've been sitting/standing (up) all day; **ne reste pas là les bras croisés** don't just stand there with your arms folded; **il est resté très timide** he has remained *ou* he is still very shy; **il est et restera toujours maladroit** he is clumsy and he always will be; **cette coutume est restée en honneur dans certains pays** this custom is still honoured in certain countries; **le centre-ville est resté paralysé toute la journée** the city centre was choked with traffic *ou* gridlocked all day → **lettre, panne¹, plan¹**

[c] *(= subsister)* to be left, remain; **rien ne reste de l'ancien château** nothing is left *ou* remains of the old castle; **c'est le seul parent qui leur reste** he's their only remaining relative, he's the only relative they have left; **c'est tout l'argent qui leur reste** that's all the money they have left; **10 km restaient à faire** there were still 10 km to go

[d] *(= durer)* to last, live on; **c'est une œuvre qui restera** it's a work which will live on *ou* which will last; **le désir passe, la tendresse reste** desire passes, tenderness lives on; **le surnom lui est resté** the nickname stayed with him, the nickname stuck

[e] **~ sur une impression** to retain an impression; **je suis resté sur ma faim** *(après un repas)* I still felt hungry; *(à la fin d'une histoire)* I felt there was something missing; **sa remarque m'est restée sur le cœur** his remark (still) rankles (in my mind); **mon déjeuner m'est resté sur l'estomac** my lunch is still sitting there; *(fig)* **ça m'est resté sur l'estomac*** it still riles me*, I still feel sore about it*; **ne restons pas sur un échec** let's not give up just because we failed

[f] **en ~ à** *(= ne pas dépasser)* to go no further than; **ils en sont restés à quelques baisers/des discussions préliminaires** they got no further than a few kisses/preliminary discussions; **les gens du village en sont restés à la bougie** the villagers are still using candles; **les pourparlers en sont restés là** they only got that far *ou* that is as far as they got in their discussions; **les choses en sont restées là jusqu'à ...** nothing more happened until ..., nothing more was done (about it) until ...; **où en étions-nous restés dans notre lecture?** where did we leave off in our reading?; **restons-en là** let's leave off there, let's leave it at that

[g] *(* = mourir)* **y ~** to die; **il a bien failli y ~** that was nearly the end of him

[2] VB IMPERS **il reste encore un peu de jour/de pain** there's still a little daylight/bread left; **il leur reste juste de quoi vivre** they have just enough left to live on; **il me reste à faire ceci** I still have this to do, there's still this for me to do; **il reste beaucoup à faire** much remains to be done, there's a lot left to do; **il nous reste son souvenir** we still have our memories of him; **il ne me reste que toi** you're all I have left; **il n'est rien resté de leur maison/des provisions** nothing remained *ou* was left of their house/of the supplies; **le peu de temps qu'il lui restait à vivre** the short time that he had left to live; **il ne me reste qu'à vous remercier** it only remains for me to thank you; **il restait à faire 50 km** there were 50 km still *ou* left to go; **est-ce qu'il vous reste assez de force pour terminer ce travail?** do you have enough strength left to finish this job?; **quand on a été en prison, il en reste toujours quelque chose** when you've been in prison something of it always stays with you; **(il) reste à savoir si/à prouver que ...** it remains to be seen if/to be proved that ...; **il reste que ... ◊ il n'en reste pas moins que ...** the fact remains (nonetheless) that ..., it is nevertheless a fact that ...; **il reste entendu que ...** it remains *ou* is still quite understood that ...

restituer [ʀɛstitɥe] ▶conjug 1◀ VT [a] *(= redonner)* [+ *objet volé*] to return, restore **(à qn** to sb); [+ *argent*] to return, refund **(à qn** to sb) [b] *(= reconstituer)* [+ *fresque, texte, inscription*] to reconstruct, restore; [+ *son*] to reproduce; **un texte enfin restitué dans son intégralité** a text finally restored in its entirety [c] *(= recréer)* to recreate; **le film restitue bien l'atmosphère de l'époque** the film successfully recreates the atmosphere of the period; **appareil qui restitue fidèlement les sons** apparatus which gives faithful sound reproduction; **il n'a pas su ~ la complexité des sentiments du héros** he wasn't able to render the complexity of the hero's feelings [d] *(= libérer)* [+ *énergie, chaleur*] to release; **l'énergie emmagasinée est entièrement restituée sous forme de chaleur** the energy stored up is entirely released in the form of heat

restitution [ʀɛstitysjɔ̃] NF [a] [*objet volé, argent*] return; **pour obtenir la ~ des territoires** to secure the return of the territories [b] [*fresque, texte, inscription*] reconstruction, restoration; [*son*] reproduction [c] [*énergie, chaleur*] release

resto* [ʀɛsto] NM (ABRÉV = **restaurant**) restaurant; **~ U** university refectory *ou* canteen *ou* cafeteria; **les ~s du cœur** charity set up to provide food for the homeless during the winter

restoroute® [ʀɛstoʀut] NM [*route*] roadside restaurant; [*autoroute*] motorway (*Brit*) *ou* highway (*US*) restaurant

restreindre [ʀɛstʀɛ̃dʀ] ▶conjug 52◀ [1] VT [+ *quantité, production, dépenses*] to restrict, limit, cut down; [+ *ambition*] to restrict, limit, curb; **nous restreindrons notre étude à quelques exemples** we will restrict our study to a few examples; **~ le crédit** to restrict credit [2] **se restreindre** VPR [a] *(dans ses dépenses, sur la nourriture)* to cut down **(sur** on) [b] *(= diminuer)* [*production, tirage*] to decrease, go down; [*espace*] to decrease, diminish; [*ambition, champ d'action*] to narrow; [*sens d'un mot*] to become more restricted; **le champ de leur enquête se restreint** the scope of their inquiry is narrowing

restreint, e [ʀɛstʀɛ̃, ɛ̃t] *(ptp de* **restreindre**) ADJ [*autorité, emploi, production, vocabulaire*] limited, restricted; [*espace, moyens, nombre, personnel*] limited; [*sens*] restricted; **~ à** confined *ou* restricted *ou* limited to → **comité, suffrage**

restrictif, -ive [ʀɛstʀiktif, iv] ADJ restrictive

restriction [ʀɛstʀiksjɔ̃] NF [a] *(= action)* restriction, limiting, limitation [b] *(= réduction)* restriction; **~s** [*personnel,*

consommation, crédit] restrictions; **~s budgétaires** budget(ary) constraints *ou* restrictions; **~s d'électricité** electricity restrictions, restrictions on the use of electricity; **prendre des mesures de ~** to adopt restrictive measures; **~s à l'exportation/importation** export/import restraints [c] *(= condition)* qualification; *(= réticence)* reservation; **~ mentale** mental reservation; **faire** *ou* **émettre des ~s** to express some reservations; **avec ~** *ou* **des ~s** with some qualification(s) *ou* reservation(s); **sans ~** [*soutien, attachement*] unqualified, unconditional; [*accepter, soutenir*] unreservedly; **approuver qch sans ~** to give one's unqualified approval to sth, accept sth without reservation; **ce régime alimentaire autorise sans ~ les fruits** this diet places no restriction on the consumption of fruit; **ce pays accueille sans ~ les immigrants** this country allows unrestricted entry to *ou* has an open door policy towards immigrants

restructuration [ʀəstʀyktyʀasjɔ̃] NF *(gén, Écon)* restructuring; **notre groupe est en pleine ~** our company is going through a major restructuring (programme); **la ~ du quartier** the reorganization of the area

restructurer [ʀəstʀyktyʀe] ▶conjug 1◀ [1] VT [+ *entreprise, industrie, secteur*] to restructure; [+ *quartier*] to reorganize [2] **se restructurer** VPR to restructure

resucée* [ʀ(ə)syse] NF [a] [*boisson*] **veux-tu une ~ de whisky?** would you like another drop *ou* shot of whisky? [b] *(fig)* [*film, musique, théorie*] rehash*

résultante [ʀezyltɑ̃t] NF *(Sci)* resultant; *(fig = conséquence)* outcome, result, consequence

▼**résultat** [ʀezylta] NM [a] *(= conséquence)* result, outcome; **cette tentative a eu des ~s désastreux** this attempt had disastrous results *ou* a disastrous outcome; **cette démarche eut pour ~ une amélioration de la situation** this measure resulted in *ou* led to an improvement in the situation; **on l'a laissé seul ... il a fait des bêtises** we left him alone, and what happens? — he goes and does something silly; **il n'y a que le ~ qui compte** the only thing that matters is the result [b] *(= chose obtenue, réalisation)* result; **c'est un ~ remarquable** it is a remarkable result *ou* achievement; **il a promis d'obtenir des ~s** he promised to get results; *(iro)* **beau ~!** well done! *(iro)*; **il essaya, sans ~, de le convaincre** he tried to convince him but to no effect *ou* avail; **le traitement fut sans ~** the treatment had no effect *ou* didn't work [c] *(= solution)* [*addition, problème*] result [d] *(= classement)* [*élection, examen*] results; **et maintenant, les ~s sportifs** and now for the sports results; **le ~ des courses** *(Sport)* the racing results; *(fig)* the upshot; **voici quelques ~s partiels de l'élection** here are some of the election results so far [e] *(Fin gén)* result; *(= chiffres)* figures; *(= bénéfices)* profit; *(= revenu)* income; *(= gains)* earnings; **~s** results; **~ bénéficiaire** profit; **~ net** net profit *ou* income *ou* earnings; **~ brut d'exploitation** gross trading profit

résulter [ʀezylte] ▶conjug 1◀ [1] VI **~ de** to result from, be the result of; **rien de bon ne peut en ~** no good can come of it; **les avantages économiques qui en résultent** the resulting economic benefits; **ce qui a résulté de la discussion est que ...** the result *ou* outcome of the discussion was that ..., what came out of the discussion was that ... [2] VB IMPERS **il résulte de tout ceci que ...** the result of all this is that ...; **il en résulte que c'est impossible** the result is that it's impossible; **qu'en résultera-t-il?** what will be the result? *ou* outcome?

▼**résumé** [ʀezyme] NM *(= texte, ouvrage)* summary; **« ~ des chapitres précédents »** "the

➤ GRAMMAIRE ACTIVE: **résultat** 53.4 **résumé** 53.4

story so far"; (*Radio, TV*) **~ des informations** news roundup; **en ~** (= *en bref*) in short, in brief; (= *pour conclure*) to sum up; (= *en miniature*) in miniature; **faire un ~ de** to sum up, give a brief summary of

▼ **résumer** [Rezyme] ▶conjug 1◀ ① VT (= *abréger*) to summarize; (= *récapituler, aussi Jur*) to sum up; (= *symboliser*) to epitomize, typify ② **se résumer** VPR a [*personne*] to sum up (one's ideas) b (= *être contenu*) **les faits se résument en quelques mots** the facts can be summed up *ou* summarized in a few words c (= *se réduire à*) **se ~ à** to amount to, come down to, boil down to; **l'affaire se résume à peu de chose** the affair amounts to *ou* comes down to nothing really

résurgence [Rezyrʒɑ̃s] NF (*Géol*) reappearance (of river), resurgence; [*idée, mythe*] resurgence

résurgent, e [Rezyrʒɑ̃, ɑ̃t] ADJ (*Géol*) [*eaux*] re-emergent

resurgir [R(ə)syrʒir] ▶conjug 2◀ VI [*cours d'eau*] to come up again, resurface; [*personne, passé, souvenir*] to resurface; [*problème, idée, débat, menace*] to resurface, re-emerge; [*conflit*] to blow up again

résurrection [Rezyrɛksjɔ̃] NF [*mort*] resurrection; (*fig = renouveau*) revival; (*Rel*) **la Résurrection** the Resurrection; **c'est une véritable ~!** he has really come back to life!

retable [Rətabl] NM altarpiece, reredos

▼ **rétablir** [Retablir] ▶conjug 2◀ ① VT a [+ *courant, communications*] to restore b [+ *démocratie, monarchie*] to restore, re-establish; [+ *droit, ordre, équilibre, confiance, forces, santé*] to restore; [+ *fait, vérité*] to re-establish; [+ *cessez-le-feu, paix*] to restore; **~ les relations diplomatiques** to restore diplomatic relations; **~ la situation** to rectify the situation, get the situation back to normal; **il était mené 5 jeux à rien mais il a réussi à ~ la situation** he was losing 5 games to love but managed to pull back c (= *réintégrer*) to reinstate; **~ qn dans ses fonctions** to reinstate sb in *ou* restore sb to their post; **~ qn dans ses droits** to restore sb's rights d (= *guérir*) **~ qn** to restore sb to health, bring about sb's recovery ② **se rétablir** VPR a [*personne, économie*] to recover; **il s'est vite rétabli** he soon recovered b (= *revenir*) [*silence, calme*] to return, be restored c (*Sport*) to pull o.s. up (*onto a ledge etc*)

▼ **rétablissement** [Retablismɑ̃] NM a [*courant, communications*] restoring; [*démocratie, monarchie, droit, ordre, équilibre, forces, santé*] restoration; [*fait, vérité*] re-establishment; [*cessez-le-feu*] restoration; **~ des relations diplomatiques** restoring diplomatic relations b [*personne, économie*] recovery; **en vous souhaitant un prompt ~** with my (*ou* our) good wishes for your swift recovery, hoping you will be better soon; **tous nos vœux de prompt ~** our best wishes for a speedy recovery c (*Sport*) **faire** *ou* **opérer un ~** to do a pull-up (*into a standing position, onto a ledge etc*)

retailler [R(ə)taje] ▶conjug 1◀ VT [+ *diamant, vêtement*] to re-cut; [+ *crayon*] to sharpen; [+ *arbre*] to (re-)prune

rétamage [Retamaʒ] NM re-coating, re-tinning (*of pans*)

rétamé, e: [Retame] (*ptp de* **rétamer**) ADJ (= *fatigué*) worn out*, knackered: (*Brit*); (= *ivre*) plastered:, sloshed:; (= *détruit, démoli*) wiped out:; (= *sans argent*) broke*; (= *mort*) **il a été ~ en un mois** he was dead within a month, he was a goner within a month:

rétamer [Retame] ▶conjug 1◀ VT a [+ *casseroles*] to re-coat, re-tin b :(= *fatiguer*) to wear out*, knacker: (*Brit*); (= *rendre ivre*) to knock out:; (= *démolir*) to wipe out:; (=

dépouiller au jeu) to clean out*; (*à un examen*) to flunk*; **se faire ~ au poker** to be cleaned out* at poker ② **se rétamer:** VPR [*candidat*] to flunk*; (= *tomber*) **se ~ (par terre)** to take a dive*, crash to the ground; **la voiture s'est rétamée contre un arbre** the car crashed into a tree

rétameur [Retamœr] NM tinker

retapage [R(ə)tapaʒ] NM [*maison, vêtement*] doing up; [*voiture*] fixing up; [*lit*] straightening

retape: [R(ə)tap] NF **faire (de) la ~** [*prostituée*] to walk the streets*, be on the game: (*Brit*); [*agent publicitaire*] to tout (around) for business; **faire de la ~ pour une compagnie de bateaux-mouches** to tout for a pleasure boat company

retaper [R(ə)tape] ▶conjug 1◀ ① VT a (* = *remettre en état*) [+ *maison, vêtement*] to do up; [+ *voiture*] to fix up; [+ *lit*] to straighten; [+ *malade, personne fatiguée*] to buck up*; **la maison a été entièrement retapée** the house has been entirely redone *ou* redecorated; **ça m'a retapé, ce whisky** that whisky has really bucked me up* b (= *dactylographier*) to re-type, type again ② **se retaper*** VPR a (= *guérir*) to get back on one's feet; **il va se ~ en quelques semaines** he'll be back on his feet in a few weeks b (= *refaire*) **j'ai dû me ~ tout le trajet à pied** I had to walk all the way back; **j'ai dû me ~ la vaisselle** I got lumbered with the washing-up again

retapisser [R(ə)tapise] ▶conjug 1◀ VT (*de papier peint*) [+ *pièce*] to repaper; (*de tissu*) [+ *fauteuil*] to reupholster; **j'ai retapissé la chambre en papier bleu** I repapered the bedroom in blue

retard [R(ə)tar] ① NM a [*personne attendue*] lateness (*NonC*); **ces ~s continuels seront punis** this constant lateness will be punished; **plusieurs ~s dans la même semaine, c'est inadmissible** it won't do being late several times in one week; (*Scol*) **il a eu quatre ~s** he was late four times; (*Scol*) **son ~ m'inquiète** I'm worried that he hasn't arrived yet; **vous avez du ~ ◊ vous êtes en ~** you're late; **vous avez deux heures de ~** *ou* **un ~ de deux heures ◊ vous êtes en ~ de deux heures** you're two hours late; **ça/il m'a mis en ~** it/he made me late; **je me suis mis en ~** I made myself late → **billet** b [*train, concurrent*] delay; **le train est en ~ sur l'horaire** the train is running behind schedule; **un ~ de trois heures a été annoncé sur la ligne Paris-Brest** there will be a delay of three hours *ou* trains will run three hours late on the Paris-Brest line; **le conducteur essayait de combler son ~** the driver was trying to make up the time he had lost; (*Sport*) **être en ~ (de 2 heures/2 km) sur le peloton** to be (2 hours/2 km) behind the pack; (*Sport*) **avoir 2 secondes de ~ sur le champion/le record** to be 2 seconds slower than *ou* behind the champion/outside the record; (*Méd*) **elle a un ~ de règles** her period's late, she's late with her period c (*Horlogerie*) **cette montre a du ~** this watch is slow; **la pendule prend du ~** the clock is slow; **la pendule prend un ~ de 3 minutes par jour** the clock loses 3 minutes a day d (= *non-observation des délais*) delay; **des ~s successifs** a series of delays; **si l'on apporte du ~ dans l'exécution d'une commande** if one is late *ou* if there is a delay in carrying out an order; **paiement en ~** (*effectué*) late payment; (*non effectué*) overdue payment, payment overdue; **vous êtes en ~ pour les inscriptions** *ou* **pour vous inscrire** you are late (in) registering; **il est toujours en ~ pour payer sa cotisation** he is always behind with his subscription; **payer/livrer qch avec ~** *ou* **en ~** to pay/deliver sth late, be late (in) paying/delivering sth; **sans ~** without delay e (*sur un programme*) delay; **nous sommes/les recherches sont en ~ sur le programme** we are/the research is behind schedule; **j'ai du**

travail/courrier en ~ I'm behind with my work/mail, I have a backlog of work/mail; **il avait un ~ scolaire considérable** he had fallen a long way behind at school; **il doit combler son ~ en anglais** he has a lot of ground to make up in English; **j'ai pris du** *ou* **je me suis mis en ~ dans mes révisions** I have fallen behind in *ou* I am behind with my revision f (= *infériorité*) [*pays, peuple*] backwardness; **il est en ~ pour son âge** he's backward for his age; **~ de croissance** [*enfant*] growth retardation; (*Écon*) slow growth; **région en ~** underdeveloped *ou* economically backward region; **ce pays a cent ans de ~ économique** *ou* **est en ~ de cent ans du point de vue économique** this country's economy is one hundred years behind, this country is economically one hundred years behind; **~ industriel** industrial backwardness; **~ mental** backwardness; **être en ~ sur son temps** *ou* **siècle** to be behind the times; **il vit avec un siècle de ~** he's a hundred years behind the times, he's living in the last century; (* *hum*) **tu es en ~ d'un métro** *ou* **d'un train!** ◊ **tu as un métro** *ou* **un train de ~!** (= *tu n'es pas au courant*) you must have been asleep!; (= *tu es lent à comprendre*) you're slow on the uptake!; (= *tu n'es pas branché*) you're behind the times!; **ils sont toujours en ~ d'une guerre** they're always fighting yesterday's battles g (*Mus*) retardation

② ADJ INV (*Pharm*) **insuline/effet ~** delayed insulin/effect

③ COMP ▶ **retard à l'allumage** (*Aut*) retarded spark *ou* ignition; (*fig*) **il a du ~ à l'allumage*** he's a bit slow on the uptake*

retardataire [R(ə)tardatɛr] ① ADJ [*arrivant*] late; [*théorie, méthode*] obsolete, outmoded ② NMF latecomer

retardateur, -trice [R(ə)tardatœr, tris] ① ADJ (*Sci, Tech*) retarding ② NM (*Photo*) self-timer; (*Chim*) retarder

retardé, e [R(ə)tarde] (*ptp de* **retarder**) ADJ (*scolairement*) backward, slow; (*intellectuellement*) retarded, backward; (*économiquement*) backward

retardement [R(ə)tardəmɑ̃] ① NM [*processus, train*] delaying; **manœuvres de ~** delaying tactics ② **à retardement** LOC ADJ [+ *engin, torpille*] with a timing device; [+ *dispositif*] delayed-action (*épith*); (*Photo*) [+ *mécanisme*] self-timing; * [+ *excuses, souhaits*] belated → **bombe** ③ **à retardement** LOC ADV [*comprendre, se fâcher, rire*] after the event, in retrospect; (*péj*) **il comprend tout à ~** he's always a bit slow on the uptake*; (*péj*) **il rit toujours à ~** it always takes him a while to see the joke

retarder [R(ə)tarde] ▶conjug 1◀ ① VT a (= *mettre en retard sur un horaire*) [+ *arrivant, arrivée*] to delay, make late; [+ *personne ou véhicule en chemin*] to delay, hold up; **une visite inattendue m'a retardé** I was delayed by an unexpected visitor; **je ne veux pas vous ~** I don't want to delay you *ou* make you late; **ne te retarde pas (pour ça)** don't make yourself late for that; **il a été retardé par les grèves** he has been delayed *ou* held up by the strikes b (= *mettre en retard sur un programme*) [+ *employé, élève*] to hinder, set back; [+ *opération, vendange, chercheur*] to delay, hold up; **ça l'a retardé dans sa mission/ses études** this has set him back in *ou* hindered him in his mission/his studies c (= *remettre*) [+ *départ, moment, opération*] to delay; [+ *date*] to put back; (*Aut*) [+ *allumage*] to retard; **~ son départ d'une heure** to put back one's departure by an hour, delay one's departure for an hour; **porte à ouverture retardée** door with a time lock; **parachute à ouverture retardée** parachute with fail-safe delayed opening

---

boxed d [+ *montre, réveil*] to put back; **~ l'horloge d'une heure** to put the clock back an hour

boxed 2 VI boxed a [*montre*] to be slow; (*régulièrement*) to lose time; **je retarde (de 10 minutes)** my watch is (10 minutes) slow, I'm (10 minutes) slow

boxed b (= *être à un stade antérieur*) **~ sur son époque** *ou* **temps** *ou* **siècle** to be behind the times boxed c * (= *être dépassé*) to be out of touch, be behind the times*; (= *n'être pas au courant*) **ma voiture? tu retardes, je l'ai vendue il y a deux ans** my car? you're a bit behind the times* *ou* you're a bit out of touch — I sold it two years ago

retâter [ʀ(ə)tɑte] ▸conjug 1◂ boxed 1 VT [+ *objet, pouls*] to feel again boxed 2 VI **~ de*** [+ *prison*] to get another taste of; [+ *métier*] to have another go at

reteindre [ʀ(ə)tɛ̃dʀ] ▸conjug 52◂ VT to dye again, redye

retéléphoner [ʀ(ə)telefɔne] ▸conjug 1◂ VI to phone again, call back; **je lui retéléphonerai demain** I'll phone him again *ou* call him back tomorrow, I'll give him another call tomorrow

retendre [ʀ(ə)tɑ̃dʀ] ▸conjug 41◂ VT boxed a [+ *câble*] to stretch again, pull taut again; [+ *peau, tissu*] to tauten; [+ *cordes de guitare, de raquette*] to (re)tighten boxed b [+ *piège, filets*] to reset, set again boxed c **~ la main à qn** to stretch out one's hand again to sb

retenir [ʀət(ə)niʀ, ʀ(ə)təniʀ] ▸conjug 22◂ boxed 1 VT boxed a (*lit, fig* = *maintenir*) [+ *personne, objet qui glisse*] to hold back; [+ *chien*] to hold back; [+ *cheval*] to rein in, hold back; **~ qn par le bras** to hold sb back by the arm; **il allait tomber, une branche l'a retenu** he was about to fall but a branch held him back; **le barrage retient l'eau** the dam holds back the water; **~ la foule** to hold back the crowd; **il se serait jeté par la fenêtre si on ne l'avait pas retenu** he would have thrown himself out of the window if he hadn't been held back *ou* stopped; **retenez-moi ou je fais un malheur!*** hold me back *ou* stop me or I'll do something I'll regret!; **une certaine timidité le retenait** a certain shyness held him back; **~ qn de faire qch** to keep sb from doing sth, stop sb doing sth; **je ne sais pas ce qui me retient de lui dire ce que je pense** I don't know what keeps me from *ou* stops me telling him what I think

boxed b (= *garder*) [+ *personne*] to keep; **~ qn à dîner** to have sb stay for dinner, keep sb for dinner; **j'ai été retenu** I was kept back *ou* detained *ou* held up; **il m'a retenu une heure** he kept me for an hour; **si tu veux partir, je ne te retiens pas** if you want to leave, I won't hold you back *ou* stop you; **c'est la maladie de sa femme qui l'a retenu à Brest** it was his wife's illness that detained him in Brest; **son travail le retenait ailleurs** his work detained *ou* kept him elsewhere; **la grippe l'a retenu au lit/à la maison** flu kept him in bed/at home; **~ qn prisonnier/en otage** to hold sb prisoner/hostage

boxed c (= *empêcher de se dissiper*) [+ *eau d'infiltration, odeur*] to retain; [+ *chaleur*] to retain, keep in; [+ *lumière*] to reflect; **cette terre retient l'eau** this soil retains water; **le noir retient la chaleur** black retains the heat *ou* keeps in the heat

boxed d (= *fixer*) [*clou, nœud*] to hold; **c'est un simple clou qui retient le tableau au mur** there's just a nail holding the picture on the wall; **un ruban retenait ses cheveux** a ribbon kept *ou* held her hair in place, her hair was tied up with a ribbon

boxed e **~ l'attention de qn** to hold sb's attention; **ce détail retient l'attention** this detail holds one's attention; (*frm*) **votre demande a retenu toute notre attention** your request has been given full consideration

boxed f (= *louer, réserver*) [+ *chambre, place, table*] to book, reserve; [+ *date*] to reserve, set aside; [+

domestique] to engage

boxed g (= *se souvenir de*) [+ *donnée, leçon, nom*] to remember; [+ *impression*] to retain; **je n'ai pas retenu son nom/la date** I can't remember his name/the date; **je retiens de cette aventure qu'il est plus prudent de bien s'équiper** I've learnt from this adventure that it's wiser to be properly equipped; **j'en retiens qu'il est pingre et borné, c'est tout** the only thing that stands out *ou* that sticks in my mind is that he's stingy and narrow-minded; **un nom qu'on retient** a name that stays in your mind, a name you remember; **retenez bien ce qu'on vous a dit** don't forget *ou* make sure you remember what you were told; **celui-là, je le retiens!** I'll remember him all right!, I won't forget him in a hurry!; **ah! toi, je te retiens***, **avec tes idées lumineuses!** you and your bright ideas!

boxed h (= *contenir, réprimer*) [+ *cri, larmes*] to hold back *ou* in, suppress; [+ *colère*] to hold back; **~ son souffle** *ou* **sa respiration** to hold one's breath; **il ne put ~ un sourire/un rire** he could not hold back *ou* suppress a smile/a laugh, he could not help smiling/laughing; **il retint les mots qui lui venaient à la bouche** he held back *ou* bit back (*Brit*) the words that came to him

boxed i (*Math*) to carry; **je pose 4 et je retiens 2** 4 down and 2 to carry, put down 4 and carry 2

boxed j (= *garder*) [+ *salaire*] to stop, withhold; [+ *possessions, bagages d'un client*] to retain

boxed k (= *prélever, retrancher*) to deduct, keep back; **ils nous retiennent 1 000 F (sur notre salaire) pour les assurances** they deduct 1,000 francs (from our wages) for insurance; **~ une certaine somme pour la retraite** to deduct a certain sum for a pension scheme; **~ les impôts à la base** to deduct taxes at source

boxed l (= *accepter*) [+ *plan, proposition*] to accept; [+ *candidature, nom*] to retain, accept; (*Jur*) **le jury a retenu la préméditation** the jury accepted the charge of premeditation; **c'est notre projet qui a été retenu** it's our project that has been accepted

boxed 2 **se retenir** VPR boxed a (= *s'accrocher*) **se ~ à qch** to hold on to sth

boxed b (= *se contenir*) to restrain o.s.; (= *s'abstenir*) to stop o.s. (**de faire** doing); (*de faire ses besoins naturels*) to hold on, hold o.s. in; **se ~ de pleurer** *ou* **pour ne pas pleurer** to hold back one's tears; **malgré sa colère, il essaya de se ~** despite his anger, he tried to restrain *ou* contain himself; **il se retint de lui faire remarquer que ...** he refrained from pointing out to him that ...

retenter [ʀ(ə)tɑ̃te] ▸conjug 1◂ VT (*gén*) to try again, make another attempt at, have another go at; [+ *épreuve, saut*] to try again; [+ *action, opération*] to reattempt; **~ sa chance** to try one's luck again; **~ de faire qch** to try to do sth again

rétention [ʀetɑ̃sjɔ̃] NF (*Méd*) retention; **~ d'eau/d'urine** retention of water/of urine; **~ d'informations** withholding information; (*Jur*) **~ administrative** detention (*of asylum seekers*)

retentir [ʀ(ə)tɑ̃tiʀ] ▸conjug 2◂ VI boxed a [*sonnerie*] to ring; [*bruit métallique, cris, détonation, explosion*] to ring out; [*écho, tonnerre*] to reverberate; **à minuit, des explosions retentirent** explosions were heard at midnight; **des tirs sporadiques ont à nouveau retenti dans la ville** sporadic gunfire rang out again in the city; **ces mots retentissent encore à mes oreilles** those words are still ringing *ou* echoing in my ears boxed b (= *résonner de*) **~ de** to ring with, be full of the sound of boxed c (= *affecter*) **~ sur** to have an effect upon, affect

retentissant, e [ʀ(ə)tɑ̃tisɑ̃, ɑ̃t] ADJ boxed a (= *fort, sonore*) [*son, voix*] ringing (*épith*); [*bruit, choc, claque*] resounding (*épith*) boxed b (= *éclatant, frappant*) [*échec, succès*] resounding (*épith*); [*scandale*] tremendous; [*faillite, procès*] spectacular; [*déclaration, discours*] sensational; **son**

film a fait un bide ~* his film was a resounding flop*

retentissement [ʀ(ə)tɑ̃tismɑ̃] NM boxed a (= *répercussion*) repercussion, (after-)effect; **les ~s de l'affaire** the repercussions of the affair boxed b (= *éclat*) stir, effect; **cette nouvelle eut un grand ~ dans l'opinion** this piece of news created a considerable stir in public opinion; **son œuvre fut sans grand ~** his work went virtually unnoticed; **l'affaire a eu un énorme ~ médiatique** the affair created a media sensation boxed c (*littér*) [*son, cloche*] ringing; [*voix*] echoing sound

retenu, e¹ [ʀət(ə)ny] (*ptp de* **retenir**) ADJ (*littér* = *discret*) [*charme, grâce*] reserved, restrained

retenue² [ʀət(ə)ny] NF boxed a (= *prélèvement*) deduction; **opérer une ~ de 10% sur un salaire** to deduct 10% from a salary; **~ pour la retraite** deductions for a pension scheme; **système de ~ à la source** system of deducting income tax at source, ≈ PAYE *ou* pay-as-you-earn system (*Brit*) boxed b (= *modération*) self-control, (self-)restraint; (= *réserve*) reserve; **avoir de la ~** to be reserved; **faire preuve de ~** to show restraint; **parler/s'exprimer sans ~** to talk/express o.s. quite openly; **rire sans ~** to laugh without restraint *ou* unrestrainedly; **il n'a aucune ~ dans ses propos** he shows no restraint in what he says; **il s'est confié à moi sans aucune ~** he confided in me quite freely *ou* unreservedly; **un peu de ~!** show some restraint!, control yourself!; **dans sa colère, elle perdit toute ~** she was so enraged that she lost all self-control boxed c (*Math*) **n'oublie pas la ~** don't forget what to carry (over) boxed d (*Scol*) detention; **être en ~** to be in detention, be kept in; **il les a mis en ~** he kept them in, he gave them detention; **il a eu deux heures de ~** he got two hours' detention, he was kept in for two hours (*after school*) boxed e (*Tech*) **la ~ du barrage** the volume of water behind the dam; **barrage à faible ~** low-volume dam; **bassin de ~** balancing *ou* compensating reservoir boxed f (*Aut* = *embouteillage*) tailback (*Brit*), (traffic) backup (*US*) boxed g (*Naut*) guest rope boxed h (*Constr*) (under)pinning

rétiaire [ʀetjɛʀ] NM (*Antiq*) retiarius

réticence [ʀetisɑ̃s] NF boxed a (= *hésitation*) hesitation, reluctance (*NonC*); **avec ~** reluctantly, grudgingly, with some hesitation; **sans ~** without (any) hesitation; **cette proposition suscite quelques ~s chez les éditeurs** publishers are a bit hesitant about *ou* are reluctant to go along with this proposal; (= *réserve*) **compte tenu des ~s manifestées par les syndicats** given the misgivings *ou* reservations expressed by the unions boxed b († = *omission*) reticence (*NonC*); **parler sans ~** to speak openly, conceal nothing

réticent, e [ʀetisɑ̃, ɑ̃t] ADJ boxed a (= *hésitant*) hesitant, reluctant; **se montrer ~** to be hesitant *ou* reluctant (**pour faire** to do) boxed b (= *réservé*) reticent

réticulaire [ʀetikylɛʀ] ADJ reticular

réticule [ʀetikyl] NM (*Opt*) reticle; (= *sac*) reticule

réticulé, e [ʀetikyle] ADJ (*Anat, Géol*) reticulate; (*Archit*) reticulated

rétif, -ive [ʀetif, iv] ADJ [*animal*] stubborn; [*personne*] rebellious, restive

rétine [ʀetin] NF retina

rétinien, -ienne [ʀetinjɛ̃, jɛn] ADJ retinal

rétinite [ʀetinit] NF retinitis

retirage [ʀ(ə)tiʀaʒ] NM (*Photo, Typo*) reprint

retiré, e [ʀ(ə)tiʀe] (*ptp de* **retirer**) ADJ boxed a (= *solitaire*) [*lieu*] remote, out-of-the-way; [*maison*] isolated; [*vie*] secluded; **vivre ~** ◊ **mener une vie ~e** to live in isolation *ou* seclusion, lead a secluded life; **il vivait ~ du reste du monde** he lived withdrawn *ou* cut off from the rest of the world; **~ quelque part dans le Béarn** living quietly somewhere in the Béarn [b] (= *en retraite*) retired; **~ des affaires** retired from business

retirer [R(ə)tire] ▸ conjug 1 ◂ [1] VT [a] (*lit, fig* = *enlever*) [+ *gants, lunettes, manteau*] to take off, remove; [+ *privilèges*] to withdraw; **~ son collier au chien** to take the dog's collar off, remove the dog's collar; **retire-lui ses chaussures** take his shoes off (for him); **retire-lui ce couteau des mains** take that knife (away) from him; **~ à qn son emploi** to take sb's job away (from them), deprive sb of their job; **~ son permis (de conduire) à qn** to take away *ou* revoke sb's (driving) licence, disqualify sb from driving; **~ une pièce de l'affiche** to take off *ou* close a play; **on lui a retiré la garde des enfants** he was deprived of custody of the children; **je lui ai retiré ma confiance** I don't trust him any more; **~ la parole à qn** to make sb stand down (*Brit*), take the floor from sb (*US*)
[b] (= *sortir*) to take out, remove (**de** from); **~ un bouchon** to pull out *ou* take out *ou* remove a cork; **~ un corps de l'eau/qn de dessous les décombres** to pull a body out of the water/sb out of *ou* out from under the rubble; **~ un plat du four/les bagages du coffre** to take a dish out of the oven/the luggage out of the boot; **ils ont retiré leur fils du lycée** they have taken their son away from *ou* removed their son from the school; **se faire ~ une dent** to have a tooth out; **je ne peux pas ~ la clé de la serrure** I can't get the key out of the lock; **retire les mains de tes poches** take your hands out of your pockets; **on lui retirera difficilement de l'idée** *ou* **de la tête qu'il est menacé*** we'll have difficulty *ou* a job convincing him that he's not being threatened
[c] (= *reprendre possession de*) [+ *bagages, billets réservés*] to collect, pick up; [+ *argent en dépôt*] to withdraw, take out; [+ *gage*] to redeem; **~ de l'argent (de la banque)** to withdraw money (from the bank), take money out (of the bank); **votre commande est prête à être retirée** your order is now awaiting collection *ou* ready for collection
[d] (= *ramener en arrière*) to take away, remove, withdraw; **~ sa tête/sa main (pour éviter un coup)** to remove *ou* withdraw one's head/one's hand (to avoid being hit); **il retira prestement sa main** he whisked *ou* snatched his hand away
[e] (= *annuler*) [+ *candidature*] to withdraw; [+ *accusation, plainte*] to withdraw, take back; **je retire ce que j'ai dit** I take back what I said; (*Pol*) **~ sa candidature** to withdraw one's candidature, stand down (*Brit*); **~ un produit du commerce** *ou* **du marché** to take a product off the market
[f] (= *obtenir*) [+ *avantages*] to get, gain *ou* derive (**de** from); **les bénéfices qu'on en retire** the profits to be had *ou* gained from it; **il en a retiré un grand profit** he profited *ou* gained greatly by it; **il n'en a retiré que des ennuis** it caused him nothing but trouble; **tout ce qu'il en a retiré, c'est ...** the only thing he has got out of it is ..., all he has gained is ...
[g] (= *extraire*) [+ *extrait, huile, minerai*] to obtain; **une substance dont on retire une huile précieuse** a substance from which a valuable oil is obtained
[h] (*Photo*) to reprint; **faire ~ des photos** to have reprints of one's photographs done

[2] **se retirer** VPR [a] (= *partir*) to retire, withdraw; (= *aller se coucher*) to retire (to bed); (= *prendre sa retraite*) to retire; (= *retirer sa candidature*) to withdraw, stand down (*Brit*) (**en faveur de** in favour of); **se ~ discrètement** to withdraw discreetly; **ils se sont retirés dans un coin pour discuter affaires** they withdrew *ou* retired to a corner to talk business; **se ~**

dans sa chambre to go *ou* withdraw (*frm*) *ou* retire (*frm*) to one's room; (*fig*) **se ~ dans sa tour d'ivoire** to take refuge *ou* lock o.s. up in an ivory tower; **ils ont décidé de se ~ à la campagne** they've decided to retire to the country; **elle s'est retirée dans un couvent** she retired *ou* withdrew to a convent
[b] (= *reculer*: *pour laisser passer qn, éviter un coup*) to move out of the way; [*troupes*] to withdraw; [*marée, mer*] to recede, go back, ebb; [*eaux d'inondation*] to recede, go down; [*glacier*] to recede; **retire-toi d'ici** *ou* **de là, tu me gênes** stand somewhere else — you're in my way
[c] (= *quitter*) **se ~ de** to withdraw from; **se ~ d'une compétition/d'un marché** to withdraw from a competition/from a market; **se ~ des affaires** to retire from business; **se ~ du monde** to withdraw from society; **se ~ de la partie** to drop out

retombant, e [R(ə)tɔ̃bɑ̃, ɑ̃t] ADJ [*moustache*] drooping; [*branches*] hanging; **plantes à port ~** hanging plants

retombée [R(ə)tɔ̃be] NF [a] **~s (radioactives** *ou* **atomiques)** (radioactive) fallout (*NonC*)
[b] (*gén pl* = *répercussion*) [*scandale*] consequence, effect; [*invention*] spin-off; **les ~s financières d'une opération** the financial spin-offs of a deal; **l'accord a eu des ~s économiques immédiates** the agreement had an immediate knock-on effect on the economy *ou* immediate economic repercussions; **le gouvernement redoute les ~s médiatiques de l'événement** the government is concerned about the effects media coverage of this event might have [c] (*Archit*) spring, springing

retomber [R(ə)tɔ̃be] ▸ conjug 1 ◂ VI [a] (= *faire une nouvelle chute*) to fall again; **le lendemain, il est retombé dans la piscine** the next day he fell into the swimming pool again; **~ dans la misère** to fall on hard times again; **~ dans le découragement** to lose heart again; **~ dans l'erreur/le péché** to fall back *ou* lapse into error/sin; **son roman est retombé dans l'oubli** his novel has sunk back into oblivion; **le pays retomba dans la guerre civile** the country lapsed into civil war again; **je vais ~ dans l'ennui** I'll start being bored again; **la conversation retomba sur le même sujet** the conversation turned once again *ou* came round again to the same subject
[b] (= *redevenir*) **~ amoureux/enceinte/malade** to fall in love/get pregnant/fall ill again; **ils sont retombés d'accord** they reached agreement again
[c] [*neige, pluie*] to fall again, come down again; **la neige retombait de plus belle** the snow was falling again still more heavily
[d] (= *tomber après s'être élevé*) [*personne*] to land; [*chose lancée, liquide*] to come down; [*gâteau, soufflé*] to collapse; [*abattant, capot, herse*] to fall back down; [*fusée, missile*] to land, come back to earth; [*conversation*] to fall away, die; [*intérêt*] to fall away, fall off; (*Pol*) [*tension*] to subside; [*vent*] to subside, die down; [*silence*] to fall *ou* descend again; (*fig*) **~ comme un soufflé** to fade away to nothing; **il est retombé lourdement (sur le dos)** he landed heavily (on his back); **elle saute bien mais elle ne sait pas ~** she can jump well but she doesn't know how to land; **le chat retombe toujours sur ses pattes** cats always land on their feet; (*fig*) **il retombera toujours sur ses pattes** *ou* **pieds** he'll always land *ou* fall on his feet; **se laisser ~ sur son oreiller** to fall back *ou* sink back onto one's pillow; (*Sport*) **laissez ~ les bras** let your arms drop *ou* fall (by your sides); **il laissa ~ le rideau** he let the curtain fall back; **l'eau retombait en cascades** the water fell back in cascades; (*fig*) **ça lui est retombé sur le nez*** it backfired on him; **le brouillard est retombé en fin de matinée** the fog fell again *ou* came down again *ou* closed

in again towards lunchtime; **l'inflation est retombée à 4%** inflation has fallen to 4%
[e] (= *pendre*) [*cheveux, rideaux*] to fall, hang (down); **de petites boucles blondes retombaient sur son front** little blond curls tumbled *ou* fell onto her forehead
[f] (= *échoir à*) **la responsabilité retombera sur toi** the responsibility will fall *ou* land on you; **les frais retomberont sur nous** we were landed* *ou* saddled with the expense; **faire ~ sur qn la responsabilité de qch/les frais de qch** to pass the responsibility for sth/the cost of sth on to sb, land* sb with the responsibility for sth/the cost of sth; **ça va me ~ dessus*** (*gén*) I'll get the blame *ou* take the flak* (for it); [*travail*] I'll get lumbered *ou* landed with it*; **le péché du père retombera sur la tête des enfants** the sins of the fathers will be visited on the sons
[g] **Noël retombe un samedi** Christmas falls on a Saturday again; **~ en enfance** to lapse into second childhood; **je suis retombé sur lui le lendemain, au même endroit** I came across him again the next day in the same place; **ils nous sont retombés dessus le lendemain** they landed* on us again the next day

retordre [R(ə)tɔRdR] ▸ conjug 41 ◂ VT [+ *câbles*] to twist again; [+ *linge*] to wring (out) again → **fil**

rétorquer [RetɔRke] ▸ conjug 1 ◂ VT to retort

retors, e [Rətɔr, ɔRs] ADJ [a] (*Tex*) **fil ~** twisted yarn [b] (= *rusé*) sly, wily, underhand

rétorsion [RetɔRsjɔ̃] NF (*frm, Jur, Pol*) retortion, retaliation; **user de ~ envers un État** to retaliate *ou* use retortion against a state → **mesure**

retouche [R(ə)tuʃ] NF [*photo, peinture*] touching up (*NonC*); [*texte, vêtement*] alteration; **faire une ~ à une photo** to touch up a photo; **faire une ~ (à une photo, une peinture)** to do some touching up; (*à un vêtement*) to make an alteration

retoucher [R(ə)tuʃe] ▸ conjug 1 ◂ [1] VT [a] (= *améliorer*) [+ *peinture, photo*] to touch up, retouch; [+ *texte, vêtement*] to alter, make alterations to; **il faudra ~ cette veste au col** this jacket will have to be altered at the neck; **on voit tout de suite que cette photo est retouchée** you can see straight away that this photo has been touched up [b] (= *toucher de nouveau*) to touch again; (= *blesser de nouveau*) to hit again [2] VI **~ à qch** to touch sth again; **s'il retouche à ma sœur, gare à lui !** if he lays hands on *ou* touches my sister again he'd better look out!; **je n'ai plus jamais retouché à l'alcool** I never touched a drop of alcohol again

retoucheur, -euse [R(ə)tuʃœr, øz] NM,F **~ (en confection)** dressmaker in charge of alterations; **~ photographe** retoucher

retour [R(ə)tur] [1] NM [a] (= *fait d'être revenu*) (*gén*) return; (*à la maison*) homecoming, return home; (= *chemin, trajet*) return (journey), way back, journey back; (= *billet*) return (ticket); **il fallait déjà penser au ~** it was already time to think about going back *ou* about the return journey; **être sur le ~ (chemin du) ~** to be on one's way back; **pendant le ~** on the way back, during the return journey (*Brit*), on our trip *ou* journey back (*Brit*); **elle n'a pas assez pour payer son ~** she hasn't enough to pay for her return trip *ou* journey (*Brit*); **(être) de ~ (de)** to be back (from); **à votre ~, écrivez-nous** write to us when you are *ou* get back; **à leur ~, ils trouvèrent la maison vide** when they got back *ou* on their return, they found the house empty; **de ~ à la maison** back home; **au ~ de notre voyage** when we got back from our trip *ou* journey (*Brit*); **à son ~ d'Afrique/du service militaire** on his return *ou* on returning from Africa/from military service → **cheval**
[b] (*à un état antérieur*) **~ à** return to; **le ~ à une vie normale** the return *ou* reversion to (a) normal life; **ils considèrent le ~ à l'emploi comme**

une priorité they believe that getting people back to work is a priority; **~ à la nature/la terre** return to nature/the land; **~ aux sources** (*gén: aux origines*) return to basics; (*à la nature*) return to the basic *ou* simple life; (*à son village natal*) return to one's roots; **~ à la normale** return to normal; **~ au calme/à l'Antiquité** return to a state of calm/to Antiquity; **son ~ à la politique** his return to politics, his political comeback

c (*= réapparition*) return; (*= répétition régulière*) [*cadence, motif, thème*] recurrence; **le ~ du printemps/de la paix** the return of spring/of peace; **on prévoit un ~ du froid** a return of the cold weather is forecast; **un ~ offensif de la grippe** a renewed outbreak of flu

d (*Comm, Poste*) [*emballage, objets invendus, récipient*] return; **à l'envoyeur** *ou* **à l'expéditeur** return to sender; **avec faculté de ~** on approval, on sale or return; (*Fin*) **clause de ~** no protest clause

e (*Jur*) **(droit de) ~** reversion

f (*littér = changement d'avis*) change of heart; (*= revirements*) **~s** reversals; **les ~s de la fortune** the turns of fortune; **un ~ soudain dans l'opinion publique** a sudden turnabout in public opinion

g (*Tech*) [*chariot de machine, pièce mobile*] return; (*= partie de bureau*) (desk) extension; (*Ordin*) **touche ~** return key

h (*Élec*) **à la terre** *ou* **à la masse** earth (*Brit*) *ou* ground (*US*) return

i (*Tennis*) return; **~ de service** return of service *ou* serve; (*Sport*) **match ~** return match, second *ou* return leg

j (*Fin*) return; **~ sur investissements** return on investments

k (*loc*) **en ~** in return; **choc** *ou* **effet en ~** backlash; **bâtiment en ~ (d'équerre)** building constructed at right angles; (*péj*) **être sur le ~*** to be over the hill*, be a bit past it* (*Brit*); **faire ~ à** to revert to; **par un juste ~ des choses, il a été cette fois récompensé** events went his way *ou* fate was fair to him this time and he got his just reward; **par un juste ~ des choses, il a été puni** he was punished, which served him right; **par ~ (du courrier)** by return (of post); **sans ~** [*partir*] for ever; **voyage sans ~** journey from which there is no return; **faire un ~ sur soi-même** to take stock of o.s., do some soul-searching → **payer**

2 COMP ► **retour d'âge** change of life ► **retour en arrière** (*Ciné, Littérat*) flashback; (*= souvenir*) look back; (*= mesure rétrograde*) retreat; **faire un ~ en arrière** to take a look back, look back; (*Ciné*) to flash back ► **retour de bâton** (*= contrecoup*) backlash; **ils ont dépensé sans compter pendant des années, maintenant c'est le ~ de bâton** they spent money recklessly for years — but now the chickens are coming home to roost ► **retour de couches** first period (after pregnancy), return of menstruation ► **retour éternel** (*Philo*) eternal recurrence ► **retour de flamme** (*dans un moteur*) backfire; (*fig*) rekindling of passion; (*feu*) **il y a eu un ~ de flamme** the flames leapt up ► **retour en force: il y a eu un ~ en force du racisme** racism is back with a vengeance; **on assiste à un ~ en force de leur parti sur la scène politique** their party is making a big comeback ► **retour de manivelle** (*lit*) kick; (*fig*) **il y aura un ~ de manivelle** it'll backfire (on them)

retourne [ʀ(ə)tuʀn] NF (*Cartes*) card turned over to determine the trump

retournement [ʀ(ə)tuʀnəmɑ̃] NM [*situation, opinion publique*] reversal (**de** of), turnaround (**de** in)

retourner [ʀ(ə)tuʀne] ►conjug 1◄ 1 VT (*avec aux avoir*) a (*= mettre dans l'autre sens*) [+ *caisse, seau*] to turn upside down; [+ *matelas*] to turn (over); [+ *carte*] to turn up *ou* over; [+ *omelette, poisson, viande*] to turn over; [+ *crêpe*]

(*avec une spatule*) to turn over; (*en lançant*) to toss; **~ un tableau/une carte contre le mur** to turn a picture/a map against the wall; (*fig*) **elle l'a retourné (comme une crêpe** *ou* **un gant)*** she soon changed his mind for him; **~ la situation** to reverse the situation, turn the situation round

b (*en remuant, secouant*) [+ *sol, terre*] to turn over; [+ *salade*] to toss; [+ *foin*] to toss, turn (over)

c (*= mettre l'intérieur à l'extérieur*) [+ *parapluie, sac, vêtement*] to turn inside out; (*Couture*) [+ *col, vêtement*] to turn; **~ ses poches pour trouver qch** to turn one's pockets inside out *ou* turn out one's pockets to find sth; **son col/revers est retourné** (*par mégarde*) his collar/lapel is turned up → **veste**

d (*= orienter dans le sens opposé*) [+ *mot, phrase*] to turn round; **~ un argument contre qn** to turn an argument back on sb *ou* against sb; **il retourna le pistolet contre lui-même** he turned the gun on himself; **~ un compliment** to return a compliment; **je pourrais vous ~ votre critique** I could criticize you in the same way

e (*= renvoyer*) [+ *lettre, marchandise*] to return, send back

f (** fig = bouleverser*) [+ *maison, pièce*] to turn upside down; [+ *personne*] to shake; **il a tout retourné dans la maison pour retrouver ce livre** he turned the whole house upside down to find that book; **la nouvelle l'a complètement retourné** the news has severely shaken him; **ce spectacle m'a retourné** seeing it gave me quite a turn*

g (*= tourner plusieurs fois*) **~ une pensée/une idée dans sa tête** to turn a thought/an idea over (and over) in one's mind; (*fig*) **~ le couteau** *ou* **le poignard dans la plaie** to twist the knife in the wound → **tourner**

2 VI (*avec aux être*) a (*= aller à nouveau*) to return, go back; **~ en Italie/à la mer** to return *ou* go back to Italy/to the seaside; **je devrai ~ chez le médecin** I'll have to go back to the doctor's; **~ en arrière** *ou* **sur ses pas** to turn back, retrace one's steps; **il retourne demain à son travail/à l'école** he's going back to work/to school tomorrow; **elle est retournée chez elle chercher son parapluie** she went back home to get her umbrella

b (*à un état antérieur*) **~ à** to return to, go back to; **~ à la vie sauvage** to revert *ou* go back to the wild state; **~ à Dieu** to return to God; **il est retourné à son ancien métier/à la physique** he's gone back to his old job/to physics

c (*= être restitué*) **la maison retournera à son frère** the house will revert to his brother

3 VB IMPERS **nous voudrions bien savoir de quoi il retourne** we should really like to know what is going on *ou* what it's all about

4 **se retourner** VPR a [*personne couchée*] to turn over; [*automobiliste, véhicule*] to turn over, overturn; [*bateau*] to capsize, keel over, overturn; **se ~ sur le dos/le ventre** to turn (over) onto one's back/one's stomach; **se ~ dans son lit toute la nuit** to toss and turn all night in bed; (*hum*) **il doit se ~ dans sa tombe!** he must be turning in his grave! (*hum*); **la voiture s'est retournée** *ou* **ils se sont retournés (dans un fossé)** the car *ou* they overturned (into a ditch); (*fig*) **laissez-lui le temps de se ~** give him time to sort himself out; (*fig*) **il sait se ~** he knows how to cope

b (*= tourner la tête*) to turn round; **partir sans se ~** to leave without looking back *ou* without a backward glance; **tout le monde se retournait sur lui** *ou* **sur son passage** everyone turned round as he went by

c (*fig*) [*situation*] to be reversed, be turned round; **se ~ contre qn** [*personne*] to turn against sb; [*acte, situation*] to backfire on sb, rebound on sb; (*Jur = poursuivre*) to take (court) action *ou* proceedings against sb; **il ne savait vers qui se ~** he didn't know who to

turn to

d (*= tordre*) [+ *pouce*] to wrench, twist

e (*littér*) **s'en ~** (*= cheminer*) to journey back; (*= partir*) to depart, leave; **il s'en retourna comme il était venu** he left as he had come; **s'en ~ dans son pays (natal)** to return to one's native country

retracer [ʀ(ə)tʀase] ►conjug 3◄ VT a (*= raconter*) [+ *histoire, vie*] to relate, recount; **le film retrace la carrière de l'artiste** the film goes back over *ou* traces the artist's career

b (*= tracer à nouveau*) [+ *trait effacé*] to redraw, draw again

rétractable [ʀetʀaktabl] ADJ (*Jur*) revocable; **crayon à pointe ~** retractable pencil; **volant ~ (en cas de choc)** collapsible steering wheel; (*Ordin*) **clavier ~** pull-out keyboard; **emballé sous film ~** shrink-wrapped

rétractation [ʀetʀaktasjɔ̃] NF [*aveux, promesse, témoignage*] retraction, withdrawal

rétracter [ʀetʀakte] ►conjug 1◄ 1 VT a (*= contracter, rentrer*) [+ *griffe*] to draw in, retract

b (*littér = revenir sur*) [+ *parole, opinion*] to retract, withdraw, take back 2 **se rétracter** VPR a (*= se retirer*) [*griffe, antenne*] to retract; (*fig littér*) **au moindre reproche, elle se rétractait** she would shrink at the slightest reproach b (*= se dédire, Jur*) to retract, withdraw one's statement; **je ne veux pas avoir l'air de me ~** I don't want to appear to back down

rétractile [ʀetʀaktil] ADJ retractile

rétraction [ʀetʀaksjɔ̃] NF (*Méd*) retraction

retraduction [ʀ(ə)tʀadyksjɔ̃] NF retranslation

retraduire [ʀ(ə)tʀadɥiʀ] ►conjug 38◄ VT (*= traduire de nouveau*) to retranslate, translate again; (*= traduire dans la langue de départ*) to translate back

retrait [ʀ(ə)tʀɛ] NM a (*= départ*) [*mer*] ebb; [*eaux, glacier*] retreat; [*candidat, candidature, troupes*] withdrawal; **on vient d'annoncer le ~ du marché de ce produit** it's just been announced that this product has been withdrawn from sale *ou* taken off the market

b [*somme d'argent*] withdrawal; [*bagages*] collection; [*objet en gage*] redemption; **le ~ des bagages peut se faire à toute heure** luggage may be collected at any time; **faire un ~ de 500F** to withdraw 500 francs; **~ à vue** withdrawal on demand

c (*= suppression*) [*demande, projet*] withdrawal; **~ du permis (de conduire)** disqualification from driving, driving ban, revocation of a driving licence; **il a eu un ~ de deux points** his licence was endorsed with two points; (*Admin*) **~ d'emploi** deprivation of office; (*Jur*) **~ de plainte** nonsuit; **les étudiants réclament le ~ du projet de loi** the students are demanding that the bill be withdrawn *ou* shelved

d (*= rétrécissement*) [*ciment*] shrinkage, contraction; [*tissu*] shrinkage; **il y a du ~** there's some shrinkage

e (*loc*) **situé en ~** set back; **se tenant en ~** standing back; **en ~ de** set back from; **une petite maison, un peu en ~ de la route** a little house, set back a bit from the road; **rester en ~** [*personne*] to stay in the background; **ces propositions sont en ~ sur les précédentes** these offers do not go as far as the previous ones; **notre chiffre d'affaires est en léger ~ par rapport aux années précédentes** our turnover is slightly down *ou* has fallen slightly compared to previous years

retraite [ʀ(ə)tʀɛt] 1 NF a (*Mil = fuite*) retreat; **battre/sonner la ~** to beat/sound the retreat; **battre en ~** to beat a retreat

b (*= cessation de travail*) retirement; **être en** *ou* **à la ~** to be retired *ou* in retirement; **travailleur en ~** retired worker, pensioner; **mettre qn à la ~** to pension sb off, superannuate sb; **mise à la ~ (d'office)** (compulsory) retirement; **mettre qn à la ~ d'office** to make sb take compulsory retirement; **prendre sa ~** to retire, go into retirement; **prendre une ~ anticipée** to retire early, take early retirement; **pour lui, c'est la ~ forcée** he has had retirement forced on him, he has had to retire early ⓒ (= *pension*) pension; **toucher** *ou* **percevoir une petite ~** to receive *ou* draw a small pension → **caisse, maison** ⓓ (*littér = refuge*) [*poète, amants*] retreat, refuge; [*ours, loup*] lair; [*voleurs*] hideout, hiding place ⓔ (*Rel = récollection*) retreat; **faire** *ou* **suivre une ~** to be in retreat, go into retreat ⓕ (*Constr*) tapering ❷ COMP ▶ **retraite des cadres** management pension ▶ **retraite par capitalisation** self-funded retirement scheme (*Brit*) *ou* plan (*US*) ▶ **retraite complémentaire** supplementary pension ▶ **retraite aux flambeaux** torchlight procession ▶ **retraite par répartition** contributory pension scheme (*Brit*) *ou* plan (*US*) ▶ **retraite des vieux**†* (old age) pension ▶ **retraite des vieux travailleurs** retirement pension

retraité, e [ʀ(ə)tʀete] ❶ ADJ ⓐ [*personne*] retired ⓑ [*déchets*] reprocessed ❷ NM,F (*old age*) pensioner; **les ~s** retired people, pensioners; **~s actifs** active retired people

retraitement [ʀ(ə)tʀetmã] NM reprocessing; **usine de ~ des déchets nucléaires** nuclear reprocessing plant

retraiter [ʀ(ə)tʀete] ▶ conjug 1 ◀ VT to reprocess

retranchement [ʀ(ə)tʀãʃmã] NM (*Mil*) entrenchment, retrenchment; (*fig*) **pousser qn dans ses derniers ~s** to drive *ou* hound sb into a corner; **poussé dans ses derniers ~s, il dut admettre les faits** he was driven into a corner and had to admit the facts

retrancher [ʀ(ə)tʀãʃe] ▶ conjug 1 ◀ ❶ VT ⓐ (= *enlever*) [+ *quantité*] to take away, subtract (**de** from); [+ *somme d'argent*] to deduct, dock, take off; [+ *passage, mot*] to take out, remove, omit (**de** from); **~ 10 de 15** to take 10 (away) from 15, subtract 10 from 15; **~ une somme d'un salaire** to deduct *ou* dock a sum from a salary; **si l'on retranche ceux qui n'ont pas de licence** if you leave out *ou* omit the non-graduates; (*hum*) **ils étaient décidés à me ~ du monde des vivants** they were set on removing me from the land of the living ⓑ (*littér = couper*) [+ *chair gangrenée*] to remove, cut off; [+ *organe malade*] to remove, cut out ⓒ (*littér = séparer*) to cut off; **son argent le retranchait des autres** his money cut him off from other people ⓓ († *Mil = fortifier*) to entrench ❷ **se retrancher** VPR ⓐ (*Mil = se fortifier*) **se ~ derrière/dans** to entrench o.s. behind/in; **se ~ sur une position** to entrench o.s. in a position ⓑ (*fig*) **se ~ dans son mutisme** to take refuge in silence; **se ~ dans sa douleur** to shut o.s. away with one's grief; **se ~ derrière la loi/le secret professionnel** to take refuge behind *ou* hide behind the law/professional secrecy

retranscription [ʀ(ə)tʀãskʀipsjɔ̃] NF (= *action*) retranscription; (= *résultat*) new transcript

retranscrire [ʀ(ə)tʀãskʀiʀ] ▶ conjug 39 ◀ VT to retranscribe

retransmettre [ʀ(ə)tʀãsmetʀ] ▶ conjug 56 ◀ VT ⓐ [+ *match, émission, concert*] (*Radio*) to broadcast, relay; (*TV*) to show, broadcast, relay; **~ qch en différé** (*Radio*) to broadcast a recording of sth; (*TV*) to show *ou* broadcast a recording of sth; **~ qch en direct** (*Radio*) to relay *ou* broadcast sth live; (*TV*) to show *ou* broadcast sth live; **retransmis par satellite** relayed by satellite ⓑ [+ *nouvelle, ordre*] to pass on

retransmission [ʀ(ə)tʀãsmisjɔ̃] NF ⓐ [*match, émission, concert*] (*Radio*) broadcast; (*TV*) broadcast, showing; **~ en direct/différé** live/

recorded broadcast; **la ~ du match aura lieu à 23 heures** the match will be shown at 11 p.m ⓑ [*nouvelle, ordre*] passing on

retravailler [ʀ(ə)tʀavaje] ▶ conjug 1 ◀ ❶ VI ⓐ (= *recommencer le travail*) to start work again; **il retravaille depuis le mois dernier** he has been back at work since last month ⓑ (= *se remettre à*) **~ à qch** to start work on sth again, work at sth again ❷ VT [+ *question*] to give (some) more thought to; [+ *discours, ouvrage*] to work on again; [+ *pâte à pain*] to knead again; [+ *argile*] to work again; [+ *minerai*] to reprocess

retraverser [ʀ(ə)tʀavɛʀse] ▶ conjug 1 ◀ VT (*de nouveau*) to recross; (*dans l'autre sens*) to cross back over

rétréci, e [ʀetʀesi] (*ptp de* **rétrécir**) ADJ [*tricot, vêtement*] shrunk, shrunken; [*pupille*] contracted; (*péj*) [*esprit*] narrow; (*Écon*) [*marché*] shrinking; (*Aut*) **«chaussée ~e»** "road narrows"

rétrécir [ʀetʀesiʀ] ▶ conjug 2 ◀ ❶ VT [+ *vêtement*] to take in; [+ *tissu*] to shrink; [+ *pupille*] to contract; [+ *conduit, orifice, rue*] to narrow, make narrower; [+ *bague*] to tighten, make smaller; (*fig*) [+ *champ d'activité, esprit*] to narrow ❷ VI [*laine, tissu*] to shrink; [*pupille*] to contract; [*rue, vallée*] to narrow, become *ou* get narrower; [*esprit*] to grow narrow; [*cercle d'amis*] to grow smaller, dwindle; (*Écon*) [*marché*] to shrink, contract; **~ au lavage** to shrink in the wash; **faire ~** [+ *tissu*] to shrink ❸ **se rétrécir** VPR → **2**

rétrécissement [ʀetʀesismã] NM [*laine, tricot*] shrinkage; [*pupille*] contraction; [*conduit, rue, vallée*] narrowing; (*Écon*) [*marché*] shrinking, contracting; [*vêtement*] taking in; (*Méd*) [*aorte, rectum*] stricture

retrempe [ʀətʀãp] NF [*acier*] requenching

retremper [ʀ(ə)tʀãpe] ▶ conjug 1 ◀ ❶ VT ⓐ (*Tech*) [+ *acier*] to requench; (*fig*) **~ son courage aux dangers du front** to try *ou* test one's courage again amid the dangers at the front ⓑ (= *réimprégner*) to resoak ❷ **se retremper** VPR [*baigneur*] to go back into the water; (*fig*) **se ~ dans l'ambiance familiale** to reimmerse o.s. in the family atmosphere

rétribuer [ʀetʀibɥe] ▶ conjug 1 ◀ VT [+ *ouvrier*] to pay; **~ le travail/les services de qn** to pay sb for their work/their services

rétribution [ʀetʀibysjɔ̃] NF (= *paiement*) payment, remuneration (*NonC*); (*littér = récompense*) reward, recompense (**de** for)

retriever [ʀetʀivœʀ] NM retriever

rétro¹* [ʀetʀo] NM ⓐ ABRÉV = **rétroviseur** ⓑ (*Billard*) screw-back stroke

rétro² [ʀetʀo] ❶ ADJ INV **la mode/le style ~** retro fashions/style; **robe ~** retro-style dress ❷ NM **le ~** retro

rétroactes [ʀetʀoakt] NMPL (*Belg = antécédents*) antecedents; **elle ignorait les ~ de l'affaire** she knew nothing about the background to the affair

rétroactif, -ive [ʀetʀoaktif, iv] ADJ retroactive, retrospective; **mesure/augmentation de salaire avec effet ~** retroactive *ou* backdated measure/pay rise; **loi à effet ~** ex post facto law; **la loi est entrée en vigueur avec effet ~ à compter du 1er octobre** the law came into force, retroactive to October 1st

rétroaction [ʀetʀoaksjɔ̃] NF retroactive *ou* retrospective effect

rétroactivement [ʀetʀoaktivmã] ADV retroactively, retrospectively

rétroactivité [ʀetʀoaktivite] NF retroactivity

rétrocéder [ʀetʀosede] ▶ conjug 6 ◀ VT (*Jur*) to retrocede, cede back

rétrocession [ʀetʀosesjɔ̃] NF (*Jur*) retrocession, retrocedence; **la ~ de Hong-Kong à la Chine** the handover of Hong Kong to China

rétroflexe [ʀetʀofleks] ADJ retroflex

rétrofusée [ʀetʀofyze] NF retrorocket

rétrogradation [ʀetʀogʀadasjɔ̃] NF (*littér = régression*) regression, retrogression; (*Admin*) [*officier*] demotion; [*fonctionnaire*] demotion, downgrading; (*Astron*) retrogradation

rétrograde [ʀetʀogʀad] ADJ ⓐ (*péj = arriéré*) [*esprit*] reactionary; [*idées, mesures, politique*] retrograde, reactionary ⓑ (= *de recul*) [*mouvement, sens*] backward, retrograde; (*Littérat*) [*rimes, vers*] palindromic; (*Astron*) retrograde; (*Billard*) **effet ~** screw-back; (*Méd*) **amnésie ~** retrograde amnesia

rétrograder [ʀetʀogʀade] ▶ conjug 1 ◀ ❶ VI ⓐ (*Aut*) to change down; **~ de troisième en seconde** to change down from third to second ⓑ (= *régresser*) (*dans une hiérarchie*) to regress, move down; (*contre le progrès*) to go backward, regress; (= *perdre son avance*) to fall back; (= *reculer*) to move back ⓒ (*Astron*) to retrograde ❷ VT [+ *officier*] to demote; [+ *fonctionnaire*] to demote, downgrade

rétropédalage [ʀetʀopedalaʒ] NM back-pedalling (*lit*)

rétroprojecteur [ʀetʀopʀoʒɛktœʀ] NM overhead projector

rétropropulsion [ʀetʀopʀopylsjɔ̃] NF reverse thrust

rétrospectif, -ive [ʀetʀospɛktif, iv] ❶ ADJ [*étude, peur*] retrospective ❷ **rétrospective** NF (*Art = exposition*) retrospective; (*Ciné = projections*) **rétrospective Buster Keaton** Buster Keaton season

rétrospectivement [ʀetʀospɛktivmã] ADV [*apparaître*] in retrospect, retrospectively; [*avoir peur, être jaloux*] in retrospect, looking back; **ces faits me sont apparus ~ sous un jour inquiétant** looking back on it *ou* in retrospect I saw the worrying side of these facts

retroussé, e [ʀ(ə)tʀuse] (*ptp de* **retrousser**) ADJ [*jupe*] hitched up; [*manche, pantalon*] rolled up; [*nez*] turned-up, snub; [*moustaches, lèvres*] curled up

retrousser [ʀ(ə)tʀuse] ▶ conjug 1 ◀ VT [+ *jupe*] to hitch up; [+ *manche, pantalon*] to roll up; [+ *lèvres*] to curl up; (*lit, fig*) **~ ses manches** to roll up one's sleeves; [*animal*] **~ ses babines** to snarl

retroussis [ʀ(ə)tʀusi] NM (= *partie retroussée*) lip

retrouvailles [ʀ(ə)tʀuvaj] NFPL (*après une séparation*) reunion; **ses ~ avec son pays natal** his homecoming, his return to his homeland; **aspirer aux ~ avec la nature** to dream of getting back to nature; (*Pol*) **les ~ franco-vietnamiennes** the renewal of ties between France and Vietnam

retrouver [ʀ(ə)tʀuve] ▶ conjug 1 ◀ ❶ VT ⓐ (= *récupérer*) [+ *objet personnel, enfant*] to find (again); [+ *fugitif, objet égaré par un tiers*] to find; **~ son chemin** to find one's way again; **on retrouva son cadavre sur une plage** his body was found on a beach; **on les a retrouvés vivants** they were found alive; **après sa maladie, il a retrouvé son poste** he got his job back again after his illness; **une chienne** *ou* **une chatte n'y retrouverait pas ses petits** ◊ **une poule n'y retrouverait pas ses poussins** it's in absolute chaos, it's an absolute shambles *ou* an unholy mess* ⓑ (= *se remémorer*) to think of, remember, recall; **je ne retrouve plus son nom** I can't think of *ou* remember *ou* recall his name ⓒ (= *revoir*) [+ *personne*] to meet (up with) again; [+ *endroit*] to be back in, see again; **je l'ai retrouvé par hasard en Italie** I met up with him again by chance in Italy, I happened to come across him again in Italy; **je l'ai retrouvé grandi/vieilli** I found him taller/looking older; **et que je ne te retrouve pas ici!** and don't let me catch *ou* find you here again!; **je serai ravi de vous ~** I'll be delighted to see *ou* meet you again boxed[d] (= *rejoindre*) to join, meet (again), see (again); **je vous retrouve à 5 heures au Café de la Poste** I'll join *ou* meet *ou* see you at 5 o'clock at the Café de la Poste; **après le pont, vous retrouverez la route de Caen** after the bridge you'll be back on the road to Caen

boxed[e] (= *recouvrer*) [+ *forces, santé, calme*] to regain; [+ *joie, foi*] to find again; ~ **le sommeil** to go *ou* get back to sleep (again); **elle mit longtemps à ~ la santé/le calme** she took a long time to regain her health/composure, it was a long time before she regained her health/composure; **très vite elle retrouva son sourire** she very soon found her smile again

boxed[f] (= *redécouvrir*) [+ *secret*] to rediscover; [+ *recette*] to rediscover, uncover; [+ *article en vente, situation, poste*] to find again; **je voudrais ~ des rideaux de la même couleur** I'd like to find curtains in the same colour again; ~ **du travail** to find work again; **il a bien cherché, mais une situation pareille ne se retrouve pas facilement** he looked around but it's not easy to come by *ou* find another job like that; **une telle occasion ne se retrouvera jamais** an opportunity like this will never occur again *ou* crop up again

boxed[g] (= *reconnaître*) to recognize; **on retrouve chez Louis le sourire de son père** you can see *ou* recognize his father's smile in Louis, you can see Louis has his father's smile; **je retrouve bien là mon fils !** that's my son all right!

boxed[h] (= *trouver, rencontrer*) to find, encounter; **on retrouve sans cesse les mêmes tournures dans ses romans** you find the same expressions all the time in his novels

boxed[2] **se retrouver** VPR boxed[a] (= *se réunir*) to meet, meet up; (= *se revoir après une absence*) to meet again; **après le travail, ils se sont tous retrouvés au café** after work they all met in the café; **ils se sont retrouvés par hasard à Paris** they met again by chance in Paris; **un club où l'on se retrouve entre sportifs** a club where sportsmen get together; **comme on se retrouve !** fancy *ou* imagine meeting *ou* seeing you here!; (*menace*) **on se retrouvera !** I'll get even with you!, I'll get my own back! (*Brit*)

boxed[b] (= *être de nouveau*) to find o.s. back; **il se retrouva place de la Concorde** he found himself back at the Place de la Concorde; **se ~ dans la même situation** to find o.s. back in the same situation; **se ~ seul** (*sans amis*) to be left on one's own *ou* with no one; (*loin des autres, de la foule*) to be alone *ou* on one's own

boxed[c] (* = *finir*) **il s'est retrouvé en prison/dans le fossé** he ended up in prison/in the ditch, he wound up* *ou* landed up* (*Brit*) in prison/in the ditch

boxed[d] (= *voir clair, mettre de l'ordre*) **il ne se** *ou* **s'y retrouve pas dans ses calculs/la numération binaire** he can't make sense of his calculations/binary notation; **on a de la peine à s'y ~, dans ces digressions/raisonnements** it's hard to find one's way through *ou* to make sense of these digressions/arguments; **allez donc vous (y) ~ dans un désordre pareil !** let's see you try and straighten out this awful mess!; **je ne m'y retrouve plus** I'm completely lost

boxed[e] (* = *rentrer dans ses frais*) **s'y ~** to break even; **les frais furent énormes mais il s'y est largement retrouvé** his costs were enormous but he did very well out of the deal; **tout ce que j'espère, c'est qu'on s'y retrouve** all I hope is that we don't lose on it *ou* that we break even; **s'il te prête cet argent c'est qu'il s'y retrouve** if he's lending you this money it's because there's something in it for him

boxed[f] (= *trouver son chemin*) **se ~** ◊ **s'y ~** to find one's way; **la ville a tellement changé que je ne m'y retrouve plus** the town has changed so much I can't find my way around any more

boxed[g] (*littér* = *faire un retour sur soi-même*) to find o.s. again

boxed[h] (= *être présent*) **ces caractéristiques se retrouvent aussi chez les cervidés** these characteristics are also found *ou* encountered in the deer family

rétrovirus [ʀetʀoviʀys] NM retrovirus

rétroviseur [ʀetʀovizœʀ] NM rear-view mirror, (driving) mirror; ~ **latéral** wing mirror (*Brit*), side-view mirror (*US*)

rets [ʀɛ] NMPL (*littér* = *piège*) snare; **prendre** *ou* **attraper qn dans ses ~** to ensnare sb; **se laisser prendre** *ou* **tomber dans les ~ de qn** to be ensnared by sb

réuni, e [ʀeyni] (*ptp de réunir*) ADJ boxed[a] (= *pris ensemble*) ~**s** (put) together, combined; **aussi fort que les Français et les Anglais ~s** as strong as the French and the English put together *ou* combined boxed[b] (*Comm* = *associés*) ~**s** associated; **les Transporteurs Réunis** Associated Carriers

réunification [ʀeynifikasjɔ̃] NF reunification

réunifier [ʀeynifje] ▶conjug 7◀ boxed[1] VT to reunify, reunite; **l'Allemagne réunifiée** reunited *ou* reunified Germany boxed[2] **se réunifier** VPR to reunify

Réunion [ʀeynjɔ̃] NF (*Géog*) **(l'île de) la ~** Réunion (Island)

réunion [ʀeynjɔ̃] NF boxed[a] [*faits, objets*] collection, gathering; [*fonds*] raising; [*amis, membres d'une famille, d'un club*] bringing together, reunion, reuniting; [*éléments, parties*] combination; (*Math*) [*ensembles*] union; **la ~ d'une province à un État** the union of a province with a state; ~ **de famille** family gathering boxed[b] [*entreprises*] merging; [*États*] union; [*fleuves*] confluence, merging; [*rues*] junction, joining; [*idées*] meeting boxed[c] (= *séance*) meeting; **notre prochaine ~ sera le 10** our next meeting will be on the 10th; **dans une ~** at *ou* in a meeting; ~ **d'information** briefing (session); ~ **syndicale** union meeting; ~ **de travail** work session; **être en ~** to be at *ou* in a meeting boxed[d] (*Sport*) ~ **cycliste** cycle rally; ~ **d'athlétisme** athletics meeting; ~ **hippique** (= *concours*) horse show; (= *course*) race meeting; ~ **sportive** sports meeting

réunionite* [ʀeynjɔnit] NF mania for meetings

réunionnais, e [ʀeynjɔnɛ, ɛz] boxed[1] ADJ of *ou* from Réunion boxed[2] **Réunionnais(e)** NM,F inhabitant *ou* native of Réunion

réunir [ʀeyniʀ] ▶conjug 2◀ boxed[1] VT boxed[a] (= *rassembler*) [+ *objets*] to gather *ou* collect (together); [+ *faits, preuves*] to put together; ~ **tout son linge en un paquet** to collect all one's washing into a bundle; ~ **des papiers par une épingle** to pin papers together, fix papers together with a pin boxed[b] (= *recueillir*) [+ *fonds*] to raise, get together; [+ *preuves*] to collect, gather (together); [*pièces de collection, timbres*] to collect boxed[c] (= *cumuler*) to combine; **ce livre réunit diverses tendances stylistiques** this book combines various styles, this book is a combination of different styles; ~ **toutes les conditions exigées** to satisfy *ou* meet all the requirements boxed[d] (= *assembler*) [+ *participants*] to gather, collect; (= *convoquer*) [+ *membres d'un parti*] to call together, call a meeting of; (= *inviter*) [+ *amis, famille*] to entertain, have over *ou* round (*Brit*); (= *rapprocher*) [+ *antagonistes, ennemis*] to bring together, reunite; [+ *anciens amis*] to bring together again, reunite; **on avait réuni les participants dans la cour** they had gathered those taking part in the yard; **ce congrès a réuni des écrivains de toutes tendances** this congress gathered *ou* brought together writers of all kinds; **nous réunissons nos amis tous les mercredis** we entertain our friends every Wednesday, we have our friends over *ou* round (*Brit*) every Wednesday; **après une brouille de plusieurs années, ce deuil les a réunis** after a quarrel which lasted several

years, this bereavement brought them together again *ou* reunited them

boxed[e] (= *raccorder*) [+ *éléments, parties*] to join; **le couloir réunit les deux ailes du bâtiment** the corridor joins *ou* links the two wings of the building

boxed[f] (= *relier*) to join (up *ou* together); ~ **deux fils** to tie two threads together; ~ **les bords d'une plaie/d'un accroc** to bring together the edges of a wound/of a tear

boxed[g] (= *rattacher à*) ~ **à** [+ *province*] to unite to

boxed[2] **se réunir** VPR boxed[a] (= *se rencontrer*) to meet, get together; **se ~ entre amis** to get together with (some) friends, have a friendly get-together; **le petit groupe se réunissait dans un bar** the little group would meet *ou* get together in a bar

boxed[b] (= *s'associer*) [*entreprises*] to combine, merge; [*États*] to unite

boxed[c] (= *se joindre*) [*États*] to unite; [*fleuves*] to flow into each other, merge; [*rues*] to join, converge; [*idées*] to unite, be united

réussi, e [ʀeysi] (*ptp de réussir*) ADJ (= *couronné de succès*) [*dîner, mariage, soirée*] successful; (= *bien exécuté*) [*mouvement*] good, well executed (*frm*); [*photo, roman*] successful; [*mélange, tournure*] effective; **c'était vraiment très ~** it really was a great success *ou* very successful; (*iro*) **eh bien, c'est ~ !** well that's just great!* (*iro*), very clever! (*iro*)

▼**réussir** [ʀeysiʀ] ▶conjug 2◀ boxed[1] VI boxed[a] [*affaire, entreprise, projet*] to succeed, be a success, be successful; [*culture, plantation*] to thrive, do well; [*manœuvre, ruse*] to pay off; **pourquoi l'entreprise n'a-t-elle pas réussi ?** why wasn't the venture a success?, why didn't the venture come off *ou* succeed?; **le culot réussit parfois où la prudence échoue** sometimes nerve succeeds *ou* works where caution fails; **la vigne ne réussit pas partout** vines don't thrive everywhere *ou* do not do well everywhere; **tout lui/rien ne lui réussit** everything/nothing goes right for him, everything/nothing works for him; **cela lui a mal réussi** ◊ **cela ne lui a pas réussi** that didn't do him any good

boxed[b] [*personne*] (*dans une entreprise*) to succeed, be successful; (*à un examen*) to pass; ~ **dans la vie** to succeed *ou* get on in life; ~ **dans les affaires/dans ses études** to succeed *ou* do well in business/in one's studies; **et leur expédition au Pôle, ont-ils réussi ? — ils n'ont pas réussi** what about their expedition to the Pole, did they succeed? *ou* did they pull it off*? — they failed; **il a réussi/il n'a pas réussi à l'examen** he passed/he failed the exam; **il a réussi dans tout ce qu'il a entrepris** he has made a success of *ou* been successful *ou* succeeded in all his undertakings; **tous leurs enfants ont bien réussi** all their children have done well; **il réussit bien en anglais/à l'école** he's a success at *ou* he does well at English/at school

boxed[c] ~ **à faire qch** to succeed in doing sth, manage to do sth; **il a réussi à les convaincre** he succeeded in convincing them, he managed to convince them; (*iro*) **cette maladroite a réussi à se brûler*** this clumsy girl has managed to burn herself *ou* has gone and burnt herself*

boxed[d] (= *être bénéfique à*) ~ **à** to agree with; **l'air de la mer/la vie active lui réussit** sea air/an active life agrees with him; **le curry ne me réussit pas** curry doesn't agree with me

boxed[2] VT boxed[a] (= *bien exécuter*) [+ *entreprise, film*] to make a success of; ~ **sa carrière** to have a successful career; ~ **sa vie** to make a success of one's life; **ce plat est facile/difficile à ~** this dish is easy/difficult to make; **elle a bien réussi sa sauce** her sauce was a great success; **le Premier ministre a réussi son examen de passage** the Prime Minister has passed the test; **vont-ils ~ leur coup ?** will they manage to carry *ou* pull it off?; **il a réussi son coup :**

▶ GRAMMAIRE ACTIVE: **réussir** 50.5

10 000 F de raflés* en 10 minutes ! he pulled the job off — 10,000 francs swiped in 10 minutes flat*; (*hum*) **je l'ai bien réussi, mon fils** I did a good job on my son (*hum*); **~ l'impossible** to manage to do the impossible; **il a réussi le tour de force** *ou* **la prouesse de les réconcilier** he miraculously managed to bring about a reconciliation between them; **elle a réussi une prouesse** she pulled off a remarkable feat; **elle a réussi son effet** she achieved the effect she wanted

  b (= *exécuter*) [+ *but, essai*] to bring off, pull off; [+ *tâche*] to bring off, manage successfully; **il a réussi deux très jolies photos** he managed two very nice photographs, he took two very successful photographs

réussite [Reysit] NF **a** [*entreprise*] success, successful outcome; [*culture, soirée*] success; **ce fut une ~ complète** it was a complete *ou* an unqualified success **b** [*personne*] success; **sa ~ sociale a été fulgurante** his rise to success was dazzling; **c'est un signe de ~ sociale** it's a sign of social success; **je me suis fait teindre les cheveux mais ce n'est pas une ~ !** I had my hair dyed but it hasn't turned out very well!; **~ scolaire** academic success; **le taux de ~ au concours est de 10%** there is a 10% success rate in the exam; **les chances de ~ de cet accord** the agreement's chances of success *ou* of succeeding; **ce n'est pas une franche ~** it's not a great success **c** (*Cartes*) patience; **faire une ~** to play patience

réutilisable [Reytilizabl] ADJ reusable; **emballage non-~** disposable *ou* non-reusable packaging

réutiliser [Reytilize] ▸conjug 1◂ VT to reuse

revaccination [R(ə)vaksinasjɔ̃] NF revaccination

revacciner [R(ə)vaksine] ▸conjug 1◂ VT to revaccinate

revaloir [R(ə)valwaR] ▸conjug 29◂ VT to pay back; **je te revaudrai ça ◊ je te le revaudrai** (*hostile*) I'll pay you back for this, I'll get even with you for this, I'll get back at you for this; (*reconnaissant*) I'll repay you some day

revalorisation [R(ə)valɔRizasjɔ̃] NF [*monnaie*] revaluation; **~ salariale** *ou* **des salaires** wage increase; **ils prônent la ~ des carrières de l'enseignement** they want to improve the image *ou* to restore the prestige of the teaching profession

revaloriser [R(ə)valɔRize] ▸conjug 1◂ VT **a** [+ *monnaie*] to revalue; [+ *titre*] to increase the value of **b** [+ *salaire*] to raise; [+ *conditions de travail*] to improve **c** (= *promouvoir*) [+ *méthode*] to promote again; [+ *valeur morale, institution, tradition*] to reassert the value of; **l'entreprise veut ~ son image** the company wants to boost its image

revanchard, e [R(ə)vɑ̃ʃaR, aRd] (*péj*) **1** ADJ [*politique*] of revenge (*especially against enemy country*); [*politicien*] who is an advocate of *ou* who advocates revenge; [*pays*] bent on revenge [*attitude, propos*] vengeful **2** NM,F advocate of revenge, revanchist (*frm*)

revanche [R(ə)vɑ̃ʃ] NF (*après défaite, humiliation*) revenge; (*Sport*) revenge match; (*Jeux*) return game; (*Boxe*) return fight *ou* bout; **prendre sa ~ (sur qn)** to take one's revenge (on sb), get one's own back (on sb)* (*Brit*); **prendre une ~ éclatante (sur qn)** to take a spectacular revenge (on sb); (*Jeux, Sport*) **donner sa ~ à qn** to let sb have *ou* give sb their revenge; **le mépris est la ~ des faibles** contempt is the revenge of the weak; **en ~** on the other hand → **charge**

revanchisme [R(ə)vɑ̃ʃism] NM (*Pol*) revanchism

rêvasser [Revase] ▸conjug 1◂ VI to daydream, let one's mind wander, muse (*littér*)

rêvasserie [Revasri] NF (= *rêve*) daydreaming

(*NonC*); (= *chimère*) (idle) dream, (idle) fancy, daydreaming (*NonC*)

rêve [Rev] NM **a** (*pendant le sommeil*) dream; (*éveillé*) dream, daydream; (*fig* = *chimère*) dream; **le ~ et la réalité** dream and reality; (*Psych*) **le ~ ◊ les ~s** dreaming, dreams; (*Psych*) **le ~ éveillé** daydreaming; **j'ai fait un ~ affreux** I had a horrible dream; **~ prémonitoire** premonitory dream; **mauvais ~** bad dream, nightmare; **faire des ~s** to dream, have dreams; **faites de beaux ~s !** sweet dreams!; **il est perdu dans ses ~s** he's (day)dreaming, he's in a world of his own; **sortir d'un ~** to come out of a dream

  b (*loc*) **c'était un beau ~ !** it was a lovely dream!; **le ~ américain** the American dream; **c'est un de mes ~s de jeunesse** it's one of the things I've always dreamt of *ou* wanted; **c'est le ~ de leur vie** it's their life-long dream; **mon ~ s'est enfin réalisé** my dream has finally come true; **voiture/maison de ~** dream car/house; **créature de ~** gorgeous *ou* lovely creature; **il fait un temps de ~ pour une balade à la campagne** it's perfect weather for a walk in the country; **il mène une vie de ~** he leads an idyllic life; **il a un corps de ~** he's got a superb body; **la voiture/la femme de ses ~s** the car/the woman of his dreams, his dream car/woman; **disparaître** *ou* **s'évanouir comme un ~** to vanish *ou* fade like a dream; **disparaître comme dans un ~** to be gone *ou* disappear in a trice; **voir/entendre qch en ~** to see/hear sth in a dream; **créer qch en ~** to dream sth up; **ça, c'est le ~*** that would be ideal *ou* (just) perfect; **une maison comme ça, ce n'est pas le ~*** it's not exactly a dream house

rêvé, e [Reve] ADJ (*ptp de* **rêver**) ADJ ideal, perfect; **c'est l'occasion ~e !** it's the ideal *ou* a golden opportunity!

revêche [Rəveʃ] ADJ [*air, ton*] surly; [*personne*] sour-tempered

réveil [Revej] NM **a** [*dormeur*] waking (up) (*NonC*), wakening (*littér*); [*personne évanouie*] coming to (*NonC*); (*fig* = *retour à la réalité*) awakening; **au ~, je vis qu'il était parti** when I woke up *ou* on waking I found he was already gone; **il a le ~ difficile** he finds it hard to wake up, he finds waking up difficult; **il eut un ~ brutal** he was rudely woken up *ou* awakened; **dès le ~, il chante** as soon as he's awake *ou* he wakes up he starts singing; **il a passé une nuit entrecoupée de ~s en sursaut** he had a bad night, waking with a start every so often; **~ téléphonique** alarm call; (*fig*) **le ~ fut pénible** he (*ou* I *etc*) had a rude awakening **b** (*fig* = *renaissance*) [*nature, sentiment, souvenir*] reawakening; [*volcan*] fresh stirrings; [*douleur*] return; **le ~ des nationalismes** the resurgence of nationalism **c** (*Mil*) reveille; **sonner le ~** to sound the reveille; **battre le ~** to wake soldiers up to the sound of drums; **~ en fanfare** reveille on the bugle; (*fig*) **ce matin, j'ai eu droit à un ~ en fanfare !** I was treated to a rowdy awakening this morning! **d** (= *réveille-matin*) alarm (clock); **mets le ~ à 8 heures** set the alarm for 8 (o'clock); **~ de voyage** travel alarm (clock)

réveillé, e [Reveje] (*ptp de* **réveiller**) ADJ (= *à l'état de veille*) awake; (* = *dégourdi*) bright, all there* (*attrib*); **à moitié ~** half asleep; **il était mal ~** he was still half asleep, he hadn't woken up properly

réveille-matin [Revejmatɛ̃] NM INV alarm clock

réveiller [Reveje] ▸conjug 1◂ **1** VT **a** [+ *dormeur*] to wake (up), waken, awaken (*littér*); (= *ranimer*) [+ *personne évanouie*] to bring round, revive; (= *ramener à la réalité*) [+ *rêveur*] to wake up, waken; **réveillez-moi à 5 heures** wake me (up) at 5 (o'clock); (*dans un hôtel*) **voulez-vous qu'on vous réveille ?** would you like a wake-up call?; **se faire ~ tous les matins**

à la même heure to be woken up every morning at the same time; **être réveillé en sursaut** to be woken (up) with a start; **faire un vacarme à ~ les morts** to make a racket that would waken the dead ■ (*PROV*) **ne réveillez pas le chat qui dort** let sleeping dogs lie (*PROV*)

  b (= *raviver*) [+ *appétit, courage*] to rouse, awaken; [+ *douleur*] (*physique*) to start up again; (*mentale*) to revive, reawaken; [+ *jalousie, rancune*] to reawaken, rouse; [+ *souvenir*] to awaken, revive, bring back

  c (= *ranimer*) [+ *membre ankylosé*] to bring some sensation *ou* feeling back into; **~ les consciences** to awaken *ou* stir people's consciences

  2 se réveiller VPR **a** [*dormeur*] to wake (up), awake, awaken (*littér*); [*personne évanouie*] to come round (*Brit*) *ou* around (*US*), come to, regain consciousness; [*paresseux, rêveur*] to wake up (**de** from); **réveille-toi !** wake up!; **se réveillant de sa torpeur** rousing himself from his lethargy; **se ~ en sursaut** to wake up with a start

  b (= *se raviver*) [*appétit, courage*] to be roused; [*douleur*] to return; [*jalousie, rancune*] to be reawakened *ou* roused; [*souvenir*] to return, come back, reawaken (*littér*)

  c (= *se ranimer*) [*nature*] to reawaken; [*volcan*] to stir again; **mon pied se réveille** the feeling's coming back into my foot, I'm getting some feeling back in my foot

réveillon [Revejɔ̃] NM **~ (de Noël/du Nouvel An)** (= *repas*) Christmas Eve/New Year's Eve dinner; (= *fête*) Christmas Eve/New Year's (Eve) party; (= *date*) Christmas/New Year's Eve

réveillonner [Revejɔne] ▸conjug 1◂ VI to celebrate Christmas *ou* New Year's Eve (*with a dinner and a party*)

▾**révélateur, -trice** [RevelatœR, tRis] **1** ADJ [*détail*] telling, revealing; [*indice, symptôme*] revealing; **film ~ d'une mode/d'une tendance** film revealing a fashion/a tendency; **c'est ~ d'un malaise profond** it reveals a deep malaise → **lapsus** **2** NM **a** (*Photo*) developer **b** (*littér*) (= *personne*) enlightener; (= *événement, expérience*) revelation; **ce conflit a été le ~ d'une crise plus profonde** this conflict revealed a much deeper crisis

révélation [Revelasjɔ̃] NF **a** [*fait, projet, secret*] revelation, disclosure **b** [*artiste*] revelation, discovery; **ce livre est une ~** this book is a revelation; **ce fut une véritable ~ !** it was quite a revelation!; **ce jeune auteur a été la ~ de l'année** this young author was the discovery of the year **c** [*sensations, talent, tendances*] revelation; **avoir la ~ de qch** to discover sth **d** (= *confidence, aveu*) disclosure, revelation; **faire des ~s importantes** to make important disclosures *ou* revelations **e** (*Rel*) revelation **f** (*Photo*) [*image*] developing

révélé, e [Revele] (*ptp de* **révéler**) ADJ (*Rel*) [*dogme, religion*] revealed

révéler [Revele] ▸conjug 6◂ **1** VT **a** (= *divulguer*) [+ *fait, projet*] to reveal, make known, disclose; [+ *secret*] to disclose, give away, reveal; [+ *opinion*] to make known; **je ne peux encore rien ~** I can't disclose *ou* reveal anything yet, I can't give anything away yet; **~ que** to reveal that; **ça l'avait révélée à elle-même** this had given her a new awareness of herself

  b (= *témoigner de*) [+ *aptitude, caractère*] to reveal, show; [+ *sentiments*] to show; **œuvre qui révèle une grande sensibilité** work which reveals *ou* displays great sensitivity; **sa physionomie révèle la bonté/une grande ambition** his features show kindness/great ambition; **son décolleté révélait la délicatesse de sa peau** her low neckline showed *ou* revealed her delicate skin

  c (= *faire connaître*) [+ *artiste*] [*imprésario*] to

revenant — revenu

discover; [œuvre] to bring to fame; (Rel) to reveal; **le roman qui l'a révélé au public** the novel that introduced him to the public
[d] (Photo) to develop

2 se révéler VPR [a] [vérité, talent, tendance]
to be revealed, reveal itself; (Rel) to reveal
o.s.; **des sensations nouvelles se révélaient à
lui** he was becoming aware of new feelings
[b] [artiste] to come into one's own; **il ne s'est
révélé que vers la quarantaine** he didn't really
come into his own until he was nearly forty
[c] (= s'avérer) **se ~ cruel/ambitieux** to show
o.s. ou prove to be cruel/ambitious; **se ~
difficile/aisé** to prove difficult/easy; **son hypothèse se révéla fausse** his hypothesis proved
(to be) ou was shown to be false

revenant, e [R(ə)vənɑ̃, ɑ̃t] NM,F ghost; **tiens,
un ~!** hello stranger!* → **histoire**

revendeur, -euse [R(ə)vɑ̃dœʀ, øz] NM,F (=
détaillant) retailer, dealer, stockist (Brit);
(d'occasion) secondhand dealer; **chez votre ~
habituel** at your local dealer ou stockist (Brit);
~ (de drogue) (drug-)pusher* ou dealer

revendicateur, -trice [R(ə)vɑ̃dikatœʀ, tʀis]
1 NM,F protester **2** ADJ **lettre revendicatrice**
letter putting forward one's claims; **déclaration revendicatrice** declaration of claims;
avoir une attitude revendicatrice to make a lot
of demands

revendicatif, -ive [R(ə)vɑ̃dikatif, iv] ADJ
[mouvement] protest (épith); **action revendicative** protest campaign; **organiser une journée
d'action revendicative** to organize a day of action ou protest (in support of one's claims);
**les syndicats ont adopté une position plus re-
vendicative** the unions have stepped up their
demands

revendication [R(ə)vɑ̃dikasjɔ̃] NF [a] (= action) claiming; **il n'y a pas eu de ~ de
l'attentat** no one claimed responsibility for
the attack [b] (Pol, Syndicats = demande) claim,
demand; **journée de ~** day of action ou of
protest (in support of one's claims); **lettre de
~** letter putting forward one's claims; **mouvement de ~** protest movement; **~s salariales/
territoriales** wage/territorial claims; **~s sociales** workers' demands; **~s d'autonomie** demands for autonomy → **catégoriel**

revendiquer [R(ə)vɑ̃dike] ▸ conjug 1 ◂ **1** VT
[a] (= demander) [+ chose due, droits] to claim,
demand; **ils passent leur temps à ~** they're
forever making demands; **~ l'égalité des salaires** to demand equal pay [b] (= assumer) [+
paternité, responsabilité] to claim; [+ attentat,
explosion] to claim responsibility for;
l'attentat n'a pas été revendiqué no one has
claimed responsibility for the attack; **il revendique son appartenance à la communauté
juive** he asserts ou proclaims his Jewish identity **2** **se revendiquer** VPR **il se revendique
(comme) Basque** he asserts ou proclaims his
Basque identity; **elle se revendiquait du féminisme** she was a feminist and proud of it

revendre [R(ə)vɑ̃dʀ] ▸ conjug 41 ◂ VT [a] (=
vendre d'occasion ou au détail) to resell, sell;
[+ actions, terres, filiale] to sell off; **acheté 50 F,
cet article est revendu ou se revend 300 F** purchased for 50 francs, this item is being resold
at 300 francs; **ça se revend facilement** that's
easily resold ou sold again; **il a revendu sa voiture pour payer ses dettes** he sold his car to
pay off his debts
[b] (= vendre davantage) **j'en ai vendu deux en
janvier et j'en ai revendu quatre en février** I
sold two in January and I sold another four
in February; **j'en ai vendu la semaine dernière
mais je n'en ai pas revendu depuis** I sold some
last week but I've sold no more since then
[c] (loc) **avoir de l'énergie/de l'intelligence à ~**
to have energy/brains to spare; **si tu veux un
tableau, on en a à ~** if you want a picture,
we've got lots of them; **des chapeaux, elle en**

a à ~ she's got more hats than she knows
what to do with

revenez-y [Rəv(ə)nezi, R(ə)vənezi] NM INV →
goût

revenir [Rəv(ə)niʀ, R(ə)vəniʀ]
▸ conjug 22 ◂
1 VERBE INTRANSITIF   **2** VERBE PRONOMINAL

1 VERBE INTRANSITIF
[a] = repasser, venir de nouveau to come back,
come again; **il doit ~ nous voir demain** he's
coming back to see us tomorrow, he's coming to see us again tomorrow; **pouvez-vous ~
plus tard?** can you come back later?; **reviens!**
je plaisantais come back! I was joking
[b] = réapparaître [saison, mode] to come
back, return; [soleil, oiseaux] to return, reappear; [fête, date] to come (round) again;
[calme, ordre] to return; [thème, idée] to recur,
reappear; **~ à la mémoire** [souvenir, idée] to
come back to mind; **cette expression revient
souvent dans ses livres** that expression often
crops up in his books; **Noël revient chaque
année à la même date** Christmas comes
(round) on the same date every year; **sa lettre
est revenue parce qu'il avait changé d'adresse**
his letter was returned ou came back because
he had changed his address
[c] = rentrer to come back, return; **~ quelque
part/de quelque part** to come back ou return
(to) somewhere/from somewhere; **~ chez soi**
to come back ou return home; **~ dans son
pays** to come back ou return to one's country;
~ en bateau/avion to sail/fly back, come back
by boat/air; **~ à la hâte** to hurry back; **~ de
voyage** to return from a trip; **en revenant de
l'école** on the way back ou home from school;
je lui téléphonerai en revenant I'll phone him
when I get back; **sa femme lui est revenue** his
wife has come back to him; **je reviens dans un
instant** I'll be back in a minute, I'll be right
back*; **on va à la piscine? — j'en reviens!** shall
we go to the swimming pool? — I've just
come back from there!
[d] = retourner **~ en arrière** (gén) to go back;
(dans le temps) **on ne peut pas ~ en arrière** you
can't turn ou put back the clock
[e] = coûter **ça revient cher** it's expensive
[f] Culin **faire ~** to brown; **« faire ~ les oignons
dans le beurre »** "brown ou fry the onions
gently in the butter"
[g]
♦ **revenir à qch** (= recommencer, reprendre) [+
études, sujet] to go back to, return to;
[+ méthode, procédé] to go back to, return to,
revert to; **~ à ses premières amours** to go back
ou return to one's first love; **~ à de meilleurs
sentiments** to return to a better frame of
mind; **~ à la religion** to come back to religion;
~ à la vie to come back to life; **on y reviendra, à
cette mode** this fashion will come back; **nous
y reviendrons dans un instant** we'll come back
to that in a moment; **n'y revenez plus!** (= ne
recommencez plus) don't do that again!; (= n'en
redemandez plus) that's all you're getting!,
don't bother coming back!; **j'en reviens toujours là, il faut ...** I still come back to this, we
must ...; **il n'y a pas à y ~** there's no going back
on it; **~ à la charge** to return to the attack
(= équivaloir à) to come down to, amount to,
boil down to; **cette hypothèse revient à une
proposition très simple** this hypothesis comes
down ou amounts to a very simple proposition; **ça revient à une question d'argent** it all
boils down to a question of money; **cela revient à dire que ...** it amounts to saying that
...; **ça revient au même** it amounts ou comes to
the same thing
(= coûter) to amount to, come to, cost; **ça revient à 100 F** it comes to ou amounts to 100
francs; **à combien est-ce que cela va vous ~?**
how much will that cost you?, how much
will that set you back?*

(Sport) **~ à la marque** ou **au score** to draw (even
ou level)
[h]
♦ **revenir à qn** [souvenir, idée] to come back to
sb; **son nom me revient maintenant** his name
has come back to me now; **ça me revient!** I've
got it now!, it's coming back to me now!
[courage, appétit, parole] to come back to sb,
return (to sb); **le courage me revint** my courage
came back to me ou returned; **l'appétit m'est
revenu** my appetite returned, I got my appetite back
[rumeur] **~ à qn** ou **aux oreilles de qn** to reach
sb's ears, get back to sb; (frm, hum) **il m'est revenu que ...** word has come back to me ou
reached me that ...
(= appartenir à) [droit, honneur, responsabilité] to
fall to sb; [biens, somme d'argent] (= échoir à) to
come ou pass to sb; (= être la part de) to come
ou go to sb; (= incomber à) **il lui revient de décider** it is for him ou up to him to decide; **ce titre lui revient de droit** this title is his by right;
cet honneur lui revient this honour is due to
him ou is his by right; **tout le mérite vous revient** all the credit goes to you, the credit is
all yours; **les biens de son père sont revenus à
l'État** his father's property passed to the state;
là-dessus, 100 F me reviennent 100 francs of
that comes to me
(* = plaire à) **il a une tête qui ne me revient pas** I
don't like the look of him; **elle ne me revient
pas du tout cette fille** I don't like that girl at all
♦ **revenir à soi** (= se rétablir) [personne] **~ à soi**
to come to, come round (Brit)
[i]
♦ **revenir de** (= se remettre de) [+ maladie] to recover from, get over; [+ syncope] to come to
after, come round from (Brit); [+ égarement,
surprise] to get over; [+ illusions] to lose, shake
off; [+ erreurs, théories] to leave behind, throw
over, put ou cast aside; **il revient de loin** it was
a close shave ou a near thing for him, he had
a close shave; **crois-tu qu'il en reviendra?** (=
qu'il en réchappera) do you think he'll pull
through?; (surprise) **je n'en reviens pas!** I can't
get over it!; **ils sont déjà revenus de ces théories**
they have already thrown over ou put aside
these theories; **elle est revenue de tout** she's
seen it all before
[j]
♦ **revenir sur** (= réexaminer) [+ affaire, problème]
to go back over; **ne revenons pas là-dessus** let's
not go back over that; **~ sur le passé** to go
back over the past → **tapis**
(= se dédire de) [+ promesse] to go back on; [+
décision] to go back on, reconsider
(Sport = rattraper) to catch up with

2 **s'en revenir** VPR † ou littér **comme il s'en revenait (du village), il aperçut un aigle** as he was
coming back (from the village), he noticed
an eagle; **il s'en revint la queue basse** he came
back with his tail between his legs; **il s'en revint, le cœur plein d'allégresse** he came away
with a joyful heart

revente [R(ə)vɑ̃t] NF resale; **valeur à la ~** resale
value; **il a été inculpé de ~ de drogue** he was
charged with drug dealing; **la ~ de l'entreprise lui a rapporté beaucoup d'argent** he made
a lot of money on the sale of the company

revenu [Rəv(ə)ny] **1** NM [particulier] income
(NonC) (de from); [État] revenue (de from);
[domaine, terre] income (de from); [capital,
investissement] yield (de from, on); **~ annuel/
brut/imposable/par habitant** annual/gross/
assessed/per capita income; (Fin) **à ~ fixe**
[valeurs] fixed-yield; **les pays à ~ élevé** high-
income countries; **famille/ménage à ~s modestes** low-income family/household; **avoir
de gros ~s** to have a large income, have substantial means; **personne sans ~s réguliers**
person who has no regular income

2 COMP ► **revenus de l'État** public revenue ► **revenu fiscal** tax revenue ► **revenu intérieur brut** gross domestic income ► **revenu minimum d'insertion** *minimum welfare payment given to those who are not entitled to unemployment benefit,* ≈ income support (*Brit*), ≈ welfare (*US*) ► **revenu national** gross national product ► **revenu net d'impôts** disposable income ► **revenus publics = revenus de l'État** ► **revenu du travail** earned income

rêver [ʀeve] ▸ conjug 1 ◂ **1** VI **a** [*dormeur*] to dream (**de**, *of, about*); **~ que** to dream that; **j'ai rêvé de toi** I dreamt about *ou* of you; **il en rêve la nuit** he dreams about it at night; **~ tout éveillé** to be lost in a daydream; **je ne rêve pas, c'est bien vrai?** I'm not imagining it *ou* dreaming, am I? — it's really true!; **tu m'as appelé? — moi? tu rêves!** did you call me? — me? you must have been dreaming! *ou* you're imagining things!; **une révolution, maintenant? vous rêvez!** a revolution now? your imagination's running away with you!; **on croit ~!** I can hardly believe it!, the mind boggles!*; **(non), mais je rêve!*** he (*ou* they *etc*) can't be serious!; **(il ne) faut pas ~*** I wouldn't count on it*; **on peut toujours ~** there's no harm in dreaming

b (= *rêvasser*) to dream, muse (*littér*), daydream; **travaille au lieu de ~!** get on with your work instead of (day)dreaming!; **~ à des jours meilleurs** to dream of better days

c (= *désirer*) to dream; **~ tout haut** to dream aloud; **~ de qch/de faire** to dream of sth/of doing; **elle rêve d'une chaumière en pleine forêt** she dreams of a cottage in the heart of a forest; **~ de réussir** to long to succeed, long for success; **~ de rencontrer la femme idéale** to dream of meeting *ou* long to meet the ideal woman; **des images qui font ~** pictures that fire the imagination; **ça fait ~ de l'entendre parler de ses voyages** hearing him talk about his travels really gets the imagination going

2 VT **a** (*en dormant*) to dream; **j'ai rêvé la même chose qu'hier** I dreamt the same (thing) as last night

b (*littér = imaginer*) to dream; **il rêve sa vie au lieu de la vivre** he's dreaming his life away instead of living it; (*péj*) **je n'ai jamais dit ça, c'est toi qui l'as rêvé!** I never said that — you must have dreamt it!

c (= *désirer*) to dream of; (*littér*) **~ mariage/succès** to dream of marriage/success; (*littér*) **il se rêve conquérant** he dreams of being a conqueror; **il ne rêve que plaies et bosses** his mind is full of heroic dreams

réverbération [ʀeveʀbeʀasjɔ̃] NF [*son*] reverberation; [*chaleur, lumière*] reflection

réverbère [ʀeveʀbɛʀ] NM (*d'éclairage*) street lamp *ou* light; (*Tech*) reflector → **allumeur**

réverbérer [ʀeveʀbeʀe] ▸ conjug 6 ◂ VT [+ *son*] to send back, reverberate; [+ *chaleur, lumière*] to reflect

reverdir [ʀ(ə)vɛʀdiʀ] ▸ conjug 2 ◂ **1** VI [*plantes*] to grow green again **2** VT (*Tech*) [*peaux*] to soak

révérence [ʀeveʀɑ̃s] NF **a** (= *salut*) [*homme*] bow; [*femme*] curtsey; **faire une ~** [*homme*] to bow; [*femme*] curtsey (**à qn** to sb); **tirer sa ~ (à qn)** (*lit*) to bow out, make one's bow (and leave); (*fig*) to take one's leave (of sb) **b** (*littér = respect*) reverence (**envers, pour** for); **~ parler**† with all due respect

révérencieux, -ieuse [ʀeveʀɑ̃sjø, jøz] ADJ (*littér*) reverent; **être peu ~ envers** to show scant respect for

révérend, e [ʀeveʀɑ̃, ɑ̃d] ADJ, NM reverend; **le Révérend Père Martin** Reverend Father Martin

révérendissime [ʀeveʀɑ̃disim] ADJ most reverend

révérer [ʀeveʀe] ▸ conjug 6 ◂ VT (*littér*) (*gén*) to revere; (*Rel*) to revere, reverence

rêverie [ʀɛvʀi] NF **a** (= *activité*) daydreaming, reverie (*littér*), musing (*littér*) **b** (= *rêve*) daydream, reverie (*littér*) **c** (*péj* = *chimère*) **~s** daydreams, delusions, illusions

revérifier [ʀ(ə)veʀifje] ▸ conjug 7 ◂ VT to double-check

revernir [ʀ(ə)vɛʀniʀ] ▸ conjug 2 ◂ VT to revarnish

▾ **revers** [ʀ(ə)vɛʀ] NM **a** [*feuille, papier*] back; [*étoffe*] wrong side; (*fig littér*) **le ~ de la charité** the reverse of charity; **prendre l'ennemi de** *ou* **à ~** to take the enemy from *ou* in the rear **b** [*médaille, pièce d'argent*] reverse, reverse side, back; **pièce frappée au ~ d'une effigie** coin struck with a portrait on the reverse; (*fig*) **c'est le ~ de la médaille** that's the other side of the coin; **toute médaille a son ~** every rose has its thorn (*PROV*)

c (*main*) back; **d'un ~ de main** (*lit*) with the back of one's hand; (*fig*) **il a balayé** *ou* **écarté nos arguments d'un ~ de (la) main** he brushed aside all our arguments, he dismissed all our arguments out of hand

d (*Tennis*) backhand; **faire un ~** to play a backhand shot; **volée de ~** backhand volley; **~ à deux mains** double-handed *ou* two-handed backhand

e (*Habillement*) [*manteau, veste*] lapel, revers; [*pantalon*] turn-up (*Brit*), cuff (*US*); [*bottes*] top; [*manche*] (turned-back) cuff; **bottes à ~** turned-down boots; **pantalons à ~** trousers with turn-ups (*Brit*) *ou* cuffs (*US*)

f (= *coup du sort*) setback; **~ (de fortune)** reverse (of fortune); **~ économiques/militaires** economic/military setbacks *ou* reverses

reversement [ʀ(ə)vɛʀsəmɑ̃] NM (*Fin*) [*excédent, somme*] putting back, paying back (**dans, sur** into); [*titre*] transfer

reverser [ʀ(ə)vɛʀse] ▸ conjug 1 ◂ VT **a** [+ *liquide*] (= *verser davantage*) to pour out some more; **reverse-moi du vin/un verre de vin** pour me (out) some more wine/another glass of wine; (= *remettre*) **reversez le vin dans la bouteille** pour the wine back into the bottle **b** (*Fin*) [+ *excédent, somme*] to put back, pay back (**dans, sur** into); [+ *titre*] to transfer

réversibilité [ʀevɛʀsibilite] NF [*pension*] revertibility; [*mouvement*] (*Chim*) reversibility

réversible [ʀevɛʀsibl] ADJ [*mouvement, vêtement, réaction chimique*] reversible; (*Jur*) revertible (**sur** to); **l'histoire n'est pas ~** history cannot be undone *ou* altered

réversion [ʀevɛʀsjɔ̃] NF (*Bio, Jur*) reversion; **pension de ~** reversion pension

revêtement [ʀ(ə)vɛtmɑ̃] NM (= *enduit*) coating; (= *surface*) [*route*] surface; (= *garniture, placage*) [*mur extérieur*] facing, cladding; [*mur intérieur*] covering; **~ (du sol)** flooring (*NonC*), floor-covering (*NonC*); **~ mural** wall-covering (*NonC*); **~ antiadhésif** [*poêle*] nonstick coating

revêtir [ʀ(ə)vetiʀ] ▸ conjug 20 ◂ **1** VT **a** (*frm, hum = mettre*) [+ *uniforme, habit*] to don (*frm*), put on, array o.s. in (*frm*)

b (= *prendre, avoir*) [+ *caractère, importance*] to take on, assume; [+ *apparence, forme*] to assume, take on; **une rencontre qui revêt une importance particulière** a meeting which is especially important; **cela ne revêt aucun caractère d'urgence** it is by no means urgent; **le langage humain revêt les formes les plus variées** human language appears in *ou* takes on the most varied forms

c (*frm, hum = habiller*) [*vêtement*] to adorn; [*personne*] **~ qn de** to dress *ou* array (*frm*) sb in; **~ un prélat des vêtements sacerdotaux** to array (*frm*) *ou* clothe a prelate in his priestly robes

d (= *couvrir, déguiser*) **~ qch de** to cloak sth in, cover sth with

e (*frm* = *investir de*) **~ qn de** [+ *dignité, autorité*] to endow *ou* invest sb with

f (*Admin, Jur*) **~ un document de sa signature/d'un sceau** to append one's signature/a seal to a document

g (*Tech*) (= *enduire*) to coat (**de** with); (= *couvrir*) [+ *route*] to surface (**de** with); [+ *mur, sol*] to cover (**de** with); **~ un mur de boiseries** to (wood-)panel a wall; **~ un mur de carreaux** to tile a wall, cover a wall with tiles; **~ de plâtre** to plaster; **~ de crépi** to face with roughcast, roughcast; **~ d'un enduit imperméable** to cover with a waterproof coating, give a waterproof coating to; **rue revêtue d'un pavage** street which has been paved over; **sommets revêtus de neige** snow-clad *ou* snow-covered summits

2 **se revêtir** VPR (= *mettre*) **se ~ de** (*frm*) to array o.s. in (*frm*), don (*frm*), dress o.s. in; (*littér*) **vers l'automne les sommets se revêtent de neige** as autumn draws near, the mountain tops don their snowy mantle (*littér*) *ou* are bedecked (*frm*) with snow

revêtu, e [ʀ(ə)vety] (*ptp de* **revêtir**) ADJ **a** (= *habillé de*) **~ de** dressed in, wearing **b** (*Tech*) [*route*] surfaced; **chemin non ~** unsurfaced road **c** (*Tech = enduit de*) **~ de** coated with

rêveur, -euse [ʀɛvœʀ, øz] **1** ADJ [*air, personne*] dreamy; **il a l'esprit ~** he's inclined to be a dreamer; **ça vous laisse ~*** it makes you wonder **2** NM,F (*lit, péj*) dreamer

rêveusement [ʀɛvøzmɑ̃] ADV (= *distraitement*) dreamily, as (if) in a dream; (= *avec perplexité*) distractedly

revient [ʀəvjɛ̃] NM → **prix**

revigorant, e [ʀ(ə)vigɔʀɑ̃, ɑ̃t] ADJ [*vent, air frais*] invigorating; [*repas, boisson*] reviving (*épith*); [*discours, promesse*] cheering, invigorating

revigorer [ʀ(ə)vigɔʀe] ▸ conjug 1 ◂ VT [*vent, air frais*] to invigorate; [*repas, boisson*] to revive, put new life into, buck up*; [*discours, promesse*] to cheer, invigorate, buck up*; **un petit vent frais qui revigore** a bracing *ou* an invigorating cool breeze; **ces mesures vont ~ l'économie locale** these measures will give a boost to the local economy

revirement [ʀ(ə)viʀmɑ̃] NM (= *changement d'avis*) change of mind, reversal (of opinion); (= *changement brusque*) [*tendances*] reversal (**de** of); [*opinion*] change (**de** in); **~ d'opinion** change *ou* U-turn *ou* turnaround in public opinion; **un ~ soudain de la situation** a sudden reversal of the situation

révisable [ʀevizabl] ADJ **a** (= *qui peut être sujet à modification*) [*contrat, salaire*] revisable; **prix ~ à la baisse/hausse** price that can be revised downwards/upwards; **prêt à taux ~** (*gén*) loan with adjustable interest rate; (*immobilier*) ≈ adjustable-rate mortgage **b** (*Jur*) [*procès*] reviewable

réviser [ʀevize] ▸ conjug 1 ◂ VT **a** [+ *procès, règlement, constitution*] to review; [+ *croyance, opinion*] to review, reappraise; **j'ai révisé mon jugement sur lui** I've revised my opinion of him **b** [+ *comptes*] to audit; [+ *moteur, installation*] to overhaul, service; [+ *montre*] to service; **faire ~ sa voiture** to have one's car serviced; **j'ai fait ~ les freins** I've had the brakes looked at **c** (= *mettre à jour*) [+ *liste, estimation*] to revise; **~ à la hausse/à la baisse** to revise upwards/downwards **d** (= *corriger*) [+ *texte, manuscrit, épreuves*] to revise; **nouvelle édition complètement révisée** new and completely revised edition **e** (*Scol*) [+ *sujet*] to revise; **~ son histoire** to revise history, do one's history revision; **commencer à ~** to start revising *ou* (one's) one's revision

réviseur [ʀevizœʀ] NM reviser; **~-comptable** independent auditor

révision [ʀevizjɔ̃] NF **a** [*procès, règlement, constitution*] review; [*croyance, opinion*] review, reappraisal **b** (= *vérification*) [*comptes*] auditing (*NonC*); [*moteur, installation*] overhaul (*NonC*), servicing (*NonC*); **~ prochaine ~ après 10 000 km** next major service after 10,000 km → **conseil** **c** (= *mise à jour*) [*liste*] revision (NonC); **~ des listes électorales** revision ou revising of the electoral register [d] (= correction) [texte, manuscrit, épreuves] revision [e] (Scol) [sujet] revising; **faire ses ~s** to do one's revision, revise

révisionnisme [Revizjɔnism] NM revisionism

révisionniste [Revizjɔnist] ADJ, NMF revisionist

revisiter [R(ə)vizite] ▸ conjug 1 ◂ VT [+ musée, ville] to revisit, visit again; [+ théorie] to reexamine; **la mode des années 30/la pièce de Molière revisitée par Anne Morand** thirties fashions/Molière's play reinterpreted by Anne Morand, a new take on thirties fashions/Molière's play by Anne Morand

revisser [R(ə)vise] ▸ conjug 1 ◂ VT to screw back again

revitalisant, e [R(ə)vitalizã, ãt] ADJ [séjour, vacances] revitalizing, restorative; [crème de soin, lotion, shampooing] revitalizing, regenerative

revitalisation [R(ə)vitalizasjɔ̃] NF revitalization

revitaliser [R(ə)vitalize] ▸ conjug 1 ◂ VT to revitalize

revivifier [R(ə)vivifje] ▸ conjug 7 ◂ VT (littér) [+ personne, souvenir] to revive

revivre [R(ə)vivR] ▸ conjug 46 ◂ [1] VI [a] (= être ressuscité) to live again; **on peut vraiment dire qu'il revit dans son fils** it's really true to say that he lives on in his son [b] (= être revigoré) to come alive again; **je me sentais ~** I felt alive again, I felt (like) a new man (ou woman); **ouf, je revis!** whew! what a relief! ou I can breathe again!* [c] (= se renouveler) [coutumes, institution, mode] to be revived [d] **faire ~** (= ressusciter) to bring back to life, restore to life; (= revigorer) to revive, put new life in ou into; (= remettre en honneur) [+ mode, époque, usage] to revive; (= remettre en mémoire) to bring back; **faire ~ un personnage/une époque dans un roman** to bring a character/an era back to life in a novel; **le grand air m'a fait ~** the fresh air put new life in me; **cela faisait ~ tout un monde que j'avais cru oublié** it brought back a whole world I thought had been forgotten [2] VT [+ passé, période] (lit) to relive, live (through) again; (en imagination) to relive, live (over) again

révocabilité [Revɔkabilite] NF [contrat] revocability; [fonctionnaire] removability

révocable [Revɔkabl] ADJ [legs, contrat] revocable; [fonctionnaire] removable, dismissible

révocation [Revɔkasjɔ̃] NF [a] (= destitution) [magistrat, fonctionnaire] removal (from office), dismissal [b] (= annulation) [legs, contrat, édit] revocation; (Hist) **la ~ de l'Édit de Nantes** the Revocation of the Edict of Nantes

revoici* [R(ə)vwasi], **revoilà*** [R(ə)vwala] PRÉP **~ Paul!** (here's) Paul again!; **me ~!** it's me again!, here I am again!; **nous ~ à la maison/en France** here we are, back home in France (again); **~ la mer** here's the sea again; **le revoilà qui se plaint!** there he goes complaining again!; **les revoilà!** there they are again!

revoir [R(ə)vwaR] ▸ conjug 30 ◂ [1] VT [a] (= retrouver) [+ personne] to see ou meet again; [+ patrie, village] to see again; **je l'ai revu deux ou trois fois depuis** I've seen him ou we've met two or three times since; **quand le revois-tu?** when are you seeing ou meeting him again?, when are you meeting again?; **au ~!** goodbye!; **au ~ Monsieur/Madame** goodbye (Mr X/ Mrs X); **dire au ~ à qn** to say goodbye to sb; **faire au ~ de la main** to wave goodbye; **ce n'était heureusement qu'un au ~** fortunately it was farewell and not adieu → **plaisir** [b] (= apercevoir de nouveau) to see again; **filez, et qu'on ne vous revoie plus ici!** clear off, and

don't show your face here again! [c] (= regarder de nouveau) to see again; **je suis allé ~ ce film** I went to (see) that film again [d] (= être à nouveau témoin de) [+ atrocités, scène] to witness ou see again; [+ conditions] to see again; **craignant de ~ augmenter le chômage** afraid of seeing unemployment increase again [e] (= imaginer de nouveau) to see again; **je le revois encore, dans sa cuisine** I can still see him there in his kitchen [f] (= réviser) [+ édition, texte] to revise; (Scol) [+ leçons] to go over again; (= examiner de nouveau) [+ position, stratégie] to review, reconsider; **édition revue et corrigée/augmentée** revised and updated/expanded edition; (fig) **l'histoire de France revue et corrigée par A. Leblanc** the history of France revised and updated ou given a new treatment by A. Leblanc; **nos tarifs/objectifs ont été revus à la baisse/hausse** our prices/targets have been revised downwards/upwards; (fig) **~ sa copie** to review one's plans, go back to the drawing board [2] **se revoir** VPR [a] (réciproque) to see each other again; **on se revoit quand?** when shall we see each other again?; **nous nous revoyons de temps en temps** we still see each other from time to time [b] (réfléchi) **je me revoyais écolier, dans mon village natal** I saw myself as a schoolboy again, back in the village where I was born

revoler [R(ə)vɔle] ▸ conjug 1 ◂ VI [oiseau, pilote] to fly again

révoltant, e [Revɔltã, ãt] ADJ revolting, appalling

révolte [Revɔlt] NF revolt, rebellion; **les paysans sont en ~** the peasants are in revolt against ... ou up in arms against ...; **adolescent en ~** rebellious adolescent; **devant ce refus, elle a eu un mouvement de ~** she bridled at this refusal; **à 17 ans, Alex était en pleine ~** at 17 Alex was going through a rebellious phase

révolté, e [Revɔlte] (ptp de **révolter**) [1] ADJ [a] [paysans, adolescent] rebellious [b] (= outré) outraged, incensed [2] NM,F rebel

révolter [Revɔlte] ▸ conjug 1 ◂ [1] VT (= indigner) to revolt, outrage, appal; **ceci nous révolte** we are revolted ou outraged by this [2] **se révolter** VPR [a] [personne] (= s'insurger) to revolt, rebel, rise up (**contre** against); (= se cabrer) to rebel (**contre** against) [b] (= s'indigner) to be revolted ou repelled ou appalled (**contre** by); **à cette vue tout mon être se révolte** my whole being revolts at this sight; **l'esprit se révolte contre une telle propagande** the mind revolts at ou is repelled ou revolted by such propaganda

révolu, e [Revɔly] ADJ [a] (littér = de jadis) [époque] past, bygone (épith), gone by; **des jours ~s** past ou bygone days, days gone by; **l'époque ~e des diligences** the bygone days of stagecoaches [b] (= fini) [époque, jours] past, in the past (attrib); **cette époque est ~e, nous devons penser à l'avenir** that era is in the past — we have to think of the future [c] (Admin = complété) **âgé de 20 ans ~s** over 20 years of age; **avoir 20 ans ~s** to be over 20 years of age; **après deux ans ~s** when two full years had (ou have) passed

révolution [Revɔlysjɔ̃] NF [a] (= rotation) revolution; **escalier à double ~** double staircase [b] (= changement: culturelle, industrielle) revolution; **~ pacifique/permanente/violente** peaceful/permanent/violent revolution; **la Révolution (française)** the French Revolution; **la ~ d'Octobre/de velours** the October/Velvet Revolution; **la ~ de palais** palace revolution ou coup; **la ~ silencieuse/verte/sexuelle** the silent/green/sexual revolution; **la ~ technologique** the technological revolution, the revolution in technology; **ce nouveau produit**

constitue une véritable ~ this new product is truly revolutionary; **notre profession a subi une véritable ~** our profession has been revolutionized ou has undergone a radical transformation [c] (= parti, forces de la révolution) **la ~** the forces of revolution [d] (loc) [rue, quartier] **être en ~** to be in turmoil; [idée, invention, procédé] **créer une petite ~** to cause a stir

┌─────────────────────────────┐
│ **LA RÉVOLUTION TRANQUILLE** │
└─────────────────────────────┘

The term **la Révolution tranquille** refers to the important social, political and cultural transition that took place in Quebec from the early 1960s. As well as rapid economic expansion and a reorganization of political institutions, there was a growing sense of pride among Québécois in their specific identity as French-speaking citizens. The Révolution tranquille is thus seen as a strong affirmation of Quebec's identity as a French-speaking province.
→ OFFICE DE LA LANGUE FRANÇAISE ; QUÉBEC

révolutionnaire [RevɔlysjɔnɛR] [1] ADJ (gén) revolutionary; (Hist) Revolutionary, of the French Revolution [2] NMF (gén) revolutionary; (Hist) Revolutionary (in the French Revolution)

révolutionner [Revɔlysjɔne] ▸ conjug 1 ◂ VT [a] (= transformer radicalement) to revolutionize [b] (* = bouleverser) [+ personnes] to stir up; **son arrivée a révolutionné le quartier** his arrival stirred up the whole neighbourhood ou caused a great stir in the neighbourhood

revolver [Revɔlvɛʀ] NM (= pistolet) (gén) pistol, (hand)gun; (à barillet) revolver; **coup de ~** pistol shot, gunshot; **tué de plusieurs coups de ~** gunned down; **microscope à ~** microscope with a revolving nosepiece; **tour ~** capstan lathe, turret lathe → **poche**[1]

revolving [Revɔlviŋ] ADJ INV **crédit ~** revolving credit

révoquer [Revɔke] ▸ conjug 1 ◂ VT [a] (= destituer) [+ magistrat, fonctionnaire] to remove from office, dismiss [b] (= annuler) [+ legs, contrat, édit] to revoke [c] (littér = contester) **~ qch en doute** to call sth into question, question sth

revoter [R(ə)vɔte] ▸ conjug 1 ◂ [1] VI to vote again [2] VT **~ un texte de loi** to vote on a bill again

revouloir* [R(ə)vulwaR] ▸ conjug 31 ◂ VT [+ pain] to want more; [+ orange] to want another; **qui en reveut?** (gén) who wants (some) more?; (nourriture) anyone for seconds?*; **tu reveux du café/un morceau de gâteau?** would you like some more coffee/another slice of cake?; **il reveut le livre** (qui est à lui) he wants his book back; (qu'on lui a déjà prêté) he wants the book again

revoyure* [R(ə)vwajyR] **◆ à la revoyure** EXCL see you!*, (I'll) be seeing you!*

revue [R(ə)vy] [1] NF [a] (= examen) review; **faire la ~ de** to review, go through; **une ~ de la presse hebdomadaire** a review of the weekly press [b] (Mil) (= inspection) inspection, review; (= parade) march-past, review [c] (= magazine) (à fort tirage, illustrée) magazine; (érudite) review, journal; **~ automobile/ de mode** car/fashion magazine; **~ littéraire/ scientifique** literary/scientific journal ou review [d] (= spectacle) (satirique) revue; (de variétés) variety show ou performance; **~ à grand spectacle** extravaganza [e] (loc) **passer en ~** (Mil) to pass in review, review, inspect; (fig = énumérer mentalement) to go over in one's mind, pass in review, go through; (= faire la liste de) to list; **être de la ~*** to lose out

2 COMP ► **revue d'armement** (*Mil*) arms inspection ► **revue de détail** (*Mil*) kit inspection ► **revue de presse** review of the press *ou* papers

révulsé, e [revylse] (*ptp de* **se révulser**) ADJ [*yeux*] rolled upwards (*attrib*); [*visage*] contorted

révulser [revylse] ▸ conjug 1 ◂ **1** VT (= *dégoûter*) to disgust; **ça me révulse** I find it repulsive *ou* disgusting **2** **se révulser** VPR [*visage*] to contort; [*yeux*] to roll upwards

révulsif, -ive [revylsif, iv] (*Méd*) **1** ADJ revulsant **2** NM revulsant, revulsive

révulsion [revylsjɔ̃] NF (*Méd, fig*) revulsion

rewriter¹ [ʀiʀajte] ▸ conjug 1 ◂ VT to edit, rewrite (*US*)

rewriter² [ʀiʀajtœʀ] NM editor, rewriter (*US*)

rewriting [ʀiʀajtiŋ] NM editing, rewriting (*US*)

Reykjavik [ʀekjavik] N Reykjavik

rez-de-chaussée [ʀed(ə)ʃose] NM INV ground floor (*surtout Brit*), first floor (*US*); **au ~** on the ground floor; **habiter un ~** to live in a ground-floor flat (*Brit*) *ou* in a first-floor apartment (*US*)

rez-de-jardin [ʀed(ə)ʒaʀdɛ̃] NM INV garden level; **appartement en ~** garden flat (*Brit*) *ou* apartment (*US*)

RF (ABRÉV = **République française**) → **république**

RFA [ɛʀɛfa] NF (ABRÉV = **République fédérale d'Allemagne**) → **république**

RG [ɛʀʒe] NMPL (ABRÉV = **renseignements généraux**) → **renseignement**

Rh (ABRÉV = **rhésus**) Rh

rhabiller [ʀabije] ▸ conjug 1 ◂ **1** VT **a** **~ qn** (*lit*) to dress sb again, put sb's clothes back on; (= *lui racheter des habits*) to fit sb out again, reclothe sb **b** [+ *édifice*] to renovate; **immeuble rhabillé façon moderne** renovated and modernized building **c** (*Tech*) [+ *montre, pendule*] to repair **2** **se rhabiller** VPR to put one's clothes back on, dress (o.s.) again; **tu peux aller te ~ !** you can forget it!*

rhapsode [ʀapsɔd] NM rhapsode

rhapsodie [ʀapsɔdi] NF rhapsody

rhème [ʀɛm] NM rheme

rhénan, e [ʀenã, an] ADJ (*Géog*) Rhine (*épith*), of the Rhine; (*Art*) Rhenish

Rhénanie [ʀenani] NF Rhineland; **la ~ Palatinat** the Rhineland-Palatinate

rhénium [ʀenjɔm] NM rhenium

rhéostat [ʀeɔsta] NM rheostat

rhésus [ʀezys] NM **a** (*Méd*) rhesus; **~ positif/ négatif** rhesus *ou* Rh positive/negative → **facteur b** (*Zool*) rhesus monkey

rhéteur [ʀetœʀ] NM (*Hist*) rhetor

rhétique [ʀetik] ADJ rhetic

rhétoricien, -ienne [ʀetɔʀisjɛ̃, jɛn] NM,F (*lit, péj*) rhetorician

rhétorique [ʀetɔʀik] **1** NF rhetoric → **figure, fleur 2** ADJ rhetorical

rhéto-roman [ʀetɔʀɔmɑ̃, an] **1** ADJ (*pl* **rhéto-romans**) [ʀetɔʀɔmɑ̃, an] ADJ Rhaeto-Romanic **2** NM (*Ling*) Rhaeto-Romanic

Rhin [ʀɛ̃] NM **le ~** the Rhine

rhinite [ʀinit] NF rhinitis (*NonC*) (*SPÉC*)

rhinocéros [ʀinɔseʀɔs] NM rhinoceros, rhino; **~ d'Asie** Indian rhinoceros; **~ d'Afrique** (African) white rhinoceros

rhinolaryngite [ʀinolaʀɛ̃ʒit] NF sore throat, throat infection, rhinolaryngitis (*NonC*) (*SPÉC*)

rhinologie [ʀinɔlɔʒi] NF rhinology

rhinopharyngé, e [ʀinofaʀɛ̃ʒe], **rhino- pharyngien, -ienne** [ʀinofaʀɛ̃ʒjɛ̃, jɛn] ADJ nose and throat (*épith*), rhinopharyngeal (*SPÉC*)

rhinopharyngite [ʀinofaʀɛ̃ʒit] NF sore throat, throat infection, rhinopharyngitis (*NonC*) (*SPÉC*)

rhinopharynx [ʀinofaʀɛ̃ks] NM nose and throat, rhinopharynx (*SPÉC*)

rhinoplastie [ʀinoplasti] NF rhinoplasty

rhizome [ʀizɔm] NM rhizome

rho [ʀo] NM (= *lettre grecque*) rho

rhodanien, -ienne [ʀɔdanjɛ̃, jɛn] ADJ Rhone (*épith*), of the Rhone → **sillon**

Rhode Island [ʀɔdajlɑ̃d] NM Rhode Island

Rhodes [ʀɔd] N Rhodes; **l'île de ~** the island of Rhodes → **colosse**

Rhodésie [ʀɔdezi] NF Rhodesia

rhodésien, -ienne [ʀɔdezjɛ̃, jɛn] **1** ADJ Rhodesian **2** **Rhodésien(ne)** NM,F Rhodesian

rhodium [ʀɔdjɔm] NM rhodium

rhododendron [ʀɔdɔdɛ̃dʀɔ̃] NM rhododendron

rhombe [ʀɔb] NM († = *losange*) rhomb, rhombus; (= *instrument*) bullroarer

rhombique [ʀɔbik] ADJ rhombic

rhomboïdal, e (*mpl* **-aux**) [ʀɔboidal, o] ADJ rhomboid

rhomboïde [ʀɔboid] NM rhomboid

Rhône [ʀon] NM (= *fleuve*) **le ~** the (river) Rhone

rhovyl® [ʀɔvil] NM Rhovyl®

rhubarbe [ʀybaʀb] NF rhubarb

rhum [ʀɔm] NM rum; **~ blanc** *ou* **agricole/brun** white/dark rum; **sorbet au ~** rum-flavoured sorbet; **glace ~-raisin** rum and raisin ice cream

rhumatisant, e [ʀymatizɑ̃, ɑ̃t] ADJ, NM,F rheumatic

rhumatismal, e (*mpl* **-aux**) [ʀymatismal, o] ADJ rheumatic

rhumatisme [ʀymatism] NM rheumatism (*NonC*); **avoir un ~** *ou* **des ~s dans le bras** to have rheumatism in one's arm; **~ articulaire** rheumatoid arthritis (*NonC*); **~ déformant** polyarthritis (*NonC*)

rhumato* [ʀymato] **1** NF ABRÉV = **rhumatologie 2** NMF ABRÉV = **rhumatologue**

rhumatologie [ʀymatɔlɔʒi] NF rheumatology

rhumatologue [ʀymatɔlɔg] NMF rheumatologist

rhume [ʀym] NM cold; **attraper un (gros) ~** to catch a (bad *ou* heavy) cold; **~ de cerveau** head cold; **~ des foins** hay fever

rhumerie [ʀɔmʀi] NF (= *distillerie*) rum distillery

rhyolit(h)e [ʀjɔlit] NF rhyolite

rhythm and blues [ʀitmɛndbluz], **rhy- thm'n'blues** [ʀitmɛnbluz] NM rhythm and blues, rhythm'n'blues

ria [ʀija] NF ria

riant, e [ʀ(i)jɑ̃, ɑ̃t] ADJ [*paysage*] pleasant; [*atmosphère, perspective*] cheerful, happy; [*visage*] cheerful, smiling, happy

RIB [ʀib] NM (ABRÉV = **relevé d'identité bancaire**) → **relevé**

ribambelle [ʀibɑ̃bɛl] NF **une ~ de** [+ *enfants*] a swarm *ou* herd *ou* flock of; [+ *animaux*] a herd of; [+ *noms*] a string of; [+ *objets*] a row of; [+ *choses à faire*] stacks of

ribaud [ʀibo] NM (†† *ou hum*) bawdy *ou* ribald fellow

ribaude†† [ʀibod] NF trollop†*, bawdy wench†

riboflavine [ʀiboflavin] NF riboflavin

ribonucléique [ʀibonykleik] ADJ **acide ~** ribonucleic acid

ribosome [ʀibozɔm] NM ribosome

ribote†* [ʀibɔt] NF merrymaking (*NonC*), revel, carousing† (*NonC*); **être en ~** ◊ **faire ~** to make merry, carouse†

ribouldingue*† [ʀibuldɛ̃g] NF spree, binge*; **deux jours de ~** a two-day spree* *ou* binge*; **faire la ~** to go on a spree *ou* a binge*

ricain, e* [ʀikɛ̃, ɛn] (*hum, péj*) **1** ADJ Yank(ee)* (*péj*) **2** **Ricain(e)** NM,F Yank(ee)*

ricanant, e [ʀikanɑ̃, ɑ̃t] ADJ [*personne, voix*] sniggering

ricanement [ʀikanmɑ̃] NM (*méchant*) snigger, sniggering (*NonC*); (*sot*) giggle, giggling (*NonC*); (*gêné*) nervous laughter (*NonC*); **j'ai entendu des ~s** I heard someone sniggering

ricaner [ʀikane] ▸ conjug 1 ◂ VI (*méchamment*) to snigger; (*sottement*) to giggle; (*avec gêne*) to laugh nervously, give a nervous laugh

ricaneur, -euse [ʀikanœʀ, øz] **1** ADJ (*méchant*) sniggering; (*bête*) giggling **2** NM,F (= *personne méchante*) sniggerer; (= *personne bête*) giggler

Richard [ʀiʃaʀ] NM Richard; **~ Cœur de Lion** Richard (the) Lionheart

richard, e* [ʀiʃaʀ, aʀd] NM,F (*péj*) rich person; **un hôtel pour ~s** a posh* hotel

riche [ʀiʃ] **1** ADJ **a** (= *nanti*) [*personne*] rich, wealthy, well-off (*attrib*); [*pays*] rich; **~ à millions** enormously wealthy; **~ comme Crésus** as rich as Croesus, fabulously rich *ou* wealthy; **faire un ~ mariage** to marry into a wealthy family, marry (into) money; **~ héritière** wealthy heiress; **nous ne sommes pas ~s** we're by no means rich, we're not very well-off

b (= *luxueux*) [*bijoux, étoffes*] rich, costly; [*coloris*] rich; [*mobilier*] sumptuous, costly; **je vous donne ce stylo, mais ce n'est pas un ~ cadeau** I'll give you this pen but it's not much of a gift; **ça fait ~*** it looks expensive *ou* posh*

c (= *consistant, fertile*) [*aliment, mélange, sujet, terre*] rich; **le français est une langue ~** French is a rich language; **c'est une ~ nature** he (*ou* she) is a person of immense resources *ou* qualities; **c'est une ~ idée*** that's a great* *ou* grand idea

d (= *abondant*) [*moisson*] rich; [*végétation*] rich, lush; [*collection*] large, rich; [*vocabulaire*] rich, wide; **il y a une documentation très ~ sur ce sujet** there is a wealth of *ou* a vast amount of information on this subject

e **~ en** [*calories, gibier, monuments*] rich in; **alimentation ~ en protéines/cellulose végétale** high-protein/high-fibre diet; **région ~ en eau/pétrole** region rich in water/oil resources; (*hum*) **je ne suis pas ~ en sucre** I'm not very well-off for sugar; **année ~ en événements spectaculaires** year full of dramatic incidents, action-packed year

f **~ de** [+ *espérances, possibilités*] full of; **c'est une expérience ~ d'enseignements** you learn a great deal from this experience, it's a tremendous learning experience; **il est revenu, ~ de souvenirs** he returned with a wealth of memories; **acteur/marché ~ de promesses** highly promising actor/market; **bibliothèque ~ de plusieurs millions d'ouvrages** library boasting several million books; **~ de cette expérience, il ...** thanks to this experience, he ...

2 NMF rich *ou* wealthy person; **les ~s** the rich, the wealthy; **de ~(s)** [*vêtements, nourriture*] fancy; (*péj*) **voiture de ~(s)** fancy *ou* flashy car **~ gosse, prêter**

richelieu [ʀiʃəljø] NM (= *chaussure*) Oxford (shoe)

richement [ʀiʃmɑ̃] ADV (*récompenser, vêtir*) richly; [*décoré, meublé*] richly, sumptuously; **~ illustré** richly *ou* lavishly illustrated, with lavish *ou* copious illustrations → **doter**

richesse [ʀiʃɛs] **1** NF **a** [*pays, personne*] wealth; **la ~ ne l'a pas changé** wealth *ou* being rich hasn't altered him; **ce n'est pas la ~, mais c'est mieux que rien*** it's not exactly the lap of luxury but it's better than nothing; **être d'une ~ insolente** to be obscenely rich; **le tourisme est notre principale (source de) ~** tourism is our greatest asset; **la ~ nationale** the country's national wealth

b [*ameublement, décor*] sumptuousness, richness; [*coloris, étoffe*] richness

[c] [aliment, collection, sol, texte] richness; [végétation] richness, lushness; **la ~ de son vocabulaire** the richness of his vocabulary, his wide ou rich vocabulary; **la ~ de cette documentation** the abundance of the information; **la ~ en calcium de cet aliment** the high calcium content of this food; **la ~ en matières premières/en gibier de cette région** the abundance of raw materials/of game in this region; **la ~ en pétrole/en minéraux du pays** the country's abundant ou vast oil/mineral resources; **une culture d'une ~ inouïe** an extraordinarily rich culture

[d] (= bien) **notre ferme, c'est notre seule ~** this farm is all we have; **la santé est une ~** good health is a great blessing ou is a boon, it's a blessing to be healthy

[2] **richesses** NF PL (= argent) riches, wealth; (= ressources) wealth; (fig = trésors) treasures; **entasser des ~s** to pile up riches; **la répartition des ~s d'un pays** the distribution of a country's wealth; **l'exploitation des ~s naturelles** the exploitation of natural resources; **les ~s de l'art tibétain** the treasures of Tibetan art; **montrez-nous toutes vos ~s** show us your treasures

richissime [ʀiʃisim] ADJ fabulously rich ou wealthy

ricin [ʀisɛ̃] NM castor oil plant → **huile**

ricocher [ʀikɔʃe] ▸ conjug 1 ◂ VI [balle de fusil] to ricochet (**sur** off); [pierre] to rebound (**sur** off); (sur l'eau) to bounce (**sur** on); **faire ~ un galet sur l'eau** to skim a pebble across the water, make a pebble bounce on the water

ricochet [ʀikɔʃɛ] NM (gén) rebound; [balle de fusil] ricochet; [caillou sur l'eau] bounce; (lit, fig) **faire ~** to rebound; **il a été blessé par ~** he was wounded by a ricocheting bullet; (fig) **par ~, il a perdu son emploi** as an indirect result he lost his job; **(s'amuser à) faire des ~s** to skim pebbles; **il a fait quatre ~s** he made the pebble bounce four times

ric-rac [ʀikʀak] ADV [a] (= très exactement) [payer] on the nail*; [b] (= de justesse) [réussir, échapper] by the skin of one's teeth; **côté finances, ce mois-ci, c'est ~** money is going to be tight this month, we'll just about make it through the month moneywise; **ça va se jouer ~** it's going to be touch and go; **j'ai eu mon train ~** I caught the train, but only just

rictus [ʀiktys] NM (grimaçant) grin; (effrayant) snarl; **~ moqueur/cruel** mocking ou sardonic/cruel grin

ride [ʀid] NF [peau, pomme] wrinkle (**de** in); [eau, sable] ripple (**de** on, in), ridge (**de** in); **les ~s de son front** the wrinkles ou lines on his forehead; **visage creusé de ~s** deeply lined face, wrinkled face; (lit, fig) **elle/ce roman n'a pas pris une ~** she/this novel hasn't aged a bit

ridé, e [ʀide] (ptp de **rider**) ADJ [peau, fruit] wrinkled; [front] furrowed; [eau, mer] rippled; **~e comme une vieille pomme** as wrinkled as a prune

rideau (pl **rideaux**) [ʀido] [1] NM [a] (= draperie) curtain; **tirer les ~x** (fermer) to draw ou close the curtains ou drapes (US), draw the curtains to; (ouvrir) to draw the curtains, pull ou draw the curtains back; (fig) **tirer le ~ sur** [+ défaut, passé] to draw a veil over; **tomber en ~*** to break down; **je me suis retrouvé en ~ en pleine campagne*** there I was, broken down in the middle of nowhere

[b] (Théât) curtain; **~ à 20 heures** the curtain rises at 8 o'clock, the curtain's at 8 o'clock; **~ !** (= cri des spectateurs) curtain!; (* fig = assez) that's enough!, I've had enough!; (fig) **le ~ est tombé sur l'affaire** the curtain came down on the affair

[c] [boutique] shutter; [cheminée] register, blower; [classeur, secrétaire] roll shutter; [appareil-photo] shutter

[d] (= écran) **~ de** [+ arbres, verdure] curtain ou screen of; [+ policiers, troupes] curtain of; [+

pluie] curtain ou sheet of; **~ de fumée** smoke screen; **~ de feu** sheet of flame ou fire

[2] COMP ▸ **rideaux bonne femme** looped curtains ou drapes (US) ▸ **rideau de douche** shower curtain ▸ **rideau de fer** ou **métallique** [boutique] metal shutter(s); [théâtre] (metal) safety curtain, fire curtain; (Hist) **le ~ de fer** the Iron Curtain; **les pays au-delà du ~ de fer** the Iron Curtain countries, the countries behind the Iron Curtain ▸ **rideaux de lit** bed hangings ou curtains

ridelle [ʀidɛl] NF [camion, charrette] slatted side

rider [ʀide] ▸ conjug 1 ◂ [1] VT [+ fruit, peau] to wrinkle; [+ front] [colère, soucis] to wrinkle; [âge] to line with wrinkles; [+ eau] to ripple, ruffle the surface of; [+ neige, sable] to ruffle ou wrinkle the surface of; (Naut) to tighten [2] **se rider** VPR [peau, fruit, visage] to become wrinkled, become lined with wrinkles; [eau, surface] to ripple, become rippled; **à ces mots, son front se rida** his forehead wrinkled ou he wrinkled his forehead at these words

ridicule [ʀidikyl] [1] ADJ [a] (= grotesque) [conduite, personne, vêtement] ridiculous, ludicrous, absurd; [prétentions] ridiculous, laughable; [superstition] ridiculous, silly; **se rendre ~ aux yeux de tous** to make o.s. (look) ridiculous ou make a fool of o.s. ou make o.s. look a fool in everyone's eyes; **ça le rend ~** it makes him look ridiculous ou (like) a fool; **ne sois pas ~** don't be ridiculous ou silly ou absurd [b] (= infime) [prix] ridiculous, ridiculously low; [quantité] ridiculous, ridiculously small

[2] NM [a] (= absurdité) ridiculousness, absurdity; **le ~ de la conversation ne lui échappait pas** he was well aware of the absurdity of the conversation; **je ne sais pas si vous saisissez tout le ~ de la situation** I don't know if you realize just how absurd ou ridiculous the situation is ou if you realize the full absurdity of the situation; **il y a quelque ~ à faire ...** it is rather ridiculous to do ...; **c'est d'un ~ achevé** it's perfectly ou utterly ridiculous; **se donner le ~ de ...** to be ridiculous enough to ... → **tourner**

[b] **le ~** ridicule; **tomber dans le ~** [personne] to make o.s. ridiculous, become ridiculous; [film] to become ridiculous; **s'exposer au ~** to expose o.s. ou lay o.s. open to ridicule; **avoir le sens du ~** to have a sense of the ridiculous; **la peur du ~** (the) fear of ridicule ou of appearing ridiculous; **le ~ ne tue pas** ridicule has never been the unmaking of anyone, ridicule never killed anyone; **tourner qn/qch en ~** to ridicule sb/sth, make sb/sth an object of ridicule; **couvrir qn de ~** to heap ridicule on sb, make sb look ridiculous, make a laughing stock of sb; **il y en a qui n'ont pas peur du ~ !** some people aren't afraid of looking ridiculous!

[3] **ridicules** NM PL (= travers) silliness (NonC), ridiculous ou silly ways, absurdities; **les ~s humains** the absurdities of human nature; **les ~s d'une classe sociale** the ridiculous ways ou the (little) absurdities of a social class

ridiculement [ʀidikylmɑ̃] ADV [bas, vêtu] ridiculously; [chanter, marcher] in a ridiculous way

ridiculiser [ʀidikylize] ▸ conjug 1 ◂ [1] VT [+ défaut, doctrine, personne] to ridicule, hold up to ridicule [2] **se ridiculiser** VPR to make o.s. (look) ridiculous, make a fool of o.s.

ridule [ʀidyl] NF fine line ou wrinkle

rien [ʀjɛ̃]

[1]	PRONOM INDÉFINI	[3]	LOC ADVERBIALE
[2]	NOM MASCULIN	[4]	ADVERBE

[1] PRONOM INDÉFINI

♦ **avec ne** (= nulle chose) nothing; **~ ne le fera reculer** nothing will make him turn back; **il n'y a ~ qui puisse m'empêcher de faire cela** there's

nothing that could prevent me from doing that; **il n'y a ~ que je ne fasse pour elle** there's nothing I wouldn't do for her; **il n'y a plus ~** there's nothing left; **on ne pouvait plus ~ pour elle** there was nothing more ou else to be done for her, nothing more could be done for her; **je n'ai ~ entendu/compris** I didn't hear/understand anything ou a thing, I heard/understood nothing; **je ne crois plus à ~** I don't believe in anything any more; **elle ne mange presque ~** she hardly eats a thing, she eats hardly anything; **il n'en sait ~** he has no idea; **je n'en sais trop ~** I haven't a clue; (dans la vie) **on n'a ~ sans ~** you only get out of life what you put into it ■ (PROV) **~ ne sert de courir, il faut partir à point** ou **temps** slow and steady wins the race (PROV) → **risquer, valoir**

♦ **avec avoir : ils n'ont ~** (possessions) they have nothing; (maladie, blessure) there's nothing wrong with them; **ça va, tu n'as ~ ?** are you OK?; **n'avoir ~ contre qn** to have nothing against sb; **il n'a ~ d'un politicien/d'un dictateur** he's got nothing of the politician/dictator in ou about him; **il n'a ~ de son père** he is nothing ou not a bit like his father; **j'en ai ~ à faire*** ou **à foutre‡** I don't give a damn‡ ou toss‡

♦ **avec être : n'être ~** [personne] to be a nobody; [chose] to be nothing; **pour lui, 50 km à vélo, ce n'est ~** he thinks nothing of cycling 50 kilometres; **n'être ~ en comparaison de ...** to be nothing compared to ...; **il n'est ~ dans l'entreprise** he's a nobody ou he's nothing in the firm; **il ne nous est ~** he's not connected with us, he's nothing to do with us; **il n'est plus ~ pour moi** he means nothing to me anymore; **il n'en est ~** it's nothing of the sort, that's not it at all; **on le croyait blessé, mais il n'en est ~** we thought he was injured but he's not at all ou he's nothing of the sort; **élever quatre enfants, ça n'est pas ~** bringing up four children is not exactly a picnic* ou is no mean feat; **tu t'es fait mal ? — non, ce n'est** ou **c'est* ~** did you hurt yourself? — no, it's nothing; **pardon ! — c'est* ~** sorry! — it doesn't matter ou it's alright; **c'est ~ de le dire*** (and) that's putting it mildly*, (and) that's an understatement

♦ **avec faire : il ne fait (plus) ~** he doesn't work (any more); **huit jours sans ~ faire** a week doing nothing; **il ne nous a ~ fait** he hasn't done anything to us; **cela ne lui fait ~** he doesn't mind ou care; **ça ne fait ~** it doesn't matter, never mind; **ça ne fait ~ si j'amène un ami ?** is it all right if I bring a friend along?; **il n'y a ~ à faire** (gén) there's nothing we can do, there's nothing to be done; (= c'est inutile) it's useless ou hopeless; **~ à faire !** it's no good!; **~ n'y fait !** nothing's any good!

♦ **en rien** (= absolument pas) cela ne nous gêne **en ~** it doesn't bother us in any way ou in the least ou at all; **il n'est en ~ responsable de la situation** he's not in any way ou at all responsible for the situation, he's not the slightest bit responsible for the situation; **ce tableau ne ressemble en ~ au reste de son œuvre** this picture is nothing like his other works

♦ **rien de + adjectif ou adverbe** nothing; **~ d'autre** nothing else; **~ de plus** nothing more ou else ou further; **~ de moins** nothing less; **~ de neuf** nothing new; **~ de plus facile** nothing easier; **il n'y a ~ eu de volé** nothing was stolen, there was nothing stolen; **nous n'avons ~ d'autre** ou **de plus à ajouter** we have nothing else ou more ou further to add; **ça n'a ~ d'impossible** it's perfectly possible; **(il n'y a) ~ de tel qu'une bonne douche chaude !** there's nothing like ou nothing to beat a nice hot shower!, you can't beat a nice hot shower!; (sans ne) **je t'achèterai le journal, ~ d'autre ?** I'll get you a newspaper — do you want anything else?; **~ de grave, j'espère ?** (après un accident, un incident) nothing serious, I hope?; **elle a fait ce qu'il fallait, ~ de plus, ~ de moins** she did all she had to, nothing more nor less ou nothing more, nothing less

b = quelque chose anything; avez-vous jamais ~ fait pour l'aider? have you ever done anything to help him?; as-tu jamais ~ lu de plus drôle? did you ever read anything quite so funny?; as-tu jamais ~ vu de pareil? have you ever seen such a thing? ou anything like it? ou the like?; sans ~ qui le prouve without anything to prove it; sans que/avant que tu en saches ~ without your knowing/before you know anything about it

c locutions intensives
♦ **deux** ou **trois fois rien** next to nothing
♦ **rien à rien**: il ne comprend ~ à ~ he hasn't got a clue
♦ **rien au monde** nothing on earth ou in the world; je ne connais ~ au monde de plus bête I can't think of anything more stupid; il ne quitterait son pays pour ~ au monde he wouldn't leave his country for anything ou for all the tea in China
♦ **rien de rien*** nothing, absolutely nothing; il ne fait ~, mais ~ de ~ he does nothing, and I mean nothing ou but nothing (at all)
♦ **rien du tout** nothing at all; une petite blessure de ~ du tout a trifling ou trivial little injury, a mere scratch; qu'est-ce que c'est que cette pomme/ce cadeau de ~ du tout? what on earth can I (ou you etc) do with this stupid little apple/present?
♦ **rien qui vaille**: ne faire/n'écrire ~ qui vaille to do/write nothing useful ou worthwhile ou of any use; ça ne me dit ~ qui vaille (= je me méfie) I don't like the look of that, that looks suspicious to me; (= ça ne me tente pas) it doesn't appeal to me in the least ou slightest

d Sport nil; (Tennis) love; ~ partout (Sport) nil all; (Tennis) love all; (Tennis) **15 à ~** 15 love; il mène par deux sets à ~ he's leading by two sets to love

e Jeux ~ ne va plus! rien ne va plus!

f
♦ **pour rien** (= inutilement) for nothing; (= sans cause) ce n'est pas pour ~ que ... it is not without cause ou good reason that ..., it's not for nothing that ...
(= pour peu d'argent) for a song, for next to nothing; on n'a ~ pour ~ everything has its price → compter, coup, être

g
♦ **rien que** (= seulement) la vérité, ~ que la vérité the truth and nothing but the truth; ~ que la chambre coûte déjà très cher the room alone already costs a great deal; ~ que dans cet immeuble, il y a eu six cambriolages in this apartment building alone there have been six burglaries; ~ qu'à le voir, j'ai deviné I guessed by just looking at him; je voudrais vous voir, ~ qu'une minute could I see you just for a minute?; je voudrais une pièce ~ que pour moi I would like a room of my own; il le fait ~ que pour l'embêter* he does it just to annoy him; c'est à moi, ~ qu'à moi it's mine and mine alone, it's mine and mine only; (iro) il voulait 500 F, ~ que ça! he wanted a mere 500 francs (iro), he just ou only wanted 500 francs (iro); elle veut être actrice, ~ que ça! she wants to be an actress, no less!

h
♦ **rien moins que** (= nullement) ~ moins que sûr anything but sure, not at all sure
(= absolument) un monument ~ moins que colossal an absolutely huge monument; il s'agit là de ~ moins qu'un crime it's nothing less than a crime; il n'est question de ~ moins que d'abattre deux forêts it will mean nothing less than chopping down two forests

i loc
♦ à signaler/déclarer nothing to report/declare; je vous remercie — de ~* thank you — you're welcome ou don't mention it ou not at all; excusez-moi! — de ~* sorry! — no bother* ou no trouble (at all); († péj) une fille de ~ a worthless girl; c'est mieux que ~ it's better than nothing; c'est ça ou ~ it's that or

nothing, take it or leave it; ce que tu fais ou ~! you may as well not bother! → comme, dire etc

2 NOM MASCULIN
a = néant nothingness
b = petite chose sans importance un ~ a mere nothing; des ~s trivia; un ~ l'effraie ◊ il a peur d'un ~ every little thing ou the slightest thing frightens him; un ~ la fait rire she laughs at every little thing ou at anything at all; un ~ l'habille she looks good in anything; j'ai failli rater le train, il s'en est fallu d'un ~ I came within a hair's breadth of missing the train; il suffirait d'un ~ pour qu'ils se réconcilient it would take nothing at all for them to make up
♦ **comme un rien**: il pourrait te casser le bras comme un ~* he could break your arm, no trouble; ces vieilles savates, ça tue l'amour comme un ~! those old slippers are a real passion killer!
♦ **pour un rien**: il pleure pour un ~ he cries at the drop of a hat; il s'inquiète pour un ~ he worries about the slightest little thing

c = petite quantité
♦ **un rien de**: with a touch ou hint of; mettez-y un ~ de muscade add a touch ou a tiny pinch of nutmeg; un ~ de vin a taste of wine; un ~ de fantaisie a touch of fantasy; avec un ~ d'ironie with a hint ou touch of irony; en un ~ de temps in no time (at all), in next to no time
d péj: désignant une personne c'est un/une ~ du tout (socialement) he/she is a nobody; (moralement) he/she is no good

3 **un rien** LOC ADV = un peu a (tiny) bit, a shade; c'est un ~ bruyant ici it's a bit ou a shade noisy in here; un ~ plus grand/petit a fraction bigger/smaller; moi pas, dit-elle un ~ insolente I'm not, she said rather insolently

4 ADVERBE
†,* = très really, not half* (Brit); il fait ~ froid ici it's damned cold• ou it isn't half cold* (Brit) here; ils sont ~ snobs they're really stuck-up*, they aren't half snobs* (Brit)

rieur, rieuse [ʀ(i)jœʀ, ʀ(i)jøz] **1** ADJ [personne] cheerful, merry; [expression, yeux] cheerful, laughing → mouette **2** NM,F les ~s se turent people stopped laughing; il avait les ~s de son côté he had people laughing with him rather than at him

rififi [ʀififi] NM (arg Crime) trouble

riflard [ʀiflaʀ] NM (Tech) (= rabot) jack plane; (= lime à métaux) rough file

rifle [ʀifl] NM rifle → vingt-deux

Riga [ʀiga] N Riga

rigaudon [ʀigodɔ̃, ʀigɔdɔ̃] NM rigadoon

rigide [ʀiʒid] ADJ **a** [armature, tige] rigid, stiff; [muscle, col, carton] stiff; **livre à couverture ~** hardback (book) **b** [caractère] rigid, inflexible; [règle] strict, hard-and-fast; [classification, éducation] strict; [morale, politique, discipline] strict, rigid; [personne] rigid

rigidement [ʀiʒidmɑ̃] ADV [élever un enfant] strictly; [appliquer un règlement] strictly, rigidly

rigidifier [ʀiʒidifje] ▶conjug 7◀ VT (lit) to make rigid ou stiff; (fig) to rigidify

rigidité [ʀiʒidite] NF **a** [armature, tige] rigidity, rigidness, stiffness; [muscle, carton, col] stiffness; **~ cadavérique** rigor mortis **b** [caractère, personne] rigidity, inflexibility; [règle, morale, politique] strictness, rigidity; [classification, éducation] strictness

rigodon [ʀigodɔ̃] NM = rigaudon

rigolade* [ʀigolad] NF **a** (= rire, amusement) il aime la ~ he likes a bit of fun ou a laugh; on a eu une bonne partie ou séance de ~ it was ou we had a good laugh* ou a lot of fun; quelle ~, quand il est entré! what a laugh* when he came in!; le dîner s'est terminé dans la plus franche ~ the dinner ended in uproarious laughter; il n'y a pas que la ~ dans

la vie having fun isn't the only thing in life; il prend tout à la ~ he thinks everything's a big joke ou laugh*, he makes a joke of everything **b** (= plaisanterie) ce procès est une (vaste) ~ this trial is a (big) joke ou farce; démonter ça, c'est une ou de la ~ taking that to pieces is child's play ou is a cinch*; ce qu'il dit là, c'est de la ~ what he says is a lot of con ou a load of hooey•; ce régime, c'est de la ~ this diet is a complete con*

rigolard, e* [ʀigolaʀ, aʀd] ADJ [air, personne] jovial; c'est un ~ he's always ready for a laugh*, he likes a good laugh*

rigole [ʀigol] NF (= canal) channel; (= filet d'eau) rivulet; (Agr = sillon) furrow; la pluie avait creusé des ~s dans le sol the rain had cut channels ou furrows in the earth; ~ d'irrigation irrigation channel; ~ d'écoulement drain

rigoler* [ʀigole] ▶conjug 1◀ VI **a** (= rire) to laugh; quand il l'a su, il a bien rigolé when he found out, he had a good laugh about it*; il nous a bien fait ~ he had us all laughing ou in stitches*; (iro) tu me fais ~ you make me laugh (iro); ne me fais pas ~ don't make me laugh; il n'y a pas de quoi ~! that's nothing to laugh about!, what's so funny?; quand tu verras les dégâts, tu rigoleras moins you'll be laughing on the other side of your face ou you won't be laughing when you see the damage **b** (= s'amuser) to have (a bit of) fun, have a (bit of a) laugh*; il aime ~ he likes a bit of fun ou a good laugh*; on a bien rigolé we had great fun ou a good laugh*; chez eux, on ne doit pas ~ tous les jours! it can't be much fun in their house! **c** (= plaisanter) to joke; tu rigoles! you're kidding!* ou joking!; je ne rigole pas I'm not joking ou kidding*; le patron est quelqu'un qui ne rigole pas the boss won't take any nonsense; il ne faut pas ~ avec ces médicaments you shouldn't mess about* ou fool about* with medicines like these; il ne faut pas ~ avec ce genre de maladie an illness like this has to be taken seriously ou can't be taken lightly; j'ai dit ça pour ~ it was only a joke, I only said it in fun ou for a laugh*

rigolo, -ote* [ʀigolo, ɔt] **1** ADJ [histoire, film] funny; [personne] funny, comical; il est ~ (plaisantin) he's funny, he's a laugh*; (original) he's comical ou funny; ce qui lui est arrivé n'est pas ~ what's happened to him is no joke ou is not funny; (iro) vous êtes ~, vous, mettez-vous à ma place! you make me laugh — put yourself in my shoes!; c'est ~, je n'avais jamais remarqué cela that's funny ou odd, I'd never noticed that; (iro) c'est ~ comme les gens sont égoïstes it's funny how selfish people can be (iro) **2** NM,F (= comique) comic, wag; (péj = fumiste) fraud, phoney; c'est un sacré ~ he likes a good laugh*, he's a real comic; (péj) c'est un (petit) ~ he's a (little) fraud **3** NM (†• = revolver) gun, rod (US)

rigorisme [ʀigoʀism] NM rigorism, austerity, rigid moral standards

rigoriste [ʀigoʀist] **1** ADJ rigoristic, austere, rigid **2** NMF rigorist, rigid moralist

rigoureusement [ʀiguʀøzmɑ̃] ADV **a** [punir, traiter] harshly; [démontrer, raisonner, sélectionner] rigorously; [appliquer, classifier] rigorously, strictly; **respecter ~ les consignes** to observe the regulations strictly **b** (= absolument) [authentique, vrai] absolutely, utterly, entirely; [exact] rigorously; [interdit] strictly; [impossible] utterly; [identique] absolutely; **ça ne changera ~ rien** that'll change absolutely nothing

rigoureux, -euse [ʀiguʀø, øz] ADJ **a** (= sévère) [discipline, punition] rigorous, harsh, severe; [mesures] rigorous, stringent, harsh; [maître, moraliste] rigorous, strict, rigid; [sélection, gestion, suivi] rigorous; [climat] rigorous, harsh; **hiver ~** hard ou harsh winter; **avoir l'esprit ~** to have a rigorous mind; **de façon rigoureuse** rigorously [b] (= exact) [méthode, raisonnement, style, examen] rigorous; [classification, définition] rigorous, strict [c] (= absolu) [interdiction, sens d'un mot] strict; **l'application rigoureuse de la loi** the strict enforcement of the law; **ce n'est pas une règle rigoureuse** it's not a hard-and-fast rule

rigueur [RigœR] NF [a] (= sévérité) [condamnation, discipline] harshness, severity, rigour; [mesures] harshness, stringency, rigour; [climat, hiver] rigour, harshness; **punir qn avec toute la ~ de la loi** to punish sb with the utmost rigour of the law; **faire preuve de ~ à l'égard de qn** to be strict ou harsh with sb, be hard on sb; **traiter qn avec la plus grande ~** to treat sb with the utmost rigour ou harshness ou severity; (littér) **les ~s du sort/de l'hiver** the rigours of fate/of winter → **arrêt, délai** [b] (= austérité) [morale] rigour, rigidity, strictness; [personne] sternness, strictness; **la politique de ~ du gouvernement** the government's austerity measures; **la ~ économique** economic austerity [c] (= précision) [pensée, raisonnement, style] rigour; [calcul] precision, exactness; [classification, définition] strictness, rigour, rigorousness; **manquer de ~** to lack rigour [d] (loc) **tenir ~ à qn** to hold it against sb; **il lui a tenu ~ de n'être pas venu** he held it against him that he didn't come; **je ne vous en tiens pas ~** I don't hold it against you; **à la ~** at a pinch, if need be; **on peut à l'extrême ~ remplacer le curry par du poivre** at a pinch ou if you really have to you can use pepper instead of curry powder; **un délit, à la ~, mais un crime non: le mot est trop fort** a minor offence possibly ou perhaps, but not a crime — that's too strong a word; **il pourrait à la ~ avoir gagné la côte, mais j'en doute** there is a faint possibility that he made it ou he may just possibly have made it back to the shore but I doubt it; **il est de ~ d'envoyer un petit mot de remerciement** it is the done thing to send a note of thanks; **la tenue de ~ est ...** the dress to be worn is ..., the accepted dress ou attire (frm) is ...; **«tenue de soirée de ~»** "evening dress", "dress: formal"; **en toute ~** strictly speaking → **délai**

rikiki [Rikiki] ADJ INV → **riquiqui**

rillettes [Rijɛt] NFPL rillettes (type of potted meat or fish); **~ pur porc** 100% pork rillettes

rillons [Rijɔ̃] NMPL pork cooked in fat and served cold

rimailler† [Rimaje] ▶conjug 1◀ VI (péj) to write doggerel, versify

rimailleur, -euse† [Rimajœr, øz] NM,F (péj) would-be poet, rhymester, poetaster†

rimaye [Rimaj] NF bergschrund

rime [Rim] NF rhyme; **~ masculine/féminine** masculine/feminine rhyme; **~ pauvre/riche** poor/rich rhyme; **~s croisées** ou **alternées** alternate rhymes; **~s plates** ou **suivies** rhyming couplets; **~s embrassées** abba rhyme scheme; **~s tiercées** terza rima; **~ pour l'œil/l'oreille** rhyme for the eye/the ear; **faire qch sans ~ ni raison** to do sth without either rhyme or reason; **cela n'a ni ~ ni raison** there's neither rhyme nor reason to it

rimer [Rime] ▶conjug 1◀ [1] VI [a] [mot] to rhyme (**avec** with); (fig) **cela ne rime à rien** it doesn't make sense, there's no sense in it; **à quoi cela rime-t-il ?** what's the point of it? ou sense in it?; **économie ne rime pas toujours avec profit** saving doesn't necessarily go together with profit, saving and profit don't necessarily go hand in hand [b] [poète] to write verse ou rhyme [2] VT to put into verse; **poésie rimée** rhyming poetry ou verse

rimeur, -euse [Rimœr, øz] NM,F (péj) rhymester, would-be poet, poetaster†

rimmel ® [Rimɛl] NM mascara

---

rinçage [Rɛ̃saʒ] NM [a] (= fait de passer à l'eau) rinsing out ou through; (pour enlever le savon) rinsing; (= opération) rinse; **cette machine à laver fait 3 ~s** this washing machine does 3 rinses; **ajouter du vinaigre dans la dernière eau de ~** add some vinegar in the final rinse [b] (pour cheveux) (colour (Brit) ou color (US)) rinse; **elle s'est fait faire un ~** she had a colour rinse

rinceau (pl rinceaux) [Rɛ̃so] NM (Archit) foliage (NonC), foliation (NonC)

rince-bouteille(s) (pl rince-bouteilles) [Rɛ̃sbutɛj] NM (= machine) bottle-washing machine; (= brosse) bottlebrush

rince-doigts [Rɛ̃sdwa] NM INV (= bol) fingerbowl; (en papier) finger wipe

rincée [Rɛ̃se] NF (= averse) downpour; (= défaite, volée) thrashing*, licking*

rincer [Rɛ̃se] ▶conjug 3◀ [1] VT [a] [+ bouteille, verre] to rinse (out); (pour enlever le savon) to rinse; **rince l'assiette** give the plate a rinse, rinse the plate [b]* (= offrir à boire) **c'est lui qui rince*** the drinks are on him [c] **se faire ~*** (par la pluie) to get drenched ou soaked; (au jeu) to get cleaned out*; **il est rincé*** he's lost everything [2] **se rincer** VPR (= laver) **se ~ la bouche** to rinse out one's mouth; **se ~ les mains/les cheveux** to rinse one's hands/one's hair; **se ~ l'œil*** to get an eyeful*; **se ~ le gosier** ou **la dalle** to wet one's whistle*

rincette* [Rɛ̃sɛt] NF nip of brandy etc, little drop of wine (ou brandy etc)

rinçure [Rɛ̃syr] NF (= eau de lavage) rinsing water; (péj = mauvais vin) plonk* (Brit), cheap wine

ring [Riŋ] NM (boxing) ring; **les champions du ~** boxing champions; **monter sur le ~** (pour un match) to go into the ring; (= faire carrière) to take up boxing

ringard[1] [Rɛ̃gar] NM (= tisonnier) poker

ringard[2], e* [Rɛ̃gar, ar] [1] ADJ (= dépassé) [personne] square*; [vêtement] dowdy, naff* (Brit); (= de piètre qualité) [film, roman, chanson] corny*; [décor] tacky*, naff* (Brit) [2] NM,F (dépassé) square*; (médiocre) loser*

ringardise* [Rɛ̃gardiz] NF [vêtement] dowdiness; **ses films/chansons sont d'une ~!** his films/songs are unbelievably corny!*

RIP [Rip] NM (ABRÉV = relevé d'identité postal) → **relevé**

ripaille†* [Ripaj] NF (= festin) feast; **faire ~** to have a feast, have a good blow-out* (Brit)

ripailler†* [Ripaje] ▶conjug 1◀ VI (= festoyer) to feast, have a good blow-out* (Brit)

ripailleur, -euse†* [Ripajœr, øz] [1] ADJ revelling [2] NM,F reveller

ripaton* [Ripatɔ̃] NM (= pied) foot

riper [Ripe] ▶conjug 1◀ [1] VI [a] (= déraper) to slip [b] (* = s'en aller) to take off [2] VT [a] (Tech = gratter) to scrape [b] (faire) **~ (= déplacer)** [+ meuble, pierre, véhicule] to slide along

ripoliner [Ripɔline] ▶conjug 1◀ VT to paint with gloss paint; **murs ripolinés de vert** walls painted in green gloss

riposte [Ripɔst] NF (= réponse) retort, riposte; (= contre-attaque) counterattack, reprisal; (Escrime) riposte; **en ~ à** in reply to; **notre ~ sera impitoyable** we will retaliate mercilessly; **il est prompt à la ~** he always has a ready answer ou a quick retort; **la ~ ne s'est pas fait attendre** the reaction was not long in coming

riposter [Ripɔste] ▶conjug 1◀ [1] VI [a] (= répondre) to answer back, riposte, retaliate; **~ à une insulte** to reply to an insult; **il riposta (à cela) par une insulte** he answered back ou retorted with an insult, he flung back an insult; **~ à une accusation par une insulte** to counter an accusation with an insult [b] (= contre-attaquer) to counterattack, retaliate; **~ à coups de grenades** to retaliate by throwing gre-

---

nades; **~ à une attaque** to counter an attack [c] (Escrime) to riposte [2] VT **~ que** to retort ou riposte ou answer back that

ripou (pl **ripous, ripoux**) [Ripu] [1] ADJ crooked [2] NM (gén) crook; (= policier) crooked cop*, bent copper* (Brit)

riquiqui* [Rikiki] ADJ INV tiny; **ça fait un peu ~** [portion] it's a bit stingy*; [manteau] it's much too small

rire [RiR] ▶conjug 36◀ [1] VI [a] (gén) to laugh; **~ aux éclats** ou **à gorge déployée** to roar with laughter, laugh one's head off; **~ aux larmes** to laugh until one cries; **~ franchement** ou **de bon cœur** to laugh heartily; **~ bruyamment** to guffaw, roar with laughter; (péj) **~ comme un bossu** ou **comme une baleine** to laugh o.s. silly, be doubled up with laughter, split one's sides (laughing); **c'est à mourir** ou **crever* de ~** it's hilarious, it's awfully funny; **la plaisanterie fit ~** the joke raised a laugh ou made everyone laugh; **ça ne me fait pas ~** I don't find it funny, I'm not amused, it doesn't make me laugh; **nous avons bien ri (de notre mésaventure)** we had a good laugh* (over our mishap); **ça m'a bien fait ~** it really made me laugh, it had me in fits*; **on va ~ : il va essayer de sauter** we're in for a laugh* — he's going to try and jump; **il vaut mieux en ~ qu'en pleurer** it's better to look on the bright side; **il a pris les choses en riant** (avec bonne humeur) he saw the funny side of it; (à la légère) he laughed it off; **il n'y a pas de quoi ~** there's nothing to laugh about, it's no laughing matter ■ (PROV) **rira bien qui rira le dernier** he who laughs last laughs longest (Brit) ou best (US) (PROV) [b] (littér) [yeux] to sparkle ou shine with happiness ou laughter; [visage] to shine with happiness [c] (= s'amuser) to have fun, have a laugh*; **il ne pense qu'à ~** he only thinks of having fun; **il passe son temps à ~ avec ses camarades** he spends his time fooling around ou playing about ou larking about (Brit) with his friends; **~ aux dépens de qn** to laugh ou have a laugh at sb's expense; **c'est un homme qui aime bien ~** he is a man who likes a bit of fun ou a good laugh*; **c'est maintenant qu'on va ~!** this is where the fun starts! → **histoire** [d] (= plaisanter) to be joking; **vous voulez ~!** you're joking!, you must be joking! ou kidding!*; **et je ne ris pas** and I'm not joking; **il a dit cela pour ~** he was only joking, he said it in fun; **il a fait cela pour ~** he did it for a joke ou laugh*; **c'était une bagarre pour ~** it was only a pretend fight, it wasn't a real fight → **mot** [e] (loc) **~ dans sa barbe** ou **tout bas** to laugh to o.s., chuckle (away) to o.s.; **~ sous cape** to laugh up one's sleeve, have a quiet laugh; **~ au nez** ou **à la barbe de qn** to laugh in sb's face; **~ du bout des dents** ou **des lèvres** to force o.s. to laugh, laugh politely; **il faisait semblant de trouver ça drôle, mais en fait il riait jaune** he pretended he found it funny but in fact he had to force himself to laugh; **quand il apprendra la nouvelle, il rira jaune** when he hears the news he won't find it funny ou he'll be laughing on the other side of his face (Brit); (iro) **vous me faites ~ !** ◊ **laissez-moi ~ !** don't make me laugh!, you make me laugh! (iro); **sans ~, c'est vrai ?** joking apart ou aside, is it true?, seriously, is it true?; **elle l'a quitté — oh ! sans ~ ?** she has left him — really? ou you're joking? (iro)

[2] **rire de** VT INDIR (= se moquer de) [+ personne, défaut, crainte] to laugh at, scoff at; **il fait ~ de lui** people laugh at him ou make fun of him, he's a laughing stock

[3] **se rire** VPR **se ~ de** (= se jouer de) [+ difficultés, épreuve] to make light of, take in one's stride; (= se moquer de) [+ menaces, recommandations] to laugh at; [+ personne] to laugh at, scoff at

4 NM (= façon de rire) laugh; (= éclat de rire) laughter (NonC), laugh; **~s** laughter; **le ~ laughter** ■ (PROV) **le ~ est le propre de l'homme** laughter is unique to man; **un gros ~** a loud laugh, a guffaw; **un ~ homérique** a hearty ou booming laugh; **un petit ~ bête** a stupid giggle ou titter; **un ~ moqueur** a mocking ou scornful laugh; (Radio, TV) **~s préenregistrés** ou **en boîte*** canned laughter; **il y eut des ~ dans la salle quand ...** there was laughter in the audience when ...; **elle a un ~ bête** she has a silly ou stupid laugh; **elle eut un petit ~ méchant** she gave a wicked little laugh, she laughed wickedly; **il eut un petit ~ de satisfaction** he gave a little chuckle of satisfaction, he chuckled with satisfaction; **les ~s l'obligèrent à se taire** the laughter forced him to stop speaking, he was laughed down → **éclater, fou**

ris¹ [Ri] NM a (Culin) **~ de veau** calf's sweetbread; (sur un menu) calves' sweetbreads b (Naut) reef

ris² [Ri] NM (littér = rire) laugh, laughter (NonC)

RISC [ɛRiɛssə] ADJ (ABRÉV = **Reduced Instruction Set Computing**) (Ordin) RISC; **technologie/système ~** RISC technology/system

risée [Rize] NF a (= moquerie) **s'exposer à la ~ générale** to lay o.s. open to ridicule; **être un objet de ~** to be a laughing stock, be an object of ridicule; **être la ~ de toute l'Europe** to be the laughing stock of Europe b (Naut) **~(s)** light breeze

risette [Rizɛt] NF (langage enfantin) little smile; **~ à qn** to give sb a nice ou little smile; **fais ~ (au monsieur)** smile nicely (at the gentleman); (fig) **être obligé de faire des ~s au patron** to have to smile politely to the boss

risible [Rizibl] ADJ (= ridicule) [attitude] laughable, ridiculous, silly; (= comique) [aventure] laughable, funny

risiblement [Rizibləmɑ̃] ADV ridiculously, laughably

▼ **risque** [Risk] NM a (gén, Jur = danger) risk; **~ calculé** calculated risk; **entreprise pleine de ~s** high-risk business; **c'est un ~ à courir** it's a risk one has to take ou run, one has to take ou run the risk; **il y a du ~ à faire cela** there's a risk in doing that, it's taking a risk doing that, it's risky doing ou to do that; **le goût du ~** a taste for danger; **ce qui paie, c'est le ~** it pays off to take risks, taking risks pays off; **on n'a rien sans ~** you don't get anywhere without taking risks, nothing ventured, nothing gained (PROV); **il y a (un) ~ d'émeute/d'épidémie** there's a risk of an uprising/an epidemic; **à cause du ~ d'incendie** because of the fire risk ou the risk of fire; **cela constitue un ~ pour la santé** that is a health hazard ou a health risk; (Fin) **~ de change** exchange risk ou exposure; **à ~** (Méd) [groupe] high-risk; (Fin) [placement] risky; **à haut ~** high-risk (épith); **pratique à ~** (high-)risk behaviour (NonC) (Brit) ou behavior (NonC) (US); **prendre des ~s** to take risks; (fig) **ne prendre aucun ~** to play (it) safe, take no risks; **prise de ~(s)** risk-taking → **assurance** b (loc: hum) **ce sont les ~s du métier** that's an occupational hazard (hum); **il n'y a pas de ~ qu'il refuse** there's no risk ou chance of his refusing; **au ~ de le mécontenter/de se tuer/de sa vie** at the risk of displeasing him/of killing himself/of his life; **c'est à tes ~s et périls** you do it at your own risk, on your own head be it! c (Assurances) risk; **bon/mauvais ~** good/bad risk

risqué, e [Riske] (ptp de **risquer**) ADJ (= hasardeux) risky, dicey* (Brit); (= licencieux) risqué, daring, off-color (US)

▼ **risquer** [Riske] ▶conjug 1◀ 1 VT a (= mettre en danger) [+ fortune, réputation, vie] to risk b (= s'exposer à) [+ ennuis, prison, renvoi] to risk; **il risque la mort** he's risking death, he

risks being killed; **tu risques gros** you're taking a big risk; **tu risques qu'on te le vole** you risk having it stolen; **qu'est-ce qu'on risque ?** (= quels sont les risques ?) what do we risk?, what are the risks? ou dangers?; (= c'est sans danger) what have we got to lose?, where's ou what's the risk?; **bien emballé, ce vase ne risque rien** packed like this the vase is ou will be quite safe; **ce vieux chapeau ne risque rien** it doesn't matter what happens to this old hat c (= tenter) to risk; **~ le tout pour le tout** ◊ **le paquet*** to risk ou chance the lot; **risquons le coup** let's chance it, let's take the chance ■ (PROV) **qui ne risque rien n'a rien** nothing ventured, nothing gained (PROV) d (= hasarder) [+ allusion, regard] to venture, hazard; **je ne risquerais pas un gros mot devant mon grand-père** I wouldn't dare to use bad language in front of my grandfather; **~ un œil au dehors** to take a peep ou a quick look outside, poke one's nose outside; (hum) **~ un orteil dans l'eau** to venture a toe in the water e **tu risques de le perdre** (éventualité) you might (well) ou could (well) lose it; (forte possibilité) you could easily lose it; (probabilité) you're likely to lose it; **il risque de pleuvoir** it could ou may (well) rain, there's a chance of rain; **le feu risque de s'éteindre** the fire may (well) go out, there's a chance the fire may go out; **avec ces embouteillages, il risque d'être en retard** with these traffic jams he's likely to be late, these traffic jams could well make him late; **on risque fort d'être en retard** we're very likely to be late; **pourquoi ~ de tout perdre ?** why should we risk losing ou take the risk of losing everything?; **ça ne risque pas (d'arriver) !** not a chance!, there's no chance ou danger of that (happening)!, that's not likely to happen!; **il ne risque pas de gagner** he hasn't got much chance of winning, there isn't much chance of him winning, he isn't likely to win

2 **se risquer** VPR **se ~ dans une grotte/sur une corniche** to venture inside a cave/onto a ledge; **se ~ dans une entreprise** to venture (up)on ou take a gamble on an enterprise; **se ~ dans une aventure dangereuse** to set out on a dangerous course; **se ~ à faire qch** to venture ou dare to do sth; **à ta place, je ne m'y risquerais pas** if I were you, I wouldn't risk it; **je vais me ~ à faire un soufflé** I'm going to try my hand ou have a go at making a soufflé

risque-tout [Riskətu] NMF INV daredevil; **elle est ~** ◊ **c'est une ~** she's a daredevil

rissole [Risɔl] NF rissole

rissoler [Risɔle] ▶conjug 1◀ 1 VT (Culin) **(faire) ~** to brown; **pommes rissolées** fried potatoes 2 VI (Culin) to brown

ristourne [RistuRn] NF (sur achat) discount; (sur cotisation) rebate; (= commission) commission; **faire une ~ à qn** to give sb a discount; **je lui ai demandé 10% de ~** I asked him for a 10% discount

ristourner [RistuRne] ▶conjug 1◀ VT a (= accorder une réduction de) to give a discount of; (= rembourser un trop-perçu de) to refund the difference of; (= donner une commission de) to give a commission of; **ils m'ont ristourné 500 F** they gave me 500 francs back; **une partie de la taxe est ristournée au pays exportateur** part of the tax is refunded to the exporting country b (Jur, Naut) [+ police d'assurance] to cancel

ristrette [RistRɛt], **ristretto** [RistRɛto] NM (Helv) strong black coffee (served in a small cup); **~s sociaux** social rituals

rital** [Rital] NM (injurieux = Italien) wop** (injurieux), Eyetie** (injurieux)

rite [Rit] NM (gén, Rel) rite; (fig = habitude) ritual; **~s sociaux** social rituals; **~s d'initiation** ou **initiatiques** initiation rites; **~ de passage** rite of passage

ritournelle [RituRnɛl] NF (Mus) ritornello; (fig) **c'est toujours la même ~** it's always the same (old) story

ritualiser [Ritɥalize] ▶conjug 1◀ VT to ritualize

ritualisme [Ritɥalism] NM ritualism

ritualiste [Ritɥalist] 1 ADJ ritualistic 2 NMF ritualist

rituel, -elle [Ritɥɛl] 1 ADJ ritual 2 NM ritual; **le ~ du départ était toujours le même** the ritual was always the same when we left

rituellement [Ritɥɛlmɑ̃] ADV (= religieusement) religiously, ritually; (hum = invariablement) invariably, unfailingly

rivage [Rivaʒ] NM shore

rival, e (mpl **-aux**) [Rival, o] ADJ, NM,F rival; **sans ~** unrivalled

▼ **rivaliser** [Rivalize] ▶conjug 1◀ VI **~ avec** [personne] to rival, compete with, vie with; [chose] to hold its own against, compare with; **~ de générosité/de bons mots avec qn** to vie with sb ou try to outdo sb in generosity/wit, rival sb in generosity/wit; **il essaie de ~ avec moi** he's trying to emulate me ou to vie with me; **ses tableaux rivalisent avec les plus grands chefs-d'œuvre** his paintings rival the greatest masterpieces ou can hold their own against the greatest masterpieces

rivalité [Rivalite] NF rivalry; **~s internes** (gén) internal rivalries; (Pol) internecine strife ou rivalries; **~s de personnes** rivalry between people

rive [Riv] NF a [mer, lac] shore; [rivière] bank; **la ~ gauche/droite de la Tamise** the north/south bank of the Thames; **la ~ gauche/droite (de la Seine)** the left/right bank (of the Seine) b (Tech) [four] lip; [toit] **planche de ~** eaves fascia

---

RIVE GAUCHE, RIVE DROITE

The terms rive gauche *and* rive droite *are social and cultural notions as well as geographical ones. The Left Bank of the Seine (ie, the southern half of Paris) is traditionally associated with the arts (especially literature), with students and with a somewhat bohemian lifestyle. The Right Bank is generally viewed as being more traditionalist, commercially-minded and conformist.*

---

rivé, e [Rive] (ptp de **river**) ADJ **~ à** [+ bureau, travail] tethered ou tied to; [+ chaise] glued ou riveted to; **les yeux ~s sur moi/la tache de sang** (with) his eyes riveted on me/the bloodstain; **rester ~ sur place** to be ou stand riveted ou rooted to the spot; **~ à la télé*** glued to the TV*

river [Rive] ▶conjug 1◀ VT a (Tech) [+ clou] to clinch; [+ plaques] to rivet together; (fig) **~ son clou à qn*** to shut sb up* b (littér = fixer) **~ qch au mur/sol** to nail sth to the wall/floor; **il la rivait au sol** he pinned her to the ground; **la haine/le sentiment qui les rivait ensemble** ou **l'un à l'autre** the hatred/the emotional bond which held them to each other

riverain, e [Riv(ə)Rɛ̃, ɛn] 1 ADJ (d'un lac) lakeside, riparian (SPÉC); (d'une rivière) riverside, riparian (SPÉC); (d'une route) **les propriétés ~es** the houses along the road; **les propriétés ~es de la Seine** the houses bordering on the Seine ou along the banks of the Seine 2 NM,F [lac] lakeside resident, riparian (SPÉC); [fleuve, rivière] riverside resident, riparian (SPÉC); [route] **les ~s se plaignent du bruit des voitures** the residents of ou in the street complain about the noise of cars; **« interdit sauf aux ~s »** "no entry except for access", "residents only"

rivet [Rivɛ] NM rivet

rivetage [Riv(ə)taʒ] NM riveting

riveter [Riv(ə)te] ▶conjug 4◀ VT to rivet (together)

➤ GRAMMAIRE ACTIVE: **risque** 42.3 **risquer** 29.3 **rivaliser** 32.2, 32.3

riveteuse [ʀiv(ə)tøz], **riveuse** [ʀivøz] NF riveting machine

rivière [ʀivjɛʀ] NF (*lit, fig*) river; (*Équitation*) water jump; **~ de diamants** diamond rivière → **petit**

rixe [ʀiks] NF brawl, fight, scuffle

Riyad [ʀijad] N Riyadh

riyal [ʀijal] NM riyal

riz [ʀi] NM rice; **~ Caroline** *ou* **à grains longs** long-grain rice; **~ à grains ronds** round-grain rice; **~ basmati** basmati rice; **~ brun** *ou* **complet** brown rice; **~ cantonais** fried rice; **~ créole** creole rice; **~ gluant** sticky rice; **~ au lait** rice pudding; **~ pilaf** pilaf(f) *ou* pilau rice; **~ sauvage** wild rice → **gâteau, paille**

rizerie [ʀizʀi] NF rice-processing factory

riziculture [ʀizikyltyʀ] NF rice-growing

rizière [ʀizjɛʀ] NF paddy-field, ricefield

RM [ɛʀɛm] NM (ABRÉV = **règlement mensuel**) → **règlement**

RMI [ɛʀɛmi] NM (ABRÉV = **revenu minimum d'insertion**) → **revenu**

RMiste, rmiste [ɛʀɛmist] NMF *person receiving welfare payment*, ≈ person on income support (*Brit*), ≈ person on welfare (*US*)

RMN [ɛʀɛmɛn] NF (ABRÉV = **résonance magnétique nucléaire**) NMR

RN [ɛʀɛn] **1** NF (ABRÉV = **route nationale**) → **route** **2** NM (ABRÉV = **revenu national**) → **revenu**

RNIS [ɛʀɛniɛs] NM (ABRÉV = **Réseau Numérique à Intégration de Service**) ISDN

robe [ʀɔb] **1** NF **a** [*femme, fillette*] dress; **~ courte/décolletée/d'été** short/low-necked/summer dress **b** [*magistrat, prélat*] robe; [*professeur*] gown; (*Hist Jur*) **la ~** the legal profession → **gens¹, homme, noblesse** **c** (= *pelage*) [*cheval, fauve*] coat **d** (= *peau*) [*oignon*] skin; [*fève*] husk **e** [*cigare*] wrapper, outer leaf **f** (= *couleur*) [*vin*] colour (*Brit*), color (*US*) **2** COMP ► **robe bain de soleil** sundress ► **robe de bal** ball gown *ou* dress ► **robe de baptême** christening *ou* baptism robe ► **robe bustier** off-the-shoulder dress ► **robe de chambre** dressing gown; (*Culin*) **pommes de terre en ~ de chambre** *ou* **des champs** baked *ou* jacket (*Brit*) potatoes, potatoes in their jackets ► **robe chasuble** pinafore dress ► **robe chaussette** = **robe tube** ► **robe chemisier** shirtwaister (dress) (*Brit*), shirtwaist (dress) (*US*) ► **robe de cocktail** cocktail dress ► **robe de communion** *ou* **de communiant(e)** first communion dress ► **robe de grossesse** maternity dress ► **robe d'hôtesse** hostess gown ► **robe d'intérieur** housecoat ► **robe kimono** kimono (dress) ► **robe de mariée** wedding dress *ou* gown ► **robe du soir** evening dress *ou* gown ► **robe tube** tube ► **robe tunique** smock

robe-manteau (*pl* **robes-manteaux**) [ʀɔbmɑ̃to] NF coat dress

roberts✲ [ʀɔbɛʀ] NMPL (= *seins*) tits✲, boobs✲

robe-sac (*pl* **robes-sacs**) [ʀɔbsak] NF sack dress

robe-tablier (*pl* **robes-tabliers**) [ʀɔbtablije] NF overall

Robin [ʀɔbɛ̃] NM Robin; **~ des Bois** Robin Hood; (*hum* = *justicier*) **c'est le ~ des Bois de la politique française** he's the Robin Hood of French politics

robin†† [ʀɔbɛ̃] NM (*péj*) lawyer

robinet [ʀɔbinɛ] NM **a** [*évier, baignoire, tonneau*] tap (*Brit*), faucet (*US*); **~ d'eau chaude/froide** hot/cold (water) tap (*Brit*) *ou* faucet (*US*); **~ mélangeur** *◊* **~ mitigeur** mixer tap (*Brit*) *ou* faucet (*US*); **~ du gaz** gas tap; **~ d'arrêt** stopcock → **problème b** (✲, *langage enfantin* = *pénis*) willy✲ (*Brit*), peter✲ (*US*)

robinetterie [ʀɔbinɛtʀi] NF (= *installations*) taps (*Brit*), faucets (*US*), plumbing (*NonC*); (= *usine*) tap (*Brit*) *ou* faucet (*US*) factory; (= *commerce*) tap (*Brit*) *ou* faucet (*US*) trade

robinier [ʀɔbinje] NM locust tree, false acacia

Robinson Crusoé [ʀɔbɛ̃sɔ̃kʀyzɔe] NM Robinson Crusoe

roboratif, -ive [ʀɔbɔʀatif, iv] ADJ (*littér*) [*climat*] bracing; [*activité*] invigorating; [*liqueur, vin*] tonic, stimulating

robot [ʀɔbo] NM (*lit, fig*) robot; **~ ménager** *ou* **de cuisine** food processor

roboticien, -ienne [ʀɔbɔtisjɛ̃, jɛn] NM,F robotics specialist

robotique [ʀɔbɔtik] NF robotics *sg*

robotisation [ʀɔbɔtizasjɔ̃] NF [*atelier, usine*] automation; **il redoute la ~ de l'humanité** he fears that human beings are being turned into robots

robotiser [ʀɔbɔtize] ► conjug 1 ◄ VT [+ *atelier, usine*] to automate; **des gens complètement robotisés** people who have been turned into robots

robre [ʀɔbʀ] NM (*Bridge*) rubber

robusta [ʀɔbysta] NM (= *café*) robusta

robuste [ʀɔbyst] ADJ [*personne, animal*] robust, sturdy; [*santé*] robust, sound; [*plante, arbre*] robust, hardy; [*voiture*] solid; [*meuble, moteur, machine*] robust; [*foi*] firm, strong; **de ~ constitution** of strong *ou* robust constitution

robustement [ʀɔbystəmɑ̃] ADV robustly, sturdily

robustesse [ʀɔbystɛs] NF [*personne, animal*] robustness, sturdiness; [*santé*] robustness, soundness; [*plante, arbre*] robustness, hardiness; [*voiture*] solidity; [*meuble, moteur, machine*] robustness; [*foi*] firmness, strength

roc¹ [ʀɔk] NM (*lit, fig*) rock → **bâtir, dur**

roc² [ʀɔk] NM (*Myth*) (*oiseau*) **~** roc

rocade [ʀɔkad] NF (= *route*) bypass; (*Mil*) communications line

rocaille [ʀɔkaj] **1** ADJ [*objet, style*] rocaille **2** NF **a** (= *cailloux*) loose stones; (= *terrain*) rocky *ou* stony ground **b** (= *jardin*) rockery, rock garden; **plantes de ~** rock plants **c** (*Constr*) **grotte/fontaine en ~** grotto/fountain in rockwork

rocailleux, -euse [ʀɔkajø, øz] ADJ [*terrain*] rocky, stony; [*style*] rugged; [*son, voix*] harsh, grating

rocambole [ʀɔkɑ̃bɔl] NF rocambole

rocambolesque [ʀɔkɑ̃bɔlɛsk] ADJ [*aventures, péripéties*] fantastic, incredible

rochassier, -ière [ʀɔʃasje, jɛʀ] NM,F rock climber

roche [ʀɔʃ] NF (*gén*) rock; **~s sédimentaires/volcaniques** sedimentary/volcanic rock(s); **~ lunaire** moon rock; **~ mère** parent rock; **la Tarpéienne** the Tarpeian Rock; (*Naut*) **fond de ~** rock bottom → **anguille, coq¹, cristal**

rocher [ʀɔʃe] NM **a** (= *bloc*) rock; (*gros, lisse*) boulder; (= *substance*) rock; **le ~ de Sisyphe** the rock of Sisyphus; **le ~ de Gibraltar** the Rock (of Gibraltar); (*Alpinisme*) **faire du ~** to go rock-climbing **b** (*Anat*) petrosal bone **c** (*en chocolat*) chocolate

rochet [ʀɔʃe] NM **a** (*Rel*) ratchet **b** (*Tech*) **roue à ~** ratchet wheel

rocheux, -euse [ʀɔʃø, øz] **1** ADJ rocky; **paroi rocheuse** rock face **2 Rocheuses** NFPL **les (montagnes) Rocheuses** the Rocky Mountains, the Rockies

rock¹ [ʀɔk] NM (*Myth*) = **roc²**

rock² [ʀɔk] (*Mus*) **1** ADJ rock **2** NM (= *musique*) rock; (= *danse*) jive, rock 'n' roll; **le ~ punk/alternatif** punk/alternative rock; **danser le ~** to rock, jive; **~ and roll** *◊* **~ 'n' roll** rock 'n' roll; **~ acrobatique** acrobatic dancing

rocker [ʀɔkœʀ] NM = **rockeur**

rockeur, -euse [ʀɔkœʀ, øz] NM,F (= *chanteur*) rock singer; (= *musicien*) rock musician, rocker; (= *fan*) rock fan, rocker

rocking-chair (*pl* **rocking-chairs**) [ʀɔkiŋ(t)ʃɛʀ] NM rocking chair

rococo [ʀɔkɔko] **1** NM (*Art*) rococo **2** ADJ INV (*Art*) rococo; (*péj*) old-fashioned, outdated

rodage [ʀɔdaʒ] NM **a** [*véhicule, moteur*] running in (*Brit*), breaking in (*US*); **« en ~ »** "running in" (*Brit*), "breaking in" (*US*); **pendant le ~** during the running-in (*Brit*) *ou* breaking-in (*US*) period; **la voiture était en ~** the car was being run in (*Brit*) *ou* broken in (*US*) **b** (*Aut*) [*soupape*] grinding **c** (= *mise au point*) **on a dû prévoir une période de ~** we had to allow some time for it to get up to speed; **ce spectacle a demandé un certain ~** the show took a little while to get over its teething troubles *ou* get into its stride; **le nouveau gouvernement est encore en ~** the new government is still cutting its teeth

rodéo [ʀɔdeo] NM (= *sport*) rodeo; (= *poursuite*) high-speed car chase; **~ (automobile ou motorisé)** *◊* **~ de voitures volées** joy riding (*NonC*)

roder [ʀɔde] ► conjug 1 ◄ VT **a** [+ *véhicule, moteur*] to run in (*Brit*), break in (*US*) **b** (*Tech*) [+ *soupape*] to grind **c** (= *mettre au point*) **il faut ~ ce spectacle/ce nouveau service** we have to let this show/this new service get into its stride, we have to give this show/this new service time to get over its teething troubles; **ce spectacle est maintenant bien rodé** the show is really running well *ou* smoothly now, all the initial problems in the show have been ironed out; **il n'est pas encore rodé** [*personne*] he hasn't quite got the hang of it yet; [*organisme*] it hasn't yet got into its stride

rôder [ʀode] ► conjug 1 ◄ VI (*au hasard*) to roam *ou* wander about; (*de façon suspecte*) to loiter *ou* lurk (*about ou around*); (= *être en maraude*) to prowl about, be on the prowl; **~ autour d'un magasin** to hang *ou* lurk around a shop; **~ autour de qn** to hang around sb

rôdeur, -euse [ʀodœʀ, øz] NM,F prowler

rodomontade [ʀɔdɔmɔ̃tad] NF (*littér*) (= *vantardise*) bragging (*NonC*), boasting (*NonC*); (= *menace*) sabre rattling (*NonC*)

Rogations [ʀɔgasjɔ̃] NFPL (*Rel*) Rogations

rogatoire [ʀɔgatwaʀ] ADJ (*Jur*) rogatory → **commission**

rogatons [ʀɔgatɔ̃] NMPL (*péj*) (= *nourriture*) scraps (of food), left-overs; (= *objets*) pieces of junk; (= *vêtements*) old rags

rogne✲ [ʀɔɲ] NF anger; **être en ~** to be (really *ou* hopping✲ (*Brit*)) mad *ou* really ratty✲ (*Brit*); **se mettre en ~** to get (really *ou* hopping✲ (*Brit*)) mad *ou* really ratty✲ (*Brit*), blow one's top✲ (*contre* at); **mettre qn en ~** to make sb (really *ou* hopping✲ (*Brit*)) mad *ou* really ratty✲ (*Brit*), make sb lose their temper; **il était dans une telle ~ que ...** he was in such a (foul) temper that ..., he was so mad✲ *ou* ratty✲ (*Brit*) that ...; **ses ~s duraient des jours** his tempers lasted for days

rogner [ʀɔɲe] ► conjug 1 ◄ VT **a** (= *couper*) [+ *ongle, page, plaque*] to trim; [+ *griffe*] to clip, trim; [+ *aile, pièce d'or*] to clip; **~ les ailes à qn** to clip sb's wings **b** (= *réduire*) [+ *prix*] to whittle down, cut down; [+ *salaire*] to cut back *ou* down, whittle down; **~ sur** [+ *dépense, prix*] to cut down on, cut back on; [+ *nourriture, sorties*] to cut down on

rognon [ʀɔɲɔ̃] NM (*Culin*) kidney; (*Géol*) nodule; (*Culin*) **~s blancs** ram's testicles

rognures [ʀɔɲyʀ] NFPL [*métal*] clippings, trimmings; [*cuir, papier*] clippings; [*ongles*] clippings, parings; [*viande*] scraps

rogomme [ʀɔgɔm] NM **voix de ~** hoarse *ou* rasping voice

rogue [ʀɔg] ADJ (= *arrogant*) haughty, arrogant

roi [ʀwa] **1** NM **a** (= *souverain, Cartes, Échecs*) king; (*Bible*) **le livre des Rois** (the Book of)

Kings; **le jour des Rois** (*gén*) Twelfth Night; (*Rel*) Epiphany; **tirer les ~s** to eat Twelfth Night cake; **le ~ n'est pas son cousin !** he's very full of himself!; **travailler pour le ~ de Prusse** to receive no reward for one's pains → **bleu, camelot, heureux** *etc*

b (*fig*) king; **le ~ des animaux/de la forêt** the king of the beasts/of the forest; **~ du pétrole** oil king; **les ~s de la finance** the kings of finance; **un des ~s de la presse/du textile** one of the press/textile barons *ou* magnates *ou* tycoons; **c'est le ~ des fromages** it's the prince of cheeses; **c'est le ~ de la resquille !*** he's a master *ou* an ace* at getting something for nothing; **tu es vraiment le ~ (des imbéciles) !*** you really are a prize idiot!*, you really take the cake (for sheer stupidity)!*; **c'est le ~ des cons**** he's an utter cretin* (*Brit*) *ou* a total asshole** (*US*); **c'est le ~ des salauds**** he's the world's biggest bastard**

2 COMP ► **les rois fainéants** (*Hist*) the last Merovingian kings ► **le Roi des Juifs** the King of the Jews ► **le Roi des Rois** the King of Kings ► **le Roi Très Chrétien** the King of France → **mage**

LES ROIS

At Epiphany, it is traditional for French people to get together and share a "galette des rois", a round, flat pastry filled with almond paste. A small figurine ("la fève") is baked inside the pastry, and the person who finds it in his or her portion is given a cardboard crown to wear. This tradition is known as "tirer les rois". In some families, a child goes under the table while the pastry is being shared out and says who should receive each portion.
---

roide [Rwad] ADJ, **roideur** [Rwadœr] NF, **roidir** [Rwadir] VT (†† *ou littér*) = **raide, raideur, raidir**

Roi-Soleil [Rwasɔlɛj] NM **le ~** the Sun King

roitelet [Rwat(ə)lɛ] NM **a** (*péj* = *roi*) kinglet, petty king **b** (= *oiseau*) wren; **~ (huppé)** goldcrest

rôle [Rol] NM **a** (*Théât, fig*) role, part; **jouer un ~** [*personne*] (*Théât*) to play a part (**dans** in); (*fig*) to put on an act; [*fait, circonstance*] to play a part (**dans** in); **premier ~** lead, leading *ou* major role *ou* part; (*fig*) **avoir le premier ~ dans une affaire** to play the leading part in an affair; **second/petit ~** supporting/minor role *ou* part; **jouer les seconds ~s** (*Ciné*) to play minor parts *ou* supporting roles; (*fig : en politique*) to play second fiddle; **~ muet** non-speaking part; **~ de composition** character part *ou* role; **savoir son ~** to know one's part *ou* lines; **distribuer les ~s** to cast the parts; **je lui ai donné le ~ de Lear** I gave him the role *ou* part of Lear, I cast him as Lear; **il joue bien son ~ de jeune cadre** he acts his role of young executive *ou* plays the part of a young executive well; **inverser** *ou* **renverser les ~s** to reverse the roles; **avoir le beau ~** to show o.s. in a good light, come off best → **jeu**

b (= *fonction, statut*) [*personne*] role, part; [*institution, système*] role, function; (= *contribution*) part; (= *devoir, travail*) job; **il a un ~ important dans l'organisation** he plays an important part *ou* he has an important part to play *ou* he has an important role in the organization; **quel a été son ~ dans cette affaire ?** what part did he play in this business?; **ce n'est pas mon ~ de vous sermonner mais ...** it isn't my job *ou* place to lecture you but ...; **en donnant cet avertissement, il est dans son ~** (*il fait ce qu'il a à faire*) in issuing this warning, he's simply doing his job; **le ~ de la métaphore chez Lawrence** the role of metaphor *ou* the part played by metaphor in Lawrence; **la télévision a pour ~ de ...** the role *ou* function of television is to ...

c (= *registre, Admin*) roll; (*Jur*) cause list; **~**

d'équipage muster (roll); **~ des impôts** tax list *ou* roll → **tour**²

rôle-titre (*pl* **rôles-titres**) [Roltitr] NM title role

roller [Rolœr] NM roller skate; **~ en ligne** rollerblade, in-line roller skate; **faire du ~** to roller-skate; **faire du ~ en ligne** to rollerblade

rollmops [Rolmɔps] NM rollmop

Rolls ® [Rols] NF (*lit*) Rolls, Rolls Royce ®; (*fig*) Rolls Royce

ROM [Rɔm] NF (ABRÉV = **Read Only Memory**) (*Ordin*) ROM

romain, e [Romɛ̃, ɛn] **1** ADJ (*gén*) Roman **2** (*Typo*) roman **3** **Romain(e)** NM,F Roman → **travail**¹ **4** **romaine** NF (*laitue*) **~e** cos (lettuce) (*Brit*), romaine (lettuce) (*US*); **(balance) ~e** steelyard; **être bon comme la ~e** (*trop bon*) to be too nice for one's own good; (*menacé*) to be in for it*

romaïque [Romaik] ADJ, NM Romaic, demotic Greek

roman¹ [Romɑ̃] **1** NM **a** (= *livre*) novel; (*fig* = *récit*) story; (*genre*) **le ~** the novel; **ils ne publient que des ~s** they only publish novels *ou* fiction; **ça n'arrive que dans les ~s** it only happens in novels *ou* fiction *ou* stories; **sa vie est un vrai ~** his life is like something out of a novel; **c'est tout un ~*** it's a long story, it's a real saga; **Éric et sa mère, c'est un vrai ~** *ou* **tout un ~ !** you could write a book about Eric and his mother!; **ça se lit comme un ~** it reads like a novel → **eau, nouveau**

b (*Littérat* = *œuvre médiévale*) romance; **~ courtois** courtly romance; **« le Roman de Renart »** "the Romance of Renart"; **« le Roman de la Rose »** "the Romance of the Rose", "the Roman de la Rose"

2 COMP ► **roman d'amour** (*lit*) love story; (*fig*) love story, (*storybook*) romance ► **roman d'analyse** psychological novel ► **roman d'anticipation** futuristic novel, science-fiction novel ► **roman d'aventures** adventure story ► **roman de cape et d'épée** swashbuckler ► **roman de chevalerie** tale of chivalry ► **roman à clés** roman à clés ► **roman d'épouvante** horror story ► **roman d'espionnage** spy thriller *ou* story ► **roman familial** (*Psych*) family romance ► **roman de gare** airport novel ► **roman historique** historical novel ► **roman de mœurs** social novel ► **roman noir** (*Hist*) Gothic novel; (*policier*) violent thriller ► **roman policier** detective novel *ou* story, whodunit* ► **roman de science-fiction** science-fiction novel ► **roman (de) série noire** thriller

roman², **e** [Romɑ̃, an] **1** ADJ (*Ling*) Romance (*épith*), Romanic; (*Archit*) Romanesque; (*en Grande-Bretagne*) Norman **2** NM (*Ling*) **le ~ (commun)** late vulgar Latin; (*Archit*) **le ~** the Romanesque

romance [Romɑ̃s] NF **a** (= *chanson*) sentimental ballad, lovesong; **les ~s napolitaines** the Neapolitan lovesongs → **pousser b** (*Littérat, Mus*) ballad, romance

romancer [Romɑ̃se] ▸ conjug 3 ◂ VT (= *présenter sous forme de roman*) to make into a novel; (= *agrémenter*) to romanticize; **histoire romancée** fictionalized history → **biographie**

romanche [Romɑ̃ʃ] ADJ, NM (*Ling*) Romans(c)h

romancier [Romɑ̃sje] NM novelist

romancière [Romɑ̃sjɛr] NF (woman) novelist

romand, e [Romɑ̃, ɑ̃d] ADJ of French-speaking Switzerland; **les Romands** the French-speaking Swiss → **suisse**

romanesque [Romanɛsk] **1** ADJ **a** [*histoire*] fabulous, fantastic; [*amours*] storybook (*épith*); [*aventures*] storybook (*épith*), fabulous; [*imagination, personne, tempérament*] romantic **b** (*Littérat*) [*traitement, récit*] novelistic; **la technique ~** the technique(s) of the novel;

œuvres ~s novels, fiction (*NonC*) **2** NM [*imagination, personne*] romantic side; **elle se réfugiait dans le ~** she took refuge in fancy

roman-feuilleton (*pl* **romans-feuilletons**) [Romɑ̃fœjtɔ̃] NM serialized novel, serial; **son histoire, c'est un vrai ~** his story is like something out of a soap opera

roman-fleuve (*pl* **romans-fleuves**) [Romɑ̃flœv] NM roman fleuve, saga

romanichel, -elle* [Romaniʃɛl] NM,F (*souvent injurieux*) gipsy, gyppo* (*injurieux*)

romanisant, e [Romanizɑ̃, ɑ̃t] **1** ADJ (*Rel*) romanist; (*Ling*) specializing in Romance languages **2** NM,F (= *linguiste*) romanist, specialist in Romance languages

romaniser [Romanize] ▸ conjug 1 ◂ VT (*gén*) to romanize

romaniste [Romanist] NMF (*Jur, Rel*) romanist; (*Ling*) romanist, specialist in Romance languages

romanité [Romanite] NF (= *civilisation*) Roman civilization; (= *pays*) Roman Empire

romano* [Romano] NMF (*injurieux*) gyppo* (*injurieux*)

roman-photo (*pl* **romans-photos**) [Romɑ̃foto] NM photo romance, photo love story; (*hum*) **une héroïne de ~** a Mills and Boon (*Brit*) *ou* Harlequin Romance (*US*) type heroine

romantique [Romɑ̃tik] **1** ADJ romantic **2** NMF romantic

romantisme [Romɑ̃tism] NM romanticism; (*Art : Littérat*) **le ~** the Romantic Movement

romarin [Romarɛ̃] NM rosemary

rombière* [Rɔ̃bjɛr] NF (*péj*) **(vieille) ~** old biddy* (*péj*)

Rome [Rom] N Rome; **la ~ antique** Ancient Rome → **tout**

Roméo [Romeo] NM Romeo

rompre [Rɔ̃pr] ▸ conjug 41 ◂ **1** VT **a** (= *faire cesser*) [+ *fiançailles, pourparlers, relations diplomatiques*] to break off; [+ *enchantement, monotonie, silence*] to break; [+ *solitude, isolement*] to put an end to; [+ *liens, contrat, traité*] to break; **~ l'équilibre** to upset the balance; **l'équilibre écologique est rompu** the ecological balance has been upset *ou* disturbed; **~ le Carême** to break Lent *ou* the Lenten fast; (*littér*) **~ le charme** to break the spell **b** (= *casser*) [+ *branche*] to break; [+ *pain*] to break (up); (*lit, fig*) **~ ses chaînes** to break one's chains; (*Naut*) **~ ses amarres** to break (loose from) its moorings; (*fig*) **il a rompu les amarres avec son pays natal** he has cut himself off completely from *ou* broken all links with his native country; **~ le front de l'ennemi** to break through the enemy front; **la mer a rompu les digues** the sea has broken (through) *ou* burst the dykes → **applaudir, glace**¹ **c** (*littér* = *habituer*) **~ qn à un exercice** to break sb in to an exercise **d** (*loc*) **~ une lance** *ou* **des lances pour qn** to take up the cudgels for sb; **~ une lance** *ou* **des lances contre qn** to cross swords with sb; (*Mil*) **~ les rangs** to fall out, dismiss; (*Mil*) **rompez (les rangs) !** dismiss!, fall out!

2 VI **a** (= *se séparer de*) **~ avec qn** to break with sb, break off one's relations with sb; **il n'a pas le courage de ~** he hasn't got the courage to break it off; **~ avec de vieilles habitudes/la tradition** to break with old habits/tradition **b** [*corde*] to break, snap; [*digue*] to burst, break **c** (*Boxe, Escrime*) to break; (*fig*) **~ en visière avec** to quarrel openly with; (*Mil*) **~ le combat** to withdraw from the engagement

3 **se rompre** VPR (= *se briser*) [*branche, câble, chaîne, corde*] to break, snap; [*digue*] to burst, break; [*vaisseau sanguin*] to burst, rupture; **il va se ~ les os** *ou* **le cou** he's going to break his neck

rompu, e [ʀɔ̃py] (*ptp de* **rompre**) ADJ [a] (= *fourbu*) ~ **(de fatigue)** exhausted, worn-out, tired out; ~ **de travail** exhausted by overwork [b] (= *expérimenté*) **être ~ aux affaires** to have wide business experience; ~ **aux privations/à la discipline** accustomed *ou* inured to hardship/to discipline; **il est ~ à toutes les ficelles du métier/au maniement des armes** he is experienced in *ou* familiar with all the tricks of the trade/the handling of firearms; ~ **aux techniques militaires/à l'art de la diplomatie** well-versed in military techniques/in the art of diplomacy → **bâton**

romsteck [ʀɔmstɛk] NM (= *viande*) rumpsteak (*NonC*); (= *tranche*) piece of rumpsteak

ronce [ʀɔ̃s] NF [a] (= *branche*) bramble branch; (= *buissons*) ~**s** brambles, thorns; (*Bot*) ~ **(des haies)** blackberry bush, bramble (bush); **il a déchiré son pantalon dans les ~s** he tore his trousers *ou* in the brambles [b] (*Menuiserie*) burr; ~ **de noyer** burr walnut; ~ **d'acajou** figured mahogany

ronceraie [ʀɔ̃sʀɛ] NF bramble patch, briar patch

Roncevaux [ʀɔ̃s(ə)vo] N Roncesvalles

ronchon, -onne [ʀɔ̃ʃɔ̃, ɔn] [1] ADJ grumpy, grouchy* [2] NM,F grumbler, grouch(er)*, grouser*

ronchonnement [ʀɔ̃ʃɔnmɑ̃] NM grumbling, grousing*, grouching*

ronchonner [ʀɔ̃ʃɔne] ▶ conjug 1 ◀ VI to grumble, grouse*, grouch* (**après** at)

ronchonneur, -euse [ʀɔ̃ʃɔnœʀ, øz] [1] ADJ grumpy, grouchy* [2] NM,F grumbler, grouser*, grouch(er)*

rond, e[1] [ʀɔ̃, ʀɔ̃d] [1] ADJ [a] (= *forme, objet*) round; (*pièce, lit*) circular, round → **dos, œil, table** [b] (= *rebondi*) [*joues, visage*] round; [*épaules, fesses*] plump, well-rounded; [*hanches*] rounded, curvaceous; [*mollet*] well-rounded; [*poitrine*] full, (well-)rounded; [*ventre*] tubby, round; [*bébé*] chubby; **une petite femme toute ~e** a plump little woman; **un petit homme ~** a chubby *ou* tubby little man [c] (= *net*) round; [*chiffre*] round number *ou* figure; **ça fait 50 F tout ~** it comes to exactly 50 francs; **ça fait un compte ~** it makes a round number *ou* figure; **être ~ en affaires** to be straightforward *ou* straight* *ou* on the level* in business matters [d] (* = *soûl*) drunk, tight*; **être ~ comme une bille** *ou* **comme une queue de pelle** to be blind *ou* rolling drunk*
[2] NM [a] (= *cercle*) circle, ring; **faire des ~s de fumée** to blow smoke rings; **faire des ~s dans l'eau** to make rings *ou* circular ripples in the water; (*en bateau*) to potter about (*Brit*) *ou* putter around (*US*) in a boat; **le verre a fait des ~s sur la table** the glass has made rings on the table [b] (= *objet*) [*cuisinière*] ring; ~ **de serviette** napkin ou serviette (*Brit*) ring; **il en est resté comme deux ~s de flan*** you could have knocked him down with a feather → **baver** [c] (* = *sou*) lolly* (*NonC*), cash* (*NonC*); **avoir des ~s** to be loaded*, be rolling in it*, have plenty of cash*; **il n'a pas le** *ou* **un ~** he hasn't got a penny (to his name) *ou* a red cent (*US*), he doesn't have two pennies *ou* cents (*US*) to rub together; **il n'a plus un** *ou* **le ~** he's (flat *ou* stony (*Brit*) *ou* stone (*US*)) broke*; **je l'ai eu pour pas un ~** it didn't cost me a penny *ou* a cent (*US*); **ça doit valoir des ~s !** that must be worth a mint!* *ou* a pretty penny!* *ou* a penny or two! [d] (*loc*) **en ~** in a circle *ou* ring; **s'asseoir/danser en ~** to sit/dance in a circle *ou* ring; **tourner en ~** (*à pied*) to walk round and round; (*en voiture*) to drive round in circles; [*enquête, discussion*] to get nowhere, go round in circles; **nous tournons en ~ depuis trois mois** we've been marking time *ou* going

round in circles for three months → **empêcheur**
[3] ADV **avaler qch tout ~** to swallow sth whole; **tourner ~** to run smoothly; **ça ne tourne pas ~ chez elle** ◊ **elle ne tourne pas ~*** she's got a screw loose*; **qu'est-ce qui ne tourne pas ~ ?*** what's the matter?, what's wrong?, what's up?*
[4] COMP ▶ **rond de jambes** (*Danse*) rond de jambe; (*fig péj*) **faire des ~s de jambes** to bow and scrape (*péj*) ▶ **rond de sorcière** (*Bot*) fairy ring

rond-de-cuir (*pl* **ronds-de-cuir**) [ʀɔ̃d(ə)kɥiʀ] NM (*péj*) penpusher (*Brit*), pencil pusher (*US*)

ronde[2] [ʀɔ̃d] NF [a] (= *tour de surveillance*) [*gardien, vigile, soldats*] rounds, patrol; [*policier*] beat, patrol, rounds; (= *patrouille*) patrol; **faire sa ~** to be on one's rounds *ou* on the beat *ou* on patrol; **sa ~ dura plus longtemps** he took longer doing his rounds; **il a fait trois ~s aujourd'hui** he has been on his rounds three times today, he has covered his beat three times today; ~ **de nuit** (= *action*) night rounds, night watch *ou* patrol; (= *soldats*) night patrol; **ils virent passer la ~** they saw the soldiers pass on their rounds → **chemin** [b] (= *danse*) round (dance), dance in a ring; (= *danseurs*) circle, ring; ~ **villageoise/enfantine** villagers'/children's dance (*in a ring*); **faites la ~** a dance round in a circle *ou* ring; **la ~ des hélicoptères dans le ciel** the helicopters coming and going in the sky; **la ~ des voitures sur la place** the constant flow of traffic round the square; (*littér*) **la ~ des saisons** the cycle of the seasons; **sa vie n'est qu'une ~ continue de fêtes et de sorties** his life is a non-stop social whirl [c] (*Mus*) semibreve (*Brit*), whole note (*US*) [d] (*Écriture*) roundhand [e] (*loc*) **à 10 km à la ~** within a 10-km radius; **à des kilomètres à la ~** for miles around; **passer qch à la ~** to pass sth round

rondeau (*pl* **rondeaux**) [ʀɔ̃do] NM (*Littérat*) rondeau; (*Mus*) rondo

ronde-bosse (*pl* **rondes-bosses**) [ʀɔ̃dbɔs] NF (= *technique*) sculpture in the round; **personnages en ~** figures in the round

rondelet, -ette [ʀɔ̃dlɛ, ɛt] ADJ [*adulte*] plumpish; [*enfant*] chubby; [*salaire, somme*] tidy (*épith*)

rondelle [ʀɔ̃dɛl] NF [a] [*carotte, saucisson*] slice, round (*Brit*); ~ **de citron/d'orange** slice of lemon/of orange; **couper en ~s** to slice, cut into slices *ou* rounds (*Brit*) [b] (= *disque de carton, plastique*) disc; [*boulon*] washer; [*bâton de ski*] basket

rondement [ʀɔ̃dmɑ̃] ADV [a] (= *efficacement*) efficiently; **il a mené ~ cette enquête/réunion** he conducted the investigation/meeting quickly and efficiently; **c'est quelqu'un qui mène ~ les affaires** he's someone who gets things done; **le film est ~ mené** the film is well-paced [b] (= *franchement*) frankly, outspokenly

rondeur [ʀɔ̃dœʀ] NF [a] [*bras, joues, personne*] plumpness, chubbiness; [*visage*] roundness, chubbiness; [*poitrine*] fullness; [*mollet*] roundness; (*hum*) **les ~s d'une femme** a woman's curves [b] (= *forme sphérique*) roundness [c] (= *bonhomie*) friendly straightforwardness, easy-going directness; **avec ~** with (an) easy-going directness

rondin [ʀɔ̃dɛ̃] NM log → **cabane**

rondo [ʀɔ̃do] NM rondo

rondouillard, e* [ʀɔ̃dujaʀ, aʀd] ADJ (*péj*) tubby, podgy (*Brit*), pudgy (*US*); **c'est un petit ~** he's a tubby *ou* podgy little guy* *ou* chap (*Brit*)

rond-point (*pl* **ronds-points**) [ʀɔ̃pwɛ̃] NM (= *carrefour*) roundabout (*Brit*), traffic circle (*US*); (*dans un nom de lieu = place*) ≈ circus (*Brit*)

Ronéo® [ʀɔneo] NF mimeo, Roneo®

ronéoter [ʀɔneɔte], **ronéotyper** [ʀɔneɔtipe] ▶ conjug 1 ◀ VT to duplicate, roneo®, mimeo

ronflant, e [ʀɔ̃flɑ̃, ɑ̃t] ADJ [*moteur*] purring; (*péj*) [*discours*] high-flown, grand(-sounding); [*titre*] grand(-sounding); [*style*] bombastic

ronflement [ʀɔ̃fləmɑ̃] NM [a] [*dormeur*] snore, snoring (*NonC*); **j'entendais des ~s** I could hear (somebody) snoring [b] [*poêle, feu*] (*sourd*) hum(ming) (*NonC*); (*plus fort*) roar, roaring (*NonC*); [*moteur*] purr(ing) (*NonC*), throbbing (*NonC*); (= *vrombissement*) roar, roaring (*NonC*)

ronfler [ʀɔ̃fle] ▶ conjug 1 ◀ VI [a] [*dormeur*] to snore [b] [*poêle, feu*] to hum; (*plus fort*) to roar; [*moteur*] (*sourdement*) to purr, throb; **faire ~ son moteur** to rev up one's engine; **il actionna le démarreur et le moteur ronfla** he pressed the starter and the engine throbbed *ou* roared into action [c] (* = *dormir*) to snore away, be out for the count* (*Brit*)

ronfleur, -euse [ʀɔ̃flœʀ, øz] [1] NM,F snorer [2] NM [*téléphone*] buzzer

ronger [ʀɔ̃ʒe] ▶ conjug 3 ◀ [1] VT [a] [*souris*] to gnaw *ou* eat away at, gnaw *ou* eat into; [*acide, pourriture, rouille, vers*] to eat into; [*mer*] to wear away, eat into; [*eczéma*] to pit; [*chien*] to gnaw (at) a bone; [*personne*] to pick a bone, gnaw (at) a bone; **les chenilles rongent les feuilles** caterpillars are eating away *ou* are nibbling (at) the leaves; **rongé par les vers** worm-eaten; **rongé par la rouille** eaten into by rust, pitted with rust; **fresques rongées par l'humidité** mildewed frescoes; [*cheval*] (*fig*) ~ **son frein** to champ at the bit → **os** [b] [*maladie*] to sap (the strength of); [*chagrin, pensée*] to gnaw *ou* eat away at; **le mal qui le ronge** the evil which is gnawing *ou* eating away at him; **rongé par la maladie** sapped by illness; **rongé par la drogue** ravaged by drugs; **le chômage, ce cancer qui ronge la société** the cancer of unemployment that is eating away at society; **une démocratie rongée de l'intérieur** a democracy that is being undermined from within
[2] **se ronger** VPR [a] **se ~ les ongles** to bite one's nails → **sang** [b] (*fig*) **elle se ronge** (*de chagrin*) she's eating her heart out, she's tormented with grief; (*d'inquiétude*) she's worrying herself sick, she's making herself sick with worry

rongeur, -euse [ʀɔ̃ʒœʀ, øz] ADJ, NM rodent

ronron [ʀɔ̃ʀɔ̃] NM [*chat*] purr(ing) (*NonC*); * [*moteur*] purr(ing) (*NonC*), hum(ming) (*NonC*); (*péj*) [*discours*] drone (*NonC*), droning (on) (*NonC*); **le ~ de la vie quotidienne** the humdrum routine of daily life

ronronnement [ʀɔ̃ʀɔnmɑ̃] NM [*chat*] purr(ing) (*NonC*); [*moteur*] purr(ing) (*NonC*), hum(ming) (*NonC*); **un ~ conformiste** stultifying conformism

ronronner [ʀɔ̃ʀɔne] ▶ conjug 1 ◀ VI [*chat*] to purr; [*moteur*] to purr, hum; (*fig*) **il ronronnait de satisfaction** he was purring with satisfaction; **ça ronronne dans ce service** things are ticking over nicely in the department

roque [ʀɔk] NM (*Échecs*) castling; **grand/petit ~** castling queen's/king's side

roquefort [ʀɔkfɔʀ] NM Roquefort (cheese)

roquer [ʀɔke] ▶ conjug 1 ◀ VI (*Échecs*) to castle; (*Croquet*) to roquet

roquet [ʀɔkɛ] NM (*péj*) (= *chien*) (nasty little) dog; (= *personne*) ill-tempered little runt*

roquette [ʀɔkɛt] NF (*Mil*) rocket; ~ **antichar** anti-tank rocket

rorqual (*pl* **rorquals**) [ʀɔʀk(w)al] NM rorqual, finback

rosace [ʀozas] NF [*cathédrale*] rose window, rosace; [*plafond*] (ceiling) rose; (*Broderie*) Tenerife motif; (= *figure géométrique*) rosette

rosacé, e [ʀɔzase] [1] ADJ (Bot) rosaceous [2] **rosacée** NF [a] (Méd) rosacea [b] (Bot) rosaceous plant; **~es** Rosaceae, rosaceous plants

rosaire [ʀɔzɛʀ] NM rosary; **réciter son ~** to say ou recite the rosary, tell one's beads†

rosat [ʀɔza] ADJ INV [miel, pommade] rose (épith); **huile ~** attar of roses

rosâtre [ʀozatʀ] ADJ pinkish

rosbif [ʀɔsbif] NM [a] (= rôti) roast beef (NonC); (à rôtir) roasting beef (NonC); **un ~** a joint of (roast) beef, a joint of (roasting) beef [b] (:†, péj = Anglais) Brit*

rose [ʀoz] [1] NF (= fleur) rose; (= vitrail) rose window; (= diamant) rose diamond ■ (PROV) **il n'y a pas de ~s sans épines** there's no rose without a thorn (PROV) → **bois, découvrir, envoyer**
[2] NM (= couleur) pink → **vieux**
[3] ADJ [a] (gén) pink; [joues, teint] pink; (= plein de santé) rosy; **~ bonbon** candy-pink; **~ saumoné** ou **saumon** salmon pink; **~ indien** hot pink; **la ville ~** Toulouse (so called because of the pink stone of which it is largely built) → **crevette, flamant**
[b] (hum = socialiste) left-wing, pink (hum)
[c] (= érotique) **messageries ~s** sex chatlines (on Minitel); **téléphone ~** sex chatlines, phone sex → **Minitel**
[d] (loc) **voir la vie** ou **tout en ~** to see life through rose-tinted ou rose-coloured glasses; **ce roman montre la vie en ~** this novel gives a rosy picture ou view of life; **tout n'est pas ~** ◊ **ce n'est pas tout ~** it's not all roses ou all rosy, it's no bed of roses; **sa vie n'était pas bien ~** his life was no bed of roses
[4] COMP ► **rose de Jéricho** resurrection plant, rose of Jericho ► **rose d'Inde** African marigold ► **rose de Noël** Christmas rose ► **rose pompon** button rose ► **rose des sables** gypsum flower ► **rose trémière** hollyhock ► **rose des vents** compass rose

rosé, e† [ʀoze] [1] ADJ [couleur] pinkish; [vin] rosé; [viande cuite] pink [2] NM (= vin) rosé (wine); (= champignon) **~ (des prés)** field mushroom

roseau (pl **roseaux**) [ʀozo] NM reed

rose-croix [ʀozkʀwa] [1] NF INV **la Rose-Croix** (= confrérie) the Rosicrucians [2] NM INV (= membre) Rosicrucian; (= grade de franc-maçonnerie) Rose-croix

rosée[2] [ʀoze] NF dew; **couvert** ou **humide de ~** [herbe, prés] dewy, covered in ou with dew; [sac de couchage, objet laissé dehors] wet with dew; (Phys) **point de ~** dew point → **goutte**

roséole [ʀozeɔl] NF (Méd = éruption) roseola

roseraie [ʀozʀɛ] NF (= jardin) rose garden; (= plantation) rose-nursery

rose-thé, rose thé (pl **roses(-)thé**) [ʀozte] [1] NF tea rose [2] ADJ (épith)

rosette [ʀozɛt] NF (= nœud) bow; (= insigne) rosette; (Archit, Art, Bot) rosette; **avoir la ~** to be an officer of the Légion d'honneur; (Culin) **~ de Lyon** type of slicing sausage → LÉGION D'HONNEUR

rosicrucien, -ienne [ʀozikʀysjɛ̃, jɛn] ADJ, NM,F Rosicrucian

rosier [ʀozje] NM rosebush, rose tree; **~ nain/grimpant** dwarf/climbing rose

rosière [ʀozjɛʀ] NF (Hist) village maiden publicly rewarded for her chastity; (hum) innocent maiden

rosiériste [ʀozjeʀist] NMF rose grower

rosir [ʀoziʀ] ► conjug 2 ◄ [1] VI [ciel, neige] to grow ou turn pink; [personne, visage] (de confusion) to go pink, blush slightly; (de santé) to get one's colour back [2] VT [+ ciel, neige] to give a pink(ish) hue ou tinge to

rosse [ʀos] [1] NF [a] (†, péj = cheval) nag [b] (: = méchant) (homme) swine*, beast*; (femme) cow:, beast*; **ah les ~s!** (the rotten) swine!:, the (rotten) beasts!* [2] ADJ (péj) [critique,

chansonnier, caricature] nasty, vicious; [coup, action] lousy*, rotten*; [femme] bitchy:; [homme] horrid; **tu as vraiment été ~ (avec lui)** you were really horrid (to him)

rossée†* [ʀose] NF thrashing, (good) hiding, hammering*

rosser [ʀose] ► conjug 1 ◄ VT [a] (= frapper) to thrash, give a (good) hiding to; **se faire ~** to get a (good) hiding ou a thrashing ou a hammering: [b] (* = vaincre) to thrash, lick*, hammer*

rosserie [ʀosʀi] NF [a] (= méchanceté: gén) horridness; [critique, chansonnier, caricature] nastiness, viciousness; [action] lousiness*, rottenness* [b] (= propos) nasty ou bitchy: remark; (= acte) lousy* ou rotten* trick

rossignol [ʀosiɲɔl] NM [a] (= oiseau) nightingale [b] (* = invendu) unsaleable article, piece of junk* [c] (= clé) picklock

rossinante† [ʀosinɑt] NF (hum) (old) jade, old nag

rostre [ʀostʀ] [1] NM (= éperon) rostrum [2] **rostres** NMPL (= tribune) rostrum

rot [ʀo] NM (= renvoi) belch, burp*; [bébé] burp; **faire** ou **lâcher un ~** to belch, burp*, let out a belch ou burp*; **le bébé a fait son ~** the baby has done his (little) burp; **faire faire son ~ à un bébé** to burp ou wind (Brit) a baby

rôt†† [ʀo] NM roast

rotatif, -ive [ʀotatif, iv] [1] ADJ rotary; **mouvement ~** rotating movement, rotary movement ou motion [2] **rotative** NF rotary press

rotation [ʀotasjɔ̃] NF [a] (= mouvement) rotation; **mouvement de ~** rotating movement, rotary movement ou motion; **corps en ~** rotating body, body in rotation; **vitesse de ~** speed of rotation; **la Terre effectue une ~ sur elle-même en 24 heures** the Earth completes a full rotation in 24 hours [b] (= alternance) [matériel, stock] turnover; [avions, bateaux] frequency (of service); **la ~ du personnel** (à des tâches successives) the rotation of staff; (= départs et embauches) the turnover of staff; **taux de ~ (du personnel)** (staff) turnover rate; **~ des cultures** rotation of crops, crop rotation; (Aviat) **15 ~s quotidiennes Paris-Lyon** 15 daily return flights between Paris and Lyon; **les médecin sont de garde par ~ tous les mois** the doctors are on duty each month on a rota basis ou system

rotatoire [ʀotatwaʀ] ADJ rotatory, rotary

roter* [ʀote] ► conjug 1 ◄ VI to burp*, belch

rôti [ʀoti] NM (Culin) (cru) joint, roasting meat (NonC); (cuit) joint, roast, roast meat (NonC); **un ~ de bœuf/porc** a joint of beef/pork; **du ~ de bœuf/porc** (cru) roasting beef/pork; (cuit) roast beef/pork

rôtie [ʀoti] NF (Can††) piece ou slice of toast

rotin [ʀotɛ̃] NM [a] (= fibre) rattan (cane); **chaise de** ou **en ~** rattan chair [b] (†,* = sou) penny, cent; **il n'a pas un ~** he hasn't got a penny ou cent to his name

rôtir [ʀotiʀ] ► conjug 2 ◄ [1] VT (Culin) (faire) **~** to roast; **poulet/agneau rôti** roast chicken/lamb; (fig) **il attend toujours que ça lui tombe tout rôti dans le bec*** he expects everything to be handed to him on a plate ou a silver platter (US) [2] VI (Culin) to roast; * [baigneur, estivants] to roast; **mettre un canard à ~** to put a duck in the oven to roast [3] **se rôtir** VPR **se ~ au soleil*** to bask in the sun

rôtisserie [ʀotisʀi] NF (dans nom de restaurant) steakhouse, grill; (= boutique) shop selling roast meat

rôtisseur, -euse [ʀotisœʀ, øz] NM,F (= traiteur) seller of roast meat; (= restaurateur) steakhouse proprietor

rôtissoire [ʀotiswaʀ] NF rotisserie, (roasting) spit

rotogravure [ʀotogʀavyʀ] NF rotogravure

rotonde [ʀotɔd] NF (Archit) rotunda; (Rail) engine shed (Brit), roundhouse (US); (dans un bus) row of seats at rear of bus; **édifice en ~** circular building

rotondité [ʀotɔdite] NF [a] (= sphéricité) roundness, rotundity (frm) [b] (hum = embonpoint) plumpness, rotundity (hum)

rotor [ʀotɔʀ] NM rotor

rotule [ʀotyl] NF [a] (Anat) kneecap, patella (SPÉC); **être sur les ~s*** to be dead beat* ou all in* [b] (Tech) ball-and-socket joint

rotulien, -ienne [ʀotyljɛ̃, jɛn] ADJ patellar → **réflexe**

roture [ʀotyʀ] NF (= absence de noblesse) common rank; [fief] roture; (= roturiers) **la ~** the commoners, the common people

roturier, -ière [ʀotyʀje, jɛʀ] [1] ADJ (Hist) common, of common birth; (fig = vulgaire) common, plebeian [2] NM,F commoner

rouage [ʀwaʒ] NM [engrenage] cog(wheel), gearwheel; [montre] part; **les ~s d'une montre** the works ou parts of a watch; **il n'est qu'un ~ dans cette organisation** he's merely a cog in this organization; **les ~s de l'État** the machinery of state; **les ~s administratifs** the administrative machinery; **organisation aux ~s compliqués** organization with complex structures

roubignoles:* [ʀubiɲɔl] NFPL (= testicules) balls:*, nuts:*

roublard, e* [ʀublaʀ, aʀd] [1] ADJ crafty, wily, artful [2] NM,F crafty ou artful devil*; **ce ~ de Paul** crafty old Paul*

roublardise* [ʀublaʀdiz] NF (= caractère) craftiness, wiliness, artfulness; (= acte, tour) crafty ou artful trick

rouble [ʀubl] NM rouble

roucoulade [ʀukulad] NF, **roucoulement** [ʀukulmɑ] NM [a] [oiseau] cooing (NonC); * [amoureux] (billing and) cooing (NonC); (péj) [chanteur] crooning (NonC)

roucouler [ʀukule] ► conjug 1 ◄ [1] VI [oiseau] to coo; * [amoureux] to bill and coo; (péj) [chanteur] to croon [2] VT (péj) [+ chanson] to croon; * [+ mots d'amour] to coo; **il lui roucoulait des mots tendres** he was whispering sweet nothings to her

roudoudou [ʀududu] NM children's sweet in the form of a small shell filled with hard confectionery

roue [ʀu] [1] NF [véhicule, loterie, moulin] wheel; [engrenage] cog(wheel), (gear)wheel; **véhicule à deux/quatre ~s** two-/four-wheeled vehicle; **~ avant/arrière** front/back wheel; (Hist) **(supplice de) la ~** (torture of) the wheel; **la ~ de la Fortune** the wheel of Fortune; **la ~ tourne!** how things change!; **faire la ~** [paon] to spread ou fan its tail; [personne] (= se pavaner) to strut about, swagger (about); (Gym) to do a cartwheel; (fête foraine) **la grande ~** the big wheel (Brit), the Ferris Wheel (US); **il s'est jeté sous les ~s de la voiture** he threw himself under the car; **son bureau est à quelques tours de ~ de la tour Eiffel** his office is a short car-ride away from the Eiffel Tower; **le coureur est revenu dans la ~ de son adversaire** the cyclist closed in right behind his opponent; **être ~ à** ou **dans ~** to be neck and neck → **bâton, chapeau, cinquième, pousser**
[2] COMP ► **roue à aubes** [bateau] paddle wheel ► **roue dentée** cogwheel ► **roue à friction** friction wheel ► **roue à godets** bucket wheel ► **roue de gouvernail** (steering) wheel, helm ► **roue hydraulique** waterwheel ► **roue libre** freewheel; **descendre une côte en ~ libre** to freewheel ou coast down a hill; **pédaler en ~ libre** to freewheel, coast (along); (fig = ne pas se surmener) **il s'est mis en ~ libre*** he's taking it easy ► **roue motrice** driving wheel; **véhicule à 4 ~s motrices** 4-wheel drive vehicle ► **roue de se-**

cours (*Aut*) spare wheel (*Brit*) *ou* tire (*US*) ► **roue de transmission** driving wheel

roué, e [ʀwe] (*ptp de* **rouer**) [1] ADJ (= *rusé*) cunning, wily, sly [2] NM,F cunning *ou* sly individual; **c'est une petite ~e** she's a cunning *ou* wily *ou* sly little minx [3] NM (*Hist* = *débauché*) rake, roué [4] **rouée** NF (*Hist* = *débauchée*) hussy

rouelle [ʀwel] NF **~ (de veau)** slice of calf's leg

rouer [ʀwe] ▶ conjug 1 ◀ VT [a] **~ qn de coups** to give sb a beating *ou* thrashing, beat sb black and blue [b] (*Hist*) [+ *condamné*] to put on the wheel

rouerie [ʀuʀi] NF (*littér*) (= *caractère*) cunning, wiliness, slyness; (= *action*) cunning *ou* wily *ou* sly trick

rouet [ʀwe] NM (*à filer*) spinning wheel

rouflaquettes* [ʀuflaket] NFPL (= *favoris*) sideburns, sideboards (*Brit*)

rouge [ʀuʒ] [1] ADJ [a] (*gén, Pol*) red → **armée²** [b] (= *incandescent*) [*métal*] red-hot; [*tison*] glowing red (*attrib*), red-hot [c] [*visage, yeux*] red; **~ de colère/confusion/honte** red *ou* flushed with anger/embarrassment/shame; **~ d'émotion** flushed with emotion; **devenir ~ comme une cerise** to blush, go quite pink, go red in the face; **il est ~ comme un coq** *ou* **un coquelicot** *ou* **un homard** *ou* **une pivoine** *ou* **une écrevisse** *ou* **une tomate** he's as red as a beetroot *ou* a lobster; **il était ~ d'avoir couru** he was red in the face *ou* his face was flushed from running [d] (= *roux*) [*cheveux, pelage*] red [2] ADV **voir ~** to see red; (*Pol*) **voter ~** to vote Communist → **fâcher** [3] NM [a] (= *couleur*) red; (*Aut*) **le feu est au ~** the lights are red; **passer au ~** [*feu*] to change to red; (= *redémarrer trop tôt*) to jump the lights; (= *ne pas s'arrêter*) to go through a red light, run a red light (*US*); (*Jeux*) **tout miser sur le ~** to put all one's chips on the red; (*Fin*) **être dans le ~*** to be in the red*; **sortir du ~*** to get out of the red* → **bordeaux** [b] (= *signe d'émotion*) **ça lui a fait monter le ~ aux joues** it made him blush; **le ~ lui monta aux joues** his cheeks flushed, he went red (in the face); **le ~ (de la confusion ou de la honte) lui monta au front** his face went red *ou* flushed *ou* he blushed (with embarrassment/with shame) [c] (= *vin*) red wine; *** boire un coup de ~*** to have a glass of red wine → **gros** [d] (= *fard*) [*joues*] rouge†, blusher; (*à lèvres*) lipstick → **bâton, tube** [e] (= *incandescence*) **fer porté** *ou* **chauffé au ~** red-hot iron [4] NMF (*péj* = *communiste*) Red* (*péj*), Commie* (*péj*) [5] COMP ► **rouge brique** ADJ INV brick red ► **rouge cerise** ADJ INV cherry-red ► **rouge à joues** rouge†, blusher; **se mettre du ~ à joues** to rouge one's cheeks†, put blusher on ► **rouge à lèvres** lipstick ► **rouge sang** ADJ INV blood red

rougeâtre [ʀuʒɑtʀ] ADJ reddish

rougeaud, e [ʀuʒo, od] ADJ red-faced; **ce gros ~ la dégoûtait** she found this fat red-faced man repellent

rouge-gorge (*pl* **rouges-gorges**) [ʀuʒgɔʀʒ] NM robin

rougeoiement [ʀuʒwamɑ̃] NM [*couchant, incendie*] red *ou* reddish glow; [*ciel*] reddening

rougeole [ʀuʒɔl] NF **la ~** (the) measles *sg*; **il a eu une très forte ~** he had a very bad bout of measles

rougeoyant, e [ʀuʒwajɑ̃, ɑ̃t] ADJ [*ciel*] reddening; [*cendres*] glowing red (*attrib*), glowing; **des reflets ~s** a glimmering red glow

rougeoyer [ʀuʒwaje] ▶ conjug 8 ◀ VI [*couchant, feu, incendie*] to glow red; [*ciel*] to turn red, take on a reddish hue

rouge-queue (*pl* **rouges-queues**) [ʀuʒkø] NM redstart

rouget [ʀuʒe] NM mullet; **~ barbet** red *ou* striped mullet, goatfish (*US*); **~ grondin** gurnard; **~ de roche** surmullet

rougeur [ʀuʒœʀ] NF [a] (= *teinte*) redness [b] [*personne*] (*due à la course, un échauffement, une émotion*) red face, flushing (*NonC*); (*due à la honte, gêne*) red face, blushing (*NonC*); [*visages, joues*] redness, flushing (*NonC*); **sa ~ a trahi son émotion/sa gêne** her red face *ou* her blushes betrayed her emotion/her embarrassment; **la ~ de ses joues** his red face *ou* cheeks, his blushing; **avoir des ~s de jeune fille** to blush like a young girl; **elle était sujette à des ~s subites** she was inclined to blush suddenly [c] (*Méd* = *tache*) red blotch *ou* patch

rough [ʀœf] NM (*Golf*) rough

rougir [ʀuʒiʀ] ▶ conjug 2 ◀ [1] VI [a] (*de honte, gêne*) to blush, go red, redden (**de** with); (*de plaisir, d'émotion*) to flush, go red, redden (**de** with); **il rougit de colère** he *ou* his face flushed *ou* reddened with anger; **à ces mots, elle rougit** she blushed *ou* went red *ou* reddened at the words; **~ jusqu'au blanc des yeux** *ou* **jusqu'aux yeux** ◊ **~ jusqu'aux oreilles** ◊ **~ jusqu'à la racine des cheveux** to go bright red, blush to the roots of one's hair; (*lit, fig*) **faire ~ qn** to make sb blush; **dire qch sans ~** to say sth without blushing *ou* unblushingly [b] (*fig = avoir honte*) **~ de** to be ashamed of; **je n'ai pas à ~ de cela** that is nothing for me to be ashamed of; **il ne rougit de rien** he's quite shameless, he has no shame; **j'en rougis pour lui** I blush for him, I'm ashamed for him [c] (*après un coup de soleil*) to go red [d] [*ciel, feuille, métal*] to become *ou* get red, redden; [*métal*] to become *ou* get red-hot; (*Culin*) [*crustacés*] to go *ou* turn red, redden; (*Agr*) [*fraises, tomates*] to redden, turn red [2] VT [+ *ciel*] to turn red, give a red glow to, redden; [+ *arbres, feuilles*] to turn red, redden; [+ *métal*] to heat to red heat, make red-hot; **~ son eau** to put a dash *ou* drop of red wine in one's water; **boire de l'eau rougie** to drink water with a few drops of red wine in it; **~ la terre de son sang** (*lit*) to stain the ground with one's blood; (*fig*) to shed one's blood; **les yeux rougis** (*par les larmes*) with red eyes, red-eyed; (*par l'alcool, la drogue*) with blood-shot eyes

rougissant, e [ʀuʒisɑ̃, ɑ̃t] ADJ [*personne, visage*] blushing; [*ciel, feuille*] reddening

rougissement [ʀuʒismɑ̃] NM (*de honte*) blush, blushing (*NonC*); (*d'émotion*) flush, flushing (*NonC*)

rouille [ʀuj] [1] NF [a] (*Bot, Chim*) rust [b] (*Culin*) spicy Provençal sauce eaten with fish [2] ADJ INV rust(-coloured), rusty

rouillé, e [ʀuje] (*ptp de* **rouiller**) ADJ [a] [*métal*] rusty, rusted; (*littér*) [*écorce, roche*] rust-coloured [b] [*personne*] (*intellectuellement*) rusty; (*physiquement*) out of practice; [*mémoire*] rusty; [*muscles*] stiff [c] (*Bot*) [*blé*] rusty

rouiller [ʀuje] ▶ conjug 1 ◀ [1] VI to rust, go *ou* get rusty; **laisser ~ qch** to let sth go *ou* get rusty [2] VT [+ *esprit, métal*] to make rusty [3] **se rouiller** VPR [*métal*] to go *ou* get rusty, rust; [*esprit, mémoire*] to become *ou* go rusty; [*corps, muscles*] to grow *ou* get stiff; [*sportif*] to get rusty, get out of practice; **mon italien se rouille** my Italian is getting a bit rusty

rouir [ʀwiʀ] ▶ conjug 2 ◀ VT, VI (**faire**) **~** to ret

rouissage [ʀwisaʒ] NM retting

roulade [ʀulad] NF [a] (*Mus*) roulade, run; [*oiseau*] trill [b] (*Culin*) **~ de veau** veal roulade [c] (*Sport*) roll; **~ avant/arrière** forward/backward roll; **faire des ~s** to do rolls

roulage [ʀulaʒ] NM († *Min* = *camionnage, transport*) haulage; (*Agr*) rolling

roulant, e [ʀulɑ̃, ɑ̃t] [1] ADJ [a] (= *mobile*) [*meuble*] on wheels → **cuisine, fauteuil, table** [b] (*Rail*) **matériel ~** rolling stock; **personnel ~** train crews [c] [*trottoir, surface transporteuse*] moving → **escalier, feu¹, pont** [d] [*route, piste*] fast [2] **roulants** NMPL (*arg Rail*) **les ~s** train crews [3] **roulante** NF (*arg Mil*) field kitchen

roulé, e [ʀule] [1] ADJ [a] [*bord de chapeau*] curved; [*bord de foulard, morceau de boucherie*] rolled; [*journal, tapis*] rolled up → **col** [b]* **elle est bien ~e** she's got all the right curves in all the right places, she's well put together [c] (*Ling*) rolled; **r ~** trilled *ou* rolled r [2] NM (= *gâteau*) Swiss roll; (= *viande*) rolled meat (*NonC*); **~ de veau** rolled veal (*NonC*); **~ au fromage** puff-pastry roll with cheese filling

rouleau (*pl* **rouleaux**) [ʀulo] [1] NM [a] (= *bande enroulée*) roll; **~ de papier/tissu/pellicule** roll of paper/material/film; **un ~ de cheveux blonds** (= *boucle*) a ringlet of blond hair; (= *cheveux roulés sur la nuque*) a coil of blond hair (*rolled at the nape of the neck*) → **bout** [b] (= *cylindre*) [*pièces, tabac*] roll; **~ de réglisse** liquorice roll [c] (= *outil, ustensile*) roller; [*machine à écrire*] platen, roller; **passer une pelouse au ~** to roll a lawn; **avoir des ~x dans les cheveux** *ou* **sur la tête** to have one's hair in curlers *ou* rollers, have curlers *ou* rollers in one's hair; **peindre au ~** to paint with a roller [d] (= *vague*) roller [e] (*Sport* = *saut*) roll [2] COMP ► **rouleau compresseur** (*lit*) steamroller, roadroller; (*fig*) steamroller, bulldozer ► **rouleau dorsal** (*Sport*) Fosbury flop ► **rouleau encreur** = **rouleau imprimeur** ► **rouleau essuie-mains** roller towel ► **rouleau imprimeur** ink roller ► **rouleau de papier hygiénique** toilet roll, roll of toilet paper *ou* tissue ► **rouleau de papyrus** papyrus scroll ► **rouleau de parchemin** scroll *ou* roll of parchment ► **rouleau à pâtisserie** rolling pin ► **rouleau de printemps** (*Culin*) spring roll ► **rouleau ventral** (*Sport*) western roll

roulé-boulé (*pl* **roulés-boulés**) [ʀulebule] NM roll; **faire un ~** to roll over, curl up; **tomber en ~** to roll (down)

roulement [ʀulmɑ̃] [1] NM [a] (= *rotation*) [*équipe, ouvriers*] rotation; **travailler par ~** to work on a rota basis *ou* system, work in rotation [b] (= *circulation*) [*train, voiture*] movement; **route usée/pneu usé par le ~** road/tyre worn through use → **bande¹** [c] (= *bruit*) [*camion, train*] rumble, rumbling (*NonC*); [*charrette*] rattle, rattling (*NonC*); **entendre le ~ du tonnerre** to hear thunder; **il y eut un ~ de tonnerre** there was a rumble *ou* peal *ou* roll of thunder; **~ de tambour** drum roll [d] [*capitaux*] circulation → **fonds** [e] (= *mouvement*) [*œil*] rolling; [*hanche*] wiggling [2] COMP ► **roulement (à billes)** ball bearings; **monté sur ~ à billes** mounted on ball bearings

rouler [ʀule] ▶ conjug 1 ◀ [1] VT [a] (= *pousser*) [+ *meuble*] to wheel (along), roll (along); [+ *chariot, brouette*] to wheel (along), trundle along; [+ *boule, tonneau*] to roll (along) [b] (= *enrouler*) [+ *tapis, tissu, carte*] to roll up; [+ *cigarette*] to roll; [+ *ficelle, fil de fer*] to wind up, roll up; [+ *viande, parapluie, mèche de cheveux*] to roll (up); **~ qn dans une couverture** to wrap *ou* roll sb (up) in a blanket; **~ un pansement autour d'un bras** to wrap *ou* wind a bandage round an arm; **~ ses manches jusqu'au coude** to roll up one's sleeves to one's elbows [c] (= *tourner et retourner*) to roll; **~ des boulettes dans de la farine** to roll meatballs in flour; **la mer roulait les galets sur la plage** the sea rolled the pebbles along the beach; (*fig*) **il roulait mille projets dans sa tête** he was turning thousands of plans over (and over) in his mind; (*littér*) **le fleuve roulait des flots boueux** the river flowed muddily along

d (= *passer au rouleau*) [+ *court de tennis, pelouse*] to roll; (*Culin*) [+ *pâte*] to roll out **e** (* = *duper*) to con‡; (*sur le prix, le poids*) to diddle* (*Brit*), do* (**sur** over); **je l'ai bien roulé** I really conned him‡, I really took him for a ride*; **elle m'a roulé de 50F** she's diddled* (*Brit*) ou done* me out of 50 francs; **se faire ~ to be conned** ou had* ou done* ou diddled* (*Brit*); **il s'est fait ~ dans la farine** he was had* **f** (= *balancer, faire bouger*) **~ les** ou **des épaules** (*en marchant*) to sway one's shoulders (as one walks along); **~ les** ou **des mécaniques** (*en marchant*) to (walk with a) swagger; (= *montrer sa force, ses muscles*) to show off one's muscles; (*intellectuellement*) to show off; **~ les** ou **des hanches** to wiggle one's hips; **~ les yeux** to roll one's eyes; (*fig*) **il a roulé sa bosse*** he's been around* → **patin, pelle** **g** (*Ling*) **~ les « r »** to roll one's r's

2 VI **a** [*voiture, train*] to go; run; **le train roulait/roulait à vive allure à travers la campagne** the train was going along/was racing (along) through the countryside; **cette voiture a très peu/beaucoup roulé** this car has a very low/high mileage; **cette voiture a 10 ans et elle roule encore** this car is 10 years old but it's still going ou running; **la voiture roule bien depuis la révision** the car is running ou going well since its service; **les voitures ne roulent pas bien sur le sable** cars don't run well on sand; **le véhicule roulait à gauche** the vehicle was driving (along) on the left; **~ au pas** (*par prudence*) to go at a walking pace, go dead slow (*Brit*); (*dans un embouteillage*) to crawl along; **le train roulait à 150 à l'heure au moment de l'accident** the train was doing 150 ou going at 150 kilometres an hour at the time of the accident; **sa voiture roule au super/au gazole** his car runs on four-star/diesel

b [*passager, conducteur*] to drive; **à 80 km à l'heure** to do 80 km per hour, drive at 80 km per hour; **on a bien roulé*** we made good time; **ça roule/ça ne roule pas bien** the traffic is/is not flowing well; **nous roulions sur la N7 quand soudain ...** we were driving along the N7 when suddenly ...; **dans son métier, il roule beaucoup** he does a lot of driving in his job; **il roule en 2CV** he drives a 2CV; **il roule en Rolls** he drives (around in) a Rolls (†, *hum*) **~ carrosse** to live in high style; (*fig* = être à la solde de qn) **~ pour qn*** to be for sb

c [*boule, bille, dé*] to roll, run; **allez, roulez!** let's roll it!*, off we go!; **une larme roula sur sa joue** a tear rolled down his cheek; **une secousse le fit ~ à bas de sa couchette** there was a jolt and he rolled off his couchette; **il a roulé en bas de l'escalier** he rolled right down the stairs; **un coup de poing l'envoya ~ dans la poussière** a punch sent him rolling in the dust; (*ivre*) **il a roulé sous la table** he was legless* ou under the table; **faire ~** [+ *boule*] to roll; [+ *cerceau*] to roll along → **pierre**

d [*bateau*] to roll; **ça roulait*** the boat was rolling quite a bit

e (* = *bourlinguer*) to knock about*; **il a pas mal roulé** he has knocked about* quite a bit, he's been around*

f [*argent, capitaux*] to turn over, circulate **g** (= *faire un bruit sourd*) [*tambour*] to roll; [*tonnerre*] to rumble

h [*conversation*] **~ sur** to turn on, be centred on

i (* = *aller bien*) **ça roule?** how's things?*, how's life?; **c'est une affaire qui roule** it's going well

j **~ sur l'or** to be rolling in money*, have pots of money*; **ils ne roulent pas sur l'or depuis qu'ils sont à la retraite** they're not exactly living in the lap of luxury ou they're not terribly well-off now they've retired

3 **se rouler** VPR **a** (*allongé sur le sol ou sur qch*) to roll (about); **se ~ par terre/dans l'herbe**

to roll (about) on the ground/in the grass; (*fig*) **se ~ par terre de rire** to roll on the ground burning ou scorching with laughter, fall about* (laughing) (*Brit*); **c'est à se ~ (par terre)** it's a scream* → **pouce**

b (= *s'enrouler*) **se ~ dans une couverture** to roll ou wrap o.s. up in a blanket; **se ~ en boule** to roll o.s. (up) into a ball

roulette [rulɛt] NF **a** [*meuble*] caster, castor; **fauteuil à ~s** armchair on casters ou castors; **ça a marché** ou **été comme sur des ~s*** [*plan*] it went like clockwork ou very smoothly; [*interview, soirée*] it went off very smoothly ou like a dream → **patin b** (= *outil*) [*pâtissier*] pastry (cutting) wheel; [*relieur*] fillet; [*couturière*] tracing wheel; [*vitrier*] steel(-wheel) glass cutter; **~ de dentiste** dentist's drill **c** (= *jeu*) roulette (= *instrument*) roulette wheel; **jouer à la ~** to play roulette; **~ russe** Russian roulette

rouleur [rulœʀ] NM (*Cyclisme*) flat racer; **c'est un bon ~** he's good on the flat; (*fig*) **quel ~ de mécaniques!‡** he likes to strut his stuff!*

roulier [rulje] NM (*Hist*) cart driver, wagoner; (*Naut*) roll-on roll-off ferry, ro-ro ferry

roulis [ruli] NM (*Naut*) roll(ing) (*NonC*); **il y a beaucoup de ~** the ship is rolling a lot; **coup de ~** roll

roulotte [rulɔt] NF caravan (*Brit*), trailer (*US*); **visitez l'Irlande en ~** tour around Ireland in a horse-drawn ou gypsy caravan

roulotté, e [rulɔte] **1** ADJ (*Couture*) rolled; **foulard ~ (à la) main** hand-rolled scarf **2** NM rolled hem

roulure [rulyʀ] NF (*péj*) slut (*péj*), trollop† (*péj*)

roumain, e [rumɛ̃, ɛn] **1** ADJ Romanian, Rumanian **2** NM (*Ling*) Romanian, Rumanian **3** **Roumain(e)** NM,F Romanian, Rumanian

Roumanie [rumani] NF Rumania, Romania

round [ʀaund] NM (*Boxe*) round

roupettes‡ [rupɛt] NFPL (= *testicules*) balls‡, nuts‡

roupie [rupi] NF **a** (= *monnaie*) rupee **b** († *) **c'est de la ~ de sansonnet** it's a load of (old) rubbish ou junk*, it's absolute trash*; **ce n'est pas de la ~ de sansonnet** it's none of your cheap rubbish ou junk*

roupiller* [rupije] ▸ conjug 1 ◂ VI (= *dormir*) to sleep; (= *faire un petit somme*) to have a snooze* ou a nap ou a kip* (*Brit*); **j'ai besoin de ~** I must get some shut-eye*; **je n'arrive pas à ~** I can't get any shut-eye*; **je vais ~** I'll be turning in*, I'm off to hit the hay*; **viens ~ chez nous** come and bed down ou kip down (*Brit*) at our place‡; **secouez-vous, vous roupillez!** pull yourself together — you're half asleep! ou you're dozing!

roupillon* [rupijɔ̃] NM snooze*, nap, kip‡ (*Brit*); **piquer** ou **faire un ~** to have a snooze* ou a nap ou a kip* (*Brit*)

rouquin, e* [ʀukɛ̃, in] **1** ADJ [*personne*] red-haired; [*cheveux*] red, carroty* (*péj*) **2** NM,F redhead **3** NM (= *vin rouge*) (cheap) red wine, red plonk* (*Brit*)

rouscailler‡ [ruskaje] ▸ conjug 1 ◂ VI to moan*, bellyache‡

rouspétance* [ruspetɑ̃s] NF (= *ronchonnement*) moaning* (*NonC*), grousing* (*NonC*), grouching* (*NonC*); (= *protestation*) moaning* (*NonC*), grumbling (*NonC*); **pas de ~!** no grumbling!

rouspéter* [ruspete] ▸ conjug 6 ◂ VI (= *ronchonner*) to moan*, grouse*, grouch*; (= *protester*) to moan*, grumble (**après, contre** at); **se faire ~ par qn** to get an earful from sb*

rouspéteur, -euse* [ruspetœʀ, øz] **1** ADJ grumpy **2** NM,F moaner*

roussâtre [rusɑtʀ] ADJ reddish, russet

rousse[1]‡ [rus] NF (*arg Crime* = *police*) **la ~** the fuzz (*arg, Crime*), the cops*

rousserolle [rus(ə)ʀɔl] NF **~ verderolle** marsh warbler; **~ effarvatte** reed warbler

roussette [rusɛt] NF (= *poisson*) dogfish; (= *chauve-souris*) flying fox; (= *grenouille*) common frog

rousseur [rusœʀ] NF **a** [*cheveux, barbe*] redness; (*orangé*) gingery colour; [*pelage, robe, feuille*] russet colour → **tache b** (*sur le papier*) **~s** brownish marks ou stains; (*sur la peau*) liver spots

roussi [rusi] NM **odeur de ~** smell of (something) burning ou scorching ou singeing; **ça sent le ~!** (*lit*) there's a smell of (something) burning ou scorching ou singeing; (*fig*) I can smell trouble

roussir [rusiʀ] ▸ conjug 2 ◂ **1** VT [*fer à repasser*] to scorch, singe; [*flamme*] to singe; **~ l'herbe** [*gelée*] to turn the grass brown ou yellow; [*chaleur*] to scorch the grass **2** VI [*feuilles, forêt*] to turn ou go brown ou russet **b** (*Culin*) **faire ~** to brown

rouste* [rust] NF (= *coups*) hiding, thrashing; (= *défaite*) hammering*; **prendre une ~** (*lit*) to get a hiding, get thrashed; (*fig*) to get a hammering*, get thrashed*; **flanquer** ou **filer une ~ à qn** (*lit*) to give sb a hiding ou thrashing; (*fig*) to give sb a hammering*, thrash sb

roustons‡ [rustɔ̃] NMPL (= *testicules*) balls‡, nuts‡

routage [ʀutaʒ] NM **a** (= *distribution*) sorting and mailing; **entreprise de ~** mailing firm ou service **b** (*Naut*) plotting a course (**de** for)

routard, e* [ʀutaʀ, aʀd] NM,F backpacker

route [ʀut] NF **a** (= *voie de communication*) road; **~ nationale** main road, ≈ A road (*Brit*), trunk road (*Brit*); **~ départementale** minor road, ≈ B road (*Brit*); **~ secondaire** minor ou secondary road; **~ de montagne** mountain road; **prenez la ~ de Lyon** take the road to Lyon ou the Lyon road; **«~ barrée»** "road closed" → **barrer, grand-route**

b (= *moyen de transport*) **la ~** road; **la ~ est plus économique que le rail** road is cheaper than rail; **la ~ est meurtrière** the road is a killer; **arriver par la ~** to arrive by road; **faire de la ~** to do a lot of mileage → **accident, blessé, code**

c (= *chemin à suivre*) way; (*Naut* = *direction, cap*) course; **je ne l'emmène pas, ce n'est pas (sur) ma ~** I'm not taking him — it's not on my way; **indiquer/montrer la ~ à qn** to point out/show the way to sb; **perdre/retrouver sa ~** to lose/find one's way

d (= *ligne de communication*) route; **~ aérienne/maritime** air/sea route; **la ~ du sel/de l'opium/des épices** the salt/opium/spice route ou trail; **la ~ de la soie** the Silk Road ou Route; **la ~ des vins** the wine trail; **la ~ des Indes** the route to India

e (= *trajet*) trip, journey (*Brit*); **bonne ~!** have a good trip! ou journey! (*Brit*); **carnet** ou **journal de ~** travel diary ou journal; **la ~ sera longue** (*gén*) it'll be a long journey; (*en voiture*) it'll be a long drive ou ride; **il y a trois heures de ~** (*en voiture*) it's a three-hour drive ou ride ou journey (*Brit*); (*à bicyclette*) it's a three-hour (cycle-)ride; **ils ont fait toute la ~ à pied/à bicyclette** they walked/cycled the whole way, they did the whole journey (*Brit*) on foot/by bicycle → **compagnon**

f (*fig* = *ligne de conduite, voie*) path, road, way; **la ~ à suivre** the path ou road to follow; **la ~ du bonheur** the road ou path ou way to happiness; **nos ~s se sont croisées** our paths crossed; **votre ~ est toute tracée** your path is set out for you; **être sur la bonne ~** (*dans la vie*) to be on the right road ou path; (*dans un problème*) to be on the right track; **remettre qn sur la bonne ~** to put sb back on the right road ou path ou way; **c'est lui qui a ouvert la ~** he's the one who opened (up) the road ou way → **faux[2]**

g (*loc*) **en ~** on the way ou journey (*Brit*), en

route; **en ~ !** let's go!, let's be off!; (*hum*) **en ~, mauvaise troupe !** off we go!; (*Naut*) **faire ~** to be under way; **en ~ pour ◊ faisant ~ vers** bound for, heading for, on its way to; **avoir plusieurs projets en ~** to have several projects on the go; **mettre en ~** [+ *machine, moteur*] to start (up); [+ *processus, projet, réforme*] to set in motion, get under way; **mettre le repas en ~** to get the meal started; **ils ont attendu longtemps avant de mettre un bébé en ~** they waited a long time before starting a family; **remettre en ~ le moteur/le processus de paix** to restart the engine/the peace process, get the engine/peace process going again; **mise en ~** [*machine*] starting up; [*processus, projet*] setting in motion; **la mise en ~ des réformes sera difficile** it will be difficult to implement the reforms *ou* to get the reforms under way; **depuis la remise en ~ des machines** since the machines have been restarted *ou* started up again; **ils envisagent la remise en ~ de l'usine** they're considering bringing the factory back into operation; **prendre la ~ avec qn** to travel with sb; **prendre la ~ ◊ se mettre en ~** to start out, set off *ou* out, get under way; **reprendre la ~ ◊ se remettre en ~** to start out again, set off *ou* out again, resume one's journey (*Brit*); **tenir la ~** [*voiture*] to hold the road; * [*matériel*] to be well-made *ou* serviceable; * [*argument, raisonnement*] to hold water; [*solution, politique*] to be viable → **tenue**

router [Rute] ▶conjug 1◀ VT **[a]** [+ *journaux*] to pack and mail **[b]** (*Naut*) to plot a course for

routeur, -euse [Rutœr, øz] **[1]** NM,F (*Naut*) route planner **[2]** NM (*Ordin*) router

routier, -ière [Rutje, jɛr] **[1]** ADJ [*carte, circulation, réseau, transport*] road (*épith*) → **gare¹** **[2]** NM (= *camionneur*) long-distance truck *ou* lorry (*Brit*) driver; (= *restaurant*) ≈ roadside café, ≈ transport café (*Brit*), ≈ truckstop (*US*); (= *cycliste*) road racer *ou* rider; (*Naut* = *carte*) route chart; († = *scout*) rover; **un vieux ~ de la politique** a wily old politician, an old hand at politics **[3]** **routière** NF (= *voiture*) touring car, tourer (*Brit*); (= *moto*) road bike; **grande routière** high-performance touring car *ou* tourer (*Brit*)

routine [Rutin] NF **[a]** (= *habitude*) routine; **la ~ quotidienne** the daily routine *ou* grind; **s'enfoncer/tomber dans la ~** to settle/fall into a routine; **par ~** as a matter of routine; **contrôle/opération de ~** routine check/operation **[b]** (*Ordin*) routine

routinier, -ière [Rutinje, jɛr] ADJ [*procédé, travail, vie*] humdrum, routine; [*personne*] routine-minded, addicted to routine (*attrib*); **il a l'esprit ~** he's completely tied to (his) routine; **c'est un travail un peu ~** the work is a bit routine *ou* humdrum; **c'est un ~** he's a creature of habit

rouvre [Ruvr] ADJ, NM (**chêne**) **~** durmast *ou* sessile oak

rouvrir [Ruvrir] ▶conjug 18◀ **[1]** VT (*gén*) to re-open; [+ *porte, yeux*] to reopen, open again; **le stade rouvrira ses portes dimanche** the stadium will reopen its doors on Sunday **[2]** VI [*magasin, musée, théâtre*] to reopen, open again **[3]** **se rouvrir** VPR [*porte*] to reopen, open again; [*plaie, blessure*] to open up again, reopen

roux, rousse² [Ru, Rus] **[1]** ADJ [*cheveux*] (*foncé*) red, auburn; (*clair*) ginger; [*barbe*] (*foncé*) red; (*clair*) ginger; [*pelage, robe, feuilles*] russet, reddish-brown → **blond, lune [2]** NM,F redhead **[3]** NM **[a]** (= *couleur*) [*cheveux*] red, auburn; [*barbe*] red; (= *orangé*) ginger; [*pelage, robe feuille*] russet, reddish-brown; **cheveux d'un ~ flamboyant** flaming red hair **[b]** (*Culin*) roux

royal, e (*mpl* **-aux**) [Rwajal, o] **[1]** ADJ **[a]** (*gén*) royal; **la famille ~e** the Royal Family *ou* royal family → **gelée, voie [b]** [*magnificence, maintien*] kingly, regal; [*cadeau, demeure, repas*]

fit for a king (*attrib*); [*salaire*] princely → **aigle, tigre [c]** (*intensif*) [*indifférence, mépris*] majestic, lofty, regal; **il m'a fichu une paix ~e*** he left me in perfect peace **[2]** NF **[a]** (* *Naut*) **la Royale** the French Navy **[b]** (*Culin*) **lièvre à la ~e** hare royale

royalement [Rwajalmɑ̃] ADV [*vivre*] in (a) royal fashion; [*recevoir, traiter*] royally, in (a) regal *ou* royal fashion; **il se moque ~ de sa situation*** he couldn't care less* *ou* he doesn't care two hoots* about his position; (*iro*) **il m'a ◊ offert 100 F d'augmentation** he offered me a princely 100-franc rise (*iro*)

royalisme [Rwajalism] NM royalism

royaliste [Rwajalist] **[1]** ADJ royalist; (*fig*) **être plus ~ que le roi** to carry things to extremes, be more Catholic than the Pope; **puisqu'on ne te demande rien, pourquoi être plus ~ que le roi ?** since you haven't been asked to do anything, why put yourself out? *ou* why be so zealous? **[2]** NMF royalist

royalties [Rwajalti] NFPL royalties; **toucher des ~** to receive royalties

royaume [Rwajom] NM (*lit*) kingdom, realm; (*fig = domaine*) domain; **le vieux grenier était son ~** the old attic was his domain; (*Rel*) **le ~ céleste** *ou* **des cieux** *ou* **de Dieu** the kingdom of heaven *ou* God; **le ~ des morts** the kingdom of the dead; **le ~ des ombres** the land of the shades, the valley of the shadows ■ (*PROV*) **au ~ des aveugles les borgnes sont rois** in the kingdom of the blind the one-eyed man is king (*PROV*)

Royaume-Uni [Rwajomyni] NM **le ~ (de Grande-Bretagne et d'Irlande du Nord)** the United Kingdom (of Great Britain and Northern Ireland)

royauté [Rwajote] NF (= *régime*) monarchy; (= *fonction, dignité*) kingship

RP [1] NM (ABRÉV = **Révérend Père**) → **révérend [2]** NF (ABRÉV = **recette principale**) → **recette [3]** NFPL (ABRÉV = **relations publiques**) PR

RPR [ɛrpeɛr] NM (ABRÉV = **Rassemblement pour la République**) *French political party*

RSVP [ɛresvepe] (ABRÉV = **répondez s'il vous plaît**) R.S.V.P.

Rte ABRÉV = **route**

RU [Ry] NM (ABRÉV = **restaurant universitaire**) → **restaurant**

ru † [Ry] NM brook, rivulet (*littér*)

ruade [Ryad] NF kick; **tué par une ~** killed by a kick from a horse; **le cheval lui a cassé la jambe d'une ~** the horse kicked *ou* lashed out at him and broke his leg; **décocher** *ou* **lancer une ~** to lash *ou* kick out

ruban [Rybɑ̃] **[1]** NM (*gén, fig*) ribbon; [*machine à écrire*] ribbon; [*couture, ourlet*] binding, tape; **le ~ (rouge)** (*de la Légion d'honneur*) ribbon *of the Légion d'Honneur*; (*fig*) **le ~ argenté du Rhône** the silver ribbon of the Rhone; **le double ~ de l'autoroute** the two *ou* twin lines of the motorway → | LÉGION D'HONNEUR | ; → **mètre, scie [2]** COMP ▶ **ruban d'acier** steel band *ou* strip ▶ **ruban adhésif** adhesive tape, sticky tape ▶ **le ruban bleu** (*Naut*) the Blue Riband *ou* Ribbon (*of the Atlantic*); (*fig*) **détenir le ~ bleu (de qch)** to be the world leader (in sth) ▶ **ruban de chapeau** hat band ▶ **ruban d'eau** (*Bot*) bur reed ▶ **ruban encreur** typewriter ribbon ▶ **ruban isolant** insulating tape ▶ **ruban perforé** (*Ordin*) paper tape

rubato [Rybato] ADV, NM rubato

rubéole [Rybeɔl] NF German measles *sg*, rubella (*SPÉC*)

Rubicon [Rybikɔ̃] NM Rubicon → **franchir**

rubicond, e [Rybikɔ̃, ɔ̃d] ADJ rubicund, ruddy

rubidium [Rybidjɔm] NM rubidium

rubis [Rybi] **[1]** NM (= *pierre*) ruby; (= *couleur*) ruby (colour); [*horloge, montre*] jewel → **payer [2]** ADJ INV ruby(-coloured)

rubrique [Rybrik] NF **[a]** (= *article, chronique*) column; **~ sportive/littéraire/des spectacles** sports/literary/entertainments column; **il tient la ~ scientifique du journal** he writes the newspaper's science column **[b]** (= *catégorie, titre*) heading, rubric; **sous cette même ~** under the same heading *ou* rubric **[c]** (*Rel*) rubric

ruche [Ryʃ] NF **[a]** (*en bois*) (bee) hive; (*en paille*) (bee) hive, skep (*SPÉC*); (= *essaim*) hive; (*fig*) **nos bureaux sont une véritable ~** *ou* **une ~ bourdonnante** our offices are a real hive of activity **[b]** (*Couture*) ruche

ruché [Ryʃe] NM (*Couture*) ruching (*NonC*), ruche

rucher [Ryʃe] NM apiary

rude [Ryd] ADJ **[a]** (= *rêche*) [*surface, barbe, peau*] rough; (= *rauque*) [*voix, sons*] harsh **[b]** [*métier, vie, combat*] hard, tough; [*montée*] stiff, tough, hard; [*adversaire*] tough; [*climat, hiver*] harsh, hard, severe; **c'est un ~ coup pour elle/notre équipe** it's a hard *ou* harsh *ou* severe blow for her/our team; **être mis à ~ épreuve** [*personne*] to be severely tested, be put through the mill; [*tissu, métal*] to receive *ou* have rough treatment; **mes nerfs ont été mis à ~ épreuve** it was a great strain on my nerves; **il a été à ~ école dans sa jeunesse** he learned life the hard way when he was young, he went to the school of hard knocks; **en faire voir de ~s à qn** to give sb a hard *ou* tough time; **en voir de ~s** to have a hard *ou* tough time (of it) **[c]** (= *fruste*) [*manières*] unpolished, crude, unrefined; [*traits*] rugged; [*montagnards*] rugged, tough **[d]** (= *sévère, bourru*) [*personne, caractère*] harsh, hard, severe; [*manières*] rough; **tu as été trop ~ avec elle** you were too hard on her **[e]** (* : *intensif*) **un ~ gaillard** a hearty fellow; **avoir un ~ appétit/estomac** to have a hearty appetite/an iron stomach; **il a une ~ veine** he's a lucky beggar* (*Brit*) *ou* son-of-a-gun* (*US*); **ça m'a fait une ~ peur** it gave me a dreadful *ou* real fright; **recevoir un ~ coup de poing** to get a real *ou* proper* (*Brit*) thump

rudement [Rydmɑ̃] ADV **[a]** [*heurter, frapper, tomber*] hard; [*répondre*] harshly; [*traiter*] roughly, harshly **[b]** (* = *très*) [*bon, content*] terribly*, awfully*, jolly* (*Brit*); [*cher, fatigant, mauvais*] dreadfully, terribly, awfully; **il a fallu ~ travailler** we had to work really hard; **elle danse ~ bien** she dances awfully *ou* jolly (*Brit*) well, she's quite a dancer; **ça me change ~ de faire ça** it's a real change *ou* quite a change for me to do that; **elle avait ~ changé** she had really changed, she hadn't half changed* (*Brit*); **il est ~ plus généreux que toi** he's a great deal *ou* darned sight* more generous than you; **j'ai eu ~ peur** it gave me a dreadful *ou* real fright

rudesse [Rydɛs] NF **[a]** [*surface, barbe, peau*] roughness; [*voix, sons*] harshness **[b]** [*métier, vie, combat, montée*] hardness, toughness; [*adversaire*] toughness; [*climat, hiver*] harshness, hardness, severity **[c]** [*manières*] crudeness; [*traits*] ruggedness; [*montagnards*] ruggedness, toughness **[d]** [*personne, caractère*] harshness, hardness, severity; [*manières*] roughness; **traiter qn avec ~** to treat sb roughly *ou* harshly

rudiment [Rydimɑ̃] **[1]** NM **[a]** (*littér = principes de base*) basics; **il n'a pas le moindre ~ d'informatique** he doesn't know the first *ou* slightest thing about computers **[b]** (*Anat, Zool*) rudiment **[2]** **rudiments** NM PL [*discipline*] rudiments; [*système, théorie*] principles; **~s d'algèbre** principles *ou* rudiments of algebra; **avoir quelques ~s de chimie** to have some basic *ou* rudimentary notions *ou* some basic knowledge of chemistry, have a rudimentary knowledge of chemistry; **avoir quelques ~s d'anglais** to have a smattering of English *ou* some basic knowledge of English; **nous n'en sommes qu'aux ~s** ◊ **on en est encore aux ~s** we're still at a rudimentary stage

rudimentaire [ʀydimɑ̃tɛʀ] ADJ (gén) rudimentary; [connaissances] rudimentary, elementary; **les installations de l'hôpital sont très ~** the hospital facilities are rather rough-and-ready ou a bit basic; **elle parle un anglais ~** she speaks basic English

rudoiement [ʀydwamɑ̃] NM (littér) rough ou harsh treatment

rudoyer [ʀydwaje] ▸conjug 8◂ VT to treat harshly

rue¹ [ʀy] NF [a] (= voie, habitants) street; **~ à sens unique** one-way street; **scènes de la ~** street scenes; **élevé dans la ~** brought up in the street(s); **être à la ~** to be on the streets; **jeter qn à la ~** to put sb out ou throw sb out (into the street); (fig, Pol) **descendre dans la ~** to take to the streets → **coin, combat, piéton, plein** etc [b] (péj = populace) **la ~** the mob

---
┌─── **RUE** ───┐

Many Paris street names are used, especially in the press, to refer to the famous institutions that have their homes there. The Ministry of Education is on the **rue de Grenelle;** *the* **rue de Solférino** *refers to Socialist Party headquarters; the* **rue d'Ulm** *is where the "École normale supérieure" is situated, and the* **rue de Valois** *is the home of the Ministry of Culture.* → QUAI
---

rue² [ʀy] NF (= plante) rue

ruée [ʀɥe] NF rush; (péj) stampede; **à l'ouverture, ce fut la ~ vers l'entrée du magasin** when the shop opened, there was a (great) rush ou a stampede for the entrance, as soon as the doors opened there was a stampede ou a mad scramble to get into the shop; **la ~ des touristes ne prend fin qu'à l'automne** the influx of tourists doesn't tail off until the autumn, the tourist invasion doesn't end until the autumn; (fig) **dès que quelqu'un prend sa retraite ou démissionne, c'est la ~** the moment someone retires or resigns there's a scramble for their job; **dans la ~, il fut renversé** he was knocked over in the rush ou stampede; **cet événement a entraîné une ~ sur le dollar** this event caused a run on the dollar; **la ~ vers l'or** the gold rush

ruelle [ʀɥɛl] NF (= rue) alley(way), lane;†† [chambre] ruelle†, space (between bed and wall); (Hist, Littérat) ruelle (room used in 17th century to hold literary salons)

ruer [ʀɥe] ▸conjug 1◂ [1] VI [cheval] to kick (out); (fig) **~ dans les brancards** to rebel, kick over the traces [2] **se ruer** VPR **se ~ sur** [+ article en vente, nourriture, personne] to pounce on; [+ emplois vacants] to fling o.s. at, pounce at; **se ~ vers** [+ porte, sortie] to dash ou rush for ou towards; **se ~ dans/hors de** [+ maison, pièce] to dash ou rush ou tear into/out of; **se ~ dans l'escalier** (monter) to tear ou dash up the stairs; (descendre) to tear down the stairs, hurl o.s. down the stairs; **se ~ à l'assaut** to hurl ou fling o.s. into the attack

ruf(f)ian [ʀyfjɑ̃] NM (littér, = aventurier) ruffian

ruflette® [ʀyflɛt] NF curtain ou heading tape

rugby [ʀygbi] NM rugby (football); **~ à quinze** Rugby Union; **~ à treize** Rugby League; **jouer au ~** ◊ **faire du ~** to play rugby

rugbyman [ʀygbiman] (pl **rugbymen** [ʀygbimɛn]) NM rugby player

rugir [ʀyʒiʀ] ▸conjug 2◂ [1] VI [fauve, mer, moteur] to roar; [vent, tempête] to howl; **~ de douleur** to howl ou roar with pain; **~ de colère** to bellow ou roar with anger; **faire ~ son moteur** to rev (up) one's engine [2] VT [+ ordres, menaces] to roar ou bellow out

rugissant, e [ʀyʒisɑ̃, ɑ̃t] ADJ roaring, howling → **quarantième**

rugissement [ʀyʒismɑ̃] NM [fauve, mer, moteur] roar, roaring (NonC); [vent, tempête] howl, howling (NonC); **~ de douleur** howl ou roar of pain; **~ de colère** roar of anger; **j'entendais des ~s de lions** I could hear lions roaring ou the roar of lions; **pousser un ~ de rage** to roar with anger

rugosité [ʀygozite] NF [a] (NonC) [écorce, surface, vin] roughness; [peau, tissu] roughness, coarseness; [sol] ruggedness, roughness, bumpiness [b] (= aspérité) rough patch, bump; **poncer les ~s** to sand down the rough areas

rugueux, -euse [ʀygø, øz] ADJ [écorce, surface, vin] rough; [peau, tissu] rough, coarse; [sol] rugged, rough, bumpy

Ruhr [ʀuʀ] NF **la ~** the Ruhr

ruine [ʀɥin] NF [a] (lit, fig = décombres, destruction, perte de fortune) ruin; **~s romaines** Roman ruins; **acheter une ~ à la campagne** to buy a ruin in the country; (péj) **~ (humaine)** (human) wreck; **en ~(s)** in ruin(s), ruined (épith); **causer la ~ de** [+ monarchie] to bring about the ruin ou downfall of; [+ carrière, réputation, santé] to ruin, bring about the ruin of; [+ banquier, entreprise] to ruin, bring ruin upon; **c'est la ~ de tous mes espoirs** that means the ruin of ou that puts paid to (Brit) all my hopes; **courir ou aller à sa ~** to be on the road to ruin, be heading for ruin; **tomber en ~** to fall in ruins → **menacer** [b] (= acquisition coûteuse) **cette voiture est une vraie ~** that car will ruin me; **50 F, c'est pas la ~!*** 50 francs won't break the bank!*

ruiner [ʀɥine] ▸conjug 1◂ [1] VT [a] [+ pays, personne] to ruin, cause the ruin of; **ça ne va pas te ~!*** it won't break* ou ruin you! [b] [+ réputation, santé] to ruin; [+ carrière] to ruin, wreck; [+ espoirs] to shatter, dash, ruin; [+ efforts] to destroy, ruin [2] **se ruiner** VPR (= dépenser tout son argent) to ruin ou bankrupt o.s.; (fig = dépenser trop) to spend a fortune; **se ~ en fleurs** to spend a fortune on flowers; **quelques conseils pour partir en vacances sans se ~** a few tips for going on holiday without spending a fortune ou breaking the bank*; **se ~ au jeu** to lose all one's money gambling

ruineux, -euse [ʀɥinø, øz] ADJ [goût] extravagant, ruinously expensive; [dépense] ruinous; [acquisition, voiture] (prix élevé) ruinous, ruinously expensive; (entretien coûteux) expensive to run (ou keep); **ce n'est pas ~!** it won't break* ou ruin us!

ruisseau (pl **ruisseaux**) [ʀɥiso] NM [a] (= cours d'eau) stream, brook; (fig) **des ~x de** [+ larmes] floods of; [+ lave, sang] streams of → **petit** [b] (= caniveau) gutter; (fig) **élevé dans le ~** brought up in the gutter; (fig) **tirer qn du ~** to pull ou drag sb out of the gutter

ruisselant, e [ʀɥis(ə)lɑ̃, ɑ̃t] ADJ [visage] streaming; [personne] dripping wet, streaming; **le mur était ~** the wall had water running down it; **son front ~ de sueur** his forehead bathed in ou dripping with sweat; **le visage ~ de larmes** his face streaming with tears, with tears streaming down his face

ruisseler [ʀɥis(ə)le] ▸conjug 4◂ VI [a] (= couler) [lumière] to stream; [cheveux] to flow, stream (**sur** over); [liquide, pluie] to stream, flow (**sur** down) [b] (= être couvert d'eau) **~ (d'eau)** [mur] to have water running down it; [visage] to stream (with water); **~ de lumière/larmes** to stream with light/tears; **~ de sueur** to drip ou stream with sweat

ruisselet [ʀɥis(ə)lɛ] NM rivulet, brooklet

ruissellement [ʀɥisɛlmɑ̃] [1] NM **le ~ de la pluie/de l'eau sur le mur** the rain/water streaming ou running ou flowing down the wall; **eaux de ~** runoff; **le ~ de sa chevelure sur ses épaules** her hair flowing ou tumbling over her shoulders; **un ~ de pierreries** a glistening ou glittering cascade of jewels; **ébloui par ce ~ de lumière** dazzled by this stream of

light [2] COMP ▸ **ruissellement pluvial** (Géol) run-off

rumba [ʀumba] NF rumba

rumeur [ʀymœʀ] NF [a] (= nouvelle imprécise) rumour; **selon certaines ~s, elle ...** rumour has it that she ..., it is rumoured that she ...; **il dément les ~s selon lesquelles le boxeur était dopé** he denies the rumours that the boxer was doped; **si l'on en croit la ~ publique, il ...** if you believe what is publicly rumoured, he ...; **faire courir de fausses ~s** to spread rumours [b] (= son) [vagues, vent] murmur(ing) (NonC); [circulation, rue, ville] hum (NonC); [émeute] rumbling; [bureau, conversation] buzz (NonC) [c] (= protestation) rumblings; **~ de mécontentement** rumblings of discontent; **une ~ s'éleva ou des ~s s'élevèrent de la foule** angry sounds rose up from the crowd

ruminant [ʀyminɑ̃] NM (Zool) ruminant

rumination [ʀyminasjɔ̃] NF (Zool) rumination

ruminer [ʀymine] ▸conjug 1◂ [1] VT (Zool) to ruminate; (fig) [+ projet] to ruminate on ou over, chew over; [+ chagrin] to brood over; [+ vengeance] to ponder, meditate; **toujours dans son coin à ~ (ses pensées)** always in his corner chewing the cud ou chewing things over ou pondering (things) [2] VI (Zool) to ruminate, chew the cud

rumsteck [ʀɔmstɛk] NM = **romsteck**

rune [ʀyn] NF (Ling) rune

runique [ʀynik] ADJ (Ling) runic

rupestre [ʀypɛstʀ] ADJ (Bot) rupestrine (SPÉC), rock (épith); (Art) rupestrian (SPÉC), rupestral (SPÉC), rock (épith); **peintures ~s** (gén) rock paintings; (dans une grotte) cave ou rock paintings

rupin, e✝ [ʀypɛ̃, in] [1] ADJ [appartement, quartier] ritzy✝, plush*, swanky*; [personne] stinking ou filthy rich✝ [2] NM,F rich person; **c'est un ~** he's rolling in it*; **les ~s** the rich

rupteur [ʀyptœʀ] NM (contact) breaker

rupture [ʀyptyʀ] [1] NF [a] (= annulation) [relations diplomatiques] breaking off, severing, rupture; [fiançailles, pourparlers] breaking off; **la ~ du traité/contrat par ce pays** this country's breaking the treaty/contract, the breach of the treaty/contract by this country; **après la ~ des négociations** after negotiations broke down, after the breakdown of ou in the negotiations; **la ~ de leurs fiançailles m'a surpris** I was surprised when they broke off their engagement [b] (= séparation amoureuse) break-up, split; **sa ~ (d')avec Louise** his split ou break-up with Louise; **~ passagère** temporary break-up [c] (= désaccord) **il est en ~ ~ avec son parti** he's at odds with his party, he disagrees with his party's line; **être en ~ avec le monde/les idées de son temps** to be at odds with the world/the ideas of one's time; **il est en ~ avec sa famille** he's estranged from his family; **cette initiative est en ~ avec la tradition** this initiative marks a break with tradition [d] (= cassure, déchirure) [câble, branche, corde, poutre] breaking; [digue] bursting, breach(ing); [veine] bursting, rupture; [organe] rupture; [tendon] rupture, tearing; **en cas de ~ du barrage** should the dam burst; **point de ~** (gén) breaking point; (Ordin) breakpoint [e] (= solution de continuité) break; **~ entre le passé et le présent** break between the past and the present; **~ de rythme** (sudden) break in (the) rhythm; **~ de ton** abrupt change in ou of tone; **la ~ d'approvisionnement provoquée par les grèves** the disruption in supplies caused by the strikes

[2] COMP ▸ **rupture d'anévrisme** aneurysmal rupture ▸ **rupture de ban** illegal return from banishment; **en ~ de ban** (Jur) illegally returning from banishment; (fig) in defiance of the accepted code of conduct; **en ~ de ban avec la société** at odds with society

► **rupture de charge** (*Transport*) transshipment ► **rupture de circuit** (*Élec*) break in the circuit ► **rupture de contrat** breach of contract ► **rupture de direction** steering failure ► **rupture d'équilibre** (*lit*) loss of balance; (*fig*) **une ~ d'équilibre est à craindre entre ces nations** an upset in the balance of power is to be feared among these states ► **rupture d'essieu** broken axle ► **rupture du jeûne** breaking of a fast ► **rupture de pente** change of incline *ou* gradient ► **rupture de séquence** (*Ordin*) jump ► **rupture de stock** stock shortage, stockout (*US*); **être en ~ de stock** to be out of stock

rural, e (*mpl* -aux) [ʀyʀal, o] [1] ADJ (*gén*) country (*épith*), rural; (*Admin*) rural; **le monde ~** (*gén*) rural society; (= *agriculteurs*) the farming community → **exode** [2] NM,F country person, rustic; **les ruraux** country people, countryfolk

ruse [ʀyz] NF [a] (*NonC*) (*pour gagner, obtenir un avantage*) cunning, craftiness, slyness; (*pour tromper*) trickery, guile; **obtenir qch par ~** to obtain sth by *ou* through trickery *ou* by guile [b] (= *subterfuge*) trick, ruse; (*lit hum*) **~ de guerre** stratagem, tactics; **avec des ~s de Sioux** with crafty tactics

rusé, e [ʀyze] (*ptp de ruser*) ADJ [*personne*] cunning, crafty, sly, wily; [*air*] sly, wily; **~ comme un (vieux) renard** as sly *ou* cunning as a fox; **c'est un ~** he's a crafty *ou* sly one

ruser [ʀyze] ▶conjug 1◀ VI (= *être habile*) (*pour gagner, obtenir un avantage*) to use cunning; (*pour tromper*) to use trickery; **ne ruse pas avec moi!** don't try and be clever *ou* smart* with me!; **il va falloir ~ si l'on veut entrer** we'll have to use a bit of cunning *ou* be a bit crafty if we want to get in

rush [ʀœʃ] NM (= *afflux*) rush; (*Ciné*) rush

russe [ʀys] [1] ADJ Russian; **boire à la ~** to drink (and cast one's glass aside) in the Russian style → **montagne, roulette** [2] NM (*Ling*)

Russian [3] **Russe** NMF Russian; **Russe blanc(he)** White Russian

Russie [ʀysi] NF Russia; **la ~ blanche** White Russia; **la ~ soviétique** Soviet Russia

russification [ʀysifikasjɔ̃] NF russianization, russification

russifier [ʀysifje] ▶conjug 7◀ VT to russianize, russify

russophile [ʀysɔfil] ADJ, NMF Russophil(e)

russophone [ʀysɔfɔn] [1] ADJ [*population, communauté, minorité*] Russian-speaking [2] NMF (= *personne*) Russian speaker

rustaud, e [ʀysto, od] [1] ADJ countrified, rustic [2] NM,F (*péj*) country bumpkin, yokel, hillbilly (*US*)

rusticité [ʀystisite] NF [a] [*manières, personne*] rustic simplicity, rusticity (*littér*) [b] (*Agr*) hardiness

rustine® [ʀystin] NF rubber repair patch (*for bicycle tyre*); (*fig*) **il ne suffira pas de coller quelques ~s pour sauver l'entreprise** it'll take more than stopgap measures *ou* cosmetic improvements to save the company

rustique [ʀystik] [1] ADJ [a] [*mobilier*] rustic; [*maçonnerie*] rustic, rusticated; **bois ~** rustic wood [b] (*littér*) [*maison*] rustic (*épith*); [*manières, vie*] rustic, country (*épith*) [c] (*Agr*) hardy [2] NM (= *style*) rustic style; **meubler une maison en ~** to furnish a house in the rustic style *ou* with rustic furniture

rustre [ʀystʀ] [1] NM [a] (*péj* = *brute*) lout, boor [b] († = *paysan*) peasant [2] ADJ brutish, boorish

rut [ʀyt] NM (= *état*) [*mâle*] rut; [*femelle*] heat; (= *période*) [*mâle*] rutting (period); [*femelle*] heat period; **être en ~** [*mâle*] to be rutting; [*femelle*] to be on (*Brit*) *ou* in (*US*) heat

rutabaga [ʀytabaga] NM swede, rutabaga (*US*)

ruthénium [ʀytenjɔm] NM ruthenium

rutilant, e [ʀytilɑ̃, ɑ̃t] ADJ (= *brillant*) brightly shining, gleaming; (= *rouge ardent*) rutilant;

vêtu d'un uniforme ~ very spick and span *ou* very spruce in his uniform

rutiler [ʀytile] ▶conjug 1◀ VI to gleam, shine brightly

rv ABRÉV = **rendez-vous**

Rwanda [ʀwɑ̃da] NM Rwanda

rwandais, e [ʀwɑ̃dɛ, ɛz] [1] ADJ Rwandan [2] **Rwandais(e)** NM,F Rwandan

rythme [ʀitm] NM [a] (*Art, Littérat, Mus*) rhythm; **marquer le ~** to beat time; (*Mus*) **au ~ de** to the beat *ou* rhythm of; **avoir le sens du ~** to have a sense of rhythm; (*Théât*) **pièce qui manque de ~** play which lacks tempo, slow-moving play [b] (= *cadence*) [*cœur, respiration, saisons*] rhythm; **interrompant le ~ de sa respiration** interrupting the rhythm of his breathing [c] (= *vitesse*) [*respiration*] rate; [*battements du cœur*] rate, speed; [*travail, vie*] tempo, pace; [*production*] rate; **à un ~ infernal/régulier** at a phenomenal *ou* terrific/steady rate; **le ~ soutenu de la croissance économique** the sustained rate of economic growth; **~ cardiaque** (rate of) heartbeat; **~ biologique** biological rhythm; **les ~s scolaires** the way the school year is organized *ou* divided up; **à ce ~-là, il ne va plus en rester** at that rate there won't be any left; **il n'arrive pas à suivre le ~** he can't keep up (the pace); **produire des voitures au ~ de 1 000 par jour** to produce cars at the rate of 1,000 a *ou* per day

rythmé, e [ʀitme] (*ptp de rythmer*) ADJ rhythmic(al); **bien ~** highly rhythmic(al)

rythmer [ʀitme] ▶conjug 1◀ VT (= *cadencer*) [+ *phrase, prose, travail*] to give rhythm to, punctuate; **les saisons rythmaient leur vie** their lives were governed by the rhythm of the seasons

rythmique [ʀitmik] [1] ADJ rhythmic(al) → **section** [2] NF (*Littérat*) rhythmics *sg*; **la (danse) ~** rhythmics *sg*

S

S¹, s¹ [ɛs] NM [a] (= lettre) S, s [b] (= figure) zig-zag; (= virages) double bend, S bend; **faire des s** to zigzag; **en s** [route] zigzagging (épith), winding; [barre] S-shaped

S² (ABRÉV = **Sud**) S

s² (ABRÉV = **seconde**) s

S' [s] → **se, si¹**

s/ ABRÉV = **sur**

SA [ɛsa] NF (ABRÉV = **société anonyme**) (gén) limited company; (ouverte au public) public limited company; **Raymond SA** Raymond Ltd (Brit), Raymond Inc. (US); (ouverte au public) Raymond plc

sa [sa] ADJ POSS → **son¹**

Saba [saba] NF Sheba; **la reine de ~** the Queen of Sheba

sabayon [sabajɔ̃] NM zabaglione

sabbat [saba] NM [a] (Rel) Sabbath [b] (* = bruit) racket, row* [c] [sorcières] (witches') sabbath

sabbatique [sabatik] ADJ (Rel, Univ) [année, congé] sabbatical; **prendre une année ~** (Univ) to take a sabbatical year ou a year's sabbatical (leave); [étudiant, employé] to take a year off ou out; **être en congé ~** (Univ) to be on sabbatical (leave); [employé] to be taking a year off ou out

sabin, e [sabɛ̃, in] [1] ADJ Sabine [2] **Sabin(e)** NM,F Sabine → **enlèvement**

sabir [sabiʀ] NM (= parlé dans le Levant) sabir; (Ling) ≈ pidgin; (péj = jargon) jargon; (incompréhensible) mumbo jumbo*; **un curieux ~ fait de français et d'arabe** a strange mixture of French and Arabic

sablage [sablaʒ] NM [allée, route] sanding; [façade] sandblasting

sable¹ [sabl] [1] NM sand; **de ~** [dune] sand (épith); [fond, plage] sandy; **vent de ~** sandstorm; **~s mouvants** quicksand(s); **ville ensevelie sous les ~s** city buried in the sands; **être sur le ~*** (sans argent) to be (stony (Brit) ou stone (US)) broke*, be skint* (Brit); (sans travail) to be out of a job, be jobless → **bac²**, **bâtir**, **grain**, **marchand** [2] ADJ INV sandy, sand-coloured (Brit) ou -colored (US)

sable² [sabl] NM (Hér) sable

sablé, e [sable] (ptp de **sabler**) [1] ADJ [a] (gâteau) shortbread biscuit (Brit) ou cookie (US) → **pâte** [b] [route] sandy, sanded

sabler [sable] ▸ conjug 1 ◂ VT [a] [+ route] to sand; [+ façade] to sandblast [b] **~ le champagne** (lit) to crack open a bottle of champagne; (fig) to celebrate with champagne

sableux, -euse [sablø, øz] [1] ADJ [alluvions, sol] sandy; [coquillages] gritty, sandy [2] **sableuse** NF (= machine) sandblaster

sablier [sablije] NM (gén) hourglass, sandglass; (Culin) egg timer

sablière [sablijɛʀ] NF (= carrière) sand quarry; (Constr) string-piece; (Rail) sand-box

sablonneux, -euse [sablɔnø, øz] ADJ sandy

sablonnière [sablɔnjɛʀ] NF sand quarry

sabord [sabɔʀ] NM (Naut) scuttle; (hum) **mille ~s!*** blistering barnacles!* (hum)

sabordage [sabɔʀdaʒ], **sabordement** [sabɔʀdəmã] NM (Naut) scuppering, scuttling; (fig) [entreprise] winding up

saborder [sabɔʀde] ▸ conjug 1 ◂ [1] VT (Naut) to scupper, scuttle; (fig) [+ entreprise] to wind up; [+ négociations, projet] to put paid to, scupper [2] **se saborder** VPR (Naut) to scupper ou scuttle one's ship; [candidat] to write o.s. off, scupper one's chances; [parti] to wind (itself) up; [entreprise] to wind (itself) up, fold; **il a décidé de se ~** (patron) he decided to wind up the company

sabot [sabo] NM [a] (= chaussure) clog → **baignoire**, **venir** [b] (Zool) hoof; **animal à ~s** hoofed animal; **le cheval lui donna un coup de ~** the horse kicked out at him [c] (* : péj) **c'est un vrai ~†** (voiture, machine) it's a piece of old junk*; **il travaille comme un ~** he's a shoddy worker; **il joue comme un ~** he's a hopeless ou pathetic* player [d] (= toupie) (whipping) top [e] (Tech) [pied de table, poteau] ferrule; **~ de frein** brake shoe; (Aut) **~ (de Denver)** wheel clamp, Denver boot (US); **mettre un ~ à une voiture** to clamp a car

sabotage [sabotaʒ] NM [a] (Mil, Pol, fig) (= action) sabotage; (= acte) act of sabotage; **~ industriel** industrial sabotage [b] (= bâclage) botching

sabot-de-Vénus (pl **sabots-de-Vénus**) [sabod(ə)venys] NM (Bot) lady's slipper

saboter [sabote] ▸ conjug 1 ◂ VT [a] (Mil, Pol, fig) to sabotage [b] (= bâcler) to make a (proper) mess of, botch; (= abîmer) to mess up, ruin

saboteur, -euse [sabotœʀ, øz] NM,F (Mil, Pol) saboteur; (= bâcleur) shoddy worker

sabotier, -ière [sabotje, jɛʀ] NM,F (= fabricant) clog-maker; (= marchand) clog-seller

sabra [sabʀa] NMF sabra

sabre [sabʀ] NM sabre (Brit), saber (US); **~ d'abordage** cutlass; **~ de cavalerie** riding sabre; **mettre ~ au clair** to draw one's sword; **charger ~ au clair** to charge with swords drawn; **le ~ et le goupillon** the Army and the Church; (Pol) **bruits de ~** sabre-rattling

sabrer [sabʀe] ▸ conjug 1 ◂ VT [a] (Mil) to sabre (Brit), saber (US), cut down; **~ le champagne** to open a bottle of champagne using a sabre; (fig) to celebrate with champagne [b] (littér = marquer) **la ride qui sabrait son front** the deep line across his brow; **dessin sabré de coups de crayon rageurs** drawing scored with angry pencil strokes [c] (* = biffer) [+ texte] to slash (great) chunks out of*; [+ passage, phrase] to cut out, scrub (out)*; [+ projet] to axe, chop* [d] (* = recaler) [+ étudiant] to flunk*; (= renvoyer) [+ employé] to fire*, sack* (Brit); **se faire ~** [étudiant] to be flunked*; [employé] to get fired* ou sacked* (Brit); to get the sack* [e] (* = critiquer) [+ devoir] to tear to pieces ou to shreds; [+ livre, pièce] to slam*, pan* [f] (* = bâcler) [+ travail] to knock off* (in a rush)

sabretache† [sabʀətaʃ] NF sabretache

sabreur [sabʀœʀ] NM (péj = soldat) fighting cock (péj); (= escrimeur) swordsman

sac¹ [sak] [1] NM [a] (gén) bag; (de grande taille, en toile) sack; (= cartable) (school) bag; (à bretelles) satchel; (pour achats) shopping bag, carrier bag (Brit); **~ (en) plastique** plastic bag; (pour aspirateur) **~ (à poussières)** dust bag, vacuum cleaner bag, Hoover® bag (Brit); **mettre en ~(s)** to bag → **course** [b] (= contenu) (gén) bag(ful); (de grande taille, en toile) sack(ful) [c] (‡ = 10 francs) **dix/trente ~s** one hundred/three hundred francs [d] (loc) **habillé comme un ~** dressed like a tramp; (péj) **ils sont tous à mettre dans le même ~** they're all as bad as each other; **l'affaire est ou c'est dans le ~*** it's in the bag*; **des gens de ~ et de corde††** gallows birds; (Rel) **le ~ et la cendre** sackcloth and ashes → **main**, **tour²** [e] (Anat) sac; **~ embryonnaire/lacrymal** embryo/lacrimal sac

[2] COMP ▸ **sac à bandoulière** shoulder bag ▸ **sac de couchage** sleeping bag ▸ **sac à dos** rucksack, backpack ▸ **sac d'embrouilles*** muddle ▸ **sac à main** handbag, purse (US), pocketbook (US) ▸ **sac à malice** bag of tricks ▸ **sac de marin** kit-bag ▸ **sac de nœuds*** = sac d'embrouilles ▸ **sac d'os** (* : péj) bag of bones ▸ **sac à ouvrage** workbag ▸ **sac de plage** beach bag ▸ **sac polochon** sausage bag ▸ **sac à provisions** shopping bag ▸ **sac à puces** (* péj = lit) fleabag* ▸ **sac reporter** organizer bag ▸ **sac de sable** (Constr, Mil) sandbag; (Boxe) punching bag, punchbag (Brit) ▸ **sac de sport** sports bag ▸ **sac à viande** (Camping) sleeping bag sheet ▸ **sac à vin*** (old) soak*, wino*, drunkard ▸ **sac de voyage** travelling bag; (pour l'avion) flight bag, carry-on bag

sac² [sak] NM **(mise à) ~** [ville] sack, sacking (NonC); [maison, pièce] ransacking (NonC); **mettre à ~** [+ ville] to sack; [+ maison, pièce] to ransack

saccade [sakad] NF jerk; **avancer par ~s** to jerk along, move along in fits and starts ou jerkily; **parler par ~s** to speak haltingly

saccadé, e [sakade] ADJ [démarche, gestes, style] jerky; [débit, respiration] spasmodic, halting; [bruit] staccato; [sommeil] fitful

saccage [sakaʒ] NM (= destruction) [pièce, bâtiment] ransacking; [jardin] wrecking; [forêt, littoral, planète] destruction; (= pillage) [pays, ville] sack, sacking (NonC); [maison] ransacking

saccager [sakaʒe] ▸ conjug 3 ◂ VT [a] (= dévaster) [+ pièce] to turn upside down, wreck; [+ jardin, bâtiment] to wreck; [+ forêt, littoral, planète] to destroy; **ils ont tout saccagé dans la maison** they turned the whole house upside down; **l'appartement était entièrement saccagé** the flat was completely wrecked; **champ saccagé par la grêle** field laid waste ou

saccageur, -euse [sakaʒœʀ, øz] NM,F (= *dévastateur*) vandal; (= *pillard*) pillager, plunderer

saccharification [sakaʀifikasjɔ̃] NF saccharification

saccharifier [sakaʀifje] ▸ conjug 7 ◂ VT to saccharify

saccharine [sakaʀin] NF saccharin(e)

saccharose [sakaʀoz] NM sucrose, saccharose

SACEM [sasɛm] NF (ABRÉV = **Société des auteurs, compositeurs et éditeurs de musique**) *French body responsible for collecting and distributing music royalties*, ≈ PRS (Brit)

sacerdoce [sasɛʀdɔs] NM (Rel) priesthood; (fig) calling, vocation

sacerdotal, e (mpl **-aux**) [sasɛʀdɔtal, o] ADJ priestly, sacerdotal

sachem [saʃɛm] NM sachem

sachet [saʃɛ] NM [bonbons, thé] bag; [levure, sucre vanillé] sachet; [drogue] (small) bag; [soupe] packet; **~ de lavande** lavender bag ou sachet; **~ d'aspirine** sachet of (powdered) aspirin; **soupe en ~(s)** packet soup; **thé en ~(s)** tea bags; **café en ~s individuels** individual sachets of coffee

sacoche [sakɔʃ] NF (gén) bag; (pour outils) toolbag; [cycliste] (de selle) saddlebag; (de porte-bagages) pannier; [écolier] (school) bag; (à bretelles) satchel; [encaisseur] (money) bag; [facteur] (post-)bag

sac-poubelle, sac poubelle (pl **sacs(-) poubelles**) [sakpubɛl] NM bin liner (Brit), garbage bag (US)

sacquer* [sake] ▸ conjug 1 ◂ VT ⓐ [+ employé] **~ qn** to fire sb, kick sb out✲, give sb the push ou the boot✲ ou the sack* (Brit); **se faire ~** to get the push✲ ou boot✲ ou sack* (Brit), get (o.s.) kicked out✲ ⓑ [+ élève] to mark (Brit) ou grade (US) strictly; **je me suis fait ~ à l'examen** the examiner gave me lousy* marks (Brit) ou grades (US) ⓒ (= *détester*) **je ne peux pas le ~** I can't stand him, I hate his guts✲

sacral, e (mpl **-aux**) [sakʀal, o] ADJ sacred

sacralisation [sakʀalizasjɔ̃] NF **la ~ des loisirs/de la famille** regarding leisure time/the family as sacred

sacraliser [sakʀalize] ▸ conjug 1 ◂ VT to regard as sacred, make sacred; **~ la réussite sociale/la famille** to regard social success/the family as sacred

sacralité [sakʀalite] NF [personne] sacred status; [institution] sacredness

sacramentel, -elle [sakʀamɑ̃tɛl] ADJ ⓐ (fig = *rituel*) ritual, ritualistic ⓑ (Rel) [rite, formule] sacramental

sacre [sakʀ] NM ⓐ [roi] coronation; [évêque] consecration; (Mus) **« le Sacre du Printemps »** "the Rite of Spring" ⓑ (Orn) saker ⓒ (Can = *juron*) (blasphemous) swearword

sacré¹, e [sakʀe] (ptp de **sacrer**) ADJ ⓐ (après n : Rel) [lieu, objet, texte] sacred, holy; [art, musique] sacred; [horreur, terreur] holy; [droit] hallowed, sacred; **le Sacré Collège** the Sacred College (of Cardinals) → **feu¹**, **union** ⓑ (après n = *inviolable*) [droit, promesse] sacred; **son sommeil, c'est ~** his sleep is sacred → **monstre** ⓒ (✲: avant n = *maudit*) blasted✲, confounded✲; **~ nom de nom !✲** hell and damnation!✲; **elle a un ~ caractère** she's got a lousy* temper ⓓ (✲: avant n = *considérable*) damned✲; **~ imbécile** he's a real idiot; **c'est un ~ menteur** he's a terrible liar; **il a un ~ toupet** he's got a ou one heck* ou hell✲ of a nerve, he's got a right cheek* (Brit); **elle a eu une ~e chance** she was damn(ed) lucky✲ ⓔ (✲: avant n : *admiration, surprise*) **~ farceur !** you old devil (you)!✲; **ce ~ Paul a encore gagné aux courses** Paul's gone and won on the horses again, the lucky devil* ② NM **le ~** the sacred

sacré², e [sakʀe] ADJ (Anat) sacral

sacrebleu [sakʀəblø] EXCL (††, hum) confound it!*, strewth! (Brit)

Sacré-Cœur [sakʀekœʀ] NM ⓐ (Rel) **le ~** the Sacred Heart; **la fête du ~** the Feast of the Sacred Heart ⓑ (= *église*) **le ~** ◊ **la basilique du ~** the Sacré-Cœur

sacrement [sakʀəmɑ̃] NM sacrament; **recevoir les derniers ~s** to receive the last rites ou sacraments; **il est mort, muni des ~s de l'Église** he died fortified with the (last) rites ou sacraments of the Church

sacrément* [sakʀemɑ̃] ADV [froid, intéressant, laid] damned✲; [jolly*, jolly✲; **j'ai eu ~ peur** I was damned✲ ou jolly* (Brit) scared; **ça m'a ~ plu** I really liked it, I liked it ever so much; **il est ~ menteur** he's a downright ou an out-and-out liar

sacrer [sakʀe] ▸ conjug 1 ◂ ① VT [+ roi] to crown; [+ évêque] to consecrate; **il a été sacré champion du monde/meilleur joueur** he was crowned world champion/best player ② VI (*, †† = *jurer*) to curse, swear

sacrificateur, -trice [sakʀifikatœʀ, tʀis] NM,F (Hist) sacrificer; **grand ~** high priest

sacrifice [sakʀifis] NM (Rel, fig) sacrifice; **~ financier/humain** financial/human sacrifice; **faire un ~/des ~** to make a sacrifice/sacrifices; **faire le ~ de sa vie/d'une journée de vacances** to sacrifice one's life/a day's holiday; **offrir qch en ~** to offer sth as a sacrifice (à to); **être prêt à tous les ~s pour qn/qch** to be prepared to sacrifice everything for sb/sth; **~ de soi** self-sacrifice → **saint**

sacrificiel, -ielle [sakʀifisjɛl] ADJ sacrificial

sacrifié, e [sakʀifje] (ptp de **sacrifier**) ADJ ⓐ [peuple, troupe] sacrificed; **les ~s du plan de restructuration** the victims of ou those who have been sacrificed in the restructuring plan ⓑ (Comm) **articles ~s** give-aways*, items given away at knockdown prices; **« prix ~s »** "giveaway prices", "rock-bottom prices", "prices slashed"

sacrifier [sakʀifje] ▸ conjug 7 ◂ ① VT ⓐ (gén) to sacrifice (à to, **pour** for); (= *abandonner*) to give up; **~ sa vie pour sa patrie** to lay down ou sacrifice one's life for one's country; **il a sacrifié sa carrière au profit de sa famille** he sacrificed his career for (the sake of) his family; **il a dû ~ ses vacances** he had to give up his holidays ⓑ (Comm) [+ marchandises] to give away (at a knockdown price) ② **sacrifier à** VT INDIR [+ mode, préjugés, tradition] to conform to ③ **se sacrifier** VPR to sacrifice o.s. (à to, **pour** for); (iro) **il ne reste qu'un chocolat ... je me sacrifie !** there's only one chocolate left ... I'll just have to eat it myself!

sacrilège [sakʀilɛʒ] ① ADJ (Rel, fig) sacrilegious; **acte ~** sacrilegious act, act of sacrilege ② NM (Rel, fig) sacrilege; **ce serait un ~ de ...** it would be (a) sacrilege to ...; **commettre un ~** to commit sacrilege; **il a coupé son vin avec de l'eau, quel ~ !** he put water in his wine, what sacrilege! ③ NMF sacrilegious person

sacripant [sakʀipɑ̃] NM (††, hum) rogue, scoundrel

sacristain [sakʀistɛ̃] NM [sacristie] sacristan; [église] sexton

sacristaine [sakʀisten] NF sacristan

sacristie [sakʀisti] NF (catholique) sacristy; (protestante) vestry → **punaise**

sacristine [sakʀistin] NF = **sacristaine**

sacro-iliaque [sakʀoiljak] ADJ sacroiliac

sacro-saint, e [sakʀosɛ̃, sɛ̃t] ADJ (lit, iro) sacrosanct

sacrum [sakʀɔm] NM sacrum

sadique [sadik] ① ADJ sadistic; (Psych) **stade ~ anal** anal stage ② NMF sadist

sadiquement [sadikmɑ̃] ADV sadistically

sadisme [sadism] NM sadism

sado* [sado] ① ADJ sadistic; **il est ~-maso** he's into S&M ② NMF sadist

sadomasochisme [sadomazɔʃism] NM sadomasochism

sadomasochiste [sadomazɔʃist] ① ADJ sadomasochistic ② NMF sadomasochist

SAE [esaø] (ABRÉV = **Society of Automotive Engineers**) SAE; **classification/numéro ~** SAE classification/number

safari [safaʀi] NM safari; **faire un ~** to go on safari

safari-photo (pl **safaris-photos**) [safaʀifɔto] NM photo(graphic) safari

safran [safʀɑ̃] ① NM ⓐ (= *couleur, Bot, Culin*) saffron; **~ des prés** autumn crocus, meadow saffron, colchium (SPÉC); **riz au ~** saffron rice ⓑ (Naut) rudder blade ② ADJ INV saffron(-coloured (Brit) ou -colored (US)); **jaune ~** saffron yellow

safrané, e [safʀane] (ptp de **safraner**) ADJ [plat, sauce] with saffron; [tissu] saffron(-coloured (Brit) ou -colored (US)), saffron (yellow); **de couleur ~e** saffron-coloured

saga [saga] NF saga

sagace [sagas] ADJ (littér) sagacious, shrewd

sagacité [sagasite] NF sagacity, shrewdness; **avec ~** shrewdly

sagaie [sage] NF assegai, assagai

sage [saʒ] ① ADJ ⓐ (= *avisé*) [conseil] sound, sensible, wise; [action, démarche, décision, précaution] wise, sensible; [personne] wise; **il serait plus ~ de ...** it would be wiser ou more sensible to ..., you (ou he etc) would be better advised to ... ⓑ (euph = *chaste*) [jeune fille] good, well-behaved; **elle n'est pas très ~** she's a bit wild ⓒ (= *docile*) [animal, enfant] good, well-behaved; **sois ~** be good, behave yourself, be a good boy (ou girl); **~ comme une image** (as) good as gold; **il a été très ~ chez son oncle** he was very well-behaved ou he behaved (himself) very well at his uncle's; **est-ce que tu as été ~ ?** have you been a good boy (ou girl)? ⓓ (= *décent, modéré*) [goûts] sober, moderate; [roman] restrained, tame; [prix] moderate; [vêtement] sensible ② NM wise man; (Antiq) sage

sage-femme (pl **sages-femmes**) [saʒfam] NF midwife

sagement [saʒmɑ̃] ADV ⓐ (= *avec bon sens*) [conseiller, agir] wisely, sensibly; [décider] wisely ⓑ (= *chastement*) properly; **se conduire ~** to be good, behave o.s. (properly) ⓒ (= *docilement*) quietly; **il est resté ~ assis sans rien dire** [enfant] he sat quietly ou he sat like a good boy and said nothing; **va bien ~ te coucher** be a good boy (ou girl) and go to bed, off you go to bed like a good boy (ou girl); **des paires de chaussures ~ alignées** pairs of shoes neatly lined up ⓓ (= *modérément*) wisely, moderately; **savoir user ~ de qch** to know how to use sth wisely ou in moderation ou moderately

sagesse [saʒɛs] NF ⓐ (= *bon sens*) [personne] wisdom, (good) sense; [conseil] soundness; [action, démarche, décision] wisdom; **faire preuve de ~** to be sensible; **il a eu la ~ de ...** he had the wisdom ou (good) sense to ..., he was wise ou sensible enough to ...; **dans son infinie ~, il m'a conseillé de ...** in his infinite wisdom, he advised me to ...; **écouter la voix de la ~** to listen to the voice of reason; **la ~ populaire/des nations** popular/traditional wisdom ⓑ (euph = *chasteté*) chastity ⓒ (= *docilité*) [enfant] good behaviour (Brit) ou behavior (US); **il est la ~ même** he's incredibly well-behaved; **il a été d'une ~ exemplaire** he has been very good, he has behaved himself very well → **dent** ⓓ (= *modération*) moderation; **savoir utiliser qch avec ~** to know how to use sth wisely ou in moderation

Sagittaire [saʒitɛʀ] NM **le ~** Sagittarius; **il est ~ ◊ il est (du signe) du ~** he's (a) Sagittarius *ou* a Sagittarian

sagittal, e (*mpl* **-aux**) [saʒital, o] ADJ sagittal

sagouin, e [sagwɛ̃, in] 1 NM a (= *singe*) marmoset b ‡ (= *homme*) (*sale*) filthy pig‡, filthy slob‡; (*méchant*) swine‡; (*incompétent*) bungling idiot* 2 **sagouine‡** NF (*sale*) filthy slob‡; (*méchante*) bitch‡‡, cow‡ (*Brit*); (*incompétente*) bungling idiot*

Sahara [saaʀa] NM **le ~** the Sahara (desert); **au ~** in the Sahara; **le ~ occidental** the Western Sahara

saharien, -ienne [saaʀjɛ̃, jɛn] 1 ADJ (= *du Sahara*) Saharan; [*chaleur, climat*] desert (*épith*); **ensemble ~** (= *costume*) safari suit 2 **saharienne** NF (= *veste*) safari jacket; (= *chemise*) safari shirt

Sahel [saɛl] NM **le ~** the Sahel

sahélien, -ienne [saeljɛ̃, jɛn] 1 ADJ Sahelian 2 **Sahélien(ne)** NM,F Sahelian

sahraoui, e [saʀawi] 1 ADJ Western Saharan 2 **Sahraoui(e)** NM,F Western Saharan

saignant, e [sɛɲɑ̃, ɑ̃t] ADJ [*plaie*] bleeding; [*entrecôte*] rare; ‡ [*critique*] scathing, savage, biting; [*mésaventure*] nasty; **je n'aime pas le ~** I don't like rare *ou* underdone meat

saignée [sɛɲe] NF a (*Méd*) (= *épanchement*) bleeding (*NonC*); (= *opération*) bloodletting (*NonC*), bleeding (*NonC*); **faire une ~ à qn** to bleed sb, let sb's blood b [*budget*] savage cut (**à, dans** in); **les ~s que j'ai dû faire sur mon salaire/mes économies pour ...** the huge holes I had to make in my salary/my savings to ...; **les ~s faites dans le pays par la guerre** the heavy losses incurred by the country in the war c (*Anat*) **la ~ du bras** the crook of the elbow d (= *sillon*) [*sol*] trench, ditch; [*mur*] groove; **faire une ~ à un arbre** to make a taphole in a tree

saignement [sɛɲmɑ̃] NM bleeding (*NonC*); **~ de nez** nosebleed

saigner [sɛɲe] ▶conjug 1◀ 1 VI a (*lit*) to bleed; **il saignait comme un bœuf*** the blood was pouring out of him; **il saignait du nez** he had a nosebleed, his nose was bleeding; (*fig*) **ça va ~ !**‡ the fur will fly!* b (*littér*) [*dignité, orgueil*] to sting; **mon cœur saigne** *ou* **le cœur me saigne encore** my heart is still bleeding 2 VT a [+ *animal*] to kill (*by bleeding*); [+ *malade*] to bleed b (= *exploiter*) to bleed; **~ qn à blanc** to bleed sb dry *ou* white; **nation/ville saignée à blanc** nation/town that has been bled dry *ou* white c [+ *arbre*] to tap 3 **se saigner** VPR **se ~ (aux quatre veines) pour qn** to bleed o.s. dry *ou* white for sb

Saïgon [saigɔ̃] N Saigon

saillant, e [sajɑ̃, ɑ̃t] 1 ADJ a [*menton*] prominent, protruding (*épith*); [*front, pommette, muscle, veine*] protruding (*épith*), prominent, protuberant; [*yeux*] bulging (*épith*); [*corniche*] projecting (*épith*) → **angle** b [*événement, point, trait*] salient, outstanding c (*Hér*) salient 2 NM (= *avancée*) salient

saillie [saji] NF a (= *aspérité*) projection; **faire ~** to project, jut out; **qui forme ~ ◊ en ~** projecting, overhanging; **rocher qui s'avance en ~** rock which sticks *ou* juts out, overhang b (*littér* = *boutade*) sally, witticism c (*Zool* = *accouplement*) covering, servicing, serving

saillir¹ [sajiʀ] ▶conjug 13◀ VI [*balcon, corniche*] to jut out, stick out, project; [*menton, poitrine, pommette*] to be prominent; [*muscle, veine*] to protrude, stand out; [*yeux*] to bulge

saillir² [sajiʀ] ▶conjug 2◀ 1 VI (*littér* = *jaillir*) to gush forth 2 VT (*Zool*) to cover, service, serve

sain, saine [sɛ̃, sɛn] ADJ a (= *en bonne santé*) healthy; [*personne, cellules*] healthy; [*constitution, dents*] healthy, sound; **être/arriver ~ et sauf** to be/arrive safe and sound; **il est sorti ~ et sauf de l'accident** he escaped unharmed *ou* un-

scathed from the accident; **~ de corps et d'esprit** (*gén*) sound in body and mind; (*dans testament*) being of sound mind; **être ~ d'esprit** to be of sound mind, be sane → **porteur** b (= *salubre, bon pour la santé*) [*climat, vie*] healthy; [*nourriture*] healthy, wholesome; **il n'est pas ~ de si peu manger** it's not good *ou* it's not healthy to eat so little; **il est ~ de rire de temps en temps** it does you good to laugh from time to time c (= *non abîmé*) [*fondations, mur*] sound; [*affaire, économie, gestion*] sound; **établir qch sur des bases ~es** to establish sth on a sound basis d (*moralement*) [*personne*] sane; [*jugement, politique*] sound, sane; [*goûts, idées*] healthy; [*lectures*] wholesome; **ce n'est pas ~ pour la démocratie/notre économie** it's not healthy for democracy/our economy e (*Naut*) [*côte*] safe

saindoux [sɛ̃du] NM lard

sainement [sɛnmɑ̃] ADV [*manger*] healthily; [*juger*] sanely; [*raisonner*] soundly; **vivre ~** to lead a healthy life, live healthily

sainfoin [sɛ̃fwɛ̃] NM sainfoin

saint, sainte [sɛ̃, sɛ̃t] 1 ADJ a (= *sacré*) [*image, semaine*] holy; **la ~e Bible** the Holy Bible; **les Saintes Écritures** the Holy Scriptures, Holy Scripture; **les ~es huiles** the holy oils; **la ~e Croix/Sainte Famille** the Holy Cross/Family; **les ~es femmes** the holy women; **la semaine ~e** Holy Week; **le mardi/mercredi ~** Tuesday/Wednesday before Easter, the Tuesday/Wednesday of Holy Week; **le jeudi ~** Maundy Thursday; **le vendredi ~** Good Friday; **le samedi ~** Holy *ou* Easter Saturday; **s'approcher de la ~e table** to take communion → **guerre, lieu¹, semaine, terre** b (*devant prénom*) Saint; **~ Pierre/Paul** Saint Peter/Paul; (*église*) **Saint-Pierre/-Paul** Saint Peter's/Paul's; (*fête*) **ils ont fêté la Saint-Pierre** they celebrated the feast of Saint Peter; (*jour*) **le jour de la Saint-Pierre ◊ à la Saint-Pierre** (on) Saint Peter's day; **à la Saint-Michel/-Martin** at Michaelmas/Martinmas → **saint-pierre** c (= *pieux*) [*pensée, personne*] saintly, godly; [*vie, action*] pious, saintly, holy; **sa mère est une ~e femme** his mother is a real saint d (* *loc*) **toute la ~e journée** the whole blessed day*; **avoir une ~e horreur de qch** to have a holy horror of sth*; **être saisi d'une ~e colère** to fly into an almighty *ou* a holy rage 2 NM,F (*lit, fig*) saint; **il veut se faire passer pour un (petit) ~** he wants to pass for a saint; **ce n'est pas un ~** he's no saint; **elle a la patience d'une ~e** she has the patience of a saint *ou* of Job; **un ~ de bois/pierre** a wooden/stone statue of a saint; **la fête de tous les ~s** All Saints' Day; **~ laïc** secular saint ■ (*PROV*) **comme on connaît ses ~s on les honore** we treat people according to their merits → **prêcher, savoir** 3 COMP ► **le saint chrême** the chrism, the holy oil ► **le Saint Empire romain germanique** the Holy Roman Empire ► **les saints de glace** the 11th, 12th and 13th of May ► **Saint-Jacques-de-Compostelle** Santiago de Compostela ► **Saint Louis** Saint Louis ► **sainte nitouche** (*péj*) (*pious ou saintly*) hypocrite; **c'est une ~e nitouche** she looks as if butter wouldn't melt in her mouth; **de ~e nitouche** [*attitude, air*] hypocritically pious ► **saint patron** patron saint ► **le saint sacrifice** the Holy Sacrifice of the Mass ► **le Saint des Saints** (*Rel*) the Holy of Holies; (*fig*) the holy of holies ► **le ~ suaire** the Holy Shroud; **le ~ suaire de Turin** the Turin Shroud ► **la sainte Trinité** the Holy Trinity ► **la Sainte Vierge** the Blessed Virgin

Saint-Barthélemy [sɛ̃baʀtelemi] 1 N (*Géog*) Saint-Barthélemy, Saint Bartholomew, Saint

Bart's 2 NF (**le massacre de) la ~** the Saint Bartholomew's Day Massacre

saint-bernard (*pl* **saint(s)-bernard(s)**) [sɛ̃bɛʀnaʀ] NM a (= *chien*) St Bernard; (*hum* = *personne*) good Samaritan

Saint-Cyr [sɛ̃siʀ] N French military academy

saint-cyrien (*pl* **saint-cyriens**) [sɛ̃siʀjɛ̃] NM (*military*) cadet (*of the Saint-Cyr academy*)

Saint-Domingue [sɛ̃dɔmɛ̃g] N Santo Domingo

Sainte-Alliance [sɛ̃taljɑ̃s] NF **la ~** the Holy Alliance

Sainte-Hélène [sɛ̃telɛn] N Saint Helena

Sainte-Lucie [sɛ̃tlysi] N Saint Lucia

saintement [sɛ̃tmɑ̃] ADV [*agir, mourir*] like a saint; **vivre ~** to lead a saintly *ou* holy life, live like a saint

Sainte-Sophie [sɛ̃tsɔfi] NF Saint Sophia

saint-esprit [sɛ̃tɛspʀi] NM (= *croix*) type of cross bearing the emblem of the Holy Ghost, sometimes worn by French Protestant women; **le Saint-Esprit** the Holy Spirit *ou* Ghost → **opération**

sainteté [sɛ̃tte] NF a [*personne*] saintliness, godliness; [*Évangile, Vierge*] holiness; [*lieu*] holiness, sanctity; [*mariage*] sanctity → **odeur** b **Sa Sainteté (le pape)** His Holiness (the Pope)

saint-frusquin† [sɛ̃fʀyskɛ̃] NM **il est arrivé avec tout son ~** he arrived with all his gear* *ou* clobber (*Brit*)*; (= *et tout le reste*) **et tout le ~** and all the rest

saint-glinglin [sɛ̃glɛ̃glɛ̃] ♦ **à la saint-glinglin*** LOC ADV **il te le rendra à la ~** he'll never give it back to you in a month of Sundays; **attendre jusqu'à la ~** to wait forever; **on ne va pas rester là jusqu'à la ~** we're not going to hang around here forever*

saint-honoré (*pl* **saint-honoré(s)**) [sɛ̃tɔnɔʀe] NM (*Culin*) Saint Honoré (*gâteau*)

Saint-Jean [sɛ̃ʒɑ̃] NF **la ~** Midsummer('s) Day; **les feux de la ~** bonfires lit to celebrate Midsummer Night

Saint-Laurent [sɛ̃lɔʀɑ̃] NM **le ~** the St Lawrence (river)

Saint-Marin [sɛ̃maʀɛ̃] NM San Marino

Saint-Nicolas [sɛ̃nikɔla] NF **la ~** St Nicholas's Day

Saint-Office [sɛ̃tɔfis] NM **le ~** the Holy Office

Saint-Père [sɛ̃pɛʀ] NM **le ~** the Holy Father

saint-pierre [sɛ̃pjɛʀ] NM INV (= *poisson*) dory, John Dory

Saint-Pierre-et-Miquelon [sɛ̃pjɛʀemiklɔ̃] N Saint Pierre and Miquelon

Saint-Sacrement [sɛ̃sakʀəmɑ̃] NM **le ~** the Blessed Sacrament; **porter qch comme le ~†** to carry sth with infinite care *ou* as if it were the Crown Jewels

Saint-Sépulcre [sɛ̃sepylkʀ] NM **le ~** the Holy Sepulchre

Saint-Siège [sɛ̃sjɛʒ] NM **le ~** the Holy See

saint-simonien, -ienne (*mpl* **saint-simoniens**) [sɛ̃simɔnjɛ̃, jɛn] ADJ, NMF Saint-Simonian

saint-simonisme [sɛ̃simɔnism] NM Saint-Simonism

Saints-Innocents [sɛ̃zinɔsɑ̃] NMPL **le jour des ~** Holy Innocents' Day

Saint-Sylvestre [sɛ̃silvɛstʀ] NF **la ~** New Year's Eve

Saint-Synode [sɛ̃sinɔd] NM **le ~** the Holy Synod

Saint-Valentin [sɛ̃valɑ̃tɛ̃] NF **la ~** (Saint) Valentine's Day

Saint-Vincent et (les) Grenadines [sɛ̃vɛ̃sɑ̃e(le)gʀənadn] NPL Saint Vincent and the Grenadines

saisi, e [sezi] (*ptp de* **saisir**) 1 ADJ (*Jur*) **tiers ~** garnishee 2 NM (*Jur*) distrainee

saisie [sezi] ① NF ⓐ [biens] seizure, distraint (SPÉC), distress (SPÉC); **opérer une ~** to make a seizure ⓑ [documents, articles prohibés] seizure, confiscation; [drogue] seizure ⓒ (= capture) capture ⓓ (Ordin) **~ de données** (gén) data capture; (sur clavier) keyboarding; **~ manuelle** (manual) data entry; **~ automatique** (gén) automatic data capture; (au scanner) optical reading ou scanning; **faire de la ~ (de données)** (gén) to capture data; (sur clavier) to key(board) data ② COMP ► **saisie conservatoire** seizure of goods (to prevent sale etc) ► **saisie immobilière** seizure of property ► **saisie mobilière** = **saisie-exécution**

saisie-arrêt (pl **saisies-arrêts**) [seziaʀɛ] NF distraint, attachment

saisie-exécution (pl **saisies-exécutions**) [seziɛgzekysjɔ̃] NF distraint (for sale by court order)

saisie-gagerie (pl **saisies-gageries**) [sezigaʒʀi] NF seizure of goods (by landlord in lieu of unpaid rent)

saisine [sezin] NF ⓐ (Jur) submission of a case to the court ⓑ (Naut = cordage) lashing

saisir [seziʀ] ▶conjug 2◀ VT ⓐ (= prendre) to take hold of, catch hold of; (= s'emparer de) to seize, grab (hold of); **~ qn à la gorge** to grab ou seize sb by the throat; **~ un ballon au vol** to catch a ball (in mid air); **il lui saisit le bras pour l'empêcher de sauter** he grabbed (hold of) ou seized his arm to stop him jumping; **ils le saisirent à bras-le-corps** they took hold of ou seized him bodily ⓑ [+ occasion] to seize (on); [+ prétexte] to seize (on); **~ sa chance** to seize one's chance; **~ l'occasion/la chance au vol** to jump at the opportunity/the chance, grasp the opportunity/the chance when it arises; **~ la balle au bond** to jump at the opportunity (while the going is good) ⓒ (= entendre) [+ nom, mot] to catch, get; (= comprendre) [+ explications] to grasp, understand, get; **il a saisi quelques noms au vol** he caught ou overheard a few names in passing; **d'un coup d'œil, il saisit ce qui se passait** he understood what was going on at a glance; **tu saisis ce que je veux dire ?** do you get it?*, do you get what I mean? ⓓ [peur] to take hold of, seize, grip; [allégresse, colère] to take hold of, come over; [malaise] to come over; **le froid l'a saisi** ou **il a été saisi par le froid en sortant** he was gripped by the cold as he went out; **il a été saisi de mouvements convulsifs** he was seized with convulsions; **saisi de joie** overcome with joy; **saisi de peur** seized ou gripped by fear, transfixed with fear; **saisi de panique/d'horreur** panic-/horror-stricken; **je fus saisi de l'envie de ...** I suddenly had the urge to ... ⓔ (= impressionner, surprendre) to strike; **la ressemblance entre les deux sœurs le saisit** he was struck by the resemblance between the two sisters; **elle fut tellement saisie que ...** she was so surprised that ... ⓕ (Jur) [+ biens] to seize, distrain (SPÉC); [+ documents, drogue] to seize, confiscate; [+ personne] to take into custody, seize ⓖ (Jur) [+ juridiction] to submit ou refer a case to; **~ le Conseil de sécurité d'une affaire** to submit ou refer a matter to the Security Council; **~ la Cour de justice** to complain to the Court of Justice; **la cour a été saisie de l'affaire** ou **du dossier** the case has been submitted ou referred to the court ⓗ (Culin) [+ viande] to seal, sear ⓘ (Ordin) [+ données] (gén) to capture; (sur clavier) to key (in), keyboard

② **se saisir** VPR **se ~ de qch/qn** to seize sth/sb, catch ou grab hold of sth/sb; **le gouvernement/le Conseil de sécurité s'est saisi du dossier** the government/Security Council has taken up the issue

saisissable [sezisabl] ADJ ⓐ [nuance, sensation] perceptible ⓑ (Jur) seizable, distrainable (SPÉC)

saisissant, e [sezisɑ̃, ɑ̃t] ① ADJ ⓐ [spectacle] gripping; [contraste, ressemblance] striking, startling; [froid] biting, piercing ⓑ (Jur) distraining ② NM (Jur) distrainer

saisissement [sezismɑ̃] NM (= émotion) shock; († = frisson de froid) sudden chill

saison [sɛzɔ̃] NF ⓐ (= division de l'année) season; **la belle/mauvaise ~** the summer/winter months; **en cette ~** at this time of year; **en toutes ~s** all (the) year round; **il n'y a plus de ~s !** there are no seasons any more! ⓑ (= époque) season; **~ des amours/des fraises/théâtrale/touristique** mating/strawberry-/theatre/tourist season; **la ~ des pluies** the rainy ou wet season; **la ~ sèche** the dry season; **la ~ des moissons/des vendanges** harvest/grape-harvesting time; **les nouvelles couleurs de la ~** the new season's colours; **nous faisons la ~ sur la Côte d'Azur** we're working on the Côte d'Azur during the season; **les hôteliers ont fait une bonne ~** hoteliers have had a good season; **haute/basse ~** high ou peak/low ou off season; **en (haute) ~ les prix sont plus chers** in the high season ou at the height of the season prices are higher; **en pleine ~** at the height ou peak of the season → **marchand, voiture** ⓒ (= cure) stay (at a spa), cure ⓓ (loc) **de ~** [fruits, légumes] seasonal; **il fait un temps de ~** the weather is right ou what one would expect for the time of year, the weather is seasonable; **faire preuve d'un optimisme de ~** to show fitting optimism; (frm) **vos plaisanteries ne sont pas de ~** your jokes are totally out of place; **hors de ~** (lit) out of season; (frm = inopportun) untimely, out of place; **hors ~** [plante] out of season (attrib); [prix] off-season (épith), low-season (épith); **prendre ses vacances hors ~** to go on holiday in the off season ou low season

saisonnalité [sɛzɔnalite] NF seasonality

saisonnier, -ière [sɛzɔnje, jɛʀ] ① ADJ [commerce, emploi, travailleur] seasonal; **variations saisonnières** seasonal variations ou fluctuations; (Psych) **dépression saisonnière** seasonal affective disorder, SAD ② NM,F (= ouvrier) seasonal worker

saké [sake] NM sake

salace [salas] ADJ (littér) salacious

salacité [salasite] NF (littér) salaciousness, salacity

salade [salad] NF ⓐ (= plante) lettuce; (= scarole) escarole; **la laitue est une ~** lettuce is a salad vegetable ⓑ (= plat) green salad; **~ de tomates/de fruits/russe** tomato/fruit/Russian salad; **~ niçoise** salade niçoise; **~ composée** mixed salad; **~ cuite** cooked salad greens; **haricots en ~** bean salad → **panier** ⓒ (* = confusion) tangle, muddle ⓓ (* = mensonge) ~s stories*; **raconter des ~s** to spin yarns, tell stories*; [représentant] **vendre sa ~** to make one's sales pitch* ⓔ [armure] sallet

saladier [saladje] NM ⓐ (= récipient) salad bowl; (= contenu) bowlful

salage [salaʒ] NM salting

▼ **salaire** [salɛʀ] NM ⓐ (mensuel, annuel) salary; (journalier, hebdomadaire) wage(s), pay; **~ horaire** hourly wage; **famille à ~ unique** single income family; (allocation) **toucher le ~ unique** ≈ to get income support (Brit); **~ de famine** ou **de misère** starvation wage; **~ minimum** minimum wage; **~ minimum agricole garanti** guaranteed minimum agricultural wage; **~ minimum interprofessionnel de croissance ◊ ~ minimum interprofessionnel garanti †** (index-linked) guaranteed minimum wage; **~ d'embauche** starting salary; **~ de base** basic pay ou salary; **~ indirect** employer's contributions; **~ brut/net** gross/net ou take-home pay; **~ nominal/réel** nominal/real wage; **~ imposa-**

-ble taxable income; (= personnes) **les petits ~s** low-wage earners; **les gros ~s** high earners → **bulletin, échelle, peine** etc ⓑ (= récompense) reward (de for); (= châtiment) reward, retribution, recompense (de for) → **peine**

salaison [salɛzɔ̃] NF ⓐ (= procédé) salting ⓑ (= viande) salt meat; (= poisson) salt fish

salamalecs* [salamalɛk] NMPL (péj) bowing and scraping; **faire des ~** to bow and scrape

salamandre [salamɑ̃dʀ] NF ⓐ (= animal) salamander ⓑ (= poêle) slow-combustion stove

salami [salami] NM salami

Salamine [salamin] N Salamis

salant [salɑ̃] ADJ M, NM **(marais) ~** (gén) salt marsh; (exploité) saltern

salarial, e (mpl **-iaux**) [salaʀjal, jo] ADJ ⓐ (= des salaires) [accord, politique, exigences, revendications] wage (épith), pay (épith) ⓑ (= des salariés) **cotisations ~es** employee contributions; **charges ~es** payroll ou wage costs → **masse**

salariat [salaʀja] NM ⓐ (= salariés) wage-earners; **le ~ et le patronat** employees and employers ⓑ (= rémunération) (au mois) payment by salary; (au jour, à la semaine) payment by wages ⓒ (= état) (being in) employment; **être réduit au ~ après avoir été patron** to be reduced to the ranks of the employees ou of the salaried staff after having been in a senior position

salarié, e [salaʀje] ① ADJ [travailleur] (au mois) salaried (épith); (à la journée, à la semaine) wage-earning; [travail, emploi] paid; **elle est ~e** she gets a salary, she's on the payroll; **travailleur non ~** non-salaried worker ② NM,F (payé au mois) salaried employee; (payé au jour, à la semaine) wage-earner; **le statut de ~** employee status; **notre entreprise compte 55 ~s** our company has 55 employees on the payroll ou has a payroll of 55 employees

salarier [salaʀje] ▶conjug 7◀ VT to put on a salary; **il préférerait se faire ~** he would prefer to have a salaried job ou to be put on a salary; **la direction a salarié cinq personnes** management have put five people on the company payroll

salaud‡ [salo] ① NM bastard‡, swine‡; **quel beau ~ !** what an absolute bastard!‡; **alors mon ~, tu ne t'en fais pas !** well you old bugger‡, you're not exactly overdoing it!; **10 000 F ? ben, mon ~ !** 10,000 francs? I'll be damned*; **tous des ~s !** they're all bastards!‡ ② ADJ **tu es ~** you're an absolute bastard‡ ou swine‡; **il a été ~ avec elle** he was a real bastard to her‡‡; **il n'a pas été ~ avec toi** he's been nice to you; **c'est ~ d'avoir fait ça** that was a shitty‡ thing to do; **sois pas ~ ! ◊ ne fais pas ton ~ !** don't be so mean!

sale [sal] ① ADJ ⓐ (= crasseux) dirty; **~ comme un cochon** ou **un porc** ou **un peigne** filthy (dirty); **oh la ~ !** you dirty girl!; **c'est pas ~ !*** it's not bad!*; **l'argent ~** dirty money → **laver** ⓑ (= ordurier) [histoire] dirty, filthy ⓒ (*: avant n = mauvais) [affaire, maladie, habitude] nasty; [guerre] dirty; **~ coup** (= mauvais tour) dirty trick; (= choc) terrible ou dreadful blow; **faire un ~ coup à qn** to play a (dirty) trick on sb; **c'est un ~ coup pour l'entreprise** it's bad news for the company, it's dealt a heavy blow to the company; **(c'est un) ~ coup pour la fanfare** it's a real blow; **~ tour** dirty trick; **~ temps** filthy* ou foul ou lousy* weather; **~ temps pour les petites entreprises** bad days ou hard times for small businesses; **~ démago‡** bloody‡ (Brit) ou goddamn* (US) demagogue; **avoir une ~ tête*** (= sembler malade) to look awful, look like death warmed up* (Brit) ou over* (US); (= faire peur) to look evil; **faire une ~ tête** (= être mécontent) to have a face like thunder; **il a fait une ~ tête** (= il était dépité) his face fell; **il m'est arrivé une ~ histoire** something awful happened to me;

► **GRAMMAIRE ACTIVE:**   **salaire** 46.2

faire le ~ travail *ou* **boulot*** to do the dirty work → **besogne, délit**

[2] NM **mettre qch au ~** to put sth in the wash; **aller/être au ~** to go/be in the wash

salé, e [sale] (*ptp de* **saler**) [1] ADJ [a] (= *contenant du sel*) [*mer, saveur*] salty; (= *additionné de sel*) [*amande, plat*] salted; [*gâteau*] (= *non sucré*) savoury (*Brit*), savory (*US*); (= *au goût salé*) salty; (= *conservé au sel*) [*poisson, viande*] salt (*épith*); [*beurre*] salted → **eau** [b] (*= grivois*) spicy, juicy, fruity*; **plaisanterie ~e** dirty joke [c] (* = *sévère*) [*punition*] stiff; [*facture*] steep [2] NM (= *nourriture*) **le ~** (*gén*) salty foods; (*par opposition à sucré*) savoury (*Brit*) *ou* savory (*US*) foods; **petit ~** (= *porc*) salt pork [3] ADV **manger ~** to like a lot of salt on one's food, like one's food well salted; **il ne peut pas manger trop ~** he can't have his food too salty

salement [salmɑ̃] ADV [a] (= *malproprement, bassement*) dirtily [b] (✷ = *très, beaucoup*) [*dur, embêtant*] damned*, bloody* (*Brit*); **j'ai ~ mal** it's damned *ou* bloody (*Brit*) painful*, it hurts like mad*; **j'ai eu ~ peur** I had a *ou* one hell of a fright*, I was damned *ou* bloody (*Brit*) scared✷

saler [sale] ▸ conjug 1 ◂ VT [a] [+ *plat, soupe*] to put salt in, salt; (*pour conserver*) to salt; [+ *chaussée*] to salt; **tu ne sales pas assez** you don't put enough salt in, you don't use enough salt [b]✷ [+ *client*] to do*, fleece; [+ *facture*] to bump up*; [+ *inculpé*] to be tough on*

saleté [salte] NF [a] (= *malpropreté*) [*lieu, personne*] dirtiness; **il est/c'est d'une ~ incroyable** he's/it's absolutely filthy [b] (= *crasse*) dirt, filth; **murs couverts de ~** walls covered in dirt *ou* filth; **vivre dans la ~** to live in filth *ou* squalor; **le chauffage au charbon fait de la ~** coal heating makes a lot of mess *ou* dirt [c] (= *ordure, impureté*) dirt (*NonC*); **il y a une ~ par terre/sur ta robe** there's some dirt on the floor/on your dress; **j'ai une ~ dans l'œil** I've got some dirt in my eye; **tu as fait des ~s partout en perçant le mur** you've made a mess all over the place drilling the wall; **enlève tes ~s de ma chambre** get your junk* *ou* rubbish (*Brit*) *ou* trash* (*US*) out of my room; **le chat a fait des ~s** *ou* **ses ~s dans le salon** the cat has made a mess in the lounge [d] (* *sans valeur*) piece of junk*; **ce réfrigérateur est une ~** *ou* **de la vraie ~** this fridge is a piece of junk*; **c'est une ~ qu'ils ont achetée hier** it's some (old) junk* *ou* rubbish (*Brit*) *ou* trash* (*US*) they bought yesterday; **chez eux, il n'y a que des ~s** their place is full of junk* *ou* trash (*US*); **il se bourre de ~s avant le repas** he stuffs himself* with junk food before meals [e] (* = *maladie*) **je me demande où j'ai bien pu attraper cette ~là** I wonder where on earth I could have caught this blasted thing*; **je récolte toutes les ~s qui traînent** I catch every blasted thing going* [f] (* = *obscénité*) dirty *ou* filthy thing (to say)*; **dire des ~s** to say filthy things*, talk dirty* [g] (* = *méchanceté*) dirty trick; **faire une ~ à qn** to play a dirty trick on sb; **on en a vu des ~s pendant la guerre** we saw plenty of disgusting things during the war [h] (* = *personne méprisable*) nasty piece of work*, nasty character [i] (*: *intensif*) **~ de virus !** this blasted virus!; **~ de guerre !** what a damned✷ *ou* bloody✷ (*Brit*) awful war!

salicylate [salisilat] NM salicylate

salicylique [salisilik] ADJ **acide ~** salicylic acid

salière [saljɛʀ] NF [a] (= *récipient*) saltcellar; (*à trous*) saltcellar (*Brit*), salt shaker (*US*) [b] [*clavicule*] saltcellar

salifère [salifɛʀ] ADJ saliferous

salification [salifikasjɔ̃] NF salification

salifier [salifje] ▸ conjug 7 ◂ VT to salify

saligaud✷ [saligo] NM (= *malpropre*) dirty *ou* filthy pig✷; (= *salaud*) swine✷, bastard✷✷

salin, e [salɛ̃, in] [1] ADJ saline [2] NM salt marsh [3] **saline** NF (= *entreprise*) saltworks; (= *salin*) salt marsh

salinité [salinite] NF salinity

salique [salik] ADJ Salic, Salian; **loi ~** Salic law

salir [saliʀ] ▸ conjug 2 ◂ [1] VT [a] [+ *lieu*] to make dirty, mess up*, make a mess in; [+ *objet*] to make dirty; **le charbon salit** coal is messy *ou* dirty [b] [+ *imagination*] to corrupt, defile; [+ *réputation*] to sully, soil, tarnish; **~ qn** to sully *ou* soil *ou* tarnish sb's reputation [2] **se salir** VPR [a] [*tissu*] to get dirty *ou* soiled; [*personne*] to get dirty; **le blanc se salit facilement** white shows the dirt (easily), white soils easily; (*lit, fig*) **se ~ les mains** to get one's hands dirty, dirty one's hands [b] (= *se déshonorer*) to sully *ou* soil *ou* tarnish one's reputation

salissant, e [salisɑ̃, ɑ̃t] ADJ [*étoffe*] which shows the dirt, which soils easily; [*travail*] dirty, messy

salissure [salisyʀ] NF (= *saleté*) dirt, filth; (= *tache*) dirty mark

salivaire [salivɛʀ] ADJ salivary

salivation [salivasjɔ̃] NF salivation

salive [saliv] NF saliva, spittle; **avaler sa ~** to gulp; **épargne** *ou* **ne gaspille pas ta ~** save your breath, don't waste your breath; **dépenser beaucoup de ~ pour convaincre qn** to have to do a lot of talking *ou* use a lot of breath to persuade sb

saliver [salive] ▸ conjug 1 ◂ VI to salivate; [*animal*] (*péj*) to drool; **ça le faisait ~** [*nourriture*] it made his mouth water; [*spectacle*] it made him drool

salle [sal] [1] NF [a] [*café, musée*] room; [*château*] hall; [*restaurant*] (dining) room; [*hôpital*] ward; (*Sport*) **en ~** [*record, athlétisme*] indoor → **fille, garçon** [b] [*Ciné, Théât*] (= *auditorium*) auditorium, theatre (*Brit*), theater (*US*); (= *cinéma*) cinema (*Brit*), movie theater (*US*); (= *public*) audience; **plusieurs ~s de quartier ont dû fermer** several local cinemas had to close down; **faire ~ comble** *ou* **pleine** [*comédien*] to play to a packed *ou* full house, have a full house; [*spectacle*] to play to a packed *ou* full house; **cinéma à plusieurs ~s** cinema with several screens; **film projeté dans la ~ 3** film showing on screen 3; **le film sort en ~** *ou* **dans les ~s mercredi prochain** the film will be in cinemas *ou* on general release next Wednesday; **sortie en ~** [*film*] cinema release

[2] COMP ▸ **salle d'armes** arms room ▸ **salle d'attente** waiting room ▸ **salle d'audience** courtroom ▸ **salle de bain(s)** bathroom ▸ **salle de bal** ballroom ▸ **salle de banquets** [*château*] banqueting hall ▸ **salle basse** lower hall ▸ **salle de billard** billiard room ▸ **salle blanche** clean room ▸ **salle du chapitre** (*Rel*) chapter room ▸ **salle de cinéma** cinema (*Brit*), movie theater (*US*) ▸ **salle de classe** classroom ▸ **salle des coffres** strongroom, vault ▸ **salle commune** [*colonie de vacances*] commonroom; [*hôpital*] ward ▸ **salle de concert** concert hall ▸ **salle de conférences** lecture *ou* conference room; (*grande*) lecture hall *ou* theatre ▸ **salle de cours** classroom ▸ **salle de douches** showerroom, showers ▸ **salle d'eau** shower-room ▸ **salle d'embarquement** (*Aviat*) departure lounge ▸ **salle d'étude(s)** prep room ▸ **salle d'exposition** (*Comm*) showroom ▸ **salle des fêtes** village hall ▸ **salle de garde** staff waiting room (*in hospital*) ▸ **salle des gardes** [*château*] guardroom ▸ **salle de jeu** (*pour enfants*) playroom, rumpus room (*US*); [*casino*] gaming room ▸ **salle**

de lecture reading room ▸ **salle des machines** engine room ▸ **salle à manger** (= *pièce*) dining room; (= *meubles*) dining-room suite ▸ **salle de montage** cutting room ▸ **salle de musculation** weights room ▸ **salle de permanence** = **salle d'étude(s)** ▸ **les salles obscures** cinemas (*Brit*), movie theaters (*US*) ▸ **salle d'opération** operating theatre (*Brit*) *ou* room (*US*) ▸ **salle des pas perdus** (waiting) hall ▸ **salle de police** guardhouse, guardroom ▸ **salle des professeurs** common room, staff room ▸ **salle de projection** film theatre ▸ **salle de réanimation** recovery room ▸ **salle de rédaction** (newspaper) office ▸ **salle de réunion** meeting room ▸ **salle de réveil** observation ward ▸ **salle de séjour** living room ▸ **salle de soins** treatment room ▸ **salle de spectacle** (= *cinéma*) cinema, movie theater (*US*); (= *théâtre*) theatre (*Brit*), theater (*US*) ▸ **salle de sport** gym ▸ **salle de travail** [*hôpital*] labour room ▸ **salle du trône** throne room ▸ **salle des ventes** saleroom, auction room

salmigondis [salmigɔ̃di] NM (*Culin, fig*) hotch-potch (*Brit*), hodgepodge (*US*)

salmis [salmi] NM salmi (*rich stew*)

salmonella [salmɔnɛla], **salmonelle** [salmɔnɛl] NF salmonella

salmonellose [salmɔneloz] NF salmonellosis

salmoniculture [salmɔnikyltyʀ] NF salmon farming

saloir [salwaʀ] NM salting-tub

Salomé [salɔme] NF Salome

Salomon [salɔmɔ̃] NM Solomon; **le jugement de ~** the judgment of Solomon; **les îles ~** the Solomon Islands

salon [salɔ̃] [1] NM [a] [*maison*] sitting *ou* living room, lounge (*Brit*); [*navire*] saloon, lounge; **coin ~** living area [b] [*hôtel*] (*pour les clients*) lounge; (*pour conférences, réceptions*) function room [c] (= *meubles*) living-room suite, (= *canapé et deux fauteuils*) three-piece suite; **~ de jardin** set of garden furniture [d] (= *exposition*) exhibition, show [e] (= *cercle littéraire*) salon; (*Littér*) **tenir ~** to hold a salon; (*hum*) **faire** *ou* **tenir ~** to have a natter*; (*péj hum*) **c'est le dernier** *ou* **l'on cause !** what a lot of chatterboxes (you are)!*

[2] COMP ▸ **Salon des Arts ménagers** *home improvements exhibition*, ≈ Ideal Home Exhibition (*Brit*) ▸ **salon d'attente** waiting room ▸ **le Salon de l'Auto** the Motor *ou* Car Show ▸ **salon de beauté** beauty salon *ou* parlour (*Brit*) *ou* parlor (*US*) ▸ **salon de coiffure** hairdressing salon ▸ **salon d'essayage** fitting room ▸ **salon funéraire** (*Can*) funeral home, funeral parlour (*Brit*) *ou* parlor (*US*) ▸ **le Salon du Livre** the Book Fair ▸ **salon particulier** private room ▸ **salon professionnel** trade fair *ou* show ▸ **salon de réception** [*maison*] reception room; [*hôtel*] function room ▸ **salon-salle à manger** living-cum-dining room (*Brit*), living room-dining room (*US*) ▸ **salon de thé** tearoom

saloon [salun] NM (*Far-West*) saloon

salop✷ [salo] NM = **salaud**

salopard✷ [salɔpaʀ] NM bastard✷✷, swine✷

salope✷✷ [salɔp] NF (= *déloyale, méchante*) bitch✷✷, cow✷ (*Brit*); (= *dévergondée, sale*) slut✷

saloper✷ [salɔpe] ▸ conjug 1 ◂ VT (= *bâcler*) to botch, bungle, make a mess of; (= *salir*) to mess up*, muck up*

saloperie✷ [salɔpʀi] NF [a] (= *chose sans valeur*) piece of junk*; **cette radio est une ~** *ou* **de la vraie ~** this radio is a piece of junk* *ou* is absolute crap✷✷; **ils n'achètent que des ~s** they only buy junk* *ou* crap✷✷; **le grenier est plein de ~s** the attic is full of junk *ou* rubbish* (*Brit*) [b] (= *mauvaise nourriture*) muck* (*NonC*), rubbish* (*NonC*) (*Brit*) **ils nous ont fait manger de la ~ ou des ~s** they gave us some awful muck *ou* rubbish (*Brit*) to eat*; **c'est bon, ces petites ~s** these little things are really good; **il se bourre de ~s avant le repas** he stuffs himself* with junk food before meals

[c] (= *maladie*) **il a dû attraper une ~** he must have caught some blasted bug*; **il récolte toutes les ~s** he gets every blasted thing going*

[d] (= *ordure*) dirt (*NonC*), mess (*NonC*), muck* (*NonC*); **quand on ramone la cheminée, ça fait des ~s ou de la ~ partout** when the chimney's swept the dirt gets everywhere; **va faire tes ~s ailleurs** go and make your mess somewhere else

[e] (= *action*) dirty trick; (= *parole*) bitchy remark*; **faire une ~ à qn** to play a dirty *ou* a lousy* trick on sb, do the dirty on sb*

[f] (= *obscénités*) **~s** dirty *ou* filthy remarks; **dire des ~s** to talk dirty*

[g] (= *crasse*) filth

salopette [salɔpɛt] NF [*ouvrier*] overall(s); [*enfant, femme*] dungarees; (*Ski*) ski pants, salopettes (*Brit*)

salpêtre [salpɛtʀ] NM saltpetre (*Brit*), saltpeter (*US*)

salpêtrer [salpetʀe] ▸ conjug 1 ◂ VT [a] (*Agr*) [+ *terre*] to add saltpetre (*Brit*) *ou* saltpeter (*US*) to [b] [+ *mur*] to cover with saltpetre (*Brit*) *ou* saltpeter (*US*); **cave salpêtrée** cellar covered with saltpetre

salpingite [salpɛ̃ʒit] NF salpingitis

salsa [salsa] NF salsa; **danser la ~** to dance *ou* do the salsa

salsifis [salsifi] NM (= *plante*) salsify, oyster-plant

SALT [salt] (ABRÉV = **Strategic Arms Limitation Talks**) SALT

saltimbanque [saltɛ̃bɑ̃k] NMF (= *acrobate*) acrobat; (= *forain*) (travelling) performer; (= *professionnel du spectacle*) entertainer

salto [salto] NM (*Sport*) somersault, flip; **~ avant/arrière** forward/backward somersault; **double ~** double somersault *ou* flip

salubre [salybʀ] ADJ [*air, climat*] healthy, salubrious (*frm*); [*logement*] salubrious (*frm*)

salubrité [salybʀite] NF [*lieu, climat*] healthiness, salubrity (*frm*), salubriousness (*frm*); **par mesure de ~** as a health measure; **~ publique** public health

saluer [salɥe] ▸ conjug 1 ◂ VT [a] (= *dire bonjour à*) to greet; **se découvrir/s'incliner pour ~ qn** to raise one's hat/bow to sb (in greeting); **~ qn** to wave to sb (in greeting); **~ qn d'un signe de tête** to nod (a greeting) to sb; **~ qn à son arrivée** to greet sb on their arrival; **saluez-le de ma part** give him my regards

[b] (= *dire au revoir à*) to say goodbye to, take one's leave of; **il nous salua et sortit** he said goodbye *ou* took his leave and went out; **il salua (le public)** he bowed (to the audience)

[c] (*Mil, Naut*) [+ *supérieur, drapeau, navire*] to salute

[d] (= *témoigner son respect pour*) [+ *ennemi vaincu, courage, héroïsme*] to salute; **~ la mémoire/les efforts de qn** to pay tribute to sb's memory/efforts; **nous saluons en vous l'homme qui a sauvé tant de vies** we salute you as the man who has saved so many lives

[e] (= *accueillir*) [+ *initiative*] to welcome; (= *acclamer*) to hail; (*Rel*) « **je vous salue, Marie** » "Hail, Mary"; **~ qch comme un succès/une victoire** to hail sth as a success/a victory; **l'événement a été salué comme historique** it was hailed as an historic event; **cette déclaration a été saluée par une ovation** this announcement was greeted with thunderous applause; (*hum*) **elle/son arrivée fut saluée par des huées** she/her arrival was greeted with *ou* by booing

salut [saly] [1] NM [a] (*de la main*) wave (of the hand); (*de la tête*) nod (of the head); (*du buste*) bow; (*Mil, Naut*) salute; **faire un ~** (*de la main*) to wave (one's hand); (*de la tête*) to nod (one's head); (*du buste*) to bow; **faire le ~ militaire** to give the military salute; **~ au drapeau** salute to the colours

[b] (= *sauvegarde*) [*personne*] (personal) safety; [*nation*] safety; **trouver/chercher son ~ dans la fuite** to find/seek safety *ou* refuge in flight; **elle n'a dû son ~ qu'à son courage** only her courage saved her; **mesures de ~ public** state security measures, measures to protect national security; **ancre ou planche de ~** sheet anchor (*fig*)

[c] (*Rel* = *rédemption*) salvation → **armée²**, **hors**

[2] EXCL [a] * (= *bonjour*) hello!, hi!*; (= *au revoir*) see you!*, bye!*, cheerio!* (*Brit*); **~, les gars!** hi guys!*; **~!** (= *rien à faire*) no thanks!

[b] (*littér*) (all) hail; **~ (à toi) puissant seigneur!** (all) hail to thee mighty lord!; **~, forêt de mon enfance!** hail (to thee), o forest of my childhood!

salutaire [salytɛʀ] ADJ [a] [*conseil*] salutary (*épith*), profitable (*épith*); [*choc, épreuve*] salutary (*épith*); [*influence*] healthy (*épith*), salutary (*épith*); [*dégoût*] healthy (*épith*); **cette déception lui a été ~** that disappointment was good for him *ou* did him some good [b] [*air*] healthy, salubrious (*frm*); [*remède*] beneficial; **ce petit repos m'a été ~** that little rest did me good *ou* was good for me

salutation [salytasjɔ̃] NF greeting, salutation (*frm*); **après les ~s d'usage** after the usual greetings

salutiste [salytist] ADJ, NMF Salvationist

Salvador [salvadɔʀ] NM **le ~** El Salvador; **au ~** in El Salvador

salvadorien, -ienne [salvadɔʀjɛ̃, jɛn] [1] ADJ Salvadorian, Salvadorean, Salvadoran [2] **Salvadorien(ne)** NM,F Salvadorian, Salvadorean, Salvadoran

salvateur, -trice [salvatœʀ, tʀis] ADJ (*littér*) saving (*épith*)

salve [salv] NF [*artillerie, roquettes*] salvo; **une ~ de 21 coups de canon** a 21-gun salute; **tirer une ~ d'honneur** to fire a salute; **une ~ d'applaudissements** a burst *ou* round of applause; **une ~ de critiques/d'injures** a volley of criticism/of abuse

Salzbourg [salzbuʀ] N Salzburg

Samarie [samaʀi] NF Samaria

samaritain, e [samaʀitɛ̃, ɛn] [1] ADJ Samaritan [2] **Samaritain(e)** NM,F Samaritan; **les Samaritains** the Samaritans; (*Bible*) **bon Samaritain** good Samaritan; (*souvent iro*) **jouer les bons Samaritains** to play the good Samaritan

samba [sɑ̃(m)ba] NF samba

samedi [samdi] NM Saturday; **nous irons ~** we'll go on Saturday; **~ nous sommes allés ...** on Saturday *ou* last Saturday we went ...; **pas ~ qui vient mais l'autre** not this (coming) Saturday but the next *ou* but the one after that; **ce ~(-ci)** ◊ **~ qui vient** this (coming) Saturday; **un ~ sur deux** every other *ou* second Saturday; **nous sommes ~ (aujourd'hui)** it's Saturday (today); **~, le 18 décembre** Saturday December 18th; **le ~ 23 janvier** on Saturday January 23rd; **~ matin/après-midi** Saturday morning/afternoon; **~ soir** Saturday evening *ou* night; **la nuit de ~** Saturday night; **dans la nuit de ~ à dimanche** on Saturday night; **l'édition de ~ ou du ~** the Saturday edition → **huit**

samit [sami] NM samite

Samoa [samɔa] NM **les îles ~** Samoa, the Samoa Islands; **les ~-occidentales/-américaines** Western/American Samoa

samoan, e [samɔɑ̃, an] [1] ADJ Samoan [2] **Samoan(e)** NM,F Samoan

samouraï [samuʀaj] NM samurai

samovar [samɔvaʀ] NM samovar

sampan(g) [sɑ̃pɑ̃] NM sampan

Samson [sɑ̃sɔ̃] NM Samson; **~ et Dalila** Samson and Delilah

SAMU [samy] NM (ABRÉV = **Service d'assistance médicale d'urgence**) ~ **social** *mobile emergency medical service for homeless people* → **service**

samuraï [samuʀaj] NM = **samouraï**

sana* [sana] NM ABRÉV = **sanatorium**

Sanaa [sanaa] N San'a, Sanaa

sanatorium [sanatɔʀjɔm] NM sanatorium, sanitarium (*US*)

sancerre [sɑ̃sɛʀ] NM Sancerre (*type of wine from the Loire valley*)

Sancho Pança [sɑ̃ʃopɑ̃sa] NM Sancho Panza

sanctification [sɑ̃ktifikasjɔ̃] NF sanctification

sanctifié, e [sɑ̃ktifje] (*ptp de* **sanctifier**) ADJ blessed

sanctifier [sɑ̃ktifje] ▸ conjug 7 ◂ VT to sanctify, hallow, bless; **~ le jour du Seigneur** to observe the Sabbath; (*Rel*) « **que ton nom soit sanctifié** » "hallowed be Thy name"

sanction [sɑ̃ksjɔ̃] NF [a] (= *condamnation*) (*Jur*) sanction, penalty; (*Écon, Pol*) sanction; (*Scol*) punishment; (*fig* = *conséquence*) penalty (**de** for); **~ administrative/disciplinaire** administrative/disciplinary action (*NonC*); **~ pénale** penalty; **~s commerciales/économiques** trade/economic sanctions; (*Écon, Pol*) **prendre des ~s to** impose sanctions (**contre, à l'encontre de** on); **prendre des ~s contre un joueur/club/ministre** to take disciplinary action against a player/club/minister; **prendre des ~s contre un élève** to punish *ou* discipline a pupil; **la ~ électorale a été sévère** the electorate's rejection was complete

[b] (= *ratification*) sanction (*NonC*), approval (*NonC*); **recevoir la ~ de qn** to obtain sb's sanction *ou* approval; **c'est la ~ du progrès** (= *conséquence*) it's the price of progress; **ce mot a reçu la ~ de l'usage** this word has been sanctioned by use

sanctionner [sɑ̃ksjɔne] ▸ conjug 1 ◂ VT [a] (= *punir*) [+ *faute, personne*] to punish; [+ *joueur, club sportif*] to take disciplinary action against; [+ *pays*] to impose sanctions on; **tout manquement à ce principe sera sévèrement sanctionné** any breach of this principle will be severely punished; **les électeurs ont sanctionné la politique du précédent gouvernement** the electorate rejected the policy of the previous government [b] (= *consacrer: gén*) to sanction, approve; [+ *loi*] to sanction; **ce diplôme sanctionne les études secondaires** this diploma marks the successful conclusion of secondary education

sanctuaire [sɑ̃ktɥɛʀ] NM [a] (*Rel* = *lieu saint*) sanctuary, shrine; [*temple, église*] sanctuary [b] (*fig littér*) sanctuary (*Pol*) sanctuary

sanctus [sɑ̃ktys] NM Sanctus

sandale [sɑ̃dal] NF sandal

sandalette [sɑ̃dalɛt] NF (light) sandal

sandiniste [sɑ̃dinist] ADJ, NMF Sandinist(a)

sandow® [sɑ̃do] NM (= *attache*) luggage elastic; (*Aviat*) catapult

sandre [sɑ̃dʀ] NM pikeperch, zander

sandwich (*pl* **sandwiches** *ou* **sandwichs**) [sɑ̃dwi(t)ʃ] NM sandwich; **~ au jambon** ham sandwich; **(pris) en ~ (entre)*** sandwiched (between); **les deux voitures l'ont pris en ~*** he was sandwiched between the two cars

sandwicherie [sɑ̃dwi(t)ʃəʀi] NF sandwich shop *ou* bar

San Francisco [sɑ̃ fʀɑ̃sisko] N San Francisco

sang [sɑ̃] NM [a] (*lit, fig*) blood; **~ artériel/veineux** arterial/venous blood; **~ contaminé** infected *ou* contaminated blood; **animal à ~ froid/chaud** cold-/warm-blooded animal; **le ~ a coulé** blood has flowed; **verser ou faire couler le ~** to shed *ou* spill blood; **cela finira dans le ~** blood will be shed; (*fig*) **il va y avoir du**

~!* the fur will fly!*; *(fig)* **avoir du ~ sur les mains** to have blood on one's hands; **son ~ crie vengeance** his blood cries (for) vengeance; **il était en ~** he was covered in *ou* with blood; **pincer qn (jusqu')au ~** to pinch sb till he bleeds *ou* till the blood comes; **mordre qn jusqu'au ~** to bite sb and draw blood; **payer son crime de son ~** to pay for one's crime with one's life; **donner son ~ pour un malade** to give *ou* donate one's blood for somebody who is ill; **donner son ~ pour sa patrie** to shed one's blood for one's country → **donneur, feu¹, noyer², pinte**

[b] (= *race, famille*) blood; **de ~ royal** of royal blood; **avoir du ~ bleu** to have blue blood, be blue-blooded; **du même ~** of the same flesh and blood; **liens du ~** blood ties, ties of blood → **prince, voix**

[c] *(loc)* **avoir le ~ chaud** (= *s'emporter facilement*) to be hotheaded; (= *être sensuel*) to be hot-blooded; **un apport de ~ neuf** an injection of new *ou* fresh blood (**dans** into); **se faire ~ ou ~ d'encre** to be worried sick *ou* stiff*; **se faire du mauvais ~** to worry, get in a state; **avoir du ~ dans les veines** to have courage *ou* guts*; **il n'a pas de ~ dans les veines** ◊ **il a du ~ de navet** *ou* **de poulet** *(manque de courage)* he's a spineless individual, he's got no guts*; *(manque d'énergie)* he's very lethargic; **il a le jeu/le jazz dans le ~** he's got gambling/jazz in his blood; **le ~ lui monta au visage** the blood rushed to his face; **bon ~ !** dammit!*; **coup de ~** (*Méd*) stroke; *(fig = colère)* **attraper un coup de ~** to fly into a rage; **mon ~ n'a fait qu'un tour** *(émotion, peur)* my heart missed *ou* skipped a beat; *(colère, indignation)* I saw red; **se ronger** *ou* **se manger les ~s** to worry (o.s.), fret; **se ronger les ~s pour savoir comment faire qch** to agonize over how to do sth; **tourner les ~s à qn** to shake sb up; **histoire à glacer le ~** bloodcurdling story; **son ~ se glaça** *ou* **se figea dans ses veines** his blood froze *ou* ran cold in his veins → **suer**

sang-froid [sɑ̃fʀwa] NM INV calm, cool*, sangfroid *(frm)*; **garder/perdre son ~** to keep/lose one's head *ou* one's cool*; **faire qch de ~** to do sth in cold blood *ou* cold-bloodedly; **répondre avec ~** to reply coolly *ou* calmly; **crime commis de ~** cold-blooded murder

sanglant, e [sɑ̃glɑ̃, ɑ̃t] ADJ *[couteau, plaie]* bloody; *[bandage, habits]* blood-soaked, bloody; *[mains, visage]* covered in blood, bloody **[b]** *[combat, guerre]* bloody **[c]** *[insulte, reproche, défaite]* cruel **[d]** *(littér = couleur)* blood-red

sangle [sɑ̃gl] NF *(gén)* strap; *[selle]* girth; *[siège]* ~s webbing; *[parachute]* ~ **d'ouverture automatique** ripcord; *(Anat)* ~ **abdominale** abdominal muscles → **lit**

sangler [sɑ̃gle] ▶ conjug 1 ◀ **[1]** VT [+ *cheval*] to girth; [+ *colis, corps*] to strap up; **sanglé dans son uniforme** done up *ou* strapped up tight in one's uniform **[2] se sangler** VPR to do one's belt up tight

sanglier [sɑ̃glije] NM (wild) boar

sanglot [sɑ̃glo] NM sob; **avec des ~s dans la voix** in a voice choked with emotion; **elle répondit dans un ~ que ...** she answered with a sob that ...; **elle essayait de me parler entre deux ~s** she tried to speak to me between sobs → **éclater**

sangloter [sɑ̃glɔte] ▶ conjug 1 ◀ VI to sob

sang-mêlé [sɑ̃mele] NMF INV *person of mixed blood*

sangria [sɑ̃gʀija] NF sangria

sangsue [sɑ̃sy] NF *(lit, fig)* leech

sanguin, e [sɑ̃gɛ̃, in] **[1]** ADJ **[a]** *[caractère, personne]* fiery; *[visage]* ruddy, sanguine *(frm)* **[b]** *(Anat)* blood *(épith)*; **produits ~s** blood products **[2] sanguine** NF **[a]** (**orange**) **~e** blood orange **[b]** (= *dessin*) red chalk drawing; (= *crayon*) red chalk, sanguine (*SPÉC*)

sanguinaire [sɑ̃ginɛʀ] **[1]** ADJ *[personne]* bloodthirsty, sanguinary *(littér)*; *[combat, dictature]* bloody, sanguinary *(littér)*; **monstre ~** bloodthirsty monster **[2]** NF (= *plante*) bloodroot, sanguinaria

sanguinolent, e [sɑ̃ginɔlɑ̃, ɑ̃t] ADJ *[crachat]* streaked with blood; *[plaie]* oozing blood *(attrib)*, bloody

Sanisette ® [sanizɛt] NF *coin-operated public toilet, Superloo* ® *(Brit)*

sanitaire [sanitɛʀ] **[1]** ADJ **[a]** *(Méd)* *[services, mesures]* health *(épith)*; *[conditions]* sanitary; **campagne ~** campaign to improve sanitary conditions → **cordon, train [b]** *(Plomberie)* **l'installation ~ est défectueuse** the bathroom plumbing is faulty; **appareil ~** bathroom *ou* sanitary appliance **[2]** NM **le ~** bathroom installations; **les ~s** (= *lieu*) the bathroom; (= *appareils*) the bathroom (suite); (= *plomberie*) the bathroom plumbing

San José [sɑ̃ʒoze] N San José

San Juan [sɑ̃ʒyɑ̃] N San Juan

sans [sɑ̃] **[1]** PRÉP **[a]** *(privation, absence)* without; **être ~ père/mère** to have no father/mother, be fatherless/motherless; **il est ~ secrétaire en ce moment** he is without a secretary at the moment, he has no secretary at the moment; **ils sont ~ argent** they have no money, they are penniless; **je suis sorti ~ chapeau ni manteau** I went out without a hat or coat *ou* with no hat or coat; **repas à 60 F ~ le vin** meal at 60 francs exclusive of wine *ou* not including wine; **on a retrouvé le sac, mais ~ l'argent** they found the bag minus the money *ou* but without the money; **être ~ abri** to be homeless

[b] *(manière, caractérisation)* without; **manger ~ fourchette** to eat without a fork; **boire ~ soif** to drink without being thirsty; **il est parti même ~ ou ~ seulement un mot de remerciement** he left without even a word of thanks; **l'histoire n'est pas ~ intérêt** the story is not devoid of interest *ou* is not without interest; **nous avons trouvé la maison ~ mal** we found his house with no difficulty *ou* with no trouble *ou* without difficulty; **la situation n'est pas ~ nous inquiéter** the situation is somewhat disturbing; **marcher ~ chaussures** to walk barefoot; **promenade ~ but** aimless walk; **une Europe ~ frontières** a Europe without borders; **je le connais, ~ plus** I know him but no more than that; **tu as aimé ce film? — ~ plus** did you like the film? — it was all right (I suppose)

[c] *(cause ou condition négative)* but for; **~ moi, il ne les aurait jamais retrouvés** but for me *ou* had it not been for me, he would never have found them; **~ cette réunion, il aurait pu partir ce soir** if it had not been for *ou* were it not for *ou* but for this meeting he could have left tonight; **~ sa présence d'esprit, il se tuait** had he not had such presence of mind *ou* without *ou* but for his presence of mind he would have been killed

[d] *(avec infin ou subj)* without; **il est entré ~ faire de bruit** he came in without making a noise *ou* noiselessly; **il est entré ~ (même ou seulement) que je l'entende** he came in without my (even) hearing him; **~ (même) que nous le sachions, il avait écrit** he had written without our (even) knowing; **je n'irai pas ~ être invité** I won't go without being invited *ou* unless I am invited; **~ que cela (ne) vous dérange** as long as *ou* provided that it doesn't put you out; **j'y crois ~ y croire** I believe it and I don't; **je ne suis pas ~ avoir des doutes sur son honnêteté** I have my doubts *ou* I am not without some doubts as to his honesty; **il ne se passe pas de jour ~ qu'il lui écrive** not a day passes without his writing to him → **attendre, dire, jamais, savoir**

[e] **non ~ peine** *ou* **mal** *ou* **difficulté** not without difficulty; **il l'a fait non ~ rechigner** he did it albeit reluctantly; **l'incendie a été maîtrisé,**

non ~ que les pompiers aient dû intervenir the fire was brought under control but not until the fire brigade were brought in

[2] ADV* **votre parapluie! vous alliez partir ~** your umbrella! you were going to go off without it; **il a oublié ses lunettes et il ne peut pas conduire ~** he's forgotten his glasses, and he can't drive without them

[3] sans ça* **sans quoi*** LOC CONJ otherwise; **si on m'offre un bon prix je vends ma voiture, ~ ça** *ou* **~ quoi je la garde** I'll sell my car if I'm offered a good price for it but otherwise *ou* if not, I'll keep it; **sois sage, ~ ça ...!** be good or else ...!

[4] COMP ▶ **sans domicile fixe** ADJ INV of no fixed abode ◊ NMF INV homeless person; **les ~ domicile fixe** the homeless ▶ **sans faute** *[téléphoner, prévenir]* without fail

sans-abri [sɑ̃zabʀi] NMF INV homeless person; **les ~** the homeless

San Salvador [sɑ̃salvadɔʀ] N San Salvador

sans-cœur [sɑ̃kœʀ] **[1]** ADJ INV heartless **[2]** NMF INV heartless person

sanscrit, e [sɑ̃skʀi, it] ADJ, NM = **sanskrit**

sans-culotte (*pl* **sans-culottes**) [sɑ̃kylɔt] NM *(Hist)* sans culotte

sans-emploi [sɑ̃zɑ̃plwa] NMF INV unemployed person; **les ~** the jobless, the unemployed; **le nombre des ~** the number of unemployed *ou* of people out of work, the jobless figure

sans-façon [sɑ̃fasɔ̃] NM INV casualness, offhandedness

sans-faute [sɑ̃fot] NM INV *(Équitation)* clear round; *(Sport)* faultless performance; **faire un ~** *(Équitation)* to do a clear round; *(Sport)* to put up a faultless performance, not to put a foot wrong; **son cursus scolaire est un ~** his academic record is impeccable; **jusqu'à présent, il a réussi un ~** *(gén)* he hasn't put a foot wrong so far; *(dans un jeu avec questions)* he has got all the answers right so far

sans-fil [sɑ̃fil] NM (= *téléphone*) cordless telephone; († = *radio*) wireless telegraphy; **le marché du ~** the cordless telephone market → **fil**

sans-filiste † (*pl* **sans-filistes**) [sɑ̃filist] NMF wireless enthusiast

sans-gêne [sɑ̃ʒɛn] **[1]** ADJ INV inconsiderate; **il est vraiment ~!** he's got a nerve!* **[2]** NM INV lack of consideration (for others), inconsiderateness; **elle est d'un ~ incroyable!** she's got an incredible nerve!* **[3]** NMF INV inconsiderate person

sans-grade [sɑ̃gʀad] NMF INV **[a]** *(Mil)* serviceman, enlisted man *(US)* **[b]** (= *subalterne*) underling, peon *(US)*; **les ~** *(dans une hiérarchie)* the underlings, the small fry; *(dans la société, un milieu)* the nobodies, the nonentities

sanskrit, e [sɑ̃skʀi, it] ADJ, NM Sanskrit

sans-le-sou* [sɑ̃l(ə)su] NMF INV **c'est un ~** he's penniless; **les ~** the have-nots

sans-logis [sɑ̃lɔʒi] NMF *(gén pl)* homeless person; **les ~** the homeless

sansonnet [sɑ̃sɔnɛ] NM starling → **roupie**

sans-papiers [sɑ̃papje] NMF INV *immigrant without the proper identity or working papers*

sans-parti [sɑ̃paʀti] NMF INV *(gén)* person who is not a member of a political party; (= *candidat*) independent (candidate)

sans-patrie [sɑ̃patʀi] NMF INV stateless person

sans-soin † [sɑ̃swɛ̃] NMF INV careless person

sans-souci † [sɑ̃susi] NMF INV carefree *ou* happy-go-lucky person

sans-travail [sɑ̃tʀavaj] NMF INV = **sans-emploi**

santal [sɑ̃tal] NM sandal, sandalwood; **bois de ~** sandalwood; **huile de ~** sandalwood oil

santé [sɑ̃te] NF **[a]** *[personne, esprit, pays]* health; **~ mentale** mental health; **en bonne/mauvaise ~** in good/bad health; **avoir des pro-**

blèmes *ou* ennuis de ~ to have health problems; la bonne ~ du franc the good health of the Franc; la mauvaise ~ financière d'une entreprise a company's poor financial health; c'est bon/mauvais pour la ~ it's good/bad for the health *ou* for you; être en pleine ~ to be in perfect health; avoir la ~ to be healthy, be in good health; (*fig* = *énergie*) il a la ~!* he must have lots of energy!; il n'a pas de ~ ◊ il a une petite ~ he's in poor health; avoir une ~ de fer to have an iron constitution; comment va la ~?* how are you doing?* *ou* keeping?* (*Brit*); meilleure ~! get well soon! → maison, raison, respirer

[b] (*Admin*) la ~ publique public health; (*Naut*) la ~ the quarantine service; (*Admin*) services de ~ health services; les dépenses de ~ health spending; le système de ~ the health system; les professions de ~ health (care) professions → ministère, ministre

[c] (*en trinquant*) à votre ~!◊~!* cheers!, (your) good health!; à la ~ de Paul! (here's) to Paul!; boire à la ~ de qn to drink to sb's health

santiag [sɑ̃tjag] NM cowboy boot

Santiago [sɑ̃tjago] N Santiago

santoméen, -enne [sɑ̃tɔmeɛ̃, ɛn] [1] ADJ of *ou* from São Tomé e Principe [2] **Santoméen(ne)** NM,F inhabitant of São Tomé e Principe

santon [sɑ̃tɔ̃] NM (ornamental) figure (*in a Christmas crib*)

São Tomé [saotɔme] N ~ et Principe São Tomé e Principe

saoudien, -ienne [saudjɛ̃, jɛn] [1] ADJ Saudi Arabian [2] **Saoudien(ne)** NM,F Saudi Arabian

saoul, e [su, sul] ADJ = soûl

saoulard, e: [sular, ard] NM,F = soûlard

sapajou [sapaʒu] NM (*Zool*) capuchin monkey, sapajou

sape [sap] NF [a] (*lit, fig* = *action*) undermining, sapping; (= *tranchée*) approach *ou* sapping trench; travail de ~ (*Mil*) sap; (*fig*) chipping away [b] (= *habits*) ~s: gear* (*NonC*), clobber: (*NonC*) (*Brit*)

saper [sape] ▶ conjug 1 ◀ [1] VT (*lit, fig*) to undermine, sap; ~ le moral à qn* to knock the stuffing out of sb* [2] se saper: VPR to get all dressed up*; il s'était sapé pour aller danser he'd got all dressed up to go dancing*; bien sapé well-dressed

saperlipopette [sapɛrlipɔpɛt] EXCL (*hum*) gad!† (*hum*), gadzooks!† (*hum*)

sapeur [sapœr] NM (*Mil*) sapper → fumer

sapeur-pompier (*pl* sapeurs-pompiers) [sapœrpɔ̃pje] NM firefighter, fireman (*Brit*)

saphène [safɛn] [1] ADJ saphenous [2] NF saphena

saphique [safik] ADJ, NM (*Littérat*) Sapphic

saphir [safir] [1] NM (= *pierre*) sapphire; (= *aiguille*) needle; [*tourne-disque*] stylus [2] ADJ INV sapphire

saphisme [safism] NM sapphism

sapide [sapid] ADJ sapid

sapidité [sapidite] NF sapidity → agent

sapience† [sapjɑ̃s] NF sapience (*frm*), wisdom

sapin [sapɛ̃] NM (= *arbre*) fir (tree); (= *bois*) fir; ~ de Noël Christmas tree; toux qui sent le ~* graveyard cough; costume en ~: wooden overcoat:; ça sent le ~ (*hum*)* he's (*ou* you've *etc*) got one foot in the grave

sapinière [sapinjɛr] NF fir plantation *ou* forest

saponacé, e [sapɔnase] ADJ saponaceous

saponaire [sapɔnɛr] NF saponin

saponification [sapɔnifikasjɔ̃] NF saponification

saponifier [sapɔnifje] ▶ conjug 7 ◀ VT to saponify

sapristi•† [sapristi] EXCL (*colère*) for God's sake!:; (*surprise*) good grief!*, (good) heavens!

saprophage [saprɔfaʒ] [1] ADJ saprophagous [2] NM saprophagous animal

saprophyte [saprɔfit] ADJ, NM (*Bio, Méd*) saprophyte

saquer• [sake] ▶ conjug 1 ◀ VT = sacquer

S.A.R. (ABRÉV = Son Altesse Royale) HRH

sarabande [sarabɑ̃d] NF (= *danse*) saraband; (* = *tapage*) racket, hullabaloo*; (= *succession*) jumble; faire la ~* to make a racket *ou* a hullabaloo*; les souvenirs/chiffres qui dansent la ~ dans ma tête the memories/figures whirling around in my head

Saragosse [saragɔs] N Saragossa

Sarajevo [sarajevo] N Sarajevo

sarbacane [sarbakan] NF (= *arme*) blowpipe, blowgun; (= *jouet*) peashooter

sarcasme [sarkasm] NM (= *ironie*) sarcasm; (= *remarque*) sarcastic remark

sarcastique [sarkastik] ADJ sarcastic

sarcastiquement [sarkastikmɑ̃] ADV sarcastically

sarcelle [sarsɛl] NF teal

sarclage [sarklaʒ] NM [*jardin, culture*] weeding; [*mauvaise herbe*] hoeing

sarcler [sarkle] ▶ conjug 1 ◀ VT [+ *jardin, culture*] to weed; [+ *mauvaise herbe*] to hoe

sarclette [sarklɛt] NF (small) hoe

sarcomateux, -euse [sarkɔmatø, øz] ADJ sarcomatoid, sarcomatous

sarcome [sarkom] NM sarcoma; ~ de Kaposi Kaposi's Sarcoma

sarcophage [sarkɔfaʒ] NM (*Antiq, Nucl, Phys*) sarcophagus

Sardaigne [sardɛɲ] NF Sardinia

sarde [sard] [1] ADJ Sardinian [2] NM (*Ling*) Sardinian [3] **Sarde** NMF Sardinian

sardine [sardin] NF [a] (= *poisson*) sardine; une boîte de ~s à l'huile a tin (*Brit*) *ou* can (*US*) of sardines in oil; serrés *ou* tassés comme des ~s (en boîte) packed *ou* squashed together like sardines (in a tin (*Brit*) *ou* can (*US*)) [b] (* *Camping*) tent peg [c] (*arg Mil*) stripe

sardinerie [sardinri] NF sardine cannery

sardinier, -ière [sardinje, jɛr] [1] ADJ sardine (*épith*) [2] NM,F (= *ouvrier*) sardine canner [3] NM (= *bateau*) sardine boat; (= *pêcheur*) sardine fisher

sardonique [sardɔnik] ADJ sardonic

sardoniquement [sardɔnikmɑ̃] ADV sardonically

sargasse [sargas] NF sargasso, gulfweed → mer

sari [sari] NM sari, saree

sarigue [sarig] NF (o)possum

SARL [ɛsaɛrɛl] NF (ABRÉV = société à responsabilité limitée) limited liability company; Raymond ~ Raymond Ltd (*Brit*), Raymond Inc. (*US*) → société

sarment [sarmɑ̃] NM (= *tige*) twining *ou* climbing stem, bine (*SPÉC*); ~ (de vigne) vine shoot

sarmenteux, -euse [sarmɑ̃tø, øz] ADJ [*plante*] climbing (*épith*); [*tige*] climbing (*épith*), twining (*épith*)

saroual [sarwal], **sarouel** [sarwɛl] NM baggy trousers (*worn in North Africa*)

sarrasin¹, e [sarazɛ̃, in] (*Hist*) [1] ADJ Saracen [2] **Sarrasin(e)** NM,F Saracen

sarrasin² [sarazɛ̃] NM (*Bot*) buckwheat

sarrau [saro] NM smock

sarriette [sarjɛt] NF savory

S.A.S. [ɛsaɛs] (ABRÉV = Son Altesse Sérénissime) HSH

sas [sas] NM [a] (*Espace, Naut*) airlock; [*écluse*] lock; [*banque*] double-entrance security door;

~ de décompression decompression airlock [b] (= *tamis*) sieve, screen

sashimi [saʃimi] NM sashimi

sassafras [sasafra] NM sassafras

sasser [sase] ▶ conjug 1 ◀ VT [+ *farine*] to sift, screen; [+ *péniche*] to take through a lock

Satan [satɑ̃] NM Satan

satané, e• [satane] ADJ blasted*, confounded*; c'est un ~ menteur! he's a damned liar!:; ~s embouteillages! blasted traffic jams!*

satanique [satanik] ADJ (= *de Satan*) satanic; (*fig*) [*plaisir, rire*] fiendish, satanic, wicked; [*ruse*] fiendish

satanisme [satanism] NM (= *culte*) Satanism; (*fig*) fiendishness, wickedness

satellisation [satelizasjɔ̃] NF [a] [*fusée*] (launching and) putting into orbit; programme de ~ satellite launching programme [b] [*pays*] satellization; la ~ de cet État est à craindre it is feared that this state will become a satellite

satelliser [satelize] ▶ conjug 1 ◀ VT [+ *fusée*] to put into orbit (round the earth); [+ *pays*] to make a satellite of, make into a satellite

satellitaire [satelitɛr] ADJ [*diffusion, système, téléphone*] satellite (*épith*) → antenne

satellite [satelit] NM [a] (*Astron, Espace, Pol*) satellite; ~ artificiel/naturel artificial/natural satellite; ~ de communication/télécommunications/radiodiffusion communications/telecommunications/broadcast satellite; ~ météorologique/d'observation weather/observation satellite; ~ antisatellite ◊ ~ d'intervention killer satellite; ~-espion spy satellite, spy-in-the-sky*; diffusion par ~ satellite broadcasting, broadcasting by satellite [b] (*en apposition*) [*chaîne, image, photo, liaison, pays, ville*] satellite (*épith*); ordinateur ~ satellite *ou* peripheral computer [c] (*aérogare*) satellite; ~ numéro 5 satellite number 5 [d] (*Tech*) (*pignon*) ~ bevel pinion

satiété [sasjete] NF satiation, satiety; (jusqu')à ~ [*répéter*] ad nauseam; [*boire/manger jusqu'à*] to eat/drink until one can eat/drink no more; j'en ai à ~ I've got more than enough

satin [satɛ̃] NM satin; ~ de laine/de coton wool/cotton satin; elle avait une peau de ~ her skin was (like) satin, she had satin(-smooth) skin

satiné, e [satine] (*ptp de* satiner) [1] ADJ [*aspect, tissu*] satiny, satin-like; [*peau*] satin (*épith*), satin-smooth; [*papier, peinture*] with a silk finish [2] NM satin finish *ou* satiny quality

satiner [satine] ▶ conjug 1 ◀ VT [+ *étoffe*] to put a satin finish on, satinize; [+ *papier, photo*] to give a silk finish to; la lumière satinait sa peau the light gave her skin a satin-like quality *ou* gloss

satinette [satinɛt] NF (*en coton et soie*) satinet; (*en coton*) sateen

satire [satir] NF (*gén*) satire; (*écrite*) satire, lampoon; faire la ~ de qch to satirize sth, lampoon sth

satirique [satirik] ADJ satirical, satiric

satiriquement [satirikmɑ̃] ADV satirically

satiriste [satirist] NMF satirist

satisfaction [satisfaksjɔ̃] NF [a] (= *contentement*) satisfaction; éprouver une certaine ~ à faire qch to feel a certain satisfaction in doing sth, get a certain satisfaction out of doing sth *ou* from doing sth; cet employé/cette lessive me donne (toute *ou* entière) ~ I'm (completely) satisfied with this employee/this washing powder; je vois avec ~ que ... I'm pleased *ou* gratified to see that ...; à la ~ générale *ou* de tous to everybody's satisfaction; à leur grande ~ to their great satisfaction; la ~ du devoir accompli the satisfaction of having done one's duty

[b] (= *sujet de contentement*) satisfaction; mon travail/mon fils me procure de grandes ~s my

job/my son gives me great satisfaction, I get a lot of satisfaction out of *ou* from my job/my son; **ma fille ne m'a donné que des ~s** my daughter has always been a (source of) great satisfaction to me; **c'est une ~ qu'il pourrait m'accorder** he might grant me that satisfaction; **~ d'amour-propre** gratification of one's self-esteem

[c] (*en réponse à une attente, des exigences*) **donner ~ à qn** to satisfy sb; **il ne faut pas donner ~ aux terroristes** we mustn't give in to the terrorists' demands; **obtenir ~** to get *ou* obtain satisfaction, get what one wants; **ils ont obtenu ~ (sur tous les points)** they got what they wanted (on all counts)

[d] (*frm = assouvissement*) [*faim, passion*] satisfaction, appeasement; [*soif*] satisfaction, quenching; [*envie*] satisfaction; [*désir*] satisfaction, gratification

[e] (*Rel*) satisfaction

satisfaire [satisfɛʀ] ▶conjug 60◀ [1] VT [+ *curiosité, personne*] to satisfy; [+ *désir*] to satisfy, fulfil (*Brit*), fulfill (*US*); [+ *faim, passion*] to satisfy, appease; [+ *soif*] to quench, satisfy; [+ *besoin, demande, revendications, goûts*] to meet, satisfy; [+ *clientèle*] to satisfy, please; **votre nouvel assistant vous satisfait-il ?** are you satisfied with your new assistant?; **j'espère que cette solution vous satisfait** I hope you find this solution satisfactory, I hope you are satisfied *ou* happy with this solution; **je suis désolé que vous n'en soyez pas satisfait** I am sorry it was not satisfactory *ou* you were not satisfied; **~ l'attente de qn** to come up to sb's expectations; (*Ind*) **arriver à ~ la demande** to keep up with demand

[2] **satisfaire à** VT INDIR [+ *désir*] to satisfy, fulfil (*Brit*), fulfill (*US*); [+ *engagement, promesse*] to fulfil (*Brit*), fulfill (*US*); [+ *demande, revendication, critères*] to meet, satisfy; [+ *condition, exigences*] to meet, fulfil (*Brit*), fulfill (*US*), satisfy; [+ *test de qualité*] to pass; **avez-vous satisfait à vos obligations militaires ?** have you completed your military service?; **cette installation ne satisfait pas aux normes** this installation does not comply with *ou* satisfy standard requirements

[3] **se satisfaire** VPR to be satisfied (*de* with); (*euph*) to relieve o.s.; **se ~ de peu** to be easily satisfied; (*hum*) **tu as vu son mari ?, elle se satisfait de peu !** have you seen her husband? she's not exactly choosy!*; **il ne se satisfait pas de mots, il a besoin d'agir** words aren't enough for him, he needs to act

satisfaisant, e [satisfəzɑ̃, ɑ̃t] ADJ (= *acceptable*) satisfactory; (= *qui fait plaisir*) satisfying; **de façon ~e** satisfactorily; **ces questions n'ont toujours pas reçu de réponses ~es** these questions have still not been answered satisfactorily; **son état est jugé ~** [*malade*] his condition is said to be satisfactory; **peu ~** [*bilan, résultats, solution, travail*] unsatisfactory

satisfait, e [satisfɛ, ɛt] (*ptp de* **satisfaire**) ADJ [*air, besoin, désir, personne*] satisfied; (*Comm*) **«~ ou remboursé»** "satisfaction or your money back"; **être ~ de** [+ *personne*] to be satisfied with; [+ *décision, solution*] to be satisfied with, be happy with *ou* about; [+ *soirée*] to be pleased with; **être ~ de soi** to be satisfied *ou* pleased with o.s.; **il est toujours très ~ de lui** he's so self-satisfied; **il est ~ de son sort** he is satisfied *ou* happy with his lot; (*iro*) **te voilà ~ !** are you satisfied?

satisfecit [satisfesit] NM INV (*Scol*) ≈ star, ≈ merit point; **je lui donne un ~ pour la façon dont il a mené l'affaire** I'll give him full marks (*Brit*) *ou* full points (*US*) for the way he conducted the business

satrape [satʀap] NM (*Hist*) satrap; (*littér = despote*) satrap, despot; (*menant grand train*) nabob

saturant, e [satyʀɑ̃, ɑ̃t] ADJ saturating; **vapeur ~e** saturated vapour

saturateur [satyʀatœʀ] NM [*radiateur*] humidifier; (*Sci*) saturator

saturation [satyʀasjɔ̃] NF (*gén, Sci*) saturation (**de** of); **arriver à ~** to reach saturation point; **à cause de la ~ des lignes téléphoniques** because the telephone lines are all engaged (*Brit*) *ou* busy (*US*); **pour éviter la ~ du réseau routier** to prevent the road network from getting clogged up *ou* becoming saturated; **j'en ai jusqu'à ~** I've had more than I can take

saturé, e [satyʀe] (*ptp de* **saturer**) ADJ [a] (*Chim*) [*solution*] saturated [b] (= *imprégné*) [*sol, terre*] saturated (**de** with) [c] (= *encombré*) [*autoroute*] heavily congested; [*marché*] saturated, glutted; (*Téléc*) [*réseau*] overloaded, saturated; [*standard, lignes*] jammed; (*Ordin*) [*mémoire*] exhausted [d] [*personne*] **je suis ~** (*par trop de travail*) I'm up to my eyes in work, I've got more work than I can cope with; **les gens sont ~s de publicité** people have had their fill of *ou* are sick of advertising; **j'ai mangé tant de fraises que j'en suis ~** I couldn't eat another strawberry, I've had so many [e] (*Peinture*) **couleur ~e** saturated colour (*Brit*) *ou* color (*US*)

saturer [satyʀe] ▶conjug 1◀ [1] VT [a] (*gén, Sci*) to saturate (**de** with); **~ les électeurs de promesses** to swamp the electors with promises [2] VI [a] [*appareil hi-fi*] to distort [b]* [*personne*] **après six heures de ce travail, je sature** after six hours of this work, I've had enough

saturnales [satyʀnal] NFPL (*lit*) Saturnalia; (*fig*) saturnalia

Saturne [satyʀn] [1] NM (*Myth*) Saturn [2] NF (*Astron*) Saturn; (*Pharm*) **extrait** *ou* **sel de saturne** lead acetate

saturnien, -ienne [satyʀnjɛ̃, jɛn] ADJ (*littér*) saturnine

saturnin, e [satyʀnɛ̃, in] ADJ saturnine

saturnisme [satyʀnism] NM lead poisoning, saturnism (*SPÉC*)

satyre [satiʀ] NM (*Myth, Zool*) satyr; (* = *obsédé*) sex maniac

satyrique [satiʀik] ADJ satyric

sauce [sos] NF [a] (*Culin*) sauce; [*salade*] dressing; (= *jus de viande*) gravy; **viande en ~** meat cooked in a sauce; **~ béarnaise/béchamel/blanche/moutarde/piquante/tomate** béarnaise/béchamel/white/mustard/piquant/tomato sauce; **~ vinaigrette** vinaigrette, French dressing (*Brit*); **~ à l'orange/aux câpres** orange/caper sauce; **~ chasseur/mousseline** sauce chasseur/mousseline; **~ madère/suprême/hollandaise** Madeira/suprême/hollandaise sauce

[b] * (= *remplissage*) padding*; (= *présentation*) **reprendre un vieux discours en changeant la ~** to take an old speech and dress it up; **c'est la même chose avec une autre ~** same meat, different gravy; **il faudrait rallonger la ~ pour ce devoir** you'll have to pad out this essay

[c] (*loc*) **à quelle ~ allons-nous être mangés ?** I wonder what fate has in store for us; **mettre qn à toutes les ~s** to make sb do any job going*; **mettre un exemple à toutes les ~s** to turn *ou* adapt an example to fit any case; **mettre la ~** (*Aut*) to step on the gas*; (*gén* = *se dépêcher*) to step on it*; (*Aut, gén*) **mettre toute la ~** to go flat out; **recevoir la ~*** to get soaked *ou* drenched

[d] (= *crayon à estomper*) soft black crayon

saucée* [sose] NF downpour; **recevoir** *ou* **prendre une ~** to get soaked *ou* drenched

saucer [sose] ▶conjug 3◀ VT [+ *assiette*] to mop up the sauce from; [+ *pain*] to use to mop up the sauce; **prends du pain pour ~** have some bread to mop up the sauce; **se faire ~*** ◊ **être saucé*** to get soaked *ou* drenched

saucier [sosje] NM sauce chef *ou* cook

saucière [sosjɛʀ] NF (*gén*) sauceboat; [*jus de viande*] gravy boat

sauciflard: [sosiflaʀ] NM (*slicing*) sausage, ≈ salami

saucisse [sosis] NF [a] (*Culin*) sausage; **~ de Morteau** type of smoked sausage; **~ de Strasbourg** type of beef sausage; **~ de Francfort** frankfurter → **attacher, chair** [b] (*Aviat*) sausage [c] (= *idiot*) **(grande) ~:** nincompoop*, great ninny*

saucisson [sosisɔ̃] NM [a] (*Culin*) sausage (*eaten cold in slices*); **~ à l'ail** garlic sausage; **~ sec** (*dry*) pork and beef sausage; **~ pur porc** 100% pork sausage → **ficeler** [b] (= *pain*) (cylindrical) loaf [c] [*poudre*] canvas tube filled with gunpowder, saucisson (*US*)

saucissonnage* [sosisɔnaʒ] NM [*livre, émission*] chopping up; **les gens se plaignent du ~ des émissions par la publicité** people are complaining about television programmes being chopped up *ou* constantly interrupted by commercial breaks

saucissonné, e* [sosisɔne] (*ptp de* **saucissonner**) ADJ (= *ligoté*) trussed up

saucissonner [sosisɔne] ▶conjug 1◀ [1] VI (†,*) (= *pique-niquer*) to (have a) picnic [2] VT [a] (*hum* = *ligoter*) [+ *personne*] to truss up [b] (= *découper*) [+ *livre, émission*] to chop up; [+ *entreprise, territoire*] to carve *ou* slice up (**en** into); **des films saucissonnés par la publicité** films chopped up by commercials

sauf[1], sauve [sof, sov] ADJ [*personne*] unharmed, unhurt; [*honneur*] intact; **il a eu la vie sauve** his life was spared; **laisser la vie sauve à qn** to spare sb's life; **il dut à sa franchise d'avoir la vie sauve** he owed his life to his frankness, it was thanks to his frankness that his life was spared → **sain**

sauf[2] [sof] PRÉP [a] (= *à part*) except, but, save (*frm*); **tout le monde ~ lui** everyone except *ou* but *ou* save (*frm*) him; **~ avis contraire** unless you hear *ou* are told otherwise, unless you hear to the contrary; **~ erreur de ma part** if I'm not mistaken; **~ imprévu** barring accidents, unless anything unforeseen happens; (*Jur*) **~ accord** *ou* **convention contraire** unless otherwise agreed; **~ dispositions contraires** except as otherwise provided; **~ cas exceptionnel** except in exceptional circumstances; **le repas était excellent ~ le dessert** *ou* **pour ce qui est du dessert** the meal was excellent except for *ou* apart from *ou* aside from (*surtout US*) the dessert

[b] (*avec conj*) **~ si** unless; **nous irons demain, ~ s'il pleut** we'll go tomorrow unless it rains; **nous sortons tout le temps ~ quand il pleut** we always go out except when it's raining; **~ que** except that

[c] (*loc: littér*) **il accepte de nous aider, ~ à nous critiquer si nous échouons** he agrees to help us even if he does (reserve the right to) criticize us if we fail; **~ le respect que je vous dois** ◊ **~ votre respect** with all due respect

sauf-conduit (*pl* **sauf-conduits**) [sofkɔ̃dɥi] NM safe-conduct

sauge [soʒ] NF (*Culin*) sage; (*ornementale*) salvia

saugrenu, e [sogʀəny] ADJ preposterous, ludicrous; **voilà une question bien ~e !** what a ridiculous question!; **quelle idée ~e !** what a ridiculous idea!

Saül [sayl] NM Saul

saulaie [sole] NF willow plantation

saule [sol] NM willow (tree); **~ blanc/pleureur** white/weeping willow

saumâtre [somɑtʀ] ADJ [*eau*] brackish; [*goût*] briny; [*humeur, impression, plaisanterie*] nasty, unpleasant; **il l'a trouvée ~*** he was not amused

saumon [somɔ̃] [1] NM [a] (*Zool*) salmon; **~ fumé** smoked salmon, lox (*US*); **~ cru mariné à l'aneth** gravadlax, gravlax, salmon marinated in dill [b] (*Tech*) pig [2] ADJ INV salmon (pink)

saumoné, e [somɔne] ADJ [*couleur*] salmon (pink) → **truite**

saumure [somyʀ] NF brine

saumuré, e [somyʀe] ADJ [hareng] pickled (in brine)

sauna [sona] NM sauna

saunier [sonje] NM (= ouvrier) worker in a salt-works; (= exploitant) salt merchant

saupiquet [sopikɛ] NM (= sauce, ragoût) spicy sauce or stew

saupoudrage [sopudʀaʒ] NM [a] (gén) sprinkling; (Culin) sprinkling, dusting [b] [crédits, subventions] spreading thinly

saupoudrer [sopudʀe] ▶ conjug 1 ◀ VT (gén) to sprinkle; (Culin) to sprinkle, dust (de with); [+ crédits] to spread thinly, give sparingly; **se les mains de talc** to sprinkle talc on one's hands; **il saupoudre sa conversation de mots anglais** he peppers ou sprinkles his conversation with English words

saupoudreuse [sopudʀøz] NF (sugar ou flour etc) dredger

saur [sɔʀ] ADJ M → hareng

saurer [sɔʀe] ▶ conjug 1 ◀ VT to smoke, cure

saurien [sɔʀjɛ̃] NM saurian; **~s** Sauria (SPÉC), saurians

saurissage [sɔʀisaʒ] NM smoking, curing

saut [so] [1] NM [a] (lit, fig = bond) jump, leap; (Sport) **~ avec/sans élan** running/standing jump; **faire un ~** to (make a) jump ou leap; **faire un ~ dans l'inconnu/le vide** to (make a) leap into the unknown/the void; **le véhicule fit un ~ de 100 mètres dans le ravin** the vehicle fell ou dropped 100 metres into the ravine; **se lever d'un ~** to jump ou leap up, jump ou leap to one's feet; **quittons Louis XIV et faisons un ~ d'un siècle** let us leave Louis XIV and jump forward a century; (fig) **progresser ou avancer par ~s** to go forward by ou in stages [b] (Sport) jumping; **épreuves de ~** jumping events → triple [c] (Géog = cascade) waterfall, falls [d] (Math, Ordin) jump [e] (loc) **faire qch au ~ du lit** to do sth as soon as one gets up ou gets out of bed; **prendre qn au ~ du lit** to find sb just out of bed (when one calls); **faire le ~** to take the plunge; **faire le grand ~** (= mourir) to pass on; **faire un ~ chez qn** to pop over ou round (Brit) to sb's place*, drop in on sb; **faire un ~ à la banque** to drop in at the bank; **il a fait un ~ jusqu'à Bordeaux** he made a flying visit to Bordeaux

[2] COMP ▶ **saut de l'ange** (Natation) swallow dive (Brit), swan dive (US) ▶ **saut de carpe** jack-knife dive, pike (Brit) ▶ **saut de chat** pas de chat ▶ **saut en chute libre** (= sport) free-fall parachuting; (= bond) free-fall jump ▶ **saut en ciseaux** scissors (jump) ▶ **saut à la corde** skipping (Brit), jumping rope (US) ▶ **saut à l'élastique** bungee jumping ▶ **saut groupé** tuck ▶ **saut de haies** hurdling ▶ **saut en hauteur** (= sport) high jump; (= bond) (high) jump ▶ **saut en longueur** (= sport) long jump; (= bond) (long) jump ▶ **saut de la mort** leap of death ▶ **saut de ligne** (Ordin) line break ▶ **saut de page** page break ▶ **saut en parachute** (= sport) parachuting, parachute jumping; (= bond) parachute jump ▶ **saut à la perche** (= sport) pole vaulting; (= bond) (pole) vault ▶ **saut périlleux** somersault ▶ **saut à pieds joints** standing jump ▶ **saut de puce : l'avion fait des ~s de puce** the plane makes several stopovers ▶ **saut en rouleau** western roll ▶ **saut de séquence** (Ordin) jump ▶ **saut à skis** (= sport) skijumping; (= bond) jump

saut-de-lit (pl sauts-de-lit) [sod(ə)li] NM negligée

saut-de-loup (pl sauts-de-loup) [sod(ə)lu] NM (wide) ditch

saut-de-mouton (pl sauts-de-mouton) [sod(ə)mutɔ̃] NM flyover (Brit), overpass (US)

saute [sot] NF sudden change; **~ de vent** sudden change (in the direction) of the wind; **~ d'humeur** sudden change of mood; **~ de température** jump in temperature; (TV) **pour empêcher les ~s d'images** to stop the picture jumping, keep the picture steady

sauté, e [sote] (ptp de **sauter**) ADJ, NM sauté; **~ de veau** sauté of veal

saute-mouton [sotmutɔ̃] NM INV leapfrog; **jouer à ~** (lit) to play leapfrog; (fig) **le scénario joue à ~ par dessus les siècles** the film script leapfrogs from one century to the next

sauter [sote] ▶ conjug 1 ◀ [1] VI [a] [personne] to jump, leap (dans into, par-dessus over); (vers le bas) to jump ou leap (down); (vers le haut) to jump ou leap (up); [oiseau] to hop; [insecte] to jump, hop; [kangourou] to jump; **~ à pieds joints** to make a standing jump; (fig) **~ à pieds joints dans qch** to jump into sth with both feet, rush headlong into sth; **~ à cloche-pied** to hop; **~ à la corde** to skip (Brit), jump rope (US); **~ à la perche** to pole-vault; **~ en parachute** (gén, Sport) to parachute, make a parachute jump; [parachutistes] to parachute, be dropped (sur over); (en cas d'accident) to bale out (Brit), bail out (US), make an emergency (parachute) jump; **~ en ciseaux** to do a scissors jump; **~ en hauteur/en longueur** to do the high/the long jump; **faire ~ un enfant sur ses genoux** to bounce ou dandle† a child on one's knee; **les cahots faisaient ~ les passagers** the passengers jolted ou bounced along over the bumps; **il sauta de la table** he jumped ou leapt (down) off ou from the table; **~ en l'air** ou **au plafond** (de colère) to hit the roof*; (de joie) to jump for joy; (de surprise, de peur) to jump (out of one's skin); (lit, fig) **~ de joie** to jump for joy

[b] (= se précipiter) **~ (à bas) du lit** to jump ou spring out of bed; **~ en selle** to jump ou leap ou spring into the saddle; **~ à la gorge de qn** to fly ou leap at sb's throat; **~ au cou de qn** to fly into sb's arms; **~ dans un taxi/un autobus** to jump ou leap into a taxi/onto a bus; **~ par la fenêtre** to jump ou leap out of the window; **~ d'un train en marche** to jump ou leap from a moving train; **~ sur une occasion/une proposition** to jump ou leap at an opportunity/an offer; **il m'a sauté dessus** he pounced on me; (fig) **saute-lui dessus* quand il sortira du bureau pour lui demander ...** grab him when he comes out of the office and ask him ...; **va faire tes devoirs, et que ça saute !*** go and do your homework and be quick about it!; **il est malade, cela saute aux yeux** he's ill — it sticks out a mile ou it's (quite) obvious; **sa malhonnêteté saute aux yeux** his dishonesty sticks out a mile ou is (quite) obvious

[c] (indiquant la discontinuité) to jump, leap; **~ d'un sujet à l'autre** to jump ou skip from one subject to another

[d] [bouchon] to pop ou fly out; [bouton] to fly ou pop off; [chaîne de vélo] to come off; * [classe, cours] to be cancelled; **faire ~ un cours** to cancel a class ou a lecture; **faire ~ une crêpe** to toss a pancake; **faire ~ une serrure** to burst ou break open a lock; (fig) **faire ~ le(s) verrou(s)** to break down the barrier(s); **faire ~ une contravention*** to get a fine taken care of ou quashed (Brit)

[e] (= exploser) [bâtiment, bombe, pont] to blow up, explode; (Élec) [fil, circuit] to fuse; [fusible] to blow; **~ sur une mine** [personne] to step on a mine; [véhicule] to go over a mine; **faire ~** [+ train, édifice] to blow up; (Élec) [+ plombs] to blow; **faire ~ une mine** (pour la détruire) to blow up a mine; (pour détruire un bâtiment) to set off a mine; **il s'est fait ~ avec les otages** he blew himself up with the hostages; **se faire ~ la cervelle*** ou **le caisson*** to blow one's brains out*; (Casino) **faire ~ la banque** to break the bank; **les plombs ont sauté** the fuses have

blown ou gone

[f] (* = être renvoyé) [directeur] to get fired, get the push* ou the sack* (Brit); [gouvernement] to get kicked out*; **faire ~ qn** (gén) to fire sb, give sb the push* ou the sack* (Brit); [+ gouvernement] to kick out*

[g] (Culin) **faire ~** to sauté, (shallow) fry

[h] (= clignoter) [paupière] to twitch; [image de télévision] to flicker, jump

[2] VT [a] (= franchir) [+ obstacle, mur] to jump (over), leap (over); **il saute 5 mètres** he can jump 5 metres; **il sauta le fossé d'un bond** he jumped ou cleared the ditch with one bound; (fig) **~ le pas** to take the plunge

[b] (= omettre) [+ étape, page, repas] to skip, miss; (Scol) **~ une classe** to skip a year; **ces caractères héréditaires peuvent ~ une génération** these hereditary characteristics can skip a generation; **on la saute ici !*** we're starving to death here!*

[c] (‡ = avoir des rapports sexuels avec) to fuck‡*, screw‡*; **elle s'est fait ~ par Pierre‡** she had it off with Pierre‡, she got laid by Pierre‡

sauterelle [sotʀɛl] NF [a] (gén) grasshopper; (= criquet) locust; (lit, fig) **nuage** ou **nuée de ~s** swarm of locusts; (fig) **(grande) ~*** beanpole (Brit), string bean (US) [b] (= fausse équerre) bevel; (= appareil de manutention) conveyor belt

sauterie† [sotʀi] NF party, thrash* (Brit); **je donne une petite ~ demain** I'm giving ou throwing a little party tomorrow

saute-ruisseau (pl saute-ruisseaux) [sotʀɥiso] NM († ou littér) errand boy, office boy (in a lawyer's office)

sauteur, -euse [sotœʀ, øz] [1] ADJ [insecte] jumping (épith); [oiseau] hopping (épith) → **scie** [2] NM,F [a] (= athlète, cheval) jumper [b] (* = fumiste) unreliable person [3] **sauteuse** NF (Culin) high-sided frying pan [b] (* = dévergondée) floozy* [4] COMP ▶ **sauteur en hauteur** high jumper ▶ **sauteur en longueur** long jumper ▶ **sauteur à la perche** pole vaulter ▶ **sauteur à skis** skijumper

sautillant, e [sotijɑ̃, ɑ̃t] ADJ [démarche] hopping, skipping; [oiseau] hopping; [enfant] skipping; (sur un pied) hopping; [musique] bouncy; [style] jumpy, jerky; **les images ~es des films d'époque** the flickering images of vintage films

sautillement [sotijmɑ̃] NM [oiseau] hopping; [enfant] skipping; (sur un pied) hopping

sautiller [sotije] ▶ conjug 1 ◀ VI [oiseau] to hop; [enfant] to skip; (sur un pied) to hop

sautoir [sotwaʀ] NM [a] (Bijouterie) chain; **~ de perles** string of pearls; **porter qch en ~** to wear sth (on a chain) round one's neck [b] (Sport) jumping pit [c] (Hér) saltire; **épées en ~** crossed swords

sauvage [sovaʒ] [1] ADJ [a] [animal, plante, fleur, lieu] wild; [peuplade] primitive, savage; **côte ~** wild coast; **enfant ~** wild child; **vivre à l'état ~** to live wild; **retourner à l'état ~** [jardin] to go wild; [animal] to revert to its wild state → **soie¹** [b] (= farouche) [animal] wild; [personne] unsociable [c] (= brutal) [cri] wild; [conduite] savage, wild; [combat] savage [d] (= illégal) [vente] unauthorized; [concurrence] unfair; [crèche, école] unofficial; [urbanisation] unplanned; [immigration, importations] illegal; [capitalisme, libéralisme] unrestrained, untrammeled; **faire du camping ~** (= illégal) to camp on unauthorized sites; (dans la nature) to camp in the wild, go wilderness camping (US); **décharge ~** illicit rubbish (Brit) ou garbage (US) dump; **il a été condamné pour affichage ~** he was prosecuted for flyposting → **grève, parking**

[2] NMF [a] (= solitaire) recluse; **vivre en ~** to live a secluded life, live as a recluse

b (= *brute*) brute, savage; **mœurs de ~s** brutish *ou* savage ways

c (= *indigène*) savage; **on n'est pas des ~s !*** we're not savages!

sauvagement [sovaʒmã] ADV [*frapper, tuer*] savagely, brutally

sauvageon, -onne [sovaʒɔ̃, ɔn] **1** NM,F little savage **2** NM wild stock (*for grafting*)

sauvagerie [sovaʒʀi] NF (= *cruauté*) savagery, savageness, brutality; (= *insociabilité*) unsociability, unsociableness

sauvagin, e [sovaʒɛ̃, in] **1** ADJ [*odeur, goût*] of wildfowl **2 sauvagine** NF wildfowl; **chasse à la ~e** wildfowling

sauve [sov] ADJ F → **sauf¹**

sauvegarde¹ [sovgaʀd] NF **a** (= *action*) [*droits, emploi, environnement*] protection, safeguarding; [*dignité, réputation*] protecting, safeguarding; [*ordre public, paix*] upholding, maintenance; (*Ordin*) saving; **sous la ~ de** under the protection of; **clause de ~** safety clause; **la ~ des droits de l'homme** the protection of human rights, safeguarding human rights; (*Ordin*) **faire la ~ d'un fichier** to save a file; (*Ordin*) **de ~** [*copie, disquette, fichier*] backup (*épith*) **b** (= *garantie*) safeguard; **être la ~ de** to safeguard, be the safeguard of *ou* for

sauvegarde² [sovgaʀd] NF (*Naut*) protective rope

sauvegarder [sovgaʀde] ▶conjug 1◀ VT [+ *droits, emploi, environnement, dignité, réputation*] to protect, safeguard; [+ *ordre public, paix*] to uphold, maintain; (*Ordin*) to save

sauve-qui-peut [sovkipø] NM INV (= *cri* of) run for your life; (= *panique*) stampede, mad rush

sauver [sove] ▶conjug 1◀ **1** VT **a** (= *épargner la mort, la faillite à*) to save; (= *porter secours à*) to rescue; **elle est sauvée !** [*malade*] she's come through!; [*accidentée, otage*] she's been rescued!; **nous sommes sauvés !*** we're saved!; **~ qn/qch de** [+ *danger, désastre*] to save *ou* rescue sb/sth from; **un mot de lui peut tout ~** a word from him can save the day *ou* situation **b** (= *sauvegarder*) [+ *biens, cargaison, mobilier*] to salvage, save, rescue; [+ *honneur, emplois, planète, processus de paix*] to save **c** (*Rel*) [+ *âme, pécheurs*] to save **d** (= *racheter*) to save, redeem; **ce sont les illustrations qui sauvent le livre** it's the illustrations which save *ou* redeem the book, the illustrations are the redeeming feature *ou* the saving grace of the book **e** (*loc*) **~ la vie à *ou* de qn** to save sb's life; **~ sa peau*** *ou* **sa tête*** to save one's skin *ou* hide*; (*fig*) **~ les meubles*** to salvage *ou* save something from the wreckage; **~ la situation** to save *ou* retrieve the situation; **~ les apparences** to keep up appearances; **~ la face** to save face; **il m'a sauvé la mise** he bailed me out, he got me out of a tight corner; **être sauvé par le gong** [*boxeur, candidat*] to be saved by the bell

2 se sauver VPR **a** (= *s'enfuir*) to run away (**de** from); (* = *partir*) to be off*, get going; **il s'est sauvé à toutes jambes** he ran away as fast as his legs could carry him; **sauve-toi*, il est déjà 8 heures** you'd better be off* *ou* get going, it's already 8 o'clock; **bon, je me sauve*** right, I'm off*; **vite, le lait se sauve*** quick, the milk's boiling over; **sauve qui peut !** run for your life! → **sauve-qui-peut**

b se ~ de [+ *danger, désastre*] to escape

sauvetage [sov(ə)taʒ] NM **a** [*personnes*] rescue; (*moral*) salvation; [*biens*] salvaging; **~ en mer/montagne** sea/mountain rescue; **le ~ des naufragés** rescuing the survivors of the shipwreck; **opérer le ~ de** [+ *personnes*] to rescue; [+ *biens*] to salvage; **de ~** [*matériel, équipe*] rescue (*épith*); **opération de ~** [*personnes*] rescue operation; [*biens*] salvage operation; (*Écon*) **plan de ~ d'une entreprise** rescue plan for a firm → **bateau, bouée, canot** etc **b** (= *tech-*

nique) **le ~** life-saving; **cours de ~** life-saving lessons

sauveteur [sov(ə)tœʀ] NM rescuer

sauvette* [sovɛt] ◆ **à la sauvette** LOC ADV (= *vite*) hastily, hurriedly; (= *en cachette*) on the sly; **ils se sont mariés à la ~** they married in haste; **la réforme a été votée à la ~** the reform was rushed through parliament; **images tournées à la ~** pictures shot on the sly; **vente à la ~** (unauthorized) street hawking *ou* peddling; **vendre qch à la ~** to hawk *ou* peddle sth on the streets (*without authorization*); **vendeur** *ou* **marchand à la ~** street hawker; **acheter son billet à un revendeur à la ~** to buy one's ticket from an unauthorized source *ou* from a ticket tout (*Brit*)

sauveur [sovœʀ] **1** ADJ M **le Dieu ~** God the Saviour (*Brit*) *ou* Savior (*US*) **2** NM saviour (*Brit*), savior (*US*); (*Rel*) **le Sauveur** the Saviour; (*hum*) **tu es mon ~ !** you're my saviour!

sauvignon [sovinɔ̃] NM Sauvignon (*type of wine from the Loire valley*)

SAV [esave] NM (ABRÉV = **service après-vente**) → **service**

savamment [savamã] ADV (= *avec érudition*) learnedly; (= *adroitement*) cleverly, skilfully (*Brit*), skillfully (*US*); (= *par expérience*) **j'en parle ~** I know what I'm talking about; **~ dosé/entretenu/orchestré** skilfully controlled/maintained/orchestrated

savane [savan] NF savannah; (* *Can*) swamp

savant, e [savã, ãt] **1** ADJ **a** (= *érudit*) [*personne*] learned, scholarly; [*édition*] scholarly; [*mot, société*] learned; **être ~ en qch** to be learned in sth; (*hum*) **c'est trop ~ pour moi** [*discussion, livre*] it's too highbrow for me; [*problème*] it's too difficult *ou* complicated for me **b** (= *habile*) [*arrangement, dosage, stratagème*] clever, skilful (*Brit*), skillful (*US*); **le ~ désordre de sa tenue** the studied carelessness of his dress **c** [*chien, puce*] performing (*épith*) **2** NM (*sciences*) scientist; (*lettres*) scholar

savarin [savaʀɛ̃] NM (*Culin*) savarin

savate* [savat] NF **a** (= *pantoufle*) worn-out old slipper; (= *chaussure*) worn-out old shoe; **être en ~s** to be in one's slippers → **traîner** **b** (* = *maladroit*) clumsy idiot *ou* oaf **c** (*Sport*) **la ~** kickboxing

savetier †† [sav(ə)tje] NM cobbler †

saveur [savœʀ] NF (*lit* = *goût*) flavour (*Brit*), flavor (*US*); (*fig* = *piment*) savour (*Brit*), savor (*US*); **sans ~** flavourless (*Brit*), flavorless (*US*); **venez déguster les ~s de notre terroir** come and taste our local specialities

Savoie [savwa] NF (= *région*) **la ~** Savoy → **biscuit**

▼ **savoir** [savwaʀ] ▶conjug 32◀ **1** VT **a** (*gén*) to know; **~ le nom/l'adresse de qn** to know sb's name/address; **c'est difficile à ~** it's difficult to know *ou* ascertain; **je ne savais quoi** *ou* **que dire/faire** I didn't know what to say/do; **oui, je (le) sais** yes, I know; **je savais qu'elle était malade** ◊ **je la savais malade** I knew (that) she was ill; **on ne lui savait pas de parents/de fortune** we didn't know whether *ou* if he had any relatives/money; (*en fait il en a*) we didn't know (that) he had any relatives/money; **savez-vous quand/comment il vient ?** do you know when/how he's coming?; **vous savez la nouvelle ?** have you heard *ou* do you know the news?; **elle sait cela par** *ou* **de son boucher** she heard it from her butcher; **tout le village sut bientôt la catastrophe** the whole village soon knew *ou* heard about the disaster; **il ne savait pas s'il devait accepter** he didn't know whether to accept (or not); **je crois ~ que ...** I believe *ou* understand that ..., I am led to believe *ou* understand that ...; **je n'en sais rien** I don't know, I have no idea; **il ment — qu'en savez-vous ?** he is lying — how do you know?; **leur politique ne marchera ja-**

mais — qu'en sais-tu ? their policy will never work — what do you know about it?; **je voudrais en ~ davantage** I'd like to know more about it; **il nous a fait ~ que ...** he informed us *ou* let us know that ...; **ça se saurait si c'était vrai** if it was true people would know about it; **ça finira bien par se ~** it'll get out in the end

b (= *avoir des connaissances sur*) to know; **~ le grec/son rôle/sa leçon** to know Greek/one's part/one's lesson; **dites-nous ce que vous savez de l'affaire** tell us what you know about *ou* of the matter; **en ~ trop (long)** to know too much; **il croit tout ~** he thinks he knows everything *ou* knows it all; (*péj*) **Monsieur** (*ou* **Madame** *ou* **Mademoiselle**) **je-sais-tout*** smart-alec(k)*, know-all; **tu en sais, des choses*** you certainly know a thing or two, don't you!; **il ne sait ni A ni B** ◊ **il ne sait rien de rien** he hasn't a clue about anything

c (*avec infin* = *être capable de*) to know how to; **elle sait lire et écrire** she can read and write, she knows how to read and write; **il ne sait pas nager** he can't swim, he doesn't know how to swim; **~ plaire** to know how to please; **il sait parler aux enfants** he's good at talking to children, he knows how to talk to children, he can talk to children; **elle saura bien se défendre** she'll be quite capable of looking after herself; **il sait y faire** he's good at getting things his own way; **il a toujours su y faire** *ou* **s'y prendre** he's always known how to go about things (the right way); **il sait écouter** he's a good listener; **il faut ~ attendre/se contenter de peu** you have to learn to be patient *ou* to wait/be content with little; (*littér hum*) **on ne saurait penser à tout** you can't think of everything; **je ne saurais vous exprimer toute ma gratitude** I shall never be able to express my gratitude; **je ne saurais pas vous répondre/vous renseigner** I'm afraid I can't answer you/give you any information; **ces explications ont su éclairer et rassurer** these explanations proved both enlightening and reassuring → **vivre**

d (= *se rendre compte de*) to know; **il ne sait plus ce qu'il dit** he doesn't know *ou* realize what he's saying, he isn't aware of what he's saying; **je ne sais plus ce que je dis** I no longer know what I'm saying; **il ne sait pas ce qu'il veut** he doesn't know what he wants, he doesn't know his own mind; **il se savait très malade** he knew he was very ill; **elle sait bien qu'il ment** she's well aware of the fact that he's lying, she knows very well *ou* full well that he's lying; **sans le ~** (= *sans s'en rendre compte*) without knowing *ou* realizing (it), unknowingly; (= *sans le faire exprès*) unwittingly, unknowingly; **c'est un artiste sans le ~** he's an artist but he doesn't know it

e (*loc*) **qui sait ?** who knows?; **et que sais-je encore** and I don't know what else; **(à) ~ si ça va lui plaire !** there's no knowing whether he'll like it or not!; **tu veux celui-ci ou celui-là, faudrait ~ !** do you want this one or that one, make up your mind, will you?; **ils vont renouveler nos contrats ou pas, faudrait ~ !** so are they going to renew our contracts or not, it's about time we knew!; **je sais ce que je sais** I know what I know; **je sais bien, mais ...** I know, but ...; **et puis, tu sais, nous serons très heureux de t'aider** and you know, we'll be very happy to help you; **il nous a emmenés je ne sais où** he took us goodness knows where; **je ne sais qui de ses amis m'a dit que ...** one of his friends, whose name I forget, told me that ...; **il y a je ne sais combien de temps qu'il ne l'a vue** it's been I don't know how long since he last saw her, I don't how long it is since he (last) saw her; **cette pièce avait je ne sais quoi de sinistre** the room had something sinister about it; **elle ne sait pas quoi faire** *ou* **elle ne sait que faire pour l'aider/le consoler** she's at a loss to know how to help him/comfort him; **il n'a**

rien voulu ~ he didn't want to know; **on ne sait jamais** you never know; **(pour autant) que je sache** as far as I know, to the best of my knowledge; **je ne l'y ai pas autorisé, que je sache** I didn't give him permission to do so, as far as I know; **pas que je sache** not as far as I know, not to my knowledge; **je ne sache pas que je vous ai invité !** I'm not aware that *ou* I didn't know that I invited you!; **sachons-le bien, si …** let's be quite clear, if …; **sachez (bien) que jamais je n'accepterai !** I'll have you know *ou* let me tell you I shall never accept!; **oui, mais sachez qu'à l'origine, c'est elle-même qui ne le voulait pas** yes, but you should know that it was she who didn't want to in the first place; **à ~** that is, namely, i.e.; *(hum)* **l'objet/la personne que vous savez sera là demain** you-know-what/you-know-who will be there tomorrow; *(frm)* **vous n'êtes pas sans ~ que …** you are not *ou* will not be unaware (of the fact) that … *(frm)*, you will not be ignorant of the fact that … *(frm)*; **il m'a su gré/il ne m'a su aucun gré de l'avoir averti** he was grateful to me/he wasn't in the least grateful to me for having warned him; **il ne savait à quel saint se vouer** he didn't know which way to turn; **si je savais, j'irais la chercher** if I knew (for sure) *ou* if I could be sure, I would go and look for her; **si j'avais su** had I known, if I had known; **elle ne savait où donner de la tête** she didn't know whether she was coming or going; **il ne savait où se mettre** he didn't know where to put himself; **tout ce que vous avez toujours voulu ~ sur …** everything you always wanted to know about … → **dieu, qui**

[2] NM **le ~** learning, knowledge

savoir-faire [savwaʀfɛʀ] NM INV *(gén)* know-how*; *(dans un métier)* expertise; **acquérir un ~** to acquire expertise; **il a beaucoup/il manque de ~ avec les enfants** he's very good/isn't very good with children

savoir-vivre [savwaʀvivʀ] NM INV manners; **il n'a aucun ~** he has no manners; **les règles du ~** the rules of (social) etiquette

savon [savɔ̃] NM [a] (= *matière*) soap *(NonC)*; (= *morceau*) bar of soap; **~ liquide/noir** liquid/soft soap; **~ à barbe/de toilette/de Marseille** shaving/toilet/household soap; **~ en paillettes/en poudre** soap flakes/powder → **bulle, pain** [b] (* = *remontrance*) **il m'a passé/j'ai reçu un (bon) ~** he gave me/I got a (real) telling-off* *ou* dressing-down*, he really tore me off a strip* *(Brit)*

savonnage [savɔnaʒ] NM soaping *(NonC)*

savonner [savɔne] ▶ conjug 1 ◀ VT [+ *enfant, linge, corps*] to soap; [+ *barbe*] to lather, soap; **~ la tête de qn*** to give sb a dressing-down*, haul sb over the coals; **~ la planche à qn*** to make life difficult for sb*; **se ~ les mains/le visage** to soap one's hands/one's face, put soap on one's hands/one's face

savonnerie [savɔnʀi] NF [a] (= *usine*) soap factory [b] (= *tapis*) Savonnerie carpet

savonnette [savɔnɛt] NF bar of (toilet) soap

savonneux, -euse [savɔnø, øz] ADJ soapy → **pente**

savourer [savuʀe] ▶ conjug 1 ◀ VT [+ *plat, boisson, plaisanterie, triomphe*] to savour *(Brit)*, savor *(US)*

savoureux, -euse [savuʀø, øz] ADJ [*plat*] delicious, very tasty; [*anecdote, moment, personne*] delightful

savoyard, e [savwajaʀ, aʀd] [1] ADJ Savoyard → **fondue** [2] **Savoyard(e)** NM,F Savoyard

sax* [saks] NM (ABRÉV = **saxophone**) sax*

Saxe [saks] NF Saxony → **porcelaine**

saxe [saks] NM (= *matière*) Dresden china *(NonC)*; (= *objet*) piece of Dresden china

saxhorn [saksɔʀn] NM saxhorn

saxifrage [saksifʀaʒ] NF saxifrage

saxo* [sakso] [1] NM (= *instrument*) sax* [2] NM,F (= *musicien*) sax player*

saxon, -onne [saksɔ̃, ɔn] [1] ADJ Saxon [2] NM *(Ling)* Saxon [3] **Saxon(ne)** NM,F Saxon

saxophone [saksɔfɔn] NM saxophone

saxophoniste [saksɔfɔnist] NMF saxophonist, saxophone player

saynète [sɛnɛt] NF playlet

sbire [sbiʀ] NM *(péj)* henchman

s/c (ABRÉV = **sous couvert de**) ≈ c/o

scabieux, -ieuse [skabjø, jøz] [1] ADJ scabious [2] **scabieuse** NF scabious

scabreux, -euse [skabʀø, øz] ADJ (= *indécent*) improper, shocking; (= *dangereux*) risky

scalaire [skalɛʀ] [1] ADJ *(Math)* scalar [2] NM (= *poisson*) angel fish, scalare

scalène [skalɛn] [1] ADJ *(Anat, Math)* scalene [2] NM **(muscle) ~** scalenus

scalp [skalp] NM (= *action*) scalping; (= *chevelure*) scalp

scalpel [skalpɛl] NM scalpel

scalper [skalpe] ▶ conjug 1 ◀ VT to scalp

scampi [skɑ̃pi] NMPL scampi

scandale [skɑ̃dal] NM [a] (= *fait choquant, affaire, Rel*) scandal; **~ financier/public** financial/public scandal; **c'est un ~ !** it's scandalous! *ou* outrageous!, it's a scandal!; **sa tenue a fait ~** people were shocked by his outfit; **son livre a fait ~** his book caused a scandal; **au grand ~ de mon père, j'ai voulu épouser un étranger** I wanted to marry a foreigner, which scandalized my father; **elle va crier au ~** she'll make a big fuss about it; **les gens vont crier au ~** there'll be an outcry; **à ~** [*couple, livre*] controversial, headline-hitting* *(épith)*; **journal à ~** scandal sheet [b] (= *scène, tapage*) scene, fuss; **faire un** *ou* **du ~** to make a scene, kick up a fuss*; **et pas de ~ !** and don't make a fuss!; **condamné pour ~ sur la voie publique** fined for disturbing the peace *ou* for creating a public disturbance

scandaleusement [skɑ̃daløzmɑ̃] ADV [*se comporter*] scandalously, outrageously, shockingly; [*cher*] scandalously, outrageously, prohibitively; [*laid, mauvais*] appallingly; [*exagéré, sous-estimé*] grossly

scandaleux, -euse [skɑ̃dalø, øz] ADJ [*conduite, prix, propos*] scandalous, outrageous, shocking; [*chronique, littérature*] outrageous, shocking; **vie scandaleuse** life of scandal, scandalous life; **c'est ~ !** it's scandalous!

scandaliser [skɑ̃dalize] ▶ conjug 1 ◀ VT to scandalize, shock deeply; **se ~ de qch** to be deeply shocked at sth, be scandalized by sth

scander [skɑ̃de] ▶ conjug 1 ◀ VT [+ *vers*] to scan; [+ *discours*] to give emphasis to; [+ *mots*] to articulate separately; [+ *nom, slogan*] to chant

scandinave [skɑ̃dinav] [1] ADJ Scandinavian [2] **Scandinave** NMF Scandinavian

Scandinavie [skɑ̃dinavi] NF Scandinavia

scandium [skɑ̃djɔm] NM scandium

scanner¹ [skanɛʀ] NM *(Opt)* (optical) scanner; *(Méd)* **(examen au) ~** scanner; **passer un ~** to have a scan

scanner² [skane] ▶ conjug 1 ◀ VT *(Ordin)* to scan

scanneur [skanœʀ] NM = **scanner¹**

scanographe [skanɔgʀaf] NM *(Méd)* scanner

scanographie [skanɔgʀafi] NF (= *science*) (body) scanning; (= *photo*) scan; **~ du cerveau** brain scan

scansion [skɑ̃sjɔ̃] NF scanning, scansion

scaphandre [skafɑ̃dʀ] NM [*plongeur*] diving suit; [*cosmonaute*] spacesuit; **~ autonome** aqualung, scuba

scaphandrier [skafɑ̃dʀije] NM (deep-sea) diver

scapulaire [skapylɛʀ] ADJ, NM *(Anat, Méd, Rel)* scapular

scarabée [skaʀabe] NM (= *insecte*) beetle, scarab *(Spéc)*; (= *bijou*) scarab

scarificateur [skaʀifikatœʀ] NM *(Méd)* scarificator; *(Agr)* scarifier

scarification [skaʀifikasjɔ̃] NF scarification

scarifier [skaʀifje] ▶ conjug 7 ◀ VT *(Agr, Méd)* to scarify

scarlatine [skaʀlatin] NF scarlet fever, scarlatina *(SPÉC)*

scarole [skaʀɔl] NF escarole

scato* [skato] ADJ ABRÉV = **scatologique**

scatologie [skatɔlɔʒi] NF scatology

scatologique [skatɔlɔʒik] ADJ scatological, lavatory *(Brit)*

sceau *(pl* **sceaux)** [so] NM (= *cachet, estampille*) seal; *(fig = marque)* stamp, mark; **mettre son ~ sur** to put one's seal to *ou* on; **apposer son ~ sur** to affix one's seal to; *(fig)* **porter le ~ du génie** to bear the stamp *ou* mark of genius; **sous le ~ du secret** under the seal of secrecy → **garde²**

scélérat, e† [selexa, at] [1] ADJ *(littér)* (= *criminel*) villainous, blackguardly†; (= *méchant*) wicked [2] NM,F *(littér = criminel)* villain, blackguard†; **petit ~ !** (you) little rascal!

scélératesse† [seleʀatɛs] NF *(littér)* (= *caractère*) villainy, wickedness; (= *acte*) villainy, villainous *ou* wicked *ou* blackguardly† deed

scellement [sɛlmɑ̃] NM [a] [*acte, document, sac*] sealing [b] *(Constr)* embedding *(NonC)* [c] *(Méd)* [*couronne, prothèse*] lute, luting

sceller [sele] ▶ conjug 1 ◀ VT [a] (= *cacheter*) [+ *acte, document, sac*] to seal [b] *(Constr)* to embed [c] *(Méd)* [+ *couronne, prothèse*] to lute [d] (= *sanctionner*) [+ *amitié, pacte, réconciliation*] to seal; **son destin était scellé** his fate was sealed

scellés [sele] NMPL seals; **apposer** *ou* **mettre les ~ sur une porte** to put the seals on a door, affix the seals to a door; **lever les ~** to take the seals off; **mettre** *ou* **placer qch sous ~** to put *ou* place sth under seal

scellofrais® [sɛlɔfʀɛ] NM clingfilm® *(Brit)*, clingwrap *(Brit)*, Saran Wrap® *(US)*

scénario [senaʀjo] NM [a] *(Ciné, Théât = plan)* scenario; *(Ciné = découpage et dialogues)* screenplay, (film) script [b] (= *évolution possible*) scenario; **ça s'est déroulé selon le ~ habituel** it followed the usual pattern; **c'est toujours le même ~*** it's always the same old ritual *ou* carry-on* *(Brit)* → **catastrophe**

scénariser [senaʀize] ▶ conjug 1 ◀ VT *(TV)* to script

scénariste [senaʀist] NMF *(Ciné)* scriptwriter

scène [sɛn] NM [a] (= *estrade*) stage; **~ tournante** revolving stage; **sortir de** ◊ **quitter la ~** to go off stage, exit; **occuper le devant de la ~** *(lit)* to be in the foreground, be at the front of the stage; *(fig)* to be in the forefront; **en fond de ~** at the back of the stage, in the background; **sur (la) ~** on stage; **il se produira** *ou* **sera sur la ~ de l'Olympia en janvier** he'll be performing *ou* appearing at the Olympia in January [b] (= *le théâtre*) **la ~** the stage; **une vedette de la ~ française** a star of the French stage; **il a quitté la ~ à 75 ans** he gave up the stage at the age of 75; **à la ~ comme à la ville** (both) on stage and off, both on and off (the) stage; **porter une œuvre à la ~** to bring a work to the stage, stage a work; **adapter un film pour la ~** to adapt a film for the stage [c] *(Ciné, Théât = division)* scene; **dans la première ~** in the first *ou* opening scene, in scene one; *(Ciné)* **~ d'action** action scene *ou* sequence; **~ d'amour** love scene; **elle m'a joué la grande ~ du deux** she made an almighty fuss [d] (= *décor*) scene; **changement de ~** scene change [e] (= *lieu de l'action*) scene; *(Ciné, Théât)* **la ~**

est *ou* se passe à Rome the scene is set in Rome

[f] (= *spectacle*) scene; **il a assisté à toute la ~** he witnessed the whole scene; **~ de panique/ de violence** scene of panic/of violence; (*Psych*) **la ~ originaire** *ou* **primitive** the primal scene

[g] (= *confrontation, dispute*) scene; **~ de jalousie/de rupture** jealous/break-up scene; **il m'a fait une ~ de jalousie** he exploded at me in a fit of jealousy; **~ de ménage** domestic fight *ou* quarrel; **faire une ~** to make a scene; **il m'a fait une ~ parce que j'avais oublié la clé** he made a scene because I had forgotten the key; **avoir une ~ (avec qn)** to have a scene (with sb)

[h] (= *domaine*) scene; **sur la ~ politique/ internationale/littéraire** on the political/ international/literary scene; **la ~ publique** the public arena; **il s'est retiré de la ~ publique** he has retired from public life

[i] (*Art* = *tableau*) scene; **~ d'intérieur/ mythologique** indoor/mythological scene; **~ de genre** genre painting

[j] **en ~** on stage; **tout le monde en ~!** everybody on stage!; **être en ~** to be on stage; **entrer en ~** (*Théât*) to come on stage; [*politicien, sportif*] to arrive on *ou* enter the scene; **c'est là que l'informatique entre en ~** this is where computing comes in; **entrée en ~** (*Théât*) entrance; (*fig*) arrival on the scene; **par ordre d'entrée en ~** in order of appearance; **mettre en ~** (*Théât*) [+ *histoire, personnage*] to present; [+ *auteur*] to stage *ou* produce the play(s) of; [+ *pièce de théâtre*] to stage, direct; (*Ciné*) [+ *film*] to direct; **mise en ~** (*Ciné*) (*Théât*) (= *production*) production; (= *art*) **il a révolutionné la mise en ~** he revolutionized directing *ou* stagecraft; **mise en ~ de Vilar** directed by Vilar; (*fig, péj*) **c'est de la mise en ~** it's all put on; **toute cette mise en ~ pour nous faire croire que ...** this whole performance was to make us believe that ... → **metteur**

scénique [senik] ADJ theatrical → **indication**

scéniquement [senikmɑ̃] ADV (*Théât*) theatrically

scénographe [senɔgraf] NMF (*Théât*) stage *ou* theatre (*Brit*) *ou* theater (*US*) designer

scénographie [senɔgrafi] NF [a] (*Art*) scenography [b] (*Théât*) stage design

scénographique [senɔgrafik] ADJ (*Théât*) [*conditions*] relating to stage *ou* theatre (*Brit*) *ou* theater (*US*) design; **quelle que soit la solution ~ retenue** whatever way the director decides to handle the scene

scepticisme [sɛptisism] NM scepticism (*Brit*), skepticism (*US*); **exprimer son ~ à l'égard de** *ou* **sur qch** to express scepticism about sth

sceptique [sɛptik] [1] ADJ sceptical (*Brit*), skeptical (*US*); **d'un air ~** sceptically (*Brit*), skeptically (*US*); **être** *ou* **se montrer ~** to be sceptical (**à l'égard de, sur, quant à** about); **ses arguments me laissent ~** his arguments don't convince me [2] NMF sceptic (*Brit*), skeptic (*US*); (*Philo*) Sceptic (*Brit*), Skeptic (*US*)

sceptre [sɛptʀ] NM (*lit, fig*) sceptre (*Brit*), scepter (*US*)

Schéhérazade [ʃeeʀazad] NF Sheherazade

schelling [ʃ(ə)liŋ] NM = **schilling**

schéma [ʃema] NM [a] (= *diagramme*) diagram, sketch; **~ de montage** assembly diagram *ou* instructions; **~ de principe** (wiring) diagram; (*Admin*) **~ d'aménagement** ◊ **~ directeur** urban development plan [b] (= *résumé*) outline; **faire le ~ de l'opération** to give an outline of the operation [c] (*Psych*) **~ corporel** body image

schématique [ʃematik] ADJ [*dessin*] diagrammatic(al), schematic; (*péj*) [*interprétation, conception*] oversimplified

schématiquement [ʃematikmɑ̃] ADV [*représenter*] diagrammatically, schematically; **il exposa l'affaire ~** he gave an outline of the

affair, he outlined the affair; **très ~, voici de quoi il s'agit** briefly, this is what it's all about

schématisation [ʃematizasjɔ̃] NF schematization; (*péj*) (over)simplification

schématiser [ʃematize] ▸conjug 1◂ VT to schematize; (*péj*) to (over)simplify

schématisme [ʃematism] NM (*péj*) over-simplicity

schème [ʃɛm] NM (*Philo*) schema; (*Art*) design, scheme

scherzando [skɛʀtsando] ADV scherzando

scherzo [skɛʀdzo] [1] NM scherzo [2] ADV scherzando

schilling [ʃiliŋ] NM schilling

schismatique [ʃismatik] ADJ, NMF schismatic

schisme [ʃism] NM (*Rel*) schism; (*Pol*) split; **faire ~** to split away

schiste [ʃist] NM (*métamorphique*) schist, shale; **~ bitumineux** oil shale; **huile de ~** shale oil

schisteux, -euse [ʃisto, øz] ADJ schistose

schizo* [skizo] NMF (ABRÉV = **schizophrène**) schizo*

schizoïde [skizoid] ADJ, NMF schizoid

schizophrène [skizɔfʀɛn] ADJ, NMF (*Méd, fig*) schizophrenic

schizophrénie [skizɔfʀeni] NF (*Méd, fig*) schizophrenia

schizophrénique [skizɔfʀenik] ADJ schizophrenic

schlague [ʃlag] NF (*Mil Hist*) **la ~** drubbing, flogging; **ils n'obéissent qu'à la ~‡** they only do as they're told if you really lay into them‡ *ou* if you give them what-for‡

schlass‡ [ʃlas] [1] ADJ INV (= *ivre*) sozzled‡, plastered‡ [2] NM (= *couteau*) knife

schlinguer‡ [ʃlɛɡe] ▸conjug 1◂ VI to pong‡, stink to high heaven*

schlitte [ʃlit] NF sledge (*for transporting wood*)

schlitter [ʃlite] ▸conjug 1◂ VT to sledge (*wood*)

schmilblik* [ʃmilblik] NM **faire avancer le ~** to help things along; **ça ne fait pas avancer le ~** that doesn't get anybody anywhere, that doesn't get us very far

schnaps [ʃnaps] NM schnap(p)s

schnock‡ [ʃnɔk] NM = **chnoque**

schnouff† [ʃnuf] NF (*arg Drogue*) dope‡

Schtroumpf [ʃtʀumf] NM Smurf

schuss [ʃus] [1] NM schuss [2] ADV **descendre (tout) ~** to schuss (down)

schwa [ʃva] NM schwa(h)

Schweppes® [ʃwɛps] NM tonic (water)

SCI [ɛssei] NF (ABRÉV = **société civile immobilière**) → **société**

sciage [sjaʒ] NM [*bois, métal*] sawing

sciatique [sjatik] [1] NF sciatica [2] ADJ sciatic

scie [si] NF [a] (= *outil*) saw; **~ à bois** wood saw; **~ circulaire** circular saw; **~ à chantourner** *ou* **découper** fretsaw; **~ électrique** power saw; **~ à guichet** panel saw; **~ à métaux** hacksaw; **~ musicale** musical saw; **~ à ruban** bandsaw; **~ sauteuse** jigsaw; **~ à chaîne** chainsaw → **dent** [b] (*péj*) (= *chanson*) repetitive song; (= *personne*) bore

sciemment [sjamɑ̃] ADV knowingly

science [sjɑ̃s] NF [a] (= *domaine scientifique*) science; **les ~s** (*gén*) the sciences; (*Scol*) science; **la ~ du beau** the science of beauty; **~s appliquées/exactes/pures/sociales/occultes** applied/exact/pure/social/occult sciences; **~s expérimentales** experimental sciences; (*Univ*) **institut des ~s sociales** institute of social science; (*Scol*) **~s naturelles†** natural science†; **~s physiques** physical science; **~s marines** *ou* **de la mer** marine science; **les ~s de la vie** the life sciences; **~s d'observation** observational sciences; **~s économiques** economics *sg*; **~s politiques** political science; (*Univ*) **Sciences Po** French school of political science → **homme**

[b] (= *art, habileté*) **la ~ de la guerre** the science *ou* art of war; **faire qch avec une ~ consommée** to do sth with consummate skill; **sa ~ des couleurs** his skilful use of colour [c] (= *érudition*) knowledge; **je n'ai pas la ~ infuse** I have no way of knowing; (*Rel*) **la ~ du bien et du mal** the knowledge of good and evil; **savoir de ~ certaine que ...** to know for a fact *ou* for certain that ...; **il faut toujours qu'il étale sa ~** he's always showing off his knowledge → **puits**

science-fiction [sjɑ̃sfiksjɔ̃] NF science fiction, sci-fi*; **film/roman de ~** science fiction *ou* sci-fi* film/novel; **c'est ça la relève de la ~** it's like something out of science fiction

scientificité [sjɑ̃tifisite] NF scientific character *ou* nature

scientifique [sjɑ̃tifik] [1] ADJ scientific [2] NMF scientist

scientifiquement [sjɑ̃tifikmɑ̃] ADV scientifically

scientisme [sjɑ̃tism] NM scientism

scientiste [sjɑ̃tist] [1] NMF adept of scientism [2] ADJ scientistic

scientologie [sjɑ̃tɔlɔʒi] NF Scientology®

scientologue [sjɑ̃tɔlɔg] ADJ, NMF Scientologist

scier [sje] ▸conjug 7◂ VT [a] [+ *bois, métal*] to saw; [+ *bûche*] to saw (up); [+ *partie en trop*] to saw off; **~ une branche pour faire des bûches** to saw (up) a branch into logs; (*fig*) **la branche sur laquelle on est assis** to dig one's own grave [b] (* = *stupéfier*) **ça m'a scié !** it bowled me over!*, it staggered me!*; **c'est vraiment sciant !** it's absolutely staggering!* [c] (* = *ennuyer*) **~ qn** to bore sb rigid* *ou* stiff*

scierie [siʀi] NF sawmill

scieur [sjœʀ] NM sawyer; **~ de long** pit sawyer

scille [sil] NF scilla

Scilly [sili] **N les îles ~** the Scilly Isles

scinder [sɛ̃de] ▸conjug 1◂ [1] VT to split (up), divide (up) (**en** in, into) [2] **se scinder** VPR to split (up) (**en** in, into)

scintigraphie [sɛ̃tigrafi] NF scintigraphy

scintillant, e [sɛ̃tijɑ̃, ɑ̃t] ADJ [*diamant, yeux*] sparkling; [*étoile, lumières*] twinkling; [*goutte d'eau*] glistening; [*esprit*] sparkling, scintillating

scintillation [sɛ̃tijasjɔ̃] NF (*Astron, Phys*) scintillation; **compteur à ~s** scintillation counter

scintillement [sɛ̃tijmɑ̃] NM [*diamant, yeux*] sparkling; [*étoile, lumières*] twinkling; [*goutte d'eau*] glistening; [*esprit*] sparkling, scintillating; **le ~ de son esprit** his scintillating mind; **le ~ de ses yeux** his sparkling eyes

scintiller [sɛ̃tije] ▸conjug 1◂ VI [*diamant, yeux*] to sparkle; [*étoile, lumières*] to twinkle; [*goutte d'eau*] to glisten; [*esprit*] to sparkle, scintillate

scion [sjɔ̃] NM (*Bot*) (*gén*) twig; (= *greffe*) scion; (*Pêche*) top piece

Scipion [sipjɔ̃] NM Scipio; **~ l'Africain** Scipio Africanus

scission [sisjɔ̃] NF [a] (= *schisme*) split, scission (*frm*); **faire ~** to split away, secede [b] (*Écon*) demerger [c] (*Bot, Phys*) fission

scissionniste [sisjɔnist] ADJ, NMF secessionist

scissipare [sisipar] ADJ fissiparous, schizo-genetic

scissiparité [sisiparite] NF fissiparousness, schizogenesis

scissure [sisyʀ] NF fissure, sulcus; **~ inter-hémisphérique** longitudinal fissure of the cerebrum; **~ latérale** *ou* **de Sylvius** fissure of Sylvius, lateral fissure

sciure [sjyʀ] NF **~ (de bois)** sawdust

scléreux, -euse [sklero, øz] ADJ sclerotic, sclerous

sclérosant, e [sklerozɑ̃, ɑ̃t] ADJ (*fig*) ossifying

sclérose [skleroz] NF [a] (*Méd*) sclerosis; **~ artérielle** hardening of the arteries, arteriosclerosis (*SPÉC*); ~ **en plaques** multiple sclerosis [b] (*fig*) ossification

sclérosé, e [skleroze] (*ptp de* **se scléroser**) ADJ (*lit*) sclerosed, sclerotic; (*fig*) ossified

scléroser [skleroze] ▶conjug 1◀ [1] **se scléroser** VPR (*Méd*) to become sclerotic *ou* sclerosed; (*fig*) to become ossified [2] VT [+ *tissus*] to cause sclerosis of

sclérotique [sklerɔtik] NF sclera, sclerotic

scolaire [skɔlɛʀ] ADJ [a] (*gén*) school (*épith*); **ses succès ~s** his success in *ou* at school; **enfant d'âge ~** child of school age; **en milieu ~** in schools; **les ~s** schoolchildren → **établissement, groupe, livret** *etc* [b] (*péj*) [*style*] unimaginative; **son livre est un peu ~ par endroits** his book is a bit starchy in places

scolairement [skɔlɛʀmɑ̃] ADV **il réussit très bien ~** he's doing very well at school

scolarisable [skɔlaʀizabl] ADJ [*handicapé*] educable, capable of attending school

scolarisation [skɔlaʀizasjɔ̃] NF [*enfant*] schooling; **la ~ d'une population/d'un pays** providing a population with schooling/a country with schools; **taux de ~** percentage of children in full-time education

scolariser [skɔlaʀize] ▶conjug 1◀ VT [+ *enfant*] to provide with schooling, send to school; [+ *pays*] to provide with schools *ou* schooling

scolarité [skɔlaʀite] NF schooling; **~ primaire/secondaire** primary/secondary schooling *ou* education; **la ~ a été prolongée jusqu'à 16 ans** the school-leaving age has been raised to 16; **pendant mes années de ~** during my school years *ou* years at school; **~ obligatoire** compulsory education *ou* schooling; (*Univ*) **service de la ~** registrar's office; **il a suivi une ~ normale** he had a normal education; **il a eu une ~ difficile** he had difficulties at school → **certificat, frais²**

scolastique [skɔlastik] [1] ADJ (*Philo, péj*) scholastic [2] NF scholasticism [3] NM (*Philo*) scholastic, schoolman; (= *séminariste*) seminarian, seminarist; (*péj*) scholastic

scoliose [skɔljoz] NF curvature of the spine, scoliosis (*SPÉC*)

scolopendre [skɔlɔpɑ̃dʀ] NF [a] (*Zool*) centipede, scolopendra (*SPÉC*) [b] (*Bot*) hart's-tongue, scolopendrium (*SPÉC*)

sconse [skɔ̃s] NM skunk (fur)

scoop* [skup] NM (*Presse*) scoop

scooter [skutœʀ] NM (motor) scooter; **~ des mers** jet ski; **~ des neiges** Skidoo®; **faire du ~** to ride a scooter

scootériste [skuterist] NMF scooter rider

scopie* [skɔpi] NF ABRÉV = **radioscopie**

scorbut [skɔʀbyt] NM scurvy

scorbutique [skɔʀbytik] [1] ADJ [*symptômes*] of scurvy, scorbutic (*SPÉC*); [*personne*] suffering from scurvy, scorbutic (*SPÉC*) [2] NMF person with *ou* suffering from scurvy

score [skɔʀ] NM (*gén, Sport*) score; (*Pol, Scol, Sport*) **faire un bon/mauvais ~** to do well/badly; **obtenir ~ de 48% aux élections** to get 48% of the votes

scorie [skɔʀi] NF (*gén pl*) [a] (*Ind*) slag (*NonC*), scoria (*NonC*), clinker (*NonC*); **~s (volcaniques)** (volcanic) scoria [b] (*fig*) dross (*NonC*)

scorpion [skɔʀpjɔ̃] NM [a] (*Zool*) scorpion; **~ d'eau** water-scorpion; **~ de mer** scorpion-fish [b] (*Astron*) **le Scorpion** Scorpio; **il est Scorpion ◊ il est (du signe) du Scorpion** he's (a) Scorpio

scotch [skɔtʃ] NM [a] (= *boisson*) scotch (whisky (*Brit*) *ou* whiskey (*US, Ir*)) [b] (= *adhésif*) **Scotch®** Sellotape® (*Brit*), Scotchtape® (*US*)

scotcher [skɔtʃe] ▶conjug 1◀ VT to sellotape (*Brit*), stick with Scotchtape® (*US*); **il reste des heures scotché* devant sa télévision** he spends hours glued to the television

scotch-terrier (*pl* **scotch-terriers**) [skɔtʃtɛʀje] NM Scottish *ou* Scotch terrier

---

scoumoune* [skumun] NF (*arg Crime*) tough *ou* rotten luck*

scout, e [skut] [1] ADJ [*camp, mouvement*] scout (*épith*); (*péj*) **avoir un côté ~** to be a bit of a boy scout [2] NM (boy) scout; **les ~s de France** French scouts [3] **scoute** NF (girl) scout

scoutisme [skutism] NM (= *mouvement*) scout movement; (= *activité*) scouting; **faire du ~** to be a scout

SCP [ɛssepe] NF (ABRÉV = **société civile professionnelle**) → **société**

SCPI [ɛssepei] NF (ABRÉV = **société civile de placement immobilier**) → **société**

Scrabble® [skʀabl] NM Scrabble®; **faire un ~** to play Scrabble®, have a game of Scrabble®

scratcher [skʀatʃe] ▶conjug 1◀ [1] VT (*Sport*) to scratch [2] **se scratcher** VPR* to get smashed up*

scriban [skʀibɑ̃] NM (*avec cabinet*) bureau bookcase; (*sans cabinet*) slant-front bureau

scribe [skʀib] NM (*péj* = *bureaucrate*) pen-pusher (*Brit*), pencil pusher (*US*); (*Hist*) scribe

scribouillard, e [skʀibujaʀ, aʀd] NM,F (*péj*) penpusher (*Brit*), pencil pusher (*US*)

scribouilleur, -euse* [skʀibujœʀ, øz] NM,F (*péj*) hack (writer), scribbler

script [skʀipt] [1] NM [a] (= *écriture*) ~ printing; **apprendre le ~** to learn how to print (letters); **écrire en ~** to print [b] (*Ciné*) (shooting) script [2] NF = **script-girl**

scripte [skʀipt] NF (*Ciné*) continuity girl

scripteur [skʀiptœʀ] NM (*Ling*) writer

script-girl (*pl* **script-girls**) [skʀiptgœʀl] NF continuity girl

scriptural, e (*mpl* **-aux**) [skʀiptyʀal, o] ADJ → **monnaie**

scrofulaire [skʀɔfylɛʀ] NF figwort

scrofule [skʀɔfyl] NF (*Méd*) scrofula; (*Hist Méd*) **~s** scrofula, king's evil

scrofuleux, -euse [skʀɔfylø, øz] ADJ [*tumeur*] scrofulous; [*personne*] scrofulous, suffering from scrofula

scrogneugneu [skʀɔɲøɲø] EXCL damnation!

scrotal, e (*mpl* **-aux**) [skʀɔtal, o] ADJ scrotal

scrotum [skʀɔtɔm] NM scrotum

scrupule [skʀypyl] NM [a] (*gén*) scruple; **avoir des ~s** to have scruples; **avoir des ~s à faire qch ◊ se faire ~ de faire qch** to have scruples *ou* misgivings *ou* qualms about doing sth; **faire taire ses ~s** to silence one's scruples; **je n'aurais aucun ~ à refuser** I wouldn't have any scruples *ou* qualms *ou* misgivings about refusing; **son honnêteté est poussée jusqu'au ~** he's scrupulously honest; **il est dénué de ~s** he has no scruples, he is completely unscrupulous, **sans ~s** [*personne*] unscrupulous, without scruples; [*agir*] unscrupulously; **vos ~s vous honorent** your scrupulousness is a credit to you; **je comprends votre ~ ou vos ~s** I understand your scruples [b] (= *par souci de*) **dans ou par un ~ d'honnêteté/d'exactitude historique** in scrupulous regard for honesty/for historical exactness

scrupuleusement [skʀypyløzmɑ̃] ADV scrupulously

scrupuleux, -euse [skʀypylø, øz] ADJ [*honnêteté, personne*] scrupulous; **peu ~** unscrupulous; **ils réclament le respect ~ des règles démocratiques** they demand that the rules of democracy be scrupulously respected

scrutateur, -trice [skʀytatœʀ, tʀis] [1] ADJ (*littér*) [*caractère, regard*] searching [2] NM (*Pol*) teller, scrutineer (*Brit*)

scruter [skʀyte] ▶conjug 1◀ VT [+ *horizon*] to scan, search, scrutinize; [+ *objet, personne*] to scrutinize, examine; [+ *pénombre*] to peer into, search

scrutin [skʀytɛ̃] NM [a] (= *vote*) ballot; **par voie de ~** by ballot; **voter au ~ secret** to vote by se-

---

cret ballot; **il a été élu au troisième tour de ~** he was elected on *ou* at the third ballot *ou* round; **dépouiller le ~** to count the votes [b] (= *élection*) poll; **le jour du ~** polling day; **ouverture/clôture du ~** start/close of polling [c] (= *modalité*) **~ de liste** list system; **~ d'arrondissement** district election system; **~ majoritaire** election on a majority basis; **~ proportionnel** proportional representation; **~ de ballottage** second ballot, second round of voting; **~ uninominal** uninominal system

sculpter [skylte] ▶conjug 1◀ VT [+ *marbre, statue*] to sculpt; [+ *meuble*] to carve, sculpt; [+ *bâton, bois*] to carve; **~ qch dans du bois** to carve sth out of wood

sculpteur [skyltœʀ] NM (= *homme*) sculptor; (= *femme*) sculptor, sculptress; **~ sur bois** woodcarver

sculptural, e (*mpl* **-aux**) [skyltyʀal, o] ADJ (*Art*) sculptural; (*fig*) [*beauté, corps, formes*] statuesque

sculpture [skyltyʀ] NF [a] (= *art, objet*) sculpture; **faire de la ~** to sculpt; **~ sur bois** woodcarving; **une ~ sur marbre/neige/glace** a marble/snow/an ice sculpture [b] (*Aut*) [*pneu*] tread (pattern); **~s** tread

Scylla [sila] NF Scylla → **Charybde**

scythe [sit] [1] ADJ Scythian [2] NM (*Ling*) Scythian [3] **Scythe** NMF Scythian

Scythie [siti] NF Scythia

SDF [ɛsdeɛf] NMF INV (ABRÉV = **sans domicile fixe**) homeless person; **les ~** the homeless

SDN [ɛsdeɛn] NF (ABRÉV = **Société des Nations**) → **société**

S.E. (ABRÉV = **Son Excellence**) HE

se [sə] PRON [a] (*réfléchi*) (*sg*) (*indéfini*) oneself; (*homme*) himself; (*femme*) herself; (*sujet non humain*) itself; (*pl*) themselves; **se regarder dans la glace** to look at o.s. in the mirror; **se raser/laver** to shave/wash; **se mouiller/salir** to get wet/dirty; **se brûler/couper** to burn/cut o.s. → **écouter, faire** [b] (*réciproque*) each other, one another; **deux personnes qui s'aiment** two people who love each other *ou* one another; **des gens qui se haïssent** people who hate each other *ou* one another [c] (*possessif*) **se casser la jambe** to break one's leg; **il se lave les mains** he is washing his hands; **elle s'est coupé les cheveux** she has cut her hair [d] (*passif*) **cela ne se fait pas** that's not done; **cela se répare/recolle facilement** it can easily be repaired/glued together again; **la vérité finira par se savoir** the truth will out in the end, the truth will finally be found out; **l'anglais se parle dans le monde entier** English is spoken throughout the world; **cela se vend bien** it sells well; **les escargots se servent dans la coquille** snails are served in their shells [e] (*impersonnel*) **il se peut que ...** it may be that ..., it is possible that ...; **comment se fait-il que ... ?** how is it that ...?

S.É. (ABRÉV = **Son Éminence**) HE

séance [seɑ̃s] NF [a] (= *réunion*) [*conseil municipal*] meeting, session; [*parlement, tribunal*] session, sitting; [*comité*] session; **être en ~** to be in session, sit; **la ~ est levée** the meeting is over; **~ extraordinaire** extraordinary meeting; **la proposition sera examinée en ~ publique** the proposal will be considered at *ou* in a public session *ou* meeting; **ils l'ont fusillé ~ tenante** they shot him there and then *ou* on the spot; **nous partirons ~ tenante** we shall leave forthwith *ou* without further ado → **suspension** [b] (= *période*) session; **~ de photographie/rééducation/gymnastique** photographic *ou* photography/physiotherapy/gymnastics session; **~ de pose** sitting; **~ de spiritisme** séance; **~ de travail** working session; **~ de torture** torture session

[c] (= *représentation*) (*Théât*) performance; **~ privée** private showing *ou* performance; **~ (de cinéma)** film; (*Ciné*) **première/dernière ~** first/last showing; **la ~ est à 21h, et le film 15 minutes plus tard** the programme starts at 9 o'clock and the film 15 minutes later

[d] (*Bourse*) day of trading, session; **après plusieurs ~s de hausse** after several sessions *ou* days of bullish trading; **en début/fin de ~** at the opening/close (of the day's trading); **l'indice a gagné 10 points en cours de ~** the index gained 10 points during (the day's) trading

[e] (* = *dispute*) scene*; **il m'a fait une ~** he made a scene*

séant¹ [seã] NM (*hum* = *derrière*) posterior (*hum*); (*frm*) **se mettre sur son ~** to sit up (*from a lying position*)

séant², **séante** [seã, seãt] ADJ (*littér* = *convenable*) seemly, fitting; **il n'est pas ~ de dire cela** it is unseemly *ou* unfitting to say such things

seau (*pl* **seaux**) [so] NM (= *récipient*) bucket, pail (*surtout US*); (= *contenu*) bucket(ful), pail(ful) (*surtout US*); **il pleut à ~x** ◊ **la pluie tombe à ~x** it's coming *ou* pouring down in buckets*, it's raining buckets*; **~ à champagne/glace** champagne/ice bucket; **~ à charbon** coal scuttle; **~ hygiénique** slop pail

sébacé, e [sebase] ADJ [*glande*] sebaceous

sébile [sebil] NF begging bowl; **tendre la ~** (*lit*) to beg; (*fig*) to bring out *ou* hold out the begging bowl

séborrhée [sebɔʀe] NF seborrhoea (*Brit*), seborrhea (*US*)

sébum [sebɔm] NM sebum

sec, sèche¹ [sɛk, sɛʃ] [1] ADJ [a] [*air, bois, climat, linge, temps, saison, toux*] dry; [*fruit*] dried; **elle le regarda partir, l'œil ~** she watched him go, dry-eyed; **j'avais la gorge sèche** my throat was dry; **il est au régime** → he's not allowed to drink alcohol → **cale¹, cinq, cul**

[b] (= *sans graisse*) [*cheveu, peau*] dry

[c] (= *maigre*) [*bras, personne*] lean; **il est comme un coup de trique* ou comme un hareng*** he's as thin as a rake

[d] (= *sans douceur*) [*rire, vin*] dry; [*style*] terse; [*cœur*] cold, hard; [*réponse*] curt; **elle a été très sèche avec moi** she was very curt with me; **il lui a écrit une lettre très sèche** he wrote him a very curt letter; **se casser avec un bruit ~** to break with a (sharp) snap, snap; **« non », dit-il d'un ton ~** "no", he said curtly; (*Sport*) **placage ~** hard tackle → **coup**

[e] (= *sans eau*) [*alcool*] neat; **il prend son whisky ~** he takes *ou* drinks his whisky neat *ou* straight

[f] (*Cartes*) **atout/valet ~** singleton trump/jack; **son valet était ~** his jack was a singleton

[g] (*Tennis*) **il a été battu en trois sets ~s** he was beaten in three straight sets

[h] (= *sans prestations supplémentaires*) **le vol ~ coûte 1 500 F** the flight-only price is 1,500 francs; **licenciement ~** compulsory lay-off *ou* redundancy (*Brit*) (*without any compensation*)

[i] * (*loc*) **je l'ai eu ~** I was really shocked; **être ou rester ~** to be stumped*; **je suis resté ~ sur ce sujet** I drew a blank on the subject

[2] ADV* [*frapper*] hard; **il boit ~** he really knocks it back*, he's a hard *ou* heavy drinker; **démarrer ~** (*Aut*) (*sans douceur*) to start (up) with a jolt *ou* jerk; (*rapidement*) to tear off; **ça démarre ~ ce soir** the evening's off to a good start; **conduire ~** to drive like a racing driver; **et lui, aussi ~, a répondu que ... et il est arrivé et reparti aussi ~** he arrived and left again just as quickly

[3] NM **tenir ou conserver qch au ~** to keep sth in a dry place; **rester au ~** to stay in the dry; **pour garder les pieds au ~** to keep your feet dry; **être à ~** [*puits, torrent*] to be dry *ou* dried-

up; (* = *être sans argent*) [*personne*] to be broke* *ou* skint* (*Brit*); [*caisse*] to be empty; **mettre à ~ un étang** [*personne*] to drain a pond; [*soleil*] to dry up a pond; (*au jeu*) **il l'a mis à ~** [+ *joueur*] he cleaned him out*, he took him to the cleaner's*

sécable [sekabl] ADJ divisible, scored

SECAM [sekam] ADJ, NM (ABRÉV = **séquentiel couleur à mémoire**) SECAM

sécant, e [sekã, ãt] [1] ADJ secant [2] **sécante** NF secant

sécateur [sekatœʀ] NM (pair of) secateurs, (pair of) pruning shears

sécession [sesesjɔ̃] NF secession; **faire ~** to secede, break away → **guerre**

sécessionniste [sesesjɔnist] ADJ, NMF secessionist; **république ~** breakaway republic

séchage [seʃaʒ] NM [*cheveux, linge*] drying; [*bois*] seasoning; **le ~ (en) machine n'est pas recommandé pour ce tissu** it is not recommended that this fabric be dried in a clothes dryer; **« ~ à plat »** "dry flat"; **vernis/colle à ~ rapide** quick-drying varnish/glue

sèche² * [sɛʃ] NF (= *cigarette*) cigarette, cig*, fag* (*Brit*)

sèche-cheveux [sɛʃʃəvø] NM INV hairdryer

sèche-linge [sɛʃlɛ̃ʒ] NM INV (= *armoire*) drying cabinet; (= *machine*) tumble-dryer

sèche-mains [sɛʃmɛ̃] NM INV hand-dryer, blower

sèchement [sɛʃmã] ADV [*répondre*] curtly

sécher [seʃe] ▸ conjug 6 ◂ [1] VT [a] (*gén*) to dry; **sèche tes larmes** dry your tears *ou* eyes; (*fig*) **~ les larmes ou les pleurs de qn** to wipe away sb's tears

[b] (*arg Scol* = *manquer*) [+ *cours*] to skip*; **il a séché l'école pendant trois jours** he skipped school* *ou* skived off school (*Brit*)* for three days

[c] ‡ **~ son verre** to drain one's glass

[2] VI [a] [*surface mouillée, peinture*] to dry (off); [*substance imbibée de liquide*] to dry (out); [*linge*] to dry; **faire ou laisser ~ du linge** ◊ **mettre du linge à ~** (*à l'intérieur*) to put *ou* hang washing up to dry; (*à l'extérieur*) to put *ou* hang washing out to dry; **« faire ~ sans essorer »** "do not spin (dry)"; **« faire ~ à plat »** "dry flat"

[b] (= *se déshydrater*) [*bois*] to dry out; [*fleur*] to dry up *ou* out; **le caoutchouc a séché** the rubber has dried up *ou* gone dry; **~ sur pied** [*plante*] to wither on the stalk; (*fig*) [*personne*] to languish; **faire ~** [+ *fleurs, fruits, viande*] to dry; [+ *bois*] to season; **boue/fleur/viande séchée** dried mud/flower/meat

[c] (*arg Scol* = *rester sec*) to be stumped*; **j'ai séché en chimie** I drew a (complete) blank *ou* I dried up* completely in chemistry

[3] **se sécher** VPR to dry o.s. (off); **se ~ les cheveux/mains** to dry one's hair/hands; **se ~ au soleil/avec une serviette** to dry o.s. in the sun/with a towel; **se ~ devant le feu** to dry o.s. *ou* dry (o.s.) off in front of the fire

sécheresse [seʃʀɛs] NF [a] [*climat, sol, style, ton*] dryness; [*réponse*] curtness; [*cœur*] coldness, hardness; **~ vaginale** vaginal dryness; **~ cutanée/oculaire** dry skin/eyes, dryness of the skin/eyes; **dire qch avec ~** to say sth curtly

[b] (= *absence de pluie*) drought; **année/période de ~** year/period of drought

sécherie [seʃʀi] NF (= *machine*) drier, dryer, drying machine; (= *installations*) drying plant

séchoir [seʃwaʀ] NM (= *local*) (*pour nourriture*) drying shed; (*pour linge*) drying room; (= *appareil*) dryer; **~ à linge** (*pliant*) clothes-horse; (*rotatif*) tumble dryer; (*à cordes*) clothes airer; **~ à chanvre/à tabac** hemp/tobacco drying shed; **~ à cheveux** hairdryer; **~ à tambour** tumble-dryer

second, e¹ [s(ə)gɔ̃, ɔ̃d] [1] ADJ [a] (*chronologiquement*) second; **la ~e fois** the second

time; **je vous le dis pour la ~e fois, vous n'aurez rien** I repeat, you'll get nothing; **~ chapitre** ◊ **chapitre ~** chapter two → **main, noce**

[b] (*hiérarchiquement*) second; **intelligence/malhonnêteté à nulle autre ~e** unparalleled intelligence/dishonesty → **couteau, marché, plan¹**

[c] (= *autre, nouveau*) second; **une ~e jeunesse** a second youth; **dans une ~e vie** in a second life; **cet écrivain est un ~ Hugo** this writer is a second Hugo; **chez lui, c'est une ~e nature** with him it's second nature → **état, habitude, souffle, vue**

[d] (= *dérivé*) [*cause*] secondary

[2] NM,F second; **le ~ de ses fils** his second son; **il a été reçu ~ (en physique)** he came *ou* was second (in physics); (*littér*) **sans ~** second to none, peerless (*littér*); (*Alpinisme*) **~ (de cordée)** second (on the rope)

[3] NM [a] (= *adjoint*) second in command; (*Naut*) first mate; (*en duel*) second

[b] (= *étage*) second floor (*Brit*), third floor (*US*); **la dame du ~** the lady on the second floor (*Brit*) *ou* the third floor (*US*)

[c] (*dans une charade*) second; **mon ~ est ...** my second is...

[4] **seconde** NF [a] (*Transport*) second class; (*billet*) second-class ticket; (*Rail*) **les ~es sont à l'avant** the second-class seats *ou* carriages are at the front *ou* in front; **voyager en ~** to travel second-class

[b] (*Scol*) **(classe de) ~e** ≈ fifth form (*Brit*) (*in secondary school*), ≈ tenth grade (*US*) (*in high school*), ≈ sophomore year (*US*) (*in high school*) → LYCÉE

[c] (*Aut*) second (gear); **être en/passer la ou en ~e** to be in/change into second (gear)

[d] (*Mus*) second

[e] (*Danse*) second (position)

[f] (*Escrime*) seconde → **seconde²**

[5] **en second** LOC ADJ, LOC ADV **officier ou capitaine en ~** first mate; **passer en ~** to be second; **sa famille passe en ~** his family comes second *ou* takes second place

secondaire [s(ə)gɔ̃dɛʀ] [1] ADJ (*gén, Chim, Scol*) secondary; (*Géol*) mesozoic, secondary†; **c'est ~** that's of secondary importance; (*Psych*) **caractères sexuels ~s** secondary sexual characteristics; (*Littérat*) **intrigue ~** subplot; **effets ~s** side effects; (*Rail*) **ligne ~** branch line → **route, secteur** [2] NM [a] (*Scol*) **le ~** secondary (school) (*Brit*) *ou* high-school (*US*) education; **les professeurs du ~** secondary school (*Brit*) *ou* high-school (*US*) teachers

[b] (*Écon*) **le ~** the secondary sector [c] (*Géol*) **le ~** the Mesozoic, the Secondary Era†

[d] (*Élec* = *enroulement*) secondary (winding)

secondairement [s(ə)gɔ̃dɛʀmã] ADV secondarily

seconde² [s(ə)gɔ̃d] NF (*gén, Géom*) second; **(attends) une ~ !** just a *ou* one second! *ou* sec!*; **à la ~ où il la vit ...** the (very) moment he saw her ..., the second he saw her ...; **avec elle, tout doit être fait à la ~** with her, things have to be done instantly → **fraction, quart**

secondement [s(ə)gɔ̃dmã] ADV second(ly)

seconder [s(ə)gɔ̃de] ▸ conjug 1 ◂ VT (*lit, fig*) to assist, aid, help; **bien secondé par ...** ably assisted by ...

secouer [s(ə)kwe] ▸ conjug 1 ◂ [1] VT [a] [+ *arbre, salade*] to shake; [+ *miettes, poussière, oppression, paresse*] to shake off; [+ *tapis*] to shake (out); **~ le joug de** [+ *dictature, tyrannie*] to throw off *ou* cast off the yoke of; **arrête de me ~ comme un prunier !*** stop shaking me!; **~ la tête** (*pour dire oui*) to nod (one's head); (*pour dire non*) to shake one's head; **l'explosion secoua l'hôtel** the explosion shook *ou* rocked the hotel; **on est drôlement secoué** (*dans un autocar*) you really get shaken about; (*dans un bateau*) you really get tossed about; **le vent secouait le petit bateau** the wind tossed the little boat about; **la ville a été**

fortement secouée par le tremblement de terre the town was rocked by the earthquake; **le malade était secoué de spasmes/sanglots** spasms/great sobs shook the patient's body, the patient was racked with *ou* by spasms/great sobs; **j'en ai rien à ~‡** I don't give a damn‡ *ou* toss‡
[b] (= *traumatiser*) to shake; **ce deuil l'a beaucoup secoué** this bereavement has really shaken him
[c] (= *ébranler*) to shake, rock; **cela a durement secoué le franc** this has severely shaken the franc; **un gouvernement secoué par des affaires de corruption** a government rocked *ou* shaken by corruption scandals
[d] (= *bousculer*) to shake up; **il ne travaille que lorsqu'on le secoue** he only works if you push him; **il faut ~ la torpeur de notre pays** this country needs to be shaken from *ou* out of its torpor; **~ les puces à qn*** (= *le réprimander*) to tell sb off* (*Brit*) sb off, give sb a telling-off *ou* a ticking-off* (*Brit*); (= *le stimuler*) to give sb a good shake; **secoue tes puces*** *ou* **ta graisse‡** (= *cesse de te morfondre*) snap out of it*; (= *fais vite*) get a move on*; **~ le cocotier** to get rid of the deadwood*
[2] **se secouer** VPR (*lit*) to shake o.s.; (* = *faire un effort*) to make an effort; (* = *se dépêcher*) to get a move on*

secourable [s(ə)kuʀabl] ADJ [*personne*] helpful → **main**

secourir [s(ə)kuʀiʀ] ▶conjug 11◀ VT [+ *blessé, pauvre*] to help, assist, aid; [+ *alpiniste, skieur*] to rescue; [+ *misère*] to help relieve *ou* ease

secourisme [s(ə)kuʀism] NM first aid; **brevet de ~** first-aid certificate; **apprendre les gestes élémentaires de ~** to learn basic first-aid skills

secouriste [s(ə)kuʀist] NMF first-aid worker

secours [s(ə)kuʀ] NM [a] (= *aide*) help, aid, assistance; **appeler qn à son ~** to call to sb for help; **demander du ~** to ask for help *ou* assistance; **crier au ~** to shout *ou* call (out) for help; **au ~!** help!; **aller au ~ de qn** to go to sb's aid *ou* assistance; **porter ~ à qn** to give sb help *ou* assistance; **le Secours catholique** *Catholic charity organization giving assistance to the poor*; **le Secours populaire** *charity organization giving assistance to the poor*
[b] (= *vivres, argent*) aid (*NonC*); **distribuer/recevoir des ~** to distribute/receive aid; **~ humanitaires** humanitarian aid *ou* assistance; (*Hist*) **société de ~ mutuel** friendly (*Brit*) *ou* benefit (*US*) society
[c] (= *sauvetage*) aid (*NonC*), assistance (*NonC*); **~ aux blessés** aid *ou* assistance for the wounded; **d'urgence** emergency aid *ou* assistance; **le ~ en montagne/en mer** mountain/sea rescue; **équipe de ~** rescue party *ou* team; **quand les ~ arrivèrent** when help *ou* the rescue party arrived; **porter ~ à un alpiniste** to rescue a mountaineer; **les premiers ~ sont arrivés très rapidement** the emergency services were soon at the scene; **apporter les premiers ~ à qn** to give first aid to sb → **poste²**
[d] (*Mil*) relief (*NonC*); **la colonne de ~** the relief column; **les ~ sont attendus** relief is expected
[e] (*Rel*) **mourir avec/sans les ~ de la religion** to die with/without the last rites
[f] (*loc*) **cela m'a été/ne m'a pas été d'un grand ~** this has been a *ou* of great help/of little help to me; **éclairage de ~** emergency lighting; **batterie de ~** spare battery → **escalier, issue, poste, roue**

secousse [s(ə)kus] NF [a] (= *cahot*) [*train, voiture*] jolt, bump; [*avion*] bump; **sans (une) ~** [*s'arrêter*] without a jolt, smoothly; [*transporter*] smoothly; **avancer par ~** to jolt along [b] (= *choc*) jerk, jolt; (= *traction*) tug, pull; **(électrique)** (electric) shock; **il a donné des ~s à la corde** he tugged the rope; **~ (tellurique** *ou* **sismique)** (earth) tremor; **il n'en fiche pas une**

~†* he never does a stroke of work [c] (= *bouleversement*) jolt, shock; **~s politiques/monétaires** political/monetary upheavals

secret, -ète [səkʀe, ɛt] [1] ADJ [a] (= *confidentiel*) [*document, rite*] secret; **garder** *ou* **tenir qch ~** to keep sth secret; **des informations classées secrètes** classified information → **agent, fonds, service**
[b] (= *caché*) [*tiroir, porte, pressentiment, vie*] secret; **nos plus secrètes pensées** our most secret *ou* our innermost thoughts; **avoir un charme ~** to have a hidden charm
[c] (= *renfermé*) [*personne*] secretive
[2] NM [a] (= *cachotterie*) secret; **c'est son ~** it's his secret; **il a gardé le ~ de notre projet** he kept our plan secret; **ne pas avoir de ~ pour qn** [*personne*] to have no secrets from sb, keep nothing from sb; [*sujet*] to have *ou* hold no secrets for sb; **confier un ~ à qn** to confide a secret to sb; **il n'en fait pas un ~** he makes no secret about *ou* of it; **~s d'alcôve** intimate talk; **un ~ d'État** a state *ou* official secret; (*fig*) **faire de qch un ~ d'État** to make a big secret of sth, act as if sth were a state secret; **« ~(-)défense »** "official secret"; **couvert par le ~(-)défense** ≈ covered by the Official Secrets Act; **~ de Polichinelle** open secret; **ce n'est un ~ pour personne que ...** it's no secret that ...
[b] (= *mécanisme, moyen*) secret; **~ industriel/de fabrication** industrial/trade secret; **le ~ du bonheur/de la réussite** the secret of happiness/of success; **une sauce/un tour de passe-passe dont il a le ~** a sauce/a conjuring trick of which he (alone) has the secret; **il a le ~ de ces plaisanteries stupides** he's got a knack for telling stupid jokes; **tiroir à ~** drawer with a secret lock; **cadenas à ~** combination lock
[c] (= *discrétion, silence*) secrecy; **demander/exiger/promettre le ~ (absolu)** to ask for/demand/promise (absolute) secrecy; **trahir le ~** to betray the oath of secrecy; **le ~ professionnel/bancaire** professional/bank secrecy; **le ~ médical** medical confidentiality; **le ~ de la confession** the seal of the confessional; **le gouvernement a gardé le ~ sur les négociations** the government has maintained silence *ou* remained silent about the negotiations → **sceau**
[d] (= *mystère*) secret; **les ~s de la nature** the secrets of nature, nature's secrets; **pénétrer dans le ~ des cœurs** to penetrate the secrets of the heart
[e] (*loc*) **dans le ~** in secret *ou* secrecy, secretly; **négociations menées dans le plus grand ~** negotiations carried out in the strictest *ou* utmost secrecy; **mettre qn dans le ~** to let sb into *ou* in on the secret, let sb in on it*; **être dans le ~** to be in on the secret, be in on it*; **je ne suis pas dans le ~ des dieux** I don't share the secrets of the powers that be; **faire ~ de tout** to be secretive about everything; **en ~** (= *sans témoins*) in secret *ou* secrecy, secretly; (= *intérieurement*) secretly, inwardly; (*Prison*) **au ~** in solitary confinement, in solitary*

secrétaire [s(ə)kʀetɛʀ] [1] NMF (*gén*) secretary; **~ médicale/commerciale/particulière/juridique** medical/business *ou* commercial/private/legal secretary; (*Pol*) **premier ~** first secretary
[2] NM (= *meuble*) writing desk, secretaire (*Brit*), secretary (*US*)
[3] COMP ▶ **secrétaire d'ambassade** embassy secretary ▶ **secrétaire de direction** executive secretary, personal assistant ▶ **secrétaire d'État** junior minister; (*US Pol = ministre des Affaires étrangères*) Secretary of State; **le ~ d'État américain au Trésor** the American Treasury Secretary ▶ **secrétaire général** secretary-general, general secretary; **le ~ général des Nations unies** the Secretary-General of the United Nations ▶ **secrétaire de mairie** ≈ town clerk (*in charge of records and legal business*) ▶ **secrétaire perpétuel**

permanent secretary (*of one of the Académies françaises*) ▶ **secrétaire de production** (*Ciné*) production secretary ▶ **secrétaire de rédaction** sub-editor (*Brit*), copy editor (*US*)

secrétariat [s(ə)kʀetaʀja] NM [a] (= *fonction officielle*) secretaryship, post *ou* office of secretary; (= *durée de fonction*) secretaryship, term (of office) as secretary; **~ d'État** (= *fonction*) post of junior minister; ≈ junior minister's office; **~ général des Nations Unies** United Nations Secretariat [b] (= *profession, travail*) secretarial work; (= *bureaux*) [*école*] (secretary's) office; [*usine, administration*] secretarial offices; [*organisation internationale*] secretariat; (= *personnel*) secretarial staff; **école de ~** secretarial college; **~ de rédaction** editorial office

secrètement [sakʀetmɑ̃] ADV [*négocier, se rencontrer*] secretly, in secret; [*espérer*] secretly

sécréter [sekʀete] ▶conjug 6◀ VT (*Bot, Physiol*) to secrete; [+ *ennui*] to exude

sécréteur, -euse *ou* **-trice** [sekʀetœʀ, øz, tʀis] ADJ secretory

sécrétion [sekʀesjɔ̃] NF secretion

sécrétoire [sekʀetwaʀ] ADJ secretory

sectaire [sektɛʀ] ADJ, NMF sectarian

sectarisme [sektaʀism] NM sectarianism

secte [sekt] NF sect

secteur [sektœʀ] NM [a] (*gén, Mil*) sector; (*Admin*) (= *zone, domaine*) area; (= *partie*) part; [*agent de police*] beat; (*Mil*) **~ postal** postal area, ≈ BFPO area (*Brit*); **dans le ~*** (= *ici*) round here; (= *là-bas*) round there; **changer de ~*** to move elsewhere; (*Admin*) **~ sauvegardé** conservation area; (*Scol*) **~ géographique** *ou* **de recrutement scolaire** catchment area (*Brit*), school district (*US*)
[b] (*Élec*) (= *zone*) local supply area; (= *circuit*) **le ~** the mains (supply); **panne de ~** local supply breakdown; **fonctionne sur pile et ~** battery or mains operated
[c] (*Écon*) **~ (économique)** (economic) sector; **~ agricole/bancaire/industriel/pétrolier** agricultural/banking/industrial/oil sector; **~ public/semi-public/privé** public *ou* state/semi-public/private sector; **le ~ nationalisé** nationalized industries; **~ d'activité** branch of industry; **~ primaire** primary sector; **~ secondaire** manufacturing *ou* secondary sector; **~ tertiaire** service industries, service *ou* tertiary sector
[d] (*Géom*) sector; **~ angulaire** sector; **~ circulaire** sector of circle; **~ sphérique** spherical sector, sector of sphere
[e] (*Ordin*) sector

section [sɛksjɔ̃] NF [a] (= *coupe: gén*) section; [*fil électrique*] gauge; **fil de petite/grosse ~** thin-/heavy-gauge wire; **prenons un tube de double** let's use a tube which is twice the bore; **dessiner la ~ d'un os/d'une tige** to draw the section of a bone/of a stem, draw a bone/a stem in section; **la ~ (de ce câble) est toute rouillée** the end (of this cable) is all rusted
[b] (*Scol*) ≈ course; **il est en ~ littéraire/scientifique** he's doing a literature/science course
[c] (*Univ*) department
[d] (*Admin*) section, department; (*Pol*) branch; **~ du Conseil d'État** department of the Council of State; **~ (du) contentieux** legal section *ou* department; **~ électorale** ward; **~ syndicale** (trade) union group
[e] (= *partie*) [*ouvrage*] section; [*route, rivière, voie ferrée*] section; (*en autobus*) fare stage → **fin²**
[f] (*Mus*) section; **~ mélodique/rythmique** melody/rhythm section
[g] (*Mil*) platoon
[h] (*Math*) section; **~ conique/plane** conic/plane section
[i] (*Méd = ablation*) severing

sectionnement [sɛksjɔnmɑ̃] NM [a] [*tube, fil,*

artère] severing [b] [circonscription, groupe] division

sectionner [sɛksjɔne] ▸conjug 1◂ [1] VT [a] [+ tube, fil, artère, membre] to sever [b] [+ circonscription, groupe] to divide (up), split (up) (en into) [2] **se sectionner** VPR [a] [tube, fil, artère, membre] to be severed [b] [circonscription, groupe] to divide ou split (up)

sectoriel, -ielle [sɛktɔrjel] ADJ sectional

sectorisation [sɛktɔrizasjɔ̃] NF division into sectors

sectoriser [sɛktɔrize] ▸conjug 1◂ VT to divide into sectors, sector

Sécu* [seky] NF (ABRÉV = **Sécurité sociale**) → **sécurité**

séculaire [sekylɛr] ADJ (= très vieux) [arbre] ancient; [croyance] age-old; (= qui a lieu tous les cent ans) [fête, jeux] centennial; **ces forêts/maisons sont quatre fois ~s** these forests/houses are four centuries old; **année ~** last year of the century

sécularisation [sekylarizasjɔ̃] NF secularization

séculariser [sekylarize] ▸conjug 1◂ VT to secularize

séculier, -ière [sekylje, jɛr] [1] ADJ [clergé, autorité] secular → **bras** [2] NM secular

secundo [sɛgɔ̃do] ADV second(ly), in the second place

sécurisant, e [sekyrizɑ̃, ɑ̃t] ADJ (gén) reassuring; [climat] of security, reassuring

sécurisation [sekyrizasjɔ̃] NF [personne] reassuring; **des opérations de ~ de la population** measures to reassure the population ou to make the population feel more secure

sécuriser [sekyrize] ▸conjug 1◂ VT [a] (= rassurer) **~ qn** to give (a feeling of) security to sb, make sb feel secure; **~ l'opinion** to reassure people; **être/se sentir sécurisé par qn/qch** to be/feel reassured by sb/sth [b] (= accroître la sécurité de) **~ les transports de fonds** to increase the security of transfers of funds; **~ l'accès à qch** to make access to sth more secure

Securit® [sekyrit] NM **verre ~** Triplex (glass)®

sécuritaire [sekyritɛr] ADJ [discours, politique] law-and-order (épith); [idéologie] that concentrates on law and order; **mesures ~s** security measures

sécurité [sekyrite] [1] NF [a] (= absence de danger) safety; (= conditions d'ordre, absence de troubles) security; **être/se sentir en ~** to be/feel safe, be/feel secure; **mettre qch en ~** to put sth in a safe place; **en toute ~** safely, in complete safety; **une fausse impression de ~** a false sense of security; **cette retraite représentait pour lui une ~** this pension meant security for him; **la ~ de l'emploi** security of employment, job security; **la ~ matérielle** material security; **assurer la ~ d'un personnage important/des ouvriers/des installations** to ensure the safety of an important person/of workers/of the equipment; **l'État assure la ~ des citoyens** the state looks after the security ou safety of its citizens; **la ~ nationale/internationale/intérieure/européenne** national/international/internal/European security; **pacte/traité de ~ collective** collective security pact/treaty; **mesures de ~** (contre incendie) safety measures ou precautions; (contre attentat) security measures; **des mesures de ~ très strictes avaient été prises** very strict security precautions ou measures had been taken, security was very tight → **ceinture, compagnie, conseil**
[b] (= mécanisme) safety catch, safety (US); **mettre la ~** [arme à feu] to put on the safety catch ou the safety (US); **de ~** [dispositif] safety (épith); (Aut) **(porte à) ~ enfants** childproof lock, child lock; **~ informatique** computer security; **assurer la ~ d'un système** to ensure

that a system is secure, ensure system security → **cran**
[c] (= service) security; **la ~ militaire** military security

[2] COMP ▶ **la sécurité civile** emergency services dealing with natural disasters, bomb disposal etc ▶ **la sécurité publique** law and order; **agent de la ~ publique** officer of the law ▶ **la sécurité routière** road safety ▶ **la Sécurité sociale** (pour la santé) ≈ the National Health Service (Brit), ≈ Medicaid (US); (pour vieillesse etc) ≈ the Social Security, ≈ Medicare (US); **prestations de la Sécurité sociale** ≈ Social Security benefits

---

SÉCURITÉ SOCIALE

The French public welfare system is financed by compulsory contributions paid directly from salaries and by employers. It covers essential health care, pensions and other basic benefits. In many cases, costs not covered by the **Sécurité sociale** may be met by a **mutuelle**. The deficit of the **Sécurité sociale**, popularly known as the "trou de la Sécurité sociale", has reached massive proportions in recent years, and efforts to stabilize the situation include an extra contribution from salaries, paid at source, called the "CRDS" ("contribution au remboursement de la dette sociale"). → MUTUELLE

---

sédatif, -ive [sedatif, iv] [1] ADJ sedative [2] NM sedative; **sous ~s** under sedation

sédation [sedasjɔ̃] NF sedation

sédentaire [sedɑ̃tɛr] ADJ [personne, travail, vie,] sedentary; [population] settled, sedentary; (Mil) permanently garrisoned

sédentarisation [sedɑ̃tarizasjɔ̃] NF settling process

sédentariser [sedɑ̃tarize] ▸conjug 1◂ VT to settle; **population sédentarisée** settled population

sédentarité [sedɑ̃tarite] NF [population] settled way of life; [travail] sedentary nature

sédiment [sedimɑ̃] NM (Méd, fig) sediment; (Géol) deposit, sediment

sédimentaire [sedimɑ̃tɛr] ADJ sedimentary

sédimentation [sedimɑ̃tasjɔ̃] NF sedimentation → **vitesse**

sédimenter [sedimɑ̃te] ▸conjug 1◂ VI to deposit sediment

séditieux, -ieuse [sedisjø, jøz] [1] ADJ (= en sédition) [général, troupes] insurrectionary (épith), insurgent (épith); (= agitateur) [esprit, propos, réunion] seditious [2] NM,F insurrectionary, insurgent

sédition [sedisjɔ̃] NF insurrection, sedition; **esprit de ~** spirit of sedition ou insurrection ou revolt

séducteur, -trice [sedyktœr, tris] [1] ADJ seductive [2] NM (= débaucheur) seducer; (péj = Don Juan) womanizer (péj) [3] **séductrice** NF seductress

séduction [sedyksjɔ̃] NF [a] (= charme) charm; (= action) seduction; **il a un grand pouvoir de ~** he has great charm; **scène de ~** seduction scene; **il y a toujours un jeu de ~ entre un homme et une femme** there is always an element of seduction between a man and a woman; (fig) **le pouvoir de ~ de l'argent** the lure ou seductive power of money; **leur opération de ~ en direction du public/des électeurs** the charm offensive they aimed at the public/the voters; **leurs tentatives de ~ pour se concilier l'ONU** their attempts to win over the UN [b] (= attrait) [style, projet, idéologie] appeal; **exercer une forte ~ sur qn** to have a great deal of appeal for sb; **les ~s de la vie estudiantine** the attractions ou appeal of student life [c] (Jur) [femme] seduction; [mineur] corruption

séduire [sedɥir] ▸conjug 38◂ VT [a] (par son physique, son charme) to charm; **qu'est-ce qui t'a séduit chez ou en elle ?** what attracted you to her?; **elle sait ~** she knows how to use her charms
[b] (= plaire) [style, qualité, projet] to appeal to; **une des qualités qui me séduisent le plus** one of the qualities which most appeal to me ou which I find most appealing; **ils ont essayé de nous ~ avec ces propositions** they tried to win us over ou to tempt us with these proposals; **cette idée va-t-elle les ~ ?** is this idea going to tempt them? ou appeal to them?; **leur projet/style de vie me séduit mais ...** their plan/lifestyle does appeal to me ou does have some appeal for me but ...; **essayez cette crème, vous serez séduite** try this cream, you'll love it; (= tromper) **séduit par les apparences** taken in by appearances
[c] († : sexuellement) to seduce

séduisant, e [sedɥizɑ̃, ɑ̃t] ADJ [personne, visage] attractive; [beauté] seductive; [genre de vie, projet, style, tenue] appealing, attractive

sédum [sedɔm] NM sedum

séfarade [sefarad] [1] ADJ Sephardic [2] NMF Sephardi

segment [sɛgmɑ̃] NM (gén) segment; **~ de frein** brake shoe; **~ de piston** piston ring; (Ordin) **~ de programme** segment; **~ de marché** market segment, segment of the market

segmental, e [sɛgmɑ̃tal, o] ADJ (mpl -aux) (Ling) segmental

segmentation [sɛgmɑ̃tasjɔ̃] NF (gén) segmentation

segmenter [sɛgmɑ̃te] ▸conjug 1◂ [1] VT to segment [2] **se segmenter** VPR to segment, form ou break into segments

ségrégatif, -ive [segregatif, iv] ADJ segregative

ségrégation [segregasjɔ̃] NF segregation; **~ raciale** racial segregation

ségrégationnisme [segregasjɔnism] NM racial segregation, segregationism

ségrégationniste [segregasjɔnist] [1] ADJ [manifestant] segregationist; [problème] of segregation; [troubles] due to segregation [2] NMF segregationist

ségréger [segreʒe] ▸conjug 3 ou 6◂, **ségréguer** [segrege] ▸conjug 6◂ VT to segregate; **une nation de plus en plus ségréguée** a nation that has become increasingly segregated

seiche [sɛʃ] NF (Zool) cuttlefish → **os**

séide [seid] NM (fanatically devoted) henchman

seigle [sɛgl] NM rye → **pain**

seigneur [sɛɲœr] NM [a] (Hist = suzerain, noble) lord; (fig = maître) overlord; (hum) **mon ~ et maître** my lord and master; **grand ~** great ou powerful lord; **se montrer grand ~** avec qn to behave in a lordly fashion towards sb; **faire le grand ~** to play ou act the grand ou fine gentleman; **faire le grand ~ avec qn** to lord it over sb ■ (PROV) **à tout ~ tout honneur** honour to whom honour is due (PROV) [b] (Rel) **le Seigneur** the Lord; **Notre-Seigneur Jésus-Christ** Our Lord Jesus Christ; **Seigneur Dieu !** good Lord! → **jour, vigne**

seigneurial, e [sɛɲœrjal, jo] ADJ (mpl -iaux) [château, domaine] seigniorial; [allure, luxe] lordly, stately

seigneurie [sɛɲœri] NF [a] **Votre/Sa Seigneurie** your/his Lordship [b] (= terre) (lord's) domain, seigniory; (= droits féodaux) seigniory

sein [sɛ̃] NM [a] (= mamelle) breast; **donner le ~ à un bébé** (= méthode) to breast-feed a baby, suckle ou nurse a baby; (= être en train d'allaiter) to feed a baby (at the breast), suckle ou nurse a baby; (= présenter le sein) to give a baby the breast; **prendre le ~** to take the breast; **elle était ~s nus** she was topless; (fig) **ça me ferait mal aux ~s¦** that would really get (to) me* → **faux²**, nourrir [b] (*littér*) (= *poitrine*) breast (*littér*), bosom (*littér*); (= *matrice*) womb; (*fig* = *giron, milieu*) bosom; **serrer qn/qch contre son ~** to clasp sb/sth to one's bosom; **porter un enfant dans son ~** to carry a child in one's womb; **dans le ~ de la terre/de l'église** in the bosom of the earth/of the church; **le ~ de Dieu** the bosom of the Father → **réchauffer** [c] (= *parmi, dans*) **au ~ de** within

Seine [sɛn] NF **la ~** the Seine

seine [sɛn] NF (= *filet*) seine

seing [sɛ̃] NM†† signature; (*Jur*) **acte sous ~ privé** private agreement (*document not legally certified*)

séisme [seism] NM (*Géog*) earthquake, seism (*SPÉC*); (*fig*) upheaval

séismique [seismik] ADJ = **sismique**

séismographe [seismɔgraf] NM = **sismographe**

séismologie [seismɔlɔʒi] NF = **sismologie**

seize [sɛz] ADJ INV, NM INV sixteen; **film tourné en ~ millimètres** film shot in sixteen millimetres; *pour locutions voir* **six**

seizième [sɛzjɛm] ADJ, NMF sixteenth; (*Sport*) **~s de finale** first round (*of 5-round knockout competition*); **le ~ (arrondissement)** the sixteenth arrondissement (*wealthy area in Paris*); **être très ~** to be typical of the sixteenth arrondissement, ≈ be a Sloane Ranger* (*Brit*) ou a preppy* (*US*); *pour locutions voir* **sixième**

seizièmement [sɛzjɛmmɑ̃] ADV in the sixteenth place, sixteenth

séjour [seʒuʀ] NM [a] (= *visite*) stay; **faire un ~ de trois semaines à Paris** to stay (for) three weeks in Paris, have a three-week stay in Paris; **faire un ~ à l'étranger** to spend time abroad; **j'ai fait plusieurs ~s en Australie** I've been to Australia several times; **c'est mon deuxième ~ aux États-Unis** it's my second stay in ou trip to the United States, it's the second time I've been to the United States; **il a fait trois ~s en prison** he has been in prison three times before, he has had three spells in prison; **elle a fait plusieurs ~s à l'hôpital** she has had several stays ou spells in hospital; (*Pol*) **~ officiel** official visit; **le ministre était en ~ privé en France** the minister was on a private holiday (*Brit*) ou on vacation (*US*) in France; **il a fait un ~ linguistique en Irlande** he went to Ireland on a language course → **interdit¹, permis, taxe** [b] (= *salon*) living room, lounge (*Brit*); **~ double** living-cum-dining room (*Brit*), living room-dining room (*US*) → **salle** [c] (*littér*) (= *endroit*) abode (*littér*), dwelling place (*littér*); (= *demeure temporaire*) sojourn (*littér*); **le ~ des dieux** the abode ou dwelling place of the gods

séjourner [seʒuʀne] ▶ conjug 1 ◀ VI [*personne*] to stay; [*eau, neige*] to lie; **~ chez qn** to stay with sb

sel [sɛl] [1] NM [a] (*gén, Chim*) salt; **sans ~** [*biscottes, pain, régime*] salt-free (*épith*); **je mange sans ~** I don't put salt on my food → **gros, poivre** [b] (*fig*) (= *humour*) wit; (= *piquant*) spice; **la remarque ne manque pas de ~** it's quite a witty remark; **c'est ce qui fait tout le ~ de l'aventure** that's what gives the adventure its spice; (*littér*) **ils sont le ~ de la terre** they are the salt of the earth → **grain** [2] **sels** NMPL (*à respirer*) smelling salts [3] COMP ▶ **sel d'Angleterre** = **sel d'Epsom** ▶ **sel attique** Attic salt ou wit ▶ **sels de bain** bath salts ▶ **sels biliaires** bile salts ▶ **sel de céleri** celery salt ▶ **sel de cuisine** cooking salt ▶ **sel d'Epsom** Epsom salts ▶ **sel fin = sel de table** ▶ **sel gemme** rock salt ▶ **sel marin** ou **de mer** sea salt ▶ **sels minéraux** mineral salts ▶ **sel de table** table salt

sélacien, -ienne [selasjɛ̃, jɛn] ADJ, NM selachian

select* [selɛkt] ADJ INV, **sélect, e*** [selɛkt] ADJ [*personne*] posh*, high-class; [*clientèle, club, endroit*] select, posh*

sélecteur [selɛktœʀ] [1] NM [*ordinateur, poste de télé, central téléphonique*] selector; [*motocyclette*] gear lever [2] ADJ **comité ~** selection committee

sélectif, -ive [selɛktif, iv] ADJ selective

sélection [selɛksjɔ̃] NF [a] (= *action*) selection; (*Bio*) **~ naturelle** natural selection; (*Scol, Univ*) **il y a une ~ (à l'entrée)** admission is by selective entry; **faire** ou **opérer** ou **effectuer une ~ parmi** to make a selection from among [b] (= *choix, gamme*) [*articles, produits, œuvres*] selection [c] (= *choix*) selection; (= *équipe*) (*gén*) team; (*Ftbl, Rugby etc*) line-up; **la ~ française au festival de Cannes** the French films selected to be shown at the Cannes film festival; **comité de ~** selection committee; **il a plus de 20 ~s à son actif en équipe nationale** he's been selected over 20 times for the national team, he's been capped more than 20 times (*Brit*), he has more than 20 caps to his credit (*Brit*); **match de ~** trial match; **épreuves de ~** (selection) trials, heats

sélectionné, e [selɛksjɔne] (*ptp de* **sélectionner**) [1] ADJ = *soigneusement choisi*) specially selected, choice (*épith*) [2] NM,F (*Ftbl etc*) selected player; (*Athlétisme*) selected competitor; **les ~s** (*Ftbl, Rugby*) the line-up; **figurer parmi les ~s** to be in the line-up

sélectionner [selɛksjɔne] ▶ conjug 1 ◀ VT to select (**parmi** from (among)); **un film sélectionné à Cannes** a film selected at the Cannes film festival; (*Ftbl, Rugby*) **il a été sélectionné trois fois en équipe nationale** he was selected three times for the national team, he was capped three times (*Brit*)

sélectionneur, -euse [selɛksjɔnœʀ, øz] NM,F (*Sport*) selector

sélectivement [selɛktivmɑ̃] ADV selectively

sélectivité [selɛktivite] NF (*Radio*) selectivity

sélénite [selenit] [1] ADJ moon (*épith*) [2] **Sélénite** NMF moon-dweller

sélénium [selenjɔm] NM selenium

self [sɛlf] [1] NM (* = *restaurant*) self-service restaurant, cafeteria [2] NF (*Élec*) (= *propriété*) self-induction; (= *bobine*) self-induction coil

self-control [sɛlfkɔ̃tʀol] NM self-control

self-inductance [sɛlfɛ̃dyktɑ̃s] NF self-inductance

self-induction [sɛlfɛ̃dyksjɔ̃] NF self-induction

self-made-man [sɛlfmɛdman] (*pl* **self-made-men** [sɛlfmɛdmɛn]) NM self-made man

self-service (*pl* **self-services**) [sɛlfsɛʀvis] NM (*gén*) self-service; (= *restaurant*) self-service restaurant, cafeteria

selle [sɛl] [1] NF [a] (*Cyclisme, Équitation*) saddle; **monter sans ~** to ride bareback; **se mettre en ~** to mount, get into the saddle; **mettre qn en ~** (*lit*) to put sb in the saddle; (*fig*) to give sb a boost ou a leg-up; **se remettre en ~** (*lit*) to remount, get back into the saddle; (*fig*) to get back in the saddle; (*lit, fig*) **être bien en ~** to be firmly in the saddle → **cheval** [b] (*Boucherie*) saddle [c] (*Art*) [*sculpteur*] turntable [d] **êtes-vous allé à la ~ aujourd'hui?** have your bowels moved today? [2] **selles** NFPL (*Méd*) stools, motions

seller [sele] ▶ conjug 1 ◀ VT to saddle

sellerie [sɛlʀi] NF (= *articles, métier, selles*) saddlery; (= *lieu de rangement*) tack room, harness room, saddle room

sellette [sɛlɛt] NF [a] (*pour sculpteur*) turntable; (*pour statue, pot de fleur*) stand [b] (*Constr*) cradle [c] (*loc*) **être/mettre qn sur la ~** to be/put sb in the hot seat

sellier [selje] NM saddler

✔ selon [s(ə)lɔ̃] PRÉP [a] (= *conformément à*) in accordance with; **agir ~ sa conscience** to follow the dictates of one's conscience, act accord-

---

ing to one's conscience; **~ la volonté de qn** in accordance with sb's wishes; **~ la formule** ou **l'expression consacrée** as the saying goes [b] (= *en proportion de, en fonction de*) according to; **vivre ~ ses moyens** to live within one's means; **donner ~ ses moyens** to give according to one's means; **le nombre varie ~ la saison** the number varies (along with ou according to the season); **c'est ~ le cas/les circonstances** it all depends on the individual case/on the circumstances; **c'est ~*** it (all) depends; **il acceptera ou n'acceptera pas, ~ son humeur** he may or may not accept, depending on ou according to his mood ou how he feels [c] (= *suivant l'opinion de*) according to; **~ lui** according to him; **~ ses propres termes** in his own words; **~ moi, c'est une mauvaise idée** in my opinion, it's a bad idea; **qui la cassé? — ~ toi?** who broke it? — who do you think? [d] (*loc*) **~ toute apparence** to all appearances; **~ toute vraisemblance** in all probability; **~ que** according to ou depending on whether

Seltz [sɛls] NF → **eau**

semailles [s(ə)maj] NFPL (= *action*) sowing (*NonC*); (= *période*) sowing period; (= *graine*) seed, seeds

semaine [s(ə)mɛn] NF [a] (*gén*) week; **la première ~ de mai** the first week in ou of May; **en ~** during the week, on weekdays; **louer à la ~** to let by the week; **dans 2 ~s à partir d'aujourd'hui** 2 weeks ou a fortnight (*Brit*) (from) today; **la ~ de 39 heures** the 39-hour (working) week; **à la ~ prochaine!** I'll see you (ou talk to you) next week! → **courant, fin²** [b] (= *salaire*) week's wages ou pay, weekly wage ou pay; (= *argent de poche*) week's ou weekly pocket money [c] (*Publicité*) week; **~ publicitaire/commerciale** publicity/business week; **la ~ du livre/du bricolage** book/do-it-yourself week; **la ~ contre la faim** feed the hungry week; **la ~ contre le SIDA** AIDS week; (*hum*) **c'est sa ~ de bonté!*** it must be charity week!* (*hum*) [d] (*Bijouterie*) (= *bracelet*) (seven-band) bracelet; (= *bague*) (seven-band) ring [e] (*loc*) **il te le rendra la ~ des quatre jeudis** he'll never give it back to you in a month of Sundays; **faire la ~ anglaise** to work ou do a five-day week; (*Mil*) **être de ~** to be on duty (*for the week*); **officier de ~** officer on duty (*for the week*), officer of the week; **gestion à la petite ~** short-sighted management; **trafiquants à la petite ~** small-time dealers

semainier, -ière [s(ə)menje, jɛʀ] [1] NM,F (= *personne*) person on duty (*for the week*) [2] NM (= *agenda*) desk diary; (= *meuble*) chest of (seven) drawers, semainier; (= *bracelet*) (seven-band) bracelet

sémanticien, -ienne [semɑ̃tisjɛ̃, jɛn] NM,F semantician, semanticist

sémantique [semɑ̃tik] [1] ADJ semantic [2] NF semantics *sg*

sémaphore [semafɔʀ] NM (*Naut*) semaphore; (*Rail*) semaphore signal

semblable [sɑ̃blabl] [1] ADJ [a] (= *similaire*) similar; **~ à** like, similar to; **dans un cas ~** in a similar case; **je ne connais rien de ~** I've never come across anything like it; **une maison ~ à tant d'autres** a house like any other, a house like so many others ou similar to so many others; **il a prononcé un discours très ~ à celui de l'année dernière** he delivered a speech very much like ou very much in the same vein as last year's; **en cette circonstance, il a été ~ à lui-même** on this occasion he behaved true to form ou as usual; **elle était là, ~ à elle-même** she was there, the same as ever [b] (*avant n* = *tel*) such; **de ~s calomnies sont inacceptables** such calumnies ou calumnies of this kind are unacceptable [c] (= *qui se ressemblent*) **~s** alike; **les deux frè-**

▶ GRAMMAIRE ACTIVE: **selon** 33.2, 53.3, 53.5

res étaient ~s (en tout) the two brothers were alike (in every way) → triangle

[2] NMF fellow creature; **aimer son ~** to love one's fellow creatures ou fellow men; (péj) **toi et tes ~s** you and your kind (péj), you and people like you (péj); **il n'a pas son ~** there's no-one like him

semblablement [sãblabləmã] ADV similarly, likewise

semblant [sãblã] NM [a] (= apparence) **un ~ de calme/bonheur/vie/vérité** a semblance of calm/happiness/life/truth; **un ~ de réponse** some vague attempt at a reply; **un ~ de soleil** a glimmer of sun; **un ~ de sourire** the shadow ou ghost of a smile; **nous avons un ~ de jardin** we've got a garden of sorts; **pour redonner un ~ de cohérence à leur politique** to make their policy look more consistent [b] (loc) **faire ~ de dormir/lire** to pretend to be asleep/to be reading; **il a fait ~ de ne pas me voir** he pretended not to see me, he acted as if he didn't see me; **il fait ~** he's pretending; **il fait ~ de rien*, mais il entend tout** he's pretending to take no notice but he can hear everything

▼ **sembler** [sãble] ▸conjug 1 ◂ [1] VB IMPERS [a] (= paraître) **il semble bon/inutile de ...** it seems a good idea/useless to ...; **il semblerait qu'il ne soit pas venu** it would seem ou appear that he didn't come, it looks as though ou as if he didn't come [b] (= estimer) **il peut te ~ démodé de ...** it may seem ou appear old-fashioned to you to ...; **c'était lundi, il me semble** I think it was on Monday; **il me semble que ...** it seems ou appears to me that ...; **il me semble que oui/que non** I think so/I don't think so; **il me semble que tu n'as pas le droit de ...** it seems ou appears to me that you don't have the right to ...; **comme bon me/te semble** as I/you see fit, as I/you think best ou fit; **ils se marieront quand bon leur semblera** they will get married when they see fit; **prenez qui/ce que bon vous semble** take who/what you please ou wish [c] (= croire) **il me semble que** I think (that); **il me semblait bien que je l'avais posé là** I really thought ou did think I had put it down here; **il me semble revoir mon grand-père** it's as though I were seeing my grandfather again; **il me semble vous l'avoir déjà dit** I think ou I have a feeling I've already told you [d] (= loc) **je vous connais, ce me semble†** methinks I know you†, it seems to me that I know you; **je suis déjà venu ici, me semble-t-il** it seems to me (that) I've been here before, I seem to have been here before; **il a, semble-t-il, essayé de me contacter** apparently he tried to contact me; **à ce qu'il me semble, notre organisation est mauvaise** to my mind ou it seems to me (that) our organization is bad, our organization seems bad to me; (frm, hum) **que vous en semble ?** what do you think (of it)?

[2] VI to seem; **la maison lui sembla magnifique** the house seemed magnificent to him; **il semblait content/nerveux** he seemed (to be) ou appeared ou looked happy/nervous; **elle me semble bien fatiguée** she seems ou looks very tired to me; **vous me semblez bien pessimiste !** you do sound ou seem very pessimistic!; **il ne semblait pas convaincu** he didn't seem (to be) convinced, he didn't look ou sound convinced; **les frontières de la science semblent reculer** the frontiers of science seem ou appear to be retreating; **tout semble indiquer que leur départ fut précipité** all the signs are that they left in a hurry; **mes arguments ne semblent pas l'avoir convaincu** apparently he has not been convinced by my arguments

semé, e [s(ə)me] (ptp de semer) ADJ **questions ~es de pièges** questions full of pitfalls; **la route de la démocratie est ~e d'embûches/n'est pas ~e de roses** the road to democracy is

fraught with difficulties/is not easy; **mer ~e d'écueils** sea scattered ou dotted with reefs; **robe ~e de pierreries** dress studded with gems; **récit ~ d'anecdotes** story interspersed ou sprinkled with anecdotes; **tissu ~ de fleurs** flowery material; **gazon ~ de fleurs** lawn dotted with flowers; **campagne ~e d'arbres** countryside dotted with trees; **la vie est ~e de joies et de peines** life is full of joys and sorrows

sème [sɛm] NM seme

semelle [s(ə)mɛl] NF [a] [chaussure] sole; **~s (intérieures)** insoles; **~s compensées** platform soles; **chaussures à ~s compensées** ou **à plate-forme** platform shoes; **~s de plomb** lead boots; (fig) **j'avais des ~s de plomb** my feet felt like lead weights; **c'est de la vraie ~*** [viande] it's as tough as old boots* (Brit) ou shoe leather (US), it's like leather → **battre, crêpe²** [b] (= loc) **il n'a pas avancé/reculé d'une ~** he hasn't moved forward/moved back (so much as) a single inch ou an inch; **il ne m'a pas quitté** ou **lâché d'une ~** he didn't leave me for a single second, he stuck to me like a leech; **ne le lâche pas d'une ~ !** don't let him out of your sight! [c] (Tech) [rail] base plate pad; [machine] bedplate; [fer à repasser] sole plate; [ski] running surface

semence [s(ə)mãs] NF [a] (Agr, fig) seed; **blé/pommes de terre de ~** seed corn/potatoes [b] (= sperme) semen, seed (littér) [c] (= clou) tack [d] (Bijouterie) **~ de diamants** diamond sparks; **~ de perles** seed pearls

semer [s(ə)me] ▸conjug 5 ◂ VT [a] (= répandre) [+ discorde, graines] to sow; [+ confusion, terreur] to spread; [+ clous, confettis] to scatter; [+ faux bruits] to spread, disseminate (frm); **~ la panique** to spread panic; **ils ont semé la mort dans la région** they brought death and destruction to the region; **~ le doute dans l'esprit de qn** to sow doubts in sb's mind; **~ ses propos de citations** to intersperse ou sprinkle one's remarks with quotations ■ (PROV) **qui sème le vent récolte la tempête** he who sows the wind shall reap the whirlwind (PROV) [b] (* = perdre) [+ mouchoir] to lose; [+ poursuivant] to lose, shake off

semestre [s(ə)mɛstʀ] NM [a] (= période) half-year, six-month period; **tous les ~s** every six months, twice yearly ou a year; **taxe payée par ~** tax paid half-yearly; **pendant le premier/second ~ (de l'année)** during the first/second half of the year, during the first/second six-month period (of the year) [b] (Univ) semester [c] (= loyer) half-yearly ou six months' rent; **je vous dois un ~** I owe you six months' ou half a year's rent [d] [rente, pension] half-yearly payment

semestriel, -ielle [s(ə)mɛstʀijɛl] ADJ [a] [assemblée] six-monthly; [revue, bulletin] biannual; [résultats] half-yearly [b] (Univ) [examen] end-of-semester; [cours] one-semester (épith) [c] [rente, pension] half-yearly

semestriellement [s(ə)mɛstʀijɛlmã] ADV (gén) half-yearly; (Univ) every ou each semester; **les montants sont fixés ~** the amounts are set every six months

semeur, -euse [s(ə)mœʀ, øz] NM,F sower; **~ de trouble(s)** troublemaker; **~ de discorde** sower of discord; **la Semeuse** symbolic figure of a female sower that appears on some French coins

semi- [səmi] PRÉF (dans les mots composés à trait d'union, le préfixe reste invariable au pluriel) semi-; **~autonome/-professionnel** semi-autonomous/-professional

semi-aride [səmiaʀid] ADJ semiarid

semi-automatique [səmiɔtɔmatik] ADJ semi-automatic

semi-auxiliaire [səmiɔksiljɛʀ] [1] ADJ semiauxiliary [2] NM semiauxiliary verb

semi-chenillé, e [səmi(ə)nije] [1] ADJ half-tracked [2] NM half-track

semi-circulaire [səmisiʀkylɛʀ] ADJ semicircular

semi-conducteur, -trice [səmikɔdyktœʀ, tʀis] [1] ADJ [propriétés, cristaux] semiconducting [2] NM semiconductor

semi-conserve [səmikɔsɛʀv] NF semi-preserve

semi-consonne [səmikɔsɔn] NF semiconsonant

semi-fini, e [səmifini] ADJ semi-finished; **produits ~s** semi-finished goods ou products

semi-liberté [səmilibɛʀte] NF [prisonnier] ≈ partial release; **les animaux vivent en ~** the animals live in relative liberty

sémillant, e [semijã, ãt] ADJ (= alerte, vif) [personne] vivacious, spirited; [allure, esprit] vivacious; (= fringant) dashing (épith)

séminaire [seminɛʀ] NM (Rel) seminary; (Univ) seminar; (Rel) **grand ~** (theological) seminary; **petit ~** Catholic secondary school

séminal, e (mpl -aux) [seminal, o] ADJ (Bio) seminal

séminariste [seminaʀist] NM seminarian, seminarist

séminifère [seminifɛʀ] ADJ seminiferous

semi-nomade [səminɔmad] [1] ADJ seminomadic [2] NMF seminomad

semi-nomadisme [səminɔmadism] NM seminomadism

semi-officiel, -elle [səmiɔfisjɛl] ADJ semi-official

sémiologie [semjɔlɔʒi] NF (Ling, Méd) semiology

sémiologique [semjɔlɔʒik] ADJ semiological

sémiologue [semjɔlɔg] NMF semiologist

sémioticien, -ienne [semjɔtisjɛ, jɛn] NM,F semiotician

sémiotique [semjɔtik] [1] ADJ semiotic [2] NF semiotics sg

semi-ouvré, e [səmiuvʀe] ADJ semifinished

semi-perméable [səmipɛʀmeabl] ADJ semipermeable

semi-précieux, -ieuse [səmipʀesjø, jøz] ADJ [pierre] semiprecious

semi-produit [səmipʀɔdɥi] NM semifinished product

semi-public, -ique [səmipyblik] ADJ semipublic

sémique [semik] ADJ semic; **acte ~** semic ou meaningful act

Sémiramis [semiʀamis] NF Semiramis

semi-remorque [səmiʀ(ə)mɔʀk] [1] NM (= camion) articulated lorry (Brit), artic* (Brit), trailer truck (US) [2] NF (= remorque) trailer (Brit), semitrailer (US)

semis [s(ə)mi] NM (= plante) seedling; (= opération) sowing; (= terrain) seedbed, seed plot; (= motif) pattern, motif

sémite [semit] [1] ADJ Semitic [2] **Sémite** NMF Semite

sémitique [semitik] ADJ Semitic

sémitisme [semitism] NM Semitism

semi-voyelle [səmivwajɛl] NF semivowel

semoir [səmwaʀ] NM [a] (= machine) sower, seeder; **~ à engrais** muckspreader, manure spreader [b] (= sac) seed-bag, seed-lip

semonce [səmɔs] NF reprimand; (Naut) **coup de ~** (Naut) warning shot across the bows; (fig) warning; (Pol) **un coup de ~ pour le gouvernement** a warning shot across the government's bows

semoule [s(ə)mul] NF **~ (de blé dur)** (gén) semolina; (pour couscous) couscous; **~ de maïs** corn meal → **gâteau, sucre**

sempiternel, -elle [sãpitɛʀnɛl] ADJ [plaintes, reproches] eternal (épith), never-ending

➤ GRAMMAIRE ACTIVE: **sembler** 33.2, 53.4, 53.5

sempiternellement [sɑ̃piternelmɑ̃] ADV
eternally

sénat [sena] NM (*gén, Hist*) senate; (*Pol*) **le Sénat** the Senate; **le Sénat américain** the American Senate → SÉNAT

☐ **SÉNAT**

The **Sénat**, *the upper house of the French parliament, sits at the Palais du Luxembourg in Paris. One third of its members, known as "sénateurs", are elected for a nine-year term every three years by an electoral college consisting of "députés" and other electoral representatives. The* **Sénat** *has a wide range of powers but is overruled by the "Assemblée nationale" in cases of disagreement.*
→ ASSEMBLÉE NATIONALE ; DÉPUTÉ ; ÉLECTIONS

---

sénateur [senatœr] NM senator → train

sénatorial, e (*mpl* **-iaux**) [senatɔrjal, jo]
[1] ADJ (*commission*) senatorial; [*mission, rapport*] Senate (*épith*); **la majorité ~e** the majority in the Senate [2] NFPL **les (élections) ~es** (*gén*) the senatorial elections; (*aux USA*) the Senate elections → ÉLECTIONS

sénatus-consulte (*pl* **sénatus-consultes**)
[senatyskɔ̃sylt] NM (*Antiq, Hist*) senatus consultum

séné [sene] NM senna

sénéchal (*pl* **-aux**) [seneʃal, o] NM (*Hist*) seneschal

séneçon [sənsɔ̃] NM groundsel

Sénégal [senegal] NM Senegal

sénégalais, e [senegalɛ, ɛz] [1] ADJ Senegalese [2] **Sénégalais(e)** NM,F Senegalese

Sénèque [senɛk] NM Seneca

sénescence [senesɑ̃s] NF senescence

sénescent, e [senesɑ̃, ɑ̃t] ADJ senescent

sénevé [senve] NM (= *plante*) wild mustard; (= *graine*) wild mustard seed

sénile [senil] ADJ (*péj, Méd*) senile

sénilité [senilite] NF senility

senior [senjɔr] ADJ, NMF (*Sport*) senior; **les ~s** (= *personnes de plus de 50 ans*) the over-fifties

senne [sɛn] NF = **seine**

sens [sɑ̃s] [1] ADJ (= *goût, vue etc*) sense; **les ~** the senses; **avoir le ~ de l'odorat/de l'ouïe très développé** to have a highly developed *ou* a very keen sense of smell/of hearing; **reprendre ses ~** to regain consciousness; **sixième ~** sixth sense → **organe**
[b] (= *instinct*) sense; **avoir le ~ du rythme/de l'humour/du ridicule** to have a sense of rhythm/of humour/of the ridiculous; **il n'a aucun ~ moral/pratique** he has no moral/practical sense; **avoir le ~ des réalités** to have a sense of reality; **avoir le ~ de l'orientation** to have a (good) sense of direction; **avoir le ~ des responsabilités/des valeurs** to have a sense of responsibility/of moral values; **avoir le ~ des affaires** to have business acumen *ou* good business sense, have a good head for business
[c] (= *avis, jugement*) sense; **ce qu'il dit est plein de ~** what he is saying makes (good) sense *ou* is very sensible; **il n'a pas de ~** that doesn't make (any) sense; **il a perdu le ~ (commun)** he's lost his hold on common sense; **bon ~** common sense; **homme de (bon) ~** man of (good) sense; **le bon ~ voudrait qu'il refuse** the sensible thing would be for him to refuse, the sensible thing for him to do would be to refuse; **c'est une question de bon ~** it's a matter of common sense; **interprétations qui défient le bon ~** interpretations that fly in the face of common sense; **ça semble de bon ~** it seems to make sense; **c'est le bon ~ même de ...** it's only common sense *ou* it only makes sense to ...; **cela tombe sous le ~** it's (perfectly) obvious, it stands to reason; **à mon ~** to my mind, in my opinion, the way I see it → **abonder, dépit**

[d] (= *signification*) [*parole, geste*] meaning; **ce qui donne un ~ à la vie/à son action** what gives (a) meaning to life/to what he did; **au ~ propre/figuré** in the literal *ou* true/figurative sense; **au ~ large/strict du terme** in the general/strict sense of the word; **dans tous les ~ du terme** in every sense of the word; **dans le bon ~ du terme** in the best sense of the word; **faire ~** to make sense; **qui n'a pas de ◊ dépourvu de ~ ◊ vide de ~** meaningless, which has no meaning; **en un (certain) ~** in a (certain) sense; **en ce ~ que ...** in the sense that ...; **la culture, au ~ où il l'entend** culture, as he understands it → **double, faux(-)sens**

[e] (= *direction*) direction; **aller** *ou* **être dans le bon/mauvais ~** to go *ou* be in the right/wrong direction, go the right/wrong way; **mesurer/fendre qch dans le ~ de la longueur** to measure/split sth along its length *ou* lengthwise *ou* lengthways; **ça fait dix mètres dans le ~ de la longueur** it's ten metres in length; **dans le ~ de la largeur** across its width, in width, widthwise; **dans le ~ du bois** with the grain (of the wood); **arriver/venir en ~ contraire** *ou* **inverse** to arrive/come from the opposite direction; **aller en ~ contraire** to go in the opposite direction; **dans le ~ des aiguilles d'une montre** clockwise; **dans le ~ inverse des aiguilles d'une montre** anticlockwise (*Brit*), counterclockwise (*US*); **dans le ~ de la marche** facing the front (of the train), facing the engine; **il retourna la boîte dans tous les ~ avant de l'ouvrir** he turned the box this way and that before opening it; (*fig*) **ça va** *ou* **part dans tous les ~** it's going all over the place; **une voie de circulation a été mise en ~ inverse sur ...** there is a contraflow system in operation on ...; **la circulation dans le ~ Paris-province/dans le ~ province-Paris** traffic out of Paris/into Paris

[f] (= *ligne directrice*) **il a répondu dans le même ~** he replied more or less in the same way *ou* along the same lines; **il a agi dans le même ~** he acted along the same lines, he did more or less the same thing; **j'ai donné des directives dans ce ~** I've given instructions to that effect *ou* end; **dans quel ~ allez-vous orienter votre politique ?** along what lines are you going to direct your policy?; **cette réforme va dans le bon ~** this reform is a step in the right direction; **le ~ de l'histoire** the course of history

[2] **sens dessus dessous** LOC ADV (*lit, fig*) **être/mettre ~ dessus dessous** to be/turn upside down

[3] **sens devant derrière** LOC ADV back to front, the wrong way round

[4] COMP ► **sens giratoire** (*Aut*) roundabout (*Brit*), traffic circle (*US*); **la place est en ~ giratoire** the square forms a roundabout ► **sens interdit** (*Aut*) one-way street; **vous êtes en ~ interdit** you are in a one-way street, you are going the wrong way (up a one-way street) ► **sens unique** (*Aut*) one-way street; **à ~ unique** [*rue*] one-way; [*concession*] one-sided

sensass* [sɑ̃sas] ADJ INV fantastic*, terrific*, sensational

sensation [sɑ̃sasjɔ̃] NF [a] (= *perception*) sensation; (= *impression*) feeling, sensation; **il eut une ~ d'étouffement** he felt he was suffocating; **éprouver une ~ de bien-être** to have a feeling of well-being; **éprouver une ~ de faim/froid** to feel cold/hungry; **avoir une ~ de malaise** (*psychologiquement*) to feel ill at ease; (*physiquement*) to feel weak; **~ de brûlure** burning sensation; **ça laisse une ~ de fraîcheur** [*déodorant*] it leaves you feeling refreshed; **~ de liberté/plénitude/puissance** feeling *ou* sense of freedom/bliss/power; **j'ai la ~ de l'avoir déjà vu** I have a feeling I've seen him before; **quelle ~ cela te procure-t-il ?** how does it make you feel?, what kind of sensation does it give you?; **les amateurs de ~s**

fortes thrill-seekers, people who like big thrills
[b] (= *effet*) **faire ~** to cause *ou* create a sensation; **à ~** [*littérature, roman*] sensational; **la presse à ~** the tabloid *ou* gutter (*péj*) press; **journal à ~** tabloid (newspaper), scandal sheet

sensationnalisme [sɑ̃sasjɔnalism] NM sensationalism

sensationnel, -elle [sɑ̃sasjɔnɛl] [1] ADJ (* = *merveilleux*) fantastic*, terrific*, sensational; (= *qui fait sensation*) sensational [2] NM **le ~** the sensational; **des journalistes à l'affût du ~** journalists on the lookout for sensational stories

sensé, e [sɑ̃se] ADJ [*question, personne, mesure*] sensible; **tenir des propos ~s** to talk sense

sensément [sɑ̃semɑ̃] ADV sensibly; **je ne peux ~ pas lui proposer cela** it would be unreasonable of me to suggest that to him

sensibilisateur, -trice [sɑ̃sibilizatœr, tris] [1] ADJ sensitizing [2] NM sensitizer

sensibilisation [sɑ̃sibilizasjɔ̃] NF [a] (*personnes*) **la ~ de l'opinion publique à ce problème est récente** public opinion has only recently become sensitive *ou* alive to this problem; **campagne de ~** public awareness campaign, consciousness-raising campaign; **mener des actions de ~ à l'écologie** to attempt to raise public awareness of ecological issues [b] (*Bio, Photo*) sensitization

sensibilisé, e [sɑ̃sibilize] (*ptp de* **sensibiliser**) ADJ **◆ sensibilisé à** (*gén*) sensitive *ou* alive to; **~ aux problèmes sociaux** socially aware; **~ aux problèmes de santé** aware of health issues

sensibiliser [sɑ̃sibilize] ▸ conjug 1 ◂ VT [a] **~ qn** to make sb sensitive (**à** to); **~ l'opinion publique à un problème** to heighten public awareness of a problem, make the public aware of a problem [b] (*Bio, Photo*) to sensitize

sensibilité [sɑ̃sibilite] NF [a] [*personne*] (*gén*) sensitivity, sensitiveness; [*artiste*] sensibility, sensitivity; **être d'une grande ~** to be extremely sensitive; **faire preuve d'une ~ exacerbée** to be hypersensitive; **certaines scènes peuvent heurter la ~ des plus jeunes** some scenes may be unsuitable for a younger audience [b] (*Pol*) **il a une ~ de gauche/de droite** his sympathies lie with the left/the right; **les maires, toutes ~s politiques confondues, sont d'accord** mayors of all political tendencies agree [c] [*instrument, muscle, pellicule, marché, secteur*] sensitivity

▼ **sensible** [sɑ̃sibl] ADJ [a] (= *impressionnable*) [*personne*] sensitive (**à** to); **film déconseillé aux personnes ~s** film not recommended for people of a nervous disposition; **elle a le cœur ~** she is tender-hearted; **être ~ au charme de qn** to be susceptible to sb's charm; **j'ai été très ~ à ses attentions** I was touched by how considerate he was; **les gens sont de plus en plus ~s à la qualité du cadre de vie** people are more and more aware of the importance of their surroundings; **il est très ~ à la poésie** he has a great feeling for poetry; **il est peu ~ à ce genre d'argument** he's unlikely to be convinced by that kind of argument; **ils ne sont pas du tout ~s à notre humour** they don't appreciate our sense of humour at all; **l'opinion publique est très ~ aux problèmes des réfugiés** public opinion is very much alive to the refugees' problems → **âme, point¹**
[b] (= *notable*) [*hausse, changement, progrès*] appreciable, noticeable, palpable (*épith*); **la différence n'est pas ~** the difference is hardly noticeable *ou* appreciable; **de façon ~** appreciably
[c] (= *tangible*) perceptible; **le vent était à peine ~** the wind was scarcely *ou* hardly perceptible; **~ à la vue/l'ouïe** perceptible to the eye/the ear
[d] [*blessure, organe, peau*] sensitive; **avoir l'ouïe ~** to have sensitive *ou* keen hearing; **~ au chaud/froid** sensitive to (the) heat/cold;

➤ GRAMMAIRE ACTIVE: sensible 49

être ~ de la bouche/gorge to have a sensitive mouth/throat
[e] (= qui varie) ~ à [marché, secteur] sensitive to; **les valeurs (les plus) ~s à l'évolution des taux d'intérêt** shares that are (most) sensitive to fluctuating interest rates
[f] (= difficile) [dossier, projet, secteur] sensitive; [établissement scolaire, quartier] problem (épith); **zone** ~ (= quartier) problem area; (Mil) sensitive area
[g] (Tech) [balance, baromètre, papier] sensitive → **corde**
[h] (Mus) (note) ~ leading note
[i] (Philo) **intuition** ~ sensory intuition; **un être** ~ a sentient being; **le monde** ~ the physical world, the world as perceived by the senses

sensiblement [sãsibləmã] ADV [a] (= presque) approximately, more or less; **être ~ du même âge/de la même taille** to be approximately ou more or less the same age/the same height [b] (= notablement) appreciably, noticeably, markedly

sensiblerie [sãsibləri] NF (= sentimentalité) sentimentality, mawkishness; (= impressionnabilité) squeamishness

sensitif, -ive [sãsitif, iv] [1] ADJ (Anat) [nerf] sensory; (littér) oversensitive [2] **sensitive** NF (Bot) sensitive plant

sensoriel, -ielle [sãsɔrjɛl] ADJ sensory, sensorial; **organe** ~ sense organ, sensory organ

sensorimoteur, -trice [sãsɔrimɔtœr, tris] ADJ sensorimotor

sensualisme [sãsɥalism] NM (Philo) sensualism

sensualiste [sãsɥalist] (Philo) [1] ADJ sensualist, sensualistic [2] NMF sensualist

sensualité [sãsɥalite] NF (gén) sensuality; [langage, style] sensuousness

sensuel, -uelle [sãsɥɛl] ADJ (gén) sensual; [langage, style] sensuous

sensuellement [sãsɥɛlmã] ADV sensually

sent-bon [sãbɔ̃] NM INV (langage enfantin) perfume

sente [sãt] NF (littér) (foot)path

sentence [sãtãs] NF (= verdict) sentence; (= adage) maxim

sentencieusement [sãtãsjøzmã] ADV sententiously

sentencieux, -ieuse [sãtãsjø, jøz] ADJ sententious

senteur [sãtœr] NF (littér) scent, perfume → **pois**

senti, e [sãti] (ptp de sentir) ADJ (= sincère) heartfelt, sincere; **quelques vérités bien ~es** a few home truths; **quelques mots bien ~s** (bien choisis) a few well-chosen ou well-expressed words; (de blâme) a few well-chosen words; **un discours bien** ~ a well-delivered ou heartfelt speech

sentier [sãtje] NM (lit) (foot)path; (fig) path; **sortir des ~s battus** to go ou venture off the the beaten track; **hors** ou **loin des ~s battus** off the beaten track; (littér) **les ~s de la gloire** the path to glory; (lit, fig) **être sur le ~ de la guerre** to be on the warpath; (Pol) **le Sentier lumineux** the Shining Path → **randonnée**

▼ **sentiment** [sãtimã] NM [a] (= émotion) feeling, sentiment (frm); ~ **de pitié/tendresse/haine** feeling of pity/tenderness/hatred; ~ **de culpabilité** feeling of guilt, guilty feeling; **avoir de bons/mauvais ~s à l'égard de qn** to be well-/ill-disposed towards sb; **bons ~s** finer feelings; **dans ce cas, il faut savoir oublier les ~s** in this case, we have to put sentiment to one side ou to disregard our own feelings; **prendre qn par les ~s** to appeal to sb's feelings; (souvent iro) **ça n'empêche pas les ~s*** that doesn't mean we (ou they etc) don't love each other
[b] (= sensibilité) **le** ~ feeling, emotion; **être ca-**

pable de ~ to be capable of emotion; **être dépourvu de** ~ to be devoid of all feeling ou emotion; **jouer/danser avec** ~ to play/dance with feeling; **agir par** ~ to be guided by ou listen to one's feelings; (péj) **faire du** ~ to sentimentalize; be sentimental; **tu ne m'auras pas au ~*** you won't get round me like that, you can't sweet-talk me*
[c] (= conscience) **avoir le** ~ **de** to be aware of; **elle avait le** ~ **très vif de sa valeur** she was keenly aware of her worth, she had a keen sense of her worth; **avoir le** ~ **que quelque chose va arriver** to have a feeling that something is going to happen
[d] (formule de politesse) **transmettez-lui nos meilleurs ~s** give him our best wishes → **agréer**
[e] (littér = opinion) feeling; **quel est votre** ~ ? what are your feelings ou what is your feeling (about that)?

sentimental, e [sãtimãtal, o] (mpl -aux) [1] ADJ [a] (= tendre) [personne] romantic [b] (= affectif) [raisons, voyage] sentimental; **cette bague a pour moi une grande valeur ~e** this ring is of great sentimental value to me [c] (= amoureux) [aventure, vie] love (épith); **sur le plan** ~ (dans horoscope) on the romantic ou love front; **sa vie était un échec sur le plan** ~ as far as relationships were concerned, his life was a failure; **il a des problèmes sentimentaux** he has problems with his love life; **déception ~e** disappointment in love; **drame** ~ tragic love story [d] (péj) [chanson, film, personne] sentimental, soppy*; **ne sois pas si** ~ don't be so soft ou soppy* ou sentimental [2] NM,F sentimentalist; **c'est un grand** ~ he's a great romantic

sentimentalement [sãtimãtalmã] ADV sentimentally; (péj) soppily*

sentimentalisme [sãtimãtalism] NM sentimentalism

sentimentalité [sãtimãtalite] NF sentimentality; (péj) soppiness*

sentinelle [sãtinɛl] NF sentry, sentinel (littér); (Mil) **être en** ~ to be on sentry duty, stand sentry; (fig) **mets-toi en** ~ **à la fenêtre** stand guard ou keep watch at the window

sentir [sãtir] ▶ conjug 16 ◀ [1] VT [a] (= percevoir) (par l'odorat) to smell; (au goût) to taste; (au toucher, contact) to feel; ~ **un courant d'air** to feel a draught; ~ **son cœur battre/ses yeux se fermer** to feel one's heart beating/one's eyes closing; **il ne sent pas la différence entre le beurre et la margarine** he can't taste ou tell the difference between butter and margarine; **elle sentit une odeur de gaz/de brûlé** she smelled ou (Brit) gas/burning; **on sent qu'il y a de l'ail dans ce plat** you can taste the garlic in this dish, you can tell there's garlic in this dish; **il ne sent jamais le froid/la fatigue** he never feels the cold/feels tired; **elle sentit qu'on lui tapait sur l'épaule** she felt somebody tapping her on the shoulder; **je suis enrhumé, je ne sens plus rien** I have a cold and can't smell anything ou and I've lost my sense of smell; (fig) **je ne sens plus mes doigts** (de froid) I have lost all sensation in my fingers, I can't feel my fingers; **je ne sens plus mes jambes** (de fatigue) my legs are dropping off* (Brit), my legs are folding under me (US); (fig) ~ **l'écurie** to get the smell ou scent of home in one's nostrils; **je ne le sens pas, ce type*** I don't like the look of him; **je le sens mal ce voyage*** I'm not (at all) happy about this trip
[b] (= dégager une certaine odeur) to smell; (= avoir un certain goût) to taste; ~ **bon/mauvais** to smell good ou nice/bad; ~ **des pieds/de la bouche** to have smelly feet/bad breath; **son manteau sent la fumée** his coat smells of smoke; **ce poisson commence à** ~ this fish is beginning to smell; **ce thé sent le jasmin** (goût) this tea tastes of jasmine; (odeur) this tea smells of jasmine; **la pièce sent le**

renfermé/le moisi the room smells stale/musty; **ça ne sent pas la rose !*** that doesn't smell too good!
[c] (= dénoter) to be indicative of, reveal, smack of; **une certaine arrogance qui sent la petite bourgeoisie** a certain arrogance indicative of ou which reveals ou suggests a middle-class background
[d] (= annoncer) **ça sent le fagot/l'autoritarisme** it smacks of heresy/of authoritarianism; **ça sent le piège** there's a trap ou catch; **ça sent la pluie/la neige** it looks ou feels like rain/snow; **ça sent l'orage** there's a storm in the air; **ça sent le printemps** spring is in the air; **ça sent la punition** someone's in for a telling off*, someone's going to be punished; **cela sent la poudre** things could flare up → **roussi, sapin**
[e] (= avoir conscience de) [+ changement, fatigue] to feel, be aware ou conscious of; [+ importance de qch] to be aware ou conscious of; (= apprécier) [+ beauté, élégance de qch] to appreciate; (= pressentir) [+ danger, difficulté] to sense; **il sentait la panique le gagner** he felt panic rising within him; **sentant le but proche ...** sensing the goal was at hand ...; **il ne sent pas sa force** he doesn't know ou realize his own strength; **elle sent maintenant le vide causé par son départ** now she is feeling the emptiness left by his departure; **sentez-vous la beauté de ce passage ?** do you feel ou appreciate the beauty of this passage?; **le cheval sentait (venir) l'orage** the horse sensed the storm (coming); **nul besoin de réfléchir, cela se sent** there's no need to think about it — you can feel ou sense it; **c'est sa façon de** ~ **(les choses)** that's the way he feels (about things); ~ **que** to be aware ou conscious that; (= pressentir) to sense that; **il sentit qu'il ne reviendrait jamais** he sensed ou felt that he would never come back (again); **faire** ~ **son autorité** to make one's authority felt; **faire** ~ **la beauté d'une œuvre d'art** to bring out ou demonstrate the beauty of a work of art; **il m'a fait** ~ **que j'étais de trop** he let me know I wasn't wanted
[f] (* = supporter) **il ne peut pas le ~*** he can't stand ou bear (the sight of) him
[2] **se sentir** VPR [a] [personne] **se** ~ **mal** (physiquement) to feel ill ou unwell ou sick, not to feel very well; (psychologiquement) to be unhappy; **se** ~ **bien** (physiquement, psychologiquement) to feel good; **se** ~ **mieux/fatigué** to feel better/tired; **se** ~ **revivre/rajeunir** to feel o.s. coming alive again/growing young again; **il ne se sent pas la force/le courage de le lui dire** he doesn't feel strong/brave enough to tell him; **ne pas se** ~ **de joie** to be beside o.s. with joy; **il ne se sent plus !*** he really thinks he's arrived!; **non, mais tu ne te sens plus !*** ou **tu ne te sens pas bien !*** are you out of your mind!*
[b] (= être perceptible) [effet] to be felt, show; **cette amélioration/augmentation se sent** this improvement/increase can be felt ou shows; **les effets des grèves vont se faire** ~ **à la fin du mois** the effect of the strikes will be felt ou will show at the end of the month
[c] (= se supporter) **ils ne peuvent pas se ~*** they can't stand ou bear each other
[d] * (= être d'accord) **tu te sens pour aller faire un tour ?** do you feel like going for a walk?

seoir [swar] ▶ conjug 26 ◀ (frm) [1] VI (= convenir) ~ **à qn** to become sb [2] VB IMPERS **il sied de/que** it is proper ou fitting to/that; **comme il sied** as is proper ou fitting; **il lui sied/ne lui sied pas de faire** it befits ou becomes/ill befits ou ill becomes him to do

Séoul [seul] N Seoul

sep [sɛp] NM = **cep**

sépale [sepal] NM sepal

séparable [separabl] ADJ separable (de from); **deux concepts difficilement ~s** two concepts which are difficult to separate

➤ **GRAMMAIRE ACTIVE:** **sentiment** 33.1

séparateur, -trice [separatœʀ, tʀis] **1** ADJ separating (*épith*), separative; **pouvoir ~ de l'œil/d'un instrument d'optique** resolving power of the eye/of an optical instrument **2** NM (*Élec, Tech*) separator; (*Ordin*) delimiter; **~ d'isotopes** isotope separator

séparation [separasjɔ̃] NF **a** (= *dissociation*) [*éléments, gaz, liquides*] separation; **~ isotopique** *ou* **des isotopes** isotope separation **b** (= *division*) [*territoire*] division, splitting **c** [*amis, parents*] separation; **une longue ~ avait transformé leurs rapports** a long (period of) separation had changed their relationship; **après cinq ans de ~** after five years' separation; **au moment de la ~** [*manifestants*] when they dispersed; [*convives*] when they parted; (*Jur*) **~ de corps** legal separation; **~ de fait** de facto separation; **~ à l'amiable** voluntary separation **d** [*notions, services*] separation; (*Pol*) **la ~ des pouvoirs** the separation of powers; (*Pol*) **la ~ de l'Église et de l'État** the separation of the Church and the State; (*Jur*) **mariés sous le régime de la ~ de biens** married under separation of property **e** (= *démarcation*) division, partition; **mur de ~** separating *ou* dividing wall; **un paravent sert de ~ entre les deux parties de la pièce** a screen separates the two parts of the room **f** (= *distinction*) dividing line; **il faut établir une ~ très nette entre ces problèmes** you must draw a very clear dividing line between these problems

séparatisme [separatism] NM (*Pol, Rel*) separatism

séparatiste [separatist] ADJ, NMF (*Pol*) separatist; (*Hist* US = *sudiste*) secessionist; **mouvement/organisation ~** separatist movement/organization

séparé, e [separe] (*ptp de* **séparer**) ADJ **a** (= *distinct*) [*analyses, entités, mondes, notions, paix*] separate; **ces colis feront l'objet d'un envoi ~** these parcels will be sent separately; **accord ~** separate agreement; **ils dorment dans deux chambres ~es** they sleep in separate rooms; (*Pol*) **le développement ~** (*racial*) separate development **b** [*personnes*] (*Jur* = *désuni*) separated; (*gén* = *éloigné*) parted (*attrib*), apart (*attrib*); **vivre ~** to live apart, be separated (**de** from)

séparément [separemɑ̃] ADV separately

séparer [separe] ▶ conjug 1 ◀ **1** VT **a** (= *détacher*) (*gén*) to separate; [+ *écorce, peau, enveloppe*] to pull off, pull away (**de** from); (= *extraire*) [+ *éléments, gaz, liquides*] to separate (out) (**de** from); **~ la tête du tronc** to separate *ou* sever the head from the trunk; **~ la noix de sa coquille** to separate the nut from its shell; **~ le grain du son** to separate the grain from the bran; **~ un minerai de ses impuretés** to separate an ore from its impurities; (*Culin*) **séparez les blancs des jaunes** separate the whites from the yolks; (*Bible*) **~ le bon grain de l'ivraie** to separate the wheat from the chaff **b** (= *diviser*) to part, split, divide; **~ un territoire (en deux) par une frontière** to split *ou* divide a territory (in two) by a frontier **c** (= *désunir*) [+ *amis, alliés*] to part, drive apart; [+ *adversaires, combattants*] to separate, pull apart, part; **ils se battaient, je les ai séparés** they were fighting and I separated them *ou* pulled them apart *ou* parted them; **~ qn et ou de qn** to separate *ou* part sb from sb else; **dans cet hôpital, les hommes et les femmes sont séparés** men and women are separated in this hospital; **ils avaient séparé l'enfant de sa mère** they had separated the child from its mother; **rien ne pourra jamais nous** ~ nothing will ever come between us *ou* drive us apart; **la vie les a séparés** they went their separate ways in life; **la mort les a séparés** they were parted by death **d** (= *se dresser entre*) [+ *territoires, classes*

sociales, générations] to separate; **une barrière sépare les spectateurs des** *ou* **et les joueurs** a barrier separates the spectators from the players; **un simple grillage nous séparait des lions** a wire fence was all that separated us from the lions; **une chaîne de montagnes sépare la France et** *ou* **de l'Espagne** a chain of mountains separates France from *ou* and Spain; **un seul obstacle le séparait encore du but** only one obstacle stood *ou* remained between him and his goal; **près de deux heures le séparaient de la ville** he was nearly two hours away from the city; **3 kilomètres séparent le village de la mer** the village is 3 kilometres from the sea; **les 200 mètres qui séparent la poste et la gare** the 200 metres between the post office and the station; **les six ans qui séparent l'audience de la date du drame** the six years that have elapsed between the hearing and the date of the tragedy; **tout les séparait** they were worlds apart, they had nothing in common **e** (= *différencier*) [+ *questions, aspects*] to distinguish between; **~ l'érudition de** *ou* **et l'intelligence** to distinguish *ou* differentiate between learning and intelligence

2 **se séparer** VPR **a** (= *se défaire de*) **se ~ de** [+ *employé, objet personnel*] to part with; **en voyage, ne vous séparez jamais de votre passeport** keep your passport on you at all times when travelling **b** (= *s'écarter*) to divide, part (**de** from); (= *se détacher*) to split off, separate off (**de** from); **l'écorce se sépare du tronc** the bark is coming away from the trunk; **l'endroit où les branches se séparent du tronc** the place where the branches split *ou* separate off from the trunk; **le premier étage de la fusée s'est séparé (de la base)** the first stage of the rocket has split off (from the base) *ou* separated (off) from the base; **à cet endroit, le fleuve/la route se sépare en deux** at this point the river/the road forks; **les routes/branches se séparent** the roads/branches divide *ou* part; **c'est là que nos routes** *ou* **chemins se séparent** this is where we go our separate ways **c** (= *se disperser*) [*adversaires*] to separate, break apart; [*manifestants, participants*] to disperse; [*assemblée*] to break up **d** (= *se quitter*) [*convives*] to leave each other, part; [*époux*] to separate (*aussi Jur*), part, split up; **se ~ de son mari/sa femme** to part *ou* separate from one's husband/one's wife; **ils se sont séparés à l'amiable** their separation was amicable

sépia [sepja] NF (*Zool* = *sécrétion*) cuttlefish ink, sepia; (= *couleur, dessin, substance*) sepia; **(dessin à la) ~** sepia (drawing)

sept [sɛt] ADJ INV, NM INV seven; **les ~ péchés capitaux** the seven deadly sins; **les Sept Merveilles du monde** the seven wonders of the world; (*Cartes*) **les ~ familles** Happy Families; **les ~ pays les plus industrialisés** the Group of Seven (industrialized nations); **les Sept d'or** television awards; *pour locutions voir* **six**

septain [sɛtɛ̃] NM *seven-line stanza or poem*

septantaine [sɛptɑ̃tɛn] NF (*Belg, Helv*) about seventy, seventy or so; **il doit avoir la ~** he must be about seventy

septante [sɛptɑ̃t] ADJ INV (*Belg, Helv*) seventy; (*Bible*) **la version des Septante** the Septuagint

septantième [sɛptɑ̃tjɛm] ADJ, NMF (*Belg, Helv*) seventieth

septembre [sɛptɑ̃bʀ] NM September; **le mois de ~** the month of September; **le premier/dix ~ tombe un mercredi** the first/tenth of September falls on a Wednesday; **nous avons rendez-vous le premier/dix ~** we have an appointment on the first/tenth of September; **en ~** in September; **au mois de ~** in (the month of) September; **au début (du mois) de** ◊ **début ~** at the beginning of September, in

early September; **au milieu (du mois) de** ◊ **à la mi-~** in the middle of September, in mid-September; **à la fin (du mois) de ~** ◊ **fin ~** at the end of September; **pendant le mois de ~** during September; **vers la fin de ~** late in September, in late September, towards the end of September; **~ a été très froid** September was very cold; **~ prochain/dernier** next/last September

septennal, e (*mpl* **-aux**) [sɛptenal, o] ADJ (*durée*) [*mandat, période*] seven-year (*épith*); (*fréquence*) [*festival*] septennial

septennat [sɛptena] NM [*président*] seven-year term (of office); **au cours de son ~** during his time in office *ou* his presidency; **briguer un second ~** to run for a second term in office, seek a second term of office

septentrion [sɛptɑ̃tʀijɔ̃] NM (†† *littér*) north

septentrional, e (*mpl* **-aux**) [sɛptɑ̃tʀijɔnal, o] ADJ northern

septicémie [sɛptisemi] NF blood poisoning, septicaemia (*SPÉC, Brit*), septicemia (*SPÉC, US*)

septicémique [sɛptisemik] ADJ septicaemic (*Brit*), septicemic (*US*)

septicité [sɛptisite] NF septicity

septième [sɛtjɛm] **1** ADJ, NM seventh; **le ~ art** the cinema; **être au ~ ciel** to be in seventh heaven, be on cloud nine*; *pour autres locutions voir* **sixième 2** NF **a** (*Scol*) sixth year in primary school, fifth grade (*US*) **b** (*Mus*) seventh

septièmement [sɛtjɛmmɑ̃] ADV seventhly; *pour locutions voir* **sixièmement**

septique [sɛptik] ADJ [*bactérie, fièvre*] septic → **fosse**

septuagénaire [sɛptɥaʒenɛʀ] **1** ADJ septuagenarian, seventy-year-old (*épith*) **2** NMF septuagenarian, seventy-year-old man (*ou* woman)

septuagésime [sɛptɥaʒezim] NF Septuagesima

septuor [sɛptɥɔʀ] NM septet(te)

septuple [sɛptypl] **1** ADJ [*nombre, quantité, rangée*] septuple; **une quantité ~ de l'autre** a quantity seven times (as great as) the other; **en ~ exemplaire** in seven copies **2** NM (*gén, Math*) **je l'ai payé le ~/le ~ de l'autre** I paid seven times as much for it/seven times as much as the other for it; **augmenter au ~** to increase sevenfold *ou* seven times

septupler [sɛptyple] ▶ conjug 1 ◀ VTI to increase sevenfold *ou* seven times

sépulcral, e (*mpl* **-aux**) [sepylkʀal, o] ADJ [*atmosphère, voix*] sepulchral; [*salle*] tomb-like

sépulcre [sepylkʀ] NM sepulchre (*Brit*), sepulcher (*US*)

sépulture [sepyltyʀ] NF **a** († *littér* = *inhumation*) sepulture (*littér*), burial; **être privé de ~** to be refused burial **b** (= *lieu*) burial place; (= *tombe*) grave; (= *pierre tombale*) gravestone, tombstone → **violation**

séquelle [sekɛl] NF (*souvent pl*) [*maladie, accident*] after-effect; (= *conséquence*) [*guerre*] aftermath (*NonC*); **les ~s du colonialisme** the legacy of colonialism; **elle n'a gardé aucune ~ psychologique de son agression** she was not psychologically scarred by the attack; **ça a laissé des ~s** [*blessure, incident*] it had serious after-effects *ou* consequences; **la lutte entre les différents courants du parti a laissé des ~s** the struggle between the different factions has left its mark on the party

séquençage [sekɑ̃saʒ] NM (*Bio*) sequencing

séquence [sekɑ̃s] NF (*Ciné, Mus, Rel*) sequence; (*Cartes*) run; (*Ling, Ordin*) sequence, string; **~ d'ADN/d'ARN** DNA/RNA sequence; **~ génétique** gene sequence → **plan¹**

séquencer [sekɑ̃se] ▶ conjug 3 ◀ VT (*Bio*) [+ *génome*] to sequence

séquenceur [sekɑ̃sœʀ] NM sequencer

séquentiel, -ielle [sekɑ̃sjɛl] ADJ sequential; (*Ordin*) **accès ~** sequential *ou* serial access; **accomplir des tâches de façon séquentielle** to perform tasks in sequence *ou* sequentially

séquestration [sekɛstrasjɔ̃] NF a [*otage*] holding; (*Jur*) **~ (arbitraire)** false imprisonment b [*biens*] sequestration, impoundment c (*Chim, Méd*) sequestration

séquestre [sekɛstr] NM a (*Jur, Pol*) (= *action*) confiscation, impoundment, sequestration; (= *dépositaire*) depository; **mettre** *ou* **placer des biens sous ~** to sequester goods; **biens sous ~** sequestrated property; **mise sous ~** sequestration b (*Méd*) sequestrum

séquestrer [sekɛstre] ▸ conjug 1 ◂ VT a (*Jur*) [+ *personne*] to confine illegally; **les ouvriers en grève ont séquestré le directeur dans son bureau** the strikers confined the manager to his office b (= *saisir*) [+ *biens*] to sequester, impound (*pending decision over ownership*)

sequin [səkɛ̃] NM (*Hist* = *pièce d'or*) sequin

séquoia [sekɔja] NM sequoia, redwood

sérac [serak] NM serac

sérail [seraj] NM (*lit*) seraglio, serail; (*fig*) inner circle; **c'est un homme du ~** he's an establishment figure *ou* man; **il est issu du ~ politique** he's from a political background

séraphin [serafɛ̃] NM seraph

séraphique [serafik] ADJ (*Rel, fig*) seraphic

serbe [sɛrb] 1 ADJ Serbian 2 NM (*Ling*) Serbian 3 **Serbe** NMF Serb

Serbie [sɛrbi] NF Serbia; **la République de ~** the Serbian Republic

serbo-croate (*pl* serbo-croates) [sɛrbokrɔat] 1 ADJ Serbo-Croat(ian) 2 NM (*Ling*) Serbo-Croat

Sercq [sɛrk] NM Sark

séré [sere] NM (*Helv*) soft white cheese

serein, e [sərɛ̃, ɛn] ADJ a [*ciel, nuit, jour*] clear b [*âme, foi, visage, personne*] serene, calm; **je suis tout à fait ~, je suis sûr que son innocence sera prouvée** I'm quite confident, I'm sure he'll be proven innocent c (= *impartial*) [*jugement, critique*] calm, dispassionate

sereinement [sərɛnmɑ̃] ADV a [*regarder*] serenely; [*parler, attendre*] calmly; [*juger*] impartially, dispassionately; **ils envisagent l'avenir ~** they view the future with equanimity *ou* calmly

sérénade [serenad] NF a (*Mus* = concert, pièce) serenade; **donner une ~ à qn** to serenade sb b (* *hum* = charivari) racket, hullabaloo*; **faire toute une ~ à propos de qch** to make a big fuss *ou* a song and dance about sth; **c'est toujours la même ~ !** it's always the same scenario!

sérénissime [serenisim] ADJ **Son Altesse ~** His (*ou* Her) Most Serene Highness; (*Hist*) **la république ~** ◊ **la Sérénissime** the Venetian Republic, the *ou* la Serenissima

sérénité [serenite] NF a [*ciel, nuit, jour*] clearness, clarity b [*âme, foi, visage*] serenity, calmness; **elle affiche une ~ étonnante** she's incredibly serene *ou* calm; **j'ai retrouvé la ~** I feel serene *ou* calm again; **il envisage l'avenir avec une relative ~** he views the future with relative equanimity, he feels quite calm about the future c [*jugement, critique*] impartiality, dispassionateness

séreux, -euse [serø, øz] 1 ADJ serous 2 **séreuse** NF serous membrane, serosa

serf, serve [sɛr(f), sɛrv] 1 ADJ [*personne*] in serfdom (*attrib*); **condition serve** (state of) serfdom; **terre serve** land held in villein tenure 2 NM,F serf

serfouette [sɛrfwɛt] NF hoe-fork, weeding hoe

serge [sɛrʒ] NF serge

sergent[1] [sɛrʒɑ̃] NM (*Mil*) sergeant; **~-chef** staff sergeant; **~ de ville**† policeman; **~(-)fourrier** quartermaster sergeant; **~ instructeur** drill sergeant; **~-major** ≈ quartermaster sergeant (*in charge of accounts etc*)

sergent[2] [sɛrʒɑ̃] NM (= *serre-joint*) cramp, clamp

séricicole [serisikɔl] ADJ silkworm-breeding (*épith*), sericultural (*SPÉC*)

sériciculteur, -trice [serisikyltœr, tris] NM,F silkworm breeder, sericulturist (*SPÉC*)

sériciculture [serisikyltyr] NF silkworm breeding, sericulture (*SPÉC*)

série [seri] NF a (= *suite*) [*timbres*] set, series; [*clés, casseroles, volumes*] set; [*tests*] series, battery; [*accidents, ennuis, succès*] series, string; [*mesures, réformes*] series; (*beaucoup*) **(toute) une ~ de ...** a (whole) series *ou* string of ...; **meurtres en ~** serial killings; **tueur en ~** serial killer; (*hum*) **dans la ~ les ennuis continuent, la voiture est tombée en panne !** and now something else has gone wrong, the car has broken down!; (*Littérat*) (**ouvrages de**) **~ noire** crime thrillers, whodunnits*; (*fig*) **c'est la ~ noire** it's one disaster after another, it's a chain of disasters → **loi**
b (*Radio, TV*) series; **~ télévisée** television series
c (= *catégorie, Naut*) class; (*Sport* = *épreuve de qualification*) qualifying heat *ou* round; **joueur de deuxième ~** second-rank player; **film de ~ B** B film *ou* movie; **les différentes ~s du baccalauréat** the different baccalauréat options → **tête**, BACCALAURÉAT
d (*Comm, Ind*) **~ limitée/spéciale** limited/special series; (*lit, fig*) **fabrication** *ou* **production en ~** mass production; **fabriqué** *ou* **produit en ~** mass-produced; **la direction assistée est (livrée) en ~** standard features include power steering; **numéro de ~** [*véhicule*] serial number; **prix de ~** standard price; **article/voiture de ~** standard article/car; **modèle de ~** production model; **hors ~** [*table, machine*] made-to-order, custom-built; [*talent, don*] incomparable, outstanding; (*Presse*) **numéro hors ~** special issue → **fin[2]**, hors-série
e (*Chim, Math, Mus, Phon*) series; (*Billard*) break; (*Élec*) **monté en ~** connected in series; **imprimante/port ~** serial printer/port

sériel, -ielle [serjɛl] ADJ [*ordre*] serial; [*musique*] serial, twelve-note (*épith*), dodecaphonic; [*compositeur*] dodecaphonic

sérier [serje] ▸ conjug 7 ◂ VT [+ *problèmes, questions*] to classify, arrange

sérieusement [serjøzmɑ̃] ADV a (= *consciencieusement*) [*travailler*] conscientiously b (= *sans rire*) [*parler, envisager*] seriously; **elle envisage ~ de divorcer** she's seriously considering divorce; (**tu parles**) **~ ?** are you serious?, do you really mean it?; **non, il l'a dit ~** no — he was quite serious, no — he really meant it c (= *vraiment*) really; **ça commence ~ à m'agacer** it's really beginning to annoy me d (= *gravement*) [*blesser*] seriously; **l'un des reins est ~ atteint** one of the kidneys is seriously damaged

sérieux, -ieuse [serjø, jøz] 1 ADJ a (= *grave*) [*personne, air*] serious; **~ comme un pape*** deadly serious
b (= *digne de confiance*) [*personne*] reliable, dependable; (= *fiable*) [*acquéreur, promesses, raison, proposition, annonce*] genuine, serious; [*renseignement, source*] genuine, reliable; **un client ~** a good customer; **« pas ~ s'abstenir »** "no time wasters", "genuine inquiries only"
c (= *réfléchi*) [*personne*] serious, serious-minded; (= *consciencieux*) [*employé, élève, apprenti*] conscientious; [*études*] serious; [*travail, artisan*] careful, painstaking; **elle est très sérieuse dans son travail** she's a very conscientious worker; **vous annulez le rendez-vous une heure avant, ce n'est pas ~ !** you cancel the appointment just one hour beforehand — it's just not good enough!; **ça ne fait pas très ~** it doesn't look good; **partir skier pendant les examens, ce n'est vraiment pas ~ !** it's not very responsible to go off skiing during the exams!; **un nom comme ça, ça fait ~** a name like that makes a good impression *ou* is quite impressive; **si tu veux faire ~, mets un costume** if you want to be taken seriously *ou* if you want to come across, well you should wear a suit
d (= *convenable*) [*jeune homme, jeune fille*] responsible, trustworthy
e (= *qui ne plaisante pas*) serious; **ce n'est pas ~ !** ◊ **vous n'êtes pas ~ !** you can't be serious!, you must be joking!; **ce n'est pas ~, il ne le fera jamais** he doesn't really mean it — he'll never do it!; **non, il était ~** no, he was serious *ou* he meant it; **c'est ~, ce que vous dites ?** are you serious?, do you really mean that?
f (= *important*) [*conversation, livre, projet*] serious; **passons aux affaires** *ou* **choses sérieuses** let's move on to more serious matters, let's get down to business
g (= *préoccupant*) [*situation, affaire, maladie, blessure*] serious
h (*intensif*) [*coup*] serious; [*somme, différence*] considerable, sizeable; **de sérieuses chances de ...** a strong *ou* good chance of ...; **il a de sérieuses raisons de ...** he has very good reasons to ...; **je n'avais aucune raison sérieuse de penser qu'il mettrait sa menace à exécution** I had no real reason to think he would carry out his threat; **ils ont une sérieuse avance** they have a strong *ou* good *ou* sizeable lead; **ils ont un ~ retard** they're seriously behind schedule; **il pourrait avoir de ~ ennuis** he could have real *ou* serious problems; **elle a un ~ besoin d'argent/de vacances** she's in real *ou* serious need of money/of a holiday; **il devra faire de ~ efforts pour rattraper son retard** he'll have to make a real effort to catch up
2 NM a (= *gravité*) [*personne, air*] seriousness, earnestness; [*conversation, livre, projet*] seriousness; **garder son ~** to keep a straight face; **perdre son ~** to give way to laughter; **prendre qch/qn au ~** to take sth/sb seriously; **se prendre au ~** to take o.s. seriously
b (= *fiabilité*) [*personne*] reliability, dependability; [*acquéreur, promesses, intentions*] genuineness, seriousness; [*renseignement, sources*] genuineness, reliability; [*employé, élève, apprenti*] conscientiousness; **travailler avec ~** to be a conscientious worker; **il fait preuve de beaucoup de ~ dans son travail/ses études** he takes his work/his studies very seriously, he's a conscientious worker/student
c (= *sagesse*) [*jeune homme, jeune fille*] trustworthiness
d (= *caractère préoccupant*) [*situation, affaire, maladie*] seriousness

sérigraphie [serigrafi] NF (= *technique*) silkscreen printing, serigraphy (*SPÉC*); (= *estampe*) screen print, serigraph (*SPÉC*)

serin [s(ə)rɛ̃] NM (= *oiseau*) canary; (†: *péj* = *niais*) ninny*

seriner [s(ə)rine] ▸ conjug 1 ◂ VT a (*péj* = *rabâcher*) **~ qch à qn** to drum sth into sb; **tais-toi, tu nous serines !*** oh, be quiet, we're tired of hearing the same thing over and over again! b **~ (un air à) un oiseau** to teach a bird a tune (*using a bird organ*)

seringa(t) [s(ə)rɛ̃ga] NM syringa, mock orange

seringue [s(ə)rɛ̃g] NF (*Méd, Tech*) syringe

sérique [serik] ADJ serum (*épith*)

serment [sɛrmɑ̃] NM a (*solennel*) oath; **faire un ~** to take an oath; **~ sur l'honneur** solemn oath; **sous ~** on *ou* under oath; **~ d'Hippocrate** Hippocratic oath; (*Hist*) **le ~ du Jeu de paume** the Tennis Court Oath; **~ professionnel** oath of office → **prestation**, **prêter** b (= *promesse*) pledge; **échanger des ~s (d'amour)** to exchange vows *ou* pledges of love; (*fig*) **~ d'ivrogne** empty vow, vain resolution; **je te fais le ~ de ne plus jouer** I (solemnly) swear to you *ou* I'll make you a solemn promise that I'll never gamble again → **faux²**

sermon [sɛʀmɔ̃] NM (*Rel*) sermon; (*fig péj*) lecture, sermon

sermonner [sɛʀmɔne] ▸conjug 1◂ VT ~ **qn** to lecture sb, sermonize sb

sermonneur, -euse [sɛʀmɔnœʀ, øz] NM,F (*péj*) sermonizer, preacher

SERNAM [sɛʀnam] NF (ABRÉV = **Service national des messageries**) *French national parcels service*

séroconversion [seʀɔkɔ̃vɛʀsjɔ̃] NF seroconversion

sérodiagnostic [seʀɔdjagnɔstik] NM serodiagnosis

sérologie [seʀɔlɔʒi] NF serology

sérologique [seʀɔlɔʒik] ADJ serologic(al)

sérologiste [seʀɔlɔʒist] NMF serologist

séronégatif, -ive [seʀɔnegatif, iv] [1] ADJ (*gén*) seronegative; (*Sida*) HIV negative [2] NM,F (*gén*) person who is seronegative; (*Sida*) person who is HIV negative

séronégativité [seʀɔnegativite] NF (*gén*) seronegativity; (*Sida*) HIV-negative status

séropo* [seʀɔpo] ABRÉV = **séropositif, -ive**

séropositif, -ive [seʀɔpozitif, iv] [1] ADJ (*gén*) seropositive; (*Sida*) HIV positive [2] NM,F (*gén*) person who is seropositive; (*Sida*) person who is HIV positive, person with HIV

séropositivité [seʀɔpozitivite] NF (*gén*) seropositivity; (*Sida*) HIV infection, seropositivity (*SPÉC*); **quand il a appris sa ~** when he learned that he was HIV positive *ou* that he was infected with HIV

sérosité [seʀɔzite] NF serous fluid, serosity

sérothérapie [seʀɔteʀapi] NF serotherapy

serpe [sɛʀp] NF billhook, bill; **visage taillé à la ~** *ou* **à coups de ~** craggy *ou* rugged face

serpent [sɛʀpɑ̃] [1] NM [a] (*Zool*) snake; (*péj = personne*) viper (*péj*); (*Rel*) **le ~** the serpent; (*fig*) **c'est le ~ qui se mord la queue** it's a vicious circle → **charmeur, réchauffer** [b] (*Mus*) bass horn [c] (= *ruban*) ribbon; **un ~ de fumée** a ribbon of smoke; **le ~ argenté du fleuve** the silvery ribbon of the river [2] COMP ▸ **serpent d'eau** water snake ▸ **serpent à lunettes** Indian cobra ▸ **serpent de mer** (*hum Presse*) trite news story (*that journalists fall back on in the absence of more important news*) ▸ **le serpent monétaire (européen)** (*Fin*) the (European) currency snake ▸ **serpent à plumes** (*Myth*) plumed serpent ▸ **serpent à sonnettes** rattlesnake

serpentaire [sɛʀpɑ̃tɛʀ] [1] NM (= *oiseau*) secretary bird, serpent-eater [2] NF (= *plante*) snakeroot

serpenteau (*pl* **serpenteaux**) [sɛʀpɑ̃to] NM (= *animal*) young snake; (= *feu d'artifice*) serpent

serpenter [sɛʀpɑ̃te] ▸conjug 1◂ VI [*chemin, rivière*] to snake, meander, wind; [*vallée*] to wind; **la route descendait en serpentant vers la plaine** the road snaked *ou* wound (its way) down to the plain

serpentin, e [sɛʀpɑ̃tɛ̃, in] [1] ADJ (*gén*) serpentine [2] NM (= *ruban*) streamer; (*Chim*) coil [3] **serpentine** NF (*Minér*) serpentine

serpette [sɛʀpɛt] NF pruning knife

serpillière [sɛʀpijɛʀ] NF floorcloth; **passer la ~** to mop the floor

serpolet [sɛʀpɔlɛ] NM mother-of-thyme, wild thyme

serrage [seʀaʒ] NM (*gén, Tech*) [*écrou, vis*] tightening; [*joint*] clamping; [*nœud*] tightening, pulling tight → **bague, collier, vis**

serre¹ [sɛʀ] NF (*Agr*) greenhouse, glasshouse; (*attenant à une maison*) conservatory; **pousser en ~** to grow under glass; ~ **chaude** hothouse; ~ **froide** cold greenhouse → **effet**

serre² [sɛʀ] NF (= *griffe*) talon, claw

serré, e [seʀe] (*ptp de* **serrer**) [1] ADJ [a] [*chaussures, vêtement*] tight; **robe ~e à la**

taille dress fitted at the waist; **elle porte des jeans ~s** she wears tight-fitting jeans [b] [*passagers, spectateurs*] (tightly) packed; **être ~s comme des harengs** *ou* **sardines** to be packed like sardines; **mettez-vous ailleurs, nous sommes trop ~s à cette table** sit somewhere else, it's too crowded at this table → **rang** [c] [*tissu*] closely woven; [*réseau*] dense; [*écriture, mailles*] close; [*blés, herbe, forêt*] dense; [*virage*] sharp; [*style*] tight, concise; [*horaire*] tight; **une petite pluie fine et ~e** a steady drizzle; **un café (bien) ~** a (good) strong coffee; **pousser en touffes ~es** to grow in thick clumps; **nous avons un calendrier très ~** we have a very tight schedule; (*Ciné*) **plan ~** tight shot, close-up [d] (= *bloqué*) [*bandage, nœud*] tight; **trop ~** too tight; **pas assez ~** not tight enough [e] (= *contracté*) **les mâchoires/dents ~es** with set jaws/clenched teeth; **les lèvres ~es** with tight lips, tight-lipped; **les poings ~s** with clenched fists; **avoir le cœur ~** to feel a pang of anguish; **je le regardai partir, le cœur ~** I felt sick at heart as I watched him go; **avoir la gorge ~e** to have a lump in one's throat [f] [*discussion, négociations*] closely argued; [*jeu, lutte, match*] tight, close-fought; [*budget*] tight; [*prix*] keen; [*gestion*] strict; (*Sport*) **arrivée ~e** close finish; **les deux candidats sont en ballottage très ~** the two candidates are fighting it out in a very close second round, the two candidates are running neck and neck in the second round of voting; **la partie est ~e ◊ nous jouons une partie ~e** it's a tight game, we're in a tight game [2] ADV **écrire ~** to write one's letters close together, write in a cramped hand; (*fig*) **jouer ~** to play it tight, play a tight game; **vivre ~** to live on a tight budget

serre-file (*pl* **serre-files**) [sɛʀfil] NM (*Mil*) file closer, serrefile; (*Naut*) tail-end Charlie

serre-joint (*pl* **serre-joints**) [sɛʀʒwɛ̃] NM clamp, cramp

serre-livres [sɛʀlivʀ] NM INV bookend

serrement [sɛʀmɑ̃] NM [a] ~ **de main** handshake; ~ **de cœur** pang of anguish; ~ **de gorge** tightening in the throat [b] (*Min*) dam

serrer [seʀe] ▸conjug 1◂ [1] VT [a] (= *maintenir, presser*) to grip, hold tight; ~ **qch dans sa main** to clutch sth; ~ **une pipe/un os entre ses dents** to clench *ou* have a pipe/a bone between one's teeth; ~ **qn dans ses bras/contre son cœur** to clasp sb in one's arms/to one's chest; ~ **la main à** *ou* **de qn** (= *la donner*) to shake sb's hand, shake hands with sb; (= *la presser*) to squeeze *ou* press sb's hand; **se ~ la main** to shake hands; ~ **qn à la gorge** to grab sb by the throat → **kiki** [b] (= *contracter*) ~ **le poing/les mâchoires** to clench one's fist/one's jaws; ~ **les lèvres** to set one's lips; **avoir le cœur serré par l'émotion** to feel a pang of emotion; **avoir la gorge serrée par l'émotion** to be choked by emotion; **cela serre le cœur** *ou* **c'est à vous ~ le cœur de les voir si malheureux** it makes your heart bleed to see them so unhappy; ~ **les dents** (*lit*) to clench one's teeth; (*fig*) to grit one's teeth; ~ **les fesses** (= *se retenir*) to hold on; (* = *avoir peur*) to be scared stiff *ou* out of one's wits* [c] (= *comprimer*) to be too tight for; (= *mouler*) to fit tightly; **mon pantalon me serre** my trousers are too tight (for me); **cette jupe me serre (à) la taille** this skirt is too tight round the waist; **ces chaussures me serrent (le pied)** these shoes are too tight [d] (= *bloquer*) [+ *écrou, vis*] to tighten; [+ *pansement*] to wind tightly; [+ *joint*] to clamp; [+ *robinet*] to turn off tight; [+ *ceinture, lacet, nœud*] to tighten, pull tight; [+ *tendre*] to câble] to tauten, make taut, tighten; (*Naut*) [+ *voile*] to make fast, belay (*SPÉC*); ~ **les prix** to keep prices down; ~ **le frein à main** to put on the handbrake; ~ **la vis à qn*** to crack down

on sb*
[e] (= *se tenir près de*) (*par derrière*) to keep close behind; (*latéralement*) [+ *automobile, current*] to squeeze (**contre** up against); ~ **qn de près** to follow close behind sb; (*fig*) ~ **une femme de près*** to come on strong* to a woman; ~ **de près l'ennemi** to be snapping at the enemy's heels; ~ **qn dans un coin** to wedge sb in a corner; ~ **un cycliste contre le trottoir** to squeeze a cyclist against the pavement; ~ **le trottoir** to hug the kerb; (*Aut*) ~ **sa droite** to keep to the right; **ne serre pas cette voiture de trop près** don't get too close to *ou* behind that car; ~ **une question de plus près** to study a question more closely; ~ **le texte** to follow the text closely, keep close to the text; (*Naut*) ~ **la côte** to sail close to the shore, hug the shore; (*Naut*) ~ **le vent** to hug the wind [f] (* = *emprisonner*) to nab*; **se faire ~ par la police** to get nabbed* by the police [g] (= *rapprocher*) [+ *objets alignés, lignes, mots*] to close up, put close together; (*Mil*) ~ **les rangs** to close ranks; **serrez !** close ranks!; ~ **son style** to write concisely, write in a condensed *ou* concise style; **il faudra ~ les invités, la table est petite** we'll have to squeeze the guests up *ou* together as the table is so small [h] (*dial*, † = *ranger*) to put away
[2] VI (*Aut* = *obliquer*) ~ **à droite/gauche** to move in to the right-/left-hand lane; « **véhicules lents serrez à droite** » "slow-moving vehicles keep to the right"
[3] **se serrer** VPR [a] (= *se rapprocher*) **se ~ contre qn** to huddle (up) against sb; (*tendrement*) to cuddle *ou* snuggle up to sb; **se ~ autour de la table/du feu** to squeeze *ou* crowd round the table/the fire; **se ~ pour faire de la place** to squeeze up to make room; **serrez-vous un peu** squeeze up a bit → **ceinture, coude** [b] (= *se contracter*) **à cette vue, son cœur se serra** at the sight of this he felt a pang of anguish; **ses poings se serrèrent, presque malgré lui** his fists clenched *ou* he clenched his fists almost in spite of himself

serre-tête (*pl* **serre-tête(s)**) [sɛʀtɛt] NM (= *bandeau*) headband; [*cycliste, skieur*] skullcap

serrure [seʀyʀ] NF [*porte, coffre-fort, valise*] lock; (*Rail*) interlocking switch; ~ **encastrée** mortise lock; ~ **de sûreté** safety lock; ~ **à pompe** spring lock; ~ **à combinaison** combination lock; ~ **trois points** three-point security lock → **trou**

serrurerie [seʀyʀʀi] NF (= *métier*) locksmithing, locksmith's trade; (= *ferronnerie, objets*) ironwork; ~ **d'art** ornamental ironwork, wrought-iron work; **grosse ~** heavy ironwork

serrurier [seʀyʀje] NM (= *fabriquant de clés, serrures*) locksmith; (= *ferronnier*) ironsmith

sertir [sɛʀtiʀ] ▸conjug 2◂ VT [a] (= *monter*) [+ *pierre précieuse*] to set; **bague sertie de diamants** ring set with diamonds [b] (*Tech*) [+ *pièces de tôle*] to crimp

sertissage [sɛʀtisaʒ] NM [a] [*pierre précieuse*] setting [b] (*Tech*) [*pièces de tôle*] crimping

sertisseur, -euse [sɛʀtisœʀ, øz] NM,F [a] [*pierre précieuse*] setter [b] (*Tech*) [*pièces de tôle*] crimper

sertissure [sɛʀtisyʀ] NF [*pierre précieuse*] (*procédé*) setting; (= *objet*) bezel

sérum [seʀɔm] NM [a] (*Physiol*) ~ **(sanguin)** (blood) serum; ~ **artificiel** *ou* **physiologique** normal *ou* physiological salt solution [b] (*Méd*) serum; ~ **antidiphtérique/antitétanique/antivenimeux** anti-diphtheric/antitetanus/snakebite serum; ~ **de vérité** truth drug

servage [sɛʀvaʒ] NM (*Hist*) serfdom; (*fig*) bondage, thraldom

serval (*pl* **-s**) [sɛʀval] NM serval

servant, e [sɛʀvɑ̃, ɑ̃t] [1] ADJ **chevalier** *ou* **cavalier ~** escort [2] NM (*Rel*) server; (*Mil*) [*pièce d'artillerie*] server; ~ **d'autel** altar boy [3] **servante** NF (= *domestique*) servant, maid-servant

serveur [sɛʀvœʀ] NM [a] [*restaurant*] waiter; [*bar*] barman [b] (= *ouvrier*) [*machine*] feeder [c] (*Tennis*) server [d] (*Cartes*) dealer [e] (*Ordin*) server; **centre ~** service centre, retrieval centre; **~ Internet** Internet server; **~ de fichiers** file server; **~ vocal** answering service

serveuse [sɛʀvøz] NF [*restaurant*] waitress; [*bar*] barmaid

serviabilité [sɛʀvjabilite] NF helpfulness

serviable [sɛʀvjabl] ADJ helpful

service [sɛʀvis]

[1] NOM MASCULIN	[2] COMPOSÉS

[1] NOM MASCULIN

[a] = **travail** duty; [*domestique*] (domestic) service; **~ de jour/nuit** day/night duty; **on ne fume pas pendant le ~** smoking is not allowed while on duty; **un peu de vin ? — non merci, jamais pendant le ~** a little wine? — no, thank you, not while I'm on duty; **heures de ~** hours of service *ou* duty; **il est très ~(-)service*** he's a stickler for the regulations; (*Admin, Mil*) **avoir 25 ans de ~** to have completed 25 years' service; [*domestique*] **être en ~ chez qn** to be in service with sb; **10 ans de ~ chez le même maître** 10 years in service with the same master; **après 10 ans de bons et loyaux ~s** after 10 years' loyal service; **qui est de ~ cette nuit ?** who's on duty tonight?, who's on night duty?; **être en ~ commandé** to be acting under orders, be on an official assignment; **prendre/quitter son ~** to come on/off duty; **reprendre du ~** [*personne*] to come back to work; [*objet*] to have a new lease of life → **escalier, note, règlement**

♦ **au service de** : **être au ~ de** [+ *maître, Dieu*] to be in the service of; [+ *cause*] to serve; **nos conseillers sont à votre ~** our advisers are at your service; **se mettre au ~ de** [+ *maître*] to enter the service of, go into service with; [+ *cause*] to begin to serve; [+ *Dieu, État*] to place o.s. in the service of; **prendre qn à son ~** to take sb into one's service

[b] = **prestation** service; **s'assurer les ~s de qn** to enlist sb's services; **offrir** *ou* **proposer ses ~s à qn** to offer sb one's services; **nous serons obligés de nous passer de vos ~s** we will have to let you go; (*Téléc*) **~ de base d'un réseau câblé** basic range of channels available to cable television subscribers

[c] **Écon** (*au pl*) **les biens et les ~s** goods and services; (= *secteur*) **la part des ~s dans l'économie** the role of the service industries in the economy → **emploi, société**

[d] **Mil** **le ~** (*militaire ou national*) military *ou* national service; **~ civil** non-military national service; **bon pour le ~** fit for military service; **faire son ~** to do one's military *ou* national service; **~ armé** combatant service → **état**

[e] **Admin** (= *administration*) service; (= *département*) department (*US*); **les ~s d'un ministère** the departments of a ministry; **les ~s de santé/postaux** health (care)/postal services; **les ~s de police** the police department (*US*); **les ~s financiers de la Ville de Paris** the treasury department of the City of Paris; **les ~s sociaux** the social services; **le ~ social de la ville** the local social services; **~ hospitalier** hospital service; **~ de réanimation** intensive care unit; **~ du contentieux/des achats/de la communication** legal/buying/PR department; **~ consommateurs** customer service department; (*dans une entreprise*) **les ~s généraux** the maintenance department; **~ informatique** computer department; **~ de surveillance/contrôle** surveillance/monitoring service → **chef¹**

[f] **Rel = office, messe** service; **~ funèbre** funeral service

[g] = **faveur, aide** service; **rendre ~ à qn** (= *aider qn*) to do sb a service *ou* a good turn; (= *s'avérer utile*) to come in useful *ou* handy for sb, be of use to sb; **il aime rendre ~** he likes to do good turns ou be helpful; (*fig*) **rendre un petit ~ à qn** to do sb a favour, do sb a small service; **tous les ~s qu'il m'a rendus** all the favours *ou* services he has done me; **décoré pour ~s rendus pendant la guerre** decorated for services rendered during the war; **rendre un mauvais ~ à qn** to do sb a disservice; (*frm*) **qu'y-a-t-il pour votre ~ ?** how can I be of service to you?

[h] **à table, au restaurant** service; (= *pourboire*) service charge; **Marc fera le ~** Marc will serve; **passe-moi les amuse-gueules, je vais faire le ~** hand me the appetizers, I'll pass them round; **la nourriture est bonne mais le ~ est trop lent** the food is good but the service is too slow; **ils ont oublié de compter le ~** they have forgotten to include the service (charge) on the bill; **~ compris/non compris** service included/not included, inclusive/exclusive of service; (= *série de repas*) **premier/deuxième ~** first/second sitting

[i] = **assortiment** [*couverts, linge de table*] set; [*verres, vaisselle*] service, set; **~ de table** (= *linge*) set of table linen; (= *vaisselle*) set of tableware; **~ à café/thé** coffee/tea set *ou* service; **~ à liqueurs** set of liqueur glasses; **~ à poisson** (= *vaisselle*) set of fish plates; (= *couverts*) fish service; **~ à fondue** fondue set; **~ à gâteaux** (= *couverts*) set of cake knives and forks; (= *vaisselle*) set of cake plates; **~ trois pièces**: (= *sexe masculin*) wedding tackle* (*hum*)

[j] **Transport** service; **un ~ d'autocars dessert ces localités** there is a coach service to these districts; **assurer le ~ entre** to provide a service between; **~ d'hiver/d'été** winter/summer service; **~ partiel** [*autobus*] limited service; **le ~ est interrompu sur la ligne 3** service is suspended on line 3

[k] **Tennis** service; **être au ~** to have the service; **prendre le ~ (de qn)** to win the service (from sb); **il a un excellent ~** he has an excellent service *ou* serve; **~ Dupont !** Dupont to serve!; **~ canon** bullet-like serve *ou* service; **~volée** serve and volley

[l] = **fonctionnement** [*machine, installation*] operation, working; **faire le ~ d'une pièce d'artillerie** to operate *ou* work a piece of artillery

♦ **en service** [*installation, usine*] in service; **entrer en ~** to come into service; **mettre en ~** to put *ou* bring into service; **la mise en ~ des nouveaux autobus est prévue pour juin** the new buses are due to be put into service in June; **remise en ~** [*aéroport, réacteur, voie ferrée*] re-opening

♦ **hors service** [*appareil*] out of order (*attrib*); * [*personne*] shattered*, done in*

[2] COMPOSÉS
► **service après-vente** after-sales service ► **Service d'assistance médicale d'urgence** mobile emergency medical service ► **service en ligne** (*Ordin*) on-line service ► **service minimum** skeleton service ► **service d'ordre** (= *policiers*) police contingent; (= *manifestants*) team of stewards (*responsible for crowd control etc*); **pour assurer le ~ d'ordre** to maintain (good) order ► **service de presse** [*ministère, entreprise*] press relations department; (= *distribution*) distribution of review copies; (= *ouvrage*) review copy; **ce livre m'a été envoyé en ~ de presse** I got a review copy of the book ► **service public** public service; **les ~s publics** the (public) utilities; **une télévision de ~ public** a public television company ► **service régional de police judiciaire** regional crime squad ► **les services secrets** the secret service ► **service de sécurité** (*d'un pays*) security

service; **le ~ de sécurité de l'aéroport** airport security ► **les services spéciaux** the secret service ► **Service du travail obligatoire** (*Hist*) forced labour instituted in France by the Nazis during World War II

SERVICE MILITAIRE

*Until 1997, all French men over eighteen years of age were required to do ten months' **service militaire** if passed fit. The call-up could be delayed if the conscript was a full-time student in higher education. Conscientious objectors were required to do two years' public service. The entire system is now being phased out.* → COOPÉRATION
---

serviette [sɛʀvjɛt] [1] NF [a] (*en tissu*) **~ (de toilette)** (hand) towel; **~ (de table)** (table) napkin, serviette (*Brit*) → **mélanger, rond** [b] (= *cartable*) [*écolier, homme d'affaires*] briefcase [2] COMP ► **serviette de bain** bath towel ► **serviette(-)éponge** terry towel ► **serviette hygiénique** sanitary towel (*Brit*) *ou* napkin (*US*) ► **serviette en papier** paper (table) napkin, paper serviette (*Brit*) ► **serviette périodique** = serviette hygiénique ► **serviette de plage** beach towel

servile [sɛʀvil] ADJ [a] (= *obséquieux*) [*personne*] servile; [*obéissance*] slavish; [*flatterie*] fawning [b] (= *sans originalité*) [*traduction, imitation*] slavish [c] (*littér = de serf*) [*condition, travail*] servile

servilement [sɛʀvilmɑ̃] ADV [a] [*obéir, imiter, traduire, copier*] slavishly; **flatter qn ~** to fawn on sb

servilité [sɛʀvilite] NF [a] (= *obséquiosité*) servility [b] [*traduction, imitation*] slavishness [c] (*littér*) [*condition, travail*] servility

servir [sɛʀviʀ] ► conjug 14 ◄ [1] VT [a] (= *être au service de*) [+ *pays, cause*] to serve; (*emploi absolu = être soldat*) to serve (**dans** in); (*Rel*) **~ la messe** to serve mass [b] [*domestique*] [+ *patron*] to serve, wait on; **il sert comme chauffeur** he works as a chauffeur; **il servait dans la même famille depuis 20 ans** he had been in service with the same family for 20 years; **elle aime se faire ~** she likes to be waited on ■ (*PROV*) **on n'est jamais si bien servi que par soi-même** if you want something doing, do it yourself [c] (= *aider*) [+ *personne*] to be of service to, aid; **~ les ambitions/intérêts de qn** to serve *ou* aid sb's ambitions/interests; **ceci nous sert** this serves our interests; **sa prudence l'a servi auprès des autorités** his caution served him well *ou* stood him in good stead in his dealings with the authorities; **il a été servi par les circonstances** he was aided by circumstances; **il a été servi par une bonne mémoire** his memory served him well [d] (*dans un magasin*) [+ *client*] to serve, attend to; [+ *consommateur*] to serve; [+ *dîneur*] to wait on; (*chez soi, à table*) to serve; **ce boucher nous sert depuis des années** this butcher has supplied us for years, we've been going to this butcher for years; **le boucher m'a bien servi** (*en qualité*) the butcher has given me good meat; (*en quantité*) the butcher has given me a good amount for my money; **on vous sert, Madame ?** are you being served?; **on n'arrive pas à se faire ~ ici** it's difficult to get served here; **prenez, n'attendez pas qu'on vous serve** help yourself — don't wait to be served; **«Madame est servie»** "dinner is served"; **pour vous ~†** at your service; **des garçons en livrée servaient** waiters in livery waited *ou* served at table; (*fig*) **les paysans voulaient la pluie, ils ont été servis !** the farmers wanted rain — well, they've certainly got what they wanted!; (*fig*) **en fait d'ennuis, elle a été servie** she's had more than her fair share of problems [e] (*Mil*) [+ *pièce d'artillerie*] to serve

f (= *donner*) [+ *rafraîchissement, plat*] to serve; ~ **qch à qn** to serve sb with sth, help sb to sth; ~ **le déjeuner/dîner** to serve (up) lunch/dinner; **« ~ frais »** "serve chilled"; ~ **à déjeuner/dîner** to serve lunch/dinner (**à qn** to sb); ~ **à boire** to serve drinks; ~ **à boire à qn** to serve a drink to sb; ~ **le café** to serve ou pour the coffee; **on nous a servi le petit déjeuner au lit** we were served (our) breakfast in bed; **il a faim, servez-le bien** he's hungry so give him a good helping; **à table, c'est servi!** come and sit down now, it's ready!; (*fig*) **il nous sert toujours les mêmes plaisanteries** he always trots out the same old jokes ou treats us to the same old jokes; **toutes ces émissions stupides qu'ils nous servent** all these stupid programmes they expect us to watch → **soupe**

g (= *verser*) to pay; ~ **une rente/une pension/des intérêts à qn** to pay sb an income/a pension/interest

h (*Cartes*) to deal

i (*Tennis, Ping-pong, Volley*) to serve; **à vous de** ~ your service, it's your turn to serve

j ~ **à** (= *être utile à*) [+ *personne*] to be of use ou help to; [+ *usage, opération*] to be of use in, be useful for; ~ **à faire qch** to be used for doing sth; **ça m'a servi à réparer ce fauteuil** I used it to mend this armchair; **ça ne sert à rien** [*objet*] it's no use, it's useless; [*démarche*] there's no point; **cela ne sert à rien de pleurer/réclamer** it's no use ou there's no point crying/complaining, crying/complaining won't help; **à quoi sert cet objet?** what's this thing used for?; **à quoi servirait de réclamer?** what use would it be to complain?, what would be the point of complaining?; **cela ne servirait pas à grand-chose de dire ...** there's little point in saying ..., it wouldn't be much use saying ...; **est-ce que cela pourrait vous ~?** could this be (of) any use to you?, could you make use of this?; **vos conseils lui ont bien servi** your advice has been very useful ou helpful to him; **ces projecteurs servent à guider les avions** these floodlights are used to guide ou for guiding the planes; **cet instrument sert à beaucoup de choses** this instrument has many uses ou is used for many things; **cela a servi à nous faire comprendre les difficultés** this served to help us understand the difficulties; **cet héritage n'a servi qu'à les brouiller** the inheritance only served to drive a wedge between them; **ne jette pas cette boîte, ça peut toujours ~** don't throw that box away — it may still come in handy ou still be of some use; **ce mot a beaucoup servi dans les années 60** the word was much used in the sixties; **cette valise n'a jamais servi** this suitcase has never been used → **rien**

k ~ **de** (= *être utilisé comme*) [*personne*] to act as; [*ustensile, objet*] to serve as; **elle lui a servi d'interprète/de témoin** she acted as his interpreter/as a witness (for him); **cette pièce sert de chambre d'amis** this room serves as ou is used as a guest room; **cela pourrait te ~ de table** you could use that as a table, that would serve ou do as a table for you → **exemple, leçon**

2 se servir VPR **a** (*à table, dans une distribution*) to help o.s.; (*chez un fournisseur*) **se ~ chez Leblanc** to buy ou shop at Leblanc's; **se ~ en viande chez Leblanc** to buy one's meat at Leblanc's, go to Leblanc's for one's meat; **servez-vous donc de viande** do help yourself to some meat; **tu t'es mal servi** you haven't given yourself a very big portion; (*iro*) **ne te gêne pas, sers-toi!** go ahead, help yourself! (*iro*)

b **se ~ de** (= *utiliser*) [+ *outil, mot, main-d'œuvre*] to use; [+ *personne*] to use, make use of; **il sait bien se ~ de cet outil** he knows how to use this tool; **t'es-tu servi de ce vêtement?** have you ever worn this?; **il se sert de sa voiture pour aller au bureau** he uses his car to go

---

to the office; **se ~ de ses relations** to make use of ou use one's acquaintances; **il s'est servi de moi** he used me

c (*sens passif*) **ce vin se sert très frais** this wine should be served chilled

serviteur [sɛʀvitœʀ] NM (*gén*) servant; (*hum*) **en ce qui concerne votre ~ ...** as far as yours truly is concerned ... (*hum*)

servitude [sɛʀvityd] NF **a** (= *esclavage*) servitude, bondage **b** (*gén pl* = *contrainte*) constraint **c** (*Jur*) easement; ~ **de passage** right of way

servocommande [sɛʀvɔkɔmɑ̃d] NF servomechanism

servodirection [sɛʀvɔdiʀɛksjɔ̃] NF servo(-assisted) steering

servofrein [sɛʀvɔfʀɛ̃] NM servo(-assisted) brake

servomécanisme [sɛʀvɔmekanism] NM servo system

servomoteur [sɛʀvɔmɔtœʀ] NM servo-motor

servovalve [sɛʀvɔvalv] NF servo valve

ses [se] ADJ POSS → **son**[1]

sésame [sezam] NM (*Bot*) sesame; **graines de ~** sesame seeds; **pain au ~** sesame seed loaf; **« Sésame ouvre-toi »** "open Sesame"; **ce diplôme est un ~ pour l'emploi** this degree opens doors in the job market

sessile [sesil] ADJ (*Bot*) sessile → **chêne**

session [sesjɔ̃] NF **a** (*Jur, Parl*) session, sitting; (*Parl*) ~ **extraordinaire** special session **b** (*Scol, Univ*) session; **la ~ de printemps/d'automne** the spring/autumn session; ~ **d'examen** exam session; **la ~ de juin** the June exams; **la ~ de septembre** the (September) retakes ou resits (*Brit*); ~ **de rattrapage** special session of the baccalauréat for students who are unable to take the exam the first time around **c** (= *cours, stage*) course; ~ **de formation** training course

sesterce [sɛstɛʀs] NM (*Hist*) (= *monnaie*) sesterce, sestertius; (= *mille unités*) sestertium

set [sɛt] NM **a** (*Tennis*) set → **balle**[1] **b** ~ **(de table)** (= *ensemble*) set of tablemats ou place mats; (= *napperon*) tablemat, place mat

setter [sɛtɛʀ] NM setter; ~ **irlandais** Irish setter

seuil [sœj] NM **a** [*porte*] (= *marche*) doorstep; (= *entrée*) doorway, threshold†; (*fig*) threshold; **se tenir sur le ~ de sa maison** to stand in the doorway of one's house; **il m'a reçu sur le ~** he kept me on the doorstep ou at the door; **avoir la campagne au ~ de sa maison** to have the country on ou at one's doorstep; (*au* = *début*) **le ~ de** [+ *période*] the threshold of; **au ~ de la mort** at death's door; **le ~ du désert** the edge of the desert

b (*Géog, Tech*) sill

c (*fig* = *limite*) threshold; (*Psych*) threshold, limen (*SPÉC*); ~ **auditif** auditory threshold; ~ **de la douleur** pain threshold; ~ **de rentabilité** break-even point; ~ **de tolérance** threshold of tolerance; ~ **de pauvreté** poverty line ou level; **vivre en dessous du ~ de pauvreté** to live below ou beneath the poverty line; (*Bourse*) ~ **de résistance** resistance level; **le dollar est passé sous le ~ des 6 F** the dollar fell below the 6 franc level; ~ **d'imposition** tax threshold; (*Jur*) **relever les ~s sociaux** to raise the minimum number of employees required to establish works councils, delegates' committees etc

seul, e [sœl] **1** ADJ **a** (*après n ou attrib*) [*personne*] (= *sans compagnie, non accompagné*) alone (*attrib*), on one's own (*attrib*), by oneself (*attrib*); (= *isolé*) lonely; [*objet, mot*] alone (*attrib*), on its own (*attrib*), by itself (*attrib*); **être/rester ~** to be/remain alone ou on one's own ou by oneself; **laissez-moi ~ quelques instants** leave me alone ou on my own ou by myself for a moment; ~ **avec qn/ses pensées/son chagrin** alone with sb/one's thoughts/one's grief; **ils se retrouvèrent enfin ~s** they were alone (together) ou on their own ou by themselves at last; **un homme ~/une femme ~e**

---

peut très bien se débrouiller a man on his own/a woman on her own ou a single man/woman can manage perfectly well; **au bal, il y avait beaucoup d'hommes ~s** at the dance there were many men on their own; **se sentir (très) ~** to feel (very) lonely ou lonesome; ~ **au monde** alone in the world; **les amoureux sont ~s au monde** lovers behave as if they are the only ones in the world; **être ~ contre tous** to be alone against the world; **il s'est battu, ~ contre tous** he fought single-handedly; **mot employé ~** word used alone ou on its own ou by itself; **la lampe ~e ne suffit pas** the lamp alone ou on its own is not enough, the lamp is not enough on its own ou by itself; **il est tout ~** he's all alone; **il était tout ~ dans un coin** he was all by himself ou all alone in a corner; **il l'a fait tout ~** he did it all by himself ou (all) on his own; **cette tasse ne s'est pas cassée toute ~e!** this cup didn't break all by itself! → **cavalier**

b (*avant n* = *unique*) **un ~ homme/livre** (*et non plusieurs*) one man/book, a single man/book; (*à l'exception de tout autre*) only one man/book; **le ~ homme/livre** the one man/book, the only man/book, the sole man/book; **les ~es personnes/conditions** the only people/conditions; **un ~ livre suffit** one book ou a single book will do; **un ~ homme peut vous aider: Paul** only one man can help you and that's Paul; **pour cette ~e raison** for this reason alone ou only, for this one reason; **son ~ souci est de ...** his only ou sole ou one concern is to ...; **un ~ moment d'inattention** one ou a single moment's lapse of concentration; **il n'y a qu'un ~ Dieu** there is only one God, there is one God only ou alone; **une ~e fois** only once, once only; **la ~e chose, c'est que ça ferme à 6 heures** the only thing is (that) it shuts at 6

c (*en apposition*) only; ~ **le résultat compte** the result alone counts, only the result counts; **~s les parents sont admis** only parents are admitted; **~e Gabrielle peut le faire** only Gabrielle ou Gabrielle alone can do it; **~e l'imprudence peut être la cause de cet accident** only carelessness can have caused this accident; **lui ~ est venu en voiture** he alone ou only he came by car; **à eux ~s, ils ont bu dix bouteilles** they drank ten bottles between them; **je l'ai fait à moi (tout) ~** I did it (all) on my own ou (all) by myself, I did it single-handed

d (*loc*) ~ **et unique** one and only; **c'est la ~e et même personne** they're one and the same (person); ~ **de son espèce** the only one of its kind; **d'un ~ coup** (= *subitement*) suddenly; (= *en une seule fois*) in one go; **vous êtes ~ juge** you alone can judge; **à ~e fin de ...** with the sole purpose of ...; **dans la ~e intention de ...** with the one ou sole intention of ...; **du ~ fait que ...** by the very fact that ...; **à la ~e pensée de ...** at the mere thought of ...; **la ~e pensée d'y retourner la remplissait de frayeur** the mere ou very thought of going back there filled her with fear; **parler à qn ~ à ~** to speak to sb in private ou privately ou alone; **se retrouver ~ à ~ avec qn** to find o.s. alone with sb; (*fig*) **comme un ~ homme** as one man; **d'une ~e voix** with one voice

2 ADV **a** (= *sans compagnie*) **parler/rire ~** to talk/laugh to oneself; **vivre/travailler ~** to live/work alone ou by oneself ou on one's own

b (= *sans aide*) by oneself, on one's own, unaided; **faire qch (tout) ~** to do sth (all) by oneself ou (all) on one's own, do sth unaided ou single-handed; **ça va tout ~** it's all going smoothly

3 NM,F **un ~ peut le faire** (*et non plusieurs*) one man can do it, a single man can do it; (*à l'exception de tout autre*) only one man can do it; **un ~ contre tous** one (man) against all; **le ~ que j'aime** the only one I love; **vous n'êtes**

pas la ~e à vous plaindre you aren't the only one to complain, you aren't alone in complaining; **une ~e de ses peintures n'a pas été détruite dans l'incendie** only one of his paintings was not destroyed in the fire; **il n'en reste pas un ~** there isn't a single *ou* solitary one left

seulement [sœlmɑ̃] ADV a (*quantité = pas davantage*) only; **cinq personnes ~ sont venues** only five people came; **nous serons ~ quatre** there will only be four of us; **je pars pour deux jours ~** I'm only going away for two days

b (= *exclusivement*) only, alone, solely; **on ne vit pas ~ de pain** you can't live on bread alone; **ce n'est pas ~ sa maladie qui le déprime** it's not only *ou* just his illness that depresses him; **1500 F, c'est le prix de la chambre** 1,500 francs is the price for just the room *ou* is the price for the room only; **on leur permet de lire ~ le soir** they are only allowed to read at night; **il fait cela ~ pour nous ennuyer** he only does that to annoy us

c (*temps = pas avant*) only; **il vient ~ d'entrer** he's only just (now) come in; **ce fut ~ vers 10 heures qu'il arriva** he only got there at about 10 o'clock; **il est parti ~ ce matin** he left only this morning, he only left this morning

d (*en tête de proposition = mais, toutefois*) only, but; **je connais un bon chirurgien, ~ il est cher** I know a good surgeon, only *ou* but he is expensive; **j'avais tout organisé, ~ voilà, ils ne sont même pas venus** I'd organized everything, the only thing was they didn't turn up

e (*loc*) **non ~ il ne travaille pas mais (encore) il empêche les autres de travailler** not only does he not work but he stops the others working too; **non ~ le directeur mais aussi** *ou* **encore les employés** not only *ou* just the manager but the employees too *ou* as well; **non ~ il a plu, mais (encore) il a fait froid** it didn't only rain but it was cold too, it not only rained but it was also cold; (*même pas*) **on ne nous a pas ~ donné un verre d'eau** we were not even given a glass of water, we were not given so much as a glass of water; **il n'a pas ~ de quoi se payer un costume** he hasn't even got enough to buy himself a suit; **il est parti sans ~ nous prévenir** he left without so much as *ou* without even telling us; **si ~** → **si¹**

seulet, -ette †* [sœlɛ, ɛt] ADJ (*hum*) lonesome, lonely, all alone; **se sentir bien ~** to feel all alone *ou* very lonesome

sève [sɛv] NF [*arbre*] sap; (*fig*) sap, life, vigour (*Brit*), vigor (*US*); **~ ascendante/brute/descendante élaborée** rising/crude/falling elaborated sap; **les arbres sont en pleine ~** the sap has risen in the trees; **la jeunesse est débordante de ~** young people are brimming with strength and vigour

sévère [sevɛʀ] ADJ a (= *dur, strict*) [*maître, juge, climat, mesures, règlement*] severe, harsh; [*parent, éducation, ton*] strict, severe; [*jugement*] severe, harsh; [*regard, visage*] severe, stern; [*verdict*] harsh; **elle suit un régime ~** she's on a strict diet; **après une sélection ~** after a rigorous selection process; **une morale ~** a strict *ou* stern moral code; **ne soyez pas trop ~ avec elle** don't be too harsh on her *ou* strict with her; **la critique a été très ~ avec son film** the critics were very hard on his film b (= *austère*) [*style, architecture*] severe; [*traits du visage, tenue*] severe, stern; **une beauté ~** a severe beauty c (= *lourd*) [*pertes, échec*] severe, heavy

sévèrement [sevɛʀmɑ̃] ADV a (= *durement*) [*punir*] severely; [*juger, critiquer*] harshly, severely; [*contrôler, réglementer*] strictly; **les visites sont ~ contrôlées** visits are under strict control b (= *gravement*) [*éprouver, affecter*] severely; **cette ville est ~ affectée par la crise** the town has been severely hit by the crisis; **un malade ~ atteint** a severely affected patient

sévérité [severite] NF a (= *dureté, rigueur*) [*maître, juge, jugement, climat, mesures, règlement*] severity, harshness; [*parent, éducation, ton*] strictness, severity; [*regard*] severity, sternness; [*verdict*] harshness; **elle a élevé ses enfants avec une grande ~** she was very strict with her children; **il se juge avec trop de ~** he's too hard on himself; **tu manques de ~ avec lui** you're not strict enough with him, you're too soft on him b (= *austérité*) [*style, architecture*] severity; [*tenue, mœurs, traits du visage*] severity, sternness c (= *gravité*) [*pertes, échec, récession*] severity

sévices [sevis] NMPL physical cruelty (*NonC*), ill treatment (*NonC*); **~ corporels/sexuels** physical/sexual abuse (*NonC*); **faire subir des ~ à la population** to treat the population brutally *ou* cruelly; **exercer des ~ sur un enfant** (*gén*) to ill-treat a child; (*sexuels*) to abuse a child; **être victime de ~** to be ill-treated *ou* abused

Séville [sevil] N Seville

sévir [seviʀ] ▸ conjug 2 ◂ VI a (= *punir*) to act ruthlessly; **~ contre** [+ *personne, abus, pratique*] to deal ruthlessly with; **si vous continuez, je vais devoir ~** if you carry on, I shall have to deal severely with you *ou* use harsh measures b (= *exercer ses ravages*) [*virus*] to be rife; [*doctrine*] to hold sway; **ce fléau sévit encore en Asie** the illness is still rife in Asia; **la pauvreté sévissait** poverty was rampant *ou* rife; (*hum*) **il sévit à la télé/dans notre service depuis 20 ans** he's been plaguing our screens/our department for 20 years now (*hum*); (*hum*) **est-ce qu'il sévit encore à l'université?** do they still let him loose on the students? (*hum*)

sevrage [səvʀaʒ] NM a [*nourrisson, jeune animal*] weaning b (*Hort*) separation c (*Méd*) **une méthode de ~ des toxicomanes** a method of weaning addicts off drugs; **les cures de ~ des toxicomanes** drug withdrawal programmes; **pour faciliter le ~ tabagique** to make it easier for people to give up *ou* to stop smoking; **il lui faudra un ~ pharmacologique** he'll need some kind of prop *ou* substitute product to help him give up

sevrer [səvʀe] ▸ conjug 5 ◂ VT a [+ *nourrisson, jeune animal*] to wean; **~ un toxicomane** to wean an addict off drugs; **pour ~ les fumeurs** to help smokers give up b (*Hort*) to separate c (*littér = priver*) **~ qn de qch** to deprive sb of sth; **nous avons été sevrés de théâtre** we have been deprived of theatre outings

Sèvres [sevʀ] NM (= *porcelaine*) Sèvres porcelain; (= *objet*) piece of Sèvres porcelain

sexagénaire [sɛksaʒenɛʀ] 1 ADJ sixty-year-old (*épith*), sexagenarian 2 NMF sixty-year-old, sexagenarian

sexagésimal, e (*mpl* -aux) [sɛgzaʒezimal, o] ADJ sexagesimal

sexagésime [sɛgzaʒezim] NF (*Rel*) Sexagesima (Sunday)

sex-appeal [sɛksapil] NM sex appeal

sexe [sɛks] NM a (= *catégorie*) sex; **enfant de ou du ~ masculin/féminin** male/female child; **nous recherchons une personne de ~ féminin/masculin** we are looking for a woman/man; **le ~ faible/fort** the weaker/stronger sex; (*littér*) **le (beau) ~** the fair sex b (= *sexualité*) sex; **ce journal ne parle que de ~** this paper is full of nothing but sex c (= *organes génitaux*) genitals, sex organs; (= *verge*) penis

sexisme [sɛksism] NM sexism; **être accusé de ~** to be accused of sexism *ou* of being sexist

sexiste [sɛksist] ADJ, NMF sexist

sexologie [sɛksɔlɔʒi] NF sexology

sexologue [sɛksɔlɔg] NMF sexologist, sex specialist

sex-shop (*pl* **sex-shops**) [sɛksʃɔp] NM sex-shop

sex-symbol (*pl* **sex-symbols**) [sɛkssɛbɔl] NM sex symbol

sextant [sɛkstɑ̃] NM (= *instrument*) sextant; (*Math = arc*) sextant arc

sextuor [sɛkstɥɔʀ] NM (*Mus*) sextet(te)

sextuple [sɛkstypl] 1 ADJ [*nombre, quantité, rangée*] sextuple; **une quantité ~ de l'autre** a quantity six times (as great as) the other; **en ~ exemplaire** in six copies 2 NM (*gén, Math*) **je l'ai payé le ~/le ~ de l'autre** I paid six times as much for it/six times as much as the other for it; **augmenter au ~** to increase sixfold *ou* six times

sextupler [sɛkstyple] ▸ conjug 1 ◂ VTI to increase six times *ou* sixfold

sextuplés, -ées [sɛkstyple] NM,F PL sextuplets

sexualiser [sɛksɥalize] ▸ conjug 1 ◂ VT to sexualize

sexualité [sɛksɥalite] NF sexuality; **troubles de la ~** sexual problems; **avoir une ~ épanouie** to have a full sex life

sexué, e [sɛksɥe] ADJ [*mammifères, plantes*] sexed, sexual; [*reproduction*] sexual

sexuel, -elle [sɛksɥɛl] ADJ [*caractère, instinct, plaisir*] sexual; [*éducation, hormone, organe, partenaire*] sexual, sex (*épith*); [*abus, comportement, sévices*] sexual; **avoir une activité sexuelle importante** to have a very active sex life → **rapport**

sexuellement [sɛksɥɛlmɑ̃] ADV sexually → **maladie**

sexy* [sɛksi] ADJ INV sexy*

seyant, e [sɛjɑ̃, ɑ̃t] ADJ [*vêtement*] becoming; **elle portait une jupe très ~e** she was wearing a skirt that really suited her

Seychelles [seʃɛl] NFPL **les ~** the Seychelles

seychellois, e [seʃɛlwa, az] 1 ADJ of *ou* from the Seychelles 2 **Seychellois(e)** NM,F inhabitant *ou* native of the Seychelles

SF* [ɛsɛf] NF (*ABRÉV* = **science-fiction**) sci-fi*; **film/roman de SF** sci-fi* film/novel

SG [ɛsʒe] NM (*ABRÉV* = **secrétaire général**) → **secrétaire**

SGBD [ɛsʒebede] NM (*ABRÉV* = **système de gestion de bases de données**) → **système**

shabbat [ʃabat] NM = **sabbat**

shah [ʃa] NM shah

shaker [ʃɛkœʀ] NM cocktail shaker

shakespearien, -ienne [ʃɛkspiʀjɛ̃, jɛn] ADJ Shakespearian

shako [ʃako] NM shako

shampoing, shampooing [ʃɑ̃pwɛ̃] NM (= *lavage, produit*) shampoo; **faire un shampooing à qn** to give sb a shampoo, shampoo *ou* wash sb's hair; **se faire un shampooing** to shampoo one's hair; **à appliquer après chaque shampooing** apply every time after shampooing; **shampooing colorant** shampoo-in hair colourant (*Brit*) *ou* colorant (*US*); **shampooing crème** cream shampoo; **shampooing à moquette** carpet shampoo

shampouiner, shampooiner [ʃɑ̃pwine] ▸ conjug 1 ◂ VT to shampoo; **se shampooiner la tête** to shampoo one's hair

shampouineur, -euse, shampooineur, -euse [ʃɑ̃pwinœʀ, øz] 1 NM,F trainee hairdresser (*who washes hair*), junior 2 **shampouineuse** ▸ **shampooineuse** NF (= *machine*) carpet shampooer

shant(o)ung [ʃɑ̃tuŋ] NM shantung (silk)

shekel [ʃekɛl] NM shekel

shérif [ʃeʀif] NM [*western*] sheriff, marshal

sherpa [ʃɛʀpa] NM (= *guide*) Sherpa; (*Pol*) aide (*helping with preparations for summit talks*)

sherry [ʃeʀi] NM sherry

shetland [ʃɛtlɑ̃d] 1 NM (= *laine*) Shetland wool; (= *tricot*) Shetland pullover 2 **Shetland** NFPL **les ~ (les îles)** Shetland *ou* the Shetlands, the Shetland Islands; **les (îles) Shetland-du-Sud** the South Shetlands

shetlandais, e [ʃɛtlɑ̃dɛ, ɛz] 1 ADJ Shetland (*épith*) 2 **Shetlandais(e)** NM,F Shetlander

shilling [ʃiliŋ] NM shilling

shimmy [ʃimi] NM (= danse) shimmy; (Aut) shimmy

shintô [ʃinto], **shintoïsme** [ʃintɔism] NM Shinto, Shintoism

shintoïste [ʃintɔist] ADJ, NMF Shintoist

shit [ʃit] NM (arg Drogue) dope*, hash*

Shiva [ʃiva] NM = **Siva**

Shoah [ʃɔa] NF Shoah

shog(o)un [ʃɔgun] NM shogun

shoot [ʃut] NM [a] (Ftbl) shot [b] (arg Drogue) fix*; **se faire un ~ d'héroïne** to shoot up* with heroin

shooter [ʃute] ▸ conjug 1 ◂ [1] VI (Ftbl) to shoot, make a shot [2] VT **~ un penalty** to take a penalty (kick ou shot) [3] **se shooter** VPR (arg Drogue) to shoot up*; **se ~ à l'héroïne** to mainline* heroin, shoot up* with heroin; **il s'est shooté pendant dix ans** he mainlined* drugs for ten years; **je me shoote au café*** I need to have my daily fix* of coffee; **on l'a complètement shooté aux médicaments*** he's been drugged ou doped up to the eyeballs*

shopping [ʃɔpiŋ] NM shopping; **faire du ~** to go shopping; **faire son ~** to do one's shopping

short [ʃɔrt] NM **~(s)** pair of shorts, shorts; **être en ~(s)** to be in shorts ou wearing shorts → **tailler**

show [ʃo] NM show

showbiz* [ʃobiz] NM INV (ABRÉV = **show-business**) show biz*

show-business [ʃobiznɛs] NM INV show business

show-room (pl **show-rooms**) [ʃorum] NM showroom

shrapnel(l) [ʃrapnɛl] NM shrapnel

shunt [ʃœt] NM (Élec) shunt

shunter [ʃœte] ▸ conjug 1 ◂ VT (Élec) to shunt; * [+ personne, service] to bypass

SI [a] (ABRÉV = **syndicat d'initiative**) → **syndicat** [b] (ABRÉV = **Système international (d'unités)**) SI

▼ **si¹** [si] [1] CONJ [a] (éventualité, condition) if; **s'il fait beau demain (et si j'en ai ou et que j'en aie le temps), je sortirai** if it's fine tomorrow (and (if) I have time), I'll go out [b] (hypothèse) if; (Math) **si et seulement si** if and only if; **si j'avais de l'argent, j'achèterais une voiture** if I had any money ou had I any money, I would buy a car; **même s'il s'excusait, je ne lui pardonnerais pas** even if he were to apologize I wouldn't forgive him; **si nous n'avions pas été prévenus, nous serions arrivés ou nous arrivions trop tard** if we hadn't been warned, we would have arrived too late; **il a déclaré que si on ne l'augmentait pas, il partirait ou il partait** he said that if he didn't get a rise he would leave ou he was leaving; **viendras-tu? si oui, préviens-moi à l'avance** are you coming? if so ou if you are, tell me in advance → **comme** [c] (répétition = toutes les fois que) if, when; **s'il faisait beau, il allait se promener** if ou when it was nice he used to go for a walk; **si je sors sans parapluie, il pleut** if ou whenever I go out without an umbrella it always rains [d] (opposition) while, whilst (surtout Brit); **si lui est aimable, sa femme (par contre) est arrogante** while ou whereas he is very pleasant his wife (on the other hand) is arrogant [e] (exposant un fait) **s'il ne joue plus, c'est qu'il s'est cassé la jambe** if he doesn't play any more it's because he has broken his leg, the reason he no longer plays is that he has broken his leg; **c'est un miracle si la voiture n'a pas pris feu** it's a miracle (that) the car didn't catch fire; **excusez-nous ou pardonnez-nous si nous n'avons pas pu venir** please excuse ou forgive us for not being able to come

[f] (dans une interrogation indirecte) if, whether; **il ignore/se demande si elle viendra (ou non)** he doesn't know/is wondering whether ou if she'll come (or not); **il faut s'assurer si la télé marche** we must make sure that the TV is working; **vous imaginez s'ils étaient fiers!** you can imagine how proud they were!; **si je veux y aller! quelle question!** do I want to go! what a question!

[g] (en corrélation avec proposition implicite) if; **si j'avais su!** if I had only known!, had I (only) known!; **si je le tenais!** if I could (only) lay my hands on him!; **et s'il refusait?** and what if he refused?, and what if he should refuse?, and supposing he refused?; **si tu lui téléphonais?** how ou what about phoning him?, supposing ou suppose you phoned him?; **si nous allions nous promener?** what ou how about going for a walk?, what would you say to a walk?

[h] **qui peut le savoir, si ce n'est lui?** if he doesn't know, who will?; **si ce n'est elle, qui aurait osé?** if not her, who else would have dared?; **si ce n'était la crainte de les décourager** if it were not ou were it not for the fear of putting them off; **il n'avait rien emporté, si ce n'est quelques biscuits et une pomme** he had taken nothing with him apart from ou other than a few biscuits and an apple; **une des plus belles, si ce n'est la plus belle** one of the most beautiful, if not the most beautiful; **elle se porte bien, si ce n'est qu'elle est très fatiguée** she's quite well apart from the fact that she is very tired ou apart from feeling very tired

[i] (loc) **si tant est que** so long as, provided ou providing that; **invite-les tous, si tant est que nous ayons assez de verres** invite them all, so long as we have enough glasses ou if we have enough glasses that is; **ils sont sous-payés, si tant est qu'on les paie** they are underpaid, if they are paid at all; **s'il te ou vous plaît** please; **si je ne me trompe ◊ si je ne m'abuse** (frm, iro) if I'm not ou unless I'm mistaken; (frm, hum) **si j'ose dire** if I may say so; (frm) **si je puis dire** if I may put it like that; **si l'on peut dire** in a way, as it were, so to speak, in a manner of speaking; **si j'ai bien compris/entendu** if I understood correctly/heard properly; **si seulement il venait/était venu** if only he was coming/had come; **brave homme s'il en fut** a fine man if ever there was one; **si c'est ça*, je m'en vais** if that's how it is, I'm off*

[2] NM INV if; **avec des si (et des mais), on mettrait Paris en bouteille** if ifs and ands and buts and pots and pans there'd be no need for tinkers

si² [si] ADV [a] (affirmatif) **vous ne venez pas? — si/mais si/que si** aren't you coming? — yes I am/of course I am/indeed I am ou I certainly am; **vous n'avez rien mangé? — si, une pomme** haven't you had anything to eat? — yes (I have), an apple; **si, si, il faut venir** oh but you must come!; **il n'a pas voulu, moi si** he didn't want to, but I did; **il n'a pas écrit? — il semble bien ou il paraît que si** hasn't he written? — yes, it seems that he has; **je pensais qu'il ne viendrait pas, mais quand je lui en ai parlé il m'a répondu que si** I thought he wouldn't come but when I mentioned it to him he told me he would; **je croyais qu'elle ne voulait pas venir, mais il m'a dit que si** I thought she didn't want to come but he said she did; **si fait†** indeed yes

[b] (intensif = tellement) (modifiant attrib, adv) so; (modifiant épith) **un ami si gentil** such a kind friend, so kind a friend (frm); **des amis si gentils ◊ de si gentils amis** such kind friends; **il parle si bas qu'on ne l'entend pas** he speaks so low ou in such a low voice that you can't hear him; **j'ai si faim** I'm so hungry; **elle n'est pas si stupide qu'elle ne puisse comprendre ceci** she's not so stupid that she can't understand this; (iro) **il est stupide, non? — si peu!** he's stupid, isn't he? — and how!* ou too

right!*

[c] **si bien que** so that, with the result that [d] (concessif = aussi) however; **si bête soit-il ou qu'il soit, il comprendra** however stupid he is he will understand; **si rapidement qu'il progresse** however rapidly he progresses; **si adroitement qu'il ait parlé, il n'a convaincu personne** for all that he spoke very cleverly ou however cleverly he may have spoken he didn't convince anyone; **si beau qu'il fasse, il ne peut encore sortir** however good the weather is, he can't go out yet; **si peu que ce soit** however little it may be, little as ou though it may be [e] (égalité = aussi) as, so; **elle n'est pas si timide que vous croyez** she's not so ou as shy as you think; **il ne travaille pas si lentement qu'il en a l'air** he doesn't work as slowly as he seems to; **ce n'est pas si facile ou simple** it's not as simple as that

si³ [si] NM INV (Mus) B; (en chantant la gamme) ti, te

sial [sjal] NM (Géol) sial

Siam [sjam] NM Siam

siamois, e [sjamwa, waz] [1] ADJ († Géog) Siamese; [chat] Siamese; **frères ~ ◊ sœurs ~es** Siamese twins [2] NM,F [a] († Géog) Siamois(e) Siamese [b] (pl = jumeaux) Siamese twins [3] NM (= chat) Siamese

Sibérie [siberi] NF Siberia

sibérien, -ienne [siberjɛ̃, jɛn] [1] ADJ (Géog, fig) Siberian [2] **Sibérien(ne)** NM,F Siberian

sibilant, e [sibilɑ̃, ɑ̃t] ADJ (Méd) sibilant

sibylle [sibil] NF sibyl

sibyllin, e [sibilɛ̃, in] ADJ (Myth) sibylline; [phrase, personne] cryptic, sibylline (frm); **tenir des propos ~s** to talk in riddles; **de façon ou de manière ~e** cryptically

sic [sik] ADV sic

SICAV, sicav [sikav] NF INV (ABRÉV = **société d'investissement à capital variable**) (= fonds) unit trust (Brit), open-end investment trust (US), mutual fund (US); (= part) share in a unit trust (Brit) ou an open-end investment trust (US) ou a mutual fund (US); **sicav monétaire** money market fund; **sicav obligataire** bond fund; **sicav de trésorerie** cash management unit trust ou mutual fund

siccatif, -ive [sikatif, iv] ADJ, NM siccative

Sicile [sisil] NF Sicily

sicilien, -ienne [sisiljɛ̃, jɛn] [1] ADJ Sicilian [2] NM [a] (= dialecte) Sicilian [b] **Sicilien** Sicilian [3] **sicilienne** NF [a] **Sicilienne** Sicilian [b] (= danse) Siciliano, Sicilienne

SIDA, sida [sida] NM (ABRÉV = **syndrome d'immunodéficience acquise**) AIDS, Aids; **avoir le/être atteint du sida** to have/be suffering from AIDS; **le virus du sida** the AIDS virus; **la lutte contre le sida** the battle against AIDS

side-car (pl **side-cars**) [sidkar] NM (= habitacle) sidecar; (= véhicule entier) motorcycle and sidecar

sidéen, -enne [sideɛ̃, ɛn] [1] ADJ [personne] (infected) with AIDS ou Aids [2] NM,F AIDS ou Aids sufferer, person with AIDS, PWA

sidéral, e (mpl -aux) [sideral, o] ADJ sidereal

sidérant, e* [siderɑ̃, ɑ̃t] ADJ staggering*, shattering*

sidération [siderasjɔ̃] NF (Méd) sideration

sidérer [sidere] ▸ conjug 6 ◂ VT [a] (* = abasourdir) to stagger*; **cette nouvelle m'a sidéré** I was staggered* ou dumbfounded by the news; **je suis sidéré par son intelligence/son insolence** I'm dumbfounded ou amazed by his intelligence/his insolence; **la foule regardait, sidérée** the crowd watched, dumbfounded [b] (Méd) to siderate

sidérurgie [sideryrʒi] NF (= fabrication) (iron and) steel metallurgy; (= industrie) (iron and) steel industry

➤ GRAMMAIRE ACTIVE: **si** 30

sidérurgique [sideryrʒik] ADJ [procédé] (iron-and) steel-manufacturing (épith); [industrie] iron and steel (épith)

sidérurgiste [sideryrʒist] NMF (= industriel) steel manufacturer; (= ouvrier) steel worker

sidi † [sidi] NM (injurieux) North African immigrant (resident in France)

Sidon [sidɔ̃] N Sidon

siècle [sjɛkl] NM **a** (gén) century; **au 3ème ~ avant Jésus-Christ/après Jésus-Christ** in the 3rd century B.C./A.D.; **au ~ dernier** in the last century; **le Grand Siècle** the 17th century (in France), the grand siècle; **le hold-up/match du ~*** the hold-up/match of the century; **cet arbre a/ces ruines ont des ~s** this tree is/these ruins are centuries old; **après des ~s de colonisation, le pays ...** after centuries of colonial rule, the country ...; **il est né avec le ~ ◊ il a l'âge du ~** he's as old as the century → **consommation, fin², mal** **b** (= époque) age; **être de son ~/d'un autre ~** to belong to one's age/to another age; **de ~ en ~** from age to age, through the ages; **le ~ de Périclès/d'Auguste** the age of Pericles/of Augustus; **le Siècle des lumières** the (Age of) the Enlightenment; **il y a un ~ ou des ~s que nous ne nous sommes vus*** it has been ou it is years ou ages since we last saw each other **c** (Rel = monde) **le ~** the world; **les plaisirs du ~** worldly pleasures, the pleasures of the world

siège¹ [sjɛʒ] NM **a** (= meuble) seat; **~ de jardin/de bureau** garden/office chair; **le ~ des toilettes** the toilet seat; **donner/offrir un ~ à qn** to give/offer sb a seat; **prenez un ~** take a seat; **Dupont, le spécialiste du ~ de bureau** Dupont, the specialist in office seating; (Aut) **~ avant/arrière** front/back seat; (Aviat) **~ éjectable** ejector seat; (Aut) **~ baquet** bucket seat; (Aut) **~ pour bébé(s) ◊ ~-auto** baby (car) seat **b** (frm, Méd = postérieur) seat; **l'enfant se présente par le ~** the baby's in the breech position → **bain** **c** (Pol = fonction) seat; **~ vacant** vacant seat; **retrouver son ~ de député** to win back one's parliamentary seat **d** (Jur) [magistrat] bench → **magistrature** **e** (= résidence principale) [firme] head office; [parti, organisation internationale] headquarters; [assemblée, tribunal] seat; **~ social** registered office; **~ épiscopal/pontifical** episcopal/pontifical see; **cette organisation, dont le ~ est à Genève** this Geneva-based organization, this organization which is based in Geneva ou which has its headquarters in Geneva **f** (fig = centre) [maladie, passions, rébellion] seat; (Physiol) [faculté, sensation] centre (Brit), center (US)

siège² [sjɛʒ] NM [place forte] siege; **mettre le ~ devant une ville** to besiege a town; (lit, fig) **faire le ~ de** to lay siege to → **état, lever**

siéger [sjeʒe] ▶ conjug 3 et 6 ◀ VI **a** (= être en session) [assemblée, tribunal] to be in session **b** (= être membre de) **~ à** [+ conseil, comité] to sit ou be on **c** (= être situé à) [tribunal, organisme] **~ à** to have its headquarters in, be headquartered in (US) **d** (fig = résider) **voilà où siège le mal** that's where the trouble lies

sien, sienne [sjɛ̃, sjɛn] **1** PRON POSS **le ~ ◊ la sienne ◊ les ~s ◊ les siennes** [homme] his (own); [femme] hers, her own; [chose, animal] its own; [nation] its own, hers, her own; (indéf) one's own; **ce sac/cette robe est le ~/la sienne** this bag/this dress is his, this is her bag/dress; **il est parti avec une veste qui n'est pas la sienne** he left with a jacket which isn't his ou with somebody else's jacket; **le voisin est furieux parce que nos fleurs sont plus jolies que les siennes** our neighbour is furious because our flowers are nicer than his; **mes enfants sont sortis avec deux des ~s/les deux ~s** my children have gone out with two of hers/her two; **cet oiseau préfère les nids des**

autres au ~ this bird prefers other birds' nests to its own; **je préfère mes ciseaux, les ~s ne coupent pas** I prefer my scissors because hers don't cut; (emphatique) **la sienne de voiture est plus rapide*** his car is faster, his is a faster car; **de tous les pays, on préfère toujours le ~** of all countries one always prefers one's own **2** NM **a** **les choses s'arrangent depuis qu'elle y a mis du ~** things are beginning to sort themselves out since she began to pull her weight; **chacun doit être prêt à y mettre du ~** everyone must be prepared to pull his weight ou to make some more effort **b** **les ~s** (= famille) one's family, one's folks*; (= partisans) one's (own) people; **Dieu reconnaît les ~s** God knows his own ou his people **3** **siennes** NFPL **il/elle a encore fait des siennes*** he/she has (gone and) done it again*; **le mal de mer commençait à faire des siennes parmi les passagers** seasickness was beginning to claim some victims among the passengers **4** ADJ POSS († ou littér) **un ~ cousin** a cousin of his (ou hers); **il fait siennes toutes les opinions de son père** he adopts all his father's opinions

Sienne [sjɛn] N Siena → **terre**

sierra [sjera] NF sierra; **la ~ Madre/Nevada** the Sierra Madre/Nevada

Sierra Leone [sjeraleɔn(e)] NF Sierra Leone

sierra-léonien, -ienne [sjeraleɔnjɛ̃, jɛn] **1** ADJ Sierra Leonean **2** **Sierra-Léonien(ne)** NM,F Sierra Leonean

sieste [sjɛst] NF (gén) nap, snooze*; (en Espagne etc) siesta; **faire la ~** (gén) to have ou take a nap; (en Espagne etc) to have a siesta; **je vais faire une petite ~** I'm going to take a little nap; **c'est l'heure de la ~ !** it's time for a snooze!* ou an afternoon nap!

sieur [sjœr] NM **le ~ Leblanc** († †, Jur) Mr Leblanc; (péj, hum) Master Leblanc

sifflant, e [siflɑ̃, ɑ̃t] **1** ADJ [sonorité] whistling; [toux] wheezing; [prononciation] hissing, whistling **2** **sifflante** NF (consonne) **~e** sibilant

sifflement [sifləmɑ̃] NM **a** [personne, oiseau, train, bouilloire, vent] whistling (NonC); [serpent, vapeur, gaz, machine à vapeur] hissing (NonC); [voix, respiration] wheezing (NonC); [projectile] whistling (NonC), hissing (NonC); **un ~** a whistle, a hiss; **un ~ d'admiration** ou **admiratif** a whistle of admiration; **un ~ mélodieux** a tuneful whistle; **des ~s se firent entendre** there was the sound of whistling; **j'entendis le ~ aigu/les ~s de la locomotive** I heard the shrill whistle/the whistling of the locomotive; **des ~s** whistling noises, hissing noises; **~ d'oreilles** ringing in the ears **b** (gén pl = huées) booing (NonC), hissing (NonC); **il quitta la scène sous les ~s du public** he left the stage to hisses and boos from the audience, he was booed off the stage

siffler [sifle] ▶ conjug 1 ◀ **1** VI [personne] to whistle; (avec un sifflet) to blow one's ou a whistle; [oiseau, train, bouilloire, vent] to whistle; [serpent, vapeur, gaz, machine à vapeur] to hiss; [voix, respiration] to wheeze; [projectile] to whistle, hiss; **~ comme un merle** to whistle like a bird; **la balle/l'obus siffla à ses oreilles** the bullet/the shell whistled past his ears; **il siffle en respirant** he wheezes; **j'ai les oreilles qui sifflent** my ears are ringing **2** VT **a** (= appeler) [+ chien, personne] to whistle for; [+ fille] to whistle at; [+ automobiliste ou joueur en faute] to blow one's whistle at; (= signaler) [+ départ, faute] to blow one's whistle for; (Ftbl) **~ la fin du match/la mi-temps** to blow the final whistle/the half-time whistle, blow for time/for half time; **elle s'est fait ~ dans la rue** someone wolf-whistled at her in the street **b** (= huer) [+ orateur, acteur, pièce] to hiss,

boo; **se faire ~** to get booed **c** (= moduler) [+ air, chanson] to whistle **d** (‡ = avaler) to guzzle*, knock back‡

sifflet [siflɛ] NM **a** (= instrument, son) whistle; **~ à roulette** whistle; **~ à vapeur** steam whistle; **~ d'alarme** alarm whistle; **coup de ~** whistle → **couper** **b** (= huées) **~s** whistles of disapproval, hissing, booing, catcalls

siffleur, -euse [siflœr, øz] **1** ADJ [merle] whistling; [serpent] hissing; **(canard) ~** widgeon **2** NM,F (= qui sifflote) whistler; (= qui hue) hisser, booer

siffleux* [siflø] NM (Can) groundhog, woodchuck, whistler (US, Can)

sifflotement [siflɔtmɑ̃] NM whistling (NonC)

siffloter [siflɔte] ▶ conjug 1 ◀ **1** VI to whistle (a tune), **~ entre ses dents** to whistle under one's breath **2** VT [+ air] to whistle

sigillé, e [siʒile] ADJ sigillated

sigisbée † [siʒizbe] NM (hum = amant) beau †

sigle [sigl] NM (prononcé lettre par lettre) (set of) initials, abbreviation; (= acronyme) acronym

siglé, e [sigle] ADJ [objet] bearing the initials of a designer; **sac ~** designer bag; **boutons ~s ARA** buttons with the designer's initials, ARA, engraved on them

sigma [sigma] NM sigma

signal [siɲal] (pl **-aux**) [siɲal, o] NM **a** (= signe convenu) (Psych = stimulus) signal; (= indice) sign; **donner le ~ de** (lit) to give the signal for; (fig = déclencher) to be the signal ou sign for, signal; **cette émeute fut le ~ d'une véritable révolution** the riot was the signal for the start of ou signalled the outbreak of a virtual revolution; **à mon ~ tous se levèrent** when I gave the signal everyone got up; **donner le ~ du départ** (gén) to give the signal for departure; (Sport) to give the starting signal; **~ de détresse** distress signal **b** (Naut, Rail = écriteau, avertisseur) signal; (Aut = écriteau) (road) sign; (= feux) **signaux (lumineux)** traffic signals ou lights; (Rail) **~ automatique** automatic signal; (Rail) **~ d'alarme** alarm; **tirer le ~ d'alarme** (lit) to pull the alarm, pull the communication cord † (Brit); (fig) to sound the alarm ou alert; **~ sonore** ou **acoustique** sound ou acoustic signal; **~ optique/lumineux** visual/light signal; (Rail) **~ avancé** advance signal **c** (Ling, Ordin, Téléc) signal; **~ horaire** time signal; (Téléc : option) **« ~ d'appel »** "call waiting"

signalé, e [siɲale] (ptp de **signaler**) ADJ (littér = remarquable) [récompense, service] signal (littér) (épith)

signalement [siɲalmɑ̃] NM [personne, véhicule] description, particulars; **donner le ~ de qn** to describe sb

▼ **signaler** [siɲale] ▶ conjug 1 ◀ **1** VT **a** (= être l'indice de) to indicate, be a sign of; **des empreintes qui signalent la présence de qn** footprints indicating sb's presence **b** [écriteau, sonnerie] to signal; [personne] (= faire un signe) to signal; (en mettant un écriteau ou une indication) to indicate; **on signale l'arrivée d'un train au moyen d'une sonnerie** the arrival of a train is signalled by a bell ringing, a bell warns of ou signals the arrival of a train; **sur ma carte, on signale l'existence d'une source près du village** my map indicates that there's a spring near the village, on my map there's a spring marked near the village; **signalez que vous allez tourner en tendant le bras** indicate ou signal that you are turning by putting out your arm **c** [+ détail, erreur] to indicate, point out; [+ fait nouveau, perte, vol] to report; **on a signalé leur présence à Paris** they are reported to be in Paris; **on signale l'arrivée du bateau** it has been reported that the boat will arrive shortly; **rien à ~** nothing to report; **~ qn à l'attention de qn** to bring sb to sb's attention;

➤ GRAMMAIRE ACTIVE: **signaler** 47.4

~ qn à la vindicte publique to expose sb to public condemnation; **nous vous signalons en outre que ...** we would further point out to you that ...; **nous vous signalons qu'il ... for your information, he ...; je te signale que je t'attends depuis une heure!** I'd like you to know that I've been waiting for you for an hour!

2 se signaler VPR **a** (= *s'illustrer*) to distinguish o.s., stand out; **il se signale par sa bravoure** he distinguishes himself by his courage, his courage makes him stand out **b** (= *attirer l'attention*) to draw attention to o.s.; **se ~ à l'attention de qn** to attract sb's attention, bring o.s. to sb's attention

signalétique [siɲaletik] **1** ADJ [*détail*] identifying, descriptive; **fiche ~** identification sheet **2** NF means of signalling

signalisation [siɲalizasjɔ̃] NF **a** (= *balisage*) [*route, réseau*] erection of (road)signs (and signals) (**de** on); [*piste*] laying out of runway markings and lights (**de** on); [*voie*] putting signals (**de** on); **«absence de ~»** "no road markings"; (*Rail*) **~ automatique** automatic signalling; **erreur de ~** (*Aut*) signposting error; (*Rail*) signalling error; **moyens de ~** means of signalling → **feu¹, panneau b** (= *panneaux*) (*Aut*) signs; (*Rail* = *signaux*) signals; **~ routière** roadsigns and markings; (*Aut*) **~ horizontale** road markings; **~ verticale** roadsigns

signaliser [siɲalize] ▶ conjug 1 ◀ VT [+ *route, réseau*] to put up (road)signs on; [+ *piste*] to put runway markings and lights on; [+ *voie de chemin de fer*] to put signals on; **bien signalé** [+ *route*] well signposted; [+ *piste*] clearly marked; [+ *voie de chemin de fer*] with clear signals; **la frontière n'est pas toujours signalisée** the border isn't always marked

signataire [siɲatɛʀ] **1** ADJ signatory; **pays ~s** signatory countries **2** NMF [*traité, paix*] signatory; **les ~s** those signing, the signatories

signature [siɲatyʀ] NF **a** (= *action*) signing; (= *marque, nom*) signature; **avant la ~ du contrat** before the contract is signed; **les fondés de pouvoir ont la ~** the senior executives may sign for the company; **honorer sa ~** to honour one's signature; (*Jur*) **~ légalisée/ sociale** authenticated/authorized signature; **ouvrage publié sous la ~ d'un journaliste** work published under the name of a journalist **b** (= *signe distinctif*) mark; **l'attentat porte leur ~** the attack bears their mark *ou* has their name written all over it* **c** (*Typo* = *cahier*) signature

signe [siɲ] **1** NM **a** (= *geste*) (*de la main*) sign, gesture; (*de l'expression*) sign; **s'exprimer par ~s** to use signs to communicate; **langage *ou* langue des ~s** sign language; **faire un ~ à qn** to make a sign to sb, sign to sb; **un ~ de tête affirmatif/négatif** a nod/a shake of the head; **ils se faisaient des ~s** they were making signs to each other; **un ~ d'adieu/de refus** a sign of farewell/of refusal; **elle m'a fait un ~ d'adieu** she waved goodbye to me **b** (= *indice*) sign; **~ précurseur *ou* avant- coureur** portent, omen, forewarning; **elle t'a invité? c'est un ~!** she invited you? that's a good sign!; **il recommence à manger, c'est bon ~** he's beginning to eat again, that's a good sign; **c'est (un) ~ de pluie** it's a sign of rain; **c'est ~ qu'il va pleuvoir/qu'il est de retour** it shows *ou* it's a sign that it's going to rain/ that he's back; **c'est mauvais ~** it's a bad sign; **y a-t-il des ~s de vie sur Mars?** are there signs of life on Mars?; **il n'a plus jamais donné ~ de vie** we've never heard from him since; **c'est un ~ des temps** it's a sign of the times; **c'est un ~ révélateur** it's very revealing; **c'est un ~ qui ne trompe pas** the signs are unmistakable; **montrer *ou* donner des ~s de faiblesse *ou* de fatigue** [*personne*] to show signs of tiredness; [*appareil, montre*] to be on its last legs; [*coalition*] to be showing signs of strain; [*monnaie*]

to be weakening; (*Méd*) **~ clinique** clinical sign **c** (= *trait*) mark; **«~s particuliers: néant»** "distinguishing marks: none"; **~ distinctif** distinguishing feature; **leur argot est un ~ de reconnaissance** using slang is a way for them to recognize each other **d** (= *symbole*) (*gén, Ling, Math, Mus*) sign; (*Typo*) [*correcteurs*] mark; **le ~ moins/plus/égal** the minus/plus/equal(s) sign; **~ (typographique)** character; (*Mus*) **~s d'expression** expression marks; (*Mus*) **~ accidentel** accidental **e** (*Astrol*) **~ du zodiaque** sign of the zodiac; **sous quel ~ es-tu né?** what sign were you born under?, what's your sign?; **rencontre placée sous le ~ de l'amitié franco-britannique** meeting where the keynote was Franco- British friendship *ou* where the dominant theme was Franco-British friendship; **ministère qui a vécu sous le ~ du mécontentement** term of office for the government where the dominant *ou* prevailing mood was one of discontent **f** (*loc*) **faire ~ à qn** (*lit*) to make a sign to sb; (*fig* = *contacter*) to get in touch with sb, contact sb; **faire ~ à qn d'entrer** to motion sb in, make a sign for sb to come in; **de la tête, il m'a fait ~ de ne pas bouger** he shook his head to tell me not to move; **il a fait ~ à la voiture de franchir les grilles** he waved the car through the gates; **faire ~ du doigt à qn** to beckon (to) sb; **faire ~ que oui** to nod (in agreement); **faire ~ que non** (*de la tête*) to shake one's head (in disagreement *ou* disapproval); (*de la main*) to make a gesture of refusal (*ou* disagreement *ou* disapproval); **en ~ de protestation** as a sign *ou* mark of protest; **en ~ de reconnaissance** as a token of gratitude; **en ~ de respect** as a sign *ou* mark *ou* token of respect; **en ~ de solidarité/de deuil** as a sign of solidarity/of mourning **2** COMP ▶ **signe cabalistique** cabalistic sign ▶ **signe de la croix** sign of the cross; **faire le ~ de la croix** *ou* **un ~ de croix** to make the sign of the cross, cross o.s. ▶ **signes extérieurs de richesse** outward signs of wealth ▶ **signes héraldiques** coat of arms ▶ **signe de ponctuation** punctuation mark ▶ **signe de ralliement** rallying symbol

signer [siɲe] ▶ conjug 1 ◀ **1** VT **a** [+ *document, traité, œuvre d'art*] to sign; **~ la paix** to sign a peace treaty; **signez au bas de la page/en marge** sign at the bottom of the page/in the margin; (*lit, fig*) **~ un chèque en blanc** to sign a blank cheque; **~ son nom** to sign one's name; **elle signe «Malou»** she signs herself "Malou"; (*Sport*) **il a signé avec le club italien** he's signed for the Italian club; **~ d'une croix/de son vrai nom** to sign with a cross/ with one's real name; **~ de son sang** to sign in blood; **tableau non signé** unsigned painting; **œuvre signée de la main de l'artiste** work signed by the artist; **cela a signé la fin de leur collaboration** that signalled the end of their collaboration → **arrêt b** (= *être l'auteur de*) to make; **elle vient de son deuxième film** she's just made her second film; (*Sport*) **il signe le troisième but de la partie** he's scored the third goal of the match; **cravate/carrosserie signée Paul** tie/ coachwork by Paul; (*fig*) **c'est signé!*** it's obvious who did it!; (*fig*) **c'est signé Louis!*** it has Louis written all over it!* **c** (*Tech*) to hallmark **2 se signer** VPR (*Rel*) to cross o.s.

signet [siɲɛ] NM (*book*) marker, bookmark

signifiant, e [siɲifjɑ̃, jɑ̃t] **1** ADJ (*littér*) significative, meaningful **2** NM (*Ling*) signifier, signified

significatif, -ive [siɲifikatif, iv] ADJ **a** (= *révélateur*) [*exemple, mot*] significant, revealing; [*geste, sourire*] meaningful; **ces oublis sont ~s de son état d'esprit** his forgetfulness

reflects his state of mind **b** (= *visible*) [*amélioration, baisse, changement, progrès*] significant, considerable; **de manière significative** significantly **c** (= *expressif*) [*symbole*] meaningful, significant

signification [siɲifikasjɔ̃] NF **a** [*fait, chiffres*] significance (*NonC*); **une omission lourde de ~** a highly significant omission; **cette mesure n'a pas grande ~** this measure is not very significant **b** [*mot, symbole*] meaning; (*Ling*) **la ~ signification; quelle est la ~ de ce dessin?** what does this drawing mean? **c** (*Jur*) [*décision judiciaire*] notification; **~ d'actes** service of documents

significativement [siɲifikativmɑ̃] ADV [*améliorer, augmenter, réduire*] significantly, to a significant extent; [*meilleur, supérieur*] significantly; **les commentaires ont été assez ~ una- nimes** significantly, most people made the same kind of comments

signifié [siɲifje] NM (*Ling*) signified, signifié

signifier [siɲifje] ▶ conjug 7 ◀ VT **a** (= *avoir pour sens*) to mean, signify; **que signifie ce mot/son silence?** what is the meaning of this word/ his silence?, what does this word/his silence mean *ou* signify?; (*Ling*) **les symboles signi- fient** symbols convey meaning; **que signifie cette cérémonie?** what is the significance of this ceremony?, what does this ceremony signify?; **ses colères ne signifient rien** his tempers don't mean anything; **bonté ne signifie pas forcément faiblesse** kindness does not necessarily mean *ou* signify *ou* imply weak- ness *ou* is not necessarily synonymous with weakness; **cela signifie que l'automne est pro- che** it means *ou* shows that autumn is near, it marks *ou* signifies the approach of autumn; **qu'est-ce que cela signifie?** (*gén*) what's the meaning of this?; (*après remarque hostile*) what's that supposed to mean?; (*à un enfant qui fait une scène*) what's all this in aid of? **b** (*frm* = *faire connaître*) to make known; **~ ses intentions/sa volonté à qn** to make one's intentions/one's wishes known to sb, inform sb of one's intentions/one's wishes; **~ son congé à qn** (= *renvoyer qn*) to give sb notice of dismissal, give sb their notice; **son regard me signifiait tout son mépris** his look conveyed to me his utter scorn; **signifiez-lui qu'il doit se rendre à cette convocation** inform him that he is to answer this summons **c** (*Jur*) [+ *exploit, décision judiciaire*] to serve notice of (**à** on), notify (**à** to)

sikh [sik] **1** ADJ Sikh **2** Sikh NMF Sikh

silence [silɑ̃s] NM **a** (= *absence de bruits, de conversation*) silence; **garder le ~** to keep si- lent, say nothing; **faire ~** to be silent; **faire qch en ~** to do sth in silence; **réclamer le ~** to ask for silence; **il n'arrive pas à faire le ~ dans sa classe** he can't get his pupils to be quiet; **sortez vos livres et en ~!** get out your books and no talking!; **(faites) ~!** (*gén*) silence!; (*en classe*) silence!, no talking!; (*Ciné*) **~!** on **tourne** quiet everybody, action!; **il prononça son discours dans un ~ absolu** there was dead silence while he made his speech; **un ~ de mort** a deathly hush *ou* silence → **minute, pa- role b** (= *pause*) (*dans la conversation, un récit*) pause; (*Mus*) rest; **récit entrecoupé de longs ~s** account broken by lengthy pauses; **il y eut un ~ gêné** there was an embarrassed silence; **à son entrée il y eut un ~** there was a hush when he came in **c** (= *impossibilité ou refus de s'exprimer*) si- lence; **les journaux gardèrent le ~ sur cette grève** the newspapers kept silent on this strike; **promets-moi un ~ absolu** promise me you won't breathe a word; **garder un ~ absolu sur qch** to say absolutely nothing about sth, keep completely quiet about sth; **contraindre l'opposition au ~** to force the opposition to keep silent; **réduire qn au ~** to silence sb, reduce sb to silence;

acheter le ~ de qn to buy sb's silence; **briser** *ou* **rompre le** ~ to break one's silence; **passer qch sous** ~ to pass sth over in silence; **le sujet est passé sous** ~ the subject was not mentioned; **souffrir en** ~ to suffer in silence; **aimer qn en** ~ to love sb secretly; **surprise préparée dans le plus grand** ~ surprise prepared in the greatest secrecy; ~ **radio** (*lit*) radio silence, blackout; (*fig*) total silence; **le célèbre compositeur vient de sortir de 12 années de** ~ the famous composer has just broken 12 years of silence; **le ~ de la loi sur ce sujet** the lack *ou* absence of legislation on this matter → **loi**
[d] (= *paix*) silence, still(ness); **dans le grand ~ de la plaine** in the great silence *ou* stillness of the plain; **vivre dans la solitude et le ~** to live in solitary silence

silencieusement [silɑ̃sjøzmɑ̃] ADV (*se déplacer*) silently, quietly; **la cérémonie s'est déroulée** ~ the ceremony took place in silence

silencieux, -ieuse [silɑ̃sjø, jøz] [1] ADJ [a] (= *peu bruyant*) [*mouvement, pas, personne*] silent, quiet; [*moteur, machine*] quiet, noiseless; [*lieu, cloître*] silent, still; **le voyage du retour fut** ~ the return journey took place in silence [b] (= *peu communicatif*) quiet; (= *qui ne veut ou ne peut s'exprimer*) silent; **rester ~** to remain silent (**sur, à propos de** about) → **majorité** [2] NM [*arme à feu*] silencer; [*pot d'échappement*] silencer (*Brit*), muffler (*US*)

Silésie [silezi] NF Silesia

silex [silɛks] NM flint; (*Archéol*) **des (armes en) ~** flints

silhouette [silwɛt] NF [a] (= *contours*) outline, silhouette; [*voiture*] shape; **la ~ du château se détache sur le couchant** the outline *ou* silhouette of the château stands out *ou* the château is silhouetted against the sunset; **on le voyait en ~, à contre-jour** he could be seen silhouetted against the light [b] (= *personne*) figure; **je distinguais une ~ dans le brouillard** I could make out a figure in the fog; (*Mil*) **~s de tir** figure targets [c] (= *allure*) figure; **une ~ massive/élégante** a heavy/an elegant figure

silhouetter [silwete] ▶conjug 1◀ [1] VT [a] (*Art*) to outline; **l'artiste silhouetta un corps de femme** the artist outlined *ou* drew an outline of a woman's body [b] (*Photo*) to block out [2] **se silhouetter** VPR to be silhouetted; **le clocher se silhouette sur le ciel** the bell tower is silhouetted *ou* outlined against the sky

silicate [silikat] NM silicate

silice [silis] NF silica; ~ **fondue** *ou* **vitreuse** silica glass

siliceux, -euse [siliso, øz] ADJ siliceous, silicious

silicium [silisjɔm] NM silicon

silicone [silikon] NF silicone; **gel de ~** silicone gel

siliconer [silikone] ▶conjug 1◀ VT to cover with silicone; **pare-brise siliconé** silicone-coated windscreen; (*péj ou hum*) **sa poitrine siliconée** her silicone-implanted bosom

silicose [silikoz] NF silicosis

sillage [sijaʒ] NM [a] [*embarcation*] wake; [*avion à réaction*] (= *déplacement d'air*) slipstream; (= *trace*) (vapour (*Brit*) *ou* vapor (*US*)) trail; (*fig*) [*personne, animal, parfum*] trail; (*lit, fig*) **dans le ~ de qn** (following) in sb's wake; **marcher dans le ~ de qn** to follow in sb's footsteps [b] (*Phys*) wake

sillon [sijɔ̃] NM [a] [*champ*] furrow; (*littér*) **les ~s** (ploughed (*Brit*) *ou* plowed (*US*)) fields [b] (*fig* = *ride, rayure*) furrow [c] (*Anat*) fissure [d] [*disque*] groove [e] **le ~ rhodanien** the Rhone valley

sillonner [sijɔne] ▶conjug 1◀ VT [a] (= *traverser*) [*avion, bateau, routes*] to cut across, cross; **les canaux qui sillonnent la Hollande** the canals which cut across *ou* which criss-cross Hol-

land; **région sillonnée de canaux/routes** region criss-crossed by canals/roads; **des avions ont sillonné le ciel toute la journée** planes have been droning backwards and forwards *ou* to and fro across the sky all day; **des éclairs sillonnaient le ciel** flashes of lightning criss-crossed the sky; ~ **les routes** to travel the country; **les touristes sillonnent la France en été** tourists travel to every corner *ou* throughout the length and breadth of France in the summer [b] (= *creuser*) [*rides, ravins, crevasses*] to furrow; **visage sillonné de rides** face furrowed with wrinkles; **front sillonné d'une ride profonde** deeply furrowed brow

silo [silo] NM (*Aviat, Mil*) silo; ~ **à céréales** *ou* **à grains/fourrage** grain/fodder silo; **mettre en ~** to put in a silo, silo

silotage [silɔtaʒ] NM (*Tech*) ensilage

silure [silyʀ] NM silurid

silurien, -ienne [silyʀjɛ̃, jɛn] [1] ADJ Silurian [2] NM **le** ~ the Silurian

sima [sima] NM (*Géol*) sima

simagrée [simagʀe] NF (*gén pl*) fuss (*NonC*), playacting (*NonC*); **faire des ~s** to playact; **arrête tes ~s!** stop your playacting!; **elle a fait beaucoup de ~s avant d'accepter son cadeau** she made a great fuss (about it) *ou* she put on a great show of reluctance before she accepted his present

simien, -ienne [simjɛ̃, jɛn] ADJ, NM simian

simiesque [simjɛsk] ADJ monkey-like, ape-like

similaire [similɛʀ] ADJ similar (**à** to); **le rouge à lèvres, le fond de teint et produits ~s** lipstick, foundation and similar products *ou* products of a similar nature

similarité [similaʀite] NF similarity (**entre** between, **avec** with)

simili [simili] [1] PRÉF imitation (*épith*), artificial; **en ~ fourrure** fun fur (*épith*) [2] NM imitation; **bijoux en ~** imitation *ou* costume jewellery [3] NF* ABRÉV → **similigravure**

similicuir [similikɥiʀ] NM imitation leather, Leatherette®

similigravure [similigʀavyʀ] NF half-tone engraving

similitude [similityd] NF [a] (= *ressemblance*) similarity; **il y a certaines ~s entre ces méthodes** there are certain similarities between these methods [b] (*Géom*) similarity

simonie [simɔni] NF simony

simoun [simun] NM simoom, simoon

simple [sɛ̃pl] [1] ADJ [a] (= *non composé, non multiple*) [*fleur*] simple; [*nœud, cornet de glace*] single; (*Chim*) [*corps*] simple; (*Math*) [*racine*] simple; **en ~ épaisseur** in a single layer *ou* thickness → **passé**
[b] (= *peu complexe*) simple; **réduit à sa plus ~ expression** reduced to a minimum; **sa situation est loin d'être ~** his situation is far from being simple *ou* straightforward; ~ **comme bonjour** (as) easy as falling off a log* *ou* as pie*; **dans ce cas, c'est bien ~: je m'en vais*** in that case it's quite simple *ou* straightforward — I'm leaving; (*hum*) **pourquoi faire ~ quand on peut faire compliqué ?*** why not make things really complicated! (*hum*); **ce serait trop ~!** that would be too easy! *ou* too simple!; **ce n'est pas si ~** it's not as simple as that; **il y a un moyen ~ pour ...** there is an easy way of ...
[c] (= *modeste*) [*personne*] unaffected; **il a su rester ~** he hasn't let it go to his head
[d] (= *peu sophistiqué*) [*vie, goûts*] simple; [*robe, repas, style*] simple, plain; **être ~ dans sa mise** to dress simply *ou* plainly; (*hum*) **dans le plus ~ appareil** in one's birthday suit, in the altogether*
[e] (= *de condition modeste*) modest; **ce sont des gens** ~**s** they are simple folk
[f] (= *naïf*) simple; **il est un peu ~** he's a bit simple; **il est ~ d'esprit** ◊ **c'est un ~ d'esprit** he's simple-minded

[g] (= *ordinaire*) [*particulier, salarié*] ordinary; **un ~ soldat** a private
[h] (*valeur restrictive*) **une ~ formalité** a mere formality; **un ~ regard/une ~ remarque la déconcertait** just a *ou* a mere look/comment would upset her; **d'un ~ geste de la main** with a simple movement *ou* with just a movement of his hand; **par ~ curiosité** out of pure curiosity; **sur ~ présentation de votre carte d'étudiant** simply *ou* just show your student card; **vous obtiendrez des informations sur ~ appel (téléphonique)** simply pick up the phone and you will get all the information you need → **pur**

[2] NM [a] **passer du ~ au double** to double; **les prix peuvent varier du ~ au double** prices can vary by as much as 100%
[b] (*Bot*) medicinal plant, simple†
[c] (*Tennis*) singles; ~ **messieurs/dames** men's/women's *ou* ladies' singles

simplement [sɛ̃pləmɑ̃] ADV [a] (= *sans sophistication*) simply; **elle s'habille très ~** she dresses very simply; **ils vivent très ~** they lead a very simple life [b] (= *seulement*) simply, merely, just; **je vous demande ~ de me prévenir** I simply *ou* just want you to warn me, all I ask is that you warn me; **je veux ~ dire que ...** I simply *ou* merely *ou* just want to say that ... [c] (= *tout à fait*) **tout** ~ [*remarquable, insupportable, incroyable*] quite simply, just; **c'est tout ~ inadmissible** it's quite simply intolerable → **purement** [d] (= *facilement*) easily; **cela s'explique très ~** that's easily explained

simplet, -ette [sɛ̃plɛ, ɛt] ADJ [a] [*personne*] simple(-minded), ingenuous [b] [*question, raisonnement*] simplistic, naïve; [*intrigue, roman*] simple, unsophisticated

simplex [sɛ̃plɛks] NM (*Ordin*) simplex

simplicité [sɛ̃plisite] NF [a] (= *facilité*) simplicity; **un appareil d'une grande ~ d'emploi** an easy-to-use appliance, an appliance that is very easy to use; **cet exercice est d'une ~ biblique** *ou* **enfantine** this exercise is child's play *ou* is simplicity itself
[b] (= *manque de sophistication*) [*vie, goûts*] simplicity; [*robe, repas, style*] simplicity, plainness; **habillé avec ~** dressed simply; **décor d'une grande ~** very simple decor; **« c'est une vocation », dit-elle en toute ~** "it's a vocation", she said modestly; **venez dîner demain, ce sera en toute ~** come for dinner tomorrow — it won't be anything fancy; (*iro*) **il dit en toute ~ être un sculpteur de génie** he very modestly says that he's a brilliant sculptor (*iro*)
[c] (= *naïveté*) simpleness; **j'avais la ~ de croire que cela durerait toujours** I was naïve enough to think that it would last forever
[d] (= *modestie, naturel*) unaffectedness; **il manque de ~** he's rather affected

simplifiable [sɛ̃plifjabl] ADJ (*gén*) [*méthode*] that can be simplified; (*Math*) [*fraction*] reducible

simplificateur, -trice [sɛ̃plifikatœʀ, tʀis] ADJ simplifying (*épith*)

simplification [sɛ̃plifikasjɔ̃] NF simplification

simplifier [sɛ̃plifje] ▶conjug 7◀ VT (*gén, Math*) to simplify; **disons, pour ~ les choses, que ...** to simplify matters, let's say that ...; **à l'extrême** *ou* **à l'excès** ◊ **trop ~** to oversimplify; **des procédures très simplifiées** streamlined procedures

simplisme [sɛ̃plism] NM (*péj*) simplism

simpliste [sɛ̃plist] ADJ (*péj*) simplistic

simulacre [simylakʀ] NM [a] (= *action simulée*) enactment; **les acteurs firent un ~ de sacrifice humain** the actors enacted a human sacrifice [b] (*péj* = *fausse apparence*) **un ~ de justice** a pretence of justice; **un ~ de gouvernement/de procès** a sham government/trial, a mockery of a government/of a trial

simulateur, -trice [simylatœʀ, ʀis] [1] NM,F (*gén*) pretender; (= *qui feint la maladie*) malingerer [2] NM simulator; (*Aut*) **~ de conduite** (driving) simulator; (*Aviat*) **~ de vol** flight simulator

simulation [simylasjɔ̃] NF simulation; **il n'est pas malade, c'est de la ~** he isn't ill — it's all put on *ou* he's just malingering; **logiciel de ~** simulation software

simulé, e [simyle] (*ptp de simuler*) ADJ (= *feint*) [*attaque, retraite*] simulated; [*amabilité, gravité*] feigned; [*accident, suicide*] fake (*épith*); (*Tech* = *reproduit*) [*conditions, situation, essais nucléaires*] simulated; **~ sur ordinateur** computer-simulated

simuler [simyle] ▶ conjug 1 ◀ VT [a] (= *feindre*) [+ *sentiment, attaque*] to feign, simulate (*frm*); **~ une maladie** to feign illness, pretend to be ill, malinger [b] (= *avoir l'apparence de*) to simulate; **ce papier peint simule une boiserie** this wallpaper is made to look like *ou* simulates wood panelling [c] (*Ordin, Tech* = *reproduire*) to simulate [d] (*Jur*) [+ *contrat, vente*] to effect fictitiously

simultané, e [simyltane] [1] ADJ simultaneous; **la présence ~e de deux personnes dans un même lieu** the presence of two people in the same place at the same time; **de manière ~e** at the same time, simultaneously; **diffusion en ~** simultaneous broadcast; **c'était en ~** it was shown *ou* broadcast simultaneously → **traduction** [2] **simultanée** NF (*Échecs*) simultaneous, simul

simultanéisme [simyltaneism] NM (*Littérat* = *procédé narratif*) (use of) simultaneous action

simultanéité [simyltaneite] NF simultaneousness, simultaneity

simultanément [simyltanemɑ̃] ADV simultaneously

Sinaï [sinai] NM Sinai → **mont**

sinapisé [sinapize] ADJ **bain/cataplasme ~** mustard bath/poultice

sinapisme [sinapism] NM mustard poultice *ou* plaster

▼ **sincère** [sɛ̃sɛʀ] ADJ [a] (= *franc, loyal*) [*personne, aveu, paroles*] sincere; [*réponse, explication*] sincere, honest; **est-il ~ dans son amitié ?** is he sincere in his friendship?, is his friendship sincere? *ou* genuine?; **sois ~ avec toi-même** be honest with yourself [b] (= *réel*) [*repentir, amour, partisan, admiration*] sincere, genuine, true; **son chagrin est ~** he's genuinely upset, his sorrow is genuine; **un ami ~ des arts** a true *ou* genuine friend of the arts; (*formules épistolaires*) **mes ~s condoléances** my sincere *ou* heartfelt condolences; **mes regrets les plus ~s** my sincerest regrets; **mes ~ salutations** yours sincerely; **nos vœux les plus ~s** with our best wishes

sincèrement [sɛ̃sɛʀmɑ̃] ADV [a] (= *réellement*) [*espérer, croire, penser, regretter, remercier*] sincerely; [*aimer*] truly; **je vous souhaite ~ de réussir** I sincerely hope you will succeed; **je suis ~ désolé que ...** I am sincerely *ou* truly *ou* genuinely sorry that ...; **il a paru ~ étonné** he seemed genuinely surprised [b] (= *franchement*) honestly, really; **~, vous feriez mieux de refuser** to be honest you'd be better off saying no

sincérité [sɛ̃seʀite] NF [a] (= *franchise, loyauté*) [*personne, aveu, paroles*] sincerity; [*réponse, explications*] sincerity, honesty; **en toute ~** in all sincerity; **répondez-moi en toute ~** give me an honest answer [b] [*repentir, amour, admiration*] sincerity, genuineness

sinécure [sinekyʀ] NF sinecure; **ce n'est pas une ~*** it's no picnic*

sine die [sinedje] LOC ADV sine die

▼ **sine qua non** [sinekwanɔn] LOC ADJ **une condition ~** an indispensable condition, a sine qua non

Singapour [sɛ̃gapuʀ] N Singapore

singapourien, -ienne [sɛ̃gapuʀjɛ̃, jɛn] [1] ADJ Singaporean [2] **Singapourien(ne)** NM,F Singaporean

singe [sɛ̃ʒ] NM [a] (*Zool*) (*à longue queue*) monkey; (*à queue courte ou sans queue*) ape; **les grands ~s** the big apes [b] (*péj*) (= *personne laide*) horror; (= *enfant espiègle*) monkey; **c'est un vrai ~** (*très agile*) he's very agile [c] (*arg Mil* = *corned beef*) bully beef* [d] (‡ = *patron*) boss* [e] (*loc*) **faire le ~** to monkey about; **être laid comme un ~** to be as ugly as sin → **apprendre, malin, monnaie**

singer [sɛ̃ʒe] ▶ conjug 3 ◀ VT [+ *démarche, personne*] to ape, mimic, take off; [+ *sentiments*] to feign

singerie [sɛ̃ʒʀi] NF [a] (*gén pl* = *grimaces et pitreries*) antics, clowning (*NonC*); **faire des ~s** to clown about, play the fool [b] (= *simagrées*) **~s** antics [c] (= *cage*) monkey house

single [singœl] NM (= *chambre*) single room; (= *disque*) single

singleton [sɛ̃glətɔ̃] NM singleton

singulariser [sɛ̃gylaʀize] ▶ conjug 1 ◀ [1] VT to mark out, make conspicuous [2] **se singulariser** VPR (= *se faire remarquer*) to call attention to o.s., make o.s. conspicuous; **se ~ par qch** to distinguish o.s. by sth; **cette église se singularise par son étrange clocher** this church is remarkable for its strange steeple

singularité [sɛ̃gylaʀite] NF [a] (= *particularité*) singularity; **cet orchestre a pour ~ ou présente la ~ de jouer sans chef** this orchestra is unusual in that it doesn't have a conductor; **il cultive sa ~** he likes to stand out from the crowd *ou* to be different [b] (= *bizarrerie*) peculiarity; **le manuscrit présente plusieurs ~s** the manuscript is odd in several respects

singulier, -ière [sɛ̃gylje, jɛʀ] [1] ADJ [a] (= *étonnant, peu commun*) remarkable, singular (*frm*); **un visage d'une beauté singulière** a face of remarkable *ou* singular (*frm*) beauty; **c'est un personnage** he's an unusual character [b] (= *étrange*) odd, strange; **je trouve ~ qu'il n'ait pas jugé bon de ...** I find it odd *ou* strange that he didn't see fit to ...; **singulière façon de se comporter !** what a strange way to behave! [c] (*Ling*) singular [2] NM (*Ling*) singular; **au ~** in the singular; **à la deuxième personne du ~** in the second person singular

singulièrement [sɛ̃gyljɛʀmɑ̃] ADV [a] (= *étrangement*) in a peculiar way, oddly, strangely [b] (= *beaucoup, très*) [*intéressant, fort*] remarkably, extremely; **cela leur complique ~ la tâche** that makes things particularly difficult for them; **il manque ~ d'imagination** he is singularly lacking in imagination; **sa marge de manœuvre est ~ réduite** his room for manoeuvre has been greatly *ou* severely reduced; **trancher** *ou* **contraster ~ avec qch** to be in singular contrast with sth [c] (= *en particulier*) particularly, especially

sinisation [sinizasjɔ̃] NF sinicization

siniser [sinize] ▶ conjug 1 ◀ [1] VT [+ *culture, région*] to sinicize; **une population fortement sinisée** a people strongly influenced by Chinese culture [2] **se siniser** VPR to become sinicized

sinistre [sinistʀ] [1] ADJ [a] (= *de mauvais augure*) [*bruit, endroit, projet*] sinister [b] (*avant n*) [*personnage, réputation*] sinister, unsavoury (*Brit*), unsavory (*US*); **un ~ voyou/imbécile** an absolute lout/idiot; **un pénitencier de ~ réputation** a prison of evil repute; **ce pays détient le ~ record du nombre de tués sur la route** this country holds the gruesome record for road fatalities [c] (= *lugubre*) [*voix, air*] funereal; [*personne*] grim-looking; [*soirée, réunion*] grim*, deadly (boring)*; **tu es ~ ce soir !** you're in very morbid mood tonight!; **le patron est ~** the boss gives me the creeps* [2] NM (= *catastrophe*) disaster; (= *incendie*) blaze; (*Assurances* = *cas*) accident; **l'assuré doit déclarer le ~ dans les 24 heures** any (accident) claim must be notified within 24 hours; (*Assurances*) **évaluer l'importance d'un ~** to appraise the extent of the damage (*ou loss etc*)

sinistré, e [sinistʀe] [1] ADJ [*région, pays*] (disaster-)stricken (*épith*); [*secteur économique*] devastated; **zone ~e** disaster area; **ville ~e sur le plan de l'emploi** town devastated *ou* blighted by unemployment; **les personnes ~es** the disaster victims [2] NM,F disaster victim

sinistrement [sinistʀəmɑ̃] ADV in a sinister way; **nom ~ célèbre** infamous name

sinistrose [sinistʀoz] NF pessimism

Sinn Féin [sinfɛjn] NM (*Pol*) Sinn Féin

sino- [sino] PRÉF Sino-; **~américain/tibétain** Sino-American/Tibetan

sinologie [sinɔlɔʒi] NF sinology

sinologue [sinɔlɔg] NMF sinologist, specialist in Chinese affairs

sinon [sinɔ̃] CONJ [a] (*frm* = *sauf*) except, other than, save (*frm*); **on ne possède jamais rien, ~ soi-même** there is nothing one ever possesses, except (for) *ou* other than oneself; **à quoi peut bien servir cette manœuvre ~ à nous intimider ?** what can be the purpose of this manoeuvre other than *ou* if not to intimidate us?; **je ne sais pas grand-chose, ~ qu'il a démissionné** I don't know much about it, only that *ou* other than that he has resigned; **un homme courageux, ~ qu'il était un tant soit peu imprudent†** a courageous man, save† for being rather reckless [b] (*de concession* = *si ce n'est*) if not; **il faut le faire, ~ pour le plaisir, du moins par devoir** it must be done, if not for pleasure, (then) at least out of a sense of duty; **il avait leur approbation, ~ leur enthousiasme** he had their approval, if not their enthusiasm; (*frm*) **cette histoire est savoureuse, ~ très morale** this story is spicy, if not very moral; (*frm*) **ils y étaient opposés, ~ hostiles** they were opposed, if not (actively) hostile, to it [c] (= *autrement*) otherwise, or else; **fais-le, ~ nous aurons des ennuis** do it, otherwise *ou* or else we will be in trouble; **faites-le, vous vous exposerez ~ à des ennuis** do it — you're likely to get into trouble otherwise; **elle doit être malade, ~ elle serait déjà venue** she must be ill, otherwise *ou* or else she would have already come; (*pour indiquer la menace*) **fais-le, ~ ...** do it, or else ...

sinophile [sinɔfil] ADJ, NMF sinophile

sinoque‡† [sinɔk] [1] ADJ (†) crazy*, batty*, nutty* [2] NMF loony*, nutcase*

sinuer [sinɥe] ▶ conjug 1 ◀ VI (*littér*) [*rivière, route*] to meander, wind

sinueux, -euse [sinɥø, øz] ADJ [a] [*rivière*] winding (*épith*), meandering (*épith*); [*route, chemin*] winding (*épith*); [*ligne*] sinuous [b] [*pensée, raisonnement*] tortuous; **il a eu un parcours ~** his career followed a tortuous path *ou* route

sinuosité [sinɥozite] NF (*NonC*) [*route*] winding; [*rivière*] winding, meandering; [*pensée, raisonnement*] tortuousness; **les ~s du chemin/de la rivière** the twists and turns of the path/of the river; **les ~s de sa pensée** his tortuous train of thought, his convoluted thought processes; **les ~s de la politique** the tortuous course of politics

sinus¹ [sinys] NM (*Anat*) sinus; **~ frontal/maxillaire** frontal/maxillary sinus

sinus² [sinys] NM (*Math*) sine

sinusite [sinyzit] NF sinusitis (*NonC*)

sinusoïdal, e (*mpl* **-aux**) [sinyzɔidal, o] ADJ sinusoidal

sinusoïde [sinyzɔid] NF sinusoid, sine curve

Sion [sjɔ̃] N Zion

sionisme [sjɔnism] NM Zionism

sioniste [sjɔnist] ADJ, NMF Zionist

sioux [sju] [1] ADJ INV Sioux [2] NM (*Ling*) Sioux [3] **Sioux** NMF Sioux → **ruse**

siphon [sifɔ̃] NM (= *tube, bouteille, Zool*) siphon; [*évier, W-C*] U-bend; (*Spéléologie*) sump

siphonné, e: [sifɔne] (*ptp de* **siphonner**) ADJ (= *fou*) crazy*, batty*, nutty*

siphonner [sifɔne] ▶ conjug 1 ◀ VT to siphon

sire [siʀ] NM [a] (*au roi*) Sire [b] (*Hist* = *seigneur*) lord [c] **un triste ~** an unsavoury (*Brit*) *ou* unsavory (*US*) individual; **un pauvre ~†** a poor *ou* penniless fellow

sirène [siʀɛn] NF [a] (*Myth*) siren; (*à queue de poisson*) mermaid; **écouter le chant des ~s** to listen to the sirens' song; **céder à l'appel des ~s protectionnistes/nationalistes** to give in to the lure of protectionist/nationalist ideas [b] (= *appareil*) [*ambulance, bateau*] siren; [*usine*] hooter (*Brit*), siren (*US*); [*pompiers*] fire siren; **~ d'alarme** (*en temps de guerre*) air-raid siren; (*en temps de paix*) fire alarm; **la police est arrivée toutes ~s hurlantes** the police cars arrived with their sirens wailing

Sirius [siʀjys] NM Sirius

sirocco [siʀɔko] NM sirocco

sirop [siʀo] NM [a] (= *médicament*) syrup, mixture; (= *boisson*) fruit drink *ou* cordial (*Brit*); **~ d'orgeat** barley water; **~ de groseille/d'ananas/de menthe** redcurrant/pineapple/mint cordial (*Brit*) *ou* beverage (*US*); **~ d'érable** maple syrup; **~ de maïs** corn syrup; **~ contre la toux** cough mixture *ou* syrup *ou* linctus (*Brit*) [b] (*: *péj*) schmaltz*; **cette musique, c'est du ~** this music is schmaltz* *ou* very syrupy

siroter* [siʀɔte] ▶ conjug 1 ◀ VT to sip

sirupeux, -euse [siʀypø, øz] ADJ [*liquide*] syrupy; (*péj*) [*musique*] schmaltzy*, syrupy

sis, sise [si, siz] ADJ (*Admin, Jur*) located

sisal [sizal] NM sisal

sismal, e (*mpl* **-aux**) [sismal, o] ADJ **ligne ~e** path of an earthquake

sismicité [sismisite] NF seismicity

sismique [sismik] ADJ seismic → **secousse**

sismogramme [sismɔgʀam] NM seismogram

sismographe [sismɔgʀaf] NM seismograph

sismographie [sismɔgʀafi] NF seismography

sismologie [sismɔlɔʒi] NF seismology

sismologue [sismɔlɔg] NMF seismologist

sismothérapie [sismoteʀapi] NF shock therapy

sistre [sistʀ] NM sistrum

Sisyphe [sizif] NM Sisyphus → **rocher**

sitar [sitaʀ] NM sitar

sitcom [sitkɔm] NM *ou* F (ABRÉV = **situation comedy**) sitcom

site [sit] NM [a] (= *environnement*) setting; (= *endroit remarquable*) beauty spot; **dans un ~ merveilleux/très sauvage** in a marvellous/very wild setting; **~ naturel/historique** natural/historic site; **les ~s pittoresques de la région** the beauty spots of the area; **~ touristique** tourist spot *ou* attraction; **la protection des ~s** the conservation of places of interest; **~ protégé** *ou* **classé** conservation area; **« Beaumanoir, ses plages, ses hôtels, ses ~s »** "Beaumanoir for beaches, hotels and places to visit" [b] (= *emplacement*) (*industriel, militaire*) site; **~ archéologique/olympique/de production** archeological/Olympic/production site; (*Transport*) **pistes cyclables en ~ propre** separate bicycle lanes [c] (*Mil*) **(angle de) ~** (angle of) sight; **ligne de ~** line of sight [d] (*Ordin*) site; **dépannage sur ~** on-site repairs

sit-in [sitin] NM INV sit-in; **faire un ~** to stage a sit-in

sitôt [sito] [1] ADV [a] (= *dès que*) **~ couchée, elle s'endormit** as soon as she was in bed she fell asleep, she was no sooner in bed *ou* no sooner was she in bed than she fell asleep; **~ dit, ~ fait** no sooner said than done; **après**

---

la guerre immediately *ou* straight (*Brit*) *ou* right after the war, immediately the war was over (*Brit*)

[b] (*avec nég*) **il ne reviendra pas de ~** he won't be back for quite a while *ou* for (quite) some time, he won't be back in a hurry; **il a été si bien puni qu'il ne recommencera pas de ~ !** he was so severely punished that he won't be doing that again for a while! *ou* in a hurry!

[2] PRÉP (*littér*) **~ ton retour, il faudra que ...** as soon as you're back, we must ...; **~ les vacances, elle partait** she would go away as soon as the holidays started, the holidays had no sooner begun than she would go away

[3] **sitôt (après) que** LOC CONJ as soon as, no sooner than; **~ (après) que le docteur fut parti, elle se sentit mieux** as soon as the doctor had left she felt better, the doctor had no sooner left than she felt better; **~ qu'il sera guéri, il reprendra le travail** as soon as he is better he'll go back to work

sittelle [sitɛl] NF nuthatch

▼ **situation** [situasjɔ̃] NF [a] (= *emplacement*) situation, location; **la ~ de cette villa est excellente** this villa is very well situated *ou* is in an excellent location [b] (= *conjoncture, circonstances*) situation; **tu vois la ~ où je me trouve** you see the situation *ou* position I'm in; **être dans une ~ délicate** *ou* **difficile** to be in a difficult position *ou* situation; **être en ~ de faire qch** to be in a position to do sth; **~ de fait** de facto situation; **~ de famille** marital status; **~ financière/politique** financial/political situation; **étranger en ~ irrégulière** foreigner whose papers are not in order; **dans une ~ désespérée** in a desperate plight; **l'entreprise est en ~ de monopole** the company has a monopoly on the market; **faire face à une ~ d'urgence** to cope with an emergency situation; **c'est l'homme de la ~** he's the right man for the job → **comique, renverser** [c] (= *emploi*) post, job, position; **chercher une/perdre sa ~** to look for a/lose one's post *ou* job; **il a une belle ~** he has an excellent job; **il s'est fait une belle ~ dans l'édition** he's worked up to a good position in publishing [d] (*Fin* = *état*) statement of finances; **~ de trésorerie** cash flow statement [e] (*loc*) **en ~** in a real-life situation

situationnisme [situasjɔnism] NM situationism

situationniste [situasjɔnist] NMF situationist

situé, e [situe] (*ptp de* **situer**) ADJ situated; **bien/mal ~** well/poorly situated

situer [situe] ▶ conjug 1 ◀ [1] VT [a] (*lit = placer, construire*) to site, situate, locate [b] (*par la pensée*) (= *localiser*) to set, place; (* = *catégoriser*) [+ *personne*] to place; **on ne le situe pas bien*** you just can't figure him out* [2] **se situer** VPR [a] (*emploi réfléchi*) to place o.s.; **essayer de se ~ par rapport à qn/qch** to try to place o.s. in relation to sb/sth; (*Pol*) **il se situe à gauche** he's on the left, he leans towards the left [b] (= *se trouver*) (*dans l'espace*) to be situated; (*dans le temps*) to take place; (*par rapport à des notions*) to stand; **l'action/cette scène se situe à Paris** the action/this scene is set *ou* takes place in Paris; **la hausse des prix se situera entre 5% et 10%** prices will rise by between 5% and 10%, there will be price rises of between 5% and 10%; **la France se situe dans le peloton de tête** France is among the leading countries

Siva [ʃiva] NM Siva, Shiva

six [sis, *devant n commençant par consonne* si, *devant n commençant par voyelle ou h muet* siz] [1] ADJ CARDINAL INV **il y avait ~ mille personnes** there were six thousand people; **ils sont ~ enfants** there are six children; **je suis resté ~ heures/jours** I stayed six hours/days; **les ~ huitièmes de cette somme** six eighths of

---

this sum; **il a ~ ans** he is six (years old); **un enfant de ~ ans** a six-year-old (child), a child of six; **un objet de ~ F** an item costing six francs; **polygone à ~ faces** six-sided polygon; **couper qch en ~ morceaux** to cut sth into six pieces; **j'en ai pris trois, il en reste ~** I've taken three (of them) and there are six (of them) left; **il est ~ heures** it's six o'clock; **il est ~ heures du soir** it's 6 pm, it's six in the evening; **il est ~ heures du matin** it's 6 am, it's six in the morning; **il est trois heures moins ~** it is six minutes to three; **il est trois heures ~** it is six minutes past *ou* after (*US*) three; **par vingt voix contre ~** by twenty votes to six; **cinq jours/fois sur ~** five days/times out of six; **ils sont venus tous les ~** all six of them came; **ils ont porté la table à ~** the six of them carried the table; **ils ont mangé le jambon à eux ~** the six of them ate the ham, they ate the ham between the six of them; **partagez cela entre vous ~** share that among the six of you; **ils viennent à ~ pour déjeuner** there are six coming to lunch; **on peut s'asseoir à ~ autour de cette table** this table can seat six (people); **ils vivent à ~ dans une seule pièce** there are six of them living in one room; **se battre à ~ contre un/à un contre ~** to fight six against one/one against six; **entrer ~ par ~** to come in by sixes *ou* six at a time *ou* six by six; **se mettre en rangs par ~** to form rows of six

[2] ADJ ORDINAL INV **arriver le ~ septembre** to arrive on the sixth of September *ou* (on) September the sixth *ou* (on) September sixth; **Louis ~** Louis the Sixth; **chapitre/page/article ~** chapter/page/article six; **le numéro ~ gagne un lot** number six wins a prize; **il habite au numéro ~ de la rue Arthur** he lives at number six Rue Arthur

[3] NM INV [a] (= *nombre*) six; **trente-/quarante-~** thirty-/forty-six; **quatre et deux font ~** four and two are *ou* make six; **il fait mal ses ~** he writes his sixes badly; **c'est le ~ qui a gagné** number six has won; **il habite au ~ (de la rue)** he lives at number six; **il habite ~ rue de Paris** he lives at six, Rue de Paris; **nous sommes le ~ aujourd'hui** it's the sixth today; **il est venu le ~** he came on the sixth; **il est payé le ~** *ou* **tous les ~ de chaque mois** he is paid on the sixth of each month; (*Cartes*) **le ~ de cœur** the six of hearts; (*Dominos*) **le ~ et deux** the six-two; **la facture est datée du ~** the bill is dated the 6th [b] (*Pol: jusqu'en 1973*) **les Six** ◊ **l'Europe des Six** the Six, the Europe of the Six

sixain [sizɛ̃] NM = **sizain**

six-huit [sisɥit] NM INV (*Mus*) six-eight (time); **mesure à ~** bar in six-eight (time)

sixième [sizjɛm] [1] ADJ sixth; **vingt-/trente-~** twenty-/thirty-sixth; **recevoir la ~ partie d'un héritage** to receive a sixth of a bequest; **demeurer dans le ~ (arrondissement)** to live in the sixth arrondissement (*in Paris*); **habiter au ~ (étage)** to live on the sixth floor (*Brit*) *ou* the seventh floor (*US*) [2] NMF (*gén*) sixth (person); **se classer ~** to come sixth; **nous avons besoin d'un ~ pour compléter l'équipe** we need a sixth (person) to complete the team; **elle est arrivée (la) ~ dans la course** she came (in) sixth in the race [3] NM (= *portion*) sixth; **calculer le ~ d'un nombre** to work out the sixth of a number; **recevoir le ~** *ou* **un ~ d'une somme** to receive a sixth of a sum; **(les) deux ~s du budget seront consacrés à ...** two sixths of the budget will be given over to ... [4] NF (*Scol*) ≈ first form (*Brit*), ≈ sixth grade (*US*); **entrer en classe de ~** to go into the first form (*Brit*) *ou* sixth grade (*US*); **élève de ~** ≈ first form (*Brit*) *ou* sixth-grade (*US*) pupil

sixièmement [sizjɛmmɑ̃] ADV in the sixth place, sixthly

six-mâts [sima] NM INV (*Naut*) six-master

six-quatre-deux* [siskatdø] ◆**à la six-**

---

quatre-deux LOC ADV [*faire*] in a slapdash way, any old way, any old how* (*Brit*)

sixte [sikst] NF (*Mus*) sixth; (*Escrime*) sixte

Sixtine [sikstin] ADJ, NF **la (chapelle) ~** the Sistine Chapel

sizain [sizɛ̃] NM (*Littérat*) six-line stanza; (*Cartes*) packet of six packs of cards

ska [ska] NM ska

Skaï® [skaj] NM Leatherette®; **en skaï** Leatherette (*épith*)

skate(-board) [skɛt(bɔʀd)] NM skateboard; (= *activité*) **le ~** skateboarding; **faire du ~** to skateboard

sketch (*pl* **sketches**) [skɛtʃ] NM (variety) sketch → **film**

ski [ski] ① NM (= *objet*) ski; (= *sport*) skiing; **s'acheter des ~s** to buy o.s. a pair of skis *ou* some skis; **~ amont/aval** uphill/downhill ski; **aller quelque part à** *ou* **en ~s** to go somewhere on skis, ski somewhere; **faire du ~** to ski, go skiing; **aller au ~*** to go skiing; **vacances/équipement de ~** ski(ing) holiday/equipment; **chaussures/moniteur/épreuve/station de ~** ski boots/instructor/race/resort → **lunette, piste**
② COMP ► **ski acrobatique** hot-dogging, free-styling ► **ski alpin** (= *discipline*) Alpine skiing; (*opposé à ski de fond*) downhill skiing ► **ski artistique** ski ballet ► **ski sur bosses** mogul skiing ► **ski court** short ski ► **ski de descente** downhill skiing ► **ski d'été** glacier skiing ► **ski évolutif** short ski method, ski évolutif ► **ski de fond** (= *sport*) cross-country skiing, ski touring (*US*), langlauf; (= *objet*) cross-country ski ► **ski sur glacier** glacier skiing ► **ski de haute montagne** ski-mountaineering ► **ski nautique** water-skiing ► **ski nordique** Nordic skiing ► **ski de piste** downhill skiing ► **ski de randonnée = ski de fond**

skiable [skjabl] ADJ [*neige, piste*] skiable; **ils ont un grand domaine ~** they have a lot of ski slopes *ou* pistes

ski-bob (*pl* **ski-bobs**) [skibɔb] NM skibob; **faire du ~** to go skibobbing

skidoo [skidu] NM skidoo, snow scooter; **faire du ~** to skidoo; **il y est allé en ~** he went there on a skidoo *ou* on a snow scooter

skier [skje] ▶conjug 7◀ VI to ski

skieur, skieuse [skjœʀ, skjøz] NM,F skier; (*Ski nautique*) water-skier; **~ de fond** cross-country *ou* langlauf skier; **~ hors piste** off-piste skier; **deux ~s hors piste ont été tués** two people skiing off-piste were killed

skif(f) [skif] NM skiff

skin* [skin] NM skin*

skinhead [skinɛd] NM skinhead

skipper [skipœʀ] NM (*Voile*) skipper

Skopje [skɔpje] N Skopje

slalom [slalɔm] NM (= *épreuve, piste*) slalom; (= *mouvement*) slalom *ou* weaving movement; (*entre divers obstacles*) zigzag; **faire du ~** to slalom (*entre, parmi* between); **~ géant/spécial** giant/special slalom; **le ~ nautique** slalom canoeing → **descente**

slalomer [slalɔme] ▶conjug 1◀ VI (*Sport*) to slalom; **il slalomait entre les voitures** he was weaving in and out of the traffic *ou* zigzagging through the traffic; **le serveur slalomait entre les tables** the waiter was weaving between the tables

slalomeur, -euse [slalɔmœʀ, øz] NM,F slalom skier *ou* specialist *ou* racer

slave [slav] ① ADJ Slav(onic), Slavic; [*langue*] Slavic, Slavonic; **le charme ~** Slavonic charm ② **Slave** NMF Slav

slavisant, e [slavizɑ̃, ɑ̃t] NM,F Slavist

Slavonie [slavɔni] NF Slavonia

slavophile [slavɔfil] ADJ, NMF Slavophile

sleeping† [slipiŋ] NM sleeping car

slip [slip] NM ⓐ [*homme*] briefs, underpants; [*femme*] pants (*Brit*), panties (*US*), briefs; **~ de bain** [*homme*] (bathing *ou* swimming) trunks; (*bikini*) bikini bottom(s); **~ brésilien** tanga; **~ kangourou** Y-fronts; **j'ai acheté deux ~s** I bought two pairs of briefs *ou* pants; (*fig*) **se retrouver en ~*** to lose one's shirt ⓑ (*Naut*) slipway

slogan [slɔgɑ̃] NM slogan

sloop [slup] NM sloop

slovaque [slɔvak] ① ADJ Slovak ② **Slovaque** NMF Slovak

Slovaquie [slɔvaki] NF Slovakia

slovène [slɔvɛn] ① ADJ Slovene ② NM (*Ling*) Slovene ③ **Slovène** NMF Slovene

Slovénie [slɔveni] NF Slovenia

slow [slo] NM (= *danse*) slow dance; (= *musique*) slow number; (= *fox-trot*) slow fox trot; **danser un ~** to do *ou* dance a slow dance

SMAG [smag] NM (ABRÉV = **salaire minimum agricole garanti**) → **salaire**

smala* [smala] NF (*péj* = *troupe*) tribe*; **ils ont débarqué avec toute la ~** they turned up with all their family in tow

smash [sma(t)ʃ] NM (*Tennis*) smash; **faire un ~** to do a smash, smash (the ball)

smasher [sma(t)ʃe] ▶conjug 1◀ VI (*Tennis*) ① VT to smash ② VI to do a smash, smash (the ball)

SME [ɛsəmə] NM (ABRÉV = **système monétaire européen**) EMS

SMIC [smik] NM (ABRÉV = **salaire minimum interprofessionnel de croissance**) → **salaire**

smicard, e* [smikaʀ, aʀd] NM,F minimum wage earner

SMIG† [smig] NM (ABRÉV = **salaire minimum interprofessionnel garanti**) → **salaire**

smocks [smɔk] NMPL (= *fronces*) smocking (*NonC*); **robe à ~** smocked dress

smog [smɔg] NM smog

smok* [smɔk] NM (ABRÉV = **smoking**) DJ* (*Brit*), tux* (*US*)

smoking [smɔkiŋ] NM (= *costume*) dinner suit, evening suit, dress suit; (= *veston*) dinner jacket, DJ* (*Brit*), tuxedo (*US*), tux* (*US*)

SMUR [smyʀ] NM (ABRÉV = **Service médical d'urgence et de réanimation**) mobile emergency unit

smurf [smœʀf] NM (*Danse*) break dancing; **danser le ~** to break-dance

snack [snak], **snack-bar** (*pl* **snack-bars** [snakbaʀ]) NM snack bar

SNCF [ɛsɛnseɛf] NF (ABRÉV = **Société nationale des chemins de fer français**) → **société**

snif(f) [snif] EXCL boo hoo!

sniffer [snife] ▶conjug 1◀ VT (*arg Drogue*) to sniff; **~ de la cocaïne/de la colle** to sniff cocaine/glue

sniper [snajpœʀ] NM sniper

snob [snɔb] ① NMF snob ② ADJ [*personne, attitude*] snobbish; [*quartier*] snobbish, posh*

snober [snɔbe] ▶conjug 1◀ VT [+ *personne*] to snub, give the cold shoulder to; [+ *endroit, réception*] to turn one's nose up at

snobinard, e* [snɔbinaʀ, aʀd] (*péj*) ① ADJ snooty*, stuck-up*, snobbish ② NM,F stuck-up thing*, snob

snobisme [snɔbism] NM snobbery, snobbishness; **~ à l'envers** *ou* **à rebours** inverted snobbery

snowboard [snobɔʀd] NM (*Sport*) snowboard; **faire du ~** to snowboard

soap-opéra (*pl* **soap-opéras**) [sopɔpeʀa] NM soap opera

sobre [sɔbʀ] ADJ ⓐ [*personne*] (= *qui mange et boit peu*) abstemious; (= *qui ne boit pas d'alcool*) teetotal; (= *qui n'est pas ivre*) sober; **~ comme un chameau*** as sober as a judge ⓑ (= *mesuré, simple*) [*décor, style, éloquence*] sober;

[*tenue*] simple, plain; [*commentaire, vie*] simple; **~ de gestes/en paroles** sparing of gestures/of words; **des vêtements de coupe ~** clothes cut simply

sobrement [sɔbʀəmɑ̃] ADV ⓐ [*vivre*] abstemiously ⓑ (= *simplement*) [*s'habiller*] simply, plainly; [*commenter, expliquer*] simply

sobriété [sɔbʀijete] NF ⓐ [*personne*] (= *fait de boire et manger peu*) temperance; (= *fait de ne pas boire d'alcool*) abstinence ⓑ (= *simplicité*) [*style, éloquence*] sobriety; [*mise en scène, décor*] simplicity; **~ de gestes/paroles** restraint in one's gestures/words

sobriquet [sɔbʀikɛ] NM nickname

soc [sɔk] NM ploughshare (*Brit*), plowshare (*US*)

sociabilité [sɔsjabilite] NF ⓐ (*Sociol*) sociability, social nature ⓑ (= *civilité*) [*personne, caractère*] sociability

sociable [sɔsjabl] ADJ ⓐ (*Sociol*) social ⓑ (= *ouvert, civil*) [*personne, caractère*] sociable; [*milieu*] hospitable; **je ne suis pas d'humeur ~ aujourd'hui** I'm not in a sociable mood today, I don't feel like socializing today

social, e (*mpl* **-iaux**) [sɔsjal, jo] ① ADJ ⓐ [*animal, créature, rapports, conventions*] social → **science** ⓑ [*classe, questions, loi, politique, système*] social; **œuvres ~es** charity activities → **assistant, sécurité, siège** [c] (= *du travail*) **revendications ~es** workers' demands; **conflit ~** industrial *ou* trade dispute; **plan ~** restructuring programme ② NM **le ~** (= *questions*) social issues; **faire du ~** to tackle social issues

social-démocrate, sociale-démocrate (*mpl* **sociaux-démocrates**) [sɔsjaldemɔkʀat, sɔsjodemɔkʀat] ADJ, NM,F Social Democrat

social-démocratie (*pl* **social-démocraties**) [sɔsjaldemɔkʀasi] NF social democracy

socialement [sɔsjalmɑ̃] ADV socially

socialisant, e [sɔsjalizɑ̃, ɑ̃t] ADJ with socialist leanings *ou* tendencies

socialisation [sɔsjalizasjɔ̃] NF ⓐ (*Écon*) [*moyens de production*] collectivization ⓑ (*Sociol*) [*personne*] socialization

socialiser [sɔsjalize] ▶conjug 1◀ VT ⓐ (*Écon*) [+ *moyens de production*] to collectivize ⓑ (*Sociol*) [+ *personne*] to socialize

socialisme [sɔsjalism] NM socialism; **~ utopique/scientifique/révolutionnaire** utopian/scientific/revolutionary socialism; **~ d'État** state socialism

socialiste [sɔsjalist] ADJ, NMF socialist

sociétaire [sɔsjetɛʀ] NMF member (*of a society*); **~ de la Comédie-Française** (shareholding) member of the Comédie-Française

sociétal, e (*mpl* **-aux**) [sɔsjetal, o] ADJ [*changement, structure*] societal

société [sɔsjete] ① NF ⓐ (= *groupe, communauté*) society; **la ~** society; **la vie en ~** life in society; **~ sans classe** classless society; **la ~ de consommation** the consumer society; **la ~ de loisirs** the leisure society ⓑ (= *club*) [*littéraire*] society; (*sportif*) club; **~ de pêche/tir** angling/shooting club; **~ secrète/savante** secret/learned society; **la Société protectrice des animaux** ≈ the Royal Society for the Prevention of Cruelty to Animals (*Brit*), ≈ the American Society for the Prevention of Cruelty to Animals (*US*) [c] (= *firme*) company, firm; **~ financière** finance company; **~ immobilière** (= *compagnie*) property (*Brit*) *ou* real estate (*US*) company; [*copropriétaires*] housing association [d] (= *classes supérieures*) **la ~** society; **dans la bonne ~** in polite society; **la haute ~** high society [e] (= *assemblée*) company, gathering; **il y venait une ~ assez mêlée/une ~ d'artistes et d'écrivains** a fairly mixed company *ou* gathering/a company *ou* gathering of artists and writers used to come; **toute la ~ se leva**

pour l'acclamer the whole company rose to acclaim him

f (= *compagnie*) company, society (*frm*, *littér*); **rechercher/priser la ~ de qn** to seek/value sb's company *ou* society (*littér*) *ou* companionship; **dans la ~ de qn** in the company *ou* society (*frm*, *littér*) of sb → **jeu, talent¹**

2 COMP ► **société par actions** joint-stock company ► **société anonyme** (*gén*) ≈ limited (liability) company; (*ouverte au public*) ≈ public limited company ► **Société des auteurs, compositeurs et éditeurs de musique** *French body responsible for collecting and distributing music royalties,* ≈ Publishing Rights Society (*Brit*) ► **société de Bourse** brokerage *ou* broking firm ► **société à capital variable** company with variable capital ► **société civile** (*Comm*) non-trading company; (*Philo*) civil society; (*Pol*) **personne de la ~ civile** lay person ► **société civile immobilière** non-trading property (*Brit*) *ou* real estate (*US*) company ► **société civile de placement immobilier** non-trading property (*Brit*) *ou* real estate (*US*) investment trust ► **société civile professionnelle** professional partnership ► **société en commandite** limited partnership ► **société commerciale** trading company ► **société commune** joint-venture company ► **société de crédit** *ou* finance company ► **société d'économie mixte** semi-public company ► **société écran** bogus *ou* dummy company ► **société d'exploitation** development company ► **société d'investissement** investment trust; **~ d'investissement à capital variable** unit trust (*Brit*), open-end investment trust (*US*), mutual fund (*US*) ► **la société de Jésus** the Society of Jesus ► **société nationale des chemins de fer français** *French national railway company* ► **la Société des Nations** (*Hist Pol*) the League of Nations ► **société en nom collectif** general partnership ► **société en participation** joint-venture company ► **société de personnes** partnership ► **société de portefeuille** holding company ► **société de production** (*Audiov*) production company ► **société à responsabilité limitée** limited liability company ► **société de services** service company; **~ de services informatiques** software house ► **société de tempérance** temperance society

socio* [sɔsjo] NF ABRÉV = **sociologie**

sociobiologie [sɔsjobjɔlɔʒi] NF sociobiology

socioculturel, -elle [sɔsjokyltyʀɛl] ADJ sociocultural

sociodrame [sɔsjodʀam] NM sociodrama

socio-économique (*pl* socio-économiques) [sɔsjoekɔnɔmik] ADJ socioeconomic

socio-éducatif, -ive (*mpl* socio-éducatifs) [sɔsjoedykatif, iv] ADJ socioeducational

sociogéographique [sɔsjoʒeɔgʀafik] ADJ sociogeographic

sociogramme [sɔsjogʀam] NM sociogram

sociolinguistique [sɔsjolɛ̃gɥistik] **1** ADJ sociolinguistic **2** NF sociolinguistics *sg*

sociologie [sɔsjɔlɔʒi] NF sociology

sociologique [sɔsjɔlɔʒik] ADJ sociological

sociologiquement [sɔsjɔlɔʒikmɑ̃] ADV sociologically

sociologue [sɔsjɔlɔg] NMF sociologist

sociométrie [sɔsjɔmetʀi] NF sociometry

sociopolitique [sɔsjopɔlitik] ADJ sociopolitical

socioprofessionnel, -elle [sɔsjopʀofesjɔnɛl] ADJ socio-professional

socle [sɔkl] NM **a** [*statue, colonne*] plinth, pedestal, socle (SPÉC); [*lampe, vase*] base **b** (*Géog*) platform

socque [sɔk] NM (= *sabot*) clog

socquette [sɔkɛt] NF ankle sock (*Brit*), anklet (*US*)

Socrate [sɔkʀat] NM Socrates

socratique [sɔkʀatik] ADJ Socratic

soda [sɔda] NM fizzy drink (*Brit*), soda (*US*), pop*; **~ à l'orange** orangeade; **whisky ~** whisky and soda

sodé, e [sɔde] ADJ sodium (*épith*)

sodique [sɔdik] ADJ sodic

sodium [sɔdjɔm] NM sodium

Sodome [sɔdɔm] N Sodom; **~ et Gomorrhe** Sodom and Gomorrah

sodomie [sɔdɔmi] NF sodomy, buggery

sodomiser [sɔdɔmize] ▶ conjug 1 ◀ VT to bugger, have anal intercourse with

sodomite [sɔdɔmit] NM sodomite

sœur [sœʀ] NF **a** (*lit, fig*) sister; **avec un dévouement de ~** with a sister's *ou* with sisterly devotion; **la poésie, ~ de la musique** poetry, sister of *ou* to music; **peuplades/organisations ~s** sister peoples/organizations; (*littér*) **d'infortune** fellow sufferer; (*hum*) **j'ai trouvé la ~ de cette commode chez un antiquaire** I found the partner to this chest of drawers in an antique shop; **et ta ~ !*** get lost!* → **âme, lait b** (*Rel*) nun, sister; (*comme titre*) Sister; **~ Jeanne** Sister Jeanne; **elle a été élevée chez les ~s** she was convent-educated; **elle était en pension chez les ~s** she went to a convent (boarding) school; **les Petites ~s des pauvres** the Little Sisters of the Poor; **les ~s de la Charité** the Sisters of Charity → **bon¹**

sœurette* [sœʀɛt] NF little sister, kid* sister

sofa [sɔfa] NM sofa

Sofia [sɔfja] N Sofia

SOFRES [sɔfʀɛs] NF (ABRÉV = **Société française d'enquêtes par sondage**) *French public opinion poll institute,* ≈ Gallup, ≈ MORI (*Brit*)

soft [sɔft] **1** ADJ INV [*film*] soft-porn*, soft-core*; **érotisme ~** soft(-core) porn*; **l'ambiance ~ d'un salon de thé** the cosy atmosphere of a tearoom; **c'est la version ~ de son premier livre** it's the watered-down version of his first book; **la campagne électorale est plus ~ que la précédente** the electoral campaign is less aggressive than the previous one **2** NM **le ~** (*Ordin*) software; (*Ciné*) soft(-core) porn films*

software [sɔftwɛʀ] NM software

soi [swa] **1** PRON PERS **a** (*gén*) one(self); (*fonction d'attribut*) oneself; **n'aimer que ~** to love only oneself; **regarder devant/derrière ~** to look in front of/behind one; **malgré ~** in spite of oneself; **avoir confiance en ~** to be self-confident; **rester chez ~** to stay at home **b** † (= *lui*) himself; (= *elle*) herself; (= *chose*) itself; (*frm*) **il n'agissait que pour ~** he was only acting for himself *ou* in his own interests; (*évite une ambiguïté*) **elle comprenait qu'il fût mécontent de ~** she understood his not being pleased with himself; **il allait droit devant ~** he was going straight ahead **c** (*loc*) **aller de ~** to be self-evident, be obvious; **cela va de ~** it goes without saying, it's obvious, it stands to reason; **il va de ~ que ...** it goes without saying *ou* it stands to reason that ...; (= *intrinsèquement*) **en ~** in itself; **n'exister que pour ~** to exist only for oneself; **dans un groupe, on peut se rendre service entre ~** in a group, people can help each other *ou* one another (out); **être/rester ~** to be/ remain oneself → **chacun, hors, maître**

d **~-même** oneself; **on le fait ~-même** you do it yourself, one does it oneself (*frm*); (*hum*) **le respect de ~-même** self-respect; (*hum*) **Monsieur Leblanc ? — ~-même !** Mr Leblanc? — in person! *ou* none other!; *pour autres locutions voir* **même**

2 NM (*Philo, littér* = *personnalité, conscience*) self; (*Psych* = *inconscient*) id; **la conscience de ~** self-awareness, awareness of self → **en-soi, pour-soi**

soi-disant [swadizɑ̃] **1** ADJ INV so-called; **un ~ poète/professeur** a so-called *ou* would-be poet/teacher **2** ADV supposedly; **il était ~ parti à Rome** he was supposed to have left for Rome, he was supposed to have left for Rome; **il était venu ~ pour discuter** he had come to talk — or so he said, he had come ostensibly for a talk; **~ que* ...** it would appear that ..., apparently ...

soie [swa] NF **a** (*Tex*) silk; **~ sauvage/végétale** wild/vegetal silk; **~ grège/lavée** raw/washed silk → **papier, ver b** (= *poil*) [*sanglier*] bristle; **brosse en ~s de sanglier** (boar) bristle brush; **brosse à dents en ~s de nylon** nylon (bristle) tooth brush, tooth brush with nylon bristles **c** (*Tech*) [*lime, couteau*] tang

soierie [swaʀi] NF (= *tissu*) silk; (= *industrie, commerce*) silk trade; (= *filature*) silk mill

soif [swaf] NF **a** (*lit*) thirst; **avoir ~** [*personne*] to be thirsty; [*plante, terre*] to be dry *ou* thirsty; **avoir grand ~**† to be very thirsty; **ça donne ~** it makes you thirsty; **il fait ~*** I'm parched*; **jusqu'à plus ~** (*lit*) till one's thirst is quenched; (*fig*) till one can't take any more; **rester sur sa ~** (*lit*) to remain thirsty; (*fig*) to be left unsatisfied → **boire, étancher, garder mourir b** (= *désir*) **~ de** [+ *richesse, connaissances, vengeance, pouvoir*] thirst *ou* craving for; **~ de faire qch** craving to do sth

soiffard, e*† [swafaʀ, aʀd] (*péj*) **1** ADJ boozy* **2** NM,F boozer*

soignant, e [swaɲɑ̃, ɑ̃t] ADJ [*personnel*] nursing (*épith*); **équipe ~e** (team of) doctors and nurses

soigné, e [swaɲe] (*ptp de* **soigner**) ADJ **a** (= *propre*) [*personne, chevelure*] well-groomed, neat, tidy; [*ongles*] manicured, well-kept; [*mains*] well-cared-for (*épith*), well cared for (*attrib*); **peu ~** [*personne*] untidy; [*cheveux*] unkempt, untidy; [*ongles, mains*] neglected(-looking); **il est très ~ de sa personne** he is very well turned-out *ou* well-groomed **b** (= *consciencieux*) [*travail, style, présentation*] careful, meticulous; [*vitrine*] neat, carefully laid out; [*jardin*] well-kept; [*repas*] carefully prepared; **peu ~** [*travail*] careless, sloppy **c** (* : *intensif*) [*note*] massive*, whopping* (*épith*); [*punition*] stiff*; **avoir un rhume (quelque chose de)** ~ to have a real beauty* *ou* a whopper* of a cold; **la note était ~e** it was some bill*, it was a massive* *ou* whopping* bill

soigner [swaɲe] ▶ conjug 1 ◀ **1** VT **a** (= *traiter*) [+ *patient, maladie*] [*médecin*] to treat; [*infirmière, mère*] to look after, nurse; **j'ai été très bien soigné dans cette clinique** I had very good treatment *ou* I was very well looked after in this clinic; **~ les blessés** to tend *ou* nurse the wounded; **tu devrais te faire ~** you should see a doctor; **il faut te faire ~ !*** you need your head examined *ou* examining!; **rentrez chez vous pour ~ votre rhume** go back home and look after *ou* nurse that cold (of yours); **je soigne mes rhumatismes avec des pilules** I'm taking pills for my rheumatism **b** (= *entretenir*) [+ *chien, plantes, invité*] to look after; [+ *ongles, chevelure, outils, livres*] to look after, take (good) care of; [+ *cheval*] to groom; [+ *tenue, travail, repas, style, présentation*] to take care over; **~ sa clientèle** to look after one's customers; **~ son image (de marque)** to be careful about one's image; **le pays essaie de ~ son image à l'étranger** the country is trying to cultivate its image abroad **c** (* = *maltraiter*) **~ qn** to let sb have it*; **35 F le café — ils nous ont soignés !** 35 francs for a coffee — what a rip-off!* *ou* we've been had!* *ou* done!* (*Brit*); **ils lui sont tombés dessus à quatre : j'aime autant te dire qu'ils l'ont soigné** four of them laid into him — I can tell you they really let him have it* → **oignon**

2 **se soigner** VPR **a** [*personne*] (= *prendre des médicaments*) to take medicine; **se ~ par**

les plantes to take herbal medicine; **soigne-toi bien** take good care of yourself, look after yourself; (*hum*) **ils se soignent : champagne, saumon ... !** they take good care of *ou* they look after themselves (all right) — champagne, salmon, the lot!

b [*maladie*] **de nos jours, la tuberculose se soigne** these days tuberculosis can be treated; (*hum*) **ça se soigne, tu sais ! *** there's a cure for that, you know!

soigneur [swaɲœʀ] NM (*Boxe*) second; (*Cyclisme, Ftbl*) trainer

soigneusement [swaɲøzmɑ̃] ADV [*ranger, nettoyer, entretenir, éviter, choisir*] carefully; [*écrire, plier*] carefully, neatly; **~ préparé** carefully prepared, prepared with care; **il pèse ~ ses mots** he weighs his words carefully

soigneux, -euse [swaɲø, øz] ADJ **a** (= *propre, ordonné*) tidy, neat; **ce garçon n'est pas assez ~** that boy isn't tidy enough **b** (= *appliqué, minutieux*) [*travailleur*] careful, painstaking; [*travail*] careful, meticulous; [*recherche, examen*] careful; **être ~ dans son travail** to take care over one's work **c** (= *soucieux*) **être ~ de sa santé** to be careful about one's health; **être ~ de ses affaires** to be careful with one's belongings; **être ~ de sa personne** to be careful about *ou* take care over one's appearance; **être ~ de ses vêtements** to take care of *ou* look after one's clothes

soi-même [swamɛm] PRON → **même, soi**

soin [swɛ̃] **1** NM **a** (= *application*) care; (= *ordre et propreté*) tidiness, neatness; **être sans ~ ◊ n'avoir aucun ~** to be careless *ou* untidy *ou* sloppy; **faire qch sans ~** to do sth carelessly; **faire qch avec (grand) ~** to do sth with (great) care *ou* (very) carefully; **il nous évite avec un certain ~ ◊ il met un certain ~ à nous éviter** he takes great care *ou* he goes to some lengths to avoid us

b (= *charge, responsabilité*) care; **confier à qn le ~ de ses affaires** to entrust sb with the care of one's affairs; **confier à qn le ~ de faire qch** to entrust sb with the job *ou* task of doing sth; **je vous laisse ce ~** I leave this to you, I leave you to take care of this; **son premier ~ fut de ...** his first concern was to ...; (*littér*) **le ~ de son salut/avenir l'occupait tout entier** his thoughts were filled with the care of his salvation/future (*littér*)

c (= *traitement*) **le ~ du cheveu** hair care

d (*loc*) **avoir** *ou* **prendre ~ de faire qch** to take care to do sth, make a point of doing sth; **avoir** *ou* **prendre ~ de qn/qch** to take care of *ou* look after sb/sth; **il prend bien ~/grand ~ de sa petite personne** he takes good care/great care of his little self *ou* of number one*; **ayez** *ou* **prenez ~ d'éteindre** take care *ou* be sure to turn out the lights, make sure you turn out the lights; **avoir ~ que ...** to make sure that ...

2 soins NMPL **a** (= *entretien, hygiène*) care (*NonC*); (= *traitement*) treatment (*NonC*); **les ~s du ménage** *ou* **domestiques†** the care of the home; **~s esthétiques** *ou* **de beauté** beauty care; **pour les ~s des cheveux/des ongles utilisez ...** for hair-/nail-care use ...; **les ~s du visage** facial care; **~s médicaux** medical *ou* health care, medical treatment; **~s dentaires** dental treatment *ou* care; **son état demande des ~s** his condition requires treatment *ou* (medical) attention; **le blessé a reçu les premiers ~s** the injured man has been given first aid

b (= *attention*) care (and attention) (*NonC*); **l'enfant a besoin des ~s d'une mère** the child needs a mother's care (and attention); **confier qn/qch aux (bons) ~s de qn** to leave sb/sth in the hands *ou* care of sb; (*sur lettre : frm*) **aux bons ~s de** care of, c/o; **être aux petits ~s pour qn** to attend to sb's every need, wait on sb hand and foot

c (*Rel*) **donner ses ~s à qn** to minister to sb

soir [swaʀ] NM **a** (= *fin du jour*) evening; **les ~s d'automne/d'hiver** autumn/winter evenings; **le ~ descend** *ou* **tombe** night is falling, evening is closing in; **le ~ où j'y suis allé** the evening I went; **viens nous voir un de ces ~s** come and see us one evening *ou* night; **être du ~** to be a night owl*; (*littér*) **au ~ de la/de sa vie** in the evening of life/of his life (*littér*); **le grand ~** the big night; (*Pol*) the revolution → **matin**

b **repas/journal du ~** evening meal/paper; **5 heures du ~** 5 (o'clock) in the afternoon *ou* evening, 5 pm; **8 heures du ~** 8 (o'clock) in the evening, 8 o'clock at night, 8 pm; **11 heures du ~** 11 (o'clock) at night, 11 pm → **cours, robe**

c (*loc : compléments de temps*) **le ~, je vais souvent les voir** I often go to see them in the evening; **le ~, je suis allé les voir/il a plu** I went to see them/it rained in the evening; **il pleut assez souvent le ~** it quite often rains in the evening(s); **sortir le ~** to go out in the evening; **j'y vais ce ~** I'm going this evening *ou* tonight; **à ce ~ !** (I'll) see you (*ou* I'll talk to you) this evening! *ou* tonight!; **vivement ce ~ qu'on se couche*** I can't wait until bedtime, roll on bedtime* (*Brit*); **tous les ~s** *ou* **chaque ~** every evening *ou* night; **hier ~** last night, yesterday evening; **demain ~** tomorrow evening *ou* night; **dimanche ~** Sunday evening *ou* night; **hier au ~** yesterday evening; **le 17 au ~** on the evening of the 17th; **la veille au ~** the previous evening; **il est arrivé un (beau) ~** he turned up one (fine) evening

▼ **soirée** [swaʀe] NF **a** (= *soir*) evening; **bonne ~ !** have a nice evening!; **les longues ~s d'hiver** the long winter evenings **b** (= *réception*) party; **~ dansante** dance; **~ mondaine** society party → **tenue** **c** (*Ciné, Théât* = *séance*) evening performance; **donner un spectacle/une pièce en ~** to give an evening performance of a show/play; (*TV*) **~ thématique** *evening of programmes devoted to a theme*; **~ électorale** election night

soit [swa] **1** ADV (*frm* = *oui*) very well, so be it (*frm*); **eh bien, ~, qu'il y aille !** very well then, let him go! → **tant**

2 CONJ **a** (= *ou*) **~ l'un ~ l'autre** (either) one or the other; **~ avant ~ après** (either) before or after; **~ timidité, ~ mépris** *ou* **timidité ou mépris**, elle ne lui adressait jamais la parole be it (out) of *ou* whether out of shyness or contempt, she never spoke to him; **~ qu'il soit fatigué, ~ qu'il en ait assez** whether he is tired or whether he has had enough; **~ qu'il n'entende pas, ou ne veuille pas entendre** whether he cannot hear or (whether) he does not wish to hear

b (= *à savoir*) that is to say; **des détails importants, ~ l'approvisionnement, le transport, etc** important details, that is to say *ou* for instance provisions, transport, etc

c (*Math* = *posons*) **~ un rectangle ABCD** let ABCD be a rectangle; **soient deux triangles isocèles** given two isosceles triangles

soixantaine [swasɑ̃tɛn] NF **a** (= *environ soixante*) sixty or so, (round) about sixty, sixty-odd*; **il y avait une ~ de personnes/de livres** there were sixty or so *ou* about sixty people/books, there were sixty-odd* people/books; **la ~ de spectateurs qui étaient là** the sixty or so *ou* the sixty-odd* people there; **ils étaient une bonne ~** there were a good sixty of them; **il y a une ~/une bonne ~ d'années** sixty or so *ou* a good sixty years ago; **ça doit coûter une ~ de mille (francs)** that must cost sixty thousand or so francs *ou* (round) about sixty thousand francs *ou* some sixty thousand francs

b (= *soixante unités*) sixty; **sa collection n'atteint pas encore/a dépassé la ~** his collection has not yet reached/has passed the sixty mark, there are not yet sixty/are now over sixty in his collection

c (= *âge*) sixty; **approcher de la/atteindre la ~** to near/reach sixty; **un homme dans la ~** a man in his sixties; **d'une ~ d'années** [*personne*] of about sixty; [*arbre*] sixty or so years old; **elle a la ~** she's about sixty, she's sixtyish

soixante [swasɑ̃t] ADJ INV, NM INV sixty; **à la page ~** on page sixty; **habiter au ~** to live at number sixty; **les années ~** the sixties, the 60s; **~ et un** sixty-one; **~ et unième** sixty-first; **~-dix** seventy; **~-dixième** seventieth; **~ mille** sixty thousand; (*jeu, rue*) **le (numéro) ~** number sixty; (= *position sexuelle*) **un ~-neuf*** a soixante-neuf*, a sixty-nine*

soixante-huitard, e (*mpl* **soixante-huitards**) [swasɑ̃tɥitaʀ, aʀd] **1** ADJ [*personne*] who took part in the events of May 1968; [*idéologie, slogan*] inspired by the events of May 1968 **2** NM,F (*en mai 68*) participant in the events of May 1968; (*après 1968*) proponent of the ideals of May 1968 → **MAI 68**

soixantième [swasɑ̃tjɛm] ADJ, NM sixtieth

soja [sɔʒa] NM (= *plante*) soya; (= *graines*) soya beans

sol¹ [sɔl] NM (*gén*) ground; (= *plancher*) floor; (= *revêtement*) floor, flooring (*NonC*); (= *territoire, terrain, Agr, Géol*) soil; **étendu sur le ~** spread out on the ground; **posé au ~** *ou* **à même le ~** (placed) on the ground (*ou* floor); **~ carrelé/cimenté** tiled/concrete floor; **la surface au ~** the floor surface; (*Constr*) **la pose des ~s** the laying of floors *ou* of flooring; **~ natal** native soil; **sur le ~ français** on French soil; (*Aviat*) **personnel au ~** ground staff *ou* personnel; (*Aviat*) **essais/vitesse au ~** ground tests/speed; (*Sport*) **exercices au ~** floor exercises

sol² [sɔl] NM INV (*Mus*) G; (*en chantant la gamme*) so(h) → **clé**

sol³ [sɔl] NM (*Chim*) sol

sol⁴ [sɔl] NM (= *monnaie*) sol

sol-air [sɔlɛʀ] ADJ INV ground-to-air

solaire [sɔlɛʀ] **1** ADJ (*Astrol, Astron*) [*énergie, panneaux*] solar; [*crème, filtre*] sun (*attrib*) → **cadran, plexus, spectre** **2** NM (= *énergie*) **le ~** solar energy

solarisation [sɔlaʀizasjɔ̃] NF (= *chauffage*) solar heating; (*Photo*) solarization

solarium [sɔlaʀjɔm] NM solarium

soldanelle [sɔldanɛl] NF (*Bot*) (= *primulacée*) soldanella; (= *liseron*) sea bindweed

soldat [sɔlda] NM (*gén*) soldier; **(simple) ~ ◊ ~ de 2ᵉᵐᵉ classe** (*armée de terre*) private; (*armée de l'air*) aircraftman (*Brit*), basic airman (*US*); **~ de 1ᵉʳᵉ classe** (*armée de terre*) ≈ private (*Brit*), ≈ private first class (*US*); (*armée de l'air*) leading aircraftman (*Brit*), airman first class (*US*); **~ d'infanterie** infantryman; **se faire ~** to join the army, enlist; **le Soldat inconnu** the Unknown Soldier *ou* Warrior; (*fig littér*) **~ de la liberté/du Christ** soldier of liberty/of Christ; **~s de la paix** peacekeepers; **~ de plomb** tin *ou* toy soldier; **jouer aux (petits) ~s** to play (at) soldiers; (*fig*) **jouer au petit ~** to throw one's weight around → **fille**

soldate [sɔldat] NF woman soldier

soldatesque [sɔldatɛsk] (*péj*) **1** NF army rabble **2** ADJ† barrack-room (*épith*)

solde¹ [sɔld] NF **a** [*soldat, matelot*] pay **b** (*péj*) **être à la ~ de qn** to be in the pay of sb; **avoir qn à sa ~** to have sb in one's pay

solde² [sɔld] **1** NM **a** (*Fin* = *reliquat*) (*gén*) balance; (= *reste à payer*) balance outstanding; **il y a un ~ de 100 F en votre faveur** there is a balance of 100 francs in your favour; **~ débiteur/créditeur** debit/credit balance; **~ de trésorerie** cash balance; **pour ~ de (tout) compte** in settlement **b** (*Comm*) **~ (de marchandises)** remaining goods; **vente de ~s** sale, sale of reduced items; **mettre des marchandises en ~** to put goods in a sale; **vendre/acheter qch en ~** to sell (off)/buy sth at sale price; **article (vendu) en ~** sale(s) item *ou* article **2 soldes** NMPL (*parfois nfpl : pancarte*) **« ~s »** "sale"; **les ~s** the sales; **je l'ai acheté**

dans les ~s I bought it in the sales; **faire les ~s** to go to the sales; **la saison des ~s** the sales season

solder [sɔlde] ▸conjug 1◂ **1** VT **a** [+ *compte*] (= *arrêter*) to wind up, close; (= *acquitter*) to pay (off) the balance of, settle **b** [+ *marchandises*] to sell (off) at sale price; **ils soldent ces pantalons à 130 F** they are selling off these trousers at ou for 130 francs, they are selling these trousers in the sale at ou for 130 francs; **je vous le solde à 40 F** I'll let you have it for 40 francs, I'll knock it down* ou reduce it to 40 francs for you

2 se solder VPR **se ~ par** (*Comm*) [*exercice, budget*] to show; (*fig*) [*entreprise, opération*] to end in; **les comptes se soldent par un bénéfice** the accounts show a profit; **l'exercice se solde par un déficit/bénéfice de 50 millions** the end-of-year figures show a loss/profit of 50 million; **l'entreprise/la conférence s'est soldée par un échec** the undertaking/the conference ended in failure ou came to nothing

solderie [sɔldəʀi] NF discount store

soldeur, -euse [sɔldœʀ, øz] NM,F (= *propriétaire*) discount store owner; (= *entreprise*) discount store

sole[1] [sɔl] NF (= *poisson*) sole; (*Culin*) **~ meunière** sole meunière

sole[2] [sɔl] NF (*Tech*) [*four*] hearth; [*sabot, bateau*] sole

solécisme [sɔlesism] NM solecism (*in language*)

soleil [sɔlɛj] NM **a** (= *astre, gén*) sun; (*Astron, Myth*) **le Soleil** the Sun; **orienté au ~ levant/couchant** facing the rising/setting sun; **le ~ de minuit** the midnight sun; (*littér*) **les ~s pâles/brumeux de l'hiver** the pale/misty winter sun; (*fig*) **tu es mon (rayon de) ~** you are my sunshine → **coucher, lever, rayon** **b** (= *chaleur*) sun, sunshine; (= *lumière*) sun, sunshine, sunlight; **au ~** in the sun; **être assis/se mettre au ~** to be sitting in/go into the sun(shine); **vivre au ~** to live in the sun; **il y a du ~ ◊ il fait du ~ ◊ il fait ~*** the sun's shining, it's sunny; **il fait un beau ~** it's nice and sunny; **il fait un ~ de plomb** the sun is blazing down, there's a blazing sun; **être en plein ~** to be right in the sun; **rester en plein ~** to stay (out) in the sun; **c'est une plante de plein ~** this plant thrives in full sun; **des jours sans ~** sunless days; **se chercher un coin au ~** to look for a spot in the sun(shine) ou a sunny spot; **la couleur a passé au ~** the colour has faded in the sun; **coup de ~** sunburn (*NonC*); **attraper** ou **prendre un coup de ~** to get sunburned; **j'ai (pris) un coup de ~ dans le dos** I burned my back, my back is sunburned → **bain, fondre** **c** (= *motif, ornement*) sun **d** (= *feu d'artifice*) Catherine wheel **e** (= *acrobatie*) grand circle; (*fig* = *culbute*) **faire un ~** to turn ou do a somersault, somersault **f** (= *fleur*) sunflower **g** (*loc*) **se lever avec le ~** to rise with the sun, be up with the sun ou the lark (*Brit*) ■ *PROV* **le ~ brille pour tout le monde** nature belongs to everyone; **rien de nouveau** ou **neuf sous le ~** there's nothing new under the sun; **avoir du bien** ou **des biens au ~** to be the owner of property, have property; (*fig*) **se faire/avoir une place au ~** to find oneself/have a place in the sun

solennel, -elle [sɔlanɛl] ADJ (*gén*) solemn; [*promesse, ton, occasion*] solemn, formal; [*séance*] ceremonious → **communion**

solennellement [sɔlanɛlmɑ̃] ADV (*gén*) solemnly; [*offrir, ouvrir*] ceremoniously

solenniser [sɔlanize] ▸conjug 1◂ VT to solemnize

solennité [sɔlanite] NF **a** (= *caractère*) solem-

nity **b** (= *fête*) grand ou formal occasion **c** (*gén pl* = *formalité*) formality, solemnity

solénoïde [sɔlenɔid] NM solenoid

soleret [sɔlʀɛ] NM (*Hist*) solleret

Solex® [sɔlɛks] NM ≈ moped

solfège [sɔlfɛʒ] NM (= *théorie*) music theory, musical notation; (= *livre*) (music) theory book; († = *gamme*) (tonic) sol-fa; **apprendre le ~** to learn music theory ou musical notation

solfier [sɔlfje] ▸conjug 7◂ VTI to sing naming the notes

solidaire [sɔlidɛʀ] ADJ **a** [*personnes*] **être ~s** to show solidarity, stand ou stick together; **pendant les grèves les ouvriers sont ~s** during strikes workers stand ou stick together ou show solidarity; **être ~ de** to stand by, be behind; **nous sommes ~s du gouvernement** we stand by ou are behind ou are backing the government; **nous sommes ~s de leur combat** we support their struggle; **être ~ des victimes d'un régime** to show solidarity with ou stand by ou support the victims of a régime; **ils ne sont pas très ~s l'un de l'autre** they're not very supportive of each other; **ces pays se sentent ~s** these countries feel they have each others' support ou feel a sense of solidarity; **se montrer ~ de qn** to show solidarity with sb; **il rêve d'une société plus ~** he dreams of a more united society **b** [*mécanismes, pièces, systèmes*] interdependent; **cette pièce est ~ de l'autre** the two parts are interdependent; **ces trois objectifs sont étroitement ~s** these three objectives are closely interlinked **c** (*Jur*) [*contrat, engagement*] binding all parties; [*débiteurs*] jointly liable → **caution**

solidairement [sɔlidɛʀmɑ̃] ADV jointly, jointly and severally (*SPÉC*)

solidariser [sɔlidaʀize] ▸conjug 1◂ **1** VT [+ *personnes*] to unify; [+ *objets*] to interlock **2 se solidariser** VPR **se ~ avec** to show solidarity with

solidarité [sɔlidaʀite] NF **a** [*personnes*] solidarity; **~ de classe/professionnelle** class/professional solidarity; **~ ministérielle** ministerial solidarity (*whereby all ministers assume responsibility for a government's decisions*); **cesser le travail par ~ des grévistes** to come out ou stop work in sympathy with the strikers → **grève** **b** [*mécanismes, systèmes*] interdependence **c** (*Jur*) joint and several liability

solide [sɔlid] **1** ADJ **a** (= *non liquide*) [*nourriture, état, corps*] solid; (*Géom, Phys*) solid; **ne lui donnez pas encore d'aliments ~s** don't give him any solid food ou any solids yet **b** (= *robuste*) [*matériaux, construction, meuble*] solid, sturdy; [*outil*] solid, strong; [*monnaie, économie*] strong; **c'est du ~*** [*meuble*] it's solid stuff; **être ~ sur ses jambes** to be steady on one's legs; **avoir une position ~** to have a secure position **c** (= *durable, sérieux*) [*institutions, qualités, vertus*] solid, sound; [*bases*] solid, firm, sound; [*preuve, alibi, expérience, amitié*] solid, firm; [*argument, formation, culture, connaissances, raisons*] sound; **être doué d'un ~ bon sens** to have sound common sense; **ces opinions/raisonnements ne reposent sur rien de ~** these opinions/arguments have no solid ou sound foundation; **leur couple, c'est du ~*** they have a solid ou strong relationship **d** (= *vigoureux*) [*personne*] sturdy, robust; [*poigne, jambes, bras*] sturdy, solid; [*santé, poumons, cœur, esprit, psychisme*] sound; **avoir la tête ~** (*lit*) to have a hard head; (*fig*) to have a good head on one's shoulders; **il n'a plus la tête bien ~** his mind's not what it was; **il n'a pas l'estomac très ~** he has a rather weak ou delicate stomach; **il faut avoir les nerfs ~s** you need strong nerves ou nerves of steel → **rein** **e** (*intensif*) [*coup de poing*] hefty*; [*revenus*]

substantial; [*engueulade*] good, proper* (*Brit*); **il a un ~ appétit** ou **coup de fourchette*** he has a hearty appetite, he's a hearty eater; **un ~ repas le remit d'aplomb** a (good) solid meal put him back on his feet **f** (*loc*) **être ~ au poste** (*Mil*) to be loyal to one's post; (*fig*) to be completely dependable ou reliable; **~ comme un roc** as solid as a rock **2** NM (*Géom, Phys*) solid

solidement [sɔlidmɑ̃] ADV **a** [*fixer, tenir*] firmly; [*fabriquer, construire*] solidly; **résister ~** to put up a solid ou firm resistance **b** [*s'établir, s'installer*] securely, firmly, solidly; [*raisonner*] soundly; **rester ~ attaché aux traditions locales** to remain firmly attached to local traditions; **être ~ attaché à qn/qch** to be deeply attached to sb/sth; **une certitude ~ ancrée dans les esprits** a conviction firmly entrenched in people's minds; **tradition ~ établie** long ou solidly established tradition

solidification [sɔlidifikasjɔ̃] NF solidification

solidifier, se solidifier VT, VPR [sɔlidifje] ▸conjug 7◂ to solidify

solidité [sɔlidite] NF **a** (= *robustesse*) [*matériaux, construction, meuble*] solidity, sturdiness; [*outil*] solidity; **d'une ~ à toute épreuve** [*construction, meuble*] strong enough to resist anything **b** (= *stabilité*) [*institutions*] solidity, soundness; [*bases*] solidity, firmness, soundness; [*amitié, liens*] solidity, firmness; [*monnaie, économie*] strength; [*raisonnement*] soundness **c** (= *vigueur*) [*personne*] sturdiness, robustness; [*poigne, jambes, bras*] sturdiness, solidity

soliflore [sɔliflɔʀ] NM bud vase

soliloque [sɔlilɔk] NM soliloquy

soliloquer [sɔlilɔke] ▸conjug 1◂ VI to soliloquize

Soliman [sɔlimɑ̃] NM **~ le Magnifique** Suleiman the Magnificent

solipède [sɔliped] ADJ, NM solidungulate

solipsisme [sɔlipsism] NM solipsism

soliste [sɔlist] NMF soloist

solitaire [sɔlitɛʀ] **1** ADJ **a** (= *isolé*) [*passant*] solitary (*épith*), lone (*épith*); [*arbre, maison, rocher*] solitary (*épith*), lonely (*épith*), isolated; **là vivaient quelques chasseurs/bûcherons ~s** a few solitary ou lone hunters/woodcutters lived there **b** (= *désert*) [*chemin, demeure, parc*] lonely (*épith*), deserted **c** (= *sans compagnie*) [*adolescent, vieillard, vie*] solitary, lonely, lonesome (*US*); [*caractère, passe-temps*] solitary → **plaisir** **d** (*Bot*) [*fleur*] solitary → **ver** **2** NMF (= *ermite*) solitary person, recluse, hermit; (*fig* = *ours*) lone wolf, loner; **il préfère travailler en ~** he prefers to work on his own; **ascension/traversée en ~** solo climb/crossing; **course en ~** single-handed ou solo race; **partir/voyager en ~** to leave/travel alone ou on one's own; (*Naut*) **elle a fait le tour du monde en ~** she sailed single-handed ou solo around the world **3** NM **a** (= *sanglier*) old boar **b** (= *diamant*) solitaire **c** (= *jeu*) solitaire

solitairement [sɔlitɛʀmɑ̃] ADV [*souffrir*] alone; **vivre ~** to lead a solitary life

solitude [sɔlityd] NF **a** [*personne*] (= *tranquillité*) solitude; (= *manque de compagnie*) loneliness, lonesomeness (*US*); [*endroit*] loneliness; **~ morale** moral isolation; **la ~ à deux** shared solitude; **éprouver un sentiment de ~** to feel lonely; **dans les moments de grande ~** at times of great loneliness; **aimer la ~** to like being on one's own, like one's own company **b** (= *désert*) solitude; (*littér*) **les ~s glacées du Grand Nord** the icy solitudes ou wastes of the far North (*littér*)

solive [sɔliv] NF joist

sollicitation [sɔlisitasjɔ̃] NF [a] (= démarche) entreaty, appeal; **céder/répondre aux ~s de qn** to yield/respond to sb's entreaties [b] (littér: gén pl = tentation) solicitation (littér), enticement [c] (Tech = impulsion) prompting; **l'engin répondait aux moindres ~s de son pilote** the craft responded to the slightest touch (from the pilot)

solliciter [sɔlisite] ▶conjug 1◀ VT [a] (frm = demander) [+ poste, explication] to seek; [+ faveur, audience] to seek, solicit (frm) (**de qn** from sb) [b] (frm = faire appel à) [+ personne] to appeal to; **~ qn de faire qch** to appeal to sb ou request sb to do sth; **je l'ai déjà sollicité à plusieurs reprises à ce sujet** I have already appealed to him ou approached him on several occasions over this matter; **il est très sollicité** he's very much in demand [c] (= agir sur) [+ curiosité, sens de qn] to appeal to; [+ attention] to attract, solicit (frm); **les attractions qui sollicitent le touriste** the attractions that are there to tempt ou entice the tourist; **le moteur répondait immédiatement lorsque le pilote le sollicitait** the engine responded immediately to the pilot's touch; **~ un cheval** to urge a horse on

solliciteur, -euse [sɔlisitœR, øz] [1] NM,F suppliant [2] NM (Can) **~ général** Solicitor General

sollicitude [sɔlisityd] NF concern (NonC), solicitude (frm); **demander/dire qch avec ~** to ask/say sth solicitously ou with concern; **être ou se montrer plein de ~ envers qn** to be very attentive ou solicitous (frm) to(wards) sb; **toutes leurs ~s finissaient par nous agacer** we found their constant concern (for our welfare) ou their solicitude (frm) annoying in the end

solo [sɔlo] (pl **solos** ou **soli** [sɔli]) ADJ INV, NM solo; **~ de violon** violin solo; **violon/flûte ~** solo violin/flute; **jouer/chanter en ~** to play/sing a solo; **escalade en ~** solo climbing; **travailler en ~** to work on one's own; **il a décidé d'agir en ~** he decided to go it alone*; **(spectacle) ~** one-man (ou one-woman) show

sol-sol [sɔlsɔl] ADJ INV ground-to-ground

solstice [sɔlstis] NM solstice; **~ d'hiver/d'été** winter/summer solstice

solubiliser [sɔlybilize] ▶conjug 1◀ VT to make soluble

solubilité [sɔlybilite] NF solubility

soluble [sɔlybl] ADJ [a] [substance] soluble → **café** [b] [problème] soluble, solvable

soluté [sɔlyte] NM (Chim, Pharm) solution

solution [sɔlysjɔ̃] [1] NF [a] [problème, énigme, équation] (= action) solution, solving (**de** of); (= résultat) solution, answer (**de** to) [b] [difficulté, situation] (= issue) solution, answer (**de** to); (= moyens employés) solution (**de** to); **c'est une ~ de facilité** it's the easy way out; **ce n'est pas une ~ à la crise qu'ils traversent** that's no way to resolve the crisis they're in; **ce n'est pas une ~!** that won't solve anything!; **hâter la ~ d'une crise** to hasten the resolution ou settling of a crisis [c] (Chim = action, mélange) solution; **en ~** in solution [2] COMP ▶ **solution de continuité** (frm) solution of continuity (frm) ▶ **la solution finale** (Hist Pol) the Final Solution

solutionner [sɔlysjɔne] ▶conjug 1◀ VT to solve

solvabilité [sɔlvabilite] NF solvency, creditworthiness

solvable [sɔlvabl] ADJ solvent, creditworthy

solvant [sɔlvɑ̃] NM (Chim) solvent

soma [sɔma] NM soma

somali [sɔmali] [1] NM (Ling) Somali [2] **Somalis** NMPL Somalis

Somalie [sɔmali] NF (= région) Somaliland; (= État) Somalia

somalien, -ienne [sɔmaljɛ̃, jɛn] [1] ADJ Somalian [2] **Somalien(ne)** NM,F Somalian

somatique [sɔmatik] ADJ (Bio, Psych) somatic

somatisation [sɔmatizasjɔ̃] NF somatization

somatiser [sɔmatize] ▶conjug 1◀ VT to somatize; **il a tendance à ~** he tends to have psychosomatic problems

sombre [sɔ̃bR] ADJ [a] (= obscur, foncé) [ciel, nuit, pièce] dark; **il fait déjà ~** it's already dark; **bleu/vert ~** dark blue/green; (littér) **de ~s abîmes** dark abysses; (Myth) **le ~ empire** ◊ **les ~s rivages** the underworld, the nether world → **coupe²** [b] (= mélancolique) sombre (Brit), somber (US), gloomy, dismal; (= sinistre, funeste) [période] dark; **d'un air ~** sombrely (Brit), somberly (US), gloomily; **il avait le visage ~** he looked gloomy ou sombre; **de ~s pensées** sombre ou gloomy ou dark thoughts; **un ~ avenir** a dark ou gloomy ou dismal future; **les moments ou heures ~s de notre histoire** the dark moments in our history [c] (*: valeur intensive) **~ idiot/brute** absolute idiot/brute; **une ~ histoire de meurtre** a dark tale of murder; **ils se sont disputés pour une ~ histoire d'argent** they argued over a sordid financial matter [d] (Phon) [voyelle] dark

sombrement [sɔ̃bR(ə)mɑ̃] ADV [dire] sombrely (Brit), somberly (US), gloomily

sombrer [sɔ̃bRe] ▶conjug 1◀ VI [bateau] to sink, go down, founder; [empire] to founder; [fortune] to be swallowed up; [entreprise] to collapse; **sa raison a sombré** he has lost his reason, his mind has gone; **~ dans** [+ désespoir, sommeil, misère, alcool, oubli] to sink into; **évitons de ~ dans le sordide** let's not get sordid

sombrero [sɔ̃bRero] NM sombrero

sommaire [sɔmɛR] [1] ADJ [a] (= court) [exposé, explication] basic, summary (épith), brief; [réponse] brief, summary (épith); (= expéditif) [justice, procédure, exécution] summary (épith) [b] (= rudimentaire, superficiel) [connaissances, éducation] basic; [examen] brief, cursory, perfunctory; [analyse, description] brief, cursory; [instruction, réparation, repas] basic; [décoration] minimal [2] NM (= exposé) summary; (= résumé de chapitre) summary, argument; [revue] (table of) contents; **au ~ du numéro spécial** appearing in ou featured in the special issue; **au ~ de notre émission ce soir ...** in our programme tonight ...

sommairement [sɔmɛRmɑ̃] ADV [a] [exposer, juger, exécuter] summarily; **il me l'a expliqué assez ~** he gave me a fairly basic explanation of it [b] (= rudimentairement) [réparer] superficially; [meubler] basically

sommation¹ [sɔmasjɔ̃] NF (Jur) summons sg; (frm = injonction) demand; (avant de faire feu) warning; (Jur) **recevoir ~ de payer une dette** to be served notice to pay a debt; (Mil, Police) **faire les ~s d'usage** to give the standard ou customary warnings; **tirer sans ~** to shoot without warning

sommation² [sɔmasjɔ̃] NF (Math, Physiol) summation

somme¹ [sɔm] NF → **bête**

somme² [sɔm] NM (= sieste) nap, snooze; **faire un petit ~** to have a (short) nap ou a (little) snooze ou forty winks*

▼ **somme³** [sɔm] NF [a] (Math) sum; (= quantité) amount; **~ algébrique** algebraic sum; **la ~ totale** the grand total, the sum total; **faire la ~ de** to add up; **la ~ des dégâts est considérable** the (total) amount of damage ou the total damage is considerable; **une ~ de travail énorme** an enormous amount of work [b] (= d'argent) sum ou amount (of money); **dépenser des ~s folles*** to spend vast amounts ou sums of money; (intensif) **c'est une ~!** it's quite a sum!; **payer/toucher/atteindre une ~ de 1 000 F** to pay/get/fetch 1,000 francs; **pour la coquette ~ de 10 millions de francs** for the tidy sum of 10 million francs [c] (= ouvrage de synthèse) comprehensive sur-

vey; **une ~ littéraire/scientifique** a comprehensive survey of literature/of science [d] (loc) **en ~** (= tout bien considéré) all in all; (= bref) in short; **en ~, il ne s'agit que d'un incident sans importance** in fact, it's only an incident of minor importance; **en ~, vous n'en voulez plus?** in short, you don't want any more?; (frm) **~ toute** when all is said and done

sommeil [sɔmɛj] NM [a] (= fait de dormir) sleep; (= envie de dormir) drowsiness, sleepiness; **avoir ~** to be ou feel sleepy; **tomber de ~** to be asleep on one's feet, be ready ou fit to drop*; **chercher le ~** to try to sleep; **il ne pouvait pas trouver le ~** he couldn't get to sleep; **un ~ agréable l'envahissait** he was beginning to feel pleasantly sleepy; **huit heures de ~** eight hours' sleep; **avoir le ~ léger/profond** to be a light/heavy sleeper, sleep lightly/deeply; **avoir un bon ~** to be a sound sleeper; **dormir d'un ~ agité** to sleep fitfully; **un ~ profond** ou **de plomb** a heavy ou deep sleep; **le ~ paradoxal** REM sleep; **premier ~** first hours of sleep; **nuit sans ~** sleepless night; **être en plein ~** to be fast asleep; **la sonnerie du téléphone l'a tirée de son ~** she was woken (up) by the phone ringing; **il en a perdu le ~** he lost sleep over it; (littér) **le ~ éternel** ◊ **le dernier ~** eternal rest; (littér) **le ~ des morts** the sleep of the dead → **cure¹**, **dormir**, **maladie** [b] (= inactivité) **le ~ de la nature** nature's sleep (littér), the dormant state of nature; **laisser une affaire en ~** to leave a matter (lying) dormant, leave a matter in abeyance; **le ~ de la petite ville pendant l'hiver** the sleepiness of the little town during winter

sommeiller [sɔmeje] ▶conjug 1◀ VI [personne] to doze; [qualité, défaut, nature] to lie dormant → **cochon**

sommelier [sɔməlje] NM wine waiter

sommelière [sɔməljɛR] NF (= caviste) wine waitress; (Helv = serveuse) waitress

sommer¹ [sɔme] ▶conjug 1◀ VT (frm = enjoindre) **~ qn de faire qch** to command ou enjoin sb to do sth (frm); (Jur) **~ qn de** ou **à comparaître** to summon sb to appear

sommer² [sɔme] ▶conjug 1◀ VT (= additionner) to add

sommet [sɔme] NM [a] (= point culminant) [montagne] summit, top; [tour, arbre, toit, pente, hiérarchie] top; [vague] crest; [crâne] crown, vertex (SPÉC); [angle] vertex; [solide, figure, parabole] vertex, apex; (Méd) **présentation du ~** vertex presentation; **au ~ de l'échelle sociale** at the top of the social ladder; **les ~s de la gloire/des honneurs** the summits ou heights of fame/of honour; (littér, hum) **redescendons de ces ~s** let us climb down from these lofty heights (littér, hum) [b] (= cime, montagne) summit, mountain top; **l'air pur des ~s** the pure air of the summits ou the mountain tops [c] (Pol) summit; **au ~** (= réunion, discussions) summit (épith) → **conférence**

sommier [sɔmje] NM [a] [lit] **~ (à ressorts)** ◊ **~ tapissier** (s'encastrant dans le lit, fixé au lit) springing (NonC) (Brit), springs (of bedstead); (avec pieds) bed base, box springs (US); **~ (métallique)** mesh-springing (Brit), mesh-sprung bed base, mesh springs (US); **~ à lattes** slatted bed base; **~ extra-plat** metal-framed bed base [b] (Tech) [voûte] impost, springer; [clocher] stock; [porte, fenêtre] transom; [grille] lower crossbar; [orgue] windchest [c] (= registre) ledger

sommité [sɔ(m)mite] NF [a] (= personne) prominent person, leading light (**de** in); **les ~s du monde médical** leading medical experts [b] (Bot) head

somnambule [sɔmnɑ̃byl] [1] NMF sleepwalker, somnambulist (SPÉC); **marcher/agir comme un ~** to walk/act like a sleepwalker ou as if in

➤ GRAMMAIRE ACTIVE: **somme** 47.5

a trance [2] ADJ **être ~** to be a sleepwalker, sleepwalk

somnambulisme [sɔmnɑ̃bylism] NM sleep-walking, somnambulism (*SPÉC*)

somnifère [sɔmnifɛʀ] [1] NM sleeping drug, soporific; (= *pilule*) sleeping pill, sleeping tablet [2] ADJ somniferous (*frm*), sleep-inducing, soporific

somnolence [sɔmnɔlɑ̃s] NF [*personne*] sleepiness (*NonC*), drowsiness (*NonC*), somnolence (*NonC*) (*frm*); [*marché, économie*] sluggishness; **être dans un état de ~** to be in a drowsy state; « **risques de ~ attachés à ce médicament** » "this medicine can cause drowsiness"

somnolent, e [sɔmnɔlɑ̃, ɑ̃t] ADJ [*personne*] sleepy, drowsy, somnolent (*frm*); [*vie, province*] sleepy; [*faculté*] dormant, inert

somnoler [sɔmnɔle] ▸ conjug 1 ◂ VI [*personne*] to doze; [*ville*] to be sleepy; [*économie, marché*] to be sluggish

somptuaire [sɔ̃ptɥɛʀ] ADJ [a] [*loi, réforme*] sumptuary [b] [*projet, dépenses*] extravagant

somptueusement [sɔ̃ptɥøzmɑ̃] ADV [*décorer, meubler*] sumptuously, lavishly; [*illustrer*] lavishly; **il nous a reçus** he received us royally

somptueux, -euse [sɔ̃ptɥø, øz] ADJ [*habit, résidence, palais, décor*] sumptuous, magnificent; [*train de vie, illustration*] lavish; [*cadeau*] handsome, lavish; [*repas, festin*] sumptuous, lavish; **tu es somptueuse ce soir** you look magnificent tonight

somptuosité [sɔ̃ptɥozite] NF [*habit, résidence*] sumptuousness, magnificence; [*train de vie*] lavishness; [*cadeau*] handsomeness, sumptuousness; [*repas, festin*] sumptuousness, lavishness; **impressionné par la ~ des images** impressed by the sumptuous images

son¹ [sɔ̃], **sa** [sa] (*pl* **ses** [se]) ADJ POSS [a] (*homme*) his; (*emphatique*) his own; (*femme*) her; (*emphatique*) her own; (*nation*) its, her; (*emphatique*) its own, her own; **Son Altesse Royale** (*prince*) His Royal Highness; (*princesse*) Her Royal Highness; **Sa Majesté** (*roi*) His Majesty; (*reine*) Her Majesty; **Sa Sainteté le pape** His Holiness the Pope; **ce n'est pas ~ genre** he (*ou* she) is not that sort, it's not like him (*ou* her); **quand s'est passé ~ accident ?** when did he have his accident?; **~ père et sa mère** ◊ **ses père et mère** his (*ou* her) father and (his *ou* her) mother; (*emphatique*) **~ jardin à lui/à elle est une vraie jungle** his *ou* his own/her *ou* her own garden is a real jungle; **ses date et lieu de naissance** his (*ou* her) date and place of birth; **à sa vue, elle poussa un cri** she screamed at the sight of him (*ou* her); **un de ses amis** one of his (*ou* her) friends, a friend of his (*ou* hers); **~ idiote de sœur*** that stupid sister of his (*ou* hers) [b] [*objet, abstraction*] its; **l'hôtel est réputé pour sa cuisine** the hotel is famous for its food; **pour comprendre ce crime il faut chercher ~ mobile** to understand this crime we must try to find the motive; **ça a ~ importance** it has its *ou* a certain importance [c] (*à valeur d'indéfini*) one's; (*après chacun, personne*) his, her; **faire ses études** to study; **on ne connaît pas ~ bonheur** one never knows how fortunate one is, you never know how fortunate you are; **être satisfait de sa situation** to be satisfied with one's situation; **chacun selon ses possibilités** each according to his (*own*) capabilities; **personne ne sait comment finira sa vie** no-one knows how his *ou* their life will end; **quelqu'un a-t-il oublié sa veste ?** has someone left their jacket? [d] (** : valeur affective, ironique, intensive*) **il doit (bien) gagner ~ million par an** he must be (easily) earning a million a year; **avoir ~ samedi/dimanche** to have (one's) Saturday(s)/Sunday(s) off; **il a passé tout ~ dimanche à travailler** he spent the whole of ou all Sunday working; **~ M. Dupont ne me plaît pas du tout** I don't care for his (*ou* her) Mr Dupont at all;

avoir ses petites manies to have one's funny little ways; **elle a ses jours !** she has her (good and bad) days!; **il a sa crise de foie** he is having one of his bilious attacks; **cet enfant ne ferme jamais ses portes** that child never shuts the door behind him; **alors, on est content de revoir ses camarades ?** so, are you happy to see your friends again? → **sentir**

son² [sɔ̃] NM [a] (*gén, Ling, Phys*) sound; **~ articulé/inarticulé** articulate/inarticulate sound; **le timbre et la hauteur du ~ d'une cloche/d'un tambour/d'un avertisseur** the tone and pitch of (the sound of) a bell/of a drum/ of an alarm; **réveillé par le ~ des cloches/ tambours/klaxons** woken by the sound of bells/drums/horns, woken by the ringing of bells/the beat of drums/the blare of horns; **défiler au ~ d'une fanfare** to march past to the sound of a band; **elle dansait au ~ de l'accordéon** she was dancing to the accordion; **elle tressaillit au ~ de sa voix** she started at the sound of his voice; **proclamer qch à ~ de trompe** to proclaim sth from the rooftops *ou* the housetops; (*fig*) **n'entendre qu'un/ entendre un autre ~ de cloche** to hear only one/another side of the story; **j'aimerais bien entendre un autre ~ de cloche** I'd like to have a second opinion; **même ~ de cloche chez les patrons/à l'ambassade** the bosses are/the embassy is telling the same story; **c'est un autre ~ de cloche** that's quite another story ◼ (*PROV*) **qui n'entend qu'une cloche n'entend qu'un ~** you should always get both sides of the story [b] (*Ciné, Radio, TV*) sound; **baisser le ~** to turn down the sound *ou* volume; **équipe/ingénieur du ~** sound team/engineer; **synchroniser le ~ et l'image** to synchronize the sound and the picture; (*spectacle*) **~ et lumière** son et lumière (*show*) → **numérique, stéréo**

son³ [sɔ̃] NM (*Bot*) bran; **farine de ~** bran flour → **pain, poupée, tache**

sonar [sɔnaʀ] NM sonar

sonate [sɔnat] NF sonata; **~s pour piano** sonatas, sonatas for piano

sonatine [sɔnatin] NF sonatina

sondage [sɔ̃daʒ] NM [a] (= *enquête*) (*succincte*) poll; (*approfondie*) survey; **~ d'opinion** opinion poll; **~ par téléphone** telephone poll; **il remonte/baisse dans les ~s** he is going up again/down in the polls; **faire un ~** to take a poll, conduct a survey (*auprès de* among); **procéder par ~** to do a spot check → **institut** [b] (*Tech = forage*) boring, drilling; (*Mét, Naut*) sounding; (*Méd*) probing (*NonC*), probe; (*pour évacuer*) catheterization; **puits de ~** borehole

sonde [sɔ̃d] NF [a] (*Naut*) (= *instrument*) lead line, sounding line; (= *relevé : gén pl*) soundings; **naviguer à la ~** to navigate by soundings; **jeter une ~** to cast the lead → **île** [b] (*Tech : de forage*) borer, drill [c] (*Méd*) probe; (*à canal central*) catheter; (*d'alimentation*) feeding tube; **mettre une ~ à qn** to put a catheter in sb; **alimenter un malade avec une ~** to feed a patient through a tube [d] (*Aviat, Mét*) sonde; **~ aérienne** sounding balloon; **~ atmosphérique** sonde; **~ moléculaire/spatiale** molecular/space probe [e] (*Douane : pour fouiller*) probe; (*Comm : pour prélever*) taster; (*à avalanche*) pole (*for locating victims*); **~ à fromage** cheese taster

sondé, e [sɔ̃de] NM,F *person taking part in an opinion poll*; **la majorité des ~s était pour** the majority of those polled were in favour of the idea

sonder [sɔ̃de] ▸ conjug 1 ◂ VT [a] (*Naut*) to sound; (*Tech*) [+ *terrain*] to bore, drill; [+ *bagages*] to probe, search (*with a probe*); [+ *avalanche*] to probe; (*Méd*) [+ *plaie*] to probe; [+ *vessie, malade*] to catheterize; **~ l'atmosphère** to make soundings in the atmosphere; (*littér*) **il sonda l'abîme du regard** his eyes probed the depths of the abyss [b] (*fig*)

[+ *personne*] (*gén*) to sound out; (*par sondage d'opinion*) to poll; [+ *conscience, avenir*] to sound out, probe; **je l'ai sondé sur ses intentions** I sounded him out, I asked him what his intentions were; **~ les esprits** to sound out opinion; **~ l'opinion** to make a survey of (*public*) opinion → **terrain**

sondeur, -euse [sɔ̃dœʀ, øz] [1] NM (*Tech*) sounder [2] NM,F [*sondage d'opinion*] pollster

songe [sɔ̃ʒ] NM (*littér*) dream; **en ~** in a dream; **faire un ~** to have a dream ◼ (*PROV*) **~, mensonge** dreams are just illusions

songe-creux† [sɔ̃ʒkʀø] NM INV (*littér*) visionary

▼ **songer** [sɔ̃ʒe] ▸ conjug 3 ◂ [1] VI (*littér* = *rêver*) to dream

[2] VT **~ que ...** to reflect *ou* consider that ...; **ils pourraient refuser, songeait-il** they could refuse, he reflected *ou* mused; **songez que cela peut présenter de grands dangers** remember *ou* you must be aware that it can be very dangerous; **il n'avait jamais songé qu'ils puissent réussir** he had never imagined they might be successful; **cela me fait ~ que je voulais lui téléphoner** that reminds me — I wanted to phone him; **songez donc !** just imagine! *ou* think!

[3] **songer à** VT INDIR (= *considérer*) to consider, think about; **~ à se marier** *ou* **au mariage** to contemplate marriage, think of getting married; **j'y ai sérieusement songé** I gave it some serious thought; **elle songe sérieusement à s'expatrier** she's seriously thinking about *ou* considering going to live abroad; **songez-y** think it over, give it some thought; **il ne songe qu'à son avancement** all he thinks about is his own advancement; **quand on songe à tout ce gaspillage** when you think of all this waste; **il ne faut pas y ~** ◊ **inutile d'y ~** it's no use (even) thinking about it; **vous n'y songez pas !** you must be joking!, you're not serious!; **vous me faites ~ à mon frère** you remind me of my brother → **mal 3e**

songerie [sɔ̃ʒʀi] NF (*littér*) reverie

songeur, -euse [sɔ̃ʒœʀ, øz] [1] ADJ pensive; **cela me laisse ~** I just don't know what to think [2] NM,F dreamer

sonique [sɔnik] ADJ [*vitesse*] sonic; **barrière ~** sound barrier

sonnaille [sɔnaj] NF (= *cloche*) bell; (= *bruit*) ringing (*NonC*)

sonnant, e [sɔnɑ̃, ɑ̃t] ADJ [a] (= *précis*) **à 4 heures ~es** on the stroke of 4, at 4 (o'clock) sharp [b] [*horloge*] chiming, striking [c] [*voix*] resonant → **espèce**

sonné, e [sɔne] (*ptp de* **sonner**) ADJ [a] (= *annoncé*) **il est midi ~** it's past *ou* gone (*Brit*) twelve; (= *révolu*) **avoir trente ans bien ~s** to be on the wrong side of thirty* [b] (‡ = *fou*) cracked*, off one's rocker‡ (*attrib*) [c] (* = *assommé*) groggy

▼ **sonner** [sɔne] ▸ conjug 1 ◂ [1] VT [a] [+ *cloche*] to ring; [+ *tocsin, glas*] to sound, toll; [+ *clairon*] to sound; **~ trois coups à la porte** to ring three times at the door; **se faire ~ les cloches*** to get a good telling-off* *ou* ticking-off* (*Brit*); **~ les cloches à qn*** to give sb a roasting* *ou* a telling-off* [b] (= *annoncer*) [+ *messe, matines*] to ring the bell for; [+ *réveil, rassemblement, retraite*] to sound; **~ l'alarme** to sound the alarm; (*Mil*) **~ la charge** to sound the charge; **~ l'heure** to strike the hour; **la pendule sonnait 3 heures** the clock was striking 3 (o'clock) [c] (= *appeler*) [+ *portier, infirmière*] to ring for; **on ne t'a pas sonné !*** nobody asked you! [d] (= *étourdir*) [*chute, grippe*] to knock out; [*nouvelle*] to stagger*, take aback; **la nouvelle l'a un peu sonné** he was rather taken aback by the news [2] VI [a] [*cloches, téléphone*] to ring; [*réveil*] to go off; [*clairon*] to sound; [*tocsin, glas*] to sound, toll; **elle a mis le réveil à ~ pour** *ou* **à 7 heures** she set the alarm for 7 o'clock; (*Scol*) **la cloche a sonné** the bell has gone *ou* rung; **~ à toute volée** to peal (out); **les oreilles lui sonnent** his ears are ringing

b (*son métallique*) [*marteau*] to ring; [*clés, monnaie*] to jangle, jingle; **~ clair** to give a clear ring; **~ creux** (*lit*) to sound hollow; [*discours*] to have a hollow ring, ring hollow; **~ faux** (*lit*) to sound out of tune; [*rire, paroles*] to ring *ou* sound false; **~ juste** (*lit*) to sound in tune; [*déclaration*] to ring true; (*fig*) **~ bien/mal** to sound good/bad; **ce prénom sonne bien à l'oreille** that name has a nice ring to it, it's a nice-sounding name; **l'argent sonna sur le comptoir** the money clattered onto the counter

c (= *être annoncé*) [*midi, minuit*] to strike; **3 heures venaient de ~** it had just struck 3 o'clock, 3 o'clock had just struck; **la récréation a sonné** the bell has gone for break; **la messe sonne** the bells are ringing *ou* going for mass → **heure**

d (= *actionner une sonnette*) to ring; **on a sonné** the bell has just gone, I just heard the bell, somebody just rang (the bell); **~ chez qn** to ring at sb's door, ring sb's doorbell; **« ~ avant d'entrer »** "please ring before you enter"

e **faire ~** [+ *nom, mot*] to say in a resonant voice

3 sonner de VT INDIR [+ *clairon, cor*] to sound

sonnerie [sɔnʀi] NF **a** (= *son*) [*sonnette, cloches*] ringing; **la ~ du clairon** the bugle call, the sound of the bugle; **j'ai entendu la ~ du téléphone** I heard the telephone ringing; **la ~ du téléphone l'a réveillé** he was woken by the telephone (ringing); **elle sursautait à chaque ~ du téléphone** she jumped every time the phone rang; **~ d'alarme** alarm bell **b** (*Mil = air*) call; **la ~ du réveil** (the sounding of) reveille; **la ~ aux morts** the last post **c** (= *mécanisme*) [*réveil*] alarm (mechanism), bell; [*pendule*] chimes, chiming *ou* striking mechanism; (= *sonnette*) bell; **~ électrique/téléphonique** electric/telephone bell

sonnet [sɔnɛ] NM sonnet

sonnette [sɔnɛt] NF **a** (*électrique, de porte*) bell; (= *clochette*) (hand) bell; **coup de ~** ring; **je n'ai pas entendu le coup de ~** I didn't hear the bell (ring); **~ de nuit** night bell; **~ d'alarme** alarm bell; (*fig*) **tirer la ~ d'alarme** to set off *ou* sound the alarm (bell); **tirer les ~s** (*jeu d'enfants*) to ring doorbells (and run away); (*fig = démarcher*) to go knocking on doors → **serpent** [*Tech*] pile driver

sonneur [sɔnœʀ] NM **a** [*cloches*] bell ringer **b** (*Tech*) pile driver operator

sono* [sɔno] NF (ABRÉV = *sonorisation*) [*salle de conférences*] P.A. (system); [*discothèque*] sound system; **la ~ est trop forte** the sound's too loud

sonore [sɔnɔʀ] **1** ADJ **a** [*objet, surface en métal*] resonant; [*voix*] ringing (*épith*), sonorous, resonant; [*rire*] ringing (*épith*), resounding (*épith*); [*baiser, gifle*] resounding (*épith*) **b** [*salle*] resonant; [*voûte*] echoing **c** (*péj*) [*paroles, mots*] high-sounding, sonorous **d** (*Acoustique*) [*niveau, onde, vibrations*] sound (*épith*); **fond ~** (= *bruits*) background noise; (= *musique*) background music **e** (*Ciné*) [*film, effets*] sound (*épith*); **bande** *ou* **piste ~** soundtrack **f** (*Ling*) voiced **2** NF (*Ling*) voiced consonant

sonorisation [sɔnɔʀizasjɔ̃] NF **a** (*Ciné*) adding the soundtrack (**de** to), dubbing (**de** of) **b** (= *action*) [*salle de conférences*] fitting with a public address system; [*discothèque*] fitting with a sound system; (= *équipement*) [*salle de conférences*] public address system, P.A. (system); [*discothèque*] sound system **c** (*Phon*) voicing

sonoriser [sɔnɔʀize] ▶conjug 1◀ VT **a** [+ *film*] to add the soundtrack to, dub; [+ *salle de con-*

férences] to fit with a public address system *ou* a P.A. (system) **b** (*Phon*) to voice

sonorité [sɔnɔʀite] NF **a** (= *timbre, son*) [*radio, instrument de musique*] tone; [*voix*] sonority, tone; **~s** [*voix, instrument*] tones **b** (*Ling*) voicing **c** (= *résonance*) [*air*] sonority, resonance; [*salle*] acoustics *sg*; [*cirque rocheux, grotte*] resonance

sonothèque [sɔnɔtɛk] NF sound (effects) library

sonotone® [sɔnɔtɔn] NM hearing aid

sophisme [sɔfism] NM sophism

sophiste [sɔfist] NMF sophist

sophistication [sɔfistikasjɔ̃] NF sophistication; († = *altération*) adulteration

sophistique [sɔfistik] **1** ADJ sophistic **2** NF sophistry

sophistiqué, e [sɔfistike] (*ptp de* **sophistiquer**) ADJ (*gén*) sophisticated; († = *altéré*) adulterated

sophistiquer [sɔfistike] ▶conjug 1◀ **1** VT (= *raffiner*) to make (more) sophisticated; († = *altérer*) to adulterate **2 se sophistiquer** VPR to become (more) sophisticated

Sophocle [sɔfɔkl] NM Sophocles

sophrologie [sɔfʀɔlɔʒi] NF relaxation therapy

sophrologue [sɔfʀɔlɔg] NMF relaxation therapist

soporifique [sɔpɔʀifik] **1** ADJ (*lit*) soporific, sleep-inducing; (*fig péj*) soporific **2** NM sleeping drug, soporific

soprane [sɔpʀan] NMF = **soprano 3**

sopraniste [sɔpʀanist] NM (male) soprano

soprano [sɔpʀano] (*pl* **sopranos** *ou* **soprani** [sɔpʀani]) **1** ADJ **saxophone ~** soprano saxophone **2** NM (= *voix*) soprano (voice); (= *voix d'enfant*) soprano, treble **3** NMF (= *personne*) soprano; **~ dramatique/lyrique** dramatic/lyric soprano

sorbe [sɔʀb] NF sorb (apple)

sorbet [sɔʀbɛ] NM sorbet, water ice (*Brit*), sherbet (*US*); **~ au citron/à l'orange** lemon/orange sorbet

sorbetière [sɔʀbətjɛʀ] NF ice cream maker

sorbier [sɔʀbje] NM service tree, sorb; **~ des oiseleurs** European mountain ash, rowan tree

sorbitol [sɔʀbitɔl] NM sorbitol

sorbonnard, e [sɔʀbɔnaʀ, aʀd] (*péj*) **1** ADJ pedantic **2** NM,F *student or teacher at the Sorbonne*

sorcellerie [sɔʀsɛlʀi] NF witchcraft, sorcery; **c'est de la ~ !** it's magic!

sorcier [sɔʀsje] **1** NM (*lit*) sorcerer; (*fig*) **il ne faut pas être ~ pour ...** you don't have to be a wizard to ... → **apprenti 2** ADJ **ce n'est pas ~ !** it's dead easy!*

sorcière [sɔʀsjɛʀ] NF witch, sorceress; (*péj*) **vieille ~ !** old witch! *ou* hag! → **chasse¹**

sordide [sɔʀdid] ADJ **a** [*ruelle, quartier, hôtel, banlieue*] sordid, squalid; **des conditions de vie ~s** squalid living conditions **b** [*action, mentalité, avarice, égoïsme*] base; [*crime, querelle, affaire*] sordid; **le ~ de la situation** the sordidness of the situation; **épargnez-moi les détails ~s** spare me the sordid details

sordidement [sɔʀdidmã] ADV [*vivre*] in squalor; [*agir*] basely; **il a fini ~** he came to a squalid *ou* sordid end

sorgho [sɔʀgo] NM sorghum

Sorlingues [sɔʀlɛ̃g] NFPL **les (îles) ~** the Scilly Isles, the Isles of Scilly, the Scillies

sornettes† [sɔʀnɛt] NFPL twaddle, balderdash; **~ !** fiddlesticks!

sort [sɔʀ] NM **a** (= *condition*) lot; **être content** *ou* **satisfait de son ~** to be happy with one's lot (in life); **améliorer le ~ des pauvres/handicapés** to improve the lot of the poor/the handicapped; **envier le ~ de qn** to envy sb's lot

b (= *destinée*) fate; **le ~ qui l'attend** the fate that awaits him; (*hum*) **abandonner qn à son triste ~** to abandon sb to his sad fate; **sa proposition a eu** *ou* **subi le même ~ que les précédentes** his proposal met with the same fate as the previous ones; **le ~ décidera** fate will decide; **pour essayer de conjurer le (mauvais) ~** to try to ward off fate; **c'est un coup du ~** it's a stroke of fate; **faire un ~ à** (= *mettre en valeur*) to stress, emphasize; (* = *se débarrasser de*) to get rid of, get shot of* (*Brit*); [+ *plat, bouteille*] to polish off* → **caprice, ironie**

c (= *hasard*) fate; **le ~ est tombé sur lui** he was chosen by fate, it fell to him; **le ~ en est jeté** the die is cast; **tirer au ~** to draw lots; **tirer qch au ~** to draw lots for sth → **tirage**

d (= *sorcellerie*) spell; (= *malédiction*) curse; **il y a un ~ sur qn** there is a curse on sb; **jeter un ~ à** *ou* **sur qn** to put *ou* cast a spell on, put a curse *ou* jinx* on sb

sortable* [sɔʀtabl] ADJ (*gén nég*) [*personne*] presentable; **tu n'es pas ~ !** we (*ou* I) can't take you anywhere!

sortant, e [sɔʀtã, ãt] **1** ADJ [*député, maire*] outgoing (*épith*); **les numéros ~s** the numbers which come up **2** NM (= *personne : gén pl*) **les ~s** (*gén*) the outgoing crowd; (*Pol*) the outgoing deputies

sorte [sɔʀt] NF **a** (= *espèce*) sort, kind; **toutes ~s de gens/choses** all kinds *ou* sorts *ou* manner of people/things; **des vêtements de toutes (les) ~s** all kinds *ou* sorts *ou* manner of clothes; **nous avons trois ~s de fleurs** we have three kinds *ou* types *ou* sorts of flower(s); **des roches de même ~** rocks of the same sort *ou* kind *ou* type

b **une ~ de** a sort *ou* kind of; (*péj*) **une ~ de médecin/voiture** a doctor/car of sorts; **robe taillée dans une ~ de satin** dress cut out of some sort *ou* kind of satin

c (*loc*) **de la ~** (= *de cette façon*) in that way; **accoutré de la ~** dressed in that way; **il n'a rien fait de la ~** he did nothing of the kind *ou* no such thing; **de ~ à** so as to, in order to; **en quelque ~** in a way, as it were; **vous avouez l'avoir dit, en quelque ~** you are in a way *ou* as it were admitting to having said it; **en aucune ~†** not at all, not in the least; **de (telle) ~ que** ◊ **en ~ que** (*littér*) (= *de façon à ce que*) so that, in such a way that; (= *si bien que*) so much so that; **faites en ~ d'avoir fini demain** see to it *ou* arrange it *ou* arrange things so that you finish tomorrow; **faire en ~ que** to see to it that

sortie [sɔʀti] **1** NF **a** (= *action, moment*) [*personne*] exit; [*véhicule, bateau, armée occupante*] departure; (*Mil* = *mission*) sortie; (*Théât*) exit; **elle attend la ~ des artistes** she's waiting for the performers to come out; **à sa ~, tous se sont tus** when he went out *ou* left everybody fell silent; **à sa ~ du salon** when he went out of *ou* left the lounge; **il a fait une ~ remarquée** he made a dramatic exit; **il a fait une ~ discrète** he made a discreet exit, he left discreetly; (*Aviat, Mil*) **faire une ~** to make a sortie; **faire une ~ dans l'espace** to take *ou* make a space walk; (*Mil*) **tenter une ~** to attempt a sortie; **les sauveteurs ont fait 30 ~s en mer cette semaine** the lifeboatmen were called out 30 times this week; **la ~ des classes est fixée au 29 juin** the schools will close for the summer on 29th June; **à la ~ des ouvriers/bureaux/théâtres** when the workers/offices/theatres come out; **sa mère l'attend tous les jours à la ~ de l'école** his mother waits for him every day after school *ou* when school comes out *ou* finishes; **retrouvons-nous à la ~ (du concert)** let's meet at the end (of the concert); **à sa ~ de prison** when he comes (*ou* came) out of prison; **c'est sa première ~ depuis sa maladie** it's the first time he's been out since his illness; (*Théât*) **elle a**

manqué sa ~ à l'acte **2** she missed *ou* fluffed (*Brit*) her exit in act 2 → **faux²**

b (= *fin*) end; **à la ~ de l'enfance** at the end of childhood; **à la ~ de l'hiver** at the end of winter

c (= *congé*) day off; (= *promenade*) outing; (*le soir : au théâtre, au cinéma etc*) evening *ou* night out; **c'est le jour de ~ de la bonne** it's the maid's day off; **c'est le jour de ~ des pensionnaires** it's the boarders' day out; **il est de ~** [*soldat, domestique*] it's his day off; **nous sommes de ~ ce soir** we're going out tonight, we're having an evening out tonight; **ils viennent déjeuner le dimanche, cela leur fait une petite ~** they come to lunch on Sundays — it gives them a little outing *ou* it's a day out for them; **elle s'est acheté une robe du soir pour leurs ~s** she's bought herself an evening dress for when they go out *ou* have a night out; **faire une ~ en mer** to go on a boat trip (*at sea*); (*Scol*) **~ éducative** *ou* **scolaire** field-trip, school outing (*Brit*), school visit (*Brit*)

d (= *lieu*) exit, way out; **~ d'autoroute** motorway exit (*Brit*), highway exit (*US*); **~ de métro** metro exit, underground (*Brit*) *ou* subway (*US*) exit; **~ de secours** emergency exit; **~ des artistes** stage door; **« attention, ~ d'usine »** "caution, factory entrance *ou* exit"; **« ~ de camions »** "vehicle exit"; **garé devant la ~ de l'école** parked in front of the school gates *ou* entrance; **sa maison se trouve à la ~ du village** his house is at the edge of the village *ou* just as you come out of the village; **les ~s de Paris sont encombrées** the roads out of Paris are jammed; **par ici la ~!** this way out!; (*fig*) **trouver une (porte de) ~** to find a way out; **il faut se ménager une (porte de) ~** you must try to leave yourself a way out

e (= *écoulement*) [*eau, gaz*] outflow; **cela empêche la ~ des gaz** it prevents the gases from coming out *ou* escaping

f (= *emportement*) outburst; (= *remarque drôle*) sally; (= *remarque incongrue*) peculiar *ou* odd remark; **elle est sujette à ce genre de ~** she's given to that kind of outburst; **faire une ~ à qn** to let fly at sb; **faire une ~ contre qch/qn** to lash out against sth/sb

g (*Comm* = *mise en vente*) [*voiture, modèle*] launching; [*livre*] appearance, publication; [*disque, film*] release; **à la ~ du livre** when the book comes (*ou* came) out

h (*Comm*) [*marchandises, devises*] export; **~ (de capitaux)** outflow (of capital); **la ~ de l'or/des devises/de certains produits est contingentée** there are controls on gold/currency/certain products leaving the country *ou* on the export of gold/currency/certain products; **il y a eu d'importantes ~s de devises** large amounts of currency have been flowing out of *ou* leaving the country

i (*Comm, Fin* = *somme dépensée*) item of expenditure; **il y a eu plus de ~s que de rentrées** there have been more outgoings than receipts; **~s de caisse** cash payments

j (*Ordin*) output, readout; **~ (sur) imprimante** print-out

k (*Sport*) **~ en touche** going into touch; **il y a ~ en touche si le ballon touche la ligne** the ball is in touch *ou* has gone into touch if it touches the line; (*Rugby*) **ils ont marqué l'essai sur une ~ de mêlée** they scored a try straight out of the scrum; (*Ftbl*) **le ballon est allé en ~ de but** the ball has gone into touch behind the back line; **faire une ~** [*gardien de but*] to leave the goalmouth, come out of goal; **lors de la dernière ~ de l'équipe de France contre l'Angleterre** when France last played (against) England; (*Aut*) **faire une ~ de route** to go off the track

2 COMP ► **sortie de bain** bathrobe

sortilège [sɔʀtilɛʒ] NM (magic) spell

sortir¹ [sɔʀtiʀ] ► conjug 16 ◄ **1** VI (*avec aux être*)
a [*personne*] (*aller*) to go out, leave; (*venir*) to

come out, leave; (*à pied*) to walk out; (*en voiture*) to drive out, go *ou* come out; [*véhicule*] to drive out, go *ou* come out; (*Ordin*) to exit, log out; (*Théât*) to exit, leave (the stage); **~ en voiture/à bicyclette** to go out for a drive/a cycle ride, go out in one's car/on one's bike; **~ en courant** to run out; **~ en boitant** to limp out; **~ par la porte/par la fenêtre** to go *ou* get out *ou* leave by the door/by the window; **ça me sort par les yeux** *ou* **les oreilles*** I've had more than I can take (of it); **~ en mer** to put out to sea; **depuis trois jours, les bateaux ne sont pas sortis** the boats haven't been out for three days; **faites ~ ces gens** make these people go *ou* leave, get these people out; (*Scol*) **Madame, est-ce que je peux ~?** Miss, can I be excused please?; **~ de** [+ *pièce*] to go *ou* come out of, leave; [+ *région, pays*] to leave; **~ de chez qn** to go *ou* come out of sb's house, leave sb's house; **mais d'où sort-il (donc) ?** (= *il est tout sale*) where has he been!; (= *il ne sait pas la nouvelle*) where has he been (all this time)?; (= *il est mal élevé*) where was he brought up? (*iro*); (= *il est bête*) where did they find him? (*iro*); **il sortit discrètement (de la pièce)** he went out (of the room) *ou* left (the room) discreetly, he slipped out (of the room); **sors (d'ici)!** get out (of here)!; **le train sort du tunnel** the train is coming out of the tunnel; **les voiliers sortaient du port** the sailing boats were leaving the harbour; (*Théât*) **« la servante sort »** "exit the maid"; (*Théât*) **« les 3 gardes sortent »** "exeunt 3 guards"; **laisser ~ qn** to let sb out, let sb leave; **ne laissez ~ personne** don't let anybody out *ou* leave; **laisser ~ qn de** [+ *pièce, pays*] to let sb out of, let sb leave → **gond**

b (= *partir de chez soi*) to go out; **~ faire des courses/prendre l'air** to go out shopping/for some fresh air; **~ acheter du pain** to go out to buy *ou* for some bread; **dîner/déjeuner** to go out for *ou* to dinner/lunch; (*au téléphone*) **mon père est sorti, puis-je prendre un message ?** my father's gone out, can I take a message?; **ils sortent beaucoup/ne sortent pas beaucoup** they go out a lot/don't go out much; **tu ne les connais pas ? il faut ~ un peu** *ou* **le dimanche !** you don't know them? where have you been?*; **mes parents ne me laissent pas ~** my parents don't let me (go) out; **le médecin lui a permis de ~** the doctor has allowed him (to go) out; **c'est le soir que les moustiques sortent** the mosquitoes come out in the evening; **il n'est jamais sorti de son village** he has never been out of *ou* gone outside his village

c (*Comm*) [*marchandises, devises*] to leave; **tout ce qui sort (du pays) doit être déclaré** everything going out (of the country) *ou* leaving (the country) must be declared

d (= *quitter*) to leave, come out; [*élèves*] to get out; [*objet, pièce*] to come out; **le joint est sorti de son logement** the joint has come out of its socket; **~ du théâtre** to go *ou* come out of *ou* leave the theatre; **~ de l'hôpital/de prison** to come out of hospital/of prison; **quand sort-il ?** (*de prison*) when does he come *ou* get out?; (*de l'hôpital*) when is he coming out? *ou* leaving?; **je sors à 6 heures** (*du bureau, du lycée*) I finish at 6; **~ de table** to leave the table; **~ de l'eau** to come out of the water; **~ du lit** to get out of bed, get up; **~ de son lit** [*fleuve*] to overflow its banks; **~ de terre** [*plante*] to sprout; (*Rail*) **~ des rails** to go off the rails; **la voiture est sortie de la route** the car left *ou* came off the road; **~ de convalescence/d'un profond sommeil** to come out of *ou* emerge from convalescence/a deep sleep; **~ de son calme** to lose one's calm; **~ de son indifférence** to overcome one's indifference; **~ indemne d'un accident** to come out of an accident unscathed; **ce secret ne doit pas ~ de la famille** this secret must not go beyond *ou* outside family; **c'est confidentiel, ça ne doit pas ~ d'ici** it's confidential, it must not leave

this room; **~ de la récession** to get out of the recession; **il a trop de copies à corriger, il n'en sort pas** he has too many papers to correct — there's no end to them; **on n'est pas sortis de l'auberge*** we're not out of the woods yet; **cela lui est sorti de la mémoire** *ou* **de l'esprit** it slipped his mind; **ça m'est sorti de la tête** it went right out of my head → **impasse, mauvais**

e (= *fréquenter*) **~ avec qn** to go out with sb

f (*marquant le passé immédiat*) **~ de l'enfance** to leave childhood behind; **on sortait de l'hiver** it was getting near the end of winter; **il sort d'ici** he's just left; **il sort du lit** he's just got up, he's just out of bed; **on ne dirait pas qu'elle sort de chez le coiffeur !** you'd never believe she'd just had her hair done!; **il sort d'une bronchite** he's just had bronchitis, he's just recovering from a bout of bronchitis; **il sort d'une période de cafard** he's just gone through *ou* had a spell of depression; (*d'une épreuve*) **il en est sorti grandi** he came out of it a stronger person, he was better for it; **je sors de lui parler*** I've just been talking to him; **je sors d'en prendre*** I've had quite enough thank you (*iro*)

g (= *s'écarter de*) **~ du sujet/de la question** to go *ou* get off the subject/the point; **~ de la légalité** to overstep *ou* go outside *ou* go beyond the law; **~ des limites de** to go beyond the bounds of, overstep the limits of; (*Sport*) [*balle, ballon*] **~ (du jeu)** to go out (of play); [*ballon*] **~ en touche** to go into touch; (*Tennis*) **la balle est sortie** the ball is out; **cela sort de mon domaine/ma compétence** that's outside my field/my authority; **vous sortez de votre rôle** that is not your responsibility *ou* part of your brief → **ordinaire**

h (= *être issu de*) **~ d'une bonne famille/du peuple** to come from a good family/from the working class; **il sort du lycée Victor Duruy** he was (educated) at the lycée Victor Duruy; **il sort de l'université de Perpignan** he was *ou* he studied at the University of Perpignan; **pas besoin de** *ou* **il ne faut pas ~ de Polytechnique pour comprendre ça*** you don't need a Ph.D. to understand that

i (= *dépasser*) to stick out; (= *commencer à pousser*) [*blé, plante*] to come up; [*dent*] to come through; [*bouton*] to appear

j (= *être fabriqué, publié*) to come out; [*disque, film*] to be released; **le film sort sur les écrans le 2 mai** the film is on general release from 2nd May; **cette encyclopédie sort par fascicules** this encyclopaedia comes out *ou* is published in instalments; **sa robe sort de chez un grand couturier** her dress is by one of the top fashion designers

k (*Jeux, Loterie*) [*numéro, couleur*] to come up; (*Scol*) [*sujet d'examen*] to come up

l (= *provenir de*) **~ de** to come from; (*fig*) (= *résulter*) **sait-on ce qui sortira de ces entrevues !** who knows what will come (out) of these talks! *ou* what these talks will lead to!; (*fig*) **il n'est rien sorti de nos recherches** nothing came (out) of our research; **que va-t-il de tout cela ?** what will come of all this?; **des mots qui sortent du cœur** words which come from the heart, heartfelt words; **une odeur de brûlé sortait de la cuisine** a smell of burning came from the kitchen; **une épaisse fumée sortait par les fenêtres** thick smoke was pouring out of the windows

m (= *être dit*) [*propos, remarque*] **c'est sorti tout seul*** it just came out*; **il fallait que ça sorte*** I (*ou* he etc) just had to say it

2 VT (*avec aux avoir*) **a** (= *mener dehors*) [+ *personne, chien*] to take out; (* = *accompagner lors d'une sortie*) to take out; (= *expulser*) [+ *personne*] to throw out; **sortez-le !** throw him out!, get him out of here!; **va au cinéma, cela te sortira** go and see a film, that'll get you out a bit *ou* give you a change of scene

b (= *extraire*) to take out; (*Aviat*) [+ *train d'atterrissage*] to lower; **~ des vêtements d'une armoire/une voiture du garage** to get *ou* take clothes out of a wardrobe/the car out of the garage; **ils ont réussi à ~ les enfants de la grotte/le car du ravin** they managed to get the children out of the cave/the coach out of the ravine; **il sortit de sa poche un mouchoir** he took *ou* brought *ou* pulled a handkerchief out of his pocket; **~ les mains de ses poches** to take one's hands out of one's pockets; **il a sorti son passeport** he took out *ou* produced his passport; **les douaniers ont tout sorti de sa valise** the customs men took everything out of his suitcase; **sortons les fauteuils dans le jardin** let's take the armchairs out into the garden; **il nous a sorti son vieux bordeaux** he got his old claret out for us; (*lit, fig*) **il faut le ~ de là** (*d'un lieu*) we must get him out of there; (*d'une situation difficile*) we must get him out of it → **affaire 1a**

c (*Comm*) **(faire) ~** [+ *marchandises*] (*par la douane*) to take out; (*en fraude*) to smuggle out

d (= *mettre en vente*) [+ *voiture, modèle*] to bring out; [+ *livre*] to bring out, publish; [+ *disque, film*] [*artiste*] to bring out; [*compagnie*] to release; **ils viennent de ~ un nouveau logiciel** they've just brought out a new software package

e * (= *dire*) to come out with*; **il vous sort de ces réflexions !** the things he comes out with!*; **elle en a sorti une bien bonne** she came out with a good one*; **qu'est-ce qu'il va encore nous ~ ?** what will he come out with next?*; (*Journalisme* = *révéler*) **c'est ce journal qui a sorti l'affaire** this was the newspaper that first broke the story

f (* = *éliminer d'un concours*) [+ *concurrent, adversaire*] to knock out (*fig*); **il s'est fait ~ dès le premier match** he was knocked out in the first match

3 se sortir VPR **se ~ d'une situation difficile** to manage to get out of a difficult situation *ou* to extricate o.s. from a difficult situation; **la voiture est en miettes, mais il s'en est sorti sans une égratignure** the car's a write-off but he came out of it without a scratch; **tu crois qu'il va s'en ~ ?** (*il est malade*) do you think he'll pull through?; (*il est surchargé de travail*) do you think he'll ever get to *ou* see the end of it?; (*il est sur la sellette*) do you think he'll come through all right?; **avec son salaire, il ne peut pas s'en ~** he can't get by on what he earns; **va l'aider, il ne s'en sort pas** go and help him, he can't cope *ou* manage; **j'ai trop de travail, je ne m'en sors pas** I've got too much work, I can't see the end of it; **bravo, tu t'en es très bien sorti !** you've done really well!

sortir² [sɔʀtiʀ] NM (*littér*) **au ~ de l'hiver/de l'enfance** as winter/childhood draws (*ou* drew) to a close; **au ~ de la réunion** at the end of the meeting, when the meeting broke up

SOS [ɛsoɛs] NM SOS; (*Aviat, Naut*) **lancer un ~** to put out an SOS; (*fig*) **envoyer un ~ à qn** to send an SOS to sb; **~ médecins/dépannage** *etc* emergency medical/repair *etc* service

sosie [sɔzi] NM (= *personne*) double; **c'est le ~ de son frère** he's the (spitting) image of his brother

sot, sotte [so, sɔt] **1** ADJ silly, foolish, stupid ◼ (*PROV*) **il n'y a pas de ~ métier(, il n'y a que de ~tes gens)** every trade has its value; **il est facteur — il n'y a pas de ~ métier !** he's a postman — well, there's nothing wrong with that! **2** NM,F (†, *frm*) (= *niais*) fool; (= *enfant*) (little) idiot; (*Hist, Littérat*) = **bouffon** fool

sotie [sɔti] NF (*Hist Littérat*) satirical farce of 15th and 16th centuries

sot-l'y-laisse [soliles] NM INV [*volaille*] oyster (*in chicken*)

sottement [sɔtmɑ̃] ADV foolishly, stupidly

sottie [sɔti] NF = **sotie**

sottise [sɔtiz] NF **a** (= *caractère*) stupidity, foolishness; **avoir la ~ de faire** to be foolish *ou* stupid enough to do sth, have the stupidity to do sth **b** (= *parole*) silly *ou* foolish remark; (= *action*) silly *ou* foolish thing to do, folly†; (*frm*) **dire des ~s** to say silly *ou* stupid *ou* foolish things, make silly *ou* foolish remarks; **faire une ~** [*adulte*] to do a silly *ou* foolish thing, do something stupid; **faire des ~s** [*enfant*] to misbehave, be naughty

sottisier [sɔtizje] NM (= *livre*) collection of howlers*; (*Radio, TV*) collection of out-takes

sou [su] NM **a** (= *monnaie*) (*Hist*) sou, = shilling (*Brit*); (†, *Helv* = *cinq centimes*) 5 centimes; (* *Can*) cent; (*Can*) **un trente ~s :** a quarter (*US, Can*) **b** (*loc*) **un ~ est un ~** every penny counts; (*péj*) **c'est une affaire** *ou* **une histoire de gros ~s** there's big money involved; **donner/compter/économiser ~ à** *ou* **par ~** to give/count/save penny by penny; **il n'a pas le (premier) ~** ◊ **il n'a pas un ~ vaillant** he hasn't got a penny *ou* a cent (*US*) (to his name); **il est sans le** *ou* **un ~** he's penniless; **il est toujours en train de compter ses ~s** he's always counting the pennies; **ils en sont à leurs derniers ~s** they're down to their last few pennies; **dépenser jusqu'à son dernier ~** to spend every last penny; **y laisser jusqu'à son dernier ~** to lose everything, lose one's last buck* (*US*); **il n'a pas pour un ~ de méchanceté/bon sens** he hasn't got an ounce of unkindness/good sense (in him); **il n'est pas hypocrite/raciste pour un ~** *ou* **deux ~s** he isn't at all *ou* (in) the least bit hypocritical/racist; **propre/reluisant** *ou* **brillant comme un ~ neuf** (as) clean/bright as a new pin, spick and span → **appareil, cent¹, machine, près, quatre**

soubassement [subasmɑ̃] NM [*maison*] base; [*murs, fenêtre*] dado; [*colonne*] crepidoma; (*Géol*) bedrock; (*fig*) [*thèse*] basis

soubresaut [subʀəso] NM **a** (= *cahot*) jolt; **le véhicule fit un ~** the vehicle gave a jolt **b** (= *tressaillement*) (*de peur*) start; (*d'agonie*) convulsive movement; **avoir** *ou* **faire un ~** to give a start, start

soubrette [subʀɛt] NF (†, *hum* = *femme de chambre*) maid; (*Théat*) soubrette

souche [suʃ] NF **a** (*Bot*) [*arbre*] stump; [*vigne*] stock; **rester planté comme une ~** to stand stock-still → **dormir b** [*famille, race*] founder; **faire ~** to found a line; **de vieille ~** of old stock; **elle est française de ~** she's of French origin *ou* extraction **c** (*Ling*) root; **mot de ~ latine** word with a Latin root; **mot ~** root word **d** (*Bio*) [*bactéries, virus*] clone, strain; **cellule ~** original cell **e** (= *talon*) counterfoil, stub; **carnet à ~s** counterfoil book **f** (*Archit*) [*cheminée*] (chimney) stack

souci¹ [susi] NM (= *fleur*) ~ (**des jardins**) marigold; **~ d'eau** *ou* **des marais** marsh marigold

souci² [susi] NM **a** (= *inquiétude*) worry; **se faire du ~** to worry; **être sans ~** to be free of worries *ou* cares; **cela t'éviterait bien du ~** it would save *ou* spare you a lot of worry; **cela lui donne (bien) du ~** it worries him (a lot), he worries (a great deal) over it; **~s d'argent** money worries, worries about money **b** (= *préoccupation*) concern (**de** for); **avoir ~ du bien-être de son prochain** to be concerned about other people's well-being; **sa carrière est son unique ~** his career is his sole concern *ou* is all he worries about; **cet enfant est un ~ perpétuel pour ses parents** that child is a constant source of worry for his parents; **avoir le ~ de bien faire** to be concerned about doing things well; **dans le ~ de lui plaire** in his concern to please her; **nous avons fait ce choix dans un ~ de cohérence** we made this choice with a view to being consistent *ou* for the sake of consistency; **par ~ d'honnêteté** for honesty's sake; **ils produisent sans ~ de quali-**

-té they churn out products regardless of quality; **c'est le moindre** *ou* **le cadet** *ou* **le dernier de mes ~s** that's the least of my worries

soucier [susje] ▶conjug 7◀ **1 se soucier** VPR **se ~ de** to care about; **se ~ des autres** to care about *ou* for others, show concern for others; **je ne m'en soucie guère** I am quite indifferent to it; **il s'en soucie comme de sa première chemise** *ou* **comme de l'an quarante** * he doesn't give *ou* care a hoot* (about it)*, he couldn't care less (about it)*; (*littér*) **il se soucie peu de plaire** he cares little *ou* he doesn't bother whether he is liked or not; **il se soucie fort de ce qu'ils pensent** he cares very much what they think; **sans se ~ de leur réaction** without worrying about their reaction; **sans se ~ de fermer la porte à clé** without bothering to lock the door; **elle a accepté sans se ~ des conséquences** she accepted without giving any thought to the consequences; (*littér*) **se ~ que** (+ *subj*) to care that **2** VT to worry, trouble

soucieux, -ieuse [susjø, jøz] ADJ **a** (= *inquiet*) [*personne, air, ton*] concerned, worried **b être ~ de qch** to be concerned with *ou* about sth, be preoccupied with sth; **~ de son seul intérêt** concerned *ou* preoccupied solely with his own interests; **être ~ de faire** to be anxious to do; (*frm*) **~ que** concerned *ou* anxious that; **peu ~ qu'on le voie** caring little *ou* unconcerned whether he be *ou* is seen or not

soucoupe [sukup] NF saucer; **~ volante** flying saucer → **œil**

soudage [sudaʒ] NM (*avec brasure, fil à souder*) soldering; (*autogène*) welding

soudain, e [sudɛ̃, ɛn] **1** ADJ (*gén*) sudden; [*mort*] sudden, unexpected **2** ADV (= *tout à coup*) suddenly, all of a sudden; **~, il se mit à pleurer** all of a sudden he started to cry, he suddenly started to cry

soudainement [sudɛnmɑ̃] ADV suddenly, all of a sudden

soudaineté [sudɛnte] NF suddenness

Soudan [sudɑ̃] NM **le ~** the Sudan

soudanais, e [sudanɛ, ɛz] **1** ADJ Sudanese, of *ou* from (the) Sudan **2 Soudanais(e)** NM,F Sudanese, inhabitant *ou* native of (the) Sudan

soudard [sudaʀ] NM (*péj*) ruffianly *ou* roughneck soldier

soude [sud] NF **a** (*industrielle*) soda; **~ caustique** caustic soda → **bicarbonate, cristal b** (*Bot*) saltwort; (*Chim*) **(cendre de) ~†** soda ash

soudé, e [sude] (*ptp de* **souder**) ADJ **a** [*organes, pétales*] joined (together); [*couple*] close, united; [*équipe*] closely-knit **b** (*fig*) **~ au plancher/à la paroi** glued to the floor/to the wall

souder [sude] ▶conjug 1◀ **1** VT **a** (*Tech*) [+ *métal*] (*avec brasure, fil à souder*) to solder; (*soudure autogène*) to weld; [+ *plastique*] to weld, seal; **~ à chaud/froid** to hot-/cold-weld → **fer, fil, lampe b** (*Méd*) [+ *os*] to knit **c** (= *unir*) [+ *choses, organismes*] to fuse (together); (*littér*) [+ *cœurs, êtres*] to bind *ou* knit together (*littér*), unite; **l'opposition est soudée derrière lui** the opposition is united behind him; **c'est un couple très soudé** they're a very united couple; **notre équipe n'est pas assez soudée** our team isn't united enough **d** (*Culin*) [+ *bords*] to seal **2 se souder** VPR **a** (*os*) to knit together; [*vertèbres*] to fuse **b** [*équipe, parti*] to pull together, unite; (= *s'unir*) to be knit together (*littér*)

soudeur, -euse [sudœʀ, øz] **1** NM,F [*métal*] (*avec brasure, fil à souder*) solderer; (*soudure autogène*) welder **2 soudeuse** NF (= *machine*) welder

soudoyer [sudwaje] ▶conjug 8◀ VT to bribe

soudure [sudyʀ] NF **a** (*Tech*) (= *opération*) [*métal*] (*avec brasure, fil à souder*) soldering;

soufflage [suflaʒ] NM **a** (*Métal*) blowing; ~ **du verre** glass-blowing **b** (*Naut*) sheathing

soufflant, e [suflā, āt] **1** ADJ **a** **(machine)** ~**e** blower; **(radiateur)** ~ fan heater **b** (†* = *étonnant*) staggering, stunning **2** NM (*arg Crime* = *pistolet*) pistol, rod‡ (*US*)

souffle [sufl] NM **a** (= *expiration*) (*en soufflant*) blow, puff; (*en respirant*) breath; **éteindre une bougie d'un** ~ to blow a candle out; **il murmura mon nom dans un** ~ he breathed my name; **le dernier** ~ **d'un agonisant** the last breath of a dying man; **pour jouer d'un instrument à vent, il faut du** ~ you need a lot of breath *ou* puff* (*Brit*) to play a wind instrument **b** (= *respiration*) breathing; **on entendait un** ~ **dans l'obscurité** we heard (someone) breathing in the darkness; **manquer de** ~ (*lit*) to be short of breath; (*fig*) [*prose*] to be lacklustre (*Brit*) *ou* lackluster (*US*); [*campagne électorale*] to be lacklustre (*Brit*) *ou* lackluster (*US*), be lacking (in) oomph*; **son roman manque de** ~ * (= *il a du toupet*) he's got a nerve!*; **avoir le** ~ **court** to be short of breath, be short-winded; **retenir son** ~ to hold one's breath; **reprendre son** ~ to get one's breath back; **ne plus avoir de** ~ to be out of breath; **couper le** ~ **à qn** (*lit*) to wind sb; (*fig*) to take sb's breath away; (*fig*) **j'en ai eu le** ~ **coupé** it (quite) took my breath away; **c'est à vous couper le** ~ it's breathtaking, it's enough to take your breath away; **donner un** ~ **nouveau** *ou* **redonner du** ~ **à qch** to give sth a new lease of life, breathe new life into sth; **la dévaluation va redonner du** ~ **aux exportations** devaluation will give a fillip to exports; **trouver son second** ~ (*Sport*) to get one's second wind; (*fig*) to find a new lease of life → **bout, second** **c** (= *déplacement d'air*) [*incendie, ventilateur, explosion*] blast **d** (= *vent*) puff *ou* breath of air, puff of wind; **le** ~ **du vent dans les feuilles** the wind blowing through the leaves; **un** ~ **d'air faisait bruire le feuillage** a slight breeze was rustling the leaves; **il n'y avait pas un** ~ **(d'air** *ou* **de vent)** there was not a breath of air **e** (*fig* = *force créatrice*) inspiration; **le** ~ **du génie** the inspiration born of genius; (*Rel*) **le** ~ **créateur** the breath of God **f** (*Méd*) ~ **cardiaque** *ou* **au cœur** cardiac *ou* heart murmur → **bruit** **g** (*Téléc*) background noise

soufflé, e [sufle] (*ptp de* **souffler**) **1** ADJ **a** (*Culin*) soufflé (*épith*) **b** (* = *surpris*) flabbergasted*, staggered* **2** NM (*Culin*) soufflé; ~ **au fromage** cheese soufflé → **retomber**

souffler [sufle] ▶conjug 1◀ **1** VI **a** [*vent, personne*] to blow; ~ **dans un instrument à vent** to blow (into) a wind instrument; ~ **sur une bougie (pour l'éteindre)** to blow out a candle; ~ **sur sa soupe (pour la faire refroidir)** to blow on one's soup (to cool it down); ~ **sur ses doigts (pour les réchauffer)** to blow on one's fingers (to warm them up); (*lit, fig*) **voir de quel côté souffle le vent** to see which way the wind is blowing; **le vent a soufflé si fort qu'il a abattu deux arbres** the wind was so strong *ou* blew so hard that it brought two trees down; **le vent soufflait en rafales** the wind was blowing in gusts; **le vent soufflait en tempête** it was blowing a gale; **j'ai dû** ~ **dans le ballon** (*alcootest*) I was breathalyzed, they gave me a breath test; ~ **sur le feu** (*lit*) to blow on the fire; (*fig*) to add fuel to the fire; (*fig*) **il croit qu'il va y arriver en soufflant dessus** he

thinks it's going to be a cinch* **b** (= *respirer avec peine*) to puff (and blow); **il ne peut monter les escaliers sans** ~ he can't go up the stairs without puffing (and blowing); ~ **comme un bœuf** *ou* **une locomotive** *ou* **un phoque*** to puff and blow like an old steam engine **c** (= *se reposer*) to get one's breath back; **laisser** ~ **qn/un cheval** to let sb/a horse get his breath back; **il ne prend jamais le temps de** ~ he never lets up, he never stops to catch his breath; **donnez-lui un peu de temps pour** ~ (*pour se reposer*) give him time to get his breath back, give him a breather*; (*avant de payer*) give him a breather*

2 VT **a** [+ *bougie, feu*] to blow out **b** (= *envoyer*) ~ **de la fumée au nez de qn** to blow smoke in(to) sb's face; ~ **des odeurs d'ail au visage de qn** to breathe garlic over sb *ou* into sb's face; **le ventilateur soufflait des odeurs de graillon** the fan was blowing out greasy smells; **le vent leur soufflait le sable dans les yeux** the wind was blowing the sand into their eyes; (*fig*) ~ **le chaud et le froid** to blow hot and cold **c** (* = *prendre*) to pinch*, swipe*, nick* (*Brit*) (**à qn** from sb); **il lui a soufflé sa petite amie/son poste** he's pinched* his girlfriend/his job; (*Dames*) ~ **un pion** to huff a draught; (*Dames*) ~ **n'est pas jouer** huffing isn't a real move **d** [*bombe, explosion*] to destroy; **leur maison a été soufflée par une bombe** their house was destroyed by the blast from a bomb **e** (= *dire*) [+ *conseil, réponse, réplique*] to whisper (**à qn** to sb); (*fig*) **on lui a soufflé sa leçon** he was told what to say; (*Théât*) ~ **son rôle à qn** to prompt sb, give sb a prompt; ~ **qch à l'oreille de qn** to whisper sth in sb's ear; (*en classe, dans un jeu*) **on ne souffle pas !** no whispering!; **il n'a pas soufflé mot** he didn't breathe a word; **c'est lui qui m'en avait soufflé l'idée** he's the one who gave me the idea **f** (* = *étonner*) to flabbergast*, stagger*; **elle a été soufflée d'apprendre leur échec** she was flabbergasted* *ou* staggered* to hear they had failed; **leur toupet m'a soufflé** I was flabbergasted* *ou* staggered* at their nerve **g** (*Tech*) ~ **le verre** to blow glass

soufflerie [sufləʀi] NF [*orgue, forge*] bellows; (*Tech : d'aération*) ventilating fan; (*Ind*) blower; (*Aviat*) ~ **(aérodynamique)** wind tunnel

soufflet¹ [suflɛ] NM **a** [*forge*] bellows **b** (*Rail*) vestibule; (*Couture*) gusset; [*sac, classeur*] extendible gusset; [*appareil photographique, instrument de musique*] bellows; **classeur à** ~**s** accordion file

soufflet² [suflɛ] NM (*littér* = *gifle*) slap in the face

souffleter [sufləte] ▶conjug 4◀ VT (*littér*) ~ **qn** to give sb a slap in the face

souffleur, -euse [suflœʀ, øz] **1** NM **a** (*Géol*) fumarole **b** (*Zool*) (= *baleine*) blower; (= *dauphin*) bottle-nose(d) dolphin **c** (*Tech*) ~ **de verre** glass-blower **2** NM,F (*Théât*) prompter → **trou** **3 souffleuse** NF (*Can*) snowblower

souffrance [sufʀās] NF **a** (= *douleur*) suffering; ~ **physique/morale** physical/mental suffering; **les** ~**s infligées à la population** the suffering inflicted on the population; **elle est morte dans d'atroces** ~**s** she died in agony *ou* great pain **b** **être en** ~ [*marchandises, colis*] to be awaiting delivery, be held up; [*affaire, dossier*] to be pending, be waiting to be dealt with

souffrant, e [sufʀā, āt] ADJ **a** (= *malade*) [*personne*] unwell, poorly; **avoir l'air** ~ to look unwell *ou* poorly **b** (*littér*) **l'humanité** ~**e** suffering humanity; **l'Église** ~**e** the Church suffering

souffre-douleur [sufʀədulœʀ] NMF INV whipping boy, punch bag (*Brit*), punching bag (*US*)

souffreteux, -euse [sufʀətø, øz] ADJ [*personne, plante*] sickly, puny

souffrir [sufʀiʀ] ▶conjug 18◀ **1** VI **a** (*physiquement*) to suffer; **elle est en grande douleur** *ou* **is suffering a great deal**; ~ **comme un damné** to suffer torture *ou* torment(s); (*hum*) **il faut** ~ **pour être belle** you have to suffer to be beautiful, no pain no gain; **faire** ~ **qn** [*personne, blessure*] to hurt sb; **mon bras me fait** ~ my arm hurts *ou* is painful; ~ **de l'estomac/des reins** to have stomach/kidney trouble; **il souffre d'une grave maladie/de rhumatismes** he is suffering from a serious illness/from rheumatism; ~ **du froid/de la chaleur** to suffer from the cold/from the heat **b** (*moralement*) to suffer (**de** from); **faire** ~ **qn** [*personne*] to make sb suffer; [*attitude, événement*] to cause sb pain; **il a beaucoup souffert d'avoir été chassé de son pays** he has suffered a great deal from being forced to leave his country; **je souffre de le voir si affaibli** it pains *ou* grieves me to see him so weak; **j'en souffrais pour lui** I felt bad for him **c** (= *pâtir*) to suffer; **les fraises souffrent de la chaleur** strawberries suffer in the heat; **les fraises ont souffert du gel** the strawberries have suffered from *ou* have been hard hit by the frost; **sa réputation en a souffert** his reputation suffered by it; **le pays a souffert de la guerre** the country has suffered from the war **d** (* = *éprouver de la difficulté*) to have a hard time of it; **on a fini par gagner, mais ils nous ont fait** ~ *ou* **mais on a souffert** we won in the end but we had a hard time of it *ou* they gave us a rough time; **je l'ai réparé mais j'ai souffert** I fixed it, but it wasn't easy

2 VT **a** (= *éprouver*) ~ **le martyre** to go through agonies, go through hell; **sa jambe lui fait** ~ **le martyre** he goes through hell with that leg of his; ~ **mille morts** to die a thousand deaths **b** (*littér* = *supporter*) to bear; **il ne peut pas** ~ **cette fille/le mensonge/les épinards** he can't stand *ou* bear that girl/lies/spinach; **je ne peux** ~ **de te voir malheureux** I can't bear to see you unhappy; **il ne peut pas** ~ **que ...** he cannot bear that ...; **je ne souffrirai pas qu'il me donne des ordres** I won't take him giving me orders; **souffrez que je vous contredise** allow *ou* permit me to contradict you **c** (*frm* = *admettre*) to admit of, allow of; **la règle souffre quelques exceptions** the rule admits of *ou* allows of a few exceptions; **la règle ne peut** ~ **aucune exception** the rule admits of no exception; **cette affaire ne peut** ~ **aucun retard** this matter simply cannot be delayed

3 se souffrir VPR (= *se supporter*) **ils ne peuvent pas se** ~ they can't stand *ou* bear each other

soufi, e [sufi] **1** ADJ Sufi, Sufic **2** NM,F Sufi

soufisme [sufism] NM Sufism

soufrage [sufʀaʒ] NM [*vigne, laine*] sulphuration (*Brit*), sulfuration (*US*); [*allumettes*] sulphuring (*Brit*), sulfuring (*US*)

soufre [sufʀ] NM sulphur (*Brit*), sulfur (*US*); **jaune** ~ sulphur (*Brit*) *ou* sulfur (*US*) yellow; (*fig*) **sentir le** ~ to smack of heresy

soufré, e [sufʀe] ADJ **a** (= *enduit de soufre*) coated with sulphur (*Brit*) *ou* sulfur (*US*) **b** (= *jaune*) sulphur (*Brit*) *ou* sulfur (*US*) yellow

soufrer [sufʀe] ▶conjug 1◀ VT [+ *vigne*] to (treat with) sulphur (*Brit*) *ou* sulfur (*US*); [+ *allumettes*] to sulphur (*Brit*) *ou* sulfur (*US*); [+ *laine*] to sulphurate (*Brit*) *ou* sulfurate (*US*)

soufrière [sufʀijɛʀ] NF sulphur (*Brit*) *ou* sulfur (*US*) mine; (*Géog*) **la Soufrière** the Soufrière

souhait [swɛ] NM wish; **formuler des** ~**s pour qch** to express one's best wishes for sth; **les** ~**s de bonne année** New Year greetings, good wishes for the New Year; **tous nos** ~**s de réussite** our best wishes for your success; **à vos** ~**s!** bless you!, gesundheit! (*US*); **la viande**

était rôtie à ~ the meat was done to perfection *ou* done to a turn; **le vin était fruité à ~** the wine was delightfully fruity; **tout marchait à ~** everything went perfectly *ou* went like a dream; (*hum*) **une chanson niaise à ~** an incredibly silly song

souhaitable [swetabl] ADJ desirable; **ce n'est guère ~** it is not really to be desired; **sa présence n'a pas été jugée ~** his presence was deemed undesirable

▼ **souhaiter** [swete] ▸ conjug 1 ◂ VT [a] (= *espérer*) [+ *réussite, changements*] to wish for; **~ que** to hope that; **il est à ~ que ...** it is to be hoped that ...; **ce n'est pas à ~** it's not really to be desired; **je souhaite qu'il réussisse** I hope he succeeds; **je souhaite réussir** I hope to succeed; **~ pouvoir étudier/partir à l'étranger** to hope to be able to study/go abroad; **je le souhaitais différent/plus affectueux** I wished he were different/more affectionate; **je souhaiterais parler à Jean** I'd like to speak to Jean, please; **à quelle heure souhaitez-vous partir?** what time would you like to leave?; (*dans une offre d'emploi*) « **anglais souhaité** » "knowledge of English desirable"

[b] (= *exprimer ses vœux*) **~ à qn le bonheur/la réussite** to wish sb happiness/success; **je vous souhaite bien des choses** all the best; **~ à qn de réussir** to wish sb success; (*iro*) **je vous souhaite bien du plaisir !** (and the) best of luck to you! (*iro*); **~ la bonne année/bonne chance à qn** to wish sb a happy New Year/(the best of) luck; **je vous la souhaite bonne et heureuse !** here's hoping you have a really good New Year!; **je ne souhaite à personne de connaître une telle horreur** I wouldn't wish such an awful thing on anybody; **tout ce que je souhaite, c'est que tu sois heureux** all I want is for you to be happy

souiller [suje] ▸ conjug 1 ◂ VT (*littér*) [+ *drap, vêtement*] to soil, dirty; [+ *atmosphère*] to pollute; [+ *réputation, pureté, âme*] to sully, tarnish; **souillé de boue** spattered with mud; **~ ses mains du sang des innocents** to stain one's hands with the blood of innocents

souillon [sujɔ̃] NF slattern, slut

souillure [sujyʀ] NF (*littér*) (*lit*) stain; (*fig*) blemish, stain; **la ~ du péché** the stain of sin

souk [suk] NM [a] (= *marché*) souk [b]* (= *désordre*) **c'est le ~ ici !** this place is absolute chaos!; (= *tintamarre*) **c'est fini, ce ~ ?** will you stop that racket?

soul [sul] (*Mus*) [1] ADJ INV soul (*épith*) [2] NF *ou* NM soul

soûl, soûle [su, sul] [1] ADJ (= *ivre*) drunk, drunken (*épith*); **~ comme une bourrique*** *ou* **un Polonais*** *ou* **une grive** blind drunk*, (as) drunk as a lord (*surtout Brit*) [2] NM (= *à satiété*) **manger tout son ~** to eat one's fill; **chanter tout son ~** to sing one's heart out; **elle a ri/pleuré tout son ~** she laughed/cried till she could laugh/cry no more

soulagement [sulaʒmɑ̃] NM relief; **j'ai éprouvé un immense ~** I felt an immense sense of relief, I felt immensely relieved; **un murmure de ~ parcourut la foule** the crowd murmured in relief; **ça a été un ~ d'apprendre que ...** it was a relief *ou* I was (*ou* we were *etc*) relieved to learn that ...; **cette annonce a été accueillie avec ~** the announcement came as a relief; **à mon grand ~** to my great relief

soulager [sulaʒe] ▸ conjug 3 ◂ [1] VT [a] [+ *personne*] (*physiquement*) to relieve; (*moralement*) to relieve, soothe; [+ *douleur*] to relieve, soothe; [+ *maux*] to relieve; [+ *conscience*] to ease; **ça le soulage de s'étendre** it relieves the pain when he stretches out; **ça le soulage de prendre ces pilules** these pills bring him relief; **buvez, ça vous soulagera** drink this — it'll make you feel better; **être soulagé d'avoir fait qch** to be relieved that one has done *ou* to have done sth; **cet aveu**

l'a soulagé this confession made him feel better *ou* eased his conscience; **cela me soulage d'un grand poids** it's a great weight off my mind; **~ les pauvres/les déshérités** to bring relief to *ou* relieve the poor/the underprivileged; **si ça peut te ~, sache que tu n'es pas le seul dans ce cas** if it's any consolation you should know that you're not the only one in this situation; **mets de la crème, ça soulage** put some cream on, it's soothing; **pleure un bon coup, ça soulage !** have a good cry, it'll make you feel better!

[b] (= *décharger*) [+ *personne*] to relieve (**de** of); (*Archit*) [+ *mur, poutre*] to relieve the strain on; (*hum*) **~ qn de son portefeuille** to relieve sb of their wallet (*hum*)

[2] **se soulager** VPR [a] (= *se décharger d'un souci*) to find relief, ease one's feelings, make o.s. feel better; (= *apaiser sa conscience*) to ease one's conscience; **elle se soulageait en lui prodiguant des insultes** she found relief in *ou* eased her feelings by throwing insults at him; **leur conscience se soulage à bon marché** their consciences can be eased at little expense

[b] (*euph* = *uriner*) to relieve o.s.

soûlant, e* [sulɑ̃, ɑ̃t] ADJ wearing; **tu es ~ avec tes questions** you're wearing me out *ou* tiring me out with your questions

soûlard, e‡ [sular, aʀd], **soûlaud, e‡** [sulo, od] NM,F drunkard, old soak‡

soûler [sule] ▸ conjug 1 ◂ [1] VT [a] (* = *rendre ivre*) **~ qn** [*personne*] to get sb drunk; [*boisson*] to make sb drunk

[b] * (= *fatiguer*) **~ qn** to make sb's head spin *ou* reel; **tu nous soûles avec tes questions** you're driving us mad with all your questions; **~ qn de** [+ *théories*] to make sb's head spin *ou* reel with; [+ *questions, conseils*] to wear *ou* tire sb out with; [+ *luxe, sensations*] to intoxicate sb with; **chaque fois qu'il vient, il nous soûle de paroles** every time he comes, he wears us out with all his talking

[c] (= *griser qn*) [*parfum*] to go to sb's head, intoxicate sb; [*vent, vitesse, théories*] to intoxicate sb, make sb's head spin *ou* reel

[2] **se soûler** VPR (* = *s'enivrer*) to get drunk; **se ~ à la bière/au whisky** to get drunk on beer/on whisky; **se ~ la gueule‡** to get blind drunk*, get pissed*‡ (*Brit*); **se ~ de** [+ *bruit, vitesse, vent, parfums*] to get drunk on; [+ *sensations*] to make o.s. drunk with *ou* on

soûlerie [sulʀi] NF (*péj*) drunken binge

soulèvement [sulɛvmɑ̃] NM [a] (= *révolte*) uprising [b] (*Géol*) upthrust, upheaval

▼ **soulever** [sul(ə)ve] ▸ conjug 5 ◂ [1] VT [a] (= *lever*) [+ *fardeau, malade, couvercle, rideau*] to lift (up); **~ qn de terre** to lift sb (up) off the ground; **cela me soulève le cœur** [*odeur*] it makes me feel sick *ou* want to heave*, it turns my stomach; [*attitude*] it makes me sick, it turns my stomach; **odeur/spectacle qui soulève le cœur** nauseating *ou* sickening smell/sight; (*fig*) **cette déclaration a permis de ~ un coin du voile** this declaration has thrown a little light on the matter

[b] (= *remuer*) [+ *poussière*] to raise; **le véhicule soulevait des nuages de poussière** the vehicle sent up *ou* raised clouds of dust; **le bateau soulevait de grosses vagues** the boat was making great waves; **le vent soulevait les vagues/le sable** the wind whipped up the waves/blew *ou* whipped up the sand

[c] (= *indigner*) to stir up; (= *pousser à la révolte*) to stir up *ou* rouse (to revolt); (= *exalter*) to stir; **~ l'opinion publique (contre qn)** to stir up *ou* rouse public opinion (against sb)

[d] (= *provoquer*) [+ *enthousiasme, colère*] to arouse; [+ *protestations, applaudissements*] to raise; [+ *difficultés, questions*] to raise, bring up

[e] (= *évoquer*) [+ *question, problème*] to raise, bring up

[f] (‡ = *voler*) **~ qch (à qn)** to pinch* *ou* swipe‡

sth (from sb); **il lui a soulevé sa femme** he stole his wife

[2] **se soulever** VPR [a] (= *se lever*) [*personne*] to lift o.s. up; [*poitrine*] to heave; **soulève-toi pour que je redresse ton oreiller** lift yourself up *ou* sit up a bit so that I can plump up your pillow; **il s'est soulevé sur un bras** he raised himself on one elbow

[b] [*véhicule, couvercle, rideau*] to lift; [*vagues, mer*] to swell (up); **à cette vue, son cœur se souleva** his stomach turned at the sight

[c] (= *s'insurger*) to rise up (**contre** against)

soulier [sulje] NM shoe; **~s bas/plats** low-heeled/flat shoes; **~s montants** ankle boots; **~s de marche** walking shoes; (*fig*) **être dans ses petits ~s** to feel awkward *ou* ill at ease

soulignage [sulɲaʒ], **soulignement** [sulɲmɑ̃] NM underlining

▼ **souligner** [sulɲe] ▸ conjug 1 ◂ VT [a] (*lit*) to underline; (*fig* = *accentuer*) to accentuate, emphasize; **~ qch d'un trait double** to underline sth twice, double underline sth; **~ qch en rouge** to underline sth in red; **~ ses yeux de noir** to put on black eye-liner; **ce tissu à rayures soulignait son embonpoint** that striped material emphasized *ou* accentuated his stoutness [b] (= *faire remarquer*) to underline, stress, emphasize; **il souligna l'importance de cette rencontre** he underlined *ou* stressed *ou* emphasized the importance of this meeting

soûlographe* [sulɔgʀaf] NMF (*hum*) lush*, piss artist‡ (*Brit*), boozer* (*Brit*)

soûlographie* [sulɔgʀafi] NF (*hum*) drunkenness, boozing* (*Brit*)

soumettre [sumɛtʀ] ▸ conjug 56 ◂ [1] VT [a] (= *dompter*) [+ *pays, peuple*] to subject, subjugate; [+ *personne*] to subject; [+ *rebelles*] to put down, subdue, subjugate

[b] (= *asservir*) **~ qn à** [+ *maître, loi*] to subject sb to

[c] (= *astreindre*) **~ qn à** [+ *traitement, formalité, régime, impôt*] to subject sb to; **~ qch à** [+ *traitement, essai, taxe*] to subject sth to; **être soumis à des règles strictes** to be subject to strict rules; **soumis aux droits de douane** dutiable, subject to (customs) duty; **soumis à l'impôt** subject to tax(ation), taxable

[d] (= *présenter*) [+ *idée, cas, manuscrit*] to submit (**à** to); **~ une idée/un projet/une question à qn** to submit an idea/a plan/a matter to sb, put an idea/a plan/a matter before sb; **~ un document à la signature** to submit a document for signature; **~ un projet de loi à référendum** to submit *ou* put a bill to referendum

[2] **se soumettre** VPR [a] (= *obéir*) to submit (**à** to)

[b] **se ~ à** [+ *traitement, formalité*] to submit to; [+ *entraînement, régime*] to submit to, subject o.s. to

soumis, e [sumi, iz] (*ptp de* **soumettre**) ADJ (= *docile*) [*personne, air*] submissive; **fille ~e**† ≈ registered prostitute

soumission [sumisjɔ̃] NF [a] (= *obéissance*) submission (**à** to); **il est toujours d'une parfaite ~ à leur égard** he is always totally submissive to their wishes; **il exigeait de moi une totale ~** he demanded that I submit completely to him, he demanded my complete submission [b] (= *reddition*) submission; **ils ont fait leur ~** they have submitted (**à** to) [c] (*Comm*) tender; **faire une ~ pour un contrat** to tender for a contract; **~ cachetée** sealed bid

soumissionnaire [sumisjɔnɛʀ] NMF (*Comm*) bidder, tenderer

soumissionner [sumisjɔne] ▸ conjug 1 ◂ VT (*Comm*) to bid for, tender for

soupape [supap] NF valve; **moteur 16 ~s** 16-valve engine; **~ d'admission/d'échappement** inlet/exhaust valve; **~s en tête/latérales** overhead/side valves; (*lit, fig*) **~ de sûreté** *ou* **de sécurité** safety valve

---

➤ GRAMMAIRE ACTIVE: **souhaiter** 28.1, 31, 50.1, 50.3   **soulever** 53.2, 53.6   **souligner** 53.6

soupçon [supsɔ̃] NM a (= suspicion) suspicion; **conduite exempte de tout ~** conduct above suspicion; **personne à l'abri de** ou **au-dessus de tout ~** person free from ou person above all ou any suspicion; **de graves ~s pèsent sur lui** he's under serious suspicion; **avoir des ~s (sur)** to have one's suspicions (about), be suspicious (about); **j'en avais le ~!** I suspected as much!; **sa femme eut bientôt des ~s** his wife soon became suspicious; **des difficultés dont il n'avait pas ~** difficulties of which he had no inkling ou no suspicion b (= petite quantité) [assaisonnement, maquillage, vulgarité] hint, touch; [vin, lait] drop

soupçonnable [supsɔnabl] ADJ (gén nég) that arouses suspicion(s); **il est peu ~ de sympathies racistes** he can hardly be accused of being a racist

soupçonner [supsɔne] ▶ conjug 1 ◀ VT to suspect; **il est soupçonné de vol** he is suspected of theft; **on le soupçonne d'y avoir participé** ◊ **on soupçonne qu'il y a participé** he is suspected of having taken part in it; **il soupçonnait un piège** he suspected a trap; **vous ne soupçonnez pas ce que ça demande comme travail** you've no idea how much work it involves

soupçonneux, -euse [supsɔnø, øz] ADJ suspicious; **il me lança un regard ~** he gave me a suspicious glance, he glanced at me suspiciously

soupe [sup] 1 NF a (Culin) soup; **~ à l'oignon/aux légumes/de poisson** onion/vegetable/fish soup → **cheveu, marchand, plein** b (hum = nourriture) grub*, nosh‡; **à la ~!** grub's up!‡, come and get it! c (*: Ski) porridge* d (loc) **il a eu droit à la ~ à la grimace** he was given a frosty reception when he got home; **il est (très) ~ au lait** ◊ **c'est une ~ au lait** he flies off the handle easily, he's very quick-tempered; **par ici la bonne ~!** roll up! roll up!; (fig) **il est allé à la ~*** he has taken a backhander*; (fig) **servir la ~ à qn** to crawl to sb* 2 COMP ▶ **soupe populaire** (= lieu) soup kitchen; (= nourriture) free meals; (fig) **se retrouver à la ~ populaire** to end up penniless ▶ **soupe primitive** (Bio) primeval soup

soupente [supɑ̃t] NF cupboard (Brit) ou closet (US) (under the stairs)

souper [supe] 1 NM supper (= Belg, Can, Helv = dîner) dinner, supper 2 ▶ conjug 1 ◀ VI a (lit) to have supper; (Belg, Can, Helv) to have dinner ou supper; **après le spectacle, nous sommes allés ~** after the show we went for supper b **j'en ai soupé de ces histoires!** I'm sick and tired* ou I've had a bellyful‡ of all this fuss!

soupeser [supǝze] ▶ conjug 5 ◀ VT (lit) to weigh in one's hand(s), feel the weight of; (fig) to weigh up

soupière [supjɛʀ] NF (soup) tureen

soupir [supiʀ] NM a (gén) sigh; **~ de satisfaction** sigh of satisfaction, satisfied sigh; **pousser un ~ de soulagement** to give ou heave a sigh of relief; **pousser un gros ~** to let out ou give a heavy sigh, sigh heavily; **« oui », dit-il dans un ~** "yes", he said with a sigh ou he sighed; (littér) **rendre le dernier ~** to breathe one's last (littér); (littér) **l'objet de ses ~s** the object of his desire b (Mus) crotchet rest (Brit), quarter(-note) rest (US) → **quart**

soupirail (pl -aux) [supiʀaj, o] NM (small) basement window (gen with bars)

soupirant [supiʀɑ̃] NM († ou hum) suitor† (aussi hum), wooer† (aussi hum)

soupirer [supiʀe] ▶ conjug 1 ◀ VI to sigh; **~ d'aise** to sigh with contentment, heave a contented sigh; (littér) **~ après** ou **pour qch/qn** to sigh for sth/sb (littér), yearn for sth/sb; **« j'ai tout perdu », soupira-t-il** "I've lost everything," he sighed; **... dit-il en soupirant** ... he said with a sigh ou he sighed

souple [supl] ADJ a (= flexible) [corps, membres, poignet] supple; [branche, tige, lame] flexible, pliable; [plastique] soft; [cuir, peau, cheveux] supple; [trait] gentle; [brosse à dents, lentilles cornéennes] soft; [col] soft, floppy; **il est ~ comme un verre de lampe** he's as stiff as a board; (Aut) **avoir une conduite ~** to be a smooth driver → **disque, échine** b (= accommodant) [personne, caractère, esprit] flexible, adaptable; [discipline, forme d'expression, règlement] flexible; **horaires ~s** flexible hours c (= gracieux, fluide) [corps, silhouette] lithe, lissom (littér); [démarche, taille] lithe, supple; [style] fluid, flowing (épith); **~ comme un chat** ou **une chatte** as agile as a cat

souplement [supləmɑ̃] ADV [utiliser] flexibly; **les mesures sont appliquées plus ~ dans ce pays** the measures are applied with greater flexibility in this country

souplesse [suples] NF a (= flexibilité) [corps, membres] suppleness; [branche, tige, lame] flexibility, pliability; [plastique] softness; [cuir] suppleness; **pour entretenir la ~ de la peau/des cheveux** to keep the skin/the hair supple; **d'une grande ~ d'utilisation** very easy to use; **je manque de ~** I'm not very supple b (= adaptabilité) [personne, caractère, esprit] flexibility, adaptability; [discipline, forme d'expression, règlement] flexibility; **il manque de ~** he's quite inflexible; **il faut introduire plus de ~ dans les horaires** we must bring in more flexible working hours c (= grâce, fluidité) [corps, silhouette] litheness, lissomness (littér); [démarche, taille] litheness, suppleness; [style] fluidity; **faire qch en ~** to do sth smoothly; **un démarrage en ~** a smooth start

souquenille [suknij] NF (Hist) smock

souquer [suke] ▶ conjug 1 ◀ 1 VT (= serrer) to tighten 2 VI (= ramer) **~ ferme** ou **dur** to pull hard (at the oars)

sourate [suʀat] NF sura

source [suʀs] NF a (= point d'eau) spring; **~ thermale/d'eau minérale** hot ou thermal/mineral spring → **couler, eau** b (= foyer) source; **~ de chaleur/d'énergie** source of heat/of energy; **~ lumineuse** ou **de lumière** source of light, light source; **~ sonore** source of sound c [cours d'eau] source; **cette rivière prend sa ~ dans le Massif central** this river has its source in the Massif Central d (= origine) source; **~ de ridicule/d'inspiration** source of ridicule/of inspiration; **~ de revenus** source of income; **l'argent est la ~ de tous les maux** money is the root of all evil; **cette voiture est une ~ de tracas** this car causes me a lot of trouble; **de ~ sûre** ◊ **de bonne ~** from a reliable source, on good authority; **tenir qch de ~ sûre** to have sth on good authority, get sth from a reliable source; **de ~ généralement bien informée** from a usually well-informed ou accurate source; **de ~ officielle** ou **autorisée** from an official source; **citer ses ~s** to quote one's sources; (Ordin) **langage/programme/fichier ~** source language/program/file; (Ling) **langue ~** departure ou source language → **retenue²**, **retour**

sourcier, -ière [suʀsje, jɛʀ] NM,F water diviner → **baguette**

sourcil [suʀsi] NM (eye)brow; **aux ~s épais** heavy-browed, beetle-browed → **froncer**

sourcilier, -ière [suʀsilje, jɛʀ] ADJ superciliary → **arcade**

sourciller [suʀsije] ▶ conjug 1 ◀ VI **il n'a pas sourcillé** he didn't turn a hair ou bat an eyelid; **écoutant sans ~ mes reproches** listening to my reproaches without turning a hair ou batting an eyelid

sourcilleux, -euse [suʀsijø, øz] ADJ (= pointilleux) finicky; (littér = hautain) haughty

sourd, e [suʀ, suʀd] 1 ADJ a [personne] deaf; **~ d'une oreille** deaf in one ear; **être ~ comme un pot*** to be as deaf as a post; **faire la ~e oreille** to turn a deaf ear (à to) → **naissance** b **~ à** [+ conseils, prières] deaf to; [+ vacarme, environnement] oblivious of ou to; **rester ~ aux appels de qn** to remain deaf to sb's appeals c [son, voix] muffled, muted; [couleur] muted, subdued; (Phon) [consonne] voiceless, unvoiced; **chambre ~e** anechoic room → **lanterne** d [douleur] dull; [désir, angoisse, inquiétude] muted, gnawing; [colère] subdued, muted e (= caché) [lutte] silent, hidden; **se livrer à de ~es manigances** to be engaged in hidden manoeuvring 2 NM,F deaf person; **les ~s** the deaf; **taper** ou **frapper** ou **cogner comme un ~*** to bang with all one's might; **crier** ou **hurler comme un ~*** to yell at the top of one's voice ou for all one is worth → **dialogue, pire** 3 **sourde** NF (Phon) voiceless ou unvoiced consonant

sourdement [suʀdəmɑ̃] ADV (= avec un bruit assourdi) dully; (littér = secrètement) silently; **le tonnerre grondait ~ au loin** there was a muffled rumble of thunder ou thunder rumbled dully in the distance

sourdine [suʀdin] NF a [trompette, violon] mute; **jouer en ~** to play softly ou quietly; **on entendait une musique en ~** there was music playing softly in the background b (fig) **en ~** [faire, suggérer] on the quiet, quietly; **mettre une ~ à** [+ prétentions] to tone down; [+ enthousiasme] to dampen, mute; **mettre en ~** [+ débat] to relegate to the background; [+ idée, querelle] to pass over; **mets-là en ~!** put a sock in it!‡, shut your mouth!‡

sourdingue‡ [suʀdɛ̃g] ADJ deaf

sourd-muet, sourde-muette (mpl sourds-muets) [suʀmɥe, suʀd(ə)mɥet] 1 ADJ deaf-and-dumb 2 NM,F deaf-mute, deaf-and-dumb person

sourdre [suʀdʀ] VI (littér) [source] to rise; [eau] to spring up, rise; [émotions] to well up, rise

souriant, e [suʀjɑ̃, jɑ̃t] ADJ [visage] smiling; [personne] cheerful; [pensée, philosophie] benign, agreeable; **la standardiste est très ~e** the receptionist is always smiling ou is very cheerful

souriceau (pl souriceaux) [suʀiso] NM young mouse

souricière [suʀisjɛʀ] NF (lit) mousetrap; (fig) trap; (Police) **établir une ~** to set a trap

sourire [suʀiʀ] 1 NM smile; **le ~ aux lèvres** with a smile on his lips; **avec le ~** [accueillir qn] with a smile; [travailler] cheerfully; **gardez le ~!** keep smiling!; (lit, fig) **avoir le ~** to have a smile on one's face; **il avait un ~ jusqu'aux oreilles** he was grinning from ear to ear; **faire** ou **adresser un ~ à qn** to give sb a smile; **faire des ~s à qn** to keep smiling at sb; **être tout ~** to be all smiles; **un large ~** (chaleureux) a broad smile; (amusé) a (broad) grin, a broad smile → **coin**

2 ▶ conjug 36 ◀ VI a (gén) to smile (à qn at sb); **~ à la vie** to delight in living; **~ aux anges** [personne] to have a great beam ou vacant grin on one's face; [bébé] to smile happily in one's sleep; (lit) **cette remarque les fit ~** this remark made them smile ou brought a smile to their faces; (fig) **ce projet fait ~** this project is laughable; **il est difficile d'en ~** it's nothing to smile about; **je souris de le voir si vaniteux** it makes me smile to see how vain he is; **il sourit de nos efforts** he laughs at our efforts, our efforts make him smile; **il ne faut pas ~ de ces menaces** these threats can't just be laughed ou shrugged off b **~ à** (= plaire à) to appeal to; (= être favorable à) to smile on, favour (Brit), favor (US); **cette idée ne me sourit guère** that idea doesn't appeal to me, I don't fancy that idea* (Brit); **l'idée de faire cela ne me sourit pas** I don't

relish the thought of doing that, the idea of doing that doesn't appeal to me; **la chance lui souriait** luck smiled on him; **tout lui sourit** everything goes his way

souris¹ [suʀi] NF a (= *animal*) mouse; **~ blanche** white mouse; **~ grise** house mouse; (*fig*: *pour espionner*) **je voudrais bien être une petite ~** I'd love to be a fly on the wall → **gris, jouer, trotter** b (⚹ = *femme*) chick*; **~ d'hôtel** sneak thief (*operating in hotels*) c [*gigot*] knuckle-joint; **~ d'agneau** knuckle of lamb d (*Ordin*) mouse

souris²†† [suʀi] NM (= *sourire*) smile

sournois, e [suʀnwa, waz] 1 ADJ [*personne, regard, air*] sly, shifty; [*méthode, attaque, manœuvres*] underhand; [*douleur, virus, maladie*] insidious 2 NM,F sly person; **c'est un petit ~** he's a sly little devil*

sournoisement [suʀnwazmɑ̃] ADV [*agir, regarder*] slyly; **il s'approcha ~ de lui** he stole *ou* crept stealthily up to him

sournoiserie [suʀnwazʀi] NF (*littér*) [*personne, regard, air*] slyness, shiftiness; [*méthode, attaque*] underhand nature

▼ **SOUS** [su] 1 PRÉP a (*position*) under, underneath, beneath; (*atmosphère*) in; **~ terre** under the ground, underground; **~ le canon** *ou* **le feu de l'ennemi** under enemy fire; **nager ~ l'eau** to swim under water; **s'abriter ~ un arbre/un parapluie** to shelter under *ou* underneath *ou* beneath a tree/an umbrella; **porter son sac ~ le bras** to carry one's bag under one's arm; **dormir ~ la tente** to sleep under canvas *ou* in a tent; **une mèche dépassait de ~ son chapeau** a lock of hair hung down from under her hat; **vous trouverez le renseignement ~ tel numéro/telle rubrique** you will find the information under such-and-such a number/such-and-such a heading; **~ des dehors frustes/une apparence paisible, il ...** beneath *ou* under his rough/peaceful exterior, he ...; **se promener ~ la pluie/~ le soleil** to take a walk in the rain/in the sunshine; **le village est plus joli ~ la lune/la clarté des étoiles** the village is prettier in the *ou* by moonlight/by starlight; **le pays était ~ la neige** the country was covered with *ou* in snow → **clé, coup, manteau** *etc*
b (*temps*) (= à *l'époque de*) under; (= *dans un délai de*) within; **~ le règne/le pontificat de ...** under *ou* during the reign/the pontificate of ...; **~ Charles X** under Charles X; **~ la Révolution/la Ve République** at the time of *ou* during the Revolution/the Vth Republic; **~ peu** shortly, before long; **~ huitaine/quinzaine** within a week/two weeks *ou* a fortnight (*Brit*)
c (*cause*) under; **~ l'influence de qn/qch** under the influence of sb/sth; **le rocher s'est effrité ~ l'action du soleil/du gel** the rock has crumbled away due to the action of the sun/of the frost; **plier ~ le poids de qch** to bend beneath *ou* under the weight of sth
d (*manière*) **examiner une question ~ tous ses angles** *ou* **toutes ses faces** to examine every angle *ou* facet of a question, look at a question from every angle; **~ un faux nom/une identité d'emprunt** under a false name/an assumed identity; **~ certaines conditions, j'accepte** I accept on certain conditions; **~ ce rapport** on that score, in this *ou* that respect; **il a été peint ~ les traits d'un berger** he was painted as a shepherd *ou* in the guise of a shepherd
e (*dépendance*) under; **être ~ les ordres de qn** to be under sb's orders; **~ un régime capitaliste/socialiste** under a capitalist/socialist régime; **la valise est ~ sa garde** the suitcase is in his care; **se mettre ~ la protection/la garde de qn** to commit o.s. to sb's protection/care; **l'affaire est ~ sa direction** he is running *ou* managing the affair, the affair is under his management; **l'affaire est ~ sa responsabilité** the affair is his responsibility *ou* comes within his sphere of respon-

sibility
f (*Méd*) **il est ~ calmants/antibiotiques** he's on tranquilizers/antibiotics
g (*Tech*) **câble ~ gaine** sheathed *ou* encased cable; **(emballé) ~ plastique** plastic-wrapped; **~ tube** in (a) tube; **(emballé) ~ vide** vacuum-packed
h (*Ordin*) **travailler ~ DOS®/UNIX®** to work in DOS®/UNIX®

2 PRÉF (*pour les composés les plus fréquents, voir à l'ordre alphabétique*) a (*infériorité*) **c'est du ~-Chagall/de la ~-littérature** it's pseudo-Chagall/pseudo-literature; **il fait du ~-Giono** he's a sort of substandard Giono
b (*subordination*) sub-; **~-catégorie** sub-category; (*Écon*) **~-agence** sub-branch
c (*insuffisance*) **~-industrialisé** underindustrialized; **~-peuplement** underpopulation; **les dangers de la ~-productivité** the dangers of underproductivity; **~-rémunéré** underpaid; **la région est ~-urbanisée** the region is insufficiently urbanized

sous-alimentation [suzalimɑ̃tasjɔ̃] NF undernourishment, malnutrition

sous-alimenté, e [suzalimɑ̃te] ADJ undernourished, underfed

sous-amendement [suzamɑ̃dmɑ̃] NM amendment to an amendment

sous-bibliothécaire [subiblijɔtekɛʀ] NMF assistant librarian, sub-librarian

sous-bois [subwa] NM INV undergrowth; **se promener dans les** *ou* **en ~** to walk through the trees

sous-brigadier [subʀigadje] NM deputy sergeant

sous-chef [suʃɛf] NMF (*gén*) second-in-command; (*Admin*) **~ de bureau** deputy chief clerk; **~ de gare** deputy *ou* sub-stationmaster

sous-classe [suklas] NF sub-class

sous-comité [sukɔmite] NM subcommittee

sous-commission [sukɔmisjɔ̃] NF subcommittee

sous-consommation [sukɔ̃sɔmasjɔ̃] NF underconsumption

sous-continent [sukɔ̃tinɑ̃] NM subcontinent

sous-couche [sukuʃ] NF [*peinture*] undercoat; [*parquet, moquette*] underlay; **la ~ de glace** the underlying layer of ice

souscripteur, -trice [suskʀiptœʀ, tʀis] NM,F [*emprunt, publication*] subscriber (**de** to)

souscription [suskʀipsjɔ̃] NF (*Fin*) [*actions*] subscription, application (**de** for); [*police d'assurance*] taking out*; (= *somme*) subscription, contribution; **ouvrir une ~ en faveur de qch** to start a fund in aid of sth; **livre en ~** book sold on a subscription basis; **ce livre est offert en ~ jusqu'au 15 novembre au prix de 750 F** this book is available to subscribers until November 15th at the prepublication price of 750 francs

souscrire [suskʀiʀ] ▸ conjug 39 ◂ 1 **souscrire à** VT INDIR a [+ *emprunt, publication*] to subscribe to; [+ *émission d'actions*] to subscribe for, apply for; **il a souscrit pour 1 000 F à l'emprunt** he subscribed *ou* applied for 1,000 francs' worth of shares in the scheme b [+ *idée, opinion, projet*] to subscribe to; **c'est une excellente idée et j'y souscris** it's an excellent idea and I subscribe to it *ou* and I'm all in favour of 2 VT [+ *abonnement, assurance*] to take out; [+ *actions*] to subscribe for, apply for; [+ *emprunt*] to subscribe to; [+ *billet de commerce*] to sign; **le capital a été entièrement souscrit** the capital was fully subscribed

souscrit, e [suskʀi, it] (*ptp de* **souscrire**) ADJ **capital ~** subscribed capital

sous-cutané, e [sukytane] ADJ subcutaneous; **piqûre ~** subcutaneous injection

sous-développé, e [sudev(ə)lɔpe] ADJ underdeveloped; **les pays ~s** the underdeveloped countries

sous-développement [sudev(ə)lɔpmɑ̃] NM underdevelopment

sous-diacre [sudjakʀ] NM subdeacon

sous-directeur, -trice [sudiʀɛktœʀ, tʀis] NM,F assistant manager, sub-manager

sous-dominante [sudɔminɑ̃t] NF subdominant

sous-doué, e [sudwe] (*péj ou hum*) 1 ADJ dim 2 NM,F dimwit*

sous-effectif [suzefɛktif] NM understaffing; **en ~** (*Mil*) undermanned; [*entreprise, service*] understaffed; [*usine, police*] undermanned; **nous travaillons en ~** we are understaffed

sous-embranchement [suzɑ̃bʀɑ̃ʃmɑ̃] NM sub-branch

sous-emploi [suzɑ̃plwa] NM underemployment

sous-employer [suzɑ̃plwaje] ▸ conjug 8 ◂ VT to underuse

sous-ensemble [suzɑ̃sɑ̃bl] NM subset

sous-entendre [suzɑ̃tɑ̃dʀ] ▸ conjug 41 ◂ VT to imply, infer; **qu'est-ce qu'il sous-entend par là?** what's he trying to imply *ou* what does he mean by that?

sous-entendu, e [suzɑ̃tɑ̃dy] 1 ADJ implied, understood; **il me faut une personne jeune, ~: plus jeune que vous** I need a young person, meaning: younger than you 2 NM insinuation; (*surtout sexuel*) innuendo; **d'une voix pleine** *ou* **chargée** *ou* **lourde de ~s** (*gén*) in a voice full of hidden meaning; (*avec connotations sexuelles*) in a voice full of *ou* charged with innuendo

sous-équipé, e [suzekipe] ADJ under-equipped

sous-équipement [suzekipmɑ̃] NM lack of equipment

sous-espèce [suzɛspɛs] NF subspecies

sous-estimation [suzɛstimasjɔ̃] NF underestimate

sous-estimer [suzɛstime] ▸ conjug 1 ◂ VT to underestimate

sous-évaluation [suzevalɥasjɔ̃] NF [*bijou, meuble, monnaie*] undervaluation; [*compétence, adversaire*] underestimation

sous-évaluer [suzevalɥe] ▸ conjug 1 ◂ VT [+ *objet, entreprise, monnaie*] to undervalue; [+ *sentiment, risque, conséquence*] to underestimate

sous-exploitation [suzɛksplwatasjɔ̃] NF underexploitation, underuse

sous-exploiter [suzɛksplwate] ▸ conjug 1 ◂ VT to underexploit, underuse

sous-exposer [suzɛkspoze] ▸ conjug 1 ◂ VT to underexpose

sous-exposition [suzɛkspozisjɔ̃] NF underexposure

sous-fifre* [sufifʀ] NM underling

sous-filiale [sufiljal] NF sub-branch

sous-gouverneur [suguvɛʀnœʀ] NM deputy governor

sous-groupe [sugʀup] NM subgroup

sous-homme [suzɔm] NM subhuman

sous-informé, e [suzɛ̃fɔʀme] ADJ poorly informed

sous-jacent, e [suʒasɑ̃, ɑ̃t] ADJ [*terrain, couche*] subjacent, underlying; [*raison, problème*] underlying

sous-lieutenant [suljøt(ə)nɑ̃] NM (*armée de terre*) second lieutenant; (*marine*) sub-lieutenant; (*aviation*) pilot officer (*Brit*), second lieutenant (*US*)

sous-locataire [sulɔkatɛʀ] NMF subtenant

sous-location [sulɔkasjɔ̃] NF (= *action*) subletting; (= *logement*) house *ou* apartment that is sublet

sous-louer [sulwe] ▸ conjug 1 ◂ VT to sublet

sous-main [sumɛ̃] NM INV desk blotter; (*fig*) **en ~** [*agir, négocier*] secretly, behind the scenes

➤ GRAMMAIRE ACTIVE: **SOUS** 53.6

sous-maîtresse [sumɛtʀɛs] NF brothel-keeper, madam

sous-marin, e [sumaʀɛ̃, in] **1** ADJ [pêche, chasse] underwater (épith); [végétation, faune] submarine (épith), underwater (épith); [câble] undersea (épith) → **plongée, plongeur** **2** NM **a** (lit) submarine; **~ nucléaire d'attaque** nuclear hunter-killer (submarine), nuclear attack submarine; **~ de poche** pocket ou midget submarine **b** (= espion) mole

sous-marinier [sumaʀinje] NM submariner

sous-marque [sumaʀk] NF sub-brand

sous-médicalisé, e [sumedikalize] ADJ [population, région] underprovided with medical care; [hôpital] with inadequate medical facilities

sous-menu [sumǝny] NM (Ordin) sub-menu

sous-ministre [suministʀ] NM (Can) deputy minister

sous-multiple [sumyltipl] NM submultiple

sous-nappe [sunap] NF undercloth

sous-nutrition [sunytʀisjɔ̃] NF malnutrition

sous-off* [suzɔf] NM (ABRÉV = **sous-officier**) non-com*

sous-officier [suzɔfisje] NM non-commissioned officer, NCO

sous-ordre [suzɔʀdʀ] NM **a** (Zool) suborder **b** (= subalterne) subordinate, underling

sous-payer [supeje] ▸ conjug 8 ◂ VT to underpay

sous-peuplé, e [supœple] ADJ underpopulated

sous-peuplement [supœplǝmɑ̃] NM underpopulation

sous-pied [supje] NM (under)strap

sous-plat (pl **sous-plats**) [supla] NM (Belg = dessous-de-plat) table mat (for hot serving dishes)

sous-préfecture [supʀefɛktyʀ] NF sub-prefecture

sous-préfet [supʀefɛ] NM sub-prefect

sous-préfète [supʀefɛt] NF (= fonctionnaire) sub-prefect; (= épouse) sub-prefect's wife

sous-production [supʀɔdyksjɔ̃] NF underproduction

sous-produit [supʀɔdɥi] NM (Ind) by-product; (péj) inferior product

sous-programme [supʀɔgʀam] NM subroutine, subprogram

sous-prolétaire [supʀɔletɛʀ] NMF member of the urban underclass

sous-prolétariat [supʀɔletaʀja] NM underclass

sous-pull [supyl] NM thin poloneck jersey

sous-qualifié, e [sukalifje] ADJ [emploi, main-d'œuvre] underqualified

sous-secrétaire [sus(ǝ)kʀetɛʀ] NM **~ d'État** Under-Secretary

sous-secrétariat [sus(ǝ)kʀetaʀja] NM (= fonction) post of Under-Secretary; (= bureau) Under-Secretary's office

sous-seing [susɛ̃] NM INV (Jur) private agreement (that has not been legally certified)

soussigné, e [susiɲe] ADJ, NM,F undersigned; **je ~, Dupont Charles-Henri, déclare que ...** I the undersigned, Charles-Henri Dupont, certify that ...; **les (témoins) ~s** we the undersigned

sous-sol [susɔl] NM (Géol) subsoil, substratum; [maison] basement; [magasin] basement, lower ground floor; **les richesses de notre ~** our mineral resources; **parking en ~** underground car park; **~ total** full basement

sous-tasse [sutas] NF (Belg, Helv) saucer

sous-tendre [sutɑ̃dʀ] ▸ conjug 41 ◂ VT (Géom) to subtend; (fig) to underlie, underpin; **l'idéologie qui sous-tend toutes ces publicités** the underlying ideology behind all these advertisements

sous-titrage [sutitʀaʒ] NM subtitling (NonC)

sous-titre [sutitʀ] NM [journal, livre] subheading, subhead; [film] subtitle

sous-titrer [sutitʀe] ▸ conjug 1 ◂ VT to subtitle; **en version originale sous-titrée** in the original (version) with subtitles

soustractif, -ive [sustʀaktif, iv] ADJ subtractive

soustraction [sustʀaksjɔ̃] NF **a** (Math) subtraction; **faire la ~ de** [+ somme] to take away, subtract; **et il faut encore déduire les frais de réparation : faites la ~ vous-même** and then you have to deduct repair costs — you can work it out for yourself ou you can do the sum yourself **b** (frm = vol) removal, abstraction

soustraire [sustʀɛʀ] ▸ conjug 50 ◂ **1** VT **a** (gén, Math = défalquer) to subtract, take away (**de** from) **b** (frm) (= dérober) to remove, abstract; (= cacher) to conceal, shield (**à** from); **~ qn à la justice/à la colère de qn** to shield sb from justice/from sb's anger; (Jur) **à la compétence de** to exclude from the jurisdiction of **2** **se soustraire** VPR (frm) **se ~ à** [+ devoir] to shirk; [+ obligation, corvée] to escape, shirk; [+ autorité] to elude, escape from; [+ curiosité] to conceal o.s. from, escape from; [+ regards, vue] to conceal o.s. from; **se ~ à la justice** to elude justice; (en s'enfuyant) to abscond; **quelle corvée ! comment m'y ~ ?** what a chore! how can I get out of it?

sous-traitance [sutʀɛtɑ̃s] NF subcontracting

sous-traitant [sutʀɛtɑ̃] NM subcontractor

sous-traiter [sutʀete] ▸ conjug 1 ◂ **1** VI [maître d'œuvre] to subcontract work ou jobs, contract out work; [exécutant] to be subcontracted; **son entreprise sous-traite pour une grosse société** his company does contract work for a big firm **2** VT [+ affaire, tâche] to subcontract, contract out; **cette marque sous-traite la fabrication des vêtements** this company contracts out ou subcontracts clothes manufacturing

sous-utiliser [suzytilize] ▸ conjug 1 ◂ VT [+ capacités, réseau] to underuse

sous-ventrière [suvɑ̃tʀijɛʀ] NF [cheval] girth, bellyband; (fig) **manger à s'en faire péter* la ~** to stuff o.s.

sous-verre [suvɛʀ] NM (= encadrement) clip frame; (= image encadrée) clip-framed picture

sous-vêtement [suvɛtmɑ̃] NM item of underwear, undergarment; **~s** underwear

soutache [sutaʃ] NF (Couture) frog, braid

soutane [sutan] NF cassock, soutane; (fig) **prendre la ~** to enter the Church; (péj = le clergé) **la ~** priests, the cloth

soute [sut] NF [navire] hold; **~ (à bagages)** [bateau, avion] baggage hold; **~ à charbon** coal bunker; **~ à munitions** ammunition store; **~ à mazout** oil tank; **~ à bombes** bomb bay

soutenable [sut(ǝ)nabl] ADJ [opinion] tenable, defensible; **ce film est d'une violence difficilement ~** this film is almost unbearably violent

soutenance [sut(ǝ)nɑ̃s] NF (Univ) **~ de thèse** ≈ viva (voce) (Brit), defense (US)

soutènement [sutɛnmɑ̃] NM **travaux de ~** support(ing) works; **ouvrage de ~** support(ing) structure; **mur de ~** retaining ou breast wall

souteneur [sut(ǝ)nœʀ] NM (= proxénète) pimp, procurer

▸**soutenir** [sut(ǝ)niʀ] ▸ conjug 22 ◂ **1** VT **a** (= servir d'appui à) [+ personne, toit, mur] to support, hold up; [médicament, traitement] to sustain; **on lui a fait une piqûre pour ~ le cœur** they gave him an injection to sustain his heart ou to keep his heart going; **ses jambes peuvent à peine le ~** his legs can hardly support him, he can hardly stand; **prenez un peu d'alcool, cela soutient** have a little drink — it'll give you a lift* ou keep you going **b** (= aider) [+ gouvernement, parti, candidat] to

support, back; [+ famille] to support; **~ le franc/l'économie** to support ou bolster the franc/the economy; **elle soutient les enfants contre leur père** she takes the children's part ou she stands up for the children against their father; **son amitié/il les a beaucoup soutenus dans leur épreuve** his friendship/he was a real support ou prop to them in their time of trouble, his friendship was something/he was someone for them to lean on in their time of trouble; **~ le moral des troupes** to keep the troops' morale up ou high **c** (= faire durer) [+ attention, conversation, effort] to keep up, sustain; [+ réputation] to keep up, maintain **d** (= résister à) [+ assaut, combat] to stand up to, withstand; [+ siège] to withstand; [+ regard] to bear, support; **~ la comparaison avec** to bear ou stand comparison with, compare (favourably) with **e** (= affirmer) [+ opinion, doctrine] to uphold, support; (= défendre) [+ droits] to uphold, defend; (Univ) **~ sa thèse** to attend ou have one's viva (Brit), defend one's dissertation (US); **c'est une doctrine que je ne pourrai jamais ~** it is a doctrine which I shall never be able to support ou uphold; **elle soutient toujours le contraire de ce qu'il dit** she always maintains the opposite of what he says; **il a soutenu jusqu'au bout qu'il était innocent** he maintained to the end that he was innocent; **il m'a soutenu (mordicus) qu'il avait écrit*** he swore (blind) that he'd written

2 **se soutenir** VPR **a** (= se maintenir) (sur ses jambes) to hold o.s. up, support o.s.; (dans l'eau) to keep (o.s.) afloat ou up; **il n'arrivait plus à se ~ sur ses jambes** his legs could no longer support him, he could no longer stand **b** (fig) **ça peut se ~** it's a tenable point of view; **un tel point de vue ne peut se ~** a point of view like that is indefensible ou untenable; **l'intérêt se soutient jusqu'à la fin** the interest is kept up ou sustained ou maintained right to the end **c** (= s'entraider) to stand by each other; **dans la famille, ils se soutiennent tous** the family all stand by each other ou stick together

soutenu, e [sut(ǝ)ny] (ptp de **soutenir**) ADJ (= châtié) [style, langue] formal, elevated; (= constant, assidu) [attention, effort] sustained, unflagging; [travail] sustained; (= intense) [couleur] strong; [marché] buoyant

souterrain, e [suteʀɛ̃, ɛn] **1** ADJ [parking, laboratoire, autoroute, explosion] underground; [cours d'eau, galerie] subterranean, underground; [action, influence] subterranean; **économie ~e** underground economy → **passage** **2** NM (= passage) (gén) underground ou subterranean passage; (pour piétons) underpass, subway (Brit); (= cave) underground ou subterranean room; (Archéol) souterrain

▸**soutien** [sutjɛ̃] NM **a** (= aide) support; **~ financier** financial backing; **~ logistique/moral** logistical/moral support; (Scol) **cours de ~** remedial course; **~ en français** extra teaching in French; **apporter son ~ à qn/qch** to give sb/ sth one's support; **psychothérapie de ~** supportive psychotherapy; (Mil) **unité de ~** support ou reserve unit **b** (= personne) (gén) support, prop; [parti] supporter; **tu es mon seul ~** you're my only support; **l'un des ~s du régime** one of the mainstays of the regime; (Admin) **être ~ de famille** to be the main wage-earner in the family **c** (= action) [voûte] supporting; **~ des prix** price support

soutien-gorge (pl **soutiens-gorge**) [sutjɛ̃gɔʀʒ] NM bra; **~ d'allaitement** nursing bra

soutier [sutje] NM (Naut) coal-trimmer

soutif* [sutif] NM (ABRÉV = **soutien-gorge**) bra

soutirage [sutiʀaʒ] NM [vin] decanting

soutirer [sutiʀe] ▸ conjug 1 ◂ VT **a** (= prendre) **~ qch à qn** [+ argent] to squeeze ou get sth out

---

➤ **GRAMMAIRE ACTIVE:** **soutenir** 40.2, 53.2, 53.5   **soutien** 38.1, 38.2, 40.2

of sb; [+ *promesse*] to extract sth from sb, worm sth out of sb **b** [+ *vin*] to decant, rack

souvenance [suv(ə)nɑ̃s] NF (*littér*) recollection; **avoir ~ de** to recollect, have a recollection of; (*frm*) **à ma ~** as I recall

▼ **souvenir** [suv(ə)niʀ] **1** NM **a** (= *réminiscence*) memory; (= *mémoires écrits*) **~s** memoirs; **elle a gardé de lui un bon/mauvais ~** she has good/bad memories of him; **ce n'est plus qu'un mauvais ~** it's just a bad memory now; **je n'ai qu'un vague ~ de l'incident/de l'avoir rencontré** I have only a vague ou dim recollection of the incident/of having met him ou of meeting him; **raconter des ~s d'enfance/de guerre** to recount memories of one's childhood/of the war; **si mes ~s sont exacts** if my memory serves me right ou correctly, if memory serves; (*Psych*) **~-écran** screen memory

b (*littér* = *fait de se souvenir*) recollection, remembrance (*littér*); **avoir le ~ de qch** to remember sth; **garder** ou **conserver le ~ de qch** to remember sth, retain the memory of sth; **perdre le ~ de qch** to lose all recollection of sth; **évoquer le ~ de qn** to recall ou evoke the memory of sb; (*frm*) **je n'ai pas ~ d'avoir ...** I have no recollection ou memory of having ...; **en ~ de** [+ *personne disparue*] in memory ou remembrance of; [+ *occasion*] in memory of; **en ~ du passé** for old times' sake

c (= *objet à valeur sentimentale*) keepsake, memento; (*pour touristes, marque d'un événement*) souvenir; **photo** ~ souvenir photo; **garder qch comme ~ (de qn)** to keep sth as a memento (of sb); **cette cicatrice est un ~ de la guerre** this scar is a souvenir from the war; **cette montre est un ~ de famille** this watch is a family heirloom; **boutique** ou **magasin de ~s** souvenir shop

d (= *formule de politesse*) **amical** ou **affectueux ~** yours (ever); (*sur une carte*) **meilleur** ou **amical ~ de Rome** greetings from Rome; **mon bon ~ à Jean** ◊ **transmettez mon meilleur ~ à Jean** remember me to Jean, (give my) regards to Jean; **rappelez-moi au bon ~ de votre mère** remember me to your mother, give my (kind) regards to your mother; **croyez à mon fidèle ~** yours ever, yours sincerely

2 se souvenir ▶ conjug 22 ◀ VPR to remember; **se ~ de qn** to remember sb; **se ~ de qch/d'avoir fait qch/que ...** to remember ou recall ou recollect sth/doing sth/that ...; **il a plu tout l'été, tu t'en souviens ?** ou **tu te souviens ?*** it rained all summer, do you remember?, it rained all summer, remember?*; **elle lui a donné une leçon dont il se souviendra** she taught him a lesson he won't forget (in a hurry); **souvenez-vous qu'il est très puissant** bear in mind ou remember that he is very powerful; **souviens-toi de ta promesse !** remember your promise!; **autant que je m'en souvienne ...** as ou so far as I (can) remember ...; **tu m'as fait me ~ que ...** (*littér*) ◊ **tu m'as fait ~ que ...** you have reminded me that ...; (*menace*) **je m'en souviendrai !** I won't forget!

3 VB IMPERS (*littér*) **il me souvient d'avoir entendu raconter cette histoire** I recollect ou recall ou remember having heard ou hearing that story

souvent [suvɑ̃] ADV often; **le plus ~, ça marche bien** more often than not it works well; **il ne vient pas ~ nous voir** he doesn't come to see us often, he doesn't often come and see us; **on se voit ~ ces derniers temps** we have seen a lot of each other recently; **il se trompe plus ~ qu'à son tour** he's very often mistaken; **bien ~** very often; **peu ~** seldom

souverain, e [suv(ə)ʀɛ̃, ɛn] **1** ADJ **a** (*État, puissance*) sovereign; [*assemblée, cour, juge*] supreme; **le ~ pontife** the Supreme Pontiff, the Pope **b** (= *suprême*) sovereign; **le ~ bien** the sovereign good; **remède ~ contre qch** sovereign remedy against sth **c** (*intensif*) [*mépris*] supreme **2** NM,F **a** (= *monarque*) sovereign,

monarch; **~ absolu/constitutionnel** absolute/constitutional monarch; **la ~e britannique** the British sovereign, the Queen **b** (*fig*) sovereign; **s'imposer en ~** to reign supreme; **la philosophie est la ~e des disciplines de l'esprit** philosophy is the most noble ou the highest of the mental disciplines **3** NM **a** (*Jur, Pol*) **le ~** the sovereign power **b** (*Hist Brit* = *monnaie*) sovereign

souverainement [suv(ə)ʀɛnmɑ̃] ADV **a** (= *intensément*) supremely; **ça me déplaît ~** I dislike it intensely **b** (= *en tant que souverain*) with sovereign power

souveraineté [suv(ə)ʀɛnte] NF sovereignty

souverainiste [suv(ə)ʀɛnist] ADJ, NMF (*Can*) Quebec separatist

soviet† [sɔvjɛt] NM soviet†; **le Soviet suprême** the Supreme Soviet†; (*péj*) **les Soviets*** the Soviets†

soviétique [sɔvjetik] **1** ADJ Soviet **2 Soviétique** NMF Soviet citizen

soviétisation [sɔvjetizasjɔ̃] NF sovietization

soviétiser [sɔvjetize] ▶ conjug 1 ◀ VT to sovietize

soviétologue [sɔvjetɔlɔg] NMF Kremlinologist

sovkhoze [sɔvkoz] NM sovkhoz

soya [sɔja] NM = **soja**

soyeux, -euse [swajø, øz] **1** ADJ silky **2** NM silk manufacturer (*of Lyons*), silk merchant (*of Lyons*)

SPA [ɛspea] NF (ABRÉV = **Société protectrice des animaux**) ≈ R.S.P.C.A., ≈ A.S.P.C.A. (*US*)

spacieusement [spasjøzmɑ̃] ADV spaciously; **~ aménagé** spaciously laid out; **nous sommes ~ logés** we have ample room where we are staying

spacieux, -ieuse [spasjø, jøz] ADJ spacious, roomy

spadassin [spadasɛ̃] NM (*littér*, † = *mercenaire*) hired killer ou assassin; († = *bretteur*) swordsman

spaghetti [spageti] NM **des ~s** spaghetti; **~s bolognaise** spaghetti Bolognaise; **un ~** a strand of spaghetti → **western**

spahi [spai] NM (*Hist, Mil*) Spahi (*soldier of native cavalry corps of French army in North Africa*)

sparadrap [spaʀadʀa] NM Band-Aid ®, plaster (*Brit*)

Spartacus [spaʀtakys] NM Spartacus

spartakiste [spaʀtakist] NMF Spartacist

Sparte [spaʀt] N Sparta

spartiate [spaʀsjat] **1** ADJ (*Hist, fig*) Spartan **2** NMF (*Hist*) **Spartiate** Spartan **3 spartiates** NFPL (= *chaussures*) Roman sandals

spasme [spasm] NM spasm

spasmodique [spasmɔdik] ADJ spasmodic

spasmophile [spasmɔfil] **1** ADJ ≈ tetany (*épith*) **2** NMF ≈ person suffering from tetany

spasmophilie [spasmɔfili] NF ≈ tetany

spath [spat] NM (*Minér*) spar; **~ fluor** fluorspar, fluorite (*US*)

spatial, e (*mpl* -iaux) [spasjal, jo] ADJ (*opposé à temporel*) spatial; (*Espace*) space (*épith*) → **combinaison, engin, station**

spatialisation [spasjalizasjɔ̃] NF spatialization

spatialiser [spasjalize] ▶ conjug 1 ◀ VT to spatialize

spatialité [spasjalite] NF spatiality

spationaute [spasjonot] **1** NM astronaut, spaceman **2** NF astronaut, spacewoman

spationef [spasjonɛf] NM spaceship, spacecraft

spatiotemporel, -elle [spasjotɑ̃pɔʀɛl] ADJ spatiotemporal

spatule [spatyl] NF **a** (= *ustensile*) [*peintre, cuisinier*] spatula; **doigts en ~** spatula-shaped fingers **b** (= *bout*) [*ski, manche de cuiller*] tip **c** (= *oiseau*) spoon-bill

speaker [spikœʀ] NM (*Radio, TV*) (= *annonceur*) announcer; (= *journaliste*) newscaster, newsreader; (*Pol Brit et US*) **le ~** the Speaker

speakerine† [spikʀin] NF (*Radio, TV*) (= *annonceuse*) announcer; (= *journaliste*) newsreader, newscaster

spécial, e (*mpl* -iaux) [spesjal, jo] **1** ADJ **a** (= *spécifique*) special; **une (émission) ~e élections** an election special; (*Ciné*) **le prix ~ du jury** the special jury prize; **crème ~ visage** face cream → **édition, envoyé, service b** (= *bizarre*) peculiar; (*euph*) **il a des mœurs un peu ~es** he's that way inclined* (*euph*); **il est très ~** he's very peculiar ou odd; **la cuisine japonaise, c'est ~** Japanese food is not to everybody's taste **2 spéciale** NF (= *huître*) top-quality oyster; (*Rallye*) (**épreuve) ~e** special stage

spécialement [spesjalmɑ̃] ADV (= *plus particulièrement*) especially, particularly; (= *tout exprès*) specially; **pas ~ intéressant** not particularly ou especially interesting; **tu es pressé ? — pas ~*** are you in a hurry? — not really ou especially; **c'est très intéressant, ~ vers la fin** it is very interesting, especially ou particularly towards the end; **on l'a choisi ~ pour ce travail** he was specially chosen for this job; **~ construit pour cet usage** specially built for this purpose

spécialisation [spesjalizasjɔ̃] NF specialization; (*Univ*) **faire une ~ en qch** to specialize in sth

spécialisé, e [spesjalize] (*ptp de* **spécialiser**) ADJ [*travail, personne, ouvrage, revue*] specialized; **être ~ dans** [*personne*] to be a specialist in; [*entreprise*] to specialize in → **ouvrier**

spécialiser [spesjalize] ▶ conjug 1 ◀ **1 se spécialiser** VPR to specialize (**dans** in) **2** VT to specialize

spécialiste [spesjalist] NMF (*gén, Méd*) specialist; **c'est un ~ de la gaffe*** he's always putting his foot in it*; **lecteur/public non ~** non-specialist reader/audience

spécialité [spesjalite] NF (*gén, Culin*) speciality (*Brit*), specialty (*US*); (*Univ* = *branche*) special field, specialism (*Brit*); **~ pharmaceutique** patent medicine; **~ médicale** area of medical specialization; **sa ~, c'est la chirurgie** he specializes in surgery; (*Culin*) **~s régionales** regional specialties; (*Culin*) **« la ~ du chef »** "the chef's special ou speciality"; **il est le meilleur dans sa ~** he's the best in his field; **les gaffes, c'est sa ~** he's always putting his foot in it; **il a la ~ de faire ...*** he has a special ou particular knack of doing ..., he specializes in doing ...

spécieusement [spesjøzmɑ̃] ADV speciously

spécieux, -ieuse [spesjø, jøz] ADJ specious

spécification [spesifikasjɔ̃] NF specification

spécificité [spesifisite] NF specificity

spécifier [spesifje] ▶ conjug 7 ◀ VT (= *préciser*) to specify, state; (= *indiquer, mentionner*) to state; **veuillez ~ le modèle que vous désirez** please specify the model that you require; **en passant votre commande, n'oubliez pas de ~ votre adresse** when placing your order, don't forget to state your address; **a-t-il spécifié l'heure ?** did he specify ou state the time?; **j'avais bien spécifié qu'il devait venir le matin** I had stated specifically that he should come in the morning

▼ **spécifique** [spesifik] ADJ specific

spécifiquement [spesifikmɑ̃] ADV (= *tout exprès*) specifically; (= *typiquement*) typically

spécimen [spesimɛn] NM (= *échantillon, exemple*) specimen; (= *exemplaire publicitaire*) specimen ou sample copy; **~ de signature** specimen signature; (*iro*) **c'est un drôle de ~*** he's an odd character ou a queer fish* (*Brit*)

▼ **spectacle** [spɛktakl] NM **a** (= *vue, tableau*) sight; (*grandiose, magnifique*) sight, spectacle; **au ~ de** at the sight of; (*péj*) **se donner** ou **s'offrir en ~ (à qn)** to make a spectacle ou an exhibition of o.s. (in front of sb); **une vieille dame qui assistait au ~ de la foule/de la rue** an old lady who was watching the crowd/the bustle of the street

b (= *représentation* : *Ciné, Théât*) show; (= *branche*) **le ~** show business, show biz*; **les arts du ~** the performing arts; (= *rubrique*) **«~s »** "entertainment"; **le ~ va commencer** the show is about to begin; **un ~ lyrique** an opera; **un ~ dramatique** a play; **~ de variétés** variety show; **aller au ~** to go to a show; **donner un ~** to put on a show; **donner un ~ de danse/marionnettes** to put on a dance/ puppet show; **l'industrie du ~** the entertainment(s) industry; **film à grand ~** epic (film); **procès-~** show trial; **politique-~** showbiz politics → **salle**

spectaculaire [spɛktakylɛʀ] ADJ spectacular

spectateur, -trice [spɛktatœʀ, tʀis] NM,F [*événement, accident*] onlooker, witness; [*œuvre d'art*] viewer; (*Sport*) spectator; (*Ciné, Théât*) member of the audience; (*Ciné, Théât*) **les ~s** the audience; (*fig*) **traverser la vie en ~** to go through life as an onlooker *ou* a spectator; **allons-nous assister en ~s impuissants à cette horreur ?** are we just going to stand by helplessly and watch this horrific spectacle?

spectral, e (*mpl* **-aux**) [spɛktʀal, o] ADJ **a** (= *fantomatique*) ghostly, spectral **b** (*Phys*) spectral → **analyse**

spectre [spɛktʀ] NM **a** (= *fantôme*) ghost; (*fig*) spectre (*Brit*), specter (*US*); **comme s'il avait vu un ~** as if he'd seen a ghost; **le ~ du chômage** the spectre of unemployment; **brandir le ~ de la guerre civile** to raise the spectre of civil war **b** (*Phys*) spectrum; (*fig* = *éventail*) [*thèmes, partis politiques*] spectrum; **~ d'absorption/de masse/de résonance** absorption/mass/ resonance spectrum; **~ solaire** solar spectrum **c** (*Pharm*) spectrum; **antibiotique à large ~** broad-spectrum antibiotic

spectrogramme [spɛktʀɔgʀam] NM spectrogram

spectrographe [spɛktʀɔgʀaf] NM spectrograph

spectrographie [spɛktʀɔgʀafi] NF spectrography

spectromètre [spɛktʀɔmɛtʀ] NM spectrometer

spectrométrie [spɛktʀɔmetʀi] NF spectrometry

spectroscope [spɛktʀɔskɔp] NM spectroscope

spectroscopie [spɛktʀɔskɔpi] NF spectroscopy

spectroscopique [spɛktʀɔskɔpik] ADJ spectroscopic

spéculaire [spekylɛʀ] **1** ADJ (*gén*) specular; **écriture/image ~** mirror writing/image **2** NF (*Bot*) Venus's looking-glass

spéculateur, -trice [spekylatœʀ, tʀis] NM,F speculator; (*Bourse*) **~ à la baisse** bear; **~ à la hausse** bull

spéculatif, -ive [spekylatif, iv] ADJ (*Fin, Philo*) speculative

spéculation [spekylasjɔ̃] NF (*gén*) speculation; **~ à la baisse/à la hausse** bear/bull operation; **~ boursière/immobilière** stock-market/ property (*Brit*) *ou* real-estate (*US*) speculation; **ce ne sont que des ~s (hasardeuses)** it's pure speculation *ou* conjecture; **cela a relancé les ~s sur l'éventualité d'un accord** this prompted new speculation about the possibility of an agreement

spéculer [spekyle] ▸ conjug 1 ◂ VI **a** (*Bourse*) to speculate (**sur** in); **~ à la hausse/à la baisse** to bull/bear (*Philo*) to speculate (**sur** on, about); (*fig* = *tabler sur*) **~ sur** to bank on, rely on

spéculum [spekylɔm] NM speculum

speech* [spitʃ] NM (= *laïus*) speech (*after a dinner, toast*); **faire un ~** to make a speech; **elle nous a fait son ~ sur le machisme** she gave us her speech *ou* spiel* on male chauvinism

speed* [spid] **1** ADJ (= *agité*) hyper*; **elle est très ~** she's really hyper* **2** NM (*arg Drogue*) speed

speedé, e* [spide] ADJ (= *agité*) hyper*, hyped up*

spéléo* [speleo] **1** NF ABRÉV = **spéléologie 2** NMF ABRÉV = **spéléologue**

spéléologie [speleɔlɔʒi] NF **a** (= *étude*) speleology; (= *exploration*) caving, potholing (*Brit*), spelunking (*US*)

spéléologique [speleɔlɔʒik] ADJ [*recherche*] speleological; [*expédition*] caving (*épith*), potholing (*Brit*) (*épith*), spelunking (*US*) (*épith*)

spéléologue [speleɔlɔg] NMF (= *spécialiste*) speleologist; (= *explorateur*) caver, potholer (*Brit*), spelunker (*US*)

spencer [spensœʀ] NM short jacket, spencer; (*Mil*) mess jacket

spermaceti [spɛʀmaseti] NM spermaceti

spermatique [spɛʀmatik] ADJ spermatic; **cordon ~** spermatic cord

spermatogénèse [spɛʀmatɔʒenɛz] NF spermatogenesis

spermatozoïde [spɛʀmatɔzɔid] NM sperm, spermatozoon

sperme [spɛʀm] NM semen, sperm

spermicide [spɛʀmisid] **1** ADJ spermicide (*épith*), spermicidal **2** NM spermicide

spermogramme [spɛʀmɔgʀam] NM semen analysis

sphaigne [sfɛɲ] NF peat *ou* bog moss

sphénoïde [sfenɔid] NM sphenoid bone

sphère [sfɛʀ] NF (*Astron, fig*) sphere; **~ céleste/ terrestre** celestial/terrestrial sphere; **~ d'influence/d'activité** sphere of influence/of activity; **dans toutes les ~s de la vie privée/ publique** in all spheres of private/public life; **les hautes ~s de l'État** the higher *ou* highest echelons *ou* levels of government; **il évolue dans les hautes ~s** he moves in influential circles

sphéricité [sfeʀisite] NF sphericity

sphérique [sfeʀik] ADJ spherical → **calotte**

sphéroïde [sfeʀɔid] NM spheroid

sphincter [sfɛktɛʀ] NM sphincter

sphinx [sfɛks] NM **a** (*Art, Myth, fig*) sphinx; (*Myth*) **le Sphinx** the Sphinx; **sourire de ~** sphinx-like smile **b** (*Zool*) hawkmoth (*Brit*), sphinx moth (*US*)

spi [spi] NM = **spinnaker**

spina-bifida [spinabifida] NM INV spina bifida

spinal, e (*mpl* **-aux**) [spinal, o] ADJ spinal

spinnaker [spinakɛʀ] NM spinnaker

spiral, e (*mpl* **-aux**) [spiʀal, o] **1** ADJ spiral **2** NM (**ressort**) **~** hairspring **3** **spirale** NF spiral; **s'élever/tomber en ~e** to spiral up(wards)/down(wards); **la ~e de l'inflation** *ou* **inflationniste** the inflationary spiral → **cahier**

spiralé, e [spiʀale] ADJ spiral (*épith*)

spirante [spiʀɑ̃t] ADJ F, NF (**consonne**) **~** spirant, fricative

spire [spiʀ] NF [*hélice, spirale*] (single) turn; [*coquille*] whorl; [*ressort*] spiral

spirite [spiʀit] ADJ, NMF spiritualist

spiritisme [spiʀitism] NM spiritualism

spiritualiser [spiʀitɥalize] ▸ conjug 1 ◂ VT to spiritualize

spiritualisme [spiʀitɥalism] NM spiritualism

spiritualiste [spiʀitɥalist] **1** ADJ spiritualist(ic) **2** NMF spiritualist

spiritualité [spiʀitɥalite] NF spirituality

spirituel, -elle [spiʀitɥɛl] ADJ **a** (= *vif, fin*) [*personne, remarque*] witty **b** (*Philo, Rel*) [*chef, maître, père, fils, pouvoir*] spiritual; **musique spi-** rituelle sacred music; **concert ~** concert of sacred music; **le ~ et le temporel** the spiritual and the temporal

spirituellement [spiʀitɥɛlmɑ̃] ADV **a** [*remarquer*] wittily **b** (*Philo, Rel*) spiritually

spiritueux, -euse [spiʀitɥø, øz] **1** ADJ spirituous **2** NM spirit; **les ~** spirits

spiroïdal, e (*mpl* **-aux**) [spiʀɔidal, o] ADJ spiroid

spleen [splin] NM (*littér*) melancholy, spleen †† ; **avoir le ~** to feel melancholy

splendeur [splɑ̃dœʀ] NF **a** [*paysage, réception, résidence*] magnificence, splendour (*Brit*), splendor (*US*); **ce tapis est une ~** this carpet is quite magnificent; **les ~s de l'art africain** the splendours of African art; **quelle ~ !** it's magnificent! **b** (= *gloire*) glory, splendour (*Brit*), splendor (*US*); **du temps de sa ~** in the days of its (*ou* his *etc*) glory *ou* splendour; (*iro*) **dans toute sa/leur ~** in all its/their splendour *ou* glory **c** (*littér* = *éclat, lumière*) brilliance, splendour (*Brit*), splendor (*US*)

splendide [splɑ̃did] ADJ [*temps, journée*] splendid, gorgeous, glorious; [*soleil*] glorious; [*réception, résidence, spectacle*] splendid, magnificent; [*femme*] magnificent, gorgeous; **~ isolement** splendid isolation; **tu as un teint** *ou* **une mine ~** you look wonderful

splendidement [splɑ̃didmɑ̃] ADV splendidly, magnificently

splénétique † [splenetik] ADJ (*littér*) splenetic

spoiler [spɔjlɛʀ] NM (*Aut*) spoiler

spoliateur, -trice [spɔljatœʀ, tʀis] **1** ADJ [*loi*] spoliatory **2** NM,F despoiler

spoliation [spɔljasjɔ̃] NF despoilment (**de** of)

spolier [spɔlje] ▸ conjug 7 ◂ VT to despoil (**de** of)

spondaïque [spɔ̃daik] ADJ spondaic

spondée [spɔ̃de] NM spondee

spongieux, -ieuse [spɔ̃ʒjø, jøz] ADJ (*gén, Anat*) spongy

spongiforme [spɔ̃ʒifɔʀm] ADJ spongiform

sponsor [spɔ̃sɔʀ] NM sponsor

sponsorisation [spɔ̃sɔʀizasjɔ̃] NF sponsoring

sponsoriser [spɔ̃sɔʀize] ▸ conjug 1 ◂ VT to sponsor; **se faire ~ par une société** to get sponsorship from a company

spontané, e [spɔ̃tane] ADJ (*gén*) spontaneous; [*candidature, témoignage*] unsolicited → **génération**

spontanéité [spɔ̃taneite] NF spontaneity

spontanément [spɔ̃tanemɑ̃] ADV spontaneously

Sporades [spɔʀad] NFPL **les ~** the Sporades

sporadicité [spɔʀadisite] NF sporadic nature *ou* occurrence

sporadique [spɔʀadik] ADJ sporadic

sporadiquement [spɔʀadikmɑ̃] ADV sporadically

sporange [spɔʀɑ̃ʒ] NM spore case, sporangium (*SPÉC*)

spore [spɔʀ] NF spore

sport [spɔʀ] **1** NM **a** (= *activité*) sport; **faire du ~** to do sport; **~ individuel/d'équipe** *ou* **collectif** individual/team sport; **~ en salle/de plein air** indoor/outdoor sport; **~ de compétition/de combat** competitive/combat sport; **~ de loisir** recreational sport; **les ~s d'hiver** winter sports; **aller aux ~s d'hiver** to go on a winter sports holiday; **~s nautiques/ mécaniques** water/motor sports; (*fig*) **~ cérébral** mental exercise; **la corruption/la fraude fiscale est devenue un véritable ~ national** corruption/tax fraud has become a national pastime; (*Scol*) (**section**) **~-études** special course in secondary school for athletically-gifted pupils; **de ~** [*vêtements, terrain, voiture*] sports (*épith*) **b** (* = *action*) **il va y avoir du ~ !** we're going to see some fun!* *ou* action!*; **faire ça, c'est**

vraiment du ~ it's no picnic*; **faire qch pour le ~** to do sth for the hell of it* [2] ADJ INV [a] (= *décontracté*) [*vêtement, coupe*] casual [b] († = *chic, fair-play*) sporting, fair

sportif, -ive [spɔrtif, iv] [1] ADJ [a] [*épreuve, journal, résultats*] sports (*épith*); [*pêche, marche*] competitive (*épith*); **pratiquer une activité sportive** to play *ou* practise a sport [b] [*personne, jeunesse*] athletic, fond of sports (*attrib*); [*allure, démarche*] athletic; **elle a une conduite sportive** she handles a car like a rally driver [c] [*attitude, mentalité, comportement*] sporting, sportsmanlike; **faire preuve d'esprit ~** to be sportsmanlike [2] NM sportsman [3] **sportive** NF sportswoman

sportivement [spɔrtivmɑ̃] ADV sportingly

sportivité [spɔrtivite] NF sportsmanship

spot [spɔt] [1] NM [a] (*Phys*) light spot; [*Élec*] scanning spot; [*radar*] blip [b] (= *lampe, Ciné, Théât*) spotlight, spot [c] (= *publicité*) **~ (publicitaire)** commercial, advert* (*Brit*), ad* [2] ADJ INV (*Écon*) [*crédit, marché, prix*] spot (*épith*)

spoutnik [sputnik] NM sputnik

sprat [sprat] NM sprat

spray [sprɛ] NM (= *aérosol*) spray, aerosol; **déodorant en ~** spray(-on) deodorant

sprint [sprint] NM (*de fin de course*) (final) sprint, final spurt; (= *épreuve*) sprint; **battu au ~ (final)** beaten in the (final) sprint → **piquer 1f**

sprinter¹ [sprinte] ▸ conjug 1 ◂ VI to sprint; (*en fin de course*) to put on a final spurt

sprinter² [sprintœr] NM, **sprinteur, -euse** [sprintœr, øz] NM,F sprinter; (*en fin de course*) fast finisher

squale [skwal] NM shark

squame [skwam] NF (*Méd*) scale, squama (*SPÉC*)

squameux, -euse [skwamø, øz] ADJ (*Méd*) squamous, squamose; (*littér*) scaly

square [skwar] NM public garden(s)

squash [skwaʃ] NM squash; **faire du ~** to play squash

squat* [skwat] NM (= *logement*) squat

squatter¹ [skwatœr] NM squatter

squatter² [skwate], **squattériser** [skwaterize] ▸ conjug 1 ◂ VT (= *loger*) to squat (in)

squatteur [skwatœr] NM = **squatter¹**

squaw [skwo] NF squaw

squeezer [skwize] ▸ conjug 1 ◂ VT [a] (*au bridge*) to squeeze [b] (* = *évincer*) to bypass

squelette [skəlɛt] NM (*lit, fig*) skeleton; **après sa maladie, c'était un vrai ~** after his illness he was just a bag of bones *ou* he was like a skeleton; **c'est un ~ ambulant*** he's a walking skeleton; (= *scandale*) **un ~ dans le placard*** a skeleton in the cupboard (*Brit*) *ou* closet (*US*)

squelettique [skəletik] ADJ [*personne, arbre*] scrawny; [*exposé*] sketchy, skimpy; (*Anat*) skeletal; **d'une maigreur ~** all skin and bone; **il est ~** he's an absolute skeleton, he's all skin and bone; **des effectifs ~s** a skeleton staff

Sri Lanka [srilɑ̃ka] NM Sri Lanka

sri-lankais, e [srilɑ̃kɛ, ɛz] [1] ADJ Sri-Lankan [2] **Sri-Lankais(e)** NM,F Sri-Lankan

SRPJ [ɛsɛrpeʒi] NM (ABRÉV = **service régional de la police judiciaire**) ≈ regional crime squad, ≈ CID (*Brit*)

S.S. [ɛsɛs] [1] NF [a] (ABRÉV = **Sécurité sociale**) → **sécurité** [b] (ABRÉV = **Sa Sainteté**) HH [2] NM (= *soldat*) SS

SSII [ɛsɛsii] NF (ABRÉV = **société de service et d'ingénierie en informatique**) computer engineering and maintenance company

St (ABRÉV = **Saint**) St

stabilisant [stabilizɑ̃] NM (*Chim*) stabilizer

stabilisateur, -trice [stabilizatœr, tris] [1] ADJ stabilizing [2] NM (*Tech*) [*véhicule*] anti-roll device; [*navire, vélo*] stabilizer; [*avion*] (*horizontal*) tailplane; (*vertical*) fixed fin; (*Chim : pour aliments*) stabilizer

stabilisation [stabilizasjɔ̃] NF stabilization

stabiliser [stabilize] ▸ conjug 1 ◂ [1] VT [+ *situation, prix*] to stabilize; [+ *terrain*] to consolidate; (*Aut*) **à 90 km/h en vitesse stabilisée** at a constant 90 km/h → **accotement** [2] **se stabiliser** VPR [*situation, prix, cours*] to stabilize, become stabilized; [*courbe de graphe*] to plateau; [*personne*] (*physiquement*) to find one's balance; (*dans la vie*) to settle down

stabilité [stabilite] NF stability; **~ des prix** price stability; **~ monétaire/économique/politique** monetary/economic/political stability

stable [stabl] ADJ [*monnaie, gouvernement, personne*] (*Chim, Phys*) stable; [*position, échelle*] stable, steady; **~ sur ses jambes** steady on one's legs

stabulation [stabylasjɔ̃] NF [*bétail*] stalling; [*chevaux*] stabling; [*poissons*] storing in tanks

staccato [stakato] [1] ADV staccato [2] NM staccato passage

stade [stad] NM [a] (*sportif*) stadium [b] (= *période, étape*) stage; **à ce ~** at this stage; **à ce ~ de la maladie** at this stage in the development of the disease; **il en est resté au ~ de l'adolescence** he never got beyond adolescence *ou* the adolescent phase; (*Psych*) **~ oral/anal/génital** oral/anal/genital stage

staff¹ [staf] NM [a] (= *personnel*) staff [b] (*Méd* = *réunion de travail*) staff meeting

staff² [staf] NM (= *plâtre*) staff

staffeur [stafœr] NM plasterer (*working in staff*)

▼ **stage** [staʒ] NM (= *période*) training period, internship (*US*); (= *cours*) training course; [*avocat*] articles; **~ de perfectionnement** advanced training course; **~ de formation (professionnelle)** vocational (training) course; **~ en entreprise** work experience scheme *ou* placement; **~ d'insertion (professionnelle)** *training scheme for the young unemployed to help them find work*; **~ de réinsertion** retraining course; **~-parking*** useless training course; **~ d'initiation** introductory course; **~ pédagogique** teaching practice; **il a fait son ~ chez Maître Legrand** he did his articles in Mr Legrand's practice *ou* chambers; **faire son ~ chez Mr Legrand**; **faire ~ ou suivre un ~** to undergo a period of training, go on a (training) course; **faire un ~ d'informatique** (*gén*) to go on a computing course; (*sur son lieu de travail*) to have in-service *ou* in-house training in computing

stagflation [stagflasjɔ̃] NF stagflation

stagiaire [staʒjɛr] [1] NMF trainee, intern (*US*) [2] ADJ (*épith*); **professeur ~** student *ou* trainee teacher

stagnant, e [stagnɑ̃, ɑ̃t] ADJ (*lit, fig*) stagnant

stagnation [stagnasjɔ̃] NF (*lit, fig*) stagnation; **marché en ~** stagnating market

stagner [stagne] ▸ conjug 1 ◂ VI (*lit, fig*) to stagnate

stakhanovisme [stakanɔvism] NM Stakhanovism

stakhanoviste [stakanɔvist] [1] ADJ Stakhanovist [2] NMF Stakhanovite

stalactite [stalaktit] NF stalactite

stalag [stalag] NM stalag

stalagmite [stalagmit] NF stalagmite

Staline [stalin] NM Stalin

stalinien, -ienne [stalinjɛ̃, jɛn] ADJ, NM,F Stalinist

stalinisme [stalinism] NM Stalinism

stalle [stal] NF [*cheval*] stall, box; (*Rel*) stall

stance [stɑ̃s] NF († = *strophe*) stanza; (= *poème*) **~s** *type of verse form (of lyrical poem)*

stand [stɑ̃d] NM [*exposition*] stand; [*foire*] stall; **~ (de tir)** [*foire*] (*Sport*) shooting range; (*Mil*) firing range; (*Sport*) **~ de ravitaillement** pit

standard¹ [stɑ̃dar] NM (*Téléc*) switchboard

standard² [stɑ̃dar] [1] NM [a] (= *norme*) standard; **~ de vie** standard of living [b] (*Mus*) (jazz) standard [2] ADJ INV (*Comm, Tech*) standard (*épith*) → **échange**

standardisation [stɑ̃dardizasjɔ̃] NF standardization

standardiser [stɑ̃dardize] ▸ conjug 1 ◂ VT to standardize

standardiste [stɑ̃dardist] NMF switchboard operator; **demandez à la ~** ask the operator

stand-by [stɑ̃dbaj] [1] ADJ INV stand-by (*épith*); **en ~** on stand-by [2] NM INV stand-by passenger

standing [stɑ̃diŋ] NM standing; **immeuble de grand ~** block of luxury flats (*Brit*) *ou* apartments (*US*)

staphylocoque [stafilɔkɔk] NM staphylococcus; **~ doré** staphylococcus aureus

star [star] NF (*Ciné*) star; **c'est une ~ du journalisme/de la politique** he's (*ou* she's) a big name in journalism/in politics; **~ du tennis** top name in tennis, star tennis player

starking [starkiŋ] NF starking (apple)

starlette [starlɛt] NF starlet

star-system (*pl* star-systems) [starsistɛm] NM star system

START [start] (ABRÉV = **Strategic Arms Reduction Talks**) START

starter [startɛr] NM [a] (*Aut*) choke; **mettre le ~** to pull the choke out; **marcher au ~** to run with the choke out; **~ automatique** automatic choke [b] (*Sport*) starter

starting-block (*pl* starting-blocks) [startiŋblɔk] NM starting block; **être dans les ~s** to be on the starting blocks

starting-gate (*pl* starting-gates) [startiŋget] NM starting gate

stase [staz] NF stasis

stat* [stat] NF (ABRÉV = **statistique**) stat*; **faire des ~s** to do stats*

station [stasjɔ̃] NF [a] (= *lieu d'arrêt*) **~ (de métro)** (underground (*Brit*) *ou* subway (*US*) station; **~ (d'autobus)** (bus) stop; **~ (de chemin de fer)** halt; **~ de taxis** taxi rank [b] (= *poste, établissement*) station; **~ d'observation/de recherches** observation/research station; **~ agronomique/météorologique** agricultural research/meteorological station; **~ d'épuration** water-treatment plant; **~ de pompage** pumping station; **~ géodésique** geodesic *ou* geodetic station; **~ d'émission** *ou* **émettrice** transmitting station; **~ (de) radar** radar tracking station; **~ de radio** radio station; **~ spatiale/orbitale** space/orbiting station; **~ d'essence** service *ou* filling station, petrol (*Brit*) *ou* gas (*US*) station; **~ de lavage** carwash [c] (= *site*) site (*Bot, Zool*) station; **~ préhistorique** prehistoric site; (*Bot*) **une ~ de gentianes** a gentian station [d] (*de vacances*) resort; **~ balnéaire/climatique** sea *ou* seaside/health resort; **~ de ski** *ou* **de sports d'hiver** winter sports *ou* (winter) ski resort; **~ de montagne** *ou* **d'altitude** mountain resort; **~ thermale** thermal spa [e] (= *posture*) posture, stance; **~ verticale** upright position; **la ~ debout lui est pénible** he finds standing upright painful [f] (= *halte*) stop; **faire des ~s prolongées devant les vitrines** to linger in front of the shop windows [g] (*Rel*) station; **les ~s de la Croix** the Stations of the Cross [h] (*Marine*) station [i] (*Astron*) stationary point [j] (*Ordin*) **~ d'accueil** docking station; **~ de travail** workstation

> GRAMMAIRE ACTIVE: **stage** 46.1

stationnaire [stasjɔnɛʀ] ⊡ ADJ stationary; (*Méd*) **son état est ~** his condition is stable; (*Phys*) **ondes ~s** standing waves; **l'hélicoptère était en vol ~** the helicopter was hovering overhead ⊡ NM (*Naut*) station ship

stationnement [stasjɔnmɑ̃] NM ⓐ (*véhicule*) parking; **~ alterné** parking on alternate sides; **~ bilatéral/unilatéral** parking on both sides/on one side only; **« ~ gênant »** "limited parking"; **« ~ réglementé »** "restricted parking"; **« ~ interdit »** "no parking", "no waiting"; (*sur autoroute*) "no stopping"; **« ~ payant »** (*avec parcmètres*) "meter zone"; (*avec tickets*) "parking with ticket only"; **en ~** (*véhicule*) parked; (*Mil*) stationed → **disque, feu**¹ ⓑ (*Can = parking*) car park (*Brit*), parking lot (*US*)

stationner [stasjɔne] ▸ conjug 1 ◂ VI ⓐ (= *être garé*) to be parked; (= *se garer*) to park ⓑ (= *rester sur place*) [*personne*] to stay, remain ⓒ (*Mil*) **armes nucléaires/troupes stationnées en Europe** nuclear weapons/troops stationed in Europe

station-service (*pl* **stations-service(s)**) [stasjɔ̃sɛʀvis] NF service *ou* filling station, petrol (*Brit*) *ou* gas (*US*) station

statique [statik] ⊡ ADJ static ⊡ NF statics *sg*

statiquement [statikmɑ̃] ADV statically

statisme [statism] NM stasis

statisticien, -ienne [statistisjɛ̃, jɛn] NM,F statistician

statistique [statistik] ⊡ NF (= *science*) **la ~** statistics *sg*; (= *données*) **des ~s** statistics; **une ~** a statistic ⊡ ADJ statistical; **données ~s** statistical data

statistiquement [statistikmɑ̃] ADV statistically

stator [statɔʀ] NM stator

statuaire [statɥɛʀ] ⊡ NF statuary ⊡ ADJ statuary ⊡ NM (*littér*) sculptor

statue [staty] NF statue; **rester immobile comme une ~** to stand as still as a statue, stand stock-still; **elle était là ~ du désespoir** she was the picture of despair; **changé en ~ de sel** (*Bible*) turned into a pillar of salt; (*fig*) transfixed, rooted to the spot

statuer [statɥe] ▸ conjug 1 ◂ VI to give a verdict; **~ sur** to rule on, give a ruling on; **~ sur le cas de qn** to decide sb's case

statuette [statɥɛt] NF statuette

statufier [statyfje] ▸ conjug 7 ◂ VT (= *immortaliser*) to erect a statue to; (= *pétrifier*) to transfix, root to the spot

statu quo [statykwo] NM INV status quo

stature [statyʀ] NF (= *taille*) stature; (*fig* = *calibre*) calibre (*Brit*), caliber (*US*); **de haute ~** of (great) stature; **cet écrivain est d'une tout autre ~** this writer is in a different league altogether

statut [staty] ⊡ NM (= *position*) status; **~ social/fiscal/juridique** social/tax/legal status; **avoir/obtenir le ~ de salarié** to be on/be put on the payroll; **il a obtenu le ~ de réfugié politique** he has been given *ou* granted political refugee status ⊡ **statuts** NMPL (= *règlement*) statutes

statutaire [statɥtɛʀ] ADJ statutory; **horaire ~** regulation *ou* statutory number of working hours

statutairement [statɥtɛʀmɑ̃] ADV in accordance with the statutes *ou* regulations, statutorily

Ste (ABRÉV = **Sainte**) St

Sté (ABRÉV = **société**) **et ~** and Co.

steak [stɛk] NM steak; **~ au poivre** steak au poivre, peppered steak; **~ tartare** steak tartar(e); **~ frites** steak and chips (*Brit*) *ou* French fries (*US*); **~ haché** minced beef (*Brit*), ground beef (*US*); **~ de thon** tuna steak

stéarine [stearin] NF stearin

stéatite [steatit] NF steatite

steeple [stipœl] NM **~(-chase)** (*Athlétisme, Équitation*) steeplechase; **le 3 000 mètres ~** the 3,000 metres steeplechase

stèle [stɛl] NF stele

stellaire [stelɛʀ] ⊡ ADJ stellar ⊡ NF stitchwort

stem(m) [stɛm] NM (*Ski*) stem; **faire du ~** to stem

stencil [stɛnsil] NM (*pour polycopie*) stencil

sténo [steno] ⊡ NMF (ABRÉV = **sténographe**) shorthand typist, steno* (*US*) ⊡ NF (ABRÉV = **sténographie**) shorthand; **prendre une lettre en ~** to take a letter (down) in shorthand

sténodactylo¹ [stenodaktilo], **sténodactylographe**† [stenodaktilɔgʀaf] NMF shorthand typist

sténodactylo² [stenodaktilo], **sténodactylographie**† [stenodaktilɔgʀafi] NF shorthand typing

sténographe† [stenɔgʀaf] NMF shorthand typist, stenographer (*US*)

sténographie [stenɔgʀafi] NF shorthand, stenography

sténographier [stenɔgʀafje] ▸ conjug 7 ◂ VT to take down in shorthand

sténographique [stenɔgʀafik] ADJ shorthand (*épith*), stenographic

sténopé [stenɔpe] NM (*Photo*) pinhole

sténotype [stenɔtip] NF stenotype

sténotypie [stenɔtipi] NF stenotypy

sténotypiste [stenɔtipist] NMF stenotypist

stentor [stɑ̃tɔʀ] NM ⓐ (= *homme*) stentor; **une voix de ~** a stentorian voice ⓑ (*Zool*) stentor

steppe [stɛp] NF steppe

stercoraire [stɛʀkɔʀɛʀ] NM skua

stère [stɛʀ] NM stere

stéréo [stereo] ⊡ NF (ABRÉV = **stéréophonie**) stereo; **émission (en) ~** programme in stereo; **enregistrement (en) ~** stereo recording; **c'est en ~** it's in stereo ⊡ ADJ INV (ABRÉV = **stéréophonique**) stereo; **son ~** stereo sound

stéréophonie [stereɔfɔni] NF stereophony

stéréophonique [stereɔfɔnik] ADJ stereophonic

stéréoscope [stereɔskɔp] NM stereoscope

stéréoscopie [stereɔskɔpi] NF stereoscopy

stéréoscopique [stereɔskɔpik] ADJ stereoscopic

stéréotype [stereɔtip] NM (*lit, fig*) stereotype

stéréotypé, e [stereɔtipe] ADJ stereotyped

stérile [steʀil] ADJ ⓐ [*personne*] sterile, infertile; [*animal, plante, union*] sterile; [*terre, sol*] barren ⓑ (= *aseptique*) [*milieu, compresse, flacon*] sterile ⓒ [*sujet, réflexions, pensées*] sterile; [*discussion, effort, débat*] fruitless, futile; [*écrivain, artiste*] unproductive

stérilet [steʀilɛ] NM coil, I.U.D., intra-uterine device

stérilisant, e [steʀilizɑ̃, ɑ̃t] ADJ (*lit*) sterilizing; (*fig*) unproductive, fruitless

stérilisateur [steʀilizatœʀ] NM sterilizer

stérilisation [steʀilizasjɔ̃] NF sterilization

stériliser [steʀilize] ▸ conjug 1 ◂ VT to sterilize; **lait stérilisé** sterilized milk

stérilité [steʀilite] NF ⓐ [*personne*] infertility, sterility; [*animal, plante, union*] sterility; [*terre, sol*] barrenness ⓑ [*milieu, compresse, flacon*] sterility ⓒ [*sujet, réflexion, pensées*] sterility; [*discussion, débat, effort*] fruitlessness, futility; [*écrivain, artiste*] lack of creativity

sterling [stɛʀliŋ] ADJ INV, NM INV sterling → **livre**²

sterne [stɛʀn] NF tern; **~ arctique** Arctic tern

sternum [stɛʀnɔm] NM breastbone, sternum (*SPÉC*)

stéroïde [steʀɔid] ⊡ NM steroid ⊡ ADJ steroidal

stéthoscope [stetɔskɔp] NM stethoscope

Stetson® [stɛtsɔn] NM Stetson®

steward [stiwart] NM steward, flight attendant

stick [stik] NM [*colle*] stick; (*Hockey*) stick; (= *groupe de parachutistes*) stick; **déodorant en ~** stick deodorant

stigmate [stigmat] NM ⓐ (= *marque, Méd*) mark, scar; (*Rel*) **~s** stigmata; (*fig*) **~s du vice/de la bêtise** marks of vice/of stupidity ⓑ (= *orifice*) (*Zool*) stigma, spiracle; (*Bot*) stigma

stigmatisation [stigmatizasjɔ̃] NF (*Rel*) stigmatization; (= *blâme*) condemnation, denunciation

stigmatiser [stigmatize] ▸ conjug 1 ◂ VT ⓐ (= *blâmer*) to denounce, condemn; **stigmatisé comme égoïste/criminel** stigmatized *ou* branded as an egoist/a murderer ⓑ (*Méd*) to mark, scar

stimulant, e [stimylɑ̃, ɑ̃t] ⊡ ADJ stimulating ⊡ NM (*physique*) stimulant; (*intellectuel*) stimulus, spur, incentive; (= *drogue*) upper*

stimulateur [stimylatœʀ] NM **~ cardiaque** pacemaker

stimulation [stimylasjɔ̃] NF stimulation; (*Écon*) **mesures de ~ de la demande** measures to stimulate *ou* boost demand

stimuler [stimyle] ▸ conjug 1 ◂ VT [+ *personne*] to stimulate, spur on; [+ *économie, croissance, demande*] to stimulate, boost; [+ *appétit*] to stimulate; **cet élève a besoin d'être stimulé sans arrêt** this pupil needs constant stimulation

stimulus [stimylys] (*pl* **stimuli** [stimyli]) NM (*Physiol, Psych*) stimulus

stipendié, e [stipɑ̃dje] (*ptp de* **stipendier**) ADJ (*littér, péj*) hired

stipendier [stipɑ̃dje] ▸ conjug 7 ◂ VT (*littér, péj*) to hire, take into one's pay

stipulation [stipylasjɔ̃] NF stipulation

stipuler [stipyle] ▸ conjug 1 ◂ VT [*clause, loi, condition*] to state, stipulate; (= *faire savoir expressément*) to stipulate, specify

STO [esteo] NM (ABRÉV = **Service du travail obligatoire**) → **service**

stock [stɔk] NM ⓐ (*Comm*) stock; (*fig*) stock, supply; **~ d'or** gold reserves; **faire des ~s** to stock up (**de** on); **avoir qch en ~** to have *ou* keep sth in stock; **prends un crayon, j'en ai tout un ~** take a pencil, I've got a whole stock of them; **dans la limite des ~s disponibles** while stocks last; **~s stratégiques/régulateurs** strategic/regulatory stocks → **rupture** ⓑ (*Bio*) stock

stockage [stɔkaʒ] NM ⓐ (= *accumulation*) stocking; (= *entreposage*) storage; **le ~ de l'énergie** energy storage; **le ~ des déchets radioactifs** the storage of nuclear waste ⓑ (*Ordin*) storage

stock-car (*pl* **stock-cars**) [stɔkkaʀ] NM (= *sport*) stock-car racing; (= *voiture*) stock car; **une course de ~** a stock-car race

stocker [stɔke] ▸ conjug 1 ◂ VT (= *accumuler*) to stock; (= *entreposer*) to store; (*péj: pour spéculer, amasser*) to stockpile; (*Ordin*) **~ (sur mémoire)** to store (in the memory)

Stockholm [stɔkɔlm] N Stockholm

stockiste [stɔkist] NMF (*Comm*) stockist (*Brit*), dealer (*US*); (*Aut*) agent

stoïcien, -ienne [stɔisjɛ̃, jɛn] ADJ, NM,F stoic

stoïcisme [stɔisism] NM (*Philo*) Stoicism; (*fig*) stoicism

stoïque [stɔik] ⊡ ADJ stoical, stoic ⊡ NMF (*gén*) stoic; (*Philo*) Stoic

stoïquement [stɔikmɑ̃] ADV stoically

stomacal, e (*mpl* **-aux**) [stɔmakal, o] ADJ stomach (*épith*), gastric

stomatologie [stɔmatɔlɔʒi] NF stomatology

stomatologiste [stɔmatɔlɔʒist], **stomatologue** [stɔmatɔlɔg] NMF stomatologist

stop [stɔp] **1** EXCL a ~! stop!; (*en servant qn*) **tu me diras ~ — ~!** say when — when!; **il faut savoir dire ~** you have to know when to say no; **après deux ans sans vacances, j'ai dit ~!** after two years without a holiday, I said enough is enough! b (*Téléc*) stop **2** NM a (*Aut*) (= *panneau*) stop *ou* halt sign; (= *feu arrière*) brake-light b* (ABRÉV = **auto-stop**) **faire du ~** to hitch(hike), thumb* a lift *ou* a ride; **faire le tour de l'Europe en ~** to hitch round Europe; **il a fait du ~ pour rentrer chez lui** ◊ **il est rentré chez lui en ~** he hitched (a lift) home; **j'ai pris deux personnes en ~** I picked up two hitchhikers; **je l'ai pris en ~** I gave him a lift *ou* ride

stop and go [stɔpɛndɡo] NM INV (*Écon*) stop and go; **politique de ~** stop-go policy

stoppage [stɔpaʒ] NM invisible mending

stopper [stɔpe] ▶conjug 1◀ **1** VI to halt, stop **2** VT a (= *arrêter*) to stop, halt b (*Couture*) [+ *bas*] to mend; **faire ~ un vêtement** to get a garment (invisibly) mended

stoppeur, -euse [stɔpœʀ, øz] NM,F a (*Couture*) invisible mender b (* = *auto-stoppeur*) hitchhiker c (*Ftbl*) fullback

store [stɔʀ] NM (*en plastique, bois, tissu*) blind; [*magasin*] (*en toile*) awning, shade; (*en métal*) shutters; **~ vénitien** *ou* **à lamelles orientables** Venetian blind b (= *voilage*) net curtain

strabisme [strabism] NM squinting (*Brit*), strabismus (*SPÉC*); **~ divergent** divergent squint; **~ convergent** convergent strabismus (*SPÉC*); **il souffre d'un léger ~** he is slightly cross-eyed, he suffers from a slight strabismus (*SPÉC*), he has a slight squint (*Brit*)

stradivarius [stradivaʀjys] NM Stradivarius

strangulation [stʀɑ̃ɡylasjɔ̃] NF strangulation

strapontin [strapɔ̃tɛ̃] NM (*Aut, Théât*) jump seat, foldaway seat; (*fig = position subalterne*) minor role

Strasbourg [strazbuʀ] N Strasbourg

strasbourgeois, e [strazbuʀʒwa, waz] **1** ADJ of *ou* from Strasbourg **2** **Strasbourgeois(e)** NM,F inhabitant *ou* native of Strasbourg

strass [stras] NM (*lit*) paste; (*fig péj*) show, gloss; **broche/collier en ~** paste brooch/necklace

stratagème [strataʒɛm] NM stratagem

strate [strat] NF stratum

stratège [strateʒ] NM (*Mil, fig*) strategist

stratégie [strateʒi] NF strategy; **~ de communication/de vente** communication/selling strategy; **~ d'entreprise** corporate strategy

stratégique [strateʒik] ADJ strategic

stratégiquement [strateʒikmɑ̃] ADV strategically

stratification [stratifikasjɔ̃] NF stratification

stratifié, e [stratifje] (*ptp de* **stratifier**) **1** ADJ stratified; (*Tech*) laminated **2** NM laminate; **en ~** laminated

stratifier [stratifje] ▶conjug 7◀ VT to stratify

stratigraphie [stratigrafi] NF (*Géol*) stratigraphy

stratocumulus [stratokymylys] NM INV stratocumulus

stratosphère [stratɔsfɛʀ] NF stratosphere

stratosphérique [stratɔsferik] ADJ stratospheric

stratus [stratys] NM INV stratus

streptocoque [stʀɛptɔkɔk] NM streptococcus

streptomycine [stʀɛptɔmisin] NF streptomycin

stress [stres] NM (*gén, Méd*) stress; **être dans un état de ~ permanent** to be under constant stress

stressant, e [stresɑ̃, ɑ̃t] ADJ [*situation, vie, métier*] stressful

stresser [strese] ▶conjug 1◀ **1** VT to put under stress, stress out*; **cette réunion m'a complètement stressé** the meeting really stressed me out*, I felt completely stressed after the meeting; **être stressé** to be under stress; **se sentir stressé** to feel stressed; **les cadres stressés d'aujourd'hui** today's stressed(-out) executives **2** **se stresser** VPR to get stressed

stretch [stretʃ] **1** ADJ INV stretch (*épith*), stretchy **2** NM **Stretch**® stretch fabric; **jupe en Stretch** stretch skirt

stretching [stretʃiŋ] NM (*Sport*) stretches; **faire du ~** to do stretches; **cours de ~** stretch class

striation [strijasjɔ̃] NF striation

strict, e [strikt] ADJ a (= *astreignant, étroit*) [*obligation, sens*] strict; [*interprétation*] literal; (*Math*) strict; **au sens ~ du terme** in the strict sense of the word; **la ~e observation du règlement** the strict observance of the rules b (= *sévère*) [*discipline, maître, morale, principes*] strict; **il est très ~ sur la ponctualité** he is a stickler for punctuality, he's very strict about punctuality; **il était très ~ avec nous** *ou* **à notre égard** he was very strict with us c (= *absolu*) **c'est son droit le plus ~** it is his most basic right; **le ~ nécessaire/minimum** the bare essentials/minimum; **c'est la ~e vérité** it is the plain *ou* simple truth; **dans la plus ~e intimité** in the strictest privacy d (= *sobre*) [*tenue*] severe, plain; [*coiffure*] austere, severe; **un uniforme/costume très ~** a very austere *ou* plain uniform/suit

strictement [striktəmɑ̃] ADV a (= *rigoureusement*) [*confidentiel, personnel*] strictly; **les sanctions seront ~ appliquées** the sanctions will be strictly enforced; (*Math*) **~ inférieur/supérieur** strictly lesser/greater b (= *sévèrement*) strictly; **il a été élevé très ~** he had a very strict upbringing c (= *sobrement*) plainly

stricto sensu [striktosɛ̃sy] LOC ADV strictly speaking

strident, e [stridɑ̃, ɑ̃t] ADJ shrill, strident; (*Phon*) strident

stridulation [stridylasjɔ̃] NF stridulation, chirring (*NonC*)

striduler [stridyle] ▶conjug 1◀ VI to stridulate, chirr

strie [stri] NF (*de couleur*) streak; (*en relief*) ridge; (*en creux*) groove; (*Anat, Géol*) stria

strié, e [strije] ADJ a [*coquille, roche, tige*] striated b (*Anat*) [*muscle*] striated; **corps ~** (*corpus*) striatum

strier [strije] ▶conjug 7◀ VT (*de couleurs*) to streak; (*en relief*) to ridge; (*en creux*) to groove; (*Anat, Géol*) to striate; **cheveux striés de blanc** hair streaked with grey; **l'orage striait le ciel d'éclairs** lightning ripped through the sky → **muscle**

string [strin] NM (= *sous-vêtement*) G-string; (= *maillot de bain*) tanga

striptease, strip-tease (*pl* **strip-teases**) [striptiz] NM (= *spectacle*) striptease; **faire un ~** to do a striptease; **faire du ~** to be a striptease artist, be a stripper

strip-teaseur, -euse (*mpl* **strip-teaseurs**) [striptizœʀ, øz] NM,F stripper, striptease artist

striure [strijyʀ] NF [*couleurs*] streaking (*NonC*); **la ~** *ou* **les ~s de la pierre** the ridges *ou* grooves in the stone

stroboscope [strɔbɔskɔp] NM stroboscope

stroboscopique [strɔbɔskɔpik] ADJ stroboscopic, strobe (*épith*); **lumière ~** strobe lighting

strontium [strɔ̃sjɔm] NM strontium

strophe [strɔf] NF (*Littérat*) verse, stanza; (*Théât Grec*) strophe

structural, e (*mpl* **-aux**) [stryktyral, o] ADJ structural

structuralisme [stryktyralism] NM structuralism

structuraliste [stryktyralist] ADJ, NMF structuralist

structurant, e [stryktyrɑ̃, ɑ̃t] ADJ [*principe*] founding; [*expérience*] formative → **gel**

structuration [stryktyrasjɔ̃] NF structuring

structure [stryktyr] NF a (= *architecture, lit, fig*) structure; **la ~ familiale** the family structure; **~s d'accueil** (*gén*) facilities; [*hôpital*] reception facilities; **la ~ des dépenses s'est modifiée** spending patterns have changed; (*Ling*) **~ profonde/superficielle** *ou* **de surface** deep/surface structure; **~ mentale** mindset; **réformes de ~** structural reforms b (= *organisme*) organization

structuré, e [stryktyre] (*ptp de* **structurer**) ADJ structured

structurel, -elle [stryktyrɛl] ADJ structural

structurellement [stryktyrɛlmɑ̃] ADV structurally; **cette entreprise est ~ déficitaire** the way the company is structured means it's bound to run up debts

structurer [stryktyre] ▶conjug 1◀ **1** VT to structure, to give structure to **2** **se structurer** VPR [*parti*] to develop a structure; [*enfant*] to form

strychnine [striknin] NF strychnine

stuc [styk] NM stucco; **en ~** stucco (*épith*)

studette [stydɛt] NF small studio flat (*Brit*) *ou* apartment (*surtout US*)

studieusement [stydjøzmɑ̃] ADV studiously

studieux, -ieuse [stydjø, jøz] ADJ [*personne*] studious; [*vacances*] study (*épith*); **passer une soirée studieuse** to spend an evening studying

studio [stydjo] NM a (*d'habitation*) studio flat (*Brit*) *ou* apartment (*surtout US*); (*d'artiste*) studio b (*Ciné, TV: de prise de vues*) studio; (= *salle de cinéma*) film theatre (*Brit*) *ou* theater (*US*); **tourner en ~** to film *ou* shoot in the studio; **~ d'enregistrement** recording studio; (*TV*) **à vous les ~!** and now back to the studio!

stupéfaction [stypefaksjɔ̃] NF (= *étonnement*) amazement, astonishment, stupefaction; **à la ~ générale** to everyone's astonishment *ou* amazement

stupéfaire [stypefɛʀ] ▶conjug 60◀ VT to stun, astound, dumbfound

stupéfait, e [stypefɛ, ɛt] (*ptp de* **stupéfaire**) ADJ stunned, dumbfounded, astounded (*de qch* at sth); **~ de voir que ...** astounded *ou* stunned to see that ...

stupéfiant, e [stypefjɑ̃, jɑ̃t] **1** ADJ (= *étonnant*) astounding, staggering; (*Méd*) stupefying, stupefacient (*SPÉC*) **2** NM drug, narcotic, stupefacient (*SPÉC*) → **brigade**

stupéfié, e [stypefje] (*ptp de* **stupéfier**) ADJ staggered, dumbfounded

stupéfier [stypefje] ▶conjug 7◀ VT (= *étonner*) to stagger, astound; (*Méd, littér*) to stupefy

stupeur [stypœʀ] NF (= *étonnement*) astonishment, amazement; (*Méd*) stupor; **être frappé de ~** to be dumbfounded *ou* stunned; **c'est avec ~ que j'appris la nouvelle** I was stunned when I heard the news; **à la ~ générale** to everyone's astonishment *ou* amazement

stupide [stypid] ADJ (= *inepte*) stupid; (= *hébété*) stunned, bemused; (= *imprévisible*) [*accident*] stupid, silly; **c'est ~, j'ai oublié!** how stupid of me, I forgot!

stupidement [stypidmɑ̃] ADV stupidly

stupidité [stypidite] NF (= *caractère*) stupidity; (= *parole*) stupid thing to say; (= *acte*) stupid thing to do; **c'est une vraie ~** *ou* **de la ~** that's a really stupid *ou* silly *ou* foolish thing to say (*ou* do)

stupre† [stypʀ] NM (*littér*) debauchery, depravity

stups* [styp] NMPL (ABRÉV = **stupéfiants**) → **brigade**

style [stil] **1** NM **a** ·(gén, Art, Littérat, Sport) style; **meubles/reliure de ~** period furniture/binding; **meubles de ~ Directoire/Louis XVI** Directoire/Louis XVI furniture; **je reconnais bien là son ~** that is just his style; **ce n'est pas son ~** (vêtements) it's not his style; (comportement étonnant) it's not like him; (fig) **ou quelque chose de ce ~** or something along those lines; **cet athlète a du ~** this athlete has style; **offensive/opération de grand ~** full-scale ou large-scale offensive/operation → **exercice**

b (= pointe, Bot) style; [cylindre enregistreur] stylus; [cadran solaire] style, gnomon; (Hist = poinçon) style, stylus

2 COMP ► **style direct** (Ling) direct speech ► **style indirect** (Ling) indirect ou reported speech; **~ indirect libre** indirect free speech ► **style journalistique** journalistic style, journalese (péj) ► **style télégraphique** telegraphic style ► **style de vie** lifestyle

stylé, e [stile] ADJ [domestique, personnel] perfectly trained

stylet [stilɛ] NM (= poignard) stiletto, stylet; (Méd) stylet; (Zool) proboscis, stylet

stylisation [stilizasjɔ̃] NF stylization

styliser [stilize] ▶conjug 1◀ VT to stylize; **colombe/fleur stylisée** stylized dove/flower

stylisme [stilism] NM (= métier) dress designing; (= snobisme) concern for style

styliste [stilist] NMF (= dessinateur industriel) designer; (= écrivain) stylist; **~ de mode** clothes ou dress designer

stylisticien, -ienne [stilistisjɛ̃, jɛn] NM,F stylistician, specialist in stylistics

stylistique [stilistik] **1** NF stylistics sg **2** ADJ [analyse, emploi] stylistic

stylo [stilo] NM pen; **~-bille** ◊ **~ à bille** ball-point (pen), Biro ® (Brit), Bic ® (US); **~ à encre ou (à) plume ou à réservoir** fountain pen; **~-feutre** felt-tip pen; **~ à cartouche** cartridge pen

stylographe† [stilɔgʀaf] NM fountain pen

Styx [stiks] NM **le ~** the Styx

su, e [sy] (ptp de **savoir**) **1** ADJ known **2** NM **au su de** → **vu**

suaire [sɥɛʀ] NM (littér = linceul) shroud, winding sheet; (fig) shroud → **saint**

suant, suante [sɥɑ̃, sɥɑ̃t] ADJ (= en sueur) sweaty; (= ennuyeux) [livre, cours] deadly (dull)*; **ce film est ~*** this film is a real drag! ou is deadly*; **ce qu'il est ~ !*** what a drag! ou a pain (in the neck)* he is!

suave [sɥav] ADJ [personne, manières, voix, regard] suave, smooth; [musique, parfum] sweet; [couleurs] mellow; [formes] smooth

suavement [sɥavmɑ̃] ADV [s'exprimer] suavely

suavité [sɥavite] NF [personne, manières, voix, regard] suavity, smoothness; [musique, parfum] sweetness; [couleurs] mellowness; [formes] smoothness

subaigu, -uë [sybegy] ADJ subacute

subalterne [sybaltɛʀn] **1** ADJ [rôle] subordinate, subsidiary; [employé, poste] junior (épith); **officier ~** subaltern **2** NMF subordinate, inferior

subantarctique [sybɑ̃taʀktik] ADJ subantarctic

subaquatique [sybakwatik] ADJ subaquatic, underwater (épith)

subarctique [sybaʀktik] ADJ subarctic

subconscient, e [sypkɔ̃sjɑ̃, jɑ̃t] ADJ, NM subconscious

subdiviser [sybdivize] ▶conjug 1◀ **1** VT to subdivide (**en** into) **2 se subdiviser** VPR to be subdivided, be further divided (**en** into)

subdivision [sybdivizjɔ̃] NF (gén) subdivision; [classeur] section

subéquatorial, e (mpl **-iaux**) [sybekwatɔʀjal, jo] ADJ subequatorial

subir [sybiʀ] ▶conjug 2◀ VT **a** (= être victime de) [+ affront] to be subjected to, suffer; [+ violences, attaque, critique] to undergo, suffer, be subjected to; [+ perte, défaite, dégâts] to suffer, sustain; [+ choc] to suffer; **faire ~ un affront/des tortures à qn** to subject sb to an insult/to torture; **faire ~ des pertes/une défaite à l'ennemi** to inflict losses/defeat on the enemy

b (= être soumis à) [+ charme] to be subject to, be under the influence of; [+ influence] to be under; [+ peine de prison] to serve; [+ examen] to undergo, go through; [+ opération, interrogatoire] to undergo; **~ les effets de qch** to be affected by sth; **~ la loi du plus fort** to be subjected to the law of the strongest; **~ les rigueurs de l'hiver** to undergo ou be subjected to the rigours of winter; **faire ~ son influence à qn** to exert an influence over sb; **faire ~ un examen à qn** to put sb through ou subject sb to an examination, make sb undergo an examination

c (= endurer) to suffer, put up with, endure; **il faut ~ et se taire** you must suffer in silence; **il va falloir le ~ pendant toute la journée*** we're going to have to put up with him all day; **on subit sa famille, on choisit ses amis** you can pick your friends but not your family

d (= recevoir) [+ modification, transformation] to undergo, go through; **les prix ont subi une hausse importante** there has been a considerable increase in prices, prices have undergone a considerable increase

subit, e [sybi, it] ADJ sudden

subitement [sybitmɑ̃] ADV suddenly, all of a sudden

subito (presto)* [sybito(pʀɛsto)] LOC ADV (= brusquement) all of a sudden; (= immédiatement) at once

subjectif, -ive [sybʒɛktif, iv] ADJ subjective; **un danger ~** a danger which one creates for oneself

subjectivement [sybʒɛktivmɑ̃] ADV subjectively

subjectivisme [sybʒɛktivism] NM subjectivism

subjectiviste [sybʒɛktivist] **1** ADJ subjectivistic **2** NMF subjectivist

subjectivité [sybʒɛktivite] NF subjectivity

subjonctif, -ive [sybʒɔ̃ktif, iv] ADJ, NM subjunctive; **au ~** in the subjunctive

subjuguer [sybʒyge] ▶conjug 1◀ VT [+ auditoire] to captivate, enthrall; (littér) [+ esprits, personne malléable] to render powerless; † [+ peuple vaincu] to subjugate; **être subjugué par le charme/la personnalité de qn** to be captivated by sb's charm/personality

sublimation [syblimasjɔ̃] NF (Chim, Psych) sublimation

sublime [syblim] **1** ADJ (gén) sublime; [personne] magnificent, wonderful; **~ de dévouement** sublimely dedicated; (Hist) **la Sublime Porte** the Sublime Porte **2** NM **le ~** the sublime

sublimé, e [syblime] (ptp de **sublimer**) **1** ADJ sublimate(d) **2** NM sublimate

sublimement [syblimmɑ̃] ADV sublimely

sublimer [syblime] ▶conjug 1◀ VT (Psych) to sublimate; (Chim) to sublimate, sublime

subliminaire [sybliminɛʀ], **subliminal, e** (mpl **-aux** [sybliminal, o]) ADJ subliminal

sublimité [syblimite] NF (littér) sublimeness (NonC), sublimity

sublingual, e (mpl **-aux**) [syblɛ̃gwal, o] ADJ sublingual; **comprimé ~** tablet to be dissolved under the tongue

submergé, e [sybmɛʀʒe] (ptp de **submerger**) ADJ **a** [terres, plaine] flooded, submerged; [récifs] submerged **b** (fig = débordé, dépassé) swamped, snowed under; **~ de** [+ appels téléphoniques, commandes] snowed under ou swamped ou inundated with; [+ douleur, plaisir, inquiétude] overwhelmed ou overcome with; **~ de travail** snowed under ou swamped with work, up to one's eyes (Brit) ou ears (US) in work; **nous étions complètement ~s** we were completely snowed under, we were up to our eyes (Brit) ou ears (US) in it*

submerger [sybmɛʀʒe] ▶conjug 3◀ VT (lit = inonder) [+ terres, plaine] to flood, submerge; [+ barque] to submerge; (fig) **~ qn** [foule] to engulf sb; [ennemi] to overwhelm sb; [émotion] to overcome sb, overwhelm sb; **le standard est submergé d'appels** the switchboard is inundated ou flooded ou swamped with calls; **les hôpitaux sont submergés de blessés** the hospitals are overflowing with wounded people; **les policiers furent submergés par la foule** the police were engulfed in ou by the crowd; **ils nous submergeaient de travail** they swamped ou inundated us with work

submersible [sybmɛʀsibl] **1** ADJ (Bot) [plante] submerged **2** NM (Naut) submersible

submersion [sybmɛʀsjɔ̃] NF [terres] flooding, submersion; (Méd) **mort par ~** death by drowning

subodorer [sybɔdɔʀe] ▶conjug 1◀ VT (hum = soupçonner) [+ irrégularité, malversation] to scent; **il subodora quelque chose de pas très catholique** he smelt a rat

subordination [sybɔʀdinasjɔ̃] NF subordination; **je m'élève contre la ~ de cette décision à leurs plans** I object to this decision being subject to their plans; (Ling) **relation** ou **rapport de ~** relation of subordination → **conjonction**

subordonné, e [sybɔʀdɔne] (ptp de **subordonner**) **1** ADJ (gén, Ling) subordinate (**à** to); (Ling) **proposition ~e** dependent ou subordinate clause **2** NM,F subordinate **3** **subordonnée** NF (Ling) dependent ou subordinate clause

subordonner [sybɔʀdɔne] ▶conjug 1◀ VT **a** (dans une hiérarchie) **~ qn à** to subordinate sb to; **accepter de se ~ à qn** to agree to subordinate o.s. to sb, accept a subordinate position under sb **b** (Ling) to subordinate; **~ qch à** (= placer au second rang) to subordinate sth to; (= faire dépendre de) **nous subordonnons notre décision à ses plans** our decision will be subject to his plans; **leur départ est subordonné au résultat des examens** their departure is subject to ou depends on the exam results

subornation [sybɔʀnasjɔ̃] NF (Jur) [témoins] bribing, subornation (SPÉC)

suborner [sybɔʀne] ▶conjug 1◀ VT (Jur) [+ témoins] to bribe, suborn (SPÉC); (littér) [+ jeune fille] to lead astray, seduce

suborneur† [sybɔʀnœʀ] NM seducer

subreptice [sybʀɛptis] ADJ [moyen] stealthy, surreptitious; (Jur) **acte ~** subreption

subrepticement [sybʀɛptismɑ̃] ADV stealthily, surreptitiously

subrogation [sybʀɔgasjɔ̃] NF (Jur) subrogation

subrogé, e [sybʀɔʒe] (ptp de **subroger**) **1** ADJ (Jur) **~(-)tuteur** surrogate guardian; (Ling) **langage ~** subrogate language **2** NM,F (Jur) surrogate

subroger [sybʀɔʒe] ▶conjug 3◀ VT (Jur) to subrogate, substitute

subsaharien, -ienne [sybsaaʀjɛ̃, jɛn] ADJ [désert, pays] sub-Saharan → **Afrique**

subséquemment [sypsekamɑ̃] ADV (†, Jur) subsequently

subséquent, e [sypsekɑ̃, ɑ̃t] ADJ (†, Jur, Géog) subsequent

subside [sybzid] NM grant; **les modestes ~s**

qu'il recevait de son père the small allowance he received from his father

subsidiaire [sybzidjɛʀ] ADJ [*raison, motif*] subsidiary → **question**

subsidiairement [sybzidjɛʀmɑ̃] ADV subsidiarily

subsidiarité [sybzidjaʀite] NF (*Pol*) subsidiarity; (*Europe*) **le principe de ~** the principle of subsidiarity

subsistance [sybzistɑ̃s] NF [a] (= *moyens d'existence*) subsistence; **assurer la ~ de sa famille/de qn** to support *ou* maintain *ou* keep one's family/sb; **assurer sa (propre) ~** to keep *ou* support o.s.; **ma ~ était assurée** I had enough to live on; **pour toute ~** *ou* **tous moyens de ~, ils n'avaient que deux chèvres** their sole means of subsistence was two goats; **ils tirent leur ~ de certaines racines** they live on certain root crops; **elle contribue à la ~ du ménage** she contributes towards the maintenance of the family *ou* towards the housekeeping money; **économie/agriculture de ~** subsistence economy/agriculture [b] (*Mil*) **militaire en ~** seconded serviceman

subsistant, e [sybzistɑ̃, ɑ̃t] [1] ADJ remaining (*épith*) [2] NM (*Mil*) seconded serviceman

subsister [sybziste] ▶conjug 1◀ VI [*personne*] (= *ne pas périr*) to live on, survive; (= *se nourrir, gagner sa vie*) to live, stay alive, subsist; (= *rester*) [*erreur, vestiges*] to remain; **ils ont tout juste de quoi ~** they have just enough to live on *ou* to keep body and soul together; **le doute subsiste** *ou* **il subsiste un doute quant à** *ou* **sur** there is still some doubt as to, there remains some doubt as to; **du château primitif, il ne subsiste que l'aile gauche** only the left wing of the original castle remains intact

subsonique [sybsɔnik] ADJ subsonic

substance [sypstɑ̃s] NF (*gén, Philo*) substance; **la ~ de notre discussion** the substance *ou* gist of our discussion; **c'était un discours sans ~ ◊ ce discours manquait de ~** the speech had no substance to it; (*Anat*) **~ blanche/grise** white/grey matter; **~ étrangère** foreign substance *ou* matter (*NonC*); **le lait est une ~ alimentaire** milk is a food; **en ~** in substance; **voilà, en ~, ce qu'ils ont dit** here is, in substance, what they said, here is the gist of what they said

substantialité [sypstɑ̃sjalite] NF substantiality

substantiel, -ielle [sypstɑ̃sjɛl] ADJ (*gén, Philo*) substantial

substantiellement [sypstɑ̃sjɛlmɑ̃] ADV substantially

substantif, -ive [sypstɑ̃tif, iv] [1] ADJ [*proposition*] noun (*épith*); [*emploi*] nominal, substantival; [*style*] nominal [2] NM noun, substantive

substantifique [sypstɑ̃tifik] ADJ (*hum*) **la ~ moelle** the very substance

substantivation [sypstɑ̃tivasjɔ̃] NF nominalization, substantivization

substantivement [sypstɑ̃tivmɑ̃] ADV nominally, as a noun, substantively

substantiver [sypstɑ̃tive] ▶conjug 1◀ VT to nominalize, substantivize

substituer [sypstitɥe] ▶conjug 1◀ [1] VT [a] (= *remplacer*) **~ qch/qn à** to substitute sth/sb for; [b] (*Jur*) [+ *legs*] to entail [2] **se substituer** VPR **se ~ à qn** (*en l'évinçant*) to substitute o.s. for sb; (*en le représentant*) to substitute for sb, act as a substitute for sb; **l'adjoint s'est substitué au chef** the deputy is substituting for the boss

substitut [sypstity] NM (= *magistrat*) deputy public prosecutor (*Brit*), assistant district attorney (*US*); (= *succédané*) substitute (**de** for); (*Ling*) pro-form substitute; (*Psych*) **~ maternel** substitute mother; **~ de repas** meal replacement

substitutif, -ive [sypstitytif, iv] ADJ (*Méd*) **traitement ~** replacement therapy; **traitement hormonal ~** hormone replacement therapy

substitution [sypstitysjɔ̃] NF (*gén, Chim*) (*intentionnelle*) substitution (**à** for); (*accidentelle*) [*vêtements, bébés*] mix-up (**de** of, in); **il y a eu ~ d'enfants** the babies were switched; **produit de ~** substitute (product); **produit ou drogue de ~ à l'héroïne** heroin substitute; **traitement de ~** treatment of drug addicts with substitute drugs; **hormones de ~** replacement hormones; **énergies de ~** alternative (sources of) energy; **carburant de ~** substitute fuel; (*dans l'emploi*) **effet de ~** substitution effect → **mère, peine**

substrat [sypstʀa], **substratum†** [sypstʀatɔm] NM (*Géol, Ling, Philo*) substratum

subsumer [sypsyme] ▶conjug 1◀ VT to subsume

subterfuge [syptɛʀfyʒ] NM subterfuge; **user de ~s** to use subterfuge

subtil, e [syptil] ADJ [a] (= *sagace*) [*personne, esprit, intelligence*] subtle, discerning; [*réponse, calcul*] subtle; **c'est un négociateur ~** he's a skilful negotiator [b] (= *raffiné*) [*nuance, distinction*] subtle, fine; [*parfum, goût, raisonnement*] subtle; **un ~ mélange d'autorité et de tendresse** a subtle blend of authority and tenderness; **c'est trop ~ pour moi** it's too subtle for me

subtilement [syptilmɑ̃] ADV subtly, in a subtle way

subtilisation [syptilizasjɔ̃] NF spiriting away

subtiliser [syptilize] ▶conjug 1◀ [1] VT (= *dérober*) to steal, spirit away (*hum*); **il s'est fait ~ sa valise** his suitcase has been spirited away (*hum*) *ou* stolen [2] VI (*littér = raffiner*) to subtilize

subtilité [syptilite] NF [a] (= *sagacité*) [*personne, esprit, intelligence, réponse*] subtlety [b] (= *raffinement*) [*nuance, distinction*] subtlety, nicety; [*raisonnement*] subtlety; **des ~s** subtleties, niceties; **les ~s de la langue française** the subtleties of the French language

subtropical, e (*mpl -aux*) [sybtʀɔpikal, o] ADJ subtropical; **régions ~es** subtropical regions, subtropics

suburbain, e [sybyʀbɛ̃, ɛn] ADJ suburban

subvenir [sybvəniʀ] ▶conjug 22◀ ✦ **subvenir à** VT INDIR [+ *besoins*] to provide for, meet; [+ *frais*] to meet, cover; **~ aux besoins de sa famille** to provide for *ou* support one's family; **~ à ses propres besoins** to support o.s.

subvention [sybvɑ̃sjɔ̃] NF (*gén*) grant; (*pour baisser les prix de vente*) subsidy

subventionner [sybvɑ̃sjɔne] ▶conjug 1◀ VT (*gén*) to grant funds to; (*pour baisser les prix de vente*) to subsidize; **école subventionnée** grant-maintained school; **théâtre subventionné** subsidized theatre

subversif, -ive [sybvɛʀsif, iv] ADJ subversive

subversion [sybvɛʀsjɔ̃] NF subversion

subversivement [sybvɛʀsivmɑ̃] ADV subversively

subvertir [sybvɛʀtiʀ] ▶conjug 2◀ VT [+ *structure, valeurs*] to subvert

suc [syk] NM [*plante*] sap; [*viande, fleur, fruit*] juice; (*fig littér*) [*œuvre*] pith, meat; **~s digestifs** *ou* **gastriques** gastric juices

succédané [syksedane] NM (= *substitut*) substitute (**de** for); (= *médicament*) substitute, succedaneum (*SPÉC*); (*péj = imitation*) **un ~ de ... ** a pale imitation of ...

succéder [syksede] ▶conjug 6◀ [1] **succéder à** VT INDIR [+ *directeur, roi*] to succeed; [+ *période, chose, personne*] to succeed, follow; (*Jur*) [+ *titres, héritage*] to inherit, succeed to; **~ à qn à la tête d'une entreprise** to succeed sb *ou* take over from sb at the head of a firm; **des prés succédèrent aux champs de blé** cornfields were followed *ou* replaced by meadows,

cornfields gave way to meadows; **le rire succéda à la peur** fear gave way to laughter

[2] **se succéder** VPR to follow one another, succeed one another; **ils se succédèrent de père en fils** son followed father; **les mois se succédèrent** month followed month; **les échecs se succédèrent** one failure followed another; **trois gouvernements se sont succédé en trois ans** there have been three successive governments in three years; **les visites se sont succédé toute la journée dans la chambre du malade** visitors filed in and out of the patient's room all day

succès [syksɛ] NM [a] (= *réussite*) [*entreprise, roman*] success; **~ militaires/sportifs** military/sporting successes; **félicitations pour votre ~** congratulations on your success; **le ~ ne l'a pas changé** success hasn't changed him; **~ d'estime** succès d'estime, praise from the critics (*with poor sales*); **avoir du ~ auprès des femmes** to be successful with women

[b] (= *livre*) success, bestseller; (= *chanson, disque*) success, hit*; (= *film, pièce*) box-office success, hit*; **~ de librairie** bestseller; **tous ses livres ont été des ~** all his books have been bestsellers, every one of his books was a success; **~ commercial** commercial success; **~ d'audience** success *ou* hit* with the audience(s), ratings success

[c] (= *conquête amoureuse*) **~ (féminin)** conquest; **son charme lui vaut de nombreux ~** numerous women have fallen for his charms

[d] (*loc*) **avec ~** successfully; **avec un égal ~** equally successfully, with equal success; **sans ~** unsuccessfully, without success; **pour ce film, c'est le ~ assuré** *ou* **garanti** this film is sure to be a success; **à ~** [*auteur, livre*] successful, bestselling; **film à ~** hit film*, blockbuster*; **chanson/pièce à ~** hit*, successful song/play; **roman à ~** successful novel, bestseller; **avoir du ~ ◊ être un ~** to be successful, be a success; **cette pièce a eu un grand ~** *ou* **beaucoup de ~** *ou* **un ~ fou*** the play was a great success *ou* was very successful *ou* was a smash hit*; **ce chanteur a eu un ~ monstre*** this singer was a big hit*

successeur [syksesœʀ] NM (*gén*) successor

successif, -ive [syksesif, iv] ADJ successive

succession [syksesjɔ̃] NF [a] (= *enchaînement, série*) succession; **la ~ des saisons** the succession *ou* sequence of the seasons; **toute une ~ de visiteurs/malheurs** a whole succession *ou* series of visitors/misfortunes [b] (= *transmission de pouvoir*) succession; (*Jur*) (= *transmission de biens*) succession; (= *patrimoine*) estate, inheritance; **partager une ~** to share an estate *ou* an inheritance; (*Jur*) **la ~ est ouverte** ≈ the will is going through probate; **~ vacante** estate in abeyance; **par voie de ~** by right of inheritance *ou* succession; **prendre la ~ de** [+ *ministre, directeur*] to succeed, take over from; [+ *roi*] to succeed; [+ *maison de commerce*] to take over → **droit³, guerre**

successivement [syksesivmɑ̃] ADV successively

successoral, e (*mpl -aux*) [syksesɔʀal, o] ADJ **droits successoraux** inheritance tax

succinct, e [syksɛ̃, ɛ̃t] ADJ [*écrit*] succinct; [*repas*] frugal; **soyez ~** be brief; **il a été très ~** he was very brief

succinctement [syksɛ̃tmɑ̃] ADV [*raconter*] succinctly; [*manger*] frugally

succion [sy(k)sjɔ̃] NF (*Phys, Tech*) suction; (*Méd*) [*plaie*] sucking; **bruit de ~** sucking noise

succomber [sykɔ̃be] ▶conjug 1◀ VI [a] (= *mourir*) to die, succumb (*frm*); **~ à ses blessures** to die from *ou* succumb to one's injuries [b] (= *être vaincu*) to succumb (*frm*); (*par tentations*) to succumb, give way; **~ sous le nombre** to be overcome by numbers; **~ à** [+ *tentation*] to succumb *ou* yield *ou* give way to; [+ *promesses*] to succumb to; [+ *charme*] to succumb to, fall under; [+ *fatigue, désespoir,*

sommeil] to give way to, succumb to; (*littér: lit, fig*) **~ sous le poids de qch** to yield *ou* give way beneath the weight of sth; **ce gâteau était trop tentant, j'ai succombé!** this cake was so tempting I just couldn't resist!; **la ville a succombé sous les assauts répétés de l'armée** the town fell under the repeated attacks of the army

succube [sykyb] NM succubus

succulence [sykylɑ̃s] NF (*littér*) succulence

succulent, e [sykylɑ̃, ɑ̃t] ADJ [a] (*Bot*) [*plante*] succulent [b] (= *délicieux*) [*fruit, rôti*] succulent; [*mets, repas*] delicious; [*récit*] juicy* [c] (†† = *juteux*) succulent

succursale [sykyʀsal] NF [*magasin, firme*] branch → **magasin**

sucer [syse] ▸ conjug 3 ◂ VT [a] (*lit*) to suck; **toujours à ~ des bonbons** always sucking sweets; **ces pastilles se sucent** these tablets are to be sucked; **~ son pouce/ses doigts** to suck one's thumb/one's fingers; **ce procès lui a sucé toutes ses économies*** this lawsuit has bled him of all his savings; **~ qn jusqu'à la moelle* ou jusqu'au dernier sou*** to suck sb dry*, bleed sb dry*; **se ~ la poire‡ ou la pomme‡** to neck‡, kiss passionately; (*hum*) **on voit bien qu'il ne suce pas de la glace!*** he really knocks it back!‡ [b] (‡ = *boire*) to tipple*, booze*; **cette voiture suce beaucoup** this car guzzles* a lot of petrol (*Brit*) *ou* gas (*US*) [c]‡‡ (*fellation*) to suck off‡‡; (*cunnilingus*) to go down on‡‡

sucette [syset] NF (= *bonbon*) lollipop, lolly (*Brit*); (= *tétine*) comforter, dummy (*Brit*), pacifier (*US*)

suceur, -euse [sysœʀ, øz] [1] NM [a] (*Zool*) **(insecte) ~** sucking insect [b] [*aspirateur*] nozzle [2] NM,F (*fig*) **~ de sang** bloodsucker [3] **suceuse** NF (= *machine*) suction dredge

suçon* [sysɔ̃] NM love bite* (*Brit*), hickey* (*US*); **faire un ~ à qn** to give sb a love bite (*Brit*) *ou* a hickey (*US*)

suçoter [sysɔte] ▸ conjug 1 ◂ VT to suck

sucrage [sykʀaʒ] NM [*vin*] sugaring, sweetening

sucrant, e [sykʀɑ̃, ɑ̃t] ADJ sweetening; **c'est très ~** it's very sweet

sucrase [sykʀaz] NF sucrase

sucre [sykʀ] [1] NM [a] (= *substance*) sugar; (= *morceau*) lump of sugar, sugar lump; **prendre deux ~s dans son café** to take two lumps of sugar *ou* two sugars in one's coffee; **combien de ~s?** how many sugars (do you take)?; **fraises au ~** strawberries sprinkled with sugar; **chewing-gum sans ~** sugarless *ou* sugar-free chewing gum; **cet enfant n'est pas en ~ quand même!** for goodness sake, the child won't break!; (*fig*) **être tout ~ tout miel** to be all sweetness and light; **mon petit trésor en ~** my little honey-bun *ou* sugarplum; (*Canada*) **partie de ~** sugaring-off party → **casser** [b] (= *unité monétaire*) sucre [2] COMP ► **sucre de betterave** beet sugar ► **sucre brun** brown sugar ► **sucre candi** sugar candy ► **sucre de canne** cane sugar ► **sucre cristallisé** (coarse) granulated sugar ► **sucre d'érable** (*Can*) maple sugar ► **sucre glace** icing sugar (*Brit*), confectioners' sugar (*US*) ► **sucres lents** complex sugars ► **sucre en morceaux** lump *ou* cube sugar ► **sucre d'orge** (= *substance*) barley sugar; (= *bâton*) stick of barley sugar ► **sucre en poudre** fine granulated sugar, caster sugar (*Brit*) ► **sucres rapides** simple sugars ► **sucre roux** brown sugar ► **sucre semoule** = **sucre en poudre** ► **sucre vanillé** vanilla sugar

┌─ **LE TEMPS DES SUCRES** ─┐

Maple sugar and syrup production is an important traditional industry in Quebec, and the sugar harvest is a time for festivities in rural areas. The local community traditionally gets together for a celebration with music and dancing, and boiling maple sugar is thrown into the snow where it hardens into a kind of toffee known as "tire".

sucré, e [sykʀe] (*ptp de* **sucrer**) [1] ADJ [a] [*fruit, saveur, vin*] sweet; [*jus de fruits, lait condensé*] sweetened; **eau ~e** sugar water; **ce thé est trop ~** this tea is too sweet, there's too much sugar in this tea; **prenez-vous votre café ~?** do you take sugar (in your coffee)?; **tasse de thé bien ~e** well-sweetened cup of tea, cup of nice sweet tea; **non ~** unsweetened [b] (*péj*) [*ton*] sugary, honeyed; [*air*] sickly-sweet; **elle fait sa ~e** she's turning on the charm [2] NM **le ~ et le salé** sweet and savoury food; **je préfère le ~ au salé** I prefer sweet things to savouries

sucrer [sykʀe] ▸ conjug 1 ◂ [1] VT [a] [+ *boisson*] to sugar, put sugar in, sweeten; [+ *produit alimentaire*] to sweeten; **le miel sucre autant que le sucre lui-même** honey sweetens as much as sugar, honey is as good a sweetener as sugar; **on peut ~ avec du miel** honey may be used as a sweetener *ou* may be used to sweeten things; **sucrez à volonté** sweeten *ou* add sugar to taste; (*fig*) **~ les fraises*** to be a bit doddery* [b] (‡ = *supprimer*) **~ son argent de poche à qn** to stop sb's pocket money; **il s'est fait ~ ses heures supplémentaires** he's had his overtime money stopped; **il s'est fait ~ son permis de conduire** he had his driving licence taken away; **ils m'ont sucré mes vacances à la dernière minute** I was told at the last minute I couldn't have my holiday

[2] **se sucrer** VPR [a] (* *lit* = *prendre du sucre*) to help o.s. to sugar, have some sugar [b] (‡ *fig* = *s'enrichir*) to line one's pockets*

sucrerie [sykʀəʀi] NF [a] (= *bonbon*) sweet (*Brit*), candy (*US*); **~s** sweets, sweet things; **aimer les ~s** to have a sweet tooth, like sweet things [b] (= *usine*) sugar house; (= *raffinerie*) sugar refinery; (*Can*) (maple) sugar house

Sucrette ® [sykʀɛt] NF artificial sweetener

sucrier, -ière [sykʀije, ijɛʀ] [1] ADJ [*industrie, betterave*] sugar (*épith*); [*région*] sugar-producing [2] NM [a] (= *récipient*) sugar basin, sugar bowl; **~ (verseur)** sugar dispenser *ou* shaker [b] (= *industriel*) sugar producer

sud [syd] [1] NM [a] (= *point cardinal*) south; **le vent du ~** the south wind; **un vent du ~** a south(erly) wind, a southerly (*Naut*); **le vent tourne/est au ~** the wind is veering south(wards) *ou* towards the south/is blowing from the south; **regarder vers le ~** *ou* **dans la direction du ~** to look south(wards) *ou* towards the south; **au ~** (= *situation*) in the south; (*direction*) to the south, south(wards); **au ~ de** south of, to the south of; **la maison est (exposée) au ~/exposée plein ~** the house faces (the) south *ou* southwards/due south, the house looks south(wards)/due south [b] (= *régions*) south; **le ~ de la France** ◇ **le Sud** the South of France; **l'Europe/l'Italie du Sud** Southern Europe/Italy; **le Pacifique Sud** the South Pacific; **les mers du Sud** the South Seas; (*Pol*) **le dialogue Nord-Sud** the North-South dialogue → **Amérique, Corée, croix** [2] ADJ INV [*région, partie*] southern; [*entrée, paroi*] south; [*versant, côte*] south(ern); [*côté*] south(ward); [*direction*] southward, southerly (*Mét*); **il habite (dans) la banlieue ~** he lives in the southern suburbs → **hémisphère, pôle**

sud-africain, e [sydafʀikɛ̃, ɛn] (*mpl* **sud-africains**) [sydafʀikɛ̃, ɛn] [1] ADJ South African [2] **Sud-Africain(e)** NM,F South African

sud-américain, e [sydameʀikɛ̃, ɛn] (*mpl* **sud-américains**) [1] ADJ South American [2] **Sud-Américain(e)** NM,F South American

sudation [sydasjɔ̃] NF sweating, sudation (*SPÉC*)

sudatoire [sydatwaʀ] ADJ sudatory

sud-coréen, -enne (*mpl* **sud-coréens**) [sydkɔʀeɛ̃, ɛn] [1] ADJ South Korean [2] **Sud-Coréen(ne)** NM,F South Korean

sud-est [sydɛst] [1] ADJ INV south-east; [*banlieue*] south-eastern; [*côte*] south-east(ern) [2] NM south-east; **le Sud-Est asiatique** South-East Asia; **aller dans le Sud-Est (de la France)** to go to the south-east (of France); **au ~ de Rome** (*à l'extérieur*) south-east of Rome; (*dans la ville*) in the south-east of Rome; **regarder vers le ~** to look south-east(wards) *ou* towards the southeast; **en direction du ~** in a south-easterly direction; **vent du** *ou* **de ~** southeasterly (wind), southeaster

sudiste [sydist] (*Hist US*) [1] NMF Southerner [2] ADJ Southern

sudorifère [sydɔʀifɛʀ] ADJ = **sudoripare**

sudorifique [sydɔʀifik] ADJ, NM sudorific

sudoripare [sydɔʀipaʀ] ADJ sudoriferous, sudoriparous; **glande ~** sweat gland

sud-ouest [sydwɛst] [1] ADJ INV south-west; [*banlieue*] south-western; [*côte*] south-west(ern) [2] NM southwest; **aller dans le Sud-Ouest (de la France)** to go to the south-west (of France); **au ~ de Rome** (*à l'extérieur*) south-west of Rome; (*dans la ville*) in the south-west of Rome; **regarder vers le ~** to look south-west(wards) *ou* towards the south-west; **en direction du ~** in a south-westerly direction; **vent du** *ou* **de ~** southwesterly (wind), southwester

sud-sud-est [sydsydɛst] NM, ADJ INV south-southeast

sud-sud-ouest [sydsydwɛst] NM, ADJ INV south-southwest

sud-vietnamien, -ienne (*mpl* **sud-vietnamiens**) [sydvjetnamjɛ̃, jɛn] [1] ADJ South Vietnamese [2] **Sud-Vietnamien(ne)** NM,F South Vietnamese

suédé, e [sɥede] ADJ, NM suede

Suède [sɥɛd] NF Sweden

suède [sɥɛd] NM (= *peau*) suede; **en** *ou* **de ~** suede

suédine [sɥedin] NF suedette

suédois, e [sɥedwa, waz] [1] ADJ Swedish → **allumette, gymnastique** [2] NM (*Ling*) Swedish [3] **Suédois(e)** NM,F Swede

suée* [sɥe] NF sweat; **prendre** *ou* **attraper une bonne ~** to work up a good sweat; **à l'idée de cette épreuve, j'en avais la ~** I was in a (cold) sweat at the thought of the test*; **je dois aller le voir, quelle ~!** I've got to go and see him — what a drag!* *ou* pain!*

suer [sɥe] ▸ conjug 1 ◂ [1] VI [a] (= *transpirer*) to sweat; (*fig* = *peiner*) to sweat* (*sur* over); **~ de peur** to be in a cold sweat; **~ à grosses gouttes** to sweat profusely; **~ sur une dissertation** to sweat over an essay* [b] (= *suinter*) [*murs*] to ooze, sweat (*de* with) [c] (*Culin*) **faire ~** to sweat [d] (*loc*) **faire ~ qn** (*lit*) [*médicament*] to make sb sweat; (*fig*) **tu me fais ~*** you're a pain (in the neck)* *ou* a drag*; **on se fait ~ ici*** it's such a drag here*; **ce qu'on se fait ~ à ses cours*** his classes are such a drag*; **je me suis fait ~ à le réparer*** I sweated blood to repair that; (*péj*) **faire ~ le burnous** to use sweated labour, exploit native labour [2] VT [a] [+ *sueur, sang*] to sweat; (*fig*) **~ sang et eau** *ou* **pour faire qch** to sweat blood to get sth done, sweat blood over sth [b] [+ *humidité*] to ooze [c] (= *révéler, respirer*) [+ *pauvreté, misère, avarice, lâcheté*] to exude, reek of; **cet endroit sue l'ennui** this place reeks of boredom [d] († = *danser*) **en ~ une** to shake a leg*

sueur [sɥœʀ] NF sweat (*NonC*); **en ~** in a sweat, sweating; **être en ~** to be bathed in sweat; **à la ~ de son front** by the sweat of one's brow; **donner des ~s froides à qn** to put sb in a cold sweat; **j'en avais des ~s froides** I was in a cold sweat about it; (*fig*) **vivre de la ~ du peuple** to live off the backs of the people

Suez [sɥɛz] N Suez; **le canal de ~** the Suez Canal; **le golfe de ~** the Gulf of Suez

suffire [syfiʀ] ▸conjug 37◂ **1** VI **a** (= être assez) [somme, durée, quantité] to be enough, be sufficient, suffice; **cette explication ne (me) suffit pas** this explanation isn't enough ou isn't sufficient (for me) ou won't do; **cinq hommes suffisent (pour ce travail)** five men will do (for this job); **un rien suffirait pour ou à bouleverser nos plans** it would only take the smallest thing to upset our plans → **peine b** (= satisfaire, combler) **~ à** [+ besoins] to meet; [+ personne] to be enough for; **ma femme me suffit** ou **suffit à mon bonheur** my wife is all I need to make me happy, my wife is enough to make me happy; **il ne suffit pas aux besoins de la famille** he does not meet the needs of his family; **il ne peut ~ à tout** he can't manage (to do) everything, he can't cope with everything; **les week-ends, il ne suffisait plus à servir les clients** at weekends he couldn't manage to serve all the customers by himself **c** (loc) **ça suffit** that's enough, that'll do; **(ça) suffit!** that's enough!, that will do!; **comme ennuis, ça suffit (comme ça)** we've had enough trouble as it is thank you very much; **ça ne te suffit pas de l'avoir tourmentée?** isn't it enough for you to have tormented her?; **ça suffira pour aujourd'hui** that's enough for today ou for one day

2 VB IMPERS **a** (avec de) **il suffit de s'inscrire pour devenir membre** all you have to do to become a member is sign up; **il suffit de (la) faire réchauffer et la soupe est prête** just heat (up) the soup and it's ready (to serve); **il suffit d'un accord verbal pour conclure l'affaire** a verbal agreement is sufficient ou is enough ou will suffice (frm) to conclude the matter; **il suffisait d'y penser** it's obvious when you think about it; (intensif) **il suffit d'un rien pour l'inquiéter** it only takes the smallest thing to worry him, the smallest thing is enough to worry him; **il suffit d'une fois: on n'est jamais trop prudent** once is enough — you can never be too careful **b** (avec que) **il suffit que vous leur écriviez** all you have to do is write to them; **il suffit que tu me dises comment me rendre à l'aéroport** all you have to do is tell me how to get to the airport; **il suffit qu'il ouvre la bouche pour que tout le monde se taise** he has only to open his mouth and everyone stops talking; **il suffit qu'il soit démotivé pour faire du mauvais travail** if he feels the least bit demotivated he doesn't produce very good work **3** se suffire VPR **se ~ (à soi-même)** [pays, personne] to be self-sufficient; **la beauté se suffit (à elle-même)** beauty is sufficient unto itself (littér); **ils se suffisent (l'un à l'autre)** they have each other and don't need anyone else

suffisamment [syfizamɑ̃] ADV sufficiently, enough; **~ fort/clair** sufficiently strong/clear, strong/clear enough; **être ~ vêtu** to have enough clothes on; **lettre ~ affranchie** letter with enough stamps on; **~ de nourriture/d'argent** sufficient ou enough food/money; **y a-t-il ~ à boire?** is there enough ou sufficient to drink?; **nous ne sommes pas ~ nombreux** there aren't enough of us

suffisance [syfizɑ̃s] NF **a** (= vanité) self-importance, smugness **b** (littér) **avoir sa ~ de qch** † ◊ **avoir qch en ~** to have sth in plenty, have a sufficiency of sth†; **il y en a en ~** there is sufficient of it; **des livres, il en a sa ~** † ou **à sa ~** he has books aplenty ou in abundance

suffisant, e [syfizɑ̃, ɑ̃t] ADJ **a** (= adéquat) sufficient; (Scol) [résultats] satisfactory; **c'est ~ pour qu'il se mette en colère** it's enough to make him lose his temper; **je n'ai pas la place/la somme ~e** I haven't got sufficient ou enough room/money; **500 F, c'est amplement** ou **plus que ~** 500 francs is more than enough → **condition, grâce b** (= prétentieux)

[personne, ton] self-important, smug; **faire le ~** to put on airs

suffixal, e [syfiksal, o] ADJ suffixal

suffixation [syfiksasjɔ̃] NF suffixation

suffixe [syfiks] NM suffix

suffixer [sufikse] ▸conjug 1◂ VT to suffix, add a suffix to; **mot suffixé** word with a suffix

suffocant, e [syfɔkɑ̃, ɑ̃t] ADJ **a** [fumée, chaleur] suffocating, stifling **b** (= étonnant) staggering

suffocation [syfɔkasjɔ̃] NF (= action) suffocation; (= sensation) suffocating feeling; **il avait des ~s** he had fits of choking

suffoquer [syfɔke] ▸conjug 1◂ **1** VI (lit) to choke, suffocate, stifle (**de** with); **~ de** [+ rage, indignation] to choke with **2** VT **a** [fumée] to suffocate, choke, stifle; [colère, joie] to choke; **les larmes la suffoquaient** she was choking with tears **b** (= étonner) [nouvelle, comportement de qn] to stagger; **la nouvelle nous a suffoqués** we were staggered by the news

suffragant [syfʀagɑ̃] ADJ M, NM (Rel) suffragan

suffrage [syfʀaʒ] **1** NM **a** (Pol = voix) vote; **~s exprimés** valid votes; **le parti obtiendra peu de/beaucoup de ~s** the party will poll badly/heavily, the party will get a poor/good share of the vote **b** (= approbation) [public, critique] approval (NonC), approbation (NonC); **accorder son ~ à qn/qch** to give one's approval to sb/sth; **ce livre a remporté tous les ~s** this book met with universal approval; **cette nouvelle voiture mérite tous les ~s** this new car deserves everyone's approval **2** COMP ► **suffrage censitaire** suffrage on the basis of property qualification ► **suffrage direct** direct suffrage ► **suffrage indirect** indirect suffrage ► **suffrage restreint** restricted suffrage ► **suffrage universel** universal suffrage ou franchise

suffragette [syfʀaʒɛt] NF suffragette

▼ **suggérer** [syɡʒeʀe] ▸conjug 6◂ VT (gén) to suggest; [+ solution, projet] to suggest, put forward; **~ une réponse à qn** to suggest a reply to sb; **je lui suggérai que c'était moins facile qu'il ne pensait** I suggested to him ou I put it to him that it was not as easy as he thought; **~ à qn une solution** to put forward ou suggest ou put a solution to sb; **j'ai suggéré d'aller au cinéma/que nous allions au cinéma** I suggested going to the cinema/that we went to the cinema; **elle lui a suggéré de voir un médecin** she suggested he should see a doctor; **mot qui en suggère un autre** word which brings another to mind

se suffire VPR **se ~ (à soi-même)** [pays, personne] to be self-sufficient; **la beauté se suffit (à elle-même)** beauty is sufficient unto itself (littér); **ils se suffisent (l'un à l'autre)** they have each other and don't need anyone else

suggestibilité [syɡʒɛstibilite] NF suggestibility

suggestible [syɡʒɛstibl] ADJ suggestible

suggestif, -ive [syɡʒɛstif, iv] ADJ (= évocateur, indécent) suggestive

▼ **suggestion** [syɡʒɛstjɔ̃] NF suggestion; **faire une ~** to make a suggestion

suggestionner [syɡʒɛstjɔne] ▸conjug 1◂ VT to influence by suggestion

suggestivité [syɡʒɛstivite] NF suggestiveness

suicidaire [sɥiside] **1** ADJ (lit, fig) suicidal **2** NMF person with suicidal tendencies

suicide [sɥisid] NM (lit, fig) suicide; (fig) **c'est un** ou **du ~!** it's suicide!; **opération** ou **mission ~** suicide mission; **attaque/commando ~** suicide attack/commando squad; **~ collectif/rituel** group/ritual suicide; **pousser qn au ~** to push sb to suicide; **ce serait un véritable ~ politique** it would be political suicide → **tentative**

suicidé, e [sɥiside] (ptp de se suicider) **1** ADJ who has committed suicide **2** NM,F (= personne) suicide

suicider (se) [sɥiside] ▸conjug 1◂ **1** se suicider VPR to commit suicide **2** VT* (= tuer) **ils ont**

suicidé le témoin they made it look as if the witness had committed suicide

suie [sɥi] NF soot → **noir**

suif [sɥif] NM tallow; **~ de mouton** mutton suet; (arg Crime) **chercher du ~ à qn** to needle sb*; (arg Crime) **il va y avoir du ~** there's going to be trouble

sui generis [sɥiʒeneʀis] LOC ADJ sui generis; **l'odeur ~ d'un hôpital** the distinctive ou peculiar ou characteristic smell of a hospital; (hum) **odeur ~** foul smell

suint [sɥɛ̃] NM [laine] suint

suintant, e [sɥɛ̃tɑ̃, ɑ̃t] ADJ [pierre, roche, mur] oozing, sweating

suintement [sɥɛ̃tmɑ̃] NM [eau] seepage; [sève] oozing; [mur] oozing, sweating; [plaie, ulcère] weeping; **des ~s sur le mur** moisture oozing out of the wall; **le ~ des eaux entraîne des fissures** water seepage causes cracks to form

suinter [sɥɛ̃te] ▸conjug 1◂ VI [eau] to seep; [sève] to ooze; [mur] to ooze, sweat; [plaie] to weep; **des gouttes de pluie suintent du plafond** rainwater is seeping through the ceiling

Suisse [sɥis] **1** NF (= pays) Switzerland; **~ romande/allemande** ou **alémanique** French-speaking/German-speaking Switzerland **2** NMF (= personne) Swiss; **~ romand** French-speaking Swiss; **~ allemand** German-speaking Swiss, Swiss German; (fig) **boire/manger en ~**† to drink/eat alone

suisse [sɥis] **1** ADJ Swiss; **~ romand** Swiss French; **~ allemand** Swiss German **2** NM **a** (= bedeau) ≈ verger **b** [Vatican] Swiss Guard **c** (Can) chipmunk

Suissesse [sɥisɛs] NF Swiss (woman)

▼ **suite** [sɥit] NF **a** (= escorte) retinue, suite **b** (= nouvel épisode) continuation, following episode; (= second roman, film) sequel; (= rebondissement d'une affaire) follow-up; (= reste) remainder, rest; **voici la ~ de notre feuilleton** here is the next episode in ou the continuation of our serial; **ce roman/film a une ~** there is a sequel to this novel/film; (Presse) **voici la ~ de l'affaire que nous évoquions hier** here is the follow-up to ou further information on the item we mentioned yesterday; **la ~ du film/du repas/de la lettre était moins bonne** the remainder ou the rest of the film/the meal/the letter was not so good; **la ~ au prochain numéro** (journal) to be continued (in the next issue); (*: fig) we'll talk about this later; **~ et fin** concluding ou final episode; **la ~ des événements devait lui donner raison** what followed was to prove him right; **le projet n'a pas eu de ~** the project came to nothing; **attendons la ~** (d'un repas) let's wait for the next course; (d'un discours) let's see what comes next; (d'un événement) let's (wait and) see how it turns out; **lisez donc la ~** please read on **c** (= aboutissement) result; (= prolongements) **~s** [maladie] effects; [accident] results; [affaire, incident] consequences, repercussions; **la ~ logique de qch** the obvious ou logical result of sth; **cet incident a eu des ~s fâcheuses/n'a pas eu de ~s** the incident has had annoying consequences ou repercussions/has had no repercussions; **il est mort des ~s de ses blessures/d'un cancer** he died as a result of his injuries/died of cancer; **mourir des ~s d'un accident de cheval** to die following a riding accident **d** (= succession, Math) series; (Ling) sequence; **~ de** [personnes, maisons] succession ou string ou series of; [événements] succession ou train of; (Comm) **article sans ~** discontinued line **e** (frm = cohérence) coherence; **il y a beaucoup de ~ dans son raisonnement/ses réponses** his reasoning is/his replies are very coherent; **ses propos n'avaient guère de ~** what he said lacked coherence ou consistency; **travailler avec ~** to work steadily; **des propos sans ~** disjointed words; **il a de la ~ dans les idées** (réfléchi, décidé) he's very single-

---

► GRAMMAIRE ACTIVE: **suggérer** 28.1, 42.3   **suggestion** 28   **suite** 44.1, 47.1

minded; (*iro: entêté*) he's not easily put off → **esprit**

[f] (= *appartement*) suite

[g] (*Mus*) suite; **~ instrumentale/orchestrale** instrumental/orchestral suite

[h] (*loc*) **(comme) ~ à votre lettre/notre entretien** further to your letter/our conversation; **à la ~** (= *successivement*) one after the other; (= *derrière*) **mettez-vous à la ~** join on at the back, go to *ou* join the back of the queue (*Brit*) *ou* line (*US*); **à la ~ de** (*objet, personne*) behind; (= *événement*) **à la ~ de sa maladie** following his illness; **entraîner qn à sa ~** (*lit*) to drag sb along behind one; (*fig*) **entraîner qn à sa ~ dans une affaire** to drag sb into an affair; **de ~*** (= *immédiatement*) at once; **je reviens de ~*** I'll be right *ou* straight (*Brit*) back; (= *d'affilée*) **boire trois verres de ~** to drink three glasses in a row *ou* one after another; **pendant trois jours de ~** for three days in succession; **il est venu trois jours de ~** he came three days in a row *ou* three days running; **il n'arrive pas à dire trois mots de ~** he can't string two words together; (= *à cause de*) **par ~ de** owing to, as a result of; (= *par conséquent*) **par ~** consequently, therefore; (= *ensuite*) **par la ~** afterwards, subsequently; **donner ~ à** [+ *projet*] to pursue, follow up; [+ *demande, commande, lettre*] to follow up; **ils n'ont pas donné ~ à notre lettre** they have taken no action concerning our letter, they have not followed up our letter; **faire ~ à** [+ *événement*] to follow; [+ *chapitre*] to follow (after); [+ *bâtiment*] to adjoin; **prendre la ~ de** [+ *directeur*] to succeed, take over from; [+ *entreprise*] to take over → **ainsi, tout**

suivant[1], e [sɥivɑ̃, ɑ̃t] [1] ADJ [a] (*dans le temps*) following, next; (*dans une série*) next; **le mardi ~ je la revis** I saw her again the following Tuesday; **vendredi et les jours ~s** Friday and the following days; **le malade ~ était très atteint** the next patient was very badly affected; **«voir page ~e»** "see next page" [b] (= *ci-après*) following; **faites l'exercice ~** do the following exercise

[2] NM,F [a] (= *prochain*) (*dans une série*) next (one); (*dans le temps*) following (one), next (one); **(au) ~!** next (please)!; **cette année fut mauvaise et les ~es ne le furent guère moins** that year was bad and the following ones were scarcely any better; **pas jeudi prochain, le ~** not this (coming) Thursday, the one after (that); **je descends à la ~e*** I'm getting off at the next stop [b] (*littér* = *membre d'escorte*) attendant

[3] **suivante** NF (*Théât*) handmaiden, lady-in-waiting; †† companion

suivant[2] [sɥivɑ̃] PRÉP (= *selon*) according to; **~ son habitude** as usual, as is (*ou* was) his wont; **~ l'usage** according to custom; **~ l'expression consacrée** as the saying goes, as they say; **~ les jours/les cas** depending on the day/the circumstances; **découper ~ le pointillé** cut along the dotted line; **~ un axe** along an axis; **~ que ...** according to whether ...

suiveur, -euse [sɥivœʀ, øz] [1] ADJ [*véhicule*] following behind (*attrib*) [2] NM [a] (*Sport*) (official) follower (*of a race*) [b] (= *imitateur*) imitator; **ils n'innovent pas, ce ne sont que des ~s** they don't innovate, they just follow along [c] († = *dragueur*) **elle se retourna, son ~ avait disparu** she turned round and the man who was following her had disappeared; **elle va me prendre pour un ~** she'll think I'm the sort who follows women

suivi, e [sɥivi] (*ptp de* **suivre**) [1] ADJ [a] (= *régulier*) [*travail*] steady; [*correspondance*] regular; (= *constant*) [*qualité*] consistent; [*effort*] consistent, sustained; (*Comm*) [*demande*] constant, steady; (= *cohérent*) [*conversation, histoire, raisonnement*] coherent; [*politique*] consistent

[b] (*Comm*) [*article*] in general production (*attrib*)

[c] (= *apprécié*) **très ~** [*cours*] well-attended; [*mode, recommandation*] widely adopted; [*exemple*] widely followed; **le match était très ~** a lot a people watched the match; **cours peu ~** poorly-attended course; **mode peu ~e** fashion that has a limited following; **exemple peu ~** example which is not widely followed; **procès très ~** trial that is being closely followed by the public; **feuilleton très ~** serial with a large following

[2] NM (= *accompagnement*) [*dossier, travaux, négociations*] monitoring; **assurer le ~ de** [+ *affaire*] to follow through; [+ *produit en stock*] to go on stocking; **il n'y a pas eu de ~** there was no follow-up; **~ médical** aftercare, follow-up treatment; **assurer le ~ pédagogique des élèves** to provide pupils with continuous educational support; **assurer le ~ psychologique des victimes** to provide victims with counselling

suivisme [sɥivism] NM (*Pol*) follow-my-leader attitude

suiviste [sɥivist] [1] ADJ [*attitude, politique*] follow-my-leader (*épith*) [2] NMF person with a follow-my-leader attitude

suivre [sɥivʀ] ▶ conjug 40 ◀ [1] VT [a] (*gén*) (= *accompagner, marcher derrière, venir après*) to follow; **elle le suit comme un petit chien** *ou* **un caniche** *ou* **un toutou*** she follows him (around) like a little dog; **il me suit comme mon ombre** he follows me about like a shadow; **ralentis, je ne peux pas (te) ~** slow down, I can't keep up (with you); **pars sans moi, je te suis** go on without me and I'll follow (on); **si vous voulez bien me ~** if you'll just follow me, come this way please; **~ qn de près** (*garde du corps*) to stick close to sb; [*voiture, coureur*] to follow close behind sb; **faire ~ qn** to have sb followed; **suivez le guide!** this way, please!; (*fig*) **son image me suit sans cesse** his image is constantly with me; **cette préposition est toujours suivie de ...** this preposition is always followed by ...; **il la suivit des yeux** *ou* **du regard** he followed her with his eyes, his eyes followed her; (*iro*) **certains députés, suivez mon regard, ont ...** certain deputies, without mentioning any names *ou* no names mentioned, have ...; (*Tennis, Golf*) **~ sa balle** to follow through; (*dans le temps*) **l'été suit le printemps** summer follows spring *ou* comes after spring; **le mariage sera suivi d'une réception** the wedding ceremony will be followed by a reception; **le jour qui suivit son arrivée** the day following *ou* after his arrival, the day after he arrived; **suivent deux mois d'intense activité** two months of intense activity will follow → **aimer, lettre, trace**

[b] (*dans une série*) to follow; **la maison qui suit la mienne** the house after mine → **jour**

[c] (= *longer*) [*personne*] to follow, keep to; [*route, itinéraire*] to follow; **suivez la N7 sur 10 km** keep to *ou* go along *ou* follow the N7 for 10km; **prenez la route qui suit la Loire** take the road which goes alongside *ou* which follows the Loire; (*fig*) **~ une piste** to follow up a clue; (*fig*) **ces deux amis ont suivi des voies bien différentes** the two friends have gone very different ways; **découpez en suivant le pointillé** cut along the dotted line; **suivez les flèches** follow the arrows

[d] (= *se conformer à*) [+ *exemple, mode, conseil, consigne*] to follow; **~ un régime** to be on a diet; **il me fait ~ un régime sévère** he has put me on a strict diet; **~ son instinct** to follow one's instinct *ou* one's nose*; **il suit son idée** he does things his (own) way; **il se leva et chacun suivit son exemple** he stood up and everyone else followed suit; **on n'a pas voulu le ~** we didn't want to follow his advice; **je ne vous suivrai pas sur ce terrain** I won't follow you down that road; **tout le monde vous suivra** everybody will back you up *ou* support you; **la maladie/l'enquête suit son cours** the illness/the inquiry is running *ou* taking its

course; **laisser la justice ~ son cours** to let justice take its course; **~ le mouvement** to follow the crowd; **si les prix augmentent, les salaires doivent ~** if prices rise, salaries must do the same → **marche[1], traitement**

[e] (*Scol*) [+ *classe, cours*] (= *être inscrit à*) to attend, go to; (= *être attentif à*) to follow; (= *assimiler*) [+ *programme*] to keep up with

[f] (= *observer l'évolution de*) [+ *carrière de qn, affaire, match*] to follow; [+ *feuilleton*] to follow, keep up with; **~ un malade/un élève** to follow *ou* monitor the progress of a patient/a pupil; **~ la messe** to follow (the) mass; **elle suit de près l'actualité** she keeps abreast of *ou* up with the news; **il se fait ~ ou il est suivi par un médecin** he's seeing a doctor; **j'ai suivi ses articles avec intérêt** I've followed his articles with interest; [*feuilleton*] **«à ~ »** "to be continued"; **(c'est une) affaire à ~** watch this space, it's worth keeping an eye on

[g] (*Comm* = *avoir en stock*) [+ *article*] to (continue to) stock; **nous ne suivons plus cet article** this is a discontinued line

[h] (= *comprendre*) [+ *argument, personne, exposé*] to follow; **jusqu'ici je vous suis** I'm with you *ou* I follow you so far; **il parlait si vite qu'on le suivait mal** he spoke so fast he was difficult to follow; **là, je ne vous suis pas très bien** I don't really follow you *ou* I'm not really with you there

[i] (*Jeux*) [+ *numéro, cheval*] to follow

[2] VI [a] [*élève*] (= *être attentif*) to pay attention; **suivez avec votre voisin** share with the person sitting next to you

[b] [*élève*] (= *assimiler le programme*) to keep up, follow; **elle suit bien en physique** she's keeping up well in physics

[c] (*Cartes*) to follow; (*Poker*) **je suis** I'm in, count me in

[d] **faire ~ son courrier** to have one's mail forwarded; (*sur enveloppe*) **«faire ~»** "please forward"

[e] (= *venir après*) to follow; **lisez ce qui suit** read what follows; **les enfants suivent à pied** the children are following on foot; **les personnes dont les noms suivent** the following people; **comme suit** as follows

[3] VB IMPERS **il suit de ce que vous dites que ...** it follows from what you say that ...

[4] **se suivre** VPR [a] (*dans une série*) to follow each other; **ils se suivaient sur l'étroit sentier** [*deux personnes*] they were walking one behind the other along the narrow path; [*plusieurs personnes*] they were walking one behind the other *ou* in single file along the narrow path; **leurs enfants se suivent (de près)** there's not much of an age difference between their children; **trois démissions qui se suivent** three resignations in a row *ou* in close succession

[b] (*dans le bon ordre*) to be in (the right) order; **les pages ne se suivent pas** the pages are not in (the right) order, the pages are in the wrong order

sujet, -ette [syʒɛ, ɛt] [1] ADJ **~ à** [+ *vertige, mal de mer*] prone to; [+ *lubies, sautes d'humeur*] subject to, prone to; [+ *impôt, modification*] liable to, subject to; **question sujette à controverse** *ou* **polémique** controversial issue; **~ aux accidents** accident-prone; **il était ~ aux accidents les plus bizarres** he used to have the strangest accidents; **~ à faire qch** liable *ou* inclined *ou* prone to do sth; **il n'est pas ~ à faire des imprudences** he is not one to do anything careless; **~ à caution** [*renseignement, nouvelle*] unconfirmed; [*moralité, vie privée, honnêteté*] questionable; **je vous dis ça mais c'est ~ à caution** I'm telling you that but I can't guarantee it's true

[2] NM,F (= *gouverné*) subject

[3] NM [a] (= *matière, question, thème*) subject (*de for*); **un excellent ~ de conversation** an excellent topic (of conversation); **revenons à notre ~** let's get back to the subject at hand;

c'était devenu un ~ de plaisanterie it had become a standing joke ou something to joke about; **ça ferait un bon ~ de comédie** that would be a good subject ou theme for a comedy; **bibliographie par ~s** bibliography arranged by subject; **~ d'examen** examination question; **quel ~ ont-ils donné ?** what did you have to write about?; **distribuer les ~s** to give out the examination papers; **votre dissertation est hors ~** your essay is off the point; **faire du hors ~** to wander off the point → **or¹, vif** |b| (= motif, cause) **~ de mécontentement** cause ou grounds for dissatisfaction; **il n'avait vraiment pas ~ de se mettre en colère/se plaindre** he really had no cause to lose his temper/for complaint; **il a ~ de se plaindre** he has every reason to complain; **protester/réclamer sans ~** to protest/complain without good cause

|c| (= individu) subject; (Ling) **le ~ parlant** the speaker; **les rats qui servent de ~s (d'expérience)** the rats which serve as experimental subjects; **son frère est un ~ brillant/un ~ d'élite** his brother is a brilliant/an exceptionally brilliant student; **un mauvais ~** (= enfant) a bad boy; (= jeune homme) a bad sort ou lot (Brit)

|d| (Ling, Mus, Philo) subject; **~ grammatical/réel/apparent** grammatical/real/apparent subject; **nom/pronom ~** noun/pronoun subject

|e| (Mus, Peinture) subject

|f| (= figurine) figurine; **des petits ~s en ivoire** small ivory figurines

|g| (Jur) **~ de droit** holder of a right

|h| (= à propos de) **au ~ de** about, concerning; **que sais-tu à son ~ ?** what do you know about him?; **au ~ de cette fille, je peux vous dire que ...** about ou concerning that girl, I can tell you that ...; **à ce ~, je voulais vous dire que ...** on that subject ou about which, I wanted to tell you that ...; **c'est à quel ~ ?** can I ask what it's about?

sujétion [syʒesjɔ̃] NF |a| (= asservissement) subjection; **maintenir un peuple dans la ~ ou sous sa ~** to keep a nation in subjection; **tomber sous la ~ de qn** to fall into sb's power ou under sb's sway; (littér = asservissement) **~ aux passions/au désir** subjection to passions/to desire |b| (= obligation, contrainte) constraint; **les enfants étaient pour elle une ~** the children were a real constraint to her ou were like a millstone round her neck; **des habitudes qui deviennent des ~s** habits which become compulsions; (Scol) **indemnité de ~ spéciale** bonus paid to teachers working in schools in problem areas

sulfamides [sylfamid] NMPL sulpha drugs, sulphonamides (SPÉC)

sulfatage [sylfataʒ] NM (vigne) spraying (with copper sulphate ou sulfate (US))

sulfate [sylfat] NM sulphate, sulfate (US); **~ de cuivre** copper sulphate

sulfaté, e [sylfate] ADJ (ptp de **sulfater**) ADJ sulphated

sulfater [sylfate] ▶conjug 1◀ VT [+ vigne] to spray (with copper sulphate ou sulfate (US))

sulfateuse [sylfatøz] NF |a| (Agr) (copper sulphate ou sulfate (US)) spraying machine |b| (arg Crime = mitraillette) machine gun, MG*

sulfite [sylfit] NM sulphite, sulfite (US)

sulfure [sylfyʀ] NM |a| (Chim) sulphide, sulfide (US); **~ de fer/mercure** iron/mercuric sulphide; **~ de carbone** carbon disulphide |b| (= presse-papier) millefiore glass paperweight

sulfuré, e [sylfyʀe] (ptp de **sulfurer**) ADJ sulphurated, sulfurated (US), sulphurized, sulphuretted; **hydrogène ~** hydrogen sulphide ou sulfide (US), sulphuretted ou sulfuretted (US) hydrogen

sulfurer [sylfyʀe] ▶conjug 1◀ VT to sulphurate, sulphurize

sulfureux, -euse [sylfyʀø, øz] ADJ |a| (Chim) sulphurous; **anhydride ou gaz ~** sulphur dioxide; **source sulfureuse** sulphur spring |b| (= diabolique) [personnage, réputation] nefarious; [propos] heretical; [charme] demonic

sulfurique [sylfyʀik] ADJ sulphuric; **acide ~** sulphuric acid; **anhydride ~** sulphur trioxide

sulfurisé, e [sylfyʀize] ADJ **papier ~** greaseproof paper

sulky [sylki] NM (Courses) sulky

sultan [syltɑ̃] NM sultan

sultanat [syltana] NM sultanate

sultane [syltan] NF |a| (= épouse) sultana |b| (= canapé) couch

sumac [symak] NM sumach (Brit), sumac (US)

Sumatra [symatʀa] N Sumatra

sumérien, -ienne [symeʀjɛ̃, jɛn] |1| ADJ Sumerian |2| NM (Ling) Sumerian |3| **Sumérien(ne)** NM,F Sumerian

summum [sɔ(m)mɔm] NM [gloire, civilisation] acme, climax; [bêtise, hypocrisie] height

sumo [symo] NM (= lutteur) sumo wrestler; (= lutte) sumo (wrestling)

sumotori [symotɔʀi] NM sumo wrestler

sunnisme [synism] NM Sunni

sunnite [synit] ADJ, NMF Sunni

sup¹* [syp] ADJ (ABRÉV = **supplémentaire**) **heures ~** overtime; **faire des heures ~** to do overtime; **être payé en heures ~** to be paid overtime

sup²* [syp] ADJ (ABRÉV = **supérieur**) **Sup de Co** grande école for business students → **école, lettres, math**

super¹ [sypɛʀ] NM (ABRÉV = **supercarburant**) four-star (petrol) (Brit), extra (US), premium (US), super (US); **~ plombé** super leaded petrol; **~ sans plomb** super unleaded (petrol)

super²* [sypɛʀ] ADJ INV (= sensationnel) terrific*, great*, fantastic*

super-* [sypɛʀ] PRÉF (dans les mots composés à trait d'union, le préfixe reste invariable) |a| (avant adj) **~cher/-chic** ultra-expensive/ultra-chic; **c'est ~intéressant** it's so interesting; **il est ~sympa** he's really nice |b| (avant nom) **une ~moto** a fantastic* motorbike; **un ~flic** a supercop*

superbe [sypɛʀb] |1| ADJ |a| (= splendide) [temps, journée] superb, glorious, gorgeous; [femme, enfant] beautiful; [homme] handsome; [maison, cheval, corps, yeux] superb, beautiful; [résultat, salaire, performance, vue, voix] superb, magnificent; **tu as une mine ~** you look wonderful; (littér) **~ d'indifférence** superbly indifferent |b| (littér = orgueilleux) arrogant, haughty |2| NF (littér) arrogance, haughtiness; **il a perdu de sa ~** he's no longer quite so high and mighty

superbement [sypɛʀbəmɑ̃] ADV (= magnifiquement) superbly, wonderfully, beautifully; (= orgueilleusement) **il m'a ~ ignorée** he loftily ignored me

superbénéfice [sypɛʀbenefis] NM immense profit

supercarburant [sypɛʀkaʀbyʀɑ̃] NM high-octane petrol (Brit), high-octane ou high-test gasoline (US)

superchampion, -ionne [sypɛʀʃɑ̃pjɔ̃, jɔn] NM,F (sporting) superstar

supercherie [sypɛʀʃəʀi] NF trick, trickery (NonC); **il s'aperçut de la ~** he saw through the trick; **user de ~s pour tromper qn** to trick sb; **~ littéraire** literary hoax ou fabrication

supérette [sypɛʀɛt] NF mini-market, superette (US)

superfétation [sypɛʀfetasjɔ̃] NF (littér) superfluity

superfétatoire [sypɛʀfetatwaʀ] ADJ (littér) superfluous, supererogatory (littér)

superficialité [sypɛʀfisjalite] NF superficiality

superficie [sypɛʀfisi] NF (= aire) (surface) area; (= surface) surface; [terrain] area; **couvrir une ~ de** to cover an area of; **un appartement d'une ~ de 80 m²** an apartment of 80 square metres;

(fig) **s'en tenir à la ~ des choses** to skim the surface of things

superficiel, -ielle [sypɛʀfisjɛl] ADJ (gén) superficial; [idées, esprit, personne] superficial, shallow; [beauté] superficial, skin-deep; [modification] cosmetic; (= près de la surface) [couche de liquide] superficial, upper; (= fin) [couche de peinture] thin → **tension**

superficiellement [sypɛʀfisjɛlmɑ̃] ADV superficially

superfin, e [sypɛʀfɛ̃, in] ADJ [beurre, produit] top-quality (épith); [qualité] top (épith), superior

superflu, e [sypɛʀfly] |1| ADJ |a| (= pas nécessaire) [précaution, travail] unnecessary; **il est ~ d'insister** there is no point (in) insisting |b| (= en trop) [discours, détails, explications] superfluous, redundant; [kilos] surplus; [poils] unwanted; **un brin d'humour ne serait pas ~** a bit of humour wouldn't go amiss; **il n'est pas ~ de rappeler que ...** it's worth bearing in mind that ... |2| NM **le ~** (gén) non-essentials; (= produits de luxe) luxuries; **distinguer le ~ de l'indispensable** to differentiate between essentials and non-essentials; **maintenant, je peux m'offrir le ~** now I can afford to spend money on luxuries; **débarrasser son style du ~** to pare down one's style

superfluité [sypɛʀflyite] NF (littér) superfluity

superforme* [sypɛʀfɔʀm] NF **être en ~** (moralement) to feel great*; (physiquement) to be in great shape*; **c'est la ~** (morale) I'm (ou he's etc) feeling great*; (physique) I'm (ou he's etc) in great shape*

superforteresse [sypɛʀfɔʀtəʀɛs] NF superfortress

super-géant [sypɛʀʒeɑ̃] NM (Ski) super-giant slalom

supergrand* [sypɛʀgʀɑ̃] NM superpower

super-huit [sypɛʀɥit] ADJ INV, NM INV super-8; **caméra ~** super-8 camera

▼ **supérieur, e** [sypeʀjœʀ] |1| ADJ |a| (dans l'espace : gén) upper (épith); [planètes] superior; **dans la partie ~e du clocher** in the highest ou upper ou top part of the bell tower; **la partie ~e de l'objet** the top part of the object; **le feu a pris dans les étages ~s** fire broke out on the upper floors; **montez à l'étage ~** go to the next floor up ou to the floor above, go up to the next floor; **mâchoire/lèvre ~e** upper jaw/lip; **le lac Supérieur** Lake Superior

|b| (dans un ordre) [vitesse] higher, greater; [nombre] higher, greater, bigger; [classes sociales] upper (épith); [niveaux, échelons] upper (épith), topmost; [animaux, végétaux] higher (épith); (Scol) **passer dans la classe ~e** to go up to the next class; (Rel) **Père ~** Father Superior; (Rel) **Mère ~e** Mother Superior; (Mil) **commandement ~** senior command; **à l'échelon ~** on the next rung up; (aux enchères) **faire une offre ~e** to make a higher bid; **forces ~es en nombres** forces superior in number → **cadre, enseignement, mathématique, officier¹**

|c| (= excellent, qui prévaut) [intérêts, principe] higher (épith); [intelligence, esprit] superior; **produit de qualité ~e** product of superior quality; **des considérations d'ordre ~** considerations of a higher order

|d| (= hautain) [air, ton, regard] superior

|e| **~ à** [nombre] greater ou higher than, above; [somme] greater ou bigger than; [production] greater than, superior to; **intelligence/qualité ~e à la moyenne** above-average ou higher than average intelligence/quality; **il a obtenu un score nettement ~ à la moyenne nationale** he scored well above the national average; **il est d'une taille ~e à la moyenne** he's of above average height; **des températures ~es à 300°** temperatures in excess of ou higher than ou of more than 300°; **parvenir à un niveau ~ à ...** to reach a higher level than ...; **il est d'un niveau bien ~ à celui de son adversaire** he is of a far higher stand-

▶ GRAMMAIRE ACTIVE: **supérieur** 32.2

ard than his opponent; **il se croit ~ à tout le monde** he thinks he's better than *ou* superior to everybody else; **être ~ à qn (dans une hiérarchie)** to be higher up than sb (in a hierarchy), be sb's superior; *(aux enchères)* **faire une offre ~e à celle de qn** to outbid sb

2 NM,F *(Admin, Mil, Rel)* superior; **mon ~ hiérarchique direct** my immediate superior

3 NM *(Univ)* **le ~** higher education

supérieurement [sypeRjœRmɑ̃] ADV *[exécuter qch, dessiner]* exceptionally well; **~ doué/ ennuyeux** exceptionally gifted/boring

supériorité [sypeRjɔRite] NF a (= prééminence) superiority; **~ militaire/ technologique** military/technological superiority; **nous avons la ~ du nombre** we outnumber them, we are superior in number(s); **ce pays s'est révélé d'une écrasante ~ sur ses adversaires** this country has turned out to be overwhelmingly superior to its enemies b (= condescendance) superiority; **air de ~** superior air, air of superiority; **sourire de ~** superior smile; **avoir un sentiment de ~** to feel superior → **complexe**

superlatif, -ive [sypeRlatif, iv] 1 ADJ superlative 2 NM superlative; **~ absolu/relatif** absolute/relative superlative; **au ~*** in the superlative; *(fig)* **il m'ennuie au ~*** I find him extremely boring

superlativement [sypeRlativmɑ̃] ADV superlatively

superléger [sypeRleʒe] ADJ, NM *(Sport)* light welterweight

superman [sypeRman] *(pl* **supermans** *ou* **supermen** [sypeRmɛn]) NM superman; *(péj)* **il aime jouer les ~s** *ou* **supermen** he likes to let everybody know what a great guy* he is

supermarché [sypeRmaRʃe] NM supermarket

supernova [sypeRnɔva] *(pl* **supernovae** [sypeRnɔve]) NF supernova

superpétrolier [sypeRpetRɔlje] NM supertanker

superphosphate [sypeRfɔsfat] NM superphosphate

superposable [sypeRpozabl] ADJ *(gén)* that may be superimposed, superimposable *(à* on); *[éléments de mobilier]* stacking *(épith)*

superposé, e [sypeRpoze] *(ptp de* **superposer**) ADJ *[visions, images]* superimposed; **il y avait plusieurs couches ~es** there were several layers; **des blocs ~s** blocks one on top of the other → **lit**

superposer [sypeRpoze] ▸ conjug 1 ◂ 1 VT a (= empiler) *[+ blocs, briques, éléments de mobilier]* to stack; **~ des couches de peinture** to apply several layers of paint; **~ les consignes aux consignes** to give one instruction after another b (= faire chevaucher) *[+ cartes, clichés]* to superimpose; *[+ figures géométriques]* to superpose; **~ qch à** to superimpose *ou* superpose sth on 2 **se superposer** VPR a *[clichés photographiques, images]* to be superimposed (on one another) b (= s'ajouter) *[couches de sédiments]* to be superposed; *[éléments de mobilier]* to be stackable

superposition [sypeRpozisjɔ̃] NF a (= action) *[blocs]* stacking; *[cartes, clichés, visions]* superimposition; *[figures géométriques]* superposing b *(Photo)* superimposition; **la ~ de ces couches de sédiments** the way these strata of sediment are superposed; **la ~ de plusieurs influences** the cumulative effect of several influences

superpréfet [sypeRpRefe] NM superprefect *(in charge of a region)*

superproduction [sypeRpRɔdyksjɔ̃] NF *(Ciné)* spectacular, blockbuster

superprofit [sypeRpRɔfi] NM immense profit

superpuissance [sypeRpɥisɑ̃s] NF superpower

supersonique [sypeRsɔnik] 1 ADJ supersonic → **bang** 2 NM supersonic aircraft

superstitieusement [sypeRstisjøzmɑ̃] ADV superstitiously

superstitieux, -ieuse [sypeRstisjø, jøz] 1 ADJ superstitious 2 NM,F superstitious person

superstition [sypeRstisjɔ̃] NF superstition; **il a la ~ du chiffre 13** he's superstitious about the number 13

superstrat [sypeRstRa] NM *(Ling)* superstratum

superstructure [sypeRstRyktyR] NF *(gén)* superstructure

supertanker [sypeRtɑ̃kœR] NM supertanker

superviser [sypeRvize] ▸ conjug 1 ◂ VT to supervise, oversee

superviseur [sypeRvizœR] NM a (= personne) supervisor b *(Ordin)* supervisor

supervision [sypeRvizjɔ̃] NF supervision

superwelter [sypeRwɛlter] ADJ, NM light middleweight

superwoman [sypeRwuman] *(pl* **superwomans** *ou* **superwomen** [sypeRwumɛn]) NF superwoman

supin [sypɛ̃] NM supine

supinateur [sypinatœR] 1 ADJ supine 2 NM (= muscle) supinator

supination [sypinasjɔ̃] NF *[main]* supination

supplanter [syplɑ̃te] ▸ conjug 1 ◂ 1 VT to supplant; **le disque compact a supplanté le microsillon** the compact disc has replaced the record 2 **se supplanter** VPR to supplant one another

suppléance [sypleɑ̃s] NF (= poste) supply post *(Brit)*, substitute post *(US)*; (= action) temporary replacement; **faire des ~s** to take supply posts, do supply *(Brit) ou* substitute *(US)* teaching

suppléant, e [sypleɑ̃, ɑ̃t] 1 ADJ *(gén)* deputy *(épith)*, substitute *(épith) (US)*; *[professeur]* supply *(épith) (Brit)*, substitute *(épith) (US)*; **médecin ~** locum *(Brit)*, replacement doctor *(US)*; **verbe ~** substitute verb 2 NM,F (= professeur) supply *(Brit) ou* substitute *(US)* teacher; (= juge) deputy (judge); *(Pol)* deputy; (= médecin) locum *(Brit)*, replacement doctor *(US)*; **pendant les vacances, on fait appel à des ~s** during the holidays we take on relief *ou* temporary staff

suppléer [syplee] ▸ conjug 1 ◂ 1 VT a (= ajouter) *[+ mot manquant]* to supply, provide; *[+ somme complémentaire]* to make up, supply b (= compenser) *[+ lacune]* to fill in; *[+ manque, défaut]* to make up for, compensate for c *(frm = remplacer)* *[+ professeur]* to stand in for, replace; *[+ juge]* to deputize for; *(littér)* **la machine a suppléé l'homme dans ce domaine** men have been replaced by machines in this area 2 **suppléer à** VT INDIR (= compenser) *[+ défaut, manque]* to make up for, compensate for; (= remplacer) *[+ chose, personne, qualité]* to substitute for

supplément [syplemɑ̃] NM a (= surcroît) **un ~ de travail/salaire** extra *ou* additional work/ pay; **avoir droit à un ~ de 300 F** to be allowed a supplement of 300 francs *ou* a 300-franc supplement, be allowed an extra *ou* an additional 300 francs; **demander un ~ d'information** to ask for additional *ou* further *ou* supplementary information; **~ d'imposition** additional tax b *[journal, dictionnaire]* supplement; **~ illustré** illustrated supplement c *(à payer) (au théâtre, au restaurant)* extra charge, supplement; *(dans le train pour prolongement de trajet)* excess fare; *(sur trains spéciaux)* supplement; **~ de 1ère classe** supplement for travelling 1st class, 1st-class supplement; **sans ~ de prix** without additional charge *ou* surcharge; **payer un ~ pour excès de bagages** to pay (for) excess luggage, pay

excess on one's luggage

d **en ~** extra; **le vin est en ~** wine is extra, an additional charge is made for wine; **le tableau de bord en bois est en ~** the wooden dashboard is an optional extra

e *[angle]* supplement

supplémentaire [syplemɑ̃tɛR] ADJ *[dépenses, crédits, retards]* additional, further *(épith)*; *[travail, vérifications]* additional, extra *(épith)*; *[trains, autobus]* relief *(épith)*; *[angle]* supplementary; *(Mus)* **lignes ~s** ledger lines; **accorder un délai ~** to grant an extension of the deadline, allow additional time; **faire des/10 heures ~s** to work *ou* do overtime/10 hours' overtime; **les heures ~s sont bien payées** you get well paid for (doing) overtime, overtime hours are well-paid

supplétif, -ive [sypletif, iv] 1 ADJ additional 2 NM *(Mil)* back-up soldier; **les ~s** the back-up troops

suppliant, e [syplijɑ̃, ijɑ̃t] 1 ADJ *[regard, voix]* beseeching, imploring; *[personne]* imploring 2 NM,F suppliant, supplicant

supplication [syplikasjɔ̃] NF *(gén)* plea, entreaty; *(Rel)* supplication

supplice [syplis] 1 NM a (= peine corporelle) form of torture, torture *(NonC)*; *(peine capitale)* **le (dernier) ~** execution, death; **conduire qn au ~** to take sb to be executed; **le ~ de la roue** (torture on) the wheel; **le ~ du fouet** flogging, the lash; **le ~ du collier** necklacing b (= souffrance) torture; **~s moraux** moral tortures *ou* torments; **éprouver le ~ de l'incertitude** to be tormented by uncertainty; **cette lecture est un (vrai) ~!** reading this is absolute torture! c *(loc)* **être au ~** *(appréhension)* to be in agonies *ou* on the rack; *(gêne, douleur)* to be in misery; **mettre qn au ~** to torture sb 2 COMP ▸ **supplice chinois** Chinese torture *(NonC)* ▸ **le supplice de la Croix** the Crucifixion ▸ **supplice de Tantale** *(lit)* torment of Tantalus; *(fig)* **c'est un vrai ~ de Tantale** it's so frustrating

supplicié, e [syplisje] *(ptp de* **supplicier**) NM,F victim of torture, torture victim; **les corps/ cris des ~s** the bodies/cries of the torture victims

supplicier [syplisje] ▸ conjug 7 ◂ VT *(lit, fig)* to torture; *(à mort)* to torture to death

supplier [syplije] ▸ conjug 7 ◂ VT to implore, beseech *(frm)*, entreat *(frm) (de faire* to do); **~ qn à genoux** to beseech *ou* implore *ou* entreat sb on one's knees; **tais-toi, je t'en supplie!** will you please be quiet!; **il m'a suppliée de rester** he begged me to stay

supplique [syplik] NF petition; **présenter une ~ au roi** to petition the king, bring a petition before the king

support [sypɔR] NM a *(gén = soutien)* support; (= béquille, pied) prop, support; *[instruments de laboratoire, outils, livre]* stand b (= moyen) medium; (= aide) aid; **~ publicitaire** advertising medium; **conférence faite à l'aide d'un ~ écrit/magnétique/visuel** lecture given with the help of a written text/a tape/ visual aids; **les différents ~s d'information** the different media through which information is transmitted; **~ pédagogique** teaching aid c *(Peinture)* *[dessin]* support; *(Math)* *[vecteur]* directed line segment; *(Ordin)* *[information codée]* medium; **passer du ~ papier au ~ informatique** to go from using paper *ou* hard copy to using computers; **les chaînes d'ADN, ~ de l'hérédité** DNA sequences, the carriers of genetic information; **le symbole est le ~ du concept** the symbol is the physical medium through which the concept is expressed

supportable [sypɔRtabl] ADJ *[douleur, température]* bearable; *[conduite]* tolerable; (* = passable, pas trop mauvais) tolerable, passable

▼ **supporter**[1] [sypɔRte] ▸ conjug 1 ◂ 1 VT a (= endurer) *[+ maladie, solitude, revers]* to bear, endure, put up with; *[+ douleur]* to bear, endure;

[+ *conduite, ingratitude*] to tolerate, put up with; [+ *recommandations, personne*] to put up with, bear; **il ne pouvait plus ~ la vie** life had become unbearable for him; **il supportait leurs plaisanteries avec patience** he patiently put up with their jokes; **la mort d'un être cher est difficile à ~** the death of a loved one is hard to bear; **il va falloir le ~ pendant toute la journée !** we're going to have to put up with him all day long!; **elle supporte tout d'eux, sans jamais rien dire** she puts up with everything they do without a word; **je ne supporte pas ce genre de comportement/qu'on me parle sur ce ton** I won't put up with *ou* stand for *ou* tolerate this sort of behaviour/being spoken to in that tone of voice; **je ne peux pas ~ l'hypocrisie** I can't bear *ou* abide *ou* stand hypocrisy; **je ne peux pas les ~** I can't bear *ou* stand them; **je ne supporte pas de voir ça** I can't bear seeing *ou* to see that, I can't stand seeing that

[b] (= *subir*) [+ *frais*] to bear; [+ *conséquences, affront, malheur*] to suffer, endure; **il m'a fait ~ les conséquences de son acte** he made me suffer the consequences of his action

[c] (= *servir de base à*) to support, hold up

[d] (= *résister à*) [+ *température, conditions atmosphériques, épreuve*] to withstand; **verre qui supporte la chaleur** heatproof *ou* heat-resistant glass; **il a bien/mal supporté l'opération** he took the operation well/badly; **il ne supporte pas l'alcool** he can't take alcohol; **elle ne supporte pas la vue du sang** she can't bear *ou* stand the sight of blood *ou* seeing blood; **il ne supporte pas la chaleur** he can't take *ou* stand *ou* bear the heat; **je ne supporte pas les épinards** (= *je ne les aime pas*) I can't stand spinach; (= *ils me rendent malade*) spinach doesn't agree *ou* disagrees with me; **lait facile à ~** easily-digested milk; **tu as de la chance de ~ l'ail** you're lucky being able to eat garlic; **ce roman ne supporte pas l'examen** this novel does not stand up to analysis; **cette règle ne supporte aucune exception** this rule admits of no exception

[e] (*Ordin, Pol, Sport*) to support

[f] * **on supporte un gilet, par ce temps** you can do with a cardigan in this weather; **je pensais avoir trop chaud avec un pull, mais on le supporte** I thought I'd be too hot with a pullover but I can do with it after all

[2] **se supporter** VPR (= *se tolérer*) **ils ne peuvent pas se ~** they can't stand *ou* bear each other

supporter[2] [sypɔʀtɛʀ] NM, **supporteur, -trice** [sypɔʀtœʀ, tʀis] NM,F (*Pol, Sport*) supporter

supposé, e [sypoze] (*ptp de supposer*) ADJ (= *présumé*) [*nombre, total*] estimated; [*meurtrier*] alleged; (*Jur*) [*père*] putative; [*nom*] assumed; (= *faux*) [*testament, signature*] forged; (= *prétendu*) **l'auteur ~ de cet article** the presumed *ou* alleged author of this article; **un ~ âge d'or** a supposed *ou* so-called golden age

▼ **supposer** [sypoze] ▶ conjug 1 ◀ VT [a] (*à titre d'hypothèse*) to suppose, assume; **supposons une nouvelle guerre** (let's) suppose another war broke out; **supposez que vous soyez malade** suppose you were ill; **en supposant que◊ à ~ que** supposing (that), assuming (that); (*Sci*) **pour les besoins de l'expérience, la pression est supposée constante** for the purposes of the experiment the pressure is taken to be *ou* assumed (to be) constant; **supposons une ligne A-B** let there be a line A-B

[b] (= *présumer*) to suppose, assume; **~ qn amoureux/jaloux** to imagine *ou* suppose sb to be in love/jealous; **je lui suppose une grande ambition** I imagine him to have great ambition; **on vous supposait malade** we thought you were ill; **je ne peux que le ~** I can only make a supposition, I can only surmise; **cela laisse ~ que ...** it leads one to suppose that ...;

je suppose que tu es contre I assume *ou* I suppose *ou* I presume you are against it

[c] (= *impliquer, présupposer*) to presuppose; (= *suggérer, laisser deviner*) to imply; **la gestation suppose la fécondation** gestation presupposes fertilization; **cela suppose du courage** that takes courage; **ta réponse suppose que tu n'as rien compris** your reply implies *ou* indicates that you haven't understood a thing

[d] (*Jur*) [+ *testament, signature*] to forge

supposition [sypozisjɔ̃] NF supposition, assumption; **on ne peut que faire des ~s** we can only surmise, we can only make suppositions *ou* assumptions; **je l'ignore, c'est une simple ~** I don't know, I'm just guessing *ou* it's pure conjecture on my part; **une ~ que ...*** supposing ...; (*Jur*) let us suppose ...

suppositoire [sypozitwaʀ] NM suppository

suppôt [sypo] NM (*littér*) henchman; **~ de Satan** *ou* **du diable** fiend, hellhound; **les ~s d'un tyran/de l'impérialisme** the lackeys of a tyrant/of imperialism

suppression [sypʀesjɔ̃] NF [a] (= *fait d'enlever, d'abolir*) [*mot, clause*] deletion, removal; [*mur, obstacle*] removal; [*avantage, crédits*] withdrawal; [*loi, taxe, peine de mort*] abolition; [*libertés*] suppression; [*discrimination, concurrence, pauvreté, chômage, douleur, fatigue*] elimination; **la ~ des inégalités** the elimination *ou* abolition of inequalities; **faire des ~s dans un texte** to make some deletions in a text; **il y a eu 7 000 ~s d'emplois** ou **d'effectifs** 7,000 jobs were axed *ou* shed [b] [*avion, train, vol*] cancellation; **pour éviter la ~ des petites lignes de province** to prevent small regional lines being taken out of service [c] [*témoin gênant*] elimination [d] (*Jur*) **~ de part** *ou* **d'enfant** concealment of birth; **~ d'état** *depriving someone of the means to prove their civil status*

supprimer [sypʀime] ▶ conjug 1 ◀ [1] VT [a] (= *enlever, abolir*) [+ *mot, clause*] to delete, remove (**de** from); [+ *mur, obstacle*] to remove; [+ *emploi, poste*] to axe, shed; [+ *crédits, avantage*] to withdraw; [+ *loi, taxe*] to do away with, abolish; [+ *libertés*] to suppress; [+ *peine de mort*] to abolish; [+ *publication*] to ban; [+ *document*] to suppress; [+ *discrimination, inégalité, concurrence, pauvreté, chômage*] to do away with, put an end to, eliminate; **ce fortifiant aide à ~ la fatigue** this tonic helps to eliminate tiredness; **ce médicament supprime la douleur** this medicine is a pain-killer; **on ne parviendra jamais à ~ la douleur** we shall never succeed in doing away with *ou* in eliminating pain; **cette technique supprime des opérations inutiles** this technique does away with *ou* cuts out unnecessary operations; **il faut ~ les intermédiaires** we must cut out the middleman; **l'avion supprime les distances** air travel shortens distances; **~ qch à qn** to deprive sb of sth; **~ les permissions aux soldats** to put a stop *ou* an end to the soldiers' leave; **on lui a supprimé sa prime/pension** he's had his bonus/pension stopped; **~ qch de son alimentation** to cut sth out of one's diet, eliminate sth from one's diet

[b] [+ *avion, train, vol*] to cancel; **la ligne a été supprimée** the line was taken out of service

[c] (= *tuer*) [+ *témoin gênant*] to do away with, eliminate

[2] **se supprimer** VPR to take one's own life

suppurant, e [sypyʀɑ̃, ɑ̃t] ADJ suppurating

suppuration [sypyʀasjɔ̃] NF suppuration

suppurer [sypyʀe] ▶ conjug 1 ◀ VI to suppurate

supputation [sypytasjɔ̃] NF [a] [*dépenses, frais*] calculation, computation; [*chances, possibilités*] calculation [b] (*frm* = *prévision*) guess, prognostication (*frm*); **ce ne sont que des ~s** this is just a guess

supputer [sypyte] ▶ conjug 1 ◀ VT [+ *dépenses, frais*] to calculate, compute; [+ *chances, possibilités*] to calculate; **je suppute que ...** I presume that ..., my guess is that ...

supra- [sypʀa] PRÉF supra...; **une autorité ~humaine** a suprahuman *ou* superhuman authority

supra [sypʀa] ADV above; **voir ~** see above

supraconducteur, -trice [sypʀakɔ̃dyktœʀ, tʀis] [1] ADJ superconductive, superconducting (*épith*) [2] NM superconductor

supraconductivité [sypʀakɔ̃dyktivite] NF superconductivity

supraliminaire [sypʀaliminɛʀ] ADJ supraliminal

supranational, e (*mpl -aux*) [sypʀanasjɔnal, o] ADJ supranational

supranationalisme [sypʀanasjɔnalism] NM supranationalism

supranationaliste [sypʀanasjɔnalist] ADJ supranationaliste

supranationalité [sypʀanasjɔnalite] NF **il craint de voir l'Europe basculer dans la ~** he's afraid that Europe will end up as a supranational state

suprasegmental, e (*mpl -aux*) [sypʀasegmɑ̃tal, o] ADJ suprasegmental

suprasensible [sypʀasɑ̃sibl] ADJ suprasensitive

supraterrestre [sypʀatɛʀɛstʀ] ADJ superterrestrial

suprématie [sypʀemasi] NF supremacy

suprématisme [sypʀematism] NM Suprematism

suprême [sypʀɛm] [1] ADJ (= *supérieur*) [*chef, autorité, cour*] supreme; (= *très grand, ultime*) [*raffinement, élégance, effort, ennui*] extreme; [*indifférence*] sublime; [*affront*] ultimate; **bonheur ~, notre chambre a vue sur la mer** joy of joys, our room overlooks the sea; **au ~ degré** to the highest degree; **le pouvoir ~** the supreme power; **le moment/l'heure ~** (= *la mort*) the moment/the hour of reckoning → **sauce**, **soviet** [2] NM (*Culin*) **~ de volaille** chicken supreme

suprêmement [sypʀɛmmɑ̃] ADV supremely

sur[1] [syʀ] [1] PRÉP [a] (*position*) on, upon (*frm*); (= *sur le haut de*) on top of, on; (*avec mouvement*) on, onto; (= *dans*) in; (= *par-dessus*) over; (= *au-dessus de*) above; **il y a un sac ~ la table/une affiche ~ le mur** there's a bag on the table/a poster on the wall; **mettre une annonce ~ un tableau** to put a notice (up) on a board; **il a laissé tous ses papiers ~ la table** he left all his papers (lying) on the table; **je n'ai pas d'argent/la lettre ~ moi** I haven't got any money on me/the letter on *ou* with me; **se promener ~ la rivière** to go boating on the river; **il y avait beaucoup de circulation ~ la route** there was a lot of traffic on the road; **~ ma route** *ou* **mon chemin** on my way; (*Radio*) **~ les grandes/petites ondes** on long/short wave; **elle rangea ses chapeaux ~ l'armoire** she put her hats away on top of the wardrobe; **pose ta valise ~ une chaise** put your case (down) on a chair; **elle a jeté son sac ~ la table** she threw her bag onto the table; **retire tes livres de ~ la table** take your books from *ou* off the table; **il grimpa ~ le toit** he climbed (up) onto the roof; **une chambre (qui donne) ~ la rue** a room that looks out onto the street; **il n'est jamais monté ~ un bateau** he's never been in *ou* on a boat; **~ la place (du marché)** in the (market) square; **la clé est restée ~ la porte** the key was left in the door; **lire qch ~ le journal*** to read sth in the paper; **chercher qch ~ une carte** to look for sth on a map; **des orages sont prévus ~ l'Alsace** storms are forecast in Alsace; **il a 1 500 F ~ son compte** he has 1,500 francs in his account; **livraison gratuite ~ Paris** free delivery in *ou* within Paris; **il neige ~ Paris/~ toute l'Europe** snow is falling on *ou* in Paris/over the whole of Europe, it's snowing in Paris/all over Europe; **mettre du papier d'aluminium ~ un plat/un couvercle ~ une casserole** to put silver foil over a dish/a lid on a saucepan; **un pont ~ la rivière** a bridge across *ou* on *ou* over the river; *(fig)* **s'endormir ~ un livre/son travail** to fall asleep over a book/over *ou* at one's work; **elle a acheté des poires ~ le marché** she bought some pears at the market; **~ terre et ~ mer** on land and (at) sea; **s'étendre ~ 3 km** to spread over 3 km; **« travaux ~ 5 km »** "roadworks for 5 km"; *(fig)* **vivre les uns ~ les autres** to live on top of each other; **gravure ~ bois/verre** wood/glass engraving → **appuyer, pied, place** *etc*

[b] *(direction)* to, towards; **tourner ~ la droite** to turn (to the) right; **l'église est ~ votre gauche** the church is on *ou* to your left; **revenir ~ Paris** to return to Paris; **les vols ~ Lyon** flights to Lyons; **concentrer son attention ~ un problème** to concentrate on a problem, focus one's attention on a problem; **fermez bien la porte ~ vous** be sure and close the door behind *ou* after you

[c] *(temps: proximité, approximation)* **il est arrivé ~ les 2 heures** he came (at) about *ou* (at) around 2; **il va ~ la quarantaine** he's getting on for *(Brit)* *ou* going on *(US)* forty; **la pièce s'achève ~ une réconciliation** the play ends with a reconciliation; **il est ~ le départ** ◊ **il est ~ le point de partir** he's just going, he's (just) about to leave; **~ le moment** *ou* **~ le coup, je n'ai pas compris** at the time *ou* at first I didn't understand; **~ une période de 3 mois** over a period of 3 months; **juger les résultats ~ une année** to assess the results over a year; **boire du café ~ de la bière** to drink coffee on top of beer

[d] *(cause)* on, by; **~ invitation/commande** by invitation/order; **~ présentation d'une pièce d'identité** on presentation of identification; **nous l'avons nommé ~ la recommandation/les conseils de Marc** we appointed him on Marc's recommendation/advice; **~ un signe/une remarque du patron, elle sortit** at the boss's signal/at a word from the boss, she left

[e] *(moyen, manière)* on; **ils vivent ~ son salaire/ses économies** they live on *ou* off his salary/his savings; **rester ~ la défensive/ses gardes** to stay on the defensive/one's guard; **travailler ~ écran** to work on screen; **renseignements disponibles ~ Minitel** information available on Minitel; **choisir ~ catalogue** to choose from a catalogue; **chanter** *ou* **entonner qch ~ l'air de la Marseillaise** to sing sth to the tune of the Marseillaise; *(Mus)* **fantaisie ~ un air de Brahms** fantasy on an air by *ou* from Brahms; *(Mus)* **~ le mode mineur** in the minor key *ou* mode

[f] *(matière, sujet)* on, about; **conférence/renseignements ~ la Grèce/la drogue** lecture/information on *ou* about Greece/drug addiction; **roman/film ~ Louis XIV** novel/film about Louis XIV; **questionner** *ou* **interroger qn ~ qch** to question sb about *ou* on sth; **gémir** *ou* **se lamenter ~ ses malheurs** to lament (over) *ou* bemoan one's misfortunes; **être ~ un travail** to be occupied with a job, be (in the process of) doing a job; **être ~ un projet** to be working on a project; **être ~ une bonne affaire/une piste/un coup*** to be onto a bargain/on a trail/in on a job*; **« réductions importantes ~ les chaussures »** "big discounts on shoes"; **il touche une commission de 10% ~ les ventes** he gets a 10% commission on sales

[g] *(rapport de proportion)* out of, in; *(prélèvement)* from; *(mesure)* by; **~ douze verres, six sont ébréchés** out of twelve glasses six are chipped; **un homme ~ dix** one man in (every) *ou* out of ten; **neuf fois ~ dix** nine times out of ten; **il a une chance ~ deux de réussir** he has a fifty-fifty chance of success; **il y a une chance ~ dix pour que cela arrive** there's a one in ten chance that it will happen; *(Scol, Univ)* **il mérite 7 ~ 10** he deserves 7 out of 10; **un jour/un vendredi ~ trois** every third day/Friday; **il vient un jour/mercredi ~ deux** he comes every other day/Wednesday; **les cotisations sont retenues ~ le salaire** con-

tributions are deducted from salaries; **la cuisine fait 2 mètres ~ 3** the kitchen is *ou* measures 2 metres by 3

[h] *(accumulation)* after; **faire faute ~ faute** to make one mistake after another; **il a eu rhume ~ rhume** he's had one cold after another *ou* the other → **coup**

[i] *(influence, supériorité)* over, on; **avoir de l'influence/de l'effet ~ qn** to have influence on *ou* over/an effect on sb; **avoir des droits ~ qn/qch** to have rights over sb/to sth; **cela a influé ~ sa décision** that has influenced *ou* had an influence on his decision; **elle n'a aucun pouvoir ~ lui** she has no hold *ou* influence over him

[2] **sur ce** LOC ADV (= *sur ces mots*) so saying, with this *ou* that; **~ ce, il est sorti** whereupon *ou* upon which he went out; **~ ce, il faut que je vous quitte** and now I must leave you

sur²,e [syr] ADJ (= *aigre*) sour

sur... [syr] PRÉF over...; **~actif** overactive; **~diplômé** overqualified

▼ **sûr, e** [syr] [1] ADJ [a] **~ de** [+ *résultats, succès*] sure *ou* certain of; [+ *allié, réflexes, moyens*] sure of; [+ *fait, diagnostic, affirmation*] sure *ou* certain of *ou* about; **il avait le moral et était ~ du succès** he was in good spirits and was sure *ou* certain *ou* confident of success; **s'il s'entraîne régulièrement, il est ~ du succès** if he trains regularly he's sure of success; **il est ~/il n'est pas ~ de venir** he's/he's not sure *ou* certain that he'll be able to come; **il est ~ de son fait** *ou* **coup*** *(qu'il réussira)* he's sure *ou* confident he'll pull it off; *(qu'il a raison)* he's sure he's right; **~ de soi** self-assured, self-confident, sure of oneself; **elle n'est pas ~e d'elle(-même)** she's lacking in self-assurance *ou* self-confidence, she's not very sure of herself; **j'en étais ~ !** I knew it!, just as I thought!; **j'en suis ~ et certain** I'm positive (about it), I'm absolutely sure *ou* certain (of it); **soyez-en ~** you can depend upon it, you can be sure of it

[b] (= *certain*) certain, sure; **la chose est ~e** that's certain, that's for sure *ou* certain; **ce** *ou* **il n'est pas ~ qu'elle aille au Maroc** it's not definite *ou* certain that she's going to Morocco; **est-ce si ~ qu'il gagne ?** is he so certain *ou* sure to win?; **c'est ~ et certain** that's absolutely certain; **ça, c'est ~** that's for sure; **ce n'est pas (si) ~*** not necessarily; **c'est le plus ~ moyen de réussir** it is the surest way to succeed; **ce qui est ~, c'est qu'ils ...** one thing is for sure — they ...; **à coup ~** definitely, without a doubt; **tenir qch pour ~** to be sure about sth; **il tient pour ~ que ...** he's sure that ...; **pour ~ !** absolutely!; **à coup ~ il ne viendra pas** he definitely won't come, there's no way he'll come

[c] (= *sans danger*) [*quartier, rue*] safe; **peu ~** unsafe; **il est plus ~ de ne pas compter sur lui** it's safer not to rely on him; **le plus ~ est de mettre sa voiture au garage** the safest thing is to put your car in the garage; **en lieu ~** in a safe place; **en mains ~es** in safe hands

[d] (= *digne de confiance*) [*personne*] reliable, trustworthy; [*renseignements, diagnostic, entreprise*] reliable; [*valeurs morales, raisonnement*] sound; [*remède, moyen*] reliable, sure; [*dispositif, arme, valeurs boursières*] safe; [*investissement*] sound, safe; [*main, pied, œil*] steady; [*goût, instinct*] reliable, sound; **le temps n'est pas assez ~ pour une ascension** the weather's not reliable enough to go climbing; **avoir la main ~e** to have a steady hand; **raisonner sur des bases peu ~es** to argue on unsound *ou* shaky premises; **nous apprenons de source ~e que ...** we have been informed by a reliable source that ...; **peu ~** [*allié*] unreliable, untrustworthy; [*renseignements*] unreliable; [*moyen, méthode*] unreliable, unsafe

[2] ADV* **~ qu'il y a quelque chose qui ne tourne pas rond** there must be something wrong; **tu penses qu'il viendra ? — pas ~** do

you think he'll come? — I'm not so sure → **bien, pour**

surabondamment [syrabɔ̃damɑ̃] ADV *(littér)* [*expliquer*] in excessive detail; **~ décoré de** overabundantly decorated with; **ce thème a été ~ exploité** this theme has been dealt with more than amply; **~ informé** over-informed

surabondance [syrabɔ̃dɑ̃s] NF (= *quantité excessive*) overabundance, superabundance; (= *grande abondance*) profusion

surabondant, e [syrabɔ̃dɑ̃, ɑ̃t] ADJ (= *trop abondant*) overabundant, superabundant; (= *très abondant*) **recevoir un courrier ~** to receive a huge amount of mail

surabonder [syrabɔ̃de] ▶conjug 1◀ VI [a] [*richesses, plantes, matières premières*] to be overabundant; **une station où surabondent les touristes** a resort overflowing with tourists; **des circulaires où surabondent les fautes d'impression** circulars riddled *ou* littered with printing errors; **un port où surabondent les tavernes** a port with an inordinate number *ou* a plethora *(frm)* of taverns [b] *(littér)* **~ de** *ou* **en** to abound with *ou* in; **~ de richesses** to have an overabundance of riches, have overabundant riches

suractivé, e [syraktive] ADJ superactivated

suractivité [syraktivite] NF superactivity

suraigu, -uë [syregy] ADJ very high-pitched, very shrill

surajouter [syraʒute] ▶conjug 1◀ VT to add; **raisons auxquelles se surajoutent celles-ci** reasons to which one might add the following; **ornements surajoutés** superfluous ornaments

suralimentation [syralimɑ̃tasjɔ̃] NF [a] [*personne*] *(thérapeutique)* feeding up; *(par excès)* overeating [b] [*animal*] fattening [c] [*moteur*] supercharging, boosting

suralimenter [syralimɑ̃te] ▶conjug 1◀ [1] VT [a] [+ *personne*] to feed up [b] (= *engraisser*) [+ *animal*] to fatten [c] [+ *moteur*] to supercharge, boost; **moteur diesel suralimenté** supercharged diesel engine [2] **se suralimenter** VPR to overeat

suranné, e [syrane] ADJ [*idées, mode*] outmoded, outdated, antiquated; [*beauté, tournure, style*] outdated, outmoded

surarmement [syrarmamɑ̃] NM (= *action*) stockpiling of weapons; (= *armes*) massive stock of weapons

surarmer [syrarme] ▶conjug 1◀ VT *(surtout passif)* **pays surarmé** country with a massive stock of weapons

surate [syrat] NF = **sourate**

surbaissé, e [syrbese] *(ptp de* **surbaisser***)* ADJ [*plafond*] lowered; [*voûte*] surbased; [*châssis*] underslung; [*voiture*] low-slung; *(Rail)* **plancher ~** platform-height floor

surbaissement [syrbesmɑ̃] NM *(Archit)* surbasement

surbaisser [syrbese] ▶conjug 1◀ VT [+ *plafond*] to lower; [+ *voûte*] to surbase; [+ *voiture, châssis*] to make lower

surbooké, e [syrbuke] ADJ double-booked, overbooked

surbooking [syrbukiŋ] NM double booking, overbooking

surboum †* [syrbum] NF party

surbrillance [syrbrijɑ̃s] NF *(Ordin)* **mettre qch en ~** to highlight sth; **texte en ~** highlighted text

surcapacité [syrkapasite] NF overcapacity

surcapitalisation [syrkapitalizasjɔ̃] NF overcapitalization

surcharge [syrʃarʒ] NF [a] [*véhicule*] overloading [b] (= *poids en excédent*) extra load, excess load; [*cheval de course*] weight handicap; **~ pondérale** excess weight; **~ électrique** overload; **une tonne de ~** an extra *ou* excess load of a ton; **les passagers/marchandises en ~** the excess *ou* extra passengers/goods; **prendre des**

passagers en ~ to take on excess passengers; **ascenseur en** ~ overloaded lift (*Brit*) *ou* elevator (*US*); **payer un supplément pour une ~ de bagages** to pay (for) excess luggage, pay excess on one's luggage [c] (*fig*) **cela me cause une ~ de travail** it gives me extra work; **la ~ des programmes scolaires** the overloaded school syllabus; **il y a une ~ de détails/ d'ornements** there is a surfeit *ou* an overabundance of detail/of ornamentation [d] (= *ajout manuscrit ou imprimé*) [*document, chèque*] alteration; [*timbre-poste*] surcharge, overprint

surcharger [syʀʃaʀʒe] ▶ conjug 3 ◀ VT [+ *voiture, cheval, mémoire*] to overload; [+ *timbre*] to surcharge; [+ *mot écrit*] to alter; (*Élec*) [+ *circuit*] to overload; (*Écon*) [+ *marché*] to overload, glut; ~ **qn de travail/d'impôts** to overload *ou* overburden sb with work/with taxes; **je suis surchargé (de travail)** I'm overloaded *ou* snowed under with work; **emploi du temps surchargé** crowded timetable; **programmes scolaires surchargés** overloaded syllabuses; **classes surchargées** overcrowded classes; **train surchargé** overcrowded train; **palais surchargé de dorures** palace smothered in gilt; **manuscrit surchargé de corrections** manuscript covered *ou* littered with corrections

surchauffe [syʀʃof] NF (*Écon*) overheating; (*Tech*) superheating; (*Phys*) superheat; **il y a une ~ de l'économie** the economy is overheating

surchauffé, e [syʀʃofe] (*ptp de* **surchauffer**) ADJ [*pièce*] overheated; (*Phys, Tech*) superheated; (= *exalté*) overexcited; **le procès s'est déroulé dans une ambiance ~e** the trial took place in a highly charged atmosphere; **les esprits étaient ~s** emotions were running very high *ou* were at fever pitch

surchauffer [syʀʃofe] ▶ conjug 1 ◀ VT [+ *pièce*] to overheat; (*Phys, Tech*) to superheat

surchoix [syʀʃwa] ADJ INV [*viande*] prime (*épith*), top-quality; [*produit, fruit*] top-quality

surclasser [syʀklase] ▶ conjug 1 ◀ VT to outclass

surcompensation [syʀkɔ̃pɑ̃sasjɔ̃] NF (*Psych*) overcompensation

surcomposé, e [syʀkɔ̃poze] ADJ double-compound

surcompression [syʀkɔ̃pʀesjɔ̃] NF [*gaz*] supercharging

surcomprimer [syʀkɔ̃pʀime] ▶ conjug 1 ◀ VT [+ *gaz*] to supercharge

surconsommation [syʀkɔ̃sɔmasjɔ̃] NF overconsumption

surcontrer [syʀkɔ̃tʀe] ▶ conjug 1 ◀ VT (*Cartes*) to redouble

surcote [syʀkɔt] NF overvaluation

surcoter [syʀkɔte] ▶ conjug 1 ◀ VT to overvalue

surcouper [syʀkupe] ▶ conjug 1 ◀ VT (*Cartes*) to overtrump

surcoût [syʀku] NM extra *ou* additional cost *ou* expenditure

surcroît [syʀkʀwa] NM [a] **cela lui a donné un ~ de travail/d'inquiétudes** it gave him additional *ou* extra work/worries; **ça lui a valu un ~ de respect** this won him even more respect; **par (un) ~ d'honnêteté/de scrupules** through an excess of honesty/of scruples, through excessive honesty/scrupulousness [b] (= *de plus*) **de** *ou* **par ~** what is more, moreover; **il est avare et paresseux de** *ou* **par ~** he's miserly and idle to boot, he's miserly and what's more he's idle

surdéveloppé, e [syʀdevlɔpe] ADJ overdeveloped

surdéveloppement [syʀdevlɔpmɑ̃] NM overdevelopment

surdimensionné, e [syʀdimɑ̃sjɔne] ADJ [*chantier, équipement*] inordinately large; **le réservoir est ~ par rapport à nos besoins** the reservoir is far too big for our needs

surdimutité [syʀdimytite] NF deaf-and-dumbness

surdité [syʀdite] NF deafness; ~ **verbale** word deafness

surdosage [syʀdozaʒ] NM (*Méd*) overdosage

surdose [syʀdoz] NF (*lit, fig*) overdose

surdoué, e [syʀdwe] [1] ADJ [*enfant*] gifted, exceptional (*US*) [2] NM,F gifted *ou* exceptional (*US*) child

sureau (*pl* **sureaux**) [syʀo] NM elder (tree); **baies de ~** elderberries

sureffectif [syʀefɛktif] NM overmanning (*NonC*), overstaffing (*NonC*); **personnel en ~** excess staff

surélévation [syʀelevasjɔ̃] NF (= *action*) raising, heightening; (= *état*) extra height

surélever [syʀel(ə)ve] ▶ conjug 5 ◀ VT [+ *plafond, étage*] to raise, heighten; [+ *mur*] to heighten; ~ **une maison d'un étage** to heighten a house by one storey; **rez-de-chaussée surélevé** raised ground floor, ground floor higher than street level

sûrement [syʀmɑ̃] ADV [a] (= *sans risques, efficacement*) [*cacher qch, progresser*] in safety; [*attacher*] securely; [*fonctionner*] safely; **l'expérience instruit plus ~ que les livres** experience is a surer teacher than books → **lentement** [b] (= *vraisemblablement*) **il viendra ~** he's sure to come; ~ **qu'il a été retenu*** he must have been held up; **tu connais ~ des gens importants** you must know some important people; **ça lui plaira ~** she's bound to like it, I'm sure she'll like it; **il me trouve ~ trop sévère** no doubt he thinks I'm being too harsh [c] ~ **pas** (= *pas du tout*) certainly not; (= *peut-être pas*) **il n'est ~ pas très intelligent, mais ...** he might not be very clever but ...; **ce n'est ~ pas difficile** it can't be that difficult

suremploi [syʀɑ̃plwa] NM overemployment

surenchère [syʀɑ̃ʃɛʀ] NF [a] (*Comm*) (*sur prix fixé*) overbid; (= *enchère plus élevée*) higher bid; **faire une ~ (sur)** to make a higher bid (than); **une douzaine de ~s successives firent monter le prix** a dozen bids one after the other put up the price; **faire une ~ de 1 000 F** to bid 1,000 francs more *ou* higher (**sur** than), bid 1,000 francs over the previous bid *ou* bidder [b] (*fig* = *exagération, excès*) **la presse, royaume de la ~** the press, where overstatement is king; **faire de la ~** to try to outdo one's rivals; **la ~ électorale** political one-upmanship; **une ~ de violence** a build-up of violence

surenchérir [syʀɑ̃ʃeʀiʀ] ▶ conjug 2 ◀ VI (= *offrir plus qu'un autre*) to bid higher; (= *élever son offre*) to raise one's bid; (*lors d'élections*) to try to outdo each other (**de** with); ~ **sur une offre** to bid higher than an offer, top a bid*; ~ **sur qn** to bid higher than sb, outbid *ou* overbid sb

surenchérisseur, -euse [syʀɑ̃ʃeʀisœʀ, øz] NM,F (higher) bidder

surencombré, e [syʀɑ̃kɔ̃bʀe] ADJ [*rue*] overcrowded; [*lignes téléphoniques*] overloaded

surencombrement [syʀɑ̃kɔ̃bʀəmɑ̃] NM [*rue*] overcrowding; [*lignes téléphoniques*] overloading

surendetté, e [syʀɑ̃dete] ADJ overburdened with debt

surendettement [syʀɑ̃dɛtmɑ̃] NM excessive debt

surentraînement [syʀɑ̃tʀɛnmɑ̃] NM overtraining

surentraîner VT, **se surentraîner** VPR [syʀɑ̃tʀene] ▶ conjug 1 ◀ to overtrain

suréquipement [syʀekipmɑ̃] NM overequipment

suréquiper [syʀekipe] ▶ conjug 1 ◀ VT to overequip

surestarie [syʀestaʀi] NF (*Jur*) demurrage

surestimation [syʀestimasjɔ̃] NF [*importance, forces, capacité, frais*] overestimation; [*tableau,*

maison à vendre] overvaluation; **la ~ des devis est fréquente** estimates are often inflated *ou* made too high

surestimer [syʀestime] ▶ conjug 1 ◀ [1] VT [+ *importance, forces, frais*] to overestimate; [+ *tableau, maison à vendre*] to overvalue [2] **se surestimer** VPR to overestimate one's abilities

suret, -ette [syʀɛ, ɛt] ADJ [*goût*] sharp, tart

sûreté [syʀte] NF [a] (= *sécurité*) safety; **complot contre la ~ de l'État** plot against state security; **pour plus de ~** as an extra precaution, to be on the safe side; **être en ~** to be in safety, be safe; **mettre qn/qch en ~** to put sb/sth in a safe *ou* secure place; **de ~** [*serrure, verrou*] safety (*épith*); **c'est une ~ supplémentaire** it's an extra precaution; **20 ans de réclusion assortis d'une peine de ~ de 13 ans** a 20-year prison sentence with a minimum recommendation of 13 years [b] (= *exactitude, efficacité*) [*renseignements, méthode*] reliability → **cour, prudence** [c] (= *précision*) [*coup d'œil, geste*] steadiness; [*goût*] reliability, soundness; [*réflexe, diagnostic*] reliability; **il a une grande ~ de main** he has a very sure hand; ~ **d'exécution** sureness of touch [d] (= *dispositif*) safety device; **mettre la ~ à une arme** to put the safety catch *ou* lock on a gun → **cran** [e] (= *garantie*) assurance, guarantee; **demander/donner des ~s à qn** to ask sb for/ give sb assurances *ou* a guarantee; (*Jur*) ~ **individuelle** protection against unlawful detention; ~ **personnelle** guaranty; ~ **réelle** security [f] (*Police*) **la Sûreté (nationale)** the (French) criminal investigation department, ≈ the CID (*Brit*), ≈ the FBI (*US*)

surévaluation [syʀevalɥasjɔ̃] NF overvaluation

surévaluer [syʀevalɥe] ▶ conjug 1 ◀ VT to overvalue

surexcitable [syʀeksitabl] ADJ overexcitable

surexcitation [syʀeksitasjɔ̃] NF overexcitement

surexcité, e [syʀeksite] (*ptp de* **surexciter**) ADJ (= *enthousiaste, énergique*) overexcited; (= *énervé*) all worked up; **il me parlait d'une voix ~e** he spoke to me in a very excited voice

surexciter [syʀeksite] ▶ conjug 1 ◀ VT to overexcite

surexploitation [syʀeksplwatasjɔ̃] NF [*terre*] overexploitation; [*main-d'œuvre*] gross exploitation

surexploiter [syʀeksplwate] ▶ conjug 1 ◀ VT [+ *terres, ressources*] to overexploit; [+ *main-d'œuvre*] to grossly exploit; [+ *thème, idée*] to overdo

surexposer [syʀekspoze] ▶ conjug 1 ◀ VT to overexpose

surexposition [syʀekspozisjɔ̃] NF overexposure

surf [sœʀf] NM [a] (= *activité*) surfing; **faire du ~** to surf, go surfing; ~ **sur neige** snowboarding; **faire du ~ sur neige** to snowboard, go snowboarding [b] (= *objet*) **(planche de) ~** surfboard; ~ **des neiges** snowboard

surface [syʀfas] [1] NF [a] (*gén, Géom*) surface; (= *aire*) [*champ, chambre*] surface area; **de ~** [*politesse*] superficial; [*modifications*] cosmetic; [*eaux, température*] surface (*épith*); **navire de ~** surface vessel; **réseau/installations de ~** above-ground *ou* overground network/ installations; **en ~** [*nager, naviguer*] at the surface; [*travailler, apprendre*] superficially; **tout en ~** [*personne*] superficial, shallow; **faire ~** to surface; (*lit, fig*) **refaire ~** to resurface; **le plongeur est remonté à la ~** the diver came back up to the surface; **l'appartement fait 100 mètres carrés de ~** the flat has a surface area of 100 square metres; **il ne voit que la ~ des choses** he can't see below the surface; **il**

dispose d'une ~ **financière rassurante** he has a sound financial base, his financial situation is sound; (*fig, Fin*) **avoir de la ~*** to have great standing → **technicien**
[b] (*Comm*) **grande ~** hypermarket
[2] COMP ► **surface de but** (*Ftbl*) goal area ► **surface de chauffe** heating surface ► **surface corrigée** (*Admin*) amended area (*calculated on the basis of amenities etc for assessing rent*) ► **surface habitable** living space ► **surface porteuse** (*Aviat*) aerofoil (*Brit*), airfoil (*US*) ► **surface de réparation** (*Ftbl*) penalty area ► **surface de séparation** (*Phys*) interface ► **surface au sol** floor surface ► **surface de sustentation** (*Aviat*) = **surface porteuse** ► **surface utile** (*Constr*) floor space ► **surface de vente** (*Comm*) sales area ► **surface de voilure** sail area

surfacturation [syRfaktyRasjɔ̃] NF [*produit, prestations*] overbilling; [*client*] overcharging; **ils ont procédé à une ~ systématique des travaux** they systematically overcharged for the building work

surfacturer [syRfaktyRe] ▶ conjug 1 ◀ VT [+ *produit, prestations*] to overbill; [+ *client*] to overcharge; **il a surfacturé de 10% ses prestations** he overcharged customers by 10% for his services

surfaire [syRfɛR] ▶ conjug 60 ◀ VT [+ *réputation, auteur*] to overrate; [+ *marchandise*] to overprice

surfait, e [syRfɛ, ɛt] (*ptp de* **surfaire**) ADJ [*ouvrage, auteur*] overrated; **c'est très ~** it's highly overrated

surfer [sœRfe] ▶ conjug 1 ◀ VI (*Sport*) to surf, go surfing; (*Ordin*) to surf; **~ sur Internet** to surf (on) the Internet; **le Premier ministre a longtemps surfé sur la vague des opinions favorables** the Prime Minister has been riding on a wave of popularity for a long time; **ces industriels surfent sur la vague écologique** these industrialists are cashing in on the ecology trend *ou* have jumped on the green bandwagon

surfeur, -euse [sœRfœR, øz] NM,F surfer

surfil [syRfil] NM (*Couture*) oversewing, overcasting

surfilage [syRfilaʒ] NM (*Couture*) oversewing, overcasting

surfiler [syRfile] ▶ conjug 1 ◀ VT (*Couture*) to oversew, overcast

surfin, e [syRfɛ̃, in] ADJ [*beurre, produit*] top-quality (*épith*); [*qualité*] top (*épith*), superior

surgélation [syRʒelasjɔ̃] NF deep-freezing, fast-freezing

surgelé, e [syRʒele] [1] ADJ deep-frozen; **produits ~s** frozen foods [2] NM **les ~s** (deep-) frozen food; **magasin de ~s** freezer centre

surgeler [syRʒəle] ▶ conjug 1 ◀ VT to deep-freeze, fast-freeze

surgénérateur [syRʒeneratœR] ADJ M, NM (**réacteur**) = fast breeder (reactor)

surgeon [syRʒɔ̃] NM (*Bot*) sucker

surgir [syRʒiR] ▶ conjug 2 ◀ VI [a] [*animal, véhicule en mouvement, spectre*] to appear suddenly; [*montagne, navire*] to loom up (suddenly); [*plante, immeuble*] to shoot up, spring up; **deux hommes ont surgi de derrière un camion** two men suddenly appeared *ou* came out from behind a truck [b] [*problèmes, difficultés*] to arise, crop up; [*dilemme*] to arise; **des obstacles surgissent de toutes parts** obstacles are cropping up all over the place; **cela a fait ~ plusieurs questions** this raised several questions

surgissement [syRʒismã] NM (*littér*) [*animal, véhicule en mouvement, spectre*] sudden appearance; [*montagne, navire*] sudden looming up; [*plante, immeuble*] shooting up, springing up

surhausser [syRose] ▶ conjug 1 ◀ VT (*gén, Archit*) to raise

surhomme [syRɔm] NM superman

surhumain, e [syRymɛ̃, ɛn] ADJ superhuman

surimi [syRimi] NM surimi; **bâtonnets de ~** crab *ou* ocean sticks

surimposé, e [syRɛ̃poze] (*ptp de* **surimposer**) ADJ (*Géol*) superimposed; (*Fin*) overtaxed

surimposer [syRɛ̃poze] ▶ conjug 1 ◀ VT (*Fin*) to overtax

surimposition [syRɛ̃pozisjɔ̃] NF [a] (*Fin*) overtaxation [b] (*Géol*) epigenesis

surimpression [syRɛ̃pResjɔ̃] NF (*Photo*) double exposure; (*fig*) [*idées, visions*] superimposition; **en ~** superimposed; **on voyait apparaître un visage en ~** a face appeared superimposed (on it)

surin ‡ [syRɛ̃] NM (= *couteau*) knife

Surinam, Suriname [syRinam] NM Surinam

surinamais, e [syRiname, ɛz] [1] ADJ Surinamese [2] **Surinamais(e)** NM,F Surinamese

surinfecter (se) [syRɛ̃fɛkte] ▶ conjug 1 ◀ VPR to develop a secondary infection

surinfection [syRɛ̃fɛksjɔ̃] NF secondary infection

surinformation [syRɛ̃fɔRmasjɔ̃] NF information overload; **le public est victime d'une ~ quotidienne** the public are subjected to information overload every day

surinformé, e [syRɛ̃fɔRme] ADJ [*personne*] suffering from information overload; **dans notre monde ~** in today's world of information overload

surintendance [syRɛ̃tãdãs] NF (*Hist*) superintendency

surintendant [syRɛ̃tãdã] NM (*Hist*) **~ (des finances)** superintendent (of finances)

surinvestir [syRɛ̃vɛstiR] ▶ conjug 2 ◀ VT (*Fin*) to overinvest (**dans** in); (*Psych*) to invest too much of o.s. in

surinvestissement [syRɛ̃vɛstismã] NM (*Écon, Psych*) overinvestment

surir [syRiR] ▶ conjug 2 ◀ VI [*lait, vin*] to turn sour, (go) sour

surjet [syRʒɛ] NM [a] (*Couture*) overcast seam; **point de ~** overcast stitch [b] (*Chir*) continuous suture

surjeter [syRʒəte] ▶ conjug 4 ◀ VT (*Couture*) to overcast

sur-le-champ [syRləʃã] ADV immediately, at once, right away, straightaway (*Brit*)

surlendemain [syRlãd(ə)mɛ̃] NM **le ~ de son arrivée** two days after his arrival; **il est mort le ~** he died two days later; **il revint le lendemain et le ~** he came back the next day and the day after (that); **le ~ matin** two days later in the morning

surligner [syRliɲe] ▶ conjug 1 ◀ VT to highlight

surligneur [syRliɲœR] NM highlighter (pen)

surmédiatisation [syRmedjatizasjɔ̃] NF [*affaire, événement*] excessive media coverage; **la ~ de l'affaire a entraîné des polémiques** the excessive coverage given to the case in the media caused controversy; **il y a un risque de ~** there's a danger of media overkill

surmédiatisé, e [syRmedjatize] ADJ [*affaire, événement*] that has received too much media exposure *ou* coverage

surmédicalisation [syRmedikalizasjɔ̃] NF [*problème, cas, grossesse*] excessive medicalization; [*population, pays*] overprovision of medical care (**de** to)

surmédicaliser [syRmedikalize] ▶ conjug 1 ◀ VT [+ *problème, cas*] to overmedicalize; [+ *population, pays*] to overprovide with medical care

surmenage [syRmənaʒ] NM [a] (= *action de surmener qn*) overworking, overtaxing; **éviter le ~ des élèves** to avoid overworking schoolchildren *ou* pushing schoolchildren too hard [b] (= *action de se surmener*) overwork(ing); **éviter à tout prix le ~** to avoid

overwork(ing) *ou* overtaxing o.s. at all costs [c] (= *état maladif*) overwork; **souffrant de ~** suffering from (the effects of) overwork; **le ~ intellectuel** mental fatigue; **~ physique** overexertion

surmené, e [syRməne] (*ptp de* **surmener**) ADJ (*par le travail*) overworked; **je suis vraiment ~ en ce moment** I've got an awful lot on my plate at the moment

surmener [syRməne] ▶ conjug 5 ◀ [1] VT [+ *personne*] to overwork, overtax; [+ *animal*] to overtax [2] **se surmener** VPR (*gén*) to overwork *ou* overtax (o.s.), push o.s. too hard; (*physiquement*) to overexert o.s.

surmoi [syRmwa] NM superego

surmontable [syRmɔ̃tabl] ADJ surmountable; **obstacle difficilement ~** obstacle that is difficult to surmount *ou* overcome

surmonter [syRmɔ̃te] ▶ conjug 1 ◀ [1] VT [a] (= *être au-dessus de*) to surmount, top; **surmonté d'un dôme/clocheton** surmounted *ou* topped by a dome/bell-turret; **un clocheton surmontait l'édifice** the building was surmounted *ou* topped by a bell-turret [b] (= *vaincre*) [+ *obstacle, difficultés*] to overcome, get over, surmount; [+ *dégoût, peur*] to overcome, get the better of, fight down [2] **se surmonter** VPR [*personne*] to master o.s., control o.s.; **la peur peut se ~** fear can be overcome

surmortalité [syRmɔRtalite] NF comparatively high deathrate; **il y a eu une ~ masculine de 12%** the deathrate was 12% higher among men

surmultiplié, e [syRmyltiplije] [1] ADJ **vitesse ~e** overdrive [2] **surmultipliée** NF overdrive; (*fig*) **passer la ~e** to get a move on*, step on it*

surnager [syRnaʒe] ▶ conjug 3 ◀ VI [*huile, objet*] to float (on the surface); [*sentiment, souvenir*] to linger on

surnatalité [syRnatalite] NF comparatively high birthrate

surnaturel, -elle [syRnatyRɛl] [1] ADJ (*gén*) supernatural; (= *inquiétant*) uncanny, eerie [2] NM **le ~** the supernatural

surnom [syRnɔ̃] NM (*gén*) nickname; [*roi, héros*] name; **« le Courageux », ~ du roi Richard** "the Brave", the name by which King Richard was known

surnombre [syRnɔ̃bR] NM surplus; **en ~** [*effectifs, personnel*] surplus (*épith*), excess (*épith*); **nous étions en ~** there were too many of us; **plusieurs élèves en ~** several pupils too many; **nous étions en ~** there were too many of us; **Marie, qui était arrivée à l'improviste, était en ~** Marie, who had turned up unexpectedly, was one too many; **ils ont fait sortir les spectateurs en ~** they asked the excess spectators to leave

surnommer [syRnɔme] ▶ conjug 1 ◀ VT **~ qn « le gros »** to nickname sb "fatty"; **~ un roi « le Fort »** to give a king the name "the Strong"; **cette infirmité l'avait fait ~ « le Crapaud »** this disability had earned him the nickname of "the Toad"; **le roi Richard surnommé « le Courageux »** King Richard known as *ou* named "the Brave"

surnotation [syRnɔtasjɔ̃] NF (*Scol*) overmarking (*Brit*), overgrading (*US*)

surnoter [syRnɔte] ▶ conjug 1 ◀ VT (*Scol*) to overmark (*Brit*), overgrade (*US*)

surnuméraire [syRnymeRɛR] ADJ, NMF supernumerary; **embryons ~s** spare *ou* surplus embryos

suroffre [syRɔfR] NF (*Jur*) higher offer *ou* bid

suroît [syRwa] NM (= *vent*) south-wester, sou'wester; (= *chapeau*) sou'wester; **vent de ~** south-westerly wind

surpassement [syRpasmã] NM (*littér*) **~ de soi** surpassing (of) oneself

surpasser [syʀpase] ▶conjug 1◀ 1 VT a (= l'emporter sur) [+ concurrent, rival] to surpass, outdo; **~ qn en agilité/connaissances** to surpass sb in agility/knowledge; **sa gloire surpassait en éclat celle de Napoléon** his glory outshone that of Napoleon b (= dépasser) to surpass; **le résultat surpasse toutes les espérances** the result surpasses ou is beyond all our hopes 2 **se surpasser** VPR to surpass o.s., excel o.s.; **le cuisinier s'est surpassé aujourd'hui** the cook has excelled ou surpassed himself today; (iro) **encore un échec, décidément tu te surpasses!** failed again — you're really excelling ou surpassing yourself!

surpaye [syʀpɛj] NF [salariés, marchands] overpayment; **la ~ des marchandises** paying too much for goods

surpayer [syʀpeje] ▶conjug 8◀ VT [+ employé] to overpay; [+ marchandise] to pay too much for

surpêche [syʀpɛʃ] NF overfishing

surpeuplé, e [syʀpœple] ADJ overpopulated

surpeuplement [syʀpœpləmã] NM overpopulation

surpiquer [syʀpike] ▶conjug 1◀ VT to topstitch

surpiqûre [syʀpikyʀ] NF topstitch

sur-place, surplace [syʀplas] NM **faire du ~** (= ne pas avancer) (à vélo) to do a track-stand; (en voiture) (= être immobilisé) to be stuck; (= avancer très lentement) to move at a snail's pace; [oiseau] to hover; (= ne pas progresser) [enquête] to hang fire, mark time; [négociations] to be getting nowhere, stall; [projet] to be getting nowhere; **notre économie fait du ~** our economy is stagnating ou is stalling

surplis [syʀpli] NM surplice

surplomb [syʀplɔ̃] NM overhang; **en ~** overhanging

surplombant, e [syʀplɔ̃bã, ãt] ADJ overhanging (épith)

surplomber [syʀplɔ̃be] ▶conjug 1◀ 1 VI to overhang; (Tech) to be out of plumb 2 VT to overhang

surplus [syʀply] NM a (= excédent non écoulé) surplus (NonC); **vendre le ~ de son stock** to sell off one's surplus stock; **avoir des marchandises en ~** to have surplus goods b (= reste non utilisé) **il me reste un ~ de clous/de papier dont je ne me suis pas servi** I've got some nails/paper left over ou some surplus nails/paper that I didn't use; **avec le ~ (de bois), je vais essayer de me faire une bibliothèque** with what's left over (of the wood) ou with the leftover ou surplus (wood) I'm going to try to build myself a bookcase; **ce sont des ~ qui restent de la guerre/de l'exposition** they're left over ou it's surplus from the war/the exhibition; **~ américains** American army surplus c (= d'ailleurs) **au ~** moreover, what is more

surpopulation [syʀpɔpylasjɔ̃] NF overpopulation

surprenant, e [syʀpʀənã, ãt] ADJ surprising; **il n'y a rien de ~ à cela** that's not at all surprising; **cette tendance n'est guère ~e** this trend hardly comes as a surprise ou is hardly surprising; **chose ~e, il n'a jamais répondu** surprisingly (enough), he never replied; **de façon ~e** surprisingly

surprendre [syʀpʀãdʀ] ▶conjug 58◀ 1 VT a (= prendre sur le fait) [+ voleur] to surprise, catch in the act b (= découvrir) [+ secret, complot] to discover; [+ conversation] to overhear; [+ regard, sourire complice] to intercept; **je crus ~ en lui de la gêne** I thought I detected signs of some embarrassment in him c (= prendre au dépourvu) (par attaque) [+ ennemi] to surprise; (par visite inopinée) [+ amis, voisins] to catch unawares, catch on the hop* (Brit); **~ des amis chez eux** to drop in unex-

pectedly on friends, pay a surprise visit to friends; **espérant la ~ au bain** hoping to catch her while she was in the bath d [pluie, marée, nuit] to catch out; **se laisser ~ par la marée** to be caught (out) by the tide; **se laisser ~ par la pluie** to be caught in the rain; **se laisser ~ par la nuit** to be overtaken by darkness e (= étonner) [nouvelle, conduite] to surprise; **tu me surprends** you amaze me; **cela me surprendrait fort** that would greatly surprise me; **cela m'a agréablement surpris** I was pleasantly surprised; **cela semble te ~** you seem ou look surprised; **il a réussi, ce qui n'est pas pour nous ~** he succeeded, which is hardly surprising ou which hardly comes as a surprise; **cette question a de quoi ou peut ~** this question may seem surprising f (littér) **~ la vigilance de qn** to catch sb out; **~ la bonne foi de qn** to betray sb's good faith; **~ la confiance de qn**† to win sb's trust fraudulently 2 **se surprendre** VPR **se ~ à faire qch** to catch ou find o.s. doing sth

surpression [syʀpʀesjɔ̃] NF (gén) extremely high pressure; (Tech) overpressure

surprime [syʀpʀim] NF (Assurances) additional premium

surpris, e[1] [syʀpʀi, iz] (ptp de **surprendre**) ADJ [air, regard] surprised; **~ de qch** surprised at sth; **~ de me voir là/que je sois encore là** surprised at seeing me there ou to see me there/ that I was still there; **il va être désagréablement ~** he has an unpleasant surprise in store for him, he's in for an unpleasant surprise; **j'ai été le premier ~ de cette victoire** this victory came as a real surprise to me; **vous ne seriez pas ~ si je vous disais que ...** it wouldn't surprise you ou come as a surprise to you if I told you that ...

surprise[2] [syʀpʀiz] NF a (= étonnement) surprise; **regarder qn avec ~** to look at sb with ou in surprise; **muet de ~** speechless with surprise; **avoir la ~ de voir que ...** to be surprised to see that ...; **avoir la bonne/mauvaise ~ de constater que ...** to be pleasantly/unpleasantly surprised to find that ...; **à ma grande ~** much to my surprise, to my great surprise; **à la ~ générale** to everybody's surprise; **avec lui, on va de ~ en ~** it's one surprise after another with him; **créer la ~** to create a stir ou a sensation b (= cause d'étonnement, cadeau) surprise; **il a été réélu sans ~ avec 64% des suffrages** his re-election with 64% of the votes came as no surprise to anyone; **victoire sans ~** unsurprising victory; **c'est un film/scénario sans ~** it's a rather unexciting film/script; **voyage sans ~** uneventful ou unremarkable journey; **prix sans ~** (all-)inclusive price; **avec cette firme, c'est sans ~** you always know what you're getting with this company; **avec ça, pas de (mauvaises) ~s!** you'll have no nasty ou unpleasant surprises with this!; **il m'a apporté une petite ~** he brought me a little surprise; **quelle bonne ~!** what a nice ou pleasant ou lovely surprise!; (Culin) **« la ~ du chef »** "the chef's surprise" c **par ~** [attaquer] by surprise; **il m'a pris par ~** he took me by surprise, he caught me off guard ou unawares d (en apposition) **attaque-~** surprise attack; (Sport) **échappée-~** sudden breakaway; **grève-~** unofficial strike; **invité-~** surprise guest; **visite-~** surprise visit; **voyage-~** [homme politique] unexpected trip ou visit

surprise-partie† (pl **surprises-parties**) [syʀpʀizpaʀti] NF party

surproduction [syʀpʀɔdyksjɔ̃] NF overproduction

surproduire [syʀpʀɔdɥiʀ] ▶conjug 38◀ VT to overproduce

surprotéger [syʀpʀɔteʒe] ▶conjug 6 et 3◀ VT to overprotect

surpuissant, e [syʀpɥisã, ãt] ADJ [voiture, moteur] ultra-powerful

surqualification [syʀkalifikasjɔ̃] NF overqualification; **malgré sa ~, il a accepté le poste** despite the fact that he was overqualified, he accepted the job

surqualifié, e [syʀkalifje] ADJ overqualified

surréalisme [syʀʀealism] NM surrealism

surréaliste [syʀʀealist] 1 ADJ [écrivain, peintre] surrealist; [tableau, poème] surrealist, surrealistic; (= bizarre) surreal, surrealistic 2 NMF surrealist

surréel, -elle [syʀʀeel] ADJ surreal

surrégénérateur [syʀʀeʒeneʀatœʀ] NM = surgénérateur

surrégime [syʀʀeʒim] NM **être ou tourner en ~** [voiture, moteur] to be over-revving; [économie] to be overheating

surrénal, e (mpl **-aux**) [sy(ʀ)ʀenal, o] 1 ADJ suprarenal 2 **surrénales** NFPL (glandes) **~es** suprarenals

surreprésentation [sy(ʀ)ʀəpʀezãtasjɔ̃] NF [catégorie de personnes] over-representation

surreprésenté, e [sy(ʀ)ʀəpʀezãte] ADJ [catégorie de personnes] over-represented

sur-réservation (pl **sur-réservations**) [syʀʀezɛʀvasjɔ̃] NF double booking, overbooking

sursalaire [syʀsalɛʀ] NM bonus, premium

sursaturé, e [syʀsatyʀe] ADJ a (Sci) [solution] supersaturated b (Écon) [marché] saturated

sursaut [syʀso] NM a (= mouvement brusque) start, jump; (= élan, accès) **d'énergie/ d'indignation** (sudden) burst ou fit of energy/ of indignation; **se réveiller en ~** to wake up with a start ou jump; **elle a eu un ~** she gave a start, she jumped; **l'élève a eu un ~ au troisième trimestre** the pupil put on a spurt in the third term

sursauter [syʀsote] ▶conjug 1◀ VI to start, jump, give a start; **faire ~ qn** to make sb jump, give sb a start; **~ de peur** to jump with fright

surseoir [syʀswaʀ] ▶conjug 26◀ ◆ **surseoir à** VT INDIR [+ publication, délibération] to defer, postpone; [+ poursuites, jugement, sentence, exécution] to stay; **~ à l'exécution d'un condamné** to grant a stay of execution ou a reprieve to a condemned man

sursis [syʀsi] NM a (Jur) [condamnation à mort] reprieve; **peine avec ~ ou assortie du ~** suspended ou deferred sentence; **il a eu deux ans avec ~** he was given a two-year suspended ou deferred sentence; **~ à exécution ou d'exécution** stay of execution; **~ avec mise à l'épreuve** conditional discharge b (Mil) – **(d'incorporation)** deferment c (= temps de répit) reprieve; **c'est un mort en ~** he's a condemned man, he's living under a death sentence ou on borrowed time; **gouvernement/ entreprise en ~** government/company living on borrowed time; **demander un ~ de paiement** to ask for an extension (on the deadline for a debt); **on a eu un ~ de trois jours** we got three days' grace

sursitaire [syʀsitɛʀ] 1 ADJ (Mil) deferred (épith); (Jur) with a suspended ou deferred sentence 2 NM (Mil) deferred conscript

surtaxe [syʀtaks] NF (Fin) surcharge; [lettre mal affranchie] surcharge; [envoi exprès] additional charge, surcharge; **~ à l'importation** import surcharge

surtaxer [syʀtakse] ▶conjug 1◀ VT to surcharge

surtension [syʀtãsjɔ̃] NF (Élec) overvoltage

surtitre [syʀtitʀ] NM surtitle

surtitrer [syʀtitʀe] ▶conjug 1◀ VT [+ opéra, pièce de théâtre] to surtitle; **« surtitré »** "with surtitles"; **l'opéra était surtitré** the opera had surtitles

surtout[1] [syʀtu] ADV [a] (= avant tout, d'abord) above all; (= spécialement) especially, particularly; **rapide, efficace et ~ discret** quick, efficient and above all discreet; **il est assez timide, ~ avec les femmes** he's quite shy, especially *ou* particularly with women; **j'aime ~ les romans, mais je lis aussi de la poésie** I particularly like novels, but I also read poetry; **dernièrement, j'ai ~ lu des romans** lately I've been reading mostly *ou* mainly novels; **j'aime les romans, ~ les romans policiers** I like novels, especially *ou* particularly detective novels; **le poulet, je l'aime ~ à la broche** I like chicken best (when it's) spit-roasted
[b] **~ que*** especially as *ou* since
[c] (*intensif*) **~, n'en parle pas!** don't forget, mum's the word!; **~ pas maintenant** certainly not now; **je ne veux ~ pas vous déranger** the last thing I want is to disturb you, I certainly don't want to disturb you; **~ pas!** certainly not!; **~ ne vous mettez pas en frais** whatever you do, don't go to any expense; (*iro*) **ne m'aide pas, ~!** don't help me, will you!

surtout[2] [syʀtu] NM [a] († = manteau) greatcoat† [b] (= milieu de table) centrepiece (*Brit*), centerpiece (*US*), epergne (*SPÉC*)

survaloriser [syʀvalɔʀize] ▶conjug 1◀ VT [+ personne] to overrate, over-value; [+ critère, fonction] to attach too much importance to

surveillance [syʀvejɑ̃s] [1] NF [a] (= garde) [enfant, élève, bagages] watch; **sous la ~ attentive de qn** under the watchful eye of sb; **laisser un enfant sans ~** to leave a child unsupervised
[b] (*Mil, Police*) [personne, maison] surveillance; [frontières] surveillance, monitoring; [cessez-le-feu] monitoring, supervision; **~ aérienne** air surveillance; **sous la ~ de la police** ◊ **sous ~ policière** under police surveillance; **mission/service de ~** surveillance mission/personnel; **société de ~** security firm; **navire/avion en ~** ship/plane carrying out surveillance; (*lit, fig*) **placer qn/qch sous haute ~** to keep a close watch on sb/sth
[c] (= contrôle) [éducation, études, réparation, construction] supervision; (*Scol, Univ*) [examen] invigilation; **déjouer ou tromper la ~ de ses gardiens** to slip by *ou* evade the guards; **l'enseignant qui assure la ~ de l'épreuve** the teacher invigilating
[d] (= fait d'épier) [personne, mouvement, proie] watch; (*Sport*) watch; **exercer une ~ continuelle/une étroite ~ sur** to keep a constant/a close watch over
[2] COMP ▶ **surveillance à distance** remote electronic surveillance ▶ **surveillance électronique** electronic surveillance; (*Méd*) electronic monitoring ▶ **surveillance légale** legal surveillance (*of impounded property*)

surveillant, e [syʀvejɑ̃, ɑ̃t] NM,F [prison] warder (*Brit*), guard (*US*); [usine, chantier] supervisor, overseer; [magasin] shopwalker; (*Méd*) head nurse, charge nurse; (*Scol: aux examens*) invigilator (*Brit*), proctor (*US*); **~ (d'étude)** supervisor; (*Scol*) **~ général**† chief supervisor; (*Scol*) **~ d'internat** dormitory supervisor, dormitory monitor (*US*); (*Méd*) **~e générale** nursing officer, matron (*Brit*)

surveillé, e [syʀveje] (*ptp de surveiller*) ADJ → liberté

surveiller [syʀveje] ▶conjug 1◀ [1] VT [a] (= garder) [+ enfant, élève, bagages] to watch, keep an eye on; [+ prisonnier] to keep watch over, keep (a) watch on; [+ malade] to watch over, keep watch over
[b] (= contrôler) [+ éducation, études de qn, récréation] to supervise; [+ réparation, construction] to supervise, oversee; (*Scol, Univ*) [+ examen] to invigilate; **surveille la soupe** keep an eye on the soup, watch the soup; **surveille la cuisson du rôti** watch the roast; **je surveille l'heure, il ne faut pas être en retard** I'm keeping an eye on the time, we mustn't be late

[c] (= défendre) [+ locaux] to keep watch on; [+ territoire] to watch over, keep watch over; [+ frontières, espace aérien] to monitor; [+ cessez-le-feu] to monitor, supervise
[d] (= épier) [+ personne, mouvements, proie] to watch; [+ adversaire] (*Mil*) to keep watch on; (*Sport*) to watch; **se sentant surveillé, il partit** feeling he was being watched, he left; **~ qn de près** to keep a close eye *ou* watch on sb; **~ qn du coin de l'œil** to watch sb out the corner of one's eye
[e] (= être attentif à) **~ son langage/sa tension/sa ligne** to watch one's language/one's blood pressure/one's figure; **tu devrais ~ ta santé** you should look after your health
[2] **se surveiller** VPR to keep a check *ou* a watch on o.s.; **il devrait se ~, il grossit de plus en plus** he ought to watch himself because he's getting fatter and fatter; **ils sont obligés de se ~ devant les enfants** they have to watch themselves *ou* be careful in front of the children

survenir [syʀvəniʀ] ▶conjug 22◀ VI [événement] to take place; [incident, complications, retards] to occur, arise; [personne] to appear, arrive (unexpectedly); **s'il survenait quelque chose de nouveau** if anything new comes up; **s'il survient des complications ...** should any complications arise ...

survenue [syʀvəny] NF [personne] unexpected arrival *ou* appearance; [maladie] onset; [mutations, symptômes] appearance

survêt* [syʀvɛt] NM (ABRÉV = **survêtement**) tracksuit, sweat suit, sweats*

survêtement [syʀvɛtmɑ̃] NM [sportif] tracksuit, sweat suit; [alpiniste, skieur] overgarments

survie [syʀvi] NF [malade, accidenté, auteur, amitié, entreprise, mode] survival; (*Rel: dans l'au-delà*) afterlife; **ce médicament lui a donné quelques mois de ~** this drug has given him a few more months to live; **une ~ de quelques jours, à quoi bon, dans son état?** what's the use of prolonging his life for a few more days in his condition?; **de ~** [instinct, réflexe] survival (épith); **équipement/combinaison/couverture de ~** survival equipment/suit/blanket; **radeau de ~** life-raft; **maintenir qn en ~** to keep sb alive artificially; **ses chances de ~ sont importantes** he has *ou* stands a good chance of survival *ou* surviving

survirer [syʀviʀe] ▶conjug 1◀ VI (*Aut*) to oversteer

survireur, -euse [syʀviʀœʀ, øz] ADJ (*Aut*) **voiture survireuse** car which oversteers

survitrage [syʀvitʀaʒ] NM double-glazing

survivance [syʀvivɑ̃s] NF (= vestige) relic, survival; **cette coutume est une ~ du passé** this custom is a survival *ou* relic from the past; (*littér*) **de l'âme** survival of the soul (after death), afterlife

survivant, e [syʀvivɑ̃, ɑ̃t] [1] ADJ surviving [2] NM,F (= rescapé, *Jur*) survivor; **des sœurs, la ~e ...** the surviving sister ...; **un ~ d'un âge révolu** a survivor from a past age

survivre [syʀvivʀ] ▶conjug 46◀ [1] VI [a] (= continuer à vivre : *lit, fig*) to survive; (*après accident*) **va-t-il ~?** will he live? *ou* survive?; **il n'avait aucune chance de ~** he had no chance of survival *ou* surviving; **~ à** [+ accident, maladie, humiliation] to survive; **rien ne survivait de leurs anciennes coutumes** nothing survived of their old customs [b] (= vivre plus longtemps que) **~ à** [personne] to outlive; [œuvre, idée] to outlive, outlast [2] **se survivre** VPR (= se perpétuer) **se ~ dans** [+ œuvre, enfant, souvenir] to live on in [b] (péj) [auteur] to outlive one's talent; [aventurier] to outlive one's time

survol [syʀvɔl] NM **le ~ de** (*lit*) flying over; [livre] skimming through, skipping through; [question] skimming over; **faire un ~ à basse altitude** to make a low flight

survoler [syʀvɔle] ▶conjug 1◀ VT (*lit*) to fly over; [+ livre] to skim through, skip through; [+ question] to skim over

survoltage [syʀvɔltaʒ] NM (*Élec*) boosting

survolté, e [syʀvɔlte] ADJ [a]* (= surexcité) [foule] over-excited; [ambiance] electric, highly charged [b] (*Élec*) stepped up, boosted

sus [sy(s)] ADV [a] (*Admin*) **en ~** in addition; **en ~ de** in addition to, over and above [b] (††, *hum*) **courir ~ à l'ennemi** to rush upon the enemy; **~ à l'ennemi!** at them!; **~ au tyran!** death to the tyrant!

susceptibilité [syseptibilite] NF [a] (= sensibilité) touchiness (*NonC*), sensitiveness (*NonC*); **afin de ménager ou de ne pas froisser les ~s** so as not to offend people's susceptibilities *ou* sensibilities; **être d'une grande ~** to be extremely touchy, be hypersensitive [b] (*Phys*) **~ magnétique** magnetic susceptibility

susceptible [syseptibl] ADJ [a] (= ombrageux) touchy, thin-skinned, sensitive
[b] (= de nature à) **ces axiomes ne sont pas ~s de démonstration** *ou* **d'être démontrés** these axioms cannot be proved; **texte ~ d'être amélioré ou d'améliorations** text open to improvement *ou* that can be improved upon; **ces gens ne sont pas ~s d'éprouver du chagrin** these people are not susceptible to grief; **des conférences ~s de l'intéresser** lectures liable *ou* likely to be of interest to him *ou* that may well be of interest to him
[c] (= en mesure de) **est-il ~ de le faire?** (capacité) is he able to do it?, is he capable of doing it?; (hypothèse) is he likely to do it?; **il est ~ de gagner** he may well win, he is liable to win; **un second ~ lui aussi de prendre l'initiative des opérations** a second-in-command who is also in a position to *ou* who is also able to direct operations

susciter [sysite] ▶conjug 1◀ VT [a] (= donner naissance à) [+ admiration, intérêt] to arouse; [+ passions, jalousies, haine] to arouse, incite; [+ controverse, critiques, querelle] to give rise to, provoke; [+ obstacles] to give rise to, create [b] (= provoquer volontairement) to create; **~ des obstacles/ennuis à qn** to create obstacles/difficulties for sb; **~ des ennemis à qn** to make enemies for sb

suscription [syskʀipsjɔ̃] NF (*Admin*) address

susdit, e [sysdi, dit] ADJ (*Jur*) aforesaid

sus-dominante [sysdɔminɑ̃t] NF submediant

sushi [suʃi] NM sushi

susmentionné, e [sysmɑ̃sjɔne] ADJ (*Admin*) above-mentioned, aforementioned

susnommé, e [sysnɔme] ADJ, NM,F (*Admin, Jur*) above-named

suspect, e [syspɛ(kt), ɛkt] [1] ADJ [a] (= louche) [individu, conduite, colis] suspicious; **sa générosité m'est** *ou* **me paraît ~e** his generosity seems suspect *ou* suspicious to me; **il est mort dans des conditions ~es** he died in suspicious circumstances
[b] (= douteux) [opinion, témoignage] suspect; [viande, poisson] suspect; **elle était ~e aux yeux de la police** the police were suspicious of her; **pensées ~es à la majorité conservatrice** thoughts which the conservative majority find suspect
[c] (= soupçonné) **les personnes ~es** those under suspicion
[d] **~ de** suspected of; **ils sont ~s de collusion avec l'ennemi** they are suspected of collusion with the enemy; **Leblanc, pourtant bien peu ~ de royalisme, a proposé que ...** Leblanc, though hardly likely to be suspected of royalism, did propose that ...
[2] NM,F suspect; **principal ~** chief *ou* prime suspect

suspecter [syspɛkte] ▶conjug 1◀ VT [+ personne] to suspect; [+ bonne foi, honnêteté] to suspect, have (one's) suspicions about, ques-

suspendre

tion; **~ qn de faire qch** to suspect sb of doing sth; **on le suspecte de sympathies gauchistes** he is suspected of having leftist sympathies

suspendre [syspɑ̃dʀ] ▸ conjug 41 ◂ 1 VT a (= *accrocher*) [+ *vêtements*] to hang up; [+ *lampe, décoration*] to hang, suspend (**à** from); [+ *hamac*] to sling (up); **~ qch à** [+ *clou, crochet, portemanteau*] to hang sth on; **~ un lustre au plafond par une chaîne** to hang ou suspend a chandelier from the ceiling on ou by ou with a chain; **~ un hamac à des crochets/à deux poteaux** to sling a hammock between two hooks/between two posts b (= *interrompre*) [+ *publication, combat, paiement, mouvement de grève, transactions*] to suspend; [+ *récit, négociations, relations diplomatiques*] to break off; [+ *audience, séance*] to adjourn; [+ *permis de conduire*] to suspend; [+ *jugement*] to suspend, defer; [+ *décision*] to postpone, defer; [+ *recherche, projet*] to suspend, break off; (Bourse) **~ la cotation d'une action** to suspend a share c (= *destituer*) [+ *prélat, fonctionnaire*] to suspend; (= *mettre à pied*) [+ *joueur*] to suspend; **~ qn de ses fonctions** to suspend sb from office 2 **se suspendre** VPR **se ~ à** [+ *branche, barre*] to hang from (**par** by); **les enfants se suspendaient aux jupes de leur mère** the children were hanging onto their mother's skirt

suspendu, e [syspɑ̃dy] (*ptp de* **suspendre**) ADJ a (= *accroché*) **vêtement ~** à garment hanging on; **lustre ~ à** light hanging ou suspended from; **benne ~e à un câble/dans le vide** skip suspended by a cable/in mid air; **montre ~e à une chaîne** watch hanging on a chain; **être ~ aux lèvres de qn** to be hanging on sb's every word ou on sb's lips; **chalets ~s au-dessus d'une gorge** chalets perched ou suspended over a gorge → **jardin, pont** b (= *interrompu*) [*séance*] adjourned; [*jugement*] suspended, deferred; [*fonctionnaire, magistrat*] suspended c (Aut) **voiture bien/mal ~e** car with good/ poor suspension

suspens [syspɑ̃] NM a (= *en attente*) **en ~** [*projet, travail*] in abeyance; **question laissée en ~** question that has been shelved; **laisser une affaire en ~** to leave an affair in abeyance b (= *dans l'incertitude*) **en ~** in suspense; **tenir les lecteurs en ~** to keep the reader in suspense c (= *en suspension*) **en ~** [*poussière, flocons de neige*] in suspension; **en ~ dans l'air** hanging ou suspended in the air d (*littér* = *suspense*) suspense

suspense [syspɛns, syspɑ̃s] NM [*film, roman*] suspense; **un moment de ~** a moment's suspense; **un ~ angoissant** an agonizing feeling of suspense; **film à ~** suspense film, thriller

suspenseur [syspɑ̃sœʀ] 1 ADJ M suspensory 2 NM suspensor

suspensif, -ive [syspɑ̃sif, iv] ADJ (Jur) suspensive

suspension [syspɑ̃sjɔ̃] 1 NF a [*vêtements*] hanging; [*lampe, décoration*] hanging, suspending b (= *interruption*) [*publication, combats, paiement, permis de conduire*] suspension; [*récit*] breaking off; [*audience, séance*] adjournment; **le juge a ordonné la ~ de l'audience** the judge ordered that the hearing be adjourned; **il a eu un an de ~ de permis** he had his driving licence suspended for a year; **la ~ des relations diplomatiques entre les deux pays** the breaking off ou suspension of diplomatic relations between the two countries c (= *fait de différer*) [*jugement*] suspension, deferment; [*décision*] postponement, deferment d [*prélat, fonctionnaire*] suspension; [*joueur*] suspension; **prononcer la ~ de qn pour 2 ans** to suspend sb for 2 years; **~ à vie** lifetime ban e (Aut) suspension; **~ active/hydraulique** active/hydraulic suspension f (= *lustre*) ceiling light

g (= *installation, système*) suspension; **~ florale** hanging basket h (Chim) suspension 2 **en suspension** LOC ADJ [*particule, poussière*] in suspension, suspended; **en ~ dans l'air** [*poussière*] hanging ou suspended in the air; **en ~ dans l'air** ou **dans le vide** [*personne, câble*] hanging ou suspended in mid-air 3 COMP ▸ **suspension d'audience** adjournment ▸ **suspension des hostilités** suspension of hostilities ▸ **suspension de paiement** suspension of payment(s) ▸ **suspension des poursuites** suspension of proceedings ▸ **suspension de séance** = **suspension d'audience**

suspensoir [syspɑ̃swaʀ] NM athletic support, jockstrap

suspicieusement [syspisjøzmɑ̃] ADV suspiciously

suspicieux, -ieuse [syspisjø, jøz] ADJ suspicious

suspicion [syspisjɔ̃] NF suspicion; **avoir de la ~ à l'égard de qn** to be suspicious of sb, have one's suspicions about sb; **regard plein de ~** suspicious look; (Jur) **~ légitime** reasonable suspicion (*about the fairness of a trial*)

sustentateur, -trice [systɑ̃tatœʀ, tʀis] ADJ (Aviat) lifting; **surface sustentatrice** aerofoil (Brit), airfoil (US)

sustentation [systɑ̃tasjɔ̃] NF (Aviat) lift; (Aviat) **plan de ~** aerofoil (Brit), airfoil (US); (Géom) **polygone** ou **base de ~** base; **train à ~ magnétique** magnetic levitation train, maglev train

sustenter [systɑ̃te] ▸ conjug 1 ◂ 1 VT († = *nourrir*) to sustain; (fig) **la lecture sustente l'esprit** reading nourishes the mind 2 **se sustenter** VPR (hum, frm) to take sustenance (hum, frm)

sus-tonique [systɔnik] ADJ (Mus) supertonic

susurrement [sysyʀmɑ̃] NM [*personne*] whisper, whispering; [*eau*] murmuring

susurrer [sysyʀe] ▸ conjug 1 ◂ VTI [*personne*] to whisper; [*eau*] to murmur; **il lui susurrait des mots doux à l'oreille** he whispered sweet nothings in her ear; **les mauvaises langues susurrent qu'il a fait de la prison** malicious gossips are putting it about that he has been to prison; **on susurre qu'il a été impliqué** it's whispered that ou the whisper is that he was involved

susvisé, e [sysvize] ADJ (Admin) abovementioned, aforementioned

suture [sytyʀ] NF (Anat, Bot, Méd) suture → **point²**

suturer [sytyʀe] ▸ conjug 1 ◂ VT to suture (SPÉC), stitch up

Suva [syva] N Suva

suzerain, e [syz(ə)ʀɛ̃, ɛn] 1 NM,F suzerain, overlord 2 ADJ suzerain

suzeraineté [syz(ə)ʀɛnte] NF suzerainty

svastika [svastika] NM swastika

svelte [svɛlt] ADJ [*personne*] svelte, slender; [*édifice, silhouette*] slender, slim

sveltesse [svɛltɛs] NF slenderness

SVP [ɛsvepe] (ABRÉV = **s'il vous plaît**) please

swahili, e [swaili] 1 ADJ Swahili(an) 2 NM (Ling) Swahili 3 **Swahili(e)** NM,F Swahili

swazi, e [swazi] 1 ADJ Swazi 2 **Swazi(e)** NM,F Swazi

Swaziland [swazilɑ̃d] NM Swaziland

sweat [swit, swɛt] NM sweatshirt

sweater [switœʀ, swɛtœʀ] NM sweater

sweat-shirt (pl **sweat-shirts**) [switʃœʀt, swɛtʃœʀt] NM sweatshirt

sweepstake [swipstɛk] NM sweepstake

swing [swiŋ] NM (= *musique*) swing; (= *danse*) jive; **danser le ~** to jive

swinguer* [swiŋe] ▸ conjug 1 ◂ VI to swing*; **ça swingue !** it's really swinging!*

sympathie

sybarite [sibaʀit] NMF sybarite

sybaritique [sibaʀitik] ADJ sybaritic

sybaritisme [sibaʀitism] NM sybaritism

sycomore [sikɔmɔʀ] NM sycamore (tree)

sycophante [sikɔfɑ̃t] NM (littér = *délateur*) informer

syllabation [si(l)labasjɔ̃] NF syllabication, syllabification

syllabe [si(l)lab] NF syllable; **~ ouverte/fermée** open/closed syllable; **~ finale/muette/accentuée** final/silent/accented ou stressed syllable; **il n'a pas prononcé une ~** he didn't say a single word

syllabique [si(l)labik] ADJ syllabic

syllabisme [si(l)labism] NM syllabism

syllogisme [silɔʒism] NM syllogism

syllogistique [silɔʒistik] 1 ADJ syllogistic 2 NF syllogistics sg

sylphe [silf] NM sylph

sylphide [silfid] NF sylphid; (= *femme*) sylphlike creature; **sa taille de ~** her sylphlike figure

sylvestre [silvɛstʀ] ADJ forest (épith), silvan (littér) → **pin**

sylvicole [silvikɔl] ADJ forestry (épith)

sylviculteur, -trice [silvikyltœʀ, tʀis] NMF forester

sylviculture [silvikyltyʀ] NF forestry, silviculture (SPÉC)

symbiose [sɛ̃bjoz] NF (lit, fig) symbiosis; **en ~** in symbiosis

symbiotique [sɛ̃bjɔtik] ADJ symbiotic

symbole [sɛ̃bɔl] NM a (gén) symbol; **une ville(-)symbole/des années(-)symbole de la liberté** a city that has come to symbolize/years that have come to symbolize freedom; **la colombe, ~ de la paix** the dove, symbol of peace b (Rel) Creed; **le Symbole des apôtres** the Apostles' Creed; **le ~ de saint Athanase** the Athanasian Creed

symbolique [sɛ̃bɔlik] 1 ADJ (gén) symbolic(al); (= *très modique*) [*donation, augmentation, amende*] token (épith), nominal; [*cotisation, contribution, dommages-intérêts*] nominal; (= *sans valeur*) [*solution*] cosmetic; **c'est un geste purement ~** it's a purely symbolic gesture, it's just a token gesture; **logique ~** symbolic logic → **franc²** 2 NF (= *science*) symbolics sg; (= *système de symboles*) symbolic system; **la ~ des rêves** the symbolism of dreams, dream symbolism

symboliquement [sɛ̃bɔlikmɑ̃] ADV symbolically

symbolisation [sɛ̃bɔlizasjɔ̃] NF symbolization

symboliser [sɛ̃bɔlize] ▸ conjug 1 ◂ VT to symbolize

symbolisme [sɛ̃bɔlism] NM (gén) symbolism; (Littérat) Symbolism

symboliste [sɛ̃bɔlist] ADJ, NMF Symbolist

symétrie [simetʀi] NF (gén) symmetry (**par rapport à** in relation to); **centre/axe de ~** centre/axis of symmetry

symétrique [simetʀik] 1 ADJ symmetrical (**de** to, **par rapport à** in relation to) 2 NM [*muscle, point*] symmetry 3 NF [*figure plane*] symmetrical figure

symétriquement [simetʀikmɑ̃] ADV symmetrically

sympa* [sɛ̃pa] ADJ INV (ABRÉV = **sympathique**) [*personne, soirée, robe*] nice; [*endroit, ambiance*] nice, friendly; **un type vachement ~** a really nice guy* ou bloke* (Brit); **sois ~, prête-le-moi** be a pal* and lend it to me; **ce n'est pas très ~ de sa part** that's not very nice of him

▼ **sympathie** [sɛ̃pati] NF a (= *amitié*) liking; **ressentir de la ~ à l'égard de qn** to (rather) like sb, feel drawn to ou towards sb; **se prendre de ~ pour qn** to take a liking to sb; **j'ai beaucoup de ~ pour lui** I like him a great deal; **il inspire la ~** he's very likeable, he's a

▸ GRAMMAIRE ACTIVE: **sympathie** 51.4

likeable sort; **s'attirer la ~ de qn** to win sb over; **n'ayant que peu de ~ pour cette nouvelle théorie** having little time for this new theory

b (= *affinité*) friendship; **la ~ qui existe entre eux** the friendship there is between them, the affinity they feel for each other; **des relations de ~ les unissaient** they were united by friendship; **il n'y a guère de ~ entre ces factions/personnes** there's no love lost between these factions/people; **être en ~ avec qn** to be at one with sb (*frm*)

c (= *compassion*) sympathy; (*frm* = *condoléances*) sympathy; **ce drame lui a attiré la ~ du public** the tragedy earned him the sympathy of the public; **croyez à notre ~** please accept our deepest *ou* most heartfelt sympathy, you have our deepest sympathy; (*pour deuil*) **témoignages de ~** expressions of sympathy

d (= *tendance*) sympathy; **on le suspecte de ~ avec le nazisme** he is suspected of having Nazi sympathies *ou* leanings; **il ne cache pas ses ~s communistes** he doesn't hide his communist sympathies

sympathique [sɛ̃patik] **1** ADJ **a** (= *agréable, aimable*) [*personne*] likeable, nice; [*geste, accueil*] friendly, kindly; [*soirée, réunion, ambiance*] pleasant, friendly; [*plat*] good, nice; [*appartement*] nice, pleasant; **il m'est (très) ~** ◊ **je le trouve (très) ~** I like him (very much), I think he's (very) nice; **elle est d'un caractère peu ~** she is rather unfriendly; **il a une tête ~*** he has a friendly *ou* nice face **b** (*Anat*) sympathetic **2** NM (*Anat*) **le (grand) ~** the sympathetic nervous system

sympathiquement [sɛ̃patikmɑ̃] ADV [*accueillir, traiter*] in a friendly manner; **ils ont ~ offert de nous aider** they have kindly offered to help us; **ils nous ont ~ reçus** they gave us a friendly reception

sympathisant, e [sɛ̃patizɑ̃, ɑ̃t] (*Pol*) **1** ADJ sympathizing (*épith*) **2** NM,F sympathizer

sympathiser [sɛ̃patize] ▸ conjug 1 ◂ VI (= *bien s'entendre*) to get on (well) (**avec** with); (= *se prendre d'amitié*) to hit it off* (**avec** with); (= *fréquenter*) **ils ne sympathisent pas avec les voisins** they don't have much contact with *ou* much to do with* the neighbours; **je suis heureux de voir qu'il sympathise avec Lucien** I'm pleased to see he gets on (well) with Lucien; **ils ont tout de suite sympathisé** they took to each other immediately, they hit it off* straight away; **il sympathise avec l'extrême droite** he has sympathies *ou* he sympathizes with the far right

symphonie [sɛ̃fɔni] NF (*Mus, fig*) symphony; **~ concertante** symphonia concertante

symphonique [sɛ̃fɔnik] ADJ symphonic → **orchestre, poème**

symphoniste [sɛ̃fɔnist] NMF symphonist

symposium [sɛ̃pozjɔm] NM symposium

symptomatique [sɛ̃ptɔmatik] ADJ (*Méd*) symptomatic; (= *révélateur*) significant; **~ de** symptomatic of

symptomatiquement [sɛ̃ptɔmatikmɑ̃] ADV symptomatically

symptomatologie [sɛ̃ptɔmatɔlɔʒi] NF symptomatology

symptôme [sɛ̃ptom] NM (*Méd*) symptom; (= *signe, indice*) sign, symptom

synagogue [sinagɔg] NF synagogue

synapse [sinaps] NF [*neurones*] synapse, synapsis; [*gamètes*] synapsis

synarchie [sinaʀʃi] NF synarchy

synchro* [sɛ̃kʀo] **1** ADJ ABRÉV = **synchronisé, e 2** NF ABRÉV = **synchronisation**

synchrone [sɛ̃kʀon] ADJ synchronous

synchronie [sɛ̃kʀɔni] NF synchronic level, synchrony

synchronique [sɛ̃kʀɔnik] ADJ [*linguistique, analyse*] synchronic → **tableau**

synchroniquement [sɛ̃kʀɔnikmɑ̃] ADJ synchronically

synchronisation [sɛ̃kʀɔnizasjɔ̃] NF synchronization

synchronisé, e [sɛ̃kʀɔnize] (*ptp de* **synchroniser**) ADJ synchronized

synchroniser [sɛ̃kʀɔnize] ▸ conjug 1 ◂ VT to synchronize

synchroniseur [sɛ̃kʀɔnizœʀ] NM (*Élec*) synchronizer; (*Aut*) synchromesh

synchroniseuse [sɛ̃kʀɔnizøz] NF (*Ciné*) synchronizer

synchronisme [sɛ̃kʀɔnism] NM [*oscillations, dates*] synchronism; (*Philo*) synchronicity; **avec un ~ parfait** with perfect synchronization

synchrotron [sɛ̃kʀɔtʀɔ̃] NM synchrotron; **rayonnement ~** synchrotron radiation

synclinal, e [sɛ̃klinal, o] **1** ADJ synclinal **2** NM syncline

syncope [sɛ̃kɔp] NF **a** (= *évanouissement*) blackout, fainting fit, syncope (*SPÉC*); **avoir une ~** to have a blackout, faint, pass out **b** (*Mus*) syncopation **c** (*Ling*) syncope

syncopé, e [sɛ̃kɔpe] ADJ **a** (*Littérat, Mus*) syncopated **b** (* = *stupéfait*) staggered, flabbergasted*

syncrétique [sɛ̃kʀetik] ADJ syncretic

syncrétisme [sɛ̃kʀetism] NM syncretism

syndic [sɛ̃dik] NM (*Hist*) syndic; (*Jur*) receiver; **~ (d'immeuble** *ou* **de copropriété)** managing agent; (*Jur, Fin*) **~ de faillite** official assignee, trustee (in bankruptcy), judicial factor (*US*)

syndical, e [*mpl* -aux] [sɛ̃dikal, o] ADJ (*Ind*) (trade-)union (*épith*); **le mouvement ~** the trade-union (*Brit*) *ou* labor-union (*US*) movement; **conseil ~ d'un immeuble** ≈ management committee of a block of flats (*Brit*) *ou* of an apartment building (*US*) → **central, chambre, tarif**

syndicalisation [sɛ̃dikalizasjɔ̃] NF unionization

syndicaliser [sɛ̃dikalize] ▸ conjug 1 ◂ VT to unionize; **un secteur fortement syndicalisé** a highly unionized sector

syndicalisme [sɛ̃dikalism] NM (= *mouvement*) trade unionism; (= *activité*) (trade-)union activities; (= *doctrine politique*) syndicalism; **faire du ~** to participate in (trade-)union activities, be a (trade-)union activist

syndicaliste [sɛ̃dikalist] **1** NMF (= *responsable d'un syndicat*) (trade) union official, trade unionist; (= *doctrinaire*) syndicalist **2** ADJ [*chef*] trade-union (*épith*); [*doctrine, idéal*] unionist (*épith*)

syndicat [sɛ̃dika] **1** NM **a** [*travailleurs*] (trade) union; [*employeurs*] union, syndicate; [*producteurs agricoles*] union; **~ de mineurs/de journalistes** miners'/journalists' union; **~ du crime** crime syndicate **b** (*non professionnel*) association → **2 2** COMP ▸ **syndicat de banques** banking syndicate ▸ **syndicat de communes** association of communes ▸ **syndicat financier** syndicate of financiers ▸ **syndicat d'initiative** tourist (information) office *ou* bureau *ou* centre ▸ **syndicat interdépartemental** association of regional authorities ▸ **syndicat de locataires** tenants' association ▸ **syndicat ouvrier** trade union ▸ **syndicat patronal** employers' syndicate, federation of employers, bosses' union* ▸ **syndicat de propriétaires** (*gén*) association of property owners; (*d'un même immeuble*) householders' association

syndicataire [sɛ̃dikatɛʀ] **1** ADJ of a syndicate **2** NMF syndicate member

syndiqué, e [sɛ̃dike] (*ptp de* **syndiquer**) **1** ADJ belonging to a (trade) union; **ouvrier ~** union member; **est-il ~ ?** is he in a *ou* the union?, is

he a union man *ou* member?; **les travailleurs non ~s** non-union *ou* non-unionized workers **2** NM,F union member

syndiquer [sɛ̃dike] ▸ conjug 1 ◂ **1** VT to unionize **2 se syndiquer** VPR (= *se grouper*) to form a trade union, unionize; (= *adhérer*) to join a trade union

syndrome [sɛ̃dʀom] NM syndrome; **~ chinois** China syndrome; **le ~ de Down** Down's syndrome; **~ prémenstruel** premenstrual syndrome; **~ d'immunodéficience acquise** acquired immuno-deficiency syndrome

synecdoque [sinekdɔk] NF synecdoche

synérèse [sineʀez] NF (*Ling*) synaeresis; (*Chim*) syneresis

synergie [sineʀʒi] NF synergy, synergism; **travailler en ~** to work in synergy (**avec** with)

synergique [sineʀʒik] ADJ synergetic

synesthésie [sinestezi] NF synaesthesia

synode [sinɔd] NM synod

synodique [sinɔdik] ADJ (*Astron*) synodic(al); (*Rel*) synod(ic)al

synonyme [sinɔnim] **1** ADJ synonymous (**de** with) **2** NM synonym

synonymie [sinɔnimi] NF synonymy

synonymique [sinɔnimik] ADJ synonymic(al)

synopsis [sinɔpsis] NF (*Ciné*) synopsis

synoptique [sinɔptik] ADJ synoptic; **les (Évangiles) ~s** the synoptic gospels

synovial, e [*mpl* -iaux] [sinɔvjal, jo] ADJ synovial

synovie [sinɔvi] NF synovia → **épanchement**

synovite [sinɔvit] NF synovitis

syntactique [sɛ̃taktik] ADJ = **syntaxique**

syntagmatique [sɛ̃tagmatik] **1** ADJ syntagmatic, phrasal **2** NF syntagmatic analysis

syntagme [sɛ̃tagm] NM (word) group, phrase, syntagm (*SPÉC*); **~ adjectival** adjunctive phrase, adjunct; **~ nominal** nominal group, noun phrase; **~ verbal** verb phrase

syntaxe [sɛ̃taks] NF (*Ling, Ordin*) syntax; **erreur de ~** syntax error

syntaxique [sɛ̃taksik] ADJ syntactic

synthé* [sɛ̃te] NM (ABRÉV = **synthétiseur**) synth*

synthèse [sɛ̃tez] NF synthesis; **faire la ~ d'un exposé** to summarize the major points of a talk; **de ~** [*sucre, arôme*] synthetic; **produit de ~** product of synthesis; **protéique** protein synthesis; (*Ordin*) **~ vocale/de la parole** voice/speech synthesis → **esprit, image**

synthétique [sɛ̃tetik] **1** ADJ **a** [*textile, fibre*] synthetic, man-made; [*résine, caoutchouc, revêtement*] synthetic; **matières ~s** synthetic materials, synthetics; **c'est de la fourrure ~** it's fake fur *ou* fun fur **b** (= *artificiel*) [*images, voix, son*] synthetic **c** (= *qui envisage la totalité*) [*exposé*] that gives an overall picture (of a subject); [*ouvrage*] that takes a global perspective; **avoir l'esprit ~** to be good at synthesizing information; **avoir une vision ~ des choses** to (be able to) see the overall picture; **présenter un sujet de façon ~** to give an overall picture of a subject **2** NM (*Tex*) synthetics; **c'est du ~** it's synthetic; **vêtement/chaussures en ~** garment/shoes made of synthetic material

synthétiquement [sɛ̃tetikmɑ̃] ADV synthetically

synthétiser [sɛ̃tetize] ▸ conjug 1 ◂ VT to synthetize, synthesize

synthétiseur [sɛ̃tetizœʀ] NM synthesizer; **~ de (la) parole** speech synthesizer

syntonie [sɛ̃tɔni] NF (*Psych*) syntonia; (*Phys*) syntonism

syntoniser [sɛ̃tɔnize] ▸ conjug 1 ◂ VT to syntonize, tune

syntoniseur [sɛ̃tɔnizœʀ] NM tuner

syphilis [sifilis] NF syphilis

syphilitique [sifilitik] ADJ, NMF syphilitic

syriaque [siʀjak] ① ADJ Syriac (*épith*) ② NM (*Ling*) Syriac

Syrie [siʀi] NF Syria

syrien, -ienne [siʀjɛ̃, jɛn] ① ADJ Syrian; **République arabe syrienne** Syrian Arab Republic ② **Syrien(ne)** NM,F Syrian

systématique [sistematik] ① ADJ [*opposition, classement, esprit*] systematic; [*soutien, aide*] unconditional; **opposer un refus ~ à qch** to refuse sth systematically; **avec l'intention ~ de nuire** systematically intending to harm; **il est trop ~** he's too dogmatic, his views are too set; **chaque fois qu'elle est invitée quelque part il l'est aussi, c'est ~** every time she's invited somewhere, he's automatically invited too ② NF (*gén*) systematics *sg*; (*Bio*) taxonomy

systématiquement [sistematikmɑ̃] ADV systematically

systématisation [sistematizasjɔ̃] NF systematization

systématiser [sistematize] ▸ conjug 1 ◂ ① VT [+ *recherches, mesures*] to systematize; **il n'a pas le sens de la nuance, il systématise (tout)** he has no sense of nuance — he systematizes

everything ② **se systématiser** VPR to become the rule

système [sistɛm] ① NM [a] (*gén*) (= *structure*) system; **~ de vie** way of life, lifestyle; (= *institution*) **entrer dans le ~** to join *ou* enter the system; (*Ling*) **~ casuel** case system; (*Méd*) **troubles du ~** systemic disorders → **esprit**
[b] (= *moyen*) system; **il connaît un ~ pour entrer sans payer** he's got a system for getting in without paying; **il connaît le ~** he knows the system; **le meilleur ~, c'est de se relayer** the best plan *ou* system is to take turns
[c] (*loc*) **par ~** [*agir*] in a systematic way; [*contredire*] systematically; **il me tape** *ou* **court** *ou* **porte sur le ~!** he gets on my nerves* *ou* wick* (*Brit*)
② COMP ▸ **système ABS** ABS ▸ **système d'alarme** alarm system ▸ **système d'alimentation** (*électrique*) electricity supply system; (*en eau*) water supply system ▸ **système D*** resourcefulness; **recourir au ~ D** to rely on one's own resources, fend for o.s. ▸ **système décimal** decimal system ▸ **système de défense** (*Mil*) defence system; (*Physiol*) defence mechanism ▸ **système d'éducation** education system ▸ **système d'équations** system of equa-

tions ▸ **système expert** expert system ▸ **système d'exploitation** operating system ▸ **système de gestion de bases de données** database management system ▸ **système immunitaire** immune system ▸ **Système international d'unités** International System of Units ▸ **système métrique** metric system ▸ **système monétaire européen** European monetary system ▸ **système nerveux** nervous system; **~ nerveux central/périphérique** central/peripheral nervous system ▸ **système pénitentiaire** prison *ou* penal system ▸ **système pileux** : **avoir un ~ pileux très développé** to have a lot of body hair ▸ **système respiratoire** respiratory system ▸ **système de santé** health system ▸ **système de sécurité sociale** social security system ▸ **système solaire** solar system ▸ **système de traitement de l'information** data-processing system

systémique [sistemik] ① ADJ systemic ② NF systems analysis

systole [sistɔl] NF systole

systolique [sistɔlik] ADJ systolic

syzygie [siziʒi] NF syzygy

T

T, t¹ [te] NM **a** (= *lettre*) T, t; **en T** [*table, immeuble*] T-shaped; **bandage/antenne/équerre en T** T-bandage/-aerial/-square **b** (*Méd*) **T4** T4

t² **a** (ABRÉV = **tonne**) t **b** (ABRÉV = **tome**) vol.

t' [t] → **te, tu**

ta [ta] ADJ POSS → **ton¹**

ta, ta, ta [tatata] EXCL (stuff and) nonsense!, rubbish!

tabac [taba] **1** NM **a** (= *plante, produit*) tobacco; (= *couleur*) buff, tobacco (brown); (= *magasin*) tobacconist's (shop) (*Brit*), tobacco *ou* smoke shop (*US*) → **blague, bureau, débit** **b** (**: loc*) **passer qn à ~** to beat sb up, do sb over* (*Brit*); **faire un ~** to be a big hit *ou* a roaring success, hit it big* (*US*); **c'est toujours le même ~** it's always the same old thing; **quelque chose du même ~** something like that; **coup de ~** squall → **passage** **2** ADJ INV buff, tobacco (brown) **3** COMP ► **tabac blond** light *ou* mild *ou* Virginia tobacco ► **tabac brun** dark tobacco ► **tabac à chiquer** chewing tobacco ► **tabac gris** shag ► **tabac à priser** snuff

tabagie [tabaʒi] NF (= *lieu enfumé*) smoke-filled room; (*au Canada* = *bureau de tabac*) tobacconist's (shop) (*Brit*), tobacco *ou* smoke shop (*US*); **ce bureau, quelle ~!** it's really smoky in this office!

tabagique [tabaʒik] **1** ADJ [*consommation, publicité*] tobacco (*épith*) **2** NMF chain smoker

tabagisme [tabaʒism] NM addiction to smoking, nicotine addiction; **~ passif** passive smoking; **lutte contre le ~** anti-smoking campaign

tabasco® [tabasko] NM (*Culin*) Tabasco (sauce)®

tabasser* [tabase] ▸conjug 1◂ **1** VT (= *passer à tabac*) **~ qn** to beat sb up, do sb over* (*Brit*); **se faire ~** to get beaten up, get one's face smashed in* (par by) **2 se tabasser** VPR (= *se bagarrer*) to have a fight *ou* punch-up* (*Brit*)

tabatière [tabatjɛʀ] NF **a** (= *boîte*) snuffbox; **~ anatomique** anatomical snuffbox **b** (= *lucarne*) skylight → **fenêtre**

T.A.B.D.T. [teabedete] NM (ABRÉV = **vaccin antityphoïdique et anti-paratyphoïdique A et B, antidiphtérique et tétanique**) *vaccine against typhoid, paratyphoid A and B, diphtheria and tetanus*

tabellion [tabeljɔ̃] NM (*hum péj*: = *notaire*) lawyer

tabernacle [tabɛʀnakl] NM (*Rel*) tabernacle

tablar(d) [tablaʀ] NM (*Helv* = *étagère*) shelf

tablature [tablatyʀ] NF (*Mus*) tablature

table [tabl] **1** NF **a** (= *meuble*) table; **~ de salle à manger/de cuisine/de billard** dining-room/kitchen/billiard table; **~ de** *ou* **en bois/marbre** wooden/marble table → **dessous, carte, tennis** **b** (*pour le repas*) **être à ~** to be having a meal, be eating; **nous étions huit à ~** there were eight of us at *ou* round the table; (*au restaurant*) **une ~ pour quatre** a table for four; **à ~!** come and eat!, dinner (*ou* lunch *etc*) is ready!; **mettre** *ou* (*littér*) **dresser la ~** to lay *ou* set the table; **débarrasser** *ou* (*littér*) **desservir la ~** to clear the table; **passer à ~** ◊ **se mettre à ~*** to sit down to eat, sit down at the table; **présider la ~** to sit at the head of the table; **recevoir qn à sa ~** to have sb to lunch (*ou* dinner *etc*); **se lever de ~** to get up *ou* rise (*frm*) from the table; **quitter la ~** ◊ **sortir de ~** to leave the table; **~ de 12 couverts** table set for 12; **linge/vin/propos de ~** table linen/wine/talk

c (= *tablée*) table; **toute la ~ éclata de rire** everyone round the table *ou* the whole table burst out laughing; **soldats et officiers mangeaient à la même ~** soldiers and officers ate at the same table

d (= *nourriture*) **une ~ frugale** frugal fare (*NonC*); **avoir une bonne ~** to keep a good table; **aimer (les plaisirs de) la ~** to enjoy one's food

e (= *tablette avec inscriptions*) **~ de marbre** marble tablet; **les Tables de la Loi** the Tables of the Law; (*Antiq*) **la Loi des Douze Tables** the Twelve Tables

f (= *liste*) table; **~ de logarithmes/de multiplication** log/multiplication table; **~ de vérité** truth table; **~ alphabétique** alphabetical table; **il sait sa ~ de 8** he knows his 8 times table

g (*Géol* = *plateau*) tableland, plateau

h (*loc*) (*Philo*) **~ rase** tabula rasa; **faire ~ rase** to make a clean sweep (**de** of); **on a fait ~ rase du passé** we put the past behind us; (*Police*) **se mettre à ~*** to talk, come clean*; **tenir ~ ouverte** to keep open house

2 COMP ► **table à abattants** drop-leaf table ► **table anglaise** gate-legged table ► **table d'architecte** drawing board ► **table d'autel** altar stone ► **table basse** coffee table, occasional table ► **table de bridge** card *ou* bridge table ► **table à cartes** (*Naut*) chart house ► **table de chevet** bedside table, night stand *ou* table (*US*) ► **table de communion** communion table ► **table de conférence** conference table ► **table de cuisson** hob ► **table à dessin** drawing board ► **table à digitaliser** digitizer ► **table d'écoute** wire-tapping set; **mettre qn sur ~ d'écoute** to tap sb's phone ► **tables gigognes** nest of tables ► **table d'harmonie** sounding board ► **table d'honneur** top table ► **table d'hôte** table d'hôte; **faire ~ d'hôte** to serve table d'hôte dinners, serve dinner for residents ► **table de jeu** gaming table ► **table de lancement** launch(ing) pad ► **table à langer** changing table ► **table de lecture** [*chaîne haute fidélité*] turntable ► **table de malade** bedtable ► **table des matières** (table of) contents ► **table de Mendeleïev** Mendeleyev's periodic table ► **table de mixage** mixing desk ► **la table des négociations** the negotiating table ► **table de nuit** = table de chevet ► **table d'opération** operating table ► **table d'orientation** viewpoint indicator ► **table à ouvrage** worktable ► **table de ping-pong** table-tennis table ► **table pliante** folding table ► **table de Pythagore** Pythagorean table ► **table à rallonges** extending table ► **table à repasser** ironing board ► **table ronde** (*lit*) round table; (*fig*) round table, panel ► **la Table ronde** (*Hist*) the Round Table ► **table roulante** trolley (*Brit*), cart (*US*) ► **table de survie** life table ► **tables de tir** range tables ► **table de toilette** (*pour lavabo*) washstand; (= *coiffeuse*) dressing table ► **table tournante** séance table ► **table traçante** (*Ordin*) (graph) plotter ► **table de travail** work table

tableau (*pl* **tableaux**) [tablo] **1** NM **a** (= *peinture*) painting; (= *reproduction, gravure*) picture; **exposition de ~x** art exhibition → **galerie**

b (*fig* = *scène*) picture, scene; **le ~ l'émut au plus haut point** he was deeply moved by the scene; **un ~ tragique/idyllique** a tragic/an idyllic picture *ou* scene; **le ~ changeant de la vallée du Rhône** the changing landscape of the Rhone valley

c (*Théât*) scene; **acte un, premier ~** act one, scene one

d (= *description*) picture; **un ~ de la guerre** a picture *ou* depiction of war; **il m'a fait un ~ très noir de la situation** he drew a very black picture of the situation for me

e (*Scol*) **~ (noir)** (black)board; **~ blanc** (white)board; **aller au ~** (*lit*) to go up to the blackboard; (= *se faire interroger*) to be asked questions (*on a school subject*)

f (= *support mural*) [*sonneries*] board; [*fusibles*] box; [*clés*] rack, board

g (= *panneau*) board; (*Rail*) train indicator; [*bateau*] escutcheon, name board; **~ des départs/arrivées** departure(s)/arrival(s) board; **~ des horaires** timetable

h (= *carte, graphique*) table, chart; (*Ordin*: *fait par tableur*) spreadsheet; **~ généalogique/chronologique** genealogical/chronological table *ou* chart; **~ des conjugaisons** conjugation table, table of conjugations; **présenter qch sous forme de ~** to show sth in tabular form

i (*Admin* = *liste*) register, list; **~ de l'ordre des avocats** ≈ register of the association of barristers; **médicament au ~ A/B/C** class A/B/C drug (*according to French classification of toxicity*)

j (*loc*) **vous voyez (d'ici) le ~!** you can (just) imagine!; **pour compléter** *ou* **achever le ~** complete the picture; (*fig*) **jouer** *ou* **miser sur les deux ~x** to back both horses (*fig*); **il a gagné sur les deux/sur tous les ~x** he won on both/on all counts

2 COMP ► **tableau d'affichage** (*gén*) notice board; (*Sport*) scoreboard ► **tableau d'amortissement** depreciation schedule ► **tableau d'avancement** (*Admin*) promotion table ► **tableau de bord** [*voiture*] dashboard; [*avion, bateau*] instrument panel; (*fig*) (performance) indicators ► **tableau de chasse** [*chasseur*] bag; [*aviateur*] tally of kills; [*séducteur*] list of conquests; **ajouter qch à son ~ de chasse** to add sth to one's list of successes ► **tableau clinique** clinical picture ► **tableau électronique** (*gén*) electronic noticeboard; (*Sport*) electronic scoreboard ► **tableau d'honneur** merit *ou* prize list (*Brit*), honor roll (*US*); **être inscrit au ~ d'honneur** to appear on the merit *ou* prize list (*Brit*), make the honor roll (*US*); **au ~ d'honneur du sport français cette semaine, Luc Legrand ...** pride of place in French sport this ·week goes to Lúc Legrand ... ► **tableau de maître** masterpiece ► **tableau de marche** schedule ► **tableau de service** (*gén*) work notice board; (= *horaire de service*) duty roster ► **tableau synchronique** synchronic table of events *etc* ► **tableau synoptique** synoptic table ► **tableau vivant** (*Théât*) tableau (vivant)

tableautin [tablotɛ̃] NM little picture

tablée [table] NF table (of people); **toute la ~ éclata de rire** the whole table *ou* everyone round the table burst out laughing

tabler [table] ▸conjug 1◂ ♦ **tabler sur** VT INDIR **~ sur qch** to count *ou* bank on sth; **il avait tablé sur une baisse des taux** he had counted *ou* banked on the rates going down; **table sur ton travail plutôt que sur la chance** rely on your work rather than on luck

tablette [tablɛt] NF [a] (= *plaquette*) [*chocolat*] bar; [*médicament*] tablet; [*chewing-gum*] stick; [*métal*] block; **~ de bouillon** stock cube [b] (= *planchette, rayon*) [*lavabo, radiateur, cheminée*] shelf; [*secrétaire*] flap; **~ à glissière** pull-out flap [c] (*Archéol, Hist: pour écrire*) tablet; **~ de cire/d'argile** wax/clay tablet; (*hum*) **je vais l'inscrire sur mes ~s** I'll make a note of it; (*hum*) **ce n'est pas écrit sur mes ~s** I have no record of it [d] (*Ordin*) tablet; **~ graphique** graphic tablet

tableur [tablœʀ] NM spreadsheet (program)

tablier [tablije] NM [a] (*Habillement*) (*gén*) apron; [*ménagère*] (*sans manches*) apron, pinafore; (*avec manches*) overall; [*écolier*] overall, smock; **rendre son ~** [*domestique*] to hand *ou* give in one's notice; [*homme politique*] to resign, step down; **ça lui va comme un ~ à une vache*** [*vêtement*] it looks really weird on him; [*poste*] he's totally out of place in that job; (*Culin*) **~ de sapeur** tripe in breadcrumbs [b] [*pont*] roadway [c] (*Tech = plaque protectrice*) [*cheminée*] (flue-)shutter; [*magasin*] (iron *ou* steel) shutter; [*machine-outil*] apron; [*scooter*] fairing (*Aut : entre moteur et habitacle*) bulkhead

tabloïd(e) [tablɔid] ADJ, NM tabloid

tabou, e [tabu] [1] ADJ (= *sacré, frappé d'interdit*) taboo; (*fig = intouchable*) [*personnage*] untouchable; **sujet ~** taboo subject; **une société où la sexualité reste ~(e)** a society where sexuality is still taboo [2] NM taboo; **briser un ~** to break a taboo

taboulé [tabule] NM tabbouleh

tabouret [tabuʀɛ] NM (*pour s'asseoir*) stool; (*pour les pieds*) footstool; **~ de piano/de bar** piano/bar stool

tabulaire [tabylɛʀ] ADJ tabular

tabulateur [tabylatœʀ] NM tab key, tabulator

tabulation [tabylasjɔ̃] NF tabulation; **poser des ~s** to set tabs

tabulatrice [tabylatʀis] NF tabulator (*for punched cards*)

tabuler [tabyle] ▸conjug 1◂ VT to tabulate, tabularize, tab

tac [tak] NM [a] (= *bruit*) tap; **le ~ ~ des mitrailleuses** the rat-a-tat(-tat) of the machine guns → **tic-tac** [b] **il répond *ou* riposte du ~ au ~** he always has a ready answer; **il lui a répondu du ~ au ~ que ...** he came back at him immediately *ou* as quick as a flash that ...

tache [taʃ] [1] NF [a] (= *moucheture*) [*fruit*] mark; [*léopard*] spot; [*plumage, pelage*] mark(ing), spot; [*peau*] blotch, mark; (*fig*) **faire ~** to jar, stick out like a sore thumb; **les ~s**

des ongles the white marks on the finger-nails [b] (= *salissure*) stain, mark; **~ de graisse** greasy mark, grease stain; **~ de brûlure/de suie** burn/sooty mark; **des draps couverts de ~s** sheets covered in stains; **sa robe n'avait pas une ~** her dress was spotless; **il a fait une ~ à sa cravate** he got a stain on his tie; **tu t'es fait une ~** you've got a stain on your shirt (*ou* dress *ou* tie *etc*) [c] (*littér = flétrissure*) blot, stain; **c'est une ~ à sa réputation** it's a blot *ou* stain on his reputation; **sans ~** [*vie, réputation*] spotless, unblemished → **agneau, pur** [d] (= *impression visuelle*) patch, spot; **le soleil parsemait la campagne de ~s d'or** the sun scattered patches of gold over the countryside; **des ~s d'ombre çà et là** patches of shadow here and there [e] (*Peinture*) spot, blob; **~ de couleur** patch of colour [f] (‡ = *nullité*) jerk‡

[2] COMP ► **tache d'encre** (*sur les doigts*) ink stain; (*sur le papier*) (ink) blot *ou* blotch ► **tache d'huile** oily mark, oil stain; (*fig*) **faire ~ d'huile** to spread, gain ground ► **tache jaune** (*de l'œil*) yellow spot (of the eye) ► **tache originelle** (*Rel*) stain of original sin ► **tache de rousseur** freckle; **visage couvert de ~s de rousseur** freckled face, face covered in freckles ► **tache de sang** bloodstain ► **tache solaire** (*Astron*) sunspot ► **tache de son** = **tache de rousseur** ► **tache de vin** (*sur la nappe*) wine stain; (*sur la peau* = *envie*) strawberry mark

tâche [taʃ] NF [a] (= *besogne*) task, work (*NonC*); (= *mission*) task, job; (*Ordin*) task; **il a la lourde ~ de ...** he has the difficult task of ...; **il a pour ~ de ...** his task is to ...; **assigner une ~ à qn** to give *ou* set (*Brit*) sb a task; **s'atteler à une ~** to get down to work; (*Ordin*) **~ de fond** *ou* **d'arrière-plan** background task → **ménager²** [b] (*loc*) **à la ~** [*payer*] by the piece; **ouvrier à la ~** pieceworker; **travail à la ~** piecework; **être à la ~** to be on piecework; (*fig*) **je ne suis pas à la ~*** I'll do it in my own good time; **mourir à la ~** to die in harness; (†, *littér*) **prendre à ~ de faire qch** to set o.s. the task of doing sth, take it upon o.s. to do sth

tachéomètre [takeɔmɛtʀ] NM (= *théodolite*) tacheometer, tachymeter

tachéométrie [takeɔmetʀi] NF tacheometry

tacher [taʃe] ▸conjug 1◂ [1] VT [a] [*encre, vin*] to stain; [*graisse*] to mark, stain; **le café tache** coffee stains (badly) *ou* leaves a stain; **taché de sang** bloodstained [b] (*littér = colorer*) [+ *pré, robe*] to spot, dot; [+ *peau, fourrure*] to spot, mark; **pelage blanc taché de noir** white coat with black spots *ou* markings, white coat flecked with black [c] († = *souiller*) to tarnish, sully [2] **se tacher** VPR [a] (= *se salir*) [*personne*] to get stains on one's clothes, get o.s. dirty; [*nappe, tissu*] to get stained *ou* marked; **tissu qui se tache facilement** fabric that stains *ou* marks easily [b] (= *s'abîmer*) [*fruits*] to become marked

tâcher [taʃe] ▸conjug 1◂ [1] **tâcher de** VT INDIR (= *essayer de*) **~ de faire qch** to try *ou* endeavour (*frm*) to do sth; **tâchez de venir avant samedi** try to *ou* try and come before Saturday; **et tâche de ne pas recommencer!*** and make sure *ou* mind it doesn't happen again!; **~ moyen de faire qch*** to try to do sth [2] **tâche qu'il n'en sache rien*** make sure that he doesn't get to know about it

tâcheron [taʃ(ə)ʀɔ̃] NM [a] (*péj*) drudge; **un ~ de la littérature/politique** a literary/political drudge *ou* hack [b] (= *ouvrier*) (*dans le bâtiment*) jobber; (*agricole*) pieceworker

tacheter [taʃ(ə)te] ▸conjug 4◂ VT [+ *peau, fourrure*] to spot, speckle; [+ *tissu, champ*] to spot, dot, fleck; **pelage blanc tacheté de brun**

white coat with brown spots *ou* markings, white coat flecked with brown

tachisme [taʃism] NM (= *art abstrait*) tachisme

tachiste [taʃist] ADJ, NMF tachiste

Tachkent [taʃkɛnt] N Tashkent

tachycardie [takikaʀdi] NF tachycardia

tachygraphe [takigʀaf] NM tachograph, black box

tachymètre [takimɛtʀ] NM (*Aut*) tachometer

Tacite [tasit] NM Tacitus

tacite [tasit] ADJ tacit; (*Jur*) **~ reconduction** renewal of contract by tacit agreement

tacitement [tasitmɑ̃] ADV tacitly

taciturne [tasityʀn] ADJ taciturn, silent

tacle [takl] NM (*Sport*) tackle; **faire un ~** to make a tackle; **faire un ~ à qn** to tackle sb

taco [tako] NM (*Culin*) taco

tacot* [tako] NM (= *voiture*) jalopy*, old rattle-trap*, banger* (*Brit*)

tact [takt] NM [a] (= *délicatesse*) tact; **avoir du ~** to have tact, be tactful; **homme de ~/sans ~** tactful/tactless man; **faire qch avec/sans ~** to do sth tactfully/tactlessly; **manquer de ~** to be tactless, be lacking in tact [b] († = *toucher*) touch, tact ††

tacticien, -ienne [taktisjɛ̃, jɛn] NM,F tactician

tactile [taktil] ADJ tactile; **affichage ~** touch-sensitive display

tactique [taktik] [1] ADJ tactical [2] NF (*gén*) tactics; **changer de ~** to change (one's) tactics; **il y a plusieurs ~s possibles** there are several different tactics one might adopt; **la ~ de l'adversaire est très simple** the opponent's tactics are very simple

tactiquement [taktikmɑ̃] ADV tactically

tadjik [tadʒik] [1] ADJ Tadzhiki [2] NM (*Ling*) Tadzhiki [3] **Tadjik** NMF Tadzhik, Tadjik, Tajik

Tadjikistan [tadʒikistɑ̃] NM Tadzhikistan

tadorne [tadɔʀn] NM **~ de Bellon** shelduck

tænia [tenja] NM = **ténia**

taffe‡ [taf] NF [*cigarette*] drag*, puff; [*pipe*] puff

taffetas [tafta] NM (*Tex*) taffeta; **robe de ~** taffeta dress; **~ (gommé)** sticking plaster (*Brit*), bandaid®

tag [tag] NM (= *graffiti*) tag

Tage [taʒ] NM **le ~** the Tagus

tagine [taʒin] NM = **tajine**

tagliatelles [taljatɛl] NFPL tagliatelle (*NonC*)

taguer [tage] ▸conjug 1◂ VTI (= *faire des graffiti*) to tag

tagueur, -euse [tagœʀ, øz] NM,F tagger

Tahiti [taiti] NF Tahiti

tahitien, -ienne [taisjɛ̃, jɛn] [1] ADJ Tahitian [2] **Tahitien(ne)** NM,F Tahitian

taïaut †† [tajo] EXCL tallyho!

taie [tɛ] NF [a] **~ (d'oreiller)** pillowcase, pillowslip; **~ de traversin** bolster case [b] (*Méd*) opaque spot, leucoma (*SPÉC*)

taïga [tajga] NF taiga

taillable [tajabl] ADJ **~ et corvéable (à merci)** (*Hist*) subject to tallage; (*fig*) [*employé, main-d'œuvre*] who can be exploited at will

taillade [tajad] NF (*dans la chair*) gash, slash; (*dans un tronc d'arbre*) gash

taillader [tajade] ▸conjug 1◂ VT to slash, gash; **se ~ les poignets** to slash one's wrists

taillanderie [tajɑ̃dʀi] NF (= *fabrication*) edge-tool making; (= *outils*) edge-tools

taillandier [tajɑ̃dje] NM edge-tool maker

taille¹ [taj] NF [a] (= *hauteur*) [*personne, cheval, objet*] height; **être de petite ~** [*personne*] to be short *ou* small; [*animal*] to be small; **homme de petite ~** short *ou* small man; **homme de ~ moyenne** man of average *ou* medium height; **homme de grande ~** tall man; **ils sont de la même ~** ◊ **ils ont la même ~** they're the same height; **il a atteint sa ~ adulte** he's fully grown

[b] (= *grosseur, volume*) size; **de petite ~** small; **de ~ moyenne** medium-sized; **de grande ~** large, big; **un chien de belle ~** quite a big *ou* large dog; **le paquet est de la ~ d'une boîte à chaussures** the parcel is the size of a shoebox; (*Ordin*) **~ de mémoire** memory capacity

[c] (*Comm = mesure*) size; **les grandes/petites ~s** large/small sizes; **« 40** size 40; **« ~ unique »** "one size (fits all)"; **il ne reste plus de ~s moyennes** there are no medium sizes *ou* mediums left; **il lui faut la ~ au-dessous/au-dessus** he needs the next size down/up, he needs one *ou* a size smaller/larger; **deux ~s au-dessous/au-dessus** two sizes smaller/larger; **ce pantalon n'est pas à sa ~** these trousers aren't his size, these trousers don't fit him; **avez-vous quelque chose dans ma ~ ?** do you have anything in my size?; **si je trouvais quelqu'un de ma ~** if I found someone my size; **avoir la ~ mannequin** to have a perfect figure

[d] (*loc*) **à la ~ de** in keeping with; **c'est un poste/sujet à la ~ de ses capacités** *ou* **à sa ~** it's a job/subject in keeping with *ou* which matches his capabilities; **il a trouvé un adversaire à sa ~** he's met his match; **être de ~ à faire qch** to be up to doing sth, be quite capable of doing sth; **il n'est pas de ~** (*pour une tâche*) he isn't up *ou* equal to it; (*face à un concurrent, dans la vie*) he doesn't measure up; **de ~** [*erreur*] serious, major; [*objet*] sizeable; [*surprise, concession, décision*] big; [*difficulté, obstacle*] huge, big; **la gaffe est de ~ !** it's a major blunder!; **l'enjeu est de ~** the stakes are high

[e] (= *partie du corps*) waist; (= *partie du vêtement*) waist, waistband; **elle n'a pas de ~** she has no waist(line), she doesn't go in at the waist; **avoir la ~ fine** to have a slim waist, be slim-waisted; **avoir une ~ de guêpe** to have an hour-glass figure, have a wasp waist; **avoir la ~ bien prise** to have a neat waist(line); **prendre qn par la ~** to put one's arm round sb's waist; **ils se tenaient par la ~** they had their arms round each other's waists; **avoir de l'eau jusqu'à la ~** to be in water up to one's waist, be waist-deep in water; **robe serrée à la ~** dress fitted at the waist; **robe à ~ basse/haute** low-/high-waisted dress; **pantalon (à) ~ basse** low-waisted trousers, hipsters → **tour²**

taille² [taj] NF [a] [*pierre précieuse*] cutting; [*pierre*] cutting, hewing; [*bois*] carving; [*verre*] engraving; [*crayon*] sharpening; [*arbre, vigne*] pruning, cutting back; [*haie*] trimming, clipping, cutting; [*tissu*] cutting (out); [*cheveux, barbe*] trimming; **diamant de ~ hexagonale/en étoile** diamond with a six-sided/star-shaped cut → **pierre** [b] (= *taillis*) **~s** coppice [c] (= *tranchant*) [*épée, sabre*] edge; **il a reçu un coup de ~** he was hit with the sharp edge of the sword → **frapper** [d] (*Chir*) cystotomy [e] (*Hist = redevance*) tallage, taille [f] (*Min = galerie*) tunnel

taillé, e [taje] (*ptp de* **tailler**) ADJ [a] (= *bâti*) [*personne*] **il est ~ en athlète** he's built like an athlete, he has an athletic build [b] (= *destiné à*) [*personne*] **pour être/faire** cut out to be/do; **~ pour qch** cut out for sth [c] (= *coupé*) [*arbre*] pruned; [*haie*] clipped, trimmed; [*moustache, barbe*] trimmed; **crayon ~ en pointe** pencil sharpened to a point; **verre/ cristal ~** cut glass/crystal; **costume bien ~** well-cut suit; **il avait les cheveux ~s en brosse** he had a crew-cut; **visage ~ à la serpe** rough-hewn *ou* craggy features → **âge**

taille-crayon (*pl* **taille-crayons**) [tajkRɛjɔ̃] NM pencil sharpener

taille-douce (*pl* **tailles-douces**) [tajdus] NF [a] (*technique, tableau*) line-engraving; **gravure en ~** line-engraving

taille-haie (*pl* **taille-haies**) [tajɛ] NM hedge trimmer

tailler [taje] ▸conjug 1◂ [1] VT [a] (= *couper*) [+ *pierre précieuse*] to cut; [+ *pierre*] to cut, hew; [+ *bois*] to carve; [+ *verre*] to engrave; [+ *crayon*] to sharpen; [+ *arbre, vigne*] to prune, cut back; [+ *haie*] to trim, clip, cut; [+ *tissu*] to cut (out); [+ *barbe, cheveux*] to trim; **~ qch en pointe** to cut sth to a point; **bien taillé** [*haie*] neatly trimmed *ou* clipped; [*moustache*] neatly trimmed; [*crayon*] well-sharpened; **~ un if en cône** to trim *ou* clip a yew tree into a cone shape → **serpe**

[b] (= *confectionner*) [+ *vêtement*] to make; [+ *statue*] to carve; [+ *tartines*] to cut, slice; (*Alpinisme*) [+ *marche*] to cut; **il a un rôle taillé à sa mesure** *ou* **sur mesure** the role is tailor-made for him

[c] (*loc*) **~ une bavette*** to have a natter* (*Brit*) *ou* a rap* (*US*); († *ou littér*) **~ des croupières à qn** to make difficulties for sb; **~ une armée en pièces** to hack an army to pieces; **il s'est fait ~ en pièces par les journalistes** the journalists tore him to pieces; **il préférerait se faire ~ en pièces plutôt que de révéler son secret** he'd go through fire *ou* he'd suffer tortures rather than reveal his secret; **~ un costard** *ou* **une veste à qn*** to run sb down behind their back*; **attention ! tu vas te faire ~ un short*** careful! you'll get flattened!*; **~ la route*** to hit the road*

[2] VI [a] [*vêtement, marque*] **~ petit/grand** to be cut on the small/large side

[b] (= *couper*) **~ dans la chair** *ou* **dans le vif** to cut into the flesh; **~ dans les dépenses** to make cuts in expenditure

[3] **se tailler** VPR [a] (= *se couper*) **se ~ la moustache** to trim one's moustache; **elle s'est taillé une robe dans un coupon de taffetas** she made a dress for herself from a remnant of taffeta

[b] (= *se faire*) **se ~ une belle part de marché** to carve o.s. *ou* corner a large share of the market; **il s'est taillé une réputation d'honnêteté/ de manager** he has earned a reputation for honesty/as a manager; **se ~ un beau** *ou* **franc succès** to be a great success; **se ~ la part du lion** to take the lion's share; **se ~ un empire/ une place** to carve out an empire/a place for o.s.

[c] (‡ = *partir*) to beat it*, clear off*, split*; **taille-toi !** beat it!*, clear off!*; **allez, on se taille !** come on, let's split!*; **il est onze heures, je me taille** it's eleven o'clock, I'm off*; **j'ai envie de me ~ de cette boîte** I want to get out of this place

tailleur [tajœʀ] [1] NM [a] (= *couturier*) tailor; **~ pour dames** ladies' tailor [b] (= *costume*) (lady's) suit; **~-pantalon** trouser suit (*Brit*), pantsuit (*surtout US*); **un ~ Chanel** a Chanel suit [c] **en ~** [*assis*], [*s'asseoir*] cross-legged [2] COMP ▸ **tailleur de diamants** diamond-cutter ▸ **tailleur à façon** bespoke tailor (*Brit*), custom tailor (*US*) ▸ **tailleur de pierre(s)** stone-cutter ▸ **tailleur de verre** glass engraver ▸ **tailleur de vignes** vine pruner

taillis [taji] NM copse, coppice, thicket; **dans les ~** in the copse *ou* coppice *ou* thicket

tain [tɛ̃] NM [a] [*miroir*] silvering; **glace sans ~** two-way mirror [b] (*Tech = bain*) tin bath

T'ai-pei [tajpe] N Taipei, T'ai-pei

taire [tɛʀ] ▸conjug 54◂ [1] **se taire** VPR [a] (= *être silencieux*) [*personne*] to be silent *ou* quiet; (*littér*) [*nature, forêt*] to be silent, be still; [*vent*] to be still; [*bruit*] to disappear; **les élèves se taisaient** the pupils kept *ou* were quiet *ou* silent; **taisez-vous !** be quiet!, stop talking!; **ils ne voulaient pas se ~** they (just) wouldn't stop talking or be quiet *ou* keep quiet; **les dîneurs se sont tus** the diners stopped talking, the diners fell silent; **l'orchestre s'était tu** the orchestra had fallen silent *ou* was silent

[b] (= *s'abstenir de s'exprimer*) to keep quiet, remain silent; **dans ces cas il vaut mieux se ~** in these cases it's best to keep quiet *ou* to remain silent *ou* to say nothing; **il sait se ~** he

can keep a secret; **se ~ sur qch** to say nothing *ou* keep quiet about sth; **tais-toi !*** (= *ne m'en parle pas*) don't talk to me about it!

[2] VT [a] (= *passer sous silence*) [+ *fait, vérité, raisons*] to keep silent about; **une personne dont je tairai le nom** a person who shall be *ou* remain nameless; **~ la vérité, c'est déjà mentir** not telling the truth is as good as lying; **il a préféré ~ le reste de l'histoire** he preferred not to reveal the rest of the story

[b] (= *garder pour soi*) [+ *douleur, amertume*] to conceal, keep to o.s.; **son chagrin** to hide one's grief

[3] VI **faire ~** [+ *témoin gênant, opposition, récriminations*] to silence; [+ *craintes, désirs*] to suppress; [+ *scrupules, réticences*] to overcome; **fais ~ les enfants** make the children keep *ou* be quiet, make the children shut up*

taiseux, -euse [tɛzø, øz] (*Belg, Can*) [1] ADJ taciturn [2] NM,F taciturn person

Taiwan, Taïwan [tajwan] N Taiwan

taiwanais, e, taïwanais, e [tajwanɛ, ɛz] [1] ADJ Taiwanese [2] **Taiwanais(e)** ♦ **Taïwanais(e)** NM,F Taiwanese

tajine [taʒin] NM (= *récipient*) earthenware cooking pot; (= *plat cuisiné*) North African stew

talc [talk] NM [*toilette*] talc, talcum powder; (*Chim*) talc(um)

talé, e [tale] ADJ [*fruits*] bruised

talent¹ [talɑ̃] NM [a] (= *disposition, aptitude*) talent; **il a des ~s dans tous les domaines** he's multitalented; **un ~ littéraire** a literary talent; **il n'a pas le métier d'un professionnel mais un beau ~ d'amateur** he's not a professional but he's a talented amateur; (*hum*) **montrez-nous vos ~s*** show us what you can do; **décidément, vous avez tous les ~s !** what a talented young man (*ou* woman *etc*) you are!; **ses ~s d'imitateur/d'organisateur** his talents *ou* gifts as an impersonator/as an organizer

[b] **le ~** talent; **avoir du ~** to have talent, be talented; **avoir beaucoup de ~** to have a great deal of talent, be highly talented; **auteur de (grand) ~** (highly) talented author

[c] (= *personnes douées*) **~s** talent (*NonC*); **encourager les jeunes ~s** to encourage young talent; **faire appel aux ~s disponibles** to call on (all) the available talent

[d] (*iro*) **il a le ~ de se faire des ennemis** he has a talent *ou* gift for making enemies

talent² [talɑ̃] NM (= *monnaie*) talent

talentueusement [talɑ̃tɥøzmɑ̃] ADV with talent

talentueux, -euse [talɑ̃tɥø, øz] ADJ talented

taler [tale] ▸conjug 1◂ VT [+ *fruits*] to bruise

taleth [talet] NM = **talith**

talion [taljɔ̃] NM → **loi**

talisman [talismɑ̃] NM talisman

talismanique [talismanik] ADJ talismanic

talith [talit] NM tallith

talkie-walkie (*pl* **talkies-walkies**) [tokiwoki] NM walkie-talkie

talle [tal] NF (*Agr*) sucker

taller [tale] ▸conjug 1◂ VI (*Agr*) to sucker, put out suckers

Tallin [talin] N Tallin(n)

Talmud [talmyd] NM **le ~** the Talmud

talmudique [talmydik] ADJ Talmudic

talmudiste [talmydist] NM Talmudist

taloche [talɔʃ] NF [a] (* = *gifle*) cuff, clout* (*Brit*); **flanquer une ~ à qn** to cuff *ou* clout* (*Brit*) sb, give sb a cuff *ou* clout* (*Brit*) [b] (*Constr*) float

talocher [talɔʃe] ▸conjug 1◂ VT [a] (* = *gifler*) to cuff, clout* (*Brit*) [b] (*Constr*) to float

talon [talɔ̃] [1] NM [a] (*Anat*) [*cheval, chaussure*] heel; **être sur les ~s de qn** to be hot on sb's heels; **tourner les ~s** to turn on one's heel (and walk away) → **estomac, pivoter** [b] (= *croûton, bout*) [*jambon, fromage*] heel; [*pain*] crust, heel [c] [*pipe*] spur [d] [*chèque*] stub, counterfoil; [*carnet à souche*] stub [e] (*Cartes*) talon [f] (*Mus*) [*archet*] heel [g] [*ski*] tail [2] COMP ► **talon d'Achille** Achilles' heel ► **talons aiguilles** stiletto heels ► **talons bottier** medium heels ► **talons compensés** wedge heels ► **talons hauts** high heels; **des chaussures à ~s hauts** high-heeled shoes, high heels ► **« talon-minute »** "heel bar" ► **talons plats** flat heels; **chaussures à ~s plats** flat shoes, flatties* (*Brit*), flats* (*US*) ► **talon rouge** (*Hist*) aristocrat

talonnade [talɔnad] NF (*Rugby*) heel; (*Ftbl*) back-heel

talonnage [talɔnaʒ] NM heeling

talonner [talɔne] ►conjug 1◄ [1] VT [a] (= *suivre*) [+ *fugitifs, coureurs*] to follow (hot) on the heels of; **talonné par qn** hotly pursued by sb [b] (= *harceler*) [+ *débiteur, entrepreneur*] to hound; [*faim*] to gnaw at [c] (= *frapper du talon*) [+ *cheval*] to kick, spur on; (*Rugby*) **~ (le ballon)** to heel (the ball) [2] VI (*Naut*) to touch *ou* scrape the bottom with the keel; **le bateau talonne** the boat is touching the bottom

talonnette [talɔnɛt] NF [*chaussures*] heelpiece; [*pantalon*] binding

talonneur [talɔnœʀ] NM (*Rugby*) hooker

talquer [talke] ►conjug 1◄ VT to put talcum powder *ou* talc on

talqueux, -euse [talkø, øz] ADJ talcose

talus [taly] [1] NM [a] [*route, voie ferrée*] embankment; [*terrassement*] bank, embankment [b] (*Mil*) talus [2] COMP ► **talus continental** (*Géol*) continental slope ► **talus de déblai** excavation slope ► **talus d'éboulis** (*Géol*) scree ► **talus de remblai** embankment slope

talweg [talvɛg] NM = **thalweg**

tamanoir [tamanwaʀ] NM anteater

tamarin [tamaʀɛ̃] NM [a] (= *animal*) tamarin [b] (= *fruit*) tamarind [c] = **tamarinier** [d] = **tamaris**

tamarinier [tamaʀinje] NM tamarind (tree)

tamaris [tamaʀis], **tamarix** [tamaʀiks] NM tamarisk

tambouille* [tãbuj] NF (*péj = nourriture*) grub*; **faire la ~** to cook the grub*; **ça, c'est de la bonne ~ !** that's what I call food!

tambour [tãbuʀ] [1] NM [a] (= *instrument de musique*) drum → **roulement** [b] (= *musicien*) drummer [c] (*à broder*) embroidery hoop, tambour [d] (= *porte*) (*sas*) tambour; (*à tourniquet*) revolving door(s) [e] (= *cylindre*) [*machine à laver, treuil, roue de loterie*] drum; [*moulinet*] spool; [*montre*] barrel; **moulinet à ~ fixe** fixed-spool reel → **frein** [f] (*Archit*) [*colonne, coupole*] drum [g] (*loc*) **~ battant** briskly; **sans ~ ni trompette** without any fuss, unobtrusively; **il est parti sans ~ ni trompette** he left quietly, he slipped away unobtrusively [h] (*Ordin*) drum; **~ magnétique** magnetic drum [2] COMP ► **tambour de basque** tambourine ► **tambour d'église** tambour ► **tambour de frein** brake drum ► **tambour plat** side drum ► **tambour de ville** (*Hist*) ≈ town crier ► **tambour à timbre** snare drum

tambourin [tãbuʀɛ̃] NM (= *tambour de basque*) tambourine; (= *tambour haut et étroit*) tambourin

tambourinage [tãbuʀinaʒ] NM drumming (*NonC*)

tambourinaire [tãbuʀinɛʀ] NM (= *joueur de tambourin*) tambourin player; (*Hist* = *tambour de ville*) ≈ town crier

tambourinement [tãbuʀinmã] NM drumming (*NonC*)

tambouriner [tãbuʀine] ►conjug 1◄ [1] VI (*avec les doigts*) to drum; **~ contre** *ou* **à/sur** to drum (one's fingers) against *ou* at/on; **la pluie tambourinait sur le toit** the rain was beating down *ou* drumming on the roof; **~ à la porte**

to hammer at the door [2] VT [a] (= *jouer*) [+ *marche*] to drum *ou* beat out [b] († = *annoncer*) [+ *nouvelle, décret*] to cry (out); (*fig*) **~ une nouvelle** to shout a piece of news from the rooftops

tambour-major (*pl* **tambours-majors**) [tãbuʀmaʒɔʀ] NM drum major

Tamerlan [tamɛʀlã] NM Tamburlaine, Tamerlane

tamil [tamil] ADJ, NMF = **tamoul**

tamis [tami] NM (*gén*) sieve; (*à sable*) riddle, sifter; [*raquette*] (= *surface*) head; (= *cordage*) strings; **raquette grand ~** large-headed racket; **passer au ~** [+ *farine, plâtre*] to sieve, sift; [+ *sable*] to riddle, sift; (*fig*) [+ *campagne, bois*] to comb, search, scour; [+ *personnes*] to vet thoroughly; [+ *dossier*] to sift *ou* search through; **~ moléculaire** molecular sieve

tamisage [tamizaʒ] NM [*farine, plâtre*] sifting, sieving; [*sable*] riddling, sifting

Tamise [tamiz] NF **la ~** the Thames

tamiser [tamize] ►conjug 1◄ VT [a] [+ *farine, plâtre*] to sift, sieve; [+ *sable*] to riddle, sift; **farine tamisée** sifted flour [b] (= *voiler*) [+ *lumière*] to filter

tamoul, e [tamul] [1] ADJ Tamil [2] NM (*Ling*) Tamil [3] **Tamoul(e)** NM,F Tamil

tampon [tãpɔ̃] [1] NM [a] (*pour boucher*) (*gén*) stopper, plug; (*en bois*) plug, bung; (*en coton*) wad, plug; (*pour hémorragie, règles*) tampon; (*pour nettoyer une plaie*) swab; (*pour étendre un liquide, un vernis*) pad; **rouler qch en ~** to roll sth (up) into a ball → **vernir** [b] (*Menuiserie = cheville*) (wall-)plug [c] (*pour timbrer*) (= *instrument*) (rubber) stamp; (= *cachet*) stamp; **le ~ de la poste** the postmark; **apposer** *ou* **mettre un ~ sur qch** to stamp sth, put a stamp on sth [d] (*Rail, fig* = *amortisseur*) buffer; **servir de ~ entre deux personnes** to act as a buffer between two people [e] (*Chim*) **(solution) ~** buffer (solution) [2] ADJ INV **État/zone ~** buffer state/zone; (*Ordin*) **mémoire ~** buffer (memory) [3] COMP ► **tampon buvard** blotter ► **tampon encreur** inking-pad ► **tampon hygiénique** tampon ► **tampon Jex**® Brillo pad® ► **tampon à nettoyer** cleaning pad ► **tampon à récurer** scouring pad, scourer

tamponnement [tãpɔnmã] NM [a] (= *collision*) collision, crash [b] (*Méd*) [*plaie*] tamponade, tamponage [c] (*Tech*) [*mur*] plugging

tamponner [tãpɔne] ►conjug 1◄ [1] VT [a] (= *essuyer*) [+ *plaie*] to mop up, dab; [+ *yeux*] to dab (at); [+ *front*] to mop, dab; [+ *surface à sécher, à vernir*] to dab [b] (= *heurter*) [+ *train, véhicule*] to ram (into), crash into [c] (*avec un timbre*) [+ *document, lettre*] to stamp; **faire ~ un reçu** to have a receipt stamped [d] (*Tech* = *percer*) [+ *mur*] to plug, put (wall-)plugs in [2] **se tamponner** VPR [a] (= *s'essuyer*) [+ *yeux*] to dab; [+ *front*] to mop; **se ~ le visage avec un coton** to dab one's face with a piece of cotton wool [b] (= *se heurter*) (*accident*) to crash into each other; (*exprès*) to ram each other [c] (*loc*) **je m'en tamponne (le coquillard)** I don't give a damn*

tamponneuse [tãpɔnøz] ADJ F → **auto**

tamponnoir [tãpɔnwaʀ] NM masonry drill bit

tam-tam (*pl* **tam-tams**) [tamtam] NM [a] (= *tambour*) tomtom [b] (* = *battage, tapage*) fuss; **faire du ~ autour de** [+ *affaire, événement*] to make a lot of fuss *ou* a great ballyhoo* *ou* hullaballoo* about

tan [tã] NM tan (for tanning)

tancer [tãse] ►conjug 3◄ VT (*littér*) to scold, berate, rebuke

tanche [tãʃ] NF tench

tandem [tãdɛm] NM (= *bicyclette*) tandem; (*fig* = *duo*) pair, duo; **travailler en ~** to work in tandem

tandis [tãdi] ♦**tandis que** LOC CONJ (*simultanéité*) while, whilst (*frm*), as; (*pour marquer le contraste, l'opposition*) whereas, while, whilst (*frm*)

tandoori, tandouri [tãduʀi] NM tandoori; **poulet ~** tandoori chicken

tangage [tãgaʒ] NM [*navire, avion*] pitching; (*Naut*) **il y a du ~** the boat's pitching

Tanganyika [tãganika] NF Tanganyika; **le lac ~** Lake Tanganyika

tangence [tãʒãs] NF tangency

tangent, e [tãʒã, ãt] [1] ADJ [a] (*Géom*) tangent, tangential; **~ à** tangent *ou* tangential to [b] (* = *qui se fait de justesse*) close, touch-and-go (*attrib*); **on est passé mais c'était ~** we made it but it was a near *ou* close thing *ou* it was touch-and-go; **il était ~** he was a borderline case; **il a eu son examen mais c'était ~** he passed his exam by the skin of his teeth *ou* but it was a near thing [2] **tangente** NF (*Géom*) tangent; (*fig*) **prendre la ~e*** (= *partir*) to make off*, make o.s. scarce; (= *éluder*) to dodge the issue, wriggle out of it

tangentiel, -ielle [tãʒãsjɛl] ADJ tangential

tangentiellement [tãʒãsjɛlmã] ADV tangentially

Tanger [tãʒe] N Tangier(s)

tangerine [tãʒ(ə)ʀin] NF tangerine

tangible [tãʒibl] ADJ tangible

tangiblement [tãʒibləmã] ADV tangibly

tango [tãgo] [1] ADJ INV tangerine [2] NM [a] (= *danse*) tango; **danser le ~** to tango, do the tango [b] (= *boisson*) beer with grenadine [c] (= *couleur*) tangerine

tanguer [tãge] ►conjug 1◄ VI [a] [*navire, avion*] to pitch; **l'embarcation tanguait dangereusement** the boat pitched dangerously [b] (= *vaciller*) to reel; **tout tanguait autour de lui** (*gén*) everything around him was reeling; (*dans une pièce*) the room was spinning [c] (= *tituber*) to reel, sway; **des marins ivres tanguaient dans la rue** drunken sailors were reeling *ou* swaying along the street

tanière [tanjɛʀ] NF [*animal*] den, lair; [*malfaiteur*] lair; [*poète, solitaire*] (= *pièce*) den; (= *maison*) hideaway, retreat

tanin [tanɛ̃] NM tannin

tank [tɑ̃k] NM tank

tanker [tãkœʀ] NM tanker

tankiste [tãkist] NM member of a tank crew

tannage [tanaʒ] NM tanning

tannant, e [tanã, ãt] ADJ [a] (* = *ennuyeux*) maddening*, sickening*; **il est ~ avec ses remarques idiotes** his stupid remarks are enough to drive you mad* [b] (*Tech*) tanning

tannée* [tane] NF [a] (* = *coups, défaite*) hammering*; **(se) prendre une ~** to get hammered* [b] (*Tech*) (spent) tanbark

tanner [tane] ►conjug 1◄ VT [a] [+ *cuir*] to tan; [+ *visage*] to weather; **visage tanné** weather-beaten face; **~ le cuir à qn** to give sb a hammering*, tan sb's hide* [b] (* = *harceler*) **~ qn** to badger sb, pester sb; (= *ennuyer*) to drive sb mad*, drive sb up the wall*; **ça fait des semaines qu'il me tanne pour aller voir ce film** he's been badgering *ou* pestering me for weeks to go and see that film

tannerie [tanʀi] NF (= *endroit*) tannery; (= *activité*) tanning

tanneur [tanœʀ] NM tanner

tannin [tanɛ̃] NM = **tanin**

tannique [tanik] ADJ [*acide, vin*] tannic

tant [tã]
ADVERBE

Lorsque tant s'emploie dans des locutions figées commençant par un autre mot, telles que si tant est que, tous tant qu'ils sont etc, cherchez au premier mot.

a = tellement

● *avec verbe* so much; **il mange ~!** he eats so much! *ou* such a lot!; **il l'aime ~!** he loves him so much!; **j'ai ~ marché que je suis épuisé** I've walked so much that I'm exhausted; **tu m'en diras** *ou* **vous m'en direz ~!** really! ■ (*PROV*) **~ va la cruche à l'eau qu'à la fin elle se casse** people who play with fire must expect to get burnt

● *avec adjectif, participe* so; **il est rentré ~ le ciel était menaçant** he went home because the sky looked so overcast, the sky looked so overcast that he went home; **cet enfant ~ désiré** this child they had longed for so much; **le jour ~ attendu arriva** the long-awaited day arrived

● **tant de** + *nom ou pronom singulier* [+ *temps, eau, argent*] so much; [+ *gentillesse, mauvaise foi*] such, so much; **fait avec ~ d'habileté** done with so much *ou* such skill; **elle a ~ de sensibilité** she's so sensitive, she has such sensitivity; **il a ~ de mal** *ou* **de peine à se décider** he has so much *ou* such trouble making up his mind; **il gagne ~ et ~ d'argent qu'il ne sait pas quoi en faire** he earns so much money *ou* such a lot (of money) that he doesn't know what to do with it all; **il y avait ~ de brouillard qu'il n'est pas parti** it was so foggy *ou* there was so much fog about that he didn't go

● **tant de** + *nom ou pronom pluriel* [+ *choses, livres, arbres, gens*] so many; **~ de fois** so many times, so often; **comme ~ d'autres** like so many others; **~ de précautions semblaient suspectes** it seemed suspicious to take so many precautions; **des gens comme il y en a ~** ordinary people; **c'est une histoire comme il y en a ~** it's a familiar story

● **tant il est vrai que ...** since ..., as ...; **le dialogue sera difficile, ~ il est vrai que les attentats ont altéré les relations entre les deux pays** dialogue will not be easy, as *ou* since the bombings have damaged the relationship between the two countries; **il sera difficile de sauver l'entreprise, ~ il est vrai que sa situation financière est désastreuse** the financial situation is so disastrous that it will be difficult to save the company

b quantité non précisée so much; **gagner ~ par mois** to earn so much a month, earn such-and-such an amount a month; **il devrait donner ~ à l'un, ~ à l'autre** he should give so much to one, so much to the other; **~ pour cent** so many per cent

c comparaison = autant **les enfants, ~ filles que garçons** the children, both girls and boys *ou* girls as well as boys *ou* (both) girls and boys alike; **ses œuvres ~ politiques que lyriques** both his political and his poetic works; **il criait ~ qu'il pouvait** he shouted as loud as he could *ou* for all he was worth; (*littér*) **je n'aime rien ~ que l'odeur des sous-bois** there is nothing I love more than woodland smells; **ce n'est pas ~ leur maison qui me plaît que leur jardin** it's not so much their house that I like as their garden; **~ que ça?** that much?, as much as that?; **pas ~ que ça** not that much; **tu la paies ~ que ça?** do you pay her that much? *ou* as much as that?; **je ne l'ai pas vu ~ que ça pendant l'été** I didn't see him (all) that much during the summer

d expressions figées

● **tant bien que mal**: **la centrale nucléaire continue de fonctionner ~ bien que mal** the nuclear power station is still more or less operational; **ils résistent ~ bien que mal à l'influence de la publicité** they resist the influence of advertising as best they can; **il essaie, ~ bien que mal, d'égayer l'atmosphère** he's doing his best to liven things up; **la plupart survivent ~ bien que mal avec leurs économies** most of them manage to get by on what they've saved

● **tant et plus**: **il y en a ~ et plus** [*eau, argent*] there is a great deal; [*objets, personnes*] there are a great many; **il a protesté ~ et plus, mais**

sans résultat he protested for all he was worth *ou* over and over again but to no avail

◆ **tant et si bien que** so much so that, to such an extent that; **il a fait ~ et si bien qu'elle l'a quitté** he finally succeeded in making her leave him

◆ **tant mieux** (= *à la bonne heure*) good; (*avec une certaine réserve*) so much the better, that's fine; **~ mieux pour lui** good for him

◆ **tant pis** (= *ça ne fait rien*) never mind, (that's) too bad; (= *peu importe, qu'à cela ne tienne*) (that's just) too bad; **~ pis pour lui** (that's just) too bad for him; **je ne peux pas venir — ~ pis pour toi!** I can't come — tough!

◆ **tant qu'à** + *infinitif* : **~ qu'à faire, allons-y maintenant** we might *ou* may as well go now; **~ qu'à faire, tu aurais pu ranger la vaisselle** you could have put away the dishes while you were at it; **j'aurais préféré être mince, beau et riche, ~ qu'à faire** I would have preferred to have been slim, handsome and rich for that matter; **~ qu'à faire, je préfère payer tout de suite** (since I have to pay) I might *ou* may as well pay right away; **~ qu'à faire, faites-le bien** if you're going to do it, do it properly; **~ qu'à marcher, allons en forêt** if we have to walk *ou* if we are walking, let's go to the woods

◆ **tant s'en faut** not by a long way, far from it, not by a long shot *ou* chalk (*Brit*); **il n'a pas la gentillesse de son frère, ~ s'en faut** he's not nearly as *ou* he's nothing like as nice as his brother, he's not as nice as his brother — not by a long way *ou* shot

◆ **tant soit peu** : **s'il est ~ soit peu intelligent il saura s'en tirer** if he is (even) remotely intelligent *ou* if he has the slightest grain of intelligence he'll be able to get out of it; **si vous craignez ~ soit peu le froid, restez chez vous** if you feel the cold at all *ou* the slightest bit, stay at home; **il est un ~ soit peu prétentieux** he's ever so slightly *ou* he's just a little bit pretentious

◆ **tant que** (= *aussi longtemps que*) as long as; **~ qu'elle aura de la fièvre, elle restera au lit** while *ou* as long as she has a temperature she'll stay in bed; **~ que tu n'auras pas fini tes devoirs, tu resteras à la maison** you'll have to stay indoors until you've finished your homework; (**tout va bien**) **~ qu'on a la santé!*** (you're all right) as long as you've got your health! ■ (*PROV*) **~ qu'il y a de la vie, il y a de l'espoir** where there's life, there's hope (*PROV*)

(= *pendant que*) while; **~ que vous y êtes, achetez les deux volumes** while you are about it *ou* at it, buy both volumes; **~ que vous êtes ici, donnez-moi un coup de main*** seeing (as) *ou* since you're here, give me a hand; **je veux une moto — pourquoi pas une voiture ~ que tu y es!*** I want a motorbike — why not a car while you're at it!*

◆ **en tant que** (= *comme*) as; **en ~ qu'ami de la famille** as a family friend; **en ~ que tel** as such

tantale [tɑ̃tal] NM **a** (*Myth*) **Tantale** Tantalus → **supplice** **b** (*Chim*) tantalum

tante [tɑ̃t] NF (= *parente*) aunt, auntie*; (‡ = *homosexuel*) queer‡, fairy‡, fag‡ (*US*); **la ~ Marie** Aunt *ou* Auntie* Marie; **~ à héritage** rich (childless) aunt; († = *mont de piété*) **ma ~*** uncle's‡, the pawnshop

tantième [tɑ̃tjɛm] **1** NM (= *pourcentage*) percentage; (*d'une copropriété*) percentage share; (= *jeton de présence*) director's percentage of profits **2** ADJ **la ~ partie de qch** such (and such) a proportion of sth

tantine [tɑ̃tin] NF (*langage enfantin*) auntie*

tantinet* [tɑ̃tinɛ] NM **un ~ fatigant/ridicule** a tiny bit tiring/ridiculous; **un ~ de** a tiny bit of

tantôt [tɑ̃to] ADV **a** (= *cet après-midi*) this afternoon; (†† = *tout à l'heure*) shortly; **mardi ~** †* on Tuesday afternoon **b** (= *parfois*) **à pied, ~ en voiture** sometimes on foot, sometimes by car; (*littér*) **~ riant, ~ pleurant** now laughing, now crying

tantouse‡, tantouze‡ [tɑ̃tuz] NF (= *homosexuel*) queer‡, fairy‡, fag‡ (*US*)

tantrique [tɑ̃trik] ADJ Tantric

tantrisme [tɑ̃trism] NM Tantrism

Tanzanie [tɑ̃zani] NF Tanzania; **la République unie de ~** the United Republic of Tanzania

tanzanien, -ienne [tɑ̃zanjɛ̃, jɛn] **1** ADJ Tanzanian **2** **Tanzanien(ne)** NM,F Tanzanian

TAO [teao] NF (ABRÉV = **traduction assistée par ordinateur**) machine-aided translation

Tao [tao] NM Tao

taoïsme [taoism] NM Taoism

taoïste [taoist] ADJ, NM,F Taoist

taon [tɑ̃] NM horsefly, gadfly

tapage [tapaʒ] **1** NM **a** (= *vacarme*) row, racket; **faire du ~** to kick up* *ou* make a row, make a racket **b** (= *battage*) fuss, talk; **ils ont fait un tel ~ autour de cette affaire que ...** there was so much fuss made about *ou* so much talk over this affair that ... **2** COMP ▶ **tapage nocturne** (*Jur*) disturbance of the peace (*at night*); **porter plainte pour ~ nocturne** to make a complaint about the noise at night

tapageur, -euse [tapaʒœr, øz] ADJ **a** (= *bruyant*) [*enfant, hôtes*] noisy, rowdy **b** (= *peu discret, voyant*) [*publicité*] obtrusive; [*élégance, toilette*] flashy, loud, showy; [*luxe*] ostentatious; (= *qui fait scandale*) **liaison tapageuse** lurid affair

tapant, e [tapɑ̃, ɑ̃t] ADJ **à 8 heures ~(es)** at 8 (o'clock) sharp, on the stroke of 8, at 8 o'clock on the dot*

tapas [tapas] NFPL tapas

tape [tap] NF (= *coup*) slap; **il m'a donné une grande ~ dans le dos** he slapped me hard on the back; **petite ~ amicale** friendly little tap

tapé, e¹ [tape] (*ptp de* **taper**) ADJ **a** [*fruit*] = *talé*) bruised; * [*personne*] (= *marqué par l'âge*) wizened **b** (* = *fou*) cracked*, bonkers‡ (*Brit*)

tape-à-l'œil [tapalœj] (*péj*) **1** ADJ INV [+ *décoration, vêtements*] flashy, showy **2** NM INV **c'est du ~** it's all show

tapecul, tape-cul (*pl* **tape-culs**) [tapky] NM (= *voile*) jigger; (* = *balançoire*) see-saw; (* = *voiture*) rattletrap*, bone-shaker* (*Brit*); (* = *trot assis*) close trot; **faire du ~** to trot close

tapée²* [tape] NF **une ~ de** ◊ **des ~s de** loads of*, masses of*

tapement [tapmɑ̃] NM banging (*NonC*), banging noise

tapenade [tap(a)nad] NF tapenade (*savoury spread made with pureed olives*)

taper [tape] ▶ conjug 1 ◀ **1** VT **a** (= *battre*) [+ *tapis*] to beat; * [+ *enfant*] to slap, smack; (= *claquer*) [+ *porte*] to bang, slam; **~ le carton*** to have a game of cards

b (= *frapper*) **~ un coup/deux coups à la porte** to knock once/twice at the door, give a knock/two knocks at the door; (*péj*) **~ un air sur le piano** to bang *ou* thump out a tune on the piano

c (*à la machine, sur un ordinateur*) to type (out); **apprendre à ~ à la machine** to learn (how) to type; **elle tape bien** she types well, she's a good typist; **elle tape 60 mots à la minute** her typing speed is 60 words a minute; **tapé à la machine** typed, typewritten; **lettre tapée sur ordinateur** letter done on computer; (*sur Minitel*) **tapez 36 15, code ...** type in 36 15, code ...; **tape sur la touche « Retour »** hit *ou* press "Return"

d (* = *demander de l'argent*) **il tape tous ses collègues** he scrounges* *ou* cadges (*Brit*) off all his colleagues; **~ qn de 500 F** to scrounge* *ou* cadge (*Brit*) 500 francs off sb

2 VI **a** (= *frapper*) **~ sur un clou** to hit a nail; **~ sur la table** to bang *ou* rap on the table; (*péj*) **~ sur un piano** to bang *ou* thump away on a piano; **~ sur qn*** to thump sb; **~ sur la gueule de qn‡** to belt sb‡; (*fig*) **~ sur le ventre**

de *ou* **à qn*** to be a bit pushy with sb*, be overfamiliar with sb; **~ à la porte/au mur** to knock on the door/on the wall; **il tapait comme un sourd** he was thumping away for all he was worth; **il tape (dur), le salaud*** the bastard's got one hell of a punch‡; **~ dans un ballon** to kick a ball about *ou* around
b (* = *dire du mal de*) **~ sur qn** to run sb down*, have a go at sb* (behind their back)
c (* = *entamer*) **~ dans** [+ *provisions, caisse*] to dig into*
d (= *être fort, intense*) [*soleil*] to beat down; * [*vin*] to go to one's head; **ça tape fort aujourd'hui!*** the sun's beating down today, it's scorching hot today
e (‡ = *sentir mauvais*) to stink*, pong‡ (*Brit*)
f (*loc*) **~ des pieds** to stamp one's feet; **~ des mains** to clap one's hands; (*fig*) **se faire ~ sur les doigts*** to be rapped over the knuckles; **il a tapé à côté*** he was wide of the mark; **~ sur les nerfs** *ou* **le système de qn*** to get on sb's nerves *ou* wick* (*Brit*); **~ dans l'œil de qn*** to take sb's fancy; **elle lui a tapé dans l'œil*** he took a fancy to her, she took his fancy; **~ dans le tas*** (*bagarre*) to pitch into the crowd; (*repas*) to tuck in*, dig in* → **mille**[1]
3 **se taper** VPR **a** (‡ = *prendre*) [+ *repas*] to put away*; [+ *corvée*] to get landed with*; [+ *importun*] to get landed* *ou* lumbered* (*Brit*) with; **je me taperais bien un petit cognac** I could murder a brandy*, I'd love a brandy; **on s'est tapé les 10 km à pied** we did the whole 10 km on foot; (*sexuellement*) **se ~ qn*** to have it off with sb‡
b (*loc*) **se ~ sur les cuisses de contentement*** to slap one's thighs with satisfaction; **il y a de quoi se ~ le derrière*** *ou* **le cul‡ par terre** it's damned* *ou* bloody‡ (*Brit*) ridiculous; **c'est à se ~ la tête contre les murs** it's enough to drive you up the wall*; **se ~ la cloche*** to feed one's face‡, have a blow-out* (*Brit*) *ou* nosh-up* (*Brit*); **il peut toujours se ~**‡ he knows what he can do‡; **se ~ sur le ventre*** to be buddies* *ou* pals*; **il s'en tape complètement*** he couldn't give a damn‡

tapette [tapet] NF **a** (*petite tape*) little tap **b** (*pour tapis*) carpet beater; (*pour mouches*) flyswatter **c** (*pour souris*) mousetrap **d** (†* = *langue*) **il a une bonne ~** *ou* **une de ces ~** he's a real chatterbox* **e** (‡ = *homosexuel*) queer‡, poof‡ (*Brit*), fag‡ (*US*)

tapeur, -euse* [tapœʀ, øz] NM,F (= *emprunteur*) cadger*

tapin‡ [tapɛ̃] NM **a** **faire le ~** ‡ to be on the game‡ (*Brit*), hustle* (*US*) **b** († = *tambour*) drummer

tapiner‡ [tapine] ▸conjug 1◂ VI to be on the game‡ (*Brit*), hustle* (*US*)

tapineuse‡ [tapinøz] NF streetwalker, hustler* (*US*)

tapinois [tapinwa] NM **en ~** [*s'approcher*] stealthily, furtively; [*agir*] on the sly

tapioca [tapjɔka] NM tapioca

tapir [tapiʀ] NM (= *animal*) tapir

tapir (se) [tapiʀ] ▸conjug 2◂ VPR (= *se blottir*) to crouch; (= *se cacher*) to hide away; (= *s'embusquer*) to lurk; **maison tapie au fond de la vallée** house hidden away at the bottom of the valley

tapis [tapi] **1** NM **a** [*sol*] (*gén*) carpet; (*petit*) rug; (= *natte*) mat; (*dans un gymnase*) mat; **~ mécanique** machine-woven carpet; (*Gym*) **exercices au ~** floor exercises → **marchand** **b** [*meuble*] cloth; [*table de jeu*] baize (*NonC*), cloth, covering; **le ~ vert des tables de conférence** the green baize *ou* covering of conference tables; (*Casino*) **le ~ brûle** place your stakes **c** (*fig*) **~ de verdure/neige** carpet of greenery/snow **d** (*loc*) **aller au ~** to go down for the count; (*lit, fig*) **envoyer qn au ~** to floor sb; **mettre une entreprise au ~** to sink a company; **mettre** *ou*

porter sur le ~ [+ *affaire, question*] to lay on the table, bring up for discussion; **être/revenir sur le ~** to come up/come back up for discussion
2 COMP ► **tapis à bagages** (*dans un aéroport*) carousel ► **tapis de bain** bath mat ► **tapis de billard** baize (*NonC*) ► **tapis de bombes** carpet of bombs ► **tapis de chœur** altar carpet ► **tapis de couloir** runner ► **tapis de haute laine** long-pile carpet ► **tapis d'Orient** oriental carpet ► **tapis persan** Persian carpet ► **tapis de prière** prayer mat ► **tapis ras** short-pile carpet ► **tapis rouge** red carpet; **dérouler le ~ rouge** to roll out the red carpet ► **tapis roulant** (*pour colis, marchandises*) conveyor belt; (*pour piétons*) moving walkway, travelator; (*pour bagages*) carousel ► **tapis de selle** saddle-cloth ► **tapis de sol** (*Camping*) ground-sheet; (*Gym*) (*exercise*) mat ► **tapis de souris** (*Ordin*) mouse mat ► **tapis de table** table cover ► **tapis végétal** ground cover ► **tapis volant** magic *ou* flying carpet

tapis-brosse (*pl* **tapis-brosses**) [tapibʀɔs] NM doormat

tapissé, e [tapise] (*ptp de* **tapisser**) ADJ **~ de neige** [*sol*] carpeted with snow; [*sommet*] snow-clad, covered in snow; **mur ~ de photos/d'affiches** wall covered *ou* plastered with photos/with posters; **murs ~s de livres** walls lined with books; **~ de lierre/de mousse** ivy-/moss-clad; **carrosse ~ de velours** carriage with velvet upholstery

tapisser [tapise] ▸conjug 1◂ VT **a** [*personne*] (*de papier peint*) to (wall)paper; (*Culin*) [+ *plat, moule*] to line; **~ un mur/une pièce de tentures** to hang a wall/a room with drapes, cover a wall/a room with hangings; **~ un mur d'affiches/de photos** to plaster *ou* cover a wall with posters/with photos **b** [*tenture, papier*] to cover, line; [*mousse, neige, lierre*] to carpet, cover; [*Anat, Bot*] [*membranes, tissus*] to line; **le lierre tapissait le mur** the wall was covered with ivy

tapisserie [tapisʀi] NF **a** (= *tenture*) tapestry; (= *papier peint*) wallpaper; (= *activité*) tapestry-making; **faire ~** [*subalterne*] to stand on the sidelines; [*danseur*] to be a wallflower, sit out; **j'ai dû faire ~ pendant que ma femme dansait** I had to sit out while my wife was dancing **b** (= *broderie*) tapestry; (= *activité*) tapestry-work; **faire de la ~** to do tapestry work; **fauteuil recouvert de ~** tapestried armchair; **pantoufles en ~** embroidered slippers; **les ~s d'Aubusson/des Gobelins** the Aubusson/Gobelins tapestries → **point**[2]

tapissier, -ière [tapisje, jɛʀ] NM,F (= *fabricant*) tapestry-maker; (= *commerçant*) upholsterer; **~-décorateur** interior decorator

tapon† [tapɔ̃] NM **en ~** in a ball; **mettre en ~** to roll (up) into a ball

tapotement [tapɔtmɑ̃] NM (*sur la table*) tapping (*NonC*); (*sur le piano*) plonking (*NonC*)

tapoter [tapɔte] ▸conjug 1◂ **1** VT [+ *joue*] to pat; [+ *baromètre*] to tap; **~ sa cigarette pour faire tomber la cendre** to flick (the ash off) one's cigarette **2** VI **~ sur** *ou* **contre** to tap on; (*nerveusement*) to drum one's fingers on; **~ sur un clavier d'ordinateur** to tap away at a computer keyboard

tapuscrit [tapyskʀi] NM typescript

taquet [takɛ] NM (= *coin, cale*) wedge; (= *cheville, butée*) peg; (*pour enrouler un cordage*) cleat; [*machine à écrire*] stop; (*Ordin*) **~ de tabulation** tab stop

taquin, e [takɛ̃, in] ADJ [*caractère, personne*] teasing (*épith*); [*sourire*] mischievous, cheeky; **il est très ~** ◊ **c'est un ~** he's a real tease

taquiner [takine] ▸conjug 1◂ VT [*personne*] to tease; [*fait, douleur*] to bother, worry; (*hum*) **~ le goujon** to do a bit of fishing; (*hum*) **~ le cochonnet** to have a game of petanque; (*hum*) **~ la muse** to dabble in poetry, court the Muse

(*hum*) **ils n'arrêtent pas de se ~** they're always teasing each other

taquinerie [takinʀi] NF teasing (*NonC*); **agacé par ses ~s** annoyed by his teasing

tarabiscoté, e [taʀabiskɔte] ADJ [*meuble*] (over-)ornate, fussy; [*style*] involved, (over-)ornate, fussy; [*explication*] (overly) involved

tarabuster [taʀabyste] ▸conjug 1◂ VT [*personne*] to badger, pester; [*fait, idée*] to bother, worry; **il m'a tarabusté pour que j'y aille** he badgered *ou* pestered me to go

tarama [taʀama] NM taramasalata

taratata [taʀatata] EXCL (stuff and) nonsense!, rubbish!

taraud [taʀo] NM (*Tech*) tap

taraudage [taʀodaʒ] NM (*Tech*) tapping; **~ à la machine/à la main** machine-/hand-tapping

tarauder [taʀode] ▸conjug 1◂ VT (*Tech*) [+ *plaque, écrou*] to tap; [+ *vis, boulon*] to thread; (*fig*) [*insecte*] to bore into; [*remords, angoisse*] to pierce

taraudeur, -euse [taʀodœʀ, øz] **1** NM,F (= *ouvrier*) tapper **2** **taraudeuse** NF (= *machine*) tapping-machine; (à *fileter*) threader

Tarawa [taʀawa] N Tarawa

tard [taʀ] **1** ADV (*dans la journée, dans la saison*) late; **plus ~** later (on); **il est ~** it's late; **il se fait ~** it's getting late; **se coucher/travailler ~** to go to bed/work late; **travailler ~ dans la nuit** to work late (on) into the night; **il vint nous voir ~ dans la matinée/journée** he came to see us late in the morning *ou* in the late morning/late in the day; **il vous faut arriver jeudi au plus ~** you must come on Thursday at the latest; **c'est un peu ~ pour t'excuser** it's a bit late in the day to apologize, it's a bit late to apologize now; **pas plus ~ qu'hier** only yesterday; **pas plus ~ que la semaine dernière** just *ou* only last week, as recently as last week; **remettre qch à plus ~** to put sth off till later, postpone sth → **jamais, mieux, tôt**
2 NM **sur le ~** (*dans la vie*) late (on) in life, late in the day (*fig*); (*dans la journée*) late in the day

tarder [taʀde] ▸conjug 1◂ VI **a** (= *différer, traîner*) to delay; **~ à entreprendre qch** to put off *ou* delay starting sth; **ne tardez pas (à le faire)** don't delay, do it without delay; **~ en chemin** to loiter *ou* dawdle on the way; **sans (plus) ~** without (further) delay *ou* ado; **pourquoi tant ~?** why delay it *ou* put it off so long?
b (= *se faire attendre*) [*réaction, moment*] to be a long time coming; [*lettre*] to take a long time (coming), be a long time coming; **l'été tarde (à venir)** summer is a long time coming; **sa réponse a trop tardé** his reply took too long
c (*loc nég*) **ça ne va pas ~** it won't be long (coming); **ça n'a pas tardé** it wasn't long (in) coming; **leur réaction ne va pas ~** they won't take long to react; **il est 2 heures: ils ne vont pas ~** it's 2 o'clock — they won't be long (now); **ils n'ont pas tardé à être endettés** before long they were in debt, it wasn't long before long they were in debt; **il n'a pas tardé à s'en apercevoir** it didn't take him long to notice, he noticed soon enough; **ils n'ont pas tardé à réagir** ◊ **leur réaction n'a pas tardé** they didn't take long to react; **l'élève ne tarda pas à dépasser le maître** the pupil soon outstripped the teacher
d (= *sembler long*) **le temps** *ou* **le moment me tarde d'être en vacances** I can't wait to be on holiday
2 VB IMPERS (*littér*) **il me tarde de le revoir/que ces travaux soient finis** I am longing *ou* I can't wait to see him again/for this work to be finished

tardif, -ive [taʀdif, iv] ADJ (*gén*) late; [*regrets, remords*] belated; **rentrer à une heure tardive** to come home late at night; **cette prise de**

conscience a été tardive this realization was slow in coming

tardivement [taʀdivmɑ̃] ADV (= à une heure tardive) [rentrer] late; (= après coup, trop tard) [s'apercevoir] belatedly

tare [taʀ] NF [a] (= contrepoids) tare; **faire la ~** to allow for the tare [b] (= défaut) [personne, marchandise] defect (**de** in, of); [cheval] vice; [société, système] flaw (**de** in), defect (**de** of); (Méd) **~ héréditaire** hereditary defect; (hum) **ce n'est pas une ~!** it's not a sin! ou crime!

taré, e [taʀe] [1] ADJ [a] [enfant, animal] with a defect [b] (péj) [régime, politicien] tainted, corrupt; (= pervers) **il faut être ~ pour faire cela** you have to be sick to do that*; (= fou) **il est complètement ~, ce type!** that guy's completely crazy* ou out to lunch!* [2] NM,F (Méd) degenerate; (péj) **regardez-moi ce ~!** look at that cretin*

tarentelle [taʀɑ̃tɛl] NF tarantella

tarentule [taʀɑ̃tyl] NF tarantula

tarer [taʀe] ▸ conjug 1 ◂ VT (Comm) to tare, allow for the tare

targette [taʀʒɛt] NF (= verrou) bolt

targuer (se) [taʀge] ▸ conjug 1 ◂ VPR (= se vanter) **se targuer de qch** to boast about sth; **se targuer de ce que ...** to boast that ...; **se targuer d'avoir fait qch** to pride o.s. on having done sth; **il se targuant d'y parvenir aisément ...** boasting that he would easily manage it ...

targui, e [taʀgi] [1] ADJ Tuareg [2] **Targui(e)** NM,F Tuareg

tarière [taʀjɛʀ] NF [a] (Tech) (pour le bois) auger; (pour le sol) drill [b] (Zool) drill, ovipositor (SPÉC)

tarif [taʀif] [1] NM (= tableau) price list, tariff (Brit); (= prix) (gén) rate; (Transport) fare; **consulter/afficher le ~ des consommations** to check/put up the price list for drinks ou the bar tariff (Brit); **le ~ postal pour l'étranger/le ~ des taxis va augmenter** overseas postage rates/taxi fares are going up; **payé au ~ syndical** paid according to union rates, paid the union rate; **quels sont vos ~s?** (réparateur) how much do you charge?; (profession libérale) what are your fees?; **est-ce le ~ habituel?** is this the usual ou going rate?; **voyager à plein ~/à ~ réduit** to travel at full/at reduced fare; **billet plein ~/à ~ réduit** (Transport) full-fare/reduced-fare ticket; (Ciné, Théât) full-price/reduced-price ticket; **«~s réduits pour étudiants»** "special prices for students", "student concessions" (Brit); **envoyer une lettre au ~ lent** ou **économique** ≈ to send a letter second class, ≈ to send a letter by second-class mail ou post (Brit); (hum) **500 F d'amende/deux mois de prison, c'est le ~!** a 500-franc fine/two months' prison is what you get!

[2] COMP ▸ **tarif de base** (gén) standard ou basic rate; (Publicité) open rate, transient rate (US) ▸ **tarif dégressif** (gén) tapering charges; (Publicité) earned rate ▸ **tarif étudiant** (pour transports) student fare; (pour loisirs) student concession ▸ **tarif extérieur commun** (Europe) common external tariff ▸ **tarif jeunes** (pour transports) youth ou under-26 fare ▸ **tarif de nuit** night ou off-peak rate

tarifaire [taʀifɛʀ] ADJ tariff (épith)

tarifer [taʀife] ▸ conjug 1 ◂ VT to fix the price ou rate for; **marchandises tarifées** fixed-price goods

tarification [taʀifikasjɔ̃] NF (= action) setting ou fixing of prices (**de** for); (= prix) prices; **nouvelle ~ à compter du 23 mai** new prices as of 23rd May

tarin [taʀɛ̃] NM [a] (‡ = nez) nose, conk‡ (Brit), snoot‡ (US) [b] (= oiseau) siskin

tarir [taʀiʀ] ▸ conjug 2 ◂ [1] VI [a] [cours d'eau, puits, ressource] to run dry, dry up; [larmes] to dry (up); [pitié, conversation, imagination] to dry up [b] [personne] **il ne tarit pas sur ce sujet** he

can't stop talking about it, he's unstoppable* on that subject; **il ne tarit pas d'éloges sur elle** he never stops ou he can't stop singing her praises [2] VT (lit, fig) to dry up; (littér) **~ les larmes de qn** to dry sb's tears [3] **se tarir** VPR [source] to run dry, dry up; [rentrées d'argent, imagination] to dry up

tarissement [taʀismɑ̃] NM [cours d'eau, puits] drying up; [gisement, ressource] depletion; [commandes, débouchés, offre, demande] drying up

tarmac [taʀmak] NM (Aviat) tarmac

tarot [taʀo] NM (= jeu) tarot; (= paquet de cartes) tarot (pack)

Tarse [taʀs] NM Tarsus

tarse [taʀs] NM (Anat, Zool) tarsus

tarsien, -ienne [taʀsjɛ̃, jɛn] ADJ tarsal

Tartan® [taʀtɑ̃] NM (= revêtement) Tartan®; (= piste) tartan track

tartan [taʀtɑ̃] NM (= tissu) tartan

tartane [taʀtan] NF (Naut) tartan

tartare [taʀtaʀ] [1] ADJ [a] (Hist) Tartar [b] (Culin) **sauce ~** tartar(e) sauce → **steak** [2] NMF (Hist) **Tartare** Tartar

tarte [taʀt] [1] NF [a] (Culin) tart; **~ aux fruits/à la crème** fruit/cream tart; **~ aux pommes** apple tart; **~ Tatin** tarte Tatin, ≈ apple upside-down tart; (fig péj) **~ à la crème** (= formule vide) pet theme; (= comique, comédie) slapstick (comedy); **c'est pas de la ~**‡ it's no joke*, it's no easy matter [b] (‡ = gifle) clout, clip round the ear [2] ADJ INV * (= laid) [personne] plain-looking; [chaussures, vêtement] tacky*, naff* (Brit); (= bête) stupid, daft* (Brit); **j'ai l'air ~ dans cette robe** I look stupid in this dress

tartelette [taʀtəlɛt] NF tartlet, tart

Tartempion* [taʀtɑ̃pjɔ̃] NM thingumabob*, so-and-so*, what's-his (ou -her)-name; **un ~ quelconque** someone or other

tartignol(l)e* [taʀtiɲɔl] ADJ [personne, film] stupid, daft* (Brit); [vêtement, chaussures] tacky*

tartine [taʀtin] NF [a] (= tranche) slice ou piece of bread; (beurrée) slice of bread and butter; (à la confiture) slice of bread and jam; **le matin, on mange des ~s** in the morning we have bread and butter; **tu as déjà mangé trois ~s, ça suffit** you've already had three slices ou three pieces of bread, that's enough; **couper des tranches de pain pour faire des ~s** to cut (slices of) bread for buttering; **~ au ou de miel** slice ou piece of bread and honey; **~ grillée et beurrée** piece of toast and butter [b] (* fig = lettre, article) **il en a mis une ~** he wrote reams; **il y a une ~ dans le journal à propos de ...** there's a great spread in the paper about ...

tartiner [taʀtine] ▸ conjug 1 ◂ VT [+ pain] to spread (**de** with); [+ beurre] to spread; **pâté de foie/fromage à ~** liver/cheese spread; **pâte à ~** spread; **~ du pain de beurre** to butter bread; (fig) **il en a tartiné plusieurs pages*** he went on about it for several pages

tartre [taʀtʀ] NM [dents, tonneau] tartar, scale; [chaudière, bouilloire] scale, fur (Brit)

tartrique [taʀtʀik] ADJ **acide ~** tartaric acid

tartu(f)fe [taʀtyf] NM (sanctimonious) hypocrite [2] ADJ hypocritical; **il est un peu ~** he's something of a hypocrite

tartu(f)ferie [taʀtyfʀi] NF hypocrisy

Tarzan [taʀzɑ̃] NM Tarzan; (* fig) muscleman

tas [tɑ] [1] NM [a] (= amas) pile, heap; **mettre en ~** to make a pile of, put into a heap, heap ou pile up [b] **un** ou **des ~ de*** (= beaucoup de) loads of*, heaps of*, lots of; **il connaît un ~ de choses/gens** he knows loads* ou heaps* ou lots of things/people; **il y avait tout un ~ de gens** there was a whole load* of people there; **j'ai appris des ~ de choses sur lui** I found out a lot about him; **il m'a raconté un ~ de mensonges** he told me a pack of lies; **~ de**

crétins!* you load ou bunch of idiots!* [c] (* : loc) **tirer dans le ~** to fire into the crowd; **foncer dans le ~** to charge in; **dans le ~, on en trouvera bien un qui sache conduire** we're bound to find ONE who can drive; **dans le ~, tu trouveras bien un stylo qui marche** you're bound to find ONE pen that works; **j'ai acheté des cerises, tape** ou **pioche dans le ~** I've bought some cherries so dig in* ou tuck in* ou help yourself [d] (= par la pratique) **apprendre un métier sur le ~** to learn a trade on the job ou as one goes along; **il a appris/s'est formé sur le ~** he learned/was trained on the job; **formation sur le ~** on-the-job training → **grève**

[2] COMP ▸ **tas de boue*** (= voiture) heap*, wreck*, banger* (Brit) ▸ **tas de charge** (Archit) tas de charge ▸ **tas de ferraille** scrapheap; **cette voiture/ce vélo, c'est un vrai ~ de ferraille!*** that car/that bike's only fit for the scrapheap ▸ **tas de fumier** dung ou manure heap ▸ **tas d'ordures** rubbish (Brit) ou garbage (US) heap

Tasmanie [tasmani] NF Tasmania

tasmanien, -ienne [tasmanjɛ̃, jɛn] [1] ADJ Tasmanian [2] **Tasmanien(ne)** NM,F Tasmanian

Tasse [tɑs] NM **le ~** Tasso

tasse [tɑs] NF cup; **~ de porcelaine** china cup; **~ à thé** teacup; **~ à café** coffee cup; **~ de thé** cup of tea; (hum) **ce n'est pas ma ~ de thé** it's not my cup of tea → **boire**

tassé, e [tɑse] (ptp de **tasser**) ADJ [a] (= affaissé) [façade, mur] that has settled ou sunk ou subsided; [vieillard] shrunken; **~ sur sa chaise** slumped on his chair [b] (= serrés) **~s** [spectateurs, passagers] packed (tight) [c] **bien ~*** (= fort) [whisky] stiff (épith); (= bien rempli) [verre] well-filled, full to the brim (attrib); **café bien ~** good strong coffee; **trois kilos bien ~s** a good three kilos; **il a 50 ans bien ~s** he's well into his fifties, he's well over fifty

tasseau (pl **tasseaux**) [tɑso] NM (= morceau de bois) piece ou length of wood; (= support) bracket

tassement [tɑsmɑ̃] NM [a] [sol, neige] packing down [b] [mur, terrain] settling, subsidence; **~ de la colonne (vertébrale)** compression of the spinal column [c] (= diminution) **le ~ des voix en faveur du candidat** the drop ou fall-off in votes for the candidate; **un ~ de l'activité économique** a downturn ou a slowing down in economic activity

tasser [tɑse] ▸ conjug 1 ◂ [1] VT [a] (= comprimer) [+ sol, neige] to pack down, tamp down; [+ foin, paille] to pack; **~ des vêtements dans une valise** to cram clothes into a suitcase; **~ le contenu d'une valise** to push down the contents of a case; **~ le tabac dans sa pipe** to pack ou tamp down the tobacco in one's pipe; **~ des prisonniers dans un camion** to cram ou pack prisoners into a truck [b] (Sport) [+ concurrent] to box in

[2] **se tasser** VPR [a] (= s'affaisser) [façade, mur, terrain] to sink, subside; [vieillard, corps] to shrink; [demande] to slow down [b] (= se serrer) to bunch up; **on s'est tassé à dix dans la voiture** ten of us crammed into the car; **tassez-vous, il y a encore de la place** bunch ou squeeze up, there's still room [c] (= s'arranger) to settle down; **ne vous en faites pas, ça va se ~** don't worry — things will settle down ou iron themselves out* [d] (‡ = engloutir) [+ petits fours, boissons] to down*, get through*

taste-vin [tastəvɛ̃] NM INV (wine-)tasting cup

tata [tata] NF (langage enfantin = tante) auntie*; (‡ = homosexuel) queer‡, fairy‡, poof‡ (Brit), fag‡ (US)

tatami [tatami] NM tatami

tatane* [tatan] NF shoe

tatar, e [tataʀ] **1** ADJ Ta(r)tar **2** NM (Ling) Ta(r)tar **3** **Tatar(e)** NM,F Ta(r)tar

tâter [tate] ▸conjug 1◂ **1** VT **a** (= palper) [+ objet, étoffe, pouls] to feel; **~ qch du bout des doigts** to feel ou explore sth with one's fingertips; **marcher en tâtant les murs** to feel ou grope one's way along the walls
b (= sonder) [+ adversaire, concurrent] to try (out); **~ l'opinion** to sound ou test out opinion; (fig) **~ le terrain** to find out how the land lies, put out feelers, find out the lie (Brit) ou lay (US) of the land
2 **tâter de** VT INDIR **a** (†, littér = goûter à) [+ mets] to taste, try
b (= essayer, passer par) to sample, try out; **~ de la prison** to sample prison life, have a taste of prison; **il a tâté de tous les métiers** he's had a go at* ou he's tried his hand at lots of jobs
3 **se tâter** VPR **a** (après une chute) to feel o.s. (for injuries); (pensant avoir perdu qch) to feel one's pocket(s); **il se releva, se tâta: rien de cassé** he got up and felt himself but there was nothing broken
b (* = hésiter) to be in (Brit) ou of (US) two minds; **viendras-tu? — je ne sais pas, je me tâte** are you coming? — I don't know, I haven't made up my mind

tâte-vin [tatvɛ̃] NM INV = **taste-vin**

tati(e) [tati] NF (langage enfantin) auntie*

tatillon, -onne [tatijɔ̃, ɔn] ADJ finicky, pernickety (Brit), persnickety (US); **il est ~ ◊ c'est un ~** he's very finicky ou pernickety (Brit)

tâtonnant, e [tatɔnɑ̃, ɑ̃t] ADJ [geste, main] groping (épith); [style] hesitant; **leurs recherches étaient ~es** they were feeling their way in their research

tâtonnement [tatɔnmɑ̃] NM (gén pl = essai) trial and error (NonC), experimentation (NonC); **après bien des ~s** after a lot of trial and error; **procéder par ~(s)** to proceed by trial and error; **les premiers ~s d'une technique** the first tentative steps in a new technique

tâtonner [tatɔne] ▸conjug 1◂ VI **a** (pour se diriger) to grope ou feel one's way (along), grope along; (pour trouver qch) to grope ou feel around ou about **b** (fig = essayer) to grope around; (par méthode) to proceed by trial and error

tâtons [tatɔ̃] **à tâtons** LOC ADV **avancer à ~** (lit) to grope along, grope ou feel one's way along; (fig) to feel one's way along; (lit, fig) **chercher qch à ~** to grope ou feel around for sth

tatou [tatu] NM armadillo

tatouage [tatwaʒ] NM (= action) tattooing; (= dessin) tattoo; **son dos est couvert de ~s** his back is covered with ou in tattoos

tatouer [tatwe] ▸conjug 1◂ VT to tattoo; **se faire ~ le dos** to have one's back tattooed; **mon chat est tatoué à l'oreille** my cat has a tattoo in its ear (for identification)

tatoueur, -euse [tatwœʀ, øz] NM,F tattooer

tau [to] NM INV **a** (= lettre grecque) tau **b** (Hér) tau cross, Saint Anthony's cross

taudis [todi] NM **a** (= logement) hovel; (pl) (Admin) slums; (fig: en désordre) **ta chambre est un vrai ~** your room's a real pigsty

taulard, -arde: [tolaʀ, aʀd] NM,F convict, con:

taule: [tol] NF **a** (= prison) jail, clink:, nick: (Brit); **être en ~** to be inside*, be in the nick: (Brit); **aller en ~** to go down*, get banged up: (Brit); **mettre ou foutre: qn en ~** to put sb in jail; **il a fait de la ~** he's done time ou a stretch*, he's been inside*; **il a eu cinq ans de ~** he's been given a five-year stretch* ou five years in the nick: (Brit) **b** (= chambre) room

taulier, -ière: [tolje, jɛʀ] NM,F (hotel) boss*

taupe [top] NF **a** (= animal, fig = espion) mole; (= fourrure) moleskin; (fig péj) **une vieille ~** an old crone ou hag, an old bag: → **myope**
b (arg Scol = classe) advanced maths class preparing for the Grandes Écoles

taupin [topɛ̃] NM **a** (= animal) click beetle, elaterida (SPÉC) **b** (arg Scol) maths student preparing for the Grandes Écoles

taupinière [topinjɛʀ] NF (= tas) molehill; (= galeries, terrier) mole tunnel; (fig péj = immeuble, bureaux) rabbit warren

taureau (pl **taureaux**) [tɔʀo] NM **a** (= animal) bull; **~ de combat** fighting bull; **il avait une force de ~** he was as strong as an ox; **une encolure ou un cou de ~** a bull neck; **prendre le ~ par les cornes** to take the bull by the horns **b** (Astron) **le Taureau** Taurus; **il est Taureau ◊ il est (du signe) du Taureau** he's (a) Taurus → **course**

taurillon [tɔʀijɔ̃] NM bull-calf

taurin, e [tɔʀɛ̃, in] ADJ bullfighting (épith)

tauromachie [tɔʀɔmaʃi] NF bullfighting, tauromachy (SPÉC)

tauromachique [tɔʀɔmaʃik] ADJ bullfighting (épith)

tautologie [totɔlɔʒi] NF tautology

tautologique [totɔlɔʒik] ADJ tautological

taux [to] NM **a** (Fin) rate; **~ actuariel (brut)** annual percentage rate; **~ de base bancaire** minimum ou base ou prime (US) lending rate; **~ de change** exchange rate, rate of exchange; **~ court/moyen/long** short-term/medium-term/long-term rate; **~ de croissance** growth rate; **~ d'escompte** discount rate; **~ d'intérêt** interest rate, rate of interest; **~ officiel d'escompte** bank rate; **~ de prêt** lending rate; **~ de TVA** VAT rate; **prêt à ~ zéro** interest-free loan
b (Stat) rate; **~ de natalité/mortalité** birth/death ou mortality rate; **~ de chômage** unemployment rate; **~ de réussite** (à un examen) pass rate; (TV) **~ d'audience** audience figures; (Radio) **~ d'écoute** audience figures; (Ciné, Théât) **~ de fréquentation** attendance ou audience figures
c (Méd, Sci = niveau, degré) [cholestérol, sucre] level; **~ de pollution/radioactivité** level of pollution/radioactivity, pollution/radioactivity level; **~ d'invalidité** degree of disability; **~ de compression** [moteur] compression ratio

tavelé, e [tav(ə)le] (ptp de **taveler**) ADJ [fruit] marked; **visage ~ de taches de son** face covered in freckles; **visage ~ par la petite vérole** pockmarked face, face pitted with pockmarks

taveler [tav(ə)le] ▸conjug 4◂ **1** VT [+ fruit] to mark **2** **se taveler** VPR [fruit] to become marked

tavelure [tav(ə)lyʀ] NF mark

taverne [tavɛʀn] NF (Hist) inn, tavern; (Can) tavern, beer parlor (Can)

tavernier, -ière [tavɛʀnje, jɛʀ] NM,F (Hist, hum) innkeeper

taxable [taksabl] ADJ (gén) taxable; (à la douane) liable to duty, dutiable

taxateur, -trice [taksatœʀ, tʀis] NM,F (Admin) taxer; **(juge) ~** taxing master

taxation [taksasjɔ̃] NF **a** (= imposition) [marchandise, service, particuliers] taxing, taxation; **seuil de ~** tax threshold **b** (Admin, Comm) [valeur] fixing (the rate); [marchandise] fixing the price; (Jur) [dépens] taxation; **~ d'office** estimation of tax(es)

taxe [taks] **1** NF **a** (= impôt, redevance) tax; (à la douane) duty; **~s locales/municipales** local/municipal taxes; **toutes ~s comprises** inclusive of tax; **hors ~(s)** [boutique, article] duty-free; (sur facture) exclusive of VAT; [prix] before tax (attrib) **b** (Admin, Comm = tarif) statutory price; **vendre des marchandises à la ~/plus cher que la ~** to sell goods at/for more than the statutory price **c** (Jur) [dépens] taxation, assessment **2** COMP ▸ **taxes d'aéro-**port** airport tax(es) ▸ **taxe d'apprentissage** apprenticeship tax (paid by French employers to finance apprenticeships) ▸ **taxe d'habitation** local tax paid by residents, ≈ council tax (Brit) ▸ **taxe professionnelle** local tax on businesses, ≈ business rate (Brit) ▸ **taxe de raccordement** (Télec) connection fee ▸ **taxe de séjour** tourist tax ▸ **taxe à ou sur la valeur ajoutée** ≈ sales tax, value-added tax (Brit)

taxer [takse] ▸conjug 1◂ VT **a** (= imposer) [+ marchandises, service] to put ou impose a tax on, tax; (à la douane) to impose ou put duty on; [+ personne, entreprise] to tax; **produits taxés à 5,5%** products taxed at 5.5%; **~ qn d'office** to assess sb for tax ou taxation (purposes) **b** (Admin, Comm) [+ valeur] to fix (the rate of); [+ marchandise] to fix the price of; (Jur) [+ dépens] to tax, assess **c** (: = voler) to pinch*, nick: (Brit); **il l'a taxé au supermarché** he pinched* ou nicked: (Brit) it from the supermarket **d** (: = prendre) **je peux te ~ une cigarette?** can I pinch a cigarette?; **il m'a taxé 100 F** he got 100 francs out of me* **e** **~ qn de qch** (= le qualifier de qch) to call sb sth; (= l'accuser de qch) to accuse sb of sth, tax sb with sth (frm); **une méthode que l'on a taxée de charlatanisme** a method which has been referred to as charlatanism; **on le taxe d'avarice** he's accused of miserliness ou of being a miser

taxi [taksi] NM **a** (= voiture) taxi, (taxi)cab; **~-brousse** bush taxi; (en apposition) **bateau-/vélo-~** boat/bicycle taxi ~ **chauffeur**, station **b** (: = chauffeur) cabby* (Brit), taxi ou cab driver; **elle fait (le) ~** she's a cabby*, she's a taxi ou cab driver; (fig) **j'en ai assez de faire le ~** I'm fed up* driving everyone around

taxidermie [taksidɛʀmi] NF taxidermy

taxidermiste [taksidɛʀmist] NMF taxidermist

taxi-girl (pl **taxi-girls**) [taksigœʀl] NF (= danseuse) taxigirl

taximètre [taksimɛtʀ] NM (taxi)meter

taxinomie [taksinɔmi] NF taxonomy

taxinomique [taksinɔmik] ADJ taxonomic(al)

taxinomiste [taksinɔmist] NMF taxonomist

taxiphone® [taksifɔn] NM payphone, public (tele)phone

taxiway [taksiwe] NM taxiway

taxonomie [taksɔnɔmi] NF = **taxinomie**

taxonomique [taksɔnɔmik] ADJ = **taxinomique**

taylorisation [tɛlɔʀizasjɔ̃] NF Taylorization

tayloriser [tɛlɔʀize] ▸conjug 1◂ VT [+ production] to Taylorize; **usine taylorisée** mass production factory

taylorisme [tɛlɔʀism] NM Taylorism

TB (ABRÉV = **très bien**) VG

TBB [tebebe] NM (ABRÉV = **taux de base bancaire**) → **taux**

Tbilissi [tbilisi] N Tbilisi

Tchad [tʃad] NM **le ~** Chad; **le lac ~** Lake Chad

tchadien, -ienne [tʃadjɛ̃, jɛn] **1** ADJ Chad **2** **Tchadien(ne)** NM,F Chad

tchador [tʃadɔʀ] NM chador

tchao [tʃao] EXCL bye!, ciao!, cheerio! (Brit)

tchatche: [tʃatʃ] NF (gén) talk; (péj) yacking*; **il a une de ces ~s!** he's got the gift of the gab!*

tchatcher: [tʃatʃe] ▸conjug 1◂ VI (péj) to yack*; **il ne fait que ~** he never stops yacking*, all he does is yak yak yak*

tchécoslovaque [tʃekɔslɔvak] **1** ADJ Czechoslovak(ian) **2** **Tchécoslovaque** NMF Czechoslovakian

Tchécoslovaquie [tʃekɔslɔvaki] NF Czechoslovakia

Tchekhov [tʃekɔv] NM Chek(h)ov

tchèque [tʃɛk] **1** ADJ Czech; **la République ~**

the Czech Republic [2] NM (Ling) Czech [3] **Tchèque** NMF Czech

Tchernobyl [tʃɛrnɔbil] N Chernobyl

tchétchène [tʃetʃɛn] [1] ADJ Chechen [2] **Tchétchène** NMF Chechen

Tchétchénie [tʃetʃeni] NF Chechnya

tchin(-tchin) [tʃin(tʃin)] EXCL cheers!

TD [tede] NM (ABRÉV = **travaux dirigés**) (Univ) → **travail**¹

TDF [tedeef] NF (ABRÉV = **Télédiffusion de France**) ≈ IBA (Brit), ≈ FCC (US)

te [tə] PRON PERS [a] (objet direct ou indirect) you; **te l'a-t-il dit?** did he tell you?; **t'en a-t-il parlé?** did he speak to you about it? **b** (réfléchi) yourself; **si tu te poses des questions** if you ask yourself questions; **tu t'es fait mal?** did you hurt yourself?; (souvent non traduit) **comment te sens-tu?** how do you feel?; **tu devrais te doucher** you should have a shower; **va te laver les dents/les mains** go and brush your teeth/wash your hands

té¹ [te] NM (= règle) T-square; (= ferrure) T(-shaped) bracket; **fer en ~** T-shaped iron

té² [te] EXCL (dial) well! well!, my!

TEC [tɛase] NF (ABRÉV = **tonne équivalent charbon**) TCE

technétium [tɛknesjɔm] NM technetium

technicien, -ienne [tɛknisjɛ̃, jɛn] NM,F technician; **il est ~ en électronique** he's an electronics engineer; (Admin) **~ de surface** cleaning operative; **~ de (la) télévision** television technician; **c'est un ~ de la politique/finance** he's a political/financial expert ou wizard

technicité [tɛknisite] NF [recherche, sujet, langage] technical nature; [personne] technical skill; **produit de haute ~** technically advanced ou high-tech product

technico-commercial, e (mpl **technico-commerciaux**) [tɛknikokɔmɛrsjal, jo] ADJ, NM,F (**agent**) ~ technical salesman; (**ingénieur**) ~ sales engineer

Technicolor® [tɛknikɔlɔr] NM Technicolor®; **film en ~** Technicolor film, film in Technicolor

technique [tɛknik] [1] ADJ technical → **contrôle**, **escale**, **incident** [2] NF [a] (méthode) technique; **il n'a pas la (bonne) ~*** he hasn't got the knack* ou the right technique; **c'est toute une ~!** it's quite an art!; **manquer de ~** to lack technique [b] (= aire de la connaissance) **la ~** technology [3] NM (enseignement) **le ~** technical education, industrial arts (US); **il est professeur dans le ~** he's a technical teacher

techniquement [tɛknikmɑ̃] ADV technically

techno¹ [tɛkno] ADJ, NF (Mus) techno; **la (musique) ~** techno (music)

techno²* [tɛkno] NF ABRÉV = **technologie**

technocrate [tɛknɔkrat] NMF technocrat

technocratie [tɛknɔkrasi] NF technocracy

technocratique [tɛknɔkratik] ADJ technocratic

technocratisme [tɛknɔkratism] NM [gestionnaire] technocratic attitude; [institution] technocratic ethos

technologie [tɛknɔlɔʒi] NF (gén) technology; (Scol) subject area covering basic technological skills taught in French schools; **~ de pointe** ou **avancée** leading-edge ou advanced technology; **~ de l'information** information technology; **la haute ~** high technology; **~ des systèmes automatisés** automated systems technology

technologique [tɛknɔlɔʒik] ADJ technological; **révolution ~** technological revolution

technologiquement [tɛknɔlɔʒikmɑ̃] ADV technologically

technologue [tɛknɔlɔg] NMF technologist

technophobe [tɛknɔfɔb] NMF technophobe

technopole [tɛknɔpɔl] NF town with high-tech industrial research and development facilities

technopôle [tɛknopol] NM science and technology park (with research facilities)

technostructure [tɛknostryktyr] NF technostructure

teck [tɛk] NM teak

teckel [tekɛl] NM dachshund

tectonique [tɛktɔnik] [1] ADJ tectonic [2] NF tectonics sg; **~ des plaques** plate tectonics

Te Deum [tedeɔm] NM INV Te Deum

tee [ti] NM tee; **partir du ~** to tee off

tee-shirt [tiʃœrt] NM T-shirt, tee shirt

Téflon® [tefl5] NM Teflon®

Tegucigalpa [tegusigalpa] N Tegucigalpa

tégument [tegymɑ̃] NM (Bot, Zool) (in)tegument

Téhéran [teerɑ̃] N Teheran

teigne [tɛɲ] NF [a] (Zool) moth, tinea (SPÉC) [b] (Méd) ringworm, tinea (SPÉC) [c] (fig péj) (= homme) bastard*‡, swine‡ (Brit); (= femme) shrew, vixen; **mauvais** ou **méchant comme une ~** as nasty as anything

teigneux, -euse [tɛɲø, øz] ADJ (Méd) suffering from ringworm; **il est ~** (lit) he has ou is suffering from ringworm; (péj = pouilleux) he's scabby*; (péj = acariâtre) he's very cantankerous, he's real ornery* (US)

teindre [tɛ̃dr] ▶conjug 52◀ [1] VT [+ vêtement, cheveux] to dye; (littér) to tint, tinge [2] **se teindre** VPR [a] **se ~ (les cheveux)** to dye one's hair; **se ~ la barbe/la moustache** to dye one's beard/one's moustache [b] (littér = se colorer) **les montagnes se teignaient de pourpre** the mountains took on a purple hue ou tinge ou tint, the mountains were tinged with purple

teint¹ [tɛ̃] NM [a] (= couleur de peau) (permanent) complexion, colouring (Brit), coloring (US); (momentané) colour (Brit), color (US); **avoir le ~ frais** to be looking well; **~ de rose/de porcelaine** rosy/porcelain complexion [b] (= couleur d'un tissu) **grand ~** [couleur] fast; [tissu] colourfast (Brit), colorfast (US); **bon ~** [couleur] fast; [syndicaliste] staunch, dyed-in-the-wool → **fond**

teint², **e**¹ [tɛ̃, tɛ̃t] (ptp de **teindre**) ADJ [cheveux, laine] dyed; (péj) **elle est ~e** her hair is dyed, she dyes her hair

teinte² [tɛ̃t] NF (= nuance) shade, hue, tint; (= couleur) colour (Brit), color (US); (fig) tinge, hint; **pull aux ~s vives** brightly-coloured sweater; **avec une ~ de tristesse dans la voix** with a tinge ou hint of sadness in his voice

teinté, e [tɛ̃te] (ptp de **teinter**) ADJ [bois] stained; [verre] tinted; **crème ~e** tinted day cream; **table ~e acajou** mahogany-stained table; **blanc ~ de rose** white with a hint of pink; **discours ~ de puritanisme** speech tinged with puritanism

teinter [tɛ̃te] ▶conjug 1◀ [1] VT [+ papier, verre] to tint; [+ meuble, bois] to stain; **un peu d'eau teintée de vin** a little water with a hint of wine ou just coloured with wine [2] **se teinter** VPR (littér) **se ~ d'amertume** to become tinged with bitterness; **les sommets se teintèrent de pourpre** the peaks took on a purple tinge ou hue ou tint, the peaks were tinged with purple

teinture [tɛ̃tyr] NF [a] (= colorant) dye; (= action) dyeing; (fig, littér) **une ~ de philosophie** a nodding acquaintance with philosophy [b] (Pharm) tincture; **~ d'arnica/d'iode** tincture of arnica/of iodine

teinturerie [tɛ̃tyrri] NF (= métier, industrie) dyeing; (= magasin) (dry) cleaner's

teinturier, -ière [tɛ̃tyrje, jɛr] NM,F (qui nettoie) dry cleaner; (qui teint) dyer

tek [tɛk] NM = **teck**

tel, telle [tɛl] [1] ADJ [a] (similitude) (sg: avec nom concret) such, like; (avec nom abstrait) such; (pl) such; **une telle ignorance/réponse est inexcusable** such ignorance/such an answer is inexcusable; **~ père, ~ fils** like father like son; **nous n'avons pas de ~s orages en Europe** we don't get such storms ou storms like this in Europe; **as-tu jamais rien vu de ~?** have you ever seen such a thing?, have you ever seen anything like it?; **s'il n'est pas menteur, il passe pour ~** perhaps he isn't a liar but that's the reputation he has; **il a filé ~ un zèbre** he was off like a shot; **~s sont ces gens que vous croyiez honnêtes** that's what the people you thought were honest are really like; (frm) **prenez telles décisions qui vous sembleront nécessaires** take such decisions as you deem ou whatever decisions you deem necessary; **telles furent ses dernières paroles** those ou such (frm) were his last words; **il est le patron, en tant que ~** ou **comme ~ il aurait dû agir** he is the boss and as such he ought to have taken action, he's the boss and in that capacity he should have acted; **~ il était enfant, ~ je le retrouve** thus he was as a child, and thus he has remained; (littér) **le lac ~ un miroir** the lake like a mirror ou mirror-like → **rien**

b (valeur d'indéfini) such-and-such; **~ et ~** such-and-such; **venez ~ jour/à telle heure** come on such-and-such a day/at such-and-such a time; **telle quantité d'arsenic peut tuer un homme et pas un autre** a given quantity of arsenic can kill one man and not another; **telle ou telle personne vous dira que ...** someone ou somebody or other will tell you that ...; **j'ai lu dans ~ ou ~ article que ...** I read in some article or other that ...; **~ enfant qui se croit menacé devient agressif** any child that feels threatened will become aggressive; **l'on connaît ~ bureau où ...** there's ou I know a certain office ou one office where ...

c **~ que** like, (such ou the same ou just) as; (énumération) like, such as; **il est resté ~ que je le connaissais** he is still the same ou just as he used to be, he's stayed just as I remember him; **un homme ~ que lui doit comprendre** a man like him ou such a man as he (frm) must understand; **~ que je le connais, il ne viendra pas** if I know him, he won't come; **~ que vous me voyez, je reviens d'Afrique** I'm just back from Africa; **~ que vous me voyez, j'ai 72 ans** you wouldn't think it to look at me but I'm 72; **restez ~ que vous êtes** stay (just) as you are; **là il se montre ~ qu'il est** now he's showing himself in his true colours ou as he really is; **les métaux ~s que l'or, l'argent et le platine** metals like ou such as gold, silver and platinum; (littér) **le ciel à l'occident ~ qu'un brasier** the western sky like a fiery furnace

d **il a acheté la maison telle quelle** ou **telle que*** he bought the house (just) as it was ou stood; **laissez tous ces dossiers ~s quels** ou **~s que*** leave all those files as they are ou as you find them; (sur objet en solde) **« à vendre ~ quel »** "sold as seen" (Brit), "sold as is" (US); **il m'a dit: « sortez d'ici ou je vous sors »**, **~ que!*** he said to me "get out of here or I'll throw you out" — just like that!

e (intensif) (sg: avec nom concret) such a; (avec nom abstrait) such; (pl) such; **on n'a jamais vu (une) telle cohue** you've never seen such a crush; **c'est une telle joie de l'entendre!** what a joy ou it's such a joy to hear him!

f (avec conséquence) **de telle façon** ou **manière** in such a way; **ils ont eu de ~s ennuis avec leur voiture qu'ils l'ont vendue** they had such (a lot of) trouble with ou so much trouble with their car that they sold it; **de telle sorte que** so that; **à telle(s) enseigne(s) que** so much so that → **point**¹

[2] PRON INDÉF **~ vous dira qu'il faut voter oui, ~ autre ...** one will tell you you must vote yes, another ...; **si ~ ou ~ vous dit que ...** if some-

body *ou* anybody tells you that ... ■ (*PROV*) **~ est pris qui croyait prendre** it's the biter bit ■ (*PROV*) **~ qui rit vendredi, dimanche pleurera** you can be laughing on Friday but crying by Sunday → **un**

tél. (ABRÉV = **téléphone**) tel.

télé* [tele] **[1]** NF ABRÉV = **télévision** [a] (= *organisme*) TV; **il travaille à la ~** he works on TV [b] (= *programmes*) TV; **qu'est-ce qu'il y a à la ~ ce soir?** what's on TV *ou* the box* *ou* telly* (*Brit*) tonight?; **son mari est passé à la ~** her husband has been *ou* appeared on TV [c] (= *poste*) TV, telly* (*Brit*); **allume la ~** turn on the TV *ou* the telly* (*Brit*) **[2]** NM ABRÉV = **téléobjectif**

téléachat [teleaʃa] NM teleshopping (*NonC*), armchair shopping (*NonC*)

téléacteur, -trice [teleaktœʀ, tʀis] NM,F telesales operator *ou* clerk

téléalarme [telealaʀm] NF remote alarm

télébenne [teleben] NF = **télécabine**

téléboutique® [telebutik] NF phone shop

télécabine [telekabin] NF cable car

télécarte® [telekaʀt] NF phonecard

téléchargement [teleʃaʀʒəmɑ̃] NM downloading

télécharger [teleʃaʀʒe] VTI to download

télécinéma [telesinema] NM (= *appareil*) telecine

télécommande [telekɔmɑ̃d] NF remote control

télécommander [telekɔmɑ̃de] ▶ conjug 1 ◀ VT (*Tech*) to operate by remote control; **un complot télécommandé de l'étranger** a plot masterminded from abroad

télécommunication [telekɔmynikasjɔ̃] NF telecommunications; **réseau de ~(s)** telecommunications *ou* telecoms network; **les ~s sont en pleine expansion** the telecommunications industry is booming

télécoms* [telekɔm] NFPL (ABRÉV = **télécommunications**) **les ~** telecommunications, the telecommunications industry; **ingénieur télécom(s)** telecommunications engineer

téléconférence [telekɔ̃feʀɑ̃s] NF (= *méthode*) teleconferencing; (= *discussion*) teleconference, conference call

télécopie [telekɔpi] NF (= *procédé*) fax; (= *document*) fax; **transmettre par ~** to send by fax, fax

télécopieur [telekɔpjœʀ] NM fax (machine)

télédétection [teledeteksjɔ̃] NF remote sensing; **satellite de ~** remote-sensing satellite

télédiffuser [teledifyze] ▶ conjug 1 ◀ VT to broadcast by television

télédiffusion [teledifyzjɔ̃] NF television broadcasting; **Télédiffusion de France** *French broadcasting authority*, ≈ Independent Broadcasting Authority (*Brit*), ≈ Federal Communications Commission (*US*)

télédistribution [teledistʀibysjɔ̃] NF cable broadcasting

téléenseignement [teleɑ̃seɲmɑ̃] NM distance learning

téléférique [teleferik] NM (= *installation*) cableway; (= *cabine*) cable-car

téléfilm [telefilm] NM television *ou* TV film, made-for-TV movie

télégénique [teleʒenik] ADJ telegenic

télégestion [teleʒɛstjɔ̃] NF remote management

télégramme [telegram] NM telegram, wire, cable

télégraphe [telegraf] NM telegraph

télégraphie [telegrafi] NF (= *technique*) telegraphy; **~ optique** signalling; **~ sans fil†** wireless telegraphy†

télégraphier [telegrafje] ▶ conjug 7 ◀ VT [+ *message*] to telegraph, wire, cable; **tu devrais**

lui ~ you should send him a telegram *ou* wire *ou* cable, you should wire (to) him *ou* cable him

télégraphique [telegrafik] ADJ [a] [*poteau, fils*] telegraph (*épith*); [*alphabet, code*] Morse (*épith*); [*message*] telegram (*épith*), telegraphed, telegraphic; **adresse ~** telegraphic address [b] (*fig*) [*style, langage*] telegraphic

télégraphiste [telegrafist] NMF (= *technicien*) telegrapher, telegraphist; (= *messager*) telegraph boy

téléguidage [telegidaʒ] NM remote control

téléguider [telegide] ▶ conjug 1 ◀ VT [a] (*Tech*) to operate by remote control; **voiture téléguidée** remote-controlled *ou* radio-controlled car; **engin téléguidé** guided missile [b] (*fig*) (= *manipuler*) [+ *personne, organisation*] to control (from a distance); (= *diriger*) [+ *action, complot, campagne de presse*] to mastermind

téléimprimeur [teleɛ̃pʀimœʀ] NM teleprinter

téléinformatique [teleɛ̃fɔʀmatik] NF telecomputing, remote computing

téléjournal [teleʒuʀnal] NM (*Helv* = *journal télévisé*) television news (bulletin)

télékinésie [telekinezi] NF telekinesis

télémaintenance [telemɛ̃t(ə)nɑ̃s] NF remote maintenance

télémanipulation [telemanipylasjɔ̃] NF remote control handling

Télémaque [telemak] NM Telemachus

télémark [telemaʀk] NM (= *discipline*) telemark skiing; (= *virage*) telemark turn; **skis ~** telemark skis

télémarketing [telemaʀketiŋ] NM telemarketing

télématique [telematik] **[1]** ADJ [*serveur, service, réseau*] data communications (*épith*) **[2]** NF computer telephone integration, CTI, telematics *sg*

télémètre [telemɛtʀ] NM (*Mil, Photo*) rangefinder

télémétrie [telemetʀi] NF telemetry

télémétrique [telemetʀik] ADJ telemetric(al)

téléobjectif [teleɔbʒɛktif] NM telephoto lens

téléologie [teleɔlɔʒi] NF teleology

téléologique [teleɔlɔʒik] ADJ teleologic(al)

télépaiement [telepɛmɑ̃] NM electronic payment

télépathe [telepat] **[1]** ADJ telepathic **[2]** NMF telepathist

télépathie [telepati] NF telepathy

télépathique [telepatik] ADJ telepathic

télépéage [telepeaʒ] NM *motorway toll system based on electronic tagging of cars*

téléphérage [telefeʀaʒ] NM transport by cableway

téléphérique [teleferik] NM = **téléférique**

▼ **téléphone** [telefɔn] **[1]** NM (= *système*) telephone; (= *appareil*) (tele)phone; (= *service*) **le ~ marche très bien dans notre pays** our country has an excellent telephone service; **avoir le ~** to be on the (tele)phone (*Brit*), have a (tele)phone; (= *numéro*) **donne-moi ton ~*** give me your phone number; **demande-le-lui au** *ou* **par ~** phone him (and ask) about it, give him a call about it; **on vous demande au ~** there's someone on the phone for you, you're wanted on the phone; **j'ai eu un coup de ~ de Richard** I had *ou* got a phone call from Richard; **j'avais Jean au ~ quand on nous a coupés** I was on the phone to Jean when we were cut off; **je l'ai/il est au ~** I have him/he's on the phone; **tu peux me donner les renseignements par ~** you can give me the information over the phone; **réserver par ~** to reserve by telephone, make a (tele)phone booking; **coup de ~** (phone) call; **donner** *ou* **passer un coup de ~ à qn** to phone sb, call sb, give sb a call *ou* ring (*Brit*), ring sb up (*Brit*); **il faut que je te donne un coup de ~** I've got to

make a phone call; **recevoir un coup de ~ (de qn)** to get a (phone) call (from sb); **jouer au ~** to play Chinese whispers → **abonné, numéro**

[2] COMP ► **téléphone arabe** bush telegraph; **apprendre qch par le ~ arabe** to hear sth through the grapevine *ou* on the bush telegraph ► **téléphone automatique** automatic telephone system ► **téléphone de brousse** = **téléphone arabe** ► **téléphone à cadran** dial (tele)phone ► **téléphone à carte (magnétique)** cardphone ► **téléphone cellulaire** cellular (tele-)phone ► **téléphone interne** internal (tele)phone ► **téléphone à manivelle** magneto telephone ► **téléphone mobile** mobile (tele)phone ► **téléphone de poche** pocket (tele)phone ► **téléphone portable** portable (tele)phone ► **téléphone public** public (tele)phone, pay-phone ► **téléphone rose** (= *service*) telephone sex line, phone sex chatline; (= *concept*) telephone sex ► **le téléphone rouge** (*Pol*) the hot line; **il l'a appelé par le ~ rouge** he called him on the hot line ► **téléphone sans fil** cordless (tele)phone ► **téléphone à touches** push-button (tele)phone ► **téléphone de voiture** car phone

▼ **téléphoner** [telefɔne] ▶ conjug 1 ◀ VT [a] [+ *message*] to give by (tele)phone; **il m'a téléphoné la nouvelle** he phoned me and told me the news; **téléphone-lui de venir** phone him and tell him to come; **télégramme téléphoné** telegram sent by telephone [b] (* *fig* = *être prévisible*) **leur manœuvre était téléphonée** you could see what they were up to from a mile off*; (*Sport*) **ses passes/attaques sont téléphonées** his passes/attacks are telegraphed **[2]** VI to (tele)phone; **~ à qn** to (tele)phone sb, call *ou* ring (*Brit*) sb (up); **où est Paul? — il téléphone** where's Paul? — he's on the phone *ou* he's making a call; **j'étais en train de ~ à Paul** I was on the phone to Paul; **je téléphone beaucoup, je n'aime pas écrire** I phone people a lot *ou* I use the phone a lot as I don't like writing **[3]** se **téléphoner** VPR to (tele)phone each other

téléphonie [telefɔni] NF telephony; **~ sans fil** wireless telephony, radiotelephony

téléphonique [telefɔnik] ADJ telephone (*épith*)

téléphoniquement [telefɔnikmɑ̃] ADV by telephone, telephonically

téléphoniste [telefɔnist] NMF [*poste*] telephonist (*Brit*), (telephone) operator; [*entreprise*] switchboard operator

téléphotographie [telefɔtɔgʀafi] NF telephotography

téléprompteur [telepʀɔ̃ptœʀ] NM Autocue® (*Brit*), Teleprompter® (*US*)

téléreportage [teleʀ(ə)pɔʀtaʒ] NM (= *activité*) television reporting; **un ~** a television report; **le car de ~** the outside-broadcast coach

télescopage [teleskɔpaʒ] NM [*véhicules*] concertinaing (*NonC*); [*trains*] telescoping (*NonC*), concertinaing (*NonC*)

télescope [teleskɔp] NM telescope; **~ spatial** space telescope

télescoper [teleskɔpe] ▶ conjug 1 ◀ **[1]** VT [+ *véhicule*] to smash up; [+ *faits, idées*] to mix up, jumble together **[2]** se **télescoper** VPR [*véhicules*] to concertina; [*trains*] to telescope, concertina; [*souvenirs*] to become confused *ou* mixed up

télescopique [teleskɔpik] ADJ telescopic

téléscripteur [teleskʀiptœʀ] NM teleprinter, Teletype® (machine)

télésecrétariat [telesekʀetaʀja] NM secretarial teleworking

téléservice [telesɛʀvis] NM on-line *ou* remote services

télésiège [telesjɛʒ] NM chairlift

➤ GRAMMAIRE ACTIVE: **téléphone** 27.7 **téléphoner** 27.1, 27.2

téléski [teleski] NM (ski) lift, (ski) tow; **~ à fourche** T-bar tow; **~ à archets** T-bar lift

téléspectateur, -trice [telespɛktatœʀ, tʀis] NM,F (television *ou* TV) viewer

télésurveillance [telesyʀvɛjãs] NF electronic surveillance; **caméra de ~** security *ou* surveillance camera

Télétel® [teletɛl] NM electronic telephone directory

télétexte [teletɛkst] NM Teletext®, Viewdata®

Téléthon [teletɔ̃] NM Telethon

télétraitement [teletʀɛtmã] NM (*Ordin*) teleprocessing

télétransmission [teletʀãsmisjɔ̃] NF remote transmission

télétravail [teletʀavaj] NM teleworking, telecommuting

télétravailler [teletʀavaje] ▸conjug 1◂ VI to telework, telecommute

télétravailleur, -euse [teletʀavajœʀ, øz] NM,F teleworker, telecommuter

Télétype® [teletip] NM teleprinter, Teletype® (machine)

télévangéliste [televãʒelist] NMF televangelist, television *ou* TV evangelist

télévendeur, -euse [televãdœʀ, øz] NM,F telesales operator

télévente [televãt] NF (= *technique*) telephone selling, telesales; (= *action*) telephone sales

téléviser [televize] ▸conjug 1◂ VT to televise → **journal**

téléviseur [televizœʀ] NM television (set), TV (set)

télévision [televizjɔ̃] NF **a** (= *organisme, technique*) television, TV; **la ~ par satellite** satellite television *ou* TV; **la ~ câblée** *ou* **par câble** cable television *ou* TV, cablevision (*US*); **~ (à) haute définition** high definition television *ou* TV, HDTV; **~ 16/9ème** wide-screen television; **~ payante** pay television *ou* TV; **il travaille pour la ~ allemande** he works for German television

b (= *programmes*) television, TV; **à la ~** on television *ou* TV; **il est passé à la ~** [*personne*] he has been *ou* appeared on television *ou* TV; [*film*] it has been on television *ou* TV; **regarder la ~** to watch television *ou* TV; **la ~ du matin** breakfast television *ou* TV → **carte, interactif**

c (= *chaîne*) television channel; **les ~s étrangères** foreign channels; **~ privée** independent *ou* private channel

d (= *poste*) television (set); **~ (en) noir et blanc/couleur** black-and-white/colour television

télévisuel, -elle [televizɥɛl] ADJ television (*épith*), televisual

télex [telɛks] NM INV telex; **envoyer qch par ~** to telex sth

télexer [telɛkse] ▸conjug 1◂ VT to telex

télexiste [telɛksist] NMF telex operator

tellement [tɛlmã] ADV **a** (= *si*) (*avec adj ou adv*) so; (*avec compar*) so much; **il est ~ gentil** he's so nice; **~ mieux/plus fort/plus beau** so much better/stronger/more beautiful; **j'étais ~ fatigué que je me suis couché immédiatement** I was so tired (that) I went straight to bed; (*nég, avec subj: littér*) **il n'est pas ~ pauvre qu'il ne puisse ...** he's not so poor that he cannot ...

b (= *tant*) so much; (= *tant de*) **~ de gens** so many people; **~ de temps** so much time, so long; **il a ~ insisté que ...** he insisted so much that ..., he was so insistent that ...; **il travaille ~ qu'il se rend malade** he works so much *ou* hard (that) he's making himself ill; (*nég, avec subj: littér*) **il ne travaille pas ~ qu'il ait besoin de repos** he does not work to such an extent *ou* so very much that he needs rest

c (*introduisant une causale = tant*) **on ne le comprend pas, ~ il parle vite** he talks so fast

(that) you can't understand him; **il trouve à peine le temps de dormir, ~ il travaille** he works so much *ou* hard that he hardly finds time to sleep

d (*avec nég = pas très, pas beaucoup*) **pas ~ fort/lentement** not (all) that strong/slowly, not so (very) strong/slowly; **il ne travaille pas ~** he doesn't work (all) that much *ou* hard, he doesn't work so (very) much *ou* hard; **cet article n'est plus ~ demandé** this article is no longer very much in demand; **ce n'est plus ~ à la mode** it's not really *ou* all that fashionable any more; **cela ne se fait plus ~** people no longer do that very much; **tu aimes le cinéma ? — pas ~** do you like the cinema? — not (all) that much *ou* not particularly *ou* not especially; **y allez-vous toujours ? — plus ~, maintenant qu'il y a le bébé** do you still go there? — not (very) much *ou* not all that much now that there's the baby; **on ne la voit plus ~** we don't really see (very) much of her any more

tellure [telyʀ] NM tellurium

tellurique [telyʀik] ADJ telluric → **secousse**

téloche* [telɔʃ] NF TV, box*, telly* (*Brit*); **à la ~** on TV, on the box* *ou* telly (*Brit*), on the (boob)tube* (*US*)

téméraire [temeʀɛʀ] ADJ [*action, entreprise, personne*] rash, reckless, foolhardy; [*jugement*] rash; **~ dans ses jugements** rash in one's judgments; (*hum*) **courageux** *ou* **audacieux, mais pas ~ !*** brave maybe, but not foolhardy!

témérairement [temeʀɛʀmã] ADV [*entreprendre*] rashly, recklessly; [*décider, juger*] rashly

témérité [temeʀite] NF [*action, entreprise*] rashness, recklessness, foolhardiness; [*jugement*] rashness; [*personne*] (= *imprudence*) recklessness, foolhardiness, rashness; (= *audace*) temerity; **avoir la ~ de faire qch** to have the temerity to do sth

témoignage [temwaɲaʒ] NM **a** (*en justice*) (= *déclaration*) testimony (*NonC*), evidence (*NonC*); (= *faits relatés*) evidence (*NonC*); **recueillir des ~s** to gather evidence; **d'après le ~ de M. Lebrun** according to Mr Lebrun's testimony *ou* evidence, according to the evidence of *ou* given by Mr Lebrun; **j'étais présent lors de son ~** I was present when he gave evidence *ou* gave his testimony; **ces ~s sont contradictoires** these are contradictory pieces of evidence; **c'est un ~ écrasant/irrécusable** the evidence is overwhelming/incontestable; **porter** *ou* **rendre ~ de qch** to testify to sth, bear witness to sth; **rendre ~ au courage de qn** to praise sb's courage → **faux²**

b (= *récit, rapport*) account, testimony; **ce livre est un merveilleux ~ sur notre époque** this book gives a marvellous account of the age we live in

c (= *attestation*) **~ de probité/de bonne conduite** evidence (*NonC*) *ou* proof (*NonC*) of honesty/of good conduct; **invoquer le ~ de qn pour prouver sa bonne foi** to call on sb's evidence *ou* testimony to prove one's good faith; **en ~ de quoi ...** in witness whereof ...

d (= *manifestation*) expression; **~ d'amitié/de reconnaissance** (= *geste*) expression *ou* gesture of friendship/of gratitude; (= *cadeau*) token *ou* mark of friendship/of gratitude; **leurs ~s de sympathie nous ont touchés** we were touched by their expressions *ou* gestures of sympathy; **en ~ de ma reconnaissance** as a token *ou* mark of my gratitude; **le ~ émouvant de leur confiance** the touching expression of their trust

témoigner [temwaɲe] ▸conjug 1◂ **1** VI (*Jur*) to testify; **~ en faveur de qn/contre qn** to testify *ou* give evidence in sb's favour/against sb; **~ en justice** to testify in court; **~ de vive voix/par écrit** to give spoken/written evidence, testify in person/in writing

2 VT **a** (= *attester que*) **~ que ...** to testify that ...; **il a témoigné qu'il ne l'avait jamais vu** *ou* **ne l'avoir jamais vu** he testified that he had never seen him

b (= *faire preuve de, faire paraître*: *gén*) to show, display; [+ *reconnaissance*] to show, evince (*frm*); **~ un goût pour qch** to show *ou* display a taste *ou* liking for sth; **~ de l'aversion à qn** to show *ou* evince (*frm*) dislike of sb

c (= *démontrer*) **~ que ...** to show that ...; **~ de qch** to show sth; **son attitude témoigne de sa préoccupation** *ou* **qu'il est préoccupé** his attitude shows how preoccupied he is; **tout cela témoigne que les temps changent** all this shows how times change

3 témoigner de VT INDIR **a** (= *confirmer*) to testify to, bear witness to; **~ de Dieu** to bear witness to God; **je peux en ~** I can testify to that, I can bear witness to that (*frm*)

b (= *manifester*) to indicate, attest, bespeak (*frm*); **ce livre témoigne d'une certaine originalité** this book indicates *ou* attests *ou* bespeaks (*frm*) a certain originality

témoin [temwɛ̃] **1** NM **a** (*gén, Jur*: *personne*) witness; [*duel*] second; (*à un mariage*) (*gén*) witness; **c'est le ~ du marié** he's the best man; **~ auriculaire** earwitness; **~ oculaire** eyewitness; **~ direct/indirect** direct/indirect witness; **~ de moralité** character witness, character reference (*person*); **~ gênant** embarrassing witness; (*Jur*) **être ~ à charge/à décharge** to be (a) witness for the prosecution/for the defence; **être ~ de** [+ *crime, scène*] to witness, be a witness to; [+ *la sincérité de qn*] to vouch for; **prendre qn à ~ (de qch)** to call sb to witness (to *ou* of sth); **parler devant ~(s)** to speak in front of witnesses; **faire qch sans ~** to do sth unwitnessed; **cela doit être signé devant ~** this must be signed in front of a witness; **il a été entendu comme ~ dans l'affaire Lebrun** he was a witness in the Lebrun case; **que Dieu m'en soit ~** as God is my witness; **Dieu m'est ~ que je n'ai pas voulu le tuer** as God is my witness, I didn't mean to kill him; **les Témoins de Jéhovah** Jehovah's Witnesses; **ces lieux ~s de notre enfance** these places which witnessed our childhood → **faux²**

b (= *preuve*) evidence (*NonC*), testimony; **ces ruines sont le ~ de la férocité des combats** these ruins are (the) evidence of *ou* a testimony to the fierceness of the fighting; **ils sont les ~s d'une époque révolue** they are the survivors of a bygone age; **la région est riche, ~ les constructions nouvelles qui se dressent partout** the region is rich — witness the new buildings going up everywhere

c (*Sport*) baton; **passer le ~** to hand on *ou* pass the baton

d (*Géol*) outlier; [*excavations*] dumpling → **butte**

e (*Constr*: *posé sur une fente*) telltale

f (= *borne*) boundary marker

g (*lampe*) **~** warning light

2 ADJ (*après n*) control (*épith*); **animaux/sujets ~s** control animals/subjects; **appartement ~** show-flat (*Brit*), model apartment (*US*); **réalisation ~** pilot *ou* test development → **lampe**

tempe [tãp] NF (*Anat*) temple; **avoir les ~s grisonnantes** to have greying temples, be going grey at the temples

tempera [tãpera] ◆**a tempera** LOC ADJ in *ou* with tempera

tempérament [tãperamã] NM **a** (= *constitution*) constitution; **~ robuste/faible** strong/weak constitution; **se tuer** *ou* **s'esquinter le ~*** to wreck one's health; **~ sanguin/lymphatique** sanguine/lymphatic constitution; **~ nerveux** nervous disposition

b (= *nature, caractère*) disposition, temperament, nature; **elle a un ~ actif/réservé** she is of *ou* has an active/a reserved disposition; **~ romantique** romantic nature *ou* tempera-

ment; **moqueur par ~** naturally given to *ou* disposed to mockery; **avoir du ~** to have a strong personality; **c'est un ~** he (*ou* she) has a strong personality
[c] (= *sensualité*) sexual nature; **être de ~ ardent/froid** to have a passionate/cold nature; **avoir du ~** to be hot-blooded *ou* highly sexed [d] (*Comm*) **vente à ~** hire purchase (*Brit*), installment plan (*US*); **acheter qch à ~** to buy sth on hire purchase (*Brit*) *ou* on an installment plan (*US*); **trop d'achats à ~ l'avaient mis dans une situation difficile** too many hire purchase commitments (*Brit*) *ou* too many installment purchases (*US*) had got him into a difficult situation
[e] (*Mus*) temperament

tempérance [tɑ̃peʀɑ̃s] NF temperance → **société**

tempérant, e [tɑ̃peʀɑ̃, ɑ̃t] ADJ temperate

température [tɑ̃peʀatyʀ] NF [a] (*Mét, Phys*) temperature; **les ~s sont en hausse/en baisse** temperatures are rising/falling; **~ d'ébullition/de fusion** boiling/melting point; **~ absolue** *ou* **en degrés absolus** absolute temperature; **lavage à basse/haute** temperature wash [b] (= *chaleur du corps*) temperature; **animaux à ~ fixe/variable** warm-blooded/cold-blooded animals; **avoir** *ou* **faire de la ~** to have a temperature, be running a temperature; **prendre la ~ de** [+ *malade*] to take the temperature of; (*fig*) [+ *auditoire, groupe*] to sound out → **courbe, feuille**

tempéré, e [tɑ̃peʀe] (*ptp de* **tempérer**) ADJ [*climat, zone*] temperate; (*Mus*) tempered

tempérer [tɑ̃peʀe] ▸ conjug 6 ◂ VT [+ *froid, rigueur du climat*] to temper; (*littér*) [+ *peine, douleur*] to soothe, ease; (*littér*) [+ *ardeur, sévérité*] to temper

tempête [tɑ̃pɛt] NF [a] (*lit*) storm, gale, tempest (*littér*); **~ de neige** snowstorm, blizzard; **~ de sable** sandstorm → **briquet¹, semer, souffler** [b] (*fig* = *agitation*) storm; **une ~ dans un verre d'eau** a storm in a teacup (*Brit*), a tempest in a teapot (*US*); **cela va déchaîner des ~s** that's going to raise a storm; **il est resté calme dans la ~** he remained calm in the midst of the storm; **les ~s de l'âme** inner turmoil [c] (= *déchaînement*) **une ~ d'applaudissements** a storm of applause, thunderous applause (*NonC*); **une ~ d'injures** a storm of abuse

tempêter [tɑ̃pete] ▸ conjug 1 ◂ VI to rant and rave (**contre** about), rage (**contre** against)

tempétueux, -euse [tɑ̃petɥø, øz] ADJ (*littér*) [*région, côte*] tempestuous (*littér*), stormy; [*vie, époque*] tempestuous, stormy, turbulent

temple [tɑ̃pl] NM [a] (*Hist, littér*) temple [b] (*Rel*) (Protestant) church; **l'Ordre du Temple** ◊ **le Temple** the Order of the Temple

templier [tɑ̃plije] NM (Knight) Templar

tempo [tempo] NM (*Mus*) tempo; (*fig*) tempo, pace

temporaire [tɑ̃pɔʀɛʀ] ˈ ADJ [*personnel, mesures, crise*] temporary; **nomination à titre ~** temporary appointment, appointment on a temporary basis → **travail¹**

temporairement [tɑ̃pɔʀɛʀmɑ̃] ADV temporarily

temporal, e [mpl -aux] [tɑ̃pɔʀal, o] (*Anat*) [1] ADJ temporal [2] NM temporal (bone)

temporalité [tɑ̃pɔʀalite] NF (*Ling, Philo*) temporality

temporel, -elle [tɑ̃pɔʀɛl] ADJ [a] (*Rel*) (= *non spirituel*) worldly, temporal; (= *non éternel*) temporal; **biens ~s** temporal *ou* worldly goods, temporals [b] (*Ling, Philo*) temporal

temporellement [tɑ̃pɔʀɛlmɑ̃] ADV temporally

temporisateur, -trice [tɑ̃pɔʀizatœʀ, tʀis] [1] ADJ [*tactique*] delaying (*épith*), stalling (*épith*); [*effet*] delaying (*épith*) [2] NM,F (= *personne*) temporizer [3] NM (*Tech*) timer

temporisation [tɑ̃pɔʀizasjɔ̃] NF (= *attentisme*) delaying, stalling, playing for time; (*Tech*) time delay

temporiser [tɑ̃pɔʀize] ▸ conjug 1 ◂ [1] VI to delay, stall, play for time [2] VT (*Tech*) to delay

temps¹ [tɑ̃]

| [1] NOM MASCULIN | [2] COMPOSÉS |

[1] **NOM MASCULIN**
[a] = *passage des ans* **le ~** time; (*personnifié*) **le Temps** (Old) Father Time; **l'usure du ~** the ravages of time; **avec le ~, ça s'arrangera** it'll all be forgotten with *ou* in time; **il faut laisser** *ou* **donner du ~ au ~** you must give these things time → **tuer**

[b] = *durée* **time**; **cela prend trop de ~** it takes (up) too much time, it's too time-consuming; **la blessure mettra du ~ à guérir** the wound will take (some) time to heal; **il a mis beaucoup de ~ à se préparer** he took a long time to get ready; **la jeunesse n'a qu'un ~** youth doesn't last; **travailler à plein ~** *ou* **à ~ plein/à ~ partiel** to work full-time/part-time; **(travail à) ~ choisi** flexitime; **en peu de ~** in a short time; **peu de ~ avant/après Noël** shortly before/after Christmas; **je l'ai vu peu de ~ après** I saw him a short time after(wards), I saw him shortly after(wards); **dans peu de ~** before (very) long; **pendant ce ~(-là)** meanwhile, in the meantime; **il y a beau ~ que je le sais** I've known that for a long time → **depuis, hors, quelque**

[c] = *portion de temps* **time**; **s'accorder un ~ de réflexion** to give o.s. time to think; **avoir le ~ (de faire)** to have time (to do); **je n'ai pas le ~** I haven't got (the) time; **je n'ai pas le ~ de faire** I haven't got the time *ou* I can't spare the time to do it; **vous avez tout votre ~** you have all the time in the world *ou* plenty of time *ou* all the time you need; **avoir** *ou* **se donner** *ou* **prendre du bon ~** to enjoy o.s., have a good time; **(donnez-moi) le ~ de m'habiller et je suis à vous** just give me time *ou* a moment to get dressed and I'll be with you; **faire son ~** [*soldat*] to serve one's time (in the army); [*prisonnier*] to do *ou* serve one's time; (*fig*) **il a fait son ~** [*personnage*] he has had his day; [*objet*] it has had its day; **je me suis arrêté juste le ~ de prendre un verre** I stopped just long enough for a drink *ou* to have a drink; **il passe son ~ à la lecture** *ou* **à lire** he spends his time reading; **passer tout son ~ à faire qch/à qch** to spends all one's time doing sth/on sth; **il faut bien passer le ~** you've got to pass the time somehow; **cela fait passer le ~** it passes the time; **comme le ~ passe!** how time flies!; **perdre du/son ~ (à faire qch)** to waste time/waste one's time (doing sth); **il n'y a pas de ~ à perdre** there's no time to lose ▪ (*PROV*) **le ~ perdu ne se rattrape jamais** time and tide wait for no man (*PROV*); **prendre le ~ de faire** to find time to do; **prendre le ~ de vivre** to make time to enjoy life; **prenez donc votre ~** do take your time; **il a pris son ~!** he took his time (over *ou* about it)!; **le ~ presse** time is short, time presses ▪ (*PROV*) **le ~ c'est de l'argent** time is money (*PROV*) → **clair, devant, plupart**

[d] = *moment précis* **time**; **il est ~ de partir** it's time to go, it's time we left; **il est** *ou* **il serait (grand) ~ qu'il parte** it's (high) time he went, it's time for him to go; **le ~ est venu de supprimer les frontières** the time has come to abolish frontiers; **ce n'est ni le ~ ni le lieu de discuter** this is neither the time nor the place for discussions; **il était ~!** (= *ce n'est pas trop tôt*) not before time!, about time too!; (*c'était juste*) it came in the nick of time!; **il n'est plus ~ de se plaindre** the time for complaining is past *ou* over; **il n'est que ~ de s'en préoccuper** it's high time we started worrying about it ▪ (*PROV*) **il y a un ~ pour tout** there's a right time for everything → **chaque**

[e] = *époque* **time, times**; (= *saison*) **le ~ des moissons/des vacances** harvest/holiday time; **les ~ modernes** modern times; **au** *ou* **du ~ où ... ◊ dans le ~ où ... ◊ du ~ que ...** (*littér*) in the days when ..., at the time when ...; **au ~ de la marine à voile** in the days of sailing ships; **ces derniers ~ ◊ ces ~ derniers** lately, recently, of late; **dans les derniers ~ du colonialisme** towards the end of the colonial period; **les premiers ~** at the beginning, at first, at the outset; **dans les premiers ~ de la crise** at the beginning of the crisis; **dans les ~ anciens** in ancient times *ou* days; **en ~ de guerre/paix** in wartime/peacetime; **en ~ de crise** in times of crisis; **en un ~ où ...** at a time when ...; **en ces ~ troublés** (*actuellement*) in these troubled times; (*dans le passé*) in those troubled times; **les ~ ont bien changé** times have changed; **le ~ n'est plus où ...** gone are the days when ...; **il fut un ~ (frm) où l'on pensait que...** time was *ou* there was a time when people thought that ...; **c'était le bon ~** those were the days; **dans le** *ou* **au bon vieux ~** in the good old days; **quels ~ nous vivons!** what times we live in!; **les ~ sont durs!** times are hard! → **ancien, nuit, signe**

[f] = *époque délimitée par rapport à qn* **time(s), day**; **du ~ de Néron** in Nero's time *ou* day, at the time of Nero; **au ~ des Tudors** in Tudor times, in the days of the Tudors; **de mon ~** in my day *ou* time; **dans mon jeune ~** in my younger days; **être de son ~** (*homme*) to be a man of his time; (*femme*) to be a woman of her time; **les jeunes de notre ~** young people today

[g] = *phase* **l'opération s'est déroulée en trois ~** there were three phases to the operation; **dans un premier ~** at first, to start *ou* begin with; **dans un deuxième ~** subsequently

[h] *marquant un rythme* (*Mus*) beat; (*Gym*) [*exercice, mouvement*] stage; **~ fort/faible** strong/weak beat; (*fig*) **les ~ forts et les ~ faibles d'un roman** the powerful and the weak moments of a novel; (*Mus*) **~ frappé** downbeat; **trois ~** three beats to the bar; **à deux/trois ~** in duple/triple time; **~ de valse** waltz time → **deux**

[i] (*Ling*) [*verbe*] tense; **~ simple/composé** simple/compound tense; **~ surcomposé** double-compound tense; **adverbe/complément de ~** adverb/complement of time, temporal adverb/complement → **concordance**

[j] (*Tech*) **moteur à 4 ~** 4-stroke engine; **un 2 ~** a 2-stroke

[k] (*Sport*) [*coureur, concurrent*] time; **le skieur a réalisé un très bon ~** the skier achieved a very good time; **dans les meilleurs ~** among the best times

[l] *expressions figées*
♦ **à temps** in time; **j'arrive à ~!** I've come just in time!
♦ **à temps perdu** in my (*ou* your *etc*) spare time
♦ **au temps pour moi!** my mistake!
♦ **ces temps-ci** these days
♦ **dans ce temps-là ◊ en ce temps-là** at that time
♦ **dans le temps** in the old days, in the past, formerly
♦ **dans les temps** : **être dans les ~** (*Sport*) to be within the time limit; (*travail*) to be on schedule; (*fig* = *pas en retard*) to be in time; **il ne reste que 12 jours avant la fin, mais nous sommes dans les ~** there are only 12 days left, but we're on schedule; **cette commande sera livrée dans les ~** the order will be delivered on time
♦ **de tout temps** from time immemorial, since the beginning of time
♦ **de temps à autre ◊ de temps en temps** from time to time, now and again, every now and then
♦ **du temps que** (* = *pendant que*) **du ~ que tu y es, rapporte des fruits** while you're at it* *ou*

about it*, get some fruit
♦ **en temps et en heure** in due course
♦ **en temps et lieu** in due course, at the proper time (and place)
♦ **en temps** + *adjectif*: **en ~ normal** *ou* **ordinaire** usually, under normal circumstances; **en ~ opportun** at the appropriate time; **en ~ voulu** *ou* **utile** in due time *ou* course
♦ **entre temps** = entre-temps
♦ **par les temps qui courent** these days, nowadays
♦ **pour un temps** for a time *ou* while
♦ **tout le temps** all the time; **l'air est presque tout le ~ pollué** the air is polluted almost all the time; **il se plaint tout le ~** he complains all the time, he's forever complaining; **je ne vis pas tout le ~ à Rome** I don't live in Rome all the time

2 COMPOSÉS
► **temps d'accès** (*Ordin*) access time ► **temps d'arrêt** pause, halt; **marquer un ~ d'arrêt** to pause ► **temps astronomique** (*Sci*) mean *ou* astronomical time ► **temps atomique** (*Phys*) atomic time ► **temps de cuisson** cooking time ► **temps différé** (*Ordin*) batch mode ► **temps libre** spare time; **comment occupes-tu ton ~ libre?** what do you do in your spare time? ► **temps mort** (*Ftbl, Rugby*) injury time (*NonC*), stoppage for injury; (*fig*) (*dans le commerce, le travail*) slack period; (*dans la conversation*) lull ► **temps de parole** (*dans une émission*) air time ► **temps partagé** (*Ordin*) time-sharing; (*Ordin*) **utilisation en ~ partagé** time-sharing ► **temps de pose** (*Photo*) exposure *ou* value index ► **temps de réaction** reaction time ► **temps réel** (*Ordin*) real time; **ordinateur exploité en ~ réel** real-time computer ► **temps de réponse** response time ► **temps de saignement** (*Méd*) bleeding time ► **temps sidéral** (*Astron*) sideral time ► **temps solaire vrai** apparent *ou* real solar time ► **temps universel** universal time

temps² [tã] NM (= *conditions atmosphériques*) weather; **quel ~ fait-il?** what's the weather like?; **il fait beau/mauvais** ~ the weather's fine/bad; **le ~ s'est mis au beau** the weather has turned fine; **le ~ se gâte** the weather is changing for the worse; **par ~ pluvieux/mauvais ~** in wet/bad weather; **sortir par tous les ~** to go out in all weathers; **avec le ~ qu'il fait!** in this weather!; **il fait un ~ de chien*** the weather's awful *ou* lousy*; **~ de saison** seasonable weather; **il faisait un beau ~ sec** (*pendant une période*) it was beautiful dry weather; (*ce jour-là*) it was a lovely dry day; **le ~ est lourd aujourd'hui** it's very humid *ou* close (*Brit*) today; (*fig*) **prendre le ~ comme il vient** to take things as they come → **air¹**

tenable [t(ə)nabl] ADJ (*gén nég*) [*température, situation*] bearable; [*position*] tenable; **il fait trop chaud ici, ce n'est pas ~** it's too hot here, it's unbearable; **quand ils sont ensemble, ce n'est plus ~** when they're together it becomes *ou* they become unbearable

tenace [tənas] ADJ **a** (= *persistant*) [*douleur, rhume*] stubborn, persistent; [*maladie, toux, rumeur, souvenir*] persistent; [*croyance, préjugés*] deep-seated, deep-rooted, stubborn; [*espoir, illusions*] tenacious, stubborn; [*rancune, méfiance*] lingering; [*odeur, parfum*] lingering, persistent; [*tache*] stubborn **b** (= *têtu, obstiné*) [*quémandeur*] persistent; [*chercheur*] dogged, tenacious; [*résistance, volonté*] tenacious, stubborn

ténacité [tenasite] NF **a** (= *persistance*) [*douleur, rhume*] stubbornness, persistence; [*croyance, préjugés*] deep-seated nature, stubbornness; [*rumeur, souvenir, odeur, parfum*] persistence; [*espoir, illusion*] tenacity, stubbornness **b** (= *entêtement, obstination*) [*quémandeur*] persistence; [*chercheur*] tenacity; [*résistance, volonté*] tenacity, doggedness; **avec**

~ persistently, tenaciously, doggedly; **ils ont fait preuve de ~** they were persistent *ou* tenacious **c** (*Tech*) tenacity, toughness

tenaille [t(ə)naj] NF **a** (*gén pl*) [*menuisier, bricoleur*] pliers, pincers; [*forgeron*] tongs; [*cordonnier*] nippers, pincers **b** (*Mil*) [*fortification*] tenaille, tenail; (*manœuvre*) **prendre en ~** to catch in a pincer movement; **mouvement de ~** pincer movement

tenailler [tənaje] ▶conjug 1◀ VT [*remords, inquiétude*] to torture, torment; **la faim le tenaillait** hunger gnawed at him; **le remords le tenaillait** he was racked with remorse; **l'inquiétude le tenaillait** he was desperately worried

tenancier [tənãsje] NM **a** [*maison de jeu, hôtel, bar*] manager **b** [*ferme*] tenant farmer; (*Hist*) [*terre*] (feudal) tenant

tenancière [tənãsjɛʀ] NF [*maison close*] brothel-keeper, madam; [*maison de jeu, hôtel, bar*] manageress

tenant, e [tənã, ãt] **1** ADJ **chemise à col ~** shirt with an attached collar *ou* with collar attached → **séance** **2** NM **a** (*gén pl* = *partisan*) [*doctrine*] supporter, upholder (**de** of), adherent (**de** to); [*homme politique*] supporter **b** (*Sport*) [*coupe*] holder; **le ~ du titre** the titleholder, the reigning champion **c** (*loc*) **les ~s et (les) aboutissants d'une affaire** the ins and outs of a question; **d'un seul ~** [*terrain*] all in one piece; **100 hectares d'un seul ~** 100 unbroken *ou* uninterrupted hectares **d** (*Hér*) supporter

▼ **tendance** [tãdãs] NF **a** (= *inclination, Psych*) tendency; **~s refoulées/inconscientes** repressed/unconscious tendencies; **la ~ principale de son caractère est l'égoïsme** the chief tendency in his character *ou* his chief tendency is selfishness; **manifester des ~s homosexuelles** to show homosexual leanings *ou* tendencies; **~ à l'exagération/à s'enivrer** tendency to exaggerate *ou* to exaggeration/to get drunk **b** (= *opinions*) [*parti, politicien*] leanings, sympathies; [*groupe artistique, artiste*] leanings; [*livre*] drift, tenor; **il est de ~ gauchiste/surréaliste** he has leftist/surrealist leanings; **à quelle ~ (politique) appartient-il?** what are his (political) leanings? *ou* sympathies?; **les députés, toutes ~s confondues ...** deputies from across the political spectrum *ou* on all sides ... **c** (= *évolution*) [*art, langage, système économique ou politique*] trend; **~s démographiques** population trends; **~ à la hausse/baisse** [*prix*] upward/downward trend, rising/falling trend; [*température*] upward/downward trend; **la récente ~ à la baisse des valeurs mobilières** the recent downward *ou* falling trend in stocks and shares; **les ~s actuelles de l'opinion publique** the current trends in public opinion → **indicateur** **d** (*loc*) **avoir ~ à** [+ *paresse, exagération*] to have a tendency to, tend towards; **avoir ~ à s'enivrer/être impertinent** to have a tendency to get drunk/to be impertinent, tend to get drunk/to be impertinent; **cette roue a ~ à se bloquer** this wheel tends *ou* has a tendency *ou* is inclined to lock; **le temps a ~ à se gâter vers le soir** the weather tends to deteriorate towards the evening; **en période d'inflation, les prix ont ~ à monter** in a period of inflation, prices tend *ou* have a tendency *ou* are inclined to go up; **j'aurais ~ à penser que ...** I'd be inclined to think that ...

tendanciel, -ielle [tãdãsjɛl] ADJ underlying

tendancieusement [tãdãsjøzmã] ADV tendentiously

tendancieux, -ieuse [tãdãsjø, jøz] ADJ tendentious

tender [tãdɛʀ] NM (*Rail*) tender

tendeur [tãdœʀ] NM (= *dispositif*) [*fil de fer*] wire-strainer; [*ficelle de tente*] runner; [*chaîne de bicyclette*] chain-adjuster; [*porte-bagages*]

bungee (cord *ou* rope); **~ de chaussures** shoe-stretcher

tendineux, -euse [tãdinø, øz] ADJ [*viande*] stringy; (*Anat*) tendinous

tendinite [tãdinit] NF tendinitis (*NonC*)

tendon [tãdɔ̃] NM tendon, sinew; **~ d'Achille** Achilles' tendon

tendre¹ [tãdʀ] ▶conjug 41◀ **1** VT **a** (= *raidir*) [+ *corde, câble, corde de raquette*] to tighten, tauten; [+ *corde d'arc*] to brace, draw tight; [+ *arc*] to bend, draw back; [+ *ressort*] to set; [+ *muscles*] to tense; [+ *pièce de tissu*] to stretch, pull *ou* draw tight; **~ la peau d'un tambour** to brace a drum; **~ le jarret** to flex one's leg muscles; (*littér*) **~ son esprit vers ...** to bend one's mind to ... **b** (= *installer, poser*) [+ *tapisserie, tenture*] to hang; [+ *piège*] to set; **~ une bâche sur une remorque** to pull a tarpaulin over a trailer; **~ une chaîne entre deux poteaux** to hang *ou* fasten a chain between two posts; **~ ses filets** (*lit*) to set one's nets; (*fig*) to set one's snares; **~ un piège/une embuscade (à qn)** to set a trap/an ambush (for sb) **c** († *littér* = *tapisser*) **~ une pièce de tissu** to hang a room with material; **~ une pièce de soie bleue** to line the walls of a room with blue silk **d** (= *avancer*) **~ le cou** to crane one's neck; **~ l'oreille** to prick up one's ears; **~ la joue** to offer one's cheek; (*fig*) **~ l'autre joue** to turn the other cheek; **~ la gorge au couteau** to put *ou* lay one's head on the block; **~ le poing** to raise one's fist; **~ la main** (*pour attraper, mendier*) to hold out one's hand; **~ la main à qn** (*pour saluer*) to hold out one's hand to sb; (*pour aider*) to lend *ou* offer sb a helping hand; (*pour se réconcilier*) to hold out *ou* extend the hand of friendship to sb; **~ le bras** to stretch out one's arm; **il me tendit les bras** he stretched out his arms to me; **~ une main secourable** to offer a helping hand; (*lit, fig*) **~ le dos** to brace oneself **e** (= *présenter, donner*) **~ qch à qn** [+ *briquet, objet demandé*] to hold sth out to *ou* for sb; [+ *cigarette offerte, bonbon*] to offer sth to sb; **il lui tendit un paquet de cigarettes** he held out a packet of cigarettes to him; **il lui tendit un bonbon/une cigarette** he offered him a sweet/a cigarette; (*fig*) **~ une perche à qn** to throw sb a line

2 se **tendre** VPR [*corde*] to become taut, tighten; [*rapports*] to become strained

3 VI **a** (= *avoir tendance à*) **~ à qch/à faire qch** to tend towards sth/to do sth; **le langage tend à se simplifier** language tends to become simpler; **la situation tend à s'améliorer** the situation seems to be improving; (*sens affaibli*) **ceci tend à prouver/confirmer que ...** this seems *ou* tends to prove/confirm that ... **b** (*littér* = *viser à*) **~ à qch/à faire** to aim at sth/to do; **cette mesure tend à faciliter les échanges** this measure aims to facilitate *ou* at facilitating exchanges; **~ à** *ou* **vers la perfection** to strive towards perfection, aim at perfection **c** (*Math*) **~ vers l'infini** to tend towards infinity

tendre² [tãdʀ] **1** ADJ **a** (= *délicat*) [*peau, pierre, bois*] soft; [*haricots, viande*] tender; **crayon à mine ~** soft-(lead) pencil; **un steak bien ~** a nice tender steak; [*cheval*] **avoir la bouche ~** to be tender-mouthed; (*littér*) **couché dans l'herbe ~** lying in the sweet grass *ou* the fresh young grass; (*littér*) **~s bourgeons/fleurettes** tender shoots/little flowers; **depuis sa plus ~ enfance** from his earliest days; (*hum*) **dans ma ~ enfance** in my innocent childhood days; **~ comme la rosée** wonderfully tender → **âge** **b** (= *affectueux*) [*ami, amitié*] loving; [*amour*] tender; [*regard, mot*] tender, loving; **~ aveu** tender confession; **il la regardait d'un air ~ he**

looked at her tenderly *ou* lovingly, he gave her a tender *ou* loving look; **dire des mots ~s à qn** to say tender *ou* loving things to sb; **ne pas être ~ pour** *ou* **avec qn*** to be hard on sb c (= *cher*) [+ *ami, époux*] dear; **à mon ~ époux** to my dear(est) husband d [*couleur*] soft, delicate; **rose/vert/bleu ~** soft *ou* delicate pink/green/blue 2 NMF **c'est un ~** he's tender-hearted *ou* soft-hearted; **en affaires, ce n'est pas un ~*** he's a tough businessman

tendrement [tɑ̃dʀəmɑ̃] ADV [*aimer*] tenderly; [*regarder, embrasser*] tenderly, lovingly; **époux ~ unis** loving couple

tendresse [tɑ̃dʀɛs] NF a (= *affection*) tenderness; **un geste de ~** a tender *ou* loving gesture; **privé de ~ maternelle** denied maternal affection; **avoir** *ou* **ressentir** *ou* **éprouver de la ~ pour qn** to feel tenderness *ou* affection for sb b (= *câlineries*) ~s tokens of affection, tenderness (*NonC*); **combler qn de ~s** to overwhelm sb with tenderness *ou* with tokens of (one's) affection; (*sur lettre*) **mille ~s** lots of love, much love c (= *penchant*) **n'avoir aucune ~ pour qn** to have no fondness for sb; **il avait gardé des ~s royalistes** he had retained (his) royalist sympathies

tendreté [tɑ̃dʀəte] NF [*viande*] tenderness; [*bois, métal*] softness

tendron [tɑ̃dʀɔ̃] NM a (*Culin*) **~ de veau** tendron of veal (*Brit*), plate of veal (*US*) b (= *pousse, bourgeon*) (tender) shoot c († *hum* = *jeune fille*) young *ou* little girl

tendu, e [tɑ̃dy] (*ptp de* **tendre¹**) ADJ a (= *raide*) [*corde, toile*] tight, taut; [*muscles*] tensed; [*ressort*] set; [*Ling*] [*voyelle, prononciation*] tense; **tir ~** (*Mil*) straight shot; (*Ftbl*) straight kick; **la corde est trop ~e/bien ~e** the rope is too tight *ou* taut/is taut; **la corde est mal ~e** the rope is slack *ou* isn't tight *ou* taut enough b (= *appliqué*) [*esprit*] concentrated c (= *empreint de nervosité*) [*rapports, relations*] strained, fraught; [*personne*] (*gén*) tense; (= *nerveux, inquiet*) strained; [*situation*] tense, fraught; [*climat, ambiance*] tense, strained; **il entra, le visage ~** he came in looking tense; **avant le match il était ~** he was all keyed-up before the match d (= *en avant, pointé*) **les bras ~s** with arms outstretched, with outstretched arms; **s'avancer la main ~e** to come forward with one's hand held out; **la politique de la main ~e à l'égard de ...** a policy of friendly cooperation with ... *ou* friendly exchanges with ...; **le poing ~** with one's fist raised e (= *tapissé de*) **~ de** [+ *velours, soie*] hung with; **chambre ~e de bleu/de soie bleue** bedroom with blue hangings/blue silk hangings

ténèbres [tenɛbʀ] NFPL (*littér*) [*nuit, cachot*] darkness, gloom; **plongé dans les ~** plunged in darkness; **s'avançant à tâtons dans les ~** groping his way forward in the dark(ness) *ou* gloom; **les ~ de la mort** the shades of death (*littér*); **le prince/l'empire des ~** the prince/the world of darkness; **les ~ de l'ignorance** the darkness of ignorance; **les ~ de l'inconscient** the dark regions *ou* murky depths of the unconscious; **une lueur au milieu des ~** a ray of light in the darkness *ou* amidst the gloom

ténébreux, -euse [tenebʀø, øz] ADJ a (*littér*) (= *obscur*) [*prison, forêt*] dark, gloomy; (= *mystérieux et dangereux*) [*intrigue, dessein*] dark (*épith*); (= *sombre*) [*époque, temps*] obscure; (= *incompréhensible*) [*affaire, philosophie*] dark (*épith*), mysterious b (*littér*) [*personne*] saturnine; (*hum*) **un beau ~** a man with dark, brooding good looks

Ténéré [teneʀe] NM **le ~** Ténéré

Tenerife [teneʀif] N Tenerife

teneur [tənœʀ] NF a [*traité*] terms; [*lettre*] content, terms; [*article*] content; **il n'a pu révéler la ~ exacte de leurs entretiens** he couldn't reveal the actual content *ou* the exact nature

of their conversations b [*minerai*] grade, content; [*solution*] content; **de haute/faible ~** high-/low-grade (*épith*); **~ en cuivre/alcool/matières grasses** copper/alcohol/fat content; **la forte ~ en fer d'un minerai** the high iron content of an ore, the high percentage of iron in an ore; **la ~ en hémoglobine du sang** the haemoglobin content of the blood

ténia [tenja] NM tapeworm, taenia (*SPÉC*)

▼**tenir** [t(ə)niʀ]

▶ conjug 22 ◀
1 VERBE TRANSITIF	4 VERBE TRANSITIF INDIR
2 VERBE INTRANSITIF	
3 VERBE TRANSITIF INDIR	5 VERBE IMPERSONNEL
	6 VERBE PRONOMINAL

Lorsque **tenir** *s'emploie dans des expressions figées telles que* **tenir compagnie/compte/rigueur, tenir chaud, tenir en haleine** *etc, cherchez à l'autre mot.*

1 VERBE TRANSITIF
a **avec les mains** to hold; **la clé qu'il tient à la main** *ou* **dans sa main** the key that he's holding *ou* that he's got in his hand; **il tient son fils par la main** he's holding his son's hand; **elle le tenait par le cou** (*pour l'empêcher de s'enfuir*) she had got him by the neck; (*par affection*) she had her arm around his neck
b **= maintenir dans un certain état** to keep; (*maintenir dans une certaine position*) to hold, keep; **~ les yeux fermés/les bras levés** to keep one's eyes shut/one's arms raised *ou* up; **le café le tient éveillé** coffee keeps him awake; **elle tient ses enfants très propres** she keeps her children very neat; **~ qch en place/en position** to hold *ou* keep sth in place/in position; **ses livres sont tenus par une courroie** his books are held (together) by a strap; **il m'a tenu la tête sous l'eau** he held my head under the water; **~ la porte à qn** to hold the door open for sb
c **Mus = garder** [+ *note*] to hold; **~ l'accord** to stay in tune
d **= avoir, détenir** [+ *voleur, maladie*]* to have, have caught; [+ *vérité, preuve, solution*] to hold, have; (*littér*) **faire ~ qch à qn** [+ *lettre, objet*] to transmit *ou* communicate sth to sb; (*menace*) **si je le tenais!** if I could get my hands *ou* lay hands on him!; **nous le tenons** (*lit*) (= *nous l'avons attrapé*) we've got *ou* caught him; (= *il ne peut se dérober*) we've got him (where we want him); **je tiens le mot de l'énigme/la clé du mystère** I've found *ou* got the secret of the riddle/the key to the mystery; **parfait, je tiens mon article/mon sujet** great, now I have my article/my subject; **je tiens un de ces rhumes!*** I've got *ou* caught a nasty cold; **qu'est-ce qu'il tient!*** ◊ **il en tient une bonne!*** (= *il est ivre*) he's plastered* *ou* loaded!* (*US*); (= *il est idiot*) he's such a wally* (*Brit*) *ou* clot* (*Brit*)! ■ (*PROV*) **un tiens vaut mieux que deux tu l'auras** (*PROV*) **mieux vaut ~ que courir** a bird in the hand is worth two in the bush (*PROV*)
e **Comm = avoir en stock** [+ *article, marchandise*] to stock, keep
f **= avoir le contrôle de** [+ *enfant, classe*] to have under control, keep under control *ou* on a tight rein; [+ *pays*] to have under one's control; **il tient (bien) sa classe** he has *ou* keeps his class (well) under control, he controls his class well; **les enfants sont très tenus** the children are held very much in check *ou* are kept on a very tight rein; **les soldats tiennent la plaine** the soldiers are holding the plain, the soldiers control the plain
g **= gérer** [+ *hôtel, magasin*] to run, keep; [+ *comptes, registre, maison, ménage*] to keep
h **= faire que qch ait lieu** [+ *séance, réunion, conférence*] to hold → **langage, propos, raisonnement** *etc*
i **= occuper** [+ *place, largeur*] to take up; [+ *rôle*] to fulfill; [+ *emploi*] to hold; **tu tiens trop de place!** you're taking up too much room!;

le camion tenait toute la largeur/la moitié de la chaussée the lorry took up the whole width of/half the roadway; (*Aut*) **il tenait sa droite** he was keeping to the right; **elle a bien tenu son rôle de femme au foyer/de chef** she was the perfect housewife/manager; (*Théât, Ciné*) **elle tient le rôle d'Ophélie** she plays the role of Ophelia, she's cast as Ophelia *ou* in the role of Ophelia
j **= contenir** [*récipient*] to hold
k **= résister à, bien se comporter** **~ l'alcool*** to be able to hold *ou* take (*Brit*) one's drink; **~ la mer** [*bateau*] to be seaworthy; **~ le coup** [*personne*] to survive; [*chose*] (= *durer*) to last; **financièrement, ils n'auraient pas tenu le coup** financially they wouldn't have survived *ou* been able to hold out; **avec tout ce travail, est-ce qu'il pourra ~ le coup?** with all that work will he be able to cope?; **leur mariage tient le coup malgré tout** their marriage has survived *ou* lasted in spite of everything; **si on danse, est-ce que la moquette tiendra le coup?** if we dance, will the carpet stand up to it?
l **= respecter** [+ *promesse*] to keep; [+ *pari*] to keep to, honour (*Brit*), honor (*US*); (= *se conformer à*) [+ *planning*] to keep to; **~ le rythme** to keep up (the pace)
m **= immobiliser** **il m'a tenu dans son bureau pendant une heure** he kept me in his office for an hour; **il est très tenu par ses affaires** he's very tied (*Brit*) *ou* tied up by his business; (*littér*) **la colère le tenait** anger had him in its grip; (*littér*) **l'envie me tenait de ...** I was filled *ou* gripped by the desire to ...; **cette maladie le tient depuis deux mois** he's had this illness for two months (now)
n
♦ **tenir qch de qn** (= *avoir reçu*) [+ *renseignement, meuble, bijou*] to have (got) sth from sb; [+ *trait physique, de caractère*] to get from sb; **il tient cela de son père** he gets that from his father; **je tiens ce renseignement d'un voisin** I have *ou* I got this information from a neighbour
o
♦ **tenir qn/qch pour** (= *considérer comme*) to regard sb/sth as, consider sb/sth (as), hold sb/sth to be (*frm*); **je le tenais pour un honnête homme** I regarded him as *ou* considered him (to be) *ou* held him to be (*frm*) an honest man; **elle le tient pour responsable de l'accident** she holds him responsible *ou* considers him to be responsible for the accident; **~ pour certain** *ou* **assuré que ...** to be quite sure that ...
p
♦ **en tenir pour qch** (= *être partisan de*) [+ *solution*] to be keen on sth, be in favour (*Brit*) *ou* favor (*US*) of sth; **en ~ pour qn** (= *l'aimer*) to fancy sb* (*Brit*), be keen on sb*, have a crush on sb*; **il en tient pour l'équipe d'Irlande** he's for the Irish team
q
♦ **tiens! ◊ tenez!** (*en donnant*) here (you are); (*surprise*) **tiens, voilà mon frère!** ah *ou* hullo, there's my brother!; **tiens, tiens** well, well!, fancy that!; (*pour attirer l'attention*) **tenez, je vais vous expliquer** look, I'll explain; **tenez, ça m'écœure** you know, that sickens me

2 VERBE INTRANSITIF
a **= rester en place, en position** [*objet fixe, nœud, branche*] to hold; [*objets empilés, échafaudage*] to stay up, hold (up); **croyez-vous que le clou va ~?** do you think the nail will hold?; **l'armoire tient au mur** the cupboard is fixed to the wall; **ce chapeau ne tient pas sur ma tête** this hat won't stay on (my head); **la branche est cassée mais elle tient encore** the branch is broken but it's still attached to the tree; **il tient bien sur ses jambes** he's very steady on his legs
b **= être valable** to be on; **ça tient toujours, notre pique-nique?*** is our picnic still on?; **il**

n'y a pas de bal/match qui tienne there's no question of going to any dance/match

c = *résister* (Mil, gén) to hold out; **~ bon ou ferme** to stand fast ou firm, hold out; **il fait trop chaud, on ne tient plus ici** it's too hot — we can't stand it here any longer; **il n'a pas pu ~ : il a protesté violemment** he couldn't contain himself and protested vehemently

d = *pouvoir être contenu dans* **~ dans** ou **à** ou **en** to fit in(to); **est-ce que la caisse tiendra en hauteur?** will the box fit in vertically?; **ils ne tiendront pas dans la pièce/la voiture** the room/the car won't hold them, they won't fit into the room/the car; **à cette table, on peut ~ à huit** this table can seat eight, we can get eight round this table; **son discours tient en quelques pages** his speech takes up just a few pages, his speech is just a few pages long; **ma réponse tient en un seul mot : non** in a word, my answer is no

e = *durer* [accord, beau temps] to hold; [couleur] to be fast; [mariage] to last; [fleurs] to last (well); **sa coiffure a tenu 2 jours** her hairstyle held for 2 days

3 **tenir à** VERBE TRANSITIF INDIR

a = *aimer, être attaché à* [+ réputation, opinion de qn] to value, care about; [+ objet] to be attached to, be fond of; [+ personne] to be attached to, be fond of, care for; **il ne tenait plus à la vie** he had lost his will to live, he no longer had any desire to live; **voudriez-vous un peu de vin? — je n'y tiens pas** would you like some wine? — not really ou not particularly ou I'm not that keen* (Brit)

b = *vouloir*
◆ **tenir à** + infinitif ◊ **tenir à ce que** + subjonctif to be anxious to, be anxious that; **il tient beaucoup à vous connaître** he's very anxious ou keen (Brit) ou eager to meet you; **elle tenait absolument à parler** she insisted on speaking; **il tient à ce que nous sachions** ...; he insists ou is anxious that we should know ...; **si vous y tenez** if you really want to, if you insist; **tu viens avec nous? — si tu y tiens** are you coming with us? — if you really want me to ou if you insist

c = *avoir pour cause* to be due to, stem from; **ça tient au climat** it's because of the climate, it's due to the climate; **à quoi tient sa popularité?** what's the reason for his popularity?; **son succès tient à peu de chose** his success hangs on very little

d = *être contigu à* to adjoin; **le jardin tient à la ferme** the garden adjoins the farmhouse

4 **tenir de** VERBE TRANSITIF INDIR

= *ressembler à* [+ parent] to take after; **il tient de son père** he takes after his father; **il a de qui ~** it runs in the family; **sa réussite tient du prodige** his success is something of a miracle; **cela tient du comique et du tragique** there's something (both) comic and tragic about it, there are elements of both the comic and the tragic in it

5 VERBE IMPERSONNEL

= *dépendre de* to depend; **il ne tient qu'à vous de décider** it's up to you to decide, the decision rests with you; **il ne tient qu'à elle que cela se fasse** it's entirely up to her whether it's done; **ça ne tient qu'à lui** it doesn't depend on him alone; **à quoi cela tient-il qu'il n'écrive pas?** how is it ou why is it that he doesn't write?; **ça tient à peu de chose** it's touch and go, it's in the balance

◆ **qu'à cela ne tienne** never mind (that), that needn't matter, that's no problem

6 **se tenir** VERBE PRONOMINAL

a = *avec les mains ou une partie du corps* **il se tenait le ventre de douleur** he was clutching ou holding his stomach in pain; **se ~ à qch** to hold onto sth; **l'acrobate se tenait par les pieds** the acrobat hung on by his feet; (mutuellement) **ils se tenaient (par) la main** they were

holding hands ou holding each other by the hand; **ils se tenaient par la taille/le cou** they had their arms round each other's waists/necks

b = *être dans une position, un état* ou *un lieu* **se ~ debout/couché/à genoux** to be standing (up)/lying (down)/kneeling (down) ou on one's knees; **tiens-toi droit** (debout) stand up straight; (assis) sit up (straight); **redresse-toi, tu te tiens mal** stand up straight, you're not holding yourself properly; **tenez-vous prêts à partir** be ready to leave; **elle se tenait à sa fenêtre/dans un coin de la pièce** she was standing at her window/in a corner of the room

c = *se conduire* to behave; **il ne sait pas se ~** he doesn't know how to behave; **se ~ tranquille** to be quiet; **tiens-toi tranquille** (lit) keep still; (fig = n'agis pas) lie low; **se ~ bien/mal** (à table) to have good/bad table manners; (en société) to behave well/badly; **devant cette dame, tâche de te ~ comme il faut** ou **de bien te ~** when you meet the lady, try to behave properly; (hum) **il se tient mieux à table qu'à cheval*** he's a healthy eater, he's got a healthy appetite; (avertissement) **il n'a qu'à bien se ~** (bien se conduire) he'd better behave himself; (faire attention) he'd better watch out

d = *avoir lieu* [réunion, séance] to be held; **le marché se tient là chaque semaine** the market is held there every week

e = *être cohérent* [raisonnement] to hold together; (= être liés, solidaires) [événements, faits] to be connected ou interlinked; **tout se tient** it's all connected

f = *se retenir* (gén nég) **il ne peut se ~ de rire/critiquer** he can't help laughing/criticizing; **il ne se tenait pas de joie** he couldn't contain his joy; **tiens-toi bien!** wait till you hear the next bit!; **tu sais combien elle a gagné? tiens-toi bien : 3 millions!** do you know how much she won? wait for it! ou you won't believe it! — 3 million! → **quatre**

g

◆ **s'en tenir à** (= se limiter à) to confine o.s. to, stick to; (= se satisfaire de) to content o.s. with; **nous nous en tiendrons là pour aujourd'hui** we'll leave it at that for today; **il aimerait savoir à quoi s'en ~** he'd like to know where he stands; **je sais à quoi m'en ~ sur son compte** I know exactly who I'm dealing with, I know just the sort of man he is

h

◆ **se tenir pour** (= se considérer comme) **il se tient pour responsable** he holds himself responsible; **il ne se tient pas pour battu** he doesn't consider himself beaten; (avertissement) **tenez-vous-le pour dit!** you've been warned!, you won't be told again!

Tennessee [tenesi] NM Tennessee

tennis [tenis] **1** NM **a** (= sport) tennis; **~ sur gazon** lawn tennis; **~ sur terre battue** hardcourt tennis; **~ en salle** indoor tennis; **~ de table** table tennis **b** (= terrain) (tennis) court **c** (= partie) game of tennis; **faire un ~** to have a game of tennis, play tennis **2** NMPL (= chaussures) tennis shoes; (par extension = chaussures de gym) gym shoes, trainers (Brit), sneakers (US)

tennisman [tenisman] (pl **tennismen** [tenismɛn]) NM tennis player

tennistique [tenistik] ADJ tennis (épith)

tenon [tənɔ̃] NM (Menuiserie) tenon; **assemblage à ~ et mortaise** mortice and tenon joint

ténor [tenɔʀ] **1** NM **a** (Mus) tenor; **~ léger** light tenor **b** (fig) (Pol) leading light, big name (de in); (Sport) star player, big name **2** ADJ tenor

tenseur [tɑ̃sœʀ] NM, ADJ M (Anat, Math) tensor

tensioactif, -ive [tɑ̃sjoaktif, iv] ADJ, NM (agent) **~** surface-active agent

tensiomètre [tɑ̃sjɔmɛtʀ] NM tensiometer

tension [tɑ̃sjɔ̃] NF **a** [ressort, cordes de piano, muscles] tension; [courroie] tightness, tautness, tension; **chaîne à ~ réglable** adjustable tension chain; **corde de ~ d'une scie** tightening-cord of a saw

b (Phon) (= phase d'articulation) attack; (= état d'un phonème tendu) tension, tenseness

c (Élec) voltage, tension; **~ de 220 volts** tension of 220 volts; **à haute/basse ~** high-/low-voltage ou -tension (épith); **baisse** ou **chute de ~** voltage drop, drop in voltage; **sous ~** live; **mettre un appareil sous ~** to switch on a piece of equipment

d (Méd) **~ nerveuse** nervous tension ou strain; **~ (artérielle)** blood pressure; **avoir** ou **faire de la ~** ◊ **avoir trop de ~** to have high blood pressure; **prendre la ~ de qn** to take ou check sb's blood pressure; **baisse** ou **chute de ~** sudden drop in blood pressure

e (fig) [relations, situation] tension (de in); **~s sociales/ethniques/politiques** social/ethnic/political tensions; **~s inflationnistes/monétaires** inflationary/monetary pressures; **on note un regain de ~ dans la région** there is renewed tension in the region; **~ entre deux pays/personnes** tension ou strained relationship between two countries/people

f (= concentration, effort) **~ d'esprit** sustained mental effort; (littér) **~ vers un but/idéal** striving ou straining towards a goal/an ideal

g (Phys) [liquide] tension; [vapeur] pressure; (Tech) stress; **~ superficielle** surface tension

tentaculaire [tɑ̃takylɛʀ] ADJ (Zool) tentacular; (fig) **villes ~s** sprawling towns; **firmes ~s** monster (international) combines

tentacule [tɑ̃takyl] NM (Zool, fig) tentacle

tentant, e [tɑ̃tɑ̃, ɑ̃t] ADJ [plat] tempting; [offre, projet] tempting, attractive

tentateur, -trice [tɑ̃tatœʀ, tʀis] **1** ADJ [beauté] tempting, alluring, enticing; [propos] tempting, enticing; (Rel) **l'esprit ~** the Tempter **2** NM tempter; (Rel) **le Tentateur** the Tempter **3** **tentatrice** NF temptress

tentation [tɑ̃tasjɔ̃] NF temptation; (Rel) **la ~ de saint Antoine** the temptation of Saint Anthony; **résister à la ~** to resist temptation; **succomber à la ~** to yield ou give in to temptation

tentative [tɑ̃tativ] NF (gén) attempt, endeavour; (sportive, style journalistique) bid, attempt; **de vaines ~s** vain attempts ou endeavours; **~ d'évasion** attempt ou bid to escape, escape bid ou attempt; **~ de meurtre/de suicide** (gén) murder/suicide attempt; (Jur) attempted murder/suicide; **faire une ~ auprès de qn** (en vue de ...) to approach sb (with a view to ...)

tente [tɑ̃t] **1** NF (gén) tent; **~ de camping** (camping) tent; **coucher sous la ~** to sleep under canvas, camp out; (fig) **se retirer sous sa ~** to go and sulk in one's corner **2** COMP ▶ **tente de cirque** circus tent, marquee ▶ **tente(-)igloo** igloo tent ▶ **tente à oxygène** oxygen tent ▶ **tente de plage** beach tent

tenté, e [tɑ̃te] (ptp de **tenter**) ADJ **être ~ de faire/croire qch** to be tempted to do/believe sth

tente-abri (pl **tentes-abris**) [tɑ̃tabʀi] NF shelter tent

▼ **tenter** [tɑ̃te] ▶ conjug 1 ◀ VT **a** (= chercher à séduire) [+ personne] (gén, Rel) to tempt; **~ qn (par une offre)** to tempt sb (with an offer); **ce n'était pas cher, elle s'est laissée ~** it wasn't expensive and she let herself be tempted; **se laisser ~ par une offre** to be tempted by an offer; **qu'est-ce qui te tente comme gâteau?*** what kind of cake do you feel like?; **qu'est-ce que ça te dit?*; un match de tennis, ça te tenterait?** do you feel like ou do you fancy* (Brit) a game of tennis?, how about a game of tennis?; **tu peux venir si ça te tente** you can come if you feel like it; **c'est vraiment ~ le diable** it's really tempting fate ou Providence; **il ne faut pas ~**

le diable don't tempt fate, don't push your luck*

[b] (= *risquer*) [+ *expérience, démarche*] to try, attempt; **on a tout tenté pour le sauver** they tried everything to save him; **on a tenté l'impossible pour le sauver** they attempted the impossible to save him; **~ le tout pour le tout** to risk one's all; **~ la** *ou* **sa chance** to try one's luck; **~ le coup*** to have a go* *ou* a bash*, give it a try* *ou* a whirl*; **~ l'aventure** to take the plunge, try one's luck

[c] (= *essayer*) **~ de faire qch** to attempt *ou* try to do sth; **je vais ~ de le convaincre** I'll try to *ou* try and convince him

tenture [tɑ̃tyʀ] NF [a] (= *tapisserie*) hanging; **~ murale** wall covering [b] (= *grand rideau*) hanging, curtain, drape (*US*); (*derrière une porte*) door curtain [c] (*de deuil*) funeral hangings

tenu, e[1] [t(ə)ny] (*ptp de* **tenir**) ADJ [a] (= *entretenu*) **bien ~** [*enfant*] well *ou* neatly turned out; [*maison*] well-kept, well looked after; [*comptes, registres*] well-kept, tidy; **mal ~** [*enfant*] poorly turned out, untidy; [*maison*] poorly kept, poorly looked after; [*comptes, registres*] badly kept, untidy [b] (= *strictement surveillé*) **leurs filles sont très ~es** their daughters are kept on a tight rein *ou* are held very much in check [c] (= *obligé*) **être ~ de faire qch** to be obliged to do sth, have to do sth; **être ~ au secret professionnel** to be bound by professional secrecy → **impossible** [d] (*Mus*) [*note*] held, sustained [e] (*Bourse*) [*valeurs*] firm, steady

ténu, e [teny] ADJ (*littér*) [a] [*point, particule, fil*] fine; [*brume*] thin; [*voix*] thin, reedy [b] [*raison*] tenuous, flimsy; [*nuance, cause*] tenuous, subtle; [*souvenir, espoir*] faint

tenue[2] [t(ə)ny] [1] NF [a] [*maison*] upkeep, running; [*magasin*] running; [*classe*] handling, control; [*séance*] holding; (*Mus*) [*note*] holding, sustaining; **la ~ des livres de comptes** the book-keeping; **~ fautive de la plume** wrong way of holding one's pen [b] (= *conduite*) (good) manners, good behaviour (*Brit*) *ou* behavior (*US*); **bonne ~ en classe/à table** good behaviour in class/at (the) table; **avoir de la ~** to have good manners, know how to behave (o.s.); **allons! un peu de ~!** come on, behave yourself! *ou* watch your manners! [c] (= *qualité*) [*journal*] standard, quality; **publication qui a de la ~** publication of a high standard, quality publication [d] (= *maintien*) posture; **mauvaise ~ d'un écolier** bad posture of a schoolboy [e] (*Bourse*) performance; **la bonne/mauvaise ~ du franc face au dollar** the good/poor performance of the franc against the dollar [f] (= *habillement, apparence*) dress, appearance; (= *vêtements, uniforme*) dress; **leur ~ négligée** their sloppy dress *ou* appearance; **en ~ négligée** wearing *ou* in casual clothes; **ce n'est pas une ~ pour aller au golf!** that's no way to dress to play golf!; **« ~ correcte exigée »** "strict dress code"; **~ d'intérieur** indoor clothes; **en ~ légère** (*d'été*) wearing *ou* in light clothing; (*osée*) scantily dressed *ou* clad; **en petite ~** scantily dressed *ou* clad; (*hum*) **en ~ d'Adam** (*ou* **d'Ève**) in one's birthday suit*; **en grande ~** in full dress (uniform); **des touristes en ~ estivale/d'hiver** tourists in summer/winter clothes; **se mettre en ~** to get dressed; (*Mil*) **être en ~** to be in uniform; **les policiers en ~** uniformed policemen, policemen in uniform; (*Mil*) **~ camouflée** *ou* **de camouflage/de campagne** camouflage/combat dress

[2] COMP ► **tenue de combat** battle dress ► **tenue de route** road holding ► **tenue de service** uniform ► **tenue de soirée** formal *ou* evening dress; **« ~ de soirée de rigueur »** ≈ "black tie" ► **tenue de sport** sports clothes, sports gear ► **tenue de ville**

[*homme*] lounge suit (*Brit*), town suit (*US*); [*femme*] town dress *ou* suit ► **tenue de vol** flying gear

ténuité [tenɥite] NF (*littér*) [a] [*point, particule, fil*] fineness; [*brume*] thinness; [*voix*] thinness, reediness [b] [*raison*] tenuousness, tenuity, flimsiness; [*nuance, cause*] tenuousness, tenuity, subtlety

tenure [tənyʀ] NF (*Hist, Jur*) tenure

TEP [teəpe] (ABRÉV = **tonne équivalent pétrole**) TOE

tequila [tekila] NF tequila

ter [tɛʀ] [1] ADJ (*dans une adresse*) **il habite au 10 ~** he lives at (number) 10b [2] ADV (*Mus*) three times, ter

tératogène [teʀatɔʒɛn] ADJ teratogenic

tératologie [teʀatɔlɔʒi] NF teratology

tératologique [teʀatɔlɔʒik] ADJ teratological

terbium [tɛʀbjɔm] NM terbium

tercet [tɛʀsɛ] NM (*Poésie*) tercet, triplet

térébenthine [teʀebɑ̃tin] NF turpentine; **nettoyer à l'essence de ~** *ou* **à la ~** to clean with turpentine *ou* turps* (*Brit*) *ou* turp (*US*)

térébinthe [teʀebɛ̃t] NM terebinth

Tergal ® [tɛʀgal] NM Terylene ®

tergiversations [tɛʀʒivɛʀsasjɔ̃] NFPL prevarication, equivocation; **après des semaines de ~** after weeks of prevarication; **trêve de ~!** stop beating about the bush!, stop prevaricating!

tergiverser [tɛʀʒivɛʀse] ▶conjug 1◀ VI to prevaricate, equivocate, shilly-shally; **cessez donc de ~!** stop beating about the bush!, stop prevaricating!

terme [tɛʀm] [1] NM [a] (*Ling = mot, expression*) term; (*Math, Philo = élément*) term; **~ de marine/de métier** nautical/professional term; **aux ~s du contrat** according to the terms of the contract; **en ~s clairs/voilés/flatteurs** in clear/veiled/flattering terms; **en d'autres ~s** in other words; **il ne l'a pas dit en ces ~s** he didn't put it like that; **il raisonne en ~s d'efficacité** he thinks in terms of efficiency; **... et le ~ est faible** ... and that's putting it mildly, ... and that's an understatement; **moyen ~** (*gén*) middle course; (*Logique*) middle term → **acception, force**

[b] (= *date limite*) time limit, deadline; (*littér* = *fin*) [*vie, voyage, bail*] end, term (*littér*); **passé ce ~** after this date; **se fixer un ~ pour ...** to set o.s. a time limit *ou* a deadline for ...; **arriver à ~** [*délai, mandat, contrat*] to expire; [*opération*] to reach its *ou* a conclusion; [*paiement*] to fall due; **mettre un ~ à qch** to put an end *ou* a stop to sth; **mener qch à (son) ~** to bring sth to completion, carry sth through (to completion); **arrivé au ~ de sa vie** having reached the end *ou* the term (*littér*) of his life; **prévisions à court/moyen/long ~** (*gén*) short-/medium-/long-term forecasts; (*Mét*) short-/medium-/long-range forecasts; **ce sera rentable à court/moyen/long ~** it will be profitable in the short/medium/long term; **à ~, c'est ce qui arrivera** this is what will happen eventually *ou* in the long run *ou* in the end

[c] (*Méd*) **à ~** [*accouchement*] full term; [*naître*] at term; **être à ~** [*femme enceinte*] to be at full term; **avant ~** [*naître, accoucher*] prematurely; **bébé né/naissance avant ~** premature baby/birth; **un bébé né deux mois avant ~** a baby born two months premature, a two-months premature baby; **elle a dépassé le ~ de trois jours** she's three days overdue

[d] (*loyer*) (= *date*) term, date for payment; (= *période*) quarter, rental term *ou* period; (= *somme*) (quarterly) rent (*NonC*); **payer à ~ échu** to pay at the end of the rental term, pay a quarter *ou* term in arrears; (= *loyer*) **le (jour du) ~** the quarterday; **il a un ~ de retard** he's one quarter *ou* one payment behind (with his rent); **devoir/payer son ~** to owe/pay one's rent

[e] (*Bourse, Fin*) **à ~** forward; **acheter/vendre à ~** to buy/sell forward; **transaction à ~** (*Bourse de marchandises*) forward transaction; (*Bourse des valeurs*) settlement bargain; **crédit/emprunt à court/long ~** short-term *ou* short-dated/long-term *ou* long-dated credit/loan, short/long credit/loan → **marché**

[2] **termes** NMPL (= *relations*) terms; **être en bons/mauvais ~s avec qn** to be on good *ou* friendly/bad terms with sb; **ils sont dans les meilleurs ~s** they are on the best of terms

terminaison [tɛʀminɛzɔ̃] NF (*Ling*) ending; (*Anat*) **~s nerveuses** nerve endings

terminal, e (*mpl* **-aux**) [tɛʀminal, o] [1] ADJ [*élément, bourgeon, phase de maladie*] terminal; (*Scol*) **classe ~e** final year, ≈ upper sixth (form) (*Brit*), twelfth grade (*US*), ≈ senior year (*US*); **élève de ~e** ≈ upper sixth former (*Brit*), senior (*US*), twelfth grader (*US*); **malade au stade ~** *ou* **en phase ~e** terminally ill patient [2] NM [a] (= *aérogare*) (air) terminal [b] [*pétrole, marchandises*] terminal; **~ pétrolier** oil terminal; **~ maritime** shipping terminal [c] (= *ordinateur*) terminal; **~ intelligent/passif** smart *ou* intelligent/dumb terminal; **~ vocal** vocal terminal; **~ de paiement électronique** electronic payment terminal; **~ point de vente** point-of-sale *ou* POS terminal [3] **terminale** NF (*Scol*) → [1]

terminer [tɛʀmine] ▶conjug 1◀ [1] VT [a] (= *clore*) [+ *débat, séance*] to bring to an end *ou* to a close, terminate [b] (= *achever*) [+ *travail*] to finish (off), complete; [+ *repas, temps d'exil*] to end, finish; [+ *récit, débat*] to finish, close, end; **il termina en nous remerciant** he finished (up *ou* off) *ou* he ended by thanking us; **nous avons terminé la journée/soirée chez un ami/par une promenade** we finished off *ou* ended the day/evening at a friend's house/with a walk; **~ ses jours à la campagne/à l'hôpital** to end one's days in the country/in hospital; **~ un repas par un café** to finish off *ou* round off *ou* end a meal with a coffee; **~ un livre par quelques conseils pratiques** to end a book with a few pieces of practical advice; **en avoir terminé avec un travail** to be finished with a job; **j'en ai terminé avec eux** I am *ou* have finished with them, I have done with them; **pour ~ je dirais que ...** in conclusion *ou* to conclude I would say that ..., and finally I would say that ...; **j'attends qu'il termine** I'm waiting for him to finish, I'm waiting till he's finished [c] (= *former le dernier élément de*) **le café termina le repas** the meal finished *ou* ended with coffee, coffee finished off the meal; **un bourgeon termine la tige** the stalk ends in a bud

[2] **se terminer** VPR [a] (= *prendre fin*) [*rue, domaine*] to end, terminate (*frm*); [*affaire, repas*] to (come to an) end; **les vacances se terminent demain** the holidays finish *ou* (come to an) end tomorrow; **le parc se termine ici** the park ends here; **ça s'est bien/mal terminé** it ended well/badly, it turned out well *ou* all right/badly (in the end); **alors ces travaux, ça se termine?** (*gén*) well, is the work just about complete? *ou* done?; (*impatience*) when's the work going to be finished? [b] (= *s'achever sur*) **se ~ par** to end with; **la thèse se termine par une bibliographie** the thesis ends with a bibliography; **la soirée se termina par un jeu** the evening ended with a game; **ces verbes se terminent par le suffixe « ir »** these verbs end in the suffix "ir" [c] (= *finir en*) **se ~ en** to end in; **les mots qui se terminent en « ation »** words which end in "ation"; **cette comédie se termine en tragédie** this comedy ends in tragedy; **se ~ en pointe** to taper to a point, end in a point

terminologie [tɛʀminɔlɔʒi] NF terminology

terminologique [tɛʀminɔlɔʒik] ADJ terminological

terminologue [tɛʀminɔlɔg] NMF terminologist

terminus [tɛʀminys] NM [autobus, train] terminus; **~! tout le monde descend!** (last stop!) all change!

termite [tɛʀmit] NM termite, white ant

termitière [tɛʀmitjɛʀ] NF termites' nest, termitarium (SPÉC)

ternaire [tɛʀnɛʀ] ADJ ternary

terne [tɛʀn] ADJ [teint] lifeless, colourless (Brit), colorless (US); [regard] lifeless, lacklustre (Brit), lackluster (US); [personne] dull, drab, colourless (Brit), colorless (US); [style, conversation] dull, drab, lacklustre (Brit), lackluster (US); [couleur, journée, vie] dull, drab; [cheveux] dull, lifeless

terni, e [tɛʀni] (ptp de ternir) ADJ (lit, fig) tarnished

ternir [tɛʀniʀ] ▸conjug 2 ◂ 1 VT a [+ métal, glace] to tarnish b [+ mémoire, honneur, réputation] to stain, tarnish, sully 2 **se ternir** VPR [métal, glace] to tarnish, become tarnished; [réputation] to become tarnished ou stained

ternissement [tɛʀnismɑ̃] NM [métal] tarnishing

ternissure [tɛʀnisyʀ] NF (= aspect) [argenterie, métal, glace] tarnish, tarnished condition; (= tache) tarnished ou dull spot

terrain [tɛʀɛ̃] 1 NM a (= relief) ground, terrain (SPÉC, littér); (= sol) soil, ground; **~ caillouteux/vallonné** stony/hilly ground; **~ meuble/lourd** loose/heavy soil ou ground; **c'est un bon ~ pour la culture** it's (a) good soil for cultivation → **accident, glissement, tout-terrain**
b (Ftbl, Rugby) pitch, field; (avec les installations) ground; (Courses, Golf) course; (Basket, Volley, Hand-ball) court; **sur le ~** on the field; **disputer un match sur ~ adverse/sur son propre ~** to play an away/a home match
c (= étendue de terre) land (NonC); (= parcelle) plot (of land), piece of land; (à bâtir) site; **~ à lotir** land for dividing into plots; **«~ à bâtir»** "site ou building land for sale"; **une maison avec deux hectares de ~** a house with two hectares of land; **le prix du ~ à Paris** the price of land in Paris
d (Géog, Géol: souvent pl) formation; **les ~s primaires/glaciaires** primary/glacial formations
e (Mil = lieu d'opérations) terrain; (gagné ou perdu) ground; **en ~ ennemi** on enemy ground ou territory; **disputer le ~** (Mil) to fight for every inch of ground; (fig) to fight every inch of the way; (lit, fig) **céder/gagner/perdre du ~** to give/gain/lose ground; **céder du ~ à l'ennemi** to lose ou yield ground to the enemy, fall back before the enemy; **ils finiront par céder du ~** (négociateurs) in the end they'll make concessions; **l'épidémie cède du ~ devant les efforts des médecins** the epidemic is receding before the doctors' efforts; **la livre a cédé/gagné du ~** the pound has lost/gained ground (**par rapport à** against); **reconnaître le ~** (lit) to reconnoitre the terrain; (fig) to see how the land lies, get the lie (Brit) ou lay (US) of the land; (fig) **sonder** ou **tâter le ~** to test the ground, put out feelers; **avoir l'avantage du ~** (lit) to have territorial advantage; (fig) to have the advantage of being on (one's) home ground; **préparer/déblayer le ~** to prepare/clear the ground; **aller/être sur le ~** to go out into/be out in the field; (Pol) **de ~** [politicien] grass-roots; (Ind) **le nouveau P.D.G. est un homme de ~** the new managing director has a practical rather than an academic background ou has done his stint at the coalface (fig, Brit)
f (fig = domaine) ground; **être sur son ~** to be on home ground ou territory; **trouver un ~ d'entente** to find common ground ou an area of agreement; **chercher un ~ favorable à la discussion** to seek an area conducive to

(useful) discussion; **je ne le suivrai pas sur ce ~** I can't go along with him there ou on that, I'm not with him on that; **être en** ou **sur un ~ mouvant** to be on uncertain ground; **être sur un ~ glissant** to be on slippery ou dangerous ground; **le journaliste s'aventura sur un ~ brûlant** the journalist ventured onto dangerous ground ou brought up a highly sensitive ou ticklish issue; **l'épidémie a trouvé un ~ très favorable chez les réfugiés** the epidemic found an ideal breeding ground amongst the refugees; (Méd) **~ allergique** conditions likely to produce allergies; (Méd) **il a un mauvais ~** he's quite susceptible to illness; (Méd) **il a un ~ arthritique** he's quite susceptible to arthritis

2 COMP ▸ **terrain d'atterrissage** landing ground ▸ **terrain d'aviation** airfield ▸ **terrain de camping** campsite, camping ground ▸ **terrain de chasse** hunting ground ▸ **terrain d'exercice** training ground ▸ **terrain de jeu** playing field ▸ **terrain de manœuvre** (Mil) training ground; (= domaine) stomping ground ▸ **terrain militaire** army ground ▸ **terrain de sport** sports ground ▸ **terrain de tennis** tennis court ▸ **terrain de tir** shooting ou firing range ▸ **terrain vague** waste ground (NonC), wasteland (NonC)

terra incognita [teʀaɛ̃kɔɡnita] (pl **terrae incognitae** [teʀaɛ̃kɔɡnite]) NF (littér) terra incognita

terrasse [teʀas] NF a [parc, jardin] terrace; **cultures en ~s** terrace cultivation; (Géog) **~ fluviale** river terrace b [appartement] terrace; (sur le toit) terrace roof; **toiture en ◊ toit-~** flat roof c [café] terrace, pavement (area); **j'ai aperçu Charles attablé à la ~ du Café Royal** I saw Charles sitting at the terrace of the Café Royal ou outside the Café Royal; **à la** ou **en ~** outside; **il refusa de me servir à la** ou **en ~** he refused to serve me outside d (Constr = métier) excavation work; **faire de la ~** to do excavation work

terrassement [teʀasmɑ̃] NM a (= action) excavation; **travaux de ~** excavation work; **engins de ~** earth-moving ou excavating equipment b (= terres creusées) **~s** excavations, earthworks; [voie ferrée] embankments

terrasser [teʀase] ▸conjug 1 ◂ VT a [adversaire] to floor, bring down; [attaque] to bring down; [fatigue] to overcome; [émotion, nouvelle] to overwhelm; [maladie] to strike down; **cette maladie l'a terrassé** this illness laid him low; **terrassé par une crise cardiaque** struck down ou felled by a heart attack b (Tech) to excavate, dig out; (Agr) to dig over

terrassier [teʀasje] NM unskilled road worker, navvy (Brit)

terre [tɛʀ] 1 NF a (= planète) earth; (= monde) world; **la planète Terre** (the) planet Earth; (Rel) **sur la ~ comme au ciel** on earth as it is in heaven; **Dieu créa le Ciel et la Terre** God created the Heavens and the Earth, God created Heaven and Earth; **il a parcouru la ~ entière** he has travelled the world over, he has travelled all over the world ou globe; **prendre à témoin la ~ entière** to take the world as one's witness; **tant qu'il y aura des hommes sur la ~** as long as there are men on (the) earth; **être seul sur (la) ~** to be alone in the world; **il ne faut pas s'attendre au bonheur sur (cette) ~** happiness is not to be expected in this world ou on this earth; (fig) **redescendre** ou **revenir sur ~** to come (back) down to earth → **remuer, sel, ventre**
b (sol, surface) ground, land; (= matière) earth, soil; (pour la poterie) clay; **pipe/vase en ~** clay pipe/vase; **ne t'allonge pas par ~, la ~ est humide** don't lie on the ground — it's damp, don't lie down — the ground is damp; **une ~ fertile/aride** a fertile/an arid ou a barren soil; **retourner/labourer la ~** to turn over/work the soil; **travailler la ~** to work the

soil ou land; **planter un arbre en pleine ~** to plant a tree in the ground; **être à ~** [lutteur] to be down; (lit, fig) **il ne faut pas frapper quelqu'un qui est à ~** you shouldn't kick a man when he's down ou somebody when they're down; **poser qch à** ou **par ~** to put sth (down) on the ground; **jeter qch à** ou **par ~** to throw sth (down) on the ground, throw sth to the ground; **cela fiche** ou **flanque tous nos projets par ~*** that really messes up all our plans, that puts paid to all our plans (Brit); **mettre qn en ~** to bury sb; **mettre qch en ~** to put sth into the soil; **cinq mètres sous ~** five metres underground; (fig) **être à six pieds sous ~** to be six feet under, be pushing up the daisies*; **j'aurais voulu rentrer sous ~** (de honte) I wished the ground would swallow me up, I could have died* → **chemin, motte, ver**
c (= étendue, campagne) **~(s)** land (NonC); **une bande** ou **langue de ~** a strip ou tongue of land; **des ~s à blé** wheat-growing land; **il a acheté un bout** ou **un lopin de ~** he's bought a piece ou patch ou plot of land; **~s cultivées** cultivated land; **~s en friche** ou **en jachère/incultes** fallow/uncultivated land
d (par opposition à mer) land (NonC); **sur la ~ ferme** on dry land, on terra firma; **apercevoir la ~** to sight land; (Naut) **~!** land ho!; (Naut) **aller à ~** to go ashore; **dans les ~s** inland; **aller/voyager par (voie de) ~** to go/travel by land ou overland; **toucher ~** [navire, avion] to land
e (= propriété, domaine) land (gén NonC); **la ~** land; **une ~** an estate; **il a acheté une ~ en Normandie** he's bought an estate ou some land in Normandy; **vivre sur/de ses ~s** to live on/off one's lands ou estates; **se retirer sur ses ~s** to go and live on one's country estate; **la ~ est un excellent investissement** land is an excellent investment
f (= pays, région) land, country; **sa ~ natale** his native land ou country; **la France, ~ d'accueil** France, (the) land of welcome; **~s lointaines/australes** distant/southern lands; **la Terre promise** the Promised Land
g (Élec) earth (Brit), ground (US); **mettre** ou **relier à la ~** to earth (Brit), ground (US) → **pris**

2 COMP ▸ **la Terre Adélie** the Adélie Coast, Adélie Land ▸ **terre d'asile** country of refuge ou asylum ▸ **terre battue** beaten earth; **sol en ~ battue** beaten-earth floor; (Tennis) **jouer sur ~ battue** to play on a hard court ▸ **terre brûlée** (fig) politique de la ~ brûlée scorched earth policy ▸ **terre de bruyère** heath-mould, heath-peat ▸ **terre cuite** (pour briques, tuiles) baked clay; (pour jattes, statuettes) terracotta; **objets en ~ cuite ◊ ~s cuites** terracotta ware (NonC); **une ~ cuite** a terracotta (object) ▸ **terre d'exil** land ou country of exile ▸ **la Terre de Feu** Tierra del Fuego ▸ **terre à foulon** fuller's earth ▸ **terre glaise** clay ▸ **terre noire** (Géog) chernozem ▸ **terre à potier** potter's clay ▸ **terres rares** (Chim) rare earths ▸ **la Terre sainte** the Holy Land ▸ **terre de Sienne** sienna ▸ **terre végétale** topsoil ▸ **terres vierges** virgin lands

terre à terre, terre-à-terre [tɛʀatɛʀ] ADJ INV [esprit] matter-of-fact; [personne] down-to-earth; [préoccupations] mundane, workaday, prosaic

terreau [tɛʀo] NM (soil-based) compost; **~ de feuilles** leaf mould; **les rumeurs trouvent ici un ~ très favorable** this is an ideal breeding ground for rumours

terre-neuvas [tɛʀnœva] NM INV (= bateau) fishing boat (for fishing off Newfoundland); (= marin) fisherman, trawlerman (who fishes off Newfoundland)

Terre-Neuve [tɛʀnœv] NF Newfoundland

terre-neuve [tɛʀnœv] NM INV (= chien) Newfoundland terrier; (hum = personne) good Samaritan

terre-neuvien, -ienne (*mpl* **terre-neuviens**) [tɛʀnœvjɛ̃, jɛn] [1] ADJ Newfoundland (*épith*) [2] **Terre-Neuvien(ne)** NM,F Newfoundlander

terre-neuvier (*pl* **terre-neuviers**) [tɛʀnœvje] NM = **terre-neuvas**

terre-plein (*pl* **terre-pleins**) [tɛʀplɛ̃] NM (*Mil*) terreplein; (*Constr*) platform; (*sur chaussée*) ~ **(central)** central reservation (*Brit*), median strip (*US*)

terrer [tɛʀe] ▶ conjug 1 ◀ [1] **se terrer** VPR [a] [*personne poursuivie*] to flatten o.s., crouch down; [*criminel*] to lie low, go to ground *ou* earth; [*personne peu sociable*] to hide (o.s.) away; **terrés dans la cave pendant les bombardements** hidden *ou* buried (away) in the cellar during the bombings [b] [*lapin, renard*] (*dans son terrier*) to go to earth *ou* ground; (*contre terre*) to crouch down, flatten itself [2] VT (*Agr*) [+ *arbre*] to earth round *ou* up; [+ *pelouse*] to spread with soil; [+ *semis*] to earth over; (*Tech*) [+ *drap*] to full

terrestre [tɛʀɛstʀ] ADJ [a] [*faune, flore, transports, habitat*] land (*épith*); [*surface, magnétisme*] earth's (*épith*), terrestrial, of earth; (*Mil*) **effectifs ~s** land forces; **missile ~** land-based missile → **croûte, écorce, globe** [b] (= *d'ici-bas*) [*biens, plaisirs, vie*] earthly, terrestrial → **paradis**

terreur [tɛʀœʀ] NF [a] (= *peur*) terror (*gén NonC*); **avec ~** with terror *ou* dread; **vaines ~s** vain *ou* empty fears; **le dentiste était ma grande ~** the dentist was my greatest fear, I was terrified of the dentist; **il vivait dans la ~ d'être découvert/de la police** he lived in terror of being discovered/of the police; **faire régner la ~** to conduct *ou* impose a reign of terror; **semer la ~** to spread terror; **climat/régime de ~** climate/reign of terror [b] (= *terrorisme*) terror; (*Hist*) **la Terreur** the (Reign of) Terror [c] (* *hum* = *personne*) terror; **petite ~** little terror *ou* horror; **jouer les ~s** to play the tough guy*; **on l'appelait Joe la ~** he was known as Joe, the tough guy*; **c'est la ~ de la ville** he's the terror of the town

terreux, -euse [tɛʀø, øz] ADJ [a] [*goût, odeur*] earthy [b] [*semelles, chaussures*] muddy; [*mains*] grubby, soiled; [*salade*] gritty, dirty [c] [*teint*] sallow, muddy; [*ciel*] muddy, leaden, sullen

terrible [tɛʀibl] [1] ADJ [a] (= *effroyable*) [*accident, maladie, châtiment*] terrible, dreadful, awful; [*arme*] terrible [b] (= *terrifiant, féroce*) [*guerrier, air, menaces*] terrible, fearsome [c] (*intensif*) [*vent, force, pression, bruit*] terrific, tremendous; [*colère, erreur*] terrible; **c'est un ~ menteur** he's a terrible *ou* an awful liar; **c'est ~ ce qu'il peut manger** he can eat an incredible amount [d] (= *affligeant, pénible*) terrible, dreadful, awful; **c'est ~ d'en arriver là** it's terrible *ou* awful *ou* dreadful to come to this; **le (plus) ~, c'est que ...** the (most) terrible *ou* awful thing about it is that ...; **il est ~, avec sa manie de toujours vous contredire** he's got a dreadful habit of always contradicting you; **c'est ~ de devoir toujours tout répéter** it's awful *ou* dreadful always having to repeat everything → **enfant** [e] (* = *formidable*) [*film, soirée, personne*] terrific*, great*, tremendous*; **ce film n'est pas ~** this film is nothing special *ou* nothing to write home about *ou* no great shakes* [2] ADV **ça marche ~!** it's working fantastically (well)* *ou* really great*

terriblement [tɛʀibləmɑ̃] ADV [a] (= *extrêmement*) terribly, dreadfully, awfully [b] († = *affreusement*) terribly†

terrien, -ienne [tɛʀjɛ̃, jɛn] [1] ADJ [a] (= *qui possède des terres*) landed (*épith*), landowning (*épith*); **propriétaire ~** landowner, landed proprietor [b] (= *rural*) rural, country; **vertus**

---

terriennes virtues of the soil *ou* land; **avoir une vieille ascendance terrienne** to come of old country stock [2] NM [a] (= *paysan*) man of the soil, countryman [b] (= *habitant de la Terre*) Earthman, earthling [c] (*Naut*) landsman [3] **terrienne** NF [a] (= *paysanne*) countrywoman [b] (= *habitante de la Terre*) Earthwoman, earthling [c] (*Naut*) landswoman

terrier [tɛʀje] NM [a] (= *tanière*) [*lapin, taupe*] burrow, hole; [*renard*] earth; [*blaireau*] set [b] (= *chien*) terrier

terrifiant, e [tɛʀifjɑ̃, jɑ̃t] ADJ [a] (= *effrayant*) terrifying [b] (*sens affaibli*) [*progrès, appétit*] fearsome, incredible; **c'est ~ comme il a maigri/grandi!** it's frightening how much weight he's lost/how much he's grown!

terrifier [tɛʀifje] ▶ conjug 7 ◀ VT to terrify

terril [tɛʀi(l)] NM (*coal*) tip, slag heap

terrine [tɛʀin] NF (= *pot*) earthenware vessel, terrine; (*Culin*) (= *récipient*) terrine; (= *pâté*) pâté, terrine; **~ du chef** chef's special pâté; **~ de lapin/de légumes** rabbit/vegetable terrine *ou* pâté

territoire [tɛʀitwaʀ] NM (*gén, Pol, Zool*) territory; [*département, commune*] area; [*évêque, juge*] jurisdiction; **~s d'outre-mer** (French) overseas territories → **aménagement, surveillance**

territorial, e (*mpl* **-iaux**) [tɛʀitɔʀjal, jo] [1] ADJ [a] [*puissance*] land (*épith*); [*intégrité, modifications*] territorial; **eaux ~es** territorial waters; **armée ~e** Territorial Army [b] (*Jur: opposé à personnel*) territorial [2] NM (*Mil*) Territorial [3] **territoriale** NF (*Mil*) Territorial Army

territorialement [tɛʀitɔʀjalmɑ̃] ADV territorially; (*Jur*) **être ~ compétent** to have jurisdiction

territorialité [tɛʀitɔʀjalite] NF (*Jur*) territoriality

terroir [tɛʀwaʀ] NM [a] (*Agr*) soil; **vin qui a un goût de ~** wine which has a taste *ou* tang of its soil [b] (*fig* = *région rurale*) land; **accent du ~** country *ou* rural accent; **cuisine du ~** country cooking; **mots du ~** words with a rural flavour; **il sent son ~** he is very much of his native heath *ou* soil; **poète du ~** poet of the land

terrorisant, e [tɛʀɔʀizɑ̃, ɑ̃t] ADJ terrifying

terroriser [tɛʀɔʀize] ▶ conjug 1 ◀ VT to terrorize

terrorisme [tɛʀɔʀism] NM terrorism

terroriste [tɛʀɔʀist] ADJ, NMF terrorist

tertiaire [tɛʀsjɛʀ] [1] ADJ (*Écon, Géol, Méd*) tertiary [2] NM **le ~** (*Géol*) the Tertiary; (*Écon*) the service *ou* tertiary sector

tertiarisation [tɛʀsjaʀizasjɔ̃], **tertiarisation** [tɛʀsjaʀizasjɔ̃] NF expansion *ou* development of the service sector

tertio [tɛʀsjo] ADV third(ly)

tertre [tɛʀtʀ] NM (= *monticule*) hillock, mound, knoll (*littér*); **~ (funéraire)** (burial) mound

tes [te] ADJ POSS → **ton¹**

tessiture [tesityʀ] NF [*voix*] tessitura; [*instrument*] range

tesson [tesɔ̃] NM **~ (de bouteille)** shard, sliver *ou* piece of broken glass *ou* bottle

test¹ [tɛst] [1] NM (*gén*) test; **faire passer un ~ à qn** to give sb a test; **soumettre qn à des ~s** to subject sb to tests, test sb; **~ d'intelligence** IQ test; **~ d'orientation professionnelle** vocational *ou* occupational test; **~ d'aptitude/psychologique** *ou* **de personnalité** aptitude/personality test; **~ de grossesse/d'allergie** pregnancy/allergy test → **dépistage** [2] ADJ **groupe-/région-~** test group/area

test² [tɛst] NM (*Zool*) test

test³ [tɛst] NM = **têt**

testable [tɛstabl] ADJ testable

testament [tɛstamɑ̃] [1] NM [a] (*Rel*) **l'Ancien/le Nouveau Testament** the Old/the New Testa-

---

ment [b] (*Jur*) will, testament (*Jur*); **mourir sans ~** to die intestate *ou* without leaving a will; **ceci est mon ~** this is my last will and testament; (*hum*) **il peut faire son ~*** he can *ou* he'd better make out his will → **coucher, léguer** [c] (*fig*) [*homme politique, artiste*] legacy; **~ politique** political legacy [2] COMP ► **testament par acte public, testament authentique** will dictated to notary in the presence of witnesses ► **testament mystique** will written *ou* dictated by testator, signed by him, and handed to notary in a sealed envelope, before witnesses ► **testament olographe** will written, dated and signed by the testator ► **testament secret** = **testament mystique**

testamentaire [tɛstamɑ̃tɛʀ] ADJ **dispositions ~s** clauses *ou* provisions of a will, devises (*SPÉC*); **donation ~** bequest, legacy; **héritier ~** legatee; (*de biens immobiliers*) devisee → **exécuteur**

testateur [tɛstatœʀ] NM testator, legator; (*léguant des biens immobiliers*) devisor

testatrice [tɛstatʀis] NF testatrix, legator; (*léguant des biens immobiliers*) devisor

tester¹ [tɛste] ▶ conjug 1 ◀ VT [+ *personne, produit, connaissances*] to test; **produit testé en laboratoire** laboratory-tested product; **cosmétiques non testés sur animaux** cosmetics that have not been tested on animals, non-animal-tested cosmetics; **il cherchait à ~ ma détermination** he was testing my resolve

tester² [tɛste] ▶ conjug 1 ◀ VI (*Jur*) to make (out) one's will

testeur [tɛstœʀ] NM (= *personne, machine*) tester

testiculaire [tɛstikylɛʀ] ADJ testicular

testicule [tɛstikyl] NM testicle, testis (*SPÉC*)

test-match (*pl* **test-match(e)s**) [tɛstmatʃ] NM (*Rugby*) rugby international

testostérone [tɛstɔsteʀɔn] NF testosterone

têt [tɛ(t)] NM (*Chim*) **~ à rôtir** roasting dish *ou* crucible; **~ à gaz** beehive shelf

tétanie [tetani] NF tetany

tétanique [tetanik] ADJ [*convulsions*] tetanic; [*patient*] tetanus (*épith*), suffering from tetanus (*attrib*)

tétanisation [tetanizasjɔ̃] NF [*muscle*] tetanization

tétaniser [tetanize] ▶ conjug 1 ◀ VT (*Méd*) to tetanize; **muscle qui se tétanise** muscle that becomes tetanized; (*fig*) **il était tétanisé par la peur** he was paralyzed with fear; **le public était tétanisé de surprise** the audience was stunned

tétanos [tetanos] NM (= *maladie*) tetanus, lockjaw; (= *contraction*) tetanus; **~ musculaire** *ou* **physiologique** tetanus (of a muscle); **vaccin contre le ~** tetanus vaccine

têtard [tɛtaʀ] NM tadpole

---

tête [tɛt]

[1] NOM FÉMININ	[2] COMPOSÉS

[1] NOM FÉMININ

[a] **Anat** [*personne, animal*] head; (= *chevelure*) hair (*NonC*); **être ~ nue** ◊ n'avoir rien sur la ~ to be bareheaded, have nothing on one's head; **avoir mal à la ~** to have a headache; **j'ai la ~ lourde** my head feels heavy; **sa ~ brune/bouclée** his brown/curly hair; **avoir la ~ sale/propre** to have dirty/clean hair; **veau à deux ~s** two-headed calf; **se tenir la ~ à deux mains** to hold one's head in one's hands; **tomber la ~ la première** to fall headfirst; **c'est à se cogner** *ou* **se taper la ~ contre les murs** it's enough to drive you up the wall*; **j'en donnerais ma ~ à couper** I would stake my life on it; **faire une** *ou* **la ~ au carré à qn*** to smash sb's face in*, knock sb's block off*; **tenir ~ à qn/qch** to stand up to sb/sth

♦ **tête baissée** (*lit*) **courir** *ou* **foncer ~ baissée** to rush *ou* charge headlong; (*fig*) **y aller ~**

baissée to charge in blindly; **se jeter** *ou* **donner** ~ **baissée dans** [+ *entreprise, piège*] to rush headlong into

♦ **la tête basse** : **marcher la** ~ **basse** to walk along with one's head bowed; (*fig*) **il est reparti la** ~ **basse** he left hanging his head

♦ **la tête haute** (*fig*) **aller** *ou* **marcher la** ~ **haute** to walk with one's head held high, carry one's head high; **battu aux élections, il peut néanmoins se retirer la** ~ **haute** beaten in the elections he can nevertheless withdraw with his head held high

♦ **de la tête aux pieds** from head to foot *ou* toe, from top to toe

♦ **coup de tête** (*lit*) head-butt; (*fig*) sudden impulse; **donner un coup de** ~ **à qn** to headbutt sb; **donner des coups de** ~ **contre qch** to bang one's head against sth; (*fig*) **agir sur un coup de** ~ to act on impulse → **tête-à-tête**

[b] fig = vie mettre à prix la ~ de qn to put a price on sb's head; réclamer la ~ de qn to demand sb's head; jurer sur la ~ de qn to swear on sb's life; risquer sa ~ to risk one's neck; sauver sa ~ to save one's skin *ou* neck; il y va de sa ~ his life is at stake

[c] = visage, expression face; il a une ~ sympathique he has a nice *ou* friendly face; il a une ~ sinistre he has a sinister look about him, he looks an ugly customer; il a une bonne ~ he looks a decent sort; quand il a appris la nouvelle il a fait une (drôle de) ~ ! he pulled a face when he heard the news!, you should have seen his face when he heard the news!; il en fait une ~ ! what a face!, just look at his face!; faire la ~ to sulk, have the sulks* (*Brit*); tu as vu la ~ qu'il a ! *ou* sa ~ ! have you seen his face!; je connais cette ~-là ! I know that face!; mettre un nom sur une ~ to put a name to a face; il a ou c'est une ~ à claques* he has got the sort of face you'd love to smack *ou* that just asks to be smacked; jeter *ou* lancer à la ~ de qn que ... to hurl in sb's face that ..; c'est à la ~ du client* it depends on the person; il fait son prix à la ~ du client he charges what he feels like → enterrement, payer *etc*

[d] = personne head; ~ couronnée crowned head; de nouvelles ~s new faces; des ~s connues familiar faces; des ~s vont tomber heads will roll; avoir ses ~s* to have one's favourites; le repas coûtera 150 F par ~ (de pipe:*) the meal will cost 150 francs a head *ou* 150 francs per person *ou* 150 francs apiece

[e] = animal 20 ~s de bétail 20 head of cattle

[f] mesure head; il a une ~/demi-~ de plus que moi he's a head taller/half a head taller than me; (*Courses*) gagner d'une ~ to win by a head

[g] = partie supérieure [*clou, marteau*] head; [*arbre*] top; ~ d'ail head of garlic; ~ d'artichaut artichoke head; ~ d'épingle pinhead; gros comme une ~ d'épingle no bigger than a pinhead; (*Anat*) ~ de l'humérus head of the humerus

[h] = partie antérieure [*train, procession*] front, head; (*Mil*) [*colonne, peloton*] head; (= première place) [*liste, chapitre, classe*] top, head; l'équipe conserve la ~ du classement the team retains its lead; prendre la ~ to take the lead; prendre la ~ du cortège to lead the procession, take one's place at the head of the procession; être la ~ d'un mouvement to be the leader of a movement; être la ~ d'une affaire to head up a business

♦ **à la tête de** : **à la** ~ **du cortège** at the head of the procession; **tué à la** ~ **de ses troupes** killed leading his troops *ou* at the head of his troops; **être à la** ~ **d'un mouvement** (= *diriger*) to be at the head of a movement/of a business, head (up) a movement/a business; **se trouver à la** ~ **d'une petite fortune/de deux maisons** to find o.s. the owner *ou* possessor of a small fortune/of two houses

♦ **de tête** (*Sport, fig*) **il est dans le peloton de** ~ he's among the leaders; (*Rail*) **voiture de** ~

front coach; (*Presse*) **article de** ~ leading article, leader (column)

♦ **en tête** : **ils sont entrés dans la ville, musique en** ~ they came into the town led *ou* headed by the band; (*Rail*) **on monte en** ~ **ou en queue ?** shall we get on at the front or (at) the back?; **être en** ~ to be in the lead *ou* in front; **dans les sondages, il arrive largement en** ~ he's well ahead in the polls

♦ **en tête de** : **en** ~ **de phrase** at the beginning of the sentence; **monter dans le métro en** ~ **de ligne** to get on the metro at the beginning of the line; **être** *ou* **venir en** ~ **de liste** to head the list, come at the head *ou* top of the list; **il arrive en** ~ **du scrutin** he's leading in the elections

[i] = facultés mentales avoir (toute) sa ~ to have (all) one's wits about one; n'avoir rien dans la ~ to be empty-headed; où ai-je la ~ ? whatever am I thinking of?; avoir une petite ~ to be dim-witted; alors, petite ~ !* well, dimwit!*; avoir *ou* être une ~ sans cervelle *ou* de linotte ◊ être ~ en l'air to be scatterbrained, be a scatterbrain; avoir de la ~ to have a good head on one's shoulders; ce type-là, c'est une ~* that guy's really brainy*; femme/homme de ~ level-headed *ou* capable woman/man; avoir la ~ bien faite to have a good mind; avoir la ~ sur les épaules to be level-headed; calculer qch de ~ to work sth out in one's head; chercher qch dans sa ~ to search one's memory for sth; mettre *ou* fourrer* qch dans la ~ de qn to put sth into sb's head; se mettre dans la ~ que (= s'imaginer) to get it into one's head that; se mettre dans la ~ de faire qch (= décider) to take it into one's head to do sth; j'ai la ~ vide my mind is a blank *ou* has gone blank; avoir la ~ à ce que l'on fait to have one's mind on what one is doing; avoir la ~ ailleurs to have one's mind on other matters *ou* elsewhere; n'en faire qu'à sa ~ to do (exactly) as one pleases, please o.s., go one's own (sweet) way; il me prend la ~: he drives me nuts* *ou* mad; la géométrie, ça me prend la ~: geometry does my head in:; les maths, quelle prise de ~ !* maths does my head in!:; j'y réfléchirai à ~ reposée I'll think about it when I've got a quiet moment → creuser, monter *etc*

♦ **en tête** : **je n'ai plus le chiffre/le nom en** ~ I can't recall the number/the name, the number/the name has gone (clean) out of my head; **avoir des projets en** ~ to have plans; **se mettre en** ~ **que** (= *s'imaginer*) to get it into one's head that; **se mettre en** ~ **de faire qch** (= *décider*) to take it into one's head to do sth

[j] = tempérament avoir la ~ chaude/froide to be quick- *ou* fiery-tempered/cool-headed; garder la ~ froide to keep a cool head, remain cool, keep one's head; avoir la ~ dure to be a blockhead*; avoir *ou* être une ~ de mule* *ou* de bois* *ou* de lard* *ou* de cochon* ◊ être une ~ de pioche* to be as stubborn as a mule, be mulish *ou* pigheaded; avoir la ~ près du bonnet to be quick-tempered, have a short fuse → fort, mauvais

[k] Ftbl header; faire une ~ to head the ball

2 COMPOSÉS
► **tête d'affiche** (*Théât*) top of the bill; **être la** ~ **d'affiche** to head the bill, be top of the bill ► **tête de bielle** (*Aut*) big end ► **tête blonde*** (*fig* = *enfant*) little one ► **tête brûlée** (= *baroudeur*) desperado ► **tête chercheuse** (*lit*) homing device; (*fig* = *personne*) pioneering researcher; (= *groupe*) pioneering research group; **fusée à** ~ **chercheuse** homing rocket ► **tête de cuvée** tête de cuvée ► **tête de Delco**® (*Aut*) distributor ► **tête d'écriture** (*Ordin*) writing head ► **tête d'enregistrement** recording head ► **tête d'injection** (*Tech*) swivel ► **tête de lecture** [*pick-up*] pickup head; [*magnétophone, magnétoscope*] play-back head; (*Ordin*) reading head; (*Ordin*) ~ **de lecture-écriture** read-write head ► **tête de ligne** terminus, start of the line (*Rail*) ► **tête de liste** (*Pol*) chief candi-

date (*in list system of voting*) ► **tête de lit** bedhead ► **tête de mort** (= *emblème*) death's-head; [*pavillon*] skull and crossbones, Jolly Roger; (*Zool*) death's-head moth; (*Culin*) Gouda cheese ► **tête de nœud**:* prick*:, dickhead*: ► **tête nucléaire** nuclear warhead ► **tête d'œuf** (*péj*) egghead ► **tête pensante** brains* ► **tête de pont** (*au-delà d'un fleuve*) bridgehead; (*au-delà de la mer*) beachhead; (*fig*) bridgehead ► **tête de série** (*Tennis*) seeded player; **il était classé troisième** ~ **de série** he was seeded third; **il est** ~ **de série numéro 2** he's the number 2 seed ► **tête de Turc** whipping boy

tête-à-queue [tɛtakø] NM INV spin; **faire un** ~ [*cheval*] to turn about; [*voiture*] to spin round

tête-à-tête [tɛtatɛt] NM INV [a] (= *conversation*) tête-à-tête, private conversation; **en** ~ alone together; **discussion en** ~ discussion in private; **on a dîné en** ~ the two of us had dinner together [b] (= *service*) breakfast set for two, tea *ou* coffee set for two; (= *meuble*) tête-à-tête

tête-bêche [tɛtbɛʃ] ADV head to foot *ou* tail; **timbre** ~ tête-bêche stamp

tête-de-loup (*pl* **têtes-de-loup**) [tɛtdəlu] NF ceiling brush

tête-de-nègre [tɛtdənɛgʀ] [1] ADJ INV dark brown, chocolate brown (*Brit*) [2] NF [a] (*Culin*) chocolate-covered meringue [b] (= *champignon*) brown boletus

tétée [tete] NF (= *action*) sucking; (*repas, lait*) nursing, feed (*Brit*); **cinq** ~**s par jour** five nursings *ou* feeds (*Brit*) a day; **l'heure de la** ~ nursing *ou* feeding (*Brit*) time

téter [tete] ► conjug 6 ◄ VT [a] [+ *lait*] to suck; [+ *biberon, sein*] to suck at; ~ **sa mère** to suck at one's mother's breast; **donner à** ~ **à un bébé** to feed a baby (at the breast), suckle *ou* nurse a baby [b] * [+ *pouce*] to suck; [+ *pipe*] to suck at *ou* on

tétière [tetjɛʀ] NF [*cheval*] headstall; [*siège*] (*en tissu, dentelle*) antimacassar; (= *repose-tête*) head rest

tétine [tetin] NF [*vache*] udder, dug (*SPÉC*); [*truie*] teat, dug (*SPÉC*); [*biberon*] teat (*Brit*), nipple (*US*); (= *sucette*) comforter, dummy (*Brit*), pacifier (*US*)

téton [tetɔ̃] NM [a] (* = *sein*) breast, tit: [b] (*Tech* = *saillie*) stud, nipple

tétrachlorure [tetʀakloʀyʀ] NM tetrachloride; ~ **de carbone** carbon tetrachloride

tétracorde [tetʀakɔʀd] NM tetrachord

tétraèdre [tetʀaɛdʀ] NM tetrahedron

tétraédrique [tetʀaedʀik] ADJ tetrahedral

tétralogie [tetʀalɔʒi] NF tetralogy; **la Tétralogie de Wagner** Wagner's Ring

tétramètre [tetʀamɛtʀ] NM tetrameter

tétraphonie [tetʀafɔni] NF quadrophonia

tétraphonique [tetʀafɔnik] ADJ quadraphonic

tétraplégie [tetʀapleʒi] NF tetraplegia

tétraplégique [tetʀapleʒik] ADJ, NMF quadraplegic, tetraplegic

tétrapode [tetʀapɔd] NM tetrapod

tétrarque [tetʀaʀk] NM tetrarch

tétras [tetʀɑ(s)] NM grouse; ~**-lyre** black grouse; **grand** ~ capercaillie

tétrasyllabe [tetʀasi(l)lab] [1] ADJ tetrasyllabic [2] NM tetrasyllable

tétrasyllabique [tetʀasi(l)labik] ADJ tetrasyllabic

têtu, e [tety] [1] ADJ stubborn, obstinate; ~ **comme une mule** *ou* **une bourrique** *ou* **un âne** as stubborn as a mule; **les faits sont** ~**s** there's no getting away from the facts [2] NM,F **c'est un** ~ he's stubborn

teuf-teuf (*pl* **teufs-teufs**) [tœftœf] NM a (= *bruit*) [*train*] puff-puff, chuff-chuff; [*voiture*] chug-chug b (* = *automobile*) bone-shaker, rattle-trap*; (*langage enfantin = train*) chuff-chuff, puff-puff

teuton, -onne [tøtɔ̃, ɔn] 1 ADJ (*Hist, péj, hum*) Teutonic 2 **Teuton(ne)** NM,F (*Hist, hum*) Teuton; (*péj*) **les Teutons** the Huns (*péj*)

teutonique [tøtɔnik] ADJ (*Hist, péj*) Teutonic → **chevalier**

texan, e [tɛksɑ̃, an] 1 ADJ Texan 2 **Texan(e)** NM,F Texan

Texas [teksas] NM Texas

tex-mex [tɛksmɛks] ADJ [*musique, restaurant, repas*] Tex-Mex

texte [tɛkst] NM a (= *partie écrite*) [*contrat, livre, pièce de théâtre*] text; ~ **de loi** (*adopté*) law; (*en discussion*) bill; **il y a des erreurs dans le ~** there are textual errors *ou* errors in the text; **lire Shakespeare dans le ~ (original)** to read Shakespeare in the original (text); **« ~ et illustrations de Julien Leduc »** "written and illustrated by Julien Leduc"; (*Théât*) **apprendre son ~** to learn one's lines; **il écrit lui-même le ~ de ses chansons** *ou* **ses ~s** he writes his own lyrics; **en français dans le ~** (*lit*) in French in the original (text); (*iro*) those were the very words used b (= *œuvre littéraire*) text; (*fragment*) passage, piece; ~s **choisis** selected passages; **les grands ~s classiques** the great classics; **expliquez ce ~ de Gide** comment on this passage *ou* piece from *ou* by Gide → **explication** c (*Scol* = *énoncé*) [*devoir, dissertation*] subject, topic; ~ **libre** free composition → **cahier**

textile [tɛkstil] 1 NM a (= *matière*) textile; ~s **artificiels** man-made fibres; ~s **synthétiques** synthetic *ou* man-made fibres b (*Ind*) **le ~** the textile industry, textiles 2 ADJ textile

texto* [tɛksto] ADV word for word

textuel, -elle [tɛkstɥɛl] ADJ a (= *conforme au texte*) [*traduction*] literal, word for word; [*copie*] exact; [*citation*] verbatim (*épith*), exact; **elle m'a dit d'aller me faire cuire un œuf : ~ !*** she told me to get lost — those were her very words!; **c'est ~ !** those were his (*ou* her) very *ou* exact words! b (= *du texte*) textual; [*analyse, sens*] textual

textuellement [tɛkstɥɛlmɑ̃] ADV literally, word for word, verbatim; **alors il m'a dit, ~, que j'étais un imbécile** so he told me I was a fool — those were his very words; **il m'a ~ rapporté ses paroles** he told me what the had said word for word

texture [tɛkstyʀ] NF (*gén*) texture; (= *agencement des parties*) structure; **agent de ~** texturizing agent

TF1 [teɛfœ̃] N (ABRÉV = **Télévision française un**) *independent French television channel*

TG [teʒe] NF (ABRÉV = **Trésorerie générale**) → **trésorerie**

TGV [teʒeve] NM (ABRÉV = **train à grande vitesse**) → **train**

thaï [taj] 1 NM (*Ling*) Thai 2 ADJ Thai

thaïlandais, e [tajlɑ̃dɛ, ɛz] 1 ADJ Thai 2 **Thaïlandais(e)** NM,F Thai

Thaïlande [tajlɑ̃d] NF Thailand

thalamus [talamys] NM thalamus

thalassémie [talasemi] NF thalassemia

thalasso* [talaso] NF ABRÉV = **thalassothérapie**

thalassothérapie [talasoteʀapi] NF thalassotherapy

thalle [tal] NM thallus

thallium [taljɔm] NM thallium

thallophytes [talɔfit] NFPL, NMPL thallophytes

thalweg [talvɛg] NM thalweg

Thanatos [tanatɔs] NM Thanatos

thaumaturge [tomatyʀʒ] 1 NM miracle-worker, thaumaturge (*SPÉC*), thaumaturgist (*SPÉC*) 2 ADJ miracle-working (*épith*), thaumaturgic(al) (*SPÉC*)

thaumaturgie [tomatyʀʒi] NF miracle-working, thaumaturgy (*SPÉC*)

thé [te] NM a (= *feuilles séchées, boisson*) tea; ~ **de Chine** China tea; **les ~s de Ceylan** Ceylon teas; ~ **vert/noir** green/black tea; ~ **au lait/nature** tea with milk/without milk; ~ **glacé** iced tea; ~ **au citron/au jasmin/à la menthe** lemon/jasmine/mint tea; ~ **à la bergamote** tea scented with bergamot, ≈ Earl Grey; **faire le** *ou* **du ~** to make tea; **prendre le ~** to have tea; **à l'heure du ~** at teatime → **feuille, rose, salon** b (= *arbre*) tea plant c (= *réunion*) tea party; ~ **dansant** tea dance, thé-dansant d (*Helv* = *infusion*) herbal tea, tisane

théâtral, e (*mpl* -**aux**) [teɑtʀal, o] ADJ a [*œuvre, situation*] theatrical, dramatic; [*rubrique, chronique*] stage (*épith*), theatre (*Brit*) (*épith*), theater (*US*) (*épith*); [*saison*] theatre (*Brit*) (*épith*), theater (*US*) (*épith*); [*représentation*] stage (*épith*), theatrical b (*péj*) [*air, personne*] theatrical, histrionic; **ses attitudes ~es m'agacent** his theatricals *ou* histrionics irritate me

théâtralement [teɑtʀalmɑ̃] ADV (*lit*) theatrically; (*péj*) histrionically

théâtralisation [teɑtʀalizasjɔ̃] NF [*roman*] dramatization; (*péj*) **la ~ de ses discours politiques** the way he turns his political speeches into theatrical performances

théâtraliser [teɑtʀalize] ▸conjug 1◂ VT to dramatize

théâtralité [teɑtʀalite] NF (*littér*) theatricality

théâtre [teɑtʀ] NM a (= *genre artistique*) theatre (*Brit*), theater (*US*); (= *ensemble de techniques*) drama, theatre (*Brit*), theater (*US*); (= *activité, profession*) stage, theatre (*Brit*), theater (*US*); **faire du ~** (*comme acteur*) to be a stage actor, be on the stage; (*comme metteur en scène*) to be in the theatre; **elle a fait du ~** she has appeared on the stage, she has done some acting; **elle veut faire du ~** she wants to go on the stage; **je n'aime pas le ~ à la télévision** I do not like televised stage dramas *ou* stage productions on television; **c'est du ~ filmé** it's a filmed stage production, it's a film of the play; **ce n'est pas du bon ~** it doesn't make good theatre; **technique** *ou* **art du ~** stagecraft; **cours de ~** drama lessons; ~ **d'essai** experimental theatre *ou* drama; **le ~ musical** musicals; **il fait du ~ d'amateur** he's involved in *ou* he does some amateur dramatics; **un roman adapté pour le ~** a novel adapted for the stage *ou* the theatre → **critique²** b (= *genre littéraire*) drama, theatre (*Brit*), theater (*US*); (= *œuvres théâtrales*) plays, dramatic works, theatre (*Brit*), theater (*US*); **le ~ de Sheridan** Sheridan's plays *ou* dramatic works, the theatre of Sheridan; **le ~ classique/élisabéthain** the classical/Elizabethan theatre, classical/Elizabethan drama; **le ~ antique** (*gén*) ancient theatre; (*grec*) Greek theatre; **le ~ de caractères/de situation** the theatre of character/of situation; **le ~ de l'absurde** the theatre of the absurd; **le ~ de boulevard** light comedies (*as performed in the theatres of the Paris Boulevards*) → **pièce** c (= *lieu, entreprise*) theatre (*Brit*), theater (*US*); ~ **de rue** street theatre; ~ **de marionnettes/de verdure** puppet/open-air theatre; ~ **d'ombres** shadow theatre; ~ **de guignol** ≈ Punch and Judy show; **il ne va jamais au ~** he never goes to the theatre, he is not a theatregoer; **le ~ est plein ce soir** it's a full house tonight, the performance is sold out tonight d (= *lieu d'affrontement, de phénomène*) **homme/femme de ~** man/woman of the theatre; **les gens de ~** theatre *ou* stage people; **accessoires / costumes / décors de ~** stage props / costumes / sets; **artifices de ~** stage

tricks; **directeur de ~** theatre *ou* stage director; **festival de ~** drama festival; **voix/gestes de ~** theatrical *ou* histrionic *ou* stagey* voice/gestures; **coup de ~** (*Théât*) coup de théâtre; (*gén*) dramatic turn of events → **agence, troupe** e (*péj*) (= *exagération*) theatricals, histrionics; (= *simulation*) playacting; **c'est du ~** it's just playacting f [*événement, crime*] scene; **les Flandres ont été le ~ de combats sanglants** Flanders was the scene of bloody fighting; (*Mil*) **le ~ des opérations** the theatre of operations; **les émeutes ont eu pour ~ la capitale** the riots took place in the capital, the capital was the scene of the riots *ou* rioting

théâtreux, -euse* [teɑtʀø, øz] NM,F (*hum*) Thespian; (*péj*) second-rate *ou* ham actor

thébaïde [tebaid] NF (*littér*) solitary retreat

thébain, e [tebɛ̃, ɛn] 1 ADJ Theban 2 **Thébain(e)** NM,F Theban

Thèbes [tɛb] N Thebes

théier [teje] NM tea plant

théière [tejɛʀ] NF teapot

théine [tein] NF theine

théisme [teism] NM a (*Rel*) theism b (*Méd*) tea poisoning

théiste [teist] 1 ADJ theistic(al), theist 2 NMF theist

thématique [tematik] 1 ADJ (*gén*) thematic; [*voyelle*] thematic; [*chaîne de télévision*] specialized; [*exposition, supplément d'un journal*] thematic, based on a theme (*attrib*); **index ~** subject index 2 NF set of themes

thème [tɛm] NM a (= *sujet : gén, Littérat, Mus*) theme; [*débat*] theme, subject; **le ~ de composition d'un peintre** a painter's theme; **ce livre propose plusieurs ~s de réflexion** this book raises several issues b (*Scol* = *traduction*) translation (*into a foreign language*), prose (*translation*); ~ **allemand/espagnol** German/Spanish prose (translation), translation into German/Spanish c (*Ling*) stem, theme; ~ **nominal/verbal** noun/verb stem *ou* theme d (*Astrol*) ~ **astral** birth chart

théocratie [teɔkʀasi] NF theocracy

théocratique [teɔkʀatik] ADJ theocratic

Théocrite [teɔkʀit] NM Theocritus

théodicée [teɔdise] NF theodicy

théodolite [teɔdɔlit] NM theodolite

théogonie [teɔgɔni] NF theogony

théologal, e (*mpl* -**aux**) [teɔlɔgal, o] ADJ → **vertu**

théologie [teɔlɔʒi] NF theology; **études de ~** theological studies; **faire sa ~** to study theology *ou* divinity

théologien, -ienne [teɔlɔʒjɛ̃, jɛn] NM,F theologian, theologist

théologique [teɔlɔʒik] ADJ (*Rel*) theological

Théophraste [teɔfʀast] NM Theophrastus

théorbe [teɔʀb] NM theorbo

théorème [teɔʀɛm] NM theorem; **le ~ d'Archimède/de Pythagore** Archimedes'/Pythagoras' theorem

théoricien, -ienne [teɔʀisjɛ̃, jɛn] NM,F theoretician, theorist

▼ **théorie¹** [teɔʀi] NF (= *doctrine, hypothèse*) theory; **la ~ et la pratique** theory and practice; **en ~** in theory; **la ~, c'est bien joli, mais ...** theory *ou* theorizing is all very well but ...; ~ **des catastrophes/du chaos/des jeux/des ensembles** catastrophe/chaos/game/set theory

théorie² [teɔʀi] NF (*littér* = *procession*) procession, file

théorique [teɔʀik] ADJ theoretical; **c'est une liberté toute ~** it's a purely theoretical freedom

théoriquement [teɔʀikmɑ̃] ADV theoretically, in theory; ~, **c'est vrai** in theory *ou* theoretically it's true

➤ GRAMMAIRE ACTIVE: théorie 53.2

théorisation [teɔʀizasjɔ̃] NF theorization

théoriser [teɔʀize] ▶conjug 1◀ 1 VI to theorize (**sur** about) 2 VT to theorize about

théosophe [teɔzɔf] NMF theosophist

théosophie [teɔzɔfi] NF theosophy

théosophique [teɔzɔfik] ADJ theosophic

thérapeute [teʀapøt] NMF therapist

thérapeutique [teʀapøtik] 1 ADJ [usage, effet, avortement] therapeutic; **essais ~s** drug trials; **les moyens ~s actuels** current methods of treatment 2 NF (= branche de la médecine) therapeutics sg; (= traitement) therapy

thérapie [teʀapi] NF (Méd) therapy, treatment; (Psych) therapy; **~ de groupe/comportementale** group/behavioural therapy; **~ génique** gene therapy; **suivre une ~** to undergo ou have therapy

thermal, e (mpl **-aux**) [teʀmal, o] ADJ [source] thermal, hot; **cure ~e** water cure; **faire une cure ~e** to take the waters; **eaux ~es** hot springs; **établissement ~** hydropathic ou water-cure establishment; **station ~e** spa; **ville ~e** spa town

thermalisme [teʀmalism] NM (= science) balneology; (= cures) water cures

thermes [teʀm] NMPL (Hist) thermae; (= établissement thermal) thermal baths

thermidor [teʀmidɔʀ] NM Thermidor (11th month of French Republican calendar)

thermidorien, -ienne [teʀmidɔʀjɛ̃, jɛn] 1 ADJ of the 9th Thermidor 2 NM,F revolutionary of the 9th Thermidor

thermie [teʀmi] NF (Phys) therm

thermique [teʀmik] ADJ [unité, équilibre] thermal; [énergie] thermic; **moteur ~** heat engine; **carte ~** temperature map; **ascendance ~** thermal, thermal current → **central**

thermocautère [teʀmokotɛʀ] NM diathermy, electro-cautery

thermochimie [teʀmoʃimi] NF thermochemistry

thermocouple [teʀmokupl] NM thermocouple, thermoelectric couple

thermodynamique [teʀmodinamik] 1 NF thermodynamics sg 2 ADJ thermodynamic(al)

thermoélectricité [teʀmoelɛktʀisite] NF thermoelectricity

thermoélectrique [teʀmoelɛktʀik] ADJ thermoelectric(al); **couple ~** thermoelectric couple, thermocouple; **effet ~** thermoelectric ou Seebeck effect; **pile ~** thermopile, thermoelectric pile

thermoformage [teʀmofɔʀmaʒ] NM thermal compression moulding

thermoformé, e [teʀmofɔʀme] ADJ thermally moulded

thermogène [teʀmoʒɛn] ADJ → **ouate**

thermographe [teʀmogʀaf] NM thermograph

thermographie [teʀmogʀafi] NF thermography

thermoluminescence [teʀmolyminesɑ̃s] NF thermoluminescence

thermomètre [teʀmomɛtʀ] NM thermometer; **le ~ indique 38°** the thermometer is (standing) at ou is showing 38°; **le ~ monte** the temperature is rising, the thermometer is showing a rise in temperature; **~ à mercure/à alcool** mercury/alcohol thermometer; **~ à maxima et minima** maximum and minimum thermometer; **~ médical** clinical thermometer; **le ~ de l'opinion publique** the barometer ou gauge of public opinion

thermométrie [teʀmometri] NF thermometry

thermométrique [teʀmometrik] ADJ thermometric(al)

thermonucléaire [teʀmonykleɛʀ] ADJ thermonuclear

thermopile [teʀmopil] NF thermopile

thermoplastique [teʀmoplastik] ADJ thermoplastic

thermopropulsion [teʀmopʀopylsjɔ̃] NF thermal propulsion

Thermopyles [teʀmopil] NFPL **les ~** Thermopylae

thermorégulateur, -trice [teʀmoʀegylatœʀ, tʀis] ADJ thermotaxic, thermoregulation (épith)

thermorégulation [teʀmoʀegylasjɔ̃] NF thermotaxis, thermoregulation (épith)

thermorésistant, e [teʀmoʀezistɑ̃, ɑ̃t] ADJ (gén) heat-resistant; [plastique] thermosetting

thermos® [teʀmos] NM ou NF (**bouteille**) ~ vacuum ou Thermos® flask (Brit) ou bottle (US)

thermoscope [teʀmoskɔp] NM thermoscope

thermosiphon [teʀmosifɔ̃] NM thermosiphon

thermosphère [teʀmosfɛʀ] NF thermosphere

thermostat [teʀmosta] NM thermostat; **préchauffez le four, ~ 7** preheat the oven to gas mark 7

thermothérapie [teʀmoteʀapi] NF (deep) heat treatment, thermotherapy

thésard, e* [tezaʀ, aʀd] NM,F Ph.D. student

thésaurisation [tezoʀizasjɔ̃] NF hoarding (of money); (Écon) building up of capital

thésauriser [tezoʀize] ▶conjug 1◀ 1 VI to hoard money 2 VT to hoard (up)

thésauriseur, -euse [tezoʀizœʀ, øz] NM,F hoarder (of money)

thésaurus [tezoʀys] NM thesaurus (dictionary of specialized terms)

thèse [tɛz] NF a (= doctrine) thesis, argument; **pièce/roman à ~** play/novel expounding a philosophical or social message, pièce/roman à thèse (SPÉC) b (Univ) thesis; **~ de doctorat (d'État)** Ph.D., doctoral thesis (Brit), doctoral dissertation (US); **~ de 3ème cycle** ≈ M.A. ou M.Sc. thesis, ≈ Master's thesis → **soutenance, soutenir** c (Philo) thesis; **~, antithèse, synthèse** thesis, antithesis, synthesis d (= théorie) theory, possibility; **selon la ~ officielle, il ...** the official line is that he ...; **la ~ du suicide a été écartée** suicide has been ruled out

Thésée [teze] NM Theseus

Thessalie [tesali] NF Thessaly

thessalien, -ienne [tesaljɛ̃, jɛn] 1 ADJ Thessalian 2 **Thessalien(ne)** NM,F Thessalian

Thessalonique [tesalɔnik] N Thessalonica

thibaude [tibod] NF anti-slip undercarpeting (NonC), carpet underlay (NonC); **moquette sur ~** fitted carpet (Brit) ou wall-to-wall carpet (US) with underlay

Thimbou [timbu] N Thimbu

Thomas [tɔma] NM Thomas; **saint ~** Saint Thomas; **je suis comme saint ~, je ne crois que ce que je vois** I'm a real doubting Thomas, I'll believe it when I see it, seeing is believing; **saint ~ d'Aquin** (Saint) Thomas Aquinas

thomisme [tɔmism] NM Thomism

thomiste [tɔmist] 1 ADJ Thomistic(al) 2 NMF Thomist

thon [tɔ̃] NM (Zool) tuna, tunny (fish) (Brit); (en boîte) tuna(-fish) (NonC); **~ blanc** long fin tuna; **~ rouge** blue fin tuna; **~ en miettes** flaked tuna; **~ au naturel/à l'huile** tuna(-fish) in brine/in oil

thonier [tɔnje] NM tuna boat

Thor [tɔʀ] NM Thor

Thora, Torah [tɔʀa] NF **la ~** the Torah

thoracique [tɔʀasik] ADJ [cavité, canal] thoracic; **capacité ~** respiratory ou vital capacity → **cage**

thorax [tɔʀaks] NM thorax

thorium [tɔʀjɔm] NM thorium

Thrace [tʀas] NF Thrace

thrène [tʀɛn] NM threnody

thrombine [tʀɔ̃bin] NF thrombin

thrombocyte [tʀɔ̃bɔsit] NM thrombocyte

thrombose [tʀɔ̃boz] NF thrombosis

Thucydide [tysidid] NM Thucydides

Thulé [tyle] N Thule

thulium [tyljɔm] NM thulium

thune [tyn] NF a (†* = pièce) 5-franc piece b (‡ = argent) **de la ~ ◊ des ~s** cash*, dosh‡ (Brit); **j'ai plus une ~** I'm flat ou stony (Brit) broke; **il se fait pas mal de ~(s)** he makes loads of ou a pile of money*

thuriféraire [tyʀifeʀɛʀ] NM (Rel) thurifer; (fig littér) flatterer, sycophant

thuya [tyja] NM thuja

thym [tɛ̃] NM thyme; **~ sauvage** wild thyme

thymique [timik] ADJ (Méd, Psych) thymic

thymus [timys] NM thymus

thyroïde [tiʀɔid] 1 ADJ thyroid (épith) 2 NF (**glande**) ~ thyroid (gland)

thyroïdien, -ienne [tiʀɔidjɛ̃, jɛn] ADJ thyroid (épith)

thyroxine [tiʀɔksin] NF thyroxin

thyrse [tiʀs] NM (Bot, Myth) thyrsus

tiare [tjaʀ] NF tiara

Tibère [tibɛʀ] NM Tiberius

Tibériade [tibeʀjad] N **le lac de ~** Lake Tiberias, the Sea of Galilee

Tibesti [tibɛsti] NM **le (massif du) ~** the Tibesti (Massif)

Tibet [tibɛ] NM Tibet

tibétain, e [tibetɛ̃, ɛn] 1 ADJ Tibetan 2 NM (Ling) Tibetan 3 **Tibétain(e)** NM,F Tibetan

tibia [tibja] NM (Anat = os) tibia (SPÉC), shinbone; (= partie antérieure de la jambe) shin; **donner un coup de pied dans les ~s à qn** to kick sb in the shins

Tibre [tibʀ] NM **le ~** the Tiber

tic [tik] NM a (facial) (facial) twitch ou tic; (du corps) twitch, mannerism, tic; (= manie) habit, mannerism; **~ (nerveux)** nervous twitch ou tic; **~ verbal** ou **de langage** verbal tic; **c'est un ~ chez lui** (manie) it's a habit with him; (geste) it's a tic he has; **il est plein de ~s** he never stops twitching b (Vét = déglutition) cribbing (NonC), crib-biting (NonC)

ticket [tikɛ] 1 NM a (= billet) ticket; **~ de métro/consigne/vestiaire** underground (Brit) ou subway (US)/left-luggage/cloakroom ticket b (‡† = 10 francs) 10-franc note c **j'ai le ou un ~ avec sa sœur** I've made a hit with his sister* d (Pol) ticket 2 COMP ▶ **ticket d'alimentation** ≈ ration card, food stamp (US) ▶ **ticket de caisse** sales slip ou receipt ▶ **ticket d'entrée** (entrance) ticket; **leur ~ d'entrée sur le marché européen** their ticket into the European market ▶ **ticket modérateur** patient's contribution (towards cost of medical treatment) ▶ **ticket de quai** platform ticket ▶ **ticket de rationnement** ≈ ration card

ticket-repas (pl **tickets-repas**) [tikɛʀapa] NM luncheon voucher (Brit), ≈ meal ticket (US)

Ticket-Restaurant® (pl **Tickets-Restaurant**) [tikɛʀɛstɔʀɑ̃] NM = **ticket-repas**

tic-tac [tiktak] NM INV ticking, tick-tock; **faire ~** to tick, go tick tock

tie-break (pl **tie-breaks**) [tajbʀɛk] NM tie break; **il a remporté le premier set au ~** he won the first set on ou in a tie-break

tiédasse [tjedas] ADJ (péj) lukewarm, tepid

tiède [tjɛd] 1 ADJ a (= refroidi) [boisson, bain] (désagréablement) lukewarm, tepid; (agréablement) warm; (= doux) [vent, saison, température] mild, warm; [atmosphère] balmy; **salade ~** warm salad b (= sans conviction) [sentiment, foi, accueil] lukewarm, half-hearted, tepid; [chrétien, militant] half-hearted, lukewarm; **tu lui as propo-**

sé ? — **oui, mais il était plutôt ~** did you suggest it to him? — yes, but he wasn't very enthusiastic

2 NMF (*péj*) lukewarm *ou* half-hearted individual; (*Pol*) **des mesures qui risquent d'effaroucher les ~s** measures likely to scare the wets

3 ADV **elle boit son café ~** she drinks her coffee lukewarm, she doesn't like her coffee too hot; **ils boivent leur bière ~** they drink their beer (luke)warm; **je n'aime pas boire ~** I don't like drinking things when they're lukewarm; (*dans une recette*) **servir ~/à peine ~** serve warm/just warm

tièdement [tjɛdmɑ̃] ADV [*accueillir*] in a lukewarm way, half-heartedly; **~ soutenu par son parti** with the half-hearted support of his party

tiédeur [tjedœʀ] NF a [*bain*] tepidness; [*vent, saison, température*] mildness, warmth; [*atmosphère*] balminess; **les premières ~s du printemps** the first warm days of spring; **la ~ du vent/de la nuit** the warm wind/night air b [*sentiment, foi, accueil*] lukewarmness, half-heartedness, tepidness; [*chrétien, militant*] half-heartedness, lukewarmness; **la ~ du public à l'égard du référendum** the public's lack of enthusiasm for *ou* half-hearted attitude towards the referendum

tiédir [tjediʀ] ▸ conjug 2 ◂ 1 VI a (= *refroidir*) to cool (down); **laisser ~ un café trop chaud** to let a cup of coffee cool down b (= *se réchauffer*) to grow warm(er); **faire ~ de l'eau** to warm *ou* heat up some water; **dans un bol, versez le lait tiédi** pour the warmed milk into a bowl c (= *faiblir*) [*sentiment, foi, ardeur*] to cool (off); **l'enthousiasme tiédit avec le temps** enthusiasm wanes with time 2 VT a (= *réchauffer*) to warm (up) b (= *rafraîchir*) to cool (down)

tien, tienne [tjɛ̃, tjɛn] 1 PRON POSS **le tien** ◊ **la tienne** ◊ **les tiens** ◊ **les tiennes** yours; (†, *Rel*) thine; **ce sac n'est pas le ~** this bag is not yours, this is not your bag; **mes fils sont stupides comparés aux ~s** my sons are stupid compared to yours; **à la ~ne !*** your (good) health!, cheers!; (*iro*) **tu vas faire ce travail tout seul ? — à la ~ne !*** you're going to do the job all by yourself? — good luck to you!; *pour autres locutions voir* **sien** 2 NM a **il n'y a pas à distinguer le ~ du mien** what's mine is yours — see **sien** b **les ~s** your family, your (own) folks*; **toi et tous les ~s** you and yours; *pour autres locutions voir* **sien** 3 ADJ POSS († *ou hum*) **un ~ cousin** a cousin of yours

tierce¹ [tjɛʀs] 1 NF a (*Mus*) third; **~ majeure/mineure** major/minor third b (*Cartes*) tierce; **~ majeure** tierce major c (*Typo*) final proof d (*Rel*) terce e (*Escrime*) tierce f (= *unité de temps*) sixtieth of a second 2 ADJ → **tiers**

tiercé, e [tjɛʀse] 1 ADJ (*Hér*) tiercé, tierced → **rime** 2 NM *French triple forecast system for horse-racing*, tierce (*Austral*); **réussir le ~ dans l'ordre/dans le désordre** *ou* **dans un ordre différent** to win on the tiercé with the right placings/without the right placings; **un beau ~** a good win on the tiercé; **toucher** *ou* **gagner le ~** to win the tiercé; (*lit, fig*) **le ~ gagnant** the three winners, the first three

tierceron [tjɛʀsəʀɔ̃] NM tierceron

tiers, tierce² [tjɛʀ, tjɛʀs] 1 ADJ third; (*Math*) **b tierce** b triple dash; **une tierce personne** a third party; (*Europe*) **pays ~** third country; (*Typo*) **tierce épreuve** final proof; (*Jur*) **~ porteur** endorsee; (*Jur*) **tierce opposition** opposition by third party (*to outcome of litigation*)

2 NM a (= *fraction*) third; **le premier ~/les deux premiers ~ de l'année** the first third/the first two thirds of the year; **j'ai lu le** *ou* **un ~/les deux ~ du livre** I have read a third/two thirds of the book; **j'en suis au ~** I'm a third of the way through; **les deux ~ des gens pensent que ...** the majority of people think that ...; **l'article est trop long d'un ~** the article is a third too long *ou* over length, the article is too long by a third; **remplissez la casserole aux deux ~** fill the pan two-thirds full; **la ville était détruite aux deux ~** two thirds of the city was destroyed

b (= *troisième personne*) third party *ou* person; (= *étranger, inconnu*) outsider; (*Jur*) third party; **il a appris la nouvelle par un ~** he learnt the news through a third party *ou* through an outsider; **l'assurance ne couvre pas les ~** the insurance does not cover third party risks; **il se moque du ~ comme du quart†** he doesn't care a fig *ou* a hoot* *ou* a damn* → **assurance**

c (= *troisième élément, Logique*) **principe du ~ exclu** law of excluded middle

3 COMP ▸ **le Tiers État** NM (*Hist*) the third estate ▸ **tiers ordre** (*Rel*) third order ▸ **tiers payant** direct payment by insurers (*for medical treatment*) ▸ **tiers provisionnel** provisional *ou* interim payment (*of tax*)

tiers-arbitre, tiers arbitre (*pl* **tiers(-)arbitres**) [tjɛʀaʀbitʀ] NM independent arbitrator

Tiers-Monde [tjɛʀmɔ̃d] NM **le ~** the Third World

tiers-mondisme [tjɛʀmɔ̃dism] NM third-worldism

tiers-mondiste [tjɛʀmɔ̃dist] 1 ADJ (= *du Tiers-Monde*) Third-World (*épith*); (= *en faveur du Tiers-Monde*) supporting the Third World 2 NMF (= *spécialiste*) specialist of the Third World; (= *partisan*) supporter of the Third World

tiers-point (*pl* **tiers-points**) [tjɛʀpwɛ̃] NM (*Archit*) crown; (= *lime*) saw-file

tif* [tif] NM (*gén pl*) hair; **~s** hair

TIG [teiʒe] NM (ABRÉV = **travaux d'intérêt général**) → **travail¹**

tige [tiʒ] NF a [*fleur, arbre*] stem; [*céréales, graminées*] stalk; **fleurs à longues ~s** long-stemmed flowers; **(arbre de) haute/basse ~** standard/half-standard tree; **~ aérienne/souterraine** overground/underground stem b (= *plant*) sapling c [*colonne, plume, démarreur*] shaft; [*botte, chaussette, bas*] leg (part); [*chaussure*] ankle (part); [*clé, clou*] shank; [*pompe*] rod; **chaussures à ~** boots; **~ de métal** metal rod; **~ de culbuteur** pushrod; **~ de forage** drill pipe d (†, *littér*) [*arbre généalogique*] stock; **faire ~** to found a line e (* = *cigarette*) cig*, smoke*, fag* (*Brit*)

tignasse [tiɲas] NF (= *chevelure mal peignée*) shock of hair, mop (of hair); (* = *cheveux*) hair

Tigre [tigʀ] NM **le ~** the Tigris

tigre [tigʀ] NM a (= *animal*) tiger; **~ royal** *ou* **du Bengale** Bengal tiger b (= *homme cruel*) monster; **~ de papier** paper tiger; (*Écon*) **les ~s asiatiques** the tiger economies, the Asian tigers

tigré, e [tigʀe] ADJ a (= *tacheté*) spotted (*de* with); [*cheval*] piebald b (= *rayé*) striped, streaked; **chat ~** tabby (cat)

tigresse [tigʀɛs] NF (= *animal*) tigress; (= *harpie*) tigress, hellcat*

tilbury [tilbyʀi] NM tilbury

tilde [tild(e)] NM tilde

tillac [tijak] NM (*Hist Naut*) upper deck

tilleul [tijœl] NM (= *arbre*) lime (tree), linden (tree); (= *infusion*) lime(-blossom) tea; **(vert) ~** lime green

tilt [tilt] NM (*Jeux*) tilt sign *ou* signal; **faire ~** (*lit*) to show tilt; (* *fig*) **ce mot a fait ~ dans mon esprit** the word rang a bell; **soudain, ça a fait ~*** it suddenly clicked, the penny suddenly dropped

timbale [tɛ̃bal] NF a (*Mus*) kettledrum; **les ~s** the timpani, the timps*, the kettledrums b (= *gobelet*) (metal) cup (*without handle*), (metal) tumbler c (*Culin*) (= *moule*) timbale (mould); (= *mets*) **~ de langouste** lobster timbale

timbalier [tɛ̃balje] NM timpanist

timbrage [tɛ̃bʀaʒ] NM a (= *affranchissement*) [*lettre, envoi*] stamping; **dispensé de ~** postage paid (*Brit*), post paid (*US*) b (= *apposition d'un cachet*) [*document, acte*] stamping; [*lettre, envoi*] postmarking

timbre [tɛ̃bʀ] 1 NM a (= *vignette*) stamp; **~(-poste)** (postage) stamp; **~ neuf/oblitéré** new/used stamp; **marché** *ou* **Bourse aux ~s** stamp market; **~s antituberculeux/anti-cancéreux** TB/cancer research stamps; (*Méd*) **~ (thérapeutique)** patch; **à la nicotine** *ou* **antitabac*** nicotine patch → **collection** b (= *marque*) stamp; **mettre** *ou* **apposer son ~ sur** to put one's stamp on, affix one's stamp to; **~ sec/humide** embossed/ink(ed) stamp → **droit³** c (= *instrument*) stamp; **~ de caoutchouc/de cuivre** rubber/brass stamp d (*Mus*) [*tambour*] snares e (= *son*) [*instrument, voix*] timbre, tone; [*voyelle*] timbre; **avoir le ~ voilé** to have a muffled voice; **voix qui a du ~** sonorous *ou* resonant voice; **voix sans ~** voice lacking in resonance f (= *sonnette*) bell

2 COMP ▸ **timbre fiscal** excise *ou* revenue *ou* fiscal stamp ▸ **timbre horodateur** time and date stamp ▸ **timbre de quittance** receipt stamp

timbré, e [tɛ̃bʀe] (*ptp de* **timbrer**) 1 ADJ a (*Admin, Jur*) [*document, acte*] stamped, bearing a stamp (*attrib*) → **papier** b [*voix*] resonant, sonorous; [*sonorité*] resonant; **voix bien ~e** beautifully resonant voice; **mal ~** lacking in resonance c (* = *fou*) cracked*, nuts* 2 NM,F (* = *fou*) loony*, nutcase*, head case*

timbre-amende (*pl* **timbres-amendes**) [tɛ̃bʀamɑ̃d] NM *stamp purchased to pay a fine for a parking offence*

timbre-prime (*pl* **timbres-primes**) [tɛ̃bʀpʀim] NM trading stamp

timbre-quittance (*pl* **timbres-quittances**) [tɛ̃bʀkitɑ̃s] NM receipt stamp

timbrer [tɛ̃bʀe] ▸ conjug 1 ◂ VT a (= *affranchir*) [+ *lettre, envoi*] to stamp, put a stamp (*ou* stamps) on; **«joindre une enveloppe timbrée»** "send a stamped addressed envelope *ou* an sae" (*Brit*), "send a self-addressed envelope" (*US*) b (= *apposer un cachet sur*) [+ *document, acte*] to stamp; [+ *lettre, envoi*] to postmark; **lettre timbrée de** *ou* **à Paris** letter with a Paris postmark, letter postmarked Paris

timbre-taxe (*pl* **timbres-taxes**) [tɛ̃bʀtaks] NM postage-due stamp

timide [timid] ADJ a (= *gauche*) [*personne, air, sourire, voix, amoureux*] shy, timid, bashful; **ne sois pas si ~, approche !** don't be shy, come over here!; **faussement ~** coy; **d'une voix ~** shyly, in a shy voice; **c'est un grand ~** he's awfully shy b (= *hésitant*) [*personne, critique, réponse, tentative*] timid, timorous; [*réforme*] timid; [*politique, reprise économique*] tentative; **une ~ amélioration de l'économie** a slight *ou* faint improvement in the economy; **des mesures ~** half measures; **des protestations bien ~s** half-hearted protests; **le soleil fera de ~s apparitions au nord** there will be intermittent sunshine in the north

timidement [timidmɑ̃] ADV a (= *gauchement*) shyly, timidly; **il l'a abordée ~** he approached her shyly *ou* timidly; **..., demanda-t-il ~** ..., he asked shyly b (= *légèrement*) **l'activité a ~ repris** business has picked up slightly; **la région s'ouvre ~ au tourisme** the region is tentatively opening up to tourism

timidité [timidite] NF a (= pusillanimité) [personne, critique, réponse, tentative] timidity, timorousness; [entreprise, style] timidity; **étant donné la ~ de la reprise économique** given the fact that there has been only a slight ou faint improvement in the economy b (= embarras) [personne, air, sourire, voix, amoureux] shyness, timidity, bashfulness; **avec ~** shyly, timidly; **il n'a pas osé, par ~** he was too shy to dare, he didn't dare, he was too shy

timing [tajmiŋ] NM timing

timon [timɔ̃] NM [char] shaft; [charrue] beam; [embarcation] tiller

timonerie [timɔnʀi] NF a (Naut) (= poste, service) wheelhouse; (= marins) wheelhouse crew b (Aut) steering and braking systems

timonier [timɔnje] NM a (Naut) helmsman, steersman b (= cheval) wheel-horse, wheeler

timoré, e [timɔʀe] ADJ (gén) [caractère, personne] timorous, fearful; (Rel, littér) [conscience] over-scrupulous

tinctorial, e (mpl -iaux) [tɛ̃ktɔʀjal, jo] ADJ [opération, produit] tinctorial (SPÉC), dyeing (épith); **matières ~es** dyestuffs; **plantes ~es** plants used in dyeing

tinette [tinɛt] NF (pour la vidange) sanitary tub; (arg Mil = toilettes) **~s** latrines

tintamarre [tɛ̃tamaʀ] NM racket, din, hullabaloo*; **faire du ~** to make a racket ou din; **on a entendu un ~ de klaxons** we heard horns blaring

tintement [tɛ̃tmɑ̃] NM [cloche] ringing, chiming; [clochette] tinkling, jingling; [sonnette] ringing; [objets métalliques, pièces de monnaie] jingling, chinking; [verres entrechoqués] clinking; [verre frotté] ringing; **~ d'oreilles** ringing in the ears, tinnitus (SPEC)

tinter [tɛ̃te] ▸ conjug 1 ◂ 1 VI [cloche] to ring, chime; [clochette] to tinkle, jingle; [sonnette] to ring; [objets métalliques, pièces de monnaie] to jingle, chink; [verres entrechoqués] to clink; [verre frotté] to ring; **faire ~** [+ cloche] to ring; [+ pièces de monnaie] to jingle; [+ verres] to clink; **trois coups tintèrent** the bell rang ou chimed three times; **les oreilles me tintent** my ears are ringing, there's a ringing in my ears; (fig) **les oreilles ont dû vous ~** your ears must have been burning 2 VT [+ cloche, heure, angélus] to ring; [+ messe] to ring for

tintin: [tɛ̃tɛ̃] EXCL nothing doing!*, no way!*; **faire ~** to go without

tintinnabuler [tɛ̃tinabyle] ▸ conjug 1 ◂ VI (littér) to tinkle, tintinnabulate (littér)

Tintoret [tɛ̃tɔʀɛ] NM **le ~** Tintoretto

tintouin: [tɛ̃twɛ̃] NM a (= tracas) bother, worry; **quel ~ pour y aller** it was such a hassle* getting there; **donner du ~ à qn** to give sb a lot of trouble; **se donner du ~** to go to a lot of trouble; **et tout le ~** and all the rest, and what have you* b († = bruit) racket, din

TIP [tip] NM (ABRÉV = **titre interbancaire de paiement**) → **titre**

tipi [tipi] NM te(e)pee

Tipp-Ex® [tipɛks] NM Tipp-Ex® (Brit), liquid paper® (US), White out® (US)

tique [tik] NF (= parasite) tick

tiquer [tike] ▸ conjug 1 ◂ VI a [personne] to make ou pull (Brit) a face, raise an eyebrow; **sans ~** without turning a hair ou batting an eyelid ou raising an eyebrow b [cheval] to crib(-bite), suck wind

tiqueté, e [tik(ə)te] ADJ (littér) speckled, mottled

TIR [tiʀ] NMPL (ABRÉV = **transports internationaux routiers**) TIR

tir [tiʀ] 1 NM a (= discipline sportive ou militaire) shooting; **~ au pistolet/à la carabine** pistol/rifle shooting → **stand** b (= action de tirer) firing (NonC); **en position de ~** in firing position; **commander/déclencher le ~** to order/set off ou open the firing; **puissance/vitesse de ~ d'une arme** fire-power/firing speed of a gun; **des ~s d'exercice** practice rounds; **des ~s à blanc** firing blank rounds ou blanks; **secteur ou zone de ~ libre** free-fire zone; **corriger ou rectifier ou ajuster le ~** (lit) to adjust the fire; (fig) to make some adjustments c (= manière de tirer) firing; (trajectoire des projectiles) fire; **arme à ~ automatique/rapide** automatic/rapid-firing gun; **arme à ~ courbe/tendu** gun with curved/flat trajectory fire; (lit, fig) **~s croisés** crossfire; **être pris sous des ~s croisés** to be caught in the crossfire; **~ groupé** (lit) grouped fire; (fig) (= série d'attaques) combined attack; (= série de succès) string of successes; **un ~ groupé de mesures/films** a string of measures/films; **plan/angle/ligne de ~** plane/angle/line of fire → **table** d (= feu, rafales) fire (NonC); **stoppés par un ~ ou des ~s de mitrailleuses/d'artillerie** halted by machine-gun/artillery fire; **~ de roquettes** rocket fire; **~ de harcèlement** harassing fire; **~s de sommation** warning shots e (Boules) shot (at another bowl); (Ftbl) shot; **~ au but** (gén) shot at goal; (de pénalité) penalty kick; **épreuve des ~s au but** penalty shootout f (= stand) **~ (forain)** shooting gallery, rifle range g (Espace = lancement) launch 2 COMP ▸ **tir d'appui** = **tir de soutien** ▸ **tir à l'arbalète** crossbow archery ▸ **tir à l'arc** archery ▸ **tir de barrage** barrage fire ▸ **tir au pigeon** clay pigeon shooting ▸ **tir de soutien** support fire

tirade [tiʀad] NF (Théât) monologue, speech; (fig, péj) tirade

tirage [tiʀaʒ] 1 NM a [chèque] drawing; [vin] drawing off; [carte] taking, drawing b (Photo, Typo) printing; **faire le ~ de clichés/d'une épreuve** to print negatives/a proof; **~ à la main** hand-printing; **un ~ sur papier glacé** a print on glazed paper; **~ par contact/inversion** contact/reversal print c [journal] circulation; [livre] (= nombre d'exemplaires) (print) run; (= édition) edition; **~ de luxe/limité** de luxe/limited edition; **cet auteur réalise de gros ~s** this author's works have huge print runs ou are printed in great numbers; **quel est le ~ de cet ouvrage?** how many copies of this work were printed?; **les gros ~s de la presse quotidienne** the high circulation figures of the daily press; **magazine à faible ~** small-circulation magazine; **~ de 2 000 exemplaires** run ou impression of 2,000 copies d [cheminée] draught (Brit), draft (US); **avoir du ~** to draw well, have a good draught; **cette cheminée a un bon/mauvais ~** this chimney draws well/badly e (Loterie) draw; **le ~ des numéros gagnants** the draw for the winning numbers f (* = désaccord) friction; **il y avait du ~ entre eux** there was some friction between them g [métaux] drawing 2 COMP ▸ **tirage à part** off-print ▸ **tirage au sort** drawing lots; **procéder par ~ au sort** to draw lots; **le gagnant sera désigné par ~ au sort** the winner will be chosen by drawing lots; **le ~ au sort des équipes de football** the selection ou choice of the football teams by drawing lots

tiraillement [tiʀajmɑ̃] 1 NM a (sur une corde) tugging (NonC); b [douleur] [intestin] gnawing pain; [peau, muscles] tightness; **~s d'estomac** gnawing pains in the stomach 2 **tiraillements** NMPL (= hésitations) agonizing indecision (NonC); (= conflits) friction (NonC), conflict (NonC); **après quelques ~s, les deux groupes se sont mis d'accord** after some tussling, the two groups came to an agreement

tirailler [tiʀaje] ▸ conjug 1 ◂ 1 VT a [+ corde, moustache, manche] to pull at, tug at; **~ qn par le bras ou la manche** to pull ou tug at sb's sleeve b [douleurs] to gnaw at, stab at; **douleurs qui tiraillent l'estomac** gnawing pains in the stomach; **des élancements lui tiraillaient l'épaule** he had sharp ou shooting ou stabbing pains in his shoulder c [doutes, remords] to tug at, plague, pester; [choix, contradictions] to beset, plague; **être tiraillé entre plusieurs possibilités** to be torn between several possibilities; **la crainte et l'ambition le tiraillaient** he was torn between fear and ambition 2 VI (en tous sens) to shoot wild; (Mil : par tir de harcèlement) to fire at random; **ça tiraillait de tous côtés dans le bois** there was firing on all sides in the wood

tirailleur [tiʀajœʀ] NM a (Mil, fig) skirmisher; **se déployer/avancer en ~s** to be deployed/advance as a skirmish contingent b (Hist Mil : originaire des colonies) soldier, infantryman

tiramisu [tiʀamisu] NM tiramisu

Tirana [tiʀana] N Tirana

tirant [tiʀɑ̃] NM a (= cordon) (draw) string; (= tirette) [botte] bootstrap; (= partie de la tige) [chaussure] facing b (Constr) [arcades] tie-rod; [comble] tie-beam; [pont] **~ d'air** headroom c (Naut) **~ (d'eau)** draught (Brit), draft (US); **navire de faible ~ d'eau** ship with a shallow draught; **~ avant/arrière** draught (Brit) ou draft (US) at the bows/stern; **avoir six mètres de ~ (d'eau)** to draw six metres of water; **~ d'air** [navire] clearance height

tire¹: [tiʀ] NF (= voiture) wagon*, car; **vieille ~** old rattletrap* ou crate* ou banger* (Brit)

tire² [tiʀ] NF **vol à la ~** picking pockets; **voleur à la ~** pickpocket

tire³ [tiʀ] NF (Can) (= caramel) toffee, taffy (Can, US); (= sirop d'érable) molasses, maple candy; **~ d'érable** maple toffee ou taffy (Can, US); **~ sur la neige** taffy-on-the-snow (Can, US)

tiré, e [tiʀe] (ptp de **tirer**) 1 ADJ a (= tendu) [traits, visage] drawn, haggard; **avoir les traits ~s** to look drawn ou haggard; **les cheveux ~s en arrière** with one's hair pulled back; **~ à quatre épingles** impeccably ou well turned-out, done up ou dressed up to the nines*; (fig) **~ par les cheveux** far-fetched → **couteau** b (Fin) **la personne ~e** the drawee c (= bas) **prix ~s** rock-bottom prices 2 NM (Fin) drawee; (Mus) down-bow 3 **tirée** NF (= long trajet) long haul, long trek; (= quantité) **une ~e de** a load* of, heaps* ou tons* of 4 COMP ▸ **tiré à part** ADJ, NM off-print

tire-au-cul: [tiʀoky] NMF INV = **tire-au-flanc**

tire-au-flanc* [tiʀoflɑ̃] NMF INV skiver* (Brit), layabout, shirker

tire-bonde (pl **tire-bondes**) [tiʀbɔ̃d] NM bung-drawer

tire-botte (pl **tire-bottes**) [tiʀbɔt] NM (pour se chausser) boot-hook; (pour se déchausser) bootjack

tire-bouchon, tirebouchon (pl **tire(-)bouchons**) [tiʀbuʃɔ̃] NM (= ustensile) corkscrew; (= mèche de cheveux) corkscrew curl; **en ~** corkscrew (épith); **cochon avec la queue en ~** pig with a corkscrew ou curly tail; **avec ses chaussettes en ~** with his socks all crumpled ou wrinkled

tire-bouchonner, tirebouchonner [tiʀbuʃɔne] ▸ conjug 1 ◂ 1 VT [+ mèche] to twiddle, twirl 2 VI [pantalon] to crumple (up); [chaussettes] to become crumpled ou wrinkled; **pantalon tire-bouchonné** crumpled trousers 3 **se tire-bouchonner** VPR* (de rire) to fall about laughing* (Brit), be in stitches*

tire-clou (pl **tire-clous**) [tiʀklu] NM nail puller

tire-d'aile [tiʀdɛl] ▸ **à tire-d'aile** LOC ADV [voler] swiftly; **passer à ~** to pass by in full flight; **s'envoler à ~** to take flight in a flurry of feathers; (fig) **le temps s'enfuit à ~** time flies past

tire-fesses* [tiʀfɛs] NM INV (*gén, à perche*) ski tow; (*à archet*) T-bar tow

tire-fond (*pl* **tire-fond(s)**) [tiʀfɔ̃] NM (*avec anneau*) long screw with ring attachment; (*Rail*) sleeper (*Brit*) *ou* tie (*US*) screw

tire-jus* [tiʀʒy] NM INV nose-wipe*, snot-rag*

tire-laine †† [tiʀlɛn] NM INV footpad ††

tire-lait (*pl* **tire-laits**) [tiʀlɛ] NM breast-pump

tire-larigot* [tiʀlaʀigo] ♦ **à tire-larigot** LOC ADV [*boire, manger*] to one's heart's content, like there's no tomorrow; **il téléphone à ~** he's forever *ou* continually telephoning

tire-ligne (*pl* **tire-lignes**) [tiʀliɲ] NM drawing pen

tirelire [tiʀliʀ] NF **a** (= *récipient*) moneybox; (*en forme de cochon*) piggy bank; **casser la ~** to break open the piggy bank; **il a une ~ à la place du cœur** all he ever thinks about is money **b*** (= *estomac, ventre*) belly*, gut(s)*; (= *tête*) nut*, noddle*, bonce* (*Brit*); (= *visage*) face

▼ **tirer** [tiʀe] ▸ conjug 1 ◂ **1** VT **a** (= *amener vers soi*) [*pièce mobile, poignée, corde*] to pull; [*manche, robe*] to pull down; [*chaussette*] to pull up; **ne tire pas, ça risque de tomber/ça va l'étrangler** don't pull or it'll fall/it'll strangle him; **~ les cheveux à qn** to pull sb's hair; **~ l'aiguille** to ply the needle; (*lit*) **~ qch à soi** to pull sth to(wards) one; (*fig*) **~ un texte/auteur à soi** to turn a text/an author round to suit one
b [+ *rideaux*] to draw; [+ *tiroir*] to pull open; [+ *verrou*] (= *fermer*) to slide to, shoot; (= *ouvrir*) to draw; **tire la porte** pull the door to; **as-tu tiré le verrou ?** have you bolted the door?; **elle avait les cheveux tirés en arrière** she had her hair pulled back (from her face)
c [+ *personne*] to pull; **~ qn par le bras** to pull sb's arm, pull sb by the arm; **~ qn par la manche** to tug *ou* pluck sb's sleeve; **~ qn de côté** *ou* **à l'écart** to draw sb aside, take sb on one side
d (= *haler, remorquer*) [+ *véhicule, charge*] to pull, draw; [+ *navire, remorque*] to tow; [+ *charrue*] to draw, pull; **une charrette tirée par un tracteur** a cart drawn *ou* pulled by a tractor, a tractor-drawn cart; **carrosse tiré par huit chevaux** carriage drawn by eight horses → **jambe, patte**
e (= *retirer, extraire*) [+ *épée, couteau*] to draw, pull out; [+ *vin, cidre*] to draw; [+ *conclusions, morale, argument, idée, thème*] to draw; [+ *plaisir, satisfaction*] to draw, derive (**de** from); **~ une substance d'une matière première** to extract a substance from a raw material; **~ le jus d'un citron** to extract the juice from a lemon, squeeze the juice from a lemon *ou* out of a lemon; **~ un son d'un instrument** to get a sound out of *ou* draw a sound from an instrument; **~ un objet d'un tiroir/d'un sac** to pull an object out of a drawer/a bag; **~ son chapeau/sa casquette à qn** to raise one's hat/ one's cap to sb; **~ de l'argent d'une activité/ d'une terre** to make money from an activity/a piece of land; **il a tiré 40 000 F de sa vieille voiture** he managed to get 40,000 francs for his old car; **savoir ~ qch de la vie/d'un moment** (to know how) to get sth out of life/a moment; **~ qch de qn** to obtain sth from sb, get sth out of sb; **~ de l'argent de qn** to get money out of sb; **on ne peut rien en ~** (*enfant têtu*) you can't do anything with him; (*personne qui refuse de parler*) you can't get anything out of him; **~ qn du sommeil** to arouse sb from sleep; **~ qn du lit** to get *ou* drag sb out of bed; **~ qn de son travail** to take *ou* drag sb away from his work; **ce bruit le tira de sa rêverie** this noise brought him out of *ou* roused him from his daydream; **~ des larmes/ gémissements à qn** to draw tears/moans from sb
f (= *délivrer*) **~ qn de prison/des décombres/ d'une situation dangereuse** to get sb out of prison/the rubble/a dangerous situation; **~ qn**

du doute to remove *ou* dispel sb's doubts; **~ qn de l'erreur** to disabuse sb; **~ qn de la misère/de l'obscurité** to rescue sb from poverty/from obscurity; **il faut le ~ de là** we'll have to help him out → **affaire, embarras**
g (*indiquant l'origine*) **~ son origine d'une vieille coutume** to have an old custom as its origin; **mots tirés du latin** words taken *ou* derived from (the) Latin; **~ son nom de** to take one's name from; **pièce tirée d'un roman** play taken from *ou* adapted from *ou* derived from a novel; **on tire de l'huile des olives** oil is extracted from olives; **l'opium est tiré du pavot** opium is obtained from the poppy
h (*Jeux*) [+ *billet, numéro, loterie*] to draw; [+ *carte*] to take, draw; **~ qch au sort** to draw lots for sth; **qui est-ce qui donne ? on tire ?** whose deal is it? shall we pick a card?; (*à l'Épiphanie*) **~ les rois** to cut the Twelfth Night cake; **~ la fève** to win the charm → **carte, court¹**
i (*Photo, Typo*) to print; **ce journal est tiré à 100 000 exemplaires** this paper has a circulation of 100,000; **~ un roman à 8 000 exemplaires** to print 8,000 copies of a novel; **tirons quelques épreuves de ce texte** let's run off *ou* print a few proofs of the text; (*fig*) **tiré à des centaines d'exemplaires** turned out *ou* churned out by the hundred; **se faire ~ le portrait*** (*photographier*) to have one's photograph taken; (*dessiner*) to have one's portrait drawn → **bon²**
j (= *tracer*) [+ *ligne, trait*] to draw; [+ *plan*] to draw up → **plan¹**
k [+ *coup de feu, balle*] to fire; [+ *flèche*] to shoot; [+ *boule*] to throw (*so as to hit another or the jack*); [+ *feu d'artifice*] to set off; [+ *gibier*] to shoot; **il a tiré plusieurs coups de revolver sur l'agent** he fired several shots at the policeman, he shot *ou* fired at the policeman several times; **~ le canon** to fire the cannon; **la balle a été tirée avec un gros calibre** the bullet was fired from a large-bore gun; **il a tiré un faisan** he shot a pheasant; (*sexuellement*) **~ un coup**** to have a bang**, have it off**
l (*Ftbl*) to shoot; **~ un corner/un pénalty** to take a corner/a penalty
m [+ *chèque, lettre de change*] to draw; **~ de l'argent sur son compte** to draw money out of one's account, withdraw money from one's account; **prête-moi ta carte bleue pour que j'aille ~ de l'argent** lend me your credit card so that I can go and get some money out
n (*Naut*) **~ 6 mètres** to draw 6 metres of water; **~ un bord** *ou* **une bordée** to tack
o (* = *passer*) to get through; **encore une heure/un mois à ~** another hour/month to get through; **~ deux ans de prison/de service** to do two years in prison *ou* a two-year stretch*/two years in the army; **voilà une semaine de tirée** that's one week over with
p (* = *voler*) to pinch*, nick* (*Brit*); **il s'est fait ~ son blouson** he got his jacket pinched* *ou* nicked* (*Brit*)
q (*Tech*) [+ *étirer*] [+ *métal*] to draw
r (= *limiter aussi bas que possible*) [+ *délais*] to get down to an absolute minimum; **~ ses prix** to sell at rock-bottom prices
s (*dial* = *traire*) [+ *vache*] to milk
2 VI **a** (= *faire feu*) to fire; (= *se servir d'une arme à feu, viser*) to shoot; **il leur donna l'ordre de ~** he gave the order for them to fire; **apprendre à ~** to learn to shoot; **~ à l'arbalète/à la carabine** to shoot with a crossbow/a rifle; **savez-vous ~ à l'arc ?** can you use a bow (and arrow)?; **le canon tirait sans arrêt** the cannon fired continuously; **~ en l'air** to fire into the air; **~ à vue** to shoot on sight; **~ à balles (réelles)/à blanc** to fire (real) bullets/blanks; **~ sans sommation** to shoot without warning; **il lui a tiré dans le dos** (*lit*) he shot him in the back; (*fig*) he stabbed him in the back; (*fig*) **~ dans les jambes** *ou* **pattes*** **de qn*** to make life difficult for sb

b (*Sport, Ftbl*) to shoot, take a shot; (*Boules*) to throw (*one boule at another or at the jack*); **~ au but** (*gén*) to take a shot at goal, shoot at goal; (*pénalité*) to take a penalty kick
c (*Presse*) **à 10 000 exemplaires** to have a circulation of 10,000
d [*cheminée, poêle*] to draw; **la cheminée tire bien** the chimney draws well
e [*moteur, voiture*] to pull; **le moteur tire bien en côte** the engine pulls well on hills
f [*points de suture, sparadrap*] to pull; **le matin, j'ai la peau qui tire** my skin feels tight in the morning
3 **tirer à** VT INDIR **a** (= *aller vers*) **~ à sa fin** [*journée*] to be drawing to a close; [*épreuve*] to be nearly over; [*provisions*] to be nearly finished; **la voiture tire à gauche** the car pulls to the left; **~ au flanc*** *ou* **au cul*** to skive* (*Brit*), shirk → **ligne¹**
b (= *entraîner*) **~ à conséquence** to matter; **cela ne tire pas à conséquence** it's of no consequence, it doesn't matter
4 **tirer sur** VT INDIR **a** [+ *corde, poignée*] to pull at *ou* on, tug at; **~ sur les rênes** to pull in *ou* on the reins; (*fig*) **~ sur la ficelle*** *ou* **la corde*** to push one's luck*, go too far, overstep the mark
b (= *approcher de*) [+ *couleur*] to border on, verge on; **il tire sur la soixantaine** he's getting on for (*Brit*) *ou* going on sixty
c (= *faire feu sur*) to shoot at, fire (a shot *ou* shots) at; **il m'a tiré dessus** he shot *ou* fired at me; (*fig* = *critiquer*) **ils tirent sans cesse sur les médias** they're always criticizing the media; (*fig*) **ne tirez pas sur le pianiste** he's (*ou* I'm *etc*) doing his (*ou* my *etc*) best; **se ~ dessus** (*lit*) to shoot *ou* fire at each other; (*fig = se critiquer, se quereller*) to shoot each other down → **boulet**
d (= *aspirer*) [+ *pipe*] to pull at, draw on; [+ *cigarette, cigare*] to puff at, draw on, take a drag at*
e (= *prélever*) **ils tirent sur leur épargne pour maintenir leur niveau de vie** they're drawing on their savings to maintain their standard of living
5 **se tirer** VPR **a** **se ~ de** (= *échapper à*) [+ *danger, situation*] to get (o.s.) out of; **il s'est tiré sans dommage de l'accident** he came out of the accident unharmed; **sa voiture était en mille morceaux mais lui s'en est tiré*** his car was smashed to pieces but he escaped unharmed; **il est très malade mais je crois qu'il va s'en ~** he's very ill but I think he'll pull through; **la première fois il a eu un sursis mais cette fois il ne va pas s'en ~ si facilement** the first time he got a suspended sentence but he won't get off so lightly this time; **il s'en est tiré avec une amende** he got off with a fine; **il s'en est tiré avec une jambe cassée** he got out of it with a broken leg → **affaire, flûte, patte**
b **bien/mal se ~ de qch** [+ *tâche*] to manage *ou* handle sth well/badly, make a good/bad job of sth; **comment va-t-il se ~ de ce sujet/ travail ?** how will he get on with *ou* cope with this subject/job?; **les questions étaient difficiles mais il s'en est bien tiré** the questions were difficult but he managed *ou* handled them well *ou* coped very well with them; **on n'a pas beaucoup d'argent mais on s'en tire** we haven't got a lot of money but we get by *ou* we manage; **on s'en tire tout juste** we just scrape by, we just (about) get by
c (* = *déguerpir*) to push off*, shove off*, clear off*; **allez, on se tire** come on, let's be off *ou* push off* *ou* clear off*
d (* = *toucher à sa fin*) [*période, travail*] to be nearly over; **ça se tire** the end is in sight
e (= *être tendu*) [*traits, visage*] to become drawn

tiret [tiʀɛ] NM (= *trait*) dash; († = *trait d'union*) hyphen

tirette [tiʀɛt] NF **a** [*bureau, table*] (*pour écrire*) (writing) leaf; (*pour ranger** *des crayons*) (pencil)

> GRAMMAIRE ACTIVE: **tirer** 53.4

tray; (pour soutenir un abattant) support; [fermeture à glissière] pull, tab [b] (Belg = fermeture à glissière) zip (Brit), zipper (US) [c] [cheminée] damper [d] (= cordon) [sonnette] bell-pull; [rideaux] (curtain) cord ou pull

tireur, -euse [tiʀɶʀ, øz] [1] NM,F [a] (avec arme à feu) ~ **embusqué** sniper; ~ **isolé** lone gunman; ~ **d'élite** marksman, sharpshooter; **c'est un bon** ~ he's a good shot; **concours ouvert aux** ~**s débutants et entraînés** shooting competition open to beginners and advanced classes [b] (Boules) player who tries to dislodge the opponents' bowls [c] (= photographe) printer [d] (= escrimeur) ~ **d'épée ou d'armes** swordsman, fencer [e] **tireuse** ou ~ **de cartes** fortune-teller [2] NM [chèque, lettre de change] drawer [3] **tireuse** NF [a] (Tech) (hand) pump; **bière à la tireuse** draught beer; **vin à la tireuse** wine from the barrel [b] (Photo) contact printer

tiroir [tiʀwaʀ] NM [a] [table, commode] drawer; ~ **(à) secret** secret drawer; **roman/pièce à ~s** novel/play made up of episodes, roman/ pièce à tiroirs (SPÉC) → **fond, nom** [b] (Tech) slide valve

tiroir-caisse (pl **tiroirs-caisses**) [tiʀwaʀkɛs] NM till, cash register

tisane [tizan] NF (= boisson) herb(al) tea; ~ **de tilleul/de menthe** lime(-blossom)/mint tea; (hum) **c'est de la ~*** it's really watery

tisanière [tizanjɛʀ] NF (= pot) teapot (for making herbal tea); (= tasse) (large) teacup (for herbal tea)

tison [tizɔ̃] NM brand → **allumette, Noël**

tisonner [tizɔne] ▸ conjug 1 ◂ VT to poke

tisonnier [tizɔnje] NM poker

tissage [tisaʒ] NM weaving; **usine de** ~ cloth ou weaving mill

tisser [tise] ▸ conjug 1 ◂ [1] VT [a] (lit) to weave; **l'araignée tisse sa toile** the spider spins its web ou **métier** [b] (fig) [+ liens] to forge; [+ réseau de relations] to build up; [+ intrigue] to weave [2] **se tisser** VPR [liens] to be forged; [amitié, complicité] to grow

tisserand, e [tisʀɑ̃, ɑ̃d] NM,F weaver

tisseur, -euse [tisɶʀ, øz] NM,F weaver

tissu [tisy] [1] NM [a] (Tex) fabric, material, cloth; **c'est un** ~ **très délicat** it's a very delicate fabric ou material; **acheter du ~/trois mètres de** ~ **pour faire une robe** to buy some material ou fabric/three metres of material ou fabric to make a dress; **choisir un** ~ **pour faire une robe** to choose material to make a dress, choose a dress fabric ou material; ~ **imprimé/à fleurs** printed/floral-patterned material ou fabric; ~ **synthétique** synthetic material ou fabric; ~**s d'ameublement** soft furnishings; **étoffe à ~ lâche/serré** loosely-/finely-woven material ou fabric ou cloth [b] (fig péj) **un** ~ **de mensonges/contradictions** a web ou tissue of lies/contradictions; **un ~ d'intrigues** a web of intrigue; **un** ~ **d'horreurs/ d'obscénités/d'inepties** a catalogue of horrors/of obscenities/of blunders [c] (Anat, Bot) tissue; ~ **sanguin/osseux/ cicatriciel** blood/bone/scar ou cicatricial (SPÉC) tissue [d] (Sociol) fabric; **le** ~ **social/industriel/urbain** the social/industrial/urban fabric [2] COMP ▸ **tissu-éponge** NM (pl **tissus-éponge**) (terry) towelling (NonC) (Brit) ou toweling (NonC) (US)

tissulaire [tisylɛʀ] ADJ (Bio) tissue (épith); **culture** ~ tissue culture

Titan [titɑ̃] NM Titan; **les** ~**s** the Titans; **œuvre/travail de** ~ titanic work/task

titane [titan] NM titanium

titanesque [titanɛsk] , **titanique** [titanik] ADJ titanic

Tite-Live [titliv] NM Livy

titi [titi] NM ~ **(parisien)** Parisian street urchin

Titien [tisjɛ̃] NM **le** ~ Titian

titillation [titijasjɔ̃] NF (littér, hum) titillation

titiller [titije] ▸ conjug 1 ◂ VT (littér, hum) (= exciter) to titillate; (= chatouiller légèrement) to tickle; (= agacer pour provoquer) to tease, goad; **l'envie le titillait de devenir comédien** he was quite taken with the idea of becoming an actor

titisme [titism] NM (Hist) Titoism

titiste [titist] ADJ, NMF (Hist) Titoist

titrage [titʀaʒ] NM [a] [alliage] assaying; [solution] titration [b] (Ciné) titling

titre [titʀ(ə)] NM [a] [œuvre] title; [chapitre] heading, title; (Jur) [code] title; (= manchette de journal) headline; (= journal) newspaper; **les (gros) ~s** the headlines; ~ **sur cinq colonnes à la une** five-column front page headline; (Typo) ~ **courant** running head; **les principaux ~s de la presse parisienne** the major Parisian newspapers; (Typo) **(page de)** ~ title page; ~ **budgétaire** budgetary item [b] (honorifique, de fonctions professionnelles) title; (= formule de politesse) form of address; (littér = nom) title, name; ~ **nobiliaire** ou **de noblesse** title; **conférer à qn le** ~ **de maréchal/ prince** to confer the title of marshal/prince on sb; **il ne mérite pas le** ~ **de citoyen** he doesn't deserve to be called a citizen [c] (Sport) title [d] **en** ~ (Admin) titular; (Jur) [propriétaire] legal; (Comm) [fournisseur] appointed; (hum) [maîtresse] official; **le champion du monde en** ~ the world title-holder [e] (= document) title; (= certificat) certificate; (= reçu) receipt; ~ **de créance** evidence ou proof of debt; ~ **de pension** pension book; ~ **de propriété** title deed; ~ **de séjour** residence permit; ~ **de transport** ticket; ~ **de paiement** order to pay, remittance; ~ **universel de paiement** universal payment order; ~ **interbancaire de paiement** payment slip allowing automatic withdrawal from a bank account [f] (Bourse, Fin) security; **acheter/vendre des ~s** to buy/sell securities ou stock; ~**s cotés/non cotés** listed/unlisted securities; ~ **de Bourse** ◊ ~ **boursier** stock-exchange security, stock certificate; ~ **d'obligation** debenture (bond); ~ **participatif** non-voting share (in a public sector enterprise); ~ **au porteur** bearer bond ou share; ~**s d'État** government securities; ~**s nominatifs** registered securities [g] (= preuve de capacité, diplôme) (gén) qualification; (Univ) degree, qualification; ~**s universitaires** academic ou university qualifications; **nommer/recruter sur ~s** to appoint/ recruit according to qualifications; **il a tous les ~s (nécessaires) pour enseigner** he is fully qualified ou he has all the necessary qualifications to teach [h] (littér, gén pl = droit, prétentions) **avoir des ~s à la reconnaissance de qn** to have a right to sb's gratitude; **ses ~s de gloire** his claims to fame [i] [or, argent, monnaie] fineness; [solution] titre; **or/argent au** ~ standard gold/silver; ~ **d'alcool** ou **alcoolique** alcohol content [j] (loc) **à ce** ~ (= en cette qualité) as such; (= pour cette raison) on this account, therefore; **à quel** ~ **?** on what grounds?; **au même** ~ in the same way; **il y a droit au même** ~ **que les autres** he is entitled to it in the same way as the others; **à aucun** ~ on no account; **nous ne voulons de lui à aucun** ~ we don't want him on any account; **à des ~s divers** ◊ **à plusieurs ~s** ◊ **à plus d'un** ~ on several accounts, on more than one account; **à double** ~ on two accounts; **à** ~ **privé/personnel** in a private/ personal capacity; **à** ~ **permanent/provisoire** on a permanent/temporary basis, permanently/provisionally; **à** ~ **exceptionnel** ou **d'exception** (dans ce cas) exceptionally, in this exceptional case; (dans certains cas) in exceptional cases; **à** ~ **d'ami/de client fidèle** as a friend/a loyal customer; **à** ~ **gratuit** freely,

free of charge; **à** ~ **gracieux** free of ou without charge; **à** ~ **lucratif** for payment; **à** ~ **d'essai** on a trial basis; **à** ~ **d'exemple** as an example, by way of example; (frm) **à** ~ **onéreux** against payment; **à** ~ **indicatif** for information only; **il travaille à** ~ **de secrétaire** he works as a secretary; **à** ~ **consultatif** [collaborer] in an advisory ou a consultative capacity; **on vous donne 1500 F à** ~ **d'indemnité** we are giving you 1,500 francs by way of indemnity ou as an indemnity → **juste**

titré, e [titʀe] (ptp de **titrer**) ADJ [a] (= noble) [personne] titled; [terres] carrying a title (attrib) [b] (Tech) [liqueur] standard

titrer [titʀe] ▸ conjug 1 ◂ VT [a] (gén ptp = anoblir) to confer a title on [b] (Chim) [+ alliage] to assay; [+ solution] to titrate [c] [+ livre, œuvre d'art] to title; (Ciné) to title [d] (Presse) to run as a headline; ~ **sur 2/5 colonnes : « Défaite de la Droite »** to run a 2/5-column headline: "Defeat of the Right" [e] [alcool, vin] ~ **10°/38°** to be 10°/38° proof (on the Gay Lussac scale); ≈ to be 17°/66° proof

titrisation [titʀizasjɔ̃] NF securitization

titubant, e [titybɑ̃, ɑ̃t] ADJ [personne] (de faiblesse, fatigue) staggering; (d'ivresse) staggering, reeling; [démarche] unsteady

tituber [titybe] ▸ conjug 1 ◂ VI [personne] (de faiblesse, fatigue) to stagger (along); (d'ivresse) to stagger (along), reel (along); **il avança vers nous/sortit de la cuisine en titubant** he came staggering ou tottering towards us/out of the kitchen, he staggered ou tottered towards us/ out of the kitchen; **nous titubions de fatigue** we were so tired that we could hardly keep upright, we were so tired we were staggering ou stumbling along

titulaire [titylɛʀ] [1] ADJ [a] (Admin) [professeur] with tenure; **être** ~ to have tenure [b] **être** ~ **de** (Univ) [+ chaire] to occupy, hold; (Pol) [+ portefeuille] to hold; **être** ~ **de** to be entitled to; [+ permis, diplôme, carte, compte] to hold, have [c] (Rel) [évêque] titular (épith); **saint/patron** ~ **d'une église** (titular) saint/patron of a church [2] NMF (Admin) [poste] incumbent; (Jur) [droit] person entitled (**de** to); [permis, bail, compte bancaire, carte de crédit] holder; [+ passeport] holder, bearer

titularisation [titylaʀizasjɔ̃] NF [enseignant, fonctionnaire] appointment to a permanent post; [professeur d'université] granting of tenure; [sportif] signing up as a full team member; **sa** ~ **a été refusée** his application for a permanent post ou for tenure was refused

titulariser [titylaʀize] ▸ conjug 1 ◂ VT [+ enseignant, fonctionnaire] to give a permanent appointment to; [+ professeur d'université] to give tenure to; [+ sportif] to sign up (as a full team member)

TMS [teɛmɛs] NMPL (ABRÉV = **troubles musculo-squelettiques**) RSI

TNT [teɛnte] NM (ABRÉV = **trinitrotoluène**) TNT

toast [tost] NM [a] (= pain grillé) slice ou piece of toast; **un** ~ **beurré** a slice ou piece of buttered toast [b] (= discours) toast; ~ **de bienvenue** welcoming toast; **porter un** ~ **en l'honneur de qn** to drink (a toast) to sb, toast sb

toasteur [tostɶʀ] NM toaster

toboggan [tɔbɔɡɑ̃] NM [a] (= traîneau) toboggan; **faire du** ~ to go tobogganing; **piste de** ~ toboggan run [b] (= glissière, jeu) slide; [piscine] waterslide; **faire du** ~ (une fois) to go on a slide; (plusieurs fois) to play on a slide [c] (Tech : pour manutention) chute; (Aviat) emergency chute; (Aut = viaduc) flyover (Brit), overpass (US)

toc¹ [tɔk] [1] EXCL [a] (= bruit) ~ ~! knock knock!, rat-a-tat(-tat)! [b] (* = repartie) **et** ~! (en s'adressant à qn) so there!*; (en racontant la réaction de qn) and serves him (ou her etc) damned ou jolly (Brit) well right!* [2] ADJ (* =

fou) **il est ~ ~, celui-là!** he's cracked* *ou* nuts*!, he's got a screw loose!*

toc² [tɔk] **1** NM **c'est du ~** (= *imitation, faux*) it's (a) fake; (= *camelote*) it's trash *ou* junk; **en ~** [*bijou*] fake **2** ADJ INV (= *imitation*) fake; (= *camelote*) rubbishy, trashy; **ça fait ~** (= *imité, faux*) it looks fake; (= *camelote*) it looks cheap *ou* rubbishy, it's junk

tocante* [tɔkãt] NF watch, ticker* (*Brit*)

tocard, e: [tɔkaʀ, aʀd] **1** ADJ [*meubles, décor*] cheap and nasty, trashy* **2** NM (= *personne*) dead loss*, useless twit*, washout*; (= *cheval*) (old) nag (*péj*)

toccata [tɔkata] NF toccata

tocsin [tɔksɛ̃] NM alarm (bell), tocsin (*littér*); **sonner le ~** to ring the alarm, sound the tocsin (*littér*)

toge [tɔʒ] NF **a** (*Hist*) toga; **~ virile/prétexte** toga virilis/praetexta **b** (*Jur, Scol*) gown

Togo [tɔgo] NM Togo

togolais, e [tɔgɔlɛ, ɛz] **1** ADJ of *ou* from Togo **2** **Togolais(e)** NM,F native of Togo

tohu-bohu [tɔybɔy] NM (= *désordre*) jumble, confusion; (= *agitation*) hustle (and bustle); (= *tumulte*) hubbub, commotion

toi [twa] PRON PERS **a** (*sujet, objet*) you; **~ et lui, vous êtes tous les deux aussi têtus** you're both as stubborn as one another; **si j'étais ~, j'irais** if I were you *ou* in your shoes I'd go; **il n'obéit qu'à ~** you are the only one he obeys, he obeys only you; **il a accepté, ~ non** *ou* **pas ~** he accepted but you didn't *ou* but not you; **c'est enfin ~!** here you are at last!; **qui l'a vu? ~?** who saw him? did you?; **~ mentir? ce n'est pas possible** YOU tell a lie? I can't believe it; **~ qui sais tout, explique-moi** you're the one who knows everything so explain to me; **va devant, c'est ~ qui connais le chemin** you go first, you know the way *ou* you're the one who knows the way; **~, tu n'as pas à te plaindre** you have no cause to complain; **pourquoi ne le ferais-je pas, tu l'as bien fait, ~!** why shouldn't I do it? YOU did it, didn't you?; **tu l'as vu, ~?** did you see him?, have you seen him?; **t'épouser, ~? jamais!** marry you? never!; **~, je te connais** I know you; **aide-moi, ~!** you there* ou hey you*, give me a hand!; **~, tu m'agaces! ◊ tu m'agaces, ~!** you really get on my nerves!; **~, pauvre innocent, tu n'as rien compris!** you, poor fool, haven't understood a thing!, you poor fool — you haven't understood a thing!

b (*avec vpr: souvent non traduit*) **assieds-~!** sit down!; **mets-~ là!** stand over there!; **~, tais-~!** you be quiet!; **montre-~ un peu aimable!** be nice!

c (*avec prép*) you, yourself; **à ~ tout seul, tu ne peux pas le faire** you can't do it on your own *ou* by yourself; **cette maison est-elle à ~?** does this house belong to you?, is this house yours?; **tu n'as même pas une chambre à ~ tout seul?** you don't even have a room of your own? *ou* a room to yourself?; **tu ne penses qu'à ~** you only think of yourself, you think only of yourself; **je compte sur ~** I'm counting on you

d (*dans des comparaisons*) you; **il me connaît mieux que ~** (*qu'il ne te connaît*) he knows me better than (he knows) you; (*que tu ne me connais*) he knows me better than you (do); **il est plus/moins fort que ~** he is stronger than/ not so strong as you; **il a fait comme ~** he did what you did, he did the same as you

toile [twal] **1** NF **a** (= *tissu*) (*gén*) cloth (*NonC*); (*grossière, de chanvre*) canvas (*NonC*); (*pour pneu*) canvas (*NonC*); **grosse ~** (rough *ou* coarse) canvas; **~ de lin/de coton** linen/ cotton (cloth); **en ~ ◊ de ~** [*draps*] linen; [*pantalon, blazer*] (heavy) cotton; [*sac*] canvas; **en ~ tergal** in Terylene fabric; **~ caoutchoutée/plastifiée** rubberized/plastic-coated cloth; **relié ~** cloth bound; **~ d'amiante/métallique** asbestos/metal cloth; **~**

imprimée printed cotton, cotton print; **reliure ~** cloth binding → **chanson, village**

b (= *morceau*) piece of cloth; **poser qch sur une ~** to put sth on a piece of cloth; (* = *draps*) **se mettre dans les ~s** to hit the hay* *ou* the sack*

c (*Art*) (= *support*) canvas; (= *œuvre*) canvas, painting; **il expose ses ~s chez Legrand** he exhibits his canvasses *ou* paintings at Legrand's; **une ~ de maître** an old master; **gâcher** *ou* **barbouiller de la ~** to daub on canvas

d (*Naut* = *ensemble des voiles*) sails; **faire de la/réduire la ~** to make/take in sail; **navire chargé de ~s** ship under canvas, ship under full sail

e [*araignée*] web; **la ~ de l'araignée** the spider's web; **une belle ~ d'araignée** a beautiful spider's web; **grenier plein de ~s d'araignées** attic full of cobwebs

f (* = *film*) film, movie (*surtout US*); **se faire une ~** to go and see a film, go to a movie (*surtout US*)

2 COMP ► **toile d'avion** aeroplane cloth *ou* linen ► **toile de bâche** tarpaulin; **une parka en ~ de bâche** a heavy canvas parka ► **toile cirée** oilcloth ► **toile émeri** emery cloth ► **toile de fond** (*Théât*) backdrop, backcloth; (*fig*) **un moulin avec un lac en ~ de fond** a windmill with a lake in the background; **une histoire d'amour, avec en ~ de fond la guerre** a love story set against the backdrop of the war ► **toile goudronnée** tarpaulin, tarp ► **toile de Jouy** ≈ Liberty print ► **toile de jute** hessian ► **toile à matelas** ticking ► **toile à sac** sacking, sackcloth ► **toile de tente** (*Camping*) canvas; (*Mil*) tent sheet ► **toile à voile** sailcloth

toilerie [twalʀi] NF (= *fabrication*) textile manufacture (*of cotton, linen, canvas etc*); (= *commerce*) textile trade; (= *atelier*) textile mill

toilettage [twaletaʒ] NM [*chien*] grooming; [*texte de loi*] tidying up; (*enseigne*) **« ~ pour chiens » ◊ « salon de ~ »** "grooming parlour"

toilette [twalɛt] **1** NF **a** (= *ablutions*) **faire sa ~** to have a wash, get washed; (= *habillage*) **être à sa ~** to be dressing, be getting ready; **faire une grande ~/une ~ rapide** *ou* **un brin de ~** to have a thorough/quick wash; **faire une ~ de chat** to give o.s. a lick and a promise *ou* a cat-lick (*Brit*); **~ intime** personal hygiene; **elle passe des heures à sa ~** she spends hours getting ready *ou* washing and dressing *ou* at her toilet (*frm*); **la ~ des enfants prend toujours du temps** it always takes a long time to get the children washed *ou* ready; **une lotion pour la ~ de bébé** a cleansing lotion for babies; **produits de ~** toiletries; **j'ai oublié mes affaires de ~** I've forgotten my toothbrush and things; **faire la ~ d'un mort** to lay out a corpse; **la ~ d'un condamné à mort** the washing of a prisoner before execution; **(table de) ~** (*pour lavabo*) washstand; (= *coiffeuse*) dressing table → **cabinet, gant, trousse**

b (= *nettoyage*) [*voiture*] cleaning; [*maison, monument*] facelift; **faire la ~ de** [+ *voiture*] to clean; [+ *monument, maison*] to give a facelift to, tart up* (*Brit*) (*hum*); [+ *texte*] to tidy up, polish up

c [*animal*] **faire sa ~** to wash itself; **faire la ~ de son chien** to groom one's dog

d (= *habillement, parure*) clothes; **en ~ de bal** wearing a ballgown; **~ de mariée** wedding *ou* bridal dress *ou* gown; **être en grande ~** to be (dressed) in all one's finery, be all dressed up; **aimer la ~** to like clothes; **elle porte bien la ~** she wears her clothes well

e (= *costume*) outfit; **elle a changé trois fois de ~!** she's changed her outfit *ou* clothes three times!; **«nos ~s d'été»** "summer wear *ou* outfits"; **on voit déjà les ~s d'été** you can already see people in summer outfits *ou* clothes

f (*Boucherie*) **~ (de porc)** pig's caul

g (*Tech*) reed casing

2 **toilettes** NFPL (= *W.-C.*) toilet, bathroom (*US*); (*publiques*) public lavatory *ou* conveniences (*Brit*), restroom (*US*); **aller aux ~s** to go to the toilet; (*dans un lieu public*) **où sont les ~s?** (*gén*) where's the toilet? *ou* the restroom? (*US*); (*pour femmes*) where's the ladies' room? *ou* the ladies?* (*Brit*); (*pour hommes*) where's the men's room? *ou* the gents?* (*Brit*)

toiletter [twalete] ►conjug 1◄ VT [+ *chien, chat*] to groom; [+ *texte de loi*] to tidy up, polish up

toiletteur, -euse [twaletœʀ, øz] NM,F groomer; **~ pour chiens** dog groomer

toi-même [twamɛm] PRON → **même**

toise [twaz] NF **a** (= *instrument*) height gauge; **passer qn à la ~** to measure sb's height; **il est passé à** *ou* **sous la ~** he had his height measured **b** (*Hist* = *mesure*) toise, ≈ 6 ft

toiser [twaze] ►conjug 1◄ VT **a** (= *regarder avec dédain*) to look up and down, eye scornfully; **ils se toisèrent** they looked each other up and down **b** (†, *littér* = *évaluer*) to estimate

toison [twazɔ̃] NF **a** [*mouton*] fleece; **la Toison d'or** the Golden Fleece **b** (= *chevelure*) (*épaisse*) mop; (*longue*) mane **c** (= *poils*) abundant growth

toit [twa] NM **a** (*gén*) roof; **~ de chaume/de tuiles/d'ardoises** thatched/tiled/slate roof; **~ plat** *ou* **en terrasse/en pente** flat/sloping roof; **habiter sous les ~s** to live in an attic flat (*Brit*) *ou* apartment (*US*) (*with a sloping ceiling*); **le ~ du monde** the roof of the world; **voiture à ~ ouvrant** car with a sunroof; **double ~** [*tente*] fly sheet → **crier b** (*fig* = *maison*) **avoir un ~** to have a roof over one's head, have a home; **chercher un ~** to look for somewhere to live; **être sans ~** to have no roof over one's head, have nowhere to call home *ou* one's own; **sous le ~ de qn** under sb's roof, in sb's house; **vivre sous le même ~** to live under the same roof; **vivre sous le ~ paternel** to live in the paternal home; **recevoir qn sous son ~** to have sb as a guest in one's house

toiture [twatyʀ] NF roof, roofing

tokai [tɔkɛ], **tokaï** [tɔkaj], **tokay** [tɔkɛ] NM Tokay

Tokyo [tɔkjo] N Tokyo

tôlard, e: [tolaʀ, aʀd] NM,F = **taulard**

tôle¹ [tol] NF (= *matériau*) sheet metal (*NonC*); (= *pièce*) steel (*ou* iron) sheet; **~ d'acier/ d'aluminium** sheet steel/aluminium; **~ étamée** tinplate; **~ galvanisée/émaillée** galvanized/ enamelled iron; (*Aut*) **~ froissée** dented bodywork; **~ ondulée** (*lit*) corrugated iron; (*fig* = *route*) rugged dirt track

tôle²: [tol] NF = **taule**

Tolède [tɔlɛd] N Toledo

tôlée [tole] ADJ F **neige ~** crusted snow

tolérable [tɔleʀabl] **1** ADJ [*comportement, retard*] tolerable; [*douleur, attente*] tolerable, bearable; **cette attitude n'est pas ~** this attitude is intolerable *ou* cannot be tolerated **2** NM **c'est à la limite du ~** it's barely tolerable

tolérance [tɔleʀɑ̃s] NF **a** (= *compréhension, largeur d'esprit*) tolerance (**à l'égard de, envers** toward(s)); **faire preuve de ~** to be tolerant (**à l'égard de, envers** with) **b** (= *liberté limitée*) **c'est une ~, pas un droit** it's tolerated rather than allowed as of right; (*Comm : produits hors taxe*) **il y a une ~ de 2 litres d'alcool/200 cigarettes** there's an allowance of 2 litres of spirits/200 cigarettes; **~ orthographique/ grammaticale** permitted departure in spelling/grammar → **maison c** (*Méd, Tech*) tolerance; **~ aux antibiotiques** antibiotic tolerance; **~ immunitaire** immunological tolerance → **marge d** (*Hist, Rel*) toleration

tolérant, e [tɔleʀɑ̃, ɑ̃t] ADJ tolerant; **il est trop ~ avec ses élèves** he's too lenient *ou* easygoing with his pupils

tolérantisme [tɔleʀɑ̃tism] NM (Hist Rel) tolerationism

tolérer [tɔleʀe] ▶conjug 6◀ VT [a] (= ne pas sévir contre) [+ culte, pratiques, abus, infractions] to tolerate; (= autoriser) to allow; **ils tolèrent un excédent de bagages de 15 kg** they allow 15 kg (of) excess baggage
[b] (= supporter) [+ comportement, excentricités, personne] to put up with, tolerate; [+ douleur] to bear, endure, stand; **ils ne s'aimaient guère : disons qu'ils se toléraient** they didn't like each other much — you could say that they put up with ou tolerated each other; **je ne ~ai pas cette impertinence** I will not stand for ou put up with ou tolerate this impertinence; **il tolérait qu'on l'appelle par son prénom** he allowed people to call him by his first name; **il ne tolère pas qu'on le contredise** he won't tolerate being contradicted
[c] (Bio, Méd) [organisme] to tolerate; (Tech) [matériau, système] to tolerate; **il ne tolère pas l'alcool** he can't tolerate ou take alcohol, alcohol doesn't agree with him

tôlerie [tolʀi] NF [a] (= fabrication) sheet metal manufacture; (= commerce) sheet metal trade; (= atelier) sheet metal workshop [b] (= tôles) [voiture] panels, coachwork (NonC); [bateau, chaudière] plates, steelwork (NonC)

tolet [tɔlɛ] NM rowlock, thole

tôlier¹ [tolje] NM (= industriel) sheet iron ou steel manufacturer; **(ouvrier-)tôlier** sheet metal worker; **~ en voitures** panel beater

tôlier², -ière: [tolje, jɛʀ] NM,F = **taulier**

tollé [tɔ(l)le] NM general outcry ou protest; **ce fut un ~ (général)** there was a general outcry

Tolstoï [tɔlstɔj] NM Tolstoy

toluène [tɔlyɛn] NM toluene

TOM [tɔm] NM (ABRÉV = **territoire d'outre-mer**) → **territoire**

tomahawk [tɔmaok] NM tomahawk

tomaison [tɔmɛzɔ̃] NF volume numbering

tomate [tɔmat] NF [a] (= plante) tomato (plant); (= fruit) tomato; **~s farcies** stuffed tomatoes; **~s en grappes** vine tomatoes; **~s (à la) provençale** tomatoes (à la) Provençale; **~s cerises/vertes** cherry/green tomatoes; (fig) **il va recevoir des ~s** he'll get a hostile reception → **rouge** [b] (= boisson) pastis with grenadine

tombal, e (mpl **tombals** ou **tombaux**) [tɔ̃bal, o] ADJ [dalle] funerary; (littér = funèbre) tomb-like, funereal (épith); **inscription ~e** tombstone inscription → **pierre**

tombant, e [tɔ̃bɑ̃, ɑ̃t] ADJ [draperies] hanging (épith); [épaules] sloping (épith); [moustache, paupières] drooping (épith); [bouche] down-turned, turned down at the corners (attrib); [oreilles de chien] floppy → **nuit**

tombe [tɔ̃b] NF [a] (gén) grave; (avec monument) tomb; (= pierre) gravestone, tombstone; **aller sur la ~ de qn** to visit sb's grave; **froid comme la ~** cold as the tomb; **muet** ou **silencieux comme la ~** (as) silent as the grave ou tomb → **recueillir**, **retourner** [b] (loc) **suivre qn dans la ~** to follow sb to the grave; (littér) **descendre dans la ~** to go to one's grave → **pied**

tombeau (pl **tombeaux**) [tɔ̃bo] NM [a] (lit) tomb; **mettre qn au ~** to commit sb to the grave, entomb sb; **mise au ~** entombment [b] (fig) (= endroit lugubre ou solitaire) grave, tomb; (= ruine) [espérances, amour] death (NonC); (= lieu du trépas) grave; **jusqu'au ~** to the grave; **descendre au ~** to go to one's grave; **cette pièce est un ~** this room is like a grave ou tomb; (secret) **je serai un vrai ~** my lips are sealed, I'll be as silent as the grave [c] **à ~ ouvert** at breakneck speed

tombée [tɔ̃be] NF **(à) la ~ de la nuit** (at) nightfall; **(à) la ~ du jour** (at) the close of the day

tomber¹ [tɔ̃be]

> ▶conjug 1◀
> [1] VERBE INTRANSITIF   [2] VERBE TRANSITIF
> Lorsque **tomber** s'emploie dans des locutions figées telles que **tomber** malade/amoureux, tomber d'accord, tomber de sommeil, tomber en désuétude etc, cherchez au nom ou à l'adjectif.

[1] VERBE INTRANSITIF

avec aux être

[a] de la station debout   to fall (over ou down); **il est tombé et s'est cassé la jambe** he fell (over ou down) and broke his leg; **le chien l'a fait ~** the dog knocked him over ou down; **~ par terre** to fall down, fall to the ground; **~ de (tout) son haut** to fall ou crash ou topple to the ground, fall headlong; **se laisser ~ dans un fauteuil** to drop ou fall into an armchair
[b] de la position verticale   [arbre, bouteille, poteau] to fall (over ou down); [chaise, pile d'objets] to fall (over); [échafaudage, mur] to fall down, collapse; **faire ~** (gén) to knock down; (en renversant) to knock over
[c] d'un endroit élevé   [personne, objet] to fall (down); [avion] to fall; (fig, littér = pécher) to fall; **attention! tu vas ~** careful! you'll fall!; **dans ou à l'eau** to fall into the water; **~ d'un arbre** to fall from a tree, fall out of a tree; **~ d'une chaise/d'une échelle** to fall off a chair/off a ladder; **~ de bicyclette/de cheval** to fall off one's bicycle/from ou off one's horse; **~ à bas de son cheval** to fall from ou off one's horse; **~ du cinquième étage** to fall from the fifth floor; **~ de haut** (lit) to fall from a height; (fig) to come down with a bump; **il est tombé sur la tête!*** he's got a screw loose* → **ciel**, **lune**
[d] = se détacher   [feuilles, fruits] to fall; [cheveux] to fall (out); **ramasser des fruits tombés** to pick up fruit that has fallen, pick up windfalls; **le journal tombe (des presses) à 6 heures** the paper comes off the press at 6 o'clock; **la nouvelle vient de ~ à l'instant** the news has just this minute broken; **un télex vient de ~** a telex has just come through; **la plume me tombe des mains** the pen is falling from my hand; **faire ~** (en lâchant) to drop; **porte le vase sur la table sans le faire ~** carry the vase to the table without dropping it
[e] = s'abattre, descendre   [eau, lumière] to fall; [neige, pluie] to fall, come down; [brouillard] to come down; **il tombe de la neige** it's snowing; **qu'est-ce qu'il tombe!*** it's coming down in buckets!*, it's tipping it down* (Brit); **l'eau tombait en cascades** the water was cascading down; **il tombe quelques gouttes** it's raining slightly, there are a few drops of rain (falling), it's spitting (with rain) (Brit) ou sprinkling lightly (US); **la nuit tombe** night is falling, it's getting dark; **la foudre est tombée deux fois/tout près** the lightning has struck twice/nearby
[f] = baisser   [fièvre] to drop; [vent] to drop, abate, die down; [baromètre] to fall; [jour] to draw to a close; [voix] to drop, fall away; [prix, nombre, température] to fall (à to, de by); [colère, conversation] to die down, drop; [exaltation, assurance, enthousiasme] to fall away; **le dollar est tombé à 5F** the dollar has fallen ou dropped to 5 francs; **les prix ne sont jamais tombés aussi bas** prices have reached a new low ou an all-time low, prices have never fallen so low; (fig) **ils sont tombés bien bas** they've sunk really low; **faire ~** [+ température, vent, prix] to bring down
[g] = disparaître   [obstacle, objection] to disappear; [poursuites] to lapse; [record] to fall; (Cartes) **l'as et le roi sont tombés** the ace and king have gone ou have been played; **faire ~ les atouts** to force out the trumps

[h] = pendre, descendre   [draperie, robe, chevelure] to fall, hang; [pantalon] to hang; [moustaches] to droop; [épaules] to slope; **ses cheveux lui tombaient sur les épaules** his hair fell to ou hung down to his shoulders; **les rideaux tombaient jusqu'au plancher** the curtains hung down to the floor; **sa jupe tombe bien** her skirt hangs nicely ou well
[i] = échoir   [date, choix, sort] to fall; [verdict, sanction] to be pronounced; **Pâques tombe tard cette année** Easter falls late this year; **Noël tombe un mardi** Christmas falls on a Tuesday; **les deux concerts tombent le même jour** the two concerts fall on the same day
[j] = arriver, se produire   **il est tombé en pleine réunion/scène de ménage** he walked straight into a meeting/a domestic row; **je tombe toujours aux heures de fermeture** I always manage to come at closing time; **bien/mal ~** (moment) to come at the right/wrong moment; (chance) to be lucky/unlucky; **ça tombe bien** that's fortunate ou convenient; **ça tombe à point** ou **à pic*** that's perfect timing; **ça ne pouvait pas mieux ~** that couldn't have come at a better time; **il est vraiment bien/mal tombé avec son nouveau patron** he's really lucky/unlucky ou he's really in luck/out of luck with his new boss; **si ça tombe, il viendra même pas:** he may not even come → **juste**
[k] = être tué   [combattant] to fall
[l] = être vaincu   [ville, régime, garnison] to fall; **faire ~ le gouvernement** to bring down the government, bring the government down
[m] * = être arrêté   to be ou get busted: ou nicked: (Brit)

♦ **laisser tomber** [+ objet que l'on porte] to drop; [+ amis, activité] to drop; [+ métier] to drop, give up, chuck in*; [+ fiancé] to jilt, throw over*; [+ vieux parents] to let down, leave in the lurch; **il a voulu faire du droit mais il a vite laissé ~** he wanted to do law but he soon gave it up ou dropped it; **la famille nous a bien laissé ~** the family really let us down ou left us in the lurch; **laisse ~!*** (gén) forget it!; (nuance d'irritation) give it a rest!*

♦ **tomber dans** [+ état] **~ dans la misère** to become destitute; **~ dans l'alcool/la drogue** to take to drinking/to drugs; **~ dans le coma** to fall into a coma; **son œuvre est tombée dans l'oubli** his work fell into oblivion; **ce roman tombe dans le mélo/la vulgarité** the novel tends to lapse into melodrama/vulgarity; **~ dans l'excès** to lapse into excess; **~ dans l'excès inverse** to go to the opposite extreme; **~ d'un excès dans un autre** to go from one extreme to another; (fig hum) **le tennis, il est tombé dedans quand il était petit** he learnt how to play tennis almost as soon as he could walk → **domaine**, **pomme**, **piège** etc

♦ **tomber sur** [regard] to fall ou light upon; [conversation] to come round to (= rencontrer par hasard) [+ personne] to run ou bump into; (= trouver par hasard) [+ objet, piste, détail] to come across ou upon; **j'ai eu la chance de ~ sur un spécialiste** I was lucky enough to come across a specialist; **en prenant cette rue, vous tombez sur le boulevard/la gare** if you go along this street, you'll come out onto the boulevard/you'll find the station; **je suis tombé sur une vieille photo** I came across ou upon an old photo → **bec**, **os** (= échoir à) **on a tiré au sort et c'est tombé sur moi** we drew straws and I was the lucky winner (iro); **et il a fallu que ça tombe sur moi!** it (just) had to be me! (* = arriver à l'improviste) [personne] to land on*; **il nous est tombé dessus le jour de Noël** he landed on us on Christmas day*; **une quantité de problèmes leur est tombée dessus** they had a whole series of problems; **la maladie, ça peut** vous ~ dessus n'importe quand you can fall ill any time; **quand la solitude vous tombe dessus ... when you suddenly find yourself alone ...**; **je ne voulais pas d'une nouvelle relation amoureuse, ça m'est tombé dessus** I didn't want to have another love affair, it just happened (* = *attaquer*) to set about*, go for*; (= *critiquer*) to go for*; **il m'est tombé sur le râble** ou **le paletot** ou **le dos** he laid into me*, he went for me*; **ils nous sont tombés dessus à huit contre trois** eight of them laid into the three of us

② VERBE TRANSITIF

avec auxiliaire avoir

a * = *vaincre* ~ **qn** (*Sport*) to throw sb; (* *Pol*) to beat sb; (= *séduire*) **il les tombe toutes** he's a real ladykiller

b * = *enlever* ~ **la veste** to take off one's jacket; ~ **le masque** to drop the mask

tomber² [tɔ̃be] NM **a** (*littér*) **au ~ du jour** ou **de la nuit** at nightfall **b** [*vêtement, étoffe*] **le ~ de ce tissu/de cette robe** the way the material/the dress hangs

tombereau (*pl* **tombereaux**) [tɔ̃bʀo] NM (= *charrette*) tipcart; (= *contenu*) cartload; (*pour terrassement*) dump truck, dumper-truck; (*fig*) **des ~x de** masses of

tombeur [tɔ̃bœʀ] NM (= *lutteur*) thrower; (* = *don Juan*) ladykiller, Casanova; **le ~ du tenant du titre/du sénateur** the man who defeated the title holder/the senator

tombola [tɔ̃bɔla] NF tombola, raffle

Tombouctou [tɔ̃buktu] N Timbuktoo

tome [tɔm] NM (= *division*) part, book; (= *volume*) volume

tomette [tɔmɛt] NF = **tommette**

tomme [tɔm] NF tomme (cheese)

tommette [tɔmɛt] NF (red, hexagonal) floor-tile

tomographie [tɔmɔgʀafi] NF tomography

tom-pouce [tɔmpus] NM (= *nain*) Tom Thumb, dwarf, midget

ton¹ [tɔ̃], **ta** [ta] (*pl* **tes** [te]) ADJ POSS **a** (*possession, relation*) your; (*emphatique*) your own; († *Rel*) thy; ~ **fils et ta fille** your son and (your) daughter; (*Rel*) **que ta volonté soit faite** Thy will be done; *pour autres locutions voir* **son¹** **b** (*valeur affective, ironique, intensive*) **tu as de la chance d'avoir ~ samedi!** you're lucky to have Saturday(s) off!; ~ **Paris est devenu très bruyant** your beloved Paris is getting very noisy; **tu vas avoir ta crise de foie si tu manges ça** you'll upset your stomach if you eat that; **ferme donc ta porte!** shut the door behind you!; *pour autres locutions voir* **son¹**

ton² [tɔ̃] NM **a** (= *hauteur de la voix*) pitch; (= *timbre*) tone; (= *manière de parler*) tone (of voice); ~ **aigu/grave** shrill/low pitch; ~ **nasillard** twang; **d'un ~ détaché/brusque/pédant** in a detached/an abrupt/a pedantic tone (of voice); **d'un ~ sec** curtly; **avec un ~ de supériorité** in a superior tone; **sur le ~ de la conversation/plaisanterie** conversationally/jokingly, in a conversational/joking tone (of voice); **le ~ est à la conciliation/à la prudence** the prevailing mood is one of conciliation/of caution, conciliation/caution is the order of the day; **hausser le ~** (*lit*) to raise one's voice; (*fig*) (= *se fâcher*) to raise one's voice; (= *être arrogant*) to adopt an arrogant tone; **baisser le ~** (*lit*) to lower one's voice; (*fig*) to soften ou moderate one's tone; **baisse un peu le ~!** pipe down!*; (*fig*) **faire baisser le ~ à qn** to bring sb down a peg (or two); **les débats ont changé de ~** the tone of the debates has changed; (*fig*) **il devra changer de ~** he'll have to change his tune; **ne me parle pas sur ce ~!** don't use that tone (of voice) with me!, don't you talk to me like that!; **ne le prenez pas sur ce ~** don't take it like that; **alors là, si vous le prenez sur ce ~** well if that's the way you're

going to take it, well if you're going to take it like that; **dire/répéter sur tous les ~s** to say/repeat in every possible way

b (*Mus = intervalle*) tone; [*morceau*] key; [*instrument à vent*] crook; (= *hauteur d'un instrument*) pitch; **le ~ de si majeur** the key of B major; **passer d'un ~ à un autre** to change from one key to another; **il y a un ~ majeur entre do et ré** there is a whole ou full tone between C and D; **prendre le ~** to tune up (de to); **donner le ~** to give the pitch; **sortir du ~** to go out of tune; **il/ce n'est pas dans le ~** he/it is not in tune; **le ~ est trop haut pour elle** it's set in too high a key for her, it's pitched too high for her

c (*Ling, Phon*) tone; **langue à ~s** tone language

d (= *style*) tone; **le ~ soutenu de son discours** the elevated tone of his speech; (= *manière de se comporter*) **le bon ~** good manners, good form (*Brit*); **plaisanteries/remarques de bon ~** jokes/remarks in good taste; **il est de bon ~ de ...** it's considered polite to ..., it is good manners ou form (*Brit*) to ...; **plaisanteries de mauvais ~** tasteless jokes; **être dans le ~** to fit in; **il s'est vite mis dans le ~** he soon fitted in; **donner le ~** to set the tone; (*en matière de mode*) to set the fashion

e (= *couleur, nuance*) shade, tone; **être dans le ~** to tone in, match; **la ceinture n'est pas du même ~** ou **dans le même ~ que la robe** the belt doesn't match the dress; **~s chauds** warm tones ou shades; **~s dégradés** gradual shadings; ~ **sur ~** in matching tones

tonal, e (*mpl* **tonals**) [tɔnal] ADJ (*Ling, Mus*) tonal

tonalité [tɔnalite] NF **a** (*Mus*) (= *système*) tonality; (= *ton*) key; (*Phon*) [*voyelle*] tone **b** (= *fidélité*) [*poste, amplificateur*] tone **c** (= *timbre, qualité*) [*voix*] tone; (*fig*) [*texte, impression*] tone; [*couleurs*] tonality **d** (*Téléc*) dialling tone (*Brit*), dial tone (*US*); **je n'ai pas la ~** I'm not getting the dialling tone

tondeur, -euse [tɔ̃dœʀ, øz] **1** NM,F (*gén*) shearer **2** NF (*à cheveux*) clippers; (*pour les moutons*) shears; (*Tex: pour les draps*) shears; **tondeuse (à gazon)** (lawn)mower; **tondeuse à main/à moteur** hand-/motor-mower; **tondeuse électrique** (*pour le gazon*) electric (lawn)mower; (*pour les cheveux*) electric clippers

tondre [tɔ̃dʀ] ▶ conjug 41 ◀ VT **a** [+ *mouton, toison*] to shear; [+ *gazon*] to mow; [+ *haie*] to clip, cut; [+ *caniche, poil*] to clip; [+ *cheveux*] to crop; [+ *drap, feutre*] to shear **b** * ~ **qn** (= *couper les cheveux à*) to cut sb's hair; (= *escroquer*) to fleece sb; (*au jeu*) to clean sb out; **je vais me faire** ~ I'm going to get my hair cut really short → **laine**

tondu, e [tɔ̃dy] (*ptp de* **tondre**) ADJ [*cheveux, tête*] (closely-)cut; [*personne*] with closely-cropped hair, close-cropped; [*pelouse, sommet*] closely-cropped → **pelé**

Tonga [tɔ̃ga] NM Tonga; **les îles ~** Tonga

tongs [tɔ̃g] NFPL (= *sandales*) flip-flops, thongs (*US*)

tonicité [tɔnisite] NF **a** (*Méd*) [*tissus*] tone, tonicity (*SPÉC*), tonus (*SPÉC*) **b** [*air, mer*] tonic ou bracing effect

tonifiant, e [tɔnifjɑ̃, jɑ̃t] **1** ADJ [*air*] bracing, invigorating; [*massage, lotion*] toning (*épith*), tonic (*épith*), stimulating; [*lecture, expérience*] stimulating **2** NM tonic

tonifier [tɔnifje] ▶ conjug 7 ◀ VT [+ *muscles*] to tone (up); [+ *esprit, personne*] to stimulate; [+ *peau*] to tone; [+ *cheveux*] to put new life into; **cela tonifie l'organisme** it tones up the whole system

tonique [tɔnik] **1** ADJ **a** [*médicament, vin, boisson*] tonic **b** [*air, froid*] invigorating, bracing; [*idée, expérience, lecture*] stimulating **c** (*Ling*) [*syllabe, voyelle*] tonic, accented →

accent ② NM (*Méd, fig*) tonic; (= *lotion*) toning lotion; ~ **du cœur** heart tonic ③ NF (*Mus*) tonic, keynote

tonitruant, e [tɔnitʀyɑ̃, ɑ̃t] ADJ [*voix*] thundering, booming (*épith*)

tonitruer [tɔnitʀye] ▶ conjug 1 ◀ VI to thunder

Tonkin [tɔ̃kɛ̃] NM Tonkin

tonkinois, e [tɔ̃kinwa, waz] **1** ADJ Tonkinese **2** **Tonkinois(e)** NM,F Tonkinese

tonnage [tɔnaʒ] NM [*navire*] tonnage, burden; [*port, pays*] tonnage; ~ **brut/net** gross/net tonnage

tonnant, e [tɔnɑ̃, ɑ̃t] ADJ [*voix, acclamation*] thunderous, thundering (*épith*)

tonne [tɔn] NF **a** (= *unité de poids*) (metric) ton, tonne; **une ~ de bois** a ton ou tonne (*Brit*) of wood; ~ **américaine** ou **courte** short ou net ton; ~ **anglaise** ou **longue** ou **forte** long ou gross ou imperial ton; **~-kilomètre** ton kilometre; **un navire de 10 000 ~s** a 10,000-ton ou -tonne (*Brit*) ship, a ship of 10,000 tons ou tonnes (*Brit*); **un (camion de) 5 ~s** a 5-ton truck, a 5-tonner*; ~ **équivalent charbon** ton coal equivalent; ~ **équivalent pétrole** ton oil equivalent; **ses plaisanteries pèsent des ~s** his jokes are very laboured ou heavy-handed **b** (* = *énorme quantité*) **des ~s de** ◊ **une** ~ **de** tons of*, loads of*; **il y en a des** ~ there are tons* ou loads* of them; **des gens comme lui, (il n') y en a pas des ~s** you don't come across people like him every day; **en faire des ~s** to overdo it, go over the top* **c** (*Tech = récipient*) tun; (*Naut = bouée*) tun-buoy

tonneau (*pl* **tonneaux**) [tɔno] NM **a** (= *récipient*) barrel, cask; (= *contenu*) barrel(ful), cask(ful); **vin au** ~ wine from the barrel ou cask; **vieillir en** ~ to age in the barrel ou cask; **le ~ de Diogène** Diogenes' tub; **le ~ des Danaïdes** (*Myth*) the Danaides' jar; (*fig*) **c'est le ~ des Danaïdes** (= *gouffre financier*) it's a bottomless pit; (= *tâche sans fin*) it's a Sisyphean task; (*péj*) **être du même ~** to be of the same kind → **perce** **b** (*Aviat*) hesitation flick roll (*Brit*), hesitation snap roll (*US*) **c** (*Aut*) somersault; **faire un** ~ to roll over, somersault; **leur voiture a fait trois ~x** their car rolled (over) ou somersaulted three times **d** (*Naut*) ton; ~ **de jauge brute** gross register ton; **un bateau de 1 500 ~x** a 1,500-ton ou -tonne (*Brit*) ship

tonnelet [tɔnlɛ] NM keg, (small) cask

tonnelier [tɔnəlje] NM cooper

tonnelle [tɔnɛl] NF (= *abri*) bower, arbour (*Brit*), arbor (*US*); (*Archit*) barrel vault

tonnellerie [tɔnɛlʀi] NF cooperage

tonner [tɔne] ▶ conjug 1 ◀ **1** VI **a** [*canons, artillerie*] to thunder, boom, roar **b** [*personne*] to thunder, rage, inveigh (**contre** against) **2** VB IMPERS to thunder; **il tonne** it's thundering; **il a tonné vers 2 heures** there was some thunder about 2 o'clock; **il tonnait sans discontinuer** the thunder rumbled continuously

tonnerre [tɔnɛʀ] **1** NM **a** (= *détonation*) thunder; († = *foudre*) thunderbolt; **j'entends le ~ qui gronde** I can hear thunder; **coup de ~** thunderbolt; (*fig*) **comme un coup de ~ dans un ciel serein** ou **bleu** like a bolt from the blue; **un bruit/une voix de ~** a noise/a voice like thunder, a thunderous noise/voice; **un ~ d'applaudissements** thunderous applause; **le ~ des canons** the roar ou the thundering of the guns **b** (* : *valeur intensive*) **du ~** terrific*, fantastic*; **ça marchait du ~** it was going great guns* ou tremendously well; **un livre du ~ de Dieu** one ou a hell of a book*, a fantastic book* **2** EXCL ~! **† ye gods!**† †; **mille ~s !** ◊ ~ **de Brest !** shiver me timbers!* † (*aussi hum*); ~ **de Dieu!** hell and damnation!*, hell's bells!*

tonsure [tɔ̃syʀ] NF (*Rel*) tonsure; (* = *calvitie*) bald spot ou patch; **porter la** ~ to wear the tonsure

tonsuré, e [tɔ̃syʀe] (*ptp de* **tonsurer**) [1] ADJ tonsured [2] NM (*péj* = *moine*) monk

tonsurer [tɔ̃syʀe] ▶conjug 1◀ VT to tonsure

tonte [tɔ̃t] NF [a] (= *action*) [*moutons*] shearing; [*haie*] clipping; [*gazon*] mowing [b] (= *laine*) fleece [c] (= *époque*) shearing-time

tontine [tɔ̃tin] NF (*Fin, Jur*) tontine

tonton [tɔ̃tɔ̃] NM (*langage enfantin*) uncle

tonus [tɔnys] NM [a] (*Physiol*) tone, tonus (*SPÉC*); ~ **musculaire** muscle tone, muscular tonus (*SPÉC*); ~ **nerveux** nerve tone [b] (*fig* = *dynamisme*) energy, dynamism; (*au travail*) drive; **redonner du ~ à l'économie** to give the economy a boost; **ce shampoing donnera du ~ à vos cheveux** this shampoo will put new life into your hair

top [tɔp] [1] NM [a] (= *signal électrique*) beep; (*Radio*) **au 4ᵉᵐᵉ ~ il sera midi** at the 4th stroke it will be twelve o'clock [b] (*Courses*) **donner le ~ (de départ)** to give the starting signal; **attention, ~, partez!** *ou* **~ départ!** on your marks, get set, go! [c] ~ **10/30** *etc* top 10 *ou* ten/30 *ou* thirty *etc*; (*Mus*) **le ~ 50** the top 50 (*singles*), ≈ the singles charts; **numéro un du ~ 50** number one in the charts [d] (* = *le mieux*) **c'est le ~!** it's the best!; **être au ~** [*athlète, chercheur*] to be the best in one's field; **être au ~ de sa forme** to be in tip-top condition *ou* shape, be in great shape* [2] ADJ ~ **secret** top secret; ~ **modèle** top model [*athlète, chercheur*] **être au ~ niveau** to be at the top of one's field

topaze [tɔpaz] [1] NF topaz; ~ **brûlée** burnt topaz [2] ADJ INV (= *couleur*) topaz; **liquide ~** topaz-coloured liquid

toper [tɔpe] ▶conjug 1◀ VI **tope-là!** ◊ **topez-là!** let's shake on it!, done!, you're on!*, it's a deal!*

topiaire [tɔpjɛʀ] ADJ, NF (**art**) ~ topiary

topinambour [tɔpinãbuʀ] NM Jerusalem artichoke

topique [tɔpik] [1] ADJ (*frm*) [*argument, explication*] pertinent; [*citation*] apposite; [*remède, médicament*] topical, local [2] NM (*Méd*) topical *ou* local remedy; (*Philo*) topic [3] NF (*Philo*) topics *sg*

topless* [tɔplɛs] [1] ADJ [*bar, serveuse*] topless [2] NM **faire du ~** to go topless

topo* [tɔpo] NM (= *exposé, rapport*) rundown*; (*péj* = *laïus*) spiel*; **faire un ~ sur qch** to give a rundown* on sth; **c'est toujours le même ~** it's always the same old story*; **tu vois un peu le ~?** get the picture?

topographe [tɔpɔgʀaf] NM topographer

topographie [tɔpɔgʀafi] NF (= *technique*) topography; (= *configuration*) layout, topography; † (= *description*) topographical description; (= *croquis*) topographical plan

topographique [tɔpɔgʀafik] ADJ topographic(al)

topographiquement [tɔpɔgʀafikmã] ADV topographically

topoguide [tɔpogid] NM topographical guide

topologie [tɔpɔlɔʒi] NF topology

topologique [tɔpɔlɔʒik] ADJ topologic(al)

topométrie [tɔpɔmetʀi] NF topometry

toponyme [tɔpɔnim] NM place name, toponym (*SPÉC*)

toponymie [tɔpɔnimi] NF (= *étude*) toponymy (*SPÉC*), study of place names; (= *noms de lieux*) toponymy (*SPÉC*), place names

toponymique [tɔpɔnimik] ADJ toponymic

toquade [tɔkad] NF (*péj*) (*pour qn*) infatuation, crush*; (*pour qch*) fad, craze; **avoir une ~ pour qn** to have a crush on sb*, be infatuated with sb

toquante* [tɔkãt] NF = **tocante**

toquard, e* [tɔkaʀ, aʀd] ADJ, NM = **tocard, e**

toque [tɔk] NF (*en fourrure*) fur hat; [*juge, jockey*] cap; ~ **de cuisinier** chef's hat; (= *chef cuisinier*) **l'une des ~s les plus renommées** one of the most famous chefs

toqué, e* [tɔke] [1] ADJ crazy*, cracked*, nuts* (*attrib*); **être ~ de qn** to be crazy *ou* mad *ou* nuts about sb* [2] NM,F loony‡, nutcase*, nutter‡ (*Brit*)

toquer* [tɔke] ▶conjug 1◀ VI to tap, rap; ~ **(à la porte)** to tap *ou* rap at the door

toquer (se)* [tɔke] ▶conjug 1◀ VPR **se toquer de qn** to lose one's head over sb, go crazy over sb*; **se toquer de qch** to go crazy over sth

Tor [tɔʀ] NM = **Thor**

Torah [tɔʀa] NF = **Thora**

torche [tɔʀʃ] NF [a] (= *flambeau*) torch; ~ **électrique** (electric) torch (*Brit*), flashlight (*US*); **être transformé en ~ vivante** to be turned into a human torch; (*Parachutisme*) **se mettre en ~** to candle [b] (*Ind* = *torchère*) flare

torche-cul‡ [*pl* **torche-culs**] [tɔʀʃəky] NM toilet paper, bog-paper‡ (*Brit*); (*fig, †* = *écrit*) drivel (*NonC*)

torchée* [tɔʀʃe] NF (= *correction*) hammering, thrashing

torcher [tɔʀʃe] ▶conjug 1◀ [1] VT [a]* [+ *assiette*] to wipe (clean); [+ *jus*] to mop up [b]‡ [+ *derrière*] to wipe; ~ **un bébé** to wipe a baby's bottom [c] (*péj*) [+ *travail, rapport*] (= *produire*) to toss off; (= *bâcler*) to make a mess of, botch (up); **rapport/article bien torché** well-written report/article [2] **se torcher‡** VPR [a] (= *s'essuyer*) **se ~ (les fesses)** to wipe one's bottom; (*fig*) **je m'en torche** (= *je m'en moque*) I don't give *ou* care a damn* [b]‡ (= *boire*) **il s'est torché la bouteille de vodka** he polished off* *ou* downed* the bottle of vodka; **il était complètement torché** (= *saoul*) he was completely pissed‡ (*Brit*) *ou* wasted‡ (*US*)

torchère [tɔʀʃɛʀ] NF [a] (*Ind*) flare [b] (= *candélabre*) torchère; (= *chandelier*) candelabrum; (= *vase*) cresset

torchis [tɔʀʃi] NM cob (*for walls*)

torchon [tɔʀʃɔ̃] NM [a] (*gén*) cloth; (*pour épousseter*) duster (*Brit*), dustcloth (*US*); (*à vaisselle*) tea towel, dish towel; **coup de ~** (= *bagarre*) scrap; (= *épuration*) clear-out; **donner un coup de ~** (*ménage*) to give a room a dust, flick a duster over a room; (*vaisselle*) to give the dishes a wipe; (*fig: épuration*) to have a clear-out; (*fig*) **le ~ brûle** there's a running battle (going on) (*entre* between) *ou* **mélanger** [b] (*péj*) (= *devoir mal présenté*) mess; (= *écrit sans valeur*) drivel (*NonC*), tripe* (*NonC*); (= *mauvais journal*) rag; **ce devoir est un ~** this homework is a mess

torchonner* [tɔʀʃɔne] ▶conjug 1◀ VT (*péj*) [+ *travail*] to do a rushed job on; **un devoir torchonné** a slipshod *ou* badly done piece of homework

tordant, e* [tɔʀdã, ãt] ADJ hilarious; **il est ~** he's a scream*

tord-boyaux*† [tɔʀbwajo] NM INV rotgut*, hooch* (*US*)

tordre [tɔʀdʀ] ▶conjug 41◀ [1] VT [a] (*entre ses mains*) to wring; (*pour essorer*) to wring (out); [+ *tresses*] to wind; (*Tex*) [+ *brins, laine*] to twist; [+ *bras, poignet*] to twist; (*sur étiquette*) « **ne pas ~** » "do not wring"; **sa robe était à ~** (*très mouillée*) her dress was wringing wet; ~ **le cou à un poulet** to wring a chicken's neck; (*fig*) **je vais lui ~ le cou*** I'll wring his neck (for him); ~ **le cou à une rumeur** to put an end to *ou* kill a rumour; **cet alcool vous tord les boyaux*** this stuff is real rot-gut‡; **la peur lui tordait l'estomac** his stomach was churning with fear [b] (= *plier*) [+ *barre de fer*] to twist; [+ *cuiller, branche de lunette*] to bend [c] (= *déformer*) [+ *traits, visage*] to contort, twist; **une joie sadique lui tordait la bouche** his mouth was twisted into a sadistic leer; **la colère lui tordait le visage** his face was twisted *ou* contorted with anger; ~ **le nez (devant**

qch)* to screw up one's face in disgust (at sth) [2] **se tordre** VPR [a] [*personne*] **se ~ de douleur** to be doubled up with pain; **se ~ (de rire)** to be doubled up *ou* creased up (*Brit*) with laughter; **c'est à se ~ (de rire)!** it's hilarious!; **ça les a fait se ~ de rire** it had them in stitches*; **mon estomac se tord** I've got a terrible pain in my stomach [b] [*barre, poteau*] to bend; [*roue*] to buckle, twist; [*racine, tronc*] to twist round, writhe (*littér*) [c] (= *se faire mal à*) **se ~ le pied/le poignet/la cheville** to twist one's foot/one's wrist/one's ankle; **se ~ les mains (de désespoir)** to wring one's hands (in despair)

tordu, e [tɔʀdy] (*ptp de* **tordre**) [1] ADJ [*nez*] crooked; [*jambes*] bent, crooked; [*tronc*] twisted; [*règle, barre*] bent; [*roue*] bent, buckled, twisted; [*idée*] weird; [*raisonnement*] twisted; **avoir l'esprit ~** to have a warped mind; **être (complètement) ~‡** to be off one's head*, be round the bend* (*Brit*) *ou* the twist* (*Brit*); **il m'a fait un coup ~** he played a dirty trick on me [2] NM,F‡ (= *fou*) loony*, nutcase*; (= *crétin*) twit*

tore [tɔʀ] NM (*Géom*) torus; (*Archit*) torus, tore; ~ **magnétique** magnetic core; ~ **de ferrite** ferrite core

toréador [tɔʀeadɔʀ] NM toreador

toréer [tɔʀee] ▶conjug 1◀ VI (*ponctuellement*) to fight *ou* work a bull; (*habituellement*) to be a bullfighter

torero [tɔʀeʀo] NM bullfighter, torero

torgnole* [tɔʀɲɔl] NF clout, wallop*; **flanquer* une ~ à qn** to clout* *ou* wallop* sb

toril [tɔʀil] NM bullpen

tornade [tɔʀnad] NF tornado; **entrer comme une ~** to come in like a whirlwind

toron [tɔʀɔ̃] NM (= *brin*) strand

torpédo [tɔʀpedo] NF† open tourer (*Brit*), open touring car (*US*)

torpeur [tɔʀpœʀ] NF torpor; **faire sortir** *ou* **tirer qn de sa ~** to bring sb out of his torpor

torpide [tɔʀpid] ADJ (*littér, Méd*) torpid

torpillage [tɔʀpijaʒ] NM (*lit, fig*) torpedoing

torpille [tɔʀpij] NF [a] (*Mil*) (*sous-marine*) torpedo; (= *bombe*) ~ **(aérienne)** (aerial) torpedo [b] (= *poisson*) torpedo

torpiller [tɔʀpije] ▶conjug 1◀ VT (*lit, fig*) to torpedo

torpilleur [tɔʀpijœʀ] NM torpedo boat

torréfacteur [tɔʀefaktœʀ] NM [a] (= *appareil*) [*café, malt, cacao*] roaster; [*tabac*] toasting machine [b] (= *commerçant*) coffee merchant

torréfaction [tɔʀefaksjɔ̃] NF [*café, malt, cacao*] roasting; [*tabac*] toasting

torréfier [tɔʀefje] ▶conjug 7◀ VT [+ *café, malt, cacao*] to roast; [+ *tabac*] to toast; **café torréfié** roast(ed) coffee

torrent [tɔʀã] NM [a] (= *cours d'eau*) torrent; ~ **de montagne** (fast-flowing) mountain stream, mountain torrent [b] (= *écoulement rapide*) ~ **de lave** torrent *ou* flood of lava; ~ **de boue** torrent of mud; **des ~s d'eau** (*pluie*) torrential rain; (*inondation*) torrents of water; **il pleut à ~s** it's pouring (= *grande abondance*) **un ~ de** [+ *injures, paroles*] a torrent *ou* stream *ou* flood of; [+ *musique*] a flood of; **des ~s de** [+ *fumée, lumière, larmes*] streams of

torrentiel, -elle [tɔʀãsjɛl] ADJ [*eaux, régime, pluie*] torrential

torrentueux, -euse [tɔʀãtɥø, øz] ADJ (*littér*) [a] [*cours d'eau*] torrential, surging (*épith*) [b] (*fig*) [*vie*] hectic; [*discours*] torrent-like

torride [tɔʀid] ADJ (= *très chaud*) [*région, climat*] torrid; [*journée, chaleur*] scorching, torrid; (= *sensuel, ardent*) [*scène d'amour, ambiance*] torrid

tors, torse¹ [tɔʀ, tɔʀs] [1] ADJ [*fil*] twisted; [*colonne*] wreathed; [*pied de verre*] twist (*épith*); [*jambes*] crooked, bent [2] NM (*Tech*) twist

torsade [tɔʀsad] NF [fils] twist; (Archit) cable moulding; (Tricot) cable-stitch; **~ de cheveux** twist ou coil of hair; **en ~** [embrasse, cheveux] twisted; **colonne à ~s** cabled column; **pull à ~s** cable(-knit ou -stitch) sweater → **point²**

torsader [tɔʀsade] ▸ conjug 1 ◂ VT [+ frange, corde, cheveux] to twist; **colonne torsadée** cabled column; **pull torsadé** cable(-knit ou -stitch) sweater

torse² [tɔʀs] NM (gén) chest; (Anat, Sculp) torso; **~ nu** stripped to the waist, bare-chested; **se mettre ~ nu** to strip to the waist → **bomber**

torsion [tɔʀsjɔ̃] NF (= action) twisting; (Phys, Tech) torsion; **exercer sur qn une ~ du bras** to twist sb's arm back; **moment de ~** torque → **couple**

▼ **tort** [tɔʀ] NM [a] (= action, attitude blâmable) fault; **il a un ~, c'est de trop parler** his one fault is that he talks too much; **il a le ~ d'être trop jeune** the only trouble with him is that he's too young; **il a eu le ~ d'être impoli avec le patron** he made the mistake of being rude to the boss; **je n'ai eu qu'un seul ~, celui de t'écouter** the only mistake I made was to listen to you; **ils ont tous les ~s de leur côté** the fault is entirely on their side, they are completely in the wrong; (Jur) **les ~s sont du côté du mari/cycliste** the fault lies with the husband/cyclist, the husband/cyclist is at fault; **avoir des ~s envers qn** to have wronged sb; **il n'a aucun ~** he's not at fault, he's in no way to blame; **il a reconnu ses ~s** he acknowledged ou admitted that he had done something wrong; **vous avez refusé ? c'est un ~** did you refuse? — you were wrong (to do that) ou you shouldn't have (done that); **tu ne le savais pas ? c'est un ~** you didn't know? — you should have ou that was a mistake ou that was unfortunate

[b] (= dommage, préjudice) wrong; **redresser un ~** to right a wrong; **faire ou causer du ~ à qn** ◊ **faire ou porter ~ à qn†** to harm sb, do ou cause sb harm; **ça ne fait de ~ à personne** it doesn't harm ou hurt anybody; **il s'est fait du ~** he has harmed himself, he has done himself no good; **cette mesure va faire du ~ aux produits laitiers** this measure will harm ou be harmful to ou be detrimental to the dairy industry; **il ne me ferait pas ~ d'un centime†** he wouldn't do me out of a penny → **redresseur**

[c] **à ~** wrongly; **soupçonner/accuser qn à ~** to suspect/accuse sb wrongly; **c'est à ~ qu'on l'avait dit malade** he was wrongly ou mistakenly said to be ill; **à ~ ou à raison** rightly or wrongly; **dépenser à ~ et à travers** to spend wildly, spend money like water; **il parle à ~ et à travers** he's blathering, he's saying any old thing*

[d] **être/se mettre/se sentir dans son ~** to be/put o.s./feel o.s. in the wrong; **mettre qn dans son ~** to put sb in the wrong; **être en ~** to be in the wrong ou at fault; (Aut) **il venait de ma droite, j'étais dans mon ~** he was coming from the right, I was at fault

[e] **avoir ~** to be wrong; **il a ~ de se mettre en colère** he's wrong ou it's wrong of him to get angry; **il n'a pas tout à fait ~ de dire que ...** he's not altogether ou entirely wrong in saying that ...; **elle a grand ou bien ~ de le croire** she's very wrong to believe it; **tu aurais bien ~ de te gêner !** you'd be quite wrong to bother yourself!; **on aurait ~ de croire que ...** it would be wrong to think ou believe that ... → **absent**

[f] **donner ~ à qn** (= blâmer) to lay the blame on sb, blame sb; (= ne pas être d'accord avec) to disagree with sb; **les statistiques donnent ~ à son rapport** statistics show ou prove his report to be wrong ou inaccurate; **les événements lui ont donné ~** events proved him wrong ou showed that he was wrong

torticolis [tɔʀtikɔli] NM stiff neck, torticollis (SPÉC); **avoir/attraper un ~** to have/get a stiff neck

tortillard [tɔʀtijaʀ] NM (hum péj = train) local train

tortillement [tɔʀtijmɑ̃] NM [serpent] writhing; [ver] wriggling, squirming; [personne] (en dansant, en se débattant etc) wriggling; (d'impatience) fidgeting, wriggling; (d'embarras, de douleur) squirming; **elle marchait avec un léger ~ des hanches** she wiggled her hips slightly as she walked

tortiller [tɔʀtije] ▸ conjug 1 ◂ [1] VT [+ corde, mouchoir] to twist; [+ cheveux, cravate] to twiddle (with); [+ moustache] to twirl; [+ doigts] to twiddle; **il tortillait son chapeau entre ses mains** he was fiddling with his hat [2] VI [a] (= remuer) **~ des hanches** to wiggle one's hips; **~ des fesses ou du derrière*** to wiggle one's bottom [b] (* = tergiverser) **il n'y a pas à ~** there's no wriggling out of it [3] **se tortiller** VPR [a] [serpent] to writhe; [ver] to wriggle, squirm; [personne] (en dansant, en se débattant etc) to wiggle; (d'impatience) to fidget, wriggle; (d'embarras, de douleur) to squirm; **se ~ comme une anguille ou un ver** to wriggle like a worm ou an eel, squirm like an eel [b] [fumée] to curl upwards; [racine, tige] to curl, writhe

tortillon [tɔʀtijɔ̃] NM [a] (Dessin) stump, tortillon [b] **~ (de papier)** twist (of paper)

tortionnaire [tɔʀsjɔnɛʀ] NM, ADJ torturer; **les militaires ~s seront jugés** the army torturers will be taken to court

tortue [tɔʀty] NF [a] (Zool: terrestre) tortoise; **~ d'eau douce** terrapin; **~ marine ou de mer** turtle → **île, luth** [b] (= personne lente) slowcoach (Brit), slowpoke (US); **avancer comme une ~** to crawl along at a snail's pace [c] (Hist Mil) testudo, tortoise

tortueusement [tɔʀtyøzmɑ̃] ADV windingly, tortuously

tortueux, -euse [tɔʀtyø, øz] ADJ [a] (= sinueux) [chemin, escalier] winding, twisting, tortuous (littér); [rivière] winding [b] (péj) [esprit] tortuous; [langage, discours, raisonnement] tortuous, convoluted; [manœuvres, conduite] devious

torturant, e [tɔʀtyʀɑ̃, ɑ̃t] ADJ agonizing

torture [tɔʀtyʀ] NF (lit) torture (NonC); (fig) torture (NonC), torment; **c'est une ~ atroce** it's an appalling form ou kind of torture; **instruments de ~** instruments of torture; **chambre ou salle de(s) ~s** torture chamber; **sous la ~** under torture; **cette attente fut pour elle une véritable ~** it was real torture for her to wait around like that; (fig) **mettre qn à la ~** to torture sb, make sb suffer

torturer [tɔʀtyʀe] ▸ conjug 1 ◂ [1] VT [a] (lit) [+ prisonnier, animal] to torture; (fig) **le doute/la crainte/le remords le torturait** he was racked with ou by doubt/fear/remorse; **la faim le torturait** hunger was gnawing at his belly; **cette pensée le torturait** he was tormented by the thought [b] (littér = dénaturer) [+ texte] to distort, torture (littér); **son visage était torturé par le chagrin** his face was twisted ou racked with grief; **sa poésie torturée, déchirante** his tormented, heartrending poetry [2] **se torturer** VPR (= se faire du souci) to fret, worry o.s. sick (**pour** over); **se ~ le cerveau ou l'esprit** to rack ou cudgel one's brains

torve [tɔʀv] ADJ [regard, œil] menacing, grim

tory (pl **tories** ou **torys**) [tɔʀi] ADJ, NM Tory

toscan, e [tɔskɑ̃, an] [1] ADJ Tuscan [2] NM (Ling) Tuscan

Toscane [tɔskan] NF Tuscany

tôt [to] ADV [a] (= de bonne heure) early; **se lever/se coucher (très) ~** to get up/go to bed (very) early; **il se lève ~** he's an early riser, he gets up early; **il arrive toujours ~ le jeudi** he's always early on Thursdays; **venez ~ dans la matinée/soirée** come early (on) in the morning/evening ou in the early morning/evening; **~ dans l'année** early (on) in the year, in the early part of the year; **~ le matin, il**

n'est pas très lucide he's not very clear-headed first thing (in the morning) ou early in the morning; **il n'est pas si ~ que je croyais** it's not as early as I thought; **Pâques tombe ~ cette année** Easter falls early this year → **avenir**

[b] (= avant un moment déterminé, habituel ou prévu) soon, early; **il est un peu (trop) ~ pour le juger** it's a little too soon ou early to judge him; **si tu étais venu une heure plus ~, tu l'aurais rencontré** if you'd come an hour sooner ou earlier you would have met him; **elle m'avait téléphoné une semaine plus ~** she'd called me a week earlier; **ce n'est pas trop ~ !** and about time too!*

[c] (= vite) soon, early; **si seulement vous me l'aviez dit plus ~ !** if only you'd told me sooner! ou earlier!; **il n'était pas plus ~ parti que la voiture est tombée en panne** no sooner had he set off ou he had no sooner set off than the car broke down; **venez le plus ~ possible** come as early ou as soon as you can; **le plus ~ sera le mieux** the sooner the better; **je ne m'attendais pas à le revoir si ~** I didn't expect to see him (again) so soon; **cette soirée, je ne l'oublierai pas de si ~ !** I won't forget that party in a hurry!; **une occasion pareille ne se représentera pas de si ~** you don't get an opportunity like that every day

[d] **avoir ~ fait de** (+ infin) : **il a eu ~ fait de s'en apercevoir !** he was quick ou it didn't take him long to notice it!, it wasn't long before he noticed it!; **il aura ~ fait de s'en apercevoir !** it won't be long before he notices it!, it won't take him long to notice it!

[e] **au plus ~** : **il peut venir jeudi au plus ~** Thursday is the earliest ou soonest he can come; **c'est au plus ~ en mai qu'il prendra la décision** it'll be May at the earliest that he takes ou he'll take the decision, he'll decide in May at the earliest; **il faut qu'il vienne au plus ~** he must come as soon as possible ou as soon as he possibly can

[f] **~ ou tard** sooner or later

total, e [tɔtal, o] (mpl -aux) [1] ADJ [a] (= complet : gén) total, complete; [contrôle] complete; [ruine, désespoir] utter (épith), total; **grève ~e** all-out strike; **l'arrêt ~ des hostilités** the complete ou total cessation of hostilities; **dans la confusion la plus ~e** in utter ou total confusion → **guerre**

[b] (= global) [hauteur, coût, revenu] total; **la somme ~e est plus élevée que nous ne pensions** the total (sum ou amount) is higher than we thought; **la longueur ~e de la voiture** the overall length of the car

[2] ADV **~, il a tout perdu** the net result ou outcome was that he lost everything

[3] NM [a] (= quantité) total (number); (= résultat) total; **le ~ s'élève à 150 F** the total amounts to 150 francs; **le ~ de la population** the total (number of the) population; (Fin) **~ général** grand total; **faire le ~** to work out the total; (fig) **si on fait le ~, ils n'ont pas réalisé grand-chose** if you add it all up ou together they didn't achieve very much

[b] **au ~** (lit) in total; (fig) all things considered, all in all

[4] **totale*** NF [a] (Méd) (total) hysterectomy; **on lui a fait la ~e** she had her works out‡

[b] **la ~e** (= tout ce qu'on peut imaginer) the works*; (= le comble) **alors là, c'est la ~e !** that's the last straw!

totalement [tɔtalmɑ̃] ADV totally

totalisateur, -trice [tɔtalizatœʀ, tʀis] [1] ADJ [appareil, machine] adding (épith) [2] NM adding machine; (Ordin) accumulator; (Aut) **~ kilométrique** kilometre counter, ≈ mileometer

totalisation [tɔtalizasjɔ̃] NF adding up, addition

totaliser [tɔtalize] ▸ conjug 1 ◂ VT [a] (= additionner) to add up, total, totalize [b] (= avoir au total) to total, have a total of; **à eux deux**

▸ GRAMMAIRE ACTIVE: **tort** 29.2, 39.1, 41

ils **totalisent** 60 ans de service between the two of them they have a total of 60 years' service *ou* they total 60 years' service; **le candidat qui totalise le plus grand nombre de points** the candidate with the highest total *ou* who gets the highest number of points

totalitaire [tɔtaliter] ADJ (*Pol*) [*régime*] totalitarian; (*Philo*) [*conception*] all-embracing, global

totalitarisme [tɔtalitaʀism] NM totalitarianism

totalité [tɔtalite] NF [a] (*gén*) **la ~ de** all of; **la ~ du sable/des livres** all (of) the sand/the books; **la ~ du livre/de la population** all the book/the population, the whole *ou* entire book/population; **la ~ de son salaire** his whole *ou* entire salary, all of his salary; **la ~ de ses biens** all of his possessions; **vendu en ~ aux États-Unis** all sold to the USA; **édité en ~ par Dubosc** published entirely by Dubosc; **pris dans sa ~** taken as a whole *ou* in its entirety; **j'en connais la quasi-~** I know virtually all of them *ou* just about all of them; **la presque ~ de la population** almost the entire population [b] (*Philo*) totality

totem [tɔtɛm] NM (*gén*) totem; (= *poteau*) totem pole

totémique [tɔtemik] ADJ totemic

totémisme [tɔtemism] NM totemism

toto: [tɔto] NM (= *pou*) louse, cootie* (*US*)

toton [tɔtɔ̃] NM teetotum

touage [twaʒ] NM (*Naut*) warping, kedging

touareg, -ègue [twaʀɛg] [1] ADJ Tuareg [2] NM (*Ling*) Tuareg ♦ **Touareg** ♦ **Touarègue** NM,F Tuareg

toubib: [tubib] NM doctor; **elle est ~** she's a doctor; **aller chez le ~** to go and see the doctor

toucan [tukɑ̃] NM toucan

touchant[1] [tuʃɑ̃] PRÉP (= *au sujet de*) concerning, with regard to, about

touchant[2], e [tuʃɑ̃, ɑ̃t] ADJ (= *émouvant*) [*histoire, lettre, situation, adieux*] touching, moving; (= *attendrissant*) [*geste, reconnaissance, enthousiasme*] touching; **~ de naïveté/d'ignorance** touchingly naïve/ignorant

touche [tuʃ] NF [a] [*piano, ordinateur*] key; [*téléphone, télécommande, lave-vaisselle*] button; [*instrument à corde*] fingerboard; [*guitare*] fret; (*Ordin*) **~ de fonction/programmable** function/user-defined key; (*Téléc*) **~ bis** redial button [b] (*Peinture*) (= *tache de couleur*) touch, stroke; (*fig* = *style*) [*peintre, écrivain*] touch; **appliquer la couleur par petites ~s** to apply the colour with small strokes *ou* in small touches *ou* dabs, dab the colour on; **finesse de ~ d'un peintre/auteur** deftness of touch of a painter/an author; **une ~ exotique** an exotic touch; **une ~ de gaieté** a touch *ou* note of gaiety; **avec une ~ d'humour** with a hint *ou* suggestion *ou* touch of humour; **mettre la dernière ~** *ou* **la ~ finale à qch** to put the finishing touches to sth [c] (*Pêche*) bite; **avoir** *ou* **faire une ~** (*lit*) to get a bite; * (= *séduire*) **faire une ~** to make a hit*; **avoir la ~*** ◊ **avoir fait une ~*** to have made a hit* (**avec** with) [d] (*Escrime*) hit, touch [e] (*Sport*) (= *sortie*) touch; (= *ligne*) touchline; (= *remise en jeu*) (*Ftbl*) (*Hand-ball*) throw-in; (*Rugby*) line-out; (*Basket*) return to play; (*Hockey*) roll-in; **botter en ~** to kick into touch; **envoyer** *ou* **mettre la balle en ~** to kick the ball into touch; **le ballon est sorti en ~** the ball has gone into touch; **coup de pied en ~** (*Ftbl*) **jouer la ~** to play for time (*by putting the ball repeatedly into touch*); (*Rugby*) **il a trouvé la ~** he found touch; **rester sur la ~** (*lit*) to stay on the bench; (*fig*) **être mis/rester sur la ~** to be put/stay on the sidelines → **juge**

[f] (* = *allure*) look, appearance; **quelle drôle de ~!** what a sight!*, what does he (*ou* she *etc*) look like!*; **il a une de ces ~s!** you should see the way he dresses!; **il a la ~ de quelqu'un qui sort de prison** he looks as though he's just out of prison → **pierre**

touche-à-tout [tuʃatu] NMF INV, ADJ INV **c'est un ~** ◊ **il est ~** (= *enfant*) his little fingers are *ou* he's into everything; (= *dilettante*) he dabbles in everything

touche-pipi* [tuʃpipi] NM INV **jouer à ~** [*enfants*] to play doctors and nurses; [*adultes*] to pet*, make out* (*US*)

toucher[1] [tuʃe] ▸ conjug 1 ◂ [1] VT [a] (*pour sentir, prendre*) (*gén*) to touch; (*pour palper*) [+ *fruits, tissu, enflure*] to feel; **il me toucha l'épaule** he touched my shoulder; **« prière de ne pas ~ »** "please do not touch"; **pas touche!*** hands off!*; **il n'a pas touché un verre de vin depuis son accident** he hasn't touched a drop of wine since his accident; **je n'avais pas touché une raquette/touché une carte depuis 6 mois** I hadn't picked up a racket/touched a pack of cards for 6 months; (*fig*) **~ la main à qn** to give sb a quick handshake → **bois, doigt**

[b] (= *entrer en contact avec*) to touch; **il ne faut pas que ça touche (le mur/le plafond)** it mustn't touch (the wall/the ceiling); (*Lutte*) **il lui fit ~ le sol des épaules** he got his shoulders down on the floor; **l'avion toucha le sol** the plane touched down *ou* landed; **au football on ne doit pas ~ le ballon (de la main)** in football you mustn't touch the ball (with your hand) *ou* you mustn't handle the ball → **fond, terre**

[c] (= *être proche de*) (*lit*) to adjoin; (*fig*) [*affaire*] to concern; **son jardin touche le nôtre** his garden (ad)joins ours *ou* is adjacent to ours; (*fig*) **une personne qui vous touche de près** someone close to you

[d] (= *atteindre*) (*lit, fig*) [+ *adversaire, objectif*] to hit; (*Boxe*) **il l'a touché au menton/foie** he hit him on the chin/in the stomach; **il s'affaissa, touché d'une balle en plein cœur** he slumped to the ground, hit by a bullet in the heart; **deux immeubles ont été touchés par l'explosion** two buildings have been hit *ou* damaged by the explosion; **touché!** (*Escrime*) touché!; (*bataille navale*) hit!; **il n'a pas touché une balle pendant ce match** he didn't hit a single ball throughout the match; (*fig*) **il voudrait ~ un public plus large** he'd like to reach a wider audience

[e] (= *contacter*) to reach, get in touch with, contact; **où peut-on le ~ par téléphone?** where can he be reached *ou* contacted by phone?, where can one get in touch with him by phone?

[f] (= *faire escale à*) [+ *port*] to put in at, call at, touch

[g] (= *recevoir*) [+ *prime, allocation, traitement*] to receive, get; [+ *chèque*] to cash; (*Mil*) [+ *ration, équipement*] to draw; (*Scol*) [+ *fournitures*] to receive, get; **~ le tiercé/le gros lot** to win the tiercé/the jackpot; **~ le chômage*** to be on the dole*; **il touche une petite retraite** he gets a small pension; **il touche sa pension le 10 du mois** he draws *ou* gets his pension on the 10th of the month; **il est allé à la poste ~ sa pension** he went to draw (out) *ou* collect his pension at the post office; **à partir du mois prochain, ils toucheront 1 000 F par mois/des primes** as from next month they'll get *ou* they'll be paid 1,000 francs a month/bonuses; **il a fini le travail mais n'a encore rien touché** he's finished the work but he hasn't been paid yet

[h] (= *émouvoir*) [*drame, deuil*] to affect, shake; [*scène attendrissante*] to touch, move; [*critique, reproche*] to have an effect on; **cette tragédie les a beaucoup touchés** this tragedy affected them greatly *ou* has shaken them very badly; **rien ne le touche** there is nothing that can

move him; **votre cadeau/geste nous a vivement touchés** we were deeply touched by your gift/gesture → **corde, vif**

[i] (= *concerner*) to affect; **ce problème ne nous touche pas** this problem doesn't affect *ou* concern us; **le chômage touche surtout les jeunes** unemployment affects the young especially; **ils n'ont pas été touchés par la dévaluation** they haven't been affected *ou* hit by devaluation

[2] **toucher à** VT INDIR [a] [+ *objet dangereux, drogue*] to touch; [+ *capital, économies*] to break into, touch; **n'y touche pas!** don't touch!; **« prière de ne pas ~ aux objets exposés »** "please do not touch the exhibits", "kindly refrain from handling the exhibits"; **~ à tout** [*enfant*] to touch everything, fiddle with everything; (*fig*) [*amateur curieux*] to try one's hand at everything; **elle n'a pas touché à son déjeuner/au fromage** she didn't touch her lunch/the cheese; **on n'a pas touché au fromage** we haven't touched the cheese, the cheese hasn't been touched; **il n'a jamais touché à un fusil** he's never handled a gun

[b] (= *malmener*) [+ *personne*] to touch, lay a finger on; (= *porter atteinte à*) [+ *réputation, légende*] to question; **s'il touche à cet enfant/à ma sœur, gare à lui!** if he lays a finger on *ou* touches that child/my sister, he'd better watch out!; **touche pas à ma bagnole!*** hands off my car!; (*Pol*) **~ aux intérêts d'un pays** to interfere with a country's interests; **la réforme touche au statut des salariés/au principe du droit d'asile** the reform affects the status of employees/the right of asylum

[c] (= *modifier*) [+ *règlement, loi, tradition*] to meddle with; [+ *mécanisme*] to tamper with; [+ *monument, site classé*] to touch; **quelqu'un a touché au moteur** someone has tampered with the engine; **on peut rénover sans ~ à la façade** it's possible to renovate without touching the façade *ou* interfering with the façade; **c'est parfait, n'y touche pas** it's perfect, don't change a thing

[d] (= *concerner*) [+ *intérêts*] to affect; [+ *problème, domaine*] to touch, have to do with; **tout ce qui touche à l'enseignement** everything connected with *ou* to do with teaching

[e] (= *aborder*) [+ *période, but*] to near, approach; [+ *sujet, question*] to broach, come onto; **je touche ici à un problème d'ordre très général** here I am coming onto *ou* broaching a problem of a very general nature; **vous touchez là à une question délicate** that is a very delicate matter you have raised *ou* broached; **nous touchons au but** we're nearing our goal, our goal is in sight; **l'hiver/la guerre touche à sa fin** *ou* **son terme** winter/the war is nearing its end *ou* is drawing to a close; (*fig, littér*) **~ au port** to be within sight of home → **air**

[f] (= *être en contact avec*) to touch; (= *être contigu à*) to border on, adjoin; (= *confiner à*) to verge on, border on; **le jardin touche à la forêt** the garden adjoins the forest *ou* borders on the forest; **cela touche à la folie/pornographie** that verges *ou* borders on madness/pornography

[3] **se toucher** VPR [a] (*mutuellement*) to touch; **leurs mains se touchèrent** their hands touched; **les deux lignes se touchent** the two lines touch; **nos deux jardins se touchent** our two gardens are adjacent (to each other); **les deux villes se sont tellement développées qu'elles se touchent presque** the two towns have been developed to such an extent that they almost meet; **ils ont passé une nuit ensemble sans se ~** they spent the night together without touching each other

[b] **il se toucha le front** (*lit*) he touched his forehead; (*pour indiquer que qn est fou*) he screwed a finger against his temple

[c] (*, *euph* = *se masturber*) to play with* *ou* touch o.s.

toucher² [tuʃe] NM a (= sens) (sense of) touch b (= action, manière de toucher) touch; (= impression produite) feel; **doux au ~** soft to the touch; **cela a le ~ de la soie** it feels like silk, it has the feel of silk; **s'habituer à reconnaître les objets au ~** to become used to recognizing objects by touch ou feel(ing); **on reconnaît la soie au ~** you can tell silk by the feel of it c (Mus) touch d (Méd) (internal) examination; **~ rectal/vaginal** rectal/vaginal examination e (Sport) **avoir un bon ~ de balle** to have a nice touch

touche-touche* [tuʃtuʃ] ADV [trains, voitures] **être à ~** to be nose to tail

toucouleur [tukulœʀ] 1 ADJ Toucouleur, Tukulor 2 **Toucouleur** NMF member of the Toucouleur ou Tukulor people

touée [twe] NF (Naut) (= câble) warp, cable; (= longueur de chaîne) scope

touer [twe] ▶conjug 1◀ VT (Naut) to warp, kedge

toueur [twœʀ] NM warping tug

touffe [tuf] NF [herbe] tuft, clump; [arbres, buissons] clump; [cheveux, poils] tuft; [fleurs] cluster, clump (de of); **~ de lavande** lavender bush, clump of lavender

touffeur† [tufœʀ] NF (littér) suffocating ou sweltering heat (NonC)

touffu, e [tufy] ADJ a (= épais) [barbe, sourcils] bushy; [arbres] with thick ou dense foliage; [haie] thick, bushy; [bois, maquis, végétation] dense, thick b [roman, style] dense

touillage* [tujaʒ] NM stirring

touiller* [tuje] ▶conjug 1◀ VT [+ sauce, café] to stir; [+ salade] to toss

toujours [tuʒuʀ] ADV a (= tout le temps) always; (péj = sempiternellement) forever, always, all the time; **je l'avais ~ cru célibataire** I (had) always thought he was a bachelor; **je t'aimerai ~** I'll always love you, I'll love you forever; **je déteste et détesterai ~ l'avion** I hate flying and always will; **la vie se déroule ~ pareille** life goes on the same as ever; **il est ~ à* ou en train de critiquer** he's always ou forever criticizing; **cette rue est ~ encombrée** this street is always ou constantly jammed with traffic; **les saisons ~ pareilles** the never-changing seasons; **il n'est pas ~ très ponctuel** he's not always ou invariably on time; **il est ~ à l'heure** he's always ou invariably on time; **il fut ~ modeste** he was always ou ever (littér) modest; **les journaux sont ~ plus pessimistes** the newspapers are more and more pessimistic; **les jeunes veulent ~ plus d'indépendance** young people want more and more ou still more independence; **comme ~** as ever, as always; **ce sont des amis de ~** they are lifelong friends; **il est parti pour ~** he's gone forever ou for good; **presque ~** almost always → **depuis** b (= encore) still; **bien qu'à la retraite il travaillait ~** although he had retired he was still working ou he had kept on working; **j'espère ~ qu'elle viendra** I keep hoping ou I'm still hoping she'll come; **ils n'ont ~ pas répondu** they still haven't replied; **est-ce que Paul est rentré ? — non il est ~ à Paris/non ~ pas** is Paul back? — no, he's still in Paris/no not yet ou no he's still not back; **il est ~ le même/~ aussi désagréable** he's (still) the same as ever/(still) as unpleasant as ever c (intensif) anyway, anyhow; **écrivez ~, il vous répondra peut-être** write anyway ou anyhow ou you may as well write — he (just) might answer; **il vient ~ un moment où ...** there must ou will come a time when ...; **buvez ~ un verre avant de partir** at least have a drink before you go; **c'est ~ pas toi qui l'auras** at any rate it won't be you that gets it*; **où est-elle ? — pas chez moi ~ !** where is she? — not at my place anyway! ou at any rate!; **je trouverai ~ (bien) une excuse** I always think up an excuse; **passez à la gare, vous aurez ~ bien un train** go (along) to the station — you're sure ou bound to get a train ou there's bound to be a train; **tu peux ~ courir !* ou te fouiller !*** you haven't got a chance! ou a hope! (Brit); **il aime donner des conseils, mais ~ avec tact** he likes to give advice but he always does it tactfully; **vous pouvez ~ crier, il n'y a personne** shout as much as you like ou shout by all means — there's no one about; **il était peut-être là, ~ est-il que je ne l'ai pas vu** he may well have around, but the fact remains ou that doesn't alter the fact that I didn't see him; **cette politique semblait raisonnable, ~ est-il qu'elle a échoué** the policy seemed reasonable but the fact remains it was a failure ou but it still failed; **c'est ~ ça de pris*** that's something anyway, (well) at least that's something; **ça peut ~ servir** it might come in handy some day → **causer²**

toundra [tundʀa] NF tundra

toupet [tupɛ] NM a [cheveux] tuft (of hair), quiff (Brit); (postiche) toupee b (* = culot) nerve*, cheek* (Brit); **avoir du ~** to have a nerve* ou a cheek* (Brit); **il avait le ~ de prétendre que ...** he had the nerve* ou cheek* (Brit) to make out that ...; **il ne manque pas de ~ !** he's got a nerve!* ou cheek!* (Brit)

toupie [tupi] NF a (= jouet) (spinning) top; **~ à musique** humming-top **b** (péj = femme désagréable) **vieille ~** silly old trout* c (Tech) [menuisier] spindle moulding-machine; [plombier] turn-pin; (= bétonnière) cement mixer

tour¹ [tuʀ] 1 NF a (= édifice) tower; (Hist = machine de guerre) siege tower; (= immeuble très haut) tower block, high-rise building; (Ordin) tower; (fig, péj) **c'est une vraie ~ ◊ il est gros comme une ~** he's massive ou enormous b (Échecs) castle, rook 2 COMP ► **la tour de Babel** the Tower of Babel; (fig) **c'est une ~ de Babel** it's a real Tower of Babel ► **tour de contrôle** (Aviat) control tower ► **la tour Eiffel** the Eiffel Tower ► **tour de forage** drilling rig, derrick ► **tour de guet** watchtower, look-out tower ► **tour hertzienne** radio mast ► **tour d'ivoire** (fig) ivory tower; **enfermé dans sa ou une ~ d'ivoire** shut away in an ivory tower ► **la tour de Londres** the Tower of London ► **la tour de Pise** the Leaning Tower of Pisa

---

tour² [tuʀ]

1 NOM MASCULIN	2 COMPOSÉS

1 NOM MASCULIN

a **= parcours, exploration** **faire le ~ de** [+ parc, pays, circuit, montagne] to go round; [+ magasins] to go round, look round; [+ possibilités] to explore; [+ problème] to consider from all angles; **~ de ville** (pour touristes) city tour; **le ~ du parc prend bien une heure** it takes a good hour to walk around the park; **si on faisait le ~ ?** shall we go round (it)? ou walk round (it)?; **faire le ~ du cadran** [aiguille] to go round the clock; [dormeur] to sleep (right) round the clock; **faire le ~ du monde** to go round the world; **faire un ~ d'Europe** to go on a European tour, tour Europe; **faire un ~ d'Europe en auto-stop** to hitch-hike around Europe; **ils ont fait un ~ du monde en bateau** they sailed round the world; **la route fait (tout) le ~ de leur propriété** the road goes (right) round their estate; **faire le ~ du propriétaire** to look round ou go round ou over one's property; **je vais te faire faire le ~ du propriétaire** I'll show you over ou round the place; **faire le ~ des invités** to do the rounds of the guests; **la bouteille/plaisanterie a fait le ~ de la table** the bottle/joke went round the table; **on en a vite fait le ~** [lieu] there's not much to see; [livre, théorie] there isn't much to it; [personne] there isn't much to him (or her etc) → **repartir**

b **= excursion** trip, outing; (= promenade) (à pied) walk, stroll; (en voiture) run, drive, ride, spin*; (en vélo) ride; (en bateau) trip; **allons faire un (petit) ~ à pied** let's go for a (short) walk ou stroll; **faire un ~ de manège ou de chevaux de bois** to have a ride on a merry-go-round; **faire un ~ en ville/sur le marché** to go for a walk round town/round the market; **faire un ~ en Italie** to go for a trip round Italy; **un ~ de jardin/en voiture vous fera du bien** a walk ou stroll round the garden/a run ou drive (in the car) will do you good

c **= parcours sinueux** (littér) **la rivière fait des ~s et des détours** the river meanders along ou winds its way in and out, the river twists and turns (along its way)

d **dans un ordre, une succession** turn, go; **c'est votre ~** it's your turn; **à ton ~ (de jouer)** (gén) (it's) your turn ou go; (Échecs, Dames) (it's) your move; **attendre/perdre son ~** to wait/miss one's turn; **prendre/passer son ~** to take/miss one's turn ou go; **parler à son ~** to speak in turn; **ils parleront chacun à leur ~** they will each speak in turn; **attends, tu parleras à ton ~** wait — you'll have your turn to speak; **chacun son ~ !** wait your turn!; **nous le faisons chacun à notre ~** (= deux personnes) we do it in turn, we take turns at it; (plusieurs personnes) we take turns at it, we do it by turns; **c'est au ~ de Marc de parler** it's Marc's turn to speak; **à qui le ~ ?** whose turn ou go is it?, who is next?; (lit, fig) **votre ~ viendra** your turn will come → **faveur, souvent**

♦ **à tour de rôle** alternately, in turn; **ils vinrent à ~ de rôle nous vanter leurs mérites** they each came in turn to sing their own praises; **ils sont de garde à ~ de rôle** they take turns being on duty

♦ **tour à tour** alternately, in turn; **le temps était ~ à ~ pluvieux et ensoleillé** the weather was alternately wet and sunny; **elle se sentait ~ à ~ optimiste et désespérée** she felt optimistic and despairing by turns

e Pol **~ (de scrutin)** ballot; **élu au premier/second ~** elected in the first/second round; **un troisième ~ social** a post-election backlash (of social unrest); (Sport) **ils ont été éliminés au premier ~ de la Coupe d'Europe** they were eliminated in the first round of the European Cup

f **= circonférence** [partie du corps] measurement; [tronc, colonne] girth; [visage] contour, outline; [surface] circumference; [bouche] outline; (= périphérie) **le ~ des yeux** the area around the eyes; **~ de tête** (= mensuration) head measurement; (pour chapeau) hat size; **quel est son ~ de taille ?** what's his waist measurement?, what size waist is he?; **~ de poitrine** [homme] chest measurement; [femme] bust measurement; **~ de hanches** hip measurement; **mesurer le ~ d'une table** to measure round a table, measure the circumference of a table; **la table fait 3 mètres de ~** the table measures 3 metres round (the edge); **le tronc a 3 mètres de ~** the trunk measures 3 metres round ou has a girth of 3 metres

g **= rotation** [roue, hélice] turn, revolution; [écrou, clé] turn; [axe, arbre] revolution; **l'hélice a fait deux ~s** the propeller turned ou revolved twice; (Aut) **régime de 2 000 ~s (minute)** speed of 2,000 revs ou revolutions per minute; **donner un ~ de clé** to turn the key, give the key a turn; (Cyclisme) **battre un concurrent d'un ~ de roue** to beat a competitor by a wheel's turn; **faire un ~/plusieurs ~s sur soi-même** to spin round once/several times (on oneself); **faire un ~ de valse** to waltz round the floor; **après quelques ~s de valse** after waltzing round the floor a few times; (Culin) **donnez 4 ~s à la pâte** roll and fold the dough 4 times, turning it as you go → **double, quart**

♦ **à tour de bras** [frapper, taper] with all one's strength ou might; (fig) [composer, produire] prolifically; [critiquer] with a vengeance; **il écrit des chansons à ~ de bras** he writes songs by the dozen, he runs off ou churns out songs one after the other; **il prescrit des antibiotiques** à ~ de bras he hands out antibiotics like candy; l'industrie textile licenciait à ~ de bras the textile industry was laying people off left, right and centre

[h] = disque un 33 ~s an LP; un 45 ~s a single; un 78 ~s a 78

[i] = tournure [situation, conversation] turn, twist; (= expression) ~ (de phrase) turn of phrase; la situation prend un ~ dramatique/désagréable the situation is taking a dramatic/an unpleasant turn ou twist; un certain ~ d'esprit a certain turn ou cast of mind

[j] = exercice [acrobate] feat, stunt; [jongleur, prestidigitateur] trick; ~ d'adresse feat of skill, skilful trick; ~s d'agilité acrobatics; ~ de cartes card trick; et le ~ est joué ! and there you have it!, and Bob's your uncle!* (Brit); c'est un ~ à prendre ! it's just a knack one picks up!; avoir plus d'un ~ dans son sac to have more than one trick up one's sleeve

[k] = duperie trick; faire ou jouer un ~ à qn to play a trick on sb; un ~ pendable a rotten trick; un sale ~ ◊ un ~ de cochon* ou de salaud* a dirty ou lousy trick*, a mean trick; je lui réserve un ~ à ma façon ! I'll pay him back in my own way! → jouer

[2] COMPOSÉS

► tour de chant song recital ► tour de cou (= ruban) choker; (= fourrure) fur collar; (= mensuration) collar measurement; faire du 39 de ~ de cou to take a size 39 collar ► tour de force (lit) feat of strength, tour de force; (fig) amazing feat ► le Tour de France (= course cycliste) the Tour de France; (Hist) le ~ de France d'un compagnon a journeyman's tour of France ► tour de garde spell ou turn of duty; mon prochain ~ de garde est à 8 heures my next spell ou turn of duty is at 8 o'clock ► tour d'honneur (Sport) lap of honour ► tour d'horizon (fig) (general) survey ► tour de lit (bed) valance ► tour de main (= adresse) dexterity; avoir/acquérir un ~ de main to have/pick up a knack; en un ~ de main in no time at all ► tour de manivelle (lit) turn of the handle; (Ciné) le premier ~ de manivelle est prévu pour octobre the cameras should begin rolling in October ► tour de piste (Sport) lap; (dans un cirque) circuit of the ring) ► tour de reins : souffrir d'un ~ de reins to suffer from a strained ou sprained back; attraper un ~ de reins to strain one's back ► tour de table (Fin) capital structure; (dans une réunion) procéder à un ~ de table to seek the views of all those present; la société immobilière a bouclé son ~ de table the property company has finalized its capital structure ► tour de vis (turn of a) screw; il faudra donner un ~ de vis you'll have to give the screw a turn ou tighten the screw a little; (fig) donner un ~ de vis au crédit to freeze credit, put a squeeze on credit; donner un ~ de vis aux libertés to clamp down on civil rights; ~ de vis fiscal tax squeeze; ~ de vis militaire/politique military/political crackdown ou clampdown (à l'encontre de on); → chauffe, passe-passe

---

┌─ LE TOUR DE FRANCE ─┐

The famous annual cycle race takes about three weeks to complete in daily stages ("étapes") of approximately 110 miles. The leading cyclist wears a yellow jersey, the "maillot jaune". There are a number of time trials. The route varies and is not usually confined only to France, but the race always ends on the Champs-Élysées in Paris.

---

tour³ [tuʀ] NM [a] (Tech) lathe; ~ de potier potter's wheel; objet fait au ~ object turned on the lathe; travail au ~ lathe-work; (fig littér) jambes/cuisses faites au ~ shapely legs/thighs [b] (= passe-plat) hatch

---

tourbe [tuʀb] NF (Agr) peat; ~ limoneuse alluvial peat

tourbeux, -euse [tuʀbø, øz] ADJ [a] [terrain] (= qui contient de la tourbe) peat (épith), peaty; (= de la nature de la tourbe) peaty [b] [plante] found in peat

tourbière [tuʀbjɛʀ] NF peat bog

tourbillon [tuʀbijɔ̃] NM [a] (atmosphérique) ~ (de vent) whirlwind; ~ de fumée/sable/neige/poussière swirl ou eddy of smoke/sand/snow/dust; le sable s'élevait en ~s the sand was swirling up [b] (dans l'eau) eddy; (plus important) whirlpool; l'eau faisait des ~s the water was making eddies [c] (Phys) vortex [d] (fig) whirl of pleasure, giddy round of pleasure(s); le ~ de la vie/des affaires the hurly-burly ou hustle and bustle of life/of business; il regardait le ~ des danseurs he was looking at the whirling ou swirling group of dancers; le pays plongea dans un ~ de violence the country was plunged into a maelstrom of violence

tourbillonnant, e [tuʀbijɔnɑ̃, ɑ̃t] ADJ [feuilles] swirling, eddying; [vie] whirlwind (épith); [jupes] swirling

tourbillonnement [tuʀbijɔnmɑ̃] NM [poussière, sable, feuilles mortes, flocons de neige] whirling, swirling, eddying; [danseurs] whirling, swirling, twirling; [idées] swirling, whirling

tourbillonner [tuʀbijɔne] ▶conjug 1◀ VI [poussière, sable, feuilles mortes, flocons de neige] to whirl, swirl, eddy; [danseurs] to whirl (round), swirl (round), twirl (round); [idées] to swirl (round), whirl (round)

tourelle [tuʀɛl] NF [a] (= petite tour) turret [b] (Mil, Naut) (gun) turret; [caméra] lens turret; [sous-marin] conning tower

tourière [tuʀjɛʀ] ADJ F, NF (sœur) ~ sister at the convent gate, extern sister

tourillon [tuʀijɔ̃] NM [mécanisme] bearing, journal; [canon] trunnion; [meuble] dowel

tourisme [tuʀism] NM [a] (= action de voyager) faire du ~ en Irlande to go touring round Ireland; (= action de visiter) faire du ~ dans Paris to go sightseeing in Paris [b] (= industrie) le ~ tourism, the tourist industry ou trade; le ~ d'hiver/d'été winter/summer tourism; le ~ français se porte bien the French tourist industry ou trade is in good shape; ~ de masse/d'affaires mass/business tourism; ~ rural ou vert green tourism, ecotourism; ~ culturel/sexuel cultural/sex tourism; promouvoir le ~ to promote tourism in rural areas; avion/voiture de ~ private plane/car; voiture (de) grand ~ GT saloon car (Brit), 4-door sedan (US) → agence, office

touriste [tuʀist] NMF tourist; (fig) faire qch en ~ to do sth half-heartedly → classe

touristique [tuʀistik] ADJ [itinéraire, billet, activités, saison, guide] tourist (épith); [région, ville] with great tourist attractions, popular with (the) tourists (attrib); trop ~ touristy*; route ~ scenic route → menu

tourment [tuʀmɑ̃] NM (littér) (physique) agony; (moral) torment, torture (NonC); les ~s de la jalousie the torments of jealousy

tourmente [tuʀmɑ̃t] NF (= tempête) storm, gale, tempest (littér); (fig : sociale, politique) upheaval, turmoil; ~ de neige snowstorm, blizzard; ~ monétaire upheaval ou turmoil in the currency markets

tourmenté, e [tuʀmɑ̃te] (ptp de tourmenter) ADJ [a] [personne, expression, visage, esprit] tormented, tortured [b] [relief] rugged; [paysage, formes] tortured (littér); [style, art] tortured, anguished [c] (littér) [vie, mer, ciel] stormy, turbulent, tempestuous; l'histoire ~e de ce pays this country's turbulent history; nous vivons une époque ~e we're living in troubled ou turbulent times

---

tourmenter [tuʀmɑ̃te] ▶conjug 1◀ [1] VT [a] [personne] to torment; ses créanciers continuaient à le ~ his creditors continued to harass ou hound him; ~ qn de questions to plague ou harass sb with questions [b] [douleur, rhumatismes, faim] to rack, torment; [remords, doute] to rack, torment, plague; [ambition, envie, jalousie] to torment; ce qui me tourmente dans cette affaire what worries ou bothers ou bugs* me in this business [2] se tourmenter VPR to fret, worry (o.s.); ne vous tourmentez pas, ce n'était pas de votre faute don't distress ou worry yourself — it wasn't your fault; il se tourmente à cause de son fils he's fretting ou worrying about his son

tourmenteur, -euse [tuʀmɑ̃tœʀ, øz] NM,F (littér = persécuteur) tormentor

tourmentin [tuʀmɑ̃tɛ̃] NM [a] (Naut = foc) storm jib [b] (= oiseau) stormy petrel

tournage [tuʀnaʒ] NM [a] (Ciné) shooting; être en ~ en Italie to be filming in Italy, be on a shoot in Italy; pendant le ~ during the shoot, while the film was being made ou shot; l'équipe de ~ the film ou camera crew; il l'emmène sur tous ses ~s he takes her with him on all the shoots [b] (Menuiserie) turning; le ~ sur bois/métal wood-/metal-turning [c] (Naut) belaying cleat

tournailler* [tuʀnaje] ▶conjug 1◀ VI (péj) to wander aimlessly; ~ autour de to hang round

tournant, e [tuʀnɑ̃, ɑ̃t] [1] ADJ [a] [fauteuil, dispositif] swivel (épith); [feu, scène] revolving (épith) → grève, plaque, pont, table [b] [mouvement, manœuvre] encircling (épith) [c] [escalier] spiral (épith); (littér) [ruelle, couloir] winding, twisting [2] NM [a] (= virage) bend; prendre bien/mal son ~ to take a bend well/badly, corner well/badly; cette entreprise a bien su prendre le ~ this company has managed the change ou switch well, this company has adapted well to the new circumstances; attendre qn au ~* to wait for the chance to trip sb up ou catch sb out (Brit); avoir ou rattraper qn au ~* to get even with sb, get one's own back on sb (Brit) [b] (= changement) turning point; ~ décisif watershed; les ~s de l'histoire/de sa vie the turning points in history/in his life; c'est à la 50ème minute qu'a eu lieu le ~ du match the decisive ou turning point of the match came in the 50th minute; il arrive à un ~ de sa carrière he's coming to a turning point in his career; au ~ du siècle at the turn of the century; un ~ de la politique française a watershed in French politics; marquer un ~ to be a turning point

tourné, e¹ [tuʀne] (ptp de tourner) ADJ [a] bien ~ [personne] shapely, with a good figure; [jambes] shapely; [taille] neat, trim; [compliment, poème, expression] well-turned; [article, lettre] well-worded, well-phrased [b] mal ~ [article, lettre] badly expressed ou phrased ou worded; [expression] unfortunate; avoir l'esprit mal ~ to have a dirty mind [c] [lait, vin] sour; [poisson, viande] off (attrib), high (attrib); [fruits] rotten, bad [d] (Menuiserie) [pied, objet] turned

tournebouler* [tuʀnəbule] ▶conjug 1◀ VT [+ personne] to put in a whirl; ~ la cervelle à qn to turn sb's head ou brain, put sb's head in a whirl; il en était tourneboulé (mauvaise nouvelle) he was very upset by it; (heureuse surprise) his head was in a whirl over it

tournebroche [tuʀnəbʀɔʃ] NM roasting spit, rotisserie; poulet au ~ spit-roasted chicken

tourne-disque (pl tourne-disques) [tuʀnədisk] NM record player

tournedos [tuʀnədo] NM tournedos

tournée² [tuʀne] NF [a] (= tour) [conférencier, artiste] tour; [représentant, livreur, représentant] round; ~ de conférences/théâtrale lecture/theatre tour; ~ d'inspection round ou tour of inspection; partir/être en ~ [artiste, troupe de *théâtre*] to set off on/be on tour; [*livreur, représentant*] to set off on/be on one's rounds; **faire une ~ électorale** to go on a campaign tour *ou* the campaign trail; **faire la ~ de** [+ *magasins, musées, cafés*] to do the rounds of, go round; **faire la ~ des grands ducs*** to go out on the town *ou* on a spree; **faire la ~ des popotes*** to go on a tour of inspection

b (= *consommations*) round (of drinks); **payer une/sa ~** to buy *ou* stand a/one's round (of drinks); **c'est ma ~** it's my round; **il a payé une ~ générale** he paid for drinks all round; **c'est la ~ du patron** the drinks are on the house

c (* = *raclée*) hiding, thrashing

tournemain [turnəmɛ̃] ◆ **en un tournemain** LOC ADV in no time at all, in the twinkling of an eye, (as) quick as a flash

tourner [turne] ▶ conjug 1 ◀ 1 VT a [+ *manivelle, clé, poignée*] to turn; [+ *sauce*] to stir; [+ *salade*] to toss; [+ *page*] to turn (over); **tournez s.v.p** please turn over, P.T.O.; **~ et retourner** [+ *chose*] to turn over and over; [+ *pensée, problème*] to turn over and over (in one's mind), mull over → **dos, page, talon**

b (= *diriger, orienter*) [+ *appareil, tête, yeux*] to turn; **elle tourna son regard** *ou* **les yeux vers la fenêtre** she turned her eyes towards the window; **~ la tête à droite/à gauche** to turn one's head to the right/to the left; **quand il m'a vu, il a tourné la tête** when he saw me he looked away *ou* he turned his head away; **~ les pieds en dedans/en dehors** to turn one's toes *ou* feet in/out; **tourne le tableau de l'autre côté/contre le mur** turn the picture the other way round/round to face the wall; (*littér*) **~ ses pas vers** to wend one's way towards; (*littér*) **~ ses pensées/efforts vers** to turn *ou* bend one's thoughts/efforts towards *ou* to → **bride, casaque**

c (= *contourner*) (*Naut*) [+ *cap*] to round; [+ *armée*] to turn, outflank; [+ *obstacle*] to round; (*fig* = *éluder*) [+ *difficulté, règlement*] to get round *ou* past; **~ la loi** to get round the law, find a loophole in the law; **il vient de ~ le coin de la rue** he has just turned the corner; (*Rugby*) **~ la mêlée** to turn the scrum, wheel the scrum round

d (*frm* = *exprimer*) [+ *phrase, compliment*] to turn; [+ *demande, lettre*] to phrase, express

e (= *transformer*) **il a tourné l'incident en plaisanterie** he made light of the incident, he made a joke out of the incident; **~ qn/qch en ridicule** to make sb/sth a laughing stock, ridicule sb/sth, hold sb/sth up to ridicule; **il tourne tout à son avantage** he turns everything to his (own) advantage → **dérision**

f (*Ciné*) **~ une scène** [*cinéaste*] to shoot *ou* film a scene; [*acteur*] to act in *ou* do a scene; **~ un film** (= *faire les prises de vues*) to shoot a film; (= *produire*) to make a film; (= *jouer*) to make *ou* do a film; **ils ont dû ~ en studio** they had to do the filming in the studio → **extérieur, silence**

g (*Tech*) [+ *bois, ivoire*] to turn; [+ *pot*] to throw

h (*loc*) **~ le cœur** *ou* **l'estomac à qn**† to turn sb's stomach, make sb heave; **~ la tête à qn** [*vin*] to go to sb's head; [*succès*] to go to *ou* turn sb's head; [*personne*] to turn sb's head → **2a**

2 VI a [*manège, compteur, aiguille d'horloge*] to turn, go round; [*disque, cylindre, roue*] to turn, revolve; [*pièce sur un axe, clé, danseur*] to turn; [*toupie*] to spin; [*taximètre*] to tick away; [*usine, moteur*] to run; **~ sur soi-même** to turn round on o.s.; (*très vite*) to spin round and round; **la grande aiguille tourne plus vite que la petite** the big hand goes round faster than the small one; **l'heure tourne** time's getting on; **les éléphants tournent sur la piste** the elephants move round the ring; **~ comme une toupie** to spin like a top; **tout d'un coup, j'ai vu tout ~** all of a sudden my head began to

spin *ou* swim; **usine qui tourne à plein (régime)** factory working at full capacity *ou* flat out*; **la machine à laver tourne surtout la nuit** the washing machine runs mostly at night; (*Comm*) **ce représentant tourne sur Lyon** this sales representative covers Lyons; **son spectacle va ~ dans le Midi cet été** his show is on tour in the South of France this summer; **faire ~ le moteur** to run the engine; (*Spiritisme*) **faire ~ les tables** to hold seances, do table-turning; **c'est elle qui va faire ~ l'affaire** she's going to manage *ou* run the business; **faire ~ la tête à qn** [*compliments, succès*] to go to sb's head; **ça me fait ~ la tête** [*vin*] it goes to my head; [*bruit, altitude*] it makes my head spin, it makes me dizzy *ou* giddy → **ours, ralenti, rond, vide** etc

b (*Ordin*) [*programme*] to work; **arriver à faire ~ un programme** to get a program working *ou* to work; **ça tourne sur quelles machines?** which machines does it work on?, which machines is it compatible with?

c ~ **autour de** (*gén*) to turn *ou* go round; [*terre, roue*] to revolve *ou* go round; [*chemin*] to wind *ou* go round; [*oiseau*] to wheel *ou* circle *ou* fly round; [*mouches*] to buzz *ou* fly round; [*prix*] to be around *ou* about (*Brit*); ~ **autour de la piste** to go round the track; ~ **autour de qn** (*péj*) (= *importuner*) to hang round sb; (*pour courtiser*) to hang round sb; (*par curiosité*) to hover round sb; **un individu tourne autour de la maison depuis une heure** somebody has been hanging round outside the house for an hour; [*discussion, sujet*] ~ **autour de** *ou* **sur qch** to centre *ou* focus on; **l'enquête tourne autour de ces trois suspects/de cet indice capital** the inquiry centres on *ou* around these three suspects/this vital clue; **le prix doit ~ autour de 80 000 F** the price must be around 80,000 francs *ou* in the 80,000 franc mark *ou* in the region of 80,000 francs → **pot**

d (= *changer de direction*) [*vent, opinion*] to turn, shift, veer (round); [*chemin, promeneur*] to turn; **la chance a tourné** his (*ou* her *etc*) luck has turned; **la voiture a tourné à gauche** the car turned left *ou* turned off to the left; **tournez à droite au prochain feu rouge** turn right *ou* take a right at the next traffic lights

e (= *évoluer*) **bien ~** to turn out well; **mal ~** [*farce, entreprise*] to go wrong, turn out badly; [*personne*] to go to the dogs*, turn out badly; **ça va mal ~** no good will come of it, it'll end in trouble; **si les choses avaient tourné autrement** if things had turned out *ou* gone differently; **~ à l'avantage de qn** to turn to sb's advantage; **le débat tournait à la polémique** the debate was becoming increasingly heated; **le temps a tourné au froid/à la pluie** the weather has turned cold/rainy *ou* wet; **le ciel tournait au violet** the sky was turning purple; **~ au drame/au tragique** to take a dramatic/tragic turn; **la discussion a tourné en** *ou* **à la bagarre** the argument turned *ou* degenerated into a fight; **sa bronchite a tourné en pneumonie** his bronchitis has turned *ou* developed into pneumonia → **bourrique**

f [*lait*] to turn (sour); [*poisson, viande*] to go off, go bad; [*fruits*] to go rotten *ou* bad; [*vin*] (**au vinaigre**) to turn (vinegary); **la chaleur a fait ~ le lait** the milk's gone sour in the heat

g (*loc*) **j'ai la tête qui tourne** ◊ **la tête me tourne** my head's spinning; **~ de l'œil*** to pass out, faint → **court, rond** etc

3 **se tourner** VPR **se ~ du côté de** *ou* **vers qn/qch** to turn towards sb/sth; **se ~ vers qn pour lui demander de l'aide** to turn to sb for help; **se ~ vers une profession/la politique/une question** to turn to a profession/to politics/to a question; **une société tournée vers l'avenir** a forward-looking company; **se ~ contre qn** to turn against sb; **se ~ et se retourner dans son lit** to toss and turn in bed; **de quelque côté que l'on se tourne** whichever way one turns;

tourne-toi (de l'autre côté) turn round *ou* the other way → **pouce**

tournesol [turnəsɔl] NM a (*Bot*) sunflower → **huile** b (*Chim*) litmus

tourneur, -euse [turnœr, øz] 1 NM,F (*Tech*) turner; **~ sur bois/métaux** wood/metal turner 2 ADJ → **derviche**

tournevis [turnəvis] NM screwdriver; **usine ~** screwdriver plant → **cruciforme**

tournicoter* [turnikɔte], **tourniquer** [turnike] ▶ conjug 1 ◀ VI (*péj*) to wander aimlessly; **~ autour de qn** (= *importuner, courtiser*) to hang round sb; (*par curiosité*) to hover round sb

tourniquet [turnike] NM a (= *barrière*) turnstile; (= *porte*) revolving door b (*Tech*) **~ (hydraulique)** reaction turbine; (*d'arrosage*) (lawn-)sprinkler c (= *présentoir*) revolving stand d (*Méd*) tourniquet e (*arg Mil*) court-martial; **passer au ~** to come up before a court-martial

tournis [turni] NM a (*Vét*) sturdy b *** avoir le ~** to feel dizzy *ou* giddy; **ça/il me donne le ~** it/he makes my head spin, it/he makes me (feel) dizzy *ou* giddy

tournoi [turnwa] NM a (*Hist*) tournament, tourney b (*Sport*) tournament; **~ d'échecs/de tennis** chess/tennis tournament; (*fig littér*) **~ d'éloquence/d'adresse** contest of eloquence/of skill; (*Rugby*) **le Tournoi des cinq nations** the Five Nations Championship; **disputer** *ou* **faire un ~** to play in *ou* enter a tournament

tournoiement [turnwamã] NM a [*danseurs*] whirling, twirling; [*eau, fumée*] swirling, eddying, whirling; [*feuilles mortes*] swirling, eddying; **les ~s des danseurs** the whirling (of the) dancers; **des ~s de feuilles** swirling *ou* eddying leaves b [*oiseaux*] wheeling

tournoyer [turnwaje] ▶ conjug 8 ◀ VI [*danseurs*] to whirl (round), twirl (round); [*eau, fumée*] to swirl, eddy; [*boomerang*] to spin; [*papiers*] to flutter around; [*oiseaux*] to wheel, circle; [*feuilles mortes*] to swirl *ou* eddy around; [*abeille, moustique*] to fly around (in circles); **faire ~** [*danseur, canne*] to twirl; [*robe*] to swirl; **les feuilles tombaient en tournoyant** the leaves were twirling *ou* whirling down; **la fumée s'élevait en tournoyant** the smoke spiralled up; **tout s'est mis à ~ et je me suis évanoui** everything started to spin and I fainted

tournure [turnyr] NF a (= *tour de phrase*) turn of phrase; (= *forme*) form; **~ négative/impersonnelle** negative/impersonal form; **la ~ précieuse de ses phrases** the affected way (in which) he phrases his sentences b (= *apparence*) **la ~ des événements** the turn of events; **la ~ que prenaient les événements** the way the situation was developing, the turn events were taking; **la situation a pris une mauvaise/meilleure ~** the situation took a turn for the worse/for the better; **donner une autre ~ à une affaire** to put a matter in a different light, put a new face on a matter; **prendre ~** to take shape c **~ d'esprit** turn *ou* cast of mind d († = *allure*) bearing; **il a une belle ~** he carries himself well, he has a very upright bearing

touron [turɔ̃] NM *kind of nougat*

tour-opérateur (*pl* tour-opérateurs) [turɔperatœr] NM tour operator

tourte [turt] 1 ADJ (* = *bête*) dense*, thick* (*Brit*) 2 NF (*Culin*) pie; **~ à la viande/au poisson** meat/fish pie

tourteau[1] (*pl* tourteaux) [turto] NM (*Agr*) oilcake, cattle-cake; (*Hér*) roundel; (*Culin*) **~ fromagé** *round spongecake made with fromage frais*

tourteau[2] (*pl* tourteaux) [turto] NM (= *crabe*) common *ou* edible crab

tourtereau (*pl* tourtereaux) [turtəro] NM (= *oiseau*) young turtledove; (= *amoureux*) **~x** lovebirds

tourterelle [tuʀtəʀɛl] NF turtledove; **gris ~** dove ou soft grey

tourtière [tuʀtjɛʀ] NF (à tourtes) pie tin; (à tartes) pie dish ou plate

tous [(adj) tu ou (pron) tus] → **tout**

toussailler [tusaje] ▸ conjug 1 ◂ VI to have a bit of a cough; **arrête de ~!** stop coughing and spluttering like that!

Toussaint [tusɛ̃] NF **la ~** All Saints' Day; **nous partirons en vacances à la ~** we're going on holiday at the beginning of November; **il fait un temps de ~** it's real November weather, it's grim cold weather

┌─────────────────────┐
│ **TOUSSAINT**   │
└─────────────────────┘

All Saints' Day (November 1) is a public holiday in France. It is the day when people traditionally visit cemeteries to lay heather and chrysanthemums on the graves of relatives and friends.

tousser [tuse] ▸ conjug 1 ◂ VI [a] [personne] to cough; **ne sors pas, tu tousses encore un peu** don't go out — you've still got a bit of a cough [b] [moteur] to splutter, cough

toussotement [tusɔtmɑ̃] NM (slight) coughing (NonC)

toussoter [tusɔte] ▸ conjug 1 ◂ VI (Méd) to have a bit of a ou a slight cough; (pour avertir, signaler) to cough softly, give a little cough; **je l'entendais ~ dans la pièce à côté** I could hear him coughing in the next room; **il toussote, je vais lui faire prendre du sirop** he's got a bit of a ou a slight cough — I'm going to give him some cough mixture

─────────────────────────

tout, toute [tu, tut]

┌──┐
│ *mpl* **tous**; *fpl* **toutes**   │
│ ① ADJECTIF   ③ PRONOM INDÉFINI   │
│   QUALIFICATIF   ④ ADVERBE   │
│ ② ADJECTIF INDÉFINI ⑤ NOM MASCULIN   │
│ *Lorsque* **tout** *fait partie d'une expression figée telle que* **à tout bout de champ, de tout repos, en tout cas, tout le temps** *etc, cherchez au premier nom.* │
└──┘

① ADJECTIF QUALIFICATIF
[a] = complet, entier, total

♦ **tout, toute** + article ou possessif ou démonstratif : **~ le, ~e la** all (the), the whole (of the); **~ le reste** (all) the rest; **il a ~ le temps/l'argent qu'il lui faut** he has all the time/the money he needs; **~e la France regardait le match** the whole of ou all France was watching the match; **pendant ~ le voyage** during the whole (of the) trip, throughout the trip; **il a plu ~e la nuit/~e une nuit** it rained all night (long) ou throughout the night/for a whole night; **il a plu ~e cette nuit** it rained all (of) ou throughout last night; **il a dépensé ~ son argent** he has spent all (of) his money; **mange ~e ta viande** eat up your meat, eat all (of) your meat; **il a passé ~es ses vacances à lire** he spent the whole of ou all (of) his holidays reading; **il courait de ~e la vitesse de ses petites jambes** he was running as fast as his little legs would carry him

♦ **tout le monde** everybody, everyone; **~ le monde le dit/le sait** everybody says so/knows; **la nature appartient à ~ le monde** the countryside belongs to everybody; **ils veulent vivre/être comme ~ le monde** they want to live/be like everybody else; **il ne fait jamais comme ~ le monde** he always has to be different

♦ **tout, toute** + nom : **il a lu ~ Balzac** he has read the whole of ou all of Balzac; **elle a visité ~ Londres** she has been round the whole of London; **le ~-Londres/-Rome** the London/ Rome smart set, everybody who is anybody in London/Rome; **en ~e illégalité** quite illegally; **donner ~e satisfaction** to give complete satisfaction, be entirely ou completely satisfactory

[b] = seul, unique only; **c'est ~ l'effet que ça lui fait** that's all the effect ou the only effect it has on him; **cet enfant est ~e ma joie** this child is my only ou sole joy, all my joy in life lies with this child; **c'est là ~ le problème** that's the whole problem, that's just where the problem lies; **~ le secret est dans la rapidité** the whole secret lies in speed; **pour ~ mobilier, il avait un lit et une table** all he had in the way of furniture ou the only furniture he had was a bed and a table

② ADJECTIF INDÉFINI
[a]

♦ **tout, toute** + nom singulier (= n'importe quel) any, all; **~e personne susceptible de nous aider** any person ou anyone able to help us; **une empreinte digitale, un cheveu, ~e indice qui pourrait être utile** a fingerprint, a hair, any clue that might be useful; **~e trace d'agitation a disparu** all ou any trace of agitation has gone; **~ autre (que lui) aurait deviné** anybody ou anyone (but him) would have guessed; **à ~ âge** at any age, at all ages; **pour ~ renseignement, téléphoner ...** for all information, ring ...

♦ **tout un chacun** everybody, everyone; **comme ~ un chacun, il a le droit de ...** like everybody else, he has a right to ...; **le fait que ~ un chacun puisse librement donner son avis** the fact that anybody can freely express their opinion

[b]

♦ **tous, toutes (les)** + nom pluriel (= chaque) every; **tous les jours/ans/mois** every day/year/ month; **tous les deux jours/mois** every other ou second day/month, every two days/months; **tous les 10 mètres** every 10 metres; **~es les trois heures** every three hours, at three-hourly intervals
(= l'ensemble, la totalité des) all, every; **~es les personnes que nous connaissons** all the people ou everyone ou everybody (that) we know; **~es les fois que je le vois** every time I see him; **il avait ~es les raisons d'être mécontent** he had every reason to be ou for being displeased; **tous les hommes sont mortels** all men are mortal; **courir dans tous les sens** to run all over the place; **film (pour) tous publics** film suitable for all audiences; **des individus de ~es tendances/ tous bords** people of all tendencies/shades of opinion; (servant à récapituler) (frm) **le saut en hauteur, la course, le lancer du javelot, ~es disciplines qui exigent ...** the high jump, running, throwing the javelin, all (of them) disciplines requiring ...

♦ **tous, toutes (les)** + numéral (= ensemble) **tous (les) deux** both (of them), the two of them, each (of them); **tous (les) trois/quatre** three/four (of them); **ils sont arrivés tous les six hier soir** all six of them arrived last night

③ PRONOM INDÉFINI
[a] = l'ensemble des choses everything, all; (sans discrimination) anything; **il a ~ organisé** he organized everything, he organized it all; **on ne peut pas ~ faire** you can't do everything; **~ va bien** all's (going) well, everything's fine; **son travail, ses enfants, ~ l'exaspère** his work, the children, everything annoys him; **~ lui est bon** everything is grist to his mill (pour to); **ses enfants mangent de ~** her children will eat anything; **il vend de ~** he sells anything and everything; **il est capable de ~** he's capable of anything; **il a ~ pour réussir** he's got everything going for him; (iro) **il a ~ pour plaire*** he's got nothing going for him; **il est capable d'improviser un discours sur ~ et n'importe quoi** he can improvise a speech on just about anything; **il promet ~ et son contraire** he makes the wildest promises; **au cours du débat, on a entendu ~ et son contraire** the discussion was a real ragbag of ideas

♦ **avoir tout de** + nom : **elle a ~ d'une star** she's every inch a star; **avec ce chapeau, elle a ~ d'une sorcière** she looks just like a witch in that hat; **ça a ~ d'un canular** it's obviously a

practical joke; **l'organisation a ~ d'une secte** the organization is nothing less than a sect

♦ **à tout va*** [licencier, investir, recruter] like mad; [libéralisme, communication, consommation] unbridled; **à l'époque, on construisait à ~ va** at that time there were buildings going up everywhere; **il répète à ~ va ce que tu lui as raconté** he's going round telling everyone what you told him

♦ **ce n'est pas tout de** + infinitif (= ça ne suffit pas) **ce n'est pas ~ d'en parler** there's more to it than just talking about it; **ce n'est pas ~ de faire son métier, il faut le faire bien** it's not enough just to do your job, you have to do it well

♦ **en tout** (= au total) in all; **nous étions 16 (personnes) en ~** there were 16 of us in all; **ça coûte 1 000 F en ~** it costs 1,000 francs in all ou in total
(= en tous points) **cette pratique est en ~ contraire aux droits de l'homme** this practice is a violation of human rights in every respect; **leurs programmes politiques s'opposent en ~** their political programmes clash in every way

♦ **en tout et pour tout** all in all; **il lui reste trois jours/150 F en ~ et pour ~** he only has a total of three days/150 francs left; **j'avais une valise en ~ et pour ~** all I had was a suitcase

♦ **... et tout (et tout)*** ... and everything; **j'avais préparé le dîner, fait le ménage et ~ et ~** I'd made the dinner, done the housework and everything; **je lui avais expliqué et ~, mais il n'a pas compris** I'd explained and everything, but he didn't understand; **avec les vacances et ~, je n'ai pas eu le temps** what with the holidays and all*, I didn't have time

♦ avec **être** : **c'est ~ that's all; **ce sera ~?** will that be all?, (will there be) anything else?; **et ce n'est pas ~!** and that's not all!, and there's more to come!; **c'est pas ~ ça*, mais il est tard** all this is very nice, but it's getting late; **être ~ pour qn** to be everything to sb

♦ **pour tout dire** : **cette idée audacieuse avait surpris et pour ~ dire n'avait pas convaincu** this daring idea surprised everybody and, to be honest, wasn't convincing; **il est vaniteux, égoïste, pour ~ dire c'est un sale type** he's vain, he's selfish, in a word he's a swine

♦ **tout ce qui** ◊ **tout ce que** : **~ ce que je sais, c'est qu'il est parti** all I know is that he's gone; **c'est ~ ce qu'il m'a dit/laissé** that's all he told me/left me; **~ ce que le pays compte de sportifs/savants** all the country has in the way of sportsmen/scientists, the country's entire stock of sportsmen/scientists; **est-ce que vous avez ~ ce dont vous avez besoin?** ou **ce qu'il vous faut?** have you everything ou all (that) you need?; **ne croyez pas ~ ce qu'il raconte** don't believe everything he tells you; **~ ce qui lui appartient** everything ou all that belongs to him ■ **~ ce qui brille n'est pas or** all that glitters is not gold (PROV)

♦ **tout ce qu'il y a de** + adjectif (= extrêmement) most; **il a été ~ ce qu'il y a de gentil/serviable** he was most kind/obliging, he couldn't have been kinder/more obliging; **des gens ~ ce qu'il y a de plus distingué(s)** most distinguished people; **c'était ~ ce qu'il y a de chic** it was the last word in chic ou the ultimate in chic

♦ **tout est là** : **la persévérance, ~ est là** all that counts is perseverance, perseverance is all that matters

[b]

♦ **tous, toutes** (= l'ensemble des personnes) all; **tous ou ~es tant qu'ils en sont** all of them, every single one of them; **tous sont arrivés** they have all arrived; **il les déteste tous** ou **~es** he hates them all ou all of them; **écoutez bien tous!** listen, all of you!; **tous ensemble** all together; **il parle en leur nom à tous** he's speaking for them all ou for all of them; **film pour tous** film suitable for all audiences

♦ *pronom personnel* + **tous** *ou* **toutes** : nous avons tous nos défauts we all *ou* all of us have our faults; nous mourrons tous we shall all die; vous ~es qui m'écoutez all of you who are listening to me; il s'attaque à nous tous he's attacking us all *ou* all of us

[c] locutions   ~ a une fin there is an end to everything, everything comes to an end; ~ est bien qui finit bien all's well that ends well; ~ finit par des chansons everything ends with a song; ~ passe, ~ casse nothing lasts for ever ■ (*PROV*) ~ vient à point à qui sait attendre everything comes to he who waits (*PROV*)

[4] ADVERBE

> *S'accorde en genre et en nombre devant un adjectif féminin qui commence par une consonne ou un h aspiré.*

[a]

♦ **tout** + *adjectif* (= *très*) very; (= *entièrement*) quite; il est ~ étonné he's very *ou* most surprised; c'est une ~e jeune femme she's a very young woman; elles étaient ~ heureuses/~es contentes they were very *ou* extremely happy/pleased; les ~es premières années the very first *ou* early years; c'est ~ autre chose that's quite another matter; c'est une ~ autre histoire that's quite another story; il a mangé sa viande ~e crue he ate his meat quite *ou* completely raw; c'est ~ naturel it's perfectly *ou* quite natural; ~e petite, elle aimait la campagne as a (very) small child she liked the country

♦ **tout** + *article* + *nom* : c'est ~ le contraire it's quite the opposite *ou* the very opposite; avec toi c'est ~ l'un ou ~ l'autre there's no in-between with you, you see everything in black and white

♦ **tout** (+ *préposition*) + *nom* : être ~ yeux/oreilles to be all eyes/ears; (*hum*) je suis ~ ouïe ! I'm all ears!; ~ (en) laine/coton all wool/cotton; il était ~ à son travail he was entirely taken up by *ou* absorbed in his work; habillé ~ en noir dressed all in black, dressed entirely in black; un style ~ en nuances a very subtle style, a style full of nuances; un jeu ~ en douceur a very delicate style of play; il était ~ en sueur he was dripping with sweat; elle était ~ en larmes she was in floods of tears; le jardin est ~ en fleurs the garden is a mass of flowers

♦ **tout** + *adverbe* : ~ près *ou* à côté very near *ou* close; ~ là-bas right over there; ~ en bas de la colline right at the bottom of the hill; ~ au fond right at the bottom, at the very bottom; ~ simplement *ou* bonnement quite simply; je vois cela ~ autrement I see it quite differently; je le sais ~ autant que toi I know it as well as you do, I'm as aware of it as you are; j'aime ça ~ aussi peu que lui I like that as little as he does; ~ plein* de cartes postales loads* of postcards; il est gentil/mignon ~ plein* he's really very *ou* really awfully* nice/sweet

♦ **tout** + *verbe* : tu t'es ~ sali you've got yourself all dirty; tu as ~ sali tes habits you've got your clothes all dirty

[b] = *déjà*   ~ prêt ◊ ~ préparé ready-made; phrases ~es faites ready-made *ou* set *ou* standard phrases; idées ~es faites preconceived ideas, unquestioning ideas

[c]

♦ **tout** en + *participe présent* (*simultanéité*) ~ en marchant/travaillant as *ou* while you walk/work, while walking/working; elle tricotait ~ en regardant la télévision she was knitting while watching television; je suis incapable de travailler ~ en écoutant de la musique I can't work and listen to music at the same time

(*opposition*) ~ en prétendant le contraire il voulait être élu (al)though he pretended otherwise he wanted to be elected; ~ en reconnaissant ses mérites je ne suis pas d'accord avec lui (al)though *ou* even though I recognize his strengths I don't agree with him

[d]

♦ **tout** + *nom ou adjectif* + **que** (*concession*) ~

---

médecin qu'il soit even though *ou* although he's a doctor, I don't care if he's a doctor; ~e malade qu'elle se prétende however ill *ou* no matter how ill she says she is; leur appartement, ~ grand qu'il est, ne suffira pas however large *ou* no matter how large their flat is, it won't be enough

[e] expressions figées

♦ **tout à fait** quite, entirely, altogether; ce n'est pas ~ la même chose it's not quite the same thing; c'est ~ à fait faux/exact it's quite *ou* entirely wrong/right; il est ~ à fait charmant he's absolutely *ou* quite charming; je suis ~ à fait d'accord avec vous I'm in complete agreement with you, I agree completely *ou* entirely with you; vous êtes d'accord ? — ~ à fait ! do you agree? — absolutely!

♦ **tout à l'heure** (= *plus tard*) later, in a short *ou* little while; (= *peu avant*) just now, a short while ago, a moment ago; je repasserai ~ à l'heure I'll come back later; ~ à l'heure tu as dit que ... (*à l'instant*) you said just now that ...; (*il y a plus longtemps*) you said earlier that ...; à ~ à l'heure ! see you later!

♦ **tout de suite** straightaway, at once, immediately; j'ai ~ de suite compris que ... I understood straightaway that ...; alors, tu es prêt ? — ~ de suite ! are you ready then? — just a second!; vous le voulez pour quand ? — pas ~ de suite when do you want it for? — there's no rush; ce n'est pas pour ~ de suite (= *ce n'est pas près d'arriver*) it won't happen overnight; (= *c'est assez improbable*) it's hardly likely to happen

[5] NOM MASCULIN

[a] = *ensemble*   whole; ces éléments forment un ~ these elements make up a whole; acheter/vendre/prendre le ~ to buy/sell/take the (whole) lot *ou* all of it (*ou* them); (*Rel*) le grand Tout the Great Whole; jouer *ou* tenter *ou* risquer le ~ pour le ~ to stake one's all

[b]

♦ *avec* **être** (= *l'essentiel*) le ~ est qu'il parte à temps the main *ou* most important thing is that he leaves in time; le ~ c'est de faire vite the main thing is to be quick about it; c'est pas le ~* mais j'ai du travail this is all very well but I've got work to do; ce n'est pas le ~ de s'amuser, il faut travailler we can't just enjoy ourselves, we must get down to work

[c] dans une charade   mon ~ est un roi de France my whole *ou* all is a king of France

[d]

♦ **du tout** (*en réponse*) (pas) du ~ ! not at all!; il n'y a pas de pain du ~ there's no bread at all; il n'y a plus du ~ de pain there's no bread left at all; je n'entends/ne vois rien du ~ I can't hear/see a thing, I can't hear/see anything at all; sans s'inquiéter du ~ without worrying at all

♦ **du tout au tout** (= *complètement*) completely; il avait changé du ~ au ~ he had changed completely; la situation s'est modifiée du ~ au ~ the situation has completely changed

---

tout-à-l'égout [tutalegu] NM INV (= *système*) mains drainage (*NonC*); (= *tuyau*) main sewer

Toutankhamon [tutãkamɔ̃]   NM Tutankhamen, Tutankhamun

toutefois [tutfwa] ADV however; sans ~ que cela les retarde without that delaying them, however; si ~ il est d'accord if he agrees, that is

tout-en-un [tutãœ̃] ADJ INV all-in-one

toute-puissance (*pl* **toutes-puissances**) [tutpɥisãs] NF omnipotence (*NonC*)

tout-fou* (*pl* **tout-fous**) [tufu] [1] ADJ M overexcited [2] NM il fait son ~ he's a bit overexcited

toutim* [tutim] NM et (tout) le ~ the whole caboodle*, the whole lot (*Brit*)

toutou [tutu]   NM (*langage enfantin*) doggie, bow-wow (*langage enfantin*); suivre qn/obéir à

---

qn comme un ~ to follow sb about/obey sb as meekly as a lamb

Tout-Paris [tupaʀi] NM le ~ the Paris smart set, the tout-Paris; le ~ artistique assistait au vernissage the artistic elite of Paris attended the preview of the exhibition

tout-petit (*pl* **tout-petits**) [tup(ə)ti] NM toddler, tiny tot; jeu pour les ~s game for the very young *ou* for toddlers *ou* tiny tots

tout-puissant, **toute-puissante** (*mpl* **tout-puissants**) [tupɥisã, tutpɥisãt] [1] ADJ almighty, omnipotent, all-powerful [2] NM le Tout-Puissant the Almighty

tout-terrain (*pl* **tout-terrains**) [tuterɛ̃] [1] ADJ [*véhicule*] four-wheel drive (*épith*), cross-country (*épith*); vélo ~ mountain bike; moto ~ trail bike [2] NM le ~ (*Sport*) (*en voiture*) cross-country racing; (*en vélo*) mountain biking; (*en moto*) trail-biking; faire du ~ (*en voiture*) to go cross-country racing; (*en vélo*) to go mountain-biking; (*en moto*) to go trail-biking

tout(-)va [tuva]   ♦ à tout(-)va LOC ADV left, right and centre

tout-venant [tuv(ə)nã]   NM INV (= *charbon*) raw coal; (= *articles, marchandises*) le ~ the run-of-the-mill *ou* ordinary stuff

toux [tu] NF cough; ~ grasse/sèche/nerveuse loose/dry/nervous cough → **quinte**

toxémie [tɔksemi] NF blood poisoning, toxaemia (*Brit*), toxemia (*US*)

toxicité [tɔksisite] NF toxicity

toxico* [tɔksiko]   NMF (ABRÉV = **toxicomane**) junkie*

toxicodépendance [tɔksikodepãdãs]   NF drug-dependency

toxicodépendant, **e** [tɔksikodepãdã, ãt] NM,F drug-dependent

toxicologie [tɔksikɔlɔʒi] NF toxicology

toxicologique [tɔksikɔlɔʒik]   ADJ toxicological

toxicologue [tɔksikɔlɔg] NMF toxicologist

toxicomane [tɔksikɔman]   [1] ADJ drug-addicted, addicted to drugs [2] NMF drug addict

toxicomaniaque [tɔksikɔmanjak]   ADJ (*habitude, pratique*) (drug) addiction-related

toxicomanie [tɔksikɔmani] NF drug addiction

toxicose [tɔksikoz] NF toxicosis

toxine [tɔksin] NF toxin

toxique [tɔksik]   [1] ADJ toxic; substance ~ pour l'organisme substance that is toxic *ou* poisonous to the system [2] NM toxin, poison

toxoplasme [tɔksoplasm] NM toxoplasma

toxoplasmose [tɔksoplasmoz]   NF toxoplasmosis

TP [tepe] [1] NM [a] (ABRÉV = **Trésor public**) → **trésor** [b] (ABRÉV = **travaux pratiques**) (*Univ*) practical [2] NF (ABRÉV = **trésorerie principale**) → **trésorerie** [3] NMPL (ABRÉV = **travaux publics**) → **travail¹**

TPE [tepeə] NM (ABRÉV = **terminal de paiement électronique**) EFTPOS

TPG [tepeʒe]   NM (ABRÉV = **trésorier-payeur général**) → **trésorier**

TPV [tepeve]   NM (ABRÉV = **terminal point de vente**) POST

trac¹ [trak] NM (*Théât, en public*) stage fright; (*aux examens*) (exam) nerves; avoir le ~ (*Théât, en public*) (*sur le moment*) to have stage fright; (*à chaque fois*) to get stage fright; (*aux examens*) (*sur le moment*) to be nervous; (*à chaque fois*) to get nervous, get (an attack *ou* fit of) nerves; ficher le ~ à qn* to give sb a fright, put the wind up sb* (*Brit*)

trac² [trak]   ♦ tout à trac LOC ADV [*dire, demander*] right out of the blue

traçage [trasaʒ]   NM [a] [*ligne, triangle, plan, chiffre, mot*] drawing; [*courbe de graphique*] plotting [b] [*route, piste*] (= *déblaiement*) opening up; (= *balisage*) marking out [c] (*Min*) heading [d] (*Tech*) tracing

traçant, e [tRasɑ̃, ɑ̃t] ADJ [a] [*racine*] running, creeping [b] [*obus, balle*] tracer (*épith*) → **table**

tracas [tRaka] [1] NM (*littér†* = *embarras*) bother, upset; **se donner bien du ~** to give o.s. a great deal of trouble [2] NMPL (= *soucis, ennuis*) worries

tracasser [tRakase] ▸conjug 1◂ [1] VT (*gén*) to worry, bother; [*administration*] to harass, bother; **qu'est-ce qui te tracasse?** what's bothering *ou* worrying *ou* bugging* you? [2] **se tracasser** VPR (= *se faire du souci*) to worry, fret; **ne te tracasse pas pour si peu!** don't worry *ou* fret over a little thing like that!

tracasserie [tRakasRi] NF (*gén pl*) harassment; **j'en ai assez de toutes ces ~s administratives!** I'm fed up with all this irritating red tape!; **à la suite de cette loi, beaucoup d'étrangers ont subi des ~s administratives** in the aftermath of this law many foreigners were hassled* *ou* harassed by the authorities

tracassier, -ière [tRakasje, jɛR] ADJ [*fonctionnaire, bureaucratie*] pettifogging

trace [tRas] [a] (= *empreinte*) [*animal, fugitif, pneu*] tracks; **la ~ du renard diffère de celle de la belette** the fox's tracks differ from those of the weasel; **suivre une ~ de blaireau** to follow some badger tracks; **~s de doigt** (*sur disque, meuble*) finger marks; **~s de pas** footprints; **~s de pneus** tyre tracks
[b] (= *chemin frayé*) track, path; (*Ski*) track; **s'ouvrir une ~ dans les broussailles** to open up a track *ou* path through the undergrowth; (*Alpinisme, Ski*) **faire la ~** to be the first to ski (*ou* walk *etc*) on new snow; **on voyait leur ~ dans la face nord** we could see their tracks on the north face; (*Ski*) **~ directe** direct descent
[c] (= *marque*) [*sang*] trace; [*brûlure, encre*] mark; [*outil*] mark; [*blessure, maladie*] mark; **~s de freinage** brake marks; **~s d'effraction** signs of a break-in; **il n'y avait pas de ~ écrite** nothing had been put down in writing; **la victime portait des ~s de coups au visage** there were bruises on the victim's face; **le corps ne présentait aucune ~ de violence** there were no signs of violence on the body; (*littér*) **les ~s de la souffrance** the marks of suffering; **des ~s de fatigue se lisaient sur son visage** his face showed signs of tiredness *ou* bore the marks of tiredness; **cet incident avait laissé une ~ durable/profonde dans son esprit** the incident had left an indelible/a definite mark on his mind
[d] (= *indice*) **trace**; **il n'y avait pas ~ des documents volés/du fugitif dans l'appartement** there was no trace of the stolen documents/ of the fugitive in the flat; **on ne trouve pas ~ de cet événement dans les journaux** there's no trace of this event to be found in the papers
[e] (= *vestige: gén pl*) [*bataille, civilisation*] trace; (= *indice*) [*bagarre*] sign; **on voyait encore les ~s de son passage** there was still evidence that he had recently passed by; **retrouver les ~s d'une civilisation disparue** to discover the traces *ou* signs of a lost civilisation
[f] (= *quantité minime*) [*poison, substance*] trace; **on y a trouvé de l'albumine à l'état de ~** traces of albumen have been found; **il ne montrait nulle ~ de repentir/de chagrin** he showed no trace of regret/of sorrow *ou* no sign(s) of being sorry/of sorrow; **sans une ~ d'accent étranger** without a *ou* any trace of a foreign accent; **il parlait sans la moindre ~ d'émotion dans la voix** he spoke without the slightest trace *ou* hint of emotion in his voice
[g] (*loc*) **disparaître sans laisser de ~s** [*personne*] to disappear without trace; [*tache*] to disappear completely without leaving a mark; **être sur les ~s** *ou* **la ~ de** (+ *fugitif*) to be on the trail of; [+ *complot, document*] to be on the track of; **perdre la ~ d'un fugitif** to lose track of *ou* lose the trail of a fugitive; **retrouver la ~ d'un fugitif** to pick up the trail of a fu-

gitive again; (*fig*) **marcher sur** *ou* **suivre les ~s de qn** to follow in sb's footsteps; **suivre à la ~** [+ *gibier, fugitif*] to track; **les journalistes la suivaient à la ~** reporters followed her wherever she went; (*iro*) **on peut le suivre à la ~!** you can always tell when he has been here!

tracé [tRase] NM [a] (= *plan*) [*réseau routier ou ferroviaire, installations*] layout, plan; [*frontière*] line; **corriger le ~ de la frontière entre deux pays** to redraw the border between two countries [b] (= *parcours*) [*ligne de chemin de fer, autoroute*] route; [*rivière*] line, course; [*itinéraire*] course; (= *contour*) [*côte, crête*] line [c] (= *graphisme*) [*dessin, écriture*] line

tracer [tRase] ▸conjug 3◂ [1] VT [a] (= *dessiner*) [+ *ligne, triangle, plan, trait*] to draw; [+ *courbe de graphique*] to plot; (= *écrire*) [+ *chiffre, mot*] to write; (*fig*) **~ le tableau d'une époque** to draw *ou* paint the picture of a period
[b] [+ *frontière*] to mark out; [+ *route, piste*] (= *frayer*) to open up; [+ *baliser*] to mark out; (*fig*) **~ le chemin** *ou* **la voie à qn** to show sb the way; **son avenir est tout tracé** his future is all mapped out; **~ une frontière entre ce qui est possible et ce qui est souhaitable** to mark a boundary between what is possible and what is desirable; **le parcours d'une autoroute** to mark out the path of a motorway
[c] (= *définir*) [+ *programme d'action*] to outline; **~ les grandes lignes d'un projet** to give a broad outline of a project
[2] VI [a] (⁑ = *aller vite*) to belt along*, shift* (*Brit*); **il trace sur ses rollers/sa moto!** he really belts along* on those roller skates/on that motorbike!; **allez, trace!** *ou* **que ça trace!** get a move on!*
[b] (*Bot*) to creep (horizontally)

traceur, -euse [tRasœR, øz] [1] ADJ (*Sci*) [*substance*] tracer (*épith*) [2] NM (= *appareil enregistreur*) pen; (*Sci*) tracer; **~ radioactif** radioactive tracer; (*Ordin*) **~ (de courbes)** (graph) plotter; **~ de cartes** chart plotter

trachéal, e (*mpl* -**aux**) [tRakeal, o] ADJ tracheal

trachée [tRaʃe] NF [a] (*Anat*) **~(-artère)** windpipe, trachea (*SPÉC*) [b] (*Zool*) trachea

trachéen, -enne [tRakeɛ̃, ɛn] ADJ (*Zool*) tracheal

trachéite [tRakeit] NF tracheitis (*NonC*); **avoir une ~** *ou* **faire de la ~** to have tracheitis

trachéotomie [tRakeɔtɔmi] NF tracheotomy

trachome [tRakom] NM trachoma

traçoir [tRaswaR] NM [*dessinateur, graveur*] scriber; [*jardinier*] drill marker

tract [tRakt] NM leaflet, handout

tractable [tRaktabl] ADJ [*caravane*] towable

tractation [tRaktasjɔ̃] NF (*gén péj*) negotiation, dealings, bargaining (*NonC*)

tracté, e [tRakte] ADJ tractor-drawn

tracter [tRakte] ▸conjug 1◂ VT to tow

tracteur, -trice [tRaktœR, tRis] [1] ADJ [*véhicule*] towing; **force tractrice** [*cours d'eau*] tractive force [2] NM tractor

traction [tRaksjɔ̃] NF [a] (*Sci, gén* = action, *mouvement*) traction; **être en ~** to be in traction; (*Sci*) **résistance à la ~** tensile strength; **effort de ~** tensile stress; (*Sport*) **faire des ~s** (*en se suspendant*) to do pull-ups; (*au sol*) to do push-ups *ou* press-ups (*Brit*) [b] (= *mode d'entraînement d'un véhicule*) traction, haulage; (*Rail*) traction; **~ animale/mécanique** animal/ mechanical traction *ou* haulage; **à ~ animale** drawn *ou* hauled by animals; **à ~ mécanique** mechanically drawn; **~ à vapeur/électrique** steam/electric traction; (*Aut*) **~ arrière** rear-wheel drive; (*Aut*) **~ avant** (= *dispositif*) front-wheel drive; (= *voiture*) car with front-wheel drive [c] (*Rail* = *service*) **la ~** the engine and driver section; **service du matériel et de la ~** mechanical and electrical engineer's department

tractopelle [tRaktɔpɛl] NM backhoe

tractus [tRaktys] NM (*Anat*) tract; **~ digestif** digestive tract

tradition [tRadisjɔ̃] NF [a] (*gén*) tradition; (*Rel*) **la Tradition** Tradition; **la ~ orale** the oral tradition; **pays de ~ catholique/musulmane** Catholic/Muslim country; **il est de ~ de faire/que** (+ *subj*) it is a tradition *ou* traditional to do/that; **fidèle à la ~** true to tradition; **c'était bien dans la ~ française** it was very much in the French tradition; **par ~** traditionally; **ce pays a une longue ~ artistique/de violence** this country has a long artistic tradition/a long history of violence [b] (*Jur* = *livraison*) tradition, transfer

traditionalisme [tRadisjɔnalism] NM traditionalism

traditionaliste [tRadisjɔnalist] [1] ADJ traditionalist(ic) [2] NM,F traditionalist

traditionnel, -elle [tRadisjɔnɛl] ADJ [*pratique, interprétation, opinion*] traditional; (* = *habituel*) good old* (*épith*), usual; **sa traditionnelle robe noire*** her good old* *ou* usual black dress

traditionnellement [tRadisjɔnɛlmɑ̃] ADV traditionally; (= *habituellement*) as always, as usual; **~ vêtue de noir** dressed in black as always *ou* as is (*ou* was) her wont (*hum*); **un électorat ~ favorable à la droite** an electorate who have traditionally voted for the Right

traducteur, -trice [tRadyktœR, tRis] [1] NM,F translator; **~-interprète** translator-interpreter [2] NM (*Ordin*) translator

traduction [tRadyksjɔ̃] NF [a] (= *action, opération, technique*) translation, translating (**de** from, **dans, en** into); (*Scol* = *exercice*) translation; **la ~ de ce texte a pris trois semaines** it took three weeks to translate the text; **école d'interprétariat et de ~** institute of translation and interpreting; **c'est une ~ assez libre** it's a fairly free translation *ou* rendering; **une excellente ~ de Proust** an excellent translation of Proust; **~ fidèle/littérale** faithful *ou* accurate/literal translation; **~ automatique** machine *ou* automatic translation; **~ assistée par ordinateur** machine-aided translation; **~ simultanée** simultaneous translation; **ce mot a plusieurs ~s différentes en anglais** this word can be translated in several different ways in English; **il publie son troisième roman en ~ française** his third novel is being published in a French translation; **son œuvre est disponible en ~** his work is available in translation; **ce poème perd beaucoup à la ~** this poem loses a lot in translation
[b] (*fig* = *interprétation*) [*sentiments*] expression; **la ~ concrète de ses promesses électorales se fait attendre** it's taking a long time for his election promises to be translated into concrete action

traduire [tRadɥiR] ▸conjug 38◂ VT [a] [+ *mot, texte, auteur*] to translate (**en, dans** into); **traduit de l'allemand** translated from (the) German; **comment se traduit ce mot en anglais?** how does this word translate into English?
[b] (= *exprimer*) to convey, render, express; (= *rendre manifeste*) to be the expression of; **les mots traduisent la pensée** words convey *ou* render *ou* express thought; **ce tableau traduit un sentiment de désespoir** this picture conveys *ou* expresses a feeling of despair; **sa peur se traduisait par une grande volubilité** his fear found expression in great volubility; **cela s'est traduit par une baisse du pouvoir d'achat** the effect of this was a drop in buying power, it was translated into a drop in buying power
[c] (*Jur*) **~ qn en justice/en correctionnelle** to bring sb before the courts/before the criminal court

traduisible [tRadɥizibl] ADJ translatable; **ce titre est difficilement ~** this title is difficult to translate, this title does not translate easily

Trafalgar [tRafalgaR] NM Trafalgar; **coup de ~** underhand trick

trafic [tʀafik] NM [a] (péj) (= commerce clandestin) traffic; (= activité) trafficking; († = commerce) trade (de in); ~ **d'armes** arms dealing, gunrunning; **faire le ou du ~ d'armes** to be engaged in arms dealing ou gunrunning; ~ **de stupéfiants** ou **de drogue** drug trafficking; **faire du ~ de stupéfiants** ou **de drogue** [gros trafiquant] to traffic in drugs; [revendeur] to deal in drugs; ~ **d'enfants/de voitures volées** trafficking ou trade in children/in stolen cars [b] (fig = activités suspectes) dealings; (* = manigances) funny business*, goings-on*; (Hist) ~ **des bénéfices** selling of benefices; (Jur) ~ **d'influence** influence peddling; **il se fait ici un drôle de ~*** there's some funny business going on here*, there are some strange goings-on here* [c] (Aut, Aviat, Rail) traffic; ~ **maritime/routier/aérien/ferroviaire** sea/road/air/rail traffic; **ligne à fort ~** line carrying dense ou heavy traffic; **(de) marchandises/(de) voyageurs** goods/passenger traffic; ~ **fluide/dense sur le périphérique** light/heavy traffic on the ring road; **le ~ est perturbé sur la ligne 6 du métro parisien** there are delays ou problems on line 6 of the Paris metro; ~ **téléphonique** telephone traffic

traficoter* [tʀafikɔte] ▶ conjug 1 ◀ [1] VT [a] (= altérer) [+ vin] to doctor*; [+ moteur] to tamper ou fiddle with; ~ **les comptes** to fiddle ou cook* (Brit) the books [b] (= réparer) [+ serrure, transistor, robinet] to mend, fix [c] (= faire) **qu'est-ce qu'il traficote dans la cuisine?** what's he up to ou doing in the kitchen? [2] VI (péj) to traffic

trafiquant, e [tʀafikã, ãt] NM,F (péj) trafficker; ~ **de drogue** drug trafficker; ~ **d'armes** arms dealer, gunrunner; **c'est un ~ de voitures volées** he deals in stolen cars

trafiquer [tʀafike] ▶ conjug 1 ◀ [1] VI (péj) to traffic, trade (illicitly); ~ **de son influence** to use one's influence to corrupt ends; († hum) ~ **de ses charmes** to offer one's charms for sale [2] VT* [a] (= altérer) [+ vin] to doctor*; [+ moteur] to tamper ou fiddle with; [+ document] to tamper with; [+ chiffres] to fiddle, doctor; **compteur trafiqué** meter that has been tampered with [b] (= réparer) [+ serrure, appareil] to mend, fix [c] (= gonfler) [+ moteur] to soup up* [d] (= manigancer) **mais qu'est-ce que tu trafiques?** what are you up to?

tragédie [tʀaʒedi] NF (gén, Théât) tragedy; (fig) ~ **humaine/familiale** human/family tragedy; **la manifestation a tourné à la ~** the demonstration ended in tragedy; **ce n'est pas une ~!*** it's not the end of the world!

tragédien [tʀaʒedjɛ̃] NM tragedian, tragic actor

tragédienne [tʀaʒedjɛn] NF tragedienne, tragic actress

tragicomédie [tʀaʒikɔmedi] NF (Théât, fig) tragi-comedy

tragicomique [tʀaʒikɔmik] ADJ (Théât, fig) tragi-comic

tragique [tʀaʒik] [1] ADJ (lit, fig) tragic; **ce n'est pas ~!*** it's not the end of the world! [2] NM [a] (= auteur) tragedian, tragic author [b] (= genre) **le ~** tragedy [c] (= caractère dramatique) [situation] tragedy; **le ~ de la condition humaine** the tragedy of the human condition; **la situation tourne au ~** the situation is taking a tragic turn; **prendre qch au ~** to act as if sth were a tragedy, make a tragedy out of sth

tragiquement [tʀaʒikmã] ADV tragically

trahir [tʀaiʀ] ▶ conjug 2 ◀ [1] VT [a] [+ ami, patrie, cause, idéal] to betray; [+ promesse, engagement] to break; ~ **la confiance/les intérêts de qn** to betray sb's confidence/interests; **sa rougeur l'a trahie** her blushes gave her away ou betrayed her
[b] (= révéler, manifester) [+ secret, émotion] to betray, give away; ~ **sa pensée** to betray ou reveal one's thoughts; **son intonation trahissait sa colère** his intonation betrayed his anger
[c] (= lâcher) [forces, santé] to fail; **ses forces l'ont trahi** his strength failed him; **ses nerfs l'ont trahi** his nerves let him down ou failed him
[d] (= mal exprimer: gén) to misrepresent; [+ vérité] to distort; **ces mots ont trahi ma pensée** those words misrepresented what I had in mind; **ce traducteur/cet interprète a trahi ma pièce** this translator/this performer has given a totally false rendering of my play
[2] **se trahir** VPR to betray o.s., give o.s. away; **il s'est trahi par cette question** his question gave him away, by asking this question he gave himself away; **sa peur se trahissait par un flot de paroles** his fear betrayed itself in a great flow of words

trahison [tʀaizɔ̃] NF (gén) betrayal, treachery (NonC); (Jur, Mil = crime) treason; **il est capable des pires ~s** he is capable of the worst treachery → **haut**

train [tʀɛ̃] [1] NM [a] (Rail) train; ~ **omnibus/express/rapide** slow ou stopping/fast/express train; ~ **direct** fast ou non-stop train; ~ **à vapeur/électrique** steam/electric train; ~ **de marchandises/voyageurs** goods/passenger train; ~ **auto-couchettes** car-sleeper train, ≈ Motorail (Brit); ~**s supplémentaires** extra trains; ~ **à supplément** fast train (on which one has to pay a supplement); **c'est un ~ à supplément** you have to pay a supplement on this train; **le ~ de Paris/Lyon** the Paris/Lyons train; ~ **à grande vitesse** high-speed train; **les ~s de neige** the winter-sports trains; **il est dans ce ~** he's on ou aboard this train; **mettre qn dans le ~** ou **au ~*** to see sb to the train, see sb off on the train ou at the station; **voyager par le ~ ◊ prendre le ~** to travel by rail ou train, take the train; **attraper/rater le ~ de 10h50** to catch/miss the 10.50 train; **monter dans** ou **prendre le ~ en marche** (lit) to get on the moving train; (fig) to jump on ou climb onto the bandwagon
[b] (allure) pace; **ralentir/accélérer le ~** to slow down/speed up, slow/quicken the pace; **aller son ~** to carry along; **aller son petit ~** to go along at one's own pace; **l'affaire va son petit ~** things are chugging ou jogging along (nicely); **aller bon ~** [affaire, travaux] to make good progress; [voiture] to go at a good pace, make good progress; **aller grand ~** to make brisk progress, move along briskly; **les langues des commères allaient bon ~** the old wives' tongues were wagging away ou were going nineteen to the dozen (Brit); **mener/suivre le ~** to set/follow the pace; **mener grand ~** (= dépenser beaucoup) to live in grand style, spend money like water; **il allait à un ~ d'enfer** he was going flat out*, he was tearing along*; **à un ~ de sénateur** ponderously; **au** ou **où il travaille** (at) the rate he's working; **au** ou **du ~ où vont les choses ◊ à ce ~-là** the rate things are going, at this rate → **fond**
[c] **être en ~** (= en action) to be under way; (= de bonne humeur) to be in good spirits; **mettre qn en ~** (= l'égayer) to put sb in good spirits; **mettre un travail en ~** (= le commencer) to get a job under way ou started; **je suis long à me mettre en ~ le matin** it takes me a long time to get going* in the morning; **mise en ~** [travail] starting (up), start; (Typo) make-ready; (= exercices de gym) warm-up; **être/se sentir en ~** (= en bonne santé) to be/feel in good form ou shape; **elle ne se sent pas très en ~** she doesn't feel too good ou too bright*
[d] **être en ~ de faire qch** to be doing sth; **être en ~ de manger/regarder la télévision** to be eating/watching television; **j'étais juste en ~ de manger** I was (right) in the middle of eating, I was just eating; **on l'a pris en ~ de voler** he was caught stealing
[e] (= file) [bateaux, mulets] train, line; (Mil) **le ~ (des équipages)** ≈ the (Army) Service Corps; ~ **de bois (de flottage)** timber raft; (Espace) ~ **spatial** space train
[f] (Tech = jeu) ~ **d'engrenages** train of gears; ~ **de pneus** set of (four) tyres
[g] (Admin = série) batch; ~ **d'arrêtés/de mesures** batch of decrees/of measures; **un premier ~ de réformes** a first batch ou set of reforms
[h] (= partie: Aut) ~ **avant/arrière** front/rear wheel-axle unit; [animal] ~ **de devant** forequarters; ~ **de derrière** hindquarters
[i] (* = derrière) backside*, rear (end)*; **recevoir un coup de pied dans le ~** to get a kick in the pants* ou up the backside: → **filer, magner**
[2] COMP ► **train d'atterrissage** undercarriage, landing gear ► **train fantôme** ghost train ► **train de maison**† (= domestiques) household, retainers†; (= dépenses, installation) (household) establishment ► **train mixte** goods and passenger train ► **train d'ondes** wave train ► **train postal** mail train ► **train sanitaire** hospital train ► **train de sonde** drilling bit and pipe ► **train de vie** lifestyle, style of living; **le ~ de vie de l'État** the government's rate of expenditure

traînailler [tʀenaje] ▶ conjug 1 ◀ VI [a] (= être lent) to dawdle, dillydally [b] (= vagabonder) to loaf ou hang about

traînant, e [tʀenã, ãt] ADJ [voix, accent] drawling (épith); [robe, aile] trailing (épith); [démarche] shuffling (épith)

traînard, e [tʀenaʀ, aʀd] NM,F (péj) (gén) slowcoach* (Brit), slowpoke* (US); (toujours en queue d'un groupe) straggler

traînasser [tʀenase] ▶ conjug 1 ◀ VI = **traînailler**

traîne [tʀen] NF [a] [robe] train [b] (Pêche) dragnet; **pêche à la ~** dragnet fishing [c] (fig) **être à la ~** (en remorque) to be in tow; (*: en retard, en arrière) to lag behind

traîneau (pl traîneaux) [tʀeno] NM [a] (= véhicule) sleigh, sledge (Brit), sled (US); **promenade en ~** sleigh ride [b] (Pêche) dragnet

traînée [tʀene] NF [a] (= laissée par un véhicule, un animal) trail, tracks; [humidité, sang] (sur un mur) streak, smear; (= bande, raie: dans le ciel, sur un tableau) streak; ~ **de brouillard** wisps of fog; ~ **de poudre** powder trail; **la nouvelle s'est répandue** ou **propagée comme une ~ de poudre** the news spread like wildfire [b]: (péj = femme de mauvaise vie) slut, hussy† [c] (Tech = force) drag

traînement [tʀenmã] NM [jambes, pieds] trailing, dragging; [voix] drawl

traîne-misère [tʀenmizɛʀ] NM INV wretch

traîne-patins* [tʀenpatɛ̃] NM INV = **traîne-savates**

traîner [tʀene] ▶ conjug 1 ◀ [1] VT [a] (= tirer) [+ sac, objet lourd, personne] to pull, drag; ~ **un meuble à travers une pièce** to pull ou drag a piece of furniture across a room; ~ **qn par les pieds** to drag sb along by the feet; ~ **les pieds** (lit) to drag one's feet, shuffle along; (fig = hésiter) to drag one's feet; ~ **la jambe** ou **la patte*** to limp, hobble; **elle traînait sa poupée dans la poussière** she was trailing ou dragging her doll through the dust; (fig) ~ **ses guêtres*** to knock around*; **il a traîné ses guêtres en Afrique*** he knocked around Africa*; (fig) ~ **la savate*** to bum around:; (fig) ~ **qn dans la boue** ou **fange** to drag sb ou sb's name through the mud; (fig) ~ **un boulet** to have a millstone round one's neck
[b] (= emmener: péj) to drag; **elle est obligée de ~ ses enfants partout** she has to trail ou drag her children along (with her) everywhere; **il traîne toujours une vieille valise avec lui** he's always dragging ou lugging* an old suitcase around with him; ~ **de vieilles idées/des conceptions surannées** to cling to old ideas/to outdated conceptions
[c] (= subir) **elle traîne cette bronchite depuis**

janvier this bronchitis has been with her *ou* plaguing her since January; **elle traîne un mauvais rhume** she's got a bad cold she can't get rid of *ou* shake off; **~ une existence misérable** to drag out a wretched existence [d] (= *faire durer*) to drag out, draw out; **~ les choses en longueur** to drag things out [e] **(faire) ~** [+ *mots*] to drawl; [+ *fin de phrase*] to drag out, drawl; **(faire) ~ sa voix** to drawl [2] VI [a] [*personne*] (= *rester en arrière*) to lag *ou* trail behind; (= *aller lentement*) to dawdle; (*péj* = *errer*) to hang about; **~ en chemin** to dawdle on the way; **~ dans les rues** to roam the streets, hang about the streets; **elle laisse ses enfants ~ dans la rue** she lets her children hang about the street(s); **il traîne pour se préparer** he dawdles when he gets dressed, he takes ages to get dressed; **~ en peignoir dans la maison** to trail round *ou* hang about in one's dressing-gown in the house; **~ au lit** to lounge in bed; **on est en retard, il ne s'agit plus de ~** we're late — we must stop hanging around *ou* dawdling; **~ dans les cafés** to hang around the cafés; **après sa maladie, il a encore traîné 2 ans** after his illness he lingered on for 2 years [b] [*chose*] (= *être éparpillé*) to lie about *ou* around; **ses livres traînent sur toutes les chaises** his books are lying about on all the chairs; **ne laisse pas ~ ton argent/tes affaires** don't leave your money/your things lying about *ou* around; **des histoires/idées qui traînent partout** stories/ideas that float around everywhere; **elle attrape tous les microbes qui traînent** *ou* **tout ce qui traîne** she catches anything that's going [c] (= *durer trop longtemps*) to drag on; **un procès qui traîne** a case which is dragging on; **une maladie qui traîne** a lingering illness, an illness which drags on; **la discussion a traîné en longueur** the discussion dragged on for ages *ou* dragged on and on; **ça n'a pas traîné !*** that wasn't long coming!; **il n'a pas traîné (à répondre)*** he was quick (with his answer), his answer wasn't long in coming, he replied immediately; **~ ne ~ pas, je vous mettrai tous à la porte*** he'll throw you all out before you know what's happening *ou* where you are; **faire ~ qch en longueur** to drag sth out; **doctrine où traînent des relents de fascisme** doctrine which still has a whiff of fascism about it [d] [*robe, manteau*] to trail; **ta ceinture/ton lacet traîne par terre** your belt/your shoelace is trailing *ou* dragging on the ground [3] **se traîner** VPR [a] [*personne fatiguée*] to drag o.s.; [*train, voiture*] to crawl along; **on se traînait à 20 à l'heure** we were crawling along at 20; **se ~ par terre** to crawl on the ground; **avec cette chaleur, on se traîne** it's all you can do to drag yourself around in this heat; **elle a pu se ~ jusqu'à son fauteuil** she managed to drag *ou* haul herself (over) to her chair; **je ne peux même plus me ~** I can't even drag myself about any more; (*fig*) **se ~ aux pieds de qn** to grovel at sb's feet [b] [*conversation, journée, hiver*] to drag on

traîne-savates* [tʀɛnsavat] NM INV (= *vagabond*) tramp, bum*; (= *traînard*) slowcoach (*Brit*), slowpoke (*US*)

training [tʀɛniŋ] NM [a] (= *entraînement*) training; **~ autogène** autogenic training [b] (= *chaussure*) trainer; (= *survêtement*) tracksuit top

train-train, traintrain [tʀɛtʀɛ̃] NM INV humdrum routine; **le ~ de la vie quotidienne** the humdrum routine of everyday life, the daily round

traire [tʀɛʀ] ▶ conjug 50 ◀ VT [+ *vache*] to milk; [+ *lait*] to draw; **machine à ~** milking machine

▼ **trait** [tʀɛ] [1] NM [a] (= *ligne*) (*en dessinant*) stroke; (*en soulignant, dans un graphique*) line; **faire un trait** *ou* **tracer un ~** to draw a line; **tirer**

un ~ sur son passé to make a complete break with one's past, sever all connections with one's past; **tirons un ~ sur cette affaire** let's put this business behind us; **ta promotion ? tu peux tirer un ~ dessus !** your promotion? you can forget about it! *ou* kiss it goodbye!*; (*Art*) **dessin au ~** line drawing; (*Art*) **le ~ est ferme** the line is firm; (*lit, fig*) **d'un ~ de plume** with one stroke of the pen; **~ de repère** reference mark; **biffer qch d'un ~** to score *ou* cross sth out, put a line through sth; **copier** *ou* **reproduire qch ~ pour ~** to copy sth line by line, make a line for line copy of sth; (*fig*) **ça lui ressemble ~ pour ~** that's just *ou* exactly like him, that's him all over; **les ~s d'un dessin/portrait** the lines of a drawing/portrait; **dessiner qch à grands ~s** to sketch sth roughly, make a rough sketch of sth; **décrire qch à grands ~s** to describe sth in broad outline; **il l'a décrit en ~s vifs et émouvants** he drew a vivid and moving picture of it [b] (= *élément caractéristique*) feature, trait; **c'est un ~ de cet auteur** this is a (characteristic) trait *ou* feature of this author; **les ~s dominants d'une époque/œuvre** the dominant features of an age/a work; **avoir des ~s de ressemblance avec** to have certain features in common with; **il tient ce ~ de caractère de son père** this trait comes to him from his father, he gets that from his father [c] (= *acte révélateur*) **~ de générosité/courage/perfidie** act of generosity/courage/wickedness [d] († = *projectile*) arrow, dart; (*littér* = *attaque malveillante*) taunt, gibe; **filer** *ou* **partir comme un ~** to be off like a shot; **~ mordant** biting taunt; **un ~ satirique/d'ironie** a shaft of satire/of irony (*littér*); **les ~s de la calomnie** the darts of slander (*littér*) [e] (= *courroie*) trace [f] (= *traction*) **animal** *ou* **bête/cheval de ~** draught (*Brit*) *ou* draft (*US*) animal/horse [g] (*Mus*) virtuosic passage [h] (*Rel*) tract [i] (= *gorgée*) gulp, draught (*Brit*), draft (*US*); **d'un ~** [*dire*] in one breath; [*boire*] in one gulp, at one go; [*dormir*] uninterruptedly, without waking; **boire qch à longs** *ou* **grands ~s** to take big *ou* large gulps of sth [j] (*Ling*) **~ distinctif** distinctive feature [k] (*Échecs*) **avoir le ~** to have the move; **en début de partie les blancs ont toujours le ~** at the start of the game white always has first move; **il avait le ~** it was his move, it was his turn to move [l] **avoir ~ à** to relate to, be connected with, have to do with, concern; **tout ce qui a ~ à cette affaire** everything relating to *ou* connected with *ou* (having) to do with *ou* concerning this matter [2] **traits** NMPL (= *physionomie*) features; **avoir des ~s fins/réguliers** to have delicate/regular features; **avoir les ~s tirés/creusés** to have drawn/sunken features [3] COMP ▶ **trait (d'esprit)** flash *ou* shaft of wit, witticism ▶ **trait de génie** brainwave, flash of inspiration *ou* genius ▶ **trait de lumière** (*lit*) shaft *ou* ray of light; (*fig*) flash of inspiration, sudden revelation (*NonC*) ▶ **trait de scie** cutting-line ▶ **trait d'union** (*Typo*) hyphen; (*fig*) link

traitable [tʀɛtabl] ADJ [a] (*littér*) [*personne*] accommodating, tractable (*frm*) [b] [*sujet, matière*] manageable

traitant, e [tʀɛtɑ̃, ɑ̃t] ADJ [a] [*shampooing*] medicated → **médecin** [b] (*Espionnage*) **(officier) ~** contact

traite [tʀɛt] NF [a] (= *trafic*) **~ des Noirs** slave trade; **~ des Blanches** white slave trade [b] (*Comm* = *billet*) draft, bill; **tirer/escompter une ~** to draw/discount a draft; **~ de cavalerie** accommodation bill, kite [c] (= *parcours*) stretch; **d'une (seule) ~** [*parcourir*] in one go, without stopping on the way; [*dire*] in one

breath; [*boire*] in one gulp, at one go; [*dormir*] uninterruptedly, without waking [d] [*vache*] milking; **~ mécanique** machine milking; **l'heure de la ~** milking time

traité [tʀɛte] NM [a] (= *livre*) treatise; (*Rel* = *brochure*) tract [b] (= *convention*) treaty; **~ de paix** peace treaty; **le ~ de Versailles/Paris** the Treaty of Versailles/Paris; **conclure/ratifier un ~** to conclude/ratify a treaty

traitement [tʀɛtmɑ̃] NM [a] (= *manière d'agir*) treatment; **~ de faveur** special *ou* preferential treatment; **le ~ social du chômage** social measures for fighting unemployment [b] (*Méd*) treatment; **suivre/prescrire un ~ douloureux** to undergo/prescribe painful treatment *ou* a painful course of treatment; **hormonal** (*gén*) hormone therapy; (*après la ménopause*) hormone replacement therapy; **~ chirurgical** surgery; **~ de fond** (*lit*) long term (course of) treatment; **le problème du chômage nécessite un ~ de fond** what is required is a sustained approach to tackling unemployment; **~ de choc** (*lit*) intensive (course of) treatment; (*fig*) shock treatment; **être en ~ (à l'hôpital)** to be having treatment (in hospital); **être sous ~** to be undergoing treatment; **les nouveaux ~s de** *ou* **contre la stérilité** new ways of treating sterility; **les médicaments utilisés dans le ~ du cancer** cancer drugs, drugs used in the treatment of cancer [c] (= *rémunération*) salary, wage; (*Rel*) stipend; **toucher un bon ~** to get a good wage *ou* salary [d] (*Tech*) [*matières premières, déchets*] processing, treating [e] (*Ordin*) processing; **le ~ (automatique) de l'information** *ou* **des données** (automatic) data processing; **~ de texte** (= *technique*) word-processing; (= *logiciel*) word-processing package; **machine** *ou* **système de ~ de texte** word processor; **~ par lots** batch processing; **~ d'images/du signal** image/(digital) signal processing

▼ **traiter** [tʀɛte] ▶ conjug 1 ◀ [1] VT [a] [+ *personne, animal*] to treat; (= *soigner*) [+ *malade, maladie*] to treat; **~ qn bien/mal/comme un chien** to treat sb well/badly/like a dog; **~ qn d'égal à égal** to treat sb as an equal; **~ qn en enfant/malade** to treat sb as *ou* like a child/an invalid; **~ durement qn** to be hard on sb, give sb a hard time; **les congressistes ont été magnifiquement traités** the conference members were entertained magnificently *ou* treated royally; **se faire ~ pour une affection pulmonaire** to undergo treatment for *ou* be treated for lung trouble; **cette infection se traite facilement** this infection is easily treated [b] (= *qualifier*) **~ qn de fou/menteur** to call sb a fool/a liar; **~ qn de tous les noms** to call sb all the names imaginable *ou* all the names under the sun; **ils se sont traités de voleur(s)** they called each other thieves; **je me suis fait ~ d'imbécile** they called me a fool [c] (= *examiner, s'occuper de*) [+ *question*] to treat, deal with; (*Art*) [+ *thème, sujet*] to treat; (*Comm*) [+ *affaire*] to handle, deal with; (*Jur*) [+ *dossier, plainte*] to deal with; (*Mil*) [+ *objectif*] to handle; **il n'a pas traité le sujet** he hasn't dealt with the subject; (*Bourse*) **le volume des affaires traitées a augmenté** the volume of trading has increased; (*Bourse*) **le dollar se traitait à 5 F en fin de séance** the dollar was trading at 5 francs at the close; **les valeurs qui se traitent à Paris** shares that are traded on the Paris stock exchange [d] (*Tech*) [+ *cuir, minerai, pétrole*] to treat, process; [+ *déchets*] to process; (*Ordin*) [+ *données*] to process; **non traité** untreated [e] (*Agr*) [+ *cultures*] to treat, spray; [+ *aliments*] to treat; **fruits non traités** unsprayed fruit [2] **traiter de** VT INDIR to deal with, treat of (*frm*); **le livre/romancier traite des problèmes de la drogue** the book/novelist deals with *ou* treats of (*frm*) the problems of drugs

3 VI (= *négocier, parlementer*) to negotiate, make ou do* a deal; **~ avec qn** to negotiate ou deal with sb, have dealings with sb; **les pays doivent ~ entre eux** countries must deal ou have dealings with each other

traiteur [tʀɛtœʀ] NM caterer; **épicier-~** grocer and caterer

traître, traîtresse [tʀɛtʀ, tʀɛtʀɛs] **1** ADJ **a** [*personne*] treacherous, traitorous; [*allure*] treacherous; [*douceur, paroles*] perfidious, treacherous; **être ~ à une cause/à sa patrie** to be a traitor to a cause/to one's country, betray a cause/one's country **b** (*fig = dangereux*) [*animal*] vicious; [*vin*] deceptive; [*escalier, virage*] treacherous; **le soleil est ~ aujourd'hui** the sun is hotter than it looks today **c** (*loc*) **il n'a pas dit un ~ mot** he didn't breathe a word **2** NM **a** (= *gén*) traitor; (*Théât*) villain; (*hum*) **le ~, il complotait pour m'offrir cette robe!** he's a sly one, he was planning to buy me this dress all along! **b** († = *perfide*) scoundrel† **c prendre/attaquer qn en ~** to take/attack sb off-guard, play an underhand trick/make an insidious attack on sb; **je ne veux pas vous prendre en ~** I want to be up front with you; **un coup en ~** a stab in the back **3 traîtresse** NF traitress

traîtreusement [tʀɛtʀøzmɑ̃] ADV treacherously

traîtrise [tʀɛtʀiz] NF **a** (= *caractère*) treachery, treacherousness **b** (= *acte*) piece ou act of treachery; (= *danger*) treacherousness (*NonC*), peril

trajectoire [tʀaʒɛktwaʀ] NF (*gén*) trajectory; [*projectile*] path; **la ~ de la balle passa très près du cœur** the bullet passed very close to the heart; **~ de vol** flight path; **les deux hommes n'ont pas du tout la même ~ politique** the two men have followed very different paths in politics ou have pursued very different political careers

trajet [tʀaʒɛ] NM **a** (= *distance à parcourir*) distance; (= *itinéraire*) route; (= *parcours, voyage*) trip, journey (*Brit*); (= *par mer*) voyage; **un ~ de 8 km** a distance of 8 km; **le ~ aller/retour** the outward/return trip ou journey (*Brit*); **choisir le ~ le plus long** to choose the longest route ou way; **elle fait à pied le court ~ de son bureau à la gare** she walks the short distance from her office to the station; **il a une heure de ~ pour se rendre à son travail** it takes him an hour to get to work; **elle a dû refaire le ~ en sens inverse** she had to walk (ou drive *etc*) back; **faire le ~ de Paris à Lyon en voiture/train** to do the trip ou the journey (*Brit*) from Paris to Lyon by car/train; **le ~ par mer est plus intéressant** the sea voyage ou crossing is more interesting; **il prend l'autobus puis termine son ~ en métro** he takes the bus and goes the rest of the way on the metro; (*fig*) **quel ~ il a parcouru depuis son dernier roman!** what a distance ou a long way he has come since his last novel! **b** (*Anat*) [*nerf, artère*] course; [*projectile*] path

tralala* [tʀalala] **1** NM (= *luxe, apprêts*) fuss (*NonC*), frills; (= *accessoires*) trimmings; **faire du ~** to make a lot of fuss; **en grand ~** with all the works*, with a great deal of fuss; **avec tout le ~** with all the frills ou trimmings; **et tout le ~** and the whole kit and caboodle*, and the whole shebang* (*US*) **2** EXCL ha ha!; **~! j'ai gagné!** ha ha! I've won!

tram [tʀam] NM = **tramway**

tramail (*pl* **tramails**) [tʀamaj] NM trammel (net)

trame [tʀam] NF **a** [*tissu*] weft, woof; **usé jusqu'à la ~** threadbare **b** [*roman*] framework; [*vie*] web **c** (*Typo = quadrillage*) screen; (*TV = lignes*) frame **d** (*Géog*) network, system; **la ~ urbaine** the urban network ou system

tramer [tʀame] ▸conjug 1◂ VT **a** [+ *évasion, coup d'État*] to plot; [+ *complot*] to hatch, weave; **il se trame quelque chose** there's something brewing **b** (*Tex*) to weave **c** (*Typo, Photo*) to screen; **cliché tramé** half-tone

traminot [tʀamino] NM tram(way) (*Brit*) ou streetcar (*US*) worker

tramontane [tʀamɔ̃tan] NF tramontana

tramp [tʀap] NM (*Naut*) tramp

trampoline [tʀɑ̃pɔlin] NM trampoline; **faire du ~** to go ou do trampolining

tramway [tʀamwɛ] NM (= *moyen de transport*) tram(way); (= *voiture*) tram(car) (*Brit*), streetcar (*US*)

tranchant, e [tʀɑ̃ʃɑ̃, ɑ̃t] **1** ADJ **a** [*couteau, arête*] sharp; **du côté ~/non ~** with the sharp ou cutting/blunt edge **b** (*fig*) [*personne, ton*] assertive, peremptory, curt **2** NM **a** [*couteau*] sharp ou cutting edge; **avec le ~ de la main** with the edge of one's hand → **double b** (= *instrument*) [*apiculteur*] scraper; [*tanneur*] fleshing knife **c** (*fig*) [*argument, réprimande*] force, impact

tranche [tʀɑ̃ʃ] NF **a** (= *portion*) [*pain, jambon*] slice; [*bacon*] rasher; **~ de bœuf** beefsteak; **~ de saumon** salmon steak; **~ napolitaine** neapolitan slice; **en ~s** sliced, in slices; **couper en ~s** to slice, cut into slices; (*Ordin*) **~ de silicium** silicon wafer; **ils s'en sont payé une ~*** they had a great time* ou a whale of a time*, they had great fun ou a lot of fun **b** (= *bord*) [*livre, pièce de monnaie, planche*] edge → **doré c** (= *section*) (*gén*) section; (*Fin*) [*actions, bons*] block, tranche; [*crédit, prêt*] instalment; (*Admin*) [*revenus*] bracket; [*imposition*] band, bracket; (*Loterie*) **~ (d'émission*)** issue; (*Admin*) **~ d'âge/de salaires** age/wage bracket; (*TV, Radio*) **~ horaire** (time) slot; **~ de temps** period of time; **~ de vie** slice of life; **la première ~ des travaux** the first phase of the work **d** (*Boucherie = morceau*) **~ grasse** silverside; **bifteck dans la ~** ≈ piece of silverside steak

tranché, e¹ [tʀɑ̃ʃe] (*ptp de* **trancher**) ADJ **a** (= *coupé*) [*pain, saumon*] sliced **b** (= *distinct*) [*couleurs*] clear, distinct; [*limite*] clear-cut, definite; [*opinion*] clear-cut, cut-and-dried

tranchée² [tʀɑ̃ʃe] NF **a** (*gén, Mil = fossé*) trench → **guerre b** (*Sylviculture*) cutting

tranchées [tʀɑ̃ʃe] NFPL (*Méd*) colic, gripes, tormina *pl* (*SPÉC*); **~ utérines** after-pains

tranchefile [tʀɑ̃ʃfil] NF [*reliure*] headband

trancher [tʀɑ̃ʃe] ▸conjug 1◂ **1** VT **a** (= *couper*) [+ *corde, nœud, lien*] to cut, sever; **~ le cou** ou **la tête à qn** to cut off ou sever sb's head; **~ la gorge à qn** to cut ou slit sb's throat; **le prisonnier s'est tranché la gorge** the prisoner slit ou cut his throat; (*littér*) **la mort** ou **la Parque tranche le fil des jours** death severs ou the Fates sever the thread of our days → **nœud, vif b** (†, *frm = mettre fin à*) [+ *discussion*] to conclude, bring to a close; **~ court** ou **net** to bring things to an abrupt conclusion; **tranchons là** let's close the matter there **c** (= *résoudre*) [+ *question, difficulté*] to settle, decide, resolve; (*sans complément = décider*) to take a decision; **un différend** to settle a disagreement; **le juge a dû ~/a tranché que ...** the judge has to make a ruling/ruled that ...; **il ne faut pas avoir peur de ~** you mustn't be afraid of taking decisions; **le gouvernement a tranché en faveur de ce projet** the government has decided ou has come out in favour of this plan **2** VI (= *faire contraste*) [*couleur*] to stand out clearly (**sur, avec** against); [*trait, qualité*] to contrast strongly ou sharply (**sur, avec** with); **cette vallée sombre tranche sur le paysage environnant** this dark valley stands out against the surrounding countryside; **la journée du dimanche a tranché sur une semai-**

ne très agitée Sunday formed a sharp contrast to a very busy week; **son silence tranchait avec** ou **sur l'hystérie générale** his silence was in stark contrast to the general mood of hysteria

tranchet [tʀɑ̃ʃɛ] NM [*bourrelier, sellier*] leather knife; [*plombier*] hacking knife

trancheuse [tʀɑ̃ʃøz] NF (*à bois*) cutter; (*de terrassement*) trencher; (*à pain, à jambon*) slicer

tranchoir [tʀɑ̃ʃwaʀ] NM **a** (*Culin*) (= *plateau*) trencher†, platter; (= *couteau*) chopper **b** (= *poisson*) zanclus

tranquille [tʀɑ̃kil] ADJ **a** (= *calme*) [*eau, mer, air*] quiet, tranquil (*littér*); [*sommeil*] gentle, peaceful, tranquil (*littér*); [*vie, journée, vacances, endroit, quartier*] quiet, peaceful, tranquil (*littér*); **un coin ~** a quiet corner; **un ~ bien-être l'envahissait** a feeling of quiet ou calm well-being crept over him; **c'est l'heure la plus ~ de la journée** it's the quietest ou most peaceful time of day; **aller/entrer d'un pas ~** to walk/go in calmly; **ils mènent une petite vie bien ~** they have a nice quiet life **b** (= *serein*) [*courage, conviction*] quiet, calm; **avec une ~ assurance** with quiet ou calm assurance **c** (= *paisible*) [*tempérament, personne*] quiet, placid; [*voisins, enfants, élèves*] quiet; **il veut être ~** he wants to have some peace (and quiet); **rester/se tenir ~** to keep ou stay/be quiet; **nous étions bien ~s et il a fallu qu'il nous dérange** we were having a nice quiet ou peaceful time and he came to disturb us; **j'aime être ~ après le repas** I like to (have) some peace (and quiet) after my meal; **ferme la porte, tu seras plus ~ pour travailler** close the door, it'll be quieter for you to work; **laisser qn ~** to leave sb in peace, give sb a bit of peace; **laisser qch ~** to leave sth alone ou in peace; **laisse-le donc ~, tu vois bien qu'il travaille/qu'il est moins fort que toi** leave him in peace ou let him be — you can see he's working/he's not as strong as you are; **laissez-moi ~ avec vos questions** stop bothering me with your questions; **il est ~ comme Baptiste** he's got nothing to worry about → **père d** (= *sans souci*) **être ~** to feel ou be easy in one's mind; **tu peux être ~** you needn't worry, you can set your mind at rest; **soyez ~, tout ira bien** don't worry — everything will be all right; **je ne suis pas ~ lorsqu'il est sur la route** I worry when he's out on the road; **je serais plus ~ si j'avais un poste stable** I'd feel easier in my mind if I had a steady job; **pouvoir dormir ~** (*lit*) to be able to sleep easy (in one's bed); (= *être rassuré*) **tu peux dormir ~** you can rest easy, you needn't worry; **comme ça, nous serons ~s** that way our minds will be at rest; **maintenant je peux mourir ~** now I can die in peace; **il a l'esprit ~** his mind is at rest ou at ease; **pour avoir l'esprit ~** to set one's mind at rest, to feel easy in one's mind; **avoir la conscience ~** to be at peace with one's conscience, have a clear conscience **e** (= *certain*) **être ~ (que ...)** to be sure (that ...); **il n'ira pas, je suis ~** he won't go, I'm sure of it; **tu peux être ~ que ...** you may be sure that ..., rest assured that ...; **soyez ~, je me vengerai** don't (you) worry ou rest assured — I shall have my revenge **f** (*Pharm*) **baume ~** soothing balm; **vin ~** still wine **g** (* = *facilement*) easily; **il l'a fait en trois heures ~** he did it in three hours easily ou no trouble*; **il a gagné en trois sets, ~** he won easily in three sets; (= *sans risque*) **tu peux y aller ~** you can go there quite safely

tranquillement [tʀɑ̃kilmɑ̃] ADV **a** (= *paisiblement*) [*dormir, vivre*] peacefully; [*jouer*] quietly; (= *sereinement*) [*affirmer, annoncer*] calmly; **~ installé dans un fauteuil** sitting quietly in an armchair; **il attendait ~ son tour** he calmly ou quietly waited his turn; **on peut y**

aller ~, ça ne risque plus rien* we can go ahead safely — there's no risk now b (= *sans se presser*) **vous pouvez y aller ~ en deux heures** you can get there easily *ou* without hurrying in two hours c (= *sans être dérangé*) [*travailler*] in peace, quietly; **j'aimerais pouvoir lire ~** I'd like to have a quiet read, I'd like to read in peace *ou* quietly

tranquillisant, e [tʀãkiliza, ãt] 1 ADJ [*nouvelle*] reassuring; [*effet, produit*] soothing, tranquillizing 2 NM (*Méd*) tranquillizer

tranquilliser [tʀãkilize] ▶ conjug 1 ◀ 1 VT ~ **qn** to reassure sb, set sb's mind at rest; **je suis tranquillisé** I'm reassured *ou* relieved 2 **se tranquilliser** VPR to set one's mind at rest; **tranquillise-toi, il ne lui arrivera rien** calm down *ou* take it easy, nothing will happen to him

tranquillité [tʀãkilite] NF a [*eau, mer*] quietness, tranquillity (*littér*); [*sommeil*] gentleness, peacefulness, tranquillity (*littér*); [*vie, journée, vacances, endroit*] quietness, peacefulness, tranquillity (*littér*) b [*courage, conviction, assurance*] quietness; [*personne*] quietness, peacefulness c (= *paix*) peace, tranquillity (*littér*); **en toute ~** without being bothered *ou* disturbed; **ils ont cambriolé la villa en toute ~** they burgled the house without being disturbed (at all) *ou* without any disturbance; **troubler la ~ publique** to disturb the peace; **travailler dans la ~** to work in peace; **il tient beaucoup à sa ~** all he wants is to be left in peace; **je n'ai pas eu un seul moment de ~** I haven't had a moment's peace d (= *absence d'inquiétude*) **~ (d'esprit)** peace of mind; **~ matérielle** material security; **en toute ~** with complete peace of mind, free from all anxiety; **vous pouvez le lui confier en toute ~** you can entrust it to him with absolute confidence

trans... [tʀãz] PRÉF trans...; **ligne ~(-)Pacifique** trans-Pacific route; **réseau de communication ~européen** trans-European communications network; **une éducation ~culturelle** a cross-cultural education

transaction [tʀãzaksjɔ̃] NF a (*Comm*) transaction; **~s commerciales/financières/boursières** commercial/financial/stock exchange transactions *ou* dealings b (*Jur* = *compromis*) settlement, compromise c (*Ordin*) transaction

transactionnel, -elle [tʀãzaksjɔnɛl] ADJ (*Ordin*) transactional; (*Jur*) compromise (*épith*), settlement (*épith*); **formule transactionnelle** compromise formula; **règlement ~** compromise settlement; (*Psych*) **analyse ~le** transactional analysis

transafricain, e [tʀãzafʀikɛ̃, ɛn] ADJ transafrican

transalpin, e [tʀãzalpɛ̃, in] ADJ transalpine

transamazonien, -ienne [tʀãzamazɔnjɛ̃, jɛn] ADJ trans-Amazonian; **(autoroute) transamazonienne** trans-Amazonian highway

transaméricain, e [tʀãzameʀikɛ̃, ɛn] ADJ transamerican

transaminase [tʀãzaminaz] NF transaminase

transat [tʀãzat] 1 NM (ABRÉV = **transatlantique**) (= *chaise longue*) deckchair; (*pour bébé*) bouncer chair, bouncing cradle 2 NF (ABRÉV = **course transatlantique**) **~ en solitaire** single-handed transatlantic race; **~ en double** two-man (*ou* two-woman) transatlantic race

transatlantique [tʀãzatlãtik] 1 ADJ transatlantic; **course ~** transatlantic race 2 NM (= *paquebot*) transatlantic liner; (= *fauteuil*) deckchair

transbahuter* [tʀãsbayte] ▶ conjug 1 ◀ 1 VT to shift, lug along*, hump along* (*Brit*) 2 **se transbahuter** VPR to traipse along*

transbordement [tʀãsbɔʀdəmã] NM (*Naut,*

Rail) [*marchandises*] tran(s)shipment, transfer; [*passagers*] transfer; **quai de ~** transfer dock

transborder [tʀãsbɔʀde] ▶ conjug 1 ◀ VT (*Naut, Rail*) [*+ marchandises*] to tran(s)ship, transfer; [*+ passagers*] to transfer

transbordeur [tʀãsbɔʀdœʀ] NM **(pont) ~** transporter bridge

transcanadien, -ienne [tʀãskanadjɛ̃, jɛn] 1 ADJ trans-Canada (*épith*) 2 **Transcanadienne** NF **la Transcanadienne** the Trans-Canada highway

Transcaucasie [tʀãskokazi] NF Transcaucasia

transcendance [tʀãsãdãs] NF (*Philo*) transcendence, transcendency; (*littér*, †) (= *excellence*) transcendence (*littér*); (= *fait de se surpasser*) self-transcendence (*littér*)

transcendant, e [tʀãsãdã, ãt] ADJ a (*littér* = *sublime*) [*génie, mérite*] transcendent (*littér*); **ce n'est pas ~*** [*film, livre*] it's nothing special*, it's nothing to write home about* b (*Philo*) transcendent(al); **être ~ à** to transcend c (*Math*) transcendental

transcendantal, e (*mpl* **-aux**) [tʀãsãdãtal, o] ADJ transcendental

transcendantalisme [tʀãsãdãtalism] NM transcendentalism

transcender [tʀãsãde] ▶ conjug 1 ◀ 1 VT to transcend 2 **se transcender** VPR to transcend o.s.

transcodage [tʀãskɔdaʒ] NM (*Ordin*) compiling; (*TV*) transcoding

transcoder [tʀãskɔde] ▶ conjug 1 ◀ VT (*Ordin*) [*+ programme*] to compile; (*TV*) to transcode

transcodeur [tʀãskɔdœʀ] NM (*Ordin*) compiler; (*TV*) transcoder

transcontinental, e (*mpl* **-aux**) [tʀãskɔ̃tinãtal, o] ADJ transcontinental

transcriptase [tʀãskʀiptaz] NF **~ inverse** reverse transcriptase

transcripteur [tʀãskʀiptœʀ] NM transcriber

transcription [tʀãskʀipsjɔ̃] NF a (= *fait de copier*) copying out, transcribing, transcription b (= *copie*) transcript c (= *translittération*) transcription, transliteration; **~ en braille** braille transcription d (*Mus, Ling, Bio*) transcription; **~ phonétique** phonetic transcription; **~ génétique** genetic transcription

transcrire [tʀãskʀiʀ] ▶ conjug 39 ◀ VT a (= *copier*) to copy out, transcribe b (= *translittérer*) to transcribe, transliterate c (*Mus, Ling, Bio*) to transcribe d (= *restituer*) [*+ ambiance, réalité*] to translate

transdermique [tʀãsdɛʀmik] ADJ [*substance*] transdermal; **timbre autocollant ~** skin *ou* transdermal (*SPÉC*) patch

transdisciplinaire [tʀãsdisiplinɛʀ] ADJ interdisciplinary

transducteur [tʀãsdyktœʀ] NM transducer

transduction [tʀãsdyksjɔ̃] NF (*Bio*) transduction

transe [tʀãs] 1 NF (= *état second*) trance; **être en ~** to be in a trance; **entrer en ~** (*lit*) to go into a trance; (*fig* = *s'énerver*) to go into a rage, see red* 2 **transes** NFPL (= *affres*) agony; **être dans les ~s** to be in *ou* suffer agony, go through agony; **être dans les ~s de l'attente/des examens** to be in agonies of anticipation/over the exams

transept [tʀãsɛpt] NM transept

transférable [tʀãsfeʀabl] ADJ transferable

transfèrement [tʀãsfɛʀmã] NM [*prisonnier*] transfer; **~ cellulaire** transfer by prison van

transférer [tʀãsfeʀe] ▶ conjug 6 ◀ VT a [*+ fonctionnaire, assemblée, bureaux*] to transfer, move; [*+ joueur, prisonnier*] to transfer; **~ la production dans une autre usine** to transfer *ou* switch production to another factory; **nos bureaux sont transférés au 5 rue de Lyon** our offices have transferred *ou* moved to 5 rue de

Lyon b (*Ordin, Télec*) to transfer; **faire ~ ses appels à un autre numéro** to have one's calls transferred to another number c [*+ dépouille mortelle, reliques*] to transfer, translate d (*Fin*) [*+ capitaux*] to transfer, move; (*Comptab: par virement*) to transfer e (*Jur*) [*+ propriété, droit*] to transfer, convey (*SPÉC*) f (*Psych*) to transfer (**sur** onto)

transfert [tʀãsfɛʀ] NM a [*fonctionnaire, assemblée, bureau, prisonnier, joueur*] transfer; **demander son ~ dans une filiale** to ask to be transferred to *ou* for a transfer to a subsidiary company; **il est décédé pendant son ~ à l'hôpital** he died while he was being taken to hospital; (*Écon*) **~ de technologie** transfer of technology, technology transfer; (*Méd*) **~ d'embryon** embryo transfer b (*Ordin, Télec*) transfer; **~ (électronique) de données** (electronic) data transfer; **~ d'appel** call forwarding c [*dépouille mortelle, reliques*] transfer, translation (*littér*) d (*Fin, Comptab*) transfer; **~ de fonds** transfer of funds; **tranferts sociaux** welfare transfers e (*Jur*) [*propriété, droit*] transfer, conveyance f (= *décalcomanie*) transfer (*Brit*), decal (*US*) g (*Psych*) transference; **faire un ~ sur qn** to transfer onto sb

transfiguration [tʀãsfigyʀasjɔ̃] NF transfiguration; (*Rel*) **la Transfiguration** the Transfiguration

transfigurer [tʀãsfigyʀe] ▶ conjug 1 ◀ VT (= *transformer*) to transform, transfigure (*frm*); (*Rel*) to transfigure

transfo* [tʀãsfo] NM ABRÉV = **transformateur**

transformable [tʀãsfɔʀmabl] ADJ [*structure*] convertible; [*aspect*] transformable; (*Rugby*) [*essai*] convertible

transformateur, -trice [tʀãsfɔʀmatœʀ, tʀis] 1 ADJ [*processus*] transformation (*épith*); [*action*] transforming (*épith*); **pouvoir ~** power to transform 2 NM transformer

transformation [tʀãsfɔʀmasjɔ̃] NF a (= *modification*) [*personne, caractère, pays*] change, alteration; (*radicale*) transformation; [*vêtement*] alteration; (*Bot, Zool*) [*larve, embryon*] transformation; (*Chim, Phys*) [*énergie, matière*] conversion; **travaux de ◊ ~s** alterations; **subir des ~s** (*gén*) to be changed, undergo changes; (*plus radical*) to be transformed; (*Chim, Phys*) to be converted; **opérer des ~s sur qch** to change sth; (*plus radical*) to transform sth; **depuis son mariage, nous assistons chez lui à une véritable ~** since he married we've seen a real transformation in him *ou* a complete change come over him → **industrie** b (*Rugby*) conversion; **il a réussi la ~** he converted the try c (*Géom, Math, Ling*) transformation

transformationnel, -elle [tʀãsfɔʀmasjɔnɛl] ADJ transformational

transformer [tʀãsfɔʀme] ▶ conjug 1 ◀ 1 VT a (= *modifier*) [*+ personne, caractère, pays*] to change, alter; (= *changer radicalement, améliorer*) to transform; [*+ matière première*] to convert; [*+ vêtement*] to alter, remake; **on a transformé toute la maison** we've made massive alterations to the house, we've transformed the house; **on a mis du papier peint et la pièce en a été transformée** we put up wallpaper and it has completely altered the look of the room *ou* it has transformed the room; **le bonheur/son mariage l'a transformé** happiness/being married has transformed him *ou* made a new man of him; **rêver de ~ la société/les hommes** to dream of transforming society/mankind; **depuis qu'il va à l'école, il est transformé** he's been a different child since he started school b (= *convertir*) **~ qn/qch en** to turn sb/sth into; **~ la houille en énergie** to convert coal into energy; **~ du plomb en or** to turn *ou* change *ou* transmute lead into gold; **on a transformé la grange en atelier** the barn has been converted *ou* turned *ou* made into a studio; **elle a transformé leur maison en palais** she has transformed their house into a palace [c] (*Rugby*) [+ *essai*] to convert; (*fig*) **maintenant il faut ~ l'essai** now they (*ou we etc*) must consolidate their (*ou our etc*) gains *ou* ram their (*ou our etc*) advantage home [d] (*Géom, Math, Ling*) to transform

[2] **se transformer** VPR [a] (= *changer, évoluer*) [*personne, pays*] to change, alter; **la manifestation risque de se ~ en émeute** the demonstration could well turn into a riot [b] (= *se métamorphoser*: *gén*) to be transformed (**en** into); [*énergie, matière*] to be converted (**en** into); **la chenille se transforme en papillon** the caterpillar turns into a butterfly; **la ville s'est étonnamment transformée en deux ans** the town has been transformed over the last two years *ou* has undergone amazing changes in two years; **il s'est transformé depuis qu'il a ce poste** there's been a real transformation *ou* change in him *ou* a real change has come over him since he has had this job

transformisme [trɑ̃sfɔrmism] NM transformism

transformiste [trɑ̃sfɔrmist] [1] ADJ, NMF (= *évolutionniste*) transformist [2] NM (= *artiste qui se change très rapidement*) quick-change artist; (= *travesti*) drag artist

transfrontalier, -ière [trɑ̃sfrɔ̃talje, jɛr] ADJ cross-border

transfuge [trɑ̃sfyʒ] NMF (*Mil, Pol*) renegade

transfusé, e [trɑ̃sfyze] (*ptp de* **transfuser**) ADJ [*produit*] transfused; **personne ~e** person who has had a blood transfusion

transfuser [trɑ̃sfyze] ▶conjug 1◀ VT [+ *sang, liquide*] to transfuse; [+ *malade*] to give a blood transfusion to; (*fig, littér*) to transfuse (*littér*) (**à** into), instil (**à** into), impart (**à** to)

transfuseur [trɑ̃sfyzœr] NM transfuser

transfusion [trɑ̃sfyzjɔ̃] NF ~ (**sanguine**) (blood) transfusion; **faire une ~ à qn** to give sb a blood transfusion; **centre de ~ sanguine** blood transfusion centre

transfusionnel, -elle [trɑ̃sfyzjɔnɛl] ADJ [*système*] blood transfusion (*épith*); **il a été contaminé par voie transfusionnelle** he contracted the disease through a contaminated blood transfusion

transgénique [trɑ̃sʒenik] ADJ transgenic

transgresser [trɑ̃sgrese] ▶conjug 1◀ VT [+ *règle, code*] to infringe, contravene; [+ *interdit*] to defy; [+ *tabou*] to break; [+ *ordre*] to disobey, go against, contravene; **~ la loi** to break the law

transgresseur [trɑ̃sgresœr] NM (*littér*) transgressor (*littér*)

transgression [trɑ̃sgresjɔ̃] NF [*règle, code*] infringement, contravention; [*interdit*] defiance; [*ordre*] disobedience, contravention; [*tabou, loi*] breaking; **~ marine** encroachment of the sea

transhumance [trɑ̃zymɑ̃s] NF transhumance

transhumant, e [trɑ̃zymɑ̃, ɑ̃t] ADJ transhumant

transhumer [trɑ̃zyme] ▶conjug 1◀ VTI to move to summer pastures

transi, e [trɑ̃zi] (*ptp de* **transir**) ADJ **être ~ (de froid)** to be numb with cold *ou* chilled to the bone *ou* frozen to the marrow, be perished (*Brit*); **être ~ de peur** to be paralyzed by fear, be transfixed *ou* numb with fear → **amoureux**

transiger [trɑ̃ziʒe] ▶conjug 3◀ VI [a] (*dans un différend*) to compromise, come to terms *ou* an agreement [b] (*fig*) **~ avec sa conscience** to come to terms *ou* to a compromise with one's conscience, make a deal with one's conscience; **~ avec le devoir** to make a compromise with duty; **ne pas ~ sur l'honneur/le devoir** to make no compromise in matters of honour/of duty; **je me refuse à**

~ sur ce point I refuse to compromise on this point, I am adamant on this point

transir [trɑ̃zir] ▶conjug 2◀ VT (*littér*) [*froid*] to chill to the bone, numb, freeze to the marrow; [*peur*] to paralyze, transfix, numb

transistor [trɑ̃zistɔr] NM (= *élément, poste de radio*) transistor; **~ à effet de champ** field-effect transistor, FET

transistorisation [trɑ̃zistɔrizasjɔ̃] NF transistorization

transistoriser [trɑ̃zistɔrize] ▶conjug 1◀ VT to transistorize; **transistorisé** transistorized

transit [trɑ̃zit] NM transit; **en ~** [*marchandises, voyageurs*] in transit; **de ~** [*document, port, zone*] transit (*épith*); **le ~ intestinal** digestion, intestinal transit (*SPÉC*); **les fibres alimentaires favorisent le ~ intestinal** high-fibre foods relieve constipation *ou* facilitate regular bowel movements

transitaire [trɑ̃zitɛr] [1] ADJ [*pays*] of transit; [*commerce*] which is done in transit [2] NMF forwarding *ou* freight agent; **~s en douane** customs clearance agents

transiter [trɑ̃zite] ▶conjug 1◀ [1] VT [+ *marchandises*] to pass *ou* convey in transit [2] VI to pass in transit (**par** through)

transitif, -ive [trɑ̃zitif, iv] ADJ (*Ling, Math, Philo*) transitive

transition [trɑ̃zisjɔ̃] NF (*gén, Art, Ciné, Mus, Sci*) transition (**vers** to, towards, **entre** between); **période/gouvernement de ~** transitional *ou* transition period/government; **mesure de ~** transitional measure *ou* step; **sans ~, il enchaîna avec la météo** he moved straight onto the weather forecast; **une tribu passée sans ~ de l'âge de fer au vingtième siècle** a tribe who've gone straight from the Iron Age into the twentieth century; **l'auteur passait sans ~ du tragique au comique** the writer switched abruptly from tragedy to comedy

transitionnel, -elle [trɑ̃zisjɔnɛl] ADJ transitional

transitivement [trɑ̃zitivmɑ̃] ADV transitively

transitivité [trɑ̃zitivite] NF (*Ling, Philo*) transitivity

transitoire [trɑ̃zitwar] ADJ [a] (= *fugitif*) transitory, transient [b] (= *provisoire*) [*régime, mesures*] transitional, provisional; [*fonction*] interim (*épith*), provisional; **à titre ~** provisionally

transitoirement [trɑ̃zitwarmɑ̃] ADV [a] (= *de manière fugitive*) transitorily, transiently [b] (= *provisoirement*) provisionally

Transjordanie [trɑ̃sʒɔrdani] NF (*Hist*) Transjordan

translation [trɑ̃slasjɔ̃] NF [a] (*Admin*) [*tribunal, évêque*] translation (*frm*), transfer; (*Jur*) [*droit, propriété*] transfer, conveyance; (*littér*) [*dépouille, cendres*] translation (*littér*); (*Rel*) [*fête*] transfer, translation (*frm*) [b] (*Géom, Sci*) translation; **mouvement de ~** translatory movement; **la ~ de la Terre autour du soleil** the rotation *ou* the orbit of the Earth around the Sun

translit(t)ération [trɑ̃sliterasjɔ̃] NF transliteration

translit(t)érer [trɑ̃slitere] ▶conjug 6◀ VT to transliterate

translocation [trɑ̃slɔkasjɔ̃] NF (*Bio*) translocation

translucide [trɑ̃slysid] ADJ translucent

translucidité [trɑ̃slysidite] NF translucence, translucency

transmanche [trɑ̃smɑ̃ʃ] ADJ INV [*liaison, trafic*] cross-Channel (*épith*)

transmetteur [trɑ̃smetœr] NM (*Téléc, Bio*) transmitter; (*Naut*) **~ d'ordres** speaking tube

▼ **transmettre** [trɑ̃smetr] ▶conjug 56◀ VT [a] (= *léguer*) [+ *biens, secret, autorité*] to hand down, pass on; [+ *qualité, recette*] to pass on; **sa mère**

lui avait transmis le goût de la nature his mother had passed her love of nature on to him; **c'est une recette qui se transmet de mère en fille** it's a recipe that's passed down from mother to daughter; **un savoir-faire que l'on se transmet de génération en génération** knowledge that is passed down from generation to generation [b] (= *transférer*) [+ *autorité, pouvoir*] to pass on, hand over, transmit (*frm*) [c] (= *communiquer*) [+ *message, ordre, renseignement*] to pass on; (= *faire parvenir*) [+ *lettre, colis*] to send on, forward; **ils se sont transmis tous les renseignements nécessaires** they exchanged all the necessary information; **veuillez ~ mes amitiés à Paul** kindly give *ou* convey my best wishes to Paul; **veuillez ~ mon meilleur souvenir à Paul** kindly give my regards to *ou* remember me to Paul; **d'accord, je transmettrai*** OK, I'll pass on the message [d] (*Téléc*) [+ *signal*] to transmit, send; (*Radio, TV*) [+ *émission, discours*] to broadcast; **~ sur ondes courtes** (*Téléc*) to transmit on short wave; (*Radio, TV*) to broadcast on short wave [e] (*Sport*) [+ *ballon*] to pass; [+ *flambeau*] to hand over, pass on [f] (*Sci*) [+ *énergie, impulsion*] to transmit [g] (*Méd*) [+ *maladie*] to pass on, transmit (**à** to); [+ *microbe*] to transmit (**à** to); **cette maladie se transmet par contact** the disease is passed on *ou* transmitted by contact; **une maladie qui se transmet sexuellement** a sexually transmitted disease, a disease transmitted by sexual contact; **il risque de ~ son rhume aux autres** he may pass on his cold to the others

transmigration [trɑ̃smigrasjɔ̃] NF transmigration

transmigrer [trɑ̃smigre] ▶conjug 1◀ VI to transmigrate

transmissibilité [trɑ̃smisibilite] NF transmissibility

transmissible [trɑ̃smisibl] ADJ [a] (*Jur*) [*patrimoine, droit, caractère*] transmissible, transmittable; **ce document est ~ par fax** this document can be sent by fax [b] (*Méd*) [*maladie*] transmittable; **virus ~ par voie sanguine** virus that can be transmitted by the blood → **maladie**

transmission [trɑ̃smisjɔ̃] NF [a] (= *legs*) [*biens, secret, tradition*] handing down, passing on; [*qualité, recette*] passing on; **grâce à la ~ de ce savoir de génération en génération** because this knowledge has been passed down from generation to generation [b] (= *transfert*) [*autorité, pouvoir*] passing on, handing over, transmission; (*Pol*) **~ des pouvoirs** handing over *ou* transfer of power [c] (= *communication*) [*message, ordre, renseignement*] passing on; (= *remise*) [*lettre, colis*] sending on, forwarding; **la ~ du savoir** transmission of knowledge; (*Ordin*) **~ des données** data transmission; **~ de pensées** thought transmission, telepathy; (*hum*) **c'est de la ~ de pensée !** you (*ou he etc*) must be telepathic! [d] (*Téléc*) [*signal*] transmission; (*Radio, TV*) [*émission, discours*] broadcasting; (*Mil* = *service*) **les ~s** ≈ the Signals (corps) [e] (*Sport*) [*ballon*] passing [f] (*Sci*) [*énergie, impulsion*] transmission; (*Aut, Tech*) **les organes de ~** ◊ **la ~** the parts of the transmission system, the transmission; (*Aut*) **~ automatique** automatic transmission → **arbre, courroie** [g] (*Méd*) [*maladie*] passing on, transmission; [*microbe*] passing on; **le mode de ~ du virus** the mode of transmission of the virus

transmuer [trɑ̃smɥe] ▶conjug 1◀ VT (*Chim, littér*) to transmute

transmutabilité [trɑ̃smytabilite] NF transmutability

transmutation [trɑ̃smytasjɔ̃] NF (*Chim, Phys, littér*) transmutation

➤ GRAMMAIRE ACTIVE: **transmettre** 48.2, 49, 50.1

transmuter [trɑ̃smyte] ▶conjug 1◀ VT = transmuer

transnational, e (*mpl* **-aux**) [trɑ̃snasjɔnal, o] ADJ transnational

transocéanique [trɑ̃zɔseanik] ADJ transoceanic

Transpac® [trɑ̃spak] NM packet switch network, ≈ PSS (*Brit*)

transparaître [trɑ̃sparɛtr] ▶conjug 57◀ VI to show (through); **laisser ~ un sentiment** to let an emotion show (through), betray an emotion; **il n'a rien laissé ~ de ses intentions** he gave no sign of what his intentions were

transparence [trɑ̃sparɑ̃s] NF a [*verre, porcelaine, papier, tissu*] transparency; [*eau, ciel*] transparency, limpidity; [*regard, yeux*] limpidity, clearness; [*teint, peau*] transparency, translucency; **regarder qch par ~** to look at sth against the light; **voir ~** to see sth showing through; **éclairé par ~** with the light shining through b [*allusion, sentiment, intentions, texte, âme, personne*] transparency; [*négociations, comptes*] openness; **réclamer la ~ du financement des partis politiques** to call for openness in the financing of political parties; **société dotée de la ~ fiscale** = partnership; **adopter une politique de ~** to adopt a policy of openness; **~ financière** financial accountability c (*Ciné*) back projection

transparent, e [trɑ̃sparɑ̃, ɑ̃t] 1 ADJ a (= translucide) [*verre, porcelaine*] transparent; [*papier, tissu*] transparent, see-through; [*teint, peau*] transparent, translucent b (= limpide) [*eau, ciel*] transparent, limpid; [*regard, yeux*] limpid, clear c (= clair, sans secret) [*allusion, sentiment, intentions*] transparent, evident; [*négociations, comptes*] open; [*âme, personne*] transparent; **nous sommes pour une gestion ~e** we favour complete openness where management is concerned; (*Écon*) **société ~e** ≈ partnership 2 NM a (= écran) transparent screen; (*pour rétroprojecteur*) b (*Archit*) openwork motif c (= feuille réglée) ruled sheet (*placed under writing paper*)

transpercer [trɑ̃spɛrse] ▶conjug 3◀ VT a (*gén*) to pierce; (*d'un coup d'épée*) to run through, transfix; (*d'un coup de couteau*) to stab; [*épée, lame*] to pierce; [*balle*] to go through; (*fig*) **transpercé de douleur** pierced by sorrow; **~ qn du regard** to give sb a piercing look b [*froid, pluie*] to go through, pierce; **malgré nos chandails, le froid nous transperçait** despite our sweaters, the cold was going *ou* cutting straight through us; **la pluie avait finalement transpercé ma pèlerine/la toile de tente** the rain had finally come through *ou* penetrated my cape/the tent canvas

transpiration [trɑ̃spirasjɔ̃] NF (= processus) perspiration, perspiring; (*Bot*) transpiration; (= sueur) perspiration, sweat; **être en ~** to be perspiring *ou* sweating *ou* in a sweat

transpirer [trɑ̃spire] ▶conjug 1◀ VI a (*lit*) to perspire, sweat; (*Bot*) to transpire; * **il transpire des mains/pieds** his hands/feet perspire *ou* sweat, he has sweaty hands/feet; **~ à grosses gouttes** to be running *ou* streaming with sweat; **~ sur un devoir*** to sweat over an exercise* b (*fig*) [*secret, projet, détails*] to come to light, leak out, transpire; **rien n'a transpiré** nothing transpired (**de** from)

transplant [trɑ̃splɑ̃] NM (*Bio*) transplant

transplantable [trɑ̃splɑ̃tabl] ADJ transplantable

transplantation [trɑ̃splɑ̃tasjɔ̃] NF [*arbre, peuple, traditions*] transplantation, transplanting; (*Méd* = *technique*) transplantation; (= intervention) transplant; **~ cardiaque/du rein** heart/kidney transplant

transplanté, e [trɑ̃splɑ̃te] (*ptp de* **transplanter**) NM,F (*Méd*) (*gén*) receiver of a transplant; (= patient à l'hôpital) transplant patient; **les ~s**

du cœur people who have received heart transplants

transplanter [trɑ̃splɑ̃te] ▶conjug 1◀ VT (*Bot, Méd, fig*) to transplant; **se ~ dans un pays lointain** to uproot o.s. and move to a distant country, resettle in a distant country

transpolaire [trɑ̃spɔlɛr] ADJ transpolar

transport [trɑ̃spɔr] 1 NM a (à la main, à dos) carrying; (avec un véhicule) [*marchandises, passagers*] transport, transportation (*surtout US*); **~ de voyageurs** transport of passengers; **un car se chargera du ~ des bagages** the luggage will be taken *ou* transported by coach; **pour faciliter le ~ des blessés** to facilitate the transport of the injured, enable the injured to be moved more easily; (*Mil*) (= action) troop transportation; (= navire, train) troop transport; **~ de fonds** transfer of funds; **endommagé pendant le ~** damaged in transit; **mode de ~** means *ou* mode of transport; **matériel/frais de ~** transportation *ou* transport equipment/costs; **~ maritime** *ou* **par mer** shipping, sea transport; **~ maritime à la demande** tramping; **~ en ambulance** ambulance transport; **~ ferroviaire** rail transport, transport by rail; **~ aérien** *ou* **par air** *ou* **par avion** air transport; **~(s) maritime(s)** sea transport; **~(s) routier(s)** road haulage *ou* transport; **~ par hélicoptère** helicopter transport; **entreprise de ~(s)** haulage company, trucking company (*US*) **~ avion, moyen**
b (*Tech*) [*énergie, son*] carrying
c (= transfert) [*traditions, conflit*] carrying, bringing; [*thème, idée*] carrying over, transposition
d (*littér* = *élan*) transport; (avec) **des ~s de joie/d'enthousiasme** (with) transports of delight/of enthusiasm; **~ de colère** fit of rage *ou* anger; **embrasser qn avec ~** to embrace sb enthusiastically; **~s amoureux** amorous transports
2 **transports** NMPL transport, transportation (*surtout US*); **les ~s publics** *ou* **en commun** public transport *ou* transportation (*US*); **prendre les ~s en commun** to use public transport; **elle passe trois heures par jour dans les ~s en commun pour aller travailler** she spends three hours a day commuting to work; **~s urbains** city *ou* urban transport; **~s fluviaux** transport by inland waterway; **mal des ~s** travel-sickness (*Brit*), motion sickness (*US*); **médicament contre le mal des ~s** travel sickness drug (*Brit*), anti-motion-sickness drug (*US*)
3 COMP ▶ **transport au cerveau**† seizure, stroke ▶ **transport de justice**, **transport sur les lieux** (*Jur*) visit by public prosecutor's office to the scene of a crime

transportable [trɑ̃spɔrtabl] ADJ [*marchandise*] transportable; [*blessé, malade*] fit to be moved (*attrib*)

transportation [trɑ̃spɔrtasjɔ̃] NF [*condamnés*] transportation

transporter [trɑ̃spɔrte] ▶conjug 1◀ 1 VT a (à la main, à dos) to carry; (avec un véhicule) [*+ marchandises, voyageurs*] to transport, carry; (*Tech*) [*+ énergie, son*] to carry; **le train transportait les écoliers/touristes** the train was carrying schoolchildren/tourists, the train had schoolchildren/tourists on board; **le train a transporté les soldats/le matériel au camp de base** the train took *ou* transported the soldiers/the equipment to base camp; **on a transporté le blessé à l'hôpital** the injured man was taken to hospital; **on l'a transporté d'urgence à l'hôpital** he was rushed to hospital; **~ qch par mer** to ship sth, transport sth by sea; **~ des marchandises par terre/train/avion** to transport goods by land/train/plane; **ils ont dû ~ tout le matériel à bras** they had to move all the equipment by hand, they had to carry all the equipment; **le sable/vin est transporté par péniche** the sand/wine is transported by barge; **elle transportait une**

forte somme d'argent she was carrying a large sum of money (on her); **ce roman nous transporte dans un autre monde/siècle** this novel transports us into another world/century; **on se retrouve transporté au seizième siècle** we find ourselves transported back to the sixteenth century
b (= transférer) [*+ traditions, conflit*] to carry, bring; [*+ thème, idée*] to carry over, transpose; **~ la guerre/la maladie dans un autre pays** to spread war/disease into another country; **~ un fait divers à l'écran** to bring a news item to the screen; **dans sa traduction, il transporte la scène à Moscou** in his translation, he shifts the scene to Moscow
c (*littér* = *exalter*) to carry away, send into raptures; **~ qn de joie** to send sb into transports of delight *ou* into raptures; **être** *ou* **se sentir transporté de joie/d'admiration** to be beside o.s. with joy/with admiration; **transporté de fureur** beside o.s. with fury; **cette musique m'a transporté** the music carried me away; **se laisser ~ par la musique** to let o.s. be carried away by the music
2 **se transporter** VPR (= se déplacer) to go, betake o.s. (*frm*), repair (*frm*); (*Jur*) **le parquet s'est transporté sur les lieux** the public prosecutor's office visited the scene of the crime; **se ~ quelque part par la pensée** to let one's imagination carry one away somewhere

transporteur, -euse [trɑ̃spɔrtœr, øz] 1 ADJ **navire ~ de marchandises en vrac** bulk carrier; **(navires) ~s de pétrole/gaz/produits chimiques** oil/gas/chemical tankers; **bande transporteuse** conveyor belt 2 NM a (= entrepreneur, entreprise) carrier, haulage contractor, haulier (*Brit*); (*Jur*) carrier; **~ aérien** airline company; **~ routier** road haulage contractor, road haulier (*Brit*); **~ maritime** shipping agent *ou* company; **~ de fonds** security company (*transporting money*), ≈ Securicor® (*Tech* = *appareil*) conveyor c (*Chim, Bio*) carrier

transposable [trɑ̃spozabl] ADJ **roman facilement ~ à l'écran** novel that can easily be adapted for the screen *ou* that lends itself to screen adaptation; **ces résultats/idées sont ~s dans d'autres domaines** these results/ideas can be applied to other areas

transposée [trɑ̃spoze] ADJ F, NF (*Math*) (**matrice) ~** transpose

transposer [trɑ̃spoze] ▶conjug 1◀ VTI to transpose; **~ un roman à l'écran** to adapt a novel for the screen; **ils ont transposé l'action dans les années 30** they have transposed the action to the 1930s

transposition [trɑ̃spozisjɔ̃] NF transposition; **la ~ en droit français d'une directive européenne** the adaptation of a European directive to French law; **la ~ d'un roman à l'écran** the adaptation of a novel for the screen

transpyrénéen, -enne [trɑ̃spireneɛ̃, ɛn] ADJ trans-Pyrenean

transrhénan, e [trɑ̃srenɑ̃, an] ADJ trans-rhenane

transsaharien, -ienne [trɑ̃(s)saarjɛ̃, jɛn] ADJ trans-Saharan

transsexualisme [trɑ̃(s)sɛksyalism] NM transsexualism

transsexualité [trɑ̃(s)sɛksyalite] NF transsexuality

transsexuel, -elle [trɑ̃(s)sɛksyel] ADJ, NM,F transsexual

transsibérien, -ienne [trɑ̃(s)siberjɛ̃, jɛn] 1 ADJ trans-Siberian 2 NM **le ~** the Trans-Siberian Railway

transsubstantiation [trɑ̃(s)sypstɑ̃sjasjɔ̃] NF transubstantiation

transsudation [trɑ̃(s)sydasjɔ̃] NF transudation

transsuder [trɑ̃(s)syde] ▶conjug 1◀ VI to transude

Transvaal [trɑ̃sval] NM **le ~** the Transvaal

transvasement [trɑ̃svazmɑ̃] NM decanting

transvaser [trɑ̃svaze] ▶ conjug 1 ◀ VT to decant

transversal, e (*mpl* **-aux**) [trɑ̃sversal, o] ADJ [*coupe, fibre, pièce*] cross (*épith*), transverse (SPÉC); [*chemin*] which runs across *ou* at right angles; [*vallée*] transverse; (*Naut*) [*cloison*] horizontal; **rue ~e** side street; **axe ~ ◊ (route) ~e** cross-country link, cross-country trunk road (*Brit*) *ou* highway (*US*); (*Rail*) [*ligne*] **~e** (*entre deux régions*) cross-country line; (*entre deux villes*) Intercity line; **moteur ~** transverse engine; **thème ~** cross-disciplinary theme; **relations ~es** lateral relations; **l'organisation ~e des entreprises** horizontal management structure in companies → **barre**

transversalement [trɑ̃sversalmɑ̃] ADV across, crosswise, transversely (SPÉC)

transverse [trɑ̃svers] ADJ (*Anat*) transverse

transvestisme [trɑ̃svestism] NM = **travestisme**

transvider [trɑ̃svide] ▶ conjug 1 ◀ VT to transfer to another container

Transylvanie [trɑ̃silvani] NF Transylvania

trapèze [trapez] NM [a] (*Géom*) trapezium (*Brit*), trapezoid (*US*) [b] (*Sport*) trapeze; **~ volant** flying trapeze; **faire du ~** to perform on the trapeze [c] (*Anat*) **(muscle) ~** trapezius (muscle)

trapéziste [trapezist] NMF trapeze artist

trapézoèdre [trapezɔedr] NM (*Minér*) trapezohedron

trapézoïdal, e (*mpl* **-aux**) [trapezɔidal, o] ADJ trapezoid (*épith*)

trapézoïde [trapezɔid] ADJ, NM (os) **~** trapezoid

Trappe [trap] NF (= *monastère*) Trappist monastery; (= *ordre*) Trappist order

trappe [trap] NF [a] (*dans le plancher*) trap door; (*Tech: d'accès, d'évacuation*) hatch; (*Théât*) trap door; (*Aviat: pour parachutistes*) exit door; (*fig*) **mettre qn à la ~** to give sb the push*; **passer à la ~** [*projet*] to be written off*; [*personne*] to be given the push*, be shown the door [b] (= *piège*) trap

trappeur [trapœr] NM trapper, fur trader

trappiste [trapist] NM Trappist (monk)

trapu, e [trapy] ADJ [a] [*personne*] squat, stocky, thickset; [*maison*] squat [b] (*arg Scol* = *calé*) [*élève*] brainy*; [*question, problème*] tough, hard, stiff; **une question ~e** a stinker* of a question, a really tough question, a poser; **il est ~ en latin** he's terrific* at Latin

traque [trak] NF **la ~ (du gibier)** (the) tracking (of game)

traquenard [traknar] NM (= *piège*) trap; (*fig*) [*grammaire, loi*] pitfall, trap; **tomber dans un ~** to fall into a trap

traquer [trake] ▶ conjug 1 ◀ VT [+ *gibier*] to track (down); [+ *fugitif*] to track down, run to earth, hunt down; (*fig, littér*) [+ *abus, injustice*] to hunt down; (= *harceler*) [*journalistes, percepteur*] to hound, pursue; **air/regard de bête traquée** look/gaze of a hunted animal; **c'était maintenant un homme traqué** he was now a hunted man

traquet [trake] NM (= *oiseau*) **~ (pâtre)** stonechat; **~ (motteux)** wheatear

traqueur, -euse [trakœr, øz] NM,F (*Chasse*) tracker

trauma [troma] NM (*Méd, Psych*) trauma

traumatique [tromatik] ADJ traumatic

traumatisant, e [tromatizɑ̃, ɑ̃t] ADJ traumatic

traumatiser [tromatize] ▶ conjug 1 ◀ VT to traumatize

traumatisme [tromatism] NM trauma; **~ crânien** cranial trauma (SPÉC), head injury; **psychologique** (psychological) trauma; **subir un ~** to undergo *ou* suffer a traumatic experience; **provoquer un ~ chez qn** to traumatize sb

traumatologie [tromatɔlɔʒi] NF traumatology; **service de ~** trauma unit

traumatologique [tromatɔlɔʒik] ADJ traumatological

traumatologiste [tromatɔlɔʒist(ə)], **traumatologue** [tromatɔlɔg] NMF trauma specialist, accident and emergency specialist

travail¹ (*pl* **-aux**) [travaj, o] [1] NM [a] (= *labeur*) **le ~** work; **~ intellectuel** brainwork, intellectual *ou* mental work; **~ manuel** manual work *ou* labour (*NonC*); **ce mouvement demande des semaines de ~** it takes weeks of work to perfect this movement; **il est en plein ~** he's right in the middle of something; **son ardeur au ~** his enthusiasm for work; **se mettre au ~** to get down to work; **allez, au ~!** (it's) time to get down to work!; **observer qn au ~** to watch sb at work, watch sb working; **avoir du ~/beaucoup de ~** to have (some) work/a lot of work to do; **j'ai un ~ fou en ce moment*** I'm up to my eyes in work at the moment*, I'm snowed under with work at the moment*; **horaire/vêtements de ~** work schedule/clothes; **conditions/méthodes/groupe/déjeuner de ~** working conditions/methods/group/lunch; **le ~ c'est la santé*** work is good for you; **à ~ égal, salaire égal** equal pay for equal work; **améliorer la communication, c'est tout un ~!** improving communications is quite a task!

[b] (= *tâche*) work (*NonC*), job; (= *ouvrage*) work (*NonC*); **c'est un ~ de spécialiste** (*difficile à faire*) it's a job for a specialist; (*bien fait*) it's the work of a specialist; **c'est le ~ de l'électricien** I'm not touching it — that's the electrician's job; **fais-le tout seul, c'est ton ~** do it yourself, it's your job; **commencer/achever/interrompre un ~** to start/complete/interrupt a piece of work *ou* a job; **ce n'est pas du ~!** (= *c'est mal fait*) that's shoddy work!; (= *ce n'est pas fatigant*) (do you) call that work!; **et voilà le ~!** not bad, eh?; **les travaux de la commission seront publiés** the committee's work *ou* deliberations *ou* findings will be published; **il est l'auteur d'un gros ~ sur le romantisme** he has written a major work on romanticism; **travaux scientifiques/de recherche** scientific/research work; **travaux sur bois** woodwork; **travaux sur métal** metalwork; **les travaux de la ferme** farm work; **les gros travaux ◊ les travaux de force** the heavy work; **travaux de réfection/de réparation/de construction** renovation/repair/building work; **travaux de plomberie** plumbing work; **travaux d'aménagement** alterations, alteration work; **faire faire des travaux dans la maison** to have some work done in the house; **entreprendre de grands travaux d'assainissement/d'irrigation** to undertake large-scale sanitation/irrigation work; **les grands travaux présidentiels/européens** the major projects undertaken by the president/by the European Union; **« pendant les travaux, le magasin restera ouvert »** "business as usual during alterations", "the shop will remain open (as usual) during alterations"; **il y a des travaux (sur la chaussée)** the road is up, there are roadworks in progress; **« attention! travaux! »** "caution! work in progress!"; (*sur la route*) "roadworks (*Brit*) *ou* roadwork (*US*) ahead!" → **inspecteur**

[c] (= *métier, profession*) job, occupation; (= *situation*) work (*NonC*), job, situation; (= *activité rétribuée*) **le ~** work (*NonC*); **avoir un ~ intéressant/lucratif** to have an interesting/a highly paid job; **apprendre un ~** to learn a job; **être sans ~ ◊ ne pas avoir de ~** to be out of work *ou* without a job *ou* unemployed; **chercher/trouver du ~** to look for/find work *ou* a job; **~ à mi-temps/à plein temps** part-time/full-time work; **~ temporaire** temporary job *ou* work (*NonC*); **~ de bureau** office work; **~ d'équipe** *ou* **en équipe** team work; **~ en équipes** shift work; **~ précaire** casual labour; **~ en**

usine factory work; (*Ind*) **cesser le ~** to stop work, down tools; **reprendre le ~** to go back to work

[d] (*Écon: opposé au capital*) labour (*Brit*), labor (*US*); **l'exploitation du ~** the exploitation of labour; **association capital-~** cooperation between workers and management *ou* workers and the bosses*; **les revenus du ~** earned income; **le monde du ~** the world of work

[e] (= *facture*) work (*NonC*); **dentelle d'un ~ très fin** finely-worked lace; **sculpture d'un ~ délicat** finely-wrought sculpture; **c'est un très joli ~** it's a very nice piece of handiwork *ou* craftsmanship *ou* work; **~ soigné** *ou* **d'artiste/d'amateur** quality/amateurish workmanship (*NonC*); **c'est du beau** *ou* **joli ~!** (*iro*) nice work!* (*iro*), well done!* (*iro*)

[f] (= *façonnage*) [*bois, cuir, fer*] working; (*Peinture*) **le ~ de la pâte** working the paste; **le ~ du marbre requiert une grande habileté** working with marble requires great skill

[g] [*machine, organe*] work; **~ musculaire** muscular effort, work of the muscles

[h] (= *effet*) [*gel, érosion, eaux*] work; (= *évolution*) [*bois*] warp, warping; [*vin, cidre*] working; **le ~ de l'imagination/l'inconscient** the workings of the imagination/the unconscious; **le ~ du temps** the work of time

[i] (*Phys*) work; **unité de ~** unit of work

[j] (*Méd = accouchement*) labour (*Brit*), labor (*US*); **femme en ~** woman in labour; **le ~ n'a pas encore commencé** she hasn't gone into labour yet, labour hasn't started yet → **salle**

[2] COMP ▶ **travaux agricoles** agricultural *ou* farm work ▶ **travaux d'aiguille** needlework ▶ **travaux d'approche** (*Mil*) sapping *ou* approach works; (*fig*) initial overtures (**auprès de** to); **tu as fait des travaux d'approche auprès du patron pour ton augmentation?** have you broached the subject of a rise with the boss? ▶ **un travail de bénédictin** (*fig*) a painstaking task ▶ **travail à la chaîne** assembly-line work ▶ **travaux des champs** = **travaux agricoles** ▶ **travaux dirigés** (*Univ*) tutorial (class) (*Brit*), section (of a course) (*US*) ▶ **travail de forçat** (*fig*) hard labour (*fig*); **c'est un ~ de forçat** it's hard labour ▶ **travaux forcés** (*Jur*) hard labour; **être condamné aux travaux forcés** (*lit*) to be sentenced to hard labour; (*fig*) **dans cette entreprise c'est vraiment les travaux forcés** it's real slave labour in this company ▶ **un travail de fourmi** (*fig*) a long, painstaking job ▶ **les travaux d'Hercule** the labours of Hercules ▶ **travaux d'intérêt général** community work carried out by young people, ≈ community service (*Brit*) ▶ **travaux manuels** (*Scol*) handicrafts ▶ **travaux ménagers** housework ▶ **travail au noir** (*gén*) undeclared work; (*en plus d'un autre*) moonlighting ▶ **travaux pratiques** (*Scol, Univ*) (*gén*) practical work; (*en laboratoire*) lab work (*Brit*), lab (*US*) ▶ **travaux préparatoires** [*projet de loi*] preliminary documents ▶ **travaux publics** civil engineering; **ingénieur des travaux publics** civil engineer → **entreprise** ▶ **un travail de Romain** a Herculean task ▶ **travaux d'utilité collective** (paid) community work (*done by the unemployed*), ≈ employment training (*Brit*), ≈ YTS (*Brit*)

travail² (*pl* **travails**) [travaj] NM (= *appareil*) trave

travaillé, e [travaje] (*ptp de* **travailler**) ADJ [a] (= *façonné*) [*bois, cuivre*] worked, wrought [b] (= *fignolé*) [*style, phrases*] polished, studied; [*meuble, ornement*] intricate, finely-worked; (*Tennis*) **une balle très ~e** a ball with a lot of spin [c] (= *tourmenté*) **~ par le remords/la peur/la jalousie** tormented by remorse/fear/jealousy [d] (= *ouvré*) **heures ~es** hours worked; **le nombre de journées non ~es** the number of days not worked

▼ **travailler** [travaje] ▶ conjug 1 ◀ [1] VI [a] (= *faire sa besogne*) to work; **~ dur** to work hard; **~**

➤ GRAMMAIRE ACTIVE: **travailler** 46.2

comme un forçat/une bête de somme to work like a galley slave/a horse *ou* a Trojan; **il aime ~ au jardin** he likes working in the garden; **je vais ~ un peu à la bibliothèque** I'm going to do some work in the library; **faire ~ sa tête** *ou* **sa matière grise** to set one's mind *ou* the grey matter to work; **va ~** (go and) do some work; **fais ~ ta tête!** get your brain working!, use your head!; **faire ~ ses bras** to exercise one's arms; **~ du chapeau*** to be a bit cracked* *ou* nuts* *ou* touched* (*Brit*); **~ pour le roi de Prusse** to receive no reward for one's pains

b (= *exercer un métier*) to work; **~ en usine/à domicile** to work in a factory/at *ou* from home; **~ 39 heures par semaine** to work a 39-hour week; **~ dans les assurances/l'enseignement** to work in insurance/education; **~ aux pièces** to do piecework; **tu pourras te l'offrir quand tu travailleras** you'll be able to buy *ou* afford it once you start work; **dans ce pays on fait ~ les enfants à huit ans** in this country they put children to work at the age of eight *ou* they make children work from the age of eight; **il a commencé à ~ chez Legrand hier** he started work *ou* he went to work at Legrand's yesterday; **sa femme travaille** his wife goes out to work, his wife works; **on finit de ~ à 17 heures** we finish *ou* stop work at 5 o'clock → **temps**[1]

c (= *s'exercer*) [*artiste, acrobate*] to practise, train; [*boxeur*] to have a workout, train; [*musicien*] to practise; [+ *enfant*] **son père le fait ~ tous les soirs** his father makes him work every evening → **filet**

d (= *agir, fonctionner*) [*firme, argent*] to work; **l'industrie travaille pour le pays** industry works for the country; **~ à perte** to work *ou* be working at a loss; **faites ~ votre argent** make your money work for you; **le temps travaille pour/contre eux** time is on their side/against them

e [*métal, bois*] to warp; [*vin, cidre*] to work, ferment; [*pâte*] to work, rise; (*fig*) [*imagination*] to work

2 VT a (= *façonner*) [+ *matière, verre, fer*] to work, shape; **~ la terre** to work *ou* cultivate the land; **~ la pâte** (*Culin*) to knead *ou* work the dough; (*Peinture*) to work the paste

b (= *potasser*) [+ *branche, discipline*] to work at *ou* on; [+ *morceau de musique*] to work on, practise; [+ *rôle, scène*] to work on; (= *fignoler*) [+ *style, phrase*] to polish up, work on; (*Sport*) [+ *mouvement, coup*] to work on; **~ son anglais** to work on one's English; **~ le chant/piano** to practise singing/the piano; **~ son piano/violon** to do one's piano/violin practice; (*Tennis*) **~ une balle** to put some spin on a ball

c (= *agir sur*) [+ *personne*] to work on; **~ l'opinion/les esprits** to work on public opinion/people's minds; **~ qn au corps** (*Boxe*) to punch *ou* pummel sb around the body; (*fig*) to put pressure on sb, pressurize sb

d (= *faire s'exercer*) [+ *taureau, cheval*] to work

e (= *préoccuper*) [*doutes, faits*] to worry; (= *tourmenter*) [*douleur, fièvre*] to torment; **cette idée/ce projet le travaille** this idea/this plan is very much on his mind; **le ventre me travaille** I have pains in my stomach

3 **travailler à** VT INDIR [+ *livre, projet*] to work on; [+ *cause, but*] to work for; (= *s'efforcer d'obtenir*) to work towards; **~ à la perte de qn** to work towards sb's downfall, endeavour to bring about sb's downfall

travailleur, -euse [tʀavajœʀ, øz] 1 ADJ (= *consciencieux*) hard-working, painstaking, diligent (*frm*)

2 NM,F a (*gén*) worker; **un bon/mauvais ~ ◊ une bonne/mauvaise travailleuse** a good/bad worker

b (= *personne consciencieuse*) (hard) worker

3 NM (= *personne exerçant un métier*) worker; **les ~s** the workers, working people; **les revendications des ~s** the claims made by the workers; **le problème des ~s étrangers** the problem of immigrant labour *ou* workers; **~ en situation irrégulière** illegal worker

4 **travailleuse** NF (= *meuble*) worktable

5 COMP ► **travailleur agricole** agricultural *ou* farm worker ► **travailleur clandestin** illegal *ou* clandestine worker ► **travailleur à domicile** homeworker ► **travailleuse familiale** home help ► **travailleur de force** labourer ► **travailleur frontalier** cross-border worker ► **travailleur indépendant** self-employed person, freelance worker ► **travailleur intellectuel** non-manual *ou* intellectual worker ► **travailleur manuel** manual worker ► **travailleur au noir** moonlighter ► **travailleur précaire** casual worker, worker on a casual contract ► **travailleur saisonnier** seasonal worker *ou* labourer ► **travailleur salarié** salaried employee, employee on a permanent contract ► **travailleur social** social worker ► **travailleur temporaire** temporary worker

travaillisme [tʀavajism] NM Labour philosophy, Labour brand of socialism

travailliste [tʀavajist] 1 ADJ Labour 2 NMF Labour Party member; **il est ~** he is Labour, he supports Labour; **les ~s** Labour, the Labour Party

travailloter [tʀavajɔte] ►conjug 1◄ VI (*péj*) to work a little

travée [tʀave] NF a (= *section*) [*mur, voûte, rayon, nef*] bay; [*pont*] span b (*Tech* = *portée*) span c (= *rangée*) [*église, amphithéâtre*] row (of benches); [*théâtre*] row (of seats); **les ~s du fond manifestèrent leur mécontentement** the back rows showed their displeasure

traveller [tʀavlœʀ] NM ABRÉV = **traveller's chèque** *ou* **check**

traveller's chèque, traveller's check [tʀavlœʀ(s)ʃɛk] NM traveller's cheque (*Brit*), traveler's check (*US*)

travelling [tʀavliŋ] NM (*Ciné*) (= *dispositif*) dolly, travelling platform; (= *mouvement*) tracking; **~ avant/arrière/latéral** tracking in/out/sideways; **~ optique** zoom shots; **faire un ~** to track, dolly

travelo* [tʀavlo] NM (= *travesti*) drag queen*

travers[1] [tʀavɛʀ] NM (= *défaut*) failing, fault; **chacun a ses petits ~** everyone has his little failings *ou* faults; **tomber dans le ~ qui consiste à faire ...** to make the mistake of doing ...

travers[2] [tʀavɛʀ] NM a (= *sens diagonal, transversal*) **en ~** across, crosswise; **en ~ de** across; **couper/scier en ~** to cut/saw across; **pose la planche en ~** lay the plank across *ou* crosswise; **un arbre était en ~ de la route** there was a tree lying across the road; **le véhicule dérapa et se mit en ~ (de la route)** the vehicle skidded and stopped sideways on *ou* stopped across the road; **se mettre en ~ (des projets de qn)** to stand in the way (of sb's plans) → **tort**

b (*Naut*: *navire*) **en ~ ◊ par le ~** abeam, on the beam; **vent de ~** wind on the beam; **mettre un navire en ~ ◊ se mettre en ~** to heave to; **s'échouer en ~** to run aground on the beam

c **au ~** through; **au ~ de** through; **la palissade est délabrée: on voit au ~/le vent passe au ~** the fence is falling down and you can see (right) through/the wind comes (right) through; **au ~ de ses mensonges, on devine sa peur** through his lies you can tell he's frightened; (*fig*) **passer au ~** to escape; **le truand est passé au ~** the criminal slipped through the net *ou* escaped; **passer au ~ d'une corvée** to get out of doing a chore; **tout le monde a eu la grippe mais je suis passé au ~** everyone had flu but I managed to avoid *ou* escape it

d **de ~** (= *pas droit*) crooked, askew; (= *à côté*) **répondre de ~** to give a silly answer; **comprendre de ~** to misunderstand; (= *mal*) **aller** *ou* **marcher de ~** to be going wrong; **avoir la bouche/le nez de ~** to have a crooked mouth/nose; [*ivrogne*] **marcher de ~** to stagger *ou* totter along; **planter un clou de ~** to hammer a nail in crooked; **il répond toujours de ~** he never gives a straight *ou* proper answer; [*véhicule*] **se mettre de ~** to stop sideways on; **elle a mis son chapeau de ~** she has put her hat on crooked, her hat is not on straight; **il a l'esprit un peu de ~** he's slightly odd; **il lui a jeté un regard** *ou* **il l'a regardé de ~** he looked askance at him, he gave him a funny look; **il a avalé sa soupe de ~ ◊ sa soupe est passée de ~** his soup has gone down the wrong way; **tout va de ~ chez eux en ce moment** everything is going wrong *ou* nothing is going right for them at the moment; **il prend tout de ~** he takes everything the wrong way *ou* amiss

e **à ~** [+ *vitre, maille, trou, foule*] through; [+ *campagne, bois*] across, through; **voir qn à ~ la vitre** to see sb through the window; **ce n'est pas opaque, on voit à ~** it's not opaque — you can see through it; **le renard est passé à ~ le grillage** the fox went through the fence; **sentir le froid à ~ un manteau** to feel the cold through a coat; **passer à ~ champs/bois** to go through *ou* across fields *ou* across country/through woods; **la couche de glace est mince, tu risques de passer à ~** the ice is thin — you could fall through; **juger qn à ~ son œuvre** to judge sb through his work; **à ~ les siècles** through *ou* across the centuries; **à ~ les divers rapports, on entrevoit la vérité** through the various reports we can get some idea of the truth; (*lit, fig*) **passer à ~ les mailles du filet** to slip through the net

f (*Boucherie*) **~ (de porc)** sparerib of pork

traversable [tʀavɛʀsabl] ADJ which can be crossed, traversable (*frm*); **rivière ~ à gué** fordable river

traverse [tʀavɛʀs] NF a (*Rail*) sleeper (*Brit*), tie (*US*) b (= *pièce, barre transversale*) strut, crosspiece c (= *raccourci*) **chemin de ~ ◊ ~†** road which cuts across, shortcut

traversée [tʀavɛʀse] 1 NF a [*rue, mer, pont*] crossing; [*ville, forêt, tunnel*] going through; **la ~ des Alpes/de l'Atlantique en avion** the crossing of the Alps/of the Atlantic by plane; **la ~ de la ville en voiture peut prendre deux heures** driving through the town can take two hours, it can take two hours to cross the town by car; **faire la ~ d'un fleuve à la nage** to swim across a river; **faire la ~ de Dieppe à Newhaven** to cross from Dieppe to Newhaven

b (*Naut* = *trajet*) crossing c (*Alpinisme*) (= *course*) through-route; (= *passage*) traverse; (*Ski*) **descendre en ~** to traverse 2 COMP ► **traversée du désert** [*politicien, parti, artiste*] time (spent) in the wilderness; **après une ~ du désert de cinq ans, il est revenu au pouvoir** after spending five years in the political wilderness, he returned to power

traverser [tʀavɛʀse] ►conjug 1◄ VT a [*personne, véhicule*] [+ *rue, pont*] to cross; [+ *chaîne de montagnes, mer*] to cross, traverse (*littér*); [+ *ville, forêt, tunnel*] to go through; **~ une rivière à la nage** to swim across a river; **~ une rivière en bac** to take a ferry across a river, cross a river by ferry; **~ (une rivière) à gué** to ford a river, wade across a river; **il traversa le salon à grands pas** he strode across the living room; **avant de ~, assurez-vous que la chaussée est libre** before crossing, make sure that the road is clear

b [*pont, route*] to cross, run across; [*tunnel*] to cross under; [*barre, trait*] to run across; **le fleuve/cette route traverse tout le pays** the river/this road runs *ou* cuts right across the country; **ce tunnel traverse les Alpes** this tunnel crosses under the Alps; **un pont traverse le Rhône en amont de Valence** a bridge crosses *ou* there is a bridge across the Rhone upstream from Valence; **une cicatrice lui tra-**

versait le front he had a scar (right) across his forehead, a scar ran right across his forehead c (= percer) [projectile, infiltration] to go ou come through; ~ qch de part en part to go right through sth; les clous ont traversé la semelle the nails have come through the sole; la pluie a traversé la tente the rain has come through the tent; une balle lui traversa la tête a bullet went through his head; il s'effondra, la cuisse traversée d'une balle he collapsed, shot through the thigh; une douleur lui traversa le poignet a pain shot through his wrist; ça ne m'a jamais traversé l'esprit it never occurred to me ou crossed my mind d (= passer à travers) ~ la foule to make one's way through the crowd e (dans le temps) [+ période] to go ou live through; [+ crise] to pass ou go through, undergo; sa gloire a traversé les siècles his glory travelled down the ages

traversier, -ière [tʀavɛʀsje, jɛʀ] 1 ADJ a [rue] which runs across b (Naut) [navire] cutting across the bows c (Mus) → flûte 2 NM (Can) ferryboat

traversin [tʀavɛʀsɛ̃] NM [lit] bolster

travertin [tʀavɛʀtɛ̃] NM travertin(e)

travesti, e [tʀavɛsti] (ptp de travestir) 1 ADJ déguisé: gén) disguised; [acteur] playing a female role; [rôle] female (played by man) → bal 2 NM a (= acteur) actor playing a female role; (= artiste de cabaret) female impersonator, drag artist; (= homosexuel) transvestite; numéro de ~ drag act b (= déguisement) fancy dress; en ~ in fancy dress

travestir [tʀavɛstiʀ] ▶conjug 2◀ 1 VT a (= déguiser) [+ personne] to dress up; [+ acteur] to cast in a female role; ~ un homme en femme to dress a man up as a woman b [+ vérité, paroles] to misrepresent 2 se travestir VPR (pour un bal) to put on fancy dress; (Théât) to put on a woman's costume; (pour un numéro de cabaret) to put on drag; (Psych) to dress as a woman, cross-dress; se ~ en Arlequin to dress up as Harlequin

travestisme [tʀavɛstism] NM (Psych) transvestism

travestissement [tʀavɛstismɑ̃] NM a (= action) [personne] (gén) dressing-up; (Psych) cross-dressing; [vérité, paroles] travesty, misrepresentation b (= habit) fancy dress (NonC)

traviole* [tʀavjɔl] ◆de traviole* LOC ADV skew-whiff*, crooked; être/mettre de ~ to be/put skew-whiff* ou crooked; il comprend tout de ~ he gets hold of the wrong end of the stick every time*, he gets in a muddle about everything; elle fait tout de ~ she does everything wrong; tout va de ~ en ce moment/dans ce service everything's going wrong these days/in this department

trayeur, -euse [tʀɛjœʀ, øz] 1 NM,F milker 2 trayeuse NF (= machine) milking machine

trébuchant, e [tʀebyʃɑ̃, ɑ̃t] ADJ (= chancelant) [démarche, ivrogne] tottering (épith), staggering (épith); [diction, voix] halting (épith) → espèce

trébucher [tʀebyʃe] ▶conjug 1◀ VI (lit, fig) to stumble; faire ~ qn to trip sb up; ~ sur ou contre [+ racine, pierre] to stumble over, trip against; [+ mot, morceau difficile] to stumble over

trébuchet [tʀebyʃɛ] NM a (= piège) bird-trap b (= balance) assay balance

tréfilage [tʀefilaʒ] NM wiredrawing

tréfiler [tʀefile] ▶conjug 1◀ VT to wiredraw

tréfilerie [tʀefilʀi] NF wireworks

tréfileur [tʀefilœʀ] NM (= ouvrier) wireworker, wiredrawer

tréfileuse [tʀefiløz] NF (= machine) wiredrawing machine

trèfle [tʀɛfl] NM a (Bot) clover; ~ à quatre feuilles four-leaf clover; ~ blanc/rouge white/red clover; ~ cornu trefoil; ~ d'eau bogbean

b (Cartes) clubs; jouer ~ to play a club ou clubs; le 8 de ~ the 8 of clubs c (Aut) (carrefour en) ~ cloverleaf (junction ou intersection) d (Archit) trefoil e (= emblème de l'Irlande) le ~ the shamrock; (Rugby) le Trèfle (irlandais) the Irish team

tréflière [tʀefliljɛʀ] NF field of clover

tréfonds [tʀefɔ̃] NM (littér) le ~ de the inmost depths of; ébranlé jusqu'au ~ deeply ou profoundly shaken, shaken to the core; dans le ou au ~ de mon cœur deep down in my heart; dans le ou au ~ de son âme in the depths of his soul

treillage [tʀɛjaʒ] NM (sur un mur) lattice work, trellis(work); (= clôture) trellis fence; ~ en voûte trellis archway

treillager [tʀɛjaʒe] ▶conjug 3◀ VT [+ mur] to trellis, lattice; [+ fenêtre] to lattice; treillagé de rubans criss-crossed with tape

treille [tʀɛj] NF (= tonnelle) vine arbour (Brit) ou arbor (US); (= vigne) climbing vine → jus

treillis[1] [tʀɛji] NM (en bois) trellis; (en métal) wire-mesh; (Constr) lattice work

treillis[2] [tʀɛji] NM (Tex) canvas; (Mil = tenue de combat) battledress, combat uniform; (= tenue d'exercice) fatigues

treize [tʀɛz] ADJ INV, NM INV thirteen; il m'en a donné ~ à la douzaine he gave me a baker's dozen; vendre des huîtres ~ à la douzaine to sell oysters at thirteen for the price of twelve; le (nombre) ~ porte malheur thirteen is unlucky; pour autres locutions voir six

treizième [tʀɛzjɛm] ADJ, NMF thirteenth; ~ mois (de salaire) (bonus) thirteenth month's salary; pour autres locutions voir sixième

treizièmement [tʀɛzjɛmmɑ̃] ADV in the thirteenth place

trekking [tʀekin] NM (= activité) trekking (NonC); (= randonnée) trek; faire un ~ to go on a trek; faire du ~ to go trekking

tréma [tʀema] NM dieresis; i ~ i dieresis

trémail (pl trémails) [tʀemaj] NM = tramail

tremblant, e [tʀɑ̃blɑ̃, ɑ̃t] 1 ADJ [personne, membre, main] trembling, shaking; [voix] trembling, shaky, quavering, tremulous; [lèvres] trembling; [lumière] trembling, flickering, quivering; il vint me trouver, ~ he came looking for me in fear and trembling; il se présenta ~ devant son chef he appeared trembling ou shaking before his boss; ~ de froid shivering ou trembling with cold; ~ de peur trembling ou shaking ou shivering with fear; ~ de colère quivering with rage 2 tremblante NF (Vét) la ~e (du mouton) scrapie

tremble [tʀɑ̃bl] NM aspen

tremblé, e [tʀɑ̃ble] (ptp de trembler) ADJ a [écriture, dessin] shaky; [voix] trembling, shaky, tremulous, quavering (épith); [note] quavering (épith) b (Typo) (filet) ~ wavy ou waved rule

tremblement [tʀɑ̃bləmɑ̃] 1 NM a [personne] (de froid, de fièvre) shiver, trembling (NonC), shaking (NonC); (de peur, d'indignation, de colère) trembling (NonC), shaking (NonC); (de fatigue) trembling (NonC); un ~ le parcourut a shiver ran through him; il fut saisi d'un ~ convulsif he suddenly started shivering ou trembling violently; j'ai été prise de ~s incontrôlables I was shaking ou trembling uncontrollably b [feuille] trembling (NonC), fluttering (NonC); [main] trembling (NonC), shaking (NonC); [menton] quivering (NonC); [paupières] fluttering (NonC); [lèvres] trembling (NonC) c [lumière, lueur] trembling (NonC), flickering (NonC), quivering (NonC); [flamme] trembling (NonC), flickering (NonC), wavering (NonC); [reflet] shimmering (NonC) d [voix] trembling (NonC), shaking (NonC), quavering (NonC); [son] trembling (NonC), quavering (NonC); avec des ~s dans la voix in a trembling ou quavering ou shaky voice

e [bâtiment, vitres, plancher, terre] shaking (NonC), trembling (NonC) f (loc) et tout le ~* the whole (kit and) caboodle* 2 COMP ► tremblement de terre earthquake; léger ~ de terre earth tremor

trembler [tʀɑ̃ble] ▶conjug 1◀ VI a [personne] (de froid, de fièvre) to shiver, tremble, shake (de with); (de peur, d'indignation, de colère) to tremble, shake (de with); (de fatigue) to tremble (de with); il tremblait de tout son corps ou de tous ses membres he was shaking ou trembling all over; ~ comme une feuille to shake ou tremble like a leaf b [feuille] to tremble, flutter; [main] to tremble, shake; [menton] to quiver; [paupières] to flutter; [lèvres] to tremble c [lumière, lueur] to tremble, flicker, quiver; [flamme] to tremble, flicker, waver; [reflet] to shimmer d [voix] to tremble, shake, quaver; [son] to quaver e [bâtiment, vitres, plancher] to shake, tremble; faire ~ le sol to make the ground tremble, shake the ground; la terre a tremblé the ground shook; la terre a encore tremblé en Arménie there has been another earthquake in Armenia f (= avoir peur) to tremble; ~ pour qn/qch to fear for sb/sth; ~ à la pensée ou à l'idée de qch to tremble at the (very) thought of sth; il fait ~ ses subordonnés he strikes fear (and trembling) into his subordinates, his subordinates live in dread of him; il tremble devant son patron he lives in fear (and trembling) of his boss; il tremble de l'avoir perdu he's terrified that he might have lost it; je tremble qu'elle ne s'en remette pas I'm terrified she might not recover

tremblotant, e [tʀɑ̃blɔtɑ̃, ɑ̃t] ADJ [personne, main] trembling, shaking; [voix] quavering (épith), tremulous; [flamme] trembling (épith), flickering (épith), wavering (épith); [lumière] trembling (épith), quivering (épith), flickering (épith)

tremblote* [tʀɑ̃blɔt] NF avoir la ~ (de froid) to have the shivers*; (de peur) to have the jitters*; [vieillard] to have the shakes*

tremblotement [tʀɑ̃blɔtmɑ̃] NM a [personne, main] trembling (NonC), shaking (NonC) b [voix] quavering (NonC), trembling (NonC); avec un ~ dans sa voix with a tremble in his voice c [lumière, lueur, flamme] flickering (NonC)

trembloter [tʀɑ̃blɔte] ▶conjug 1◀ VI a [personne, mains] to tremble ou shake (slightly) b [voix] to quaver, tremble c [lumière, lueur, flamme] to flicker, waver

trémie [tʀemi] NF a (Tech = entonnoir) [concasseur, broyeur, trieuse] hopper b (= mangeoire) feedbox c (Constr) [cheminée] hearth cavity ou space; [escalier] stair cavity

trémière [tʀemjɛʀ] ADJ F → rose

trémolo [tʀemolo] NM [instrument] tremolo; [voix] quaver, tremor; avec des ~s dans la voix with a quaver ou tremor in one's voice

trémoussement [tʀemusmɑ̃] NM wriggling (NonC), jigging about (Brit) (NonC)

trémousser (se) [tʀemuse] ▶conjug 1◀ VPR to wriggle, jig about (Brit); se trémousser sur sa chaise to wriggle ou jig about (Brit) on one's chair; marcher en se trémoussant to wriggle as one walks

trempage [tʀɑ̃paʒ] NM [linge, graines, semences] soaking; [papier] damping, wetting

trempe [tʀɑ̃p] NF a (Tech) [acier] (= processus) quenching; (= qualité) temper; de bonne ~ well-tempered b [personne, âme] calibre (Brit), caliber (US); un homme de sa ~ a man of his calibre ou of his moral fibre c (Tech = trempage) [papier] damping, wetting; [peaux] soaking d* (= correction) walloping*, hiding*;

(= *gifle*) slap, clout* (Brit); **flanquer une ~ à qn** to slap *ou* clout* (Brit) sb

trempé, e [trɑ̃pe] (*ptp de* **tremper**) ADJ [a] (= *mouillé*) [*vêtement, personne*] soaked, drenched; **~ de sueur** bathed *ou* soaked in *ou* streaming with sweat; **~ jusqu'aux os** *ou* **comme une soupe*** wet through, soaked to the skin; **visage ~ de pleurs** face bathed in tears [b] (Tech) [*acier, verre*] tempered; (fig) **caractère bien ~** sturdy character

tremper [trɑ̃pe] ▸conjug 1◂ [1] VT [a] (= *mouiller*) to soak, drench; **la pluie a trempé sa veste/le tapis** the rain has soaked *ou* drenched his jacket/the carpet; **je me suis fait ~** I got soaked *ou* drenched [b] (= *plonger*) [+ *mouchoir, plume*] to dip (**dans** into, in); [+ *pain, biscuit*] to dip, dunk (**dans** in); **~ sa main dans l'eau** to dip one's hand in the water; **il a trempé ses lèvres** he just took a sip; **il n'aime pas qu'on lui trempe la tête dans l'eau** he doesn't like having his head ducked in the water [c] (Tech) [+ *métal, lame*] to quench → **acier** [d] (*littér* = *aguerrir, fortifier*) [+ *personne, caractère, âme*] to steel, strengthen

[2] VI [a] [*tige de fleur*] to stand in water; [*linge, graines, semences*] to soak; **tes manches trempent dans ton assiette !** your sleeves are trailing in your plate! [b] (**faire**) **~** [+ *linge, graines*] to soak; [+ *aliments*] to soak, steep; [+ *papier*] to damp, wet; [+ *tige de fleur*] to stand in water; **mettre le linge à ~** to soak the washing, put the washing to soak; **faire ~ des légumes secs** to soak pulses [c] (*fig péj* = *participer*) **~ dans** [+ *crime, affaire, complot*] to take part in, have a hand in, be involved in

[3] **se tremper** VPR (= *prendre un bain rapide*) to have a quick dip; (= *se mouiller*) to get (o.s.) soaked *ou* soaking wet, get drenched; **je ne fais que me ~** I'm just going for a quick dip

trempette [trɑ̃pet] NF [a]* (= *baignade*) **faire ~** to have a (quick) dip [b] (Can : Culin) dips

tremplin [trɑ̃plɛ̃] NM [a] [*piscine*] diving-board, springboard; [*gymnase*] springboard; (Ski) ski-jump [b] (fig) springboard; **servir de ~ à qn** to be a springboard for sb

trémulation [tremylasjɔ̃] NF (Méd) tremor

trench-coat (*pl* trench-coats) [trɛ̃ʃkot] NM trench coat

trentaine [trɑ̃tɛn] NF (= *âge, nombre*) about thirty, thirty or so; **il a la ~** he's about thirty, he's thirty-ish; **il approche de la ~** he's coming up to *ou* he's nearly thirty

trente [trɑ̃t] [1] ADJ INV, NM INV thirty; **les années ~** the (nineteen) thirties → **concile, guerre, tour, six** [2] COMP ▸ **trente et un** (lit, Cartes) thirty-one; **être/se mettre sur son ~ et un*** to be wearing/put on one's Sunday best *ou* one's glad rags*, be/get all dressed up to the nines*, be/get dressed to kill* → **glorieux**

trente-et-quarante [trɑ̃tekarɑ̃t] NM INV (Jeux) trente et quarante

trentenaire [trɑ̃t(ə)nɛr] ADJ thirty-year; (**concession**) **~** thirty-year lease; (**personne**) **~** thirty-year-old (person)

trente-six [trɑ̃tsis] [1] ADJ INV (lit) thirty-six; (* = *beaucoup*) umpteen* **il y en a ~ modèles** there are umpteen* models; **il n'y a pas ~ possibilités** there aren't all that many choices; **faire ~ choses en même temps** *ou* **à la fois** (try to) do too many things at once, (try to) do a hundred things at once; **j'ai ~ mille choses à faire** I've a thousand and one things to do; **voir ~ chandelles*** to see stars [2] NM INV thirty-six; **tous les ~ du mois*** once in a blue moon

trente-sixième [trɑ̃tsizjɛm] ADJ thirty-sixth; **être dans le** *ou* **au ~ dessous** to be in the depths of depression

trentième [trɑ̃tjɛm] ADJ, NMF thirtieth; *pour locutions voir* **sixième**

trépan [trepɑ̃] NM (Méd) trephine, trepan; (Tech) trepan

trépanation [trepanasjɔ̃] NF (Méd) trephination, trepanation

trépané, e [trepane] (*ptp de* **trépaner**) [1] NMF (Méd) patient who has undergone trephination *ou* trepanation [2] ADJ **être ~** to have undergone trephination *ou* trepanation

trépaner [trepane] ▸conjug 1◂ VT (Méd) to trephine, trepan

trépas [trepa] NM (littér) demise, death → **vie**

trépassé, e [trepase] (*ptp de* **trépasser**) ADJ (littér) deceased, dead; **les ~s** the departed; (Rel) **le jour** *ou* **la fête des Trépassés** All Souls' (Day)

trépasser [trepase] ▸conjug 1◂ VI (littér) to pass away, depart this life

trépidant, e [trepidɑ̃, ɑ̃t] ADJ [*plancher*] vibrating, quivering; [*machine*] vibrating, throbbing; [*rythme*] pulsating (*épith*), thrilling (*épith*); [*vie*] hectic, busy

trépidation [trepidasjɔ̃] NF [*moteur, navire, train*] vibration; (Méd) trembling; (fig) [*ville*] hustle and bustle

trépider [trepide] ▸conjug 1◂ VI [*plancher*] to vibrate, reverberate; [*machine*] to vibrate, throb

trépied [trepje] NM (gén) tripod; (*dans l'âtre*) trivet

trépignement [trepiɲmɑ̃] NM stamping (of feet) (NonC)

trépigner [trepiɲe] ▸conjug 1◂ VI to stamp one's feet; **d'impatience/d'enthousiasme** to stamp (one's feet) with impatience/with enthusiasm; **~ de colère** to stamp one's feet with rage, be hopping mad*

trépointe [trepwɛ̃t] NF welt

tréponème [treponɛm] NM treponema

très [trɛ] ADV [a] (*avec adj*) very, most; (*devant certains ptp etc*) (very) much, greatly, highly; **~ intelligent/difficile** very *ou* most intelligent/difficult; **il est ~ conscient de ...** he is very much aware of ... *ou* very conscious of ...; **~ admiré** greatly *ou* highly *ou* (very) much admired; **~ industrialisé/automatisé** highly industrialized/automatized; **c'est un garçon ~ travailleur** he's a very hard-working lad, he's a very hard worker; **elle est ~ grande dame** she is very much the great lady *ou* every bit a great lady; **avoir ~ peur/faim** to be very frightened/hungry; **elle a été vraiment ~ aimable** she was really most *ou* very kind; **c'est ~ nécessaire** it's most *ou* absolutely essential; **ils sont ~ amis/~ liés** they are great friends/very close (friends); **je suis ~, ~ content** I'm very, very *ou* terribly, terribly* pleased; **j'ai ~ envie de le rencontrer** I would very much like to meet him, I'm very *ou* most anxious to meet him; **un jeune homme ~ comme il faut** a well brought-up young man, a very respectable young man; **un hebdomadaire ~ lu dans les milieux économiques** a magazine that's widely read *ou* that's read a lot in economic circles; **être ~ à la page*** *ou* **dans le vent*** to be very *ou* terribly with-it*; **je ne suis jamais ~ à mon aise avec lui** I never feel very *ou* particularly *ou* terribly* comfortable with him; **êtes-vous fatigué ? — ~/pas ~** are you tired? — very *ou* terribly*/not very *ou* not terribly* [b] (*avec adv*) very; **~ peu de gens** very few people; **c'est ~ bien écrit/fait** it's very well written/done; **il est ~ en avant/arrière** (*sur le chemin*) he is well *ou* a long way ahead/behind; (*dans une salle*) he is well forward *ou* a long way to the front/well back *ou* a long way back; **~ bien, si vous insistez** all right *ou* very well, if you insist; **~ bien, je vais le lui expliquer** all right *ou* fine* *ou* very good *ou* O.K.*, I'll explain to him; **travailler le samedi ?**

~ peu pour moi ! work on Saturday? not likely!* *ou* not me! → **peu**

trésor [trezɔr] NM [a] (= *richesses enfouies*) treasure (NonC); (Jur: *trouvé*) treasure-trove; (fig = *chose, personne, vertu précieuse*) treasure; **découvrir un ~** to find some treasure *ou* a treasure-trove; **course** *ou* **chasse au/chercheur de ~** treasure hunt/hunter [b] (= *petit musée*) treasure-house, treasury; **le ~ de Notre-Dame** the treasure-house of Notre-Dame [c] (*gén pl* = *richesses*) treasure; **les ~s du Louvre/de l'océan** the treasures *ou* riches of the Louvre/of the ocean; (hum) **je vais chercher dans mes ~s** I'll look through my treasures *ou* precious possessions [d] (= *abondance*) **des ~s de dévouement/de patience** a wealth of devotion/of patience, boundless devotion/patience; **dépenser des ~s d'ingéniosité** to expend boundless ingenuity [e] (= *ouvrage*) treasury [f] (Admin, Fin = *ressources*) [*roi, État*] exchequer, finances; [*organisation secrète*] finances, funds; (= *service*) **le Trésor (public)** the public revenue department, ≈ the Treasury (Brit), ≈ the Treasury Department (US) → **bon²** [g] (*affectif*) **mon (petit) ~** my (little) treasure, my precious; **tu es un ~ de m'avoir acheté ce livre** you're a (real) treasure for buying me this book [h] (Fin) **~ de guerre** war chest

trésorerie [trezɔrri] NF [a] (= *bureaux*) [*association*] accounts department; [*Trésor public*] **Trésorerie (générale** *ou* **principale)** ≈ public revenue office [b] (= *gestion*) accounts; **leur ~ est bien/mal tenue** their accounts are well/badly kept → **moyen** [c] (= *argent disponible*) finances, funds; **difficultés** *ou* **problèmes de ~** cash shortage, cash (flow) problems, shortage of funds; **~ nette** net liquid assets [d] (= *fonction de trésorier*) treasurership

trésorier, -ière [trezɔrje, jɛr] NM,F (gén) [*club, association*] treasurer; (Admin) **~-payeur général** paymaster (for a *département*); (Fin) **~ d'entreprise** company treasurer

tressage [tresaʒ] NM [a] [*cheveux, rubans*] plaiting, braiding (US); [*paille, fil*] plaiting; [*câble, corde, cordon*] twisting [b] [*panier, guirlande*] weaving

tressaillement [tresajmɑ̃] NM [a] (= *frémissement*) (*de plaisir*) thrill, quiver; (*de peur*) shudder; (*de douleur*) wince; **des ~s parcoururent l'animal** the animal twitched [b] (= *sursaut*) start [c] [*plancher, véhicule*] shaking (NonC), vibration

tressaillir [tresajir] ▸conjug 13◂ VI [a] (= *frémir*) (*de plaisir*) to thrill, quiver; (*de peur*) to shudder, shiver; (*de douleur*) to wince; [*muscle, personne* *ou* *animal à l'agonie*] to twitch; **son cœur tressaillait** his heart was fluttering [b] (= *sursauter*) to start, give a start; **faire ~ qn** to startle sb, make sb jump [c] [*plancher, véhicule*] to shake, vibrate

tressautement [tresotmɑ̃] NM (= *sursaut*) start, jump; (= *secousses*) [*voyageurs*] jolting (NonC), tossing (NonC); [*objets*] shaking (NonC)

tressauter [tresote] ▸conjug 1◂ VI [a] (= *sursauter*) to start, jump; **faire ~ qn** to startle sb, make sb jump [b] (= *être secoué*) [*voyageurs*] to be jolted, tossed about; [*objets*] to be shaken about, jump about; **faire ~ les voyageurs** to toss the passengers about; **les tasses tressautent sur le plateau** the cups are shaking *ou* jumping about on the tray

tresse [tres] NF [a] (= *cheveux*) plait, braid (US); **se faire des ~s** to plait (Brit) *ou* braid (US) one's hair [b] (= *cordon*) braid (NonC) [c] (Archit = *motif*) strapwork

tresser [trese] ▸conjug 1◂ VT [a] [+ *cheveux, rubans*] to plait, braid (US); [+ *paille, fil*] to plait; [+ *câble, corde, cordon*] to twist; **chaussu-**

res en cuir tressé lattice-work leather shoes **b** [+ *panier, guirlande*] to weave; (*fig*) **~ des couronnes** *ou* **des lauriers à qn** to praise *ou* laud sb to the skies, sing sb's praises

tréteau (*pl* **tréteaux**) [tʀeto] NM **a** (= *support*) trestle; **table à ~x** trestle table **b** (*Théât fig*) **les ~x** the boards, the stage; **monter sur les ~x** to go on the boards *ou* the stage

treuil [tʀœj] NM winch, windlass

treuiller [tʀœje] ▶ conjug 1 ◀ VT to winch up

trêve [tʀɛv] NF **a** (*Mil, Pol*) truce; (*Sport*) midwinter break; (*Hist*) **~ de Dieu** truce of God; (*hum*) **~ des confiseurs** Christmas *ou* New Year (political) truce **b** (= *répit*) respite, rest; **s'accorder une ~** to allow o.s. a (moment's) respite *ou* a rest; (*littér*) **faire ~ à** [+ *disputes, travaux*] to rest from **c** **~ de** (= *assez de*) **~ de plaisanteries/polémique** enough of this joking/arguing; **~ de plaisanteries, tu veux vraiment te marier avec lui ?** joking apart, do you really want to marry him? **d** **sans ~** (= *sans cesse*) unremittingly, unceasingly, relentlessly

trévise [tʀeviz] NF radicchio lettuce

tri [tʀi] NM **a** (*gén*) sorting out; [*fiches, lettres, dossiers, linge*] sorting; [*personnes*] selection; [*wagons*] shunting, marshalling; (= *calibrage*) grading; (= *tamisage*) sifting; **le ~ sélectif des ordures ménagères** the selective sorting of household waste; **faire le ~ de** (*gén*) to sort out; [+ *lettres, fiches, dossiers*] to sort; [+ *personnes*] to select; [+ *wagons*] to marshal; [+ *déchets*] to sort through; (*en calibrant*) to grade; (*en tamisant*) to sift; **faire le ~ entre les rumeurs et les faits** to sift *ou* separate fact from rumour; **le chômage m'a permis de faire le ~ entre mes vrais et mes faux amis** when I became unemployed I found out who my real friends were; **on a procédé à des ~s successifs pour sélectionner les meilleurs candidats** they used a series of selection procedures to sift out the best candidates **b** (*Poste*) sorting; (*Ordin*) sort, sorting; **postal** sorting of mail; **le (bureau de) ~** the sorting office

tri... [tʀi] PRÉF tri...; **~acétate** triacetate

triacide [tʀiasid] NM triacid

triade [tʀijad] NF triad

triage [tʀijaʒ] NM = **tri** ; →**gare**[1]

trial [tʀijal] NM motocross, scrambling (*Brit*); **faire du ~** to do motocross, go scrambling (*Brit*) → **moto**

triangle [tʀijɑ̃gl] NM (*Géom, Mus*) triangle; **en ~** in a triangle; **~ isocèle/équilatéral/ rectangle/scalène** isosceles/equilateral/rightangled/scalene triangle; **~s semblables/égaux** similar/equal triangles; **~ quelconque** ordinary triangle; **soit un ~ quelconque ABC** let ABC be any triangle; (*Aut*) **~ de signalisation** warning triangle; **le ~ des Bermudes** the Bermuda Triangle; **le Triangle d'or** the Golden Triangle

triangulaire [tʀijɑ̃gylɛʀ] **1** ADJ [*section, voile, prisme*] triangular; [*débat, tournoi*] threecornered; (*Hist*) **commerce** *ou* **trafic ~** triangular slave trade **2** NF (= *élection*) threecornered (election) contest *ou* fight

triangulation [tʀijɑ̃gylasjɔ̃] NF triangulation

trianguler [tʀijɑ̃gyle] ▶ conjug 1 ◀ VT to triangulate

trias [tʀijɑs] NM (= *terrain*) trias; (= *période*) **le ~** the Triassic, the Trias

triasique [tʀijazik] ADJ Triassic

triathlète [tʀi(j)atlɛt] NMF triathlete

triathlon [tʀi(j)atlɔ̃] NM triathlon

triatomique [tʀiatɔmik] ADJ triatomic

tribal, e (*mpl* **-aux**) [tʀibal, o] ADJ tribal

tribalisme [tʀibalism] NM (*littér*) tribalism

tribasique [tʀibazik] ADJ tribasic

tribo-électricité [tʀiboelɛktʀisite] NF triboelectricity

tribo-électrique [tʀiboelɛktʀik] ADJ triboelectric

triboluminescence [tʀibolyminesɑ̃s] NF triboluminescence

tribord [tʀibɔʀ] NM starboard; **à ~** to starboard, on the starboard side; **hauban ~ arrière** aft starboard shroud

tribu [tʀiby] NF (*gén*) tribe; (*fig*) clan; **chef de ~** tribal chief

tribulations [tʀibylasjɔ̃] NFPL (*littér* = *mésaventures*) tribulations, trials, troubles

tribun [tʀibœ̃] NM (*Hist romaine*) tribune; (= *orateur*) powerful orator; (*littér* = *défenseur*) tribune (*littér*)

tribunal (*pl* **-aux**) [tʀibynal, o] **1** NM **a** (*lit*) court; **~ judiciaire/d'exception** judicial/special court; **~ révolutionnaire/militaire** revolutionary/military tribunal; **porter une affaire devant les tribunaux** to bring a case before the courts; **déposer une plainte auprès des tribunaux** to instigate legal proceedings; **comparaître devant un ~** to appear before a court; **traduire qn devant un ~** to bring sb to court *ou* justice; **traduire qn devant un ~ militaire** to court-martial sb; **affaire renvoyée d'un ~ à l'autre** case referred from one court to another **b** (*fig*) **le ~ des hommes** the justice of men; **être jugé par le ~ suprême** *ou* **de Dieu** to appear before the judgment seat of God; **être condamné par le ~ de l'histoire** to be condemned by the judgment of history, be judged and condemned by history; **s'ériger en ~ du goût/des mœurs** to set o.s. up as an arbiter of (good) taste/of morals

2 COMP ▶ **tribunal administratif** *tribunal dealing with internal disputes in the French civil service* ▶ **tribunal arbitral** arbitration court, court of arbitration ▶ **tribunal de commerce** commercial court ▶ **tribunal des conflits** jurisdictional court ▶ **tribunal correctionnel** ≈ magistrates' court (*dealing with criminal matters*) ▶ **tribunal pour enfants** juvenile court ▶ **tribunal de grande instance** ≈ county court ▶ **le Tribunal de l'Inquisition** the Tribunal of the Inquisition ▶ **tribunal d'instance** ≈ magistrates' court (*dealing with civil matters*) ▶ **tribunal pénal international** international criminal court ▶ **tribunal de police** police court ▶ **tribunal de première instance†** = tribunal de grande instance

tribune [tʀibyn] **1** NF **a** (*pour le public*) [*église, assemblée, tribunal*] gallery; [*stade, champ de courses*] (*couverte*) stand; **~ d'honneur** ◊ **~ officielle** VIP stand; **les ~s du public/de la presse** the public/press gallery; **les applaudissements des ~s** applause from the stands; **il avait une ~** he had a seat in the stand; (*Parl*) **~ du public** visitors' gallery **b** (*pour un orateur*) platform, rostrum; **monter à la ~** to mount the platform *ou* rostrum, stand up to speak; (*Parl = parler*) to address the House, take the floor **c** (*fig = débat*) forum; **~ radiophonique** radio forum; **offrir une ~ à la contestation** to offer a forum *ou* platform for protest; **~ libre d'un journal** opinion column in *ou* of a newspaper; **organiser une ~ sur un sujet d'actualité** to organize an open forum *ou* a free discussion on a topical issue; **se présenter à l'élection pour avoir une ~ afin de faire connaître ses vues** to stand for election to give o.s. a platform from which to publicize one's views

2 COMP ▶ **tribune d'orgue** organ loft

tribut [tʀiby] NM (*lit, fig*) tribute; (= *argent*) **payer ~ au vainqueur** to pay tribute to the conqueror; **ils ont payé un lourd ~ à la maladie/guerre** disease/war has cost them dear, disease/war has taken a heavy toll (among them); (*littér*) **payer ~ à la nature** to go the way of all flesh, pay the debt of nature

tributaire [tʀibytɛʀ] ADJ **a** (= *dépendant*) **être ~ de** to be dependent *ou* reliant on **b** (*Géog*) **être ~ de** to be a tributary of, flow into; **rivière ~** tributary **c** (*Hist = qui paie tribut*) tributary; **être ~ de qn** to be a tributary of sb, pay tribute to sb

tric [tʀik] NM = **trick**

tricard [tʀikaʀ] NM (*arg*) (*Crime*) ex-convict prohibited from entering certain French cities; (*fig*) **il est ~ dans le milieu du cyclisme** he's an outcast in the cycling world

tricentenaire [tʀisɑ̃t(ə)nɛʀ] **1** ADJ threehundred-year-old (*épith*) **2** NM tercentenary, tricentennial

tricéphale [tʀisefal] ADJ (*littér*) three-headed

triceps [tʀisɛps] ADJ, NM (**muscle**) **~ triceps** (muscle); **~ brachial/crural** brachial/crural triceps

triche* [tʀiʃ] NF cheating; **c'est de la ~** it's cheating *ou* a cheat

tricher [tʀiʃe] ▶ conjug 1 ◀ VI (*gén*) to cheat; **~ au jeu** to cheat at gambling; **~ sur son âge** to lie about *ou* cheat over one's age; **~ sur le poids/la longueur** to cheat over *ou* on the weight/the length, give short weight/short measure; **~ sur les prix** to cheat over the price, overcharge; **~ en affaires/en amour** to cheat in business/in love; **on a dû ~ un peu : un des murs est en contre-plaqué** we had to cheat a bit — one of the walls is plywood

tricherie [tʀiʃʀi] NF (= *tromperie*) cheating (*NonC*); **gagner par ~** to win by cheating; **c'est une ~** *ou* **de la ~** it's cheating *ou* a cheat; (= *astuce*) **on s'en tire avec une petite ~** we get round the problem by cheating a bit

tricheur, -euse [tʀiʃœʀ, øz] NM,F (*gén*) cheat; (*en affaires*) swindler, trickster, cheat

trichloréthylène [tʀiklɔʀetilɛn] NM trichlorethylene, trichloroethylene

trichomonas [tʀikɔmɔnɑs] NM trichomonad

trichrome [tʀikʀom] ADJ (*Tech*) three-colour (*épith*) (*Brit*), three-color (*épith*) (*US*), trichromatic

trichromie [tʀikʀɔmi] NF (*Tech*) three-colour (*Brit*) *ou* three-color (*US*) process

trick [tʀik] NM (*Bridge*) seventh trick

tricolore [tʀikɔlɔʀ] ADJ (*gén*) three-coloured (*Brit*), three-colored (*US*), tricolour(ed) (*frm, Brit*), tricolor(ed) (*frm, US*); (= *aux couleurs françaises*) red, white and blue; **le drapeau ~** the (French) tricolour; (*fig*) **le chauvinisme ~** French *ou* Gallic chauvinism; (*Sport*) **l'équipe ~*** ◊ **les ~s*** the French team

tricorne [tʀikɔʀn] NM three-cornered hat, tricorn(e)

tricot [tʀiko] NM **a** (= *vêtement*) sweater, jersey, jumper (*Brit*); **~ de corps** vest (*Brit*), undershirt (*US*); **emporte des ~s** take some woollens *ou* woollies* (*Brit*) with you **b** (= *technique*) knitting (*NonC*); (= *ouvrage*) (*gén*) knitting (*NonC*); (*Comm*) knitwear (*NonC*); **faire du ~** to knit, do some knitting; **~ jacquard** Jacquard knitwear; **~ plat** ordinary knitting, knitting on 2 needles; **~ rond** knitting on 4 needles → **point**[2] **c** (= *tissu*) knitted fabric; **en ~** knitted; **vêtements de ~** knitwear

tricotage [tʀikɔtaʒ] NM knitting

tricoter [tʀikɔte] ▶ conjug 1 ◀ **1** VT [+ *vêtement, maille*] to knit; **écharpe tricotée (à la) main** hand-knit(ted) scarf **2** VI **a** (*lit*) to knit; **~ serré/lâche** to be a tight/loose knitter; **~ à la main** to knit by hand; **~ à la machine** to machine-knit → **aiguille, laine, machine b** (* *fig*) [*cycliste*] to pedal fast, twiddle* (*Brit*); [*danseur*] to prance about *ou* jig about like crazy *ou* like a mad thing* (*Brit*); **~ des jambes** [*fugitif*] to run like mad*; [*danseur*] to prance about *ou* jig about madly*; [*bébé*] to kick its legs

tricoteur, -euse [tʀikɔtœʀ, øz] 1 NM,F knitter; **~ de filets** netmaker 2 **tricoteuse** NF (= machine) knitting machine; (= meuble) tricoteuse

trictrac [tʀiktʀak] NM (Hist) (= jeu) backgammon; (= partie) game of backgammon; (= plateau) backgammon board

tricycle [tʀisikl] NM [enfant] tricycle; **faire du ~** to ride a tricycle; **~ à moteur** motorized tricycle

tridactyle [tʀidaktil] ADJ tridactyl, tridactylous

trident [tʀidɑ̃] NM (Myth) trident; (Pêche) trident, fish-spear; (Agr) three-pronged fork

tridimensionnel, -elle [tʀidimɑ̃sjɔnɛl] ADJ three-dimensional

trièdre [tʀi(j)ɛdʀ] 1 ADJ trihedral 2 NM trihedron

triennal, e (mpl **-aux**) [tʀijenal, o] ADJ [prix, foire, élection] triennial, three-yearly; [charge, mandat, plan] three-year (épith); [magistrat, président] elected ou appointed for three years; (Agr) **assolement ~** three-year rotation of crops

trier [tʀije] ▸ conjug 7 ◂ VT a (= classer) (gén) to sort out; [+ lettres, fiches] to sort; [+ wagons] to marshal; [+ fruits] to sort; (en calibrant) to grade b (= sélectionner) [+ grains, visiteurs] to sort out; [+ candidats] to select, pick; [+ lentilles] to pick over; (en tamisant) to sift; (fig) **triés sur le volet** hand-picked; **il raconte un peu n'importe quoi, il faut ~** he talks a lot of nonsense sometimes, you have to decide what to listen to; (hum) **mets ça sur la table, on va ~** say what you want to say and we'll decide

trieur, trieuse [tʀijœʀ, tʀijøz] 1 NM,F personne) sorter; (en calibrant) grader; **~ de minerai/de légumes** ore/vegetable grader 2 NM (= machine) sorter; **~ de grains** grain sorter; **~-calibreur** [fruits] sorter; [œufs] grader, grading machine 3 **trieuse** NF (= machine) sorter; [ordinateur, photocopieur] sorting machine

trifolié, e [tʀifɔlje] ADJ trifoliate, trifoliated

trifouiller* [tʀifuje] ▸ conjug 1 ◂ 1 VT to rummage about in, root about in 2 VI to rummage about, root about; **il trifouillait dans le moteur** he was poking about* in the engine

triglycéride [tʀigliseʀid] NM triglyceride

triglyphe [tʀiglif] NM triglyph

trigo* [tʀigo] NF (ABRÉV = **trigonométrie**) trig*

trigonométrie [tʀigɔnɔmetʀi] NF trigonometry

trigonométrique [tʀigɔnɔmetʀik] ADJ trigonometric(al)

trijumeau (pl **trijumeaux**) [tʀiʒymo] ADJ M, NM (**nerf**) **~** trigeminal ou trifacial nerve

trilatéral, e (mpl **-aux**) [tʀilateʀal, o] ADJ a (Géom) trilateral, three-sided b (Écon) [accords] tripartite; **la (commission) ~e** the Trilateral Commission

trilingue [tʀilɛ̃g] ADJ [dictionnaire, secrétaire] trilingual; **il est ~** he's trilingual, he speaks three languages

trille [tʀij] NM [oiseau, flûte] trill; **faire des ~s** to trill

trillion [tʀiljɔ̃] NM trillion

trilobé, e [tʀilɔbe] ADJ [feuille] trilobate; [ogive] trefoil (épith)

trilogie [tʀilɔʒi] NF trilogy

trimaran [tʀimaʀɑ̃] NM trimaran

trimard†* [tʀimaʀ] NM road; **prendre le ~** to take to ou set out on the road

trimarder†* [tʀimaʀde] ▸ conjug 1 ◂ 1 VI (= vagabonder) to walk the roads, be on the road 2 VT (= transporter) to lug* ou cart* along

trimardeur, -euse†* [tʀimaʀdœʀ, øz] NM,F (= vagabond) tramp, hobo (US)

---

trimbal(l)age* [tʀɛ̃balaʒ], **trimbal(l)ement*** [tʀɛ̃balmɑ̃] NM [bagages, marchandises] carting ou lugging around*

trimbal(l)er* [tʀɛ̃bale] ▸ conjug 1 ◂ 1 VT* [+ bagages, marchandises] to lug* ou cart* around; (péj) [+ personne] to trail along; [+ rhume] to carry around; **qu'est-ce qu'il trimballe !:** he's as dumb ou thick (Brit) as they come:* 2 **se trimbal(l)er:** VPR to trail along; **on a dû se ~ en voiture jusque chez eux** we had to trail over to their place in the car; **il a fallu que je me trimballe jusqu'à la gare avec mes valises** I had to trail all the way to the station with my suitcases

trimer* [tʀime] ▸ conjug 1 ◂ VI to slave away; **faire ~ qn** to keep sb's nose to the grindstone, drive sb hard, keep sb hard at it*

trimestre [tʀimɛstʀ] NM a (= période) (gén, Comm) quarter; (Scol) term; (Scol) **premier/ second/troisième ~** autumn/winter/summer term; **payer par ~** to pay quarterly b (= loyer) quarter, quarter's rent; (= frais de scolarité) term's fees; (= salaire) quarter's income

trimestriel, -elle [tʀimɛstʀijɛl] ADJ [publication] quarterly; [paiement] three-monthly, quarterly; [fonction, charge] three-month (épith), for three months (attrib); (Scol) [bulletin, examen] end-of-term (épith), termly (épith)

trimestriellement [tʀimɛstʀijɛlmɑ̃] ADV [payer] on a quarterly ou three-monthly basis, every quarter, every three months; [publier] quarterly; (Scol) once a term

trimètre [tʀimɛtʀ] NM trimeter

trimoteur [tʀimɔtœʀ] NM three-engined aircraft

tringle [tʀɛ̃gl] NF a (Tech) rod; **~ à rideaux** curtain rod ou rail b (Archit = moulure) tenia

tringler [tʀɛ̃gle] ▸ conjug 1 ◂ VT a (Tech) to mark with a line b (**: sexuellement) to lay:, screw:*; **se faire ~** to get laid:

trinidadien, -ienne [tʀinidjɛ̃, jɛn] 1 ADJ Trinidadian 2 **Trinidadien(ne)** NM,F Trinidadian

trinitaire [tʀinitɛʀ] ADJ, NMF (Rel) Trinitarian

trinité [tʀinite] NF a (= triade) trinity; **la Trinité** (= dogme) the Trinity; (= fête) Trinity Sunday; **à la Trinité** on Trinity Sunday; **la sainte Trinité** the Holy Trinity → **Pâques** b (Géog) **Trinité-et-Tobago** Trinidad and Tobago; **(l'île de) la Trinité** Trinidad

trinitrobenzène [tʀinitʀobɛ̃zɛn] NM trinitrobenzene

trinitrotoluène [tʀinitʀotɔlɥɛn] NM trinitrotoluene, trinitrotoluol

trinôme [tʀinom] NM (Math) trinomial

trinquer [tʀɛ̃ke] ▸ conjug 1 ◂ VI a (= porter un toast) to clink glasses; (= boire) to drink; **~ à qch** to drink to sth; **~ à la santé de qn** to drink sb's health b (* = être puni) to take the rap*; **il a trinqué pour les autres** he took the rap for the others* c (= être endommagé) to be damaged; **c'est l'aile qui a trinqué** the wing got the worst of the damage d (†* = trop boire) to booze* e († = se heurter) to knock ou bump into one another

trinquet [tʀɛ̃kɛ] NM (Naut) foremast

trinquette [tʀɛ̃kɛt] NF (Naut) fore(-topmast) staysail

trio [tʀijo] NM (Mus) trio; (= groupe) threesome, trio; (Courses) **~ urbain** system of betting on three horses in any order

triode [tʀijɔd] NF triode

triolet [tʀijɔlɛ] NM (Mus) triplet; (Hist Littérat) triolet

triomphal, e (mpl **-aux**) [tʀijɔ̃fal, o] ADJ [marche] triumphal; [succès] triumphant, resounding; [entrée, accueil, geste, air] triumphant; (Hist romaine) triumphal; **son élection ~e** his triumphant election

---

triomphalement [tʀijɔ̃falmɑ̃] ADV [accueillir, saluer] in triumph; [annoncer] triumphantly

triomphalisme [tʀijɔ̃falism] NM triumphalism; **ne faisons pas de ~** let's not gloat

triomphaliste [tʀijɔ̃falist] ADJ [discours, slogan] triumphalist; **sur un ton ~** gloatingly, exultantly

triomphant, e [tʀijɔ̃fɑ̃, ɑ̃t] ADJ triumphant; **l'Église ~e** the Church triumphant

triomphateur, -trice [tʀijɔ̃fatœʀ, tʀis] 1 ADJ [parti, nation] triumphant 2 NM,F (= vainqueur) triumphant victor 3 NM (Hist romaine) triumphant general

triomphe [tʀijɔ̃f] NM a (Mil, Pol, Sport, gén) triumph; **cet acquittement représente le ~ de la justice/du bon sens** this acquittal represents the triumph of ou is a triumph for justice/common sense b (Hist romaine, gén = honneurs) triumph; **en ~** in triumph; **porter qn en ~** to bear ou carry sb in triumph, carry sb shoulder-high (in triumph) → **arc** c (= exultation) triumph; **air/cri de ~** air/cry of triumph, triumphant air/cry d (= succès) triumph; **cette pièce/cet artiste a remporté ou fait un ~** this play/this artist has been ou had a triumph success; **ce film/livre est un vrai ~** this film/book is a triumphant success; **j'ai le ~ modeste** I'm not one to boast; **le public lui a fait un ~** the audience gave him an ovation

triompher [tʀijɔ̃fe] ▸ conjug 1 ◂ 1 VI a (militairement) to triumph; (aux élections, en sport, gén) to triumph, win; [cause, raison] to prevail, be triumphant; **faire ~ une cause** to bring ou give victory to a cause; **ses idées ont fini par ~** his ideas eventually prevailed ou won the day → **vaincre** b (= crier victoire) to exult, rejoice c (= exceller) to triumph, excel; [acteur] **~ dans un rôle** to give a triumphant performance in a role 2 **triompher de** VT INDIR [+ ennemi] to triumph over, vanquish; [+ concurrent, rival] to triumph over, overcome; [+ obstacle, difficulté] to triumph over, surmount, overcome; [+ peur, timidité] to conquer, overcome

trip* [tʀip] NM (arg Drogue) trip (arg); **il est en plein ~** ◊ **il fait un ~** he's tripping; (fig) **c'est pas mon ~** it's not my thing* ou my scene*; **elle est dans son ~ végétarien** she's going through a vegetarian phase at the moment

tripaille: [tʀipaj] NF (péj) guts*, innards

triparti, e [tʀipaʀti] ADJ (Bot, Pol = à trois éléments) tripartite; (Pol = à trois partis) three-party (épith)

tripartisme [tʀipaʀtism] NM three-party government

tripartite [tʀipaʀtit] ADJ = **triparti**

tripatouillage* [tʀipatujaʒ] NM (péj) a (= remaniement) [texte] fiddling about* (de with); [comptes, résultats électoraux] fiddling* (de with); [statistiques] fiddling, juggling (de with) b (= opération malhonnête) fiddle*; **~ électoral** election rigging

tripatouiller* [tʀipatuje] ▸ conjug 1 ◂ VT (péj) a (= remanier) [+ texte] to fiddle about with*; [+ comptes, résultats électoraux] to fiddle*, tamper with; [+ statistiques] to fiddle with, massage* b (= tripoter) [+ objet] to fiddle ou mess about with*, toy with; [+ moteur, moto, machine] to tinker with*; [+ personne] to paw*

tripatouilleur, -euse* [tʀipatujœʀ, øz] NM,F (péj) a (= touche-à-tout) fiddler*; (= affairiste) grafter* (péj)

tripe [tʀip] 1 **tripes** NFPL a (Culin) tripe; **~s à la mode de Caen/à la lyonnaise** tripe à la mode de Caen/à la Lyonnaise b (* = intestins) guts*; **rendre ~s et boyaux** to be as sick as a dog*; [comédien] **il joue avec ses ~s** he puts his heart and soul into it; **ça vous prend aux ~s** it gets you right there*; **c'est un spectacle qui vous remue les ~s** it's a gut-wrenching performance 2 NF (* fig = fibre) avoir la ~ républicaine/royaliste to be a republican/a royalist through and through ou to the core

triperie [tRipRi] NF (= *boutique*) tripe shop; (= *commerce*) tripe trade

tripette* [tRipet] NF → **valoir**

triphasé, e [tRifaze] **1** ADJ three-phase **2** NM three-phase current

triphtongue [tRiftɔ̃g] NF triphthong

tripier, -ière [tRipje, jeR] NM,F tripe butcher

triplace [tRiplas] ADJ, NM three-seater

triplan [tRiplɑ̃] NM triplane

triple [tRipl] **1** ADJ **a** (= *à trois éléments ou aspects*) triple; (= *trois fois plus grand*) treble, triple; **le prix est ~ de ce qu'il était** the price is three times ou treble what it was, the price has trebled; **faire qch en ~ exemplaire** to make three copies of sth, do sth in triplicate; **ce livre, je l'ai en ~** I've got three copies of this book; **il faut que l'épaisseur soit ~** three thicknesses are needed, a treble thickness is needed; **avec ~ couture** triple stitched; **avec ~ semelle** with a three-layer sole; **l'inconvénient est ~** ◊ **il y a un ~ inconvénient** there are three disadvantages, the disadvantages are threefold; **naissance ~** birth of triplets; **prendre une ~ dose** to take three times the dose, take a triple dose (**de** of)
b (*intensif*) **c'est un ~ idiot** he's a prize idiot; **~ idiot!** you stupid idiot! ou fool!
2 NM **9 est le ~ de 3** 9 is three times 3; **manger/gagner le ~ (de qn)** to eat/earn three times as much (as sb ou as sb does); **celui-ci pèse le ~ de l'autre** this one weighs three times as much as the other ou is three times ou treble the weight of the other; **c'est le ~ du prix normal/de la distance Paris-Londres** it's three times ou treble the normal price/the distance between Paris and London; **on a mis le ~ de temps à le faire** it took three times as long ou treble the time to do it
3 COMP ► **la Triple Alliance** the Triple Alliance ► **triple saut** triple jump ► **triple saut périlleux** triple somersault → **croche, entente, galop, menton**

triplé, e [tRiple] (*ptp de* **tripler**) **1** NM **a** (*Courses*) [*chevaux*] treble (*betting on three different horses in three different races*) **b** (*Sport*) [*athlète*] triple success; (*Ftbl*) hat trick; **il a réussi un beau ~** [*athlète*] he came first in three events; [*footballeur*] he scored a hat trick; [*équipe*] **réussir le ~ dans le 4 000 mètres** to win the first three places ou come 1st, 2nd and 3rd in the 4,000 metres **2** **triplés** NMPL (= *bébés*) triplets; (= *garçons*) boy triplets **3** **triplées** NFPL (= *bébés*) girl triplets

triplement [tRipləmɑ̃] **1** ADV **a** (= *pour trois raisons*) in three ways **b** (= *à un degré triple*) trebly, three times over **2** NM [*prix, bénéfices, nombre*] trebling, tripling, threefold increase (**de** in); **cette politique s'est traduite par un ~ de l'endettement public** this policy has caused national debt to treble ou triple, this policy has brought about a threefold increase in the national debt

tripler [tRiple] ▸conjug 1◂ **1** VT (*gén*) to treble, triple; (*Scol, Univ*) [+ *classe*] to do for the third time; **il tripla la dose** he made the dose three times as big, he tripled ou trebled the dose; **~ la longueur/l'épaisseur de qch** to treble ou triple the length/the thickness of sth, make sth three times as long/thick; **~ sa mise** to treble one's stake **2** VI to triple, treble, increase threefold; **~ de valeur/de poids/de volume** to treble in value/in weight/in volume; **le chiffre d'affaires a triplé en un an** turnover has tripled ou trebled in a year; **la population de la ville a triplé depuis la guerre** the town's population has tripled ou trebled since the war, there has been a threefold increase in the town's population since the war

triplette [tRiplet] NF (*Boules*) threesome

Triplex® [tRipleks] NM (= *verre*) laminated safety glass, Triplex® (*Brit*)

triplex [tRipleks] NM (= *appartement*) three-storey apartment ou flat (*Brit*), triplex (*US*)

triploïde [tRiploid] ADJ triploid

tripode [tRipɔd] **1** ADJ tripodal; **mât ~** tripod (mast) **2** NM tripod

Tripoli [tRipɔli] N Tripoli

triporteur [tRipɔRtœR] NM delivery tricycle

tripot [tRipo] NM (*péj*) dive*, joint*

tripotage* [tRipɔtaʒ] NM (*péj*) **a** (= *attouchements*) [*personne, partie du corps*] groping*, feeling up* **b** (= *manigances*) jiggery-pokery* (*NonC*); **~s électoraux** election rigging

tripotée* [tRipɔte] NF **a** (= *correction*) belting*, hiding*, thrashing **b** (= *grand nombre*) **une ~ de ...** loads* of ..., lots of ...; **avoir toute une ~ d'enfants** to have a whole string of children*

tripoter* [tRipɔte] ▸conjug 1◂ (*péj*) **1** VT **a** [+ *objet, fruit*] to fiddle with, finger; (*machinalement*) [+ *montre, stylo, bouton*] to fiddle with, play with, toy with; **se ~ le nez/la barbe** to fiddle with one's nose/one's beard; **elle tripotait nerveusement ses bagues** she was playing with ou fiddling with her rings nervously **b** [+ *personne, partie du corps*] to grope*, feel up* **se faire ~** to be groped*, be felt up* **se ~** to play with o.s. **2** VI **a** (= *fouiller*) to root about, rummage about; **~ dans les affaires de qn/dans un tiroir** to root about ou rummage about in sb's things/in a drawer **b** (= *trafiquer*) to be involved in some shady business

tripoteur, -euse* [tRipɔtœR, øz] NM,F (*péj*) (= *affairiste*) shark*, shady dealer*; (= *peloteur*) groper*

tripous, tripoux [tRipu] NMPL *dish (from Auvergne) of sheep's offal and sheep's feet*

triptyque [tRiptik] NM **a** (*Art, Littérat*) triptych **b** (*Admin* = *classement*) triptyque

triquard [tRikaR] NM → **tricard**

trique [tRik] NF cudgel; (*fig*) **il les mène à la ~** he's a real slave driver; **donner des coups de ~ à** to cudgel, thrash; **maigre ou sec comme un coup de ~** as skinny as a rake; **avoir la ~**⁑ to have a hard-on⁑

trirectangle [tRiRektɑ̃gl] ADJ trirectangular

trirème [tRiRem] NF trireme

trisaïeul (*pl* **trisaïeuls**) [tRizajœl, ø] NM great-great-grandfather

trisaïeule [tRizajœl] NF great-great-grandmother

trisannuel, -elle [tRizanɥel] ADJ [*fête, plante*] triennial

trisection [tRiseksjɔ̃] NF (*Géom*) trisection

trisomie [tRizɔmi] NF trisomy; **~ 21** Down's syndrome, trisomy 21

trisomique [tRizɔmik] **1** ADJ trisomic **2** NMF trisome; **~ 21** person with Down's syndrome

trisser (se)⁑ [tRise] ▸conjug 1◂ VPR (= *partir*) to clear off*, skedaddle*

trissyllabe [tRisi(l)lab] ADJ, NM = **trisyllabe**

trissyllabique [tRisi(l)labik] ADJ = **trisyllabique**

Tristan [tRistɑ̃] NM Tristan, Tristram; **~ et Iseu(l)t** Tristan and Isolde

triste [tRist] ADJ **a** (= *malheureux, affligé*) [*personne*] sad, unhappy; [*regard, sourire*] sad, sorrowful; **d'un air ~** sadly, with a sad look; **d'une voix ~** sadly, in a sad ou sorrowful voice; **un enfant à l'air ~** a sad-looking ou an unhappy-looking child; **les animaux en cage ont l'air ~** caged animals look sad ou miserable; **être ~ à l'idée** ou **à la pensée de partir** to be sad at the idea ou thought of leaving; **elle était ~ de voir partir ses enfants** she was sad to see her children go

b (= *sombre, maussade*) [*personne*] sad, gloomy; [*pensée*] sad, depressing; [*couleur, temps, journée*] dreary, depressing, dismal; [*paysage*] bleak, dreary; **il aime les chansons ~s** he likes sad ou melancholy songs; **~ à pleurer** terribly sad; **~ à mourir** [*personne, ambiance, musique*] utterly depressing; **il est ~ comme un bonnet de nuit** he's as miserable as sin; **son père est un homme ~** his father is a rather joyless man; **avoir** ou **faire ~ mine** ou **figure** to cut a sorry figure, look a sorry sight; **faire ~ mine** ou **figure à qn** to give sb a cool reception, greet sb unenthusiastically → **vin**

c (= *attristant, pénible*) [*nouvelle, épreuve, destin*] sad; **depuis ces ~ événements** since these sad events took place; **c'est une ~ nécessité** it's a painful necessity, it's sadly necessary; **c'est la ~ réalité** that's the grim ou sad reality; **il se lamente toujours sur son ~ sort** he's always bewailing his unhappy ou sad fate; **ce furent des mois bien ~s** these were very sad ou unhappy months; **ce pays détient le ~ record de l'alcoolisme** this country holds the unenviable record for having the highest rate of alcoholism; **il aura le ~ privilège d'annoncer ...** he'll have the dubious privilege of announcing ...; **c'est ~ à dire mais ...** it's sad to say but ...; **~ chose que ...** it is sad that ...; **depuis son accident, il est dans un ~ état** (ever) since his accident he has been in a sad ou sorry state; **c'est pas ~!*** (= *c'est amusant*) it's a laugh a minute!*; (= *c'est difficile*) it's really tough!*, it's no joke!*; (= *c'est la pagaille*) it's a real mess! → **abandonner**

d (*avant n*: *péj* = *lamentable*) **quelle ~ époque!** what sad times we live in!; **une ~ réputation/affaire** a sorry reputation/business; **un ~ sire** ou **personnage** an unsavoury ou dreadful individual; **ses ~s résultats à l'examen** his wretched ou deplorable exam results

tristement [tRistəmɑ̃] ADV **a** (= *d'un air triste*) sadly, sorrowfully **b** (= *de façon lugubre*) sadly, gloomily, glumly **c** (*valeur intensive, péjorative*) sadly, regrettably; **~ célèbre** notorious (**pour** for); **c'est ~ vrai** it's sad but true

▼ **tristesse** [tRistes] NF **a** (= *caractère, état*) [*personne, pensée*] sadness, gloominess; [*couleur, temps, journée*] dreariness; [*paysage*] sadness, bleakness, dreariness; **il sourit toujours avec une certaine ~** there is always a certain sadness in his smile; **enclin à la ~** given to melancholy, inclined to be gloomy ou sad **b** (= *chagrin*) sadness (*NonC*), sorrow; **avoir un accès de ~** to be overcome by sadness; **les ~s de la vie** life's sorrows, the sorrows of life; **c'est avec une grande ~ que nous apprenons son décès** it is with deep sadness ou sorrow that we have learned of his death

tristounet, -ette* [tRistune, et] ADJ [*temps, nouvelles*] gloomy, depressing; **il avait l'air ~** he looked a bit down in the mouth* ou down in the dumps*

trisyllabe [tRisi(l)lab] **1** ADJ trisyllabic **2** NM trisyllable

trisyllabique [tRisi(l)labik] ADJ trisyllabic

trithérapie [tRiteRapi] NF triple therapy

tritium [tRitjɔm] NM tritium

Triton [tRitɔ̃] NM (*Myth*) Triton

triton¹ [tRitɔ̃] NM (= *mollusque*) triton; (= *amphibien*) newt

triton² [tRitɔ̃] NM (*Mus*) tritone, augmented fourth

trituration [tRityRasjɔ̃] NF **a** (= *broyage*) grinding up, trituration (*SPÉC*); **bois de ~** wood pulp **b** [*pâte*] pummelling, kneading **c** (= *manipulation*) manipulation

triturer [tRityRe] ▸conjug 1◂ VT **a** (= *broyer*) [+ *sel, médicament, fibres*] to grind up, triturate (*SPÉC*) **b** (= *malaxer*) [+ *pâte*] to pummel, knead; **ce masseur vous triture les chairs** this masseur really pummels you **c** (= *manipuler*) [+ *objet*] to fiddle with; **elle triturait nerveusement son mouchoir** she was twisting her

► GRAMMAIRE ACTIVE: **tristesse** 51.4

handkerchief nervously; **se ~ la cervelle*** ou **les méninges*** to rack ou cudgel one's brains*

triumvir [tʀijɔmviʀ] NM triumvir

triumviral, e (mpl **-aux**) [tʀijɔmviʀal, o] ADJ triumviral

triumvirat [tʀijɔmviʀa] NM triumvirate

trivalence [tʀivalɑ̃s] NF trivalence, trivalency

trivalent, e [tʀivalɑ̃, ɑ̃t] ADJ trivalent

trivalve [tʀivalv] ADJ trivalve

trivial, e (mpl **-iaux**) [tʀivjal, jo] ADJ a (= vulgaire) [langage, plaisanterie, manières] coarse, crude b (= commun) [objet, acte] mundane, commonplace; [détail] trivial

trivialement [tʀivjalmɑ̃] ADV a (= vulgairement) [appeler] coarsely, crudely b (= banalement) trivially, tritely

trivialité [tʀivjalite] NF a (= vulgarité) [langage, plaisanterie, manières] coarseness, crudeness b (= banalité) [objet, acte] mundanity; [détail] triviality c (= remarque vulgaire) coarse ou crude remark; (= remarque banale) commonplace ou trite remark; (= détail vulgaire) coarse ou crude detail; (= détail banal) mundane ou trivial detail

troc [tʀɔk] NM (= échange) exchange; (= système) barter; **l'économie de ~** the barter economy; **faire du ~** to barter; **on a fait un ~** we did a swap; **le ~ de qch contre qch d'autre** bartering ou exchanging ou swapping sth for sth else

trochaïque [tʀɔkaik] ADJ trochaic

trochée [tʀɔʃe] NM trochee

trochlée [tʀɔkle] NF trochlea

troène [tʀɔɛn] NM privet

troglodyte [tʀɔglɔdit] NM (Ethnol) cave dweller; (fig) troglodyte; (Orn) wren

troglodytique [tʀɔglɔditik] ADJ (Ethnol) troglodytic (SPÉC), cave-dwelling (épith); **habitation ~** cave dwelling, cave-dweller's settlement

trogne* [tʀɔɲ] NF (= visage) mug*, face

trognon [tʀɔɲɔ̃] [1] NM [fruit] core; [chou] stalk; **~ de pomme** apple core; **jusqu'au ~*** to be well and truly had*; **mon petit ~*** sweetie pie* [2] ADJ INV (* = mignon) [enfant, objet, vêtement] cute*, lovely

Troie [tʀwa] N Troy; **la guerre/le cheval de ~** the Trojan War/Horse

troïka [tʀɔika] NF (gén, Pol) troika

trois [tʀwa] [1] ADJ INV a (= nombre) three; (= troisième) third; **volume/acte ~** volume/act three; **le ~ (janvier)** the third (of January); **Henri III** Henry the Third; (Littérat) **« Les Trois Mousquetaires »** "The Three Musketeers"; → **ménage**; pour autres locutions voir **six** et **fois** b (= quelques) **je pars dans ~ minutes** I'm off in a couple of ou a few minutes; **il n'a pas dit ~ mots** he hardly opened his mouth ou said a word → **cuiller, deux** [2] NM INV three; (= troisième) third; (Cartes, Dés) three; **c'est ~ fois rien** (égratignure, cadeau) it's nothing at all, it's hardly anything; **ça coûte ~ fois rien** it costs next to nothing; **et de ~!** that makes three!; pour autres locutions voir **six** [3] COMP ► **les trois coups** (Théât) the three knocks (announcing beginning of play) ► **les trois ordres** (Hist) the three estates ► **trois quarts** three-quarters; **portrait de ~ quarts** three-quarter(s) portrait; **j'ai fait les ~ quarts du travail** I've done three-quarters of the work; **les ~ quarts des gens l'ignorent** the great majority of people ou most people don't know this; **aux ~ quarts détruit** almost totally destroyed → **trois-quarts, dimension, étoile, glorieux, grâce, temps**

trois-deux [tʀwadø] NM INV (Mus) three-two time

trois-huit [tʀwaɥit] NM INV a (Mus) three-eight (time) b (Ind) **faire les ~** to operate

three eight-hour shifts, operate round the clock in eight-hour shifts

troisième [tʀwazjɛm] [1] ADJ, NMF third; **le ~ sexe** the third sex; **le ~ âge** (= période) retirement (years); (= groupe social) senior citizens; **personne du ~ âge** senior citizen; **~ cycle d'université** graduate school; **étudiant de ~ cycle** graduate ou post-graduate (Brit) student; **être** ou **faire le ~ larron dans une affaire** to take advantage of the other two quarrelling over something; pour autres locutions voir **sixième** [2] NF a (Scol) (classe de) ~ fourth form ou year (Brit), 8th grade (US) b (Aut) third (gear); **en ~** in third (gear)

troisièmement [tʀwazjɛmmɑ̃] ADV third(ly), in the third place

trois-mâts [tʀwama] NM INV (Naut) three-master

trois-pièces [tʀwapjɛs] NM INV (= complet) three-piece suit; (= appartement) three-room flat (Brit) ou apartment (surtout US)

trois-portes [tʀwapɔʀt] NF INV (Aut) two-door hatchback

trois-quarts [tʀwakaʀ] NM INV a (= manteau) three-quarter (length) coat b (Rugby) three-quarter; **il joue ~ aile** he plays wing three-quarter; **~ centre** centre three-quarter; **la ligne des ~** the three-quarter line c (= violon) three-quarter violin

trois-quatre [tʀwakatʀ] NM INV (Mus) three-four time

troll [tʀɔl] NM troll

trolley [tʀɔlɛ] NM (= dispositif) trolley(-wheel); (* = bus) trolley bus

trolleybus [tʀɔlɛbys] NM trolley bus

trombe [tʀɔ̃b] NF a (Mét) waterspout; (= pluie) **une ~ d'eau** ◊ **des ~s d'eau** a cloudburst, a downpour; **des ~s de lave/débris** streams ou torrents of lava/debris b **entrer/sortir/passer en ~** to sweep in/out/by like a whirlwind; **démarrer en ~** [voiture] to take off at top speed, roar off; (fig) to get off to a flying start

trombine* [tʀɔ̃bin] NF (= visage) face, mug* (péj); (= tête) nut*

trombinoscope* [tʀɔ̃binɔskɔp] NM a (= photographie collective) group photo b (= annuaire de l'Assemblée nationale) register, with photographs, of French deputies, ≈ rogues' gallery* of MPs (Brit) ou representatives (US)

tromblon [tʀɔ̃blɔ̃] NM a (Mil: Hist) blunderbuss; [fusil lance-roquettes] grenade launcher b (* = chapeau) hat

trombone [tʀɔ̃bɔn] NM a (Mus) (= instrument) trombone; (= tromboniste) trombonist, trombone (player); **~ à coulisse/à pistons** slide/valve trombone; **~ basse** bass trombone b (= agrafe) paper clip

tromboniste [tʀɔ̃bɔnist] NMF trombonist, trombone (player)

trompe [tʀɔ̃p] [1] NF a (Mus) trumpet, horn; († = avertisseur, sirène) horn; **~ de chasse** hunting horn; **~ de brume** fog horn → **son²** b (Zool) [éléphant] trunk, proboscis (SPÉC); [insecte] proboscis; [tapir] snout, proboscis (SPÉC); (* = nez) proboscis (hum), snout* c (Tech) **~ à eau/mercure** water/mercury pump d (Archit) squinch [2] COMP ► **trompe d'Eustache** Eustachian tube ► **trompe de Fallope** ou **utérine** Fallopian tube

trompe-la-mort [tʀɔ̃plamɔʀ] NMF INV death-dodger

trompe-l'œil [tʀɔ̃plœj] NM INV a (Art) trompe-l'œil; **peinture en ~** trompe-l'œil painting; **décor en ~** decor done in trompe-l'œil; **peint en ~ sur un mur** painted in trompe-l'œil on a wall b (= esbroufe) eyewash (Brit)*, hogwash (US); **c'est du ~** it's all eyewash (Brit)* ou hogwash (US)

▼ **tromper** [tʀɔ̃pe] ► conjug 1 ◄ [1] VT a (= duper) to deceive, trick, fool; (= être infidèle à) [+ époux] to be unfaithful to, deceive, cheat on*; **~ qn sur qch** to deceive ou mislead sb about ou over sth; **on m'a trompé sur la marchandise** I was misled; **~ sa femme** to cheat on* one's wife, be unfaithful; **elle trompait son mari avec le patron** she was having an affair with her boss behind her husband's back; **une femme trompée** a woman who has been deceived; **cela ne trompe personne** that doesn't fool anybody; **il trompe son monde** he's fooling everybody around him b (= induire en erreur par accident) [personne] to mislead; [symptômes] to deceive, mislead; **les apparences trompent** appearances are deceptive ou misleading; **c'est ce qui vous trompe** that's where you're mistaken ou wrong; **c'est un signe qui ne trompe pas** it's a clear ou an unmistakable sign c (= déjouer) [+ poursuivants] [personne] to elude, escape from, outwit; [manœuvre] to fool, trick; **~ la vigilance de qn** (pour entrer ou sortir) to slip past sb's guard; **il a trompé la vigilance du gardien de but** he managed to slip the ball past the goalkeeper d (= décevoir) **~ l'attente/l'espoir de qn** to fall short of ou fail to come up to sb's expectations/one's hopes; **être trompé dans son attente/ses espoirs** to be disappointed in one's expectations/one's hopes; **~ la faim/la soif** to stave off one's hunger/thirst; **pour ~ le temps** to kill time; **pour ~ l'ennui** ou **son ennui** to keep boredom at bay; **pour ~ leur longue attente** to while away their long wait

[2] **se tromper** VPR a (= faire erreur) to make a mistake, be mistaken; **se ~ de 15 F dans un calcul** to be 15 francs out (Brit) ou off (US) in one's calculations; **tout le monde peut se ~** anybody can make a mistake; **se ~ sur les intentions de qn** to be mistaken about sb's intentions, misjudge ou mistake sb's intentions; **on pourrait s'y ~** ◊ **c'est à s'y ~** you'd hardly know the difference; **ne vous y trompez pas, il arrivera à ses fins** make no mistake, he'll get what he wants; **si je ne me trompe** if I'm not mistaken, unless I'm very much mistaken b **se ~ de route/chapeau** to take the wrong road/hat; **se ~ d'adresse** (lit) to get the wrong address; (fig) **tu te trompes d'adresse** ou **de porte** you've come to the wrong place, you've got the wrong person; **se ~ de jour/date** to get the day/date wrong

tromperie [tʀɔ̃pʀi] NF a (= duperie) deception, deceit, trickery (NonC); **il y a eu ~ sur la marchandise** the goods are not what they were described to be b (littér = illusion) illusion

trompeter [tʀɔ̃pete] ► conjug 4 ◄ VT (péj) [+ nouvelle] to trumpet abroad, shout from the housetops

trompette [tʀɔ̃pɛt] [1] NF a (Mus) trumpet; **~ de cavalerie** bugle; **~ d'harmonie/à pistons/chromatique/naturelle** orchestral/valve/chromatic/natural trumpet; **~ basse/bouchée** bass/muted trumpet; (Bible) **la ~ du Jugement (dernier)** the last Trump; (littér) **la ~ de la Renommée** the Trumpet of Fame; **avoir la queue en ~** to have a turned-up tail → **nez, tambour** b (= coquillage) trumpet shell [2] NM (= trompettiste) trumpeter, trumpet (player); (Mil) bugler

trompette-de-la-mort (pl **trompettes-de-la-mort**) [tʀɔ̃pɛtdəlamɔʀ] NF (= champignon) horn of plenty

trompettiste [tʀɔ̃petist] NMF trumpet player, trumpeter

trompeur, -euse [tʀɔ̃pœʀ, øz] [1] ADJ a (= hypocrite) [personne, paroles, discours] deceitful b (= fallacieux) [distance, profondeur, virage] deceptive; **les apparences sont trompeuses** appearances are deceptive ou misleading

[2] NM,F deceiver ∎ (*PROV*) **à ~, ~ et demi** every rogue has his match

trompeusement [tʀɔ̃pøzmɑ̃] ADV (= *hypocritement*) deceitfully; (= *faussement*) deceptively

tronc [tʀɔ̃] [1] NM [a] [*arbre*] trunk; [*colonne*] shaft, trunk; (*Géom*) [*cône, pyramide*] frustum; (*Anat*) [*nerf, vaisseau*] trunk, mainstem; **~ d'arbre** tree trunk; **~ de cône/pyramide** truncated cone/pyramid [b] (*Anat = thorax et abdomen*) trunk; [*cadavre mutilé*] torso [c] (= *boîte*) (collection) box; **le ~ des pauvres** the poor box [2] COMP ► **tronc commun** (*Scol*) common-core syllabus

troncation [tʀɔ̃kasjɔ̃] NF (*Ling*) truncating; (*Ordin*) truncation; **recherche par ~ à droite/gauche** search by truncating a word on the right/left

troncature [tʀɔ̃katyʀ] NF (*Minér*) truncation

tronche‡ [tʀɔ̃ʃ] NF (= *visage*) mug‡; (= *tête*) nut*, noggin‡ (*US*); **faire** ou **tirer la ~** (*ponctuellement*) to make a face; (*durablement*) to sulk; **il a une sale ~** he's got a nasty face, he's a nasty-looking customer*; **il lui a envoyé un coup de poing dans la ~** he punched him in the face ou the kisser‡ ou the gob‡ (*Brit*); **il a fait une drôle de ~ quand je lui ai dit ça** you should have seen the look on his face when I told him that

tronçon [tʀɔ̃sɔ̃] NM [a] [*tube, colonne, serpent*] section [b] [*route, voie*] section, stretch; [*convoi, colonne*] section; [*phrase, texte*] part

tronconique [tʀɔ̃kɔnik] ADJ like a flattened cone ou a sawn-off cone

tronçonnage [tʀɔ̃sɔnaʒ], **tronçonnement** [tʀɔ̃sɔnmɑ̃] NM [*tronc*] sawing ou cutting up; [*tube, barre*] cutting into sections

tronçonner [tʀɔ̃sɔne] ▸conjug 1 ◂ VT [+ *tronc*] to saw ou cut up; [+ *tube, barre*] to cut into sections; (*Culin*) to cut into small pieces; **le film a été tronçonné en épisodes** the film was divided up into episodes

tronçonneuse [tʀɔ̃sɔnøz] NF chain saw

trône [tʀon] [1] NM [a] (= *siège, fonction*) throne; **~ pontifical** papal throne; **placer qn/monter sur le ~** to put sb on/come to ou ascend the throne; **chasser du ~** to dethrone, remove from the throne; **le ~ et l'autel** King and Church [b] (‡ *hum* = W.-C.) throne* (*hum*); **être sur le ~** to be on the throne*

trôner [tʀone] ▸conjug 1 ◂ VI [a] [*roi, divinité*] to sit enthroned, sit on the throne [b] (= *avoir la place d'honneur*) [*personne*] to sit enthroned; [*chose*] to sit imposingly; (*péj* = *faire l'important*) to lord it; **la photo dédicacée de son joueur préféré trônait sur son bureau** the signed photograph of his favourite player had pride of place on his desk

tronquer [tʀɔ̃ke] ▸conjug 1 ◂ VT [a] (= *couper*) [+ *colonne, statue*] to truncate [b] (= *retrancher*) [+ *citation, texte*] to truncate, shorten; [+ *détails, faits*] to abbreviate, cut out; **version tronquée** shortened ou truncated version

trop [tʀo] [1] ADV [a] (*avec vb = à l'excès*) too much; (*devant adv, adj*) too; **beaucoup** ou **bien ~** [*manger, fumer, parler*] far ou much too much; **beaucoup** ou **bien par** (*littér*) **~** (*avec adj*) far too, much too, excessively; **il a ~ mangé/bu** he has had too much to eat/drink, he has eaten/drunk too much; **elle en a déjà bien ~ dit** she has said far ou much too much already; **je suis exténué d'avoir ~ marché** I'm exhausted from having walked too far ou too much; **il a ~ travaillé** he has worked too hard, he has done too much work; **vous en demandez ~** you're asking for too much; **elle a ~ peu dormi** she hasn't had enough sleep, she's had too little sleep; **il faut régler le problème sans ~ attendre** ou **tarder** we must solve the problem quickly ou without too much delay; **tu as ~ conduit** you've been driving (for) too long; **il ne faut pas ~ aller le voir** we mustn't go to visit him too often, we mustn't overdo the visits; **en faire ~** ◊ **aller beaucoup ~ loin** to go overboard*, go too far, overdo it; **elle en fait ~ pour qu'on la croie vraiment malade** she makes so much fuss it's difficult to believe she's really ill; **un ~ grand effort l'épuiserait** too great an effort would exhaust him; **des restrictions ~ sévères aggraveraient la situation économique** excessively severe restrictions would aggravate the economic situation; **la maison est ~ grande pour eux** the house is too large for them; **la pièce est ~ chauffée** the room is overheated; **une ~ forte dose** an overdose; **tu conduis bien ~ vite/lentement** you drive far too fast/slowly; **vous êtes ~ (nombreux)/~ peu (nombreux)** there are too many/too few of you

[b] **~ de** (*quantité*) too much; (*nombre*) too many; **j'ai acheté ~ de pain/d'oranges** I've bought too much bread/too many oranges; **n'apportez pas de pain, il y en a déjà ~** don't bring any bread — there's too much already; **n'apportez pas de verres, il y en a déjà ~** don't bring any glasses — there are too many already; **s'il te reste ~ de dollars, vends-les moi** if you have dollars left over ou to spare, sell them to me; **nous avons ~ de personnel** we are overstaffed; **il y a ~ de monde dans la salle** the hall is overcrowded ou overfull, there are too many people in the hall; **j'ai ~ de travail** I'm overworked, I've got too much work (to do); **~ de bonté/d'égoïsme** excessive kindness/selfishness; **nous n'avons pas ~ de place chez nous** we haven't got very much room ou (all) that much* room at our place; **on peut le faire sans ~ de risques/de mal** it can be done without too much risk/difficulty; **ils ne seront pas ~ de deux pour faire ça** it'll take at least the two of them to do it

[c] (*introduisant une conséquence*) **~ ... pour** (*avec verbe*) too much ... to; (*devant adj, adv*) too ... to; **elle a ~ de travail pour partir en week-end** she has too much work to go away for the weekend; **il n'aura pas ~ de problèmes pour rentrer à Paris** he won't have too much difficulty getting back to Paris; **il se donne ~ peu de mal pour trouver du travail** he's not making enough effort to find work; **le village est ~ loin pour qu'il puisse y aller à pied** the village is too far for him to walk there; **il est bien ~ idiot pour comprendre** he's far too stupid ou too much of an idiot to understand; **c'est ~ beau pour être vrai!** it's too good to be true!; **les voyages à l'étranger sont ~ rares pour ne pas en profiter** trips abroad are too rare to be missed

[d] (*intensif*) **j'ai oublié mes papiers, c'est vraiment ~ bête** how stupid (of me) ou it's too stupid for words — I've forgotten my papers; **c'est ~ drôle!** it's too funny for words!, it's hilarious!, how funny!; **c'est par ~ injuste** (*littér*) it's too unfair for words!; **il y a vraiment par ~ de gens égoïstes** there are far too many selfish people about; **il n'est pas ~ satisfait/mécontent du résultat** he's not over-pleased ou too satisfied ou too pleased/not too unhappy ou dissatisfied with the result; **vous êtes ~ aimable** you are too ou most kind; **cela n'a que ~ duré** it's gone on (far) too long already; **je ne le sais que ~** I know only too well, I'm only too well aware of that; **je ne sais ~ que faire** I am not too ou quite sure what to do ou what I should do, I don't really know what to do; **cela ne va pas ~ bien** things are not going so ou terribly well; **je n'ai pas ~ confiance en lui** I haven't much ou all that much* confidence in him; **je n'en sais ~ rien** I don't really know; **il n'aime pas ~ ça*** he doesn't like it overmuch ou (all) that much*, he isn't too keen (*Brit*) ou overkeen (*Brit*) (on it); **c'est ~!** ◊ **c'en est ~!** ◊ **c'est ~!** that's going too far!, enough is enough!; **elle est ~, ta copine!*** your girlfriend's too much!* → **tôt**

[e] **de ~** ◊ **en ~**: **il y a une personne/deux personnes de ~** ou **en ~ dans l'ascenseur** there's one person/there are two people too many in the lift; **s'il y a du pain en ~, j'en emporterai** if there's any bread (left) over ou any bread extra ou any surplus bread I'll take some away; **il m'a rendu 2 F de ~** ou **en ~** he gave me back 2 francs too much; **ces 5 F sont de ~** that's 5 francs too much; **l'argent versé en ~** the excess payment; **il pèse 3 kg de ~** he's 3 kg overweight; **ce régime vous fait perdre les kilos en ~** this diet will help you lose those extra pounds; **si je suis de ~, je peux m'en aller!** if I'm in the way ou not welcome I can always leave!; **cette remarque est de ~** that remark is uncalled-for; **un petit café ne serait pas de ~** a cup of coffee wouldn't go amiss; **il a bu un verre** ou **un coup* de ~** he's had a drink ou one* too many; **tu manges/bois de ~*** you eat/drink too much

[2] NM excess, surplus; **le ~ d'importance accordé à ...** the excessive importance attributed to ...

trope [tʀɔp] NM (*Littérat*) trope

trophée [tʀɔfe] NM trophy; **~ de chasse** hunting trophy

tropical, e (*mpl* -aux) [tʀɔpikal, o] ADJ tropical

tropicaliser [tʀɔpikalize] ▸conjug 1 ◂ VT [+ *matériel*] to tropicalize

tropique [tʀɔpik] [1] ADJ [*année*] tropical [2] NM (*Géog = ligne*) tropic; **~ du Cancer/Capricorne** tropic of Cancer/Capricorn [3] **tropiques** NMPL (= *zone*) tropics; **le soleil des ~s** the tropical sun; **vivre sous les ~s** to live in the tropics

tropisme [tʀɔpism] NM (*Bio*) tropism

troposphère [tʀɔpɔsfɛʀ] NF troposphere

trop-perçu (*pl* **trop-perçus**) [tʀɔpɛʀsy] NM (*Admin, Comm*) excess (tax) payment, overpayment (of tax)

trop-plein (*pl* **trop-pleins**) [tʀɔplɛ̃] NM [a] (= *excès d'eau*) [*réservoir, barrage*] overflow; [*vase*] excess water; (= *tuyau d'évacuation*) overflow (pipe); (= *déversoir*) overflow outlet [b] (= *excès de contenu*) [*grains, terre, informations*] excess, surplus; **le ~ de terre** the excess earth [c] (*fig*) **~ d'amour/d'amitié** overflowing love/friendship; **~ de vie** ou **d'énergie** surplus ou boundless energy; **déverser le ~ de son cœur/âme** to pour out one's heart/soul

troquer [tʀɔke] ▸conjug 1 ◂ VT (= *échanger*) to swap, exchange; (*Comm*) to trade, barter (**contre, pour** for); **elle a troqué son sari pour un jean** she swapped her sari for a pair of jeans

troquet* [tʀɔke] NM (small) café

trot [tʀo] NM [*cheval*] trot; **petit/grand ~** jog/full trot; **~ de manège** dressage trot; **~ assis/enlevé** close/rising trot; **course de ~ attelé** trotting race; **course de ~ monté** *trotting race under saddle*; (*lit*) **aller au ~** to trot along; **vas-y, et au ~!*** off you go, at the double ou and be quick about it!; (*lit,* * *: fig*) **partir au ~** to set off at a trot; **prendre le ~** to break into a trot

Trotski [tʀɔtski] NM Trotsky

trotskisme, trotskysme [tʀɔtskism] NM Trotskyism

trotskiste, trotskyste [tʀɔtskist] ADJ, NMF Trotskyist, Trotskyite (*péj*)

trotte* [tʀɔt] NF **il y a** ou **ça fait une ~ (d'ici au village)** it's a fair distance (from here to the village); **on a fait une (jolie) ~** we've come a good way, we covered a good distance

trotter [tʀɔte] ▸conjug 1 ◂ [1] VI [a] [*cheval, cavalier*] to trot [b] (*fig*) [*personne*] (= *marcher à petits pas*) to trot about (ou along); (= *marcher beaucoup*) to run around, run hither and thither; [*souris, enfants*] to scurry (about), scamper (about); [*bébé*] to toddle along; **un air/une idée qui vous trotte dans** ou **par la tête** ou **la cervelle** a tune/an idea which keeps running through your head [2] **se trotter*** VPR (= *se sauver*) to dash (off)

trotteur, -euse [tʀɔtœʀ, øz] **1** NM,F (= *cheval*) trotter, trotting horse **2** NM **a** (= *chaussure*) flat shoe **b** (*pour apprendre à marcher*) baby-walker **3** **trotteuse** NF (= *aiguille*) sweep *ou* second hand

trottin †† [tʀɔtɛ̃] NM (dressmaker's) errand girl

trottinement [tʀɔtinmɑ̃] NM [*cheval*] jogging; [*souris*] scurrying, scampering; [*personne*] trotting; [*bébé*] toddling

trottiner [tʀɔtine] ▶conjug 1◀ VI [*cheval*] to jog along; [*souris*] to scurry *ou* scamper about *ou* along; [*personne*] to trot along; [*bébé*] to toddle along

trottinette [tʀɔtinɛt] NF (= *jouet*) (child's) scooter; (* = *voiture*) mini (car); **faire de la ~** to ride a scooter

trottoir [tʀɔtwaʀ] NM **a** (= *accotement*) pavement (*Brit*), sidewalk (*US*); **~ roulant** moving walkway, travelator (*Brit*); **se garer le long du ~** to park alongside the kerb; **changer de ~** (*pour éviter qn*) to cross the street **b** (*péj*) **faire le ~*** to be a streetwalker *ou* a hooker*, be on the game* (*Brit*); **elle s'est retrouvée sur le ~** she ended up as a prostitute *ou* on the streets

trou [tʀu] **1** NM **a** (*gén, Golf*) hole; (= *terrier*) hole, burrow; [*flûte*] (finger-)hole; [*aiguille*] eye; **par le ~ de la serrure** through the key-hole; (*Théât*) **le ~ du souffleur** the prompt box; **faire un ~** (*dans le sol*) to dig *ou* make a hole; (*dans une haie*) to make a hole *ou* a gap; (*dans un mur avec une vrille*) to bore *ou* make a hole; (*en perforant: dans le cuir, papier*) to punch *ou* make a hole; (*avec des ciseaux, un couteau*) to cut a hole; (*en usant, frottant*) to wear a hole (**dans** in); (*Golf*) **faire un ~ en un** to get a hole in one; (*Golf*) **un 9/18 ~s** a 9-hole/an 18-hole course; **il a fait un ~ à son pantalon** (*usure*) he has (worn) a hole in his trousers; (*brûlure, acide*) he has burnt a hole in his trousers; (*déchirure*) he has torn a hole in his trousers; **ses chaussettes sont pleines de ~s** *ou* **ont des ~s partout** his socks are in holes *ou* are full of holes; **sol/rocher creusé de ~s** ground/rock pitted with holes; **le ~ dans la couche d'ozone** the hole in the ozone layer **b** (*fig*) (= *moment de libre*) gap; (= *déficit*) deficit; (*Sport*) (= *trouée*) gap, space; **un ~ (de 10 millions) dans la comptabilité** a deficit (of 10 million) in the accounts; (*Sport*) **faire le ~** to break *ou* burst through; **il y a des ~s dans ma collection** there are some gaps in my collection; **il y a des ~s dans son témoignage** there are gaps in *ou* things missing from his account of what happened; **il a des ~s en physique** there are gaps in his knowledge of physics; **cela a fait un gros ~ dans ses économies** it made quite a hole in his savings; **le ~ de la Sécurité sociale** the deficit in the Social Security budget; **j'ai un ~ demain dans la matinée, venez me voir** I have a gap in my schedule tomorrow morning so come and see me; **j'ai un ~ d'une heure** I have an hour free; **j'ai eu un ~ (de mémoire)** my mind went blank; (*Scol*) **texte à ~s** cloze test **c** (*Anat*) foramen; **~ optique** optic foramen; **~s intervertébraux** intervertebral foramina; **~ vertébral** vertebral canal *ou* foramen → **œil** **d** (*péj* = *localité*) place, hole* (*péj*); **ce village est un ~** this village is a real hole* *ou* dump*; **il n'est jamais sorti de son ~** he has never been out of his own backyard; **chercher un petit ~ pas cher** to look for a little place that's not too expensive; **un ~ perdu** *ou* **paumé*** a dead-and-alive hole*, a god forsaken hole* *ou* dump* **e** (*loc*) **(se) faire son ~*** to make a niche for o.s.; **vivre tranquille dans son ~** to live quietly in one's little hideaway *ou* hidey-hole* (*Brit*); (= *prison*) **mettre/être au ~*** to put/be in clink* *ou* in the nick (*Brit*)*; **quand on sera dans le ~*** when we're dead and buried *ou* dead and gone, when we're six feet under* → **boire**

2 COMP ▶ **trou d'aération** airhole, (air) vent ▶ **trou d'air** (*Aviat*) air pocket ▶ **trou de balle**** (*lit, fig*) arse-hole** (*Brit*), asshole** (*US*) ▶ **trou du chat** (*Naut*) lubber's hole ▶ **trou de cigarette** cigarette burn ▶ **trou du cul**** = **trou de balle** ▶ **trou d'homme** manhole ▶ **trou de nez*** nostril ▶ **trou noir** (*Astron*) black hole; (*fig* = *désespoir*) **c'était le ~ noir** I (*ou* *he* etc) was in the depths of despair ▶ **trou normand** glass of spirits, often Calvados, drunk between courses of a meal ▶ **trou d'obus** shell-hole, shell-crater ▶ **trou de souris** mousehole; **elle était si gênée qu'elle serait rentrée dans un ~ de souris** she was so embarrassed that she wished the ground would swallow her up ▶ **trou de ver** wormhole

troubadour [tʀubaduʀ] NM troubadour

troublant, e [tʀublɑ̃, ɑ̃t] ADJ (= *déconcertant*) disturbing, disquieting, unsettling; (= *sexuellement provocant*) disturbing, arousing

trouble¹ [tʀubl] **1** ADJ **a** [*eau, vin*] unclear, cloudy, turbid (*littér*); [*regard*] misty, dull; [*image*] blurred, misty, indistinct; [*photo*] blurred, out of focus; **avoir la vue ~** to have blurred vision → **pêcher¹** **b** (= *impur, équivoque*) [*personnage, rôle*] shady, suspicious, dubious; [*atmosphère, passé*] shady; [*affaire*] shady, murky, fishy; [*désir*] dark (*épith*); [*joie*] perverse (*épith*); (= *vague, pas franc*) [*regard*] shifty, uneasy; **une période ~ de l'histoire** a murky chapter *ou* period in history **2** ADV **voir ~** to have blurred vision, see things dimly *ou* as if through a mist

trouble² [tʀubl] NM **a** (= *agitation, remue-ménage*) tumult, turmoil; (= *zizanie, désunion*) discord, trouble **b** (= *émeute*) **~s** unrest (*NonC*), disturbances, troubles; **~s politiques/sociaux** political/social unrest (*NonC*) *ou* disturbances *ou* upheavals; **des ~s ont éclaté dans le sud du pays** rioting has broken out *ou* disturbances have broken out in the south of the country; **~s à l'ordre public** disturbance *ou* breach of the peace → **fauteur** **c** (= *émoi affectif ou sensuel*) (inner) turmoil, agitation; (= *inquiétude, désarroi*) distress; (= *gêne, perplexité*) confusion, embarrassment; **le ~ étrange qui s'empara d'elle** the strange feeling of turmoil *ou* agitation which overcame her; **le ~ profond causé par ces événements traumatisants** the profound distress caused by these traumatic events; (*littér*) **le ~ de son âme/cœur** the tumult *ou* turmoil in his soul/heart; **le ~ de son esprit** the agitation in his mind, the turmoil his mind was in; **dominer/se laisser trahir par son ~** to overcome/give o.s. away by one's confusion *ou* embarrassment; **semer le ~ dans l'esprit des gens** to sow confusion in peoples' minds **d** (*gén pl: Méd*) trouble (*NonC*), disorder; **~s physiologiques/psychiques** physiological/psychological trouble *ou* disorders; **~s respiratoires/cardiaques** respiratory/heart ailments *ou* disorders; **~s du sommeil** sleeping disorders; **il a des ~s de la vision** he has trouble with his (eye)sight *ou* vision; **elle souffre de ~s de la mémoire** she has memory problems; **~s de la personnalité** *ou* **du caractère** personality problems *ou* disorders; **~s du comportement** behavioural problems; **~s du langage** speech difficulties; **~s musculo-squelettiques** repetitive strain injury, RSI; (*Psych*) **~ obsessionnel compulsif** obsessive-compulsive disorder; **ce n'est qu'un ~ passager** it's only a passing disorder

trouble-fête [tʀubləfɛt] NMF INV spoilsport, killjoy*; **jouer les ~** to be a spoilsport *ou* killjoy*

troubler [tʀuble] ▶conjug 1◀ **1** VT **a** (= *perturber*) [+ *ordre*] to disturb, disrupt; [+ *sommeil, tranquillité, silence*] to disturb; [+ *représentation, réunion*] to disrupt; [+ *jugement, raison, esprit*] to cloud; [+ *digestion*] to upset; ~

l'ordre public to disturb public order, cause a breach of public order, disturb the peace; **en ces temps troublés** in these troubled times **b** [+ *personne*] (= *démonter, impressionner*) to disturb, disconcert; (= *inquiéter*) to trouble, perturb; (= *gêner, embrouiller*) to bother, confuse; (= *émouvoir*) to disturb, unsettle; (= *exciter sexuellement*) to arouse; **elle le regarda, toute troublée** she looked at him, all of a tremble *ou* all in a fluster; **ce film/cet événement l'a profondément troublé** this film/this event has disturbed him deeply; **la perspective d'un échec ne le trouble pas du tout** the prospect of failure doesn't perturb *ou* trouble him in the slightest; **il y a quand même un détail qui me trouble** there's still a detail which is bothering *ou* confusing me; **cesse de parler, tu me troubles (dans mes calculs)** stop talking — you're disturbing me *ou* putting me off (in my calculations); **~ un candidat** to disconcert a candidate, put a candidate off; **~ (les sens de) qn** to disturb *ou* agitate sb **c** (= *brouiller*) [+ *eau*] to make cloudy *ou* muddy *ou* turbid (*littér*); [+ *vin*] to cloud, make cloudy; [+ *atmosphère*] to cloud; [+ *ciel*] to darken, cloud; (*TV*) [+ *image*] to blur; **les larmes lui troublaient la vue** tears clouded *ou* blurred her vision

2 **se troubler** VPR **a** (= *devenir trouble*) [*eau*] to cloud, become cloudy *ou* muddy *ou* turbid (*littér*); [*temps*] to become cloudy *ou* overcast; [*ciel*] to become cloudy *ou* overcast, darken; [*lignes, images, vue*] to become blurred **b** (= *perdre contenance*) to become flustered; **il se trouble facilement lorsqu'il doit parler en public** he's easily flustered when he has to speak in public; **il répondit sans se ~** he replied calmly

troué, e¹ [tʀue] (*ptp de trouer*) ADJ **bas/sac ~** stocking/bag with a hole *ou* with holes in it; **avoir une chaussette ~e** to have a hole in one's sock; **ce sac est ~** this bag has a hole *ou* holes (in it); **ses chaussettes sont toutes ~es** *ou* **~es de partout** his socks are full of holes; **ce seau est ~ de partout** *ou* **comme une passoire** this bucket's like a sieve; **corps ~ comme une passoire** *ou* **comme une écumoire** body riddled with bullets; **son gant ~ laissait passer son pouce** his thumb stuck *ou* poked out through a hole in his glove

trouée² [tʀue] NF **a** [*haie, forêt, nuages*] gap, break (**de** in); **~ de lumière** shaft of light **b** (*Mil*) breach; **faire une ~** to make a breach, break through **c** (*Géog* = *défilé*) gap; **la ~ de Belfort** the Belfort Gap

trouer [tʀue] ▶conjug 1◀ VT **a** [+ *vêtement*] to make *ou* wear a hole in; [+ *ticket*] to punch (a hole in); (= *transpercer*) to pierce; **il a troué son pantalon** (*avec une cigarette*) he's burnt a hole in his trousers; (*dans les ronces*) he's torn *ou* ripped a hole in his trousers; (*par usure*) he's worn a hole in his trousers; **ces chaussettes se sont trouées très vite** these socks soon got holes in them; **~ qch de part en part** to pierce sth through, pierce a hole right through sth; **après le bombardement, les rues étaient trouées de cratères** after the bombing, the streets were pockmarked with craters; **des immeubles troués par les obus** buildings full of gaping shellholes; **~ la peau à qn*** to put a bullet in sb; **se faire ~ la peau*** to get a bullet in one's hide* **b** (*fig* = *traverser*) [+ *silence, nuit*] to pierce; **une fusée troua l'obscurité** a rocket pierced the darkness; **le soleil troue les nuages** the sun's breaking through the clouds **c** (*fig* = *parsemer: gén ptp*) to dot; **la plaine trouée d'ombres** the plain dotted with shadows

troufignon †** [tʀufiɲɔ̃] NM (= *derrière*) backside*, arse** (*Brit*), ass** (*US*); (= *anus*) arsehole** (*Brit*), asshole** (*US*)

troufion* [tʀufjɔ̃] NM soldier, squaddie*;

quand j'étais ~ when I was in the army *ou* was a soldier

trouillard, e: [tʀujaʀ, aʀd] (*péj*) [1] ADJ yellow*, chicken* (*attrib*), yellow-bellied: [2] NM,F yellowbelly*

trouille: [tʀuj] NF **avoir la ~** to be scared stiff* *ou* to death; **j'ai eu la ~ de ma vie** I got the fright of my life *ou* a hell of a fright*; **flanquer** *ou* **ficher la ~ à qn** to scare the pants off sb*, put the wind up sb* (*Brit*)

trouillomètre: [tʀujɔmɛtʀ] NM **avoir le ~ à zéro** to be scared witless*

troupe [tʀup] NF [a] (*Mil, Scoutisme*) troop; (*Mil*) **la ~** (= *l'armée*) the army; (= *les simples soldats*) the troops, the rank and file; **les ~s** the troops; **~s de choc/de débarquement** shock/landing troops; **lever des ~s** to raise troops; **faire intervenir la ~** to call *ou* bring in the army; **réservé à la ~** reserved for the troops; **il y avait de la ~ cantonnée au village** there were some army units billeted in the village → **enfant, homme** [b] [*chanteurs, danseurs*] troupe; **~ (de théâtre)** (theatre *ou* drama) company [c] [*gens, animaux*] band, group, troop; **se déplacer en ~** to go about in a band *ou* group *ou* troop

troupeau (*pl* **troupeaux**) [tʀupo] NM [*bœufs, chevaux*] (*dans un pré*) herd; (*transhumant*) drove; [*moutons, chèvres*] flock; [*éléphants, buffles, girafes*] herd; [*oies*] gaggle; (*péj*) [*touristes, prisonniers*] herd (*péj*); (*Rel*) **le ~ du Seigneur** the Lord's flock

troupier [tʀupje] [1] NM († = *soldat*) private [2] ADJ → **comique**

trousse [tʀus] NF [a] (= *étui*) (*gén*) case, kit; [*médecin, chirurgien*] instrument case; [*écolier*] pencil case *ou* wallet; **~ à aiguilles** needle case; **~ à couture** sewing case *ou* kit; **~ de maquillage** (= *mallette*) vanity case *ou* bag; (= *sac*) make-up bag; **~ à outils** toolkit; **~ à ongles** nail kit, manicure set; **~ de secours** first-aid kit; **~ de toilette** *ou* **de voyage** (= *sac*) toilet bag, sponge bag; (= *mallette*) travelling case, grip [b] (*loc*) **aux ~s de** hot on the heels of, on the tail of; **les créanciers/policiers étaient à ses ~s** the creditors/policemen were on his tail *ou* hot on his heels; **avoir la police aux ~s** to have the police on one's tail *ou* hot on one's heels

trousseau (*pl* **trousseaux**) [tʀuso] NM [a] **~ de clés** bunch of keys [b] (= *vêtements, linge*) [*mariée*] trousseau; [*écolier*] outfit

troussequin [tʀuskɛ̃] NM [a] (*Équitation*) cantle [b] (= *outil*) = **trusquin**

trousser [tʀuse] ▷ conjug 1 ◁ VT [a] (*Culin*) [+ *volaille*] to truss [b] († = *retrousser*) [+ *robe, jupes*] to pick *ou* tuck up; **se ~** to pick *ou* tuck up one's skirts [c] (†, *hum*) [+ *femme*] to tumble† [d] († = *expédier*) [+ *poème, article, discours*] to dash off, throw together; **compliment bien troussé** well-phrased compliment

trousseur† [tʀusœʀ] NM (*hum*) **~ de jupons** womanizer, ladykiller

trou-trou (*pl* **trou(s)-trou(s)**) [tʀutʀu] NM (*Tricot*) row of holes through which ribbon is passed; (*Couture*) lace trimming through which ribbon is passed; **chemisier à trous-trous** openwork blouse

trouvaille [tʀuvaj] NF (= *objet*) find; (= *idée, métaphore, procédé*) stroke of inspiration, brainwave (*Brit*); (= *mot*) coinage; (*iro*) **quelle est sa dernière ~?** what's his latest brainwave?

▼ trouver [tʀuve] ▷ conjug 1 ◁ [1] VT [a] (*en cherchant*) [+ *objet, emploi, main-d'œuvre, renseignement*] to find; **je ne le trouve pas** I can't find it; **où peut-on le ~?** where can he be found?, where is he to be found?; **on lui a trouvé une place dans un lycée** he was found a place in a lycée, they found him a place *ou* a place for him in a lycée; **est-ce qu'ils trouveront le chemin?** will they find the way? *ou*

their way?; **~ le temps/l'énergie/le courage de faire qch** to find (the) time/the energy/the courage to do sth; **comment avez-vous trouvé un secrétaire si compétent?** how did you come by *ou* find such a competent secretary?; **elle a trouvé en lui un ami sûr/un associé compétent** she has found in him a faithful friend/a competent partner; **~ son maître** to find one's master

[b] (= *rencontrer par hasard*) [+ *document, information, personne*] to find, come across; [+ *difficultés*] to meet with, come across, come up against; [+ *idée, plan*] to hit on; **on trouve cette plante sous tous les climats humides** this plant is found *ou* is to be found in all damp climates; **~ la mort (dans un accident)** to meet one's death (in an accident)

[c] (= *découvrir*) to find; (*avec attribut du complément*) **~ qch cassé/vide** to find sth broken/empty; **je l'ai trouvé en train de pleurer** I found him crying; **je ne lui trouve aucun défaut** I can find no fault with him; **mais qu'est-ce qu'elle lui trouve?** what on earth does she see in him?

[d] **~ à** (+ *infin*): **~ à manger/boire** to find something to eat/drink; **~ à se distraire/à s'occuper** to find a way to amuse/occupy o.s., find something to amuse/occupy o.s. with; **il trouve toujours à faire dans la maison** he can always find something to do in the house; **si tu trouves à te garer dans ma rue ...** if you manage to find a parking space in my street ...; **elle trouvera bien à les loger quelque part** she's bound to find somewhere to put them up; **il n'a rien trouvé à répondre** he couldn't think of anything to say in reply → **redire**

[e] (= *penser, juger*) to think, find; **~ que** to find *ou* think that; **elle trouve qu'il fait trop chaud ici** she finds it too hot (in) here; **~ qch à son goût/trop cher** to find sth to one's liking/too expensive; **je trouve cela trop sucré/lourd** I find it too sweet/heavy, it's too sweet/heavy for me; **il a trouvé bon de nous écrire** he saw fit to write to us; **~ le temps long** to find that time passes slowly *ou* hangs heavy on one's hands; **je le trouve fatigué** I think he looks tired; **tu lui trouves bonne mine?** do you think he's looking well?; **comment l'as-tu trouvé?** what did you think of him?, how did you find him?; **vous la trouvez sympathique?** do you like her?, do you think she's nice?; **trouvez-vous ça normal?** do you think that's right?; **tu trouves ça drôle!** ◊ **tu trouves que c'est drôle!** so you think that's funny!, so you find that funny!; **vous trouvez?** (do) you think so?

[f] (= *imaginer, inventer*) [+ *solution, prétexte, moyen*] to find, come up with; (*énigme*) **comment as-tu fait pour ~?** how did you work it out?; **j'ai trouvé!** I've got it!*; **solution/explication/excuse toute trouvée** ready-made solution/explanation/excuse; **c'est un sujet tout trouvé pour ta rédaction** it's an obvious topic for your essay; **formule bien trouvée** clever *ou* happy phrase; (*iro*) **tu as trouvé ça tout seul?** did you work it out all by yourself? (*iro*); **où est-il allé ~ ça?** where (on earth) did he get that idea from?, whatever gave him that idea? → **moyen, remède** *etc*

[g] (= *rendre visite à*) **aller/venir ~ qn** to go/come and see sb; **quand il a des ennuis, c'est moi qu'il vient ~** when he has problems, it's me he comes to

[h] (= *éprouver*) **~ (du) plaisir à qch/à faire qch** to take pleasure in sth/in doing sth, enjoy sth/doing sth; **~ une consolation dans le travail** to find consolation in work *ou* in working

[i] (*loc*) **ne pas ~ ses mots** to be at a loss for words; **~ le sommeil** to get to sleep, fall asleep; **il a trouvé à qui parler** he met his match; **il va ~ à qui parler** he'll get more than he bargained for; **cet objet n'avait pas trouvé d'amateur** no one had expressed *ou* shown

any interest in the object; **tu as trouvé ton bonheur dans ce bric-à-brac?** can you find what you're after *ou* what you're looking for in this jumble?; **je la trouve mauvaise!*** *ou* **saumâtre!*** I don't like it at all, I think it's a bit off* (*Brit*) → **compte, grâce, preneur** *etc*

[2] **se trouver** VPR [a] (= *être dans une situation*) [*personne*] to find o.s.; [*chose*] to be; **il se trouva nez à nez avec Paul** he found himself face to face with Paul; **la question se trouva reléguée au second plan** the question was relegated to the background; **la voiture se trouva coincée entre ...** the car was jammed between ...; **nous nous trouvons dans une situation délicate** we are in a delicate situation; **je me suis trouvé dans l'impossibilité de répondre** I found myself unable to reply; **il se trouve dans l'impossibilité de venir** he's unable to come, he's not in a position to come; **il se trouve dans l'obligation de partir** he has to *ou* is compelled to leave

[b] (= *être situé*) [*personne*] to be; [*chose*] to be, be situated; **son nom ne se trouve pas sur la liste** his name isn't on *ou* doesn't appear on the list; **je me trouvais près de l'entrée** I was (standing *ou* sitting *etc*) near the entrance; **il ne fait pas bon se ~ dehors par ce froid** it's not pleasant to be out in this cold; **la maison se trouve au coin de la rue** the house is (situated) *ou* stands on the corner of the street; **où se trouve la poste?** where is the post office?; **les toilettes se trouvent près de l'entrée** the toilets are (situated) near the entrance

[c] (= *pouvoir être trouvé*) **un crayon, ça se trouve facilement** you can find a pencil anywhere; **ça ne se trouve pas sous le pas** *ou* **le sabot d'un cheval** it's not easy to find *ou* to come by

[d] (= *se sentir*) to feel; **se ~ bien** (*dans un fauteuil etc*) to be *ou* feel comfortable; (*santé*) to feel well; **il se trouve mieux en montagne** he feels better in the mountains; **elle se trouvait bien dans ce pays** she was happy in this country; **se ~ mal** (= *s'évanouir*) to faint, pass out; **elle s'est trouvée mal à cause de la chaleur/en entendant la nouvelle** she fainted *ou* passed out in the heat/on hearing the news; **se ~ bien/mal d'avoir fait qch** to be glad/to regret having done sth; **il s'en est bien trouvé** he benefited from it; **il s'en est mal trouvé** he lived to regret it; (*iro*) **je me suis trouvé!** a fine *ou* right* fool I looked!

[e] (= *se juger*) **il se trouve beau dans son nouveau costume** he thinks he looks good in his new suit; **tu te trouves malin** *ou* **intelligent/spirituel?** I suppose you think that's clever/funny!

[f] (*exprimant la coïncidence: souvent avec infin*) **se ~ être/avoir ...** to happen to be/have ...; **elles se trouvaient avoir la même robe** it turned out that they had *ou* they happened to have the same dress; **pour une fois, ils se trouvaient d'accord** for once they happened to agree

[g] (= *découvrir sa personnalité, son style*) **à cette époque, l'artiste ne s'était pas encore trouvé** at this time, the artist hadn't yet developed his own distinctive style

[3] **se trouver** VPR IMPERS [a] (*événement fortuit*) **il se trouve que c'est moi** it happens to be me, it's me as it happens; **il s'est trouvé que j'étais là quand ...** I happened *ou* chanced to be there when ..., it so happened that I was there when ...; **il se trouvait qu'elle avait menti** it turned out that she had been lying

[b] **il se trouve** (+ *nom*) (= *il y a*) **il se trouve toujours des gens qui disent ...** *ou* **pour dire ...** there are always people *ou* you'll always find people who will say ...; **il se trouvera peut-être des journalistes pour l'approuver** there'll probably be *ou* there may (well) be some journalists who approve

[c] * **ils sont sortis, si ça se trouve** they may well be out, they're probably out; **si ça se**

> ━ GRAMMAIRE ACTIVE: **trouver** 33.2, 53.5

trouve, il ne viendra pas maybe he won't come

trouvère [truver] NM trouvère

troyen, -enne [trwajɛ̃, ɛn] [1] ADJ (*Antiq*) Trojan [2] **Troyen(ne)** NM,F (*Antiq*) Trojan

truand, e [tryɑ̃, ɑ̃d] [1] NM (= *gangster*) gangster, mobster (*US*); (= *escroc*) crook [2] NM,F († = *mendiant*) beggar

truander: [tryɑ̃de] ▸ conjug 1 ◂ [1] VT to swindle, do:; **se faire ~** to be swindled *ou* done: [2] VI to cheat

trublion [tryblijɔ̃] NM troublemaker, agitator

▼ **truc¹** [tryk] NM [a] (* = *moyen, combine*) way, trick; **il a trouvé le ~ (pour le faire)** he's got the hang* of it; **il n'a pas encore compris le ~** he hasn't got the hang* of it yet; **avoir le ~** to have the knack; **cherche un ~ pour venir me voir** try to find some way of coming to see me; **on le connaît, leur ~** we know what they're up to* *ou* playing at*, we're onto their little game*; **les ~s du métier** the tricks of the trade; **j'ai un ~ infaillible contre les taches** I've got just the thing for getting rid of stains, I know a great way of getting rid of stains [b] (= *tour*) [*prestidigitateur*] trick; (= *trucage*: *Ciné, Théât*) trick, effect; **c'est impressionnant mais ce n'est qu'un ~** it's impressive but it's only a trick *ou* an effect; **il y a un ~!** there's a trick in it! [c] (* = *chose, idée*) thing; **on m'a raconté un ~ extraordinaire** I've been told an extraordinary thing; **j'ai pensé (à) un ~** I've thought of something, I've had a thought; **il y a un tas de ~s à faire** there's a heap of things to do*; **je lui ai offert un petit ~ pour son anniversaire** I gave him a little something for his birthday; **il a dit un ~ dans ce style** he said something along those lines *ou* something of the sort; **le ski, c'est pas mon ~** skiing isn't my thing*; **la médecine/l'équitation, c'est son ~** he's really into* medicine/horseriding [d] (* = *machin*) (*dont le nom échappe*) thingumajig*, thingummy*, whatsit*; (*inconnu, jamais vu*) contraption, thing, thingumajig*; (= *chose bizarre*) thing; **c'est quoi, ce ~-là?** what's that thing? *ou* thingumajig?*; **méfie-toi de ces ~s-là** be careful of *ou* beware of those things [e] (: = *personne*) **Truc (Chouette)** ◊ **Machin Truc** what's-his-(*ou* her-) name*, what-d'you-call-him (*ou* -her)*

truc² [tryk] NM (*Rail*) truck, waggon

trucage [tryka3] NM = **truquage**

truchement [tryʃmɑ̃] NM [a] **par le ~ de qn** through (the intervention *ou* agency of) sb; **par le ~ de qch** with the aid of sth [b] (††, *littér* = *moyen d'expression, intermédiaire*) medium, means of expression

trucider* [tryside] ▸ conjug 1 ◂ VT (*hum*) to knock off:, bump off:; **je vais me faire ~ si jamais j'arrive en retard!** I'll get killed* *ou* I'll get my head bitten off* if I arrive late!

trucmuche: [trykmyʃ] NM [a] (= *chose*) thingumajig*, thingummy*, whatsit* [b] (= *personne*) **Trucmuche** what's-his-(*ou* her-) name*, what-d'you-call-him (*ou* -her)*

truculence [trykylɑ̃s] NF [*langage*] vividness, colourfulness (*Brit*), colorfulness (*US*); [*style*] colourfulness (*Brit*), colorfulness (*US*); **la ~ de ce personnage** the liveliness *ou* verve of this character

truculent, e [trykylɑ̃, ɑ̃t] ADJ [*langage*] vivid, colourful (*Brit*), colorful (*US*); [*style*] colourful (*Brit*), colorful (*US*); [*personnage*] colourful (*Brit*), colorful (*US*), larger-than-life (*épith*), larger than life (*attrib*)

truelle [tryɛl] NF [*maçon*] trowel; (*Culin*) **~ à poisson** fish slice

truffe [tryf] NF [a] (*Bot*) truffle; **~ noire/blanche** black/white truffle [b] (*Culin*) **~s (au chocolat)** (chocolate) truffles [c] (= *nez du chien*) nose;

(* = *nez*) nose, conk* (*Brit*), hooter* (*Brit*) [d] (* = *idiot*) nitwit*, twit*

truffer [tryfe] ▸ conjug 1 ◂ VT [a] (*Culin*) to garnish with truffles [b] (= *remplir*) **~ qch de** to pepper sth with; **truffé de citations** peppered *ou* larded with quotations; **truffé de fautes** *ou* **d'erreurs** riddled with mistakes; **région truffée de mines** area littered with mines; **truffé de pièges** bristling with traps; **pièce truffée de micros** room bristling with hidden bugging devices; **film truffé d'effets spéciaux** film laden with special effects

truffier, -ière [tryfje, jɛR] [1] ADJ [*région*] truffle (*épith*); [*chêne*] truffle-producing; **chien ~** truffle hound [2] **truffière** NF truffle field

truie [trɥi] NF (*Zool*) sow

truisme [trɥism] NM (*littér*) truism

truite [trɥit] NF trout *inv*; **~ saumonée** salmon trout; **~ de mer** sea trout; **~ arc-en-ciel** rainbow trout; (*Culin*) **~ meunière** truite *ou* trout meunière → **bleu**

truité, e [trɥite] ADJ [a] (= *tacheté*) [*cheval*] mottled, speckled; [*chien*] spotted, speckled [b] (= *craquelé*) [*porcelaine*] crackled

trumeau (*pl* **trumeaux**) [trymo] NM [a] [*pilier*] pier; [*entre portes, fenêtres*] pier; [*panneau ou glace*] pier glass; [*cheminée*] overmantel [b] (*Culin*) shin of beef

truquage [tryka3] NM [a] [*serrure, verrou*] adapting, fixing; [*cartes, dés*] fixing; [*élections*] rigging, fixing*; [*combat*] fixing* [b] († = *falsification*) [*dossier*] doctoring*; [*comptes*] fiddling*; [*œuvre d'art, meuble*] faking; (*Ciné*) **le ~ d'une scène** using special effects in a scene [c] (*Ciné*) **un ~ très réussi** a very successful effect; **~s optiques** optical effects *ou* illusions; **~s de laboratoire** lab effects

truqué, e [tryke] (*ptp de* **truquer**) ADJ [*élections*] rigged; [*combat*] fixed*; [*cartes, dés*] fixed*; (*Ciné*) **une scène ~e** a scene involving special effects

truquer [tryke] ▸ conjug 1 ◂ VT [a] [+ *serrure, verrou, cartes*] to fix*; [+ *dés*] to load; [+ *combat, élections*] to rig, fix*; (*Ciné*) **une scène** to use special effects in a scene [b] († = *falsifier*) [+ *dossier*] to doctor*; [+ *comptes*] to fiddle*; [+ *œuvre d'art, meuble*] to fake

truqueur, -euse [trykœR, øz] NM,F [a] (= *fraudeur*) cheat [b] (*Ciné*) special effects man (*ou* woman)

truquiste [trykist(ə)] NM = **truqueur b**

trusquin [tryskɛ̃] NM marking gauge

trust [trœst] NM (= *cartel*) trust; (= *grande entreprise*) corporation → **antitrust**

truster [trœste] ▸ conjug 1 ◂ VT [+ *secteur du marché*] to monopolize, corner; [+ *produit*] to have the monopoly of, monopolize; (* = *accaparer*) to monopolize; **ils ont trusté les médailles aux derniers Jeux olympiques** they carried off all the medals *ou* they made a clean sweep of the medals at the last Olympic Games

trypanosome [tRipanozom] NM trypanosome

trypanosomiase [tRipanozomjaz] NF trypanosomiasis

TSA [teɛsa] NF (ABRÉV = **technologie des systèmes automatisés**) → **technologie**

tsar [dzaR] NM tsar, czar, tzar

tsarévitch [dzaRevitʃ] NM tsarevich, czarevich, tzarevich

tsarine [dzaRin] NF tsarina, czarina, tzarina

tsarisme [dzaRism] NM tsarism, czarism, tzarism

tsariste [dzaRist] ADJ tsarist, czarist, tzarist

tsé-tsé [tsetse] NF (**mouche**) **~** tsetse fly

TSF† [teɛsɛf] NF (ABRÉV = **télégraphie sans fil**) (= *procédé*) wireless telegraphy; (= *radio*) wireless, radio; (= *poste*) wireless; **à la ~** on the radio *ou* wireless

---

T(-)shirt [tiʃœRt] NM = **tee(-)shirt**

tsigane [tsigan] [1] ADJ (Hungarian) gypsy *ou* gipsy, tzigane; **violoniste/musique ~** (Hungarian) gypsy violinist/music [2] NM (*Ling*) Romany [3] **Tsigane** NMF (Hungarian) Gypsy *ou* Gipsy, Tzigane

tsoin-tsoin*, **tsouin-tsouin*** [tswɛ̃tswɛ̃] EXCL boom-boom!

tss-tss [tsts] EXCL tut-tut!

TSVP (ABRÉV = **tournez s'il vous plaît**) PTO

TTC [tetese] (ABRÉV = **toutes taxes comprises**) inclusive of (all) tax

TU [tey] NM (ABRÉV = **temps universel**) UT → **temps**

tu, t'* [ty, t] [1] PRON PERS you (*as opposed to vous: familiar form of address*); (*Rel*) thou; **t'as* de la chance** you're lucky [2] NM **employer le tu** to use the "tu" form; **dire tu à qn** to address sb as "tu"; **être à tu et à toi avec qn*** to be on first-name terms with sb, be a great pal of sb*

tuant, tuante* [tɥɑ̃, tɥɑ̃t] ADJ (= *fatigant*) killing, exhausting, (= *énervant*) exasperating, tiresome

tub [tœb] NM (= *bassin*) (bath)tub; (= *bain*) bath

tuba [tyba] NM (*Mus*) tuba; (*Sport*) snorkel, breathing tube; **~ d'orchestre** bass tuba

tubage [tyba3] NM (*Méd*) intubation, cannulation

tubaire [tybɛR] ADJ (*Méd*) tubal

tubard, e: [tybaR, aRd] (ABRÉV = **tuberculeux**) (*péj*) [1] ADJ suffering from TB [2] NM,F TB case

tube [tyb] NM [a] (= *tuyau*) (*gén, de mesure, en verre*) tube; (*de canalisation, tubulure, métallique*) pipe; [*canon*] barrel; **~ capillaire** capillary tube; **~ à essai** test tube; **~ lance-torpilles** torpedo tube; **~ au néon** neon tube; (*Élec*) **~ redresseur** vacuum diode; **~ régulateur de potentiel** triode; (*Élec, TV, Ordin*) **~ cathodique** cathode ray tube; **~ à vide** vacuum valve *ou* tube; **~ électronique** electronic valve *ou* tube [b] (= *emballage*) *aspirine, dentifrice, peinture*] tube; **~ de rouge (à lèvres)** lipstick; **en ~** in a tube [c] (*Anat, Bot* = *conduit*) **~ digestif** digestive tract, alimentary canal; **~s urinifères/séminaux** urinary/seminiferous tubules; **~ pollinique** pollen tube [d] (* = *chanson à succès*) hit; **le ~ de l'été** the summer hit, the hit-song of the summer [e] (= *vêtement*) **jupe ~** tube skirt; **pull ~** skinny-rib (sweater *ou* jumper) [f] (*† = téléphone*) **donner un coup de ~ à qn** to give sb a buzz* *ou* a tinkle* [g] (* † = *haut-de-forme*) topper* [h] (*loc*) **marcher à pleins ~s** [*moteur*] to be running full throttle *ou* at maximum revs; **il a mis sa chaîne hi-fi à pleins ~s** he turned his stereo on full blast*; **délirer* ou déconner: à pleins ~s** to be raving mad*, be off one's head* *ou* rocker:

tubercule [tybɛRkyl] NM (*Anat, Méd*) tubercle; (*Bot*) tuber; **~s quadrijumeaux** corpora quadrigemina, quadrigeminal *ou* quadrigeminate bodies

tuberculeux, -euse [tybɛRkylø, øz] [1] ADJ [a] (*Méd*) tuberculous, tubercular; **être ~** to suffer from tuberculosis *ou* TB, have tuberculosis *ou* TB [b] (*Bot*) tuberous, tuberose [2] NM,F tuberculosis *ou* tubercular *ou* TB patient

tuberculine [tybɛRkylin] NF tuberculin

tuberculinique [tybɛRkylinik] ADJ [*test*] tuberculinic, tuberculin

tuberculose [tybɛRkyloz] NF tuberculosis, TB; **~ pulmonaire** pulmonary tuberculosis; **~ osseuse** tuberculosis of the bones

tubéreux, -euse [tybeRø, øz] [1] ADJ tuberous [2] **tubéreuse** NF (*Bot*) tuberose

tubérosité [tybeRozite] NF (*Anat*) tuberosity

tubulaire [tybylɛR] ADJ tubular

---

tubulé, **e** [tybyle] ADJ [*plante*] tubulate; [*flacon*] tubulated

tubuleux, -euse [tybylø, øz] ADJ tubulous, tubulate

tubulure [tybylyʀ] NF **a** (= *tube*) pipe **b** (*Tech*) (= *ouverture*) tubulure; (= *tubes*) **~s** piping; (*Aut*) **~ d'échappement/d'admission** exhaust/inlet manifold; **~ d'alimentation** feed *ou* supply pipe

TUC [tyk] **1** NMPL (ABRÉV = **travaux d'utilité collective**) → **travail** **2** NMF = **tucard, e**

tucard, e [tykaʀ, aʀd] NM,F, **tuciste** [tysist] NMF (paid) community worker (*otherwise unemployed*), ≈ employment trainee (*Brit*), ≈ YTS trainee (*Brit*)

tudieu†† [tydjø] EXCL zounds!†, 'sdeath!†

tué, e [tɥe] (*ptp de* **tuer**) NM,F (*dans un accident, au combat*) person killed; **les ~s** the dead, those killed; **il y a eu cinq ~s** there were five (people) killed *ou* five dead

tue-mouche [tymuʃ] **1** NM INV (*Bot*) (**amanite**) **~** fly agaric **2** ADJ **papier** *ou* **ruban ~(s)** fly-paper

tuer [tɥe] ▸ conjug 1 ◂ **1** VT **a** [+ *personne, animal*] to kill; (*à la chasse*) to shoot; (*Bible*) **tu ne tueras point** thou shalt not kill; **~ qn à coups de pierre/sb** to stone/stab *ou* knife sb to death; **~ qn d'une balle** to shoot sb dead; **l'alcool tue** alcohol can kill *ou* is a killer; **la route tue des milliers de gens chaque année** thousands of people are killed on the roads every year; **se faire ~** to get killed; **il était prêt à se faire ~ pour son pays** he was prepared to die for his country; (*Psych*) **~ le père** to kill the father; **cet enfant me tuera** this child will be the death of me; (*fig*) **il est à ~!** you (*ou* I) could kill him!; **il n'a jamais tué personne!** he wouldn't hurt a fly, he's quite harmless; **ça n'a jamais tué personne** ◊ **ça ne va pas te ~** it won't kill you; **quelle odeur! ça tue les mouches à 15 pas!*** what a stink!* it's enough to kill a man at twenty paces!; **un culot pareil, ça me tue!*** he's (*ou* she's *etc*) got a nerve!; **ça m'a tué d'apprendre qu'ils divorçaient*** I was flabbergasted* *ou* staggered when I heard that they were getting divorced ◊ **poule cleaning** **b** (= *ruiner*) to kill; (= *exténuer*) to exhaust, wear out; **la bureaucratie tue toute initiative** bureaucracy kills (off) all initiative; **les supermarchés n'ont pas tué le petit commerce** supermarkets have not killed off small traders; **ce rouge tue tout leur décor** this red kills (the effect of) their whole decor; **ces escaliers/querelles me tuent** these stairs/quarrels will be the death of me; **~ qch dans l'œuf** to nip sth in the bud; **~ le temps** to kill time

2 **se tuer** VPR **a** (*l'un l'autre*) to kill each other; **séparez-les, ils vont se ~!** pull them apart, they're going to kill each other! **b** (*soi-même, par accident*) to be killed; **il s'est tué en montagne/en voiture** he was killed in a mountaineering/car accident **c** (= *se suicider*) to kill o.s.; **il s'est tué d'une balle dans la tête** he put a bullet through his head, he shot himself in the head **d** (= *s'épuiser*) **se ~ au travail** ◊ **se ~ à la tâche** to work o.s. to death, kill o.s. with work; **se ~ à répéter/expliquer qch à qn** to repeat/explain sth to sb until one is blue in the face, wear o.s. out repeating/explaining sth to sb

tuerie [tyʀi] NF (= *carnage*) slaughter, carnage

tue-tête [tytɛt] ◆ **à tue-tête** LOC ADV **crier/chanter à ~** to shout/sing at the top of one's voice, shout/sing one's head off*

tueur, tueuse [tɥœʀ, tɥøz] **1** NM,F **a** (= *assassin*) killer; (*fig = personne impitoyable*) shark; **~ à gages** hired *ou* professional killer, contract killer, hitman*; **~ en série** serial killer **b** (= *chasseur*) **~ de lions/d'éléphants** lion-/elephant-killer **2** NM (*d'abattoir*) slaughterman, slaughterer

tuf [tyf] NM (*Géol*) (*volcanique*) tuff; (*calcaire*) tufa

tuf(f)eau [tyfo] NM tufa

tuilage [tɥilaʒ] NM [*opérations*] overlapping

tuile [tɥil] NF **a** (*lit*) tile; **~ creuse** *ou* **romaine** *ou* **ronde** curved tile; **~ faîtière** ridge tile; **~s mécaniques** industrial *ou* interlocking tiles; **couvrir un toit de ~s** to tile a roof; **toit de ~s** tiled roof; **~s de pierre/d'ardoise** stone/slate tiles; **nous préférons la ~ à l'ardoise** we prefer tiles to slate **b** (* = *coup de malchance*) stroke *ou* piece of bad luck; **quelle ~!** what rotten luck!, what a pain!*; **il vient de m'arriver une ~** I've just had a piece of bad luck **c** (*Culin*) (thin sweet) biscuit (*Brit*) *ou* cookie (*US*)

tuiler [tɥile] ▸ conjug 1 ◂ VT [+ *opérations*] to overlap

tuilerie [tɥilʀi] NF (= *fabrique*) tilery; (= *four*) tilery, tile kiln

tuilier, -ière [tɥilje, jɛʀ] **1** ADJ tile (*épith*) **2** NM,F tile maker *ou* manufacturer

tulipe [tylip] NF (= *fleur*) tulip; (= *lampe*) tulip-shaped lamp; **verre ~** tulip glass

tulipier [tylipje] NM tulip tree

tulle [tyl] NM tulle; **robe de ~** tulle dress; (*Méd*) **~ gras** sofra-tulle

tuméfaction [tymefaksjɔ̃] NF (= *effet*) swelling *ou* puffing up, tumefaction (*SPÉC*); (= *partie tuméfiée*) swelling

tuméfier [tymefje] ▸ conjug 7 ◂ **1** VT to cause to swell, tumefy (*SPÉC*); **visage/œil tuméfié** puffed-up *ou* swollen face/eye **2** **se tuméfier** VPR to swell up, puff up, tumefy (*SPÉC*)

tumescence [tymesɑ̃s] NF tumescence

tumescent, e [tymesɑ̃, ɑ̃t] ADJ tumescent

tumeur [tymœʀ] NF tumour (*Brit*), tumor (*US*) (**de** of), growth (**de** in); **~ bénigne/maligne** benign/malignant tumour; **~ au cerveau** brain tumour

tumoral, e (*mpl* **-aux**) [tymɔʀal, o] ADJ tumorous, tumoral

tumorectomie [tymɔʀɛktɔmi] NF lumpectomy

tumulte [tymylt] NM **a** (= *bruit*) [*foule*] commotion; [*voix*] hubbub; [*acclamations*] thunder, tumult; **un ~ d'applaudissements** thunderous applause, a thunder of applause; (*littér*) **le ~ des flots/de l'orage** the tumult of the waves/of the storm; **la réunion s'est achevée dans un ~ général** the meeting ended in uproar *ou* in pandemonium **b** (= *agitation*) [*affaires*] hurly-burly; [*passions*] turmoil, tumult; [*rue, ville*] hustle and bustle (**de** in, of), commotion (**de** in)

tumultueusement [tymyltɥøzmɑ̃] ADV stormily, turbulently, tumultuously

tumultueux, -euse [tymyltɥø, øz] ADJ [*séance*] stormy, turbulent, tumultuous; [*foule*] turbulent, agitated; (*littér*) [*flots, bouillonnement*] turbulent; [*vie, période, jeunesse*] stormy, turbulent; [*passion*] tumultuous, turbulent

tumulus [tymylys] NM burial mound, tumulus (*SPÉC*), barrow (*SPÉC*)

tune [tyn] NF = **thune**

tuner [tynɛʀ] NM (= *amplificateur*) tuner

tungstène [tœ̃kstɛn] NM tungsten, wolfram

tunique [tynik] NF **a** [*soldat, écolier*] tunic; [*prêtre*] tunicle, tunic; [*femme*] (*droite*) tunic; (*à forme ample*) smock; (*longue*) gown; (*Myth*) **la ~ de Nessus** the shirt of Nessus **b** (*Anat*) tunic, tunica; (*Bot*) tunic; **~ de l'œil** tunica albuginea of the eye

Tunis [tynis] N Tunis

Tunisie [tynizi] NF Tunisia

tunisien, -ienne [tynizjɛ̃, jɛn] **1** ADJ **a** (*de Tunisie*) Tunisian **b** (**T-shirt**) **~** Grandad-style T-shirt **2** **Tunisien(ne)** NM,F Tunisian

tunnel [tynɛl] NM **a** (*lit*) (*gén*) tunnel; (*Hort*) tunnel; **~ ferroviaire/routier** railway/road tunnel; **~ aérodynamique** wind tunnel; **le ~ sous la Manche** the Channel Tunnel, the Chunnel* → **effet** **b** (*fig*) tunnel; **voir le bout du ~** to see (the) light at the end of the tunnel

tunnelier [tynəlje] NM (= *ouvrier*) tunneller (= *machine*) mole

TUP [typ] NM (ABRÉV = **titre universel de paiement**) → **titre**

tuque [tyk] NF (*Can*) woollen cap, tuque (*Can*)

turban [tyʀbɑ̃] NM turban

turbin* [tyʀbɛ̃] NM (= *emploi*) work; **aller au ~** to go off to work; **se remettre au ~** to get back to work; **après le ~** after work

turbine [tyʀbin] NF turbine; **~ hydraulique** water *ou* hydraulic turbine; **~ à réaction/à impulsion** reaction/impulse turbine; **~ à vapeur/à gaz** steam/gas turbine

turbiner* [tyʀbine] ▸ conjug 1 ◂ VI to graft (away)*, slog away*, slave away; **faire ~ qn** to make sb work, keep sb at it* *ou* with his nose to the grindstone*

turbo [tyʀbo] **1** ADJ INV **a** (*Aut*) turbo **b** (*Ordin*) **~ pascal/C** turbo pascal/C **2** NM (= *moteur*) turbo; (*fig*) **mettre le ~*** to get a move on*, step on it* **3** NF (= *voiture*) turbo, turbo-car

turbocompresseur [tyʀbokɔ̃pʀesœʀ] NM turbocharger; **~ de suralimentation** turbo-supercharger

turbodiesel [tyʀbodjezɛl] ADJ, NM turbodiesel

turbomoteur [tyʀbomotœʀ] NM turbine engine

turbopompe [tyʀbopɔ̃p] NF turbopump, turbine-pump

turbo-prof* (*pl* **turbo-profs**) [tyʀbopʀof] NMF teacher commuting long distances

turbopropulseur [tyʀbopʀopylsœʀ] N turbo-prop

turboréacteur [tyʀboʀeaktœʀ] NM turbojet (engine); **~ à double flux** bypass turbojet *ou* engine

turbot [tyʀbo] NM turbot

turbotrain [tyʀbotʀɛ̃] NM turbotrain

turbulence [tyʀbylɑ̃s] NF **a** (= *dissipation*) boisterousness, unruliness **b** (= *agitation*) (*gén Sci*) turbulence (*NonC*); (*Aviat*) **entrer dans une zone de ~s** to go into an area of turbulence; (*fig*) **le franc traverse une nouvelle période de turbulence** the franc is going through a new period of turbulence; **~s politiques/sociales** political/social unrest

turbulent, e [tyʀbylɑ̃, ɑ̃t] ADJ **a** (= *agité*) [*enfant, élève*] unruly, boisterous, obstreperous; [*jeunesse, foule*] unruly, turbulent; [*époque*] turbulent **b** (*littér = tumultueux*) [*passion*] turbulent, stormy; (*Sci*) turbulent

turc, turque [tyʀk] **1** ADJ Turkish; **à la turque** (= *accroupi, assis*) cross-legged; [*cabinets*] seatless; (*Mus*) alla turca → **bain, café, fort, tête** **2** NM **a** (= *personne*) **Turc** Turk; (*Hist*) **le Grand Turc** the Sultan; (*Hist, fig*) **les Jeunes Turcs** the Young Turks **b** (*Ling*) Turkish **3** **Turque** NF Turkish woman

turcophone [tyʀkɔfɔn] **1** ADJ Turkish-speaking **2** NMF Turkish speaker

turf [tyʀf] NM **a** (*Sport*) (= *terrain*) racecourse; (= *activité*) **le ~** racing, the turf **b** (*arg Crime* = *prostitution*) **le ~** streetwalking; **aller au ~** to go and walk the streets **c** (‡ = *travail*) **aller au ~** to go off to work

turfiste [tyʀfist] NMF racegoer

turgescence [tyʀʒesɑ̃s] NF turgescence

turgescent, e [tyʀʒesɑ̃, ɑ̃t] ADJ turgescent

turgide [tyʀʒid] ADJ (*littér*) swollen

turista* [tyʀista] NF ≈ Delhi belly*, Montezuma's revenge*; **avoir/attraper la ~** to have/get Montezuma's revenge*

turkmène [tyʀkmɛn] **1** ADJ Turkoman, Turkman **2** NM (*Ling*) Turkmen, Turk(o)man **3** **Turkmène** NMF Turkoman, Turkman

Turkménistan [tyʀkmenistã] NM Turkmenistan

turlupiner* [tyʀlypine] ▶ conjug 1 ◀ VT to bother, worry; **ce qui me turlupine** what bugs me* ou worries me

turlute [tyʀlyt] NF a (Can) hummed tune b‡ blow-job*‡; **faire une ~ à qn** to give sb a blow-job‡‡

turluter [tyʀlyte] ▶ conjug 1 ◀ (Can) 1 VT [+ chanson] to hum 2 VI to hum a tune

turne* [tyʀn] NF a († péj = logement) digs* b (Scol = chambre) room

turpitude [tyʀpityd] NF a (caractère) turpitude b (gén pl = acte) base act

Turquie [tyʀki] NF Turkey

turquoise [tyʀkwaz] NF, ADJ INV turquoise

tutélaire [tyteleʀ] ADJ (littér = protecteur) tutelary, protecting (épith); (Jur = de la tutelle) tutelary

tutelle [tytɛl] NF a (Jur) [mineur] guardianship, wardship; [aliéné] guardianship; **avoir la ~ de qn** to be sb's guardian; **mettre qn en ~** to put sb in the care of a guardian; **enfant en ~** child under guardianship; **être placé sous ~ judiciaire** to be made a ward of court b (= contrôle financier, administratif, politique) supervision; (= protection) tutelage, protection; **~ administrative/de l'État** administrative/state supervision; **organisme de ~** regulator, regulating body; **autorité de ~** regulatory authority; (Admin) **ministère de ~** ministry in charge; (Pol) **régime de ~** trusteeship; (Pol) **territoires sous ~** trust territories; **pays sous la ~ de l'ONU** country under UN trusteeship; **mettre sous ~** to put under supervision; **la banque a été mise sous ~** control of the bank has been put in the hands of trustees; **être sous la ~ de qn** (dépendant) to be under sb's supervision; (protégé) to be in sb's tutelage; **tenir** ou **garder en ~** [+ pays] to hold sway over; [+ personne] to keep a tight rein on; **exercer sa ~ sur** to control

tuteur, -trice [tytœʀ, tʀis] 1 NM,F (Jur, fig littér = protecteur) guardian; (Univ) tutor; **~ légal/testamentaire** legal/testamentary guardian; **~ ad hoc** specially appointed guardian 2 NM (Agr) stake, support

tuteurage [tytœʀaʒ] NM (Agr) staking

tuteurer [tytœʀe] ▶ conjug 1 ◀ VT (Agr) to stake (up)

tutoiement [tytwamã] NM use of (the familiar) "tu" (instead of "vous")

There are no hard-and-fast rules about when to use "tu" or "vous" to address people. Small children can be addressed as "tu", and will often reply using the "tu" form as well. In informal contexts among young people of the same age, "tu" is often used even at first meeting. Among the older generation, "vous" is standard until people know each other well; some older married couples even use the "vous" form to address their spouse. As a general rule for non-native speakers, "vous" should always be used to address adults until the other person uses "tu", or asks permission to do so.

tutorat [tytɔʀa] NM (Scol) guidance; (Univ) tutorial system

tutoyer [tytwaje] ▶ conjug 8 ◀ VT a (lit) **~ qn** to use (the familiar) "tu" when speaking to sb, address sb as "tu" (instead of "vous") b (fig littér) to be on familiar ou intimate terms with c (* = frôler) **le cheval a tutoyé l'obstacle** the horse brushed the fence; **le nombre des chômeurs tutoie la barre des trois millions** unemployment is nearing the three million mark

tutti frutti [tutifʀuti] LOC ADJ INV [glace] tutti-frutti

tutti quanti [tutikwãti] ◆ **et tutti quanti** LOC ADV and all the rest (of them), and all that lot* ou crowd*

tutu [tyty] NM tutu, ballet skirt

Tuvalu [tuvaly] N Tuvalu

tuyau (pl **tuyaux**) [tɥijo] 1 NM a (gén, rigide) pipe, length of piping; (flexible, en caoutchouc, vendu au mètre) length of rubber tubing, rubber tubing (NonC); [pipe] stem; **il me l'a dit dans le ~ de l'oreille*** he whispered it to me b (Habillement = pli) flute c * (= conseil) tip; (= renseignement) gen* (NonC); **quelques ~x pour le bricoleur** a few tips for the do-it-yourself enthusiast; **il nous a donné des ~x sur leurs activités/projets** he gave us some gen* on their activities/plans; **~ crevé** useless tip 2 COMP ▶ **tuyau d'alimentation** feeder pipe ▶ **tuyau d'arrosage** hosepipe, garden hose ▶ **tuyau de cheminée** chimney pipe ou flue ▶ **tuyau de descente** (pluvial) downpipe, fall pipe; [lavabo, W-C] wastepipe ▶ **tuyau d'échappement** exhaust (pipe), tailpipe ▶ **tuyau de gaz** gas pipe ▶ **tuyau d'orgue** (Géol, Mus) organ pipe ▶ **tuyau de pipe** stem of a pipe; **avoir les artères en ~ de pipe** to have hardened arteries ▶ **tuyau de poêle** stovepipe; (*†) (chapeau en) **~ de poêle** stovepipe hat; **quelle famille ~ de poêle** ‡! (à problèmes) what a mixed-up family!*; (incestueuse) everybody sleeps with everybody in that family! ▶ **tuyau de pompe** pump pipe

tuyautage [tɥijɔtaʒ] NM a [linge] fluting, goffering b (* = renseignement) tipping off

tuyauter [tɥijɔte] ▶ conjug 1 ◀ VT a [+ linge] to flute, goffer; **un tuyauté** a fluted frill b * **~ qn** (= conseiller) to give sb a tip; (= mettre au courant) to give sb some gen*, put sb in the know*, give sb the tip-off*

tuyauterie [tɥijɔtʀi] NF a [machines, canalisations] piping (NonC); [orgue] pipes

tuyère [tɥijeʀ] NF [turbine] nozzle; [four, haut fourneau] tuyère, twyer; **~ d'éjection** exhaust ou propulsion nozzle

TV [teve] (ABRÉV = **télévision**) TV

TVA [tevea] NF (ABRÉV = **taxe sur la valeur ajoutée**) VAT

TVHD [teve'aʃde] NF (ABRÉV = **télévision haute définition**) HDTV

tweed [twid] NM tweed

twin-set (pl **twin-sets**) [twinset] NM twinset

twist [twist] NM (= danse) twist

twister [twiste] ▶ conjug 1 ◀ VI (Danse) to twist

tympan [tɛ̃pã] NM a (Anat) eardrum, tympanum (SPÉC); **bruit à vous déchirer** ou **crever les ~s** earsplitting noise → **caisse** b (Archit) tympan(um) c (Tech = pignon) pinion

tympanique [tɛ̃panik] ADJ (Anat) tympanic

tympanon [tɛ̃panɔ̃] NM (Mus) dulcimer

type [tip] 1 NM a (= modèle) type; **il y a plusieurs ~s de bicyclettes** there are several types of bicycle; **une pompe du ~ B5** a pump of type B5, a type B5 pump; **une pompe du ~ réglementaire** a regulation-type pump; **une voiture (de) ~ break** an estate-type (Brit) ou station-wagon-type (US) car; **«convient à tous les ~s de peau»** "suitable for all skin types"; **certains ~s humains** certain human types; **avoir le ~ oriental/nordique** to be Oriental-/Nordic-looking, have Oriental/Nordic looks; **un beau ~ de femme/d'homme** a fine specimen of womanhood ou manhood; **c'est le ~ d'homme à faire cela** he's the type ou sort of man who would do that; **plusieurs opérations de ce ~ ont déjà eu lieu** several operations of that nature ou kind ou type have already taken place; **des contrats d'un ~ nouveau** new types of contract; **rien ne peut justifier ce ~ de comportement** nothing can justify that kind ou type of behaviour; **pour étudier certains ~s de comportements** to study certain behaviour patterns; **ce** ou **il/elle n'est pas mon ~** he/she is not my type ou sort b (= exemple) classic example; **c'est le ~ (parfait** ou **même) de l'intellectuel/du vieux garçon** he's the typical intellectual/bachelor, he's a perfect ou classic example of the intellectual/of the bachelor; **c'est le ~ même de la machination politique** it's a classic example of political intrigue c (* = individu) guy*, chap* (Brit), bloke* (Brit); († = individu remarquable) character; (= amant) boyfriend; **un sale ~** a nasty character, a nasty piece of work*; **quel sale ~!** he's such a swine* ou bastard*‡! → **chic** d (Typo) typeface; (Numismatique) type 2 ADJ INV typical, classic; (Stat) standard; **l'erreur/le politicien ~** the typical ou classic mistake/politician; **l'exemple/la situation ~** the typical ou classic example/situation; **lettre/contrat ~** standard letter/contract → **écart**

typé, e [tipe] (ptp de **typer**) ADJ a (physiquement) **une femme brune et très ~e** a dark-haired woman with the characteristic features of her race; **elle est allemande mais pas très ~e** she's German but she doesn't look typically German ou doesn't have typical German looks b [attitudes, goûts] typical, characteristic; **les personnages fortement ~s de la commedia dell'arte** the stock characters of the commedia dell'arte

typer [tipe] ▶ conjug 1 ◀ VT a (= caractériser) **auteur/acteur qui type son personnage** author/actor who brings out the features of the character well; **un personnage bien typé** a character well rendered as a type b (Tech) to stamp, mark

typesse ‡‡ [tipɛs] NF (péj) female* (péj)

typhique [tifik] 1 ADJ (= du typhus) typhous; (= de la typhoïde) typhoid; **bacille ~** typhoid bacillus 2 NMF typhoid sufferer

typhoïde [tifɔid] ADJ, NF (fièvre) **~** typhoid (fever)

typhoïdique [tifɔidik] ADJ typhic

typhon [tifɔ̃] NM typhoon

typhus [tifys] NM typhus (fever)

typique [tipik] ADJ a (gén, Bio) typical (de of); **sa réaction est ~** his reaction is typical (of him) ou true to form ou type; **un cas ~ de ...** a typical case of ...; **il a encore oublié, c'est ~!** he's forgotten again — typical! b† [musique, orchestre] Latin American

typiquement [tipikmã] ADV typically

typo* [tipɔ] 1 NF ABRÉV = **typographie** 2 NM ABRÉV = **typographe**

typographe [tipɔɡʀaf] NMF (gén) typographer; (= compositeur à la main) hand compositor

typographie [tipɔɡʀafi] NF a (= procédé d'impression) letterpress (printing); (= opérations de composition, art) typography b (= aspect) typography

typographique [tipɔɡʀafik] ADJ [procédé, impression] letterpress (épith); [opérations, art] typographic(al); **erreur** ou **faute ~** typographic(al) ou printer's error, misprint, typo*; **argot ~** typographers' jargon; **cet ouvrage est une réussite ~** this work is a success typographically ou as regards typography

typographiquement [tipɔɡʀafikmã] ADV [imprimer] by letter-press; **livre ~ réussi** book that is a success typographically ou successful as regards typography

typolithographie [tipolitɔɡʀafi] NF typolithography

typologie [tipɔlɔʒi] NF typology

typologique [tipɔlɔʒik] ADJ typological

Tyr [tiʀ] N Tyre

tyran [tiʀã] NM (lit, fig) tyrant; **c'est un ~ domestique** he's a tyrant at home

tyranneau (*pl* **tyranneaux**) [tiʀano] NM (*hum, péj*) petty tyrant

tyrannie [tiʀani] NF (*lit, fig*) tyranny; **la ~ de la mode/d'un mari** the tyranny of fashion/ of a husband; **exercer sa ~ sur qn** to tyrannize sb, wield one's tyrannical powers over sb

tyrannique [tiʀanik] ADJ [*personne, régime, pouvoir*] tyrannical; **il est ~ envers** *ou* **avec ses étudiants** he bullies his students

tyranniquement [tiʀanikmɑ̃]   ADV tyranni- cally

tyranniser [tiʀanize] ▸conjug 1◂ VT to bully, tyrannize; **un élève tyrannisé par ses camara- des d'école** a pupil bullied by his class- mates

tyrannosaure [tiʀanɔzɔʀ]   NM tyrannosaur, tyrannosaurus

tyrien [tiʀjɛ̃] ADJ M **rose ~** Tyrian purple

Tyrol [tiʀɔl] NM **le ~** the Tyrol

tyrolien, -ienne [tiʀɔljɛ̃, jɛn]   1 ADJ Tyrolean

→ **chapeau** 2   **Tyrolien(ne)** NM,F Tyrolean 3   **tyrolienne** NF a (= *chant*) yodel, Tyro- lienne b (*Alpinisme*) (= *technique*) Tyrolean traverse; (= *pont*) rope bridge

Tyrrhénienne [tiʀenjɛn] NF → **mer**

tzar [dzaʀ]   NM, **tzarévitch** [dzaʀevitʃ] NM, **tzarine** [dzaʀin]   NF = **tsar, tsarévitch, tsarine**

tzigane [dzigan] ADJ, NMF = **tsigane**

U

U, u [y] NM (= *lettre*) U, u; **poutre en U** U(-shaped) beam; **vallée en U** U-shaped valley; **disposer des tables en U** to arrange tables in a U-shape

ubac [ybak] NM (*Géog*) north(-facing) side, ubac (*SPÉC*)

ubiquité [ybikɥite] NF ubiquity; **avoir le don d'~** to be ubiquitous, be everywhere at once (*hum*)

ubuesque [ybyɛsk] ADJ (= *grotesque*) grotesque; (*Littérat*) Ubuesque

UDF [ydeef] NF (ABRÉV = **Union pour la démocratie française**) *French political party*

UE [yə] NF a (ABRÉV = **Union européenne**) EU b (ABRÉV = **unité d'enseignement**) → **unité**

UEFA [yefa] NF (ABRÉV = **Union of European Football Associations**) UEFA; **la coupe de l'~** the UEFA cup

UEM [yaɛm] NF (ABRÉV = **Union économique et monétaire**) EMU

UEO [yəo] NF (ABRÉV = **Union de l'Europe occidentale**) WEU

UER† [yəɛʁ] NF (ABRÉV = **Unité d'enseignement et de recherche**) → **unité**

UFR [yefɛʁ] NF (ABRÉV = **Unité de formation et de recherche**) → **unité**

UHF [yaʃef] NF (ABRÉV = **ultra-high frequency**) UHF

uhlan [ylɑ̃] NM uhlan

UHT [yaʃte] NF (ABRÉV = **ultra-haute température**) UHT

ukase [ykɑz] NM = **oukase**

Ukraine [ykʁɛn] NF **l'~** the Ukraine

ukrainien, -ienne [ykʁɛnjɛ̃, jɛn] 1 ADJ Ukrainian 2 NM (*Ling*) Ukrainian 3 **Ukrainien(ne)** NM,F Ukrainian

ukulélé [jukulele] NM ukulele

ulcération [ylseʁasjɔ̃] NF ulceration

ulcère [ylsɛʁ] NM **~ à l'estomac** stomach ulcer; **~ variqueux** varicose ulcer

ulcérer [ylseʁe] ▶ conjug 6 ◀ VT a (= *révolter*) to sicken, appal; **le verdict/cette accusation l'a ulcéré** he was outraged by *ou* appalled at the verdict/the accusation; **être ulcéré (par l'attitude de qn)** to be sickened *ou* appalled (by sb's attitude) b (*Méd*) to ulcerate; **plaie ulcérée** festering *ou* ulcerated wound

ulcéreux, -euse [ylseʁø, øz] ADJ ulcerated, ulcerous

uléma [ylema] NM ulema

ULM [yɛlɛm] NM (ABRÉV = **ultra-léger motorisé**) microlight, microlite; **faire de l'~** to go microlighting

ulmaire [ylmɛʁ] NF (= *plante*) meadowsweet

Ulster [ylstɛʁ] NM Ulster

ultérieur, e [ylteʁjœʁ] ADJ later, subsequent; **à une date ~e** at a later date; **cela devrait faire l'objet de discussions ~es** this should be the subject of later *ou* future discussions; **la question sera abordée dans une phase ~e (des négociations)** the question will be discussed at a later stage (of the negotiations)

ultérieurement [ylteʁjœʁmɑ̃] ADV later, subsequently

ultimatum [yltimatɔm] NM ultimatum; **envoyer** *ou* **adresser un ~ à qn** to present sb with an ultimatum

ultime [yltim] ADJ [*étape, avertissement, réunion, hommage*] last, final; [*recours, chance*] last; [*objectif, responsabilité*] ultimate; [*tentative*] last(-ditch), final

ultra [yltʁa] 1 NM (= *réactionnaire*) extreme reactionary; (= *extrémiste*) extremist; (*Hist*) **Ultra(-royaliste)** ultra(-royalist) 2 PRÉF (*dans les mots composés à trait d'union, le préfixe reste invariable*) **~-chic/-long** ultra-chic/-long; **~-conservateur/-nationaliste/-orthodoxe** ultra-conservative/-nationalist/-orthodox; **~-court** (*gén*) ultra-short; (*Radio*) **ondes ~-courtes** ultra-high frequency; **~-plat** [*boîtier, montre*] slimline; **~-fin** [*tranche*] wafer-thin; [*poudre, texture*] ultra-fine; [*collant, tissu*] sheer

ultra-confidentiel, -ielle [yltʁakɔ̃fidɑ̃sjɛl] ADJ (*gén, sur un dossier*) top secret

ultra-léger, ultraléger, -ère [yltʁaleʒe, ɛʁ] ADJ [*équipement*] ultra-light; [*cigarette*] ultra-mild; [*tissu, vêtement*] very light → **ULM**

ultra-libéral, ultralibéral, e (*mpl* **-aux**) [yltʁalibeʁal, o] 1 ADJ [*idéologie, politique*] ultra-free market (*épith*); [*personne*] who advocates an ultra-free market 2 NM,F ultra-free marketeer

ultra-libéralisme, ultralibéralisme [yltʁalibeʁalism] NM doctrine of the ultra-free market

ultramicroscope [yltʁamikʁɔskɔp] NM ultramicroscope

ultramicroscopique [yltʁamikʁɔskɔpik] ADJ ultramicroscopic

ultramoderne [yltʁamɔdɛʁn] ADJ (*gén*) ultra-modern; [*équipement*] high-tech, hi-tech, state-of-the-art (*épith*)

ultramontain, e [yltʁamɔ̃tɛ̃, ɛn] (*Rel*) 1 ADJ ultramontane 2 NMPL **les ~s** ultramontanists, ultramontanes

ultra-rapide, ultrarapide [yltʁaʁapid] ADJ [*bateau, ordinateur*] high-speed (*épith*); (*dans un restaurant*) **formule ~** express menu

ultrasecret, -ète [yltʁasəkʁɛ, ɛt] ADJ top secret

ultra-sensible, ultrasensible [yltʁasɑ̃sibl] ADJ [*appareil, balance, dossier, problème*] ultrasensitive; [*personne, peau*] hypersensitive; **film** *ou* **pellicule ~** high-speed film

ultrason [yltʁasɔ̃] NM ultrasonic sound; **les ~s** ultrasound (*NonC*)

ultrasonique [yltʁasɔnik], **ultrasonore** [yltʁasɔnɔʁ] ADJ ultrasonic

ultraviolet, -ette [yltʁavjɔlɛ, ɛt] 1 ADJ ultraviolet 2 NM ultraviolet ray; **faire des séances d'~s** to have sunbed sessions

ululation [ylylasjɔ̃] NF, **ululement** [ylylmɑ̃] NM = **hululement**

ululer [ylyle] ▶ conjug 1 ◀ VI = **hululer**

Ulysse [ylis] NM Ulysses

---

un, une [œ̃, yn]

1	ARTICLE INDÉFINI	4 NOM MASCULIN INV
2	PRONOM	5 NOM FÉMININ
3	ADJECTIF	

Lorsque **un, une** *s'emploient dans des locutions figées telles que* **pour un rien, un de ces jours, il n'en rate pas une** *etc, cherchez au nom ou au verbe.*

1 ARTICLE INDÉFINI

a **gén** a, an (*devant voyelle*); (= *un, une quelconque*) some; **ne venez pas un dimanche** don't come on a Sunday; **le témoignage d'un enfant n'est pas valable** a child's evidence *ou* the evidence of a child is not valid; **un chien sent tout de suite si quelqu'un a peur de lui** dogs know straight away when you're afraid of them; **c'est l'œuvre d'un poète** it's the work of a poet; **retrouvons-nous dans un café** let's meet in a café; **un jour/soir il partit** one day/evening he went away; **un jour, tu comprendras** one day *ou* some day you'll understand; **passez un soir** drop in one *ou* some evening; **une fois, il est venu avec un ami et …** once he came with a friend and …

b **avec nom abstrait** avec une grande sagesse/violence with great wisdom/violence, very wisely/violently; **des hommes d'un courage sans égal** men of unparalleled courage; **un amour qui frôlait la passion** a love which bordered on passion

c **avec nom propre** a, an; **ce n'est pas un Picasso** (*hum*) [*personne*] he's no Picasso, he's not exactly a Picasso; [*tableau*] it's not a Picasso; **un certain M. Legrand** a (certain) Mr Legrand, one Mr Legrand; **on a élu un (nommé** *ou* **certain) Dupont** they've appointed a man called Dupont; **c'est encore un Kennedy qui fait parler de lui** that's yet another Kennedy in the news; **il a le talent d'un Hugo** he has the talent of a Hugo; **cet enfant sera un Paganini** this child will be another Paganini

d **intensif** elle a fait une scène ! *ou* une de ces scènes ! she made a dreadful scene! *ou* such a scene!; j'ai une faim/une soif ! *ou* une de ces faims/une de ces soifs ! I'm so hungry/thirsty!, I'm starving/parched!; il est d'un sale ! *ou* d'une saleté ! he's so dirty!, he's filthy!

2 PRONOM

a **gén** one; **un seul** (just) one; **pas un (seul)** not one; (*emphatique*) not a single one; **six contre un** six against one; **prêtez-moi un de vos livres** lend me one of your books; **une des trois a dû mentir** one of the three must have been lying; **il est un des rares qui m'ont écrit** he's one of the few (people) who wrote to me; **c'est un de ces enfants qui s'ennuient partout** he's the kind of child *ou* one of those children who gets bored wherever he goes; **un à qui je voudrais parler, c'est Jean** there's one person I'd like to speak to and that's John, one person I'd like to speak to is John ■ (*PROV*) **un(e) de perdu(e), dix de retrouvé(e)s** there are plenty more fish in the sea

◆ **comme pas un*** : il est arrogant/bête comme pas un he's as arrogant/stupid as they come;

elle chante/danse comme pas une she's a great* singer/dancer

♦ **et d'un*** (= *voilà une chose faite, terminée*) that's one done *ou* finished *ou* out of the way

♦ **et d'une !*** (= *d'abord*) for a start!; **personne ne t'a forcé de venir, et d'une !** no one forced you to come for one thing!, for a start no one forced you to come!

♦ **un(e) à un(e) ◊ un(e) par un(e)** one by one; **ajouter les œufs un par un** add the eggs one by one *ou* one at a time; **pris un par un, ces indices ne font pas une preuve** taken individually, these clues do not constitute proof

b

♦ *avec le pronom* **en**

(= *personne*) **en voilà un qui ne se gêne pas !** well, he's got a nerve!; **j'en connais un qui sera content !** I know someone *ou* somebody *ou* one person who'll be pleased!; **il n'y en a pas eu un pour m'aider** nobody lifted a finger to help me

(= *chose*) **prête-m'en un** lend me one (of them); **il n'en reste qu'une** there's only one left; **j'en ai vu un très joli, de chapeau*** I've seen a very nice hat

(= *histoire*) **il m'en a raconté une drôle sur le directeur** he told me a really funny story about the manager → **bon¹**

c **avec article défini** **l'un d'eux ◊ l'un d'entre eux** one of them; **l'une des meilleures chanteuses** one of the best singers; **les uns disent ..., les autres répondent ...** some say ..., others reply ...; **l'un après l'autre** one after the other; **serrés l'un contre l'autre** huddled together; **elles étaient assises en face l'une de l'autre** they were sitting opposite one another *ou* each other; **ils sont belges l'un et l'autre** *ou* **l'un comme l'autre** they're both Belgian, both of them are Belgian; **l'une et l'autre solution sont acceptables** either solution is acceptable, both solutions are acceptable; **malgré ce que peuvent dire les uns et les autres** despite what some *ou* other people may say; **prenez l'un ou l'autre** take either one, take one or the other → **ni**

♦ **l'un dans l'autre** (= *tout bien considéré*) all in all; **l'un dans l'autre il s'y retrouve** all in all he manages to break even; **l'un dans l'autre, cela fera dans les 2 000 F** it'll come to around 2,000 francs in all

♦ **l'un l'autre ◊ les uns les autres** one another, each other; **ils se regardaient l'un l'autre** they looked at one another *ou* at each other; **ils s'invitent régulièrement les uns les autres** they have each other round regularly; *(Bible)* **aimez-vous les uns les autres** love one another

3 ADJECTIF

a **numéral cardinal** one; **vingt/trente et un ans** twenty-/thirty-one years; **il reviendra dans un an ou deux** he'll come back in a year or two; **il n'y a pas une seule voiture dans les rues** there's not a single car in the streets; **dix heures une (minute)** one minute past ten; **sans un (sou)*** penniless, broke*; *(Sport)* **ils ont gagné deux à un** they won two-one; *(fig)* **un partout, (la) balle au centre !*** we're even! → **fois, moins**

b **numéral ordinal** **page/chapitre un** page/chapter one; **en deux mille un** in two thousand and one

c **= formant un tout** **le Dieu un et indivisible** the one and indivisible God

♦ **c'est tout un** it's all one, it's one and the same thing; **pour moi c'est tout un** as far as I'm concerned it amounts to the same thing

4 NOM MASCULIN INV

= chiffre one; **un et un font deux** one and one are two; **compter de un à cent** to count from one to a hundred; **tu écris mal tes un** you don't write your ones very clearly; *(aux dés)* **j'ai fait deux un** I've got two ones; **il habite au 1, rue Léger** he lives at number 1, rue Léger; **le cavalier ne faisait qu'un avec son cheval** horse and rider were as one; **les deux frères ne font qu'un** the two brothers are like one person

---

5 **une** NF Presse **la une** the front page; **cet accident fait la une des journaux** the accident made the front pages *ou* the headlines; *(TV)* **la Une** channel one; *(au restaurant)* **l'addition de la une !** bill for table number one please!; *(Mil)* **une, deux ! une, deux !** left, right! left, right!; **à la une, à la deux !** with a one and a two and a three!; **il n'a fait ni une ni deux, il a accepté** he accepted without a second's hesitation *ou* like a shot; **il n'a fait ni une ni deux et il est parti** he left there and then *ou* without further ado → **colonne**

unanime [ynanim] ADJ [*témoins, sentiment, vote*] unanimous; **de l'avis ~ des observateurs** in the unanimous view of the observers; **~s pour** *ou* **à penser que** unanimous in thinking that; **la presse et les politiques sont ~s à condamner ce meurtre** the press and politicians are unanimous in condemning this murder; **de manière ~** unanimously

unanimement [ynanimmã] ADV unanimously, with one accord

unanimisme [ynanimism] NM a (= *accord*) universal consensus; **il dénonçait l'~ de la presse** he condemned the way in which the papers were all taking the same line b *(Littérat)* unanimism, unanism

unanimiste [ynanimist] 1 ADJ [*discours*] that reflects generally held beliefs; **une idéologie ~** an ideology to which the majority of people subscribe 2 NMF *(Littérat)* unanimist

unanimité [ynanimite] NF unanimity; **vote acquis à l'~** unanimous vote; **ils ont voté à l'~ pour** they voted unanimously for; **élu/voté à l'~** elected/voted unanimously; **élu à l'~ moins une voix** elected with only one vote against *ou* with only one dissenting vote; **il y a ~ pour dire que ...** the unanimous opinion is that ..., everyone agrees that ...; **cette décision a fait l'~** the decision was approved unanimously; **il fait l'~** there is general agreement about him; **il fait l'~ contre lui** everybody disapproves of him

unau [yno] NM unau, two-toed sloth

UNEDIC [ynedik] NF (ABRÉV = **Union nationale pour l'emploi dans l'industrie et le commerce**) *French national organization managing unemployment benefit schemes*

UNEF [ynɛf] NF (ABRÉV = **Union nationale des étudiants de France**) *French national students' union*

une-pièce [ynpjɛs] NM **(maillot de bain) ~** one-piece swimsuit

UNESCO [ynɛsko] NF (ABRÉV = **United Nations Educational, Scientific and Cultural Organization**) UNESCO

uni, e [yni] *(ptp de unir)* ADJ a (= *sans ornements*) [*tissu, jupe*] plain, self-coloured *(Brit)*; [*couleur*] plain, solid *(US)*; **tissu de couleur ~e** plain *ou* self-coloured *(Brit)* fabric; **l'imprimé et l'~** printed and plain *ou* self-coloured *(Brit)* ou material, prints and solids *(US)* b (= *soudé*) [*couple, amis*] close; [*famille*] close(-knit); **ils sont ~s comme les deux doigts de la main** *ou* **ils sont très ~s** they're very close; **ils forment un couple très ~** they're a very close couple; *(frm)* **~s par les liens du mariage** united in marriage, married; **présenter un front ~ contre l'adversaire** to present a united front to the enemy; **nous devons rester ~s** we must stay *ou* stand united c (= *uniforme, lisse*) [*surface*] smooth, even; [*mer*] calm, unruffled; *(littér)* **une vie ~e et sans nuages** a serene, untroubled life

UNICEF [ynisef] NF *ou rare* NM (ABRÉV = **United Nations Children's Fund**) *(anciennt :* ABRÉV = **United Nations International Children's Emergency Fund**) UNICEF

unicellulaire [yniselylɛʀ] ADJ unicellular

unicité [ynisite] NF uniqueness, unicity *(SPÉC)*

---

unicolore [ynikɔlɔʀ] ADJ plain, self-coloured *(Brit)*

unidimensionnel, -elle [ynidimãsjɔnɛl] ADJ one-dimensional, unidimensional

unidirectionnel, -elle [ynidiʀɛksjɔnɛl] ADJ unidirectional

unidose [ynidoz] 1 ADJ single-dose *(épith)* 2 NF single dose

unième [ynjɛm] ADJ **vingt/trente et ~** twenty-/thirty-first

unièmement [ynjɛmmã] ADV **vingt/trente et ~** in the twenty-/thirty-first place

unificateur, -trice [ynifikatœʀ, tʀis] ADJ unifying

unification [ynifikasjɔ̃] NF [*pays, système, parti*] unification; **~ européenne** European unification; **l'~ allemande** *ou* **de l'Allemagne** the unification of Germany; **l'~ monétaire** monetary union

unifier [ynifje] ▸ conjug 7 ◂ VT a [+ *pays, systèmes*] to unify; [+ *parti*] to unify, unite; **l'Allemagne unifiée** united *ou* unified Germany; **des pays qui s'unifient lentement** countries that are slowly becoming unified b [+ *procédures, tarifs*] to standardize

uniforme [ynifɔʀm] 1 ADJ [*vitesse, mouvement*] regular, uniform; [*terrain, surface*] even; [*style, couleur, ciel, paysage*] uniform; [*vie, conduite*] unchanging, uniform 2 NM uniform; **être en ~** to be in uniform; [*étudiant*] to be wearing one's uniform; **policier en ~** uniformed police officer; **en grand ~** in dress uniform, in full regalia; **endosser/quitter l'~** to join/leave the forces; **servir sous l'~** to be in the army; **il y avait beaucoup d'~s à ce dîner** there were a great many officers at the dinner; **~ scolaire** school uniform

uniformément [ynifɔʀmemã] ADV uniformly, regularly; **le temps s'écoule ~** time goes steadily by; **répartissez le caramel ~ dans le moule** spread the caramel evenly around the mould; **appliquer ~ la crème** apply the cream evenly; **un ciel ~ bleu/gris** a uniformly blue/grey sky; *(Phys)* **vitesse ~ accélérée** uniform change of speed

uniformisation [ynifɔʀmizasjɔ̃] NF standardization

uniformiser [ynifɔʀmize] ▸ conjug 1 ◂ VT [+ *mœurs, tarifs*] to standardize; [+ *teinte*] to make uniform

uniformité [ynifɔʀmite] NF [*vitesse, mouvement*] regularity, uniformity, steadiness; [*terrain, surface*] evenness; [*style, vie, conduite, ciel, paysage*] uniformity

unijambiste [yniʒɑ̃bist] 1 ADJ one-legged 2 NMF one-legged man (*ou* woman)

unilatéral, e (*mpl* **-aux**) [ynilateral, o] ADJ *(gén, Bot, Jur)* unilateral → **stationnement**

unilatéralement [ynilateralmã] ADV unilaterally

unilingue [ynilɛ̃g] ADJ unilingual

uniment [ynimã] ADV *(littér = uniformément)* smoothly; *(† = simplement)* **(tout) ~** (quite) plainly

uninominal, e (*mpl* **-aux**) [yninɔminal, o] ADJ **scrutin ~** voting for a single member *(attrib)*

union [ynjɔ̃] 1 NF a (= *alliance*) [*États, partis, fortunes*] union; **en ~ avec** in union with ■ *(PROV)* **l'~ fait la force** united we stand, divided we fall, strength through unity b (= *mariage*) union; **deux enfants sont nés de cette ~** two children were born of this union c (= *juxtaposition*) [*éléments, couleurs*] combination, blending → **trait** d (= *groupe*) association, union; **l'Union sportive de Strasbourg** the Strasbourg sports club 2 COMP ► **union charnelle** union of the flesh ► **union conjugale** marital union ► **union de consommateurs** consumers' association ► **union douanière** customs union ► **Union de l'Europe occidentale** Western European Union ► **Union économique et monétaire** Economic and Monetary Union ► **Union européenne** European Union ► **l'union libre** cohabitation ► **union monogame** (*Zool*) pair-bonding ► **union mystique** (*Rel*) mystic union ► **Union des républiques socialistes soviétiques** Union of Soviet Socialist Republics ► **union sacrée** (*Hist*) union sacrée (*united front presented by the French against the enemy in 1914*); (*fig*) **l'~ sacrée des syndicats contre la nouvelle loi** the trade unions' united front against the new law ► **l'Union soviétique** the Soviet Union ► **Union sportive** sports club *ou* association

unionisme [ynjɔnism] NM (*gén*) unionism; (*Hist*) Unionism

unioniste [ynjɔnist] ADJ, NMF (*gén*) unionist; (*Hist*) Unionist

unipare [ynipar] ADJ uniparous

unipersonnel, -elle [ynipɛrsɔnɛl] ☐ ADJ (*Ling*) impersonal ☐ NM (= *verbe*) impersonal verb

unipolaire [ynipɔlɛr] ADJ unipolar

▼ **unique** [ynik] ADJ ⓐ (= *seul*) only; **mon ~ souci/espoir** my only *ou* sole (*frm*) *ou* one concern/hope; **fils/fille ~** only son/daughter; **c'est un fils/une fille ~** he's/she's an only child; (*Pol*) **système à parti ~** one-party system; **le candidat ~ du parti** the party's sole candidate; **ce n'est pas un cas ~** this is not an isolated case; **croire en un Dieu ~** to believe in one God; **en France/en Europe** unique *ou* the only one of its kind in France/in Europe; **l'argent est son ~ sujet de préoccupation** money is the only thing he cares about; **deux aspects d'un même ~ problème** two aspects of one and the same problem; **rayon à prix ~** department where all items are at one price; (*dans un cinéma*) **"places : prix ~ 40 F"** "all seats 40 francs" → **monnaie, salaire, sens, seul** ⓑ (*après nom* = *exceptionnel*) [*livre, talent*] unique; **il est/c'est ~ en son genre** he's/it's one of a kind; **c'est un livre/une expérience ~ en son genre** it's a truly *ou* an absolutely unique book/experience; **il se croit ~** he thinks he's unique; **~ au monde** quite unique; **un paysage ~ au monde** a landscape that is quite unique; (*Art*) **c'est une pièce ~** it's unique ⓒ (* = *impayable*) priceless*; **il est ~ ce gars-là !** that guy's priceless!*

uniquement [ynikmɑ̃] ADV ⓐ (= *exclusivement*) only, solely, exclusively; **tu ne fais que du secrétariat ? — pas ~** do you only have secretarial duties? — not exclusively; **il était venu ~ pour me voir** he had come just to see me, he had come for the sole purpose of seeing me; **il pense ~ à l'argent** he only ever thinks of money, he thinks only of money, money is all he ever thinks about ⓑ (= *simplement*) only, merely, just; **c'était ~ par curiosité** it was only *ou* just *ou* merely out of curiosity

unir [ynir] ▸conjug 2◂ ☐ VT ⓐ (= *associer*) [+ *États, partis, fortunes*] to unite (à with); **~ ses forces** to join forces; **le sentiment commun qui les unit** the shared feeling which unites them ⓑ (= *marier*) **~ (en mariage)** to marry; **le prêtre qui les a unis** the priest who married them; (*Rel*) **ce que Dieu a uni** whom God has joined together; **ils ont voulu ~ leurs destinées** they wanted to get married ⓒ (= *juxtaposer, combiner*) [+ *couleurs, qualités*] to combine (à with); **il unit l'intelligence au courage** he combines intelligence with courage ⓓ (= *relier*) [+ *continents, villes*] to link, join up ☐ **s'unir** VPR ⓐ (= *s'associer*) [*pays, partis, fortunes*] to unite (à, avec with); **s'~ contre un ennemi commun** to unite against a common

enemy ⓑ (= *se marier*) to get married; **des jeunes gens qui vont s'~** a young couple who are going to be married ⓒ (= *s'accoupler*) **s'~ dans une étreinte fougueuse** to come together in a passionate embrace ⓓ (= *se combiner*) [*mots, formes, couleurs, qualités*] to combine (à, avec with)

unisexe [yniseks] ADJ INV unisex

unisexué, e [ynisɛksɥe] ADJ (*Bio, Bot*) unisexual

unisson [ynisɔ̃] NM (*Mus*) unison; **à l'~** [*chanter*] in unison; **répondre à l'~** to answer as one; **ils ont dit à l'~ que ...** they all said that ...; **les deux présidents sont à l'~ sur ce problème** the two presidents are of one mind about this problem; **l'Espagne s'est mise à l'~ de ses partenaires européens** Spain has come into line with its European partners

unitaire [yniter] ☐ ADJ (*Comm, Math, Phys*) unitary, unit (*épith*); (*Pol*) unitarian; (*Rel*) Unitarian; **prix ~** unit price ☐ NMF (*Rel*) Unitarian

unitarien, -ienne [ynitarjɛ̃, jɛn] ADJ, NM,F (*Pol*) unitarian; (*Rel*) Unitarian

unitarisme [ynitarism] NM (*Pol*) unitarianism; (*Rel*) Unitarianism

unité [ynite] NF ⓐ (= *cohésion*) unity; **l'~ nationale** national unity; **~ de vues** unity *ou* unanimity of views; **l'~ d'action des syndicats** the united action of the unions; **réaliser l'~ européenne** to build a united Europe; (*Littérat*) **les trois ~s** the three unities; **~ de lieu/de temps/d'action** unity of place/of time/of action; **roman qui manque d'~** novel lacking in unity *ou* cohesion ⓑ (*gén, Comm, Math* = *élément*) unit; **~ de mesure/de poids** unit of measure/of weight; **~ administrative** administrative unit; **~ monétaire** monetary unit; **~ monétaire européenne** European monetary *ou* currency unit; **~ de compte** unit of account; **~ de compte européenne** European Unit of Account; **~ lexicale** lexical item; **la colonne des ~s** the units column; **antibiotique à 100 000 ~s** antibiotic with 100,000 units; **prix de vente à l'~** unit selling price, selling price per item; **nous ne les vendons pas à l'~** we don't sell them singly *ou* individually ⓒ (= *troupe*) unit; (= *bateau*) ship; (*Mil*) **rejoindre son ~** to go back to *ou* rejoin one's unit; **~ mobile de police** mobile police unit; **~ de combat** combat *ou* fighting unit; **~ d'élite** crack unit ⓓ (= *établissement, service*) unit; **~ de production/fabrication** production/manufacturing unit; (*Méd*) **~ de soins palliatifs** care unit for the terminally ill ⓔ (*Univ*) **~ de formation et de recherche ◊ d'enseignement et de recherche†** university department; **~ d'enseignement ◊ ~ de valeur†** ≈ credit, ≈ course unit ⓕ (*Ordin*) **~ arithmétique et logique** arithmetic logic unit; **~ centrale** mainframe, central processing unit; **~ de commande** control unit; **~ de (lecteur de) disquettes** disk drive unit; **~ périphérique de sortie** output device ⓖ (* = *dix mille francs*) ten thousand francs; **32 ~s** 320,000 francs

univalve [ynivalv] ADJ univalve (*épith*)

univers [ynivɛr] NM (*gén*) universe; (= *milieu, domaine*) world; **dans tout l'~** throughout the world; **son ~ se borne à son travail** his work is his whole world; (*Ling*) **l'~ du discours** the universe of discourse; **l'~ mathématique** the world of mathematics; **~ virtuel** virtual world, world of virtual reality; **l'~ impitoyable de la mode** the cut-throat world of fashion → **face**

universalisation [yniversalizasjɔ̃] NF universalization

universaliser [yniversalize] ▸conjug 1◂ VT to universalize

universalisme [yniversalism] NM (*Rel*) Universalism; (*Philo*) universalism

universaliste [yniversalist] ADJ, NMF (*Rel*) Universalist; (*Philo*) universalist

universalité [yniversalite] NF universality

universaux [yniverso] NMPL **les ~ (du langage)** (language) universals; (*Philo*) **les ~** the universals

universel, -elle [yniversɛl] ADJ ⓐ (*gén*) universal; **esprit ~** polymath; **c'est un homme ~** he's a polymath, he's a man of vast knowledge; **produit de réputation universelle** world-famous product, product which is universally renowned; **il a une réputation universelle d'honnêteté** he is well-known for his honesty, his honesty is universally recognized → **exposition, légataire, suffrage** ⓑ (= *aux applications multiples*) [*outil, appareil*] universal, all-purpose (*épith*) → **pince, remède**

universellement [yniversɛlmɑ̃] ADV universally; **des valeurs ~ partagées** universally shared values; **un auteur ~ connu** an author known throughout the world; **il est ~ reconnu comme le plus grand paysagiste français** he is universally recognized as the greatest French landscape artist

universitaire [yniversiter] ☐ ADJ [*vie étudiante, restaurant*] university (*épith*); [*études, milieux, carrière, diplôme*] university (*épith*), academic → **année, centre, cité** ☐ NMF academic

université [yniversite] NF university; **entrer à l'~** to start university; **entrée à l'~** university entrance; **depuis son entrée à l'~** since he started university; **du troisième âge** university of the third age, u3a, post-retirement *ou* senior citizens' university; **~ d'été** (*Univ*) summer school; (*Pol* = *rencontre*) party conference; (= *session de formation*) summer school organized by a political party for young or potential members

univitellin, e [ynivitelɛ̃, in] ADJ **jumeaux ~s** identical *ou* monozygotic (*SPÉC*) twins

univocité [ynivɔsite] NF (*Math, Philo*) univocity

univoque [ynivɔk] ADJ [*mot*] univocal; [*relation*] one-to-one

Untel, Unetelle [œ̃tɛl, yntɛl] NM so-and-so; **Monsieur ~** Mr so-and-so

upérisation [yperizasjɔ̃] NF ultra heat treatment

upériser [yperize] ▸conjug 1◂ VT to sterilize at ultrahigh temperature; **upérisé** ultra heat treated; **lait upérisé** UHT milk

UPF [ypeɛf] NF (ABRÉV = **Union pour la France**) *French political party*

uppercut [ypɛrkyt] NM uppercut

upsilon [ypsilɔn] NM upsilon

uranifère [yranifɛr] ADJ uranium-bearing

uranium [yranjɔm] NM uranium; **~ enrichi** enriched uranium

uranoscope [yranɔskɔp] NM (*Zool*) stargazer

Uranus [yranys] ☐ NM (*Myth*) Uranus ☐ NF (*Astron*) Uranus

urbain, e [yrbɛ̃, ɛn] ADJ ⓐ (= *de la ville*) (*gén*) urban; [*transports*] city (*épith*), urban ⓑ (*littér* = *poli*) urbane

urbanisation [yrbanizasjɔ̃] NF urbanization

urbaniser [yrbanize] ▸conjug 1◂ VT to urbanize; **région fortement urbanisée** heavily built-up *ou* highly urbanized area; **la campagne environnante s'urbanise rapidement** the surrounding countryside is quickly becoming urbanized *ou* is becoming rapidly built up → **zone**

urbanisme [yrbanism] NM town planning

urbaniste [yrbanist] ☐ NMF town planner ☐ ADJ = **urbanistique**

urbanistique [yʀbanistik] ADJ [*réglementation, impératifs*] town-planning (*épith*), urbanistic; **nouvelles conceptions ~s** new concepts in town planning

urbanité [yʀbanite] NF (= *politesse*) urbanity

urbi et orbi [yʀbietɔʀbi] LOC ADV (*Rel*) urbi et orbi; (*fig*) **proclamer qch ~** to proclaim sth from the rooftops

urée [yʀe] NF urea

urémie [yʀemi] NF uraemia (*Brit*), uremia (*US*); **faire de l'~** to get uraemia (*Brit*) ou uremia (*US*)

urémique [yʀemik] ADJ uraemic (*Brit*), uremic (*US*)

uretère [yʀ(ə)tɛʀ] NM ureter

urétral, e [yʀetʀal, o] (*mpl* -aux) ADJ urethral

urètre [yʀɛtʀ] NM urethra

urgence [yʀʒɑ̃s] NF a [*décision, départ, situation*] urgency; **il y a ~** it's urgent, it's a matter of (great) urgency; **y a-t-il ~ à ce que nous fassions ...?** is it urgent for us to do ...?; **il n'y a pas (d')~** there's no rush, it's not urgent; **c'est une ~ absolue** it's a matter of the utmost urgency; **d'~** [*mesures, situation, aide*] emergency (*épith*); **procédure d'~** emergency procedure; (*Pol*) **déclencher la procédure d'extrême ~** to invoke emergency powers; **transporté d'~ à l'hôpital** rushed to hospital (*Brit*), rushed to the hospital (*US*); **être opéré d'~** to have an emergency operation; **on l'a appelé d'~** he was asked to come immediately; **à envoyer d'~** to be sent immediately, for immediate dispatch; **convoquer d'~ les actionnaires** to call an emergency meeting of the shareholders; **faire qch d'~** to do sth urgently; **il faut le faire de toute ~** it's very ou extremely urgent; **faire qch dans l'~** (= *très vite*) to do sth in a rush; (= *dans un état d'urgente nécessité*) to do sth urgently ou as a matter of urgency; **affaire à traiter en première ~** question to be dealt with as a matter of the utmost urgency ou as (a) top priority → **cas, état**

b (= *cas urgent*) emergency; **service/salle des ~s** emergency department/ward, casualty department/ward (*Brit*)

urgent, e [yʀʒɑ̃, ɑ̃t] ADJ [*besoin, problème*] urgent, pressing; [*mesure, réunion*] emergency (*épith*); [*appel, réforme*] urgent; **c'est ~** it's urgent; **rien d'~** nothing urgent; **l'~ est de ...** the most urgent thing is to ...; **il est ~ de réparer le toit** the roof is in urgent need of repair ou needs repairing urgently; **il est ~ qu'une décision soit prise** a decision must be taken urgently ou as a matter of urgency; **avoir un besoin ~ de capitaux** to need capital urgently, be in urgent need of capital; **de façon ~e** urgently

urger* [yʀʒe] ▶conjug 3◀ VI **ça urge!** it's urgent!; **je dois lui téléphoner mais ça urge pas** ou **il n'y a rien qui urge** I've got to phone him but there's no rush ou it's not urgent

urinaire [yʀinɛʀ] ADJ urinary

urinal (*pl* -aux) [yʀinal, o] NM (bed) urinal

urine [yʀin] NF urine (*NonC*); **sucre dans les ~s** sugar in the urine

uriner [yʀine] ▶conjug 1◀ VI to urinate, pass ou make water (*SPÉC*)

urinifère [yʀinifɛʀ] ADJ uriniferous

urinoir [yʀinwaʀ] N (public) urinal

urique [yʀik] ADJ uric

urne [yʀn] NF a (*Pol*) **~ (électorale)** ballot box; **aller** ou **se rendre aux ~s** to vote, go to the polls; **le verdict des ~s** the result of the polls b (= *vase*) urn; **~ funéraire** funeral urn

urogénital, e [yʀoʒenital, o] (*mpl* -aux) ADJ urogenital

urographie [yʀɔgʀafi] NF intravenous pyelogram

urologie [yʀɔlɔʒi] NF urology

urologue [yʀɔlɔg] NMF urologist

ursidés [yʀside] NMPL ursids

URSS [yʀs] NF (*Hist*) (ABRÉV = **Union des républiques socialistes soviétiques**) USSR

URSSAF [yʀsaf] NF (ABRÉV = **Union pour le recouvrement des cotisations de la Sécurité sociale et des allocations familiales**) social security contribution collection agency

ursuline [yʀsylin] NF Ursuline

urticaire [yʀtikɛʀ] NF nettle rash, hives, urticaria (*SPÉC*); **faire** ou **avoir des crises d'~** to suffer from nettle rash; **donner de l'~ à qn** (*lit*) to bring sb out in a rash; (*‚ fig*) to make sb's skin crawl

urticant, e [yʀtikɑ̃, ɑ̃t] ADJ urticant

urubu [yʀyby] NM buzzard

Uruguay [yʀygwɛ] NM (= *pays*) Uruguay; (= *fleuve*) Uruguay river

uruguayen, -enne [yʀygwajɛ̃, ɛn] 1 ADJ Uruguayan 2 **Uruguayen(ne)** NM,F Uruguayan

US [yɛs] NF (ABRÉV = **Union sportive**) → **union**

US(A) [yɛs(a)] NMPL (ABRÉV = **United States (of America)**) US(A)

us †† [ys] NMPL **~ (et coutumes)** customs

usage [yzaʒ] NM a (= *utilisation*) use; **apprendre l'~ de la boussole** to learn how to use a compass; **elle fait un ~ immodéré de parfum** she uses (far) too much ou an excessive amount of perfume; **abîmé par l'~** damaged through constant use; **elle nous laisse l'~ de son jardin** she lets us use her garden, she gives us ou allows us the use of her garden; **l'~ de stupéfiants** drug use ou abuse; **dépénaliser l'~ des drogues douces** to decriminalize (the use of) soft drugs → **faux²**

b (= *exercice, pratique*) [*membre, langue*] use; [*faculté*] use, power; **perdre l'~ de ses yeux/membres** to lose the use of one's eyes/limbs; **perdre l'~ de la parole** to lose the power of speech

c (= *fonction, application*) [*instrument*] use; **outil à ~s multiples** multi-purpose tool; **document à ~ interne** document for internal use only; (*Méd*) **à ~ externe** for external use (only); **à ~ unique** [*matériel stérile, seringues*] single-use; **servir à divers ~s** to have several uses, serve several purposes; **moquette/pile à ~ intensif** heavy-duty carpeting/battery → **valeur**

d (= *coutume, habitude*) custom; **un ~ qui se perd** a vanishing custom, a custom which is dying out; **c'est l'~** it's the done thing, it's the custom; **ce n'est pas l'~ (de)** it's not done (to), it's not the custom (to); **entrer dans l'~ (courant)** [*objet, mot*] to come into common ou current use; [*mœurs*] to become common practice; **contraire aux ~s** contrary to common practice ou to custom; **il n'est pas dans les ~s de la compagnie de faire cela** the company is not in the habit of doing that, it is not the usual policy of the company to do that, it is not customary for the company to do that; **il était d'~** ou **c'était un ~ de** it was customary ou a custom ou usual to; **formule d'~** set formula; **après les compliments/recommandations d'~** after the usual ou customary compliments/recommendations

e (*Ling*) **l'~** usage; **expression consacrée par l'~** expression fixed by usage; **l'~ écrit/oral** written/spoken usage; **l'~ décide** (common) usage decides → **bon¹**

f (*littér* = *politesse*) **avoir de l'~** to have breeding; **manquer d'~** to lack breeding, be lacking in the social graces; **il n'a pas l'~ du monde** he lacks savoir-faire ou the social graces

g (*loc*) **vous verrez à l'~ comme c'est utile** you'll see when you use it how useful it is; **ça s'assouplira à l'~** it will soften with use; **son français s'améliorera à l'~** his French will improve with practice; **à l'~ de** for use of, for; **à son ~ personnel** ◊ **pour son propre ~** for his personal use; **notice à l'~ de** notice for (the attention of); **à l'~ des écoles** [*émission*] for schools; [*manuel*] for use in schools; **en ~**

[dispositif, mot] in use; **hors d'~** [*éclairage, installation*] out of service; [*véhicule, machine à laver*] broken down; **mettre hors d'~** to put out of action; **avoir l'~ de qch** (= *droit d'utiliser*) to have the use of sth; (= *occasion d'utiliser*) **en aurez-vous l'~?** will you have any use for it?; **ces souliers ont fait de l'~** these shoes have lasted a long time, I've (ou we've *etc*) had good use out of these shoes; **faire ~ de** [+ *pouvoir, droit*] to exercise; [+ *permission, avantage, objet, thème*] to make use of; [+ *violence, force, procédé*] to use, employ; [+ *expression*] to use; **faire ~ de son arme** to use one's gun; **faire (un) bon/mauvais ~ de qch** to put sth to good/bad use, make good/bad use of sth

usagé, e [yzaʒe] ADJ (= *qui a beaucoup servi*) [*pneu, habits*] worn, old; (= *d'occasion*) used, secondhand; (*qui ne peut plus être utilisé*) [*seringue, préservatif, ticket, pile*] used; **quelques ustensiles ~s** some old utensils; **huiles ~es** waste oil

usager, -ère [yzaʒe, ɛʀ] NM,F user; **~ des transports en commun/du téléphone** public transport/telephone user; **~ de la route** road user; **~ de drogue** drug user; **les ~s de la langue française** French (language) speakers

usant, e‚ [yzɑ̃, ɑ̃t] ADJ (= *fatigant*) [*travail*] exhausting, wearing; [*personne*] tiresome, wearing; **il est ~ avec ses discours** he wears ou tires you out with his talking

usé, e [yze] (*ptp de* **user**) ADJ a (= *détérioré*) [*objet*] worn; [*vêtement, tapis*] worn, worn-out; (*Nucl Phys*) [*combustibles*] spent; (*fig*) [*personne*] (= *épuisé*) worn-out; (*par le stress*) burnt-out; **un parti/homme politique ~ par le pouvoir** a party/politician jaded by too many years in power; **~ jusqu'à la corde** threadbare → **eau** b (= *banal*) [*thème, expression*] hackneyed, well-worn; [*plaisanterie*] well-worn

user [yze] ▶conjug 1◀ 1 VT a (= *détériorer*) [+ *outil, roches*] to wear away; [+ *vêtements*] to wear out; **~ un manteau jusqu'à la corde** to wear out a coat, wear a coat threadbare; (*hum*) **ils ont usé leurs fonds de culottes sur les mêmes bancs** they were at school together b (*fig* = *épuiser*) [+ *personne, forces*] to wear out; [+ *nerfs*] to wear down; [+ *influence*] to weaken, sap; **la maladie l'avait usé** illness had worn him out c (= *consommer*) [+ *essence, charbon*] to use, burn; [+ *papier, huile, eau*] to use; **il use deux paires de chaussures par mois** he gets through two pairs of shoes (in) a month

2 VI (*littér* = *se comporter*) **en ~ mal/bien avec** ou **à l'égard de qn** to treat ou use (*littér*) sb badly/well

3 **user de** VT INDIR (= *utiliser*) [+ *pouvoir, patience, droit*] to exercise; [+ *charme, influence, liberté*] to use; [+ *autorité*] to use, exercise; [+ *permission, avantage*] to make use of; [+ *violence, force, procédé*] to use, employ; [+ *expression, mot*] to use; (*littér*) [+ *objet, thème*] to make use of; **ce journaliste a usé de moyens déloyaux pour obtenir cette information** this journalist used underhand means to get this information; **usant de douceur** using gentle means; **il en a usé et abusé** he has used and abused it; **il faut en ~ avec parcimonie** it should be used sparingly

4 **s'user** VPR [*tissu, vêtement, semelle*] to wear out; [*sentiments, passion*] to wear off; **mon manteau s'use** my coat's showing signs of wear; **elle s'use les yeux à trop lire** she's straining her eyes by reading too much; **elle s'est usée au travail** she wore herself out with work; **c'est ce que tout le monde s'use à lui dire** it's what everyone's been telling him all this time ou over and over again

usinage [yzinaʒ] NM (= *façonnage*) machining; (= *fabrication*) manufacturing

usine [yzin] 1 NF factory; **un copain de l'~** ou **d'~** a friend from the works ou factory; **travail**

en ~ factory work; (*fig*) **ce bureau est une vraie ~!** this office is a hive of activity!; (*fig*) **l'~ à rêves hollywoodienne** the Hollywood dream factory; **ce pays est une véritable ~ à champions*** this country churns out one champion after the other → **cheminée, travailler**

2 COMP ► **usine d'armement** arms *ou* armaments factory ► **usine d'assemblage** assembly plant ► **usine atomique** atomic energy *ou* power station, atomic plant ► **usine automatisée** automated factory ► **usine d'automobiles** car factory *ou* plant ► **usine à gaz** (*lit*) gasworks; (*fig*) huge labyrinthine system ► **usine d'incinération (d'ordures ménagères)** (household waste) incineration plant ► **usine de fabrication** manufacturing plant ► **usine métallurgique** ironworks ► **usine de montage** assembly plant ► **usine de pâte à papier** paper mill ► **usine de production** production plant ► **usine de raffinage** refinery ► **usine de retraitement (des déchets nucléaires)** (nuclear waste) reprocessing plant ► **usine sidérurgique** steelworks, steel mill ► **usine textile** textile plant *ou* factory, mill ► **usine de traitement des ordures** sewage works *ou* farm *ou* plant

usiner [yzine] ▸conjug 1◂ **1** VT (= *façonner*) to machine; (= *fabriquer*) to manufacture **2** VI (* = *travailler dur*) **ça usine dans le coin !** they're hard at it round here!*

usinier, -ière† [yzinje, jɛʀ] ADJ [*vie, monde*] factory (*épith*); [*faubourg*] industrial; **bâtiments ~s** factories

usité, e [yzite] ADJ in common use, common; **un temps très/peu ~** a very commonly-used/a rarely-used tense; **le moins ~** the least (commonly) used; **ce mot n'est plus ~** this word is no longer used *ou* in use

ustensile [ystɑ̃sil] NM (*gén* = *outil, instrument*) implement; (= *attirail*) **~s*** implements, tackle (*NonC*), gear (*NonC*); **~ (de cuisine)** (kitchen) utensil; **~s de ménage** household cleaning stuff *ou* things; **~s de jardinage** gardening tools *ou* implements; **qu'est-ce que c'est que cet ~ ?*** what's that gadget? *ou* contraption?

usuel, -elle [yzɥɛl] **1** ADJ [*objet*] everyday (*épith*), ordinary; [*mot, expression, vocabulaire*] everyday (*épith*); **dénomination ~le d'une plante** common name for *ou* of a plant; **il est ~ de faire** it is usual to do, it is common practice to do; **c'est un ~** it's on the open shelf; **c'est un ~** it's on the open shelves

usuellement [yzɥɛlmɑ̃] ADV ordinarily, commonly

usufruit [yzyfʀɥi] NM usufruct; **avoir l'~ de qch** to hold sth in usufruct

usufruitier, -ière [yzyfʀɥitje, jɛʀ] ADJ, NM,F usufructuary

usuraire [yzyʀɛʀ] ADJ [*taux, prêt*] usurious

usure¹ [yzyʀ] NF **a** (= *processus*) [*vêtement*] wear (and tear); [*objet*] wear; [*terrain, roche*] wearing away; [*forces, énergie*] wearing out; (*Ling*) [*mot*] weakening; **~ normale** fair wear and tear; **résiste à l'~** wears well, hard-wearing; **subir l'~ du temps** to be worn away by time; **résister à l'~ du temps** to stand the

test of time; (*Pol*) **c'est l'~ du pouvoir** it's the wearing effect of being in power; **~ de la monnaie** debasement of the currency; **on l'aura à l'~*** we'll wear him down in the end → **guerre b** (= *état*) [*objet, vêtement*] worn state

usure² [yzyʀ] NF (= *intérêt*) usury; **prêter à ~** to lend at usurious rates of interest; (*fig littér*) **je te le rendrai avec ~** I will pay you back (with interest), I will get my own back (on you) with interest (*Brit*)

usurier, -ière [yzyʀje, jɛʀ] NM,F usurer

usurpateur, -trice [yzyʀpatœʀ, tʀis] **1** ADJ [*tendance, pouvoir*] usurping (*épith*) **2** NM,F usurper

usurpation [yzyʀpasjɔ̃] NF [*pouvoir, honneur, titre, nom*] usurpation; (*littér = empiètement*) encroachment

usurpatoire [yzyʀpatwaʀ] ADJ usurpatory

usurper [yzyʀpe] ▸conjug 1◂ **1** VT [+ *pouvoir, honneur, titre, nom, réputation*] to usurp; **il a usurpé le titre de docteur en médecine** he wrongfully took *ou* assumed the title of Doctor of Medicine; **sa réputation n'est pas usurpée** he well deserves his reputation **2** VI (*littér = empiéter*) **~ sur** to encroach (up)on

ut [yt] NM (*Mus*) C → **clé**

Utah [yta] NM Utah

utérin, e [yteʀɛ̃, in] ADJ (*Anat, Jur*) uterine

utérus [yteʀys] NM womb, uterus; **location** *ou* **prêt d'~** womb-leasing → **col**

utile [ytil] **1** ADJ **a** [*objet, appareil, action*] useful; [*aide, conseil*] useful, helpful (**à qn** to *ou* for sb); **livre ~ à lire** useful book to read; **« adresses ~s »** "useful addresses"; **cela vous sera certainement ~** that'll certainly be of use to you; **veux-tu que je lui en parle ? — ce ne sera pas ~** do you want me to speak to him about it? — that won't be necessary; **ça peut toujours être ~** it could always come in handy; **ton parapluie m'a été bien ~ ce matin** your umbrella came in very handy (for me) this morning; **est-il vraiment ~ d'y aller** *ou* **que j'y aille ?** do I really need to go?, is there really any point in (my) going?; **il est ~ de rappeler que ...** it's worth remembering that ...; **il n'a pas jugé ~ de prévenir la police** he didn't think it was *ou* he didn't deem it necessary to tell the police, he didn't think it was worth telling the police; (*Écon*) **la vie ~ d'un bien** the productive life of an asset → **charge, temps¹, voter**

b [*collaborateur, relation*] useful; **il adore se rendre ~** he loves to make himself useful; **puis-je vous être ~ ?** can I be of help?, can I do anything for you?

2 NM **l'~** what is useful → **joindre**

utilement [ytilmɑ̃] ADV (= *avec profit*) profitably, usefully; **conseiller ~ qn** to give sb useful advice; **une bibliographie vient très ~ compléter l'article** there is a very helpful bibliography at the end of the article, the article is accompanied by a very useful bibliography; **ces mesures ont ~ contribué au redressement du pays** these measures were effective in putting *ou* helped put the country back on its feet

utilisable [ytilizabl] ADJ usable; **est-ce encore**

~ ? [*cahier, vêtement*] can it still be used?, is it still usable?; [*appareil*] is it still usable? *ou* working?; **facilement ~** easy to use; **ces listes incomplètes sont difficilement ~s** it's hard to use these incomplete lists; **une carte de crédit ~ dans le monde entier** a credit card that can be used throughout the world

utilisateur, -trice [ytilizatœʀ, tʀis] NM,F [*appareil*] user; (*Comm, Ordin*) **~ final** end user

utilisation [ytilizasjɔ̃] NF (*gén*) use; (*Culin*) [*restes*] using (up); **notice d'~** instructions for use

utiliser [ytilize] ▸conjug 1◂ VT **a** (= *employer*) (*gén*) to use; [+ *appareil, système*] to use, utilize; [+ *force, moyen*] to use, employ; **produit facile à ~** user-friendly product, product that is easy to use; (*sur un emballage*) **« à ~ avant le ... »** "use by ..." **b** (= *tirer parti de*) [+ *personne*] to use; [+ *incident*] to use, make use of; (*Culin*) [+ *restes*] to use (up); **savoir ~ les compétences** to know how to make the most of *ou* make use of people's abilities; **~ qch au mieux** to make the most of sth, use sth to its best advantage

utilitaire [ytilitɛʀ] **1** ADJ utilitarian → **véhicule 2** NM (*Ordin*) utility

utilitarisme [ytilitaʀism] NM utilitarianism

utilitariste [ytilitaʀist] ADJ, NMF (*Philo*) utilitarian

utilité [ytilite] NF (= *caractère utile*) usefulness; (= *utilisation possible*) use; **je ne conteste pas l'~ de cet appareil** I don't deny the usefulness of this apparatus; **cet outil a son ~** this tool has its uses; **cet outil peut avoir son ~** this tool might come in handy *ou* useful; **d'une grande ~** very useful, of great use *ou* usefulness *ou* help; **ce livre ne m'est pas d'une grande ~** this book isn't much use *ou* help *ou* a great deal of use *ou* help to me; **de peu d'~** of little use *ou* help; **d'aucune ~** (of) no use *ou* help; **sans ~** useless; **auras-tu l'~ de cet objet ?** can you make use of this object?, will you have any use for this object?; **de quelle ~ est-ce que cela peut (bien) vous être ?** what earthly use is it to you?, what on earth can you use it for?; (*Jur*) **reconnu** *ou* **déclaré d'~ publique** state-approved; **jouer les ~s** (*Théât*) to play small *ou* bit parts; (*fig*) to play second fiddle

utopie [ytɔpi] NF **a** (= *genre, ouvrage, idéal politique*) utopia, Utopia **b** (= *idée, plan chimérique*) utopian view (*ou* idea etc); **~s** utopianism, utopian views *ou* ideas; **ceci est une véritable ~** that's sheer utopianism; **c'est de l'~ !** it's just a pipedream!, it's all pie in the sky!

utopique [ytɔpik] ADJ utopian, Utopian → **socialisme**

utopisme [ytɔpism] NM Utopianism

utopiste [ytɔpist] NMF utopian, Utopian

UV [yve] **1** NF (ABRÉV = **unité de valeur**) († *Univ*) → **unité 2** NM (ABRÉV = **ultraviolet**) ultraviolet ray; **filtre UVA/UVB** UVA/UVB filter

uvulaire [yvylɛʀ] ADJ uvular

uvule [yvyl] NF (= *luette*) uvula

V

V¹, v¹ [ve] NM (= *lettre*) V, v; **en V** V-shaped; **moteur en V** V-engine; **encolure en V** V-neck; **décolleté en V** V-neckline; **le V de la victoire** the victory sign, the V for victory → **vitesse**

V², v² (ABRÉV = **voir, voyez**) V

V³ (ABRÉV = **volt**) V

va [va] → **aller**

vacance [vakɑ̃s] **1** NF **a** (*Admin*) [*poste*] vacancy **b** (*Jur*) **~ de succession** abeyance of succession; **~ du pouvoir** power vacuum **2** **vacances** NFPL **a** (*gén*) holiday(s) (*Brit*), vacation (*US*); (*Univ*) vacation; **les grandes ~s ◊ les ~s d'été** the summer holiday(s) (*Brit*) *ou* vacation (*US*); (*Univ*) the long vacation; **les ~s scolaires/de Noël/d'hiver** the school/ Christmas/winter holiday(s) (*Brit*) *ou* vacation (*US*); **~s de ou à la neige** winter sports holiday(s) (*Brit*) *ou* vacation (*US*); **~s actives** activity holiday(s) (*Brit*) *ou* vacation (*US*); **maison/ lieu de ~s** holiday (*Brit*) *ou* vacation (*US*) home/spot; **au moment de partir en ~s, nous ...** just as we were about to set off on (our) holiday (*Brit*) *ou* vacation (*US*), we ...; **aller en ~s en Angleterre** to go on holiday (*Brit*) *ou* vacation (*US*) to England; **il n'a jamais pris de ~s** he has never taken a holiday (*Brit*) *ou* vacation (*US*); **prendre ses ~s en une fois** to take all one's holiday (*Brit*) *ou* vacation (*US*) at once; **avoir droit à 5 semaines de ~s** to be entitled to 5 weeks' holiday (*Brit*) *ou* vacation (*US*); **j'ai besoin de ~s/de quelques jours de ~s** I need a holiday (*Brit*) *ou* vacation (*US*)/a few days' holiday (*Brit*) *ou* vacation (*US*); (*hum*) **il est parti ? ça va nous faire des ~s!** has he gone? that'll give us a break! → **colonie, devoir** **b** (*Jur*) **~s judiciaires** recess, vacation; **~s parlementaires** parliamentary recess

vacancier, -ière [vakɑ̃sje, jɛʀ] NM,F holidaymaker (*Brit*), vacationer (*US*)

vacant, e [vakɑ̃, ɑ̃t] ADJ **a** [*poste, siège*] vacant; [*appartement*] unoccupied, vacant **b** (*Jur*) [*biens, succession*] in abeyance

vacarme [vakaʀm] NM racket, row, din; **faire du ~** to make a racket *ou* row *ou* din; **il y avait un ~ de klaxons** horns were blaring; **il y avait un ~ continuel de camions** trucks roared past constantly; **il démarra dans un ~ assourdissant** he set off with a deafening roar

vacataire [vakatɛʀ] NMF temporary replacement, stand-in; (*Univ*) part-time lecturer (on contract); **il est ~** he's on a temporary contract

vacation [vakasjɔ̃] **1** NF **a** (= *temps de travail*) [*expert, notaire, commissaire de police*] session; [*médecin*] shift; [*enseignant*] (= *travail*) supply work; (= *honoraires*) fee; (= *vente aux enchères*) auction; **faire des ~s** to work on a short-term basis; **être payé à la ~** to be paid on a sessional basis **b** **~ (radio)** radio contact time **2** **vacations** NFPL (= *vacances judiciaires*) recess, vacation

vaccin [vaksɛ̃] NM (= *substance*) vaccine; (= *vaccination*) vaccination, inoculation; **faire un ~ à**

qn to give sb a vaccination *ou* an inoculation; **~ contre la grippe** flu vaccine; (*fig*) **un ~ contre qch** a safeguard against sth

vaccinal, e (*mpl* **-aux**) [vaksinal, o] ADJ [*essai, efficacité*] vaccine (*épith*); **complication ~e** complication arising from a vaccination; **taux de couverture ~e** vaccination rate

vaccinateur, -trice [vaksinatœʀ, tʀis] **1** ADJ vaccinating (*épith*), inoculating (*épith*) **2** NM,F vaccinator, inoculator

vaccination [vaksinasjɔ̃] NF vaccination, inoculation; **~ contre la rage** *ou* **antirabique/ contre l'hépatite B** rabies/hepatitus B vaccination

vaccine [vaksin] NF (= *maladie*) cowpox, vaccinia (*SPÉC*); († = *inoculation*) inoculation of cowpox; **fausse ~** false vaccinia

vacciner [vaksine] ▶ conjug 1 ◀ VT (*Méd*) to vaccinate, inoculate (**contre** against); **se faire ~** to have a vaccination *ou* an inoculation, get vaccinated *ou* inoculated; **les personnes vaccinées** the people who have been vaccinated; (*fig*) **être vacciné contre qch*** [+ *amour, tentation, illusion*] to be cured of sth; [+ *critiques*] to be immune to sth; **merci, maintenant je suis vacciné !*** thanks, I've learnt my lesson! *ou* I'm cured of that! → **majeur**

vaccinostyle [vaksinɔstil] NM scarificator

vachard, e [vaʃaʀ, aʀd] ADJ (= *méchant*) nasty, rotten*, mean

vache [vaʃ] **1** NF **a** (*Zool*) cow; (= *cuir*) cowhide; **~ laitière** dairy cow; **~ marine** sea cow; (*Vét*) **maladie de la ~ folle** mad cow disease → **plancher¹** **b** (‡ *péj* = *police*) **les ~s** the pigs, the filth‡ → **mort¹** **c** (‡ = *personne méchante*) (*femme*) bitch‡*, cow‡; (*homme*) swine*, sod‡; **ah les ~s !** the bastards!‡* → **peau** **d** (‡ : *intensif*) **une ~ de surprise/bagnole** a *ou* one hell of a surprise/car‡ **e** (*loc*) **comme une ~ qui regarde passer les trains** vacantly; **il parle français comme une ~ espagnole*** he absolutely murders the French language; **manger de la ~ enragée** to go through hard *ou* lean times, have a very hard *ou* lean time of it; **période de ~s grasses/ maigres pour l'économie française** good *ou* prosperous/lean *ou* hard times for the French economy; **donner des coups de pied en ~ à qn** to kick sb slyly; **faire un coup en ~ à qn** to play a dirty trick on sb, do the dirty on sb‡; **ah la ~ !‡** (*surprise, admiration*) wow!*, blimey!* (*Brit*); (*douleur, indignation*) hell!‡, damn (me)!‡

2 ADJ (* = *méchant, sévère*) rotten*, mean; **il est ~** he's really rotten* *ou* mean, he's a (rotten) swine* *ou* sod‡ (*Brit*); **elle est ~** she's really rotten* *ou* mean, she's a (mean *ou* rotten) cow‡ (*Brit*); **il n'a pas été ~ avec toi** he was quite kind *ou* good to you; **c'est ~ pour eux** it's really rotten for them*

3 COMP ▶ **vache à eau** (canvas) water bag ▶ **vache à lait*** (*péj*) cash cow, milch cow (*péj*) ▶ **vache sacrée** (*lit, fig*) sacred cow

vachement* [vaʃmɑ̃] ADV (= *très*) really; **~ bon/difficile** really *ou* damned‡ *ou* bloody‡ (*Brit*) good/hard; **on s'est ~ dépêchés** we rushed like mad* *ou* hell‡; **ça m'a ~ aidé** it helped me no end*, it was a big help; **c'est ~ important pour moi** it's really important to me; **il était ~ bien, ce film !** it was a brilliant film!; **il est ~ plus grand qu'elle** he's a hell of a lot bigger than she is‡; **il pleut ~** it's pouring (down), it's tipping it down* (*Brit*)

vacher [vaʃe] NM cowherd

vachère [vaʃɛʀ] NF cowgirl

vacherie [vaʃʀi] NF **a*** (= *méchanceté*) [*personne, remarque*] rottenness*, meanness; (= *action*) dirty trick*; (= *remarque*) nasty *ou* bitchy‡ remark; **faire une ~ à qn** to play a dirty* *ou* mean trick on sb; **dire des ~s** to make nasty remarks **b** (‡ : *intensif*) **c'est une sacrée ~, cette maladie** it's a hell of a nasty illness‡; **cette ~ d'appareil ne veut pas marcher** this damned‡ *ou* blasted* *ou* bloody‡ (*Brit*) machine won't work; **quelle ~ de temps !** what damned‡ *ou* blasted* *ou* bloody‡ (*Brit*) awful weather! **c** († = *étable*) cowshed, byre

vacherin [vaʃʀɛ̃] NM (= *glace*) vacherin; (= *fromage*) vacherin cheese

vachette [vaʃɛt] NF **a** (= *jeune vache*) young cow **b** (= *cuir*) calfskin

vacillant, e [vasijɑ̃, ɑ̃t] ADJ **a** [*jambes, démarche*] unsteady, shaky, wobbly; [*lueur, flamme*] flickering (*épith*) **b** [*santé, mémoire*] shaky, failing; [*raison*] failing; [*courage*] wavering, faltering; [*caractère*] indecisive, wavering (*épith*)

vacillation [vasijasjɔ̃] NF = **vacillement**

vacillement [vasijmɑ̃] NM **a** [*personne, blessé, ivrogne*] swaying; [*bébé, meuble*] wobbling; [*poteau*] swaying; [*flamme, lumière*] flickering **b** [*résolution, courage*] faltering, wavering; [*raison*] failure; [*santé, mémoire*] shakiness

vaciller [vasije] ▶ conjug 1 ◀ VI **a** (= *chanceler*) [*personne*] to sway (to and fro); [*blessé, ivrogne*] to sway, reel; [*bébé*] to wobble; **~ sur ses jambes** to be unsteady on one's legs, sway (to and fro); **il s'avança en vacillant vers la porte** he reeled *ou* staggered towards the door **b** [*poteau*] to sway (to and fro); [*meuble*] to wobble; **il lui semblait que les murs vacillaient autour d'elle** she felt as if the room was spinning around her **c** [*flamme, lumière*] to flicker **d** [*résolution, courage*] to falter, waver; [*raison, intelligence*] to fail; [*santé, mémoire*] to be shaky, be failing; **il vacillait dans ses résolutions** he wavered in his resolve

va-comme-je-te-pousse [vakɔmʒtəpus] ◆ **à la va-comme-je-te-pousse*** LOC ADV in a slapdash manner, any old how*

vacuité [vakɥite] NF (*littér* = *vide*) vacuity (*littér*), emptiness; (*intellectuelle, spirituelle*) vacuity, vacuousness

vacuole [vakɥɔl] NF (*Bio*) vacuole

vade-mecum [vademekɔm] NM INV (*littér*) handbook, vade mecum

vadrouille [vadʀuj] NF [a] (* = balade) ramble, jaunt; **partir en ~** to go on a ramble ou jaunt; **être en ~** to be out on a ramble; **elle est toujours en ~ à l'étranger** she's always off gallivanting abroad ou around the world [b] (Can = balai) mop

vadrouiller* [vadʀuje] ▶conjug 1◀ VI to rove around ou about; **dans les rues de Paris** to knock* ou rove about the streets of Paris

Vaduz [vadyz] N Vaduz

va-et-vient [vaevjɛ̃] NM INV [a] [personnes, véhicules] comings and goings; **il y a beaucoup de ~ dans ce café** it's a very busy café, there are a lot of comings and goings in this café; **j'en ai assez de ce ~ incessant dans mon bureau** I'm sick of this constant stream of people coming in and out of my office; **faire le ~ entre** [personne, train, bus] (lit) to go to and fro ou backwards and forwards between; [bateau] to ply between; **le dossier a fait le ~ d'un bureau à l'autre** the file has been passed backwards and forwards from one office to the other; (fig) **l'interprète faisait le ~ entre les deux langues** the interpreter was switching back and forth between the two languages [b] [piston, pièce] (**mouvement de**) ~ (gén) to and fro (motion), backwards and forwards motion; (verticalement) up-and-down movement [c] (Élec) (= circuit) two-way wiring (NonC) ou wiring system; (= interrupteur) two-way switch [d] (= gond) helical hinge; **porte à ~** swing door [e] (= bac) (small) ferryboat

vagabond, e [vagabɔ̃, ɔ̃d] [1] ADJ [peuple, vie] wandering (épith); [imagination] roaming (épith), roving (épith), restless; **son humeur ~e** his restless mood [2] NM,F (péj = rôdeur) tramp, vagrant; (littér = personne qui voyage beaucoup) wanderer, vagabond

vagabondage [vagabɔ̃daʒ] NM [a] (= errance) wandering, roaming; **leurs ~s à travers l'Europe** their wanderings across Europe; (littér) **le ~ de son imagination** the meanderings of his imagination [b] (Jur, péj = vie sans domicile fixe) vagrancy

vagabonder [vagabɔ̃de] ▶conjug 1◀ VI [personne] to roam, wander; [imagination, esprit] to wander, roam; **à travers l'Europe** to roam the length and breadth of Europe, wander across Europe

vagin [vaʒɛ̃] NM vagina

vaginal, e [mpl -aux) [vaʒinal, o] ADJ vaginal → **frottis**

vaginisme [vaʒinism] NM vaginismus

vaginite [vaʒinit] NF vaginitis (NonC)

vagir [vaʒiʀ] ▶conjug 2◀ VI [bébé] to wail, cry

vagissant, e [vaʒisɑ̃, ɑ̃t] ADJ wailing, crying

vagissement [vaʒismɑ̃] NM wail, cry

vague¹ [vag] [1] ADJ [a] (= imprécis) [renseignement, geste] vague; [notion, idée] vague, hazy; [sentiment, forme] vague, indistinct; (= distrait) [air, regard] faraway (épith), vague, (= ample) [robe, manteau] loose(-fitting); **j'ai le ~ sentiment que ...** I have a vague feeling that ...; **un ~ cousin** some distant cousin; **il avait un ~ diplôme** he had a diploma of sorts ou some kind of (a) diploma → **nerf, terrain**

[2] NM [a] (littér) [forme] vagueness, indistinctness; [passions, sentiments] vagueness [b] (= vagueness) **nous sommes dans le ~** things are rather unclear to us; **il est resté dans le ~** he kept it all ou he remained rather vague; **la police a préféré rester dans le ~ quant aux causes de cet incident** the police preferred not to give any details about the causes of the incident; **laisser qn dans le ~** to keep sb guessing, keep sb in the dark; **laisser qch dans le ~** to leave sth up in the air; **regarder dans le ~** to stare into space; **les yeux perdus dans le ~** with a faraway look in his

eyes; **~ à l'âme** melancholy; **avoir du ~ à l'âme** to feel melancholic

vague² [vag] NF [a] (lit) wave; **~ de fond** (lit) groundswell; (fig) groundswell of opinion; **le multimédia est une ~ de fond qui déferle sur le monde** multimedia is a tidal wave sweeping over the world; **faire des ~s** (lit, fig) to make waves; **surtout, pas de ~s!** whatever you do, don't rock the boat! → **déferlante** [b] (fig = déferlement) wave; **~ d'enthousiasme/de tendresse** wave ou surge of enthusiasm/of tenderness; **la première ~ d'immigrants/de départs en vacances** the first wave of immigrants/of holiday departures; **~ d'attentats/d'arrestations** wave of bombings/of arrests; **~ de criminalité** crime wave; (Mil) **~ d'assaut** wave of assault; **~ de chaleur** heatwave; **~ de froid** cold spell ou snap → **nouveau** [c] (= émanations) wave; **une ~ de gaz se propagea jusqu'à nous** a smell of gas drifted ou wafted up to us [d] (fig = ondulation) (Archit) waved motif; [chevelure] wave; [blés, fougères] wave, undulation (littér); **effet de ~** ripple effect

vaguelette [vaglɛt] NF wavelet, ripple

vaguement [vagmɑ̃] ADV vaguely; **ils sont ~ parents** they're vaguely related; **sourire ~ ironique** vaguely ou faintly ironic smile; **il était ~ inquiet** he was slightly ou vaguely worried; **à 18 ans, elle pensait ~ devenir professeur** when she was 18, she toyed with the idea of becoming a teacher; **il était ~ question d'organiser une réunion** there was vague talk of planning a meeting; **on entendait ~ parler dans le couloir** muffled voices could be heard in the corridor

vaguemestre [vagmɛstʀ] NM (Mil, Naut) officer responsible for the delivery of mail

vaguer [vage] ▶conjug 1◀ VI (littér = errer) [personne] to wander, roam; **laisser ~ son imagination/son regard** to let one's imagination/one's eyes wander

vahiné [vaine] NF Tahitian woman, wahine

vaillamment [vajamɑ̃] ADV bravely, courageously, valiantly

vaillance [vajɑ̃s] NF (= courage) courage, bravery; (au combat) gallantry, valour (Brit), valor (US); **avec ~** courageously, valiantly

vaillant, e [vajɑ̃, ɑ̃t] ADJ [a] (littér = courageux) brave, courageous; (au combat) valiant, gallant ■ (PROV) **à cœur ~ rien d'impossible** nothing is impossible to a willing heart (PROV) → **sou** [b] (= vigoureux) [personne] vigorous, hale and hearty, robust; [monnaie, économie] healthy; **je ne me sens pas très ~** I'm feeling a bit under the weather*, I don't feel too good

vaille que vaille [vajkəvaj] LOC ADV → **valoir**

vain, e [vɛ̃, vɛn] [1] ADJ [a] (= sans fondement) [paroles, promesse] empty, hollow, vain (épith); [craintes, espoir, plaisirs] vain (épith), empty; **pour lui la loyauté n'est pas un ~ mot** loyalty is not an empty word for him, the word loyalty really means something to him [b] (= frivole) [personne] shallow, superficial [c] (= infructueux) [effort, tentative, attente] vain (épith), in vain (attrib), futile, fruitless; [regrets, discussion] vain (épith), idle (épith); **son sacrifice n'aura pas été ~** his sacrifice will not have been in vain; **il est ~ d'essayer de ...** it is futile to try to ... [d] (littér = vaniteux) [personne] vain

[2] **en vain** LOC ADV in vain; **elle essaya en ~ de s'en souvenir** she tried vainly ou in vain to remember; **ce ne fut pas en ~ que ...** it was not in vain that ...; **je réessayai, mais en ~** I tried again, but in vain ou but to no avail; (frm) **invoquer le nom de Dieu en ~** to take the Lord's name in vain

[3] COMP ▶ **vaine pâture** (Jur) common grazing land

vaincre [vɛ̃kʀ] ▶conjug 42◀ VT [a] [+ rival, concurrent] to defeat, beat; [+ armée, ennemi] to defeat, vanquish (littér), conquer; **les meilleurs ont fini par ~** the best men finally won; **à ~ sans péril, on triomphe sans gloire** triumph without peril brings no glory; **nous vaincrons** we shall overcome [b] [+ obstacle, préjugé, maladie, sentiment] to overcome; [+ chômage] to conquer; **vaincu par le sommeil** overcome by sleep

vaincu, e [vɛ̃ky] (ptp de vaincre) [1] ADJ beaten, defeated, vanquished (littér); **s'avouer ~** to admit defeat, confess o.s. beaten; **il part d'avance** he feels he's beaten ou defeated before he begins [2] NM,F defeated man (ou woman); **les ~s** the vanquished (littér), the defeated; **malheur aux ~s!** woe to the vanquished! (littér); **mentalité/attitude de ~** defeatist mentality/attitude

vainement [vɛnmɑ̃] ADV vainly, in vain; **j'ai ~ essayé de lui expliquer** I tried in vain to explain to him, I tried to explain to him (but) to no avail

vainqueur [vɛ̃kœʀ] [1] NM (à la guerre) victor, conqueror; (en sport) winner; [concours, élection] winner; **le ~ de l'Everest** the conqueror of Everest; **les ~s de cette équipe** the conquerors of this team; **les ~s de cette compétition** the winners of this competition; **accueillir qn en ~** to welcome sb as a conquering hero; **il est sorti ~ des élections** he emerged victorious from the election, he emerged as the winner of the election; **ce film est le grand ~ du festival** this film scooped all the awards at the festival [2] ADJ M victorious, triumphant

vair [vɛʀ] NM vair; **la pantoufle de ~** the glass slipper

vairon¹ [vɛʀɔ̃] NM (= poisson) minnow

vairon² [vɛʀɔ̃] ADJ M **yeux ~s** (cerclés de blanc) wall eyes; (de couleur différente) eyes of different colours (Brit) ou colors (US), wall eyes

vaisseau (pl vaisseaux) [vɛso] NM [a] (Naut) vessel (frm), ship; **~ amiral** flagship; **~ de guerre** warship; **~ fantôme** ghost ship; (Mus) « **le Vaisseau fantôme** » "the Flying Dutchman"; **~ spatial** spaceship → **brûler, capitaine, enseigne, lieutenant** [b] (Anat) vessel; **~ sanguin/lymphatique/capillaire** blood/lymphatic/capillary vessel [c] (Bot) vessel; **plante à ~x** vascular plant [d] (Archit) nave

vaisselier [vɛsəlje] NM (= meuble) dresser

vaisselle [vɛsɛl] NF (= plats) crockery; (= plats à laver) dishes; (= lavage) dishes, washing-up (Brit); **~ de porcelaine** china; **~ de faïence** earthenware; **~ plate** (gold ou silver) plate; **faire la ~** to do the dishes ou the washing-up (Brit), wash up (Brit); **la ~ était faite en deux minutes** the dishes were done ou the washing-up (Brit) was done in two minutes → **eau**

VAL [val] NM (ABRÉV = **véhicule automatique léger**) automated (driverless) train

val (pl vals ou vaux) [val, vo] NM (gén dans noms de lieux) valley; **le Val de Loire** the Val de Loire, the Loire Valley; **le Val d'Aoste** Valle d'Aosta → **mont**

valable [valabl] ADJ [a] (= valide) [contrat, passeport] valid; **billet ~ un an** a ticket valid for one year; « **offre ~ jusqu'au 31 mai** » "offer valid until 31st May" [b] (= acceptable, recevable) [excuse, raison] valid, legitimate; [loi, critère, théorie, motif] valid; **elle n'a aucune raison ~ de le faire** she has no good ou valid reason for doing it; **ce n'est ~ que dans certains cas** it is only valid ou it only holds ou applies in certain cases; **ce que j'ai dit reste ~ dans ce cas aussi** what I said is valid ou applies in this case as well [c] (= de qualité) [œuvre, solution, commentaire] worthwhile; [auteur, équipements] decent; [concurrent] worthy → **interlocuteur** [d] (= rentable) worthwhile; **financièrement, ce**

n'est pas ~ it's not financially viable, it's not worthwhile financially

valablement [valabləmã] ADV a (= *légitimement*) validly, legitimately; **ce billet ne peut pas être ~ utilisé** this ticket isn't valid; **ne pouvant ~ soutenir que ...** not being able to uphold legitimately ou justifiably that ... b (= *de façon satisfaisante*) **pour en parler ~, il faut être spécialiste** you need to be a specialist to be able to make valid comments ou to have anything worth saying about it

Valais [vale] NM **le ~** Valais

valaisan, -anne [valezã, an] 1 ADJ of ou from Valais 2 **Valaisan(ne)** NM,F inhabitant ou native of Valais

valdinguer* [valdɛge] ▶conjug 1 ◀ VI (= *tomber*) **aller ~** [*personne*] to fall flat on one's face*, go sprawling; **les boîtes ont failli ~ (par terre)** the boxes nearly came crashing down ou nearly went flying*; **envoyer ~ qn** (*lit*) to send sb flying; (*fig*) to tell sb to clear off* ou buzz off*, send sb off with a flea in his ear* (*Brit*); **envoyer ~ qch** to send sth flying*; **j'ai bien envie de tout envoyer ~!** I'd like to jack it all in!*

valence [valãs] NF (*Ling, Phys*) valency (*Brit*), valence (*US*); **~-gramme** gramme-equivalent

valériane [valerjan] NF valerian

valet [vale] 1 NM a (= *domestique*) (man)servant; (*Hist*) [*seigneur*] valet; (*péj Pol*) lackey (*péj*); **premier ~ de chambre du roi** king's first valet; (*Théât*) **~ de comédie** manservant (part ou role); (*Théât*) **jouer les ~s** to play servant parts ou roles b (*Cartes*) jack, knave; **~ de cœur** jack ou knave of hearts c (= *cintre*) (**de nuit**) valet d (*Tech*) **~ (de menuisier)** (woodworker's) clamp 2 COMP ▶ **valet d'âtre** companion set ▶ **valet de chambre** manservant, valet ▶ **valet de chiens** (hunt) kennel attendant ▶ **valet d'écurie** groom, stableboy, stable lad (*Brit*) ▶ **valet de ferme** farmhand ▶ **valet de pied** footman

valetaille [valtaj] NF († ou péj) menials, flunkeys†

valétudinaire [valetydinɛʀ] ADJ, NMF (*littér*) valetudinarian

valeur [valœʀ] 1 NF a (= *prix*) value, worth; (*Fin*) [*devise, action*] value, price; (*Comm*) **~ marchande** market value; (*Poste*) **en ~ déclarée** value declared; (*Écon*) **~ ajoutée** added value; **~ d'usage/d'échange** use/exchange value, value in use/in exchange; **~ nominale** ou **faciale** face ou nominal value, face amount (*US*); **~ vénale** monetary value; **quelle est la ~ de cet objet/du franc?** what is this object/the franc worth?, what is the value of this object/the franc?; **prendre/perdre de la ~** to go up/down in value, lose/gain in value; **la ~ intrinsèque de qch** the intrinsic value ou worth of sth; **cette monnaie/cette pièce n'a plus de ~** this currency/this coin is worthless; **estimer la ~ d'un terrain/d'un tableau à 800 000 F** to value a piece of land/a picture at 800,000 francs, put the value ou estimate the value of a piece of land/of a picture at 800,000 francs; **ces tableaux sont de même ~** ou **ont la même ~** these pictures are of equal value ou have the same value ou are worth the same amount; **manuscrit d'une ~ inestimable** priceless manuscript → **taxe** b (*Bourse*: gén pl = titre) security; **~s mobilières** securities, stocks and shares; **~s disponibles** liquid assets; **~s de premier ordre** ou **de tout repos** ou **de père de famille** gilt-edged ou blue-chip securities, gilts → **bourse, refuge, vedette** c (= *qualité*) [*personne, auteur*] worth, merit; [*roman, tableau*] value, merit; [*science, théorie*] value; (= *courage*) valour (*Brit*), valor (*US*); **la ~ de cette méthode/découverte reste à prouver** the value of this method/discovery is still to be proved; **estimer** ou **juger qn/qch à sa (juste) ~** to estimate ou judge sb/sth at his/its

true value ou worth; **son œuvre n'est pas sans ~** his work is not without value ou merit; **ce meuble n'a qu'une ~ sentimentale** this piece of furniture has sentimental value only; **accorder** ou **attacher de la ~ à qch** to value sth, place value on sth → **jugement** d (*Jeux, Math, Mus*) value; **la ~ affective/poétique/symbolique** the emotive/poetic/symbolic value; (*Math*) **~ absolue** absolute value; **en ~ absolue/relative, le prix des voitures a diminué** in absolute/relative terms the price of cars has gone down; **donnez-lui la ~ d'un verre à liqueur/d'une cuiller à café** give him the equivalent of a liqueur glass/a teaspoonful e (*loc*) **de ~** [*bijou, meuble*] valuable, of value; **objets de ~** valuables, articles of value; **professeur/acteur de ~** teacher/actor of considerable merit; **sans ~** [*objet, témoignage*] worthless, valueless; **mettre en ~** [+ *bien, patrimoine, terrain*] to develop, exploit; [+ *détail, caractéristique*] to bring out, highlight, emphasize; [+ *yeux, jambes*] to set off, enhance; [+ *taille*] to emphasize; [+ *objet décoratif*] to set off, show (off) to advantage; [+ *personne*] to show to advantage ou in a flattering light; **se mettre en ~** to show o.s. off to advantage; **ce chapeau te met en ~** that hat (of yours) is very flattering ou becoming, that hat really suits you; **son discours a mis en ~ l'importance de la culture/le rôle des syndicats** in his speech he emphasized the importance of culture/the role of the unions; **mise en ~** [*terrain, ressources naturelles, patrimoine*] development; [*forêt*] exploitation; [*meuble, tableau*] setting-off; [*détail, caractéristique, mot*] emphasizing, highlighting

2 **valeurs** NFPL (*morales, intellectuelles*) values; **échelle** ou **hiérarchie des ~s** scale of values; **système de ~s** value system; **nous n'avons pas les mêmes ~s** we don't have ou share the same values

valeureusement [valœʀøzmã] ADV (*littér*) valiantly, valorously (*littér*)

valeureux, -euse [valœʀø, øz] ADJ (*littér*) valiant, valorous (*littér*)

validation [validasjɔ̃] NF [*passeport, billet*] validation; [*document*] authentication; [*décision*] ratification; [*bulletin*] validation, stamping

valide [valid] ADJ a [*personne*] (= *non blessé ou handicapé*) able, able-bodied; (= *en bonne santé*) fit, well (*attrib*); [*membre*] good (*épith*); **la population ~** the able-bodied population; **se sentir assez ~ pour faire** to feel fit ou well enough to do, feel up to doing b [*billet, carte d'identité*] valid

valider [valide] ▶conjug 1 ◀ VT [+ *passeport, billet*] to validate; [+ *document*] to authenticate; [+ *décision*] to ratify; (*Jeux*) **faire ~ un bulletin** to get a coupon validated ou stamped; **l'élection ne sera validée que si le taux de participation est suffisant** the election will only be valid if the turnout is high enough

validité [validite] NF [*billet, élection, argument, accord*] validity; **quelle est la durée de ~ de votre passeport?** how long is your passport valid for?

valise [valiz] NF (suit)case, bag; **faire sa ~** ou **ses ~s** (*lit*) to pack; (*fig* = *partir*) to pack one's bags, pack up and leave; **la ~ (diplomatique)** the diplomatic bag ou pouch (*US*); **avoir des ~s sous les yeux*** to have bags under one's eyes → **boucler**

Valkyrie [valkiʀi] NF Valkyrie, Walkyrie

vallée [vale] NF (*Géog*) valley; **les gens de la ~** the lowland people; **~ suspendue/en U/glaciaire** hanging/U-shaped/glaciated valley; **~ sèche** ou **morte** dry valley; **la ~ de la Loire/du Nil** the Loire/Nile valley; **la Vallée des Rois/Reines** the Valley of the Kings/Queens; (*fig littér*) **la vie est une ~ de larmes** life is a vale of tears (*littér*); **la ~ de la mort** (*Bible*) the

valley of the shadow of death; (*Géog*) Death Valley

vallon [valɔ̃] NM small valley

vallonné, e [valɔne] ADJ undulating, hilly

vallonnement [valɔnmã] NM undulation

valoche* [valɔʃ] NF case, bag

▼ **valoir** [valwaʀ]

▶conjug 29◀
1 VERBE INTRANSITIF   3 VERBE PRONOMINAL
2 VERBE TRANSITIF
---

1 VERBE INTRANSITIF

a **valeur marchande** [*propriété, bijou*] to be worth; **~ 1 000 F** to be worth 1,000 francs; **ça vaut combien?** (*gén*) how much is it worth?; (*à un commerçant*) how much is it?; **~ de l'argent** to be worth a lot of money; **ça vaut bien 2 000 F** (*estimation*) it must easily be worth 2,000 francs; (*jugement*) it's well worth 2,000 francs; **~ cher/encore plus cher** to be worth a lot/still more; (*fig*) **ça alors, ça vaut mille!*** that's priceless!* → **pesant**

♦ **à ~** (*Comm*) to be deducted, on account; **paiement/acompte à ~ sur ...** payment/deposit to be deducted from ...; **500 F à ~ sur votre prochaine facture** 500 francs credit against your next bill → **à-valoir**

♦ **faire valoir** (= *exploiter*) [+ *domaine*] to farm; [+ *titres, capitaux*] to invest profitably

b **qualités** **que vaut cet auteur/cette émission/le nouveau maire?** is this author/this programme/the new mayor any good?; **que valent ses promesses?** what are his promises worth?; **cette pièce vaut surtout par son originalité** the chief ou principal merit of this play is its originality; **prendre une chose pour ce qu'elle vaut** to take a thing for what it's worth; **ça vaut ce que ça vaut*, mais j'ai entendu dire que ...** take this for what it's worth, but I've heard that ...; **il a conscience de ce qu'il vaut** he's aware of his worth, he knows his (own) worth; **leur fils ne vaut pas cher!** their son's no good!; **il ne vaut pas la corde pour le pendre** he's not worth bothering with!; **sa dernière pièce ne valait pas grand-chose** his last play wasn't particularly good, his last play wasn't up to much* (*Brit*); **ce tissu/cette marchandise ne vaut rien** this material/this article is no good; **votre argument ne vaut rien** your argument is worthless; **cet outil ne vaut rien** this tool is useless ou no good ou no use; **ce climat ne vaut rien pour les rhumatismes** this climate is no good for rheumatism; **ça/il ne vaut pas tripette*** ou **un clou*** ou **un pet de lapin*** it's/he's a dead loss* → **rien**

♦ **faire valoir** (= *mettre en avant*) [+ *droit*] to assert; [+ *fait*] to emphasize; [+ *argument*] to put forward; [+ *caractéristique*] to highlight, bring out; **je lui fis ~ que ...** I impressed upon him that ..., I pointed out to him that ...; **il peut faire ~ ses droits à la retraite** he is eligible for retirement; **il s'entoure de gens faibles/ignorants parce que ça le fait ~** he surrounds himself with weak/ignorant people because it makes him appear stronger/more intelligent; **se faire ~** to sell o.s.; **il ne sait pas se faire ~** he doesn't know how to sell himself → **faire-valoir**

♦ **valoir mieux** (= *avoir plus de qualités, être meilleur*) **tu vaux mieux que lui** you're better than he is ou than him; **c'est un travail sans intérêt, tu vaux mieux que ça!** it's not a very good job, you're cut out ou made for better things!; **cet endroit vaut mieux que sa réputation** this place is better than its reputation allows; **ils ne valent pas mieux l'un que l'autre** they're both as bad as each other (= *être préférable*) **dans ce cas, il vaut mieux refuser** ou **mieux vaut refuser** in that case, it's better to refuse; **il vaudrait mieux que vous refusiez** you had ou you'd better refuse, you would ou you'd do better to refuse; **ça vaut mieux comme ça** it's better that way; **avertis-le, ça vaut mieux**

➤   GRAMMAIRE ACTIVE: **valoir** 28.1, 29.2

I'd tell him if I were you, it would be better if you told him; **il vaut mieux le prévenir** we'd (*ou* you'd *etc*) better tell him; **j'aurais dû lui téléphoner** — oui, il aurait mieux valu I should have phoned him — yes, you should (have) *ou* yes, that would have been the best thing to do; **je le fais tout de suite** — **il vaudrait mieux (pour toi)!** I'll do it straight away — you'd better!; **il vaut mieux entendre ça que d'être sourd!*** what a stupid thing to say! → **mieux**

♦ **vaille que vaille** somehow; **la police assurait vaille que vaille un semblant d'ordre** the police somehow managed to maintain order; **pendant la révolution, les gens ont continué à vivre vaille que vaille** during the revolution people somehow managed to go on living their lives

c = **être valable** to hold, apply, be valid; **ceci ne vaut que dans certains cas** this only holds *ou* applies *ou* is only valid in certain cases; **la décision vaut pour tout le monde** the decision applies to everyone

d = **équivaloir à** **la campagne vaut bien la mer** the countryside is just as good *ou* is every bit as good as the seaside; (*Mus*) **une blanche vaut deux noires** one minim (*Brit*) *ou* half note (*US*) is equivalent to two crochets (*Brit*) *ou* quarter notes (*US*); (*Bridge*) **un as vaut quatre points** an ace is worth four points; **il vaut largement son frère** he is every bit as good as his brother; **ce nouveau médicament/traitement ne vaut pas le précédent** this new medicine/treatment is not as good as *ou* isn't a patch on* (*Brit*) the previous one; **cette méthode en vaut une autre** it's as good a method as any; **tout ça ne vaut pas la mer/la liberté** this is all very well but it's not like the seaside/having one's freedom; **rien ne vaut un bon bain chaud** there's nothing like a nice warm bath, there's nothing to beat a nice warm bath; **ça ne vaut pas la réflexion qu'il m'a faite hier** you should have heard what he said to me yesterday; **ça vaut pas René*, tu sais ce qu'il m'a fait?** that's nothing on René* — do you know what he did to me?

e = **justifier** to be worth; (= **mériter**) to deserve; **Lyon vaut (bien) une visite/le déplacement** *ou* **voyage** Lyons is (well) worth a visit/the journey; (*hum*) **une soirée pareille, ça valait le voyage*** it was well worth going to a party like that; **ça valait bien un merci** he (*ou* they *etc*) could have said thank you; **un service en vaut un autre** one good turn deserves another → **coup, détour, peine**

2 VERBE TRANSITIF

♦ **valoir qch à qn** (= **rapporter, procurer**) to earn sb sth; **ceci lui a valu des louanges/des reproches** this earned *ou* brought him praise/ criticism; **les soucis/ennuis que nous a valus cette affaire!** the worry/trouble that this business has caused us!; **qu'est-ce qui nous vaut l'honneur de cette visite?** to what do we owe the honour of this visit?; **l'incident lui a valu d'être accusé d'imprudence** the incident meant he was accused of carelessness; **un bon rhume, c'est tout ce que ça lui a valu de sortir sous la pluie** all he got for going out in the rain was a bad cold; **l'inaction ne lui vaut rien** it isn't good for him to remain inactive; **ça ne lui a rien valu** it didn't do him any good

3 **se valoir** VERBE PRONOMINAL

= **être équivalents** **ces deux candidats/ méthodes se valent** there's not much to choose between the two applicants/methods, the two applicants/methods are of equal merit; **aux échecs, nous nous valons** (*en bien*) we're just as good as each other at chess, we're equally good at chess; (*en mal*) we're both as bad as each other at chess; **ça se vaut*** it's all the same; **et pour le prix? — ça se vaut** and pricewise? — there's hardly any difference

valorisant, e [valɔʀizɑ̃, ɑ̃t] ADJ status-enhancing (*épith*); **des responsabilités ~es pour eux** (*à leurs propres yeux*) responsibilities that give them a sense of self-worth; (*aux yeux des autres*) responsibilities that give them a certain amount of prestige; **tâches peu ~es** menial tasks

valorisation [valɔʀizasjɔ̃] NF a (*Écon, Fin*) (= **mise en valeur**) [*région, terrain, patrimoine*] development; (= **augmentation de la valeur**) [*produit, monnaie, titres*] increase in value b (= **augmentation du mérite, du prestige**) [*diplôme, compétences*] increased prestige; [*profession, activité*] improved status; [*personne*] improved standing; (*Psych*) self-actualization (*SPÉC*) c (*Écol*) [*déchets*] recovering

valoriser [valɔʀize] ▸ conjug 1 ◂ 1 VT a (*Écon, Fin*) [+ *région, patrimoine, capital*] to develop; [+ *produit, titre*] to increase the value of; **ces aménagements vont ~ la maison** these improvements will increase the value of the house; **le yen est fortement valorisé sur le marché des changes** the yen has risen sharply on the foreign exchange market b (= **donner plus de prestige à**) [+ *diplôme*] to increase the prestige of; [+ *personne*] to increase the standing of; [+ *profession*] to enhance the status of; **pour ~ l'image de l'entreprise** to enhance the image of the company c (*Écol*) [+ *déchets*] to recover d (= **évaluer la valeur de**) [+ *entreprise*] to value 2 **se valoriser** VPR [*immeuble, monnaie, titres*] to increase in value; [*personne*] to increase one's standing

valse [vals] NF a (= *danse, air*) waltz; **~ lente/viennoise** slow/Viennese waltz; **~ musette** waltz (*to accordion accompaniment*) b (*fig = remplacement fréquent*) **la ~ des prix** constant price rises; **la ~ des ministres** *ou* **des portefeuilles** the ministerial musical chairs; **~-hésitation** pussyfooting* (*NonC*)

valser [valse] ▸ conjug 1 ◂ VI a (= *danser*) to waltz b (* *fig* = *faire tomber*) **envoyer ~ qch/qn** to send sth/sb flying; **il est allé ~ contre le mur** he went flying against the wall; **faire ~ l'argent** to spend money like water, throw money around; **faire ~ les étiquettes** *ou* **les prix*** to jack up* the prices; **faire ~ les ministres/les employés** to play musical chairs with ministerial/staff posts

valseur, -euse [valsœʀ, øz] 1 NM,F (*Danse*) waltzer 2 **valseuses**‡ NFPL (= *testicules*) balls*‡

valve [valv] NF (*Bot, Élec, Tech, Zool*) valve; **~ cardiaque** heart valve

valvulaire [valvylɛʀ] ADJ (*Anat, Méd*) valvular

valvule [valvyl] NF (*Anat, Tech*) valve; (*Bot*) valvule; **~ mitrale** mitral valve

vamp [vɑ̃p] NF vamp

vamper* [vɑ̃pe] ▸ conjug 1 ◂ VT to vamp

vampire [vɑ̃piʀ] NM a (= *fantôme*) vampire b (*fig,†*) (= *escroc*) vampire, bloodsucker c (*Zool*) vampire bat

vampirique [vɑ̃piʀik] ADJ vampiric

vampiriser [vɑ̃piʀize] ▸ conjug 1 ◂ VT (*lit*) to suck the blood of; (*fig*) to suck the lifeblood out of

vampirisme [vɑ̃piʀism] NM vampirism

van[1] [vɑ̃] NM (= *panier*) winnowing basket

van[2] [van] NM (= *véhicule*) horse-box (*Brit*), horse trailer (*US*)

vanadium [vanadjɔm] NM vanadium

Vancouver [vɑ̃kuvɛʀ] N Vancouver; **l'île de ~** Vancouver Island

vandale [vɑ̃dal] 1 NMF vandal; (*Hist*) Vandal 2 ADJ vandal (*épith*); (*Hist*) Vandalic

vandaliser [vɑ̃dalize] ▸ conjug 1 ◂ VT to vandalize

vandalisme [vɑ̃dalism] NM vandalism; **acte de ~** act of vandalism; **c'est du ~!** it's vandalism!

vandoise [vɑ̃dwaz] NF dace, chub

vanesse [vanɛs] NF vanessa

vanille [vanij] NF (*Bot, Culin*) vanilla; **crème/glace à la ~** vanilla cream/ice cream

vanillé, e [vanije] ADJ [*sucre, thé*] vanilla (*épith*); [*parfum*] vanilla-scented

vanillier [vanije] NM vanilla plant

vanilline [vanilin] NF vanillin

vanilliné, e [vaniline] ADJ [*sucre*] flavoured with vanillin

vanité [vanite] NF a (= *fatuité*) vanity, conceit; **avoir la ~ de croire que ...** to be conceited enough to think that ...; **il avait des petites ~s d'artiste** he had the little conceits of an artist; **je le dis sans ~** I say it with all due modesty *ou* without wishing to boast; **tirer ~ de** to pride o.s. on; **elle n'a jamais tiré ~ de sa beauté** she has never been conceited about her beauty; **blesser qn dans sa ~** to wound sb's pride; **flatter la ~ de qn** to flatter sb's ego b (*littér*) [*paroles, promesse*] emptiness, hollowness, vanity; [*craintes, espoir, plaisirs*] vanity, emptiness; [*personne*] shallowness, superficiality; [*effort, tentative, attente*] vanity, futility, fruitlessness; [*regrets, discussion*] vanity, uselessness; (*Bible*) **~, ~, tout n'est que ~** vanity of vanities, all is vanity c (*Art*) vanitas

vaniteusement [vanitøzmɑ̃] ADV vainly, conceitedly

vaniteux, -euse [vanitø, øz] 1 ADJ vain, conceited 2 NM,F vain *ou* conceited person

vanity-case (*pl* **vanity-cases**) [vanitikɛz] NM vanity case

vannage [vanaʒ] NM (*Agr*) winnowing

vanne [van] NF a [*écluse*] (lock) gate, sluice (gate); [*barrage, digue*] floodgate, (sluice) gate; [*moulin*] (weir) hatch; [*canalisation*] gate; (*Aut*) **~ thermostatique** thermostat; (*fig*) **ouvrir les ~s** (= *laisser passer ou s'exprimer librement*) to open the floodgates; * (= *pleurer*) to turn on the waterworks* b (* = *remarque*) dig*, jibe; **envoyer une ~ à qn** to have a dig at sb*, jibe at sb

vanneau (*pl* **vanneaux**) [vano] NM peewit, lapwing; **~ huppé** Northern lapwing

vanner [vane] ▸ conjug 1 ◂ VT a (*Agr*) to winnow b (* = *fatiguer*) to do in*, knacker (out)‡ (*Brit*); **je suis vanné** I'm dead-beat* *ou* knackered‡ (*Brit*)

vannerie [vanʀi] NF (= *métier*) basketry, basketwork; (= *objets*) wickerwork, basketwork

vanneur, -euse [vanœʀ, øz] NM,F winnower

vannier [vanje] NM basket maker, basket worker

vantail (*pl* **-aux**) [vɑ̃taj, o] NM [*porte*] leaf; [*armoire*] door; **porte à double ~** *ou* **à (deux) vantaux** stable door (*Brit*), Dutch door (*US*)

vantard, e [vɑ̃taʀ, aʀd] 1 ADJ boastful 2 NM,F boaster, braggart

vantardise [vɑ̃taʀdiz] NF (= *caractère*) boastfulness; (= *action*) boasting (*NonC*), bragging (*NonC*); (= *propos*) boast

vanter [vɑ̃te] ▸ conjug 1 ◂ 1 VT [+ *personne*] to praise, sing the praises of; [+ *qualité, méthode, avantage*] to speak highly of, praise, vaunt (*frm*); **~ la marchandise** to peddle one's wares; **film dont on vante les mérites** much-praised film 2 **se vanter** VPR a (= *fanfaronner*) to boast, brag; **sans (vouloir) me ~** without wishing to blow my own trumpet, without wishing to boast *ou* brag, I don't want to boast b (= *se targuer*) **se ~ de** to pride o.s. on; **se ~ d'avoir fait qch** to pride o.s. on having done sth; **il se vante de (pouvoir) faire ...** he boasts he can *ou* will do ...; (*iro*) **il ne s'en est pas vanté** he kept quiet about it; **il n'y a pas de quoi se ~** there's nothing to be proud of *ou* to boast about; **et il s'en vante!** and he's proud of it!

Vanuatu [vanwatu] N Vanuatu

va-nu-pieds [vanypje] NMF INV (péj) tramp, beggar

vapes: [vap] NFPL **tomber dans les ~** to fall into a dead faint, pass out; **être dans les ~** (= évanoui) to be out for the count* ou out cold*; (= étourdi par un choc) to be woozy* ou in a daze; (= abruti par le travail) to be punch-drunk ou in a daze; (= distrait) to have one's head in the clouds

vapeur [vapœʀ] [1] NF [a] (littér = brouillard) haze (NonC), vapour (Brit) (NonC), vapor (US) (NonC) [b] (d'eau) steam, (water) vapour (Brit) ou vapor (US); **~ atmosphérique** atmospheric vapour; (Tech) **à ~** steam (épith); **repassage à la ~** steam-ironing; (Culin) (**cuit à la**) **~ steamed** [c] (= émanation: Chim, Phys) vapour (Brit) (NonC), vapor (US) (NonC); **~s** (nocives) fumes; **~ d'essence** petrol (Brit) ou gasoline (US) fumes; **~ saturante** saturated vapour; **~ sèche** dry steam [d] (†: gén pl = malaises) **~s** vapours†; (bouffées de chaleur) **avoir ses ~s** to have hot flushes (Brit) ou flashes (US); (†: malaise) to have the vapours† [e] (gén pl = griserie) **les ~s de l'ivresse/de la gloire** the heady fumes of intoxication/of glory [f] (loc) **aller à toute ~** (navire) to sail full steam ahead; (* fig) to go at full speed, go full steam ahead (fig) → **renverser** [2] NM (= bateau) steamship, steamer

vapo* [vapo] NM ABRÉV = **vaporisateur**

vaporeusement [vapɔʀøzmɑ̃] ADV vaporously

vaporeux, -euse [vapɔʀø, øz] ADJ [tissu, robe] diaphanous, gossamer (épith) (littér); (littér) [lumière, atmosphère] hazy, misty, vaporous; [nuage, cheveux] gossamer (épith) (littér); (Art) **lointain ~** sfumato background

vaporisateur [vapɔʀizatœʀ] NM (à parfum) spray, atomizer; (Agr) spray; (Tech) vaporizer; **parfum en ~** perfume in a spray bottle ou in an atomizer

vaporisation [vapɔʀizasjɔ̃] NF [a] [parfum, insecticide, surface] spraying; **une ~ suffit** one spray is enough [b] (Phys) vaporization

vaporiser [vapɔʀize] ▸conjug 1◂ [1] VT [a] [+ parfum, insecticide, surface] to spray; **vaporisez le produit sur la plaie** spray the product onto the wound [b] (Phys) to vaporize [2] **se vaporiser** VPR (Phys) to vaporize

vaquer [vake] ▸conjug 1◂ [1] **vaquer à** VT INDIR (= s'occuper de) to attend to, see to; **~ à ses occupations** to attend to one's affairs, go about one's business [2] VI [a] († = être vacant) to stand ou be vacant [b] (Admin = être en vacances) to be on vacation

varan [vaʀɑ̃] NM varanus

varappe [vaʀap] NF (= sport) rock-climbing; (= ascension) (rock) climb; **faire de la ~** to go rock-climbing

varapper [vaʀape] ▸conjug 1◂ VI to rock-climb

varappeur, -euse [vaʀapœʀ, øz] NM,F (rock-) climber

varech [vaʀɛk] NM wrack, kelp, varec

vareuse [vaʀøz] NF [pêcheur, marin] pea jacket; (d'uniforme) tunic; (de ville) jacket

variabilité [vaʀjabilite] NF [a] [temps, humeur] changeableness, variableness [b] (Math, Sci) variability

variable [vaʀjabl] [1] ADJ [a] (= incertain) [temps] variable, changeable, unsettled; [humeur] changeable, variable; [vent] variable; **le baromètre est au ~** the barometer is at ou reads "change" [b] (= susceptible de changements) [montant, allocation, part] variable; [dimensions, modalités, formes] adaptable, variable; (Math, Sci) [grandeur, quantité, facteur] variable; (Ling) [forme, mot] inflectional, inflected (épith); (Fin) **à revenu ~** variable yield (épith); **l'effet est (très) ~ selon les individus** the effect varies (greatly) from person to person ou according to the in-

dividual; **mot ~ en genre** word that is inflected ou marked for gender → **foyer, géométrie** [c] (au pl = varié) [résultats, réactions] varied, varying (épith) [2] NF (Chim, Ling, Math, Phys, Stat) variable; **~ aléatoire/continue/discrète** random/continuous/discrete variable; (Ordin) **~ entière/numérique** integer/numeric variable

variance [vaʀjɑ̃s] NF (Sci) variance

variante [vaʀjɑ̃t] NF (gén) variant (de of), variation (de on); (Ling, Littérat) variant (de of)

variateur [vaʀjatœʀ] NM **~ de vitesse** speed variator; **~ (de lumière)** dimmer

variation [vaʀjasjɔ̃] NF [a] (= écart, changement) variation (de in); **les ~s de (la) température** variations in (the) temperature, temperature variations; **~s climatiques** climatic ou climate variations; **les ~s orthographiques/phonétiques au cours des siècles/selon les régions** spelling/phonetic variations ou variants throughout the centuries/from region to region; **les ~s du mode de vie au cours des siècles** the changes in life-style through the centuries; (Écon) **corrigé des ~s saisonnières** seasonally adjusted, adjusted for seasonal variations; **~s monétaires** currency fluctuations; **~s hormonales** hormonal fluctuations; **~s d'humeur** mood swings; **les ~s de l'opinion** swings ou changes in public opinion; **subir** ou **connaître de fortes ~s** to vary ou fluctuate considerably [b] (Mus) variation; **~s pour piano** variations for piano; (hum) **~s sur un thème connu** variations on the same old theme ou on a well-worn theme

varice [vaʀis] NF (Méd) varicose vein, varix (SPÉC) → **bas²**

varicelle [vaʀisɛl] NF chickenpox, varicella (SPÉC)

varicosité [vaʀikozite] NF varicosity

varié, e [vaʀje] (ptp de **varier**) ADJ [a] (= non monotone) [style, existence, paysage] varied, varying (épith); [programme, menu] (= qu'on change souvent) varying (épith); (= diversifié) varied; **un travail très ~** a very varied job; (Mil) **en terrain ~** on irregular terrain; (Mus) **air ~** theme with ou and variations [b] (littér = non uni) [tissu, couleur] variegated [c] (= divers) [résultats] various, varying (épith), varied; [produits, sujets, objets] various; **hors-d'œuvre ~s** selection of hors d'œuvres, hors d'œuvres variés; **avoir recours à des arguments ~s** to use various arguments; **on rencontre les opinions les plus ~es** you come across the most varied ou diverse opinions on the subject

varier [vaʀje] ▸conjug 7◂ [1] VI [a] (= changer) to vary, change; (Math) **faire ~ une fonction** to vary a function; **pour ~ un peu** for a bit of a change, for a bit of variety [b] (= différer) to vary; **son témoignage n'a pas varié** he stuck to his story; **ma réponse ne variera pas** I will not change my reply; **les prix varient de 90 à 150 F/entre 90 et 150 F** prices vary from 90 to 150 francs/between 90 and 150 francs; **le taux peut ~ du simple au double** rates can vary by as much as 100%; **les tarifs varient selon les pays** prices vary from country to country; **le dosage varie en fonction de l'âge et du poids** the dose varies according to age and weight [c] (Ling) [mot, forme] to be inflected; **ce mot varie en genre et en nombre** this word inflects in gender and number [d] (= changer d'opinion) **ils varient souvent dans leurs opinions sur ...** their opinions often vary on the subject of ...; **elle n'a jamais varié sur ce point** she has never changed her opinion on that [2] VT [a] [+ style, vie] (= changer) to vary; (= rendre moins monotone) (Mus) to vary, lend ou give variety to; (iro) **pour ~ les plaisirs** just for a pleasant change (iro); **elle variait souvent sa coiffure/le menu** she often changed her hair

style/the menu [b] (= diversifier) [+ thèmes, produits] to vary, diversify

variété [vaʀjete] [1] NF [a] (= diversité) variety; **étonné par la grande ~ des produits/opinions** surprised at the great variety ou the wide range of products/opinions; **aimer la ~** to like variety; **~ des langues** language variety [b] (Bot, Zool) variety; (= aspect, forme) variety, type; **il cultive exclusivement cette ~ de rose** he only grows this variety of rose; **on y rencontrait toutes les ~s de criminels/de costumes** there you could find every possible variety ou type of criminal/of costume [2] **variétés** NFPL (Littérat) miscellanies; (Music hall) variety show; (Radio, TV = musique) light music (NonC); **émission/spectacle/théâtre de ~s** variety programme/show/hall

variole [vaʀjɔl] NF smallpox, variola (SPÉC)

variolé, e [vaʀjɔle] ADJ pockmarked

varioleux, -euse [vaʀjɔlø, øz] [1] ADJ suffering from smallpox, variolous (SPÉC) [2] NM smallpox case, patient suffering from smallpox

variolique [vaʀjɔlik] ADJ smallpox (épith), variolous (SPÉC)

variomètre [vaʀjɔmɛtʀ] NM variometer

variqueux, -euse [vaʀikø, øz] ADJ [ulcère] varicose

varlope [vaʀlɔp] NF trying-plane

varloper [vaʀlɔpe] ▸conjug 1◂ VT to plane (down)

Varsovie [vaʀsɔvi] N Warsaw

vasculaire [vaskylɛʀ] ADJ (Anat, Bot) vascular; **système ~ sanguin** blood-vascular system

vascularisation [vaskylaʀizasjɔ̃] NF (= processus) vascularization; (= réseau) vascularity

vascularisé, e [vaskylaʀize] ADJ vascular

vase¹ [vaz] [1] NM (à fleurs, décoratif) vase, bowl; **en ~ clos** (vivre, croître) in isolation, cut off from the world, in seclusion; [étudier, discuter] behind closed doors; (Hort) **taillé en ~** cut in the shape of a vase, vase-shaped → **goutte** [2] COMP ▸ **vases communicants** communicating vessels ▸ **vase d'expansion** (Aut) expansion bottle ou tank ▸ **vase de nuit** chamber(pot) ▸ **vases sacrés** (Rel) sacred vessels

vase² [vaz] NF (= boue) silt, mud, sludge (on riverbed)

vasectomie [vazɛktɔmi] NF vasectomy

vaseline [vaz(ə)lin] NF Vaseline®, petroleum jelly

vaseux, -euse [vazø, øz] ADJ [a] (= boueux) muddy, silty, sludgy [b] (* = fatigué) in a daze; **je me sens un peu ~** I'm in a bit of a daze, I feel a bit out of it* [c]* (= confus) [raisonnement] woolly, muddled; [explication] muddled; (= médiocre) [astuce, plaisanterie] pathetic*, lousy*

vasière [vazjɛʀ] NF [marais salant] tidal reservoir; (= fonds vaseux) (tidal) mud flats; (= parc à moules) mussel bed

vasistas [vazistas] NM [porte] (opening) window, fanlight; [fenêtre] fanlight

vasoconstricteur [vazokøstʀiktœʀ] [1] ADJ M vasoconstrictor (épith) [2] NM vasoconstrictor

vasoconstriction [vazokøstʀiksjɔ̃] NF vasoconstriction

vasodilatateur [vazodilatatœʀ] [1] ADJ M vasodilator (épith) [2] NM vasodilator

vasodilatation [vazodilatasjɔ̃] NF vasodil(at)ation

vasomoteur, -trice [vazomɔtœʀ, tʀis] ADJ vasomotor (épith)

vasouillard, e* [vazujaʀ, aʀd] ADJ [personne] in a daze; [raisonnement] woolly, muddled; [explication] muddled

vasouiller* [vazuje] ▸conjug 1◂ VI [*personne*] to flounder; [*opération, affaire*] to struggle along, limp along

vasque [vask] NF (= *bassin, lavabo*) basin; (= *coupe*) bowl

vassal, e (*mpl* **-aux**) [vasal, o] NM,F (*Hist, fig*) vassal

vassaliser [vasalize] ▸conjug 1◂ VT [+ *pays*] to reduce to the status of a vassal state

vassalité [vasalite] NF, **vasselage** [vaslaʒ] NM (*Hist, fig*) vassalage

vaste [vast] ADJ a [*surface, édifice, salle*] vast, immense, enormous, huge; [*vêtement*] huge, enormous; [*organisation, groupement*] vast, huge; **à la tête d'un ~ empire industriel** at the head of a vast ou huge industrial empire; **de par le ~ monde** throughout the whole wide world b [*connaissances, érudition, ambitions*] vast, immense; [*génie, culture*] immense; [*domaine, sujet*] wide(-ranging), huge, vast; [*problème*] wide-ranging, far-reaching; **un homme d'une ~ culture** an extremely cultured man, a man of immense learning, a highly cultured man; **ce sujet est trop ~** this subject is far too wide(-ranging) ou vast c (* : *intensif*) **c'est une ~ rigolade** ou **plaisanterie** ou **fumisterie** it's a huge ou an enormous joke

va-t-en-guerre [vatɑ̃gɛʀ] NM INV warmonger

Vatican [vatikɑ̃] NM **le ~** the Vatican

vaticane [vatikan] ADJ F [*politique, bibliothèque, grottes*] Vatican

vaticinateur, -trice [vatisinatœʀ, tʀis] NM,F (*littér*) vaticinator (*frm, littér*)

vaticination [vatisinasjɔ̃] NF (*littér*) vaticination (*frm, littér*); (*péj*) **~s** pompous predictions ou prophecies

vaticiner [vatisine] ▸conjug 1◂ VI (*littér* = *prophétiser*) to vaticinate (*frm, littér*); (*péj*) to make pompous predictions ou prophecies

va-tout [vatu] NM INV **jouer son ~** to stake ou risk one's all

Vaud [vo] NM **le canton de ~** the canton of Vaud

vaudeville [vod(ə)vil] NM vaudeville, light comedy; **ça tourne au ~** it's turning into a farce

vaudevillesque [vod(ə)vilɛsk] ADJ vaudeville (*épith*); (*fig*) farcical

vaudevilliste [vod(ə)vilist] NM writer of vaudeville

vaudois, e [vodwa, waz] 1 ADJ (*Hist*) Waldensian; (*Géog*) Vaudois, of ou from the canton of Vaud 2 NM,F (*Hist*) Waldensian; (*Géog*) **Vaudois(e)** Vaudois

vaudou [vodu] 1 NM **le (culte du) ~** voodoo 2 ADJ INV voodoo (*épith*)

vau-l'eau [volo] ♦**à vau-l'eau** LOC ADV (*lit*) with the stream ou current; (*fig*) **aller** ou **s'en aller à ~** to be on the road to ruin, go to the dogs*; **voilà tous mes projets à ~ !** there are all my plans in ruins! ou down the drain!*

vaurien, -ienne [voʀjɛ̃, jɛn] 1 NM,F (= *voyou*) good-for-nothing; (= *garnement*) little devil*; **petit ~ !** little devil!* 2 NM (*Naut*) small yacht ou sailing boat

vautour [votuʀ] NM (*Zool, fig*) vulture

vautrer (se) [votʀe] ▸conjug 1◂ VPR a (= *se rouler*) **se vautrer dans** [+ *boue, vice, obscénité, oisiveté*] to wallow in; (*fig littér*) **se vautrer dans la fange** to wallow in the mire b (= *s'avachir*) **se vautrer dans un fauteuil** to loll ou slouch in an armchair; **se vautrer sur** [+ *tapis, canapé*] to sprawl on; **vautré à plat ventre** ou **par terre** sprawling ou sprawled (flat) on the ground; **vautré dans l'herbe/sur le tapis** sprawling ou sprawled in the grass/on the carpet

vauvert [voveʀ] → **diable**

vaux [vo] NMPL → **val**

va-vite [vavit] ♦**à la va-vite*** LOC ADV in a rush ou hurry; **faire qch à la ~** to rush sth, do sth in a rush ou hurry

VDQS (ABRÉV = **vin délimité de qualité supérieure**) VDQS (*label guaranteeing quality and origin of wine*)

> **VDQS**
> VDQS, on a bottle of French wine, indicates that it contains wine from an approved regional vineyard. It is the second highest French wine classification after "AOC", and is followed by "vin de pays". Unlike the previous categories, "vin de table" or "vin ordinaire" is table wine of unspecified origin, and is often blended. → AOC

veau (*pl* **veaux**) [vo] NM a (*Zool*) calf; **~ marin** seal; (*Bible*) **le Veau d'or** the golden calf; **adorer le Veau d'or** to worship Mammon; **tuer le ~ gras** to kill the fatted calf; **~ de lait** ou (**élevé) sous la mère** suckling calf → **pleurer** b (*Culin*) veal; **escalope/côte de ~** veal escalope/chop; **foie/pied/tête de ~** calf's liver/foot/head; **rôti de ~** roast veal → **marengo** c (= *cuir*) calfskin ou **velours** d (* : *péj*) (= *personne*) sheep; (= *cheval*) nag (*péj*); (= *automobile*) tank* (*péj*)

vécés* [vese] NMPL **les ~** the toilet

vecteur [vɛktœʀ] 1 ADJ M (*Astron, Géom*) **rayon ~** radius vector 2 NM (*Math*) vector; (*Mil = véhicule*) carrier; (*Bio*) [*virus*] carrier, vector (*SPÉC*); (*fig*) vehicle, medium; (*Math*) **~ glissant** sliding vector; **les médias, ~s de l'information** the media, conveyor ou carrier of information

vectoriel, -elle [vɛktɔʀjɛl] ADJ [*espace, produit, fonction, image, ordinateur*] vector (*épith*); **calcul ~** vector analysis

vectoriser [vɛktɔʀize] ▸conjug 1◂ VT (*Ordin*) to vectorize

vécu, e [veky] (*ptp de* **vivre**) 1 ADJ [*histoire, aventure*] real(-life) (*épith*), true(-life) (*épith*); [*roman*] real-life (*épith*), based on fact (*attrib*); (*Philo*) [*temps, durée*] lived; **échec mal ~** failure that is hard to come to terms with; **un licenciement mal ~ peut mener à une dépression** redundancy can lead to depression if the person cannot come to terms with it 2 NM (*Philo*) **le ~** real life; **ce que le lecteur veut, c'est du ~** what the reader wants is real-life ou actual experience

vedettariat [vədetaʀja] NM (= *état*) stardom; (= *vedettes*) stars

vedette [vədɛt] NF a (= *artiste, personnage en vue*) star; **les ~s de l'écran/du cinéma** screen/film stars; **une ~ de la politique** a leading figure ou a big name in politics; **joueur ~** star ou top player; **mannequin ~** top model; **présentateur ~** star presenter; (*fig*) **produit-~** leading product, flagship product; **l'émission ~ d'une chaîne** the flagship (programme) of a channel; (*Bourse*) **valeurs** ou **titres ~s** leaders b (*Ciné, Théât = première place*) **avoir la ~** to top the bill, have star billing; (*fig*) **avoir** ou **tenir la ~ (de l'actualité)** to be in the spotlight, make the headlines; (*fig*) **pendant toute la soirée, il a eu la ~** he was in the limelight ou was the centre of attraction all evening; **avec, en ~, Lulu** [*film, pièce*] starring Lulu; [*concert, gala*] with Lulu as top of the bill; **mettre qn en ~** (*Ciné, Théât*) to give sb star billing; (*fig*) to push sb into the limelight, put the spotlight on sb; **partager la ~ avec qn** (*Ciné, Théât*) to share star billing with sb, top the bill alongside sb; (*fig*) to share the limelight ou spotlight with sb; **il passe en ~ américaine** he's the support (act); (*fig*) **ravir la ~ à qn** to steal the show from sb; **jouer les ~s*** to act like a star c (= *embarcation*) launch; (*Mil*) patrol boat; (= *munie de canons*) gun boat; **~ lance-torpilles** motor torpedo boat; **~ lance-missiles** missile-carrying launch d (†† *Mil = guetteur*) sentinel

vedettisation [vədetizasjɔ̃] NF **la ~ de qn** pushing sb into the limelight, putting the spotlight on sb

védique [vedik] ADJ, NM Vedic

védisme [vedism] NM Vedaism

végétal, e (*mpl* **-aux**) [veʒetal, o] 1 ADJ [*graisses, teintures, huiles*] vegetable (*épith*); [*biologie, histologie, fibres, cellules*] plant (*épith*); [*sol*] rich in humus; [*ornementation*] plant-like → **règne** 2 NM vegetable, plant

végétalien, -ienne [veʒetaljɛ̃, jɛn] ADJ, NM,F vegan

végétalisme [veʒetalism] NM veganism

végétarien, -ienne [veʒetaʀjɛ̃, jɛn] ADJ, NM,F vegetarian

végétarisme [veʒetaʀism] NM vegetarianism

végétatif, -ive [veʒetatif, iv] ADJ (*Bot, Physiol*) vegetative; **vie végétative** (*Méd*) vegetative life; (*fig péj*) vegetable-like existence

végétation [veʒetasjɔ̃] NF a (*Bot*) vegetation b (*Méd*) **~s (adénoïdes)** adenoids; **se faire opérer des ~s** to have one's adenoids removed ou out*

végéter [veʒete] ▸conjug 6◂ VI a (*péj*) [*personne*] to vegetate; [*affaire*] to stagnate b (*Agr*) (= *être chétif*) to grow poorly, be stunted; († = *pousser*) to grow, vegetate

véhémence [veemɑ̃s] NF (*littér*) vehemence; **la ~ de ses propos** the vehemence of his words; **avec ~** [*protester, refuser, dénoncer*] vehemently; **plaider avec ~ en faveur de** ou **pour qch** to make a passionate plea for sth

véhément, e [veemɑ̃, ɑ̃t] ADJ (*littér*) vehement; **d'un ton ~** vehemently

véhémentement [veemɑ̃tmɑ̃] ADV (*littér*) vehemently

véhiculaire [veikylɛʀ] ADJ (*Ling*) **langue ~** lingua franca, common language

véhicule [veikyl] NM a (= *moyen de transport, agent de transmission*) vehicle; **~ automobile/utilitaire/industriel** motor/commercial/industrial vehicle; **~ spatial** spacecraft b (*fig*) vehicle, medium; **le langage est le ~ de la pensée** language is the vehicle ou medium of thought c (*Rel*) **petit/grand ~** Hinayana/Mahayana Buddhism d (*Pharm*) vehicle

véhiculer [veikyle] ▸conjug 1◂ VT [+ *marchandises, troupes*] to convey, transport; [+ *substance, idées*] to convey, serve as a vehicle for; [+ *information, images*] to convey; [+ *virus*] to carry

veille [vɛj] NF a (= *état*) wakefulness; (= *période*) period of wakefulness; **en état de ~** in a waking state, awake; **entre la ~ et le sommeil** between waking and sleeping; **nuit de ~** (*sans dormir*) sleepless night; **en ~** [*machine, ordinateur*] in sleep mode b (= *garde*) (night) watch; **homme de ~** (night) watch; **prendre la ~** to take one's turn on watch; **nuit de ~** (*en montant la garde*) night on watch; (*auprès d'un malade*) all-night vigil; **faire de la ~ technologique** to monitor technological development c (= *jour précédent*) **la ~** the day before; **la ~ au soir** the previous evening, the night ou evening before; **la ~ de Pâques/de l'examen** the day before Easter/the exam; **la ~ de Noël/du jour de l'an** Christmas/New Year's Eve; **la ~ de sa mort** on the eve of his death, on the day before his death → **demain** d (*fig*) **à la ~ de** [+ *guerre, révolution*] on the eve of; **tu es à la ~ de commettre une grave injustice/une grosse erreur** you are on the brink ou verge of committing a grave injustice/of making a big mistake; **ils étaient à la ~ d'être renvoyés/de manquer de vivres** they were on the point of being dismissed/of running out of supplies

veillée [veje] NF [a] (= période) evening (spent in company); (= réunion) evening gathering ou meeting; **faire une ~ autour d'un feu de camp** to spend the evening around a campfire; **il se souvient de ces ~s d'hiver** he remembers those winter evening gatherings; **~ d'armes** (Hist) knightly vigil; **il régnait une ambiance de ~ d'armes** it felt like the night before a battle [b] [malade] vigil; **~ funèbre** wake, funeral vigil; **~ pascale** Easter vigil; **~ de prières** prayer vigil

veiller [veje] ▸conjug 1 ◂ [1] VI [a] (= ne pas se coucher) to stay up, sit up; **~ tard** to stay ou sit up late; **~ au chevet d'un malade** to sit up ou keep a vigil at the bedside of a sick person; **~ auprès du mort** to keep watch ou vigil over the body
[b] (= être de garde) to be on watch; (= rester vigilant) to be watchful, be vigilant
[c] (= être en état de veille) to be awake
[d] (= faire la veillée) to spend the evening in company
[2] VT [+ mort, malade] to watch over, sit up with; (fig) **on veille les morts ici!** it's pitch dark in here!
[3] VT INDIR [a] **~ à** [+ intérêts, approvisionnement] to attend to, see to, look after; **~ au bon fonctionnement d'une machine** to make sure that a machine is working properly; **~ à ce que ...** to see to it that ..., make sure that ...; **veillez à ce que tout soit prêt** make sure that ou ensure that everything is ready; (fig) **~ au grain** to keep an eye open for trouble ou problems, look out for squalls (fig)
[b] **~ sur** [+ personne, santé, bonheur de qn] to watch over, keep a watchful eye on; [+ trésor, lieu] to watch over, guard

veilleur [vɛjœʀ] NM [a] **~ (de nuit)** (night) watchman [b] (Mil) look-out

veilleuse [vɛjøz] NF [a] (= lampe) night light; (Aut) sidelight; **mettre en ~** [+ lampe] to dim; [+ projet] to put on the back burner; (Aut) **mettre ses phares** ou **se mettre en ~s** (= allumer) to put one's sidelights on; (= baisser) to switch to sidelights; **mets-la en ~!:** (= tais-toi!) shut your face!:, put a sock in it!* (Brit) (= du calme!) cool it!: [b] (= flamme) pilot light

veinard, e* [vɛnaʀ, aʀd] [1] ADJ lucky, jammy: (Brit) [2] NM,F lucky devil* ou dog*, jammy so-and-so: (Brit)

veine [vɛn] NF [a] (Anat) vein; **~ coronaire/pulmonaire** coronary/pulmonary vein; **~ cave** vena cava; **~ porte** portal vein → **ouvrir, saigner, sang**
[b] (= nervure) vein; (= filon) [houille] seam, vein; [minerai non ferreux] vein; [minerai de fer] lode, vein
[c] (fig = inspiration) inspiration; **~ poétique/dramatique** poetic/dramatic inspiration; **sa ~ est tarie** his inspiration has dried up; **de la même ~** in the same vein; **être en ~** to be inspired; **être en ~ de patience/bonté/confidences** to be in a patient/benevolent/confiding mood ou frame of mind
[d] (* = chance) luck; **c'est une ~** that's a bit of luck, what a bit of luck; **c'est une ~ que ...** it's lucky that ...; **un coup de ~** a stroke of luck; **pas de ~!** hard ou bad ou rotten* luck!; **avoir de la ~** to be lucky; **il n'a pas de ~** (dans la vie) he has no luck; (aujourd'hui) he's out of luck; **ce type a de la ~** that fellow's a lucky devil* ou dog*; **avoir une ~ de cocu:** ou **pendu:** to have the luck of the devil*; **il a eu de la ~ aux examens** he was lucky ou in luck at the exams, his luck was in at the exams; **il n'a pas eu de ~ aux examens** he was unlucky in the exams, his luck was out at the exams; (iro) **c'est bien ma ~!** that's just my luck!

veiné, e [vɛne] (ptp de **veiner**) ADJ [a] [bras, peau] veined, veiny; **bras à la peau ~e** arm with the veins apparent on the skin [b] [bois] grained; [marbre] veined; **marbre ~ de vert** marble with green veins, green-veined marble

veiner [vɛne] ▸conjug 1 ◂ VT (aspect du bois) to grain; (aspect du marbre) to vein; **les stries qui veinent le marbre** the veins that can be seen in marble; **les nervures qui veinent une feuille** the pattern of veins on a leaf

veineux, -euse [vɛnø, øz] ADJ [a] [système, sang] venous [b] [bois] grainy; [marbre] veined

veinule [venyl] NF (Anat) veinlet, venule (SPÉC); (Bot) venule

veinure [venyʀ] NF [bois] graining; [pierre] veining; **la ~ du marbre** the veins ou veining of the marble

vêlage [vɛlaʒ] NM (Géog, Zool) calving

vélaire [velɛʀ] ADJ, NF **(consonne/voyelle) ~** velar (consonant/vowel)

vélarisation [velaʀizasjɔ̃] NF velarization

vélariser [velaʀize] ▸conjug 1 ◂ VT to velarize

Velcro® [vɛlkʀo] NM Velcro®; **bande/fermeture ~** Velcro strip/fastening

veld(t) [vɛlt] NM veld(t)

vêlement [vɛlmɑ̃] NM = **vêlage**

vêler [vɛle] ▸conjug 1 ◂ VI to calve

vélin [velɛ̃] NM (= peau) vellum; **(papier) ~** vellum (paper)

véliplanchiste [veliplɑ̃ʃist] NMF windsurfer

vélique [velik] ADJ sails (épith); **point ~** centre of effort

vélite [velit] NM (Hist) velite

velléitaire [veleitɛʀ] [1] ADJ irresolute, indecisive, wavering (épith) [2] NM waverer

velléité [veleite] NF vague desire, vague impulse; **ces mesures ont découragé toute ~ de changement** these measures have discouraged any thought of change; **il a des ~s de carrière littéraire** he has a vague desire to take up a literary career

vélo [velo] NM bike, cycle; **~ de course** racing bike ou cycle, racer; **~ d'appartement** exercise bike; **~ tout-chemin** hybrid bike; **~ tout-terrain** mountain bike; **faire du ~ tout-terrain** to go mountain-biking; (= vélo) stunt bike; **faire du ~-cross** to go stunt-riding; **être à ou en ~** to be on a bike; **venir à ou en ~** to come by bike ou on a bike; **il sait faire du ~** he can ride a bike; **je fais beaucoup de ~** I cycle a lot, I do a lot of cycling; **on va faire un peu de ~** we're going out (for a ride) on our bikes; **à cinq ans, il allait déjà à ~** he could already ride a bike at five; **on y va à ou en ~?** shall we go by bike? ou on our bikes?, shall we cycle there?; **il a un (petit) ~ dans la tête*** he's got a screw loose*, he isn't all there*

véloce [velos] ADJ (littér) swift, fleet (littér)

vélocipède†† [velosiped] NM velocipede

vélocité [velosite] NF [a] (Mus) nimbleness, swiftness; **exercices de ~** five-finger exercises [b] (Tech) velocity; (littér = vitesse) swiftness, fleetness (littér)

vélodrome [velodʀom] NM velodrome

vélomoteur [velomotœʀ] NM moped

vélomotoriste [velomotoʀist] NMF moped rider

véloski [veloski] NM skibob

velours [v(ə)luʀ] NM [a] (= tissu) velvet; **~ de coton/de laine** cotton/wool velvet; **~ côtelé** ou **à côtes** corduroy, cord; **~ frappé** crushed velvet; (fig) **il joue sur du ~** he's sitting pretty* → **main** [b] (= velouté) velvet; **le ~ de la pêche** the bloom of the peach; **le ~ de sa joue** the velvety texture of her cheek, her velvet(y) cheek; **voix/yeux/peau de ~** velvet(y) voice/eyes/skin; **ce potage/cette crème est un vrai ~** this soup/this cream dessert is velvety-smooth; **agneau/veau ~** (lambskin)/(calfskin) suede → **œil, patte¹**

velouté, e [velute] (ptp de **velouter**) [1] ADJ [a] (Tex) brushed; (à motifs) with a raised vel-

vet pattern [b] (= doux) [joues] velvety (épith), velvety, velvet-smooth; [pêche] velvety, downy; [crème, potage, vin] smooth, velvety; [lumière, regard] soft, mellow; [voix] velvet-smooth, mellow [2] NM [a] (= douceur) [joues] smoothness; [pêche] smoothness, downiness; [lumière, regard] softness; [voix] mellowness [b] (Culin) (= sauce) velouté sauce; (= potage) velouté; **~ de tomates/d'asperges** cream of tomato/asparagus soup

velouter [velute] ▸conjug 1 ◂ [1] VT [a] [+ papier] to put a velvety finish on [b] [+ joues, pêche] to give a velvet(y) texture to; [+ vin, crème, potage] to make smooth; [+ lumière, regard] to soften, mellow; [+ voix] to mellow; **le duvet qui veloutait ses joues** the down that gave a velvet softness to her cheeks [2] **se velouter** VPR [joues, pêche] to take on a velvety texture; [regard] to soften; [voix] to mellow

veloutex, -euse [velutø, øz] ADJ velvet-like, velvety

Velpeau® [vɛlpo] ADJ → **bande¹**

velu, e [vəly] ADJ [main] hairy; [plante] hairy, villous (SPÉC)

velum, vélum [veləm] NM canopy

Vélux® [velyks] NM skylight, Velux window®

venaison [vənɛzɔ̃] NF venison

vénal, e [venal, o] ADJ [a] [personne] venal, mercenary; [activité, amour] venal [b] (Hist) [office] venal → **valeur**

vénalité [venalite] NF venality

vendable [vɑ̃dabl] ADJ saleable, marketable; **ces produits seront difficilement ~s** these products will be difficult to sell

vendange [vɑ̃dɑ̃ʒ] NF (parfois pl = récolte) wine harvest, grape harvest ou picking; (= raisins récoltés) grapes (harvested), grape crop; (gén pl = période) grape harvest ou picking (time); **pendant les ~s** during the grape harvest ou picking (time); **faire la ~ ou les ~s** to harvest ou pick the grapes; **~ tardive** late vintage

vendangeoir [vɑ̃dɑ̃ʒwaʀ] NM grape-picker's basket

vendanger [vɑ̃dɑ̃ʒe] ▸conjug 3 ◂ [1] VT [+ vigne] to gather ou pick ou harvest grapes from; [+ raisins] to pick, harvest [2] VI (= faire la vendange) to pick ou harvest the grapes; (= presser le raisin) to press the grapes

vendangeur, -euse [vɑ̃dɑ̃ʒœʀ, øz] [1] NM,F grape-picker; **vendangeuse** NF (= machine) grape harvester; (Bot) aster

Vendée [vɑ̃de] NF **la ~** the Vendée; **les guerres de ~** pro-royalist uprising in the Vendée during the French revolution

vendéen, -enne [vɑ̃deɛ̃, ɛn] [1] ADJ of ou from the Vendée [2] **Vendéen(ne)** NM,F inhabitant ou native of the Vendée

vendémiaire [vɑ̃demjɛʀ] NM Vendémiaire (1st month of French Republican calendar)

venderesse [vɑ̃dʀɛs] NF (Jur) vendor

vendetta [vɑ̃deta] NF vendetta

vendeur, -euse [vɑ̃dœʀ, øz] [1] NM [a] (dans un magasin) shop assistant (Brit), salesclerk (US); (dans un grand magasin) sales assistant, salesman, shop assistant (Brit); **« cherchons 2 ~s, rayon librairie »** "2 sales assistants required for our book department" [b] (= marchand) seller, salesman; **~ ambulant** street peddler; **~ de journaux** newsvendor, newspaper seller; **~ à domicile** door-to-door salesman → **sauvette** [c] (Comm = chargé des ventes) salesman; (fig) **c'est un excellent ~** he's an excellent salesman, he has a flair for selling [d] (Jur) vendor, seller; (Écon) seller; **je ne suis pas ~** I'm not selling; **il serait ~** he'd be ready ou willing to sell; **les pays ~s de cacao** the cocoa-selling countries
[2] **vendeuse** NF [a] (dans un magasin) shop assistant (Brit), salesclerk (US); (dans un grand

magasin) sales assistant, saleswoman, shop assistant *(Brit)*; *(jeune)* salesgirl **b** *(= marchande)* seller, saleswoman; **vendeuse de glaces** ice-cream seller **3** ADJ *[slogan]* effective

vendre [vɑ̃dʀ] ▸conjug 41◂ **1** VT **a** *[+ marchandise, valeurs]* to sell **(à** to); **~ qch à qn** to sell sb sth, sell sth to sb; **~ au détail/au poids/au mètre/au kilo** to sell retail/by weight/by the metre/by the kilo; **elle vend des foulards à 400 F** she sells scarves for *ou* at 400 francs; **il m'a vendu un tableau 3 000 F** he sold me a picture for 3,000 francs; **l'art de ~** salesmanship, the art of selling; **elle vend cher** her prices are high, she's expensive; *(Comm)* **ces affiches publicitaires font ~** these advertising posters get things sold *ou* are boosting sales; **~ qch aux enchères** to sell sth by auction; **~ sa part d'une affaire** to sell (out) one's share of a business; **«(maison/terrain) à ~»** "(house/land) for sale"; *(Bible)* **~ son droit d'aînesse pour un plat de lentilles** to sell one's birthright for a mess of potage → **perte, prix** *etc*

b *(péj)* *[+ droit, charge]* to sell; **~ son âme/honneur** to sell one's soul/honour; **~ son silence** to be paid for one's silence; **il vendrait père et mère pour réussir/pour ce tableau** he would sell his grandmother to succeed/for this picture **c** *(= faire payer)* **ils nous ont vendu très cher ce droit/cet avantage** they made us pay dear *ou* dearly for this right/this advantage; **~ chèrement sa vie** *ou* **sa peau*** to sell one's life *ou* one's skin dearly **d** *(* = trahir)* *[+ personne, complice]* to sell **e** *(loc)* **~ la peau de l'ours (avant de l'avoir tué)** to count one's chickens (before they are hatched) → **mèche**

2 se vendre VPR **a** *[marchandise]* to sell, be sold; **se ~ à la pièce/douzaine** to be sold singly/by the dozen; **ça se vend bien** it sells well; **ses romans vendent comme des petits pains** his novels are selling like hot cakes; **ouvrage/auteur qui se vend bien** work/author that sells well **b** *[personne]* *(aussi péj)* to sell o.s.; **se ~ à un parti/l'ennemi** to sell o.s. to a party/the enemy

vendredi [vɑ̃dʀədi] NM Friday; **Vendredi** *(= personnage de Robinson Crusoé)* Man Friday; **c'était un ~ treize** it was Friday the thirteenth; *pour autres locutions voir* **samedi**

vendu, e [vɑ̃dy] *(ptp de* **vendre)** **1** ADJ *[fonctionnaire, juge]* corrupt → **adjuger 2** NM *(péj)* Judas, mercenary traitor

venelle [vənɛl] NF alley

vénéneux, -euse [venenø, øz] ADJ *[plante, champignon, fleur]* poisonous; *(littér)* *[charme, beauté]* deadly; *[idée, plaisir]* pernicious, harmful

vénérable [venerabl] **1** ADJ *(littér, hum = respectable)* venerable; *(hum = très vieux)* *[personne, chose]* **(d'un âge) ~** venerable, ancient **2** NM *(Rel)* Venerable; *(Franc-Maçonnerie)* Worshipful Master

vénération [venerasjɔ̃] NF *(Rel)* veneration; *(gén = grande estime)* veneration, reverence; **avoir de la ~ pour qn** to venerate *ou* revere sb

vénérer [venere] ▸conjug 6◂ VT *(Rel)* to venerate; *(gén)* to venerate, revere

vénerie [venʀi] NF **a** *(= art)* venery *(SPÉC)*, hunting **b** *(= administration)* **la ~** the Hunt

vénérien, -ienne [venerjɛ̃, jɛn] **1** ADJ **a** *(Méd)* venereal → **maladie b** *(†† = sexuel)* venereal†, sexual **2** NM *(= malade)* V.D. patient, person with V.D. *ou* venereal disease

vénérologie [venerɔlɔʒi] NF venereology

vénérologue [venerɔlɔg] NMF venereologist

Vénétie [venesi] NF Venetia

veneur [vənœʀ] NM *(Hist)* huntsman, venerer†; **grand ~** master of the royal hounds

Venezuela [venezɥela] NM Venezuela

vénézuélien, -ienne [venezɥeljɛ̃, jɛn] **1** ADJ Venezuelan **2 Vénézuélien(ne)** NM,F Venezuelan

vengeance [vɑ̃ʒɑ̃s] NF revenge, vengeance; **soif/désir de ~** thirst/desire for revenge *ou* vengeance; **tirer ~ de qch** to get revenge for sth; **exercer sa ~ sur** to take (one's) revenge on; **préparer sa ~ contre qn** to plan (one's) revenge on sb; **crier ~** to cry out for revenge *ou* vengeance; **agir par ~** to act out of revenge *ou* vengeance; **assouvir une ~ personnelle** to satisfy a desire for personal revenge; **de petites ~s** petty acts of revenge *ou* vengeance; **la ~ divine** divine retribution *ou* vengeance; *(hum)* **ma ~ sera terrible !** my revenge will be terrible! ▪ *(PROV)* **la ~ est un plat qui se mange froid** revenge is a dish best eaten cold *(PROV)*

venger [vɑ̃ʒe] ▸conjug 3◂ **1** VT **a** *[+ personne, honneur, mémoire]* to avenge **(de** for) **b** *[+ injustice, affront]* to avenge; **rien ne vengera cette injustice** nothing will avenge this injustice, there is no revenge for this injustice **2 se venger** VPR to avenge o.s., take (one's) revenge *ou* vengeance; **se ~ de qn** to take revenge *ou* vengeance on sb, get one's own back on sb; **se ~ de qch** to avenge o.s. for sth, take one's revenge for sth; **il l'a fait pour se ~** he did it out of revenge; **je me vengerai** I shall get *ou* have *ou* take my revenge, I shall be avenged; **je n'ai pas pris de fromage mais je me vengerai sur les fruits** I haven't had any cheese but I'll make up for it with the fruit

vengeur, -geresse [vɑ̃ʒœʀ, ʒ(ə)ʀɛs] **1** ADJ *[personne, geste, lettre]* vengeful **2** NM,F avenger

véniel, -elle [venjɛl] ADJ *[faute, oubli]* venial *(littér)*, pardonable, excusable → **péché**

venimeux, -euse [vənimø, øz] ADJ **a** *(lit)* *[serpent, piqûre]* venomous, poisonous **b** *(fig)* *[personne, voix]* venomous, vicious; *[remarque, haine]* venomous, vicious; **une langue venimeuse** a poisonous *ou* venomous *ou* vicious tongue

venin [vənɛ̃] NM **a** *(lit)* venom, poison; **~ de serpent** snake venom; **crochets à ~** poison fangs **b** *(fig)* venom, viciousness; **jeter** *ou* **cracher son ~** to spit out one's venom; **répandre son ~ contre qn** to pour out one's venom against sb; **paroles pleines de ~** venomous words, words full of venom *ou* viciousness

venir [v(ə)niʀ]

▸conjug 22◂
1 VERBE INTRANSITIF   **3** VERBE IMPERSONNEL
2 VERBE AUXILIAIRE   **4** VERBE PRONOMINAL

1 VERBE INTRANSITIF

a **dans l'espace** to come; **je viens !** I'm coming!; **venez ! venez !** come on! come on!; **viens voir !** come and see!; **je viens dans un instant** I'll be there in a moment; **quand doit-il ~ ?** when is he coming?; **comment est-il venu ?** — **en avion/en voiture** how did he get here? — by plane/by car; **le voisin est venu** the man from next door came round *ou* called; **il est venu à moi pour me demander si ...** he came to ask me if ...; **il ne vient jamais aux réunions** he never comes to meetings; **il vient chez nous tous les jeudis** he comes (round) to our house every Thursday; **il venait sur nous l'air furieux** he bore down on us looking furious; **le camion venait droit sur nous** the lorry was coming straight at us *ou* heading straight for us *ou* was bearing down on us; **il vint vers moi** he came up to *ou* towards me → **monde**

♦ **faire venir** *[+ médecin, plombier]* to send for, call; **le patron l'a fait ~ dans son bureau** the boss called him into his office; **tu nous as fait ~ pour rien** you got us to come *ou* you made us come for nothing; **il fait ~ son vin de Provence** he has *ou* gets his wine sent from Provence; *(hum)* **on va prendre l'apéritif, ça les fera peut-être ~** let's have a drink, then they'll

turn up; **ferme la fenêtre, tu vas faire ~ les moustiques** shut the window or you'll attract the mosquitoes *ou* bring in the mosquitoes

♦ **venir à** *ou* **jusqu'à** + *nom (= atteindre)* *(vers le haut)* to come up to, reach (up to); *(vers le bas)* to come down to, reach (down to); *(en longueur, en superficie)* to come to, reach; **l'eau nous venait aux genoux** the water came up to our knees, we were knee-deep in water; **il me vient à l'épaule** he comes up to my shoulder; **la forêt vient jusqu'à la route** the forest comes right up to the road

b ♦ **venir de** *(provenance, cause)* to come from; *(Ling)* to derive from; **ils viennent de Paris** *(en voyage)* they're coming from Paris; *(origine)* they come *ou* are from Paris; **ce produit vient du Maroc** this product comes from Morocco; **l'épée lui vient de son oncle** *(il l'a reçue en cadeau)* he got the sword from his uncle; *(il en a hérité)* the sword was passed down to him by his uncle; **ces troubles viennent du foie** this trouble comes *ou* stems from the liver; **cette substance vient d'un coquillage** this substance comes from shellfish; **ceci vient de son imprudence** this is the result of his carelessness, this comes from his being careless; **d'où vient que ... ?** how is it that ...?, what is the reason that ...?; **de là vient que ...** the result of this is that ...; **d'où vient cette hâte soudaine ?** why the hurry all of a sudden?; **ça vient de ce que ...** it comes *ou* results *ou* stems from the fact that ...

c = **se débloquer, se détacher** **j'ai tiré et la poignée est venue toute seule** I pulled the handle and it just came off in my hands; **une fois que tu as mouillé le papier peint, ça vient tout seul** once you've dampened the wallpaper, it comes off all by itself

d = **arriver, survenir** to come; **quand l'aube vint** when dawn came; **la nuit vient vite** night is coming (on) fast; **ceci vient à point/mal à propos** this has come (along) just at the right/wrong moment; **les idées ne viennent pas** I'm short of ideas; **une idée m'est venue (à l'esprit)** I had an idea, something occurred to me; **l'idée lui est venue de ...** it occurred to him to ...; **ça ne me serait pas venu à l'idée** *ou* **à l'esprit** that would never have occurred to me *ou* entered my head, I would never have thought of that; **dis le premier mot qui te vient à l'esprit** say the first word that comes into your head; **le bruit est venu jusqu'à nous que ...** word has reached us *ou* come to us that ...; *[personne]* **comment est-il venu au sport/à la religion ?** how did he (first) come to sport/religion?; **il ne sait pas encore nager, mais ça va ~** he can't swim yet, but it'll come; *(impatience)* **ça vient ?** come on!; **alors ce dossier, ça vient ?** so when's that file going to be ready?, how much longer have I got to wait for that file?; **et ma bière ? — ça vient !** where's my beer? — it's coming! → **tout, voir**

e **dans le temps, dans une série** to come; **ça vient avant/après** it comes before/after; **le moment viendra où ...** the time will come when ...; **l'heure est venue** *ou* **le moment est venu d'agir/de changer** the time has come to act *ou* for action/to change *ou* for change; **la semaine/l'année qui vient** the coming week/year; **samedi qui vient** this Saturday, next Saturday → **venu**

♦ **à venir** : **les années/générations à ~** the years/generations to come, future years/generations; **nous le saurons dans les jours/les mois à ~** we'll know in the next few days/months

f = **pousser** **cette plante vient bien dans un sol argileux** this plant does well in a clayey soil

g

♦ **en venir à** : **j'en viens maintenant à votre question/à cet aspect du problème** I shall now come *ou* turn to your question/to that aspect of the problem; **venons-en au fait** let's get to the point; **j'en viens à la conclusion que** ... I have come to *ou* reached the conclusion that ..., I'm coming to the conclusion that ...; **en ~ aux mains** *ou* **aux coups** to come to blows; **où voulez-vous en ~?** what are you getting *ou* driving at?; **j'en viens à me demander si** ... I'm beginning to wonder if ...; **il en est venu à mendier** he was reduced to begging, he had to resort to begging; **il en est venu à haïr ses parents** he has come to hate his parents, he has got to the stage where he hates his parents; **comment les choses en sont-elles venues là?** how did things come to this? *ou* get into this state?; **il faudra bien en ~ là** that's what it'll come to in the end

h

◆ **y venir : il y viendra, mais ne le brusquez pas** he'll come round to it *ou* to the idea, but don't rush him; **il faudra bien qu'il y vienne** he'll just have to get used to it; **et le budget? — j'y viens** and the budget? — I'm coming *ou* getting to that; *(menace)* **viens-y!** just (you) come here!; *(menace)* **qu'il y vienne!** just let him come!

2 VERBE AUXILIAIRE

a

◆ **venir** + *infinitif* (= *se déplacer pour*) **je suis venu travailler** I have come to work; **il va ~ la voir** he's going to come to *ou* and see her; **viens m'aider** come and help me; **elle doit ~ passer une semaine chez nous** she's coming to spend a week with us; **après cela ne viens pas te plaindre!** and don't (you) come and complain *ou* come complaining afterwards!

b

◆ **venir de** + *infinitif* (*passé récent*) **il vient d'arriver** he has just arrived; **elle venait de se lever** she had just got up

c

◆ **venir à** + *infinitif* : **s'il venait à mourir** if he were to die, if he should die; **s'il venait à passer par là** if he should (happen *ou* chance to) go that way; **quand l'eau vint à manquer** when the water started running out; **vint à passer un officier** an officer happened to pass by

3 VERBE IMPERSONNEL

a = arriver, survenir   **il vient beaucoup d'enfants** a lot of children are coming, there are a lot of children coming; **il lui est venu des boutons*** he came out in spots; **il ne lui viendrait pas à l'idée** *ou* **à l'esprit que j'ai besoin d'aide** it wouldn't occur to him *ou* enter his head *ou* cross his mind that I might need help; **il m'est venu un doute** I had a doubt

b temps   **il vient un moment/une heure où** ... the time/the hour comes when ...

c éventualité   **s'il vient à pleuvoir/neiger** if it should (happen to) rain/snow

4 **s'en venir** VERBE PRONOMINAL

† *ou littér* = **venir** to come, approach; **il s'en venait tranquillement** he was approaching unhurriedly; **il s'en vint nous voir** he came to see us

Venise [vəniz] N Venice

vénitien, -ienne [venisjɛ̃, jɛn] **1** ADJ Venetian → **lanterne**, **store 2** **Vénitien(ne)** NM,F Venetian

vent [vã] **1** NM **a** (*gén*) wind; **~ du nord/d'ouest** North/West wind; **le ~ du large** the sea breeze; **il y a** *ou* **il fait du ~** it's windy, there's a wind blowing; (*lit, fig*) **le ~ tourne** the wind is turning; **un ~ d'orage** a stormy wind; **un ~ à décorner les bœufs** a fierce gale, a howling wind; **coup de ~** (*Naut*) gale; **un coup** *ou* **une rafale de ~ a emporté son chapeau** a gust of wind blew his hat off; **entrer en coup de ~** to burst in, come bursting in; **flotter/claquer au ~** to flutter/flap in the wind; **elle courait cheveux au ~** she was running along with her hair streaming in the wind; **observer d'où vient le ~** (*lit*) to see

which way the wind blows; (*fig*) to see which way the wind blows *ou* how the land lies; (*fig*) **il a senti le ~ du boulet** he had a narrow escape; **être en plein ~** to be exposed to the wind; **marché/atelier en plein ~** outdoor market/workshop; **rapide comme le ~** swift as the wind, like the wind → **moulin**

b (*fig* = *tendance*) **le ~ est à l'optimisme** there's a (general) mood of optimism, there's optimism in the air; **un ~ de révolte/contestation** a wind of revolt/protest; **un ~ de panique soufflait sur les marchés financiers** a wave of panic swept the financial markets

c (*euph,†* = *gaz intestinal*) wind (*NonC*); **il a des ~s** he has wind; **lâcher un ~** to break wind

d (*Naut, Chasse*) **au ~ (de)** to windward (of); **sous le ~ (de)** to leeward (of); (*Naut*) **venir au ~** to turn into the wind; **chasser au ~** *ou* **dans le ~** to hunt upwind; **~ arrière/debout** *ou* **contraire** rear/head wind; **avoir le ~ debout** to head into the wind; **aller contre le ~** to go into the wind; **avoir le ~ arrière** *ou* **en poupe** to have the wind astern, sail *ou* run before the wind; (*fig*) **il a le ~ en poupe** he has the wind in his sails, he's on a roll*; **l'entreprise a le ~ en poupe** the company is on a roll*; **prendre le ~** (*lit*) to test the wind; (*fig*) to test the waters; **avoir bon ~** to have a fair wind; **bon ~!** (*Naut*) fair journey!; (* = *fichez le camp*) good riddance!

e (*loc*) **les quatre ~s** the four winds; **aux quatre ~s ◊ à tous les ~s** to the four winds, to all (four) points of the compass; **être dans le ~*** to be trendy; **c'est du ~*** it's just hot air*; **du ~!*** (= *allez-vous-en*) off with you!; **avoir ~ de** to get wind of; (*gén hum*) **quel bon ~ vous amène?** what brings you here?; **elle l'a fait contre ~s et marées** she did it against all the odds *ou* despite all the obstacles; **je le ferai contre ~s et marées** I'll do it come hell or high water; **faire du ~** [*éventail*] to create a breeze; (*sur le feu*) to fan the flame, blow up the fire; (*péj = inefficace*) **il fait beaucoup de ~ mais c'est tout** he's always busying about but he doesn't do anything; **avoir du ~ dans les voiles*** (= *être ivre*) to be three sheets in the wind*, be half-seas over* (*Brit*)

2 COMP ► **vent coulis** draught (*Brit*), draft (*US*) ► **vent solaire** (*Astron*) solar wind

ventail (*pl* -**aux**) [vãtaj, o] NM (= *visière*) ventail

vente [vãt] **1** NF **a** (= *action*) sale; **la ~ de cet article est interdite** the sale of this article is forbidden; **bureau de ~** sales office; **être en ~ libre** (*gén*) to be freely sold, have no sales restrictions; **médicament en ~ libre** over-the-counter medicine; **en ~ dès demain** available *ou* on sale (as) from tomorrow; **en ~ dans toutes les pharmacies/chez votre libraire** available *ou* on sale at all chemists/at your local bookshop; **tous les articles exposés sont en ~** all (the) goods on show are for sale; **mettre en ~** [+ *produit*] to put on sale; [+ *maison, objet personnel*] to put up for sale; **mise en ~** [*maison*] putting up for sale; [*produit*] putting on sale; **les articles en ~ dans ce magasin** the goods on sale in this store; **nous n'en avons pas la ~** we have no demand *ou* sale for that, we can't sell that → **crédit, point¹, sauvette** etc

b (*Comm*) (= *transaction*) sale; (= *technique*) selling; **avoir l'expérience de la ~** to have sales experience, have experience in selling; **s'occuper de la ~** (*dans une affaire*) to deal with the sales; **il a un pourcentage sur les ~s** he gets a percentage on sales; **directeur/direction/service des ~s** sales director/management/department

c (**aux enchères**) (*auction*) sale, auction; **courir les ~s** to do the rounds of the sales *ou* auctions → **hôtel, salle**

d (*Bourse*) selling; **la livre vaut 10 F à la ~** the selling rate for (the pound) sterling is 10 francs → **terme**

2 COMP ► **vente ambulante** (*dans les rues*) street vending *ou* peddling; (*dans un train*) trolley service ► **vente par adjudication** sale by auction ► **vente de charité** charity sale *ou* bazaar, jumble sale ► **vente par correspondance** mail-order selling ► **vente par courtage** direct selling ► **vente directe** direct selling *ou* sales ► **vente à domicile** door-to-door *ou* house-to-house selling ► **vente judiciaire** auction by order of the court ► **vente paroissiale** church sale *ou* bazaar ► **vente publique** public sale ► **vente par téléphone** telephone sales, telesales, telemarketing → **tempérament**

venté, e [vãte] (*ptp de* **venter**) ADJ windswept, windy

venter [vãte] ▶ conjug 1 ◀ VB IMPERS (*littér*) **il vente** the wind is blowing, it is windy → **pleuvoir**

venteux, -euse [vãtø, øz] ADJ [*lieu*] windswept, windy; [*temps*] windy

ventilateur [vãtilatœʀ] NM (*gén*) fan; (*dans un mur, une fenêtre*) ventilator, fan; (*Ciné*) wind machine; **~ électrique** electric fan; **~ à hélice/à turbine** blade/turbine ventilator; **~ de plafond** ceiling fan → **courroie**

ventilation [vãtilasjɔ̃] NF **a** (= *aération*) ventilation; **il y a une bonne ~ dans cette pièce** this room is well ventilated, this room has good ventilation **b** (*Méd*) **~ respiratoire** respiratory ventilation; **~ artificielle/assistée** artificial/assisted ventilation **c** (*Jur* = *évaluation*) separate valuation; (*Comptab*) [*sommes*] breaking down; (= *répartition*) [*subventions, aides*] allocation, distribution; **voici la ~ des ventes pour cette année-là** here is the breakdown of sales for that year

ventiler [vãtile] ▶ conjug 1 ◀ VT **a** (= *aérer*) [+ *pièce, tunnel*] to ventilate; **pièce bien/mal ventilée** well/poorly ventilated room **b** (*Méd*) to ventilate **c** (= *décomposer*) [+ *total, chiffre, somme*] to break down; (*Jur*) [+ *produit d'une vente*] to value separately; (= *répartir*) [+ *touristes, élèves*] to divide up (into groups); **~ les dépenses entre différents comptes** to spread the expenses over different accounts

ventôse [vãtoz] NM Ventôse (*6th month of French Republican calendar*)

ventouse [vãtuz] NF **a** (*Méd*) cupping glass; **poser des ~s à qn** to place cupping glasses on sb, cup sb **b** (*Zool*) sucker **c** (= *dispositif adhésif*) suction disc, suction pad; (*pour déboucher*) plunger; **faire ~** to cling, adhere; **porte-savon à ~** suction-grip soap holder, self-adhering soap holder → **voiture d** (*Tech* = *ouverture*) airhole, air-vent

ventral, e (*mpl* -**aux**) [vãtral, o] ADJ ventral → **parachute, rouleau**

ventre [vãtr] NM **a** (= *abdomen*) stomach, belly; **dormir/être étendu sur le ~** to sleep/be lying on one's stomach *ou* front; **avoir/prendre du ~** to have/be getting rather a paunch, have/be getting a bit of a tummy*; **rentrer le ~** to hold *ou* pull in one's stomach; (*fig*) **passer sur le ~ de qn** to ride roughshod over sb, walk over sb; **il faudra me passer sur le ~!** over my dead body! → **danse, plat¹**

b (= *estomac*) stomach; **se coucher le ~ vide** *ou* **creux** to go to bed hungry *ou* on an empty stomach; **ne partez pas le ~ vide!** *ou* **creux!** don't leave on an empty stomach!; **avoir le ~ plein*** to be full; **avoir mal au ~ ◊ avoir des maux de ~** to have stomach ache *ou* (a) tummy ache*; (*fig*) **ça me ferait mal au ~!*** it would sicken me!, it would make me sick! ■ (*PROV*) **affamé n'a point d'oreilles** words are wasted on a starving man; **le ~ de la terre** the bowels of the earth → **œil, reconnaissance, taper**

c (= *utérus*) womb; **quand tu étais dans le ~ de ta mère** when you were in mummy's tum-

my*
d [animal] (under)belly
e [cruche, vase] bulb, bulbous part; [bateau] belly, bilge; [avion] belly → **atterrissage**
f (Tech) **faire ~** [mur] to bulge; [plafond] to sag, bulge
g (Phys) [onde] antinode
h (loc) **courir** ou **aller ~ à terre** to go flat out* ou at top speed; **galoper ~ à terre** to gallop flat out*, go at full gallop; **nous allons voir s'il a quelque chose dans le ~** we'll see what he's made of, we'll see if he's got guts*; **il n'a rien dans le ~** he has no guts*, he's spineless; **j'aimerais bien savoir ce qu'il a dans le ~** (ce qu'il pense) I'd like to know what's going on in his mind; (quelles sont ses qualités) I'd like to see what he's made of; **ouvrir sa montre pour voir ce qu'elle a dans le ~*** to open (up) one's watch to see what it has got inside ou what's inside it; **le ~ mou de l'Europe** the soft underbelly of Europe → **cœur**

ventrebleu †† [vɑ̃trəblø] EXCL gadzooks!†, zounds!†

ventrée ·† [vɑ̃tre] NF **une ~ de pâtes** a good bellyful* of pasta; **on s'en est mis une bonne ~** we pigged* ou stuffed* ourselves on it

ventre-saint-gris †† [vɑ̃trəsɛ̃gri] EXCL gadzooks!†, zounds!†

ventriculaire [vɑ̃trikyler] ADJ ventricular

ventricule [vɑ̃trikyl] NM ventricle

ventrière [vɑ̃trijer] NF **a** (= sangle) girth; (= toile de transport) sling **b** (Constr) purlin; (Naut) bilge block

ventriloque [vɑ̃trilɔk] NMF ventriloquist; **il est ~** he can throw his voice; (de profession) he's a ventriloquist

ventriloquie [vɑ̃trilɔki] NF ventriloquy, ventriloquism

ventripotent, e [vɑ̃tripɔtɑ̃, ɑ̃t] ADJ potbellied

ventru, e [vɑ̃try] ADJ [personne] potbellied; [pot, commode] bulbous

venu, e¹ [v(ə)ny] (ptp de **venir**) ADJ **a** (= fondé, placé) [personne] **être mal ~ de faire** to be in no position to do; **elle serait mal ~e de se plaindre/refuser** she is in no position to complain/refuse, she should be the last to complain/refuse
b **bien ~** (= à propos) [événement, question, remarque] timely, apposite, opportune; **mal ~** (= inopportun) [événement, question] untimely, inapposite, inopportune; **sa remarque était plutôt mal ~e** his remark was rather out of place ou uncalled-for, his remark was a bit off*; **un empressement mal ~** unseemly ou unfitting haste; (impers) **il serait mal ~ de lui poser cette question** it would not be fitting ou it would be a bit out of place to ask him (that)
c (= développé) **bien ~** [enfant] sturdy, sturdily built; [plante, arbre] well-developed, fine; [pièce, œuvre] well-written; **mal ~** [enfant, arbre] (= chétif) stunted; (= mal conformé) malformed
d (= arrivé) **tard ~** late; **tôt ~** early; **le premier/dernier ~** the first/last to come; (fig) **il n'est pas le premier ~** he isn't just anybody; **elle n'épousera pas le premier ~** she won't marry the first man that comes along → **nouveau**

venue² [v(ə)ny] NF **a** [personne] arrival, coming; **à l'occasion de la ~ de la reine** (dans le passé) when the queen visited; (dans le futur) when the queen visits; **il a annoncé sa ~** he announced that he was coming → **allée**
b (littér = avènement) coming; **la ~ du printemps/du Christ** the coming of spring/of Christ; **lors de ma ~ au monde** when I came into the world **c** (loc: littér) **d'une seule ~** ◊ **tout d'une ~** [arbre] straight-growing (épith); **d'une belle ~** finely ou beautifully developed

Vénus [venys] NF (Astron, Myth) Venus; (fig = femme) **une ~** a venus, a great beauty → **mont**

vénus [venys] NF (= mollusque) type of clam

vépéciste [vepesist] NM (= entreprise) mail-order firm

vêpres [vɛpr] NFPL vespers; **sonner les ~** to ring the vespers bell

ver [ver] **1** NM (gén) worm; (= larve) grub; [viande, fruits, fromage] maggot; [bois] woodworm (NonC); **mangé** ou **rongé aux ~s** worm-eaten; (Méd) **avoir des ~s** to have worms; (Agr) **mes poireaux ont le ~** my leeks have been eaten ou attacked by grubs; (fig) **le ~ est dans le fruit** the rot has already set in; **tirer les ~s du nez à qn*** to worm information out of sb; **se tordre** ou **se tortiller comme un ~** to wriggle like an eel → **nu, piqué 2** COMP ► **ver d'eau** caddis worm ► **ver blanc** May beetle grub ► **ver luisant** glow-worm ► **ver de sable** sea slug ► **ver à soie** silkworm ► **ver solitaire** tapeworm; **avoir/attraper le ~ solitaire** to have/get tapeworm ► **ver de terre** (lit) earthworm; (fig péj) worm ► **ver de vase** bloodworm

véracité [verasite] NF [rapport, récit, témoin] veracity (frm), truthfulness; [déclaration, fait] truth, veracity (frm)

véranda [verɑ̃da] NF veranda(h)

verbal, e (mpl **-aux**) [verbal, o] ADJ **a** (= oral) verbal **b** (Ling) [adjectif, locution] verbal; [système, forme, terminaison] verb (épith), verbal → **groupe**

verbalement [verbalmɑ̃] ADV [dire, faire savoir] verbally, by word of mouth; [approuver, donner son accord] verbally

verbalisateur [verbalizatœr] ADJ M **l'agent doit toujours ...** an officer reporting an offence must always ...; **l'agent ~ a oublié de ...** the officer who reported ou booked* (Brit) me (ou him etc) forgot to ...

verbalisation [verbalizasjɔ̃] NF **a** (Police) reporting (by an officer) of an offence **b** (Psych) verbalization

verbaliser [verbalize] ▶ conjug 1 ◀ **1** VI **a** (Police) **l'agent a dû ~** the officer had to report ou book* (Brit) him (ou me etc) **b** (Psych) to verbalize **2** VT (Psych) to verbalize

verbalisme [verbalism] NM verbalism

verbe [verb] NM **a** (Gram) verb; **~ défectif/impersonnel** defective/impersonal verb; **~ transitif/intransitif** transitive/intransitive verb; **~ pronominal** reflexive verb; **~ actif/passif** active/passive verb, verb in the active/passive (voice); **~ d'action/d'état** action/stative verb; **~ fort** strong verb; **~ à particule** phrasal verb **b** (Rel) **le Verbe** the Word; **le Verbe s'est fait chair** the Word was made flesh; **le Verbe incarné** the Word incarnate **c** (littér = mots, langage) language, word; **la magie du ~** the magic of language ou the word **d** (littér = ton de voix) tone (of voice); **avoir le ~ haut** to speak in a high and mighty tone, sound high and mighty

verbeusement [verbøzmɑ̃] ADV verbosely

verbeux, -euse [verbø, øz] ADJ verbose, wordy, prolix

verbiage [verbjaʒ] NM verbiage

verbicruciste [verbikrysist] NMF crossword compiler, compiler of crossword puzzles

verbosité [verbozite] NF verbosity, wordiness, prolixity

verdâtre [verdɑtr] ADJ greenish

verdeur [verdœr] NF **a** (= jeunesse) vigour (Brit), vigor (US) **b** [fruit] tartness, sharpness; [vin] acidity **c** [langage] forthrightness

verdict [verdik(t)] NM (Jur, gén) verdict; (Jur) **~ de culpabilité/d'acquittement** verdict of guilty/of not guilty; **rendre** ou **prononcer un ~** to return ou bring in a verdict; **le ~ est tombé** the verdict was announced; **il attend le ~ des critiques** he's waiting for the critics' verdict

verdier [verdje] NM greenfinch

verdir [verdir] ▶ conjug 2 ◀ **1** VI [feuilles, arbres] to turn ou go green; [personne] to turn pale, blanch; **~ de peur** to turn white with fear **2** VT to turn green

verdissant, e [verdisɑ̃, ɑ̃t] ADJ (littér) [arbre, champ] greening (épith) (littér)

verdoiement [verdwamɑ̃] NM (= état) verdancy (littér), greenness; (= action) **le ~ des prés au printemps** the greening of the meadows ou the verdant hue taken on by the meadows in spring (littér)

verdoyant, e [verdwajɑ̃, ɑ̃t] ADJ verdant (littér), green

verdoyer [verdwaje] ▶ conjug 8 ◀ VI (= être vert) to be verdant (littér) ou green; (= devenir vert) to become verdant (littér) ou green

verdure [verdyr] NF **a** (= végétation) greenery (NonC), verdure (NonC) (littér); **tapis de ~** greensward (littér); **rideau de ~** curtain of greenery ou verdure (littér); **tapisserie de ~** ou **à ~s** verdure (tapestry); **je vous mets un peu de ~?** (pour un bouquet) shall I put some greenery in for you? → **théâtre b** (littér = couleur) verdure (littér), greenness **c** (= salade) lettuce

véreux, -euse [verø, øz] ADJ **a** (lit) [aliment] maggoty, worm-eaten **b** (fig) [policier, financier] corrupt; [affaire] dubious, fishy*, shady*

verge [verʒ] NF **a** († = baguette) stick, cane; (pour fouetter) **les ~s** the birch; **ce serait lui donner des ~s pour nous faire battre** that would be giving him a stick to beat us with; (Bot) **~ d'or** goldenrod **b** (Hist = insigne d'autorité) [huissier] wand; [bedeau] rod **c** (Anat) penis **d** (Tech = tringle) shank **e** (Can) yard (0,914 m)

vergé, e [verʒe] ADJ, NM [papier] **~** laid paper

vergeoise [verʒwaz] NF brown sugar (made from waste refining products)

verger [verʒe] NM orchard

vergeté, e [verʒate] ADJ [peau] stretch marked

vergeture [verʒatyr] NF stretch mark

verglaçant, e [verglasɑ̃, ɑ̃t] ADJ **pluie ~e** freezing rain

verglacé, e [verglase] ADJ icy; **les routes sont ~es** there's (black) ice on the roads, the roads are icy

verglas [vergla] NM (black) ice (on road etc); **plaque de ~** icy patch, patch of black ice

vergogne [vergɔɲ] ◆ **sans vergogne** LOC ADJ, LOC ADV [personne, concurrence] shameless; [parler, agir] shamelessly

vergue [verg] NF (Naut) yard; **grand-~** main yard; **~ de misaine** foreyard; **~ de hune** topsail yard

véridique [veridik] ADJ [récit, témoignage] truthful, true, veracious (frm); [témoin] truthful, veracious (frm); [repentir, douleur] genuine, authentic

véridiquement [veridikmɑ̃] ADV truthfully, veraciously (frm)

vérifiable [verifjabl] ADJ verifiable; **c'est aisément ~** it can easily be checked

vérificateur, -trice [verifikatœr, tris] **1** ADJ [appareil, système] checking (épith), verifying (épith) **2** NM,F controller, checker; **~ des douanes** Customs inspector; (Fin) **~ des comptes** auditor; (Can) **~ général** Auditor General; (Ordin) **~ orthographique** ou **d'orthographe** spellchecker, spelling checker **3** **vérificatrice** NF (Tech) verifier

vérification [verifikasjɔ̃] NF **a** (= contrôle) [affirmation, fait, récit, alibi] checking, verification; [adresse, renseignement, rumeur] checking; [véracité, authenticité, exactitude] ascertaining, checking; (Fin) [comptes] auditing; [poids, mesure, classement] check, checking; **procéder à** ou **effectuer plusieurs ~s** to carry out several checks; **~ faite** ou **après ~, il se trouve que ...** on checking, we find that ...; (Police) **~ d'identité** identity check; (lors d'une assemblée

générale) **~ des pouvoirs** check on proxies given to shareholders; (*Pol*) **~ du scrutin** *ou* **des votes** scrutiny of votes; **~ comptable** auditing, audit; **~ fiscale** tax investigation; **mission de ~** investigative mission
b (= *confirmation*) confirmation; [*affirmation, fait*] establishing, confirming, proving (to be true); [*axiome, témoignage*] establishing, confirming; [*soupçons, conjecture*] confirming; [*hypothèse, théorie*] confirming, proving (to be true)

vérifier [veʀifje] ▸conjug 7◂ ☐1 VT **a** (= *contrôler*) [+ *affirmation, fait, récit, alibi*] to check, verify; [+ *adresse, renseignement, rumeur, identité*] to check; [+ *véracité, authenticité, exactitude*] to ascertain, check; (*Fin*) [+ *comptes*] to audit; [+ *poids, mesure, classement*] to check; **ne vous faites pas de souci, cela a été vérifié et revérifié** don't worry — it has been checked and double-checked *ou* cross-checked; **vérifie que/si la porte est bien fermée** check that/if the door's properly closed; **~ ses freins/le niveau d'huile** to check one's brakes/the oil (level)
b (= *confirmer, prouver*) [+ *affirmation, fait*] to establish the truth of, confirm (the truth of), prove to be true; [+ *axiome*] to establish *ou* confirm the truth of; [+ *témoignage*] to establish the truth *ou* veracity (*frm*) of, confirm; [+ *soupçons, conjecture*] to bear out, confirm; [+ *hypothèse, théorie*] to bear out, confirm, prove; **cet accident a vérifié mes craintes** this accident has borne out *ou* confirmed my fears
☐2 **se vérifier** VPR [*craintes*] to be borne out, be confirmed; [*théorie*] to be borne out, be proved; **l'adage s'est encore vérifié** the old saying has once again proved true; **cette tendance se vérifie dans tous les secteurs** the tendency is clearly visible in all sectors

vérin [veʀɛ̃] NM jack; **~ hydraulique/pneumatique** hydraulic/pneumatic jack; **monté sur ~** raised on a jack

vérisme [veʀism] NM verism

vériste [veʀist] ADJ, NMF verist

véritable [veʀitabl] ADJ **a** (= *authentique*) [*argent, or, cuir, perles, larmes, colère*] real, genuine; [*ami, artiste, vocation*] real, genuine, true; **l'art/l'amour ~ se reconnaît d'emblée** true art/love is immediately recognizable **b** (= *vrai, réel*) [*identité, raisons*] true, real; [*nom*] real; **la ~ religion/joie** true religion/joy; **sous son jour ~** in his true light; **ça n'a pas de ~ fondement** it has no real foundation **c** (*intensif = qui mérite bien son nom*) real; **un ~ coquin** an absolute *ou* a real *ou* a downright rogue; **~ provocation** real *ou* downright *ou* sheer provocation; **c'est une ~ folie** it's absolute *ou* sheer madness; **c'est une ~ expédition/révolution** it's a real *ou* veritable (*frm*) expedition/revolution

véritablement [veʀitabləmɑ̃] ADV really; **est-il ~ fatigué/diplômé ?** is he really tired/qualified?; **il l'a ~ fait/rencontré** he actually *ou* really did it/met him; **ce n'est pas truqué : ils traversent ~ les flammes** it isn't fixed — they really *ou* genuinely do go through the flames; **ce n'est pas ~ un roman/dictionnaire** it's not really *ou* exactly a novel/dictionary, it's not a real *ou* proper novel/dictionary; (*intensif*) **c'est ~ délicieux** it's absolutely *ou* positively *ou* really delicious

▼**vérité** [veʀite] NF **a** (= *connaissance du vrai*) **la ~** (= *conformité aux faits*) the truth; **nul n'est dépositaire de la ~** no one has a monopoly on (the) truth; **la ~ d'un fait/principe** the truth of a fact/principle; **c'est la ~ vraie*** it's the honest truth*; **la ~ toute nue** the naked *ou* unadorned truth; **son souci de (la) ~** his desire *ou* concern for (the) truth; **dire la ~** to tell *ou* speak the truth; (*Jur, hum*) **jurez de dire la ~, toute la ~, rien que la ~** do you swear to

tell the truth, the whole truth and nothing but the truth?; **la ~ dépasse souvent la fiction** truth is often stranger than fiction ■ (*PROV*) **la ~ sort de la bouche des enfants** out of the mouths of babes and sucklings (comes forth truth) (*PROV*) ■ (*PROV*) **toute ~ n'est pas bonne à dire** some things are better left unsaid
b (= *vraisemblance, ressemblance au réel*) [*portrait*] lifelikeness, trueness to life; [*tableau, personnage*] trueness to life; **s'efforcer à la ~ en art** to strive to be true to life in art
c (= *sincérité, authenticité*) truthfulness, sincerity; **un air/un accent de ~** an air/a note of sincerity *ou* truthfulness
d (= *fait vrai, évidence*) truth; **une ~ bien sentie** a heartfelt truth; **~s éternelles/premières** eternal/first truths *ou* verities (*frm*) → **La Palice, quatre**
e (*loc*) **en ~** (= *en fait*) in fact, actually; **en ~** (*frm*) ◊ **à la ~** (= *à dire vrai*) to tell the truth, to be honest; **c'est (bien) peu de chose, en ~** it's really *ou* actually nothing very much; (*Bible*) **en ~ je vous le dis** verily I say unto you; (*frm*) **à la ~ il préfère s'amuser que de travailler** to tell the truth *ou* to be honest he prefers to enjoy himself rather than work; **j'étais à la ~ loin de m'en douter** to tell the truth *ou* to tell I was far from suspecting it; **la ~, c'est que je n'en sais rien** the truth (of the matter) is that *ou* to tell the truth I know nothing about it; **l'heure** *ou* **la minute de ~** the moment of truth → **sérum**

verjus [veʀʒy] NM verjuice

verlan [veʀlɑ̃] NM (back) slang

┌─────────────────┐
│ █ **VERLAN**
└─────────────────┘
Verlan is a particular kind of backslang that has become extremely popular among young people in France. It consists of inverting the syllables of words, and often then truncating the result to make a new word. The slang words "meuf", "keuf", "keum" and "beur" are **verlan** *renderings of the words "femme","flic", "mec" and "Arabe". The expression "laisse béton" ("forget it") is* **verlan** *for "laisse tomber", and the word* **verlan** *itself comes from the expression "à l'envers" ("back to front").*

vermeil, -eille [veʀmɛj] ☐1 ADJ [*tissu, objet*] vermilion, bright red; [*bouche*] ruby (*épith*), cherry (*épith*), ruby- *ou* cherry-red; [*teint*] rosy → **carte** ☐2 NM (= *métal*) vermeil; **cuiller/médaille de ~** silver-gilt spoon/medal

vermicelle [veʀmisɛl] NM (= *pâtes*) **~(s)** vermicelli, angel hair pasta (*US*); **potage au ~** vermicelli soup; **~ chinois** fine rice noodles

vermiculaire [veʀmikylɛʀ] ADJ (*Anat*) vermicular, vermiform; **appendice ~** vermiform appendix; **éminence ~** vermis; **contraction ~** peristalsis (*NonC*)

vermiculé, e [veʀmikyle] ADJ vermiculated

vermiculure [veʀmikylyʀ] NF (*gén pl*) vermiculation (*NonC*)

vermiforme [veʀmifɔʀm] ADJ vermiform

vermifuge [veʀmifyʒ] ADJ, NM vermifuge (*SPÉC*); **poudre ~** worm powder

vermillon [veʀmijɔ̃] ☐1 NM (= *poudre*) vermilion, cinnabar; (= *couleur*) (**rouge**) **~** vermilion, scarlet ☐2 ADJ INV vermilion, scarlet

vermine [veʀmin] NF **a** (= *parasites*) vermin (*NonC*); **couvert de ~** crawling with vermin, lice-ridden **b** (*littér, péj = racaille*) vermin; (†, *péj = vaurien*) knave†, cur†

vermisseau (*pl* **vermisseaux**) [veʀmiso] NM (= *ver*) small worm, vermicule (*SPÉC*)

Vermont [veʀmɔ̃] NM Vermont

vermoulu, e [veʀmuly] ADJ [*bois*] full of woodworm, worm-eaten; (*fig*) [*régime politique, institutions*] moth-eaten; **cette commode est ~e** there is woodworm in this chest, this chest is full of woodworm *ou* is worm-eaten

vermoulure [veʀmulyʀ] NF (= *traces*) woodworm (*NonC*), worm holes

vermout(h) [veʀmut] NM vermouth

vernaculaire [veʀnakylɛʀ] ADJ vernacular; **langue ~** vernacular

vernal, e (*mpl* **-aux**) [veʀnal, o] ADJ (*Astron, Bot*) vernal

verni, e [veʀni] (*ptp de* **vernir**) ADJ **a** [*bois*] varnished; (*fig = luisant*) [*feuilles*] shiny, glossy; **cuir ~** patent leather; **souliers ~s** patent (leather) shoes; **poterie ~e** glazed earthenware **b** (* = *chanceux*) lucky, jammy‡ (*Brit*); **il est ~** ◊ **c'est un ~** he's lucky *ou* jammy‡ (*Brit*), he's a lucky devil* *ou* dog*

vernier [veʀnje] NM vernier (scale)

vernir [veʀniʀ] ▸conjug 2◂ VT [+ *bois, tableau, cuir*] to varnish; [+ *poterie*] to glaze; [+ *ongles*] to put nail varnish on, varnish; (*Ébénisterie*) **~ au tampon** to French polish

vernis [veʀni] NM **a** [*bois, tableau, mur*] varnish; [*poterie*] glaze; **~ (à ongles)** nail varnish *ou* polish; **~ cellulosique/synthétique** cellulose/synthetic varnish; **~ au tampon** French polish **b** (= *éclat*) shine, gloss **c** (*Bot*) (**faux**) **~ du Japon** varnish tree, tree of heaven **d** (*fig*) veneer (*fig*); **un ~ de culture** a veneer of culture

vernissage [veʀnisaʒ] NM **a** [*bois, tableau, ongles, cuir*] varnishing; [*poterie*] glazing **b** (= *exposition*) private viewing, preview (*at an art gallery*)

vernissé, e [veʀnise] (*ptp de* **vernisser**) ADJ [*poterie, tuile*] glazed; (*fig = luisant*) [*feuillage*] shiny, glossy

vernisser [veʀnise] ▸conjug 1◂ VT to glaze

vernisseur, -euse [veʀnisœʀ, øz] NM,F [*bois*] varnisher; [*poterie*] glazer

vérole [veʀɔl] NF **a** (= *variole*) → **petit** **b** (‡ = *syphilis*) pox‡; **il a/il a attrapé la ~** he's got/he has caught the pox‡

vérolé, e‡ [veʀɔle] ADJ **a** (= *atteint de syphilis*) pox-ridden **b** (= *mauvais*) [*contrat*] poxy‡, lousy‡; (= *abîmé par un virus*) [*fichier, disquette*] infected by a virus

véronal [veʀɔnal] NM (*Pharm*) veronal

Vérone [veʀɔn] N Verona

véronique [veʀɔnik] NF (*Bot*) speedwell, veronica; (*Tauromachie*) veronica

verrat [veʀa] NM boar

verre [veʀ] ☐1 NM **a** (= *substance*) glass; **~ moulé/étiré/coulé** pressed/cast/drawn glass; **cela se casse** *ou* **se brise comme du ~** it's as brittle as glass → **laine, papier, pâte** **b** (= *objet*) [*vitre, cadre*] glass; [*lunettes*] lens; **mettre qch sous ~** to put sth under glass; **~ grossissant/déformant** magnifying/distorting glass; **porter des ~s** to wear glasses **c** (= *récipient*) glass; (= *contenu*) glass, glassful; (*Culin*) **ajouter un ~ de lait** ≈ add one cup of milk; **un ~ d'eau/de bière** a glass of water/of beer; **~ à bière** beer glass → **casser, noyer², tempête** **d** (= *boisson*) drink; **boire** *ou* **prendre un ~** to have a drink; **payer un ~ à qn** to buy sb a drink; **lever son ~** to raise one's glass; **boire le ~ de l'amitié** to drink a toast to friendship; **videz vos ~s !** drink up!; **un petit ~*** a quick one*, a quickie*; **il a bu un ~ de trop*** ◊ **il a un ~ dans le nez*** he's had one too many* *ou* a drop too much*, he's had one over the eight* (*Brit*)
☐2 COMP ► **verre armé** wired glass ► **verre ballon** balloon glass, brandy glass ► **verre blanc** plain glass ► **verre cathédrale** cathedral glass ► **verres de contact (souples/durs)** (soft/hard) contact lenses ► **verres correcteurs** corrective lenses ► **verre à dégustation** wine-tasting glass ► **verre à dents** tooth mug *ou* glass ► **verre dépoli** frosted glass ► **verre feuilleté** laminated glass ► **verre fumé** smoked glass ► **verres fumés** [*lunettes*] tinted lenses ► **verre incassable** unbreakable glass ► **verre de lampe** lamp glass, (lamp)

┌────────────────────────────────────┐
│ ► GRAMMAIRE ACTIVE: *vérité* 53.4 │
└────────────────────────────────────┘

chimney ► **verre à liqueur** liqueur glass; **verser la valeur d'un ~ à liqueur de ...** ≈ add two tablespoons of ... ► **verre mesureur** measuring glass ► **verre de montre** watch glass ► **verre à moutarde** (glass) mustard jar ► **verre à pied** stemmed glass ► **verres progressifs** multifocal lenses, multifocals ► **verre de sécurité** safety glass ► **verre trempé** toughened glass ► **verre à vin** wineglass ► **verre à vitre** window glass ► **verre à whisky** whisky glass *ou* tumbler

verrerie [vɛʀʀi] NF (= *usine*) glassworks *pl inv*, glass factory; (= *fabrication du verre*) glass-making; (= *manufacture d'objets*) glass-working; (= *objets*) glassware; (= *commerce*) glass trade *ou* industry

verrier [vɛʀje] [1] NM (= *ouvrier*) glassworker; (= *souffleur de verre*) glassblower; (= *artiste*) artist in glass; **maître ~** master glazier; **peintre ~** stained-glass artist [2] ADJ M (*Ind*) [*groupe, établissement*] glass-making

verrière [vɛʀjɛʀ] NF [a] (= *fenêtre*) [*église, édifice*] window [b] (= *toit vitré*) glass roof [c] (= *paroi vitrée*) glass wall [d] (*Aviat*) canopy

verroterie [vɛʀɔtʀi] NF (**bijoux en**) ~ glass jewellery (*Brit*) *ou* jewelry (*US*); **un collier de ~** a necklace of glass beads

verrou [vɛʀu] NM [a] [*porte*] bolt; **tire/pousse le ~** unbolt/bolt the door; **as-tu mis le ~?** have you bolted the door?; **~ de sécurité** (*lit*) safety *ou* security lock; (*fig*) safety net; **mettre qn sous les ~s** to put sb under lock and key; **être sous les ~s** to be behind bars → **sauter** [b] (*Tech*) [*aiguillage*] facing point lock; [*culasse*] bolt [c] (*Géol*) constriction [d] (*Mil*) stopper (*in breach*) [e] (*Ordin*) lock

verrouillage [vɛʀujaʒ] NM [a] (= *fermeture*) [*porte, fenêtre*] bolting, locking; [*culasse*] locking; (*Aut*) **~ automatique des portes** ◊ **~ centralisé** central locking [b] (= *fait de rendre inaccessible*) (*Mil*) [*brèche*] closing; [*frontière*] sealing; (*Ordin*) locking [c] (= *muselage*) **le ~ des médias** the muzzling of the media [d] (= *dispositif*) locking mechanism

verrouiller [vɛʀuje] ▶conjug 1◀ VT [a] (= *fermer*) [+ *porte, fenêtre*] to bolt; (*à clé*) to lock; [+ *culasse*] to lock [b] (= *rendre inaccessible*) (*Mil*) [+ *brèche*] to close; [+ *frontière*] to seal; **la police a verrouillé le quartier** the police cordoned off *ou* sealed (off) the area [c] (= *enfermer*) (*lit, fig*) **ses parents le verrouillent** his parents keep him locked in; (*fig*) **se ~ chez soi** to shut o.s. away at home [d] (= *bloquer*) [+ *capital, marché, processus*] to block [e] (= *contrôler*) **j'ai tout verrouillé** I've got everything under control

verrouilleur [vɛʀujœʀ] NM (*Rugby*) last man in the line-out

verrue [vɛʀy] NF (*lit*) wart; (*fig*) eyesore; **~ plantaire** verruca; **cette usine est une ~ au milieu du paysage** this factory is a blot on the landscape *ou* an eyesore in the middle of the countryside

verruqueux, -euse [vɛʀykø, øz] ADJ warty, verrucose (*US*)

vers[1] [vɛʀ] PRÉP [a] (*direction*) toward(s), to; **en allant ~ Aix/la gare** going to *ou* toward(s) Aix/ the station; **le lieu ~ lequel il nous menait** the place he was leading us to *ou* to which he was leading us; **~ la droite, la brume se levait** to *ou* toward(s) the right the mist was rising; **la foule se dirigeait ~ la plage** the crowd was making for *ou* heading towards the beach; **« ~ la plage »** "to the beach"; **elle fit un pas ~ la fenêtre** she took a step toward(s) the window; **notre chambre regarde ~ le sud/la colline** our bedroom faces *ou* looks south/faces the hills *ou* looks toward(s) the hills; **il tendit la main ~ la bouteille** he reached out for the bottle, he stretched out his hand toward(s) the bottle; **le pays se dirige droit ~ l'abîme** the country is heading straight for disaster; **c'est un pas ~ la paix/la vérité** it's a step toward(s)

(*establishing*) peace/(*finding out*) the truth; (*titre*) **« Vers une sémantique de l'anglais »** "Towards a Semantics of English"; **traduire ~ le français/l'espagnol** to translate into French/Spanish

[b] (= *aux environs de*) around; **c'est ~ Aix que nous avons eu une panne** it was (somewhere) near Aix *ou* round about Aix that we broke down; **~ 2 000 mètres l'air est frais** at around the 2,000 metres mark *ou* at about 2,000 metres the air is cool

[c] (*temps : approximation*) about, around; **~ quelle heure doit-il venir?** around *ou* about what time is he due?; **il est arrivé ~ 6 heures** he arrived (at) about *ou* around 6 o'clock; **elle a commencé à lire ~ 6 ans** she started reading at about 6 *ou* around 6; **il était ~ (les) 3 heures quand je suis rentré** it was about *ou* around 3 when I came home; **~ la fin de la soirée/de l'année** toward(s) the end of the evening/the year; **~ 1900/le début du siècle** toward(s) *ou* about 1900/the turn of the century

vers[2] [vɛʀ] NM [a] (*sg = ligne*) line; **au 3ᵉᵐᵉ ~** in line 3, in the 3rd line; **~ de dix syllabes** ◊ **~ décasyllabe** line of ten syllables, decasyllabic line; **un ~ boiteux** a short line, a hypometric line (*SPÉC*); **je me souviens d'un ~ de Virgile** I recall a line by Virgil; **réciter quelques ~** to recite a few lines of poetry [b] (*pl = poésie*) verse (*NonC*); **~ blancs/libres** blank/free verse; **~ de circonstance** occasional verse; **traduction en ~** verse translation; **faire** *ou* **écrire des ~** to write verse, versify (*péj*); **mettre en ~** to put into verse; **il fait des ~ de temps en temps** he writes a little verse from time to time; **écrire des ~ de mirliton** to write a bit of doggerel

versaillais, e [vɛʀsaje, ɛz] [1] ADJ from *ou* of Versailles; (*Hist*) **l'armée ~e** army which suppressed the Commune of 1871 [2] **Versaillais(e)** NM,F inhabitant *ou* native of Versailles; (*Hist*) **les Versaillais** the government troops who suppressed the Commune of 1871

Versailles [vɛʀsaj] N Versailles; **le château de ~** the palace of Versailles; (*fig*) **c'est ~!** [*appartement*] it's like a palace!, it's palatial!; [*événement, réception*] it's really spectacular!

versant [vɛʀsã] NM [*vallée, toit*] side; [*massif*] slopes; **les Pyrénées ont un ~ français et un ~ espagnol** the Pyrenees have a French side and a Spanish side; **le ~ nord/français de ce massif** the northern/French slopes of this range; (*fig*) **les deux ~s d'une même politique** the two sides of the same policy

versatile [vɛʀsatil] ADJ fickle, changeable, capricious

versatilité [vɛʀsatilite] NF fickleness, changeability, capriciousness

verse [vɛʀs] ▶à **verse** LOC ADV in torrents; **il pleut à ~** it's pouring down, it's coming down in torrents *ou* in buckets*

versé, e [vɛʀse] (*ptp de verser*) ADJ (= *savant, expérimenté*) **~/peu ~ dans l'histoire ancienne** (well-)versed/ill-versed in ancient history; **~/peu ~ dans l'art de l'escrime** (highly) skilled *ou* accomplished/unaccomplished in the art of fencing; **l'homme le plus ~ de France dans l'art chaldéen** the most learned man in France in the field of Chaldean art

Verseau [vɛʀso] NM (*Astron*) **le ~** Aquarius, the Water-carrier; **il est ~** ◊ **il est (du signe) du ~** he's (an) Aquarius

versement [vɛʀsəmã] NM payment; (*échelonné*) instalment, installment (*US*); **le ~ d'une somme sur un compte** the payment of a sum into an account; **par chèque/virement** payment by cheque/credit transfer; **par ~s échelonnés** in *ou* by instalments; **je veux faire un ~ sur mon compte** I want to put some money into my account, I want to make a deposit into my account; **le ~ de ces sommes se fera le mois prochain** these sums will be paid next month; **~ en espèces** cash deposit; **~ à une**

œuvre donation to a charity; **bulletin** *ou* **bordereau de ~** paying-in (*Brit*) *ou* deposit (*US*) slip; **un premier ~** *ou* **un ~ initial de 1 000 F** a first *ou* an initial payment of 1,000 francs

verser [vɛʀse] ▶conjug 1◀ [1] VT [a] [+ *liquide, grains*] to pour, tip (**dans** into, **sur** onto); (= *servir*) [+ *thé, café, vin*] to pour (out) (**dans** into); **~ le café dans les tasses** to pour the coffee into the cups; **~ des haricots (d'un sac) dans un bocal** to pour *ou* tip beans (from a bag) into a jar; **~ du vin/un verre de vin à qn** to pour sb some wine/a glass of wine; **verse-lui/-toi à boire** pour him/yourself a drink; **veux-tu ~ à boire/le vin s'il te plaît?** will you pour (out) *ou* serve the drinks/the wine please? → **huile**

[b] (= *répandre*) [+ *larmes, sang*] to shed; (= *déverser*) to pour out, scatter (**sur** onto); **~ le sang** (= *tuer*) to shed *ou* spill blood; **sans ~ une goutte de sang** without shedding *ou* spilling a drop of blood; (*littér, hum*) **~ un pleur/quelques pleurs** to shed a tear/a few tears

[c] (= *classer*) **~ une pièce à un dossier** to add an item to a file

[d] (= *payer: gén, Fin*) to pay; **~ une somme à un compte** to pay a sum of money into an account, deposit a sum of money in an account; **~ des intérêts à qn** to pay sb interest; **~ des arrhes** to put down *ou* pay a deposit; **~ une rente à qn** to pay sb a pension

[e] (= *affecter, incorporer*) **~ qn dans** to assign *ou* attach sb to; **se faire ~ dans l'infanterie** to get o.s. assigned *ou* attached to the infantry

[2] VI [a] (= *basculer*) [*véhicule*] to overturn; **il va nous faire ~ dans le fossé** he'll tip us into the ditch, we'll end up in the ditch because of him; **il a déjà versé deux fois** he has already overturned twice

[b] (= *tomber dans*) **~ dans** [+ *sentimentalité, démagogie*] to lapse into

verset [vɛʀse] NM (*Rel*) [*Bible, Coran*] verse; (= *prière*) versicle; (*Littérat*) verse

verseur, -euse [vɛʀsœʀ, øz] [1] ADJ **bouchon ~** pour-through stopper; **sucrier ~** sugar dispenser → **bec** [2] NM (= *dispositif*) pourer [3] **verseuse** NF (= *cafetière*) coffeepot

versicolore [vɛʀsikɔlɔʀ] ADJ versicolour (*Brit*), versicolor (*US*)

versificateur [vɛʀsifikatœʀ] NM writer of verse, versifier (*péj*), rhymester (*péj*)

versification [vɛʀsifikasjɔ̃] NF versification

versifier [vɛʀsifje] ▶conjug 7◀ [1] VT to put into verse; **une œuvre versifiée** a work put into verse [2] VI to write verse, versify (*péj*)

version [vɛʀsjɔ̃] NF [a] (*Scol = traduction*) translation (*into the mother tongue*), unseen (translation); **~ grecque/anglaise** Greek/English unseen (translation), translation from Greek/ English [b] (= *variante*) [*œuvre, texte*] version; **film en ~ originale** film in the original language *ou* version; **« Casablanca » en ~ originale (sous-titrée)** "Casablanca" in English (with French subtitles); **la ~ française du film** the French version of the film; **film italien en ~ française** Italian film dubbed into French; (*Aut*) **~ 4 portes** 4-door model [c] (= *modèle*) model [d] (= *interprétation*) [*incident, faits*] version; **donner sa ~ des faits** to give one's (own) version of the facts [e] (*Ordin*) version; **~ bêta** beta version

verso [vɛʀso] NM back; **au ~** on the back (of the page); **« voir au ~ »** "see over(leaf)"

verste [vɛʀst] NF verst

versus [vɛʀsys] PRÉP versus

vert, verte [vɛʀ, vɛʀt] [1] ADJ [a] (= *couleur*) green; **~ de jalousie** green with envy; **~ de rage** purple with rage; **~ de peur** white with fear; (*hum*) **les petits hommes ~s** the little green men (*hum*) → **feu**[1], **haricot**, **numéro**, **tapis** *etc*

[b] (= *pas mûr*) [*céréale, fruit*] unripe, green;

[*vin*] young; (= *frais, non séché*) [*foin, bois*] green; **être au régime ~** to be on a green-vegetable diet *ou* a diet of green vegetables → **cuir**

[c] (*fig*) [*vieillard*] vigorous, sprightly, spry; **au temps de sa ~e jeunesse** in the first bloom of his youth

[d] († = *sévère*) [*réprimande*] sharp, stiff

[e] [*propos, histoire*] spicy, saucy; **elle en a vu des ~es et des pas mûres*** she has been through it, she has had a hard *ou* rough time (of it); **il en a dit des ~es (et des pas mûres)*** he came out with some pretty risqué stuff*; **j'en ai entendu des ~es et des pas mûres sur son compte!*** you wouldn't believe the things I've heard about him! → **langue**

[f] (*Agr*) **tourisme ~** country holidays; **classe ~e** school camp; **avoir les pouces ~s** *ou* **la main ~e** to have green fingers (*Brit*), have a green thumb (*US*)

[g] (= *écologique*) green (*épith*); (*Pol*) **le parti ~** the Green Party; **les produits ~s** green products

2 NM [a] (= *couleur*) green; (*Golf*) green; **~ olive/pistache/émeraude** olive/pistachio/emerald(-green); **~ pomme/d'eau/bouteille** apple-/sea-/bottle-green; **~ amande/mousse** almond/moss green; **~ menthe** mint green; **~ sapin** forest green; **tu as du ~ sur ta jupe** you've got a green stain on your skirt; **mettre un cheval au ~** to put a horse out to grass *ou* to pasture; (*fig*) **se mettre au ~** [*vacancier*] to take a rest *ou* a refreshing break in the country; [*gangster*] to lie low *ou* hole up for a while in the country; **passer au ~** [*voiture*] to go when the lights are on green; **le feu est passé au ~** the lights turned green → **tendre²**

[b] (*Pol* = *écologistes*) **les Verts** the Greens

3 **verte** NF († * = *absinthe*) absinth(e)

vert-de-gris [vɛʀdəgʀi] **1** NM INV verdigris; (*péj*) **les ~** (= *soldats allemands*) German soldiers (*during the Second World War*) **2** ADJ INV grey(ish)-green

vert-de-grisé, e (*mpl* **vert-de-grisés**) [vɛʀdəgʀize] ADJ coated with verdigris; (*fig*) grey(ish)-green

vertébral, e (*mpl* **-aux**) [vɛʀtebʀal, o] ADJ vertebral → **colonne**

vertébré, e [vɛʀtebʀe] ADJ, NM vertebrate

vertèbre [vɛʀtebʀ] NF vertebra; **se déplacer une ~** to slip a disc, dislocate a vertebra (*SPÉC*); **~s cervicales/lombaires** cervical/lumbar vertebrae

vertement [vɛʀtəmɑ̃] ADV [*rappeler à l'ordre, répliquer*] sharply, in no uncertain terms; [*critiquer, réagir*] strongly; **se faire ~ réprimander** to get a severe dressing-down, be hauled over the coals

vertex [vɛʀtɛks] NM (*Anat*) vertex

vertical, e (*mpl* **-aux**) [vɛʀtikal, o] **1** ADJ (*gén, Écon*) [*ligne, plan, éclairage*] vertical; [*position du corps, station*] vertical, upright → **avion**, **concentration 2 verticale** NF [a] **la ~e** the vertical; **à la ~e** [*s'élever, tomber*] vertically; **falaise à la ~e** vertical *ou* sheer cliff; **écarté de la ~e** off the vertical [b] (= *ligne, Archit*) vertical line [3] NM (*Astron*) vertical circle

verticalement [vɛʀtikalmɑ̃] ADV [*monter*] vertically, straight up; [*descendre*] vertically, straight down

verticalité [vɛʀtikalite] NF verticalness, verticality

vertige [vɛʀtiʒ] NM [a] (= *peur du vide*) **le ~** vertigo; **avoir le ~** to suffer from vertigo, get dizzy *ou* giddy; **il eut soudain le ~** *ou* **fut soudain pris de ~** he suddenly felt dizzy *ou* giddy, he was suddenly overcome by vertigo; **un précipice à donner le ~** a precipice that would make you (feel) dizzy *ou* giddy; **cela me donne le ~** it makes me feel dizzy *ou* giddy, it gives me vertigo; **ces chiffres donnent le ~** these figures make your head swim *ou* spin

[b] (= *étourdissement*) dizzy *ou* giddy spell, dizziness (*NonC*), giddiness (*NonC*); **avoir un ~** to have a dizzy *ou* giddy spell *ou* turn; **être pris de ~s** to get dizzy *ou* giddy turns *ou* spells

[c] (= *égarement*) fever; **les spéculateurs étaient gagnés par ce ~** the speculators had caught this fever; **le ~ de la gloire** the intoxication of glory; **d'autres, gagnés eux aussi par le ~ de l'expansion ...** others, who had also been bitten by the expansion bug ... *ou* who had also caught the expansion fever ...; **le ~ de la violence** the heady lure of violence

vertigineusement [vɛʀtiʒinøzmɑ̃] ADV [*monter, chuter*] at a dizzying rate; **les prix augmentent ~** prices are rising at a dizzying rate, prices are rocketing *ou* are going sky-high*

vertigineux, -euse [vɛʀtiʒinø, øz] ADJ [a] [*plongée, descente*] vertiginous, breath-taking; [*précipice*] breathtakingly high; [*vitesse, hauteur*] breathtaking, dizzy (*épith*), giddy (*épith*) [b] (= *très rapide*) breathtaking; **une hausse/baisse vertigineuse** a spectacular *ou* dramatic rise/fall [c] (*Méd*) vertiginous

vertigo [vɛʀtigo] NM (*Vét*) (blind) staggers

vertu [vɛʀty] NF [a] (*gén* = *morale*) virtue; **les ~s bourgeoises** the bourgeois virtues; **les (quatre) ~s cardinales** the (four) cardinal virtues; **~s théologales** theological virtues; (= *anges*) **Vertus** Virtues; **femme** *ou* **dame** (*hum*) **de petite ~** † woman of easy virtue → **nécessité**, **parer¹**, **prix**

[b] (*littér*) (= *pouvoir*) power; (= *propriété*) property; (*littér* = *courage*) courage, bravery; **~ curative/magique** healing/magic power; **les ~s thérapeutiques du chocolat** the healing properties of chocolate; **les ~s pédagogiques d'un débat** the educational qualities of a debate

[c] **en ~ de** in accordance with; **en ~ des pouvoirs qui me sont conférés** in accordance with *ou* by virtue of the powers conferred upon me; **en ~ de l'article 4 de la loi** in accordance *ou* compliance with article 4 of the law; **en ~ de quoi pouvez-vous exiger ... ?** by what right can you demand ...?; **en ~ de quoi je déclare ...** in accordance with which I declare ..., by virtue of which I declare ...

vertueusement [vɛʀtɥøzmɑ̃] ADV virtuously

vertueux, -euse [vɛʀtɥø, øz] ADJ virtuous

vertugadin [vɛʀtygadɛ̃] NM (*Hist* = *vêtement*) farthingale

verve [vɛʀv] NF [a] (= *esprit, éloquence*) witty eloquence; **être en ~** to be in brilliant form; **il nous a raconté l'entrevue avec ~** he gave us a spirited account of the interview [b] (*littér* = *fougue, entrain*) verve, vigour (*Brit*), vigor (*US*), zest; **la ~ de son style** the verve *ou* vigour of his style

verveine [vɛʀvɛn] NF (= *plante*) vervain, verbena; (= *tisane*) verbena tea; (= *liqueur*) vervain liqueur

vésical, e (*mpl* **-aux**) [vezikal, o] ADJ vesical

vésicant, e [vezikɑ̃, ɑ̃t] ADJ vesicant, vesicatory

vésicatoire [vezikatwaʀ] ADJ, NM vesicatory

vésiculaire [vezikylɛʀ] ADJ vesicular

vésicule [vezikyl] NF (*Méd* = *organe*) vesicle; (= *ampoule*) blister; (*Bot*) vesicle; **la ~ (biliaire)** the gall-bladder; **~s séminales** seminal vesicles

vésiculeux, -euse [vezikylø, øz] ADJ = **vésiculaire**

Vespa® [vɛspa] NF Vespa®

vespasienne [vɛspazjɛn] NF urinal (*in the street*)

vespéral, e (*mpl* **-aux**) [vɛspeʀal, o] **1** ADJ (*littér*) evening (*épith*) **2** NM (*Rel*) vesperal

vesse-de-loup (*pl* **vesses-de-loup**) [vɛsdəlu] NF (*Bot*) puffball

vessie [vesi] NF (*Anat*) bladder, vesica (*SPÉC*); (*animale : utilisée comme sac*) bladder; **~ nata-** toire swim bladder; **elle veut nous faire prendre des ~s pour des lanternes*** she would have us believe that the moon is made of green cheese, she's trying to pull the wool over our eyes

Vesta [vɛsta] NF Vesta

vestale [vɛstal] NF (*Hist*) vestal; (*fig littér*) vestal, vestal virgin

veste [vɛst] NF [a] (= *habit*) jacket; **~ droite/croisée** single-/double-breasted jacket; **~ de pyjama** pyjama jacket *ou* top; **~ d'intérieur** smoking jacket [b] (* *loc*) **ramasser** *ou* **(se) prendre une ~** (*dans une élection*) to be beaten hollow; **retourner sa ~** to change sides

vestiaire [vɛstjɛʀ] NM [a] [*théâtre, restaurant*] cloakroom; [*stade, piscine*] changing-room; **la dame du ~** the cloakroom attendant *ou* lady; **réclamer son ~** to collect one's things from the cloakroom; **au ~! au ~!*** get off!; **il a dû laisser sa fierté/ses convictions au ~** he had to forget his pride/his convictions [b] (= *meuble*) (armoire-)vestiaire locker

vestibulaire [vɛstibylɛʀ] ADJ vestibular

vestibule [vɛstibyl] NM [a] [*maison*] hall; [*hôtel*] lobby; [*église*] vestibule [b] (*Anat*) vestibule

vestige [vɛstiʒ] NM (= *objet*) relic; (= *fragment*) trace; [*coutume, splendeur, gloire*] vestige, remnant; **~s** [*ville*] remains, vestiges; [*civilisation, passé*] vestiges, remnants; **~s archéologiques/antiques** arch(a)eological/classical remains; **les ~s de leur armée décimée** the remnants of their decimated army; **les ~s de la guerre** the vestiges of war

vestimentaire [vɛstimɑ̃tɛʀ] ADJ **modes/styles ~s** fashions/styles in clothing *ou* clothes; **dépenses ~s** clothing expenditure, expenditure on clothing; **élégance ~** sartorial elegance; **ses goûts ~s** his taste in clothes; **code ~** dress code; **ces fantaisies ~s n'étaient pas de son goût** these eccentricities of dress were not to his taste; **il se préoccupait beaucoup de détails ~s** he was very preoccupied with the details of his dress; **sa fonction exigeait une tenue ~ adéquate** his position required that he dress appropriately

veston [vɛstɔ̃] NM jacket → **complet**

Vésuve [vezyv] NM Vesuvius

vêtement [vɛtmɑ̃] NM [a] (= *article d'habillement*) garment, item *ou* article of clothing; (= *ensemble de vêtements, costume*) clothes, clothing (*NonC*); (*frm* = *manteau, veste*) coat; (*Comm*) **le ~** (= *industrie*) the clothing industry, the rag trade*, the garment industry (*US*); **le ~ masculin évolue** men's clothes are changing; **c'est un ~ très pratique** it's a very practical garment *ou* item of clothing *ou* article of clothing

[b] **~s** clothes; **où ai-je mis mes ~s ?** where did I put my clothes? *ou* things?*; **emporte des ~s chauds** take (some) warm clothes *ou* clothing; **porter des ~s de sport/de ville** to wear sports/town clothes *ou* gear*; **acheter des ~s de bébé** to buy baby garments *ou* clothes; **il portait des ~s de tous les jours** he was wearing ordinary *ou* everyday clothes; **~s sacerdotaux** vestments; **~s de travail/de deuil** working/mourning clothes; **~s du dimanche** Sunday clothes, Sunday best (*parfois hum*)

[c] (= *rayon de magasin*) (rayon) **~s** clothing department; **~s pour dames** ladies' wear (*NonC*); **~s pour hommes** menswear (*NonC*); **~s de sport** sportswear (*NonC*); **~s de ski** skiwear (*NonC*); **~s de bébé** babywear (*NonC*)

[d] (= *parure*) garment (*fig*); **le langage est le ~ de la pensée** language clothes thought

vétéran [veteʀɑ̃] NM (*Mil*) veteran, old campaigner; (*fig*) veteran, old hand*; (*Sport*) veteran; (= *personne expérimentée*) **un ~ de l'enseignement primaire** an old hand* at primary teaching

vicier [visje] ▶conjug 7 ◀ VT a [+ atmosphère] to pollute, taint; [+ sang] to contaminate, taint b (fig) [+ rapports] to taint; [+ esprit, ambiance] to taint, pollute c [+ élection] to invalidate; [+ acte juridique] to vitiate, invalidate

vicieusement [visjøzmɑ̃] ADV a (= sournoisement) cunningly, slyly b (= lubriquement) [regarder] lecherously, lustfully

vicieux, -ieuse [visjø, jøz] 1 ADJ a (= pervers) [personne, penchant] lecherous, perverted; [air, regard, geste] depraved, licentious b (littér = dépravé) depraved, vice-ridden, vicious (littér) c (= rétif) [cheval] restive, unruly d (= sournois) [attaque, balle, coup, question] nasty → **cercle** e (= fautif) [prononciation, expression] incorrect, wrong 2 NM,F pervert; **c'est un petit ~** he's a little lecher; **un vieux ~** a dirty old man, an old lecher

vicinal, e (mpl -aux) [visinal, o] ADJ **chemin ~** by-road, byway

vicissitudes [visisityd] NFPL (= infortunes) vicissitudes; (littér = variations, événements) vicissitudes, vagaries; **les ~ de la vie** the vicissitudes ou the trials and tribulations of life; **il a connu bien des ~** he has had his ups and downs

vicomte [vikɔ̃t] NM viscount

vicomté [vikɔ̃te] NF viscountcy, viscounty

vicomtesse [vikɔ̃tɛs] NF viscountess

victime [viktim] NF (gén) victim; (accident, catastrophe) casualty, victim; (Jur) aggrieved party, victim; **être ~ de** [+ escroc, accident, calomnie] to be the victim of; **il a été ~ de son imprudence/imprévoyance** he was the victim of his own imprudence/lack of foresight; **il est mort, ~ d'une crise cardiaque** he died of a heart attack; **l'incendie a fait de nombreuses ~s** the fire claimed many casualties ou victims; **l'attentat n'a pas fait de ~s** there were no casualties ou no one was hurt in the bomb attack; **l'entreprise est ~ de la concurrence/de son succès** the company is a victim of the competition/the victim of its own success; **~s de guerre** war victims; **les ~s de la route** (gén) road casualties; (= morts) road deaths ou fatalities

victoire [viktwaʀ] NF (gén) victory; (Sport) win, victory; (Boxe) **~ aux points** win on points; **~ à la Pyrrhus** Pyrrhic victory; **crier** ou **chanter ~** to crow (over one's victory); **ne criez pas ~ trop tôt** don't count your chickens before they're hatched

Victoria [viktɔʀja] 1 NF Victoria; **le lac ~** Lake Victoria 2 NM (Géog) Victoria

victoria [viktɔʀja] NF (Hist = voiture, Bot) victoria

victorien, -ienne [viktɔʀjɛ̃, jɛn] ADJ, NM,F Victorian

victorieusement [viktɔʀjøzmɑ̃] ADV (gén) victoriously; [combattre, résister, défendre] successfully

victorieux, -ieuse [viktɔʀjø, jøz] ADJ [général, campagne, armée, parti] victorious; [équipe] winning (épith), victorious; [air, sourire] triumphant; **son parti est sorti ~ des élections** his party emerged victorious from the elections

victuailles [viktɥaj] NFPL food, victuals (littér)

vidage [vidaʒ] NM a [récipient] emptying b (* = expulsion) kicking out*, chucking out* c (Ordin) dump; **~ de mémoire** memory ou storage dump

vidame [vidam] NM (Hist) vidame

vidange [vidɑ̃ʒ] NF a [fosse, tonneau, réservoir] emptying; (Aut) oil change; **entreprise de ~** sewage disposal business; (Aut) **faire la ~** to change the oil, do an ou the oil change → **bouchon, huile** b (= matières) **~s** sewage c (= dispositif) [lavabo] waste outlet

vidanger [vidɑ̃ʒe] ▶conjug 3 ◀ VT a [+ réservoir, fosse d'aisance] to empty b [+ huile, eau] to drain (off), empty out

vidangeur [vidɑ̃ʒœʀ] NM cesspool emptier

vide [vid] 1 ADJ a (lit) (gén) empty; (= disponible) [appartement, siège] empty, vacant; (Ling) [élément] empty; (Comm) **bouteilles ~s** empty bottles, empties* → **case, ensemble, estomac, main** b (fig) (= sans intérêt, creux) [journée, heures] empty; (= stérile) [discussion, paroles, style] empty, vacuous; **sa vie était ~** his life was empty ou a void; **passer une journée ~** to spend a day with nothing to do, spend an empty day → **tête** c **~ de** empty ou (de)void of; **~ de sens** [mot, expression] meaningless, empty ou (de)void of (all) meaning; [paroles] meaningless, empty; **les rues ~s de voitures** the streets empty of cars; **elle se sentait ~ de tout sentiment** she felt (de)void ou empty of all feeling

2 NM a (= absence d'air) vacuum; **le ~ absolu** an absolute vacuum; **pompe à ~** vacuum pump; **faire le ~ dans un récipient** to create a vacuum in a container; **sous ~** under vacuum; **emballé sous ~** vacuum-packed; **emballage sous ~** vacuum packing → **nature, tube** b (= trou) (entre objets) gap, empty space; (Archit) void; (Constr) **~ sanitaire** underfloor space c (= abîme) drop; (= l'espace) **le ~** the void; **être au-dessus du ~** to be over ou above a drop; **tomber dans le ~** to fall into empty space ou into the void; **j'ai peur/je n'ai pas peur du ~** I am/I am not afraid of heights, I have no head/I have a good head for heights d (= néant) emptiness; **le ~ de l'existence** the emptiness of life; **regarder dans le ~** to gaze ou stare into space ou emptiness e (fig = manque) **un ~ douloureux dans son cœur** an aching void in one's heart; **son départ/sa mort laisse un grand ~** his departure/his death leaves a great void ou vacuum; **~ juridique** gap in the law f (loc) **faire le ~ autour de soi** to isolate o.s., drive everyone away; **faire le ~ autour de qn** to isolate sb completely, leave sb on his own; **faire le ~ dans son esprit** to empty one's mind; **parler dans le ~** (sans objet) to talk vacuously; (personne n'écoute) to talk to a brick wall, waste one's breath; [camion] **repartir à ~** to go off again empty; **tourner à ~** [moteur] to run in neutral; [engrenage, mécanisme] to turn without gripping; [personne] to be unable to think straight; **la politique sociale actuelle tourne à ~** the current social policy is not producing results → **nettoyage, passage**

vidé, e* [vide] (ptp de vider) ADJ (= fatigué) [personne] worn out, dead beat*, all in*

vidéaste [videast] NMF video director; **~ amateur** amateur video-maker

vidéo [video] 1 ADJ INV video; **caméra/jeu/ signal ~** video camera/game/signal; **images/ film/bande/cassette ~** video images/film/ tape/cassette; **système de surveillance ~** video surveillance system 2 NF video; **faire de la ~** to make videos; **film disponible en ~** film available ou out on video; **service de ~ à la demande** video on demand service

vidéocassette [videokasɛt] NF video cassette

vidéoclip [videoklip] NM (= chanson) video

vidéoclub [videoklœb] NM videoclub

vidéocommunication [videokɔmynikasjɔ̃] NF video communication

vidéoconférence [videokɔ̃feʀɑ̃s] NF videoconference, teleconference

vidéodisque [videodisk] NM videodisk

vidéofréquence [videofʀekɑ̃s] NF video frequency

vidéogramme [videogʀam] NM video recording

vidéographie [videogʀafi] NF videotext; **~ interactive** Videotex®

vidéolecteur [videolɛktœʀ] NM videodisk player

vide-ordures [vidɔʀdyʀ] NM INV rubbish chute (Brit), garbage chute (US)

vidéosurveillance [videosyʀvejɑ̃s] NF video surveillance; **caméra/système de ~** video surveillance camera/system

vidéotex® [videotɛks] ADJ INV, NM INV videotex®

vidéothèque [videotɛk] NF video library

vidéotransmission [videotʀɑ̃smisjɔ̃] NF video transmission

vide-poche (pl vide-poches) [vidpɔʃ] NM (= récipient) tidy; (Aut) side pocket

vide-pomme (pl vide-pommes) [vidpɔm] NM apple-corer

vider [vide] ▶conjug 1 ◀ 1 VT a [+ récipient, réservoir, meuble, pièce] to empty; [+ étang, citerne] to empty, drain; **~ un appartement de ses meubles** to empty ou clear a flat of its furniture; **~ un étang de ses poissons** to empty ou clear a pond of fish; **~ un tiroir sur la table/dans une corbeille** to empty a drawer (out) onto the table/into a wastebasket; (Ordin) **~ la corbeille** to empty the waste; (en consommant) **ils ont vidé 3 bouteilles** they emptied ou drained 3 bottles; **il vida son verre et partit** he emptied ou drained his glass and left; (en emportant) **ils ont vidé tous les tiroirs** they cleaned out ou emptied all the drawers b [+ contenu] to empty (out); **~ l'eau d'un bassin** to empty the water out of a basin; **va ~ les ordures** go and empty (out) the rubbish; **~ des déchets dans une poubelle** to empty waste into a dustbin c (= faire évacuer) [+ lieu] to empty, clear; **la pluie a vidé les rues** the rain emptied ou cleared the streets d (= quitter) **~ les lieux** to quit ou vacate the premises e (= évider) [+ poisson, poulet] to gut, clean out; [+ pomme] to core f († = régler) [+ querelle, affaire] to settle g (Équitation) [+ cavalier] to throw; **~ les arçons/les étriers** to leave the saddle/the stirrups h (* = expulser) [+ trouble-fête, indésirable] to throw out, chuck out*; **~ qn d'une réunion/ d'un bistro** to throw ou chuck* sb out of a meeting/of a café i (= épuiser) to wear out; **ce travail m'a vidé*** this work has worn me out; **travail qui vous vide l'esprit** occupation that leaves you mentally drained ou exhausted j (loc) **~ son sac*** to come out with it*; **~ l'abcès** to root out the evil; **~ son cœur** to pour out one's heart

2 **se vider** VPR [récipient, réservoir, bassin, salle] to empty; **les eaux sales se vident dans l'égout** the dirty water empties ou drains into the sewer; **ce réservoir se vide dans un canal** this reservoir empties into a canal; **en août, la ville se vide (de ses habitants)** in August, the town empties (of its inhabitants); **se ~ de son sang** to bleed to death; **nos campagnes se vident** our rural areas are becoming empty of people ou deserted

videur [vidœʀ] NM [boîte de nuit] bouncer*

viduité [vidɥite] NF (Jur) [femme] widowhood, viduity (SPÉC); [homme] widowerhood, viduity (SPÉC); **délai de ~** minimum legal period of widowhood (ou widowerhood)

vie [vi]

1 NOM FÉMININ	2 COMPOSÉS

1 NOM FÉMININ

a Bio life; (Rel) **la Vie** the Life; **le respect de la ~** respect for life; **la ~ animale/végétale** animal/plant life; **donner la ~** to give birth (à to); **donner/risquer sa ~ pour** to give/risk one's life for; **avoir la ~ dure** [*personne, animal*] to have nine lives; [*préjugé, superstition*] to die hard; **être entre la ~ et la mort** to be at death's door; **avoir droit de ~ et de mort sur qn** to have the power of life and death over sb; **passer de ~ à trépas** to pass on; **faire passer qn de ~ à trépas** to dispatch sb into the next world; **sans ~** [*personne, corps*] (= *mort*) lifeless; (= *évanoui*) insensible; **rappeler qn à/revenir à la ~** to bring sb back to life/come back to life; **tôt/tard dans la ~** early/late in life; **attends de connaître la ~ pour juger** wait until you know (something) about life before you pass judgment → **fleuve, question**

♦ **en vie** alive; **être en ~** to be alive; **être bien en ~** to be well and truly alive, be alive and kicking*; **rester en ~** to stay or remain alive; **maintenir qn en ~** to keep sb alive; **ce journal, ils sont fiers de l'avoir maintenu en ~** they're proud of having kept this newspaper going *ou* afloat

[b] = *animation* life; **être plein de ~** to be full of life; **un film/portrait plein de ~** a lively film/ portrait; **donner de la ~ à qch** ◊ **mettre de la ~ dans qch** to liven sth up; **sa présence met de la ~ dans la maison** he brings some life *ou* a bit of life into the house, he livens the house up; **sans ~** [*regard*] lifeless, listless; [*rue, quartier*] dead (*attrib*)

[c] = *existence* life; **~ sentimentale/conjugale/ professionnelle** love/married/professional life; **la ~ militaire** life in the services; **la ~ de famille/ d'étudiant** family/student life; **la ~ de pêcheur** the life of a fisherman; **la ~ intellectuelle à Paris** intellectual life in Paris, the intellectual life of Paris; **(mode de) ~** way of life, lifestyle; **dans la ~ courante** in everyday life; **avoir la ~ facile** to have an easy life; **une ~ difficile** *ou* **dure** a hard life; **mener la ~ dure à qn** to give sb a hard time (of it), make life hard for sb; **il a** *ou* **mène une ~ sédentaire** he has a sedentary lifestyle, he leads a sedentary life; **faire la ~*†** (= *se débaucher*) to live it up, lead a life of pleasure; (* = *faire une scène*) to make a scene; **chaque fois, elle me fait la ~*** she goes on (and on) at me every time; **il en a fait une ~ quand ... he kicked up a real fuss* when** ..., he made a real scene when ...; **faire une ~ impossible à qn** to make sb's life intolerable *ou* impossible (for them); **mener joyeuse ~** to have a happy life; **il poursuivit sa petite ~** he carried on with his day-to-day existence *ou* his daily affairs; **elle a refait sa ~ avec lui** she made a new life with him; **depuis, il a refait sa ~** since then he's started a new life; **sa femme l'a quitté et il n'a jamais refait sa ~** his wife left him and he never met anyone else; **il a la bonne** *ou* **belle ~** he's got it easy, he has an easy *ou* a cushy* life; **c'est la belle ~!** this is the life!; **c'était la belle ~!** those were the days!; **ce n'est pas une ~!** it's a rotten* *ou* hard life!; **c'est la ~!** that's life!; **quelle ~!** what a life!; **la ~ est ainsi faite!** such is life!, that's life!; **la ~ continue** life goes on → **actif, rose, vivre**

[d] *Écon* **(le coût de) la ~** the cost of living; **la ~ augmente** the cost of living is rising *ou* going up; **ils manifestent contre la ~ chère** they are demonstrating against the high cost of living → **gagner, niveau**

[e] = *durée* life(time); **il a habité ici toute sa ~** he lived here all his life; **des habits qui durent une ~** clothes that last a lifetime; **faire qch une fois dans sa ~** to do sth once in one's life(time); **une occasion pareille n'arrive qu'une fois dans la ~** such an opportunity happens only once in a lifetime; **de ma ~ (*frm*) je n'ai vu un homme aussi grand** never (in my life) have I seen such a tall man, I have never (in my life) seen such a tall man; **tu as la ~ devant toi** you've got your whole life ahead of you → **jamais**

♦ **à vie** for life; **condamné à la prison à ~** sentenced to life imprisonment; **cet accident l'a marqué à ~** this accident marked him for life; **il est nommé à ~** he has a life appointment;

directeur/président (nommé) à ~ life director/ president, director/president for life; **un emploi à ~, ça n'existe plus** there's no such thing as a job for life any more

♦ **à la vie (et) à la mort** [*amitié, fidélité*] undying (*épith*); **amis à la ~ à la mort** friends for life; **entre nous, c'est à la ~ et à la mort** we have sworn eternal friendship, we are friends for life; **rester fidèle à qn à la ~ à la mort** to remain faithful to sb to one's dying day

♦ **pour la vie** for life; **il est infirme pour la ~** he'll be an invalid for the rest of his life; **amis pour la ~** friends for life, lifelong friends; **quand on est marié, c'est pour la ~** a marriage is for life; **quand on est bête, c'est pour la ~** once an idiot, always an idiot; (*tatouage*) **à Lulu pour la ~** Lulu forever

[f] = *biographie* life (story); **écrire/lire une ~ de qn** to write/read sb's life story; **j'ai lu la ~ de Bach** I read Bach's life story *ou* the story of Bach's life; **elle m'a raconté toute sa ~** she told me her whole life story, she told me the story of her life

[2] COMPOSÉS
► **vie de bâton de chaise** riotous *ou* wild existence ► **vie de bohème** bohemian life *ou* lifestyle ► **vie de château : mener la ~ de château** to live a life of luxury ► **vie de garçon** bachelor's life *ou* existence ► **vie de patachon*** disorderly way of life *ou* lifestyle ► **vie privée** private life → **enterrer**

vieil [vjɛj] ADJ M → **vieux**

vieillard [vjɛjaʀ] NM old man; **les ~s** the elderly, old people → **asile, hospice**

vieille¹ [vjɛj] ADJ F, NF → **vieux**

vieille² [vjɛj] NF (= *poisson*) wrasse

vieillerie [vjɛjʀi] NF (= *objet*) old-fashioned thing; (= *idée*) old *ou* stale idea; **aimer les ~s** to like old *ou* old-fashioned things *ou* stuff; (*hum*) **j'ai mal au dos — c'est la ~*** I've got backache — it's old age

vieillesse [vjɛjɛs] NF [a] (= *période*) old age; (= *fait d'être vieux*) old age; **mourir de ~** to die of old age; **dans sa ~** in his old age → **assurance, bâton** [b] (= *vieillards*) **la ~** the old, the elderly, the aged → **jeunesse** [c] [*choses*] age, oldness

vieilli, e [vjeji] (*ptp de* **vieillir**) ADJ = *marqué par l'âge* aged, grown old (*attrib*); (= *suranné*) [*mot, expression*] dated, old-fashioned; (*Mode*) [*cuir*] distressed (*épith*); **vin ~ en cave** wine aged in the cellar; **une population ~e** an ageing *ou* aged population; **je l'ai trouvé ~** I thought he'd aged; **visage prématurément ~** face that has prematurely aged

vieillir [vjejiʀ] ▶conjug 2◀ [1] VI [a] (= *prendre de l'âge*) [*personne, maison, organe*] to grow *ou* get old; [*population*] to age; **~ dans un métier** to grow old in a job; **savoir ~** to grow old gracefully; **l'art de ~** the art of growing old gracefully; **il a bien/mal vieilli** [*personne*] he has/has not aged well; [*film*] it has/has not stood the test of time, it has not/has become dated [b] (= *paraître plus vieux*) to age; **il a vieilli de 10 ans en quelques jours** he aged (by) 10 years in a few days; **je la trouve très vieillie** I find she has aged a lot; **il ne vieillit pas** he doesn't get any older [c] (= *passer de mode*) [*auteur, mot, doctrine*] to become (out)dated [d] (*Culin*) [*vin, fromage*] to age; **vieilli en fûts de chêne** aged *ou* matured in oak (casks)

[2] VT [a] (*coiffure, maladie*) to put years on sb, make sb look older; **cette coiffure vous vieillit** that hair style puts years on you *ou* makes you look older [b] (*par fausse estimation*) **~ qn** to make sb older than he (really) is; **vous me vieillissez de 5 ans** you're making me out to be 5 years older than I (really) am

[3] **se vieillir** VPR to make o.s. look older

vieillissant, e [vjejisɑ̃, ɑ̃t] ADJ [*personne*] ageing, who is growing old; [*œuvre*] ageing, which is becoming (out)dated

vieillissement [vjejismɑ̃] NM [a] [*personne, population, maison, institution*] ageing; **le ~ fait perdre à la peau son élasticité** ageing *ou* the ageing process makes the skin lose its elasticity [b] [*mot, doctrine, œuvre*] becoming (out)dated [c] [*vin, fromage*] ageing; **~ forcé** artificial ageing

vieillot, -otte [vjejo, ɔt] ADJ [a] (= *démodé*) antiquated, quaint [b] (= *vieux*) old-looking

vielle [vjɛl] NF hurdy-gurdy

Vienne [vjɛn] N (*en Autriche*) Vienna; (*en France*) Vienne

viennois, e [vjɛnwa, waz] [1] ADJ (*d'Autriche*) Viennese; (*de France*) of *ou* from Vienne; **café/chocolat ~** coffee/hot chocolate with whipped cream → **pain** [2] **Viennois(e)** NM,F (*d'Autriche*) Viennese; (*de France*) native *ou* inhabitant of Vienne

viennoiserie [vjɛnwazʀi] NF (= *ensemble des produits*) Viennese pastries (*croissants, brioches etc*); (= *magasin*) Viennese pastry shop; (= *commerce*) Viennese pastry trade

Vientiane [vjɛntjan] N Vientiane

vierge [vjɛʀʒ] [1] NF [a] (= *pucelle*) virgin [b] (*Rel*) **la (Sainte) Vierge** the (Blessed) Virgin; **la Vierge (Marie)** the Virgin (Mary); **la Vierge immaculée** the Immaculate Virgin, Immaculate Mary; (= *statue*) **une Vierge romane/ gothique** a Romanesque/Gothic (statue of the) Virgin → **fil** [c] (*Astron*) **la Vierge** Virgo; **il est Vierge** ◊ **il est (du signe) de la Vierge** he's (a) Virgo

[2] ADJ [a] [*personne*] virgin (*épith*); **rester/être ~** to remain/be a virgin [b] [*ovule*] unfertilized [c] [*feuille de papier*] blank, virgin (*épith*); [*film*] unexposed; [*bande magnétique, disquette*] blank; [*casier judiciaire*] clean; [*terre, neige*] virgin (*épith*); (*Sport*) [*sommet*] unclimbed → **huile, laine, vigne** *etc* [d] (*littér = exempt*) **~ de** free from, unsullied by; **~ de tout reproche** free from (all) reproach; **~ de connaissances/d'expérience** with absolutely no knowledge/experience

Vierges [vjɛʀʒ] NFPL **les îles ~** the Virgin Islands

Viêtnam, Viêt Nam [vjetnam] NM Vietnam; (*Hist*) **~ du Nord/du Sud** North/South Vietnam

vietnamien, -ienne [vjetnamjɛ̃, jɛn] [1] ADJ Vietnamese [2] NM (*Ling*) Vietnamese [3] **Vietnamien(ne)** NM,F Vietnamese; (*Hist*) **Vietnamien(ne) du Nord/Sud** North/South Vietnamese

vieux [vjø], **vieille** [vjɛj] (*devant nm commençant par une voyelle ou un h muet* **vieil** [vjɛj]) (*mpl* **vieux** [vjø]) [1] ADJ [a] (= *âgé*) old; **très ~** ancient, very old; **un vieil homme** an old man; **une vieille femme** an old woman; **c'est un homme déjà ~** he's already an old man; **les vieilles gens** old people, the aged *ou* elderly; **un ~ retraité** an old-age pensioner; **il est plus ~ que moi** he's older than I am; **~ comme comme le monde** *ou* **Hérode** *ou* **mes robes*** (*hum*) *ou* **les chemins** as old as the hills; **histoire vieille de vingt ans** story which goes back twenty years; **il se fait ~** he's getting old, he's getting on (in years) → **jour, os** [b] (= *ancien*) [*demeure, bijoux, meuble*] old; **une belle vieille demeure** a fine old house; **un vin ~** an old wine; **un pays de vieille civilisation** a country with an age-old civilization; **~ français** Old French; **vieil anglais** Old English; **c'est déjà ~ tout ça!** that's all old hat!* [c] (= *expérimenté*) [*marin, soldat, guide*] old, seasoned; **un ~ loup de mer** an old sea dog → **briscard, renard, singe** [d] (= *usé*) [*objet, maison, vêtement*] old; **ce pull est très ~** this sweater is ancient *ou* very old; **~ papiers** waste paper; **~ journaux** old

(news)papers
e (*avant le n*) (= *de longue date*) [*ami, habitude*] old; [*amitié*] long-standing; (= *passé*) [*coutumes*] old, ancient; **un vieil ami** an old friend, a friend of long standing; **vieille famille** old *ou* ancient family; **c'est une vieille histoire** it's ancient history *ou* an old story; **nous avons beaucoup de ~ souvenirs en commun** we share a lot of old memories; **c'est la vieille question/le ~ problème** it's the same old question/problem; **traîner un ~ rhume** to have a cold that is dragging on → **date**

f (*avant le n*) (= *de naguère*) old; (= *précédent*) old, former, previous; **la vieille génération** the older generation; **mon vieil enthousiasme** my old *ou* former *ou* previous enthusiasm; **ma vieille voiture était plus confortable que la nouvelle** my old *ou* previous car was more comfortable than the one I've got now; **le ~ Paris/Lyon** old Paris/Lyons; **la vieille France/Angleterre** France/England of bygone days *ou* of yesteryear; **ses vieilles craintes se réveillaient** his old fears were aroused once more → **école, temps¹**

g (*péj: intensif*) **vieille peau*** old bag*; **~ jeton*** old misery*; **espèce de ~ satyre!*** dirty old man!*; **n'importe quel ~ bout de papier fera l'affaire** any old bit of paper will do → **bique, chameau, chnoque** *etc*

2 NM **a** (= *personne*) old man; **les ~** the old *ou* aged *ou* elderly, old people; **tu fais partie des ~ maintenant** you're one of the old folks* now; **il a des manies/idées de ~** he acts/thinks like an old man; **c'est de la musique de ~** that's music for old people; **un ~ de la vieille*** one of the old brigade; (= *père*) **mon** *ou* **le ~*** my *ou* the old man*; (= *parents*) **ses ~*** his folks*; **comment ça va, mon ~?*** how are you, old boy?* (*Brit*) *ou* mate* (*Brit*) *ou* old buddy?* (*US*); **mon (petit) ~*, tu vas m'expliquer ça** listen you, you're going to give me an explanation; **ça, mon ~, c'est ton problème!*** that's your problem mate* (*Brit*) *ou* man* (*US*); (*exprimant la surprise*) **ils m'ont augmenté de 500 F — ben mon ~!** they've given me a 500 franc rise — well I never! → **petit**

b **préférer le ~ au neuf** to prefer old things to new → **neuf²**

c *** sa mère a pris un bon** *ou* **sacré coup de ~** her mother has really aged; **ça lui a donné un coup de ~** (*à une personne*) it put years on him; **cette nouvelle technique donne un terrible coup de ~ à la précédente** this new technique means the old one is now totally out of date

3 **vieille** NF old woman; (= *mère*) **ma** *ou* **la vieille:** my *ou* the old woman? *ou* lady?*; **alors, ma vieille, tu viens?*** are you coming then, old girl?*; (*hum: à un homme*) are you coming then, old man? *ou* old chap?* (*Brit*) *ou* old boy?* (*Brit*); **comment ça va, ma vieille?*** how are you, old girl?* → **petit**

4 ADV (*vivre*) to an old age, to a ripe old age; (*s'habiller*) **elle s'habille trop ~** she dresses too old; **ce manteau fait ~** this coat makes you look old

5 COMP ► **vieux beau** (*péj*) ageing beau ► **vieille branche** (*fig, ††* *ou* *hum*) old fruit* (*Brit*) *ou* bean* (*hum*) ► **le Vieux Continent** the Old World ► **vieille fille†** spinster, old maid; **elle est très vieille fille** she's very old-maidish ► **vieille France** ADJ INV [*personne*] with old-world values ► **vieux garçon†** bachelor; **des habitudes de ~ garçon** bachelor ways ► **la vieille garde** the old guard; (*fig*) **la vieille garde conservatrice du parti** the conservative old guard in the party ► **vieux jeu** ADJ INV [*idées*] old hat (*attrib*), outmoded; [*personne*] behind the times (*attrib*), old-fashioned; [*vêtement*] old-fashioned, out-of-date (*épith*), out of date (*attrib*) ► **vieilles lunes** (= *temps passé*) olden days; (= *idées dépassées*) old-fashioned ideas ► **le Vieux Monde** the Old World ► **vieil or** ADJ INV,

NM old gold ► **vieux rose** ADJ INV, NM old rose

vif, vive¹ [vif, viv] **1** ADJ **a** (= *plein de vie*) [*enfant, personne*] lively, vivacious; [*mouvement, rythme, style*] lively, animated, brisk; (= *alerte*) sharp, quick (*attrib*); [*imagination*] lively, keen; [*intelligence*] keen, quick; **il a l'œil** *ou* **le regard ~** he has a sharp *ou* keen eye; **à l'esprit ~** quick-witted; **eau vive** (fresh) running water, flowing water → **haie, mémoire¹**

b (= *brusque, emporté*) [*personne*] sharp, brusque, quick-tempered; [*ton, propos, attitude*] sharp, brusque, curt; **il s'est montré un peu ~ avec elle** he was rather sharp *ou* brusque *ou* curt with her; **le débat prit un tour assez ~** the discussion took on a rather acrimonious turn

c (= *profond*) [*émotion*] keen (*épith*), intense, strong; [*souvenirs*] vivid; [*impression*] vivid, intense; [*plaisirs, désir*] intense, keen (*épith*); [*déception*] acute, keen (*épith*), intense; **j'ai le sentiment très ~ de l'avoir vexé** I have the distinct feeling that I've offended him

d (= *fort, grand*) [*goût*] strong, distinct; [*chagrin, regret*] deep, great; [*critiques, réprobation*] strong, severe; **une vive satisfaction** a great *ou* deep feeling of satisfaction, deep *ou* great satisfaction; **une vive impatience** great impatience; **il lui fit de ~s reproches** he severely reprimanded him; **un ~ penchant pour ...** a strong liking *ou* inclination for ...; **à vive allure** at a brisk pace; (*formules de politesse*) **avec mes plus ~s remerciements** with my most profound thanks; **c'est avec un ~ plaisir que ...** it is with very great pleasure that ...

e (= *cru, aigu*) [*lumière, éclat*] bright, brilliant; [*couleur*] bright, vivid, brilliant; [*froid*] biting, bitter; [*douleur*] sharp; [*vent*] keen, biting, bitter; [*ongles, arête*] sharp; **l'air ~ les revigorait** the bracing air revived them; **rouge ~** bright red, vivid *ou* brilliant red; **il faisait un froid très ~** it was bitterly cold

f (= *à nu*) [*pierre*] bare; [*joints*] dry

g († = *vivant*) alive; **être brûlé/enterré ~** to be burnt/buried alive; **de vive voix** [*renseigner, communiquer, remercier*] personally, in person; **il vous le dira de vive voix** he'll tell you himself *ou* in person → **chaux, mort², œuvre** *etc*

2 NM **a** (*loc*) **à ~** [*chair*] bared; [*plaie*] open; **avoir les nerfs à ~** to have frayed nerves, be on edge; **être touché** *ou* **piqué au ~** to be cut to the quick; **tailler** *ou* **couper** *ou* **trancher dans le ~** (*lit*) to cut into the flesh; (*fig* = *prendre une décision*) to take drastic action; **entrer dans le ~ du sujet** to get to the heart of the matter; **sur le ~** [*peindre, décrire*] from life; **scènes/photos prises sur le ~** scenes shot/photos taken from real life; **faire un reportage sur le ~** to do a live *ou* an on-the-spot broadcast; **voici quelques réactions prises sur le ~** now for a few on-the-spot reactions

b (*Pêche*) live bait (*NonC*); **pêcher au ~** to fish with live bait

c (*Jur* = *personne vivante*) living person; **donation entre ~s** donation inter vivos → **mort²**

vif-argent [vifarʒɑ̃] NM INV (*Chim*) quicksilver; **il a du ~ dans les veines† ◊ c'est du ~†** he is a real live wire*

vigie [viʒi] NF **a** (*Naut*) (= *matelot*) look-out, watch; (= *poste*) [*mât*] look-out post, crow's-nest; [*proue*] look-out post; **être en ~** to be on watch **b** (*Rail*) = **de frein** brake cabin

vigilance [viʒilɑ̃s] NF [*personne, attention, soins*] vigilance; **surveiller qn avec ~** to keep a very close watch on sb; **tromper la ~ de qn** to give sb the slip; **rien d'important n'a échappé à leur ~** nothing of importance escaped their notice *ou* attention; **une extrême ~ s'impose** we (*ou* they *etc*) must be extremely vigilant; **l'absorption d'alcool entraîne une baisse de la ~** drinking alcohol affects your concentration

vigilant, e [viʒilɑ̃, ɑ̃t] ADJ [*personne*] vigilant, watchful; [*attention, soins*] vigilant; **essaie**

d'être plus ~ quand tu conduis try and drive more carefully

vigile¹ [viʒil] NF (*Rel*) vigil

vigile² [viʒil] NM (*Hist*) watch; (= *veilleur de nuit*) (night) watchman; [*police privée*] vigilante

vigne [viɲ] **1** NF **a** (= *plante*) vine; **être dans les ~s du Seigneur†** to be in one's cups → **cep, feuille, pied b** (= *vignoble*) vineyard; **des champs de ~** vineyards; (= *activité*) **la ~ rapporte** wine-growing isn't very profitable; **les produits de la ~** the produce of the vineyards → **pêche¹ 2** COMP ► **vigne vierge** Virginia creeper

vigneau (*pl* **vigneaux**) [viɲo] NM winkle

vigneron, -onne [viɲ(ə)ʀɔ̃, ɔn] NM,F wine grower

vignette [viɲɛt] NF **a** (*Art* = *motif*) vignette **b** († = *illustration*) illustration **c** (*Comm* = *timbre*) (manufacturer's) label *ou* seal; (*sur un médicament*) price label on medicines for reimbursement by Social Security; (*Aut*) ~ (**automobile**) ≈ (road) tax disc (*Brit*), ≈ (annual) license tag (*US*)

vignoble [viɲɔbl] NM vineyard; (= *ensemble de vignobles*) **le ~ français/bordelais** the vineyards of France/Bordeaux

vignot [viɲo] NM = **vigneau**

vigogne [vigɔɲ] NF (*Zool*) vicuna; (*Tex*) vicuna (wool)

vigoureusement [viguʀøzmɑ̃] ADV [*taper, frotter*] vigorously, energetically; [*protester, résister*] vigorously; [*peindre, écrire*] vigorously, with vigour

vigoureux, -euse [viguʀø, øz] ADJ **a** (= *robuste*) [*personne*] vigorous, sturdy; [*cheval*] sturdy; [*corps*] robust, vigorous; [*bras, mains*] strong, powerful; [*poignée de main*] vigorous; [*santé*] robust; [*plante*] sturdy, robust; **manier la hache d'un bras ~** to wield the axe vigorously *ou* with vigour; **il est encore ~ pour son âge** he's still hale and hearty *ou* still vigorous for his age **b** (= *énergique*) [*esprit, style, dessin*] vigorous; [*sentiment, passion*] strong; [*résistance, protestations*] vigorous, strenuous; **donner de ~ coups de poing à qch** to deal sth sturdy *ou* strong *ou* energetic blows

vigueur [vigœʀ] **1** NF **a** [*personne*] sturdiness, vigour (*Brit*), vigor (*US*); [*corps*] robustness, vigour (*Brit*), vigor (*US*); [*bras, mains*] strength; [*santé*] robustness; [*plante*] sturdiness, robustness; **dans toute la ~ de la jeunesse** in the full vigour of youth

b [*sentiment, passion*] strength; [*esprit, résistance, protestations*] vigour (*Brit*), vigor (*US*); **sans ~** without vigour; **se débattre avec ~** to defend o.s. vigorously *ou* with vigour; **donner de la ~ à** to invigorate; **~ intellectuelle** intellectual vigour; **s'exprimer/protester avec ~** to express o.s./protest vigorously

c [*coloris, style, dessin*] vigour (*Brit*), vigor (*US*), energy

2 **en vigueur** LOC ADJ, LOC ADV [*loi, dispositions*] in force; [*terminologie, formule*] current, in use; **entrer en ~** to come into force *ou* effect; **en ~ depuis hier** in force as of *ou* from yesterday; **faire entrer en ~** to bring into force *ou* effect, implement; **cesser d'être en ~** to cease to apply

VIH [veiaʃ] NM (ABRÉV = **virus de l'immunodéficience humaine**) HIV

Viking [vikiŋ] NM Viking

vil, e [vil] ADJ **a** (*littér* = *méprisable*) vile, base **b** († = *non noble*) low(ly) **c** († = *sans valeur*) [*marchandises*] worthless, cheap; **métaux ~s** base metals **d** **à ~ prix** [*acheter, vendre*] at a very low price, for next to nothing

vilain, e [vilɛ̃, ɛn] **1** ADJ **a** (= *laid*) [*personne, visage*] ugly(-looking); [*vêtement*] ugly, unattractive; [*couleur*] nasty; **elle n'est pas ~e** she's not bad-looking, she's not unattractive;

(*Littérat, fig*) **le ~ petit canard** the ugly duckling; **1 000 F d'augmentation, ce n'est pas ~** a 1,000 francs pay rise — that's not bad [b] (= *mauvais*) [*temps*] bad, lousy*; [*odeur*] nasty, bad; **il a fait ~ toute la semaine*** we've had bad *ou* lousy* weather all week [c] (= *grave, dangereux*) [*blessure, affaire*] nasty, bad; **une ~e plaie** a nasty wound [d] (= *méchant*) [*action, pensée*] wicked; [*enfant, conduite*] naughty, bad; **~s mots** naughty *ou* wicked words; **c'est un ~ monsieur** *ou* **coco*** he's a nasty customer *ou* piece of work*; **il a été ~** he was a naughty boy; **il a été ~ au cinéma/avec sa grand-mère** he was naughty at the cinema/with his grandmother, he played up at the cinema/played his grandmother up; **jouer un ~ tour à qn** to play a nasty *ou* naughty trick on sb [2] NM [a] (*Hist*) villein, villain [b] (= *méchant: garçon*) naughty *ou* bad boy; **oh le (gros) ~!** what a naughty boy (you are)! [c] (*: *loc*) **il va y avoir du ~ ◊ ça va tourner au ~ ◊ ça va faire du ~** things are going to get nasty, it's going to turn nasty [3] **vilaine** NF (= *méchante*) naughty *ou* bad girl; **oh la (grosse) ~e!** what a naughty girl (you are)!

vilainement [vilɛnmɑ̃] ADV wickedly

vilebrequin [vilbʀəkɛ̃] NM (= *outil*) (bit-) brace; (*Aut*) crankshaft

vilement [vilmɑ̃] ADV (*littér*) vilely, basely

vilenie [vil(ə)ni], **vilénie** [vileni] NF (*littér*) (= *caractère*) vileness, baseness; (= *acte*) villainy, vile *ou* base deed

vilipender [vilipɑ̃de] ▶conjug 1◀ VT (*littér*) to revile, vilify, inveigh against

villa [villa] NF [a] (= *maison*) (= *maison de plaisance*) villa; (= *pavillon*) (detached) house; (*Antiq*) **les ~s romaines** Roman villas [b] (= *impasse privée*) ≈ mews

village [vilaʒ] NM (= *bourg, habitants*) village; **~ de toile** tent village; **~ de vacances** ◊ **~ club** holiday (*Brit*) *ou* vacation (*US*) village; **~ olympique** Olympic village; **le ~ planétaire** the global village → **idiot**

villageois, e [vilaʒwa, waz] [1] ADJ [*atmosphère, coutumes*] village (*épith*), rustic (*épith*); **un air ~** a rustic air [2] NM (= *résident*) villager, village resident [3] **villageoise** NF (= *résidente*) villager, village resident

ville [vil] [1] NF [a] (= *cité, habitants*) town; (*plus importante*) city; **la ~ de Paris** the city of Paris; **la ~ d'Albi** the town of Albi; **le plus grand cinéma de la ~** the biggest cinema in town; **en ~ ◊ à la ~** in town, in the city; **à la ~ comme à la scène** (*comédien*) on stage and off; (*acteur de cinéma*) on screen and off; **à la ~, c'est quelqu'un de charmant** in real life he's perfectly charming; **aller en ~** to go into town; **habiter la ~** to live in a (*ou* the) town *ou* city; **une ~ de province** a provincial town; **sa ~ d'attache était Genève** Geneva was his home-base [b] (= *quartier*) **~ basse/haute** lower/upper (part of the) town; **vieille ~** old (part of) town [c] (= *municipalité*) local authority, town *ou* city council; **dépenses assumées par la ~** local authority spending *ou* expenditure; **l'eau de la ~** tap water [d] (= *vie urbaine*) **la ~** town *ou* city life, the town *ou* city; **aimer la ~** to like town *ou* city life *ou* the town *ou* city; **les gens de la ~** townspeople, townsfolk, city folk; **vêtements de ~** town wear *ou* clothes

[2] COMP ▶ **ville champignon** mushroom town ▶ **ville d'eaux** spa (town) ▶ **la Ville éternelle** the Eternal City ▶ **ville forte** fortified town ▶ **ville industrielle** industrial town *ou* city ▶ **la Ville lumière** the City of Light, Paris ▶ **ville nouvelle** new town ▶ **ville ouverte** open city ▶ **Ville sainte** Holy City ▶ **ville satellite** satellite town ▶ **ville universitaire** university town *ou* city

ville-dortoir (*pl* **villes-dortoirs**) [vildɔʀtwaʀ] NF dormitory (*Brit*) *ou* bedroom (*US*) town

villégiature [vi(l)leʒjatyʀ] NF [a] (= *séjour*) holiday (*Brit*), vacation (*US*); **être en ~ quelque part** to be on holiday (*Brit*) *ou* vacation (*US*) *ou* to be holidaying (*Brit*) *ou* vacationing (*US*) somewhere; **aller en ~ dans sa maison de campagne** to go for a holiday (*Brit*) *ou* vacation (*US*) *ou* to holiday (*Brit*) *ou* vacation (*US*) in one's country home [b] (**lieu de**) **~** (holiday (*Brit*) *ou* vacation (*US*)) resort

villeux, -euse [vilø, øz] ADJ villous

villosité [vilozite] NF villus; **~s** villi

Vilnius [vilnjys] N Vilnius

vin [vɛ̃] NM [a] (= *boisson*) wine; **~ blanc/rouge/rosé** white/red/rosé wine; **~ gris** pale rosé wine; **~ jaune** *wine produced in the Jura region of France, similar to a light Spanish sherry*; **~ mousseux/de coupage** sparkling/blended wine; **~ ordinaire** *ou* **de table/de messe** ordinary *ou* table/altar *ou* communion wine; **~ nouveau** new wine; **grand ~** ◊ **~ fin** vintage wine; **un petit ~ blanc** a nice little white wine; **~ chaud** mulled wine; **~ cuit** fortified wine; **~ doux** sweet wine; **~ délimité de qualité supérieure** *label guaranteeing quality and origin of a wine* ■ (*PROV*) **quand le ~ est tiré, il faut le boire** once the first step is taken there's no going back → **lie, pays, table** [b] (= *réunion*) **~ d'honneur** reception (*where wine is served*) [c] (= *liqueur*) **~ de palme/de canne** palm/cane wine [d] (*loc*) **être entre deux ~s** to be tipsy; **avoir le ~ gai/triste** to get merry/maudlin when one drinks

vinaigre [vinɛgʀ] NM [a] (= *condiment*) vinegar; **~ de vin/d'alcool/de cidre/de Xérès** wine/spirit/cider/sherry vinegar → **mère, mouche** [b] (*loc*) **tourner au ~** to turn sour; **faire ~*** to hurry up, get a move on

vinaigrer [vinegʀe] ▶conjug 1◀ VT to season with vinegar; **la salade/sauce est trop vinaigrée** there's too much vinegar on the salad/in the sauce

vinaigrerie [vinɛgʀəʀi] NF (= *fabrication*) vinegar-making; (= *usine*) vinegar factory

vinaigrette [vinegʀɛt] NF French dressing, vinaigrette, oil and vinegar dressing; **tomates (en** *ou* **à la) ~** tomatoes in French dressing *ou* in oil and vinegar dressing, tomatoes (in) vinaigrette

vinaigrier [vinegʀije] NM [a] (= *fabricant*) vinegar-maker; (= *commerçant*) vinegar dealer [b] (= *flacon*) vinegar cruet *ou* bottle

vinasse [vinas] NF (*, *péj*) plonk* (*Brit*) (*péj*), cheap wine; (*Tech*) vinasse

vindicatif, -ive [vɛ̃dikatif, iv] ADJ vindictive

vindicte [vɛ̃dikt] NF **~ publique** (*gén*) public condemnation; (*Jur*) prosecution and conviction; **désigner qn à la ~ publique** *ou* **populaire** to expose sb to public condemnation

vineux, -euse [vinø, øz] ADJ [a] [*couleur, odeur, goût*] of wine, winey; [*pêche*] wine-flavoured, that tastes win(e)y; [*haleine*] wine-laden (*épith*), that smells of wine; [*teint*] purplish, red; **d'une couleur vineuse** wine-coloured, the colour of wine; **rouge ~** wine-red [b] (= *riche en alcool*) with a high alcohol content; **région vineuse** rich wine-growing area

vingt [vɛ̃], vɛ̃t *en liaison et dans les nombres de 22 à 29*] [1] ADJ INV, NM INV twenty; **je te l'ai dit ~ fois** I've told you a hundred times; **il n'avait plus son cœur/ses jambes de ~ ans** he no longer had the heart/the legs of a young man *ou* of a twenty-year-old; **~ dieux!†*** ye gods!†; **il mérite ~ sur ~** he deserves full marks; *pour autres locutions voir* **six, soixante** [2] COMP ▶ **vingt-quatre heures** twenty-four hours; **~-quatre heures sur ~-quatre** round the clock, twenty-four hours a day ▶ **vingt et**

un (= *nombre*) twenty-one; (= *jeu*) **le ~-et-un** pontoon, vingt-et-un, twenty-one (*US*)

vingtaine [vɛ̃tɛn] NF **une ~** about twenty, twenty or so, (about) a score; **une ~ de personnes** about twenty people, twenty people or so; **un jeune homme d'une ~ d'années** a young man of around *ou* about twenty *ou* of twenty or so

vingt-deux [vɛ̃tdø] ADJ INV, NM INV twenty-two; **~ !*** watch out!; **~ (voilà) les flics !*** watch out! it's the fuzz!* (= *carabine*) **22 Long Rifle** .22 rifle, point two two rifle; (*Rugby*) **la ligne des ~ ◊ les ~** the 22-metre line → **renvoi, renvoyer**

vingtième [vɛ̃tjɛm] [1] ADJ twentieth; **la ~ partie** the twentieth part; **au ~ siècle** in the twentieth century [2] NM twentieth, twentieth part

vinicole [vinikɔl] ADJ [*industrie*] wine (*épith*); [*région*] wine-growing (*épith*), wine-producing (*épith*); [*établissement*] wine-making (*épith*)

vinifère [vinifɛʀ] ADJ viniferous

vinification [vinifikasjɔ̃] NF [*raisin*] wine-making (process); [*sucres*] vinification

vinifier [vinifje] ▶conjug 7◀ VT [+ *moût*] to convert into wine

vinyle [vinil] NM vinyl; **il collectionne les vieux ~s** he collects old (vinyl) records; **son album est sorti en ~ en 1959** his album came out on vinyl in 1959

vinylique [vinilik] ADJ [*peinture*] vinyl (*épith*)

vioc* [vjɔk] NMF = **vioque**

viol [vjɔl] NM [*personne*] rape; [*temple*] violation, desecration; **au ~!** rape!; **~ collectif** gang rape

violacé, e [vjɔlase] (*ptp de* **violacer**) [1] ADJ purplish, mauvish; **rouge/rose ~** purplish red/pink [2] **violacée** NF (*Bot*) **les ~es** the violaceae

violacer [vjɔlase] ▶conjug 3◀ [1] VT to make *ou* turn purple *ou* mauve [2] **se violacer** VPR to turn *ou* become purple *ou* mauve, take on a purple hue (*littér*)

violateur, -trice [vjɔlatœʀ, tʀis] NM,F [*profanateur*] [*tombeau*] violator, desecrator; [*lois*] transgressor

violation [vjɔlasjɔ̃] NF [a] [*traité, loi*] violation, breaking; [*constitution*] violation; [*droit*] violation, infringement; [*promesse*] breaking; (*Jur*) **~ du secret professionnel** breach *ou* violation of professional secrecy; **de nombreuses ~s de cessez-le-feu** numerous violations of the ceasefire [b] [*temple*] violation, desecration; [*frontières, territoire*] violation; (*littér*) [*consciences*] violation; (*Jur*) **~ de domicile** forcible entry (*into a person's home*); (*Jur*) **~ de sépulture** violation *ou* desecration of graves

violâtre [vjɔlɑtʀ] ADJ purplish, mauvish

viole [vjɔl] NF viol; **~ d'amour** viola d'amore; **~ de gambe** viola da gamba, bass viol

violemment [vjɔlamɑ̃] ADV [*réagir, frapper, agresser*] violently; **ces mesures ont été ~ critiquées** these measures have been severely *ou* strongly criticized; **ils ont protesté ~ contre cette interdiction** they have protested vigorously *ou* strongly against this ban

violence [vjɔlɑ̃s] NF [a] [*personne, colère, coup, choc*] violence; **~ verbale** verbal abuse; **mouvement de ~** violent impulse; **répondre à la ~ par la ~** to meet violence with violence [b] [*odeur, parfum*] pungency; [*orage, vent, tempête*] violence, fierceness; [*pluie*] violence; [*douleur*] intensity; [*poison*] virulence; [*exercice, effort*] violence, strenuousness; [*remède*] drastic nature [c] (= *acte*) act of violence; **commettre des ~s contre qn** to commit acts of violence against sb; **l'enfant a subi des ~s** the child has suffered physical abuse; **faire subir des ~s sexuelles à qn** to abuse sb sexually; **inculpé de ~(s) à agent** found guilty of assaulting a police officer *ou* of assault on a police officer **d** (= *contrainte*) **faire ~ à qn** to do violence to sb; **faire ~ à une femme†** to use a woman violently†; **se faire ~** to force o.s.; **faire ~ à** [+ *sentiments*] to offend, savage, desecrate; **obtenir qch par la ~** to get sth by force → **doux**

violent, e [vjɔlɑ̃, ɑ̃t] ADJ **a** (= *brutal*) [*personne, colère, coup, choc, sport*] violent; **il s'est montré ~ avec elle** he was violent with her; **c'est un ~** he's a violent man → **non, mort'**, **révolution b** (= *intense*) [*odeur, parfum*] pungent, strong; [*couleur*] harsh; [*orage, vent, tempête*] violent, fierce; [*pluie*] violent; [*sentiment, passion, désir, dégoût*] violent, intense; [*douleur*] intense; [*poison*] virulent; [*exercice, effort*] violent, strenuous; [*remède*] drastic; **~ besoin de s'affirmer** intense *ou* urgent need to assert o.s.; **saisi d'une peur ~e** seized by a violent *ou* rabid fear; **une ~e migraine** a severe migraine **c** (* = *excessif*) **c'est un peu ~!** it's a bit much!*, that's going a bit far!*

violenter [vjɔlɑ̃te] ▸ conjug 1 ◂ VT **a** [+ *femme*] to assault (sexually); **elle a été violentée** she has been sexually assaulted **b** (*littér*) [+ *texte, désir*] to do violence to, desecrate

violer [vjɔle] ▸ conjug 1 ◂ VT **a** [+ *traité, loi*] to violate, break; [+ *constitution, cessez-le-feu*] to violate; [+ *droit*] to violate, infringe; [+ *promesse, serment*] to break **b** [+ *sépulture, temple*] to violate, desecrate; [+ *frontières, territoire*] to violate; **~ le domicile de qn** to force an entry into sb's home **c** (= *abuser de*) [+ *personne*] to rape, ravish† (*littér*), violate (*littér*); **se faire ~** to be raped **d** (*littér*) [+ *consciences*] to violate

violet, -ette [vjɔle, ɛt] **1** ADJ purple, violet **2** NM (= *couleur*) purple, violet; **le ~ lui va bien** purple suits him; **porter du ~** to wear purple; **peindre qch en ~** to paint sth purple; (*Peinture*) **un tube de ~** a tube of purple; **robe d'un ~ assez pâle** pale purple dress **3** **violette** NF (*Bot*) violet; **violette odorante** sweet violet; **violette de Parme** Parma violet

violeur, -euse [vjɔlœr, øz] NM,F rapist

violine [vjɔlin] ADJ dark purple, deep purple

violon [vjɔlɔ̃] NM **a** (= *instrument d'orchestre*) violin, fiddle*; (*de violoneux*) fiddle → **accorder, pisser b** (= *musicien d'orchestre*) violin, fiddle*; [*orchestre*] **le premier ~** the leader, the first violin; [*quatuor*] **the first violin *ou* fiddle*; **les premiers/seconds ~s** (= *groupe*) the first/second violins; (*fig*†) **payer les ~s (du bal)** to pick up the bill *ou* tab* → **vite c** (* = *prison*) cells, slammer*, nick* (*Brit*); **conduire qn au ~** to take sb to the cells; **passer la nuit au ~** to spend the night in the cells *ou* the slammer* *ou* the nick* (*Brit*) **d** **~ d'Ingres** (artistic) hobby

violoncelle [vjɔlɔ̃sɛl] NM cello, violoncello (*SPÉC*)

violoncelliste [vjɔlɔ̃selist] NMF cellist, cello player, violoncellist (*SPÉC*)

violoneux [vjɔlɔnø] NM (*de village, péj*) fiddler*

violoniste [vjɔlɔnist] NMF violinist, violin player

vioque [vjɔk] NMF (= *vieillard*) old person, old timer*; (= *père*) **le ~** my *ou* the old man*; (= *mère*) **la ~** my *ou* the old woman* *ou* lady*; **mes ~s** my folks*

viorne [vjɔrn] NF (*Bot*) viburnum

VIP [veipe] NMF (ABRÉV = **Very Important Person**) VIP

vipère [viper] NF adder, viper; **~ aspic** asp; **cette femme est une ~** that woman's a (real) viper → **langue, nœud**

vipereau (*pl* **vipereaux**) [vip(ə)ro] NM young viper

vipérin, e [viperɛ̃, in] **1** ADJ (*Zool*) viperine; (*fig*) [*propos*] vicious, poisonous **2** **vipérine** NF **a** (*Bot*) viper's bugloss **b** (*Zool*) (**couleuvre**) **~e** viperine snake (*SPÉC*), grass snake

virage [viraʒ] NM **a** (= *action*) [*avion, véhicule, coureur, skieur*] turn; (*Aviat*) **faire un ~ sur l'aile** to bank; (*Aut*) **prendre un ~ sur les chapeaux de roues** to take a bend *ou* curve (*US*) on two wheels *ou* on one's hub caps; **prendre un ~ à la corde** to hug the bend *ou* curve (*US*); (*Ski*) **~ parallèle** parallel turn **b** (*Aut* = *tournant*) bend; **~ en épingle à cheveux** hairpin bend; **~ en S** S-bend, S-curve (*US*); **« ~s sur 3 km »** "bends for 3 km"; **~ relevé** banked corner; **accélérer dans les ~s** to accelerate round the bends *ou* curves (*US*); **cette voiture prend bien les ~s** this car corners well; **il a pris son ~ trop vite** he went into *ou* took the bend *ou* curve (*US*) too fast **c** (= *changement*) change in policy *ou* of direction; **le ~ européen du gouvernement britannique** the British government's change of policy *ou* direction over Europe, the change in the British government's European policy; **amorcer un ~ à droite** to take a turn to the right; **un ~ à 180 degrés de la politique française** a U-turn in French politics; **savoir prendre le ~** to adapt to meet new circumstances **d** (= *transformation*) (*Chim*) [*papier de tournesol*] change in colour; (*Photo*) **~ à l'or/au cuivre** gold/copper toning; (*Méd*) **~ d'une cuti-réaction** positive reaction of a skin test

virago [virago] NF virago

viral, e [viral, o] ADJ (*mpl* -**aux**) viral

vire [vir] NF [*paroi rocheuse*] ledge

virée* [vire] NF (*en voiture*) drive, ride, spin*; (*de plusieurs jours*) trip, tour; (*à pied*) walk; (*de plusieurs jours*) walking *ou* hiking tour; (*à vélo, moto*) ride; (*de plusieurs jours*) trip; **faire une ~** to go for a ride (*ou* walk, drive etc); **faire une ~ en voiture** to go for a drive, go for a ride *ou* spin* in the car; **on a fait une ~ en Espagne** we went on a trip *ou* tour round Spain; **faire une ~ dans les bars/boîtes de nuit** to go round *ou* do* the bars/nightclubs; **leur ~ dans les pubs s'est mal terminée** their pub-crawl* ended badly

virelai [virlɛ] NM (*Littérat*) virelay

virement [virmɑ̃] NM **a** (*Fin*) **~ (bancaire)** (bank *ou* giro (*Brit*)) transfer; **~ postal** postal *ou* giro (*Brit*) transfer; **faire un ~ (d'un compte sur un autre)** to make a (credit) transfer (from one account to another); **j'ai fait un ~ de 5 000 F sur son compte** I transferred 5,000 francs to his account; **~ automatique** automatic transfer; **~ permanent** standing order **b** (*Naut*) **~ de bord** tacking

virer [vire] ▸ conjug 1 ◂ **1** VI **a** (= *changer de direction*) [*véhicule, avion, bateau*] to turn; (*Aviat*) **~ sur l'aile** to bank; (*littér*†) **à tout vent** to be as changeable as a weathercock **b** (*Naut*) **~ de bord** to tack; **~ vent devant** to go about; **~ vent arrière** to wear; **~ sur ses amarres** to turn at anchor; **~ au cabestan** to heave at the capstan **c** (= *tourner sur soi-même*) to turn (around) **d** (= *changer de couleur, d'aspect*) [*couleur*] to turn, change; (*Photo*) [*épreuves*] to tone; (*Méd*) [*cuti-réaction*] to come up positive

2 **virer à** VT INDIR (= *devenir*) **le bleu vire au violet** the blue is turning purple *ou* is changing to purple; [*temps*] **~ au froid/à la pluie/au beau** to turn cold/rainy/fine *ou* fair; **~ à l'aigre** to turn sour; **l'ambiance vire au drame** things are taking a dramatic turn; **le film vire à la farce** the film lapses into farce, the film turns into a farce *ou* becomes farcical; (*Pol*) **cette région a viré à droite** this region has swung to the right; (*Fin*) **~ au rouge** [*comptes, résultats*] to go *ou* slip into the red; **les indicateurs (financiers) virent au rouge** indicators have dropped sharply; **il a viré à l'intello*** he's become a bit of an intellectual

3 VT **a** (*Fin*) to transfer; **~ 1 000 F sur *ou* à un compte** to transfer 1,000 francs into an account

b * (= *expulser*) to kick out*, chuck out*; (= *renvoyer*) to fire*, sack* (*Brit*); **~ qn d'une réunion** to kick *ou* chuck sb out of a meeting*; **se faire ~** (= *se faire expulser*) to get o.s. kicked *ou* thrown out (**de** of); (= *se faire renvoyer*) to be fired*, get the sack* (*Brit*) **c** (* = *jeter*) to kick out*, throw out, get rid of; **il a viré les vieux fauteuils au grenier** he's chucked* *ou* thrown the old chairs in the loft **d** (*Méd*) **il a viré sa cuti(-réaction)*** he gave a positive skin test, his skin test came up positive; (*fig*) **il a viré sa cuti*** he changed totally

vireux, -euse [virø, øz] ADJ (*littér*) noxious; **amanite vireuse** amanita virosa

virevoltant, e [virvɔltɑ̃, ɑ̃t] ADJ [*danseuse*] twirling, pirouetting; [*cheval*] pirouetting; [*jupons*] twirling

virevolte [virvɔlt] NF [*danseuse*] twirl, pirouette; [*cheval*] demivolt, pirouette; (*fig* = *volteface*) about-turn, volte-face; **les ~s élégantes de la danseuse** the elegant twirling of the dancer

virevolter [virvɔlte] ▸ conjug 1 ◂ VI [*danseuse*] to twirl around, pirouette; [*cheval*] to do a demivolt, pirouette

Virgile [virʒil] NM Virgil

virginal, e [virʒinal, o] **1** ADJ (*littér*) virginal, maidenly (*littér*); **d'une blancheur ~e** virgin white **2** NM (*Mus*) virginal, virginals

Virginie [virʒini] NF (*Géog*) Virginia; **~ Occidentale** West Virginia

virginité [virʒinite] NF **a** (*lit*) virginity, maidenhood (*littér*); **garder/perdre sa ~** to keep/lose one's virginity **b** (*fig littér*) [*neige, aube, âme*] purity; **il voulait rendre à ce lieu sa ~** he wished to restore this place to its untouched *ou* virgin quality; (*hum*) **se refaire une ~** to restore one's image

virgule [virgyl] NF **a** (= *ponctuation*) comma; **mettre une ~** to put a comma in; (*fig*) **sans y changer une ~** without changing a (single) thing, without touching a single comma; **c'est exactement ce qu'il m'a dit, à la ~ près** that's exactly what he said to me, word for word; **à quelques ~s près, le texte n'a pas été modifié** apart from the odd comma, the text hasn't been changed at all; **moustaches en ~** curled moustache **b** (*Math*) (decimal) point; **(arrondi à) 3 chiffres après la ~** (correct to) 3 decimal places; **5 ~ 2** 5 point 2; **~ fixe/flottante** fixed/floating decimal (point)

viril, e [viril] ADJ [*attributs, apparence*] male, masculine; [*attitude, courage, langage, traits*] manly, virile; [*prouesses, amant*] virile; **force ~e** virile *ou* manly strength; **amitiés ~es** male friendships; **elle fait un peu ~** she's a bit mannish; (*Sport*) **jeu ~** aggressive style → **âge, membre, toge**

virilement [virilmɑ̃] ADV in a manly *ou* virile way

virilisant, e [virilizɑ̃, ɑ̃t] ADJ [*médicament*] that provokes male characteristics, virilizing

virilisation [virilizasjɔ̃] NF (*Méd*) virilism

viriliser [virilize] ▸ conjug 1 ◂ VT (*Bio*) to give male characteristics to; (*en apparence*) [+ *femme*] to make appear mannish *ou* masculine; [+ *homme*] to make (appear) more manly *ou* masculine

virilisme [virilism] NM virility; (*Méd.*) virilism

virilité [virilite] NF [*attributs, apparence, formes*] masculinity; [*attitude, courage, langage, traits*] manliness, virility; [*prouesses, amant*] virility; **il se sent menacé dans sa ~** his masculinity feels threatened; **manquer de ~** to be unmanly

virole [virɔl] NF **a** (= *bague*) ferrule; **couteau à ~ tournante** pocket knife with a safety catch **b** (*Tech* = *moule*) collar

viroler [virɔle] ▸ conjug 1 ◂ VT **a** [+ *couteau, parapluie*] to ferrule, fit with a ferrule **b** (*Tech*) to place in a collar

virologie [viʀɔlɔʒi] NF virology

virologique [viʀɔlɔʒik] ADJ virological

virologiste [viʀɔlɔʒist], **virologue** [viʀɔlɔg] NMF virologist

virose [viʀoz] NF viral infection

virtualité [viʀtɥalite] NF [a] [marché, sens, revenu] potentiality [b] (Philo, Phys, Ordin) virtuality

virtuel, -elle [viʀtɥɛl] [1] ADJ [a] (= potentiel) [candidat, marché, sens, revenu] potential; **tout cela est très ~** all that is purely theoretical [b] (Philo, Phys, Ordin) virtual; **mémoire/réalité virtuelle** virtual memory/reality → **image** [2] NM (Ordin) **le ~** virtual reality

virtuellement [viʀtɥɛlmɑ̃] ADV [a] (littér = en puissance) potentially [b] (= pratiquement) virtually; **c'était ~ fini** it was virtually finished, it was as good as finished [c] (Ordin) **visiter ~ le Louvre** to make a virtual reality tour of the Louvre

virtuose [viʀtɥoz] [1] NMF (Mus) virtuoso; (= personne douée) master, virtuoso; **~ du violon** violin virtuoso; **~ de la plume/du pinceau** master of the pen/of the brush, brilliant writer/painter [2] ADJ virtuoso

virtuosité [viʀtɥozite] NF virtuosity; (Mus) **exercices de ~** exercises in virtuosity; **avec ~** masterfully; **il a interprété ce morceau avec ~** he gave a virtuoso performance (of this piece), he played this piece brilliantly

virulence [viʀylɑ̃s] NF [a] (Méd) virulence [b] (fig) [critique, opposition, campagne de presse] virulence, viciousness; **avec ~** virulently

virulent, e [viʀylɑ̃, ɑ̃t] ADJ [a] (Méd) virulent [b] (fig) [critique, opposition, déclaration, personne] virulent, vicious

virus [viʀys] NM (Méd, Ordin) virus; **~ de la rage/du sida** rabies/AIDS virus; **~ de l'immunodéficience humaine** human immunodeficiency virus; (fig) **le ~ de la danse/du jeu** the dancing/gambling bug*; **attraper le ~ du jeu** to be ou get bitten by the gambling bug*

vis [vis] [1] NF [a] (gén) screw; **~ à bois** wood screw; **~ à métaux** metal screw; **~ à tête plate/à tête ronde** flat-headed/round-headed screw; **~ à ailettes** wing nut → **cruciforme, pas¹, serrer, tour²** [b]† (escalier à) **~** spiral staircase [2] COMP ► **vis d'Archimède** Archimedes' screw ► **vis sans fin** worm screw, endless screw ► **vis micrométrique** micrometer screw ► **vis platinées** (Aut) (contact) points ► **vis de pressoir** press screw ► **vis de serrage** binding ou clamping screw

visa [viza] NM (= formule, sceau) stamp; (sur un passeport) visa; **~ d'entrée/de sortie/de transit** entry/exit/transit visa; **~ touristique** ou **de tourisme** tourist visa; (Ciné) **~ de censure** (censor's) certificate; (Ciné) **~ d'exploitation** distribution number; (fig) **~ pour ...** passport to ...; (Fin) **carte Visa®** Visa® card

visage [vizaʒ] [1] NM [a] (lit = figure, fig = expression, personne, aspect) face; **au ~ pâle/joufflu** pale-faced/chubby-faced; **un ~ connu/ami** a known/friendly face; **je lui trouve bon ~** he looks well (to me); **sans ~** faceless; **le vrai ~ de ...** the true face of ...; **un homme à deux ~s** a two-faced man; **un problème aux multiples ~s** a multifaceted problem; **à ~ humain** [capitalisme, entreprise] with a human face; **le nouveau ~ du parti/pays** the new face of the party/country; **donner un nouveau ~ à** [+ ville] to give a new look to; [+ entreprise, parti] to change the face of; **elle changea de ~** her face ou expression changed; **l'Europe a changé de ~** the face of Europe has changed → **soin** [b] (loc) **agir/parler à ~ découvert** to act/speak openly; **faire bon ~** to put a good face on it; (littér) **faire bon ~ à qn** (= l'accueillir chaleureusement) to give sb a warm welcome; (avec hypocrisie) to put on a show of friendli-

ness for sb; **montrer son vrai ~** to show one's true colours (Brit) ou colors (US) [2] COMP ► **Visage pâle** paleface

visagiste® [vizaʒist] NMF (coiffeur) **~** (hair) stylist; (esthéticienne) **~** beautician

vis-à-vis [vizavi] [1] PRÉP [a] (= en face de) **~ de** opposite; **~ de la gare** opposite the station [b] (= comparé à) **~ de** beside, next to, against; **mes ennuis ne sont pas graves ~ des siens** my problems aren't serious beside ou next to his [c] **~ de** (= envers) towards, vis-à-vis; (= à l'égard de) as regards, with regard to, vis-à-vis; **être sincère ~ de soi-même** to be frank with oneself; **être méfiant ~ de ce genre d'évolution** to be wary of such developments; **~ de cette proposition** with regard to this proposal; **j'en ai honte ~ de lui** I'm ashamed of it in front of ou before him [2] ADV (= face à face) face to face; **leurs maisons se font ~** their houses face ou are opposite each other [3] NM INV [a] (= position) **en ~** facing ou opposite each other; **des immeubles en ~** buildings facing ou opposite each other; **ils étaient assis en ~** they were sitting opposite each other, they were sitting face to face [b] (= tête-à-tête) encounter, meeting; **un ~ ennuyeux** a tiresome encounter ou meeting [c] (= personne faisant face) person opposite; (aux cartes) (= partenaire) partner; (= homologue) opposite number, counterpart [d] (= bâtiment) **immeuble sans ~** building with an open outlook; **avoir une école pour ~** to have a school opposite, look out over a school [e] (= canapé) tête-à-tête

viscéral, e (mpl **-aux**) [viseʀal, o] ADJ [a] (Anat) visceral [b] (fig) [haine, peur, besoin] deeprooted, visceral (frm); [rejet] instinctive; [attachement] passionate; **réaction ~e** gut reaction

viscéralement [viseʀalmɑ̃] ADV [attaché] passionately; [hostile] instinctively; **détester ~ qch** to have a deep ou visceral (frm) loathing of sth; **réagir ~ à qch** to have a gut reaction to sth; **~ jaloux** pathologically jealous

viscère [viseʀ] NM (internal) organ; **~s** intestines, entrails, viscera (SPÉC)

viscose [viskoz] NF viscose

viscosité [viskozite] NF [liquide] viscosity; [surface gluante] stickiness, viscosity

visée [vize] NF [a] (avec une arme) taking aim (NonC), aiming (NonC); (Arpentage) sighting; **pour faciliter la ~, ce fusil comporte un dispositif spécial** to help you to (take) aim ou to help your aim, this rifle comes equipped with a special device → **ligne¹** [b] (gén pl = dessein) aim, design; **avoir des ~ sur qn/qch** to have designs on sb/sth; **ses ~s ambitieuses** his ambitious aims; **les ~s expansionnistes d'un pays** the expansionist aims ou ambitions of a country; **~s coupables** wicked designs

viser¹ [vize] ▸ conjug 1 ◂ [1] VT [a] [+ objectif] to aim at ou for; [+ cible] to aim at [b] (= ambitionner) [+ effet] to aim at; [+ carrière] to aim at, set one's sights on [c] (= concerner) [mesure] to be aimed at, be directed at; [remarque] to be aimed ou directed at, be meant ou intended for; **cette mesure vise tout le monde** this measure applies to everyone, everyone is affected by this measure; **il se sent visé** he feels he's being got at* [d] (‡ = regarder) to take a look at, have a dekko‡ (Brit) at; **vise un peu ça !** just take a look ou have a dekko‡ (Brit) at that! [2] VI [a] [tireur] to aim, take aim; **~ juste** (lit) to aim accurately; (fig) not to miss the mark; **~ trop haut/trop bas** to aim (too) high/(too) low; **~ à la tête/au cœur** to aim for the head/the heart [b] (= ambitionner) **~ haut/plus haut** to set one's sights high/higher, aim high/higher

[3] **viser à** VT INDIR (= avoir pour but de) **~ à qch/à faire** to aim at sth/to do; **scène qui vise à provoquer le rire** scene which sets out to raise a laugh ou to make people laugh; **mesures qui visent à la réunification de la majorité** measures which are aimed at reuniting ou which aim ou are intended to reunite the majority

viser² [vize] ▸ conjug 1 ◂ VT (Admin) [+ passeport] to visa; [+ document] to stamp; **faire ~ un passeport** to have a passport visaed

viseur [vizœʀ] NM [a] [arme] sights; [caméra, appareil photo] viewfinder; (Photo) **~ à cadre lumineux** collimator viewfinder [b] (Astron = lunette) telescopic sight

Vishnou, Vishnu [viʃnu] NM Vishnu

visibilité [vizibilite] NF (gén, Sci) visibility; **bonne/mauvaise ~** good/poor ou bad visibility; **~ nulle** nil ou zero visibility; **ce pare-brise permet une très bonne ~** this windscreen gives excellent visibility; **manque de ~** (lit) lack of visibility; (fig) lack of foresight; **sans ~** [pilotage, virage, atterrissage] blind (épith); **piloter sans ~** to fly blind

visible [vizibl] [1] ADJ [a] (= qui peut être vu) visible; **~ à l'œil nu/au microscope** visible to the naked eye/under a microscope → **iceberg** [b] (= évident, net) [embarras, surprise] obvious, visible; [amélioration, progrès] clear, visible; [réparation, reprise] obvious; **sa déception était ~** his disappointment was obvious ou visible, you could see his disappointment ou that he was disappointed; **il ne veut pas le faire, c'est ~** he obviously doesn't want to, he doesn't want to, that's obvious ou apparent ou clear; **il est ~ que ...** it is obvious ou apparent ou clear that ... [c] (= en état de recevoir) **Monsieur est-il ~?** is Mr X (ou Lord X etc) able to receive visitors?, is Mr X (ou Lord X etc) receiving visitors?; **elle n'est pas ~ le matin** she's not at home to visitors ou not in to visitors in the morning [2] NM **le ~** what is visible, the visible

visiblement [vizibləmɑ̃] ADV (= manifestement) visibly, obviously; **il était ~ inquiet** he was visibly ou obviously worried; **~, c'est une erreur** obviously ou clearly it's a mistake [b] (= de façon perceptible à l'œil) visibly, perceptibly

visière [vizjeʀ] NF [casquette, képi] peak; [casque] visor; (pour le soleil) eyeshade; **mettre sa main en ~** to shade one's eyes with one's hand → **rompre**

visioconférence [vizjokɔ̃feʀɑ̃s] NF videoconference, teleconference

vision [vizjɔ̃] NF [a] (= faculté) (eye)sight, vision; (= perception) vision, sight; **une ~ défectueuse** defective (eye)sight ou vision; **le mécanisme de la ~** the mechanism of vision ou sight; **pour faciliter la ~** to aid (eye)sight ou vision; **~ nette/floue** clear/hazy vision; **porter des lunettes pour la ~ de loin** to wear glasses for distance vision → **champ** [b] (= conception) view; **c'est une ~ idyllique des choses** it's an idyllic view of things; **avoir une ~ globale** ou **d'ensemble d'un problème** to have a global view of a problem; **nous partageons la même ~ des choses** we see things (in) the same way [c] (= image, apparition, mirage) vision; **tu as des ~s*** you're seeing things [d] (= spectacle) sight; **~ d'horreur** horrific sight ou scene; **après l'attentat, l'aéroport offrait une ~ d'apocalypse** after the bomb attack the airport was a scene of apocalyptic horror ou was like a scene from the apocalypse

visionnage [vizjɔnaʒ] NM viewing

visionnaire [vizjɔnɛʀ] ADJ, NMF visionary

visionner [vizjɔne] ▸ conjug 1 ◂ VT to view

visionneuse [vizjɔnøz] NF viewer (for transparencies or film)

visiophone [vizjɔfɔn] NM videophone, viewphone

visiophonie [vizjɔfɔni] NF video tele-conferencing

Visitation [vizitasjɔ̃] NF (*Rel*) **la ~** the Visitation

visite [vizit] **1** NF **a** (= *fait de visiter*) visiting, going round; (*à la prison, l'hôpital*) **heures/jour de ~ ou des ~s** visiting hours/day; **la ~ du château a duré deux heures** it took two hours to visit ou go round (*Brit*) ou go through (*US*) the château → **droit³**
b (= *tournée, inspection*) visit; **au programme il y a des ~s de musée** there are museum visits on the programme; **~ accompagnée** ou **guidée** guided tour; (*hum*) **ces ~s nocturnes au garde-manger** these nocturnal visits ou trips to the pantry
c (*chez une connaissance*) visit; **une courte ~** a short visit, a call; **une ~ de politesse** a courtesy call ou visit; **une ~ de remerciements** a thank-you visit; **être en ~ chez qn** to be paying sb a visit, be on a visit to sb; **rendre ~ à qn** to pay sb a visit, call on sb, visit sb; **je vais lui faire une petite ~** I'm going to pay him a (little) visit, I'm going to call on him; **rendre à qn sa ~** to return sb's visit, pay a return visit; **avoir ou recevoir la ~ de qn** to have a visit from sb; **vos ~s se font de plus en plus rares** you should come and visit more often; **ses ~s étaient rares** he rarely visited → **carte**
d (= *visiteur*) **nous avons des ~s** we've got visitors ou company ou guests; **j'ai une ~ dans le salon** I have a visitor ou I have company in the lounge; **nous attendons de la ~ ou des ~s** we're expecting visitors ou company ou guests; (*hum*) **tiens, nous avons de la ~** hey, we've got company ou guests
e [*chef d'État*] visit; **en ~ officielle au Japon** on an official visit to Japan
f [*médecin hospitalier avec étudiants*] ward round; [*médecin de ville*] **~ (à domicile)** (house)call, visit; **il ne fait pas de ~s à domicile** he doesn't make housecalls; **~ de contrôle** follow-up visit; **la ~** (*chez le médecin*) (medical) consultation; (*Mil*) (*quotidienne*) sick parade; (*d'entrée*) medical (examination) (*Brit*), physical examination (*US*); **aller à la ~** to go to the surgery (for a consultation); [*recrue*] **passer à la ~** (*médicale*) to have a medical (*Brit*) ou physical (*US*) examination; **l'heure de la ~ dans le service** the time when the doctor does his ward round(s)
g (*Comm*) visit, call; (*d'expert*) inspection; **j'ai reçu la ~ d'un représentant** I had a visit ou call from a representative, a representative called (on me)
2 COMP ► **visite du diocèse** = **visite épiscopale** ► **visite domiciliaire** (*Jur*) house search ► **visite de douane** customs inspection ou examination ► **visite épiscopale** (*Rel*) pastoral visitation

visiter [vizite] ▸ conjug 1 ◂ VT **a** (*en touriste, curieux*) [+ *pays, ville*] to visit; [+ *château, musée*] to visit, go round (*Brit*) ou through (*US*); **~ une maison** (*à vendre*) to look over a house, view a house; **il me fit ~ sa maison/son laboratoire** he showed me round (*Brit*) ou through (*US*) his house/his laboratory; **il nous a fait ~ la maison que nous envisagions d'acheter** he showed us round (*Brit*) ou through (*US*) ou over (*Brit*) the house we were thinking of buying; **le monument le plus visité de Paris** the most visited monument in Paris
b (*en cherchant qch*) [+ *bagages*] to examine, inspect; [+ *boutiques*] to go round (*Brit*) ou round; [+ *recoins*] to search (in); [+ *armoire*] to go through, search (in); (*Admin*) [+ *navire*] to inspect; (*hum*) [+ *coffre-fort*] to visit (*hum*), pay a visit to (*hum*); **leur maison a été visitée plusieurs fois** they've been burgled ou they've had burglars several times
c (*par charité*) [+ *malades, prisonniers*] to visit

d [*médecin, représentant, inspecteur*] to visit, call on
e (*Rel*) to visit
f († = *fréquenter*) [+ *voisins, connaissances*] to visit, call on

visiteur, -euse [vizitœR, øz] **1** NM,F (*gén*) visitor; (*Sport*) **les ~s** the visiting ou away team → **infirmier, médical 2** COMP ► **visiteur des douanes** customs inspector ► **visiteur de prison** prison visitor

vison [vizɔ̃] NM (= *animal, fourrure*) mink; (= *manteau*) mink (coat)

visonnière [vizɔnjɛR] NF (*Can*) mink farm, minkery (*Can*)

visqueux, -euse [viskø, øz] ADJ **a** [*liquide*] viscous, thick; [*pâte*] sticky, viscous; (*péj*) [*surface, objet*] sticky, goo(e)y*, viscous **b** (*fig péj*) [*personne, manière*] slimy, smarmy (*Brit*)

vissage [visaʒ] NM screwing (on ou down)

visser [vise] ▸ conjug 1 ◂ VT **a** (*au moyen de vis*) [+ *plaque, serrure*] to screw on; [+ *couvercle*] to screw down ou on; **ce n'est pas bien vissé** it's not screwed down properly; **~ un objet sur qch** to screw an object on to sth; **vissé devant la télé*** glued* to the television; **il est resté vissé sur sa chaise*** he never got out of his chair; **le chapeau vissé sur la tête** with his hat jammed hard ou tight on his head **b** (*en tournant*) [+ *couvercle, bouchon, écrou*] to screw on; **ce couvercle se visse** this is a screw-on lid, this lid screws on; **ce n'est pas bien vissé** [*bouchon*] it's not screwed on ou down properly; [*écrou*] it's not screwed down properly **c** (* = *être strict avec*) [+ *élève, subordonné*] to keep a tight rein on, crack down on*; **toi, je vais te ~!** things are going to get tough for you around here!

visseuse [visøz] NF screwing machine

Vistule [vistyl] NF **la ~** the Vistula

visu [vizy] ◆ **de visu** LOC ADV with one's own eyes; **s'assurer de qch de ~** to check sth with one's own eyes ou for oneself

visualisation [vizɥalizasjɔ̃] NF (*gén*) visualization; (*Ordin*) display → **console, écran**

visualiser [vizɥalize] ▸ conjug 1 ◂ VT **a** (*Tech*) to visualize; (*Ordin*) to display **b** (= *voir, se représenter*) to visualize; **j'ai du mal à ~ la scène** it's hard for me to visualize what happened

visuel, -elle [vizɥɛl] **1** ADJ (*gén*) visual; **troubles ~s** eye trouble (*NonC*) → **champ, mémoire 2** NM,F **cet écrivain est un ~** visual images predominate in the writings of this author **3** NM (*Ordin*) visual display unit, VDU; (*Publicité*) visual; **~ graphique** graphical display unit

visuellement [vizɥɛlmɑ̃] ADV visually

vit† [vi] NM (*littér*) penis

vital, e (*mpl -aux*) [vital, o] ADJ (*Bio, gén*) vital → **centre, espace, minimum**

vitalisme [vitalism] NM (*Philo*) vitalism

vitalité [vitalite] NF [*personne*] energy, vitality; [*institution, terme*] vitality; **il est plein de ~** he's full of energy ou go ou vitality; **la ~ de ces enfants est incroyable** it's incredible how much energy these children have

vitamine [vitamin] NF vitamin; **~ A/C** vitamin A/C; **alimentation riche/pauvre en ~s** food that is rich ou high/low in vitamins; **lait enrichi en ~s** vitamin-enriched milk, milk with added vitamins ou enriched with vitamins → **carence**

vitaminé, e [vitamine] ADJ with added vitamins

vitaminique [vitaminik] ADJ vitamin (*épith*)

vite [vit] **1** ADV **a** (= *à vive allure*) [*rouler, marcher*] fast, quickly; [*progresser, avancer*] quickly, rapidly, swiftly
b (= *rapidement*) [*travailler, se dérouler, se passer*] quickly, fast; (= *en hâte*) [*faire un travail*] quickly, in a rush ou hurry; **ça s'est passé si**

~, je n'ai rien vu it happened so quickly ou fast I didn't see a thing; **il travaille ~ et bien** he works quickly ou fast and well; **vous avez fait ~ pour venir** it didn't take you long to come, you were quick getting here; **ça ne va pas ~** it's slow work; **fais ~!** be quick about it!, look sharp!*; **et plus ~ que ça!** and get a move on!*, and be quick about it!; **là il (y) va un peu ~** he's being a bit hasty; **le temps passe ~** time flies; **la police est allée ~ en besogne*** the police were quick off the mark ou worked fast ou didn't waste any time; **vous allez un peu ~ en besogne*** you're going too fast, you're a bit too quick off the mark; **aller plus ~ que les violons ou la musique** to jump the gun; **c'est ~ dit*** (it's) easier said than done; **j'aurais plus ~ fait de l'écrire moi-même** it would have been quicker if I'd written it myself; **ça, c'est du ~ fait!** that's a rushed job!, that's been done too quickly!; **elle s'est tirée ~ fait*** she was off like a shot*, she took off as quick as a flash*; **il faut que tu termines ça, ~ fait (sur le gaz)*** you have to finish that, pronto*; **on prend une bière, mais ~ fait (sur le gaz)*** we'll have a beer, but just a quick one* ou a quickie*; **il l'a terminé ~ fait, bien fait** he finished it nice and quickly*; **il l'a peint ~ fait, bien fait** he gave it a quick coat of paint; **c'est du ~ fait, bien fait** it's a nice quick job → **aller**
c (= *bientôt*) soon, in no time; **elle sera ~ arrivée/guérie** she'll soon be here/better, she'll be here/better in no time; **il eut ~ fait de découvrir que ...** he soon ou quickly discovered that ..., in no time he discovered that ...; **ce sera ~ fait** it won't take long, it won't take a moment ou a second; **on a ~ fait de dire que ...** it's easy to say that ...
d (= *immédiatement*) quick; **lève-toi ~!** get up quick!; **va ~ voir!** go and see quick!; **au plus ~** as quickly as possible; **il faut le prévenir au plus ~** he must be warned as quickly ou as soon as possible; **faites-moi ça, et ~!** do this for me and be quick about it!; **~! un médecin** quick! a doctor
2 ADJ (*style journalistique : Sport*) fast

vitellus [vitelys] NM (*Bio*) vitellin

vitesse [vites] **1** NF **a** (= *promptitude, hâte*) speed, quickness, rapidity; **en ~** (= *rapidement*) quickly; (= *en hâte*) in a hurry ou rush; **faites-moi ça en ~** do this for me quickly; **faites-moi ça, et en ~!** do this for me and be quick about it!; **on va prendre un verre en ~** we'll go for a quick drink; **écrire un petit mot en ~** to scribble a hasty note; **j'ai préparé le déjeuner/cette conférence un peu en ~** I prepared lunch/this lecture in a bit of a hurry ou rush; **à toute ~ ◊ en quatrième** at full ou top speed; **il faut toujours tout faire en quatrième ~** everything always has to be done at top speed ou in a great rush; (*à la nouvelle*) **il est arrivé en quatrième ~ ou à toute ~** (on hearing the news) he came like a shot ou at the double
b [*courant, processus*] speed; [*véhicule, projectile*] speed, velocity; **aimer la ~** to love speed; **à la ~ de 60 km/h** at (a speed of) 60 km/h; **à quelle ~ allait-il? ◊ quelle ~ faisait-il?** what speed was he going at? ou doing?, how fast was he going?; **faire de la ~** to go ou drive fast; **faire une ~ (moyenne) de 60** to do an average (speed) of 60; **prendre de la ~** to gather ou increase speed, pick up speed; **gagner ou prendre qn de ~** (*lit*) to beat sb, outstrip sb; (*fig*) to beat sb to it, pip sb at the post* (*Brit*), beat sb by a nose (*US*); **entraîné par sa propre ~** carried along by his own momentum; **~ de propagation/réaction/rotation** speed of propagation/reaction/rotation; **à grande ~** at great speed; **passer une vidéo en ~ accélérée** to fast-forward a video; **faire qch à la ~ de l'éclair** to do sth with lightning speed ou as quick as a flash; **à une ~ vertigineuse** [*conduire,*

avancer] at a dizzying speed; [*augmenter, se multiplier*] at a dizzying rate; **circuler à ~ réduite** to drive at reduced speed → **course, excès, perte**

c (*Rail*) **grande/petite ~** fast/slow goods service; **expédier un colis en petite ~** to send a parcel by slow goods service; **expédier un colis en grande ~** to send a parcel express **d** (*Aut*) gear; **changer de ~** to change *ou* shift (*US*) gear; **passer les ~s** to go *ou* run through the gears; (*fig*) **passer la ~ supérieure** to quicken the pace, shift into high gear (*US*); (*fig*) **une Europe à deux ~s** a two-speed Europe; **société/justice à deux ~s** two-tier society/justice system → **boîte** **e** (*loc*) **à (la) ~ grand V** at top speed, real fast* (*US*); **il est parti à la ~ grand V** he shot off*, he went tearing off*, he left like a bullet from a gun

2 COMP ► **vitesse acquise** momentum ► **vitesse d'affichage** (*Ordin*) display speed ► **vitesse de croisière** (*lit, fig*) cruising speed ► **vitesse initiale** muzzle velocity ► **vitesse de frappe** typing speed ► **vitesse d'impression** (*Ordin*) print speed ► **vitesse de lecture** (*Ordin*) reading rate ► **vitesse de libération** escape velocity *ou* speed ► **vitesse de la lumière** speed of light ► **vitesse de pointe** maximum *ou* top speed ► **vitesse de sédimentation** sedimentation speed ► **vitesse du son** (*lit, fig*) speed of sound ► **vitesse de sustentation** minimum flying speed ► **vitesse de traitement** (*Ordin*) processing speed

viticole [vitikɔl] ADJ [*industrie*] wine (*épith*); [*région*] wine-growing (*épith*), wine-producing (*épith*); [*établissement*] wine-producing (*épith*), wine-making (*épith*); **culture ~** wine growing, viticulture (*SPÉC*)

viticulteur, -trice [vitikyltœʀ, tʀis] NM,F wine grower, viticulturist (*SPÉC*)

viticulture [vitikyltyʀ] NF wine growing, viticulture (*SPÉC*)

vitrage [vitʀaʒ] NM **a** (= *action*) glazing **b** (= *vitres*) windows; (= *cloison*) glass partition; (= *toit*) glass roof; **double ~** double glazing; **fenêtre à double ~** double-glazed window **c** (= *rideau*) net curtain; (= *tissu*) net curtaining

vitrail (*pl* **-aux**) [vitʀaj, o] NM stained-glass window, church window; **l'art du ~ ◊ le ~** the art of stained-glass window making

vitre [vitʀ] NF **a** [*fenêtre, vitrine*] (window) pane, pane (of glass); [*voiture*] window; **poser/mastiquer une ~** to put in/putty a window pane *ou* a pane of glass; **verre à ~** window glass; **laver/faire les ~s** to wash/do *ou* clean the windows; **appuyer son front à la ~** to press one's forehead against the window (pane); **les camions font trembler les ~s** the lorries make the window panes *ou* the windows rattle; **casser une ~** to break a window (pane); **~ blindée** bullet-proof window; (*Aut*) **la ~ arrière** the rear window *ou* windscreen (*Brit*) *ou* windshield (*US*); (*Aut*) **~s électriques** electric windows **b** (= *fenêtre*) **~s** windows; **fermer les ~s** to close the windows

vitré, e [vitʀe] (*ptp de* **vitrer**) **1** ADJ **a** [*porte, cloison*] glass (*épith*) → **baie²** **b** (*Anat*) **corps ~** vitreous body; **humeur ~e** vitreous humour **2** NM (*Anat*) vitreous body

vitrer [vitʀe] ► conjug 1 ◀ VT [+ *fenêtre*] to glaze, put glass in; [+ *véranda, porte*] to put windows in, put glass in

vitrerie [vitʀəʀi] NF (= *activité*) glaziery, glazing; (= *marchandise*) glass

vitreux, -euse [vitʀø, øz] ADJ **a** (*Anat*) [*humeur*] vitreous **b** (*Géol*) vitreous → **porcelaine c** (*péj* = *terne, glauque*) [*yeux*] glassy, dull; [*regard*] glassy, glazed, lacklustre (*Brit*) *ou* lackluster (*US*) (*épith*); [*surface, eau*] dull

vitrier [vitʀije] NM glazier; **ton père n'est pas ~!** I can't see through you!

vitrification [vitʀifikasjɔ̃] NF **a** (*Tech*) (*par fusion*) vitrification; (*par enduit*) glazing; **la ~ des déchets radioactifs** vitrification of nuclear waste **b** [*parquet*] sealing, varnishing

vitrifier [vitʀifje] ► conjug 7 ◀ **1** VT **a** (*Tech*) (*par fusion*) to vitrify; (*par enduit*) to glaze, put a glaze on; **déchets vitrifiés** vitrified waste **b** (= *vernir*) [+ *parquet*] to seal, varnish **2** **se vitrifier** VPR to vitrify

vitrine [vitʀin] NF **a** (= *devanture*) (shop) window; **en ~** in the window; **la ~ du boucher/de la pâtisserie** the butcher's/pastry *ou* cake (*Brit*) shop window; **faire les ~s** to dress the windows; ► **publicitaire** display case, showcase; (*fig*) **cette exposition est la ~ de l'Europe** this exhibition is Europe's showcase; **la ~ légale d'une organisation terroriste** the legal front for a terrorist organization → **lécher b** (= *meuble*) (*chez soi*) display cabinet; (*au musée*) showcase, display cabinet

vitriol [vitʀijɔl] NM (*Hist, Chim*) vitriol; (*fig*) **une critique/un style au ~** a vitriolic review/style; (*péj* = *mauvais alcool*) **du ~** firewater

vitriolage [vitʀijɔlaʒ] NM (*Tech*) vitriolization

vitrioler [vitʀijɔle] ► conjug 1 ◀ VT **a** (*Tech*) to vitriolize, treat with vitriol *ou* (concentrated) sulphuric acid **b** [+ *victime d'agression*] to throw acid *ou* vitriol at

vitrocéramique [vitʀoseʀamik] NF vitreous ceramic; **table de cuisson en ~** ceramic hob

vitupération [vitypeʀasjɔ̃] NF (= *propos*) **~s** rantings and ravings, vituperations (*frm*)

vitupérer [vitypeʀe] ► conjug 6 ◀ **1** VI to vituperate (*frm*) (**contre** against), rant and rave (**contre** about); **~ contre qn/qch** to rail against sb/sth, rant and rave about sb/sth **2** VT (*littér*) to inveigh against

vivable [vivabl] ADJ **a*** [*personne*] bearable; **il n'est pas ~** he's impossible to live with; **ce n'est pas ~!** it's intolerable! **b** [*milieu, monde*] fit to live in; **cette maison n'est pas ~** this house isn't fit to live in

vivace¹ [vivas] **1** ADJ **a** (*Bot*) hardy; **plante ~** (hardy) perennial **b** [*préjugé*] inveterate, indestructible; [*haine*] undying, inveterate; [*souvenir*] vivid; [*foi*] steadfast, undying; [*tradition*] enduring **2** NF (= *plante*) perennial

vivace² [vivatʃe] ADV, ADJ (*Mus*) vivace

vivacité [vivasite] NF **a** (= *rapidité, vie*) [*personne*] liveliness, vivacity; [*mouvement*] liveliness, briskness; [*intelligence*] keenness; [*langue, dialogues, débat*] liveliness; **~ d'esprit** quick-wittedness; **avoir de la ~** to be lively *ou* vivacious; **avec ~** [*réagir, se déplacer*] swiftly **b** (= *brusquerie*) sharpness, brusqueness; **avec ~** [*critiquer, répliquer*] sharply, brusquely **c** (= *caractère vif*) [*lumière, éclat*] brightness, brilliance; [*couleur*] vividness; [*froid*] bitterness; [*douleur*] sharpness; [*vent*] keenness **d** (= *intensité*) [*émotion, plaisir*] keenness, intensity; [*impression*] vividness

vivandière [vivɑ̃djɛʀ] NF (*Hist*) vivandière

vivant, e [vivɑ̃, ɑ̃t] **1** ADJ **a** (= *en vie*) living, alive (*attrib*), live (*épith*); **né ~** born alive; **il est encore ~** he's still alive *ou* living; **il n'en sortira pas ~** he won't come out of it alive; **expériences sur des animaux ~s** experiments on live *ou* living animals, live animal experiments; **c'est un cadavre/squelette ~** he's a living corpse/skeleton **b** (= *plein de vie*) [*regard, visage, enfant*] lively; [*ville, quartier, rue*] lively, full of life (*attrib*); [*portrait*] lifelike, true to life (*attrib*); [*dialogue, récit, film*] lively; (*fig*) [*personnage*] lifelike **c** (= *doué de vie*) [*matière, organisme*] living → **être d** (= *constitué par des êtres vivants*) [*machine, témoignage, preuve*] living; **c'est le portrait ~ de sa mère** he's the (living) image of his mother → **tableau e** (= *en usage*) [*expression, croyance, influence*] living; **une expression encore très ~e** a phrase

which is still very much alive → **langue f** (*Rel*) **le pain ~** the bread of life; **le Dieu ~** the living God

2 NM **a** (= *personne, Rel*) **les ~s** the living; **les ~s et les morts** (*gén*) the living and the dead; (*Bible*) the quick and the dead → **bon¹ b** (= *vie*) **de son ~** in his (*ou* her) lifetime, while he (*ou* she) was alive

vivarium [vivaʀjɔm] NM vivarium

vivats [viva] NM PL cheers; **il quitta la scène sous les ~** he left the stage to the cheers of the crowd

vive² [viv] EXCL **~ le roi/la France/l'amour!** long live the king/France/love!; **~ les vacances!** three cheers for *ou* hurrah for the holidays!

vive³ [viv] NF (= *poisson*) weever

vive-eau (*pl* **vives-eaux**) [vivo, vivzo] NF (**marée de**) **~** spring tide; **les vives-eaux** the spring tides

vivement [vivmɑ̃] ADV **a** (= *avec brusquerie*) sharply, brusquely **b** (= *beaucoup*) [*regretter*] deeply, greatly; [*désirer*] keenly, greatly; [*affecter, ressentir, intéresser*] deeply, keenly; **s'intéresser ~ à** to take a keen *ou* deep interest in, be keenly *ou* deeply interested in **c** (= *avec éclat*) [*colorer*] brilliantly, vividly; [*briller*] brightly, brilliantly **d** (*littér* = *rapidement*) [*agir, se mouvoir*] in a lively manner **e** (*marque un souhait*) **~ les vacances!** I can't wait for the holidays! (*Brit*) *ou* for vacation! (*US*), roll on the holidays!* (*Brit*); **~ que ce soit fini!** I'll be glad when it's all over!, roll on the end!* (*Brit*); **~ ce soir qu'on se couche!*** I can't wait until bedtime!, roll on bedtime!* (*Brit*)

viveur† [vivœʀ] NM pleasure seeker

vivier [vivje] NM (= *étang*) fishpond; (= *réservoir*) fish-tank; (*fig*) breeding ground

vivifiant, e [vivifjɑ̃, jɑ̃t] ADJ [*air, brise, promenade*] invigorating, bracing; [*ambiance, climat*] invigorating → **grâce**

vivifier [vivifje] ► conjug 7 ◀ VT **a** [+ *personne*] to invigorate, enliven; [+ *sang, plante*] to invigorate; (*fig littér*) [+ *âme*] to vitalize, quicken (*littér*); [+ *race*] to vitalize, give life to **b** (*emploi absolu*: *Rel, littér*) **l'esprit vivifie** the spirit gives life

vivipare [vivipaʀ] **1** ADJ viviparous **2** NM viviparous animal; **~s** vivipara

viviparité [vivipaʀite] NF viviparity

vivisection [visviseksjɔ̃] NF vivisection

vivoir [vivwaʀ] NM (*Can*) living room

vivoter [vivɔte] ► conjug 1 ◀ VI [*personne*] to get by (somehow), live from hand to mouth; [*entreprise*] to struggle along

vivre¹ [vivʀ] ► conjug 46 ◀ **1** VI **a** (= *être vivant*) to live, be alive; **il n'a vécu que quelques jours** he only lived a few days; **je ne savais pas qu'il vivait encore** I didn't know he was still alive *ou* living; **quand l'ambulance est arrivée, il vivait encore** he was still alive when the ambulance arrived; **quand elle arriva, il avait cessé de ~** he was dead when she arrived; **~ vieux** to live to a ripe old age, live to a great age; **il vivra centenaire** he'll live to be a hundred; **le peu de temps qu'il lui reste à ~** the little time he has left (to live); **le colonialisme a vécu** colonialism is a thing of the past, colonialism has had its day; **ce manteau a vécu*** this coat is finished *ou* has had its day; **il fait bon ~** it's good to be alive, it's a good life; (*Mil*) **qui vive?** who goes there? ■ (*PROV*) **qui vivra verra** what will be will be (*PROV*) → **âme, qui-vive b** (= *habiter*) to live; **~ à Londres/en France** to live in London/in France; **~ avec qn** to live with sb; **ils vivent ensemble/comme mari et femme** they live together/as husband and wife; **~ dans le passé/dans ses livres/dans la crainte** to live in the past/in one's books/in fear **c** (= *se comporter*) to live; **~ en paix (avec soi-même)** to be at peace (with oneself); **~ dangereusement** to live dangerously; **se**

laisser ~ to live for the day, take life *ou* each day as it comes; **laissez-les ~ !** (= *ne les tracassez pas*) let them be!; (*slogan anti-avortement*) let them live!; **être facile/difficile à ~** to be easy/difficult to live with *ou* to get on with; **ces gens-là savent ~** [*épicuriens*] those people (really) know how to live; [*personnes bien élevées*] those people know how to behave; **il faut ~ avec son temps** *ou* **son époque** you've got to move with the times → **apprendre**

[d] (= *exister*) to live; **on vit bien en France** life is good in France; **c'est un homme qui a beaucoup vécu** he's a man who has seen a lot of life; (*fig*) **elle ne vit plus depuis que son fils est pilote** she's been living on her nerves since her son became a pilot; **il ne vit que pour sa famille** he lives only for his family → **art, joie**

[e] (= *subsister*) to live (**de** on); **~ de laitages/de son traitement/de rentes** to live on dairy produce/one's salary/a private income; (*Bible*) **l'homme ne vit pas seulement de pain** man shall not live by bread alone; **~ au jour le jour** to live from day to day *ou* from hand to mouth; **~ largement** *ou* **bien** to live well; **avoir (juste) de quoi ~** to have (just) enough to live on; **ils vivent très bien avec son salaire** they live very comfortably *ou* get along very well on his salary; **il vit de sa peinture/musique** he earns his living by painting/with his music; **travailler/écrire pour ~** to work/write for a living; **il faut bien ~ !** a person has to live!, you have to live!; **faire ~ qn** [*personne*] to keep sb, support sb; **je n'aime pas ce métier mais il me fait ~** I don't like this job but it pays the bills* *ou* it's a living; **seul son amour pour ses enfants le fait ~** only his love for his children keeps him going; **~ de l'air du temps** to live on air; **~ d'amour et d'eau fraîche** to live on love alone; **~ sur sa réputation** to get by on the strength of one's reputation → **crochet**

[f] (*fig*) [*idée, rue, paysage*] to be alive; **un portrait qui vit** a lively *ou* lifelike portrait, a portrait which seems alive; **sa gloire vivra longtemps** his glory will live on *ou* will endure

[2] VT [a] (= *passer*) to live, spend; **~ des jours heureux/des heures joyeuses** to live through *ou* spend happy days/hours; **il vivait un beau roman d'amour** his life was a love story come true; **la vie ne vaut pas la peine d'être vécue** life isn't worth living

[b] (= *être mêlé à*) [+ *événement, guerre*] to live through; **nous vivons des temps troublés** we are living in *ou* through troubled times; **le pays vit une période de crise** the country is going through a period of crisis

[c] (= *éprouver intensément*) **~ sa vie** to live one's own life, live (one's life) as one pleases *ou* sees fit; **~ sa foi/son art** to live out one's faith/one's art; **~ l'instant/le présent** to live for the moment/the present; **~ son époque intensément** to be intensely involved in the period one lives in; **il a mal vécu son divorce/son adolescence/la mort de sa mère** he had a hard time of it when he got divorced/as an adolescent/when his mother died

vivre² [vivʀ] [1] NM (*littér*) **le ~ et le couvert** bed and board; **le ~ et le logement** board and lodging, room and board [2] **vivres** NMPL supplies, provisions → **couper**

vivrier, -ière [vivʀije, ijɛʀ] ADJ food-producing (*épith*)

vizir [viziʀ] NM vizier; **le grand ~** the Grand Vizier; (*hum*) **il veut être ~ à la place du ~** he wants to be top dog*

v'là [vla] PRÉP = **voilà**

vlan, v'lan [vlɑ̃] EXCL wham!, bang!; **et ~ !** **dans la figure** smack *ou* slap-bang in the face; **et ~ ! il est parti en claquant la porte** wham! *ou* bang! he slammed the door and left

VO [veo] NF (ABRÉV = **version originale**) film en VO film in the original version *ou* language;

en VO sous-titrée in the original version with subtitles

vocable [vɔkabl] NM [a] (= *mot*) term [b] (*Rel*) **église sous le ~ de saint Pierre** church dedicated to St Peter

vocabulaire [vɔkabylɛʀ] NM [a] [*dictionnaire*] vocabulary, word list; **~ français-anglais** French-English vocabulary; **~ de la photographie** dictionary *ou* lexicon of photographic terms [b] [*individu, groupe*] (= *terminologie*) vocabulary; **~ technique/médical** technical/medical vocabulary; **~ actif/passif** active/passive vocabulary; **enrichir son ~** to enrich one's vocabulary; **j'ai rayé ce mot de mon ~** that word is no longer part of my vocabulary; **quel ~ !** what language!; **surveille ton ~ !** watch *ou* mind your language!

vocal, e (*mpl* **-aux**) [vɔkal, o] ADJ [*organe, musique*] vocal; **synthèse ~e** voice *ou* speech synthesis → **corde, serveur**

vocalement [vɔkalmɑ̃] ADV vocally

vocalique [vɔkalik] ADJ vowel (*épith*), vocalic; **système ~** vowel system

vocalisation [vɔkalizasjɔ̃] NF (*Ling*) vocalization; (*Mus*) singing exercise

vocalise [vɔkaliz] NF singing exercise; **faire des ~s** to practise (one's) singing exercises

vocaliser [vɔkalize] ▸conjug 1◂ [1] VT (*Ling*) to vocalize [2] VI (*Mus*) to practise (one's) singing exercises [3] **se vocaliser** VPR (*Ling*) to become vocalized

vocalisme [vɔkalism] NM (*Ling*) (= *théorie*) vocalism; (= *système vocalique*) vowel system; [*mot*] vowel pattern

vocatif [vɔkatif] NM vocative (case)

vocation [vɔkasjɔ̃] NF [a] (*pour un métier une activité, Rel*) vocation, calling; **avoir/ne pas avoir la ~** to have/lack a vocation; **avoir la ~ de l'enseignement/du théâtre** to be cut out to be a teacher *ou* for teaching/for acting *ou* the theatre; **~ artistique** artistic calling; **~ contrariée** frustrated vocation; **rater sa ~** to miss one's vocation; (*hum*) **il a la ~** it's a real vocation for him [b] (= *destin*) vocation, calling; **la ~ maternelle de la femme** woman's maternal vocation *ou* calling; **la ~ industrielle du Japon** the industrial calling of Japan [c] (*Admin*) **avoir ~ à** *ou* **pour** to have authority to

vociférateur, -trice [vɔsiferatœʀ, tʀis] [1] ADJ vociferous [2] NM,F vociferator

vocifération [vɔsiferasjɔ̃] NF cry of rage, vociferation (*frm*); **pousser des ~s** to utter cries of rage

vociférer [vɔsifeʀe] ▸conjug 6◂ [1] VI to utter cries of rage, vociferate; **~ contre qn** to shout angrily at sb, scream at sb [2] VT [+ *insulte, ordre*] to shout (out), scream; **~ des injures** to hurl abuse, shout (out) *ou* scream insults

vocodeur [vɔkɔdœʀ] NM vocoder

vodka [vɔdka] NF vodka

▼ **vœu** (*pl* **vœux**) [vø] NM [a] (= *promesse*) vow; **faire (le) ~ de faire** to vow to do, make a vow to do; **~x de religion** religious vows; **~x de célibat** vows of celibacy; (*Rel*) **prononcer ses ~x** to take one's vows; **~ de chasteté** vow of chastity; **faire ~ de pauvreté** to take a vow of poverty

[b] (= *souhait*) wish; **faire un ~** to make a wish; **nous formons des ~x pour votre santé** we send our good wishes for your recovery *ou* health; **tous nos ~x de prompt rétablissement** our best wishes for a speedy recovery; **l'assemblée a émis le ~ que ...** the assembly expressed the wish *ou* its desire that ...; **appeler qch de ses ~x** to hope and pray for sth; **je fais le ~ qu'il me pardonne** I pray (that) he may forgive me; **tous nos ~x (de bonheur)** all good wishes *ou* every good wish for your happiness; **tous nos ~x vous accompagnent** our very best wishes go with you; **~ pieux** pious hope

[c] (*au jour de l'an*) **les ~x télévisés du président de la République** the President of the

Republic's televised New Year speech *ou* address; **il a reçu les ~x du corps diplomatique** he received New Year's greetings from the diplomatic corps; **tous nos (meilleurs *ou* bons) ~x de bonne et heureuse année ◊ meilleurs ~x** best wishes for the New Year, Happy New Year; (*sur une carte*) "Season's Greetings"

vogue [vɔg] NF [a] (= *popularité*) fashion, vogue; **la ~ de l'informatique** the vogue for computers; **connaître une ~ extraordinaire** to be extremely fashionable *ou* popular; **être en ~** to be in fashion *ou* vogue, be fashionable; **c'est la grande ~ maintenant** it's all the rage now; **ce n'est plus en ~** it's no longer fashionable, it's on the way out [b] (*dial = foire*) fair

voguer [vɔge] ▸conjug 1◂ VI (*littér*) [*embarcation, vaisseau spatial*] to sail; (*fig*) [*pensées*] to drift, wander; **nous voguions vers l'Amérique** we were sailing towards America; **l'embarcation voguait au fil de l'eau** the boat was drifting *ou* floating along on *ou* with the current; (*hum*) **vogue la galère !** come what may!

voici [vwasi] PRÉP [a] (*pour désigner: opposé à voilà*) here is, here are, this is, these are; **~ mon bureau et voilà le vôtre** here's *ou* this is my office and there's *ou* that's yours; **~ mon frère et voilà sa femme** this is *ou* here is my brother and there's *ou* that's his wife; **~ mes parents** here are *ou* these are my parents

[b] (*pour désigner: même valeur que voilà*) here is, here are, this is, these are; **~ mon frère** this is my brother; **~ le livre que vous cherchiez** here's the book you were looking for; **l'homme/la maison que ~** this (*particular*) man/house; **M. Dupont, que ~** Mr Dupont here; **il m'a raconté l'histoire que ~** he told me the following story

[c] (*pour annoncer, introduire*) here is, here are, this is, these are; **~ le printemps/la pluie** here comes spring/the rain; **~ la fin de l'hiver** the end of winter is here; **me/nous/le** *etc* **~** here I am/we are/he is *etc*; **les ~ prêts à partir** they're ready to leave, that's them ready to leave*; **nous ~ arrivés** here we are, we've arrived; **le ~ qui se plaint encore** there he goes, complaining again, that's him complaining again*; **me ~ à me ronger les sangs pendant que lui ...** (*au présent*) here am I *ou* here's me* in a terrible state while he ...; (*au passé*) there was I *ou* there was me* in a terrible state while he ...; **vous voulez des preuves, en ~** you want proof, well here you are then; **nous y ~** here we are; (*question délicate*) now we're getting there; **~ qui va vous surprendre** here's something that'll surprise you; **~ qu'il se met à pleuvoir maintenant** and now it's starting to rain; **~ ce que je compte faire** this is what I'm hoping to do; **ce qu'il m'a dit/ce dont il s'agit** this is what he told me/what it's all about; **~ comment il faut faire** this is the way to do it, this is how it's done; **~ pourquoi je l'ai fait** this *ou* that was why I did it; **~ pourquoi je l'avais supprimé** that was why I'd eliminated it; **~ que tombe la nuit** night is falling, it's getting dark

[d] (*il y a*) **~ 5 ans que je ne l'ai pas vu** it's 5 years (now) since I last saw him, I haven't seen him for the past 5 years; **il est parti ~ une heure** he left an hour ago, it's an hour since he left; **~ bientôt 20 ans que nous sommes mariés** it'll soon be 20 years since we got married, we'll have been married 20 years soon

voie [vwa] [1] NF [a] (= *chemin*) way; (*Admin* = *route, rue*) road; (= *itinéraire*) route; (*Hist*) **~ romaine/sacrée** Roman/sacred way; **par la ~ des airs** *ou* **aérienne** by air; **emprunter la ~ maritime** to go by sea; **expédier qch par ~ de mer** *ou* **maritime** to send sth by sea *ou* by ship, ship sth; **voyager par ~ de terre** *ou* **terrestre** to travel overland; **~s de communication** communication routes; **~ sans issue** no through road, cul-de-sac; **~ privée** private road; **~ à**

double sens/à sens unique two-way/one-way road

b (= *partie d'une route*) lane; « travaux — passage à ~ unique » "roadworks — single-lane traffic"; **route à ~ unique** single-lane *ou* single-track road; **route à 3/4 ~s** 3-/4-lane road; **~ réservée aux autobus/aux cyclistes** bus/cycle lane; **~ à contresens** contraflow lane; **une ~ de circulation a été mise en sens inverse sur ...** there is a contraflow system in operation on ...

c (*Rail*) track, (railway) line; **ligne à ~ unique/à 2 ~s** single-/double-track line; **ligne à ~ étroite** narrow-gauge line; **on répare les ~s** the line *ou* track is under repair; **~ montante/descendante** up/down line; **le train est annoncé sur la ~ 2** the train will arrive at platform 2

d (*Anat*) **~s digestives/respiratoires/urinaires** digestive/respiratory/urinary tract; **par ~ buccale** *ou* **orale** orally; **administrer qch par ~ nasale/rectale** to administer sth through the nose/the rectum; **évacuer qch par les ~s naturelles** to get rid of sth by the natural routes *ou* naturally; **les usagers de drogues par ~ intraveineuse** intravenous drug users; **être contaminé par ~ sexuelle** to be infected through sexual intercourse

e (*fig*) way; **la ~ du bien/mal** the path of good/evil; **la ~ de l'honneur** the honourable course; **rester dans la ~ du devoir** to keep to the line *ou* path of duty; **entrer dans la ~ des aveux** to make a confession; **ouvrir/tracer/montrer la ~** to open up/mark out/show the way; **préparer la ~ à qn/qch** to prepare *ou* pave the way for sb/sth; **continuez sur cette ~** continue in this way; **il est sur la bonne ~** he's on the right track; **l'affaire est en bonne ~** the matter is shaping *ou* going well; **mettre qn sur la ~** to put sb on the right track; **trouver sa ~** to find one's way (in life); **la ~ est toute tracée** (*pour une personne*) his career is mapped out (for him); (*pour un projet*) the way ahead is clear; **la ~ est libre** the way is clear *ou* open

f (= *filière, moyen, option*) **par des ~s détournées** by devious *ou* roundabout means; **par la ~ hiérarchique/diplomatique** through official/diplomatic channels; **faire qch par (la) ~ légale** *ou* **par les ~s légales** to follow the proper procedures for doing sth; **par ~ de conséquence** in consequence, as a result; **annoncer qch par ~ de presse** to announce sth in the press; **publicité par ~ d'affiche** poster advertising; **consulter le peuple par ~ de référendum** to consult the people in a *ou* by referendum; **recruter des cadres par ~ de concours/d'annonces** to recruit executives in open competition/through advertisements; **proposer une troisième ~** to suggest a third option

g **en ~ de** : **en ~ de réorganisation** in the process of reorganization, undergoing reorganization; **en ~ d'exécution** in (the) process of being carried out, being carried out; **en ~ de guérison** getting better, regaining one's health, on the road to recovery; **en ~ de cicatrisation** (well) on the way to healing over; **en ~ d'achèvement** (well) on the way to completion, nearing completion; **elle est en ~ de réussir** she's on the way *ou* road to success; **il est en ~ de perdre sa situation** he's on the way to losing his job, he's heading for dismissal

2 COMP ► **voie d'accès** access road ► **voie Appienne** Appian Way ► **voie de dégagement urbain** urban relief road ► **les voies de Dieu** the ways of God *ou* Providence; **les ~s de Dieu sont impénétrables** *ou* **insondables** God moves in mysterious ways ► **voie d'eau** leak ► **voie express** express way, motorway (*Brit*), freeway (*US*) ► **voie de fait** (*Jur*) assault (and battery) (*NonC*); **~ de fait simple** common assault; **se livrer à des ~s de fait sur qn** to assault sb,

commit an assault on sb ► **voie ferrée** (*Rail*) railway (*Brit*) *ou* railroad (*US*) line ► **voie de garage** (*Rail*) siding; (*fig*) **mettre sur une ~ de garage** [+ *affaire*] to shelve; [+ *personne*] to shunt to one side; (*Téléc*) **on m'a mis sur une ~ de garage** they put me on hold ► **la voie lactée** the Milky Way ► **voies navigables** waterways ► **voie de passage** major road ► **les voies de la Providence** = **les voies de Dieu** ► **la voie publique** (*Admin*) the public highway ► **voie de raccordement** slip road ► **voie rapide** = **voie express** ► **voie royale** (*fig*) **c'est la ~ royale vers** *ou* **pour** (*gén*) it's the pathway to; [+ *carrière, pouvoir*] it's the fast track to ► **les voies du Seigneur** = **les voies de Dieu**

voilà [vwala] **1** PRÉP **a** (*pour désigner : opposé à voici*) there is, there are, that is, those are; (*même sens que voici*) here is, here are, this is, these are; **voici mon bureau et ~ le vôtre** here's *ou* this is my office and that's yours; **voici mon frère et ~ sa femme** this is *ou* here's my brother and that's *ou* there's his wife; **le ~ mon frère** this is *ou* here is my brother; **le livre que vous cherchiez** (*je le tiens*) here's the book you were looking for; (*il est là-bas*) there's the book you were looking for; **l'homme/la maison que ~** that man/house (there); **M. Dupont que ~** Mr Dupont there; **il m'a raconté l'histoire que ~** he told me the following story

b (*pour annoncer, introduire*) there is, there are, that is, those are; **~ le printemps/la pluie** here comes spring/the rain; **~ la fin de l'hiver** the end of winter is here; **le ~, c'est lui** there he is, that's him; **le ~ prêt à partir** he's ready to leave, that's him ready to leave*; **le ~ qui se plaint encore** there he goes, complaining again, that's him complaining again*; **me ~ à me ronger les sangs pendant que lui ...** (*au présent*) there am I *ou* there's me* in a terrible state while he ...; (*au passé*) there was I *ou* there was me* in a terrible state while he ...; **~ ce que je compte faire** this is what I'm hoping to do; **~ ce qu'il m'a dit/ce dont il s'agit** (*je viens de le dire*) that's what he told me/what it's all about; (*je vais le dire*) this is what he told me/what it's all about; **~ comment il faut faire** that's how it's done; **~ pourquoi je l'ai fait** that's why I did it; **~ que tombe la nuit** night is falling, it's getting dark; **~ qu'il se met à pleuvoir maintenant** now it's starting to rain, here comes the rain now; **~ où je veux en venir** that's what I'm getting at, that's my point; **nous y ~** (*lieu*) here we are; (*question délicate*) now we're getting there

c (*pour résumer*) ... **et ~ pourquoi je n'ai pas pu le faire** ... and that's why *ou* that's the reason I couldn't do it; **~ ce qui fait que c'est impossible** that's what makes it impossible; **~ qui est louche** that's a bit odd *ou* suspicious; **~ qui s'appelle parler** that's what I call talking; **~ ce que c'est (que) de ne pas obéir** that's what comes of not doing as you're told, that's what happens when you don't do as you're told

d (*il y a*) **~ une heure que je l'attends** I've been waiting for him for an hour now, that's a whole hour I've been waiting for him now; **~ 5 ans que je ne l'ai pas vu** it's 5 years since I last saw him, I haven't seen him for the past 5 years; **il est parti ~ une heure** he left an hour ago, it's an hour since he left; **~ bientôt 20 ans que nous sommes mariés** it'll soon be 20 years since we got married, we'll have been married 20 years soon

e (*loc*) **~ une histoire/blague !** what a story/joke!, that's some story/joke!; **en ~ un imbécile !** there's an idiot for you!, what a fool!; **en ~ assez !** that's enough!, that'll do!; **veux-tu de l'argent ? — en ~** do you want some money? — here's some *ou* here you are; **vous voulez des preuves, en ~** you want proof, well here you are then; **~ le hic*** that's

the snag *ou* catch, there's *ou* that's the hitch; **~ tout** that's all; **et ~ tout** and that's all there is to it *ou* all there is to say, and that's the top and bottom of it* (*Brit*); **~ bien les Français !** how like the French!, isn't that just like the French!, that's the French all over!*; **(et) ne ~-t-il pas qu'il s'avise de se déshabiller** lo and behold, he suddenly decides to get undressed!, I'm blest if he doesn't suddenly decide to get undressed!; **nous ~ frais !** now we're in a mess! *ou* a nice pickle!*, that's a fine mess *ou* pickle we're in!* → **vouloir**

2 EXCL **~ ! j'arrive !** here I come!, there — I'm coming!; **ah ! ~ ! je comprends !** oh, (so) that's it, I understand!, oh, I see!; **~ autre chose !** (*incident*) that's all I need(ed)!; (*impertinence*) what a cheek!, the cheek of it!; **je n'ai pas pu le faire, et ~ !** I couldn't do it and that's all there is to it! *ou* so there!*; **~, je m'appelle M. Dupont et je suis votre nouvel instituteur** right (then), my name is Mr Dupont and I'm your new teacher; **~, tu l'as cassé !** there (you are), you've broken it!

voilage [vwalaʒ] NM (= *rideau*) net curtain; (= *tissu*) net (*NonC*), netting (*NonC*), veiling (*NonC*); [*chapeau, vêtement*] gauze (*NonC*), veiling (*NonC*)

voile¹ [vwal] NF **a** [*bateau*] sail; **~ carrée/latine** square/lateen sail; **les hautes ~s** the light *ou* upper sails, the (flying) kites; **les basses ~s** the lower sails; **navire sous ~s** ship under sail; **faire ~ vers** to sail towards; **mettre à la ~** to set sail, make way under sail; **mettre toutes ~s dehors** to raise *ou* set full sail; **arriver toutes ~s dehors** (*lit*) to draw near under *ou* in full sail; (*fig*) to make a grand entrance; (*fig*) **mettre les ~s*** to clear off*, scram*; [*bisexuel*] **marcher à ~ et à vapeur*** to be AC/DC* *ou* bi*, swing both ways* → **planche, vent, vol¹**

b (*littér* = *embarcation*) sail *inv* (*littér*), vessel **c** (= *navigation, sport*) sailing, yachting; **faire de la ~** to sail, go sailing *ou* yachting; **demain on va faire de la ~** we're going sailing *ou* yachting tomorrow; **faire le tour du monde à la ~** to sail round the world

voile² [vwal] NM **a** (= *coiffure, vêtement*) veil; **~ de deuil** (mourning) veil; **~ islamique** Islamic veil; **~ de mariée** bridal veil; **porter le ~** to wear the veil; (*Rel*) **prendre le ~** to take the veil; **sa prise de ~ a eu lieu hier** she took the veil yesterday

b [*statue, plaque commémorative*] veil **c** (= *tissu*) net (*NonC*), netting (*NonC*); **~ de coton/de tergal**® cotton/Terylene® net *ou* netting **d** (*fig* = *qui cache*) veil; **le ~ de l'oubli** the veil of oblivion; **sous le ~ de la franchise** under the veil *ou* a pretence of candour; **le ~ de mystère qui entoure cet assassinat** the veil of mystery that surrounds this murder; **jeter/tirer un ~ sur qch** to cast/draw a veil over sth; **lever le ~ sur** to unveil, lift the veil from; **soulever un coin du ~** to lift a corner of the veil **e** (*fig* = *qui rend flou*) (*gén*) veil; (*sur un liquide*) cloud; **~ de brume** veil of mist, veiling mist; **avoir un ~ devant les yeux** to have a film before one's eyes **f** (*Photo*) fog (*NonC*); **un ~ sur la photo** a shadow on the photo **g** (*Méd*) **~ au poumon** shadow on the lung; **le ~ noir/gris/rouge des aviateurs** blackout/greyout/redout **h** (*Anat*) **~ du palais** soft palate, velum **i** (*Bot*) [*champignon*] veil **j** (= *enregistrement du son*) warp

voilé¹, e¹ [vwale] (*ptp de* **voiler¹**) ADJ **a** [*femme, statue*] veiled **b** [*termes, allusion, sens*] veiled; **accusation à peine ~e** thinly disguised accusation; **il fit une allusion peu ~e à ...** he made a thinly veiled reference to ... **c** (= *flou*) [*lumière, ciel, soleil*] hazy; [*éclat*] dimmed; [*regard*] misty; [*contour*] hazy, misty; [*photo*] fogged; **les yeux ~s de larmes** his eyes misty *ou* misted (over) *ou* blurred with tears; **sa voix était un peu ~e** his voice was slightly husky

voilé², e² [vwale] (*ptp de* **voiler²**) ADJ (= *tordu*) [*roue*] buckled; [*planche*] warped

voilement [vwalmã] NM (*Tech*) [*roue*] buckle; [*planche*] warp

voiler¹ [vwale] ▶ conjug 1 ◀ **1** VT (*lit, fig, littér* = *cacher*) to veil; **les larmes voilaient ses yeux** tears dimmed his eyes, his eyes were misty with tears; **un brouillard voilait les sommets** the peaks were shrouded in fog; **la plaine était voilée de brume** the plain was shrouded *ou* veiled in mist; **je préfère lui ~ la vérité** I prefer to shield him from the truth *ou* to conceal the truth from him **2** **se voiler** VPR **a** (= *porter un voile*) **se ~ le visage** [*personne*] to wear a veil; [*musulmane*] to wear the veil; (*fig*) **se ~ la face** to close one's eyes (**devant** to) **b** (= *devenir flou*) [*horizon, soleil*] to mist over; [*ciel*] to grow hazy *ou* misty; [*regard, yeux*] to mist over, become glazed; [*voix*] to become husky

voiler² [vwale] ▶ conjug 1 ◀ **1** **se voiler** VPR [*roue*] to buckle; [*planche*] to warp **2** VT [+ *roue*] to buckle; [+ *planche*] to warp

voilerie [vwalʀi] NF sail-loft

voilette [vwalɛt] NF (hat) veil

voilier [vwalje] NM **a** (= *navire à voiles*) sailing ship; (*de plaisance*) sailing boat, sailboat (*US*); yacht; **grand ~** tall ship **b** (= *fabricant de voiles*) sailmaker; **maître(-)voilier** master sailmaker **c** (= *oiseau*) long-flight bird

voilure¹ [vwalyʀ] NF **a** [*bateau*] sails; **réduire la ~** to shorten sail; **une ~ de 1 000 m²** 1,000 m² of sail **b** [*planeur*] aerofoils; **~ tournante** rotary wing **c** [*parachute*] canopy

voilure² [vwalyʀ] NF = **voilement**

▼**voir** [vwaʀ]

▶ conjug 30 ◀

1 VERBE TRANSITIF	**4** VERBE TRANSITIF
2 VERBE INTRANSITIF	INDIR
3 LOC EXCLAMATIVE	**5** VERBE PRONOMINAL

1 VERBE TRANSITIF

a = perçevoir par la vue to see; **je vois deux arbres** I (can) see two trees; **est-ce que tu le vois?** can you see it?; **je l'ai vu de mes (propres) yeux** ◊ **je l'ai vu, de mes yeux vu** I saw it with my own eyes; **je l'ai vu comme je vous vois** I saw him as plainly as I see you now; **aller ~ un film/une exposition** to go to (see) a film/an exhibition; **c'est un film à ~** it's a film worth seeing; **à le ~ si joyeux/triste** seeing him look so happy/sad; **à le ~, on ne lui donnerait pas 90 ans** to look at him, you wouldn't think he was 90; **vous m'en voyez ravi/navré** I'm delighted/terribly sorry about that; **tu vois ce que je vois?** do you see what I see?; **~ Naples et mourir** see Naples and die; **j'ai vu la mort de près** I've looked *ou* stared death in the face → **chandelle, falloir, jour, pays**

◆ **voir** + *infinitif*: **to see; je les ai vus sauter** we saw them jump; **on a vu le voleur entrer** the thief was seen going in; **j'ai vu bâtir ces maisons** I saw these houses being built; **je voudrais la ~ travailler plus** I'd like to see her work more

b = être témoin de as-tu jamais vu pareille impolitesse? have you ever seen *ou* did you ever see such rudeness?; **il a vu deux guerres** he has lived through *ou* seen two wars; **cette maison a vu bien des drames** this house has known *ou* seen many a drama; **à ~ son train de vie, elle doit être très riche** if her lifestyle is anything to go by, she must be very rich, looking *ou* to look at her lifestyle, you'd think she was very rich; **je voudrais t'y ~!** I'd like to see you try!; **tu aurais dû refuser! — j'aurais voulu t'y ~!** I'd like to have seen you do! — I'd like to have seen what you'd have done! → **naître**

◆ **voir** + *infinitif* to see; **ce journal a vu son tirage augmenter** this newspaper has seen an increase in its circulation; **un pays qui voit renaître le fascisme** a country which is witnessing *ou* seeing the rebirth of fascism

c = découvrir, constater to see; **va ~ s'il y a quelqu'un** go and see if there's anybody there; **des meubles comme on en voit partout** ordinary furniture; **vous verrez que ce n'est pas leur faute** you'll see that they're not to blame; **il ne fera plus cette erreur — c'est à ~** he won't make the same mistake again — we'll see; **nous allons bien ~!** we'll soon find out!; **(attendons,) on verra bien** we'll see, let's wait and see; **voyez si elle accepte** see if she'll agree; **voyez comme les prix ont augmenté** see how prices have risen; **c'est ce que nous verrons!** we'll see about that!; **histoire de ~** ◊ **pour ~** just to see; (*menace*) **essaie un peu, pour ~!** just you try!; **il n'a pas de goût, il n'y a qu'à ~ comment il s'habille** he's got no taste, just look at the way he dresses; **c'est tout vu!*** that's for sure!, it's a dead cert!*; (*euph*) **si tu me trompes, moi je vais ~ ailleurs*** if you're ever unfaithful to me, I'll go and find somebody else; **va ~ ailleurs si j'y suis!*** get lost!* → **falloir**

d = imaginer, se représenter to see, imagine; **tu me vois aller lui dire ça/rester sans travailler?** can you see *ou* imagine me telling him that?/not working?; **je ne le vois pas** *ou* **je le vois mal habiter la banlieue** I (somehow) can't see *ou* imagine him living in the suburbs; **je le verrais bien dans ce rôle** I could just see him in this role; **nous ne voyons pas qu'il ait de quoi s'inquiéter** we can't see that he has any reason for worrying; **voyez-vous une solution?** can you see a solution?; **je ne vois pas le problème** I don't see what the problem is; **comment voyez-vous l'avenir?** how do you see *ou* envisage the future?; **je ne vois pas comment ils auraient pu gagner** I can't *ou* don't see how they could have won; **tu vois ça d'ici** you can just imagine it; **il va encore protester, je vois ça d'ici** he's going to start protesting again, I can see it coming; **je vois*** ma sœur, elle a trois enfants et ... take my sister, she has three children and ... → **inconvénient, noir, rose**

e = examiner, étudier [+ *problème, dossier*] to look at; [+ *leçon*] to look *ou* go over; [+ *circulaire*] to see, read; **il a encore trois malades à ~** he still has three patients to see; **il faudra la question de plus près** we'll have to look at *ou* into the question more closely, the question requires closer examination; **il faut** *ou* **il faudra ~** we'll have to see; **je verrai (ce que je dois faire)** I'll have to see, I'll think about it; **voyons un peu comment tu fais** let's see how you do it

f = juger, concevoir to see; **c'est à vous de ~ s'il est compétent** it's up to you to see *ou* to decide whether he is competent; **si elle ne revient pas travailler lundi, elle va se faire mal ~** if she doesn't come back to work on Monday, it won't look too good; **il a fait ça pour se faire bien ~ de ses collègues/des autorités** he did that to impress his colleagues/to make himself popular with the authorities; **façon** *ou* **manière de ~** view of things, outlook; **nous n'avons pas la même façon de ~ les choses** we see things differently; **voici comment on peut ~ les choses** you can look at things this way; **nous ne voyons pas le problème de la même façon** we don't see *ou* view the problem in the same way, we don't take the same view of the problem; **ne ~ aucun mal à ...** to see no harm in ...; **~ qn comme un ami** to look upon *ou* regard sb as a friend, consider sb a friend; **il ne voit que son intérêt** he only considers his own interest → **œil**

g = rencontrer [+ *médecin, avocat*] to see; **il voit le directeur ce soir** he's seeing the manager tonight; **le ministre doit ~ les délégués** the minister is to see *ou* meet the delegates; **on ne vous voit plus** we never see you these days,

you've become quite a stranger; **il la voit beaucoup** he sees a lot of her; **je l'ai assez vu*** I've had (quite) enough of him*; **aller ~** [+ *médecin, avocat*] to go and see; [+ *ami*] to go and see, call on, visit; **aller ~ qn à l'hôpital** to visit sb *ou* go and see sb in hospital; **passez me ~ quand vous serez à Paris** look me up *ou* call in and see me (*Brit*) when you're in Paris; **je suis passé le ~** I went to see him; **il vient nous ~ demain** he's coming to see us tomorrow

h = faire l'expérience de j'en ai vu d'autres! I've seen worse!; **il en a vu de dures** *ou* **de toutes les couleurs** *ou* **des vertes et des pas mûres*** he has been through the mill *ou* through some hard times, he has taken some hard knocks; **en faire ~ (de dures** *ou* **de toutes les couleurs) à qn** to give sb a hard time; **a-t-on jamais vu ça?** ◊ **on n'a jamais vu ça!** have you ever seen *ou* heard anything like it?; **on aura tout vu!** we've seen everything now!, that beats everything!; **vous n'avez encore rien vu!** you haven't seen anything yet!, you ain't seen nothing yet!* → **autre**

i = comprendre to see; **je ne vois pas ce que vous voulez dire** I don't see *ou* get *ou* understand what you mean, I don't understand your meaning; **elle ne voyait pas le côté drôle de l'aventure** she couldn't see *ou* appreciate the funny side of what had happened; **vous aurez du mal à lui faire ~ que ...** you'll find it difficult to make him see *ou* realize that ...; **je ne vois pas comment il a pu oublier** I don't see how he could forget; **tu vas le faire tout de suite, vu?*** you're going to do it straightaway, understood?

j * = supporter **elle ne peut pas le ~ (en peinture)** she can't stand (the sight of) him

k

◆ **faire voir** (= *montrer*) to show; **fais ~!** show me!, let me have a look!; **faites-moi ~ ce dessin** show me *ou* let me see the picture; **va te faire ~ (ailleurs)!*** get lost!*; **qu'il aille se faire ~ (chez les Grecs)!*** he can go to hell!*

l

◆ **voir venir** (= *attendre les événements*) to wait and see; **j'ai quelques économies, ça me permettra de ~ venir*** I've got some money put by, it should be enough to see me through*; (= *prévoir*) **on va perdre, ça je le vois venir (gros comme une maison*)** we're going to lose, I can see it coming (a mile off*); **je te vois venir* (avec tes gros sabots)** I can see what you're leading up to; (*iro*) **1 000 F pour ce vase? on t'a vu venir!*** 1,000 francs for that vase? they saw you coming!*

m

◆ **rien/quelque chose/pas grand-chose à voir avec** *ou* **dans**: **je n'ai rien à ~ dans cette affaire** this has nothing to do with me, none of this has anything to do with me; **cela n'a rien/a quelque chose à ~ avec ...** this has got nothing/something to do with ...; **son nouveau film? rien à ~ avec les précédents** his new film? it's nothing like his previous work; **le résultat n'a plus grand-chose à ~ avec le projet initial** the result bears scarcely any resemblance *ou* very little relation to the initial project

2 VERBE INTRANSITIF

a avec les yeux to see; **~ mal** to have trouble seeing; **on voit mal ici** it's difficult to see in here; **on n'y voit plus** you can't see a thing; **~ trouble** to have blurred vision; **il a vu grand** he planned things on a grand *ou* big scale, he thought big → **clair, loin, rouge**

b *: intensif **dites ~, vous connaissez la nouvelle?** tell me, have you heard the news?; **dis-moi ~ ...** tell me ...; **essaie ~!** just try it and see!, just you try it!; **regarde ~ ce qu'il a fait!** just look what he's done!

3 **voyons** LOC EXCL rappel à l'ordre **un peu de charité, voyons!** come (on) now, let's be chari-

▶ GRAMMAIRE ACTIVE: **voir** 53.2

table !; **mais voyons, il n'a jamais dit ça !** oh come on, he never said that!; **voyons ~ !** let's see now !

④ **voir à** VT INDIR [littér = veiller à] to make sure that, see (to it) that; **nous verrons à vous contenter** we shall do our best *ou* our utmost to please you; **il faudra ~ à ce qu'il obéisse** we must see *ou* make sure that he obeys

⑤ **se voir** VERBE PRONOMINAL

[a] [soi-même] **se ~ dans une glace** to see oneself in a mirror; **il ne s'est pas vu mourir** death caught him unawares; **elle se voyait déjà célèbre** she pictured herself famous already; **je me vois mal habiter** *ou* **habitant là** I can't see myself living there somehow; **tu te vois faire trois heures de trajet par jour ?** can you see yourself commuting three hours every day?; **il la trouve moche — il ne s'est pas vu !** he thinks she's ugly — has he looked in the mirror lately?

[b] [mutuellement] to see each other; **ils se voient beaucoup** they see a lot of each other; **nous essaierons de nous ~ à Londres** we shall try to see each other *ou* to meet (up) in London; **ils ne peuvent pas se ~*** they can't stand the sight of each other*

[c] [= se trouver] **se ~ contraint de** to find o.s. forced to; **je me vois dans la triste obligation de ...** sadly, I find myself obliged to ...

[d] [= être visible, évident] [tache, couleur, sentiments] to show; **la tache ne se voit pas** the stain doesn't show; **il est très intelligent — ça se voit !** he's very clever — that's obvious! → **nez**

[e] [= se produire] **cela se voit tous les jours** it happens every day, it's an everyday occurrence; **ça ne se voit pas tous les jours** it's not something you see every day, it's quite a rare occurrence; **cela ne s'est jamais vu !** it's unheard of!; **une attitude qui ne se voit que trop fréquemment** an all-too-common attitude; **des attitudes/préjugés qui se voient encore chez ...** attitudes/prejudices which are still commonplace *ou* encountered in ...

[f] [fonction passive] **ils se sont vu interdire l'accès du musée** they were refused admission to the museum; **ces outils se sont vus relégués au grenier** these tools have been put away in the attic; **je me suis vu répondre que c'était trop tard** I was told that it was too late

voire [vwaʀ] ADV [a] (frm = et même) indeed, nay† (littér); **c'est révoltant, ~ même criminel** it's disgusting, indeed even criminal; **il faudrait attendre une semaine, ~ un mois** you would have to wait a week or (perhaps) even a month; **ce sera difficile, ~ impossible** it'll be difficult, if not impossible [b] († hum = j'en doute) indeed?† (hum)

voirie [vwaʀi] NF [a] (= enlèvement des ordures) refuse (Brit) *ou* garbage (US) collection; (= dépotoir) refuse (Brit) *ou* garbage (US) dump [b] (= entretien des routes) road *ou* highway maintenance; (= service administratif) roads *ou* highways department; (= voie publique) (public) highways; **travaux de ~** road works; **les ingénieurs de la ~** highway *ou* road engineers

voisé, e [vwaze] ADJ (Phon) voiced

voisement [vwazmɑ̃] NM (Phon) voicing

voisin, e [vwazɛ̃, in] ① ADJ [a] (= proche) neighbouring (Brit), neighboring (US); (= adjacent) next; **les maisons/rues ~es** the neighbouring houses/streets; **il habite la maison ~e/la rue ~e** he lives in the house next door/ in the next street; **deux maisons ~es (l'une de l'autre)** two adjoining houses, two houses next to each other; **une maison ~e de l'église** a house next to *ou* adjoining the church; **ils se sont réfugiés dans des villages ~s** they took refuge in neighbouring villages; **les pays ~s de la Suisse** the countries bordering on *ou* adjoining Switzerland; **les années ~es de 1870** the years around 1870; **un chiffre d'affaires ~**

de 4 milliards de francs a turnover in the region of 4 billion francs

[b] (= semblable) [idées, espèces, cas] connected; **~ de** akin to, related to; **un animal ~ du chat** an animal akin to *ou* related to the cat; **dans un état ~ de la folie** in a state bordering on *ou* akin to madness

② NM,F [a] (gén) neighbour (Brit), neighbor (US); **nous sommes ~s** we're neighbours; **nos ~s d'à côté** our next-door neighbours, the people next door; **les ~s du dessus/dessous** the people (who live) above/below; **nos ~s de palier** our neighbours *ou* the people who live across the landing; **un de mes ~s de table** one of the people next to me at table, one of my neighbours at table; **je demandai à mon ~ de me passer le sel** I asked the person (sitting) next to me *ou* my neighbour to pass me the salt; (en classe) **qui est ta ~e cette année ?** who is sitting next to you this year?; **mon ~ de dortoir/de salle** the person in the bed next to mine (in the dormitory/ward); **j'étais venu en ~** I had dropped in as I lived nearby; **nos ~s européens** our European neighbours

[b] (fig littér = prochain) neighbour (Brit), neighbor (US); **envier son ~** to envy one's neighbour

voisinage [vwazinaʒ] NM [a] (= voisins) neighbourhood (Brit), neighborhood (US); **ameuter tout le ~** to rouse the whole neighbourhood; **être connu de tout le ~** to be known throughout the neighbourhood; **faire une enquête de ~** to make inquiries in the neighbourhood; **querelle/conflit de ~** quarrel/dispute between neighbours

[b] (= relations) **être en bon ~ avec qn** *ou* **entretenir des relations de bon ~ avec qn** to be on neighbourly terms with sb

[c] (= environs) vicinity; **les villages du ~** the villages in the vicinity, the villages round about; **se trouver dans le ~** to be in the vicinity; **dans le ~ immédiat du musée** in the immediate vicinity of the museum; **nous ne connaissons personne dans le ~** we don't know anyone in the neighbourhood *ou* around here

[d] (= proximité) proximity, closeness; **le ~ de la montagne** the proximity *ou* closeness of the mountains; **il n'était pas enchanté du ~ de cette usine** he wasn't very happy at having the factory so close *ou* on his doorstep

[e] (Math) [point] neighbourhood (Brit), neighborhood (US)

voisiner [vwazine] ▶ conjug 1 ◀ VI (= être près de) **~ avec qch** to be (placed) side by side with sth

voiture [vwatyʀ] NF [a] (= automobile) car, automobile (US); **ils sont venus en ~** they came by car, they drove (here); **~(-)balai** (Tour de France) broom wagon; (Métro) last train; **vol à la ~(-)bélier** ram-raiding; **~ cellulaire** prison *ou* police van (Brit), patrol *ou* police wagon (US); **~ de compétition** competition car; **~ de course** racing car; **~ décapotable** convertible; **~-école** driving-school car; **~ de formule un** Formula-One car; (Admin) **~ de grande remise** hired limousine (with chauffeur); **~ de location** rental car, rented *ou* hired (Brit) car, hire car (Brit); **~ de maître** chauffeur-driven car; **~ particulière** private car; **~ pie†** ≈ (police) patrol car, ≈ panda car (Brit); (Admin) **~ de place** taxi cab, hackney carriage (Brit); **~ de police** police car; **~ de pompiers** fire engine; (Tour de France) **~ publicitaire** promoter's *ou* sponsor's back-up vehicle; **~-radio** radio car; **~ sans chauffeur** self-drive hire car; **~ sans permis** small car for which no driving licence is required; **~ de série** production car; **~ de fonction** *ou* **de service ◊ ~ de société** company car; **~ de sport** sportscar; **~ de tourisme** saloon (Brit), sedan (US); **~ ventouse** illegally parked car (exceeding the time limit for parking)

[b] (= wagon) carriage (Brit), coach (Brit), car (US); **~ de tête/queue** front/back carriage

(Brit) *ou* coach (Brit) *ou* car (US); **~-bar** buffet car; **~-couchette** couchette; **~-lit** sleeper (Brit), Pullman (US), sleeping car (US); **~-restaurant** dining car; **en ~ !** all aboard!

[c] (= véhicule attelé, poussé) (pour marchandises) cart; (pour voyageurs) carriage, coach; (pour handicapé) wheelchair, invalid carriage (Brit); **~ à bras** handcart; **~ à cheval** horse-drawn carriage; **~ d'enfant** pram (Brit), baby carriage (US), perambulator (Brit, frm); **~ de poste** mailcoach, stagecoach; **~ des quatre saisons** costermonger's (Brit) *ou* greengrocer's (Brit) barrow, sidewalk vegetable barrow (US) → **petit**

voiturée †† [vwatyʀe] NF (hum) [choses] cartload; [personnes] carriageful, coachload

voiturer [vwatyʀe] ▶ conjug 1 ◀ VT († *ou* hum) (sur un chariot) to wheel in; (* : en voiture) to take in the car

voiturette [vwatyʀɛt] NF (d'infirme) carriage; (= petite auto) little *ou* small car

voiturier [vwatyʀje] NM (†, Jur) carrier, carter; [hôtel, casino] doorman (responsible for parking clients' cars)

voix [vwa] NF [a] (= sons) voice; **à ~ basse** in a low *ou* hushed voice; **ils parlaient à ~ basse** they were talking in hushed *ou* low voices *ou* in undertones; **à ~ haute** ◊ **à haute ~** aloud, out loud; **de crécelle/de fausset/de gorge** shrill/falsetto/throaty voice; **d'une ~ blanche** in a toneless *ou* flat voice; **d'une ~ forte** in a loud voice; **à haute et intelligible ~** loud and clear; **avoir de la ~** to have a good (singing) voice; **être** *ou* **rester sans ~** to be speechless (devant before, at); **de la ~ et du geste** by word and gesture, with words and gestures; **une ~ lui cria de monter** a voice shouted to him to come up; **donner de la ~** (= aboyer) to bay, give tongue; (* = crier) to bawl; (Ciné, TV) **~ dans le champ** *ou* **in voice-in**; **~ hors champs** *ou* **off** (Théât) voice-off; (= commentaire) voice-over; **elle commente les images en ~ off** she provides the voice-over for the pictures; **la ~ des violons** the voice of the violins → **élever, gros, portée²**

[b] (= conseil, avertissement) **~ de la conscience/raison** voice of conscience/reason; **une petite ~ m'a dit ...** something inside me said ...; **se fier à la ~ d'un ami** to rely on *ou* trust to a friend's advice; **la ~ du sang** the ties of blood, the call of the blood; **c'est la ~ du sang qui parle** he must heed the call of his blood

[c] (= opinion) voice; (Pol = suffrage) vote; **la ~ du peuple** the voice of the people, vox populi; **mettre qch aux ~** to put sth to the vote; **la proposition a recueilli 30 ~** the proposal received *ou* got 30 votes; **demander la mise au ~ d'une proposition** to ask for a vote on a proposal, ask for a proposal to be put to the vote; **avoir ~ consultative** to have consultative powers *ou* a consultative voice; **avoir ~ prépondérante** to have a casting vote; **gagner des ~** to win votes; **donner sa ~ à un candidat** to give a candidate one's vote, vote for a candidate; **le parti obtiendra peu de/beaucoup de ~** the party will poll badly/heavily; **avoir ~ au chapitre** to have a say in the matter

[d] (Mus) voice; **chanter à 2/3 ~** to sing in 2/3 parts; **fugue à 3 ~** fugue in 3 voices; **~ de basse/de ténor** bass/tenor (voice); **chanter d'une ~ fausse/juste** to sing out of tune/in tune; **~ de tête/de poitrine** head/chest voice; **être/ne pas être en ~** to be/not to be in good voice; **la ~ humaine/céleste de l'orgue** the vox humana/voix céleste on the organ

[e] (Ling) voice; **à la ~ active/passive** in the active/passive voice

vol¹ [vɔl] ① NM [a] [oiseau, avion] (gén) flight; (Zool) **~ ramé/plané** flapping/gliding flight; **faire un ~ plané** [oiseau] to glide through the air; (fig = tomber) to fall flat on one's face; (Aviat) **~ d'essai/de nuit** trial/night flight; **~ régulier/charter** scheduled/charter flight; **il y a**

8 heures de ~ entre ... it's an 8-hour flight between ...; **le ~ Paris-Londres** the Paris-London flight; **heures/conditions de ~** flying hours/conditions; **~ habité** manned flight; **~ sec** flight only; **pilote qui a plusieurs centaines d'heures de ~** pilot with several hundred hours of flying time → **haut, ravitaillement** ⓑ (*Zool* = *formation*) flock, flight; **un ~ de perdrix** a covey *ou* flock of partridges; **un ~ de canards sauvages** a flight of wild ducks; **un ~ de moucherons** a cloud of gnats ⓒ (*loc*) **à ~ d'oiseau** as the crow flies; **attraper qch au ~** [+ *ballon, objet lancé*] to catch sth as it flies past, catch sth in midair; [+ *autobus, train*] to leap onto sth as it moves off; **elle a rattrapé son chapeau au ~** she caught her hat as it went flying through the air; **saisir une occasion au ~** to leap at *ou* seize an opportunity; **saisir** *ou* **cueillir une remarque/une impression au ~** to catch a chance *ou* passing remark/impression; **tirer un oiseau au ~** to shoot (at) a bird on the wing; **en (plein) ~** in (full) flight; **prendre son ~** (*lit*) to take wing, fly off *ou* away; (*fig*) to take off ② COMP ► **vol libre** hang-gliding; **pratiquer le ~ libre** to hang-glide, go hang-gliding ► **vol relatif** (*Sport*) relative work, RW (*style of free fall parachuting*) ► **vol à voile** gliding; **faire du ~ à voile** to go gliding

vol² [vɔl] ① NM (= *délit*) theft; (*Jur*) **~ simple** theft; **~ qualifié** *ou* **aggravé** aggravated theft; **~ avec violence** robbery with violence; **~s de voiture** car thefts; (*fig*) **c'est du ~!** it's daylight robbery!, it's a rip-off!*; (*fig*) **c'est du ~ organisé** it's a racket ② COMP ► **vol à l'arraché** bag-snatching ► **vol domestique** *theft committed by an employee* ► **vol avec effraction** burglary, breaking and entering ► **vol à l'étalage** shoplifting (*NonC*) ► **vol à main armée** armed robbery ► **vol à la roulotte** theft from a vehicle ► **vol à la tire** pickpocketing (*NonC*)

volage [vɔlaʒ] ADJ [*époux, cœur*] flighty, fickle, inconstant

volaille [vɔlaj] NF (*Culin, Zool*) **une ~** a fowl; **la ~** poultry; **les ~s de la basse-cour** the farmyard poultry; **~ rôtie** roast poultry (*NonC*) *ou* fowl

volailler, -ère [vɔlaje, ɛʀ] NM,F poulterer

volant¹ [vɔlɑ̃] ① NM ⓐ (*Aut*) steering wheel; **être au ~** to be at *ou* behind the wheel; **la femme au ~** women drivers; **prendre le ~** ◊ **se mettre au ~** to take the wheel; **c'est lui qui tenait le ~** he was at *ou* behind the wheel; **un brusque coup de ~** a sharp turn of the wheel; **as du ~** crack *ou* ace driver ⓑ (*Tech = roue, régulateur*) flywheel; (*de commande*) (hand)wheel ⓒ [*rideau, robe*] flounce; **jupe à ~s** flounced skirt, skirt with flounces ⓓ (= *balle de badminton*) shuttlecock; (= *jeu*) badminton, battledore and shuttlecock† ⓔ [*carnet à souches*] tear-off portion ⓕ (= *réserve, marge*) reserve ② COMP ► **volant inclinable** tilt steering wheel ► **volant magnétique** magneto ► **volant réglable** adjustable steering wheel ► **volant de sécurité** reserve, safeguard ► **volant de trésorerie** cash reserve

volant², e [vɔlɑ̃, ɑ̃t] ADJ ⓐ (*gén, Aviat*) (= *qui vole*) flying; (*Aviat*) **le personnel ~** ◊ **les ~s** the flight *ou* flying staff → **poisson, soucoupe, tapis** etc ⓑ (*littér* = *fugace*) [*ombre, forme*] fleeting ⓒ (= *mobile, transportable*) [*pont, camp, personnel*] flying; (*Police*) (**brigade**) **~e** flying squad → **feuille**

volanté, e [vɔlɑ̃te] ADJ [*jupe*] flounced

volapük [vɔlapyk] NM Volapuk

volatil, e¹ [vɔlatil] ADJ (*Bourse, Chim*) volatile; (*littér* = *éphémère*) evanescent, ephemeral → **alcali**

volatile² [vɔlatil] NM (*gén hum*) (= *volaille*) fowl; (= *tout oiseau*) winged *ou* feathered creature

volatilisable [vɔlatilizabl] ADJ volatilizable

volatilisation [vɔlatilizasjɔ̃] NF ⓐ (*Chim*) volatilization ⓑ (= *disparition*) extinguishing, obliteration

volatiliser [vɔlatilize] ► conjug 1 ◄ ① VT (*Chim*) to volatilize ② **se volatiliser** VPR ⓐ (*Chim*) to volatilize ⓑ (= *disparaître*) to vanish (into thin air)

volatilité [vɔlatilite] NF volatility

vol-au-vent [vɔlovɑ̃] NM INV vol-au-vent

volcan [vɔlkɑ̃] NM ⓐ (*Géog*) volcano; **~ en activité/éteint** active/extinct volcano ⓑ (*fig*) (= *personne*) spitfire; (= *situation*) powder keg, volcano; **nous sommes assis sur un ~** we are sitting on a powder keg *ou* a volcano

volcanique [vɔlkanik] ADJ (*lit*) volcanic; (*fig*) [*tempérament*] explosive, fiery

volcanisme [vɔlkanism] NM volcanism

volcanologie [vɔlkanɔlɔʒi] NF vulcanology

volcanologue [vɔlkanɔlɔg] NMF vulcanologist

volée [vɔle] NF ⓐ [*oiseaux*] (= *envol, distance*) flight; (= *groupe*) flock, flight; **une ~ de moineaux/corbeaux** a flock *ou* flight of sparrows/crows; **s'enfuir comme une ~ de moineaux** to scatter in all directions; **une ~ d'enfants** a swarm of children; **prendre sa ~** (*lit*) to take wing, fly off *ou* away; (*fig* = *s'affranchir*) to spread one's wings → **haut** ⓑ (*en Suisse* = *groupe d'élèves*) (pupils in the same year) ⓒ (= *décharge, tir*) volley; **~ de flèches** flight *ou* volley of arrows; **~ d'obus** volley of shells ⓓ (= *suite de coups*) volley; **une ~ de coups** a volley of blows; **une ~ de bois vert†** (= *coups*) a volley *ou* flurry of blows; (= *réprimande*) a volley of reproaches; **administrer/recevoir une bonne ~** to give/get a sound thrashing *ou* beating ⓔ (*Ftbl, Tennis*) volley; **faire une reprise de ~** to strike the ball on the volley; (*Tennis*) **~ croisée/de face/de revers** cross-court/forehand/backhand volley ⓕ (*Archit*) **~ de marches** flight of stairs ⓖ **à la ~**: **jeter qch à la ~** to fling sth about; **semer à la ~** to sow broadcast, broadcast; **attraper la balle à la ~** to catch the ball in midair; **saisir une allusion à la ~** to pick up a passing allusion; **à la ~ ◊ à toute ~** [*gifler, lancer*] vigorously, with full force; **les cloches sonnaient à toute ~** the bells were pealing out; **il referma la porte/fenêtre à la ~** *ou* **à toute ~** he slammed the door/window shut

voler¹ [vɔle] ► conjug 1 ◄ VI ⓐ [*oiseau, avion, pilote*] to fly; **vouloir ~ avant d'avoir des ailes** to want to run before one can walk; **~ de ses propres ailes** to stand on one's own two feet, fend for o.s.; **on entendrait ~ une mouche** you could hear a pin drop ⓑ [*flèche, pierres, insultes*] to fly; **~ en éclats** to fly *ou* smash into pieces; [*neige, voile, feuille*] **~ au vent** to fly in the wind, float on the wind; [*nouvelles*] **~ de bouche en bouche** to fly from mouth to mouth, spread like wildfire; **plaisanterie qui vole bas** feeble joke; **ça ne vole pas haut!*** it's pretty low-level! ⓒ (= *s'élancer*) **~ vers qn/dans les bras de qn** to fly to sb/into sb's arms; **~ au secours de qn** to fly to sb's assistance; **il lui a volé dans les plumes*** (*physiquement*) he flew at him, he laid into him*, he went for him; (*verbalement*) he went for him; **se ~ dans les plumes*** to go for each other, fly at each other ⓓ (*littér* = *passer, aller très vite*) [*temps*] to fly; [*embarcation, véhicule*] to fly (along); **son cheval volait/semblait ~** his horse flew (along)/ seemed to fly (along)

voler² [vɔle] ► conjug 1 ◄ VT ⓐ [+ *objet*] (= *dérober*) to steal; **~ de l'argent/une idée/un baiser à qn** to steal money/an idea/a kiss from sb; **on m'a volé mon stylo** somebody stole my pen, my pen has been stolen; **se faire ~ ses bagages** to have one's luggage stolen; (*fig*) **il** **ne l'a pas volé!** he asked for it!, it serves him right!; (*fig*) **il ne l'a pas volée, cette médaille!** he worked hard for that medal! ■ (*PROV*) **qui vole un œuf vole un bœuf** once a thief, always a thief (*PROV*) ⓑ [+ *personne*] (= *dépouiller*) to rob; (= *léser*) to cheat; **~ les clients** to rob *ou* cheat customers; **~ les clients sur le poids** to cheat customers over (the) weight, give customers short measure; **le boucher ne t'a pas volé sur le poids** the butcher gave you good weight; **~ qn lors du partage** to cheat sb when sharing out; **se sentir volé** (*lors d'un spectacle interrompu*) to feel cheated *ou* robbed; **on n'est pas volé*** you get your money's worth all right*, it's good value for money

volet [vɔlɛ] NM ⓐ [*fenêtre, hublot*] shutter ⓑ [*intrados/de freinage*] split/brake flap; **~ de courbure** [*parachute*] flap ⓒ (*Aut* = *panneau articulé*) bonnet flap; (*Tech*) [*roue à aube*] paddle; **~ de carburateur** throttle valve, butterfly valve ⓓ [*triptyque*] volet, wing; [*feuillet, carte*] section → **trier** ⓔ [*trilogie, émission, plan d'action, enquête*] part; **un plan de paix en trois ~s** a three-point peace plan; **le ~ social du traité** the social chapter of the treaty; **le ~ agricole de l'accord** the section on agriculture in the agreement

voleter [vɔl(ə)te] ► conjug 4 ◄ VI [*oiseau*] to flutter about, flit about; [*rubans, flocons*] to flutter

voleur, -euse [vɔlœʀ, øz] ① ADJ **être ~** (*gén*) to be light-fingered, be a (bit of a) thief; (*commerçant*) to be a cheat *ou* swindler, be dishonest; [*animal*] to be a thief; **~ comme une pie** thievish as a magpie ② NM,F (= *malfaiteur*) thief; (= *escroc, commerçant*) swindler; **~ de grand chemin** highwayman; **~ à l'étalage** shoplifter; **~ d'enfants†** kidnapper; **au ~!** stop thief!; **~ de voitures** car thief; **se sauver comme un ~** to run off like a thief (in the night) → **tire²**

Volga [vɔlga] NF Volga

volière [vɔljɛʀ] NF (= *cage*) aviary; (*fig*) **ce bureau est une ~** this office is a proper henhouse* (*hum*)

volige [vɔliʒ] NF (= *toit*) lath

volitif, -ive [vɔlitif, iv] ADJ volitional, volitive

volition [vɔlisjɔ̃] NF volition

volley [vɔlɛ], **volley-ball** [vɔlɛbol] NM volleyball

volleyer [vɔleje] ► conjug 8 ◄ VI (*Tennis*) to volley

volleyeur, -euse [vɔlɛjœʀ, øz] NM,F (*Volley*) volleyball player; (*Tennis*) volleyer

volontaire [vɔlɔ̃tɛʀ] ① ADJ ⓐ (= *voulu*) [*acte, enrôlement, prisonnier*] voluntary; [*oubli*] intentional → **engagé** ⓑ (= *décidé*) [*personne*] wilful, headstrong; [*expression, menton*] determined ② NMF (*Mil, gén*) volunteer; **se porter ~ pour qch** to volunteer for sth; **je suis ~** I volunteer; **~ du service national à l'étranger** *person doing his military service as a civilian working abroad*

volontairement [vɔlɔ̃tɛʀmɑ̃] ADV ⓐ (= *de son plein gré*) voluntarily, of one's own free will; (*Jur* = *facultativement*) voluntarily ⓑ (= *exprès*) intentionally, deliberately; **il a dit ça ~** he said it on purpose *ou* deliberately ⓒ (= *d'une manière décidée*) determinedly

volontariat [vɔlɔ̃taʀja] NM (*gén*) voluntary participation; (*Mil*) voluntary service

volontarisme [vɔlɔ̃taʀism] NM voluntarism

volontariste [vɔlɔ̃taʀist] ADJ, NMF voluntarist

volonté [vɔlɔ̃te] NF ⓐ (= *faculté*) will; (= *souhait, intention*) wish, will (*frm*); **manifester sa ~ de faire qch** to show one's intention of doing sth; **accomplir/respecter la ~ de qn** to carry out/respect sb's wishes; **la ~ nationale** the will of the nation; **la ~ générale** the general will; **les dernières ~s de qn** the last wishes of sb; **~ de puissance** thirst for power; **~ de guérir/réussir** will to recover/succeed;

(*Rel*) **que ta** *ou* **votre ~ soit faite** Thy will be done → **indépendant, quatre**
b (= *disposition*) **bonne ~** goodwill, willingness; **mauvaise ~** lack of goodwill, unwillingness; **il a beaucoup de bonne ~ mais peu d'aptitude** he shows great willingness but not much aptitude; **il met de la bonne/mauvaise ~ à faire son travail** he goes about his work with goodwill/grudgingly, he does his work willingly/unwillingly *ou* with a good/bad grace; **il fait preuve de bonne/mauvaise ~** he has a positive/negative attitude; **paix sur la terre, aux hommes de bonne ~** peace on earth (and) goodwill to all men; **faire appel aux bonnes ~s pour construire qch** to appeal to volunteers to construct sth; **toutes les bonnes ~s sont les bienvenues** all offers of help are welcome; **avec la meilleure ~ du monde** with the best will in the world
c (= *caractère, énergie*) willpower, will; **faire un effort de ~** to make an effort of will(power); **avoir de la ~** to have willpower; **cette femme a une ~ de fer** this woman has an iron will *ou* a will of iron; **réussir à force de ~** to succeed through sheer will(power) *ou* determination; **échouer par manque de ~** to fail through lack of will(power) *ou* determination; **faire preuve de ~** to display willpower
d (*loc*) **pain/café à ~»** "as much bread/coffee as you like *ou* want"; **«sucrer à ~»** "sweeten to taste"; **vous pouvez le prendre ou le laisser à ~** you can take it or leave it as you wish *ou* just as you like; **nous avons de l'eau à ~** we have as much water as we want, we have plenty of water; **vin à ~ pendant le repas** as much wine as one wants *ou* unlimited wine with the meal; (*Comm*) **billet payable à ~** promissory note payable on demand; **il en fait toujours à sa ~** he always does things his own way, he always does as he pleases *ou* likes, he always suits himself → **feu¹**

▼ **volontiers** [vɔlɔ̃tje] ADV **a** (= *de bonne grâce*) gladly, willingly; **je l'aiderais ~** I would gladly *ou* willingly help him; **voulez-vous dîner chez nous ? — ~** would you like to eat with us? — I'd love to *ou* with pleasure **b** (= *naturellement*) readily, willingly; **il lit ~ pendant des heures** he'll happily *ou* willingly read for hours on end; **on croit ~ que ...** people readily believe that ..., people are apt *ou* quite ready to believe that ...; **il est ~ pessimiste** he's given to pessimism, he's pessimistic by nature

volt [vɔlt] NM volt

voltage [vɔltaʒ] NM voltage

voltaïque [vɔltaik] ADJ voltaic, galvanic

voltaire [vɔltɛʀ] NM **(fauteuil) ~** Voltaire chair

volte [vɔlt] NF (*Équitation*) volte

volte-face [vɔltfas] NF INV **a** (*lit*) **faire ~** (= *se retourner*) to turn round **b** (*fig = changement d'opinion*) about-turn, U-turn, volte-face (*frm*); **faire une ~** to do an about-turn *ou* a U-turn

volter [vɔlte] ▸ conjug 1 ◂ VI (*Équitation*) **faire ~ un cheval** to make a horse circle

voltige [vɔltiʒ] NF (*Équitation*) trick riding; (*Aviat*) **~ (aérienne)** aerobatics, stunt flying; (*Gym*) **faire de la ~** to do acrobatics; (*Gym*) **(haute) ~** acrobatics; (*fig*) **c'est de la (haute) ~ intellectuelle** it's mental gymnastics; **c'était un exercice de haute ~ monétaire** it was an example of financial wizardry

voltiger [vɔltiʒe] ▸ conjug 3 ◂ VI [*oiseaux*] to flit about, flutter about; [*objet léger*] to flutter about

voltigeur [vɔltiʒœʀ] NM **a** (= *acrobate*) acrobat; (= *pilote*) stunt pilot *ou* flier **b** (*Hist, Mil*) light infantryman

voltmètre [vɔltmɛtʀ] NM voltmeter

volubile [vɔlybil] ADJ **a** [*personne, éloquence*] voluble **b** (*Bot*) voluble

volubilis [vɔlybilis] NM convolvulus, morning glory

volubilité [vɔlybilite] NF volubility; **parler avec ~** to talk volubly

volucompteur® [vɔlykɔ̃tœʀ] NM (volume) indicator

volumateur, -trice [vɔlymatœʀ, tʀis] ADJ [*shampooing, mousse*] that gives body to the hair

volume [vɔlym] NM **a** (= *livre, tome*) volume **b** (*gén, Art, Géom, Sci* = *espace, quantité*) volume; **~ moléculaire/atomique** molecular/atomic volume; **~ d'eau d'un fleuve** volume of water in a river; **eau oxygénée à 20 ~s** 20-volume hydrogen peroxide; **le ~ des exportations/transactions** the volume of exports/trade; **le marché est en baisse de 7% en ~** the volume of the market has fallen 7%; [*gros objets*] **faire du ~** to be bulky, take up space **c** (= *intensité*) [*son*] volume; **~ de la voix/radio** volume of the voice/radio; **~ sonore** (*pour enregistrement*) sound level; (*mesure de pollution*) noise level

volumétrique [vɔlymetʀik] ADJ volumetric

volumineux, -euse [vɔlyminø, øz] ADJ [*catalogue, dictionnaire, dossier*] bulky, voluminous; [*courrier*] voluminous; [*paquet*] bulky

volumique [vɔlymik] ADJ (*Phys*) **masse ~** density; **poids ~** specific weight, weight per unit volume

volupté [vɔlypte] NF (*sensuelle*) sensual delight, sensual *ou* voluptuous pleasure; (*morale, intellectuelle*) exquisite delight *ou* pleasure

voluptueusement [vɔlyptɥøzmɑ̃] ADV voluptuously

voluptueux, -euse [vɔlyptɥø, øz] ADJ voluptuous

volute [vɔlyt] NF **a** [*colonne, grille, escalier*] volute, scroll; [*fumée*] curl, wreath; [*vague*] curl; **en ~** voluted, scrolled **b** (= *mollusque*) volute

volve [vɔlv] NF volva

vomi [vɔmi] NM vomit

vomique [vɔmik] ADJ F → **noix**

vomiquier [vɔmikje] NM nux vomica (*tree*)

vomir [vɔmiʀ] ▸ conjug 2 ◂ VT **a** [+ *aliments*] to vomit, bring up; [+ *sang*] to spit, bring up **b** (*sans compl*) to be sick, vomit, throw up; **il a vomi partout** he was sick everywhere; **ça te fera ~** it'll make you vomit *ou* be sick; **avoir envie de ~** to feel sick; (*fig*) **ça donne envie de ~ ◊ c'est à ~** it makes you *ou* it's enough to make you sick, it's nauseating **c** (*fig*) [+ *lave, flammes*] to belch forth, spew forth; [+ *injures, haine*] to spew out **d** (*fig = détester*) to loathe, abhor; **il vomit les intellectuels** he has a loathing for *ou* loathes intellectuals

vomissement [vɔmismɑ̃] NM **a** (= *action*) vomiting (*NonC*); **il fut pris de ~s** he (suddenly) started vomiting **b** (= *matières*) vomit (*NonC*)

vomissure [vɔmisyʀ] NF vomit (*NonC*)

vomitif, -ive [vɔmitif, iv] ADJ, NM (*Pharm*) emetic, vomitory

vorace [vɔʀas] ADJ [*animal, personne, curiosité*] voracious; **appétit ~** voracious *ou* ravenous appetite; **plantes ~s** plants which deplete the soil

voracement [vɔʀasmɑ̃] ADV voraciously

voracité [vɔʀasite] NF voracity, voraciousness

vortex [vɔʀtɛks] NM (*littér*) vortex

vos [vo] ADJ POSS → **votre**

Vosges [voʒ] NFPL **les ~** the Vosges

vosgien, -ienne [voʒjɛ̃, jɛn] **1** ADJ Vosges (*épith*), of *ou* from the Vosges **2** **Vosgien(ne)** NM,F inhabitant *ou* native of the Vosges

VOST (ABRÉV = **version originale sous-titrée**) → **version**

votant, e [vɔtɑ̃, ɑ̃t] NM,F voter

votation [vɔtasjɔ̃] NF (*Helv*) voting

vote [vɔt] NM **a** (= *approbation*) [*projet de loi*] vote (**de** for); [*loi, réforme*] passing; [*crédits*] voting; **après le ~ du budget** after the budget was voted **b** (= *suffrage, acte, opération*) vote; (= *ensemble des votants*) voters; **le ~ socialiste** Socialist voters, the Socialist vote; **~ de confiance** vote of confidence; **~ à main levée** vote by a show of hands; **~ à bulletin secret/par correspondance** secret/postal vote *ou* ballot; **~ par procuration** proxy vote; **~ direct/indirect** direct/indirect vote; **~ blanc/nul** blank/spoilt ballot paper; **~ utile** tactical vote; **~ bloqué** *single vote on a bill containing several government amendments*; **~ de confiance** vote of confidence; **procéder** *ou* **passer au ~** to proceed to a vote, take a vote → **bulletin, bureau, droit³**

voter [vɔte] ▸ conjug 1 ◂ VI to vote; **~ à main levée** to vote by a show of hands; **~ à droite/pour X** to vote for the right/for X; **~ libéral** to vote liberal; **~ utile** to vote tactically; **~ pour/contre qch** to vote for/against sth; **j'ai voté contre** I voted against it; **~ sur une motion** to vote on a motion; **j'ai voté blanc** I cast a blank vote **2** VT (= *adopter*) [+ *projet de loi*] to vote for; [+ *loi, réforme*] to pass; [+ *crédits*] to vote; **~ la censure** to pass a vote of censure; **~ la reconduction d'une grève** to vote to continue a strike; **ne pas ~** [+ *amendement*] to vote out; **~ la mort du roi** to vote to execute the king, vote for the king's death

votif, -ive [vɔtif, iv] ADJ votive

votre (*pl* **vos**) [vɔtʀ, vo] ADJ POSS your; (*emphatique*) your own; (†, *Rel*) thy; **laissez ~ manteau et vos gants au vestiaire** (*à une personne*) leave your coat and gloves in the cloakroom; (*à plusieurs personnes*) leave your coats and gloves in the cloakroom; **un de vos livres** one of your books, a book of yours; **je vous accorde ~ lundi** you may have Monday off; **Votre Excellence/Majesté** Your Excellency/Majesty; *pour autres locutions voir* **son, ton**

vôtre [votʀ] **1** PRON POSS **le ~ ◊ la ~ ◊ les ~s** yours; **ce sac n'est pas le ~** this bag isn't yours, this isn't your bag; **nos enfants sont sortis avec les ~s** our children are out with yours; **à la (bonne) ~ !** your (good) health!, cheers!; (*fig*) **vous voulez y aller quand même — à la (bonne) ~ !** you still want to go? — rather you than me!; *pour autres locutions voir* **sien 2** NMF **a** **j'espère que vous y mettrez du ~** I hope you'll pull your weight *ou* do your bit* → **sien b** **les ~s** your family, your folks*; **vous et tous les ~s** you and all those like you, you and your kind (*péj*); **bonne année à vous et à tous les ~s** Happy New Year to you and yours; **nous pourrons être des ~s ce soir** we shall be able to join your party *ou* join you tonight → **sien 3** ADJ POSS (*littér*) yours; **son cœur est ~ depuis toujours** his (*ou* her) heart has always been yours; **amicalement ~** best wishes → **sien**

vouer [vwe] ▸ conjug 1 ◂ VT **a** (*Rel*) **~ qn à Dieu/à la Vierge** to dedicate sb to God/to the Virgin Mary → **savoir b** (= *promettre*) to vow; **il lui a voué un amour éternel** he vowed his undying love to her **c** (= *consacrer*) to devote; **~ son temps à ses études** to devote one's time to one's studies; **se ~ à une cause** to dedicate o.s. *ou* devote o.s. to a cause **d** (*gén ptp* = *condamner*) to doom; **projet voué à l'échec** project doomed to *ou* destined for failure; **famille vouée à la misère** family doomed to poverty

▼ **vouloir¹** [vulwaʀ]

▸ conjug 31 ◂
| 1 VERBE TRANSITIF | 2 VERBE TRANSITIF |
| 3 VERBE PRONOMINAL | INDIR |

1 VERBE TRANSITIF
a (= *exiger, être décidé à obtenir*) [+ *objet, augmentation, changement*] to want; **~ faire qch** to

want to do sth; ~ que qn fasse qch/que qch se fasse to want sb to do sth/sth to be done; **je veux que tu viennes tout de suite** I want you to come at once; **il veut absolument venir/qu'elle parte/ce jouet** he is set on coming/on her leaving/on having that toy, he is determined to come/(that) she should leave/to have that toy; **il ne veut pas y aller/qu'elle y aille** he doesn't want to go/her to go ■ (PROV) ~, **c'est pouvoir** ■ (PROV) **quand on veut, on peut** where there's a will there's a way (PROV); **qu'est-ce qu'ils veulent maintenant?** what do they want now?; **il sait ce qu'il veut** he knows what he wants; **il veut sans ~** he only half wants to; **tu l'as voulu** you asked for it; **tu l'auras voulu** it'll have been your own fault, you'll have brought it on yourself; **elle fait de lui ce qu'elle veut** she does what she likes with him, she twists him round her little finger

◆ **en vouloir*** (= vouloir gagner, réussir) **il en veut** he wants to win; **l'équipe de France en veut ce soir** the French team is raring to go* ou is out to win tonight

b = désirer, souhaiter **voulez-vous à boire/manger?** would you like something to drink/eat?; **tu veux quelque chose à boire?** would you like ou do you want something to drink?; **comment voulez-vous votre poisson, frit ou poché?** how would you like your fish — fried or poached?; **je ne veux pas qu'il se croie obligé de ...** I wouldn't like ou I don't want him to feel obliged to ...; **je voulais vous dire ...** I meant to tell you ...; **il voulait partir hier mais ...** he wanted ou meant ou intended to leave yesterday but ...; **il ne voulait pas vous blesser** he didn't want ou mean to hurt you; **sans ~ vous vexer** no offence (meant); **qu'il le veuille ou non** whether he likes it or not; **ça va comme tu veux?*** is everything all right ou OK?*; **veux-tu que je te dise** ou **raconte pourquoi ...?** shall I tell you why ...?; **que lui voulez-vous?** what do you want with him?; **qu'est-ce qu'il me veut, celui-là?*** what does he want (from me)? → **bien, mal**

◆ **avec comme** : **comme tu veux** (ou vous voulez) as you like ou wish ou please; **bon, comme tu voudras** all right, have it your own way ou suit yourself; **comme vous voulez, moi ça m'est égal** just as you like ou please ou wish, it makes no difference to me

◆ **avec si** : **si tu veux** ◊ **si vous voulez** if you like, if you want (to); **oui, si on veut** (= dans un sens, d'un côté) yes, if you like; **s'il voulait, il pourrait être ministre** if he wanted (to), he could be a minister, he could be a minister if he so desired; **s'il voulait (bien) nous aider, cela gagnerait du temps** it would save time if he'd help us; **s'ils veulent garder leur avance, ils ne peuvent se permettre de relâcher leur effort** if they want to keep their lead they can't afford to reduce their efforts

◆ **en veux-tu en voilà*** : **il y a eu des discours en veux-tu en voilà** there were speeches galore; **elle a des dettes en veux-tu en voilà** she's up to her ears ou eyes in debt*; **on lui a proposé des stages en veux-tu en voilà** they've offered him one course after another

◆ **sans le vouloir** unintentionally, inadvertently; **si je t'ai vexé, c'était sans le ~** if I offended you it was unintentional ou I didn't mean to

◆ **vouloir de qch** (avec de partitif = désirer) [+ nourriture] **je n'en veux plus** I don't want any more; [+ gâteau] **est-ce que tu en veux?** do you want some?, would you like some? → **2**

c au conditionnel **je voudrais un stylo/écrire/qu'il m'écrive** I would like a pen/to write/him to write to me; **il aurait voulu être médecin mais ...** he would have liked to be a doctor ou he would like to have been a doctor but ...; **je ne voudrais pas abuser** I don't want to impose; **je voudrais/j'aurais voulu que vous voyiez sa tête!** I wish you could see/could have seen his face!; **je voudrais qu'il soit plus énergique** ◊ **je lui vou-**

drais plus d'énergie (frm) I wish he was a bit more energetic; **je voudrais bien voir ça!** I'd like to see that! → **voir 1b**

d exprimant l'impuissance **que voulez-vous** ◊ **que veux-tu** ◊ **qu'est-ce que vous voulez** ◊ **qu'est-ce que tu veux** what can you do?, what do you expect?; **que veux-tu, c'est comme ça, on n'y peut rien** what can you do? ou what do you expect? that's the way it is and there's nothing we can do about it; **qu'est-ce que tu veux que je te dise?** j'ai perdu what can I say? ou what do you want me to say? I lost

e = consentir à **ils ne voulurent pas nous recevoir** they wouldn't see us, they weren't willing to see us; **le moteur ne veut pas partir** the engine won't start; **le feu n'a pas voulu prendre** the fire wouldn't light ou catch; **il joue bien quand il veut** he plays well when he wants to ou has a mind to ou when he puts his mind to it

◆ **bien vouloir** : **je veux bien le faire/qu'il vienne** (s'il le faut vraiment) I don't mind doing it/if he comes; (il n'y a pas d'inconvénient) I'm quite happy to do it/for him to come; (enthousiaste) I'm happy ou I'll be happy to do it/for him to come; **je voudrais bien y aller** I'd really like ou I'd love to go; **si tu voulais bien le faire, ça nous rendrait service** if you'd be kind enough to do it, you'd be doing us a favour; **tu veux bien leur dire que ...** would you please tell them that ...; **je veux bien encore un peu de café** I'd like some more coffee; **encore un peu de thé?** — **je veux bien** more tea? — yes, please; **nous en parlerons plus tard, si vous le voulez bien** we'll talk about it later, if you don't mind; **je veux bien le croire mais ...** I'd like to take his word for it but ...; **moi je veux bien, mais ...** fair enough*, but ...

f formules de politesse **voudriez-vous avoir l'obligeance** ou **l'amabilité de ...** would you be so kind as to ...; **veuillez croire à toute ma sympathie** please accept my deepest sympathy; **voulez-vous me prêter ce livre?** will you lend me this book?; **voudriez-vous fermer la fenêtre?** would you mind closing the window?; **si vous voulez bien me suivre** (come) this way, please → **agréer**

g à l'impératif: ordre **veux-tu (bien) te taire!** will you (please) be quiet!; **veuillez quitter la pièce immédiatement** please leave the room at once; **veux-tu bien arrêter!** will you please stop it!, stop it will you ou please!

h = chercher à, essayer de **elle voulut se lever mais elle retomba** she tried to get up but she fell back; **en voulant m'aider, il a fait échouer mon projet** by trying to help he ruined my project; **il veut se faire remarquer** he wants to be noticed, he's out to be noticed

i = escompter, demander **~ qch de qn to** want sth from sb; **que voulez-vous de moi?** what do you want from me?; **~ un certain prix de qch** to want a certain price for sth; **j'en veux 1 000 F** I want 1,000 francs for it

j = s'attendre à **comment voulez-vous que je sache?** how should I know?, how do you expect me to know?; **avec 3 000 F par mois, comment veux-tu qu'elle s'en sorte?** how do you expect her to manage on 3,000 francs a month?; **il a tout, pourquoi voudriez-vous qu'il réclame?** he's got everything so why should he complain?; **que voulez-vous qu'on y fasse?** what do you expect us (ou them etc) to do about it?

k

◆ **en vouloir à qn** to have something against sb, have a grudge against sb; **les deux frères s'en veulent à mort** the two brothers absolutely hate each other ou are at daggers drawn; **en ~ à qn de qch** to hold sth against sb; **il m'en veut beaucoup d'avoir fait cela** he holds a tremendous grudge against me for having done

that; **il m'en veut d'avoir fait rater ce projet** he holds it against me that I made the plan fail; **il m'en veut de mon incompréhension** he holds the fact that I don't understand against me, he resents the fact that I don't understand; **je m'en veux d'avoir accepté** I could kick myself* ou I'm so annoyed with myself for accepting; **accepter cela? je m'en voudrais!** accept that? not on your life!; **ne m'en veuillez pas** ◊ **ne m'en voulez pas*** don't hold it against me; **tu ne m'en veux pas?** no hard feelings?; **je ne t'en veux pas** I'm not angry with you

◆ **en vouloir à qch** to be after sth; **il en veut à son argent** he's after her money; **ils en voulaient à sa vie** they wanted him dead; **ils en voulaient à sa réputation** they wanted to ruin his reputation

l = affirmer to claim; **une philosophie qui veut que l'homme soit ...** a philosophy which claims that man is ...; **la légende veut qu'il soit né ici** according to legend he was born here

◆ **je veux!** : **ça te dirait d'aller à la mer? — je veux!** would you like to go to the seaside? — that would be great!* ou you bet!*; **tu vas lui demander? — je veux!** are you going to ask him? — you bet (I am)!

m sujet chose = requérir to need, require; **cette plante veut un sol riche** this plant needs ou requires a rich soil; **l'usage veut que ...** custom requires that ...; **comme le veut la loi** according to the law, as the law requires; **comme le veut la tradition** according to tradition

n = faire [destin, sort] **le hasard voulut que ...** as luck would have it ...; **le malheur a voulu qu'il prenne cette route** he had the misfortune to take this road

o

◆ **vouloir dire** to mean → **dire**

2 **vouloir de** VERBE TRANSITIF INDIR

gén nég, interrog = accepter **~ de qn/qch** to want sb/sth; **on ne veut plus de lui ou on n'en veut plus au bureau** they don't want him ou won't have him in the office any more; **je ne veux pas de lui comme chauffeur** I don't want him ou won't have him as a driver; **voudront-ils de moi dans leur nouvelle maison?** will they want me in their new house?; **je l'accompagnerai si elle veut de moi** I'll go with her if she'll have me; **elle ne veut plus de ce chapeau** she doesn't want this hat any more

3 **se vouloir** VERBE PRONOMINAL

= vouloir être, prétendre être **ce journal se veut objectif** this newspaper likes to think it's ou is meant to be objective; **son discours se veut rassurant** what he says is meant to be reassuring; **cette peinture se veut réaliste** this painting is supposed to be realistic

vouloir² [vulwaʀ] NM **a** (littér = volonté) will **b** **bon ~** goodwill; **mauvais ~** reluctance; **avec un mauvais ~ évident** with obvious reluctance; **attendre le bon ~ de qn** to wait on sb's pleasure; **cette décision dépend du bon ~ du ministre** this decision depends on the minister's goodwill

voulu, e [vuly] (ptp de **vouloir**) ADJ **a** (= requis) required, requisite; **il n'avait pas l'argent ~** he didn't have the required ou requisite money ou the money required; **au moment ~** at the required moment; **en temps ~** in due time ou course; **produire l'effet ~** to produce the desired effect; **le temps ~** the time required **b** (= volontaire) deliberate, intentional; **c'est ~*** it's done on purpose, it's intentional ou deliberate

vous [vu] **1** PRON PERS **a** (sujet, objet) you; (pl de tu, toi) you; (valeur indéfinie) **les gens qui viennent ~ poser des questions** people who come asking questions ou who come and ask you questions; **~ avez bien répondu tous les deux** you both answered well, the two of you answered well; **et lui, ~ êtes aussi têtus l'un**

que l'autre you are both as stubborn as each other; **si j'étais ~, j'accepterais** if I were you *ou* in your shoes I'd accept; **eux ont accepté, ~ pas** *ou* **pas ~** they accepted but you didn't, they accepted but not you; **~ parti(s), je pourrai travailler** once you've gone *ou* with you out of the way, I'll be able to work; **c'est enfin ~** ◊ **voilà enfin** here you are at last; **qui l'a vu ? ~ ?** who saw him? (did) you?; **je ~ ai demandé de m'aider** I asked you to help me; **elle n'obéit qu'à ~** you're the only one *ou* ones she obeys

[b] (*emphatique : insistance, apostrophe*) (*sujet*) you, you yourself *sg*, you yourselves *pl*; (*objet*) you; **~ tous écoutez-moi** listen to me all of you *ou* the lot of you*; **~, ~ n'avez pas à ~ plaindre** you have no cause to complain; **pourquoi ne le ferais-je pas : ~ l'avez bien fait, ~ !** why shouldn't I do it — you did (it)! *ou* you yourself *ou* you yourselves did it!; **~, mentir ?, ce n'est pas possible** you, tell a lie? I can't believe it; **alors ~, ~ ne partez pas ?** so what about you — aren't you going?; **~, aidez-moi !** you (there) *ou* hey you, give me a hand!; **je ~ demande à ~ parce que je ~ connais** I'm asking you because I know you; **je ~ connais, ~ !** I know you!; **~, ~ m'agacez ! ◊ ~ m'agacez, ~ !** you're getting on my nerves!; **~, je vois que ~ n'êtes pas bien** it's obvious to me that you're not well

[c] (*emphatique avec qui, que*) **c'est ~ qui avez raison** it's you who is (*ou* are) right; **~ tous qui m'écoutez** all of you listening to me; **et ~ qui détestiez le cinéma, ~ avez bien changé** and (to think) you were the one who hated the cinema *ou* you used to say you hated the cinema — well you've certainly changed!

[d] (*avec prép*) you; **à ~ quatre ~ pourrez le porter** with four of you *ou* between (the) four of you you'll be able to carry it; **cette maison est-elle à ~ ?** does this house belong to you?, is this house yours?; **~ n'avez pas une chambre à ~ tout seul/tout seuls ?** you don't even have a room to yourself *ou* of your own/to yourselves *ou* of your own?; **c'est à ~ de décider** it's up to you to decide; **l'un de ~ ou d'entre ~ doit le savoir** one of you must know; **de ~ à moi** between you and me; **~ ne pensez qu'à ~** you think only of yourself (*ou* yourselves)

[e] (*dans comparaisons*) you; **il me connaît mieux que ~** (*mieux qu'il ne vous connaît*) he knows me better than (he knows) you; (*mieux que vous ne me connaissez*) he knows me better than you do; **il est plus/moins fort que ~** he's stronger than you/not as strong as you (are); **il a fait comme ~** he did as *ou* what you did, he did the same as you

[f] (*avec vpr : souvent non traduit*) **~ êtes-~ bien amusé(s) ?** did you have a good time?; **je crois que ~ ~ connaissez** I believe you know each other; **servez-~ donc** do help yourself (*ou* yourselves); **ne ~ disputez pas** don't fight; **asseyez-~ donc** do sit down

[2] NM **dire ~ à qn** to call sb "vous"; **le ~ est de moins en moins employé** (the form of address) "vous" *ou* the "vous" form is used less and less frequently

vous-même (*pl* **vous-mêmes**) [vumɛm] PRON → **même**

vousseau [vuso], **voussoir** [vuswaʀ] NM voussoir

voussure [vusyʀ] NF (= *courbure*) arching; (= *partie cintrée*) arch; (*Archit* = *archivolte*) archivolt

voûte [vut] [1] NF (*Archit*) vault; (= *porche*) archway; **~ en plein cintre/d'arête** semi-circular/groined vault; **~ en ogive/en berceau** rib/barrel vault; **~ en éventail** fan-vaulting (*NonC*); **en ~** vaulted; **la ~ d'une caverne** the vault of a cave; (*fig*) **une ~ d'arbres** an archway of trees → **clé** [2] COMP ► **la voûte céleste** the vault *ou* canopy of heaven ► **voûte crânienne** dome of the skull, vault

of the cranium (*SPÉC*) ► **la voûte étoilée** the starry vault *ou* dome ► **voûte du palais** *ou* **palatine** roof of the mouth, hard palate ► **voûte plantaire** arch (of the foot)

voûté, e [vute] (*ptp de* **voûter**) ADJ [a] [*cave, plafond*] vaulted, arched [b] [*dos*] bent; [*personne*] stooped; **être ~** ◊ **avoir le dos ~** to be stooped, have a stoop

voûter [vute] ▶ conjug 1 ◀ VT [a] (*Archit*) to arch, vault [b] [+ *personne, dos*] to make stooped; **la vieillesse l'a voûté** age has given him a stoop; **il s'est voûté avec l'âge** he has become stooped with age

vouvoiement [vuvwamɑ̃] NM addressing sb as "vous", using the "vous" form; **entre eux, le ~ reste de rigueur** they still address each other as "vous"

vouvoyer [vuvwaje] ▶ conjug 8 ◀ VT **~ qn** to address sb as "vous", use the "vous" form with sb

vox populi [vɔkspɔpyli] NF vox populi, voice of the people

voyage [vwajaʒ] NM [a] (*gén*) journey, trip; (*par mer*) voyage; **le ~** ◊ **les ~s** travelling (*Brit*), traveling (*US*); **il aime les ~s** he likes travel *ou* travelling; **les ~s le fatiguent** travelling tires him; **le ~ l'a fatigué** the journey tired him; **j'ai fait un beau ~** I had a very nice trip; **les ~s de Christophe Colomb** the voyages *ou* journeys of Christopher Columbus; **les fatigues du ~** the strain of the journey; **il est en ~** he's away; **il est absent — il est parti en ~** he's away — he's gone (off) on a trip; **au moment de partir en ~** just as he (*ou* I *etc*) was setting off on his (*ou* my *etc*) journey *ou* travels; **il reste 3 jours de ~** there are still 3 days' travelling left, the journey will take another 3 days (to do); **lors de notre ~ en Espagne** on our trip to Spain, during *ou* on our travels in Spain; **frais/souvenirs de ~** travel expenses/souvenirs; **~ aller/retour** outward/return journey; **~ d'affaires/d'agrément/d'études** business/pleasure/study *ou* field trip; **~ d'information** fact-finding trip; **~ autour du monde** round-the-world trip; **faire un ~ autour du monde** to go round the world; **~ de noces** honeymoon; **~ organisé** *ou* **à forfait** package tour *ou* holiday (*Brit*); **le grand ~** (*littér, euph*) the last great journey (*littér*) (*euph*); **faire le grand ~** to pass away ■ (*PROV*) **les ~s forment la jeunesse** travel broadens the mind → **agence, bon¹, sac¹**

[b] (= *course*) trip, journey; **faire 2 ~s pour transporter qch** to make 2 trips *ou* journeys to transport sth; **j'ai dû faire le ~ de Grenoble une seconde fois** I had to make the trip *ou* journey from Grenoble a second time [c] (*Drogue*) trip

voyager [vwajaʒe] ▶ conjug 3 ◀ VI [a] (= *faire des voyages*) to travel; **comment as-tu voyagé ?** how did you travel?; **j'ai voyagé en avion/par mer/en 1ʳᵉ classe** I travelled by air/by sea/1st class; **aimer ~** to like travelling; **il a beaucoup voyagé** he has travelled widely *ou* a great deal, he has done a lot of travelling ■ (*PROV*) **qui veut ~ loin ménage sa monture** he who takes it slow and steady goes a long way [b] (*Comm*) to travel; **~ pour un quotidien parisien** to travel for a Paris daily paper [c] [*chose*] to travel; **cette malle a beaucoup voyagé** this trunk has travelled a great deal *ou* has done a lot of travelling; **ces vins/denrées voyagent mal/bien** these wines/goods travel badly/well; **ce paquet s'est abîmé en voyageant** this package has been damaged in transit

voyageur, -euse [vwajaʒœʀ, øz] [1] ADJ (*littér*) [*humeur, tempérament*] wayfaring (*littér*) → **commis, pigeon** [2] NM,F (= *explorateur, Comm*) traveller (*Brit*), traveler (*US*); (= *passager*) traveller (*Brit*), traveler (*US*), passenger; **c'est un grand ~** he travels a lot; **~ de commerce** (*Admin*) ◊ **~, représentant, placier** commercial traveller, sales representative

voyagiste [vwajaʒist] NM tour operator

voyance [vwajɑ̃s] NF clairvoyance

voyant, e [vwajɑ̃, ɑ̃t] [1] ADJ [*couleurs*] loud, gaudy, garish [2] NM,F (= *illuminé*) visionary, seer; (= *personne qui voit*) sighted person; **les ~s** the sighted [3] **voyante** NF **~e** (**extralucide**) clairvoyant [4] NM [a] (= *signal*) **~** (**lumineux**) (*gén*) indicator light; (*d'alerte*) warning light; **~ d'essence/d'huile** petrol/oil warning light [b] [*arpenteur*] levelling rod *ou* staff

voyelle [vwajɛl] NF vowel; **~ orale/nasale/cardinale/centrale** oral/nasal/cardinal/central vowel; **point ~** vowel point

voyeur, -euse [vwajœʀ, øz] NM,F voyeur; (*qui se cache*) Peeping Tom

voyeurisme [vwajœʀism] NM voyeurism

voyou [vwaju] [1] NM [a] (= *délinquant*) lout, hoodlum, hooligan, yobbo* (*Brit*) [b] (= *garnement, enfant*) rascal, brat*; **espèce de petit ~ !** you little rascal! [2] ADJ loutish; **un air ~** a loutish manner; **il avait l'air un peu ~** he looked like a bit of a lout

voyoucratie [vwajukʀasi] NF **la ~** (*au gouvernement*) the government of things

VPC [vepese] NF (ABRÉV = **vente par correspondance**) → **vente**

vrac [vʀak] ◆ **en vrac** LOC ADV (= *au poids, sans emballage, au détail*) loose; (= *en gros*) in bulk *ou* quantity; (*fig* = *en désordre*) in a jumble, higgledy-piggledy; **acheter du vin en ~** to buy wine in bulk; **il a tout mis en ~ dans la valise** he jumbled everything into the case, he filled the case any old how; **il a cité en ~ Hugo, Balzac et Baudelaire** he quoted Hugo, Balzac and Baudelaire at random

vrai, vraie [vʀɛ] [1] ADJ [a] (*après n = exact*) [*récit, fait*] true; (*Art, Littérat*) [*couleurs, personnage*] true; **ce que tu dis est ~** what you say is true *ou* right; **c'est dangereux, c'est ~** (*frm*) **il est ~, mais ...** it's dangerous, it's true *ou* certainly, but ...; **le tableau, tristement ~, que cet auteur peint de notre société** the picture, sadly only too true (to life), which this author paints of our society; **tu as fini, pas ~ ?*** you've finished, right?* *ou* haven't you?; **tu veux venir aussi, pas ~ ?*** you want to come too, right?* *ou* don't you?; **c'est beau, pas ~ ?*** it's lovely, isn't it?; **c'est pas ~ !*** (*dénégation*) it just isn't true!; (*surprise*) I don't believe it!; (*consternation*) **c'est pas ~ ! j'ai encore oublié mes clés !*** oh no, I don't believe it! I've forgotten my keys again!; **il est pas ~, ce type !*** that guy's unbelievable!; **il n'en est pas moins ~ que ...** it's nonetheless *ou* nevertheless true that ...; **ce n'est que trop ~** it's only too true; **et cela est si ~ qu'une rencontre est prévue pour demain** and to prove it a meeting has been planned for tomorrow → **trop, vérité**

[b] (*gén avant nom = réel*) real; **ce sont ses ~s cheveux** that's his own hair; **une ~e blonde** a real *ou* genuine blonde; **un ~ Picasso** a real *ou* genuine Picasso; **son ~ nom c'est Charles** his real name is Charles; **des bijoux en or ~** real gold jewellery; **lui c'est un cheik, un ~ de ~*** he's a sheik — the real thing *ou* the genuine article; **un ~ socialiste** a true socialist

[c] (*avant nom : intensif*) real; **c'est un ~ fou !** he's really *ou* completely mad!; **c'est une ~e mère pour moi** she's a real mother to me; **un ~ chef-d'œuvre/héros** a real masterpiece/hero

[d] (*avant nom = bon*) real; **c'est le ~ moyen de le faire** that's the real way to do it

[e] (*Sci*) **le temps solaire ~** true solar time; **le jour ~** true time

[2] NM [a] (= *la vérité*) **le ~** the truth; **il y a du ~ dans ce qu'il dit** there's some truth *ou* there's an element of truth in what he says; **distinguer le ~ du faux** to distinguish truth from falsehood *ou* the true from the false; **être dans le ~** to be right → **plaider**

[b] (*loc*) **il dit ~** he's right (in what he says), it's true what he says; **à ~ dire ◊ à dire (le) ~**

to tell (you) the truth, in (actual) fact, actual-ly; **en ~*** in real life; (*gén langage enfantin*) **pour de ~*** for real*, really, seriously; **c'est pour de ~?*** is it for real?*, do you (or they *etc*) really mean it?; **au ~** (*littér*) ◊ **de ~††** in (actual) fact

3 ADV **faire ~** [*décor, perruque*] to look real *ou* like the real thing; [*peintre, artiste*] to strive for realism, paint (*ou* draw *etc*) realistically; **~†, quelle honte!** oh really, how shameful!

vrai-faux, vraie-fausse (*mpl* **vrais-faux**) [vʀɛfo, vʀɛfos] ADJ **a** (*délivré par une autorité*) **~ passeport/visa** false passport/visa (*issued by the state authorities to government agents etc*) **b** (= *truqué*) [*entretien*] faked; [*journal télévisé*] mock (*épith*); (= *usurpateur*) [*chirurgien, savant*] bogus (*épith*), phoney (*épith*)

vraiment [vʀɛmɑ̃] ADV **a** (= *véritablement*) re-ally; **nous voulons ~ la paix** we really do want peace; **s'aiment-ils ~?** do they really (and tru-ly) love each other? **b** (*intensif*) really; **il est ~ idiot** he's a real idiot, he's really stupid; **~, il exagère!** really, he's going too far!; **je ne sais ~ pas quoi faire** I really *ou* honestly don't know what to do; **oui ~, c'est dommage** yes, it's a real shame; **vous trouvez? — ah oui, ~!** do you think so? — oh yes, definitely! **c** (*de doute*) really?, is that so?; **il est parti — ~?** he has gone — (has he) really?

vraisemblable [vʀɛsɑ̃blabl] ADJ [*hypothèse, in-terprétation*] likely; [*situation, intrigue*] plau-sible, convincing; [*excuse, histoire*] **peu ~** im-probable, unlikely; **il est (très) ~ que ...** it's (highly *ou* most) likely *ou* probable that ...

vraisemblablement [vʀɛsɑ̃blabləmɑ̃] ADV probably, in all likelihood *ou* probability, very likely; **viendra-t-il? — ~/~ pas** will he come? — probably/probably not; **la fin, ~ proche, des hostilités** the end of hostilities, which looks imminent *ou* is likely to come very soon

vraisemblance [vʀɛsɑ̃blɑ̃s] NF [*hypothèse, in-terprétation*] likelihood; [*situation romanesque*] plausibility, verisimilitude; **selon toute ~** in all likelihood, in all probability

vraquier [vʀakje] NM bulk carrier

V/Réf (ABRÉV = **votre référence**) your ref

vrille [vʀij] NF **a** (*Bot*) tendril **b** (*Tech*) gimlet **c** (= *spirale*) spiral; (*Aviat*) spin, tailspin; **escalier en ~** spiral staircase; (*Aviat*) **descente en ~** spiral dive; (*Aviat*) **descendre en ~** to spi-ral downwards, come down in a spin; (*Aviat*) **se mettre en ~** to go into a tailspin

vrillé, e [vʀije] (*ptp de* **vriller**) ADJ [*tige*] tendrilled; [*fil*] twisted

vriller [vʀije] ▶ conjug 1 ◀ **1** VT to bore into, pierce **2** VI (*Aviat*) to spiral, spin; [*fil*] to be-come twisted

vrombir [vʀɔ̃biʀ] ▶ conjug 2 ◀ VI [*moteur*] (*régulièrement*) to throb; (*après une accélération*) to roar; [*insecte*] to buzz, hum; **faire ~ son mo-teur** to rev one's engine

vrombissement [vʀɔ̃bismɑ̃] NM [*moteur*] (*régu-lier*) humming (*NonC*); (*après accélération*) roar; [*insecte*] buzzing (*NonC*), humming (*NonC*)

vroum [vʀum] EXCL brum! brum!

VRP [veeʀpe] NM (ABRÉV = **voyageur, repré-sentant, placier**) sales rep* → **voyageur**

vs (ABRÉV = **versus**) vs, v

VSNE [veesɛnə] NM (ABRÉV = **volontaire du servi-ce national à l'étranger**) → **volontaire**

VSOP [veesɔpe] ADJ (ABRÉV = **very superior old pale**) VSOP

VTC [vetese] NM (ABRÉV = **vélo tout-chemin**) → **vélo**

VTT [vetete] NM (ABRÉV = **vélo tout-terrain**) → **vélo**

vu¹, vue¹ [vy] (*ptp de* **voir**) **1** ADJ **a** (* = *compris*) all right?, got it?*, under-stood?; **c'est bien vu?** all clear?*, is that quite clear?; **vu?** O.K.?*, right?*; **c'est tout vu** it's a foregone conclusion → **ni** **b** (= *jugé*) **balle/**

passe bien vue well-judged ball/pass; **re-marque bien vue** judicious remark; **c'était bien vu de sa part** what he said was spot-on* **c** (= *considéré*) **bien vu** [*personne*] well thought of, highly regarded; **mal vu** [*personne*] poorly thought of; **il est mal vu du patron** the boss thinks poorly of him *ou* has a poor opinion of him; **ici c'est bien/mal vu de porter une cravate** it's the done thing here *ou* it's good form (*Brit*)/it's not the done thing *ou* it's bad form (*Brit*) to wear a tie here **2** NM **au vu et au su de tous** openly and publicly → **déjà**

▼vu² [vy] **1** PRÉP (*gén, Jur*) in view of; **vu la situa-tion, cela valait mieux** it was better, in view of *ou* considering *ou* given the situation **2** CONJ* **vu que** in view of the fact that, see-ing *ou* considering that; **vu qu'il était tard, nous avons abandonné la partie** seeing *ou* considering how late it was, we abandoned the game

▼vue² [vy] NF **a** (= *sens*) sight, eyesight; **perdre la ~** to lose one's (eye)sight; **troubles de la ~** sight trouble; **il a une bonne ~** he has good eyesight, his eyesight is good; **il a la ~ basse** *ou* **courte** he's short-sighted *ou* near-sighted (*US*); **une politique à courte ~** a short-sighted policy; **don de seconde** *ou* **double ~** gift of se-cond sight

b (= *regard*) **détourner la ~** to look away, avert one's gaze; (*littér*) **porter la ~ sur qn/qch** to cast one's eyes over sb/sth, look in sb's direction/in the direction of sth; **s'offrir à la ~ de tous** to present o.s. for all to see; **il l'a fait à la ~ de tous** he did it in full view of every-body; **à première ~** at first sight; (*lit, fig*) **per-dre qch de ~** to lose sight of sth; **perdre qn de ~** (*lit*) to lose sight of sb; **il ne faut pas perdre de ~ que ...** we mustn't lose sight of the fact that ...; **perdre/ne pas perdre un ami de ~** to lose touch/keep in touch with a friend; **il lui en a mis plein la ~*** he really impressed her; **il a essayé de m'en mettre plein la ~*** he really tried to impress me

c (= *panorama*) view; **de cette colline, on a une très belle ~ de la ville** there's a very good view *ou* you get a very good view of the town from this hill; **avec ~ imprenable** with an open *ou* unobstructed view *ou* outlook; **ces immeubles nous bouchent la ~** those build-ings block our view; **cette pièce a ~ sur la mer** this room looks out onto the sea; **chambre avec ~ sur la montagne** room with a view of the mountains; **de là, on avait une ~ de profil de la cathédrale** from there you had a side view of the cathedral; **~ cavalière** (*lit*) bird's eye view; (*fig*) overview; **avoir une ~ cavalière d'une situation/période** to have an overview of a situation/period → **perte, point¹**

d (= *spectacle*) sight; **la ~ du sang l'a fait s'évanouir** the sight of the blood made him faint; **à la ~ de** at the sight of; **à sa ~ elle s'est mise à rougir** when she saw him she began to blush

e (= *image*) view; **des ~s de Paris** views of Paris; **un film de 36 ~s** a 36-exposure film; **ils nous ont montré des ~s prises pendant leurs vacances** they showed us some photos they'd taken on their holidays; **~ de la ville sous la neige** view of the town in the snow → **prise**

f (= *opinion*) **~s** views; **exprimer ses ~s sur un sujet** to air one's views on a subject; **de courtes ~s** short-sighted views → **échange**

g (= *conception*) view; **il a une ~ pessimiste de la situation** he has a pessimistic view of the situation; **donner une ~ d'ensemble** to give an overall view *ou* an overview; **c'est une ~ de l'esprit** that's a purely theoretical view → **point¹**

h (= *projet*) **~s** plans; (*sur qn ou ses biens*) de-signs; **la société a des ~s sur cet immeuble** the company has its eye on that building; **elle a des ~s sur lui** (*pour un projet*) she has her eye on him; (= *elle veut l'épouser*) she has designs on him, she has her eye on him

i (*Jur = fenêtre*) window

j (*loc*) **à ~** (*Aviat*) [*piloter, atterrir*] visually; [*atterrissage, navigation*] visual; (*Fin : payable*) at sight *ou* on demand; **dépôt à ~** demand *ou* sight deposit; **changement à ~** (*Théât*) trans-formation scene; (*fig*) (sudden) transforma-tion; **tirer à ~** to shoot on sight; **naviguer à ~** (*lit*) to navigate visually; (*fig*) to play it by ear; **à ~ d'œil** (= *rapidement*) before one's very eyes; (= *par une estimation rapide*) at a quick glance; **il maigrit à ~ d'œil** he seems to be get-ting thinner before our very eyes *ou* by the minute*; **à ~ de nez*** roughly*, at a rough guess; **de ~** by sight; **je le connais de ~** I know him by sight; **en ~** (*lit, fig*) (= *proche*) in sight; (= *en évidence*) (**bien**) **en ~** conspicuous; (= *cé-lèbre*) **très/assez en ~** very much/much in the public eye; **il a mis sa pancarte bien en ~** he put his placard in a prominent *ou* a conspicu-ous position *ou* where everyone could see it; **c'est un des hommes politiques les plus en ~** he's one of the most prominent *ou* best-known men in politics; **avoir un poste en ~** to have one's sights on a job; **avoir un collabora-teur en ~** to have an associate in mind; **avoir en ~ de faire** to have it in mind to do, plan to do; **il a acheté une maison en ~ de son maria-ge** he has bought a house with his marriage in mind; **il s'entraîne en ~ de la course de dimanche/de devenir champion du monde** he's training with a view to the race on Sunday/ becoming world champion; **il a dit cela en ~ de le décourager** he said that with the idea of *ou* a view to discouraging him → **changement, garder, tirer**

Vulcain [vylkɛ̃] NM Vulcan

vulcain [vylkɛ̃] NM (= *papillon*) red admiral

vulcanisation [vylkanizasjɔ̃] NF vulcanization

vulcaniser [vylkanize] ▶ conjug 1 ◀ VT to vul-canize

vulcanologie [vylkanɔlɔʒi] NF vulcanology

vulcanologue [vylkanɔlɔg] NMF vulcanolo-gist

vulgaire [vylgɛʀ] **1** ADJ **a** (= *grossier*) [*langage, personne*] vulgar, coarse; [*genre, dé-cor*] vulgar, crude **b** (= *prosaïque*) [*réalités, problèmes*] commonplace, everyday; mun-dane **c** (= *usuel, banal*) common, popular; **nom ~** common *ou* popular name; **langues ~s** common languages → **latin d** (*littér,†* = *du peuple*) common; **esprit ~** common mind; **l'opinion ~** the common opinion **e** (*avant n* = *quelconque*) ordinary; **~ escroc** common swindler; **un ~ bout de bois** an ordinary piece of wood; **de la ~ matière plastique** ordinary plastic, common *ou* garden plastic (*Brit*), garden-variety plastic (*US*) **2** NM (†, *hum* = *peuple*) **le ~** the common herd; (= *la vulgarité*) **tomber dans le ~** to lapse into vulgarity

vulgairement [vylgɛʀmɑ̃] ADV **a** (= *gros-sièrement*) vulgarly, coarsely **b** (= *couramment*) [*dénommer*] popularly, common-ly; **le fruit de l'églantier, ~ appelé** *ou* **que l'on appelle ~ gratte-cul** the fruit of the wild rose, commonly known as *ou* called haws

vulgarisateur, -trice [vylgaʀizatœʀ, tʀis] NM,F popularizer

vulgarisation [vylgaʀizasjɔ̃] NF populariza-tion; **~ scientifique** scientific popularization; **c'est un ouvrage de ~ scientifique** it's a book that makes science accessible to the layman *ou* the general public; **ouvrage de ~ scientifique** popular scientific work

vulgariser [vylgaʀize] ▶ conjug 1 ◀ VT **a** [+ *ouvrage*] to popularize **b** (*littér* = *rendre vulgaire*) to coarsen; **cet accent la vulgarise** this accent makes her sound coarse

vulgarisme [vylgaʀism] NM vulgarism

vulgarité [vylgaʀite] NF **a** (= *grossièreté*) vul-garity, coarseness (*NonC*); **des ~s** vulgarities **b** (*littér* = *terre à terre*) commonplaceness, ordinariness

> GRAMMAIRE ACTIVE : **vu** 44.1 **vue** 35.1, 35.2

vulgate [vylgat] NF vulgate

vulgum pecus[*] [vylgɔmpekys] NM (*hum*) **le ~** the hoi polloi, the common herd

vulnérabilité [vylnerabilite] NF vulnerability

vulnérable [vylnerabl] ADJ (*gén, Cartes*) vulnerable

vulnéraire [vylnerɛr] NF (*Bot*) kidney vetch, ladies' fingers

vulvaire [vylvɛr] 1 ADJ (*Anat*) vulvar 2 NF (*Bot*) stinking goosefoot

vulve [vylv] NF vulva

vulvite [vylvit] NF vulvitis

vumètre [vymɛtr] NM recording level gauge

Vve ABRÉV = **veuve**

W

W¹, **w** [dubləve] NM (= *lettre*) W, w
W² (ABRÉV = **Watt**) W
wagnérien, -ienne [vagneʀjɛ̃, jɛn] ① ADJ Wagnerian ② NM,F Wagnerian
wagon [vagɔ̃] ① NM [a] (*Rail = véhicule*) (*de marchandises*) truck, wagon (*Brit*), freight car (*US*); (*de voyageurs*) carriage (*Brit*), car (*US*) [b] (= *contenu*) truckload, wagonload; **un plein ~ de marchandises** a truckful *ou* truckload of goods; (*fig*) **il y en a tout un ~*** there are stacks of them*, there's a whole pile of them* ② COMP ► **wagon à bestiaux** cattle truck *ou* wagon ► **wagon frigorifique** refrigerated van ► **wagon de marchandises** goods truck, freight car (*US*) ► **wagon de voyageurs** passenger carriage (*Brit*) *ou* car (*US*)
wagon-citerne (*pl* **wagons-citernes**) [vagɔ̃sitɛʀn] NM tanker, tank wagon
wagon-couchettes (*pl* **wagons-couchettes**) [vagɔ̃kuʃɛt] NM couchette car *ou* carriage, ≈ sleeping car
wagon-foudre (*pl* **wagons-foudres**) [vagɔ̃fudʀ] NM (wine) tanker *ou* tank wagon
wagon-lit (*pl* **wagons-lits**) [vagɔ̃li] NM sleeper (*Brit*), Pullman (*US*)
wagonnet [vagɔnɛ] NM small truck
wagon-poste (*pl* **wagons-postes**) [vagɔ̃pɔst] NM mail van
wagon-réservoir (*pl* **wagons-réservoirs**) [vagɔ̃ʀezɛʀvwaʀ] NM = **wagon-citerne**
wagon-restaurant (*pl* **wagons-restaurants**) [vagɔ̃ʀɛstɔʀɑ̃] NM restaurant *ou* dining car
wahhabisme [waabism] NM Wa(h)habism
wahhabite [waabit] ADJ, NMF Wa(h)habi
Walhalla [valala] NM Valhalla
Walkman® [wɔkman] NM Walkman®, personal stereo
walkyrie [valkiʀi] NF (*Myth*) Valkyrie; (*fig hum*)

amazon
wallaby (*pl* **wallabies**) [walabi] NM wallaby
wallingant, e [walɛ̃gɑ̃, ɑ̃t] NM,F (*Belg : péj*) Walloon separatist
Wallis-et-Futuna [walisefutuna] N Wallis and Futuna Islands
wallon, -onne [walɔ̃, ɔn] ① ADJ Walloon ② NM (*Ling*) Walloon ③ **Wallon(ne)** NM,F Walloon
Wallonie [walɔni] NF Wallonia
wapiti [wapiti] NM wapiti
warrant [vaʀɑ̃] NM [a] [*magasins généraux*] warrant, warehouse warrant *ou* receipt, bond warrant; [*port*] dock *ou* deposit warrant [b] (*Bourse*) warrant
Washington [waʃiŋtɔn] ① N (= *ville*) Washington D.C ② NM (= *État*) Washington (State)
wassingue [vasɛ̃g] NF floorcloth
water-closet(s)† [watɛʀklozɛt] NM(PL) = **waters**
Waterloo [watɛʀlo] N Waterloo; **la bataille de ~** the Battle of Waterloo; (*fig*) **il a connu son ~ quand ...** he met his Waterloo when ...
water-polo [watɛʀpolo] NM water polo
waterproof [watɛʀpʀuf] ADJ INV [*montre, mascara*] waterproof
waters† [watɛʀ] NMPL toilet, loo* (*Brit*), lavatory; **où sont les ~ ?** where's the toilet?
waterzoï [watɛʀzɔj] NM (*Belg : Culin*) dish made with chicken or fish in a cream sauce
watt [wat] NM watt
wattheure [watœʀ] NM watt hour
wattman† [watman] NM tram driver
W-C, WC [vese] NMPL (ABRÉV = **water-closet(s)**) = **waters**
Web [wɛb] NM INV **le ~** the (Worldwide) Web

weber [vebɛʀ] NM weber
week-end (*pl* **week-ends**) [wikɛnd] NM weekend; **partir en ~** to go away for the weekend; **partir en ~ prolongé** to go away on *ou* for a long weekend
Weimar [vajmaʀ] N Weimar; **la république de ~** the Weimar Republic
Wellington [wɛliŋtɔn] N Wellington
welter [wɛltɛʀ] NM → **poids**
western [wɛstɛʀn] NM western; **~-spaghetti** ◊ **~ italien** spaghetti western
Westphalie [vɛsfali] NF Westphalia
whisky (*pl* **whiskies**) [wiski] NM (*écossais*) whisky; (*américain, irlandais*) whiskey; **~ soda** whisky and soda
whist [wist] NM whist
white-spirit [wajtspiʀit] NM white-spirit
Wight [wait] N **l'île de ~** the Isle of Wight
wigwam [wigwam] NM wigwam
williams [wiljams] NF (**poire**) **~** Williams pear
winch [win(t)ʃ] NM (*Naut*) winch
Winchester [winʃestɛʀ] NF (**carabine**) **~** Winchester (rifle)
Windhoek [windɔk] N Windhoek
Wisconsin [viskɔnsin] NM Wisconsin
wishbone [wiʃbon] NM (*Naut*) wishbone
wisigoth, e [vizigo, ɔt] ① ADJ Visigothic ② **Wisigoth(e)** NM,F Visigoth
wisigothique [vizigɔtik] ADJ Visigothic
wolfram [vɔlfʀam] NM wolfram
wolof [wɔlɔf] ① ADJ Wolof ② NM (*Ling*) Wolof ③ **Wolof** NMF Wolof
woofer [wufœʀ] NM woofer
Wyoming [wajɔmiŋ] NM Wyoming
wysiwyg [wiziwig] ADJ (ABRÉV = **what you see is what you get**) (*Ordin*) WYSIWYG

X

X, **x** [iks] NM [a] (= *lettre*) X, x; (*Math*) x; (*Bio*) **chromosome X** X-chromosome; (*Math*) **l'axe des x** the x axis; **croisés en X** forming an x; **ça fait x temps que je ne l'ai pas vu*** I haven't seen him for ages; **je te l'ai dit x fois** I've told you umpteen* times; (*Jur*) **plainte contre X** action against person or persons unknown; **Monsieur X** Mr X; **elle a accouché sous X** she gave her baby up as soon as it was born; **les enfants nés sous X** children whose mothers gave them up at birth; **film (classé) X** X(-rated) film, 18 film → **rayon** [b] (*arg Univ*) **l'X** the École Polytechnique; **un X** a student of the École Polytechnique

Xavier [gzavje] NM Xavier

xénon [gzenɔ̃] NM xenon

xénophobe [gzenɔfɔb] [1] ADJ xenophobic [2] NMF xenophobe

xénophobie [gzenɔfɔbi] NF xenophobia

Xénophon [gzenɔfɔ̃] NM Xenophon

xérès [gzeʀɛs] [1] NM (= *vin*) sherry [2] **Xérès** N (= *ville*) Jerez

Xerxès [gzeʀksɛs] NM Xerxes

xi [ksi] NM xi

xylographe [gzilɔgʀaf] NM xylographer

xylographie [gzilɔgʀafi] NF (= *technique*) xylography; (= *gravure*) xylograph

xylographique [gzilɔgʀafik] ADJ xylographic

xylophage [gzilɔfaʒ] [1] ADJ [*insecte*] woodboring (*épith*), xylophagous (*SPÉC*) [2] NM woodborer, xylophage (*SPÉC*)

xylophène® [gzilɔfɛn] NM wood preservative

xylophone [gzilɔfɔn] NM xylophone

Y

y¹, Y¹ [igrɛk] NM (= lettre) Y, y; (Bio) **chromosome Y** Y-chromosome; (Math) **l'axe des y** the y axis

y² (ABRÉV = **yen**) Y

y² [i] **1** ADV (indiquant le lieu) there; **restez-y** stay there; **nous y avons passé 2 jours** we spent 2 days there; **il avait une feuille de papier et il y dessinait un bateau** he had a sheet of paper and he was drawing a ship on it; **avez-vous vu le film?** — **j'y vais demain** have you seen the film? — I'm going (to see it) tomorrow; **les maisons étaient neuves, personne n'y avait habité** the houses were new and nobody had lived in them; **la pièce est sombre, quand on y entre, on n'y voit rien** the room is dark and when you go in you can't see a thing; **j'y suis, j'y reste** here I am and here I stay; (fig) **ah! j'y suis!** (comprendre) oh, I understand!; (se rappeler) oh, I remember!; **vous y allez, à ce dîner?*** are you going to that dinner then?; **je suis passé le voir mais il n'y était pas** I stopped by to see him but he wasn't there → **aller, avoir**

2 PRON PERS **a** (gén se rapportant à des choses) it; **vous serez là?** — **n'y comptez pas** you'll be there? — it's highly unlikely ou I doubt it; **n'y pensez plus** forget (about) it; **à votre place, je ne m'y fierais pas** if I were you I wouldn't trust it; **il a plu alors que personne ne s'y attendait** it rained when no one was expecting it to; **il y trouve du plaisir** he enjoys it

b (loc) **elle s'y connaît** she knows all about it, she's an expert; **il faudra vous y faire** you'll just have to get used to it; **je n'y suis pour rien** it's nothing to do with me, I had no part in it; **je n'y suis pour personne** I'm not in to anyone; **ça y est! c'est fait!** that's it, it's done!; **ça y est, il a cassé le verre** there you are, he's broken the glass; **ça y est, il a signé le contrat** that's it, he's signed the contract; **ça y est oui!, je peux parler?** is that it then? ou have you finished then? can I talk now?; **ça y est, tu es prêt?** — **non ça n'y est pas** is that it then, are you ready? — no I'm not; **ça y est pour quelque chose** it has something to do with it → **avoir, comprendre, voir** etc

c (* = il) (aussi iro) **c'est-y pas gentil?** isn't it nice?; **y en a qui exagèrent** some people ou folk go too far; **du pain? y en a pas** bread? there's none ou there isn't any

yacht ['jɔt] NM yacht; **~ de course/croisière** racing/cruising yacht

yacht-club (pl **yacht-clubs**) ['jɔtklœb] NM yacht club

yachting† ['jɔtiŋ] NM yachting; **faire du ~** to go out on one's yacht, go yachting

yacht(s)man† ['jɔtman] (pl **yacht(s)men** ['jɔtmɛn]) NM yacht owner, yachtsman

yack ['jak] NM = **yak**

Yahvé ['jave] NM Yahveh

yak ['jak] NM yak

yakusa ['jakuza] NM yakuza

Yalta ['jalta] N Yalta; **la conférence/les accords de ~** the Yalta conference/agreement

Yamoussoukro ['jamusukro] N Yamoussoukro

yang ['jãg] NM yang

Yang-Tsê Kiang ['jãgtsekjãg] NM Yangtze (Kiang)

yankee ['jãki] ADJ, NMF Yankee

Yaoundé ['jaunde] N Yaoundé

yaourt ['jaurt] NM yog(h)urt; **~ nature/maigre** natural/low-fat yog(h)urt; **~ aux fruits/à la grecque** fruit/Greek yog(h)urt; **~ à boire** yog(h)urt drink; **~ brassé** thick creamy yog(h)urt

yaourtière ['jaurtjɛr] NF yoghurt-maker

yard ['jard] NM yard

yatagan ['jatagã] NM yataghan

yearling ['jœrliŋ] NM (= cheval) yearling

Yémen ['jemɛn] NM **le ~** the Yemen; **Nord-/Sud-~** North/South Yemen; **au ~** in Yemen

yéménite ['jemenit] **1** ADJ Yemeni **2** **Yéménite** NMF Yemeni

yen ['jɛn] NM (Fin) yen

yéti ['jeti] NM yeti

yeuse ['jøz] NF holm oak, ilex

yeux ['jø] pl de **œil**

yéyé, yé-yé† [jeje] **1** ADJ INV **musique ~** French pop music of the 1960s; **les années ~** the sixties; **la mode ~** the sixties' look **2** NM **le ~** French pop music of the 1960s **3** NMF INV (= chanteur) French pop singer of the 1960s; (= jeune) teenage pop fan of the 1960s

yiddish ['jidiʃ] ADJ, NM Yiddish

Yi king ['jikiŋ] NM I Ching

yin ['jin] NM yin

ylang-ylang [ilãilã] NM ylang-ylang, ilang-ilang

yod ['jɔd] NM yod

yoga ['jɔga] NM yoga; **faire du ~** to do yoga

yogi ['jɔgi] NM yogi

yogourt, yoghourt ['jɔgurt] NM = **yaourt**

yole ['jɔl] NF skiff

Yom Kippour ['jɔmkipur] NM Yom Kippur

yorkshire, yorkshire-terrier (pl **yorkshire-terriers**) ['jɔrkʃœrtɛrje] NM Yorkshire terrier, yorkie*

yougoslave ['jugɔslav] **1** ADJ Yugoslav, Yugoslavian **2** **Yougoslave** NMF Yugoslav, Yugoslavian

Yougoslavie ['jugɔslavi] NF Yugoslavia

youp ['jup] EXCL hup!; **allez ~, dégagez!** come on, get a move on!

youpala ['jupala] NM baby bouncer

youpi ['jupi] EXCL yippee

youpin, e*‡ ['jupɛ̃, in] NM,F (injurieux) Yid‡ (injurieux)

yourte ['jurt] NF yurt

youyou ['juju] NM (Naut) dinghy

yo-yo, yoyo® ['jojo] NM INV (= jouet) yo-yo; (Fin) **les mouvements de yoyo du dollar** the wild fluctuations of the dollar; (fig) **jouer au ~** ◊ **faire le yoyo** to yo-yo

ypérite [iperit] NF mustard gas, yperite (SPÉC)

ytterbium [itɛrbjɔm] NM ytterbium

yttrium [itrijɔm] NM yttrium

yuan ['jyan] NM yuan

yucca ['juka] NM yucca

Yukon ['jykɔ̃] NM **le ~** (= fleuve) the Yukon (River); **le (territoire du) ~** the Yukon (Territory)

yuppie (pl **yuppies**) ['jupi] NM yuppie, yuppy

Z

Z, z [zɛd] NM (*lettre*) Z, z → **A**

ZAC [zak] NF (ABRÉV = **zone d'aménagement concerté**) → **zone**

Zacharie [zakaʀi] NM (= *prophète*) Zechariah; (= *père de Jean-Baptiste*) Zachariah

ZAD [zad] NF (ABRÉV = **zone d'aménagement différé**) → **zone**

Zagreb [zagʀɛb] N Zagreb

Zaïre [zaiʀ] NM **le ~** (= *pays*) Zaire; (= *fleuve*) the Zaire (River)

zaïre [zaiʀ] NM (= *monnaie*) zaire

zaïrois, -oise [zaiʀwa, waz] [1] ADJ Zairean, Zairian [2] **Zaïrois(e)** NM,F Zairean, Zairian

zakouski [zakuski] NMPL zakuski, zakouski

Zambèze [zɑ̃bɛz] NM **le ~** the Zambezi (River)

Zambie [zɑ̃bi] NF Zambia

zambien, -ienne [zɑ̃bjɛ̃, jɛn] [1] ADJ Zambian [2] **Zambien(ne)** NM,F Zambian

zanzi [zɑ̃zi] NM dice game

Zanzibar [zɑ̃zibaʀ] N Zanzibar

zapper [zape] ▶conjug 1◀ VI (*à la télévision*) to channel-hop, zap; (*à la radio*) to flick from one channel to the next

zappeur, -euse [zapœʀ, øz] NM,F (*TV*) zapper, channel-hopper

zapping [zapiŋ] NM (*TV*) zapping, channel-hopping

Zarathoustra [zaʀatustʀa] NM Zarathustra

zazou, e [zazu] [1] ADJ **la jeunesse ~(e)** young jazz-swingers of the 1940s; **tenue ~e** zoot suit [2] NMF (*parfois péj*) ≈ hepcat*

zébi [zebi] NM → **peau**

zèbre [zɛbʀ] NM (= *animal*) zebra; (* = *individu*) guy*, bloke* (*Brit*); **un drôle de ~** an oddball*, an odd bod* (*Brit*); **filer** *ou* **courir comme un ~** to run like the wind

zébrer [zebʀe] ▶conjug 6◀ VT (*lignes régulières*) to stripe; (*lignes irrégulières*) to streak (**de** with); **ciel zébré d'éclairs** sky streaked with lightning; **allée zébrée d'ombre et de lumière** lane dappled with light and shade

zébrure [zebʀyʀ] NF (*animal*) stripe, streak; [*coup de fouet*] weal, welt; (= *éclair*) streak

zébu [zeby] NM zebu

Zélande [zelɑ̃d] NF Zealand

zélateur, -trice [zelatœʀ, tʀis] NM,F (*gén*) champion, partisan (*péj*); zealot (*péj*); (*Rel*) Zealot

zélé, e [zele] ADJ zealous

zèle [zɛl] NM zeal; **avec ~** zealously, with zeal; (*péj*) **faire du ~** to be over-zealous; **faire preuve de/manquer de ~** to show/lack enthusiasm; **pas de ~!** don't overdo it!; **pousser le ~ jusqu'à faire qch** to go to the extreme of doing sth, go so far as to do sth → **excès, grève**

zélote [zelɔt] NM (*Hist*) Zealot

zen [zɛn] [1] NM ADJ INV (*lit*) Zen; **jardin ~** Zen garden; (*fig = serein*) **rester ~*** to remain unfazed*; (* *fig = dépouillé*) **c'est ~, chez lui !/cette pièce !** his place/this room is very minimalist! [2] NM Zen

zénana [zenana] NM → **peau**

zénith [zenit] NM (*lit, fig*) zenith; **le soleil est au ~** *ou* **à son ~** the sun is at its zenith *ou* height; **au ~ de la gloire** at the zenith *ou* peak of glory

zénithal, e [zenital, o] ADJ zenithal; **éclairage ~** overhead natural lighting

Zénon [zenɔ̃] NM Zeno

ZEP [zɛp] NF [a] (ABRÉV = **zone d'éducation prioritaire**) → **zone** [b] (ABRÉV = **zone d'environnement protégé**) → **zone**

zéphyr [zefiʀ] NM (*vent*) zephyr; (*Myth*) **Zéphyr** Zephyr(us)

zéphyrien, -ienne [zefiʀjɛ̃, jɛn] ADJ (*littér*) zephyr-like (*littér*)

zeppelin [zɛplɛ̃] NM zeppelin

zéro [zeʀo] NM [a] (*gén, Math*) zero, nought (*Brit*); (*compte à rebours*) zero; (*dans un numéro de téléphone*) 0, zero (*US*); **les enfants de ~ à cinq ans** children up to the age of five; **sur une échelle de ~ à dix** on a scale of zero *ou* nought (*Brit*) to ten; **recommencer à ~** ◊ **repartir de** *ou* **à ~** to start from scratch again, go back to square one; **remettre à ~** [*compteur, chronomètre*] to reset; **il n'avait rien compris, j'ai dû tout reprendre à ~** he hadn't understood a thing, I had to start all over again from scratch; **tout ça, pour moi, c'est ~, je veux des preuves*** as far as I'm concerned that's worthless *ou* a waste of time — I want some proof; **les avoir à ~⁑** to be scared out of one's wits*, be scared stiff* → **compteur, moral, partir¹, réduire**

[b] (*température*) freezing (point), zero (centigrade); **3 degrés au-dessus de ~** 3 degrees above freezing (point) *ou* above zero; **3 degrés au-dessous de ~** 3 degrees below freezing (point) *ou* below zero, 3 degrees below*, minus 3 (degrees centigrade); **~ absolu** absolute zero

[c] (*Rugby, Ftbl*) zero, nil (*Brit*), nothing (*US*); (*Tennis*) love; (*Tennis*) **mener par 2 jeux/sets à ~** to lead (by) 2 games/sets to love; **~ à ~ ou ~ partout à la mi-temps** no score at half time; **gagner par 2 (buts) à ~** to win 2 nil (*Brit*) *ou* 2 nothing (*US*), win by 2 goals to zero *ou* nil (*Brit*) *ou* nothing (*US*); **la France avait ~ à la mi-temps** France hadn't scored *ou* had no score by half time

[d] (*Scol*) zero, nought (*Brit*); **~ de conduite** bad mark (*Brit*) *ou* grade (*US*) for behaviour *ou* conduct; **~ pointé** (*Scol*) nothing, nought (*Brit*) (*counted in the final average mark*); (*fig*) **le gouvernement mérite un ~ pointé** the government deserves nothing out of 20; (*fig*) **mais en cuisine, ~ (pour la question)*** but as far as cooking goes he's (*ou* she's) useless *ou* a dead loss*

[e] (* = *personne*) dead loss*, washout*

[2] ADJ **~ heure** (*gén*) midnight; (*heure GMT*) zero hour; **~ heure trente** (*gén*) half past midnight; (*heure GMT*) zero thirty hours; **il a fait ~ faute** he didn't make any mistakes, he didn't make a single mistake; (*Ind*) **~ défaut/stock** zero defect/stock; **j'ai eu ~ point** I got no marks (*Brit*) *ou* points (*US*) (at all), I got zero;

ça m'a coûté ~ franc ~ centime* I got it for nothing; **en ski, le risque ~ n'existe pas** in skiing there's no such thing as zero risk; **taux de croissance ~** zero growth; (*Nucl*) **le point ~** ground zero; (*Mil*) **l'option ~** the zero option

zeste [zɛst] NM [a] [*citron, orange*] peel (*NonC*); (*en cuisine*) zest (*NonC*), peel (*NonC*); **avec un ~ de citron** with a piece of lemon peel [b] (*fig = pointe*) [*ironie*] touch, hint; **un ~ de folie/d'humour** a touch of madness/humour

zêta [(d)zeta] NM zeta

zeugma [zøgma], **zeugme** [zøgm] NM zeugma

Zeus [zøs] NM Zeus

zézaiement [zezɛmɑ̃] NM lisp

zézayer [zezeje] ▶conjug 8◀ VI to lisp

ZI [zɛdi] NF (ABRÉV = **zone industrielle**) → **zone**

zibeline [ziblin] NF sable

zidovudine [zidɔvydin] NF zidovudine

zieuter⁑ [zjøte] ▶conjug 1◀ VT (*longuement*) to eye; (*rapidement*) to have a squint at*, have a dekko at⁑ (*Brit*)

zig*† [zig] NM = **zigoto**

ziggourat [zigurat] NF ziggurat, zik(k)urat

zigoto*† [zigɔto], **zigomar*†** [zigɔmaʀ] NM guy*, bloke* (*Brit*), chap* (*Brit*), geezer* †; **c'est un drôle de ~** he's a bit of an oddball*; **faire le ~** to mess *ou* muck (*Brit*) around

zigouiller* [ziguje] ▶conjug 1◀ VT to do in*; **se faire ~** to get bumped off*

zigounette* [zigunɛt] NF (*hum ou langage enfantin*) willy* (*Brit*), peter* (*US*)

zigue*† [zig] NM = **zig**

zigzag [zigzag] NM zigzag; **route en ~** windy *ou* winding *ou* zigzagging road; **faire des ~s** [*route*] to zigzag; [*personne*] to zigzag along; **avoir fait** *ou* **eu une carrière en ~** to have had a chequered career

zigzaguer [zigzage] ▶conjug 1◀ VI to zigzag (along)

Zimbabwe [zimbabwe] NM Zimbabwe

zimbabwéen, -enne [zimbabweɛ̃, ɛn] [1] ADJ Zimbabwean [2] **Zimbabwéen(ne)** NM,F Zimbabwean

zinc [zɛ̃g] NM [a] (= *métal*) zinc [b] (* = *avion*) plane [c] (* = *comptoir*) bar, counter; **boire un coup sur le ~** to have a drink at the bar

zinguer [zɛ̃ge] ▶conjug 1◀ VT [+ *toiture, acier*] to coat with zinc

zingueur [zɛ̃gœʀ] NM zinc worker; **plombier-~** plumber and zinc worker

zinnia [zinja] NM zinnia

zinzin* [zɛ̃zɛ̃] [1] ADJ cracked*, nuts*, barmy* (*Brit*) [2] NM [a] (= *fou*) nutcase*, loony* (*Brit*) [b] (= *machin*) thingummy(jig)* (*Brit*), thingamajig (*US*), what's-it* (*Brit*) [3] **zinzins*** NMPL (*arg Bourse*) institutional investors

zip® [zip] NM zip; **poche fermée par un ~** zip(ped) pocket

zippé, e [zipe] (*ptp de* **zipper**) ADJ zip-up (*épith*), with a zip

zipper [zipe] ▶conjug 1◀ VT to zip up

zircon [ziRkɔ̃] NM zircon

zirconium [ziRkɔnjɔm] NM zirconium

zizanie [zizani] NF ill-feeling; **mettre** ou **semer la ~ dans une famille** to set a family at loggerheads, stir up ill-feeling in a family

zizi* [zizi] NM (hum, langage enfantin = pénis) willy* (Brit) (hum), peter* (US) (hum)

zloty [zlɔti] NM zloty

zob*: [zɔb] NM (= pénis) dick*:, prick*:, cock*:

Zodiac® [zɔdjak] NM rubber ou inflatable dinghy

zodiacal, e (mpl **-aux**) [zɔdjakal, o] ADJ [constellation, signe] of the zodiac; [lumière] zodiacal

zodiaque [zɔdjak] NM zodiac → **signe**

zombi(e) [zɔ̃bi] NM zombie

zona [zona] NM shingles sg, herpes zoster (SPÉC); **avoir un ~** to have shingles

zonage [zonaʒ] NM (Urbanisme, Ordin) zoning

zonard, e: [zonaR, aRd] NM,F (= marginal) dropout*

zone [zon] ☐ NF ⓐ (gén, Sci) zone, area; (Transport) travel zone; (Agr) **~ d'élevage** cattle-breeding area; **~ de pêche** fishing zone; **~ d'influence (d'un pays)** sphere ou zone of influence (of a country); **la ~ des combats** the combat zone; (Mét) **~ de haute/basse pression** area of high/low pressure; **~ franc/ sterling** franc/sterling area; **hors ~ franc** [pays] that does not belong to the franc area; (Scol) **~s A, B et C** three zones in France where schools take mid-term breaks and Easter holidays at different times to avoid overcrowding in the transport system and at holiday resorts; **dans cette affaire, des ~s d'ombre subsistent encore** some aspects of this business remain very unclear; (fig) **de deuxième/troisième ~** second-/ third-rate; (Mil) **arriver sur ~** to arrive at the scene of the action

ⓑ * **la ~** (= quartiers pauvres) the slum belt; (= marginalité) the dropout lifestyle; **c'est la ~ !** it's the pits!*; **enlève ce bric-à-brac de ton jardin, ça fait ~*** get rid of that junk in your garden, it looks like a tip *

☐ COMP ► **zone d'activités** business park, enterprise zone ► **zone d'aménagement concerté** urban development zone ► **zone d'aménagement différé** future develop-

ment zone ► **la zone des armées** the war zone ► **zone artisanale** industrial estate (Brit) ou park (US) for small businesses ► **zone bleue** ≈ restricted parking zone ou area ► **zone dangereuse** danger zone ► **zone démilitarisée** demilitarized zone ► **zone de dépression** ou **dépressionnaire** (Météo) trough of low pressure ► **zone de dialogue** (Ordin) dialogue box ► **zone d'éducation prioritaire** area targeted for special help in education ► **zone d'environnement protégé** environmentally protected zone, ≈ SSSI (Brit) ► **zone érogène** erogenous zone ► **zone d'exclusion** (Mil) exclusion zone; **~ d'exclusion aérienne** no-fly zone ► **zone franche** free zone ► **zone frontalière** border area ou zone ► **zone industrielle** industrial estate (Brit) ou park (US) ► **zone inondable** flood-risk area ► **zone interdite** off-limits area, no-go area; **~ interdite à la navigation** area which is closed to shipping ► **zone libre** (Hist France) unoccupied France; **passer/se réfugier en ~ libre** to enter/take refuge in the unoccupied zone ► **zone de libre-échange** free trade zone ou area ► **zone monétaire** monetary zone ► **zone occupée** (Hist France) occupied zone ► **zone piétonne** ou **piétonnière** pedestrian precinct ► **zone à risque** (catastrophes naturelles) disaster-prone area; (criminalité) high-risk area ► **zone tampon** (Mil) buffer zone; (Ordin) buffer ► **zone de turbulences** (Aviat) area of turbulence; (fig) trouble spot ► **zone urbaine** urban area ► **zone à urbaniser en priorité**† (Admin) urban development zone

zoner [zone] ►conjug 1◄ ☐ VT to zone ☐ VI*: [marginal] to bum around*

zoo [zo(o)] NM zoo

zoologie [zɔɔlɔʒi] NF zoology

zoologique [zɔɔlɔʒik] ADJ zoological

zoologiste [zɔɔlɔʒist], **zoologue** [zɔɔlɔg] NMF zoologist

zoom [zum] NM (= objectif) zoom lens; (= effet) zoom; **faire un ~ sur** to zoom in on; **~ avant/ arrière** zoom in/out; **faire un ~ avant/arrière** to zoom in/out

zoomer [zume] ►conjug 1◄ VI to zoom in (**sur** on)

zoomorphe [zɔɔmɔRf] ADJ zoomorphic

zoophile [zɔɔfil] ☐ ADJ zoophilic ☐ NMF zoophilist

zoophilie [zɔɔfili] NF (= perversion) zoophilia

zootechnicien, -ienne [zɔɔtɛknisjɛ̃, jɛn] NMF zootechnician

zootechnique [zɔɔteknik] ADJ zootechnic

zoreille* [zɔRɛj] NMF person from metropolitan France living in the overseas territories

Zoroastre [zɔRɔastR] NM Zoroaster, Zarathustra

zoroastrisme [zɔRɔastRism] NM Zoroastrianism, Zoroastrism

zou* [zu] EXCL (**allez**) **~ !** (= partez) off with you!, shoo!*; (= dépêchez-vous) get a move on!*; **et ~, les voilà partis !** zoom, off they go!*

zouave [zwav] NM Zouave, zouave; **faire le ~*** to play the fool, fool around

zouk [zuk] NM zouk

zoulou, e [zulu] ☐ ADJ Zulu ☐ NM (Ling) Zulu ☐ **Zoulou(e)** NM,F Zulu

Zoulouland [zululɑ̃d] NM Zululand

zozo* [zozo] NM (= naïf) nit(wit)*, ninny*; (= individu) guy, bloke (Brit)

zozoter* [zozɔte] ►conjug 1◄ VI to lisp

ZUP† [zyp] NF (ABRÉV = **zone à urbaniser en priorité**) → **zone**

zut* [zyt] EXCL (= c'est embêtant) damn!*, darn (it)!*; (= ça suffit !) (do) shut up!*; **je te dis ~ !** get lost!*; **je fais ce que je veux, ~ alors !** I'll do what I want, for goodness' sake!; **et puis ~ à la fin ! j'abandonne !** what the heck*, I give up!; **avoir un œil qui dit ~ à l'autre** to be cross-eyed

zwanze [zwɑ̃z] NF (Belg) joke

zwanzer [zwɑ̃ze] ►conjug 1◄ VI (Belg) to joke

zygomatique [zigɔmatik] ☐ ADJ zygomatic; **os/arcade ~** zygomatic bone/arch ☐ NM zygomatic major (muscle) (SPÉC); (hum) **se dérouiller les ~s*** to have a good laugh

zygote [zigɔt] NM zygote

zyklon [ziklɔ̃] NM (gaz) **~** ◊ **~ B** Zyklon B

zymase [zimɑz] NF zymase

LANGUAGE IN USE
GRAMMAIRE ACTIVE

First Edition
by
Beryl T. Atkins and Hélène M. A. Lewis
New Edition
by
Diana Feri   Hélène Bernaert   Christine Penman

INTRODUCTION

This **LANGUAGE IN USE** supplement is divided into 27 topics, providing thousands of structures to facilitate self-expression and communication in French.

Using a key word in the message you wish to convey as a starting point, **Language in Use** shows you other possible ways of expressing the same message and provides you with a repertoire from which to choose the most appropriate formulation for the situation you are dealing with. The core translation which follows each phrase acts as a point of reference rather than as a direct equivalent and we have also provided guidance as to whether a phrase should be used in a familiar or formal context, whether it expresses the message directly or indirectly, or in a tentative or assertive manner.

Language in Use has been compiled using our vast linguistic databases of contemporary French and English. The examples have been selected from a wide variety of different sources: fiction and non-fiction, magazines and newspapers, business and personal correspondence, and spoken material gathered from real-life conversations and radio and television programmes. This means you can always be sure that the phrases and grammatical structures you choose are idiomatic and up-to-date.

Several hundred dictionary entries are linked to **Language in Use** by means of cross-references which show the topic number and section in **Language in Use** where that dictionary entry occurs. To help you further, the word is underlined in the **Language in Use** section so that you can locate it quickly and easily. This linking of the main text with **Language in Use** allows you to navigate directly from a single-concept word in the dictionary to further, more diverse means of expression in context.

INTRODUCTION

La **GRAMMAIRE ACTIVE** ROBERT & COLLINS est divisée en 27 chapitres qui présentent plusieurs milliers de structures syntaxiques couvrant l'essentiel des besoins de communication entre francophones et anglophones.

Elle permet de s'exprimer directement dans la langue étrangère au lieu de procéder à la traduction à partir du mot ou de la locution, tels qu'ils figurent dans la partie dictionnaire. L'usager part ici d'un thème de réflexion ou du message qu'il cherche à communiquer et trouve dans le chapitre concerné un vaste éventail de possibilités d'expression dans la langue étrangère. De brèves indications dans sa langue maternelle, dont la fonction n'est pas de traduire mais de servir de points de repère, l'informeront sur le registre (familier ou soutenu) ou la nature (hésitante ou assurée, directe ou indirecte) du message.

Les exemples de la **Grammaire active** ont été tirés d'une très vaste base de données informatisée en langue française et en langue anglaise. Ces exemples ont été sélectionnés dans un grand nombre de sources différentes, allant de la littérature à la correspondance personnelle, en passant par les magazines, les journaux, ainsi que la langue parlée telle qu'on l'entend à la télévision et à la radio. Ils garantissent ainsi l'authenticité absolue des structures grammaticales et des expressions idiomatiques qui sont proposées.

Plusieurs centaines de mots-clés du dictionnaire sont suivis d'un renvoi à une rubrique de la **Grammaire active**. Ces renvois avertissent l'usager qu'il trouvera dans le recueil d'expressions grammaticales des possibilités d'expression supplémentaires qui complètent l'information contenue dans les articles bilingues. Afin de vous aider à repérer facilement dans la **Grammaire active** le mot faisant l'objet d'un renvoi, celui-ci est souligné.

1   SUGGESTIONS

1.1   Making suggestions

Tentatively

+ **Si je peux me permettre une suggestion**, je crois qu'il faudrait ...
  = *if I may make a <u>suggestion</u>*
+ **À votre place,** je me renseignerais
  = *if I were you*
+ **Si j'étais vous**, je resterais
  = *if I were you*
+ **À mon avis**, il faudrait les inviter
  = *in my <u>opinion</u>*
+ **Personnellement**, j'en parlerais à ses parents
  = *<u>personally</u> (speaking)*

More assertively

+ **Vous pourriez** remettre cela à plus tard
  = *you <u>could</u>*
+ **Rien ne vous empêche de** profiter des soldes
  = *there's nothing to stop you*
+ **Essayez quand même de** lui en parler
  = *still, try to*
+ **Vous feriez mieux de** prendre vos vacances en septembre
  = *you'd do <u>better</u> to*
+ **Vous auriez intérêt à** prendre l'avion à Genève
  = *you'd be <u>well-advised</u> to*
+ **Vous feriez bien d'**aller voir sur place
  = *you'd do <u>well</u> to*
+ **N'oubliez pas de** répondre à sa lettre
  = *don't <u>forget</u> to*
+ **Vous devriez** appeler un médecin
  = *you <u>ought</u> to*
+ **Je propose que** nous nous mett**ions** *(subj)* au travail tout de suite
  = *I <u>suggest</u> that*
+ **Voici mes suggestions**: présenter le projet au Conseil, ...
  = *my <u>suggestions</u> are (as follows):*
+ **Je suggère que vous** commenc**iez** *(subj)* immédiatement *(formal)*
  = *I <u>suggest</u> that you*

Using direct questions

+ **Est-ce que vous avez songé à** faire appel à un entraîneur ?
  = *have you <u>thought</u> of*
+ **Avez-vous pensé à** reprendre vos études ?
  = *have you <u>thought</u> of*
+ **Que diriez-vous d'**un bon repas ?
  = *what would you <u>say</u> to*
+ **Est-ce que cela ne vous tente pas de** partir en Italie ?
  = *doesn't the <u>idea</u> of ... tempt you?*
+ **Puis-je faire une suggestion ?** Il me semble que ... *(formal)*
  = *can I make a <u>suggestion</u>?*

In an impersonal way

Tentatively

+ **Et si** on se passait un film ? *(spoken)*
  = *how about*
+ **Peut-être faudrait-il** discuter de ce problème
  = *<u>perhaps</u> we <u>should</u>*
+ **Il vaudrait peut-être mieux** en rester là
  = *<u>perhaps</u> it would be <u>better</u> to*

+ **Pourquoi ne pas** lui téléphoner?
  = *why not*
+ **Ce ne serait pas une mauvaise idée de** revendre la maison
  = *it wouldn't be a bad <u>idea</u> to*
+ **On pourrait** adopter une autre méthode
  = *we <u>could</u>*

More assertively

+ **Il serait souhaitable de** conserver cette procédure de vote
  = *it would be <u>desirable</u> to*
+ **Il serait préférable de ne pas** trop attendre
  = *it would be <u>preferable</u> not to*
+ **Il serait bon de** réunir le Conseil
  = *it would be a good <u>idea</u> to*
+ **Ce serait une excellente idée de** rediffuser ce document
  = *it would be an excellent <u>idea</u> to*
+ **Il n'y a qu'à** lui demander son avis
  = *all you have to do is*
+ **Il conviendrait de** contacter l'entreprise dès maintenant *(formal)*
  = *it would be <u>advisable</u> to*

1.2   Asking for suggestions

+ **Qu'est-ce que tu ferais à ma place ?**
  = *what would you do if you were me?*
+ **Comment procéderais-tu** *or* **t'y prendrais-tu ?**
  = *how would you proceed?*
+ **Qu'est-ce que vous proposez** pour résoudre ce problème ?
  = *what do you <u>suggest</u>*
+ **Avez-vous une idée de** ce que l'on pourrait faire ?
  = *have you any <u>ideas</u> about*
+ **Que fait-on dans ces cas-là ?**
  = *what does one do in such cases?*
+ **Peut-être avez-vous une meilleure solution ?**
  = *<u>perhaps</u> you have a <u>better</u> <u>solution</u>?*

2   ADVICE

2.1   Asking for advice

+ **À ma place que feriez-vous ?**
  = *if you were me, what would you do?*
+ **Que fait-on dans ces cas-là ?**
  = *what does one do in such cases?*
+ **Que me conseillez-vous de faire ?**
  = *what do you <u>advise</u> me to do?*
+ **Que dois-je faire** dans l'immédiat ?
  = *what do I have to do*
+ **J'aimerais avoir votre opinion sur** ce dossier
  = *I'd like your <u>opinion</u> on*
+ **Quel est votre avis sur** le droit d'ingérence humanitaire ?
  = *what is your <u>opinion</u> on*
+ **Je voudrais vous demander conseil : pensez-vous que je devrais** offrir des fleurs à notre hôtesse ?
  = *I'd like your <u>advice</u>: do you think I <u>should</u>*
+ **Je vous serais très reconnaissant de bien vouloir me conseiller sur** la marche à suivre *(formal, written style)*
  = *I <u>should</u> be most <u>grateful</u> for your <u>advice</u> on*

2.2   Giving advice

+ Fais comme si de rien n'était, **c'est ce que tu as de mieux à faire** *(spoken)*
  = *it's the <u>best</u> thing you can do*

◆ **Moi, je trouve que tu devrais** carrément déménager *(spoken)*
  = *I think you should*

◆ **Un conseil :** il faut découvrir cet endroit le matin quand la ville est encore fraîche
  = *a word of advice:*

◆ **Tu as (tout) intérêt à** t'y prendre aussitôt que possible
  = *you'd be well-advised to*

◆ Si vous vivez une passion, au moins taisez-la. **Surtout ne** l'écrivez **pas**
  = *whatever you do, don't*

◆ **Si j'ai un conseil à vous donner, c'est de** ne pas trop tarder à renvoyer ces papiers
  = *if I could give you one piece of advice, it would be to*

◆ **Vous auriez tort de ne pas** en profiter
  = *you'd be quite wrong not to*

◆ **Je trouve que tu devrais** essayer de passer ton permis de conduire
  = *I think you should*

◆ **À mon avis, tu devrais** te montrer plus enthousiaste
  = *in my opinion, you should*

◆ **À votre place, je** me renseignerais auprès de l'association des parents d'élèves
  = *if I were you, I'd*

◆ **Si j'étais vous, je** téléphonerais sans plus tarder
  = *if I were you, I'd*

◆ **Je ne saurais trop vous recommander d'**être discret à ce sujet
  = *I cannot advise you strongly enough to*

| More tentatively |

◆ **Pourquoi ne pas** téléphoner à Martine ? Ça lui ferait plaisir
  = *why not*

◆ **Est-ce que tu as pensé à** un cours de recyclage ?
  = *have you thought of*

◆ **Ce ne serait pas une mauvaise idée de** partir avant l'heure de pointe
  = *it wouldn't be a bad idea to*

◆ **Vous feriez mieux de** vous adresser à un autre musée
  = *you'd do better to*

◆ Nous n'avons plus de 45 mais **vous pourriez peut-être** essayer du 44
  = *perhaps you could*

◆ **Je me demande si vous ne devriez pas** attendre quelques jours
  = *I wonder if you should perhaps*

◆ **Il est déconseillé de** se promener du côté du port après la tombée de la nuit
  = *it is inadvisable to*

◆ **Il serait peut-être bon de** changer de ton à défaut de changer de politique
  = *perhaps it would be a good idea to*

◆ **Il nous semble peu prudent d'**engager des fonds aussi importants dans cette affaire
  = *it doesn't seem very wise to us*

◆ **Il serait judicieux de** publier ce document avant la fin de l'année
  = *it would be wise to*

◆ **Puis-je me permettre de suggérer que** vous changiez *(subj)* d'itinéraire au retour ?
  = *may I suggest that you*

| **2.3** Giving warnings |

◆ **Méfiez-vous de** ces faux amis
  = *beware of*

◆ **Si vous ne** réservez **pas** maintenant, **vous courez le risque de** ne pas avoir de billet
  = *if you don't ... you run the risk of*

◆ **Tu vas avoir des ennuis** de santé **si** tu continues à fumer autant
  = *you're going to have problems if*

◆ **Je vous préviens :** interdiction de stationner entre 13 et 16 heures, sinon gare au PV
  = *I am warning you:*

◆ **Je vous préviens que** je ne vous accorderai pas un jour de délai
  = *I warn you that*

◆ **Je vous avertis que** je commence à en avoir assez de vos absences répétées
  = *I warn you that*

◆ **Ce serait de la folie de** s'engager dans cette direction
  = *it would be madness to*

◆ **Si vous** ne voulez pas vous allier, **très bien, mais** ne venez pas vous plaindre de ce qui vous arrivera
  = *if you ... (that's) fine, but*

| **3** | OFFERS |

| **3.1** Direct offers |

◆ **Je ferais volontiers** ce voyage avec toi
  = *I'd gladly*

◆ **Je suis prêt à** poursuivre le travail commencé avec lui
  = *I'm prepared to*

◆ **Je peux** passer vous prendre chez vous, **si vous voulez**
  = *I can ... if you want*

◆ **Je pourrais** venir étudier la question sur place
  = *I could*

◆ **N'hésitez pas à** nous poser des questions
  = *don't hesitate to*

◆ **Laissez-moi au moins** payer les fleurs!
  = *at least let me*

| **3.2** Indirect offers |

◆ **Je serais (très) heureux de** vous rendre ce service
  = *I'd be very happy to*

◆ **Cela me ferait très plaisir de** vous emmener
  = *it would be a pleasure to*

◆ **Je ne demande pas mieux que de** participer à ce projet
  = *I'd be only too happy to*

◆ **Nous pourrions peut-être** déjeuner ensemble
  = *perhaps we could*

| **3.3** Using direct questions |

◆ **Cela te dirait de** visiter la Maison-Blanche ?
  = *how would you like to*

◆ **Et si je** passais l'aspirateur ?
  = *what if I*

◆ **Est-ce que je peux** vous renseigner ?
  = *can I*

◆ **Est-ce que vous voulez que j'aille** *(subj)* vous chercher un journal?
  = *do you want me to go*

◆ **Voudriez-vous que nous avancions** *(subj)* la réunion ?
  = *would you like us to*

◆ **Puis-je** vous être utile ?
  = *can I*

◆ **Souhaitez-vous que nous** poursuivions *(subj)* les expériences en cours ?
  = *do you want us to*

◆ **Aimeriez-vous que je** m'en charge *(subj)* pour vous?
  = *would you like me to*

4 REQUESTS

Tentatively

- **Est-ce que cela vous dérangerait beaucoup de** me céder votre place?
  = would you _mind_ awfully
- **Est-ce que cela vous ennuierait beaucoup de** me déposer chez moi?
  = would you _mind_ terribly
- **Cela me rendrait service si vous pouviez** me le prêter
  = it would be of _help_ (to me) if you could
- **Cela m'arrangerait si vous pouviez** payer tout de suite
  = it would _suit_ me (nicely) if you could
- **Nous aimerions** connaître vos heures d'ouverture
  = we would _like_ to
- **Nous souhaiterions** clarifier quelques détails (formal)
  = we _wish_ to
- **Puis-je vous demander de (bien vouloir)** me fournir quelques renseignements? (formal)
  = _can_ I _ask_ you, please, to
- **Je voudrais** connaître les horaires des trains suivants
  = I'd _like_ to

More assertively

- **Est-ce que vous pourriez** nous donner un mode d'emploi?
  = _could_ you
- **Est-ce que vous pouvez** nous donner un exemple de prix?
  = _can_ you
- **Je dois vous demander de** procéder à une enquête
  = I must _ask_ you to
- **Nous comptons sur vous pour** terminer ce travail rapidement
  = we are _counting_ on you to
- **J'insiste pour que** le rapport **soit** (subj) substantiel et motivé
  = I _insist_ on ... being

In writing

- **Vous serait-il possible de** me dire où il faut s'adresser?
  = _could_ you _possibly_
- **Auriez-vous l'amabilité de** nous transmettre le texte?
  = would you be so _kind_ as to
- **Seriez-vous assez aimable pour** m'indiquer la marche à suivre?
  = would you be so _kind_ as to
- **Je vous remercie de bien vouloir** me faire parvenir ces renseignements
  = I would _appreciate_ it if you would
- **Je vous prie de bien vouloir** attendre avant de remettre votre rapport
  = _please_
- **Je vous serais reconnaissant de bien vouloir** leur envoyer ce document
  = I would be _grateful_ if you would
- **Je vous saurais gré de bien vouloir** rectifier cette erreur
  = I should be _grateful_ if you would
- **Nous vous serions obligés de bien vouloir** nous faire part de vos décisions
  = we should be _obliged_ if you would
- **Veuillez avoir l'obligeance de** remplir ces formulaires
  = please be so _kind_ as to
- **Vous êtes prié de bien vouloir** régulariser votre situation
  = we _request_ that you

5 COMPARISONS

5.1 Objective comparisons

- Cette nouvelle structure offrirait, **par comparaison avec** l'ancienne, souplesse et personnalisation de la gestion
  = by _comparison_ with
- Quant au poisson, il offre, **en comparaison de** la viande, l'intérêt d'être peu gras
  = by _comparison_ with
- ... un chiffre non négligeable, **comparé à** l'investissement initial
  = _compared_ with
- C'est tout de même un pays riche **si on le compare à** l'ensemble du monde
  = if one _compares it_ with
- Il y a des événements **bien plus** tragiques **que de** perdre une finale de Coupe d'Europe
  = much _more_ ... than
- La progression, **par rapport à** l'année précédente, est importante
  = _compared_ to
- Sa nouvelle maison **ressemble à** l'ancienne mais en moins grand
  = _resembles_
- **Cela fait penser à** du marbre mais en plus brillant
  = it _reminds_ one of
- C'est un jardin qui peut, **par constraste avec** l'agitation environnante, évoquer ceux de Kyoto
  = when _contrasted_ with
- Cet appartement donne sur un joli jardin **tandis que** or **alors que** l'autre donne sur une cour
  = _whereas_

5.2 Making favourable/unfavourable comparisons

- Ce vin **est de très loin supérieur à** l'autre
  = is by far _superior_ to
- Ce fromage **est bien supérieur à** celui que vous venez de goûter
  = is far _superior_ to
- **Je préfère** le sud de la France **à** la Bretagne pour ce qui est du climat
  = I _prefer_ ... to
- L'élève **dépasse** le maître
  = _surpasses_
- Le film **est loin d'être aussi** intéressant **que** le roman dont on l'a tiré
  = is far from being as ... as
- Cette nouvelle adaptation du roman **est loin de valoir** la version en noir et blanc réalisée en 1939
  = is a long way from _equalling_
- Les danseurs d'aujourd'hui **n'arrivent pas à la cheville de** ceux des années 30
  = can't hold a candle to

5.3 Comparing similar things

- **On a souvent comparé** Eugène Delacroix **à** Victor Hugo
  = ... has often been _compared_ to ...
- La presse locale n'a pas hésité à **faire un rapprochement entre** le limogeage du ministre de la Justice **et** cet assassinat
  = make the _connection_ between ... and
- Le camp militaire qui se trouve à l'entrée de la ville est **comparativement** peu peuplé
  = _comparatively_
- La composition des images **rappelle** les tableaux des peintres préraphaélites anglais
  = _recalls_

◆ Tous les deux se sont retrouvés sur un banc d'assises, **mais la ressemblance s'arrête là**
   = *but that's where the* <u>*similarity*</u> *ends*

◆ Leurs taux de scolarisation **sont comparables à** ceux des pays développés
   = *are* <u>*comparable*</u> *with*

◆ Nous avons trouvé un fromage **qui est l'équivalent** grec **de** la mozzarella
   = *which is the* <u>*equivalent*</u> *of*

◆ Cette somme **correspond à** six mois de salaire
   = <u>*corresponds*</u> *to*

◆ Ces deux articles **valent pratiquement le même prix**
   = *cost practically the* <u>*same*</u>

◆ Un peuple qui n'a pas de mémoire n'a pas d'avenir. **Il en est de même des** formations politiques
   = *the* <u>*same*</u> *is true of*

◆ **C'est plus ou moins la même chose**
   = *it's more or less the* <u>*same*</u> *thing*

◆ **Cela revient au même**
   = *it* <u>*amounts*</u> *to the* <u>*same*</u> *thing*

5.4   Comparing dissimilar things

◆ **Ce qui distingue** notre langue **des** langues anciennes, **c'est** l'ordre et la construction de la phrase
   = *what* <u>*distinguishes*</u> *... from ... is*

◆ **Ce qui différencie** les cafés arabica **des** robusta, **c'est** leur teneur en caféine
   = *what* <u>*distinguishes*</u> *... from ... is*

◆ **Il n'y a aucune comparaison possible entre** l'équipement des deux armées
   = *there is no possible* <u>*comparison*</u> *to be drawn between*

◆ **On ne peut pas comparer** la situation de quelqu'un qui vit à la campagne **à** celle d'un banlieusard
   = *you can't* <u>*compare*</u> *... with*

◆ Ces vignerons vivent de productions à faible rendement **qui n'ont rien de comparable avec** celles des Charentes
   = *which are in no way* <u>*comparable*</u> *to*

◆ Leur motivation, leur travail **ne se ressemblent vraiment en rien** mais ils ont en commun le fait d'être anglais
   = *have really nothing in* <u>*common*</u>

6   OPINION

6.1   Asking for opinions
Tentatively

◆ **J'aimerais connaître votre avis** *or* **votre opinion sur** ce problème
   = *I'd like (to know) your* <u>*opinion*</u> *on*

◆ **Je voudrais savoir ce que vous pensez de** son travail
   = *I'd like to know what you* <u>*think*</u> *of*

◆ **J'aimerais connaître votre réaction face à** ce brusque changement
   = *I'd like (to know) your* <u>*reaction*</u> *to*

◆ **Est-ce que vous pourriez me donner votre avis** *or* **votre opinion sur** cette émission ?
   = *could you give me your* <u>*opinion*</u> *on*

◆ **Pourriez-vous me dire ce que vous pensez de** leur politique ?
   = *could you tell me what you* <u>*think*</u> *of*

More directly

◆ **À votre avis** *or* **Selon vous**, faut-il donner plus de liberté aux jeunes ?
   = *in your* <u>*opinion*</u>

◆ **Est-ce que vous avez une opinion sur** la publicité ?
   = *do you have any* <u>*opinion*</u> *on*

◆ **Quelle est votre opinion sur** la situation internationale ?
   = *what's your* <u>*opinion*</u> *on*

◆ **Que pensez-vous de** sa façon d'agir ?
   = *what do you* <u>*think*</u> *of*

6.2   Expressing opinions

◆ **Il me semble que** vous vous trompez
   = *I* <u>*think*</u>

◆ **J'ai l'impression que** ses parents ne la comprennent pas
   = *I have a* <u>*feeling*</u>

◆ **Je suppose que** vous n'avez pas besoin de mes conseils
   = *I* <u>*suppose*</u>

◆ **J'imagine que** ce n'est pas très facile
   = *I* <u>*imagine*</u>

◆ **Si vous voulez mon opinion**, cette décision n'est pas raisonnable
   = *if you want my* <u>*opinion*</u>

◆ **Je ne peux pas m'empêcher de penser que** c'est délibéré
   = *I can't help* <u>*thinking*</u>

◆ **Sans vouloir vous contredire, il me semble que** nous nous rapprochons d'une solution
   = *without wishing to contradict you, it* <u>*seems*</u> *to me that*

◆ **Je dois dire que** je ne suis pas satisfait
   = *I must* <u>*say*</u> *that*

More directly

◆ **Je crains qu'il ne soit** *(subj)* trop tard maintenant
   = *I* <u>*fear*</u> *that it is*

◆ **À mon avis**, il n'a pas changé
   = *in my* <u>*opinion*</u>

◆ **Selon moi** *or* **D'après moi** *or* **Pour moi,** il a fait une erreur
   = *in my* <u>*view*</u>

◆ **Personnellement**, je ne le soutiendrais pas
   = <u>*personally*</u>

◆ **En ce qui me concerne** *or* **Pour ma part** *or* **Quant à moi**, je suis content de son travail
   = *as far as I am* <u>*concerned*</u> *or for my part*

◆ **Je pense** *or* **Je crois que** ce sera possible
   = *I* <u>*think*</u> *or* <u>*believe*</u>

◆ **J'estime qu'**il faut reprendre cette discussion
   = *I* <u>*think*</u>

◆ **Je trouve que** le racisme est criminel
   = *I* <u>*think*</u>

◆ **Je considère que** cette réforme est une amélioration
   = *I* <u>*feel*</u>

◆ Il faut changer radicalement le système. **C'est du moins mon opinion**
   = *at least that is my* <u>*opinion*</u>

With more conviction

◆ **Je suis sûr que** nous pouvons trouver une solution
   = *I am* <u>*sure*</u>

◆ **Je suis certain qu'**il est tout à fait sincère
   = *I am* <u>*certain*</u>

◆ **Je suis persuadé qu'**il y a d'autres solutions
   = *I am* <u>*convinced*</u>

◆ **Je suis convaincu que** nous pouvons réussir
   = *I am* <u>*convinced*</u>

6.3   Avoiding expressing one's opinion

◆ **Il est difficile de** débattre de ces questions
   = *it is* <u>*difficult*</u> *to*

+ **Je préférerais ne pas avoir à me prononcer** là-dessus
    = I'd rather not _comment_
+ **Il m'est difficile de donner un avis (définitif) sur** ce point
    = I find it _difficult_ to _express_ a (definite) _opinion_ on
+ **Je n'ai pas d'opinion bien précise à** ce sujet
    = I have no definite _opinion_ on
+ **Je n'ai jamais vraiment réfléchi à** ce problème
    = I have never really thought about
+ **Je ne me suis jamais vraiment posé la question**
    = I have never really asked myself that _question_
+ **Je ne me le suis jamais demandé**
    = I have never thought about it
+ **Je ne suis pas à même de dire s'**il a eu raison
    = I am not in a _position_ to say whether
+ **Tout dépend de** ce que vous entendez par là
    = it all _depends_ on

7   LIKES, DISLIKES AND PREFERENCES

7.1   Asking what someone likes

+ **Qu'est-ce que vous aimez le plus** or **préférez** : la mer ou la montagne ?
    = which do you _like better_ or _prefer_
+ **Est-ce que vous aimeriez** faire une partie de tennis cet après-midi ?
    = would you _like_ to
+ **Est-ce que cela vous plaît de** vivre en ville ?
    = do you _like_
+ **Est-ce que cela vous plairait** or **ferait plaisir d'**aller à cette exposition ?
    = would you _like_ to

7.2   Saying what you like

+ **Cela ne me déplaît pas d'**être seule, je ne m'ennuie jamais
    = I don't _dislike_
+ **J'aime que** les choses **soient** (subj) à leur place
    = I _like_ ... to be
+ **J'éprouve du plaisir à** marcher dans les vagues
    = I take _pleasure_ in
+ La visite de la cathédrale **m'a beaucoup plu**
    = I _liked_ ... very much
+ **Ce que j'aime par-dessus tout, c'est** une soirée entre amis
    = what I _like most_ of all is
+ **Pour moi, rien ne vaut** un grand verre d'eau fraîche pour se désaltérer
    = as far as I'm concerned, there's nothing _like_
+ **Rien de tel qu'**une bonne soirée au théâtre !
    = there's nothing _like_

7.3   Saying what you dislike

+ **Je n'ai aucun plaisir à** travailler dans de telles conditions
    = I don't find it at all _pleasant_ to
+ Sa façon d'agir **ne me plaît pas du tout**
    = I don't _like_ ... at all
+ **Il m'est pénible de** me trouver à côté de cet homme qui a fait tant de mal à ma famille
    = I find it hard to
+ Sa façon de parler **me déplaît au plus haut point**
    = I _dislike_ ... intensely
+ **J'ai horreur de** la médiocrité
    = I _loathe_

+ **Je ne peux pas supporter qu'**on me mente (subj)
    = I can't _stand_
+ **Ce que je déteste le plus, c'est d'**attendre le bus sous la pluie
    = what I _hate_ most is

7.4   Saying what you prefer

+ **J'aime autant que** nous y all**ions** (subj) ensemble
    = I'd _rather_
+ Les critiques ne m'émeuvent pas mais **je préférerais** les recevoir directement plutôt que de façon anonyme
    = I'd _prefer_ to
+ Vendredi **me conviendrait mieux**
    = would _suit_ me _better_
+ **Cela m'arrangerait que** vous ven**iez** (subj) plutôt vendredi
    = it would _suit_ me _better_ if
+ **Je préfère** créer du nouveau **plutôt que de** modifier de l'ancien
    = I _prefer_ to ... than to
+ **Ce que je préfère chez** Matisse, **ce sont** ses dessins, les encres, les fusains
    = what I _like best_ about ... are
+ La lecture est **une de mes** activités **favorites** or **préférées**
    = one of my _favourite_

7.5   Expressing indifference

+ Cette idée **ne m'emballe pas**
    = I'm not _thrilled_ by
+ **Ça m'est égal**
    = it's all the _same_ to me
+ **C'est comme vous voudrez**
    = as you _wish_
+ Une beauté classique **me laisse froid**
    = leaves me _cold_
+ **Cela n'a pas la moindre importance**
    = it doesn't _matter_ in the _least_
+ **Je n'ai pas de préférence**
    = I have no _preference_ either way
+ **Peu importe**
    = I don't _mind_

8   INTENTIONS AND DESIRES

8.1   Asking what someone intends to do

+ **Qu'est-ce que vous comptez faire** pour mettre un terme à leurs difficultés ?
    = what are you _planning_ to do
+ **Qu'est-ce que vous envisagez de faire** pour les aider ?
    = what are you _thinking_ of doing
+ **Qu'allez-vous faire** dans les prochains mois ?
    = what are you going to do
+ **Quelles sont vos intentions** à son égard ?
    = what do you _intend_ to do
+ **Avez-vous l'intention de** faire de nouvelles propositions ?
    = do you _intend_ to
+ **Est-ce que vous pensez** retravailler ensemble ?
    = are you _thinking_ of
+ **Comptez-vous** faire un reportage ?
    = are you _planning_ to
+ **J'aimerais savoir ce que vous comptez** obtenir
    = I would _like_ to know what you _intend_ to

8.2 Saying what someone intends or wants to do

Tentatively

- **Il songe à** poursuivre ses études
  = *he is thinking of*
- **J'envisage de** simplifier les procédures
  = *I am thinking of*
- **Il projette de** restaurer un vieux château
  = *he is planning to*
- **Nous nous proposons de** publier des textes intégraux de romans étrangers
  = *we intend to*
- **Nous prévoyons de** partir en voyage le mois prochain
  = *we are planning to*
- **Je voudrais** m'entretenir avec lui le plus rapidement possible
  = *I would like to*
- **J'ai l'intention de** porter plainte
  = *I intend to*

More assertively

- **Je désire** faire connaître mes opinions
  = *I wish to*
- **Je veux** monter mon propre cabinet
  = *I want do*
- **J'ai décidé de** faire appel de ce jugement
  = *I have decided to*
- **Nous sommes (bien) décidés à** prendre des décisions radicales
  = *we have (definitely) made up our minds to*
- **Il est résolu à** apporter son soutien financier
  = *he is determined to*
- **Elle a pris la résolution de** coopérer davantage
  = *she has made up her mind to*
- **Nous voulons à tout prix** trouver du travail
  = *we want to ... at all costs*
- **Je vais** passer quelques semaines en Albanie
  = *I am going to*

8.3 Saying what someone does not intend or want to do

- **Elle n'envisage pas de** s'arrêter là
  = *she is not thinking of*
- **Nous ne comptons pas** rester ici longtemps
  = *we don't intend to*
- **Il n'est pas dans mes intentions de** démissionner
  = *it is not my intention to*
- **Je n'ai pas l'intention** or **la moindre intention de** faire un effort financier
  = *I have no or not the slightest intention of*
- **Nous ne voulons pas** dormir ici
  = *we do not want to*
- **Je suis (bien) décidé à ne pas** me laisser faire
  = *I firmly intend not to*
- **Je refuse de** mettre le nez dehors par ce froid
  = *I refuse to*
- **Il n'est pas question que** je vende *(subj)* la voiture
  = *there is no question of*
- **Je m'oppose formellement à ce que nous** y allions *(subj)*
  = *I am totally opposed to our*

8.4 Saying what someone would like to do

- **J'ai envie d'**aller au cinéma ce soir
  = *I feel like*
- **Nous aurions aimé** pouvoir le féliciter nous-mêmes
  = *we would have liked to*

- **J'aimerais** écrire un livre
  = *I would like to*
- **Je voudrais** réaliser un second film
  = *I would like to*
- **Je voudrais que** l'entrée **soit** *(subj)* repeinte avant Noël
  = *I would like ... to be*
- **Il souhaiterait** développer les contrats avec les entreprises
  = *he would like to*
- **Il est à souhaiter qu'il** dispose *(subj)* de moyens suffisants
  = *it is to be hoped that he*
- **Je forme le souhait que** les liens entre nos deux associations se développent *(subj)* *(formal)*
  = *it is my desire that*
- **Il faut espérer que** tout se déroulera comme prévu
  = *it is to be hoped that*
- **Elle rêve de** faire du cinéma
  = *she dreams of*

9 PERMISSION

9.1 Asking for permission

- **Est-ce qu'on peut** or **peut-on fumer** dans ce bureau ?
  = *is smoking allowed?*
- **Est-ce que vous accepteriez que** je vous raccompagne *(subj)* ?
  = *would you allow me to*
- **Est-ce que je pourrais** me faire photographier avec vous ?
  = *could I*
- **Je voulais vous demander si** je pourrais arriver un peu plus tard demain matin
  = *I wanted to ask you if I could*
- **J'espère que cela ne vous ennuiera pas si** je change quelques détails dans ce compte-rendu
  = *I hope you won't mind if I*
- **J'aimerais bien** participer au stage, **si cela ne vous dérange pas**
  = *I'd like to ... if you don't mind*
- **À ce sujet, puis-je vous demander de** m'accorder une petite entrevue ?
  = *may I ask you to*
- **Voyez-vous un inconvénient à ce que** ces productions **soient** *(subj)* subventionnées sur fonds publics ?
  = *do you have any objection to ... being*
- **Nous serait-il possible de** vous inviter à ce festival en novembre ?
  = *may we*

9.2 Giving permission

- **Vous pouvez** utiliser la photocopieuse, **si vous voulez**
  = *you can ... if you want*
- **Je n'y vois pas d'inconvénient**
  = *I have nothing against it*
- **Je vous permets de** partir une heure plus tôt
  = *I'll allow you to*
- **Je vous autorise à** partir plus tôt
  = *you have my permission to*
- **Je vous en prie, faites comme vous jugez nécessaire**
  = *please do what you feel you need to*
- **Je consens à ce que** vous lui en parliez *(subj)* directement
  = *I give you my permission to*

9.3 Refusing permission

+ **Il n'en est pas question**
  = *there is no question of it*
+ **Vous ne pouvez pas** voir le directeur sans rendez-vous
  = *you can't*
+ **Je ne vous permets pas de** *or* **ne vous autorise pas à** photographier l'usine
  = *I cannot allow you to* or *give you permission to*
+ **Je préférerais que vous ne** lui en parl**iez** *(subj)* **pas**
  = *I'd prefer you not to*
+ **Je refuse catégoriquement de vous laisser** partir
  = *I absolutely refuse to let you*
+ **Je vous interdis formellement de** communiquer avec nos concurrents
  = *I positively forbid you to*
+ **Je regrette de ne pouvoir consentir à** ce projet
  = *I regret that I cannot consent to*
+ **Je m'oppose absolument à ce que nous** leur expédi**ions** *(subj)* cette commande sans garantie
  = *I am totally opposed to our*
+ **Je crains d'être dans l'obligation de vous décevoir** *(formal)*
  = *I am afraid I must disappoint you*

9.4 Saying that permission has been granted

+ **Ils le laissent** boire du café bien qu'il n'ait *(subj)* que trois ans
  = *they let him*
+ **On m'a permis de** régler la machine à laver en plusieurs versements
  = *they've allowed me to*
+ **Il m'a dit que je pouvais** prendre sa voiture
  = *he said I could*
+ **On permet** *or* **autorise** une marge d'erreur
  = *... is permissible*

9.5 Saying that permission has been refused

+ **Défense d'entrer** *or* **Entrée interdite**
  = *no entry*
+ **Il m'est interdit** *or* **défendu de** boire de l'alcool
  = *I have been forbidden to*
+ **L'alcool m'est interdit**
  = *I am forbidden ...*
+ **...le dimanche, jour où il est défendu de** s'occuper à rien de sérieux
  = *it is forbidden to*
+ **Mon médecin m'interdit de** fumer
  = *forbids me to*
+ **Il est formellement interdit de** parler au conducteur
  = *... is strictly forbidden*
+ **Vous ne devez en aucun cas** ouvrir la porte
  = *on no account must you*

10 OBLIGATION

10.1 Saying what someone must do

+ **On demande que** les patients **soient** *(subj)* à l'heure
  = *... are requested to be*
+ **Il faut que** le travail **soit** *(subj)* terminé vendredi
  = *... must be*
+ **Le financement doit être** assuré par d'autres ressources
  = *... must be*
+ **Il faut (absolument)** faire quelque chose
  = *you (really) must*
+ **Il est obligatoire de** réserver pour prendre le TGV
  = *... is obligatory*

+ **Il est indispensable de** trouver d'urgence une solution
  = *it is essential to*
+ **On exige que** les candidats **aient** *(subj)* de solides connaissances en algèbre
  = *... are required to have*
+ **Cela m'oblige à** *or* **me force à** venir tous les jours
  = *I have to ... because of that*
+ **Vous êtes obligé de** venir
  = *you have to*
+ **Je suis forcé de** partir pour Londres
  = *I am forced to*
+ **Vous prendrez** deux de ces comprimés chaque matin
  = *(you must) take*
+ **Vous devez (impérativement)** payer vos impôts pour le quinze
  = *you (really) must*
+ **Il est indispensable que** vos lecteurs en **soient** *(subj)* informés
  = *it is essential that ... are*
+ **Je ne peux faire autrement que d'**accepter
  = *I have no choice but to*
+ **Je n'ai pas le choix**
  = *I have no choice*

More formally

+ **Elle s'est trouvée obligée de** rester deux heures de plus
  = *she was obliged to*
+ **Il s'est vu contraint de** suivre un traitement médical intensif
  = *he was compelled to*
+ **Il me faut** leur donner les mesures de l'appartement
  = *I have to*
+ **Je me vois dans l'obligation de** solliciter un nouveau prêt
  = *I am obliged to*
+ **J'ai le devoir de** *or* **Il est de mon devoir de** vous informer que votre demande a été rejetée *(written)*
  = *it is my duty to*

10.2 Enquiring if one is obliged to do something

+ **Est-ce qu'on doit** consulter un spécialiste avant de suivre un régime ?
  = *must one*
+ **Est-ce qu'il faut** s'en tenir à ce document ?
  = *does one have to*
+ **Est-ce que j'ai vraiment besoin de** prendre un parapluie ?
  = *do I really need to*
+ **Est-ce que je suis obligé** *or* **forcé de** venir avec vous ?
  = *do I have to*
+ **Faut-il vraiment que je** chois**isse** *(subj)* un nouveau nom ?
  = *do I really have to*
+ **Est-il nécessaire de** faire autant de bruit pour si peu ?
  = *does one have to*
+ **Est-il obligatoire de** présenter sa carte d'identité ?
  = *does one have to*

10.3 Saying what someone is not obliged to do

+ **On n'a pas besoin de** crier pour se faire entendre
  = *one doesn't have to*
+ **Il n'est pas obligatoire d'**avoir ses papiers d'identité sur soi
  = *it is not compulsory to*
+ **Il n'est pas nécessaire de** téléphoner pour confirmer
  = *it is not necessary to*
+ **Il n'est pas indispensable de** suivre la recette traditionnelle
  = *it is not essential to*
+ **Ce n'est pas la peine de** traduire tout le premier chapitre
  = *it is not worth*

◆ **Vous n'êtes pas obligé** *or* **forcé d'**aller voir un médecin
= *you don't <u>have</u> to*

◆ **Je ne vous oblige pas à** y aller
= *I am not <u>forcing</u> you to*

◆ **Ne vous sentez pas obligé de** venir la voir
= *do not feel <u>obliged</u> to*

◆ **Je ne vous demande pas de** faire des photocopies toute la journée
= *I am not asking you to*

10.4 Saying what someone must not do

◆ **On n'a pas le droit de** fumer dans les lieux publics
= *... is not <u>allowed</u>*

◆ **Il est interdit** *or* **défendu de** conduire sans permis
= *... is <u>forbidden</u>*

◆ **Il ne faut pas** être agressif
= *you <u>mustn't</u>*

◆ **Nous ne tolérerons** aucun retard
= *we will not <u>tolerate</u>*

◆ **Vous ne pouvez pas** vous absenter plus de trois jours par mois
= *you cannot*

◆ **Je ne vous permets pas de** me parler sur ce ton
= *I will not <u>allow</u> you to*

◆ **Je t'interdis** *or* **Je te défends d'**y aller seul
= *I <u>forbid</u> you to*

◆ **Surtout ne** lui en parlez **pas**
= *whatever you do, do not*

11 AGREEMENT

11.1 Agreeing with a statement

◆ **Vous avez bien** *or* **entièrement raison**
= *you are quite or absolutely <u>right</u>*

◆ **Je suis entièrement de votre avis**
= *I <u>agree</u> with you entirely*

◆ **Je suis entièrement d'accord** (avec vous)
= *I entirely <u>agree</u>*

◆ Dans l'ensemble, **nous sommes d'accord avec** l'orientation du projet
= *we <u>agree</u> with*

◆ **Nous sommes du même avis que vous sur** ce point
= *we <u>feel</u> the <u>same</u> as you on*

◆ **Je partage votre inquiétude sur** les risques d'une guerre commerciale
= *I <u>share</u> your concern over*

◆ **Je partage votre enthousiasme pour** les possibilités offertes par les nouvelles technologies de communication
= *I <u>share</u> your enthusiasm for*

◆ **Je conviens que** c'est là un discours difficile
= *I <u>admit</u> that*

◆ **Je comprends très bien que** tu **aies** (*subj*) pitié de Laura
= *I fully <u>understand</u> that*

◆ **Je vous accorde que** les hommes politiques valent beaucoup mieux que leur image électorale
= *I <u>concede</u> that*

◆ **Comme vous l'avez fait remarquer, il est vrai** *or* **exact que** nous n'avons pas toutes les données nécessaires
= *as you <u>pointed</u> out, it is <u>true</u> that*

◆ **Je ne puis que vous donner raison**
= *I cannot but <u>agree</u> with you*

11.2 Agreeing to a proposal

◆ **C'est une bonne idée**
= *it's a good <u>idea</u>*

◆ **Je trouve que tu as raison de** prendre tes congés maintenant
= *I think you're <u>right</u> to*

◆ **Je suis d'accord pour que vous** y **alliez** (*subj*) à pied
= *I <u>agree</u> that you should*

◆ **J'accepte** la proposition du commissaire
= *I <u>accept</u>*

◆ **J'accepte de** consulter un expert, comme vous l'avez suggéré
= *I <u>agree</u> to*

◆ Votre proposition **nous plaît beaucoup**
= *we <u>like</u> ... very much*

◆ La coopération des deux entreprises, **c'est exactement ce dont nous avons besoin**
= *is <u>exactly</u> what we need*

◆ **Nous donnons notre accord à** la réfection des locaux
= *we <u>agree</u> to*

◆ **Il est entendu que** la nouvelle taxe sera appliquée de façon dégressive
= *it is <u>agreed</u> that*

◆ **Je ne manquerai pas d'**appuyer votre demande
= *I shall not <u>fail</u> to*

◆ **Je suis heureux d'apporter mon soutien à** cette proposition
= *I am <u>happy</u> to <u>support</u>*

◆ **Je souscris à** beaucoup de ces analyses et propositions
= *I <u>subscribe</u> to*

11.3 Agreeing to a request

◆ **Je serais enchanté** *or* **ravi d'**aller chercher votre tante à la gare
= *I shall be <u>delighted</u> to*

◆ La date retenue **me convient parfaitement**
= *<u>suits</u> me perfectly*

◆ **Je suis prêt à** aller déjeuner en sa compagnie à sa sortie de prison
= *I am <u>prepared</u> to*

◆ **Je** quitterai **donc** l'appartement le 22, **comme vous me l'avez demandé**
= *I shall ..., then, ... as you requested*

◆ **Il est entendu que** les négociations couvriront les questions en suspens
= *it is <u>agreed</u> that*

<u>In writing</u>

◆ **J'accepte avec grand plaisir** votre aimable invitation
= *I have great <u>pleasure</u> in <u>accepting</u>*

◆ **C'est avec grand plaisir que j'accepte** votre aimable invitation
= *it is with great <u>pleasure</u> that I <u>accept</u>*

◆ Nous prenons bonne note de votre commande, **que nous honorerons dans les plus brefs délais**
= *which we will process as quickly as possible*

◆ **Je tiens à vous assurer que je suivrai vos instructions à la lettre**
= *be <u>assured</u> that I will follow your instructions to the letter*

◆ **Nous essayerons de nous conformer à vos désirs**
= *we shall endeavour to meet your requirements*

12 DISAGREEMENT

12.1 Disagreeing with a statement

◆ **Je suis désolé** *or* **Je suis navré de** devoir vous contredire
= *I am <u>sorry</u> to*

◆ **Je ne partage pas votre point de vue** là-dessus
= *I do not <u>share</u> your point of view*

◆ **Je ne suis pas d'accord avec** cette manière de voir
= *I do not <u>agree</u> with*

♦ **Je vois les choses (tout à fait) différemment**
  = *I see things (quite) differently*

More assertively

♦ **C'est faux**
  = *it's wrong*
♦ **Vous vous trompez**
  = *you are mistaken*
♦ **Vous faites erreur**
  = *you are mistaken*
♦ **Vous avez tort de** refuser
  = *you are wrong to*
♦ **Je rejette (totalement)** cette idée
  = *I (totally) reject*
♦ **Je suis contre** la violence sous toutes ses formes
  = *I'm against*
♦ **Je suis (catégoriquement) opposé à** une idée négative de l'Europe
  = *I am (categorically) opposed to*
♦ **Je ne peux pas accepter** cette condamnation globale
  = *I cannot accept*
♦ **Je n'admets pas que** l'on me **dise** *(subj)* pour qui je dois voter
  = *I will not allow ... to tell*
♦ **Je nie (catégoriquement)** l'avoir jamais rencontré
  = *I (categorically) deny*

12.2   **Disagreeing with a proposal**

♦ **Il n'est plus possible de** travailler comme avant
  = *it is no longer possible to*
♦ **Il est impossible de** fixer un calendrier précis
  = *it is impossible to*
♦ **Je ne suis pas d'accord avec** ces changements
  = *I do not agree with*
♦ **Je ne suis pas d'accord pour que** le problème **soit** *(subj)* posé en ces termes
  = *I do not agree that ... should be*
♦ **Je crains fort de ne pouvoir approuver** cette décision *(written)*
  = *I am afraid I cannot approve*

More assertively

♦ **Je ne peux pas accepter** les actions brutales et précipitées
  = *I cannot accept*
♦ **Je suis contre** le protectionnisme
  = *I am against*
♦ **Je suis opposé à** toute censure
  = *I am opposed to*
♦ **Je refuse** son licenciement
  = *I refuse to allow*
♦ **Je refuse qu'on diffuse** *(subj)* cette séquence
  = *I refuse to allow*
♦ **Il est hors de question que** je le leur **dise** *(subj)*
  = *it is out of the question that ... should tell*
♦ **Je mettrai mon veto à** ce projet
  = *I shall veto*

12.3   **Refusing a request**

Tentatively

♦ **Je ne pourrai malheureusement pas** jouer ce soir
  = *unfortunately, I won't be able to*
♦ **Il m'est difficile de** procéder à une estimation
  = *I find it difficult to*

♦ **Je ne suis pas en mesure de** prendre de nouveaux engagements
  = *I'm not in a position to*

More assertively

♦ **Il est hors de question que nous** accept**ions** *(subj)*
  = *it is out of the question that we should*
♦ **Je refuse de** les faire travailler pour rien
  = *I refuse to*
♦ **Je n'accepterai pas d'**assumer cette responsabilité
  = *I will not agree to*

In writing

♦ **Il m'est (vraiment) impossible de** répondre à votre demande
  = *it is (really) impossible for me to*
♦ **Je dois malheureusement décliner** votre invitation
  = *unfortunately, I must decline*
♦ **Nous avons le regret de vous informer que vous ne pourrez** assister au procès
  = *we regret to inform you that you will be unable to*
♦ **Nous regrettons de ne pouvoir** donner suite à votre requête
  = *we regret that we are unable to*
♦ **Je regrette sincèrement de ne pas être en mesure d'**apporter les garanties réclamées
  = *I sincerely regret that I am not in a position to*
♦ **Je suis au regret de ne pouvoir** appuyer votre demande
  = *I regret that I am unable to*

---

13   **APPROVAL**

♦ **Quelle excellente idée !**
  = *what an excellent idea!*
♦ **Vous avez bien fait de** laisser vos bagages à la consigne de la gare
  = *you were right to*
♦ **J'ai bien aimé** la mise en scène de la pièce
  = *I liked*
♦ La mise en scène de la pièce **m'a beaucoup plu**
  = *I liked ... very much*
♦ **J'ai beaucoup apprécié** la gentillesse avec laquelle il a proposé de nous aider
  = *I greatly appreciated*
♦ Je pense que cette initiative de l'administration **est une très bonne chose**
  = *is a very good thing*
♦ **Je trouve que vous avez raison de** souligner cette différence
  = *I think you are right to*
♦ **Je trouve que vous n'avez pas tort de** chercher à étendre la gamme de vos produits
  = *I think you are not wrong in*
♦ **Nous sommes favorables à** la création d'emplois et au développement de l'activité portuaire
  = *we are favourable to*
♦ **Nous sommes en faveur d'**une solution négociée
  = *we are in favour of*
♦ **Le plus grand mérite de** ce petit livre pratique **est de** donner pour chaque cas des adresses utiles
  = *the greatest merit of ... is to*

More formally

♦ Tout renfort **est le bienvenu**
  = *is welcome*

- De nombreuses voix se sont, **à juste titre**, élevées pour protester contre cette scandaleuse manipulation
  = _rightly_
- Mon voisin de table reproche **avec raison** aux meilleures maisons de servir du thé en sachet
  = _rightly_
- **On ne peut qu'admirer** l'art avec lequel Oscar Wilde a mis en scène son destin
  = one cannot but _admire_
- **J'approuve sans réserve** les mesures prises par le ministre de l'Économie
  = I _approve_ unreservedly
- **Nous apportons notre soutien aux** mesures prises par le secrétaire général des Nations unies
  = we give our _support_ to

14 DISAPPROVAL

- **Tu n'aurais pas dû** lui parler sur ce ton
  = you shouldn't have
- **Vous auriez mieux fait de** partir sans rien dire
  = you would have done better to
- **Je désapprouve** toute discrimination, qu'elle frappe les femmes ou les minorités
  = I _disapprove_ of
- **Je trouve qu'il a eu tort d'**emprunter tant d'argent
  = I feel he was _wrong_ to
- **Je condamne** quiconque s'y oppose
  = I _condemn_
- **Je ne supporte pas** une telle arrogance
  = I can't _stand_
- **Je ne comprends pas comment on peut** fermer les yeux sur ce problème
  = I don't understand how people can
- **Je déplore** son manque de sérieux
  = I _deplore_
- **Je suis profondément déçu par** son attitude désinvolte
  = I am deeply _disappointed_ by
- **Je proteste contre** la façon dont nous avons été traités
  = I _protest_ against
- **Je suis farouchement opposé à** ce projet
  = I am fiercely _opposed_ to
- **Je suis consterné d'apprendre que** personne n'est allé vous chercher à l'aéroport
  = I am _dismayed_ to hear that
- Cette idée **me déplaît profondément**
  = I _dislike_ ... intensely
- **On ne peut que regretter** une telle légèreté
  = ... is only to be _regretted_
- **Il est dommage que** nul ne se **soit** _(subj)_ demandé si cet organisme ne pouvait pas continuer à travailler en province
  = it is a _pity_ that
- **Il est regrettable que** cet aspect essentiel de la recherche **soit** _(subj)_ à ce point délaissé par l'industrie pharmaceutique
  = it is _regrettable_ that
- **De quel droit** la presse s'érige-t-elle en censeur ?
  = what gives ... the right to
- La qualité de ce produit **laisse à désirer**
  = leaves a lot to be desired

15 CERTAINTY, PROBABILITY, POSSIBILITY AND CAPABILITY

15.1 Expressing certainty

In an impersonal way

- **Il est certain que** les discusssions ont été longues et parfois délicates
  = it is _certain_ that
- **Il est évident que** la situation est loin d'être simple
  = _evidently_
- **Il ne fait aucun doute que** les gâteaux allégés vont connaître un réel succès
  = there is no _doubt_ that
- **Il est indéniable que** nous vivons une période de moindre croissance
  = it is _undeniably_ true that
- **Il est incontestable que** le président a, en la matière, un rôle important à jouer
  = ... _unquestionably_ has
- **Il faut bien reconnaître que** nous utilisons souvent les locutions sans en connaître l'histoire ou le sens exact
  = one must _recognize_ that
- **Il faut bien admettre que** le texte, là encore, n'est pas très clair
  = it has to be _admitted_ that
- **De toute évidence**, on pourrait dépenser moins pour soigner aussi bien
  = quite _obviously_
- **Le doute n'est plus permis :** la reprise ne se manifestera pas à temps
  = there is no longer any _doubt_:
- **Il n'y a aucun doute :** il a réussi à avoir ce qu'il voulait, mais à quel prix ...
  = there is no _doubt_ about it
- **Il va sans dire que** nous vous livrerons dès que possible
  = it goes without saying that

More directly

- **Je suis sûr** or **certain que** le facteur est déjà passé
  = I am _sure_ or _certain_ that
- Je suis **sûr** or **certain d'**avoir rangé cette facture dans ce tiroir
  = I am _sure_ or _certain_ that
- **J'ai la certitude qu'**il nous a menti
  = I am _certain_ that
- **Je suis persuadé qu'**un changement d'air lui ferait le plus grand bien
  = I am _convinced_ that

15.2 Expressing probability

- **Il est probable que** les résultats ne seront pas affichés avant demain matin
  = _probably_
- Les résultats ne seront **probablement** pas affichés avant demain matin
  = _probably_
- **Il a dû** tomber en panne or Il est **sans doute** tombé en panne
  = he _must_ have
- **Vous devriez** recevoir ce chèque sous peu
  = you _should_
- Ce chèque **devrait** vous parvenir sous peu
  = _should_
- **On dirait que** le temps va changer
  = it looks as though
- **Je pense** prendre quelques jours de congé la semaine prochaine
  = I am thinking of

◆ **Il est bien possible qu'**il n'**ait** *(subj)* jamais reçu cette lettre
= it is quite _possible_ that

◆ **Il se pourrait bien qu'**il y **ait** *(subj)* des retards à cause de la grève
= it is quite _possible_ that

◆ **Il me semble que** l'on voit moins de boucheries chevalines à Paris
= it _strikes_ me that

◆ Il a changé de voiture, **paraît-il** or **à ce qu'il paraît**
= it seems

◆ **Tout semble indiquer qu'**il s'agit des salariés qui manifestaient hier
= everything _seems_ to indicate that

15.3 Expressing possibility

◆ Il s'agit **peut-être** d'une erreur
= _perhaps_

◆ **Il est peut-être** déjà trop tard pour téléphoner
= _perhaps_ it's

◆ **Peut-être qu'il est** déjà trop tard pour téléphoner
= _maybe_ it's

◆ La situation **peut** changer du jour au lendemain
= _can_

◆ **Est-il possible qu'**il **ait** *(subj)* été arrêté sans que personne n'en ait rien su?
= is it _possible_ that

◆ **Il n'est pas impossible qu'**il **ait** *(subj)* changé d'avis
= it is not _impossible_ that

◆ **Il se peut que** nous pass**ions** *(subj)* par Paris au retour
= we _might_

◆ **Il se pourrait très bien qu'**il décide *(subj)* un jour de tout quitter
= he _may_ well

15.4 Expressing capability

◆ **Savez-vous** vous servir de la nouvelle machine?
= _do you know how to_

◆ **Il sait** nager
= he _can_

◆ **Je comprends** le français
= I _understand_

◆ **Je vois** un grand mur blanc
= I _can_ see

◆ **Je peux** investir jusqu'à mille francs
= I _can_

◆ **J'arrive à** aller la voir deux ou trois fois par semaine
= I _manage_ to

◆ **Je peux tout juste** le comprendre
= I _can_ just

◆ Les candidats doivent **être capables de** traduire des textes scientifiques
= be _capable_ of

◆ **Il m'est possible de** me libérer pour 17 heures
= I _could_

◆ **Nous sommes à même de** proposer des prix très bas
= we are in a _position_ to

---

16 DOUBT, IMPROBABILITY, IMPOSSIBILITY AND INCAPABILITY

16.1 Expressing doubt

In an impersonal way

◆ **On ne sait pas exactement** ce qui se passe durant ce processus
= we don't _know_ _exactly_

◆ Les traductions récentes **ne sont pas forcément** les meilleures
= are not _necessarily_

◆ **Il n'est pas sûr qu'**elle or **Il n'est pas certain qu'**elle **soit** *(subj)* malade
= we don't _know_ for _sure_ that

◆ **On ne sait pas au juste** qui a inventé cette façon de s'habiller
= we don't _know_ exactly

◆ **Le doute subsiste quant au** nombre exact des victimes
= some _doubt_ remains as to

◆ **Rien ne permet de penser qu'**il **soit** *(subj)* un mafieux
= one has no _cause_ to think that ... is

More directly

◆ **Je ne suis pas sûr** or **Je ne suis pas certain qu'**il y **ait** *(subj)* du monde ce soir
= I am not _sure_ or _certain_ whether

◆ **Je ne suis pas sûr d'**avoir or **Je ne suis pas certain d'**avoir raison
= I am not _sure_ or _certain_ if

◆ **Nous nous demandons si** nous devons accepter leurs propositions
= we _wonder_ if

◆ **Je doute fort qu'**ils t'**aient** *(subj)* cru
= I very much _doubt_ whether

◆ **Je doute de** sa sincérité
= I _question_

◆ **Je doute de** l'avoir jamais vu
= I _doubt_ if

◆ **Nous sommes encore dans l'incertitude quant à** l'application de cet accord
= we are still _uncertain_ as to

16.2 Expressing improbability

◆ **Cela m'étonnerait que** l'on vous répond**e** *(subj)*
= it would _surprise_ me if

◆ **Elles ne risquent pas d'**avoir le prix Nobel d'économie
= they are not _likely_ to

◆ Il ne changera **probablement pas** d'avis
= _probably_ not

◆ **Il y a peu de chances que** ce programme **soit** *(subj)* réalisé
= there is not much _chance_ of

◆ **Il est peu probable qu'**il **ait** *(subj)* changé d'avis
= it is _unlikely_ that

◆ **Il serait étonnant que** ces déclarations **soient** *(subj)* entendues
= it would be _surprising_ if

◆ **Il ne semble pas que** les médecins lui **aient** *(subj)* administré des calmants
= it does not _look_ as if

◆ **Il n'est guère probable que** les négociations about**issent** *(subj)*
= it is hardly _likely_ that

◆ **Il est douteux que** ma proposition **soit** *(subj)* retenue
= it is _doubtful_ whether

◆ **Je crains fort que** nous n'arriv**ions** *(subj)* pas à nous entendre
= I very much _fear_ that

16.3 Expressing impossibility

◆ **Il n'est pas possible que** or **Il est impossible que** les renseignements **soient** *(subj)* faux
= it is not _possible_ that or it is _impossible_ that

◆ **Il n'y a aucune chance que** nous termin**ions** *(subj)* cette traduction à temps
= there is no _chance_ of

◆ **Nous n'avons aucune chance de** trouver un emploi
  = *we have no <u>chance</u> of*

◆ Le trajet **n'est pas faisable** en voiture
  = *<u>cannot</u> be done*

◆ **Il ne peut s'agir de** la même personne
  = *it <u>cannot</u> be*

◆ **Il m'est impossible de** m'absenter la semaine prochaine
  = *it is <u>impossible</u> for me to*

◆ **Il est absolument exclu que** nous équilibr**ions** *(subj)* nos comptes
  = *it is absolutely out of the <u>question</u> that*

◆ **Je suis malheureusement dans l'impossibilité de** tenir mes engagements
  = *unfortunately, I am <u>unable</u> to*

16.4   Expressing incapability

◆ **Je ne peux pas** tout contrôler
  = *I <u>cannot</u>*

◆ **Il ne sait pas** présenter les plats
  = *he does not <u>know</u> how to*

◆ **Je ne sais pas comment** la décrire
  = *I do not <u>know</u> how to*

◆ **Je n'arrive pas à** *or* **Je ne parviens pas à** trouver une explication
  = *I <u>cannot</u> (<u>manage</u> to)*

◆ **Il est incapable de** prendre une décision
  = *he is <u>incapable</u> of*

◆ **Il n'a pas les aptitudes requises pour** ce travail
  = *he does not have the necessary <u>aptitude</u> for*

◆ **Il m'est impossible de** jouer ce rôle
  = *it is <u>impossible</u> for me to*

◆ **Je suis dans l'impossibilité de** répondre
  = *I am <u>unable</u> to*

17   EXPLANATIONS

17.1   Emphasizing the reason for something

◆ C'est un endroit à la mode **à cause du** marché aux puces qui s'y est installé
  = *<u>because</u> of*

◆ Ils ont réussi à s'en sortir **grâce à** leur dynamisme
  = *<u>thanks</u> to*

◆ Je n'en ai pas parlé **parce que** le temps me manque
  = *<u>because</u>*

◆ Je suis très inquiet **car** nous n'avons pas commencé à discuter des solutions
  = *<u>as</u>*

◆ **Comme** il se faisait tard, elle a pris un taxi
  = *<u>as</u>*

◆ Le marché des changes est délocalisé, **puisque** les échanges se font par terminaux informatiques
  = *<u>since</u>*

◆ **Étant donné qu'**il *or* **Puisqu'**il n'est pas là, je dois faire son travail à sa place
  = *<u>given</u> that or <u>since</u>*

◆ **Vu** *or* **Étant donné** la situation actuelle, on ne peut pas espérer d'amélioration prochaine
  = *<u>given</u>*

◆ J'ai commencé à jouer du rock à seize ans. **Voilà pourquoi** je m'implique dans ce que je joue
  = *that's <u>why</u>*

◆ **La raison de son refus** *or* **La raison pour laquelle il a refusé, c'est qu'**il doit partir ce soir
  = *the <u>reason</u> for his refusal or that he refused is that*

◆ **C'est pour cette raison que** j'ai accepté d'y aller
  = *it is for this <u>reason</u> that*

◆ C'est la hausse du dollar qui **a provoqué** cette crise
  = *has <u>brought</u> about*

More formally

◆ Il était absent **pour raisons de** santé
  = *for ... <u>reasons</u>*

◆ Le vol AF232 a été retardé **en raison des** conditions météorologiques
  = *<u>owing</u> to*

◆ Les importations ont progressé **par suite de** l'ouverture des frontières
  = *as a <u>result</u> of*

◆ **C'est grâce à** l'émission **qu'**il a pu être identifié
  = *it was <u>thanks</u> to ... that*

◆ La bataille risque de s'arrêter **faute de** munitions
  = *for <u>lack</u> of*

◆ Le drame **vient de ce qu'**elle s'est habituée à vivre au-dessus de ses moyens
  = *is the <u>result</u> of*

◆ La violence **provient de** cette mise en scène brutale
  = *comes from*

◆ Son engagement politique **tient à** une philosophie
  = *<u>stems</u> from*

◆ L'affaire **remonte à** la plainte d'un automobiliste
  = *goes back to*

◆ Le retard **est lié à** des problèmes techniques
  = *is <u>linked</u> to*

◆ **Il attribue** ce résultat **à** la flexibilité du marché du travail
  = *he <u>attributes</u> ... to*

◆ **Étant donné que** les chiffres sont approximatifs, on ne peut se fier à ces résultats
  = *given that*

17.2   Emphasizing the result of something

◆ Je dois partir ce soir ; **je ne pourrai donc pas** venir avec vous samedi
  = *<u>so</u> I won't be able to*

◆ Le débat sur ce chapitre n'est pas achevé, **si bien que** les négociations ont de sérieuses chances de se poursuivre
  = *<u>so</u> much <u>so</u> that*

◆ Les erreurs de conception se sont accumulées, **de telle sorte que** le projet a pris un sérieux retard
  = *<u>so</u> much <u>so</u> that*

◆ Le sol de cette dépression est entièrement argileux, **par conséquent** imperméable
  = *<u>consequently</u>*

◆ Cette législation **a eu pour conséquence** d'encourager les mères à rester célibataires
  = *has <u>resulted</u> in*

◆ La haine **résulte de** l'incompréhension
  = *is the <u>result</u> of*

◆ Les grèves ont été nombreuses ces derniers mois ; **il en résulte que** la production a diminué dans ce secteur
  = *as a <u>result</u>*

18 **APOLOGIES**

18.1 Apologizing for one's actions

+ **Excusez-moi d'**arriver en retard
  = _sorry_ I

+ **Pardonnez-moi de** dire une autre banalité
  = excuse me for

+ **Je suis désolé qu'**on vous **ait** (subj) dérangé pour rien
  = I'm _sorry_

+ **Je suis vraiment navré de** ce malentendu
  = I'm really _sorry_ about

+ **Je regrette de** vous contredire **mais** ce mot est bien d'origine espagnole
  = I'm _sorry_ to ... but

+ **Je reconnais que** ce rapport contient un certain nombre de termes inutilement agressifs
  = I _admit_ that

+ **Je vous prie d'excuser** le décousu de cette lettre
  = please _excuse_

+ **Veuillez m'excuser de** vous déranger ainsi
  = please _excuse_ me for

+ **Soyez assuré que** cet incident ne se reproduira pas
  = let me _assure_ you that

+ **Nous tenons à vous présenter nos excuses pour** les difficultés que vous avez rencontrées
  = we wish to _apologize_ for

18.2 Apologizing for being unable to do something

+ **Je suis vraiment désolé de ne pas pouvoir** vous fournir immédiatement ces renseignements
  = I'm really _sorry_ I can't

+ **Il m'est malheureusement impossible d'**arriver avant 8 heures
  = _unfortunately_, it's _impossible_ for me to

+ **Je regrette infiniment mais** ce document ne peut être consulté que sur place
  = I am terribly _sorry_ but

+ **Nous regrettons de ne pouvoir** faire suite à votre demande _(written)_
  = we _regret_ that we are _unable_ to

+ **J'ai le regret de ne pouvoir** accepter votre aimable invitation _(written)_
  = I _regret_ that I am _unable_ to

+ **Nous sommes au regret de** vous informer que vous ne serez pas autorisé à assister au procès _(written)_
  = we _regret_ to

18.3 Admitting responsibility

+ Je me rends compte que **je n'aurais jamais dû** laisser la porte ouverte
  = I should never have

+ **Je reconnais que j'ai eu tort de** lui communiquer votre adresse
  = I _admit_ that I was _wrong_ to

+ **Si seulement je ne leur avais pas** déjà promis que nous passerions nos vacances avec eux!
  = if only I hadn't

+ **J'assume l'entière responsabilité de** cette affaire
  = I _accept_ full _responsibility_ for

18.4 Disclaiming responsibility

+ **Je t'assure que je n'ai pas fait exprès de** déchirer la couverture de ce livre
  = II assure you I didn't ... on _purpose_

+ **J'avais cru bien faire en** expédiant immédiatement ce chèque
  = I thought I was doing the right thing by

+ **J'essayais simplement de** vous éviter des problèmes
  = I was simply trying to

+ **Je suis sûr que vous comprendrez les raisons qui nous ont poussés à** augmenter nos tarifs
  = I'm sure you will understand the reasons we had to

+ **Je ne voulais pas vous ennuyer** avec tous ces détails
  = I didn't want to trouble you

+ **Je vous assure que je ne pouvais pas faire autrement**
  = I (can) assure you I could not do otherwise

+ **J'avais pourtant cru comprendre que** je pouvais me garer devant la maison
  = but I thought

+ **Vous comprendrez, j'espère, que** nous ne sommes pas responsables de ce retard qui est dû à la grève de la poste
  = I trust you will understand that

+ **Permettez-moi au moins de vous expliquer**...
  = at least allow me to _explain_

19 **JOB APPLICATIONS**

19.1 Starting the letter

+ **Je me réfère à votre annonce** parue aujourd'hui dans le Quotidien du Midi, et **vous serais reconnaissant de bien vouloir m'envoyer des renseignements plus complets** sur ce poste, ainsi qu'un dossier de candidature
  = with _reference_ to your _advertisement_ ... I would be _grateful_ if you would send me _further information_

+ **Votre annonce** parue dans La Gazette Alsacienne a **retenu toute mon attention et je me permets de poser ma candidature pour le poste d'**ingénieur que vous offrez
  = I saw your _advertisement_ ... and would like to _apply_ for the _post_ of

+ Je souhaite vivement travailler en France pendant les vacances universitaires et **vous serais très reconnaissant de me faire savoir s'il me serait possible d'obtenir un emploi** dans votre société
  = I would be most _grateful_ if you could tell me if there is any _possibility_ of _work_

19.2 Detailing your experience and giving your reasons for applying

+ **J'ai travaillé pendant trois ans comme** secrétaire de direction pour une société parisienne **et je maîtrise** divers traitements de texte et tableurs
  = I _worked_ for three years as ... and have a good command of

+ **Je travaille depuis cinq ans** dans une société d'import-export de New York, **ce qui m'a permis d'acquérir une connaissance approfondie des** techniques de vente et du marché américain
  = I have been _working_ for five years ..., during which time I have acquired in-depth _knowledge_ of

+ **Je parle couramment anglais, j'ai de bonnes connaissances en allemand et je lis le suédois**
  = I speak fluent English, good German and have a reading _knowledge_ of Swedish

+ **Mon salaire actuel est de ... par an et j'ai cinq semaines de congés payés**
  = my current _salary_ is ... per annum with five weeks' paid leave

Jane FELDON
179 Curzon Road
London N10 4EA

Service du Personnel[1]
International Bank
18 rue La Boétie
75008 Paris

Paris, le 20 mai 1998

Messieurs,

Suite à votre annonce dans *The Guardian* de ce jour, je vous propose ma candidature au poste de cambiste.

Vous verrez dans mon CV ci-joint que je viens de recevoir mon diplôme de gestion, au titre duquel j'ai suivi un stage de six semaines au bureau des changes de la Bradley's Bank à Londres. Je ne doute pas que cette expérience et mon excellente connaissance des langues européennes me donnent précisément le profil requis par le poste à pourvoir au sein de l'International Bank. Par ailleurs, j'envisage très sérieusement de poursuivre ma carrière dans le milieu bancaire, et ce particulièrement en France, où je pourrai mettre à profit ma connaissance du français.

N'hésitez pas à me contacter pour de plus amples renseignements. Je suis à votre disposition pour un entretien dès que vous le souhaiterez.

Je vous prie de croire, Messieurs, à l'assurance de mes salutations distinguées,

Jane Feldon

Jane Feldon

P. J. : CV

[1] *This address is appropriate if you are writing to a company. However, if you are writing to the holder of a particular post, you should write:*

Monsieur le Directeur
des ressources humaines
International Bank
18 rue la Boétie
75008 Paris

In this case, you should begin your letter with:
Monsieur le Directeur
des ressources humaines,
and repeat this in the closing formula instead of Messieurs.

If you know the name of the person, you should write:
Monsieur Jean-Bertrand Raynaud
or
Madame Anne-Marie Ormal
Directeur des ressources humaines
International Bank *etc.*

Your letter should then begin:
Monsieur, ... *or* Madame, ...

See sections 20 - 21 *for more information on letter writing.*

[1] *People with British or American qualifications applying for jobs in a French-speaking country might use some form of wording such as* équivalence baccalauréat (3 A-levels), équivalence licence de lettres (BA Hons) *etc*

CURRICULUM VITAE

GASTIN Sylvie
29, rue La Quintinie
75015 Paris
1 45 33 09 85 (répondeur)
Nationalité française
26 ans, mariée, 1 enfant

FORMATION[1]
1995 : Diplôme de secrétaire bilingue, délivré par l'École de commerce de Poitiers
1994 : Licence de langues étrangères appliquées (anglais et italien), Université de Poitiers - mention bien
1990 : Baccalauréat (langues) - mention assez bien

EXPÉRIENCE PROFESSIONNELLE
depuis 10/03/97 : Adjointe au Directeur du service Exportation, Agriventes, La Rochelle
08/10/95 - 30/01/97 : Secrétaire de direction, France-Exportations, Cognac

AUTRES RENSEIGNEMENTS
Langues étrangères : anglais (courant), italien (courant), espagnol (notions)
Stage d'informatique dans le cadre de la formation continue, 1997
Nombreux voyages aux États-Unis et en Italie
Permis de conduire

◆ **Je suis désireux de travailler en France afin de perfectionner** mes connaissances en français **et d'acquérir** une certaine expérience de l'hôtellerie
= *I wish to work in France in order to perfect ... and to acquire*

◆ **Un intérêt très vif pour** le domaine des télécommunications **m'incite à poser ma candidature pour** ce poste
= *I have a keen interest in ..., which is why I wish to apply for*

◆ **Ma formation de** comptable **et mon expérience de** la gestion des stocks **m'incitent à penser que je suis à même de vous assurer une collaboration efficace pour ce poste**
= *I believe that my training as ... and my experience in ... make me particularly suited to this position*

19.3 Closing the letter

◆ **Je serai disponible à partir de** la fin du mois d'avril
= *I will be available from*

◆ **Je demeure à votre entière disposition pour toute information complémentaire**
= *I would be delighted to supply any further information you may require*

◆ **Je serai heureux de vous rencontrer lors d'un entretien** à la date qui vous conviendra
= *I will be happy to attend an interview*

◆ **Je vous remercie dès à présent de** l'attention que vous voudrez bien porter à ma candidature
= *thank you in advance for*

◆ **Dans l'attente de votre réponse**, je vous prie d'agréer, Monsieur le Directeur, l'expression de mes salutations distinguées
= *I look forward to hearing from you*

19.4 Asking for and giving references

◆ Monsieur Jean Legrand sollicite un emploi de réceptionniste dans notre hôtel et il a donné votre nom comme référence. **Nous vous serions reconnaissants de bien vouloir nous faire savoir si vous le recommandez pour ce poste**
= *we should be grateful if you could let us know if you would recommend him for this position*

◆ **Votre réponse sera considérée comme strictement confidentielle**
= *your reply will be treated in the strictest confidence*

◆ **C'est avec grand plaisir que je vous recommande** Madame Marion Lebrun pour le poste de responsable du logement
= *I can warmly recommend*

19.5 Accepting and refusing

◆ Je vous remercie de votre lettre du 19 mars et **serai très heureux de me rendre à vos bureaux**, avenue Parmentier, **pour un entretien** le 12 mai à 15 heures
= *I will be glad to attend for interview at your offices*

◆ **J'ai le plaisir de vous confirmer que j'accepte le poste** d'expert-comptable que vous m'offrez
= *I have pleasure in confirming my acceptance of the post*

◆ **Votre offre m'intéresse très vivement mais je souhaiterais renégocier le salaire** que vous proposez avant de donner une réponse définitive
= *I am very interested in your offer but I would like to renegotiate the salary*

◆ **Après examen très attentif de votre offre, je me vois malheureusement dans l'obligation de la décliner**
= *after giving it very careful consideration, I regret that I must decline your offer*

20 COMMERCIAL CORRESPONDENCE

20.1 Making an enquiry

◆ **Nous avons remarqué dans votre annonce parue dans** le numéro de février de « Campagnes de France » **que** vous produisez une gamme d'articles de pêche
= *we note from your advertisement in ... that*

◆ **Nous vous serions reconnaissants de** nous adresser *or* faire parvenir une documentation complète sur cette gamme, y compris vos tarifs actuels, les remises consenties et vos délais de livraison
= *we should be grateful if you would*

20.2 Replying to an enquiry

◆ **Suite à votre demande, nous avons le plaisir de** vous adresser notre dernier catalogue
= *further to your request, we have pleasure in*

◆ **En réponse à** votre lettre du 10 juin, **veuillez trouver ci-joint** une documentation sur notre gamme de produits ainsi que notre liste de prix qui sont fermes jusqu'au 31 août
= *in reply to ..., please find enclosed*

◆ **Si vous désirez** des renseignements plus précis, **n'hésitez pas à nous contacter**
= *if you require ..., please do not hesitate to contact us*

20.3 Placing an order

◆ **Je vous remercie de** votre documentation et **vous serais obligé de** m'expédier les articles suivants dans les plus brefs délais
= *thank you for .... I should be grateful if you would*

◆ **Veuillez trouver ci-joint** un bon de commande pour 500 articles Réf PS788
= *please find enclosed*

◆ **Nous espérons que vous voudrez bien** nous consentir la remise de 10 % pour grosses quantités qui figure dans vos tarifs
= *we trust you will*

◆ **Cette commande tient compte de** la remise de 10 % que vous consentez sur les commandes en gros
= *this order takes into account*

20.4 Delivery

◆ **Nous vous remercions de votre commande** en date du 10 mai **que nous exécuterons dans les plus brefs délais**
= *thank you for your order ..., which will be despatched as soon as possible*

◆ **Nous procéderons à l'expédition de votre commande dès que possible**
= *we shall deliver your order as soon as possible*

◆ **Nos délais de livraison sont de** cinq semaines à partir de la date de réception de la commande
= *our delivery times are*

◆ **En raison d'**une pénurie de matières premières, **nous regrettons de ne pouvoir vous livrer avant** fin avril
= *owing to ... we regret that we are unable to deliver your order before*

20.5 Complaining

◆ **Nous n'avons pas encore reçu livraison de** la commande que nous avons passée le 20 mars dernier (voir bon de commande n° 3496)
= *we have not yet had delivery of*

◆ **Nous tenons à vous signaler que** les articles que vous nous avez livrés ne sont pas de la qualité habituelle
= *we wish to draw it to your attention that*

LA MAISON RUSTIQUE

FABRICATION DE MOBILIER
ZONE INDUSTRIELLE DE DAMPIERRE
B.P. 531 – 17015 DAMPIERRE CEDEX
TÉL: 06 28 42 37

V/Réf. - HL/SA 50746
N/Réf. - MB/AL 16064
Objet : envoi de documentation

Cuisines d'hier et d'aujourd'hui
3, place du Petit-Marché
16042 Nimeuil

Dampierre, le 3 novembre 1997

Messieurs,

Nous vous remercions de votre lettre du 30 octobre, ainsi que de votre demande de renseignements concernant notre gamme de sièges de cuisine.

Nous vous prions de trouver ci-joint une documentation complète, accompagnée de nos tarifs. Toutefois, nous nous permettons d'attirer votre attention sur nos nouveaux modèles « Saintonge », qui semblent convenir particulièrement à vos besoins. Ces modèles sont actuellement offerts à des prix très avantageux.

Nous nous tenons à votre entière disposition pour toute demande de renseignements supplémentaires et vous prions d'agréer, Messieurs, l'assurance de nos sentiments dévoués.

Le Directeur commercial

Jean Leclerc

Jean Leclerc

PJ : 1 documentation complète

Maison Duquesnois
Porcelaine et Orfèvrerie
14 rue Montpensier–84000 Poitiers

Madame Marianne Legrand
3, chemin des Princesses
16010 Granbourg

Poitiers, le 27 mai 1998

Madame,

Nous vous remercions de votre lettre du 21 mai, qui a retenu notre meilleure attention.

Malheureusement, nous ne suivons plus le modèle qui vous intéresse, et sommes donc au regret de ne pouvoir vous satisfaire.

Nous vous prions d'agréer, Madame, l'assurance de nos sentiments respecteux.

Le Directeur

Gérard Marquet

Gérard Marquet

- **Malheureusement,** les marchandises ont été endommagées en transit
  = *unfortunately*
- Les dix articles livrés **correspondent** à la référence LS59 de votre catalogue **et non à** la référence LS58 que nous avons commandée
  = *correspond to ... and not to ...*

20.6 Payment

- **Veuillez trouver ci-joint notre facture** d'un montant de ... relative à cet envoi
  = *please find <u>enclosed</u> our <u>invoice</u>*
- **Nous vous serions reconnaissants de nous faire parvenir cette somme dans les meilleurs délais**
  = *we should be <u>grateful</u> if you would <u>remit</u> <u>payment</u> of this <u>sum</u> at your earliest convenience*
- **Vous trouverez ci-joint un chèque d'un montant de** ... en règlement de votre facture n° HM307
  = *please find <u>enclosed</u> a cheque for (the <u>sum</u> of)*
- **Nous vous serions obligés de nous accorder un délai de paiement de 30 jours supplémentaires**
  = *we should be <u>obliged</u> if you would extend the <u>payment</u> <u>due</u> date by 30 days*
- **J'ai été très surpris de constater que vous me facturez** chaque article 39F **au lieu des** 35F mentionnés dans votre catalogue
  = *I was very surprised to note that you had <u>invoiced</u> me ... instead of*
- **Nous regrettons de devoir vous signaler une erreur qui s'est glissée dans votre facture**
  = *we regret to have to point out that there has been an error in your <u>invoice</u>*

21 GENERAL CORRESPONDENCE

21.1 Starting a letter

| To a friend or acquaintance |

- **Je te remercie de** ta lettre qui est arrivée ce matin
  = *<u>thanks</u> for*
- **J'ai été très contente d'avoir de tes nouvelles**
  = *it was lovely to <u>hear</u> from you*
- **Je suis désolé de ne pas vous avoir répondu plus vite** : je suis actuellement débordé de travail et n'ai que peu de moments de loisirs
  = *(I'm) sorry I didn't <u>reply</u> earlier*
- **Voilà bien longtemps que je ne vous ai pas donné de nouvelles.** C'est pourquoi je vous envoie un petit mot rapide
  = *it's been ages since I was last in touch*

| In formal correspondence |

- **Je vous serais reconnaissant de** me faire savoir si vous avez en librairie un roman intitulé ...
  = *I would be <u>grateful</u> if you would*
- **Je vous prie de** m'envoyer quatre exemplaires de votre numéro 310 et je joins à cette lettre un chèque d'un montant de ...
  = *<u>please</u>*
- **Suite à** notre conversation téléphonique de ce matin, **je vous écris pour** vous demander de bien vouloir m'expédier ...
  = *<u>further</u> to ..., I am <u>writing</u> to*

- **Ayant appris que** vous organisez des stages de voile, **je vous serais reconnaissant de me faire savoir** s'il vous reste des places pour débutants début juillet
  = *I believe that ... and I would be <u>grateful</u> if you would let me know*

21.2 Ending a letter (before the closing formulae)

- **Embrasse** Jérôme et Laure pour moi
  = *<u>love</u> to*
- Paul **vous embrasse** tous les deux
  = *sends his <u>love</u> to*
- **Dis bonjour à** Françoise pour moi
  = *say <u>hello</u> to*
- **Ecris-moi** si tu trouves une petite minute
  = *<u>write</u> to me*
- **N'oublie pas de nous donner de tes nouvelles** de temps en temps
  = *don't forget to give us your news*
- **N'hésitez pas à m'écrire** si je peux vous être utile
  = *do not <u>hesitate</u> to <u>write</u> to me*
- **Transmettez**, s'il vous plaît, **mes amitiés à** votre sœur
  = *give my <u>regards</u> to*
- Hélène **me charge de vous transmettre ses amitiés**
  = *asked me to give you her <u>regards</u>*
- **Veuillez transmettre mon meilleur souvenir à** votre mère
  = *please give my best <u>regards</u> to*

21.3 Enquiring about and booking accommodation

- **Je vous serais reconnaissant de bien vouloir** m'envoyer les tarifs de vos chambres
  = *I would be <u>grateful</u> if you would*
- **Je désirerais** retenir une chambre avec douche
  = *I wish to*
- **Je voudrais** retenir une chambre pour deux personnes ainsi qu'une chambre à deux lits pour mes enfants
  = *I would like to*
- **Veuillez me faire savoir**, par retour du courrier si possible, **si** vous avez une chambre pour une personne en demi-pension pour la semaine du 4 au 11 juillet
  = *please let me know ... if*
- **Veuillez m'indiquer** le montant des arrhes que je dois verser pour la réservation
  = *please <u>advise</u>*
- **Veuillez confirmer** par télécopie la réservation suivante : une chambre à deux lits ...
  = *please <u>confirm</u>*
- **Il est possible que nous** arrivions *(subj)* à une heure tardive
  = *we might*
- **Nous devrions normalement** arriver en début de soirée
  = *we should*

21.4 Confirming and cancelling a booking

- **Je vous confirme par ce courrier** ma réservation
  = *this is to <u>confirm</u>*
- Pour des raisons indépendantes de ma volonté, **je me vois contraint d'annuler** la réservation que j'avais faite au nom de ... pour la semaine du 4 au 11 juillet
  = *I am obliged to <u>cancel</u>*
- **Je vous serais reconnaissant de bien vouloir reporter ma réservation du** 3 septembre **au** 7 septembre
  = *I would be <u>grateful</u> if you would <u>change</u> my <u>booking</u> from ... to*

Strasbourg, le 15 mars 1998

Chère Laurence,

Un grand merci pour le livre sur les poissons d'Europe que tu m'as envoyé. C'est exactement le type d'ouvrage qu'il me fallait : il devrait m'aider énormément dans mes recherches de traductions. Je ferai en sorte de te le rendre lors de mon passage à Angers courant juin, si du moins tu n'en as pas besoin d'ici là.

Es-tu toujours d'accord pour louer un bateau cet été ? Je te donnerai bientôt un coup de fil pour discuter de cela.

Grosses bises,

Orléans, le 23 février 1998

Chers Sophie et Daniel,

Voilà un bon moment que nous ne nous sommes pas vus : comment allez-vous ?

Je vous écris en fait pour vous demander un renseignement. En effet, nous avons l'intention de passer une semaine dans le Vaucluse en août et je me suis rappelée l'enthousiasme avec lequel vous parliez du gîte que vous aviez loué à Carpentras deux années de suite. Pourriez-vous m'en donner les coordonnées pour que je puisse éventuellement faire une réservation ?

J'espère que tout va bien à Brest et que nous nous reverrons bientôt.

Bien amicalement,

Anne-Laure

Standard opening and closing formulae

OPENING FORMULAE	CLOSING FORMULAE
Used when the person is not personally known to you	
Monsieur, Madame,	Je vous prie de croire, [...], à l'assurance de mes salutations distinguées.
Mademoiselle,	**used by a man only** Veuillez agréer, [...], l'expression de mes sentiments les meilleurs.
	man to woman only Je vous prie d'accepter, [...], l'expression de mes respectueux hommages.
Used when the person is known to you personally	
Cher Monsieur, Chère Madame, Chère Mademoiselle,	Croyez, [...], à l'expression de mes sentiments les meilleurs.

To acquaintances and friends

OPENING FORMULAE	CLOSING FORMULAE
Still fairly formal	
Cher Monsieur, Chère Madame, Chère Mademoiselle,	Recevez, je vous prie, mes meilleures amitiés. Je vous envoie mes bien amicales pensées. Je vous adresse à tous deux mon très amical souvenir.
Fairly informal: 'tu' or 'vous' forms could be used	
Cher Patrick, Chère Sylvie, Chers Chantal et Jean-Claude,	Bien amicalement Cordialement Amitiés

To close friends and family

OPENING FORMULAE	CLOSING FORMULAE
	'tu' or 'vous' can be used, though 'tu' is more likely in all these expressions
Cher Franck, Chère tante Jacqueline, Mon cher Jean, Ma très chère Ingrid, Chers grands-parents, Mon cher cousin,	Je t'embrasse bien affectueusement Bien à toi Bien des choses à tous Bons baisers À bientôt Salut!

Writing to a firm or an institution (see also 20)

OPENING FORMULAE	CLOSING FORMULAE
Messieurs, *(to a firm)*	Je vous prie d'agréer, [...], l'assurance de mes sentiments distingués.
Monsieur, *(to a man)*	Veuillez accepter, [...], l'expression de mes sentiments distingués.
Madame, *(to a woman)*	

To a person in an important position

OPENING FORMULAE	CLOSING FORMULAE
Very formal	
Monsieur le Directeur *(or le Maire etc)*, Madame le Professeur *(or le Consul etc)*,	Je vous prie d'agréer, [...], l'assurance de ma considération distinguée **or used by a man only:** de mes sentiments respectueux *or* de mes sentiments dévoués.
Used only if the person is well known to you	
Cher Monsieur, Chère Madame,	Veuillez croire, [...], à l'assurance de mes sentiments les meilleurs. Je vous prie d'accepter, [...], l'expression de mes salutations distinguées. **or, used by a man only:** de mes sentiments distingués.
Cher Collègue, Chère Collègue, *(to someone in the same profession)*	**used by a man only:** Croyez, [...], à l'assurance de mes sentiments les meilleurs.

22 THANKS

* **Merci de** m'avoir fait confiance
  = _thank_ you for
* **C'est vraiment très gentil de votre part de** nous avoir invités
  = it is really very _kind_ of you to
* **Je vous remercie de** m'avoir réservé une place
  = _thank_ you for
* **Remercie-le** de ma part **pour** son accueil
  = _thank_ him ... for
* **Je ne sais comment vous remercier de** votre aide
  = I don't know how to thank you for
* **Je vous écris pour vous remercier de tout cœur d'**avoir pensé à nous
  = I am writing to express my _heartfelt_ _thanks_ for
* **Transmettez mes remerciements à** vos collègues
  = please _thank_
* **Nous vous sommes extrêmement reconnaissants d'**être venu
  = we are extremely _grateful_ to you for
* **Je vous adresse mes plus vifs remerciements pour ...**
  = my most _sincere_ _thanks_ for
* **Je tiens à vous exprimer notre gratitude pour** le soutien que vous nous avez apporté
  = I wish to express our _gratitude_ for

23 BEST WISHES

23.1 General expressions *(used on special occasions only)*

* **Meilleurs vœux** + *such expressions as « de bonheur », « à l'occasion de votre départ en retraite », « de prompt rétablissement », « de réussite » etc*
  = _best_ wishes
* **Tous mes vœux** + *such expressions as « de bonheur », « à l'occasion de votre départ en retraite », « de prompt rétablissement », « de réussite » etc*
  = my _best_ wishes
* **Je vous présente mes meilleurs vœux** à l'occasion de
  = I send you my _best_ wishes
* **Transmettez-lui tous mes vœux de ...**
  = give him my _best_ wishes for ...
* **Je vous souhaite de passer d'excellentes vacances**
  = I _hope_ you have an excellent holiday
* **J'espère (de tout cœur) que vous ferez bon voyage**
  = I (really) _hope_ you have a good trip

23.2 Season's greetings

NB : in France cards are usually sent for New Year rather than Christmas, and may be sent in the first few weeks of January

* **Joyeux Noël et Bonne Année!**
  = _Merry_ _Christmas_ and (a) _Happy_ _New_ _Year_!
* **Joyeuses fêtes!**
  = _Season's_ Greetings!
* **Bonne et heureuse année!**
  = _Happy_ _New_ _Year_!
* Paul et moi **vous adressons tous nos vœux pour la nouvelle année**
  (used at New Year only)
  = send you our _best_ _wishes_ for the _New_ Year
* **Je vous présente mes meilleurs vœux pour 1998**
  = I _wish_ you all the _best_ for 1998

23.3 Birthday greetings

* **Bon** or **Joyeux anniversaire !**
  = _happy_ _birthday_!
* **Je vous souhaite un bon** or **un joyeux anniversaire**
  = I _wish_ you a _happy_ _birthday_

23.4 Get well wishes

+ J'ai été désolé d'apprendre que vous êtes souffrant et **vous adresse tous mes vœux de prompt rétablissement**
  = I _wish_ you all the _best_ for a _speedy_ _recovery_
+ **Je vous souhaite** de tout cœur **un prompt rétablissement**
  = I _wish_ you a _speedy_ _recovery_
+ **J'espère** de tout cœur **que vous serez très bientôt rétabli**
  = I _hope_ you will be _better_ soon

23.5 Wishing someone luck

+ **Je vous adresse tous mes vœux de succès** dans votre nouvelle entreprise
  = I _wish_ you every _success_
+ **Je vous souhaite tout le succès que vous méritez** dans votre nouvelle carrière
  = I _wish_ you all the _success_ you rightly deserve
+ **Je te souhaite bonne chance**, de notre part à tous, pour tes examens
  = I _wish_ you good _luck_

23.6 Congratulations

+ **Toutes mes félicitations pour** ton succès au permis de conduire
  = my _congratulations_ on
+ **Je vous félicite de tout cœur pour** votre succès
  = warmest _congratulations_ on
+ **Je vous adresse mes plus sincères félicitations pour** la réussite de votre projet
  = my most _sincere_ _congratulations_ on
+ **Je tiens à te dire combien je suis heureux que** tu aies (subj) obtenu ce poste
  = I want you to know how _happy_ I am that
+ Je vous écris pour vous dire que **je me réjouis de votre succès**
  = I am _delighted_ about your _success_

24 ANNOUNCEMENTS

24.1 Announcing a birth

+ Claude et Anne-Marie Bernard **ont la joie de vous annoncer la naissance de** Thérèse, le 21 mars 1998 à Toulon
  = are _happy_ to _announce_ the _birth_ of
+ **J'ai le plaisir de t'annoncer que** Marie et Jean-Paul ont eu un petit garçon le 4 avril. Ils l'ont appelé Vincent. Tout s'est bien passé et la famille est ravie
  = I am delighted to tell you that

... and responding

+ **Nous vous félicitons de l'heureuse arrivée de** Thérèse et souhaitons au bébé santé et prospérité
  = _congratulations_ on the _arrival_ of
+ David et moi **sommes heureux d'apprendre la naissance de** Vincent et espérons faire bientôt sa connaissance
  = were delighted to learn of the _birth_ of

24.2 Announcing an engagement

+ Monsieur et Madame Simon **sont heureux d'annoncer les fiançailles de** leur fille Élodie avec M. Thomas Corbel
  = are pleased to _announce_ the _engagement_ of

+ Élodie et Thomas **viennent d'annoncer leurs fiançailles.** Ils n'ont pas encore fixé la date du mariage mais nous nous réjouissons tous de leur bonheur
  = have just got _engaged_

... and responding

+ **Nous nous réjouissons avec vous des fiançailles d'**Élodie et de Thomas. Transmettez tous nos vœux de bonheur aux jeunes fiancés
  = we are as delighted as you are about the _engagement_ of
+ **C'est avec beaucoup de joie que j'ai appris vos fiançailles avec** Thomas. Je vous adresse à tous deux mes vœux de bonheur les plus sincères
  = I was very _happy_ to learn of your _engagement_ to

24.3 Announcing a marriage

+ Monsieur et Madame André Kervella **ont l'honneur de vous faire part du mariage de** leur fille Isabelle avec M. Christian Minguy
  = are _happy_ to _announce_ the _marriage_ of
+ **J'ai la joie de t'annoncer qu'**Isabelle et Christian **se sont mariés** samedi dernier. La cérémonie a eu lieu à l'église de Lanvéoc
  = I am pleased to tell you that ... got _married_

... and responding

+ Monsieur et Madame Paul Gestin **félicitent** Monsieur et Madame André Kervella **à l'occasion du prochain mariage de** leur fille Isabelle
  = would like to _congratulate_ ... on the _marriage_ of ...
+ **Nous présentons toutes nos félicitations aux jeunes mariés et leur souhaitons beaucoup de bonheur et de prospérité**
  = our _congratulations_ and best _wishes_ for happiness and prosperity to the young couple
+ J'ai été très heureuse d'apprendre par ta lettre le mariage de Laetitia et de Yann. **Je leur souhaite tout le bonheur possible**
  = I _wish_ them every possible _happiness_

24.4 Announcing a death

+ M. et Mme Pierre Desmas et leurs enfants **ont la douleur de vous faire part du décès de** Mme Joseph Benard née Marie-Anne Chevalier
  = _regret_ to _announce_ the _death_ of
+ **Nous avons la grande tristesse de vous faire part du décès de** notre mère, survenu soudainement le 8 septembre. Le service religieux et l'inhumation ont eu lieu dans la plus stricte intimité
  = it is with deep _sorrow_ that we _announce_ the _death_ of
+ **C'est avec beaucoup de peine que je t'écris pour t'annoncer que** mon père est décédé la semaine dernière
  = I am very _sad_ to have to write and tell you that

... and responding

+ **J'ai été bouleversé d'apprendre** la disparition de ta sœur
  = I was terribly _upset_ to hear about ...
+ **Je tiens à te dire combien je pense à toi en ces moments douloureux**
  = I'd like you to know that I am _thinking_ of you at this _sad_ time
+ Monsieur et Madame Paul Lambert **vous prient d'accepter l'expression de leur plus profonde sympathie et vous adressent leurs plus sincères condoléances à l'occasion du deuil qui vient de vous frapper** (formal)
  = send their deepest _sympathy_ and offer you their most sincere _condolences_ on your _loss_

24.5   Announcing a change of address

+ **Nous vous prions de bien vouloir noter que notre nouvelle adresse sera**, à partir du 10 décembre 1998 : 10 rue Colbert, 29200 Brest
   = *we wish to <u>inform</u> you that our new <u>address</u> will be*

25   INVITATIONS

25.1   Formal invitations

+ Madame Paul Ambre et Madame Michel Potet **recevront après la cérémonie religieuse** au Relais des Glycines, route de Marleroy, Fontanes. RSVP
   = *<u>request</u> the <u>pleasure</u> of your <u>company</u> afterwards*

+ Les éditions Roget **ont le plaisir de vous inviter à** un cocktail à l'occasion de la sortie du premier livre de la collection Espoir, le lundi 9 août à partir de 18 h 30
   = *have <u>pleasure</u> in <u>inviting</u> you to*

+ Monsieur et Madame André Bureau **prient Madame Labadie de leur faire le plaisir de venir dîner le** mercredi 27 octobre à 20 heures
   = *<u>request</u> the <u>pleasure</u> of the <u>company</u> of Mme Labadie at dinner on*

+ **Pour les 20 ans de sa fille Joséphine, Madame Gérard Lamarche recevra chez elle**, le 24 novembre à partir de 19 h
   = *Madame Gérard Lamarche has <u>pleasure</u> in <u>inviting</u> you to <u>celebrate</u> her daughter Josephine's 20th birthday*

... and responding

+ Monsieur Pierre Quentin **regrette profondément de ne pouvoir assister au** vin d'honneur organisé à l'occasion du mariage de Paul et Nathalie, d'autres obligations ne lui permettant pas de quitter Paris
   = *very much <u>regrets</u> that he cannot <u>attend</u>*

+ Mademoiselle Charlotte Leblanc **accepte avec grand plaisir de se rendre au** cocktail organisé le 9 août par les éditions Roget
   = *has great <u>pleasure</u> in <u>accepting</u> your <u>invitation</u> to*

+ Madame Jeanne Labadie **remercie** Monsieur et Madame André Bureau **pour leur aimable invitation à** dîner **qu'elle accepte avec le plus grand plaisir/qu'elle regrette vivement de ne pouvoir accepter** en raison d'un autre engagement
   = *<u>thanks</u> ... for their <u>kind</u> <u>invitation</u>, which she is <u>delighted</u> to <u>accept</u>/deeply <u>regrets</u> she is <u>unable</u> to <u>accept</u>*

+ Monsieur Jacques Dalbret **assistera avec plaisir à** la réception organisée à l'occasion des 20 ans de Joséphine
   = *will be <u>happy</u> to <u>attend</u>*

25.2   Less formal invitations

+ **Est-ce que cela te dirait d'**aller passer la journée à Nantes? *(spoken)*
   = *would you <u>like</u> to*

+ Pour fêter les fiançailles de Geneviève et de Xavier, nous organisons une réception à l'Hôtel de France, à Saint-Martin le 2 septembre à 20 heures et **serions très heureux si vous pouviez vous joindre à nous**
   = *would be <u>delighted</u> if you could join us*

+ Michèle et Philippe doivent venir déjeuner dimanche prochain et **nous espérons que vous pourrez être des nôtres**
   = *we <u>hope</u> you can join us*

+ Lorsque vous passerez à Lyon, **vous nous feriez très plaisir si vous pouviez nous consacrer une soirée** pour que nous dînions ensemble
   = *we would be <u>delighted</u> if you could spend an evening with us*

+ Nous projetons de passer le mois de juillet à Montpellier et **serions très heureux de vous y accueillir** quelques jours
   = *we would be very <u>happy</u> to have you*

... and responding

Accepting

+ **Je vous remercie de** votre aimable invitation **et me fais une joie de venir** à votre réception
   = *<u>thank</u> you for ... I am looking forward to coming*

+ **Je viendrai avec plaisir** déjeuner avec vous dimanche prochain
   = *I will be <u>happy</u> to come*

+ Nous pensons passer le week-end de la Pentecôte à Lyon et **nous vous téléphonerons pour essayer de vous voir**
   = *we will call you to see if we can meet up*

+ **Votre invitation** à Montpellier **nous a fait très plaisir et nous espérons passer un week-end avec vous** vers le 14 juillet
   = *we were <u>delighted</u> to receive your <u>invitation</u> ... and hope to spend a weekend with you*

Declining

+ **C'est très gentil à vous de m'inviter** pour votre soirée de samedi, **mais je me vois malheureusement obligé de refuser**, car j'ai déjà accepté une invitation pour ce soir-là
   = *it was very kind of you to <u>invite</u> me ... but I am afraid I have to <u>decline</u>*

+ **J'aimerais beaucoup passer un week-end chez vous, mais malheureusement,** aucune des dates que vous me proposez ne me convient
   = *I would love to spend a weekend with you but <u>unfortunately</u>*

+ **Malheureusement, je ne peux pas me libérer** le mois prochain. Peut-être pourrions-nous nous voir en octobre
   = *<u>unfortunately</u>, I can't get away*

26   ESSAY WRITING

26.1   The broad outline of the essay

Introductory remarks

+ **Tout le monde s'accorde à penser que** le chômage est un des principaux maux de notre société. **Il convient donc d'examiner** les mesures qui pourraient être prises pour le combattre
   = *everyone <u>agrees</u> that .... So we should <u>examine</u>*

+ Peut-on lire l'œuvre d'un philosophe quand on sait qu'il a été nazi? **Telle est la question soulevée par** l'article de ...
   = *such is the <u>question</u> <u>raised</u> by*

+ **Il est bien connu que** la voiture pollue. **La question est de savoir si** nous pourrions un jour nous passer de ce mode de transport
   = *it is a well-known <u>fact</u> that ... the <u>question</u> is whether*

+ Les adolescents d'aujourd'hui ne lisent pas beaucoup. **Ceci est interprété tantôt comme** une crise passagère, **tantôt comme** un signe du déclin du message imprimé
   = *some <u>interpret</u> this as ..., others as ...*

+ **Nous vivons dans un monde où** la paix est constamment menacée
   = *we live in a world in which*

+ **Un problème souvent évoqué** or **dont il est souvent question est celui de** la corruption des milieux d'affaires
   = *a much-discussed <u>problem</u> is that of*

+ **L'histoire nous fournit de nombreux exemples de** génies incompris à leur époque puis reconnus par la postérité
   = *history provides us with countless <u>examples</u> of*

+ **Cette question est depuis longtemps au cœur du** débat sur l'éducation
   = *this <u>question</u> has long been at the <u>heart</u> of*

Developing the argument

- **La première constatation qui s'impose, c'est que** le roman va au-delà d'une simple enquête policière
  = *the first <u>point</u> to note is that*

- **Prenons comme point de départ** le rôle que le gouvernement a joué dans l'élaboration de ces programmes
  = *<u>let</u> us take ... as a <u>starting point</u>*

- **En premier lieu, examinons** ce qui fait obstacle à la paix
  = *<u>firstly</u>, <u>let</u> us <u>examine</u>*

- **Il serait utile d'examiner** la façon dont l'auteur a abouti à ces conclusions
  = *it would be useful to <u>examine</u>*

- **Il convient tout d'abord de se pencher sur** les circonstances de la parution de ce livre
  = *it is worth first of all turning one's <u>attention</u> to*

- **Selon l'auteur**, la psychanalyse **ne serait pas** un obstacle à la créativité
  = *<u>according</u> to the author ... isn't*

- **Il est significatif que** ce conflit **soit** (*subj*) le produit d'une politique africaine moderne
  = *it is <u>significant</u> that ... is*

- **Pour illustrer** l'association lucrative des vedettes de sport et des grandes entreprises, **il suffit de prendre un exemple**
  = *in order to <u>illustrate</u> ... we only need to take an <u>example</u>*

- Un second exemple **marque l'importance de** ce thème
  = *<u>underlines</u> the importance of*

- Un examen des origines de la laïcité **nous permettra peut-être de mieux comprendre** les bases de ce conflit
  = *will perhaps <u>allow</u> us better to understand*

The other side of the argument

- **Après avoir étudié** la progression de l'action, **considérons maintenant** le style
  = *after <u>studying</u> ... <u>let</u> us now <u>consider</u>*

- **Il faut maintenant s'interroger sur** la motivation de l'auteur dans le choix du contexte historique
  = *one must now <u>question</u>*

- **Venons-en maintenant à** l'analyse des retombées politiques
  = *now <u>let</u> us come to*

- **Ce qui vaut pour** le héros **s'applique également aux** personnages secondaires
  = *what goes for ... <u>applies</u> <u>equally</u> to*

- **Il convient maintenant d'analyser** les arguments de ceux qui préconisent une législation plus stricte
  = *it is worth now <u>analysing</u>*

- Le principe de laïcité de l'enseignement est-il compatible avec le port de certains signes religieux ? **C'est ce que nous allons étudier dans la seconde partie de cette analyse**
  = *... is what we are going to study in the second part of this <u>analysis</u>*

- **Plus encore que** la pollution, **c'est** le bruit qui provoque la colère de nombreux citadins
  = *even more than ... it is*

- **On pourrait objecter que** l'œuvre littéraire n'est pas séparable de son contexte
  = *one could <u>object</u> that*

The balanced view

- **Au terme de cette analyse, il faut cependant faire remarquer que** le chômage n'est pas le seul facteur en cause. **Il faudrait également examiner** ...
  = *at the end of this <u>analysis</u>, it is, <u>however</u>, necessary to <u>point</u> out that .... It is <u>equally</u> necessary to <u>examine</u>*

- **Mais le meilleur moyen de** limiter la pollution, **c'est encore d'**examiner comment on pourrait réduire les transports routiers
  = *but the best way of ... is to*

- **Enfin, il faut nous poser cette question :** la famine est-elle vraiment une fatalité?
  = *<u>finally</u>, we must <u>ask</u> ourselves whether*

In conclusion

- **Quelles conclusions tirer de cette analyse?**
  = *what <u>conclusions</u> can be drawn from this <u>analysis</u>?*

- **Le problème se résume donc à ceci :** dans un monde dominé par l'audiovisuel, le théâtre a-t-il encore une chance de survivre ?
  = *the <u>problem</u>, then, <u>boils</u> down to this:*

- L'expérience des dix dernières années **prouve** *or* **démontre que** le travail des organisations bénévoles n'est pas vain mais qu'il ne suffit pas
  = *<u>proves</u> or <u>demonstrates</u> that*

- **En dernière analyse**, c'est l'identité personnelle dans ce qu'elle a de plus secret qui est menacée
  = *in the <u>final analysis</u>*

- **En somme**, c'est la singularité du style qui constitue l'originalité profonde de l'auteur
  = *in short*

- **En définitive**, les réformateurs devraient mieux prendre en compte les leçons des expériences passées
  = *when all is <u>said</u> and done*

26.2 Constructing a paragraph

Assessing an idea

- **On peut avancer** plusieurs arguments différents
  = *one can <u>put</u> forward*

- **Plusieurs arguments viennent renforcer** cette idée
  = *there are several <u>arguments</u> in <u>support</u> of*

- **Examinons** les origines du problème **ainsi que** certaines des solutions suggérées
  = *let us <u>examine</u> ... as well as*

- **On peut noter** *or* **mentionner en passant que** l'auteur ne fait jamais allusion à ce problème
  = *it may be <u>noted</u> or <u>mentioned</u> in passing that*

- **Sans nous appesantir** *or* **nous attarder sur** les détails, **notons toutefois que** le rôle du Conseil de l'ordre a été déterminant
  = *without dwelling on the details, let us <u>note</u>, <u>however</u>, that*

- **Comme nous le verrons plus en détail par la suite**, ce sont surtout les personnages secondaires qui font progresser l'action
  = *as we shall see in more detail later*

- **Nous reviendrons plus loin sur cette question, mais signalons déjà** l'absence totale d'émotion dans ce passage
  = *we shall come back to this <u>question</u> later, but let us <u>point</u> out at this stage*

- **Avant d'aborder** la question du style, **mentionnons brièvement** le choix des métaphores
  = *before <u>tackling</u> ... let us <u>mention</u> briefly*

Establishing parallels

- Qui sont les pauvres d'aujourd'hui ? **D'une part**, il y a ceux qui naissent pauvres, et **d'autre part,** il y a ceux qui le deviennent
  = *on the one <u>hand</u> ... on the other (hand)*

- Les préjugés anticommunistes **d'un côté**, anticapitalistes **de l'autre** ne sont pas morts
  = *on the one <u>hand</u> ... on the other (hand)*

- **Les premiers** disposent du pouvoir. **Les seconds** font la grève
  = *the <u>former</u> .... the <u>latter</u> ...*

◆ L'Éducation nationale fait l'objet de critiques continuelles et **il en va de même pour** la Sécurité sociale
  = the _same_ is true of

◆ **De même que** les étudiants se demandent à quoi leurs études vont leur servir, **de même,** les professeurs s'interrogent sur leur rôle
  = in the _same_ way that ... so, too ...

◆ **Nous ne pouvons dissocier** ce facteur **de** la décision mentionnée plus haut
  = we cannot _dissociate_ ... from

◆ **Nous reprenons ainsi une idée suggérée antérieurement**
  = thus, we are again taking up an idea suggested earlier

Adding or detailing

◆ **De plus,** il s'agit là d'un progrès tout à fait remarquable
  = what is _more_

◆ **En outre**, il faut noter que les employés sont mal payés
  = _furthermore_

◆ Il faut **également** dire que le népotisme est parfois encouragé par les entreprises elles-mêmes
  = _equally_

◆ **Ajoutons à cela** or **Il faut ajouter à cela** or **À cela s'ajoute** un sens remarquable du détail
  = let us _add_ to this or _added_ to this

◆ **À cet égard** or **À ce propos**, il faut noter une détérioration dans la qualité de l'enseignement
  = in this respect or in this connection

◆ **De même**, on pourrait suggérer que le style de l'auteur manque d'originalité
  = by the _same_ _token_

◆ **D'ailleurs**, la Russie veut croire que sa contribution permettrait de rendre le système plus efficace
  = _moreover_

◆ **Pour ce qui est des** personnages secondaires, ils sont, eux aussi, remarquablement vivants
  = as for the

◆ **En ce qui concerne** la pollution chimique, il faut reconnaître qu'elle constitue aussi un grave danger
  = as far as ... is _concerned_

◆ **Quant aux** émissions sportives, elles suivent toujours le même modèle précis
  = as for the

◆ Plusieurs catégories professionnelles ont été oubliées, **notamment** or **parmi lesquelles** les employés de bureaux et les réceptionnistes
  = _notably_ or among whom

◆ **Ces enfants** d'origine étrangère **connaissent** parfois **de graves problèmes** de scolarité, **problèmes qui** doivent retenir toute l'attention des enseignants
  = these children ... have serious problems ..., which

Enumerating

◆ Différentes formules sont offertes au client : voyage à forfait, **ou bien** hébergement chez l'habitant, **ou encore** demi-pension, **ou enfin** camping dans un village de vacances
  = or ... or even ... or _finally_

◆ Faut-il inclure dans les statistiques les handicapés ? **Ou bien** doit-on exclure les jeunes ? **Ou encore** est-il nécessaire d'analyser le mode de vie en plus des revenus ?
  = or ... or even ...

◆ **Du** parti communiste à l'extrême droite, **tous** sont d'accord pour condamner cet acte de terrorisme
  = from ... to ..., all ...

◆ **Parmi** ces grands auteurs, on peut citer **(tout) d'abord** Racine, **ensuite** Corneille, **enfin** Molière
  = amongst ... first (of all) ... then ... and _finally_

◆ **En premier lieu**, il convient d'examiner attentivement chaque offre, **puis** il faut sélectionner les plus intéressantes **et, en dernier lieu,** entrer en contact avec les différents candidats
  = in the first _instance_ ... then ... and _finally_

◆ Ceci est dû essentiellement à trois facteurs : **premièrement**, l'originalité du projet, **deuxièmement**, la rapidité avec laquelle il a été réalisé, **troisièmement**, la faiblesse des coûts
  = _firstly_ ... _secondly_ ... _thirdly_

Opposing

◆ Nombreux sont les régimes autoritaires qui ont bénéficié à l'origine du soutien de la majorité de la population. **Néanmoins**, ces régimes ont mal vieilli
  = _nevertheless_

◆ Ces éléments militent en faveur de l'apparition de plusieurs conventions collectives dans les milieux sportifs. **Cependant**, chacun le pressent : les enjeux ne sont pas que sociaux
  = _however_

◆ **Malgré** ses airs d'enfant de chœur, cet homme fut un redoutable chef de guerre
  = _despite_

◆ **Malgré tout**, il est impossible de nier que le système néerlandais est coûteux
  = _despite_ everything

◆ **En dépit de** ces maladresses, le spectacle possède un charme indéniable
  = _despite_

Introducing one's own point of view

◆ **À mon avis** or **Selon moi** or **D'après moi**, ce chapitre est le meilleur du livre
  = in my _opinion_

◆ **En ce qui me concerne** or **Pour ma part**, je déplore l'évolution actuelle de la politique sociale
  = as far as I am _concerned_

◆ **Personnellement**, ce qui me frappe le plus dans cette affaire, c'est que l'origine de ces fonds est encore inexpliquée
  = _personally_

◆ **Je suis d'avis que** la télévision a un effet néfaste sur l'éducation des enfants
  = I am of the _opinion_ that

◆ **Je soutiens qu'**on n'a jamais répondu clairement aux questions posées
  = I _maintain_ that

◆ **Je pense que** l'auteur fait ici preuve d'ironie
  = I think

Introducing someone else's point of view

◆ **Selon l'auteur** or **D'après l'auteur,** le motif principal du crime est la jalousie
  = _according_ to the author

◆ **Comme le soulignent** les experts, il est nécessaire de réduire les coûts de production de 7 %
  = _as_ ... _stress_

◆ **Comme le laisse entendre** l'auteur, certains détails n'ont pas été révélés au public
  = _as_ ... gives us to understand

◆ Le budget du ministère est, **dit-il** or **affirme-t-il**, conforme aux prévisions
  = he says or affirms

◆ **Il dit/pense/croit/affirme/déclare que** ce système présente de nombreux avantages
  = he _says_/_thinks_/_believes_/_maintains_/_declares_ that

+ L'auteur **attire notre attention sur** l'ampleur de ce changement
  = *draws our <u>attention</u> to*
+ **Il nous rappelle** les bouleversements qui ont suivi ce projet de loi
  = *he <u>reminds</u> us of*
+ **Il insiste sur le fait que/souligne que/soutient que** ces rivalités
  internes sont la principale cause de l'échec du mouvement
  = *he insists on the fact that/<u>stresses</u> that/<u>maintains</u> that*
+ **Elle prétend que** ce travail ne nécessite aucune recherche
  = *she <u>claims</u> that*
+ **Il voudrait nous faire croire que** cette rébellion n'a eu aucune
  conséquence grave
  = *he would have us <u>believe</u> that*
+ **Selon la version officielle**, l'épidémie est maintenant endiguée
  = *<u>according</u> to the official version*

| Introducing an example |

+ **Prenons le cas de** Louis dans « le Nœud de vipères »
  = *(let us) take the <u>case</u> of*
+ **Il suffit de prendre pour exemple** le cinéma muet des années vingt
  = *one need only take as an <u>example</u>*
+ Le cas de l'agroalimentaire **en est un exemple frappant**
  = *is a striking <u>example</u> of this*
+ L'augmentation de la délinquance **illustre bien** les conséquences
  de cette crise chez les jeunes
  = *is a good <u>illustration</u> of*

| Introducing a quotation or source |

+ **Selon** *or* **D'après** les auteurs du rapport , « l'important n'est pas de
  nourrir l'Afrique mais de la faire reverdir »
  = *<u>according</u> to*
+ « La raison du plus fort est toujours la meilleure », **constate/
  affirme/observe** La Fontaine
  = *notes/asserts/<u>observes</u>*
+ **Comme l'a fait remarquer** le président, « la croissance économique
  dépend du taux d'investissement »
  = *<u>as</u> ... pointed out*
+ Chénier **avait écrit** : « l'art ne fait que des vers, le cœur seul est
  poète » et Musset **reprend la même idée lorsqu'il dit** : « Ah,
  frappe-toi le cœur, c'est là qu'est le génie »
  = *had written: ... echoes the <u>same</u> idea when he says:*
+ **Selon les paroles de** Duhamel, « le romancier est l'historien du
  présent »
  = *in the <u>words</u> of*
+ Dans un article récemment publié dans le journal « Le Temps », **nous
  trouvons cette remarque de** Thomas Gordon : « ... »
  = *we find this remark by*
+ Dans son étude sur le folklore vendéen, Jean Dumur **observe** ...
  = *<u>observes</u>*

| Concluding |

+ **De toute façon**, nous sommes au pied du mur
  = *in any case*
+ **Bref** *or* **En un mot**, il refuse de se prononcer
  = *<u>basically</u>* or *in a <u>word</u>*
+ **En somme**, il faut nuancer cette affirmation
  = *in <u>short</u>*
+ Il convient de signaler, **pour conclure**, l'exceptionnelle qualité des
  textes retenus
  = *in <u>conclusion</u>*
+ **En définitive**, ce dont le monde a besoin c'est d'un style de vie et
  de consommation plus sobre
  = *when all is <u>said</u> and done*

| 26.3 | The mechanics of the argument

| Stating facts |

+ **Il est exact que** les trains arrivent en général à l'heure, sauf quand il
  gèle
  = *it is <u>true</u> that*
+ **On constate** chez les cadres une forte motivation
  = *... is <u>noticeable</u>*
+ **On observe** un repli sur les valeurs sûres
  = *... can be <u>observed</u>*
+ **On peut noter que** l'essentiel des dépenses de santé est financé
  par des cotisations sociales
  = *we can <u>see</u> that*
+ Ce mode de calcul des rémunérations **fait l'objet de** négociations
  entre patronat et syndicats
  = *is the <u>object</u> of*
+ **Il s'agit d'**une mesure de défense prise face à une initiative jugée
  hostile
  = *it is a*
+ **Rappelons les faits**. Victoria l'Américaine débarque à Londres en
  1970 et réussit rapidement à s'imposer sur la scène musicale
  = *let's <u>recall</u> the <u>facts</u>*
+ Le New York Times **rapporte que** l'islam est la religion qui connaît
  aujourd'hui la plus forte croissance aux États-Unis
  = *<u>reports</u> that*

| Making a supposition |

+ Si on trouve ces fossiles à l'intérieur des terres, **on peut supposer
  que** jadis la mer recouvrait cette région
  = *one can <u>assume</u> that*
+ **Il est peu probable que** la diminution de l'ensoleillement dans la
  région **ait** *(subj)* eu des conséquences sur la croissance des plantes
  = *it is <u>unlikely</u> that*
+ **Il pourrait y avoir** une guerre commerciale si nous n'instaurons pas
  le libre accès aux marchés
  = *there <u>could</u> be*
+ Dans les milieux diplomatiques, **on évoque la possibilité d'**un
  durcissement de l'embargo
  = *there is <u>mention</u> of the <u>possibility</u> of*
+ L'ampleur des destructions **permet de penser que** d'énormes
  quantités d'essence ont pris feu
  = *<u>leads</u> us to <u>think</u> that*
+ Le film **laisse supposer que** tout peut devenir spectacle
  = *would have one <u>suppose</u> that*

| Expressing a certainty |

+ **Il est certain que** le chômage contribue à alimenter l'exclusion
  = *it is <u>certain</u> that*
+ **Il est évident que** toutes les régions devront jouer leur rôle sur le
  plan national
  = *it is <u>obvious</u> that*
+ La partie la plus originale de son livre réside **incontestablement**
  dans son analyse des arts populaires
  = *<u>indisputably</u>*
+ Il existe **indéniablement** un art de penser, de vivre, qui est commun
  à toute l'Europe
  = *<u>undoubtedly</u>*
+ **Il est indéniable que** c'est un problème
  = *it cannot be <u>denied</u> that*
+ **Tout le monde s'accorde à penser que** le conflit est loin d'être fini
  = *everyone <u>agrees</u> that*

+ **Il ne fait aucun doute qu'**il a du talent
   = there is no _doubt_ that
+ **Il est clair que** cette maison est inhabitée depuis des mois
   = _clearly_

Expressing doubt

+ **Il semble que** quelqu'un a essayé d'entrer par la fenêtre
   = it _seems_ that
+ **Il est possible** or **Il se peut que** je me **sois** (subj) trompé
   = it is _possible_ that
+ **Peut-être** est-ce or C'est **peut-être** une meilleure idée
   = _perhaps_
+ L'auteur s'est **sans doute** inspiré de contes orientaux
   = _probably_
+ Les rebelles **se seraient regroupés** près de la ville, **ce qui expliquerait** la psychose de peur qui prévaut encore
   = _allegedly_ regrouped ..., which would _explain_
+ Chaque témoignage **remet en question** ce qui paraissait établi quelques minutes plus tôt
   = _calls_ back into _question_

Conceding a point

+ Écrire un texte sans la lettre « e » semble une gageure impossible. **C'est pourtant** la règle que Lenoir s'impose pour tout un roman
   = and _yet it is_
+ Les héritiers ont du mal à se mettre d'accord. Ils sont **toutefois** unanimes sur un point : la propriété restera dans la famille
   = _however_
+ **Bien qu'**étudiés or **Quoiqu'**étudiés depuis de nombreuses années, les cyclones tropicaux comportent encore beaucoup d'inconnues
   = _though_
+ **Bien que** quelques blindés **aient** (subj) pris position dans la ville, la situation est restée relativement calme
   = _although_
+ On ne sait pas grand-chose de son enfance. **Toujours est-il qu'**il entre en apprentissage alors qu'il n'a pas quinze ans
   = the _fact_ remains that
+ **Quel que soit** (subj) le style retenu pour la mise en scène, l'atmosphère de la pièce est toujours un peu lugubre
   = _whatever_
+ **On ne peut nier que** l'intrigue **soit** (subj) quelque peu échevelée
   = it cannot be _denied_ that
+ **Le moins que l'on puisse** (subj) **dire est qu'**entre les principales organisations professionnelles agricoles, le courant ne passait pas
   = the _least_ one can say is that
+ Ces faits sont **sans doute** vrais, **mais** restent quand même peu crédibles
   = no _doubt_ ... but
+ **Certes** un encart publicitaire coûte très cher, **mais** il permet de mieux vendre
   = _certainly_ ... but
+ **Tout en reconnaissant que** les grands ensembles ont permis de loger des milliers de sans-abri, **il faut néanmoins admettre que** les conditions de vie y sont souvent déplorables
   = while _recognizing_ that ... one must, _however, admit_ that
+ La mort de ce coureur automobile, **pour** tragique **qu'**elle **soit** (subj), donne à réfléchir sur ce qui pousse certains à risquer leur vie
   = ... _though_ it may be
+ Si on supposait depuis longtemps qu'il y avait eu corruption, **ce n'est que récemment que** les archives ont confirmé ces suppositions
   = it is only recently that

Emphasizing particular points

+ **Il convient de souligner** l'importance de ces recherches
   = it is _worth stressing_
+ **Il faut bien préciser que** ce produit est commercialisé depuis des années
   = it is _important_ to _point_ out that
+ **C'est à ce niveau qu'**il faut chercher des solutions
   = it is at this level that
+ **C'est une question de** temps et non pas d'argent
   = it is a _question_ of
+ Ce dossier délicat **met en lumière** les oppositions entre la nécessaire maîtrise des dépenses de santé et la diffusion souhaitable des progrès thérapeutiques
   = _brings_ to _light_
+ Peu de gens ont vu cette émission, **d'autant plus qu'**elle est passée tard le soir
   = _especially since_
+ Il est important de se faire vacciner contre le tétanos, **à plus forte raison lorsque** l'on manipule régulièrement des objets rouillés
   = and all the _more so_ when
+ **Bien loin de** renier ses origines, il n'avait jamais rompu ses liens avec sa patrie
   = far from
+ Quel choc pour les spectateurs ! **Non (pas) que** le film **soit** (subj) sanglant, **mais** son crescendo est redoutable
   = not that ... is ... but
+ **Non seulement** les objectifs ont été atteints, **mais** ils ont été dépassés
   = not only ... but
+ Ce plat délicieux, facile à préparer, économique **qui plus est**, a tout pour nous séduire
   = and _moreover_
+ J'irais **même jusqu'à dire que** c'est un chef d'œuvre
   = I would even go _so_ far as to say that
+ **N'oublions pas que**, sur Terre, la gravité pilote absolument tous les phénomènes
   = let us not _forget_ that
+ De l'enthousiasme : **voilà précisément ce qui** leur fait défaut
   = that's _precisely_ what

Moderating a statement

+ **Sans vouloir critiquer** cette façon de procéder, **il semble cependant qu'**une autre méthode pourrait avoir de meilleurs résultats
   = I have no wish to _criticize_ ... but it _seems_ that
+ L'auteur a certainement raison **dans l'ensemble, mais certains détails mériteraient d'être revus**
   = ... on the _whole_, but some details require to be reviewed
+ **Une mise au point serait souhaitable**
   = some clarification would be desirable
+ **Sans attacher trop d'importance à ces détails, il semble pourtant qu'**une révision du texte serait utile
   = without wishing to attach too much _importance_ to these details, I do _think_ that
+ **Il serait injuste de** reprocher à l'auteur son manque d'expérience
   = it would be unfair to
+ « La sévérité de la presse est à la mesure de la démocratie. » Certains philosophes **nuancent** ces propos en précisant que ...
   = _qualify_
+ **Il faut néanmoins nuancer** l'affirmation selon laquelle l'Europe serait exagérément protectionniste
   = one has, _nevertheless_, to _qualify_

Indicating agreement

- Beaucoup de gens s'inquiètent de l'évolution du chômage, et **effectivement** *or* **en effet,** la situation est préoccupante
  = *indeed*
- **Il faut reconnaître que** les résultats sont décevants
  = *one has to recognize*
- Sa description de l'événement **est exacte en tous points**
  = *is accurate on all points*
- L'explication qu'il en donne **est tout à fait convaincante**
  = *is totally convincing*
- **Comme le suggère** l'auteur, il semble indispensable d'améliorer la qualité des formations et des diplômes
  = *as ... suggests*
- **Tout semble effectivement indiquer qu'**à trente ans, les surdoués ont été rattrapés par les autres
  = *everything seems to indicate that*
- **Il serait vain de le nier :** nous allons devoir faire face à une concurrence nouvelle
  = *it would be pointless to deny it*
- **Rien n'est plus vrai que** cette description de l'exil
  = *there is nothing more accurate than*

Indicating disagreement

Tentatively

- Je me sens tenu de **formuler quelques réserves**
  = *express some reservations*
- **Je formulerais quelques objections**
  = *I would express some objections*
- Cette affirmation **me semble contestable**
  = *seems debatable to me*
- **Bien que** son raisonnement **soit** *(subj)* intéressant, **je ne partage pas** le point de vue de l'auteur
  = *although ... is ..., I do not share*
- **Quand bien même** disposerait-on d'un vaccin efficace, celui-ci ne pourrait, sans grosses difficultés, être administré sur l'ensemble de la planète
  = *even if*
- À tous ceux qui critiquent la publicité, **on peut répondre** *or* **répliquer que** c'est un nouveau genre artistique
  = *one can reply that*
- **On voit mal comment** les élèves pourraient bénéficier de cette mesure
  = *it is hard to see how*

More assertively

- Cette explication **ne mérite pas d'être retenue**
  = *does not deserve to be accepted*
- Ces faits **sont en contradiction avec** la version officielle
  = *contradict*
- Elle **réfute l'argument selon lequel** la cause principale des défaillances est la fragilité financière des entreprises
  = *she refutes the argument that*
- L'auteur **commet une grave erreur** en laissant entendre qu'un accord avait été conclu
  = *makes a serious mistake*
- Quand on dit que la catastrophe a fait 2 000 victimes, **on est très loin de la vérité**
  = *one is very far from the truth*
- **Je m'inscris en faux** *or* **Je m'élève** *or* **Je m'insurge contre** cette version des faits
  = *I protest against*

- **Il ne saurait être question de** procéder à de nouvelles élections
  = *there can be no question of*
- **Il est impossible d'accepter** ce point de vue
  = *it is impossible to accept*
- **On ne saurait approuver** cette idée qui témoigne d'un manque de réflexion
  = *one couldn't approve of*

Indicating approval

- **Heureusement,** l'auteur nous précise plus loin que ce n'est pas le cas
  = *fortunately*
- **On comprend fort bien que** les jeunes **aient** *(subj)* réagi ainsi
  = *it is perfectly understandable that*
- **La meilleure solution serait effectivement de** réviser entièrement le projet
  = *the best solution would, in fact, be to*
- Les responsables de l'enquête **ont raison d'**insister sur ce point
  = *are right to*
- L'auteur souligne ce détail **à juste titre** *or* **avec raison**
  = *rightly*
- **Il était grand temps que** ces règles **soient** *(subj)* corrigées
  = *it was high time that ... were*
- **Enfin** un ouvrage qui traite en profondeur le problème du chômage
  = *at last*
- Ce livre **est le bienvenu** car il traite d'un sujet jamais abordé jusqu'ici
  = *is welcome*

Indicating disapproval

- **Il est regrettable que** l'auteur **ait** *(subj)* négligé cet aspect du problème
  = *it is regrettable that*
- **Il serait vraiment dommage qu'**une découverte aussi importante ne **soit** *(subj)* pas reconnue à sa juste valeur
  = *it would be a great pity if*
- **Malheureusement,** cette étude est très inégale
  = *unfortunately*
- **On peut s'étonner de** la rapidité avec laquelle la réforme a été appliquée
  = *one may well be surprised at*
- Les habitants **condamnent** *or* **critiquent** ce projet d'autoroute
  = *condemn or criticize*
- **Ils reprochent aux** autorités *or* **Ils accusent** les autorités de ne pas les avoir consultés
  = *they accuse*

Making a correction

- **En réalité** *or* **En fait,** il ne s'agit pas du tout d'une fiction
  = *in reality or in actual fact*
- **Il ne s'agit pas à proprement parler de** commerce, mais plutôt de troc
  = *it is not, strictly speaking, a question of*
- **Pour rétablir les faits**, je dirai que ...
  = *to re-establish the facts*
- Bouderaient-ils leurs pays d'accueil ? **Il semble plutôt qu'**ils les connaissent mal
  = *it seems more likely that*
- Dira-t-on qu'il est ambitieux ? **Le mot est faible. Aussi le qualifiera-t-on plus justement d'**arriviste
  = *that's too weak a word ... so he would more properly be called*

Indicating the reason for something

- Cette situation **résulte d'**un malentendu
  = ... is the _result_ of

- **Plus qu'à** ses idées politiques, sa popularité **tient à** ses dons d'acteur
  = ... is _due_ more to ... than to

- **C'est pour cette raison que** tout retour en arrière est impossible
  = it is for this _reason_ that

- Le vieux château sera réparé : **en effet**, il constitue l'un des meilleurs exemples de l'architecture du XVIIe siècle
  = _because_

- On ne peut se fier à ces résultats, **étant donné que** or **attendu que** les chiffres sont approximatifs
  = _seeing_ that

- **S'il** a accepté, **c'est** certainement qu'on a fait pression sur lui
  = if he ..., it is ... _because_

- **Cela expliquerait** la baisse des ventes en février
  = this would _explain_

Indicating the consequences of something

- Cette décision **a eu d'heureuses conséquences/a eu des conséquences néfastes**
  = had positive/disastrous _consequences_

- Sa nomination **a eu pour conséquence de** créer un mécontentement considérable au sein de l'organisation
  = _resulted_ in

- Il était très mécontent de l'évolution de la politique salariale, **aussi a-t-il** donné sa démission
  = and _so_ he

- La fermeture de l'usine **entraînera** or **provoquera** or **aura pour résultat** une augmentation du chômage dans la région
  = will _bring_ about or _result_ in

- Les compagnies aériennes ont augmenté leurs tarifs, **d'où** une diminution du nombre des passagers
  = _hence_

- Le nombre de postes sera réduit à trois, **ce qui implique** or **ce qui signifie** le départ de quatre employés
  = which _means_

- Le héros n'apparaissant pas dans ce chapitre, **il s'ensuit que** les personnages secondaires occupent le premier plan
  = it _follows_ that

- **Ainsi,** la personnalité du héros se révèle beaucoup plus complexe qu'elle ne le semblait au premier abord
  = _thus_

Contrasting or comparing

- **Certains** parlent de la faillite de l'école. **À l'inverse, d'autres** proclament les progrès du système éducatif
  = some (people) ... _conversely_, others ...

- **Les uns** se proclament pour la démocratie, **les autres** vantent les bienfaits d'un régime autoritaire
  = some (people) ..., others ...

- **Il dépasse** de loin tous ses concurrents
  = he _outstrips_

- Son deuxième roman **est bien inférieur à** son premier
  = is grossly _inferior_ to

- **Il n'arrive pas à la cheville de** son rival
  = ... is head and shoulders above

- **Comparée** à ses concurrents mondiaux de l'ingénierie, l'entreprise affiche désormais l'un des plus jolis bilans de la profession
  = _compared_ to

- **Par rapport** à ses concurrents, cette entreprise est défavorisée
  = _compared_ with

- **Il n'y a pas de comparaison possible entre** ces deux œuvres
  = there is no _possible_ _comparison_ to be drawn between

27   THE TELEPHONE

27   LE TÉLÉPHONE

27.1   Getting a number

27.1   Pour obtenir un numéro

Je voudrais le 01843 46 09 37 12, s'il vous plaît

  (*zéro dix-huit quarante-trois quarante-six zéro-neuf trente-sept douze*)

Could you get me 01843 465786, please?

  (*o-one-eight-four-three four-six-five-seven-eight-six*)

Pourriez-vous me passer les renseignements, s'il

  vous plaît?

Could you give me directory enquiries (*Brit*) *ou*

  directory assistance (*US*), please?

Je voudrais le numéro de la société Europost,

  20, rue de la Marelle, à Pierrefitte

Can you give me the number of Europost,

  20, rue de la Marelle, in Pierrefitte?

Quel est l'indicatif pour la Martinique?

What is the code for Martinique?

Comment est-ce que je peux téléphoner à l'extérieur?

How do I make an outside call? *ou* How do I get an outside line?

Quel numéro dois-je faire pour l'horloge parlante?

What do I dial to get the speaking clock?

Je n'ai pas trouvé le numéro dans l'annuaire

It's not in the book

Si vous téléphonez de France en Angleterre, ne composez pas le zéro

You omit the '0' when dialling France from England

27.2   When your number answers

27.2   Quand l'abonné répond

Pourriez-vous me passer le poste 516, s'il vous plaît?

Could I have *ou* Can you give me extension 516?

Je suis bien chez M. Lambert?

Is that Mr Lambert's phone?

Je voudrais parler à M. Wolff, s'il vous plaît *or*

  Pourrais-je parler à M. Wolff, s'il vous plaît?

Could I speak to Mr Wolff, please?

Pourriez-vous me passer le docteur Henderson, s'il vous plaît?

Could you put me through to Dr Henderson, please?

Qui est à l'appareil?

Who's speaking?

Je rappellerai dans une demi-heure

I'll call back in half an hour

Puis-je laisser mon numéro pour qu'elle me rappelle?

Could I leave my number for her to call me back?

Pourriez-vous lui demander de me rappeler quand il rentrera?

Would you ask him to ring me when he gets back?

Je vous appelle d'une cabine téléphonique *or*

  Je téléphone d'une cabine

I'm ringing from a callbox (*Brit*) *ou* I'm calling from

  a paystation (*US*)

J'appelle *or* Je téléphone d'Angleterre

I'm phoning from England

27.3   Answering the telephone

27.3   Pour répondre au téléphone

Allô, c'est Anne à l'appareil

Hullo, this is Anne speaking

(*C'est Anne à l'appareil?*) Elle-même

(*Is that Anne?*) Speaking

Voulez-vous laisser un message?

Would you like to leave a message?

Puis-je lui transmettre un message?

Can I take a message for him?

Ne quittez pas

Hold the line, please *ou* Please hold

Raccrochez, je vous rappelle

Put the phone down and I'll call you back

Vous êtes en communication avec un répondeur

  automatique (*recorded message*)

This is a recorded message

Veuillez laisser votre message après le bip sonore (*recorded message*)

Please speak after the tone *or* after the beep

27.4   The switchboard operator speaks

27.4   Le standard vous répond

Hôtel des Glycines, bonjour!

Hôtel des Glycines, can I help you?

Qui est à l'appareil?

Who's calling, please?

C'est de la part de qui?

Who shall I say is calling?

Est-ce que vous connaissez le numéro du poste?

Do you know his extension number?

Je vous le passe

I'm connecting you *ou* putting you through now

J'ai quelqu'un en ligne de Tokyo qui demande Mme Thomson

I have a call from Tokyo for Mrs Thomson

J'ai Mlle Martin à l'appareil

Le docteur Roberts est sur l'autre ligne

Ne quittez pas

Ça ne répond pas

Vous êtes en ligne avec le service des ventes

I've got Miss Martin on the line for you

Dr Roberts is talking on the other line

Hold the line, please *ou* Please hold

There's no reply

You're through to our Sales Department

27.5 The operator speaks

27.5 L'opérateur vous répond

Quel numéro demandez-vous ?

D'où appelez-vous ?

Pourriez-vous répéter le numéro, s'il vous plaît ?

Raccrochez et recomposez le numéro (*recorded message*)

M. Campbell vous appelle en PCV d'Amsterdam.
   Est-ce que vous acceptez la communication ?

Vous êtes en ligne

Il n'y a pas d'abonné à ce nom (*Directory Enquiries*)

Désolé, ce numéro est sur la liste rouge

Le 01 45 77 57 84 ne répond pas

Ne quittez pas

Par suite de l'encombrement des lignes, votre appel ne peut aboutir.
   Veuillez rappeler ultérieurement (*recorded message*)

J'essaie d'obtenir votre correspondant

Ça sonne

La ligne est occupée

Il n'y a pas d'abonné au numéro que vous avez
   demandé (*recorded message*)

Le numéro de votre correspondante n'est plus attribué.
   Veuillez consulter l'annuaire ou votre centre de renseignements

Le numéro de votre correspondant a changé. Veuillez composer
   désormais le 33 42 21 70 (*recorded message*)

Toutes les lignes de votre correspondant sont occupées.
   Veuillez rappeler ultérieurement (*recorded message*)

What number do you require *ou* What number are you calling?

Where are you calling from?

Would you repeat the number, please?

Please replace the handset and try again

There's a Mr Campbell calling you from Amsterdam.
   He wishes you to accept the charges. Will you accept?

Go ahead, caller

There's no listing under that name (*aux renseignements*)

They're ex-directory (*Brit*) *ou* unlisted (*US*)

There's no reply from 01 45 77 57 84

Hold the line, please *ou* Please hold

All lines to Bristol are engaged, please try later
   (*message enregistré*)

I'm trying it for you now

It's ringing *ou* Ringing for you now

The line is engaged (*Brit*) *ou* busy (*US*)

The number you have dialled has not been
   recognized (*message enregistré*)

The number you have dialled no longer exists.
   Please consult the directory (*message enregistré*)

The number you have dialled has been changed.
   Please dial 33422170 (*message enregistré*)

The number you are calling is engaged (*Brit*) *ou*
   busy (*US*). Please try again later

27.6 Different types of call

27.6 Les différents types de communication

C'est une communication locale

C'est une communication interurbaine

Je voudrais appeler l'étranger

Je voudrais appeler Londres en PCV

Pouvez-vous me réveiller à 7 h 30 demain matin ?

It's a local call

This is a long-distance call

I want to make an international call

I want to make a reverse charge call to a London number (*Brit*) *ou*
   I want to call a London number collect (*US*)

I'd like an alarm call for 7.30 tomorrow

27.7 In case of difficulty

27.7 En cas de difficulté

Je n'arrive pas à avoir le numéro

Leur téléphone est en dérangement

On nous a coupés *or* La communication a été coupée

J'ai dû faire un faux numéro

Il y a quelqu'un d'autre sur la ligne

J'ai appelé plusieurs fois, mais ça ne répond pas

Vous m'avez donné un faux numéro

On ne m'a pas donné le bon poste *or* On s'est trompé de poste

La ligne est très mauvaise

I can't get through (at all)

Their phone is out of order

We were cut off

I must have dialled the wrong number

We've got a crossed line

I've called them several times with no reply

You gave me a wrong number

I got the wrong extension

This is a very bad line

28   LA SUGGESTION

28.1   Pour faire des suggestions

- **You might like to** think it over before giving me your decision
  = *peut-être souhaitez-vous*

- **If you were to** give me the negative, **I could** get copies made
  = *si vous ... je pourrais*

- **You could** help me clear out my office, **if you don't mind**
  = *vous pourriez ... si cela ne vous ennuie pas*

- **We could** stop off in Venice for a day or two, **if you like**
  = *nous pourrions ... si vous voulez*

- I've got an idea - **let's organize** a surprise birthday party for Megan!
  = *organisons*

- **If you've no objection(s), I'll** ask them round for dinner on Sunday
  = *si vous n'avez pas d'objections, je*

- **If I were you, I'd** be very careful
  = *si j'étais vous, je*

- **If you ask me, you'd better** take some extra cash
  = *à mon avis, vous feriez bien de*

- **If you want my advice, I'd** steer well clear of them
  = *à votre place, je*

- **I'd be very careful not to** commit myself at this stage
  = *je ferais très attention à ne pas*

- **I would recommend (that) you** discuss it with him before making a decision
  = *je vous recommande de*

- **It could be in your interest to** have a word with the owner first
  = *il serait peut-être dans votre intérêt de*

- **There's a lot to be said for** living alone
  = *a beaucoup d'avantages*

Directement

- **I suggest that** *ou* **I'd like to suggest that** you take a long holiday
  = *je suggère que*

- **We propose that** half the fee be paid in advance, and half on completion
  = *nous proposons que*

- **It is quite important that** you develop her sense of fun and adventure
  = *il est très important que*

- I cannot put it too strongly: **you really must** see a doctor
  = *il faut absolument que vous*

Moins directement

- **Say you were to** approach the problem from a different angle
  = *et si vous*

- In these circumstances, **it might be better to** wait
  = *il vaudrait peut-être mieux*

- **It might be a good thing** *ou* **a good idea to** warn her about this
  = *ce serait peut-être une bonne idée de*

- **Perhaps it might be as well to** look now at the issues
  = *il serait peut-être bon de*

- **Perhaps you should** take up birdwatching
  = *vous devriez peut-être*

- **If I may make a suggestion**, a longer hemline might suit you better
  = *si je peux me permettre une suggestion*

- **Might I be allowed to offer a little advice?** - talk it over with a solicitor before you go any further
  = *puis-je me permettre de vous donner un conseil ?*

- **If I may be permitted to remind you of** one of the golden rules of journalism
  = *puis-je me permettre de vous rappeler*

- **If I might be permitted to suggest something**, installing bigger windows would make the office much brighter
  = *si je puis me permettre une suggestion*

En posant une question

- **How do you fancy** a holiday in Australia? *(familier)*
  = *ça vous tente ...*

- I was thinking of inviting her to dinner. **How about it?** *(familier)*
  = *qu'est-ce que vous en dites ?*

- **What would you say to** a trip up to town next week?
  = *que diriez-vous de*

- **Would you like to** go away on a second honeymoon?
  = *aimeriez-vous*

- **What if** you try ignoring her and see if that stops her complaining?
  = *et si*

- What you need is a change of scene. **Why not** go on a cruise or to a resort?
  = *pourquoi ne pas*

- **Suppose** *ou* **Supposing** you left the kids with Joe and came out with me?
  = *et si*

- **What do you think about** taking calcium supplements?
  = *que pensez-vous de*

- **Have you ever thought of** starting up a magazine of your own?
  = *avez-vous déjà songé à*

- **Would you care to** have lunch with me? *(soutenu)*
  = *voudriez-vous*

28.2   Pour demander des idées

- **What would you do if you were me?**
  = *que feriez-vous à ma place ?*

- **Have you any idea how I should** go about it to get the best results?
  = *avez-vous une idée sur la façon dont je devrais*

- I've no idea what to call our pet snake: **have you any suggestions?**
  = *avez-vous des suggestions ?*

- I can only afford to buy one of them: **which do you suggest?**
  = *que feriez-vous à ma place ?*

- **I wonder if you could suggest** where we might go for a few days?
  = *je me demande si vous pourriez me donner une idée :*

29   LE CONSEIL

29.1   Pour demander un conseil

- What would you do **if you were me?**
  = *à ma place*

- Would a pear tree grow in this situation? If not, **what would you recommend?**
  = *que conseillez-vous*

- **Do you think I ought to** tell the truth if he asks me where I've been?
  = *pensez-vous que je devrais*

- **What would you advise me to do** in the circumstances?
  = *que me conseilleriez vous de faire*

- **Would you advise me to** seek promotion within this firm or apply for another job?
  = *à votre avis, dois-je*

- I'd like *ou* **I'd appreciate your advice on** personal pensions
  = *j'aimerais avoir votre avis sur*

- **I'd be grateful if you could advise me on** how to treat this problem
  = *je vous serais reconnaissant si vous pouviez me donner votre avis sur*

29.2 Pour donner un conseil

De manière impersonnelle

* **It might be wise** ou **sensible** ou **a good idea to** consult a specialist
  = il serait peut-être _prudent_ de
* **It might be better to** think the whole thing over before making any decisions
  = il _vaudrait_ peut-être mieux
* **You'd be as well to** state your position at the outset, so there is no mistake
  = vous feriez bien de
* **You would be well-advised to** invest in a pair of sunglasses if you're going to Morocco
  = vous feriez bien de
* **You'd be ill-advised to** have any dealings with this firm
  = vous auriez _tort_ de
* **It would certainly be advisable to** book a table
  = il serait _prudent_ de
* **It is in your interest** ou **your best interests to** keep your dog under control if you don't want it to be reported
  = il est dans votre _intérêt_ de
* **Do be sure to** read the small print before you sign anything
  = prenez soin de
* **Try to avoid** getting her back up; she'll only make your life a misery
  = essayez d'_éviter_ de
* **Whatever you do, don't** drink the local schnapps
  = quoi qu'il arrive, ne ... pas

De manière plus personnelle

* **If you ask me, you'd better** take some extra cash
  = à mon _avis_, vous feriez mieux de
* **If you want my advice, I'd** steer well clear of them
  = à votre _place_, je
* **If you want my opinion, I'd** go by air to save time
  = à votre _place_, je
* **In your shoes** ou **If I were you, I'd** be thinking about moving on
  = à votre _place_, je
* **Take my advice** and don't rush into anything
  = suivez mon _conseil_
* **I'd be very careful not to** commit myself at this stage
  = je ferais très _attention_ à ne pas
* **I think you ought to** ou **should** seek professional advice
  = je crois que vous _devriez_
* **My advice would be to** have nothing to do with them
  = je vous _conseillerais_ de
* **I would advise you to** pay up promptly before they take you to court
  = je vous _conseille_ de
* **I would advise against** calling in the police unless they threaten you
  = je _déconseillerais_ de
* **I would strongly advise you to** reconsider this decision
  = je vous _conseille_ vivement de
* **I would urge you to** reconsider selling the property
  = je ne saurais trop vous _conseiller_ de
* **Might I offer a little advice?** - talk it over with a solicitor before you go any further _(soutenu)_
  = puis-je me permettre de vous donner un _conseil_ ?

29.3 Pour lancer un avertissement

* It's really none of my business but **I don't think you should** get involved
  = je ne crois pas que vous _devriez_

* **A word of caution:** watch what you say to him if you want it to remain a secret
  = un petit _conseil_ :
* **I should warn you that** he's not an easy customer to deal with
  = je vous _préviens_ que
* **Take care not to** burn your fingers
  = faites _attention_ à ne pas
* **Make sure that** ou **Mind that** ou **See that you don't** say anything they might find offensive
  = surtout, _évitez_ de
* **I'd think twice about** sharing a flat with the likes of him
  = je _réfléchirais_ à deux fois avant de
* **It would be sheer madness to** attempt to drive without your glasses
  = ce serait de la folie que de
* **You risk** a long delay in Amsterdam **if** you come back by that route
  = vous _risquez_ ... si
* **I am afraid I must refuse**
  = je crains de devoir refuser
* **I cannot possibly comply with** this request
  = je ne peux pas accéder à
* **It is unfortunately impracticable for us** to commit ourselves at this stage
  = il nous est _malheureusement_ impossible de
* In view of the proposed timescale, **I must reluctantly decline to** take part
  = je me vois _malheureusement_ obligé de refuser de

30 PROPOSITIONS

De façon directe

* **I would be delighted to** help out, **if I may**
  = je serais très _heureux_ de ... si vous le souhaitez
* **It would give me great pleasure to** invite your mother to dinner on Saturday
  = cela me ferait très _plaisir_ de
* **We would like to offer you** the post of Sales Director
  = nous _voudrions_ vous _offrir_
* **I hope you will not be offended if I offer** a contribution towards your expenses
  = j'espère que vous ne m'en _voudrez_ pas si j'_offre_
* **Do let me know if I can** help in any way
  = prévenez-moi si
* **If we can** be of any further assistance, **please do not hesitate to** contact us _(soutenu)_
  = si nous _pouvons_ ... n'hésitez pas à

En posant une question

* **Say we were to** offer you a 10% increase plus a company car, **how would that sound?**
  = mettons que ... qu'en _dites_-vous ?
* **What if I were to** call for you in the car?
  = et _si_ je
* **Could I** give you a hand with your luggage?
  = est-ce que je _peux_
* **Shall I** pick you up from work on Friday afternoon?
  = _voulez_-vous que je
* **Is there anything I can do to** help you find suitable accommodation?
  = _puis_-je

- **May** *ou* **Can I offer you** a drink?
  = *puis-je vous offrir*
- **Would you like me to** find out more about it for you?
  = *voulez-vous que je*
- **Would you allow me to** pay for dinner, at least?
  = *me permettez-vous de*

31   DEMANDES

- **Would you please** drop by on your way home and pick up the papers you left here?
  = *pourriez-vous*
- **Could you please** try to keep the noise down while I'm studying?
  = *pourriez-vous*
- **Would you mind** look**ing** after Hannah for a couple of hours tomorrow?
  = *cela vous ennuierait-il de*
- **Could I ask you to** watch out for anything suspicious in my absence?
  = *puis-je vous demander de*

À l'écrit

- **I should be grateful if you could** confirm whether it would be possible to increase my credit limit to £5000
  = *je vous serais reconnaissant de bien vouloir*
- **We should be glad to** receive your reply by return of post
  = *nous souhaiterions*
- **We would ask you not to** use the telephone for long-distance calls
  = *nous vous prions de ne pas*
- **You are requested to** park at the rear of the building
  = *vous êtes prié de*
- **We look forward to** receiv**ing** confirmation of your order within 14 days
  = *dans l'attente de*
- **Kindly inform us if** you require alternative arrangements to be made
  = *veuillez nous faire savoir si*

De façon plus indirecte

- **I would rather you didn't** breathe a word to anyone about this
  = *je préférerais que vous ne ... pas*
- **I would appreciate it if you could** let me have copies of the best photographs
  = *je vous serais reconnaissant si vous pouviez*
- **I was hoping that you might** find time to visit your grandmother
  = *j'espérais que vous pourriez*
- **I wonder whether you could** spare a few pounds till I get to the bank?
  = *est-ce qu'il vous serait possible de*
- **I hope you don't mind if I** borrow your exercise bike for half an hour
  = *j'espère que cela ne vous ennuie pas que*
- **It would be very helpful** *ou* **useful if you could** have everything ready a week in advance
  = *cela me etc rendrait service si vous pouviez*
- **If it's not too much trouble, would you** pop my suit into the dry cleaners on your way past?
  = *si cela ne vous dérange pas trop, pourriez-vous*
- **You won't forget** to lock up before you leave, **will you?**
  = *vous n'oublierez pas de*

32   LA COMPARAISON

32.1   Objectivement

- The streets, although wide for a Chinese city, are narrow **compared with** English streets
  = *comparé à*
- The bomb used to blow the car up was small **in** *ou* **by comparison with** those often used nowadays
  = *par rapport à*
- **In contrast to** the opulence of the Kirov, the Northern Ballet Theatre is a modest company
  = *par contraste avec*
- The loss of power because of the lower octane rating of paraffin **as opposed to** petrol is about fifteen per cent
  = *par opposition à*
- **Unlike** other loan repayments, those to the IMF cannot simply be rescheduled
  = *à la différence de*
- **If we set** the actual cost **against** our estimate, we can see how inaccurate the estimate was
  = *si nous comparons ... à*
- **Whereas** house thieves often used to make off only with video recorders, they now also tend to empty the fridge
  = *alors que*
- Property rights are conferred on both tenants and home owners; **the former** are common, **the latter** are private
  = *les premiers ..., les seconds ...*
- Anglophone Canadians have a distinctive structure to their society, which **differentiates** it **from** other anglophone societies
  = *différencie ... de*

32.2   Comparaisons favorables

- Silverlight was, indeed, **far superior to** him intellectually
  = *bien supérieur à*
- The Australians are far bigger and stronger than us - **we can't compete with** their robot-like style of play
  = *nous ne pouvons pas rivaliser avec*
- St Petersburg **has the edge over** Moscow and other central cities in availability of some foods
  = *est légèrement supérieur à*
- Michaela was astute beyond her years and altogether **in a class of her own**
  = *unique en son genre*

32.3   Comparaisons défavorables

- Joseph's amazing technicolour dreamcoat **is not a patch on** some of the jerseys now being worn by the country's leading goalkeepers
  = *n'est rien à côté de*
- The chair he sat in **was nowhere near as** comfortable **as** his own
  = *était loin d'être aussi ... que*
- The parliamentary opposition **is no match for** the government
  = *ne peut pas rivaliser avec*
- Commercially-made ice-cream **is far inferior to** the home-made variety
  = *est très inférieur à*
- The sad truth is that, as a poet, **he was never in the same class as** his friend
  = *il n'a jamais pu rivaliser avec*
- Ella doesn't rate anything that **doesn't measure up to** Shakespeare
  = *n'est pas du niveau de*
- Her brash charms **don't bear comparison with** Marlene's sultry sex appeal
  = *n'est pas comparable à*

32.4 Pour comparer deux choses semblables

- The new system costs **much the same as** the old one
  = *pratiquement la <u>même</u> chose que*
- When it comes to quality, **there's not much to choose between** them
  = *il n'y a pas grande <u>différence</u> entre*
- **There is essentially no difference between them**
  = *il n'y a pas de <u>différence</u> fondamentale entre eux*
- The impact was **equivalent to** 250 hydrogen bombs exploding
  = <u>équivalent</u> à
- In 1975, Spanish workers had longer hours than most Europeans but now they are **on a par with** the French
  = *sur un pied d'<u>égalité</u> avec*
- In Kleinian analysis, the psychoanalyst's role **corresponds to** that of mother
  = <u>correspond</u> à
- The immune system **can be likened to** a complicated electronic network
  = *peut être <u>comparé</u> à*
- **There was a close resemblance between** her **and** her son
  = *... et ... se <u>ressemblaient</u> beaucoup*
- **It's swings and roundabouts** - what you win in one round, you lose in another
  = *c'est du <u>pareil</u> au <u>même</u>*

32.5 Pour opposer deux choses non comparables

- **You can't compare** bacteria levels in cooked food **with** those in raw vegetables
  = *vous ne pouvez pas <u>comparer</u> ... à*
- All the muffins in England **cannot compare with** her scones
  = *ne sauraient être <u>comparés</u> à*
- **There's no comparison between** Waddle now **and** Waddle three years ago
  = *on ne peut <u>comparer</u> ... à*
- His book **has little in common with** those approved by the Party
  = *n'a pas grand-chose en <u>commun</u> avec*
- Here we are, practically twins, except **we have nothing in common**
  = *nous n'avons rien en <u>commun</u>*
- The modern army **bears little resemblance to** the army of 1940
  = *ne <u>ressemble</u> guère à*

33 L'OPINION

33.1 Pour demander l'opinion de quelqu'un

- **What do you think of** the new Managing Director?
  = *que <u>pensez</u>-vous de*
- **What is your opinion on** women's rights?
  = *quelle est votre <u>opinion</u> sur*
- **What are your thoughts on** the way forward?
  = *quel est votre <u>avis</u> sur*
- **What is your attitude to** people who say there is no such thing as sexual inequality?
  = *quelle est votre <u>attitude</u> à l'égard de*
- **What are your own feelings about** the way the case was handled?
  = *quel est votre <u>sentiment</u> sur*
- **How do you see** the next stage developing?
  = *à votre <u>avis</u>, comment*
- **How do you view** an event like the Birmingham show in terms of the cultural life of the city?
  = *comment <u>percevez</u>-vous*

- **I would value your opinion on** how best to set this all up
  = *je voudrais avoir votre <u>avis</u> sur*
- **I'd be interested to know what your reaction is to** the latest report on food additives
  = *j'aimerais connaître votre <u>réaction</u> face à*

33.2 Pour exprimer son opinion

- **In my opinion**, eight years as President is enough and sometimes too much for any man to serve in that capacity
  = *à mon <u>avis</u>*
- **As I see it**, everything depended on Karlov being permitted to go to Finland
  = <u>selon</u> moi
- **I feel that** there is an epidemic of fear about cancer which is not helped by the regular flow of publicity about the large numbers of people who die of it
  = *je <u>trouve</u> que*
- **Personally, I believe** the best way to change a government is through the electoral process
  = <u>personnellement</u>, je <u>crois</u> que
- **It seems to me that** the successful designer leads the public
  = *il me <u>semble</u> que*
- **I am under the impression that** he is essentially a man of peace
  = *j'ai l'<u>impression</u> que*
- **I have an idea that** you are going to be very successful
  = *j'ai <u>idée</u> que*
- **I am of the opinion that** the rules should be looked at and refined
  = *je suis d'<u>avis</u> que*
- **I'm convinced that** we all need a new vision of the future
  = *je suis <u>convaincu</u> que*
- **I daresay** there are so many names that you get them mixed up once in a while
  = *j'<u>imagine</u> que*
- We're prepared to prosecute the company, which **to my mind** has committed a criminal offence
  = *à mon <u>avis</u>*
- Most parts of the black market activity, **from my point of view**, is not, strictly speaking, illegal
  = *d'<u>après</u> moi*
- **As far as I'm concerned**, Barnes had it coming to him
  = *en ce qui me <u>concerne</u>*
- It's a matter of mutual accommodation, nothing more. **That's my view of the matter**
  = *telle est mon <u>opinion</u> sur la question*
- **It is our belief that** to be proactive is more positive than being reactive
  = *nous <u>croyons</u> que*
- **If you ask me**, there's something odd going on
  = *si vous voulez mon <u>avis</u>*
- **If you want my opinion**, if you don't do it soon, you'll lose the opportunity altogether and you'll be sorry
  = *si vous voulez mon <u>opinion</u>*

33.3 Pour répondre sans exprimer d'opinion

- Would I say she had been a help? **It depends what you mean by** help
  = *cela dépend de ce que vous entendez par*
- It could be seen as a triumph for capitalism but **it depends on your point of view**
  = *c'est une question de <u>point</u> de vue*

- **It's hard** ou **difficult to say whether** I identify with the hippy culture or not
  = *il est difficile de dire si*
- **I'm not in a position to comment on whether** the director's accusations are well-founded
  = *je ne suis pas à même de dire si*
- **I'd prefer not to comment on** operational decisions taken by the service in the past
  = *je préférerais ne pas me prononcer sur*
- **I'd rather not commit myself** at this stage
  = *je préférerais ne pas m'engager*
- **I don't have any strong feelings about which of the two companies** we should use for the job
  = *je n'ai pas d'opinion bien arrêtée sur le choix de l'entreprise*
- **This isn't something I've given much thought to**
  = *je n'y ai pas vraiment réfléchi*
- **I know nothing about** the workings of the female mind
  = *j'ignore tout de*

34   LES GOÛTS ET PRÉFÉRENCES

34.1   Pour demander ce que quelqu'un aime

- **Would you like to** visit the castle, while you are here?
  = *aimerais-tu*
- **How would you feel about** asking Simon to join us?
  = *et si on*
- **What do you like** doing best when you're on holiday?
  = *que préfères-tu*
- **What's your favourite** film?
  = *quel est ton ... préféré ?*
- **Which of the two** proposed options **do you prefer?**
  = *entre les deux ..., lequel préfères-tu ?*
- We could either go to Rome or stay in Florence - **which would you rather** do?
  = *que préférerais-tu*

34.2   Pour dire ce que l'on aime

- **I'm very keen on** gardening
  = *j'aime beaucoup le*
- **I'm very fond of** white geraniums and blue petunias
  = *j'adore*
- **I really enjoy** a good game of squash after work
  = *j'apprécie vraiment*
- **There's nothing I like more than** a quiet night in with a good book
  = *rien de tel que*
- **I have a weakness for** rich chocolate gateaux
  = *j'ai un faible pour*
- **I have a soft spot for** the rich peaty flavours of Islay malt
  = *j'ai un faible pour*

34.3   Pour dire ce qu'on n'aime pas

- Acting **isn't really my thing** - I'm better at singing
  = *n'est pas mon truc*
- Watching football on television **isn't my favourite** pastime
  = *n'est pas mon ... favori*
- Some people might find it funny but **it's not my kind of** humour
  = *ce n'est pas mon genre de*
- I enjoy playing golf but tennis is **not my cup of tea**
  = *ce n'est pas ma tasse de thé*

- Sitting for hours on motorways **is not my idea of fun**
  = *ça ne m'amuse pas de*
- The idea of walking home at 11 o'clock at night **doesn't appeal to me**
  = *ne me dit rien*
- **I've gone off the idea of** cycling round Holland
  = *j'ai renoncé à l'idée de*
- **I can't stand** ou **can't bear** the thought of seeing him
  = *je ne supporte pas*
- **I am not enthusiastic about** growing plants directly in greenhouse soil because of the risk of soil diseases
  = *je ne suis guère enthousiasmé par l'idée de*
- **I'm not keen on** seafood
  = *je n'aime pas beaucoup*
- **I don't like the fact that** he always gets away with not helping out
  = *je n'apprécie pas trop le fait que*
- **What I hate most is** waiting in queues for buses
  = *ce que je déteste le plus, c'est de*
- **I dislike** laziness since I'm such an energetic person myself
  = *me déplaît*
- **There's nothing I dislike more than** having to go to work in the dark
  = *il n'y a rien qui me déplaise plus que de*
- **I have a particular aversion to** the religious indoctrination of schoolchildren
  = *j'ai une aversion particulière pour*
- **I find it intolerable that** people like him should have so much power
  = *je trouve intolérable que*

34.4   Pour dire ce qu'on préfère

- **I'd prefer to** ou **I'd rather** wait until I have enough money to go by air
  = *je préférerais* ou *j'aimerais mieux*
- **I'd prefer not to** ou **I'd rather not** talk about it
  = *je préférerais ne pas* ou *j'aimerais mieux ne pas*
- **I'd prefer you to** ou **I'd rather you** put your comments in writing
  = *je préférerais* ou *j'aimerais mieux que tu*
- **I'd prefer you not to** ou **I'd rather you didn't** invite him
  = *je préférerais* ou *j'aimerais mieux que tu ne ... pas*
- **I like** the blue curtains **better than** ou **I prefer** the blue curtains **to** the red ones
  = *j'aime mieux ... que ...* ou *je préfère ... à ...*

34.5   Pour exprimer l'indifférence

- **It makes no odds whether you have** a million pounds or nothing, we won't judge you on your wealth
  = *que vous ayez ..., ça n'a aucune importance*
- **I really don't care what** you tell her as long as you tell her something
  = *ce que ... m'est complètement égal*
- **It's all the same to me whether** he comes or not
  = *peu m'importe que*
- **I don't mind at all** - let's do whatever is easiest
  = *cela m'est complètement égal*
- **It doesn't matter which** method you choose to use
  = *peu importe le*
- **I don't feel strongly about** the issue of privatization
  = *... m'est indifférent*
- **I have no particular preference**
  = *je n'ai pas de préférence*

35   L'INTENTION ET LA VOLONTÉ

35.1   Pour demander ce que quelqu'un compte faire

+ **Do you intend to** *ou* **Will you** take the job?
  = *as-tu l'intention de*

+ What flight **do you intend to** take?
  = *as-tu l'intention de*

+ **Did you mean to** *ou* **intend to** tell him about it, or did it just slip out?
  = *avais-tu l'intention de*

+ **What do you intend to do** *ou* **What are your intentions?**
  = *qu'as-tu l'intention de faire ?*

+ **What do you propose to do** with the money?
  = *qu'est-ce que tu penses faire*

+ **What did you have in mind for** the rest of the programme?
  = *qu'est-ce que tu avais prévu pour*

+ **Have you anyone in mind for** the job?
  = *as-tu quelqu'un en vue pour*

35.2   Pour exprimer ses intentions

+ **We're toying with the idea of** releasing a compilation album
  = *nous songeons à*

+ **I'm thinking of** retiring next year
  = *je pense*

+ **I'm hoping to** go and see her when I'm in Paris
  = *j'espère*

+ **What I have in mind is to** start a small software business
  = *ce que je pense faire c'est de*

+ I studied history, **with a view to** becoming a politician
  = *en vue de*

+ We bought the land **in order to** farm *ou* **for the purpose of** farming it
  = *afin de*

+ **We plan to** move *ou* **We are planning on** moving next year
  = *nous projetons de*

+ **Our aim in** *ou* **Our object in** buying the company **is to** provide work for the villagers
  = *le but que nous nous sommes fixé en … est de*

+ **I aim to** reach Africa in three months
  = *je compte*

Avec plus de conviction

+ **I am going to** *ou* **I intend to** sell the car as soon as possible
  = *je vais ou j'ai l'intention de*

+ **I have made up my mind to** *ou* **I have decided to** go to Japan
  = *j'ai décidé de*

+ **I intended him to** be a poet but he chose to be an accountant
  = *je voulais qu'il*

+ I went to London, **intending to** visit her *ou* **with the intention of** visiting her, but she was away on business
  = *dans l'intention de*

+ **We have every intention of** winning a sixth successive championship
  = *nous sommes décidés à*

+ **I have set my sights on** recapturing the title
  = *je suis déterminé à*

+ **My overriding ambition is to** overthrow the President
  = *j'ai pour principale ambition de*

+ **I resolve to** do everything in my power to bring the affair to an end
  = *je suis résolu à*

35.3   Pour exprimer ce qu'on n'a pas l'intention de faire

+ **I don't mean to** offend you, but I think you're wrong
  = *je ne veux pas*

+ **I don't intend to** pay unless he completes the job
  = *je n'ai pas l'intention de*

+ **I have no intention of** accepting the post
  = *je n'ai pas du tout l'intention de*

+ **We are not thinking of** advertising this post at the moment
  = *nous n'envisageons pas de*

35.4   Pour exprimer ce que l'on désire faire

+ **I'd like to** see the Sistine Chapel some day
  = *j'aimerais*

+ **I want to** work abroad when I leave college
  = *je veux*

+ **We want her to** be an architect when she grows up
  = *nous voulons qu'elle*

+ **I'm keen to** see more students take up zoology
  = *j'aimerais vraiment*

Avec davantage d'enthousiasme

+ **I'm dying to** leave and make my fortune in Paris *(familier)*
  = *je meurs d'envie de*

+ **My ambition is to** go straight from being an enfant terrible to a grande dame
  = *j'ai pour ambition de*

+ **I long to** go to Australia but I can't afford it
  = *j'ai très envie de*

+ **I insist on** speaking to the manager
  = *j'exige de*

35.5   Pour exprimer ce que l'on ne veut pas faire

+ **I would prefer not to** *ou* **I would rather not** have to speak to her about this
  = *j'aimerais mieux ne pas ou je préférerais ne pas*

+ **I wouldn't want to** have to change my plans just because of her
  = *je n'aimerais pas*

+ **I don't want to** *ou* **I have no wish to** *ou* **I have no desire to** take the credit for something I didn't do
  = *je ne veux pas ou je n'ai pas du tout l'intention de*

+ **I refuse to** be patronized by the likes of her
  = *je refuse de*

36   LA PERMISSION

36.1   Pour demander la permission de faire quelque chose

+ **Can I** *ou* **Could I** borrow your car this afternoon?
  = *puis-je ou pourrais-je*

+ **Can I have the go-ahead to** order the supplies?
  = *est-ce que j'ai le feu vert pour*

+ **Are we allowed to** say what we're up to or is it top secret at the moment?
  = *avons-nous le droit de*

+ **Would it be all right if** I arrived on Monday instead of Tuesday?
  = *est-ce que cela vous dérangerait si*

+ **Would it be possible for us to** leave the car in your garage for a week?
  = *est-ce qu'il nous serait possible de*

◆ We leave tomorrow. **Is that all right by you**?
= est-ce que cela vous _convient_ ?

◆ **Do you mind if** I come to the meeting next week?
= cela ne vous _ennuie_ pas que

◆ **Would it bother you if** I invited him?
= cela vous _ennuierait-il si_

◆ **Would you let me** come into partnership with you?
= me _permettriez_-vous de

◆ **Would you have any objection to** sailing at once?
= verriez-vous un _inconvénient_ à ce que

◆ **With your permission, I'd like to** ask some questions
= si vous le _permettez_, j'aimerais

[Avec moins d'assurance]

◆ **Is there any chance of** borrowing your boat while we're at the lake?
= est-ce qu'il serait _possible_ de

◆ **I wonder if I could possibly** use your telephone?
= je me demande s'il serait _possible_ de

◆ **Might I be permitted to** suggest the following ideas? _(soutenu)_
= _puis_-je me _permettre_ de

◆ **May I be allowed to** set the record straight? _(soutenu)_
= est-ce qu'il m'est _permis_ de

[36.2] **Pour donner la permission**

◆ **You can** have anything you want
= vous _pouvez_

◆ **You are allowed to** visit the museum, as long as you apply in writing to the Curator first
= vous avez le _droit_ de

◆ **It's all right by me if** you want to skip the Cathedral visit
= je n'ai pas d'_objection_ à ce que

◆ **You have my permission to** be absent for that week
= je vous _autorise_ à

◆ **There's nothing against her** going there with us
= rien ne l'empêche de

◆ The Crown **was agreeable to** having the case called on March 23
= _consentit_ à ce que

◆ **I do not mind if** my letter is forwarded to the lady concerned
= je ne vois pas d'_inconvénient_ à ce que

◆ **You have been authorized to** use force to protect relief supply routes
= on vous _autorise_ à

◆ **We should be happy to allow you to** inspect the papers here _(soutenu)_
= nous vous _autorisons volontiers_ à

[Avec plus d'insistance]

◆ If you need to keep your secret, **of course you must** keep it
= bien sûr, il faut

◆ **By all means** charge a reasonable consultation fee
= n'_hésitez_ pas à

◆ **I have no objection at all to your** quoting me in your article
= je n'ai pas d'_objection_ à ce que vous

◆ **We would be delighted to** have you
= c'est avec _plaisir_ que nous

[36.3] **Pour refuser la permission**

◆ **You can't** _ou_ **you mustn't** go anywhere near the research lab
= vous ne _devez_ pas

◆ **I don't want you to** see that Milner again
= je ne _veux_ pas que tu

◆ **I'd rather you didn't** give them my name
= j'aimerais autant que tu ne ... pas

◆ **I wouldn't want you to** be asking around about them too much
= je n'aimerais pas que tu

◆ **You're not allowed to** leave the ship until relieved
= vous n'avez pas le _droit_ de

◆ **I've been forbidden to** swim for the moment
= on m'a _interdit_ de

◆ **I've been forbidden** alcohol **by** my doctor
= m'a _interdit_

◆ **I couldn't possibly allow you to** pay for all this
= je ne _peux_ pas vous _laisser_

◆ **You must not** enter the premises without the owners' authority
= vous ne _devez_ pas

◆ **We cannot allow** the marriage **to** take place
= nous ne _pouvons_ pas permettre que

[De façon plus énergique]

◆ **I absolutely forbid you to** take part in any further search
= je vous _interdis_ formellement de

◆ **You are forbidden to** contact my children
= je vous _interdis_ de

◆ Smoking **is strictly forbidden** at all times
= il est strictement _interdit_ de

◆ **It is strictly forbidden to** carry weapons in this country
= il est strictement _interdit_ de

◆ **We regret that it is not possible for you to** visit the castle at the moment, owing to the building works _(à l'écrit)_
= nous sommes au _regret_ de vous informer que vous ne pouvez pas

[37] **L'OBLIGATION**

[37.1] **Pour exprimer ce que l'on est obligé de faire**

◆ Go and see Pompeii - **it's a must!** _(familier)_
= c'est à ne pas _manquer_

◆ You need to be very good, **no two ways about it** _(familier)_
= tu n'as pas le _choix_

◆ **You've got to** _ou_ **You have to** be back before midnight
= vous _devez_

◆ **You need to** _ou_ **You must** have an address in Prague before you can apply for the job
= il _faut_ que vous

◆ I have no choice: this is how **I must** live and I cannot do otherwise
= je _dois_

◆ **He was forced to** ask his family for a loan
= il a été _obligé_ de

◆ Jews **are obliged to** accept the divine origin of the Law
= sont tenus de

◆ A degree **is indispensable** for future entrants to the profession
= est _indispensable_

◆ Party membership **is an essential prerequisite of** a successful career
= est la condition _sine qua non_ pour

◆ **It is essential to** know what the career options are before choosing a course of study
= il est _essentiel_ de

◆ A dog collar **is a requirement of** law
= est _exigé_ par

◆ Wearing the kilt **is compulsory** for all those taking part
= est _obligatoire_

◆ One cannot admit defeat, **one is driven to** keep on trying
= on est <u>contraint à</u>

◆ **We have no alternative but to** fight
= nous n'avons pas le <u>choix</u>, nous <u>devons</u>

◆ Three passport photos **are required** (soutenu)
= il <u>faut</u> fournir

Soldiers **must not fail to** take to arms against the enemy (soutenu)
= se <u>doivent</u> de

◆ **You will** go directly to the headmaster's office and wait for me there (soutenu)
= allez

37.2 Pour savoir si l'on est obligé de faire quelque chose

◆ **Do I have to** ou **Have I got to** be home by midnight?
= est-ce je <u>dois</u>

◆ **Does one have** ou **need to** book in advance?
= <u>faut</u>-il

◆ **Is it necessary to** look at the problem across the continent?
= est-il <u>nécessaire</u> de

◆ **Ought I to** tell my colleagues?
= <u>devrais</u>-je

◆ **Should I** tell my boyfriend about my fantasy to paint his face and dress him in my petticoat?
= <u>devrais</u>-je

◆ **Am I meant to** ou **Am I expected to** ou **Am I supposed to** fill in this bit of the form?
= est-ce que je suis <u>censé</u>

37.3 Pour exprimer ce que l'on n'est pas obligé de faire

◆ **I don't have to** ou **I haven't got to** be home so early now the nights are lighter
= je ne suis pas <u>obligé</u> de

◆ **You don't have to** ou **You needn't** go there if you don't want to
= vous n'êtes pas <u>obligé</u> de

◆ **You are not obliged to** ou **You are under no obligation to** invite him
= rien ne vous <u>oblige</u> à

◆ **It is not necessary** ou **compulsory** ou **obligatory to** have a letter of acceptance but it does help
= il n'est pas <u>nécessaire</u> de

◆ The Revenue **does not expect you to** pay the assessed amount
= n'<u>exige</u> pas que vous

37.4 Pour exprimer ce que l'on ne doit pas faire

◆ **On no account must you** be persuaded to give up the cause
= vous ne <u>devez</u> en aucun cas

◆ **You are not allowed to** sit the exam more than three times
= on n'a pas le <u>droit</u> de

◆ Smoking **is not allowed** in the dining room
= il n'est pas <u>permis</u> de

◆ **You mustn't** show this document to any unauthorized person
= vous ne <u>devez</u> pas

◆ These are tasks **you cannot** ignore, delegate or bungle
= que l'on ne peut pas se <u>permettre</u> de

◆ **You're not supposed to** ou **You're not meant to** use this room unless you are a club member
= vous n'êtes pas <u>censé</u>

De façon plus énergique

◆ **It is forbidden to** bring cameras into the gallery
= il est <u>interdit</u> de

◆ **I forbid you to** return there
= je vous <u>interdis</u> de

◆ **You are forbidden to** talk to anyone while the case is being heard
= il vous est <u>interdit</u> de

◆ **Smoking is forbidden** ou **is prohibited** ou **is not permitted** in the dining room
= il est <u>interdit</u> de

38 L'ACCORD

38.1 Pour exprimer l'accord avec ce qui est dit

◆ **I fully agree with you** ou **I totally agree with you** on this point
= je suis entièrement d'<u>accord</u> avec vous

◆ **We are in complete agreement** on this
= nous sommes entièrement d'<u>accord</u>

◆ **I entirely take your point** about the extra vehicles needed
= je suis entièrement de votre <u>avis</u> à propos de

◆ **I think we see completely eye to eye** on this issue
= je pense que nous avons exactement le même point de vue

◆ **You're quite right in** pointing at the distribution system as the main problem
= vous avez <u>raison</u> de

◆ **We share your views** on the proposed expansion of the site
= nous <u>partageons</u> votre point de vue

◆ **As you have quite rightly pointed out**, we still have a long way to go
= comme vous l'avez fait remarquer

◆ **I have to concede that** the results are quite eye-catching
= je dois <u>reconnaître</u> que

◆ **I have no objection to this** being done
= je n'ai pas d'<u>objection</u> à ce que

◆ **I agree up to a point**
= je suis d'<u>accord</u> dans une certaine mesure

De façon familière

◆ Go for a drink instead of working late? **Sounds good to me!**
= je suis <u>partant</u> !

◆ **That's a lovely thought**
= comme ça serait bien !

◆ **I'm all for** encouraging a youth section in video clubs such as ours
= je suis tout à fait pour

◆ **I couldn't agree with you more**
= je suis tout à fait d'<u>accord</u> avec vous

De façon plus soutenue

◆ **I am delighted to wholeheartedly endorse** your campaign
= je suis <u>heureux</u> d'apporter mon <u>soutien</u> sans réserve à

◆ **Our conclusions are entirely consistent with** your findings
= nos conclusions viennent confirmer

◆ Independent statistics **corroborate** those of your researcher
= <u>corroborent</u>

◆ **We applaud** the group's decision to stand firm on this point
= nous <u>approuvons</u>

38.2 Pour exprimer l'accord avec ce qui est proposé

◆ This certainly **seems the right way to go about it**
= semble être la bonne façon de procéder

◆ **I will certainly give my backing to** such a scheme
= je ne manquerai pas d'apporter mon <u>soutien</u> à

◆ **It makes sense to** enlist helping hands for the final stages
= il semble logique de

◆ **We certainly welcome** this development in Stirling
   = *nous nous <u>réjouissons</u> de*

De façon plus familière

◆ **It's a great idea**
   = *c'est une idée formidable*

◆ Cruise control? **I like the sound of that**
   = *ça me paraît une bonne idée*

◆ **I'll go along with** Ted's proposal that we open the club up to
   women
   = *je suis d'<u>accord</u> avec*

De façon plus soutenue

◆ This solution **is most acceptable** to us
   = *paraît tout à fait <u>acceptable</u>*

◆ The proposed scheme **meets with our approval**
   = *nous <u>approuvons</u>*

◆ This is a proposal which **deserves our wholehearted support**
   = *mérite pleinement notre <u>soutien</u>*

◆ **We assent to** *ou* **We give our assent to** your plan to develop the
   site
   = *nous donnons notre <u>accord</u> à*

38.3   Pour exprimer l'accord avec ce qui est demandé

◆ Of course **I'll be happy to** organize it for you
   = *je serai <u>heureux</u> de*

◆ **I'll do as you suggest** and send him the documents
   = *je suivrai votre <u>conseil</u>*

◆ **There's no problem about** getting tickets for him
   = *nous n'aurons aucun mal à*

De façon plus soutenue

◆ Reputable builders **will not object to** this reasonable request
   = *ne feront pas <u>objection</u> à*

◆ **We should be delighted to** cooperate with you in this enterprise
   = *nous serions <u>enchantés</u> de*

◆ An army statement said it **would comply with** the ceasefire
   = *<u>respecterait</u>*

◆ **I consent to** the performance of such procedures as are
   considered necessary
   = *je donne mon <u>assentiment</u> à*

39   LE DÉSACCORD

39.1   Pour exprimer le désaccord avec ce qui est dit

◆ I'm afraid **he's quite wrong** if he's told you that vasectomies can't be
   reversed
   = *se <u>trompe</u>*

◆ **You're wrong in thinking that** I haven't understood
   = *vous avez <u>tort</u> de penser que*

◆ **I cannot agree with you** on this point
   = *je ne suis pas du tout d'<u>accord</u> avec vous*

◆ **We cannot accept the view that** R and D spending or rather the
   lack of it explains the decline of Britain
   = *nous ne pouvons <u>accepter</u> l'<u>opinion</u> selon laquelle*

◆ To say we should forget about it, no **I cannot go along with that**
   = *je ne suis pas du tout d'<u>accord</u> là-dessus*

◆ **We must agree to differ on this one**
   = *nous devons reconnaître que nos <u>opinions</u> <u>divergent</u>*

◆ I think **it might be better if you thought it over again**
   = *il vaudrait mieux que vous reconsidériez la question*

Avec plus d'insistance

◆ **This is most emphatically not the case**
   = *cela n'est absolument pas le cas*

◆ **I entirely reject** his contentions
   = *je <u>rejette</u> absolument*

◆ **We explicitly reject** the implication in your letter
   = *nous <u>rejetons</u> catégoriquement*

◆ **I totally disagree with** the previous two callers
   = *je ne suis pas du tout d'<u>accord</u> avec*

39.2   Pour exprimer le désaccord avec ce qui est proposé

Avec force

◆ **I'm dead against** this idea *(familier)*
   = *je suis tout à fait <u>contre</u>*

◆ **Right idea, wrong approach** *(familier)*
   = *c'était une bonne idée, mais ils etc s'y sont mal pris*

◆ **I will not hear of** such a thing
   = *je ne veux pas entendre parler de*

◆ **It is not feasible to** change the schedule at this late stage
   = *il est <u>impensable</u> de*

◆ This **is not a viable alternative**
   = *ce n'est pas <u>faisable</u>*

◆ Running down the street shouting "Eureka" has emotional appeal
   but **is the wrong approach**
   = *n'est pas la bonne manière de s'y prendre*

Avec moins d'insistance

◆ **I'm not too keen on** this idea
   = *ne me <u>plaît</u> pas beaucoup*

◆ **I don't think much of** this idea
   = *je n'<u>aime</u> pas beaucoup*

◆ **This doesn't seem to be the right way of** dealing with the problem
   = *cela ne semble pas être la bonne manière de*

◆ While we are grateful for the suggestion, **we are unfortunately
   unable to** implement this change *(soutenu)*
   = *nous ne sommes <u>malheureusement</u> pas à même de*

◆ **I regret that I am not in a position to** accept your kind offer
   (soutenu)
   = *je suis <u>désolé</u> de ne pas être en mesure de*

39.3   Pour exprimer le désaccord avec ce qui est
        demandé

◆ **I wouldn't dream of** doing a thing like that
   = *<u>jamais</u> je ne*

◆ I'm sorry but **I can't** do it
   = *il m'est <u>impossible</u> de*

◆ **I cannot in all conscience** leave those kids in that atmosphere
   = *je ne peux pas, en conscience*

Avec plus de force

◆ **This is quite out of the question** for the time being
   = *cela est hors de <u>question</u>*

◆ **I won't agree to** *ou* **I can't agree to** any plan that involves your
   brother
   = *je m'<u>oppose</u> à*

◆ **I refuse point blank to** have anything to do with this affair
   = *je <u>refuse</u> net de*

... et de façon plus soutenue

- **I am afraid I must refuse**
  = je crains de devoir _refuser_

- **I cannot possibly comply with** this request
  = je ne peux pas _accéder_ à

- **It is impracticable for us to** commit ourselves at this stage
  = il nous est difficile de

- In view of the proposed timescale, **I must reluctantly decline to** take part
  = je me vois malheureusement obligé de _refuser_ de

40   L'APPROBATION

40.1   Pour approuver ce qui a été dit

- **I couldn't agree** (with you) **more**
  = je suis entièrement de votre _avis_

- **I couldn't have put it better myself,** even if I'd tried
  = c'est _exactement_ ce que j'aurais dit moi-même

- We must oppose terrorism, whatever its source. - **Hear, hear!**
  = _bravo_ !

- **I endorse** his feelings regarding the situation (soutenu)
  = je _partage_

40.2   Pour approuver une proposition

- **It's just the job!** (familier)
  = c'est _exactement_ ce qu'il nous faut !

- **This is just the sort of thing I wanted**
  = c'est _exactement_ ce que je voulais

- **This is exactly what I had in mind** when I asked for the plan to be drawn up
  = c'est _précisément_ ce que j'avais à l'esprit

- Thank you for sending the draft agenda: **I like the look of it very much**
  = il a l'air très bien

- **We are all very enthusiastic about** ou **very keen on** his latest set of proposals
  = nous accueillons avec _enthousiasme_

- **I shall certainly give it my backing**
  = je _soutiendrai_ certainement cela

- Any game which is as enjoyable as this **meets with my approval**
  = a mon _approbation_

- Skinner's plan **deserves our total support** ou **our wholehearted approval**
  = mérite tout notre _soutien_

- **There are considerable advantages in** the alternative method you propose
  = comporte de nombreux avantages

- **We recognize** the merits of this scheme
  = nous _reconnaissons_

- **We view** your proposal to extend the site **favourably**
  = nous voyons d'un œil _favorable_

- This project **is worthy of our attention**
  = mérite notre attention

40.3   Pour approuver une idée

- **You're quite right to** wait before making such an important decision
  = vous avez _raison_ de

- **I entirely approve of** the idea
  = j'_approuve_ entièrement

- **I'd certainly go along with that!**
  = je suis tout à fait pour !

- **I'm very much in favour of** that sort of thing
  = je suis vraiment pour

40.4   Pour approuver une action

- **I applaud** Noble's perceptive analysis of the problems
  = j'_approuve_

- **I have a very high opinion of** their new teaching methods
  = j'ai une très haute opinion de

- **I have a very high regard for** the work of the Crown Prosecution Service
  = je tiens en haute _estime_

- **I think very highly of** the people who have been leading thus far
  = j'ai une grande _estime_ pour

- **I certainly admire** his courage in telling her exactly what he thought of her
  = j'_admire_ beaucoup

- **I must congratulate you on** the professional way you handled the situation
  = je dois vous _féliciter_ de

41   LA DÉSAPPROBATION

- **This doesn't seem to be the right way of** going about it
  = je ne pense pas que ce soit la bonne façon de

- **I don't think much of** what this government has done so far
  = ne me dit rien qui vaille

- **I can't say I'm pleased about** what has happened
  = je ne peux pas dire que je sois vraiment satisfait de

- As always, Britain **takes a dim view of** sex
  = voit d'un mauvais œil

- **We have a low opinion of** ou **poor opinion of** opportunists like him
  = nous n'avons pas une bien haute _opinion_ de

Plus directement

- **I'm fed up with** having to wait so long for payments to be made
  = j'en ai _assez_ de

- **I've had (just) about enough of** this whole supermodel thing
  = j'en ai vraiment _assez_ de

- **I can't bear** ou **stand** people who smoke in restaurants
  = je ne _supporte_ pas

- **He was quite wrong to** repeat what I said about her
  = il a eu _tort_ de

- **I cannot approve of** ou **support** any sort of testing on live animals
  = je _réprouve_

- **We are opposed to** all forms of professional malpractice
  = nous nous _opposons_ à

- **We condemn** any intervention which could damage race relations
  = nous _condamnons_

- **I must object to** the tag "soft porn actress"
  = je _dois_ protester contre

- **I'm very unhappy about** your (idea of) going off to Turkey on your own
  = ne me _plaît_ pas du tout

- **I strongly disapprove of** such behaviour
  = je _désapprouve_ complètement

42 LA CERTITUDE, LA PROBABILITÉ, LA POSSIBILITÉ ET LA CAPACITÉ

42.1 La certitude

- **She was bound to** discover that you and I had talked
  = *il était à prévoir qu'elle allait*
- **It is inevitable that they will** get to know of our meeting
  = *ils vont inévitablement*
- **I'm sure** ou **certain (that)** he'll keep his word
  = *je suis sûr que*
- **I'm positive** ou **convinced (that)** it was your mother I saw
  = *je suis sûr et certain que*
- **We now know for certain** ou **for sure that** the exam papers were seen by several students before the day of the exam
  = *nous savons maintenant avec certitude que*
- **I made sure** ou **certain that** no one was listening to our conversation
  = *je me suis assuré que*
- From all the evidence **it is clear that** they were planning to take over
  = *il est clair que*
- **It is indisputable that** there are budgerigars in the UK that are harbouring illness
  = *il est incontestable que*
- **It is undeniable that** racial tensions in Britain have been increasing in recent years
  = *il est incontestable que*
- **There is no doubt that** the talks will be a landmark in the new political agenda
  = *il ne fait aucun doute que*
- **There can be no doubt about** the objective of the animal liberationists
  = *ne fait aucun doute*
- This crisis has demonstrated **beyond all (possible) doubt** that effective political control must be in place before the creation of such structures
  = *sans le moindre doute*
- Her pedigree **is beyond dispute** ou **question**
  = *ne fait aucun doute*
- **You have my absolute assurance that** this is the case
  = *je peux vous garantir que*
- **I can assure you that** I have had nothing to do with any dishonest trading
  = *je peux vous assurer que*
- **Make no mistake about it** - I will return when I have proof of your involvement
  = *soyez certain que*

42.2 La probabilité

- **There is a good** ou **strong chance that** they will agree to the deal
  = *il y a de fortes chances pour que*
- **It seems highly likely that** it was Bert who spilled the beans
  = *il y a de fortes chances pour que*
- **The chances** ou **the odds are that** he will play safe in the short term
  = *il y a fort à parier que*
- **The probability is that** your investment will be worth more in two years' time
  = *il est fort probable que*
- If parents tell a child that she is bright, then she will, **in all probability**, see herself as bright and behave as such
  = *selon toute probabilité*

- You will **very probably** be met at the airport by one of our men
  = *très probablement*
- **It is highly probable that** American companies will face retaliation abroad
  = *il est très probable que*
- **It is quite likely that** you will get withdrawal symptoms at first
  = *il est probable que*
- **The likelihood is that** the mood of mistrust and recrimination will intensify
  = *il est très probable que*
- The person indicted is, **in all likelihood**, going to be guilty as charged
  = *selon toute probabilité*
- **There is reason to believe that** the books were stolen from the library
  = *il y a lieu de croire que*
- **He must** know of the paintings' existence
  = *il doit*
- The talks **could very well** spill over into tomorrow
  = *pourraient très bien*
- The cheque **should** reach you by Saturday
  = *devrait*

42.3 La possibilité

- The situation **could** change from day to day
  = *pourrait*
- Britain **could perhaps** play a more positive role in developing policy
  = *pourrait peut-être*
- **I venture to suggest (that)** a lot of it is to do with him
  = *je me permets de suggérer que*
- **It is possible that** a premonition is triggered when a random image happens to coincide with the later event
  = *il est possible que*
- **It is conceivable that** the British economy is already in recession
  = *il est possible que*
- **It is well within the bounds of possibility that** England could be beaten
  = *il est très possible que*
- **It may be that** the whole battle will have to be fought over again
  = *il se peut que*
- **It may be (the case) that** they got your name from the voters' roll
  = *il se peut que*
- **There is an outside chance that** the locomotive may appear in the Gala
  = *il existe une très faible chance pour que*
- **There is a small chance that** your body could reject the implants
  = *il y a un risque que*

42.4 Pour exprimer ce que l'on est capable de faire

- Our Design and Print Service **can** supply envelopes and package your existing literature
  = *peut*
- Applicants must **be able to** use a word processor
  = *être capables de*
- When it came to raising the spirits of the sleep-deprived ravers at Glastonbury, Ultramarine **were more than up to the job**
  = *ont vraiment été à la hauteur de la tâche*
- He is **qualified to** teach physics
  = *il a les qualifications requises pour*

43 L'INCERTITUDE, L'IMPROBABILITÉ, L'IMPOSSIBILITÉ ET L'INCAPACITÉ

43.1 L'incertitude

- **I doubt if** ou **It is doubtful whether** he knows where it came from
  = je _doute_ que
- **There is some doubt surrounding** his exact whereabouts
  = le _doute_ subsiste quant à
- **I have my doubts about** replacing private donations with taxpayers' cash
  = j'ai des _doutes_ quant à
- **It isn't known for sure** ou **It isn't certain** where she is
  = on ne _sait_ pas exactement
- Sometimes you stay in your room for three, four, five days at a time, **you couldn't say for sure**
  = on ne _sait_ pas exactement
- It's all still up in the air - **we won't know for certain** until the end of next week
  = nous serons dans l'_incertitude_
- You're asking why I should do such an extraordinary thing and **I'm not sure** ou **certain that** I really know the answer
  = je ne suis pas _sûr_ ou _certain_ que
- **I'm not convinced that** you can teach people to think sideways on problems
  = je ne suis pas _convaincu_ que
- **We are still in the dark about** where the letter came from
  = nous _ignorons_ toujours
- **It is touch and go whether** base rates have to go up
  = il n'est pas _certain_ que
- **I'm wondering if** I should offer to help them out
  = je me _demande_ si

43.2 L'improbabilité

- You have **probably not** yet seen the document I am referring to
  = vous n'avez _probablement_ pas
- **It is highly improbable that**, in the past 30 years, meteor fireballs have changed the noise they have been making for billennia
  = il est très peu _probable_ que
- **It is very doubtful whether** the expedition will reach the summit
  = il est peu _probable_ que
- **In the unlikely event that** the room was bugged, the music would scramble their conversation
  = si jamais
- **It was hardly to be expected that** the course of democratization would always run smoothly
  = on ne _pouvait_ guère s'attendre à ce que

43.3 L'impossibilité

- **There can be no** return to earlier standards
  = il est _impossible_ de
- Nowadays Carnival **cannot** happen **without** the police telling us where to walk and what direction to walk in
  = ne _peut_ ... sans que
- This is not to say that academic judgement is sacrosanct: since academic judgement is not uniform, **this cannot be the case**
  = ce n'est pas _possible_
- **I couldn't possibly** invite George and not his wife
  = je ne _pourrais_ pas
- **The new law rules out any possibility of** exceptions
  = exclut toute _possibilité_ de
- He said **there was no question of** him representing one half of the Arab world against the other
  = il n'était pas _question_ que

- A West German spokesman said **it was out of the question that** these weapons would be based in Germany
  = il était hors de _question_ que
- **There is not (even) the remotest chance that** ou **There is absolutely no chance that** he will succeed
  = il n'y a pas la moindre _chance_ que
- The idea of trying to govern twelve nations from one centre **is unthinkable**
  = est _inconcevable_
- Since we had over 500 applicants, **it would be quite impossible to** interview them all
  = il serait tout à fait _impossible_ de

43.4 Pour exprimer ce que l'on est incapable de faire

- **I can't** drive, I'm afraid
  = je ne _sais_ pas
- **I don't know how to** use a word processor
  = je ne _sais_ pas
- The army **has been unable to** suppress the political violence in the area
  = n'a pas _pu_
- The congress had shown itself **incapable of** real reform
  = _incapable_ de
- His fellow-directors **were not up** to running the business without him
  = n'étaient pas _capables_ de
- He called all the gods to help lift the giant's leg and free Thor, but even together they **were not equal** to the task
  = n'étaient pas à la _hauteur_
- I'm afraid the task proved (to be) **beyond his capabilities** ou **abilities**
  = trop _difficile_ pour lui
- I would like to leave him but sometimes I feel the effort **is beyond me**
  = est au-_dessus_ de mes _forces_
- **He simply couldn't cope with** the stresses of family life
  = il ne _pouvait_ pas faire face à
- Far too many women accept that they're **hopeless at** ou **no good at** managing money
  = totalement _incapables_ de
- **I'm not in a position to** say now how much substance there is in the reports
  = je ne suis pas en _mesure_ de
- **It is quite impossible for me to** describe the confusion and horror of the scene
  = je suis dans l'_impossibilité_ de

44 L'EXPLICATION

44.1 Donner les raisons de quelque chose

- He was sacked **for the simple reason that** he just wasn't up to it any more
  = pour la simple _raison_ que
- **The reason that** we are still so obsessed by him is simply that he was the one person we had who knew what was what
  = la _raison_ pour laquelle
- He said he could not be more specific **for** security **reasons**
  = pour des _raisons_ de
- Students have been arrested recently **because of** suspected dissident activities
  = en _raison_ de

- Parliament has prevaricated, **largely because of** the unwillingness of the main opposition party to support the changes
  = _essentiellement en raison de_
- Teachers in the eastern part of Germany are assailed by fears of mass unemployment **on account of** their communist past
  = _du fait de_
- Morocco has announced details of the austerity package it is adopting **as a result of** pressure from the International Monetary Fund
  = _par suite de_
- They are facing higher costs **owing to** rising inflation
  = _par suite de_
- The full effects will be delayed **due to** factors beyond our control
  = _en raison de_
- **Thanks to** their generosity, the charity can afford to buy new equipment
  = _grâce à_
- What also had to go was the notion that some people were born superior to others **by virtue of** their skin colour
  = _en raison de_
- Tax collection was often carried out **by means of** illegal measures
  = _au moyen de_
- He shot to fame **on the strength of** a letter he had written to the Queen
  = _grâce à_
- The King and Queen's defence of old-fashioned family values has acquired a poignancy **in view of** their inability to have children
  = _vu_
- The police have put considerable pressure on the Government to toughen its stance **in the light of** recent events
  = _étant donné_
- **In the face of** this continued disagreement, the parties have asked for the polling to be postponed
  = _face à_
- His soldiers had so far been restraining themselves **for fear of** harming civilians
  = _de crainte de_
- Babies have died **for want of** _ou_ **for lack of** proper medical attention
  = _faute de_
- I refused her a divorce, **out of** spite I suppose
  = _par_
- The warder was freed unharmed **in exchange for** the release of a colleague
  = _en échange de_
- The court had ordered his release, **on the grounds that** he had already been acquitted of most charges against him
  = _sous prétexte que_
- I am absolutely for civil disobedience **on moral grounds**
  = _pour des raisons_
- It is unclear why they initiated this week's attack, **given that** negotiations were underway
  = _étant donné que_
- **Seeing that** he had a police escort, the only time he could have switched containers was en route to the airport
  = _étant donné que_
- **As** these bottles are easy to come by, you can have one for each purpose
  = _comme_
- International intervention was appropriate **since** tensions had reached the point where there was talk of war
  = _puisque_
- Yet she was not deaf, **for** she started at the sound of a bell _(littér)_
  = _puisque_

- I'm naturally disappointed this is not quite enough to win on the first ballot. **So** I confirm it is my intention to let my name go forward to the second ballot
  = _donc_
- What the Party said was taken to be right, **therefore** anyone who disagreed must be wrong
  = _par conséquent_
- **Following** last weekend's rioting in central London, Conservatives say some left-wing Labour MPs were partly to blame
  = _à la suite de_
- **The thing is** that once you've retired there's no going back
  = _c'est que_

44.2 Pour expliquer la cause ou l'origine de quelque chose

- The serious dangers to your health **caused by** _ou_ **brought about by** cigarettes are now better understood
  = _provoqué par_
- When the picture was published recently, **it gave rise to** _ou_ **led to** speculation that the three were still alive and being held captive
  = _cela a donné lieu à_
- The army argues that security concerns **necessitated** the demolitions
  = _rendaient ... nécessaires_
- This lack of recognition **was at the root of** the dispute which led to their march
  = _était à l'origine de_
- **I attribute** all this mismanagement **to** the fact that the General Staff in London is practically non-existent
  = _j'attribue ... à_
- This unrest **dates from** colonial times
  = _remonte à_
- The custom **goes back to** pre-Christian days
  = _remonte à_

45 L'EXCUSE

45.1 Pour s'excuser

- **I'm really sorry**, Steve, **but** we won't be able to come on Saturday
  = _je suis vraiment désolé ... mais_
- **I'm sorry that** your time has been wasted
  = _je suis désolé que_
- **I am sorry to have to** say this to you but you're no good
  = _je suis désolé de_
- **Apologies if** I seemed obsessed with private woes last night
  = _toutes mes excuses si_
- **I must apologize for** what happened. Quite unforgivable
  = _je vous prie de m'excuser pour_
- **I owe you an apology.** I didn't think you knew what you were talking about
  = _je vous dois des excuses_
- The general back-pedalled, saying that **he had had no intention of** offending the German government
  = _il n'avait aucunement l'intention de_
- **Please forgive me for** feeling sorry for myself
  = _veuillez me pardonner de_
- **Please accept our apologies** if this has caused you any inconvenience _(soutenu)_
  = _nous vous prions d'accepter nos excuses_
- **Do forgive me for** being a little abrupt _(soutenu)_
  = _veuillez m'excuser de_

45.2 Pour accepter la responsabilité de quelque chose

- **I admit** I submitted the second gun for inspection, in the knowledge that you had used my own for the killing
  = *je reconnais*
- **I have no excuse for** what happened
  = *je n'ai aucune excuse pour*
- **It is my fault that** our marriage is on the rocks
  = *c'est ma faute si*
- The Government **is not entirely to blame but neither is it innocent**
  = *tout cela n'est pas entièrement la faute de ... mais il n'est pas non plus innocent*
- **I should never have** let him rush out of the house in anger
  = *je n'aurais jamais dû*
- Oh, but **if only I hadn't** made Freddy try to get my bag back!
  = *si seulement je n'avais pas*
- I hate to admit that the old man was right, but **I made a stupid mistake**
  = *je me suis grossièrement trompé*
- **My mistake was in** failing to push my concerns and convictions
  = *j'ai fait l'erreur de*
- **My mistake was to** arrive wearing a jacket and polo-neck jumper
  = *j'ai fait l'erreur de*
- In December the markets raced ahead, and I missed out. **That was my mistake**
  = *ça a été une erreur de ma part*

45.3 Pour exprimer des regrets

- **I'm very upset about** her decision but when only one partner wants to make an effort you're fighting a losing battle
  = *je suis très contrarié de*
- **It's just a bit of a shame that**, on close inspection, the main vocalists look like Whitney Houston and Lionel Richie
  = *c'est bien dommage que*
- **I feel awful** but I couldn't stand by and watch him make a fool of himself, someone had to tell him to shut up
  = *je suis vraiment désolé*
- **I'm afraid I can't** help you very much
  = *j'ai bien peur de ne pouvoir*
- **It is a pity that** my profession can make money out of the misfortunes of others
  = *il est dommage que*
- **It is unfortunate that** the matter should have come to a head when the Western allies may be on the brink of military engagement
  = *il est regrettable que*
- **I very much regret that** we have been unable to reach agreement
  = *suis navré que*
- The accused **bitterly regrets** this incident and it won't happen again
  = *regrette amèrement*
- **We regret to inform you that** the post of Editor has now been filled *(style écrit)*
  = *nous sommes au regret de vous informer que*

45.4 Pour rejeter toute responsabilité

- **I didn't do it on purpose**, it just happened
  = *je ne l'ai pas fait exprès*
- Sorry, Nanna. **I didn't mean to** upset you
  = *je n'avais pas l'intention de*
- Excuse me, but **I was under the impression that** these books were being written for women
  = *j'avais l'impression que*

- **We are simply trying to** protect the interests of our horses and owners
  = *nous essayons tout simplement de*
- I know how this hurt you but **I had no choice**. I had to put David's life above all else
  = *je n'avais pas le choix*
- **We were obliged to** accept their conditions
  = *nous avons été obligés de*
- We are unhappy with 1.5%, but under the circumstances **we have no alternative but to** accept
  = *nous ne pouvions faire autrement que de*
- **I had nothing to do with** the placing of any advertisement
  = *je n'avais rien à voir avec*
- A Charlton spokesman assured Sheffield supporters that **it was a genuine error** and there was no intention to mislead them
  = *c'était vraiment une erreur*

46 **LES DEMANDES D'EMPLOI**

46.1 Pour commencer la lettre

- **In reply to your advertisement** for a Trainee Manager in today's Guardian, I would be grateful if you would send me further details of the post.
  = *me référant à votre annonce*
- **I wish to apply for the post of** bilingual correspondent, as advertised in this week's Euronews
  = *je me permets de poser ma candidature au poste de*
- **I am writing to ask if there is any possibility of work in your company**
  = *je vous serais reconnaissant de me faire savoir s'il me serait possible d'obtenir un emploi dans votre entreprise*
- **I am writing to enquire about the possibility of joining your company on work placement** for a period of 3 months
  = *je vous serais reconnaissant de me faire savoir s'il me serait possible d'effectuer un stage rémunéré dans votre entreprise*

46.2 Pour parler de son expérience professionnelle et exposer ses motivations

- **I have** three **years' experience of** office work
  = *j'ai ... années d'expérience en*
- **I am familiar with word processors**
  = *je connais divers logiciels de traitement de texte*
- **As well as speaking fluent** English, **I have a working knowledge of** German **and a reading knowledge of** Swedish
  = *je parle couramment ..., possède de bonnes connaissances en ... et lis le*
- **I am currently working in** this field
  = *je travaille actuellement dans*
- **As you will see from my CV,** I have worked in Belgium before
  = *comme l'indique mon CV*
- **Although I have no experience of** this type of work, **I have** had other holiday jobs and can supply references from my employers, if you wish
  = *bien que je n'aie pas d'expérience dans ... j'ai*
- **My current salary is** ... per annum and I have four weeks' paid leave
  = *mon salaire actuel est de*
- **I would like to change jobs** to broaden my experience
  = *j'aimerais changer de situation*
- **I would like to make better use of** my languages
  = *j'aimerais pratiquer davantage*

89 Short Street
Glossop
Derbys SK13 4AP

The Personnel Director
Norton Manufacturing Ltd
Sandy Lodge Industrial Estate
Northants NN10 8QT

3 February 1998

Dear Sir or Madam[1],

With reference to your advertisement in the Guardian of 2 February 1998, I wish to apply for the post of Export Manager in your company.

I am currently employed as Export Sales Executive for United Engineering Ltd. My main role is to develop our European business by establishing contact with potential new distributors and conducting market research both at home and abroad.

I believe I could successfully apply my sales and marketing skills to this post and therefore enclose my curriculum vitae for your consideration. Please do not hesitate to contact me if you require further details. I am available for interview at any time.

I look forward to hearing from you.

Yours faithfully,

Janet Lilly

Janet Lilly

[1] Si l'on pose sa candidature à un poste à l'étranger, l'emploi de formules telles que "French equivalent of A-Levels (Baccalauréat Langues)" est conseillé.

[1] Quand on ne sait pas si la personne à qui on s'adresse est un homme ou une femme, il convient d'utiliser la présentation ci-contre.

Toutefois, si l'on connaît le nom de la personne, la présentation suivante est préférable :

Mr Leonard Easdon
ou
Mrs Emma Gault
Personnel Director
Norton Manufacturing Ltd *etc.*

Pour commencer votre lettre, la formule à employer est la suivante :
"Dear Sir" *ou* "Dear Madam"

Toute lettre commençant ainsi doit se terminer par la formule "Yours faithfully" suivie de la signature.
Pour plus de détails, voir pages 50-51.

CURRICULUM VITAE

Name:	Kate Maxwell
Address:	12 Poplar Avenue, Leeds LS12 9DT, England
Telephone:	0113 246 6648
Date of Birth:	2.2.73
Marital Status:	Single
Nationality:	British
Qualifications[1]:	Diploma in Business Management, Liverpool College of Business Studies (1997) BA Honours in French with Hispanic Studies (Upper 2nd class), University of York (1996) A-Levels: English (B), French (A), Spanish (A), Geography (C) (1991) O-Levels: in 8 subjects (1989)
Employment History:	Sales Assistant, Langs Bookshop, York (summer 1997) English Assistant, Lycée Victor Hugo, Nîmes, France (1994-95) Au Pair, Nantes, France (summer 1992) Campsite courier, Peniscola, Spain (summer 1991)
Other Information:	I enjoy reading, the cinema, skiing and amateur dramatics. I hold a clean driving licence and am a non-smoker.
References:	Mr John Jeffries General Reference Langs Bookshop York YT5 2PS	Ms Teresa González Department of Spanish University of York York YT4 3DE

46.3   Pour terminer la lettre

- **I will be available from** the end of April
  = *je serai <u>disponible</u> à partir de*
- **I am available for interview** at any time
  = *je me tiens à votre <u>disposition</u> pour un <u>entretien</u>*
- **I would be glad to supply further details**
  = *je me tiens à votre <u>disposition</u> pour tout complément d'<u>information</u>*
- **Please do not hesitate to contact me** for further information
  = *n'hésitez pas à me contacter*
- **Please do not contact my current employer**
  = *je vous serais <u>reconnaissant</u> de ne pas contacter mon <u>employeur</u> actuel*
- **I enclose** a stamped addressed envelope for your reply
  = *veuillez trouver <u>ci-joint</u>*

46.4   Comment demander et rédiger des références

- In my application for the position of German lecturer, I have been asked to provide the names of two referees and **I wondered whether you would mind if I gave your name** as one of them
  = *je vous serais <u>reconnaissant</u> de me permettre de donner votre nom*
- Ms Lane has applied for the post of Marketing Executive with our company and has given us your name as a reference. **We would be grateful if you would let us know whether you would recommend her for this position**
  = *nous vous serions <u>reconnaissants</u> de bien vouloir nous dire si vous la <u>recommandez</u> pour ce poste*
- **Your reply will be treated in the strictest confidence**
  = *votre <u>réponse</u> sera considérée comme strictement confidentielle*
- I have known Mr Chambers for four years in his capacity as Sales Manager and **can warmly recommend him for the position**
  = *c'est avec plaisir que je vous le <u>recommande</u> pour ce poste*

46.5   Pour accepter ou refuser une offre d'emploi

- Thank you for your letter of 20 March. **I will be pleased to attend for interview** at your Manchester offices on Thursday 7 April at 10am
  = *je serai très heureux de me rendre à l'<u>entretien</u>*
- **I would like to confirm my acceptance of** the post of Marketing Executive
  = *je désire <u>confirmer</u> que j'accepte*
- **I would be delighted to accept this post. However,** would it be possible to postpone my starting date until 8 May?
  = *c'est avec <u>plaisir</u> que j'<u>accepterais</u> ce poste. Toutefois*
- **I would be glad to accept your offer; however,** the salary stated is somewhat lower than what I had hoped for
  = *c'est avec <u>plaisir</u> que j'<u>accepterais</u> votre <u>offre</u>; toutefois,*
- Having given your offer careful thought, **I regret that I am unable to accept**
  = *j'ai le <u>regret</u> de devoir la <u>refuser</u>*

47   LA CORRESPONDANCE COMMERCIALE

47.1   Demandes de renseignements

- **We see** *ou* note from your advertisement in the latest edition of the Healthy Holiday Guide that you are offering cut-price salmon fishing holidays in Scotland, and **would be grateful if you would send us** full details of prices and dates available between 14 July and 30 August
  = *nous vous serions <u>reconnaissants</u> de bien vouloir nous <u>envoyer</u>*

- I read about the Association for Improvements in the Maternity Services in the NCT newsletter and would be very interested to learn more about your activities. **Please send me details of membership**
  = *je vous serais <u>reconnaissant</u> de bien vouloir m'<u>envoyer</u> de plus amples <u>renseignements</u> sur*
- **In response to your enquiry of** 8 March, **we have pleasure in enclosing** full details on our activity holidays in Cumbria, **together with** our price list
  = *<u>suite</u> à votre lettre du ..., nous vous prions de trouver <u>ci-joint</u> ... ainsi que*
- **Thank you for your enquiry about** the Association for the Conservation of Energy. **I have enclosed** a leaflet explaining our background, as well as a list of the issues we regularly campaign on. **Should you wish** to join ACE, a membership application form is also enclosed
  = *nous vous <u>remercions</u> de votre demande de <u>renseignements</u> concernant ... Veuillez trouver <u>ci-joint</u> ... ainsi que ... Si vous désirez*

47.2   Commandes

- **We would like to place an order for** the following items, in the sizes and quantities specified below
  = *nous aimerions passer <u>commande</u> de*
- **Please find enclosed our order no.** 3011 for ...
  = *veuillez trouver notre <u>commande</u> nº*
- **The enclosed order** is based on your current price list, assuming our usual discount of 5% on bulk orders
  = *la <u>commande</u> ci-jointe*
- **I wish to order** a can of "Buzz off!" wasp repellent, as advertised in the July issue of Gardeners' Monthly **and enclose a cheque for** £2.50
  = *je désire <u>commander</u> ... et vous envoie un chèque de*
- **Thank you for your order of** 16 June, which will be dispatched within 30 days
  = *nous vous <u>remercions</u> de votre <u>commande</u> en date du*
- **We acknowledge receipt of your order no.** 3570 and advise that the goods will be dispatched within 7 working days
  = *nous <u>accusons</u> <u>réception</u> de votre <u>commande</u> nº*
- **We regret that the goods you ordered are temporarily out of stock**
  = *nous <u>regrettons</u> de vous dire que les articles que vous avez <u>commandés</u> sont temporairement épuisés*
- **Please allow 28 days for delivery**
  = *veuillez compter un <u>délai</u> de 28 jours pour la <u>livraison</u>*

47.3   Livraisons

- **Our delivery time is** 60 days from receipt of order
  = *nos <u>délais</u> de <u>livraison</u> sont de*
- **We await confirmation of your order**
  = *nous attendons <u>confirmation</u> de votre <u>commande</u>*
- **We confirm that the goods were dispatched on** 4 September
  = *nous <u>confirmons</u> que les <u>marchandises</u> ont été <u>expédiées</u> le*
- **We cannot accept responsibility for** goods damaged in transit
  = *nous ne pouvons accepter aucune <u>responsabilité</u> pour*

47.4   Pour se plaindre

- **We have not yet received** the items ordered on 22 January (our order no.2263 refers)
  = *nous n'avons pas encore reçu <u>livraison</u> de*
- **We wish to draw your attention to** an error in the consignment received on 18 November
  = *nous désirons vous <u>signaler</u>*

Flowers To Go
117 Rollesby Road
Beccles NR6 9DL
☎ 61 654 31 71

Ms Sharon McNeillie
41 Courthill Street
Beccles NR14 8TR

18 January 1998

Dear Ms McNeillie,

Special Offer! 5% discount on orders received in January!

Thank you for your recent enquiry. We can deliver fresh flowers anywhere in the country at very reasonable prices. Our bouquets come beautifully wrapped, with satin ribbons, attractive foil backing, a sachet of plant food and, of course, your own personalized message. For that special occasion, we can even deliver arrangements with a musical greeting, the ideal surprise gift for birthdays, weddings or Christmas!

Whatever the occasion, you will find just what you need to make it special in our latest brochure, which I have pleasure in enclosing, along with our current price list. All prices include delivery within the UK.

During the promotion, a discount of 5% will apply on all orders received before the end of January, so hurry!

We look forward to hearing from you.

Yours sincerely,

Daisy Duckworth

Daisy Duckworth
Promotions Assistant

Carrick Foods Ltd
Springwood Industrial estate
Alexandra Road
Sheffield S11 5GF

Ms J Chalmers
Department of English
Holyrood High School
Mirlees Road
Sheffield S19 7KL

14 April 1998

Dear Ms Chalmers,

Thank you for your letter of 7 April enquiring if it would be possible to arrange a group visit to our factory. We would of course be delighted to invite you and your pupils to take part in a guided factory tour. You will be able to observe the process from preparation through to canning, labelling and packaging of the final product ready for dispatch. Our factory manager will be available to answer pupils' questions at the end of the tour.

I would be grateful if you could confirm the date of your proposed visit, as well as the number of pupils and teachers in the party, at your earliest convenience.

Thank you once again for your interest in our company. I look forward to meeting you.

Yours sincerely,

George Whyte

George Whyte

- **Unfortunately**, the goods were damaged in transit
  = *malheureusement*

- **The goods received differ significantly from the description in your catalogue**
  = *les articles livrés ne correspondent pas à la description qui en est donnée dans votre catalogue*

- If the goods are not received by 20 October, **we shall have to cancel our order**
  = *nous nous verrons contraints d'annuler notre commande*

47.5 Règlement

- **The total amount outstanding is ...**
  = *la somme qui reste à régler s'élève à*

- **We would be grateful if you would attend to this account immediately**
  = *nous vous serions reconnaissants de bien vouloir régler cette somme dans les plus brefs délais*

- **Please remit payment by return**
  = *veuillez nous faire parvenir ce règlement par retour du courrier*

- Full payment **is due within** 14 working days from receipt of goods
  = *est dû sous*

- **We enclose** a cheque for ... **in settlement of your invoice no.** 2003L/58
  = *veuillez trouver ci-joint ... en règlement de votre facture n°*

- We must point out an error in your account and **would be grateful if you would adjust your invoice** accordingly
  = *nous vous serions reconnaissants de rectifier votre facture*

- This mistake was due to an accounting error, and **we enclose a credit note for** the sum involved
  = *nous vous prions de trouver ci-joint un avoir pour*

- **Thank you for your cheque** for ... in settlement of our invoice
  = *nous vous remercions de votre chèque*

- **We look forward to doing further business with you in the near future**
  = *Nous espérons vous compter à nouveau parmi nos clients*

48 LA CORRESPONDANCE GÉNÉRALE

voir page 51

see page 51

48.1 Pour commencer une lettre

Pour écrire à quelqu'un que l'on connaît

- **Thank you** *ou* **Thanks for your letter**, which arrived yesterday
  = *merci pour votre lettre*

- **It was good** *ou* **nice** *ou* **lovely to hear from you**
  = *cela m'a fait plaisir d'avoir de vos nouvelles*

- **I felt I must write a few lines** just to say hello
  = *je vous envoie ce petit mot*

- **I'm sorry I haven't written for so long**, and hope you'll forgive me; I've had a lot of work recently and ...
  = *je suis désolé de ne pas vous avoir écrit depuis si longtemps*

- **This is a difficult letter for me to write**, and I hope you will understand how I feel
  = *je ne sais par où commencer cette lettre*

Pour écrire à un organisme

- **I am writing to ask whether** you (have in) stock a book entitled ...
  = *je vous écris pour demander si*

- **Please send me** ... I enclose a cheque for ...
  = *je vous prie de m'envoyer*

- When I left your hotel last week, I think I may have left a beige raincoat in my room. **Would you kindly** let me know whether it has been found
  = *je vous serais très reconnaissant de bien vouloir*

- I have seen the details of your summer courses, and **wish to know whether** you still have any vacancies on the Beginners' Swedish course
  = *je désirerais savoir si*

À quelqu'un que l'on connaît personnellement

DÉBUT DE LETTRE	FIN DE LETTRE
Dear Mr Brown	**Formule habituelle**
Dear Mrs Drake	
Dear Mr & Mrs Charlton	Yours sincerely
Dear Miss Baker	
Dear Ms Black	**Plus amical**
Dear Dr Armstrong	
Dear Professor Lyons	With all good wishes
Dear Sir Gerald	Yours sincerely
Dear Lady Mcleod	
Dear Andrew	With kindest regards
Dear Margaret	Yours sincerely

À une connaissance ou à un(e) ami(e)

DÉBUT DE LETTRE	FIN DE LETTRE
Dear Alison	**Formule habituelle**
Dear Annie and George	
Dear Uncle Eric	Yours sincerely
Dear Mrs Newman	
Dear Mr and Mrs Jones	**Plus amical**
My dear Miss Armitage	
	With best wishes
	Yours sincerely
	With kindest regards
	Yours sincerely
	With all good regards
	Yours sincerely
	Plus familier
	With best wishes
	Yours ever
	Kindest regards
	With best wishes
	As always

226 Wilton Street
Leicester LE8 7SP

20th November 1997

Dear Hannah,

Sorry I haven't been in touch for a while.
It's been hectic since we moved house and we're still unpacking! Anyway, it's Leah's first birthday on the 30th and I wondered if you and the kids would like to come to her party that afternoon.
We were planning to start around 4 o'clock and finish around 5.30 or so. I've invited a clown and a children's conjuror, mainly for the entertainment of the older ones. With a bit of luck, you and I might get a chance to catch up on all our news!

Drop me a line or give me a ring if you think you'll be able to make it over on the 30th. It would be lovely if you could all come!

Hoping to hear from you soon. Say hello to Danny, Paul and Jonathan for me.

Love,

Jackie

14 Apsley Grove
Aberdeen AB4 7LP
Scotland

14th April 1998

Dear Hélène and Michel,

I arrived back in Britain last night, just before midnight. My flight from Paris was delayed by over four hours and I was quite exhausted by the time we finally landed. Still, I have the weekend ahead to recover before going back to work on Monday!

I just wanted to thank you for all your warmth and hospitality, which made my stay with you truly unforgettable. I took hundreds of photographs, as you know, and I plan to get them developed as soon as possible and put the best ones in an album. I'll send you some, too, of course.

Remember that you're more than welcome to come and stay with me here any time. I'd be really glad to have you both and it would give me a chance to repay you for all your kindness.

Keep in touch and take care!

With love from *Sandra*

Les tableaux ci-dessous présentent quelques exemples-types de formules épistolaires.

Lettres commerciales

DÉBUT DE LETTRE	FIN DE LETTRE
à une entreprise Dear Sirs	**Formule habituelle** Yours faithfully
à un homme Dear Sir	
à une femme Dear Madam	
à une personne que l'on ne connaît pas Dear Sir or Madam	

À un(e) ami(e) proche, à un(e) parent(e)

DÉBUT DE LETTRE	FIN DE LETTRE
Dear Victoria My dear Albert Dear Aunt Eleanor Dear Granny and Grandad Dear Mum and Dad My dear Elizabeth Dearest Norman My dearest Mother My dearest Dorinda My darling Augustus	**Formule habituelle** With love from Love from **Plus familier** Love to all Love from us all Yours All the best **Plus affectueusement** With much love from Lots of love from Much love, as always All my love

48.2 Pour terminer une lettre *(avant la formule de politesse)*

À une connaissance

- **Gerald joins me in sending** very best wishes to you all
  = *Gerald se joint à moi pour vous <u>adresser</u>*
- **Irene sends her kindest regards**
  = *Irene me charge de vous <u>transmettre</u> ses <u>amitiés</u>*
- **Please remember me to** your wife - I hope she is well
  = *mon meilleur <u>souvenir</u> à*
- If there is anything else I can do, **please don't hesitate to get in touch** again
  = *n'hésitez pas à me <u>contacter</u>*
- **I look forward to hearing from you**
  = *j'attends votre réponse avec impatience*

À un(e) ami(e)

- **Say hello to Martin for me**
  = *dis <u>bonjour</u> à Martin pour moi*
- **Give my warmest regards to Vincent**
  = *<u>transmets</u> toutes mes <u>amitiés</u> à Vincent*
- **Doreen asks me to give you her best wishes**
  = *Doreen me charge de te <u>transmettre</u> ses <u>amitiés</u>*
- **Do write** when you have a minute
  = *<u>écris</u>-moi*
- **Do let us have your news** from time to time
  = *donne-nous de tes <u>nouvelles</u>*
- **Hoping to hear from you before too long**
  = *j'espère avoir bientôt de tes nouvelles*
- Rhona **sends her love**/Raimond **sends his love**
  = *t'<u>embrasse</u>*
- **Give my love to** Daniel and Leah, and tell them how much I miss them
  = *<u>embrasse</u> de ma part*
- Jodie and Carla **send you a big hug**
  = *t'<u>embrassent</u> très fort*

48.3 L'organisation des voyages

- **Please send me details of** your prices
  = *veuillez m'<u>adresser</u> le détail de*
- **Please advise** availability of dates between 1 August and 30 September
  = *veuillez me faire savoir*
- **Please let me know by return of post if** you have one single room with bath, half board, for the week commencing 3 October
  = *veuillez me faire savoir par retour du courrier si*
- **I would like to book** bed-and-breakfast accommodation with you
  = *je souhaite <u>réserver</u>*
- **Please consider this a firm booking** and hold the room until I arrive
  = *je <u>confirme</u> ma réservation*
- **Please confirm the following by fax**: one single room with shower for the nights of 20-23 October 1995
  = *veuillez <u>confirmer</u> par fax la <u>réservation</u> suivante :*
- **I am afraid I must ask you to alter my booking from** 25 August **to** 3 September. I hope this will not cause too much inconvenience
  = *je me vois obligé de vous demander de <u>reporter</u> ma <u>réservation</u> du ... au*
- **I am afraid I must cancel the booking** made with you for 5 September
  = *je me vois <u>contraint</u> d'<u>annuler</u>*

49   LES REMERCIEMENTS

- **Please accept our sincere thanks for** all your help and support
  = *recevez nos plus <u>sincères</u> <u>remerciements</u>*
- **I am writing to thank you** *ou* **to say thank you for** allowing me to quote your experience in my article on multiple births following fertility treatment
  = *je vous écris pour vous <u>remercier</u> de*
- **We greatly appreciated** your support during our period of captivity
  = *nous avons été très <u>sensibles</u> à*
- Your advice and understanding **were much appreciated**
  = *je vous suis très <u>reconnaissant</u> de*

De façon plus familière

- Just a line to say **thanks for** the lovely book which arrived today
  = *<u>merci</u> pour*
- **It was really nice of you to** remember my birthday
  = *c'était très <u>gentil</u> de ta part de*
- **(Would you) please thank him from me**
  = *<u>remerciez</u>-le pour moi*
- **I can't thank you enough for** finding my watch
  = *je ne sais pas comment vous <u>remercier</u> d'avoir*

De la part d'un groupe

- **Thank you on behalf of** the Wigtown Business Association for ...
  = *au nom de ..., <u>merci</u> pour*
- **We send our heartfelt thanks to** him and Olive and we hope that we shall continue to see them at future meetings of the group
  = *nous adressons nos plus vifs <u>remerciements</u> à*
- **I am instructed by** our committee **to tender our sincere thanks for** your assistance at our recent Valentine Social *(soutenu)*
  = *je suis chargé de vous adresser nos plus <u>sincères</u> <u>remerciements</u> pour*

À l'attention d'un groupe

- **A big thank you to** everyone involved in the show this year *(familier)*
  = *un grand <u>merci</u> à*
- **Please convey to everybody my warmest thanks and deepest appreciation**, and ask them to forgive me for not writing letters to each individual
  = *<u>transmettez</u> à tous mes <u>remerciements</u> les plus vifs et l'expression de ma <u>reconnaissance</u>*
- **We must express our appreciation to** the University of Durham Research Committee for providing a grant
  = *nous sommes extrêmement <u>reconnaissants</u> à*
- **I should like to extend my grateful thanks to** all the volunteers who helped make it such an enjoyable event
  = *je souhaite adresser mes <u>remerciements</u> à*

50   LES VŒUX

NB: Dans la section suivante, [...] pourrait être « a Merry Christmas and a Happy New Year », « a happy birthday », « a speedy recovery » etc.

50.1 Expressions passe-partout

- **I hope you have** a lovely holiday/a safe and pleasant journey/a successful trip
  = *je vous <u>souhaite</u>*

* With love and best wishes for [...]
    = meilleurs _vœux_ de
* With all good wishes for [...], from (+ signature)
    = (avec) tous mes _vœux_ de
* (Do) give my best wishes to your mother for a happy and healthy retirement
    = _transmettez_ mes meilleurs _vœux_ de ... à
* Len joins me in sending you all our very best wishes for a successful new career
    = ... se joint à moi pour vous adresser nos meilleurs _vœux_ de

50.2 À l'occasion de Noël et du Nouvel An

NB: en GB et aux USA il est traditionnel d'envoyer des cartes de vœux pour Noël et le Nouvel An avant le 25 décembre

* Merry Christmas and a Happy New Year
    = _Joyeux_ _Noël_ et _Bonne_ _Année_
* With season's greetings and very best wishes from (+ signature)
    = _bonnes_ _fêtes_ de fin d'_année_ et meilleurs _vœux_
* A Merry Christmas to you all, and best wishes for health, happiness and prosperity in the New Year
    = _Joyeux_ _Noël_ à tous et meilleurs _vœux_ de santé et de prospérité pour la Nouvelle _Année_
* May I send you all our very best wishes for 1999
    = nous vous présentons nos meilleurs _vœux_ pour 1999

50.3 À l'occasion d'un anniversaire

* All our love and best wishes on your 21st birthday, from Mum, Dad, Kerry and the cats
    = nous te _souhaitons_ un très heureux _anniversaire_ avec toute notre affection
* This is to send you our fondest love and very best wishes on your eighteenth birthday, from Aunt Alison and Uncle Paul
    = nous t'_adressons_ tous nos _vœux_ de _bonheur_ pour tes 18 ans. Bien affectueusement
* Wishing you a happy birthday for next Wednesday. See you at the party, love Hannah
    = je te _souhaite_ un très bon _anniversaire_ pour mercredi
* I am writing to wish you many happy returns (of the day). Hope your birthday brings you everything you wished for. Love from Grandma and Grandpa
    = un très _joyeux_ _anniversaire_

50.4 Pour envoyer des vœux de rétablissement

* Sorry (to hear) you're ill - get well soon! (familier)
    = j'espère que tu seras bientôt _rétabli_
* I was very sorry to learn that you were ill, and send you my best wishes for a speedy recovery (soutenu)
    = je vous adresse tous mes _vœux_ de prompt _rétablissement_

50.5 Pour souhaiter bonne chance à quelqu'un

NB: Dans la section suivante, [...] pourrait être « interview », « driving test », « exam » etc.

* I thought I'd drop you a line to send you best wishes for your [...]
    = bonne _chance_ pour ton
* Good luck for your [...]. I hope things go well for you on Friday
    = bonne _chance_ pour ton
* Sorry to hear you didn't get the job - better luck next time!
    = je suis sûr que tu _réussiras_ la prochaine fois

* Sorry you're leaving us. Good luck in your future career
    = bonne _chance_ pour
* We all wish you the best of luck in your new job
    = bonne _chance_ pour

50.6 Pour féliciter quelqu'un

Oralement

* You're doing a great job! Good for you! Keep it up!
    = _bravo_!
* You're pregnant? Congratulations! When's the baby due?
    = _félicitations_!
* You've finished the job already? Well done!
    = _bravo_!
* All I can say is well done for complaining and congratulations on getting the backdated money
    = c'est bien d'avoir ... je vous _félicite_ d'avoir

Par écrit

* We all send you our love and congratulations on such an excellent result
    = nous vous adressons toutes nos _félicitations_ pour
* This is to send you our warmest congratulations and best wishes on [...]
    = toutes nos _félicitations_ pour
* Allow me to offer you my heartiest congratulations on a well-deserved promotion
    = permettez-moi de vous _féliciter_ de tout cœur pour

51 LES FAIRE-PART

51.1 Comment annoncer une naissance

De façon familière

* Julia Archer gave birth to a healthy 6lb 5oz baby son, Andrew, last Monday
    = a le _plaisir_ de vous _annoncer_ la _naissance_ de
* Lisa had a baby boy, 7lb 5oz, last Saturday. Mother and baby are both doing well
    = La mère et l'enfant se portent bien

Officiellement

* Graham and Susan Anderson (née McDonald) are delighted to announce the birth of a daughter, Laura Anne, on 11th October, 1997, at the Royal Maternity Hospital, Glasgow (dans une lettre ou un journal)
    = ont la _joie_ de vous faire part de la _naissance_ de
* At the Southern General Hospital, on 1st December, 1997, to Paul and Diane Kelly a son, John (dans un journal)
    = Paul et Diane Kelly ont la _joie_ d'_annoncer_ la _naissance_ de John

... et comment répondre

* Congratulations (to you both) on the birth of your son, and best wishes to Alexander for good health and happiness throughout his life
    = toutes nos _félicitations_ à l'occasion de la _naissance_ de
* We were delighted to hear about the birth of Stephanie, and send our very best wishes to all of you
    = nous avons été très _heureux_ d'apprendre la _naissance_ de

51.2   Comment annoncer des fiançailles

De façon familière

+ **I'm sure you'll be delighted to learn that** Harry and I **got engaged** last Saturday
    = *je suis sûre que tu seras <u>heureux</u> d'apprendre que ... nous sommes <u>fiancés</u>*

+ **I'm happy to be able to tell you that** James and Valerie **have** at last **become engaged**
    = *je suis <u>heureux</u> de t'apprendre que ... se sont <u>fiancés</u>*

Officiellement

+ **It is with much pleasure that the engagement is announced between** Michael, younger son of Professor and Mrs Perkins, York, **and** Jennifer, only daughter of Dr and Mrs Campbell, Aberdeen *(dans un journal)*
    = *nous avons le <u>plaisir</u> de vous annoncer les <u>fiançailles</u> de ... et de ...*

+ **Both families are happy to announce the engagement of** Lorna Thompson, eldest daughter of Mark and Elaine Thompson **to** Brian Gordon, only son of James and Mary Gordon *(dans un journal)*
    = *les familles ... et ... sont <u>heureuses</u> de vous annoncer les <u>fiançailles</u> de ... et ...*

+ Mr and Mrs Levison **have much pleasure in announcing the engagement of** their daughter Marie **to** Mr David Hood, Canada *(dans un journal)*
    = *ont le <u>plaisir</u> de vous annoncer les <u>fiançailles</u> de ... et ...*

... et comment répondre

+ **Congratulations to you both on your engagement**, and very best wishes for a long and happy life together
    = *<u>félicitations</u> à tous deux pour vos <u>fiançailles</u>*

+ **I was delighted to hear of your engagement**, and wish you both all the best for your future together
    = *j'ai été très <u>heureux</u> d'apprendre vos <u>fiançailles</u>*

51.3   Comment annoncer un mariage

De façon familière

+ Louise and Peter **have decided to get married** on the 4th June
    = *ont décidé de se <u>marier</u>*

+ **I'm getting married** in June, to a wonderful man named Lester Thompson
    = *je me <u>marie</u>*

+ **We've finally set the date for** the 19th May, 1994
    = *nous avons finalement fixé la date au*

Officiellement

+ Mr and Mrs William Morris **are delighted to announce the marriage of** their daughter Sarah to Mr Jack Bond, in St. Francis Church, Whitley Bay, on 5th January 1998 *(dans une lettre ou un journal)*
    = *sont heureux de vous annoncer le <u>mariage</u> de*

+ **At Netherlee Parish Church, on 1st October, 1994, by Rev. I Doherty**, Alison, daughter of Ian and Mary Johnstone, Netherlee, to Derek, son of Ray and Lorraine Gilmore, Bishopbriggs *(dans un journal)*
    = *on nous prie d'annoncer le <u>mariage</u> de Mademoiselle Alison Johnstone, fille de Monsieur et Madame Ian Johnstone avec Monsieur Derek Gilmore, fils de Monsieur et Madame Ray Gilmore, en l'église de Netherlee, le 1er octobre 1997. La cérémonie a été <u>célébrée</u> par le Révérend I. Doherty*

... et comment répondre

+ **Congratulations on your marriage**, and best wishes to you both for your future happiness
    = *(toutes mes) <u>félicitations</u> à l'occasion de votre <u>mariage</u>*

+ **We were delighted to hear about your daughter's marriage to** Iain, and wish them both all the best for their future life together
    = *nous avons été très heureux d'apprendre le <u>mariage</u> de votre fille et de ...*

51.4   Comment annoncer un décès

Dans une lettre personnelle

+ My husband **died suddenly** last year
    = *... est <u>mort</u> subitement*

+ **It is with great sadness that I have to tell you that** Joe's father **passed away** three weeks ago
    = *c'est avec la plus grande <u>tristesse</u> que je dois t'annoncer que ... est <u>décédé</u>*

Officiellement *(dans un journal)*

+ **Suddenly**, at home, in Newcastle-upon-Tyne, on Saturday 2nd July, 1994, Alan, aged 77 years, **the beloved husband of** Helen and **loving father of** Matthew
    = *... son épouse et ... son fils ont la <u>douleur</u> de vous faire part du <u>décès</u> brutal*

+ Mavis Ann, wife of the late Gavin Birch, **passed away peacefully** in the Western Infirmary on 4th October, aged 64 years. **No flowers, please**
    = *... s'est <u>éteinte</u> paisiblement ... Ni fleurs ni couronnes*

+ **It is with deep sadness that** the Fife Club **announces the death of** Mr Tom Levi, who died in hospital on May 19 after a stroke
    = *c'est avec la plus profonde <u>tristesse</u> que ... vous annonce le <u>décès</u> de*

... et comment répondre

+ I was terribly upset to hear of Jim's death, and am writing to send you **all warmest love and deepest sympathy**
    = *toute mon amitié et ma plus profonde <u>sympathie</u>*

+ **Deepest sympathy on the loss of** a good friend to you and all of us
    = *toutes mes <u>condoléances</u> à l'occasion de la <u>perte</u> de*

+ My husband and I **were greatly saddened to learn of the passing of** Dr Smith, and send you and your family our most sincere condolences
    = *c'est avec la plus grande <u>tristesse</u> que ... avons appris le <u>décès</u> de*

+ **We wish to extend our deepest sympathy on your sad loss to you and your wife**
    = *nous vous adressons à votre épouse et à vous-même nos plus sincères <u>condoléances</u>*

51.5   Pour annoncer un changement d'adresse

+ We are moving house next week. **Our new address** as of 4 December 1997 **will be** 41 Acacia Avenue, BN7 2BT Barnton
    = *notre nouvelle <u>adresse</u> ... sera*

52   LES INVITATIONS

52.1   Les invitations officielles

- Mr and Mrs James Waller **request the pleasure of your company at the marriage of** their daughter Mary Elizabeth to Mr Richard Hanbury at St Mary's Church, Frampton on Saturday, 21st August, 1998 at 2 o'clock and afterwards at Moor House, Frampton
  = *ont le plaisir de vous <u>inviter</u> à l'occasion du mariage de*
- The Warden and Fellows of Hertford College, Oxford **request the pleasure of the company of** Miss Charlotte Young and partner **at a dinner** to mark the anniversary of the founding of the College
  = *ont le plaisir de <u>convier</u> ... à un dîner*
- Margaret and Gary Small **request the pleasure of your company at a reception** (*ou* dinner) to celebrate their Silver Wedding, on Saturday 12th November, 1998, at 8pm at Norton House Hotel, Edinburgh
  = *ont le plaisir de vous <u>inviter</u> à une <u>réception</u> (ou un dîner)*

... et comment répondre

- **We thank you for your kind invitation to** the marriage of your daughter Annabel on 20th November, **and have much pleasure in accepting**
  = *nous vous remercions de votre aimable <u>invitation</u> au ... et nous faisons une joie d'<u>accepter</u>*
- **We regret that we are unable to accept your invitation to** the marriage of your daughter on 6th May
  = *nous regrettons de ne pouvoir <u>accepter</u> votre <u>invitation</u> au*

52.2   Les invitations plus intimes

- **We are celebrating** Rosemary's engagement to David by holding a dinner dance at the Central Hotel on Friday 11th February, 1998, **and very much hope that you will be able to join us**
  = *nous <u>fêtons</u> ... et espérons de tout cœur que vous pourrez vous <u>joindre</u> à nous*
- **We** are giving a dinner party next Saturday, and **would be delighted if you and your wife could come**
  = *nous serions heureux si votre femme et vous pouviez être des nôtres*
- **I'm planning a** 25th **birthday party** for my nephew - **hope you'll be able to make it**
  = *j'<u>organise</u> une <u>soirée</u> d'anniversaire ... j'espère que vous pourrez venir*
- **I'm having a party** next week for my 18th - **come along, and bring a friend**
  = *j'<u>organise</u> une <u>soirée</u> ... <u>joins</u>-toi à nous et amène un de tes amis*

52.3   Invitations à se joindre à quelqu'un

- **Why don't you come down** for a weekend and let us show you Sussex?
  = *pourquoi ne viendriez-vous pas*
- **Would you be interested in** coming with us to the theatre next Friday?
  = *est-ce que cela vous dirait de*
- **Would you and Gordon like to come** to dinner next Saturday?
  = *voulez-vous venir ... Gordon et toi ?*
- **Would you be free for** lunch next Tuesday?
  = *seriez-vous <u>libre</u> pour*
- **Perhaps we could** meet for coffee some time next week?
  = *peut-être pourrions-nous*

52.4   Pour accepter une invitation

- **I'd love to** meet up with you tomorrow
  = *je serais <u>heureux</u> de*
- **It was good of you to invite me**, I've been longing to do something like this for ages
  = *c'était très <u>gentil</u> à vous de m'<u>inviter</u>*
- **Thank you for your invitation to** dinner - **I look forward to it very much**
  = *<u>merci</u> pour votre <u>invitation</u> ... je me fais une joie de venir*

52.5   Pour refuser une invitation

- **I'd love to come, but I'm afraid** I'm already going out that night
  = *j'aimerais beaucoup venir mais <u>malheureusement</u>*
- **I'm terribly sorry, but I won't be able to come to** your party
  = *je suis <u>désolé</u> mais je ne pourrai pas venir à*
- **I wish I could come, but unfortunately** I have something else on
  = *j'aimerais pouvoir venir, mais <u>malheureusement</u>*
- **Unfortunately, it's out of the question** for the moment
  = *<u>malheureusement</u>, c'est impossible*
- It was very kind of you to invite me to your dinner party next Saturday. **Unfortunately I will not be able to accept**
  = *je ne peux <u>malheureusement</u> pas <u>accepter</u>*
- **Much to our regret, we are unable to accept** (*soutenu*)
  = *nous sommes au <u>regret</u> de devoir <u>refuser</u>*

52.6   Sans donner de réponse précise

- **I'm not sure** what I'm doing that night, but I'll let you know either way before the end of the week
  = *je ne suis pas <u>sûr</u>*
- **It all depends on whether** I can get a sitter for Rosie at short notice
  = *cela <u>dépend</u> : oui, si*
- **I'm afraid I can't really make any definite plans** until I know when Alex will be able to take her holidays
  = *je ne peux <u>malheureusement</u> pas m'<u>engager</u>*
- It looks as if we might be going abroad with Jack's company in August so **I'd rather not commit myself** to a holiday yet
  = *je préférerais ne pas m'<u>engager</u>*

53   LA DISSERTATION

53.1   Les grandes lignes de l'argument

Pour introduire un sujet

De façon impersonnelle

- **It is often said** *ou* **asserted** *ou* **claimed that** the informing "grass" is named after the song Whispering Grass, but the tag long predates the ditty
  = *on <u>dit</u> bien souvent que*
- **It is a truth universally acknowledged that** the use and abuse of the Queen's English is stirring up a hornet's nest
  = *tout le monde s'<u>accorde</u> à <u>dire</u> que*
- **It is a truism** *ou* **a commonplace (to say) that** American accents are infinitely more glamorous than their British counterparts
  = *l'<u>opinion</u> selon laquelle ... est un lieu commun*
- **It is undeniably true that** Gormley helped to turn his members into far more sophisticated workers
  = *il est <u>indéniable</u> que*
- **It is a well-known fact that** in this age of technology, it is computer screens which are responsible for many illnesses
  = *tout le monde <u>sait</u> que*

+ **It is sometimes forgotten that** much Christian doctrine comes from Judaism
  = on *oublie* parfois que
+ **It would be naïve to suppose that** in a radically changing world these 50-year-old arrangements can survive
  = il serait *naïf* de croire que
+ **It would hardly be an exaggeration to say that** the friendship of both of them with Britten was among the most creative in the composer's life
  = on peut *dire* presque sans *exagérer* que
+ **It is hard to open a newspaper nowadays without reading that** TV is going to destroy reading and that electronic technology has made the written word obsolete
  = de nos jours, il est presque *impossible* d'ouvrir un journal sans lire que
+ **First of all, it is important to try to understand** some of the systems and processes involved in order to create a healthier body
  = tout d'abord, il est *important* de *comprendre*
+ **It is in the nature of** classics in sociological theory **to** make broad generalizations about such things as societal evolution
  = c'est un *trait* *caractéristique* des ... que de
+ **It is often the case that** early interests lead on to a career
  = il est souvent *vrai* que

De façon personnelle

+ **By way of introduction, let me** summarize the background to this question
  = en *guise* *d'introduction,* j'aimerais
+ **I would like to start with** a very sweeping statement
  = je *commencerai* par
+ **Before going into the issue of** criminal law, **I wish first to summarize** how Gewirth derives his principles of morality and justice
  = *avant* d'*étudier* en détail le *problème* de ... je voudrais *résumer*
+ **Let us look at** what self-respect in your job actually means
  = *examinons*
+ **We commonly think of** people **as** isolated individuals but, in fact, few of us ever spend more than an hour or two of our waking hours alone
  = nous *considérons* *généralement* ... en tant que
+ **What we are mainly concerned with here is** the conflict between what the hero says and what he actually does
  = ce qui nous *préoccupe* ici, c'est
+ **We live in a world in which** the word "equality" is bandied about
  = nous vivons dans un monde où

Pour évoquer des concepts ou des problèmes

+ **The concept of** controlling disease-transmitting insects by genetic means isn't new
  = l'*idée* de
+ **The idea of** getting rich without too much effort has universal appeal
  = l'*idée* de
+ **The question of whether** Hamlet was insane has long occupied critics
  = la *question* de *savoir* si
+ Why they were successful where their predecessors had failed **is a question that has been much debated**
  = est un *problème* souvent débattu
+ **One of the most striking features** ou **aspects of this issue** ou **topic** ou **question is** the way (in which) it arouses strong emotions
  = l'un des *aspects* les plus frappants de ce *problème*, c'est

+ **There are a number of issues** on which China and Britain openly disagree
  = il existe un certain nombre de *questions*

Pour faire des généralisations

+ **People** who work outside the home **tend to believe that** parenting is an easy option
  = les gens ont *tendance* à penser que
+ **There's** always **a tendency for people to** exaggerate your place in the world
  = les gens ont *tendance* à
+ Many gardeners **have a tendency to** anthropomorphize plants
  = ont *tendance* à
+ Fate **has a propensity to** behave in the same way to people of similar nature
  = a une *propension* à
+ **For the (vast) majority of people**, literature is a subject which is studied at school but which has no relevance to life as they know it
  = pour la *plupart* des gens
+ **For most of us**, the thought of the alternative to surviving into extreme old age is worse than surviving
  = pour la *plupart* d'entre nous
+ History provides **numerous examples** ou **instances of** misguided national heroes who did more harm than good in the long run
  = de nombreux *exemples* de

Pour être plus précis

+ The Meters' work with Lee Dorsey **in particular** merits closer inspection
  = en *particulier*
+ **One particular issue** raised by Narayan was, suppose Grant at the time of his conviction was old enough to be hanged, what would have happened?
  = un *problème particulier*
+ **A more specific point** relates to using the instrument in figure 6.6 as a way of challenging our hidden assumptions about reality
  = un *aspect* plus *spécifique*
+ **More specifically**, he accuses Western governments of continuing to supply weapons and training to the rebels
  = plus *précisément*

53.2 Pour présenter une thèse

Remarques d'ouverture

+ **First of all, let us consider** the advantages of urban life
  = tout d'*abord examinons*
+ **Let us begin with an examination of** the social aspects of this question
  = *commençons* par *examiner*
+ **The first thing that needs to be said is that** the author is presenting a one-sided view
  = tout d'*abord*, il faut dire que
+ **What should be established at the very outset is that** we are dealing with a practical rather than philosophical issue
  = la *première* *constatation* qui s'impose est que

Pour délimiter le débat

+ In the next section, **I will pursue the question of** whether the expansion of the Dutch prison system can be explained by Box's theory
  = je *développerai* le *problème* de

- **I will then deal with the question of** whether or not the requirements for practical discourse are compatible with criminal procedure
  = je _traiterai_ _ensuite_ du _problème_ de
- We must distinguish between the psychic and the spiritual, and **we shall see how** the subtle level of consciousness is the basis for the spiritual level
  = nous _verrons_ comment
- **I will confine myself to** giving an account of certain decisive facts in my militant career with Sartre
  = je me _contenterai_ de
- In this chapter, **I shall largely confine myself to** a consideration of those therapeutic methods that use visualization as a part of their procedures
  = j'_étudierai_ essentiellement
- **We will not concern ourselves here with** the Christian legend of St James
  = nous ne nous _préoccuperons_ pas ici de
- **Let us now consider** to what extent the present municipal tribunals differ from the former popular tribunals in the above-mentioned points
  = _examinons_ _maintenant_
- **Let us now look at** the types of corporatism that theorists developed to clarify the concept
  = _abordons_ _maintenant_

Pour exposer les problèmes

- **The main issue under discussion is** how the party should re-define itself if it is to play any future role in Hungarian politics
  = le _problème_ _principal_ est
- **A second, related problem is that** business ethics has mostly concerned itself with grand theorising
  = _problème_ _annexe_ :
- **The issue at stake here is** one of misrepresentation or cheating
  = ce dont il s'_agit_ ici est
- **An important aspect of** Milton's imagery **is** the play of light and shade
  = un des _aspects_ importants de ... est
- **It is worth mentioning here that** when this was first translated, the opening reference to Heidegger was entirely deleted
  = il faut _mentionner_ ici que
- **Finally, there is the argument that** castrating a dog will give it a nasty streak
  = _enfin_, on peut dire que

Pour mettre un argument en doute

- In their joint statement, the two presidents use tough language to condemn violence but **is there any real substance in what's been agreed?**
  = leur accord a-t-il un contenu réel ?
- This is a question which **merits close(r) examination**
  = mérite un _examen_ plus attentif
- The unity of the two separate German states **raises fundamental questions for** Germany's neighbours
  = _soulève_ des _problèmes_ _fondamentaux_ pour
- The failure to protect our fellow Europeans **raises fundamental questions on** the role of the armed forces
  = _soulève_ des _questions_ _essentielles_ quant à
- **This raises once again the question of** whether a government's right to secrecy should override the public's right to know
  = cela _soulève_ à nouveau la _question_ de savoir
- **This poses the question of** whether it is possible for equity capital to be cheap and portfolio capital to be expensive simultaneously
  = cela pose la _question_ de savoir

Pour analyser les problèmes

- **It is interesting to consider why** this scheme has opened so successfully
  = il est intéressant d'_examiner_ pourquoi
- **On the question of** whether civil disobedience is likely to help end the war, Chomsky is deliberately diffident
  = sur la _question_ de
- **We are often faced with the choice between** our sense of duty **and** our own personal inclinations
  = nous sommes souvent contraints de faire un choix entre ... et
- **When we speak of** realism in music, **we do not at all have in mind** the illustrative bases of music
  = quand nous _parlons_ de ..., nous ne _pensons_ pas à
- **It is reasonable to assume that** most people living in industrialized societies are to some extent contaminated by environmental poisons
  = on peut raisonnablement _penser_ que

Pour étayer un argument

- **An argument in support of** this approach **is that** it produces results
  = le fait que ... est un _argument_ en _faveur_ de
- **In support of his theory**, Dr Gold notes that most oil contains higher-than-atmospheric concentrations of helium-3
  = pour _appuyer_ sa _théorie_
- **This is the most telling argument in favour of** an extension of the right to vote
  = c'est l'_argument_ le plus éloquent en _faveur_ de
- **The second reason for advocating** this course of action **is that** it benefits the community at large
  = une autre _raison_ de _soutenir_ ... est que
- **The third, more fundamental, reason for** looking to the future **is that** we need a successful market
  = la troisième _raison_, plus _essentielle_, de ... est que
- Confidence in capitalism seems to be at a post-war low. **The fundamental reason for** this contradiction seems to me quite simple
  = la _raison_ _essentielle_ de

53.3 Pour présenter une antithèse

Pour critiquer quelque chose ou pour s'y opposer

- **In actual fact, the idea of** there being a rupture between a so-called old criminology and an emergent new criminology **is somewhat misleading**
  = en _réalité_, l'_idée_ _selon_ laquelle ... est quelque peu trompeuse
- In order to argue this, I will show that Wyeth's **position is untenable**
  = le _point_ de vue de ... est _indéfendable_
- **It is claimed, however,** that the strict Leboyer method is not essential for a less traumatic birth experience
  = on _affirme_ _cependant_
- **This need not mean that** we are destined to suffer for ever. **Indeed, the opposite may be true**
  = cela ne veut pas dire que ... il se peut même que le _contraire_ soit _vrai_
- Many observers, though, **find it difficult to share his opinion that** it could mean the end of the Tamil Tigers
  = ne partagent guère son _opinion_ _selon_ laquelle
- **On the other hand**, there is a competing principle in psychotherapy that should be taken into consideration
  = d'un autre _côté_
- The judgement made **may well be true but** the evidence given to sustain it is unlikely to convince the sceptical
  = est peut-être _juste, mais_

- Reform **is all very well, but** it is pointless if the rules are not enforced
  = c'est bien joli, *mais*
- The case against the use of drugs in sport rests primarily on the argument that ... **This argument is weak, for two reasons**
  = cet *argument* manque de solidité, pour deux *raisons*
- According to one theory, the ancestors of vampire bats were fruit-eating bats. But **this idea** *ou* **argument does not hold water**
  = cette *idée* ou cet *argument* ne *tient* pas
- The idea **does not stand up to** historical scrutiny
  = ne *résiste* pas à
- **This view does not stand up** if we examine the known facts about John
  = ce *point* de vue ne *tient* pas
- **The trouble with the idea that** social relations are the outcome of past actions **is not that** it is wrong, **but rather that** it is uninformative
  = le *problème* que pose l'*idée* *selon* laquelle ... n'est pas que ... mais plutôt que
- **The difficulty with this view is that** he bases the principle on a false premise
  = là où son *point* de vue *pèche*, c'est que
- **The snag with** such speculations **is that** too much turns on one man or event
  = l'*inconvénient* que présente ... est que
- Removing healthy ovaries **is entirely unjustified in my opinion**
  = est totalement *injustifié selon* moi

Pour proposer une alternative

- **Another approach may be to** develop substances capable of blocking the effects of the insect's immune system
  = une manière *différente* d'*aborder* le *problème* serait de
- **Another way of looking at that claim is to** note that Olson's explanations require little knowledge of the society in question
  = on peut *envisager* le *problème* sous un autre *angle* en
- **However, the other side of the coin is** the fact that an improved self-image can lead to prosperity
  = cependant, il y a le *revers* de la *médaille*, à savoir que
- **It is more accurate to speak of** new criminologies rather than of a single new criminology
  = il est plus *juste* de parler de
- **Paradoxical though it may seem**, computer models of mind can be positively humanising
  = aussi *paradoxal* que cela puisse paraître

53.4   Pour présenter une synthèse

Pour évaluer les arguments exposés

- **How can we reconcile** these two apparently contradictory viewpoints?
  = comment *réconcilier*
- **On balance**, making money honestly is more profitable than making it dishonestly
  = à tout prendre
- Since vitamins are expensive, **one has to weigh up the pros and cons**
  = il faut *peser* le *pour* et le *contre*
- **The benefits of** partnership in a giant trading market will almost certainly **outweigh the disadvantages**
  = les *avantages* de ... l'emportent sur les *inconvénients*
- **The two perspectives are not mutually exclusive**
  = ces deux *points* de vue ne sont pas totalement incompatibles

Pour sélectionner un argument particulier

- Dr Meaden's theory **is the most convincing explanation**
  = est l'*explication* la plus *convaincante*
- **The truth** *ou* **fact of the matter is that** in a free society you can't turn every home into a fortress
  = la *vérité* est que
- But **the truth is that** Father Christmas has a rather mixed origin
  = la *vérité* est que
- This is an exercise that on paper might not seem to be quite in harmony, but **in actual fact** this is not the position
  = en *réalité*
- **When all is said and done, it must be acknowledged that** a purely theoretical approach to social issues is sterile
  = en *fin* de compte, il faut reconnaître que

Pour résumer les arguments

- In this chapter, **I have demonstrated** *ou* **shown that** the Cuban alternative has been undergoing considerable transformations
  = j'ai *montré* que
- **This shows how**, in the final analysis, adhering to a particular theory on crime is at best a matter of reasoned choice
  = cela *démontre* comment
- **The overall picture shows that** prison sentences were relatively frequent
  = cette vue d'ensemble *montre* que
- **To recap** *ou* **To sum up, then**, (we may conclude that) there are in effect two possible solutions to this problem
  = en *résumé*, on peut *conclure* que
- **To sum up this chapter** I will offer two examples
  = *pour résumer* ce chapitre
- **To summarize**, we have seen that the old industries in Britain had been hit after the First World War by a deteriorating international position
  = en *résumé*
- Habermas's argument, **in a nutshell**, is as follows
  = en *bref*
- But **the key to the whole argument is** a single extraordinary paragraph
  = la clé du problème ... se trouve dans
- **To round off this section** on slugs, gardeners may be interested to hear that there are three species of predatory slugs in the British Isles
  = *pour clore* cette section

Pour tirer des conclusions

- **From all this, it follows that** it is impossible to extend those kinds of security measures to all potential targets of terrorism
  = il *découle* de tout cela que
- This, of course, **leads to the logical conclusion that** those who actually produce do have a claim to the results of their efforts
  = nous amène *logiquement* à *conclure* que
- **There is only one logical conclusion we can reach**, which is that we ask our customers what they think of our marketing programme
  = on ne peut *aboutir* qu'à une seule *conclusion logique*
- **The inescapable conclusion is that** the criminal justice system has a hand in creating the reality we see
  = la *conclusion inéluctable* à laquelle on *aboutit* est que
- **We must conclude that** there is no solution to the problem of defining crime
  = nous devons *conclure* que
- **In conclusion**, the punishment model of deterrence is highly unsatisfactory
  = *pour conclure*

- **The upshot of all this is that** GIFT is more likely to be readily available than IVF
  = *le résultat de tout cela est que*
- **So it would appear that** ESP is not necessarily limited to the right hemisphere of the brain
  = *il semblerait donc que*
- **This only goes to show that** a good man is hard to find, be he black or white
  = *cela prouve bien que*
- **The lesson to be learned is that** the past, especially a past lived in impotence, can be enslaving
  = *la leçon que l'on peut en tirer est que*
- **At the end of the day**, the only way the drug problem will be beaten is when people are encouraged not to take it
  = *en fin de compte*
- **Ultimately, then**, these critics are significant
  = *en définitive*

53.5   Pour rédiger un paragraphe

Pour ajouter quelque chose

- **In addition**, the author does not really empathize with his hero
  = *de plus*
- This award-winning writer, **in addition to being** a critic, biographer and poet, has written 26 crime novels
  = *outre qu'il est*
- But this is only part of the picture. **Added to this** are fears that a major price increase would cause riots
  = *s'ajoute à cela ...*
- **An added** complication **is that** the characters are not aware of their relationship to one another
  = *un autre ... est*
- **Also**, there is the question of language
  = *par ailleurs*
- **The question also arises as to** how this idea can be put into practice
  = *se pose aussi la question de savoir*
- Politicians, **as well as** academics and educationalists, tend to feel strongly about the way in which history is taught
  = *ainsi que*
- But, **over and above that**, each list contains fictitious names or addresses
  = *en plus de cela*
- **Furthermore**, ozone is, like carbon dioxide, a greenhouse gas
  = *en outre*

Pour comparer

- **Compared with** the heroine, Alison is an insipid character
  = *comparé à*
- **In comparison with** the Czech Republic, the culture of Bulgaria is less westernized
  = *en comparaison de*
- This is a high percentage for the English Midlands but low **by comparison with** some other parts of Britain
  = *par comparaison avec*
- **On the one hand**, there is no longer a Warsaw Pact threat. **On the other (hand)**, the positive changes could have negative side-effects
  = *d'un côté ... de l'autre*
- **Similarly**, a good historian is not obsessed by dates
  = *de même*
- There can only be one total at the bottom of a column of figures and **likewise** only one solution to any problem
  = *pareillement*

- What others say of us will translate into reality. **Equally**, what we affirm as true of ourselves will likewise come true
  = *de même*
- There will now be a change in the way we are regarded by our partners, and, **by the same token**, the way we regard them
  = *du même coup*
- **There is a fundamental difference between** adequate nutrient intake **and** optimum nutrient intake
  = *il existe une différence fondamentale entre ... et*

Pour relier deux éléments

- **First of all** *ou* **Firstly**, I would like to outline the benefits of the system
  = *tout d'abord*
- In music we are concerned **first and foremost** with the practical application of controlled sounds relating to the human psyche
  = *en tout premier lieu*
- **In order to understand** the conflict between the two nations, **it is first of all necessary to** know something of the history of the area
  = *pour comprendre ... il faut tout d'abord*
- **Secondly**, it might be simpler to develop chemical or even nuclear warheads for a large shell than for a missile
  = *deuxièmement*
- **In the first/second/third place**, the objectives of privatization were contradictory
  = *premièrement, deuxièmement, troisièmement*
- **Finally,** there is the argument that castrating a dog will give it a nasty streak
  = *enfin*

Pour exprimer une opinion personnelle

- **In my opinion**, the government is underestimating the scale of the epidemic
  = *à mon avis*
- **My personal opinion is that** the argument lacks depth
  = *personnellement, je pense que*
- This is a popular viewpoint, but **speaking personally**, I cannot understand it
  = *personnellement*
- **Personally**, I think that no one can appreciate ethnicity more than black or African people themselves
  = *personnellement*
- **For my part**, I cannot agree with the leadership on this question
  = *pour ma part*
- **My own view is that** what largely determines the use of non-national workers are economic factors rather than political ones
  = *je trouve que*
- **In my view**, it only perpetuates the very problem that it sets out to address
  = *à mon idée*
- Although the author argues the case for patriotism, **I feel that** he does not do it with any great personal conviction
  = *je crois que*
- **I believe that** people do understand that there can be no quick fix for Britain's economic problems
  = *je crois que*
- **It seems to me that** what we have is a political problem that needs to be solved at a political level
  = *il me semble que*
- **I would maintain that** we have made a significant effort to ensure that the results are made public
  = *je soutiens que*

Pour présenter l'opinion de quelqu'un d'autre

+ **He claims** *ou* **maintains that** intelligence is conditioned by upbringing
  = il _soutient_ que

+ Bukharin **asserts that** all great revolutions are accompanied by destructive internal conflict
  = _affirme_ que

+ The communique **states that** some form of nuclear deterrent will continue to be needed for the foreseeable future
  = _affirme_ que

+ **What he is saying is that** the time of the highly structured political party is over
  = il _dit_ que

+ His admirers **would have us believe that** watching this film is more like attending a church service than having a night at the pictures
  = voudraient nous faire _croire_ que

+ **According to** the report, poverty creates a climate favourable to violence
  = _selon_

Pour donner un exemple

+ **To take another example**: many thousands of people have been condemned to a life of sickness and pain because ...
  = pour prendre un autre _exemple_

+ Let us consider, **for example** *ou* **for instance**, the problems faced by immigrants arriving in a strange country
  = par _exemple_

+ His meteoric rise **is the most striking example yet of** voters' disillusionment with the record of the previous government
  = est l'_exemple_ le plus frappant de

+ The case of Henry Howey Robson **serves to illustrate** the courage exhibited by young men in the face of battle
  = _illustre_ bien

+ Just consider, **by way of illustration**, the difference in amounts accumulated if interest is paid gross, rather than having tax deducted
  = pour _illustrer_

+ **A case in point is** the decision to lift the ban on contacts with the republic
  = ... est un bon _exemple_

+ **Take the case of** the soldier returning from war
  = prenons le _cas_ de

+ As the Prime Minister **remarked,** the Channel Tunnel will greatly benefit us all
  = comme l'a fait _remarquer_

53.6 Les mécanismes de la discussion

Pour présenter une supposition

+ They telephoned the president to put pressure on him. And **that could be interpreted as** trying to gain an unconstitutional political advantage
  = on pourrait _interpréter_ cela comme

+ Retail sales in Britain rose sharply last month. This was higher than expected and **could be taken to mean that** inflationary pressures remain strong
  = laisse _supposer_ que

+ **It might well be prudent to** find some shelter for the night rather than sleep in the van
  = il serait sans _doute_ prudent de

+ These substances do not remain effective for very long. This is **possibly** because they work against the insects' natural instinct to feed
  = _peut-être_

+ She had become a definite security risk and **it is not beyond the bounds of possibility that** murder may have been considered
  = il n'est pas _impossible_ que

+ I am somewhat reassured by Mr Fraser's assertion, which **leads one to suppose that** on that subject he is in full agreement with Catholic teaching
  = nous amène à _supposer_ que

+ It is **probably** the case that all long heavy ships are vulnerable
  = _probablement_

+ After hearing nothing from the taxman for so long, most people **might reasonably assume that** their tax affairs were in order
  = seraient en droit de _supposer_ que

+ **One could be forgiven for thinking that** because the substances are chemicals, they'd be easy to study
  = il serait excusable de penser que

+ Thus, **I venture to suggest that** very often when visions are mentioned in the literature of occultism, self-created visualizations are meant
  = j'oserais même dire que

Pour exprimer la certitude

Voir aussi 42. La certitude

+ **It is clear that** any risk to the human foetus is very low
  = il est _clair_ que

+ Whatever may be said about individual works, the early poetry as a whole is **indisputably** a poetry of longing
  = _indiscutablement_

+ Yet, **undeniably**, this act of making it a comprehensible story does remove it one degree further from reality
  = _indéniablement_

+ **There can be no doubt that** the Earth underwent a dramatic cooling which destroyed the environment and lifestyle of these creatures
  = il ne fait aucun _doute_ que

+ **It is undoubtedly true that** over the years there has been a much greater emphasis on safer sex
  = il est _indéniable_ que

+ **As we all know**, adultery is far from uncommon
  = comme nous le savons tous

+ **One thing is certain**: no one can claim that ESP has never helped make money
  = une chose est _sûre_

+ **It is (quite) certain that** unless peace can be brought to this troubled land, no amount of aid will solve the long-term problems of the people
  = il est _certain_ que

Pour exprimer le doute

Voir aussi 43. L'incertitude

+ **It is doubtful whether**, in the present repressive climate, anyone would be brave or foolish enough to demonstrate publicly
  = il n'est pas _sûr_ que

+ **It remains to be seen whether** the security forces will try to intervene
  = (il) reste à savoir si

+ Once in a while I think about all that textbook Nietzsche and I **wonder whether** anyone ever truly understood a word of it
  = je me _demande_ si

+ **I have (a few) reservations about** the book
  = j'émettrais quelques _réserves_ sur

+ Since it spans a spectrum of ideologies, **it is by no means certain that** it wil stay together
  = il n'est pas du tout _certain_ que

- **It is questionable whether** media coverage of terrorist organizations actually affects terrorism
  = il n'est pas _sûr_ que
- **This raises the whole question of** exactly when men and women should retire
  = cela _soulève_ la _question_ de savoir
- The crisis **sets a question mark against** the Prime Minister's stated commitment to intervention
  = remet en _question_
- Both these claims are **true up to a point** and they need to be made
  = vrai dans une certaine _mesure_

Pour marquer l'accord

Voir aussi 38. L'accord

- **I agree wholeheartedly with** the opinion that smacking should be outlawed
  = je suis entièrement d'_accord_ avec
- **One must acknowledge that** China's history will make change more painful
  = il faut _reconnaître_ que
- **It cannot be denied that** there are similarities between these two approaches
  = il est _indéniable_ que
- Courtney - **rightly in my view** - is strongly critical of the snobbery and elitism that is all too evident in these circles
  = à _juste_ titre, selon moi
- Preaching was considered an important activity, **and rightly so** in a country with a high illiteracy rate
  = (et) à _juste_ titre

Pour marquer le désaccord

Voir aussi 39. Le désaccord

- **I must disagree with** Gordon's article on criminality: it is dangerous to suggest that to be a criminal one must look like a criminal
  = je ne suis pas d'_accord_ avec
- He was not a lovable failure but rather, a difficult man who succeeded. **It is hard to agree**
  = on peut difficilement être d'_accord_
- As a former teacher **I find it hard to believe that** there is no link at all between screen violence and violence on the streets
  = il m'est difficile de croire que
- The strength of their feelings **is scarcely credible**
  = est peu _crédible_
- Her claim to have been the first to discover the phenomenon **defies credibility**
  = n'est pas _crédible_
- Nevertheless, **I remain unconvinced by** Milton
  = je ne suis toujours pas _convaincu_ par
- Many do not believe that water contains anything remotely dangerous. Sadly, **this is far from the truth**
  = c'est loin d'être vrai
- To say that everyone requires the same amount of a vitamin is as stupid as saying we all have blonde hair and blue eyes. **It simply isn't true**
  = c'est complètement _faux_
- His remarks were not only highly offensive to black and other ethnic minorities but **totally inaccurate**
  = tout à fait _inexactes_
- Stomach ulcers are often associated with good living and a fast-moving lifestyle. **(But) in reality** there is no evidence to support this belief
  = (mais) en _réalité_

- This version of a political economy **does not stand up to close scrutiny**
  = ne _tient_ pas lorsqu'on l'examine attentivement

Pour souligner un argument

- Nowadays, there is **clearly** less stigma attached to unmarried mothers
  = de toute _évidence_
- Evidence shows that ..., so once again **the facts speak for themselves**
  = les _faits_ parlent d'eux-mêmes
- **Few will argue with the principle that** such a fund should be set up
  = on ne saurait remettre en _question_ l'idée que
- Hyams **supports this claim** by looking at sentences produced by young children learning German
  = _appuie_ cette affirmation
- This issue **underlines** the dangers of continuing to finance science in this way
  = _souligne_
- **The most important thing is to** reach agreement from all sides
  = le plus _important_ est de
- Perhaps **the most important aspect of** cognition is the ability to manipulate symbols
  = l'aspect le plus _important_ de

Pour mettre un détail en valeur

- **It would be impossible to exaggerate the importance of** these two volumes for anyone with a serious interest in the development of black gospel music
  = on ne saurait _exagérer_ l'importance de
- The symbolic importance of Jerusalem for both Palestinians and Jews is almost **impossible to overemphasize**
  = on ne saurait _sous_-estimer
- **It is important to be clear that** Jesus does not identify himself with Yahweh
  = il faut bien savoir que
- **It is significant that** Mandalay seems to have become the central focus in this debate
  = le _fait_ que ... est _révélateur_
- **It should not be forgotten that** many of those now in exile were close to the centre of power until only one year ago
  = il ne faut pas oublier que
- **It should be stressed that** the only way pet owners could possibly contract such a condition from their pets is by eating them
  = il faut _souligner_ que
- **There is a very important point here and that is that** the accused claims that he was with Ms Martins all evening on the night of the crime
  = on trouve ici une remarque très _importante_, à savoir que
- At the beginning of his book Mr Cviic **makes a telling point**
  = fait une remarque _importante_
- Suspicion is **the chief feature of** Britain's attitude to European theatre
  = la _caractéristique_ principale de
- **In order to focus attention on** Hobson's distinctive contributions to macroeconomics, these wider issues are neglected here
  = afin d'_attirer_ l'_attention_ sur
- These statements **are interesting in that** they illustrate different views
  = sont _intéressants_ du _fait_ que

Language in Use

Contents

French-English

		Page
	Introduction	3
1	Suggestions	4
2	Advice	4
3	Offers	5
4	Requests	6
5	Comparisons	6
6	Opinion	7
7	Likes, dislikes and preferences	8
8	Intentions and desires	8
9	Permission	9
10	Obligation	10
11	Agreement	11
12	Disagreement	11
13	Approval	12
14	Disapproval	13
15	Certainty, probability, possibility and capability	13
16	Doubt, improbability, impossibility and incapability	14
17	Explanations	15
18	Apologies	16
19	Job applications	16
20	Correspondence: commercial	18
21	general	20
22	Thanks	22
23	Best Wishes	22
24	Announcements	23
25	Invitations	24
26	Essay Writing	24
27	The telephone	31

Grammaire active

Table des matières

anglais-français

		Page
	Introduction	3
27	Le téléphone	31
28	La suggestion	33
29	Le conseil	33
30	Propositions	34
31	Demandes	35
32	La comparaison	35
33	L'opinion	36
34	Les goûts et préférences	37
35	L'intention et la volonté	38
36	La permission	38
37	L'obligation	39
38	L'accord	40
39	Le désaccord	41
40	L'approbation	42
41	La désapprobation	42
42	La certitude, la probabilité, la possibilité et la capacité	43
43	L'incertitude, l'improbabilité, l'impossibilité et l'incapacité	44
44	L'explication	44
45	L'excuse	45
46	Les demandes d'emploi	46
47	La correspondance: commerciale	48
48	générale	50
49	Les remerciements	52
50	Les vœux	52
51	Les faire-part	53
52	Les invitations	55
53	La dissertation	55

ENGLISH-FRENCH DICTIONARY

DICTIONNAIRE ANGLAIS-FRANÇAIS

A

A, a[1] [eɪ] [1] N [a] (= *letter*) A, a *m*; **A for Able** ≈ A comme André; **to know sth from A to Z** connaître qch de A à Z; **he doesn't know A from B** il est ignare; (*in house numbers*) **24a** 24 bis; **to get from A to B** aller d'un endroit à un autre; (*Brit Aut*) **on the A4** sur la (route) A4, ≈ sur la nationale 4 [b] (*Mus*) la *m* → **key** [c] (*Scol*) excellent (*de 15 à 20 sur 20*) [d] (*Elec*) (ABBR = **ampere(s)**) A [2] COMP ► **A-1** ADJ super* ► **A3 (paper)** N (papier *m*) A3 *m* ► **A4 (paper)** N (papier *m*) A4 *m* ► **A and M college** N (*US*) ≈ école *f* supérieure d'agriculture ► **A-bomb** N bombe *f* A or atomique ► **A levels** NPL (*Brit Scol*) ≈ baccalauréat *m*; **to do an A level in geography** ≈ passer l'épreuve de géographie au baccalauréat ► **A-line dress** N robe *f* trapèze *inv* ► **the A-list** N le gratin, le dessus du panier; **to be on the A-list** faire partie du gratin ► **A number 1** ADJ (*US*) = A-1 ► **A-OK*** ADJ = A-1 ► **A-road** N (*Brit*) ≈ route *f* nationale → ROADS ► **A-side** N [*of record*] face *f* A ► **A-test** N essai *m* nucléaire ► **A to Z**® N (*pl* **A to Zs**) plan *m* avec répertoire des rues; **a Glasgow A to Z** ◊ **an A to Z of Glasgow** un plan de Glasgow avec répertoire des rues

a[2] [eɪ, ə] INDEF ART (*before vowel or mute h:* "an") [a] un, une; **a tree** un arbre; **an apple** une pomme; **such a hat** un tel or pareil chapeau; **so large a country** un si grand pays [b] (*def art in French*) le, la, les; **he smokes a pipe** il fume la pipe; **to set an example** donner l'exemple; **I have read a third of the book** j'ai lu le tiers du livre; **we haven't a penny** nous n'avons pas le sou; **a woman hates violence** les femmes détestent la violence [c] (*absent in French*) **she was a doctor** elle était médecin; **as a soldier** en tant que soldat; **my uncle, a sailor ...** mon oncle, qui est marin ...; **to ~ the attempt to do sth** renoncer à faire qch; **she's a widow** elle est veuve; **what a pleasure!** quel plaisir!; **what a lovely day!** quelle belle journée!; **to make a fortune** faire fortune [d] un(e) certain(e); **I have heard of a Mr Gordon who ...** j'ai entendu parler d'un certain M. Gordon qui ... [e] le *or* la même; **they are much of an age** ils sont du même âge; **they are of a size** ils sont

de la même grandeur [f] (= *a single*) un(e) seul(e); **to empty a glass at a draught** vider un verre d'un trait; **at a blow** d'un seul coup [g] (*with abstract nouns*) du, de la, des; **to make a noise/a fuss** faire du bruit/des histoires [h] **a few survivors** quelques survivants; **a lot of** *or* **a great many flowers** beaucoup de fleurs [i] (= *per*) **£4 a person** *or* **head** 4 livres par personne; **3 francs a kilo** 3 F le kilo; **twice a month** deux fois par mois; **twice a year** deux fois par an *or* l'an; **80km an hour** 80 kilomètres-heure, 80 kilomètres à l'heure

AA [eɪ'eɪ] N [a] (*Brit*) (ABBR = **Automobile Association**) société de dépannage [b] (ABBR = **Alcoholics Anonymous**) → **alcoholic** [c] (*US Univ*) (ABBR = **Associate in Arts**) ≈ DEUG *m* de lettres

AAA [ˌeɪeɪ'eɪ] N [a] (*Brit*) ABBR = **Amateur Athletics Association** [b] (*US*) [ˈtrɪplˌeɪ] (ABBR = **American Automobile Association**) société de dépannage

Aachen [ˈɑːxən] N Aix-la-Chapelle

A & E [ˌeɪandˈiː] N (ABBR = **Accident and Emergency**) → **accident**

aardvark [ˈɑːdvɑːk] N (*Zool*) oryctérope *m*

Aaron [ˈɛərən] N Aaron *m*

AAU [ˌeɪeɪˈjuː] N (*US*) (ABBR = **Amateur Athletic Union**) association d'athlétisme amateur

AAUP [ˌeɪeɪjuːˈpiː] N ABBR = **American Association of University Professors**

AB [eɪ'biː] N [a] (ABBR = **able(-bodied) seaman**) → **able** [b] (*US*) (ABBR = **Bachelor of Arts**) **to have an AB in French** ≈ avoir une licence de français → **bachelor**; → DEGREE

ABA [ˌeɪbiːˈeɪ] N ABBR = **Amateur Boxing Association**

aback [əˈbæk] ADV **to be taken ~** être interloqué *or* décontenancé

abacus [ˈæbəkəs] N (*pl* **abacuses** *or* **abaci** [ˈæbəsaɪ]) [a] boulier *m*, abaque *m* [b] (*Archit*) abaque *m*

Abadan [ˌæbəˈdæn] N Abadan

abaft [əˈbɑːft] (*Naut*) [1] ADV sur *or* vers l'arrière [2] PREP en arrière de, sur l'arrière de

abalone [ˌæbəˈləʊnɪ] N ormeau *m*, haliotide *f*

abandon [əˈbændən] [1] VT [a] (= *forsake*) [+ *person, car*] abandonner; (*fig*) **to ~ o.s. to** [+ *despair, pleasure*] s'abandonner à, se laisser aller à; [+ *sleep*] s'abandonner à; **to ~ o.s. to one's fate** accepter son destin [b] [+ *property, right, project, idea, principles, pretence*] renoncer à; [+ *course of action*] abandonner, renoncer à; **to ~ the attempt to do sth** renoncer à faire qch; (*Ftbl etc*) **play was ~ed** le match a été interrompu *or* reporté [c] (*Jur*) [+ *cargo*] faire (acte de) délaissement de; (*Naut*) **to ~ ship** abandonner le navire; (*Jur*) **to ~ any claim** renoncer à toute prétention [2] N (*NonC*) abandon *m*; **to dance with ~** danser avec abandon; **with (gay) ~** avec (une belle) désinvolture

abandoned [əˈbændənd] ADJ [a] (= *forsaken*) [*person, place*] abandonné [b] (= *dissolute*) débauché [c] (= *wild*) [*dancing*] frénétique; [*emotion*] éperdu

abandonment [əˈbændənmənt] N (*lit, fig*) abandon *m*; (*Jur*) [*of action*] désistement *m*; [*of property, right*] cession *f*; [*of cargo*] délaissement *m*

abase [əˈbeɪs] VT (= *humiliate*) [+ *person*] mortifier, humilier; (= *degrade*) [+ *person*] abaisser, avilir; [+ *person's qualities, actions*] rabaisser, ravaler; **to ~ o.s. so far as to do** s'abaisser *or* s'humilier jusqu'à faire

abasement [əˈbeɪsmənt] N (*NonC*) (= *moral decay*) dégradation *f*, avilissement *m*; (= *humiliation*) humiliation *f*, mortification *f*

abashed [əˈbæʃt] ADJ confus

abate [əˈbeɪt] [1] VI [*storm, emotions, pain*] s'apaiser, se calmer; [*noise, flood*] baisser; [*violence*] se calmer; [*fever*] baisser, décroître; [*wind*] se modérer; (*Naut*) mollir; **the crime wave shows no sign of abating** on n'enregistre aucune baisse du taux de criminalité [2] VT [+ *tax*] baisser; (*Jur*) [+ *writ*] annuler; [+ *sentence*] remettre

abatement [əˈbeɪtmənt] N (*NonC*) (*gen*) réduction *f*; (*Fin*) **~ of the levy** abattement *m* sur le prélèvement → **noise**

abattoir [ˈæbətwɑːʳ] N abattoir *m*

abbess [ˈæbɪs] N abbesse *f*

abbey [ˈæbɪ] N abbaye *f*; **Westminster Abbey** l'abbaye *f* de Westminster

abbot [ˈæbət] N abbé *m*, (Père *m*) supérieur *m*

abbr., abbrev. (ABBR = **abbreviation, abbreviated**) abrév.

abbreviate [əˈbriːvɪeɪt] VT abréger (**to** en), raccourcir

abbreviation [əˌbriːvɪˈeɪʃən] N abréviation *f*

ABC [ˌeɪbiːˈsiː] [1] N [a] (= *alphabet*) abc *m*, alphabet *m*; **it's as easy** *or* **simple as ~*** c'est simple comme bonjour [b] ABBR = **Associated British Cinemas** [c] (ABBR = **Australian Broadcasting Commission**) [d] (ABBR = **American Broadcasting Corporation**) ABC *f* [2] **ABCs** NPL **the ~s of sth** le b a ba de qch

ABD [ˌeɪbiːˈdiː] N (*US Univ*) (ABBR = **all but dissertation**) étudiant(e) n'ayant plus que sa thèse à rédiger pour compléter son doctorat; **she was still ~ after four years** au bout de quatre ans, elle n'avait toujours pas rédigé sa thèse

abdicate [ˈæbdɪkeɪt] [1] VT [+ *right*] renoncer à, abdiquer; [+ *post, responsibility*] se démettre de; **to ~ the throne** renoncer à la couronne, abdiquer [2] VI abdiquer

abdication [ˌæbdɪˈkeɪʃən] N [*of king*] abdication *f*, renonciation *f*; [*of mandate etc*] démission *f* (**of** de); [*of right*] renonciation *f* (**of** à), désistement *m* (**of** de)

abdomen [ˈæbdəmən, æbˈdəʊmen] N (*Med*) abdomen *m*

abdominal [æbˈdɒmɪnl] [1] ADJ abdominal [2] **abdominals** NPL abdominaux *mpl*

abduct [æbˈdʌkt] VT enlever, kidnapper

abduction [æb'dʌkʃən] N enlèvement m, rapt m → **child**

abductor [æb'dʌktər] N [a] (= kidnapper) ravisseur m, -euse f [b] (Anat) abducteur m

abed† [ə'bed] ADV (liter) au lit, couché ; **to lie ~** rester couché

Abel ['eɪbl] N Abel m

Aberdonian [,æbə'dəʊnɪən] [1] N habitant(e) m(f) or natif m, -ive f d'Aberdeen [2] ADJ d'Aberdeen

aberrant [ə'berənt] ADJ (Bio, fig) aberrant, anormal

aberration [,æbə'reɪʃən] N (lit, fig) aberration f

abet [ə'bet] VT encourager, soutenir ; **to ~ sb in a crime** aider qn à commettre un crime → **aid**

abetter, abettor [ə'betər] N complice mf

abeyance [ə'beɪəns] N (NonC) [law, custom] **to be in ~** ne pas être en vigueur ; **to fall into ~** tomber en désuétude ; **the question is in ~** la question reste en suspens

abhor [əb'hɔː] VT abhorrer → **nature**

abhorrence [əb'hɒrəns] N horreur f (of de), aversion f (of pour) ; **to hold in ~** ◊ **have an ~ of** avoir horreur de, avoir en horreur

abhorrent [əb'hɒrənt] ADJ odieux

abide [ə'baɪd] (pret, ptp abided or abode) [1] VT [a] (neg only = tolerate) **I can't ~ her** je ne peux pas la supporter or la souffrir ; **I can't ~ living here** je ne supporte pas de vivre ici [b] (liter = await) attendre [2] VI† (= endure) durer ; (= live) demeurer

▶ **abide by** VT FUS [+ rule, decision] respecter ; [+ consequences] accepter, supporter ; [+ promise] rester or demeurer fidèle à ; [+ resolve] maintenir, s'en tenir à ; **they agreed to ~ by the terms of the contract** ils ont accepté de se conformer aux termes du contrat ; **I ~ by what I said** je maintiens ce que j'ai dit

abiding [ə'baɪdɪŋ] ADJ (liter) constant, éternel → **law**

Abidjan [,æbɪ'dʒɑːn] N Abidjan

ability [ə'bɪlɪtɪ] N [a] (gen) aptitude f (**to do** à faire), capacité f (**to do** pour faire) ; **people have lost confidence in the government's ~ to keep inflation in check** les gens ne croient plus que le gouvernement est capable de maîtriser l'inflation ; **the virus's ~ to infect the cells of the human immune system** la capacité du virus à infecter les cellules du système immunitaire humain ; **to have faith in sb's/one's ~ or abilities** croire en qn/en soi ; **to the best of one's ~ or abilities** de son mieux ; **he has the ~ to bring out the best in people** avec lui, les gens donnent le meilleur d'eux-mêmes ; (Fin, Jur) **~ to pay** solvabilité f ; (Fin, Jur) **~ to pay tax** capacité f or faculté f contributive [b] (NonC = talent) talent m ; **a person of great ~** une personne de grand talent ; **he has a certain artistic ~** il a un certain don or talent artistique ; **her drama teacher spotted her ~** son professeur d'art dramatique a découvert son talent [c] (Scol etc) **abilities** (= mental powers) compétences fpl

abject ['æbdʒekt] ADJ [a] (= wretched) [misery, poverty] noir ; **the ~ state of sth** l'état lamentable de qch [b] (= servile) [person, obedience, surrender] servile ; **an ~ apology** de plates excuses fpl [c] (= contemptible) [person, stupidity] méprisable ; [failure] lamentable

abjectly ['æbdʒektlɪ] ADV [apologize] platement ; **he has ~ failed** il a lamentablement échoué ; **to be ~ poor** être dans une misère noire ; **~ miserable** profondément malheureux

abjure [əb'dʒʊər] VT [+ one's rights] renoncer (publiquement or par serment) à ; **to ~ one's religion** abjurer sa religion, apostasier

Abkhaz [æb'kɑːz], **Abkhazi** [æb'kɑːzɪ] [1] ADJ

abkhaze [2] N (pl **Abkhaz**) [a] (= person) Abkhaze mf [b] (Ling) abkhaze m

Abkhazia [æb'kɑːzɪə] N l'Abkhazie f

Abkhazian [æb'kɑːzɪən] = **Abkhaz**

ablative ['æblətɪv] [1] N ablatif m ; **in the ~** à l'ablatif ; **~ absolute** ablatif m absolu [2] ADJ ablatif

ablaze [ə'bleɪz] ADJ [a] (lit) en feu, en flammes ; **to set sth ~** [person] mettre le feu à qch ; [spark, fire] embraser (liter) qch ; **to be ~** flamber [b] (fig) **his eyes were ~ with anger** ses yeux lançaient des éclairs ; **~ with light** resplendissant de lumière ; **the garden is ~ with colour** c'est une débauche de couleurs dans le jardin

able ['eɪbl] [1] ADJ [a] **to be ~ to do** (= have means or opportunity) pouvoir faire ; (= know how to) savoir faire ; (= be capable of) être capable de faire ; (= in position to) être en mesure de or à même de faire ; **I wasn't ~ to help him** je n'ai pas pu l'aider ; **I ran fast and so was ~ to catch the bus** en courant vite j'ai réussi à attraper l'autobus ; **he is ~ to read and write** il sait lire et écrire ; **~ to pay** en mesure de payer ; **you are better ~ to do it than he is** vous êtes mieux à même de le faire que lui ; **she was hardly ~ to see** (due to darkness, fog etc) elle arrivait à peine à voir ; (due to poor eyesight) elle voyait à peine [b] (= clever) capable, compétent ; **an ~ man** un homme très capable or très compétent ; **she is one of our ablest pupils** c'est une de nos meilleures élèves [c] (Med = healthy) sain ; (Jur) **~ in body and mind** sain de corps et d'esprit

[2] COMP ▶ **able-bodied** ADJ (gen = not disabled) valide ; (Mil) [recruit] bon pour le service ▶ **able-bodied seaman** N = **able seaman** ▶ **able-minded** ADJ (= not mentally handicapped) sain d'esprit ; (= intelligent) intelligent ▶ **able rating** N (Brit Naut) matelot m breveté ▶ **able seaman** N (pl **able seamen**) (Naut) matelot m breveté or de deuxième classe

ablution [ə'bluːʃən] N (Rel) ablution f ; (hum) **to perform one's ~s** faire ses ablutions

ably ['eɪblɪ] ADV (= competently) de façon très compétente ; (= skilfully) habilement ; **he was ~ assisted by his brother** son frère l'assistait avec compétence ; **he did it perfectly ~** il s'en est tiré d'une manière tout à fait compétente

ABM [,eɪbiː'em] N (ABBR = **antiballistic missile**) → **antiballistic**

abnegate ['æbnɪgeɪt] VT [+ responsibility] nier ; [+ one's rights] renoncer à ; [+ one's religion] abjurer

abnegation [,æbnɪ'geɪʃən] N (= denial) reniement m, désaveu m (of de) ; (= renunciation) renoncement m (of à) ; (also self-~) abnégation f

abnormal [æb'nɔːməl] ADJ anormal

abnormality [,æbnɔː'mælɪtɪ] N [a] (gen, Bio, Psych) anomalie f ; (Med) difformité f, malformation f ; **genetic abnormalities** anomalies fpl génétiques [b] (NonC) caractère m anormal, anormalité f

abnormally [æb'nɔːməlɪ] ADV anormalement ; **a city with an ~ high rate of HIV infection** une ville présentant un taux anormalement élevé de séropositivité ; **the cells were growing ~** les cellules se développaient de manière anormale

aboard [ə'bɔːd] [1] ADV [a] (Aviat, Naut = on) à bord ; **to go ~** (s')embarquer, monter à bord ; **to take ~** embarquer ; **all ~!** (on train, bus, car) en voiture! ; (on ship) tout le monde à bord! ; (fig) **to take an idea ~** adopter une idée (b) (Naut = alongside) le long du bord ; **close ~** bord à bord [2] PREP (Aviat, Naut) à bord de ; **~ the train/bus** dans le train/le bus ; **~ ship** à bord

abode [ə'bəʊd] [1] VB pret, ptp of **abide** [2] N (= home) demeure f ; (Jur) **place of ~** domicile m ; (Jur) **right of ~** droit m de résidence ; **to take**

up one's ~ élire domicile ; **the ~ of the gods** le séjour des dieux → **fixed**, **humble**

abolish [ə'bɒlɪʃ] VT [+ practice, custom, slavery, apartheid, tax] abolir ; [+ law] abroger, abolir

abolishment [ə'bɒlɪʃmənt] N = **abolition**

abolition [,æbəʊ'lɪʃən] N abolition f

abolitionist [,æbəʊ'lɪʃənɪst] N (Hist) abolitionniste mf, antiesclavagiste mf

abominable [ə'bɒmɪnəbl] [1] ADJ abominable [2] COMP ▶ **the abominable snowman** N l'abominable homme m des neiges

abominably [ə'bɒmɪnəblɪ] ADV [treat, behave, suffer] abominablement, d'une manière abominable ; **~ rude/cruel** d'une grossièreté/cruauté abominable ; **it's ~ cold** il fait un froid de loup

abominate [ə'bɒmɪneɪt] VT abominer, abhorrer

abomination [ə,bɒmɪ'neɪʃən] N abomination f ; (liter) **I hold him in ~** je l'ai en abomination, je l'abomine ; **this coffee is an ~** ce café est abominable

Aboriginal [,æbə'rɪdʒənl] (in Austral) [1] ADJ aborigène (australien) [2] N = **Aborigine**

aboriginal [,æbə'rɪdʒənl] [1] ADJ [person] autochtone, aborigène ; [plant, animal] aborigène [2] N (= person) autochtone mf, aborigène mf ; (= plant) plante f aborigène ; (= animal) animal m aborigène

Aborigine [,æbə'rɪdʒɪnɪ] N (in Austral) Aborigène mf (australien)

abort [ə'bɔːt] [1] VI (Med, fig) avorter ; (Mil, Space) échouer ; (Comput) abandonner [2] VT (Med) faire avorter ; (Comput) abandonner ; (Space) [+ mission, operation] abandonner, interrompre ; (fig) [+ deal, agreement, plan] faire échouer ; **an ~ed coup** une tentative avortée de coup d'État, un coup d'État manqué ; **an ~ed attempt** une tentative avortée [3] N (Comput) abandon m

abortion [ə'bɔːʃən] [1] N [a] (Med) (gen) avortement m ; (= termination) avortement m, interruption f volontaire de grossesse ; **to have an ~** (se faire) avorter [b] (fig) [of plans, scheme, mission] (= abandoning) abandon m ; (= failure) échec m [2] COMP ▶ **abortion law reform** N réforme f de la loi sur l'avortement ▶ **abortion pill** N (Med) pilule f abortive

abortionist [ə'bɔːʃənɪst] N avorteur m, -euse f → **backstreet**

abortive [ə'bɔːtɪv] ADJ [a] (= unsuccessful) [attempt] avorté ; [coup, operation, mission] avorté, manqué ; [plan] qui a échoué [b] (Med) [method] abortif, d'avortement

abortively [ə'bɔːtɪvlɪ] ADV en vain

abound [ə'baʊnd] VI [fish, resources etc] abonder ; [river, town, area etc] abonder (**in** en), regorger (**in** de)

about [ə'baʊt]

When **about** *is an element in a phrasal verb, eg* **bring about, come about, turn about, wander about,** *look up the verb.*

[1] ADV [a] (= approximately) à peu près, environ ; **there were ~ 30** il y en avait environ or à peu près 25 ; **and now there are ~ 30** il y en avait environ or à peu près 25 et à présent il y en a une trentaine ; **it's ~ 11 o'clock** il est environ or à peu près 11 heures ; **~ 11 o'clock** vers 11 heures ; (emphatic) **it's ~ time!** il est (grand) temps! ; **it's ~ time to go** il est presque temps de partir ; **she's ~ as old as you** elle a à peu près votre âge ; **that's ~ it** or **all** c'est à peu près tout ; **I've had ~ enough!*** je commence à en avoir assez !

[b] (= here and there) çà et là ; **shoes lying ~** des chaussures qui traînent (çà et là) ; **to throw one's arms ~** gesticuler, agiter les bras en tous sens

[c] (= near, in circulation) par ici ; **he's somewhere ~** il est quelque part par ici, il est dans les parages ; **is anyone ~?** il y a quelqu'un ? ; **there was nobody ~** il n'y avait personne ;

there's a lot of flu ~ il y a beaucoup de cas de grippe en ce moment; **there is a rumour ~ that ...** le bruit court que ...; **she's up and ~ again** elle est de nouveau sur pied; **you should be out and ~!** ne restez donc pas enfermé!

d (= *all round*) **all** ~ tout autour; **to glance ~** jeter un coup d'œil autour de soi

e (= *opposite direction*) **to turn sth (the other way)** ~ retourner qch; (*fig*) **it's the other way** ~ c'est le contraire; (*Brit Mil*) ~ **turn!** ◊ ~ **face!** demi-tour, marche!; (*Naut*) **to go** *or* **put** ~ virer de bord → **ready, right**

f (*in phrases*) **to be ~ to do** être sur le point de faire, aller faire; **I was ~ to go out when ...** j'étais sur le point de sortir *or* j'allais sortir quand ...; **the film is just ~ to start** le film va commencer

2 PREP a (= *concerning*) au sujet de, concernant, à propos de; ~ **it** en (*before vb*); **I heard nothing ~ it** je n'en ai pas entendu parler; **what is it ~?** de quoi s'agit-il?; **I know what it's all** ~ je sais de quoi il retourne; **to speak ~ sth** parler de qch; **well, what ~ it?*** (= *does it matter?*) et alors?*; (= *what do you think?*) alors, qu'est-ce que tu en penses?; **what ~ me?** et moi alors?*; **how** *or* **what ~ going to the cinema?*** et si on allait au cinéma?; **how** *or* **what ~ a coffee?*** et si on prenait un café?

b (= *near to*) près de; (= *somewhere in*) quelque part dans; **I dropped it ~ here** je l'ai laissé tomber par ici *or* près d'ici; **round ~ the Arctic Circle** près du Cercle polaire; **(somewhere) ~ the house** quelque part dans la maison

c (= *round*) autour de; **the trees (round) ~ the pond** les arbres qui entourent l'étang; **the countryside (round) ~ Edinburgh** la campagne autour d'Édimbourg

d (= *with, on*) **I've got it ~ me somewhere** je l'ai quelque part sur moi; **to have drugs ~ one's person** avoir de la drogue sur soi

e (*describing characteristics*) **there's something sinister ~ him** il a quelque chose de sinistre, il a un côté sinistre; **there's something interesting ~ him** il a un côté intéressant; **there's something charming ~ him** il a un certain charme; **there's something odd ~ all this** il y a quelque chose qui cloche là-dedans

f (= *occupied with*) **what are you ~?** que faites-vous?, qu'est-ce que vous fabriquez?*; **I don't know what he's ~** je ne sais pas ce qu'il fabrique*; **mind what you're ~!** faites (un peu) attention!; **while we're ~ it** pendant que nous y sommes

about-face [ə'baʊt'feɪs], **about-turn** [ə'baʊt-'tɜːn] **1** VI (*Mil*) faire demi-tour; (*fig*) faire volte-face **2** N (*Mil*) demi-tour *m*; (*fig*) volte-face *f*; **to do an** ~ faire demi-tour; (*fig*) faire volte-face

above [ə'bʌv]

> When **above** *is an element in a phrasal verb, eg* **get above***, look up the verb.*

1 ADV a (= *overhead, higher up*) au-dessus, en haut; **from** ~ d'en haut; **the view from** ~ la vue d'en haut; **the flat** ~ l'appartement *m* au-dessus *or* du dessus; **the powers** ~ (= *of higher rank*) les autorités *fpl* supérieures; (= *in heaven*) les puissances *fpl* célestes; **orders from** ~ des ordres *mpl* venant d'en haut; **a warning from** ~ un avertissement (venu) d'en haut

b (= *more*) **boys of 16 and** ~ les garçons à partir de 16 ans, les garçons de 16 ans et plus; **seats are available at 80 francs and** ~ il y a des places à partir de 80 F → **over**

c (= *earlier: in book etc*) ci-dessus, plus haut; **as** ~ comme ci-dessus, comme plus haut; **the address as** ~ l'adresse *m* ci-dessus

d (= *upstream*) en amont, plus haut

2 PREP a (= *higher than, superior to*) au-dessus de, plus haut que; ~ **it** plus haut; ~ **the horizon** au-dessus de l'horizon; ~ **all (else)** par-dessus tout, surtout; **he put his**

hands ~ **his head** il a levé les mains au-dessus de sa tête; **he values honesty ~ everything else** pour lui, il n'y a rien de plus important que l'honnêteté, il place l'honnêteté au-dessus de tout → **average**

b (= *more than*) plus de; **children ~ seven years of age** les enfants de plus de sept ans *or* au-dessus de sept ans; **it will cost ~ £10** ça coûtera plus de 10 livres; **temperatures ~ 40 degrees** des températures supérieures à 40 degrés; **wage rises of 3% ~ inflation** des augmentations de salaire supérieures de 3% à l'inflation → **over**

c (= *beyond*) au-delà de; **that is quite ~ me*** ceci me dépasse; **this book is ~ me*** ce livre est trop compliqué pour moi → **head**

d (= *too proud, honest etc for*) **he is ~ such behaviour** il est incapable de se conduire ainsi; **he's not ~ stealing/theft** il irait jusqu'à voler/jusqu'au vol; **he's not ~ playing with the children** il ne dédaigne pas de jouer avec les enfants; **they're not ~ changing the rules to suit their own purposes** ils iraient jusqu'à modifier les règles en leur faveur; **he thought he was ~ failure** (*gen*) il croyait être infaillible; (*in specific situation, theft etc*) il pensait qu'il ne pouvait pas échouer; **to get ~ o.s.** avoir des idées de grandeur

e (= *over*) **I couldn't hear what she was saying ~ the barking** les aboiements m'empêchaient d'entendre ce qu'elle disait

f (= *upstream from*) en amont de, plus haut que

g (= *north of*) au nord de, au-dessus de

3 ADJ mentionné ci-dessus, précité; **the ~ decree** le décret précité

4 N **the ~ is a photo of ...** ci-dessus nous avons une photo de ...; **please translate the ~** veuillez traduire ce qui se trouve au-dessus

5 COMP ► **above board** ADJ [*person, action*] régulier, correct ♦ ADV cartes sur table ► **above ground** ADJ [*lit*] au-dessus du sol, à la surface; (*Tech*) extérieur (-eure *f*); (*US* fig*) déclaré ► **above-mentioned** ADJ susmentionné, précité ► **above-named** ADJ susnommé

abracadabra [ˌæbrəkə'dæbrə] EXCL abracadabra!

abrade [ə'breɪd] VT user en frottant *or* par le frottement; [+ *skin etc*] écorcher, érafler; (*Geol*) éroder

Abraham ['eɪbrəhæm] N Abraham *m*

abrasion [ə'breɪʒən] (*frm*) N a (*Med*) [*of skin*] écorchure *f*; [*of teeth*] abrasion *f* b (*NonC*) (= *damage*) abrasion *f*

abrasive [ə'breɪsɪv] **1** ADJ a (*lit*) [*substance, surface*] abrasif b (*fig*) [*person, personality, manner, speech*] caustique; [*voice*] acerbe; [*wit*] corrosif **2** N abrasif *m*

abrasively [ə'breɪsɪvlɪ] ADV [*say, reply*] d'une voix acerbe; **he was ~ aggressive** il a été d'une agressivité caustique

abreaction [ˌæbrɪ'ækʃən] N abréaction *f*

abreast [ə'brest] ADV a [*horses, vehicles, ships*] de front; [*people*] de front, côte à côte; **to walk three ~** marcher trois de front; (*Naut*) **(in) line** ~ en ligne de front; ~ **of sb/sth** (= *in line with*) à la hauteur de qn/qch; **to draw ~ of sb/sth** arriver à la hauteur de qn/qch b (*fig*) ~ **of sth** (= *aware of*) au courant de qch; **to keep ~ of sth** se tenir au courant de qch; **to be ~ of the times** être de son temps, marcher avec son temps

abridge [ə'brɪdʒ] VT [+ *book*] abréger; [+ *article, speech*] raccourcir, abréger; [+ *interview*] écourter; [+ *text*] réduire

abridgement [ə'brɪdʒmənt] N a (= *shortened version*) résumé *m*, abrégé *m* b (*NonC*) diminution *f*, réduction *f*

abroad [ə'brɔːd] ADV a (= *in foreign country*) à l'étranger; **to go/be ~** aller/être à l'étranger; **news from ~** nouvelles *fpl* de l'étranger →

home b (= *far and wide*) au loin; (= *in all directions*) de tous côtés, dans toutes les directions); **scattered** ~ éparpillé de tous côtés *or* aux quatre vents; **there is a rumour ~ that ...** le bruit circule *or* court que ... → **noise**

c († = *out of doors*) (au) dehors, hors de chez soi

abrogate ['æbrəʊgeɪt] VT (*frm*) abroger, abolir

abrogation [ˌæbrəʊ'geɪʃən] N (*frm*) abrogation *f*

abrupt [ə'brʌpt] ADJ a (= *sudden*) [*change, rise, fall*] soudain, brusque; [*resignation, dismissal*] soudain; [*movement, turn*] brusque; [*departure*] précipité; **to come to an ~ end** se terminer brusquement; **to bring an ~ end to sth** mettre brusquement fin *or* un terme à qch; (*lit, fig*) **to come to an ~ halt** *or* **stop** s'arrêter brusquement b (= *brusque*) [*person, manner, comment*] abrupt c (= *steep*) [*hillside, precipice*] abrupt, raide

abruptly [ə'brʌptlɪ] ADV a (= *suddenly*) [*stop, move, turn*] brusquement b (= *brusquely*) [*say, ask*] abruptement c (= *steeply*) [*rise*] en pente raide

abruptness [ə'brʌptnɪs] N a (= *suddenness*) soudaineté *f*; (= *haste*) précipitation *f* b (= *brusqueness*) [*of person, behaviour*] brusquerie *f* c (= *steepness*) **the ~ of the slope** la pente raide

ABS [ˌeɪbiː'es] **1** N (ABBR = **anti-lock braking system**) ABS *m* **2** COMP ► **ABS brakes** NPL freins *mpl* ABS

abscess ['æbses] N abcès *m*

abscond [əb'skɒnd] VI s'enfuir, prendre la fuite (**from** de)

absconder [əb'skɒndə'] N fugitif *m*, -ive *f*; (*from prison*) évadé(e) *m(f)*

absconding [əb'skɒndɪŋ] **1** ADJ en fuite **2** N fuite *f*; [*of prisoner*] évasion *f*

abseil ['æbseɪl] (*Brit*) **1** VI descendre en rappel **2** N (descente *f* en) rappel *m*; ~ **device** descendeur *m*

abseiling ['æbseɪlɪŋ] N (*Brit*) (descente *f* en) rappel *m*

absence ['æbsəns] **1** N a (= *being away*) absence *f*; (*Jur*) non-comparution *f*, défaut *m*; **during/in the ~ of sb** pendant/en l'absence de qn; (*Jur*) **sentenced in his ~** condamné par contumace; ~ **makes the heart grow fonder** l'éloignement renforce les sentiments; (*Admin*) ~ **without leave** absence *f* irrégulière; **an ~ of three months** une absence de trois mois → **conspicuous, leave, unauthorized** b (*NonC* = *lack*) manque *m*, défaut *m*; **in the ~ of accurate information** faute de données précises **2** COMP ► **absence of mind** N (= *distraction*) distraction *f*; (= *forgetfulness*) absence *f*

absent ['æbsənt] **1** ADJ a (= *away*) absent (**from** de); **to be** ~ *or* **go** ~ **without leave** être absent sans permission; **to ~ friends!** (buvons) à la santé des absents! b (= *inattentive*) distrait c (= *lacking*) **his name was ~ from the list** son nom n'était pas sur la liste **2** [æb'sent] VT **to ~ o.s.** s'absenter (**from** de) **3** COMP ► **absent-minded** ADJ [*person*] (*gen*) distrait; (= *forgetful*) absent; [*air, manner*] absent, distrait ► **absent-mindedly** ADV (= *distractedly*) distraitement; (= *inadvertently*) par inadvertance ► **absent-mindedness** N (= *distraction*) distraction *f*; (= *forgetfulness*) absence *f*

absentee [ˌæbsən'tiː] **1** N absent(e) *m(f)*; (*habitual*) absentéiste *mf* **2** COMP ► **absentee ballot** N (*US Pol*) vote *m* par correspondance ► **absentee landlord** N propriétaire *mf* absentéiste ► **absentee rate** N (*Ind, Scol*) taux *m* d'absentéisme ► **absentee voter** (*US*) N (*US*) électeur *m*, -trice *f* qui vote par correspondance

absenteeism [ˌæbsən'tiːɪzəm] N absentéisme *m*

absently ['æbsəntlɪ] ADV distraitement

absinth(e) ['æbsɪnθ] N absinthe f

absolute ['æbsəlu:t] **1** ADJ (= complete, unqualified) [refusal, command, majority, silence, poverty] absolu; (Jur) [proof] irréfutable, formel; **an ~ truth** une vérité absolue; **she has ~ faith** or **confidence in him** elle lui fait entièrement confiance; **it's an ~ necessity** c'est indispensable; **it's an ~ fact that ...** c'est un fait indiscutable or il est indiscutable que ...; **in ~ terms** dans l'absolu; (Pol etc) **~ veto** veto m formel; (Jur) **the divorce was made ~** le (jugement de) divorce a été prononcé **b** (used for emphasis) **it's an ~ scandal** c'est un véritable scandale, c'est vraiment scandaleux; **that's ~ nonsense** or **rubbish*** c'est absurde, c'est une absurdité; **it was an ~ nightmare*** c'était un vrai cauchemar; **an ~ idiot*** un parfait crétin* **c** (= unlimited) [power] absolu, souverain; [monarch] absolu **d** (Math, Phys) [value] absolu; (Chem) [alcohol] absolu, anhydre **2** N absolu m **3** COMP ▶ **absolute liability** N (Fin, Jur) responsabilité f objective ▶ **absolute pitch** N (Mus) oreille f absolue ▶ **absolute zero** N (Phys) zéro m absolu

absolutely [,æbsə'lu:tlɪ] ADV **a** (= completely) absolument; **I ~ agree** je suis absolument or tout à fait d'accord; **to be ~ right** avoir entièrement raison; **to lie ~ still** rester parfaitement immobile, faire le mort; **~ everything** absolument tout; **it's ~ scandalous*** c'est un véritable scandale, c'est scandaleux; (expressing agreement) **~!** absolument!; (expressing disagreement) **~ not!** jamais de la vie!, sûrement pas! **b** ['æbsəlu:tlɪ] (Gram) absolument; **verb used ~** verbe m employé absolument

absolution [,æbsə'lu:ʃən] N absolution f; (in liturgy) **the Absolution** l'absoute f

absolutism ['æbsəlu:tɪzəm] N (Pol) absolutisme m; (Rel) prédestination f

absolve [əb'zɒlv] VT (from sin, of crime) absoudre (from, of de); (Jur) acquitter (of de); (from obligation, oath) décharger, délier (from de)

absorb [əb'sɔ:b] VT **a** (lit, fig) absorber; [+ sound, shock] amortir; **to ~ surplus stocks** absorber les surplus **b** **to become ~ed in one's work/in a book** s'absorber dans son travail/dans la lecture d'un livre; **to be ~ed in a book** être plongé dans un livre; **to be completely ~ed in one's work** être tout entier à son travail

absorbency [əb'sɔ:bənsɪ] N pouvoir m absorbant; (Chem, Phys) absorptivité f

absorbent [əb'sɔ:bənt] **1** ADJ absorbant **2** N absorbant m **3** COMP ▶ **absorbent cotton** N (US) coton m hydrophile

absorbing [əb'sɔ:bɪŋ] ADJ (lit) absorbant; (fig) [book, film] passionnant, captivant; [work] absorbant

absorption [əb'sɔ:pʃən] N **a** (Phys, Physiol) absorption f; (Aut) [of shock] amortissement m; (fig) [of person into group etc] absorption f, intégration f **b** (fig) concentration f (d'esprit); **his ~ in his studies prevented him from ...** ses études l'absorbaient à tel point qu'elles l'empêchaient de ...

absquatulate* [æb'skwɒtʃəleɪt] VI se tirer‡, mettre les voiles‡

abstain [əb'steɪn] VI (gen, Rel, Pol) s'abstenir (**from, from doing** de faire); (from alcohol) s'abstenir complètement (de l'usage) des boissons alcoolisées

abstainer [əb'steɪnəʳ] N **a** (also **total ~**) personne f qui s'abstient de toute boisson alcoolisée **b** (Pol) abstentionniste mf

abstemious [əb'sti:mɪəs] ADJ (frm) [person] sobre, frugal; [meal] frugal

abstemiousness [əb'sti:mɪəsnɪs] N (NonC) (frm) [of person] (from drinking) sobriété f; (from eating) frugalité f; [of meal] frugalité f

abstention [əb'stenʃən] N (from voting) abstention f; (from drinking) abstinence f; (Parl etc) **400 votes with 3 ~s** 400 voix et 3 abstentions

abstinence ['æbstɪnəns] N (gen, Rel) abstinence f (**from** de); (from alcohol: also **total ~**) abstention f de toute boisson alcoolisée

abstinent ['æbstɪnənt] ADJ sobre, tempérant; (Rel) abstinent

abstract ['æbstrækt] **1** ADJ [idea, number, noun, art, artist] abstrait; **~ expressionism** expressionnisme m abstrait **2** N **a** (Philos) abstrait m; (= idea) abstraction f; **in the ~** dans l'abstrait **b** (= summary) (for thesis, conference) résumé m, abrégé m; (Fin) **~ of accounts** extrait m de compte **c** (= work of art) œuvre f abstraite **3** [æb'strækt] VT **a** (gen, Chem = remove) extraire (**from** de) **b** (= steal) soustraire (**sth from sb** qch à qn), dérober **c** (= summarize) [+ book] résumer

abstracted [æb'stræktɪd] ADJ [person] (= absent-minded) distrait; (= preoccupied) préoccupé, absorbé

abstractedly [æb'stræktɪdlɪ] ADV distraitement

abstraction [æb'strækʃən] N **a** (= act of removing) extraction f; (hum = stealing) appropriation f **b** (= absent-mindedness) distraction f; **with an air of ~** d'un air distrait **c** (= concept) idée f abstraite, abstraction f

abstruse [æb'stru:s] ADJ abstrus

abstruseness [æb'stru:snɪs] N caractère m abstrus

absurd [əb'sɜ:d] **1** ADJ absurde; **it's ~!** c'est absurde! **2** N (Philos) absurde m

absurdist [əb'sɜ:dɪst] ADJ [writer] de l'absurde; [humour] absurde; [book, play] fondé sur l'absurde

absurdity [əb'sɜ:dɪtɪ] N absurdité f

absurdly [əb'sɜ:dlɪ] ADV [demand, laugh] de façon ridicule; [expensive, young, rich] ridiculement; **~ funny** d'un humour qui confine à l'absurde

ABTA ['æbtə] N (ABBR = **Association of British Travel Agents**) ≈ Syndicat m national des agences de voyage

Abu Dhabi [,æbu:'dɑ:bɪ] N Abou Dhabi

abundance [ə'bʌndəns] N **a** (= plenty) abondance f, profusion f; **in ~** en abondance **b** (= wealth) opulence f, aisance f; **to live in ~** vivre dans l'abondance

abundant [ə'bʌndənt] ADJ abondant; **there is ~ proof that he is guilty** les preuves de sa culpabilité abondent

abundantly [ə'bʌndəntlɪ] ADV abondamment, copieusement; **to grow ~** pousser à foison; **it was ~ clear that ...** il était tout à fait clair que ...; **he made it ~ clear to me that ...** il m'a fait comprendre or m'a bien précisé que ...

abuse [ə'bju:z] **1** VT **a** (= misuse) [+ privilege] abuser de **b** (= insult) injurier, insulter; (= ill-treat) (gen) maltraiter; (Sociol, Jur) faire subir des mauvais traitements à; (sexually) faire subir des sévices sexuels à **2** [ə'bju:s] N **a** (of power, authority) abus m; **the system is open to ~** le système présente des risques d'abus **b** (= unjust practice) abus m; **to remedy ~s** réprimer les abus **c** (NonC = curses, insults) insultes fpl, injures fpl; (= ill-treatment) (gen) mauvais traitements mpl (of infligés à); (Sociol, Jur) maltraitance f; (sexual) abus m sexuel, sévices mpl sexuels

abuser [ə'bju:zəʳ] N **a** (gen) **~s of the system** les gens qui exploitent le système **b** (Sociol, Jur) auteur m de sévices; (also **sex ~**) auteur m de sévices sexuels

Abu Simbel [,æbu:'sɪmbl] N Abou Simbel

abusive [əb'ju:sɪv] ADJ **a** (= offensive) [speech, words] injurieux; **to use ~ language to sb** injurier qn; (= rude) **he was very ~** il s'est montré très grossier **b** (Sociol, Jur) [parents] qui exercent des sévices sur leurs enfants; **children from an ~ home** les enfants maltraités par leurs parents **c** (= wrongly used) abusif, mauvais

abusively [əb'ju:sɪvlɪ] ADV [refer to] injurieusement; **to shout/scream ~ at sb** crier/hurler des insultes à qn

abut [ə'bʌt] VI **to ~ on** confiner à, être contigu (-guë f) à

abutment [ə'bʌtmənt] N (Archit) contrefort m, piédroit m; (esp on bridge) butée f

abuzz [ə'bʌz] ADJ **the office was ~ with the news** la nouvelle courait dans tout le bureau

abysmal [ə'bɪzməl] ADJ [taste, quality] épouvantable, catastrophique*; **~ ignorance** ignorance f crasse; **his work was quite ~** son travail était tout à fait exécrable

abysmally [ə'bɪzməlɪ] ADV [bad, low, unsuccessful] atrocement; [play] atrocement mal; **~ ignorant** d'une ignorance crasse; **the government has failed ~** le gouvernement a échoué lamentablement

abyss [ə'bɪs] N (lit, fig) abîme m, gouffre m; (in sea) abysse m

Abyssinia [,æbɪ'sɪnɪə] N l'Abyssinie f

Abyssinian [,æbɪ'sɪnɪən] **1** ADJ abyssinien, abyssin (rare) **2** N Abyssinien(ne) m(f), Abyssin(e) m(f) (rare); **the ~ Empire** l'empire m d'Éthiopie

AC [eɪ'si:] N (ABBR = **alternating current**) → **alternating**

a/c N (ABBR = **account**) C, compte m

acacia [ə'keɪʃə] N acacia m

Acad ABBR = **academy, academic**

academe ['ækədi:m], **academia** [,ækə'di:mɪə] N (NonC) le monde universitaire

academic [,ækə'demɪk] **1** ADJ **a** (= of studying, colleges) (Univ) universitaire; (Scol) scolaire; [failure, progress] scolaire; **~ freedom** liberté f de l'enseignement **b** (= theoretical) théorique, spéculatif; **~ debate** discussion f sans portée pratique or toute théorique **c** (= scholarly) [style, approach] intellectuel **d** (= of no practical use) **that's all quite ~** ◊ **it's an ~ question** c'est (une question) purement théorique; **out of purely ~ interest** par simple curiosité **e** [art, portrait] académique **2** N (= university teacher) universitaire mf **3** COMP ▶ **academic advisor** N (US) directeur m, -trice f d'études ▶ **academic dean** N (US) ≈ président(e) m(f) de faculté ▶ **academic dress** N toge f et toque f de professeur (or d'étudiant) ▶ **academic gown** N toge f de professeur (or d'étudiant) ▶ **academic officers** NPL (US) personnel m enseignant et cadres mpl administratifs ▶ **academic rank** N (US) grade m ▶ **academic year** N année f universitaire

academically [,ækə'demɪkəlɪ] ADV [competent] sur le plan scolaire; [sound] intellectuellement; **~ gifted** doué pour les études; **~ qualified** possédant des diplômes universitaires

academicals [,ækə'demɪkəlz] NPL toge f et toque f de professeur (or d'étudiant)

academician [ə,kædə'mɪʃən] N académicien(ne) m(f)

academy [ə'kædəmɪ] **1** N **a** (= private college) école f privée, collège m, pensionnat m; **military/naval ~** école f militaire/navale; **~ of music** conservatoire m → **police** **b** (= society) académie f, société f; **the (Royal) Academy** l'Académie f Royale → **French** **2** COMP ▶ **Academy Award** N oscar m

acanthus [ə'kænθəs] N (pl **acanthuses** or **acanthi** [ə'kænθaɪ]) acanthe f

ACAS, **Acas** [ˈeɪkæs] N (ABBR = **Advisory, Conciliation and Arbitration Service**) organisme d'arbitrage des conflits du travail

acc. N (Banking) ABBR = **account**

accede [ækˈsiːd] VI a (= agree) **to ~ to** [+ request] agréer, donner suite à ; [+ suggestion] agréer, accepter b (= gain position) entrer en possession ; **to ~ to office** entrer en fonction ; **to ~ to the throne** monter sur le trône c (= join) adhérer, se joindre (**to** à)

accelerate [ækˈseləreɪt] 1 VT [+ movement, growth] accélérer ; [+ work] activer ; [+ events] précipiter, hâter ; **to ~ the process of reform/modernization** accélérer le processus de réformes/de modernisation 2 VI (esp Aut) accélérer

accelerated [ækˈseləreɪtɪd] ADJ (Econ) [depreciation, increments etc] accéléré ; (US Univ) **~ program** cursus m intensif

acceleration [ækˌseləˈreɪʃən] 1 N accélération f ; (Fin) **repayment by ~** remboursement m par déchéance du terme 2 COMP ► **acceleration clause** N (Fin) clause f d'accélération

accelerator [ækˈseləreɪtəʳ] N (Aut) accélérateur m ; **to step on the ~** appuyer sur l'accélérateur or le champignon*

accelerometer [ækˌseləˈrɒmɪtəʳ] N accéléromètre m

accent [ˈæksənt] 1 N a (= intonation, pronunciation) accent m ; **to speak French without an ~** parler français sans accent b (= stress on part of word) accent m (tonique) c (= written mark) accent m → **acute** d (liter = way of speaking) **~s** accents mpl, paroles fpl ; **in ~s of rage** avec des accents de rage (dans la voix) 2 [ækˈsent] VT a (= emphasize) [+ word] accentuer, mettre l'accent sur ; [+ syllable] accentuer b (fig = make prominent) accentuer, mettre en valeur

accentuate [ækˈsentjʊeɪt] VT (= emphasize) [+ inequality, hostility, tendency] accentuer ; [+ physical feature] faire ressortir ; (= draw attention to) attirer l'attention sur

accentuation [ækˌsentjʊˈeɪʃən] N accentuation f

▼ **accept** [əkˈsept] VT a [+ gift, invitation, apology] accepter ; [+ goods] prendre livraison de ; [+ excuse, fact, report, findings] admettre, accepter ; [+ one's duty] se soumettre à ; [+ one's fate] se résigner à ; [+ task] se charger de, accepter ; (Comm) [+ bill] accepter ; **I ~ that ...** je conviens que ... ; **it is generally** or **widely ~ed that ...** il est généralement admis que ... b (= allow) [+ action, behaviour] admettre, accepter c (Med) [+ transplanted organ] assimiler

acceptability [əkˌseptəˈbɪlɪtɪ] N a (gen) **the organization's new-found international ~** le fait que cette organisation soit depuis peu cautionnée or admise par la communauté internationale b (Ling) acceptabilité f

acceptable [əkˈseptəbl] ADJ a (= reasonable) [offer, suggestion] acceptable (also Ling) ; (morally) [behaviour] admissible ; **I hope you will find this ~** j'espère que cela vous conviendra ; **if this offer is ~ to you** si la présente offre est à votre convenance b (= welcome) bienvenu, opportun ; [gift] qui fait plaisir ; **the money was most ~** l'argent était vraiment le bienvenu

acceptably [əkˈseptəblɪ] ADV a (= properly) [behave, treat] de façon acceptable, d'une manière décente ; (= sufficiently) **~ accurate/safe** d'une précision/sécurité satisfaisante ; **noise levels were ~ low** les niveaux sonores étaient suffisamment bas pour être tolérables b (= adequately) [play] à peu près comme il faut, d'une manière convenable

▼ **acceptance** [əkˈseptəns] 1 N a [of invitation, gift] acceptation f ; [of proposal] consentement m (**of** à) ; (Comm) [of bill] acceptation f ;

(Comm, Jur) [of delivered goods] réception f b (= approval) réception f favorable, approbation f ; **the idea met with general ~** l'idée a reçu l'approbation générale 2 COMP ► **acceptance house** N banque f d'acceptation

acceptation [ˌæksepˈteɪʃən] N a (= meaning) acception f, signification f b (= approval) approbation f

accepted [əkˈseptɪd] ADJ accepté ; [fact] reconnu ; [idea] répandu ; [behaviour, pronunciation] admis ; **... in the ~ sense of the word ...** dans le sens usuel or courant du mot

acceptor [əkˈseptəʳ] N (Comm) accepteur m

access [ˈækses] 1 N a (NonC) (= way of approach) accès m, abord m ; (Jur) (= through lane etc) droit m de passage ; (into property) droit m d'accès ; (= permission to use, see) accès m ; **easy of ~** d'accès facile, facilement accessible ; **~ to his room is by a staircase** on accède à sa chambre par un escalier ; **to give ~ to ...** donner accès à ... ; **to have ~ to sb** avoir accès auprès de qn, avoir ses entrées chez qn ; **to have (right of) ~ to papers** avoir accès à des documents ; **to have ~ to (an) education** avoir accès or droit à l'éducation ; **these children now have ~ to (an) education** ces enfants peuvent désormais bénéficier d'une scolarisation → **gain**

b (= way of entry) **there is another ~ to this room** cette pièce a un autre accès c (Jur: in divorce) droit m de visite d (Comput) **~ port/time** port m/temps m d'accès → **random** e (= sudden outburst) [of anger, remorse, melancholy] accès m ; [of generosity] élan m

2 VT (Comput) [+ file etc] accéder à 3 COMP ► **access course** N (Univ) cours intensif permettant aux personnes sans baccalauréat d'accéder aux études supérieures ► **access road** N route f d'accès ; [of motorway] bretelle f d'accès or de raccordement ; (to motorway) **there is an ~ road for Melun** Melun est raccordé (à l'autoroute)

accessary [ækˈsesərɪ] 1 N complice mf ; **~ before/after the fact** complice mf par instigation/par assistance 2 ADJ complice (**to** de)

accessibility [ækˌsesɪˈbɪlɪtɪ] N accessibilité f

accessible [ækˈsesəbl] ADJ a [place] accessible, d'accès facile ; [knowledge] à la portée de tous, accessible ; [person] accessible, d'un abord facile b (= able to be influenced) ouvert, accessible (**to** à)

accession [ækˈseʃən] 1 N a (= gaining of position) accession f (**to** à) ; (to fortune, property) accession f (**to** à), entrée f en possession (**to** de) ; **~ (to the throne)** avènement m b (= addition, increase) accroissement m, augmentation f ; **the ~ of new members to the party** l'adhésion f de membres nouveaux au parti c (= consent) accord m, assentiment m ; (Jur, Pol: to a treaty etc) adhésion f d (in library, museum) nouvelle acquisition f 2 VT [+ library book etc] mettre au catalogue

accessorize [ækˈsesəraɪz] VT accessoiriser

accessory [ækˈsesərɪ] 1 ADJ a (= additional) accessoire, auxiliaire b (Jur) = **accessary 2** 2 N a (Comm, Tech, Dress, Theat etc) accessoire m ; **car accessories** accessoires mpl d'automobile ; **toilet accessories** objets mpl de toilette b (Jur) = **accessary 1**

accidence [ˈæksɪdəns] N (Ling) morphologie f flexionnelle ; (Philos) accident m

accident [ˈæksɪdənt] 1 N a (= mishap, disaster) accident m ; **to meet with** or **have an ~** avoir un accident ; **road ~** accident m de la route or de la circulation ; **~s in the home** accidents mpl domestiques ; (fig) **it's an ~ waiting to happen** c'est une bombe à retardement b (= unforeseen event) événement m fortuit, accident m ; (= chance) hasard m, chance f ; **by**

~ [injure, break] accidentellement ; [meet, find] par hasard ; **it's no ~ that ...** ce n'est pas un hasard si ... c (Philos) accident m

2 COMP ► **Accident and Emergency Unit** N (service m des) urgences fpl ► **accident figures** NPL nombre m des accidents ► **accident insurance** N assurance f (contre les) accidents ► **accident prevention** N (in home, factory) prévention f des accidents ; (Aut) prévention f routière ► **accident-prone** ADJ **to be ~prone** être sujet aux accidents, attirer les accidents ► **accident protection** N (Aut) prévention f routière ► **accident statistics** NPL statistiques fpl des accidents ► **Accident Unit** N = **Accident and Emergency Unit**

accidental [ˌæksɪˈdentl] 1 ADJ a (= happening by chance) [shooting, poisoning, overdose, death] accidentel ; **the ~ discovery of the explosives** la découverte fortuite des explosifs ; **the cure was an ~ discovery** le traitement a été découvert par hasard b (= of secondary importance) [effect, benefit] secondaire, accessoire c (Mus, Philos) accidentel 2 N (Mus) accident m 3 COMP ► **accidental damage** N (Insurance) accident(s) m(pl) ► **accidental injury** N (Insurance) accident m

accidentally [ˌæksɪˈdentəlɪ] ADV [shoot, kill] accidentellement ; **it was discovered quite ~** on l'a découvert par hasard ; (hum) **~ on purpose*** comme par hasard

acclaim [əˈkleɪm] 1 VT (= applaud) acclamer ; **to ~ sb king** proclamer qn roi 2 N acclamations fpl ; **it met with great public/critical ~** cela a été salué unanimement par le public/les critiques

acclamation [ˌækləˈmeɪʃən] N acclamation f ; **to be elected/nominated by ~** être élu/nommé par acclamation

acclimate [əˈklaɪmət] VT (US) = **acclimatize**

acclimatization [əˌklaɪmətaɪˈzeɪʃən], **acclimation** (US) [ˌæklaɪˈmeɪʃən] N (lit) acclimatation f ; (fig: to new situation etc) accoutumance f (**to** à)

acclimatize [əˈklaɪmətaɪz], **acclimate** (US) [əˈklaɪmət] 1 VT (lit, fig) acclimater (**to** à) 2 VI (to new place, climate) s'acclimater (**to** à) ; **to ~ to a new job** s'accoutumer or se faire à un nouveau travail

acclivity [əˈklɪvɪtɪ] N montée f

accolade [ˈækəʊleɪd] N accolade f ; (fig) marque f d'approbation

accommodate [əˈkɒmədeɪt] VT a (= provide lodging or housing for) loger ; (= contain) [car] contenir ; [house] contenir, recevoir ; **the hotel/room can ~ 60 people** l'hôtel/la salle peut recevoir or accueillir 60 personnes b (= supply) équiper (**sb with sth** qn de qch), fournir (**sb with sth** qch à qn) ; (= satisfy) [+ demand etc] accéder à ; **to ~ sb with a loan** consentir un prêt à qn ; **I think we can ~ you** je crois que nous pouvons satisfaire à votre demande c (= adapt) [+ plans, wishes] accommoder, adapter (**to** à) ; **to ~ o.s. to sth** s'adapter à qch, s'accommoder à qch

accommodating [əˈkɒmədeɪtɪŋ] ADJ (= obliging) obligeant ; (= easy to deal with) accommodant, conciliant

accommodation [əˌkɒməˈdeɪʃən] 1 N a [of person] logement m ; (US) **~s** logement m ; **"~ (to let)"** « appartements or chambres à louer » ; **we have no ~ (available)** nous n'avons pas de place, c'est complet ; **there is no ~ for children** on n'accepte pas les enfants ; **"office ~ to let"** « bureaux à louer » → **seating** b (= compromise) compromis m c (Anat, Psych) accommodation f d (Fin) prêt m, crédit m ; **to take ~** contracter un emprunt, faire un prêt 2 COMP ► **accommodation address** N adresse f (utilisée uniquement pour la *correspondance*), boîte *f* à lettres ► **accommodation bill** N (*Comm*) billet *m* or effet *m* de complaisance ► **accommodation bureau** N agence *f* de logement ► **accommodation ladder** N (*Naut*) échelle *f* de coupée ► **accommodation officer** N responsable *mf* de l'hébergement ► **accommodation road** N route *f* à usage restreint ► **accommodation train** N (*US Rail*) (train *m*) omnibus *m*

accompaniment [əˈkʌmpənɪmənt] N accompagnement *m*, complément *m*; (*Mus*) accompagnement *m*; (*Culin*) accompagnement *m*, garniture *f*; **they marched to the ~ of a military band** ils ont défilé au son d'une fanfare militaire

accompanist [əˈkʌmpənɪst] N (*Mus*) accompagnateur *m*, -trice *f*

accompany [əˈkʌmpənɪ] VT [a] (= *escort*) accompagner, suivre; **accompanied by** accompagné de or par [b] (*fig*) accompagner; **cold accompanied by fever** rhume *m* accompagné de fièvre; **~ing letter** lettre *f* d'accompagnement [c] (*Mus*) accompagner (**on** à)

accomplice [əˈkʌmplɪs] N complice *mf*; **to be an ~ to** or **in a crime** tremper dans un crime, être complice d'un crime

accomplish [əˈkʌmplɪʃ] VT accomplir, exécuter; [+ *task*] accomplir, achever; [+ *desire*] réaliser; [+ *journey*] effectuer; **to ~ one's object** arriver à ses fins

accomplished [əˈkʌmplɪʃt] ADJ [*person*] (*gen*) doué; [*musician, skater etc*] accompli; [*performance*] accompli, parfait; **she's very ~** elle est très douée; **an ~ pianist** un pianiste accompli

accomplishment [əˈkʌmplɪʃmənt] N [a] (= *achievement*) œuvre *f* accomplie, projet *m* réalisé [b] (= *skill*) talent *m*; **a woman of many ~s** une femme aux multiples talents or très talentueuse [c] (= *completion*) **on ~ of the project** quand le projet aura été mené à bien

accord [əˈkɔːd] [1] VT [+ *favour, status, right, honour, privilege*] accorder (**to** à); [+ *respect*] témoigner; **to ~ priority to** accorder la priorité à; **to ~ great importance to sth** accorder beaucoup d'importance à qch; **she insisted she ~ed the same treatment as her male colleagues** elle a insisté pour avoir droit au même traitement que ses collègues masculins; **he was ~ed a hero's welcome** il a été accueilli en héros [2] VI s'accorder, concorder (**with** avec) [3] N [a] (*NonC* = *agreement*) consentement *m*, accord *m*; **of his own ~** de lui-même; **the problem disappeared of its own ~** le problème s'est résolu tout seul; **with one ~** d'un commun accord; **to be in ~** être d'accord avec [b] (= *treaty*) traité *m*, pacte *m*

accordance [əˈkɔːdəns] N accord *m* (**with** avec), conformité *f* (**with** à); **in ~ with** conformément à, suivant, en accord avec; **to be in ~ with** être conforme à, correspondre à

▼ **according** [əˈkɔːdɪŋ] ADV [a] (*gen*) **~ to** selon; **~ to him they've gone** selon lui or d'après lui ils sont partis; **classified ~ to size** classés par ordre de grandeur; **everything went ~ to plan** tout s'est passé comme prévu; **~ to what he says ...** d'après ce qu'il dit ...; **to act ~ to the law** agir conformément à la loi [b] **~ as** selon que (+ *subj*), suivant que (+ *indic*)

accordingly [əˈkɔːdɪŋlɪ] ADV [a] (= *appropriately*) [*act, pay, plan*] en conséquence [b] (= *consequently*) par conséquent

accordion [əˈkɔːdɪən] [1] N accordéon *m* [2] COMP ► **accordion file** N (*US*) dossier *m* à soufflet ► **accordion pleat** N pli *m* (en) accordéon

accordionist [əˈkɔːdɪənɪst] N accordéoniste *mf*

accost [əˈkɒst] VT accoster, aborder; (*Jur*) accoster

account [əˈkaʊnt] [1] N [a] (*Comm, Fin*) compte *m*; **to open an ~** ouvrir un compte; **put it on my ~** (*in shop*) vous le mettrez à or sur mon compte; (*in hotel*) vous le mettrez sur mon compte or sur ma note; (*Banking*) **to pay a sum into one's ~** verser une somme à son compte; (*at shop*) **I have an ~ with them** ils me font crédit; **in ~ with** en compte avec; **~s payable** comptes *mpl* clients, comptes *mpl* créditeurs; **~s receivable** comptes *mpl* fournisseurs, effets *mpl* à recevoir; **"to ~ rendered"** «facture non payée»; **on ~** à compte; **payment on ~** acompte *m*, à-valoir *m*, paiement *m* à compte; **to pay £50 on ~** verser un acompte de 50 livres; **cash or ~?** (*in hotel, bar*) vous payez comptant ou je le mets sur votre note?; (*in shop*) vous payez comptant ou je le mets sur votre compte?; (*Advertising*) **they have the Michelin ~** ce sont eux qui font la publicité de Michelin → **bank²**, **current**, **settle²** [b] **~s** (= *calculation*) comptabilité *f*, comptes *mpl*; (= *department*) (*service m*) comptabilité *f*; **to do/keep the ~s** faire/tenir la comptabilité or les comptes [c] (*NonC* = *benefit*) profit *m*, avantage *m*; **to turn** or **put sth to (good) ~** mettre qch à profit, tirer parti de qch [d] (= *explanation*) compte rendu *m*, explication *f*; **to call sb to ~ for having done** demander des comptes à qn pour avoir fait; **to be held to ~ for sth** devoir rendre des comptes pour qch; **he gave a good ~ of himself** il s'en est bien tiré, il a fait bonne impression; (*fig*) **to settle** or **square ~s with sb** régler son compte à qn [e] (= *report*) compte rendu *m*; **to give an ~ of sth** faire le compte rendu de qch or un exposé sur qch; **by her own ~** d'après ce qu'elle dit, d'après ses dires; **by all ~s** d'après l'opinion générale, au dire de tous [f] (*NonC* = *importance, consideration*) importance *f*, valeur *f*; **a man of no ~** un homme sans importance; **your statement is of no ~ to them** ils n'attachent aucune importance or valeur à votre déclaration; **to take ~ of sth/sb ◊ to take sth/sb into ~** tenir compte de qch/qn; **these facts must be taken into ~** ces faits doivent entrer en ligne de compte; **to leave sth out of ◊ to take no ~ of sth** ne pas tenir compte de qch; **to take little ~ of sth** faire peu de cas de qch; **that is of little ~ to them** ils ne s'en soucient guère, cela leur importe peu [g] **on ~ of** à cause de; **on no ◊ not on any ~** en aucun cas, sous aucun prétexte; **on her ~** à cause d'elle; **on this** or **that ~** pour cette raison; **I was worried on her ~** je m'inquiétais pour elle; **don't leave on my ~** ne partez pas à cause de moi [2] VT estimer, juger; **to ~ o.s. lucky** s'estimer heureux; **to ~ sb (to be) innocent** considérer qn comme innocent [3] COMP ► **account book** N livre *m* de comptes ► **account day** N (*St Ex*) terme *m*, jour *m* de liquidation ► **account executive** N (*Advertising*) responsable *mf* du budget ► **account holder** N (*Banking*) titulaire *mf* d'un compte ► **accounts department** N (*service m*) comptabilité *f*

► **account for** VT FUS [a] (= *explain, justify*) [+ *expenses*] rendre compte de, justifier de; [+ *one's conduct*] justifier; [+ *circumstances*] expliquer; **poor sanitation ~s for the recent outbreaks of disease** les mauvaises conditions d'hygiène expliquent les récentes épidémies; **there's no ~ing for tastes** des goûts et des couleurs on ne dispute pas (*PROV*), chacun son goût (*PROV*); **everyone is ~ed for** on n'a oublié personne; (*after accident etc*) **three people have not yet been ~ed for** trois personnes n'ont pas encore été retrouvées [b] (= *represent*) représenter; **this ~s for 10% of the total** ceci représente 10% du chiffre

total; **the Greens ~ for 10% of the vote** les Verts totalisent or représentent 10% des voix; **this area ~s for most of the country's mineral wealth** cette région produit or possède la plus grande partie des ressources minières du pays [c] (= *kill, destroy*) (*shooting etc*) tuer; (*Fishing* = *catch*) attraper; **he ~ed for four enemy planes** il a abattu quatre avions ennemis

accountability [ə,kaʊntəˈbɪlɪtɪ] N responsabilité *f*; (*financial*) responsabilité *f* financière

accountable [əˈkaʊntəbl] ADJ responsable (**for** de); **to be ~ to sb for sth** être responsable de qch or répondre de qch devant qn; **he is not ~ for his actions** (= *need not account for*) il n'a pas à répondre de ses actes; (= *is not responsible for*) il n'est pas responsable de ses actes

accountancy [əˈkaʊntənsɪ] N (= *subject*) comptabilité *f*; (= *profession*) profession *f* de comptable; **to study ~** faire des études de comptable or de comptabilité

accountant [əˈkaʊntənt] N comptable *mf*; **~'s office** agence *f* comptable

accounting [əˈkaʊntɪŋ] [1] N comptabilité *f* [2] COMP ► **accounting period** N exercice *m* comptable ► **accounting policy** N politique *f* comptable ► **accounting practices** NPL pratique *f* comptable ► **accounting year** N = accounting period

accouterments [əˈkuːtərmənts] NPL (*US*) = accoutrements

accoutred [əˈkuːtəd] ADJ (*esp Mil*) équipé (**with** de)

accoutrements [əˈkuːtrəmənts], **accouterments** (*US*) [əˈkuːtərmənts] NPL (*Mil*) équipement *m*; (*gen*) attirail *m*

accredit [əˈkredɪt] VT [a] (= *credit*) [+ *rumour*] accréditer; **to ~ sth to sb** attribuer qch à qn; **he is ~ed with having discovered the site** on lui attribue la découverte de ce site [b] [+ *representative, ambassador*] accréditer (**to** auprès de) → **accredited**

accreditation [ə,kredɪˈteɪʃn] [1] N (*US Scol, Univ*) habilitation *f* [2] COMP ► **accreditation officer** N (*US Scol*) inspecteur *m* d'académie

accredited [əˈkredɪtɪd] ADJ [*person*] accrédité, autorisé; [*opinion, belief*] admis, accepté; [*agent*] accrédité; (*Univ, Scol*) **~ institution** établissement scolaire ou universitaire dont les diplômes sont reconnus par l'État; **~ representative** représentant *m* accrédité (**to** auprès de)

accretion [əˈkriːʃən] N [a] (= *increase, growth*) accroissement *m* (*organique*) [b] (= *result of growth: Geol etc*) concrétion *f*, addition *f*; [*of wealth etc*] accroissement *m*, accumulation *f*

accruals [əˈkruːəlz] NPL (*Fin*) compte *m* de régularisation (du passif)

accrue [əˈkruː] [1] VI [a] [*money, advantages*] revenir (**to** à) [b] (*Fin*) [*interest*] courir [2] COMP ► **accrued alimony** N (*Jur*) pension *f* alimentaire due ► **accrued charges** NPL (*Fin*) charges *fpl* à payer ► **accrued expenses** NPL (*Fin*) frais *mpl* à payer ► **accrued income** N recettes *fpl* échues ► **accrued interest** N intérêts *mpl* courus

accumulate [əˈkjuːmjʊleɪt] [1] VT accumuler [2] VI s'accumuler; **to allow interest to ~** laisser courir les intérêts

accumulation [ə,kjuːmjʊˈleɪʃən] N [a] (*NonC*) accumulation *f*; (*Fin*) [*of capital*] accroissement *m*; [*of interest*] accumulation *f* [b] (= *objects accumulated*) amas *m*, tas *m*

accumulative [əˈkjuːmjʊlətɪv] ADJ qui s'accumule; (*Fin*) cumulatif

accumulator [əˈkjuːmjʊleɪtər] N [a] (*Elec*) accumulateur *m*, accus* *mpl* [b] (*Brit* = *bet*) report *m*

accuracy [ˈækjʊrəsɪ] N [*of figures, clock*] exactitude *f*; [*of aim, shot, story, report*] précision *f*;

[*of translation*] exactitude *f*, fidélité *f*; [*of judgement, assessment*] justesse *f*

accurate ['ækjʊrɪt] ADJ [*information, figures, description*] exact; [*typist*] bon; [*missile*] précis; [*measurement, clock, assessment, prediction*] juste; [*translation, account, memory*] fidèle; [*spelling*] correct; **his father or, to be ~, his stepfather ...** son père ou, pour être exact, son beau-père ...; **the newspaper is well-known for its ~ reporting** ce journal est réputé pour l'exactitude de ses informations; **the tests are 90% ~** ces tests sont fiables à 90%; **the scales were ~ to half a gram** la balance avait une précision de l'ordre du demi-gramme

accurately ['ækjʊrɪtlɪ] ADV [*reflect, report, tell*] exactement, avec exactitude; [*calculate, predict, reproduce*] exactement; [*describe, measure, draw*] avec précision; [*type, spell*] correctement; [*translate*] fidèlement

accursed [ə'kɜːst], **accurst** [ə'kɜːst] ADJ († *or liter*) maudit

accusal [ə'kjuːzl] N accusation *f*

accusation [ˌækjʊ'zeɪʃən] N accusation *f*; (*Jur*) accusation *f*, plainte *f*; (*Jur*) **to bring an ~ against sb** porter plainte *or* déposer (une) plainte contre qn

accusative [ə'kjuːzətɪv] [1] N accusatif *m*; **in the ~** à l'accusatif [2] ADJ accusatif

accusatory [ə'kjuːzətərɪ] ADJ accusateur (-trice *f*)

accuse [ə'kjuːz] VT accuser (**sb of sth** qn de qch); **they ~d him of stealing the car** *or* **of having stolen the car** ils l'ont accusé d'avoir volé la voiture; (*Jur*) **they stand ~d of murder** ils sont accusés de meurtre

accused [ə'kjuːzd] N (*pl* **accused**) (*Jur*) accusé(e) *m(f)*, inculpé(e) *m(f)*

accuser [ə'kjuːzə^r] N accusateur *m*, -trice *f*

accusing [ə'kjuːzɪŋ] ADJ accusateur (-trice *f*)

accusingly [ə'kjuːzɪŋlɪ] ADV d'une manière accusatrice

accustom [ə'kʌstəm] VT habituer, accoutumer (**sb to sth** qn à qch, **sb to doing** qn à faire); **to ~ o.s. to** s'habituer à, s'accoutumer à

accustomed [ə'kʌstəmd] ADJ [a] (= *used*) habitué, accoutumé (**to à, to do, to doing** à faire); **to become** *or* **get ~ to sth/to doing** s'habituer *or* s'accoutumer à qch/à faire; **I am not ~ to such treatment** je n'ai pas l'habitude qu'on me traite (*subj*) de cette façon [b] (= *usual*) habituel, coutumier

AC/DC [ˌeɪsiːˈdiːsiː] [1] N (ABBR = **alternating current/direct current**) → **alternating**, **direct** [2] ADJ **he's ~*** il marche à voile et à vapeur*

ace [eɪs] [1] N [a] (*Cards, Dice, Dominoes*) as *m*; (*Tennis = shot*) ace *m*; **~ of diamonds** as *m* de carreau [b] (*fig*) **to have** *or* **keep an ~ up one's sleeve** avoir une carte maîtresse *or* un atout en réserve; (*Brit*) **to have the ~ in one's hand** ◊ **to have an ~ in the hole*** avoir un atout en réserve; **to play one's ~** jouer sa meilleure carte; **to hold all the ~s** avoir tous les atouts en main; **to come within an ~ of sth** être à deux doigts de qch → **clean** [c] (= *pilot, racing driver etc*) as *m*; (*US fig*) **he's ~s*** il est super* [2] ADJ super*; **an ~ driver** un as du volant [3] COMP ► **Ace Bandage**® N (*US*) bande *f* Velpeau®

acerbic [ə'sɜːbɪk] ADJ [*taste*] âpre; [*wit, humour*] acerbe, caustique

acerbity [ə'sɜːbɪtɪ] N âpreté *f*, aigreur *f*

acetate ['æsɪteɪt] N acétate *m*

acetic [ə'siːtɪk] ADJ acétique; **~ acid** acide *m* acétique

acetone ['æsɪtəʊn] N acétone *f*

acetylene [ə'setɪliːn] [1] N acétylène *m* [2] COMP ► **acetylene burner** N chalumeau *m* à acétylène ► **acetylene lamp** N lampe *f* à acétylène ► **acetylene torch** N = **acetylene**

burner ► **acetylene welding** N soudure *f* à l'acétylène

ache [eɪk] [1] VI faire mal, être douloureux; **my head ~s** j'ai mal à la tête; **to be aching all over** (*after exercise*) être courbaturé; (*from illness*) avoir mal partout; **it makes my heart ~** cela me brise *or* me fend le cœur; **her heart ~d for them** elle souffrait pour eux; (*fig*) **to be aching** *or* **to ~ to do** mourir d'envie de faire, brûler de faire [2] N [a] (*physical*) douleur *f*, souffrance *f*; **all his ~s and pains** toutes ses douleurs, tous ses maux; **he's always complaining of ~s and pains** il se plaint toujours d'avoir mal partout → **toothache** [b] (*fig*) peine *f* → **heartache**

achieve [ə'tʃiːv] [1] VT (*gen*) accomplir, réaliser; [+ *aim, standard*] atteindre, parvenir à; [+ *success*] obtenir; [+ *fame*] parvenir à; [+ *victory*] remporter; **what they have ~d** ce qu'ils ont accompli *or* réalisé; **how did you ~ that?** comment est-ce que vous avez réussi à faire ça?; **to ~ something in life** arriver à quelque chose dans la vie; **I feel I've really ~d something today** j'ai l'impression d'avoir fait quelque chose de valable aujourd'hui → **underachieve** [2] VI (= *be successful*) réussir

achievement [ə'tʃiːvmənt] [1] N [a] (= *success, feat*) exploit *m*, réussite *f* [b] (*Scol*) **the level of ~** le niveau des élèves [c] (*NonC* = *completion*) accomplissement *m*, réalisation *f* [2] COMP ► **achievement test** N (*Scol*) test *m* de niveau (*dans les écoles primaires*)

achiever [ə'tʃiːvə^r] N (= *successful person*) gagneur *m*, -euse *f*; **high-/low-~** sujet *m* doué/peu doué

Achilles [ə'kɪliːz] [1] N Achille *m* [2] COMP ► **Achilles' heel** N (*fig*) talon *m* d'Achille ► **Achilles' tendon** N (*Anat*) tendon *m* d'Achille

aching ['eɪkɪŋ] ADJ douloureux, endolori; (*fig*) **to have an ~ heart** avoir le cœur gros

achingly ['eɪkɪŋlɪ] ADV [*funny, sad, beautiful*] à pleurer

achromatic [ˌeɪkrəʊ'mætɪk] ADJ achromatique

achy* ['eɪkɪ] ADJ [*legs, muscles, joints*] douloureux; **I feel ~ all over** j'ai mal partout

acid ['æsɪd] [1] N [a] acide *m* [b] (*Drugs**) acide* *m*; **to drop ~** prendre de l'acide* [c] **Acid = Acid house** [2] ADJ [a] (= *sour*) acide [b] (*fig = sharp*) [*person*] revêche; [*voice*] aigre; [*remark*] mordant, acide [3] COMP ► **acid drop** N bonbon *m* acidulé ► **acid head*** N (*Drugs*) drogué(e) *m(f)* au LSD ► **Acid house** N acid music *f* ► **Acid house party** N acid party *f* ► **acid jazz** N acid jazz *m* ► **acid-proof** ADJ résistant aux acides ► **acid rain** N pluies *fpl* acides ► **acid rock** N (*Mus*) acid rock *m* ► **acid test** N (*fig*) test *m*; (*fig*) **to pass the ~ test** passer le test

acidic [ə'sɪdɪk] ADJ acide

acidify [ə'sɪdɪfaɪ] VT acidifier

acidity [ə'sɪdɪtɪ] N (*Chem, fig*) acidité *f*

acidly ['æsɪdlɪ] ADV acidement, d'un ton acide

acidulous [ə'sɪdjʊləs] ADJ acidulé

ack-ack ['æk'æk] [1] N défense *f* contre avions, DCA *f* [2] COMP ► **ack-ack fire** N tir *m* de DCA ► **ack-ack guns** NPL canons *mpl* antiaériens *or* de DCA

acknowledge [ək'nɒlɪdʒ] VT [a] (= *admit*) avouer, admettre; [+ *error*] reconnaître, avouer; **to ~ sb as leader** reconnaître qn pour chef; **to ~ o.s. beaten** s'avouer vaincu *or* battu [b] (*also* ~ **receipt of**) [+ *letter, parcel*] accuser réception de; **to ~ a gift from sb** remercier qn pour *or* d'un cadeau [c] (= *express thanks for*) [+ *person's action, services, help*] manifester sa gratitude pour, se montrer reconnaissant de; [+ *applause, cheers*] saluer pour [d] (= *indicate recognition of*) [+ *greeting*] répondre à; **I smiled at him but he didn't even ~ me** je lui ai souri mais il a fait comme s'il ne me voyait pas; **he didn't even**

~ my presence il a fait comme si je n'étais pas là; (*Jur*) **to ~ a child** reconnaître un enfant

acknowledged [ək'nɒlɪdʒd] ADJ [*leader, expert etc*] reconnu (de tous); [*child*] reconnu; [*letter*] dont on a accusé réception

acknowledgement [ək'nɒlɪdʒmənt] N [a] (*NonC*) reconnaissance *f*; [*of one's error etc*] aveu *m*; **in ~ of your help** en reconnaissance *or* en remerciement de votre aide [b] [*of money*] reçu *m*, récépissé *m*, quittance *f*; [*of letter*] accusé *m* de réception; (*in preface etc*) **~s** remerciements *mpl*; **to quote without ~** faire une citation sans mentionner la source

ACLU [ˌeɪsiːel'juː] N (ABBR = **American Civil Liberties Union**) Ligue *f* des droits de l'homme

acme ['ækmɪ] N point *m* culminant

acne ['æknɪ] N acné *f*

acolyte ['ækəʊlaɪt] N acolyte *m*

aconite ['ækənaɪt] N aconit *m*

acorn ['eɪkɔːn] [1] N (*Bot*) gland *m* [2] COMP ► **acorn cup** N cupule *f*

acoustic [ə'kuːstɪk] [1] ADJ acoustique → **coupler** [2] COMP ► **acoustic feature** N (*Phon*) trait *m* distinctif acoustique ► **acoustic feedback** N (*Recording*) effet *m* Larsen, réaction *f* acoustique ► **acoustic guitar** N guitare *f* acoustique ► **acoustic hood** N (*Comput*) capot *m* insonorisant ► **acoustic phonetics** N (*NonC: Phon*) phonétique *f* acoustique ► **acoustic regeneration** N = **acoustic feedback** ► **acoustic screen** N (*in office*) cloison *f* insonorisante

acoustically [ə'kuːstɪkəlɪ] ADV [*poor, perfect*] du point de vue de l'acoustique; [*play*] en acoustique

acoustics [ə'kuːstɪks] N [a] (*Phys*: + *sg vb*) acoustique *f* [b] [*of room etc*] (+ *pl vb*) acoustique *f*

ACPO ['ækpəʊ] N ABBR = **Association of Chief Police Officers**

acquaint [ə'kweɪnt] VT [a] (= *inform*) **to ~ sb with sth** aviser qn de qch, renseigner qn sur qch; **to ~ sb with the situation** mettre qn au courant *or* au fait de la situation [b] **to be ~ed with** [+ *person, subject*] connaître; [+ *fact*] savoir, être au courant de; **to become** *or* **get ~ed with sb** faire la connaissance de qn; **to become ~ed with the facts** prendre connaissance des faits; **to get ~ed** faire connaissance

acquaintance [ə'kweɪntəns] N [a] (*NonC*) connaissance *f*; **to make sb's ~** faire la connaissance de qn, faire connaissance avec qn; **to improve upon ~** gagner à être connu; **to have some ~ with French** avoir une certaine connaissance du français, savoir un peu le français; **a person of my ~** une connaissance → **claim** [b] (= *person*) relation *f*, connaissance *f*; **to have a wide circle of ~s** avoir des relations très étendues; **she's an ~ of mine** je la connais un peu, c'est une de mes relations; **old ~s** de vieilles connaissances *fpl*

acquaintanceship [ə'kweɪntənsʃɪp] N relations *fpl*, cercle *m* de connaissances; **a wide ~** de nombreuses relations *fpl*

acquiesce [ˌækwɪ'es] VI acquiescer, consentir; **to ~ in an opinion** se ranger à une opinion *or* à un avis; **to ~ in a proposal** donner son accord *or* son assentiment à une proposition

acquiescence [ˌækwɪ'esns] N consentement *m*, assentiment *m*

acquiescent [ˌækwɪ'esnt] ADJ consentant

acquire [ə'kwaɪə^r] VT [+ *house, car, knowledge, money, fame, experience*] acquérir; [+ *language*] apprendre; [+ *habit*] prendre, contracter; [+ *reputation*] se faire; **to ~ a taste for sth** prendre goût à qch; (*hum*) **she has ~d a new husband** elle s'est dotée d'un nouveau mari

acquired [ə'kwaɪəd] [1] ADJ acquis; **~ characteristic** caractère *m* acquis; **it's an ~ taste** on finit par aimer ça, c'est un goût qui s'acquiert

2 COMP ► **acquired immune deficiency syndrome** N syndrome *m* immunodéficitaire acquis

acquirement [əˈkwaɪəmənt] N (*NonC*) acquisition *f* (**of** de)

acquirer [əˈkwaɪərəʳ] N (*Fin*) acquéreur *m*

acquisition [ˌækwɪˈzɪʃən] N (*gen, Ling*) acquisition *f*; (* = person) recrue *f* (**to** pour); (*Fin*) **~ of holdings** prise *f* de participation

acquisitive [əˈkwɪzɪtɪv] ADJ (*for money*) âpre au gain; (= *greedy*) avide (**of** de); **~ instinct** instinct *m* de possession; **to have an ~ nature** avoir l'instinct de possession très développé

acquisitiveness [əˈkwɪzɪtɪvnɪs] N instinct *m* de possession, goût *m* de la propriété

acquit [əˈkwɪt] VT a (*Jur*) acquitter, décharger (**of** de) b **to ~ o.s. well in battle** bien se conduire *or* se comporter au combat; **it was a difficult job but he ~ted himself well** c'était une tâche difficile mais il s'en est bien tiré c [+ debt] régler, s'acquitter de

acquittal [əˈkwɪtl] N a (*Jur*) acquittement *m* b [of debt] acquittement *m*

acre [ˈeɪkəʳ] N ≈ demi-hectare *m*, ≈ arpent† *m*, ≈ acre *f*; **he owns a few ~s in Sussex** il possède de quelques hectares dans le Sussex; (*fig*) **the rolling ~s of the estate** la vaste étendue du domaine; (*fig*) **~s of*** des kilomètres et des kilomètres de → **god**

acreage [ˈeɪkərɪdʒ] N aire *f*, superficie *f*; **what ~ have you?** combien avez-vous d'hectares?; **to farm a large ~** cultiver *or* exploiter de grandes superficies

acrid [ˈækrɪd] ADJ (*lit*) âcre; (*fig*) [remark, style] acerbe, mordant

Acrilan® [ˈækrɪlæn] N Acrilan® *m*

acrimonious [ˌækrɪˈməʊnɪəs] ADJ acrimonieux

acrimoniously [ˌækrɪˈməʊnɪəslɪ] ADV avec acrimonie

acrimony [ˈækrɪmənɪ] N acrimonie *f*

acrobat [ˈækrəbæt] N acrobate *mf*

acrobatic [ˌækrəʊˈbætɪk] ADJ acrobatique

acrobatics [ˌækrəʊˈbætɪks] NPL (*lit*) acrobatie *f*; (*fig*) acrobaties *fpl*; (*lit*) **to do ~** faire des acrobaties *or* de l'acrobatie; (*fig*) **political/linguistic ~** des acrobaties *fpl* politiques/linguistiques

acronym [ˈækrənɪm] N acronyme *m*

Acropolis [əˈkrɒpəlɪs] N Acropole *f*

across [əˈkrɒs]

> When **across** is an element in a phrasal verb, eg **come across, run across, stumble across**, look up the verb.

1 PREP a (= from one side to other of) d'un côté à l'autre de; **~ it** d'un côté à l'autre; **a bridge ~ the river** un pont sur le fleuve; **to walk ~ the road** traverser la rue b (= on other side of) de l'autre côté de; **~ it** de l'autre côté; **he lives ~ the street (from me/him)** il habite en face (de chez moi/lui); **the shop ~ the road** le magasin d'en face, le magasin de l'autre côté de la rue; **territories ~ the sea** territoires *mpl* d'outre-mer; **from ~ the Channel** de l'autre côté de la Manche, d'outre-Manche c (= crosswise over) en travers de, à travers; **~ it** en travers; **to go ~ the fields** *or* **~ country** aller *or* prendre à travers champs; **a plank ~ a door** une planche en travers d'une porte; **with his arms folded ~ his chest** les bras croisés sur la poitrine d (*fig*) **they cut salaries ~ the board** ils ont réduit les salaires de tout le monde *or* à tous les niveaux; **prices fell ~ the board** les prix ont chuté partout

2 ADV (= from one side to other) **the river is 5km ~** le fleuve a 5 km de large; **the plate is 30cm ~** l'assiette fait 30 cm de diamètre; **to help sb ~** aider qn à traverser; (*fig*) **to get sth ~** faire comprendre qch (**to sb** à qn); **~ from** en face de

acrostic [əˈkrɒstɪk] N acrostiche *m*

acrylic [əˈkrɪlɪk] ADJ, N acrylique *m*

act [ækt] 1 N a (= deed) acte *m*; **in the ~ of doing** en train de faire; **caught in the ~** pris sur le fait *or* en flagrant délit b (*Jur*) loi *f* c [of play] acte *m*; (in circus etc) numéro *m*; (*Theat*) **they're a brilliant ~** ils font un numéro superbe; (*fig*) **a class ~** (= person) un crack*, un as*; **he's a class ~*** c'est un crack* *or* un as*; **it was a class ~*** (= performance etc) c'était génial*; **she'll be a hard *or* tough ~ to follow** il sera difficile de l'égaler; **he's just putting on an ~** il joue la comédie; (*fig*) **it's just an ~** c'est du cinéma; (*fig*) **to get in on the ~*** s'imposer; (*fig*) **to get one's ~ together*** se ressaisir, se reprendre en main

2 VI a (= do sth) agir; **the government must ~ now** le gouvernement doit agir immédiatement *or* prendre des mesures immédiates; **you have ~ed very generously** vous avez été très généreux; **to ~ for the best** faire pour le mieux; **to ~ on sb's behalf** ◊ **to ~ for sb** agir au nom de qn, représenter qn; (*Admin*) **the Board, ~ing by a majority** le conseil statuant à la majorité; (*Admin*) **~ing on a proposal from the Commission** sur proposition de la Commission b (= behave) agir, se comporter; **to ~ like a fool** agir *or* se comporter comme un imbécile c (*Theat*) jouer; **have you ever ~ed before?** avez-vous déjà fait du théâtre (*or* du cinéma)?; **she's not crying, she's only ~ing** elle ne pleure pas, elle fait semblant *or* elle joue la comédie d (= serve) servir, faire office (**as** de); **the table ~s as a desk** la table sert de bureau; **she ~s as his assistant** elle lui sert d'assistante e [medicine, chemical] (= have an effect) agir (**on** sur)

3 VT (*Theat*) [+ part] jouer, tenir; **to ~ Hamlet** jouer *or* tenir le rôle d'Hamlet, incarner Hamlet; (*Theat, fig*) **to ~ the part of ...** tenir le rôle de ...; (*fig*) **to ~ the fool*** *or* **~ stupid*** faire l'idiot(e)

4 COMP ► **Act of Congress** N loi *f* (adoptée par le Congrès) ► **act of faith** N acte *m* de foi ► **act of God** N catastrophe *f* naturelle ► **Act of Parliament** N loi *f* (adoptée par le Parlement) ► **act of war** N acte *m* de guerre ► **Acts of the Apostles** NPL (*Rel*) Actes *mpl* des Apôtres

► **act on** VT FUS = **act upon**

► **act out** VT SEP [+ event] faire un récit mimé de; [+ fantasies] vivre; [+ emotions] exprimer, mimer

► **act up*** VI [person] se conduire mal; **the car has started ~ing up** la voiture s'est mise à faire des caprices

► **act upon** VT FUS [+ advice, suggestion] suivre, se conformer à; [+ order] exécuter; **I ~ed upon your letter at once** j'ai fait le nécessaire dès que j'ai reçu votre lettre

acting [ˈæktɪŋ] 1 ADJ **~ headmaster** directeur *m* suppléant; **~ president/head of department/police superintendent** etc président *m*/chef *m* de section/commissaire *m* etc par intérim 2 N (*Cine, Theat* = performance) jeu *m*, interprétation *f*; **his ~ is very good** il joue très bien; **I like his ~** j'aime son jeu; **he has done some ~** il a fait du théâtre (*or* du cinéma)

actinic [ækˈtɪnɪk] ADJ actinique

actinium [ækˈtɪnɪəm] N actinium *m*

action [ˈækʃən] 1 N a (*NonC*) action *f*; **to put into ~** [+ plan] mettre à exécution; [+ one's principles, a suggestion] mettre en action *or* en pratique; **the time has come for ~** il est temps d'agir; **they want a piece** *or* **slice of the ~*** *or* **their share of the ~*** ils veulent être dans le coup*; **let's go where the ~ is*** allons là où ça se passe quelque chose*; **to take ~** agir, prendre des mesures; **to go into ~** entrer en action, passer à l'action → **1g**; **he needs prodding into ~** il faut le pousser pour qu'il agisse *or* qu'il passe à l'action; **telephone out of ~** appareil *m* en dérangement; **machine out of ~** machine *f* hors d'usage *or* hors service; (*lit, fig*) **to put sth out of ~** mettre qch hors d'usage *or* hors service; **his illness put him out of ~ for six weeks** sa maladie l'a mis hors de combat pendant six semaines; **through** *or* **by volcanic** etc **~** sous l'action des volcans etc b (= deed) acte *m*, action *f*; **to judge sb by his ~s** juger qn sur ses actes; **to suit the ~ to the word** joindre le geste à la parole; **~s speak louder than words** les actes sont plus éloquents que les paroles c (= effect) [of medicine, chemical] effet *m* d (*Theat*) [of play] intrigue *f*, action *f*; (*Cine*) **~!** moteur!; **the ~ (of the play) takes place in Greece** l'action (de la pièce) se passe en Grèce; **there's not enough ~ in the play** la pièce manque d'action e (*Jur*) procès *m*, action *f* en justice; **~ for damages/libel** procès *m* *or* action *f* en dommages-intérêts/en diffamation; **to bring an ~ against sb** intenter une action *or* un procès contre qn, poursuivre qn en justice f (*Tech*) mécanisme *m*, marche *f*; [of piano] action *f*, mécanique *f*; [of clock etc] mécanique *f* g (*Mil*) combat *m*; **to go into ~** [unit, person] aller *or* marcher au combat; [army] engager le combat; **killed in ~** tué à l'ennemi *or* au combat, tombé au champ d'honneur (*frm*); **he saw (some) ~ in North Africa** il a combattu *or* il a vu le feu en Afrique du Nord → **enemy**

2 VT (*Admin*) exécuter

3 COMP ► **action committee** N comité *m* d'action ► **action film** N film *m* d'action ► **action group** N groupe *m* d'action ► **action man** N (*pl* action men) aventurier *m* ► **action movie** N (*esp US*) = **action film** ► **action-packed** ADJ [film] plein d'action; [week-end] bien rempli ► **action painting** N tachisme *m* ► **action replay** N (*Brit TV Sport*) répétition *f* immédiate d'une séquence; (= slow-motion) ralenti *m* ► **action stations** NPL (*Mil*) postes *mpl* de combat; (*Mil, fig*) **~ stations!** à vos postes!

actionable [ˈækʃnəbl] ADJ [claim] recevable; [person] passible de poursuites

activate [ˈæktɪveɪt] 1 VT (also *Chem, Tech*) activer; (*Phys*) rendre radioactif 2 COMP ► **activated sludge** N boues *fpl* radioactives

activation [ˌæktɪˈveɪʃən] N (*NonC*) activation *f*

active [ˈæktɪv] 1 ADJ a [person, life, population] actif; [mind, imagination] vif, actif; [file, case] en cours; **~ volcano** volcan *m* en activité; **to take an ~ part in sth** prendre une part active à qch; **to be an ~ member of** *or* **be ~ in an organization** être un membre actif d'une organisation; **to give ~ consideration to sth** soumettre qch à une étude attentive; **we're giving ~ consideration to the idea of doing ...** nous examinons sérieusement la possibilité *or* le projet de faire ...; **in ~ employment** en activité; (*Med*) **~ childbirth** accouchement *m* sauvage *or* accroupi b (*Brit Mil*) **the ~ list** l'armée *f* active; **to be on the ~ list** être en activité (de service) c (*Gram*) **~ voice** voix *f* active, actif *m*; **in the ~ (voice)** à la voix active d (*Comm*) **~ assets** capital *m* productif; **~ money** monnaie *f* *or* argent *m* en circulation; **~ partner** partenaire *m* actif; **Germany has an ~ trade balance** l'Allemagne a une balance commerciale excédentaire

2 COMP ► **active duty** N (*esp US Mil*) = **active service** ► **active ingredient** N principe *m* actif ► **active service** N (*Brit Mil*) service *m* actif; **on ~ service** en campagne; **he saw ~ service in Italy and Germany** il a servi en Italie et en Allemagne ► **active suspension** N (*Aut*) suspension *f* active

actively ['æktɪvlɪ] ADV [campaign, support, promote, involve] activement; [encourage, discourage] vivement; [consider] sérieusement; **to be ~ seeking employment** rechercher activement un emploi

activism ['æktɪvɪzəm] N activisme m

activist ['æktɪvɪst] N activiste mf

activity [æk'tɪvɪtɪ] **1** N **a** (NonC) [of person] activité f; [of town, port] mouvement m **b** **activities** activités fpl, occupations fpl; **business activities** activités fpl professionnelles **2** COMP ► **activity holiday** N vacances fpl actives, vacances fpl à thème ► **activity method** N (Scol) méthode f active

actor ['æktər] N acteur m, comédien m

actress ['æktrɪs] N actrice f, comédienne f

actual ['æktjʊəl] **1** ADJ **a** (= real) [number, cost, reason] réel; [figures] exact; **there is no ~ contract** il n'y a pas vraiment or à proprement parler de contrat; **to take an ~ example ...** pour prendre un exemple concret ...; **an ~ fact** un fait réel; **in ~ fact** en fait; **you met an ~ film star*** vous avez rencontré une vraie star de cinéma?; **the film used the ~ people involved as actors** pour jouer dans ce film, on a fait appel à des gens qui avaient eux-mêmes vécu les événements; **~ size** grandeur f nature; **~ size: 15cm** taille réelle: 15 cm; **his ~ words were ...** les mots exacts qu'il a employés étaient ... **b** (= proper) **the ~ film doesn't start till 8.55** le film ne commence qu'à 20 h 55; **this is the ~ house** (as opposed to its outbuildings) voici la maison elle-même; (previously mentioned) voici la maison en question **2** **actuals** NPL (Fin) chiffres mpl réels **3** COMP ► **actual bodily harm** N (Jur) coups mpl et blessures fpl ► **actual total loss** N (Insurance) perte f totale absolue

actuality [ˌæktjʊˈælɪtɪ] N **a** (NonC) réalité f; **in ~** en réalité **b** **actualities** réalités fpl, conditions fpl réelles or actuelles

actualize ['æktjʊəlaɪz] VT réaliser; (Philos) actualiser

actually ['æktjʊəlɪ] ADV **a** (gen) en fait; (= truth to tell) en fait, à vrai dire; **~ I don't know him at all** en fait or à vrai dire je ne le connais pas du tout; **his name is Smith, ~** en fait, il s'appelle Smith; **the person ~ in charge is ...** la personne véritablement responsable or la personne responsable en fait, c'est ...; **~ you were quite right** en fait or au fond vous aviez entièrement raison; **I don't ~ feel like going** au fond je n'ai pas envie d'y aller, je n'ai pas vraiment envie d'y aller; **I'm in the middle of something ~** en fait, je suis en train de faire quelque chose; **~, before I forget, she asked me to give you this** au fait, avant que je n'oublie (subj) or que j'oublie (subj), elle m'a demandé de te donner ça; **I bet you've never done that!** — **I have** je parie que tu n'as jamais fait ça! — en fait, si; **so, you're a doctor?** — **a surgeon, ~** donc, vous êtes médecin? — chirurgien, plutôt **b** (= truly, even: often showing surprise) vraiment; **are you ~ going to buy it?** est-ce que tu vas vraiment l'acheter?; **if you ~ own a house** si vous êtes vraiment or bel et bien propriétaire d'une maison; **what did he ~ say?** qu'est-ce qu'il a dit exactement or au juste?; **did it ~ happen?** est-ce que ça s'est vraiment or réellement passé?; **it's ~ taking place right now** ça se produit en ce moment même

actuarial [ˌæktjʊˈɛərɪəl] ADJ actuariel; **~ expectation** espérance f mathématique; **~ tables** tableaux mpl d'espérance de vie

actuary ['æktjʊərɪ] N actuaire mf

actuate ['æktjʊeɪt] VT [+ device] mettre en marche

acuity [əˈkjuːɪtɪ] N acuité f

acumen ['ækjʊmen] N flair m, perspicacité f; **business ~** sens m aigu des affaires

acupressure ['ækjʊpreʃər] N shiatsu m

acupuncture ['ækjʊpʌŋktʃər] N acupuncture f, acuponcture f

acupuncturist [ˌækjʊˈpʌŋktʃərɪst] N acupuncteur m, -trice f, acuponcteur m, -trice f

acute [əˈkjuːt] **1** ADJ **a** (= extreme) [situation, problem, shortage] grave; [embarrassment] profond; [anxiety, pain] vif; **to live in ~ poverty** vivre dans une extrême pauvreté **b** (= keen, perceptive) [person] perspicace; [observer, mind] perspicace, pénétrant; [powers of observation] pénétrant; [intelligence] aigu (-guë f); **to have an ~ awareness of sth** être pleinement conscient de qch; **to have ~ hearing** avoir l'oreille fine; **to have an ~ sense of smell** avoir l'odorat très développé **c** (Med) [appendicitis, leukaemia, case] aigu (-guë f); **~ beds** lits mpl réservés aux urgences **d** (Ling) **e** = e accent aigu **2** COMP ► **acute accent** N (Ling) accent m aigu ► **acute angle** N (Geom) angle m aigu ► **acute-angled** ADJ acutangle

acutely [əˈkjuːtlɪ] ADV **a** (= extremely) [embarrassing, unhappy, difficult] extrêmement; [aware, conscious] pleinement **b** (= strongly) [feel, suffer] intensément **c** (= perceptively) [observe] avec perspicacité

acuteness [əˈkjuːtnɪs] N **a** (Med) violence f **b** [of person] perspicacité f; [of senses] finesse f

AD [eɪˈdiː] N **a** (ABBR = **Anno Domini**) ap. J-C **b** (US Mil) (ABBR = **active duty**) → **active**

ad* [æd] N (ABBR = **advertisement**) (= announcement) annonce f; (Comm) pub* f → **small**

A/D [eɪˈdiː] (ABBR = **analogue-digital**) → **analogue**

adage ['ædɪdʒ] N adage m

Adam ['ædəm] **1** N Adam m; **I don't know him from ~*** je ne le connais ni d'Ève ni d'Adam; **it's as old as ~** c'est vieux comme le monde, ça remonte au déluge **2** COMP ► **Adam's apple** N pomme f d'Adam

adamant ['ædəmənt] ADJ inflexible; **to be ~ that ...** maintenir catégoriquement que ...

adamantly ['ædəməntlɪ] ADV [say, refuse] catégoriquement; [opposed] résolument

adapt [əˈdæpt] **1** VT [+ device, room, plan, idea] adapter (**sth to sth** qch à qch); **to ~ o.s.** s'adapter, se faire (**to** à); **to ~ a novel for television** adapter un roman pour la télévision **2** VI s'adapter; **to ~s easily** il s'adapte bien or à tout; **she's very willing to ~** elle est très accommodante

adaptability [əˌdæptəˈbɪlɪtɪ] N [of person] faculté f d'adaptation

adaptable [əˈdæptəbl] ADJ adaptable

adaptation [ˌædæpˈteɪʃən] N adaptation f (**of** de, **to** à)

adapted [əˈdæptɪd] ADV adapté (**for, to** à, **from** de)

adapter [əˈdæptər] **1** N **a** (= device) adaptateur m; (Brit Elec) prise f multiple **b** (= person) adaptateur m, -trice f **2** COMP ► **adapter ring** N (Phot) bague f d'adaptation

adaption [əˈdæpʃən] N = adaptation

adaptive [əˈdæptɪv] ADJ [mechanism, process] d'adaptation; **the human body is remarkably ~** le corps humain s'adapte remarquablement bien; **to have an ~ approach to business** avoir une grande capacité d'adaptation en affaires

adaptor [əˈdæptər] N = adapter

ADC [eɪdiːˈsiː] N **a** (ABBR = **aide-de-camp**) → **aide** **b** (ABBR = **analogue-digital converter**) → **analogue**

▼ **add** [æd] VT **a** ajouter (**to** à); **~ some more pepper** ajoutez encore or rajoutez un peu de poivre; **to ~ insult to injury ...** (et) pour comble ...; **that would be ~ing insult to injury** ce serait vraiment dépasser la mesure or aller trop loin; **~ed to which** or **this ...** ajoutez à cela que ... → **added** **b** (Math) [+ figures]

additionner; [+ column of figures] totaliser **c** (= say besides) ajouter (**that** que); **there is nothing to ~** il n'y a rien à ajouter
► **add in** VT SEP [+ details] inclure, ajouter; [+ considerations] faire entrer en ligne de compte
► **add on** **1** VT SEP rajouter **2** **~-on** N, ADJ → **add-on**
► **add to** VT FUS [+ amount, numbers] augmenter; [+ anxiety, danger] accroître, ajouter à
► **add together** VT SEP [+ figures] additionner; [+ advantages, drawbacks] faire la somme de
► **add up** **1** VI [figures, results] se recouper; (Math) **these figures don't ~ up (right)** or **won't ~ up** ces chiffres ne font pas le compte (exact); (fig) **it all ~s up*** tout concorde, tout s'explique; (fig) **it doesn't ~ up*** cela ne rime à rien, il y a quelque chose qui cloche **2** VT SEP **a** [+ figures] additionner; **to ~ up a column of figures** totaliser une colonne de chiffres **b** [+ advantages, reasons] faire la somme de
► **add up to** VT FUS [figures] s'élever à, se monter à; (* fig = mean) signifier, se résumer à

added ['ædɪd] ADJ [advantage, benefit] supplémentaire; (on packets) **"no ~ colouring/salt"** « sans adjonction de colorants/de sel »

addendum [əˈdendəm] N (pl **addenda** [əˈdendə]) addendum m

adder ['ædər] N **a** (= snake) vipère f **b** (= machine) additionneur m

addict ['ædɪkt] **1** N (Med) intoxiqué(e) m(f); (fig) fanatique mf; **he's an ~ now** il ne peut plus s'en passer; **he's a yoga ~*** c'est un fanatique or un mordu* du yoga, il est accro* au yoga **~ drug, heroin 2** [əˈdɪkt] VT **to ~ o.s. to** devenir dépendant de

addicted [əˈdɪktɪd] ADJ adonné (**to** à); **to become ~ to ...** s'adonner à ...; **to ~ to drink/drugs** adonné à la boisson/aux stupéfiants; **he's ~ to drugs** c'est un toxicomane; **he's ~ to cigarettes** c'est un fumeur invétéré; (fig) **to be ~ to football*** se passionner pour le football, être un mordu* or un fana* du football

addiction [əˈdɪkʃən] N goût m (**to** pour); (Med) dépendance f, accoutumance f (**to** à); **this drug causes ~** cette drogue crée une dépendance or un effet d'accoutumance → **drug**

addictive [əˈdɪktɪv] ADJ **a** (Med, Psych) [drug] qui crée une dépendance or une accoutumance; **cigarettes are highly ~** les cigarettes créent une forte dépendance; **~ habit** dépendance f; **people with ~ personalities** les gens qui deviennent facilement dépendants **b** (fig = enjoyable) **crosswords/these biscuits are ~** les mots croisés/ces biscuits, c'est comme une drogue

adding ['ædɪŋ] N (NonC) = **addition a**; **~ machine** machine f à calculer

Addis Ababa ['ædɪsˈæbəbə] N Addis-Abeba

addition [əˈdɪʃən] N **a** (Math etc) addition f **b** (to tax, income, profit) surcroît m (**to** de); (= fact of adding) adjonction f; **in ~** de plus, de surcroît; **in ~ to** en plus de; **there's been an ~ to the family** la famille s'est agrandie; **he is a welcome ~ to our team** son arrivée enrichit notre équipe; **this is a welcome ~ to the series/collection** etc ceci enrichit la série/la collection etc

additional [əˈdɪʃənl] ADJ additionnel; (= extra) supplémentaire, de plus; (Fin) **~ benefits** avantages mpl supplémentaires; (Fin) **~ charge** supplément m de prix; (Jur) **~ agreement** accord m complémentaire

additionality [əˌdɪʃəˈnælɪtɪ] N (in EU) additionnalité f

additionally [əˈdɪʃnəlɪ] ADV **a** (= further) [worry, burden] davantage **b** (= moreover) en outre, de plus

additive ['ædɪtɪv] ADJ, N additif m; **~-free** sans additifs

addled ['ædld] ADJ (*lit*) [*egg*] pourri ; (*fig*) [*brain*] embrouillé

addle-headed· ['ædl'hedɪd] ADJ écervelé, brouillon

add-on ['ædɒn] **1** N **a** (*Comput*) accessoire *m* **b** (*Telec*) conférence *f* à trois **2** ADJ **a** (*Comput*) [*component, equipment, memory*] complémentaire **b** (*Aviat*) ~ **fare** tarif *m* complémentaire

▼ **address** [ə'dres] **1** N **a** [*of person*] (*on letter etc*) adresse *f* ; **to change one's** ~ changer d'adresse *or* de domicile ; **he has left this** ~ il n'est plus à cette adresse → **name** **b** (*Comput, Ling*) adresse *f* **c** (= *speech*) discours *m*, allocution *f* → **public** **d** (= *way of speaking*) conversation *f* ; (= *way of behaving*) abord *m* **e** **form** *or* **manner of** ~ titre *m* (*à employer en s'adressant à qn*) **f** (†, *liter*) ~**es** cour *f*, galanterie *f* ; **to pay one's** ~**es to a lady** faire la cour à une dame **2** VT **a** (= *put address on*) [+ *envelope, parcel*] mettre *or* écrire l'adresse sur ; (= *direct*) [+ *speech, writing, complaints*] adresser (**to** à) ; **this is** ~**ed to you** [*letter etc*] ceci vous est adressé ; [*words, comments*] ceci s'adresse à vous ; **to** ~ **o.s. to a task** s'atteler à une tâche ; **to** ~ **(o.s. to) an issue** aborder un problème **b** (= *speak to*) s'adresser à ; [+ *crowd*] haranguer ; (= *write to*) adresser un écrit à ; **he** ~**ed the meeting** il a pris la parole devant l'assistance ; **don't** ~ **me as "Colonel"** ne m'appelez pas « Colonel » → **chair** **3** COMP ► **address book** N carnet *m* d'adresses

addressee [,ædre'si:] N destinataire *mf* ; (*Ling*) allocutaire *mf*

addresser [ə'dresə'] N expéditeur *m*, -trice *f*

addressing [ə'dresɪŋ] N (*Comput*) adressage *m*

Addressograph® [ə'dresəʊgrɑ:f] N (*US*) machine à imprimer les adresses

addressor [ə'dresə'] N = **addresser**

adduce [ə'dju:s] VT (*frm*) [+ *proof, reason*] apporter, fournir ; [+ *authority*] invoquer, citer

adductor [ə'dʌktə'] N (*Anat*) adducteur *m*

Adelaide ['ædəleɪd] N Adélaïde

Aden ['eɪdn] N Aden ; **the Gulf of** ~ le golfe d'Aden

adenoidal ['ædɪnɔɪdl] ADJ adénoïde ; **in an** ~ **voice** en parlant du nez

adenoids ['ædɪnɔɪdz] NPL végétations *fpl* (adénoïdes)

adept ['ædept] **1** N expert *m* (**in, at** en) **2** [ə'dept] ADJ expert (**in, at** à, en, dans, **at doing** à faire), compétent (**in** en) ; **he's** ~ **with numbers** il manie bien les chiffres

adequacy ['ædɪkwəsɪ] N [*of reward, punishment, amount*] caractère *m* adéquat ; [*of description*] à-propos *m* ; [*of person*] compétence *f*, capacité *f* ; [*Ling*] adéquation *f*

adequate ['ædɪkwɪt] ADJ **a** (*gen*) adéquat ; [*amount, supply*] suffisant, adéquat ; [*tool*] adapté (**to sth** à qch), qui convient (**to sth** à qch) ; **to be** ~ **for sb's needs** répondre aux besoins de qn ; **to be** ~ **to the task** [*person*] être à la hauteur de la tâche ; **to be** ~ **to do sth** être adéquat pour faire qch ; **there are no words** ~ **to express my gratitude** les mots ne suffisent pas pour exprimer ma gratitude **b** (= *not outstanding*) [*performance, essay*] acceptable **c** [*Ling*] adéquat

adequately ['ædɪkwɪtlɪ] ADV de manière adéquate ; **I speak Turkish** ~ mes connaissances en turc sont suffisantes

adhere [əd'hɪə'] VI **a** (= *stick*) adhérer, coller (**to** à) **b** (= *be faithful to*) **to** ~ **to** [+ *party*] adhérer à, donner son adhésion à ; [+ *rule*] obéir à ; [+ *resolve*] persister dans, maintenir ; **the plan must be** ~**d to** il faut se conformer au plan

adherence [əd'hɪərəns] N adhésion *f* (**to** à)

adherent [əd'hɪərənt] N (= *sympathizer*) sympathisant(e) *m(f)*, partisan *m* ; (= *member of group*) adhérent(e) *m(f)* ; [*of religion, doctrine*] adepte *mf*

adhesion [əd'hi:ʒən] N (*lit, Med, Tech*) adhérence *f* ; (*fig* = *support*) adhésion *f*

adhesive [əd'hi:zɪv] **1** ADJ [*paper, label, stamp*] adhésif, collant ; [*dressing, plaster, properties*] adhésif → **self** **2** N adhésif *m* **3** COMP ► **adhesive tape** N (*Med*) sparadrap *m* ; (*Stationery*) ruban *m* adhésif, scotch® *m*

ad hoc [,æd'hɒk] **1** ADJ [*decision, solution, arrangement, measure, approach, payment*] ad hoc *inv* ; ~ **committee** comité *m* ad hoc ; **on an** ~ **basis** de manière ad hoc **2** ADV de manière ad hoc

adieu [ə'dju:] N, EXCL (*pl* **adieus** *or* **adieux** [ə'dju:z]) adieu *m* ; (*frm*) **to bid sb** ~† faire ses adieux à qn

ad infinitum [,ædɪnfɪ'naɪtəm] ADV à l'infini

ad interim [,æd'ɪntərɪm] **1** ADV par intérim **2** ADJ (*Jur*) [*judgement*] provisoire

adipose ['ædɪpəʊs] ADJ adipeux

adiposity [,ædɪ'pɒsɪtɪ] N adiposité *f*

adjacent [ə'dʒeɪsənt] ADJ (*Math*) [*angle*] adjacent ; [*street, room, building*] adjacent (**to** à) ; [*territory*] limitrophe

adjectival [,ædʒek'taɪvəl] ADJ adjectif, adjectival

adjectivally [,ædʒek'taɪvəlɪ] ADV [*use*] adjectivement

adjective ['ædʒektɪv] N adjectif *m*

adjoin [ə'dʒɔɪn] **1** VT être contigu à **2** VI se toucher, être contigu

adjoining [ə'dʒɔɪnɪŋ] ADJ voisin, attenant ; **the room** ~ **the kitchen** la pièce à côté de *or* attenant à la cuisine ; **in the** ~ **room** dans la pièce voisine *or* d'à côté

adjourn [ə'dʒɜ:n] **1** VT ajourner, reporter (**to, for, until** à) ; **to** ~ **sth until the next day** ajourner *or* remettre *or* reporter qch au lendemain ; **to** ~ **sth for a week** remettre *or* renvoyer qch à huitaine ; **to** ~ **a meeting** (= *break off*) suspendre la séance ; (= *close*) lever la séance **2** VI **a** (= *break off*) suspendre la séance ; (= *close*) lever la séance ; **the meeting** ~**ed** on a suspendu *or* levé la séance ; **Parliament** ~**ed** (= *concluded debate*) la séance de la Chambre a été levée ; (= *interrupted debate*) la Chambre a suspendu *or* interrompu la séance ; (= *recessed*) les vacances parlementaires ont commencé **b** (= *move*) se retirer (**to** dans, à), passer (**to** à) ; **to** ~ **to the drawing room** passer au salon

adjournment [ə'dʒɜ:nmənt] **1** N [*of meeting*] suspension *f*, ajournement *m* ; [*of case*] remise *f*, renvoi *m* ; (*Parl*) **to move the** ~ demander la clôture **2** COMP ► **adjournment debate** N (*Parl*) ≈ débat *m* de clôture

adjudge [ə'dʒʌdʒ] VT **a** (= *pronounce, declare*) déclarer ; **he was** ~**d the winner** il a été déclaré gagnant **b** (*Jur*) (= *pronounce*) prononcer, déclarer ; (= *decree*) décider ; (= *award*) [+ *costs, damages*] adjuger, accorder (**to sb** à qn) ; **to** ~ **sb bankrupt** déclarer qn en faillite ; **the court** ~**d that …** le tribunal a décidé que … ; **the court shall** ~ **costs** le tribunal statue sur les frais

adjudicate [ə'dʒu:dɪkeɪt] **1** VT [+ *competition*] juger ; [+ *claim*] décider **2** VI (*frm*) se prononcer (**upon** sur)

adjudication [ə,dʒu:dɪ'keɪʃən] N **a** jugement *m*, décision *f* (*du juge etc*) **b** (*Jur*) ~ **of bankruptcy** déclaration *f* de faillite

adjudicator [ə'dʒu:dɪkeɪtə'] N juge *m* (*d'une compétition etc*)

adjunct ['ædʒʌŋkt] **1** N **a** (= *thing*) accessoire *m* ; (= *person*) adjoint(e) *m(f)*, auxiliaire *mf* **b** (*Gram*) adjuvant *m* **2** ADJ **a** (= *added,*

connected) accessoire, complémentaire **b** (= *subordinate*) [*person*] subordonné, auxiliaire

adjure [ə'dʒʊə'] VT adjurer, supplier (**sb to do** qn de faire)

adjust [ə'dʒʌst] **1** VT **a** [+ *height, speed, flow, tool*] ajuster, régler ; [+ *knob, lever, length of clothes*] ajuster ; [+ *machine, engine, brakes*] régler, mettre au point ; [+ *formula, plan, production, terms*] ajuster, adapter (**to** à) ; (*Admin*) [+ *salaries, wages, prices*] réajuster, rajuster ; (= *correct*) [+ *figures etc*] rectifier ; [+ *differences*] régler ; [+ *hat, tie, clothes*] rajuster ; **you can** ~ **the seat to three different heights** on peut régler *or* ajuster le siège à trois hauteurs différentes ; (*TV*) **do not** ~ **your set** ne changez pas le réglage de votre téléviseur ; **to** ~ **sth to meet requirements** adapter qch aux conditions requises ; **the terms have been** ~**ed in your favour** on a ajusté les conditions en votre faveur ; **we have** ~**ed all salaries upwards/downwards** nous avons réajusté tous les salaires à la hausse/à la baisse ; **figures** ~**ed for seasonal variation(s)** données corrigées des variations saisonnières ; **to** ~ **o.s. to a new situation** s'adapter à une situation nouvelle ; **to** ~ **o.s. to new demands** faire face à de nouvelles exigences **b** (*Insurance*) **to** ~ **a claim** régler une demande d'indemnité **2** VI [*person*] s'adapter (**to** à) ; [*device, machine*] se régler, s'ajuster ; **the seat** ~**s to various heights** on peut régler *or* ajuster le siège à différentes hauteurs

adjustability [ə,dʒʌstə'bɪlɪtɪ] N (*NonC*) [*of seat, lamp*] possibilité *f* de réglage

adjustable [ə'dʒʌstəbl] **1** ADJ **a** (= *movable*) [*strap, chair, height, angle*] réglable ; [*rate*] ajustable ; [*dates, hours*] flexible ; (*Scol, Univ*) ~ **timetable** horaire *m* aménagé **2** COMP ► **adjustable spanner** N (*Brit*) clé *f* universelle

adjusted [ə'dʒʌstɪd] ADJ (*Psych*) **badly/well/normally** ~ mal/bien/normalement adapté

adjuster [ə'dʒʌstə'] N expert *m* (en assurances)

adjustment [ə'dʒʌstmənt] N (*to height, speed, knob, lever, machine, engine*) réglage *m* ; (*to clothes*) retouches *fpl* ; (*to plan, terms etc*) ajustement *m* (**to** de) ; (*to wages, prices etc*) réajustement *m*, rajustement *m* (**to** de) ; **the text needs a lot of** ~ ce texte a vraiment besoin d'une mise au point ; (*psychologically, socially*) **to make** ~**s** s'adapter (**to** à) ; **"exchange flat for house — cash** ~**"** « échangerais appartement contre maison : règlement de la différence au comptant »

adjustor [ə'dʒʌstə'] N = **adjuster**

adjutant ['ædʒətənt] N **a** (*Mil*) adjudant-major *m* **b** (*also* ~ **bird**) marabout *m*

Adlerian [æd'lɪərɪən] ADJ de Adler

ad lib [æd'lɪb] **1** ADV (*continue*) ad libitum, à volonté ; (*Mus*) ad libitum **2** N **ad-lib** (*Theat*) improvisation(s) *f(pl)*, paroles *fpl* improvisées ; (= *witticism*) mot *m* d'esprit impromptu **3** ADJ [*speech, performance, comment*] improvisé, impromptu **4** VI (*Theat etc*) improviser **5** VT (*: gen, also Theat*) [+ *speech, joke*] improviser

Adm. **a** (ABBR = **Admiral**) Am **b** (ABBR = **Admiralty**)

adman· ['ædmæn] N (*pl* **-men**) publicitaire *mf*

admass ['ædmæs] **1** N masse(s) *f(pl)* **2** COMP [*culture, life*] de masse, de grande consommation

admin· ['ædmɪn] N ABBR = **administration a**

administer [əd'mɪnɪstə'] **1** VT **a** (= *manage*) [+ *business, company*] gérer, administrer ; [+ *sb's affairs, funds*] gérer ; [+ *property*] régir ; [+ *public affairs, department, country*] administrer **b** (= *dispense*) [+ *alms*] distribuer (**to** à) ; [+ *justice*] rendre, dispenser ; [+ *punishment, sacraments, medicine, drug, relief*] administrer (**to** à) ; **to** ~ **the law** appliquer la loi ; **to** ~ **an oath to sb** faire prêter serment à qn ; **the oath has been** ~**ed to the witness** le témoin a prêté serment [2] COMP ► **administered price** N (US) prix m imposé (par le fabricant)

administrate [əd'mɪnɪˌstreɪt] VT gérer, administrer

administration [ədˌmɪnɪ'streɪʃən] [1] N [a] (NonC = management) [of business, company, public affairs, department, country] administration f; [of funds] gestion f; (= paperwork) administration f; (Jur) [of estate, inheritance] curatelle f; **his new job involves a lot of ~** son nouveau poste est en grande partie administratif [b] (esp US Pol) (= government) gouvernement m; (= ministry) ministère m; **under previous ~s** sous les gouvernements précédents [c] (NonC) [of justice, remedy, sacrament] administration f; [of oath] prestation f [2] COMP ► **administration order** N (Jur) ordonnance instituant l'administrateur judiciaire d'une succession ab intestat

administrative [əd'mɪnɪstrətɪv] [1] ADJ [work, post, staff] administratif; [skills] d'administrateur; [costs, expenses] d'administration; **~ machinery** rouages mpl administratifs [2] COMP ► **administrative assistant** N assistant(e) m(f) chargé(e) des tâches administratives ► **administrative court** N (US Jur) tribunal m administratif ► **administrative law** N droit m administratif ► **administrative officer** N employé(e) m(f) chargé(e) des tâches administratives

administratively [əd'mɪnɪstrətɪvlɪ] ADV d'un point de vue administratif

administrator [əd'mɪnɪstreɪtər] N [of business, public affairs etc] administrateur m, -trice f; (Jur) [of estate, inheritance] curateur m, -trice f

admirable [ˈædmərəbl] ADJ admirable, excellent

admirably [ˈædmərəblɪ] ADV admirablement

admiral [ˈædmərəl] N [a] (Naut) amiral m (d'escadre); **Admiral of the Fleet** ≈ Amiral m de France [b] (= butterfly) vanesse f, paon-de-jour m → **red**

admiralty [ˈædmərəltɪ] [1] N amirauté f [2] COMP ► **Admiralty Board** N (Brit) ≈ ministère m de la Marine ► **admiralty court** N (US Jur) tribunal m maritime

admiration [ˌædmə'reɪʃən] N admiration f (of, for pour); **to be the ~ of ...** faire l'admiration de ...

▼ **admire** [əd'maɪər] VT admirer

admirer [əd'maɪərər] N [a] admirateur m, -trice f [b] († = suitor) soupirant† m

admiring [əd'maɪərɪŋ] ADJ admiratif

admiringly [əd'maɪərɪŋlɪ] ADV avec admiration

admissibility [ədˌmɪsə'bɪlɪtɪ] N admissibilité f; (Jur, Fin) recevabilité f

admissible [əd'mɪsəbl] ADJ [a] (Jur) [document, appeal, witness] recevable; **to rule a piece of evidence ~** déclarer une preuve recevable; **~ as evidence/in court** recevable comme preuve/devant le tribunal [b] (= acceptable) [behaviour, subject] acceptable

admission [əd'mɪʃən] [1] N [a] (= entry) (to organization, university, school, hospital) admission f; (to museum, zoo, theatre) entrée f; **"~ free"** « entrée gratuite »; **"no ~ to minors"** « entrée interdite aux mineurs »; **a visa is necessary for ~ to this country** il faut un visa pour entrer dans ce pays; **~ to a school** admission f à une école; **to gain ~ to sb** trouver accès auprès de qn; **to gain ~ to a school/club** être admis dans une école/un club; **to grant sb ~ to a society** admettre qn dans une association [b] (= person admitted) entrée f [c] (Jur) [of evidence etc] acceptation f, admission f [d] (= confession) aveu m; **by** or **on one's own ~** de son propre aveu; **it's an ~ of guilt** en fait, c'est un aveu

[2] COMP ► **admission fee** N droits mpl d'admission ► **admissions form** N (US Univ) dossier m d'inscription ► **admissions office** N (US Univ) service m des inscriptions ► **admissions officer** N (Univ) responsable mf du service des inscriptions

▼ **admit** [əd'mɪt] [1] VT [a] (= let in) [+ person] laisser entrer, faire entrer; [+ light, air] laisser passer, laisser entrer; **children not ~ted** entrée interdite aux enfants; **this ticket ~s two** ce billet est valable pour deux personnes [b] (= have space for) [halls, harbours etc] contenir, (pouvoir) recevoir [c] (= acknowledge, recognize) reconnaître, admettre (that que); **to ~ the truth of sth** reconnaître or admettre que qch est vrai; **he ~ted that this was the case** il a reconnu or admis que tel était le cas; **I must ~ that ...** je dois reconnaître or admettre que ...; **I must ~ I was wrong** ◊ **I was wrong I ~** je reconnais que j'ai eu tort, j'ai eu tort, j'en conviens [d] [criminal, wrongdoer] avouer (that que); [+ crime, murder etc] reconnaître avoir commis; **he ~ted stealing the books** il a reconnu avoir volé les livres; **you'll never get him to ~ it** vous ne le lui ferez jamais avouer or reconnaître; **to ~ one's guilt** reconnaître sa culpabilité, s'avouer coupable [e] [+ claim] faire droit à; (Jur) **to ~ sb's evidence** admettre comme valable le témoignage de qn, prendre en considération les preuves fournies par qn

[2] COMP ► **admitting office** N (US Med) service m des admissions

► **admit of** VT FUS admettre, permettre; **it ~s of no delay** cela n'admet or ne peut souffrir aucun retard → **excuse**

► **admit to** VT FUS reconnaître; [+ crime] reconnaître avoir commis; **to ~ a feeling of ...** avouer avoir un sentiment de ...

admittance [əd'mɪtəns] N droit m d'entrée, admission f (to sth à qch), accès m (to sth à qch, to sb auprès de qn); **I gained ~ to the hall** on m'a laissé entrer dans la salle; **I was denied** or **refused ~** on m'a refusé l'entrée; **~: £5** droit d'entrée: 5 livres; **"no ~"** « accès interdit au public »; **no ~ except on business** accès interdit à toute personne étrangère au service

admittedly [əd'mɪtɪdlɪ] ADV **~ this is true** il faut reconnaître or convenir que c'est vrai; **it's only a theory, ~, but ...** il est vrai que ce n'est qu'une théorie, mais ...

admixture [əd'mɪkstʃər] N mélange m, incorporation f; **X with an ~ of Y** X additionné de Y

admonish [əd'mɒnɪʃ] VT [a] (= reprove) admonester, réprimander (for doing pour avoir fait, about, for pour, à propos de) [b] (= warn) avertir, prévenir (against doing de ne pas faire), mettre en garde (against contre); (Jur) avertir [c] (= exhort) exhorter, engager (to do à faire) [d] (liter = remind) **to ~ sb of a duty**† rappeler qn à un devoir

admonishment [əd'mɒnɪʃmənt] N (frm) [a] (= rebuke) remontrance f, réprimande f [b] (= warning) avertissement m

admonition [ˌædmə'nɪʃən] N [a] (= rebuke) remontrance f, admonestation f [b] (= warning) avertissement m, admonition f; (Jur) avertissement m

ad nauseam [ˌæd'nɔːsɪæm] ADV [repeat] ad nauseam, à satiété; [do] jusqu'à saturation, à satiété; **to talk ~ about sth** raconter des histoires à n'en plus finir sur qch

adnominal [æd'nɒmɪnl] ADJ, N (Ling) adnominal m

ado [ə'duː] N agitation f; **much ~ about nothing** beaucoup de bruit pour rien; **without further** or **more ~** sans plus de cérémonie

adobe [ə'dəʊbɪ] [1] N pisé m [2] COMP ► **adobe wall** N mur m d'adobe

adolescence [ˌædəʊ'lesns] N adolescence f

adolescent [ˌædəʊ'lesnt] ADJ, N adolescent(e) m(f)

Adonis [ə'dəʊnɪs] N (Myth, fig) Adonis m

adopt [ə'dɒpt] VT [a] [+ child] adopter [b] [+ idea, method] adopter; [+ career] choisir; (Pol) [+ motion] adopter; [+ candidate] choisir; (Jur, Admin) [+ wording] retenir

adopted [ə'dɒptɪd] ADJ [child] adopté; [country] d'adoption, adoptif; **~ son** fils m adoptif; **~ daughter** fille f adoptive

adoption [ə'dɒpʃən] [1] N [of child, country, law] adoption f; [of career, idea, method] choix m; **a Londoner by ~** un Londonien d'adoption [2] COMP ► **adoption agency** N organisme spécialisé dans les adoptions

adoptive [ə'dɒptɪv] ADJ [parent, child] adoptif; [country] d'adoption

adorable [ə'dɔːrəbl] ADJ adorable

adorably [ə'dɔːrəblɪ] ADV **she is ~ sweet** elle est absolument adorable; **he's ~ innocent** il est d'une naïveté charmante

adoration [ˌædə'reɪʃən] N adoration f

adore [ə'dɔːr] VT adorer

adoring [ə'dɔːrɪŋ] ADJ [expression] d'adoration; [eyes] remplis d'adoration; **his ~ wife** sa femme qui est en adoration devant lui

adoringly [ə'dɔːrɪŋlɪ] ADV avec adoration

adorn [ə'dɔːn] VT [+ room] orner (with de); [+ dress] orner, parer (with de); **to ~ o.s.** se parer

adornment [ə'dɔːnmənt] N [a] (in room) ornement m; (on dress) parure f [b] (NonC) décoration f

ADP [ˌeɪdiː'piː] N (ABBR = automatic data processing) → **automatic**

adrate* [ˈædreɪt] N tarif m publicitaire or des annonces

adrenal [ə'driːnl] [1] ADJ surrénal [2] N (also ~ gland) surrénale f

adrenalin(e) [ə'drenəlɪn] N adrénaline f; (fig) **he felt the ~ flowing** il a senti son pouls s'emballer

Adriatic [ˌeɪdrɪ'ætɪk] [1] ADJ [coast] adriatique [2] N **~ (Sea)** (mer f) Adriatique f

adrift [ə'drɪft] ADV, ADJ (Naut) à la dérive; (fig) à l'abandon; **to go ~** [ship] aller à la dérive; (fig) **to be (all) ~** divaguer; (fig) **to turn sb ~** laisser qn se débrouiller tout seul; (fig) **to come ~*** [wire, connection] se détacher; [plans] tomber à l'eau; (Sport) **to be five points/seconds ~ of ...** être cinq points/secondes derrière ...

adroit [ə'drɔɪt] ADJ adroit, habile

adroitly [ə'drɔɪtlɪ] ADV adroitement, habilement

adroitness [ə'drɔɪtnɪs] N adresse f, dextérité f

adspeak* [ˈædspiːk] N style m or jargon m de publicité

ADT [ˌeɪdiː'tiː] N (US, Can) ABBR = **Atlantic Daylight Time**

adulate [ˈædjʊleɪt] VT aduler, flagorner

adulation [ˌædjʊ'leɪʃən] N adulation f

adulatory [ˌædjʊ'leɪtərɪ, (US) 'ædʒələtɔːrɪ] ADJ élogieux

adult [ˈædʌlt] [1] N adulte mf; (Cine etc) **~s only** réservé aux adultes, interdit aux moins de 18 ans [2] ADJ [a] [person, animal] adulte; **we were very ~ about it** nous nous sommes comportés en adultes [b] [film, book] pour adultes (seulement) [3] COMP ► **adult classes** NPL cours mpl pour adultes ► **adult education, adult learning** N enseignement m pour adultes ► **adult literacy** N alphabétisation f des adultes

adulterate [ə'dʌltəreɪt] [1] VT frelater, falsifier; **~d milk** lait m falsifié [2] ADJ [ə'dʌltərɪt] [goods, wine] falsifié, frelaté

adulteration [əˌdʌltə'reɪʃən] N frelatage m, falsification f

► **LANGUAGE IN USE:** **admire** 13 **admit** 15.1, 18.1, 18.3, 26.3

adulterer [ə'dʌltərər] N adultère *m*

adulteress [ə'dʌltərɪs] N femme *f* adultère

adulterous [ə'dʌltərəs] ADJ adultère

adultery [ə'dʌltərɪ] N adultère *m*

adulthood ['ædʌlthʊd] N âge *m* adulte

adumbrate ['ædʌmbreɪt] VT esquisser, ébaucher ; [+ *event*] faire pressentir, préfigurer

ad val. ['æd'væl] ADJ, ADV (*Comm*) ABBR = **ad valorem**

ad valorem [ædvə'lɔːrəm] ADJ, ADV (*Comm*) ad valorem, sur la valeur

▼ **advance** [əd'vɑːns] **1** N **a** (= *progress, movement forward*) avance *f*, marche *f* en avant ; [*of science, ideas*] progrès *mpl* ; (*Mil*) avance *f*, progression *f* ; **with the ~ of (old) age** avec l'âge ; **to make ~s in technology** faire des progrès en technologie **b** (*NonC*) **in ~** [*book, warn, prepare, announce*] à l'avance ; [*thank, pay, decide*] à l'avance, d'avance ; **to send sb on in ~** envoyer qn en avant ; **£10 in ~** 10 livres d'avance ; **he arrived in ~ of the others** il est arrivé en avance sur les autres ; **to be in ~ of one's time** être en avance sur *or* devancer son époque ; **a week in ~** une semaine à l'avance ; (*Rail*) **luggage in ~** bagages *mpl* enregistrés **c** (*in prices, wages*) hausse *f*, augmentation *f* (**in** de) **d** (= *sum of money*) avance *f* (**on** sur) ; **an ~ against security** une avance sur nantissement **2 advances** NPL (= *overtures of friendship*) avances *fpl* ; **to make ~s to sb** faire des avances à qn **3** VT **a** (= *move forward*) [+ *date, time*] avancer ; (*Mil*) [+ *troops*] avancer ; [+ *work, knowledge, project*] faire progresser *or* avancer ; [+ *interest, growth*] développer ; [+ *cause*] promouvoir ; (= *promote*) [+ *person*] élever, promouvoir (**to** à) **b** (= *suggest, propose*) [+ *reason, explanation*] avancer ; [+ *opinion*] avancer, émettre **c** (= *pay on account*) avancer, faire une avance de ; (= *lend*) prêter **d** (*US Pol*) [+ *campaign*] organiser **4** VI **a** (= *go forward*) avancer, s'avancer (**on, towards** vers) ; [*army*] avancer (**on** sur) ; (*during a battle*) [*troops*] se porter en avant ; **he ~d upon me** il est venu vers *or* a marché sur moi ; **the advancing army** l'armée *f* en marche **b** (= *progress*) [*work, civilization, mankind*] progresser, faire des progrès ; [*person*] (*in rank*) recevoir de l'avancement ; (*Mil*) monter en grade **c** (= *rise*) [*prices*] monter, augmenter **5** COMP ► **advance booking** N "**~ booking advisable**" « il est conseillé de louer les places à l'avance » ; **~ booking (office)** (guichet *m* de) location *f* ► **advance copy** N [*of book*] exemplaire *m* de lancement ; [*of speech*] texte *m* distribué à l'avance (*à la presse*) ► **advance deposit** N dépôt *m* préalable ► **advance factory** N usine-pilote *f* ► **advance guard** N (*Mil*) avant-garde *f* ► **advance man** N (*pl* **advance men**) (*US Pol*) organisateur *m* (*de campagne électorale*) ► **advance notice** N préavis *m*, avertissement *m* ► **advance party** N (*Mil*) groupe *m* de reconnaissance ; (*fig*) éclaireurs *mpl* ► **advance payment** N (*Fin*) paiement *m* anticipé *or* par anticipation ► **advance post** N (*Mil*) poste *m* avancé ► **advance publicity** N publicité *f* d'amorçage ► **advance warning** N = **advance notice**

advanced [əd'vɑːnst] **1** ADJ [*student, society, ideas, stage*] avancé ; [*child*] avancé, en avance ; [*disease*] à un stade avancé ; [*level, studies, class*] supérieur (-eure *f*) ; [*test, skill*] poussé ; [*design*] sophistiqué ; [*equipment*] de pointe ; **~ mathematics/physics** cours *m* supérieur de mathématiques/physique ; **he is very ~ for his age** il est très avancé *or* très en avance pour son âge ; **at an ~ age** à un âge avancé ; **~ in years** d'un âge avancé ; **a man of ~ years** un homme d'âge avancé ; **the day/season is well ~** la journée/saison est bien avancée **2** COMP ► **advanced gas-cooled reactor** N (*Nucl Phys*) réacteur *m* à gaz avancé ► **Advanced level** N (*Brit Scol: frm*) = **A level** ; → A ► **advanced standing** N (*US Univ*) **to receive ~ standing** ≈ être admis par équivalence

advancement [əd'vɑːnsmənt] N **a** (= *improvement*) progrès *m*, avancement *m* **b** (= *promotion*) avancement *m*, promotion *f*

advantage [əd'vɑːntɪdʒ] **1** N **a** avantage *m* ; **to have an ~ over sb** ◊ **to have the ~ of sb** avoir un avantage sur qn ; **that gives you an ~ over me** cela vous donne un avantage sur moi ; **to get the ~ of sb** prendre l'avantage sur qn (**by doing** en faisant) ; **to have the ~ of numbers** avoir l'avantage du nombre (**over** sur) ; **to take ~ of sb** profiter de qn ; [*employer etc*] exploiter qn ; (*sexually*) abuser de qn ; **I took ~ of the opportunity** j'ai profité de l'occasion ; **to turn sth to (one's) ~** tirer parti de qch, tourner qch à son avantage ; **I find it to my ~** j'y trouve mon compte ; **it is to his ~ to do it** c'est dans son intérêt de le faire ; **to the best** le plus avantageusement possible ; **this dress shows her off to ~** cette robe l'avantage **b** (*Tennis*) avantage *m* ; (*Rugby*) **to play the ~ rule** laisser jouer la règle de l'avantage **2** VT avantager ; **~d** (= *wealthy*) privilégié

advantageous [ˌædvən'teɪdʒəs] ADJ avantageux (**to** pour)

advantageously [ˌædvən'teɪdʒəslɪ] ADV de façon avantageuse

advent ['ædvənt] **1** N **a** venue *f*, avènement *m* **b** (*Rel*) **Advent** l'Avent *m* **2** COMP ► **Advent Calendar** N calendrier *m* de l'Avent ► **Advent Sunday** N dimanche *m* de l'Avent

Adventist ['ædvəntɪst] N adventiste *mf*

adventitious [ˌædvən'tɪʃəs] ADJ fortuit, accidentel ; (*Bot, Med*) adventice

adventure [əd'ventʃər] **1** N aventure *f* ; **to have an ~** avoir une aventure **2** VI s'aventurer, se risquer (**on** dans) **3** COMP [*story, film*] d'aventures ► **adventure holiday** N (*Brit*) circuit *m* aventure ► **adventure playground** N (*Brit*) aire *f* de jeux

adventurer [əd'ventʃərər] N aventurier *m*

adventuress [əd'ventʃərɪs] N aventurière *f*

adventurism [əd'ventʃərɪzəm] N aventurisme *m*

adventurist [əd'ventʃərɪst] **1** N (*Pol: also* **political ~**) aventuriste *mf* ; (*Comm*) aventurier *m*, -ière *f* **2** ADJ (*Pol*) aventuriste ; (*Comm*) sans scrupules

adventurous [əd'ventʃərəs] ADJ [*person*] aventureux, audacieux ; [*journey*] aventureux, hasardeux

adventurously [əd'ventʃərəs.lɪ] ADV aventureusement, audacieusement

adverb ['ædvɜːb] N adverbe *m*

adverbial [əd'vɜːbɪəl] ADJ adverbial

adverbially [əd'vɜːbɪəlɪ] ADV [*use*] adverbialement

adversarial [ˌædvə'seərɪəl] ADJ [*politics*] de confrontation ; **the ~ system** le système de débat contradictoire

adversary ['ædvəsərɪ] N adversaire *mf*

adverse ['ædvɜːs] ADJ [*effect, reaction, consequences*] négatif ; [*conditions, comment, decision*] défavorable ; [*publicity, weather*] mauvais ; [*wind*] contraire ; **~ weather conditions** conditions *fpl* météorologiques défavorables

adversely ['ædvɜːslɪ] ADV défavorablement ; **to affect sth ~** avoir un effet défavorable sur qch ; **to comment ~ on sth** faire des commentaires défavorables sur qch

adversity [əd'vɜːsɪtɪ] **1** N **a** (*NonC*) adversité *f* ; **in ~** dans l'adversité **b** (= *event*) malheur *m*

advert[1] [əd'vɜːt] VI (*frm*) **to ~ to sth** faire référence à qch, se référer à qch

advert[2]* ['ædvɜːt] N (*Brit*) (ABBR = **advertisement**) (= *announcement*) annonce *f* (publicitaire) ; (*Comm*) publicité *f*, pub* *f*

advertise ['ædvətaɪz] **1** VT **a** (*Comm etc*) [+ *goods*] faire de la publicité pour ; **I've seen that soap ~d on television** j'ai vu une publicité pour ce savon à la télévision **b** (*in newspaper etc*) **to ~ a flat (for sale)** mettre *or* insérer une annonce pour vendre un appartement ; **I saw it ~d in a shop window** j'ai vu une annonce là-dessus dans une vitrine **c** (= *draw attention to*) afficher ; **don't ~ your ignorance!** inutile d'afficher votre ignorance ! ; **don't ~ the fact that ...** essaie de ne pas trop laisser voir que ..., ne va pas crier sur les toits que ... **2** VI **a** (*Comm*) faire de la publicité *or* de la réclame ; **it pays to ~** la publicité paie **b** chercher par voie d'annonce ; **to ~ for a flat/a secretary** faire paraître une annonce pour trouver un appartement/une secrétaire

▼ **advertisement** [əd'vɜːtɪsmənt] N **a** (*Comm*) réclame *f*, publicité *f* ; (*TV*) spot *m* publicitaire ; (*Cine, Press, Rad, TV*) **~s** publicité *f* ; **I saw an ~ for that soap in the papers** j'ai vu une réclame *or* une publicité pour ce savon dans les journaux ; **I made tea during the ~s** j'ai fait le thé pendant que passait la publicité ; (*in newspaper etc*) **he's not a good ~** *or* **an ~ for his school** il ne constitue pas une bonne réclame pour son école **b** (*private: in newspaper etc*) annonce *f* ; (*Brit*) **~ column** petites annonces *fpl* ; **to put an ~ in a paper** mettre une annonce dans un journal ; **I got it through an ~** je l'ai eu par *or* grâce à une annonce ► **classified, small** **c** (*NonC*) réclame *f*, publicité *f* ; (*fig*) **his arrival received no ~** son arrivée n'a pas été annoncée → **self**

advertiser ['ædvətaɪzər] N annonceur *m*

advertising ['ædvətaɪzɪŋ] **1** N (= *activity*) publicité *f* ; (= *advertisements*) réclames *fpl* ; **a career in ~** une carrière dans la publicité **2** COMP [*firm, work*] publicitaire ► **advertising agency** N agence *f* de publicité ► **advertising campaign** N campagne *f* publicitaire ► **advertising manager** N directeur *m*, -trice *f* de la publicité ► **advertising medium** N support *m* publicitaire ► **advertising rates** NPL tarifs *mpl* publicitaires ► **advertising revenues** NPL recettes *fpl* publicitaires ► **Advertising Standards Authority** N (*Brit*) ≈ Bureau *m* de vérification de la publicité → **jingle**

advertorial [ˌædvə'tɔːrɪəl] **1** N publireportage *m* **2** ADJ de publireportage

▼ **advice** [əd'vaɪs] N **a** (*NonC*) conseils *mpl*, avis *m* ; **a piece of ~** un avis, un conseil ; **to seek ~ from sb** demander conseil à qn ; **to take medical/legal ~** consulter un médecin/un avocat ; **to take** *or* **follow sb's ~** suivre le(s) conseil(s) de qn ; (*Press*) **~ column** courrier *m* du cœur **b** (*Comm* = *notification*) avis *m* ; **as per ~ of** *or* **from ...** suivant avis de ... ; **~ note** avis *m* ; **~ of dispatch** avis *m* d'expédition

advisability [əd.vaɪzə'bɪlɪtɪ] N opportunité *f* (**of sth** de qch, **of doing** de faire)

▼ **advisable** [əd'vaɪzəbl] ADJ conseillé, recommandé ; **it is ~ to be vaccinated** il est conseillé de se faire vacciner ; **I do not think it ~ for you to come** je ne vous conseille pas de venir

▼ **advise** [əd'vaɪz] **1** VT **a** (= *give advice to*) conseiller, donner des conseils à (**sb on** *or* **about sth** qn sur *or* à propos de qch) ; **to ~ sb to do sth** conseiller à qn de faire qch, recommander à qn de faire qch ; **to ~ sb against sth** déconseiller qch à qn ; **to ~ sb against doing** conseiller à qn de ne pas faire **b** (= *recommend*) [+ *course of action*] recommander ; **I shouldn't ~ you to see him** je ne vous conseillerais *or* recommanderais pas d'aller le voir ; **you would be well/ill ~d to wait** vous feriez bien/vous auriez tort d'attendre c (= *inform*) **to ~ sb of sth** aviser *or* informer qn de qch, faire part à qn de qch 2 COMP ► **advising bank** N (*Fin*) banque *f* notificatrice

advisedly [əd'vaɪzɪdlɪ] ADV en connaissance de cause

advisement [əd'vaɪzmənt] N (*US*) **to take sth under ~** considérer qch avec soin

adviser, advisor [əd'vaɪzəʳ] N conseiller *m*, -ère *f*; (*Scol Admin*) **French/maths ~** conseiller *m*, -ère *f* pédagogique de français/de maths → **educational, legal, spiritual**

advisory [əd'vaɪzərɪ] 1 ADJ [*group, board, role, work*] consultatif; [*service*] de conseils; **in an ~ capacity** à titre consultatif 2 COMP ► **advisory committee** N (*Pol*) comité *m* consultatif ► **advisory opinion** N (*Jur*) avis *m* consultatif de la cour

advocacy ['ædvəkəsɪ] N [*of cause etc*] plaidoyer *m* (*of* en faveur de)

advocate ['ædvəkɪt] 1 N a (= *upholder*) [*of cause etc*] défenseur *m*, avocat(e) *m(f)*; **to be an ~ of** être partisan(e) de; **to become the ~ of** se faire le champion (*or* la championne) de → **devil** b (*Scot Jur*) avocat *m* (plaidant) → **lord**; → LAWYER 2 ['ædvəkeɪt] VT recommander, préconiser

advt (ABBR = **advertisement**) publicité *f*

adz(e) [ædz] N herminette *f*, doloire *f*

AEA [ˌeɪiː'eɪ] N (*Brit*) (ABBR = **Atomic Energy Authority**) ≈ CEA *m*

AEC [ˌeɪiː'siː] N (*US*) (ABBR = **Atomic Energy Commission**) ≈ CEA *m*

AEEU [ˌeɪiːiː'juː] N (*Brit*) (ABBR = **Amalgamated Engineering and Electrical Union**) *syndicat*

Aegean [iː'dʒiːən] ADJ égéen; **~ (Sea)** (mer *f*) Égée *f*; **the ~ Islands** les îles *fpl* de la mer Égée

Aegeus [iː'dʒiːəs] N Égée *m*

aegis, egis (*US*) ['iːdʒɪs] N égide *f*; **under the ~ of ...** sous l'égide de ...

aegrotat [ˈaɪɡrəʊˌtæt] N (*Brit Univ*) équivalence *f* d'obtention d'un examen (*accordée à un bon étudiant malade*)

Aeneas [iː'niːəs] N Énée *m*

Aeneid [ɪ'niːɪd] N Énéide *f*

aeolian [iː'əʊlɪən] ADJ éolien; **~ harp** harpe *f* éolienne

Aeolus ['iːələs] N Éole *m*

aeon ['iːən] N temps *m* infini, période *f* incommensurable; **through ~s of time** à travers des éternités

aerate ['ɛəreɪt] VT [+ *liquid*] gazéifier; [+ *blood*] oxygéner; [+ *soil*] retourner; **~d water** eau *f* gazeuse

aerial ['ɛərɪəl] 1 ADJ a (= *in the air*) aérien b (= *immaterial*) irréel, imaginaire 2 N (*esp Brit: Telec etc*) antenne *f* → **indoor** 3 COMP ► **aerial cableway** N téléphérique *m* ► **aerial camera** N appareil *m* photo pour prises de vues aériennes ► **aerial input** N puissance *f* reçue par l'antenne ► **aerial ladder** N (*US*) échelle *f* pivotante ► **aerial mast** N mât *m* d'antenne ► **aerial photograph** N photographie *f* aérienne ► **aerial railway** N téléphérique *m* ► **aerial survey** N levé *m* aérien ► **aerial tanker** N ravitailleur *m* en vol

aerie ['ɛərɪ] N (*esp US*) aire *f* (*d'aigle etc*)

aero... ['ɛərəʊ] PREF aéro...

aerobatics [ˌɛərəʊ'bætɪks] NPL acrobatie(s) *f(pl)* aérienne(s)

aerobic [ɛə'rəʊbɪk] ADJ (*Chem*) aérobic; [*exercises*] d'aérobic

aerobics [ɛə'rəʊbɪks] N (*NonC*) aérobic *f*; **to do ~** faire de l'aérobic

aerodrome ['ɛərədrəʊm] N (*Brit*) aérodrome *m*

aerodynamic [ˌɛərəʊdaɪ'næmɪk] ADJ aérodynamique

aerodynamically [ˌɛərəʊdaɪ'næmɪkəlɪ] ADV

[*efficient*] d'un point de vue aérodynamique; [*designed, built*] de façon aérodynamique

aerodynamics [ˌɛərəʊdaɪ'næmɪks] N (*NonC*) aérodynamique *f*

aero-engine ['ɛərəʊˌendʒɪn] N aéromoteur *m*

aerofoil ['ɛərəʊfɔːl], **airfoil** (*US*) N (*Aviat*) plan *m* de sustentation

aerogram ['ɛərəʊɡræm] N a (= *air letter*) aérogramme *m* b (= *radio telegram*) radiotélégramme *m*

aerograph ['ɛərəʊɡræf] N météorographe *m*

aerolite ['ɛərəlaɪt] N aérolithe *m*

aeromodelling ['ɛərəʊˌmɒdlɪŋ] N aéromodélisme *m*

aeronaut ['ɛərənɔːt] N aéronaute *mf*

aeronautic(al) [ˌɛərə'nɔːtɪk(əl)] 1 ADJ aéronautique 2 COMP ► **aeronautic(al) engineering** N aéronautique *f*

aeronautics [ˌɛərə'nɔːtɪks] N (*NonC*) aéronautique *f*

aeroplane ['ɛərəpleɪn] N (*Brit*) avion *m*

aerosol ['ɛərəsɒl] 1 N a (= *system*) aérosol *m* b (= *container, contents*) bombe *f* 2 COMP [*insecticide, paint*] en aérosol, en bombe; [*perfume*] en atomiseur

aerospace ['ɛərəʊspeɪs] ADJ [*industry, project*] aérospatial

Aeschylus ['iːskələs] N Eschyle *m*

Aesculapius [ˌiːskjʊ'leɪpɪəs] N Esculape *m*

Aesop ['iːsɒp] N Ésope *m*; **~'s Fables** les fables *fpl* d'Ésope

aesthete, esthete (*US*) ['iːsθiːt] N esthète *mf*

aesthetic(al), esthetic(al) (*US*) [iːs-'θetɪk(əl)] ADJ esthétique

aesthetically, esthetically (*US*) [iːs'θetɪkəlɪ] ADV esthétiquement

aestheticism, estheticism (*US*) [iːs'θetɪsɪzəm] N esthétisme *m*

aesthetics, esthetics (*US*) [iːs'θetɪks] N (*NonC*) esthétique *f*

aether ['iːθəʳ] N = **ether**

aetiology [ˌiːtɪ'ɒlədʒɪ] N étiologie *f*

AEU [ˌeɪiː'juː] N (*Brit*) (ABBR = **Amalgamated Engineering Union**) *ancien syndicat*

a.f. [eɪ'ef] N (ABBR = **audio frequency**) audiofréquence *f*

AFA [ˌeɪef'eɪ] N (*Brit*) ABBR = **Amateur Football Association**

afar [ə'fɑːʳ] ADV (*liter*) au loin; **from ~** de loin

AFB [ˌeɪef'biː] N (*US Mil*) ABBR = **Air Force Base**

AFC [ˌeɪef'siː] N a (ABBR = **Association Football Club**) AFC b ABBR = **automatic frequency control**

AFDC [ˌeɪefdiː'siː] N (*US Admin*) ABBR = **Aid to Families with Dependent Children**

affability [ˌæfə'bɪlɪtɪ] N affabilité *f*, amabilité *f*

affable ['æfəbl] ADJ affable

affably ['æfəblɪ] ADV avec affabilité, affablement

affair [ə'fɛəʳ] N a (= *event*) affaire *f*; **it was a scandalous ~** ce fut un scandale; **it was an odd ~ altogether** c'était vraiment (une histoire *or* une affaire) bizarre; **~ of honour** affaire *f* d'honneur; **the Suez ~** l'affaire *f* de Suez b (*esp Brit* = *concern*) affaire *f*; **this is not her ~** ce n'est pas son affaire, cela ne la regarde pas; **that's my ~** c'est mon affaire, ça ne me regarde que moi; **it's not your ~ what I do in the evenings** ce que je fais le soir ne te regarde pas c (= *business of any kind*) **~s** affaires *fpl*; **in the present state of ~s** les choses étant ce qu'elles sont, étant donné les circonstances actuelles; **it was a dreadful state of ~s** la situation était épouvantable; **~s of state** affaires *fpl* d'État; **to put one's ~s in order** (= *business*) mettre de l'ordre dans ses affaires; (= *belongings*) mettre ses affaires en ordre; **your pri-**

vate **~s don't concern me** votre vie privée ne m'intéresse pas; **she never interferes with his business ~s** elle n'intervient jamais dans ses activités professionnelles *or* dans ses affaires → **current, foreign** d (*also* **love ~**) liaison *f*, aventure *f*; **to have an ~ with sb** avoir une liaison *or* une aventure avec qn e (* = *material object*) affaire *f*, chose *f*

affect [ə'fekt] 1 VT a (= *have effect on*) [+ *result, experiment, numbers*] avoir un effet *or* des conséquences sur, modifier; [+ *decision, career, the future*] influer sur; (*Jur*) avoir une incidence sur; (= *have detrimental effect on*) [+ *person*] atteindre, toucher; [+ *conditions, substance, health*] détériorer; **this will certainly ~ the way we approach the problem** cela va certainement influer sur la façon dont nous aborderons le problème; **you mustn't let it ~ you** ne te laisse pas décourager *or* abattre par ça b (= *concern*) concerner, toucher; **this decision ~s all of us** cette décision nous concerne tous; **it does not ~ me personally** cela ne me touche pas personnellement c (*emotionally* = *move*) émouvoir, affecter; (= *sadden*) affecter, toucher; **she was deeply ~ed by the news** elle a été très affectée *or* touchée par la nouvelle d [*disease*] [+ *organ, powers of recuperation*] attaquer, atteindre; [*drug*] agir sur e (= *feign*) [+ *ignorance, surprise*] affecter, feindre f († *or frm* = *have liking for*) affectionner; **she ~s bright colours** elle a une prédilection pour *or* elle affectionne les couleurs vives 2 N ['æfekt] (*Psych*) affect *m*

affectation [ˌæfek'teɪʃən] N a (= *pretence*) affectation *f*, simulation *f*; **an ~ of interest/indifference** une affectation d'intérêt/d'indifférence b (= *artificiality*) affectation *f*, manque *m* de naturel; **her ~s annoy me** ses manières affectées *or* ses poses *fpl* m'agacent

affected [ə'fektɪd] ADJ (= *insincere*) [*person, behaviour*] affecté, maniéré; [*accent, clothes*] affecté; **to be ~** [*person*] poser

affectedly [ə'fektɪdlɪ] ADV avec affectation, d'une manière affectée

affecting [ə'fektɪŋ] ADJ touchant, émouvant

affection [ə'fekʃən] N a (*NonC* = *fondness*) affection *f*, tendresse *f* (*for, towards* pour); **to win sb's ~(s)** se faire aimer de qn, gagner l'affection *or* le cœur de qn; **I have a great ~ for her** j'ai beaucoup d'affection pour elle b (*Med*) affection *f*, maladie *f*

affectionate [ə'fekʃnɪt] ADJ [*person, tone*] affectueux, tendre; [*memories*] tendre; (*letter-ending*) **your ~ daughter** votre fille affectionnée

affectionately [ə'fekʃnɪtlɪ] ADV affectueusement; (*letter-ending*) **yours ~** (bien) affectueusement (à vous)

affective [ə'fektɪv] ADJ affectif (*also Ling*)

affidavit [ˌæfɪ'deɪvɪt] N (*Jur*) déclaration *f* écrite sous serment; **to swear an ~** (*to the effect that*) déclarer par écrit sous serment (que)

affiliate [ə'fɪlɪeɪt] 1 VT affilier (*to, with* à); **to ~ o.s.** s'affilier (*to, with* à); (*Comm*) **~d company** (*gen*) filiale *f*; (*on balance sheet*) société *f* liée *or* apparentée 2 [ə'fɪlɪət] N membre *m* affilié

affiliation [əˌfɪlɪ'eɪʃən] 1 N a (*Comm etc*) affiliation *f* b (*Jur*) attribution *f* de paternité c (= *connection*) affiliation *f*, attaches *fpl* 2 COMP ► **affiliation order** N jugement *m* en constatation de paternité ► **affiliation proceedings** NPL action *f* en recherche de paternité

affinity [ə'fɪnɪtɪ] N a (*gen, Bio, Chem, Ling, Math, Philos*) affinité *f* (*with, to* avec, *between* entre); (= *connection, resemblance*) ressemblance *f*, rapport *m*; **the ~ of one thing to an-**

other la ressemblance d'une chose avec une autre [b] (*Jur* = *relationship*) affinité *f* (**to, with** avec) [c] (= *liking*) attrait *m*, attraction *f* (**with, for** pour); **there is a certain ~ between them** ils ont des affinités

affirm [ə'fɜːm] VT affirmer, soutenir (**that** que)

affirmation [,æfə'meɪʃən] N affirmation *f*, assertion *f*

affirmative [ə'fɜːmətɪv] [1] N (*Ling*) affirmatif *m*; **in the ~** à l'affirmatif; (*gen*) **to answer in the ~** répondre affirmativement *or* par l'affirmative [2] ADJ affirmatif; **if the answer is ~** si la réponse est affirmative, si la réponse est positive; (*US Pol, Ind*) **~ action** mesures *fpl* de discrimination positive

---

AFFIRMATIVE ACTION

Ce terme désigne les mesures de discrimination positive prises aux États-Unis dans les années 60 en faveur des femmes et des minorités ethniques. À l'instigation de l'administration Kennedy, les catégories sous-représentées ont bénéficié d'un système de quotas en matière d'emploi et pour les inscriptions universitaires. En 1972, la loi sur l'égalité de l'emploi (Equal Employment Opportunities Act) a institué une commission chargée de faire respecter ces mesures. En réaction, certains groupes majoritaires (hommes et Blancs, par exemple), qui s'estimaient lésés par cette discrimination à l'envers, se sont mobilisés pour faire assouplir la politique de quotas.

---

affirmatively [ə'fɜːmətɪvlɪ] ADV affirmativement

affix [ə'fɪks] [1] VT [+ *seal, signature*] apposer, ajouter (**to** à); [+ *stamp*] coller (**to** à) [2] ['æfɪks] N (*Gram*) affixe *m*

afflict [ə'flɪkt] VT affliger; **to be ~ed by** *or* **with** gout être affligé *or* souffrir de la goutte

affliction [ə'flɪkʃən] N [a] (*NonC*) affliction *f*, détresse *f*; **people in ~** les gens dans la détresse [b] **the ~s of old age** les misères *fpl* de la vieillesse

affluence ['æfluəns] N (= *plenty*) abondance *f*; (= *wealth*) richesse *f*; **to rise to ~** parvenir à la fortune

affluent ['æfluənt] [1] ADJ (= *plentiful*) abondant; (= *wealthy*) riche; **to be ~** vivre dans l'aisance; **the ~ society** la société d'abondance [2] N (*Geog*) affluent *m*

afflux ['æflʌks] N [a] (*Med*) afflux *m* [b] (*of people etc*) affluence *f*, afflux *m*

afford [ə'fɔːd] VT (*following can, could, be able to*) **to be able to ~** to buy sth avoir les moyens d'acheter qch; **I can't ~ a new hat** je ne peux pas m'offrir *or* me payer* un nouveau chapeau; **he can well ~ a new car** il a tout à fait les moyens de s'acheter une nouvelle voiture; (*fig*) **he can't ~ (to make) a mistake** il ne peut pas se permettre de (faire) une erreur; **I can't ~ the time to do it** je n'ai pas le temps de le faire ~ ill [b] (= *provide*) fournir, procurer; **to ~ sb great pleasure** procurer un grand plaisir à qn; **this will ~ me an opportunity to say** ceci me fournira l'occasion de dire

affordable [ə'fɔːdəbl] ADJ abordable; **easily ~** très abordable

afforest [æ'fɒrɪst] VT reboiser

afforestation [æ,fɒrɪs'teɪʃən] N boisement *m*; **~ policy** politique *f* de boisement

affranchise [æ'fræntʃaɪz] VT affranchir

affray [ə'freɪ] N échauffourée *f*, rixe *f*

affricate ['æfrɪkɪt] N (*Phon*) affriquée *f*

affright [ə'fraɪt] (†, *liter*) [1] VT effrayer, terrifier [2] N effroi *m*, épouvante *f*

affront [ə'frʌnt] [1] VT [a] (= *insult*) faire un affront à, outrager [b] (= *face*) affronter, braver [2] N affront *m*, insulte *f*

Afghan ['æfgæn] [1] ADJ afghan [2] N [a] Afghan(e) *m(f)* [b] (*Ling*) afghan *m* [c] (*also* **~ hound**) lévrier *m* afghan

Afghani [æf'gænɪ] [1] ADJ afghan [2] N [a] (= *person*) Afghan(e) *m(f)* [b] (*Ling*) afghan *m*

Afghanistan [æf'gænɪstæn] N l'Afghanistan *m*

aficionado [ə,fɪʃjə'nɑːdəʊ] N **he's an ~ of jazz** *or* **a jazz ~** c'est un fana* *or* un mordu* du jazz

afield [ə'fiːld] ADV **far ~** [*be*] au loin; [*go*] loin; **countries further ~** pays *mpl* plus lointains; **very far ~** très loin; **too far ~** trop loin; **to explore farther ~** pousser plus loin l'exploration; (*fig*) **to go farther ~ for help/support** chercher plus loin de l'aide/un soutien

afire [ə'faɪə] ADJ, ADV (*liter*) (*lit*) en feu, embrasé (*liter*); (*fig*) enflammé (**with** de)

aflame [ə'fleɪm] (*liter*) [1] [a] (= *on fire*) en flammes [b] (*with light, colour*) embrasé (*liter*); **to be ~ with colour** briller de vives couleurs, flamboyer [c] (*emotionally*) [*cheeks*] enflammé; **she was ~ with anger/pride** elle était enflammée de colère/d'orgueil; **his heart was ~ with passion** son cœur était enflammé par la passion [2] ADV (*with light, colour*) **to set sth ~** embraser qch

AFL-CIO [,eɪef'el,siː'aɪ'əʊ] (ABBR = **American Federation of Labor and Congress of Industrial Organizations**) *fédération des syndicats indépendants américains*

afloat [ə'fləʊt] [1] ADV [a] (= *on water*) **to stay** *or* **keep ~** [*person*] garder la tête hors de l'eau; [*object*] surnager; [*boat*] rester à flot; **to set/keep a boat ~** mettre/maintenir un bateau à flot; **the largest passenger ship ~** le plus grand paquebot en exploitation [b] (= *on board ship*) sur l'eau, en mer; **service ~** service *m* à bord; **to serve ~** servir en mer [c] (= *solvent*) **to stay** *or* **keep ~** [*person, company*] se maintenir à flot; **to set a business/scheme ~** lancer une affaire/un projet [d] (= *in circulation*) **to be ~** [*rumour*] circuler, être en circulation [e] (*Fin*) **to keep bills ~** faire circuler des effets [2] ADJ (*Comm*) **~ price** prix *m* à flot *or* à bord

aflutter [ə'flʌtə] ADJ **to set sb's heart ~** faire battre le cœur de qn

afocal ['eɪ,fəʊkəl] ADJ (*Phot*) afocal

afoot [ə'fʊt] ADV [a] (= *in progress*) **there is something ~** il se prépare quelque chose; **there is a plan ~ to do** on a formé le projet *or* on envisage de faire [b] (†, *liter*) [*go, come*] à pied; **to be ~** être sur pied

afore [ə'fɔː] CONJ (†† *or dial*) avant que de, avant que; **he went ~** avant que de partir, avant qu'il ne parte

aforementioned [ə,fɔː'menʃənd], **aforenamed** [ə'fɔːneɪmd], **aforesaid** [ə'fɔːsed] ADJ (*Jur etc*) susdit, susmentionné

aforethought [ə'fɔːθɔːt] ADJ prémédité → **malice**

afoul [ə'faʊl] ADV (*esp US*) **to run ~ of sb** se mettre qn à dos, s'attirer le mécontentement de qn; **to run ~ of a ship** entrer en collision avec un bateau

afp [,eɪef'piː] N (ABBR = **alpha-fetoprotein**) AFP *f*

afraid [ə'freɪd] ADJ [a] (= *frightened*) **to be ~** avoir peur; **don't be ~!** n'ayez pas peur!, ne craignez rien!; **to look ~** avoir l'air effrayé; **to be ~ of sb/sth** avoir peur de qn/qch, craindre qn/qch; **you have nothing to be ~ of** vous n'avez aucune raison d'avoir peur; **he is not ~ of hard work** il n'a pas peur de travailler dur; **she's furious — I was ~ of that** elle est furieuse — c'est ce que je craignais; **I am ~ of hurting him** *or* **that I might hurt him** j'ai peur *or* je crains de lui faire mal; **I am ~ he will** *or* **might hurt me** je crains *or* j'ai peur qu'il (ne) me fasse mal; **I am ~ to go** *or* **of going** je n'ose pas y aller, j'ai peur d'y aller; **to be ~ for sb/sth** avoir peur pour qn/qch; **to be ~ for one's life** craindre pour sa vie → **shadow** [b] (*expressing polite regret*) **I'm ~ I can't do it** je regrette *or* je suis désolé, (mais) je ne pourrai pas le faire; **I am ~ I shall not be able to come**

je suis désolé de ne pouvoir venir, je crains de ne pas pouvoir venir; **are you going?** — **I'm ~ not/I'm ~ so** vous y allez? — hélas non/hélas oui; **it's a bit stuffy in here, I'm ~** je regrette *or* je suis désolé, mais on étouffe un peu ici

afresh [ə'freʃ] ADV de nouveau; **to start ~** recommencer

Africa ['æfrɪkə] N l'Afrique *f* → **south**

African ['æfrɪkən] [1] ADJ africain → **south** [2] N Africain(e) *m(f)* [3] COMP ► **African-American** ADJ afro-américain ♦ N Afro-Américain(e) *m(f)* ► **African elephant** N éléphant *m* d'Afrique ► **African National Congress** N Congrès *m* national africain ► **African violet** N saintpaulia *m*

Afrikaans [,æfrɪ'kɑːns] [1] N (*Ling*) afrikaans *m* [2] ADJ afrikaans

Afrikaner [,æfrɪ'kɑːnə] [1] N Afrikaner *mf* [2] ADJ afrikaner

afro ['æfrəʊ] [1] ADJ **to go ~** s'africaniser; **~ hair style** coiffure *f* afro* [2] COMP ► **Afro-American** ADJ afro-américain ♦ N Afro-Américain(e) *m(f)* ► **Afro-Asian** ADJ afro-asiatique ► **Afro-Caribbean** ADJ afro-antillais

aft [ɑːft] (*Naut*) [1] ADV sur *or* à *or* vers l'arrière; **wind dead ~** vent *m* en poupe, vent *m* arrière [2] ADJ [*cabin, deck, engine*] arrière

after ['ɑːftə]

When **after** is an element in a phrasal verb, eg **ask after, look after, take after**, look up the verb.

[1] PREP [a] (*time*) après; **~ that** après cela, après ça; **~ dinner** le dîner → **6**; **~ this date** passé cette date; **~ a week/ten minutes** au bout d'une semaine/de dix minutes; **shortly ~ 10 o'clock** peu après 10 heures; **it was ~ 2 o'clock** il était plus de 2 heures; (*US*) **it was 20 ~ 3** il était 3 heures 20; **~ seeing her** après l'avoir vue; **~ which he sat down** après quoi il s'est assis; **~ what has happened** après ce qui s'est passé → **day, hour** [b] (*order*) après; **the noun comes ~ the verb** le substantif vient après le verbe; **~ Germany, America is Britain's second-biggest customer** l'Amérique est le plus gros client de la Grande-Bretagne après l'Allemagne; **~ you, sir** après vous, Monsieur; **~ you with the salt*** passez-moi le sel s'il vous plaît (quand vous aurez fini) [c] (*place*) **come in and shut the door ~ you** entrez et (re)fermez la porte (derrière vous); **he shut the door ~ her** il a refermé la porte derrière elle [d] **~ all** après tout; **to succeed ~ all** réussir malgré *or* après tout; **~ all, no one made him go** après tout, personne ne l'a obligé à aller; **~ all, you'd expect her to say that** évidemment, il n'est pas étonnant qu'elle dise ça; **it's only two days, ~ all** après tout *or* au fond, ça fait seulement deux jours [e] (*often expressing surprise*) après; **~ all I said to him** après tout ce que je lui ai dit; **~ all I've done for you!** après tout ce que j'ai fait pour toi!, quand je pense à tout ce que j'ai fait pour toi!; **~ all that happened, it's not surprising** avec tout ce qui est arrivé *or* quand on pense à tout ce qui est arrivé ça n'a rien d'étonnant [f] (*succession*) **day ~ day** jour après jour, tous les jours; (*for*) **kilometre ~ kilometre** sur des kilomètres et des kilomètres; **kilometre ~ kilometre of forest** des kilomètres et des kilomètres de forêt; **you tell me lie ~ lie** tu me racontes mensonge sur mensonge; **she gave one excuse ~ another** elle a avancé une excuse après l'autre; **time ~ time** maintes (et maintes) fois; **she ate three biscuits, one ~ the other** elle a mangé trois biscuits l'un après l'autre *or* d'affilée; **they went out one ~ the other** (= *individually*) ils sont sortis les uns

après les autres ; (= *in a line*) ils sont sortis à la file
g (*manner = according to*) ~ **El Greco** d'après Le Gréco ; ~ **the old style** à la vieille mode, à l'ancienne → **heart, name**
h (*pursuit, inquiry*) **to be** ~ **sb/sth** chercher qn/qch ; (*after loss, disappearance etc*) rechercher qn/qch ; **the police are** ~ **him for this robbery** il est recherché par la police or la police est à ses trousses pour ce vol ; **she's a green hat** elle cherche or voudrait un chapeau vert ; **what are you** ~ ? (= *want*) qu'est-ce que vous voulez or désirez ? ; (= *have in mind*) qu'avez-vous en tête ? ; **I see what he's** ~ je vois où il veut en venir ; (*fig* = *nagging*) **she's always** ~ **her children*** elle est toujours après ses enfants*
2 ADV (*place, order, time*) après, ensuite ; **for years** ~ pendant des années après cela ; **soon** ~ bientôt après ; **the week** ~ la semaine d'après, la semaine suivante ; **what comes** ~? qu'est-ce qui vient ensuite ?, et ensuite ?
3 CONJ après (que) ; ~ **he had closed the door, she spoke** après qu'il eut fermé la porte, elle parla ; ~ **he had closed the door, he spoke** après avoir fermé la porte, il a parlé
4 ADJ **in** ~ **years** plus tard (dans la vie), par la suite
5 NPL (*Brit* = *dessert*) ~**s*** le dessert
6 COMP ► **after-dinner drink** N digestif *m* ► **after-dinner speaker** N orateur *m* (de fin de repas) ; **he's a good ~-dinner speaker** il fait de très bonnes allocutions or de très bons discours (de fin de repas) ► **after-hours drinking** N consommation *f* de boissons après la fermeture des pubs (or du pub) → **hour** ► **after-image** N image *f* rémanente ► **after-lunch** ADJ **to have an ~-lunch nap** faire la sieste ► **after-sales service** N (*Comm*) service *m* après-vente ► **after-school** ADJ [*activities etc*] extrascolaire ; **~-school club** (*Brit*) or **center** (*US*) garderie *f* ► **after-sun** ADJ [*lotion, cream*] après-soleil ♦ N (= *lotion*) lotion *f* après-soleil ; (= *cream*) crème *f* après-soleil ► **after-tax** ADJ après impôts ► **after-treatment** N (*Med*) soins *mpl* ; (*Tex*) apprêt *m*

afterbirth ['ɑːftɜːb:θ] N (*Med*) placenta *m*

afterburner ['ɑːftɜːbɜːnəʳ], **afterburning** ['ɑːftɜːbɜːnɪŋ] N postcombustion *f*

aftercare ['ɑːftɜːkɛəʳ] N [*of convalescent*] postcure *f* ; [*of appliance, product*] entretien *m* ; (*prisoner*) ~ assistance *f* (aux anciens détenus)

afterdeck ['ɑːftɜːdɛk] N (*Naut*) arrière-pont *m*, pont *m* arrière

aftereffects ['ɑːftɜːrɪˌfɛkts] NPL [*of events etc*] suites *fpl*, répercussions *fpl* ; [*of treatment*] réaction *f* ; [*of illness*] séquelles *fpl* ; (*Psych*) after-effect *m*

afterglow ['ɑːftɜːgləʊ] N [*of setting sun*] dernières lueurs *fpl*, derniers reflets *mpl* ; [*of person*] (*after exercise*) sensation *f* de bien-être

afterlife ['ɑːftɜːlaɪf] N vie *f* future

aftermath ['ɑːftɜːmæθ] N suites *fpl*, conséquences *fpl*, séquelles *fpl* ; **the** ~ **of war** le contrecoup or les conséquences de la guerre

afternoon ['ɑːftɜː'nuːn] **1** N après-midi *m* or *f* ; **in the** ~ ◊ ~**s*** l'après-midi ; **at 3 o'clock in the** ~ à 3 heures de l'après-midi ; **on Sunday** ~**(s)** le dimanche après-midi ; **every** ~ **of the 2 December** l'après-midi du 2 décembre, le 2 décembre dans l'après-midi ; **he will go this** ~ il ira cet après-midi ; **good ~!** (*on meeting sb*) bonjour ! ; (*on leaving sb*) au revoir ! ; **have a nice ~!** bon après-midi ! ; **in the early** ~ tôt dans l'après-midi ; **this** ~ cet après-midi ; **tomorrow/yesterday** ~ demain/hier après-midi ; **the next** or **following** ~ l'après-midi suivant ; **the** ~ **before** l'après-midi précédent ; **every Sunday** ~ le dimanche après-midi ; **one summer** ~ (par) un après-midi d'été

2 COMP [*lecture, class, train, meeting etc*] (de) l'après-midi ► **afternoon performance** N (*Theat*) matinée *f* ► **afternoon tea** N thé *m* (de cinq heures)

afterpains ['ɑːftɜːpeɪnz] NPL tranchées *fpl* utérines

aftershave ['ɑːftɜːʃeɪv] N (lotion *f*) après-rasage *m inv*

aftershock ['ɑːftɜːʃɒk] N [*of earthquake*] réplique *f*

aftertaste ['ɑːftɜːteɪst] N (*lit, fig*) arrière-goût *m*

afterthought ['ɑːftɜːθɔːt] N pensée *f* après coup ; **I had an** ~ cela m'est venu après coup ; **I had ~s** or **an** ~ **about my decision** j'ai eu après coup des doutes sur ma décision ; **the window was added as an** ~ la fenêtre a été ajoutée après coup

afterward(s) ['ɑːftɜːwəd(z)] ADV après, ensuite, plus tard, par la suite

afterword ['ɑːftɜːwɜːd] N postface *f*

AG [eɪ'dʒiː] N **a** ABBR = **Adjutant General** **b** (ABBR = **Attorney General**) → **attorney**

Aga® ['ɑːgə] N (*Brit*) grand fourneau de cuisine en fonte

again [ə'gen] ADV **a** (= *once more*) de nouveau ; **here we are ~!** nous revoilà !, nous voilà de nouveau ! ; **it's him ~!** c'est encore lui ! ; **~ and ◊ time and** ~ à plusieurs reprises, maintes et maintes fois ; **I've told you ~ and** ~ je te l'ai dit et répété (je ne sais combien de fois) ; **start all over** ~ recommencez au début or à partir du début, reprenez au commencement ; **he had to count them over** ~ il a dû les recompter ; **he was soon well** ~ il s'est vite remis ; **she is home** ~ elle est rentrée chez elle, elle est de retour chez elle ; **what's his name ~?** comment s'appelle-t-il déjà ? ; **to begin** ~ recommencer ; **to see** ~ revoir → **now**
b (*with neg*) **not ...** ~ ne ... plus ; **I won't do it** ~ je ne le ferai plus ; **never** ~ jamais plus, plus jamais ; **I won't do it ever** ~ je ne le ferai plus jamais ; **never ~!** c'est bien la dernière fois ! ; (*iro*) **not ~!** encore !
c **as much** ~ deux fois autant ; **he is as old ~ as Christine** il a deux fois l'âge de Christine
d (*emphatic = besides, moreover*) là encore, encore une fois ; **but there** ~ mais là encore ; **then** ~ ◊ **and** ~ d'autre part, d'un autre côté ; **~, it is not certain that ...** et d'ailleurs or et encore il n'est pas sûr que ...

▼ against [ə'genst]

When **against** is an element in a phrasal verb, eg **go against, run up against, take against**, look up the verb.

PREP **a** (*indicating opposition*) contre ; **Tyson's fight ~ Bruno** le combat entre Tyson et Bruno, le combat opposant Tyson à Bruno ; **an upsurge in racism ~ immigrants** une montée du racisme contre les immigrants ; **a demonstration ~ the government's reforms** une manifestation contre les réformes du gouvernement ; **he did it ~ my wishes** il l'a fait contre mon gré ; **~ the law** (*adj*) contraire à la loi ♦ (*adv*) contrairement à la loi ; (*lit, fig*) **there's no law ~ it** il n'y a pas de loi qui s'y oppose ; **I've got nothing ~ him/it** je n'ai rien contre lui/ rien contre (cela) ; **conditions are ~ us** les conditions nous sont défavorables or sont contre nous ; **to be ~ capital punishment** être contre la peine de mort ; **I'm ~ helping him at all** je ne suis pas d'avis qu'on l'aide (*subj*) ; **I'm ~ it** je suis contre (cela) ; **to be (dead) ~ sth** être (farouchement) opposé à qch ; **~ all comers** envers et contre tous ; **now we're up ~ it!** nous voici au pied du mur ! ; **~ my will** (= *despite myself*) malgré moi, à contrecœur ; (= *despite my opposition*) malgré moi, contre ma volonté ; **to work ~ time** or **the clock** travailler contre la montre, faire la course contre la montre (*fig*) → **grain, odds, vote**
b (*indicating collision, impact*) contre, sur ; **to hit one's head ~ the mantelpiece** se cogner la

tête contre la cheminée ; **the truck ran ~ a tree** le camion s'est jeté contre or a percuté un arbre
c (*indicating support*) contre ; **to lean ~ a wall** s'appuyer contre un mur or au mur ; **push the chairs right back ~ the wall** repoussez les chaises tout contre le mur ; **he leaned ~ it** il s'y est appuyé → **up**
d (= *in contrast to*) contre, sur ; **~ the light** à contre-jour ; **the trees stood out ~ the sunset** les arbres se détachaient sur le (soleil) couchant
e (*indicating comparison*) (**as**) ~ contre, en comparaison de ; **my rights as ~ his** mes droits comparés aux siens ; **the strength of the pound (as) ~ the dollar** la fermeté de la livre par rapport au dollar ; **the pound is down ~ the franc** la livre a baissé par rapport au franc ; **~ that, it might be said ...** en revanche or par contre on pourrait dire ... → **over, word**
f **numbered tickets are available ~ this voucher** on peut obtenir des billets numérotés contre remise de ce bon ; **~ presentation of documents** sur présentation des pièces justificatives
g (*in preparation for*) en vue de, en prévision de, pour ; **preparations ~ sb's return** préparatifs *mpl* pour le retour or en prévision du retour de qn ; **to have the roof repaired ~ the rainy season** faire réparer le toit en prévision de la saison des pluies

Agamemnon [ˌægə'memnən] N Agamemnon *m*

agape [ə'geɪp] ADJ, ADV bouche bée

agar(-agar) [ˌeɪgɑː'eɪgɑːʳ] N agar-agar *m*, gélose *f*

agaric [ə'gærɪk] N agaric *m*

agate ['ægət] N agate *f*

agave [ə'geɪvɪ] N agavé *m*

age [eɪdʒ] **1** N **a** (= *length of life*) âge *m* ; **what's her ~?** ◊ **what ~ is she?** quel âge a-t-elle ? ; **when I was your ~** quand j'avais ton âge ; **I have a daughter your ~** or **the same ~ as you** j'ai une fille de votre âge ; **be** or **act your ~!** allons, sois raisonnable ! ; **he is ten years of ~** il a dix ans ; **you don't look your ~** vous ne faites pas votre âge ; **he's twice your ~** il a le double de votre âge ; **we are of an ~** nous sommes du même âge ; (*Jur etc*) **to be under ~** être mineur ; **to be of ~** être majeur ; **to come of ~** (*lit*) atteindre sa majorité ; (*fig*) [*issue, idea*] faire son chemin ; (*Jur*) ~ **of consent** âge *m* de consentement → **middle**
b (= *latter part of life*) vieillesse *f*, âge *m* ; **the infirmities of** ~ les infirmités *fpl* de la vieillesse or de l'âge → **old**
c (*Geol etc*) âge *m* ; (*Hist, Literat*) époque *f*, siècle *m* → **enlightenment, stone**
d (*gen pl*:* = *long time*) **I haven't seen him for ~s** il y a un siècle que je ne le vois plus, il y a une éternité que je ne l'ai vu ; **she stayed for ~s** or **for an** ~ elle est restée (là) pendant une éternité or un temps fou
2 VI vieillir, prendre de l'âge ; **she had ~d beyond her years** elle paraissait or faisait maintenant plus que son âge ; **to ~ well** [*wine*] s'améliorer en vieillissant ; [*person*] vieillir bien ; **he has ~d a lot** il a beaucoup vieilli, il a pris un coup de vieux
3 VT **a** vieillir ; **this dress ~s you** cette robe vous vieillit
b [+ *wine etc*] laisser vieillir
c [+ *accounts*] classer par antériorité or par ancienneté ; **to ~ inventories** classer or analyser le stock par date d'entrée
4 COMP d'âge ► **age allowance** N (*Brit Tax*) abattement *m* vieillesse ► **age bracket** N = **age group** ► **age discrimination** N (*US*) discrimination *f* pour raisons d'âge, âgisme *m* ► **age group** N tranche *f* d'âge ; **the 40-50 ~ group** la tranche d'âge de 40 à 50 ans, les 40 à 50 ans ► **age limit** N limite *f* d'âge ► **age-old** ADJ séculaire, antique ► **age range** N children in the ~ **range 12-14** les enfants (âgés) de 12 à 14 ans

aged [eɪdʒd] **1** ADJ **a** âgé de ; **a boy ~ ten** un garçon (âgé) de dix ans **b** ['eɪdʒɪd] (= *old*) âgé, vieux (vieille *f*), vieil (*m before vowel*) **2** **the aged** NPL les personnes *fpl* âgées ; **the ~ and infirm** les gens *mpl* âgés et infirmes

ageing ['eɪdʒɪŋ] **1** ADJ [*person*] vieillissant, qui se fait vieux (vieille *f*) ; [*hairstyle etc*] qui fait paraître plus vieux (vieille *f*) **2** N vieillissement *m*

ageism ['eɪdʒɪzəm] N âgisme *m*

ageist ['eɪdʒɪst] **1** ADJ faisant preuve d'âgisme **2** N personne *f* faisant preuve d'âgisme

ageless ['eɪdʒlɪs] ADJ [*person*] sans âge ; [*beauty*] toujours jeune

agency ['eɪdʒənsɪ] N **a** (*Comm*) agence *f*, bureau *m* ; (*Govt*) organisme *m* ; **this garage has the Citroën ~** ce garage est le concessionnaire Citroën ; **he has the sole ~ for ...** il a l'exclusivité de ... ; **~ agreement** contrat *m* de représentation → **advertising, news, tourist** **b** (= *means*) intermédiaire *m*, entremise *f* ; **through** or **by the ~ of friends** par l'intermédiaire or l'entremise d'amis, grâce à des amis ; **through the ~ of water** par l'action de l'eau

agenda [ə'dʒendə] N ordre *m* du jour, programme *m* ; **on the ~** à l'ordre du jour ; (*fig*) **to set the ~** donner le ton ; (*fig*) **to have an ~** avoir une idée en tête

agent ['eɪdʒənt] N **a** (*Comm*) (= *person*) agent *m*, concessionnaire *mf* (**of, for** de) ; (= *firm*) concessionnaire *m* ; **for Ford cars** concessionnaire *m* Ford → **foreign, free, special** **b** (= *thing, person, also Ling*) agent *m* → **chemical, principal**

agentive ['eɪdʒəntɪv] N (*Ling*) agentif *m*

agent provocateur [,æʒɑ̃prə,vɒkə'tɜːr] N agent *m* provocateur

agglomerate [ə'glɒməreɪt] **1** VT agglomérer **2** VI s'agglomérer **3** ADJ aggloméré

agglomeration [ə,glɒmə'reɪʃən] N agglomération *f*

agglutinate [ə'gluːtɪneɪt] **1** VT agglutiner **2** VI s'agglutiner **3** ADJ agglutiné ; (*Ling*) agglutinant **4** COMP ▶ **agglutinating language** N (*Ling*) langue *f* agglutinante

agglutination [ə,gluːtɪ'neɪʃən] N agglutination *f*

agglutinative [ə'gluːtɪnətɪv] ADJ [*substance, language*] agglutinant

aggrandize [ə'grændaɪz] VT agrandir, grandir

aggrandizement [ə'grændɪzmənt] N agrandissement *m* ; [*of influence*] accroissement *m*

aggravate ['ægrəveɪt] VT **a** [+ *illness*] aggraver, (faire) empirer ; [+ *quarrel, situation*] envenimer ; [+ *pain*] augmenter ; (*Jur*) **~d assault** coups *mpl* et blessures **b** (= *annoy*) exaspérer, agacer

aggravating ['ægrəveɪtɪŋ] ADJ **a** (= *worsening*) [*circumstances*] aggravant **b** (= *annoying*) exaspérant, agaçant

aggravation [,ægrə'veɪʃən] N **a** (*NonC* = *exacerbation*) [*of problem, situation, illness*] aggravation *f* **b** (= *annoyance*) contrariété *f* ; **I don't need all this ~** je pourrais me passer de toutes ces contrariétés ; **the ~ of having to do sth** la contrariété d'avoir à faire qch

aggregate ['ægrɪgɪt] **1** N **a** ensemble *m*, total *m* ; **in the ~** dans l'ensemble, en somme ; **on ~** ≈ au total des points (*dans le groupe de sélection*) **b** (*Constr, Geol*) agrégat *m* **2** ADJ global, total ; **~ value** valeur *f* totale or globale **3** ['ægrɪgeɪt] VT **a** (= *gather together*) agréger, rassembler **b** (= *amount to*) s'élever à, former un total de **4** VI s'agréger, s'unir en un tout

aggression [ə'greʃən] N (*also Psych*) agression *f* ; (= *aggressiveness*) agressivité *f* → **non-aggression**

aggressive [ə'gresɪv] ADJ [*person, behaviour, speech*] agressif ; [*salesman, ad etc*] accrocheur ;

(*Mil etc*) [*tactics, action*] offensif ; (*Psych*) agressif

aggressively [ə'gresɪvlɪ] ADV agressivement

aggressiveness [ə'gresɪvnɪs] N agressivité *f*

aggressor [ə'gresər] N agresseur *m*

aggrieved [ə'griːvd] ADJ (= *angry*) fâché, contrarié ; (= *unhappy*) chagriné, mécontent → **party**

aggro* ['ægrəʊ] N (*Brit*) (ABBR = **aggravation**) (= *emotion*) agressivité *f* ; (= *physical violence*) grabuge* *m* ; (= *hassle*) embêtements *mpl*

aghast [ə'gɑːst] ADJ atterré (**at** de), frappé d'horreur

agile ['ædʒaɪl] ADJ agile, leste

agility [ə'dʒɪlɪtɪ] N agilité *f*, souplesse *f*

Agincourt [ædʒɪn,kɔːt] N Azincourt

aging ['eɪdʒɪŋ] N, ADJ = **ageing**

agio ['ædʒɪəʊ] N agio *m*

agiotage ['ædʒətɪdʒ] N agiotage *m*

agism ['eɪdʒɪzəm] N = **ageism**

agist ['eɪdʒɪst] N, ADJ = **ageist**

agitate ['ædʒɪteɪt] **1** VT **a** [+ *liquid*] agiter, remuer **b** (= *excite, upset*) perturber **2** VI **to ~ for/against sth** faire campagne or mener une campagne en faveur de/contre qch

agitated ['ædʒɪteɪtɪd] ADJ inquiet (-ète *f*), agité ; **to be very ~** être dans tous ses états

agitatedly ['ædʒɪteɪtɪdlɪ] ADV avec agitation

agitation [,ædʒɪ'teɪʃən] N **a** [*of person*] agitation *f* ; **in a state of ~** agité **b** (= *social unrest*) agitation *f*, troubles *mpl* ; (= *deliberate stirring up*) campagne *f* (**for** pour, **against** contre) **c** [*of liquid*] agitation *f*, mouvement *m*

agitator ['ædʒɪteɪtər] N **a** (= *person*) agitateur *m*, -trice *f*, fauteur *m* (de troubles) **b** (= *device*) agitateur *m*

agitprop ['ædʒɪt,prɒp] **1** N agit-prop *f inv* **2** ADJ agit-prop *inv*

aglow [ə'gləʊ] ADJ [*sky*] embrasé (*liter*) ; [*fire*] rougeoyant, incandescent ; **the sun sets the mountain ~** le soleil embrase la montagne ; (*fig*) **~ with pleasure/health** rayonnant de plaisir/de santé

AGM [,eɪdʒi:'em] N (*Brit*) (ABBR = **annual general meeting**) AG *f*, assemblée *f* générale

Agnes ['ægnɪs] N Agnès *f*

agnostic [æg'nɒstɪk] ADJ, N agnostique *mf*

agnosticism [æg'nɒstɪsɪzəm] N agnosticisme *m*

ago [ə'gəʊ] ADV il y a ; **a week ~** il y a huit jours ; **how long ~?** il y a combien de temps (de cela) ? ; **a little while ~** il y a peu de temps ; **he left ten minutes ~** il est sorti il y a dix minutes or depuis dix minutes ; **as long ~ as 1950** déjà en 1950, dès 1950 ; **no longer ~ than yesterday** pas plus tard qu'hier → **long**

agog [ə'gɒg] ADJ en émoi ; **to be (all) ~ (with excitement) about sth** être en émoi à cause de qch ; **to set ~** mettre en émoi ; **to be ~ to do** griller d'envie or être impatient de faire, brûler de faire ; **~ for news** impatient d'avoir des nouvelles

agonize ['ægənaɪz] VI **to ~ over** or **about sth** se tourmenter à propos de qch ; **to ~ over how to do sth** se ronger les sangs pour savoir comment faire qch

agonized ['ægənaɪzd] ADJ atroce, d'angoisse

agonizing ['ægənaɪzɪŋ] ADJ [*death*] atroce ; [*feeling, decision, choice*] déchirant

agonizingly ['ægənaɪzɪŋlɪ] ADV atrocement

agony ['ægənɪ] **1** N (= *mental pain*) angoisse *f*, supplice *m* ; (= *physical pain*) douleur *f* atroce ; **it was ~** la douleur était atroce ; **death ~** agonie *f* ; **to suffer agonies** souffrir le martyre or mille morts ; **to be in an ~ of impatience** mourir d'impatience ; **to be in ~** souffrir le martyre → **prolong** **2** COMP ▶ **agony aunt*** N (*Brit Press*) rédactrice de la rubrique du courrier du cœur ▶ **agony column*** N (*Brit Press*) courrier

m du cœur ▶ **agony uncle*** N (*Brit Press*) rédacteur de la rubrique du courrier du cœur

agoraphobia [,ægərə'fəʊbɪə] N agoraphobie *f*

agoraphobic [,ægərə'fəʊbɪk] ADJ agoraphobe

AGR [,eɪdʒi:'ɑːr] N (ABBR = **advanced gas-cooled reactor**) → **advanced**

agrammatical [,eɪgrə'mætɪkəl] ADJ agrammatical

agraphia [,eɪ'græfɪə] N agraphie *f*

agrarian [ə'greərɪən] **1** ADJ [*reform, laws*] agraire ; **Agrarian Revolution** réforme(s) *f(pl)* agraire(s) **2** N (*Pol Hist*) agrarien(ne) *m(f)*

▼ **agree** [ə'griː] **1** VT **a** (= *consent*) consentir (**to do** à faire), accepter (**to do** de faire) ; [+ *statement, report*] accepter or reconnaître la véracité de ; **he ~d to do it** il a consenti à or accepté de le faire
b (= *admit*) reconnaître, admettre (**that** que) ; **I ~ (that) I was wrong** je reconnais or conviens que je me suis trompé
c (= *come to an agreement*) convenir (**to do** de faire), se mettre d'accord (**to do** pour faire) ; [+ *time, price*] se mettre d'accord sur, convenir de ; (= *be of same opinion*) être d'accord (**with** avec, **that** que) ; **everyone ~s that we should stay** tout le monde s'accorde à reconnaître que nous devrions rester ; **they ~d (amongst themselves) to do it** ils ont convenu de le faire, ils se sont mis d'accord or se sont accordés pour le faire ; **it was ~d** c'était convenu ; **to ~ to disagree** or **differ** en rester là, accepter que chacun reste sur ses positions ; **I ~ that it's difficult** je conviens que c'est difficile, je suis d'accord, c'est difficile ; **the delivery was three days later than ~d** la livraison a été effectuée trois jours après la date convenue ; (*Jur*) **unless otherwise ~d** sauf accord contraire, sauf convention contraire

2 VI **a** (= *hold same opinion*) être d'accord (**with** avec), être du même avis (**with** que) ; **I (quite) ~** je suis (tout à fait) d'accord ; **I don't ~ (at all)** je ne suis pas (du tout) d'accord ; **I ~ about trying again tomorrow** je suis d'accord avec l'idée de ressayer demain ; **they all ~d in finding the play dull** tous ont été d'accord pour trouver la pièce ennuyeuse, tous ont été d'avis que la pièce était ennuyeuse ; **she ~s with me that it is unfair** elle est d'accord avec moi pour dire or elle trouve comme moi que c'est injuste ; **he entirely ~s with me** il est tout à fait d'accord or en plein accord avec moi ; **I can't ~ with you there** je ne suis absolument pas d'accord avec vous sur ce point ; **I don't ~ with children smoking** je n'admets pas que les enfants fument (*subj*)
b (= *come to terms*) se mettre d'accord (**with** avec) ; (= *get on well*) s'entendre (bien), s'accorder (bien) ; **to ~ about** or **on sth** se mettre d'accord sur qch, convenir de qch ; **we haven't ~d about the price/about where to go** nous ne nous sommes pas mis d'accord sur le prix/sur l'endroit où aller, nous n'avons pas convenu du prix/de l'endroit où aller ; **they ~d as to** or **on how to do it/as to what it should cost** ils sont tombés or se sont mis d'accord sur la manière de le faire/sur le prix que cela devrait coûter → **agreed**
c **to ~ to a proposal** accepter une proposition, donner son consentement or son adhésion à une proposition ; **he won't ~ to that** il ne sera jamais d'accord, il n'acceptera pas ; **I ~ to your marriage/your marrying her** je consens à votre mariage/à ce que vous l'épousiez ; **he ~d to the project** il a donné son adhésion au projet
d [*ideas, stories, assessments*] concorder, coïncider (**with** avec) ; **his explanation ~s with what I know** son explication correspond à ce que je sais ; **these statements do not ~ with each other** ces affirmations ne concordent pas
e (*Gram*) s'accorder (**with** avec, **in** en)

f (= *suit the health of*) **sea air ~s with invalids** l'air marin est bon pour les malades *or* réussit aux malades; **the heat does not ~ with her** la chaleur l'incommode; **onions don't ~ with me** les oignons ne me réussissent pas

agreeable [ə'griːəbl] ADJ **a** (= *pleasant, friendly*) agréable; **she was always ~ to them** elle était toujours agréable avec eux **b** (*frm = willing*) **if you are ~, we can start immediately** si vous le voulez bien *or* si vous y consentez, nous pouvons commencer immédiatement; **to be ~ to ~ (doing) sth** consentir volontiers à (faire) qch; **I am quite ~** volontiers; **I am quite ~ to doing it** je le ferai très volontiers **c** (*frm = acceptable*) **we can start the work tomorrow, if that's ~** nous pouvons commencer le travail demain si vous n'y voyez pas d'inconvénient; **is that ~ to you?** est-ce que cela vous convient?, cela vous agrée-t-il? (*frm*)

agreeably [ə'griːəblɪ] ADV [*chat, spend time*] agréablement; [*say, smile*] aimablement; **~ surprised** agréablement surpris

▼ **agreed** [ə'griːd] ADJ **a** d'accord; **we are ~** nous sommes d'accord (**about** au sujet de, à propos de, **on** sur); **the ministers were ~** les ministres sont tombés d'accord **b** [*time, place, amount*] convenu; **it's all ~** c'est tout décidé *or* convenu; **as ~** comme convenu; **it's ~ that ...** il est convenu que ... (+ *indic*); **(is that) ~?** entendu?, d'accord? **~!** entendu!, d'accord!

agreement [ə'griːmənt] N **a** (= *mutual understanding*) accord *m*, harmonie *f*; **to be in ~ on a subject** être d'accord sur un sujet; **by (mutual) ~** (= *both thinking same*) d'un commun accord; (*without quarrelling*) à l'amiable **b** (= *arrangement, contract*) accord *m*; (*Pol, frm*) pacte *m*; **to come to an ~** parvenir à une entente, tomber d'accord; **to sign an ~** signer un accord; **the Helsinki ~** les accords *mpl* d'Helsinki → **gentleman** **c** (*Gram*) accord *m*

agribusiness [ˈægrɪˌbɪznɪs] N agro-industries *fpl*

agricultural [ˌægrɪ'kʌltʃərəl] **1** ADJ [*policy, production, machinery*] agricole; [*subsidy*] à l'agriculture; [*method*] d'agriculture; [*reform*] de l'agriculture; [*exporter, exports*] de produits agricoles **2** COMP ► **agricultural college** N école *f* d'agriculture ► **agricultural engineer** N ingénieur *m* agronome ► **agricultural expert** N expert *m* agronome ► **agricultural show** N exposition *f* agricole ► **agricultural worker** N travailleur *m* agricole

agricultur(al)ist [ˌægrɪ'kʌltʃər(ə)lɪst] N agronome *mf*; (= *farmer*) agriculteur *m*

agriculture [ˈægrɪˌkʌltʃəʳ] N agriculture *f*; **Minister/Ministry of Agriculture** (*Brit*) ◇ **Secretary/Department of Agriculture** (*US*) ministre *m*/ministère *m* de l'Agriculture

agrifoodstuffs [ˈægrɪˈfuːdstʌfs] NPL agro-alimentaire *m*

agrobiology [ˌægrəʊbaɪ'ɒlədʒɪ] N agrologie *f*

agrochemical [ˌægrəʊ'kemɪkəl] **1** ADJ agrochimique **2** N produit *m* chimique à usage agricole; [*industry*] ~s agrochimie *f*

agronomist [ə'grɒnəmɪst] N agronome *mf*

agronomy [ə'grɒnəmɪ] N agronomie *f*

aground [ə'graʊnd] ADV, ADJ [*ship*] échoué; **to be ~** toucher le fond; **to be fast ~** être bien échoué; **to run ~** s'échouer, se jeter à la côte

ague†† [ˈeɪgjuː] N (*Med*) fièvre *f*

ah [ɑː] EXCL ah!

aha [ɑː'hɑː] EXCL ah, ah!

Ahasuerus [əˌhæzjʊ'ɪərəs] N Assuérus *m*

ahead [ə'hed]

*When **ahead** is an element in a phrasal verb, eg* **book ahead, draw ahead, fire ahead, go ahead, look up the verb**.

ADV **a** (*in space*) en avant, devant; **stay here, I'll go on ~** restez ici, moi je vais en avant *or* devant; (*lit, fig*) **to get ~** prendre de l'avance; (*Naut, also fig*) **full speed ~!** en avant toute! **b** (*in classification, sport etc*) en tête; **to be five points etc ~** avoir une avance de cinq points etc; **the goal put Scotland 2-1 ~** grâce à ce but, l'Écosse menait 2 à 1 **c** (*in time*) [*book*] à l'avance; **~ of time** [*decide, announce*] d'avance; [*arrive, be ready*] avant l'heure, en avance; **the project's ~ of schedule** le projet est plus avancé que prévu; **the project's two months ~ of schedule** le projet est en avance de deux mois sur le planning *or* sur le programme prévu; **~ of the meeting** avant la réunion; **two hours ~ of the next car** avec deux heures d'avance sur la voiture suivant; **he's two hours ~ of you** il a deux heures d'avance sur vous; **clocks here are two hours ~ of clocks over there** les pendules d'ici ont deux heures d'avance sur celles de là-bas, il y a un décalage horaire de deux heures entre ici et là-bas; **the months ~** les mois à venir; **there are difficult times ~** l'avenir s'annonce difficile; **to think *or* plan ~** prévoir (à l'avance); **looking *or* thinking ~ five years, what ...** essayer d'imaginer la situation dans cinq ans: qu'est-ce que ...; **to plan ~** faire des projets; (*fig*) **to be ~ of one's time** être en avance sur son temps; **what is *or* lies ~** ce que l'avenir nous réserve; **what is *or* lies ~ for him/us** ce que l'avenir lui/nous réserve

ahem [ə'hem] EXCL hum!

ahold [ə'həʊld] N (*esp US*) **to get ~ of sb** (= *contact*) contacter qn, joindre qn; (= *grab*) saisir qn; **to get ~ of sth** (= *obtain*) mettre la main sur qch; (= *grab*) saisir qch; **to get ~ of o.s.** (= *pull o.s. together*) se ressaisir; (= *control o.s.*) se maîtriser

ahoy [ə'hɔɪ] EXCL (*Naut*) ohé!; **ship ~!** ohé du navire!

AI [eɪ'aɪ] N **a** (ABBR = **artificial intelligence**) IA *f*, intelligence *f* artificielle **b** (ABBR = **artificial insemination**) IA *f*, insémination *f* artificielle **c** ABBR = **Amnesty International**

AID [ˌeɪaɪ'diː] N **a** (ABBR = **artificial insemination by donor**) IAD *f* **b** (*US*) ABBR = **Agency for International Development** **c** (*US Admin*) ABBR = **Aid to Families with Dependent Children**

aid [eɪd] **1** N (NonC) (= *help*) aide *f*, assistance *f*; (*international*) aide *f*; **by *or* with the ~ of sb** avec l'aide de qn; **by *or* with the ~ of sth** à l'aide de qch; **sale in ~ of the blind** vente *f* (de charité) au profit des aveugles; (*Brit fig*) **what is the meeting in ~ of?*** c'est dans quel but *or* en quel honneur*, cette réunion? → **first aid, mutual** **b** (= *helper*) aide *mf*, assistant(e) *m(f)*; (*gen pl = equipment, apparatus*) aide *f*; **audio-visual ~s** supports *mpl* *or* moyens *mpl* audiovisuels; **teaching ~s** outils *mpl* *or* matériel *m* pédagogique(s) → **deaf** **2** VT [+ *person*] aider; [+ *progress, recovery*] contribuer à; **to ~ one another** s'entraider, s'aider les uns les autres; **to ~ sb to do sth** aider qn à faire qch; (*Jur*) **to ~ and abet (sb)** être complice (de qn) **3** COMP ► **aid agency** N organisation *f* humanitaire ► **aid climbing** N (*Climbing*) escalade *f* artificielle

aide [eɪd] **1** N aide *mf*, assistant(e) *m(f)*; (*US Pol*) conseiller *m*, -ère *f* **2** COMP ► **aide-de-camp** N (*pl* **aides-de-camp**) aide *m* de camp ► **aide-mémoire** N (*pl* **aides-mémoire**) mémorandum *m*

AIDS, Aids, aids [eɪdz] **1** N (ABBR = **acquired immune deficiency syndrome**) sida *m* **2** COMP ► **AIDS patient** N sidéen(ne) *m(f)*, malade *mf* du sida ► **AIDS-related** ADJ associé au sida ► **AIDS-related complex** N pré-sida *m* ► **AIDS victim** N = **AIDS patient**

aigrette [eɪ'gret] N (*Bot, Zool*) aigrette *f*

AIH [ˌeɪaɪ'eɪtʃ] N (ABBR = **artificial insemination by husband**) IAC *f*

aikido [ˈaɪkɪdəʊ] N aïkido *m*

ail [eɪl] **1** VT affliger; **what ~s you?**† qu'avez-vous? **2** VI être souffrant

aileron [ˈeɪlərɒn] N (*Aviat*) aileron *m*

ailing [ˈeɪlɪŋ] ADJ souffrant; **she is always ~** elle est de santé fragile, elle a une petite santé; **an ~ company** une compagnie qui périclite

ailment [ˈeɪlmənt] N affection *f*; **all his (little) ~s** tous ses maux *mpl*

aim [eɪm] **1** N **a** **his ~ is bad** il vise mal; **to take ~ (at sb/sth)** viser (qn/qch); **to miss one's ~** manquer la cible **b** (*fig = purpose*) but *m*; **with the ~ of doing** dans le but de faire; **her ~ is to do** elle a pour but de faire, elle vise à faire; **the ~ of this policy is to ...** cette politique vise à ...; **the ~ of this government is to ...** le but que s'est fixé le gouvernement est de ...; **his ~s are open to suspicion** ses visées *or* ses ambitions sont suspectes; **political ~s** finalités *fpl* *or* buts *mpl* politiques **2** VT **a** (= *direct*) [+ *hosepipe, extinguisher*] pointer, diriger; [+ *gun*] braquer (**at** sur); [+ *missile*] pointer (**at** sur); [+ *blow*] allonger, décocher (**at** à); [+ *remark*] diriger (**at** contre); **to ~ a gun at sb** braquer un revolver sur qn, viser qn avec un revolver; (*fig*) **his remarks are ~ed at his father** ses remarques visent son père **b** (= *intend*) viser, aspirer (**to do, at doing** à faire) **3** VI viser; **to ~ at** (*lit*) viser; (*fig*) viser, aspirer à → **high**

aimless [ˈeɪmlɪs] ADJ [*person, way of life*] sans but, désœuvré; [*activity, pursuit*] qui ne mène à rien, futile

aimlessly [ˈeɪmlɪslɪ] ADV [*wander, drift*] sans but; [*chat*] à bâtons rompus

aimlessness [ˈeɪmlɪsnɪs] N **a mood of ~ and despair** une sensation d'errance (*liter*) et de désespoir; **his sense of ~** le sentiment qu'il éprouvait de ne pas avoir de but dans la vie

ain't [eɪnt] = **am not, is not, are not, has not, have not**; → **be, have**

air [ɛəʳ] **1** N **a** (*lit*) air *m*; **in the open ~** en plein air; **a change of ~** un changement d'air; **I need some ~!** j'ai besoin d'air!; **to go out for a breath of (fresh) ~** sortir prendre l'air; **to take the ~†** prendre le frais; **to transport sth by ~** transporter qch par avion; **to go by ~** aller en *or* voyager par avion; **to throw sth (up) into the ~** jeter *or* lancer qch en l'air; **the balloon rose up into the ~** le ballon s'est élevé (dans les airs); **(seen) from the ~** vu d'en haut **b** (*fig phrases*) **there's sth in the ~** il se prépare qch, il se trame qch; **it's still all in the ~** ce ne sont encore que des projets en l'air *or* de vagues projets; **all her plans were up in the ~** (= *vague*) tous ses projets étaient vagues *or* flous; **all her plans have gone up in the ~** (= *destroyed*) tous ses projets sont tombés à l'eau; **there's a rumour in the ~ that ...** le bruit court que ...; **he went up in the ~*** when he **heard the news** (*in anger*) il a bondi en apprenant la nouvelle; (*in excitement*) il a sauté d'enthousiasme en apprenant la nouvelle; **to be up in the ~ about*** ... (= *angry*) être très monté *or* très en colère à l'idée de ...; (= *excited*) être tout en émoi *or* très excité à l'idée de ...; **I can't live on ~** je ne peux pas vivre de l'air du temps; **to be walking *or* treading on ~** être aux anges, ne pas se sentir de joie; **to pull *or* pluck a figure out of the ~** donner un chiffre au hasard; (*US*) **to give sb the ~*** [*employer*] virer* *or* renvoyer qn; [*girlfriend etc*] plaquer* qn → **hot, thin** **c** **on (the) ~** (*Rad*) à la radio, sur les ondes, à l'antenne; (*TV*) à l'antenne; **you're on (the) ~**

vous êtes à l'antenne, vous avez l'antenne; **he's on (the) ~ every day** il passe tous les jours à la radio; **the station is on the ~** la station émet; **the programme goes** or **is on (the) ~ every week** l'émission passe (sur l'antenne) or est diffusée toutes les semaines; **to go off (the) ~** quitter l'antenne
d († = *breeze*) brise f, léger souffle m
e (= *manner*) air m; **with an ~ of bewilderment/superiority** d'un air perplexe/ supérieur; **with a proud ~** d'un air fier, avec une mine hautaine; **she has an ~ about her** elle a de l'allure, elle a un certain chic; **to put on ~s** ◊ **to give o.s. ~s** se donner de grands airs; **~s and graces** minauderies *fpl*; **to put on ~s and graces** minauder
f (*Mus*) air m
2 VT **a** [+ *clothes, room, bed*] aérer
b [+ *anger*] exhaler; [+ *opinions*] faire connaître; [+ *idea, proposal*] mettre sur le tapis
c (*esp US** = *broadcast*) diffuser
3 VI (*TV, Rad* = *be broadcast*) être diffusé
4 COMP ► **air alert** N alerte f aérienne ► **air ambulance** N (= *plane*) avion m sanitaire; (= *helicopter*) hélicoptère m sanitaire ► **air base** N base f aérienne ► **air bed** N (*Brit*) matelas m pneumatique ► **air brake** N (*on truck*) frein m à air comprimé; (*Aviat*) frein m aéro-dynamique, aérofrein m ► **air brick** N (*Constr*) brique f évidée or creuse ► **air bridge** N pont m aérien ► **air-brush** N aéro-graphe m ♦ VT (*lit*) retoucher à l'aérographe; (*fig*) embellir ► **air bubble** N (*in liquids*) bulle f d'air; (*in glass, metal*) soufflure f ► **air burst** N explosion f aérienne ► **air chamber** N (*Aut, Physiol*) chambre f à air ► **air chief marshal** N (*Brit*) général m d'armée aérienne ► **air commodore** N (*Brit*) général m de brigade aérienne ► **air-conditioned** ADJ climatisé ► **air conditioner** N climatiseur m ► **air conditioning** N climatisation f, air m conditionné ► **air-cooled** ADJ [+ *engine*] à refroi-dissement par air; (*US**) [+ *room*] climatisé ► **air corridor** N couloir m aérien ► **air cover** N couverture f aérienne ► **air current** N courant m atmosphérique ► **air cushion** N coussin m pneumatique; (*Tech*) matelas m or coussin m d'air ► **air cylinder** N bouteille f d'air comprimé ► **air disaster** N catastrophe f aérienne ► **air display** N meeting m aérien ► **air-dry** VT sécher à l'air ► **air duct** N (*Tech*) conduit m d'aération ► **air express** N (*US*) cargo m aérien ► **air ferry** N avion m transbordeur ► **air filter** N filtre m à air ► **air flow** N courant m atmosphérique; (*in wind tunnel*) écoulement m d'air ► **air force** N armée f de l'air, aviation f militaire ► **air-force blue** ADJ bleu gris inv ► **Air Force One** N (*US*) l'avion m présidentiel ► **air freight** N (= *goods*) fret m aérien; (= *method*) transport m aérien; **to send by ~ freight** expé-dier par voie aérienne or par avion ► **air freshener** N désodorisant m ► **air guitar** N (*hum*) guitare imaginaire dont on fait semblant de jouer en écoutant de la musique ► **air hole** N trou m d'aération ► **air hostess** N (*Brit*) hôtesse f de l'air ► **air intake** N arrivée f d'air, prise f d'air ► **air lane** N couloir m aé-rien or de navigation aérienne ► **air letter** N aérogramme m ► **air marshal** N général m de corps aérien ► **air mass** N (*Met*) masse f d'air ► **air mattress** N matelas m pneumatique ► **air miles** NPL miles *mpl* ► **air miss** N quasi-collision f ► **air pocket** N trou m or poche f d'air ► **air power** N puissance f aé-rienne ► **air pressure** N pression f atmos-phérique ► **air pump** N compresseur m, ma-chine f pneumatique ► **air purifier** N pu-rificateur m d'air ► **air raid** N attaque f aé-rienne, raid m aérien ► **air-raid precau-tions** NPL protection f passive ► **air-raid shel-ter** N abri m antiaérien ► **air-raid warden** N préposé(e) *m(f)* à la défense passive ► **air-raid warning** N alerte f (aérienne) ► **air rifle**

N carabine f à air comprimé ► **air-sea base** N base f aéronavale ► **air-sea missile** N missile m air-mer ► **air-sea rescue** N sauve-tage m en mer (*par hélicoptère etc*) ► **air shaft** N (*Min*) puits m d'aérage; (*Naut*) manche f à vent ► **air show** N (= *trade exhibition*) salon m de l'aéronautique; (= *flying display*) meeting m aérien ► **air shuttle** N navette f aérienne ► **air sock** N manche f à air ► **air space** N espace m aérien; **French ~ space** l'espace m aérien français ► **air stream** N courant m atmosphérique; (*Ling*) colonne f d'air ► **air superiority** N supériorité f aérienne ► **air suspension** N (*Aut*) suspension f pneumati-que ► **air terminal** N aérogare f ► **air ticket** N billet m d'avion ► **air time** N temps m d'antenne ► **air-to-air** ADJ (*Mil*) air-air inv, avion-avion inv ► **air-to-ground** ADJ (*Mil*) air-sol inv ► **air-to-sea** ADJ (*Mil*) air-mer inv ► **air-to-surface** ADJ = **air-to-ground** ► **air traffic control** N contrôle m du trafic aérien ► **air traffic controller** N contrôleur m, -euse f de la navigation aérienne, aiguilleur m du ciel ► **air valve** N soupape f ► **air vent** N prise f d'air ► **air vice marshal** N (*Brit*) géné-ral m de division aérienne ► **air waves†** NPL ondes *fpl* (hertziennes); **on the ~ waves** (= *on radio*) sur les ondes

airbag ['ɛəbæg] N (*Aut*) airbag® m
airborne ['ɛəbɔːn] ADJ [+ *troops*] aéroporté; **the plane was ~** l'avion avait décollé
Airbus® ['ɛəbʌs] N Airbus® m
aircraft ['ɛəkrɑːft] **1** N (*pl inv*) avion m **2** COMP ► **aircraft carrier** N porte-avions m inv
aircraft(s)man ['ɛəkrɑːft(s)mən] N (*pl -men*) (*Brit*) soldat m de deuxième classe (de l'armée de l'air)
aircrew ['ɛəkruː] N équipage m
airdrome ['ɛədrəʊm] N (*US*) aérodrome m
airdrop ['ɛədrɒp] **1** VT parachuter **2** N para-chutage m
Airedale ['ɛədeɪl] N (*also* **~ terrier**) airedale m
airfare ['ɛəfɛə'] N prix m du billet d'avion
airfield ['ɛəfiːld] N terrain m d'aviation, (petit) aérodrome m
airfoil ['ɛəfɔːl] N (*US*) = **aerofoil**
airframe ['ɛəfreɪm] N cellule f (d'avion)
airgun ['ɛəgʌn] N fusil m or carabine f à air comprimé
airhead† ['ɛəhed] N cruche† f
airily ['ɛərɪlɪ] ADV [*say, dismiss*] avec désinvoltu-re
airiness ['ɛərɪnɪs] N [*of room*] aération f, (bonne) ventilation f; (*fig*) [*of manner*] dés-involture f
airing ['ɛərɪŋ] **1** N (*fig*) **to give an idea an ~** mettre une idée sur le tapis **2** COMP ► **airing cupboard** N (*Brit*) placard-séchoir m
airless ['ɛəlɪs] ADJ **a** [*room*] privé d'air; **it is ~ in here** il n'y a pas d'air ici, cela sent le renfermé ici **b** [*weather*] lourd
airlift ['ɛəlɪft] **1** N pont m aérien **2** VT éva-cuer par pont aérien
airline ['ɛəlaɪn] N **a** (*Aviat*) compagnie f aé-rienne **b** (*diver's*) voie f d'air
airliner ['ɛəlaɪnə'] N avion m de ligne, (avion m) long-courrier or moyen-courrier m
airlock ['ɛəlɒk] N **a** (*in spacecraft, caisson etc*) sas m **b** (*in pipe*) bulle f d'air
airmail ['ɛəmeɪl] **1** N poste f aérienne; **by ~** par avion **2** VT [+ *letter, parcel*] expédier par avion **3** COMP ► **airmail edition** N édition f par avion ► **airmail letter** N lettre f par avion ► **airmail paper** N papier m pelure ► **airmail stamp, airmail sticker** N éti-quette f « par avion »
airman ['ɛəmən] **1** N (*pl -men*) aviateur m; (*Brit Aviat*) soldat m de l'armée de l'air; (*US*

Aviat) soldat m de première classe **2** COMP ► **airman first class** N (*US*) caporal m
airmobile ['ɛəməbiːl] ADJ (*US Mil*) aéroporté
airplane ['ɛəpleɪn] N (*US*) avion m
airplay ['ɛəpleɪ] N (*Rad*) temps m de passage à l'antenne; **to get a lot of ~** passer souvent à l'antenne
airport ['ɛəpɔːt] **1** N aéroport m **2** COMP ► **airport bus** N bus m de l'aéroport ► **airport lounge** N salon m d'aéroport ► **airport tax(es)** N(PL) taxes *fpl* d'aéroport
airscrew ['ɛəskruː] N (*Brit*) hélice f
airshed ['ɛəʃed] N hangar m (d'aviation)
airship ['ɛəʃɪp] N dirigeable m
airsick ['ɛəsɪk] ADJ **to be ~** avoir le mal de l'air; **I get ~** je souffre du mal de l'air
airsickness ['ɛəsɪknɪs] N mal m de l'air
airspeed ['ɛəspiːd] **1** N (*Aviat*) vitesse f relati-ve **2** COMP ► **airspeed indicator** N badin m, anémomètre m
airstrike ['ɛəstraɪk] N = **air raid**; → **air**
airstrip ['ɛəstrɪp] N piste f (d'atterrissage)
airtight ['ɛətaɪt] ADJ hermétique
airway ['ɛəweɪ] **1** N (= *route*) voie f aérienne; (= *airline company*) compagnie f aérienne; (= *ventilator shaft*) conduit m d'air **2** ► **airways** NPL voies *fpl* respiratoires
airwoman ['ɛəwʊmən] N (*pl -women*) aviatrice f; (*in air force*) auxiliaire f de l'armée de l'air
airworthiness ['ɛəwɜːðɪnɪs] N navigabilité f → **certificate**
airworthy ['ɛəwɜːðɪ] ADJ en état de navigation
airy ['ɛərɪ] **1** ADJ **a** (= *spacious*) [*room, building*] clair et spacieux **b** (= *lightweight*) [*fabric*] léger **c** (= *casual*) [*manner, gesture, wave*] désinvolte **d** (= *empty*) [*promise, idea*] en l'air **2** COMP ► **airy-fairy*** ADJ (*Brit*) [*idea, person*] farfelu
aisle [aɪl] N **a** [*of church*] (*central*) allée f cen-trale; (*side*) bas-côté m; **to take a girl up the ~**† mener une jeune fille à l'autel; (*fig*) **to walk up the ~ with sb** épouser qn **b** [*of thea-tre, cinema*] allée f; [*of plane, train, coach*] cou-loir m; (*on plane etc*) **~ seat** place f côté cou-loir
aitch [eɪtʃ] N (= *letter*) H, h m; (*Culin*) **~ bone** culotte f (de bœuf) → **drop**
Ajaccio [əˈʒæsjəʊ] N Ajaccio
ajar [əˈdʒɑː'] ADJ, ADV entrouvert, entrebâillé
Ajax ['eɪdʒæks] N Ajax m
AK ABBR = **Alaska**
AKA, aka [ˌeɪkeɪ'eɪ] (ABBR = *also known as*) alias
akimbo [əˈkɪmbəʊ] ADJ **with arms ~** les poings sur les hanches
akin [əˈkɪn] ADJ **~ to** (= *similar*) qui tient de, qui ressemble à, analogue à; (= *of same family as*) parent de, apparenté à
AL, Ala. ABBR = **Alabama**
Alabama [ˌæləˈbæmə] N l'Alabama m; **in ~** en Alabama
alabaster ['æləbɑːstə'] **1** N albâtre m **2** ADJ (*lit, fig*) d'albâtre
alacrity [əˈlækrɪtɪ] N empressement m; **with ~** avec empressement
Aladdin [əˈlædɪn] **1** N Aladin m **2** COMP ► **Aladdin's cave** N (*fig*) caverne f d'Ali Baba
Alan ['ælən] N Alain m
alarm [əˈlɑːm] **1** N **a** (= *warning*) alarme f, alerte f; **to raise the ~** donner l'alarme or l'éveil; **~s and excursions** (*Theat*) bruits *mpl* de bataille en coulisse; (*fig*) branle-bas m de combat → **burglar, clock**
b (*NonC* = *fear*) inquiétude f, alarme f; **to cause sb ~** mettre qn dans l'inquiétude, alarmer qn
c = **alarm clock**
2 VT **a** (= *frighten*) [+ *person*] alarmer, éveiller des craintes chez; [+ *animal, bird*]

effaroucher, faire peur à ; **to become** or **be ~ed** [person] prendre peur, s'alarmer ; [animal] prendre peur, s'effaroucher **b** (= warn) alerter, alarmer **3** COMP ► **alarm bell** N sonnerie f d'alarme ; (fig) **the court's decision has set ~ bells ringing in government** la décision du tribunal a alerté or inquiété le gouvernement ► **alarm call** N (Telec) appel m du service réveil ; **I'd like an ~ call (for 6am)** je voudrais être réveillé (à 6 heures) ► **alarm clock** N réveil m, réveille-matin m inv ► **alarm signal** N signal m d'alarme ► **alarm system** N système m d'alarme

alarming [ə'lɑ:mɪŋ] ADJ alarmant

alarmingly [ə'lɑ:mɪŋlɪ] ADV [rise, deteriorate] de façon alarmante ; **the deadline is ~ close** la date limite se rapproche de manière inquiétante ; **~ quickly** à une vitesse alarmante ; **an ~ high divorce rate** un taux de divorce qui atteint des niveaux alarmants ; **~, there was a sharp fall in house prices** fait alarmant, il y a eu une forte chute des prix de l'immobilier

alarmist [ə'lɑ:mɪst] ADJ, N alarmiste mf

alas [ə'læs] EXCL hélas !

Alas. ABBR = **Alaska**

Alaska [ə'læskə] N l'Alaska m ; **in ~** en Alaska ; **~ Highway** route f de l'Alaska ; **~ Range** chaîne f de l'Alaska → **bake**

Alaskan [ə'læskən] **1** ADJ de l'Alaska **2** N habitant(e) m(f) de l'Alaska

alb [ælb] N aube f (d'un prêtre)

Albania [æl'beɪnɪə] N l'Albanie f

Albanian [æl'beɪnɪən] **1** ADJ albanais **2** N **a** (= person) Albanais(e) m(f) **b** (Ling) albanais m

albatross ['ælbətrɒs] N (also Golf) albatros m ; (fig = burden) boulet m ; (fig) **to be an ~ around sb's neck** être un boulet pour qn

albeit [ɔ:l'bi:ɪt] CONJ (frm) encore que (+ subj), bien que (+ subj)

Alberta [æl'bɜ:tə] N (Geog) l'Alberta m

Albigensian [ælbɪ'dʒensɪən] **1** ADJ albigeois ; **the ~ Heresy** l'hérésie f albigeoise or cathare **2** N Albigeois(e) m(f)

albinism ['ælbɪnɪzəm] N albinisme m

albino [æl'bi:nəʊ] N albinos mf ; **~ rabbit** lapin m albinos

Albion ['ælbɪən] N Albion f

album ['ælbəm] **1** N (= book, record etc) album m **2** COMP ► **album cover** N pochette f (de disque)

albumen, **albumin** ['ælbjʊmɪn] N (= egg white) albumen m, blanc m de l'œuf ; (Bot) albumen m ; (Physiol) albumine f

albuminous [æl'bju:mɪnəs] ADJ albumineux

Alcestis [æl'sestɪs] N Alceste f

alchemical [æl'kemɪkəl] ADJ alchimique

alchemist ['ælkɪmɪst] N alchimiste m

alchemy ['ælkɪmɪ] N (lit, fig) alchimie f

alcohol ['ælkəhɒl] **1** N alcool m **2** COMP ► **alcohol abuse** N abus m d'alcool ► **alcohol abuser** N alcoolique mf ► **alcohol consumption** N consommation f d'alcool ► **alcohol content** N [of drink] teneur f en alcool ► **alcohol-free** ADJ sans alcool

alcoholic [ælkə'hɒlɪk] **1** ADJ [person] alcoolique ; [drink] alcoolisé, alcoolique **2** N alcoolique mf ; **Alcoholics Anonymous** Alcooliques mpl anonymes

alcoholism ['ælkəhɒlɪzəm] N alcoolisme m

alcopop ['ælkəpɒp] N (Brit) prémix m

alcove ['ælkəʊv] N (in room) alcôve f ; (in wall) niche f ; (in garden) tonnelle f, berceau m

aldehyde ['ældɪhaɪd] N aldéhyde m

alder ['ɔ:ldə] N aulne or aune m

alderman ['ɔ:ldəmən] N (pl -men) alderman m,

conseiller m, -ère f municipal(e) ; (Hist) échevin m

ale [eɪl] N bière f, ale f → **brown, light², pale¹**

aleatoric [ælɪə'tɒrɪk] ADJ (Mus) aléatoire

alehouse†† ['eɪl,haʊs] N taverne f

Aleppo [ə'lepəʊ] N Alep

alert [ə'lɜ:t] **1** N alerte f ; **to give the ~** donner l'alerte ; **on the ~** (gen) sur le qui-vive ; (Mil) en état d'alerte **2** ADJ **a** (= watchful) vigilant **b** (= aware) **to be ~ to sth** avoir conscience de qch **c** (= acute) [old person] alerte ; [child] éveillé ; **to be mentally ~** avoir l'esprit vif **3** VT alerter ; (fig) éveiller l'attention de (**to** sur) ; **we are now ~ed to the dangers** notre attention est maintenant éveillée sur les dangers, nous sommes maintenant sensibilisés aux dangers

alertly [ə'lɜ:tlɪ] ADV [look, watch] d'un œil alerte

alertness [ə'lɜ:tnɪs] N (NonC) **a** (= watchfulness) [of person, animal] vigilance f **b** (= liveliness) [of person] vivacité f ; **mental ~** vivacité f d'esprit

Aleutian [ə'lu:ʃən] ADJ **the ~ Islands** ◊ **the ~s** les (îles fpl) Aléoutiennes fpl

alevin ['ælɪvɪn] N alevin m

alewife ['eɪlwaɪf] N (pl -wives) (sorte f d')alose f

Alexander [ælɪg'zɑ:ndə] N Alexandre m

Alexandria [ælɪg'zɑ:ndrɪə] N Alexandrie f

alexandrine [ælɪg'zændraɪn] ADJ, N alexandrin m

ALF [eɪel'ef] N (Brit) (ABBR = **Animal Liberation Front**) mouvement de lutte en faveur du statut animal

alfalfa [æl'fælfə] N luzerne f

Alfonso [æl'fɒnsəʊ] N Alphonse m

Alfred ['ælfrɪd] N Alfred m

alfresco [æl'freskəʊ] ADJ, ADV en plein air

alga ['ælgə] N (pl **algae** ['ældʒi:]) (gen pl) algue(s) f(pl)

algal ['ælgəl] ADJ algal

algebra ['ældʒɪbrə] N algèbre f

algebraic [ældʒɪ'breɪɪk] ADJ algébrique

Algeria [æl'dʒɪərɪə] N l'Algérie f

Algerian [æl'dʒɪərɪən] **1** ADJ algérien **2** N Algérien(ne) m(f)

Algiers [æl'dʒɪəz] N Alger

Algol ['ælgɒl] N (Comput) Algol m

Algonquian [æl'gɒŋkwɪən], **Algonquin** [æl'gɒŋkwɪn] ADJ algonquin, algonkin

algorithm ['ælgərɪðəm] N (Comput, Ling) algorithme m

algorithmic [ælgə'rɪðmɪk] ADJ algorithmique

Alhambra [æl'hæmbrə] N Alhambra m

alias ['eɪlɪəs] **1** ADV alias **2** N faux nom m, nom m d'emprunt ; [of writer] pseudonyme m

Ali Baba ['ælɪ'bɑ:bə] N Ali Baba m

alibi ['ælɪbaɪ] **1** N (Police) alibi m ; (*: gen) excuse f, alibi m (hum) **2** VI (US*) trouver des excuses (**for sth** pour expliquer qch, **for doing sth** pour avoir fait qch) **3** VT (US) **to ~ sb*** trouver des excuses à qn

Alice ['ælɪs] **1** N Alice f ; **~ in Wonderland** Alice au pays des merveilles **2** COMP ► **Alice band** N (Brit) bandeau m (pour les cheveux)

alien ['eɪlɪən] **1** N **a** (from abroad) étranger m, -ère f ; **resident/non-resident ~** étranger m, -ère f résident(e)/non résident(e) **b** (from outer space) extra-terrestre mf **2** ADJ **a** (= foreign) [forces, environment, concept] étranger (**to sb/sth** à qn/qch) **b** (= from outer space) [spacecraft, species, civilization] extraterrestre ; **~ being** extraterrestre mf

alienate ['eɪlɪəneɪt] VT (also Jur) aliéner ; **this has ~d all his friends** ceci (lui) a aliéné tous ses amis ; **she has ~d all her friends** elle s'est aliéné tous ses amis (**by doing** en faisant)

alienated ['eɪlɪəneɪtɪd] ADJ (= estranged) étranger (**from** à) ; (Psych) aliéné ; **to become ~ from sb/sth** se détacher de qn/qch

alienation [eɪlɪə'neɪʃən] N **a** (= estrangement) désaffection f, éloignement m (**from** de) **b** (Jur, Psych) aliénation f

alienist ['eɪlɪənɪst] N aliéniste mf

alight¹ [ə'laɪt] VI [person] descendre (**from** de), mettre pied à terre ; [bird] se poser (**on** sur)

► **alight on** VT FUS [+ fact] apprendre par hasard ; [+ idea] tomber sur

alight² [ə'laɪt] ADJ **a** (= lit) **to be ~** [candle, fire] être allumé ; [building] être en feu ; **try and keep the fire ~** ne laissez pas éteindre le feu ; **to set sth ~** mettre le feu à qch ; (fig) **bushes ~ with fireflies** buissons mpl illuminés par des lucioles **b** (= radiant) **to be ~** [eyes] briller, pétiller ; [face] rayonner ; **his eyes were ~ with laughter** ses yeux pétillaient ; **her face was ~ with happiness** son visage rayonnait de bonheur

align [ə'laɪn] **1** VT **a** aligner, mettre en ligne ; (Tech) dégauchir **b** (Fin, Pol) aligner (**on, with** sur) ; **to ~ o.s. with sb** s'aligner sur qn **2** VI [persons] s'aligner (**with** sur) ; [objects] être alignés

alignment [ə'laɪnmənt] N (lit, fig) alignement m ; (Aut) parallélisme m → **non-alignment**

alike [ə'laɪk] **1** ADJ **to be ~** [people] se ressembler, être semblables ; **they all look ~ to me** pour moi, ils se ressemblent tous ; **no two are exactly ~** il n'y en a pas deux qui soient exactement identiques ; **the sisters were remarkably ~ in appearance** la ressemblance physique entre les sœurs était remarquable **2** ADV **a** (= in the same way) [treat, speak, think, dress] de la même façon **b** (= equally) **winter and summer ~** été comme hiver ; **the southern and northern states ~** les États du nord comme ceux du sud → **share**

alimentary [ælɪ'mentərɪ] ADJ alimentaire ; **~ canal** tube m digestif

alimony ['ælɪmənɪ] N (Jur) pension f alimentaire

aliterate [eɪ'lɪtərət] **1** N ennemi(e) m(f) de la lecture **2** ADJ antilecture

alive [ə'laɪv] ADJ **a** (= living) vivant, en vie ; (= in existence) au monde ; **to burn ~** brûler vif ; **to bury sb ~** enterrer qn vivant ; **he must be taken ~** [prisoner] il faut le prendre or capturer vivant ; **while ~, he ...** de son vivant, il ... ; **it's good to be ~** il fait bon vivre ; **no man ~ could do it** personne ne serait capable de le faire ; **to do sth as well as anyone ~** faire qch aussi bien que n'importe qui ; (lit) **to keep sb ~** maintenir qn en vie ; **to stay ~** rester en vie, survivre ; **he's going to be eaten ~ by the press** la presse ne va en faire qu'une bouchée ; **we were eaten ~ by mosquitoes** nous avons été dévorés par les moustiques **b** (fig = lively) **to bring ~** [meeting etc] animer ; [past] faire revivre ; **to keep ~** [tradition] préserver ; [memory] garder ; **to come ~** s'animer **c** (frm) **~ to** sensible à ; **I am very ~ to the honour you do me** je suis très sensible à l'honneur que vous me faites ; **to be ~ to one's interests** veiller à ses intérêts ; **to be ~ to a danger** être conscient d'un danger **d** (= alert) alerte, vif ; (= active) actif, plein de vie ; **to be ~ and kicking*** (= living) être bien en vie ; (= full of energy) être plein de vie ; **look ~!*** allons, remuez-vous !* **e** **~ with insects/tourists** etc grouillant d'insectes/de touristes etc

alkali ['ælkəlaɪ] N (pl **alkalis** or **alkalies**) alcali m

alkaline ['ælkəlaɪn] ADJ alcalin

alkalinity [ælkə'lɪnɪtɪ] N alcalinité f

alkaloid ['ælkəlɔɪd] N alcaloïde m

alkie‡, **alky**‡ [ˈælkɪ] N alcoolo* *mf*, poivrot(e)* *m(f)*

---

all [ɔːl]

1 ADJECTIVE	4 NOUN
2 PRONOUN	5 SET STRUCTURES
3 ADVERB	6 COMPOUNDS

When all is part of a set combination, eg in all seriousness/probability, beyond all doubt, of all people, look up the noun.

1 ADJECTIVE

tout (le), toute (la), tous (les), toutes (les); **~ the time** tout le temps; **~ my life** toute ma vie; **~ kinds of** toutes sortes de; **~ the others** tous (toutes) les autres; **~ that** tout cela; **~ that is irrelevant** tout cela n'a aucun rapport; **he went on about loyalty and ~ that*** il parlait de loyauté et tout ça*; **loss of appetite, sleepless nights and ~ that** la perte d'appétit, les nuits blanches, et tout le reste

Articles or pronouns often need to be added in French:

~ day toute la journée; **~ three** tous les trois; **~ three said the same** ils ont tous les trois dit la même chose; **~ three accused were found guilty of fraud** les accusés ont tous (les) trois été jugés coupables de fraude → 5

2 PRONOUN

a = everything tout; **~ or nothing** tout ou rien; **~ is well** tout va bien; **that's ~** c'est tout; **you can't see ~ of Paris in a day** on ne peut pas voir tout Paris en une journée; *BUT* **if that's ~ it is, it's not important** si ce n'est que ça, ce n'est pas bien grave

• **it all**: **he drank it ~** il a tout bu; **he's seen it ~, done it ~** il a tout vu, tout fait; **it ~ happened so quickly** tout s'est passé si vite

• **all that** (*subject of relative clause*) tout ce qui; **that's ~ that matters** c'est tout ce qui importe; **you can have ~ that's left** tu peux prendre tout ce qui reste

• **all (that)** (*object of relative clause*) tout ce que; (*after verb taking "de"*) tout ce dont; **~ I want is to sleep** tout ce que je veux, c'est dormir; **that is ~ he said** c'est tout ce qu'il a dit; **we saw ~ there was to see** nous avons vu tout ce qu'il y avait à voir; **~ I remember is ...** tout ce dont je me souviens, c'est ...; *BUT* **~ I could do not to laugh** j'ai eu toutes les peines du monde à m'empêcher de rire

b plural tous *mpl*, toutes *fpl*; **we ~ sat down** nous nous sommes tous assis; **they've invited us ~** ils nous ont tous invités; **the girls ~ knew that ...** les filles savaient toutes que ...; **they ~ came with their husbands** elles sont toutes venues avec leurs maris; **they were ~ broken** ils étaient tous cassés; **the peaches? I've eaten them ~!** les pêches? je les ai toutes mangées!; *BUT* **evening, ~!*** (*greeting people*) bonsoir, tout le monde! → each, sundry

• **all who** tous ceux qui *mpl*, toutes celles qui *fpl*; **~ who knew him loved him** tous ceux qui le connaissaient l'appréciaient; **education should be open to ~ who want it** l'éducation devrait être accessible à tous ceux qui veulent en bénéficier

• **the worst/biggest/most** *etc* **of all**: **this was the worst** *or* **biggest disappointment of ~** ça a été la plus grosse déception; **this result was the most surprising of ~** ce résultat était le plus surprenant; **best of ~, the reforms will cost nothing** et surtout, ces réformes ne coûteront rien

c

• **all of the** tout le *m*, toute la *f*, tous les *mpl*, toutes les *fpl*; **~ of the work** tout le travail; **~ of the cooking** toute la cuisine; **~ of the cakes went** tous les gâteaux ont été mangés

• **all of it**: **I gave him some soup and he ate ~ of it** je lui ai donné de la soupe et il a tout mangé; **I didn't read ~ of it** je ne l'ai pas lu en entier; **not ~ of it was true** ce n'était pas entièrement vrai

• **all of them** tous *mpl*, toutes *fpl*; **~ of them failed** ils ont tous échoué; **I love his short stories, I've read ~ of them** j'aime beaucoup ses nouvelles, je les ai toutes lues

• **all of** + *number* (= *at least*) **it took him ~ of three hours** ça lui a pris trois bonnes heures; **it weighed ~ of 30 kilos** ça pesait bien 30 kilos; (*iro* = *only*) **exploring the village took ~ of ten minutes** la visite du village a bien dû prendre dix minutes

3 ADVERB

a = entirely tout; **she was dressed ~ in white** elle était habillée tout en blanc

When used with a feminine adjective starting with a consonant, tout agrees:

she came in ~ dishevelled elle est arrivée tout ébouriffée; **she went ~ red** elle est devenue toute rouge

• **all by o.s.** ◊ **all alone** tout seul; **he had to do it ~ by himself** il a dû le faire tout seul; **she's ~ alone** elle est toute seule; **she left her daughters ~ alone in the flat** elle a laissé ses filles toutes seules dans l'appartement

b *in scores* **the score was two ~** (*tennis, squash*) les joueurs étaient à deux jeux (*or* sets) partout; (*other sports*) le score était de deux à deux; **what's the score? — two ~** quel est le score? — deux partout *or* deux à deux

4 NOUN

= utmost **I decided to give it my ~** j'ai décidé de donner mon maximum; **he puts his ~ into every game** il s'investit complètement dans chaque match

5 SET STRUCTURES

• **all along** (= *from the start*) depuis le début; (= *the whole length of*) tout le long de; **I feared that ~ along** je le craint depuis le début; **~ along the road** tout le long de la route

• **all but** (= *nearly*) presque, pratiquement; (= *all except*) tous sauf; **he's ~ but forgotten now** il est presque *or* pratiquement tombé dans l'oubli; **the party won ~ but six of the seats** le parti a remporté tous les sièges sauf six; **this would exclude ~ but those able to pay** cela exclurait tout le monde sauf ceux qui peuvent payer, cela exclurait tout ceux qui ne peuvent pas payer; *BUT* **the plant will stand ~ but the harshest winters** cette plante supportera bien le froid, à moins que l'hiver ne soit des plus rudes

• **all for**: **to be ~ for sth** être tout à fait pour qch; **I'm ~ for giving him a chance** je suis tout à fait pour lui donner une chance; **I'm ~ for it** je suis tout à fait pour*

• **all in*** (= *exhausted*) lessivé*, crevé*; **after a day's skiing I was ~ in** j'étais lessivé* *or* crevé* au bout d'une journée de ski; **you look ~ in** tu as l'air lessivé* *or* crevé* → 6

• **all in all** (= *altogether*) l'un dans l'autre; **we thought, ~ in ~, it wasn't a bad idea** nous avons pensé que, l'un dans l'autre, ce n'était pas une mauvaise idée

• **all one**: **it's ~ one** c'est du pareil au même; **it's ~ one to them** c'est du pareil au même pour eux

• **all over** (= *everywhere*) partout; **I looked for you ~ over** je vous ai cherché partout; **I'm aching ~ over** j'ai mal partout; **she was ~ over flour*** elle était couverte de farine, elle avait de la farine partout; **~ over France** partout en France; *BUT* **he was trembling ~ over** il tremblait de tous ses membres; **embroidered ~ over** recouvert de broderies; **~ over the country** dans tout le pays; **~ over the world** à travers le monde, dans le monde entier; **that's him ~ over*** c'est bien lui!, on le reconnaît bien là!

• **to be all over** (= *finished*) être fini; **it's ~ over!** c'est fini!; **it's ~ over between us** tout est fini entre nous; **it'll be ~ over with him** ce sera un homme fini

• **to be all over sb*** (= *affectionate with*): **they were ~ over each other** ils s'étaient pendus au cou l'un de l'autre; **when they hear about the money, they'll be ~ over you** quand ils sauront que tu as cet argent, ils ne vont plus te lâcher; (= *dominating*) **Celtic were ~ over Rangers*** le Celtic a complètement dominé *or* baladé* les Rangers

• **all the more**: **this was ~ the more surprising since ...** c'était d'autant plus surprenant que ...; **~ the more so since ...** d'autant plus que ...

• **all the better!** tant mieux!

• **all too**: **it was ~ too obvious he didn't mean it** on voyait bien qu'il n'en pensait rien; **the evening passed ~ too quickly** la soirée a passé bien trop rapidement

• **all up**: **it is ~ up with him*** il est fichu*

• **all very**: **that's ~ very well but ...** c'est bien beau mais ...; **it was ~ very embarrassing** c'était vraiment très gênant

• **and all**: **the dog ate the sausage, mustard and ~** le chien a mangé la saucisse, moutarde comprise, le chien a mangé la saucisse avec la moutarde et tout*; **what with the snow and ~, we didn't go** avec la neige et tout le reste, nous n'y sommes pas allés

• **as all that**: **it's not as important/urgent as ~ that** ce n'est pas si important/urgent que ça

• **for all ...** (= *despite*) malgré; **for ~ its beauty, the city may be losing its individuality** malgré sa beauté, la ville est peut-être en train de perdre son individualité; **for ~ that** malgré tout

• **for all I know ...**: **for ~ I know he could be right** il a peut-être raison, je n'en sais rien; **for ~ I know** *or* **care, they're still living together** ils vivent peut-être encore ensemble, mais c'est le dernier de mes soucis

• **if ... at all**: **they won't attempt it, if they have any sense at ~** ils ne vont pas essayer s'ils ont un peu de bon sens; **the little grammar they learn, if they study grammar at ~** le peu de grammaire qu'ils apprennent, si tant est qu'ils étudient la grammaire; **very rarely if at ~** très rarement pour ne pas dire jamais; **if at ~ possible** dans la mesure du possible

• **in all** en tout; **5 people in ~ witnessed the accident** 5 personnes en tout ont vu l'accident

• **no ... at all**: **it makes no difference at ~** ça ne fait aucune différence; **I have no regrets at ~** je n'ai aucun regret, je ne regrette rien

• **none at all**: **have you any comments? — none at ~!** vous avez des remarques à faire? — absolument aucun!

• **not ... at all** (= *not in the least*) pas ... du tout; **I don't mind at ~** ça ne me gêne pas du tout; **are you disappointed? — not at ~!** vous êtes déçu — pas du tout *or* pas le moins du monde!; **thank you! — not at ~!** merci! — de rien *or* je vous en prie!

• **not all that** (= *not so*) **it isn't ~ that far** ce n'est pas si loin que ça

• **not all there**: **he's not ~ there*** il lui manque une case*

6 COMPOUNDS

► **all-American** ADJ cent pour cent américain ► **all-around** (*US*) → **all-round** ► **all clear** N = **clear (signal)** (signal *m* de) fin *f* d'alerte; **~ clear!** (= *you can go through*) la voie est libre; (= *the alert is over*) l'alerte est passée; (*Mil*) fin d'alerte!; (*fig*) **to give sb the ~ clear** (*gen*) donner le feu vert à qn; (*doctor to patient*) dire à qn que tout va bien ► **all-conquering** ADJ [*hero, team*] qui triomphe de tous ► **all-consuming** ADJ [*passion*] dévorant ► **all-dancing*** ADJ = **all-singing** ► **all-day** ADJ qui dure toute la journée ► **all-embracing** ADJ global ► **all-fired*** ADV (*US*) **what's so ~-fired important about it?** qu'est-ce que ça a de si important? ► **All Fools' Day** N le premier avril ► **all found** ADJ logé et nourri ► **all fours** NPL **on ~ fours** à quatre pattes ► **all get-out‡** N (*US*) **angry as ~ get-out** vachement* en colère ► **All Hallows** N la Toussaint ► **all-important** ADJ de la plus haute importance, capital ► **all in** ADJ → **all 5** ► **all-in** ADJ (*Brit*) [*price*] net, tout compris *inv*; [*insurance policy*] tous risques; (*Comm*) [*tariff*] tout compris; (*Brit*) **the holiday cost £80 ~-in** les vacances ont coûté 80 livres tout compris ► **all-in-one** N combinaison *f* ◆ ADJ **an ~-in-**

one **outfit** une combinaison; **an ~-in-one sleepsuit** une grenouillère ▸ **all-inclusive** ADJ [price, rate] tout compris inv, net; [policy] tous risques ▸ **all-in wrestling** N catch m ▸ **all-metal body** N (Aut) carrosserie f toute en tôle ▸ **all-nighter** N spectacle qui dure toute la nuit ▸ **all-night pass** N (Mil) permission f de nuit ▸ **all-night service** N (Comm etc) permanence f or service m de nuit ▸ **all-night showing** N (Cine) projection ininterrompue pendant toute la nuit ▸ **all out** ADV to go ~ **out** (physically) y aller à fond; **to go ~ out for growth/monetary union** jeter toutes ses forces dans la bataille pour la croissance/l'union monétaire ▸ **all-out effort** N effort m maximum ▸ **all-out strike** N grève f totale ▸ **all-out war** N (Mil, fig) guerre f totale; **an ~-out war on inflation** une guerre contre l'inflation ▸ **all-over** ADJ (qui est) sur toute la surface ▸ **all-over pattern** N dessin or motif qui recouvre toute une surface ▸ **all-party** ADJ (Pol) multipartite, où tous les partis sont représentés ▸ **all-pervading**, **all-pervasive** ADJ [influence, presence] qui se fait sentir partout ▸ **all-points bulletin** N (US) message m à toutes les patrouilles (**on** à propos de) ▸ **all-powerful** ADJ tout-puissant ▸ **all-purpose** ADJ [flour, vehicle, cleaner] tous usages; [knife, spanner, glue] universel ▸ **all-right*** ADJ → **all-right** ▸ **all-risks insurance** N assurance f tous risques ▸ **all-round** ADJ [sportsman] complet (-ète f); [improvement] général, sur toute la ligne ▸ **all-rounder** N (Cricket) joueur m complet; (fig) **to be a good ~-rounder** être bon en tout ▸ **All Saints' Day** N (le jour de) la Toussaint ▸ **all-seater** ADJ (Brit Sport) [stadium, stand] n'ayant que des places assises ▸ **all-singing*** ADJ (Brit fig hum) polyvalent ▸ **All Souls' Day** N le jour or la fête des Morts ▸ **all-star** ADJ (Theat etc) **~-star performance, show with an ~-star cast** plateau m de vedettes ▸ **all-terrain bike** N vélo m tout-terrain, VTT m ▸ **all-terrain vehicle** N véhicule m tout-terrain ▸ **all-time** ADJ → **all-time** ▸ **all told** ADV en tout ▸ **all-weather** ADJ toute saison ▸ **all-weather court** N (Tennis) (court m en) quick® m ▸ **all-wheel-drive** N voiture f à quatre (or six etc) roues motrices ▸ **all-year-round** ADJ [sport] que l'on pratique toute l'année; [resort] ouvert toute l'année

Allah [ˈælə] N Allah m

allay [əˈleɪ] VT [+ fears] modérer, apaiser; [+ pain, thirst] soulager, apaiser; **to ~ suspicion** dissiper les soupçons

allegation [ˌælɪˈɡeɪʃən] N allégation f

allege [əˈledʒ] VT alléguer, prétendre (**that** que); **to ~ illness** prétexter or alléguer une maladie; **he is ~d to have said that ...** il aurait dit que ..., on prétend qu'il a dit que ...

alleged [əˈledʒd] ADJ (gen) présumé; [reason] allégué

▼ **allegedly** [əˈledʒɪdlɪ] ADV (esp Jur) **the crime he had ~ committed** le crime qu'il aurait commis; **~ illegal immigrants** les immigrants qui seraient en situation illégale; (= supposedly) **he's ill, ~** il est soi-disant or prétendument malade

allegiance [əˈliːdʒəns] N allégeance f (**to** à); (Brit) **the oath of ~** le serment d'allégeance

allegoric(al) [ˌælɪˈɡɒrɪk(əl)] ADJ allégorique

allegorically [ˌælɪˈɡɒrɪkəlɪ] ADV [interpret] allégoriquement; [speak, write] de façon allégorique

allegory [ˈælɪɡərɪ] N allégorie f

alleluia [ˌælɪˈluːjə] EXCL alléluia!

Allen key [ˈælənkiː], **Allen wrench** (US) [ˈælənrentʃ] N clé f à six pans

allergen [ˈælədʒen] N allergène m

allergenic [ˌæləˈdʒenɪk] ADJ allergénique

allergic [əˈlɜːdʒɪk] ADJ (Med,* fig) allergique (**to** à)

allergist [ˈælədʒɪst] N allergologue mf

allergy [ˈælədʒɪ] N allergie f (**to** à); **an ~ to dust** ◊ **a dust** ~ une allergie à la poussière

alleviate [əˈliːvɪeɪt] VT [+ pain] soulager, calmer; [+ sorrow] adoucir; [+ thirst] apaiser, calmer

alleviation [əˌliːvɪˈeɪʃən] N (NonC) [of suffering, condition, pain] soulagement m; [of poverty] réduction f; [of symptoms] atténuation f; [of sorrow] adoucissement m; [of thirst] apaisement m

alley [ˈælɪ] **1** N (between buildings) ruelle f; (in garden) allée f; (US: between counters) passage m; (fig) **this is right up my ~*** c'est tout à fait mon rayon* ▸ **blind, bowling 2** COMP ▸ **alley cat** N chat m de gouttière; **she's got the morals of an ~ cat*** elle couche à droite et à gauche*

alleyway [ˈælɪweɪ] N ruelle f

alliance [əˈlaɪəns] N [of states, persons] alliance f; **to enter into an ~** s'allier avec ...

allied [ˈælaɪd] **1** ADJ **a** (= in league) allié (**against sb/sth** contre qn/qch, **to sb/sth** à qn/qch, **with sb/sth** avec qn/qch) **b** (= associated) [industries] assimilé, apparenté; [conditions] apparenté; [subjects] connexe; **lectures on subjects ~ to health** conférences fpl sur des sujets liés à la santé; (Jur) **products** produits mpl assimilés or apparentés **c** (= coupled) **~ to** or **with sth** allié à qch; **an interest rate rise ~ with a stock market slump** une augmentation des taux d'intérêts conjuguée à une chute de la Bourse **d** (Bio) de la même famille or espèce **2** COMP ▸ **allied health professional** N (US) médecin ou infirmière dont les prestations sont remboursées par une mutuelle

alligator [ˈælɪɡeɪtər] N alligator m

alliteration [əˌlɪtəˈreɪʃən] N allitération f

alliterative [əˈlɪtərətɪv] ADJ allitératif

allocate [ˈæləʊkeɪt] VT **a** (= allot) [+ task] allouer, attribuer (**to sb** à qn); [+ money] affecter (**to** à) **b** (= apportion) répartir, distribuer (**among** parmi) **c** (Jur, Fin) ventiler

allocation [ˌæləʊˈkeɪʃən] N **a** (= allotting) affectation f; (to individual) attribution f **b** (= apportioning) répartition f **c** (= money allocated) part f, allocation f **d** (Jur, Fin) ventilation f

allograph [ˈæləʊɡrɑːf] N (Ling) allographe m

allomorph [ˈæləʊmɔːf] N (Ling) allomorphe m

allopathic [ˌæləˈpæθɪk] ADJ allopathique

allopathy [əˈlɒpəθɪ] N (NonC) allopathie f

allophone [ˈæləʊfəʊn] N (Ling) allophone m

allot [əˈlɒt] VT **a** (= allocate) attribuer, assigner (**sth to sb** qch à qn); **everyone was ~ted a piece of land** chacun a reçu un terrain en lot; **to do sth in the time ~ted (to one)** faire qch dans le temps qui (vous) est imparti or assigné; **to ~ sth to a certain use** affecter or destiner qch à un certain usage **b** (= share among group) répartir, distribuer

allotment [əˈlɒtmənt] N **a** (Brit = ground for cultivation) parcelle f or lopin m de terre (loué pour la culture), lotissement m **b** (= division of shares) partage m, lotissement m; (= distribution of shares) distribution f, part f

allotrope [ˈæləˌtrəʊp] N variété f allotropique

allottee [ˌælɒˈtiː] N (St Ex) attributaire mf

▼ **allow** [əˈlaʊ] VT **a** (= permit) permettre, autoriser; (= tolerate) tolérer, souffrir; **to ~ sb sth** permettre qch à qn; **to ~ sb to do** permettre à qn de faire, autoriser qn à faire; **to ~ sb in/out/past** etc permettre à qn d'entrer/de sortir/de passer etc; **to ~ sth to happen** laisser se produire qch; **to ~ o.s. to be persuaded** se laisser persuader; **~ us to help you** permettez que nous vous aidions, permettez-nous de vous aider; **we are not ~ed much freedom** on nous accorde peu de liberté; **smoking is not**

~ed il est interdit or défendu de fumer; **no children/dogs ~ed** interdit aux enfants/chiens; **I will not ~ such behaviour** je ne tolérerai or souffrirai pas une telle conduite **b** (= grant) [+ money] accorder, allouer; **to ~ sb £30 a month** allouer or accorder à qn 30 livres par mois; (Jur) **to ~ sb a thousand pounds damages** accorder à qn mille livres de dommages et intérêts; **to ~ space for** prévoir or ménager de la place pour; (Comm) **to ~ sb a discount** faire bénéficier qn d'une remise, consentir une remise à qn; **~ (yourself) an hour to cross the city** comptez une heure pour traverser la ville; **~ 5cm for shrinkage** prévoyez 5 cm (de plus) pour le cas où le tissu rétrécirait **c** (= agree as possible) [+ claim] admettre **d** (= concede) admettre (**that** que); **~ing that ... en admettant que ... (+ subj)

▸ **allow for** VT FUS tenir compte de; [+ money spent, funds allocated] (by deduction) déduire pour; (by addition) ajouter pour; **~ing for the circumstances** compte tenu des circonstances; **after ~ing for his expenses** déduction faite de or en tenant compte de ses dépenses; **we must ~ for the cost of the wood** il faut compter (avec) le prix du bois; **~ing for the shrinking of the material** en tenant compte du rétrécissement du tissu or du fait que le tissu rétrécit; **to ~ for all possibilities** parer à toute éventualité

▸ **allow of** VT FUS admettre, souffrir

allowable [əˈlaʊəbl] ADJ permis, admissible; (Tax) déductible; **~ against tax** déductible des impôts

allowance [əˈlaʊəns] N **a** (= money given to sb) allocation f; (for lodgings, food etc) indemnité f; (from separated husband) pension f alimentaire; (= salary) appointements mpl; (= food) ration f; (esp US = pocket money) argent m de poche; **he makes his mother an ~** il verse une rente or une pension à sa mère; **his father gives him an ~ of £500 per month** son père lui verse 500 livres par mois; **rent ~** allocation f de logement; **London ~** prime f de vie chère or indemnité f de résidence pour poste basé à Londres; **~ in kind** prestation f en nature; (Mil) **~ for quarters** indemnité f de logement → **car, clothing, family** **b** (Comm, Fin = discount) réduction f; **tax ~s** sommes fpl déductibles **c** (= concession) **you must learn to make ~s** il faut savoir faire la part des choses; **to make ~(s) for sb** (= excuse) se montrer indulgent envers qn, essayer de comprendre qn; **to make ~(s) for sth** (= allow for) tenir compte de qch, prendre qch en considération

alloy [ˈælɔɪ] **1** N alliage m **2** [əˈlɔɪ] VT (Metal) allier, faire un alliage de **3** COMP ▸ **alloy steel** N acier m allié ▸ **alloy wheels** NPL (Aut) roues fpl en alliage léger

all right [ˈɔːlˈraɪt] **1** ADJ **a** (= satisfactory) bien; **he's ~** il est bien or valable*; **do you like the champagne? — it's ~** aimez-vous ce champagne? — il n'est pas mal; **it's ~** ça va; (= don't worry) ce n'est pas grave; **is it ~ if ...?** ça vous dérange si ...?; **that's ~, don't worry** ce n'est pas grave; **is everything ~?** tout va bien?; **it's** or **that's ~ by me** d'accord; **see you later, ~?** à tout à l'heure, d'accord? **b** (= safe, well) **to be ~** (= healthy) aller bien, être en bonne santé; (= safe) être sain et sauf; **someone should see if she's ~** quelqu'un devrait aller voir si elle va bien; **the car will be ~ there overnight** la voiture ne risque rien à passer la nuit là **c** (= well-provided) **to be ~ for money/paper** etc avoir assez d'argent/de papier etc; **we're ~ for the rest of our lives** nous sommes tranquilles or nous avons tout ce qu'il nous faut pour le restant de nos jours; **I'm ~ Jack*** moi, je suis peinard*

▸ LANGUAGE IN USE: **allegedly** 26.3 **allow** 9, 10.4, 12

2 EXCL (*in approval*) ça y est !, ça va !* ; (*in agreement*) d'accord ! ; (*in exasperation*) ça va !* ; (*esp US: in triumph*) bravo !

3 ADV **a** (= *without difficulty*) sans problème ; **he's getting on ~** il se débrouille pas mal ; **did you get home ~ last night?** tu es bien rentré chez toi, hier soir ? ; **I managed that ~, but I couldn't ...** j'ai réussi à faire ça sans problème, mais je n'ai pas pu ... ; **he's doing ~ for himself** il se débrouille bien

b (= *definitely*) **he's at home ~, but he's not answering the phone** il est chez lui c'est sûr, c'est simplement qu'il ne répond pas au téléphone ; **you'll get the money back ~** vous serez remboursé, c'est sûr ; **it's warm enough ~!** il fait bien chaud, ça c'est vrai

c (*expressing agreement*) **can you help? — ~, what do you want me to do?** pouvez-vous m'aider ? — certainement, que puis-je faire pour vous ? ; **you say I was wrong; ~ but ...** vous dites que j'avais tort ; d'accord *or* admettons, mais ...

d (*summoning attention*) **~, let's get started** bon, allons-y ! ; **~, who's in charge here?** bon, qui est responsable ici ?

e (*introducing a challenge, threat*) **~, what's the joke?** bon, qu'est-ce qu'il y a de drôle ?

all-right* [ˈɔːlˈraɪt] ADJ (*US*) **an ~ guy** un type sûr *or* réglo*

allspice [ˈɔːlspaɪs] N quatre-épices *m inv*

all-time [ˈɔːlˈtaɪm] **1** ADJ sans précédent, de tous les temps ; **he's my ~ favourite** c'est mon préféré ; **"Casablanca" is one of the ~ greats** *or* **great films** « Casablanca » est l'un des plus grands films de tous les temps *or* un grand classique du cinéma ; **he's one of the ~ greats** il fait partie des plus grands ; **~ record** record *m* absolu ; **the pound has reached an ~ low** la livre a atteint le niveau le plus bas jamais enregistré ; **to be at an ~ low** être au plus bas **2** ADV **an ~ best performance** un record personnel ; **the ~ worst performance of that song** la pire interprétation qu'il y ait jamais eu de cette chanson ; **John's ~ favourite artist** l'artiste préféré de John

allude [əˈluːd] VI **to ~ to** [*person*] faire allusion à ; [*letter etc*] avoir trait à, se rapporter à

allure [əˈljʊəʳ] **1** VT (= *attract*) attirer ; (= *entice*) séduire **2** N charme *m*, attrait *m*

alluring [əˈljʊərɪŋ] ADJ séduisant, charmant

alluringly [əˈljʊərɪŋlɪ] ADV **to smile ~** avoir un sourire séduisant ; **~ mysterious** séduisant par son côté mystérieux

allusion [əˈluːʒən] N allusion *f*

allusive [əˈluːsɪv] ADJ allusif, qui contient une allusion

allusively [əˈluːsɪvlɪ] ADV par allusion

alluvia [əˈluːvɪə] NPL *of* **alluvium**

alluvial [əˈluːvɪəl] ADJ [*ground*] alluvial ; [*deposit*] alluvionnaire

alluvium [əˈluːvɪəm] N (*pl* **alluviums** *or* **alluvia**) alluvion *f*

ally [əˈlaɪ] **1** VT allier, unir (**with** avec) ; **to ~ o.s. with** s'allier avec **2** [ˈælaɪ] N (*gen*) allié(e) *m(f)* ; (*Pol*) allié(e) *m(f)* ; (*Mil Hist*) **the Allies** les Alliés *mpl*

alma mater [ˌælməˈmɑːtəʳ] N alma mater *f inv*

almanac [ˈɔːlmənæk] N almanach *m*, annuaire *m* → **nautical**

almighty [ɔːlˈmaɪtɪ] **1** ADJ **a** tout-puissant, omnipotent ; **Almighty God** Dieu Tout-Puissant ; **the ~ dollar** le dollar tout-puissant **b** (* = *tremendous*) [*row, scandal*] énorme ; **an ~ din** un vacarme de tous les diables **2** N **the Almighty** le Tout-Puissant **3** ADV* extrêmement, énormément

almond [ˈɑːmənd] **1** N amande *f* ; (*also* **~ tree**) amandier *m* ; **split ~s** amandes *fpl* effilées → **burnt**, **sugar** **2** COMP [*oil, paste*] d'amande ► **almond-eyed** ADJ aux yeux en

amande ► **almond-shaped** ADJ [*eyes etc*] en amande

almoner† [ˈɑːmənəʳ] N (*Brit*) (*lady*) **~** assistante *f* sociale (*attachée à un hôpital*)

almost [ˈɔːlməʊst] ADV presque ; **I had ~ forgotten about it** j'avais presque oublié ; **he ~ fell/died** il a failli tomber/mourir ; **you're ~ there** vous y êtes presque ; **I can ~ do it** j'arrive presque à le faire, j'y arrive presque ; **~ finished/cooked/cold** presque terminé/cuit/froid ; **~ always** presque toujours ; **he's ~ certainly been murdered** il est pratiquement certain *or* très probable qu'il a été assassiné ; **~ a month** presque un mois, près d'un mois

alms [ɑːmz] N aumône *f* ; **to give ~** faire l'aumône *or* la charité ; **~ box** tronc *m* des pauvres ; (*Hist*) **~ house** hospice *m*

aloe [ˈæləʊ] N aloès *m* → **bitter**

aloe vera [ˌæləʊˈvɪərə] N (= *plant*) aloe vera *f* ; (= *extract*) [extrait *m* d']aloès *m*

aloft [əˈlɒft] ADV (*also* **up ~**) en haut, en l'air ; (*Naut*) dans la mâture ; (*hum* = *in heaven*) au ciel

Aloha [əˈləʊə] N (*US*) **the ~ State** Hawaï *m*

alone [əˈləʊn] ADJ, ADV **a** (= *by o.s.*) seul ; **all ~** tout(e) seul(e) ; **quite ~** tout à fait seul(e) ; **you can't do it ~** vous ne pouvez pas le faire seul ; **she brought up two children** ~ elle a élevé deux enfants toute seule ; **a gunman acting ~** un bandit armé agissant seul ; **to go it ~*** faire cavalier seul ; **don't leave them ~ together** ne les laissez pas seuls ensemble ; **we'd never spent such a long time ~ together** nous n'avions jamais passé autant de temps seuls ensemble *or* en tête à tête ; **I was ~ with her/my thoughts** j'étais seul avec elle/mes pensées ; **I need to get her ~** il faut que je lui parle en tête-à-tête *or* entre quat'z'yeux*

b (= *only*) seul ; **he ~ could tell you** lui seul pourrait vous le dire ; **you ~ can do it** vous êtes le seul à pouvoir le faire ; **we are not ~ in thinking this** nous ne sommes pas les seuls à le penser ; **pride ~ prevented her from giving up** seul l'orgueil l'a empêchée d'abandonner ; **we must have gained 100 members from this ~** nous devons avoir gagné 100 membres de plus rien qu'avec cela ■ (*PROV*) **man cannot live by bread ~** l'homme ne vit pas seulement de pain ; **that charm which is hers (and hers) ~** ce charme qui lui est propre *or* qui n'appartient qu'à elle

c (= *lonely*) seul ; **I feel so ~** je me sens si seul **d** (= *in peace*) **to leave** *or* **let sb ~** laisser qn tranquille, laisser qn en paix ; **leave** *or* **let me ~!** laisse-moi tranquille !, fiche-moi la paix !* ; **leave** *or* **let him ~ to do it** laisse-le faire tout seul ; **leave** *or* **let the book ~!** ne touche pas au livre ! ; **I advise you to leave the whole business ~** je vous conseille de ne pas vous en mêler ; **leave** *or* **let well ~** le mieux est l'ennemi du bien (*PROV*)

e (*as conj*) **let ~** encore moins ; **he can't read, let ~ write** il ne sait pas lire, (et) encore moins écrire ; **he can't afford food, let ~ clothes** il n'a pas de quoi s'acheter de la nourriture, sans parler de vêtements *or* encore moins des vêtements

along [əˈlɒŋ]

> When **along** is an element in a phrasal verb, eg **go along, play along, string along**, look up the verb.

1 ADV **a** en avant ; **come ~!** allez venez !, venez donc ! ; **I'll be ~ in a moment** j'arrive tout de suite ; **she'll be ~ tomorrow** elle viendra demain ; **how is John getting ~?** et John, ça va bien ?, quelles nouvelles de John ? → **move along**

b **come ~ with me** venez avec moi ; **he came ~ with six others** il est venu accompagné de six autres ; **she escaped from the fire ~ with her baby** elle a échappé à l'incendie avec son bébé aussi ; **bring your friend ~** amène ton ami ; **~ here** par là ; (*fig*) **get ~ with you!*** (= *go*

away) fiche le camp !*, décampe !* ; (= *you can't mean it*) tu plaisantes *or* rigoles*?

c **all ~** (*space*) d'un bout à l'autre ; (*time*) depuis le début ; **I could see all ~ that he would refuse** je savais depuis le début qu'il allait refuser ; **that's what I've been saying all ~** c'est ce que je n'ai pas arrêté de dire

2 PREP le long de ; **to walk ~ the beach** se promener le long de *or* sur la plage ; **the railway runs ~ the beach** la ligne de chemin de fer longe la plage ; **the trees ~ the road** les arbres au bord de la route *or* qui bordent la route ; **they built houses ~ the river** ils ont construit des maisons le long de la rivière ; **all ~ the street** tout le long de la rue ; **somewhere ~ the way he lost a glove** il a perdu un gant en chemin *or* quelque part ; (*fig*) **somewhere ~ the way** *or* **the line*** someone made a mistake à un moment donné, quelqu'un a commis une erreur ; **to proceed ~ the lines suggested** agir *or* procéder conformément à la ligne d'action proposée

alongside [əˈlɒŋˈsaɪd] **1** PREP (= *along: also Naut*) le long de ; (= *beside*) à côté de, près de ; **to work ~ sb** travailler aux côtés de qn ; (*Naut*) **to come ~ the quay** accoster le quai ; **the road runs ~ the beach** la route longe la plage ; **to stop ~ the kerb** [*vehicle*] s'arrêter le long du trottoir ; **the car drew up ~ me** la voiture s'est arrêtée à côté de moi *or* à ma hauteur **2** ADV **a** (*Naut*) (*ships = beside one another*) bord à bord, à couple ; **to come ~** accoster ; **to make fast ~** (*quayside*) s'amarrer à *or* au quai ; (*another vessel*) s'amarrer bord à bord, s'amarrer en couple ; **to pass ~ a ship** longer un navire **b** (*people = side by side*) côte à côte

aloof [əˈluːf] ADJ **a** (= *standoffish*) [*person, character*] distant ; **he was very ~ with me** il s'est montré très distant à mon égard ; **she kept very (much) ~** elle a gardé *or* conservé ses distances **b** (= *uninvolved*) **to hold o.s.** *or* **remain ~** se tenir à l'écart (**from sb/sth** de qn/qch)

aloofness [əˈluːfnɪs] N attitude *f* distante, réserve *f*

alopecia [ˌæləˈpiːʃə] N alopécie *f*

aloud [əˈlaʊd] ADV [*read*] à haute voix, à voix haute ; [*laugh, think, wonder*] tout haut

alp [ælp] N (= *peak*) pic *m* ; (= *mountain*) montagne *f* ; (= *pasture*) alpage *m*, alpe *f* ; **the Alps** les Alpes *fpl*

alpaca [ælˈpækə] N (= *animal, wool*) alpaga *m*

alpenhorn [ˈælpənˌhɔːn] N cor *m* des Alpes

alpenstock [ˈælpənstɒk] N alpenstock *m*

alpha [ˈælfə] **1** N **a** (= *letter*) alpha *m* ; **~ particle** particule *f* alpha **b** (*Brit Scol, Univ*) ≈ très bien ; **~ plus** ≈ excellent **2** COMP ► **alpha-fetoprotein** N alpha-fœto-protéine *f* ► **alpha rhythm** N rythme *m* alpha ► **alpha wave** N onde *f* alpha

alphabet [ˈælfəbet] N alphabet *m* ; **~ soup** (*Culin*) potage *m* aux pâtes (en forme de lettres) ; (* *fig pej*) salade *f* de sigles → **deaf**, **finger**

alphabetic(al) [ˌælfəˈbetɪk(əl)] ADJ alphabétique ; **to put in alphabetical order** classer par ordre alphabétique ; **to be in alphabetical order** être dans l'ordre alphabétique

alphabetically [ˌælfəˈbetɪkəlɪ] ADV par ordre alphabétique, alphabétiquement

alphabetize [ˈælfəbətaɪz] VT classer par ordre alphabétique

alphanumeric [ˌælfənjuːˈmerɪk] ADJ alphanumérique

alpine [ˈælpaɪn] **1** ADJ [*scenery, village*] des Alpes, alpin ; [*mountain, chalet*] (= *in the Alps*) des Alpes ; (= *alpine-style*) alpin ; [*troops, skiing, skier*] alpin ; [*plant*] (*on lower slopes*) alpestre ; (*on higher slopes*) alpin ; [*meadow, pasture, climate*] alpestre **2** COMP ► **alpine hut** N refuge *m* de montagne

alpinist ['ælpınıst] N alpiniste *mf*

already [ɔːl'redı] ADV déjà ; (*esp US: expressing impatience*) **(that's) enough ~!**: maintenant, ça suffit !

alright [ɔːl'raɪt] = **all right**

Alsace ['ælsæs] N l'Alsace *f*

Alsace-Lorraine ['ælsæslɔ'reɪn] N l'Alsace-Lorraine *f*

Alsatian [æl'seɪʃən] **1** N **a** (= *person*) Alsacien(ne) *m(f)* **b** (*Brit: also* **~ dog**) chien *m* loup, berger *m* allemand **2** ADJ alsacien, d'Alsace

also ['ɔːlsəʊ] **1** ADV **a** (= *too*) aussi, également ; **her cousin ~ came** son cousin aussi est venu *or* est venu également **b** (= *moreover*) de plus, également ; **~ I must explain that ...** de plus, je dois vous expliquer que ..., je dois également vous expliquer que ... **2** COMP ► **also-ran** N (*Sport*) autre concurrent *m* (*non classé*) ; (*Racing*) cheval *m* non classé ; (* = *person*) perdant(e) *m(f)*

Alta ABBR = **Alberta**

Altamira [,æltə'miːrə] N **the ~ caves** les grottes *fpl* d'Altamira

altar ['ɒltər] **1** N (*Rel*) autel *m* ; **high ~** maître-autel *m* ; (*fig*) **he was sacrificed on the ~ of productivity** il a été immolé sur l'autel de la productivité **2** COMP ► **altar boy** N enfant *m* de chœur ► **altar cloth** N nappe *f* d'autel ► **altar piece** N retable *m* ► **altar rail(s)** N(PL) clôture *f* *or* balustre *m* (du chœur) ; (*Rel*) table *f* de communion

alter ['ɒltər] **1** VT **a** (*gen*) changer, modifier ; (*stronger*) transformer ; (= *adapt*) adapter, ajuster ; [+ *painting, poem, speech etc*] retoucher ; (*stronger*) remanier ; [+ *garment*] retoucher ; (*stronger*) transformer ; **to ~ one's plans** modifier *or* transformer ses projets ; **to ~ one's attitude** changer d'attitude (*to envers*) ; **that ~s the case** voilà qui est différent *or* qui change tout ; (*Naut*) **to ~ course** changer de cap *or* de route ; **to ~ sth for the better** changer qch en mieux, améliorer qch ; **to ~ sth for the worse** changer qch en mal, altérer qch **b** (*US* = *castrate*) châtrer, castrer **2** VI changer ; **to ~ for the better** [*circumstances*] s'améliorer ; [*person, character*] changer en mieux ; **to ~ for the worse** [*circumstances*] empirer, s'aggraver ; [*person, character*] changer en mal

alteration [,ɒltə'reɪʃən] N **a** (= *change*) (*to plan, team, rules etc*) modification *f*, changement *m* ; (*to behaviour, diet*) changement *m* ; **to make ~s to existing arrangements** apporter des modifications aux dispositions existantes ; **an ~ in the rules** une modification des règlements ; **to make ~s to a garment/text/painting** retoucher un vêtement/texte/tableau ; **textual ~s** retouches *fpl* au texte ; **climatic ~s** changements *mpl* climatiques ; **to make ~s to a team** modifier une équipe ; **the ~s to the house** les transformations *fpl* apportées à la maison ; **they're having ~s made to their house** ils font faire des travaux ; (*shop, building*) **"closed for ~s"** « fermé pour travaux » ; (*Naut*) **~ of route** (*deliberate*) changement *m* de route ; (*involuntary*) déroutement *m* **b** (*NonC* = *altering*) [*of structure, building*] transformation *f* ; [*of climate*] changements *mpl* ; [*of garment*] retouches *fpl* ; **did you see any ~ in his behaviour?** avez-vous remarqué un changement dans son comportement ? ; **"times and programmes are subject to ~"** « les horaires et les programmes peuvent être modifiés »

altercation [,ɒltə'keɪʃən] N (*frm*) altercation *f* ; **to have an ~** se disputer, avoir une altercation

alter ego ['æltər'iːgəʊ] N alter ego *m* ; **he is my ~** c'est mon alter ego

alternate [ɒl'tɜːnɪt] **1** ADJ **a** (= *successive*) [*actions, periods, colours*] alterné ; **cover with ~**

slices of tomato and mozzarella recouvrir en alternant tranches de tomate et de mozzarella ; **a week of ~ rain and sunshine** une semaine où la pluie et le beau temps ont alterné

b (= *every second*) **on ~ days** un jour sur deux ; **he works on ~ days** il travaille un jour sur deux ; **they work on ~ days** (*taking turns*) ils travaillent un jour sur deux, à tour de rôle ; **to take ~ weeks off** être en congé une semaine sur deux ; **he lives ~ months in Brussels and London** il habite un mois à Bruxelles, un mois à Londres ; **to read ~ lines** lire une ligne sur deux

c (*US*) = **alternative 1**

d (*Bot, Math*) alterne

e (*Poetry*) **~ rhymes** rimes *fpl* alternées *or* croisées

2 (*US*) remplaçant(e) *m(f)*, suppléant(e) *m(f)*

3 ['ɒltɜːneɪt] VT faire alterner, employer alternativement *or* tour à tour ; **to ~ crops** alterner les cultures, pratiquer l'assolement

4 VI **a** (= *occur etc in turns*) alterner (**with** avec), se succéder (tour à tour)

b **to ~ between French and English** passer du français à l'anglais (et vice versa) ; **he ~s between aggression and indifference** il passe de l'agressivité à l'indifférence ; **in the desert temperature ~s between boiling and freezing** dans le désert la température est tantôt torride, tantôt glaciale

c (= *interchange regularly*) se relayer, travailler (*or* jouer *etc*) en alternance

d (*Elec*) changer périodiquement de sens

alternately [ɒl'tɜːnɪtlɪ] ADV tour à tour ; **he would ~ bully and charm people** il se montrait tour à tour tyrannique et charmant, il se montrait tantôt tyrannique, tantôt charmant ; **she became ~ angry and calm** elle passait de la colère au calme, et du calme à la colère ; **I lived ~ with my mother and my grandmother** je vivais tantôt avec ma mère, tantôt avec ma grand-mère

alternating ['ɒltɜːneɪtɪŋ] ADJ alternant, en alternance ; [*movement*] alternatif ; (*Math*) **~ series** série *f* alternée ; (*Elec*) **~ current** courant *m* alternatif

alternation [,ɒltɜː'neɪʃən] N alternance *f* ; [*of emotions etc*] alternatives *fpl*

alternative [ɒl'tɜːnətɪv] **1** ADJ **a** (*gen*) autre ; (*Philos*) [*proposition*] alternatif ; (*Mil*) [*position*] de repli ; (*Tech*) de rechange ; **~ proposal** contre-proposition *f* ; **the only ~ method** la seule autre méthode, la seule autre méthode de rechange ; (*Aut*) **~ route** itinéraire *m* de délestage ; **Alternative Vote** vote *m* alternatif

b (= *non-traditional*) [*society, medicine etc*] parallèle, alternatif ; [*lifestyle*] alternatif, différent ; **~ technology** les technologies *fpl* douces ; (*US*) **~ school** école *privée ayant adopté des méthodes nouvelles* ; (*US*) **~ education** enseignement privé basé sur des méthodes nouvelles ; **~ comedian** nouveau comique *m* ; **~ comedy** nouvelle comédie *f* ; **~ (sources of) energy** (sources *fpl* d'énergie *f* de substitution

2 N (= *choice*) (*between two*) alternative *f*, choix *m* ; (*among several*) choix *m* ; (= *solution*) (*only one*) alternative *f*, seule autre solution *f* ; (*one of several*) autre solution *f*, solution *f* de rechange ; (*Philos*) terme *m* d'une alternative *or* d'un dilemme ; **she had no ~ but to accept** elle n'avait pas d'autre solution que d'accepter, elle a été obligée d'accepter ; **there's no ~** il n'y a pas le choix

alternatively [ɒl'tɜːnətɪvlɪ] ADV autrement

alternator ['ɒltɜːneɪtər] N (*Brit Elec*) alternateur *m*

▼**although** [ɔːl'ðəʊ] CONJ bien que (+ *subj*), quoique (+ *subj*) ; **~ it's raining there are 20 people here already** bien qu'il pleuve *or* malgré la pluie, il y a déjà 20 personnes ; **I'll do it, ~ I don't want to** je vais le faire bien que je

n'en aie pas envie *or* même si je n'en ai pas envie ; **~ poor they were honest** ils étaient honnêtes bien que *or* quoique *or* encore que pauvres ; **~ young he knew that ...** bien qu'il fût jeune, il savait que ..., malgré son jeune âge, il savait que ... ; **~ he might agree to go** quand bien même il accepterait d'y aller, même s'il accepte d'y aller ; (*liter*) **I will do it ~ I (should) die in the attempt** je le ferai dussé-je y laisser la vie

altimeter ['æltimiːtər] N altimètre *m*

altitude ['æltɪtjuːd] N (= *height above sea level*) altitude *f* ; [*of building*] hauteur *f* ; (*gen pl = high place*) **~s** hauteur(s) *f(pl)*, altitude *f* ; **it is difficult to breathe at these ~s** *or* **at this ~** il est difficile de respirer à cette altitude ; **~ sickness** mal *m* d'altitude *or* des montagnes

alto ['æltəʊ] **1** N **a** (*female voice*) contralto *m* ; (*male voice*) haute-contre *f* **b** (= *instrument*) alto *m* **2** ADJ (*female*) de contralto ; (*male*) de haute-contre ; (*instrument*) d'alto ; **~ clef** clef *f* d'ut ; **~ saxophone/flute** saxophone *m*/flûte *f* alto

altogether [,ɔːltə'geðər] **1** ADV **a** (= *completely*) [*stop, disappear*] complètement ; [*different*] tout à fait ; **that's another matter ~** c'est une tout autre affaire ; **it is ~ out of the question** il n'en est absolument pas question ; **you don't believe him? — no, not ~** vous ne le croyez pas ? — non, pas vraiment ; **such methods are not ~ satisfactory** de telles méthodes ne sont pas vraiment satisfaisantes ; **I'm not ~ happy about this** je n'en suis pas vraiment satisfait **b** (= *in all*) en tout ; **what do I owe you ~?** je vous dois combien en tout ?, combien vous dois-je au total ? ; **~, he played in 44 test matches** en tout, il a joué dans 44 matchs internationaux ; **taken ~** à tout prendre ; **~, it wasn't very pleasant** ce n'était somme toute pas très agréable **2** N (*hum*) **in the ~** tout nu, en costume d'Adam (*or* d'Ève)*

altoist ['æltəʊɪst] N (*Mus*) saxophoniste *mf* alto

altruism ['æltruɪzəm] N altruisme *m*

altruist ['æltruɪst] N altruiste *mf*

altruistic [,æltruː'ɪstɪk] ADJ altruiste

ALU [,eɪel'juː] N (*Comput*) (ABBR = **arithmetic logic unit**) UAL *f*

alum ['æləm] N alun *m*

alumina [ə'luːmɪnə] N alumine *f*

aluminium [,æljʊ'mɪnɪəm], **aluminum** (*US*) [ə'luːmɪnəm] **1** N aluminium *m* **2** COMP [*pot, pan etc*] en aluminium ► **aluminium bronze** N bronze *m* d'aluminium ► **aluminium foil** N papier *m* aluminium ► **aluminium oxide** N oxyde *m* d'aluminium

alumna [ə'lʌmnə] N (*pl* **alumnae** [ə'lʌmniː]) (*US*) (*Scol*) ancienne élève *f* ; (*Univ*) ancienne étudiante *f*

alumnus [ə'lʌmnəs] N (*pl* **alumni** [ə'lʌmnaɪ]) (*US*) (*Scol*) ancien élève *m* ; (*Univ*) ancien étudiant *m*

alveolar [æl'vɪələr] ADJ alvéolaire ; **~ ridge** alvéoles *fpl* dentaires

alveolus [æl'vɪələs] N (*pl* **alveoli** [æl'vɪəlaɪ]) alvéole *f*

always ['ɔːlweɪz] ADV toujours ; **he's ~ late** il est toujours en retard ; **I'll ~ love you** je t'aimerai toujours ; **I can ~ come back later** je peux toujours revenir plus tard ; **there's ~ tomorrow** demain, il fera jour ; **as/for ~** comme/pour toujours ; **office ~ open** bureau *m* ouvert en permanence → **except**

Alzheimer's disease ['æltshaɪməzdɪ,ziːz] N maladie *f* d'Alzheimer

AM [eɪ'em] (ABBR = **amplitude modulation**) AM → **modulation**

am[1] [æm] → **be**

am[2] [eɪ'em] ADV (ABBR = **ante meridiem**) du matin

► LANGUAGE IN USE: **although** 26.3

AMA [ˌeɪemˈeɪ] N ABBR = **American Medical Association**

amalgam [əˈmælgəm] N amalgame m (**of** de, entre)

amalgamate [əˈmælgəmeɪt] **1** VT [+ metals] amalgamer; [+ companies, shares] (faire) fusionner, unifier **2** VI [metals] s'amalgamer; [companies] fusionner, s'unifier; [ethnic groups] se mélanger

amalgamation [ə,mælgəˈmeɪʃən] N [of organizations, businesses, schools] fusion f (**into sth** en qch); [of regiments] amalgame m; [of legal systems] unification f; [of genres, concepts] mélange m; [of metals] amalgamation f; **the ~ of our regiment with ...** l'amalgame or le regroupement de notre régiment avec ...

amanuensis [ə,mænjʊˈensɪs] N (pl **amanuenses** [ə,mænjʊˈensiːz]) (= secretary, assistant) secrétaire mf; (= copyist) copiste mf

amaryllis [ˌæməˈrɪlɪs] N amaryllis f

amass [əˈmæs] VT [+ objects] amasser, accumuler; [+ fortune] amasser

amateur [ˈæmətə*] **1** N (also Sport) amateur m **2** COMP [painter, sports, player] amateur inv; [photography etc] d'amateur ► **amateur dramatics** NPL théâtre m amateur ► **amateur interest** N **to have an ~ interest in sth** s'intéresser à qch en amateur ► **amateur status** N statut m d'amateur

amateurish [ˈæmətərɪʃ] ADJ (pej) d'amateur, de dilettante; **the acting was rather ~** le jeu des acteurs n'était pas très professionnel

amateurishly [ˈæmətərɪʃlɪ] ADV (pej) en amateur

amateurism [ˈæmətərɪzəm] N amateurisme m (also pej), dilettantisme m

amatory [ˈæmətərɪ] ADJ (frm, liter) [feelings] amoureux; [poetry] galant; [letter] d'amour

amaze [əˈmeɪz] VT stupéfier, ébahir; (iro) **you ~ me!** pas possible!

amazed [əˈmeɪzd] ADJ [person, glance, expression] stupéfait, ébahi; **to be ~ at (seeing) sth** être stupéfait de (voir) qch; **I'd be ~** ça m'étonnerait

amazement [əˈmeɪzmənt] N stupéfaction f; **she listened in ~** elle écoutait, stupéfaite

amazing [əˈmeɪzɪŋ] ADJ incroyable, étonnant; **it's ~!** c'est incroyable!, ça alors!; (Comm) **"~ new offer"** « offre sensationnelle »

amazingly [əˈmeɪzɪŋlɪ] ADV étonnamment; **she coped ~ (well)** elle s'en est étonnamment bien tirée; **~ (enough), he got it right first time** chose étonnante, il a réussi du premier coup

Amazon [ˈæməzən] N **a** (= river) Amazone f; **the ~ Basin** le bassin amazonien or de l'Amazone; **the ~ jungle/rainforest** la jungle/la forêt amazonienne **b** (Myth) Amazone f; (pej) virago f, grande bonne femme f

Amazonia [ˌæməˈzəʊnɪə] N (Geog) l'Amazonie f

Amazonian [ˌæməˈzəʊnɪən] ADJ (Geog) amazonien

ambassador [æmˈbæsədə*] N (lit, fig) ambassadeur m; **the French ~ (to Italy)** l'ambassadeur m de France (en Italie); **~-at-large** ambassadeur m extraordinaire; **try to be an ~ for the school** essayez de vous montrer digne de or d'être un bon ambassadeur de votre école

ambassadorial [æm,bæsəˈdɔːrɪəl] ADJ d'ambassadeur, de l'ambassadeur

ambassadorship [æmˈbæsədəʃɪp] N fonction f d'ambassadeur, ambassade f

ambassadress† [æmˈbæsɪdrɪs] N (lit, fig) ambassadrice† f

amber [ˈæmbə*] **1** N ambre m **2** ADJ [jewellery] d'ambre; **~-coloured** ambré; (Brit Aut) **~ light** feu m orange; **the lights are at ~** les feux sont à l'orange

ambergris [ˈæmbəgriːs] N ambre m gris

ambi... [ˈæmbɪ] PREF ambi...

ambiance [ˈæmbɪəns] N = **ambience**

ambidextrous [ˌæmbɪˈdekstrəs] ADJ ambidextre

ambience [ˈæmbɪəns] N ambiance f, atmosphère f

ambient [ˈæmbɪənt] **1** ADJ [temperature, noise, humidity] ambiant **2** N (Phot) lumière f d'ambiance **3** COMP ► **ambient music** N musique f d'ambiance

ambiguity [ˌæmbɪˈgjuːɪtɪ] N **a** (NonC) [of word, phrase] ambiguïté f (also Ling), équivoque f; (in thought, speech = lack of clarity) ambiguïté f, obscurité f **b** (= ambiguous phrase etc) ambiguïté f, expression f ambiguë

ambiguous [æmˈbɪgjʊəs] ADJ [word, phrase] ambigu (-guë f) (also Ling), équivoque; [thought] obscur; [past] douteux, équivoque

ambiguously [æmˈbɪgjʊəslɪ] ADV [say, describe] de façon ambiguë; **~ worded** exprimé en termes ambigus

ambit [ˈæmbɪt] N [of person] sphère f d'attributions, compétence f; [of authority etc] étendue f, portée f

ambition [æmˈbɪʃən] N ambition f; **it is my ~ to ...** mon ambition est de ..., j'ai l'ambition de ...

ambitious [æmˈbɪʃəs] ADJ ambitieux; **to be ~ to do sth** ambitionner de faire qch; **to be ~ for sb** avoir de l'ambition pour qn; **my father was very ~ for me to set up my own business** mon père avait beaucoup d'ambition pour moi et voulait que je monte ma propre affaire; **to be ~ for** or **of** (frm) **sth** ambitionner qch

ambitiously [æmˈbɪʃəslɪ] ADV ambitieusement

ambivalence [æmˈbɪvələns] N ambivalence f

ambivalent [æmˈbɪvələnt] ADJ ambivalent

amble [ˈæmbl] **1** VI **a** [person] aller or marcher d'un pas tranquille; **to ~ in/out** etc entrer/sortir etc d'un pas tranquille; **to ~ along** [person] aller sans se presser; **he ~d up to me** il s'est avancé vers moi sans se presser **b** [horse] aller l'amble, ambler **2** N **a** [of person] pas m or allure f tranquille **b** [of horse] amble m

ambrosia [æmˈbrəʊzɪə] N ambroisie f

ambrosial [æmˈbrəʊzɪəl] ADJ (au parfum or au goût) d'ambroisie

ambulance [ˈæmbjʊləns] **1** N ambulance f → **flying** **2** COMP ► **ambulance chaser*** N (pej) avocat qui encourage les victimes d'accidents à engager des poursuites ► **ambulance driver** N ambulancier m, -ière f ► **ambulance man** N (pl **ambulance men**) (= driver) ambulancier m; (= nurse) infirmier m (d'ambulance); (carrying stretcher) brancardier m ► **ambulance nurse** N infirmier m, -ière f (d'ambulance) ► **ambulance train** N train m sanitaire ► **ambulance workers** NPL ambulanciers mpl

┌─────────────────────┐
│ **AMBULANCE CHASER** │
└─────────────────────┘

Aux États-Unis, le « chasseur d'ambulances » est un avocat peu scrupuleux qui incite les victimes d'accidents à engager des poursuites afin d'obtenir des dommages et intérêts, sur lesquels il touchera une commission. Par extension, l'expression désigne quiconque cherche à tirer profit du malheur des autres.

ambulatory [ˌæmbjʊˈleɪtərɪ] ADJ (US Med) ambulatoire; **~ patient/care** malade mf/ traitement m ambulatoire

ambush [ˈæmbʊʃ] **1** N embuscade f, guet-apens m; **troops in ~** troupes fpl embusquées; **to be** or **lie in ~** se tenir en embuscade; **to be** or **lie in ~ for sb** tendre une embuscade à qn → **fall** **2** VT (= wait for) tendre une embuscade à; (= attack) faire tomber dans une embuscade

ameba [əˈmiːbə] N = **amoeba**

ameliorate [əˈmiːlɪəreɪt] **1** VT améliorer **2** VI s'améliorer

amelioration [ə,miːlɪəˈreɪʃən] N amélioration f

amen [ˈɑːmen] **1** EXCL (Rel) amen, ainsi soit-il; **~ to that!** tout à fait! **2** N amen m inv; (Rel, fig) **to say ~ to ...** ◊ **to give one's ~ to ...** dire amen à ...

amenable [əˈmiːnəbl] ADJ **a** (= answerable) [person] responsable (**to sb** envers qn, **for sth** de qch); **~ to the law** responsable devant la loi **b** (= tractable, responsive) [person] maniable, souple; **he is ~ to argument** c'est un homme qui est prêt à se laisser convaincre; **~ to discipline** disciplinable; **~ to kindness** sensible à la douceur; **~ to reason** raisonnable, disposé à entendre raison **c** **~ to** (= within the scope of) qui relève de, du ressort de

amend [əˈmend] **1** VT [+ rule] amender, modifier; [Parl] amender; [+ wording] modifier; [+ mistake] rectifier, corriger; [+ habits] réformer **2** VI s'amender

amendment [əˈmendmənt] N **a** (to rule, law, constitution) amendement m (**to sth** à qch); **table an ~** présenter un amendement → **first** **b** (to contract) avenant m (**to sth** à qch) **c** (to letter, script, text) modification f **d** (NonC = changing) [of rule, law] révision f; [of behaviour] amélioration f; [of mistake] rectification f

amends [əˈmendz] NPL **to make ~** (= apologize) faire amende honorable; (by doing sth) se racheter; **to make ~ to sb for sth** dédommager qn de qch, faire réparation à qn de qch; **to make ~ for an injury** (with money) compenser un dommage; (with kindness) réparer un tort; **I'll try to make ~** j'essaierai de me racheter

amenity [əˈmiːnɪtɪ] **1** N **a** (NonC = pleasantness) [of district, climate, situation] charme m, agrément m **b** (gen pl) **amenities** (= pleasant features) agréments mpl; (= facilities) aménagements mpl, équipements mpl (locaux); (Jur) **public amenities** équipements mpl collectifs **2** **amenities**† NPL (= courtesies) civilités fpl, politesses fpl **3** COMP ► **amenity bed** N (Brit Med) lit d'hôpital réservé aux malades qui paient un supplément ► **amenity society** N (Brit) association f pour la sauvegarde de l'environnement

amenorrhoea, amenorrhea (US) [ˈeɪmenəˈrɪə] N (Med) aménorrhée f

Amerasian [ˌæməˈreɪʒən] **1** ADJ amérasien **2** N Amérasien(ne) m(f)

America [əˈmerɪkə] N l'Amérique f; **the ~s** les Amériques fpl → **north**, **united**

American [əˈmerɪkən] **1** ADJ (= of America) américain, d'Amérique; (= of US) américain, des États-Unis; [ambassador, embassy] des États-Unis; **as ~ as apple pie** typiquement américain **2** N **a** (= person) Américain(e) m(f) **b** (Ling* = American English) américain m; (US) **what's that in good** or **plain ~?** ≈ ça veut dire quoi en bon français? **3** COMP ► **American cheese** N (US) cheddar m américain ► **the American Civil War** N la guerre de Sécession ► **the American Dream** N le rêve américain ► **American English** N anglais m américain ► **American football** N (Sport) football m américain ► **American Indian** N Indien(ne) m(f) d'Amérique ♦ ADJ des Indiens d'Amérique ► **American Legion** N (US) organisme d'aide aux anciens combattants → LEGION ► **American plan** N (US: in hotels) (chambre f avec) pension f complète

┌─────────────────────┐
│ **AMERICAN DREAM** │
└─────────────────────┘

Pour beaucoup d'Américains, le « rêve américain » désigne un ensemble de valeurs et de principes inscrits dans la déclaration d'Indépendance de 1776 et qui définissent globalement une certaine conception de la vie: individualisme, ardeur au travail, égalité des chances pour tous, justice et liberté universelles. L'expression est parfois utilisée par dérision pour dénoncer le contraste entre ces idéaux et le matérialisme qui caractérise certains aspects de la vie américaine contemporaine.

Americana [əˌmerɪˈkɑːnə] N (NonC) objets ou documents appartenant à l'héritage culturel américain

americanism [əˈmerɪkənɪzəm] N américanisme m

americanize [əˈmerɪkənaɪz] VT américaniser

americium [ˌæməˈrɪsɪəm] N (Chem) américium m

Amerind [ˈæmərɪnd] N [a] Indien(ne) m(f) d'Amérique [b] (Ling) langue f amérindienne

Amerindian [ˌæməˈrɪndɪən] [1] ADJ amérindien(ne) [2] N Amérindien(ne) m(f)

amethyst [ˈæmɪθɪst] [1] N améthyste f [2] COMP [jewellery] d'améthyste; [colour] violet d'améthyste inv

Amex [ˈæmeks] N [a]® (US) ABBR = **American Express**® American Express® f; **~ card** carte f American Express® [b] (US) (ABBR = **American Stock Exchange**) Amex f (deuxième bourse américaine)

amiability [ˌeɪmɪəˈbɪlɪtɪ] N amabilité f, gentillesse f (**to, towards** envers)

amiable [ˈeɪmɪəbl] ADJ aimable, gentil

amiably [ˈeɪmɪəblɪ] ADV [chat] gentiment; [say, reply] aimablement; [nod, grin] avec amabilité

amicable [ˈæmɪkəbl] ADJ [feeling] amical; [relationship] amical, d'amitié; (Jur) **~ settlement** arrangement m à l'amiable

amicably [ˈæmɪkəblɪ] ADV amicalement; (Jur) à l'amiable

amidships [əˈmɪdʃɪps] ADV (Naut) au milieu or par le milieu du navire

amid(st) [əˈmɪd(st)] PREP parmi, au milieu de

amino acid [əˈmiːnəʊˈæsɪd] N acide m aminé, aminoacide m

Amish [ˈɑːmɪʃ] [1] NPL **the ~** les Amish mpl [2] ADJ Amish inv; **an ~ man/woman** un/une Amish

amiss [əˈmɪs] [1] ADJ **there is something ~** il y a quelque chose qui cloche; **have I said/done something ~?** j'ai dit/fait quelque chose qu'il ne fallait pas? [2] ADV **a to take sth ~** (= be offended) mal prendre qch [b]* **a little politeness wouldn't go** or **come ~** (= would be welcome) un peu de politesse ne ferait pas de mal; **a drink wouldn't go ~** un verre ne serait pas de refus [c] (= unfavourably) **to speak ~ of sb** dire du mal de qn

amity [ˈæmɪtɪ] N (frm) amitié f

Amman [əˈmɑːn] N Amman

ammeter [ˈæmɪtə'] N ampèremètre m

ammo* [ˈæməʊ] N ABBR = **ammunition**

ammonia [əˈməʊnɪə] N (gaz m) ammoniac m; (= liquid) ammoniaque f → **household, liquid**

ammonium [əˈməʊnɪəm] [1] N ammonium m [2] COMP ► **ammonium chloride** N chlorure m d'ammonium

ammunition [ˌæmjʊˈnɪʃən] [1] N munitions fpl; **round of ~** cartouche f [2] COMP ► **ammunition belt** N ceinturon m ► **ammunition dump** N dépôt m de munitions ► **ammunition pouch** N cartouchière f

amnesia [æmˈniːzɪə] N amnésie f

amnesiac [æmˈniːzɪæk] ADJ amnésique

amnesty [ˈæmnɪstɪ] [1] N amnistie f; **under an ~** en vertu d'une amnistie [2] VT amnistier [3] COMP ► **Amnesty International** N Amnesty International

amnia [ˈæmnɪə] NPL of **amnion**

amniocentesis [ˌæmnɪəʊsenˈtiːsɪs] N (pl **amniocenteses** [ˌæmnɪəʊsenˈtiːsiːz]) amniocentèse f

amnion [ˈæmnɪən] N (pl **amnions** or **amnia**) (Anat) amnios m

amniotic [ˌæmnɪˈɒtɪk] ADJ (Anat) amniotique; **~ fluid/cavity** liquide m/cavité f amniotique; **~ sac** poche f des eaux

amoeba [əˈmiːbə] N (pl **amoebas, amoebæ** [əˈmiːbiː]) amibe f

amoebic [əˈmiːbɪk] ADJ amibien; **~ dysentery** dysenterie f amibienne

amok [əˈmɒk] ADV **to run ~** (lit) être pris d'un accès or d'une crise de folie meurtrière or furieuse; (in Far East) s'abandonner à l'amok; (fig) [person] perdre tout contrôle de soi-même; [crowd] se déchaîner

among(st) [əˈmʌŋ(st)] PREP parmi, entre; **~ the crowd** parmi la foule; **divide the chocolates ~ you** partagez-vous les chocolats; **~ the lambs is one black one** parmi les agneaux il y en a un noir; **this is ~ the things we must do** ceci fait partie des choses que nous avons à faire; **settle it ~ yourselves** arrangez cela entre vous; **don't quarrel ~ yourselves** ne vous disputez pas, pas de disputes entre vous; **he is ~ those who know** il est de ces gens qui savent, il fait partie de ceux qui savent; **~ others** ◊ **~ other things** entre autres (choses); **the French** chez les Français; **to count sb ~ one's friends** compter qn parmi or au nombre de ses amis; **to be ~ friends** être entre amis; **to be sitting ~ the audience** être assis au milieu des or parmi les spectateurs

amoral [eɪˈmɒrəl] ADJ amoral

amorality [eɪmɒˈrælɪtɪ] N amoralité f

amorous [ˈæmərəs] ADJ amoureux; **to make ~ advances to** faire des avances à (connotations sexuelles)

amorously [ˈæmərəslɪ] ADV amoureusement

amorphous [əˈmɔːfəs] ADJ (also Miner) amorphe; (fig) [personality] amorphe; [style, ideas] informe, sans forme

amortization [əˌmɔːtaɪˈzeɪʃən] N amortissement m

amortize [əˈmɔːtaɪz] [1] VT [+ debt] amortir [2] COMP ► **amortized mortgage loan** N prêt m hypothécaire à remboursements périodiques

amortizement [əˈmɔːtɪzmənt] N = **amortization**

▼ **amount** [əˈmaʊnt] N [a] (= total) montant m, total m; (= sum of money) somme f; **the ~ of a bill** le montant d'une facture; (Fin, Comm) **to** or **in the ~ of** à concurrence de; **debts to the ~ of £200** dettes fpl qui se montent à 200 livres [b] (= quantity) quantité f; **I have an enormous ~ of work** j'ai énormément de travail; **quite an ~ of ...** beaucoup de ...; **any ~ of ...** quantité de ..., énormément de ...; **she's got any ~ of friends** elle a énormément or des quantités d'amis; **I've got any ~ of time** j'ai tout le temps qu'il (me) faut, j'ai tout mon temps [c] (NonC = value, importance) importance f, signification f; **the information is of little ~** ce renseignement n'a pas grande importance

► **amount to** VT FUS [a] (Math etc) [sums, figures, debts] s'élever à; **any ~ of ...** [b] (= be equivalent to) équivaloir à; **it ~s to the same thing** cela revient au même; **it ~s to stealing** cela revient or équivaut au vol; **it ~s to a change in policy** cela représente un changement de politique; **he will never ~ to much** il ne fera jamais grand-chose; **one day he will ~ to something** un jour il sera quelqu'un

amour† [əˈmʊə'] N intrigue f amoureuse†, liaison f

amour-propre [ˌæmʊəˈprɒprə] N amour-propre m

amp [æmp] N [a] (also **-ere**) ampère m; **a 13-~ plug** une prise de 13 ampères [b]* (ABBR = **amplifier**) ampli* m [c] ABBR = **ampoule**

amperage [ˈæmpərɪdʒ] N ampérage m

ampere [ˈæmpeə'] N ampère m [2] COMP ► **ampere-hour** N ampère-heure m

ampersand [ˈæmpəsænd] N esperluette f

amphetamine [æmˈfetəmiːn] N amphétamine f

amphibia [æmˈfɪbɪə] NPL amphibiens mpl

amphibian [æmˈfɪbɪən] [1] ADJ [animal, vehicle, tank] amphibie [2] N [a] (Zool) amphibie m (Mil) (= tank) char m amphibie; (= car) voiture f amphibie; (= aircraft) avion m amphibie

amphibious [æmˈfɪbɪəs] ADJ (Zool, Mil) amphibie

amphitheatre, amphitheater (US) [ˈæmfɪˌθɪətə'] N (Hist, Theat, gen) amphithéâtre m; (in mountains) cirque m

amphora [ˈæmfərə] N (pl **amphoras** or **amphorae** [ˈæmfəˌriː]) amphore f

ample [ˈæmpl] ADJ [a] (= more than adequate) [space, amount, resources] amplement suffisant (for sb/sth pour qn/qch); [parking-space, money] largement assez de; **to have ~ evidence** or **proof that ...** avoir des preuves solides que ...; **there are ~ grounds for believing that ...** on a tout lieu de croire que ...; **there is ~ justification for his behaviour** son comportement est amplement justifié; **to have ~ means** avoir de gros moyens; **there'll be ~ opportunity to discuss it later** on aura largement or amplement l'occasion d'en discuter plus tard; **to have ~ opportunities to do sth** avoir plus d'une occasion de faire qch; **to have ~ reason to do sth** avoir de solides raisons de faire qch; **there is ~ room for sb/sth** il y a largement la place pour qn/qch; **there is ~ room for improvement** il y a encore bien du chemin or bien des progrès à faire; **to have ~ time (to do sth)** avoir largement or amplement le temps (de faire qch); **to make ~ use of sth** largement utiliser qch; **she was given ~ warning** elle a été suffisamment prévenue [b] (= large) [bosom, breasts] généreux; [stomach] gros (grosse f); [waist] épais (épaisse f); [garment] ample; **her ~ cleavage** son décolleté plantureux

amplification [ˌæmplɪfɪˈkeɪʃən] N amplification f; (Jur) **~ of previous evidence** amplification f des offres de preuve

amplifier [ˈæmplɪfaɪə'] N amplificateur m, ampli* m

amplify [ˈæmplɪfaɪ] VT [+ sound, movement, force] amplifier; [+ instrument] amplifier le son de; [+ statement, idea] développer; [+ story] amplifier

amplitude [ˈæmplɪtjuːd] N [a] (Astron, Phys) amplitude f → **modulation** [b] [of style, thought] ampleur f

amply [ˈæmplɪ] ADV largement, amplement; **my patience was ~ rewarded** ma patience a été largement or amplement récompensée

ampoule, ampule (US) [ˈæmpuːl] N ampoule f (pour seringue)

ampulla [æmˈpʊlə] N (pl **ampullae** [æmˈpʊliː]) (Anat) ampoule f

amputate [ˈæmpjʊteɪt] VT amputer; **to ~ sb's arm/leg** amputer qn du bras/de la jambe

amputation [ˌæmpjʊˈteɪʃən] N amputation f; **to carry out the ~ of a limb** pratiquer l'amputation d'un membre

amputee [ˌæmpjʊˈtiː] N amputé(e) m(f)

Amsterdam [ˈæmstədæm] N Amsterdam

Amtrak [ˈæmtræk] N (in US) société mixte de transports ferroviaires interurbains pour voyageurs

amuck [əˈmʌk] ADV = **amok**

amulet [ˈæmjʊlɪt] N amulette f

amuse [əˈmjuːz] VT [a] (= cause mirth to) amuser, divertir; **to be ~d at** or **by ...** s'amuser de ...; **he was not ~d** il n'a pas trouvé ça drôle; **an ~d expression** un air amusé [b] (= entertain, occupy) distraire, amuser; **to ~ o.s. by doing sth** s'amuser à faire qch; **to ~ o.s. with sth** s'amuser avec qch/aux dépens de qn; **you'll**

have to ~ **yourselves** il va vous falloir trouver de quoi vous distraire *or* de quoi vous occuper; **to keep oneself ~d** se distraire, s'occuper

amused [ə'mjuːzd] ADJ [*person, look, smile, attitude*] amusé; **she seemed ~ at my suggestion** ma suggestion a semblé l'amuser; **I was ~ to see/hear that ...** ça m'a amusé de voir/ d'entendre que ...; **to keep sb ~** distraire qn; **to keep o.s. ~** se distraire, s'occuper; (*hum*) **we are not ~** nous ne trouvons pas cela drôle

amusedly [ə'mjuːzɪdlɪ] ADV avec amusement, d'un air amusé

amusement [ə'mjuːzmənt] ① N [a] (*NonC*) amusement *m*, divertissement *m*; **look of ~** regard *m* amusé; **to hide one's ~** dissimuler son envie de rire; **to do sth for ~** faire qch pour se distraire; (**much**) **to my ~** à mon grand amusement; **there was general ~ at this** ceci a fait rire tout le monde [b] (= *diversion, pastime*) distraction *f*; (*Brit: in arcade*) **~s** jeux *mpl* d'arcade; **a town with plenty of ~s** une ville qui offre beaucoup de distractions ② COMP ► **amusement arcade** N (*Brit*) galerie *f* de jeux *or* d'attractions ► **amusement park** N (*esp Brit = fairground*) parc *m* d'attractions

amusing [ə'mjuːzɪŋ] ADJ amusant, drôle

amusingly [ə'mjuːzɪŋlɪ] ADV [*talk, write*] d'une manière amusante; **the ~ named Susan Swishtail** cette femme au nom amusant de Susan Swishtail

amyl alcohol ['æmɪl,ælkəhɒl] N alcool *m* amylique

amylase ['æmɪleɪz] N (*Physiol*) amylase *f*

amyl nitrite ['æmɪl,naɪtraɪt] N nitrite *m* amylique

an [æn, ən, n] ① INDEF ART → **a²** ② CONJ†† si

Anabaptist [,ænə'bæptɪst] N, ADJ anabaptiste *mf*

anabolic [,ænə'bɒlɪk] ADJ anabolique; **~ steroid** stéroïde *m* anabolisant

anachronism [ə'nækrənɪzəm] N anachronisme *m*

anachronistic [ə,nækrə'nɪstɪk] ADJ anachronique

anacoluthon [,ænəkə'luːθɒn] N (*pl* **anacolutha** [,ænəkə'luːθə]) anacoluthe *f*

anaconda [,ænə'kɒndə] N eunecte *m*, anaconda *m*

Anacreon [ə'nækrɪɒn] N Anacréon *m*

anacreontic [ə,nækrɪ'ɒntɪk] ① ADJ anacréontique ② N poème *m* anacréontique

anaemia, anemia (*US*) [ə'niːmɪə] N anémie *f* → **pernicious**

anaemic, anemic (*US*) [ə'niːmɪk] N, ADJ (*Med, fig*) anémique; **to become ~** s'anémier

anaerobic [,ænə'rəʊbɪk] ADJ anaérobique

anaesthesia, anesthesia (*US*) [,ænɪs'θiːzɪə] N anesthésie *f*

anaesthetic, anesthetic (*US*) [,ænɪs'θetɪk] ① N anesthésique *m*; **under the ~** sous anesthésie; **to give sb an ~** anesthésier qn ② ADJ anesthésique

anaesthetist, anesthetist (*US*) [æ'niːsθɪtɪst] N (médecin *m*) anesthésiste *mf*

anaesthetize, anesthetize (*US*) [æ'niːsθɪtaɪz] VT anesthésier

anaglyph ['ænəglɪf] N (*Art*) anaglyphe *m*

Anaglypta® [,ænə'glɪptə] N papier *m* peint gaufré

anagram ['ænəgræm] N anagramme *f*

anal ['eɪnəl] ADJ anal; (*Psych*) **~ retentive** qui fait une fixation au stade anal; **you're so ~!** ce que tu es maniaque!

analgesia [,ænæl'dʒiːzɪə] N analgésie *f*

analgesic [,ænæl'dʒiːsɪk] ADJ, N analgésique *m*

anally ['eɪnəlɪ] ADV **~ retentive** qui fait de la fixation au stade anal

analog ['ænəlɒg] N (*US*) = **analogue**

analogic(al) [,ænə'lɒdʒɪk(əl)] ADJ analogique

analogous [ə'næləgəs] ADJ analogue (**to, with** à)

analogue ['ænəlɒg] ① N analogue *m* ② COMP ► **analogue device** N unité *f* analogique ► **analogue-digital converter** N convertisseur *m* analogique-numérique ► **analogue watch** N montre *f* à lecture analogique

analogy [ə'nælədʒɪ] N analogie *f* (**between** entre, **with** avec); **to argue from ~** raisonner par analogie; **by ~** par analogie (**with** avec)

analysand [ə'nælɪ,sænd] N (*Psych*) sujet *m* en analyse

▼ **analyse, analyze** (*US*) ['ænəlaɪz] VT [a] analyser, faire l'analyse de; (*Gram*) [+ *sentence*] faire l'analyse logique de [b] (*Psych*) psychanalyser

analyser, analyzer (*US*) ['ænəlaɪzəʳ] N analyseur *m*; **blood/image ~** analyseur *m* de sang/ d'images

▼ **analysis** [ə'næləsɪs] N (*pl* **analyses** [ə'nælɪsiːz]) [a] analyse *f*; (*Gram*) [*of sentence*] analyse *f* logique; (*fig*) **in the ultimate** *or* **last** *or* **final ~** en dernière analyse, finalement [b] (*Psych*) psychanalyse *f*; **to be in ~** poursuivre une analyse, être en cours d'analyse

analyst ['ænəlɪst] N [a] (*Chem etc*) analyste *mf* [b] (*Psych*) (psych)analyste *mf* → **news**

analytic(al) [,ænə'lɪtɪk(əl)] ADJ analytique; **~ mind** esprit *m* analytique; **~ psychology** psychologie *f* analytique *or* des profondeurs; (*Comput*) **~ engine** machine *f* de Babbage

analytically [,ænə'lɪtɪkəlɪ] ADV [*think*] d'une manière analytique; **to be ~ intelligent** avoir une intelligence analytique

analyze ['ænəlaɪz] VT (*US*) = **analyse**

analyzer ['ænəlaɪzəʳ] N (*US*) = **analyser**

anamorphosis [,ænə'mɔːfəsɪs] N (*pl* **anamorphoses** [,ænə'mɔːfə,siːz]) anamorphose *f*

anapaest, anapest (*US*) ['ænəpiːst] N anapeste *m*

anaphoric [,ænə'fɒrɪk] ADJ (*Ling*) anaphorique

anarchic(al) [æ'nɑːkɪk(əl)] ADJ anarchique

anarchism ['ænəkɪzəm] N anarchisme *m*

anarchist ['ænəkɪst] N, ADJ anarchiste *mf*

anarchistic [,ænə'kɪstɪk] ADJ anarchique

anarcho... [æ'nɑːkəʊ] PREF anarcho...; **~-syndicalism** anarcho-syndicalisme *m*

anarchy ['ænəkɪ] N anarchie *f*

anastigmatic [,ænəstɪg'mætɪk] ADJ (*Phot*) anastigmate

anathema [ə'næθɪmə] N (*Rel, fig*) anathème *m*; (*fig*) **the whole idea of exploiting people was ~ to him** il avait en abomination l'idée d'exploiter les gens

anathematize [ə'næθɪmətaɪz] VT frapper d'anathème

Anatolia [,ænə'təʊlɪə] N l'Anatolie *f*

Anatolian [,ænə'təʊlɪən] ① ADJ anatolien ② N (= *person*) Anatolien(ne) *m(f)*

anatomical [,ænə'tɒmɪkəl] ADJ anatomique

anatomically [,ænə'tɒmɪkəlɪ] ADV [*correct, different*] d'un point de vue anatomique, anatomiquement

anatomist [ə'nætəmɪst] N anatomiste *mf*

anatomize [ə'nætəmaɪz] VT disséquer

anatomy [ə'nætəmɪ] N (*Med, Sci*) anatomie *f*; (*fig*) [*of country etc*] structure *f*; (*hum*) **a delicate part of one's ~** une partie sensible de son anatomie; **he had spots all over his ~*** il avait des boutons partout, il était couvert de boutons

ANC [,eɪen'siː] N (ABBR = **African National Congress**) ANC *m*

ancestor ['ænsɪstəʳ] N (*lit*) ancêtre *mf*, aïeul *m*; (*fig*) ancêtre *m*

ancestral [æn'sestrəl] ADJ ancestral; **~ home** château *m* ancestral

ancestress† ['ænsɪstrɪs] N aïeule *f*

ancestry ['ænsɪstrɪ] N [a] (= *lineage*) ascendance *f* [b] (*NonC* = *ancestors collectively*) ancêtres *mpl*, aïeux *mpl*

anchor ['æŋkəʳ] ① N ancre *f*; (*fig*) point *m* d'ancrage; **to be** *or* **ride at ~** être à l'ancre *or* au mouillage; **to come to** *or* **drop ~** mouiller *or* jeter l'ancre; **~s away!** (*Naut*) levez l'ancre!; (*fig*) mettons les voiles!* → **cast, ride, up, weigh** ② VT mettre à l'ancre; (*fig*) ancrer, enraciner ③ VI (*Naut*) mouiller, jeter l'ancre ④ COMP ► **anchor ice** N glaces *fpl* de fond

anchorage ['æŋkərɪdʒ] ① N (*Naut*) mouillage *m*, ancrage *m* ② COMP ► **anchorage dues** NPL (*Naut*) droits *mpl* de mouillage *or* d'ancrage ► **anchorage point** N (*Aut*) point *m* d'ancrage

anchorite ['æŋkəraɪt] N anachorète *m*

anchorman ['æŋkəmæn] N (*pl* **-men**) (*esp US*) (*Rad, TV*) présentateur *m*; (*in team, organization*) pilier *m*, pivot *m*

anchorwoman ['æŋkəwʊmən] N (*pl* **-women**) (*esp US*) (*Rad, TV*) présentatrice *f*; (*in team, organization*) pilier *m*, pivot *m*

anchovy ['æntʃəvɪ] ① N anchois *m* ② COMP ► **anchovy paste** N beurre *m* d'anchois ► **anchovy sauce** N sauce *f* aux anchois, anchoïade *f*

ancient ['eɪnʃənt] ① ADJ [a] [*painting, document, custom*] ancien; **in ~ days** dans les temps anciens; **~ history** histoire *f* ancienne; **it's ~ history*** c'est de l'histoire ancienne; (*Brit*) **(scheduled as an) ~ monument** (classé) monument *m* historique; **the Ancient World** le monde *m* antique, l'Antiquité *f*; **Ancient Greece** la Grèce ancienne *or* antique; **the Ancient Greeks** les Grecs *mpl* de l'Antiquité; **Rome** la Rome antique; **~ rocks** de vieilles roches *fpl* [b] (*: gen hum*) [*person*] très vieux (vieille *f*); [*clothes, object, car*] antique, antédiluvien*; **this is positively ~** cela remonte à Mathusalem *or* au déluge; **he's getting pretty ~** il se fait vieux ② **the ancients** NPL les anciens *mpl*

anciently ['eɪnʃəntlɪ] ADV (*frm*) anciennement, autrefois

ancillary [æn'sɪlərɪ] ADJ [*service, help, forces*] auxiliaire; **~ to** subordonné à; (*hospital*) **~ workers** personnel *m* des services auxiliaires (des hôpitaux), agents *mpl* des hôpitaux; (*Brit Scol*) **~ staff** agents *mpl* d'un établissement scolaire; (*Fin, Comm*) **~ costs** frais *mpl* accessoires *or* annexes

and [ænd, ənd, nd, ən] CONJ [a] et; **a man ~ a woman** un homme et une femme; **his table ~ chair** sa table et sa chaise; **~ how!*** et comment!*; **~?** et alors?; **on Saturday ~/or Sunday** (*Admin*) samedi et/ou dimanche; (*gen*) samedi ou dimanche ou les deux [b] (*in numbers*) **three hundred ~ ten** trois cent dix; **two thousand ~ eight** deux mille huit; **two pounds ~ six pence** deux livres (et) six pence; **an hour ~ twenty minutes** une heure vingt (minutes); **five ~ three quarters** cinq trois quarts [c] (+ *infin vb*) **try ~ come** tâchez de venir; **wait ~ see** on verra bien, attendez voir [d] (*repetition, continuation*) **better ~ better** de mieux en mieux; **now ~ then** de temps en temps; **for hours ~ hours** pendant des heures et des heures; **I rang ~ rang** j'ai sonné et resonné; **he talked ~ talked/waited ~ waited** il a parlé/attendu pendant des heures; **~ so on ~ so forth** et ainsi de suite; **he goes on ~ on*** quand il commence il n'y a plus moyen de l'arrêter [e] (*with compar adj*) **uglier ~ uglier** de plus en plus laid; **more ~ more difficult** de plus en plus difficile [f] (*with neg or implied neg*) ni; **to go out without a hat ~ coat** sortir sans chapeau ni manteau; **you can't buy ~ sell here** on ne

---

► LANGUAGE IN USE: **analyse** 26.1 **analysis** 26.1

peut ni acheter ni vendre ici

g (phrases) **eggs ~ bacon** œufs mpl au bacon ; **summer ~ winter (alike)** été comme hiver ; **a carriage ~ pair** une voiture à deux chevaux

h (implying cond) **flee ~ you are lost** fuyez et vous êtes perdu, si vous fuyez vous êtes perdu

Andalucia, Andalusia [,ændəlu'si:ə] N l'Andalousie f

Andalucian, Andalusian [,ændəlu'si:ən] ADJ andalou (-ouse f)

Andean [ændɪən] ADJ des Andes, andin

Andes [ændi:z] N Andes fpl

andiron [ændaɪən] N chenet m

Andorra [,æn'dɔ:rə] N (la principauté d')Andorre f

Andorran [,æn'dɔ:rən] **1** ADJ andorran **2** N Andorran(e) m(f)

Andrew [ændru:] N André m

androgen [ændrədʒən] N (Physiol) androgène m

androgynous [æn'drɒdʒɪnəs] ADJ androgyne

androgyny [æn'drɒdʒɪnɪ] N androgynie f

android [ændrɔɪd] ADJ, N androïde m

Andromache [æn'drɒməkɪ] N Andromaque f

Andromeda [æn'drɒmɪdə] N Andromède f

androsterone [æn'drɒstə,rəʊn] N androstérone f

anecdotal [,ænɪk'dəʊtəl] ADJ anecdotique ; **his lecture was very ~** sa conférence faisait une large part à l'anecdote

anecdote [ænɪkdəʊt] N anecdote f

anemia [ə'ni:mɪə] N (US) = **anaemia**

anemic [ə'ni:mɪk] ADJ (US) = **anaemic**

anemometer [,ænɪ'mɒmɪtə'] N anémomètre m

anemone [ə'nemənɪ] N anémone f → **sea**

anent [ə'nent] PREP (Scot) concernant, à propos de

aneroid [ænərɔɪd] ADJ anéroïde ; **~ (barometer)** baromètre m anéroïde

anesthesia [,ænɪs'θi:zɪə] N (US) = **anaesthesia**

anesthesiologist [,ænɪsθi:zɪ'ɒlədʒɪst] N (US) (médecin m) anesthésiste mf

anesthetic [,ænɪs'θetɪk] N, ADJ (US) = **anaesthetic**

anesthetist [æ'ni:sθɪtɪst] N (US) = **anaesthetist**

anesthetize [æ'ni:sθɪtaɪz] VT (US) = **anaesthetize**

aneurism, aneurysm [ænjʊrɪzəm] N anévrisme m

anew [ə'nju:] ADV (liter) de nouveau ; **to be born ~** renaître ; **to start life ~ in a fresh place** recommencer sa vie ailleurs

angel [eɪndʒəl] **1** N ange m ; (* = person) ange m, amour m ; (Theat) commanditaire mf ; **~ of Darkness** ange m des Ténèbres ; **the Angel of Death** l'Ange m de la mort ; **be an ~ and fetch me my gloves** apporte-moi mes gants, tu seras un ange ; **speak** or **talk of ~s!*** quand on parle du loup (on en voit la queue) ! ; (fig) **to go where ~s fear to tread** s'aventurer en terrain dangereux → **fool, guardian 2** COMP ► **angel cake** N ≈ gâteau m de Savoie ► **angel dust*** N (Drugs) angel dust* m (Drugs), poussière f d'ange* (Drugs) ► **angel food cake** N (US) = **angel cake** ► **angel shark** N ange m de mer ► **angels-on-horseback** NPL (Brit Culin) huîtres bridées de lard servies sur toasts

Angeleno [,ændʒə'li:nəʊ] N (US) habitant(e) m(f) de Los Angeles

angelfish [eɪndʒəlfɪʃ] N (pl **angelfish**) scalaire m ; (= shark) ange m de mer

angelic [æn'dʒelɪk] ADJ angélique

angelica [æn'dʒelɪkə] N angélique f

angelical [æn'dʒelɪkəl] ADJ angélique

angelically [æn'dʒelɪkəlɪ] ADV [behave, sing] comme un or des ange(s) ; **she smiled ~** elle a eu un sourire angélique

Angelino [,ændʒe'li:nəʊ] N = **Angeleno**

angelus [ændʒɪləs] N (= prayer, bell) angélus m

anger [ængə'] **1** N colère f ; (violent) fureur f ; **to act in ~** agir sous l'empire or sous le coup de la colère, agir avec emportement ; **words spoken in ~** mots prononcés sous l'empire or sous le coup de la colère ; **to move sb to ~** mettre qn en colère ; **his ~ knew no bounds** sa colère or son emportement ne connut plus de bornes ; **in great ~** furieux **2** VT mettre en colère, irriter ; (greatly) rendre furieux ; **to be easily ~ed** se mettre facilement en colère, s'emporter facilement

angina [æn'dʒaɪnə] N angine f ; **~ (pectoris)** angine f de poitrine ; **to have ~** faire de l'angine de poitrine

angiogram [ændʒɪəʊgræm] N (Med) angiographie f

angioplasty [ændʒɪəʊ,plæstɪ] N (Med) angioplastie f

angle¹ [ængl] **1** N **a** (also Math) angle m ; **at an ~ of ...** formant un angle de ... ; **at an ~** en biais (**to** par rapport à) ; **cut at an ~** [pipe, edge] coupé en biseau ; **the building stands at an ~ to the street** le bâtiment fait angle avec la rue → **acute, right**

b (fig = aspect, point of view) angle m, aspect m ; **the various ~s of a topic** les divers aspects mpl d'un sujet ; **to study a topic from every ~** étudier un sujet sous toutes ses faces or sous tous les angles ; **his article has a new ~ on the question** son article apporte un éclairage nouveau sur la question ; **from the parents' ~** du point de vue des parents ; **let's have your ~ on it*** donnez-nous votre point de vue là-dessus or sur la question

2 VT **a*** [+ information, report] présenter sous un certain angle ; **he ~d his article towards middle-class readers** il a rédigé son article à l'intention des classes moyennes or de façon à plaire au lecteur bourgeois

b (Tennis) **to ~ a shot** croiser sa balle, jouer la diagonale

c [+ lamp etc] régler à l'angle voulu ; **she ~d the lamp towards her desk** elle a dirigé la lumière (de la lampe) sur son bureau

3 COMP ► **angle bracket** N chevron m ► **angle iron** N fer m, équerre f ► **angle of incidence** N angle m d'incidence

angle² [ængl] VI **a** (lit) pêcher à la ligne ; **to ~ for trout** pêcher la truite **b** (fig) **to ~ for sb's attention** chercher à attirer l'attention de qn ; **to ~ for compliments** chercher or quêter des compliments ; **to ~ for a rise in salary/for an invitation** chercher à se faire augmenter/à se faire inviter ; **she's angling for a husband** elle fait la chasse au mari

Anglepoise® [ænglpɔɪz] N (Brit: also **~ lamp**) lampe f d'architecte

angler [ænglə'] N pêcheur m, -euse f (à la ligne) ; **~ (fish)** lotte f de mer

Angles [ænglz] NPL (Hist) Angles mpl

Anglican [ænglɪkən] ADJ, N anglican(e) m(f) ; **the ~ Communion** la communion or la communauté anglicane

Anglicanism [ænglɪkənɪzəm] N anglicanisme m

anglicism [ænglɪsɪzəm] N anglicisme m

anglicist [ænglɪsɪst] N angliciste mf

anglicize [ænglɪsaɪz] VT angliciser

angling [ænglɪŋ] N pêche f (à la ligne)

Anglo* [ængləʊ] N = **Anglo-American**

Anglo- [ængləʊ] PREF anglo-

Anglo-American [ængləʊə'merɪkən] **1** ADJ anglo-américain **2** N (US) Anglo-Américain(e) m(f), Américain d'origine anglo-saxonne

Anglo-Asian [ængləʊ'eɪʃn] **1** ADJ britannique originaire du sub-continent indien **2** N Britannique originaire du sub-continent indien

Anglo-Catholic [ængləʊ'kæθəlɪk] ADJ, N anglo-catholique mf

Anglo-Catholicism [ængləʊkə'θɒlɪsɪzəm] N anglo-catholicisme m

Anglo-French [ængləʊ'frentʃ] **1** ADJ franco-britannique **2** N (Ling) anglo-normand m

Anglo-Indian [ængləʊ'ɪndɪən] N (= British person in India) Anglais(e) m(f) des Indes ; (= person of British and Indian descent) métis(se) m(f) d'Anglais(e) et d'Indien(ne)

Anglo-Irish [ængləʊ'aɪərɪʃ] **1** the **Anglo-Irish** NPL les Anglo-Irlandais mpl **2** ADJ anglo-irlandais

anglophile [ængləʊfaɪl] ADJ, N anglophile mf

anglophobe [ængləʊfəʊb] ADJ, N anglophobe mf

Anglo-Saxon [ængləʊ'sæksən] **1** ADJ anglo-saxon **2** N **a** (= person) Anglo-Saxon(ne) m(f) **b** (Ling) anglo-saxon m

⸻ **ANGLO-SAXON** ⸻

Langue de la famille des langues germaniques, parlée en Grande-Bretagne entre le 5ᵉ siècle et la conquête normande (1066), et dont l'anglais actuel est partiellement dérivé. Beaucoup de mots d'usage très courant, par exemple « man », « child », « eat », « love » ou « harvest » sont d'origine anglo-saxonne.

⸻

Angola [æŋ'gəʊlə] N l'Angola m

Angolan [æŋ'gəʊlən] **1** ADJ angolais **2** N Angolais(e) m(f)

angora [æŋ'gɔ:rə] **1** N **a** (= cat/rabbit) (chat m/lapin m) angora m inv ; (= goat) chèvre f angora inv **b** (= wool) laine f angora inv, angora m inv **2** ADJ [cat, rabbit etc] angora inv ; [sweater] (en) angora

angostura [æŋgə'stjʊərə] **1** N angustura f **2** COMP ► **angostura bitters®** N bitter m additionné d'angustura

angrily [æŋgrɪlɪ] ADV [say, react] avec colère ; [leave] en colère

angry [æŋgrɪ] ADJ [person] en colère, fâché (**with sb** contre qn, **at sth** à cause de qch, **about sth** à propos de qch) ; [look] furieux ; [reply] plein or vibrant de colère ; (fig) [sea] mauvais, démonté ; **to get ~** se fâcher, se mettre en colère ; **to make sb ~** mettre qn en colère ; **he was ~ at being dismissed** il était furieux d'avoir été renvoyé or qu'on l'ait renvoyé ; **in an ~ voice** sur le ton de la colère ; **you won't be ~ if I tell you?** tu ne vas pas te fâcher si je te le dis ? ; **this sort of thing makes me really ~** ce genre de chose me met hors de moi ; **there were ~ scenes when it was announced that ...** la colère de la foule a éclaté quand on a annoncé que ... ; (Literat) **~ young man** jeune homme m en colère ; **the blow left an ~ scar on his forehead** le coup lui a laissé une vilaine cicatrice au front

angst [æŋst] N angoisse f existentielle

angstrom [æŋstrəm] N angström or angstrœm m

Anguilla [æŋ'gwɪlə] N Anguilla f

anguish [æŋgwɪʃ] N (mental) angoisse f, anxiété f ; (physical) supplice m ; **to be in ~** (mentally) être dans l'angoisse or angoissé ; (physically) être au supplice, souffrir le martyre

anguished [æŋgwɪʃt] ADJ (mentally) angoissé ; (physically) plein de souffrance

angular [æŋgjʊlə'] ADJ anguleux ; [face] anguleux, osseux ; [features] anguleux ; [movement] dégingandé, saccadé

aniline [ænɪli:n] **1** N aniline f **2** COMP ► **aniline dyes** NPL colorants mpl à base d'aniline

anima [ænɪmə] N (Psych) anima m

animal ['ænɪməl] **1** N (*lit*) animal *m*; (* *pej = person*) brute *f*; **I like ~s** j'aime les animaux *or* les bêtes; **man is a social ~** l'homme est un animal sociable; (*pej*) **the ~ in him** la bête en lui, son côté bestial; **he's nothing but an ~** c'est une brute; (*fig*) **there's no such ~** ça n'existe pas; (*fig*) **they're two different ~s** ce sont deux choses complètement différentes

2 ADJ [*instinct*] animal; **~ spirits** entrain *m*, vivacité *f*; **full of ~ spirits** plein d'entrain *or* de vivacité *or* de vie

3 COMP ► **animal cracker** N (*US*) cracker en forme d'animal ► **animal experimentation** N (*NonC*) expérimentation *f* animale *or* sur les animaux ► **animal fat** N graisse *f* animale ► **animal husbandry** N (*NonC*) élevage *m* ► **the animal kingdom** N le règne animal ► **Animal Liberation Front** N (*Brit*) mouvement pour la libération des animaux ► **animal liberationist** N *militant du mouvement de libération des animaux* ► **animal lover** N *personne f qui aime les animaux* ► **animal rights** NPL droits *mpl* des animaux ► **animal rights campaigner** N défenseur *m* des droits des animaux ► **animal sanctuary** N refuge *m* pour animaux

animate ['ænɪmɪt] **1** ADJ (= *living*) vivant, animé; (*Ling*) animé **2** ['ænɪmeɪt] VT (= *make lively*) [+ *discussion*] animer, rendre vivant

animated ['ænɪmeɪtɪd] ADJ **a** (= *lively*) animé; **to become ~** s'animer; **the talk was growing ~** la conversation s'animait *or* s'échauffait **b** (*Cine*) animé; **~ film** dessin *m* animé, film *m* d'animation

animatedly ['ænɪmeɪtɪdlɪ] ADV avec animation; **he pointed ~ at the package** tout agité, il désigna le paquet

animation [ˌænɪ'meɪʃən] N **a** [*of person*] vivacité *f*, entrain *m*; [*of face*] animation *f*; [*of scene, street etc*] activité *f*, animation *f* **b** (*Cine*) animation *f* → **suspend**

animator ['ænɪmeɪtə'] N (*Cine*) animateur *m*, -trice *f*

animatronics [ˌænɪmə'trɒnɪks] N (*NonC: Cine*) animatronique *f*

animism ['ænɪmɪzəm] N animisme *m*

animist ['ænɪmɪst] ADJ, N animiste *mf*

animosity [ˌænɪ'mɒsɪtɪ] N animosité *f* (**against, towards** contre), hostilité *f* (**against, towards** envers)

animus ['ænɪməs] N **a** (*NonC*) = **animosity** **b** (*Psych*) animus *m*

anise ['ænɪs] N anis *m*

aniseed ['ænɪsiːd] **1** N graine *f* d'anis **2** COMP [*flavoured*] à l'anis

anisette [ˌænɪ'zet] N anisette *f*

Anjou [ɑ̃'ʒuː] N l'Anjou *m*

Ankara ['æŋkərə] N Ankara

ankle ['æŋkl] **1** N cheville *f* **2** COMP ► **ankle boot** N bottine *f* ► **ankle bracelet** N bracelet *m* (*porté à la cheville*) ► **ankle-deep** ADJ **he was ~-deep in water** l'eau lui montait *or* il avait de l'eau jusqu'à la cheville; **the water is ~-deep** l'eau vient (jusqu')à la cheville ► **ankle joint** N articulation *f* de la cheville ► **ankle sock** N (*Brit*) socquette *f* ► **ankle strap** N bride *f*

anklebone ['æŋklbəʊn] N astragale *m*

anklet ['æŋklɪt] N bracelet *m* or anneau *m* de cheville; (*US*) socquette *f*

ankylosis [ˌæŋkɪ'ləʊsɪs] N ankylose *f*

Ann [æn] N Anne *f*

annalist ['ænəlɪst] N annaliste *m*

annals ['ænəlz] NPL annales *fpl*; **unique in the ~ of ...** unique dans les annales de ...

Annam [æ'næm] N Annam *m*

Annapurna [ˌænə'pʊənə] N l'Annapurna *m*

Anne [æn] N Anne *f* → **queen**

anneal [ə'niːl] VT [+ *glass, metal*] recuire

annex [ə'neks] **1** VT annexer **2** ['æneks] N (= *building, document*) annexe *f*

annexation [ˌænek'seɪʃən] N (= *act*) annexion *f* (**of** de); [*of territory*] territoire *m* annexe

annexe ['æneks] N = **annex 2**

Annie Oakley: [ˌænɪ'əʊklɪ] N (*US*) billet *m* de faveur

annihilate [ə'naɪəleɪt] VT [+ *army, fleet*] anéantir; [+ *space, time*] annihiler, supprimer; [+ *effect*] annihiler; (*fig: in game, argument*) écraser

annihilation [əˌnaɪə'leɪʃən] N (*Mil*) anéantissement *m*; (*fig*) suppression *f*

anniversary [ˌænɪ'vɜːsərɪ] **1** N (= *date, event*) anniversaire *m* (**of** de) → **wedding 2** COMP ► **anniversary dinner** N dîner *m* commémoratif *or* anniversaire

Anno Domini [ˌænəʊ'dɒmɪnaɪ] ADV (*frm*) après Jésus-Christ; **~ 1965** 1965 après J.-C.

annotate ['ænəʊteɪt] VT annoter

annotation [ˌænəʊ'teɪʃən] N annotation *f*, note *f*

▼ **announce** [ə'naʊns] VT annoncer; **to ~ the birth/death of ...** faire part de la naissance/du décès de ...; **"I won't"** he **~d** « je ne le ferai pas » annonça-t-il; **it is ~d from London that ...** on apprend de Londres que ...

announcement [ə'naʊnsmənt] N (*gen*) annonce *f*; (*esp Admin*) avis *m*; [*of birth, marriage, death*] avis *m*; [*privately inserted or circulated*] faire-part *m inv*

announcer [ə'naʊnsə'] N **a** (*Rad, TV*) (*linking programmes*) speaker(ine) *m(f)*, annonceur *m*, -euse *f*; (*within a programme*) présentateur *m*, -trice *f*; (= *newsreader*) présentateur *m*, -trice *f* **b** (*at airport, station*) annonceur *m*, -euse *f*

annoy [ə'nɔɪ] VT (= *vex*) ennuyer, agacer; (= *deliberately irritate*) [+ *person, animal*] agacer, énerver; (= *inconvenience*) importuner, ennuyer; **to be/get ~ed with sb** être/se mettre en colère contre qn; **to be ~ed about sth** être contrarié par qch; **to be ~ed about a decision** être mécontent d'une décision; **to be ~ed with sb about sth** être mécontent de qn à propos de qch; **to get ~ed with a machine** se mettre en colère *or* s'énerver contre une machine; **don't get ~ed!** ne vous fâchez *or* énervez pas!; **I am very ~ed that he hasn't come** je suis très ennuyé *or* contrarié qu'il ne soit pas venu; **I am very ~ed with him for not coming** je suis très mécontent qu'il ne soit pas venu

annoyance [ə'nɔɪəns] N **a** (= *displeasure*) contrariété *f*, mécontentement *m*; **with a look of ~** d'un air contrarié *or* mécontent; **he found to his great ~ that ...** il s'est aperçu à son grand mécontentement que ... **b** (= *cause of annoyance*) tracas *m*, ennui *m*

annoying [ə'nɔɪɪŋ] ADJ agaçant *m*, (= *very irritating*) ennuyeux; **the ~ thing about it is that ...** ce qui est agaçant *or* ennuyeux dans cette histoire c'est que ...; **how ~!** que c'est agaçant *or* ennuyeux!

annoyingly [ə'nɔɪɪŋlɪ] ADV [*behave*] de façon énervante *or* agaçante; **she was ~ vague/cheerful** elle était si vague/gaie que c'était énervant *or* agaçant; **he was ~ successful** sa réussite avait quelque chose d'énervant *or* d'agaçant

annual ['ænjʊəl] **1** ADJ annuel; (*Comm etc*) **~ general meeting** assemblée *f* générale annuelle **2** N **a** (*Bot*) plante *f* annuelle → **hardy b** (= *book*) publication *f* annuelle; (*children's*) album *m* **3** COMP ► **annual ring** N (*Bot*) anneau *m* de croissance, cerne *m*

annualize ['ænjʊəlaɪz] VT annualiser

annually ['ænjʊəlɪ] ADV annuellement, tous les ans; **£5,000 ~** 5 000 livres par an

annuity [ə'njuːɪtɪ] **1** N (= *regular income*) rente *f*; (*for life*) rente *f* viagère, viager *m*; (= *investment*) viager *m*; **to invest money in an ~** placer de l'argent en viager → **defer¹, life 2** COMP ► **annuity bond** N titre *m* de rente

annul [ə'nʌl] VT [+ *law*] abroger, abolir; [+ *decision, judgement*] casser, annuler; [+ *marriage*] annuler

annulment [ə'nʌlmənt] N annulation *f*

Annunciation [əˌnʌnsɪ'eɪʃən] N Annonciation *f*

anode ['ænəʊd] N anode *f*

anodize ['ænəʊdaɪz] VT anodiser

anodyne ['ænəʊdaɪn] **1** N (*Med*) analgésique *m*, calmant *m*; (*fig liter*) baume *m* **2** ADJ (*Med*) antalgique, analgésique; (*fig liter*) apaisant

anoint [ə'nɔɪnt] VT oindre (**with** de), consacrer *or* bénir par l'onction; **to ~ sb king** sacrer qn, faire qn roi par la cérémonie du sacre; **the ~ed King** le roi consacré; (*fig*) **the press have ~ed her queen of detective fiction** la presse l'a sacrée reine du roman policier

anointing [ə'nɔɪntɪŋ] N (*Rel*) **~ of the sick** onction *f* des malades

anomalous [ə'nɒmələs] ADJ (*Med*) anormal, irrégulier; (*Gram*) anomal; (*fig*) anormal

anomaly [ə'nɒməlɪ] N anomalie *f*

anomie, anomy ['ænəʊmɪ] N (*NonC*) anomie *f*

anon¹ [ə'nɒn] ADV (†† *or hum = soon*) sous peu; **... of which more ~** ... nous y reviendrons; **see you ~** à tout à l'heure → **ever**

anon² [ə'nɒn] ADJ (ABBR = **anonymous**) anonyme; (*at end of text*) **"Anon"** « Anonyme »

anonymity [ˌænə'nɪmɪtɪ] N anonymat *m*; **to preserve one's ~** garder l'anonymat

anonymous [ə'nɒnɪməs] ADJ (*lit, fig*) anonyme; **an ~ caller claiming to represent the group** un coup de téléphone anonyme d'une personne affirmant représenter le groupe; **an ~ woman called to say that ...** une femme qui n'a pas donné son nom a appelé pour dire que ...; **to remain ~** garder l'anonymat → **alcoholic, gambler**

anonymously [ə'nɒnɪməslɪ] ADV [*send, give, publish*] anonymement; [*speak, quote, live*] sous couvert de l'anonymat

anorak ['ænəræk] N **a** (*esp Brit*) anorak *m* **b** (* = *unstylish person*) ringard(e)* *m(f)*

anorectic [ˌænə'rektɪk] ADJ = **anorexic**

anorexia [ˌænə'reksɪə] N anorexie *f*; **~ nervosa** anorexie *f* mentale

anorexic [ˌænə'reksɪk] ADJ, N anorexique *mf*

another [ə'nʌðə'] **1** ADJ **a** (= *one more*) un ... de plus, encore un; **take ~ ten** prenez-en encore dix; **to wait ~ hour** attendre une heure de plus *or* encore une heure; **I won't wait ~ minute!** je n'attendrai pas une minute de plus!; **without ~ word** sans un mot ajouter un mot, sans un mot de plus; **~ beer?** vous reprendrez bien une bière?; **in ~ 20 years** dans 20 ans d'ici; **and ~ thing ...*** (= *what's more*) et de plus ..., et d'ailleurs ...

b (= *similar*) un autre, un second; **there is not ~ book like it** ◊ **there is not ~ such book** ce livre est unique en son genre; **he will be ~ Hitler** ce sera un second *or* nouvel Hitler

c (= *different*) un autre; **that's quite ~ matter** c'est une tout autre question, c'est tout autre chose; **do it ~ time** remettez cela à plus tard, vous le ferez une autre fois

2 PRON **a** un(e) autre, encore un(e); **in one form or ~** sous une forme ou une autre; **he was opening bottles one after ~** il ouvrait des bouteilles les unes après les autres; **between or what with one thing and ~*** en fin de compte → **after, thing**

b **one ~ = each other**; → **each**

anoxia [ə'nɒksɪə] N anoxie *f*

anoxic [ə'nɒksɪk] ADJ anoxique

ANSI [ˌeɪenes'aɪ] N (*US*) (ABBR = **American National Standards Institute**) ANSI *m*, institut *m* américain de normalisation

answer ['ɑːnsə^r] **1** N **a** (= *reply*) réponse *f*; **to get** *or* **receive an ~** recevoir une réponse; **to write sb an ~** répondre à qn (par écrit); **his only ~ was to shrug his shoulders** pour toute réponse il a haussé les épaules, il a répondu par un haussement d'épaules; (*Telec*) **there's no ~** ça ne répond pas; **I knocked but there was no ~** j'ai frappé mais il n'y a pas eu de réponse *or* mais on ne m'a pas répondu; (*Comm*) **in ~ to your letter** en réponse à votre lettre; **I could find no ~** je n'ai rien trouvé à répondre; **she's got an ~ to everything** ◊ **she's always got an ~** elle a réponse à tout; (*Jur*) **~ to a charge** réponse *f* à une accusation; (*Rel*) **the ~ to my prayer** l'exaucement *m* de ma prière; (*hum*) **it's the ~ to a maiden's prayer** c'est ce dont j'ai toujours rêvé; (*hum*) **for her he was the ~ to a maiden's prayer*** c'était l'homme de ses rêves; **there's no ~ to that!** que voulez-vous répondre à ça?; **Belgium's ~ to Sylvester Stallone** le Sylvester Stallone belge; **it's the poor man's ~ to caviar** c'est le caviar du pauvre
b (= *solution*) solution *f*; **there must be an ~** il doit y avoir une solution; (*fig*) **there is no easy ~** c'est un problème difficile à résoudre, il n'y a pas de réponse toute faite; **he knows all the ~s** il a réponse à tout
2 VT **a** [+ *letter, question*] répondre à; [+ *criticism*] répondre à; (*sharply*) répliquer à; **~ me!** répondez-moi!; **to ~ the bell** *or* **door** aller *or* venir ouvrir (la porte), aller voir qui est à la porte *or* qui est là; **to ~ the bell** [*servant summoned*] répondre au coup de sonnette; **to ~ the phone** répondre au téléphone; **I didn't ~ a word** je n'ai rien répondu, je n'ai pas soufflé mot
b (= *fulfil, solve*) [+ *description*] répondre à, correspondre à; [+ *prayer*] exaucer; [+ *problem*] résoudre; [+ *need*] répondre à, satisfaire; **it ~s the purpose** cela fait l'affaire; **this machine ~s several purposes** cet appareil a plusieurs utilisations
c (*Jur*) **to ~ a charge (of assault)** répondre d'une accusation (d'agression)
d (*Naut*) **to ~ the helm** obéir à la barre
3 VI **a** (= *say, write in reply*) répondre
b (= *succeed*) [*plan etc*] faire l'affaire, réussir
c **he ~s to the name of "Baby Boy"** il répond au nom de « Baby Boy », il s'appelle « Baby Boy »; **he ~s to that description** il répond à cette description
4 COMP ► **answer-back (code)** N indicatif *m* ► **answering machine** N répondeur *m* (téléphonique) ► **answering service** N permanence *f* téléphonique
► **answer back** **1** VI, VT SEP répondre (avec impertinence) ((**to**) sb à qn); **don't ~ back!** ne réponds pas! **2** ~**-back** N → **answer**
► **answer for** VT FUS (= *be responsible for*) [+ *sb's safety etc*] répondre de; **to ~ for the truth of sth** répondre de l'exactitude de qch; **he has a lot to ~ for** il a bien des comptes à rendre

answerable ['ɑːnsərəbl] ADJ **a** (= *accountable*) [*person*] responsable (**to sb** devant qn, **for sth** de qch); **I am ~ to no one** je n'ai de comptes à rendre à personne **b** (= *having an answer*) [*question*] qui admet une réponse; [*argument*] réfutable

answerphone ['ɑːnsəfəʊn] N répondeur *m* (téléphonique)

ant [ænt] **1** N fourmi *f*; (*fig*) **to have ~s in one's pants*** ne pas (pouvoir) tenir en place **2** COMP ► **ant-heap, ant-hill** N fourmilière *f*

antacid ['ænt'æsɪd] **1** ADJ alcalin, antiacide **2** N (médicament *m*) alcalin *m*, antiacide *m*

antagonism [æn'tægənɪzəm] N antagonisme *m* (**between** entre), opposition *f* (**to** à); **to show ~ to an idea** se montrer hostile à une idée

antagonist [æn'tægənɪst] N antagoniste *mf*, adversaire *mf*

antagonistic [æn,tægə'nɪstɪk] ADJ [*force, interest*] antagonique, contraire; **to be ~ to sth** être opposé or hostile à qch; **to be ~ to sb** être en opposition avec qn; **two ~ ideas/decisions** deux idées *fpl*/décisions *fpl* antagoniques *or* antagonistes *or* opposées

antagonize [æn'tægənaɪz] VT [+ *person*] contrarier, se mettre à dos; **I don't want to ~ him** je ne veux pas le contrarier *or* me le mettre à dos

Antarctic [æn'tɑːktɪk] **1** N Antarctique *m* **2** ADJ **a** antarctique, austral **b** = **Antarctic Ocean** **3** COMP ► **Antarctic Circle** N cercle *m* Antarctique ► **Antarctic Ocean** N océan *m* Antarctique *or* Austral

Antarctica [æn'tɑːktɪkə] N l'Antarctique *m*

ante ['ænti] **1** N **a** (*Cards: in poker*) première mise *f*; (*fig*) **to raise** *or* **up the ~*** placer la barre plus haut **2** VI (*Cards*) faire une première mise; (*US** = *pay*) casquer*
► **ante up** VI (*Cards*) augmenter la mise; (*US** = *pay*) casquer*

ante... ['ænti] PREF anté..., anti...

anteater ['ænti:tə^r] N fourmilier *m*

antebellum [,ænti'beləm] ADJ (*US Hist*) d'avant la guerre de Sécession

antecedent [,ænti'si:dənt] **1** ADJ antérieur (-eure *f*) (**to** à) **2** N **a** (*Gram, Math, Philos*) antécédent *m* **b** **the ~s of sb** les antécédents de qn

antechamber ['ænti,tʃeɪmbə^r] N antichambre *f*

antedate ['ænti'deɪt] VT **a** (= *give earlier date to*) [+ *document*] antidater **b** (= *come before*) [+ *event*] précéder

antediluvian [,æntidi'lu:viən] ADJ antédiluvien; (* *hum*) [*person, hat*] antédiluvien* (*hum*)

antelope ['æntiləʊp] N (*pl* **antelope** *or* **antelopes**) antilope *f*

antenatal ['ænti'neɪtl] **1** N (= *examination*) examen *m* prénatal **2** ADJ prénatal; **~ clinic** service *m* de consultation prénatale; **to attend an ~ clinic** aller à la consultation prénatale; **~ ward** salle *f* de surveillance prénatale

antenna [æn'tenə] N (*pl* **antennas** *or* **antennae** [æn'teni:]) (*Rad, Telec, TV, Zool*) antenne *f*

antepenult [,æntipi'nʌlt] N (*Ling*) antépénultième *f*

antepenultimate [,æntipi'nʌltimit] ADJ antépénultième

ante-post [,ænti'pəʊst] (*Brit Gambling*) **1** ADJ [*bet*] engagé avant le jour de la course; **the ~ favourite** le favori d'avant la course **2** ADV **to bet ~** parier avant le jour de la course

anterior [æn'tiəriə^r] ADJ antérieur (-eure *f*) (**to** à)

anteroom ['æntirʊm] N antichambre *f*, vestibule *m*

anthem ['ænθəm] N motet *m* → **national**

anther ['ænθə^r] N anthère *f*

anthologist [æn'θɒlədʒɪst] N anthologiste *mf*

anthologize [æn'θɒlə,dʒaɪz] VT faire une anthologie de

anthology [æn'θɒlədʒɪ] N anthologie *f*

Anthony ['æntəni] N Antoine *m*

anthraces ['ænθrə,si:z] NPL of **anthrax**

anthracite ['ænθrəsaɪt] **1** N anthracite *m* **2** ADJ **~ (grey)** (gris) anthracite *inv*

anthrax ['ænθræks] N (*pl* **anthraces**) (*Med, Vet* = *disease*) charbon *m*; (*Med* = *boil*) anthrax *m*

anthropo... ['ænθrəpəʊ] PREF anthropo...

anthropoid ['ænθrəpɔɪd] ADJ, N anthropoïde *m*

anthropological [,ænθrəpə'lɒdʒɪkəl] ADJ anthropologique

anthropologist [,ænθrə'pɒlədʒɪst] N anthropologue *mf*

anthropology [,ænθrə'pɒlədʒɪ] N anthropologie *f*

anthropometry [,ænθrə'pɒmɪtrɪ] N anthropométrie *f*

anthropomorphic [,ænθrəpəʊ'mɔːfɪk] ADJ anthropomorphe, anthropomorphique

anthropomorphism [,ænθrəʊpə'mɔːfɪzəm] N anthropomorphisme *m*

anthropomorphist [,ænθrəpəʊ'mɔːfɪst] ADJ, N anthropomorphiste *mf*

anthropomorphize [,ænθrəpəʊ'mɔːfɪz] VT anthropomorphiser

anthropomorphous [,ænθrəpəʊ'mɔːfəs] ADJ anthropomorphe

anthropophagi [,ænθrəʊ'pɒfəgaɪ] NPL anthropophages *mpl*

anthropophagous [,ænθrəʊ'pɒfəgəs] ADJ anthropophage

anthropophagy [,ænθrəʊ'pɒfədʒɪ] N anthropophagie *f*

anthroposophical [,ænθrəpəʊ'sɒfɪkəl] ADJ anthroposophique

anthroposophy [,ænθrə'pɒsəfɪ] N anthroposophie *f*

anti* ['ænti] **1** ADJ **he's rather ~** il est plutôt contre **2** N **the ~s** ceux qui sont contre **3** PREP **to be ~ sth** être contre qch

anti... ['ænti] PREF anti..., contre...

anti-abortion ['æntiə'bɔːʃən] N **~ campaign** campagne *f* contre l'avortement

anti-abortionist ['æntiə'bɔːʃənɪst] N adversaire *mf* de l'avortement

anti-aircraft ['ænti'eəkrɑːft] ADJ [*gun, missile*] antiaérien; **~ defence** défense *f* contre avions, DCA *f*

anti-apartheid ['æntiə'pɑːteɪt, 'æntiə'pɑːtaɪd] ADJ anti-apartheid

anti-authority ['æntiɔː'θɒriti] ADJ contestataire

antibacterial ['æntibæk'tiəriəl] ADJ antibactérien

antiballistic ['æntibə'lɪstɪk] ADJ [*missile*] antibalistique

antibiotic ['æntibaɪ'ɒtɪk] ADJ, N antibiotique *m*

antibody ['ænti,bɒdɪ] N anticorps *m*

Antichrist ['æntikraɪst] N Antéchrist *m*

anti-Christian ['ænti'krɪstɪən] ADJ antichrétien

anticipate [æn'tisipeit] **1** VT **a** (= *expect, foresee*) prévoir, s'attendre à; **we don't ~ any trouble** nous ne prévoyons pas d'ennuis; **I ~ that he will come** je m'attends à ce qu'il vienne; **do you ~ that it will be easy?** pensez-vous que ce sera facile?; **I ~ seeing him tomorrow** je pense le voir demain; **the attendance is larger than I ~d** je ne m'attendais pas à ce que l'assistance soit aussi nombreuse; **as ~d** comme prévu
b (= *use, deal with or get before due time*) [+ *pleasure*] savourer à l'avance; [+ *grief, pain*] souffrir à l'avance; [+ *success*] escompter; [+ *wishes, objections, command, needs, request, events*] anticiper; **to ~ one's income/profits** anticiper sur son revenu/sur ses bénéfices
c (= *forestall*) **to ~ sb's doing sth** faire qch avant qn; **they ~d Columbus' discovery of America** ◊ **they ~d Columbus in discovering America** ils ont découvert l'Amérique avant Christophe Colomb
2 VI (= *act too soon*) agir avec précipitation

anticipation [æn,tisi'peɪʃən] N **a** (= *expectation, foreseeing*) attente *f* **b** (= *experiencing etc in advance*) [of *pleasure*] attente *f*; [of *grief, pain*] appréhension *f*; [of *profits, income*] jouissance *f* anticipée; **~ of sb's wishes** *etc* empressement *m* à aller au-devant des désirs *etc* de qn **c** **in ~** par anticipation, à l'avance; (*Comm*) **thanking you in ~** en vous remerciant d'avance, avec mes remerciements anticipés ; **in ~ of a fine week** en prévision d'une semaine de beau temps ; **we wait with growing ~** nous attendons avec une impatience grandissante

anticipatory [æn'tɪsɪpeɪtərɪ] ADJ (*Phon*) régressif

anticlerical [ænti'klerɪkl] ADJ, N anticlérical(e) *m(f)*

anticlericalism [ænti'klerɪkəlɪzəm] N anticléricalisme *m*

anticlimactic [æntɪklaɪ'mæktɪk] ADJ décevant

anticlimax [ænti'klaɪmæks] N [*of style, thought*] chute *f* (dans le trivial) ; **the ceremony was an ~** la cérémonie n'a pas été à la hauteur de l'attente ; **what an ~!** quelle douche froide !

anticline [ænticlaɪn] N anticlinal *m*

anticlockwise [ænti'klɒkwaɪz] ADJ, ADV (*Brit*) dans le sens inverse des aiguilles d'une montre ; **in an ~ direction** dans le sens inverse des aiguilles d'une montre

anticoagulant [æntikəʊ'ægjʊlənt] ADJ, N anticoagulant *m*

anticonvulsant [æntikən'vʌlsənt] ADJ, N antispasmodique *m*, anticonvulsivant *m*

anticorrosive [æntikə'rəʊsɪv] **1** ADJ anticorrosion *inv* **2** N produit *m* anticorrosion *inv*

antics [æntiks] NPL [*of child, animal*] cabrioles *fpl*, gambades *fpl* ; [*of clown*] bouffonneries *fpl*, singeries *fpl* ; (*pej*) **all his ~** tout le cinéma* qu'il a fait ; **he's up to his ~ again** il fait de nouveau des siennes*

anticyclone [ænti'saɪkləʊn] N anticyclone *m*

antidandruff [ænti'dændrʌf] ADJ antipelliculaire

antidazzle [ænti'dæzl] ADJ [*glass, coating*] antireflet *f inv* ; **~ headlights** phares *mpl* antiéblouissants

antidepressant [æntidɪ'presənt] N antidépresseur *m*

antidotal [ænti'dəʊtəl] ADJ antivenimeux

antidote [æntidəʊt] N (*Med, fig*) antidote *m* (**for, to** à, contre), contrepoison *m* (**for, to** de)

antidumping [ænti,dʌmpɪŋ] N antidumping *m* ; **~ agreement** convention *f* antidumping

anti-establishment [æntis'tæblɪʃmənt] ADJ contestataire

antifreeze [ænti'fri:z] N antigel *m*

anti-friction [ænti'frɪkʃən] ADJ antifriction *inv*

antigen [æntidʒən] N antigène *m*

antiglare [æntiglɛəʳ] ADJ = **antidazzle**

Antigone [æn'tɪgənɪ] N Antigone *f*

Antigua [æn'tɪgjʊə] N Antigua ; **~ and Barbuda** Antigua et Barbuda

antihero [ænti,hɪərəʊ] N (*pl* **antiheroes**) antihéros *m*

antiheroine [ænti'herəʊɪn] N antihéroïne *f*

antihistamine [ænti'hɪstəmɪn] N (produit *m*) antihistaminique *m*

anti-inflammatory [æntiɪn'flæmət(ə)rɪ] ADJ (*Med*) anti-inflammatoire

anti-inflationary [æntiɪn'fleɪʃənərɪ] ADJ anti-inflationniste

anti-interference [æntiɪntə'fɪərəns] ADJ antiparasite

anti-knock [ænti'nɒk] N antidétonant *m*

Antilles [æn'tɪliːz] N **the ~** les Antilles *fpl* ; **the Greater/the Lesser ~** les Grandes/Petites Antilles *fpl*

antilock [æntilɒk] ADJ (*Aut*) **~ braking system** système *m* antiblocage *or* ABS ; **anti-lock brakes** freins *mpl* ABS ; **~ device** dispositif *m* antiblocage

antilogarithm [ænti'lɒgərɪθəm] N antilogarithme *m*

antimacassar [æntimə'kæsəʳ] N têtière *f*, appui-tête *m*

antimagnetic [æntimæg'netɪk] ADJ antimagnétique

antimarketeer [æntimɑː'tɪəʳ] N (*Brit Pol*) adversaire *mf* du Marché commun

antimatter [ænti,mætəʳ] N antimatière *f*

antimissile [ænti'mɪsaɪl] ADJ antimissile

antimony [æntimənɪ] N antimoine *m*

anti-motion-sickness [ænti'məʊʃən'sɪknɪs] ADJ **~ tablets** comprimés *mpl* contre le mal des transports

antinuclear [ænti'njuːklɪəʳ] ADJ antinucléaire

antinuke* [ænti'njuːk] ADJ antinucléaire

Antioch [æntiɒk] N Antioche *f*

antioxidant [ænti'ɒksɪdənt] N antioxydant *m*

antipathetic [,æntipə'θetɪk] ADJ antipathique (**to** à)

antipathy [æn'tɪpəθɪ] N antipathie *f*, aversion *f* (**against, to** pour)

antipersonnel [æntipɜːsə'nel] ADJ (*Mil*) antipersonnel *inv*

antiperspirant [ænti'pɜːspɪrənt] **1** N déodorant *m* (antisudoral) **2** ADJ antisudoral

antiphony [æn'tɪfənɪ] N (*Mus*) antienne *f*

antipodean [æn,tɪpə'dɪən] ADJ (*esp Brit*) des antipodes

antipodes [æn'tɪpədiːz] NPL (*esp Brit*) antipodes *mpl*

antiquarian [,ænti'kwɛərɪən] **1** ADJ d'antiquaire ; **~ bookseller** libraire *mf* spécialisé(e) dans le livre ancien ; **~ collection** collection *f* d'antiquités **2** N **a** amateur *m* d'antiquités **b** (*Comm*) antiquaire *mf* ; **~'s shop** magasin *m* d'antiquités

antiquary [æntikwərɪ] N (= *collector*) collectionneur *m*, -euse *f* d'antiquités ; (= *student*) archéologue *mf* ; (*Comm*) antiquaire *mf*

antiquated [æntikweɪtɪd] ADJ [*factory, prison, industry*] vétuste ; [*machinery, equipment*] vétuste, archaïque ; [*system, practice*] archaïque ; [*idea, belief*] vieillot (-otte *f*) ; [*person*] vieux jeu *inv*

antique [æn'tiːk] **1** ADJ (= *very old*) [*furniture etc*] ancien ; († = *ancient*) [*civilization etc*] antique ; (* *hum*) antédiluvien* **2** N (= *sculpture, ornament etc*) objet *m* d'art (ancien) ; (= *furniture*) meuble *m* ancien ; **it's a genuine ~** c'est un objet (*or* un meuble) d'époque **3** COMP
► **antique dealer** N antiquaire *mf*
► **antique shop** N magasin *m* d'antiquités

antiqued [æn'tiːkt] ADJ [*furniture, pine*] verni à l'ancienne ; [*finish*] à l'ancienne ; [*leather*] vieilli, patiné

antiquity [æn'tɪkwɪtɪ] N **a** (*NonC* = *great age*) ancienneté *f* **b** (= *ancient times*) antiquité *f* ; **in ~** dans l'Antiquité **c** **antiquities** (= *buildings*) monuments *mpl* antiques ; (= *works of art*) objets *mpl* d'art antiques, antiquités *fpl*

anti-racism [æntɪ'reɪsɪzəm] N antiracisme *m*

anti-racist [æntɪ'reɪsɪst] ADJ antiraciste, contre le racisme

anti-religious [æntɪrɪ'lɪdʒəs] ADJ antireligieux

anti-riot [æntɪ'raɪət] ADJ antiémeute

anti-roll bar [æntɪ'rəʊlbɑːʳ] N barre *f* antiroulis, stabilisateur *m*

antirrhinum [,æntɪ'raɪnəm] N muflier *m*, gueule-de-loup *f*

anti-rust [æntɪ'rʌst] ADJ [*paint, spray etc*] antirouille *inv*

antisegregationist [ˈæntisegrəˈgeɪʃənɪst] ADJ, N antiségrégationniste *m*

anti-Semite [ænti'siːmaɪt] N antisémite *mf*

anti-Semitic [æntisɪ'mɪtɪk] ADJ antisémite

anti-Semitism [ænti'semɪtɪzəm] N antisémitisme *m*

antisepsis [,ænti'sepsɪs] N antisepsie *f*

antiseptic [,ænti'septɪk] ADJ, N antiseptique *m*

anti-skid [ænti'skɪd] ADJ antidérapant

anti-slavery [ænti'sleɪvərɪ] ADJ antiesclavagiste

anti-smoking [ænti'sməʊkɪŋ] ADJ anti-tabac

antisocial [ænti'səʊʃəl] ADJ [*person*] sauvage ; [*behaviour, activity*] antisocial, asocial ; [*habit*] antisocial ; **he arrived at an ~ hour** il est arrivé à une heure indue ; **don't be ~*, come and join us** ne sois pas si sauvage, viens nous rejoindre

antispasmodic [æntispæz'mɒdɪk] ADJ, N antispasmodique *m*

antistatic [ænti'stætɪk] ADJ antistatique

antistrike [ænti'straɪk] ADJ antigrève

antisubmarine [ænti,sʌbmə'riːn] ADJ antisous-marin

anti-tank [ænti'tæŋk] ADJ antichar (*f inv*) ; **~ mines** mines *fpl* antichars

anti-terrorist [ænti'terərɪst] ADJ antiterroriste

anti-theft [ænti'θeft] ADJ **~ device** (*Aut*) antivol *m* ; (*gen*) dispositif *m* contre le vol, dispositif *m* antivol

antithesis [æn'tɪθɪsɪs] N (*pl* **antitheses** [æn'tɪθɪsiːz]) **a** (= *direct opposite*) antithèse *f* (**to, of** de) **b** (= *contrast*) contraste *m* **c** (*Literat*) antithèse *f*

antithetic(al) [,ænti'θetɪk(əl)] ADJ antithétique

antithetically [,ænti'θetɪkəlɪ] ADV par antithèse

antitoxic [ænti'tɒksɪk] ADJ antitoxique

antitoxin [ænti'tɒksɪn] N antitoxine *f*

antitrust [ænti'trʌst] ADJ (*US*) **~ commission** commission *f* antitrust *inv* ; (*esp US*) **~ law** loi *f* antitrust *inv*

antivivisection [ænti,vɪvɪ'sekʃən] N antivivisection *f*, antivivisectionnisme *m*

antivivisectionist [ænti,vɪvɪ'sekʃənɪst] N adversaire *mf* de la vivisection

antiwrinkle [ænti'rɪŋkl] ADJ antirides *inv*

antler [æntləʳ] N merrain *m* ; **the ~s** les bois *mpl*, la ramure ; **a fine set of ~s** une belle ramure

Antony [æntənɪ] N Antoine *m*

antonym [æntənɪm] N antonyme *m*

antonymous [æn'tɒnɪməs] ADJ antonymique

antonymy [æn'tɒnɪmɪ] N antonymie *f*

antsy* [æntsɪ] ADJ (*US*) nerveux, agité

Antwerp [æntwɜːp] N Anvers

anus [eɪnəs] N anus *m*

anvil [ænvɪl] N enclume *f* ; (*fig*) **forged on the ~ of ...** forgé à la dure réalité de ...

anxiety [æŋ'zaɪətɪ] N **a** (= *concern, also Psych*) anxiété *f* ; **deep ~** angoisse *f* ; **this is a great (cause of) ~ to me** ceci m'inquiète énormément, ceci me donne énormément de soucis ; (*Psych*) **~ neurosis** anxiété *f* névrotique **b** (= *keen desire*) grand désir *m*, désir *m* ardent ; **his ~ to do well** son grand désir de réussir ; **in his ~ to be gone he left his pen behind** il était si pressé de partir qu'il en a oublié son stylo, dans son souci de partir au plus vite il a oublié son stylo

anxious [æŋkʃəs] ADJ **a** (= *worried*) [*person, face, look*] anxieux (**about sth** à propos de qch, **about doing sth** à l'idée de faire qch) ; [*feeling*] d'anxiété ; **to keep an ~ eye on sb** surveiller qn d'un œil inquiet ; **she is ~ about my health** mon état de santé l'inquiète beaucoup **b** (= *worrying*) [*time, situation, wait*] angoissant **c** (= *eager*) **to be ~ to do sth** tenir beaucoup à faire qch ; **not to be very ~ to do sth** n'avoir guère envie de faire qch ; **to be ~ that ...** tenir beaucoup à ce que ... (+ *subj*) ; **to be ~ for sth** attendre qch avec impatience ; **~ for praise** avide de louanges ; **she was ~ for him to leave** elle avait hâte qu'il s'en aille

anxiously [æŋkʃəslɪ] ADV **a** (= *worriedly*) [*say, ask*] anxieusement ; **to look ~ at sb/sth** jeter un regard anxieux à qn/qch **b** (= *eagerly*) [*wait for*] impatiemment

anxiousness [ˈæŋkʃəsnɪs] N = anxiety

any [ˈenɪ] **1** ADJ **a** (with neg and implied neg = some) **I haven't got ~ money/books** je n'ai pas d'argent/de livres ; **you haven't got ~ excuse** vous n'avez aucune excuse ; **this pan hasn't got ~ lid** cette casserole n'a pas de couvercle ; **there isn't ~ sign of life** il n'y a pas le moindre signe de vie ; **without ~ difficulty** sans la moindre difficulté ; **the impossibility of giving them ~ money/advice** l'impossibilité de leur donner de l'argent/le moindre conseil ; **I have hardly ~ money left** il ne me reste presque plus d'argent

b (in interrog sentences, clauses of cond and hypotheses) (= some) **have you got ~ butter?** avez-vous du beurre ? ; **did they find ~ survivors?** ont-ils trouvé des survivants ? ; **do you speak ~ foreign languages?** parlez-vous une ou plusieurs langues étrangères ? ; **are there ~ others?** y en a-t-il d'autres ? ; **is it ~ use trying?** est-ce que cela vaut la peine d'essayer ? ; **do you have ~ complaints?** avez-vous quelque sujet de vous plaindre ?, avez-vous à vous plaindre de quelque chose ? ; **if you see ~ children** si vous voyez des enfants ; **if you have ~ money** si vous avez de l'argent ; **he can do it if ~ man can** si quelqu'un peut le faire, c'est bien lui ; (frm) **if it is in ~ way inconvenient to you** si cela vous cause un dérangement quel qu'il soit, si cela vous cause le moindre dérangement

c (= no matter which) n'importe quel, quelconque ; (= each and every) tout ; **take ~ two points** prenez deux points quelconques ; **take ~ card you like** prenez n'importe quelle carte, prenez la carte que vous voulez ; **come at ~ time** venez à n'importe quelle heure ; **at ~ hour of the day (or night)** à toute heure du jour (ou de la nuit) ; **~ time soon** d'un moment à l'autre, très bientôt ; **~ number of ...** n'importe quelle quantité de ... ; **~ pupil who breaks the rules will be punished** tout élève qui enfreindra le règlement sera puni ; **~ actor will tell you that performing is not easy** n'importe quel acteur vous dira que ce n'est pas facile de jouer ; **he's not just ~ (old*) footballer** ce n'est pas n'importe quel footballeur ; **they're not just ~ old* trainers, they're Reeboks®** ce ne sont pas des chaussures de sport quelconques, ce sont des Reeboks® ; **they eat ~ old thing*** ils mangent n'importe quoi → **day, minute**

d (phrases) **we have ~ amount of time** nous avons tout le or notre temps ; **we have ~ amount of money** nous avons tout l'argent qu'il nous faut ; **there are ~ number of ways to do it** il y a des quantités de façons or il y a mille façons de le faire → **case, rate**

2 PRON **a** (with neg and implied neg) **she has two brothers but I haven't got ~** elle a deux frères mais moi je n'en ai pas (un seul) ; **I don't believe ~ of them has done it** je ne crois pas qu'aucun d'eux l'ait fait ; **I have hardly ~ left** il ne m'en reste presque plus

b (in interrog, cond, hypothetical constructions) **have you got ~?** en avez-vous ? ; **if ~ of you can sing** si l'un d'entre vous or si quelqu'un parmi vous sait chanter ; **if ~ of them come out** s'il y en a parmi eux qui sortent, si quelques-uns d'entre eux sortent ; **if ~ of them comes out** si l'un d'entre eux sort ; **few, if ~, will come** il viendra peu de gens — si tant est qu'il en vienne, il ne viendra pas grand-monde, voire personne

c (in affirmative sentences) **~ of those books will do** n'importe lequel de ces livres fera l'affaire

3 ADV **a** (in neg sentences) **she is not ~ more intelligent than her sister** elle n'est pas plus intelligente que sa sœur ; **I can't hear him ~ more** je ne l'entends plus ; **don't do it ~ more!** ne recommence pas ! ; **we can't go ~ further** nous ne pouvons pas aller plus loin ; **I won't wait ~ longer** je n'attendrai pas plus

longtemps ; **the room didn't look ~ too clean** la pièce ne faisait vraiment pas propre ; **without ~ more discussion they left** ils sont partis sans ajouter un mot ; **I can't imagine things getting ~ better for the unemployed** je ne pense pas que la situation puisse s'améliorer pour les chômeurs ; **~ colder and we'd have frozen to death** si la température avait encore baissé, nous serions morts de froid

b (in interrog, cond and hypothetical constructions, gen with comps) un peu ; **are you feeling ~ better?** vous sentez-vous un peu mieux ? ; **do you want ~ more soup?** voulez-vous encore de la soupe or encore un peu de soupe ? ; **if you see ~ more beautiful flower than this** si vous voyez jamais plus belle fleur que celle-ci ; **I couldn't do that ~ more than I could fly** je ne serais pas plus capable de faire cela que de voler

c (= at all) **the rope didn't help them ~*** la corde ne leur a pas servi à grand-chose or ne leur a servi à rien du tout

anybody [ˈenɪbɒdɪ] PRON **a** (with neg and implied neg = somebody) **I can't see ~** je ne vois personne ; **there is hardly ~ there** il n'y a presque personne ; **without ~ seeing him** sans que personne (ne) le voie ; **it's impossible for ~ to see him today** personne ne peut le voir aujourd'hui

b (in interrog, cond and hypothetical constructions = somebody) quelqu'un ; **was (there) ~ there?** est-ce qu'il y avait quelqu'un (là) ? ; **did ~ see you?** est-ce que quelqu'un t'a vu ?, est-ce qu'on t'a vu ? ; **~ want my sandwich?** quelqu'un veut mon sandwich ? ; **if ~ can do it, he can** si quelqu'un peut le faire c'est bien lui

c (in affirmative sentences: = no matter who) **~ who wants to do it should say so now** si quelqu'un veut le faire qu'il le dise tout de suite ; **~ could tell you** n'importe qui pourrait vous le dire ; **~ would have thought he had lost** on aurait pu croire or on aurait cru qu'il avait perdu ; **bring ~ you like** amenez qui vous voudrez ; **~ who had heard him speak would agree** quiconque l'a entendu parler serait d'accord ; **~ with any sense would know that!** le premier venu saurait cela pourvu qu'il ait un minimum de bon sens ! ; **~ but Robert** n'importe qui d'autre que or tout autre que Robert ; **~ else** n'importe qui d'autre, toute autre personne ; **~ else would have cried, but not him** un autre aurait pleuré, lui non ; **bring ~ else you like** amenez n'importe qui d'autre ; **is there ~ else I can talk to?** est-ce qu'il y a quelqu'un d'autre à qui je puisse parler ? ; **bring somebody to help us, ~ will do** amenez quelqu'un pour nous aider, n'importe qui fera l'affaire ; **he's not just ~*, he's the boss** ce n'est pas le premier venu or n'importe qui, c'est le patron

anyhow [ˈenɪhaʊ] ADV **a** (= in any case, at all events) en tout cas, de toute façon ; **whatever you say, they'll do it ~** vous pouvez dire ce que vous voulez, ils le feront de toute façon or quand même ; **you can try ~** vous pouvez toujours essayer **b** (* = carelessly, haphazardly: also ~ any old how) n'importe comment ; **he just did it ~** il l'a fait n'importe comment ; **the books were all ~ on the floor** les livres étaient tous en désordre par terre **c** (= no matter how) **do it ~ you like** faites-le comme vous voulez ; **the house was locked and I couldn't get in** la maison était fermée à clé et je n'avais aucun moyen d'entrer ; **~ I do it, it always fails** de quelque façon que je m'y prenne ça ne réussit jamais **d** (*: summing up, changing subject) bon ; **~, it's time I was going** bon, il faut que j'y aille

anymore [ˈenɪmɔːr] ADV ne ... plus ; **I couldn't trust him ~** je ne pouvais plus lui faire confiance → **any 3a**

anyone [ˈenɪwʌn] PRON = anybody

anyplace* [ˈenɪpleɪs] ADV (US) = anywhere

anyroad: [ˈenɪrəʊd] ADV (Brit) = anyhow c

anything [ˈenɪθɪŋ] PRON **a** (with neg and implied neg = something) **there isn't ~ to be done** il n'y a rien à faire ; **there wasn't ~ in the box** il n'y avait rien dans la boîte ; **we haven't seen ~ nous n'avons rien vu** ; **he won't eat meat or cheese or ~*** il ne veut manger ni viande ni fromage ni rien* ; **hardly ~** presque rien ; **without ~ happening** sans qu'il se passe (subj) rien ; **this is ~ but pleasant** ceci n'a vraiment rien d'agréable ; (reply to question) **~ but!** pas du tout !, pas le moins du monde !, tout or bien au contraire !

b (in interrog, cond and hypothetical constructions = something) **was there ~ in the box?** est-ce qu'il y avait quelque chose dans la boîte ? ; **did you see ~?** avez-vous vu quelque chose ? ; **are you doing ~ tonight?** vous faites quelque chose ce soir ?, avez-vous quelque chose de prévu pour ce soir ? ; **is there ~ in this idea?** peut-on tirer quoi que ce soit de cette idée ? ; **can ~ be done?** y a-t-il quelque chose à faire ?, peut-on faire quelque chose ? ; **can't ~ be done?** n'y a-t-il rien à faire ?, ne peut-on faire quelque chose ? ; **~ else?** (in shop) et avec ça ?*, c'est tout ce qu'il vous faut ?, ce sera tout ? ; (= have you anything more to tell me, give me etc) c'est tout ?, il y a quelque chose d'autre ? ; **have you heard ~ of her?** avez-vous de ses nouvelles ? ; **if ~ should happen to me** s'il m'arrivait quelque chose or quoi que ce soit ; **if I see ~ I'll tell you** si je vois quelque chose je te le dirai ; **he must have ~ between 15 and 20 apple trees** il doit avoir quelque chose comme 15 ou 20 pommiers ; **if ~ it's an improvement** ce serait plutôt une amélioration ; **it is, if ~, even smaller** c'est peut-être encore plus petit

c (with adj) **I didn't see ~ interesting** je n'ai rien vu d'intéressant ; **did you see ~ interesting?** tu as vu quelque chose d'intéressant ? ; **is there ~ more tiring/boring than ...?** y a-t-il rien de plus fatigant/ennuyeux que ... ?

d (= no matter what) **say ~ (at all)** dites n'importe quoi ; **take ~ you like** prenez ce que vous voudrez ; **~ else would disappoint her** s'il en était autrement elle serait déçue ; **~ else is impossible** il n'y a pas d'autre possibilité ; **I'll try ~ else** j'essaierai n'importe quoi d'autre ; **I'd give ~ to know the secret** je donnerais n'importe quoi pour connaître le secret ; **this isn't just ~** ce n'est pas n'importe quoi ; **they eat ~** (= they're not fussy) ils mangent de tout

e (*: phrases with "like", "as") **he ran like ~** il s'est mis à courir comme un dératé* or un fou ; **she cried like ~** elle a pleuré comme une Madeleine* ; **we laughed like ~** on a ri comme des fous, qu'est-ce qu'on a pu rire ! ; **they worked like ~** ils ont travaillé d'arrache-pied or comme des fous* ; **it's raining like ~** il pleut or tombe des cordes* ; **it's as big as ~** c'est très très grand ; **it was as silly as ~** c'était idiot comme tout*

anytime [ˈenɪtaɪm] ADV = any time ; → any

anyway [ˈenɪweɪ], **anyways*** (US) [ˈenɪweɪz] ADV = anyhow

anywhere [ˈenɪweər] ADV **a** (in affirmative sentences = no matter where) n'importe où, partout ; **I'd live ~ in France** je vivrais n'importe où en France ; **the oldest rock paintings ~ in North America** les peintures rupestres les plus anciennes de toute l'Amérique du Nord ; **there are more of this species in these waters than ~ in the world** il y a plus de représentants de cette espèce dans ces eaux que partout ailleurs dans le monde ; **put it down ~** pose-le n'importe où ; **you can find that soap ~** ce savon se trouve partout ; **go ~ you like** va où tu veux ; **~ you go it's the same (thing)** où qu'on aille c'est la même chose ; **~ else** partout ailleurs ; **miles from ~*** loin de tout ; **there were ~ between 200 and 300 people at the meeting** le nombre de personnes présentes à la réunion pouvait aller de 200 à 300; **the time of death could have been ~ from two to five days ago** la mort aurait pu survenir entre deux et cinq jours auparavant **b** (*in neg sentences*) nulle part; **they didn't go ~** ils ne sont allés nulle part; **we haven't been ~ this summer** nous ne sommes allés nulle part cet été; **this species is not to be found ~ else** cette espèce ne se trouve nulle part ailleurs; **we're not going ~ in particular** nous n'allons nulle part en particulier; **we can't afford to eat ~ expensive** nous ne pouvons pas nous permettre d'aller dans un restaurant cher; **that had not happened ~ in human history** cela ne s'était jamais produit dans l'histoire de l'humanité; **we aren't ~ near* Paris** nous sommes loin de Paris; **the house isn't ~ near* big enough** la maison est loin d'être assez grande; (*fig*: *in guessing etc*) **you aren't ~ near it!*** tu n'y es pas du tout!; (*fig*) **it won't get you ~** cela ne vous mènera à rien; (*fig*) **we're not getting ~** cela ne nous mène à rien; (*fig*) **I'm not earning any money, so I'm not going ~** je ne gagne pas d'argent, alors je ne vais nulle part; (*Sport etc*) **he came first and the rest didn't come ~*** il est arrivé premier et les autres étaient loin derrière **c** (*in interrog sentences*) quelque part; **have you seen it ~?** l'avez-vous vu quelque part?; **~ else?** ailleurs?

Anzac ['ænzæk] N (= *soldier*) soldat australien ou néo-zélandais

AOB, a.o.b. [eɪəʊ'biː] (ABBR = **any other business**) autres sujets *mpl* à l'ordre du jour

AOCB [eɪəʊsiː'biː] N (ABBR = **any other competent business**) = **AOB**

AONB [eɪəʊen'biː] N (*Brit*) (ABBR = **Area of Outstanding Natural Beauty**) → **area**

aorist ['eərɪst] N aoriste *m*

aorta [eɪ'ɔːtə] N (*pl* **aortas** *or* **aortae** [eɪ'ɔːtiː]) aorte *f*

aortic [eɪ'ɔːtɪk] ADJ (*Anat*) aortique

Aosta [æ'ɒstə] N Aoste

AP [eɪ'piː] (ABBR = **Associated Press**) agence de presse

apace [ə'peɪs] ADV (*frm*) rapidement, vite

Apache [ə'pætʃɪ] N (= *person*) Apache *mf*

apart [ə'pɑːt]

When **apart** *is an element in a phrasal verb, eg* **fall apart, keep apart, tear apart, tell apart, look up the verb.**

ADV **a** (= *separated*) **houses a long way ~** maisons (fort) éloignées l'une de l'autre or à une grande distance l'une de l'autre; **set equally ~** espacés à intervalles réguliers; **their birthdays were two days ~** leurs anniversaires étaient à deux jours d'intervalle; **to stand with one's feet ~** se tenir les jambes écartées → **class, world**
b (= *on one side*) à part, à l'écart; **to hold o.s. ~** se tenir à l'écart (**from** de); **joking ~** plaisanterie mise à part, blague à part*; **that ~** à part cela, cela mis à part; **~ from these difficulties** en dehors de or à part ces difficultés, ces difficultés mises à part; **~ from the fact that ...** en dehors du fait que ...
c (= *separately, distinctly*) séparément; **they are living ~ now** ils sont séparés maintenant; **he lives ~ from his wife** il est séparé de sa femme, il n'habite plus avec sa femme; **you can't tell the twins ~** on ne peut distinguer les jumeaux l'un de l'autre; **we'll have to keep those boys ~** il va falloir séparer ces garçons
d (= *into pieces*) en pièces, en morceaux; **to take ~** démonter, désassembler → **come, fall, tear**

apartheid [ə'pɑːteɪt, ə'pɑːtaɪd] N apartheid *m*; **the ~ laws** la législation permettant l'apartheid

apartment [ə'pɑːtmənt] N **a** (*esp US* = *flat*) appartement *m*; **~ building** *or* **house** (= *block*) immeuble *m* (*de résidence*); (= *divided house*)

maison *f* (divisée en appartements) **b** (*Brit*) (= *room*) pièce *f*; (= *bedroom*) chambre *f*; **a five-~ house** une maison de cinq pièces; **furnished ~s** meublé *m*

apathetic [æpə'θetɪk] ADJ apathique, indifférent

apathetically [æpə'θetɪklɪ] ADV avec apathie

apathy ['æpəθɪ] N apathie *f*, indifférence *f*

APB [eɪpiː'biː] N (*US*) (ABBR = **all-points bulletin**) message *m* à toutes les patrouilles; **to put out an ~** envoyer un message à toutes les patrouilles

ape [eɪp] **1** N (*Zool*) (grand) singe *m*; (*pej* = *person*) **big ~*** grande brute *f*; (*esp US*) **to go ~*** (= *angry*) se mettre en rogne*; (= *excited*) s'emballer* (**over** pour) → **apeshit 2** VT (*pej* = *imitate*) singer (*pej*)

APEC ['eɪpek] N (ABBR = **Asia Pacific Economic Cooperation**) APEC *f*, Coopération *f* économique Asie-Pacifique

Apennines ['æpənaɪnz] NPL Apennin *m*

aperient [ə'pɪərɪənt] ADJ, N laxatif *m*

aperitif [ə,perɪ'tiːf] N apéritif *m*

aperture ['æpətʃʊə] N (= *hole*) trou *m*, ouverture *f*; (= *gap*) brèche *f*, trouée *f*; (*Phot*) ouverture *f* (du diaphragme)

apeshit ['eɪpʃɪt] ADJ (*esp US*) **to go ~** (= *angry*) piquer une crise*; (= *excited*) devenir hystérique → **ape**

APEX ['eɪpeks] N **a** (ABBR = **Association of Professional, Executive, Clerical and Computer Staff**) *syndicat* **b** (*also* **apex**) (ABBR = **advance purchase excursion**) **~ fare/ticket** prix *m*/billet *m* APEX

apex ['eɪpeks] N (*pl* **apexes** *or* **apices**) (*Geom, Med*) sommet *m*; (*of tongue*) apex *m*, pointe *f*; (*fig*) sommet *m*, point *m* culminant

aphasia [æ'feɪzɪə] N aphasie *f*

aphasic [æ'feɪzɪk] ADJ aphasique

aphid ['eɪfɪd] N puceron *m*

aphis ['eɪfɪs] N (*pl* **aphides** ['eɪfɪdiːz]) aphidé *m*

aphonic [eɪ'fɒnɪk] ADJ **a** [*person*] aphone **b** (= *silent*) [*consonant etc*] muet

aphorism ['æfərɪzəm] N aphorisme *m*

aphoristic [æfə'rɪstɪk] ADJ aphoristique

aphrodisiac [æfrəʊ'dɪzɪæk] ADJ, N aphrodisiaque *m*

Aphrodite [æfrə'daɪtɪ] N Aphrodite *f*

apiarist ['eɪpɪərɪst] N apiculteur *m*, -trice *f*

apiary ['eɪpɪərɪ] N rucher *m*

apices ['eɪpɪsiːz] NPL of **apex**

apiece [ə'piːs] ADV (= *for each person*) chacun(e), par personne; (= *for each thing*) chacun(e), pièce *inv*

aplastic anaemia, aplastic anemia (*US*) [eɪ'plæstɪkə'niːmɪə] N (*Med*) anémie *f* aplastique

aplenty [ə'plentɪ] ADV (*liter*) en abondance

aplomb [ə'plɒm] N (*liter*) sang-froid *m*, assurance *f*

Apocalypse [ə'pɒkəlɪps] N Apocalypse *f* (*also fig*)

apocalyptic [ə,pɒkə'lɪptɪk] ADJ apocalyptique

apocopate [ə'pɒkəpeɪt] VT raccourcir par apocope

apocope [ə'pɒkəpɪ] N apocope *f*

Apocrypha [ə'pɒkrɪfə] NPL apocryphes *mpl*

apocryphal [ə'pɒkrɪfəl] ADJ apocryphe

apogee ['æpəʊdʒiː] N apogée *m*

apolitical [eɪpə'lɪtɪkəl] ADJ apolitique

Apollo [ə'pɒləʊ] N (*Myth*) Apollon *m*; (*Space*) Apollo *m*

apologetic [ə,pɒlə'dʒetɪk] ADJ [*smile, letter*] d'excuse; [*manner, tone*] contrit; **with an ~ air** d'un air contrit; **to be ~ (about sth)** se montrer très contrit (au sujet de qch); **to be profusely ~** [*person*] se confondre or se répandre

en excuses; **he didn't look in the least ~** il n'avait du tout l'air désolé

apologetically [ə,pɒlə'dʒetɪkəlɪ] ADV [*say, smile*] d'un air contrit, pour s'excuser

apologetics [ə,pɒlə'dʒetɪks] N (*NonC*) apologétique *f*

apologia [æpə'ləʊdʒɪə] N apologie *f*

apologist [ə'pɒlədʒɪst] N apologiste *mf* (**for** de)

▼ **apologize** [ə'pɒlədʒaɪz] VI s'excuser; **to ~ to sb (for sth)** s'excuser (de qch) auprès de qn, faire or présenter des excuses à qn (pour qch); **she ~d to them for her son** elle leur a demandé d'excuser la conduite de son fils; **to ~ profusely** se confondre or se répandre en excuses

apologue ['æpəlɒg] N apologue *m*

apology [ə'pɒlədʒɪ] N **a** (= *expression of regret*) excuses *fpl*; **a letter of ~** une lettre d'excuses; **to make an ~ for sth/for having done** s'excuser de qch/d'avoir fait, faire or présenter ses excuses pour qch/pour avoir fait; (*for absence at meeting*) **there are apologies from Mr Watt** M. Watt vous prie d'excuser son absence; **to send one's apologies** envoyer une lettre d'excuse, envoyer un mot d'excuse; **to offer** or **make one's apologies** présenter ses excuses; **to make no ~ or apologies for sth** assumer pleinement qch **b** (= *defence: for beliefs etc*) apologie *f* **c** (*pej*) **it was an ~ for** or **a feeble ~ for a speech/bed** en fait de or comme discours/lit c'était plutôt minable*; **he gave me an ~ for a smile** il m'a gratifié d'une sorte de grimace qui se voulait être un sourire; **we were given an ~ for a lunch** on nous a servi un soi-disant déjeuner

apoplectic [æpə'plektɪk] **1** ADJ apoplectique; (*Med, fig*) **~ fit** attaque *f* d'apoplexie **2** N apoplectique *mf*

apoplexy ['æpəpleksɪ] N **a** († = *heart attack*) apoplexie *f* **b** (*fig* = *rage*) fureur *f*

apostasy [ə'pɒstəsɪ] N apostasie *f*

apostate [ə'pɒstɪt] ADJ, N apostat(e) *m(f)*

apostatize [ə'pɒstətaɪz] VI apostasier

a posteriori ['eɪpɒs,terɪ'ɔːraɪ, 'eɪpɒs,terɪ'ɔːrɪ] ADJ, ADV a posteriori

apostle [ə'pɒsl] **1** N (*Hist, Rel, fig*) apôtre *m*; **Apostles' Creed** symbole *m* des apôtres, Credo *m*; **to say the Apostles' Creed** dire le Credo **2** COMP ► **apostle spoon** N *petite cuiller décorée d'une figure d'apôtre*

apostolate [æ'pɒstəleɪt] N apostolat *m*

apostolic [æpəs'tɒlɪk] ADJ apostolique

apostrophe [ə'pɒstrəfɪ] N (*Gram, Literat*) apostrophe *f*

apostrophize [ə'pɒstrəfaɪz] VT apostropher

apothecary [ə'pɒθɪkərɪ] N apothicaire *m*

apotheosis [ə,pɒθɪ'əʊsɪs] N (*pl* **apotheoses** [ə,pɒθɪ'əʊsiːz]) **a** (= *epitome*) archétype *m* **b** (= *high point*) apothéose *f*

appal, appall (*US*) [ə'pɔːl] VT consterner; (= *frighten*) épouvanter; **I am ~led at your behaviour** votre conduite me consterne

Appalachian [æpə'leɪʃən] ADJ, N **the ~ Mountains** ◊ **the ~s** les (monts *mpl*) Appalaches *mpl*

appall [ə'pɔːl] VT (*US*) = **appal**

appalling [ə'pɔːlɪŋ] ADJ [*sight, behaviour, weather*] épouvantable; [*suffering, crime, ignorance, poverty*] effroyable, épouvantable

appallingly [ə'pɔːlɪŋlɪ] ADV **a** (= *badly*) [*behave*] de manière épouvantable **b** (= *extremely*) [*difficult, busy*] terriblement

apparatchik [æpə'rættʃiːk] N apparatchik *m*

apparatus [æpə'reɪtəs] N (*pl* **apparatus** *or* **apparatuses**) (*also Anat*) appareil *m*; (*for filming, camping etc*) équipement *m*; (*in laboratory etc*) instruments *mpl*; (*in gym*) agrès *mpl*; **camping ~** équipement *m* de camping; **heating ~** appareil *m* de chauffage; (*in gym*) **~ work**

apparel exercices *mpl* aux agrès ; *(fig)* **the ~ of government** l'appareil *m* d'État ; *(Literat)* **critical ~** appareil *m* or apparat *m* critique

apparel (*Brit*† *or US*) [ə'pærəl] (*liter*) [1] N (*NonC*) habillement *m* [2] VT vêtir

apparent [ə'pærənt] ADJ [a] (= *seeming*) [*success, contradiction, interest*] apparent ; **the ~ coup attempt** l'apparente tentative de coup d'état [b] (= *obvious*) évident (**to sb** pour qn) ; **it is ~ that ...** il est évident que ... ; **it is ~ to me that ...** il me semble évident que ... ; **for no ~ reason** sans raison apparente → **heir**

apparently [ə'pærəntlɪ] ADV apparemment ; (= *according to rumour*) à ce qu'il paraît ; **this is ~ the case** il semble que ce soit le cas, c'est le cas apparemment ; **~, they're getting a divorce** ils sont en instance de divorce, à ce qu'il paraît ; **I thought he was coming — ~ not** je pensais qu'il venait — apparemment non *or* il semble que non ; **to be ~ calm** paraître calme ; **an ~ harmless question** une question apparemment *or* en apparence anodine ; **the murders follow an ~ random pattern** ces meurtres ont apparemment été commis au hasard

apparition [ˌæpə'rɪʃən] N (= *spirit, appearance*) apparition *f*

appeal [ə'piːl] [1] VI [a] (= *request publicly*) lancer un appel (**for sth** pour qch) ; **to ~ for the blind** lancer un appel au profit des *or* pour les aveugles ; **to ~ for calm** lancer un appel au calme ; *(Fin)* **to ~ for funds** faire un appel de fonds ; **he ~ed for silence** il a demandé le silence ; **he ~ed for tolerance** il a appelé à la tolérance ; *(Pol)* **to ~ to the country** en appeler au pays
[b] (= *beg*) faire appel (**to** à) ; **she ~ed to his generosity** elle a fait appel à sa générosité, elle en a appelé à sa générosité ; **to ~ to sb for money/help** demander de l'argent/des secours à qn ; **I ~ to you!** je vous le demande instamment !, je vous en supplie ! → **better**
[c] *(Jur)* interjeter appel, se pourvoir en appel ; **to ~ to the supreme court** se pourvoir en cassation ; *(Brit)* **to ~ against a judgement** appeler d'un jugement ; *(Brit)* **to ~ against a decision** faire appel d'une décision
[d] (= *attract*) **to ~ to sb** [*object, idea*] plaire à qn ; [*person*] plaire à qn ; **it doesn't ~ to me** cela ne m'intéresse pas, cela ne me dit rien* ; **the idea ~ed to him** cette idée l'a séduit ; **it ~s to the imagination** cela parle à l'imagination ; **does that ~?*** ça te dit ?*
[2] VT *(Jur* = *appeal against*) faire appel de
[3] N [a] (= *public call*) appel *m* ; **~ to arms** appel *m* aux armes ; *(Comm, Fin)* **~ for funds** appel *m* de fonds ; **he made a public ~ for the blind** il a lancé un appel au profit des aveugles
[b] (*by individual: for help etc*) appel *m* (**for** à) ; (*for money*) demande *f* (**for** de) ; (= *supplication*) prière *f*, supplication *f* ; **with a look of ~** d'un air suppliant *or* implorant ; **~ for help** appel *m* au secours
[c] *(Jur)* appel *m*, pourvoi *m* ; **notice of ~** infirmation *f* ; **act of ~** acte *m* d'appel ; **with no right of ~** sans appel ; **acquitted on ~** acquitté en seconde instance → **enter, lodge, lord**
[d] (= *attraction*) [*of person, object*] attrait *m*, charme *m* ; [*of plan, idea*] intérêt *m*
[4] COMP ► **Appeal Court** N *(Jur)* cour *f* d'appel ► **appeal fund** N fonds *m* d'aide (*constitué à partir de dons publics*)

appealing [ə'piːlɪŋ] ADJ (= *moving*) émouvant, attendrissant, [*look*] pathétique ; (= *begging*) suppliant, implorant ; (= *attractive*) attirant, attachant

appealingly [ə'piːlɪŋlɪ] ADV [a] (= *charmingly*) **~ naïve/modest** d'une charmante naïveté/modestie [b] (= *beseechingly*) [*look at*] d'un air implorant ; [*say*] d'un ton implorant

appear [ə'pɪəʳ] VI [a] (= *become visible*) [*person, sun etc*] apparaître, se montrer ; [*ghost, vision*] apparaître, se manifester (**to sb** à qn)

[b] (= *arrive*) arriver, se présenter ; **he ~ed from nowhere** il est apparu comme par miracle *or* comme par un coup de baguette magique ; **where did you ~ from?** d'où est-ce que tu sors ?
[c] *(Jur etc)* comparaître ; **to ~ before a court** comparaître devant un tribunal ; **to ~ on a charge of ...** être jugé pour ... ; **to ~ for sb** plaider pour qn, représenter qn ; **to ~ for the defence/for the accused** plaider pour la défense/pour l'accusé → **fail, failure**
[d] *(Theat)* **to ~ in "Hamlet"** jouer dans « Hamlet » ; **to ~ as Hamlet** jouer Hamlet ; **to ~ on TV** passer à la télévision
[e] (= *be published*) [*magazine etc*] paraître, sortir, être publié
[f] (= *seem: physical aspect*) paraître, avoir l'air ; **they ~ (to be) ill** ils ont l'air malades
[g] (= *seem: on evidence*) paraître (**that** que + *indic*) ; **he came then?** — **so it ~s** *or* **so it would ~** il est donc venu ? — il paraît que oui ; **it ~s that he did say that** il paraît qu'il a bien dit cela → **h** ; **he got the job** *or* **so it ~s** *or* **so it would ~** il a eu le poste à ce qu'il paraît, il paraît qu'il a eu le poste ; **as will presently ~** comme il paraîtra par la suite, comme on le verra bientôt ; **it's raining! — (*iro*) so it ~s!** il pleut ! — on dirait ! (*iro*)
[h] (= *seem: by surmise*) sembler (**that** que *gen* + *subj*), sembler bien (**that** que + *indic*), sembler à qn (**that** que + *indic*) ; **there ~s to be a mistake** il semble qu'il y ait une erreur ; **it ~s he did say that** il semble avoir bien dit cela, il semble bien qu'il a dit cela ; **it ~s to me they are mistaken** il me semble qu'ils ont tort ; **how does it ~ to you?** qu'en pensez-vous ?

appearance [ə'pɪərəns] N [a] (= *act*) apparition *f*, arrivée *f* ; **to make an ~** faire son apparition, se montrer, se présenter ; **to make a personal ~** apparaître en personne ; **to put in an ~** faire acte de présence ; **~ money** cachet *m*
[b] *(Jur)* **~ before a court** comparution *f* devant un tribunal
[c] *(Theat)* **since his ~ in "Hamlet"** depuis qu'il a joué dans « Hamlet » ; **in order of ~** par ordre d'entrée en scène ; **his ~ on TV** son passage à la télévision
[d] (= *publication*) parution *f*
[e] (= *look, aspect*) apparence *f*, aspect *m* ; **to have a good ~** [*person*] faire bonne figure ; **at first ~** au premier abord, à première vue ; **the ~ of the house** l'aspect *m* de la maison ; **it had all the ~s of a murder** cela avait tout l'air d'un meurtre, cela ressemblait fort à un meurtre ; **his ~ worried us** la mine qu'il avait *or* son apparence nous a inquiétés ; **~s are deceptive** il ne faut pas se fier aux apparences, les apparences peuvent être trompeuses ; **to judge by ~s** juger sur les *or* d'après les apparences ; **you shouldn't judge** *or* **go by ~s** il ne faut pas se fier aux apparences ; **for ~' sake** ◊ (**in order**) **to keep up ~s** pour sauver les apparences, pour la forme ; **to** *or* **by all ~s** selon toute apparence ; **contrary to** *or* **against all ~s** contrairement aux apparences, contre toute apparence

appease [ə'piːz] VT apaiser, calmer

appeasement [ə'piːzmənt] N apaisement *m* ; *(Pol)* apaisement, conciliation *f*

appellant [ə'pelənt] [1] N partie *f* appelante, appelant(e) *m(f)* [2] ADJ appelant

appellate [ə'pelɪt] ADJ *(US Jur)* **~ court** cour *f* d'appel ; **~ jurisdiction** juridiction *f* d'appel

appellation [ˌæpe'leɪʃən] N appellation *f*, désignation *f*

append [ə'pend] VT [+ *notes*] joindre, ajouter ; [+ *document*] joindre, annexer ; [+ *signature*] apposer ; *(Comput)* ajouter (*à la fin d'un fichier*)

appendage [ə'pendɪdʒ] N *(frm)* appendice *m*

appendectomy [ˌæpen'dektəmɪ], **appendicectomy** [ˌæpendɪ'sektəmɪ] N appendicectomie *f*

appendices [ə'pendɪsiːz] NPL *of* **appendix**

appendicitis [əˌpendɪ'saɪtɪs] N appendicite *f* ; **to have ~** avoir une (crise d')appendicite ; **was it ~?** c'était une appendicite ?

appendix [ə'pendɪks] N (*pl* **appendixes** *or* **appendices**) [a] *(Anat)* appendice *m* ; **to have one's ~ out** se faire opérer de l'appendicite [b] [*of book*] appendice *m* ; [*of document*] annexe *f*

apperception [ˌæpə'sepʃən] N aperception *f*

appertain [ˌæpə'teɪn] VI (= *belong*) appartenir (**to** à) ; (= *form part*) faire partie (**to** de) ; (= *relate*) se rapporter (**to** à), relever (**to** de)

appetite [ˈæpɪtaɪt] [1] N appétit *m* ; **he has no ~** il n'a pas d'appétit ; **to have a good ~** avoir bon appétit ; **to eat with (an) ~** manger de bon appétit ; **skiing gives one an ~** le ski ouvre l'appétit ; *(fig)* **I have no ~ for this sort of book** je n'ai pas de goût pour ce genre de livre → **spoil** [2] COMP ► **appetite depressant** N coupe-faim *m inv*

appetizer [ˈæpɪtaɪzəʳ] N (= *drink*) apéritif *m* ; (= *food*) amuse-gueule *m inv*

appetizing [ˈæpɪtaɪzɪŋ] ADJ *(lit, fig)* appétissant

appetizingly [ˈæpɪtaɪzɪŋlɪ] ADV de manière appétissante

Appian [ˈæpɪən] ADJ **the ~ Way** la voie Appienne

applaud [ə'plɔːd] VT applaudir ; *(fig)* [+ *decision, efforts*] applaudir à, approuver

applause [ə'plɔːz] N *(NonC)* applaudissements *mpl*, acclamation *f* ; **to win the ~ of ...** être applaudi *or* acclamé par ... ; **there was loud ~s** les applaudissements ont crépité ; **a round of ~** une salve d'applaudissements ; *(Theat)* **let's have a round of ~ for Lucy!** applaudissons Lucy !, un ban* pour Lucy !

apple [ˈæpl] [1] N pomme *f* ; (*also* **~ tree**) pommier *m* ; **he's/it's the ~ of my eye** je tiens à lui/j'y tiens comme à la prunelle de mes yeux ; **~ of discord** pomme *f* de discorde ; *(US)* **the (Big) Apple*** New York ■ *(PROV)* **one bad** *or* **rotten ~ can spoil the whole barrel** il suffit d'une brebis galeuse pour contaminer tout le troupeau ; *(esp US fig)* **the two things are ~s and oranges** on ne peut pas comparer deux choses si différentes → **Adam, cooking, eating**
[2] COMP ► **apple blossom** N fleur *f* de pommier ► **apple brandy** N eau-de-vie *f* de pommes ► **apple core** N trognon *m* de pomme ► **apple fritter** N beignet *m* aux pommes ► **apple-green** ADJ vert pomme *inv* ► **apple orchard** N champ *m* de pommiers, pommeraie *f* ► **apple pie** N tarte *f* aux pommes ► **apple-pie bed** N *(Brit)* lit *m* en portefeuille ► **apple-pie order** N **in ~-pie order** parfaitement en ordre ► **apple sauce** N *(Culin)* compote *f* de pommes ; *(US* fig) bobards* *mpl* ► **apple tart** N tarte *f* aux pommes ; (*individual*) tartelette *f* aux pommes ► **apple turnover** N chausson *m* aux pommes

applecart [ˈæplkɑːt] N → **upset**

applejack [ˈæpldʒæk] N *(US)* = **apple brandy**

appliance [ə'plaɪəns] N [a] (= *device*) appareil *m* ; **electrical/domestic ~s** appareils *mpl* électriques/ménagers ; **household ~** appareil *m* électroménager [b] *(Brit: also* **fire ~**) voiture *f* de pompiers [c] [*of skill, knowledge*] application *f*

applicability [ˌæplɪkə'bɪlɪtɪ] N applicabilité *f*

applicable [ə'plɪkəbl] ADJ applicable (**to** à)

applicant [ˈæplɪkənt] N (*for job*) candidat(e) *m(f)*, postulant(e) *m(f)* ; *(Jur)* requérant(e) *m(f)* ; *(Admin: for money, assistance etc)* demandeur *m*, -euse *f*

application [ˌæplɪ'keɪʃən] [1] N [a] (= *request*) demande *f* (**for** de) ; **~ for a job** candidature *f* à un poste ; **~ for membership** demande *f* d'adhésion ; **on ~** sur demande ; **to make ~ to sb for sth** s'adresser à qn pour obtenir qch ;

to submit an ~ faire une demande; **details may be had on ~ to ...** s'adresser à ... pour tous renseignements [b] (= *act of applying*) application *f* (**of sth to sth** de qch à qch); (*Pharm*) **for external ~ only** réservé à l'usage externe [c] (= *diligence*) application *f*, attention *f* [d] (= *relevancy*) portée *f*, pertinence *f*; **his arguments have no ~ to the present case** ses arguments ne s'appliquent pas au cas présent [e] (*Comput*) application *f* → **2** [2] COMP ► **application form** N (*gen: for benefits etc*) formulaire *m* de demande; (*for job*) formulaire *m* de demande d'emploi; (*for important post*) dossier *m* de candidature; (*Univ*) dossier *m* d'inscription ► **application program** N = **applications program** ► **application software** N logiciel *m* d'application ► **applications package** N (*Comput*) progiciel *m* d'application ► **applications program** N (*Comput*) (programme *m* d')application *f*

applicator ['æplɪkeɪtə'] N applicateur *m*

applied [ə'plaɪd] [1] ADJ (*gen, Ling, Math, Sci etc*) appliqué; **~ arts** arts *mpl* appliqués; **~ sciences** sciences *fpl* appliquées [2] COMP ► **applied psychology** N psychologie *f* appliquée

appliqué [æ'pliː:keɪ] [1] VT coudre (en application) [2] N (= *ornament*) application *f*; (= *end product: also* **~ work**) travail *m* d'application

▼**apply** [ə'plaɪ] [1] VT [a] [+ *paint, ointment, dressing*] appliquer, mettre (**to** sur); **to ~ heat to sth** (*Tech*) exposer qch à la chaleur; (*Med*) traiter qch par la thermothérapie; **to ~ a match to sth** mettre le feu à qch avec une allumette, allumer qch avec une allumette [b] [+ *theory*] appliquer (**to** à), mettre en pratique *or* en application; [+ *rule, law*] appliquer (**to** à); **we can't ~ this rule to you** nous ne pouvons pas appliquer cette règle à votre cas [c] **to ~ pressure on sth** exercer une pression sur qch; **to ~ pressure on sb** faire pression sur qn; (*Aut, Tech*) **to ~ the brakes** actionner les freins, freiner [d] **to ~ one's mind** *or* **o.s. to (doing) sth** s'appliquer à (faire) qch; **to ~ one's attention to ...** porter *or* fixer son attention sur ... [2] VI s'adresser, avoir recours (**to sb for sth** à qn pour obtenir qch); **~ at the office/to the manager** adressez-vous au bureau/au directeur; (*on notice*) s'adresser au bureau/au directeur; **to ~ to university** faire une demande d'inscription à l'université; (*Jur*) **right to ~ to the courts against decisions by ...** droit *m* de recours contre des décisions de ...
► **apply for** VT FUS [+ *scholarship, grant*] faire une demande de; [+ *money, assistance*] demander; **to ~ for a job** faire une demande d'emploi (**to sb** auprès de qn), poser sa candidature pour un poste; (*Jur*) **to ~ for a divorce** formuler une demande en divorce → **apply 2**, **patent**
► **apply to** VT FUS (*gen*) s'appliquer à; [*remarks*] s'appliquer à, se rapporter à; **this does not ~ to you** ceci ne s'applique pas à vous, ceci ne vous concerne pas → **apply 2**

appoggiatura [ə,pɒdʒə'tʊərə] N (*pl* **appoggiaturas** *or* **appoggiature** [ə,pɒdʒə'tʊəreɪ]) appoggiature *f*

appoint [ə'pɔɪnt] VT [a] (= *fix, decide*) [+ *date, place*] fixer [b] (= *nominate*) **to ~ sb (to a post)** nommer qn (à un poste); **to ~ sb manager** nommer qn directeur; **to ~ a new secretary** engager une nouvelle secrétaire [c] (= *ordain*) prescrire, ordonner (**that** que + *subj*), décider (**that** que + *indic*) [d] → **well**

appointed [ə'pɔɪntɪd] ADJ [*time, hour, place*] convenu; [*task*] fixé; [*representative, agent*] attitré; **at the ~ time** à l'heure convenue → **well**

appointee [əpɔɪn'tiː] N candidat(e) *m(f)* retenu(e), titulaire *mf* du poste; (*esp US*) délégué

m (*or* ambassadeur *m etc*) nommé pour des raisons politiques

appointive [ə'pɔɪntɪv] ADJ (*US*) [*position*] pourvu par nomination

appointment [ə'pɔɪntmənt] [1] N [a] (= *arrangement to meet*) rendez-vous *m*; (= *meeting*) entrevue *f*; **to make an ~ with sb** donner rendez-vous à qn, prendre rendez-vous avec qn; **to make an ~** [*two people*] se donner rendez-vous; **to keep an ~** aller *or* se rendre à un rendez-vous; **I have an ~ at 10 o'clock** j'ai (un) rendez-vous à 10 heures; (*to caller*) **do you have an ~?** vous avez (pris) rendez-vous?; **I have an ~ to see Mr Martin** j'ai rendez-vous avec M. Martin; **to meet sb by ~** rencontrer qn sur rendez-vous → **break** [b] (= *selection, nomination*) nomination *f*, désignation *f* (**to a post** à un poste); (= *office assigned*) poste *m*; (= *posting*) affectation *f*; **there are still several ~s to be made** il y a encore plusieurs postes à pourvoir; (*Comm*) **"by ~ to Her Majesty the Queen"** « fournisseur *m* de S.M. la Reine »; (*Press*) **"~s (vacant)"** « offres d'emploi » [2] COMP ► **appointments bureau**, **appointments office** N agence *f* or bureau *m* de placement

apportion [ə'pɔːʃən] VT [+ *money*] répartir, partager; [+ *land, property*] lotir; [+ *blame*] répartir; **to ~ sth to sb** assigner qch à qn

apportionment [ə'pɔːʃənmənt] N (*US Pol*) répartition *f* des sièges (par districts)

apposite ['æpəzɪt] ADJ (*frm*) pertinent, juste

apposition [,æpə'zɪʃən] N apposition *f*; **in ~** en apposition

appositional [,æpə'zɪʃənl] ADJ en apposition

appraisal [ə'preɪzəl] N évaluation *f*

appraise [ə'preɪz] VT [+ *property, jewellery*] évaluer, estimer (la valeur *or* le coût de); [+ *importance*] évaluer, apprécier; [+ *worth*] estimer, apprécier

appraiser [ə'preɪzə'] N (*US*) [*of property, value, asset*] expert *m*

appreciable [ə'priːʃəbl] ADJ appréciable, sensible

appreciably [ə'priːʃəbli] ADV sensiblement

▼**appreciate** [ə'priːʃɪeɪt] [1] VT [a] (= *assess, be aware of*) [+ *fact, difficulty, sb's attitude*] se rendre compte de, être conscient de; **to ~ sth at its true value** apprécier qch à sa juste valeur; **yes, I ~ that** oui, je comprends bien *or* je m'en rends bien compte; **I fully ~ the fact that ...** je me rends parfaitement compte du fait que ...; **they did not ~ the danger** ils ne se sont pas rendu compte du danger [b] (= *value, esteem, like*) [+ *help*] apprécier; [+ *music, painting, books*] apprécier, goûter; [+ *person*] apprécier (à sa juste valeur), faire (grand) cas de [c] (= *be grateful for*) être sensible à, être reconnaissant de; **we do ~ your kindness/your work/what you have done** nous vous sommes très reconnaissants de votre gentillesse/du travail que vous avez fait/de ce que vous avez fait; (*Comm: in letter*) **we should ~ an early reply** ◊ **an early reply would be ~d** nous vous serions obligés de bien vouloir nous répondre dans les plus brefs délais; **we deeply ~ this honour** nous sommes profondément reconnaissants de l'honneur qui nous est fait; **he felt that nobody ~d him** il avait le sentiment que personne ne l'appréciait [d] (= *raise in value*) hausser la valeur de [2] VI (*Fin etc*) [*currency*] s'apprécier; [*object, property*] prendre de la valeur

appreciation [ə,priːʃɪ'eɪʃən] N [a] (= *judgement, estimation*) appréciation *f*, évaluation *f*; (*Art, Literat, Mus*) critique *f* [b] (= *gratitude*) reconnaissance *f*; **she smiled her ~** elle a remercié d'un sourire; **in ~ of ...** en remerciement de ... [c] (*Fin*) appréciation *f*

appreciative [ə'priːʃɪətɪv] ADJ [a] (= *grateful*) [*person*] reconnaissant (**of sth** de qch) [b] (= *admiring*) [*person, murmur, laughter, whistle*] approbateur (-trice *f*); **to be ~ of sb's cooking** apprécier la cuisine de qn [c] (*frm = aware*) **to be ~ of sth** se rendre compte de qch

appreciatively [ə'priːʃɪətɪvlɪ] ADV (= *with pleasure*) avec plaisir; (= *gratefully*) avec reconnaissance

apprehend [,æprɪ'hend] VT [a] (= *arrest*) appréhender, arrêter [b] (= *fear*) redouter, appréhender

apprehension [,æprɪ'henʃən] N [a] (= *fear*) appréhension *f*, inquiétude *f* [b] (*frm = arrest*) arrestation *f*

apprehensive [,æprɪ'hensɪv] ADJ inquiet (-ète *f*), plein d'appréhension; **to be ~ for sb's safety** craindre pour la sécurité de qn; **to be ~ of danger** appréhender *or* redouter le danger

apprehensively [,æprɪ'hensɪvlɪ] ADV avec appréhension

apprentice [ə'prentɪs] [1] N apprenti·e *m(f)*; (*Archit, Mus etc*) élève *mf*; **to place sb as an ~ to ...** mettre qn en apprentissage chez ...; **plumber's/joiner's ~** apprenti *m* plombier/menuisier [2] VT mettre *or* placer en apprentissage (**to** chez), placer comme élève (**to** chez); **he is ~d to a joiner/plumber** *etc* il est en apprentissage chez un menuisier/plombier *etc*; **he is ~d to an architect** c'est l'élève d'un architecte [3] COMP ► **apprentice electrician** N apprenti *m* électricien ► **apprentice plumber** N apprenti *m* plombier

apprenticeship [ə'prentɪsʃɪp] N apprentissage *m*

apprise [ə'praɪz] VT informer (**sb of sth** qn de qch); **to be ~d of sth** être informé de *or* sur qch

appro* ['æprəʊ] N (*Brit Comm*) (ABBR = **approval**) **on ~** à *or* sous condition, à l'essai

approach [ə'prəʊtʃ] [1] VI [*person, vehicle*] (s')approcher; [*date, season, death, war*] approcher, être proche [2] VT [a] [+ *place, person*] s'approcher de; **I saw him ~ing me** je l'ai vu qui s'approchait de moi [b] (= *tackle*) [+ *problem, subject, task*] aborder; **it all depends on how one ~es it** tout dépend de la façon dont on s'y prend [c] (= *speak to*) **to ~ sb about sth** s'adresser à qn à propos de qch, aller voir qn pour qch; **a man ~ed me in the street** un homme m'a abordé dans la rue; (*fig*) **he is easy/difficult to ~** il est d'un abord facile/difficile [d] (= *get near to*) approcher de; **we are ~ing the time when ...** le jour approche où ...; **she is ~ing 30** elle approche de la trentaine, elle va sur ses 30 ans; **it was ~ing midnight** il était près de *or* presque minuit; **a colour ~ing red** une couleur voisine du rouge [3] N [a] [*of person, vehicle*] approche *f*, arrivée *f*; **the cat fled at his ~** le chat s'est enfui à son approche; **we watched his ~** nous l'avons regardé arriver [b] [*of date, season, death etc*] approche *f*; **at the ~ of Easter** à l'approche de Pâques [c] (*fig*) approche *f*, démarche *f*; **his ~ to the problem** son approche du problème, sa façon d'aborder le problème; **I like his ~ (to it)** j'aime sa façon de s'y prendre; **a new ~ to teaching French** une nouvelle approche de l'enseignement du français; **to make ~es to sb** (*gen*) faire des ouvertures *fpl* à qn, faire des démarches *fpl* auprès de qn; (*amorous*) faire des avances *fpl* à qn; (*Comm, gen*) **to make an ~ to sb** faire une proposition à qn; (*frm*) **he is easy/not easy of ~** il est d'un abord facile/difficile → **3d** [d] (= *access route: to town*) voie *f* d'accès; (*Climbing*) marche *f* d'approche; **a town easy/not easy of ~** une ville d'accès facile/difficile; **the ~ to the top of the hill** le chemin qui mè-

ne au sommet de la colline; **the station ~** les abords *mpl* de la gare
[e] (= *approximation*) ressemblance *f* (**to** à), apparence *f* (**to** de); **some ~ to gaiety** une certaine apparence de gaieté
[4] COMP ► **approach light** N (*Aviat*) balise *f* ► **approach lights** NPL (*Aviat*) balisage *m*, balises *fpl* ► **approach march** N (*Climbing*) marche *f* d'approche ► **approach road** N (*gen*) route *f* d'accès; (*to motorway*) voie *f* de raccordement, bretelle *f* ► **approach shot** N (*Golf*) approche *f* ► **approach stage** N (*Aviat*) phase *f* d'approche

approachable [ə'prəʊtʃəbl] ADJ [*place, idea, text*] accessible; [*person*] approchable, accessible

approaching [ə'prəʊtʃɪŋ] ADJ [*crisis, death, retirement, election*] prochain; [*storm, winter, date*] qui approche; **the ~ vehicle** le véhicule venant en sens inverse

approbation [ˌæprə'beɪʃən] N approbation *f*; **a nod of ~** un signe de tête approbateur

appropriate [ə'prəʊprɪt] [1] ADJ [*time, remark*] opportun; [*place, response, word, level, name*] approprié; [*treatment*] adapté; [*person, authority, department*] compétent; **to take ~ action** prendre des mesures appropriées; **he is the ~ person to ask** c'est à lui qu'il faut le demander; **she's a most ~ choice** c'est la personne idéale; **to be ~ for sb/sth** convenir à qn/qch; **what is it ~ to wear for a dinner party?** quelle est la tenue appropriée pour un dîner?; **to be ~ to sth** être approprié à qch; **an outfit ~ to the job** une tenue appropriée à l'emploi; **a job ~ to his talents** un emploi à la mesure de ses talents; **it is ~ that ...** il est opportun que ...; **it seemed ~ to end with a joke** il semblait opportun de finir par une plaisanterie; **it would not be ~ for me to comment** ce n'est pas à moi de faire des commentaires
[2] [ə'prəʊprɪeɪt] VT [a] (= *take for one's own use*) s'approprier
[b] (= *set aside for special use*) [+ *funds*] affecter (**to, for** à)

appropriately [ə'prəʊprɪtlɪ] ADV [*act, respond*] comme il faut, de façon appropriée; [*dress*] de façon appropriée; [*speak*] avec à-propos, avec pertinence; [*called, titled*] de façon appropriée; [*designed*] convenablement; **~ named** bien nommé; **~, the winner is British** comme de juste, le gagnant est britannique

appropriateness [ə'prəʊprɪtnɪs] N [*of moment, decision*] opportunité *f*; [*of remark, word*] justesse *f*

appropriation [əˌprəʊprɪ'eɪʃən] [1] N (= *act: also Jur*) appropriation *f*; (= *funds assigned*) dotation *f*; (*US Pol*) crédit *m* budgétaire
[2] COMP ► **appropriation bill** N (*US Pol*) projet *m* de loi de finances ► **Appropriations Committee** N (*US Pol*) commission des finances de la Chambre des représentants (*examinant les dépenses*)

approval [ə'pruːvəl] N approbation *f*, assentiment *m*; (*Comm*) **on ~** sous condition, à l'essai; **to give a nod of ~** ◊ **to nod one's ~** hocher la tête en signe d'approbation; **to meet with sb's ~** avoir l'approbation de qn

▼ **approve** [ə'pruːv] [1] VT [+ *action, publication, medicine, drug*] approuver; [+ *decision*] ratifier, homologuer; [+ *request*] agréer; **to be ~d by ...** recueillir or avoir l'approbation de ...; **"read and ~d"** «lu et approuvé» [2] COMP ► **approved school**† N (*Brit*) maison *f* de correction†

► **approve of** VT FUS [+ *behaviour, idea*] approuver; [+ *person*] avoir bonne opinion de; **I don't ~ of his conduct** je n'approuve pas sa conduite; **I don't ~ of your decision** je n'approuve pas or je désapprouve la décision que vous avez prise; **she doesn't ~ of drinking/smoking** elle n'approuve pas qu'on boive/fume (*subj*); **he doesn't ~ of me** il n'a pas

bonne opinion de moi; **we ~ of our new neighbours*** nos nouveaux voisins nous plaisent

approving [ə'pruːvɪŋ] ADJ approbateur (-trice *f*), approbatif

approvingly [ə'pruːvɪŋlɪ] ADV d'un air or d'un ton approbateur

approx ABBR = **approximately**

approximate [ə'prɒksɪmɪt] [1] ADJ [*time, amount, description*] approximatif; **a sum ~ to what is needed** une somme voisine or proche de celle qui est requise; **figures ~ to the nearest franc** chiffres *mpl* arrondis au franc près [2] [ə'prɒksɪmeɪt] VI être proche, se rapprocher (**to** de)

approximately [ə'prɒksɪmətlɪ] ADV [a] (= *about: with numbers*) approximativement; **we have ~ 40 pupils** nous avons approximativement 40 élèves [b] (= *roughly*) [*true*] plus ou moins; **the figures were ~ correct** les chiffres étaient à peu près corrects; **the word means ~ ...** en gros or grosso modo, ce mot veut dire ...

approximation [əˌprɒksɪ'meɪʃən] N approximation *f*

appurtenance [ə'pɜːtɪnəns] N (*gen pl*) **~s** installations *fpl*, accessoires *mpl*; **the house and its ~s** (= *outhouses etc*) l'immeuble avec ses dépendances; (*Jur* = *rights, privileges etc*) l'immeuble avec ses circonstances et dépendances or ses appartenances

APR [ˌeɪpiː'ɑː] N ABBR (= *annual(ized) percentage rate*) taux *m* annuel

après-ski [ˌæpreɪ'skiː] N (= *period*) après-ski *m*

apricot ['eɪprɪkɒt] [1] N abricot *m*; (*also* ~ **tree**) abricotier *m* [2] COMP ► **apricot jam** N confiture *f* d'abricots ► **apricot tart** N tarte *f* aux abricots

April ['eɪprəl] [1] N avril *m*; *for phrases see* **September** [2] COMP ► **April fool** N (= *person*) victime *f* d'un poisson d'avril; (= *joke*) poisson *m* d'avril; **to make an ~ fool of sb** faire un poisson d'avril à qn ► **April Fools' Day** N le premier avril ► **April showers** NPL ≈ giboulées *fpl* de mars

a priori [ˌeɪpraɪ'ɔːraɪ, ˌɑːprɪ'ɔːriː] ADJ, ADV a priori

apron ['eɪprən] N [a] (= *garment*) tablier *m*; (*fig*) **tied to his mother's ~ strings** pendu aux jupes de sa mère [b] (*Aviat*) aire *f* de stationnement [c] (*Tech*) tablier *m* [d] (*Theat: also ~ stage*) avant-scène *f* [e] (*Phot*) bande *f* gaufrée

apropos [ˌæprə'pəʊ] (*frm*) [1] ADV à propos; **~, I have often wondered what happened to him** à propos, je me suis souvent demandé ce qu'il était devenu [2] PREP **~ (of) sth** à propos de qch [3] ADJ opportun, pertinent; **it seems ~ to do that** cela semble opportun or judicieux de faire cela

apse [æps] N abside *f*

APT [ˌeɪpiː'tiː] N (*Brit: formerly*) (ABBR = **Advanced Passenger Train**) ≈ TGV *m*, ≈ train *m* à grande vitesse

apt [æpt] ADJ [a] (= *appropriate*) [*remark, comment, reply*] juste, pertinent [b] (*frm* = *inclined, tending*) **to be ~ to do sth** avoir tendance à faire qch; **he is ~ to be late** il a tendance à être en retard; (*frm*) **one is ~ to believe that ...** on croirait volontiers que ..., on pourrait croire que ...; **this is ~ to occur** il faut s'y attendre [c] (= *gifted*) [*pupil*] doué, intelligent

apt. (ABBR = **apartment**) appt

▼ **aptitude** ['æptɪtjuːd] [1] N aptitude *f* (**for** à), disposition *f* (**for** pour); **to have an ~ for learning** avoir des dispositions pour l'étude; **he shows great ~** il promet beaucoup [2] COMP ► **aptitude test** N test *m* d'aptitude

aptly ['æptlɪ] ADV [*describe, remark*] judicieusement, avec à-propos; [*called, titled*] judicieusement; **~, his place was taken by his wife** comme de juste, sa femme a pris sa place

aptness ['æptnɪs] N [a] (= *suitability*) [*of remark etc*] à-propos *m*, justesse *f* [b] (= *giftedness*) = **aptitude**

Apulia [ə'pjuːljə] N les Pouilles *fpl*

aquaculture ['ækwəˌkʌltʃər] N = **aquafarming**

aquaerobics ['ækweɪ'rəʊbɪks] N (*NonC*) aérobic *f* en piscine

aquafarming ['ækwəfɑːmɪŋ] N aquaculture *f*

aqualung ['ækwəlʌŋ] N scaphandre *m* autonome

aquamarine [ˌækwəmə'riːn] [1] N (= *stone*) aigue-marine *f*; (= *colour*) bleu vert *m inv* [2] ADJ bleu-vert *inv*

aquanaut ['ækwənɔːt] N scaphandrier *m*, plongeur *m*

aquaplane ['ækwəpleɪn] [1] N aquaplane *m* [2] VI [a] (*Sport*) faire de l'aquaplane [b] (*Brit Aut*) faire de l'aquaplaning or de l'aquaplanage

aquaplaning ['ækwəpleɪnɪŋ] N (*Brit Aut*) aquaplaning *m*, aquaplanage *m*

aquaria [ə'kweərɪə] NPL of **aquarium**

Aquarian [ə'kweərɪən] N (*personne née sous le signe du Verseau*) Verseau *m*

aquarium [ə'kweərɪəm] N (*pl* **aquariums** or **aquaria**) aquarium *m*

Aquarius [ə'kweərɪəs] N (*Astron*) le Verseau; (*Astrol*) **I'm (an) ~** je suis (du) Verseau

aquatic [ə'kwætɪk] ADJ [*animal, plant*] aquatique; [*sport*] nautique

aquatint ['ækwətɪnt] N aquatinte *f*

aqueduct ['ækwɪdʌkt] N (= *canal*) aqueduc *m*; (= *pipe*) canalisation *f* d'amenée d'eau

aqueous ['eɪkwɪəs] ADJ aqueux; **~ humour** humeur *f* aqueuse

aquiculture ['ækwɪˌkʌltʃər, 'eɪkwɪˌkʌltʃər] N = **aquafarming**

aquifer ['ækwɪfər] N (*Geog*) aquifère *m*

aquiline ['ækwɪlaɪn] ADJ [*nose, profile*] aquilin

Aquinas [ə'kwaɪnəs] N (**St**) **Thomas ~** (saint) Thomas d'Aquin

AR ABBR = **Arkansas**

Arab ['ærəb] [1] N [a] (= *person*) Arabe *mf* → **street** [b] (= *horse*) cheval *m* arabe or anglo-arabe [2] ADJ arabe; **the ~ States** les États *mpl* arabes; **the United ~ Emirates** les Émirats *mpl* arabes unis; **the ~-Israeli Wars** le conflit israélo-arabe

arabesque [ˌærə'besk] N arabesque *f*

Arabia [ə'reɪbɪə] N l'Arabie *f*

Arabian [ə'reɪbɪən] ADJ arabe, d'Arabie; **~ Desert** désert *m* d'Arabie; **~ Gulf** golfe *m* Persique; **the ~ Nights** les Mille et Une Nuits *fpl*; **~ Sea** mer *f* d'Arabie

Arabic ['ærəbɪk] [1] ADJ arabe; **~ numerals** chiffres *mpl* arabes → **gum²** [2] N (*Ling*) arabe *m*; **written ~** l'arabe *m* littéral

Arabist ['ærəbɪst] N (= *scholar*) arabisant(e) *m(f)*; (= *politician*) pro-Arabe *mf*

arabization [ˌærəbaɪ'zeɪʃən] N arabisation *f*

arabize ['ærəbaɪz] VT arabiser

arable ['ærəbl] [1] ADJ [*land*] arable, cultivable; [*farm*] agricole [2] COMP ► **arable farmer** N cultivateur *m*, -trice *f* ► **arable farming** N culture *f*

arachnid [ə'ræknɪd] **~s** arachnides *mpl*

Aramaic [ˌærə'meɪɪk] N araméen *m*

Aran ['ærən] N **the ~ Islands** les îles *fpl* d'Aran

arbiter ['ɑːbɪtər] N (= *judge*) arbitre *m*; (= *mediator*) médiateur *m*, -trice *f*; **the Supreme Court is the final ~ of any dispute over constitutional rights** la Cour suprême est l'ultime arbitre en cas de litige concernant les droits constitutionnels; (*fig*) **to be an ~ of taste/style** *etc* être une référence en matière de bon goût/de style *etc*

arbitrage ['ɑːbɪtrɪdʒ] N (*Fin, St Ex*) arbitrage *m*, opération *f* d'arbitrage

arbitrager, arbitrageur [ˈɑːbɪtræˈʒɜːr] N arbitragiste *mf*

arbitrarily [ˈɑːbɪtrərəlɪ] ADV arbitrairement

arbitrary [ˈɑːbɪtrərɪ] ADJ arbitraire

arbitrate [ˈɑːbɪtreɪt] 1 VT arbitrer, juger 2 VI arbitrer

arbitration [ˌɑːbɪˈtreɪʃən] 1 N (*also Ind*) arbitrage *m*; **to go to ~** recourir à l'arbitrage → **refer** 2 COMP ▶ **arbitration clause** N clause *f* compromissoire ▶ **arbitration tribunal** N tribunal *m* arbitral

arbitrator [ˈɑːbɪtreɪtər] N arbitre *m*, médiateur *m*, -trice *f*

arbor [ˈɑːbər] N (*US*) = **arbour**

arboreal [ɑːˈbɔːrɪəl] ADJ [*shape*] arborescent; [*animal, technique*] arboricole

arboretum [ˌɑːbəˈriːtəm] N (*pl* **arboretums** or **arboreta** [ˌɑːbəˈriːtə]) arboretum *m*

arbour, arbor (*US*) [ˈɑːbər] N tonnelle *f*, charmille† *f*

arbutus [ɑːˈbjuːtəs] N arbousier *m*

ARC [ˌeɪɑːˈsiː] N a (ABBR = **AIDS-related complex**) ARC *m*, pré-sida *m* b (ABBR = **American Red Cross**) Croix-Rouge *f* américaine

arc [ɑːk] 1 N arc *m* 2 VI a décrire un arc (de cercle); **the rocket ~ed down into the sea** la fusée a décrit un arc avant de retomber dans la mer b (*Elec*) former un arc (électrique) 3 COMP ▶ **arc lamp, arc light** N lampe *f* à arc; (*Cine, TV*) sunlight *m* ▶ **arc welding** N soudure *f* à l'arc

arcade [ɑːˈkeɪd] 1 N (= *series of arches*) arcade *f*, galerie *f*; (= *shopping precinct*) passage *m*, galerie *f* marchande; (*Brit: also* **amusement ~**) galerie *f* de jeux, salle *f* de jeux d'arcade 2 COMP ▶ **arcade game** N (*Brit*) jeu *m* vidéo, jeu *m* d'arcade

Arcadia [ɑːˈkeɪdɪə] N l'Arcadie *f*

Arcadian [ɑːˈkeɪdɪən] 1 ADJ arcadien, d'Arcadie 2 N Arcadien(ne) *m(f)*

Arcady [ˈɑːkədɪ] N (*Poetry, Literat*) l'Arcadie *f*

arcane [ɑːˈkeɪn] ADJ ésotérique, obscur

arch[1] [ɑːtʃ] 1 N a (*Archit: in church etc*) arc *m*, voûte *f*; [*of bridge etc*] arche *f* b [*of eyebrow*] arcade *f*; [*of foot*] cambrure *f*, voûte *f* plantaire → **fallen** 2 VI (s')arquer 3 VT arquer, cambrer; **the cat ~ed his back** le chat a fait le gros dos

arch[2] [ɑːtʃ] ADJ a (= *cunning*) [*glance, person*] malicieux b (= *superior*) [*look, remark*] condescendant

arch[3] [ɑːtʃ] ADJ (*gen*) grand, par excellence; **an ~ traitor** un grand traître, le traître par excellence; **an ~ villain** un parfait scélérat; **the ~ villain** le principal scélérat 2 PREF arch(i)

archaeological, archeological [ˌɑːkɪəˈlɒdʒɪkəl] ADJ archéologique

archaeologist, archeologist [ˌɑːkɪˈɒlədʒɪst] N archéologue *mf*

archaeology, archeology [ˌɑːkɪˈɒlədʒɪ] N archéologie *f*

archaic [ɑːˈkeɪɪk] ADJ archaïque

archaism [ˈɑːkeɪɪzəm] N archaïsme *m*

archangel [ˈɑːkeɪndʒəl] N archange *m*; **the Archangel Michael** l'archange *m* Michel, saint Michel archange

archbishop [ˈɑːtʃˈbɪʃəp] N archevêque *m*

archbishopric [ɑːtʃˈbɪʃəprɪk] N archevêché *m*

archdeacon [ˈɑːtʃˈdiːkən] N archidiacre *m*

archdiocese [ˈɑːtʃˈdaɪəsɪs] N archidiocèse *m*

archduchess [ˈɑːtʃˈdʌtʃɪs] N archiduchesse *f*

archduchy [ˈɑːtʃˈdʌtʃɪ] N archiduché *m*

archduke [ˈɑːtʃˈdjuːk] N archiduc *m*

arched [ɑːtʃt] ADJ [*window, alcove*] cintré; [*roof*] cintré, en voûte; [*ceiling, doorway*] voûté; [*bridge*] à arches; [*eyebrows*] voûté (*liter*); **with an ~ back** (*convex*) le dos voûté; (*concave*) la taille cambrée, les reins cambrés

arch-enemy [ˈɑːtʃˈenɪmɪ] N ennemi *m* par excellence; (*Rel*) **the Arch-enemy** Satan *m*

archeological [ˌɑːkɪəˈlɒdʒɪkəl] ADJ (*US*) = **archaeological**

archeologist [ˌɑːkɪˈɒlədʒɪst] N (*US*) = **archaeologist**

archeology [ˌɑːkɪˈɒlədʒɪ] N (*US*) = **archaeology**

archer [ˈɑːtʃər] N archer *m*

Archers [ˈɑːtʃəz] NPL (*Brit*) **The ~** feuilleton radiophonique

---

THE ARCHERS

The Archers *est un feuilleton fleuve diffusé quotidiennement depuis 1951 par la BBC (Radio 4), avec un succès constant auprès des auditeurs de tous âges. Il retrace la vie d'une famille d'un village fictif, Ambridge, et de ses institutions locales, le pub et le club de cricket en particulier. Au fil des années, l'histoire s'est enrichie de thèmes plus contemporains tels que le racisme, la drogue, les familles monoparentales ou l'ordination des femmes.*

---

archery [ˈɑːtʃərɪ] N tir *m* à l'arc

archetypal [ˈɑːkɪtaɪpəl] ADJ archétypal

archetypally [ˌɑːkɪˈtaɪpəlɪ] ADV exemplairement

archetype [ˈɑːkɪtaɪp] N archétype *m*

archetypical [ˌɑːkɪˈtɪpɪkəl] ADJ = **archetypal**

Archimedes [ˌɑːkɪˈmiːdiːz] N Archimède *m*

archipelago [ˌɑːkɪˈpelɪɡəʊ] N (*pl* **archipelagos** or **archipelagoes**) archipel *m*

archiphoneme [ˌɑːkɪˈfəʊniːm] N archiphonème *m*

architect [ˈɑːkɪtekt] N architecte *m*; (*fig*) architecte *m*, artisan *m* → **naval**

architectonic [ˌɑːkɪtekˈtɒnɪk] ADJ (*Art*) architectonique

architectural [ˌɑːkɪˈtektʃərəl] ADJ architectural

architecturally [ˌɑːkɪˈtektʃərəlɪ] ADV [*innovative, interesting*] du point de vue architectural; **~, it represents a significant advance** du point de vue architectural, ça représente un progrès important

architecture [ˈɑːkɪtektʃər] N architecture *f*

architrave [ˈɑːkɪtreɪv] N (*Archit*) architrave *f*; [*of door, window*] encadrement *m*

archive [ˈɑːkaɪv] 1 N a (*also* **~s** = *records*) archives *fpl* b (*Comput*) archive *f* 2 VT archiver 3 ADJ d'archives; **~ material/film** documentation *f*/film *m* d'archives; (*Comput*) **~ file** fichier *m* d'archives

archivist [ˈɑːkɪvɪst] N archiviste *mf*

archly [ˈɑːtʃlɪ] ADV a (= *cunningly*) malicieusement b (= *in a superior way*) avec condescendance

archness [ˈɑːtʃnɪs] N malice *f*

archpriest [ˈɑːtʃˈpriːst] N archiprêtre *m*

archway [ˈɑːtʃweɪ] N voûte *f* (d'entrée), porche *m*; (*longer*) passage *m* voûté

Arctic [ˈɑːktɪk] 1 ADJ (*Geog*) arctique; (*fig* = *very cold*) glacial 2 N **the ~** (*regions*) les régions *fpl* arctiques, l'Arctique *m* 3 COMP ▶ **Arctic Circle** N cercle *m* polaire arctique ▶ **arctic fox** N renard *m* polaire ▶ **Arctic Ocean** N océan *m* Arctique ▶ **arctic skua** N (*Orn*) labbe *m* parasite ▶ **arctic tern** N (*Orn*) sterne *f* arctique

ardent [ˈɑːdənt] ADJ a (= *enthusiastic*) [*person, opponent, feminist, desire, belief, appeal*] ardent; [*admirer, supporter*] fervent b (= *passionate*) [*lover, lovemaking*] passionné

ardently [ˈɑːdəntlɪ] ADV a (= *enthusiastically*) [*oppose, support, defend*] avec ardeur, ardemment; **she's ~ socialist** c'est une fervente socialiste b (= *passionately*) [*kiss, respond*] passionnément

ardour, ardor (*US*) [ˈɑːdər] N ardeur *f*, ferveur *f*

arduous [ˈɑːdjʊəs] ADJ [*work, conditions, journey, task*] ardu, difficile

arduously [ˈɑːdjʊəslɪ] ADV péniblement, laborieusement

arduousness [ˈɑːdjʊəsnɪs] N difficulté *f*

are [ɑːr, ər] → **be**

area [ˈeərɪə] 1 N a (= *surface measure*) superficie *f*; **this field has an ~ of 2 hectares** ce champ a une superficie de 2 hectares *or* a 2 hectares de superficie b (= *region*) région *f*; (*Mil, Pol*) (*large*) territoire *m*; (*smaller*) secteur *m*, zone *f*; **the London ~** la région londonienne *or* de Londres; **in the whole ~** dans toute la région → **sterling** c (*fig*) [*of knowledge, enquiry*] domaine *m*, champ *m*; **in this ~** dans ce domaine; **the ~s of disagreement** les zones *fpl* de désaccord d (*Brit* = *courtyard*) courette *f* en contrebas (*sur la rue*) e (*with specified function*) (= *part of room*) **dining ~** coin *m* salle à manger; **sleeping ~** coin *m* chambre; (= *part of building, housing estate etc*) **play/parking ~** aire *f* de jeux/de stationnement f (*Ftbl* = *penalty area*) surface *f* de réparation 2 COMP ▶ **area code** N (*Brit Post*) code *m* postal; (*US Telec*) indicatif *m* de zone ▶ **area manager** N directeur *m* régional ▶ **area office** N agence *f* régionale ▶ **area of outstanding natural beauty** N site *m* naturel exceptionnel

areaway [ˈeərəweɪ] N (*US*) = **area d**

arena [əˈriːnə] N (*lit, fig*) arène *f*; **the political ~** l'arène *f* politique; (*fig*) **to enter the ~** descendre dans l'arène

aren't [ɑːnt] = **are not, am not**; → **be**

areola [əˈriːələ] N (*pl* **areolas** or **areolae** [əˈriːəliː]) (*Anat*) aréole *f*

Argentina [ˌɑːdʒənˈtiːnə] N l'Argentine *f*

Argentine [ˈɑːdʒəntaɪn] 1 N a (*Geog*†) **the ~** l'Argentine *f*; **in the ~** en Argentine b = **Argentinian** 2 ADJ argentin

Argentinean [ˌɑːdʒənˈtɪnɪən] ADJ (*US*) = **Argentinian**

Argentinian [ˌɑːdʒənˈtɪnɪən] 1 ADJ argentin 2 N Argentin(e) *m(f)*

argon [ˈɑːɡɒn] N argon *m*

Argonaut [ˈɑːɡənɔːt] N Argonaute *m*

Argos [ˈɑːɡɒs] N Argos

argosy [ˈɑːɡəsɪ] N (*liter*) galion *m*

argot [ˈɑːɡəʊ] N argot *m*

arguable [ˈɑːɡjʊəbl] ADJ discutable, contestable; **it is ~ that ...** on peut soutenir que ...

arguably [ˈɑːɡjʊəblɪ] ADV **he is ~ the greatest footballer of all time** c'est sans doute le plus grand footballeur de tous les temps

argue [ˈɑːɡjuː] 1 VI a (= *dispute, quarrel*) se disputer (**with sb** avec qn, **about sth** au sujet *or* à propos de qch); **they are always arguing** ils se disputent tout le temps; **don't ~!** pas de discussion!; (*to others arguing*) **stop arguing!** arrêtez de vous disputer!; **no one can ~ with that** personne ne peut contester cela b (= *debate*) argumenter (*frm*) (**against sb** contre qn, **about sth** sur qch); **he ~d against going** il a donné les raisons qu'il avait de ne pas y aller; **they ~d (about it) for hours** ils ont discuté (à ce sujet) pendant des heures; **to ~ from sth** tirer argument de qch c (*Jur etc*) [*fact, evidence*] témoigner (**against sth** contre qch, **for, in favour of sth** en faveur de qch); **it ~s well for him** cela parle en sa faveur 2 VT a **to ~ sb into/out of doing** persuader/dissuader qn de faire; **to ~ sb into/out of a scheme** persuader/dissuader qn d'adopter un projet; **they ~d me into believing it** à force d'arguments ils sont parvenus à me le faire croire b (= *debate*) [+ *case*] discuter, débattre; **a well-~d case** une argumentation solide; **to ~**

one's way out of a situation se sortir d'une situation à force d'argumentation *or* d'arguments; *(gen pej)* **to ~ the toss*** discuter le coup*
c *(= show evidence of)* dénoter, indiquer; **it ~s a certain lack of feeling** cela dénote *or* indique un certain manque de sensibilité
d *(= maintain)* soutenir, affirmer **(that** que)
▶ **argue out** VT SEP *[+ problem]* discuter *or* débattre (à fond)

▼ **argument** ['ɑːgjʊmənt] N **a** *(= debate)* discussion *f*, débat *m*; **it is beyond ~** c'est indiscutable; **you've only heard one side of the ~** tu n'as entendu qu'une seule version de l'affaire *or* de l'histoire; **for ~'s sake** à titre d'exemple; **he is open to ~** il est prêt à écouter les arguments; **it is open to ~ that ...** on peut soutenir que ...
b *(= dispute)* dispute *f*, discussion *f*; **to have an ~** se disputer **(with sb** avec qn); *(hum)* **he has had an ~ with a tree** il s'est bagarré* avec un arbre *(hum)*
c *(= reasons advanced)* argument *m*; **his ~ is that ...** il soutient que ..., son argument est que ...; **there is a strong ~ in favour of** *or* **for doing** il y a de bonnes raisons pour faire; **there is a strong ~ in favour of his resignation** il y a de bonnes raisons pour qu'il démissionne *(subj)*; **the ~ that Europe needs Britain** le raisonnement selon lequel l'Europe a besoin de la Grande-Bretagne → **line¹**
d *(= synopsis)* sommaire *m*, argument *m*

argumentation [,ɑːgjʊmən'teɪʃən] N argumentation *f*

argumentative [,ɑːgjʊ'mentətɪv] ADJ ergoteur, raisonneur

argy-bargy* ['ɑːdʒɪ'bɑːdʒɪ] N *(pl* **-bargies)** *(Brit)* discutailleries* *fpl*; **to get caught up in an ~** se laisser entraîner dans des discussions sans fin

aria ['ɑːrɪə] N aria *f*

Ariadne [ærɪ'ædnɪ] N Ariane *f*

Arian ['eərɪən] **1** N Arien(ne) *m(f)* **2** ADJ arien

Arianism ['eərɪənɪzəm] N arianisme *m*

ARIBA [ə'riːbə] *(ABBR = Associate of the Royal Institute of British Architects)* membre *de l'institut britannique des architectes*

arid ['ærɪd] ADJ *(lit, fig)* aride

aridity [ə'rɪdɪtɪ] N *(lit, fig)* aridité *f*

Aries ['eəriːz] N *(Astron)* le Bélier; *(Astrol)* **I'm (an) ~** je suis (du) Bélier

aright [ə'raɪt] ADV bien, correctement; **did I hear ~?** ai-je bien entendu?; **to set things ~** mettre bon ordre à l'affaire

arise [ə'raɪz] *(pret* **arose,** *ptp* **arisen** [ə'rɪzn]) VI **a** *[difficulty]* survenir, surgir; *[question]* se présenter, se poser; *[cry]* s'élever; **if the question ~s** le cas échéant; **should the need ~** en cas de besoin, si le besoin s'en fait sentir; **should the occasion ~** si l'occasion se présente; **a doubt arose** un doute a surgi **b** *(= result)* résulter, provenir **(from** de) **c** *(†, liter)* *[person]* se lever; *[sun]* se lever, paraître, poindre *(liter)*

aristo* ['ærɪstəʊ] N *(Brit)* *(ABBR =* **aristocrat)** aristo* *mf*

aristocracy [ærɪs'tɒkrəsɪ] N aristocratie *f*

aristocrat ['ærɪstəkræt] N aristocrate *mf*

aristocratic [,ærɪstə'krætɪk] ADJ aristocratique

Aristophanes [,ærɪs'tɒfəniːz] N Aristophane *m*

Aristotelian [,ærɪstə'tiːlɪən] ADJ aristotélicien

Aristotelianism [,ærɪstə'tiːlɪənɪzəm] N aristotélisme *m*

Aristotle ['ærɪstɒtl] N Aristote *m*

arithmetic [ə'rɪθmətɪk] **1** N arithmétique *f* **2** [,ærɪθ'metɪk] ADJ arithmétique; *(Comput)* **~ logic unit** unité *f* arithmétique et logique; **~ mean** moyenne *f* arithmétique

arithmetical [,ærɪθ'metɪkəl] ADJ arithmétique

arithmetician [ə,rɪθmə'tɪʃən] N arithméticien(ne) *m(f)*

Ariz. ABBR = **Arizona**

Arizona [ærɪ'zəʊnə] N l'Arizona *m*

ark [ɑːk] N *(Hist)* arche *f*; *(Rel)* **Ark of the Covenant** arche *f* d'alliance; *(fig)* **it's out of the ~*** c'est vieux comme Hérode, c'est antédiluvien → **Noah**

Ark. ABBR = **Arkansas**

Arkansas ['ɑːkənsɔː] N l'Arkansas *m*

arm¹ [ɑːm] **1** N **a** *(Anat)* bras *m*; **to hold sth/sb in one's ~s** tenir qch/qn dans ses bras; **he had a coat over his ~** il avait un manteau sur le bras; **take my ~** prenez mon bras; **to give one's ~ to sb** donner *or* offrir le bras à qn; **to have sb on one's ~†** avoir qn à son bras; **on her husband's ~** au bras de son mari; **to take sb in one's ~s** prendre qn dans ses bras; **to put one's ~ round sb** passer son bras autour des épaules de qn; **~ in ~** bras dessus bras dessous; **with ~s wide apart** les bras écartés *or* en croix; **within ~'s reach** à portée de la main; **with folded ~s** les bras croisés; **at ~'s length** à bout de bras; *(fig)* **to keep sb at ~'s length** tenir qn à distance → **2**; **with open ~s** à bras ouverts; *(liter)* **in the ~s of Morpheus** dans les bras de Morphée; **the (long) ~ of the law** le bras de la justice; **a list as long as your ~*** une liste longue comme le bras*; *(fig)* **to have a long ~** avoir le bras long; *(US)* **to put the ~ on sb*** *(gen)* forcer la main à qn **(to do** pour qu'il fasse); *(= make him pay up)* faire cracher* qn; **I'd give my right ~*** *or* **I'd give an ~ and a leg* for that/to do that** je donnerais n'importe quoi pour avoir ça/pour faire ça; **they must have paid an ~ and a leg for that ◊ that must have cost them an ~ and a leg** ça a dû leur coûter les yeux de la tête* → **babe, chance, open**
b *[of river, crane, pick-up]* bras *m*; *[of spectacle frames]* branche *f* (de monture); *[of coat etc]* manche *f*; *[of armchair]* bras *m*, accoudoir *m*; **~ of the sea** bras *m* de mer

2 COMP **~'s length agreement** N *(Jur)* contrat *m* conclu dans les conditions normales du commerce ▶ **arm's length price** N *(Fin)* prix *m* fixé dans les conditions normales de la concurrence ▶ **arm-twisting*** N pressions *fpl* directes; **I don't like his ~-twisting* techniques** je n'aime pas ses façons de faire pression sur les gens ▶ **arm-wrestle** VI **to ~-wrestle with sb** faire un bras de fer avec qn ▶ **arm-wrestling** N bras *m* de fer; **an ~-wrestling match** une partie de bras de fer

arm² [ɑːm] **1** N **a** *(= weapon)* arme *f*; **under ~s** sous les armes; **in ~s** en armes; **to ~s!** aux armes!; **to call to ~s** *[rebel leader]* appeler aux armes; *[government]* appeler sous les drapeaux; **to take up ~s against sb/sth** *(lit)* prendre des armes contre qn/qch; *(fig)* s'insurger contre qn/qch; **to be up in ~s against sb/the authorities** être en rébellion ouverte contre qn/les autorités; **to be up in ~s against a decision/the cost of living** *etc* s'élever contre *or* partir en guerre contre une décision/le coût de la vie *etc*; **she was up in ~s about it** cela la mettait hors d'elle-même; **no need to get up in ~s over such a small thing!** ce n'est pas la peine de te monter *or* t'emballer pour si peu! → **man**
b *(= branch of military service)* arme *f* → **fleet¹**
c *(Her)* **~s** armes *fpl*, armoiries *fpl* → **coat**
2 VT *[+ person, nation]* armer; *(fig)* **to ~ o.s. with patience** s'armer de patience
3 VI (s')armer, prendre les armes **(against** contre)
4 COMP ▶ **arms control** N contrôle *m* des armements ▶ **arms factory** N usine *f* d'armement ▶ **arms limitation** N limitation *f* des armements ▶ **arms manufacturer** N fabricant *m* d'armes ▶ **arms race** N course *f* aux armements ▶ **arms trade** N commerce *m* des armes

Armada [ɑː'mɑːdə] N Armada *f*

armadillo [,ɑːmə'dɪləʊ] N tatou *m*

Armageddon [,ɑːmə'gedn] N *(lit, fig)* Armageddon *m*

Armalite® ['ɑːməlaɪt] N *fusil automatique rapide et ultraléger*

armament ['ɑːməmənt] N **a** *(gen pl = fighting strength)* force *f* de frappe **b** **~s** *(= weapons)* armement *m*, matériel *m* de guerre **c** *(NonC = preparation for war)* armement *m*

armature ['ɑːmətjʊəʳ] N *(gen, also Elec, Phys)* armature *f*; *(Zool)* carapace *f*

armband ['ɑːmbænd] N brassard *m*; *(for swimming)* brassard *m* gonflable; *(mourning)* brassard *m* de deuil, crêpe *m*

armchair ['ɑːmtʃɛəʳ] **1** N fauteuil *m*; *(fig)* **~ general/traveller** stratège *m*/voyageur *m* en chambre **2** COMP ▶ **armchair banking** N services *mpl* (bancaires) télématiques ▶ **armchair shopping** N *(by post, telephone)* achats par correspondance ou par téléphone; *(by computer, television)* téléachats *mpl*

armed [ɑːmd] ADJ *(lit, fig)* armé **(with** de); *[missile]* muni d'une charge explosive; *(lit)* **to go ~** porter une arme; *(fig)* **to go ~ with statistics** *etc* s'armer de statistiques *etc*; **~ to the teeth** armé jusqu'aux dents; **~ conflict/struggle** conflit *m* armé/lutte *f* armée; **the ~ forces** les forces *fpl* armées; **~ neutrality** neutralité *f* armée; **~ robbery** vol *m* *or* attaque *f* à main armée

-armed [ɑːmd] ADJ *(in compounds)* **a** *(Anat)* **long-/short-armed** aux bras longs/courts **b** *(Mil)* **nuclear-/missile-armed** armé d'engins nucléaires/de missiles

Armenia [ɑː'miːnɪə] N l'Arménie *f*

Armenian [ɑː'miːnɪən] **1** ADJ arménien **2** N **a** *(= person)* Arménien(ne) *m(f)* **b** *(Ling)* arménien *m*

armful ['ɑːmfʊl] N brassée *f*; **in ~s** à pleins bras; **he arrived with ~s of presents** il est arrivé avec des cadeaux plein les bras

armhole ['ɑːmhəʊl] N emmanchure *f*

armistice ['ɑːmɪstɪs] **1** N armistice *m* **2** COMP ▶ **Armistice Day** N le 11 novembre, l'Armistice *m*

armlet ['ɑːmlɪt] N **a** *(= armband)* brassard *m*; *(= bracelet)* bracelet *m*

armor ['ɑːməʳ] *(US)* = **armour**

armorer ['ɑːmərəʳ] N *(US)* = **armourer**

armorial [ɑː'mɔːrɪəl] **1** ADJ armorial; **~ bearings** armoiries *fpl* **2** N armorial *m*

armory ['ɑːmərɪ] N *(US)* = **armoury**

armour, armor *(US)* ['ɑːməʳ] **1** N **a** *(NonC)* *[of knight]* armure *f*; **in full ~** armé de pied en cap → **suit** **b** *(Mil)* *(NonC = armour-plating)* blindage *m*; *(collectively)* *(= vehicles)* blindés *mpl*; *(= forces)* forces *fpl* blindées **2** COMP ▶ **armour-clad** ADJ *(Mil)* blindé; *(Naut)* cuirassé, blindé ▶ **armour-piercing** ADJ *(Mil)* *[mine, gun]* antichar; *[shell, bullet]* perforant ▶ **armour-plate** N *(Mil)* blindage *m*; *(Naut)* cuirasse *f* ▶ **armour-plated** ADJ = **armour-clad** ▶ **armour-plating** N = **armour-plate**

armoured car [,ɑːməd'kɑːʳ] N voiture *f* blindée

armoured personnel carrier ['ɑːməd,pɜːsə'nel'kærɪəʳ] N véhicule *m* blindé de transport de troupes

armourer, armorer *(US)* ['ɑːmərəʳ] N armurier *m*

armoury, armory *(US)* ['ɑːmərɪ] N dépôt *m* d'armes, arsenal *m*; *(US = arms factory)* usine *f* d'armement

armpit ['ɑːmpɪt] N aisselle *f*; **to be up to one's ~s in water** avoir de l'eau jusqu'aux épaules

armrest ['ɑːmrest] N accoudoir *m*

army ['ɑːmɪ] **1** N **a** armée *f* (de terre); **to be in the ~** être dans l'armée, être militaire; **to join the ~** s'engager (dans l'armée); **to go into the ~** *[professional]* s'engager dans l'armée; *[conscript]* partir au service (militaire) → **occupation, territorial** **b** *(fig)* armée *f*

▶ LANGUAGE IN USE: **argument** 26.2

2 COMP [*life, nurse, uniform*] militaire ; [*family*] de militaires ► **army corps** N corps *m* d'armée ► **army-issue** ADJ [*rifle*] de l'armée ; **police say the grenade was ~-issue** la police dit que c'était une grenade de l'armée ► **Army List** N annuaire *m* militaire, annuaire *m* des officiers de carrière (de l'armée de terre) ► **army officer** N officier *m* (de l'armée de terre) ► **army surplus** N (*NonC*) surplus *mpl* de l'armée ► **army-surplus** ADJ [*boots, jacket etc*] des surplus de l'armée ; [*store*] de surplus (de l'armée)

Arno [ˈɑːnəʊ] N Arno *m*

aroma [əˈrəʊmə] N arôme *m*

aromatherapist [əˈrəʊməˈθerəpɪst] N aromathérapeute *mf*

aromatherapy [əˌrəʊməˈθerəpɪ] N aromathérapie *f*

aromatic [ˌærəʊˈmætɪk] **1** ADJ aromatique **2** N aromate *m*

arose [əˈrəʊz] VB *pt of* **arise**

around [əˈraʊnd]

> When **around** is an element in a phrasal verb, eg **come around**, **move around**, **potter around**, look up the verb.

1 ADV **a** autour ; **all ~** tout autour, de tous côtés ; **for miles ~** sur *or* dans un rayon de plusieurs kilomètres **b** (= *nearby*) dans les parages ; **he is somewhere ~** il est dans les parages ; **you haven't seen Susan ~, have you?** vous n'auriez pas vu Susan dans les parages, par hasard ? ; **she'll be ~ soon** elle sera bientôt là ; **is he ~?*** (est-ce qu')il est là ? ; **there's a lot of flu ~** il y a beaucoup de cas de grippe en ce moment ; **he's been ~*** (= *travelled*) il a pas mal roulé sa bosse* ; (= *experienced*) il n'est pas né d'hier *or* de la dernière pluie ; **it's been ~* for more than 20 years** ça existe depuis plus de 20 ans **2** PREP (*esp US*) **a** (= *round*) autour de ; **~ the fire** autour du feu ; **~ it** autour ; **the country ~ the town** les environs *mpl or* alentours *mpl* de la ville ; **the first building ~ the corner** le premier immeuble au coin de la rue ; **it's just ~ the corner** (*lit*) c'est juste au coin ; (*fig* = *very near*) c'est à deux pas (d'ici) ; (*in time*) c'est pour demain (*fig*) **b** (= *about*) **they are somewhere ~ the house** ils sont quelque part dans la maison **c** (= *approximately*) environ, à peu près ; **~ 2 kilos** environ *or* à peu près 2 kilos, 2 kilos environ ; **~ 1800** vers *or* aux alentours de 1800 ; **~ 10 o'clock** vers 10 heures

arousal [əˈraʊzəl] N (*sexual*) excitation *f* (sexuelle) ; [*of emotions*] éveil *m*

arouse [əˈraʊz] VT **a** (= *awaken*) réveiller, éveiller ; **to ~ sb from his sleep** tirer qn du sommeil **b** (= *cause*) [*+ suspicion, curiosity etc*] éveiller ; [*+ anger*] exciter, provoquer ; [*+ contempt*] susciter, provoquer **c** (= *stimulate*) stimuler, réveiller* ; (= *stir to action*) pousser à agir, secouer ; **that ~d him to protest** cela l'a poussé à protester ; **to ~ sb to an effort** obtenir un effort de qn

aroused [əˈraʊzd] ADJ (*sexually*) excité

arpeggio [ɑːˈpedʒɪəʊ] N arpège *m*

arr. **a** (*on timetable*) (ABBR = **arrives, arrival**) arr., arrivée **b** (*Mus*) (ABBR = **arranged**) adaptation de

arraign [əˈreɪn] VT (*Jur*) traduire en justice ; (*fig*) accuser, mettre en cause

arraignment [əˈreɪnmənt] N (*Jur*) ≈ lecture *f* de l'acte d'accusation

Arran [ˈærən] N l'île *f* d'Arran

arrange [əˈreɪndʒ] **1** VT **a** (= *put in order*) [*+ room, clothing*] arranger ; [*+ books, objects*] ranger, mettre en ordre ; [*+ flowers*] arranger, disposer ; **to ~ one's hair** arranger sa coiffure ; **a room ~d as a waiting room** une pièce aménagée en salle d'attente **b** (= *decide on*) [*+ meeting*] arranger, organi-

ser ; [*+ date*] fixer ; [*+ plans, programme*] arrêter, convenir de ; [*+ arranged marriage*] arranger ; **it was ~d that ...** il a été arrangé *or* décidé *or* convenu que ... (+ *cond*) ; **I have something ~d for tonight** j'ai quelque chose de prévu pour ce soir **c** († = *settle*) [*+ dispute*] régler, arranger **d** (*Mus*) arranger, adapter ; **to ~ sth for violin and piano** faire un arrangement de qch pour violon et piano **2** VI (= *fix details*) s'arranger (**to do** pour faire, **with sb about sth** avec qn au sujet de qch), prendre des *or* ses dispositions (**for sb to do** pour que qn fasse) ; **we have ~d for the goods to be dispatched** nous avons fait le nécessaire pour que les marchandises soient expédiées ; **to ~ for sb's luggage to be sent up** faire monter les bagages de qn ; **to ~ with sb to do** décider avec qn de faire, s'entendre avec qn pour faire **3** COMP ► **arranged marriage** N mariage *m* arrangé

arrangement [əˈreɪndʒmənt] N **a** [*of room, furniture*] arrangement *m*, agencement *m* ; [*of flowers, hair, clothing*] arrangement *m* → **flower b** (= *agreement*) arrangement *m* ; **to do sth by ~ with sb** s'entendre *or* s'arranger avec qn pour faire qch ; **larger sizes by ~** tailles *fpl* supérieures sur demande ; **price by ~** prix *m* à débattre ; **to come to an ~ with sb** parvenir à un arrangement avec qn, s'arranger *or* s'entendre avec qn (**to do sth** pour faire qch) ; **by ~ with Covent Garden** avec l'autorisation *f* de Covent Garden → **exceptional c** (= *sth decided*) arrangement *m* ; **~s** (= *plans, preparations*) dispositions *fpl*, préparatifs *mpl* ; **this ~ suited everyone** cet arrangement convenait à tous ; **I want to change the ~s we made** je veux changer les dispositions que nous avons prises ; **the ~ whereby he should visit her monthly** l'arrangement selon lequel il doit aller la voir une fois par mois ; **I write to confirm these ~s** je vous écris pour confirmer ces dispositions ; **to make ~s for a holiday** faire des préparatifs pour des vacances, organiser des vacances (à l'avance) ; **to make ~s for sth to be done** prendre des dispositions pour faire faire qch ; **can you make ~s to come tomorrow?** pouvez-vous vous arranger pour venir demain ? **d** (*Mus*) adaptation *f*, arrangement *m*

arranger [əˈreɪndʒə*] N **a** (*Mus*) arrangeur *m*, -euse *f* **b** (= *organizer*) organisateur *m*, -trice *f*

arrant [ˈærənt] ADJ (*frm*) [*fool, liar, coward*] fieffé† (*before n*) ; [*hypocrisy*] consommé, éhonté ; **his ~ stupidity** son imbécillité totale ; **that's the most ~ nonsense I've ever heard** je n'ai jamais rien entendu de plus absurde

array [əˈreɪ] **1** VT **a** (*Mil*) [*+ troops*] déployer, disposer **b** (*liter* = *clothe*) [*+ person*] revêtir (**in** de) **2** N **a** (*Mil*) rang *m*, ordre *m* ; **in battle ~** en ordre de bataille **b** [*of objects*] étalage *m* ; [*of people*] assemblée *f* ; **an ~ of solar panels** une batterie de panneaux solaires **c** (*Math etc: also Comput*) tableau *m* ; **~ of figures** tableau *m* **d** (= *ceremonial dress*) habit *m* d'apparat ; (= *fine clothes*) atours *mpl* (*iro*)

arrears [əˈrɪəz] NPL arriéré *m* ; **rent in ~** arriéré *m* de loyers ; **to get** *or* **fall into ~** accumuler des arriérés ; **she is three months in ~ with her rent** ◊ **her rent is three months in ~** elle doit trois mois de loyer, elle a un arriéré de trois mois sur son loyer ; **he fell into ~ with his mortgage/his rent** il a pris du retard dans le remboursement de son emprunt logement/ dans le paiement de son loyer ; **to be/get in ~ with one's correspondence** avoir/prendre du retard dans sa correspondance ; **~ of work** travail *m* en retard

arrest [əˈrest] **1** VT **a** [*police etc suspect*] arrêter, appréhender **b** [*+ person's attention, interest*] retenir, attirer **c** [*+ growth, development, progress*] (= *stop*)

arrêter ; (= *hinder*) entraver ; (= *retard*) retarder ; **measures to ~ inflation** des mesures pour arrêter l'inflation ; (*Med*) **to ~ (the course of) a disease** enrayer une maladie **2** N **a** [*of person*] arrestation *f* ; **under ~** en état d'arrestation ; (*Mil*) aux arrêts ; **to put sb under ~** arrêter qn ; (*Mil*) mettre qn aux arrêts ; **to make an ~** procéder à une arrestation ; (*Mil*) **open/close ~** ≈ arrêts *mpl* simples/de rigueur **b** (*Jur*) **~ of judgement** suspension *f* d'exécution d'un jugement **3** COMP ► **arrested development** N (*Med*) arrêt *m* de croissance ; (*Psych*) atrophie *f* de la personnalité ► **arresting officer** N (*Police*) *policier ayant procédé à l'arrestation* ► **arrest warrant** N mandat *m* d'arrêt

arresting [əˈrestɪŋ] ADJ (*frm* = *striking*) frappant, saisissant

arrhythmia [əˈrɪðmɪə] N (*NonC*) arythmie *f*

▼ **arrival** [əˈraɪvl] **1** N **a** (*NonC*) [*of person, vehicle, letter, parcel*] arrivée *f* ; (*Comm*) [*of goods in bulk*] arrivage *m* ; **on ~** à l'arrivée ; (*Rail etc*) **~s and departures** arrivées *fpl* et départs *mpl* **b** (= *consignment*) **an ~ of** un arrivage de ; (= *person*) **who was the first ~?** qui est arrivé le premier ? ; **a new ~** un nouveau venu, une nouvelle venue ; (*hum* = *baby*) un(e) nouveau-né(e) ; **the latest ~** le dernier arrivé **2** COMP ► **arrival board** N (*US*) = **arrivals board** ► **arrival platform** N quai *m* d'arrivée ► **arrivals board** N tableau *m* des arrivées ► **arrivals lounge** N salon *m* d'arrivée

arrive [əˈraɪv] VI **a** [*person, vehicle, letter, goods*] arriver ; **to ~ at a town** arriver à *or* atteindre une ville ; **as soon as he ~s** dès qu'il arrivera, dès son arrivée ; (*on timetable etc*) **arriving Paris (at) 14.43** arrivée *f* à Paris (à) 14 h 43 ; **to ~ (up)on the scene** survenir ; **the moment has ~d when we must go** le moment est venu pour nous de partir **b** (= *succeed in business etc*) arriver, réussir ► **arrive at** VT FUS [*+ decision, solution*] aboutir à, parvenir à ; [*+ perfection*] atteindre ; **to ~ at a price** [*one person*] fixer un prix ; [*two people*] se mettre d'accord sur un prix ; **they finally ~d at the idea of doing** ils en sont finalement venus à l'idée de faire

arrogance [ˈærəgəns] N arrogance *f*, morgue *f*

arrogant [ˈærəgənt] ADJ arrogant, plein de morgue

arrogantly [ˈærəgəntlɪ] ADV [*behave, speak*] avec arrogance ; **~ casual/careless** d'une désinvolture/insouciance arrogante

arrogate [ˈærəʊgeɪt] VT (*frm*) **a** (= *claim unjustly*) [*+ authority, right*] revendiquer à tort, s'arroger ; [*+ victory*] s'attribuer **b** (= *attribute unjustly*) attribuer injustement (**to sb** à qn)

arrow [ˈærəʊ] **1** N (= *weapon, directional sign*) flèche *f* ; **to shoot (one) off an ~** décocher une flèche **2** VT [*+ item on list etc*] cocher ; [*+ route, direction*] flécher ; (= *insert*) **to ~ sth in** indiquer l'emplacement de qch

arrowhead [ˈærəʊhed] N fer *m or* pointe *f* de flèche

arrowroot [ˈærəʊruːt] N (*Culin*) arrow-root *m* ; (*Bot*) maranta *f*

arse** [ɑːs] (*esp Brit*) **1** N cul** *m* ; **shift** *or* **move your ~!** (= *move over*) bouge ton cul !** ; (= *hurry up*) magne-toi le cul !** ; **get (up) off your ~** (= *stand up*) lève ton cul de là** ; (*fig*) bouge-toi le cul** ; (*fig*) **he doesn't know his ~ from his elbow** il comprend rien à rien* → **ass²**, **pain²** **2** VT **I can't be ~d** j'ai la flemme* ► **arse about****, **arse around**** VI déconner**

arsehole** [ˈɑːshəʊl] N (*Brit lit, also fig* = *person*) trou *m* du cul** ; **you ~!** trou du cul !**

arsenal [ˈɑːsɪnl] N arsenal *m*

arsenic [ˈɑːsnɪk] **1** N arsenic *m* **2** COMP ► **arsenic poisoning** N empoisonnement *m* à l'arsenic

arsenical [ɑːˈsenɪkəl] ADJ [*substance*] arsenical ; **~ poisoning** empoisonnement *m* à l'arsenic

arson [ˈɑːsn] N incendie *m* volontaire *or* criminel

arsonist [ˈɑːsənɪst] N (*gen*) incendiaire *mf* ; (= *maniac*) pyromane *mf*

art¹ [ɑːt] 1 N a (*NonC*) art *m* ; **~ for ~'s sake** l'art pour l'art ; **to study ~** (*gen*) faire des études d'art ; (*Univ*) faire les beaux-arts ; **the ~s** les arts *mpl* → **work** b (= *human skill*) art *m*, habileté *f* ; **the ~ of embroidering/embroidery** l'art *m* de broder/de la broderie ; **to do sth with ~** faire qch avec art *or* habileté ; **~s and crafts** artisanat *m* (d'art) → **black, fine², state** c (*Univ*) **Arts** lettres *fpl* ; **Faculty of Arts** faculté *f* des Lettres (et Sciences humaines) ; **he's doing Arts** il fait des (études de) lettres → **bachelor, master** d (= *cunning*) artifice *m*, ruse *f* ; **to use every ~ in order to do sth** user de tous les artifices pour faire qch 2 COMP ► **art collection** N collection *f* d'œuvres d'art ► **art college** N ≈ école *f* des beaux-arts ► **art deco** N art *m* déco ♦ ADJ art déco *inv* ► **art director** N (*Cine*) directeur *m*, -trice *f* artistique ► **art exhibition** N exposition *f* (d'œuvres) d'art ► **art form** N moyen *m* d'expression artistique ► **art gallery** N (= *museum*) musée *m* d'art ; (= *shop*) galerie *f* (de tableaux *or* d'art) ► **art-house** ADJ [*film, cinema*] d'art et d'essai ► **art nouveau** N art *m* nouveau, modern style *m* ► **art paper** N papier *m* couché ► **art school** N ≈ école *f* des beaux-arts ► **Arts Council** N (*Brit*) *organisme encourageant les activités culturelles* ► **Arts degree** N (*Univ*) ≈ licence *f* ès lettres ► **Arts student** N étudiant(e) *m(f)* de *or* en lettres ► **art student** N étudiant(e) *m(f)* des *or* en beaux-arts

art² [ɑːt] (††, *liter: also* **thou ~**) = **you are** ; → **be**

artefact [ˈɑːtɪfækt] N objet *m* (fabriqué), artefact *m*

Artemis [ˈɑːtɪmɪs] N Artémis *f*

arterial [ɑːˈtɪərɪəl] ADJ a (*Anat*) artériel b (*Rail*) **~ line** grande ligne *f* ; (*Aut*) **~ road** route *f* or voie *f* à grande circulation, (grande) artère *f*

arteriole [ɑːˈtɪərɪəʊl] N (*Anat*) artériole *f*

arteriosclerosis [ɑːˌtɪərɪəʊsklɪˈrəʊsɪs] N artériosclérose *f*

artery [ˈɑːtərɪ] N (*Anat*) artère *f* ; (*fig* = *road*) artère *f*, route *f* or voie *f* à grande circulation

artesian well [ɑːˈtiːzɪənwel] N puits *m* artésien

artful [ˈɑːtfʊl] ADJ rusé, malin (-igne *f*) ; **he's an ~ one*** c'est un petit malin* ; **~ dodger** roublard(e)* *m(f)*

artfully [ˈɑːtfəlɪ] ADV a (= *skilfully*) [*arranged, constructed, designed*] ingénieusement b (= *cunningly*) avec ruse

artfulness [ˈɑːtfʊlnɪs] N (= *cunning*) astuce *f*, ruse *f* ; (= *skill*) adresse *f*, habileté *f*

arthritic [ɑːˈθrɪtɪk] ADJ, N arthritique *mf*

arthritis [ɑːˈθraɪtɪs] N arthrite *f* → **rheumatoid**

arthropod [ˈɑːθrəpɒd] N arthropode *m*

Arthurian [ɑːˈθjʊərɪən] ADJ du roi Arthur, d'Arthur ; **~ legend** *or* **legends** la légende du roi Arthur, le cycle d'Arthur

artic* [ɑːˈtɪk] N (*Brit Aut*) (ABBR = **articulated lorry**) → **articulate**

artichoke [ˈɑːtɪtʃəʊk] N artichaut *m* → **globe, Jerusalem**

article [ˈɑːtɪkl] 1 N a (= *object*) objet *m* ; (*Comm*) article *m*, marchandise *f* ; **~ of clothing** pièce *f* d'habillement ; **~s of clothing** vêtements *mpl* ; **~ of food** produit *m* *or* denrée *f* alimentaire ; **~s of value** objets *mpl* de valeur b (*Press*) article *m* → **leading** c (*Jur etc*) [*of treaty, document*] article *m* ; **~s of apprenticeship** contrat *m* d'apprentissage ; **~ of faith** arti-

cle *m* de foi ; (*Rel*) **the Thirty-Nine Articles** *les trente-neuf articles de foi de l'Église anglicane* ; (*US Mil*) **~s of war** code *m* de justice militaire d (*Gram*) article *m* → **definite, indefinite** 2 VT a (= *apprentice*) (+ *trade*) mettre en apprentissage (**to** chez) ; (+ *profession*) mettre en stage (**to** chez, auprès de) b (*Jur*) stipuler 3 COMP ► **articled clerk** N (*Brit*) avocat(e) *m(f)* stagiaire

articulate [ɑːˈtɪkjʊlɪt] 1 ADJ a [*speech*] net, distinct ; [*thought*] clair, net ; [*person*] qui s'exprime bien, qui sait s'exprimer b (*Anat, Bot*) articulé 2 [ɑːˈtɪkjʊleɪt] VT a (+ *word, sentence*) articuler ; (*fig*) (+ *plan, goal*) exprimer clairement b (*Anat, Bot*) articuler 3 VI articuler 4 COMP ► **articulated lorry** N (*Brit*) semi-remorque *m*

articulately [ɑːˈtɪkjʊlɪtlɪ] ADV (= *fluently*) avec aisance ; (= *clearly*) clairement

articulation [ɑːˌtɪkjʊˈleɪʃən] N (*also Ling*) articulation *f*

articulatory phonetics [ɑːˌtɪkjʊˈleɪtərɪfəʊˈnetɪks] N (*NonC*) phonétique *f* articulatoire

artifact [ˈɑːtɪfækt] N = **artefact**

artifice [ˈɑːtɪfɪs] N a (= *stratagem*) artifice *m*, ruse *f* b (*NonC* = *cunning*) adresse *f*, art *m* c (*NonC*.† = *artificiality*) stratagème *m*

artificial [ˌɑːtɪˈfɪʃəl] 1 ADJ a (= *synthetic*) [*light, flowers*] artificiel ; [*leather, jewel*] synthétique, artificiel ; **~ climbing** escalade *f* artificielle ; **~ hair** cheveux *mpl* postiches ; **~ arm/leg** bras *m*/jambe *f* artificiel(le) ; **~ limb** prothèse *f*, membre *m* artificiel ; **~ manure** engrais *mpl* chimiques ; **~ silk** rayonne *f*, soie *f* artificielle ; **~ teeth** fausses dents *fpl*, prothèse *f* dentaire b (= *affected*) [*manner*] artificiel, affecté ; [*tears*] feint, factice ; [*smile*] forcé ; [*person*] affecté ; **it was a very ~ situation** la situation manquait de spontanéité *or* de naturel 2 COMP ► **artificial horizon** N horizon *m* artificiel ► **artificial insemination (by donor)** N insémination *f* artificielle (par un donneur) ► **artificial intelligence** N intelligence *f* artificielle ► **artificial respiration** N respiration *f* artificielle

artificiality [ˌɑːtɪfɪʃɪˈælɪtɪ] N manque *m* de naturel

artificially [ˌɑːtɪˈfɪʃəlɪ] ADV artificiellement

artillery [ɑːˈtɪlərɪ] N artillerie *f*

artilleryman [ɑːˈtɪlərɪmən] N (*pl* **-men**) artilleur *m*

artisan [ˈɑːtɪzæn] N artisan *m* ; (*collectively*) **the ~s** l'artisanat *m*

artisanal [ˈɑːtɪzənəl] ADJ artisanal

artist [ˈɑːtɪst] N a (*Art etc, also fig*) artiste *mf* → **con, piss, rip-off** b = **artiste**

artiste [ɑːˈtiːst] N (*esp Brit Cine, Theat, TV*) artiste *mf* → **variety**

artistic [ɑːˈtɪstɪk] 1 ADJ [*talent, design, heritage, freedom*] artistique ; [*person*] qui a un sens artistique 2 COMP ► **artistic director** N (*Theat*) directeur *m*, -trice *f* artistique

artistically [ɑːˈtɪstɪkəlɪ] ADV a (*Art, Mus, Theat etc*) [*gifted, successful*] du point de vue artistique b (= *attractively*) [*arranged, presented*] avec art

artistry [ˈɑːtɪstrɪ] N (*NonC*) art *m*, talent *m* artistique

artless [ˈɑːtlɪs] ADJ a (= *straightforward*) [*person, beauty*] naturel ; [*behaviour, comment, simplicity*] ingénu b (*pej* = *without art, skill*) [*object*] grossier ; [*translation*] lourd

artlessly [ˈɑːtlɪslɪ] ADV ingénument

artlessness [ˈɑːtlɪsnɪs] N (*NonC*) a (= *straightforwardness*) [*of person, beauty*] naturel *m* ; [*of behaviour, comment, simplicity*] ingénuité *f* b (*pej* = *lack of art, skill*) [*object*] grossièreté *f* ; [*translation*] lourdeur *f*

artsy* [ˈɑːtsɪ] ADJ (*US*) = **arty**

artsy-craftsy* [ˈɑːtsɪˈkrɑːftsɪ] ADJ (*US*) = **arty-crafty**

artsy-fartsy* [ˈɑːtsɪˈfɑːtsɪ] ADJ (*US*) = **arty-farty**

artwork [ˈɑːtwɜːk] N (*Publishing*) iconographie *f* ; (= *painting, sculpture*) œuvre *f* d'art ; (*US* = *objects*) objets *mpl* d'art

arty* [ˈɑːtɪ], **artsy*** (*US*) ADJ [*person*] qui se donne le genre artiste *or* bohème ; [*clothes*] de style faussement artiste

arty-crafty* [ˈɑːtɪˈkrɑːftɪ], **artsy-craftsy*** (*US*) ADJ (*pej*) [*object, style*] (exagérément) artisanal ; [*person*] qui affiche un genre artiste *or* bohème

arty-farty* [ˈɑːtɪˈfɑːtɪ], **artsy-farty*** (*US*) ADJ (*pej*) [*person*] poseur ; [*book, film*] prétentieux ; **an ~ man/woman** un poseur/une poseuse

ARV [ˌeɪɑːˈviː] N (*US Bible*) (ABBR = **American Revised Version**) *traduction américaine de la Bible*

arvee* [ɑːˈviː] N (*US*) (ABBR = **recreational vehicle**) → **recreational**

Aryan [ˈɛərɪən] 1 N Aryen(ne) *m(f)* 2 ADJ aryen

AS [eɪˈes] a ABBR = **American Samoa** b (*US*) (ABBR = **Associate in Sciences**) ≈ titulaire d'un DEUG de sciences

---

as [æz, əz]

1 CONJUNCTION	3 ADVERB
2 PREPOSITION	

For set combinations in which as *is not the first word, eg* such ... as, the same ... as, dressed/ disguised as, acknowledge as, *look up the other word.*

1 CONJUNCTION

a = *while* alors que ; **as she was falling asleep she heard a noise** elle entendit un bruit alors qu'elle commençait à s'endormir ; **he saw the accident as he was going to school** il a vu l'accident en allant à l'école ; **another policeman has been killed as fighting continued this morning** un autre policier a été tué tandis que *or* alors que les combats continuaient ce matin ; **all the jury's eyes were upon him as he continued** les jurés ne le quittaient pas des yeux tandis qu'il *or* alors qu'il continuait à parler

b with comparative **things will get more difficult as the year goes on** ça va devenir de plus en plus difficile au fur et à mesure que la fin de l'année approche ; **he grew deafer as he got older** il devenait de plus en plus sourd en vieillissant

c = *just when* (juste) au moment où, alors que ; **he came in as I was leaving** il est arrivé (juste) au moment où je partais *or* alors que je partais

d = *because* étant donné que, comme ; **as he hasn't phoned, we don't know where he is** comme il *or* étant donné qu'il n'a pas téléphoné, nous ne savons pas où il est ; **patient as she is, she'll probably put up with it** patiente comme elle est, elle arrivera probablement à le supporter

parce que *or* car *can also be used, but not at the beginning of the sentence.*

this is important as it reduces the effectiveness of the drug c'est important parce que *or* car cela diminue l'efficacité du médicament

e = *though* **long as it was, I didn't find the journey boring** bien que le trajet ait été long, je ne me suis pas ennuyé ; **unlikely/amazing as it may seem** aussi improbable/surprenant que cela paraisse ; **hard as it is to believe, ...** aussi incroyable que cela puisse paraître, ... ; **(as) important as the president is ...** pour *or* si important que soit le président ...

f indicating manner comme ; **do as you like** faites comme vous voulez ; **France, as you know, is ...** la France, comme vous le savez, est ... ; **as (is) usual** comme d'habitude, comme à l'ordinaire ; **as often happens** comme c'est souvent le cas ; **she is very gifted, as is her**

brother elle est très douée, comme son frère ; **they are fine as they are** ils sont très bien comme ça ; **I'm okay as I am** je me trouve très bien comme ça ; **knowing him as I do, I am sure he'll refuse** le connaissant comme je le connais, je suis sûr qu'il refusera ; **don't tidy up, leave it as it is** ne range rien, laisse ça comme ça ; BUT **A is to B as C is to D ◊ as A is to B so C is to D** C est à D ce que A est à B ; **the village, situated as it is near a motorway, ...** le village, étant situé non loin d'une autoroute, ...

2 PREPOSITION

a = **in the capacity of** comme ; **he works as a waiter** il travaille comme serveur ; BUT **Olivier as Hamlet** (Theat) Olivier dans le rôle de Hamlet

b = **being** en tant que ; **Napoleon, as a statesman, was ...** Napoléon, en tant qu'homme d'État, était ... ; **as a mother of five children, she is well aware ...** en tant que mère de cinq enfants, elle sait très bien ...

c = **when** **as a child, she was rather shy** (lorsqu'elle or quand elle était) enfant, elle était plutôt timide ; **as a young woman, she was very interested in politics** lorsqu'elle or quand elle était jeune, elle s'intéressait beaucoup à la politique

3 ADVERB

a = **in the way** comme ; **you'll have it by noon as agreed** vous l'aurez pour midi comme convenu ; **he came as agreed** il est venu comme convenu or prévu ; **as in all good detective stories** comme dans tout bon roman policier ; **"m" as in mother** « m » comme mère

b SET STRUCTURES

♦ **as .... as** (in comparisons of equality) aussi ... que ; **I am as tall as you** je suis aussi grand que toi ; **is it as far as that?** c'est vraiment aussi loin que ça ?

♦ **as much as** autant que ; **you ate as much as me*** or **as I did** tu as mangé autant que moi ; **you spend as much as me*** or **as I do** tu dépenses autant que moi

♦ **twice/half** etc **as ...** : **she's twice as nice as her sister** elle est deux fois plus gentille que sa sœur ; **it's half as expensive** ça coûte deux fois moins cher ; **it's twice/three times as expensive** ça coûte deux fois/trois fois plus cher

♦ **not as** or **not so ... as** pas aussi ... que ; **I am not so** or **not as ambitious as you** je ne suis pas aussi ambitieux que toi ; **it's not so** or **not as bad as all that** ce n'est pas si terrible que ça

♦ **as for** (when changing subject) quant à ; **as for her mother ...** quant à sa mère ... ; (= regarding) **as for that ...** pour ce qui est de ça ..., quant à cela ...

♦ **as from** (referring to past) depuis ; (referring to present, future) à partir de ; **as from last Tuesday** depuis mardi dernier ; **as from today/next Tuesday** à partir d'aujourd'hui or mardi prochain

♦ **as if ◊ as though** comme si ; **he was staggering as if** or **as though he'd been drinking** il titubait comme s'il avait bu ; **it was as if** or **as though he was still alive** c'était comme s'il était toujours vivant ; **it's not as if** or **as though he was nice-looking** ce n'est pas comme s'il était beau garçon

♦ **as if to** comme pour ; **as if to confirm his prediction there was a loud explosion** comme pour confirmer ses prédictions on entendit une forte explosion

♦ **as it is** (= in fact) dans l'état actuel des choses ; (= already) comme ça ; **as it is, it doesn't make much difference** dans l'état actuel des choses, ça ne fait pas grande différence ; **I've got quite enough to do as it is** j'ai bien assez à faire comme ça

♦ **as it were** pour ainsi dire, en quelque sorte ; **I have become, as it were, two people** je suis devenu, pour ainsi dire or en quelque sorte, non pas une, mais deux personnes

♦ **as of** (from past time) depuis ; (from present, future time) à partir de ; (= up to) jusqu'à ; **as of last Tuesday** depuis mardi dernier ; **as of**

today/next Tuesday à partir d'aujourd'hui/de mardi prochain ; **as of yesterday, the city has recorded 751 homicides this year** jusqu'à hier, la ville avait enregistré 751 meurtres cette année ; (= on) **the balance of your account as of 16 June** le solde de votre compte au 16 juin

♦ **as of now** pour l'instant ; **as of now, I have no definite plans** pour l'instant, je ne sais pas encore ce que je vais faire

♦ **as regards** → regard

♦ **as such** (= in itself) en soi ; (= in that capacity) en tant que tel or telle, à ce titre ; **the work as such is boring but the pay is good** le travail en soi est ennuyeux mais le salaire est correct ; **they are the best players in the world and, as such, are highly paid** ce sont les meilleurs joueurs du monde et, en tant que tels or à ce titre, ils touchent un salaire très élevé ; **he was still a novice and they treated him as such** ce n'était qu'un débutant et ils le traitaient comme tel

♦ **not/no ... as such** pas à proprement parler, pas vraiment ; **I'm not a beginner as such** je ne suis pas à proprement parler un débutant, je ne suis pas vraiment débutant ; **he had no qualifications as such** il n'avait à proprement parler aucune qualification

♦ **as to** (when changing subject) quant à ; **as to her mother ...** quant à sa mère ... ; (= regarding that) **as to that** pour ce qui est de ça, quant à cela ; (= about) **to question sb as to his intentions** interroger qn sur ses intentions ; **they should make decisions as to whether students need help** il faudrait qu'ils décident si les étudiants ont besoin d'aide (ou non) ; **he inquired as to what the problem was** il demanda ce qui n'allait pas

♦ **as yet** → yet

♦ **as you were*** (to correct oneself) non, je me trompe ; **it was in 1990 he won the trophy, as you were, 1992** c'est en 1990 qu'il a remporté la coupe, non, je me trompe, en 1992 ; (Mil) **as you were!** repos !

ASA [ˌeɪes'eɪ] a (Brit) (ABBR = **Advertising Standards Authority**) → advertising b (Brit) (ABBR = **Amateur Swimming Association**) fédération de natation c (ABBR = **American Standards Association**) **100/200 ~** 100/200 ASA

ASA/BS [ˌeɪeseɪbi'es] ABBR = **American Standards Association/British Standard**

a.s.a.p.* [ˌeɪeseɪ'piː] (ABBR = **as soon as possible**) aussitôt que possible

asbestos [æz'bestəs] 1 N amiante f, asbeste m 2 COMP ► **asbestos mat** N plaque f d'amiante

asbestosis [ˌæzbes'təʊsɪs] N asbestose f

ascend [ə'send] 1 VI monter, s'élever (**to** à, jusqu'à) ; (in time) remonter (**to** à) ; **in ~ing order** en ordre croissant 2 VT [+ ladder] monter à ; [+ mountain] gravir, faire l'ascension de ; [+ river] remonter ; [+ staircase] monter ; **to ~ the throne** monter sur le trône 3 COMP ► **ascending scale** N (Mus) gamme f ascendante or montante

ascendancy [ə'sendənsɪ] N (= influence) ascendant m, empire m (**over** sur) ; (= rise to power etc) montée f, ascension f

ascendant [ə'sendənt] 1 N (Astrol, fig) ascendant m ; (Astrol) **to be in the ~** être à l'ascendant ; (fig) **his fortunes are in the ~** tout lui sourit 2 ADJ (gen) dominant ; (Astrol) ascendant

ascension [ə'senʃən] 1 N ascension f ; (Rel) **the Ascension** l'Ascension f 2 COMP ► **Ascension Day** N l'Ascension f ► **Ascension Island** N l'île f de l'Ascension

ascensionist [ə'senʃənɪst] N ascensionniste mf

ascent [ə'sent] N [of mountain etc] ascension f ; (fig: in time) retour m ; (in rank) montée f, avancement m

ascertain [ˌæsə'teɪn] VT (gen) établir ; [+ person's age, name, address etc] vérifier ; **to ~ that sth is true** s'assurer or vérifier que qch est vrai

ascertainable [ˌæsə'teɪnəbl] ADJ vérifiable

ascertainment [ˌæsə'teɪnmənt] N constatation f, vérification f

ascetic [ə'setɪk] 1 ADJ ascétique 2 N ascète mf

asceticism [ə'setɪsɪzəm] N ascétisme m

ASCII [ˌæskiː] 1 N (ABBR = **American Standard Code for Information Interchange**) ASCII m 2 COMP ► **ASCII file** N fichier m ASCII

ascorbic acid [ə'skɔːbɪkˌæsɪd] N acide m ascorbique

ascribable [ə'skraɪbəbl] ADJ → ascribe ; attribuable, imputable (**to** à)

ascribe [ə'skraɪb] VT [+ virtue, piece of work] attribuer (**to** à) ; [+ fault, blame] imputer (**to** à)

ascription [ə'skrɪpʃən] N [of book, painting, characteristic] attribution f (**to sb/sth** à qn/qch) ; [of blame] imputation f (**to sb/sth** à qn/qch)

asdic [ˈæzdɪk] N (Brit Mil) asdic m

ASEAN [ˌeɪesiː'en] (ABBR = **Association of South-East Asian Nations**) ASEAN f

asemantic [eɪsɪ'mæntɪk] ADJ asémantique

aseptic [eɪ'septɪk] ADJ aseptique ; (Space) **~ tank** cuve f W.-C.

asexual [eɪ'seksjʊəl] ADJ a (= sexless) [person etc] asexué b (Zool) asexué ; **~ reproduction** reproduction f asexuée

asexually [eɪ'seksjʊəlɪ] ADV [reproduce] par multiplication asexuée

ASH [æʃ] (Brit) (ABBR = **Action on Smoking and Health**) comité m contre le tabagisme

ash[1] [æʃ] N (Bot: also **~ tree**) frêne m → mountain

ash[2] [æʃ] 1 N [of fire, coal, cigarette] cendre f ; (of the dead) **~es** cendres fpl ; **to reduce sth to ~es** mettre or réduire qch en cendres ; (Rel) **~es to ~es, dust to dust** tu es poussière et tu retourneras en poussière ; (Cricket) **the Ashes** trophée des matchs Australie-Angleterre → sackcloth 2 COMP ► **ash-bin** N (for ashes) cendrier m (de poêle etc) ; (for rubbish) poubelle f, boîte f à ordures ► **ash blond(e)** ADJ blond(e) cendré inv ► **ash-coloured** ADJ gris cendré inv ► **ash pan** N cendrier m (de poêle etc) ► **Ash Wednesday** N (Rel) mercredi m des Cendres

ashamed [ə'ʃeɪmd] ADJ honteux ; **to be** or **feel ~ ◊ to be ~ of o.s.** avoir honte ; **to be ~ of sb/ sth** avoir honte de qn/qch ; **it's nothing to be ~ of** il n'y a aucune raison d'en avoir honte ; **I am ~ of her** elle me fait honte, j'ai honte d'elle ; **you ought to** or **should be ~ (of yourself)!** vous devriez avoir honte ! ; **to be ~ of o.s. for doing sth** avoir honte d'avoir fait qch ; **to be ~ about sth** avoir honte de qch ; **to be ~ to do sth** avoir honte de faire qch ; **I'm too ~ to tell anyone** j'ai trop honte pour le dire à quiconque ; **I've done nothing, I'm ~ to say** à ma honte je dois dire que je n'ai rien fait, c'est honteux à dire, mais je n'ai rien fait ; **she was ~ that she had been so nasty** elle avait honte d'avoir été aussi méchante

ashcan [ˈæʃkæn] N (US) poubelle f

ashen [ˈæʃn] ADJ a (liter) (= pale) [face] terreux, livide ; (= greyish) cendré, couleur de cendre b (= of ashwood) en (bois de) frêne

Ashkenazi [ˌæʃkə'nɑːzɪ] 1 ADJ ashkénaze 2 N ashkénaze mf

Ashkenazic [ˌæʃkə'nɑːzɪk] ADJ ashkénaze

ashlar [ˈæʃlər] N pierre f de taille (équarrie)

ashman [ˈæʃmən] N (pl **-men**) (US) éboueur m

ashore [ə'ʃɔːr] ADV (= on land) à terre ; (= to the shore) vers la rive, vers le rivage ; **to go ~** débarquer, descendre à terre ; **to set** or **put sb ~** débarquer qn ; (Naut) **to run ~** s'échouer, se jeter à la côte ; **to swim ~** rejoindre la rive à la nage

ashram ['æ∫rəm] N ashram m

ashtray ['æ∫treɪ] N cendrier m

ashy ['æ∫ɪ] ADJ [a] (= ash-coloured) cendré, couleur de cendre ; (= pale) terreux, livide [b] (= covered with ashes) couvert de cendres

Asia ['eɪ∫ə] [1] N Asie f [2] COMP ► **Asia Minor** N Asie f Mineure

Asian ['eɪ∫n] [1] ADJ [a] (= from Asia) asiatique ; (Med) **~ flu** grippe f asiatique [b] (Brit = from Indian subcontinent) originaire du sous-continent indien, indo-pakistanais [2] N [a] (= person from Asia) Asiatique mf [b] (Brit = person from Indian subcontinent) personne originaire du sous-continent indien, Indo-Pakistanais(e) m(f) [3] COMP ► **Asian-American** ADJ américain d'origine asiatique ◆ N Américain(e) m(f) d'origine asiatique

Asiatic [ˌeɪsɪ'ætɪk] [1] ADJ = **Asian 1** [2] N (offensive usage) = **Asian 2**

aside [ə'saɪd]

> When **aside** is an element in a phrasal verb, eg brush aside, cast aside, put aside, stand aside, look up the verb.

[1] ADV de côté, à l'écart, à part ; **joking ~** plaisanterie or blague* à part ; (esp US) **~ from** à part [2] N (esp Theat) aparté m ; **to say sth in an ~** dire qch en aparté

asinine ['æsɪnaɪn] ADJ (frm) sot, idiot

▼ **ask** [ɑːsk] [1] VT [a] (= inquire) demander ; **to ~ sb sth** demander qch à qn ; **to ~ sb about sth** interroger qn or questionner qn or poser des questions à qn au sujet de qch ; **to ~ (sb) a question** poser une question (à qn) ; **I don't know, ~ your father** je ne sais pas, demande(-le) à ton père ; **~ him if he has seen her** demande-lui s'il l'a vue ; **~ed whether this was true, he replied ...** quand on lui a demandé si c'était vrai, il a répondu ... ; **don't ~ me!*** allez savoir !*, une fois je sais (moi) !* ; (in exasperation) **I ~ you!** je vous demande un peu !* ; **I'm not ~ing you!** (= keep quiet) je ne te demande rien (à toi) !*

[b] (= request) demander, solliciter ; (Comm) [+ price] demander ; **to ~ sb to do sth** demander à qn de faire qch, prier qn de faire qch ; **to ~ that sth (should) be done** demander que qch soit fait ; **to ~ sb for sth** demander qch à qn ; **he ~ed to go on the picnic** il a demandé à se joindre or s'il pouvait se joindre au pique-nique ; **I don't ~ much from you** je ne t'en demande pas beaucoup ; **it's not much to ~!** ce n'est pas trop demander !, ce n'est pas grand-chose ! ; **that's ~ing a lot/too much!** c'est beaucoup/trop (en) demander ! ; **that's ~ing the impossible** c'est demander l'impossible ; (Comm) **how much are they ~ing for it?** ils en demandent or veulent combien ? ; (Comm) **he is ~ing £80,000 for the house** il demande 80 000 livres or veut 80 000 livres pour la maison

[c] (= invite) inviter ; **to ~ sb to (come to) the theatre** inviter qn (à aller) au théâtre ; **to ~ sb to lunch** inviter qn à déjeuner ; **I was ~ed into the drawing room** on m'a prié d'entrer au salon ; **how about ~ing Sabine?** et si on invitait Sabine ?, et si on demandait à Sabine de venir ? ; **to ~ sb in/out/up** etc demander à qn or prier qn d'entrer/de sortir/de monter etc

[2] VI demander ; **to ~ about sth** s'informer de qch, se renseigner sur qch ; (= make enquiries) **to ~ around** demander autour de soi ; **it's there for the ~ing** il suffit de le demander (pour l'obtenir), on l'a comme on veut ; **now you're ~ing!** est-ce que je sais (moi) !*

[3] N (US) **that's a big ~*** c'est beaucoup demander

[4] COMP ► **asking price** N (Comm) prix m de départ, prix m demandé au départ

► **ask after** VT FUS [+ person] demander des nouvelles de ; **to ~ after sb's health** s'informer de la santé de qn

► **ask along** VT SEP **they didn't ~ me along** ils ne m'ont pas demandé de les accompagner

► **ask back** VT SEP [a] (on a second visit) réinviter [b] (on a reciprocal visit) **to ~ sb back** rendre son invitation à qn [c] (to one's home) **to ~ sb back for coffee** inviter qn à prendre le café

► **ask for** VT FUS [+ help, permission, money] demander ; [+ person] demander à voir ; **he ~ed for his pen back** il a demandé (qu'on lui rende) son stylo ; **they are ~ing for trouble*** ils cherchent les ennuis or les embêtements* ; **she was ~ing for it!*** (= deserved it) elle l'a bien cherché !*, elle ne l'a pas volé !* → **moon**

► **ask in** VT SEP inviter à entrer ; **to ~ sb in for a drink** inviter qn à (entrer) prendre un verre

► **ask out** VT SEP inviter à sortir ; **he ~ed her out to dinner/to see a film** il l'a invitée (à dîner) au restaurant/au cinéma

► **ask over** VT SEP inviter à (la maison) ; **let's ~ Paul over** si on invitait Paul à venir nous voir ?

► **ask round** VT SEP inviter (à la maison)

askance [ə'skɑːns] ADV **to look ~ at** (= sideways) regarder de côté ; (= suspiciously/disapprovingly) regarder d'un air soupçonneux/d'un œil désapprobateur ; **to look ~ at a suggestion** se formaliser d'une suggestion

askew [ə'skjuː] ADJ, ADV de travers, de guingois* ; (US fig) **something is ~** il y a quelque chose qui ne tourne pas rond*

aslant [ə'slɑːnt] [1] ADV de travers [2] PREP en travers de

asleep [ə'sliːp] ADJ [a] (= sleeping) endormi ; **to be ~** dormir, être endormi ; **to be fast** or **sound ~** dormir profondément or d'un sommeil profond or à poings fermés ; **to fall ~** s'endormir [b] (= numb) [finger etc] engourdi

ASLEF, Aslef ['æzlef] N (Brit) (ABBR = **Associated Society of Locomotive Engineers and Firemen**) syndicat

ASM [ˌeɪes'em] N (Theat) (ABBR = **assistant stage manager**) régisseur m adjoint

asocial [eɪ'səʊ∫əl] ADJ asocial

asp¹ [æsp] N (Zool) aspic m

asp² [æsp] N (Bot) = **aspen**

asparagus [ə'spærəgəs] [1] N (NonC) asperges fpl [2] COMP ► **asparagus fern** N asparagus m ► **asparagus spears** NPL asperges fpl ► **asparagus tips** NPL pointes fpl d'asperges

aspartame [ə'spɑːteɪm] N aspartam(e) m

ASPCA [ˌeɪespiːsiː'eɪ] N (ABBR = **American Society for the Prevention of Cruelty to Animals**) SPA américaine

aspect ['æspekt] N [a] (= facet, element) [of question, subject etc] aspect m, angle m ; **to study every ~ of a question** étudier une question sous toutes ses faces or tous ses aspects ; **seen from this ~ ...** vu sous cet angle ... [b] (liter = appearance) air m, mine f ; **of fierce ~** à la mine or à l'aspect féroce [c] (= face) [of building etc] exposition f, orientation f ; **the house has a southerly ~** la maison est exposée or orientée au midi [d] (Gram) aspect m

aspen ['æspən] N (Bot) tremble m ; **to shake** or **tremble like an ~** trembler comme une feuille

asperity [æs'perɪtɪ] N [a] (NonC) [of manner, style, voice] aspérité f ; [of person] rudesse f [b] (gen pl) [of climate, weather] rigueur(s) f(pl)

aspersion [ə'spɜː∫ən] N (untruthful) calomnie f ; (truthful) médisance f → **cast**

asphalt ['æsfælt] [1] N asphalte m [2] VT asphalter [3] COMP [road] asphalté ► **asphalt jungle** N jungle f des rues

asphyxia [æs'fɪksɪə] N asphyxie f

asphyxiate [æs'fɪksɪeɪt] [1] VT asphyxier [2] VI s'asphyxier

asphyxiation [æsˌfɪksɪ'eɪ∫ən] N asphyxie f

aspic ['æspɪk] N (Culin) gelée f (pour hors d'œuvre) ; **chicken in ~** aspic m de volaille

aspidistra [ˌæspɪ'dɪstrə] N aspidistra m

aspirant ['æspɪrənt] [1] N aspirant(e) m(f), candidat(e) m(f) (**to, after** à) [2] ADJ [artist, poet, writer] en herbe

aspirate ['æspərɪt] [1] N aspirée f [2] ADJ aspiré ; **~ h** h aspiré [3] ['æspəreɪt] VT aspirer

aspiration [ˌæspə'reɪ∫ən] N (also Ling) aspiration f

aspirational [ˌæspə'reɪ∫nl] ADJ [person] ambitieux ; [product] qui fait chic

aspirator ['æspəreɪtə] N aspirateur m

aspire [ə'paɪə] VI **to ~ after** or **to sth** aspirer or viser à qch, ambitionner qch ; **to ~ to do** aspirer à faire ; **to ~ to fame** briguer la célébrité ; **to ~ to a second car** ambitionner (d'avoir) une deuxième voiture ; **we can't ~ to that** nos prétentions ne vont pas jusque-là

aspirin ['æsprɪn] N (pl **aspirin** or **aspirins**) (= substance) aspirine f ; (= tablet) (comprimé m d')aspirine

aspiring [ə'spaɪərɪŋ] ADJ [artist, poet, writer] en herbe ; [manager, officer] potentiel

ass¹ [æs] N [a] âne m ; **she-~** ânesse f ; **~'s foal** ânon m [b] († pej) idiot(e) m(f), imbécile mf ; **he is a perfect ~** il est bête comme ses pieds* ; **to make an ~ of o.s.** se rendre ridicule, se conduire comme un idiot or imbécile ; **don't be an ~!** (action) ne fais pas l'imbécile ! ; (speech) ne dis pas de sottises !

ass² [æs] (US) [1] N cul‡ m ; **to chew sb's ~** engueuler qn‡ ; **to kiss sb's ~** lécher le cul à qn‡ ; **kiss my ~!** va te faire foutre !‡ ; **to work one's ~ off** bosser comme un dingue*, se casser le cul‡ ; **my ~!** mon cul !‡ ; **stick it** or **shove it up your ~!** tu peux te le foutre au cul !‡ ; **to have one's ~ in a sling** être dans la merde‡ ; **to get one's ~ in gear** se remuer le cul‡ ; **a piece of ~** (= sex) une baise‡ ; (= girl) une fille bonne à baiser‡ → **bust** [2] COMP ► **ass-backward‡** ADJ (= reversed) cul par-dessus tête* ; (= confused) bordélique‡ ◆ ADV (= in reverse) cul par-dessus tête* ; (= in confused manner) de façon bordélique‡ ► **ass kisser‡** N lèche-cul‡ mf inv ► **ass-wipe‡** N papier m cul‡

assail [ə'seɪl] VT (lit) attaquer, assaillir ; (fig: with questions, doubts etc) assaillir (**with** de)

assailant [ə'seɪlənt] N agresseur m, assaillant(e) m(f)

Assam [æ'sæm] N Assam m

assassin [ə'sæsɪn] N (Pol) assassin m

assassinate [ə'sæsɪneɪt] VT (Pol) assassiner

assassination [əˌsæsɪ'neɪ∫ən] N (Pol) assassinat m

assault [ə'sɔːlt] [1] N [a] (Mil, Climbing) assaut m (**on** de) ; **taken by ~** emporté or pris d'assaut ; **to make an ~ on ...** donner l'assaut à ..., aller or monter à l'assaut de ... [b] (Jur) agression f ; **~ and battery** coups mpl et blessures fpl, voies fpl de fait ; **the ~ on the old lady** l'agression dont a été victime la vieille dame ; (fig) **~ on sb's good name** atteinte f à la réputation de qn → **aggravate, common, indecent** [2] VT agresser ; (Jur = attack) se livrer à des voies de fait sur ; (= attack sexually) se livrer à des violences sexuelles sur, violenter ; (fig) **to ~ sb's sensibilities** blesser la sensibilité de qn [3] COMP ► **assault course** N (Mil) parcours m du combattant ► **assault rifle** N fusil m d'assaut

assay [ə'seɪ] [1] N essai m (d'un métal précieux etc) [2] VT [a] [+ mineral, ore] essayer [b] († = try) essayer, tenter (**to do** de faire) [3] COMP **~ office** N (US) laboratoire m d'essais (d'un hôtel des monnaies)

assemblage [ə'semblɪdʒ] N [a] (Tech = putting together) assemblage m, montage m [b] (= collection) [of things] collection f, ensemble m ; [of people] assemblée f

---

▶ **LANGUAGE IN USE:**   **ask** 4, 9.1, 26.1

assemble [ə'sembl] **1** VT [+ *objects, ideas*] assembler; [+ *people*] rassembler, réunir; (*Tech*) [+ *device, machine*] monter, assembler **2** VI se réunir, se rassembler

assembler [ə'semblə'] N (*Comput*) assembleur *m*

assembly [ə'semblɪ] **1** N **a** (= *meeting*) assemblée *f*, réunion *f*; (*Scol*) réunion de tous les élèves de l'établissement pour la prière, les annoncés etc; **in open ~** en séance publique → **unlawful b** (*Tech* = *assembling of framework, machine*) assemblage *m*, montage *m*; (= *whole unit*) assemblage *m*; **the engine ~** le bloc moteur → **tail c** (*Mil* = *call*) rassemblement *m* (*sonnerie*) **d** (*Pol*) assemblée *f* **e** (*Comput*) assemblage *m* **2** COMP ► **assembly hall** N (*for public meetings, stage shows*) salle *f* des fêtes; (*in school*) salle *f* de réunion ► **assembly language** N (*Comput*) langage *m* d'assemblage ► **assembly line** N chaîne *f* de montage ► **assembly point** N lieu *m* or point *m* de rassemblement ► **assembly room(s)** N(PL) salle *f* de réunion; [*of town hall*] salle *f* des fêtes ► **assembly shop** N atelier *m* de montage

assemblyman [ə'semblɪmən] N (*pl* **-men**) (*US*) membre *m* d'une assemblée législative

assemblywoman [ə'semblɪwʊmən] N (*pl* **-women**) (*US*) membre *m* d'une assemblée législative

assent [ə'sent] **1** N assentiment *m*, consentement *m*; **with one ~** (*two people*) d'un commun accord; (*more than two people*) à l'unanimité → **nod, royal 2** VI consentir, donner son assentiment (**to** à)

assert [ə'sɜːt] VT **a** (= *declare*) affirmer, soutenir; [+ *one's innocence*] protester de **b** (= *maintain*) [+ *claim*] défendre; [+ *one's due*] revendiquer; [+ *one's authority*] faire respecter; **to ~ o.s.** or **one's rights** faire valoir ses droits

assertion [ə'sɜːʃən] N **a** (= *statement*) affirmation *f*, assertion *f* → **self b** [*of one's rights*] revendication *f*

assertive [ə'sɜːtɪv] ADJ [*tone, voice*] assuré; [*personality*] affirmé; **~ behaviour** or **manner** assurance *f*; **~ to be ~** [*person*] avoir de l'assurance, avoir confiance en soi; **to become more ~** [*person*] prendre de l'assurance, s'affirmer

assertively [ə'sɜːtɪvlɪ] ADV avec assurance

assertiveness [ə'sɜːtɪvnɪs] **1** N assurance *f*, confiance *f* en soi **2** COMP ► **assertiveness training** N (*NonC*) stages *mpl* d'affirmation de la personnalité; **~ training course** stage *m* d'affirmation de la personnalité

assess [ə'ses] **1** VT **a** (= *estimate*) estimer, évaluer [+ *payment*] fixer or déterminer le montant de; [+ *income tax*] établir; [+ *rateable property*] calculer la valeur imposable de; [+ *damages*] fixer → **basis c** (*fig* = *evaluate*) [+ *situation*] estimer; [+ *time, amount*] estimer, évaluer; [+ *candidate*] juger (la valeur de) **2** COMP ► **assessed income** N revenu *m* imposable

assessable [ə'sesəbl] ADJ imposable; (*Fin*) **~ income** (or **profits** etc) assiette *f* de l'impôt

assessment [ə'sesmənt] **1** N **a** (= *evaluation*) [*of situation, effect, risk*] évaluation *f*; [*of prospects, chances, needs*] estimation *f*; [*of damage*] évaluation *f*, estimation *f*; **he gave his ~ of the situation** il a dit comment il voyait or jugeait la situation or ce qu'il pensait de la situation **b** (*esp Educ, Ind* = *appraisal*) [*of person*] évaluation *f*; (*on pupil's report*) appréciation *f* des professeurs; **I should be interested to hear your ~ of him** ça m'intéresserait de savoir ce que vous pensez de lui → **continuous, self c** (*Med, Psych, Sociol*) [*of patient, case*] examen *m*; **neurological ~** diagnostic *m* neurologique **d** (= *critique*) [*of book, film, play*] jugement *m*;

[*of plan, policy, idea*] opinion *f* **e** (*Fin, Tax, Jur*) [*of finances*] estimation *f*; [*of rateable property*] calcul *m* (de la valeur imposable); [*of damages*] fixation *f*; **appeals against ~s made by the taxman** opposition *f* aux estimations du fisc; **income ~** évaluation *f* du revenu; **tax ~** calcul *m* de l'impôt **2** COMP ► **assessment centre** N (*Ind*) centre *m* d'évaluation (*des demandeurs d'emploi*) ► **assessment method** N (*gen*) méthode *f* d'évaluation; (*Educ*) **the ~ method** le contrôle des connaissances; (*Univ*) le contrôle continu ► **assessment procedure** N (*Educ, Ind*) procédure *f* d'évaluation ► **assessment process** N (*Educ, Ind*) processus *m* d'évaluation

assessor [ə'sesə'] N **a** (*Jur*) (*juge m*) assesseur *m* **b** [*of property*] expert *m*; (*US*) **~ of taxes** contrôleur *m*, -euse *f* des contributions directes **c** (*in exam*) examinateur *m*, -trice *f*, correcteur *m*, -trice *f*; (*in sport*) juge *m*

asset ['æset] **1** N **a** bien *m*; **~s** biens *mpl*, avoir *m*, capital *m*; (*Comm, Fin, Jur*) actif *m*; **~s and liabilities** actif *m* et passif *m*; **their ~s amount to £1m** leur actif est d'un or s'élève à un million de livres → **liquid b** (= *advantage*) avantage *m*, atout *m*; **he is one of our greatest ~s** sa collaboration (*or* sa présence *etc*) constitue un de nos meilleurs atouts **2** COMP ► **asset-stripper** N (*Fin*) repreneur *m* d'entreprises (en faillite) ► **asset-stripping** N (*Fin*) dépeçage *m*

asseverate [ə'sevəreɪt] VT affirmer solennellement; [+ *one's innocence, loyalty*] protester de

asseveration [ə,sevə'reɪʃən] N (*frm*) affirmation *f* solennelle

asshole ['æshəʊl] N (*US lit, also fig* = *person*) trou *m* du cul

assiduity [,æsɪ'djʊɪtɪ] N assiduité *f*, zèle *m*

assiduous [ə'sɪdjʊəs] ADJ assidu

assiduously [ə'sɪdjʊəslɪ] ADV [*study, work*] assidûment; **to ~ avoid doing sth** prendre bien soin d'éviter de faire qch

assign [ə'saɪn] VT **a** (= *allot*) [+ *task, office*] assigner; [+ *date*] assigner, fixer; [+ *room*] attribuer (**to sb/sth** à qn/qch); [+ *meaning*] donner, attribuer (**to** à); **to ~ a reason for sth** donner la raison de qch; **the event is ~ed to the year 1600** on fait remonter cet événement à 1600 **b** (= *appoint*) [+ *person*] affecter (**to** à) **c** (*Jur*) [+ *property, right*] céder, faire cession de (**to sb** à qn), transférer (**to sb** au nom de qn)

assignation [,æsɪg'neɪʃən] N **a** (= *appointment*) rendez-vous *m* (*souvent galant*) **b** (= *allocation*) attribution *f*; [*of money*] allocation *f*; [*of person, room*] affectation *f* **c** (*Jur*) cession *f*, transfert *m* (de biens)

assignee [,æsaɪ'niː] N (*Jur*) cessionnaire *mf*

assignment [ə'saɪnmənt] N **a** (= *task*) mission *f*; (*Scol*) devoir *m*; (*Univ*) devoir *m*; (= *essay*) dissertation *f*; **to be on (an) ~** être en mission **b** (*NonC* = *allocation*) attribution *f*; [*of money*] allocation *f*; [*of person, room*] affectation *f* **c** (*Jur*) **~ of contract** cession *f* des droits et obligations découlant d'un or du contrat

assignor [,æsɪ'nɔː'] N (*Jur*) cédant *m*

assimilate [ə'sɪmɪleɪt] **1** VT **a** (= *absorb*) [+ *food, knowledge*] assimiler **b** (= *compare*) comparer, assimiler (**to** à), rapprocher (**to** de) **2** VI s'assimiler, être assimilé

assimilation [ə,sɪmɪ'leɪʃən] N (= *absorption*) assimilation *f*; (= *comparison*) assimilation *f* (**to** à), comparaison *f*, rapprochement *m* (**to** avec); (*Phon*) assimilation *f*

Assisi [ə'siːzɪ] N Assise

assist [ə'sɪst] **1** VT aider (**to do, in doing** à faire); **to ~ sb in/out** *etc* aider qn à entrer/sortir *etc*; **to ~ one another** s'entraider; **~ed by** avec le concours de **2** VI (= *help*) aider; **to ~ in (doing) sth** aider à (faire) qch **3** N (*Sport*) action *f* qui aide un coéquipier à marquer un

point **4** COMP ► **assisted passage** N (*Travel*) billet *m* subventionné ► **assisted place** N (*Brit Scol*) place réservée dans une école privée à un élève de milieu modeste dont les frais de scolarité sont payés par l'État ► **assisted suicide** N suicide *m* assisté

assistance [ə'sɪstəns] N aide *f*, assistance *f*; **to give ~ to sb** prêter assistance à qn; **to come to sb's ~** venir en aide à qn, porter assistance à qn; **can I be of ~?** puis-je vous aider?, puis-je vous être utile?

assistant [ə'sɪstənt] **1** N aide *mf*, auxiliaire *mf*; **(foreign language) ~** (*Scol*) assistant(e) *m(f)*; (*Univ*) lecteur *m*, -trice *f* → **shop 2** COMP adjoint, sous- ► **assistant editor** N rédacteur *m*, -trice *f* adjoint(e), assistant(e) *m(f)* de rédaction ► **assistant judge** N (*US Jur*) juge *m* assesseur ► **assistant librarian** N bibliothécaire *mf* adjoint(e) ► **assistant manager** N directeur *m*, -trice *f* adjoint(e), sous-directeur *m*, -trice *f* ► **assistant master†, assistant mistress†** N (*Brit Scol*) professeur *m* (*qui n'a pas la responsabilité d'une section*) ► **assistant priest** N vicaire *m* ► **assistant principal** N (*Scol*) directeur *m*, -trice *f* adjoint(e); (*in a French lycée*) censeur *m* ► **assistant professor** N (*US Univ*) ≈ maître *m* assistant ► **assistant secretary** N secrétaire *mf* adjoint(e), sous-secrétaire *mf* ► **assistant teacher** N (*primary*) instituteur *m*, -trice *f*; (*secondary*) professeur *m* (*qui n'a pas la responsabilité d'une section*)

assistantship [ə'sɪstəntʃɪp] N (*US Univ*) poste *m* d'étudiant(e) chargé(e) de travaux dirigés

assizes [ə'saɪzɪz] NPL (*Jur*) assises *fpl*

assn. ABBR = **association**

assoc. ABBR = **association** *and* **associated**

associate [ə'səʊʃɪɪt] **1** ADJ uni, associé; (*Jur*) **~ judge** juge *m* assesseur; (*US Jur*) **Associate Justice** juge *m* de la Cour suprême; (*US Univ*) **~ professor** ≈ maître *m* de conférences **2** N **a** (= *fellow worker*) associé(e) *m(f)*, collègue *mf*; (*Jur* = *in crime*) complice *mf*; **to be ~s in an undertaking** participer conjointement à une entreprise → **business b** [*of a society*] membre *m*, associé(e) *m(f)*; [*of learned body*] (membre *m*) correspondant *m*; (*US Univ*) **~'s degree** ≈ DEUG *m* **3** [ə'səʊʃɪeɪt] VT **a** [+ *ideas, things*] associer; **to ~ one thing with another** associer une chose à *or* avec une autre **b** **to be ~d with sth** être associé à qch; **to ~ o.s.** or **to be ~d with sb in an undertaking** s'associer à *or* avec qn dans une entreprise; **to be ~d with a plot** tremper dans un complot; **I should like to ~ myself with what has been said** je voudrais me faire l'écho de cette opinion; **I don't wish to be ~d with it** je préfère que mon nom ne soit pas mêlé à ceci **4** VI **to ~ with sb** fréquenter qn, être en relations avec qn

association [ə,səʊsɪ'eɪʃən] **1** N **a** (*NonC* = *connection*) association *f* (**with** avec), fréquentation *f* (**with** de); **in ~ with** en association avec; **by ~ of ideas** par (une) association d'idées; **to be guilty by ~** être incriminé (à cause de ses relations) **b** (= *organization*) association *f*; **to form an ~** constituer une société → **freedom c** (= *connotation*) **full of historic ~s** portant l'empreinte du passé; **this word has nasty ~s** ce mot a des connotations *fpl* désagréables **2** COMP ► **association football** N (*Brit*) football *m* (association)

associative [ə'səʊʃɪətɪv] ADJ (*Math*) associatif; (*Comput*) **~ storage** mémoire *f* associative

assonance ['æsənəns] N assonance *f*

assort [ə'sɔːt] **1** VT classer, classifier **2** VI [*colours etc*] s'assortir, aller bien (**with** avec)

assorted [ə'sɔːtɪd] ADJ **a** (= *mixed*) [*shapes, styles, colours, items*] différent; **in ~ sizes** dans toutes les tailles; **~ wild flowers** des fleurs des champs de différentes sortes **b** (= *matched*)

an oddly ~ group un groupe hétérogène ; **an strangely ~ pair** un couple qui ne semble pas bien assorti → **ill, well**

assortment [ə'sɔːtmənt] N [of objects] collection f, assortiment m ; [of people] mélange m ; **this shop has a good ~** il y a beaucoup de choix dans ce magasin, ce magasin est bien achalandé ; **an ~ of people/guests** des gens/des invités (très) divers

asst. ABBR = **assistant**

assuage [ə'sweɪdʒ] VT (liter) [+ hunger, desire, thirst] assouvir ; [+ anger, pain] soulager, apaiser ; [+ person] apaiser, calmer

▼ **assume** [ə'sjuːm] VT [a] (= accept, presume, suppose) supposer, présumer ; **assuming** or **if we ~ this to be true ...** en supposant que or supposons que ceci soit vrai ... ; **let us ~ that ...** supposons que ... (+ subj) ; **you resigned, I ~?** vous avez démissionné, je suppose or présume ? ; **you are assuming a lot** vous faites bien des suppositions [b] (= take on) [+ responsibility, burden] assumer, endosser ; [+ power, importance, possession] prendre ; [+ title, right, authority] s'arroger, s'attribuer ; [+ name] adopter, prendre ; [+ air, attitude] adopter, se donner ; **to ~ control of sth** prendre en main la direction de qch ; **to ~ the role of arbiter** assumer le rôle d'arbitre ; **to ~ a look of innocence** affecter un air d'innocence ; **to go under an ~d name** se servir d'un nom d'emprunt or d'un pseudonyme

assumption [ə'sʌmpʃən] [1] N [a] (= supposition) supposition f, hypothèse f ; **on the ~ that ...** en supposant que ... (+ subj) ; **to go on the ~ that ...** présumer que ... [b] [of power etc] appropriation f ; [of indifference] affectation f [c] (Rel) **the Assumption** l'Assomption f [2] COMP ► **Assumption Day** N (= religious festival) l'Assomption f ; (= public holiday) le 15 août

assurance [ə'ʃʊərəns] N [a] (= certainty) assurance f, conviction f ; **in the ~ that ...** avec la conviction or l'assurance que ... [b] (= self-confidence) assurance f [c] (= promise) promesse f, assurance f ; **you have my ~ that ...** je vous promets or assure que ... [d] (Brit = insurance) assurance f → **life**

▼ **assure** [ə'ʃʊəʳ] VT [a] (= tell positively) assurer ; (= convince, reassure) convaincre, assurer (**sb of sth** qn de qch) ; **it is so, I can ~ you** c'est vrai, je vous assure → **rest** [b] (= ensure) [+ happiness, success] garantir, assurer [c] (Brit = insure) assurer

assured [ə'ʃʊəd] ADJ, N assuré(e) m(f) (**of** de) ; **will you be ~ of a good salary?** aurez-vous l'assurance d'avoir un bon salaire ?

assuredly [ə'ʃʊərɪdlɪ] ADV assurément ; **most ~** sans aucun doute

Assyria [ə'sɪrɪə] N l'Assyrie f

Assyrian [ə'sɪrɪən] [1] ADJ assyrien [2] N Assyrien(ne) m(f)

AST [,eɪes'tiː] (US, Can) (ABBR = **Atlantic Standard Time**) → **Atlantic**

astatine [ˈæstətiːn] N astate m

aster [ˈæstəʳ] N aster m

asterisk [ˈæstərɪsk] [1] N astérisque m [2] VT marquer d'un astérisque

astern [əˈstɜːn] ADV (Naut) à l'arrière ; **slow ~!** (en) arrière doucement ! ; **to go** or **come ~** (using engine) faire machine arrière ; (using sail) culer ; ~ **of** à l'arrière de

asteroid [ˈæstərɔɪd] N astéroïde m

asthma [ˈæsmə] N asthme m ; ~ **sufferer** asthmatique mf

asthmatic [æsˈmætɪk] ADJ, N asthmatique mf

astigmatic [ˌæstɪgˈmætɪk] ADJ, N astigmate mf

astigmatism [æsˈtɪgmətɪzəm] N astigmatisme m

astir [əˈstɜːʳ] ADJ, ADV [a] (= excited) agité, en émoi [b] († = out of bed) debout inv, levé

ASTMS [,eɪestiːem'es] (Brit) (ABBR = **Association of Scientific, Technical and Managerial Staffs**) syndicat

astonish [əˈstɒnɪʃ] VT étonner ; (stronger) stupéfier ; (also iro) **you ~ me!** vous m'étonnez !

astonished [əˈstɒnɪʃt] ADJ étonné, stupéfait ; **I am ~ that ...** cela m'étonne or m'ahurit que ... (+ subj)

astonishing [əˈstɒnɪʃɪŋ] ADJ étonnant ; (stronger) ahurissant, stupéfiant ; **that is ~, coming from them** venant d'eux, c'est ahurissant or étonnant ; **with an ~ lack of discretion** avec un incroyable manque de discrétion

astonishingly [əˈstɒnɪʃɪŋlɪ] ADV étonnement, incroyablement ; **~ (enough), he was right** chose étonnante, il avait raison

astonishment [əˈstɒnɪʃmənt] N étonnement m, surprise f ; (stronger) ahurissement m, stupéfaction f ; **look of ~** regard m stupéfait ; **to my ~** à mon grand étonnement, à ma stupéfaction → **stare**

astound [əˈstaʊnd] VT stupéfier, étonner, ébahir

astounded [əˈstaʊndɪd] ADJ abasourdi, ébahi ; **I am ~** j'en reste abasourdi, je n'en crois pas mes yeux or mes oreilles

astounding [əˈstaʊndɪŋ] ADJ stupéfiant, ahurissant

astoundingly [əˈstaʊndɪŋlɪ] ADV [good, bad, talented] incroyablement

astrakhan [ˌæstrəˈkæn] [1] N astrakan m [2] COMP [coat] d'astrakan

astral [ˈæstrəl] [1] ADJ astral [2] COMP ► **astral projection** N projection f astrale

astray [əˈstreɪ] ADV (lit, fig) **to go ~** s'égarer ; (fig) **to lead sb ~** détourner qn du droit chemin, dévoyer qn (liter)

astride [əˈstraɪd] [1] ADJ, ADV à califourchon, à cheval ; **to ride ~** monter à califourchon [2] PREP à califourchon sur, à cheval sur

astringent [əˈstrɪndʒənt] [1] ADJ (Med) astringent ; (fig) dur, sévère ; ~ **lotion** lotion f astringente [2] N (Med) astringent m

astro... [ˈæstrəʊ] PREF astro...

astrologer [əˈstrɒlədʒəʳ] N astrologue mf

astrological [ˌæstrəˈlɒdʒɪkəl] ADJ astrologique

astrologically [ˌæstrəˈlɒdʒɪkəlɪ] ADV d'un point de vue astrologique

astrologist [əˈstrɒlədʒɪst] N astrologue mf

astrology [əˈstrɒlədʒɪ] N astrologie f

astronaut [ˈæstrənɔːt] N astronaute mf

astronautic(al) [ˌæstrəʊˈnɔːtɪk(əl)] ADJ astronautique

astronautics [ˌæstrəʊˈnɔːtɪks] N (NonC) astronautique f

astronomer [əˈstrɒnəməʳ] N astronome mf

astronomical [ˌæstrəˈnɒmɪkəl] [1] ADJ [a] (= enormous) [amount, cost, price] astronomique ; **the odds against another attack were ~** une nouvelle attaque était des plus improbables [b] (Astron) [observatory, instrument, society] d'astronomie ; [telescope, observation] astronomique [2] COMP ► **astronomical clock** N horloge f astronomique ► **astronomical unit** N unité f astronomique

astronomically [ˌæstrəˈnɒmɪkəlɪ] ADV [a] (= enormously) [rise, increase] dans des proportions astronomiques ; [high] effroyablement ; **to be ~ expensive** coûter un prix astronomique [b] (Astron) [interesting, important] d'un point de vue astronomique

astronomy [əˈstrɒnəmɪ] N astronomie f

astrophysicist [ˌæstrəʊˈfɪzɪsɪst] N astrophysicien(ne) m(f)

astrophysics [ˌæstrəʊˈfɪzɪks] N (NonC) astrophysique f

Astroturf® [ˈæstrəʊtɜːf] N gazon m artificiel

Asturian [æˈstʊərɪən] ADJ asturien

Asturias [æˈstʊərɪæs] N les Asturies fpl

astute [əsˈtjuːt] ADJ fin, astucieux, intelligent

astutely [əsˈtjuːtlɪ] ADV avec finesse, astucieusement

astuteness [əsˈtjuːtnɪs] N (NonC) finesse f, astuce f, intelligence f

Asuncion [æˌsʊntsɪˈɒn] N Asunción

asunder [əˈsʌndəʳ] ADV (liter) (= apart) écartés, éloignés (l'un de l'autre) ; (= in pieces) en morceaux

Aswan [æsˈwɑːn] [1] N Assouan [2] COMP ► **the Aswan (High) Dam** N le (haut) barrage d'Assouan

asylum [əˈsaɪləm] [1] N [a] (NonC) asile m, refuge m ; **political ~** asile m politique [b] († : also **lunatic ~**) asile m (d'aliénés)† [2] COMP ► **asylum seeker** N demandeur m, -euse f d'asile

asymmetric(al) [ˌeɪsɪˈmetrɪk(əl)] [1] ADJ asymétrique [2] COMP ► **asymmetric(al) bars** NPL (Sport) barres fpl asymétriques

asymmetry [æˈsɪmɪtrɪ] N asymétrie f

asymptomatic [ˌeɪsɪmptəˈmætɪk] ADJ asymptomatique

asynchronous [æˈsɪŋkrənəs] ADJ (Comput) asynchrone

AT [eɪˈtiː] (ABBR = **alternative technology**) → **alternative**

at [æt]

> When **at** is an element in a phrasal verb, eg **look at**, look up the verb.

[1] PREP [a] (place, position) à ; **at the table** à la table ; **at my brother's** chez mon frère ; **at home** à la maison, chez soi ; **to dry o.s. at the fire** se sécher devant le feu ; **to stand at the window** se tenir à or devant la fenêtre ; **at her heels** sur ses talons ; **to come in at the door** entrer par la porte ; **to find a gap to go in at** trouver une brèche par où passer or entrer ; **where are we at?*** (fig : progress) où en sommes-nous ? ; (US lit: position) où sommes-nous ? ; (fashion) **this is where it's at*** c'est là que ça se passe* → **hand, sea**

[b] (direction) vers, dans la direction de, sur ; **an attempt at escape** une tentative d'évasion → **jump at, laugh at**

[c] (arrival) à ; **to arrive at the house** arriver à la maison

[d] (time, frequency, order) à ; **at 10 o'clock** à 10 heures ; **at night** la nuit ; **three at a time** trois par trois, trois à la fois ; (stairs, steps) trois à trois ; **at times** de temps en temps, parfois ; **at once** (= immediately) immédiatement, tout de suite ; (= at the same time) en même temps, à la fois ; **at a time like this** à un moment pareil ; **at my time of life** à mon âge

[e] (activity) en train de, occupé à ; **at work** au travail ; **pupils at play** élèves en récréation ; **while we are at it*** pendant que nous y sommes or qu'on y est* ; **they are at it again!*** les voilà qui recommencent !, voilà qu'ils remettent ça !* ; **they are at it all day*** ils font ça toute la journée

[f] (state, condition) en ; **good/bad at languages** bon/mauvais en langues → **war**

[g] (manner) **at full speed** à toute allure ; **at 80km/h** à 80 km/h ; **he was driving at 80km/h** il faisait du 80 (à l'heure)

[h] (cause) (à cause de, à propos de ; **to be surprised at sth** être étonné de qch ; **annoyed at** contrarié par ; **angry at sb/sth** en colère contre qn/qch ; **at the request of ...** à or sur la demande or la requête de ...

[i] (rate, value, degree) à, dans, en ; **at best** au mieux ; **I cannot arrive before ten at the earliest** je n'arriverai pas avant dix heures au plus tôt ; **at first** d'abord ; **nothing at all** rien du tout ; **at all costs** à tout prix ; **he sells them at 12 francs a kilo** il les vend 12 F le kilo ; **let's leave it at that** restons-en là ; **he's only a teacher and a poor one at that** ce n'est qu'un professeur et encore assez piètre

---

[1] (* = *nagging*) **she's been at me the whole day** elle m'a harcelé *or* tanné* toute la journée ; **she was (on) at her husband to buy a new car** elle harcelait *or* tannait* son mari pour qu'il achète (*subj*) une nouvelle voiture ; **he's always (on) at me*** il est toujours après moi*

[2] COMP ► **at-home** N réception *f* (*chez soi*)

atavism ['ætəvɪzəm] N atavisme *m*

atavistic [,ætə'vɪstɪk] ADJ atavique

ataxia [ə'tæksɪə] N ataxie *f*

ataxic [ə'tæksɪk] ADJ ataxique

ATB [,eɪtiː'biː] N (ABBR = **all-terrain bike**) VTT *m*

ATC [,eɪtiː'siː] (ABBR = **Air Training Corps**) *préparation à l'école de l'air*

ate [et, eɪt] VB *pt of* **eat**

Athalia [ə'θeɪlɪə] N Athalie *f*

Athanasian [,æθə'neɪʃən] ADJ **the ~ Creed** le symbole de saint Athanase

Athanasius [,æθə'neɪʃəs] N Athanase *m*

atheism ['eɪθɪɪzəm] N athéisme *m*

atheist ['eɪθɪɪst] N athée *mf*

atheistic(al) [,eɪθɪ'ɪstɪk(əl)] ADJ athée

Athena [ə'θiːnə] N Athéna *f*

athenaeum [,æθɪ'niːəm] N association *f* littéraire (*or* culturelle)

Athene [ə'θiːnɪ] N = **Athena**

Athenian [ə'θiːnɪən] [1] N Athénien(ne) *m(f)* [2] ADJ athénien

Athens ['æθɪnz] N Athènes

athirst [ə'θɜːst] ADJ (*liter: lit, fig*) altéré, assoiffé (**for** de)

athlete ['æθliːt] [1] N (*in competitions*) athlète *mf* [2] COMP ► **athlete's foot** N (*Med*) pied *m* d'athlète

athletic [æθ'letɪk] [1] ADJ [a] (*Sport*) [*club, association, competition*] d'athlétisme ; [*activity, achievement*] athlétique [b] (= *muscular*) [*person, body, build*] athlétique [2] COMP ► **athletic coach** N (*US Scol, Univ*) entraîneur *m* (sportif) ► **athletic sports** NPL athlétisme *m* ► **athletic support(er)** N suspensoir *m*

athletically [æθ'letɪkəlɪ] ADV [a] (*Sport*) [*talented*] d'un point de vue athlétique [b] (= *agilely*) [*jump*] avec agilité

athleticism [æθ'letɪsɪzəm] N constitution *f* athlétique

athletics [æθ'letɪks] N (*NonC*) (*Brit*) athlétisme *m* ; (*US*) sport *m*

Athos ['æθɒs] N (**Mount**) **~** le mont Athos

athwart [ə'θwɔːt] [1] ADV en travers ; (*Naut*) par le travers [2] PREP en travers de ; (*Naut*) par le travers de

Atlantic [ət'læntɪk] [1] ADJ [*coast, current*] atlantique ; [*winds, island*] de l'Atlantique [2] N = **Atlantic Ocean** ; → **north** [3] COMP ► **Atlantic Charter** N Pacte *m* atlantique ► **Atlantic liner** N transatlantique *m* ► **the Atlantic Ocean** N l'Atlantique *m*, l'océan *m* Atlantique ► **the Atlantic Provinces** NPL (*Can*) les Provinces *fpl* atlantiques ► **Atlantic Standard Time** N l'heure *f* normale de l'Atlantique

Atlanticism [ət'læntɪsɪzəm] N (*Pol*) atlantisme *m*

Atlanticist [ət'læntɪsɪst] ADJ, N (*Pol*) atlantiste *mf*

Atlantis [ət'læntɪs] N l'Atlantide *f*

atlas ['ætləs] N [a] (= *book*) atlas *m* [b] (*Myth*) **Atlas** Atlas *m* ; **the Atlas Mountains** (les monts *mpl* de) l'Atlas *m*

ATM [,eɪtiː'em] N (*US*) (ABBR = **Automated Teller Machine**) GAB *m*, DAB *m*

atmosphere ['ætməsfɪə] N (*lit, Phys*) atmosphère *f* ; (*fig*) atmosphère *f*, ambiance *f* ; (*fig*) **I can't stand ~s** je ne peux pas supporter une ambiance hostile

atmospheric [,ætməs'ferɪk] [1] ADJ [a] (*Met, Phys*) atmosphérique [b] (= *evocative*) [*music, film, book*] évocateur (-trice *f*) [2] COMP ► **atmospheric pressure** N pression *f* atmosphérique

atmospherics [,ætməs'ferɪks] N [a] (*NonC: Rad, Telec* = *interference*) bruit *m* atmosphérique [b] (* = *ambience, atmosphere*) ambiance *f*, atmosphère *f*

atoll ['ætɒl] N atoll *m*

atom ['ætəm] [1] N atome *m* ; (*fig*) grain *m*, parcelle *f* ; **smashed to ~s** réduit en miettes ; **not an ~ of truth** pas la moindre parcelle de vérité ; **if you had an ~ of sense** si tu avais un gramme *or* un atome de bon sens [2] COMP ► **atom bomb** N bombe *f* atomique

atomic [ə'tɒmɪk] [1] ADJ atomique [2] COMP ► **atomic age** N ère *f* atomique ► **atomic bomb** N bombe *f* atomique ► **atomic clock** N horloge *f* atomique ► **atomic energy** N énergie *f* atomique *or* nucléaire ► **Atomic Energy Authority** (*in Brit*), **Atomic Energy Commission** (*in US*) N ≈ Commissariat *m* à l'énergie atomique ► **atomic number** N nombre *m* *or* numéro *m* atomique ► **atomic physicist** N physicien(ne) *m(f)* nucléaire ► **atomic physics** N physique *f* nucléaire ► **atomic pile** N pile *f* atomique ► **atomic-powered** ADJ (fonctionnant à l'énergie) nucléaire *or* atomique ► **atomic power station** N centrale *f* nucléaire *or* atomique ► **atomic reactor** N réacteur *m* nucléaire *or* atomique ► **atomic structure** N structure *f* atomique ► **atomic theory** N théorie *f* atomique ► **atomic warfare** N guerre *f* nucléaire *or* atomique ► **atomic weapon** N arme *f* atomique *or* nucléaire ► **atomic weight** N poids *m* *or* masse *f* atomique

atomize ['ætəmaɪz] VT pulvériser, atomiser

atomizer ['ætəmaɪzə'] N atomiseur *m*

atonal [æ'təʊnl] ADJ atonal

atonality [,eɪtəʊ'nælɪtɪ] N atonalité *f*

atone [ə'təʊn] VI **to ~ for** [+ *sin*] expier ; [+ *mistake*] racheter, réparer

atonement [ə'təʊnmənt] N (*NonC*) (*for sin, misdeed*) expiation *f* (**for sth** de qch) ; (*for mistake*) réparation *f* (**for sth** de qch) ; **in ~ for** [+ *sin, misdeed*] en expiation de ; [+ *mistake*] en réparation de ; **to make ~ for** (*for sin*) faire acte d'expiation ; **to make ~ for** [+ *mistake*] réparer ; **he was ready to make ~ for what he'd done wrong** il était prêt à réparer le mal qu'il avait fait → **day**

atonic [æ'tɒnɪk] ADJ [*syllable*] atone ; [*muscle*] atonique

atop [ə'tɒp] [1] ADV en haut, au sommet [2] PREP en haut de, au sommet de

ATP [,eɪtiː'piː] N (ABBR = **adenosine triphosphate**) ATP *m*

Atreus ['eɪtrɪəs] N Atrée *m*

Atridae [æ'trɪdiː] NPL Atrides *mpl*

atrium ['eɪtrɪəm] N (*pl* **atria**) [a] (*Anat*) orifice *m* de l'oreillette [b] (*Archit*) atrium *m* (*couvert d'une verrière*)

atrocious [ə'trəʊʃəs] ADJ [*crime*] atroce ; (* = *very bad*) [*memory, behaviour*] épouvantable ; [*weather*] épouvantable, affreux ; [*food, accent*] épouvantable, atroce

atrociously [ə'trəʊʃəslɪ] ADV [*behave, sing, play*] de façon épouvantable, atrocement mal ; **~ bad** [*film, restaurant*] horriblement mauvais

atrocity [ə'trɒsɪtɪ] N atrocité *f*

atrophy ['ætrəfɪ] [1] N atrophie *f* [2] VT atrophier [3] VI s'atrophier

att. [a] (*Comm*) ABBR = **attached** [b] ABBR = **attorney**

attaboy* ['ætəbɔɪ] EXCL (*in encouragement*) vas-y ! ; (*in congratulation*) bravo !

attach [ə'tætʃ] [1] VT [a] (= *join*) (*gen*) attacher, lier ; (*to letter*) joindre ; **document ~ed to a letter** document *m* joint à une lettre ; **the ~ed letter** la lettre ci-jointe ; (*in letter*) **I ~ a report** je joins à cette lettre un rapport de ... ; **to ~ conditions to sth** soumettre qch à des conditions ; **to ~ o.s. to a group** se joindre à un groupe, entrer dans un groupe ; (*fig*) **to be ~ed to sb/sth** (= *fond of*) être attaché à qn/qch ; **he's ~ed*** (= *married etc*) il n'est pas libre [b] (= *attribute*) [+ *value*] attacher, attribuer (**to** à) ; **to ~ credence to sth** ajouter foi à qch → **importance** [c] (*Jur*) [+ *person*] arrêter, appréhender ; [+ *goods, salary*] saisir [d] [+ *employee, troops*] affecter (**to** à) ; **he is ~ed to the Foreign Office** il est attaché au ministère des Affaires étrangères [e] (*Phys*) [*compound, atom*] fixer (**to** à) [2] VI [a] (*frm* = *belong*) être attribué, être imputé (**to** à) ; **no blame ~es to you** le blâme ne repose nullement sur vous ; **salary ~ing to a post** salaire *m* afférent à un emploi (*frm*) [b] (*Phys*) [*compound, atom*] se fixer

attaché [ə'tæʃeɪ] [1] N attaché(e) *m(f)* [2] COMP ► **attaché case** N mallette *f*, attaché-case *m*

attachment [ə'tætʃmənt] N [a] (*NonC*) fixation *f* [b] (= *accessory: for tool etc*) accessoire *m* [c] (*fig* = *affection*) attachement *m* (**to** à), affection *f* (**to** pour) [d] (*Jur*) (*on person*) arrestation *f* ; (*on goods, salary*) saisie *f* (**on** de) [e] (= *period of practical work, temporary transfer*) stage *m* ; **to be on ~** faire un stage (**to** à, auprès de, chez) [f] (*Comput*) fichier *m* adjoint

attack [ə'tæk] [1] N [a] (*gen, Mil, Sport*) attaque *f* (**on** contre) ; **to return to the ~** revenir à la charge ; **an ~ on sb's life** un attentat contre qn ; (*Jur*) un attentat à la vie de qn ; (*fig*) **to leave o.s. open to ~** prêter le flanc à la critique ; **~ is the best form of defence** le meilleur moyen de défense c'est l'attaque ; **to be under ~** (*Mil*) être attaqué (**from** par) ; (*fig*) être en butte aux attaques (**from** de) ; (*Psych*) **to feel under ~** se sentir agressé [b] (*Med sens*) crise *f* ; **~ of fever** accès *m* de fièvre ; **~ of nerves** crise *f* de nerfs → **heart** [2] VT [a] (*lit, fig*) [+ *person*] attaquer ; (*Mil*) [+ *enemy*] attaquer, assaillir ; (*fig*) **this idea ~s the whole structure of society** cette idée menace toute la structure de la société ; (*fig*) **to be ~ed by doubts** être assailli par des doutes [b] [+ *task, problem*] s'attaquer à ; [+ *poverty etc*] combattre [c] (*Chem*) [+ *metal*] attaquer [3] VI attaquer [4] COMP ► **attack dog** N chien *m* dressé pour l'attaque

attackable [ə'tækəbl] ADJ attaquable

attacker [ə'tækə'] N (*gen*) agresseur *m* ; (*Mil*) attaquant(e) *m(f)*

attagirl* ['ætəgɜːl] EXCL (*in encouragement*) vas-y ! ; (*in congratulation*) bravo !

attain [ə'teɪn] [1] VT [+ *aim, rank, age*] atteindre, parvenir à ; [+ *knowledge*] acquérir ; [+ *happiness*] atteindre à ; [+ *one's hopes*] réaliser ; **he's well on the way to ~ing his pilot's licence** il est en bonne voie pour obtenir sa licence de pilote [2] VI **to ~ to** (= *perfection*) atteindre à, toucher à ; [+ *power, prosperity*] parvenir à

attainable [ə'teɪnəbl] ADJ accessible (**by** à), à la portée (**by** de)

attainder [ə'teɪndə'] N (*Jur*) mort *f* civile → **bill**

attainment [ə'teɪnmənt] N [a] (*NonC*) [*of knowledge*] acquisition *f* ; [*of happiness*] conquête *f* ; [*of one's hopes*] réalisation *f* [b] (*gen pl* = *achievement*) travail *m*, résultats *mpl* (obtenus)

attempt [ə'tempt] [1] VT essayer, tenter (**to do** de faire) ; [+ *task*] entreprendre, s'attaquer à ; **~ed escape/murder/theft** *etc* tentative *f* d'évasion/de meurtre/de vol *etc* ; **to ~ suicide** essayer *or* tenter de se suicider

2 N **a** tentative *f*; **an ~ at escape** une tentative d'évasion; **to make one's first ~** faire sa première tentative, essayer pour la première fois; **to make an ~ at doing** or **to do** essayer de faire, chercher à faire; **to be successful at the first ~** réussir du premier coup; **he failed at the first ~** la première fois, il a échoué; **he had to give up the ~** il lui a fallu (y) renoncer; **he made no ~ to help us** il n'a rien fait pour nous aider, il n'a pas essayé de or cherché à nous aider; **to make an ~ on the record** essayer de or tenter de battre le record; **he made two ~s at it** il a essayé or tenté par deux fois de le faire; **it was a good ~ on his part but …** il a vraiment essayé mais … **b** (= *attack*) attentat *m*; **an ~ on sb's life** un attentat contre qn

▼**attend** [ə'tend] **1** VT **a** [+ *meeting, lecture*] assister à, être à; [+ *classes, course of studies*] suivre; [+ *church, school*] aller à; **the meeting was well ~ed** il y avait beaucoup de monde à la réunion → **well** **b** (= *serve, accompany*) servir, être au service de; **to ~ a patient** [*doctor*] soigner un malade; **~ed by a maid** servi par une or accompagné d'une femme de chambre; (*fig*) **a method ~ed by great risks** une méthode qui comporte de grands risques **2** VI **a** (= *be present*) être présent or là; **will you ~?** est-ce que vous y serez? **b** (= *pay attention*) faire attention (**to** à)

▶**attend on**† VT FUS = **attend upon**

▶**attend to** VT FUS (= *pay attention to*) [+ *lesson, speech*] faire attention à; [+ *advice*] prêter attention à; (= *deal with, take care of*) s'occuper de; **to ~ to a customer** s'occuper d'un client, servir un client; (*in shop*) **are you being ~ed to?** est-ce qu'on s'occupe de vous?

▶**attend upon**† VT FUS [+ *person*] être au service de

attendance [ə'tendəns] **1** N **a** service *m*; **to be in ~** être de service; **he was in ~ on the queen** il escortait la reine; (*Med*) **~ on a patient** visites *fpl* à un malade → **dance** **b** (= *being present*) présence *f*; **regular ~ at** assiduité *f* à; **is my ~ necessary?** est-il nécessaire que je sois présent or là? **c** (= *number of people present*) assistance *f*; **a large ~** une nombreuse assistance; **what was the ~ at the meeting?** combien de gens y avait-il à la réunion? **2** COMP ▶ **attendance allowance** N (*Brit*) allocation pour soins constants ▶ **attendance centre** N (*Brit Jur*) ≈ centre *m* de réinsertion ▶ **attendance officer** N (*Brit Scol*) inspecteur chargé de faire respecter l'obligation scolaire ▶ **attendance order** N (*Brit*) injonction exigeant des parents l'assiduité scolaire de leur enfant ▶ **attendance record** N **his ~ record is bad** il est souvent absent ▶ **attendance register** N (= *book*) registre *m* de(s) présence(s) ▶ **attendance sheet** N feuille *f* d'appel

attendant [ə'tendənt] **1** N **a** [*of museum etc*] gardien(ne) *m(f)*; [*of petrol station*] pompiste *mf*; (= *servant*) domestique *mf*, serviteur† *m* **b** (*US: in hospital*) garçon *m* de salle; († = *doctor*) médecin *m* (de famille) **c** (= *companion, escort*) **~s** membres *mpl* de la suite (**on** de); **the prince and his ~s** le prince et sa suite **2** ADJ **a** (= *accompanying*) [*person*] qui accompagne; **to be ~ on** or **upon sb** accompagner qn; **the ~ crowd** la foule qui était présente **b** (*frm* = *associated*) **old age and its ~ ills** la vieillesse et les maux qui l'accompagnent; **country life with all its ~ benefits** la vie à la campagne, avec tous les avantages qu'elle présente or comporte; **the ~ circumstances** les circonstances *fpl* concomitantes; **the ~ rise in prices** la hausse des prix correspondante; **~ on** or **upon sth** (= *linked to*) lié à qch; (= *due to*) dû (due *f*) à qch

attendee [ˌæten'diː] N (*esp US*) participant(e) *m(f)* (**at** à)

▼**attention** [ə'tenʃən] **1** N **a** (*NonC* = *consideration, notice, observation*) attention *f*; **may I have your ~?** puis-je avoir votre attention?; **give me your ~ for a moment** accordez-moi votre attention un instant; **he gave her his full ~** il lui a accordé toute son attention; **to call (sb's) ~ to sth** attirer l'attention (de qn) sur qch; **to pay ~ to …** faire or prêter attention à …; **to pay little/no ~ to …** prêter peu d'attention/ne prêter aucune attention à …; **to pay special ~ to …** faire tout particulièrement attention à …, prêter une attention toute particulière à …; **no ~ has been paid to my advice** on n'a fait aucun cas de or tenu aucun compte de mes conseils; **it has come to my ~ that …** j'ai appris que …; **for the ~ of Mrs C. Montgomery** à l'attention de Mme C. Montgomery; **it needs daily ~** il faut s'en occuper tous les jours; (*Comm etc*) **it shall have my earliest ~** je m'en occuperai dès que possible; **I was all ~** j'étais tout oreilles → **attract, catch, hold** **b** (= *kindnesses*) **~s** attentions *fpl*, prévenances *fpl*; **to show ~s to** avoir des égards pour; **to pay one's ~s to a woman** faire la cour à or courtiser une femme **c** (*Mil*) garde-à-vous *m*; **to stand at/come** or **stand to ~** être/se mettre au garde-à-vous; **~!** garde-à-vous! **2** COMP ▶ **attention-seeking** ADJ cherchant à attirer l'attention ♦ N désir *m* d'attirer l'attention ▶ **attention span** N **his ~ span is limited** il n'arrive pas à se concentrer très longtemps

attentive [ə'tentɪv] ADJ **a** prévenant (**to sb** envers qn), empressé (**to sb** auprès de qn); **~ to sb's interests** soucieux des intérêts de qn; **~ to detail** soucieux du détail, méticuleux **b** [*audience, spectator*] attentif (**to** à)

attentively [ə'tentɪvlɪ] ADV attentivement, avec attention; **to listen ~** écouter de toutes ses oreilles or attentivement

attentiveness [ə'tentɪvnɪs] N attention *f*, prévenance *f*

attenuate [ə'tenjʊeɪt] **1** VT **a** [+ *statement*] atténuer, modérer **b** [+ *gas*] raréfier **c** [+ *thread, line*] affiner, amincir **2** VI s'atténuer, diminuer **3** ADJ (*also* **~d**) atténué, diminué; (*fig* = *refined*) adouci, émoussé **4** COMP ▶ **attenuating circumstances** NPL circonstances *fpl* atténuantes

attenuation [əˌtenjʊ'eɪʃən] N atténuation *f*, diminution *f*

attest [ə'test] **1** VT **a** (= *certify*) attester (**that** que); (*under oath*) affirmer sous serment (**that** que); (= *prove*) attester, témoigner de; (*Jur*) [+ *signature*] légaliser **b** (= *put on oath*) faire prêter serment à **2** VI prêter serment; **to ~ to sth** attester qch, témoigner de qch **3** COMP ▶ **attested form** N (*Ling*) forme *f* attestée ▶ **attested herd** N (*Brit Agr*) cheptel *m* certifié (*comme ayant été tuberculinisé*)

attestation [ˌætes'teɪʃən] N attestation *f* (**that** que); (*Jur*) attestation *f*, témoignage *m*; [*of signature*] légalisation *f*; (= *taking oath*) assermentation *f*, prestation *f* de serment

attic ['ætɪk] **1** N grenier *m* **2** COMP ▶ **attic room** N mansarde *f*

Attica ['ætɪkə] N Attique *f*

Attila [ə'tɪlə] N Attila *m*

attire [ə'taɪəʳ] (*frm*) **1** VT vêtir, parer (**in** de); **to ~ o.s. in …** se parer de …; **elegantly ~d** vêtu avec élégance **2** N (*NonC*) vêtements *mpl*, habits *mpl*; (*ceremonial*) tenue *f*; (*hum*) atours *mpl* (*hum*); **in formal ~** en tenue de cérémonie

attitude ['ætɪtjuːd] N **a** (= *way of standing*) attitude *f*, position *f*; **to strike an ~** poser, prendre une pose affectée or théâtrale **b** (= *way of thinking*) disposition *f*, attitude *f*; **~ of mind** état *m* or disposition *f* d'esprit; **his ~ towards me** son attitude envers moi or à mon égard; **I don't like your ~** je n'aime pas l'attitude que vous prenez; **if that's your ~** si c'est ainsi or si c'est comme ça* que tu le prends **c*** **sb with ~** qn de tonique; **women with ~** des battantes

attitudinal [ˌætɪ'tjuːdɪnəl] ADJ [*change, difference*] d'attitude

attitudinize [ˌætɪ'tjuːdɪnaɪz] VI se donner des airs, adopter des attitudes affectées

attn PREP (ABBR = **(for the) attention (of)**) à l'attention de

attorney [ə'tɜːnɪ] **1** N **a** (*Comm, Jur*) mandataire *mf*, représentant(e) *m(f)*; **power of ~** procuration *f*, pouvoir *m* **b** (*US: also* **~-at-law**) avoué *m* → **district**; → LAWYER **2** COMP ▶ **Attorney General** N (*pl* **Attorneys General** *or* **Attorney Generals**) (*Brit*) ≈ Procureur Général; (*US*) ≈ Garde *m* des Sceaux, ≈ ministre *m* de la Justice

attract [ə'trækt] VT **a** [*magnet etc*] attirer; (*fig*) **to ~ sb's attention** attirer l'attention de qn; **to ~ sb's interest** éveiller l'intérêt de qn **b** (= *charm, interest*) [*person, subject, quality*] attirer, séduire; **what ~ed me to her …** ce qui m'a attiré or séduit chez elle …; **I am not ~ed to her** elle ne m'attire pas

attraction [ə'trækʃən] N (*NonC: Phys, fig*) attraction *f*; **~ of gravity** attraction *f* universelle **b** (= *pleasant thing*) attrait *m*, séduction *f*; (= *source of entertainment*) attraction *f*; **the chief ~ of this plan** l'attrait *m* principal de ce projet; **the chief ~ of the party** la grande attraction de la soirée; **one of the ~s of family life** un des charmes de la vie de famille

attractive [ə'træktɪv] ADJ **a** (= *appealing*) [*person*] séduisant, attirant; [*personality, voice, offer*] séduisant; [*features, object, prospect*] attrayant; [*sound*] agréable; [*price, salary*] intéressant, attractif; **he was immensely ~ to women** il trouvait les femmes extrêmement séduisantes; **the idea was ~ to her** elle trouvait cette idée séduisante **b** (*Phys*) attractif

attractively [ə'træktɪvlɪ] ADV [*dressed*] de façon séduisante; [*illustrated, packaged*] de façon attrayante; [*furnished*] agréablement; **~ priced** ◊ **at an ~ low price** à un prix intéressant or attractif; **~ simple** d'une simplicité séduisante

attractiveness [ə'træktɪvnəs] N [*of person*] charme *m*, beauté *f*; [*of voice, place*] charme *m*; [*of idea, plan*] attrait *m*; **physical ~** attrait *m* physique

attributable [ə'trɪbjʊtəbl] ADJ attribuable, imputable (**to** à)

▼**attribute** [ə'trɪbjuːt] **1** VT attribuer (**sth to sb** qch à qn); [+ *feelings, words*] prêter, attribuer (**to sb** à qn); [+ *crime, fault*] imputer (**to sb** à qn); **they ~ his failure to his laziness** ils attribuent son échec à sa paresse, ils mettent son échec sur le compte de sa paresse **2** ['ætrɪbjuːt] N **a** attribut *m* **b** (*Gram*) attribut *m*

attribution [ˌætrɪ'bjuːʃən] N (*gen*) attribution *f*; **~ of sth to a purpose** affectation *f* de qch à un but

attributive [ə'trɪbjʊtɪv] **1** ADJ attributif; (*Gram*) attributif **2** N attribut *m*; (*Gram*) attribut *m*

attributively [ə'trɪbjʊtɪvlɪ] ADV (*Gram*) comme épithète

attrition [ə'trɪʃən] **1** N usure *f* (*par frottement*) → **war** **2** COMP ▶ **attrition rate** N (*esp US Comm*) [*of customers*] pourcentage *m* de clients perdus; [*of subscribers*] taux *m* de désabonnement

attune [ə'tjuːn] VT (*lit, fig*) **to become ~d to** (= *used to*) s'habituer à; **tastes ~d to mine** des goûts en accord avec les miens; **to ~ o.s. to (doing) sth** s'habituer à (faire) qch; **to be ~d**

to sb's needs (= *listening*) être à l'écoute des besoins de qn

ATV [ˌeɪtiːˈviː] N (*US*) (ABBR = **all-terrain vehicle**) → **all**

atypical [ˌeɪˈtɪpɪkəl] ADJ atypique

atypically [ˌeɪˈtɪpɪkəlɪ] ADV exceptionnellement; **today, ~, he was early** exceptionnellement *or* fait inhabituel, il est arrivé en avance aujourd'hui

aubergine [ˈəʊbəʒiːn] N (*esp Brit*) aubergine *f*

auburn [ˈɔːbən] ADJ auburn *inv*

auction [ˈɔːkʃən] **1** N (vente *f* aux) enchères *fpl*, (vente *f* à la) criée *f*; **to sell by ~** vendre aux enchères *or* à la criée; **to put sth up for ~** mettre qch dans une vente aux enchères → **Dutch 2** VT (*also* **~ off**) vendre aux enchères *or* à la criée **3** COMP ► **auction bridge** N bridge *m* aux enchères ► **auction house** N société *f* de vente(s) aux enchères ► **auction room** N salle *f* des ventes ► **auction sale** N (vente *f* aux) enchères *fpl*, vente *f* à la criée

auctioneer [ˌɔːkʃəˈnɪə'] N commissaire-priseur *m*

audacious [ɔːˈdeɪʃəs] ADJ audacieux

audaciously [ɔːˈdeɪʃəslɪ] ADV audacieusement

audacity [ɔːˈdæsɪtɪ] N (*NonC*) audace *f*; **to have the ~ to do sth** avoir l'audace de faire qch

audibility [ˌɔːdɪˈbɪlɪtɪ] N audibilité *f*

audible [ˈɔːdɪbl] ADJ (*gen*) audible, perceptible; [*words*] intelligible, distinct; **she was hardly ~** on l'entendait à peine; **there was ~ laughter** des rires se firent entendre

audibly [ˈɔːdɪblɪ] ADV distinctement

audience [ˈɔːdɪəns] **1** N **a** (*NonC*) (*Theat*) spectateurs *mpl*, public *m*; (*of speaker*) auditoire *m*, assistance *f*; (*Mus, Rad*) auditeurs *mpl*; (*TV*) téléspectateurs *mpl*; (*Theat*) **the whole ~ applauded** toute la salle a applaudi; **those in the ~** les gens dans la salle, les membres de l'assistance *or* du public; **there was a big ~** les spectateurs étaient nombreux **b** (= *formal interview*) audience *f*; **to grant an ~ to sb** donner *or* accorder audience à qn **2** COMP ► **audience appeal** N **it's got ~ appeal** cela plaît au public ► **audience chamber** N salle *f* d'audience ► **audience participation** N participation *f* du public ► **audience rating** N (*Rad, TV*) indice *m* d'écoute ► **audience research** N (*Rad, TV*) études *fpl* d'opinion

audio [ˈɔːdɪəʊ] **1** ADJ acoustique **2** N* partie *f* son; **the ~'s on the blink*** il n'y a plus de son **3** COMP ► **audio book** N livre-cassette *m* ► **audio equipment** N équipement *m* acoustique ► **audio frequency** N audiofréquence *f* ► **audio recording** N enregistrement *m* sonore ► **audio system** N système *m* audio

audio- [ˈɔːdɪəʊ] PREF audio-

audio-cassette [ˈɔːdɪəʊkəˈset] N cassette *f* audio

audiometer [ˌɔːdɪˈɒmɪtə'] N audiomètre *m*

audiotronic [ˌɔːdɪəʊˈtrɒnɪk] ADJ audio-électronique

audiotyping [ˈɔːdɪəʊtaɪpɪŋ] N audiotypie *f*

audiotypist [ˈɔːdɪəʊtaɪpɪst] N audiotypiste *mf*

audiovisual [ˌɔːdɪəʊˈvɪzjʊəl] ADJ audiovisuel; **~ aids** supports *mpl* *or* moyens *mpl* audiovisuels; **~ methods** méthodes *fpl* audiovisuelles

audit [ˈɔːdɪt] **1** N audit *m*, vérification *f* des comptes **2** VT **a** [+ *accounts*] vérifier, apurer; [+ *company*] auditer; **~ed statement of accounts** état vérifié des comptes **b** (*US Univ*) **to ~ a lecture course** assister (à un cours) comme auditeur libre

auditing [ˈɔːdɪtɪŋ] N (*Fin*) **~ of accounts** audit *m* *or* vérification *f* des comptes

audition [ɔːˈdɪʃən] **1** N **a** (*Theat*) audition *f*; (*Cine, TV*) essai *m* ; **to give sb an ~** (*Theat*) auditionner qn; (*Cine*) faire faire un essai à qn **b** (*NonC: frm = power of hearing*)

ouïe *f*, audition *f* **2** VT auditionner; **he was ~ed for the part** (*Theat*) on lui a fait passer une audition *or* on l'a auditionné pour le rôle; (*Cine*) on lui a fait faire un essai pour le rôle **3** VI (*Theat*) auditionner; **he ~ed for (the part of) Hamlet** (*Theat*) il a auditionné pour le rôle de Hamlet; (*Cine, TV*) on lui a fait faire un essai pour le rôle de Hamlet

auditor [ˈɔːdɪtə'] N **a** (= *listener*) auditeur *m*, -trice *f* **b** (*Comm*) auditeur *m*, -trice *f*, vérificateur *m*, -trice *f* (des comptes) → **internal c** (*US Univ*) auditeur *m*, -trice *f* libre

auditorium [ˌɔːdɪˈtɔːrɪəm] N (*pl* **auditoriums** *or* **auditoria** [ˌɔːdɪˈtɔːrɪə]) salle *f*

auditory [ˈɔːdɪtərɪ] **1** ADJ auditif **2** COMP ► **auditory phonetics** N (*NonC*) phonétique *f* auditive

Audubon Society [ˈɔːdəbɒnsəˈsaɪətɪ] N (*US*) société *f* de protection de la nature

au fait [ˈəʊfeɪ] ADJ au courant, au fait (**with** de)

Augean Stables [ɔːˈdʒiːənˈsteɪblz] NPL **the ~** les écuries *fpl* d'Augias

auger [ˈɔːgə'] N (*Carpentry*) vrille *f*; (*Tech*) foreuse *f*

aught [ɔːt] N (††, *liter* = *anything*) **for ~ I know** (pour) autant que je sache; **for ~ I care** pour ce que ça me fait

augment [ɔːgˈment] **1** VT augmenter (**with, by** de), accroître; (*Mus*) augmenter; **~ed sixth/third** sixte *f*/tierce *f* augmentée **2** VI augmenter, s'accroître

augmentation [ˌɔːgmenˈteɪʃən] N augmentation *f*, accroissement *m*

augmentative [ɔːgˈmentətɪv] ADJ augmentatif

augur [ˈɔːgə'] **1** N augure *m* **2** VI **to ~ well/ill** être de bon/de mauvais augure (**for** pour) **3** VT (= *foretell*) prédire, prévoir; (= *be an omen of*) présager; **it ~s no good** cela ne présage *or* n'annonce rien de bon

augury [ˈɔːgjʊrɪ] N (= *omen, sign*) augure *m*, présage *m*; (= *forecast*) prédiction *f*; **to take the auguries** consulter les augures

August [ˈɔːgəst] N août *m*; *for phrases see* **September**

august [ɔːˈgʌst] ADJ (*frm*) auguste

Augustan [ɔːˈgʌstən] ADJ **a** d'Auguste; **the ~ Age** (*Latin Literat*) le siècle d'Auguste; (*English Literat*) l'époque *f* néoclassique **b** ~ **Confession** Confession *f* d'Augsbourg

Augustine [ɔːˈgʌstɪn] N Augustin *m*

Augustinian [ˌɔːgəsˈtɪnɪən] **1** ADJ augustinien, de (l'ordre de) saint Augustin **2** N augustin(e) *m(f)*

Augustus [ɔːˈgʌstəs] N (**Caesar**) ~ (César) Auguste *m*

auk [ɔːk] N pingouin *m*

Auld Lang Syne [ˌɔːldlæŋˈzaɪn] N le bon vieux temps (*chanson écossaise chantée sur le coup de minuit à la Saint-Sylvestre*)

aunt [ɑːnt] **1** N tante *f*; **yes ~** oui ma tante **2** COMP ► **Aunt Sally** N (*Brit*) (= *game*) jeu *m* de massacre; (*fig* = *person*) tête *f* de Turc

auntie*, **aunty*** [ˈɑːntɪ] N tantine* *f*, tata* *f*; **~ Mary** tante *f* Marie; (*Brit hum*) **Auntie** la BBC

au pair [ˈəʊˈpeə'] **1** ADJ (*also* **~ girl**) jeune fille *f* au pair **2** N (*pl* **au pairs**) jeune fille *f* au pair **3** VI **to ~ (for sb)** travailler au pair (chez qn)

aura [ˈɔːrə] N (*pl* **auras** *or* **aurae** [ˈɔːriː]) [*of person*] aura *f*, émanation *f*; [*of place*] atmosphère *f*, ambiance *f*

aural [ˈɔːrəl] ADJ **a** (*Anat*) auriculaire (*des oreilles*) **b** (*Educ*) ~ **comprehension (work)** compréhension *f* (orale); ~ **comprehension (test)** exercice *m* de compréhension (orale); (*Mus*) ~ **training** dictée *f* musicale

aureole [ˈɔːrɪəʊl] N (*Art, Astron*) auréole *f*

auricle [ˈɔːrɪkl] N (*Anat*) [*of ear*] pavillon *m* auriculaire, oreille *f* externe; [*of heart*] oreillette *f*

aurochs [ˈɔːrɒks] N (*pl* **aurochs**) aurochs *m*

aurora [ɔːˈrɔːrə] N (*pl* **auroras** *or* **aurorae** [ɔːˈrɔːriː]) ~ **borealis/australis** aurore *f* boréale/australe

auscultate [ˈɔːskəlteɪt] VT ausculter

auscultation [ˌɔːskəlˈteɪʃən] N auscultation *f*

auspices [ˈɔːspɪsɪz] NPL (*all senses*) auspices *mpl*; **under the ~ of ...** sous les auspices de ...

auspicious [ɔːsˈpɪʃəs] ADJ [*start*] prometteur; [*occasion, day, time*] propice; [*sign*] de bon augure

auspiciously [ɔːsˈpɪʃəslɪ] ADV favorablement, sous d'heureux auspices; **to start ~** prendre un départ prometteur

Aussie* [ˈɒzɪ] = **Australian**

austere [ɒsˈtɪə'] ADJ [*person, building, lifestyle, beauty*] austère; [*times, economic policy*] d'austérité

austerely [ɒsˈtɪəlɪ] ADV avec austérité, austèrement

austerity [ɒsˈterɪtɪ] N austérité *f*; **days** *or* **years of ~** période *f* d'austérité

Australasia [ˌɒstrəˈleɪzɪə] N l'Australasie *f*

Australasian [ˌɒstrəˈleɪzɪən] **1** ADJ d'Australasie **2** N habitant(e) *m(f)* *or* natif *m*, -ive *f* d'Australasie

Australia [ɒsˈtreɪlɪə] N (**the Commonwealth of**) ~ l'Australie *f*

Australian [ɒsˈtreɪlɪən] **1** ADJ (*gen*) australien; [*ambassador, embassy*] d'Australie; ~ **Alps** Alpes *fpl* australiennes; ~ **Antarctic Territory** Antarctique *f* australienne; ~ **Capital Territory** Territoire *m* fédéral de Canberra **2** N **a** Australien(ne) *m(f)* **b** (*Ling*) australien *m*

Austria [ˈɒstrɪə] N l'Autriche *f*; **in ~** en Autriche

Austrian [ˈɒstrɪən] **1** ADJ (*gen*) autrichien; [*ambassador, embassy*] d'Autriche **2** N Autrichien(ne) *m(f)*

Austro- [ˈɒstrəʊ] PREF austro-; **~Hungarian** austro-hongrois

AUT [ˌeɪjuːˈtiː] N (*Brit*) (ABBR = **Association of University Teachers**) syndicat

autarchy [ˈɔːtɑːkɪ] N autocratie *f*

authentic [ɔːˈθentɪk] ADJ authentique; (*Jur*) **both texts shall be deemed ~** les deux textes feront foi

authentically [ɔːˈθentɪkəlɪ] ADV **a** (= *genuinely*) [*furnished, restored*] authentiquement; **Chinese dishes** des plats authentiquement chinois, des plats chinois authentiques; **the brass has an ~ tarnished look** l'aspect terni de ce cuivre a l'air authentique **b** (= *accurately*) [*describe, depict*] de façon authentique

authenticate [ɔːˈθentɪkeɪt] VT [+ *document*] authentifier; [+ *report*] établir l'authenticité de; [+ *signature*] légaliser

authentication [ɔːˌθentɪˈkeɪʃən] N [*of document*] authentification *f*; [*of report*] confirmation *f* (de l'authenticité de)

authenticity [ˌɔːθenˈtɪsɪtɪ] N authenticité *f*

author [ˈɔːθə'] **1** N **a** (= *writer*) écrivain *m*, auteur *m*; **~'s copy** manuscrit *m* de l'auteur **b** [*of any work of art*] auteur *m*, créateur *m*; [*of plan, trouble etc*] auteur *m* **2** VT (*US*, † *Brit* = *be author of*) être l'auteur de

authoress [ˈɔːθərɪs] N femme *f* écrivain

authorial [ɔːˈθɔːrɪəl] ADJ de l'auteur

authoritarian [ˌɔːθɒrɪˈtɛərɪən] **1** ADJ autoritaire **2** N partisan(e) *m(f)* de l'autorité

authoritarianism [ˌɔːθɒrɪˈtɛərɪənɪzəm] N autoritarisme *m*

authoritative [ɔːˈθɒrɪtətɪv] ADJ **a** (= *commanding*) [*person, voice, manner*] autoritaire **b** (= *reliable*) [*person, book, guide*] faisant autorité, digne de foi; [*source*] sûr, autorisé; [*survey, study, information*] sûr, digne de foi **c** (= *official*) [*statement*] officiel

authoritatively [ɔːˈθɒrɪtətɪvlɪ] ADV **a** (= *commandingly*) [*say, nod, behave*] de façon autoritaire b (= *reliably*) [*speak, write*] avec autorité

authority [ɔ:'θɔrɪtɪ] N a (= *power to give orders*) autorité f, pouvoir m; **I'm in ~ here** c'est moi qui dirige ici; **to be in ~ over sb** avoir autorité sur qn; **those in ~** ceux qui nous dirigent b (= *permission, right*) autorisation f (*formelle*); **to give sb ~ to do sth** habiliter qn à faire qch; **to do sth without ~** faire qch sans autorisation; **she had no ~ to do it** elle n'avait pas qualité pour le faire; **on her own ~** de son propre chef, de sa propre autorité; **on whose ~?** avec l'autorisation de qui?; **to speak with ~** parler avec compétence or autorité; **to carry ~** faire autorité; **I have it on good ~ that ...** je tiens de bonne source que ...; **what is your ~?** sur quoi vous appuyez-vous (pour dire cela)?; **to say sth on the ~ of Plato** dire qch en invoquant l'autorité de Platon c (*gen pl = person or group*) **authorities** autorités fpl, corps mpl constitués, administration f; **apply to the proper authorities** adressez-vous à qui de droit or aux autorités compétentes; **the health authorities** les services mpl de la santé publique; **the public/local/district authorities** les autorités fpl publiques/locales/régionales d (= *person with special knowledge*) autorité f (**on** en matière de), expert m (**on** en); (= *book*) autorité f, source f (autorisée); **to be an ~** [*person, book*] faire autorité (**on** en matière de); **to consult an ~** consulter un avis autorisé

authorization [,ɔ:θəraɪ'zeɪʃən] N a (= *giving of authority*) autorisation f (**of, for** pour, **to do** de faire) b (= *legal right*) pouvoir m (**to do** de faire)

authorize ['ɔ:θəraɪz] VT autoriser (**sb to do** qn à faire); **to be ~d to do** avoir qualité pour faire, être autorisé à faire; **~d by custom** sanctionné par l'usage; (*Jur, Fin*) **duly ~d officer** représentant m dûment habilité

authorized ['ɔ:θəraɪzd] 1 ADJ [*person, signatory, overdraft*] autorisé; [*dealer, representative, bank*] agréé; [*signature*] social; [*biography*] officiel; (*on door*) **"~ personnel only"** «entrée réservée au personnel»; (*Jur, Fin*) **duly ~ officer** représentant m dûment habilité 2 COMP ► **authorized bank** N banque f agréée ► **authorized capital** N (*NonC*) capital m social ► **authorized dealer** N (*Comm*) distributeur m agréé ► **authorized signature** N (*Jur, Fin*) signature f sociale ► **the Authorized Version** N (*Rel*) la Bible de 1611 (*autorisée par le roi Jacques Ier*)

authorship ['ɔ:θəʃɪp] N [*of book, idea etc*] paternité f; **to establish the ~ of a book** identifier l'auteur d'un livre, établir la paternité littéraire d'un livre

autism ['ɔ:tɪzəm] N autisme m

autistic [ɔ:'tɪstɪk] ADJ autistique

auto ['ɔ:təʊ] 1 N (*US*) voiture f, auto f 2 COMP ► **Auto show** N Salon m de l'auto ► **auto worker** N ouvrier m de l'industrie automobile

auto- ['ɔ:təʊ] PREF auto-

autobank ['ɔ:təʊbæŋk] N distributeur m automatique de billets (de banque)

autobiographic(al) ['ɔ:təʊˌbaɪəʊ'græfɪk(əl)] ADJ autobiographique

autobiography [,ɔ:təʊbaɪ'ɒgrəfɪ] N autobiographie f

autocade ['ɔ:təʊkeɪd] N (*US*) cortège m d'automobiles

autocracy [ɔ:'tɒkrəsɪ] N autocratie f

autocrat ['ɔ:təʊkræt] N autocrate m

autocratic [,ɔ:təʊ'krætɪk] ADJ a (= *dictatorial*) [*person, style, behaviour, leadership*] autocratique; (*Pol*) [*leader, ruler*] absolu; [*government, regime*] autocratique

autocross ['ɔ:təʊkrɒs] N auto-cross m

Autocue® ['ɔ:təʊkju:] N (*Brit TV*) téléprompteur m

autocycle ['ɔ:təʊsaɪkl] N (*small*) cyclomoteur m; (*more powerful*) vélomoteur m

auto-da-fé ['ɔ:təʊdɑ:'feɪ] N (*pl* **autos-da-fé** ['ɔ:təʊdɑ:'feɪ]) autodafé m

autodidact ['ɔ:təʊ,daɪdækt] N (*frm*) autodidacte mf

autodrome ['ɔ:təʊdrəʊm] N autodrome m

autofocus ['ɔ:təʊfəʊkəs] N (*Phot*) autofocus m

autogenic [,ɔ:təʊ'dʒenɪk] ADJ **~ training** training m autogène

autogiro [,ɔ:təʊ'dʒaɪərəʊ] N autogire m

autograph ['ɔ:təgrɑ:f] 1 N autographe m 2 VT [+ *book*] dédicacer; [+ *other object*] signer 3 COMP ► **autograph album** N livre m or album m d'autographes ► **autograph hunter** N collectionneur m, -euse f d'autographes

autohypnosis [,ɔ:təʊhɪp'nəʊsɪs] N autohypnose f

autoimmune [,ɔ:təʊɪ'mju:n] ADJ [*reaction, response, disease*] auto-immun

autoloading [,ɔ:təʊ'ləʊdɪŋ] ADJ semi-automatique

automat ['ɔ:təmæt] N cafétéria f automatique (*munie exclusivement de distributeurs*)

automata [ɔ:'tɒmətə] NPL of **automaton**

automate ['ɔ:təmeɪt] VT automatiser; **~d teller** distributeur m automatique de billets

automatic [,ɔ:tə'mætɪk] 1 ADJ (*lit, fig*) automatique; (*Comput*) **~ data processing** traitement m automatique de l'information; (*Phot*) **~ exposure** exposition f automatique; **~ vending machine** distributeur m automatique; (*Aviat*) **on ~ pilot** en pilotage or sur pilote automatique; (*fig*) **to work/drive on ~ pilot** travailler/conduire au radar* 2 N (= *gun, washing machine*) automatique m; (= *car*) voiture f à boîte or à transmission automatique; **a Citroën ~** une Citroën à boîte or transmission automatique 3 COMP ► **automatic transmission** N (*Aut*) transmission f automatique

automatically [,ɔ:tə'mætɪkəlɪ] ADV (*lit, fig*) automatiquement; (*Jur*) **~ void** nul de plein droit

automation [,ɔ:tə'meɪʃən] N (= *technique, system, action*) automatisation f; (= *state of being automated*) automation f; **industrial ~** productique f

automaton [ɔ:'tɒmətən] N (*pl* **automatons** or **automata**) automate m

automobile ['ɔ:təməbi:l] N (*esp US*) automobile f, auto f

automobilia [,ɔ:təməʊ'bi:lɪə] NPL accessoires mpl auto

automotive [,ɔ:tə'məʊtɪv] ADJ a (*Aut*) [*industry, design*] de (l')automobile b (= *self-propelled*) automoteur

autonomous [ɔ:'tɒnəməs] ADJ autonome

autonomously [ɔ:'tɒnəməslɪ] ADV de façon autonome

autonomy [ɔ:'tɒnəmɪ] N autonomie f

autonymous [ɔ:'tɒnɪməs] ADJ (*Ling*) autonyme

autopilot ['ɔ:təʊpaɪlət] N pilote m automatique; (*lit*) **on ~** sur pilote automatique; (*fig*) **to be on ~*** marcher au radar*

autopsy ['ɔ:tɒpsɪ] N autopsie f

autoreverse [,ɔ:təʊrɪ'vɜ:s] N (*Elec, Mus*) autoreverse m, lecture f arrière automatique; **a cassette deck with ~** une platine à cassettes (avec) autoreverse

autosuggestion ['ɔ:təʊsə'dʒestʃən] N autosuggestion f

autoteller ['ɔ:təʊtelər] N (*Banking*) distributeur m automatique de billets

autotimer ['ɔ:təʊtaɪmər] N [*of oven*] programmateur m (de four)

autumn ['ɔ:təm] 1 N automne m; **in ~** en automne 2 COMP d'automne, automnal (*liter*) ► **autumn leaves** NPL (*dead*) feuilles fpl mortes; (*on tree*) feuilles fpl d'automne

autumnal [ɔ:'tʌmnəl] ADJ d'automne, automnal (*liter*)

auxiliary [ɔ:g'zɪlɪərɪ] 1 ADJ subsidiaire (**to** à), auxiliaire; (*US*) **~ police** corps m de policiers auxiliaires volontaires; (*Brit Scol*) **~ staff** personnel m auxiliaire non enseignant; (*Aviat*) **~ tank** réservoir m supplémentaire; **~ verb** verbe m auxiliaire 2 N a auxiliaire m f; **nursing ~** infirmier m, -ière f auxiliaire, aide-soignant(e) m(f); (*Mil*) **auxiliaries** auxiliaires mpl b (*Gram*) verbe m auxiliaire m

AV [eɪ'vi:] ABBR = **audiovisual**

Av. N (ABBR = **Avenue**) av.

a.v., A/V ABBR = **ad valorem**

avail [ə'veɪl] 1 VT **to ~ o.s. of** [+ *opportunity*] saisir, profiter de; [+ *right*] user de, valoir de; [+ *service*] utiliser; (*Jur*) **to ~ o.s. of the rules of jurisdiction** invoquer les règles de compétence 2 VI († *liter*) être efficace, servir; **nought ~ed** rien n'y faisait; **it ~ed him nothing** cela ne lui a servi à rien 3 N **to no ~** sans résultat, en vain; **your advice was of no ~** vos conseils n'ont eu aucun effet; **it is of no ~ to complain** il ne sert à rien de protester; **to little ~** sans grand effet or résultat; **it is of or to little ~** cela ne sert pas à grand-chose

availability [ə,veɪlə'bɪlɪtɪ] N a [*of material, people*] disponibilité f b (*US* = *validity*) validité f

▼ **available** [ə'veɪləbl] ADJ a (= *obtainable*) [*information, product, funding, accommodation*] disponible; **he is not ~ at the moment** il n'est pas libre en ce moment; **television isn't yet ~ here** on ne dispose pas encore de la télévision ici; **new treatments are becoming ~** de nouveaux traitements font leur apparition; **to be ~ for sb** être à la disposition de qn; (*Press*) **the MP was not ~ for comment yesterday** hier, le député ne s'est prêté à aucune déclaration; **~ for hire** à louer; **money ~ for spending** argent m disponible; **a car park is ~ for the use of customers** un parking est à la disposition des clients; **the guide is ~ from all good bookshops** on peut trouver ce guide dans toutes les bonnes librairies; **this service is ~ in stores everywhere** tous les magasins proposent ce service; **tickets are ~ from the box office** on peut se procurer des billets auprès du bureau de location; **to make sth ~** mettre qch à disposition; **to make sth ~ to sb** mettre qch à la disposition de qn; **to make o.s. ~** se rendre disponible; **to use every ~ means to do sth** utiliser tous les moyens disponibles pour faire qch; **the next ~ flight** le prochain vol; (*Comm*) **"other sizes/colours ~"** «existe également en d'autres tailles/couleurs»; **in the time ~** dans le temps disponible; **information ~ to patients** les informations fpl à la disposition des patients; **benefits ~ to employees** les avantages mpl dont peuvent bénéficier les employés b (= *unattached*) (*person*) libre; (*sexually*) disponible (*sexuellement*) c (*US Pol pej*) [*candidate*] honnête (*before n*)

avalanche ['ævəlɑ:nʃ] 1 N (*lit, fig*) avalanche f 2 VI tomber en avalanche 3 COMP ► **avalanche precautions** NPL mesures fpl de sécurité anti-avalanche ► **avalanche warning** N alerte f aux avalanches; (*on sign*) «attention (aux) avalanches»

avalement [aval'mɑ̃] N (*Ski*) avalement m

avant-garde ['ævɑ̃gɑ:d] 1 N (*gen, Mil*) avant-garde f 2 COMP [*dress, style*] d'avant-garde

avarice ['ævərɪs] N avarice f, cupidité f

avaricious [,ævə'rɪʃəs] ADJ avare, cupide (*liter*)

avatar ['ævətɑːʳ] N **a** (*Rel*) avatar *m* **b** (*fig = manifestation*) incarnation *f* **c** (*Comput*) avatar *m*

avdp N ABBR = **avoirdupois**

Ave N (ABBR = **Avenue**) av

Ave Maria ['ɑːveɪmə'rɪə] N avé Maria *m inv*

avenge [ə'vendʒ] VT [+ *person, thing*] venger ; **to ~ o.s.** se venger, prendre sa revanche (**on sb** sur qn)

avenger [ə'vendʒəʳ] N vengeur *m*, -eresse *f*

avenging [ə'vendʒɪŋ] ADJ vengeur (-eresse *f*) (*liter*)

avenue ['ævənjuː] N (= *private road*) avenue *f* ; (= *wide road in town*) avenue *f*, boulevard *m* ; (*fig*) route *f*

aver [ə'vɜːʳ] VT affirmer, déclarer

average ['ævərɪdʒ] **1** N **a** moyenne *f* ; **on ~** en moyenne ; **a rough ~** une moyenne approximative ; **to take an ~ of results** prendre la moyenne des résultats ; **above/below ~** au-dessus/en-dessous de la moyenne ; **to do an ~ of 70km/h** rouler à *or* faire une moyenne de 70 km/h, faire du 70 de moyenne* **b** (*Marine Insurance*) avarie *f* ; **to adjust the ~** répartir les avaries
2 ADJ [*age, wage, price*] moyen ; **the ~ American car drives 10,000 miles per year** l'automobiliste américain moyen fait 16 000 kilomètres par an ; **an ~ thirteen-year-old child could understand it** un enfant *or* n'importe quel enfant de treize ans comprendrait cela ; **£1.50 for a beer is ~** il faut compter en moyenne 1,50 livre pour une bière ; **it was an ~ piece of work** c'était un travail moyen ; **I was only ~ academically** sur le plan des études, je ne dépassais pas la moyenne
3 VT **a** (= *find the average of*) établir *or* faire la moyenne de **b** (= *reach an average of*) atteindre la moyenne de ; **we ~ eight hours' work a day** nous travaillons en moyenne huit heures par jour ; **the sales ~ 200 copies a month** la vente moyenne est de 200 exemplaires par mois ; **we ~50km/h the whole way** nous avons fait 50 km/h de moyenne sur ce trajet
► **average out** **1** VI **it'll ~ out in the end** en fin de compte ça va s'égaliser ; **our working hours ~ out at eight per day** nous travaillons en moyenne huit heures par jour **2** VT SEP faire la moyenne de

averagely ['ævərɪdʒlɪ] ADV moyennement

averager ['ævərɪdʒəʳ] N (*Marine Insurance*) répartiteur *m* d'avaries, dispatcheur *m*

averse [ə'vɜːs] ADJ ennemi (**to** de), peu disposé (**to** à) ; **to be ~ to doing sth** répugner à faire qch ; **he is ~ to getting up early** il déteste se lever tôt ; **I am not ~ to an occasional drink** je ne suis pas opposé à un petit verre de temps à autre

aversion [ə'vɜːʃən] N **a** (*NonC = strong dislike*) aversion *f* ; **he has an ~ to spiders** il a *or* éprouve de l'aversion pour les araignées ; **he has a strong ~ to work** il a horreur de travailler ; **I have an ~ to garlic** une chose que je déteste, c'est l'ail ; **he has a strong ~ to me** il ne peut pas me souffrir ; **I took an ~ to it** je me suis mis à détester cela ; **I have an ~ to him** il m'est antipathique **b** (= *object of aversion*) objet *m* d'aversion ; **my greatest ~ is ...** ce que je déteste le plus, c'est ... → **pet¹**

avert [ə'vɜːt] VT [+ *danger, accident*] prévenir, éviter ; [+ *blow*] détourner, parer ; [+ *suspicion*] écarter ; [+ *one's eyes, one's thoughts*] détourner (**from** de)

avian ['eɪvɪən] ADJ aviaire

aviary ['eɪvɪərɪ] N volière *f*

aviation [ˌeɪvɪ'eɪʃən] **1** N aviation *f* **2** COMP ► **aviation fuel** N kérosène *m* ► **aviation industry** N aéronautique *f*

aviator ['eɪvɪeɪtəʳ] **1** N aviateur *m*, -trice *f*

2 COMP ► **aviator glasses** NPL lunettes *fpl* sport

avid ['ævɪd] ADJ **a** (= *keen*) [*reader, collector, viewer*] passionné ; [*supporter, fan*] fervent **b** (= *desirous*) **~ for sth** avide de qch

avidity [ə'vɪdɪtɪ] N avidité *f* (**for** de)

avidly ['ævɪdlɪ] ADV avidement, avec avidité

Avila ['ævɪlə] N Ávila

avionics [ˌeɪvɪ'ɒnɪks] N (*NonC = science*) avionique *f* ; (*pl = circuitry*) avionique *f*

avocado [ˌævə'kɑːdəʊ] N (*Brit: also ~ pear*) avocat *m* ; (= *tree*) avocatier *m*

avocation [ˌævəʊ'keɪʃən] N **a** (= *employment*) métier *m*, profession *f* **b** (= *minor occupation*) passe-temps *m inv* favori, violon *m* d'Ingres

avocet ['ævəset] N avocette *f*

avoid [ə'vɔɪd] VT [+ *person, obstacle*] éviter ; [+ *danger*] échapper à, éviter ; **to ~ tax** (*legally*) se soustraire à l'impôt ; (*illegally*) frauder le fisc ; **to ~ doing sth** éviter de faire qch ; **~ being seen** évitez qu'on ne vous voie ; **to ~ sb's eye** fuir le regard de qn ; **to ~ notice** échapper aux regards ; **I can't ~ going now** je ne peux plus faire autrement que d'y aller, je ne peux plus me dispenser d'y aller ; **this way we ~ London** en passant par ici nous évitons Londres ; **it is to be ~ed like the plague** il faut fuir cela comme la peste → **plague**

avoidable [ə'vɔɪdəbl] ADJ évitable

avoidance [ə'vɔɪdəns] N **his ~ of me** le soin qu'il met à m'éviter ; **his ~ of his duty** ses manquements *mpl* au devoir ; **tax ~** évasion *f* fiscale

avoirdupois [ˌævədə'pɔɪz] **1** N **a** (*lit*) système *m* des poids commerciaux (*système britannique des poids et mesures*) (***** = *overweight*) embonpoint *m* **2** COMP *conforme aux poids et mesures officiellement établis* ► **avoirdupois pound** N livre *f* (453,6 grammes)

avow [ə'vaʊ] VT (*frm = proclaim*) déclarer, affirmer ; **to ~ o.s. defeated** s'avouer *or* se déclarer battu

avowal [ə'vaʊəl] N (*frm*) aveu *m*

avowed [ə'vaʊd] ADJ (*frm*) [*enemy, supporter, atheist*] déclaré ; [*aim, intention, purpose*] avoué

avowedly [ə'vaʊɪdlɪ] ADV (*frm*) de son propre aveu

avuncular [ə'vʌŋkjʊləʳ] ADJ avunculaire

AWACS ['eɪwæks] N (ABBR = **Airborne Warning and Control System**) **~ plane** (avion *m*) AWACS *m*

await [ə'weɪt] VT **a** (= *wait for*) [+ *object, event*] attendre, être dans l'attente de ; [+ *person*] attendre ; **parcels ~ing delivery** colis *mpl* en souffrance ; **long-~ed event** événement *m* longtemps attendu **b** (= *be in store for*) être réservé à, attendre ; **the fate that ~s us** le sort qui nous attend *or* qui nous est réservé

awake [ə'weɪk] (*pret* **awoke** *or* **awaked**, *ptp* **awoken** *or* **awaked**) **1** VI s'éveiller, se réveiller ; **to ~ from sleep** sortir du sommeil, s'éveiller ; (*fig*) **to ~ to one's responsibilities** prendre conscience de ses responsabilités ; (*fig*) **to ~ to the fact that ...** s'apercevoir du fait que ... ; (*fig*) **to ~ from one's illusions** revenir de ses illusions
2 VT **a** (= *wake*) [+ *person*] éveiller, réveiller **b** (= *arouse*) [+ *suspicion*] éveiller ; [+ *hope, curiosity*] éveiller, faire naître ; [+ *memories*] réveiller
3 ADJ **a** (= *not asleep*) (*before sleep*) éveillé ; (*after sleep*) réveillé ; **are you ~?** est-ce que tu dors ? ; **he was instantly ~** il s'est réveillé immédiatement ; **to keep sb ~** empêcher qn de dormir ; **to lie ~ all night** ne pas fermer l'œil de la nuit ; **she lies ~ at night worrying about it** ça la tracasse tellement qu'elle n'en dort plus ; **to shake sb ~** secouer qn pour le réveiller ; **to stay** *or* **keep ~** veiller ; **I couldn't stay** *or* **keep ~** je n'arrivais pas à rester

éveillé ; **I don't stay ~ at night worrying about that** cela ne m'inquiète pas au point de m'empêcher de dormir → **wide**
b (= *aware*) **to be ~ to sth** être conscient de qch

awaked† [ə'weɪkt] VB *pt, ptp of* **awake**

awaken [ə'weɪkən] VTI = **awake 1, 2**

awakening [ə'weɪknɪŋ] **1** N (*lit, fig*) réveil *m* ; **a rude ~** un réveil brutal **2** ADJ [*interest, passion*] naissant

award [ə'wɔːd] **1** VT [+ *prize etc*] décerner, attribuer (**to** à) ; [+ *sum of money*] allouer, attribuer (**to** à) ; [+ *dignity, honour*] conférer (**to** à) ; [+ *damages*] accorder (**to** à) **2** N **a** (= *prize*) prix *m* ; (*for bravery etc*) récompense *f*, décoration *f* ; (= *scholarship*) bourse *f* **b** (*Jur* = *judgement*) décision *f*, sentence *f* arbitrale ; (= *sum of money*) montant *m* (*or* dommages-intérêts *mpl*) accordé(s) par le juge **3** COMP ► **award ceremony**, **awards ceremony** N (*Cine, Theat, TV*) cérémonie *f* de remise des prix ► **award-winner** N (= *person*) lauréat(e) *m(f)* ; (= *work*) livre *m* (*or* film *m* etc) primé ► **award-winning** ADJ [*person, book, film*] primé

aware [ə'weəʳ] ADJ **a** (= *conscious*) conscient (**of** de) ; (= *informed*) au courant, averti (**of** de) ; **to become ~ of sth/that sth is happening** prendre conscience de *or* se rendre compte de qch/que qch se passe ; **to be ~ of sth** être conscient de qch, avoir conscience de qch ; **to be ~ that something is happening** être conscient *or* avoir conscience que quelque chose se passe ; **I am quite ~ of it** je ne l'ignore pas, j'en ai bien conscience ; **as far as I am ~** autant que je sache ; **not that I am ~ of** pas que je sache ; **to make sb ~ of sth** rendre qn conscient de qch **b** (= *knowledgeable*) informé, avisé ; **politically ~** politisé ; **socially ~** au courant des problèmes sociaux

awareness [ə'weənɪs] **1** N (*NonC*) conscience *f* (**of** de) **2** COMP ► **awareness programme** N programme *m* de sensibilisation

awash [ə'wɒʃ] ADJ (*Naut*) à fleur d'eau, qui affleure ; (= *flooded*) inondé (**with** de)

away [ə'weɪ]

*When **away** is an element in a phrasal verb, eg **boil away, die away, gabble away, get away, look up the verb.***

1 ADV **a** (= *to or at a distance*) au loin, loin ; **far ~** au loin, très loin ; **the lake is 3km ~** le lac est à 3 km (de distance) *or* à une distance de 3 km ; **~ back in the distance** très loin derrière (dans le lointain) ; **~ back in prehistoric times** dans les temps reculés de la préhistoire ; **~ back in 1600** il y a bien longtemps en 1600 ; **~ back in the 40s** il y a longtemps déjà dans les années 40 ; **keep the child ~ from the fire** tenez l'enfant loin *or* éloigné du feu ; **~ over there** là-bas au loin *or* dans le lointain, loin là-bas
b (= *absent*) **he's ~ today** (*gen*) il est absent *or* il n'est pas là aujourd'hui ; [*businessman etc*] il est en déplacement aujourd'hui ; **he is ~ in London** il est (parti) à Londres ; **when I have to be ~** lorsque je dois m'absenter ; **she was ~ before I could speak** elle était partie avant que j'aie pu parler ; (*fig*) **now she's ~ with the idea that ...** la voilà partie avec l'idée que ... ; **~!** hors d'ici ! ; **~ with you!** (= *go away*) allez-vous-en ! ; **get ~!** ◊ **~ with you!** (*disbelief*) allons ! ne dis pas de bêtises → **far, right, brush away, go away**
c (*Sport*) **they're playing ~ this week** ils jouent à l'extérieur cette semaine ; **Chelsea are ~ to Everton on Saturday** Chelsea se déplace à Everton samedi
d (= *continuously*) sans arrêt *or* interruption, continuellement ; **to be talking/working ~** parler/travailler sans arrêt
2 COMP ► **away defeat** N (*Sport*) défaite *f* à l'extérieur ► **away game, away match** N (*Sport*) match *m* à l'extérieur ► **away team** N

(*Sport*) (équipe *f* des) visiteurs *mpl*, équipe *f* jouant à l'extérieur ► **away win** N (*Sport*) victoire *f* à l'extérieur

awe [ɔː] **1** N (*fearful*) respect *m* mêlé de crainte ; (*admiring*) respect *m* mêlé d'admiration ; **to be** or **stand in ~ of sb** être intimidé par qn, être rempli du plus grand respect pour qn **2** VT inspirer un respect mêlé de crainte à ; **in an ~d voice** d'une voix (à la fois) respectueuse et intimidée **3** COMP ► **awe-inspiring** ADJ = **awesome** ► **awe-struck** ADJ (= *frightened*) frappé de terreur ; (= *astounded*) stupéfait

awesome ['ɔːsəm] ADJ (= *impressive*) impressionnant, imposant ; (= *frightening*) terrifiant ; (*esp US* = *excellent*) super*, génial*

awesomely ['ɔːsəmlɪ] ADV [*talented, complex*] terriblement ; **the streets were ~ quiet** il régnait un calme impressionnant dans les rues

awful ['ɔːfəl] **a** affreux, terrible, atroce ; **he's an ~ bore** il est assommant* ; **what ~ weather!** quel temps affreux ! or de chien !* ; **he's got an ~ cheek!** il a un de ces culots !* or un fameux culot !* ; **how ~!** comme c'est affreux !, quelle chose affreuse ! ; **it was just ~** c'était vraiment affreux ; **his English is ~** son anglais est atroce, il parle anglais comme une vache espagnole ; (= *ill*) **I feel ~** je me sens vraiment mal ; **an ~ lot of time/money** un temps/un argent fou ; **there's an ~ lot of people/cars/cream** *etc* il y a énormément de monde/voitures/crème *etc* ; **I have an ~ lot of things to do** j'ai énormément de or un tas* de choses à faire ; **he drinks an ~ lot** il boit énormément or comme un trou* **b** (= *dreadful*) [*news, crime, accident, realization*] épouvantable, terrifiant

awfully ['ɔːflɪ] ADV [*good, nice, clever*] extrêmement, vraiment ; [*bad, difficult, hot, late*] terriblement ; **an ~ big house** une énorme maison ; **I'm ~ glad** je suis absolument ravi ; **I'm ~ sorry** je suis absolument désolé ; **I'm not ~ sure** je n'en suis pas vraiment sûr ; **I don't know her ~ well** je ne la connais pas vraiment bien or très bien ; **thanks ~†** merci infiniment ; **would you mind ~ (if ...)?†** est-ce que cela vous ennuierait (si ...) ?

awfulness ['ɔːfʊlnɪs] N horreur *f* ; **the ~ of it** ce qu'il y a d'affreux or de terrible dans cette affaire, ce que cette affaire a d'affreux or de terrible

awhile [ə'waɪl] ADV (*US*) un instant, un moment ; **wait ~** attendez un peu ; **not yet ~** pas de sitôt

awkward ['ɔːkwəd] ADJ **a** (= *inconvenient, difficult*) [*question, job, task*] difficile ; [*problem, situation, stage*] délicat ; **he's at an ~ age** il est à l'âge ingrat ; **it's ~ for me** cela m'est assez

difficile, cela ne m'est pas très facile ; **tomorrow's ~ (for me); how about Thursday?** demain n'est pas très commode (pour moi) - que pensez-vous de jeudi ? ; **you've come at an ~ moment** vous tombez mal → **b** ; **to put sb in an ~ position** mettre qn dans une position délicate ; **to make things ~ for sb** rendre les choses difficiles pour qn ; **at an ~ time for sb** au mauvais moment pour qn ; **it would be ~ to postpone my trip again** il me serait difficile de reporter à nouveau mon voyage **b** (= *embarrassing*) [*silence*] gêné ; **there was an ~ moment when ...** il y a eu un moment de gêne quand ... → **a** ; **it's all a bit ~** tout ceci est un peu ennuyeux or gênant **c** (= *ill at ease*) **to be** or **feel ~ (with sb)** être mal à l'aise (avec qn) ; **I felt ~ about his hand on my knee** ça me gênait de sentir sa main sur mon genou ; **I felt ~ about touching him** ça me gênait de le toucher **d** (= *uncooperative*) [*person*] difficile, peu commode ; **he's being ~ (about it)** il fait des difficultés (à ce sujet) ; **to be ~ about doing sth** faire des difficultés pour faire qch → **customer** **e** (= *cumbersome*) [*object*] encombrant ; [*shape*] encombrant, malcommode ; **~ to carry/use** difficile à porter/utiliser **f** (= *clumsy*) [*person*] gauche, maladroit ; [*movement, gesture, phrase*] maladroit ; [*style*] gauche, emprunté ; [*position*] inconfortable

awkwardly ['ɔːkwədlɪ] ADV **a** (= *clumsily*) [*move, walk, express o.s., translate*] maladroitement, de façon maladroite ; [*fall*] mal ; [*lie*] dans une position inconfortable ; [*hang*] bizarrement ; **~ placed** mal placé **b** (= *embarrassingly*) **an ~ long silence** un long silence gêné **c** (= *embarrassedly*) [*say, behave, shake hands*] d'un air gêné or embarrassé

awkwardness ['ɔːkwədnɪs] N **a** (= *clumsiness*) gaucherie *f*, maladresse *f* **b** [*of situation*] côté *m* gênant or embarrassant **c** (= *discomfort*) embarras *m*, gêne *f*

awl [ɔːl] N alêne *f*, poinçon *m*

awning ['ɔːnɪŋ] N (*Naut*) taud *m* or taude *f*, tente *f* ; [*of shop*] banne *f*, store *m* ; [*of hotel door*] marquise *f* ; [*of tent*] auvent *m* ; (*in garden*) vélum *m*

awoke [ə'wəʊk] VB *pt of* **awake**

awoken [ə'wəʊkən] VB *ptp of* **awake**

AWOL ['eɪwɒl] (*Mil*) (ABBR = **absent without leave**) → **absent**

awry [ə'raɪ] ADJ, ADV **a** (= *askew*) de travers, de guingois* **b** (= *wrong*) de travers ; **to go ~** [*plan*] s'en aller à vau-l'eau ; [*undertaking*] mal tourner

axe, ax (*US*) [æks] **1** N hache *f* ; (*fig: in expenditure etc*) coupe *f* claire or sombre ; (*Mus* =

guitar) gratte* *f* ; (*fig*) **to have an ~ to grind** prêcher pour son saint (*fig*) ; **I've no ~ to grind** ce n'est pas mon intérêt personnel que j'ai en vue, je ne prêche pas pour mon saint ; (*fig*) **when the ~ fell** quand le couperet est tombé ; **to get** or **be given the ~** [*employee*] être mis à la porte ; [*project*] être abandonné **2** VT (*fig*) [+ *scheme, project*] annuler, abandonner ; [+ *jobs*] supprimer ; [+ *employees*] licencier ; **to ~ expenditure** réduire les dépenses, faire or opérer des coupes claires dans le budget **3** COMP ► **axe-murderer** N assassin *m* (*qui tue ses victimes à la hache*)

axeman ['æksmən] N (*pl* **-men**) (*Mus* = *guitarist*) guitariste *m* ; (*mad*) **~*** tueur *m* fou (*qui se sert d'une hache*)

axes ['æksiːz] NPL *of* **axis**

axial ['æksɪəl] ADJ axial

axiom ['æksɪəm] N axiome *m*

axiomatic [ˌæksɪəʊ'mætɪk] ADJ axiomatique ; (= *clear*) évident

axis ['æksɪs] N (*pl* **axes**) axe *m* ; (*Hist*) **the Axis (Powers)** les puissances *fpl* de l'Axe

axle ['æksl] **1** N [*of wheel*] axe *m* ; (*Aut: also* **~tree**) essieu *m* ; **front/rear ~** essieu *m* avant/arrière **2** COMP ► **axle-box** N (*Rail*) boîte *f* d'essieu ► **axle cap** N chapeau *m* de roue or de moyeu ► **axle grease** N graisse *f* à essieux ► **axle-pin** N esse *f*, clavette *f* d'essieu

ayatollah [ˌaɪə'tɒlə] N ayatollah *m*

ay(e) [aɪ] **1** PARTICLE (*esp Scot, N Engl*) oui ; (*Naut*) **~, ~ sir!** oui, commandant (or capitaine *etc*) **2** N oui *m* ; (*in voting*) **the ~s and noes** les voix *fpl* pour et contre ; **90 ~s and 2 noes** 90 voix pour et 2 contre ; **the ~s have it** les oui l'emportent

aye† [eɪ] ADV (*Scot*) toujours

AYH [ˌeɪwaɪ'eɪtʃ] N (*US*) ABBR = **American Youth Hostels**

AZ ABBR = **Arizona**

azalea [ə'zeɪlɪə] N azalée *f*

Azerbaijan [ˌæzəbaɪ'dʒɑːn] N l'Azerbaïdjan *m*

Azerbaijani [ˌæzəbaɪ'dʒɑːnɪ] **1** ADJ azerbaïdjanais **2** N Azerbaïdjanais(e) *m(f)* **b** (*Ling*) Azerbaïdjanais *m*

Azeri [ə'zɛərɪ] **1** ADJ azéri **2** N Azéri(e) *m(f)*

AZERTY, azerty [ə'zɜːtɪ] ADJ **~ keyboard** clavier *m* AZERTY

azimuth [ˈæzɪməθ] N azimut *m*

Azores [ə'zɔːz] NPL Açores *fpl*

AZT [ˌeɪzed'tiː] (ABBR = **azidothymidine**) AZT *f*

Aztec ['æztek] **1** N Aztèque *mf* **2** ADJ aztèque

azure ['eɪʒəʳ] **1** N azur *m* **2** ADJ d'azur

B

B, b [biː] **1** N **a** (= letter) B, b m; **B for Baker** ≈ B comme Berthe; (in house numbers) **number 7b** numéro m 7 ter **b** (Mus) si m → **key** **c** (Scol) bien, ≈ 14 sur 20 **d** (Cine) **B movie** or **picture**† or **film** film m de série B **e** (of record) **B side** face f B **2** COMP ► **B-girl*** N (US) entraîneuse f (de bar) ► **B-road** N (Brit) route f secondaire, route f départementale → ROADS

BA [biːˈeɪ] N (Univ) (ABBR = **Bachelor of Arts**) **to have a BA in French** avoir une licence de français → **bachelor**; → DEGREE

BAA [ˌbiːeɪˈeɪ] N (ABBR = **British Airports Authority**) → **British**

baa [bɑː] **1** N bêlement m; **~!** bé, bê! **2** VI bêler **3** COMP ► **baa-lamb** N (baby talk) petit agneau m

babble [ˈbæbl] **1** N [of baby] babil m, babillage m; [of stream] gazouillement m; **a ~ of voices** un brouhaha de voix **2** VI **a** [baby] gazouiller, babiller; [stream] jaser, gazouiller **b** (= gabble: also ~ **away**, ~ **on**) bredouiller, bafouiller*; **he was babbling about his holidays** il nous débitait des histoires à n'en plus finir sur ses vacances; **he was babbling about saving the rainforests** il nous débitait des banalités sur la sauvegarde des forêts tropicales **3** VT (also ~ **out**) bredouiller; **"don't hurt me, don't hurt me!"** he **~d** «ne me faites pas de mal, ne me faites pas de mal!» bredouilla-t-il; **he was just babbling nonsense** il était en train de débiter des absurdités

babbler [ˈbæblər] N bavard(e) m(f)

babbling [ˈbæblɪŋ] **1** ADJ [person, baby, stream] babillard **2** N = **babble 1**

babe [beɪb] N **a** (liter) bébé m, enfant mf en bas âge; **~ in arms** enfant mf au berceau or qui vient de naître; (* = inexperienced person) innocent(e) m(f); (fig) **~s in the wood(s)** des jeunes gens naïfs perdus dans un monde impitoyable **c** (esp US* = attractive woman) jolie pépée* f; **come on ~!** viens ma belle!

babel [ˈbeɪbəl] N (= noise) brouhaha m; (= confusion) tohu-bohu m → **tower**

baboon [bəˈbuːn] N babouin m

baby [ˈbeɪbɪ] **1** N **a** bébé m; **she's just had a ~** elle vient d'avoir un bébé; **the ~ of the family** le petit dernier or la petite dernière, le benjamin or la benjamine; **I've known him since he was a ~** je l'ai connu tout petit or tout bébé; **a new ~** un(e) nouveau-né(e) m(f); (pej) **don't be such a ~ (about it)** ne fais pas l'enfant!; (fig) **he was left holding the ~*** on lui a refilé le bébé*; (fig) **to throw out the ~ with the bathwater** jeter le bébé avec l'eau du bain

b (US*) (= girlfriend) copine* f, nana* f; (= man) mec* m; **come on ~!** (to woman) viens ma belle!; (to man) viens mon gars!*
c (* = special responsibility) bébé m; **the new system is his ~** le nouveau système est son bébé; **that's not my ~** je n'ai rien à voir là-dedans
d (esp US* = thing) petite merveille f

2 ADJ **~ vegetables/carrots/sweetcorn** mini-légumes mpl/-carottes fpl/-épis mpl de maïs **3** VT* [+ person] dorloter, cajoler **4** COMP [clothes etc] de bébé; [rabbit etc] bébé ► **baby-batterer** N bourreau m d'enfants ► **baby-battering** N sévices mpl à enfant(s) ► **baby-blue*** ADJ [eyes] bleu (plein d'innocence); [ribbon, car] bleu clair inv ► **baby blues*** NPL **a** (= depression) bébé blues* m **b** (= eyes) yeux mpl bleus (pleins d'innocence) ► **baby boom** N baby-boom m ► **baby boomer** N enfant mf du baby-boom ► **Baby-bouncer®** N Baby Bouncer® m ► **baby boy** N petit garçon m ► **baby brother** N petit frère m ► **baby buggy®** N (Brit) poussette f ► **baby carriage** N (US) voiture f d'enfant, landau m ► **baby-doll pyjamas** NPL baby doll m ► **baby elephant** N éléphanteau m ► **baby face** N visage m poupin ► **baby-faced** ADJ au visage poupin ► **baby food(s)** N(PL) aliments mpl pour bébés ► **baby girl** N petite fille f ► **baby grand** N (also ~ **grand piano**) (piano m) demi-queue m ► **Baby-gro®** N grenouillère f ► **baby linen** N layette f ► **baby-minder** N nourrice f (qui s'occupe des enfants pendant que les parents travaillent) ► **baby-scales** NPL pèse-bébé m ► **baby seat** N siège m pour bébés ► **baby sister** N petite sœur f ► **baby-sit** VI faire du baby-sitting ► **baby-sitter** N baby-sitter mf ► **baby-sitting** N garde f d'enfants, baby-sitting m ► **baby snatcher** N ravisseur m, -euse f d'enfant; (fig) **he/she is a ~ snatcher!** il/elle lui prend au berceau! ► **baby talk** N langage m enfantin or de bébé ► **baby tooth*** N (pl **baby teeth**) dent f de lait ► **baby-walker** N trotteur m ► **baby wipe** N lingette f (pour bébé)

babyhood [ˈbeɪbɪhʊd] N petite enfance f

babyish [ˈbeɪbɪɪʃ] ADJ puéril, enfantin

Babylon [ˈbæbɪlən] N (Geog, fig) Babylone

Babylonian [ˌbæbɪˈləʊnɪən] **1** ADJ babylonien **2** N Babylonien(ne) m(f)

baccalaureate [ˌbækəˈlɔːrɪɪt] N licence f

baccara(t) [ˈbækərɑː] N baccara m

bacchanal [ˈbækənæl] **1** ADJ bachique **2** N (= worshipper) adorateur m, -trice f de Bacchus; (= reveller) noceur* m, -euse* f; (= orgy) orgie f

bacchanalia [ˌbækəˈneɪlɪə] N (= festival) bacchanales fpl; (= orgy) orgie f

bacchanalian [ˌbækəˈneɪlɪən], **bacchic** [ˈbækɪk] ADJ bachique

Bacchus [ˈbækəs] N Bacchus m

baccy* [ˈbækɪ] N (ABBR = **tobacco**) tabac m

bachelor [ˈbætʃələr] **1** N **a** (= unmarried man) célibataire m → **confirmed** **b** (Univ) **Bachelor of Arts/of Science/of Law** licencié(e) m(f) ès lettres/ès sciences/en droit; **Bachelor of Education** licencié(e) m(f) en sciences de l'éducation; **~'s degree** ≈ licence f → DEGREE **c** (Hist) bachelier m **2** ADJ [uncle, brother etc] célibataire; [life, habits] de célibataire

3 COMP ► **bachelor flat** N garçonnière f, studio m ► **bachelor girl** N célibataire f

bachelorhood [ˈbætʃələhʊd] N (gen) vie f de garçon; (= celibacy) célibat m

bacillary [bəˈsɪlərɪ] ADJ bacillaire

bacillus [bəˈsɪləs] N (pl **bacilli** [bəˈsɪlaɪ]) bacille m

---

back [bæk]

1 NOUN		**5** INTRANSITIVE VERB	
2 ADJECTIVE		**6** COMPOUNDS	
3 ADVERB		**7** PHRASAL VERBS	
4 TRANSITIVE VERB			

1 NOUN
a of person, animal dos m; **I've got a bad ~** j'ai des problèmes de dos; **to carry sb/sth on one's ~** porter qn/qch sur son dos; **with one's ~ to the light** le dos à la lumière; **to have** or **stand** or **sit with one's ~ to sb/sth** tourner le dos à qn/qch; (lit, fig) **~ to ~** dos à dos → 6; **to be on one's ~** (lit) être (étendu) sur le dos; (* = be ill) être alité; (also fig) **behind sb's ~** derrière le dos de qn; **he went behind Mr Brown's ~ to the headmaster** il est allé voir le directeur derrière le dos de M. Brown; (fig) **as soon as he turns his ~** ◊ **as soon as his ~ is turned** dès qu'il a le dos tourné; **to fall on one's ~** tomber à la renverse or sur le dos; BUT **he stood with his ~ (up) against the wall** il était adossé au mur; **I was glad to see the ~ of him*** j'étais content de le voir partir; **to have one's ~ to the wall** (lit) être adossé au mur; (fig) être le dos au mur, être acculé

♦ **to be on sb's back*** être sur le dos de qn; **my boss is always on my ~** mon patron est toujours sur mon dos, j'ai sans arrêt mon patron sur le dos

♦ **to get off sb's back*** laisser qn tranquille, ficher la paix à qn*; **get off my ~, will you?** laisse-moi donc tranquille à la fin!, fiche-moi la paix!

♦ **to get** or **put sb's back up** hérisser qn, horripiler qn; **what gets my ~ up is the way he thinks he's always right** ce qui me hérisse or m'horripile chez lui, c'est qu'il croit qu'il a toujours raison

♦ **to live off the back of sb** exploiter qn; **the rich have always lived off the ~s of the poor** les riches ont toujours exploité les pauvres

♦ **to put one's back into sth** mettre toute son énergie dans qch; BUT **put your ~ into it!*** allons, un peu de nerf!*

♦ **to turn one's back on sb/sth** (lit, fig) **he turned his ~ on us** il nous a tourné le dos; **you can't just turn your ~ on your parents** ça ne se fait pas de tourner le dos à ses parents; **he turned his ~ on the past** il a tourné la page

♦ **on the back of** (= by means of) en profitant de; **they became immensely rich on the ~ of the property boom** ils ont fait fortune en profitant du boom immobilier

b of object [of photo, picture, dress, spoon, book] dos m; [of chair] dossier m; [of building] arrière m; [of fabric] envers m

♦ **at the back** [of building] à l'arrière, derrière;

[*of book*] à la fin ; [*of cupboard, hall, stage*] au fond ; **at the very ~** tout au fond ; **there's a car park at the ~** il y a un parking à l'arrière or derrière

♦ **at the back of** [+ *building*] derrière, à l'arrière de ; [+ *book*] à la fin de ; [+ *cupboard, hall, stage*] au fond de ; **the flour's at the ~ of the cupboard** la farine est au fond du placard ; **he's at the ~ of all this trouble** c'est lui qui est derrière tous ces problèmes ; **ambition is at the ~ of this** c'est l'ambition qui est à l'origine de tout cela → **beyond, mind**

♦ **in back** (*US*) [*of building, car*] à l'arrière, derrière ; **Chuck was in ~** Chuck était à l'arrière or derrière

♦ **in back of** (*US*) [+ *building, car*] à l'arrière de, derrière ; **in ~ of the house** à l'arrière de or derrière la maison

♦ **in the back** [*of car*] à l'arrière ; **to sit in the ~ of the car** être (assis) à l'arrière

♦ **out** or **round the back*** (*Brit*) derrière ; **the toilet's out** or **round the ~** les toilettes sont derrière

♦ **back to front** à l'envers, devant derrière ; **you've got it on ~ to front** tu l'as mis à l'envers or devant derrière

[c] [*of part of body*] [*of head*] derrière *m* ; [*of hand*] dos *m*, revers *m* ; **the ~ of one's neck** la nuque ; **I know Paris like the ~ of my hand** je connais Paris comme ma poche

[d] [Ftbl, Hockey etc] arrière *m* ; **right/left ~** arrière *m* droit/gauche

2 ADJECTIVE

[a] = *not front* [*wheel*] arrière *inv* ; **the ~ room** [*of house*] la pièce du fond ; [*of pub, restaurant*] l'arrière-salle *f*, la salle du fond ; **~ legs** [*of animal*] pattes *fpl* de derrière → **6, backroom**

[b] = *overdue* [*taxes*] arriéré ; **to owe ~ rent** devoir un arriéré de loyer

3 ADVERB

*When **back** is an element in a phrasal verb, eg come back, go back, put back, look up the verb.*

[a] [*in space, time*] (*stand*) **~!** reculez ! ; **stay well ~!** n'approchez pas ! ; **far ~** loin derrière ; **a week ~*** il y a une semaine ; **as far ~ as 1800** dès 1800, en 1800 déjà

*When followed by a preposition, **back** is often not translated.*

meanwhile, ~ in London ... pendant ce temps-là, à Londres ... ; **it all started ~ in 1980** tout a commencé en 1980 ; **I saw her ~ in August** je l'ai vue en août ; **he little suspected how worried they were ~ at home** il était loin de se douter que sa famille s'inquiétait autant ; **the house stands ~ from the road** la maison est en retrait par rapport à la route

♦ **to go back and forth** ◊ **to go back and forward** [*person*] faire des allées et venues ; [*phone calls, e-mails, letters*] être échangé

[b] = *returned*

♦ **to be back** [*person*] être rentré ; **he's not ~ yet** il n'est pas encore rentré ; **I'll be ~ at six** je serai de retour or je rentrerai à six heures ; [BUT] **as soon as I'm ~** dès mon retour ; **she's now ~ at work** elle a repris le travail ; **the electricity is ~** l'électricité est revenue, il y a à nouveau de l'électricité ; **the water is ~** il y a à nouveau de l'eau ; **everything's ~ to normal** tout est rentré à la normale, tout est rentré dans l'ordre ; (*in fashion*) **black is ~** le noir est de nouveau à la mode

♦ **... and back:** **he went to Paris and ~** il a fait le voyage de Paris aller et retour ; **the journey there and ~** le trajet aller et retour ; **you can go there and ~ in a day** tu peux faire l'aller et retour en une journée ; **he went to Lyons and then ~ to Paris** il est allé à Lyon, puis est rentré à Paris

[c] = *reimbursed* **"full satisfaction or your money ~"** « satisfait ou remboursé » ; **I got/want my money ~** j'ai récupéré/je veux récupérer mon argent, j'ai été/je veux être remboursé

---

4 TRANSITIVE VERB

[a] = *support* [+ *person, candidate, plan*] soutenir ; [+ *statement*] confirmer ; **they've found a witness to ~ his claim** ils ont trouvé un témoin qui confirme or corrobore ce qu'il a dit → **hilt**

[b] = *accompany* [+ *singer*] accompagner

[c] = *finance* [+ *person, enterprise*] financer, commanditer ; [+ *loan*] garantir ; (*Fin*) **to ~ a bill** endosser or avaliser un effet

[d] = *bet on* [+ *horse, team, contestant*] parier sur, miser sur ; **I'm ~ing Manchester to win** je parie que Manchester va gagner ; (*lit, fig*) **to ~ the wrong horse** miser sur le mauvais cheval ; **to ~ a loser** (*lit*) miser sur un perdant ; (*fig*) miser sur le mauvais cheval ; **the horse was heavily ~ed** on avait beaucoup parié sur ce cheval ; [BUT] **to ~ a horse each way** jouer un cheval gagnant et placé

[e] = *reverse* [+ *vehicle*] reculer ; [+ *train*] refouler ; **to ~ the car in/out** entrer/sortir en marche arrière ; **to ~ a car round a corner** prendre un coin de rue en marche arrière ; (*Naut*) **to ~ water** or **the oars** nager à culer

[f] = *attach backing to* [+ *rug, quilt*] doubler

5 INTRANSITIVE VERB

[a] = *move backwards* [*person, animal*] reculer ; [*vehicle*] reculer, faire marche arrière ; **to ~ in/out** [*vehicle*] entrer/sortir en marche arrière ; [*person*] entrer/sortir à reculons

[b] = *change direction* tourner ; **during the night the south wind ~ed as predicted** au cours de la nuit le vent a tourné au nord comme prévu

6 COMPOUNDS

► **back alley** N ruelle *f*, venelle *f* ► **back benches** NPL (*Brit Parl*) bancs *mpl* des députés de base → **backbencher** ► **back boiler** N (*Brit*) (petite) chaudière *f* (*à l'arrière d'une cheminée*) ► **back-breaking** ADJ [*work*] éreintant ► **back burner** N **to put sth on the ~ burner** mettre qch en veilleuse or en attente ♦ ADJ a **~ burner issue** un problème non urgent ► **back catalogue** N (*Mus*) anciens enregistrements *mpl* ► **back-cloth** N (*Brit Theat*) = backdrop ► **back-comb** VT (*Brit*) [+ *hair*] crêper ► **back copy** N (*Press*) ancien or vieux numéro *m* ► **the back country** N (*US*) la campagne profonde ► **back-country** ADJ (*US*) [*road*] de campagne ; [*expedition*] en campagne profonde ► **back cover** N [*of book, magazine*] quatrième *f* de couverture ► **back door** N porte *f* de derrière ; **to do sth by** or **through the ~ door** faire qch par des moyens détournés ; **the Government is privatizing health care through the ~ door** le gouvernement est en train de privatiser les services médicaux par des moyens détournés ; **he got into the company by** or **through the ~ door** il est entré dans la société par la petite porte ► **back-end** N [*of bus, train*] arrière *m* ; (*Brit*) **~-end of the year** arrière-saison *f* ► **back-flip** N flip-flap *m* ► **back-formation** N (*Ling*) dérivation *f* régressive ► **back garden** N (*Brit*) jardin *m* (de derrière) ; **she's in the ~ garden cutting the grass** elle est dans le jardin (de derrière) en train de tondre la pelouse ; **they were sitting in the ~ garden** ils étaient assis dans le jardin (de derrière) ► **back-heel** (*Ftbl*) N talonnade *f* ♦ VT **to ~-heel the ball** faire une talonnade ; **he ~-heeled the ball into the net** il a marqué le but d'une talonnade ► **back interest** N (*Fin*) arriérés *mpl* d'intérêts ► **back issue** N [*of magazine*] vieux or ancien numéro *m* ► **back-kitchen** N arrière-cuisine *f* ► **back-line player** N (*US Sport*) arrière *m* ► **back-lit** ADJ [*stage*] éclairé de derrière or par l'arrière ; (*Comput*) [*screen*] rétro-éclairé ► **back lot** N (*esp US*) [*of film studio*] grand terrain à l'arrière d'un studio de cinéma ► **back marker** N (*Brit Sport*) dernier *m*, -ière *f* ► **back matter** N [*of book*] appendice(s) *m(pl)* ► **back number** N [*of newspaper*

---

etc] vieux or ancien numéro *m* ; **to be a ~ number** [*person*] ne plus être dans le coup* ► **back-pack** N (*Space*) appareil *m* dorsal de survie ; (*Sport*) sac *m* à dos ► **back-packer** N routard(e) *m(f)* ► **back-packing** N **to go ~-packing** voyager sac au dos ► **back pain** N (*Med*) mal *m* or maux *mpl* de dos ► **back pass** N (*Ftbl*) passe *f* en retrait ► **back passage** N (*Brit Anat*) rectum *m* ► **back pay** N (*Ind*) rappel *m* de salaire or de traitement ; (*Mil, Naut*) rappel *m* or arriéré *m* de solde ► **back-pedal** VI rétropédaler, pédaler en arrière ; (*fig = retreat*) faire marche arrière ► **back-pedalling** N (*lit*) rétropédalage *m* ; (*fig*) reculade *f* ► **back pocket** N poche *f* arrière ► **back projection** N (*Cine*) projection *f* par transparence ► **back road** N petite route *f* de campagne ► **back-scratching** N (*NonC*) renvoi *m* d'ascenseur ► **back seat** N siège *m* or banquette *f* arrière ; (*Aut*) **in the ~ seat** sur le siège arrière, sur la banquette arrière ; **to take a ~ seat*** (*to sth*) passer au second plan (par rapport à qch) ► **back-seat driver** N **he's a ~-seat driver** il est toujours à donner des conseils (au conducteur) ► **back-shop** N arrière-boutique *f* ► **back sight** N [*of rifle*] cran *m* de mire ; (*Surv*) rétrovisée *f* ► **back straight** N (*Sport*) ligne *f* droite (*opposée à celle de l'arrivée*) ► **back street** N ruelle *f* ; (*pej*) rue *f* des quartiers pauvres ; **he grew up in the ~ streets of Leeds** il a grandi dans les quartiers pauvres de Leeds → **backstreet** ► **back stretch** N = back straight ► **back talk*** N (*NonC: US*) = backchat ► **back-to-back** ADJ dos à dos ; (*Brit*) **a row of ~-to-~ houses** une rangée de maisons adossées les unes aux autres ♦ ADV **they showed two episodes ~-to-~** ils ont passé deux épisodes de suite ► **back tooth** N (*pl* **back teeth**) molaire *f* ► **back-to-the-office report** N compte rendu *m* de mission ► **back vowel** N (*Ling*) voyelle *f* postérieure

7 PHRASAL VERBS

►**back away** VI (se) reculer ; **to ~ away from** [+ *problem*] prendre ses distances par rapport à

►**back down** VI revenir sur sa position

►**back off** **1** VI [a] (= *draw back*) reculer

[b] (*US*) **~ off*** Mom, I can make my own decisions arrête un peu, maman, je peux prendre mes propres décisions

2 VT FUS (= *withdraw*) abandonner ; **the union has ~ed off** that demand le syndicat a abandonné cette revendication

►**back on to** VT FUS [*house etc*] **the house ~s on to the golf course** l'arrière de la maison donne sur le terrain de golf

►**back out** **1** VI (*lit*) [*person*] sortir à reculons ; [*car*] sortir en marche arrière (**of** de) ; (*fig*) revenir sur ses engagements ; **at the last minute he ~ed out** à la dernière minute il a fait machine arrière

2 VT SEP [+ *vehicle*] sortir en marche arrière

►**back out of** VT FUS [+ *deal, agreement*] revenir sur ; [+ *duty, undertaking*] se soustraire à

►**back up** **1** VI [a] (= *reverse*) faire marche arrière

[b] (= *queue*) **the traffic is ~ing up for miles behind the accident** l'accident a provoqué des kilomètres de bouchon

[c] [*water*] refouler

2 VT SEP [a] (= *support*) [+ *theory, claim*] confirmer ; [+ *person*] soutenir ; **his colleagues ~ed him up** ses collègues l'ont soutenu ; **he said he had never been there and she ~ed him up** il a dit qu'il n'y était jamais allé et elle a confirmé ses dires

[b] (= *reverse*) [+ *vehicle*] faire reculer

[c] (*Comput*) [+ *file*] sauvegarder

---

backache ['bækeɪk] N mal *m* de dos ; **I've got (a) ~** j'ai mal au dos

backbencher ['bæk,bentʃə'] N (Brit Parl) député m de base

BACKBENCHER

Député de la Chambre des communes qui n'occupe aucune fonction officielle, ni au gouvernement, ni dans le cabinet fantôme. Il siège donc sur les bancs du fond de la Chambre, contrairement aux « frontbenchers », membres du gouvernement ou de l'opposition, qui sont assis aux premiers rangs. Par leur position, les **back-benchers** ne sont pas tenus de suivre aussi rigoureusement les consignes de vote de leur parti. L'expression **back benches** désigne l'ensemble des **backbenchers**, toutes appartenances confondues.

---

backbite ['bækbaɪt] VT médire de, débiner*

backbiting ['bækbaɪtɪŋ] N médisance f

backboard ['bækbɔːd] N (US Sport) panneau m

backbone ['bækbəʊn] N **[a]** [of person, animal] épine f dorsale, colonne f vertébrale ; [of fish] arête f centrale ; **English to the ~** anglais jusqu'à la moelle (des os) **[b]** (fig = main part, axis) base f, ossature f ; **to be the ~ of an organization** être or former la base or l'ossature d'une organisation ; **the economic ~ of the country** la base de l'économie du pays **[c]** (NonC: fig = strength of character) [of person] courage m, cran* m ; [of government, organization] fermeté f ; **he's got no ~** il n'a pas de cran*

backchat· ['bæktʃæt] N (NonC) impertinence f

backdate [,bæk'deɪt] VT [+ cheque] antidater ; **increase ~d to January** augmentation f avec effet rétroactif à compter de janvier

backdoor ['bækdɔː'] ADJ [loan, attempt etc] déguisé ; [methods] détourné

backdrop ['bækdrɒp] N (Theat, fig) toile f de fond

-backed [bækt] ADJ (in compounds) **[a]** (= with back) à dossier ; **low-backed chair** chaise f à dossier bas **[b]** (= with backing) doublé de ; **rubber-backed carpet** tapis m doublé de caoutchouc **[c]** (= supported by) soutenu (**by** par) ; **American-backed** soutenu par les américains

backer ['bækə'] N (= supporter) partisan(e) m(f) ; (Betting) parieur m, -euse f ; (Fin) [of bill] avaliseur m ; [of firm, play, film, business venture] commanditaire m

backfire ['bæk'faɪə'] N **[a]** (Aut) (= explosion) raté m (d'allumage) ; (= noise) pétarade f ; (US: for halting a fire) contre-feu m **[2]** VI **[a]** (Aut) pétarader, avoir un raté (d'allumage) ; (US = halt a fire) allumer un contre-feu **[b]** (fig = miscarry) [plan] avoir l'effet inverse que prévu ; **to ~ on sb** se retourner contre qn ; **his tactics could ~ (on him)** sa tactique pourrait avoir l'effet inverse or se retourner contre lui

backgammon ['bæk,gæmən] N trictrac m, jacquet m

background ['bækgraʊnd] **[1]** N **[a]** (Theat, Cine) découverte f ; [of design, fabric, picture, photo] fond m ; **in the ~** dans le fond, à l'arrière-plan → **b** ; **on a blue ~** sur fond bleu **[b]** (fig) arrière-plan m, second plan m ; **to remain in the ~** s'effacer, rester dans l'ombre ; **to keep sb in the ~** tenir qn à l'écart **[c]** (Sociol) milieu m socioculturel, cadre m de vie ; (Pol) climat m politique ; (= basic knowledge) données fpl or éléments mpl de base ; (= job experience) expérience f ; (= education) formation f ; **he has a good professional ~** il a une bonne expérience professionnelle ; **family/working-class ~** milieu m familial/ouvrier ; **what is his ~?** (social) de quel milieu est-il ? ; (professional) qu'est-ce qu'il a comme expérience (professionnelle) ? ; **from diverse ~s** venant d'horizons différents **[d]** (= circumstances) antécédents mpl ; **can you**

fill me in on the ~ to this case? (gen) pouvez-vous me résumer les éléments de cette affaire ? ; (doctor) pouvez-vous me rappeler les antécédents or le dossier médical de ce patient ? ; (= history) pouvez-vous me rappeler l'historique de cette affaire ? ; **what is the ~ to these events?** quel est le contexte de ces événements ? ; **this decision was taken against a ~ of violence** cette décision a été prise dans un climat de violence ; **the meeting took place against a ~ of growing social unrest** la réunion s'est tenue sur fond d'une agitation sociale de plus en plus virulente

[2] COMP ► **background music** N (Rad, Theat, TV) musique f de fond ; **to play sth as ~ music** passer qch en fond sonore ► **background noise** N bruit m de fond ► **background paper** N document m de référence or d'information ► **background radiation** N (Phys) radioactivité f naturelle ► **background reading** N lectures fpl générales (autour du sujet) ► **background story** N (Press) papier m d'ambiance ► **background studies** NPL (études fpl de) culture f générale

backhand ['bækhænd] **[1]** ADJ [blow] en revers ; [writing] penché à gauche ; (Tennis) **~ drive** coup m droit de dos ; **~ volley/shot** coup m/volée f de dos **[2]** N (Tennis) revers m

backhanded [,bæk'hændɪd] ADJ [shot, blow] donné du revers de la main **[b]** [action] déloyal ; [compliment] équivoque

backhander [,bæk'hændə'] N (Brit) **[a]** (= blow) revers m **[b]** (* = reproof) réprimande f, semonce f **[c]** (* = bribe) pot-de-vin m

backing ['bækɪŋ] **[1]** N **[a]** (lit) renforcement m, support m ; [of book] endossure f ; [of picture] entoilage m **[b]** (Mus) accompagnement m **[c]** (fig: Fin, Pol) soutien m **[d]** (Betting) paris mpl **[e]** (= movement) [of horse, cart etc] recul m ; [of boat] nage f à culer ; [of wind] changement m de direction (en sens inverse des aiguilles d'une montre) **[2]** COMP ► **backing group** N (Mus) groupe m (accompagnant un chanteur) ► **backing singer** N (Mus) choriste mf ► **backing store** N (Comput) mémoire f auxiliaire ► **backing vocals** NPL (Mus) chœurs mpl

backlash ['bæklæʃ] N (Tech) secousse f, saccade f ; [of explosion] contrecoup m, répercussion f ; (Pol, fig) réaction f brutale ; (fig) **there was a ~ against reforms within the party** il y a eu une réaction brutale contre les réformes au sein du parti

backless ['bæklɪs] ADJ [dress etc] dos nu inv

backlist ['bæklɪst] N (liste f des) ouvrages mpl disponibles en stock

backlog ['bæklɒg] N [of rent] arriéré m (de loyers) ; **~ of work** travail m en retard ; (Comm) **~ of orders** commandes fpl en carnet, commandes fpl inexécutées ; (Fin) **~ of accumulated arrears** accumulation f d'arriérés de paiement

backrest ['bækrest] N [of chair] dossier m

backroom ['bækrʊm] N (fig) **the ~ boys*** (gen) les travailleurs mpl de l'ombre, ceux qui restent dans la coulisse ; (= experts, scientists) les chercheurs mpl anonymes or qui travaillent dans l'ombre

backshift ['bækʃɪft] N (= period) poste m du soir ; (= workers) équipe f du soir ; **to be on the ~** faire le (poste du) soir

backside ['bæksaɪd] N (= back part) arrière m ; (* = buttocks) derrière m, postérieur* m ; (fig) **to sit on one's ~*** rester le derrière sur sa chaise*

backslapping· ['bæk,slæpɪŋ] N (fig) (grandes) démonstrations fpl d'amitié

backslash ['bækslæʃ] N (Typ) barre f oblique inversée

backslider ['bækslaɪdə'] N récidiviste mf

backsliding ['bækslaɪdɪŋ] N récidive f

backspace ['bækspeɪs] **[1]** VI revenir en arrière **[2]** COMP ► **backspace key** N = backspacer

backspacer [,bæk'speɪsə'] N touche f d'espacement or de rappel arrière

backspin ['bækspɪn] N (Tennis, Cricket etc) coupé m ; **to give a ball ~ ◊ to put ~ on a ball** couper une balle

backstage [,bæk'steɪdʒ] **[1]** ADV derrière la scène, dans les coulisses **[2]** N coulisse(s) f(pl) ; **to go ~** aller dans les coulisses

backstairs [,bæk'steəz] **[1]** N escalier m de service ; (secret) escalier m dérobé **[2]** ADJ (in servants' quarter) [work, activities] des domestiques ; **~ gossip** or **rumours** (lit) commérages mpl de domestiques ; (fig) bruits mpl de couloir ; (fig) **~ intrigue** manigances fpl ; **the government did a ~ deal with the opposition** le gouvernement a manigancé quelque chose avec l'opposition

backstitch [,bæk'stɪtʃ] **[1]** N point m arrière **[2]** VT, VI coudre en point arrière

backstop ['bækstɒp] N (Sport) (= screen, fence) grillage m ; (US Baseball*) (= person) receveur m

backstreet ['bækstriːt] **[1]** ADJ [hotel, shop] louche **[2]** COMP ► **backstreet abortion** N avortement m clandestin or illégal ► **backstreet abortionist** N faiseuse f d'anges, avorteur m, -euse f (pej)

backstroke ['bækstrəʊk] N (Swimming) dos m crawlé

backswing ['bækswɪŋ] N (Sport) swing m en arrière

backtrack ['bæktræk] VI faire marche arrière or machine arrière (fig) ; **to ~ on a promise** revenir sur une promesse ; (US) **to ~ home*** retourner chez soi

backup ['bækʌp] **[1]** N (= support) appui m, soutien m (**from sb** de qn) ; (= reserves) réserves fpl ; [of personnel, police etc] renforts mpl **[2]** ADJ **[a]** [vehicles, supplies, weapons] supplémentaire, de réserve ; [pilot, personnel, policeman] en renfort **[b]** (Comput) de sauvegarde **[3]** COMP ► **backup copy** N copie f sauvegarde ► **backup disk** N disque m sauvegarde ► **backup file** N sauvegarde f ► **backup light** N (US Aut) feu m de recul, feu m de marche arrière ► **backup store** N mémoire f auxiliaire

backward ['bækwəd] **[1]** ADJ **[a]** (= to the rear) [look, step] en arrière ; [somersault] arrière ; (fig) [step, move] rétrograde, en arrière ; **~ and forward movement** mouvement m de va-et-vient ; **~ flow** contre-courant m ; (lit, fig) **he walked out without a ~ glance** il est parti sans jeter un regard en arrière **[b]** (= retarded) [district, nation, culture] arriéré, peu avancé ; [economy] arriéré ; [technology, equipment] peu moderne ; † [child] retardé ; **to be socially/economically ~** être en retard or être arriéré sur le plan social/économique **[c]** (= reluctant) peu disposé (**in doing** à faire) ; (= hesitant) hésitant ; **he wasn't ~ in offering his opinion** il ne s'est pas fait prier pour donner son avis ; (hum) **he's never been ~ in coming forward** il n'a pas peur de se mettre en avant

[2] ADV = backwards

[3] COMP ► **backward-looking** ADJ [project, attitude] rétrograde

backwardation ['bækwə,deɪʃən] N (St Ex) report m

backwardness ['bækwədnɪs] N **[a]** [of child] retard m mental ; (Econ) retard m ; **industrial/intellectual ~** retard m industriel/intellectuel **[b]** (= reluctance, shyness) réticence f, hésitation f (**in doing** à faire)

backwards ['bækwədz] ADV **[a]** (= towards the back) en arrière ; **to fall ~** tomber en arrière or à la renverse ; **to flow ~** aller or couler à contre-courant ; **to walk ~ and forwards** marcher de long en large, aller et venir ; **to go ~**

and forwards between two places aller et venir *or* faire la navette entre deux endroits → **lean over**

b (= *back foremost*) à rebours; **to go/walk ~** aller/marcher à reculons *or* à rebours; **the car moved ~ a little** la voiture a reculé un peu

c (= *in reverse of usual way*) à l'envers, en commençant par la fin; **I know the poem ~*** je connais le poème sur le bout des doigts; **I know this road ~*** je connais cette route comme ma poche; (*fig*) **he's got it ~*** (= *misunderstood*) il a tout compris de travers

d (*fig: in time*) en arrière, vers le passé; **to look ~** jeter un regard en arrière, remonter dans le passé; **to reckon ~ to a date** remonter jusqu'à une date

e (= *retrogressively*) en rétrogradant

backwash ['bækwɒʃ] N (*Naut*) remous *m*; (*fig*) contre-coup *m* (**from** provoqué par)

backwater ['bæk,wɔːtər] N [*of pool*] eau *f* stagnante; [*of river*] bras *m* mort; (*fig = backward place*) trou *m* perdu; (*fig = peaceful spot*) (petit) coin *m* tranquille; **to live in a ~** habiter un petit coin tranquille; (*pej*) habiter un trou perdu

backwoods ['bæk,wʊdz] NPL région *f* (forestière) inexploitée; (*fig pej*) **to live in the ~** vivre dans un trou perdu

backwoodsman ['bæk,wʊdzmən] N (*pl* **-men**) pionnier *m*; (*fig pej*) rustre *m*

backyard [,bæk'jɑːd] N (*Brit*) arrière-cour *f*; (*US*) jardin *m* (de derrière); (*fig*) **in one's own ~** à sa porte

bacon ['beɪkən] **1** N lard *m* (*gén en tranches*), bacon *m*; **~ fat/rind** gras *m*/couenne *f* de lard; **~ and eggs** œufs *mpl* au lard *or* au bacon; (*fig*) **to bring home the ~*** (= *be breadwinner*) faire bouillir la marmite*; (= *achieve goal*) décrocher la timbale* → **boil¹**, **save¹**, **streaky 2** COMP ► **bacon rasher** N tranche *f* de lard ► **bacon-slicer** N coupe-jambon *m inv*

Baconian [beɪˈkəʊnɪən] ADJ baconien

bacteria [bækˈtɪərɪə] NPL *of* **bacterium**

bacterial [bækˈtɪərɪəl] ADJ bactérien

bacteriological [bæk,tɪərɪəˈlɒdʒɪkəl] ADJ bactériologique

bacteriologist [bæk,tɪərɪˈɒlədʒɪst] N bactériologiste *mf*

bacteriology [bæk,tɪərɪˈɒlədʒɪ] N bactériologie *f*

bacterium [bækˈtɪərɪəm] N (*pl* **bacteria**) bactérie *f*

bad [bæd] **1** ADJ (*compar* **worse**, *superl* **worst**) **a** (= *wicked*) [*action, habit, behaviour*] mauvais; [*person*] méchant; **it was a ~ thing to do/to say** ce n'était pas bien de faire cela/de dire cela; **it was very ~ of you to treat her like that** c'était très mal de votre part de la traiter ainsi; **it's too ~ of you** ce n'est vraiment pas bien de votre part; **you ~ boy!** vilain!, méchant!; **~ dog!** vilain chien!; **he's a ~ lot** *or* **sort** *or* **type*** c'est un mauvais sujet; (*stronger*) c'est un sale type* → **blood, breath, language b** (= *inferior, poor quality*) [*workmanship*] mauvais, de mauvaise qualité; **she speaks very ~ English** ◊ **her English is very ~** elle parle très mal l'anglais, son anglais est très mauvais; **~ quality food/material** *etc* aliments *mpl*/tissu *m* *etc* de mauvaise qualité; (*Cricket etc*) **~ light stopped play** le match a été interrompu à cause du manque de lumière → **penny c** (= *unpleasant*) [*news, weather, smell*] mauvais; **there is a ~ smell in this room** ça sent mauvais dans cette pièce; **it's a ~ business** (= *sad*) c'est une triste affaire; (= *unpleasant*) c'est une mauvaise histoire; (= *terrible*) c'est une affreuse expérience → **news d** (= *difficult, going badly*) **business is ~** les affaires vont mal; **I didn't know things were so ~ between them** je ne savais pas que les choses allaient aussi mal entre eux; **it's not so ~** ce n'est pas si mal; **it's not ~ at all** ce

n'est pas mal du tout; **(that's) too ~!** (*indignant*) c'est un peu fort!; (*sympathetic*) quel dommage!; **how is he? — (he's) not so ~** comment va-t-il? — (il ne va) pas trop mal; **she's ill? that's very ~** elle est malade? c'est bien ennuyeux; **I've had a really ~ day** j'ai eu une très mauvaise journée; (*fig, hum*) **to have a ~ hair day*** être en petite forme; **to come to a ~ end** mal finir; **she's been having a really ~ time lately** elle traverse une période très difficile; **things are going from ~ to worse** les choses vont de mal en pis

e (= *serious*) [*mistake, accident, illness*] grave; [*sprain, wound*] sérieux; **a ~ error of judgement** une grossière erreur de jugement; **a ~ cold** un mauvais *or* gros rhume; **a ~ headache** un sérieux mal de tête; **a ~ case of chickenpox/flu** une mauvaise varicelle/grippe

f (= *unfortunate*) [*idea, decision, method*] mauvais; **that's not a ~ idea!** ce n'est pas une mauvaise idée!; **it was a ~ idea to invite him** c'était une mauvaise idée (que) de l'inviter; **it wouldn't be a ~ thing (to do)** ça ne ferait pas de mal (de faire), ce ne serait pas une mauvaise idée (de faire)

g (= *unfavourable*) [*report, publicity*] mauvais; [*opinion*] mauvais, triste; [*result*] mauvais, malheureux; **~ publicity** une mauvaise publicité

h (= *ill*) **to feel ~** se sentir mal; **I didn't know she was so ~** je ne la savais pas si malade; **to have a ~ back** (*on one occasion*) avoir mal au dos; (= *have back problems*) avoir des problèmes de dos; **to have a ~ head*** avoir mal à la tête; **his ~ leg** sa mauvaise jambe, sa jambe malade

i (= *guilty, uncomfortable*) **to feel ~ about doing sth** (= *reproach oneself*) s'en vouloir d'avoir fait qch; **I feel ~ about it** je m'en veux (de l'avoir fait); **she feels very ~ about the way she treated him** elle s'en veut de l'avoir traité ainsi

j (= *decayed*) [*food*] mauvais, gâté; [*tooth*] carié; **to go ~** [*food*] se gâter, pourrir; [*milk*] tourner; [*bread*] moisir; [*teeth*] se carier

k (= *false*) [*coin, money*] faux (fausse *f*)

l (= *harmful*) (**to be**) **~ for ...** (être) mauvais pour ...; **~ for the health/the eyes** mauvais pour la santé/les yeux; **not all forms of sugar are ~ for you** toutes les formes de sucre ne sont pas mauvaises; **this is ~ for you** ce n'est pas bon pour vous; **can exercise be ~ for you?** l'exercice peut-il faire du mal?, est-ce qu'il peut être mauvais de faire de l'exercice?; **it's ~ for business** c'est mauvais pour les affaires

m (= *not clever, not good*) **to be ~ at ...** être mauvais en ...; **~ at English/spelling** mauvais en anglais/en orthographe; **I'm ~ at languages** je ne suis pas doué pour les langues; **he's ~ at remembering birthdays** il n'est pas doué pour se rappeler les anniversaires

2 N (*NonC*) mauvais *m*; **to take the good with the ~** prendre le bon avec le mauvais; **he's gone to the ~*** il a mal tourné; **I am 50p to the ~*** j'en suis de 50 pence*; (*esp US*) **I'm in ~* with him** je ne suis pas dans ses petits papiers*, je suis mal vu de lui

3 ADV (= *is obsessed by*) **he's got it ~*** (*about hobby etc*) c'est une marotte chez lui; (*about person*) il l'a dans la peau*

4 COMP ► **bad apple** N (*fig = person*) brebis *f* galeuse ► **bad claim** N (*Insurance*) réclamation *f* mal fondée ► **bad debt** N créance *f* douteuse *or* irrécouvrable ► **bad-mannered** ADJ mal élevé ► **bad-mouth*** VT débiner* ► **bad-tempered** ADJ [*person*] qui a un mauvais caractère; (*on one occasion*) de mauvaise humeur; [*look, answer*] désagréable

baddie* ['bædɪ] N méchant *m*

baddish ['bædɪʃ] ADJ pas fameux, pas brillant

bade [bæd, beɪd] VB *pt of* **bid**

badge [bædʒ] N [*of team, association*] insigne *m*; [*of an order, police*] plaque *f*; (*Mil*) insigne *m*; (*sew-on, stick-on: for jeans etc*) badge *m*; (*Scouting*) badge *m*; (*fig = symbol*) symbole *m*, signe *m* (distinctif); **his ~ of office** l'insigne *m* de sa fonction

badger ['bædʒər] **1** N (= *animal, brush*) blaireau *m*; (*US*) **the Badger State** le Wisconsin **2** VT harceler, importuner (**with** de); **to ~ sb to do sth** *or* **into doing sth** harceler qn jusqu'à ce qu'il fasse qch, tanner* (la peau à) qn pour qu'il fasse qch; **to ~ sth out of sb** soutirer qch à qn à force de le harceler **3** COMP ► **badger baiting** N déterrage *m* de blaireaux

badinage ['bædɪnɑːʒ] N (*NonC: frm*) badinage *m*

badlands ['bædlændz] NPL (*US*) bad-lands *fpl*

badly ['bædlɪ] ADV (*compar* **worse**, *superl* **worst**)

a (= *poorly*) [*behave, function, start, end, sleep, designed, taught, written*] mal; **the project was very ~ managed** le projet a été très mal géré; **~ dressed** mal habillé; **to treat sb ~** ◊ **to behave ~ towards sb** mal se comporter avec qn; **some people react ~ to this medicine** certaines personnes réagissent mal à ce médicament; **he took it very ~** il a très mal pris la chose; **to go ~** mal se passer; **things aren't going too ~** ça ne se passe pas trop mal, les choses ne vont pas trop mal; **things are going pretty ~ for me at the moment** tout va assez *or* plutôt mal pour moi en ce moment; **to do** *or* **perform ~** [*athlete*] faire une mauvaise performance; [*pupil, student, company, economy*] avoir de mauvais résultats; [*political party*] (*in opinion polls*) ne pas être populaire; (*in elections*) obtenir de mauvais résultats; **the dollar is doing ~** le dollar n'est pas très fort; **you did ~ out of it** ◊ **you came off ~** tu n'as pas été gâté; **she didn't come off too ~ in the debate** elle ne s'est pas trop mal débrouillée dans ce débat; (*financially*) **to be ~ off** être dans la gêne; (*gen*) **they're not so ~ off** ils ne s'en tirent pas si mal que ça; **to be ~ off for sth** manquer de qch

b (= *unfavourably*) **to speak ~ of sb** dire du mal de qn; **to think ~ of sb** avoir une mauvaise opinion de qn; **nobody will think ~ of you if ...** personne ne t'en voudra si ...; **to reflect ~ on sb** donner une mauvaise image de qn

c (= *seriously*) [*wound, injure*] grièvement, gravement; [*affect*] gravement; [*disrupt*] sérieusement, gravement; **his schoolwork suffered very ~ after his mother died** son travail scolaire s'est beaucoup ressenti de la mort de sa mère; **she was ~ shaken after the accident** elle a été très secouée à la suite de cet accident; **they were ~ defeated** ils ont subi une sévère *or* cuisante défaite; (*physically*) **he was ~ beaten** il a été violemment frappé; **to go ~ wrong** très mal tourner; **something is ~ wrong with him** il ne va pas bien du tout; **the ~ disabled** les grands infirmes *mfpl*, les grands invalides *mfpl*

d (= *very much*) **to want sth ~** avoir très envie de qch; **I need it ~** j'en ai absolument besoin, il me le faut absolument; **I am ~ in need of advice** j'ai grand besoin de conseils; **I ~ need a haircut** j'ai vraiment besoin de me faire couper les cheveux; **the house ~ needs a coat of paint** la maison a sacrément besoin d'un coup de peinture *or* a besoin d'un bon coup de peinture; **we need the money ~** nous avons vraiment besoin de cet argent; **they will get their ~ needed medical supplies** ils vont recevoir les médicaments qui leur font cruellement défaut

badman* ['bæd,mæn] N (*pl* **-men**) (*US*) bandit *m*; (*in movies*) méchant *m*

badminton ['bædmɪntən] N badminton *m*

badness ['bædnɪs] N (*NonC*) **a** (= *poor quality*) mauvaise qualité *f*, mauvais état *m* **b** (= *wickedness*) méchanceté *f*

Baffin ['bæfɪn] N ~ **Bay** la mer or la baie de Baffin; ~ **Island** la terre de Baffin

baffle ['bæfl] [1] VT [+ person] déconcerter, dérouter; [+ pursuers] semer; [+ plot] déjouer; [+ hope, expectation] décevoir, tromper; [+ description, explanation] échapper à, défier [2] N (Tech) déflecteur m; (Acoustics) baffle m [3] COMP ▶ **baffle-board**, **baffle-plate** N (Tech) déflecteur m; (Acoustics) baffle m

bafflement ['bæflmənt] N confusion f

baffling ['bæflɪŋ] ADJ déconcertant, déroutant

BAFTA ['bæftə] N (ABBR = **British Academy of Film and Television Arts**) Académie britannique chargée de promouvoir le cinéma et la télévision

bag [bæg] [1] N sac m; (= luggage) sac m (de voyage); (Zool) sac m, poche f; **a ~ of apples** un sac de pommes; **a ~ of sweets** un sachet de bonbons; (Brit) **a ~ of chips** un cornet de frites; (fig) **a ~ of bones** un sac d'os*; **~s** (= luggage) bagages mpl, sacs mpl (de voyage); (Brit = trousers) falzar* m, pantalon m; (Brit) **~s of** des masses de*; **paper ~** sac m en papier; **she's got ~s under the** or **her eyes** elle a des poches sous les yeux; **with ~ and baggage** avec armes et bagages; **to pack up ~ and baggage** plier bagage, prendre ses cliques et ses claques*; **the whole ~ of tricks** tout le bataclan*, tout le fourbi*; **tea/coffee ~** sachet m de thé/café; (Hunting) **to get a good ~** faire bonne chasse, faire un beau tableau; **it's not my ~** ce n'est pas mon truc*; **it's in the ~** c'est dans le sac* or dans la poche*; (US) **he was left holding the ~** il s'est retrouvé avec tout sur les bras; (pej) **she's an old ~** c'est une vieille teigne; **you stupid (old) ~!** espèce de vieille croûte! → **cat**, **moneybag**

[2] VT [a]* (= get possession of) empocher, mettre le grappin sur*; (= steal) faucher*, piquer*; (Brit) **~s I** ◊ **I ~s (that)!** moi, je le prends!; (Brit = claim in advance) **Anne has already ~ged that seat** Anne s'est déjà réservé cette place [b] (Hunting = kill) tuer [c] (also ~ **up**) [+ flour, goods] mettre en sac, ensacher [3] VI (also ~ **out**) [garment] goder [4] COMP ▶ **bag lady*** N clocharde f ▶ **bag snatcher** N voleur m, -euse f à l'arraché ▶ **bag-snatching** N vol m à l'arraché

bagatelle [,bægə'tel] N (= trifle) bagatelle f; (Mus) divertissement m; (= board game) sorte de flipper; (Billiards) billard m anglais, billard m à blouses

bagel ['beɪgl] N (Culin) petit pain rond

bagful ['bægfʊl] N sac m plein, plein sac m

baggage ['bægɪdʒ] [1] N [a] (NonC = luggage) bagages mpl; (Mil) équipement m → **bag**, **emotional** [b] († = pert girl) coquine† f [2] COMP ▶ **baggage allowance** N poids m de bagages autorisé ▶ **baggage car** N (esp US) fourgon m ▶ **baggage check** N (US = receipt) bulletin m de consigne; (= security check) contrôle m des bagages ▶ **baggage checkroom** N (US) consigne f ▶ **baggage elastic** N pieuvre f ▶ **baggage hall** N = baggage reclaim (area) ▶ **baggage handler** N bagagiste m ▶ **baggage locker** N (casier m de) consigne f automatique ▶ **baggage reclaim (area)** N (in airport) livraison f des bagages ▶ **baggage room** N consigne f ▶ **baggage train** N (Mil) train m des équipages ▶ **baggage wagon** N = baggage car

bagging ['bægɪŋ] N (Tex) toile f à sac

baggy ['bægɪ] ADJ [a] (= puffy) gonflé, bouffant [b] [jacket, coat] trop ample, flottant; (fashionably) ample; **trousers ~ at the knees** pantalon m qui fait des poches aux genoux

Baghdad ['bæg'dæd] N Bagdad

bagpiper ['bægpaɪpəʳ] N (of Scottish bagpipes) joueur m de cornemuse; (of Breton bagpipes) joueur m de biniou or de cornemuse

bagpipes ['bægpaɪps] NPL (Scottish) cornemuse f; (Breton) biniou m, cornemuse f

baguette [bæ'get] N baguette f

bah [bɑː] EXCL bah!

Baha'i [bɑ'haɪ] [1] ADJ bahaï [2] N Bahaï(e) m(f)

Bahama [bə'hɑːmə] ADJ, N **the ~ Islands** ◊ **the ~s** les Bahamas fpl

Bahamian [bə'heɪmɪən] [1] ADJ bahamien [2] N bahamien(ne) m(f)

Bahrain [bɑː'reɪn] N Bahreïn

Bahraini [bɑː'reɪnɪ] [1] ADJ bahreïni [2] N Bahreïni mf

Bahrein [bɑː'reɪn] N Bahreïn

Baikal [baɪ'kɑːl] N **Lake ~** le lac Baïkal

bail¹ [beɪl] [1] N (Jur) mise f en liberté sous caution; (= sum) caution f; (= person) caution f, répondant m; **on ~** sous caution; **to free sb on ~** mettre qn en liberté provisoire sous caution; **to go** or **stand ~ for sb** se porter or se rendre garant de qn; **to find ~ for sb** fournir une caution pour qn (pour sa mise en liberté provisoire); **to ask for/grant/refuse ~** demander/accorder/refuser la mise en liberté sous caution; **to put up ~ for sb** payer la caution de qn → **jump**, **remand**

[2] VT [a] (Jur. also ~ **out**) faire mettre en liberté provisoire sous caution [b] [+ goods] mettre en dépôt

[3] COMP ▶ **bail bandit*** N (Brit) condamné qui commet une infraction pendant qu'il est en liberté provisoire sous caution ▶ **bail bond** N (US Jur) (= document) cautionnement m; (= money) caution f ▶ **bail bondsman** N (pl **bail bondsmen**) (US Jur) garant m (d'un condamné en liberté sous caution)

▶ **bail out** VT SEP [a] = **bail² 2a** [b] (fig) (gen) sortir d'affaire; (financially) renflouer; **to ~ o.s. out** s'en sortir

bail² [beɪl] N (Cricket) **~s** bâtonnets mpl (qui couronnent le guichet)

bail³ [beɪl] [1] VT [+ boat] écoper; [+ water] vider [2] N écope f

▶ **bail out** [1] VI (Aviat) sauter (en parachute) [2] VT SEP [+ boat] écoper; [+ water] vider [3] N **~out** → **bailout**

bailee [beɪ'liː] N (Jur) dépositaire m

bailey ['beɪlɪ] N (= wall) mur m d'enceinte; (= courtyard) cour f intérieure; **Bailey bridge** pont m Bailey → **old**

bailiff ['beɪlɪf] N (Jur) huissier m; (Brit) [of estate, lands] régisseur m, intendant m; (Hist) bailli m, gouverneur m

bailiwick ['beɪlɪwɪk] N [a] (Jur) juridiction f, circonscription f [b] (esp US = speciality) domaine m

bailor ['beɪləʳ] N (Jur) déposant m

bailout ['beɪlaʊt] N [of company] sauvetage m, renflouement m

bain-marie [,beɪnmə'riː, bɛ̃mɑri] N (pl **bains-marie**) bain-marie m

bairn [bɛən] N (Scot, N Engl) enfant mf

bait [beɪt] [1] N (Fishing, Hunting) amorce f, appât m; (fig) appât m, leurre m; (lit, fig) **to rise to** or **take** or **swallow the ~** mordre à l'hameçon [2] VT [a] [+ hook] amorcer; [+ trap] appâter, garnir d'un appât [b] (= torment) tourmenter → **bear²**

baize [beɪz] N (Snooker) tapis m; **~ door** porte f matelassée

bake [beɪk] [1] VT [a] [+ food] faire cuire au four; **she ~s her own bread** elle fait son pain elle-même; **to ~ a cake** faire (cuire) un gâteau; **~d apples** pommes fpl au four → **half** [b] [+ pottery, bricks] cuire; **earth ~d by the sun** sol desséché or cuit par le soleil [2] VI [a] [bread, cakes] cuire (au four) [b] **she ~s every Tuesday** (= makes bread) elle fait du pain tous les mardis; (= bakes cakes) elle fait de la pâtisserie tous les mardis [c] [pottery etc] cuire; (fig) **we are baking in this heat*** on cuit* or on grille* par cette chaleur; **it's baking**

(hot) today!* il fait une de ces chaleurs aujourd'hui! [3] COMP ▶ **baked Alaska** N omelette f norvégienne ▶ **baked beans** NPL haricots mpl blancs à la sauce tomate ▶ **baked potato** N pomme f de terre cuite au four

bakehouse ['beɪkhaʊs] N boulangerie f (lieu de fabrication)

Bakelite® ['beɪkəlaɪt] N bakélite® f

baker ['beɪkəʳ] [1] N boulanger m, -ère f; **~'s shop** boulangerie f [2] COMP ▶ **a baker's dozen** N treize m à la douzaine

bakery ['beɪkərɪ] N boulangerie(-pâtisserie) f

bakeware ['beɪkwɛəʳ] N (NonC) plats mpl et moules mpl à gâteaux

Bakewell tart ['beɪkwel'tɑːt] N tourte f de Bakewell

baking ['beɪkɪŋ] [1] N [a] (NonC = process) cuisson f (au four); **after ~** après la cuisson; **use wholemeal flour in your ~** faites votre pain (or vos gâteaux etc) à la farine complète; **she's busy doing her ~** elle est en train de faire son pain (or des gâteaux etc) [b] (in bakery = batch of bread) fournée f [2] COMP ▶ **baking dish** N plat m allant au four ▶ **baking powder** N levure f chimique ▶ **baking sheet** N plaque f ▶ **baking soda** N bicarbonate m de soude ▶ **baking tin** N (for cakes) moule m (à gâteaux); (for tarts) moule m à tarte, tourtière f ▶ **baking tray** N plaque f de four

baksheesh ['bækʃiːʃ] N bakchich m

Balaclava, **Balaklava** [,bælə'klɑːvə] N (Geog) Balaklava; (Brit) **balaclava (helmet)** passe-montagne m

balalaika [,bælə'laɪkə] N balalaïka f

balance ['bæləns] [1] N [a] (= scales) balance f; (fig) **to be** or **hang in the ~** être en jeu; **his life was hanging in the ~** (gen) sa vie était en jeu; [sick person] il était entre la vie et la mort; (fig) **to hold the ~** faire pencher la balance → **spring**

[b] (NonC = equilibrium) équilibre m, aplomb m; (lit, fig) **to keep/lose one's ~** garder/perdre son équilibre; (lit, fig) **off ~** mal équilibré; **to throw sb off ~** (lit) faire perdre l'équilibre à qn; (fig) couper le souffle à qn; **the ~ of nature** l'équilibre m de la nature; (Jur) **when the ~ of his mind was disturbed** alors qu'il n'était pas responsable de ses actes; (fig) **to strike a ~** trouver le juste milieu; **he has no sense of ~** n'a aucun sens des proportions or de la mesure; **a nice ~ of humour and pathos** un délicat dosage d'humour et de pathétique

[c] (Comm, Fin) solde m; (also **bank ~**) solde m (d'un compte); (in bank) **what's my ~?** quelle est la position de mon compte?; **credit/debit ~** solde m créditeur/débiteur; **~ in hand** solde m créditeur; **~ carried forward** (gen) solde m à reporter; (on balance sheet) report m à nouveau; **~ due** solde m débiteur; **to pay off the ~ of an account** solder un compte; **sterling ~s** balances fpl sterling

[d] (= remainder) reste m

[e] [of clock, watch] régulateur m, balancier m

[f] **on ~** à tout prendre, tout compte fait

[2] VT [a] (= maintain equilibrium of) tenir en équilibre; (= place in equilibrium) mettre or poser en équilibre; [+ wheels] équilibrer; (fig) équilibrer, compenser; **I ~d the glass on top of the books** j'ai posé le verre en équilibre sur les livres; **the seal ~d the ball on its nose** le phoque posa le ballon en équilibre sur son nez

[b] (= compare etc) balancer, peser; [+ two arguments, two solutions] comparer; **this must be ~d against that** il faut peser le pour et le contre

[c] (= counterbalance) (in weighing, symmetrical display etc) équilibrer; (in value, amount) compenser, contrebalancer; **they ~ each other** [two objects] (in weighing) ils se font contrepoids; (in symmetrical display) ils s'équilibrent

[d] (Comm, Fin) **to ~ an account** arrêter un

compte ; **to ~ the budget** équilibrer le budget ; **to ~ the books** arrêter les comptes, dresser le bilan ; **to ~ the cash** faire la caisse

③ VI ⓐ [*two objects*] se faire contrepoids ; [*acrobat etc*] se maintenir en équilibre ; [*scales*] être en équilibre ; **to ~ on one foot** se tenir en équilibre sur un (seul) pied

ⓑ (*Comm, Fin*) [*accounts*] s'équilibrer, être en équilibre

④ COMP ► **balance of payments** N balance *f* des paiements ; **~ of payments surplus/deficit** excédent *m*/déficit *m* de la balance des paiements ► **balance of power** N (*gen*) équilibre *m* des forces ; (*in government*) équilibre *m* des pouvoirs ; **the European ~ of power** l'équilibre *m* européen ► **balance of terror** N équilibre *m* de la terreur ► **balance of trade** N (*Econ*) balance *f* commerciale ► **balance sheet** N bilan *m* ► **balance weight** N contrepoids *m*

► **balance out** VT SEP (*fig*) contrebalancer, compenser

balanced ['bælənst] ADJ (*gen*) équilibré ; **~ views** vues *fpl* sensées *or* mesurées

balancing ['bælənsɪŋ] N ⓐ (= *equilibrium*) mise *f* en équilibre, stabilisation *f* ; **to do a ~ act** (*Theat*) faire de l'équilibrisme ; (*fig*) jongler ⓑ (*Comm, Fin*) **~ of accounts** règlement *m* *or* solde *m* des comptes ; (*Comm, Fin*) **~ of the books** balances *fpl* (mensuelles)

balcony ['bælkənɪ] N ⓐ balcon *m* ⓑ (*Theat*) fauteuils *mpl* or stalles *fpl* de deuxième balcon

bald [bɔːld] ① ADJ ⓐ (*gen*) chauve ; [*tyre*] lisse ; **as ~ as a coot*** *or* **an egg*** chauve comme une boule de billard* or comme un œuf* ; **to be going ~** perdre ses cheveux, devenir chauve ⓑ [*style*] plat, sec (sèche *f*) ; **a ~ statement** une simple exposition de faits ; **a ~ lie** un mensonge flagrant *or* non déguisé ② COMP ► **bald eagle** N aigle *m* d'Amérique ► **bald-headed** ADJ chauve, à (la) tête chauve ► **bald patch** N [*of person*] (petite) tonsure *f* ; [*of animal*] place *f* dépourvue de poils ; [*of carpet etc*] coin *m* dégarni *or* pelé

baldachin ['bɔːldəkɪn], **baldachino** [ˌbældəˈkiːnəʊ] N baldaquin *m*

balderdash ['bɔːldədæʃ] N balivernes *fpl*

balding ['bɔːldɪŋ] ADJ qui devient chauve, atteint de calvitie naissante

baldly ['bɔːldlɪ] ADV [*say, state*] abruptement

baldness ['bɔːldnɪs] N [*of person*] calvitie *f* ; [*of tyre*] état *m* lisse ; [*of mountains etc*] nudité *f* ; [*of style*] platitude *f*, pauvreté *f*

bale¹ [beɪl] ① N [*of cotton, hay*] balle *f* ② VT (*also ~ up*) mettre en balles

bale² [beɪl] VT (*Naut*) = **bail³ 1**
► **bale out** = **bail out** ; → **bail³**

Balearic [ˌbælɪˈærɪk] ADJ, N **the ~ Islands** ◊ **the ~s** les (îles *fpl*) Baléares *fpl*

baleful ['beɪlfʊl] ADJ sinistre, menaçant ; **to give sb/sth a ~ look** regarder qn/qch d'un œil torve

balefully ['beɪlfəlɪ] ADV [*look*] d'un œil torve ; [*say*] d'un ton sinistre *or* menaçant

Bali ['bɑːlɪ] N Bali

Balinese [ˌbɑːlɪˈriːz] ① ADJ balinais ② N ⓐ (= *person*) Balinais(e) *m(f)* ⓑ (*Ling*) balinais *m*

balk [bɔːk] ① N (*Agr*) terre *f* non labourée ; (*Constr*) (*on ceiling*) solive *f* ; (= *building timber*) bille *f* ② VT contrecarrer ③ VI [*horse*] se dérober (**at** devant) ; **to ~ at doing sth** [*person*] regimber pour faire qch

Balkan ['bɔːlkən] ADJ, N **the ~s** les Balkans *mpl* ; **the ~ States** les États *mpl* balkaniques ; **the ~ Peninsula** la péninsule Balkanique

balkanization [ˌbɔːlkənaɪˈzeɪʃən] N balkanisation *f*

ball¹ [bɔːl] ① N ⓐ (*gen, Cricket, Golf, Hockey, Tennis*) balle *f* ; (*inflated: Ftbl etc*) ballon *m* ; (*Billiards*) bille *f*, boule *f* ; (*Croquet*) boule *f* ; **as round as a ~** rond comme une boule *or* bille ; (*US fig*) **behind the eight ~*** dans le pétrin* ; **cat curled up in a ~** chat *m* couché en rond *or* pelotonné (en boule) ; **tennis/golf etc ~** balle *f* de tennis/de golf etc ; **croquet ~** boule *f* de croquet ; (*Met*) **~ of fire** ◊ **~ lightning** éclair *m* en boule

ⓑ (*fig phrases*) (*US*) **that's the way the ~ bounces!*** c'est la vie! ; **to keep a lot of ~s in the air** faire plein de choses à la fois ; **take the ~ and run with it!** vas-y fonce!*, saisis ta chance! ; **to keep the ~ rolling** (= *maintain conversation*) alimenter la conversation ; (= *maintain activity*) maintenir le mouvement ; (= *maintain interest*) soutenir l'intérêt ; **to start** *or* **set the ~ rolling*** lancer une affaire (*or* la conversation *etc*) ; **he's got the ~ at his feet** c'est à lui de saisir cette chance ; **the ~ is with you** *or* **in your court** (c'est) à vous de jouer ; (*US*) **to have something on the ~*** en avoir là-dedans* *or* dans le ciboulot‡ ; **to be on the ~*** (= *competent*) être à la hauteur (de la situation *or* des circonstances) ; (= *alert*) être vif et le bon* ; **he's a real ~ of fire*** il est débordant d'activité ; (*US*) **the whole ~ of wax** absolument tout → **eyeball, play, tennis**

ⓒ [*of rifle etc*] balle *f* ; (*lit, fig*) **~ and chain** boulet *m* → **cannonball**

ⓓ [*of wool, string*] pelote *f*, peloton *m* ; **to wind sth up into a ~** mettre qch en pelote

ⓔ (*Culin*) [*of meat, fish*] boulette *f* ; [*of potato*] croquette *f*

ⓕ (*Tech*) bille *f* (de roulement)

ⓖ (*Anat*) **~ of the foot** (partie *f* antérieure de la) plante *f* du pied ; **~ of the thumb** (partie *f* charnue du) pouce *m* → **eyeball**

② **balls**‡ NPL (*Anat*) couilles‡ *fpl* ; (*Brit* = *nonsense*) conneries‡ *fpl*, couillonnades‡ *fpl* ; (*Brit* = *courage*) **to have ~s**‡ avoir des couilles‡ ; (*esp US*) **~s!**‡ quelles conneries!‡ ; (*fig*) **to break sb's ~s** casser les couilles‡ à qn

③ VT [+ *wool etc*] mettre en pelote, pelotonner

④ VI s'agglomérer

⑤ COMP ► **ball-and-socket joint** N (joint *m* à) rotule *f* ► **ball bearings** NPL roulement *m* à billes ► **ball boy** N (*Tennis*) ramasseur *m* de balles ► **ball cartridge** N cartouche *f* à balle ► **ball control** N (*NonC: Ftbl, Basketball etc*) contrôle *m* du ballon ► **ball game** N jeu *m* de balle (*or* ballon) ; (*US*) match *m* de base-ball ; (*fig*) **it's a whole new ~ game*** ◊ **it's not the same ~ game*** c'est une tout autre histoire ► **ball girl** N (*Tennis*) ramasseuse *f* de balles ► **ball gown** N robe *f* de bal ► **ball-point (pen)** N stylo *m* (à) bille, (pointe *f*) Bic® *m* ► **ball-shaped** ADJ sphérique ► **balls-up*‡** N (*US*) bordel‡ *m* ; **he made a ~s-up of the job** il a foutu le bordel‡ *or* salopé le boulot‡ ; (*Brit*) **the meeting was a ~s-up** la réunion a été bordélique‡

► **ball up** ① VI (*Ski etc*) botter ② VT SEP‡ **balls up**

► **balls up**‡ ① VT SEP foutre la merde‡ *or* le bordel‡ dans ; **to get/be ballsed up** être/se retrouver dans la merde jusqu'au cou‡ ② **~s-up**‡ N → **ball¹**

ball² [bɔːl] N (= *dance*) bal *m* ; **to give a ~** donner un bal ; (*lit, fig*) **to open the ~** ouvrir le bal ; **to have a ~*** s'amuser comme des fous, se marrer* → **fancy**

ballad ['bæləd] N (*Mus*) romance *f* ; (*Literat*) ballade *f*

ballast ['bæləst] ① N (*NonC*) ⓐ (*Aviat, Naut*) lest *m* ; **ship in ~** vaisseau *m* en lest ; **to sail in ~** être sur lest ⓑ [*stone, clinker*] (*Rail*) ballast *m* ② VT ⓐ (*Aviat, Naut*) lester ⓑ (*Tech*) empierrer, caillouter ; (*Rail*) ballaster

ballbreaker‡ ['bɔːlˌbreɪkər] N chieuse‡ *f*

ballcock ['bɔːlkɒk] N robinet *m* à flotteur

ballerina [ˌbæləˈriːnə] N ballerine *f*

ballet ['bæleɪ] ① N ⓐ (= *show, work of art*) ballet *m* ⓑ (*NonC* = *type of dance*) danse *f* classique ② COMP ► **ballet dancer** N danseur *m*, -euse *f* classique ► **ballet lesson** N cours *m* de danse (classique) ► **ballet school** N école *f* de danse (classique) ► **ballet shoe** N chausson *m* de danse ► **ballet skirt** N tutu *m*

balletic [ˌbæˈletɪk] ADJ [*movement, grace, style*] de danseur de ballet

ballistic [bəˈlɪstɪk] ① ADJ balistique ; **to go ~*** piquer une crise* ② COMP ► **ballistic missile** N engin *m* balistique

ballistics [bəˈlɪstɪks] N (*NonC*) balistique *f*

balloon [bəˈluːn] ① N ⓐ (*Aviat*) ballon *m*, aérostat *m* ; **navigable/captive ~** ballon *m* dirigeable/captif ; **to go up in a ~** monter en ballon ; (*fig*) **the ~ went up*** l'affaire a éclaté ; (*meteorological* *or* *weather*) ballon-sonde *m* → **barrage** ⓑ (= *toy*) ballon *m* ⓒ (*for brandy: also ~ glass*) verre *m* ballon *inv* ; (*Chem: also ~ flask*) ballon *m* ⓓ [*in drawings, comic: for speech etc*] bulle *f* ② VI ⓐ **to go ~ing** faire une (*or* des) ascension(s) en ballon ⓑ (= *swell out*) gonfler, être ballonné ③ COMP ► **balloon tyre** N pneu *m* ballon

balloonist [bəˈluːnɪst] N aéronaute *mf*

ballot ['bælət] ① N ⓐ (*Pol etc*) (= *paper*) bulletin *m* de vote ; (= *method of voting*) scrutin *m* ; (= *round of voting*) (tour *m* de) scrutin *m* ; **to vote by ~** voter par scrutin ; **first/second ~** premier/second tour *m* de scrutin ; **to take a ~** procéder à un scrutin *or* à un vote ⓑ (= *drawing of lots*) tirage *m* au sort

② VI ⓐ (*Pol etc*) voter à bulletin secret ; **union members are currently ~ing on the offer** les membres du syndicat votent actuellement sur cette proposition (à bulletins secrets) ⓑ (= *draw lots*) tirer au sort ; **to ~ for a place** tirer au sort pour avoir une place

③ VT faire voter (à bulletin secret), consulter (au moyen d'un vote à bulletin secret) ; **the union is ~ing members on strike action** le syndicat fait voter la base (à bulletin secret) sur la décision de faire grève

④ COMP ► **ballot box** N urne *f* (électorale) ► **ballot-box stuffing** N (*US Pol*) bourrage *m* des urnes ► **ballot paper** N bulletin *m* de vote ► **ballot rigging** N (*Brit*) fraude *f* électorale

balloting ['bælətɪŋ] N (*US Pol*) scrutin *m*

ballpark ['bɔːlpɑːk] ① N (*US*) stade *m* de base-ball ; (*fig*) **to be in the (right) ~** [*estimates, figures*] être dans la bonne fourchette ; **the figures were in the ~ of our estimates** les chiffres rentraient dans la fourchette de nos premières estimations ; (*estimates, figures*) **we're in the same ~** on arrive à peu près à la même somme ; **the two companies are not in the same ~** les deux sociétés ne sont pas comparables ② ADJ [*figure, estimate*] approximatif

ballplayer ['bɔːlˌpleɪər] N (*US*) joueur *m* de base-ball

ballroom ['bɔːlrʊm] ① N [*of hotel*] salle *f* de danse ; [*of mansion*] salle *f* de bal ② COMP ► **ballroom dancing** N (*NonC*) danse *f* de salon

ballsy ['bɔːlzɪ] ADJ [*person, attempt*] gonflé*

bally†* ['bælɪ] ADJ (*before n: Brit*) sacré*, satané*

ballyhoo* [ˌbælɪˈhuː] N (*pej*) (= *publicity*) battage* *m*, bourrage *m* de crâne* ; (= *nonsense*) balivernes *fpl*

balm [bɑːm] N ⓐ (*lit, fig*) baume *m* ⓑ (*Bot*) mélisse *f* officinale ; (*also* **lemon ~**) citronnelle *f*

balmy ['bɑːmɪ] ADJ ⓐ (*liter*) (= *fragrant*) embaumé, parfumé ; (= *mild*) doux (douce *f*), adoucissant ⓑ (*Bot*) balsamique

baloney* [bəˈləʊnɪ] N (*NonC: esp US*) balivernes *fpl*

balsa ['bɔːlsə] N (*also* **~ wood**) balsa *m*

balsam ['bɔːlsəm] [1] N [a] (= substance) baume m [b] (= plant) balsamine f [c] (Chem) oléorésine f [2] COMP ▶ **balsam fir** N sapin m baumier

balsamic [bɔːl'sæmɪk] ADJ [vinegar] balsamique

balti ['bɔːltɪ, 'bæltɪ] N (Culin) plat indien mijoté dans un wok

Baltic ['bɔːltɪk] [1] N **the ~** (Sea) la (mer) Baltique [2] ADJ [trade, port] de la Baltique; **the ~ States** les pays mpl baltes

baluster ['bæləstə'] N balustre m; **~s** = bannisters

balustrade [,bæləs'treɪd] N balustrade f

bamboo [bæm'buː] [1] N bambou m [2] COMP [chair, fence] de or en bambou ▶ **Bamboo Curtain** N (Pol) rideau m de bambou ▶ **bamboo shoots** NPL pousses fpl de bambou

bamboozle* [bæm'buːzl] VT [a] (= deceive) embobiner*; **I was ~d into believing he was a qualified doctor** on m'a embobiné* en me faisant croire que c'était un médecin qualifié [b] (= perplex) déboussoler*; **she was quite ~d** elle ne savait plus où elle en était, elle était complètement déboussolée*

ban [bæn] [1] N interdit m; (Comm) embargo m; **to put a ~ on sth/sb's doing sth** interdire qch/à qn de faire qch [2] VT (gen) interdire (**sth** qch, **sb from doing** à qn de faire); (= exclude) [+ person] exclure (**from** de); **Ban the Bomb Campaign** campagne f contre la bombe atomique

banal [bə'nɑːl] ADJ banal, ordinaire

banality [bə'nælɪtɪ] N banalité f

banana [bə'nɑːnə] [1] N (= fruit) banane f; (= tree) bananier m [2] ADJ **to go ~s** devenir dingue*; (= get angry) piquer une crise* [3] COMP ▶ **banana-boat** N bananier m (cargo) ▶ **banana republic** N (pej) république f bananière ▶ **banana skin** N peau f de banane; (esp Brit fig) **to slip on a ~ skin** glisser sur une peau de banane ▶ **banana split** N (Culin) banana split m inv

band¹ [bænd] [1] N (gen, Comm) bande f; (narrow) bandelette f; [of barrel] cercle m; [of metal wheel] bandage m; (leather) lanière f; [of cigar] bague f; [of hat] ruban m; (Rad) bande f; (= magnetic tape) bande f (magnétique); [of gramophone record] plage f; (Tech) bande f or courroie f de transmission; (Educ) tranche f; (Opt) **~s of the spectrum** bandes fpl du spectre; [of metal] bande f métallique; **in a narrow ~** [figures, prices etc] varier à l'intérieur d'une fourchette étroite → **elastic, frequency, rubber¹, waistband, waveband** [2] VT [+ tax, property] **to be ~ed** être réparti par tranches [3] COMP ▶ **band-saw** N (Tech) scie f à ruban
▶ **band together** VI se grouper; (= form a gang) former une bande

band² [bænd] N [a] (= group) bande f, troupe f [b] (Mus) (gen) orchestre m; (brass only) fanfare f; **members of the ~** musiciens mpl → **brass, one-man**

bandage ['bændɪdʒ] [1] N (for wound) bande f; (Med = prepared dressing) bandage m, pansement m; (blindfolding) bandeau m; **head swathed in ~s** tête f enveloppée de pansements or de bandages → **crêpe** [2] VT (also ~ **up**) [+ broken limb] bander; [+ wound] mettre un pansement or un bandage sur; [+ person] mettre un pansement or un bandage à

Band-Aid® ['bændeɪd] N pansement m adhésif; (US* fig) [measures] de fortune; **a ~ approach** une méthode qui tient du rafistolage

bandan(n)a [bæn'dænə] N foulard m

B & B [,biːən'biː] N (ABBR = **bed and breakfast**) → **bed**

bandbox ['bændbɒks] N carton m à chapeau(x); (fig) **he looked as if he had just stepped out of a ~** il avait l'air de sortir d'une boîte

bandeau ['bændəʊ] N (pl **bandeaux** ['bændəʊz]) bandeau m

banderol(e) ['bændərɒl] N (Archit, Her, Naut) banderole f

banding ['bændɪŋ] N (Brit) [of school pupils] répartition f en groupes de niveaux (dans le primaire); [of houses] répartition f par tranches

bandit ['bændɪt] N (lit, fig) bandit m → **one**

banditry ['bændɪtrɪ] N (NonC) banditisme m

bandleader ['bænd,liːdə'], **bandmaster** ['bænd,mɑːstə'] N chef m d'orchestre; (Mil etc) chef m de musique or de fanfare

bandolier [,bændə'lɪə'] N cartouchière f

bandsman ['bændzmən] N (pl **-men**) musicien m (d'orchestre or de fanfare)

bandstand ['bændstænd] N kiosque m (à musique)

bandwagon ['bænd,wægən] N (fig) **to jump** or **climb on the ~** suivre le mouvement, prendre le train en marche*

bandwidth ['bændwɪdθ] N (Comput) largeur f de bande

bandy¹ ['bændɪ] VT [+ ball, reproaches] se renvoyer; [+ jokes] échanger; **to ~ blows (with sb)** échanger des coups (avec qn); **to ~ words (with sb)** discuter (avec qn)
▶ **bandy about, bandy around** VT SEP (pej) [+ story, report] faire circuler; [+ figures, sums] avancer; **to ~ sb's name about** parler de qn; **to have one's name bandied about** faire parler de soi; **his name is being bandied about in all the newspapers** il a son nom dans tous les journaux

bandy² ['bændɪ] ADJ [a] [leg] arqué, bancal [b] (also **~-legged**) [person] bancal; [horse] arqué; **to be ~-legged** avoir les jambes arquées

bane [beɪn] N [a] fléau m, peste f; **he's/it's the ~ of my life** il/cela m'empoisonne la vie; **rain is the ~ of holiday-makers** la pluie est le fléau numéro un des vacanciers; **spots can be the ~ of a teenager's life** les boutons peuvent empoisonner la vie d'un adolescent [b] (= poison) poison m

baneful ['beɪnfʊl] ADJ (liter) funeste, fatal; [poison] mortel

banefully ['beɪnfəlɪ] ADV funestement

bang [bæŋ] [1] N [a] (= noise) [of gun, explosives] détonation f, boum m; (Aviat) bang m (supersonique); [of door] claquement m; **the door closed with a ~** la porte a claqué; **to go off with a ~** [fireworks] détoner, éclater; (* = succeed) être une réussite du tonnerre*; (esp US) **to get more ~ for the buck** or **more ~s for your bucks*** en avoir pour son argent; (fig) **to end** or **finish not with a ~ but a whimper** finir en queue de poisson
[b] (= blow) coup m (violent)
[2] ADV* **to go ~** éclater; **~ in the middle** au beau milieu, en plein milieu; **~ against the wall** tout contre le mur; **I ran ~ into a traffic jam** je suis tombé en plein dans un embouteillage; **he came ~ up against fierce opposition** il s'est brusquement trouvé face à une opposition farouche; (Brit) **to hit the target ~ on** frapper en plein dans la cible or le mille; (Brit) **his answer was ~ on** sa réponse est tombée pile; (Brit) **she arrived ~ on time** elle est arrivée à l'heure pile; **~ goes my chance of promotion** je peux faire une croix sur mes chances de promotion, je peux dire adieu à mes chances de promotion; **~ goes the fantasy of retiring at 35*** on peut dire adieu au rêve de prendre sa retraite à 35 ans
[3] EXCL (firearm) pan!; (explosion) boum!
[4] VT [a] frapper violemment; **to ~ one's fist on the table** taper du poing sur la table, frapper la table du poing; **to ~ one's head against** or **on sth** se cogner la tête contre or à qch; (fig) **talking to him is like ~ing your head against a brick wall*** autant parler à un mur

que d'essayer de discuter avec lui; **to ~ the door** (faire) claquer la porte; **he ~ed the window shut** il a claqué la fenêtre
[b] (** = have sex with) baiser**
[5] VI [a] [door] claquer; (repeatedly) battre; [fireworks] éclater; [gun] détoner
[b] **to ~ on** or **at the door** donner de grands coups dans la porte; **to ~ on the table** taper du poing sur la table, frapper la table du poing
▶ **bang about*, bang around*** VI faire du bruit or du potin*
▶ **bang away** VI [guns] tonner; [person] (= keep firing) tirer sans arrêt (**at** sur); [workman etc] faire du vacarme; **to ~ away at sth** taper sans arrêt sur qch
▶ **bang down** VT SEP poser or jeter brusquement; **to ~ down the lid** rabattre violemment le couvercle; (on telephone) **to ~ down the receiver** raccrocher brutalement
▶ **bang into** VT FUS (= collide with) se cogner contre, heurter; **the car ~ed into a tree** la voiture a heurté un arbre or est rentrée* dans un arbre
▶ **bang on*** VI continuer à laïusser*; **to ~ on about sth** laïusser* sur qch
▶ **bang out** VT SEP [+ tune] taper
▶ **bang to** VI [door, window] se fermer en claquant
▶ **bang together** VT SEP [+ objects] cogner l'un(e) contre l'autre; **I could have ~ed their heads together!*** j'en aurais pris un pour taper sur l'autre!
▶ **bang up*** VT SEP (Brit) [+ prisoner] boucler*, coffrer*
▶ **bang up against** VT FUS = **bang into**

banger ['bæŋə'] N (Brit) [a] (* = sausage) saucisse f; **~s and mash** saucisses fpl à la purée [b] (* = old car) (vieux) tacot* m, (vieille) guimbarde f [c] (= firework) pétard m

Bangkok [bæŋ'kɒk] N Bangkok

Bangladesh [,bæŋglə'deʃ] N le Bangladesh

Bangladeshi [,bæŋglə'deʃɪ] [1] ADJ du Bangladesh [2] N habitant(e) m(f) or natif m, -ive f du Bangladesh

bangle ['bæŋgl] N jonc m, bracelet m

bangs [bæŋz] NPL (US = fringe) frange f (droite)

bang-up* ['bæŋʌp] ADJ (US) formidable, impec*

banish ['bænɪʃ] VT [+ person] exiler (**from** de, **to** en, à), bannir (**from** de); [+ cares, fear] bannir, chasser

banishment ['bænɪʃmənt] N bannissement m, exil m

banister ['bænɪstə'] N = **bannister**

banjax* ['bændʒæks] VT (US) assommer

banjaxed* ['bændʒækst] ADJ nase*

banjo ['bændʒəʊ] N (pl **banjos** or **banjoes**) banjo m

bank¹ [bæŋk] [1] N [a] (= mound) [of earth, snow, flowers] talus m; (Rail = embankment) remblai m; [of road, racetrack] bord m relevé; (in horse-racing) banquette f irlandaise; (Min = coal face) front m de taille; (= pithead) carreau m; [of sand] (in sea, river) banc m; **a ~ of clouds** un amoncellement de nuages
[b] (= edge) [of river, lake] bord m, rive f; (above water level) berge f; [of canal] bord m, berge f; **the ~s** [of river, lake] le rivage; (in Paris) **the left/right ~** la Rive gauche/droite
[c] (Aviat) virage m incliné or sur l'aile
[2] VT [a] (also ~ **up**) [+ road] relever (dans un virage); [+ river] endiguer; [+ earth] amonceler; **to ~ the fire** couvrir le feu
[b] (Aviat) **to ~ an aircraft** faire faire à un avion un virage sur l'aile
[3] VI [a] [snow, clouds etc] s'amonceler
[b] (Aviat) [pilot, aircraft] virer (sur l'aile)

bank² [bæŋk] [1] N [a] (= institution) banque f; (= office) agence f (bancaire), banque f; **~ issue** banque f d'émission; **the Bank of France** la Banque de France; **the Bank of England** la

Banque d'Angleterre ; (*fig*) **it's as safe as the Bank of England** ça ne court aucun risque, c'est de tout repos → **saving**
b (*Betting*) banque *f* ; **to break the ~** faire sauter la banque
c (*Med*) banque *f* → **blood, eyebank**
2 VT [+ *money*] mettre *or* déposer en banque ; (*Med*) [+ *blood*] entreposer, conserver
3 VI **to ~ with Lloyds** avoir un compte à la Lloyds ; **who do you ~ with?** à quelle banque êtes-vous ?, où avez-vous votre compte bancaire ?
4 COMP [*cheque, credit, staff*] bancaire ► **bank acceptance** N acceptation *f* bancaire ► **bank account** N compte *m* bancaire, compte *m* en banque ► **bank balance** N solde *m* bancaire ► **bank bill** N (*US*) billet *m* de banque ; (*Brit*) effet *m* bancaire ► **bankbook** N livret *m* or carnet *m* de banque ► **bank card** N carte *f* d'identité bancaire ► **bank charges** NPL (*Brit*) frais *mpl* bancaires ► **bank clerk** N (*Brit*) employé(e) *m(f)* de banque ► **bank draft** N traite *f* de banque ► **bank employee** N employé(e) *m(f)* de banque ► **Bank Giro** N (*Brit*) (paiement *m* par) virement *m* bancaire ► **bank holiday** N jour *m* férié ► **bank loan** N crédit *m* bancaire ► **bank manager** N directeur *m* d'agence (bancaire) ; **my ~ manager** mon banquier ► **bank rate** N taux *m* d'escompte ► **bank robber** N cambrioleur *m*, -euse *f* de banque ► **bank robbery** N cambriolage *m* de banque ► **bank statement** N relevé *m* de compte ► **bank transfer** N **by ~ transfer** par virement bancaire → **job**
►**bank on** VT FUS (= *count on*) compter sur ; **you mustn't** *or* **I wouldn't ~ on it** il ne faut pas compter là-dessus

bank³ [bæŋk] **1** N **a** (= *row, tier*) [*of organ*] clavier *m* ; [*of typewriter*] rang *m* ; (*Elec*) [*of switches*] rangée *f* ; **~ of oars** rangée *f* d'avirons **b** (= *rowers' bench*) banc *m* (de rameurs) **2** VT (*Sport*) **double/single ~ed rowing** nage *f* à couple/en pointe
►**bank up** VT SEP **a** (= *arrange in tiers*) étager, disposer par étages **b** → **bank¹ 2a**

bankable ['bæŋkəbl] ADJ (*Comm*) bancable, négociable en banque ; **to be ~** [*film star etc*] être une valeur sûre

banker ['bæŋkəʳ] **1** N (*Betting, Fin*) banquier *m* **2** COMP ► **banker's card** N carte *f* d'identité bancaire ► **banker's order** N (*Brit*) prélèvement *m* automatique ► **banker's reference** N références *fpl* bancaires

banking¹ ['bæŋkɪŋ] N (*Aviat*) virage *m* sur l'aile
banking² ['bæŋkɪŋ] **1** N (*Fin*) (= *transaction*) opérations *fpl* de banque *or* bancaires ; (= *profession*) profession *f* de banquier, la banque ; **to study ~** faire des études bancaires **2** COMP ► **banking hours** NPL heures *fpl* d'ouverture des banques ► **banking house** N banque *f*, établissement *m* bancaire ; **the big ~ houses** les grandes banques *fpl* ► **banking industry** N secteur *m* bancaire

banknote ['bæŋknəʊt] N (*Brit*) billet *m* de banque

bankroll* ['bæŋkrəʊl] (*esp US*) **1** N fonds *mpl*, finances *fpl* **2** VT financer

bankrupt ['bæŋkrʌpt] **1** N **a** (*Jur*) failli(e) *m(f)* **b** (* *fig* = *penniless person*) fauché(e)* *m(f)* **2** ADJ **a** (*Jur*) failli ; **to go ~** [*person, business*] faire faillite ; **to be ~** [*person*] être en faillite ; **to be declared ~** être déclaré *or* mis en faillite **b** (* *fig* = *penniless*) fauché* **c** (= *completely lacking*) **spiritually/morally** *etc* ~ dépourvu *or* dénué de spiritualité/de moralité *etc* ; **~ of ideas** *etc* dépourvu *or* dénué d'idées *etc* **3** VT **a** (*Jur*) [*person*] mettre en faillite **b** (* *fig*) ruiner **4** COMP ► **bankrupt's certificate** N concordat *m* ► **bankrupt's estate** N actif *m* de la faillite

bankruptcy ['bæŋkrəptsɪ] **1** N **a** (*Jur*) faillite *f* **b** (* *fig* = *pennilessness*) ruine *f* **c** (*fig* = *lack*) **spiritual/moral** *etc* ~ manque *m* de spiritualité/de moralité *etc* **2** COMP ► **Bankruptcy Court** N (*Brit*) ≈ tribunal *m* de commerce ► **bankruptcy estate** N masse *f* or actif *m* de la faillite ► **bankruptcy proceedings** NPL procédure *f* de faillite

banner ['bænəʳ] **1** N bannière *f*, étendard *m* ; (*Rel, fig*) bannière *f* **2** COMP ► **banner headlines** NPL (*Press*) gros titres *mpl* ; **in ~ headlines** en gros titres, sur cinq colonnes à la une

banning ['bænɪŋ] N (= *prohibition*) [*of activity, publication, film, organization, substance*] interdiction *f* ; **the ~ of right-wing parties** l'interdiction *f* des partis de droite ; **the ~ of anti-apartheid leaders** l'interdiction *f* frappant les dirigeants du mouvement anti-apartheid ; **the ~ of cars from city centres** l'interdiction *f* de la circulation automobile dans les centre-villes ; **the ~ of three athletes from the Olympic Games** l'exclusion *f* de trois athlètes des Jeux olympiques

bannister ['bænɪstəʳ] N rampe *f* (d'escalier) ; **to slide down the ~(s)** descendre sur la rampe

banns [bænz] NPL bans *mpl* (de mariage) ; **to call the ~** publier les bans

banquet ['bæŋkwɪt] **1** N (= *ceremonial dinner*) banquet *m* ; (= *lavish meal*) festin *m* **2** VI faire un banquet, festoyer **3** COMP ► **banqueting hall** N salle *f* de(s) banquet(s)

banquette [ˌbæŋ'ket] N banquette *f*

banshee ['bænʃiː] N fée *f* (dont les cris présagent la mort)

bantam ['bæntəm] **1** N coq *m* nain, poule *f* naine **2** COMP ► **bantam-weight** N (*Boxing*) poids *m* coq

banter ['bæntəʳ] **1** N badinage *m*, plaisanteries *fpl* **2** VI badiner, plaisanter

bantering ['bæntərɪŋ] ADJ plaisantin, badin

Bantu ['bæntuː] **1** ADJ bantou **2** N (*pl* **Bantu** *or* **Bantus**) **a** (= *people*) **~(s)** Bantous *mpl* **b** (*Ling*) Bantou *m*

banyan ['bænɪən] N banian *m*

BAOR [ˌbiːeɪəʊˈɑːʳ] N (ABBR = **British Army of the Rhine**) troupes britanniques stationnées en RFA

bap [bæp] N (*Brit Culin*) petit pain *m*

baptism ['bæptɪzəm] N baptême *m* ; **~ of fire** baptême *m* du feu

baptismal [bæp'tɪzməl] **1** ADJ de baptême **2** COMP ► **baptismal font** N fonts *mpl* baptismaux ► **baptismal name** N nom *m* de baptême ► **baptismal vows** NPL vœux *mpl* du baptême

baptist ['bæptɪst] **1** N **a** baptiste *m* ; (*Saint*) **John the Baptist** saint Jean-Baptiste **b** (*Rel*) **Baptist** baptiste *mf* **2** ADJ (*Rel*) **Baptist** baptiste **3** COMP ► **the Baptist Church** N l'Église *f* baptiste

baptize [bæp'taɪz] VT (*Rel, fig*) baptiser

bar¹ [bɑːʳ] **1** N **a** (= *block, slab*) [*of metal*] barre *f* ; [*of wood*] planche *f* ; [*of gold*] lingot *m* ; [*of chocolate*] tablette *f* ; **~ of soap** savonnette *f*, pain *m* de savon ; **~ of gold** lingot *m* (d'or)
b (= *rod*) [*of window, cage*] barreau *m* ; [*of grate*] barre *f* ; [*of door*] barre *f*, bâcle *f* ; (*Sport*) barre *f* ; [*of ski-lift*] perche *f* ; [*of electric fire*] résistance *f* ; **a two-~ electric fire** un radiateur électrique à deux résistances ; **to be/put sb behind (prison) ~s** être/mettre qn derrière les barreaux → **anti-roll bar, parallel**
c [*of river, harbour*] barre *f*
d (*fig* = *obstacle*) obstacle *m* ; **to be a ~ to progress** faire obstacle au progrès → **colour**
e [*of light*] raie *f* ; [*of colour*] bande *f*
f (*NonC: Jur*) (= *profession*) barreau *m* ; (*in court*) barre *f* ; **to call** (*Brit*) *or* **admit** (*US*) **sb to the ~** inscrire qn au barreau ; **to be called** (*Brit*) *or* **admitted** (*US*) **to the ~** s'inscrire au

barreau ; **to read for the ~** préparer le barreau ; **the prisoner at the ~** l'accusé(e) *m(f)*
g (= *public house*) café *m*, bar *m* ; [*of hotel, theatre*] bar *m* ; [*of station*] café *m*, bar *m* ; [*at open-air shows etc*] buvette *f* → **coffee, public**
h (= *counter*) (*for drinks*) comptoir *m* ; **to have a drink at the ~** prendre un verre au comptoir ; (*Comm*) **sock/hat ~** rayon *m* des chaussettes/des chapeaux ; **heel ~** talon-minute *m*
i (*Mus*) mesure *f* ; (*also* **~ line**) barre *f* de mesure ; **the opening ~s** les premières mesures *fpl* → **double**
j (*Brit Mil*) barrette *f* (portée sur le ruban d'une médaille) ; (*US Mil*) galon *m*
k (*Her*) burelle *f*
l (*Met*) bar *m*
2 VT **a** (= *obstruct*) [+ *road*] barrer ; **to ~ sb's way** *or* **path** barrer le passage à qn, couper la route à qn ; **to ~ the way to progress** faire obstacle au progrès
b (= *put bars on*) [+ *window*] munir de barreaux ; **to ~ the door** mettre la barre à la porte ; (*lit, fig*) **to ~ the door against sb** barrer la porte à qn
c (= *exclude, prohibit*) [+ *person*] exclure (**from** de) ; [+ *action, thing*] défendre ; **to ~ sb from doing sth** interdire à qn de faire qch ; **many jobs were ~red to them** de nombreux emplois leur étaient interdits ; **they're ~red from the country/the pub** il leur est interdit d'entrer dans le pays/le bar ; **she ~s smoking in her house** elle défend qu'on fume (*subj*) chez elle ; (*Jur*) **to be ~red** [*contract provisions*] se prescrire → **hold**
d (= *stripe*) rayer, barrer
3 COMP ► **bar billiards** N (*NonC: Brit*) forme de billard joué dans les pubs ► **bar chart** N = **bar graph** ► **bar code** N (*Comm*) code *m* à barres, code-barre *m* ► **bar-coded** ADJ avec code à barres, avec code-barre ► **bar-code reader** N lecteur *m* de code à barres *or* de code-barre ► **bar girl*** N (*US*) entraîneuse *f* de bar ► **bar graph** N graphique *m* en barres *or* en tuyaux d'orgue

bar² [bɑːʳ] PREP sauf, à l'exception de ; **~ none** sans exception ; **~ one** sauf un(e) → **shouting**

Barabbas [bəˈræbəs] N Barabbas *m*

barb¹ [bɑːb] **1** N **a** [*of fish hook*] barbillon *m* ; [*of arrow*] barbelure *f* ; [*of feather*] barbe *f* **b** (*fig*) [*of wit etc*] trait *m* ; **the ~s of criticism** les traits *mpl* acérés de la critique **c** (*Dress*) barbette *f* **2** VT [+ *arrow*] garnir de barbelures, barbeler ; [+ *fish hook*] garnir de barbillons **3** COMP ► **barb wire** N = **barbed wire** ; → **barbed**

barb² [bɑːb] N (= *horse*) (cheval *m*) barbe *m*

Barbadian [bɑːˈbeɪdɪən] **1** ADJ barbadien **2** N Barbadien(ne) *m(f)*

Barbados [bɑːˈbeɪdɒs] N la Barbade ; **in ~** à la Barbade

barbarian [bɑːˈbɛərɪən] ADJ, N (*Hist, fig*) barbare *m*

barbaric [bɑːˈbærɪk] ADJ (*Hist, fig*) barbare, de barbare

barbarism ['bɑːbərɪzəm] N **a** (*NonC*) barbarie *f* **b** (*Ling*) barbarisme *m*

barbarity [bɑːˈbærɪtɪ] N barbarie *f*, cruauté *f* ; **the barbarities of modern warfare** la barbarie *or* les atrocités *fpl* de la guerre moderne

barbarize ['bɑːbəraɪz] VT **a** [+ *people*] ramener à l'état barbare **b** [+ *language*] corrompre

Barbarossa [ˌbɑːbəˈrɒsə] N Barberousse *m*

barbarous ['bɑːbərəs] ADJ (*Hist, Ling, fig*) barbare

barbarously ['bɑːbərəslɪ] ADV cruellement, inhumainement

Barbary ['bɑːbərɪ] **1** N la Barbarie, les États *mpl* barbaresques **2** COMP ► **Barbary ape** N magot *m* ► **the Barbary Coast** N les côtes *fpl* de Barbarie ► **Barbary duck** N canard *m* de

Barbarie ► **Barbary horse** N (cheval *m*) barbe *m*

barbecue ['bɑ:bɪkju:] (*vb: prp* **barbecuing**) **1** N barbecue *m* ; **to have a ~** faire *or* organiser un barbecue **2** VT griller au charbon de bois **3** COMP ► **barbecue sauce** N sauce *f* barbecue

barbed [bɑ:bd] **1** ADJ **a** [*arrow*] barbelé **b** (*fig*) [*words, wit*] acéré **2** COMP ► **barbed wire** N fil *m* de fer barbelé ► **barbed wire entanglements** NPL (réseau *m* de) barbelés *mpl* ► **barbed wire fence** N (haie *f* de fils) barbelés *mpl*

barbel ['bɑ:bəl] N (= *fish*) barbeau *m* ; (*smaller*) barbillon *m* ; (= *filament*) barbillon *m*

barbell ['bɑ:bel] N (*Sport*) barre *f* d'haltères

barber ['bɑ:bə^r] **1** N coiffeur *m* (pour hommes) ; (*Brit*) ~'s salon *m* de coiffure (pour hommes) ; **to go to the ~'s** aller chez le coiffeur **2** COMP ► **barber's pole** N enseigne *f* de coiffeur

barbershop ['bɑ:bəʃɒp] **1** N **a** (*US: = shop*) salon *m* de coiffure (pour hommes) **b** (*Mus*) mélodies *fpl* sentimentales (*chantées en harmonie étroite*) **2** COMP ► **barbershop quartet** N (*Mus*) groupe de quatre hommes chantant en harmonie étroite

barbican ['bɑ:bɪkən] N barbacane *f*

Barbie® ['bɑ:bɪ] N (*also* ~ **doll**) poupée *f* Barbie®

barbitone ['bɑ:bɪtəʊn] N véronal *m*

barbiturate [bɑ:'bɪtjʊrɪt] **1** N barbiturique *m* **2** COMP ► **barbiturate poisoning** N le barbiturisme

barbituric [,bɑ:bɪ'tjʊərɪk] ADJ barbiturique

barbs: [bɑ:bz] NPL (*US*) barbis: *fpl*, barbituriques *mpl*

barcarol(l)e [,bɑ:kə'rəʊl] N barcarolle *f*

Barcelona [,bɑ:sɪ'ləʊnə] N Barcelone

bard[1] [bɑ:d] N (= *minstrel*) (*esp Celtic*) barde *m* ; [*of Ancient Greece*] aède *m* ; (*Poetry, also hum* = *poet*) poète *m* ; **the Bard of Avon** le chantre d'Avon (*Shakespeare*)

bard[2] [bɑ:d] (*Culin*) **1** N barde *f* (de lard) **2** VT barder

bardic ['bɑ:dɪk] ADJ (*esp Celtic*) [*poetry etc*] du barde, des bardes

bare [bɛə^r] **1** ADJ **a** (= *naked, uncovered*) [*person, skin, sword, floor etc*] nu ; [*hill, summit*] pelé ; [*countryside, tree*] dénudé, dépouillé ; (*Elec*) [*wire*] dénudé, à nu ; **~ to the waist** nu jusqu'à la ceinture ; **in his ~ skin*** tout nu ; **he killed the wolf with his ~ hands** il a tué le loup à mains nues ; **to fight with ~ hands** se battre à main nue ; **there are ~ patches on the lawn** la pelouse est pelée par endroits ; **the dog had a few ~ patches on his back** le chien avait la peau du dos pelée par endroits ; **with his head ~** nu-tête *inv* ; **to sleep on ~ boards** coucher sur la dure ; (*fig*) **the ~ bones** les grandes lignes *fpl*, les lignes *fpl* essentielles ; (*fig*) **to strip sth down to the ~ bones** réduire qch à l'essentiel *or* à sa plus simple expression → **3** ; **she told him the ~ bones of the story** elle lui a raconté les grandes lignes *or* les lignes essentielles de l'histoire ; (*Cards*) **ace/king ~ as** *m*/roi *m* sec → **lay**

b (= *empty, unadorned*) [*garden*] dépouillé de sa végétation ; [*wall*] nu ; [*style*] dépouillé ; **a room ~ of furniture** une pièce vide ; **a ~ cupboard** un placard vide *or* dégarni ; **a ~ statement of facts** un simple énoncé des faits ; **they only told us the ~ facts** ils ne nous ont raconté que les faits à l'état brut

c (= *absolute*) **the ~ necessities (of life)** le strict nécessaire ; **to provide people with the ~ necessities of life** assurer aux gens le minimum vital ; **we're happy with the ~ necessities of life** nous nous contentons du strict minimum ; **the ~ essentials** le strict nécessaire ; **the ~ essentials of furnishing** les meubles *mpl* de base ; **a ~ majority** une faible majorité ; **the**

~ minimum le plus strict minimum

d (= *mere*) **the match lasted a ~ 18 minutes** le match n'a pas duré plus de 18 minutes ; **sales grew at a ~ two percent a year** les ventes n'ont pas augmenté de plus de deux pour cent par an

2 VT mettre à nu, découvrir ; [+ *sword*] dégainer, tirer du fourreau ; (*Elec*) [+ *wire*] dénuder, mettre à nu ; **to ~ one's teeth** [*person, animal*] montrer les dents (**at** à) ; **he ~d his teeth in a smile** il a grimacé un sourire ; **to ~ one's head** se découvrir (la tête) ; **to ~ one's soul (to sb)** mettre son cœur à nu (à qn)

3 COMP ► **bare-bones** ADJ (*esp US*) réduit à l'essentiel *or* à sa plus simple expression ► **bare-knuckle** ADJ [*fight*] à mains nues ; (*fig*) [*confrontation*] à couteaux tirés ► **bare owner** N nu(e)-propriétaire *m(f)* ► **bare ownership, bare property** N nue-propriété *f*

bareback ['bɛəbæk] ADV à cru ; **~ rider** cavalier *m*, -ière *f* qui monte à cru

barefaced [,bɛə'feɪst] ADJ [*lie, liar*] éhonté ; **it is ~ robbery** c'est un *or* du vol manifeste

barefoot(ed) [,bɛə'fʊt(ɪd)] **1** ADV nu-pieds, (les) pieds nus **2** ADJ aux pieds nus

bareheaded [,bɛə'hedɪd] **1** ADV nu-tête *inv*, (la) tête nue **2** ADJ nu-tête *inv* ; [*woman*] en cheveux†

barelegged [,bɛə'legd] **1** ADV nu-jambes, (les) jambes nues **2** ADJ aux jambes nues

barely ['bɛəlɪ] ADV **a** (= *only just*) à peine, tout juste ; **he can ~ read** c'est tout juste *or* à peine s'il sait lire, il sait tout juste *or* à peine lire ; **the temperature ~ rose above freezing** la température est à peine montée au-dessus de zéro ; **~ visible/perceptible** à peine visible/perceptible ; **her voice was ~ audible** sa voix était à peine audible, on entendait à peine sa voix ; **he was ~ able to speak** il pouvait à peine parler ; **she was ~ conscious** elle était à peine consciente ; **~ concealed** *or* **disguised resentment/contempt** une rancœur/un mépris mal dissimulé(e) ; **she had ~ begun to speak when ...** elle avait à peine commencé de parler lorsque ... ; **the car was ~ a year old** la voiture avait à peine un an ; **~ half the graduates had found jobs** à peine la moitié des diplômés avaient trouvé des emplois ; **the truce is holding, ~** la trêve est respectée, (mais) tout juste

b **a ~ furnished room** (= *poorly furnished*) une pièce pauvrement meublée ; (= *scantily furnished*) une pièce très peu meublée

c (= *plainly*) sans ambages ; **to state a fact ~** ne pas tourner autour du pot

bareness ['bɛənɪs] N [*of person*] nudité *f* ; [*of room*] dénuement *m* ; [*of furniture*] pauvreté *f* ; [*of style*] (= *poverty*) sécheresse *f*, pauvreté *f* ; (= *simplicity*) dépouillé *m*

Barents Sea ['bærənts'si:] N mer *f* de Barents

barf: [bɑ:f] VI (*US*) dégueuler:

barfly* ['bɑ:flaɪ] N (*US*) pilier *m* de bistro(t)

bargain ['bɑ:gɪn] **1** N **a** (= *transaction*) marché *m*, affaire *f* ; **to make** *or* **strike** *or* **drive a ~** conclure un marché (**with** avec) ; **it's a ~!** c'est convenu *or* entendu ! ; **a good ~** une bonne affaire ; **a ~'s a ~** on ne peut pas revenir sur un marché conclu ; (*fig*) **to keep one's side of the ~** tenir ses engagements ; **into the ~** par-dessus le marché, en plus ; **best, drive**

b (= *good buy*) occasion *f* ; **it's a (real) ~!** c'est une véritable occasion *or* affaire !

2 VI **a** (= *haggle*) **to ~ with sb** marchander avec qn ; **to ~ over an article** marchander un article

b (= *negotiate*) négocier (**with** avec) ; **to ~ with sb for sth** négocier qch avec qn

c (= *count on*) **to ~ for sth** s'attendre à qch ; **I didn't ~ for that** je ne m'attendais pas à cela ; **I got more than I ~ed for** je ne m'attendais pas à cela ; **to ~ on sth** compter sur qch ; **to ~**

on doing sth penser faire qch ; **to ~ on sb's doing sth** s'attendre à ce que qn fasse qch

3 COMP ► **bargain basement** N coin *m* des (bonnes) affaires ► **bargain-hunter** N personne *f* à l'affût des bonnes occasions ► **bargain-hunting** N chasse *f* aux (bonnes) occasions ► **bargain offer** N (*Comm*) offre *f* exceptionnelle ; **this week's ~ offer** la promotion de la semaine ► **bargain price** N prix *m* avantageux ► **bargain sale** N soldes *fpl*

bargaining ['bɑ:gənɪŋ] **1** N marchandage *m* ; **that gives us more ~ power** ceci nous met dans une position de force *or* nous donne plus d'atouts dans les négociations ► **collective** **2** COMP ► **bargaining chip** N to use sth as a **~ chip** se servir de qch comme argument dans une négociation ► **bargaining table** N table *f* de négociations

barge [bɑ:dʒ] **1** N (*on river, canal*) chaland *m* ; (*large*) péniche *f* ; (*with sail*) barge *f* ; **the admiral's ~** la vedette de l'amiral ; **motor ~** chaland *m* automoteur, péniche *f* automotrice ; **state ~** barque *f* de cérémonie **2** VI **he ~d through the crowd** il bousculait les gens pour passer **3** COMP ► **barge pole** N gaffe *f* ; (*Brit*) **I wouldn't touch it with a ~ pole*** (*revolting*) je n'y toucherais pas avec des pincettes ; (*risky*) je ne m'y frotterais pas

► **barge about, barge around** VI aller et venir comme un troupeau d'éléphants*

► **barge in** VI (= *enter*) faire irruption ; (= *interrupt*) interrompre la conversation ; (= *interfere*) se mêler de ce qui ne vous regarde pas

► **barge into** VT FUS **a** (= *knock against*) [+ *person*] rentrer dans* ; [+ *thing*] donner *or* se cogner contre ; **to ~ into a room** faire irruption dans une pièce, entrer sans façons dans une pièce **b** (= *interfere in*) [+ *discussion*] (*clumsily*) intervenir mal à propos dans ; (*rudely*) intervenir impoliment dans ; [+ *affair*] s'immiscer dans

► **barge through** VI traverser comme un ouragan

bargee [bɑ:'dʒi:] N (*Brit*) batelier *m*, marinier *m*

bargeman ['bɑ:dʒmən] N (*pl* -**men**) batelier *m*, marinier *m*

baritone ['bærɪtəʊn] **1** N (= *voice, singer, instrument*) baryton *m* **2** COMP [*voice, part*] de baryton

barium ['bɛərɪəm] **1** N baryum *m* **2** COMP ► **barium enema** N (*Med*) lavement *m* baryté ► **barium meal** N (*Med*) (bouillie *f* de) sulfate *m* de baryum

bark[1] [bɑ:k] **1** N [*of tree*] écorce *f* ; **to strip the ~ off a tree** écorcer un arbre **2** VT [+ *tree*] écorcer ; **to ~ one's shins** s'écorcher *or* s'égratigner les jambes

bark[2] [bɑ:k] **1** N [*of dog*] aboiement *m* ; [*of fox*] glapissement *m* ; (* = *cough*) toux *f* sèche ; **to let out a ~** (*lit*) aboyer ; (= *cough*) tousser ; **his ~ is worse than his bite** il fait plus de bruit que de mal, chien qui aboie ne mord pas **2** VI [*dog*] aboyer (**at** après) ; [*fox*] glapir ; [*gun*] aboyer ; (= *speak sharply*) aboyer ; (= *cough*) tousser ; **to ~ at sb** aboyer après qn ; (*fig*) **to ~ up the wrong tree** faire fausse route **3** VT **"leave me in peace!", he ~ed** « laisse-moi tranquille ! », aboya-t-il

► **bark out** VT SEP [+ *order*] glapir

bark[3] [bɑ:k] N (*liter*) barque *f* ; (*Naut*) trois-mâts *m inv or* quatre-mâts *m inv* carré

barkeeper ['bɑ:ki:pə^r] N (*US*) barman *m*, barmaid *f*

barker ['bɑ:kə^r] N [*of fairground*] bonimenteur *m*, aboyeur† *m*

barking ['bɑ:kɪŋ] **1** N [*of dog*] aboiement *m* ; [*of fox*] glapissement *m* **2** ADJ (*Brit*: *also* ~ **mad**) complètement cinglé* *or* frappé:

barley ['bɑ:lɪ] **1** N orge *f* ; **pearl ~** orge *m* perlé ; **Scotch ~** orge *m* mondé **2** EXCL (N

Engl, Scot: in games) pouce! ⟨3⟩ COMP ▶ **barley beer** N cervoise *f* ▶ **barley field** N champ *m* d'orge ▶ **barley sugar** N sucre *m* d'orge ▶ **barley water** N (*esp Brit*) ≈ orgeat *m* ▶ **barley wine** N *sorte de bière très forte et sucrée*

barleycorn ['bɑːlɪkɔːn] N grain *m* d'orge

barm [bɑːm] N levure *f* (de bière)

barmaid ['bɑːmeɪd] N (*esp Brit*) barmaid *f*

barman ['bɑːmən] N (*pl* **-men**) barman *m*

Bar Mitzvah, **bar mitzvah** [ˌbɑːˈmɪtsvə] N bar-mitsva *f*

barmy†* ['bɑːmɪ] ADJ (*Brit*) timbré*, maboul!*

barn [bɑːn] ⟨1⟩ N ⟨a⟩ grange *f*; **it's a great ~ of a house*** c'est une énorme bâtisse ⟨b⟩ (*US*) (*for horses*, *cattle*); (*for cattle*) étable *f* ⟨2⟩ COMP ▶ **barn dance** N (= *dance*) danse *f* campagnarde *or* paysanne; (= *party*) soirée *f* de danse campagnarde *or* paysanne ▶ **barn dancing** N (*NonC*) danse *f* campagnarde *or* paysanne ▶ **barn door** N **it's as big as a ~ door** c'est gros comme une maison* ▶ **barn owl** N chat-huant *m*

barnacle ['bɑːnəkl] N ⟨a⟩ (= *shellfish*) bernache *f*, anatife *m*; (*pej* = *person*) crampon* *m*; (* = *old sailor*) vieux loup de mer* *m* ⟨b⟩ (*also* = **goose**) bernache (nonnette) *f*, bernacle *f*

barney: ['bɑːnɪ] N (*Brit* = *quarrel*) prise *f* de bec*

barnstorm ['bɑːnstɔːm] VI (*Theat*) jouer sur les tréteaux; (*US Pol*) faire une tournée électorale (dans les circonscriptions rurales)

barnstormer ['bɑːnstɔːməʳ] N (*Theat*) acteur *m* ambulant; (*US Pol*) orateur *m* électoral

barnstorming ['bɑːnstɔːmɪŋ] ⟨1⟩ N (*Theat*) ≈ tournée *f* théâtrale; (*US Pol*) tournée *f* *or* campagne *f* électorale (dans les circonscriptions rurales) ⟨2⟩ ADJ* [*performance*] emballant

barnyard ['bɑːnjɑːd] ⟨1⟩ N basse-cour *f* ⟨2⟩ COMP ▶ **barnyard fowl(s)** N(PL) volaille *f*

barogram ['bærəʊgræm] N barogramme *m*

barograph ['bærəʊgrɑːf] N barographe *m*

barometer [bəˈrɒmɪtəʳ] N (*lit*, *fig*) baromètre *m*; **the ~ is showing set fair** le baromètre est au beau fixe → **aneroid**

barometric [ˌbærəʊˈmetrɪk] ADJ barométrique

baron ['bærən] N ⟨a⟩ baron *m*; (*fig*) **cattle ~** magnat *m* or gros industriel *m* du bétail; **drug(s) ~** baron *m* de la drogue; **industrial ~** magnat *m* de l'industrie, gros industriel *m* ⟨b⟩ **~ of beef** double aloyau *m* de bœuf

baroness ['bærənɪs] N baronne *f*

baronet ['bærənɪt] N (*Brit*) baronnet *m*

baronetcy ['bærənɪtsɪ] N dignité *f* de baronnet

baronial [bəˈrəʊnɪəl] ⟨1⟩ ADJ (*lit*) de baron; (*fig*) seigneurial ⟨2⟩ COMP ▶ **baronial hall** N demeure *f* seigneuriale

barony ['bærənɪ] N baronnie *f*

baroque [bəˈrɒk] ADJ, N (*Archit*, *Art*, *Mus*) baroque *m*

barque† [bɑːk] N = **bark³**

barrack¹ ['bærək] ⟨1⟩ N caserne *f*, quartier *m* → **barracks** ⟨2⟩ COMP ▶ **barrack life** N vie *f* de caserne ▶ **barrack room** N chambrée *f*; **~-room language** propos *mpl* de caserne *or* de corps de garde; (*fig*) **to be a ~-room lawyer** se promener toujours avec le code sous le bras ▶ **barrack square** N cour *f* (de caserne)

barrack² ['bærək] VT (*esp Brit*) chahuter, conspuer (*frm*)

barracks ['bærəks] ⟨1⟩ N caserne *f*, quartier *m*; **cavalry ~** quartier *m* de cavalerie; **in ~** à la caserne, au quartier → **confine**, **naval** ⟨2⟩ COMP ▶ **barracks bag** N (*US*) sac *m* (de soldat)

barracuda [ˌbærəˈkjuːdə] N (*pl* **barracuda** *or* **barracudas**) barracuda *m*

barrage ['bærɑːʒ] ⟨1⟩ N ⟨a⟩ [*of river*] barrage *m* ⟨b⟩ (*Mil*) tir *m* de barrage; (*fig*) [*of questions, re-*

proaches*] pluie *f*; [*of words*] flot *m*, déluge *m* ⟨2⟩ COMP ▶ **barrage balloon** N ballon *m* de barrage

barratry ['bærətrɪ] N (*Marine Insurance*) baraterie *f*

barred [bɑːd] ADJ [*window etc*] muni de barreaux

-barred [bɑːd] ADJ (*in compounds*) **five-barred gate** barrière *f* à cinq barreaux

barrel ['bærəl] ⟨1⟩ N ⟨a⟩ (= *cask*) [*of wine*] tonneau *m*, fût *m*; [*of cider*] futaille *f*; [*of beer*] tonneau *m*; [*of herring*] caque *f*; [*of oil*] baril *m*; [*of tar*] gonne *f*; (*small*) baril *m*; (*fig*) **to have sb over a ~*** tenir qn à sa merci; (*US*) **to pay cash on the ~** payer rubis sur l'ongle → **biscuit**, **scrape** ⟨b⟩ [*of firearm*] canon *m*; [*of fountain pen*] corps *m*; [*of key*] canon *m*; [*of lock, clock*] barillet *m*; (*fig*) **to give sb both ~s*** engueulander qn* ⟨2⟩ VT [+ *wine, cider etc*] mettre en fût (*or* en futaille *etc*) ⟨3⟩ VI (*US**) foncer*, aller à toute pompe* ⟨4⟩ COMP ▶ **barrel-chested** ADJ au torse puissant ▶ **barrel-house jazz** N (*US*) jazz *m* de bastringue ▶ **barrel organ** N orgue *m* de Barbarie ▶ **barrel-shaped** ADJ en forme de barrique *or* de tonneau; [*person*] gros (grosse *f*) comme une barrique ▶ **barrel vault** N voûte *f* en berceau

barrelhead ['bærəlhed] N (*US*) **to pay cash on the ~** payer rubis sur l'ongle

barren ['bærən] ⟨1⟩ ADJ ⟨a⟩ (†† = *infertile*) [*woman, plant, tree*] stérile ⟨b⟩ (= *dry*) [*land, landscape*] aride ⟨c⟩ (*fig*) [*film, book*] dénué *or* dépourvu d'intérêt; [*discussion, period of time*] stérile; [*lifestyle*] vide de sens; [*surroundings*] monotone; [*style*] aride, sec (sèche *f*); **his latest book is ~ of interest** son dernier livre est dénué *or* dépourvu d'intérêt; **a government ~ of new ideas** un gouvernement qui ne sait plus innover → **lande(s)** *f(pl)* ⟨3⟩ COMP ▶ **Barren Grounds**, **Barren Lands** NPL toundra *f* canadienne

barrenness ['bærənɪs] N ⟨a⟩ († = *infertility*) [*of woman, plant, tree, land*] stérilité *f* ⟨b⟩ (= *dryness*) [*of land, landscape*] aridité *f* ⟨c⟩ (*fig*) [*of film, book, surroundings*] manque *m* d'intérêt; [*lifestyle*] monotonie *f*; [*of discussion*] stérilité *f*; [*of style*] aridité *f*, sécheresse *f*

barrette [bəˈret] N (*US*) barrette *f*

barricade [ˌbærɪˈkeɪd] ⟨1⟩ N barricade *f* ⟨2⟩ VT [+ *street*] barricader; **to ~ o.s. (in)** se barricader; **police ~d them in** la police les a empêchés de sortir

barrier ['bærɪəʳ] ⟨1⟩ N barrière *f*; (*Rail: also* **ticket ~**) portillon *m* (d'accès); (*fig*) obstacle *m*, barrière *f* (**to** à); **age is no ~ to success** l'âge n'est pas un obstacle à la réussite; **a trade ~** une barrière douanière; **to put up ~s to sb/sth** dresser *or* élever des obstacles sur le chemin de qn/qch; **to break down ~s** supprimer les barrières → **language**, **sound**; ⟨2⟩ COMP ▶ **barrier contraceptive** N contraceptif *m* local ▶ **barrier cream** N crème *f* protectrice ▶ **barrier method** N méthode *f* de contraception locale ▶ **barrier reef** N barrière *f* or récif *m* de corail; **the Great Barrier Reef** la Grande Barrière (de corail *or* d'Australie)

barring ['bɑːrɪŋ] PREP excepté, sauf; **~ accidents** sauf accident, à moins d'accident(s); **~ the unforeseen** sauf imprévu

barrio ['bærɪəʊ] N (*US*) quartier *m* latino-américain

barrister ['bærɪstəʳ] N (*Brit: also* **~-at-law**) avocat *m* → ⟨LAWYER⟩

barroom ['bɑːrʊm] N (*US*) salle *f* de bar

barrow¹ ['bærəʊ] ⟨1⟩ N (*also* **wheelbarrow**) brouette *f*; (*esp Brit: also* **coster's ~**) voiture *f* des quatre saisons; (*Rail: also* **luggage ~**) diable *m*; (*also* **hand ~**) civière *f*; (*without wheels*) brancard *m*; (*Min*) wagonnet *m*; **to wheel sth in a ~** brouetter qch ⟨2⟩ COMP ▶ **barrow-boy** N marchand *m* des quatre saisons

barrow² ['bærəʊ] N (*Archeol*) tumulus *m*

Bart [bɑːt] N (*Brit*) ABBR = **baronet**

bartender ['bɑːˌtendəʳ] N (*US*) barman *m*, barmaid *f*

barter ['bɑːtəʳ] ⟨1⟩ N échange *m*, troc *m* ⟨2⟩ VT échanger, troquer (**for** contre) ⟨3⟩ VI faire un échange *or* un troc

▶ **barter away** VT [+ *rights, liberty*] vendre; [+ *one's honour*] faire trafic de

Bartholomew [bɑːˈθɒləmjuː] N Barthélemy *m*; (*Hist*) **the Massacre of St ~** (le massacre de) la Saint-Barthélemy

barytone ['bærɪtəʊn] N (*Mus*) baryton *m* (*instrument*)

basal [ˈbeɪsl] ADJ (*lit, fig*) fondamental; (*Physiol*) basal

basalt ['bæsɔːlt] N basalte *m*

bascule [ˈbæskjuːl] ⟨1⟩ N bascule *f* ⟨2⟩ COMP ▶ **bascule bridge** N pont *m* à bascule

base¹ [beɪs] ⟨1⟩ N ⟨a⟩ (= *main ingredient*) base *f*; (= *starting point*) base *f*, point *m* de départ; (*Chem, Math, Ling*) base *f*; (= *lowest part*) base *f*, partie *f* inférieure; [*of column*] base *f*, pied *m*; [*of building*] soubassement *m*; [*of cartridge, electric bulb*] culot *m*; [*of tree*] pied *m*; (*Comput*) ▶ **2/10** *etc* base 2/10 *etc* ⟨b⟩ (*Mil*) base *f* → **air** ⟨c⟩ (*Baseball*) base *f*; (*esp US fig*) **he's way off ~*** il a tort; (*fig*) **to touch ~ with sb*** reprendre contact avec qn; **we'll touch ~ this afternoon*** on se tient au courant *or* s'appelle cet après-midi; **I'll touch ~ with you about the schedule*** je t'appellerai pour discuter du programme; (*US fig*) **to touch** *or* **cover all the ~s** penser à tout ⟨2⟩ VT (*fig*) [+ *reasoning, belief, opinion*] baser, fonder (**on** sur); (*Mil etc*) **to be ~d in** *or* **on York** être basé à York; **the post will be ~d in London but will involve considerable travel** le poste sera basé à Londres mais il exigera de nombreux déplacements; **I am ~d in** *or* **on Glasgow now** je suis maintenant basé à Glasgow, j'opère maintenant à partir de Glasgow; **the company is ~d in Glasgow** l'entreprise a son siège *or* est basée à Glasgow ⟨3⟩ COMP ▶ **base camp** N (*Climbing*) camp *m* de base ▶ **base coat** N [*of paint*] première couche *f* ▶ **base form** N (*Ling*) forme *f* de base ▶ **base jumping** N base-jump *m* ▶ **base lending rate** N (*Fin*) taux *m* de base bancaire ▶ **base line** N (*Baseball*) ligne *f* des bases; (*Surv*) base *f*; [*of diagram*] ligne *f* zéro; (*Tennis*) ligne *f* de fond; (*Art*) ligne *f* de fuite ▶ **base period** N (*Stat*) période *f* de référence *or* de base ▶ **base rate** N (*Fin*) = **base lending rate** ▶ **base year** N (*Fin*) année *f* de référence

base² [beɪs] ⟨1⟩ ADJ ⟨a⟩ (= *contemptible*) [*person, behaviour, crime, betrayal, action, motive, thoughts, emotions*] vil (vile *f*), indigne; [*instincts*] bas (basse *f*); [*task*] ingrat ⟨b⟩ (*liter*) [*birth, descent*] bas (basse *f*); **of ~ descent** de basse extraction ⟨c⟩ (= *counterfeit*) [*coin*] faux (fausse *f*) ⟨d⟩ (*US*) = **bass¹ 2** ⟨2⟩ COMP ▶ **base metal** N métal *m* vil

baseball ['beɪsbɔːl] ⟨1⟩ N base-ball *or* baseball *m* ⟨2⟩ COMP ▶ **baseball cap** N casquette *f* de base(-)ball

---

BASEBALL

Sport national américain, très répandu aussi au Canada, dont certaines qualités - l'esprit de camaraderie et de compétition, par exemple - ont été popularisées par le cinéma et en viennent à symboliser l'« American way of life ».

En plus de la célèbre casquette, le base-ball est à l'origine d'un certain nombre d'expressions courantes telles que « ballpark figure » (chiffre approximatif), a « whole new ball game » (une autre histoire) ou « to first base » (franchir le premier obstacle).

---

baseboard ['beɪsbɔːd] N (*US Constr*) plinthe *f*

-based [beɪst] ADJ (*in compounds*) **to be London-based** être basé à Londres ; **an oil-based economy** une économie basée sur le pétrole ; **sea-/land-based missile** missile *m* marin/terrestre

Basel ['bɑːzəl] N Bâle

baseless ['beɪslɪs] ADJ sans fondement

baseline costs [ˌbeɪslaɪn'kɒsts] NPL (*Fin*) coûts *mpl* de base

basely ['beɪslɪ] ADV bassement, vilement

baseman ['beɪsmən] (*pl* **-men**) N (*Baseball*) gardien *m* de base

basement ['beɪsmənt] **1** N sous-sol *m* ; **in the ~** au sous-sol **2** COMP ► **basement flat** N appartement *m* en sous-sol

baseness ['beɪsnɪs] N **a** [*of person, behaviour, crime, betrayal*] ignominie *f* ; [*of action, motive, thoughts, instincts, emotions*] bassesse *f* ; [*of task*] côté *m* ingrat **b** (*liter*) **the ~ of his birth** *or* **descent** sa basse extraction

bases¹ ['beɪsiːz] NPL of **basis**

bases² ['beɪsɪz] NPL of **base¹**

bash* [bæʃ] **1** N **a** coup *m* ; (*with fist*) coup *m* de poing ; **to give sb a ~ on the nose** donner un coup de poing sur le nez de qn ; **the car bumper has had a ~** le pare-chocs est cabossé *or* bosselé **b** **to have a ~ at sth/at doing*** s'essayer à qch/à faire ; **I'll have a ~ (at it)*** ◊ **I'll give it a ~*** je vais tenter le coup ; **have a ~!*** vas-y, essaie ! **c** († = *party*) surboum† * *f* **2** VT frapper, cogner ; **to ~ one's head against a wall** se cogner la tête contre un mur ; **to ~ sb on the head** assommer qn

► **bash about***, **bash around*** VT SEP *+ person*] (= *hit*) flanquer* des coups à ; (= *ill-treat*) [*+ person*] maltraiter, rudoyer ; [*+ object*] malmener

► **bash in*** VT SEP [*+ door*] enfoncer ; [*+ hat, car*] cabosser, défoncer ; [*+ lid, cover*] défoncer ; **to ~ sb's head in*** défoncer le crâne de qn*

► **bash on*** VI continuer (**with sth** avec qch)

► **bash up*** VT SEP [*+ car*] bousiller* ; (*Brit*) [*+ person*] tabasser*

basher* [bæʃəʳ] **1** N cogneur* *m* **2** N (*in compounds*) **he's a queer-~*** il casse du pédé*

bashful ['bæʃful] ADJ timide, qui manque d'assurance

bashfully ['bæʃfəlɪ] ADV d'un air embarrassé

bashfulness ['bæʃfulnɪs] N timidité *f*

bashing* [bæʃɪŋ] **1** N rossée* *f*, raclée* *f* ; **to take a ~** [*team, regiment*] prendre une raclée* *or* une dérouillée* ; [*car, carpet etc*] en prendre un (vieux *or* sacré) coup* **2** N (*in compounds*) **union-~** dénigrement *m* systématique des syndicats → **Paki**, **queer**

BASIC, **Basic** ['beɪsɪk] N (*Comput*) basic *m*

basic ['beɪsɪk] **1** ADJ **a** (= *fundamental*) [*difficulty, principle, problem, essentials*] fondamental ; (= *elementary*) [*rule*] élémentaire ; (*Math*) **the four ~ operations** les quatre opérations fondamentales ; **~ French** le français fondamental *or* de base ; **a ~ knowledge of Russian** une connaissance de base du russe ; **~ research** recherche *f* fondamentale ; **~ vocabulary** vocabulaire *m* de base ; **~ English** l'anglais *m* fondamental ; **~ needs** besoins *mpl* essentiels **b** (= *forming starting point*) [*salary, working hours*] de base ; **a ~ suit to which one can add accessories** un petit tailleur neutre auquel on peut ajouter des accessoires ; **a ~ black dress** une petite robe noire **c** (*Chem*) basique ; **~ salt** sel *m* basique ; **~ slag** scorie *f* de déphosphoration **2** **the basics** NPL l'essentiel *m* ; **to get down to the ~s** en venir à l'essentiel ; **to get back to ~s** revenir au b.a.-ba ; **a new back-to-~s drive** une nouvelle campagne prônant un retour à la simplicité

3 COMP ► **basic airman** N (*pl* **basic airmen**) (*US*) soldat *m* de deuxième classe (de l'armée de l'air) ► **basic overhead expenditure** N (*Fin*) frais *mpl* généraux essentiels ► **basic rate** N (*Fin, Comm*) taux *m* de référence ; **~ rate of (income) tax** taux *m* de base de l'impôt sur le revenu ► **basic training** N (*Mil*) **to do one's ~ training** faire ses classes ► **basic wage** N salaire *m* de base

▼ **basically** ['beɪsɪklɪ] ADV au fond ; **it's ~ simple** au fond, c'est simple ; **it's ~ the same** c'est pratiquement la même chose ; **he's ~ lazy** au fond, il est paresseux, il est fondamentalement paresseux ; **well, ~, all I have to do is ...** eh bien, en fait, je n'ai qu'à ... ; **~ we agree** en principe *or* dans l'ensemble, nous sommes d'accord

basil ['bæzl] N (*Bot*) basilic *m*

basilica [bə'zɪlɪkə] N basilique *f*

basilisk ['bæzɪlɪsk] N (*Myth, Zool*) basilic *m*

basin ['beɪsn] N **a** (*gen*) cuvette *f*, bassine *f* ; (*for food*) bol *m* ; (*wide: for cream etc*) jatte *f* ; (*also* **washbasin**, **wash-hand ~**) lavabo *m* ; [*of lavatory*] cuvette *f* ; [*of fountain*] vasque *f* → **sugar b** (*Geog*) [*of river*] bassin *m* ; (= *valley*) cuvette *f* ; (= *harbour*) bassin *m* → **catchment**, **tidal**

basinful ['beɪsnful] N [*of milk*] bolée *f* ; [*of water*] pleine cuvette * ; **I've had a ~ (of it)*** j'en ai par-dessus la tête* *or* ras le bol* (**of** de)

basis ['beɪsɪs] **1** N (*pl* **bases**) (*lit, fig*) base *f* ; **on an ad hoc ~** de façon ad hoc, en fonction des circonstances ; **paid on a daily/day-to-day/regular ~** payé à la journée/au jour le jour/régulièrement ; **on a mileage ~** en fonction du kilométrage ; **open on a 24-hour ~** ouvert 24 heures sur 24 ; **payments are calculated on a family ~** les paiements sont calculés en prenant pour base la famille ; **on that ~** dans ces conditions ; **on the ~ of what you've told me** par suite de ce que vous m'avez dit, en me basant sur ce que vous m'avez dit ; **~ for assessing VAT** assiette *f* de la TVA **2** COMP ► **basis point** N (*Fin*) point *m* de base

bask [bɑːsk] **1** VI **to ~ in the sun** [*person*] se dorer au soleil, se prélasser au soleil ; [*animal*] se prélasser au soleil ; **to ~ in sb's favour** jouir de la faveur de qn **2** COMP ► **basking shark** N requin *m* pèlerin

basket [bɑːskɪt] **1** N (*gen*) corbeille *f* ; (*also* **shopping ~**) (*one-handled*) panier *m* ; (*deeper, two-handled*) cabas *m* ; (*also* **clothes ~**) corbeille *f* *or* panier *m* à linge (sale) ; (*also* **wastepaper ~**) corbeille *f* (à papier) ; (*on person's back*) hotte *f* ; (*on donkey*) panier *m* ; (*for game, fish, oysters*) bourriche *f* ; (*Basketball*) panier *m* ; (*on ski stick*) rondelle *f* (de ski) ; (*Econ*) **a ~ of currencies/products** un panier de devises/produits ; **a ~(ful) of eggs** un panier d'œufs ; (*Basketball*) **to make a ~** marquer un panier → **laundry**, **luncheon**, **picnic**, **workbasket 2** COMP [*handle etc*] de panier ► **basket case** N (= *country*) cas *m* désespéré ; (= *person*) **he's a ~ case** (= *crazy*) il est cinglé* ; (= *inadequate*) c'est un paumé* ; (= *nervous*) c'est un paquet de nerfs* ► **basket chair** N chaise *f* en osier ► **basket maker** N vannier *m*

basketball [bɑːskɪtbɔːl] **1** N basket(-ball) *m* **2** COMP ► **basketball player** N basketteur *m*, -euse *f*

basketry ['bɑːskɪtrɪ] N = **basketwork**

basketweave ['bɑːskɪtwiːv] N (= *cloth*) tissage *m* ; (= *cane*) tressage *m*

basketwork ['bɑːskɪtwɜːk] N vannerie *f*

Basle [bɑːl] N Bâle

basmati [bəz'mætɪ] N (*also* **~ rice**) (riz *m*) basmati *m*

Basque [bæsk] **1** N **a** Basque *m*, Basque *f* *or* Basquaise *f* **b** (*Ling*) basque *m* **2** ADJ basque ; **a ~ woman** une Basque *or* Basquaise ; **the ~**

Country le Pays basque ; **the ~ Provinces** les provinces *fpl* basques

basque [bæsk] N guêpière *f*

bas-relief ['bæsrɪˌliːf] N bas-relief *m*

bass¹ [beɪs] (*Mus*) **1** N (= *part, singer, guitar*) basse *f* ; (*also* **double ~**) contrebasse *f* → **double 2** ADJ [*voice*] de basse ; [*note*] grave ; (= *low-sounding*) bas (basse *f*), grave **3** COMP ► **bass-baritone** N baryton-basse *m* ► **bass clarinet** N clarinette *f* basse ► **bass clef** N clef *f* de fa ► **bass drum** N grosse caisse *f* ► **bass flute** N flûte *f* basse ► **bass guitar** N guitare *f* basse ► **bass guitarist** N bassiste *mf* ► **bass horn** N serpent *m* ► **bass-relief** ADJ = **bas-relief** ► **bass strings** NPL basses *fpl* ► **bass trombone** N trombone *m* basse ► **bass tuba** N tuba *m* d'orchestre ► **bass viol** N viole *f* de gambe

bass² [bæs] N (= *fish*) (*freshwater*) perche *f* ; (*sea*) bar *m*, loup *m*

basset ['bæsɪt] **1** N (*also* **~ hound**) basset *m* **2** COMP ► **basset horn** N (*Mus*) cor *m* de basset

bassi ['bæsiː] NPL of **basso**

bassist ['beɪsɪst] N bassiste *mf*

bassline ['beɪslaɪn] N (ligne *f* de) basse *f*

basso continuo [ˌbæsəʊkənˌtɪnjʊəʊ] N (*pl* **bassos** *or* **bassi continuo**) (*Mus*) basse *f* continue

bassoon [bə'suːn] N basson *m* → **double**

bassoonist [bə'suːnɪst] N basson *m*, bassoniste *mf*

basso profundo [ˌbæsəʊprəʊˈfʌndəʊ] N (*pl* **bassos** *or* **bassi profundo**) (*Mus*) basse *f* profonde

Bass Strait ['bæsstreɪt] N **the ~** le détroit de Bass

bastard ['bɑːstəd] **1** N **a** (*lit*) enfant naturel(le) *m(f)*, bâtard(e) *m(f)* **b** (: *pej* = *unpleasant person*) salaud: *m* **c** *:* **he's a lucky ~!** c'est un drôle de veinard! ; **you old ~!** sacré vieux!* ; **poor ~** pauvre type* ; **silly ~!** quel corniaud!* **2** ADJ [*child*] naturel, bâtard ; [*language, dialect*] corrompu, abâtardi ; (*Typ*) [*character*] d'un autre œil ; **~ title** faux-titre *m*

bastardized ['bɑːstədaɪzd] ADJ [*language*] corrompu, abâtardi

bastardy ['bɑːstədɪ] N (*Jur*) bâtardise *f*

baste¹ [beɪst] VT (*Sewing*) bâtir, faufiler

baste² [beɪst] VT (*Culin*) arroser

bastion ['bæstɪən] N bastion *m*

Basutoland [bə'suːtəʊlænd] N le Bas(o)utoland

bat¹ [bæt] N (*Zool*) chauve-souris *f* ; (*fig*) **an old ~*** une vieille bique* ; (*fig*) **to have ~s in the belfry*** avoir une araignée au plafond* ; **he ran like a ~ out of hell*** il a couru comme un dératé* ; **her new Ferrari goes like a ~ out of hell*** sa nouvelle Ferrari est un vrai bolide* → **blind**

bat² [bæt] **1** N **a** (*Sport etc*) (*Baseball, Cricket*) batte *f* ; (*Table Tennis*) raquette *f* ; (*fig*) **off one's own ~** de sa propre initiative, de son propre chef ; (*US*) **right off the ~** sur-le-champ ; (*Sport*) **he's a good ~** il manie bien la batte **b** (= *blow*) coup *m* **2** VI (*Baseball, Cricket*) manier la batte ; **he ~ted yesterday** il était à la batte hier ; (*fig*) **to go (in) to ~ for sb*** (= *support*) intervenir en faveur de qn **3** VT **a** [*+ ball*] frapper (*avec une batte, raquette etc*) **b** (* = *hit*) cogner*, flanquer un coup à* ; (*US fig*) **to ~ sth around** (= *discuss*) discuter de qch (à bâtons rompus)

bat³ [bæt] VT **he didn't ~ an eyelid** (*Brit*) *or* **an eye** (*US*) il n'a pas sourcillé *or* bronché ; **without ~ting an eyelid** (*Brit*) *or* **an eye** (*US*) sans sourciller *or* broncher

bat⁴: [bæt] N (*Brit* = *speed*) allure *f*

batch [bætʃ] **1** N [*of loaves*] fournée *f* ; [*of people*] groupe *m* ; [*of prisoners*] convoi *m* ; [*of recruits*] contingent *m*, fournée *f* ; [*of letters*] paquet *m*, monceau *m* ; (*Comm*) [*of goods*] lot *m* ;

[of concrete] gâchée f [2] COMP ► **batch file** N (Comput) fichier m batch ► **batch mode** N (Comput) **in ~ mode** en temps différé ► **batch-process** VT (Comput) traiter par lots ► **batch processing** N (Comput) traitement m par lots

bated ['beɪtɪd] ADJ **with ~ breath** en retenant son souffle

bath [bɑːθ] [1] N (pl **baths** [bɑːðz]) [a] bain m; (also **~ tub**) baignoire f; **to take** or **have a ~** prendre un bain; **to give sb a ~** baigner qn, donner un bain à qn; **while I was in my** or **the ~** pendant que j'étais dans or que je prenais mon bain; (in hotel) **room with (private) ~** chambre f avec salle de bains (particulière) → **blood, eyebath, Turkish** [b] (Chem, Phot, Tech) bain m; (Phot = container) cuvette f [2] **baths** NPL (for swimming) piscine f; (for washing) (établissement m de) bains(-douches) mpl; (Hist) thermes mpl [3] VT (Brit) baigner, donner un bain à [4] VI (Brit) prendre un bain [5] COMP ► **bath cube** N sels mpl de bain en cube ► **bath oil** N huile f pour le bain ► **bath salts** NPL sels mpl de bain ► **bath sheet** N drap m de bain ► **bath towel** N serviette f de bain

Bath bun ['bɑːθ,bʌn] N (Brit) ≈ pain m aux raisins

bathchair† ['bɑːθtʃɛəʳ] N fauteuil m roulant, voiture f d'infirme

bathe [beɪð] [1] VT (gen, also fig) baigner; [+ wound] laver; **to ~ one's eyes** se baigner or se bassiner les yeux; **to ~ one's feet** prendre un bain de pieds; **~d in tears** baigné de larmes; **to be ~d in sweat** être en nage; (US) **to ~ the baby** baigner l'enfant; (fig) **~d in light** baigné or inondé de lumière [2] VI (Brit) se baigner, prendre un bain (de mer ou de rivière); (US) prendre un bain (dans une baignoire) [3] N (Brit) bain m (de mer ou de rivière); **an enjoyable ~** une baignade agréable; **to take** or **have a ~** se baigner; **let's go for a ~** allons nous baigner

bather ['beɪðəʳ] N baigneur m, -euse f

bathhouse ['bɑːθhaʊs] N bains mpl publics

bathing ['beɪðɪŋ] [1] N bains mpl, baignade(s) f(pl); **~ prohibited** défense de se baigner, baignade interdite; **safe ~** baignade f sans (aucun) danger → **sea** [2] COMP ► **bathing beauty** N naïade f ► **bathing cap** N bonnet m de bain ► **bathing costume** N (Brit) maillot m (de bain) ► **bathing hut** N cabine f (de bain) ► **bathing machine** N cabine f de bains roulante ► **bathing suit** N (esp US) = **bathing costume** ► **bathing trunks** NPL (Brit) maillot m or slip m de bain, caleçon m de bain ► **bathing wrap** N peignoir m (de bain), sortie f de bain

bathmat ['bɑːθmæt] N tapis m de bain

bathos ['beɪθɒs] N (Literat) chute f du sublime au ridicule

bathrobe ['bɑːθrəʊb] N peignoir m (de bain)

bathroom ['bɑːθrʊm] [1] N salle f de bains; (esp US) **to go to** or **use the ~** aller aux toilettes [2] COMP ► **bathroom cabinet** N armoire f de toilette ► **bathroom fittings** NPL (= main fixtures) appareils mpl or installations fpl sanitaires; (= accessories) accessoires mpl de salle de bains ► **bathroom scales** NPL balance f, pèse-personne m inv

bathtub ['bɑːθtʌb] N (esp US) baignoire f; (round) tub m

bathwater ['bɑːθwɔːtəʳ] N eau f du bain

bathysphere ['bæθɪsfɪəʳ] N bathysphère f

batik [bə'tiːk] N batik m

batiste [bæ'tiːst] N batiste f

batman ['bætmən] N (pl **-men**) (Brit Mil) ordonnance f

baton ['bætən] [1] N (Mil, Mus) bâton m, baguette f; (Brit) [of policeman] matraque f; [of French traffic policeman] bâton m; [of relay race]

témoin m; (fig) **to hand on** or **pass the ~ to sb** passer le flambeau à qn [2] COMP ► **baton charge** N charge f (de police etc) à la matraque ► **baton round** N (Mil) balle f en plastique ► **baton twirler** N majorette f (menant un défilé)

bats: [bæts] ADJ toqué*, timbré*

batsman ['bætsmən] N (pl **-men**) (Cricket) batteur m

battalion [bə'tælɪən] N (Mil, fig) bataillon m

batten¹ ['bætn] [1] N (Carpentry) latte f; [of roofing] volige f; [of flooring] latte f, planche f (de parquet); (Naut) latte f (de voile); (Theat) herse f [2] VT latter; [+ roof] voliger; [+ floor] planchéier

► **batten down** VT SEP (Naut) **to ~ down the hatches** fermer les écoutilles, condamner les panneaux

batten² ['bætn] VI (= prosper illegitimately) s'engraisser (**on sb** aux dépens de qn, **on sth** de qch); (= feed greedily) se gorger, se gaver (**on** de)

batter¹ ['bætəʳ] N (Culin) (for frying) pâte f à frire; (for pancakes) pâte f à crêpes; **fried fish in ~** poisson m frit (enrobé de pâte à frire)

batter² ['bætəʳ] [1] VT [a] (= strike repeatedly) battre, frapper; [+ baby] maltraiter, martyriser; **ship ~ed by the waves** navire m battu par les vagues; **town ~ed by bombing** ville f ravagée or éventrée par les bombardements [b] (Typ) [+ type] endommager [2] VI **to ~ at the door** cogner or frapper à la porte à coups redoublés [3] N (US Sport) batteur m

► **batter about** VT SEP [+ person] rouer de coups, rosser

► **batter down** VT SEP [+ wall] démolir, abattre; (Mil) battre en brèche

► **batter in** VT SEP [+ door] enfoncer, défoncer; [+ skull] défoncer

battered ['bætəd] ADJ [hat, pan] cabossé, bosselé; [face] (lit) meurtri; (fig) buriné; [furniture, house] délabré; **~ babies** or **children** enfants mpl battus or martyrs; **~ child syndrome** syndrome m de l'enfant battu or martyr; **~ wife** femme f battue; **a ~ old car** une vieille bagnole cabossée*

batterer ['bætərəʳ] N personne qui bat son conjoint ou ses enfants → **wife**

battering ['bætərɪŋ] [1] N **the town took a dreadful ~ during the war** la ville a été terriblement éprouvée pendant la guerre; **he got such a ~** on l'a roué de coups, on l'a rossé → **baby** [2] COMP ► **battering ram** N (Mil) bélier m

battery ['bætərɪ] [1] N [a] (= guns) batterie f [b] (Elec) [of torch, radio] pile f; [of vehicle] batterie f, accumulateurs mpl [c] (= number of similar objects) batterie f; **to undergo a ~ of tests** subir une batterie de tests; **a ~ of questions** une pluie or un feu nourri de questions [d] (Agr) batterie f [e] (Jur) voie f de fait → **assault** [2] COMP ► **battery acid** N électrolyte m ► **battery charger** N (Elec) chargeur m de batterie ► **battery egg** N œuf m produit en batterie ► **battery farm** N (Brit) élevage m en batterie ► **battery fire** N (Mil) tir m par salves ► **battery hen** N poulet m d'élevage en batterie, poulet m de batterie* ► **battery lead connection** N (Aut) cosse f de batterie ► **battery-operated, battery-powered** ADJ à pile(s) ► **battery set** N (Rad) poste m à piles

battle ['bætl] [1] N [a] (Mil) bataille f, combat m; **to fight a ~** se battre, lutter (**against** contre); **to lead an army into ~** mener une armée au combat; **the Battle of Britain** la bataille d'Angleterre; **killed in ~** tué au combat [b] (fig) combat m, lutte f; **to have a ~ of wits** jouer au plus fin; **~ of wills** (partie f de) bras m de fer; **life is a continual ~** la vie est un combat perpétuel or une lutte perpétuelle; **a political ~** une lutte or un combat politique; **to do ~ for/against** lutter pour/contre; **the ~**

against crime la lutte contre le crime; **to fight sb's ~s** se battre à la place de qn; **we are fighting the same ~** nous nous battons pour la même cause; **that's half the ~*** c'est déjà pas mal*; **getting an interview is only half the ~** quand on obtient un entretien la partie n'est pas encore gagnée; **~ for control of sth/to control sth** lutte f or combat m pour obtenir le contrôle de qch/pour contrôler qch; **to lose/win the ~** perdre/gagner la bataille; **to win the ~ but lose the war** gagner une bataille mais perdre la guerre → **cancer, join, losing, Nile** [2] VI (lit, fig) se battre, lutter (**against** contre, **to do** pour faire); **sailors constantly battling with the elements** des marins luttant sans cesse contre les éléments [3] COMP ► **battle array** N **in ~ array** en ordre de bataille ► **battle cruiser** N croiseur m cuirassé ► **battle cry** N cri m de guerre ► **battle dress** N (Mil) tenue f de campagne or de combat ► **battle fatigue** N psychose f traumatique (du soldat) ► **battle lines** NPL lignes fpl de combat; (fig) **the ~ lines are drawn** chacun a choisi son camp ► **battle order** N = **battle array** ► **battle royal** N (= quarrel) bataille f en règle ► **battle-scarred** ADJ (lit) [troops, country] marqué par les combats; (fig) [person] marqué par la vie; (* hum) [furniture] endommagé, abîmé ► **battle zone** N zone f de combat

► **battle out** VT SEP **Leeds ~d it out with Manchester in the final** Leeds s'est mesuré à or avec Manchester en finale; **the three political parties ~d it out** les trois partis politiques se sont livré une bataille acharnée

battle-axe ['bætlæks] N (= weapon) hache f d'armes; (* pej = woman) virago f

battledore ['bætldɔːʳ] N (Sport) raquette f; **~ and shuttlecock** (jeu m de) volant m

battlefield ['bætlfiːld], **battleground** ['bætlgraʊnd] N (Mil, fig) champ m de bataille

battlements ['bætlmənts] NPL (= wall) remparts mpl; (= crenellation) créneaux mpl

battleship ['bætlʃɪp] N cuirassé m

battleships ['bætlʃɪps] N (NonC = game) bataille f navale

batty: ['bætɪ] ADJ (esp Brit) = **bats**

bauble ['bɔːbl] N babiole f, colifichet m; [of jester] marotte f

baud [bɔːd] (Comput) [1] N baud m [2] COMP ► **baud rate** N vitesse f en bauds

baulk [bɔːlk] = **balk**

bauxite ['bɔːksaɪt] N bauxite f

Bavaria [bə'vɛərɪə] N la Bavière

Bavarian [bə'vɛərɪən] [1] ADJ bavarois; **~ Alps** Alpes fpl bavaroises; (Culin) **~ cream** bavaroise f [2] N Bavarois(e) m(f)

bawd† [bɔːd] N (= prostitute) catin† f

bawdiness ['bɔːdɪnɪs] N paillardise f

bawdy ['bɔːdɪ] ADJ paillard

bawdyhouse†† ['bɔːdɪhaʊs] N maison f de tolérance††

bawl [bɔːl] [1] VI [a] (= shout) brailler, hurler (**at** contre) [b] (* = weep) brailler, beugler* [2] VT brailler, hurler

► **bawl out** VT SEP [a] = **bawl 2** [b] (: = scold) engueuler:

bay¹ [beɪ] N (Geog) baie f; (small) anse f; **the Bay of Biscay** le golfe de Gascogne; (US) **the Bay State** le Massachusetts

bay² [beɪ] [1] N (Bot: also **~ tree, sweet ~**) laurier(-sauce) m [2] COMP ► **bay leaf** N (pl **bay leaves**) feuille f de laurier ► **bay rum** N lotion capillaire ► **bay wreath** N couronne f de laurier

bay³ [beɪ] [1] N [a] (= alcove) renfoncement m; [of window] baie f [b] (Rail) voie f d'arrêt → **bomb, loading, parking, sick** [2] COMP ► **bay window** N bow-window m, bay-window f

bay⁴ [beɪ] [1] N (Hunting, fig) **to be at ~** être aux abois; (Hunting, fig) **to bring to ~** acculer;

(fig) **to keep** or **hold at ~** tenir à distance or en échec [2] VI aboyer (**at** à, après), donner de la voix; **to ~ at the moon** aboyer or hurler à la lune; (Brit fig) **to ~ for blood** crier vengeance; (Brit) **to ~ for sb's blood** réclamer la tête de qn (fig)

bay⁵ [beɪ] [1] ADJ [horse] bai [2] N cheval m bai; **red ~** (= horse) alezan m

Baykal [baɪˈkɑːl] N **Lake ~** le lac Baïkal

bayonet [ˈbeɪənɪt] [1] N baïonnette f → **fix** [2] VT passer à la baïonnette [3] COMP ▸ **bayonet bulb** N (Elec) ampoule f à baïonnette ▸ **bayonet charge** N charge f à la baïonnette ▸ **bayonet drill** N (NonC) ▸ **bayonet practice** N (Elec) douille f à baïonnette ▸ **bayonet-fitting bulb** N = bayonet bulb ▸ **bayonet point** N **at ~ point** à (la pointe de) la baïonnette ▸ **bayonet practice** N (NonC) exercices mpl de baïonnette ▸ **bayonet socket** N (Elec) douille f à baïonnette

bayou [ˈbaɪuː] N (US) bayou m, marécages mpl

bazaar [bəˈzɑːʳ] N (in East) bazar m; (= large shop) bazar m; (= sale of work) vente f de charité

bazoo [bəˈzuː] N (US) gueule⁑ f, bouche f

bazooka [bəˈzuːkə] N bazooka m

BB [ˈbiːˈbiː] [1] N (ABBR = **Boys' Brigade**) → **boy** [2] COMP ▸ **BB gun** N (US) carabine f à air comprimé

BBC [ˌbiːbiːˈsiː] N (ABBR = **British Broadcasting Corporation**) BBC f

BBQ [ˌbiːbiːˈkjuː] N ABBR = **barbecue**

BBS [ˌbiːbiːˈes] N (Comput) (ABBR = **bulletin board system**) BBS m, babillard m

BC [biːˈsiː] [a] (ABBR = **Before Christ**) av. J.-C. [b] (ABBR = **British Columbia**) → **British**

BCD [ˌbiːsiːˈdiː] N (Comput) (ABBR = **binary-coded decimal**) DCB f

BCG [ˌbiːsiːˈdʒiː] N (ABBR = **bacille Calmette et Guérin**) BCG m

BD [biːˈdiː] N (Univ) (ABBR = **Bachelor of Divinity**) licence de théologie

BDS [ˌbiːdiːˈes] N (Univ) (ABBR = **Bachelor of Dental Surgery**) diplôme de chirurgie dentaire

BE [biːˈiː] N (Comm) (ABBR = **bill of exchange**) → **bill**

be [biː]

pres am, is, are, pret was, were, ptp been	
[1] COPULATIVE VERB	[4] INTRANSITIVE VERB
[2] AUXILIARY VERB	[5] IMPERSONAL VERB
[3] MODAL VERB	[6] COMPOUNDS

[1] COPULATIVE VERB

[a] joining subject and predicate être; **the sky is blue** le ciel est bleu; **be good!** sois sage!; **who is that? — it's me!** qui est-ce? — c'est moi!; **she is English** elle est anglaise; **they are friendly** ils sont sympathiques; **if I were you I would refuse** à votre place or si j'étais vous, je refuserais; **and even if it were true ...** et même si c'était vrai ...

The following translations use **ce** + **être** *because they contain an article or possessive in French:*
she is an Englishwoman c'est une Anglaise; **they are friendly people** ce sont des gens sympathiques; **they are my best friends** ce sont mes meilleurs amis; **it's the most expensive** c'est le plus cher

[b] with occupation être

No article is used in French, unless the noun is qualified by an adjective.
he wants to be a doctor il veut être médecin; **she is a lawyer** elle est avocate; **she's a well-known lawyer** c'est une avocate renommée

[c] referring to health aller; **how are you?** comment allez-vous?; **I'm better now** je vais mieux maintenant; **she's none too well** elle ne va pas très bien

[d] = cost coûter; **how much is it?** combien ça coûte?; **the book is 20 francs** le livre coûte 20 F

[e] Math = equal faire; **two and two are four** deux et deux font quatre; **three times two is six** trois fois deux font six

[f] **to be cold/hot/hungry/thirsty/ashamed/right/wrong** avoir froid/chaud/faim/soif/honte/raison/tort

Note how French makes the person, not the part of the body, the subject of the sentence in the following:
my feet are cold j'ai froid aux pieds; **my hands are frozen** j'ai les mains gelées

[g] with age avoir; **how old is he?** quel âge a-t-il?; **he's 25** il a vingt-cinq ans; **she's about my age** elle a à peu près mon âge; **he will be three next week** il aura trois ans la semaine prochaine; **she was 40 on Sunday** elle a eu quarante ans dimanche

[2] AUXILIARY VERB

[a] in continuous tenses

♦ **to be** + -ing

French does not distinguish between simple and continuous actions as much as English does.
I'm coming! j'arrive!; **she's always complaining** elle se plaint constamment, elle est toujours en train de se plaindre; **what have you been doing this week?** qu'est-ce que tu as fait cette semaine?; **what's been keeping you?** qu'est-ce qui t'a retenu?; **I have just been packing my case** je viens de faire ma valise; **it's a pity you aren't coming with us — but I am coming!** c'est dommage que tu ne viennes pas avec nous — mais si, je viens!; **will you be seeing her tomorrow?** est-ce que vous allez la voir demain?

être en train de + infinitive emphasizes that one is in the middle of the action:
I haven't got time, I'm cooking the dinner je n'ai pas le temps, je suis en train de préparer le repas; **I was just writing to him when he phoned** j'étais en train de lui écrire quand il m'a appelé

The imperfect tense is used for continuous action in the past.
he was driving too fast il conduisait trop vite

♦ **have/had been ... + for/since**

French uses the present and imperfect where English uses the perfect and past perfect.
I've been waiting for you for an hour je t'attends depuis une heure, ça fait une heure que je t'attends; **I've been waiting for you since six o'clock** je t'attends depuis six heures; **I'd been at university for six weeks when my father got ill** j'étais à l'université depuis six semaines quand mon père est tombé malade

[b] in tag questions: seeking confirmation n'est-ce pas? **he's a friend of yours, isn't he?** c'est un ami à toi, n'est-ce pas?; **they were surprised, weren't they?** ils ont été surpris, n'est-ce pas or non?; **she wasn't happy, was she?** elle n'était pas heureuse, n'est-ce pas?; BUT **so it's all done, is it?** tout est fait, alors?; **you are not ill, are you?** tu n'es pas malade j'espère?

[c] in tag responses **they're getting married — oh are they?** ils vont se marier — ah bon or ah oui?; **he's going to complain about you — oh is he?** il va porter plainte contre toi — ah vraiment?; **she is pretty — no, she isn't** elle est jolie — non, je ne trouve pas

When answering questions, **oui** *or* **non** *may be used alone.*
he's always late, isn't he? — yes, he is il est toujours en retard, n'est-ce pas? — oui; **is it what you expected? — no it isn't** est-ce que c'est ce que tu t'attendais à ça? — non → **so, neither, nor**

[d] in passives être; **he was killed** il a été tué; **he was struck by a car** il a été renversé par une voiture

The passive is used less in French than in English. It is often expressed by **on** + active verb when there is no obvious agent.
the door was shut in his face on lui a fermé la porte au nez; **it is said that ...** on dit que ...

The reflexive can express the established way of doing something.
peaches are sold by the kilo les pêches se vendent au kilo; **oysters are usually eaten raw** les huîtres se mangent généralement crues

[3] MODAL VERB

[a] = will **the talks are to start tomorrow** les négociations doivent commencer demain; **they are to be married in the summer** ils doivent se marier cet été; **now the old lady has died, her house is to be sold** maintenant que la vieille dame est décédée, sa maison doit être mise en vente; **you must work harder if you are to succeed** tu dois travailler davantage si tu veux réussir

[b] = must **you are to follow these instructions exactly** tu dois suivre ces instructions scrupuleusement; **you are not to touch that** tu ne dois pas y toucher; **no, YOU are to do it!** non, c'est à toi de le faire!; **I am not to speak to him** on m'a défendu de lui parler; **this door is not to be opened** cette porte ne doit pas être ouverte, il est interdit or défendu d'ouvrir cette porte; **I wasn't to tell you his name** je ne devais pas or je n'étais pas supposé te dire son nom

[c] = should **he is to be pitied** il est à plaindre; **not to be confused with ...** à ne pas confondre avec ...; **is it to be wondered at if ...?** faut-il s'étonner si ...?

[d] = can **these birds are to be found all over the world** on trouve ces oiseaux dans le monde entier; **little traffic was to be seen** il n'y avait pas beaucoup de circulation

[e] = be destined to **this was to have serious repercussions** cela devait avoir de graves répercussions; **they were never to return** ils ne devaient jamais revenir

[f] in conditional clauses: frm **were I to** or **if I were to tell him, what could he do?** à supposer que je le lui dise, que pourrait-il faire?; **how would he react, were he to find out?** comment réagirait-il s'il venait à tout découvrir?

♦ **were it not for ...** (frm) n'eût été ...; **were it not for my friendship for him ...** n'eût été l'amitié que je lui porte ...

[4] INTRANSITIVE VERB

[a] = exist, occur, remain, be situated être; (= take place) avoir lieu; **to be or not to be** être ou ne pas être; **he is there at the moment, but he won't be there much longer** il est là en ce moment mais il ne va pas rester très longtemps; **there he was, sitting at the table** il était là, assis à la table; **be that as it may** quoi qu'il en soit; **the match is tomorrow** le match a lieu demain; BUT **Christmas Day is on a Wednesday this year** Noël tombe un mercredi cette année; **leave it as it is** laissez-le tel quel

♦ **there is/are** (= there exist(s)) il y a; **there is a mouse in the room** il y a une souris dans la pièce; **there are pigeons on the roof** il y a des pigeons sur le toit; **there was once a castle here** autrefois, il y avait un château ici; **I thought there would be problems** je pensais qu'il y aurait des problèmes; **there must be an answer** il doit y avoir une solution; **there being no alternative solution ...** comme il n'y a aucune autre solution ...; **there is nothing more beautiful** il n'y a or il n'est (liter) rien de plus beau; BUT **there were three of us** nous étions trois; **let there be light and there was light** que la lumière soit et la lumière fut

♦ **there's/there are** (pointing out sth) voilà; **there's the church** voilà l'église; **there are the others** voilà les autres; (iro) **there's democracy for you!** voilà ce qu'on appelle or c'est ce qu'on appelle de la démocratie!

♦ **here is/are** voici; **here's your key** voici ta

clé ; **here are the tickets** voici les billets ; **here you are at last!** te voici enfin !; _BUT_ **here you are!** (= _take this_) tenez _or_ tiens !

b to a place

♦ **to have been: I have already been to Paris** j'ai déjà été _or_ je suis déjà allé à Paris ; **I have been to see my aunt** je suis allé voir ma tante ; **the postman has already been** le facteur est déjà passé ; **he has been and gone** il est venu et reparti

5 IMPERSONAL VERB

a weather, temperature faire ; **it's fine/cold/dark** il fait beau/froid/nuit ; **it's 20 degrees in the shade** il fait 20 degrés à l'ombre ; _BUT_ **it's windy/foggy** il y a du vent/du brouillard

b time être ; **it's morning** c'est le matin ; **it's 6 o'clock** il est 6 heures ; **tomorrow is Friday** demain c'est vendredi ; **it is 14 June today** nous sommes le 14 juin (aujourd'hui), c'est le 14 juin (aujourd'hui)

c emphatic **it's me who does all the work** c'est moi qui fais tout le travail ; **it was me who decided to finish the relationship** c'est moi qui ai décidé de rompre ; **it was then we realised that ...** c'est alors que nous nous sommes rendu compte que ... ; **it was they who suggested that ...** ce sont eux qui ont suggéré que ... ; **it was they who had suggested that ...** c'étaient eux qui avaient suggéré que ... ; **how is it that you got back so early?** comment se fait-il que tu sois rentré si tôt ? ; **why is it that she is so popular?** pourquoi a-t-elle tant de succès ?

6 COMPOUNDS
► **the be-all and end-all** N le but suprême (of de) ; **for women today, marriage is not the be-all and end-all** pour les femmes d'aujourd'hui, le mariage n'est pas le but suprême

---

beach [biːtʃ] **1** N (_of sea_) plage _f_ ; (= _shore_) grève _f_ ; (_of lake_) rivage _m_ ; **private/sandy ~** plage _f_ privée/de sable **2** VT (+ _boat_) échouer **3** COMP ► **beach ball** N ballon _m_ de plage ► **beach buggy** N buggy _m_ ► **beach bum:** N _jeune qui passe son temps à traîner sur les plages_ ► **beach hut** N cabine _f_ de bain _or_ de plage ► **beach umbrella** N parasol _m_

beachcomber ['biːtʃˌkəʊmə'] N (= _person_) (_lit_) ramasseur _m_ d'épaves ; (_fig_ = _idler_) propre _mf_ à rien ; (= _wave_) vague _f_ déferlante

beachhead ['biːtʃhed] N (_Naut_) tête _f_ de pont

beachwear ['biːtʃwɛə'] N tenue(s) _f(pl)_ de plage

beacon ['biːkən] **1** N **a** (= _danger signal_) phare _m_, signal lumineux ; (= _lantern itself_) fanal _m_ ; (_Naut_) balise _f_ ; (_Aviat_) balise _f_, phare _m_ ; (_fig_ = _person_) figure _f_ phare ; **a moral ~** un guide moral ► **Belisha beacon, radio b** (_Hist: on hills_) feu _m_ (d'alarme) **c** (= _hill: gen in place-names_) colline _f_ **2** COMP ► **beacon light** N balise _f_ lumineuse

bead [biːd] N (_of glass, coral, amber etc_) perle _f_ ; (_of rosary_) grain _m_ ; (**string of**) **~s** collier _m_ → **tell b** (= _drop_) (_of dew_) perle _f_ ; (_of sweat_) goutte _f_ ; (= _bubble_) bulle _f_ ; **his forehead was covered in ~s of sweat** la sueur lui perlait au front **c** (_of gun_) guidon _m_ ; **to draw a ~ on** ajuster, viser

beaded ['biːdɪd] ADJ (_fabric, dress_) perlé, orné de perles ; (_fig_) **his forehead was ~ with sweat** la sueur perlait à son front

beading ['biːdɪŋ] N (_Carpentry_) baguette _f_ ; (_Archit_) chapelet _m_ ; (_Dress_) broderie _f_ perlée, garniture _f_ de perles

beadle ['biːdl] N (_Brit Univ_) appariteur _m_, huissier _m_ ; (_Rel_) bedeau _m_

beady ['biːdɪ] **1** ADJ **to watch sth with ~ eyes** regarder qch avec des yeux de fouine **2** COMP ► **beady-eyed** ADJ (_bright-eyed_) aux yeux en boutons de bottines ; (_pej_) aux yeux de fouine

---

beagle ['biːgl] **1** N beagle _m_ **2** VI chasser avec des beagles

beak [biːk] N **a** (_of bird, turtle etc_) bec _m_ ; (**:** also **~ed nose**) nez _m_ crochu **b** (_Brit_: = _judge_) juge _m_ ; (_Brit Scol_†* = _headmaster_) protal* _m_

beaker ['biːkə'] N gobelet _m_ ; (_wide_) coupe _f_ ; (_Chem_) vase _m_ à bec

beam [biːm] **1** N **a** (_Archit_) poutre _f_, solive _f_ ; (_thick_) madrier _m_ ; (_small_) poutrelle _f_, soliveau _m_ → **crossbeam**
b (_Sport: in gym_) poutre _f_
c (_Naut_) (= _transverse member_) barrot _m_ ; (= _greatest width_) largeur _f_ ; **on the ~** par le travers ; (_Naut_) **on the port ~** à bâbord ; **on the starboard ~** à tribord → **broad**
d (_Tech_) (_of scales_) fléau _m_ ; (_of engine_) balancier _m_ ; (_of plough_) age _m_ ; (_of loom_) rouleau _m_
e (_of light, sunlight_) rayon _m_, trait _m_ ; (_of lighthouse, headlight, searchlight_) faisceau _m_ (lumineux) ; (_Phys_) faisceau _m_ ; (_Aviat, Naut_) chenal _m_ de radioguidage ; **to be on/be off (the) ~** être/ne pas être dans le chenal de radioguidage ; (_fig_) **to be on (the) ~** être sur la bonne voie ; (_fig_) **to be off (the) ~** (_Brit_) ◊ **to be off the ~** (_US_) dérailler ; (_Brit fig_) **to be way off** être complètement à côté de la plaque* → **electron**
f (= _smile_) sourire _m_ épanoui

2 VI **a** (also **~ down**) (_sun_) rayonner, darder ses rayons
b (= _smile_) **she ~ed** son visage s'est épanoui en un large sourire ; **at the sight of the money she ~ed at me** elle a levé vers moi un visage épanoui _or_ rayonnant en voyant l'argent ; **her face was ~ing with joy** son visage rayonnait de joie ; **~ing with pride, she showed them her ring** rayonnante de fierté, elle leur a montré sa bague
c (_Rad, Telec_) **soon we will be ~ing into your homes via the Astra satellite** bientôt nos émissions vous parviendront chez vous grâce au satellite Astra
d (_Sci Fi_) **they ~ed up to their spaceship** ils ont été téléportés dans leur vaisseau spatial

3 VT **a** (_Rad, Telec_) (+ _message_) transmettre par émission dirigée ; **to ~ a programme to the Arab-speaking countries** diffuser un programme à l'intention des pays de langue arabe
b **"welcome" she ~ed** « bienvenue » dit-elle d'un air radieux
c (_Sci Fi_) **aliens were ~ed down to earth** des extraterrestres ont été téléportés sur terre ; **he was ~ed up into the spacecraft** il a été téléporté dans le vaisseau spatial

4 COMP (_Naut_) (_sea, wind_) de travers ► **beam balance** N balance _f_ à fléau ► **beam compass** N compas _m_ à verge ► **beam-ends** NPL (_Naut_) **on her ~-ends** couché sur le côté _or_ le flanc ; (_fig_) **to be on one's ~-ends*** être dans la dèche**:** _or_ dans la gêne

beaming ['biːmɪŋ] ADJ (_sun_) radieux, resplendissant ; (_smile, face_) rayonnant, radieux, épanoui

bean [biːn] **1** N (_Bot, Culin_) haricot _m_ ; (also **green ~**) haricot _m_ vert ; (also **broad ~**) fève _f_ ; (_of coffee_) grain _m_ ; (_US*_) (= _head_) tête _f_, tronche* _f_ ; (= _brain_) cervelle _f_ ; (_Brit_) **to be full of ~s*** être en pleine forme, péter le feu* ; (_Brit_) **to know how many ~s make five** avoir du bon sens ; (_US_) **he doesn't know ~s about it*** il n'y connaît absolument rien ; **it isn't worth a ~*** ça ne vaut pas un clou* ; **it doesn't amount to a hill or row of ~s*** ça ne vaut pas un clou ; (_Brit_) **he hasn't a ~*** il n'a pas le sou _or_ un radis* ; **it won't cost you a ~*** ça ne vous coûtera pas un centime ; **hello, old ~!**†* salut mon pote !* → **bake, kidney, spill**[1] **2** VT* frapper à la tête **3** COMP ► **bean counter*** N (_pej_) petit(e) comptable _mf_ ► **bean curd** N fromage _m_ de soja ► **bean sprouts** NPL = **beanshoots**

---

beanbag ['biːnbæg] N (_chair_) sacco _m_ ; (_for throwing_) balle _f_ lestée

beanery* ['biːnərɪ] N (_US_) gargote _f_ (_pej_)

beanfeast* ['biːnfiːst], **beano*†** ['biːnəʊ] N (_Brit_) (= _meal_) gueuleton**:** _m_ ; (= _spree_) bombe* _f_, nouba* _f_

beanpole ['biːnpəʊl] N (_lit_) perche _f_ ; (* _fig_) (grande) perche* _f_

beanshoots ['biːnʃuːts] NPL (_Culin_) germes _mpl_ de soja

beanstalk ['biːnstɔːk] N tige _f_ de haricot

bear[1] [bɛə'] (_pret_ **bore**, _ptp_ **borne**) **1** VT **a** (= _carry_) (+ _burden, arms, message_) porter ; **music borne on the wind** musique _f_ portée par le vent ; **to ~ away** emporter ; **to ~ back** rapporter ; (_fig_) **it is a cross he has to ~** c'est une croix qu'il doit porter ; **we each have our cross to ~** chacun a _or_ porte sa croix → **mind**
b (= _show_) (+ _inscription, mark, traces, signature_) porter ; **to ~ some resemblance to ...** ressembler à ... ; **to ~ no relation to ...** être sans rapport avec ..., n'avoir aucun rapport avec ...
c (= _be known by_) (+ _name_) porter
d **he bore himself like a soldier** (= _carried himself_) il avait une allure de soldat ; (= _conducted himself_) il se comportait en soldat
e (= _feel_) avoir en soi, porter ; **the love/hatred he bore her** l'amour/la haine qu'il lui portait _or_ qu'il avait à son égard ; **to ~ sb ill will** en avoir contre qn → **grudge**
f (= _bring, provide_) apporter, fournir ; **to ~ witness to sth** (_thing, result etc_) témoigner de qch ; (_person_) attester qch ; **to ~ false witness** porter un faux témoignage ; **to ~ sb company**† tenir compagnie à qn
g (= _sustain, support_) (+ _weight, person_) supporter ; **to ~ the weight of ...** supporter le poids de ... ; **to ~ comparison with ...** soutenir la comparaison avec ... ; **to ~ the expense of sth** prendre les frais de qch à sa charge ; **to ~ the responsibility for sth** assumer la responsabilité de qch
h (= _endure_) (+ _person_) supporter, souffrir ; (+ _event_) supporter ; **I cannot ~ (the sight of) that man** je ne peux pas souffrir _or_ voir cet homme ; **he can't ~ the smell of garlic** il ne supporte pas l'odeur de l'ail ; **she cannot ~ being laughed at** elle ne supporte pas qu'on se moque (_subj_) d'elle ; **his language will not ~ repeating** ses propos sont trop grossiers pour être rapportés ; **it doesn't ~ thinking about!** c'est trop affreux d'y penser ! → **brunt, grin**
i (= _produce, yield_) (+ _interest_) rapporter, produire ; (_lit, fig_) **to ~ fruit** produire des fruits ; (_Fin_) **investment which ~s 5%** placement _m_ qui rapporte 5% ; (_Fin_) **to ~ interest at 5%** produire _or_ rapporter un intérêt de 5%
j (= _give birth to_) donner naissance à, mettre au monde ; **she has borne him three daughters** elle lui a donné trois filles → **born**
k (= _push, press_) entraîner, porter ; **he was borne along by the crowd** il s'est trouvé entraîné _or_ emporté par la foule

2 VI **a** (= _move_) se diriger ; **to ~ right/left** prendre sur la droite/la gauche _or_ à droite/à gauche ; **~ towards the church** allez vers l'église ; **~ north at the windmill** prenez la direction nord au moulin ; (_Naut_) **to ~ off** virer (de bord)
b (_fruit, tree etc_) donner, produire
c (= _lean, press_) porter, appuyer (**on** sur) ; **he bore heavily on his stick** il s'appuyait lourdement sur sa canne ; (_fig_) **these taxes ~ most heavily on the poor** ces impôts pèsent le plus lourdement sur les pauvres
d (_phrases with "bring"_) **to bring one's energies to ~ on sth** consacrer _or_ mettre toute son énergie à qch ; **to bring one's mind to ~ on sth** porter son attention sur qch ; **to bring pressure to ~ on sth** exercer une pression sur qch ; **to bring pressure to ~ on sb** faire pression sur qn ; **to bring a telescope to ~ on sth** braquer

une lunette sur qch ; **to bring a gun to ~ on a target** pointer un canon sur un objectif
► **bear down** [1] VI [a] (= approach) **to ~ down on** [ship] venir sur ; [person] foncer sur [b] (= press) appuyer fermement, peser (**on** sur) [c] [woman in labour] pousser [2] VT SEP (liter) abattre, vaincre ; **borne down by adversity** abattu par l'adversité
► **bear in (up)on** VT FUS (pass only) **it was gradually borne in (up)on me that ...** la conviction s'est faite peu à peu en moi que ..., il est apparu de plus en plus évident à mes yeux que ...
► **bear on** VT FUS = bear upon
► **bear out** VT SEP confirmer, corroborer ; **to ~ sb out** ◊ **out what sb says** corroborer les dires de qn, corroborer ce que qn dit ; **the result ~s out our suspicions** le résultat confirme nos soupçons ; **you will ~ me out that ...** vous serez d'accord avec moi (pour dire) que ...
► **bear up** VI ne pas se laisser abattre or décourager ; **he bore up well after the death of his father** il a supporté courageusement la mort de son père ; **~ up!** courage ! ; **how are you? — ~ing up!*** comment ça va ? — on fait aller*
► **bear upon** VT FUS (= be relevant to) se rapporter à, avoir trait à ; (= concern) intéresser, concerner
► **bear with** VT FUS [+ person, sb's moods etc] supporter patiemment ; **~ with me a little longer** je vous demande encore un peu de patience

bear² [beəʳ] [1] N [a] (= animal) ours(e) m(f) ; (fig) **he's like a ~ with a sore head*** il est d'une humeur massacrante or de dogue, il n'est pas à prendre avec des pincettes ; (Astron) **the Great/the Little Bear** la Grande/la Petite Ourse → **grizzly, koala, polar** [b] (pej = person) ours m (pej) [c] (St Ex) baissier m [2] VT (St Ex) chercher à faire baisser [3] VI (St Ex) jouer à la baisse [4] COMP ► **bear-baiting** N combat m d'ours et de chiens ► **bear cub** N ourson m ► **bear garden** N (fig) pétaudière f ► **bear hug** N **he gave me a big ~ hug** il m'a serré très fort dans ses bras ► **bear market** N (St Ex) marché m (orienté) à la baisse, marché m baissier ► **bear pit** N fosse f aux ours ► **the Bear State** N (US) l'Arkansas m

bearable [ˈbeərəbl] ADJ supportable, tolérable

beard [bɪəd] [1] N [a] barbe f ; (small, pointed) barbiche f, bouc m ; **to have** or **wear†** a **~** porter la barbe ; **a man with a ~** un homme barbu or à la barbe, un barbu [b] [of fish, oyster] branchie f ; [of goat] barbiche f ; [of grain] barbe f, arête f ; [of hook etc] barbe f, barbelure f ; (Typ) talus m [2] VT (= face up to) affronter, braver ; **to ~ the lion in his den** aller braver le lion dans sa tanière

bearded [ˈbɪədɪd] [1] ADJ barbu ; **a ~ man** un barbu [2] COMP ► **the bearded lady** N la femme à barbe

beardless [ˈbɪədlɪs] ADJ imberbe, sans barbe ; (fig) **~ youth** (petit) jeunet m

bearer [ˈbeərəʳ] [1] N [a] [of letter, news, burden] porteur m, -euse f ; [of tradition] tenant(e) m(f) ; (at funeral) porteur m ; (= servant) serviteur m [b] [of cheque, name, title] porteur m ; [of passport] titulaire mf [c] (Agr, Bot) **a good ~** un arbre qui donne bien [d] (Constr, Tech) support m [2] COMP ► **bearer bond** N titre m au porteur ► **bearer cheque** N chèque m au porteur

bearing [ˈbeərɪŋ] [1] N [a] (= posture, behaviour) allure f ; **soldierly ~** allure f martiale ; **noble ~** allure f or maintien m noble ; **queenly ~** port m de reine [b] (= relation, aspect) relation f, rapport m ; **to have a** or **some ~ on sth** influer sur qch ; **to have no ~ on the subject** n'avoir aucun rapport avec le sujet [c] (frm) **it is beyond (all) ~** c'est absolument insupportable [d] (Naut = direction) position f ; **to take a compass ~** prendre un relèvement au compas ; **to take a ship's ~s** faire le point ; **to take** or **get**

one's **~s** s'orienter, se repérer ; (fig) **to lose one's ~s** être désorienté, perdre le nord [e] (Tech) palier m → **ball¹, main** [f] (Her) → **armorial** [2] ADJ (in compounds) **carbon-/oxygen~** etc contenant du carbone/de l'oxygène etc

bearish [ˈbeərɪʃ] [1] ADJ [a] (St Ex) [market] à la baisse ; **to be ~ (on sth)** spéculer à la baisse (sur qch) [b] [person] bourru [2] COMP ► **bearish tendency** N tendance f à la baisse, tendance f baissière

bearskin [ˈbeəskɪn] [1] N (Mil Dress) bonnet m à poil [2] COMP ► **bearskin rug** N tapis m en peau d'ours

beast [biːst] N [a] bête f, animal m ; **the king of the ~s** le roi des animaux ; **~ of burden** bête f de somme or de charge ; **~ of prey** prédateur m ; (Agr) **~s** bétail m, bestiaux mpl ; (Rel) **the Beast** l'Antéchrist m, la Bête de l'Apocalypse ; **the mark of the Beast** la marque de la Bête ; (hum) **a good thriller is a rare ~ indeed** un bon thriller est vraiment une denrée rare ; **this is a very different ~ from ...** ça n'a vraiment rien à voir avec ... → **wild** [b] (pej = person) animal m ; (cruel) brute f, chameau* m ; **a sex ~*** un maniaque sexuel

beastliness† [ˈbiːstlɪnɪs] N (NonC) (= act, quality) bestialité f ; [of language] obscénité f ; (* = unpleasantness) caractère m infect ; [of person] méchanceté f, rosserie* f

beastly† [ˈbiːstlɪ] [1] ADJ [person, conduct] bestial, brutal ; [language] obscène ; [food, sight] dégoûtant, répugnant ; (*: less strong) infect*, abominable ; [child, trick] sale, vilain (both before n) ; **what ~ weather!*** quel temps infect !*, quel sale temps ! ; **it's a ~ business*** c'est une sale affaire ; **to be ~ to sb*** être infect* avec qn, se conduire de façon abominable avec qn [2] ADV (Brit*) méchamment*, terriblement

beat [biːt] (vb: pret **beat**, ptp **beaten**) [1] N [a] [of heart, pulse] battement m ; [of drums] battement m, roulement m ; (Acoustics) battement m ; **to march to the ~ of the drum** marcher au (son du) tambour ; **80 ~s a minute** [of heart] 80 pulsations fpl par minute → **drum** [b] (Mus) temps m ; [of conductor's baton] battement m (de la mesure) ; (Jazz) rythme m ; **strong/weak ~** temps m fort/faible ; **he answered without missing a ~** il a répondu sans se démonter ; (fig) **she never misses a ~** elle a toujours un longueur d'avance [c] [of policeman] (= round) ronde f ; (= area) secteur m ; [of sentry] ronde f ; **the policeman on the ~** noticed it l'agent a remarqué pendant qu'il effectuait sa ronde ; **we need to put more officers on the ~** il faut augmenter le nombre des policiers affectés aux rondes ; **policeman on the ~** îlotier m ; (fig) **that's off my ~** cela n'est pas de mon domaine or de mon rayon* → **offbeat** [d] (Hunting) battue f [e] ‡ = **beatnik** [2] ADJ [a] (*: also **dead-~**) claqué*, crevé* [b] ‡ beatnik inv [3] VT [a] (= strike) [+ person, animal] battre, frapper ; [+ carpet] battre ; [+ eggs, cream] fouetter, battre ; [+ metal] battre ; **to ~ sth flat** aplatir qch ; **to ~ sb with a stick** donner des coups de bâton à qn ; **to ~ sb black and blue** rouer qn de coups, battre qn comme plâtre ; **to ~ sb to death** battre qn à mort ; **she ~ the flames with her jacket** elle essayait d'étouffer les flammes avec sa veste ; **to ~ a drum** battre du tambour ; (US fig) **to ~ a drum for sth*** (= publicize) faire du battage* autour de qch ; (Mil) **to ~ the retreat** battre la retraite ; (Mil, fig) **to ~ a retreat** battre en retraite ; **~ it!‡** fiche le camp !, fous le camp !‡ ; (liter: lit, fig) **to ~ one's breast** se frapper la poitrine ; **to ~ a way through sth** se frayer un passage or un chemin à travers qch ; (Hunting) **to ~ the forest/the moors** battre les bois/les landes ;

(US) **to ~ the bushes to do sth** se donner de la peine pour faire qch ; **~ing the air with its wings** battant l'air de ses ailes ; **the bird ~s its wings** l'oiseau bat des ailes ; **to ~ time** battre la mesure ; (Brit Hist) **to ~ the bounds** marquer les limites d'une paroisse (au cours d'une procession) → **dead, tattoo²**
[b] (= defeat) battre, vaincre ; **the army was ~en** l'armée a été battue ; **to ~ sb to the top of a hill** arriver au sommet d'une colline avant qn ; **to ~ sb at chess** battre qn aux échecs ; **to ~ sb into second place** reléguer qn à la seconde place, battre qn et lui prendre la première place ; **to ~ sb hollow** (Brit) or **hands down** or **into a cocked hat** battre qn à plate(s) couture(s) ; **to ~ the record** battre le record ; **to ~ the system** contourner le système ; (US) **to ~ the charge*** or **the rap‡** [accused person] se tirer d'affaire ; (fig) **to ~ sb to it** couper l'herbe sous le pied à qn, devancer qn ; **coffee ~s tea any day*** le café vaut tout le thé du monde ; **the police confess themselves ~en** la police s'avoue vaincue ; **this problem has got me ~en** or **~*** ce problème me dépasse complètement ; **if you can't ~ them, join them** si tu n'es pas sûr de les vaincre, mets-toi de leur côté ; (fig) **that ~s everything!*** ◊ **that takes some ~ing!*** ça, c'est le bouquet !*, faut le faire !* ; (fig) **his behaviour takes some ~ing*** il dépasse les bornes ; (admiring) **that will take some ~ing*** pour faire mieux, il faudra se lever de bonne heure !* ; (fig) **that ~s me*** cela me dépasse ; (fig) **it ~s me how you can speak to her*** je ne comprends pas or ça me dépasse que tu lui adresses (subj) la parole ; **can you ~ that** or **it!*** faut le faire !*
[4] VI [a] [rain, wind] battre ; [sun] (also **~ down**) taper*, cogner* ; **to ~ at the door** cogner à la porte ; **the rain was ~ing against the window** la pluie battait contre la vitre ; **the waves ~ against the cliff** les vagues battent la falaise ; (fig) **he doesn't ~ about the bush** il n'y va pas par quatre chemins, il ne tourne pas autour du pot ; **well, not to ~ about the bush, he ...** bref, il ...
[b] [heart, pulse, drum] battre ; **her heart was ~ing with joy** son cœur battait or palpitait de joie ; **with ~ing heart** le cœur battant ; **his pulse began to ~ quicker** son pouls s'est mis à battre plus fort ; **they heard the drums ~ing** ils entendaient le roulement des tambours
[c] (Naut) **to ~ (to windward)** louvoyer au plus près
[5] COMP ► **Beat Generation** N beat generation f ► **beat-up*** ADJ = beaten-up ; → **beaten**
► **beat back** VT SEP [+ enemy, flames] repousser
► **beat down** [1] VI **the rain was ~ing down** il pleuvait à verse or à seaux or à torrents ; **the sun was ~ing down** le soleil tapait* or cognait* dur → **beat** 4a [2] VT SEP [a] (= reduce) [+ prices] faire baisser ; [+ person] faire baisser ses prix à ; **I ~ him down to £8** je l'ai fait descendre à 8 livres [b] **the rain has ~en down the wheat** la pluie a couché les blés
► **beat in** VT SEP [+ door] défoncer ; **to ~ sb's brains in‡** défoncer le crâne à qn
► **beat off** VT SEP [+ attack, attacker, competition] repousser
► **beat out** VT SEP [a] [+ fire] étouffer ; **he ~ out the flames with a blanket** il a étouffé les flammes avec une couverture [b] [+ metal] marteler, étaler or amincir au marteau ; (US fig) **to ~ one's brains out*** se creuser la cervelle [c] **to ~ out the rhythm** marquer le rythme, battre la mesure [d] (esp US = beat) battre
► **beat up** [1] VT SEP [a] [+ eggs, cream] fouetter, battre ; (* fig) [+ person] passer à tabac, tabasser* [2] **~-up*** ADJ = beaten-up → **beaten** [3] **~ing-up** N = **beating**
► **beat up on*** VT FUS (US) (= hit) tabasser* ; (= bully) intimider ; (= criticize) descendre en flammes*

beaten [ˈbiːtn] [1] VB ptp of **beat** [2] ADJ [a] [metal] battu, martelé ; [earth, path] battu ;

~ track chemin *m* or sentier *m* battu ; (*lit, fig*) **off the ~ track** hors des sentiers battus **b** (= *defeated*) battu, vaincu **c** (= *exhausted*) claqué‡, crevé‡ **3** COMP ► **beaten-up*** ADJ déglingué‡, bousillé*

beater ['biːtə^r] N **a** (= *gadget*) (*for carpet*) tapette *f* ; (*for eggs* = *whisk*) fouet *m* ; (*rotary*) batteur *m* ; (*Tex*) peigne *m* → **wife b** (*Shooting*) rabatteur *m*

beatific [ˌbiːə'tɪfɪk] ADJ béatifique ; **to wear a ~ smile** sourire aux anges, arborer un sourire béat

beatification [biːˌætɪfɪ'keɪʃən] N béatification *f*

beatify [biː'ætɪfaɪ] VT béatifier

beating ['biːtɪŋ] **1** N **a** (= *punishment*) correction *f*, raclée* *f* ; (= *series of blows*) passage *m* à tabac ; **to give sb a ~** flanquer une correction *or* une raclée* à qn, passer qn à tabac ; **to get a ~** recevoir une correction *or* une raclée*, être passé à tabac **b** (*NonC*) [*of metal*] battement *m* ; [*of drums*] battement *m*, roulement *m* ; [*of carpet*] battage *m* **c** (= *defeat*) défaite *f* ; (= *rough time*) **to take a ~*** [*person*] en voir de toutes les couleurs*, passer un mauvais quart d'heure* ; (*Sport*) se faire battre à plate(s) couture(s), se faire piler* ; **the car takes a ~ on that road*** la voiture en voit de dures sur cette route → **beat 3b d** [*of wings, heart etc*] battement *m* **e** (*Shooting*) battue *f* **2** COMP ► **beating-up*** N passage *m* à tabac, raclée* *f*

beatitude [biː'ætɪtjuːd] N béatitude *f* ; **the Beatitudes** les béatitudes

beatnik ['biːtnɪk] N, ADJ beatnik *mf*

beau [bəʊ] N (*pl* **beaus** *or* **beaux**) (= *dandy*) élégant *m*, dandy *m* ; (= *suitor*) galant *m* ; (*US* = *boyfriend*) petit ami* *m*

Beaufort scale ['bəʊfət,skeɪl] N échelle *f* de Beaufort

beaut* [bjuːt] N **what a ~!** quelle merveille !*

beauteous ['bjuːtɪəs] ADJ (*liter*) = **beautiful 1**

beautician [bjuː'tɪʃən] N esthéticien(ne) *m(f)*, visagiste *mf*

beautiful ['bjuːtɪfʊl] **1** ADJ [*person, music, picture, clothes*] beau (belle *f*), bel (*m before vowel*) ; [*weather*] superbe, splendide ; [*dinner*] magnifique ; **really ~** de toute beauté **2** N **the ~** le beau

beautifully ['bjuːtɪflɪ] ADV [*sew, drive etc*] admirablement, à la perfection ; [*quiet, empty*] merveilleusement ; **that will do ~** cela convient parfaitement, c'est tout à fait ce qu'il faut

beautify ['bjuːtɪfaɪ] VT embellir, orner ; **to ~ o.s.** se faire une beauté

beauty ['bjuːtɪ] **1** N **a** (*NonC*) beauté *f* ; **to mar** *or* **spoil** *or* **ruin the ~ of sth** déparer qch ■ (*PROV*) **~ is only skin-deep** la beauté n'est pas tout ■ (*PROV*) **~ is in the eye of the beholder** la beauté est quelque chose de subjectif ; (*fig*) **the ~ of it is that* ...** le plus beau, c'est que ... ; (*fig*) **that's the ~ of it*** c'est ça qui est formidable* **b** (= *person*) beauté *f* ; **she is a ~** elle est d'une grande beauté, c'est une beauté ; **she's no ~*** ce n'est pas une beauté ; **Beauty and the Beast** la Belle et la Bête **c** * **his goal was a real ~** son but était vraiment superbe ; **isn't this car a ~!** elle est superbe, cette voiture ? **2** COMP ► **beauty competition, beauty contest** N concours *m* de beauté ► **beauty cream** N crème *f* de beauté ► **beauty editor** N rédacteur *m*, -trice *f* de la rubrique beauté ► **beauty parlour** N institut *m* or salon *m* de beauté ► **beauty preparations** NPL produits *mpl* de beauté ► **beauty queen** N reine *f* de beauté ► **beauty salon** N = **beauty parlour** ► **beauty sleep** N **off you go to bed now, you need your ~ sleep** va te coucher maintenant pour être frais et dispos demain

matin ► **beauty specialist** N esthéticien(ne) *m(f)*, visagiste *mf* ► **beauty spot** N (*on skin*) (*natural*) grain *m* de beauté ; (*applied*) mouche *f* ; (*in countryside*) site *m* superbe ► **beauty treatment** N soins *mpl* de beauté

beaux [bəʊz] NPL *of* **beau**

beaver ['biːvə^r] **1** N **a** (= *animal*) castor *m* ; (= *fur*) (fourrure *f* de) castor *m* ; (= *hat*) (chapeau *m* de) castor *m* ; **to work like a ~** travailler d'arrache-pied → **eager b** (*esp US**) foufoune*‡ *f*, chatte*‡ *f* **2** VI (*Brit fig*) **to ~ away*** **at sth** travailler d'arrache-pied à qch **3** COMP [*coat, hat*] (en poil) de castor ► **the Beaver State** N (*US*) l'Oregon *m*

Beaverboard® ['biːvəbɔːd] N (*Constr*) (panneau *m* d')aggloméré *m* (*de bois*)

bebop ['biːbɒp] N (*Mus*) be-bop *m*

becalm [bɪ'kɑːm] VT **to be ~ed** (*Naut*) être encalminé ; (*fig*) [*economy, stock market, talks*] faire du surplace

became [bɪ'keɪm] VB *pt of* **become**

▼ **because** [bɪ'kɒz] **1** CONJ parce que ; **I did it ~ you asked me to** je l'ai fait parce que tu me l'as demandé ; **I won't go out ~ it's raining** je ne sortirai pas parce qu'il pleut *or* à cause de la pluie ; **it is the more surprising ~ we were not expecting it** c'est d'autant plus surprenant que nous ne nous y attendions pas ; **if I did it, it was ~ it had to be done** je l'ai fait parce qu'il fallait bien le faire ; **~ he lied, he was punished** il a été puni pour avoir menti *or* parce qu'il avait menti ; **we are annoyed ~ the weather is bad** nous sommes contrariés parce qu'il fait mauvais ; **not ~ he was offended but ~ he was angry** non qu'il fût offusqué mais parce qu'il était furieux ; **~ he was leaving** à cause de son départ **2** PREP **~ of** à cause de, en raison de ; **~ of his age** en raison de son âge, vu son âge

bechamel [ˌbeɪʃə'mɛl] N (*also* **~ sauce**) (sauce *f*) béchamel *f*

beck[1] [bek] N **to be at sb's ~ and call** être à l'entière disposition de qn, être constamment à la disposition de qn ; **to have sb at one's ~ and call** faire marcher qn à la baguette *or* au doigt et à l'œil

beck[2] [bek] N (*N Engl*) ruisseau *m*, ru *m*

beckon ['bekən] **1** VI **a** (= *signal*) faire signe (**to sb** à qn) ; **he ~ed to her to follow him** il lui a fait signe de le suivre **b** (= *be attractive*) [*bright lights, fame*] attirer **2** VT **a** (= *signal*) faire signe à ; **he ~ed me in/back/over** *etc* il m'a fait signe d'entrer/de revenir/d'approcher *etc* **b** (= *attract*) attirer

become [bɪ'kʌm] (*pret* **became**, *ptp* **become**) **1** VI **a** (= *grow to be*) devenir, se faire ; **to ~ famous** *etc* devenir célèbre *etc* ; **to ~ old** vieillir, se faire vieux ; **to ~ thin** maigrir ; **to ~ fat** grossir ; **to ~ accustomed to ~** s'accoutumer à ..., s'habituer à ... ; **to ~ interested in ...** commencer à s'intéresser à ... ; **to ~ known** [*person*] commencer à être connu, se faire connaître ; **we are fast becoming a nation of cynics** nous nous transformons rapidement en une nation de cyniques **b** (= *acquire position of*) devenir ; **to ~ king** devenir roi ; **to ~ a doctor** devenir *or* se faire médecin **2** IMPERS VB **what has ~ of him?** qu'est-il devenu ? ; **I don't know what will ~ of her** je ne sais pas ce qu'elle va devenir **3** VT (*liter, frm*) **a** (= *suit*) aller à ; **her hat does not ~ her** son chapeau ne lui sied pas (*frm*) **b** (= *befit*) convenir à, être digne de ; **it does not ~ him to speak thus** il lui sied mal (*frm*) de parler ainsi

becoming [bɪ'kʌmɪŋ] ADJ [*behaviour, speech*] convenable, bienséant ; [*clothes, hair style*] seyant, qui va bien ; **her hat is not ~** son chapeau ne lui va pas *or* n'est pas seyant

becomingly [bɪ'kʌmɪŋlɪ] ADV **a** (= *attractively*) [*smile, blush*] de façon charmante ; **she was dressed ~ in black** elle était habillée en noir, ce qui lui allait fort bien **b** (= *suitably*) convenablement, d'une manière convenable

becquerel [ˌbekə'rel] N becquerel *m*

BEd [biː'ed] N (ABBR = **Bachelor of Education**) → **bachelor**

bed [bed] **1** N **a** (= *furniture*) lit *m* ; **a room with two ~s** une chambre à deux lits ; (*Brit*) **to book in (at a hotel) for ~ and breakfast** réserver une chambre avec le petit déjeuner (à l'hôtel) ; **to sleep in separate ~s** faire lit à part ; **to make the ~** faire le lit ; **to turn down the ~** préparer le lit (*en repliant le haut des draps*) ; **to change the ~** changer les draps (du lit) ; **to be in ~** être couché ; (*through illness*) être alité, garder le lit ; **to get into ~** se coucher, se mettre au lit ; **before ~** avant de se coucher ; **to get out of ~** se lever ; (*fig*) **to get out of ~ on the wrong side** ◊ **to get up (on) the wrong side of the ~*** (*US*) se lever du pied gauche ; **to get sb to ~** réussir à coucher qn ; **to put sb to ~** coucher qn ; **to go to ~** se coucher ; (*euph*) **to go to ~ with sb*** coucher avec qn* ; (*fig*) **to get into ~ with sb** s'allier à qn ; **to go home to ~** rentrer se coucher ■ (*PROV*) **as you make your ~ so you must lie on it** comme on fait son lit on se couche → **campbed, deathbed, feather b** (*liter*) **she was brought to ~ of a boy** †† elle accoucha d'un garçon **c** (*Press*) **to put a paper to ~*** mettre un journal sous presse ; (*Press*) **the paper has gone to ~*** le journal est sous presse ; (*fig*) **to put sth to ~** mener qch à bien **d** (= *layer*) (*Geol*) [*of coal*] couche *f*, gisement *m* ; [*of clay*] couche *f*, lit *m* ; [*of coral*] banc *m* ; [*of ore*] gisement *m* ; (*Constr*) [*of mortar*] bain *m* (de mortier) ; (*Zool*) [*of oysters*] banc *m* **e** (= *base*) (*Tech*) [*of engine*] berceau *m* ; [*of lathe*] banc *m* ; [*of machine*] base *f*, bâti *m* ; [*of truck*] plateau *m* ; (*Archit*) [*of building*] assises *fpl* ; (*Culin*) **on a ~ of lettuce/rice** sur un lit de laitue/riz **f** (= *bottom*) [*of sea*] fond *m* ; [*of river*] lit *m* **g** (*Hort*) [*of vegetables*] planche *f* ; (*square*) carré *m* ; [*of flowers*] parterre *m*, massif *m* ; (*strip*) platebande *f* ; (*oval, circular*) corbeille *f* ; (*fig*) **life is not a ~ of roses** la vie n'est pas une partie de plaisir ; (*fig*) **my job isn't exactly a ~ of roses*** mon travail n'est pas drôle tous les jours **2** VT **a** (*Hort*) **to ~ (out) plants** repiquer des plantes **b** (*Tech*) [+ *foundations*] asseoir ; **to ~ stones in mortar** cimenter *or* sceller des pierres **c** († ‡) [+ *woman*] coucher avec* **3** COMP ► **bed and board** N le gîte *or* le vivre et le couvert ► **bed and breakfast** N (*gen*) chambre *f* et petit déjeuner *m*, chambre *f* d'hôte ; **we stayed at ~ and breakfasts** *or* **~-and-breakfast places** nous avons logé dans des chambres d'hôtes ; **price for ~ and breakfast** prix *m* pour la chambre et le petit déjeuner ► **bed bath** N toilette *f* (*d'un malade*) ► **bed jacket** N liseuse *f* ► **bed linen** N (*NonC*) draps *mpl* de lit (et taies *fpl* d'oreillers), literie *f* ► **bed of nails** N (*lit*) lit *m* de clous ; (*Brit fig*) **it's a ~ of nails** c'est extrêmement pénible ► **bed pad** N (*waterproof*) alaise *f* ; (*for extra comfort*) molleton *m* ► **bed-settee** N canapé-lit *m* ► **bed-sitter, bed-sitting room** N (*Brit*) chambre *f* meublée

► **bed down 1** VI (= *go to bed*) (aller) se coucher ; (= *spend night*) coucher **2** VT [+ *children etc*] coucher

bedaub [bɪ'dɔːb] VT barbouiller (**with** de)

bedazzle [bɪ'dæzl] VT éblouir

bedbug ['bedbʌg] N punaise *f* des lits

bedchamber †† ['bed,tʃeɪmbə^r] N chambre *f* à coucher

► LANGUAGE IN USE: **because** 17.1, 26.3

bedclothes ['bedkləʊðz] NPL couvertures *fpl* et draps *mpl* (de lit)

bedcover ['bedkʌvəʳ] N couvre-lit *m*, dessus-de-lit *m inv*

-bedded ['bedɪd] ADJ (*in compounds*) **twin-bedded room** chambre *f* à deux lits

bedding ['bedɪŋ] **1** N literie *f*; (*Mil*) matériel *m* de couchage; (*for animals*) litière *f* **2** COMP ► **bedding out** N (*Hort*) repiquage *m* ► **bedding(-out) plants** NPL (*Hort*) plantes *fpl* à repiquer

bedeck [bɪ'dek] VT parer, orner (**with** de); (*slightly pej*) attifer* (**with** de)

bedevil [bɪ'devl] VT (= *confuse*) [+ *issue, person*] embrouiller; (= *torment*) [+ *person*] tourmenter, harceler; **to be ~led by** [+ *person, project*] beaucoup souffrir de

bedevilment [bɪ'devlmənt] N (= *confusion*) confusion *f*; (= *torment*) tourment *m*, harcèlement *m*

bedfellow ['bed,feləʊ] N (*lit*) **they were ~s for a night** ils ont partagé le même lit une nuit; (*fig*) **they are strange ~s** ils forment une drôle de paire *or* un drôle de couple

bedhead ['bedhed] N tête *f* de lit, chevet *m*

bedlam ['bedləm] N **a** (= *uproar*) chahut *m*; **the crowd went absolutely mad — it was ~** la foule est devenue complètement folle — c'était le cirque; **he's causing ~ at the hotel** il fait du chahut dans l'hôtel; **the room was a ~ of banging and shouting** la pièce retentissait de coups et de cris **b** (*Hist*) maison *f* de fous†

bedmate* ['bedmeɪt] N = **bedfellow**

Bedouin ['bedʊɪn] **1** N (*pl* **Bedouin** *or* **Bedouins**) Bédouin(e) *m(f)* **2** ADJ bédouin

bedpan ['bedpæn] N bassin *m* (hygiénique)

bedpost ['bedpəʊst] N colonne *f* de lit

bedraggled [bɪ'drægld] ADJ [*clothes, person*] débraillé; [*hair*] embroussaillé; (= *wet*) trempé

bedridden ['bedrɪdn] ADJ alité, cloué au lit; (*permanently*) grabataire

bedrock ['bedrɒk] N (*Geol*) soubassement *m*; (*fig*) base *f*

bedroll ['bedrəʊl] N tapis *m* de couchage

bedroom ['bedrʊm] **1** N chambre *f* (à coucher) → **spare 2** COMP ► **bedroom farce** N (*Theat*) comédie *f* de boulevard ► **bedroom scene** N ≈ scène *f* d'amour ► **bedroom slipper** N pantoufle *f* ► **bedroom suburb*** N (*US fig*) banlieue-dortoir *m* ► **bedroom suite** N chambre *f* à coucher (*mobilier*)

-bedroomed ['bedrʊmd] ADJ (*in compounds*) **a two-/four-bedroomed house** une maison avec deux/quatre chambres; **a one-bedroomed flat** un (appartement) deux-pièces

Beds N ABBR = **Bedfordshire**

bedside ['bedsaɪd] **1** N chevet *m*; **at his ~** à son chevet **2** COMP [*book, lamp*] de chevet ► **bedside manner** N [*of doctor*] comportement *m* envers les malades; **he has a good ~ manner** il sait parler à ses malades ► **bedside rug** N descente *f* de lit ► **bedside table** N table *f* de chevet *or* de nuit

bedsit* ['bedsɪt] N (*Brit*) chambre *f* meublée

bedsocks ['bedsɒks] NPL chaussettes *fpl* (de lit)

bedsore ['bedsɔːʳ] N escarre *f*

bedspread ['bedspred] N dessus-de-lit *m inv*, couvre-lit *m*

bedspring ['bedsprɪŋ] N (*US*) (= *framework*) sommier *m* à ressorts; (= *single spring*) ressort *m* de sommier

bedstead ['bedsted] N châlit *m*, bois *m* de lit

bedstraw ['bedstrɔː] N (*Bot*) gaillet *m*

bedtime ['bedtaɪm] N heure *f* du coucher; **it is ~** il est l'heure d'aller se coucher *or* d'aller au lit; **his ~ is 7 o'clock** il se couche à 7 heures; **it's past your ~** tu devrais être déjà couché **2** COMP ► **bedtime drink** N boisson *f*

chaude (*prise avant d'aller se coucher*) ► **bedtime reading** N **it's my favourite ~ reading** c'est ce que je préfère lire le soir, au lit ► **bedtime story** N **to tell a child a ~ story** raconter une histoire à un enfant avant qu'il s'endorme

bed-wetting ['bed,wetɪŋ] N (*Med*) incontinence *f* nocturne

bee [biː] **1** N **a** abeille *f*; (*fig*) **to have a ~ in one's bonnet*** avoir une idée fixe (**about** en ce qui concerne), avoir une marotte; **they crowded round him like ~s round a honeypot** ils se pressaient autour de lui comme des mouches sur un pot de confiture; **it's the ~'s knees*** c'est extra* *or* super*; **he thinks he's the ~'s knees*** il se croit sorti de la cuisse de Jupiter* → **bumblebee, busy, queen b** (*esp US* = *meeting*) réunion entre voisins ou voisines pour effectuer des activités en commun; **they have a sewing ~ on Thursdays** ils se réunissent pour coudre le jeudi → **spelling 2** COMP ► **bee eater** N (*Orn*) guêpier *m* ► **bee sting** N piqûre *f* d'abeille

Beeb* [biːb] N (*Brit*) **the ~** la BBC

beech [biːtʃ] **1** N (*also* ~ **tree**) hêtre *m*; (= *wood*) (bois *m* de) hêtre → **copper 2** COMP [*hedge, chair*] de hêtre ► **beech grove** N hêtraie *f*

beechmast ['biːtʃmɑːst] N (*NonC*) faînes *fpl* (tombées)

beechnut ['biːtʃnʌt] N faîne *f*

beechwood ['biːtʃwʊd] N (= *material*) (bois *m* de) hêtre *m*; (= *group of trees*) bois *m* de hêtres

beef [biːf] **1** N **a** (*NonC*) bœuf *m*; **roast ~** rôti *m* de bœuf, rosbif *m*; **there's too much ~ on him** il a trop de viande*, il est trop gros → **bully³, corned beef b** (*US* = *complaint*) **what's your ~?*** qu'est-ce que tu as à râler?* **2** VI (‡ = *complain*) rouspéter*, râler* (**about** contre) **3** COMP ► **beef cattle** N bœufs *mpl* de boucherie ► **beef olive** N paupiette *f* de bœuf ► **beef sausage** N ≈ saucisse *f* de Strasbourg ► **beef tea** N bouillon *m* (de viande)

► **beef up*** VT SEP [+ *speech, essay*] étoffer; [+ *team*] renforcer

beefburger ['biːf,bɜːgəʳ] N ≈ hamburger *m*

beefcake* ['biːfkeɪk] N (*hum*) monsieur-muscles* *m*

beefeater ['biːf,iːtəʳ] N (*Brit*) hallebardier *m* (*de la Tour de Londres*)

beefsteak ['biːfsteɪk] **1** N bifteck *m*, steak *m* **2** COMP ► **beefsteak tomato** N tomate *f* à farcir

beefy* ['biːfɪ] ADJ **a** (= *strong*) costaud* *inv*; (= *fat*) bien en chair **b** [*flavour*] de bœuf

beehive ['biːhaɪv] **1** N (*gen*) (*lit, fig*) ruche *f*; (= *hair style*) choucroute* *f* **2** COMP ► **the Beehive State** N (*US*) l'Utah *m*

beekeeper ['biː,kiːpəʳ] N apiculteur *m*, -trice *f*

beekeeping ['biː,kiːpɪŋ] N apiculture *f*

beeline ['biːlaɪn] N à vol d'oiseau, en ligne droite; **to make a ~ for** (= *go straight to*) se diriger tout droit *or* en droite ligne vers; (= *rush towards*) se ruer sur, filer droit sur

been [biːn] VB *ptp of* **be**

beep [biːp] **1** N (*esp Brit*) [*of watch*] bip *m*; [*of answering machine*] signal *m* sonore, bip *m* (sonore); **after the ~** après le bip *or* le signal sonore **2** VI faire bip

beeper ['biːpəʳ] N = **bleeper**

beer [bɪəʳ] **1** N bière *f*; (*Brit*) **life's not all ~ and skittles*** la vie n'est pas une partie de plaisir → **ginger 2** COMP ► **beer barrel** N tonneau *m* à *or* de bière ► **beer belly*** N bedaine* *f* (de buveur de bière) ► **beer bottle** N canette *f* (de bière) ► **beer bust** N (*US*) (= *party*) soirée *f* bière *inv*; (= *drinking spree*) soûlerie* *f* à la bière ► **beer can** N boîte *f* de bière (vide) ► **beer drinker** N buveur *m*, -euse *f* de bière ► **beer engine** N pompe *f* à bière

► **beer garden** N (*Brit*) jardin *m* attenant à un pub (*où l'on peut amener ses consommations*) ► **beer glass** N bock *m* ► **beer gut*** N = **beer belly** ► **beer pump** N = **beer engine** ► **beer-swilling*** ADJ (*pej*) qui s'envoie de la bière à tire-larigot*

beerfest ['bɪəfest] N (*US*) fête *f* de la bière

beermat ['bɪəmæt] N dessous *m* de verre, dessous *m* de bock

beery ['bɪərɪ] ADJ [*atmosphere, room, breath*] qui sent la bière; [*party, evening*] où la bière coule à flots; [*person*] un peu éméché*, parti*

beeswax ['biːzwæks] **1** N cire *f* d'abeille **2** VT [+ *floor, furniture*] cirer, encaustiquer

beet [biːt] **1** N betterave *f*; (*US*) **red ~** betterave *f* (potagère) → **sugar 2** COMP ► **beet sugar** N sucre *m* de betterave

beetle¹ ['biːtl] **1** N (*gen*) scarabée *m*; (*Zool*) coléoptère *m* → **black, Colorado, deathwatch beetle, stag 2** VI **to ~ in/through*** *etc* entrer/traverser *etc* en vitesse

► **beetle off*** VI décamper, ficher le camp*

beetle² ['biːtl] N (= *mallet*) mailloche *f*; (*heavier*) mouton *m*

beetle-browed ['biːtl,braʊd] ADJ (*bushy eyebrows*) aux sourcils broussailleux; (= *sullen*) renfrogné

beetling ['biːtlɪŋ] ADJ **~ brow** front *m* proéminent; **~ cliffs** falaises *fpl* surplombantes

beetroot ['biːtruːt] N (*Brit*) betterave *f* (potagère *or* rouge); **to go ~** devenir rouge comme une tomate, devenir cramoisi; **~ salad** salade *f* de betterave(s)

befall [bɪ'fɔːl] (*pret* **befell** [bɪ'fel], *ptp* **befallen** (*liter: only infin and 3rd pers*)) **1** VI arriver; **whatever may ~** quoi qu'il puisse arriver, quoi qu'il advienne **2** VT arriver à, échoir à; **a misfortune befell him** il lui arriva un malheur

befit [bɪ'fɪt] VT (*frm: only infin and 3rd pers*) convenir à; **it ill ~s him to speak thus** il lui convient *or* il lui sied (*frm*) mal de parler ainsi

befitting [bɪ'fɪtɪŋ] ADJ convenable, seyant; **with ~ humility** avec l'humilité qui convient *or* qui sied (*frm*)

befog [bɪ'fɒg] VT (= *puzzle*) brouiller, embrouiller; (= *obscure*) [+ *origin, meaning*] obscurcir; **she was quite ~ged** elle était dans le brouillard le plus complet

before [bɪ'fɔːʳ]

> When **before** is an element in a phrasal verb, eg **come before, go before,** look up the verb.

1 PREP **a** (*time*) avant; **I got there ~ you** je suis arrivé avant vous, je vous ai devancé; **that was ~ my time** (= *before I was here*) je n'étais pas encore là; (= *before I was born*) je n'étais pas encore né; **she died ~ I was born** elle est morte avant que je naisse *or* avant ma naissance; **I cannot do it ~ next week** je ne peux pas le faire avant la semaine prochaine; **~ Christ** avant Jésus-Christ; **the day ~ yesterday** avant-hier *m*; **he came the year ~ last** il est venu il y a deux ans; **the year ~ last was his centenary** son centenaire a eu lieu il y a deux ans; **the programme ~ last** l'avant-dernier programme *m*; **the day ~ their departure** la veille de leur départ; **two days ~ Christmas** l'avant-veille *f* de Noël; **~ it ◊ ~ now ◊ ~ then** avant (cela *or* ça), auparavant; **you should have done it ~ now** vous devriez l'avoir déjà fait; **~ long** sous peu, d'ici peu; **~ doing** avant de faire

b (*order, rank*) avant; **ladies ~ gentlemen** les dames avant les messieurs; **~ everything** avant tout

c (*place, position*) devant; **he stood ~ me** il était (là) devant moi; **~ my (very) eyes** sous mes (propres) yeux; **turn left at the junction ~ the roundabout** tournez à gauche au croisement avant le rond-point; **the question ~ us** la question qui nous occupe; **the task ~ him** la tâche qu'il a devant lui *or* qui l'attend; **he fled ~ the enemy** il s'est enfui à l'approche de

or devant l'ennemi ; (*Naut*) **to sail ~ the mast** servir comme simple matelot ; (*Naut*) **to run ~ the wind** aller *or* avoir vent arrière → **carry**
[d] (= *in presence of*) devant, en présence de ; **he said it ~ us all** il l'a dit en notre présence *or* devant nous tous ; **~ a lawyer** par-devant notaire ; **to appear ~ a court/a judge** comparaître devant un tribunal/un juge ; **he brought the case ~ the court** il a saisi le tribunal de l'affaire
[e] (= *rather than*) plutôt que ; **he would die ~ betraying his country** il mourrait plutôt que de trahir sa patrie ; **to put death ~ dishonour** préférer la mort au déshonneur
[2] ADV [a] (*time*) avant, auparavant ; **the day ~** la veille ; **the evening ~** la veille au soir ; **the week/year ~** la semaine/l'année d'avant *or* précédente ; **two days ~** l'avant-veille *f*, deux jours avant *or* auparavant ; **I have read that book** j'ai déjà lu ce livre ; **I had read it ~** je l'avais déjà lu, je l'avais lu auparavant ; **I said ~ that ...** j'ai déjà dit que ... ; **she has never met him ~** c'est la première fois qu'elle le rencontre, elle ne l'a encore jamais rencontré ; **it has never happened ~** c'est la première fois que cela arrive ; **long ~** longtemps auparavant ; **to continue as ~** faire comme par le passé ; **he should have told me ~** il aurait dû me le dire avant *or* plus tôt
[b] (*place*) avant, devant
[c] (*order*) avant ; **that chapter and the one ~** ce chapitre et le précédent *or* et celui d'avant
[3] CONJ [a] (*time*) avant de (+ *infin*), avant que (+ *ne*) (+ *subj*) ; **I did it ~ going out** je l'ai fait avant de sortir ; **go and see him ~ he goes** allez le voir avant son départ *or* avant qu'il (ne) parte ; **I ~ come/go/return** avant mon arrivée/mon départ/mon retour ; **we will need a year ~ it is finished** il nous faudra un an pour l'achever ; **it will be a long time ~ he comes again** il ne reviendra pas d'ici longtemps ; **it will be six weeks ~ the boat returns** le bateau ne reviendra pas avant six semaines ; (*fig*) **~ you could say Jack Robinson** en moins de deux, en moins de temps qu'il n'en faut pour le dire ; **~ I forget, your mother phoned** avant que je n'oublie (*subj*) *or* que j'oublie (*subj*), votre mère a téléphoné
[b] (= *rather than*) plutôt que de (+ *infin*) ; **he will die ~ he surrenders** il mourra plutôt que de se rendre
[4] COMP ► **before-and-after test** N test *m* « avant-après » ► **before-tax** ADJ [*income*] brut ; [*profit*] avant impôts

beforehand [bɪˈfɔːhænd] ADV à l'avance ; **you must tell me ~** il faut me le dire à l'avance ; **to make preparations well ~** faire des préparatifs bien à l'avance

befoul [bɪˈfaʊl] VT (*liter*: *lit, fig*) souiller (*liter*), salir

befriend [bɪˈfrend] VT (= *be friend to*) traiter en ami, donner son amitié à ; (= *help*) venir en aide à, aider

befuddle [bɪˈfʌdl] VT (= *confuse*) brouiller l'esprit *or* les idées de ; (= *make tipsy*) griser, émécher ; **~d with drink** éméché*

beg [beg] [1] VT [a] [+ *money, alms, food*] mendier
[b] [+ *favour*] solliciter, quémander ; **to ~ sb's pardon** demander pardon à qn ; **(I) ~ your pardon** (*apologizing*) je vous demande pardon ; (*not having heard*) pardon ?, vous disiez ? ; **to ~ (sb's) forgiveness** demander pardon (à qn) ; (*frm*) **I ~ to point out that ...** je me permets de (vous) faire remarquer que ..., qu'il me soit permis de faire remarquer que ... ; **I ~ to differ** permettez-moi d'être d'un autre avis, je me permets de ne pas partager cet avis ; (*frm*) **I ~ to inform you that ...** je tiens à *or* j'ai l'honneur (*frm*) de vous faire savoir que ... ; (*frm*) **to ~ leave to do** solliciter l'autorisation de faire
[c] (= *entreat*) supplier ; **to ~ (of) sb to do** sup-

plier qn de faire ; **I ~ (of) you!** je vous en supplie !, de grâce !
[d] **to ~ the question** (= *raise the question*) poser *or* soulever la question ; (= *evade the issue*) éluder la question ; (= *assume sth already proved*) présumer la question résolue
[2] VI [a] mendier, demander la charité ; **to ~ for money** mendier ; **to ~ for food** mendier de la nourriture ; **to sit up and ~** [*dog*] faire le beau ; (*fig*) **I'll have that sausage if it's going ~ging*** donne-moi cette saucisse s'il n'y a pas d'amateurs
[b] (= *entreat*) supplier ; **to ~ for mercy/help** demander grâce/de l'aide → **1c**
► **beg off** VI se faire excuser (**from** de)

began [bɪˈɡæn] VB *pt of* **begin**

beget†† [bɪˈɡet] (*pret* **begot** *or* **begat** [bɪˈɡæt], *ptp* **begotten**) VT (*lit*) engendrer ; (*fig*) engendrer, causer ; **the only begotten Son of the Father** le Fils unique engendré par le Père

begetter [bɪˈɡetəʳ] N (*frm*: *fig*) créateur *m*, -trice *f*

beggar [ˈbeɡəʳ] [1] N [a] (*also* ~ **man, ~ woman**) mendiant(e) *m(f)*, mendigot(e)* *m(f)* ; (*fig* = *very poor person*) indigent(e) *m(f)*, pauvre(sse) *m(f)* (*PROV*) **~s can't be choosers** nécessité fait loi (*PROV*) ; **~'s opera** opéra *m* de quat' sous [b] (* = *fellow*) poor ~! pauvre diable !* ; **a lucky ~** un veinard* ; **a funny little ~** un drôle de petit bonhomme [2] VT (*lit*) réduire à la mendicité ; (*fig* = *ruin*) mettre sur la paille, ruiner ; (*fig*) **to ~ description** défier toute description ; **to ~ belief** défier la raison ; **the arrogance of the man ~s belief** l'arrogance de cet homme défie la raison [3] COMP ► **beggar-my-neighbour** N (*Cards*) bataille *f* ; (*Econ*) **~-my-neighbour policy** politique *f* protectionniste

beggarly [ˈbeɡəlɪ] ADJ [*amount*] piètre, misérable ; [*existence*] misérable, sordide ; [*meal*] maigre, piètre, pauvre ; [*wage*] dérisoire, de famine

beggary [ˈbeɡərɪ] N mendicité *f*

begging [ˈbeɡɪŋ] [1] N mendicité *f* ; **to live by ~** vivre de charité *or* d'aumône → **beg** [2] ADJ **~ letter** lettre *f* quémandant de l'argent [3] COMP ► **begging bowl** N sébile *f* ; (*fig*) **to hold out a ~ bowl** tendre la main (*fig*)

begin [bɪˈɡɪn] (*pret* **began**, *ptp* **begun**) [1] VT [a] (= *start*) [+ *work*] commencer (**to do, doing** à faire) ; [+ *task*] entreprendre ; [+ *song*] commencer (à chanter), entonner ; [+ *attack*] déclencher ; [+ *packet, cake, cheese etc*] entamer ; [+ *book, letter*] [*writer*] commencer (à écrire) ; [*reader*] commencer (à lire) ; **to ~ a cheque book/a new page** commencer *or* prendre un nouveau carnet de chèques/une nouvelle page ; **to ~ a journey** partir en voyage ; **he began the day with a glass of milk** il a bu un verre de lait pour bien commencer la journée ; **to ~ the day right** bien commencer la journée, se lever du pied droit ; **to ~ life as ...** débuter dans la vie comme ... ; **that doesn't (even) ~ to compare with ...** cela n'a rien de comparable avec ... ; **it soon began to rain** il n'a pas tardé à pleuvoir ; **I'd begun to think you weren't coming** je commençais à croire que tu ne viendrais pas ; **to ~ again** recommencer (**to do** à faire) ; **"listen, darling" he began** « écoute, chérie » commença-t-il
[b] (= *originate, initiate*) [+ *discussion*] commencer, ouvrir ; [+ *conversation*] amorcer, engager ; [+ *quarrel, argument, dispute*] faire naître ; [+ *reform, movement, series of events*] déclencher ; [+ *fashion*] lancer ; [+ *custom, policy*] inaugurer ; [+ *war*] causer ; [+ *rumour*] faire naître
[2] VI [a] commencer (**with** par) ; **let's ~!** commençons !, allons-y ! ; **we must ~ at once** il faut commencer *or* nous y mettre immédiatement ; **well, to ~ at the beginning ...** bon, commençons par le commencement ... ; **it's**

~ning rather well/badly cela s'annonce plutôt bien/mal ; **to ~ in business** se lancer dans les affaires ; **just where the hair ~s** à la naissance des cheveux ; **before October ~s** avant le début octobre *or* le début du mois d'octobre ; **to ~ again** recommencer ; **he began afresh in a new country** il est reparti à zéro dans un nouveau pays ; **school ~s again on Tuesday** les cours reprennent mardi, la rentrée (des classes) est mardi ; **the classes ~ again soon** (*after short break*) les cours reprennent bientôt ; (*after summer break*) c'est bientôt la rentrée ; **~ning from Monday** à partir de lundi ; **he began in the sales department/as a clerk** il a débuté dans le service des ventes/comme employé de bureau ; **he began as a Marxist** il a commencé par être marxiste, au début *or* au départ il était marxiste ; **he began with the intention of writing a thesis** au début son intention était d'écrire *or* il avait l'intention d'écrire une thèse ; **to ~ by doing** commencer par faire ; **~ by putting everything away** commence par tout ranger ; **to ~ with sth** commencer *or* débuter par qch ; **~ with me!** commencez par moi ! ; **we only had 100 francs to ~ with** nous n'avions que 100 F pour commencer *or* au début ; **to ~ with there were only three of them but later ...** (tout) d'abord ils n'étaient que trois, mais plus tard ... ; **the spelling is wrong, to ~ with** d'abord, l'orthographe est fausse ; **~ on a new page** prenez une nouvelle page ; **the fields ~ where the garden ends** au bout du jardin il y a des champs
[b] (= *make a start*) **to ~ on** [+ *book*] commencer (à écrire *or* à lire) ; [+ *course of study*] commencer, entreprendre ; **I began on the job last week** j'ai commencé à travailler *or* j'ai débuté dans ce travail la semaine dernière
[c] [*shooting, fight, quarrel*] commencer ; [*music, noise, guns*] commencer, retentir ; [*fire*] prendre, se déclarer ; [*river*] prendre sa source ; [*road*] partir (**at** de) ; [*political party, movement, custom*] commencer, naître ; **that's when the trouble ~s** c'est alors *or* là que les ennuis commencent ; **it all began when he refused to pay** toute cette histoire a commencé *or* tout a commencé quand il a refusé de payer ; **since the world began** depuis le commencement du monde, depuis que le monde est monde

beginner [bɪˈɡɪnəʳ] N [a] (= *novice*) débutant(e) *m(f)*, novice *mf* ; **it's just ~'s luck** aux innocents les mains pleines (*PROV*) [b] (= *originator*) auteur *m*, cause *f*

beginning [bɪˈɡɪnɪŋ] [1] N [a] [*of speech, book, film, career etc*] début *m*, commencement *m* ; **from the ~** dès le début, dès le commencement ; **from ~ to end** du début à la fin ; **to start again at** *or* **from the ~** recommencer depuis le début ; **in the ~** (*gen*) au début ; (*Bible*) au commencement ; **to make a ~** commencer, débuter ; **the ~ of the academic year** la rentrée (universitaire *or* scolaire) ; **the ~ of the world** le commencement *or* l'origine *f* du monde ; **the ~ of negotiations** l'amorce *f or* l'ouverture *f* des négociations ; **it was the ~ of the end for him** ce fut pour lui le commencement de la fin ; **since the ~ of time** depuis le commencement du monde, depuis que le monde est monde
[b] (= *origin*) origine *f*, commencement *m* ; **the shooting was the ~ of the rebellion** la fusillade a été à l'origine de la révolte ; **fascism had its ~s in Italy** le fascisme prit naissance en Italie ; **to come from humble ~s** [*person*] être d'origine modeste *or* d'un milieu humble
[2] ADJ **~ learner** *or* **student** débutant(e) *m(f)*

begone†† [bɪˈɡɒn] EXCL (*liter*) partez !, hors d'ici ! (*liter*)

begonia [bɪˈɡəʊnɪə] N bégonia *m*

begot [bɪˈɡɒt] VB *pt of* **beget**

begotten [bɪˈɡɒtn] VB *ptp of* **beget**

begrimed [bɪˈɡraɪmd] ADJ (*liter*) noirci, sale

begrudge [bɪˈgrʌdʒ] VT = **grudge 1**

begrudgingly [bɪˈgrʌdʒɪŋlɪ] ADV à contre-cœur, de mauvaise grâce

beguile [bɪˈgaɪl] VT **a** (= *swindle*) abuser, duper; **to ~ sb with promises** bercer qn de promesses, endormir qn avec des promesses; **to ~ sb into doing sth** amener qn par la supercherie à faire qch; **to ~ the time (doing)** faire passer le temps (en faisant) **b** (= *charm*) séduire, captiver; (= *amuse*) distraire

beguiling [bɪˈgaɪlɪŋ] ADJ [*woman, charm*] captivant, séduisant; [*ideas, theory*] séduisant; [*story*] captivant

begum [ˈbeɪgəm] N bégum *f*

begun [bɪˈgʌn] VB ptp of **begin**

behalf [bɪˈhɑːf] N **on ~ of** (= *as representing*) de la part de, au nom de, pour; (= *in the interest of*) en faveur de, dans l'intérêt de, pour; **to come on sb's ~** venir de la part de qn; **to act on sb's ~** agir pour qn or pour le compte de qn; **he spoke on my ~** il a parlé pour moi or en mon nom; **to plead on sb's ~** plaider en faveur de qn; **he was worried on my ~** il s'inquiétait pour moi or à mon sujet

behave [bɪˈheɪv] VI **a** (= *conduct o.s.*) se conduire, se comporter; **to ~ (o.s.) well/badly** bien/mal se conduire or se comporter; **to ~ well towards sb** bien se comporter à l'égard de or envers qn, bien agir envers qn; **to ~ wisely** agir sagement; **to ~ like an honest man** se comporter or se conduire en honnête homme; **he was behaving strangely** il avait un comportement bizarre **b** (* = *conduct o.s. well*) bien se tenir; [*child*] être sage; **he knows how to ~ in society** il sait se tenir dans le monde; **~ (yourself)!** (*physical behaviour*) sois sage!, tiens-toi bien!; (*sth said*) ne dis pas n'importe quoi! **c** [*machines etc*] marcher, fonctionner; **the ship ~s well at sea** le navire tient bien la mer; **we are studying how electrons ~ within atoms** nous étudions le comportement des électrons à l'intérieur des atomes

behaviour, behavior (*US*) [bɪˈheɪvjəʳ] **1** N **a** (= *manner, bearing*) conduite *f*, comportement *m*; **to be on one's best ~** se conduire de son mieux; [*child*] se montrer d'une sagesse exemplaire **b** (= *conduct towards others*) conduite *f*, comportement *m* (**to sb, towards sb** envers qn, à l'égard de qn) **c** [*of machines*] fonctionnement *m* **2** COMP ▶ **behaviour modification** N modification *f* du comportement ▶ **behaviour patterns** NPL types *mpl* de comportement ▶ **behaviour therapy** N thérapie *f* comportementale

behavioural, behavioral (*US*) [bɪˈheɪvjərəl] ADJ **a** [*sciences, studies*] behavioriste **b** [*pattern*] de comportement; **~ problems** troubles *mpl* du comportement

behaviourism, behaviorism (*US*) [bɪˈheɪvjərɪzəm] N behaviorisme *m*

behaviourist, behaviorist (*US*) [bɪˈheɪvjərɪst] ADJ, N behavioriste *mf*

behead [bɪˈhed] VT décapiter

beheading [bɪˈhedɪŋ] N décapitation *f*

beheld [bɪˈheld] VB pt, ptp of **behold**

behemoth [bɪˈhiːmɒθ] N (= *creature*) béhémot(h) *m*; (*fig*) monstre *m* ingérable

behest [bɪˈhest] N (*frm*) commandement *m*, ordre *m*; **at the ~ of ...** sur l'ordre de ...

behind [bɪˈhaɪnd]

> When **behind** *is an element in a phrasal verb, eg* **fall behind, lag behind, stay behind,** *look up the verb.*

1 ADV **a** (= *in or at the rear*) derrière, en arrière; **to follow a long way ~/not far ~** suivre de loin/d'assez près → **fall behind**
b (= *late*) en retard; **to be ~ with one's studies/payments** être en retard dans ses études/ses paiements; **to be ~ with one's work** avoir du travail en retard, être en retard dans

son travail; **I'm too far ~ to catch up now** j'ai pris trop de retard pour me rattraper maintenant

2 PREP **a** (*lit, fig = at the back of*) derrière; **~ the table** derrière la table; **come out from ~ the door** sortez de derrière la porte; **walk close ~ me** suivez-moi de près; **she closed the door ~ her** elle a fermé la porte derrière elle; **an employee with seven years' service ~ her** une employée ayant sept ans d'ancienneté; **~ my back** (*lit*) derrière mon dos; (*fig*) derrière mon dos, à mon insu; (*fig*) **to put sth ~ one** oublier qch, refuser de penser à qch; (*Theat, fig*) **~ the scenes** dans les coulisses; (*fig*) **what is ~ this?** qu'y a-t-il là-dessous? → **bar¹, schedule**
b (*support*) **he has the Communists ~ him** il a les communistes derrière lui; **she's the one ~ this scheme** c'est elle qui est à l'origine de ce projet; **the motives ~ her decision** les motivations *fpl* profondes de sa décision
c (= *responsible for*) **who was ~ the attack?** qui est derrière cet attentat?, qui est le commanditaire de cet attentat?
d (= *less advanced than*) en retard sur, en arrière de; **her son is ~ the other pupils** son fils est en retard sur les autres élèves
e (*time*) **~ time** en retard; (*fig*) **to be ~ the times** être en retard sur son temps, ne pas être de son époque; **their youth is far ~ them** leur jeunesse est loin derrière eux

3 N (* = *buttocks*) derrière *m*, postérieur* *m*

behindhand [bɪˈhaɪndhænd] ADV en retard (**with** dans)

behold [bɪˈhəʊld] (*pret, ptp* **beheld**) VT (*liter*) voir; **~!** regardez!; **~ thy servant** voici ton serviteur; **and ~ I am with you** et voici que je suis avec vous → **lo**

beholden [bɪˈhəʊldən] ADJ (*frm*) **to be ~** être redevable (**to sb for sth** à qn de qch)

behove [bɪˈhəʊv], **behoove** (*US*) [bɪˈhuːv] IMPERS VT (*frm*) incomber, appartenir (**sb to do** à qn de faire), être du devoir or de l'intérêt (**sb to do** de qn de faire); **it ill ~s me/him** *etc* **to ...** il me/lui *etc* sied mal de ...

beige [beɪʒ] ADJ, N beige *m*

Beijing [ˈbeɪˈdʒɪŋ] N Beijing

being [ˈbiːɪŋ] N **a** (NonC = *existence*) existence *f*; **to come into ~** prendre naissance; **when the world came into ~** lorsque le monde fut créé, au moment de la naissance du monde; **to bring** or **call into ~** faire naître, susciter; **to bring a plan into ~** exécuter or réaliser un plan; **then in ~** qui existait alors **b** être *m*, créature *f*; **human ~s** les êtres *mpl* humains; **~s from outer space** des extraterrestres *mpl* **c** (= *essential nature*) être *m*, essence *f*; **with all ~ every fibre of my ~** de tout mon être; **I wanted to be an actress with every fibre of my ~** je désirais être actrice de tout mon être

Beirut [beɪˈruːt] N Beyrouth

bejewelled, bejeweled (*US*) [bɪˈdʒuːəld] ADJ [*person*] paré de bijoux; [*thing*] incrusté de joyaux; (*fig*) [*grass*] émaillé (**with** de)

belabour, belabor (*US*) [bɪˈleɪbəʳ] VT rouer de coups; (*fig: with words*) invectiver

Belarus [beləˈrʊs] N le Bélarus, la Biélorussie

Belarussian [ˌbeləˈrʌʃən] **1** ADJ bélarusse, biélorusse **2** N (= *person*) Bélarusse *mf*, Biélorusse *mf*

belated [bɪˈleɪtɪd] ADJ [*apology, greetings, measures*] tardif

belatedly [bɪˈleɪtɪdlɪ] ADV tardivement

belay [bɪˈleɪ] **1** VT **a** (*Naut*) amarrer; **~ing pin** cabillot *m* (d'amarrage) **b** (*Climbing*) assurer **2** VI (*Climbing*) assurer **3** N assurage *m*, assurance *f*

belch [beltʃ] **1** VI [*person*] avoir un renvoi, éructer **2** VT (*also* **~ forth** or **out**: *liter*) [*volcano, gun*] [+ *smoke, flames*] vomir, cracher **3** N renvoi *m*, éructation *f*

beleaguered [bɪˈliːgəd] ADJ [*city*] assiégé, investi; [*army*] cerné

belfry [ˈbelfrɪ] N beffroi *m*; [*of church*] clocher *m*, beffroi *m* → **bat¹**

Belgian [ˈbeldʒən] **1** ADJ (*gen*) belge, de Belgique; [*ambassador, embassy*] de Belgique; **~ French** le français de Belgique **2** N Belge *mf*; **the king of the ~s** le roi des Belges

belgicism [ˈbeldʒɪsɪzəm] N belgicisme *m*

Belgium [ˈbeldʒəm] N la Belgique

Belgrade [belˈgreɪd] N Belgrade

belie [bɪˈlaɪ] VT (= *fail to justify*) [+ *hopes*] démentir, tromper; (= *prove false*) [+ *words*] donner le démenti à, démentir; [+ *proverb*] faire mentir; (= *misrepresent*) [+ *facts*] donner une fausse impression or idée de

belief [bɪˈliːf] N **a** (NonC = *acceptance as true*) croyance *f* (**in** en, à); **~ in ghosts** croyance *f* aux revenants; **~ in God** croyance *f* en Dieu; **he has lost his ~ in God** il ne croit plus en Dieu, il a perdu la foi (en Dieu); **worthy of ~** digne de foi; **it is beyond** or **past (all) ~** c'est incroyable, c'est à ne pas (y) croire; **wealthy beyond ~** incroyablement riche **b** (*Rel*) (= *faith*) foi *f*; (= *doctrine*) credo *m* **c** (= *conviction*) opinion *f*, conviction *f*; **in the ~ that ...** persuadé que ..., convaincu que ...; **it is my ~ that ...** je suis convaincu or persuadé que ...; **to the best of my ~** (pour) autant que je sache → **strong d** (NonC = *trust*) confiance *f*, foi *f* (**in** en); **he has no ~ in doctors** il n'a aucune confiance dans les médecins; **he has no ~ in the future** il ne fait pas confiance à l'avenir

believable [bɪˈliːvəbl] ADJ croyable

▼ **believe** [bɪˈliːv] **1** VT **a** (= *accept truth of*) [+ *statement, account, evidence, person*] croire; **to ~ what sb says** croire ce que dit qn; **I don't ~ a word of it** je n'en crois rien or pas un mot; (*in exasperation*) **I don't ~ it!** ce n'est pas vrai!; (*in incredulity, triumph*) **I can't ~ it!** ce n'est pas possible or vrai!; **don't you ~ it!*** ne va pas croire ça!*; **and would you ~ it, he's younger than me!** et figurez-vous qu'il est plus jeune que moi!; **he could hardly ~ his eyes/ears** il en croyait à peine ses yeux/ses oreilles; **if he is to be ~d** à l'en croire, s'il faut l'en croire; **~ it or not, he ...** c'est incroyable, mais il ...; **~ me crois-moi, tu peux me croire; **~ you me*** tu peux m'en croire; (*hum*) **I ~ you, thousands wouldn't*** moi, je te crois, mais je dois être le seul!
b (= *think*) croire; **I ~ I'm right** je crois avoir raison, je crois que j'ai raison; **I don't ~ he will come** je ne crois pas qu'il viendra or qu'il vienne; **he is ~d to be ill** on le croit malade; **he is ~d to have a chance of succeeding** on lui donne des chances de succès; **that is ~d to be true** cela passe pour vrai; **I have every reason to ~ that ...** j'ai tout lieu de croire que ...; **I ~ so** je crois que oui, je le crois; **I ~ not** je crois que non, je ne le crois pas; **I don't know what to ~** je ne sais que croire or à quoi m'en tenir → **make**

2 VI **a** (*Rel*) croire, avoir la foi; **to ~ in** [+ *God*] croire en; [+ *ghosts, promises, antibiotics etc*] croire à; **to ~ in sb** croire en qn, avoir confiance en qn; **to ~ in a method** être partisan d'une méthode; **I don't ~ in doctors** je n'ai pas confiance dans les médecins; **I don't ~ in letting children do what they want** je ne suis pas d'avis qu'il faille laisser les enfants faire ce qu'ils veulent

believer [bɪˈliːvəʳ] N **a** (= *advocate*) partisan(e) *m(f)*; **a ~ in capital punishment** un partisan de la peine capitale; **I'm a great ~ in giving rewards for achievement** je suis tout à fait partisan de récompenser la réussite; **she's a firm ~ in herbal medicines** elle croit profondément aux vertus de la phytothérapie **b** (*Rel*) croyant(e) *m(f)*; **to be a ~** être croyant, avoir la foi; **to be a ~ in ghosts/in astrology** croire aux fantômes/à l'astrologie

➤ LANGUAGE IN USE: **believe** 6.2, 26.2

Belisha beacon [bɪˈliːʃəˈbiːkən] N lampadaire m (à globe orange marquant un passage pour piétons)

belittle [bɪˈlɪtl] VT [+ person, action, object] déprécier, rabaisser ; **to ~ o.s.** se déprécier

Belize [beˈliːz] N le Belize ; **in ~** au Belize

Belizean [beˈliːzɪən] **1** ADJ bélizien **2** N Bélizien(ne) m(f)

bell¹ [bel] **1** N **a** [of church, school] cloche f ; (also **handbell**) clochette f ; (on toy, cat's collar, clothes etc) grelot m ; (on cows) cloche f, clarine f ; (on goats, sheep) clochette f ; (at door) sonnette f ; (on cycle, typewriter) timbre m ; [of telephone] sonnerie f ; **great ~** bourdon m, grosse cloche f ; **the first ~ for mass was ringing** le premier coup de la messe sonnait ; (Brit) **to give sb a ~*** (= phone sb) donner or passer un coup de fil* or bigophone* à qn ; **there's the ~!** (door) on sonne!, ça sonne!* ; (telephone) le téléphone (sonne)! ; (Naut) **~s** coups mpl de cloche ; **eight ~s** huit coups mpl piqués ; **to sound four/six/eight ~s** piquer quatre/six/huit coups ; **~s and whistles*** accessoires mpl fantaisie → **answer**, **chime**, **ring²**

b [of flower] calice m, clochette f ; [of trumpet] pavillon m

2 VT mettre une cloche à ; (fig) **to ~ the cat** attacher le grelot (fig)

3 COMP ► **bell-bottomed trousers**, **bell-bottoms** NPL (pantalon m à) pattes fpl d'éléphant ; (Naut) pantalon m de marine ► **bell buoy** N bouée f à cloche ► **bell captain** N (US) chef des grooms dans un hôtel ► **bell glass** N cloche f (en verre) ► **bell heather** N bruyère f cendrée ► **bell jar** N cloche f (en verre) ► **bell pull** N [of door] poignée f de sonnette ; [of room] cordon m de sonnette ► **bell push** N bouton m de sonnette ► **bell-ringer** N sonneur m, carillonneur m ► **bell-ringing** N art du sonneur ► **bell rope** N (in belfry) corde f de cloche ; (in room) cordon m de sonnette ► **bell-shaped** ADJ en forme de cloche or de clochette ► **bell tent** N tente f conique ► **bell tower** N clocher m

bell² [bel] **1** N [of stag] bramement m **2** VI bramer

belladonna [ˌbeləˈdɒnə] N (Bot, Med) belladone f

bellboy [ˈbelbɔɪ] N groom m, chasseur m

belle [bel] N beauté f, belle f ; **the ~ of the ball** la reine du bal

bellhop [ˈbelhɒp] N (US) = **bellboy**

bellicose [ˈbelɪkəʊs] ADJ (frm) belliqueux, guerrier

bellicosity [ˌbelɪˈkɒsɪtɪ] N (frm) caractère m belliqueux

belligerence [bɪˈlɪdʒərəns], **belligerency** [bɪˈlɪdʒərənsɪ] N belligérance f

belligerent [bɪˈlɪdʒərənt] **1** N belligérant(e) m(f) **2** ADJ [person] belliqueux ; [voice, remarks, statement, policies, mood] agressif

belligerently [bɪˈlɪdʒərəntlɪ] ADV [say, ask, demand] sur un ton agressif ; [stare, look] d'un air belliqueux or agressif

bellow [ˈbeləʊ] **1** VI [animals] mugir ; [esp cow, bull] beugler, meugler ; [person] brailler, beugler* (**with** de) ; [wind, ocean] mugir **2** VT (also **~ out**) [+ song, order] brailler, hurler ; [+ blasphemies] vociférer **3** N [of animal] mugissement m ; [of esp cow, bull] beuglement m, meuglement m ; [of person] hurlement m, beuglement* m ; [of storm, ocean] mugissement m

bellows [ˈbeləʊz] NPL [of forge, organ] soufflerie f ; [of fire] soufflet m ; **a pair of ~** un soufflet

Bell's palsy [ˌbelzˈpɔːlzɪ] N (Med) paralysie f de Bell

bellwether [ˈbelˌweðəʳ] N (US) (= sheep) sonnailler m ; (fig) indicateur m

belly [ˈbelɪ] **1** N **a** (= abdomen) ventre m ; (fat) panse* f, bedaine* f ; **your eyes are bigger than your ~!** tu as les yeux plus grands que le ventre! ; **to go ~ up*** se casser la figure*

b [of container] panse f, ventre m ; [of violin] table f (d'harmonie) ; [of guitar] table f (d'harmonie), ventre m ; [of ship] ventre m ; [of sail] creux m

c (Culin) **~ of pork** poitrine f de porc

2 VT [wind] gonfler, enfler

3 VI (also **~ out**) se gonfler, s'enfler

4 COMP ► **belly button*** N nombril m ► **belly dance** N danse f du ventre ► **belly dancer** N danseuse f du ventre ► **belly flop** N (Swimming) **to do a ~ flop** faire un plat ► **belly-landing** N (Aviat) atterrissage m sur le ventre ; **to make a ~-landing** atterrir or se poser sur le ventre ► **belly laugh** N gros rire m (gras) ► **belly tank** N (Aviat) réservoir m de secours ► **belly-up*** ADV **to go ~-up** (= fail) [company] se planter*, se ramasser* ; [scheme] capoter*

bellyache [ˈbelɪeɪk] **1** N mal m de or au ventre ; **to have a ~** avoir mal au ventre **2** VI* ronchonner*, bougonner*

bellyaching* [ˈbelɪeɪkɪŋ] N ronchonnements* mpl, bougonnements* mpl

bellyband [ˈbelɪbænd] N sous-ventrière f

bellyful [ˈbelɪfʊl] N [of food] ventre m plein ; (fig) **he'd had a ~***: il en avait plein le dos*, il en avait ras le bol*

belong [bɪˈlɒŋ] VI **a** **~ to** (= be the property of) appartenir à ; **this book ~s to me** ce livre m'appartient, ce livre est à moi ; **lands which ~ to the Crown** des terres fpl qui appartiennent à la Couronne ; **the lid ~s to this box** le couvercle va avec cette boîte, c'est le couvercle de cette boîte ; **the handwriting ~s to a male** c'est une écriture masculine or d'homme ; **... but the last word ~ed to Roseanne** ... mais c'est Roseanne qui a eu le dernier mot

b (= be member, inhabitant etc) **to ~ to a society** faire partie or être membre d'une société ; **to ~ to a town** [native] être originaire or natif d'une ville ; [inhabitant] habiter une ville

c (= be in right place) être à sa place ; **to feel that one doesn't ~** se sentir étranger ; **you don't ~ here** tu n'es pas à ta place ici ; **people need to feel they ~** les gens ont besoin de sentir qu'ils ont leur place dans la société ; **to ~ together** aller ensemble ; **socks that don't ~ (together)** des chaussettes fpl qui ne vont pas ensemble ; **the book ~s on this shelf** le livre va sur ce rayon ; **put it back where it ~s** remets-le à sa place ; **murder ~s under the heading of capital crimes** le meurtre rentre dans la catégorie des crimes capitaux ; **his attitude ~s to a bygone era** c'est une attitude d'un autre âge ; **the future ~s to democracy** l'avenir est dans la démocratie

d (Jur) **this case ~ed to the Appeal Court** ce procès ressortissait à la cour d'appel

belongings [bɪˈlɒŋɪŋz] NPL affaires fpl, possessions fpl ; **personal ~** objets mpl or effets mpl personnels

Belorussia [ˌbeləʊˈrʌʃə] N = **Byelorussia**

Belorussian [ˌbeləʊˈrʌʃən] ADJ, N = **Byelorussian**

beloved [bɪˈlʌvɪd, bɪˈlʌvd] **1** ADJ bien-aimé, chéri ; **~ by all** aimé de tous ; **dearly ~ brethren ...** mes bien chers frères ... **2** N bien-aimé(e) m(f)

below [bɪˈləʊ]

When **below** is an element in a phrasal verb, eg **go below**, look up the verb.

1 PREP **a** (= under) sous ; (= lower than) au-dessous de ; **~ the bed** sous le lit ; **on the bed and ~ it** sur le lit et en dessous ; **her skirt is well ~ her knees** sa jupe est bien au-dessous du genou ; **~ average/sea level** au-dessous de la moyenne/du niveau de la mer ; **~ freezing point** au-dessous de zéro ; **~ the horizon** au-dessous de l'horizon ; **~ the surface** sous la surface ; **to be ~ sb in rank** occuper un rang inférieur à qn, être au-dessous de qn

b (river) en aval de ; **the Thames ~ Oxford** la Tamise en aval de Oxford

c (= unworthy of) **it would be ~ my dignity to speak to him** je m'abaisserais en lui parlant ; **he feels housework is ~ him** pour lui, faire le ménage c'est s'abaisser, il trouve que les tâches ménagères sont indignes de lui

2 ADV **a** (= at lower level) plus bas, en contrebas ; (= at lowest level) en bas ; (= directly underneath) au-dessous ; **you can see the town spread out ~** on voit la ville qui s'étale plus bas or en contrebas ; **the canopy of trees shades the ground ~** la voûte des arbres fait de l'ombre sur le sol au-dessous ; **~, we could see the valley** plus bas or en bas, on apercevait la vallée, on apercevait la vallée en contrebas ; **the road ~** la route en contrebas ; **a window with a view to the street ~** une fenêtre avec vue sur la rue en bas ; **lying in our bunks, she above, me ~** couchés dans nos lits superposés, elle en haut, moi en bas ; **several thousand feet ~** (from mountain top) plusieurs milliers de mètres plus bas ; (from aeroplane) plusieurs milliers de mètres au-dessous ; **down ~** plus bas, en contrebas ; **far ~** beaucoup plus bas, loin en contrebas ; **from ~** d'en bas

b (= downstairs) en bas ; **she heard two men talking ~** elle a entendu deux hommes qui parlaient en bas ; **the floor ~** l'étage m au-dessous ; **they live two floors ~** ils habitent deux étages plus bas or au-dessous ; **the people (in the flat) ~** les gens mpl (de l'appartement) du dessous or d'en dessous* ; **voices from ~** des voix fpl venant d'en bas

c (later in document) [mentioned, summarized] plus bas, ci-dessous ; **please write to me at the address ~** veuillez m'écrire à l'adresse ci-dessous ; **listed ~ are some of the books we have in stock** vous trouverez ci-dessous une liste de certains des livres que nous avons en stock ; **see ~** voir ci-dessous or plus bas ; **see the picture immediately ~** voir l'image juste ci-dessous ; **as stated ~** comme indiqué ci-dessous or plus bas

d (in hierarchy) plus bas, au-dessous

e (Naut) en bas ; **to go ~** descendre

f (Met) au-dessous ; **it will be extremely cold, with temperatures at zero or ~** il fera extrêmement froid, avec des températures tombant à zéro ou au-dessous ; **it was twenty (degrees) ~*** il faisait moins vingt

g (liter = on earth) **here ~** ici-bas

h (liter = in hell: also **down ~**) en enfer

3 COMP ► **below-the-line advertising** N publicité f hors média

belt [belt] **1** N **a** (Dress, Judo, fig) ceinture f ; (Mil etc) ceinturon m, ceinture f ; (= corset) gaine f ; (shoulder) ~ baudrier m ; (fig) **he has ten years' experience under his ~*** il a dix années d'expérience à son actif ; (Boxing, also fig) **blow below the ~** coup m bas ; **to hit below the ~** porter un coup bas ; (fig) **that was below the ~!** c'était un coup bas or un coup en traître! ; (fig) **to pull in or tighten one's ~** se serrer la ceinture ; **to be a black ~ (in judo etc)** être ceinture noire (de judo etc) ; (= punishment) **to give sb the ~** punir qn à coups d'étrivière → **safety**

b (= tract of land) région f ; **industrial ~** région f industrielle ; **the cotton ~** la région de culture du coton → **green**

c (Tech) courroie f

d (US = road) route f de ceinture

e (= region) région f

2 VT **a** (= thrash) administrer une correction à, donner une raclée* à ; (* = hit) flanquer or coller un gnon* à ; **she ~ed him (one) in the eye**: elle lui a flanqué or collé un gnon* dans l'œil

b (US) = **belt out**

3 VI (esp Brit* = rush) **to ~ in/out/across** etc entrer/sortir/traverser etc à toutes jambes or à toute blinde♥; **he ~ed down the street** il a descendu or dévalé la rue à fond de train

⁴ COMP ► **belt-and-braces** ADJ (fig) **it was a ~-and-braces job*** on a fait ça pour se donner une marge de sécurité or pour être vraiment tranquilles ► **belt bag** N banane f ► **belt pulley** N poulie f de courroie → **conveyor**

► **belt down♥** VT SEP (US) [+ drink] descendre♥, se taper♥

► **belt out*** VT SEP **to ~ out a song** chanter une chanson de tout son cœur or à pleins poumons

► **belt up** VI ⓐ (= put on seat belt) attacher sa ceinture ⓑ (Brit♥ = be quiet) la boucler♥, la fermer♥; **~ up!** la ferme !♥, boucle-la !♥

belter♥ ['beltə'] N ⓐ (= singer) chanteur ou chanteuse qui chante à pleins poumons; (= song) beuglante♥ f; (= shot, kick) boulet m (de canon); (= match, game) super match* m; (= party) super soirée* f

belting♥ ['beltɪŋ] N ⓐ (= beating) raclée* f, dérouillée♥ f; **to give sb a good ~** donner or filer une bonne raclée* or dérouillée♥ à qn

beltway ['beltweɪ] N (US: motorway-type) périphérique m

belvedere [,belvɪ'dɪə'] N belvédère m

bemoan [bɪ'məʊn] VT pleurer, déplorer

bemuse [bɪ'mjuːz] VT rendre perplexe

bemused [bɪ'mjuːzd] ADJ [person, expression, smile] perplexe

bemusedly [bɪ'mjuːzɪdlɪ] ADV [stare, gaze] d'un air perplexe; [say] sur un ton perplexe

ben [ben] (Scot) ⓵ N mont m, sommet m ⓶ COMP ► **Ben Nevis** N Ben Nevis m

bench [bentʃ] ⓵ N ⓐ (= seat) (Brit Parl) banc m; (in tiers) gradin m; (padded) banquette f; (Sport) **on the ~** sur le banc de touche → **back, Opposition**

ⓑ (Jur) **the Bench** (= court) la cour, le tribunal; (= judges collectively) les magistrats mpl; **to be raised to the ~** être nommé juge; **to be on the ~** (permanent office) être juge (or magistrat); (when in court) siéger au tribunal; **to appear before the ~** comparaître devant le tribunal; **the Bench has ruled that …** la cour a décrété que … → **king**

ⓒ (also **workbench**) [of laboratory, factory, workshop] établi m

⓶ VT (US Sport*) [+ player] exclure du jeu (souvent comme pénalisation)

⓷ COMP ► **bench lathe** N tour m à banc ► **bench mark** N (Surv) repère m de nivellement; (fig = reference point) point m de référence, repère m; (Comput) jeu m d'essai; (Stat) **the 1984 ~ mark** l'année f de référence 1984 ► **bench-mark** ADJ (Econ, Comm) **~-mark price** prix m de base or de référence; (Comput) **~-mark test** test m d'évaluation de performance ► **bench-press** VT (Weight Lifting) soulever ► **bench scientist** N expérimentateur m, -trice f ► **bench seat** N banquette f ► **bench study** N étude-pilote f ► **bench vice** N étau m d'établi

bencher ['bentʃə'] N (Brit Jur) ≈ membre m de l'ordre des avocats → **backbencher**

benchwarmer♥ ['bentʃwɔːmə'] N (US Sport) joueur m (médiocre) en réserve

bend [bend] (vb: pret, ptp **bent**) ⓵ N ⓐ [of river] coude m, détour m; [of tube, pipe] coude m; [of arm] pli m, saignée f; [of knee] pli m; [of road] virage m, coude m; (Naut = knot) nœud m de jonction; **there is a ~ in the road** la route fait un coude; (Aut) **~s for 8km** virages mpl sur 8 km; **to take a ~** [car] prendre un virage or un tournant; (Brit) **round the ~♥** tombé sur la tête*, cinglé*; (Brit) **to drive sb round the ~♥** rendre qn cinglé*

ⓑ (Med) **the ~s♥** la maladie des caissons

⓶ VT ⓐ [+ back, body] courber; [+ leg, arm] plier; [+ knee, leg] fléchir, plier; [+ head] baisser, pencher; [+ branch] courber, faire ployer; [+ light ray] réfracter; [+ rail, pipe, rod,

beam] tordre, courber; [+ bow] bander; (Naut) [+ cable] étalinguer; [+ sail] enverguer; (fig) **to ~ the rules** faire une entorse au règlement; **to ~ at right angles** couder; **to ~ out of shape** fausser, gauchir; (US fig) **to get bent out of shape*** (about sth) s'énerver (à cause de qch); **to be (all) bent out of shape*** être contrarié; **with her head bent over a book** la tête penchée or courbée sur un livre; **on ~ed knee(s)** à genoux; **to go down on ~ed knee** (to or before sb) s'agenouiller or se mettre à genoux (devant qn); **to ~ the elbow*** (= drink) lever le coude*; **to ~ o.s. to sb's will** se plier à la volonté de qn; (liter) **to ~ sb to one's will** mettre qn sous son joug; **to ~ sb's ear** (gen) accaparer (l'attention de) qn; (* pej) casser les pieds à qn* → **bent¹**

ⓑ (= direct) **all eyes were bent on him** tous les yeux or les regards étaient fixés or braqués sur lui; **the Government bent its efforts to lowering unemployment** le gouvernement a concentré ses efforts sur la lutte contre le chômage

⓷ VI [person] se courber; [branch, instrument etc] être courbé, plier; [river, road] faire un coude, tourner; [tree = submit] se soumettre, céder (**to** à); **to ~ backward/forward** se pencher en arrière/en avant

⓸ COMP ► **bend sinister** N (Her) barre f de bâtardise ► **double, hairpin**

► **bend back** ⓵ VI [wire etc] se recourber; [person] se pencher en arrière ⓶ VT SEP replier, recourber

► **bend down** ⓵ VI [person] se courber, se baisser; [tree, branch] ployer, plier ⓶ VT SEP [+ wire] replier, recourber; [+ branch] faire ployer

► **bend over** ⓵ VI [person] se pencher; (fig) **to ~ over backwards to help sb*** se mettre en quatre pour aider qn ⓶ VT SEP replier

bender♥ ['bendə'] N ⓐ (Tech) cintreuse f ⓑ **to go on a ~♥** aller se cuiter* ⓒ (= tent) hutte f (improvisée)

bendy♥ ['bendɪ] ADJ [branch] flexible; [river, road] sinueux

beneath [bɪ'niːθ] ⓵ PREP ⓐ (= under) sous; **~ the table** sous la table; (liter) **to labour ~ a burden** ployer sous un fardeau ⓑ (= lower than) au-dessous de, sous; **the town ~ the castle** la ville (située) au-dessous du château ⓒ (= unworthy of) indigne de; **it is ~ my notice** cela ne mérite pas mon attention or que je m'y arrête (subj); **he regards the critics as ~ his notice** il ne considère pas les critiques comme au-dessus des critiques; **she considered it ~ her to lie** elle pensait que mentir aurait été indigne d'elle; **she married ~ her** elle a fait une mésalliance; **they took jobs that were far ~ them** ils ont accepté des emplois qui étaient vraiment indignes d'eux ⓶ ADV dessous, au-dessous; **the flat ~** l'appartement m au-dessous or du dessous

Benedict ['benɪdɪkt] N Benoît m

Benedictine [,benɪ'dɪktɪn] ⓵ N (Rel) bénédictin(e) m(f) ⓶ ADJ (Rel) bénédictin

benedictine [,benɪ'dɪktiːn] N (= liqueur) Bénédictine f

benediction [,benɪ'dɪkʃən] N (= blessing) bénédiction f; (at table) bénédicité m; (Rel = office) salut m

benefaction [,benɪ'fækʃən] N (= good deed) bienfait m; (= gift) donation f, don m

benefactor ['benɪfæktə'] N bienfaiteur m

benefactress† ['benɪfæktrɪs] N bienfaitrice f

benefice ['benɪfɪs] N bénéfice m (Rel)

beneficence [bɪ'nefɪsəns] N ⓐ (NonC = generosity) bienfaisance f ⓑ (= act) acte m or œuvre f de bienfaisance

beneficent [bɪ'nefɪsənt] ADJ [person] bienfaisant; [thing] salutaire

beneficial [,benɪ'fɪʃəl] ADJ salutaire, avantageux (**to** pour), favorable (**to** à); **~ to health** bon pour la santé; **the change will be ~ to**

you le changement vous fera du bien or vous sera salutaire; (Jur) **~ owner** usufruitier m, -ière f

beneficially [,benɪ'fɪʃəlɪ] ADV avantageusement

beneficiary [,benɪ'fɪʃərɪ] N [of will etc] bénéficiaire mf, légataire mf; [of person] ayant droit m; [of insurance] bénéficiaire mf; (Rel) bénéficier m

benefit ['benɪfɪt] ⓵ N ⓐ (gen) bienfait m; **for the ~ of your health** dans l'intérêt de votre santé; **it's to your ~** c'est dans votre intérêt; **the book was not (of) much ~ to me, I didn't get much ~ from the book** le livre ne m'a pas beaucoup aidé or ne m'a pas été très utile; **did he get much ~ from his holiday?** est-ce que ses vacances lui ont profité or lui ont fait du bien?; **he's beginning to feel the ~ of his stay in the country** il commence à ressentir les bienfaits de son séjour à la campagne; **he had the ~ of the work I had put in** il a profité de mon travail; **a concert for the ~ of the refugees** un concert au profit des réfugiés; **we're doing all this for his ~** c'est pour lui que nous faisons tout cela; (fig) **he's not really hurt, he's just crying for your ~** il ne s'est pas vraiment fait mal, il pleure juste pour que vous fassiez attention à lui; **to give sb/get the ~ of the doubt** laisser à qn/avoir le bénéfice du doute; **the ~s of a good education** les bienfaits d'une bonne éducation

ⓑ (Admin = money) allocation f, prestation f; **unemployment ~** (formerly) allocation f (de) chômage → **sickness**; → **DSS**

ⓒ (Mus, Theat = charity performance) représentation f de bienfaisance

ⓓ **~ of clergy** (= privileges) privilège m du clergé; (= rites) rites mpl de l'Église, rites mpl religieux; **marriage without ~ of clergy** mariage non béni par l'Église

⓶ VT faire du bien à; (financially) profiter à

⓷ VI [person] se trouver bien (**from, by** de); (financially) gagner (**from** or **by doing** à faire); [work, situation] être avantagé (**from** par); **he will ~ from a holiday** des vacances lui feront du bien

⓸ COMP ► **benefit association** N (US) = **benefit society** ► **benefit club** N assurance f mutuelle, caisse f de secours mutuel ► **benefit match** N (Sport) match m au profit d'un joueur ► **benefit performance** N représentation f de bienfaisance ► **benefit society** N (US) société f de prévoyance, (société f) mutuelle f

Benelux ['benɪlʌks] N le Bénélux; **the ~ countries** les pays du Bénélux

benevolence [bɪ'nevələns] N ⓐ (NonC) (= kindness) bienveillance f; (= generosity) bienfaisance f, générosité f ⓑ (= gift, act) bienfait m ⓒ (Hist) don m forcé (au souverain)

benevolent [bɪ'nevələnt] ADJ ⓐ (= kind) bienveillant (**to** envers); **a ~ smile** un sourire bienveillant or plein de bonté ⓑ (= charitable) [organization, society] de bienfaisance; **~ fund** fonds m de secours

benevolently [bɪ'nevələntlɪ] ADV avec bienveillance or bonté

BEng [,biː'endʒ] N ABBR = **Bachelor of Engineering**

Bengal [beŋ'gɔːl] ⓵ N le Bengale; **the Bay of ~** le golfe du Bengale ⓶ COMP ► **Bengal light** N feu m de Bengale ► **Bengal tiger** N tigre m du Bengale

Bengali [beŋ'gɔːlɪ] ⓵ ADJ bengali f inv ⓶ N ⓐ (= person) Bengali mf ⓑ (Ling) bengali m

benighted [bɪ'naɪtɪd] ADJ ⓐ (fig = uncultured) [person] plongé dans (les ténèbres de) l'ignorance; [policy etc] à courte vue, aveugle ⓑ († lit) surpris par la nuit

benign [bɪ'naɪn], **benignant** [bɪ'nɪgnənt] ADJ ⓐ (= kindly) bienveillant, affable; (= beneficial) bienfaisant, salutaire; [climate] doux (douce f) [b] (= harmless) [research, substance, process] inoffensif [c] (Med) [tumour] bénin (-igne f) [d] ~ **neglect** laisser-faire m ; **a policy of ~ neglect of the economy** une politique de laisser-faire en matière économique, une politique économique non-interventionniste ; **the best thing for these moors is ~ neglect** la meilleure chose qu'on puisse faire pour cette lande, c'est de la laisser en friche

benignly [bɪˈnaɪnlɪ] ADV avec bienveillance

Benin [beˈniːn] N le Bénin

Beninese [ˌbenɪˈniːz] [1] ADJ béninois [2] N Béninois(e) m(f)

benison [ˈbenɪzn] N bénédiction f

Benjamin [ˈbendʒəmɪn] N Benjamin m

benny⁕ [ˈbenɪ] N (Drugs) (comprimé m de) benzédrine f

bent¹ [bent] [1] VB pt, ptp of **bend** [2] ADJ [a] [wire, pipe] tordu [b] (esp Brit⁕ = dishonest) véreux, ripou⁕ ; **a ~ copper** un ripou⁕ [c] (Brit pej⁕ = homosexual) homosexuel [d] **to be ~ on doing sth** être résolu or décidé à faire qch, vouloir absolument faire qch ; **he is ~ on seeing me** il veut absolument me voir ; **he is ~ on pleasure** il ne recherche que son plaisir [3] N [a] (= aptitude) dispositions fpl, aptitudes fpl (**for** pour) ; **to have a ~ for languages** avoir des dispositions pour les langues [b] (= liking) penchant m, goût m ; **to have a ~ for or towards sth** avoir du goût or un penchant pour qch ; **to follow one's ~** suivre son inclination f ; **of literary ~** tourné vers les lettres

bent² [bent] N (also ~ **grass**) agrostide f

bentwood [ˈbentwʊd] ADJ [furniture] en bois courbé

benumb [bɪˈnʌm] VT [+ limb] engourdir, endormir

benumbed [bɪˈnʌmd] ADJ (= cold) [person] transi (de froid) ; [fingers] engourdi par le froid ; (= frightened) transi de peur ; (= shocked) paralysé

Benzedrine ® [ˈbenzɪdriːn] N benzédrine f

benzene [ˈbenziːn] N benzène m

benzine [ˈbenziːn] N benzine f

benzoin¹ [ˈbenzəʊɪn] N (= resin) benjoin m ; (= shrub) styrax m (benjoin)

benzoin² [ˈbenzəʊɪn] N (Chem) benzoïne f

bequeath [bɪˈkwiːð] VT (in will) léguer (**to** à) ; (fig) [+ tradition] transmettre, léguer (**to** à)

bequest [bɪˈkwest] N legs m

berate [bɪˈreɪt] VT admonester (liter), réprimander

Berber [ˈbɜːbəʳ] [1] ADJ berbère [2] N [a] (= person) Berbère mf [b] (Ling) berbère m

bereave [bɪˈriːv] VT [a] (pret, ptp **bereft**) (= deprive) priver, déposséder (**of** de) → **bereft** [b] (pret, ptp **bereaved**) (by death) ravir (**sb of sb** qn à qn)

bereaved [bɪˈriːvd] ADJ endeuillé, affligé

bereavement [bɪˈriːvmənt] N (= loss) perte f ; (NonC = state) deuil m ; **a sad ~** une perte cruelle ; **in his ~** dans son deuil ; **owing to a recent ~** en raison d'un deuil récent

bereft [bɪˈreft] [1] VB pt, ptp of **bereave a** [2] ADJ (liter) ~ **of** privé or démuni de ; ~ **of hope** désespéré ; **he is ~ of reason** il a perdu la raison

beret [ˈbereɪ] N béret m

berg⁕ [bɜːg] N ABBR = **iceberg**

bergamot [ˈbɜːgəmɒt] N bergamote f

bergschrund [ˈbɜːkʃrʊnt] N (Climbing) rimaye f

beriberi [ˈberɪˈberɪ] N béribéri m

Bering [ˈbeɪrɪŋ] ADJ ~ **Sea/Strait** mer f/détroit m de Béring

berk⁕ [bɜːk] N (Brit) connard⁕ m, connasse⁕ f

berkelium [bɜːˈkiːlɪəm] N berkélium m

Berks N ABBR = **Berkshire**

Berlin [bɜːˈlɪn] [1] N [a] (Geog) Berlin ; **East/West ~** Berlin Est/Ouest [b] (= carriage) berlin

berline f [2] COMP ► **the Berlin Wall** N le mur de Berlin ► **Berlin wool** N laine f à broder

Berliner [bɜːˈlɪnəʳ] N Berlinois(e) m(f)

berm [bɜːm] N (US Aut) accotement m, bas-côté m

Bermuda [bɜːˈmjuːdə] [1] N les Bermudes fpl [2] COMP ► **Bermuda shorts** NPL bermuda m ► **the Bermuda Triangle** N le triangle des Bermudes

Bern [bɜːn] N Berne

Bernard [ˈbɜːnəd] N Bernard m

Bernese [ˈbɜːniːz] [1] ADJ bernois ; ~ **Oberland** Oberland m bernois [2] N Bernois(e) m(f)

berry [ˈberɪ] [1] N baie f → **brown** [2] VI **to go ~ing** aller cueillir des baies

berserk [bɜːˈsɜːk] ADJ fou furieux (folle furieuse f) ; **to go ~** devenir fou furieux, se déchaîner

berth [bɜːθ] [1] N [a] [of plane, train, ship] couchette f ; (fig) **to find a soft ~** trouver une bonne planque⁕ [b] (Naut = place for ship) mouillage m, poste m d'amarrage ; **to give a wide ~ to a ship** passer au large d'un navire ; (fig) **to give sb a wide ~** éviter qn, se tenir à une distance respectueuse de qn ; (fig) **you should give him a wide ~** vous devriez l'éviter à tout prix [2] VI (at anchor) mouiller ; (alongside) venir à quai, accoster [3] VT [+ ship] (= assign place) donner or assigner un poste d'amarrage à ; (= perform action) amarrer, faire accoster

beryl [ˈberɪl] N béryl m

beryllium [beˈrɪljəm] N béryllium m

beseech [bɪˈsiːtʃ] (pret, ptp **besought** or **beseeched**) VT (liter) [a] (= ask for) [+ permission] demander instamment, solliciter ; [+ pardon] implorer [b] (= entreat) conjurer (liter), supplier (**sb to do** qn de faire)

beseeching [bɪˈsiːtʃɪŋ] [1] ADJ [voice, look] suppliant, implorant [2] N (NonC) supplications fpl

beseechingly [bɪˈsiːtʃɪŋlɪ] ADV d'un air or d'un ton suppliant or implorant

beset [bɪˈset] (pret, ptp **beset**) VT [dangers, fears] assaillir ; [temptations] entourer ; **a path ~ with obstacles** un chemin semé d'obstacles ; ~ **with difficulties** [enterprise, journey] hérissé de difficultés ; **the difficulties ~ him** les difficultés l'assaillent (de toutes parts) ; ~ **with or by doubts** rongé or assailli par le doute

besetting [bɪˈsetɪŋ] ADJ **his ~ sin** son grand défaut

beside [bɪˈsaɪd] PREP [a] (= at the side of) à côté de, auprès de ; **she sat down ~ him** elle s'est assise à côté or auprès de lui ; **it à côté de** [b] (= compared with) à côté de [c] (= except) ~ **him, no one agreed with me** à part lui, personne n'était d'accord avec moi [d] (phrases) **that's ~ the point** cela n'a rien à voir (avec la question) ; **it's quite ~ the point to suggest that ...** il est tout à fait inutile de suggérer que ... ; **he was ~ o.s. (with anger)⁕** hors de soi ; **he was quite ~ himself with excitement⁕** il était dans un grand état d'excitation ; **he is ~ himself with joy⁕** il est transporté de joie, il ne se sent pas de joie

besides [bɪˈsaɪdz] [1] ADV [a] (= in addition) en outre, en plus, de plus ; **and many more ~** et bien d'autres encore ; **he wrote a novel and several short stories ~** il a écrit un roman et aussi plusieurs nouvelles [b] (= else) de plus, d'autre ; **there is nothing ~** il n'y a rien de plus or d'autre [c] (= moreover) d'ailleurs, du reste [2] PREP [a] (= in addition to) en plus de, en dehors de ; **others ~ ourselves** d'autres que nous ; **there were three of us ~ Jacques** nous étions trois sans compter Jacques ; ~ **this book I bought some CDs** outre ce livre, j'ai acheté des CD ; ~ **which he was unwell** sans

compter qu'il était souffrant, et en plus il était souffrant [b] (= except) excepté, hormis, en dehors de ; **no one ~ you** personne en dehors de vous or excepté vous, personne d'autre que vous ; **who ~ them could have done it?** qui aurait pu le faire cela, à part eux or sinon eux ?, qui d'autre aurait pu le faire ?

besiege [bɪˈsiːdʒ] VT [a] [+ town] assiéger, mettre le siège devant [b] (fig = surround) assaillir ; ~ **d by journalists** assailli par des journalistes [c] (fig = pester) assaillir, harceler (**with** de) ; ~ **d with questions** assailli de questions

besmear [bɪˈsmɪəʳ] VT (lit) barbouiller (**with** de), (fig) salir, souiller (liter)

besmirch [bɪˈsmɜːtʃ] VT ternir, entacher

besom [ˈbiːzəm] N balai m de bouleau

besotted [bɪˈsɒtɪd] ADJ (= drunk) abruti, hébété (**with** de) [b] (= infatuated) entiché, fou (folle f) (**with** de) [c] (= foolish) idiot, imbécile

besought [bɪˈsɔːt] VB pt, ptp of **beseech**

bespatter [bɪˈspætəʳ] VT éclabousser (**with** de)

bespeak [bɪˈspiːk] (pret **bespoke**, ptp **bespoken** or **bespoke**) VT [a] (= order) [+ goods] commander ; [+ room, place] retenir, réserver [b] (= indicate) témoigner de ; [+ weakness, fault] accuser

bespectacled [bɪˈspektɪkld] ADJ à lunettes

bespoke [bɪˈspəʊk] [1] VB pt, ptp of **bespeak** [2] ADJ (Brit) [goods] fait sur commande ; [garments] fait sur mesure ; [tailor etc] à façon ; (Comput) ~ **software** logiciel m sur mesure

bespoken [bɪˈspəʊkən] VB ptp of **bespeak**

besprinkle [bɪˈsprɪŋkl] VT (liter) (with liquid) arroser, asperger (**with** de) ; (with powder) saupoudrer (**with** de) ; (= dot with) parsemer (**with** de)

Bess [bes] N dim of **Elizabeth** (Brit Hist) **Good Queen ~** la reine Élisabeth (Iᵉʳᵉ)

Bessarabia [ˌbesəˈreɪbɪə] N la Bessarabie

▼ **best** [best] [1] ADJ (superl of **good**) le meilleur, la meilleure ; **the ~ novel he's written** le meilleur roman qu'il ait écrit ; **the ~ pupil in the class** le meilleur élève de la classe ; **Belgian beer is the ~ in the world** la bière belge est la meilleure du monde or au monde ; **the ~ route to Paris** le meilleur chemin or itinéraire pour Paris ; **the ~ thing about Spain/living abroad is ...** ce qu'il y a de mieux en Espagne/quand on vit à l'étranger, c'est ... ; **the ~ thing about her is ...** ce qu'il y a de mieux chez elle, c'est ... ; **the ~ thing to do is to wait** le mieux c'est d'attendre ; **the ~ years of one's life** les plus belles années de sa vie ; **in one's ~ clothes** vêtu de ses plus beaux vêtements ; **may the ~ man win!** que le meilleur gagne ! ; **to put one's ~ foot forward** (in walking) allonger le pas ; (= do one's best) faire de son mieux ; **she is her ~ friend** c'est sa meilleure amie ; **she's his ~ girl†⁕** c'est sa petite amie ; (fig) **the ~ part of⁕** la plus grande partie de ; **for the ~ part of an hour/month⁕** pendant près d'une heure/d'un mois ; **it took the ~ part of an hour⁕** ça m'a pris une petite heure ; (Comm: on product) ~ **before ...** à consommer de préférence avant ... ; (Cards) **to have the ~ diamond** être maître à carreau → **5** ; → **behaviour, second-best, wish**

[2] N [a] **the ~** le mieux, le meilleur ; **to do one's (level) ~ (to come)** faire tout son possible (pour venir) ; **do the ~ you can!** faites de votre mieux !, faites pour le mieux ! ; **it's the ~ I can do** je ne peux pas faire mieux ; **she's the ~ in the class at maths/drawing** elle est la meilleure de la classe en maths/en dessin ; **to get the ~ out of sb/sth** tirer le maximum de qn/qch ; **to get the ~ of the bargain** or **of it** l'emporter, avoir le dessus ; **to have** or **get the ~ of both worlds** gagner sur les deux tableaux ; **the ~ there is** ce qu'il y a de mieux ; **to save the ~ for last** garder le meilleur pour la fin ; **the ~ is yet to come** il y a mieux ; **to**

make the ~ of sth s'accommoder de qch (du mieux que l'on peut); **to make the ~ of a bad job** or **bargain** faire contre mauvaise fortune bon cœur; **to make the ~ of one's opportunities** profiter au maximum des occasions qui se présentent; **the ~ of it is that ...** le plus beau de l'affaire c'est que ...; (*Sport*) **the final is the ~ of three matches** la finale se dispute au meilleur des trois matchs; **to be the ~ of friends** être les meilleurs amis (du monde); **it's (all) for the ~** c'est pour le mieux; **to do sth for the ~** faire qch dans les meilleures intentions; **to the ~ of my ability/knowledge/ recollection** etc autant que je puisse/que je sache/que je me souvienne etc; **in one's (Sunday) ~*** endimanché, sur son trente et un; **(to keep sth) for ~*** (garder qch) pour les grandes occasions; **to look one's ~** être resplendissant; [*woman*] être en beauté; **she looks her ~ in blue** c'est le bleu qui l'avantage le plus; **to be at one's ~** (= *on form*) être en pleine forme* or en train; **the roses are at their ~ just now** les roses sont de toute beauté en ce moment; **that is Racine at his ~** voilà du meilleur Racine; **even at the ~ of times** même dans les circonstances les plus favorables; **he's not very patient (even) at the ~ of times but ...** il n'est jamais particulièrement patient mais ...; **at ~** au mieux; **even the ~ of us can make mistakes** tout le monde peut se tromper; **the ~ of plans can go astray** les meilleurs projets peuvent échouer; **he can sing with the ~ of them*** il sait chanter comme pas un*

b **all the ~!** (= *goodbye*) salut!*; (*at end of letter*) amicalement, amitiés; **all the ~ to your sister** mes amitiés à ta sœur; **all the ~ for your exam** bonne chance pour ton examen

3 ADV (*superl of* **well**) le mieux, le plus; **the ~ dressed man in Paris** l'homme le mieux habillé de Paris; **the ~ loved actor** l'acteur m le plus aimé; **I like apples ~** ce que je préfère, ce sont les pommes; **I like strawberries ~ of all** j'aime les fraises par-dessus tout; **that is the hat which suits her ~** voilà le chapeau qui lui va le mieux; **I helped him as ~ I could** je l'ai aidé de mon mieux or du mieux que j'ai pu; **he thought it ~ to accept** il a trouvé or jugé préférable d'accepter; **do as you think ~** faites à votre idée, faites pour le mieux; **you know ~** vous savez mieux que personne, c'est vous le mieux placé pour en juger, vous êtes (le) meilleur juge en la matière; **you had ~ go at once** tu ferais mieux de t'en aller tout de suite; **the ~-laid plans of mice and men oft go awry** même les projets les mieux élaborés peuvent échouer

4 VT (= *defeat, win over*) battre, l'emporter sur

5 COMP ▶ **best-before date** N (*Comm*) date f limite d'utilisation or de consommation ▶ **best boy** N (*Cine*) assistant du chef électricien ou du technicien ▶ **best man** N (*pl* **best men**) (*at wedding*) garçon m d'honneur, ≈ témoin m ▶ **best-selling** ADJ [+ *book, writer*] à succès; [+ *record*] qui remporte un grand succès

┌─────────────────────┐
BEST MAN

Choisi parmi les amis ou les proches parents du marié, le **best man** est à la fois le témoin et le garçon d'honneur. Traditionnellement responsable du bon déroulement de la journée, il doit veiller à ce que le marié soit à l'heure et à ce que les invités soient bien accueillis. Pendant la réception, il lui revient de lire les messages de félicitations, d'annoncer les orateurs, de prononcer le discours humoristique d'usage et de porter un toast aux nouveaux mariés.
└─────────────────────┘

bestial ['bestɪəl] ADJ (*lit, fig*) bestial
bestiality [,bestɪ'ælɪtɪ] N bestialité f
bestiary ['bestɪərɪ] N bestiaire m (*recueil*)

▶ **LANGUAGE IN USE:** **better** 1.1, 2.2, 7.1, 7.4, 23.4

bestir [bɪ'stɜːʳ] VT **to ~ o.s.** se remuer, se démener, s'activer

bestow [bɪ'stəʊ] VT (*frm*) **a** (= *grant*) [+ *favour, sb's hand*] accorder (**on, upon** à); [+ *title*] conférer (**on, upon** à) **b** (= *devote*) [+ *energy*] consacrer, employer (**upon** à); [+ *admiration*] accorder; **to ~ friendship on sb** prendre qn en amitié; **the attention ~ed on this boy** l'attention dont ce garçon est l'objet

bestowal [bɪ'stəʊəl] N (*NonC: frm*) octroi m

bestraddle [bɪ'strædl] VT [+ *horse, bicycle*] enfourcher; [+ *wall*] chevaucher; [+ *chair*] se mettre à califourchon sur

bestrew [bɪ'struː] (*pret* **bestrewed**, *ptp* **bestrewed** or **bestrewn** [bɪ'struːn]) VT (*liter*) parsemer, joncher (**with** de)

bestride [bɪ'straɪd] (*pret* **bestrode** [bɪ'strəʊd], *ptp* **bestridden** [bɪ'strɪdn]) VT **a** [+ *chair*] être à cheval or à califourchon sur; [+ *horse, bicycle*] enfourcher **b** [+ *brook, ditch*] enjamber

bestseller [best,seləʳ] N (= *book*) best-seller m, livre m à succès, succès m de librairie; (*Comm*) (*other article*) article m très demandé; (= *author*) auteur m à succès

bet [bet] (*pret, ptp* **bet** or **betted**) **1** VI parier (**against** contre, **on, with** avec); **to ~ 10 to 1** parier or miser à 10 contre 1; **to ~ on horses** parier or jouer aux courses; **to ~ on a horse** jouer un cheval, miser sur un cheval; **don't ~ on it!** ◊ **I wouldn't ~ on it!** ne compte pas trop dessus

2 VT **a** **to ~ £10 on a horse** parier or miser 10 livres sur un cheval; **she ~ me £10 he would refuse** elle m'a parié 10 livres qu'il refuserait

b (*fig*) **I ~ he'll come!** je te parie qu'il viendra!; **I'll ~ you anything (you like)** je te parie tout ce que tu veux; **~ you won't do it*** (je te parie que) t'es pas capable de le faire*; **you ~!** un peu!*, tu parles!*; **~ you can't!*** chiche!*; **you can ~ your boots*** or **your bottom dollar*** or **your life* that ...** tu peux parier tout ce que tu veux or parier ta chemise que ...; (*US fig*) **to ~ the ranch** or **farm on sb/sth** tout miser sur qn/qch

3 N **a** (*lit*) pari m; **to make** or **lay a ~ (on sth/sb)** parier (sur qch/qn), faire un pari (sur qch/qn); **to accept** or **take (on) a ~** accepter un pari, tenir or gager un pari; (*in casino*) **place your ~s!** faites vos jeux!; **want a ~?*** (qu'est-ce que) tu paries?*

b (*fig*) **this is your best ~** c'est ce que vous avez de mieux à faire; (*fig*) **it's a good** or **safe ~ that she'll turn up** il est à peu près certain qu'elle viendra; (*fig*) **Liverpool look a good** or **safe ~ for the championship** Liverpool a toutes les chances de gagner le championnat; (*fig*) **all ~s are off** impossible de dire ce qui va se passer ▶ **hedge**

beta ['biːtə] **1** N bêta m **2** COMP ▶ **beta blocker** N (*Med, Pharm*) bêta-bloquant m ▶ **beta-blocking** ADJ bêta-bloquant

betake [bɪ'teɪk] (*pret* **betook**, *ptp* **betaken** [bɪ'teɪkən]) VT **to ~ o.s. to ...** (s'en) aller à ..., se rendre à ...

betcha: ['betʃə] EXCL **(you) ~!** un peu!*, tu parles!*

betel ['biːtl] **1** N bétel m **2** COMP ▶ **betel nut** N noix f de bétel

Bethany ['beθənɪ] N Béthanie

bethink† [bɪ'θɪŋk] (*pret, ptp* **bethought**) VT **to ~ o.s.** réfléchir, considérer; **to ~ o.s. of sth/to do/that** s'aviser de qch/de faire/que

Bethlehem ['beθlɪhem] N Bethléem

bethought [bɪ'θɔːt] VB *pt, ptp of* **bethink**

betide [bɪ'taɪd] VTI **whatever (may) ~** quoi qu'il advienne or arrive (*subj*) → **woe**

betimes† [bɪ'taɪmz] ADV (= *early*) de bonne heure, tôt; (= *quickly*) promptement, vite; (= *in good time*) à temps, assez tôt

betoken [bɪ'təʊkən] VT (*frm*) (= *forecast*) présager, annoncer; (= *indicate*) dénoter, être signe de

betook [bɪ'tʊk] VB *pt of* **betake**

betray [bɪ'treɪ] VT **a** (= *be disloyal to*) [+ *one's country*] trahir, être traître à; [+ *friends*] trahir; [+ *spouse, partner*] tromper; (*fig*) [+ *hope* etc] trahir, décevoir; [+ *ideals, principles*] trahir; **he has ~ed our trust** il a trahi notre confiance, il a commis un abus de confiance **b** (= *give up treacherously*) [+ *person, secret*] livrer (**to** à), trahir; **to ~ sb into enemy hands** livrer qn à l'ennemi or aux mains de l'ennemi **c** (= *disclose*) [+ *fears, intentions, facts, truth*] trahir, révéler; **to ~ o.s.** se trahir; **his speech ~ed the fact that he had been drinking** on devinait à l'écouter qu'il avait bu

betrayal [bɪ'treɪəl] N [*of country, ally* etc] trahison f; [*of age, secret, plan*] divulgation f; [*of fears, intentions*] manifestation f (involontaire); [*of facts, truth*] révélation f; **a ~ of trust** un abus de confiance; **to feel a sense of ~** se sentir trahi

betrayer [bɪ'treɪəʳ] N [*of country*] traître(sse) m(f) (**of** à, envers); [*of friend*] dénonciateur m, -trice f (**of** de); **she killed her ~** elle a tué celui qui l'avait trahie

betroth [bɪ'trəʊð] VT (††, *liter*) fiancer (**to** à, avec), promettre en mariage (**to** à)

betrothal [bɪ'trəʊðəl] N (*liter*) fiançailles fpl (**to** avec)

betrothed [bɪ'trəʊðd] ADJ, N (*pl inv*: liter or hum) fiancé(e) m(f)

▼**better¹** ['betəʳ] **1** ADJ (*compar of* **good**) meilleur; **that book is ~ than this one** ce livre-là est meilleur que celui-ci; **she is a ~ dancer than her sister** ◊ **she is ~ at dancing than her sister** elle danse mieux que sa sœur; **she is ~ at dancing than at singing** elle danse mieux qu'elle ne chante; **these products are ~ for the environment** ces produits polluent moins; **he's a ~ man than his brother** il est mieux que son frère; (*hum*) **you're a ~ man than I am (Gunga Din)!** tu as plus de courage que moi!; **he's no ~ than a thief** c'est un voleur ni plus ni moins; **she's no ~ than she should be!**† (= *slightly dishonest*) ce n'est pas l'honnêteté qui l'étouffe!*; (*loose morals*) elle n'est pas d'une vertu farouche!; (*Med*) **he is much ~ now** il va or se porte bien mieux maintenant; (*Med*) **how are you? — much ~** comment allez-vous? — bien mieux; (*Med*) **he got ~ very quickly after his illness** il s'est très vite remis de sa maladie; **to grow ~** s'améliorer; **the weather is getting ~** le temps s'améliore; **this book gets ~ towards the end** ce livre s'améliore vers la fin; **his technique got ~ as he grew older** sa technique s'est affirmée avec l'âge; **his writing is ~ since he got a new pen** son écriture est meilleure depuis qu'il a un nouveau stylo; **(it's getting) ~ and ~!** (ça va) de mieux en mieux!; **that's ~!** voilà qui est mieux!; **it** or **things couldn't be ~!** ça ne pourrait pas mieux aller!; **it would be ~ to stay at home** il vaudrait mieux rester à la maison; **wouldn't it be ~ to refuse?** ne vaudrait-il pas mieux refuser?; **it is ~ not to promise anything than to let him down** il vaut mieux ne rien promettre que de le décevoir; **a ~ class of hotel** un hôtel de catégorie supérieure; **he has seen ~ days** il a connu des jours meilleurs; **this hat has seen ~ days** ce chapeau n'est plus de la première fraîcheur; (*hum*) **his ~ half*** sa moitié* (*hum*); **his ~ nature stopped him from ...** ses bons sentiments, reprenant le dessus, l'ont empêché de ...; **to appeal to sb's ~ nature** faire appel au bon cœur de qn; **to go one ~ than sb** damer le pion à qn; **the ~ part of a year/of 200 km** etc près d'un an/de 200 km etc; **to hope for ~ things** espérer mieux

2 ADV (*compar of* **well**) mieux; **he sings ~ than you** il chante mieux que toi; **he sings ~ than**

he dances il chante mieux qu'il ne danse ; **the ~ I know him the more I admire him** mieux je le connais plus je l'admire ; **I like it ~ than I used to** je l'aime mieux qu'autrefois *or* que je ne l'aimais autrefois ; **all the ~ ◊ so much the ~** tant mieux (**for** pour) ; (= *in order to*) **the ~ to see/hear** pour mieux voir/entendre ; **he was all the ~ for it** il s'en est trouvé mieux ; **it would be all the ~ for a drop of paint** un petit coup de peinture ne lui ferait pas de mal ; **they are ~ off than we are** (= *richer*) ils ont plus d'argent que nous ; (= *more fortunate*) ils sont dans une meilleure position que nous ; **he is ~ off at his sister's than living alone** il est mieux chez sa sœur que s'il vivait tout seul ; **he is ~ off where he is** il est mieux là où il est ; **I had ~ do it** (= *must do it*) il faut que je le fasse ; (= *would be preferable to do it*) il vaut mieux que je le fasse ; **hadn't you ~ speak to him?** ne vaudrait-il pas mieux que tu lui parles (*subj*) ? ; **write to her, or ~ still go and see her** écris-lui, ou mieux encore va la voir ; **~ dressed** mieux habillé ; ■ **known** plus *or* mieux connu ■ (*PROV*) **~ late than never** mieux vaut tard que jamais (*PROV*) → **know, think**

3 N **a** mieux *m* ; **it's a change for the ~** c'est une amélioration ; **for ~ or (for) worse** pour le meilleur ou pour le pire ; **to get the ~ of sb** triompher de qn ; **to get the ~ of sth** venir à bout de qch

b one's ~s ses supérieurs *mpl*

4 VT [+ *sb's achievements*] dépasser ; [+ *record, score*] améliorer ; **to ~ o.s.** améliorer sa condition

better² ['betə'] N (= *person betting*) parieur *m*, -euse *f* ; (*at races*) turfiste *mf* (*qui parie sur les chevaux*)

betterment ['betəmənt] **1** N amélioration *f* ; (*Jur*) [*of property*] plus-value *f* **2** COMP ► **betterment tax** N (*Jur*) impôt *m* sur les plus-values

betting ['betɪŋ] **1** N pari(s) *m(pl)* ; **the ~ was brisk** les paris allaient bon train ; **what is the ~ on Omar?** quelle cote fait Omar ? ; **the ~ was 2 to 1 on Baby Boy** la cote était 2 contre 1 sur Baby Boy, Baby Boy avait une cote de 2 contre 1 ; (*fig*) **the ~ is he won't succeed** il y a peu de chances (pour) qu'il réussisse **2** COMP ► **betting man** N (*pl* **betting men**) **if I were a ~ man I'd say that ...** si j'avais l'habitude de faire des paris je dirais que ... ► **betting news** N résultats *mpl* des courses ► **betting shop** N (*Brit*) bureau *m* de paris (*appartenant à un bookmaker*), ≈ bureau *m* de PMU ► **betting slip** N (*Brit*) ≈ ticket *m* de PMU ► **betting tax** N impôt *m* sur les paris

bettor ['betə'] N = **better²**

between [bɪ'twiːn] **1** PREP **a** (*of place*) entre ; **sit ~ those two boys** asseyez-vous entre ces deux garçons

b (*of order, rank*) entre ; **F comes ~ E and G** (la lettre) F se trouve *or* vient entre E et G ; **a captain comes ~ a lieutenant and a major** le grade de capitaine se situe entre celui de lieutenant et celui de commandant

c (*of time*) entre ; **~ 5 and 6 o'clock** entre 5 et 6 heures

d (*of distance, amount*) entre ; **~ 6 and 7 kilometres/litres** *etc* entre 6 et 7 kilomètres/litres *etc* ; **she is ~ 25 and 30** elle a entre 25 et 30 ans

e (= *to and from*) entre ; **the ferry goes ~ Dover and Calais** le ferry fait la navette entre Douvres et Calais

f (= *from one to other*) entre ; **you will have time to rest ~ flights** vous aurez le temps de vous reposer entre les deux vols ; **~ London and Birmingham there are several large towns** entre Londres et Birmingham il y a plusieurs grandes villes ; **the train does not stop ~ here and London** le train est direct d'ici (à) Londres, le train ne s'arrête pas entre ici et Londres ; **~ now and next week we must ...** d'ici la

semaine prochaine nous devons ...

g (*connection, relationship*) entre ; **the friendship ~ Paul and Robert** l'amitié entre Paul et Robert ; **after all there has been ~ us** après tout ce qu'il y a eu entre nous ; **no one can come ~ us** personne ne nous séparer ; **to choose ~ two hats** choisir entre deux chapeaux ; **the difference ~ them** la différence entre eux ; **the match ~ A and B** le match qui oppose (*or* opposait *etc*) A à B ; **the war ~ the two countries** la guerre entre les deux pays ; **a comparison ~ the two books** une comparaison entre les deux livres, une comparaison des deux livres ; **the distance ~ them** la distance qui les sépare (l'un de l'autre), la distance entre eux

h (*sharing*) entre ; **divide the sweets ~ the two children** partagez les bonbons entre les deux enfants ; **the four boys have five oranges ~ them** les quatre garçons ont cinq oranges en tout *or* à eux tous ; **~ ourselves** *or* **~ you and me, he is not very clever** entre nous, il n'est pas très intelligent

i (*combination, cooperation*) **the boys managed to lift the box ~ (the two of) them** à eux deux les garçons sont arrivés à soulever la caisse ; **we got the letter written ~ us** à nous tous nous avons réussi à écrire la lettre

j (*combined effect*) entre ; **~ housework and study I have no time for going out** entre le ménage et mes études je n'ai pas le temps de sortir ; **~ rage and alarm she could hardly think properly** prise entre la colère et l'inquiétude elle avait du mal à mettre de l'ordre dans ses pensées

2 ADV au milieu, dans l'intervalle ; **her visits are few and far ~** ses visites sont très espacées *or* très rares ; **rows of trees with grass in ~** des rangées *fpl* d'arbres séparées par de l'herbe ; **~ the two world wars** pendant l'entre-deux-guerres, entre les deux guerres mondiales ; **two flights with a four-hour wait in ~** deux vols avec une attente de quatre heures entre les deux

betweentimes [bɪ'twiːn,taɪmz] ADV dans l'intervalle, entre-temps

betwixt [bɪ'twɪkst] **1** PREP (††, *liter, dial*) = **between 1 2** ADV **~ and between** entre les deux, ni l'un ni l'autre

bevel ['bevəl] **1** N (= *surface*) surface *f* oblique ; (*also* **~ edge**) biseau *m* ; (= *tool: also* **~ square**) fausse équerre *f* **2** VT biseauter, tailler de biais *or* en biseau **3** COMP en biseau ► **bevel gear** N engrenage *m* conique ► **bevelled edge** N bord *m* biseauté ► **bevelled mirror** N glace *f* biseautée ► **bevel wheel** N roue *f* dentée conique

beverage ['bevərɪdʒ] N boisson *f* ; (*liter, hum*) breuvage *m*

bevvied⁑ ['bevɪd] ADJ (*Brit: also* **~ up**) soûl ; **to get ~** se soûler la gueule⁑, se biturer⁑

bevvy⁑ ['bevɪ] (*Brit*) N **a** (= *a drink*) verre *m*, pot⁑ *m* ; (= *alcohol in general*) boisson *f* ; **to go for a ~** aller prendre un verre *or* un pot⁑ ; **he fancied a few bevvies** il avait envie d'aller écluser quelques godets⁑ ; **he's back on the ~** il s'est remis à picoler⁑ **b** (= *drinking session*) beuverie *f* ; **to go out on the ~** aller picoler⁑

bevy ['bevɪ] N (*gen*) bande *f*, troupe *f* ; [*of girls, beauties*] essaim *m* ; [*of larks, quails*] volée *f* ; [*of roe deer*] harde *f*

bewail [bɪ'weɪl] VT [+ *one's lot*] se lamenter sur, déplorer ; [+ *sb's death*] pleurer

▼ beware [bɪ'weə'] VTI **to ~** prendre garde (**of sb/sth** à qn/qch, **of doing** de faire), se méfier (**of sth** de qch) ; **~ of falling** prenez garde de tomber ; **~ of being deceived ◊ ~ lest you are** *or* **lest you be deceived** (*frm*) prenez garde qu'on ne vous trompe (*subj*) ; **~ of listening to him** gardez-vous de l'écouter ; **~ (of) how you speak** faites attention à ce que vous dites, surveillez vos paroles ; **"~ of the dog"** « (attention,) chien méchant » ; **"~ of pick-**

pockets" « attention aux pickpockets » ; **"trespassers ~"** « défense d'entrer » ; (*Comm*) **"~ of imitations"** « méfiez-vous des contrefaçons »

bewhiskered [bɪ'wɪskəd] ADJ (*liter*) barbu (*or* moustachu)

bewilder [bɪ'wɪldə'] VT dérouter ; (*stronger*) abasourdir

bewildered [bɪ'wɪldəd] ADJ [*person, look*] perplexe

bewildering [bɪ'wɪldərɪŋ] ADJ déroutant, déconcertant ; (*stronger*) ahurissant

bewilderingly [bɪ'wɪldərɪŋlɪ] ADV d'une façon déroutante *or* déconcertante ; (*stronger*) d'une façon ahurissante ; **it is ~ complicated** c'est d'un compliqué déconcertant

bewilderment [bɪ'wɪldəmənt] N confusion *f*, perplexité *f* ; (*stronger*) ahurissement *m*

bewitch [bɪ'wɪtʃ] VT ensorceler, enchanter ; (*fig*) charmer, enchanter

bewitching [bɪ'wɪtʃɪŋ] ADJ [*look, smile*] enchanteur (-teresse *f*) ; [*face, person*] séduisant, ravissant

bewitchingly [bɪ'wɪtʃɪŋlɪ] ADV d'une façon séduisante *or* enchanteresse ; **~ beautiful** belle à ravir

bey [beɪ] N bey *m* ; **Hassan Bey** Hassan Bey

beyond [bɪ'jɒnd] **1** PREP **a** (*place*) au-delà de, de l'autre côté de ; **~ the Pyrenees** au-delà des Pyrénées ; **you can't go ~ the barrier** vous ne pouvez pas aller au-delà de la barrière, vous ne pouvez pas dépasser la barrière ; **~ the convent walls** en dehors des *or* par-delà les murs du couvent ; **the countries ~ the sea** les pays *mpl* au-delà des mers, les pays *mpl* d'outre-mer

b (*in time*) plus de ; **she won't stay much ~ a month** elle ne restera pas beaucoup plus d'un mois ; **~ next week/June** au-delà de *or* après la semaine prochaine/juin ; **it was ~ the middle of June** on avait dépassé la mi-juin ; **~ bedtime** passé l'heure du coucher

c (= *surpassing, exceeding*) au-dessus de ; **a task ~ her abilities** une tâche au-dessus de ses capacités ; **this work is quite ~ him** ce travail le dépasse complètement ; **it was ~ her to pass the exam** réussir à l'examen était au-dessus de ses forces ; **maths is quite ~ me** les maths, ça me dépasse⁎ ; **it's ~ me why he hasn't left her⁎** je ne comprends pas *or* ça me dépasse⁎ qu'il ne l'ait pas quittée ; **~ my reach** hors de ma portée ; **~ doubt** (*adj*) hors de doute, indubitable ♦ (*adv*) à n'en pas douter, indubitablement ; **that is ~ human understanding** cela dépasse l'entendement humain ; **he is ~ caring** il ne s'en fait plus du tout ; **~ repair** irréparable ; **~ his means** au-dessus de ses moyens → **compare, grave¹, help**

d (*with neg or interrog*) sauf, excepté ; **he gave her no answer ~ a grunt** il ne lui a répondu que par un grognement, pour toute réponse il a émis un grognement

2 ADV au-delà, plus loin, là-bas ; **the year 2000 and ~** l'an 2000 et au-delà ; **the room ~** la pièce d'après ; **the lands ~** les terres *fpl* lointaines

3 N au-delà *m* ; (*fig*) **in** *or* **at the back of ~** au diable⁎, en pleine cambrousse⁎ ; **the great Beyond** l'au-delà

bezant ['bezənt] N besant *m*

bezel ['bezl] **1** N [*of chisel*] biseau *m* ; [*of gem*] facette *f* ; [*holding gem*] chaton *m* ; [*holding watch glass*] portée *f* **2** VT tailler en biseau

bezique [bɪ'ziːk] N bésigue *m*

BFPO [,biːefpiː'əʊ] N (*Brit Mil*) ABBR = **British Forces Post Office**

bhaji ['baːdʒɪ] N (*pl* **bhaji**) bhaji *m* (*beignet indien à base de légumes*)

bhangra ['bæŋgrə] N *musique de danse de la communauté indo-pakistanaise du Royaume-Uni, combinant rythmes pop et traditionnels*

Bhutan [buː'taːn] N le Bhoutan

Bhutanese [ˌbuːtəˈniːz] **1** ADJ bhoutanais **2** N (= *person*) Bhoutanais(e) *m(f)*

bi* [baɪ] ADJ (= *bisexual*) bi*

bi... [baɪ] PREF bi...

Biafra [bɪˈæfrə] N le Biafra

Biafran [bɪˈæfrən] **1** ADJ biafrais **2** N Biafrais(e) *m(f)*

biannual [baɪˈænjʊəl] ADJ semestriel

bias [ˈbaɪəs] **1** N **a** (= *inclination*) tendance *f*, inclination *f* (**towards** à), penchant *m* (**towards** pour); (= *prejudice*) préjugé *m*, parti pris (**towards** pour, **against** contre), prévention *f* (**towards** en faveur de, **against** contre); (*Jur*) distorsion *f*; **a strong ~ towards** ... un penchant marqué pour ...; **he is without ~** il n'a aucun parti pris, il est sans préjugés **b** (*Sewing*) biais *m*; **cut on the ~** coupé dans le biais **c** (*Sport*) [*of bowls*] (= *weight*) poids placé à l'intérieur d'une boule; (= *swerve*) déviation *f* **2** VT (= *give inclination*) influencer (**towards** en faveur de, **against** contre); (= *prejudice*) prévenir (**towards** en faveur de, **against** contre) **3** COMP ► **bias binding** N biais *m* (*ruban*)

bias(s)ed [ˈbaɪəst] ADJ [*person, jury*] qui n'est pas impartial; [*judgement*] qui n'est pas objectif; [*report*] déformé, tendancieux

bib [bɪb] N **a** [*of child*] bavoir *m* **b** [*of apron*] bavette *f*; (*fig*) **in her best ~ and tucker*** sur son trente et un

Bible [ˈbaɪbl] **1** N (*lit*) Bible *f*; (*fig*) bible *f*, évangile *m* ► **holy** **2** COMP ► **Bible-basher*** N prédicateur *m*, -trice *f* frénétique* ► **Bible-bashing*** N **he really likes ~-bashing** il brandit sa Bible à tout va*; **a ~-bashing preacher** un prêcheur qui brandit sa Bible à tout va* ► **the Bible Belt** N (*US*) les États du sud des USA, profondément protestants ► **Bible class** N (*Scol*) classe *f* d'instruction religieuse; (*Rel*) catéchisme *m* ► **Bible college** N université *f* de théologie ► **Bible oath** N serment *m* (prêté) sur la Bible ► **Bible school** N (*US*) cours *m* d'été d'instruction religieuse ► **Bible stories** NPL histoires *fpl* tirées de la Bible ► **Bible study** N étude *f* de la Bible; (*in group*) lecture *f* commentée de la Bible ► **Bible-thumper*** N (*pej*) = **Bible-basher** ► **Bible-thumping*** N = **Bible-bashing**

biblical [ˈbɪblɪkəl] ADJ biblique

biblio... [ˈbɪblɪəʊ] PREF biblio...

bibliographer [ˌbɪblɪˈɒɡrəfəʳ] N bibliographe *mf*

bibliographic(al) [ˌbɪblɪəʊˈɡræfɪk(əl)] ADJ bibliographique

bibliography [ˌbɪblɪˈɒɡrəfɪ] N bibliographie *f*

bibliomania [ˌbɪblɪəʊˈmeɪnɪə] N bibliomanie *f*

bibliomaniac [ˌbɪblɪəʊˈmeɪnɪæk] N bibliomane *mf*

bibliophile [ˈbɪblɪəʊfaɪl] N bibliophile *mf*

bibulous [ˈbɪbjʊləs] ADJ adonné à la boisson; [*look*] aviné; [*evening, party*] bien arrosé

bicameral [baɪˈkæmərəl] ADJ bicaméral; **~ system** bicamér(al)isme *m*

bicarb* [ˈbaɪkɑː] N (ABBR = **bicarbonate of soda**) bicarbonate *m* (de soude)

bicarbonate [baɪˈkɑːbənɪt] **1** N bicarbonate *m* **2** COMP ► **bicarbonate of soda** N bicarbonate *m* de soude

bicentenary [ˌbaɪsenˈtiːnərɪ] ADJ, N bicentenaire *m*

bicentennial [ˌbaɪsenˈtenɪəl] ADJ, N (*US*) bicentenaire *m*

bicephalous [baɪˈsefələs] ADJ bicéphale

biceps [ˈbaɪseps] N (*pl inv*) biceps *m*

bichloride [ˈbaɪklɔːraɪd] N bichlorure *m*

bichromate [ˈbaɪkrəʊmɪt] N bichromate *m*

bicker [ˈbɪkəʳ] VI (= *quarrel*) se chamailler; **they are always ~ing** ils sont toujours à se chamailler *or* toujours en bisbille*

bickering [ˈbɪkərɪŋ] **1** N chamailleries *fpl* **2** ADJ **a** [*person*] querelleur **b** [*stream*] murmurant; [*flame*] tremblotant, vacillant

bickie* [ˈbɪkɪ] N (*Brit: esp baby talk*) petit gâteau *m*, biscuit *m*

bicuspid [baɪˈkʌspɪd] **1** ADJ bicuspide **2** N (*dent f*) prémolaire *f*

bicycle [ˈbaɪsɪkl] **1** N bicyclette *f*, vélo *m*; **to ride a ~** faire de la bicyclette *or* du vélo → **racing** **2** VI† faire de la bicyclette, aller à bicyclette **3** COMP [*lamp, chain, wheel*] de bicyclette, de vélo ► **bicycle bell** N sonnette *f* de bicyclette ► **bicycle clip** N pince *f* de cycliste ► **bicycle kick** N (*Ftbl*) coup *m* de pied retourné ► **bicycle pump** N pompe *f* à bicyclette ► **bicycle rack** N (*on ground*) râtelier *m* à bicyclettes; (*on car*) porte-vélos *m inv* ► **bicycle rickshaw** N vélo-pousse *m* ► **bicycle shed** N abri *m* à bicyclettes ► **bicycle shop** N magasin *m* de cycles ► **bicycle touring** N (*Sport*) cyclotourisme *m*

bicyclist† [ˈbaɪsɪklɪst] N cycliste *mf*

bid [bɪd] (*pret* **bade** *or* **bid**, *ptp* **bidden** *or* **bid**) **1** VT **a** (*liter* = *command*) ordonner, enjoindre (*liter*) (**sb to do** à qn de faire); **he was ~den to come** on lui a ordonné de venir; **do what I ~ you** fais ce que je te dis *or* t'ordonne **b** (= *say*) dire; **to ~ sb good morning** dire bonjour à qn; **to ~ sb welcome** souhaiter la bienvenue à qn → **farewell** **c** (†† = *invite*) inviter, convier **d** (= *offer*) [+ *amount*] offrir, faire une offre de; (*at auction*) faire une enchère de; **he is ~ding 2,000 francs for the painting** il fait une offre *or* une enchère de 2 000 francs pour ce tableau; **I did not ~ (high) enough** je n'ai pas offert assez; **the one that ~s most** le plus offrant **e** (*Cards*) demander; **he ~ three spades** il a demandé trois piques **2** VI **a** (= *make an offer*) faire une offre, proposer un prix; **to ~ for sth** faire une offre pour qch; (*at auction*) faire une enchère pour qch; **to ~ against sb** renchérir sur qn; (*US Comm*) **to ~ on** [+ *contract etc*] soumissionner **b** (*phrases*) **to ~ for power/fame** viser *or* ambitionner le pouvoir/la gloire; (*liter*) **to ~ fair to do sth** sembler devoir faire qch, promettre de faire qch; **everything ~s fair to be successful** tout semble annoncer *or* promettre le succès **3** N **a** (*Comm*) offre *f*; (*at auction*) enchère *f*; **to make a ~ for** faire une offre pour; (*at auction*) faire une enchère pour; **a high ~** une forte enchère; **a higher ~** une surenchère; **to make a higher ~** surenchérir **b** (*Cards*) demande *f*, annonce *f*; **to raise the ~** monter; (*Bridge*) **to make no ~** passer parole; **"no ~"** « parole », « passe » **c** (= *attempt*) tentative *f*; **escape/suicide ~** tentative *f* d'évasion/de suicide; **to make a ~ for power** tenter de s'emparer du pouvoir; **to make a ~ for freedom** tenter de s'évader; **he scaled the wall in a ~ for freedom** il a escaladé le mur pour tenter de s'évader; **in a desperate ~ for a better life abroad** tentant désespérément de trouver une vie meilleure à l'étranger; **to make a ~ to do sth** tenter de faire qch; **she tried acupuncture in a ~ to stop smoking** elle a essayé l'acupuncture pour tenter d'arrêter de fumer **4** COMP ► **bid bond** N caution *f* de soumission ► **bid price** N (*St Ex*) cours *m* d'achat

biddable [ˈbɪdəbl] ADJ **a** [*child*] docile, obéissant **b** (*Cards*) **~ suit** couleur *f* demandable

bidden [ˈbɪdn] VB *ptp of* **bid**

bidder [ˈbɪdəʳ] N (*at sale*) enchérisseur *m*, offrant *m*; (*Fin*) soumissionnaire *m*; **the highest ~** (*at sale*) le plus offrant; (*Fin*) le soumissionnaire le plus offrant; **the lowest ~** (*at sale*) le moins offrant; (*Fin*) le soumissionnaire le moins disant; **successful ~** adjudicataire *mf*; **there were no ~s** personne n'a fait d'offre

bidding [ˈbɪdɪŋ] **1** N **a** (*NonC*) (*at sale*) enchère(s) *f(pl)*; **~ up** surenchères *fpl*; **~ was brisk** les enchères étaient vives; **the ~ is closed** l'enchère est faite, c'est adjugé; (*at sale*) **to raise the ~** surenchérir **b** (*NonC*) (*Cards*) enchères *fpl*; (*Bridge*) **to open the ~** ouvrir (les enchères) **c** († = *order*) ordre *m*, commandement *m*; **at whose ~?** sur l'ordre de qui?; **I did his ~** j'ai fait ce qu'il m'a ordonné *or* demandé; **at sb's ~** sur l'ordre *or* l'injonction de qn; **he needed no second ~** il ne se l'est pas fait dire deux fois **2** COMP ► **bidding war** N (*Fin*) guerre *f* des enchères

biddy [ˈbɪdɪ] N **old ~** vieille bonne femme *f*

bide [baɪd] **1** VI († *or liter or dial*) = **abide 2** **2** VT **a** **to ~ one's time** se réserver, attendre son heure *or* le bon moment **b** († *or liter or dial*) = **abide 1**

bidet [ˈbiːdeɪ] N bidet *m*

bidirectional [baɪdɪˈrekʃənl] ADJ (*Comput*) bidirectionnel

biennial [baɪˈenɪəl] **1** ADJ **a** (= *happening every two years*) biennal, bisannuel **b** (= *lasting two years*) biennal **c** (*Bot*) bisannuel **2** N (*Bot*) bisannuel *m*

bier [bɪəʳ] N (*for coffin*) brancards *mpl* (de cercueil); (*for corpse*) bière *f*

biff†* [bɪf] **1** N coup *m* de poing, baffe* *f*; (*onomatopoeia*) **~!** vlan!, pan! **2** VT cogner sur, flanquer une baffe à*; **to ~ sb on the nose** flanquer* son poing dans *or* sur la figure de qn

bifocal [ˈbaɪfəʊkəl] **1** ADJ bifocal, à double foyer **2** **bifocals** NPL lunettes *fpl* à double foyer

bifurcate [ˈbaɪfɜːkeɪt] **1** VI bifurquer **2** ADJ à deux branches

bifurcation [ˌbaɪfɜːˈkeɪʃən] N bifurcation *f*, embranchement *m*

big [bɪg] **1** ADJ **a** (*in size*) [*person, fruit, parcel, book*] gros (grosse *f*); [*person, building, tree*] grand; **a ~ fellow** un grand gaillard; **a ~ man** un homme grand et fort; **to grow** *or* **~ger** grossir; (= *taller*) grandir; **a ~ stick** un gros bâton → **stick**; **~ with child** grosse, enceinte → **drum** **b** (*in age*) grand, aîné; **a ~ boy/girl** un grand garçon/une grande fille; **my ~ brother** mon grand frère, mon frère aîné; **to grow** *or* **get ~ger** grandir; **to be a ~ brother to sb** servir de conseiller à qn → **3**; (*lit, fig*) **you're a ~ boy/girl now!** tu es un grand garçon/une grande fille maintenant!; **I am ~ enough to know ...** je suis assez grand pour savoir ... **c** (= *important*) grand, important, marquant, remarquable; **a ~ man** un grand homme, un homme marquant *or* remarquable *or* important; **what's the ~ hurry?*** il n'y a pas le feu!*; **he's a ~ fish*** c'est un gros poisson*; **he's a ~ fish** *or* (*US*) **frog in a small pond** c'est une gloire locale; (*fig* = *fashionable*) **boots are ~ this year*** les bottes sont in‡ cette année; **this is my/his ~ day** c'est le grand jour (pour moi/lui); **a ~ event** un événement marquant; **to have ~ ideas** voir grand; **a ~ lie** un gros mensonge; **the ~ger they are, the harder they fall** plus haut ils sont arrivés, plus dure sera la chute; **to do things in a ~ way** faire les choses en grand; **a tragedy? that's rather a ~ word** une tragédie? c'est un bien grand mot **d** (* = *grand*) [*words*] ambitieux; **~ talk** fanfaronnades *fpl*, grands discours *mpl*; **to get/be too ~ for one's boots** attraper/avoir la grosse tête*; **he's got a ~ head** il est crâneur*, il a la grosse tête*; **he's got a ~ mouth** il ne sait pas se taire *or* la boucler*; **why can't you keep your ~ mouth shut!** pas moyen que tu te taises!*, tu aurais mieux fait de la boucler!‡ → **3, bigmouth** **e** (= *generous*) grand, généreux; **a heart as ~**

as yours un cœur aussi grand *or* aussi généreux que le vôtre; (*iro*) **that's ~ of you!** quelle générosité! (*iro*); **to be ~ on:** [+ *person*] adorer, être un fan* de; [+ *thing*] être grand amateur *or* un fana* de

2 ADV **to talk ~** fanfaronner, se faire mousser*; **to act ~** frimer*, faire l'important; **to go over ~:** avoir un succès fou *or* monstre*; **to make it ~** avoir un succès fou*; **his speech went down ~ with his audience:** ses auditeurs ont été emballés* par son discours

3 COMP ► **big band** N (*Mus*) big band *m*, grand orchestre *m* (*des années 40-50*) ► **big bang** N (*Phys*) big-bang *or* big bang *m*; (*Brit St Ex*) **the Big Bang** le Big Bang (*informatisation de la Bourse de Londres*) ► **Big Ben** N (*Brit*) Big Ben *m* ► **big-boned** ADJ bien *or* fortement charpenté ► **Big Brother** N (*Pol etc*) Big Brother *m*, l'État *m* omniprésent; **Big Brother is watching you** on vous espionne ► **big bug:** N grosse légume* *f*, huile* *f* ► **big business** N (*NonC*) les grandes entreprises *fpl*, les grandes firmes *fpl*; **the lottery has become ~ business** la loterie rapporte beaucoup d'argent *or* rapporte gros; **tourism in Hong Kong is ~ business** le tourisme est un secteur florissant à Hong-Kong ► **big cat** N grand félin *m* ► **big cheese:** N grosse légume* *f*, huile* *f* ► **the big city** N la grande agglomération ► **the Big Dipper** N (*US Astron*) la Grande Ourse ► **big dipper** N [*of fairground*] montagnes *fpl* russes ► **the Big Eight** N (*US Univ*) les grandes universités du Midwest ► **big end** N (*Aut*) tête *f* de bielle ► **the Big Four** N (*Pol*) les Quatre (Grands); (*Brit Comm*) les quatre grandes banques anglaises ► **big game** N gros gibier *m*; **~ game hunter** chasseur *m* de gros gibier ► **game hunting** chasse *f* au gros (gibier) ► **big-hearted** ADJ au grand cœur; **to be ~-hearted** avoir bon cœur, avoir du cœur; **a ~-hearted fellow** un homme de cœur ► **big-mouthed** ADJ fort en gueule*; **to be ~-mouthed:** être fort en gueule*, avoir une grande gueule* ► **big name** N (= *authority*) grand nom *m*; (*person*) **he's a ~ name in politics** c'est un grand nom de la politique ► **big noise:** N (*Brit*) grand ponte* *m*; **she's a ~ noise in linguistics** c'est un grand ponte* de la linguistique ► **big one:** N (= *a thousand dollars*) (*billet m de*) mille dollars *mpl* ► **big science** N la recherche scientifique à gros budget ► **big shot*** N grand ponte* *m* ► **big-sounding** ADJ [*idea, plan etc*] prétentieux; [*name*] ronflant, pompeux ► **the Big Ten** N → **the Big Eight** ► **big-ticket** ADJ (*US*) **~-ticket item** *or* **purchase** gros achat *m* ► **big time** N **to make the ~ time** percer ► **big-time*** ADJ [*politician, industrialist*] de première catégorie; [*part, role*] de premier plan; [*farming*] sur une grande échelle; **~-time gambler** flambeur* *m* ♦ ADV **you screwed up ~-time!*** tu as cafouillé quelque chose de bien !* ► **big toe** N gros orteil *m* ► **big top** N (= *circus*) cirque *m*; (= *main tent*) grand chapiteau *m* ► **big wheel** N (*in fairground etc*) grande roue *f*; (* = *important person*) huile* *f* → **apple, deal¹**

bigamist ['bɪgəmɪst] N bigame *mf*

bigamous ['bɪgəməs] ADJ bigame

bigamy ['bɪgəmɪ] N bigamie *f*

biggie: ['bɪgɪ] N (= *success*) (*song, record*) tube* *m*; (*film*) succès *m*; (= *anything important*) **now it's the ~** maintenant, on passe aux choses sérieuses

biggish* ['bɪgɪʃ] ADJ assez *or* relativement grand

bighead* ['bɪghed] N crâneur* *m*, -euse* *f*

bigheaded [ˌbɪg'hedɪd] ADJ crâneur*

bight [baɪt] N **a** (*Geog*) baie *f*, anse *f*; (*larger*) golfe *m* **b** [*of rope*] boucle *f*

bigmouth* ['bɪgmaʊθ] N grande gueule* *f*; **he is just a ~** il a *or* c'est une grande gueule*

---

bigot ['bɪgət] N (*Philos, Pol*) fanatique *mf*, sectaire *mf*; (*Rel*) bigot(e) *m(f)*

bigoted ['bɪgətɪd] ADJ (*Rel*) bigot; (*Pol etc*) [*person*] fanatique, sectaire; [*attitude, devotion*] fanatique

bigotry ['bɪgətrɪ] N (*NonC*) (*Rel*) bigoterie *f*; (*Philos, Pol etc*) fanatisme *m*, sectarisme *m*

bigwig* ['bɪgwɪg] N grosse légume* *f*, huile* *f*

Bihar [bɪ'hɑːʳ] N le Bihar

bijou ['biːʒuː] ADJ (*Brit*) **"~ residence for sale"** « maison à vendre, véritable bijou »

bike [baɪk] **1** N (ABBR = **bicycle**) vélo *m*; (= *motorbike*) moto *f*; (*Brit*) **on your ~!*** (= *go away*) dégage !*; (= *no way*) tu plaisantes !* **2** VI* faire du vélo; **to ~ to work** aller au travail à vélo; **to ~ 10km** faire 10 km à vélo **3** COMP ► **bike shed** N abri *m* à bicyclettes ► **bike rack** N (*on floor*) râtelier *m* à bicyclettes; (*on car roof*) porte-vélos *m inv* ► **bike shop** N magasin *m* de cycles

biker* ['baɪkəʳ] N motard(e) *m(f)*

bikeway ['baɪkweɪ] N piste *f* cyclable

bikini [bɪ'kiːnɪ] **1** N bikini® *m* **2** COMP ► **bikini bottom(s)*** N(PL) bas *m* de bikini® ► **bikini briefs, bikini pants** NPL mini-slip *m* ► **bikini top** N haut *m* de bikini®

bilabial [baɪ'leɪbɪəl] **1** ADJ bilabial **2** N bilabiale *f*

bilateral [baɪ'lætərəl] ADJ bilatéral

bilaterally [baɪ'lætərəlɪ] ADJ bilatéralement

bilberry ['bɪlbərɪ] N myrtille *f*, airelle *f*

bile [baɪl] **1** N **a** (*Physiol*) bile *f* **b** (*fig* = *anger*) mauvaise humeur *f* **c** (*Hist* = *choler*) bile *f* **2** COMP ► **bile duct** N canal *m* biliaire ► **bile stone** N calcul *m* biliaire

bilevel ['baɪlevl] ADJ sur *or* à deux niveaux

bilge [bɪldʒ] N **a** (*Naut*) (= *rounded part of hull*) bouchain *m*, renflement *m*; (= *bottom of hold*) fond *m* de cale, sentine *f* **b** (*also* = **water**) eau *f* de cale *or* de sentine **c** (: = *nonsense*) idioties *fpl*, foutaises: *fpl*

bilharzia [bɪl'hɑːzɪə], **bilharziasis** [ˌbɪlhɑː'zaɪəsɪs] N bilharziose *f*

bilingual [baɪ'lɪŋgwəl] ADJ bilingue

bilingualism [baɪ'lɪŋgwəlɪzəm] N bilinguisme *m*

bilious ['bɪlɪəs] ADJ **a** (*Med*) bilieux; **~ attack** crise *f* de foie **b** (*fig*) maussade, irritable

biliousness ['bɪlɪəsnɪs] N (*NonC*: *Med*) affection *f* hépatique

bilk [bɪlk] VT (*esp US*) [+ *creditor*] filouter, blouser*; **to ~ sb's efforts** mettre des bâtons dans les roues à qn

Bill [bɪl] N (*dim of* **William**) Guillaume *m*

bill¹ [bɪl] **1** N **a** (*for product, work done*) facture *f*; (*for gas etc*) note *f*; (*of restaurant*) addition *f*; (*of hotel*) note *f*; **have you paid the milk ~?** as-tu payé le lait ?; **a pile of ~s in the post** une pile de factures dans le courrier; **may I have the ~ please** l'addition (*or* la note) s'il vous plaît; **put it on my ~ please** mettez-le sur ma note, s'il vous plaît; **the factory has a high wages ~** l'usine a d'importantes sorties en salaires, le poste salaires est élevé dans l'entreprise → **foot, pay, settle²** **b** (= *written statement*) état *m*, liste *f* **c** (*Comm, Fin etc*) effet *m*, traite *f*; **to meet a ~** faire honneur à un effet; **to draw a ~ on …** tirer une traite sur …; (*Fin*) **~s receivable** effets *mpl* à recevoir; **exchequer ~** bon *m* du Trésor → **endorse** **d** (*US* = *banknote*) billet *m* (de banque); **5-dollar ~** billet *m* de 5 dollars **e** (*Parl*) projet *m* de loi; **to propose/pass/throw out a ~** présenter/voter/rejeter un projet de loi; (*Brit*) **the ~ passed the Commons** le projet de loi a été voté par la Chambre des communes **f** (*Jur*) plainte *f*, requête *f* **g** (= *poster, advertisement*) (*Theat etc*) affiche *f*; [*of house for sale*] écriteau *m*; (= *public notice*)

---

placard *m*; **to head** *or* **top the ~** être en vedette, être en tête d'affiche; (*fig*) **to fit** *or* **fill the ~** (*gen*) faire l'affaire; (*for job*) avoir le profil; **we need someone with leadership qualities, and she fits the ~ perfectly** il nous faut quelqu'un qui ait des qualités de chef et elle fait tout à fait l'affaire *or* elle a le profil requis; **she fits the ~ as a leader** elle a tout à fait le profil d'un chef → **handbill, stick**

2 VT **a** [+ *goods*] facturer; **to ~ sb for sth** envoyer la facture de qch à qn **b** [+ *play*] mettre à l'affiche, annoncer; **he is ~ed to play Hamlet** il est à l'affiche dans le rôle de Hamlet

3 COMP ► **bill of attainder** N décret *m* de confiscation de biens et de mort civile ► **bill of costs** N état *m* de frais ► **bill of entry** N (*Customs*) déclaration *f* d'entrée en douane ► **bill of exchange** N (*Comm*) lettre *f* de change; **foreign ~ of exchange** traite *f* sur l'étranger ► **bill of fare** N menu *m*, carte *f* (du jour) ► **bill of goods** N (*US*) **to sell sb a ~ of goods:** rouler* qn ► **bill of health** N (*Naut*) patente *f* (de santé) → **clean** ► **bill of indictment** N acte *m* d'accusation ► **bill of lading** N (*Comm*) connaissement *m* ► **bill of quantities** N (*Constr*) métré *m* (*devis*) ► **bill of rights** N déclaration *f* des droits; (*US Hist*) **the Bill of Rights** la Déclaration des droits ► **bill of sale** N acte *m* *or* contrat *m* de vente

---

BILL OF RIGHTS

Ensemble des dix premiers amendements ajoutés à la Constitution américaine en 1791 et qui définissent les droits individuels des citoyens et les pouvoirs respectifs du gouvernement fédéral et des États. Ainsi le premier amendement garantit la liberté de culte et de réunion et la liberté de la presse, le second le droit au port d'armes, le sixième le droit à un procès équitable.
→ *FIFTH AMENDMENT*

---

bill² [bɪl] **1** N **a** [*of bird*] bec *m* → **scissor** **b** (*Geog*) promontoire *m*, bec *m*; **Portland Bill** la presqu'île de Portland **2** VI [*birds*] se becqueter; (*lit, fig*) **to ~ and coo** roucouler

bill³ [bɪl] N **a** (= *tool*) serpe *f* **b** (*Hist* = *weapon*) hache *f* d'armes

billboard ['bɪlbɔːd] N panneau *m* d'affichage

billet¹ ['bɪlɪt] **1** N (*Mil*) (= *document*) billet *m* de logement; (= *accommodation*) cantonnement *m* (chez l'habitant); (*fig*) **a cushy ~:** un fromage*, une planque* **2** VT (*Mil*) **to ~ a soldier (on sb)** loger un soldat (chez qn), cantonner un soldat (chez qn); **to ~ soldiers on a town** cantonner des soldats dans une ville

billet² ['bɪlɪt] N [*of wood etc*] billette *f* (*also Archit*)

billeting ['bɪlɪtɪŋ] **1** N (*Mil*) cantonnement *m* **2** COMP ► **billeting officer** N chef *m* de cantonnement

billfold ['bɪlfəʊld] N (*US*) portefeuille *m*

billhook ['bɪlhʊk] N serpette *f*

billiard ['bɪljəd] N (*NonC*) **~s** (jeu *m* de) billard *m*; **to have a game of ~s** faire une partie de billard **2** COMP ► **billiard ball** N boule *f* de billard ► **billiard cue** N queue *f* de billard ► **billiard table** N (table *f* de) billard *m*

billing¹ ['bɪlɪŋ] N **a** [*of posters*] affichage *m* **b** (*Theat*) **to get top** *or* **star/second ~** figurer en tête d'affiche/en deuxième place à l'affiche

billing² ['bɪlɪŋ] N (*lit, fig*) **~ and cooing** roucoulements *mpl*

billing³ ['bɪlɪŋ] N (*Comm*) facturation *f*

Billingsgate ['bɪlɪŋzgeɪt] N *ancien marché au poisson du quartier de Billingsgate à Londres*

billion ['bɪljən] N (pl **billion** or **billions**) (= thousand million) milliard m ; (Brit† = million million) billion m

billionaire [,bɪljə'nɛər] N milliardaire mf

billow ['bɪləʊ] **1** N (liter) **the ~s** les flots mpl (liter) **2** VI [sail] se gonfler ; [cloth] onduler ; [smoke] s'élever en tourbillons or en volutes, tournoyer
► **billow out** VI [sail etc] se gonfler

billowy ['bɪləʊɪ] ADJ [sea] houleux, agité ; [waves] gros (grosse f) ; [sail] gonflé (par le vent) ; [smoke] en (grosses) volutes

billposter ['bɪl,pəʊstər], **billsticker** ['bɪl,stɪkər] N colleur m d'affiches, afficheur m

billy¹ ['bɪlɪ] N (US = club) matraque f

billy² ['bɪlɪ] N (also ~ **can**) gamelle f

billy goat ['bɪlɪgəʊt] **1** N bouc m **2** COMP ► **billy goat beard** N bouc m (barbe)

billy-ho•, billy-o• ['bɪlɪhəʊ] N **like ~** [laugh] à gorge déployée ; [run] à toutes jambes

bimbo• ['bɪmbəʊ] N (pl **bimbos** or **bimboes**) (pej) ravissante idiote f

bimetallic [,baɪmɪ'tælɪk] ADJ bimétallique

bimetallism [baɪ'metəlɪzəm] N bimétallisme m

bimonthly ['baɪ'mʌnθlɪ] **1** ADJ (= twice a month) bimensuel ; (= every two months) bimestriel **2** ADV deux fois par mois, tous les deux mois

bin [bɪn] **1** N **a** [of coal, corn] coffre m ; [of bread] boîte f ; (larger) huche f **b** (Brit: Wine) casier m (à bouteilles) **c** (Brit: also **dustbin, rubbish ~**) boîte f à ordures, poubelle f **2** VT (• = throw away) mettre or jeter à la poubelle **3** COMP ► **bin bag** N (grand) sac m poubelle ► **bin end** N (Wine) fin f de série ► **bin liner** N sac m poubelle

binary ['baɪnərɪ] **1** ADJ binaire **2** N (= the binary system) système m binaire ; **in ~** en binaire **3** COMP ► **binary code** N (Comput) code m binaire ► **binary form** N (Mus) forme f binaire ► **binary notation** N (Math) numération f binaire ► **binary number** N (Math) nombre m binaire ► **binary star** N (Astron) étoile f double ► **binary system** N (Math) système m binaire

bind [baɪnd] (pret, ptp **bound**) **1** VT **a** (= fasten) [+ thing] attacher ; [+ two or more things] attacher, lier ; [+ person, animal] lier, attacher (**to** à) ; [+ prisoner] ligoter ; **he bound the files (together) with string** il a attaché or lié (ensemble) les dossiers avec une ficelle ; **bound hand and foot** pieds et poings liés ; **bound by gratitude to sb** attaché à qn par la reconnaissance ; **to be bound together** [people, ideas] être liés **b** (= encircle) entourer (**with** de), ceindre (liter) (**with** de) ; (Med) [+ artery] ligaturer ; [+ wound] bander **c** [+ book] relier ; **bound in calf** relié (en) veau **d** (= oblige, pledge) obliger, contraindre (**sb to do** à faire) ; **to ~ o.s. to sth/to do sth** s'engager à qch/à faire qch ; **to ~ sb to a promise** astreindre qn à tenir une promesse ; **to ~ sb to an oath** lier par (un) serment ; **to ~ sb as an apprentice (to)** mettre qn en apprentissage (chez) → **bound³** **e** (= stick together) (also Chem, Phys) lier ; (Med) [+ bowels] resserrer ; (Culin) **~ the mixture with an egg** lier la préparation avec un œuf **2** VI [rule] être obligatoire ; [agreement] engager ; [machinery] se coincer, (se) gripper **3** N **a** (Mus) liaison f **b** (Brit•) = nuisance) **what a ~ you've got to go** quelle barbe• que tu doives partir ; **this meeting is a terrible ~** cette réunion me casse les pieds• ; **to be in a ~** être dans le pétrin•, être coincé
► **bind down** VT SEP (fig) obliger, contraindre, astreindre (**sb to do** qn à faire) ; **to be bound**

down (to do) être obligé or contraint (de faire), être astreint (à faire)
► **bind on** VT SEP attacher (avec une corde etc) **2** VI• rouspéter•, geindre• (**about** à propos de)
► **bind over** VT SEP (esp Brit Jur) mettre en liberté conditionnelle ; **to ~ sb over to keep the peace** relaxer qn sous condition qu'il ne trouble (subj) pas l'ordre public ; **he was bound over for six months** on l'a relaxé sous peine de comparaître en cas de récidive dans les six mois
► **bind to** VT FUS (Chem) se lier à
► **bind together** VT SEP (lit) [+ sticks] lier ; (fig) [+ people] unir
► **bind up** VT SEP [+ wound] panser, bander ; (fig) lier, attacher ; **his money is bound up in shares** son argent est immobilisé dans des actions ; **your life is bound up in hers** votre existence est étroitement liée à la sienne ; **their fate is closely bound up with that of the other hostages** leur sort est étroitement lié à celui des autres otages ; **the future of their country is inextricably bound up with Europe** l'avenir de leur pays est inextricablement lié à celui de l'Europe ; **to be totally bound up with sb** se dévouer entièrement à qn ; **to be totally bound up with one's work** se donner corps et âme à son travail

binder ['baɪndər] N **a** (Agr) (= machine) lieuse f ; (= person) lieur m, -euse f → **bookbinder** **b** (for papers) classeur m → **ring¹, spring** **c** (Med etc) bandage m **d** (Constr) (= cement, mortar) liant m, agglomérant m ; (= joist) entrait m **e** (US = agreement in deal) engagement m, option f d'achat

bindery ['baɪndərɪ] N atelier m de reliure

binding ['baɪndɪŋ] **1** N **a** [of book] reliure f → **cloth, half** **b** (Tex = tape) extrafort m → **bias** **c** [of skis] fixation f **2** ADJ **a** [rule] obligatoire ; [agreement, promise] qui lie, qui engage ; [price] ferme ; **to be ~ on sb** lier qn, engager qn ; **a promise is ~** on est lié par une promesse ; (Jur: of agreement) **~ effect** force f obligatoire ; (Jur) **measure ~ on each contracting party** mesure f exécutoire pour chaque partie contractante **b** (Med) [food etc] constipant ; (Constr) agglomérant

bindweed ['baɪndwi:d] N liseron m

binge [bɪndʒ] **1** VI (gen) faire des excès ; (on alcohol) se soûler, boire avec frénésie ; (on food) manger à l'excès ; (spending) dépenser comme un fou ; **to ~ on chocolate** s'empiffrer• de chocolat ; **to ~ on chartreuse** se soûler à la chartreuse **2** N **a drinking ~** une beuverie ; **to go on a ~ = to binge** → 1

bingo ['bɪŋgəʊ] **1** N bingo m **2** EXCL **~!•** euréka !•

binman ['bɪnmæn] N (pl **-men**) (= dustman) boueux m, éboueur m

binnacle ['bɪnəkl] N (Naut) habitacle m

binocular [bɪ'nɒkjʊlər] **1** ADJ binoculaire **2** **binoculars** NPL jumelle(s) f(pl)

binomial [baɪ'nəʊmɪəl] ADJ, N (Math) binôme m ; **~ distribution** distribution f binomiale ; **the ~ theorem** le théorème (de binôme) de Newton

bint• [bɪnt] N (Brit) nana• f

binuclear [baɪ'nju:klɪər] ADJ binucléaire

bio... ['baɪəʊ] PREF bio...

biochemical ['baɪəʊ'kemɪkəl] ADJ biochimique

biochemist ['baɪəʊ'kemɪst] N biochimiste mf

biochemistry ['baɪəʊ'kemɪstrɪ] N biochimie f

biodegradable ['baɪəʊdɪ'greɪdəbl] ADJ biodégradable

biodiversity [,baɪəʊdaɪ'vɜːsətɪ] N biodiversité f

biodynamic [,baɪəʊdaɪ'næmɪk] ADJ biodynamique

bioengineering [,baɪəʊ,endʒɪ'nɪərɪŋ] N bio-ingénierie f

bioethics [,baɪəʊ'eθɪks] N (NonC) bioéthique f

biofeedback [,baɪəʊ'fi:dbæk] N biofeedback m

biofuel ['baɪəʊfjʊəl] N biocarburant m

biogenesis ['baɪəʊ'dʒenɪsɪs] N biogenèse f

biographer [baɪ'ɒgrəfər] N biographe mf

biographic(al) [,baɪəʊ'græfɪk(əl)] ADJ biographique

biography [baɪ'ɒgrəfɪ] N biographie f

biological [,baɪə'lɒdʒɪkəl] **1** ADJ (gen) biologique ; [detergent, washing powder] aux enzymes **2** COMP ► **biological clock** N horloge f biologique ► **biological diversity** N diversité f biologique ► **biological father** N père m biologique ► **biological mother** N mère f biologique ► **biological parents** NPL parents mpl biologiques ► **biological warfare** N guerre f biologique ► **biological weapons** NPL armes fpl biologiques

biologically [,baɪəʊ'lɒdʒɪkəlɪ] ADV biologiquement

biologist [baɪ'ɒlədʒɪst] N biologiste mf

biology [baɪ'ɒlədʒɪ] N biologie f

biomass ['baɪəʊmæs] N biomasse f

biome ['baɪəʊm] N biome m

biomechanics [,baɪəʊmɪ'kænɪks] N (NonC) biomécanique f

biomedical [,baɪəʊ'medɪkəl] ADJ biomédical

biometrics [,baɪə'metrɪks], **biometry** [baɪ'ɒmɪtrɪ] N (NonC) biométrie f

bionic [baɪ'ɒnɪk] ADJ bionique

bionics [baɪ'ɒnɪks] N (NonC) bionique f

biophysical [,baɪəʊ'fɪzɪkəl] ADJ biophysique

biophysicist [,baɪəʊ'fɪzɪsɪst] N biophysicien(ne) m(f)

biophysics [,baɪəʊ'fɪzɪks] N (NonC) biophysique f

biopic• ['baɪəʊ,pɪk] N film m biographique

biopsy ['baɪɒpsɪ] N biopsie f

biorhythm ['baɪəʊrɪðəm] N biorythme m

biosphere ['baɪəsfɪər] N biosphère f

biosynthesis [,baɪəʊ'sɪnθɪsɪs] N biosynthèse f, anabolisme m

biosynthetic [,baɪəʊ,sɪn'θetɪk] ADJ biosynthétique

biota [baɪ'əʊtə] N biote m

biotechnology [,baɪəʊtek'nɒlədʒɪ] N biotechnologie f

biotic [baɪ'ɒtɪk] ADJ biotique

biowarfare ['baɪəʊ'wɔːfeə'] N guerre f biologique

bipartisan [,baɪ'pɑːtɪzæn] ADJ biparti or bipartite ; **~ politics** politique f qui fait l'unanimité

bipartite [baɪ'pɑːtaɪt] ADJ (Bio, Pol) biparti or bipartite ; (Jur) [document] rédigé en double

biped ['baɪped] ADJ, N bipède m

biplane ['baɪpleɪn] N (avion m) biplan m

bipolar [baɪ'pəʊlər] ADJ bipolaire

bipolarization [baɪ,pəʊləraɪ'zeɪʃən] N bipolarisation f

bipolarize [baɪ'pəʊləraɪz] VT bipolariser

birch [bɜːtʃ] **1** N (also ~ **tree**) bouleau m ; (also ~ **wood**) (bois m de) bouleau m ; (for whipping) verge f, fouet m ; (Jur) **the ~** la peine du fouet (avec les verges) → **silver** **2** VT fouetter **3** COMP de bouleau ► **birch plantation** N boulaie f, plantation f de bouleaux

birching ['bɜːtʃɪŋ] N peine f du fouet (avec les verges)

bird [bɜːd] **1** N **a** oiseau m ; (Culin) volaille f ; **they shot six ~s** ils ont abattu six oiseaux or six pièces de gibier (à plumes) ; **young** or **little ~** petit oiseau m, oisillon m ; (liter) **~ of ill omen** oiseau m de mauvais augure or de malheur ■ (PROV) **a ~ in the hand is worth two**

in the bush un tiens vaut mieux que deux tu l'auras (*PROV*) ∎ (*PROV*) ~**s of a feather flock together** qui se ressemble s'assemble (*PROV*); **they're ~s of a feather** (*gen*) ils se ressemblent beaucoup; (*pej*) ils sont à mettre dans le même sac; **a little ~ told me*** mon petit doigt me l'a dit; (*fig*) **to give sb the ~†*** (*Theat, Sport*) huer *or* siffler qn; (= *send sb packing*) envoyer bouler* *or* paître* qn; (*Theat*) **to get the ~†*** se faire siffler *or* huer; **for the ~s†** (= *worthless*) nul*; (= *silly*) débile*; (*hum*) **he'll have to be told about the ~s and the bees** il va falloir lui expliquer que les bébés ne naissent pas dans les choux → **early, jailbird, kill**

[b] († = *fellow*) oiseau* *m* (*pej*), type* *m*; **he's a queer ~** c'est un drôle d'oiseau* *or* de numéro*; **he's a cunning old ~** c'est un vieux singe *or* rusé

[c] (*Brit*† = *girl*) nana* *f*, gonzesse* *f*; **I've split up with my ~** j'ai rompu avec ma nana* *or* ma gonzesse*

[d] († = *prison*) **five years' ~** cinq ans de taule*; **to do ~** faire de la taule*

[2] COMP ► **bird bath** N vasque *f* (*pour les oiseaux*) ► **bird brain*** N (*pej*) étourneau *m*, tête *f* de linotte ► **bird-brained*** ADJ qui a une cervelle d'oiseau, écervelé ► **bird call** N cri *m* d'oiseau ► **bird dog** N (*US*) chien *m* de chasse (*le gibier à plume*) ► **bird fancier** N aviculteur *m*, -trice *f* ► **bird feeder** N mangeoire *f*, trémie *f* ► **bird-like** ADJ [*eyes, features*] d'oiseau ► **bird nesting** N to go ~**nesting** aller dénicher les oiseaux ► **bird of paradise** N oiseau *m* de paradis ► **bird of passage** N (*lit, fig*) oiseau *m* de passage ► **bird of prey** N oiseau *m* de proie ► **bird sanctuary** N réserve *f* ornithologique ► **birds' eggs** NPL œufs *mpl* d'oiseaux ► **bird's eye** N (*Bot*) petit chêne *m* ► **bird's-eye view** N (*fig*) vue *f* d'ensemble, vue *f* générale; (*lit*) **a ~'s-eye view of Paris** Paris vu d'avion → **bird's foot** N pl **bird's foots** (*Bot*) pied-d'oiseau *m* ► **bird's nest** N nid *m* d'oiseau(x) ► **bird's-nest soup** N (*Culin*) soupe *f* aux nids d'hirondelles ► **bird table** N (*in garden*) mangeoire *f* ► **bird-watcher** N ornithologue *mf* amateur ► **bird-watching** N ornithologie *f* (pratiquée en amateur); **to go ~-watching** aller observer les oiseaux

birdcage ['bɜːdkeɪdʒ] N cage *f* à oiseaux; (*large*) volière *f*

birdie ['bɜːdɪ] [1] N [a] (*baby talk*) (gentil) petit oiseau *m*; (*for photo*) **watch the ~!** le petit oiseau va sortir! [b] (*Golf*) birdie *m* [2] VT (*Golf*) **to ~ a hole** faire un birdie

birdlime ['bɜːdlaɪm] N glu *f*

birdseed ['bɜːdsiːd] N (*NonC*) graines *fpl* (*pour les oiseaux*)

birdsong ['bɜːdsɒŋ] N chant *m* des oiseaux

biretta [bɪˈretə] N barrette *f*

biriani [ˌbɪrɪˈɑːnɪ] N = **biryani**

birling ['bɜːlɪŋ] N (*US*) sport *m* de bûcheron, consistant à faire tourner avec les pieds, sans tomber, un tronc d'arbre flottant

Biro® ['baɪərəʊ] N (*Brit*) stylo *m* (à) bille, Bic® *m*

▼ **birth** [bɜːθ] [1] N [a] (= *being born*) naissance *f*; (*also* **childbirth**) accouchement *m*, couches *fpl*; [*of animal*] mise *f* bas; **at ~** à la naissance; **during the ~** pendant l'accouchement; **to give ~ to** [*woman*] donner naissance à; [*animal*] mettre bas; **blind/deaf from** *or* **since ~** aveugle/sourd de naissance; **the village/country of one's ~** son village/pays natal → **childbirth, place, premature**

[b] (= *parentage*) naissance *f*, extraction *f*; **Scottish by ~** écossais de naissance; **of good ~** bien né, de bonne famille; **of humble ~** de basse extraction

[c] (*fig*) [*of movement, idea*] naissance *f*, éclosion *f*; [*of new era*] naissance *f*, commence-

ment *m*; [*of trend, project*] naissance *f*, lancement *m*; [*of phenomenon*] apparition *f*

[2] COMP ► **birth certificate** N (*original*) acte *m* de naissance; (*copy*) extrait *m* de naissance ► **birth control** N régulation *f or* contrôle *m* des naissances; ~ **control pill** = **birth pill** ► **birth defect** N défaut *m* de naissance ► **birth father** N père *m* biologique, géniteur *m* ► **birth mother** N mère *f* biologique, génitrice *f* ► **birth parents** NPL parents *mpl* biologiques, géniteurs *mpl* ► **birth pill** N pilule *f* contraceptive ► **birth rate** N (taux *m* de) natalité *f*

birthdate ['bɜːθdeɪt] N date *f* de naissance

▼ **birthday** ['bɜːθdeɪ] [1] N anniversaire *m*; **what did you get for your ~?** qu'est-ce que tu as eu pour ton anniversaire? → **happy** [2] COMP ► **birthday cake** N gâteau *m* d'anniversaire ► **birthday card** N carte *f* d'anniversaire ► **Birthday Honours** N (*Brit*) = **Honours List** ~ **honour**; → HONOURS LIST ► **birthday party** N **she is having a ~ party** elle a organisé une petite fête *or* une soirée pour son anniversaire ► **birthday present** N cadeau *m* d'anniversaire ► **birthday suit*** N (*hum*) **in one's ~ suit** en costume d'Adam (*or* d'Ève)*, dans le plus simple appareil (*hum*)

birthing ['bɜːθɪŋ] [1] ADJ [*equipment, room*] d'accouchement [2] COMP ► **birthing chair** N chaise *f* d'accouchement ► **birthing pool** N piscine *f or* bassin *m* d'accouchement ► **birthing stool** N tabouret *m* d'accouchement

birthmark ['bɜːθmɑːk] N tache *f* de vin

birthplace ['bɜːθpleɪs] N (*gen, Admin*) lieu *m* de naissance; (= *house*) maison *f* natale; **the ~ of civilization** le berceau de la civilisation

birthright ['bɜːθraɪt] N (*lit*) [*of firstborn*] droit *m* d'aînesse; (*fig*) **it is the ~ of every Englishman** c'est un droit que chaque Anglais a *or* acquiert à sa naissance

birthstone ['bɜːθstəʊn] N pierre *f* porte-bonheur

biryani [ˌbɪrɪˈɑːnɪ] N biriani *m*

biscuit ['bɪskɪt] [1] N [a] (*Brit*) petit gâteau *m* sec, biscuit *m*; **that takes the ~!*** ça c'est le bouquet!*; **he takes the ~!*** il décroche le pompon!* → **digestive, ship, water** [b] (*US*) biscuit *m* sec [2] ADJ (*also* **~-coloured**) (couleur) biscuit *m* inv, beige [3] COMP ► **biscuit barrel** N boîte *f* à biscuits ► **biscuit-firing** N (*Pottery*) dégourdi *m* ► **biscuit ware** N (*Pottery*) biscuit *m*

bisect [baɪˈsekt] [1] VT couper *or* diviser en deux; (*Math*) couper en deux parties égales [2] VI [*road etc*] bifurquer

bisection [baɪˈsekʃən] N (*Math*) division *f* en deux parties égales; [*of angle*] bissection *f*

bisector [baɪˈsektər] N (*Math*) bissectrice *f*

bisexual ['baɪˈseksjʊəl] ADJ [a] [*person*] bisexuel [b] (*Bio, Zool*) bisexué

bishop ['bɪʃəp] N [a] (*Rel*) évêque *m*; (*as term of address*) Monseigneur [b] (*Chess*) fou *m*

bishopric ['bɪʃəprɪk] N (= *diocese*) évêché *m*; (= *function*) épiscopat *m*

bismuth ['bɪzməθ] N bismuth *m*

bison ['baɪsn] N (*pl inv*) bison *m*

bisque [bɪsk] N (*Culin, Sport*) bisque *f*; (*Pottery*) biscuit *m*

bissextile [bɪˈsekstaɪl] [1] N année *f* bissextile [2] ADJ bissextile

bistable [baɪˈsteɪbl] ADJ (*Comput*) bistable

bistoury ['bɪstʊrɪ] N bistouri *m*

bistre ['bɪstər] ADJ, N bistre *m*

bistro ['biːstrəʊ] N petit restaurant *m* (*style bistrot*)

bit[1] [bɪt] N [a] [*of horse*] mors *m*; (*lit, fig*) **to get** *or* **take the ~ between one's teeth** prendre le mors aux dents → **champ**[1] [b] (= *tool*) mèche *f* → **brace, centre**

bit[2] [bɪt] [1] N [a] (= *piece*) [*of bread*] morceau *m*; [*of paper, string*] bout *m*; [*of book, talk etc*] passage *m*; (= *tiny amount*) peu *m*; **a ~ of garden** un bout de jardin, un tout petit jardin; **a tiny little ~** un tout petit peu; **there's a ~ of the soldier in him** il y a un peu du soldat en lui; **a ~ of advice** un petit conseil; **a ~ of news** une nouvelle; **a ~ of luck** une chance; **what a ~ of luck!*** quelle chance *or* veine!*; **in ~s and pieces** (= *broken*) en morceaux, en miettes; (= *dismantled*) en pièces détachées; (*fig*) (*plan, scheme*) en ruines; **bring all your ~s and pieces*** apporte toutes tes petites affaires; **~s and bobs** petites affaires *fpl*; **to come to ~s** (= *break*) s'en aller *or* tomber en morceaux; (= *dismantle*) se démonter; **he went to ~s*** il a craqué*; **~ by ~** (= *gradually*) petit à petit; (= *piecemeal*) par morceaux; **and a ~ over** et même un peu plus; **to do one's ~** fournir sa part d'effort; **he's got a ~ on the side†** il a une maîtresse; **for him, I was just a ~ on the side†** pour lui, je n'étais qu'une aventure

[b] (*phrases*) **a ~** un peu; **a ~ of money** un peu d'argent; **it is** *or* **that is a ~ much** (= *expensive*) c'est un peu exagéré!; (= *unfair*) c'est un peu fort*!; **a good ~** *or* **quite a ~ of money** pas mal d'argent; **he paid a good ~ for it** ça lui a coûté assez cher (*lit*); **I'm a ~/a little ~/a good ~ late** je suis un peu/un petit peu/très en retard; **it's a ~ good ~ further than we thought** c'est bien *or* beaucoup plus loin que nous ne pensions; **a good ~ bigger** bien *or* beaucoup plus grand; **every ~ as good as** tout aussi bon que; **every ~ of the wall** le mur tout entier; **he's every ~ a soldier** il est militaire jusqu'à la moelle; **I'm a ~ of a socialist** je suis un peu socialiste sur les bords*; **he seems to be a ~ of an expert** il a l'air de s'y connaître (pas mal); **she's a ~ of a liar** elle est un brin *or* un tantinet menteuse; **it was a ~ of a shock** ça (nous) a plutôt fait un choc; **that's a ~ of all right!** c'est super* *or* chouette!*; **he's/she's a ~ of all right!** (= *attractive*) il/elle est plutôt bien balancé(e)*; **that's a ~ thick!** ça c'est un peu fort *or* violent!*; **not a ~** pas du tout; **not a ~ of it!** pas du tout!, pas le moins du monde!; **it's not a ~ of use** cela ne sert strictement *or* absolument à rien; **he wasn't a ~ the wiser** *or* **the better for it** il n'en était pas plus avancé → **much**

[c] (*of time*) **after a ~** après un moment; **a good** *or* **quite a ~** un bon bout de temps*; **wait a ~** attendez un instant *or* un peu

[d] († = *coin*) pièce *f* → **threepenny, two**

[e] (*Comput*) bit *m*

[2] ADJ (*Theat*) **~ part** petit rôle *m*, panne* *f* (*Theat*)

[3] COMP ► **bit-map** (*Comput*) N [a] (*NonC* = *mode*) mode point *m* [b] (*also* **~-map(ped) image**) image *f* en mode point ◆ ADJ (*also* **~-mapped**) [*graphics*] en mode point, par points; **~-map font** N police *f* en mode point *or* par points ► **bit player*** N (*Theat, Cine, fig*) figurant(e) *m(f)*

bit[3] [bɪt] VB *pt of* **bite**

bitch [bɪtʃ] [1] N [a] (*dog*) chienne *f*; (*canines generally*) femelle *f*; (*fox*) renarde *f*; (*wolf*) louve *f*; **terrier ~** terrier *m* femelle [b] (†* *pej* = *woman*) garce* *f*; **she's a ~** elle est rosse*, c'est une garce*; **that ~ of a car** cette putain de bagnole*; **that ~ of a job** cette saloperie de boulot*; **it's a ~** c'est la merde*; **life's a ~ (and then you die)** chienne de vie* [c] (*esp US* = *complaint*) **what's your ~?** qu'est-ce que tu as à râler?* [2] VI (* = *complain*) rouspéter*, râler*; **to ~ about sb** dire du mal de qn

bitching† ['bɪtʃɪŋ] ADJ (*esp US*) du tonnerre*

bitchy* ['bɪtʃɪ] ADJ rosse*, vache*; **to be ~ to sb** être vache* avec qn; **he was ~ about it** il a été vache* (à ce sujet); **that was a ~ thing to do** c'était (un coup) vache*

bite [baɪt] (*vb: pret* **bit**, *ptp* **bitten**) [1] N [a] [*of dog etc*] morsure *f*; [*of snake, insect*] piqûre *f*;

face covered in (insect) ~s visage couvert de piqûres d'insectes → **bark²**, **fleabite**

[b] (= piece bitten off) bouchée f; (= something to eat) morceau m, quelque chose (à manger); **in two ~s** en deux bouchées; **chew each ~ carefully** mâchez bien chaque bouchée; **to take a ~ out of** (lit) [+ apple etc] manger une bouchée de; (esp US fig) [+ savings, budget] faire un trou dans; (fig) **to get a second** or **another ~ at the cherry** ◊ **to have two ~s at the cherry** avoir une seconde chance

[c] * **a ~ (to eat)** un casse-croûte; **I'll get a ~ on the train** je mangerai un morceau dans le train; **come and have a ~** venez manger un morceau

[d] (Fishing) touche f; **I haven't had a ~ all day** je n'ai pas eu une seule touche aujourd'hui; **got a ~?** ça a mordu?

[e] [of sauce etc] piquant m; (fig) **there's a ~ in the air** l'air est piquant; **his speech didn't have much ~** son discours manquait de mordant

[2] VT [person, animal] mordre; [snake, insect] piquer, mordre; **to ~ one's nails** se ronger les ongles; **to ~ sth in two** couper qch en deux d'un coup de dents; **to ~ one's lips/fingers** se mordre les lèvres/les doigts; (lit, fig) **to ~ one's tongue** se mordre la langue; (fig) **to ~ one's lip** tenir sa langue; (hum) **it won't ~ (you)!** ça ne mord pas!; (fig) **what's biting you?** qu'est-ce que tu as à râler?; **to ~ the bullet** serrer les dents (fig); (lit, fig) **to ~ the dust** mordre la poussière; (fig) **to ~ the hand that feeds one** cracher dans la soupe; (PROV) **once bitten twice shy** chat échaudé craint l'eau froide (PROV); **to be bitten with** the desire to do sth mourir d'envie de faire qch; **to get bitten** (= be cheated) se faire avoir, se faire rouler

[3] VI [dog] mordre; [fish] mordre (à l'hameçon); [insect] piquer; [cold, frost, wind] mordre, pincer; [cogs] s'engrener; [anchor, screw] mordre; **to ~ into sth** [person] mordre (dans) qch; [acid] mordre sur qch

[4] COMP ► **bite-size(d)** ADJ (lit) [piece of food] petit; [biscuit, chocolate bar] miniature; **~-size(d) cheeses** mini-fromages mpl; **~-size(d) chunks** petits morceaux mpl; **cut the food into ~-size(d) chunks** coupez la nourriture en petits morceaux; (fig) **~-size(d) chunks of information** informations fpl brèves de lecture aisée; **classical music in ~-size(d) chunks** des extraits de musique classique

► **bite back** [1] VI (= respond) réagir, rendre la pareille [2] VT SEP [+ words, retort] ravaler

► **bite off** VT SEP arracher d'un coup de dent(s); **she bit off a piece of apple** elle a mordu dans la pomme; (fig) **he has bitten off more than he can chew** il a eu les yeux plus grands que le ventre, il a visé trop haut; (fig) **to ~ sb's head off** rembarrer qn (brutalement)

► **bite on** VT FUS mordre

► **bite through** VT FUS [+ tongue, lip] mordre (de part en part); [+ string, thread] couper or casser avec les dents

biter ['baɪtə'] N **the ~ bit** tel est pris qui croyait prendre

biting ['baɪtɪŋ] ADJ [cold] âpre, mordant; [winter] dur, rude; [wind] piquant, cinglant; (fig) [style, wit, remarks] mordant, caustique; **~ irony** ironie f mordante or cinglante; **~ sarcasm** sarcasme m acerbe or mordant; **~ insects** insectes mpl piqueurs or voraces

bitingly ['baɪtɪŋlɪ] ADV [speak] d'un ton mordant or caustique

bitten ['bɪtn] VB ptp of **bite**

bitter ['bɪtə'] [1] ADJ [a] [taste] amer, âpre; (fig) **it was a ~ pill (to swallow)** la pilule était dure à avaler

[b] [cold, weather] glacial; [wind] cinglant; [winter] rude, rigoureux

[c] [person] amer; [critic, criticism] acerbe; [dis-

appointment, reproach, tears] amer; [fate, sorrow] pénible, cruel; [hatred] acharné, profond; [opposition, protest] violent; [remorse] cuisant; [sight, look] amer, plein d'amertume; [suffering] âpre, cruel; [tone] amer; (fig) **to the ~ end** jusqu'au bout; **his ~ enemy** son ennemi acharné; **he was always a ~ enemy of corruption** il a toujours été un adversaire acharné de la corruption; **I feel (very) ~ about the whole business** toute cette histoire me remplit d'amertume; **~ and twisted** aigri

[2] N [a] (Brit = beer) sorte de bière brune anglaise

[b] (Pharm) amer m

[3] **bitters** NPL (= drink) bitter m, amer m; **gin and ~s** cocktail m au gin et au bitter

[4] COMP ► **bitter aloes** NPL aloès m (médicinal) ► **bitter lemon** N Schweppes® m au citron ► **bitter orange** N orange f amère, bigarade f

bitterly ['bɪtəlɪ] ADV [regret, weep] amèrement; [say, think] avec amertume; [criticize, denounce, reproach] âprement; [oppose, contest, fight] farouchement; [ashamed] profondément; **~ disappointed** amèrement déçu; **~ jealous** atrocement jaloux; **to be ~ resentful of sb's success** en vouloir amèrement à qn de son succès; **opinions are ~ divided** les avis sont profondément partagés; **it's ~ cold** il fait un froid de canard; **on a ~ cold day** par une journée glaciale

bittern ['bɪtɜːn] N (Orn) butor m

bitterness ['bɪtənɪs] N (NonC: gen) amertume f; [of opposition etc] violence f

bittersweet ['bɪtəswiːt] [1] ADJ (lit, fig) aigredoux (-douce f) [2] N (Bot) douce-amère f; (fig) amère douceur f

bitty ['bɪtɪ] ADJ (Brit) décousu

bitumen ['bɪtjumən] N bitume m

bituminous [bɪ'tjuːmɪnəs] ADJ bitumineux

bivalent ['baɪ'veɪlənt] ADJ (Bio, Chem) bivalent

bivalve ['baɪvælv] ADJ, N bivalve m

bivouac ['bɪvʊæk] [1] N bivouac m [2] VI bivouaquer

bi-weekly ['baɪ'wiːklɪ] [1] ADJ (= twice in a week) bihebdomadaire; (US = fortnightly) bimensuel [2] ADV (= twice a week) deux fois par semaine; (US = fortnightly) tous les quinze jours

biz [bɪz] N (ABBR = **business**) → **show**

bizarre [bɪ'zɑː'] ADJ bizarre

bk [a] ABBR = **book** [b] ABBR = **bank**

BL [biː'el] [a] (ABBR = **British Library**) → **British** [b] (ABBR = **Bachelor of Law**) → **bachelor**

blab [blæb] [1] VI (= tell secret) manger le morceau; [b] (= chatter) jaser [2] VT (also ~ **out**) [+ secret] laisser échapper, aller raconter

blabber ['blæbə'] VI (also ~ **on**) = **blab 1a**

blabbermouth ['blæbə,maʊθ] N (pej) grande bouche f, grande gueule f

black [blæk] [1] ADJ [a] [hair, clouds, coffee etc] noir; **eyes as ~ as sloes** des yeux noirs comme (du) jais, des yeux de jais; (fig) ~ **and blue** couvert de bleus; **to beat sb ~ and blue** battre qn comme plâtre, rouer qn de coups; ~ **bread** pain m de seigle; ~ **gold** (= oil) l'or m noir; (on invitation) **"~ tie"** « smoking », « cravate noire » → **4**; → **belt, coal, jet², pitch¹, pot¹**

[b] [race, skin] noir; ~ **man** Noir m; ~ **woman** Noire f; **Black American** Noir(e) m(f) américain(e); ~ **art** art m nègre; (US Univ) ~ **college** université f noire; ~ **consciousness** conscience f de la négritude; **Black English** l'anglais m des Noirs américains; (US) **Black Nationalism** mouvement m nationaliste noir; **Black Studies** études fpl afro-américaines → **4**

[c] (= dark) obscur, noir; **it is as ~ as pitch** il fait noir comme dans un four

[d] (= dirty) noir, sale; **his hands were ~** il avait les mains noires; **he was as ~ as a sweep** il

était noir de la tête aux pieds

[e] (fig) (= wicked) [crime, action] noir; [thought] mauvais; (= gloomy) [thoughts, prospects] noir; [grief] intense, violent; [rage] noir; [despair] sombre; (= angry) furieux, menaçant; **he looked as ~ as thunder** il avait l'air furibond; **to look ~** avoir l'air hors de soi; **to give sb a ~ look** lancer un regard noir à qn; **I got some ~ looks from John** j'ai eu des regards noirs de la part de John, John m'a lancé des regards noirs; (fig) ~ **in the face** noir de fureur; **you can scream till you're ~ in the face but ...** tu peux toujours t'égosiller or t'époumoner mais ...; (liter) **a ~ deed** un crime, un forfait (liter); **he painted their conduct in the ~est colours** il a présenté leur conduite sous les couleurs les plus noires; **he's not as ~ as he's painted** il n'est pas aussi mauvais qu'on le dit; **things are looking ~** les choses se présentent très mal; **it's a ~ outlook** or **things are looking ~ for him** ses affaires se présentent très mal; **a ~ day on the roads** une sombre journée sur les routes; **it's a ~ day for England** c'est un jour (bien) triste pour l'Angleterre; (stronger) c'est un jour de deuil pour l'Angleterre; (Ind) ~ **goods** marchandises fpl boycottées; ~ **economy** économie f parallèle or souterraine

[2] N [a] (= colour) noir m, couleur f noire; (mourning) deuil m; (Roulette etc) noire m; **dressed in ~** habillé de noir; **to wear ~ for sb** porter le deuil de qn; **there it is in ~ and white** c'est écrit noir sur blanc; (Art) ~ **and white** dessin m en noir et blanc; (fig) **to swear that ~ is white** (obstinate person) se refuser à l'évidence, nier l'évidence; (liar) mentir effrontément; (Fin) **to be in the ~** être créditeur → **lampblack**

[b] (= person) Noir(e) m(f)

[c] (= darkness) ténèbres fpl, obscurité f; (outdoors only) nuit f noire

[3] VT [a] (= blacken) noircir; [+ shoes] cirer; **to ~ one's face** se noircir le visage; **to ~ sb's eye (for him)** pocher l'œil à qn

[b] (Brit Ind) [+ cargo, firm, goods] boycotter

[4] COMP ► **Black Africa** N l'Afrique f Noire ► **black art(s)** N(PL) magie f noire, sciences fpl occultes ► **black-ball** N vote m contre ◊ VT blackbouler ► **black bass** N achigan m ► **black beetle** N cafard m, cancrelat m ► **black books** NPL **she was in his ~ books** elle n'était pas dans ses petits papiers*, elle était mal vue (de lui) ► **black box** N (Aviat) boîte f noire or enregistreuse; (= mysterious device) boîte f noire ► **black cab** N (Brit) taxi m anglais ► **black cap** N (Orn) fauvette f à tête noire; (Brit Jur Hist) bonnet m noir (que mettait un juge avant de prononcer la peine de mort) ► **black comedy** N comédie f noire ► **Black Country** N Pays m noir (région industrielle des Midlands) ► **Black Death** N (Hist) peste f noire ► **black eye** N œil m poché or au beurre noir*; **to give sb a ~ eye** pocher l'œil à qn ► **Black Forest** N Forêt-Noire f ► **Black Forest gateau** N forêt-noire f ► **Black Friar** N frère m prêcheur, dominicain m ► **black frost** N gel m ► **black grouse** N tétras-lyre m, coq m de bruyère ► **black-headed gull** N mouette f rieuse ► **black-hearted** ADJ mauvais, malfaisant ► **black hole** N (Astron, also fig) trou m noir; (Brit Hist) **the Black Hole of Calcutta** le cachot de Calcutta ► **black humour** N humour m noir ► **black ice** N verglas m ► **black knight** N (Comm) chevalier m noir ► **black magic** N magie f noire ► **Black Maria** N (Brit) panier m à salade* ► **black mark** N (fig) **that gets a ~ mark** c'est zéro*; **that's a ~ mark for** or **against him** c'est un mauvais point pour lui ► **black market** N marché m noir; **on the ~ market** au marché noir ► **black marketeer** N profiteur m, -euse f (vendant au marché noir) ► **black mass** N messe f noire ► **Black Muslim** N Musulman(e) noir(e) m(f),

Black Muslim *mf* ► **black nightshade** N (*Bot*) morelle *f* noire ► **Black Panthers** NPL (*Hist*) Panthères *fpl* noires ► **Black Papers** NPL (*Brit Scol*) livres blancs sur le système éducatif ► **black pepper** N poivre *m* noir ► **Black Power (movement)** N Black Power *m*, pouvoir *m* noir ► **the Black Prince** N (*Brit Hist*) le Prince Noir ► **black pudding** N (*Brit*) boudin *m* noir ► **Black Rod** N (*Brit Parl*) membre de la Chambre des lords chargé de convoquer les Communes lors de l'ouverture de la session parlementaire ► **the Black Sea** N la mer Noire ► **Black September** N (*Pol*) Septembre *m* noir ► **black sheep** N **the ~ sheep of the family** la brebis galeuse (de la famille) ► **black spot** N (*also* **accident ~ spot**: *Brit*) point *m* noir ► **black-tie** ADJ [*dinner, function*] habillé, en smoking → **1a** ► **black velvet** N cocktail de champagne et de stout ► **Black Watch** N (*Brit Mil*) Black Watch *mpl* (*régiment écossais*) ► **black widow** N (*Zool*) veuve *f* noire

► **black out** N VI (= *faint*) s'évanouir [2] VT SEP [a] (*in wartime*) [+ *town, building*] faire le black-out dans ; (*in peacetime*) **a power cut ~ed out the building** une panne d'électricité a plongé l'immeuble dans l'obscurité (totale) ; (*Theat*) **to ~ out the stage** faire l'obscurité sur scène [b] (= *censor*) censurer [3] **~out** N → blackout

blackamoor†† ['blækəmuəʳ] N nègre† *m*

blackberry ['blækbərɪ] N mûre *f* ; **~ bush** mûrier *m*, ronce *f*

blackberrying ['blækbərɪɪŋ] N **to go ~** aller cueillir des mûres

blackbird ['blækbɜːd] N merle *m*

blackboard ['blækbɔːd] N tableau *m* (noir) ; **~ duster** chiffon *m* ; **the ~ jungle** la loi de la jungle (dans les classes) ; **~ rubber** frottoir *m*

blackcock ['blækkɒk] N (= *male black grouse*) tétras-lyre *m*, coq *m* de bruyère

blackcurrant [,blæk'kʌrənt] N (= *fruit, bush*) cassis *m*

blacken ['blækən] [1] VT [a] (*with dirt, soot, dust*) noircir, salir ; **his hands were ~ed with filth** il avait les mains noires de crasse [b] (*with paint, cosmetics etc*) noircir, barbouiller de noir [c] (*with smoke, by fire*) noircir ; **~ed remains** restes *mpl* calcinés [d] (*fig* = *discredit*) salir, noircir, ternir [2] VI [*sky*] noircir, s'assombrir ; [*furniture*] noircir, devenir noir

blackfly ['blækflaɪ] N puceron *m* noir

blackguard† ['blægɑːd] N canaille *f*, fripouille *f*

blackguardly† ['blægɑːdlɪ] ADJ [*deed, person*] infâme, ignoble

blackhead ['blækhed] N (*Med*) point *m* noir

blacking ['blækɪŋ] N [a] [*of shoes*] cirage *m* (noir) ; [*of stoves*] pâte *f* à noircir [b] [*of goods, cargo*] boycottage *m*

blackish ['blækɪʃ] ADJ tirant sur le noir, noirâtre (*pej*)

blackjack ['blækdʒæk] [1] N (= *flag*) pavillon *m* noir (*des pirates*) ; (= *drinking vessel*) pichet *m* ; (*Min*) blende *f* ; (*US* = *weapon*) matraque *f* ; (*Cards*) black-jack *m*, ≈ vingt-et-un *m* [2] VT (= *beat*) matraquer ; (= *coerce*) contraindre sous la menace (**sb into doing** qn à faire)

blacklead ['blækled] [1] N mine *f* de plomb, graphite *m* [2] VT [+ *stove*] frotter à la mine de plomb

blackleg ['blækleg] (*Brit Ind*) [1] N jaune *m*, briseur *m* de grève [2] VI briser la grève

blacklist ['blæklɪst] [1] N liste *f* noire [2] VT [+ *person*] mettre sur la liste noire ; [+ *book*] mettre à l'index (*lit, fig*)

blackmail ['blækmeɪl] [1] N chantage *m* ; **emotional ~** chantage *m* affectif [2] VT faire chanter, faire du chantage auprès de ; **to ~ sb into doing sth** forcer qn par le chantage à faire qch

blackmailer ['blækmeɪləʳ] N maître-chanteur *m*

blackness ['blæknɪs] N [*of colour, substance*] couleur *f or* teinte *f* noire, noir *m* ; [*of night*] obscurité *f*, ténèbres *fpl* ; [*of hands, face*] saleté *f*, crasse *f*

blackout ['blækaut] N [a] (= *amnesia*) trou *m* de mémoire ; (= *fainting*) étourdissement *m*, évanouissement *m* ; **to have a ~** avoir un étourdissement, s'évanouir [b] [*of lights*] panne *f* d'électricité ; (*during war*) black-out *m* ; (*Theat*) obscurcissement *m* de la scène → news

blackshirt ['blækʃɜːt] N (*Pol*) chemise *f* noire

blacksmith ['blæksmɪθ] N (*shoes horses*) maréchal-ferrant *m* ; (*forges iron*) forgeron *m*

blackthorn ['blækθɔːn] N (*Bot*) épine *f* noire, prunellier *m*

blacktop ['blæktɒp] N (*US*) bitume *m*

blackwater fever [,blækwɔːtəˈfiːvəʳ] N fièvre *f* bilieuse hémoglobinurique

bladder ['blædəʳ] [1] N (*Anat*) vessie *f* ; (*Bot*) vésicule *f* ; (*Ftbl etc*) vessie *f* (*de ballon*) → gall[1] [2] COMP ► **bladder kelp, bladder wrack** N fucus *m* vésiculeux

bladderwort ['blædəwɔːt] N utriculaire *f*

blade [bleɪd] [1] N [a] [*of knife, tool, weapon, razor*] lame *f* ; [*of chopper, guillotine*] couperet *m* ; [*of tongue*] dos *m* ; [*of oar*] plat *m*, pale *f* ; [*of spade*] fer *m* ; [*of turbine*] aube *f* ; [*of propeller*] pale *f*, aile *f* ; [*of windscreen wiper*] caoutchouc *m*, balai *m* ; [*of grass, maize*] brin *m* ; [*of cereal*] pousse *f* ; [*of leaf*] limbe *m* ; **wheat in the ~** blé *m* en herbe → shoulder [b] (*liter* = *sword*) lame *f* [c] († = *gallant*) gaillard *m* ; **a gay ~** un joyeux luron

-bladed ['bleɪdɪd] ADJ (*in compounds*) **two-bladed knife** canif *m* à deux lames

blaeberry ['bleɪbərɪ] N (*Brit*) myrtille *f*, airelle *f*

blag‡ [blæg] VT (*Brit*) [+ *ticket*] obtenir à esbroufe* (**out of** *or* **off sb** de qn) ; **he ~ged his way into the nightclub** il est entré dans la boîte de nuit à esbroufe*

blah* [blɑː] [1] N boniment *m*, blablabla* *m* ; **~, ~, ~** bla, bla, bla* ; (*US*) **the ~s** le cafard‡ [2] ADJ (*US*) barbant‡, peu attrayant

blamable ['bleɪməbl] ADJ blâmable

blame [bleɪm] [1] VT [a] (= *fix responsibility on*) **to ~ sb for sth** ◊ **to ~ sth on sb*** rejeter la responsabilité de qch sur qn, mettre qch sur le dos de qn* ; **I'm not to ~** ce n'est pas ma faute ; **you have only yourself to ~** ◊ **you have no one but yourself to ~** tu ne peux t'en prendre qu'à toi-même, tu l'auras cherché ; **who/what is to ~** *or* **whom/what are we to ~ for this accident?** à qui/à quoi attribuer cet accident ? → workman

[b] (= *censure*) condamner, blâmer ; **to ~ sb for doing** reprocher à qn de faire ; **to ~ sb for sth** reprocher qch à qn ; **to ~ o.s. for sth/for having done sth** se reprocher qch/d'avoir fait qch ; **he was greatly to ~ for doing that** il a eu grand tort de faire cela ; **you can't ~ him for wanting to leave** vous ne pouvez lui reprocher de vouloir s'en aller ; **he's leaving — you can't ~ him!** il part — on ne peut pas lui en vouloir *or* je le comprends !

[2] N [a] (= *responsibility*) faute *f*, responsabilité *f* ; **to put** *or* **lay** *or* **place** *or* **throw the ~ for sth on sb** rejeter la responsabilité de qch sur qn ; **to bear** *or* **take the ~ (for sth)** supporter la responsabilité (de qch)

[b] (= *censure*) blâme *m*, reproches *mpl* ; **without ~** exempt de blâme, irréprochable

blameless ['bleɪmlɪs] ADJ irréprochable

blamelessly ['bleɪmlɪslɪ] ADV [*behave, live*] de façon irréprochable

blameworthy ['bleɪmwɜːðɪ] ADJ [*action*] répréhensible ; [*person*] blâmable

blanch [blɑːntʃ] [1] VT (*gen, Agr, Culin*) blanchir ; **~ed almonds** amandes *fpl* (é)mondées *or* épluchées [2] VI [*person*] blêmir

blancmange [bləˈmɒnʒ] N (*esp Brit*) blancmanger *m*

bland [blænd] ADJ [*taste, food*] fade ; [*book, film*] fade, terne ; [*person, character*] terne, falot ; [*smile, expression*] terne

blandish ['blændɪʃ] VT flatter, cajoler

blandishment ['blændɪʃmənt] N (*gen pl*) flatterie(s) *f(pl)*

blandly ['blændlɪ] ADV [*say, reply*] platement ; [*smile*] mollement

blank [blæŋk] [1] ADJ [a] [*paper*] blanc (blanche *f*) ; [*page*] blanc (blanche *f*), vierge ; [*map*] muet ; [*cheque*] en blanc ; (*fig*) **to give sb a ~ cheque (to do)** donner à qn carte blanche (pour faire) ; **~ cartridge** cartouche *f* à blanc ; **~ space** blanc *m*, (espace *m*) vide *m* ; **~ form** formulaire *m*, imprimé *m* (à remplir) ; (*on form*) **please leave ~** laisser en blanc s.v.p.

[b] (= *unrelieved*) [*wall*] aveugle ; [*silence, darkness*] profond ; [*refusal, denial*] absolu, net ; (= *empty*) [*life etc*] dépourvu d'intérêt, vide ; (= *expressionless*) [*face*] sans expression ; [*look*] sans expression, vide ; (= *puzzled*) déconcerté, dérouté ; **to look ~** (= *expressionless*) être sans expression ; (= *puzzled*) avoir l'air interdit ; **a look of ~ astonishment** un regard ébahi ; **his mind went ~** il a eu un blanc

[c] (*Poetry*) **~ verse** vers *mpl* blancs *or* non rimés

[2] N [a] (= *void*) blanc *m*, (espace *m*) vide *m* ; (*fig* = *gap*) lacune *f*, trou *m* ; **she left several ~s in her answers** elle a laissé plusieurs de ses réponses en blanc ; **your departure has left a ~** votre départ a laissé un vide ; **my mind was a ~** j'avais la tête vide, j'ai eu un blanc

[b] (= *form*) formulaire *m* ; **telegraph ~** formule *f* de télégramme

[c] [*of target*] but *m* ; (*Dominoes*) blanc *m* ; [*of coin, medal, record*] flan *m* ; [*of key*] ébauche *f* ; (= *cartridge*) cartouche *f* à blanc ; (*fig*) **to draw a ~** (= *fail in search etc*) échouer, faire chou blanc ; (*mentally*) avoir un trou ; (*Dominoes*) **double ~** double blanc *m*

[3] VT* [+ *person*] snober

► **blank out** VT SEP [+ *feeling, thought*] faire abstraction de

blanket ['blæŋkɪt] [1] N couverture *f* ; [*of snow etc*] couche *f* ; [*of fog*] manteau *m*, nappe *f* ; [*of smoke*] nuage *m* ; **born on the wrong side of the ~**† illégitime, adultérin† → electric, wet [2] ADJ [*ban, condemnation*] général ; [*bombing*] intensif ; [*coverage*] complet (-ète *f*) [3] VT [a] [*snow*] recouvrir ; [*fog, smoke*] recouvrir, envelopper [b] [+ *sounds*] étouffer, assourdir [c] (*Naut*) déventer [4] COMP ► **blanket bath** N toilette *f* (*de malade alité*) ; **to give sb a ~ bath** faire la toilette de qn dans son lit ► **blanket cover** N **this insurance policy gives ~ cover** cette police d'assurances couvre tous les risques *or* est tous risques ► **blanket finish** N arrivée *f* très serrée *or* dans un mouchoir ► **blanket stitch** N point *m* de feston ► **blanket-stitch** VTI border au point de feston

► **blanket out** VT noyer

blankety-blank* ['blæŋkɪtɪ'blæŋk] ADJ (*euph*) = blinking 1

blankly ['blæŋklɪ] ADV [a] (= *expressionlessly*) **to look** *or* **stare ~ at sb/sth** fixer qn/qch le regard vide *or* d'un air absent [b] (= *uncomprehendingly*) [*look at, stare at, say*] d'un air ébahi

blankness ['blæŋknɪs] N (*NonC: in eyes, face*) air *m* mort, absence *f* d'expression ; [*of life*] vide *m*

blare [bleəʳ] [1] N (*gen*) vacarme *m* ; [*of hooter, car horn*] bruit *m* strident ; [*of radio, music*] beuglement *m* ; [*of trumpet*] sonnerie *f* [2] VI (*also* **~ out**) [*music, horn etc*] retentir ; [*loud voice*] trompeter, claironner; [*radio*] beugler ③ VT (*also ~ out*) [*+ music*] faire retentir

blarney* ['blɑːnɪ] ① N boniment* *m*, bobards* *mpl*; (*fig*) **he's kissed the Blarney stone** c'est un beau parleur ② VT [*+ person*] enjôler, embobeliner* ③ VI manier la flatterie

blasé ['blɑːzeɪ] ADJ blasé (**about** de)

blaspheme [blæs'fiːm] VTI blasphémer (**against** contre)

blasphemer [blæs'fiːmər] N blasphémateur *m*, -trice *f*

blasphemous ['blæsfɪməs] ADJ [*person*] blasphémateur (-trice *f*); [*words*] blasphématoire

blasphemously ['blæsfɪməslɪ] ADV de façon blasphématoire

blasphemy ['blæsfɪmɪ] N blasphème *m*; **to utter ~** blasphémer; **it is ~ to say that** c'est blasphémer que de dire cela

blast [blɑːst] ① N ⓐ (= *sound*) [*of bomb*] explosion *f*; [*of space rocket*] grondement *m*, rugissement *m*; [*of trumpets etc*] fanfare *f*, sonnerie *f*; [*of whistle, car horn*] coup *m* strident; **a ~ on the siren** un coup de sirène; **to blow a ~ on the bugle** donner un coup de clairon; **a radio on at full ~*** une radio à plein(s) tube(s)*; **the heating was on at full ~*** le chauffage était au maximum; **hearing those old records was a ~ from the past*** entendre ces vieux disques nous ramenait des années en arrière; **a letter from Paul! what a ~ from the past!*** une lettre de Paul! ça me ramène aux années en arrière! ⓑ (= *explosion*) explosion *f*; (= *shock wave*) [*of bomb etc*] souffle *m*; (= *gust*) [*of furnace*] souffle *m* (d'air chaud); [*of explosion*] victimes *fpl* de l'explosion; (*lit, fig*) **at full ~** à plein; **~ of air/steam** jet *m* d'air/de vapeur; **~ of wind** coup *m* de vent, rafale *f* ⓒ (*liter = wind*) → **icy** ⓓ (* = *fun*) fête *f*, foire *f*; **to have a ~** faire la foire; **it was a ~** ça a été le pied*; **to get a ~ out of sth** trouver qch marrant* ② VT ⓐ [*lightning*] [*+ tree*] foudroyer; (*with explosive*) [*+ rocks*] faire sauter; (= *blight*) [*+ plant*] détruire; (*fig*) [*+ reputation, hopes, future*] anéantir, briser; (*verbally*) attaquer à boulets rouges *or* violemment ⓑ (= *shoot*) **he ~ed the policeman with a shotgun** il a tiré sur le policier avec un fusil de chasse ⓒ (* = *criticize*) éreinter; **"it's a disgrace", he ~ed** c'est une honte », fulmina-t-il ⓓ (= *shoot out*) [*+ air, water*] souffler ③ EXCL (*Brit*) la barbe!*; **~ him!** il est embêtant *or* empoisonnant!* ④ COMP ► **blast effect** N effet *m* de souffle ► **blast furnace** N haut fourneau *m* ► **blast-off** N (*Space*) lancement *m*, mise *f* à feu

► **blast away** VI [*music, band*] brailler; [*gun*] retentir; **to ~ away with a rifle/shotgun** *etc* tirer continuellement avec un fusil/fusil de chasse *etc*

► **blast off** ① VI [*rocket etc*] être mis à feu; (*US fig*)* partir ② **~-off** N → **blast**

► **blast out** ① VI [*music, radio*] brailler ② VT SEP [*+ song, tune*] brailler

blasted ['blɑːstɪd] ADJ ⓐ [*heath*] désolé, desséché; [*tree*] foudroyé, frappé par la foudre; (*fig*) [*hopes*] anéanti ⓑ (* = *annoying*) fichu* (*before n*); **he's a ~ nuisance** c'est un enquiquineur*, il nous enquiquine*

blasting ['blɑːstɪŋ] N (*Tech*) minage *m*; **"~ in progress"** « attention, tir de mines »; **to give sb a ~ for sth/for having done sth** attaquer violemment qn pour qch/pour avoir fait qch

blastoderm ['blæstəʊdɜːm] N blastoderme *m*

blatancy ['bleɪtənsɪ] N (= *flagrance*) caractère *m* flagrant, évidence *f*; (= *showiness*) aspect *m* criard *or* voyant

blatant ['bleɪtənt] ADJ [*injustice, lie etc*] criant, flagrant; [*bully, social climber*] éhonté; [*coward,*

thief] fieffé; **a ~ liar** un menteur éhonté, un fieffé menteur

blatantly ['bleɪtntlɪ] ADV [*false, untrue, unfair*] manifestement; [*sexist, prejudiced*] ouvertement; [*disregard, encourage*] de façon éhontée; **it's ~ obvious that ...** il n'est que trop évident que ..., il se manifeste que ...

blather* ['blæðər] ① VI raconter *or* débiter des bêtises, parler à tort et à travers; (*Scot* = chat*) bavarder ② N ⓐ (*NonC*) bêtises *fpl*, blabla* *m*; (*Scot* = chat*) causette *f*; (*Scot*) **to have a ~*** bavarder, causer ⓑ (= *person*) **she's a ~*** elle dit n'importe quoi, elle dit tout ce qui lui passe par la tête

blatherskite‡ ['blæðəskaɪt] N (= *chatterbox*) moulin *m* à paroles; (*NonC: US = nonsense*) bêtises *fpl*

blaze¹ [bleɪz] ① N ⓐ (= *cheering fire*) (belle) flambée *f*; (= *conflagration*) incendie *m*; (= *light from fire*) lueur *f* des flammes *or* du brasier; **forest ~** incendie *m* de forêt; **all in a ~** en flammes ⓑ (= *shine*) [*of gems, beauty etc*] éclat *m*, splendeur *f*; **~ of day** éclat *m* du jour; **~ of light** torrent *m* de lumière; **~ of colour** flamboiement *m* de couleur(s); **in a ~ of glory** auréolé de gloire ⓒ (= *outburst*) [*of rage, passion etc*] explosion *f*, flambée *f*; **in a ~ of anger he killed her** dans le feu de la colère *or* dans une explosion de colère il l'a tuée ② **blazes‡** NPL **go to ~s!** va te faire voir!*; **what the ~s!** qu'est-ce que ça peut bien fiche!*; **how the ~s!** comment diable!; **what the ~s have you done now?** qu'est-ce que tu as encore fichu?*; **like ~s** comme un fou *or* dingue*, furieusement; **he ran like ~s** il a filé comme un zèbre; **he worked like ~s** il a travaillé comme une brute *or* un dingue* ③ VI ⓐ [*fire*] flamber; [*sun*] flamboyer, darder ses rayons ⓑ [*colour*] flamboyer; [*jewel, light*] resplendir, jeter un vif éclat; [*anger*] éclater; (*fig*) resplendir (**with** de); **a garden blazing with colour** un jardin resplendissant de couleurs

► **blaze abroad** VT SEP (*liter*) [*+ news etc*] crier sur tous les toits

► **blaze away** VI [*fire etc*] flamber (toujours); [*soldiers, guns*] maintenir un feu nourri (**at** contre)

► **blaze down** VI [*sun*] flamboyer, darder ses rayons

► **blaze forth** VI (*liter*) [*sun*] apparaître soudain (dans tout son éclat); [*anger*] éclater

► **blaze out** VI [*sun*] apparaître soudain; [*light*] ruisseler; [*anger, hatred*] éclater

► **blaze up** VI [*fire*] s'enflammer, s'embraser (*liter*); (*fig*) [*person*] éclater, s'emporter; [*anger*] éclater

blaze² [bleɪz] ① N ⓐ (= *mark*) [*of horse etc*] étoile *f*; [*of tree*] encoche *f* ② VT [*+ tree*] faire une encoche à; **to ~ a trail** (*lit*) frayer *or* le chemin; (*fig*) montrer la voie, faire un travail de pionnier

blazer ['bleɪzər] N blazer *m*

blazing ['bleɪzɪŋ] ADJ ⓐ [*building etc*] en feu, en flammes; [*torch*] enflammé; [*sun*] éclatant, ardent; (*fig*) [*eyes*] flamboyant, qui jette des éclairs; [*jewel*] étincelant; [*colour*] très vif ⓑ (*: *also ~ angry*) furibond, furibard*

blazon ['bleɪzn] ① N (*Her*) blason *m* ② VT (*Her*) blasonner; (*fig: also ~ abroad, ~ forth*) [*+ virtues, story*] proclamer, claironner

bldg ABBR = **building**

bleach [bliːtʃ] ① N décolorant *m*; (= *liquid*) eau *f* décolorante; (**household**) ~ eau *f* de Javel ② VT ⓐ [*sun, bleach bones, hair etc*] blanchir; **~ing agent** produit *m* à blanchir, décolorant *m* ⓑ [*+ hair*] décolorer, oxygéner; **~ing powder** (chlorure *m*) décolorant *m* ⓑ [*+ hair*] décolorer, oxygéner; **to ~ one's hair** se décolorer *or* s'oxygéner les cheveux; **~ed hair** cheveux *mpl* décolorés *or* oxygénés ⓒ (*Phot*) [*+ image*] blanchir ③ VI

blanchir

► **bleach out** VT SEP [*+ colour*] enlever

bleachers ['bliːtʃəz] N (*US*) gradins *mpl* (*de stade en plein soleil*)

bleak¹ [bliːk] N (= *fish*) ablette *f*

bleak² [bliːk] ADJ [*country, landscape*] morne, désolé; [*room*] nu, austère; [*weather, wind*] froid, glacial; (*fig*) [*existence*] sombre, désolé; [*prospect*] triste, morne; [*smile*] pâle; [*voice, tone*] monocorde, morne; **it looks** *or* **things look rather ~ for him** les choses se présentent plutôt mal pour lui

bleakly ['bliːklɪ] ADV [*look*] d'un air désolé, sombrement; [*speak*] d'un ton morne, sombrement

bleakness ['bliːknɪs] N [*of landscape*] aspect *m* morne *or* désolé; [*of room, furnishings*] austérité *f*; [*of weather*] froid *m*, rigueurs *fpl*; [*of prospects, future*] aspect *m* sombre *or* décourageant

blearily ['blɪərɪlɪ] ADV [*look*] avec un regard trouble

bleary ['blɪərɪ] ADJ ⓐ [*eyes*] (*from sleep, fatigue*) trouble, voilé; (*from illness*) chassieux; (*from tears, wind etc*) larmoyant; **~-eyed** aux yeux troubles (*or* chassieux *or* larmoyants) ⓑ [*outline*] indécis, vague

bleat [bliːt] ① VI ⓐ [*sheep*] bêler; [*goat*] bêler, chevroter ⓑ [*person, voice*] bêler, chevroter; (* = *talk nonsense*) débiter des idioties, débloquer‡; (‡ = *complain*) se plaindre (**about** de); **what are you ~ing about?‡** qu'est-ce que tu as à te lamenter? ② VT (*also ~ out*) dire d'une voix bêlante, chevroter ③ N [*of sheep*] bêlement *m*; [*of voice, goat*] bêlement *m*, chevrotement *m*

bleb [bleb] N [*of skin*] cloque *f*, ampoule *f*; [*of glass, water*] bulle *f*

bled [bled] VB *pt, ptp of* **bleed**

bleed [bliːd] ① VI ⓐ saigner, perdre du sang; **his nose is ~ing** il saigne du nez; **the wound bled profusely** la plaie saignait copieusement; (*liter*) **his heart is ~ing** son cœur saigne; (*gen iro*) **my heart ~s for you** tu me fends le cœur (*iro*), tu vas me faire pleurer (*iro*) → **death** ⓑ [*plant*] pleurer, perdre sa sève ② VT (*Med*) [*+ person*] saigner, faire une saignée à; [*+ brakes, radiator*] purger ⓑ (* *fig = get money from*) tirer de l'argent à, faire casquer‡; **to ~ sb dry** *or* **white** saigner qn à blanc ③ N saignement *m* → **nosebleed**

bleeder ['bliːdər] N ⓐ (*Med* = haemophiliac*) hémophile *mf* ⓑ (*Brit‡*) gars* *m*; **poor ~!** le pauvre gars!*; **lucky ~!** veinard!*

bleeding ['bliːdɪŋ] ① N ⓐ (= *taking blood from*) saignée *f*; (= *losing blood*) saignement *m*; (*more serious*) hémorragie *f*; **~ from the nose** saignement *m* de nez; **to stop the ~** arrêter l'hémorragie ⓑ [*of plant*] écoulement *m* de sève ② ADJ ⓐ [*wound*] saignant; [*person*] qui saigne, ensanglanté; (*pej*) **~ heart** (= *person*) âme *f* sensible; (*fig, pej*) **~-heart Liberal** libéral(e) *m(f)* au grand cœur ⓑ (*Brit‡* = *bloody*) maudit (*before n*); **that ~ car** cette maudite voiture ③ ADV (*Brit‡* = *bloody*) vachement‡, fichtrement‡

bleep [bliːp] ① N ⓐ (*Rad, TV* = *noise*) top *m* ⓑ (* = *pager*) bip *m* ② VI [*transmitter*] émettre des signaux ③ VT (*: *in hospital etc*) biper

bleeper ['bliːpər] N (= *pager*) bip *m*

blemish ['blemɪʃ] ① N (= *defect*) défaut *m*, imperfection *f*; (*on fruit*) tache *f*; (*fig*) (*moral*) souillure *f* (*liter*), tare *f*; (*inborn*) défaut *m*; **there's a ~ in this cup** cette tasse a un défaut; (*fig*) **to find a ~ in sth** trouver à redire à qch; **a ~ on his reputation** une tache *or* une souillure (*liter*) à sa réputation; **without (a) ~** (*lit*) sans imperfection, (*fig*) sans tache, sans souillure (*liter*) ② VT [*+ beauty etc*] gâter; [*+ reputation, honour*] ternir, flétrir

blemished ['blemɪʃt] ADJ [*+ fruit*] talé, meurtri, abîmé; [*+ skin*] abîmé

blench [blentʃ] VI [a] (= *flinch*) sursauter; **without ~ing** sans sourciller, sans broncher [b] (= *turn pale*) pâlir or blêmir (de peur)

blend [blend] [1] N (= *mixture*) [*of tea, whisky, wine etc*] mélange m; [*of colours, styles*] mariage m; [*of cultures*] fusion f; [*of qualities*] ensemble m; **an excellent ~ of tea** un excellent mélange de thés, un excellent thé; (= *coffee*) **Brazilian ~** café m du Brésil; **"our own ~"** «mélange (spécial de la) maison»
[2] VT (*also ~ in*) mélanger, mêler (**with** à, avec), faire un mélange (**sth with sth** de qch avec qch); [+ *teas, coffees etc*] mélanger, faire un mélange; [+ *wines*] couper, mélanger; [+ *qualities*] joindre, unir (**with** à); [+ *ideas*] fusionner; [+ *colours, styles*] fondre, mêler
[3] VI (*also ~ in, ~ together*) se mêler, se mélanger (**with** à, avec), former un mélange (**with** avec), se confondre (**into** en); [*voices, perfumes*] se confondre, se mêler; [*styles*] se marier, s'allier; [*ideas, political parties, races*] fusionner; [*colours*] (= *shade into one another*) se fondre; (= *go well together*) aller bien ensemble; **the colours ~ (in) well** les couleurs vont bien ensemble

blended ['blendɪd] ADJ **a ~ tea/wine** un mélange de thés/vins; **~ whisky** du whisky blended or de mélange

blender ['blendər] N (= *machine*) (Tech) malaxeur m; (Culin) mixer m

blenny ['blenɪ] N (= *fish*) blennie f

bless [bles] (*pret, ptp* **blest** or **blessed** [blest]) VT [*God, priest, person, fate*] bénir; **God ~ the king!** Dieu bénisse le roi!; **to be ~ed with** avoir la chance de posséder, être doté de; **God did not ~ them with ...** Dieu ne leur accorda pas le bonheur d'avoir ...; **Nature ~ed him with ...** la Nature l'a doué de ...; **I was never ~ed with children** je n'ai jamais connu le bonheur d'avoir des enfants; (*iro*) **she'll ~ you for this!** elle va te bénir!*; **~ you!** mille fois merci!, tu es un ange!; (*sneezing*) à vos souhaits!; **and Paul, ~ him** or **~ his heart, had no idea that ...** et ce brave Paul (dans son innocence) ne savait pas que ...; **~ his little heart!** qu'il est mignon!; **~ my soul!**† mon Dieu!, Seigneur!†; **well, I'm ~ed!*** par exemple!, ça alors!*; **I'm** or **I'll be ~ed if I remember!*** c'est bien le diable* si je m'en souviens!

blessed ['blesɪd] [1] ADJ **a** (Rel) (= *holy*) béni, saint; (= *beatified*) bienheureux; **Blessed Virgin** Sainte Vierge f; **Blessed Sacrament** Saint Sacrement m; **~ be God!** (que) Dieu soit béni!; **the Blessed John of ...** le bienheureux Jean de ...; **the Blessed Elizabeth the Good** la bienheureuse Élisabeth la Bonne [b] (Rel, liter = *happy*) bienheureux, heureux; **~ are the pure in heart** bienheureux or heureux ceux qui ont le cœur pur; **of ~ memory** d'heureuse mémoire [c] (*liter = giving joy*) [*thing*] béni; [*person*] cher [d] (* *Brit**: *for emphasis*) sacré* (*before* n), satané (*before* n); **that child is a ~ nuisance!** cet enfant, quelle peste or quel poison!; **the whole ~ day** toute la sainte journée; **every ~ evening** tous les soirs que le bon Dieu fait* [2] **the Blessed** NPL les bienheureux mpl

blessedly ['blesɪdlɪ] ADV (*liter*) [*cool, quiet*] merveilleusement; [*brief*] fort heureusement

blessedness ['blesɪdnɪs] N (Rel) béatitude f; (= *happiness*) bonheur m, félicité f

blessing ['blesɪŋ] N [a] (= *divine favour*) grâce f, faveur f; (= *prayer*) bénédiction f; (*at meal*) bénédicité m; (= *approval*) bénédiction f; **with God's ~ we shall succeed** nous réussirons par la grâce de Dieu; **the priest pronounced the ~** le prêtre a donné la bénédiction; (*at meal*) **to ask a** or **the ~** dire le bénédicité; (*fig*) **the plan had his ~*** il avait donné sa bénédiction à ce projet* [b] (= *benefit*) bien m, bienfait m; **the ~s of civilization** les bienfaits de la civilisation; **what a ~ that the weather was fine!**

quelle chance qu'il ait fait beau!, heureusement qu'il a fait beau!; **this rain has been a real ~*** cette pluie a été une vraie bénédiction*; **it was a ~ in disguise** à quelque chose malheur est bon (PROV) → **count**[1]

blest [blest] (*liter*) [1] VB *pt, ptp* of **bless** [2] ADJ heureux

blether ['bleðər] = **blather**

blew [blu:] VB *pt* of **blow**[1]

blight [blaɪt] [1] N [*of cereals*] rouille f, charbon m; [*of potato*] mildiou m; [*of rose*] rouille f; [*of fruit trees*] cloque f; **this marriage was a ~ on his happiness** ce mariage a terni son bonheur; **she's been a ~ on his life** elle a gâché son existence; **what a ~ that woman is!*** cette femme est un vrai fléau or une véritable plaie!*; **urban ~** dégradation f urbaine [2] VT [*disease*] [+ *plants*] rouiller; [+ *wind*] saccager; (*fig*) [+ *hopes*] anéantir, détruire; [+ *career, life*] gâcher, briser; [+ *future*] gâcher

blighter†* ['blaɪtər] N (Brit) type* m, bonne femme f; **a funny ~** un drôle de numéro*; **silly ~** imbécile mf; **lucky ~!** quel(le) veinard(e)*!; **you ~!** espèce de chameau!*

Blighty†* ['blaɪtɪ] N (Brit Mil) l'Angleterre f

blimey* ['blaɪmɪ] EXCL (Brit) mince alors!*, merde alors!*

blimp [blɪmp] N [a] (Brit) **a (Colonel) Blimp*** une (vieille) culotte de peau (*pej*) [b] (*esp US Aviat*) petit dirigeable m de reconnaissance

blind [blaɪnd] [1] ADJ [a] (= *unable to see*) [*person*] aveugle; **a ~ man** un aveugle; **a ~ boy** un garçon aveugle; **to go ~** perdre la vue, devenir aveugle; **the accident left him ~** cet accident l'a rendu aveugle, il a perdu la vue dans cet accident; **~ in one eye** borgne; **in the left eye** aveugle de l'œil gauche; **~ from birth** aveugle de naissance; **(as) ~ as a bat** myope comme une taupe; **to be struck ~** être frappé de cécité; (*fig*) **to be ~ with rage/tears** être aveuglé par la rage/par les larmes ■ (PROV) **there's none so ~ as them that won't see** il n'est pire aveugle que celui qui ne veut pas voir
[b] (*fig = unwilling to see*) [*person*] aveugle; **love is ~** l'amour est aveugle; **to be ~ to sb's faults** ne pas voir les défauts de qn; **to be ~ to the consequences of one's actions** ne pas se rendre compte des conséquences de ses actes; **I am not ~ to that consideration** cela ne m'échappe pas; **to turn a ~ eye (to sth)** fermer les yeux (sur qch) → **colour**
[c] (= *unthinking*) [*panic, obedience*] aveugle; **~ faith (in sth)** foi f aveugle (en qch)
[d] (*Aut, Aviat = without visibility*) [*flying, landing, corner, turning*] sans visibilité; **on sb's ~ side** hors du champ visuel de qn
[e] (= *without openings*) [*building, wall, window*] aveugle
[f] (*: *for emphasis*) **she never takes a ~ bit of notice (of sb/sth)** elle n'écoute jamais (qn/qch); **it won't make a ~ bit of difference** ça ne changera strictement rien; **it's not a ~ bit of use** ça ne sert strictement à rien
[2] VT aveugler, rendre aveugle; [*sun, light*] aveugler, éblouir; (*fig*) aveugler, empêcher de voir; **the war ~ed** les aveugles mpl de guerre; **her love ~ed her to his faults** son amour l'aveuglait au point qu'elle ne voyait pas ses défauts → **science**
[3] N [a] [*of window*] store m; **to lower/raise the ~s** baisser/lever les stores → **Venetian** [b] (= *pretence*) paravent m; **this action is only a ~** cette action n'est qu'un paravent [c] **to go on a ~*** (aller) se soûler la gueule* [d] (*Hunting*) affût m
[4] **the blind** NPL les aveugles mpl; (*fig*) **it's the ~ leading the ~** c'est un aveugle qui conduit un aveugle
[5] ADV [a] (*Aut, Aviat*) **to drive/fly ~** conduire/voler sans visibilité

[b] (*Culin*) **to bake sth ~** cuire qch à blanc
[c] (= *categorically*) **to swear ~ that ...*** jurer ses grands dieux que ...
[d] (*Brit*) **~ drunk*** complètement bourré*
[6] COMP ► **blind alley** N (*lit, fig*) impasse f ► **blind corner** N virage m sans visibilité ► **blind date** N (= *meeting*) rendez-vous m arrangé (*avec quelqu'un qu'on ne connaît pas*); (= *person*) inconnu(e) m(f) (*avec qui on a rendez-vous*); **on a ~ date** lors d'un rendez-vous arrangé; **to go on a ~ date** sortir avec qn qu'on ne connaît pas; **to go on a ~ date with sb** aller à un rendez-vous arrangé avec qn ► **blind man's buff** N colin-maillard m ► **blind spot** N (*Anat*) tache f aveugle; (*in road*) section f sans visibilité; (*in car, plane*) angle m mort; (*fig*) **to have a ~ spot about sth** ne rien comprendre à qch; **computers are a ~ spot with me** je ne comprends rien aux ordinateurs; **he has a ~ spot where she's concerned** il ne voit pas ses défauts ► **blind-stitch** N point m perdu ♦ VI coudre à points perdus ► **blind test** N (*Marketing*) test m (en) aveugle

blinder ['blaɪndər] N [a] (US) œillère f [b] (*Brit*) **to play a ~*** jouer merveilleusement bien

blindfold ['blaɪndfəʊld] [1] VT bander les yeux à or de [2] N bandeau m [3] ADJ (*also ~ed*) aux yeux bandés [4] ADV (*also ~ed*) les yeux bandés; **(it's so easy) I could do it ~** (c'est si facile que) je le ferais les yeux bandés

blinding ['blaɪndɪŋ] ADJ [*light*] aveuglant; [*pain*] fulgurant

blindingly ['blaɪndɪŋlɪ] ADV **it is ~ obvious** c'est d'une évidence flagrante, ça saute aux yeux

blindly ['blaɪndlɪ] ADV [a] (= *unseeingly*) [*grope, stumble, shoot*] à l'aveuglette; **she stared ~ at the wall** elle fixait le mur comme si elle ne le voyait pas [b] (= *unquestioningly*) [*follow, accept, obey*] aveuglément; **a ~ obedient follower** un disciple inconditionnel

blindness ['blaɪndnɪs] N cécité f; (*fig*) aveuglement m (**to** devant); **~ to the truth** refus m de voir la vérité → **colour**

blindworm ['blaɪndwɜ:m] N orvet m

blini(s) ['blɪnɪ(z)] NPL blinis mpl

blink [blɪŋk] [1] N [*of eyes*] clignotement m (des yeux), battement m des paupières; [*of sun*] (*petit*) rayon m; [*of hope*] lueur f; (= *glimpse*) coup m d'œil; (*fig*) **in the ~ of an eye** en un clin d'œil; **my telly's on the ~*** ma télé est détraquée [2] VI [a] cligner des yeux; (*half-close*) plisser les yeux [b] [*light*] vaciller [3] VT **to ~ one's eyes** cligner des yeux; **to ~ back the tears** refouler les larmes (d'un battement de paupières)

blinker ['blɪŋkər] N [a] (*Brit*) **~s** œillères fpl; (*Aut*) feux mpl de détresse, clignotants mpl; (*fig*) **to wear ~s** avoir des œillères [b] (*also ~ light*) (*feu m*) clignotant m

blinkered ['blɪŋkəd] ADJ (*Brit*) [a] (*pej = narrowminded*) [*person, approach, attitude*] borné; [*view*] étroit; **to be ~** [*person*] avoir des œillères; **to be ~ to sth** ◊ **to have a ~ view of sth** or **approach to sth** voir qch avec des œillères [b] [*horse*] qui porte des œillères

blinking ['blɪŋkɪŋ] ADJ (*Brit**) sacré* (*before* n); **~ idiot** espèce f d'idiot [2] N [*of eyes*] clignement m (d'yeux); [*of light*] vacillement m

blintz(e) [blɪnts] N (*US Culin*) sorte de crêpe fourrée

blip [blɪp] N [a] (*on radar etc*) spot m; (= *beep*) bip m [b] (*on graph*) petite déviation f; (*fig* = *aberration*) petite anomalie f (*passagère*)

bliss [blɪs] N [a] (Rel) béatitude f; (*gen*) félicité f, bonheur m suprême or absolu [b] (* *fig*) **what ~ to collapse into a chair!** quelle volupté de se laisser tomber dans un fauteuil!; **the concert was ~** le concert était divin; **it's ~!** c'est merveilleux!, c'est divin!

► **bliss out**: VT SEP (*esp US*) **to be ~ed out** être au septième ciel

blissful ['blɪsfʊl] ADJ (*Rel, gen*) bienheureux ; (* = *wonderful*) divin, merveilleux

blissfully ['blɪsfʊlɪ] ADV [*smile*] d'un air béat ; [*happy, quiet, ignorant, unaware*] parfaitement

blister ['blɪstə^r] **1** N (*on skin*) ampoule *f*, cloque *f* ; (*on paintwork*) cloque *f* ; (*in glass*) bulle *f* **2** VI [*skin*] se couvrir de cloques ; [*paintwork*] cloquer ; [*metal, glass*] former des soufflures **3** VT [+ *paint*] faire cloquer **4** COMP ► **blister pack** N (*for pills etc*) plaquette *f* ; (*for pens, plugs etc*) blister *m* ► **blister-packed** ADJ [*pills etc*] en plaquette ; [*pens, plugs etc*] sous blister

blistered ['blɪstəd] ADJ [*skin, feet, hands*] couvert d'ampoules ; [*paintwork*] cloqué

blistering ['blɪstərɪŋ] **1** N [*of skin*] formation *f* d'ampoules ; [*of paint*] boursouflage *m* **2** ADJ **a** (= *scorching*) [*heat*] torride ; [*day*] torride, de canicule ; [*sun*] brûlant ; **a ~ pace** *or* **speed** une vitesse foudroyante **b** (= *scathing*) [*attack, criticism, speech*] cinglant

blithe [blaɪð] ADJ (*liter*) joyeux, allègre

blithely ['blaɪðlɪ] ADV allègrement

blithering* ['blɪðərɪŋ] ADJ ► **idiot** crétin fini* ; **you ~ idiot!** espèce d'idiot !

blithesome ['blaɪðsəm] ADJ = **blithe**

BLitt [biː'lɪt] ABBR = **Bachelor of Literature**

blitz [blɪts] **1** N (*Mil*) attaque *f* éclair *inv* ; (*Aviat*) bombardement *m* (aérien) ; (*Brit Hist*) **the Blitz** le Blitz ; (*fig*) **to have a ~ on sth*** s'attaquer à qch **2** VT **a** (*Mil*) bombarder ; **~ed houses** maisons *fpl* bombardées **b** (* *fig* = *go to work on*) s'attaquer à

blitzed: [blɪtst] ADJ (* = *drunk*) bourré*

blitzkrieg ['blɪtskriːg] N **a** (*Mil Hist*) guerre *f* éclair **b** (* *fig* = *attack*) attaque *f* éclair ; **an advertising ~** une intense campagne publicitaire

blizzard ['blɪzəd] N tempête *f* de neige ; (*in Arctic*) blizzard *m* ; (*fig*) avalanche *f*

bloated ['bləʊtɪd] ADJ **a** (= *swollen*) [*stomach, body, corpse*] gonflé ; [*face*] bouffi **b** (*after eating*) **to feel ~** se sentir ballonné **c** (= *overlarge*) [*bureaucracy*] hypertrophié ; [*budget, ego*] démesuré **d** (= *self-important: also* ~ **with pride**) [*person*] gonflé d'orgueil

bloater ['bləʊtə^r] N hareng *m* saur *or* fumé

blob [blɒb] N (= *drop: gen*) (grosse) goutte *f* ; [*of ink*] pâté *m*, tache *f* ; (= *stain*) tache *f*

bloc [blɒk] N **a** (*Pol*) bloc *m* **b** **en ~** en bloc, en gros

block [blɒk] **1** N **a** [*of stone*] bloc *m* ; [*of wood*] bille *f* ; [*of blacksmith, butcher, executioner*] billot *m* ; [*of chocolate*] tablette *f* ; **~s** (= *toy*) cubes *mpl*, jeu *m* de construction ; **a ~ of ice cream** un litre (*or* demi-litre *etc*) de glace ; **butcher's ~** billot *m* de boucher ; (*US*) **on the ~** [*buy*] aux enchères ; [*pay*] rubis sur l'ongle ; **to die on the ~** périr sur le billot *or* l'échafaud → **chip** **b** [*of buildings*] pâté *m* (de maisons) ; (*Brit*) **a ~ of flats** un immeuble ; **to take a stroll round the ~** faire le tour du pâté de maisons, faire un tour dans le coin ; (*US*) **she lived three ~s away** elle habitait trois rues plus loin **c** (= *part of prison, hospital etc*) quartier *m*, pavillon *m* ; (= *of factory etc*) bâtiment *m* **d** (= *obstruction*) [*of traffic*] embouteillage *m* ; [*of pipe*] obstruction *f* ; (*Med, Psych*) blocage *m* ; (*fig*) **I've got a (mental) ~ about that whole period** j'ai un trou (de mémoire), je n'ai aucun souvenir de cette période ; (*fig: frightened etc*) **I couldn't do it — I had a mental ~ about it** je n'ai pas pu le faire, c'est plus fort que moi ; **he's/I've got a ~** [*writer*] c'est le vide *or* blocage total → **roadblock** **e** [*of tickets*] série *f* ; [*of shares*] tranche *f* ; [*of seats*] groupe *m*

f (*Brit Typ*) cliché *m* (*plaque*) **g** (*also* ~ **and tackle**) palan *m*, moufles *mpl* **h** (* = *head*) caboche* *f*, ciboulot: *m* → **knock off** **i** (*Brit* = *writing pad*) bloc-notes *m* ; (*also* **artist's ~**) bloc *m* à dessein **j** (*Comput*) sélection *f* **k** (*Fin*) [*of shares*] paquet *m* ; (*larger*) bloc *m* **l** (*also* **starting ~**) **to be first/fast off the (starting) ~s** être le premier à/ne pas attendre pour se lancer

2 VT **a** [+ *pipe etc*] boucher, bloquer ; [+ *road*] bloquer, barrer ; [+ *harbour, wheel*] bloquer ; [+ *progress, traffic*] entraver, gêner ; (*Ftbl*) [+ *opponent*] gêner ; [+ *transaction, credit, negotiations*] bloquer ; (*Med*) [+ *pain*] anesthésier, neutraliser ; **the leaves ~ed the drain** les feuilles mortes ont bouché *or* bloqué le puisard ; **to ~ sb's way** barrer le chemin à qn ; (*Ftbl etc*) **to ~ the ball** bloquer (la balle) **b** [+ *title, design*] graver au fer **c** (*Comput*) sélectionner **3** VI [*wheel*] (se) bloquer **4** COMP ► **block association** N association *f* de copropriétaires (*d'un immeuble*) ► **block booking** N réservation *f* groupée *or* en bloc ► **block capitals** NPL = **block letters** ► **block diagram** N (*Comput, Geog*) bloc-diagramme *m* ; (*Elec*) schéma *m* (de principe) ► **block grant** N (*Brit Admin*) dotation *f* *or* enveloppe *f* gouvernementale (*accordée aux autorités locales*) ► **block letters** NPL majuscules *fpl*, capitales *fpl* ; **in ~ letters** en majuscules ► **block release** N (*Brit Educ*) système *m* de stages de formation alternant avec l'activité professionnelle ► **block system** N (*Rail*) bloc-système *m*, bloc *m* automatique à signaux lumineux ► **block vote** N (*Pol, Ind*) vote *m* groupé ► **block voting** N (*Pol, Ind*) (pratique *f* du) vote *m* groupé

► **block in** VT SEP (= *sketch out*) esquisser

► **block off** VT SEP [+ *part of road etc*] interdire, condamner ; (*accidentally*) obstruer

► **block out** VT SEP **a** (= *obscure*) [+ *view*] boucher ; [+ *light*] empêcher de passer **b** (*from mind*) [+ *thoughts, idea*] refouler, repousser **c** (= *sketch*) [+ *scheme, design*] ébaucher

► **block up** VT SEP [+ *gangway*] encombrer ; [+ *pipe etc*] bloquer, boucher ; [+ *window, entrance*] murer, condamner ; [+ *hole*] boucher, bloquer ; (*Comput*) [+ *text*] sélectionner

blockade [blɒ'keɪd] **1** N (*Mil*) blocus *m* ; (*fig*) barrage *m* ; **under** = en état de blocus ; **to break/raise the ~** forcer/lever le blocus ; **to run a ~** forcer un blocus **2** VT **a** (*Mil*) [+ *town, port*] bloquer, faire le blocus de ; (*fig*) bloquer, obstruer **b** (*US*) [+ *traffic*] bloquer ; [+ *street*] encombrer **3** COMP ► **blockade runner** N briseur de blocus

blockage ['blɒkɪdʒ] N (*gen*) obstruction *f* ; (*Med*) obstruction *f*, blocage *m* ; (*intestinal*) occlusion *f* ; (*mental*) blocage *m* ; (*fig*) bouchon *m*

blockbuster* ['blɒk,bʌstə^r] N (= *bomb*) bombe *f* de gros calibre ; (= *film*) film *m* à grand succès ; (= *book*) best-seller *m* ; (= *argument*) argument *m* massue ; **he's a real ~** il est d'une efficacité à tout casser*

blockhead* ['blɒkhed] N (*pej*) imbécile *mf*, crétin(e)* *m(f)*

blockhouse ['blɒkhaʊs] N (*Mil*) casemate *f*, blockhaus *m*

bloke* [bləʊk] N (*Brit*) type* *m*, mec: *m*

blokey* ['bləʊkɪ], **blok(e)ish*** ['bləʊkɪʃ] ADJ (*Brit*) [*behaviour, activity*] de mec* ; [*man*] macho* ; **a ~ sense of humour** un humour typiquement masculin

blond(e) [blɒnd] **1** ADJ blond **2** N blond(e) *m(f)* → **ash²**, **platinum** **3** COMP ► **blonde bombshell*** N blonde *f* explosive

blood [blʌd] **1** N **a** (*NonC*) sang *m* ; **to beat/whip sb till the ~ comes** battre/fouetter qn jusqu'au sang ; **it's like trying to get ~ out**

of *or* **from a stone** c'est comme si on parlait à un mur ; **to give** *or* **donate ~** donner son sang ; **bad ~** animosité *f* ; **there is bad ~ between them** le torchon brûle (entre eux) ; (*liter*) **his ~ will be on your head** vous aurez sa mort sur la conscience ; (*fig*) **to have ~ on one's hands** avoir du sang sur les mains ; (*in conflict, war*) **to spill** *or* **shed ~** faire couler le sang ; **the ~ rushed to his face** le sang lui est monté au visage ; **it makes my ~ boil** cela me fait bouillir ; **my ~ was boiling** je bouillais (de rage) ; **his ~ is up** il est très monté ; **he's out for ~*** il cherche quelqu'un sur qui passer sa colère ; **to be out for** *or* **after sb's ~*** vouloir la peau* de qn ; **I've already apologized! what do you want, ~?*** je me suis déjà excusé ! qu'est-ce que tu veux, que je me mette à genoux ? ; **you make my ~ run cold** vous me donnez le frisson ; **his ~ ran cold** son sang s'est figé *or* s'est glacé dans ses veines ; **the ties of ~** les liens *mpl* du sang ■ (*PROV*) **~ is thicker than water** la voix du sang est la plus forte ; **it's in his ~** il a cela dans le sang ; **of Irish ~** de sang irlandais ; **he believes in putting ~, sweat and tears into any job he does** il se donne à fond dans tout ce qu'il fait ; (*fig*) **this firm needs new** *or* **fresh** *or* **young ~** cette maison a besoin d'un *or* de sang nouveau → **blue, cold, flesh, sweat**

b († = *dashing young man*) petit-maître† *m* **c** (*US*: = *blood brother*) frère *m* **2** VT (*Hunting*) [+ *hounds*] acharner, donner le goût du sang à ; (*fig*) [+ *troops*] donner le baptême du feu à

3 COMP ► **blood-and-thunder** ADJ (*Brit*) **a ~-and-thunder speech** un discours mélodramatique ; **~-and-thunder novel** roman *m* à sensation ► **blood bank** N (*Med*) banque *f* du sang ► **blood bath** N (*fig*) bain *m* de sang, massacre *m* ► **blood blister** N pinçon *m* ► **blood brother** N frère *m* de sang ► **blood-caked** ADJ couvert de sang coagulé ► **blood cell** N cellule *f* sanguine ; **red/white ~ cell** globule *m* rouge/blanc ► **blood clot** N caillot *m* de sang ► **blood corpuscle** N globule *m* sanguin ► **blood count** N (*Med*) numération *f* globulaire ► **blood donor** N donneur *m*, -euse *f* de sang ► **blood doping** N dopage *m* par autotransfusion ► **blood feud** N vendetta *f* ► **blood group** N (*Med*) groupe *m* sanguin ► **blood grouping** N (*Med*) recherche *f* du groupe sanguin ► **blood heat** N température *f* du sang ► **blood lust** N soif *f* de sang ► **blood money** N prix *m* du sang ► **blood orange** N (*orange f*) sanguine *f* ► **blood plasma** N plasma *m* sanguin ► **blood poisoning** N septicémie *f* ► **blood pressure** N → **blood pressure** ► **blood pudding** N (*US*) boudin *m* noir ► **blood-red** N, ADJ rouge *m* sang *inv* ► **blood relation** N parent(e) *m(f)* (*par le sang*) ► **blood sausage** N (*US*) = **blood pudding** ► **blood sports** NPL sports *mpl* sanguinaires ► **blood sugar** N sucre *m* dans le sang ; **~ sugar level** taux *m* de sucre dans le sang ► **blood test** N (*Med*) analyse *f* *or* examen *m* de sang ► **blood transfusion** N transfusion *f* sanguine ► **blood type** N = **blood group** ► **blood vessel** N vaisseau *m* sanguin → **burst**

bloodcurdling ['blʌdkɜːdlɪŋ] ADJ à (vous) figer *or* tourner* le sang, qui (vous) fige le sang

bloodhound ['blʌdhaʊnd] N (= *dog*) limier *m* ; (* = *detective*) détective *m*, limier *m*

bloodied ['blʌdɪd] ADJ sanglant, ensanglanté ; (*fig*) **~ but unbowed** vaincu mais sa fierté intacte

bloodily ['blʌdɪlɪ] ADV [*kill*] d'une manière sanglante ; [*defeat, repress*] dans le sang

bloodiness ['blʌdɪnɪs] N (*lit*) état *m* sanglant

bloodless ['blʌdlɪs] ADJ **a** (= *pallid*) [*face, lips*] blême, exsangue ; (*liter*) **b** (= *without bloodshed*) [*coup, revolution, victory*] sans effusion de sang ; (*Brit Hist*) **the Bloodless Revolution** *la révolution de 1688-89 en Angleterre*

bloodlessly ['blʌdlɪslɪ] ADV sans effusion de sang

bloodletting ['blʌd,letɪŋ] N (*Med*) saignée *f*

bloodline ['blʌdlaɪn] N lignée *f*

bloodmobile ['blʌdmə,bi:l] N (*US*) centre *m* mobile de collecte du sang

blood pressure ['blʌdpreʃəʳ] N tension *f* (artérielle) ; **to have high/low ~** faire de l'hypertension/hypotension ; **to take sb's ~** prendre la tension de qn ; (*Med*) **his ~ went up/down** sa tension a monté/a baissé ; (*fig*) **his ~ shot up at the news** il a failli avoir une attaque en apprenant la nouvelle

bloodshed ['blʌdʃed] N effusion *f* de sang, carnage *m* ; **without ~** sans effusion de sang

bloodshot ['blʌdʃɒt] ADJ [*eyes*] injecté (de sang) ; **to become ~** s'injecter de sang

bloodstain ['blʌdsteɪn] N tache *f* de sang

bloodstained ['blʌdsteɪnd] ADJ taché de sang, ensanglanté

bloodstock ['blʌdstɒk] N (*NonC*) bêtes *fpl* de race (pure) or de sang

bloodstone ['blʌdstəʊn] N (*Miner*) héliotrope *m*

bloodstream ['blʌdstri:m] N système *m* sanguin

bloodsucker ['blʌd,sʌkəʳ] N (*lit, fig*) sangsue *f*

bloodthirstiness ['blʌd,θɜ:stɪnɪs] N [*of person, animal*] soif *f* de sang ; [*of book, story*] cruauté *f*, caractère *m* sanguinaire

bloodthirsty ['blʌd,θɜ:stɪ] ADJ [+ *person, animal*] assoiffé de sang, sanguinaire ; [+ *disposition, tale*] sanguinaire

bloody ['blʌdɪ] **1** ADJ **a** (*lit*) sanglant, ensanglanté ; [*battle, history*] sanglant ; (= *blood-coloured*) rouge, rouge sang *inv* ; **a ~ nose** un nez en sang ; **to give sb a ~ nose** (*in contest*) donner or infliger un camouflet à qn ; (*in war*) faire subir une défaite à qn ; **with ~ hands** les mains couvertes de sang or ensanglantées ; **a ~ sun** un soleil rouge sang ; **~ mary** vodka *f* (au) jus de tomate, bloody mary *m* **b** (*Brit⁂*) foutu⁑ (*before n*), sacré⁑ (*before n*) ; **this ~ machine won't start!** cette bon Dieu⁑ de machine or cette foutue⁑ machine refuse de démarrer ! ; **shut the ~ door!** veux-tu fermer la porte ! ; **it's a ~ nuisance** ce que c'est emmerdant⁑ ; **you ~ fool!** espèce de con⁑ ; **you've got a ~ cheek or nerve!** tu charries !⁑ ; **those ~ doctors!** ces bon Dieu⁑ de médecins !, ces foutus⁑ médecins ! ; **~ hell!** merde alors ! ; **it's a ~ miracle he wasn't killed!** c'est un sacré* miracle qu'il en ait réchappé ! **c** († * = *awful*) affreux, atroce ; **we had a perfectly ~ evening with them** ils nous ont fait passer une soirée (drôlement) barbante*

2 ADV (*Brit⁂*) vachement⁑ ; **not ~ likely!** tu te fous de moi !⁑ ; **I've ~ (well) lost it!** je l'ai perdu nom de Dieu !⁑

3 VT ensanglanter, souiller de sang (*liter*)

4 COMP ► **bloody-minded*** ADJ (*Brit*) [*person*] qui fait toujours des difficultés ; [*attitude*] buté ; **he's being ~-minded** il le fait pour emmerder le monde⁑ ► **bloody-mindedness*** N **out of sheer ~-mindedness** (rien que) pour emmerder le monde⁑

bloom [blu:m] **1** N **a** fleur *f* **b** (*NonC*) [*of flower, plant*] floraison *f* ; (*fig*) épanouissement *m*, floraison *f* ; **in ~** [*tree*] en fleurs ; [*flower*] éclos ; **in full ~** [*tree*] en pleine floraison ; [*flower*] épanoui ; **roses in full ~** roses *fpl* épanouies ; **to burst** or **come into ~** fleurir, s'épanouir ; (*fig liter*) **in the ~ of her youth** dans la fleur de sa jeunesse, en pleine jeunesse **c** [*of fruit, skin*] velouté *m* ; **the ~ had gone from her cheek** ses joues avaient perdu leurs fraîches couleurs **2** VI [*flower*] éclore ; [*tree*] fleurir ;

[*person*] être florissant ; **~ing with health** resplendissant de santé

bloomer ['blu:məʳ] **1** N* bévue *f*, gaffe *f* ; **to make a ~** faire une gaffe, mettre les pieds dans le plat **2** **bloomers** NPL (*Dress*) culotte *f* bouffante

blooming ['blu:mɪŋ] ADJ (*Brit*) **a** [*tree*] en fleur, fleuri ; [*looks, health*] florissant **b*** = **blinking 1**

blooper⁑ ['blu:pəʳ] N (*esp US*) gaffe *f*

blossom ['blɒsəm] **1** N **a** (*NonC*) floraison *f*, fleur(s) *f(pl)* ; **a spray of ~** une petite branche fleurie, un rameau en fleur(s) ; **tree in ~** arbre *m* en fleur(s) ; **pear trees in full ~** poiriers *mpl* en pleine floraison ; **to come into ~** fleurir, s'épanouir ; **peach ~** fleur *f* de pêcher → **orange** **b** (= *flower*) fleur *f* **2** VI fleurir ; [*person*] s'épanouir ; (*fig*) **to ~ (out) into** devenir

blot [blɒt] **1** N [*of ink*] tache *f*, pâté *m* ; (*fig*) tache *f*, souillure *f* (*liter*) ; **a ~ on his character** or **on his escutcheon** une tache à sa réputation ; **to be a ~ on the landscape** déparer le paysage **2** VT **a** (= *spot with ink*) tacher, faire des pâtés sur ; (*Brit fig*) **you've really ~ted your copybook*** ta réputation en a pris un coup* **b** (= *dry*) [+ *ink, page*] sécher **3** COMP ► **blotting-pad** N (bloc *m*) buvard *m* ► **blotting-paper** N (papier *m*) buvard *m*

► **blot out** VT SEP [+ *words*] biffer, rayer ; [+ *memories*] effacer ; [*fog etc*] [+ *view*] voiler, masquer ; [*sound*] étouffer, couvrir

blotch [blɒtʃ] **1** N **a** (*on skin*) (= *mark*) tache *f*, marbrure *f* ; (= *spot*) bouton *m* **b** [*of ink, colour*] tache *f* **2** VT [+ *paper, written work*] tacher, barbouiller, faire des taches sur ; **~ed with** taché de, couvert de taches de

blotchy ['blɒtʃɪ] ADJ [*skin, complexion*] marbré, couvert de taches or de marbrures ; [*drawing, written work*] couvert de taches, barbouillé

blotter ['blɒtəʳ] N **a** (= *block*) (bloc *m*) buvard *m* ; (= *sheet*) buvard *m* ; (*also* **hand ~**) tampon *m* buvard, (= *desk pad*) sous-main *m inv* **b** (*US* = *notebook*) registre *m*

blotto⁑ ['blɒtəʊ] ADJ bourré⁑, bituré⁑

blouse [blaʊz] N [*of woman*] corsage *m*, chemisier *m* ; [*of workman, artist, peasant*] blouse *f*, sarrau *m* ; (*US Mil*) vareuse *f*

blouson ['blu:zɒn] N blouson *m*

blow¹ [bləʊ] (*vb: pret* **blew**, *ptp* **blown**) **1** N **a** **to give a ~** (*through mouth*) souffler ; (*through nose*) se moucher **b** (= *wind*) coup *m* de vent, bourrasque *f* **c** (*Drugs**) (*Brit* = *marijuana*) herbe* *f* ; (*US* = *cocaine*) coke* *f*

2 VT **a** [*wind*] [+ *ship*] pousser ; [+ *leaves*] chasser, faire voler ; **the wind blew the ship off course** le vent a fait dévier le navire (de sa route) or a dérouté le navire ; **a gust of wind blew her hat off** un coup de vent a fait s'envoler son chapeau ; **the wind blew the chimney down** le vent a fait tomber or a renversé la cheminée ; **the wind blew away the clouds** le vent a chassé or dispersé les nuages ; **the wind blew the door open/shut** un coup de vent a ouvert/fermé la porte ; **it was ~ing a gale** le vent soufflait en tempête ; **it's ~ing great guns*** il fait un vent à décorner les bœufs* → **ill**

b (= *drive air into*) [+ *fire*] souffler sur ; [+ *bellows*] faire marcher ; **to ~ one's nose** se moucher ; **to ~ an egg** vider un œuf (*en soufflant dedans*) ; **to ~ smoke in sb's face** (*lit*) souffler la fumée à la figure de qn ; (*US fig*) induire qn en erreur ; (*US*) **to ~ smoke up sb's ass⁑** lécher le cul de qn*

c (= *make by blowing*) [+ *bubbles*] faire ; [+ *glass*] souffler ; **to ~ a kiss** envoyer un baiser ; **to ~ smoke rings** faire des ronds de fumée

d [+ *trumpet, horn*] jouer de, souffler dans ; **the referee blew his whistle** l'arbitre a sifflé → **whistle** ; (*fig*) **to ~ one's own trumpet** or (*US*) **horn** se faire mousser*, chanter ses propres

louanges ; **he blew the dust off the record** il a enlevé la poussière du disque en soufflant dessus

e (*Brit Drugs*) **to ~ grass⁑** fumer de l'herbe

f (= *destroy*) [+ *safe*] faire sauter ; (*lit*) **to ~ a fuse** faire sauter un plomb or un fusible ; **to ~ a tyre** [*driver, vehicle*] crever ; **the car blew a tyre** la voiture a crevé ; (*Aut*) **to ~ a gasket** griller or casser un joint de culasse ; (*fig*) **to ~ a gasket*** or (*US*) **one's cork*** or (*US*) **one's stack*** or **one's top*** or **a fuse*** piquer une crise* ; **that blew the lid off the whole business*** c'est cela qui a fait découvrir le pot aux roses ; **the whole plan has been ~n sky-high*** tout le projet a volé en éclats ; (*fig*) **to ~ sth out of the water*** réduire qch à néant

g (⁑ = *spend extravagantly*) [+ *wages, money*] claquer* ; **I blew £20 on a new hat** j'ai claqué* 20 livres pour un nouveau chapeau

h (* = *spoil, fail*) rater, gâcher ; **he blew it (with her)** il a tout loupé* or raté (avec elle) ; (*US*) **to ~ one's lines** s'emmêler les pinceaux*

i (*esp US*⁑⁑ = *fellate*) tailler une pipe à⁑

j (*phrases*) **to ~ sb's mind⁑** (= *astound*) en boucher un coin à qn*, en mettre plein la vue à qn* ; (*Brit*) **to ~ the gaff⁑** (= *reveal a secret*) vendre la mèche ; (= *leave*) mettre les voiles* ; (*Brit*) **to ~ the gaff on sb⁑** dénoncer or vendre qn ; **he realized he was ~n⁑** il a compris qu'il était grillé*⁑ ; **~ the expense!⁑** tant pis pour la dépense !, au diable la dépense !⁑ ; **well, I'm ~ed!⁑** ça alors !*, par exemple ! ; **I'll be ~ed⁑ if I'll do it!** pas question que je le fasse !, je veux être pendu si je le fais !⁑ ; **~ it!⁑** la barbe !*, zut !*

3 VI **a** [*wind*] souffler ; **the wind was ~ing hard** le vent soufflait très fort, il faisait grand vent ; **the wind was ~ing from the south** le vent soufflait du sud ; (*fig*) **to see which way the wind ~s** regarder or voir de quel côté souffle le vent ; **she ~s hot and cold with me** avec moi elle souffle le chaud et le froid ; **the government has been ~ing hot and cold on the subject of peace talks** le gouvernement souffle le chaud et le froid en ce qui concerne les pourparlers de paix

b (= *move with wind*) **the door blew open/shut** un coup de vent a ouvert/a fermé la porte ; **his hat blew out of the window** son chapeau s'est envolé par la fenêtre ; **the question/agreement is ~ing in the wind*** la question/l'accord est dans l'air

c [*whistle*] retentir ; [*foghorn*] mugir ; **when the whistle ~s** au coup de sifflet

d (= *breathe out hard*) souffler ; (= *breathe hard*) [*person*] souffler, être à bout de souffle ; [*animal*] souffler ; **to ~ on one's fingers** souffler dans ses doigts ; **to ~ on one's soup** souffler sur sa soupe → **puff**

e [*whale*] souffler (par les évents)

f [*fuse, light bulb*] sauter ; [*tyre*] éclater

g (⁑ = *leave*) filer*

4 EXCL* la barbe !*, zut !*

5 COMP ► **blow-dry** N brushing *m* ♦ VT **to ~-dry sb's hair** faire un brushing à qn ► **blow dryer** N sèche-cheveux *m inv* ► **blow job⁑** N pipe⁑ *f* ; **to give sb a ~ job** tailler une pipe à qn⁑ ► **blow-up** N explosion *f* ; (⁑ = *quarrel*) engueulade⁑ *f*, prise *f* de bec* ; (*Phot**) agrandissement *m*

► **blow away⁑** VT SEP (*esp US*) (= *kill*) descendre*, flinguer⁑ ; (= *defeat*) écraser, battre à plate(s) couture(s) ; (= *surprise*) sidérer

► **blow down 1** VI [*tree, fence etc*] être abattu par le vent, tomber **2** VT SEP [*wind*] faire tomber ; [*person*] faire tomber (en soufflant)

► **blow in 1** VI (* = *turn up*) s'amener*, débarquer* ; (*unexpectedly*) arriver or débarquer* à l'improviste **2** VT SEP [+ *door, window*] enfoncer ; (*hum*) **look what the wind's ~n in!** regardez qui s'amène !*

► **blow off 1** VI **a** [*hat*] s'envoler **b** (*Brit*⁑) lâcher un pet, péter **2** VT SEP **a** [+ *hat*] emporter **b** [+ *air*] laisser échapper, lâcher ;

(fig) **to ~ off steam*** se défouler*

► **blow out** ① VI *[light]* s'éteindre; *[tyre]* éclater; *[fuse]* sauter ② VT SEP **a** [+ *light*] éteindre; [+ *candle*] souffler; **the storm blew itself out** la tempête a fini par s'apaiser **b** (= *puff out*) [+ *one's cheeks*] gonfler **c** **to ~ one's brains out** se faire sauter or se brûler la cervelle; **to ~ sb's brains out** faire sauter la cervelle à qn **d** *(esp US* = let down, reject)* [+ *person*] envoyer balader*, laisser tomber ③ **~-out** N → **blow-out**

► **blow over** ① VI *[storm, dispute]* se calmer ② VT SEP [+ *tree*] renverser, abattre

► **blow up** ① VI **a** *[bomb]* exploser, sauter; *(fig)* **the whole thing has ~n up** tout a été fichu en l'air; **his allegations could ~ up in his face** ses allégations pourraient se retourner contre lui **b** *[wind]* se lever; *[storm]* se préparer **c** *(*: with anger, indignation)* exploser*, sauter au plafond*; **to ~ up at sb** s'emporter contre qn, se mettre en colère contre qn **d** (= *start up*) *[affair, crisis]* se déclencher ② VT SEP **a** [+ *mine*] (faire) exploser, faire sauter; [+ *building, bridge*] faire sauter **b** [+ *tyre*] gonfler; *(fig)* **~n up with pride** gonflé or bouffi d'orgueil; **the media blew up the story** les médias ont grossi l'affaire **c*** [+ *photo*] agrandir; [+ *event*] exagérer **d** *(‡ = reprimand)* [+ *person*] passer un (bon) savon à* ③ **~-up** N → **blow¹**

blow² [bləʊ] ① N **a** *(lit)* (= *impact*) coup *m*; *(with fist)* coup *m* de poing; **to come to ~s** en venir aux mains; **at one ~** du premier coup; *(fig)* **to cushion** or **soften the ~** amortir le choc → **strike** **b** *(fig = sudden misfortune)* coup *m*, malheur *m*; **it was a terrible ~ for them** cela a été un coup terrible pour eux ② COMP ► **blow-by-blow** ADJ *(fig)* **he gave me a ~-by-~ account** il ne m'a fait grâce d'aucun détail

blow³ [bləʊ] VI *(††, liter) [flowers]* fleurir, s'épanouir

blower [ˈbləʊəʳ] N **a** *[of grate]* tablier *m* or rideau *m* de cheminée; *[of ventilation]* ventilateur *m* (soufflant), machine *f* à vent; *(Min)* jet *m* de grisou **b** *(Brit†‡ = telephone)* bigophone* *m*; **to get on the ~ to sb** passer un coup de bigophone‡ à qn → **glassblower**

blowfly [ˈbləʊflaɪ] N mouche *f* à viande

blowgun [ˈbləʊgʌn] N *(US)* sarbacane *f*

blowhard* [ˈbləʊhɑːd] N *(US)* vantard(e) *m(f)*

blowhole [ˈbləʊhəʊl] N *[of whale]* évent *m*; *(Tech)* évent *m*, bouche *f* d'aération; *(Metal)* **~s** soufflures *fpl*

blowlamp [ˈbləʊlæmp] N *(Brit)* lampe *f* à souder, chalumeau *m*

-blown [bləʊn] ADJ *(in compounds)* → **fly**, **wind-blown**

blow-out [ˈbləʊaʊt] N **a** *[of tyre]* éclatement *m*; **he had a ~** il a eu un pneu qui a éclaté **b** *(Elec)* **there's been a ~** les plombs ont sauté **c** *[of gas well, oil well]* jaillissement *m* **d** *(‡ = meal)* gueuleton‡ *m*; **to have a ~** faire un gueuleton‡ or une bouffe‡

blowpipe [ˈbləʊpaɪp] N (= *weapon*) sarbacane *f*; *(Chem, Ind)* chalumeau *m*; *(in glass-making)* canne *f* (de souffleur), fêle *f*

blowsy [ˈblaʊzɪ] ADJ *[woman]* débraillé

blowtorch [ˈbləʊtɔːtʃ] N lampe *f* à souder, chalumeau *m*

blowy* [ˈbləʊɪ] ADJ venté, venteux

blowzy [ˈblaʊzɪ] ADJ = **blowsy**

BLT [ˌbiːelˈtiː] N *(ABBR* = **bacon, lettuce and tomato**) **a ~ sandwich** un sandwich bacon, laitue, tomate

blub [blʌb] VI *(Brit* = *cry)* pleurer comme un veau

blubber [ˈblʌbəʳ] ① N *[of whale]* blanc *m* de baleine ② VI *(‡ = cry)* pleurer comme un veau; **stop ~ing!** arrête de chialer !‡

blubbery [ˈblʌbərɪ] ADJ (= *fat*) plein de graisse

bludgeon [ˈblʌdʒən] ① N gourdin *m*, matraque *f* ② VT matraquer, assener un coup de gourdin or de matraque à; *(fig)* **he ~ed me**

into doing it il m'a forcé la main (pour que je le fasse)

blue [bluː] ① ADJ **a** bleu; **to go** or **turn ~** devenir bleu; **~ with cold** bleu de froid; *(lit)* **to be ~ in the face** avoir le visage cyanosé; **you can talk till you are ~ in the face*** tu peux toujours parler; **you can shout till you're ~ in the face*, nobody will come** tu auras beau crier or tu pourras crier tout ce que tu voudras*, personne ne viendra; **I've told you till I'm ~ in the face*** je me tue à te le dire; **once in a ~ moon** tous les trente-six du mois; *(liter)* **the wide** or **wild ~ yonder** l'inconnu *m*; **like a ~ streak*** *[run, go]* comme une flèche, au triple galop; **to have a ~ fit‡** piquer une crise* → **4**; → **black**, **murder**, **true** **b** (* = *miserable*) cafardeux, triste; **to feel ~** broyer du noir, avoir le cafard; **to be in a ~ funk** avoir la frousse* or la trouille* **c** (* = *obscene*) *[talk, language]* cochon*, obscène; *[book, film]* porno* *inv* ② N **a** (= *colour*) bleu *m*, azur *m* → **navy**, **Prussian**, **sky** **b** (= *sky*) azur *m* *(liter)*, ciel *m*; *(fig)* **to come out of the ~** *(gen)* être complètement inattendu; *[pleasant thing]* tomber du ciel; **to go off into the ~** (= *into the unknown*) partir à l'aventure; (= *out of touch*) disparaître de la circulation* → **bolt** **c** *(liter = sea)* **the ~** la mer, les flots *mpl* **d** (* = *depression*) **the ~s** le cafard; **to have the ~s** avoir le cafard, broyer du noir **e** *(Mus)* **the ~s** le blues **f** *(Brit Univ)* **the Dark/Light Blues** l'équipe *f* d'Oxford/de Cambridge; **he got his ~ for rugby** = il est dans l'équipe (universitaire) de rugby *(surtout à Oxford et Cambridge)* **g** *(in washing)* bleu *m* ③ VT *(Brit†* = *squander)* [+ *inheritance, fortune, money*] croquer*, dilapider; **to ~ money on sth** dilapider de l'argent pour acheter qch ④ COMP ► **blue-arsed fly‡*** N *(Brit)* **to run about** or **around like a ~-arsed fly** courir dans tous les sens, ne plus savoir où donner de la tête ► **blue baby** N enfant *m* bleu ► **Blue Beret** N béret *m* bleu ► **blue-black** ADJ noir bleuté *inv* ► **blue blood** N sang *m* bleu or noble ► **blue-blooded** ADJ de sang noble, aristocratique ► **blue book** N *(Brit Parl)* livre *m* bleu; *(US Scol etc)* cahier *m* d'examen ► **blue cheese** N *(fromage m)* bleu *m* ► **blue chips, blue-chip securities** NPL valeurs *fpl* de premier ordre, placements *mpl* de tout repos or de père de famille ► **blue collar worker** N col *m* bleu ► **blue-eyed** ADJ aux yeux bleus; *(fig)* **the ~-eyed boy** le chouchou*, le chéri ► **blue fin tuna, blue fin tunny** N thon *m* rouge ► **Blue Flag** N *(on beach)* drapeau *m* bleu ► **the Blue Hen State** N *(US)* le Delaware ► **blue jeans** NPL blue-jean(s) *m(pl)* ► **blue law*** N *(US)* loi limitant les activités publiques le dimanche ► **blue-pencil** VT corriger ► **Blue Peter** N **a** *(Naut)* pavillon *m* de partance **b** *(Brit TV)* émission télévisée pour enfants ► **blue riband, blue ribbon** *(US)* *(Naut)* **the ~ riband** or **ribbon** le ruban bleu ◆ ADJ *[event, competition]* de très haut niveau; *[prize]* prestigieux; *[committee, panel]* éminent ► **blue rinse** N rinçage *m* bleuté; **the ~ rinse brigade** les rombières* *fpl* ► **blue-rinsed** ADJ [+ *hair*] aux reflets bleutés; [+ *woman*] à la chevelure bleutée ► **blue shark** N requin *m* bleu ► **blue-sky** ADJ *(US)* *[stock, bond]* douteux; *[project, research]* sans but pratique; **~-sky laws** lois protégeant le public contre les titres douteux ► **blue tit** N mésange *f* bleue ► **blue whale** N baleine *f* bleue

┌─────────────┐
│ **BLUE PETER** │
└─────────────┘

Célèbre émission télévisée pour enfants dont les programmes vont du documentaire sur des sujets intéressant les enfants à la recette de cuisine et à

la confection d'objets artisanaux. Les badges **Blue Peter** récompensent les spectateurs qui participent aux émissions ou se rendent utiles à la communauté.

Bluebeard [ˈbluːbɪəd] N Barbe-Bleue *m*

bluebell [ˈbluːbel] N jacinthe *f* des bois; *(Scot* = *harebell)* campanule *f*

blueberry [ˈbluːbərɪ] N myrtille *f*

bluebird [ˈbluːbɜːd] N *(Orn)* oiseau *m* bleu

bluebottle [ˈbluːbɒtl] N **a** mouche *f* bleue or à viande **b** *(Bot)* bleuet *m* **c** *(†‡ = policeman)* poulet* *m*, flic* *m*

bluegrass [ˈbluːgrɑːs] ① N *(US Bot)* pâturin *m* des champs ② COMP ► **bluegrass music** N musique *f* bluegrass ► **the Bluegrass State** N le Kentucky

blueish [ˈbluːɪʃ] ADJ = **bluish**

blueness [ˈbluːnɪs] N bleu *m*

blueprint [ˈbluːprɪnt] N *(print, process)* bleu *m*; *(US* = *Ozalid)* ozalid® *m*; *(fig)* plan *m*, projet *m* (**for** de)

bluestocking † [ˈbluːˌstɒkɪŋ] N *(fig)* bas-bleu *m*

bluesy [ˈbluːzɪ] ADJ *(Mus)* dans le style du blues

bluey* [ˈbluːɪ] ① ADJ (= *bluish*) bleuté; **~ green** vert bleuâtre or bleuté; **~ grey** gris bleu ② N *(Austral‡* = *redhead)* rouquin(e)* *m(f)*

bluff¹ [blʌf] ① ADJ **a** *[person]* carré, direct **b** *[cliff, coast]* à pic, escarpé ② N (= *headland*) promontoire *m*

bluff² [blʌf] ① VI *(also Cards)* bluffer* ② VT [+ *person*] bluffer*, donner le change à; **we ~ed him into believing ...** nous l'avons si bien bluffé qu'il a cru ...; **he ~ed his way through (it)** il y est allé au culot **b** *(Cards)* [+ *opponent*] bluffer* ③ N *(esp Cards)* bluff *m*; *(fig)* **he called my ~** il m'a pris au mot; **let's call his ~** on va le mettre au pied du mur

bluffer [ˈblʌfəʳ] N bluffeur *m*, -euse *f*

bluish [ˈbluːɪʃ] ADJ tirant sur le bleu; *(pej)* bleuâtre; **~ grey** gris bleuté; **~ white** blanc bleuté or aux reflets bleus

blunder [ˈblʌndəʳ] ① N (= *gaffe*) bévue *f*, impair *m*, gaffe* *f*; (= *error*) faute *f*, bourde *f*; **to make a ~** faire une bévue or un impair or une gaffe*; **social ~** impair *m* ② VI **a** (= *make mistake*) faire une bourde or une faute **b** (= *move clumsily*) avancer d'un pas maladroit; **to ~ in/out** *etc* entrer/sortir *etc* d'un pas maladroit; **to ~ against** or **into sth** buter or se cogner contre qch; **he ~ed his way through his speech** il s'est embrouillé dans son discours; *(fig)* **to ~ into sth** s'engager par erreur dans qch ③ VT [+ *affair, business*] gâcher, saboter

blunderbuss [ˈblʌndəbʌs] N tromblon *m*, espingole *f*

blunderer [ˈblʌndərəʳ] N gaffeur *m*, -euse *f*

blundering [ˈblʌndərɪŋ] ① ADJ *[person]* gaffeur*, maladroit; *[words, act]* maladroit, malavisé ② N maladresse *f*

blunt [blʌnt] ① ADJ **a** *[blade, knife]* émoussé, peu tranchant; *[pencil]* mal taillé, épointé; *[point, needle]* émoussé, épointé; *(Jur, Police)* **with a ~ instrument** avec un instrument contondant **b** *(fig* = *outspoken)* *[person]* brusque; *[fact]* brutal; **he was very ~** il n'a pas mâché ses mots ② VT [+ *blade, knife, point, sword*] émousser; [+ *pencil, needle*] épointer; *(fig)* [+ *palate, feelings*] émousser

bluntly [ˈblʌntlɪ] ADV *[speak]* sans ménagements, sans mettre de gants

bluntness [ˈblʌntnɪs] N **a** *[of blade, knife]* manque *m* de tranchant; *[of needle, pencil]* pointe *f* émoussée **b** (= *frankness*) franc-parler *m*; (= *brusqueness*) brusquerie *f*

blur [blɜːʳ] ① N **a** (= *smear, blot*) tache *f*, bavure *f* **b** (= *vague form*) masse *f* indistincte; **a**

~ **of colours and forms** une masse confuse de couleurs et de formes; **a ~ of movement** un mouvement confus; **the evening passed in a ~** la soirée a passé dans une sorte de brouillard $\boxed{c}$ (= *mist: on mirror etc*) buée *f* $\boxed{2}$ VT $\boxed{a}$ [+ *shining surface*] embuer, troubler; [+ *writing, inscription*] estomper, effacer; [+ *view, outline*] estomper $\boxed{b}$ [+ *sight, judgement*] troubler, brouiller; **eyes ~red with tears** yeux *mpl* voilés de larmes $\boxed{c}$ (*fig*) [+ *distinction, boundary*] brouiller, rendre flou $\boxed{3}$ VI [*vision*] se voiler

blurb [blɜːb] N notice *f* publicitaire; [*of book*] (texte *m* de) présentation *f*, texte *m* de couverture (*or* au volet de jaquette)

blurred [blɜːd] $\boxed{1}$ ADJ [*photo, image, outline, inscription*] flou; [*eyesight*] troublé; **to become ~** s'estomper; **the issue is threatening to become ~** on risque de perdre de vue le vrai problème; **class distinctions are becoming ~** les distinctions entre les classes s'estompent; **his memory of what happened was rather ~** il avait un souvenir assez flou de ce qui s'était passé $\boxed{2}$ COMP ► **blurred vision** N vue *f* trouble

blurry* [blɜːrɪ] ADJ [*photo, image, outline, inscription*] flou; [*eyesight*] troublé

blurt [blɜːt] VT (*also* ~ **out**) [+ *word*] lâcher, jeter; [+ *information, secrets*] laisser échapper, lâcher étourdiment *or* à l'étourdie

blush [blʌʃ] $\boxed{1}$ VI $\boxed{a}$ rougir, devenir rouge (**with** de); **to ~ deeply** rougir très fort, devenir tout rouge, piquer un fard*; **to ~ to the roots of one's hair** *or* **up to the ears** rougir jusqu'aux oreilles $\boxed{b}$ (*fig* = *be ashamed*) rougir, avoir honte; **I ~ for him** j'ai honte pour lui; **I ~ to say so** je rougis de le dire $\boxed{2}$ N rougeur *f*; **with a ~** en rougissant; **without a ~** sans rougir; (*liter*) **the first ~ of dawn** les premières rougeurs *fpl* de l'aube; (*liter*) **the ~ of the rose** l'incarnat *m* de la rose (*liter*); **at the first ~** (= *at first sight*) au premier aspect, de prime abord → **spare**

blusher [blʌʃəʳ] N fard *m* à joues

blushing [blʌʃɪŋ] ADJ (*with shame*) le rouge au front; (*from embarrassment*) le rouge aux joues; (*hum*) **the ~ bride** la mariée rougissante

bluster [blʌstəʳ] $\boxed{1}$ VI $\boxed{a}$ [*wind*] faire rage, souffler violemment *or* en rafales; [*storm*] faire rage, se déchaîner $\boxed{b}$ (= *rage*) tempêter, fulminer (**at sb** contre qn); [*boast*] fanfaronner $\boxed{2}$ N (*NonC* = *boasting*) fanfaronnade(s) *f(pl)*

blusterer [blʌstərəʳ] N fanfaron(ne) *m(f)*, bravache *m*

blustering [blʌstərɪŋ] $\boxed{1}$ ADJ fanfaron $\boxed{2}$ N (*NonC* = *boasting*) fanfaronnades *fpl*

blustery [blʌstərɪ] ADJ [*wind*] de tempête, qui souffle en rafales; [*weather, day*] venteux, à bourrasques

Blu-Tack® [bluːtæk] N pâte *f* adhésive, Patafix® *m*

Blvd N (ABBR = **Boulevard**) Bd, Bld

BM N ABBR = **British Museum**

BMA [ˌbiːemˈeɪ] N (ABBR = **British Medical Association**) ≈ ordre *m* des médecins

BMus (ABBR = **Bachelor of Music**) diplômé(e) *m(f)* des études musicales

BMX [ˌbiːemˈeks] N ABBR = **bicycle motorcross** $\boxed{a}$ (= *sport*) bicross *m* $\boxed{b}$ (*also* ~ **bike**) (vélo *m* de) bicross *m*

BO* [biːˈəʊ] $\boxed{a}$ (ABBR = **body odour**) odeur *f* corporelle; **he's got BO** il sent la transpiration $\boxed{b}$ (*US*) ABBR = **box office**

boa [bəʊə] $\boxed{1}$ N (= *snake, fur or feather wrap*) boa *m* $\boxed{2}$ COMP ► **boa constrictor** N (boa *m*) constricteur *m*

Boadicea [ˌbəʊədɪˈsiːə] N Boadicée *f*

boar [bɔːʳ] $\boxed{1}$ N (*wild*) sanglier *m*; (= *male pig*) verrat *m*; **young (wild) ~** marcassin *m*; (*Culin*)

~**'s head** hure *f* (de sanglier) $\boxed{2}$ COMP ► **boar-hunting** N chasse *f* au sanglier

board [bɔːd] $\boxed{1}$ N $\boxed{a}$ (= *piece of wood*) planche *f*; († *or hum* = *table*) table *f*; (*Theat*) **the ~s** les planches *fpl*, la scène; (*fig*) **it is all quite above ~** c'est tout ce qu'il y a de plus régulier, c'est tout à fait dans les règles; (*fig*) **across the ~** systématiquement → **breadboard, chessboard, diving, tread** *etc* $\boxed{b}$ (*NonC* = *cardboard*) carton *m* (*NonC*); (= *piece of board: for games*) tableau *m* $\boxed{c}$ (*NonC* = *provision of meals*) pension *f*; (*Brit*) ~ **and lodging** (chambre *f* avec) pension *f*; (*Brit*) **full ~** pension *f* complète → **bed, half** $\boxed{d}$ (= *group of officials, council*) conseil *m*, comité *m*, commission *f*; (*Fin, Ind*) **he is on the ~ (of directors)** ◊ **he has a seat on the ~ (of directors)** il siège au conseil d'administration; **medical ~** commission *f* médicale $\boxed{e}$ (*NonC: Aviat, Naut*) bord *m*; (*lit*) **to come (or go) on ~** monter à bord, embarquer; **to take goods on ~** embarquer des marchandises; **on ~ the Queen Elizabeth** à bord du Queen Elizabeth; **on ~ (ship)** à bord; (*fig*) **to go by the ~** [*plan, attempt*] échouer; [*principles, hopes, dreams*] être abandonné; [*business, firm*] aller à vau-l'eau; **to take sth on ~*** (= *take note of*) prendre note de qch; (= *accept responsibility for*) prendre qch sur soi; (= *undertake*) assumer qch; (*fig*) **welcome on ~!** bienvenue (dans notre équipe)!
$\boxed{2}$ VT $\boxed{a}$ (= *go on to*) [+ *ship, plane*] monter à bord de; (*Naut*) (*in attack*) monter à l'abordage de, prendre à l'abordage; (*for inspection*) arraisonner; [+ *train, bus*] monter dans $\boxed{b}$ (= *cover with boards*) couvrir *or* garnir de planches, planchéier $\boxed{c}$ (= *feed, lodge*) prendre en pension *or* comme pensionnaire
$\boxed{3}$ VI $\boxed{a}$ (= *lodge*) **to ~ with sb** être en pension chez qn $\boxed{b}$ [*passengers*] embarquer; **your flight is now ~ing** l'embarquement a commencé; "**flight A123 is now ~ing at gate 3**" «vol A123: embarquement immédiat porte 3»
$\boxed{4}$ COMP (*Ind, Comm*) [*decision etc*] du conseil d'administration ► **board game** N jeu *m* de société (*se jouant sur un tableau*) ► **board meeting** N (*Ind, Comm*) réunion *f* du conseil d'administration ► **board of directors** N conseil *m* d'administration ► **board of education** N (*US Scol*) ≈ conseil *m* d'établissement ► **board of examiners** N (*Scol, Univ*) jury *m* d'examen ► **board of governors** N (*Brit Scol*) ≈ conseil *m* d'établissement (*d'un lycée ou d'un IUT*) ► **board of health** N (*US*) service *m* municipal d'hygiène; (*Mil*) conseil *m* de révision ► **board of inquiry** N commission *f* d'enquête ► **board of managers** N (*Brit Scol*) ≈ conseil *m* d'établissement (*d'une école primaire*) ► **board of pardons** N (*US Jur*) commission *f* de remises de peine ► **board of parole** N (*US Jur*) commission *f* de mise en liberté surveillée ► **board of regents** N ≈ conseil *m* de trustees ► **Board of Trade** N (*in Brit*) ≈ ministère *m* du Commerce ► **board of trade** N (*US*) chambre *f* de commerce ► **board of trustees** N (*US Univ*) ≈ conseil *m* d'université ► **board room** N salle *f* de conférence; (*in large organization*) salle *f* du conseil ► **board school** N (*Hist*) école *f* communale

►**board out** VT SEP [+ *person*] mettre en pension (**with** chez)
►**board up** VT SEP [+ *door, window*] condamner (à l'aide de planches)

boarded-up [ˌbɔːdɪdˈʌp] ADJ **a ~ window/door** une fenêtre/porte condamnée

boarder [bɔːdəʳ] N pensionnaire *mf*; **to take in ~s** prendre des pensionnaires $\boxed{b}$ (*Brit Scol*) interne *mf*, pensionnaire *mf* → **day**

boarding [bɔːdɪŋ] $\boxed{1}$ N $\boxed{a}$ [*of floor*] planchéiage *m*; [*of fence*] planches *fpl* [*of ship,*

plane] embarquement *m*; (*Naut*) (*in attack*) abordage *m*; (*for inspection*) arraisonnement *m* $\boxed{2}$ COMP ► **boarding card** N (*Brit Aviat, Naut*) carte *f* d'embarquement ► **boarding house** N pension *f* (de famille); (*Scol*) internat *m*; **to live at a ~ house** vivre dans une *or* en pension ► **boarding officer** N officier *m* chargé de l'arraisonnement ► **boarding party** N (*Naut*) section *f* d'abordage ► **boarding pass** N = **boarding card** ► **boarding school** N pension *f*, pensionnat *m*; **to send a child to ~ school** mettre un enfant en pension; **to be at ~ school** être en pension

boardwalk [bɔːdwɔːk] N (*US*) passage *m* en bois, trottoir *m* en planches; (*on beach*) promenade *f* (en planches)

boarhound [bɔːhaʊnd] N vautre *m*; **pack of ~s** vautrait *m*

boast [bəʊst] $\boxed{1}$ N rodomontade *f*, fanfaronnade *f*; **it is their ~ that they succeeded** ils se vantent *or* ils s'enorgueillissent d'avoir réussi; **it is their ~ that no one went hungry** ils se vantent que personne n'ait eu faim $\boxed{2}$ VI se vanter (**about, of** de); **without ~ing or without wishing to ~, I may say that ...** sans (vouloir) me vanter, je peux dire que ...; **that's nothing to ~ about** il n'y a pas de quoi se vanter $\boxed{3}$ VT être fier de posséder, se glorifier d'avoir; **the church ~s a fine organ** l'église est fière de posséder un bel orgue

boaster [bəʊstəʳ] N vantard(e) *m(f)*, fanfaron(ne) *m(f)*

boastful [bəʊstfʊl] ADJ [*person, words*] fanfaron, vantard

boastfully [bəʊstfʊlɪ] ADV en se vantant, avec forfanterie

boasting [bəʊstɪŋ] N vantardise *f*, fanfaronnade(s) *f(pl)*

boat [bəʊt] $\boxed{1}$ N (*gen*) bateau *m*; (= *small light boat*) embarcation *f*; (= *ship*) navire *m*, bâtiment *m*; (= *vessel*) vaisseau *m*; (= *liner*) paquebot *m*; (= *rowing-boat*) barque *f*, canot *m*; (= *sailing-boat*) voilier *m*; (= *barge*) chaland *m*, péniche *f*; **to go by ~** prendre le bateau; **to cross the ocean by ~** traverser l'océan en bateau *or* en paquebot; **to take the ~ at Dover** s'embarquer à *or* prendre le bateau à Douvres; (*fig*) **we're all in the same ~** nous sommes tous logés à la même enseigne, nous sommes tous dans la même galère → **burn¹, lifeboat, miss¹, rock¹**
$\boxed{2}$ VI **to go ~ing** aller faire une partie de canot; **to ~ up/down the river** remonter/descendre la rivière en bateau
$\boxed{3}$ COMP ► **boat deck** N pont *m* des embarcations ► **boat hook** N gaffe *f* ► **boat people** NPL boat people *mpl* ► **boat race** N course *f* d'aviron, régate(s) *f(pl)*; **the Boat Race** la course d'aviron (*entre les universités d'Oxford et de Cambridge*) ► **boat-shaped** ADJ en forme de bateau ► **boat train** N train *m* (qui assure la correspondance avec le ferry)

boatbuilder [bəʊtˌbɪldəʳ] N constructeur *m* naval *or* de bateaux

boatbuilding [bəʊtˌbɪldɪŋ] N (*NonC*) construction *f* navale

boater [bəʊtəʳ] N (= *hat*) canotier *m*

boatful [bəʊtfʊl] N [*of goods*] cargaison *f*; [*of people*] plein bateau *m*, cargaison *f* (*hum*)

boathouse [bəʊthaʊs] N hangar *m* or abri *m* à bateaux

boating [bəʊtɪŋ] $\boxed{1}$ N canotage *m* $\boxed{2}$ COMP [*club, accident*] de canotage ► **boating holiday** N vacances *fpl* en bateau ► **boating trip** N excursion *f* en bateau

boatload [bəʊtləʊd] N [*of goods etc*] cargaison *f*; [*of people*] plein bateau *m*, cargaison *f* (*hum*)

boatman [bəʊtmən] N (*pl* **-men**) (= *boat-hire proprietor*) loueur *m* de canots; (*actually rowing*) passeur *m*

boatswain ['bəʊsn] **1** N maître m d'équipage **2** COMP ► **boatswain's chair** N sellette f ► **boatswain's mate** N second maître m ► **boatswain's pipe** N sifflet m

boatyard ['bəʊtjɑːd] N chantier m naval

Bob [bɒb] N (dim of Robert) Bob m; (Brit) **~'s your uncle!*** le tour est joué !

bob¹ [bɒb] **1** VI **a** to **~ (up and down)** (in the air) pendiller; (in water) danser sur l'eau; **to ~ for apples** essayer d'attraper avec les dents des pommes flottant sur l'eau **b** (= curtsy) faire une (petite) révérence **2** N **a** (= curtsy) (petite) révérence f; (= nod) (bref) salut m de tête; (= jerky movement) petite secousse f, petit coup m; [of weight] [of pendulum] poids m; [of plumbline] plomb m; (= float) bouchon m **3** VI (Fishing) pêcher à la ligne flottante

► **bob down** VI **a** (= duck) baisser la tête; (straight) se baisser subitement **b** (‡ = be quiet) la fermer‡

► **bob up** VI remonter brusquement

bob²* [bɒb] **1** N (pl inv: Brit) shilling m; **five ~** cinq shillings mpl; **he's not short of a ~ or two** il n'est pas à court d'argent; **that must be worth a few ~!** ça doit coûter un saint de la tête! **2** COMP ► **bob-a-job** N (Brit) collecte organisée par les scouts en échange de petits travaux à domicile ► **bob-a-job week** N (Brit) semaine de la collecte organisée par les scouts en échange de petits travaux à domicile

bob³ [bɒb] **1** N (= curl) boucle f; (gen = short haircut) coiffe f courte; (= haircut: chin-length all round) coupe f au carré; (= horse's tail) queue f écourtée **2** VT [+ hair] couper au carré; [+ horse's tail] écourter

bob⁴ [bɒb] N (= sleigh: also **~sled, ~sleigh**) bobsleigh m, bob m; (= runner) patin m

bobbin ['bɒbɪn] **1** N [of thread, wire] bobine f; [of sewing machine] bobine f; [of lace] fuseau m **2** COMP ► **bobbin lace** N dentelle f aux fuseaux

bobble ['bɒbl] **1** N **a** (Brit = pom-pom) pompon m **b** (US* = mistake etc) cafouillage* m **2** VT (US* = handle ineptly) cafouiller* **3** COMP ► **bobble hat** N (Brit) bonnet m à pompon

Bobby ['bɒbɪ] N dim of Robert

bobby* ['bɒbɪ] N (= policeman) flic* m

bobby-dazzler†* [ˌbɒbɪˈdæzlə*] N (Brit) (= object) truc m sensas†* inv; (= girl) jolie pépée†* f

bobby pin ['bɒbɪpɪn] N (esp US) pince f à cheveux

bobbysocks, bobbysox* ['bɒbɪsɒks] NPL (US) socquettes fpl

bobbysoxer* ['bɒbɪsɒksə*] N (US) minette* f (des années 40)

bobcat ['bɒbkæt] N (US) lynx m

bobtail ['bɒbteɪl] N (= tail) queue f écourtée; (= horse/dog) cheval m/chien m écourté

bobtailed ['bɒbteɪld] ADJ écourté

Boche‡ [bɒʃ] (pej) **1** N Boche* m (pej) **2** ADJ boche* (pej)

bock [bɒk] N (US: also **~ beer**) **a** (NonC) bière f bock **b** (= glass of beer) bock m

bod‡ [bɒd] N **a** (Brit = person) type* m → **oddbod b** (= body) physique m, corps m

bodacious‡ [ˌbɒˈdeɪʃəs] ADJ (US) fabuleux*

bode [bəʊd] **1** VI **to ~ well (for)** être de bon augure (pour); **it ~s ill (for)** cela ne présage rien de bon (pour) **2** VT présager, augurer

bodega [bəʊˈdiːgə] N (US) épicerie f portoricaine

bodge* [bɒdʒ] (Brit) = **botch**

bodice ['bɒdɪs] **1** N **a** [of dress] corsage m; [of peasant's dress] corselet m **b** (= undergarment) cache-corset m **2** COMP ► **bodice-ripper*** N roman m rose sur fond historique ► **bodice-ripping*** ADJ ~-ripping

novel/film roman m/film m rose sur fond historique

-bodied ['bɒdɪd] ADJ (in compounds) → **able, full**

bodily ['bɒdɪlɪ] **1** ADV (lift) à bras-le-corps; (carry) dans ses etc bras; **the explosion flung him ~ to the ground** l'explosion l'a plaqué au sol **2** ADJ (need, comfort) matériel; (pain) physique; **~ functions** fonctions fpl physiologiques; **~ fluids** fluides mpl organiques; **~ illness** troubles mpl physiques; **~ injury** blessure f corporelle; **~ harm** blessures fpl → **actual, grievous**

bodkin ['bɒdkɪn] N **a** (= big darning needle) aiguille f à repriser; (for threading tape) passe-lacet m; (for leather) alène f (†† = hairpin) épingle f à cheveux

body² ['bɒdɪ] **1** N **a** [of man, animal] corps m; **just enough to keep ~ and soul together** juste assez pour subsister; **to belong to sb ~ and soul** appartenir à qn corps et âme → **sound²** **b** (= corpse) cadavre m, corps m **c** (= main part of structure) [of dress] corsage m, corps m (de robe); [of car] carrosserie f; [of plane] fuselage m; [of ship] coque f; [of church] nef f; [of camera] boîtier m; [of speech, document] fond m, corps m; **in the ~ of the hall** au centre de la salle **d** (= mass, force) **~ of troops** corps m de troupes; **the main ~ of the army** le gros de l'armée; **the great ~ of readers** la masse des lecteurs; **a large ~ of people** une masse de gens, une foule nombreuse; **a large ~ of information** une importante documentation; **a large ~ of literature on ...** une abondante bibliographie sur ...; **in a ~** en masse; **taken in a ~** pris ensemble, dans leur ensemble; **the ~ politic** le corps politique; **legislative ~** corps m législatif; **a large ~ of water** une grande étendue d'eau; **a strong ~ of evidence** une forte accumulation de preuves; **a strong ~ of opinion was against it** une grande partie de l'opinion était contre **e** * (= man) bonhomme* m; (= woman) bonne femme* f; **an inquisitive old ~** une vieille fouine; **a pleasant little ~** une gentille petite dame **f** (Phys etc = piece of matter) corps m; **heavenly ~** corps m céleste → **foreign g** (NonC) [of wine, paper] corps m; **a white wine with some ~** un vin blanc qui a du corps; **to give one's hair ~** donner du volume à ses cheveux **h** (= garment) body m **2** COMP ► **body armour** N (NonC) gilet m d'armes ► **body bag** N (esp Mil) housse f mortuaire ► **body belt** N ceinture f d'haltérophilie or de force ► **body blow** N (Boxing) coup m au corps; (fig: disappointment) coup m dur ► **body building** N culturisme m; **~-building exercises** exercices mpl de culturisme or de musculation ► **body-check** (Sport) N body-check m (on à) ◆ VT faire un body-check à ► **body clock** N horloge f biologique ► **body corporate** N (Jur) personne f morale ► **body count** N **to do a ~ count** (of those present) compter les présents; (of fatalities) compter le nombre des morts ► **body double** N doublure f ► **body fascism** N discrimination fondée sur l'apparence physique ► **body fluids** NPL fluides mpl organiques ► **body image** N schéma m corporel ► **body language** N (lit) langage m du corps; (fig) **the ~ language is good between the two leaders** le courant passe bien entre les deux leaders ► **body lotion** N lait m corporel or pour le corps ► **body mike** N (on clip) micro m cravate inv; (clandestine) micro m caché ► **body odour** N odeur f corporelle ► **body piercing** N piercing m ► **body popping** N (NonC) smurf m ► **body repairs** NPL (Aut) travaux mpl de carrosserie ► **body repair shop** N (Aut) = **body shop** ► **body scanner**

N scanner m, scanographe m ► **body search** N fouille f corporelle; **to carry out a ~ search on sb** fouiller qn; **to submit to** or **undergo a ~ search** se faire fouiller ► **body shop** N (Aut) atelier m de carrosserie ► **body snatcher** N (Hist) déterreur m, -euse f de cadavres ► **body stocking** N combinaison f de danse ► **body-surf** VI faire du body(-surf) ► **body-surfing** N (NonC) body(-surf) m ► **body swerve** N (Sport) écart m ► **body warmer** N gilet m matelassé

bodybuilder ['bɒdɪˌbɪldə*] N (Aut) carrossier m; (= food) aliment m énergétique; (= person) culturiste mf; (= apparatus) extenseur m

bodyguard ['bɒdɪgɑːd] N (= person) garde m du corps; (= group) gardes mpl du corps

bodyshell ['bɒdɪʃel] N (Aut) carrosserie f, caisse f

bodysuit ['bɒdɪsuːt] N combinaison f

bodywork ['bɒdɪwɜːk] N (Aut) carrosserie f

Boeotia [bɪˈəʊʃɪə] N la Béotie

Boeotian [bɪˈəʊʃɪən] ADJ béotien

Boer ['bəʊə*] **1** N Boer mf; **the ~ War** la guerre des Boers **2** ADJ boer (f inv)

boffin* ['bɒfɪn] N (Brit) expert m

boffo‡ ['bɒfəʊ] ADJ (US) sensationnel

bog [bɒg] **1** N **a** marais m, marécage m; [of peat] tourbière f **b** (Brit‡ = lavatory) chiottes‡ fpl **2** VT (also **~ down**: gen pass) [+ cart etc] embourber, enliser; (lit, fig) **to be** or **get ~ged down** s'embourber, s'enliser (**in** dans) **3** COMP ► **bog oak** N chêne m des marais ► **bog paper‡** N (Brit) PQ‡ m ► **bog roll‡** N (Brit) (= roll) rouleau m de PQ‡; (NonC = paper) PQ‡ m; **there's no ~ roll** il n'y a pas de PQ‡ ► **bog-standard*** ADJ (Brit) ordinaire

bogey ['bəʊgɪ] N **a** (frightening) démon m; (= bugbear) bête f noire; (fig) **this a ~ for them** c'est leur bête noire **b** (Golf) bogey or bogée m **c** (‡: in nose) crotte f de nez **2** VT (Golf) **to ~ a hole** faire un bogey

bogeyman ['bəʊgɪmæn] N (pl **-men**) croque-mitaine m, père m fouettard

boggle ['bɒgl] **1** VI **a** (= be alarmed, amazed) être ahuri; **the mind ~s!** on croit rêver!; **stories that make the mind ~** des histoires à dormir debout **b** (= hesitate) hésiter (**at** à), reculer (**at** devant) **2** VT (US) **to ~ sb's mind** époustoufler qn

boggy ['bɒgɪ] ADJ (ground) marécageux, bourbeux, tourbeux

bogie ['bəʊgɪ] N (Rail) bogie m; (esp Brit = trolley) diable m

Bogotá [ˌbɒgəˈtɑː] N Bogotá

bogus ['bəʊgəs] ADJ faux (fausse f); **a ~ marriage** un mariage blanc; **measures to deter ~ asylum seekers** des mesures fpl visant à décourager les faux demandeurs d'asile

bogy ['bəʊgɪ] N = **bogey**

Bohemia [bəʊˈhiːmɪə] N la Bohème

Bohemian [bəʊˈhiːmɪən] **1** N **a** (Geog) Bohémien(ne) m(f) **b** († = gipsy) bohémien(ne) m(f) **c** (= artist, writer etc) bohème mf **2** ADJ **a** (Geog) bohémien; († = gipsy) bohémien **c** [artist, surroundings] bohème; **~ life** la (vie de) bohème

bohemianism [bəʊˈhiːmɪənɪzəm] N (vie f de) bohème f

boho* ['bəʊhəʊ] ADJ, N branché(e)* m(f)

▼ **boil¹** [bɔɪl] **1** VI **a** [water etc] bouillir; **the kettle is ~ing** l'eau bout (dans la bouilloire); **to begin to ~** se mettre à bouillir, entrer en ébullition; **to ~ fast/gently** bouillir à gros bouillons/à petits bouillons; **to let the kettle/the vegetables ~ dry** laisser s'évaporer complètement l'eau de la bouilloire/des légumes; (Culin) **the potatoes were ~ing** les pommes de terre bouillaient → **pot¹ b** [sea] bouillonner; (fig) [person] bouillir (**with** de); **he was ~ing with rage** il bouillait (de rage) → **boiling**; → **blood**

② VT ⓐ [+ *water*] faire bouillir ; (= *bring to the boil*) amener à ébullition

ⓑ [+ *food*] (faire) cuire à l'eau, (faire) bouillir ; **~ed bacon** lard *m* bouilli ; **~ed beef** bœuf *m* bouilli, pot-au-feu *m* ; **~ed egg** œuf *m* à la coque ; **~ed ham** jambon *m* cuit ; **~ed potatoes** pommes *fpl* à l'anglaise or à l'eau ; (*Brit*) **~ed sweet** bonbon *m* à sucer, ≈ berlingot *m* → **hard, soft**

ⓒ [+ *washing*] **to ~ the whites** faire bouillir le (linge) blanc ; **~ed shirt*** chemise *f* empesée

③ N **on the ~** (*lit*) bouillant, qui bout ; (* *fig*) [*situation, project*] en ébullition ; **off the ~** (*lit*) qui ne bout plus ; (* *fig*) [*situation*] en voie d'apaisement ; [*project*] au ralenti ; **to bring sth to the** (*Brit*) or **a** (*US*) **~** faire bouillir qch ; **to come to the** (*Brit*) or **a** (*US*) **~** venir à ébullition ; **to go off the ~** (*lit*) cesser de bouillir ; (* *fig*) [*person*] baisser ; **to bring a situation to the ~** amener une situation au point critique

④ COMP ► **boil-in-a-bag, boil-in-the-bag** ADJ que l'on cuit dans le sachet

► **boil away** VI ⓐ (= *go on boiling*) (continuer de) bouillir ⓑ (= *evaporate completely*) s'évaporer, se réduire (par ébullition)

► **boil down** ① VI ⓐ (*lit*) [*jam etc*] se réduire ⓑ (* *fig*) se ramener, revenir (**to** à) ; **all the arguments ~ down to this** tous les arguments se résument or reviennent or se ramènent à ceci ; **it all ~s down to the same thing** tout cela revient absolument au même ② VT SEP ⓐ (*lit*) [+ *sauce etc*] faire réduire (par ébullition) ⓑ (* *fig*) [+ *text*] réduire (**to** à), abréger

► **boil over** VI ⓐ [*water*] déborder ; [*milk*] se sauver, déborder ; **the pot ~ed over** la casserole a débordé ⓑ (*with rage*) bouillir (**with** de) ; **their anger ~ed over into violence** leur colère a dégénéré en violence

► **boil up** VI (*lit*) [*milk*] monter ; **anger was ~ing up in him** la moutarde lui montait au nez

boil² [bɔɪl] N (*Med*) furoncle *m*, clou *m*

boiler [ˈbɔɪləʳ] ① N ⓐ (*for hot water, steam*) chaudière *f* ; (*Brit: for washing clothes*) lessiveuse *f* ; (= *pan*) casserole *f* → **double, potboiler** ⓑ (= *fowl*) poule *f* à faire au pot ② COMP ► **boiler house** N bâtiment *m* des chaudières ► **boiler room** N (*gen*) salle *f* des chaudières ; (*Naut*) chaufferie *f*, chambre *f* de chauffe ► **boiler suit** N (*Brit*) bleu(s) *m(pl)* (de travail or de chauffe)

boilermaker [ˈbɔɪləˌmeɪkəʳ] N chaudronnier *m*

boilermaking [ˈbɔɪləˌmeɪkɪŋ] N grosse chaudronnerie *f*

boilerman [ˈbɔɪləmæn] N (*pl* **-men**) (*Tech*) chauffeur *m*

boiling [ˈbɔɪlɪŋ] ① N [*of water etc*] ébullition *f* ② ADJ ⓐ [*water, oil*] bouillant ; (*Brit fig*) **the whole ~ lot*** tout le bataclan*, tout le bazar* ; **it's ~ (hot) today*** il fait une chaleur terrible aujourd'hui ; **I'm ~ (hot)!*** je meurs de chaleur ! ⓑ (* *fig* = *angry*) bouillant de colère, en rage ; **he is ~** il bout de colère ⓒ (*Culin*) **~ beef** bœuf *m* pour pot-au-feu ; **~ fowl** poule *f* à faire au pot ③ ADV ► **hot** (*lit*) tout bouillant, (*fig*) → **2** ④ COMP ► **boiling point** N point *m* d'ébullition ; (*fig*) **at ~ point** en ébullition

boisterous [ˈbɔɪstərəs] ADJ [*person, crowd, behaviour*] tapageur, turbulent ; [*game*] tumultueux ; (*fig*) [*wind*] furieux

boisterously [ˈbɔɪstərəslɪ] ADV tumultueusement

boisterousness [ˈbɔɪstərəsnɪs] N [*of person, crowd, behaviour*] gaieté *f* turbulente ; [*of game*] tumulte *m*

bold [bəʊld] ① ADJ ⓐ (= *brave*) [*person, action*] hardi, intrépide ; **to grow ~** s'enhardir ; **a ~ step** une démarche osée or audacieuse ; **a ~ stroke** un coup d'audace → **face** ⓑ [*person, look*] (= *forward*) hardi, effronté (*pej*) ; (= *not shy*) assuré ; (*frm*) **to be** or **make so ~ as to do sth** avoir l'audace de faire qch ; (*frm*) **to make**

~ with sth prendre la liberté de se servir de qch ; (*frm*) **if I may make so ~ ...** si je peux me permettre de faire remarquer ... ; **as ~ as brass** d'une impudence peu commune, culotté* ⓒ (*Art, Literat* = *striking*) hardi, vigoureux ; **to bring out in ~ relief** faire ressortir vigoureusement ; **to paint in ~ strokes** [*artist*] avoir une touche puissante ⓓ (*Typ*) en grasse, gras (grasse *f*) ② N (*NonC: Typ*) caractères *mpl* gras ; **in ~** en (caractères) gras

boldly [ˈbəʊldlɪ] ADV ⓐ (= *bravely*) hardiment, audacieusement ⓑ (= *confidently, not shyly*) [*declare, announce, claim*] avec assurance ; [*gaze*] effrontément ; **to smile ~** sourire avec assurance ⓒ (= *strikingly*) **~ patterned/checked** à grands motifs/carreaux ; **~ coloured** (*one colour*) de couleur voyante ; (*contrasting colours*) de couleurs voyantes

boldness [ˈbəʊldnɪs] N ⓐ (= *braveness, daring*) [*of person, action, plan, idea*] audace *f* ; [*of gaze*] audace *f*, aplomb *m* ⓑ [*of colour, design*] vigueur *f*

bole [bəʊl] N fût *m*, tronc *m* (d'arbre)

bolero [bəˈlɛərəʊ] N ⓐ (= *music, dance*) boléro *m* ⓑ [ˈbɒlərəʊ] (*also* **~ jacket**) boléro *m*

boletus [bəʊˈliːtəs] N (*pl* **boletuses** or **boleti** [bəʊˈliːtaɪ]) bolet *m*

bolide [ˈbəʊlaɪd] N (*Astron*) bolide *m*

Bolivia [bəˈlɪvɪə] N la Bolivie

Bolivian [bəˈlɪvɪən] ① ADJ (*gen*) bolivien ; [*ambassador, embassy*] de Bolivie ② N Bolivien(ne) *m(f)*

boll [bəʊl] ① N graine *f* (*du cotonnier, du lin*) ② COMP ► **boll weevil** N anthonome *m* (*du cotonnier*)

bollard [ˈbɒləd] N [*of quay*] bollard *m* ; (*Brit*) [*of road*] borne *f*

bollix* [ˈbɒlɪks] VT (*US: also* **~ up**) = **ball(s) up 1** ; → **ball¹**

bollocking** [ˈbɒləkɪŋ] N engueulade* *f* ; **to give sb a ~** engueuler qn* ; **I got a real ~ from him** il m'a bien engueulé*

bollocks** [ˈbɒləks] N (*Brit*) = **balls** ; → **ball¹**

Bollywood* [ˈbɒlɪwʌd] N Bollywood *m* (*le Hollywood du cinéma indien, à Bombay*)

Bologna [bəˈləʊnjə] N Bologne

bolognese [bɒləˈnjeɪz] ADJ ► **sauce** sauce *f* bolognaise

boloney* [bəˈləʊnɪ] N = **baloney**

Bolshevik [ˈbɒlʃəvɪk] ① N Bolchevik *mf* ② ADJ bolchevique

Bolshevism [ˈbɒlʃəvɪzəm] N bolchevisme *m*

Bolshevist [ˈbɒlʃəvɪst] N, ADJ bolcheviste *mf*

bolshie*, bolshy* [ˈbɒlʃɪ] (*Brit pej*) ① N (*Pol*) rouge *mf* ② ADJ (*Pol*) rouge ; (*fig*) **he's rather ~** il ne pense qu'à enquiquiner le monde*, c'est un mauvais coucheur ; **he turned ~** il a commencé à râler*

bolster [ˈbəʊlstəʳ] ① N ⓐ [*of bed*] traversin *m* ⓑ (*Constr*) racinal *m*, sous-poutre *f* ② VT (*also* **~ up**) [+ *person, morale*] soutenir (**with** par)

bolt [bəʊlt] ① N ⓐ [*of door, window*] verrou *m* ; [*of lock*] pêne *m* ; (*Tech: for nut*) boulon *m* ; [*of crossbow*] carreau *m* ; [*of rifle*] culasse *f* mobile ; (*Climbing: also* **expansion ~**) piton *m* à expansion ⓑ [*of cloth*] rouleau *m* ⓒ (= *lightning*) éclair *m* ; (*fig*) **a ~ from the blue** un coup de tonnerre → **shoot** ⓓ (= *dash*) fuite *f* soudaine, départ *m* brusque ; **he made a ~ for the door** il a fait un bond or a bondi vers la porte ; **to make a ~ for it*** filer* or se sauver à toutes jambes ② ADV ► **upright** droit comme un piquet or comme un i ③ VI ⓐ (= *run away*) [*horse*] s'emballer ; [*person*] filer*, se sauver ⓑ (= *move quickly*) se précipiter, foncer* ; **he ~ed along the corridor** il a enfilé le couloir à toutes jambes ⓒ [*plant*] monter

④ VT ⓐ [+ *food*] engouffrer, engloutir ⓑ [+ *door, window*] verrouiller, fermer au verrou ; **~ the door!** mettez or poussez le(s) verrou(s) ! ⓒ (*Tech*) [+ *beams*] boulonner ⓓ (*US** = *stop*) abandonner, laisser tomber ⑤ COMP ► **bolt cutters** NPL coupe-boulons *m* ► **bolt-hole** N (*Brit*) [*of animal*] terrier *m*, trou *m* ; [*of person*] abri *m*, refuge *m*

► **bolt in** ① VI (= *rush in*) entrer comme un ouragan ② VT SEP (= *lock in*) enfermer au verrou

► **bolt on** VT SEP (*Tech*) boulonner

► **bolt out** VI (= *rush out*) sortir comme un ouragan

bolus [ˈbəʊləs] N (*pl* **boluses**) (*Med*) bol *m*

bomb [bɒm] ① N ⓐ (= *explosive device*) bombe *f* ; **letter/parcel ~** lettre *f*/paquet *m* piégé(e) ; **the Bomb** la bombe atomique ; (*fig*) **to put a ~ under sb*** secouer (les puces à) qn* ; (*Brit*) **his party went like a ~*** sa réception a été (un succès) du tonnerre* ; (*Brit*) **this car goes like a ~*** elle file, cette bagnole* ; (*Brit*) **the car cost a ~*** la bagnole* a coûté les yeux de la tête → **A, car, H** ⓑ (*US** = *flop*) fiasco *m*, bide* *m* ② VT [+ *town*] bombarder → **dive¹** ③ VI ⓐ (*esp US** = *flop*) être un fiasco or un bide* ⓑ (* = *go quickly*) **to ~ along** foncer, bomber* ; **we ~ed down the road** nous avons foncé le long de la rue ; **we ~ed down to London** nous avons bombé* jusqu'à Londres ④ COMP ► **bomb aimer** N (*Aviat* = *person*) bombardier *m* ► **bomb attack** N attentat *m* à la bombe ► **bomb bay** N soute *f* à bombes ► **bomb crater** N (*Geog*) entonnoir *m* ► **bomb disposal** N déminage *m* ; **~ disposal expert** démineur *m* ; (*Mil*) artificier *m* ; **~ disposal squad** or **unit** équipe *f* de déminage ► **bomb factory** N fabrique *f* de bombes ► **bomb scare** N alerte *f* à la bombe ► **bomb shelter** N abri *m* (antiaérien) ► **bomb site** N lieu *m* bombardé

► **bomb out** VT SEP [+ *house*] détruire par un bombardement ; **the family was ~ed out** la famille a dû abandonner sa maison bombardée ; **~ed out families** familles *fpl* sinistrées (*par un bombardement*)

bombard [bɒmˈbɑːd] VT (*Mil, Phys, fig*) bombarder (**with** de)

bombardier [ˌbɒmbəˈdɪəʳ] N (*Mil*) caporal *m* d'artillerie ; (*Aviat*) bombardier (*aviateur*)

bombardment [bɒmˈbɑːdmənt] N bombardement *m*

bombast [ˈbɒmbæst] N grandiloquence *f*, boursouflure *f*

bombastic [bɒmˈbæstɪk] ADJ [*style, person*] grandiloquent, pompeux

bombastically [bɒmˈbæstɪkəlɪ] ADV [*speak*] avec grandiloquence, avec emphase ; [*write*] dans un style ampoulé

Bombay [bɒmˈbeɪ] ① N Bombay ② COMP ► **Bombay duck** N (*Culin*) poisson *m* salé (*indien*)

bombazine [ˈbɒmbəziːn] N bombasin *m*

bombed* [bɒmd] ADJ (*esp US*) (= *drunk*) bourré* ; (= *on drugs*) défoncé*

bomber [ˈbɒməʳ] ① N (= *aircraft*) bombardier *m* ; (*terrorist*) plastiqueur *m* ② COMP ► **bomber command** N commandement *m* tactique aérien ► **bomber jacket** N blouson *m* d'aviateur ► **bomber pilot** N pilote *m* de bombardier

bombing [ˈbɒmɪŋ] ① N (*Aviat*) bombardement *m* ; (*by terrorist*) attentat *m* à la bombe → **dive¹** ② ADJ [*raid, mission, plane*] de bombardement

bombproof [ˈbɒmpruːf] ADJ ⓐ (*lit*) [*bunker etc*] à l'épreuve des bombes ⓑ (* *fig*) indestructible

bombshell ['bɒmʃel] N a (Mil†) obus m
b (fig = shock) **to come like a ~** faire l'effet
d'une bombe; **this news was a ~** la nouvelle a
fait l'effet d'une bombe; (fig) **to drop a** or
one's ~ lâcher une bombe* (fig) c* **she's a
real ~** c'est une fille canon !*

bombsight ['bɒmsaɪt] N viseur m de bombardement

bona fide ['bəʊnə'faɪdɪ] ADJ [member, traveller,
student etc] authentique, vrai; [offer] sérieux

bona fides ['bəʊnə'faɪdɪz] N bonne foi f

bonanza [bə'nænzə] 1 N (= windfall) aubaine
f; (= boom) boom m; (US Min) riche filon m; **a
property/sales ~** un boom immobilier sur les
ventes; **the North Sea oil ~** la manne pétrolière de la mer du Nord 2 COMP ► **the Bonanza State** N (US) le Montana ► **bonanza
year** N année f exceptionnelle

Bonaparte ['bəʊnəpɑːt] N Bonaparte m

bonbon ['bɒnbɒn] N bonbon m

bonce [bɒns] N (Brit = head) tronche* f

bond [bɒnd] 1 N a (= agreement) engagement m, contrat m; **to enter into a ~** s'engager (**to do** à faire)
b (= link) lien(s) m(pl), attachement m; **to
break a ~ with the past** rompre les liens avec
le passé; **~s** (= chains) fers mpl, chaînes fpl; (fig
= ties) liens mpl; **marriage ~s** liens mpl conjugaux → **pair**
c (Comm, Fin) bon m, titre m
d (NonC: Comm = custody of goods) entreposage m (en attendant le paiement de la taxe); **to
put sth into ~** entreposer qch en douane; **to
take goods out of ~** dédouaner des marchandises
e (= adhesion between surfaces) adhérence f
f (Constr) appareil m
g (Chem) liaison f
h (also ~ **paper**) papier m à lettres de luxe
2 VT a (Comm) [+ goods] entreposer
b (= stick) coller; [+ bricks] liaisonner
c (Fin) lier (par une garantie financière)
d (= place under bond) placer sous caution m;
(= put up bond for) se porter caution pour
3 VI a (= stick together) coller
b (Psych) se lier; **to ~ with one's baby** s'attacher à son bébé; (fig) **we ~ed immediately**
nous nous sommes tout de suite liés d'amitié, nous avons tout de suite sympathisé
4 COMP ► **bonded labour** N (NonC: Brit)
travail m non rémunéré (pour le compte d'un
créancier) ► **bonded warehouse** N entrepôt
m des douanes ► **bond market** N (Fin) marché m obligataire

bondage ['bɒndɪdʒ] 1 N a (lit) esclavage m,
servage m b **to be in ~ to sb** être la serf
de qn b (fig) esclavage m, asservissement m;
the ~ of dieting/heroin addiction l'esclavage
que représentent les régimes/que représente
l'héroïnomanie c (= sexual practice) bondage
m 2 COMP [gear, magazine] de bondage

bondholder ['bɒnd,həʊldə'] N (Fin) porteur m
d'obligations or de bons

bonding ['bɒndɪŋ] N a (Constr) liaison f; [of
wood, plastic etc] collage m; (Elec) système m or
circuit m régulateur de tension b (Psych)
formation f de liens affectifs; (in general
parlance) action f de sympathiser

bondsman ['bɒndzmən] N (pl -**men**) (Hist) serf
m, esclave m; (Jur) garant m, caution f

bone [bəʊn] 1 N a os m; [of fish] arête f; **~s**
[of the dead] ossements mpl, os mpl; (= dice)
dés mpl (à jouer); **to cut costs to the ~** réduire
les coûts au strict minimum; **chilled** or **frozen
to the ~** transi de froid, glacé jusqu'à la
moelle (des os); (hum) **my old ~s** mes vieux
os, ma vieille carcasse*; **to have a ~ to pick
with sb** avoir un compte à régler avec qn; **he
made no ~s about saying what he thought** il
n'a pas hésité à dire ce qu'il pensait; **he made
no ~s about it** il n'y est pas allé par quatre
chemins or avec le dos de la cuiller*; **there

are no ~s broken (lit) il n'y a rien de cassé;
(fig) il y a plus de peur que de mal, il n'y a
rien de grave; **he won't make old ~s** il ne fera
pas de vieux os; **that was a bit close** or **near to
the ~** [remark] c'était un peu limite; **to work
one's fingers to the ~*** s'user au travail,
s'épuiser à la tâche → **anklebone, bag, feel,
skin**
b (NonC = substance) os m; **a handle (made)
of ~** un manche en os
c [of corset] baleine f
2 VT [+ meat, fowl] désosser; [+ fish] ôter les
arêtes de
3 COMP [buttons, handle etc] en os ► **bone-
chilling** ADJ à vous glacer le sang ► **bone
china** N porcelaine f tendre ► **bone-dry** ADJ
absolument sec (sèche f) ► **bone-idle**;
bone-lazy* ADJ fainéant, paresseux comme
une couleuvre ► **bone marrow** N (Anat)
moelle f osseuse ► **bone meal** N engrais m
(de cendres d'os) ► **bone of contention** N
pomme f de discorde ► **bone-shaker*** N (=
car) vieille guimbarde f, tacot* m; (= dilapidated cycle) vieux clou* m ► **bone structure**
N (NonC: gen) ossature f; [of face] ossature f de
la tête

► **bone up**: VT SEP, **bone up on**: VT FUS [+
subject] bûcher*, potasser*, bosser*

boned [bəʊnd] ADJ a [meat] désossé; [fish]
sans arêtes b [corset] baleiné

bonehead ['bəʊnhed] N crétin(e)* m(f), abru-
ti(e)* m(f)

boneheaded; ['bəʊn,hedɪd] ADJ idiot, abruti*

boneless ['bəʊnlɪs] ADJ [meat] désossé, sans
os; [fish] sans arêtes

boner ['bəʊnə'] N a (US; = blunder) gaffe f,
bourde f; **to pull a ~** faire une gaffe*, mettre
les pieds dans le plat b (= erection) **to have a
~*** bander**

boneyard* ['bəʊnjɑːd] N (US) cimetière m

bonfire ['bɒnfaɪə'] 1 N feu m (de joie); (for
rubbish) feu m (de jardin) 2 COMP ► **Bonfire
Night** N (Brit) le 5 novembre
→ GUY FAWKES NIGHT

bong [bɒŋ] N a (= sound) bong m b (; =
pipe) bong m

bongo (drum) ['bɒŋgəʊ(drʌm)] N (tambour
m) bongo m

bonhomie ['bɒnɒmiː] N bonhomie f

bonk [bɒŋk] 1 N a (* = hit) coup m; (with
hand) beigne; f, pain* m b (Brit; = sex) **to have
a ~;** s'envoyer en l'air; 2 VI (Brit; = have
sex) s'envoyer en l'air; 3 VT a (* = hit)
frapper, filer un coup à*; (with hand also) filer
une beigne* or un pain* à b (Brit; = have sex
with) s'envoyer*, sauter; 4 EXCL bang

bonkers; ['bɒŋkəz] ADJ cinglé*, dingue*

bonking ['bɒŋkɪŋ] N (NonC: Brit) partie f de
jambe en l'air;

Bonn [bɒn] N Bonn

bonnet ['bɒnɪt] N a (= hat) [of woman]
chapeau m; [of child] béguin m, bonnet m →
bee, sun b [Brit Aut] capot m c (Archit)
auvent m; [of chimney] capuchon m d (Naut)
bonnette f

bonny ['bɒnɪ] ADJ (esp N Engl, Scot) joli, beau
(belle f)

bonsai ['bɒnsaɪ] N (pl inv) bonsaï m

bonus ['bəʊnəs] 1 N prime f, bonus m; (Brit
Fin) dividende m exceptionnel; (Educ, cycle
racing) bonification f; **~ of 500 francs** 500
francs de prime; (fig) **as a ~** en prime →
incentive 2 COMP ► **bonus issue** N (Fin)
émission f d'actions gratuites ► **bonus
point** N (in game, quiz etc) point m (en prime)
► **bonus share** N action f gratuite

bony ['bəʊnɪ] ADJ a (Anat) [tissue] osseux; (fig)
[knee, person] anguleux, maigre, décharné
b [fish] plein d'arêtes; [meat] plein d'os

boo [buː] 1 EXCL hou !, peuh !; **he wouldn't
say ~ to a goose*** il n'ose jamais ouvrir le

bec* 2 VT [+ actor, play] huer, siffler; **to be
~ed off the stage** sortir de scène sous les
huées or les sifflets 3 VI huer 4 N huée f

boob* [buːb] 1 N a (Brit = mistake) gaffe
f; (= silly person) ballot* m, nigaud(e) m(f)
b (= breast) sein m, nichon; m 2 VI (Brit)
gaffer 3 COMP ► **boob job**; N **to have a ~
job** se faire refaire les seins ► **boob tube*** N
(Dress = sun top) bain m de soleil; (US = TV set)
télé f

boo-boo* ['buːbuː] N boulette; f, bourde f

booby ['buːbɪ] 1 N nigaud(e) m(f), bêta(sse)*
m(f) 2 COMP ► **booby hatch** N (Naut) écou-
tillon m; (US; pej = mental hospital) cabanon;
m, maison f de fous* ► **booby prize** N prix
m de consolation (décerné au dernier)
► **booby trap** N traquenard m; (Mil) objet
m piégé ► **booby-trapped** ADJ [car, door etc]
piégé

boodle†; ['buːdl] N (= money) oseille; f, pèze;
m; (US = bribe) pot-de-vin m; (US) **the whole ~**
le tout, tous les trucs*

booger* ['buːgə'] N (US) crotte f de nez

boogie* ['buːgɪ] 1 N (= dance) **to have a ~**
guincher*; **to go for a ~** aller guincher* or se
trémousser* 2 VI guincher*

boogie-woogie ['buːgɪ,wuːgɪ] N boogie-
woogie m

boohoo* [,buː'huː] 1 VI pleurnicher, brailler*
2 EXCL ouin ! ouin !

booing ['buːɪŋ] N (NonC) huées fpl; (Theat)
sifflets mpl

book [bʊk] 1 N a livre m, bouquin* m; **the
(Good) Book** la Bible → **bank², telephone,
textbook**
b (= chapter) [of Bible etc] livre m; [of poem]
chant m; (Bible) **the Book of Job/Kings** etc le
livre de Job/des Rois etc
c (also **exercise ~**) cahier m → **notebook**
d [of tickets, stamps, cheques etc] carnet m; **~
of matches** pochette f d'allumettes → **chequebook, passbook**
e (Comm, Fin) (account) **~s** livre m de
comptes; **to keep the ~s of a firm** tenir la
comptabilité or les comptes d'une entreprise;
the ~s and records la comptabilité
f [of club, society] registre m; **to be on the ~s
of an organization** être inscrit à une organisation; **to take one's name off the ~s** donner sa
démission
g (Betting) **to keep a ~ on sth** prendre les paris sur qch; **to make a ~** (= take bets) inscrire
les paris; (= bet) parier; **to open** or **start a ~
(on sth)** ouvrir les paris (sur qch)
h (= libretto) [of opera etc] livret m
i (Comm) **~ of samples** album m or jeu m
d'échantillons
j (phrases) **to bring sb to ~** obliger qn à rendre des comptes; **by the ~** selon les règles; **to
close the ~ on sth** considérer qch comme une
affaire classée; **to go by the ~** ◊ **to stick to the
~** appliquer strictement le règlement; **to be
in sb's bad** or **black ~s** être mal vu de qn; **I
am in his good ~s*** je suis dans ses petits papiers*, il m'a à la bonne;; (fig) **in my ~** **he's
unreliable** à mon avis or d'après moi on ne
peut pas se fier à lui; **he knew the district like
a ~** il connaissait la région comme sa poche;
that's one for the ~ or **~s!*** c'est à marquer
d'une pierre blanche !, il faut faire une croix à
la cheminée !; **already on the ~s** [regulation
etc] qui figure déjà dans les textes; [member
etc] déjà inscrit au registre; **to go on the ~s**
[law] entrer en vigueur → **suit, throw**
2 VT a [+ seat] louer; [+ room, sleeper, table]
retenir, réserver; (Brit) [+ ticket] prendre; **to ~
one's seat in advance** louer sa place à l'avance
or d'avance; (Theat) **tonight's performance is
~ed up** or **fully ~ed** on joue à bureaux fermés
or à guichets fermés ce soir; **the hotel is ~ed
up** or **fully ~ed (until September)** l'hôtel est
complet (jusqu'en septembre); **I'm ~ed for tomorrow lunch** je suis pris demain à déjeuner;

(*Rail*) **to ~ sb through to Birmingham** assurer à qn une réservation jusqu'à Birmingham ; **I've ~ed (up) my holiday** j'ai fait les réservations pour mes vacances → **solid**

b (*Comm, Fin*) [+ *order*] inscrire, enregistrer ; **to ~ goods to sb's account** inscrire des marchandises au compte de qn

c (*Police*) [+ *driver etc*] donner *or* mettre un procès-verbal *or* P.-V.* à ; (*Ftbl*) [+ *player*] montrer un carton jaune à ; **to be ~ed for speeding** attraper une contravention pour excès de vitesse ; (*Ftbl*) **to be ~ed** recevoir un carton jaune

3 VI (*at hotel*) (*on arrival*) se présenter à la réception ; (= *reserve in advance*) réserver une chambre

4 COMP ► **book club** N cercle *m* de lecture, club *m* du livre ► **book ends** NPL serre-livres *m inv* ► **book fair** N salon *m* du livre ► **book jacket** N jaquette *f* ► **book-keeper** N comptable *mf* ► **book-keeping** N comptabilité *f* ► **book knowledge, book learning** N connaissances *fpl* livresques ► **book lover** N bibliophile *mf* ► **book post** N tarif *m* livres ► **book review** N compte rendu *m* de livre ► **book token** N (*Brit*) bon-cadeau *m* (*négociable en librairie*), chèque-livre *m*

► **book in** (*Brit*) **1** VI (*at hotel etc*) (*on arrival*) se présenter à la réception ; (= *reserve in advance*) réserver une chambre **2** VT SEP (*at reception*) se présenter à la réception ; (= *reserve room for*) réserver une chambre pour

► **book up** (*Brit*) **1** VI réserver **2** VT SEP retenir, réserver ; **the school ~ed up all the seats on the coach** l'école a réservé toutes les places dans le car ; **the tour is ~ed up** on ne prend plus d'inscriptions pour l'excursion ; **the hotel is ~ed up** *or* **fully ~ed until September** l'hôtel est complet jusqu'en septembre ; **I'm very ~ed up** je suis très pris → **book 2a**

bookable ['bʊkəbl] ADJ (*Brit*) **a** [*seat etc*] qu'on peut retenir *or* réserver *or* louer ; **seats are ~ in advance** on peut retenir ses places à l'avance) ; **seats ~ from 6 June** location (des places) ouverte dès le 6 juin **b** (*Sport*) [*offence*] passible d'un avertissement

bookbinder ['bʊkbaɪndəʳ] N relieur *m*, -euse *f*

bookbinding ['bʊkbaɪndɪŋ] N (*NonC*) reliure *f*

bookcase ['bʊkkeɪs] N bibliothèque *f* (*meuble*)

Booker Prize ['bʊkə,praɪz] N (*Brit*) **the ~** le Booker Prize

---

BOOKER PRIZE

Prix littéraire britannique créé en 1969 par un industriel (M. Booker) pour récompenser une œuvre de fiction écrite par un romancier originaire du Royaume-Uni, d'Irlande ou du Commonwealth. La cérémonie de remise du prix est diffusée en direct à la télévision, et le choix du jury suscite souvent des controverses.

---

bookie* ['bʊkɪ] N book* *m*, bookmaker *m*

▼ **booking** ['bʊkɪŋ] **1** N **a** (*esp Brit*) réservation *f* ; **to make a ~** louer, réserver, faire une réservation **b** (*Ftbl*) **there were three ~s at the game** il y a eu trois cartons jaunes lors de ce match **2** COMP ► **booking clerk** N (*Brit Rail etc*) préposé(e) *m(f)* aux réservations ► **booking fee** N frais *mpl* de location ► **booking office** N (*Brit: Rail, Theat*) (bureau *m* de) location *f*

bookish ['bʊkɪʃ] ADJ [*person*] studieux, scolaire (*pej*) ; [*word, phrase*] livresque

booklet ['bʊklɪt] N brochure *f*, plaquette *f*

bookmaker ['bʊkmeɪkəʳ] N bookmaker *m*

bookmaking ['bʊkmeɪkɪŋ] **1** N (*NonC*) métier *m* de bookmaker **2** COMP ► **bookmaking firm** N bookmaker *m*

bookmark ['bʊkmɑːk] N marque-page *m*, signet *m*

bookmobile ['bʊkməˌbiːl] N (*US*) bibliobus *m*

bookplate ['bʊkpleɪt] N ex-libris *m*

bookrest ['bʊkrest] N lutrin *m*

bookseller ['bʊkˌseləʳ] N libraire *mf* → **secondhand**

bookshelf ['bʊkʃelf] N étagère *f* (à livres) ; (*in bookcase*) rayon *m* (de bibliothèque)

bookshop ['bʊkʃɒp] N (*esp Brit*) librairie *f* → **secondhand**

bookstall ['bʊkstɔːl] N (*Brit: in station, airport*) kiosque *m* à journaux ; [*of secondhand books*] étalage *m* de bouquiniste

bookstand ['bʊkstænd] N (*US*) **a** (= *bookrest, lectern*) lutrin *m* **b** (= *bookstall: in station, airport*) kiosque *m* à journaux ; **to hit the ~s** [*book*] sortir en librairie

bookstore ['bʊkstɔːʳ] N (*esp US*) librairie *f*

bookworm ['bʊkwɜːm] N (*fig*) rat *m* de bibliothèque

Boolean ['buːlɪən] ADJ booléen

boom¹ [buːm] **1** N **a** (= *barrier: across river etc*) barrage *m* (*de radeaux, de chaînes etc*), bôme *f* **b** [*of boat*] gui *m* ; (*Tech: also* **derrick ~**) bras *m* ; [*of crane*] flèche *f* ; [*of microphone, camera*] perche *f*, girafe *f*

boom² [buːm] **1** N (= *sound*) [*of sea, waves*] grondement *m*, mugissement *m* ; [*of wind*] mugissement *m*, hurlements *mpl* ; [*of guns, thunder*] grondement *m* ; [*of storm*] rugissement *m* ; [*of organ*] ronflement *m* ; [*of voices*] rugissement *m*, grondement *m* ; (*Aviat*) **sonic ~** bang *m* supersonique **2** VI **a** [*sea*] gronder, mugir ; [*wind*] hurler, mugir (*sourdement*) ; [*thunder*] gronder, rouler **b** (*also ~ out*) [*organ*] ronfler ; [*guns*] tonner, gronder ; [*voice*] retentir ; [*person*] tonner, tonitruer **3** VT **"never!" he ~ed** « jamais ! » dit-il d'une voix tonitruante *or* retentissante **4** COMP ► **boom box*** N (*US*) ghetto-blaster *m*

boom³ [buːm] **1** VI **a** (*Comm*) [*trade*] être en expansion *or* en plein essor ; **business is ~ing** les affaires prospèrent

b (*Comm, Fin, St Ex*) [*prices*] monter en flèche **2** VT (*US**) [+ *market, sales*] développer ; (= *publicize*) [+ *person, place*] promouvoir

3 N (*Comm*) (*in business, transactions*) montée *f* en flèche, boom *m* ; (*for firm*) forte progression *f* ; (*for product*) popularité *f*, vogue *f* ; (*Comm, Econ, Fin, St Ex*) boom *m* ; **a property ~** un boom sur l'immobilier ; **an export ~** un boom sur les exportations **4** COMP ► **boom and bust** ADJ = **boom-bust** ► **boom baby** N bébé *m* du baby-boom ► **boom-bust** ADJ (*Econ*) [*economy, market*] en dents de scie ; **the ~-bust pattern of the economy in recent years** l'évolution *f* en dents de scie de l'économie ces dernières années ; **property is a ~-bust business** l'immobilier est un marché en dents de scie, l'immobilier connaît des hauts et des bas ► **boom town** N ville *f* en plein développement, ville *f* champignon

boomerang ['buːməræŋ] **1** N (*lit, fig*) boomerang *m* **2** VI (*fig*) [*words, actions*] faire boomerang

booming ['buːmɪŋ] ADJ [*sound*] retentissant ; [*voice*] tonitruant, retentissant

boomlet ['buːmlɪt] N (*Econ*) expansion *f* de faible amplitude

boon [buːn] **1** N **a** (= *blessing*) bénédiction* *f*, aubaine *f* ; **it would be a ~ if he went** quelle aubaine s'il s'en allait ; **this new machine is a great ~** cette nouvelle machine est une bénédiction* ; **it is a ~ to me** cela m'est très précieux **b** (†† = *favour*) faveur *f* **2** COMP ► **boon companion**† N joyeux compère *m*, compagnon *m* de virée

boondocks* ['buːndɒks] NPL (*US*) **the ~** le bled* (*pej*)

boondoggle⁑ ['buːndɒgl] VI (*US*) **a** (= *work uselessly*) passer son temps à des tâches se-

condaires **b** (*esp Pol*) créer des emplois bidon*

boonies⁑ ['buːnɪz] NPL (*US*) = **boondocks**

boor [bʊəʳ] N (*coarse*) rustre *m* ; (*ill-mannered*) malotru(e) *m(f)*, butor *m*

boorish ['bʊərɪʃ] ADJ rustre, grossier

boorishly ['bʊərɪʃlɪ] ADV [*behave*] en rustre, avec grossièreté ; [*speak*] sans tact

boorishness ['bʊərɪʃnɪs] N manque *m* de savoir-vivre, grossièreté *f*

boost [buːst] **1** N **to give sb a ~ (up)** (*lit*) soulever qn par derrière *or* par en dessous ; (*fig: also* **give a ~ to sb's morale**) remonter le moral à qn ; **to give sb/a product a ~** (= *do publicity for*) faire du battage* pour qn/un produit **2** VT **a** (*Elec*) survolter ; (*Aut*) [+ *engine*] suralimenter ; (*Space*) [+ *spacecraft*] propulser **b** (*Comm, Ind etc* = *increase*) [+ *price*] hausser, faire monter ; [+ *output, productivity*] accroître, développer ; [+ *sales, product*] promouvoir, faire monter en flèche ; [+ *confidence etc*] renforcer ; (*Econ*) **to ~ the economy** donner du tonus à l'économie **c** (= *do publicity for*) [+ *person, product*] faire de la réclame *or* du battage* pour

booster ['buːstəʳ] **1** N (*Elec*) (= *device*) survolteur *m* ; (= *charge*) charge *f* d'appoint ; (*Rad*) amplificateur *m* ; (*Rail*) booster *m* ; (*Space: also ~* **rocket**) fusée *f* de lancement, booster *m* ; (*Med: also ~* **shot, ~ dose**) (piqûre *f* de) rappel *m* ; (*US** = *supporter*) supporter *m* actif *or* enthousiaste **2** COMP ► **booster cushion** N (*Brit Aut*) rehausseur *m* ► **booster seat** N rehausseur *m*

boot¹ [buːt] **1** N **a** (*gen*) botte *f* ; (*also* **ankle ~**) bottine *f*, boot *m* ; [*of soldier, workman etc*] (*grosse*) chaussure *f*, brodequin *m* ; (*Brit fig*) **the ~ is on the other foot** les rôles sont renversés ; **to quake** *or* **shake** *or* **tremble** *or* **shiver in one's ~s** trembler comme une feuille ; (*Brit fig*) **to fill one's ~s with sth** se remplir les poches de qch ; **his heart was in his ~s** il avait la mort dans l'âme ; (*fig*) **to give sb the ~**⁑ flanquer* qn à la porte, sacquer* qn ; **to get** *or* **be given the ~**⁑ être flanqué* à la porte, être sacqué* ; (*Brit*) **to put the ~ in**⁑ (*attack physically*) rentrer dans le chou⁑ des gens ; (*fig*) enfoncer le couteau dans la plaie ; (*Brit fig*) **to put the ~ into sb/sth**⁑ débiner* *or* éreinter qn/qch ; (*Brit*) **Boots**† garçon *m* d'hôtel → **bet, big, die¹, lick**

b (*Brit*) [*of car etc*] coffre *m*, malle *f* (*arrière*)

2 VT **a** (* = *kick*) donner *or* flanquer* des coups de pied à ; (*lit, fig*) **to ~ sb out** flanquer* qn à la porte

b (*Comput: also ~* **up**) amorcer

3 COMP ► **boot boy*** N (*Brit*) skinhead *m* (*qui porte des rangers*) ► **boot camp** N (*US Mil*) camp *m* d'entraînement (*pour nouvelles recrues*) ► **boot-polish** N cirage *m* ► **boot sale** N = **car-boot sale** ; → **car** ► **boot-scraper** N décrottoir *m*

boot² [buːt] N **to ~** par-dessus le marché, en plus, de plus, par surcroît ; **and his insolence to ~** sans parler de son insolence

bootblack† ['buːtblæk] N cireur *m* (de chaussures)

bootee [buː'tiː] N [*of baby*] petit chausson *m* (*tricoté*) ; [*of woman*] bottillon *m*

booth [buːð] N [*of fair*] baraque *f* (*foraine*) ; [*of cinema, language laboratory, telephone etc*] cabine *f* ; [*of restaurant*] box *m* ; (*also* **voting ~**) isoloir *m*

bootlace ['buːtleɪs] N lacet *m* (de chaussure) ; **to pull o.s. up by one's (own) ~s** se faire tout seul, se hisser à la force du poignet

bootleg* ['buːtleg] **1** VI faire de la contrebande d'alcool *or* de boissons alcoolisées **2** VT vendre *or* importer en contrebande, fabriquer illicitement **3** ADJ [*spirits*] de contrebande ; [*software, tape, copy, edition*] pirate

[4] N (= *illicit recording*) enregistrement *m* pirate

bootlegger: ['buːtlegəʳ] N bootlegger *m*

bootless ['buːtlɪs] ADJ [a] (= *without boots*) sans bottes [b] (*liter* = *to no avail*) infructueux

bootlicker: ['buːtlɪkəʳ] N lèche-botte* *mf inv*

bootmaker ['butmeɪkəʳ] N bottier *m*

bootstrap ['butstræp] N [a] (*lit*) tirant *m* de botte; **to pull o.s. up by one's (own) ~s** se faire tout seul, se hisser à la force du poignet; (*Austral*) **he's British/a republican** *etc* **to his ~s** il est britannique/républicain *etc* jusqu'au bout des ongles [b] (*Comput*) programme *m* amorce, amorce *f*

booty ['buːtɪ] N butin *m*

booze: [buːz] [1] N (*NonC*) boisson(s) *f(pl)* alcoolisée(s); **bring the ~** apporte à boire; **I'm going to buy some ~** je vais acheter à boire; **to go on the ~** se mettre à picoler*; **he's on the ~** il picole*; **he's off the ~** il ne boit plus [2] VI picoler* [3] COMP ► **booze-up** N (*Brit*) beuverie *f*, (partie *f* de) soûlographie* *f*

boozer: ['buːzəʳ] N [a] (= *drunkard*) soûlard(e) *m(f)* [b] (*Brit* = *pub*) bistro(t)* *m*

boozy: ['buːzɪ] ADJ [*person*] pochard*, soûlard*; **a ~ party** une (partie de) soûlographie*

bop[1] ['bɒp] [1] N [a] (*Mus*) bop *m* [b] (= *dance*) **to have a ~**: guincher* [2] VI guincher*

bop[2]: ['bɒp] VT (= *hit*) cogner*, taper
► **bop off** VI (*US*) filer

bo-peep ['bəʊ'piːp] N cache-cache *m*; **Little Bo-Peep** la petite bergère (*chanson enfantine*)

boraces ['bɔːrəˌsiːz] NPL *of* **borax**

boracic [bə'ræsɪk] ADJ borique

borage ['bɒrɪdʒ] N bourrache *f*

borax ['bɔːræks] N (*pl* **boraxes** *or* **boraces**) borax *m*

Bordeaux [bɔː'dəʊ] N [a] (*Geog*) Bordeaux; **native of ~** Bordelais(e) *m(f)* [b] (= *wine*) bordeaux *m*

bordello [bɔː'deləʊ] N maison *f* de tolérance

border ['bɔːdəʳ] [1] N [a] (= *edge, side*) [*of lake*] bord *m*, rive *f*; [*of woods, field*] lisière *f*, bordure *f*
[b] (= *boundary, frontier*) frontière *f*, limite *f*; **within the ~s of** dans les limites *or* frontières de ..., à l'intérieur des frontières de ...; **to escape over the ~** s'enfuir en passant la frontière; **on the ~s of France** aux frontières françaises → **Borders**
[c] (*in garden*) bordure *f*, platebande *f* → **herbaceous**
[d] (= *edging*) [*of carpet, dress*] bord *m*; [*of picture*] encadrement *m*, cadre *m*; [*of notepaper*] **black ~** liseré *m* noir
[2] VT [a] [*trees etc*] (= *line edges of*) border; (= *surround*) entourer, encadrer
[b] **France ~s Germany** la France touche à l'Allemagne, la France et l'Allemagne ont une frontière commune
[3] COMP [*state, post*] frontière *inv*; [*zone, town*] frontière *inv*, frontalier; [*search*] à la frontière ► **border dispute** N différend *m* sur une question de frontière(s) ► **border guard** N garde-frontière *mf* ► **border incident** N incident *m* de frontière ► **bordering countries** NPL pays *mpl* avoisinants *or* limitrophes ► **border patrol** N (*US Police*) patrouille *f* frontalière ► **border police** N police *f* de l'air et des frontières ► **border raid** N incursion *f* ► **border taxes** NPL taxes *fpl* douanières
► **border (up)on** VT FUS [a] [*country etc*] être limitrophe de, avoisiner; **the two countries ~ (up)on one another** les deux pays ont une frontière commune *or* se touchent; **his estate ~s (up)on mine** sa propriété et la mienne se touchent [b] (*fig* = *come near to being*) être voisin *or* proche de, frôler; **to ~ (up)on insanity** être voisin de *or* frôler la folie; **it ~s (up)on fanaticism** cela touche au fanatisme, cela frise

le fanatisme; **with a boldness ~ing (up)on insolence** avec une hardiesse qui frise l'insolence

borderer ['bɔːdərəʳ] N frontalier *m*, -ière *f*

borderland ['bɔːdəlænd] N région *f* limitrophe

borderline ['bɔːdəlaɪn] [1] N ligne *f* de démarcation [2] COMP ► **borderline case** N cas *m* limite

Borders ['bɔːdəz] NPL (*Brit Geog*) **the ~** la région du sud-est de l'Écosse

bore[1] [bɔːʳ] [1] VT [a] [+ *hole*] percer; [+ *well*] forer, creuser; [+ *tunnel*] creuser, percer [b] [+ *rock*] forer [2] VI forer, sonder; **to ~ for oil** forer (le sous-sol) pour extraire du pétrole, rechercher du pétrole par sondage *or* forage [3] N [a] (*also* **~hole**) trou *m* de sonde [b] [*of tube, pipe, shot, gun, wind instrument*] calibre *m*; **a 12-~ shotgun** ◊ **a 12-~**[*] un fusil de (calibre) 12

bore[2] [bɔːʳ] [1] N [a] (= *person*) raseur* *m*, -euse *f*, casse-pieds* *mf inv*, importun(e) *m(f)*; **what a ~ he is!** ce qu'il peut être ennuyeux *or* raseur!* [b] (†* = *nuisance, annoyance*) corvée *f*; **it's a frightful ~** quelle corvée!*, quelle corvée!; **what a ~ this meeting is!** quelle corvée, cette réunion! [2] VT ennuyer, assommer; **to ~ sb rigid** *or* **stiff** *or* **stupid** *or* **silly** *or* **to death** *or* **to tears** ◊ **to ~ the pants off sb**: pomper l'air à qn*

bore[3] [bɔːʳ] VB *pt of* **bear**[1]

bore[4] [bɔːʳ] N (= *tidal wave*) mascaret *m*

bored [bɔːd] ADJ [*person*] qui s'ennuie; [*look*] de quelqu'un qui s'ennuie; **to be ~ (with doing sth)** s'ennuyer (à faire qch); **I am ~ with this work/book/film** ce travail/livre/film m'ennuie; **to be ~ rigid** *or* **stiff** *or* **stupid** *or* **silly** *or* **to death** *or* **to tears** s'ennuyer à mourir, s'emmerder*

boredom ['bɔːdəm] N ennui *m*; **his ~ with the whole proceedings** l'ennui que lui inspirait toute cette cérémonie

borehole ['bɔːhəʊl] N → **bore**[1] 3a

borer ['bɔːrəʳ] N [a] (*Tech* = *tool*) (*for wood*) vrille *f*, foret *m*; (*for metal cylinders*) alésoir *m*; (*for a well, mine*) foret *m*, sonde *f*; (= *person*) foreur *m*, perceur *m* [b] (*Zool* = *insect*) insecte *m* térébrant

boric ['bɔːrɪk] ADJ borique

boring[1] ['bɔːrɪŋ] [1] N [*of tunnel*] percement *m*; [*of well*] forage *m*; [*of wood*] perçage *m*; [*of metal*] perçage *m*, alésage *m* (*Tech*) [2] COMP ► **boring machine** N (*gen*) perforatrice *f*; (*for metal cylinders*) alésoir *m*

boring[2] ['bɔːrɪŋ] ADJ [*person, place, job, life, film, book*] ennuyeux; [*colour, taste, food*] fade; [*clothes*] sans originalité

boringly ['bɔːrɪŋlɪ] ADV [*speak, write etc*] de façon ennuyeuse; **it was ~ predictable** c'était tout ce qu'il y a de plus prévisible

born [bɔːn] [1] ADJ [a] né; **to be ~** naître; **to be ~ again** renaître → **2**; **~ in Paris** né à Paris; **the town where he was ~** la ville où il est né, sa ville natale; **Napoleon was ~ in 1769** Napoléon est né *or* naquit en 1769; **three sons ~ to her** trois fils nés d'elle; **every baby ~ into the world** tout enfant qui vient au monde; **when he was ~** quand il est né; **she was ~ blind/deaf** elle est née aveugle/sourde, elle est aveugle/sourde de naissance; **the baby was ~ dead** l'enfant était mort-né; **he was ~ evil** c'est de la mauvaise graine*; **he was ~ stupid** il a toujours été stupide; **a Parisian ~ and bred** un Parisien de souche; (*fig*) **he wasn't ~ yesterday*** il n'est pas né d'hier *or* de la dernière pluie; **in all my ~ days*** de toute ma vie; **~ of poor parents** né de parents pauvres; **people ~ to riches** ceux qui naissent riches; **poets are ~, not made** on naît poète, on ne le devient pas; **qualities ~ in him** qualités *fpl* innées (en lui); (*fig*) **misfortunes ~ of war** malheurs *mpl* dûs à la guerre; **anger ~ of frustration** colère *f* issue

de la frustration; **there's one ~ every minute*** je (*or il etc*) tombe toujours dans le panneau* → **first, highborn, lowborn, newborn, silver, stillborn**
[b] (= *innate*) **a ~ poet** un poète-né; **a ~ actress** une actrice-née; **~ fool** parfait idiot *m* → **loser**
[2] COMP ► **born-again** ADJ **~-again Christian** évangéliste *mf*; (*fig* = *convert*) **he's a ~-again cyclist/socialist** *etc* il s'est converti au cyclisme/socialisme *etc*

-born [bɔːn] ADJ (*in compounds*) **Chicago-born** originaire de Chicago, né à Chicago; **Australian-born** originaire d'Australie, né en Australie

borne [bɔːn] VB *ptp of* **bear**[1]

...borne [bɔːn] ADJ (*in compounds*) **airborne** [*assault, troops*] aérien; [*supplies*] transporté par air; **seaborne** [*assault, troops, traffic*] maritime; [*supplies*] transporté par mer; **waterborne** [*disease*] véhiculé par l'eau

Borneo ['bɔːnɪəʊ] N Bornéo *f*; **in ~** à Bornéo

boron ['bɔːrɒn] N bore *m*

borough ['bʌrə] N municipalité *f*; (*in London*) arrondissement *m*; (*Brit Parl*) circonscription *f* électorale urbaine

borrow ['bɒrəʊ] VT [+ *money, word, book*] emprunter (**from** à); (*fig*) [+ *idea etc*] emprunter (**from** à), adapter (**from** de); **a ~ed word** un mot d'emprunt; **a word ~ed from Greek** un mot emprunté au grec; (*US*) **to ~ trouble** voir toujours tout en noir; (*Math: in subtraction*) **~ 1** je retiens 1

borrower ['bɒrəʊəʳ] N emprunteur *m*, -euse *f*

borrowing ['bɒrəʊɪŋ] [1] N (*Fin, Ling*) emprunt *m* [2] COMP ► **borrowing rate** N (*Econ, Fin*) taux *m* d'intérêt des emprunts

borsch(t) [bɔːʃt] N borscht *or* bortch *m*

borstal† ['bɔːstəl] [1] N (*Brit Jur*) ≈ maison *f* de redressement† [2] COMP ► **borstal boy** N jeune délinquant *m*

borzoi ['bɔːzɔɪ] N (*lévrier m*) barzoï *m*

bosh†* [bɒʃ] N niaiseries *fpl*

bosk [bɒsk], **bosket** ['bɒskɪt] N (= *plantation*) bosquet *m*; (= *thicket*) fourré *m*

bos'n ['bəʊsn] N = **boatswain**

Bosnia ['bɒznɪə] [1] N la Bosnie [2] COMP ► **Bosnia-Herzegovina** N la Bosnie-Herzégovine

Bosnian ['bɒznɪən] [1] ADJ bosniaque [2] N Bosniaque *mf*

bosom ['buzəm] [1] N [*of person*] poitrine *f*, seins *mpl*; [*of dress*] corsage *m*; (*fig*) sein *m*, milieu *m*; **in the ~ of the family** au sein de la famille; (*liter*) **the ~ of the earth** les entrailles *fpl* (*liter*) de la terre [2] COMP ► **bosom friend** N ami(e) *m(f)* intime *or* de cœur

bosomy ['buzəmɪ] ADJ à la poitrine généreuse

Bosphorus ['bɒsfərəs], **Bosporus** ['bɒspərəs] N **the ~** le Bosphore

bosquet ['bɒskɪt] N = **bosk**

BOSS [bɒs] N (*in South Africa*) ABBR = **Bureau of State Security**

boss[1]* [bɒs] [1] N patron(ne) *m(f)*, chef *m*; [*of gang etc*] caïd* *m*; (*US Pol*) chef *m* (du parti); **to be one's own ~** être son propre patron; **we'll have to show him who's ~** il va falloir lui montrer qui commande ici; **who's the ~ round here?** qui est le chef ici?; **it's his wife who's the ~** c'est sa femme qui porte la culotte* [2] VT [+ *person*] mener, régenter; [+ *organization*] diriger, mener; faire marcher [3] ADJ (*US* = *terrific*) formidable, terrible
► **boss about***, **boss around*** VT SEP [+ *person*] mener à la baguette, régenter

boss[2] [bɒs] [1] N (= *knob*) [*of shield*] ombon *m*; (*Archit*) bossage *m*; (*Tech*) mamelon *m*, bossage *m*; [*of propeller*] moyeu *m* [2] COMP ► **boss-eyed*** ADJ **to be ~-eyed** loucher

bossa nova [ˌbɒsə'nəʊvə] N bossa-nova *f*

bossiness* ['bɒsɪnɪs] N autoritarisme m

bossy* ['bɒsɪ] ADJ autoritaire, tyrannique ; **she's very ~** elle mène tout le monde à la baguette, c'est un vrai gendarme*

Boston ['bɒstən] 1 N Boston 2 COMP ▸ **Boston baked beans** NPL (US) haricots blancs cuits avec du petit salé et de la mélasse ▸ **Boston ivy** N (US) vigne f vierge

Bostonian [bɒsˈtəʊnɪən] N Bostonien(ne) m(f)

bosun ['bəʊsn] N = **boatswain**

botanic(al) [bəˈtænɪk(əl)] ADJ botanique ; ~ **garden(s)** jardin m botanique

botanical [bəˈtænɪkəl] N (gen pl: Med) médicament m à base de plantes

botanist ['bɒtənɪst] N botaniste mf

botanize ['bɒtənaɪz] VI herboriser

botany ['bɒtənɪ] 1 N (NonC) botanique f 2 COMP ▸ **botany wool** N laine f mérinos

botch [bɒtʃ] 1 VT (also ~ **up**) (= repair crudely) rafistoler* ; (= bungle) bâcler, saboter ; **a ~ed job*** un travail bâclé or de cochon* 2 N (also ~-**up**) **to make a ~ of sth** bâcler or saboter qch

both [bəʊθ] 1 ADJ les deux, l'un(e) et l'autre ; ~ **books are his** les deux livres sont à lui, les livres sont à lui tous les deux ; **on ~ sides** des deux côtés, de part et d'autre ; **to hold sth in ~ hands** tenir qch à or des deux mains ; (fig) **you can't have it ~ ways*** il faut choisir
2 PRON tous (les) deux m, toutes (les) deux f, l'un(e) et l'autre m(f) ; ~ (**of them**) **were there** ◊ **they were ~ there** ils étaient là tous les deux ; **from ~ of us** de nous deux ; ~ **of us agree** nous sommes d'accord tous les deux ; ~ **alike** l'un comme l'autre
3 ADV ~ **this and that** non seulement ceci mais aussi cela, aussi bien ceci que cela ; ~ **you and I saw him** nous l'avons vu vous et moi, nous l'avons vu (nous) l'avons vu ; ~ **Paul and I came** Paul et moi sommes venus tous les deux ; **she was ~ laughing and crying** elle riait et pleurait à la fois ; **he can ~ read and write** il sait et lire et écrire

bother ['bɒðəʳ] 1 VT (= annoy) ennuyer ; (= pester) harceler ; (= worry) inquiéter, ennuyer ; **don't ~ me!** laisse-moi tranquille !, fiche-moi la paix !*, ne viens pas m'embêter !* ; **don't ~ him with your problems** ne l'embête pas* or ne l'ennuie pas avec tes problèmes ; **I'm sorry to ~ you** je m'excuse de vous déranger ; **does it ~ you if I smoke?** ça vous ennuie or dérange que je fume (subj) or si je fume ? ; **to ~ o.s. about sth** se tracasser au sujet de qch, se mettre martel en tête au sujet de qch ; **to be ~ed about sb/sth** se faire du souci or s'inquiéter au sujet de qn/qch ; **which do you prefer? — I'm not ~ed*** lequel tu préfères ? — ça m'est égal ; **it doesn't ~ me*** ça m'est égal ; **to get (all hot and) ~ed*** (**about sth**) se mettre dans tous ses états (à propos de qch) ; **I can't be ~ed going out** or **to go out** je n'ai pas le courage de sortir ; **are you going? — no, I can't be ~ed** tu y vas ? — non, je n'en ai pas envie or non, ça me casse les pieds* ; **his leg ~s him a lot** sa jambe le fait pas mal souffrir ; ~ **that child!** quelle barbe ce gosse !*
2 VI se donner la peine (**to do** de faire) ; **please don't ~ to get up!** ne vous donnez pas la peine de vous lever ! ; **you needn't ~ to come** ce n'est pas la peine de venir ; **don't ~ about me/about my lunch** ne vous occupez pas de moi/de mon déjeuner, ne vous tracassez pas pour moi/pour mon déjeuner ; **I'll do it — please don't ~** je vais le faire — non ce n'est pas la peine or ne vous donnez pas cette peine ; **why ~?** à quoi bon ?
3 N* a (= nuisance) barbe* f ; **what a ~ it all is!** quelle barbe !* b (NonC = problems) ennui m, embêtement* m ; **she's having** or **she's in a spot of ~** elle a des ennuis or des embêtements* en ce moment ; **we had a spot** or **bit of ~ with the car** on a eu un petit embêtement* avec la voiture

c (= effort) mal m ; **to go to (all) the ~ of doing sth** se donner beaucoup de mal pour faire qch ; **it's not worth (going to) the ~ of ...** ça ne vaut pas la peine de ... ; **it is no ~ (at all)** il n'y a pas de problème ; **he found it without any ~** il l'a trouvé sans aucune difficulté ; **he is no ~ to look after** il est facile à garder ; **save yourself a lot of ~ and have it done professionally** épargnez-vous beaucoup de mal et laissez les professionnels s'en occuper
d (Brit* = violence) bagarre* f, baston‡ m or f
4 EXCL (esp Brit*) flûte !*, la barbe !*

botheration †* [ˌbɒðəˈreɪʃən] EXCL flûte !*, la barbe !*

bothersome* ['bɒðəsəm] ADJ ennuyeux, gênant

Bothnia ['bɒθnɪə] N **Gulf of ~** golfe m de Botnie

Botswana [ˌbɒtˈswɑːnə] N le Botswana

bottle ['bɒtl] 1 N a (= container, contents) bouteille f ; (also **perfume ~**) flacon m ; (also **medicine ~**) flacon m, fiole f ; (wide-mouthed) bocal m ; (goatskin) outre f ; (of stone) cruche f, cruchon m ; (for beer) canette f ; (also **baby's ~**) biberon m ; **wine ~** bouteille f à vin ; **a ~ of wine** boire une bouteille de vin ; **we'll discuss it over a ~** nous en discuterons en prenant un verre ; **he is too fond of the ~** il aime trop la bouteille* ; **to take to the ~*** se mettre à boire or picoler‡ ; **her husband's on the ~*** son mari picole* ; **child brought up on the ~** enfant m élevé or nourri au biberon → **hot, ink**
b (Brit* fig) **he's got a lot of ~** il a un drôle de cran* ; **to lose one's ~** perdre courage
2 VT [+ wine] mettre en bouteille(s) ; [+ fruit] mettre en bocal or en conserve ; (fig) **to ~ it**‡ se dégonfler*
3 COMP ▸ **bottle bank** N conteneur m de collecte du verre usagé ▸ **bottle blonde** N (pej) fausse blonde f ▸ **bottled beer** N bière f en canette ▸ **bottled fruit** N fruits mpl en bocal or en conserve ▸ **bottled gas** N gaz m en bouteille ▸ **bottled wine** N vin m en bouteille(s) ▸ **bottle-feed** VT nourrir au biberon ▸ **bottle glass** N verre m à bouteilles ▸ **bottle-green** N, ADJ vert m bouteille inv ▸ **bottle-opener** N décapsuleur m, ouvre-bouteille m ▸ **bottle party** N soirée f (où chacun apporte une bouteille) ▸ **bottle rack** N porte-bouteilles m inv, casier m à bouteilles ▸ **bottle-top** N capsule f
▸ **bottle out**‡ VI (Brit) se dégonfler*
▸ **bottle up** VT SEP (fig) [+ feelings etc] contenir, refouler

bottlebrush ['bɒtlbrʌʃ] 1 N rince-bouteille(s) m inv 2 COMP ▸ **bottlebrush moustache** N moustache f en brosse

bottleneck ['bɒtlnek] N (lit) goulot m ; (fig) [road] rétrécissement m de la chaussée ; [traffic] embouteillage m, bouchon m ; [production etc] goulet m d'étranglement

bottler ['bɒtləʳ] N (= company) société f de mise en bouteille or d'embouteillage

bottle-washer ['bɒtlˌwɒʃəʳ] N laveur m, -euse f de bouteilles, plongeur m, -euse f → **cook**

bottom ['bɒtəm] 1 N a [of box] (outside) bas m ; (inside) fond m ; [of glass, well] fond m ; [of dress, heap, page] bas m ; [of tree, hill] pied m ; [of sea, lake, river] fond m ; [of garden] fond m, bas m ; [of chair] siège m, fond m ; [of ship] carène f ; (on label) **"~"** « bas » ; **at the ~ of page ten** en or au bas de la page dix ; **at the ~ of the hill** au pied or au bas de la colline ; **the name at the ~ of the list** le nom en bas de la liste ; (fig) **he's at the ~ of the list** il est en queue de liste ; **to be at the ~ of the heap** or **pile** être en bas de l'échelle ; **to be (at the) ~ of the class** être le dernier de la classe ; (fig) **to knock the ~ out of an argument** démolir un argument ; (Fin) **the ~ has fallen out of the**

market le marché s'est effondré ; **the ~ fell out of his world*** son monde s'est effondré or a basculé ; **at the ~ of the table** en bout de table, au bout de la table ; **the ship went to the ~** le navire a coulé ; **the ship touched the ~** le navire a touché le fond ; **to go ~ up** (= capsize) se renverser ; **the ship was floating ~ up** le navire flottait la quille en l'air
b (= buttocks) derrière m, postérieur* m ; ~**s up!**‡ cul sec !
c (fig = origin, foundation) base f, origine f ; **at ~** au fond ; **to be at the ~ of sth** être à l'origine de qch ; **to get to the ~ of a mystery** aller jusqu'au fond d'un mystère ; **we can't get to the ~ of it** impossible de découvrir le fin fond de cette histoire or affaire → **heart**
2 ADJ [shelf] du bas, inférieur (-eure f) ; [step, rung etc] premier ; [price] le plus bas ; [part of garden etc] du fond ; ~ **dollar** dernier dollar m → **bet** ; (Brit) **to put sth away in one's ~ drawer** mettre qch de côté pour son trousseau ; ~ **floor** [of building] rez-de-chaussée m ; (Aut) ~ **gear** première f (vitesse) ; ~ **half** [of box] partie f inférieure ; [of class, list] deuxième moitié f ; (US) ~ **land** terre f alluviale ; (US) ~ **lands** plaine f alluviale ; **the ~ line** (Fin) le résultat financier ; (fig) l'essentiel m ; **the ~ right-hand corner** le coin en bas à droite ; (US Culin) ~ **round** gîte m à la noix → **rock**
3 COMP ▸ **bottom-up** ADJ ~-**up design/ information** conception f/information f ascendante ; ~-**up planning** planification f de bas en haut or de la base au sommet, planification f pyramidale
▸ **bottom out*** VI [figures, sales, graph] atteindre son niveau plancher ; [recession] atteindre son plus bas niveau

bottomless ['bɒtəmlɪs] ADJ [pit, well] sans fond ; [supply] inépuisable ; **he's a ~ pit*** il a un appétit d'ogre

bottommost ['bɒtəmməʊst] ADJ le plus bas

bottomry ['bɒtəmrɪ] N (Marketing) hypothèque f à la grosse aventure

botulism ['bɒtjʊlɪzəm] N botulisme m

bouclé [buːˈkleɪ] 1 N (laine f or tissu m) bouclette f 2 ADJ en laine or en tissu bouclette

boudoir ['buːdwɑːʳ] N boudoir m

bouffant ['buːfɒn] 1 N (hairdo) coiffure f bouffante 2 ADJ [hairdo] bouffant

bougainvill(a)ea [ˌbuːɡənˈvɪlɪə] N bougainvillée f, bougainvillier m

bough [baʊ] N (liter) rameau m, branche f

bought [bɔːt] pt, ptp of **buy**

bouillon ['buːjɒn] 1 N bouillon m, consommé m 2 COMP ▸ **bouillon cube** N bouillon cube m

boulder ['bəʊldəʳ] 1 N rocher m (rond), grosse pierre f ; (smaller) (gros) galet m 2 COMP ▸ **boulder clay** N (Geol) dépôt m (argileux) erratique

boulevard ['buːləvɑːʳ] N boulevard m

bounce [baʊns] 1 VI a [ball] rebondir ; [person] bondir (**into** dans, **out of** hors de) ; **to ~ in/out** etc [person] entrer/sortir etc d'un bond ; **the child ~d up and down on the bed** l'enfant faisait des bonds sur le lit ; **the car ~d along the road** la voiture faisait des bonds sur la route ; **the ball ~d down the stairs** la balle a rebondi de marche en marche ; **to ~ off sth** [light, sound etc] se réverbérer sur qch ; **the heat/light ~d off the white walls** la chaleur/lumière se réverbérait sur les murs blancs, les murs blancs réverbéraient la chaleur/lumière
b * [cheque] être sans provision, être refusé pour non-provision
c (= be returned) [e-mail message] être retourné or renvoyé à l'expéditeur
2 VT a [+ ball] faire rebondir ; [+ light, heat etc] renvoyer, réverbérer ; **use a mirror to ~ light onto the subject's face** servez-vous d'un miroir pour renvoyer or réverbérer la lumière sur le visage du sujet ; **they ~ radio waves off**

the moon ils émettent des ondes radio qui se réverbèrent sur la surface de la lune ; (fig) **to ~ one's ideas off sb*** soumettre ses idées à qn, tester ses idées sur qn* ; (fig) **to ~ sb into doing sth** pousser qn à faire qch

b (* = eject) [+ person] vider*, flanquer* à la porte (out of de)

c * [+ cheque] refuser

3 N **a** (= rebound) [of ball] bond m, rebond m

b (= springiness) **there's not much ~ in this pitch** les balles ne rebondissent pas bien sur ce terrain

c (NonC) **this ball hasn't much ~ left** cette balle ne rebondit plus beaucoup ; **to give your hair ~** pour donner du volume à vos cheveux ; (fig) **he's got plenty of ~*** il a beaucoup d'allant, il est très dynamique

► **bounce back** VI se remettre très vite

bouncer ['baʊnsə'] N (at pub, dance hall etc) videur m

bouncing ['baʊnsɪŋ] ADJ **a beautiful ~ baby** un beau bébé qui respire la santé

bouncy ['baʊnsɪ] **1** ADJ [ball, mattress] élastique ; [hair] vigoureux ; [person] dynamique, plein d'allant **2** COMP ► **bouncy castle** N château m gonflable (servant de trampoline géant pour enfants)

bound¹ [baʊnd] **1** N (lit, fig) **~s** limite(s) f(pl), bornes fpl ; **his ambition knows no ~s** son ambition est sans bornes ; **to keep within ~s** (fig) rester dans la juste mesure, user de modération ; (lit) rester dans les limites ; (Mil) **to break ~s** violer la consigne ; **within the ~s of probability** dans les limites du probable ; **within the ~s of possibility** dans la limite du possible ; **to go over** or **pass over the ~s** dépasser les bornes ; **out of ~s** (place etc) dont l'accès est interdit ; (Scol) interdit aux élèves ; (Sport) hors du terrain, sorti ; **it's out of ~s to soldiers** c'est interdit or consigné aux soldats **2** VT (gen pass) [+ country] borner ; **~ed by** borné or limité par

bound² [baʊnd] **1** N bond m, saut m ; **at a ~** d'un saut, d'un bond → **leap 2** VI [person] bondir, sauter ; [horse] bondir, faire un bond or des bonds ; **to ~ in/away/back** etc entrer/partir/revenir etc en bondissant or d'un bond ; **the horse ~ed over the fence** le cheval sauta la barrière (d'un bond)

bound³ [baʊnd] **1** VB pt, ptp of **bind**

2 ADJ **a** lié, attaché ; (Ling) [morpheme] lié ; **~ hand and foot** pieds mpl et poings mpl liés → **earthbound, icebound, spellbound**

b [book etc] relié ; **~ in boards** cartonné

c (fig = obliged) obligé, tenu ; (= sure) sûr, certain ; **you are not ~ to do it** vous n'êtes pas obligé de le faire ; **to be ~ by law/an oath etc to do sth** être tenu par la loi/un serment à faire qch ; **I am ~ to confess** je suis forcé d'avouer ; **to feel ~ to do sth** se sentir obligé de faire qch ; **you're ~ to do it** (= obliged to) vous êtes tenu or obligé de le faire ; (= sure to) vous le ferez sûrement ; **he's ~ to say so** (= obliged to) il est de son devoir de le dire, il doit le dire ; (= sure to) il le dira sûrement, il ne manquera pas de le dire ; **it is ~ to rain** il va sûrement pleuvoir, il ne peut pas manquer de pleuvoir ; **it was ~ to happen** cela devait arriver, c'était à prévoir → **duty, honour**

d (= destined) **~ for** [person] en route pour ; [parcel] à destination de ; [train] en direction de, à destination de ; [ship, plane] à destination de, en route pour ; (= about to leave) en partance pour ; **ship ~ for Australia** (before sailing) navire m en partance pour l'Australie ; (en route) navire m à destination de or en route pour l'Australie ; **where are you ~ for?** où allez-vous ?

-bound [baʊnd] ADJ (in compounds) **Australia-bound** à destination de l'Australie ; **Paris-bound traffic** la circulation dans le sens province-Paris → **northbound, outward**

boundary ['baʊndərɪ] **1** N limite f, frontière f ; (Cricket) **to score a ~** envoyer une balle jusqu'aux limites du terrain **2** COMP ► **boundary changes** NPL (Brit Pol) **to make ~ changes** effectuer un redécoupage des circonscriptions, redécouper la carte des circonscriptions ► **Boundary Commission** N (Brit Pol) organisme chargé du redécoupage des circonscriptions ► **boundary line** N ligne f frontière inv or de démarcation ; (Sport: gen) limites fpl du terrain ; (Basketball) ligne f de touche ► **boundary-stone** N borne f, pierre f de bornage (Jur)

bounden duty ['baʊndən'djuːtɪ] N devoir m impérieux

bounder†* ['baʊndə'] N (esp Brit) butor m, goujat m

boundless ['baʊndlɪs] ADJ [space] infini ; [trust] illimité ; [ambition, devotion] sans bornes

bounteous ['baʊntɪəs], **bountiful** ['baʊntɪfʊl] ADJ [harvest] abondant ; [rain] bienfaisant ; [person] généreux

bounty ['baʊntɪ] **1** N **a** (NonC = generosity) générosité f, libéralité f **b** (= gift) don m ; (= reward) prime f **2** COMP ► **bounty-fed farmers** NPL agriculteurs mpl qui ne vivent que de subventions ► **bounty hunter** N chasseur m de primes

bouquet ['bʊkeɪ] **1** N **a** [of flowers] bouquet m **b** [of wine] bouquet m **2** COMP ► **bouquet garni** N (pl **bouquets garnis**) (Culin) bouquet garni m

Bourbon ['bʊəbən] N (Hist) Bourbon m

bourbon ['bɜːbən] N (US) (whisky) bourbon m

bourgeois ['bʊəʒwɑː] **1** ADJ bourgeois **2** N (pl inv) bourgeois(e) m(f)

bourgeoisie [ˌbʊəʒwɑːˈziː] N bourgeoisie f

bout [baʊt] N **a** (= period) période f ; [of malaria etc] attaque f, accès m ; **~ of rheumatism** crise f de rhumatisme ; **~ of fever** accès m de fièvre ; **a ~ of bronchitis** une bronchite ; **a ~ of flu** une grippe ; **he's had several ~s of illness** il a été malade plusieurs fois ; **a ~ of work(ing)** une période de travail intensif ; **drinking ~** beuverie f **b** (Boxing, Wrestling) combat m ; (Fencing) assaut m

boutique [buːˈtiːk] N (= shop) boutique f (de mode ou d'objets branchés) ; (= within a store) **hat/teenage ~** rayon m des chapeaux/des jeunes

bovine ['bəʊvaɪn] ADJ (lit, fig) bovin ; **~ spongiform encephalopathy** encéphalopathie f spongiforme bovine

bovver boots* ['bɒvəˌbuːts] NPL (Brit) rangers mpl

bow¹ [bəʊ] **1** N **a** (= weapon etc) arc m ; **to draw the ~** tirer à l'arc → **crossbow, longbow, string b** (Mus) archet m **c** (= curve) [of rainbow etc] arc m → **saddlebow d** (= knot) [of ribbon etc] nœud m **2** VI (Mus) manier l'archet **3** COMP ► **bow and arrow** N [of child's game] arc m et flèches, jeu m de tir à l'arc ► **bow compass** N compas m à balustre ► **bow-legged** ADJ aux jambes arquées ► **bow legs** NPL jambes fpl arquées ► **bow tie** N nœud m papillon ► **bow window** N bow-window m (en arc-de-cercle)

bow² [baʊ] **1** N (with head) salut m ; (with body) révérence f ; **to make a (deep) ~** saluer (bas) ; **to make a ~ to sb** faire un salut à qn, saluer qn ; **to give sb a gracious ~** adresser un gracieux salut à qn ; (fig) **to make one's ~ (as a pianist etc)** faire ses débuts (de pianiste etc) ; **to take a ~** saluer

2 VI (in greeting) saluer, incliner la tête ; **to ~ to sb** saluer qn ; **to ~ and scrape** faire des courbettes → **bowing²**

b (= bend) [branch etc] (in wind) fléchir, se courber ; (under weight) ployer ; [person] se courber

c (fig = submit) s'incliner (**before, to** devant, **under** sous), se soumettre (**before, to** à, **under**

sous) ; **to ~ before the storm** laisser passer l'orage ; (iro) **we must ~ to your greater knowledge** nous devons nous incliner devant votre grand savoir ; **to ~ to sb's opinion** se soumettre à l'opinion de qn ; **to ~ to the inevitable** s'incliner devant les faits or devant l'inévitable ; **to ~ to the majority** s'incliner devant la majorité

3 VT courber ; **to ~ one's back** courber le dos ; **to ~ one's knee** fléchir le genou ; **to ~ one's head** pencher or courber la tête ; **his head was ~ed in thought** il méditait la tête penchée ; **to ~ one's consent** signifier son consentement par une inclination de tête ; **to ~ sb in/out** faire entrer/faire sortir qn en saluant ; **to ~ o.s. out** saluer pour prendre congé

► **bow down 1** VI (lit, fig) s'incliner (**to sb** devant qn) **2** VT SEP (lit) faire plier, courber ; (fig) écraser, briser

► **bow out** VI (fig) tirer sa révérence (fig) → **bow²**

bow³ [baʊ] **1** N **a** (often pl) [of ship] avant m, proue f ; **~s** à l'avant, en proue ; **on the port ~** par bâbord devant ; **on the starboard ~** par tribord devant **b** (= oarsman) nageur m de l'avant **2** COMP ► **bow doors** NPL (on ferry) porte(s) f(pl) d'étrave ► **bow wave** N lame f or vague f d'étrave

Bow Bells ['bəʊˈbelz] NPL les cloches fpl de l'église de St-Mary-le-Bow (à Londres) ; **born within the sound of ~** né en plein cœur de Londres → COCKNEY

bowdlerization [ˌbaʊdləraɪˈzeɪʃən] N expurgation f

bowdlerize ['baʊdləraɪz] VT [+ book] expurger

bowel ['baʊəl] **1** N (gen pl: Anat) [of person] intestin(s) m(pl) ; [of animal] boyau(x) m(pl), intestin(s) m(pl) ; **to empty** or **relieve one's ~s** déféquer ; (fig) **~s** entrailles fpl ; **~s of the earth** entrailles fpl de la terre → **move, movement 2** COMP ► **bowel cancer** N cancer m des intestins ► **bowel complaint** N dérangement m intestinal

bower ['baʊə'] N (= arbour) tonnelle f ; (††, liter = cottage) chaumière f ; [of lady] boudoir m

bowing¹ ['bəʊɪŋ] N (Mus) technique f d'archet ; (marked on score) indications fpl d'archet ; **his ~ was very sensitive** il avait un coup d'archet très délicat ; **to mark the ~** indiquer or introduire les coups d'archet

bowing² ['baʊɪŋ] N **~ and scraping** salamalecs mpl, courbettes fpl → **bow²**

bowl¹ [bəʊl] N **a** (= container) (gen) bol m ; (larger) saladier m, jatte f ; (for water) cuvette f ; (for fruit) coupe f ; (of beggar) sébile f ; (US Sport) championnat m, coupe f ; **a ~ of milk** un bol de lait ; **a ~ of water** une cuvette d'eau ; **a ~ of punch** un bol de punch → **finger, salad, sugar b** [of wineglass] coupe f ; [of pipe] fourneau m ; [of spoon] creux m ; [of lamp] globe m ; [of lavatory, sink] cuvette f **c** (Geog) bassin m, cuvette f

bowl² [bəʊl] **1** N (Sport) boule f ; **(game of) ~s** (Brit) (jeu m de) boules fpl ; (in Provence) pétanque f, boules fpl ; (US = skittles) bowling m **2** VI **a** (Brit) jouer aux boules ; (US) jouer au bowling ; (in Provence) jouer à la pétanque ; (Cricket) lancer (la balle) (**to** à) **b** **to ~ down the street** [person, car] descendre la rue à bonne allure ; **to ~ along** ◊ **to go ~ing along** [car] rouler bon train **3** VT **a** (Sport) [+ bowl, hoop] faire rouler ; [+ ball] lancer **b** (Cricket) [+ ball] servir ; [+ batsman] (also **~ out**) éliminer (en lançant la balle contre les guichets)

► **bowl down*** VT SEP renverser

► **bowl out** VT SEP → **bowl² 3b**

► **bowl over** VT SEP **a** [+ ninepins] renverser, faire tomber **b** [fig etc] (in wind) stupéfier, sidérer* ; **to be ~ed over (by)** (surprise) rester stupéfait or abasourdi or sidéré* (devant) ; (emotion) être bouleversé (par) ; **she was ~ed over by him** (= impressed) il l'a éblouie

bowler[1] ['bəʊləʳ] N (*Brit*) joueur *m*, -euse *f* de boules ; (*US*) joueur *m*, -euse *f* de bowling ; (*in Provence*) joueur *m*, -euse *f* de pétanque, bouliste *mf* ; (*Cricket*) lanceur *m*, -euse *f* (de la balle)

bowler[2] ['bəʊləʳ] N (*Brit: also* ~ **hat**) (chapeau *m*) melon *m*

bowline ['bəʊlɪn] N (= *knot*) nœud *m* de chaise ; (= *rope*) bouline *f*

bowling ['bəʊlɪŋ] **1** N bowling *m* **2** COMP ► **bowling alley** N bowling *m* ► **bowling green** N terrain *m* de boules (*sur gazon*) ► **bowling match** N (*Brit*) concours *m* de boules ; (*US*) concours *m* de bowling ; (*in Provence*) concours *m* de pétanque

bowman ['bəʊmən] N (*pl* -**men**) (*Archery*) archer *m*

bowsprit ['bəʊsprɪt] N beaupré *m*

bowstring ['bəʊstrɪŋ] N corde *f*

bow-wow ['baʊwaʊ] **1** N (*baby talk*) toutou *m* **2** ['baʊˈwaʊ] EXCL ouah, ouah !

box[1] [bɒks] **1** N [a] boîte *f* ; (= *crate*) caisse *f* ; (*also* **cardboard** ~) (boîte *f* en) carton *m* ; (= *casket*) coffret *m* ; († = *trunk*) malle *f* ; **a** ~ **of matches/chocolates** une boîte d'allumettes/de chocolats ; (*esp Brit* = *television*) **(on) the** ~* (à) la télé* ; (*US*) **to be first out of the** ~ **with sth** être le premier à faire qch ; (*US*) **to come out of the** ~ **with sth** se lancer dans qch ; (*Brit*) **to be out of one's** ~* (*through drink*) être pété* ; (*through drugs*) être défoncé* ; (= *crazy*) être débile* → **icebox, letterbox, toolbox** [b] (*for money*) caisse *f* ; (*in church*) tronc *m* → **strongbox** [c] (*Aut, Tech*) [of axle, steering] carter *m* → **axle, gearbox** [d] (*Theat*) loge *f* ; [of coachman] siège *m* (du cocher) ; (*Jur*) (for jury, press) banc *m* ; (*also* **witness-**~) barre *f* ; (*in stable*) box *m* → **horsebox, sentry, signal** [e] (*also* **wine** ~) cubitainer® *m* [f] (*Sport = protection*) coquille *f* [g] (*Brit* = *road junction*) zone *f* (de carrefour) d'accès réglementé **2** VT mettre en boîte *or* en caisse *etc* **3** COMP ► **box calf** N box(-calf) *m* ► **box camera** N appareil *m* (photographique) (*rudimentaire*) ► **boxed set** N coffret *m* ► **box file** N boîte *f* à archives ► **box girder** N (*Constr*) poutre-caisson *f* ► **box junction** N (*Brit*) = **1g** ► **box kite** N cerf-volant *m* cellulaire ► **box lunch** N panier-repas *m* ► **box number** N (*Post: in newspaper*) référence *f* d'annonce → **post office** ► **box pleat** N (*Sewing*) pli *m* creux ► **box spring** N sommier *m* à ressorts ► **box stall** N (*US*) box *m*

► **box in** VT SEP [+ *bath, sink*] encastrer ; (*fig*) **to feel** ~**ed in** se sentir confiné *or* à l'étroit ; **house** ~**ed in by tall buildings** maison *f* coincée entre de grands immeubles

► **box off** VT SEP compartimenter

► **box up** VT SEP mettre en boîte ; (*fig*) enfermer

box[2] [bɒks] **1** VI (*Sport*) boxer, faire de la boxe ; (*Brit fig*) **to** ~ **clever** bien manœuvrer **2** VT [a] (*Sport*) boxer avec, boxer* [b] **to** ~ **sb's ears** chauffer les oreilles à qn, gifler *or* claquer qn, flanquer* une claque *or* une gifle à qn **3** N **a** ~ **on the ear** une claque, une gifle

box[3] [bɒks] **1** N (*Bot*) buis *m* **2** COMP en *or* de buis

boxboard ['bɒksbɔ:d] N carton *m* d'emballage

boxcar ['bɒkskɑːʳ] N (*Rail*) wagon *m* (de marchandises) couvert

boxer[1] ['bɒksəʳ] **1** N (*Sport*) boxeur *m* **2** **boxers** NPL = **boxer shorts** **3** COMP ► **boxer shorts** NPL boxer-short *m*

boxer[2] ['bɒksəʳ] N (= *dog*) boxer *m*

boxing ['bɒksɪŋ] **1** N boxe *f* **2** COMP [*gloves, match*] de boxe ► **boxing ring** N ring *m* (de boxe)

Boxing Day ['bɒksɪŋdeɪ] N (*Brit*) le lendemain de Noël

BOXING DAY

Boxing Day *est un jour férié en Grande-Bretagne ; il est fixé le 26 décembre, ou le 27 si Noël tombe un samedi. C'était à l'origine le jour où l'on donnait les étrennes (une « boîte de Noël » ou « Christmas box ») au facteur et aux artisans. Aujourd'hui, cette journée est surtout consacrée aux sports, au repos ou à la poursuite des festivités de Noël.*

---

box office ['bɒksɒfɪs] (*Theat*) **1** N (= *office*) bureau *m* de location ; (= *window*) guichet *m* (de location) ; **this show will be good** ~ ce spectacle fera recette **2** COMP ► **box-office attraction** N spectacle *m* à (grand) succès ► **box-office receipts** NPL recette *f* ► **box-office success** N pièce *f* etc qui fait courir les foules *or* qui fait recette ; (= *film*) succès *m* au box-office

boxroom ['bɒksrʊm] N (*Brit*) débarras *m*

boxwood ['bɒkswʊd] N buis *m*

boxy* ['bɒksɪ] ADJ [*building*] en forme de boîte, qui ressemble à une boîte ; [*car*] en forme de caisse à savon

boy [bɔɪ] **1** N [a] (= *child*) garçon *m*, enfant *m* ; (= *young man*) jeune *m* (homme *m*), garçon *m* ; (= *son*) fils *m*, garçon *m* ; (*Scol*) élève *m*, garçon *m* ; **little** ~ petit garçon *m*, garçonnet *m* ; **beggar** ~ petit mendiant *m* ; **English** ~ petit *or* jeune Anglais *m* ; **come here, my** ~ viens ici mon petit *or* mon grand ; **bad** ~! ◊ **naughty** ~! vilain! ; **the Jones** ~ le petit Jones ; **I lived here as a** ~ j'habitais ici quand j'étais petit *or* enfant ; **he knew me from a** ~ il me connaissait depuis mon (*or* son) enfance, il me connaissait depuis tout petit ; ~**s will be** ~**s!** les garçons, on ne les changera jamais! ; **he was as much a** ~ **as ever** il était toujours aussi gamin ; (*Scol*) **sit down,** ~**s** (*to small boys*) asseyez-vous, mes enfants ; (*to sixth formers etc*) asseyez-vous, messieurs *or* mes amis → **choirboy, day, old, page**[2] [b] (* = *fellow*) **my dear** ~ mon cher (ami) ; **old** ~ mon vieux ; **the old** ~ (= *boss*) le patron ; (= *father*) le paternel* ; **a night out with the** ~**s** une sortie avec les copains → **wide** [c] (= *native servant*) boy *m* **2** EXCL bigre ! **3** COMP ► **boy band** N (*Brit Mus*) boys band *m* ► **boy-meets-girl story** N (*film, novel etc*) histoire *f* romantique conventionnelle ► **boy racer*** N (*Brit*) jeune fou *m* du volant ► **Boys' Brigade** N (*Brit*) organisation de scoutisme ► **boy scout**† N (*Catholic*) scout *m* ; (*non-Catholic*) éclaireur *m* ► **the boys in blue** NPL (*Brit*) les défenseurs *mpl* de l'ordre ► **boy soprano** N soprano *m* ► **boy wonder*** N jeune prodige *m*

boycott ['bɔɪkɒt] **1** VT [+ *person, product, place*] boycotter **2** N boycottage *m*, boycott *m*

boyfriend ['bɔɪfrend] N petit ami *m*

boyhood ['bɔɪhʊd] N enfance *f*, adolescence *f*

boyish ['bɔɪɪʃ] ADJ [*male's behaviour*] d'enfant, de garçon ; [*smile*] gamin ; (*pej*) enfantin, puéril (puérile *f*) ; [*tomboyish*] [*girl*] garçonnier ; [*behaviour*] garçonnier, de garçon ; **he looks very** ~ il fait très jeune ; **his** ~ **good looks** son air de beau garçon

boyishly ['bɔɪɪʃlɪ] ADV comme un garçon ; ~ **cut hair** cheveux *mpl* coupés à la garçonne

boyo* ['bɔɪəʊ] N (*Brit dial*) gars* *m* ; **listen,** ~ écoute, mon gars*

boysenberry ['bɔɪzənbərɪ] N boysenberry *f* (variété de mûre)

bozo: ['bəʊzəʊ] N (*esp US*) bozo* *m*, drôle de type: *m*

BP [biːˈpiː] N ABBR = **blood pressure**

Bp ABBR = **Bishop**

bpi [ˌbiːpiːˈaɪ] N (*Comput*) (ABBR = **bits per inch**) bits *mpl* par pouce

bps [ˌbiːpiːˈes] N (*Comput*) (ABBR = **bits per second**) bits *mpl* par seconde

BR [biːˈɑːʳ] N (*formerly*) (ABBR = **British Rail**) → **British**

bra [brɑː] N (ABBR = **brassière**) soutien-gorge *m* ; **half-cup** ~ balconnet *m*, soutien-gorge *m* pigeonnant

Brabant [brəˈbænt] N le Brabant

brace [breɪs] **1** N [a] attache *f*, agrafe *f* ; (*Med*) appareil *m* orthopédique ; (*Constr*) entretoise *f*, étrésillon *m* ; (*US Mil**) garde-à-vous *m* rigide ; (*for teeth*) ~**(s)** appareil *m* dentaire *or* orthodontique ; (*Tech*) ~ **(and bit)** vilebrequin *m* (à main) [b] (*pl inv* = *pair*) [of animals, pistols] paire *f* [c] (*Mus, Typ: also* ~ **bracket**) accolade *f* **2** **braces** NPL (*Brit Dress*) bretelles *fpl* **3** VT [a] (= *support, strengthen*) soutenir, consolider ; [+ *structure*] entretoiser, étrésillonner ; [+ *beam*] armer (**with** de), soutenir [b] **to** ~ **o.s.** (*lit*) s'arc-bouter ; (*fig*) rassembler ses forces (**to do** à faire), fortifier son âme (**to do** pour faire) ; **he** ~**d his leg against the door** il a bloqué la porte avec sa jambe ; ~ **yourself for the news!** tenez-vous bien que je vous raconte (*subj*) la nouvelle ! *or* que je vous en dise une bien bonne!* [c] [*climate etc*] fortifier, tonifier

► **brace up 1** VT SEP [+ *person*] revigorer, remonter ; **to** ~ **o.s. up** rassembler ses forces (**to do** pour faire) ; (*by having a drink*) reprendre des forces (*hum*) **2** EXCL ~ **up!** du courage !

bracelet ['breɪslɪt] N [a] bracelet *m* [b] ~**s**: (= *handcuffs*) menottes *fpl*, bracelets *mpl* (*hum*)

bracer: ['breɪsəʳ] N (= *drink*) remontant *m*

bracing ['breɪsɪŋ] ADJ [*air, climate*] fortifiant, tonifiant ; **a** ~ **wind** un vent vivifiant

bracken ['brækən] N (*NonC*) fougère *f*

bracket ['brækɪt] **1** N [a] (= *angled support*) support *m* ; [of shelf] tasseau *m*, équerre *f* ; (*Archit*) console *f*, corbeau *m* [b] [of lamp] fixation *f* [c] (= *small shelf*) rayon *m*, étagère *f* [d] (*Typ*) (*also* **round** ~) parenthèse *f* ; (*also* **square** ~) crochet *m* ; (*Mus, Typ: also* **brace** ~, **curly** ~) accolade *f* ; **in** ~**s** entre parenthèses [e] (*fig* = *group*) tranche *f* ; **the lower/upper income** ~ la tranche des petits/des gros revenus ; **he's in the £30,000-a-year** ~ il est dans la tranche (de revenus) des 30 000 livres par an ; **price** ~ fourchette *f* de prix ; **tax** ~ tranche *f* d'imposition ; **age** ~ classe *f* d'âge **2** VT [a] (*Typ*) [+ *sentence etc*] mettre entre parenthèses *or* entre crochets [b] (= *join by brackets*) réunir par une accolade ; (*fig: also* ~ **together**) [+ *names, persons*] mettre dans le même groupe *or* dans la même catégorie ; [+ *candidates etc*] mettre ex aequo, accoler ; (*fig* = *link in one's mind*) mettre dans le même sac ; (*Scol, Sport*) ~**ed first** premiers ex aequo [c] (*Mil*) [+ *target*] encadrer **3** COMP ► **bracket lamp** N applique *f*

bracketing ['brækətɪŋ] N (*Gram*) parenthétisation *f*

brackish ['brækɪʃ] ADJ [*water, taste*] saumâtre

brad [bræd] **1** N semence *f*, clou *m* de tapissier **2** COMP ► **brad awl** N poinçon *m*

brae [breɪ] N (*Scot*) pente *f*, côte *f*

brag [bræg] **1** VI se vanter (**about, of** de) **2** VT **to** ~ **that one has done sth** se vanter d'avoir fait qch **3** N [a] (= *boast*) vantardise *f*, fanfaronnades *fpl* [b] = **braggart** [c] (*Cards*) jeu de cartes semblable au poker

braggart ['brægət] N vantard(e) *m(f)*, fanfaron(ne) *m(f)*

bragging ['brægɪŋ] N vantardise *f* (**about** à propos de)

Brahma ['brɑːmə] N [a] (= *god*) Brahmâ *m* [b] (*US Zool*) zébu *m* américain

Brahman ['brɑːmən] N (pl **Brahmans**) [a] (= person) brahmane m [b] = **Brahma** b

Brahmaputra [ˌbrɑːməˈpuːtrə] N Brahmâpoutre m, Brahmâputra m

Brahmin ['brɑːmɪn] N (pl **Brahmin** or **Brahmins**) = **Brahman** a

braid [breɪd] [1] VT [a] (esp US) (= plait) tresser, natter; (= interweave) entrelacer (**with** avec) [b] (= trim with braid) [+ clothing, material] galonner, soutacher [2] N [a] (esp US = plait of hair) tresse f, natte f [b] (NonC = trimming) soutache f, ganse f, galon m; (Mil) galon m; **gold ~** galon m d'or or doré

braided ['breɪdɪd] ADJ galonné

Braille [breɪl] [1] N braille m [2] ADJ braille inv

brain [breɪn] [1] N [a] (Anat) cerveau m; (fig) cerveau m, tête f; (Anat, Culin) **~s** cervelle f; (fig) **he's got that on the ~!** il ne pense qu'à ça!; (fig) **he's got politics on the ~** il n'a que la politique en tête; **his ~ reeled** la tête lui a tourné; **to beat sb's ~s out** estourbir qn*; **to blow sb's ~s out** brûler la cervelle à qn; (Culin) **calves' ~** cervelle f de veau → **pick, rack**[1]
[b] (fig: gen pl = intelligence) **~s** intelligence f; **he's got ~s** il est intelligent; **he's the ~s of the family** c'est le cerveau de la famille
[2] VT (*= knock out) [+ person] assommer
[3] COMP [disease] du cerveau, cérébral; [operation] au cerveau ► **brain-box*** N tête* f, cerveau m ► **brain-child** N idée f personnelle, invention f personnelle; **it's his ~-child** c'est lui qui l'a inventé ► **brain damage** N lésions fpl cérébrales ► **brain dead** ADJ (Med) dans un coma dépassé; (*= stupid) balourd ► **brain death** N (Med) mort f cérébrale ► **brain drain** N exode m or fuite f des cerveaux ► **brain fever** N fièvre f cérébrale ► **brain pan** N boîte f crânienne ► **brain scan** N scanographie f du cerveau, scanner m cérébral ► **brain scanner** N scanner m, tomodensitomètre m ► **brains trust** N (= panel of experts) groupe m d'experts or de spécialistes; (US = advisory experts: also ~ **trust**) brain-trust m ► **brain surgeon** N neurochirurgien(ne) m(f) ► **brain teaser** N casse-tête f ► **brain trust** N (US) → **brains trust** ► **brain tumour** N tumeur f au cerveau ► **brain wave** N (Brit) idée f géniale, inspiration f ► **brain waves** NPL (Psych) ondes fpl cérébrales

brainless ['breɪnlɪs] ADJ [person] sans cervelle, stupide; [idea] stupide; **to be ~** [person] n'avoir rien dans la tête

brainpower ['breɪnpaʊə'] N intelligence f

brainstorm ['breɪnstɔːm] [1] N (Med) congestion f cérébrale; (Brit fig = sudden aberration) moment m d'aberration; (US = brilliant idea) idée f géniale [2] VI faire du remue-méninges, faire du brainstorming [3] VT explorer

brainstorming ['breɪnstɔːmɪŋ] [1] N remue-méninges m, brainstorming m [2] COMP ► **brainstorming session** N (séance f de) brainstorming m, séance f de remue-méninges

brainwash ['breɪnwɒʃ] VT faire un lavage de cerveau à; **he was ~ed into believing that ...** on a réussi à lui faire croire or à lui mettre dans la tête que ...

brainwashing ['breɪnwɒʃɪŋ] N [of prisoners etc] lavage m de cerveau;* [of public etc] bourrage* m de crâne, intox* f

brainwork ['breɪnwɜːk] N travail m intellectuel

brainy* ['breɪnɪ] ADJ intelligent, doué

braise [breɪz] VT (Culin) braiser

brake[1] [breɪk] N (Bot) (= bracken) fougère f; (= thicket) fourré m

brake[2] [breɪk] N (= vehicle) break m

brake[3] [breɪk] [1] N (Aut etc) frein m; **to put on** or **apply the ~s** freiner; (fig) **to act as a ~ on** sb's activities mettre un frein aux activités de qn → **handbrake, slam on** [2] VI freiner [3] COMP ► **brake band** N bande f de frein ► **brake block** N sabot m or patin m de frein ► **brake disc** N disque m de frein ► **brake drum** N tambour m de frein ► **brake fluid** N liquide m de freins, lockheed® m ► **brake horsepower** N puissance f au frein or effective ► **brake lever** N frein m à main ► **brake light** N (of car) stop m ► **brake lining** N garniture f de frein ► **brake pad** N plaquette f de frein ► **brake pedal** N pédale f de frein ► **brake shoe** N mâchoire f de frein ► **brake-van** N (Brit Rail) fourgon m à frein

brakeman ['breɪkmən] N (pl **-men**) (US Rail) chef m de train

braking ['breɪkɪŋ] [1] N freinage m [2] COMP ► **braking distance** N distance f de freinage ► **braking power** N puissance f de freinage

bramble ['bræmbl] N [a] (= thorny shrub) roncier m, roncière f [b] (= blackberry) (bush) ronce f des haies, mûrier m sauvage; (berry) mûre f (sauvage)

brambling ['bræmblɪŋ] N (= bird) pinson m du nord

bran [bræn] [1] N son m (de blé) [2] COMP ► **bran loaf** N pain m au son ► **bran mash** N bran m or son m mouillé ► **bran tub** N (Brit) pêche f miraculeuse (jeu)

branch [brɑːntʃ] [1] N [a] [of tree, candelabra] branche f; [of river] bras m, branche f; [of mountain chain] ramification f; [of road] embranchement m; [of railway] bifurcation f, raccordement m; [of pipe] branchement m; [of family] rameau m, branche f; (Ling) rameau m; [of subject, science etc] branche f; (Admin) division f, section f; (Mil) **he did not belong to their ~ of the service** il n'appartenait pas à leur arme → **olive, root**
[b] (Comm) [of store] succursale f; [of company] succursale f, filiale f; [of bank] agence f, succursale f; [of police force] antenne f [of industry] branche f, secteur m
[c] (Comput) branchement m
[d] (US = stream) ruisseau m
[2] VI [a] [tree] se ramifier
[b] [road] bifurquer; [river] se diviser; **the road ~es off the main road at ...** la route quitte la grand-route à ...
[3] COMP ► **branch depot** N (Comm) dépôt m auxiliaire ► **branch line** N (Rail) ligne f secondaire ► **branch manager** N (gen) directeur m de succursale etc; [of bank] directeur m d'agence or de succursale ► **branch office** N succursale f; [of bank] agence f, succursale f ► **branch water*** N (US) eau f plate
► **branch off** VI [road] bifurquer
► **branch out** VI [person, company] étendre ses activités; **the firm is ~ing out into the publishing business** la compagnie étend ses activités à l'édition

branching ['brɑːntʃɪŋ] [1] N (Gram) branchement m, arborescence f [2] COMP ► **branching rules** NPL règle f de formation d'arbre

brand [brænd] [1] N [a] (Comm = trademark: also ~ **name**) marque f (de fabrique); **that rum is an excellent ~** c'est une excellente marque de rhum
[b] (= mark) [of cattle, property] marque f; [of prisoner] flétrissure f; (fig = stigma) marque f, stigmate m
[c] (also ~**ing-iron**) fer m à marquer
[d] (= burning wood) tison m → **firebrand**
[e] (†, liter = sword) glaive m (liter), épée f
[2] VT [+ cattle, property] marquer; (fig) [+ person] cataloguer (**as** comme); (fig) **he was ~ed (as) a traitor** on l'a catalogué comme traître; **to ~ sth on sb's memory** graver qch dans la mémoire de qn
[3] COMP ► **brand acceptance** N (Comm) accueil m réservé à une (or la) marque ► **brand awareness** N (Comm) notoriété f de (la) marque ► **branded goods** NPL (Comm) produits mpl de marque ► **brand image** N (Comm) image f de marque ► **branding-iron** N fer m à marquer ► **brand loyalty** N (Comm) fidélité f à la marque ► **brand-new** ADJ tout neuf (toute neuve f), flambant neuf (neuve f)

brandish ['brændɪʃ] VT brandir

brandy ['brændɪ] [1] N cognac m; **~ and soda** fine f à l'eau; **plum ~** eau-de-vie f de prune or de quetsche [2] COMP ► **brandy butter** N beurre sucré et aromatisé au cognac ► **brandy snap** N (Culin) cornet m croquant

brash [bræʃ] ADJ (pej) [a] (= overconfident) [person] effronté, culotté*; [behaviour, style] impertinent [b] (= bold) [colour] criard; [perfume] qui cocotte*

brashly ['bræʃlɪ] ADV (pej) [say, behave] avec outrecuidance; **to be ~ confident** or **assertive** faire preuve d'outrecuidance

brashness ['bræʃnɪs] N (NonC: pej) [a] (= overconfidence) [of person] outrecuidance f [b] (= boldness) [of colour] aspect m criard

Brasilia [brəˈzɪljə] N Brasilia

brass [brɑːs] [1] N [a] (NonC) cuivre m (jaune), laiton m → **bold**
[b] (= tablet) plaque f mortuaire (en cuivre)
[c] (= object/ornament of brass) objet m/ornement m en cuivre; **to do/clean the ~(es)** faire/astiquer les cuivres; (Mus) **the ~** les cuivres mpl; **the (top) ~*** les huiles* fpl
[d] (NonC: ‡) (= impudence) toupet* m, culot* m; (Brit = money) pognon* m
[2] COMP [ornament etc] en or de cuivre ► **brass band** N fanfare f, orchestre m de cuivres ► **brassed-off:** ADJ (Brit) **to be ~ed-off with sth** en avoir ras le bol* de qch ► **brass farthing*** N **it's not worth a ~ farthing** cela ne vaut pas un clou* or un pet de lapin* → **care** ► **brass foundry** N fonderie f de cuivre ► **brass hat** N (Mil) huile* f ► **brass knuckles** NPL coup m de poing américain ► **brass monkey:** N (Brit) **it's ~ monkey weather** or **~ monkeys** ◊ **it's cold enough to freeze the balls off a ~ monkey** on se les gèle:, on caille: ► **brass neck:** N **he's got a ~ neck** il a du toupet* or du culot* ► **brass plate** N plaque f de cuivre; [of church] plaque f mortuaire or commémorative ► **brass ring** N (US fig) **to go** or **reach for the ~ ring*** essayer de décrocher la timbale* ► **brass rubbing** N (= action) décalquage m par frottement; (= object) décalque m ► **brass tacks*** NPL **to get down to ~ tacks** en venir aux faits or aux choses sérieuses

brasserie ['bræsərɪ] N brasserie f

brassica ['bræsɪkə] N (Bot) crucifère f, brassicacée f

brassie ['brɑːsɪ] N (Golf) = **brassy** 2

brassière† ['bræsɪə'] N soutien-gorge m

brassware ['brɑːswɛə'] N (NonC) chaudronnerie f d'art, dinanderie f

brassy ['brɑːsɪ] [1] ADJ [a] (= yellow) [hair] d'un blond cuivré artificiel [b] (= harsh) [sound] métallique; [voice] claironnant; [laugh] éclatant [c] (pej = flashy) [woman] à l'allure tapageuse [d] (* pej = impudent) [person] culotté* [2] N (Golf) brassie m

brat [bræt] N (pej) (sale) môme* mf, (sale) gosse* mf; **all these ~s** toute cette marmaille*; **one of his ~s** un de ses gosses*

Bratislava [ˌbrætɪˈslɑːvə] N Bratislava

bratpack ['brætpæk] N jeunes loups mpl

bravado [brəˈvɑːdəʊ] N (pl **bravados** or **bravadoes**) bravade f

brave [breɪv] [1] ADJ [a] [person, smile, attempt, action] courageux, brave; **to be as ~ as a lion** être courageux comme un lion, être intrépide; **be ~!** du courage!; **be ~ and tell her** prends ton courage à deux mains et va lui dire → **face** [b] (liter = fine) beau (belle f), élé-

gant; (*iro*) **it's a ~ new world!** on n'arrête pas le progrès! (*iro*) **2** N **a** **the bravest of the ~** des braves parmi les braves **b** (= *Indian warrior*) guerrier *m* indien, brave *m* **3** VT [+ *danger, person, sb's anger*] braver, affronter

►**brave out** VT SEP **to ~ it out** faire face à la situation

bravely ['breɪvlɪ] ADV [*fight, struggle, try, speak, smile*] bravement; **the flag was flying ~** le drapeau flottait fièrement

bravery ['breɪvərɪ] N (*NonC*) courage *m*, bravoure *f*

bravo ['brɑːˈvəʊ] EXCL, N (*pl* **bravoes** *or* **bravos**) bravo *m*

bravura [brɑːˈvʊərə] N (*also Mus*) bravoure *f*

brawl [brɔːl] **1** VI se bagarrer*, se quereller **2** N rixe *f*, bagarre *f*; **drunken ~** querelle *f* d'ivrognes

brawling ['brɔːlɪŋ] **1** ADJ bagarreur*, querelleur **2** N rixe *f*, bagarre *f*

brawn [brɔːn] N **a** (*Brit Culin*) fromage *m* de tête **b** (= *muscle*) muscle(s) *m(pl)*; (= *strength*) muscle *m*; **to have plenty of ~** être bien musclé, avoir du muscle; (*hum*) **he is all ~ and no brain** il est tout en muscles et sans cervelle

brawny ['brɔːnɪ] ADJ [*arms*] musculeux; [*person*] musclé

bray [breɪ] **1** N [*of ass*] braiment *m*; [*of trumpet*] sonnerie *f*, son *m* éclatant **2** VI [*ass*] braire; [*trumpet*] sonner

braze [breɪz] VT souder (au laiton)

brazen ['breɪzn] **1** ADJ **a** (*pej* = *shameless*) [*person, action, attitude, lie*] effronté; **I'm ~ about asking for things** je ne me gêne pas pour demander; **they are ~ about their sales tactics** ils ne font pas mystère de leur stratégie de vente; **a ~ hussy** une dévergondée **b** (= *made of brass*) en or de laiton **c** (*liter* = *brass-coloured*) [*light, sun*] cuivré **d** (= *harsh*) [*sound*] métallique **2** VT **to ~ it out** crâner* **3** COMP ►**brazen-faced** ADJ effronté

brazenly ['breɪznlɪ] ADV effrontément

brazier¹ ['breɪzɪəʳ] N [*of fire*] brasero *m*

brazier² ['breɪzɪəʳ] N (= *craftsman*) chaudronnier *m*

Brazil [brəˈzɪl] N le Brésil

brazil [brəˈzɪl] N (*also* **~ nut**) noix *f* du Brésil

Brazilian [brəˈzɪlɪən] **1** ADJ brésilien, du Brésil **2** N Brésilien(ne) *m(f)*

BRCS [ˌbiːɑːsiːˈes] N (ABBR = **British Red Cross Society**) → **British**

breach [briːtʃ] **1** N **a** (*Jur etc* = *violation*) infraction *f*, manquement *m* (**of** à); [*of rules, order, discipline, law, security*] infraction *f*; [*of friendship, good manners*] manquement *m* (**of** à); **~ of contract** rupture *f* de contrat; **a ~ of decorum** un manquement au protocole; **~ of faith** déloyauté *f*; **~ of the peace** atteinte *f* à l'ordre public; (*US Pol*) **~ of privilege** atteinte *f* portée aux prérogatives parlementaires; **~ of professional secrecy** violation *f* du secret professionnel; **~ of trust** abus *m* de confiance
b (= *estrangement*) brouille *f*, désaccord *m*
c (= *gap: in wall etc*) brèche *f*, trou *m*; (*Mil*) **to make a ~ in the enemy's lines** percer les lignes ennemies; (*fig*) **to step into the ~** s'engouffrer dans la brèche
2 VT **a** [+ *wall*] ouvrir une brèche dans, faire une trouée dans; (*Mil*) [+ *enemy lines, defences*] percer **b** [+ *security*] violer
3 VI [*whale*] sauter hors de l'eau

bread [bred] **1** N **a** pain *m*; **a loaf of ~** un pain, une miche de pain; **new ~** pain *m* frais; **~ fresh from the oven** du pain sortant du four; **an invalid on a diet of ~ and milk** un invalide qui se nourrit de pain et de lait; **to**

put sb on (dry) ~ and water mettre qn au pain (sec) et à l'eau; (*Rel*) **the ~ and wine** les (deux) espèces *fpl*; (*Rel*) **to break ~** [*congregation*] recevoir la communion; [*priest*] administrer la communion; **~ and butter** du pain et du beurre → **2**
b (*fig phrases*) **writing is his ~ and butter** sa plume est son gagne-pain, il vit de sa plume; **to earn one's ~** gagner son pain *or* sa vie; **to take the ~ out of sb's mouth** ôter à qn le pain de la bouche; **he knows which side his ~ is buttered** il sait où est son intérêt; **to throw** *or* **cast one's ~ upon the water(s)** agir de façon désintéressée; **~ and circuses** du pain et des jeux → **brown, gingerbread, slice**
c (⁂ = *money*) fric* *m*, oseille* *f*
2 COMP ►**bread-and-butter** ADJ (*fig*) [*job etc*] alimentaire; (= *reliable*) [*player etc*] sur qui l'on peut compter ►**bread-and-butter letter** N lettre *f* de château, lettre *f* de remerciements (*pour hospitalité reçue*) ►**bread-and-butter pudding** N pudding *m* (*à base de pain beurré*) ►**bread line** N (*US*) file *f* d'attente pour la soupe populaire; (*Brit*) **to be on the ~ line*** vivre en-dessous du seuil de pauvreté ►**bread poultice** N cataplasme *m* à la mie de pain ►**bread pudding** N pudding *or* pouding *m* ►**bread sauce** N sauce *f* à la mie de pain

breadbasket ['bred,bɑːskɪt] **1** N corbeille *f* à pain; (*fig* = *granary*) grenier *m*; (⁂ = *stomach*) estomac *m* **2** ADJ (*Econ etc*) fondamental

breadbin ['bredbɪn] N boîte *f* à pain; (*larger*) huche *f* à pain

breadboard ['bredbɔːd] N planche *f* à pain; (*Comput, Elec*) montage *m* expérimental

breadbox ['bredbɒks] N (*US*) = **breadbin**

breadcrumb ['bredkrʌm] N miette *f* de pain; (*Culin: as topping*) **~s** chapelure *f*; **fried in ~s** pané

breaded ['bredɪd] ADJ [*cutlet, fillet*] pané

breadfruit ['bredfruːt] N (*pl* **breadfruit** *or* **breadfruits**) (= *tree*) arbre *m* à pain, artocarpe *m*; (= *fruit*) fruit *m* de l'arbre à pain

breadknife ['brednaɪf] N (*pl* **-knives**) couteau *m* à pain

breadstick ['bredstɪk] N longuet *m*, gressin *m*

breadth [bretθ] N **a** (= *width*) largeur *f*; **this field is 100 metres in ~** ce champ a 100 mètres de large → **hair's breadth b** (*fig*) [*of mind, thought*] largeur *f*; [*of style*] ampleur *f*; [*Art*] largeur *f* d'exécution; (*Mus*) jeu *m* large; (*Mus*) **~ of tone** ampleur *f* du son

breadthwise ['bretθwaɪz] ADV en largeur, dans la largeur

breadwinner ['bred,wɪnəʳ] N soutien *m* de famille

break [breɪk] (*vb: pret* **broke**, *ptp* **broken**) **1** N **a** (= *fracture*) cassure *f*, rupture *f*; (*fig*) [*of relationship*] rupture *f*, brouille *f*; **he spoke of the need for a ~ with the past** il a dit qu'il fallait rompre avec le passé
b (= *gap*) (*in wall*) trouée *f*, brèche *f*; (*in rock*) faille *f*; (*in line*) interruption *f*, rupture *f*
c (= *interruption, interval*) interruption *f*, pause *f*; (*in TV programme etc*) interruption *f*; (*in conversation*) interruption *f*; (*in journey*) arrêt *m*; (*Brit Scol*) récréation *f*; (*Gram, Typ*) points *mpl* de suspension; **I need a ~** (= *few minutes*) j'ai besoin d'une pause; (= *holiday*) j'ai besoin de vacances; (= *change*) j'ai besoin de me changer les idées; **to take a ~** (= *few minutes*) faire une pause; (= *holiday*) prendre des vacances; (= *change*) se changer les idées; **six hours without a ~** six heures de suite, six heures d'affilée; (*Rad, TV* = *advertisements*) **after the ~** après la publicité; (*Rad*) **a ~ in transmission** une interruption (due à un incident technique); (*Elec*) **~ in circuit** rupture *f* de circuit; **a ~ in the clouds** une éclaircie; **a ~ in the weather** un changement de temps; **with a ~ in her voice** d'une voix entrecoupée

d (*liter*) **at ~ of day** *or* **dawn** au point du jour, à l'aube
e (⁂ = *escape: also* **~out**) évasion *f*; **to make a ~ for it** prendre la fuite; **he made a ~ for the door** il s'est élancé vers la porte
f (⁂ = *luck, opportunity*) chance *f*, veine* *f*; **to have a good/bad ~** avoir une période de veine*/de déveine*; **he's had all the ~s** il a eu toutes les veines*; **she got her first big ~ in the Broadway play "Sarafina"** elle a percé dans « Sarafina », une pièce montée à Broadway; **to give sb a ~** *or* **an even ~** donner une chance à qn; **give me a ~!*** (= *leave me alone*) fichez-moi la paix!*
g (*Sport*) (*Snooker*) série *f*; (*Tennis*) **to have a ~ of serve** *or* **service** prendre le service de son adversaire, faire le break
h (= *vehicle*) break *m*
2 VT **a** (= *smash, fracture, tear*) [+ *cup, chair, stick*] casser, briser; [+ *shoelace*] casser; [+ *bone*] casser, fracturer; [+ *skin*] entamer, écorcher; **to ~ sth in two** casser qch en deux; **the child has broken all his toys** l'enfant a cassé *or* brisé tous ses jouets; **to ~ one's neck** se rompre *or* se casser le cou → **breakneck**; (*fig*) **I'll ~ his neck if I catch him doing that again*** si je l'y reprends, je lui tords le cou*; **to ~ one's leg** se casser la jambe; (*Theat*) **~ a leg!*** merde!*; **the bone is not broken** il n'y a pas de fracture; **his skin is not broken** il ne s'est pas écorché; **to ~ open** [+ *door*] enfoncer, forcer; [+ *packet*] ouvrir; [+ *lock, safe*] fracturer, forcer; (*US*) **to ~ ground on a new building** commencer la construction d'un nouveau bâtiment; (*fig*) **to ~ new** *or* **fresh ground** innover, faire œuvre de pionnier; (*lit*) **to ~ one's back** se casser la colonne vertébrale; **he almost broke his back trying to lift the stone** il s'est donné un tour de reins en essayant de soulever la pierre; **he's ~ing his back to get the job finished in time** il s'échine à finir le travail à temps; (*Brit fig*) **to ~ the back of a task** faire le plus dur *or* le plus gros d'une tâche; **to ~ sb's heart** briser le cœur de qn; **to ~ one's heart over sth** avoir le cœur brisé par qch; **it ~s my heart to think that ...** cela me brise le cœur de penser que ... → **ball¹, barrier, bone, bread, code, ice, path¹, record, surface, wind¹**
b (*fig* = *fail to observe*) [+ *promise*] manquer à; [+ *treaty*] violer; [+ *commandment*] désobéir à; **to ~ the law** violer la loi; **to ~ a vow** rompre un serment; **to ~ an appointment with sb** (= *cancel*) annuler un rendez-vous avec qn; (= *stand sb up*) faire faux bond à qn, poser un lapin* à qn → **bound¹, camp¹, cover, faith, jail, parole, rank¹, Sabbath**
c (= *weaken*) [+ *health*] abîmer, détériorer; [+ *courage, spirit*] abattre, briser; [+ *strike*] briser; [+ *rebellion*] mater; [+ *horse*] dresser; (*Mil*) [+ *officer*] casser; **to ~ sb** (*morally*) causer la perte de qn; (*financially*) ruiner qn; **this will make or ~ him** (*financially*) cela fera sa fortune ou sa ruine; (*morally*) cela sera son salut ou sa perte; **to ~ sb of a habit** faire perdre une habitude à qn; **to ~ a habit** se débarrasser *or* se défaire d'une habitude; (*Betting*) **to ~ the bank** faire sauter la banque; (*fig*) **it won't ~ the bank*** cela ne va pas te (*or* nous *or* les *etc*) ruiner
d (= *interrupt*) [+ *silence, spell, fast*] rompre; (*Elec*) [+ *current, circuit*] couper; (*Tennis*) **to ~ sb's serve** *or* **service** prendre le service de qn; **to ~ one's journey** faire une étape (*or* des étapes); **to ~ the thread of a story** couper le fil d'un récit
e (= *soften*) [+ *fall, blow*] amortir, adoucir; **the wall ~s the force of the wind** le mur coupe le vent
f [+ *news*] révéler, annoncer; **try to ~ it to her gently** essayez de le lui annoncer avec ménagement
g (*Naut*) [+ *flag, signal*] déployer, déferler

③ VI **a** (= *fracture*) (*gen*) (se) casser, se briser; [*stick, rope*] se casser, se rompre; [*bone*] se casser, se fracturer; (*fig*) [*heart*] se briser; **to ~ in two** se casser en deux

b (= *disperse*) [*clouds*] se disperser, se dissiper; [*troops*] rompre les rangs; [*ranks*] se rompre

c (= *escape*) se libérer (**from** de); **to ~ free** se libérer, se dégager; **to ~ loose** [*person, animal*] s'échapper (**from** de); [*boat*] rompre ses amarres, partir à la dérive

d [*storm*] éclater, se déchaîner; [*wave*] déferler; **she tried to reach the house before the storm broke** elle a essayé d'atteindre la maison avant que l'orage éclate (*subj*) → **water**

e [*news, story*] éclater, se répandre

f (= *weaken, change*) [*health*] se détériorer; [*voice*] (*boy's*) muer; (*in emotion*) se briser, s'étrangler (**with** sous le coup de); [*weather*] se gâter; **the heat wave was ~ing** la vague de chaleur touchait à sa fin; **he broke under torture** il a craqué sous la torture; **his courage** or **spirit broke** son courage l'a abandonné

g (*in relationship, friendship*) **to ~ with sb** rompre avec qn

h (*Boxing*) se dégager

i [*dawn*] poindre; [*day*] se lever, poindre

j (*financially*) **to ~ even** rentrer dans ses fonds

k (= *pause*) **we broke for lunch** nous nous sommes arrêtés or nous avons fait une pause pour le déjeuner

l (*Ling*) [*vowel*] se diphtonguer

m (*Sport*) [*ball*] dévier

④ COMP ► **break dancer** N smurfeur *m*, -euse *f* ► **break dancing** N smurf *m* ► **break-even point** N (*Comm*) seuil *m* de rentabilité ► **break-in** N cambriolage *m* ► **break point** N (*Tennis*) balle *f* de break; (*Comput*) point *m* de rupture ► **break-up** N [*of ship*] dislocation *f*; [*of ice*] débâcle *f*; [*of friendship*] rupture *f*; [*of empire*] démembrement *m*; [*of political party*] scission *f*, schisme *m*

► **break away** ① VI **a** [*piece of cliff, railway coach*] se détacher (**from** de); [*boat*] rompre ses amarres, partir à la dérive; (*lit, fig*) **to ~ away from a group** se séparer d'un groupe; **to ~ away from routine** sortir de la routine **b** (*Ftbl*) déborder; (*Racing*) s'échapper, se détacher du peloton ② VT SEP (*lit, fig*) détacher (**from** de) ③ **~away** ADJ, N → **breakaway**

► **break down** ① VI **a** (= *fail, cease to function*) [*vehicle, machine*] tomber en panne; [*health*] se détériorer; [*argument*] s'effondrer; [*resistance*] céder; [*negotiations, plan*] échouer; **after negotiations broke down ...** après l'échec *m* or la rupture des négociations ... **b** (= *weep*) fondre en larmes, éclater en sanglots ② VT SEP **a** (= *demolish*) démolir, mettre en morceaux; [*+ door*] enfoncer; (*fig*) [*+ opposition*] briser **b** (= *analyse*) [*+ accounts*] analyser, détailler; [*+ sales figures, costs*] ventiler; (*Chem*) [*+ substance*] décomposer; **he broke down his argument into three points** il a décomposé son raisonnement en trois points ③ **~down** N, COMP → **breakdown**

► **break forth** VI (*liter*) [*light, water*] jaillir; [*storm*] éclater; **to ~ forth into song** se mettre à chanter, entonner un chant

► **break in** ① VI **a** (= *interrupt, intrude*) interrompre; **to ~ in (up)on sb/sth** interrompre qn/qch **b** (= *enter illegally*) entrer par effraction ② VT SEP **a** [*+ door*] enfoncer; [*+ cask*] défoncer **b** (= *tame, train*) [*+ horse*] dresser; (*esp US*) [*+ engine, car*] roder; **it took a month to ~ in my new running shoes** cela a pris un mois avant que mes nouvelles chaussures de course se fassent; **it will take you six months before you're broken in* (to the job)** vous mettrez six mois à vous faire au métier ③ **~-in** N → **break**

► **break into** VT FUS **a** (= *enter illegally*) [*+ house*] entrer par effraction dans; **to ~ into a**

safe fracturer or forcer un coffre-fort; **to ~ into the cashbox** forcer la caisse **b** (= *use part of*) [*+ savings*] entamer; **to ~ into a new box of sth** entamer une nouvelle boîte de qch **c** (*Comm etc*) **to ~ into a new market** percer sur un nouveau marché; **she finally broke into films after an acclaimed singing career** elle a fini par percer au cinéma après une brillante carrière de chanteuse **d** (= *begin suddenly*) **to ~ into song** se mettre à chanter; **she broke into a smile** elle s'est mise à sourire; **he broke into a long explanation** il s'est lancé dans une longue explication; **to ~ into a trot** [*horse*] prendre le trot; **to ~ into a run** se mettre à courir

► **break off** ① VI **a** [*piece, twig*] se détacher net, se casser net **b** (= *stop*) s'arrêter (**doing** de faire); **he broke off in mid-sentence** il s'est arrêté au milieu d'une phrase; **to ~ off from work** faire une pause **c** (= *end relationship*) rompre (**with** sb avec qn) **d** (*Snooker*) commencer la partie ② VT SEP **a** (*gen*) casser, détacher; [*+ piece of chocolate*] casser **b** (= *end, interrupt*) [*+ engagement, negotiations*] rompre; [*+ habit*] rompre avec, se défaire de; [*+ work*] interrompre, cesser

► **break out** ① VI **a** [*epidemic, fire*] éclater, se déclarer; [*storm, war, argument*] éclater; **to ~ out in spots** se couvrir de boutons; **to ~ out into a sweat** suer, prendre une suée*; (*from fear etc*) commencer à avoir des sueurs froides; **he broke out into a stream of insults** il a déversé un chapelet d'injures **b** (= *escape*) s'échapper, s'évader (**of** de) ② VT FUS [*+ champagne etc*] sortir ③ **~out** N → **breakout**

► **break through** ① VI (*Mil*) faire une percée; [*sun*] percer les nuages ② VT FUS [*+ defences, obstacles*] enfoncer, percer; **to ~ through sb's reserve** faire sortir qn de sa réserve; **to ~ through the crowd** se frayer un passage à travers la foule ③ **~through** N → **breakthrough**

► **break up** ① VI **a** [*ice*] craquer, se fêler; [*road*] être défoncé; [*ship in storm*] se disloquer; [*partnership*] cesser, prendre fin; [*health*] se détériorer; **the weather is ~ing up** le temps se gâte; **their marriage broke up** leur couple s'est brisé; **to ~ up with sb** rompre avec qn **b** (= *disperse*) [*clouds, crowd, meeting*] se disperser; [*group*] se disperser, se séparer; [*friends*] se quitter, se séparer; (*Brit*) **the schools ~ up tomorrow** les vacances (scolaires) commencent demain **c** (*US** = *laugh*) se tordre de rire ② VT SEP **a** (*lit*) mettre en morceaux, morceler; [*+ house*] démolir; [*+ ground*] ameublir; [*+ road*] défoncer; **to ~ sth up into three pieces** casser qch en trois morceaux **b** (*fig*) [*+ coalition*] briser, rompre; [*+ empire*] démembrer; **to ~ up a marriage/a home** désunir un couple/les membres d'une famille; **to do sth to ~ up one's day** faire qch pour faire une coupure dans la journée **c** (= *disperse*) [*+ crowd, meeting*] disperser; **~ it up!** séparez-vous!; (*said by policeman*) circulez!; **police used tear gas to ~ up the demonstration** la police a utilisé du gaz lacrymogène pour disperser les manifestants **d** (*US** = *make laugh*) donner le fou rire à ③ **a** **~-up** → **break** **b** **~ing-up** → **breaking**

breakable ['breɪkəbl] ① ADJ cassable, fragile ② **breakables** NPL objets *mpl* fragiles

breakage ['breɪkɪdʒ] N (*in chain*) rupture *f*; [*of glass, china*] casse *f*, bris *m*; **to pay for ~s** payer la casse

breakaway ['breɪkə,weɪ] ① N (*separating*) séparation *f* (**from** d'avec), rupture *f* (**from** avec); (*Sport*) échappée *f*; (*Boxing*) dégagement *m* ② ADJ [*group, movement*] séparatiste, dissident; (*Pol*) [*state, region*] séparatiste

breakdown ['breɪkdaʊn] ① N **a** [*of machine, vehicle, electricity supply*] panne *f* **b** [*of communications etc*] rupture *f*; [*of railway system etc*] interruption *f* (subite) de service; (*fig*) [*of*

moral values etc] érosion *f*, dégradation *f* **c** (*Med*) (*mental*) dépression *f* nerveuse; (*physical*) effondrement *m* **d** (= *analysis*) analyse *f*; (*into categories*) décomposition *f* (**into** en); [*of sales figures, costs etc*] ventilation *f*; **give me a ~ of these results** faites-moi l'analyse de ces résultats ② COMP [*gang, service*] de dépannage ► **breakdown truck, breakdown van** N (*Brit Aut*) dépanneuse *f*

breaker ['breɪkər] N **a** (= *wave*) brisant *m* **b** [*of cars*] (= *person*) casseur *m*; (= *business*) casse *f*; **to send to the ~s** [*+ ship, car*] envoyer à la casse → **housebreaker, lawbreaker** **c** (= *machine*) concasseur *m*, broyeur *m* → **ice-breaker** **d** (= *CB user*) cibiste *mf*

breakfast ['brekfəst] ① N petit déjeuner *m*; **to have ~** déjeuner, prendre le (petit) déjeuner → **wedding** ② VI déjeuner (**off, on** de) ③ COMP ► **breakfast bar** N bar *m* américain (*dans une cuisine américaine*) ► **breakfast cereals** fpl céréales fpl ► **breakfast cloth** N nappe *f* (ordinaire) ► **breakfast cup** N déjeuner *m* (tasse) ► **breakfast meeting** N (*Comm*) petit déjeuner *m* d'affaires ► **breakfast room** N salle *f* à manger (*où l'on prend le petit déjeuner*) ► **breakfast set** N service *m* à petit déjeuner ► **breakfast table** N **they were still sitting at the ~ table** ils étaient encore assis à la table du petit déjeuner ► **breakfast TV** N la télévision du matin

breaking ['breɪkɪŋ] ① N [*of cup, chair*] bris *m*; [*of bone, limb*] fracture *f*; (*Jur*) [*of window, seals*] bris *m*; [*of promise*] manquement *m* (**of** à); [*treaty, law*] violation *f* (**of** de); [*of commandment*] désobéissance *f* (**of** à); [*of silence, spell*] rupture *f*; [*of journey*] interruption *f* (**of** de) ② COMP ► **breaking and entering** N (*Jur*) effraction *f* ► **breaking-point** N (*Tech*) point *m* de rupture; **to try sb's patience to ~-point** pousser à bout la patience de qn; **she has reached ~-point** elle est à bout, elle n'en peut plus; (*Pol etc*) **the situation has reached ~-point** la situation a atteint le point de rupture ► **breaking strain, breaking stress** N (*Tech*) point *m* de rupture ► **breaking-up** N [*of school, college*] début *m* des vacances, fin *f* des cours; [*of meeting etc*] clôture *f*, levée *f*

breakneck ['breɪknek] ADJ **at ~ speed** [*run*] à une allure folle, à fond de train; [*drive*] à une allure folle, à tombeau ouvert

breakout ['breɪkaʊt] N évasion *f*

breakthrough ['breɪkθru:] N (*Mil*) percée *f*; (*in research etc*) découverte *f* capitale

breakwater ['breɪk,wɔ:tər] N brise-lames *m inv*, digue *f*

bream [bri:m] N (*pl inv*) brème *f*

breast [brest] ① N **a** (= *chest*) [*of man, woman*] poitrine *f*; [*of animal*] poitrine *f*, poitrail *m*; (*Culin*) [*of chicken*] blanc *m* → **beat, clean** **b** [*of woman*] sein *m*, mamelle† (*liter*); [*of man*] sein *m*; **baby at the ~** enfant *mf* au sein **c** (*Min*) front *m* de taille → **chimney** ② VT **a** (= *face*) [*+ waves, storm, danger*] affronter **b** [*+ hill*] atteindre le sommet de; (*Sport*) **to ~ the tape** franchir la ligne d'arrivée (le premier) ③ COMP ► **breast cancer** N cancer *m* du sein ► **breast enlargement** N augmentation *f* mammaire ► **breast-fed** ADJ nourri au sein ► **breast-feed** VT allaiter, donner le sein à ♦ VI allaiter ► **breast-feeding** N allaitement *m* maternel or au sein ► **breast milk** N lait *m* maternel ► **breast-pocket** N poche *f* de poitrine ► **breast-stroke** N brasse *f*; **to swim ~-stroke** nager la brasse

breastbone ['brestbəʊn] N (*Anat*) sternum *m*; [*of bird*] bréchet *m*

breastplate ['brestpleɪt] N (= *armour*) plastron *m* (de cuirasse); [*of priest*] pectoral *m*

breastwork ['brestwɜ:k] N (*Mil*) parapet *m*; (*Naut*) rambarde *f*

breath [breθ] [1] N [a] haleine f, souffle m, respiration f; **bad ~** mauvaise haleine f; **to have bad ~** avoir mauvaise haleine; (esp Brit) **to get one's ~ back** reprendre haleine, retrouver son souffle; **to catch one's ~** retenir son souffle; **out of ~** à bout de souffle, essoufflé, hors d'haleine; **to take ~** respirer, reprendre haleine; **to take a deep ~** respirer à fond; (fig) **take a deep ~!** accroche-toi bien!*; (fig) **to take sb's ~ away** couper le souffle à qn; **save your ~!** inutile de perdre or gaspiller ta salive!; **to be short of ~** avoir le souffle court; **to gasp for ~** haleter; **to stop for ~** s'arrêter pour reprendre haleine; **below** or **beneath** or **under one's ~** [say, talk] à voix basse, tout bas; **to laugh under one's ~** rire sous cape; **to say sth (all) in one ~** dire qch d'un trait; (fig) **it was the ~ of life to him** c'était (toute) sa vie, cela lui était aussi précieux que la vie même; **his last** or **dying ~** son dernier soupir; **with one's dying ~** en mourant; (liter) **to draw one's last ~** rendre l'âme, rendre le dernier soupir → **hold, same, waste**
[b] (air in movement) souffle m; **there wasn't a ~ of air** il n'y avait pas un souffle d'air; **to go out for a ~ of (fresh) air** sortir prendre l'air; (fig) **a ~ of fresh air** une bouffée d'air frais; **a little ~ of wind** un (léger) souffle d'air; (fig) **not a ~ of scandal** pas le moindre soupçon de scandale
[2] COMP ► **breath test** N (Aut) alcootest® m, éthylotest m ► **breath-test** VT faire subir l'alcootest® à

breathable ['bri:ðəbl] ADJ [air, atmosphere] respirable; [fabric, garment] aéré, qui respire

breathalyse, breathalyze (US) ['breθəlaɪz] VT (esp Brit) faire subir l'alcootest® à

Breathalyser®, Breathalyzer® (US) ['breθəlaɪzə'] N alcootest® m, éthylomètre m

breathe [bri:ð] [1] VI [person, fabric, garment] respirer; **to ~ deeply** or **heavily** (after running etc) haleter, souffler (fort); (in illness) respirer péniblement; **to ~ hard** souffler (fort), haleter; (fig) **to ~ freely** or **again** or **more easily** (pouvoir) respirer; (= be alive) **she is still breathing** elle respire encore; **red wine should be allowed to ~ before drinking** il faut faire respirer le vin rouge avant de le boire; (fig) **to ~ down sb's neck** talonner qn; **Newcastle are breathing down Liverpool's neck at the top of the table** Newcastle talonne Liverpool en haut du classement; **I've got the bank manager breathing down my neck** j'ai le directeur de la banque sur le dos
[2] VT [+ air] respirer; **to ~ one's last (breath)** rendre le dernier soupir; **to ~ air into sth** insuffler de l'air or souffler dans qch; **to ~ new life into sb** redonner goût à la vie or du courage à qn; (fig) **to ~ fire over** or **about sth** fulminer contre qch
[b] (= utter) [+ sigh] pousser; [+ prayer] murmurer; **to ~ a sigh of relief** pousser un soupir de soulagement; **don't ~ a word (about it)!** n'en dis rien à personne!, motus (et bouche cousue)!
[c] (Ling) aspirer
► **breathe in** VI, VT SEP aspirer, inspirer
► **breathe out** VI, VT SEP expirer

breather ['bri:ðə'] N [a] (= short rest) moment m de repos or répit; **to give sb a ~** laisser souffler qn [b] (= fresh air) **let's go (out) for a ~** sortons prendre l'air

breathing ['bri:ðɪŋ] [1] N [a] respiration f, souffle m; [of singer, flautist etc] respiration f; **heavy ~** respiration f bruyante [b] (Ling) aspiration f; (Greek Gram) **rough/smooth ~** esprit m rude/doux [2] COMP ► **breathing apparatus** N appareil m respiratoire ► **breathing space** N (fig) **to give sb a ~ space** donner à qn le temps de souffler or un moment de répit

breathless ['breθlɪs] ADJ [a] (= out of breath) (from exertion) essoufflé, à bout de souffle,

hors d'haleine; (from illness) qui a du mal à respirer; [voice] essoufflé; **to make sb ~** essouffler qn; **~ from doing sth** essoufflé d'avoir fait qch; **at a ~ pace** à une allure folle [b] (emotionally) [excitement] fébrile; **she was ~ with excitement** elle avait le souffle coupé par l'excitation; **he was ~ with anticipation** il retenait son souffle

breathlessly ['breθlɪslɪ] ADV (lit) [say, ask] en haletant, à bout de souffle; (fig = excitedly) [wait, watch] en retenant son souffle

breathlessness ['breθlɪsnɪs] N difficulté f respiratoire

breathtaking ['breθteɪkɪŋ] ADJ stupéfiant, à vous couper le souffle

breathtakingly ['breθteɪkɪŋlɪ] ADV **~ beautiful** d'une beauté à vous couper le souffle; **~ simple** d'une simplicité stupéfiante

breathy ['breθɪ] ADJ [voice] voilé

bred [bred] [1] VB pt, ptp of **breed** [2] ADJ (in compounds) **well-~** bien élevé → **country, ill**

breech [bri:tʃ] [1] N [a] [of gun] culasse f [b] (Med) **~ (birth** or **delivery)** accouchement m par le siège; **he was a ~*** il s'est présenté par le siège [2] VT [+ gun] munir d'une culasse

breechblock ['bri:tʃblɒk] N bloc m de culasse

breechcloth ['bri:tʃklɒθ] N (US) pagne m (d'étoffe)

breeches ['brɪtʃɪz] [1] NPL **(pair of) ~** (also **knee ~**) haut-de-chausses m; (also **riding ~**) culotte f (de cheval); **his wife wears the ~** c'est sa femme qui porte la culotte [2] ['bri:tʃɪz] COMP ► **breeches buoy** N (Naut) bouée-culotte f

breechloader ['bri:tʃləʊdə'] N (Mil) arme f qui se charge par la culasse

breed [bri:d] (pret, ptp **bred**) [1] VT [+ animals] élever, faire l'élevage de; †† [+ children] élever; (fig = give rise to) [+ hatred, resentment, violence, confusion, despair] engendrer; **he ~s horses** il fait l'élevage des chevaux, il élève des chevaux; **to ~ in/out a characteristic** acquérir/faire perdre une caractéristique (par la sélection); **to be bred for sth/to do sth** [animals] être élevé pour qch/pour faire qch; [people] être conditionné pour qch/pour faire qch → **born, cross, familiarity** [2] VI [animals] se reproduire, se multiplier; **they ~ like rabbits** ils se multiplient comme des lapins [3] N (Zool) (= race) race f, espèce f; (within race) type m; (Bot) espèce f; (fig) sorte f, espèce f → **crossbreed, half**

breeder ['bri:də'] N [a] (Phys: also **~ reactor**) sur(ré)générateur m [b] (Agr etc = person) éleveur m, -euse f → **cattle, plant, stockbreeder**

breeding ['bri:dɪŋ] [1] N [a] (= reproduction) reproduction f, procréation f [b] (Agr = raising) élevage m → **cattle** [c] (= upbringing) **(good) ~** (bonne) éducation f, bonnes manières fpl, savoir-vivre m; **to lack ~** manquer de savoir-vivre or d'éducation [d] (Phys) surrégénération f [2] COMP ► **breeding ground** N (lit) zone f de reproduction; (fig) **~ ground for revolution/germs** terrain m propice à la révolution/aux microbes; (fig) **~ ground for talent/revolutionaries** pépinière f de talents/de révolutionnaires ► **breeding season** N [of animals] saison f des amours

breeks [bri:ks] NPL (Scot) pantalon m

breeze[1] [bri:z] [1] N (= wind) brise f; **gentle ~** petite brise f, brise f légère; **stiff ~** vent m frais; **there is quite a ~** cela souffle → **sea** [b]* **it's a ~** c'est facile comme tout, c'est fastoche*; **to do sth in a ~** faire qch les doigts dans le nez* [2] VI **to ~ in/out** etc (jauntily) entrer/sortir etc d'un air dégagé; (briskly) entrer/sortir etc en coup de vent; **to ~ through sth*** faire qch les doigts dans le nez*

breeze[2] [bri:z] [1] N (= cinders) cendres fpl (de charbon) [2] COMP ► **breeze block** N (Brit) parpaing m (de laitier)

breezeway ['bri:zweɪ] N (US) passage couvert reliant deux bâtiments

breezily ['bri:zɪlɪ] ADV jovialement

breezy ['bri:zɪ] ADJ [a] (= windy) [day] de brise; [place] venteux, éventé; **it's ~ today** il y a du vent aujourd'hui [b] (= cheery) [person, manner] pétulant; [style] pétulant, enlevé; [melody] enjoué; [clothes] gai → **bright**

Bren carrier ['bren,kærɪə'] N = **Bren gun carrier**

Bren gun ['brengʌn] N (Mil) fusil-mitrailleur m

Bren gun carrier ['brengʌn,kærɪə'] N (Mil) chenillette f (pour fusil-mitrailleur)

brent goose [,brent'gu:s] N bernache f cravant

brethren ['breðrɪn] NPL [a] (††, Rel) frères mpl [b] (= fellow members) [of trade union etc] camarades mpl

Breton ['bretən] [1] ADJ breton [2] N [a] Breton(ne) m(f) [b] (Ling) breton m

breve [bri:v] N (Typ) brève f; (Mus) double ronde f

brevet ['brevɪt] N (esp Mil) brevet m

breviary ['bri:vɪərɪ] N bréviaire m

brevity ['brevɪtɪ] N (= shortness) brièveté f; (= conciseness) concision f; (= abruptness) [of reply] laconisme m; (= manner) brusquerie f ■ (PROV) **~ is the soul of wit** les plaisanteries les plus courtes sont les meilleures

brew [bru:] [1] N [a] [of beer] brassage m; (= amount brewed) brassin m → **home** [b] [of tea] infusion f; [of herbs] tisane f; (hum) **what's this ~* in the jug?** qu'est-ce que c'est que ce liquide or cette mixture dans la cruche? [2] VT [+ beer] brasser; [+ tea] faire infuser, préparer; [+ punch] préparer, mélanger; (fig) [+ scheme, mischief, plot] tramer, mijoter* [3] VI [a] (= make beer) brasser, faire de la bière [b] [beer] fermenter; [tea] infuser; (fig) [storm] couver, se préparer; [plot] se tramer; **there's trouble ~ing** il y a de l'orage dans l'air, ça va barder*; **something's ~ing** il se trame quelque chose [4] COMP ► **brew-up*** N (Brit) **let's have a ~-up** on va se faire du thé
► **brew up** [1] VI [a] (Brit* = make tea) faire du thé [b] [storm, dispute] se préparer, couver [2] **~-up*** N → **brew**

brewer ['bru:ə'] [1] N brasseur m [2] COMP ► **brewer's droop‡** N (NonC: Brit hum) impuissance f (passagère) due à l'alcool; **to get ~'s droop** bander mou‡

brewery ['bru:ərɪ] N brasserie f (fabrique)

briar ['braɪə'] N = **brier**

bribe [braɪb] [1] N pot-de-vin m; **to take a ~** se laisser corrompre or acheter, accepter un pot-de-vin; **to offer a ~** faire une tentative de corruption, offrir un pot-de-vin; **I'll give the child a sweet as a ~ to be good** je donnerai un bonbon à l'enfant pour qu'il se tienne tranquille [2] VT acheter, soudoyer; [+ witness] suborner; **to ~ sb into silence** acheter le silence de qn; **to ~ sb to do sth** soudoyer or corrompre qn pour qu'il fasse qch; **to let o.s. be ~d** se laisser soudoyer

bribery ['braɪbərɪ] N corruption f; (Jur) [of witness] subornation f; (Jur) **~ and corruption** corruption f; **open to ~** corruptible

bric-à-brac ['brɪkəbræk] N (NonC) bric-à-brac m; **~ dealer** brocanteur m

brick [brɪk] [1] N [a] (Constr) brique f; **made of ~** en brique(s); **it has not damaged the ~s and mortar** ça n'a pas endommagé les murs; **to put one's money into ~s and mortar** investir dans la pierre or l'immobilier ■ (PROV) **you can't make ~s without straw** à l'impossible nul n'est tenu (PROV); **he came down on me like a ton of ~s!*** il m'est tombé sur le râble!*, il m'a passé un de ces savons!*; (fig) **you might as well talk to a ~ wall*** autant parler à un mur; (fig) **to run one's head**

against *or* **come up against a ~ wall** se heurter à un mur ; *(fig)* **to drop a ~*** faire une gaffe* *or* une bourde* → **built**, **cat** [*Brit* = *toy*] cube *m* (de construction) [c] **a ~ of ice cream** une glace (empaquetée) [d] (↑* = *person*) type *m* sympa*, fille *f* sympa* ; **be a ~!** sois sympa* or chic ! [2] COMP [*house*] en brique(s) ► **brick-built** ADJ en brique(s) ► **brick-kiln** N four *m* à briques ► **brick red** N, ADJ (rouge *m*) brique *inv*
► **brick in** VT SEP = **brick up**
► **brick off** VT SEP [+ *area*] (em)murer
► **brick up** VT SEP [+ *door*, *window*] murer

brickbat ['brɪkbæt] N *(lit)* morceau *m* de brique ; (* *fig*) critique *f*

brickie* ['brɪkɪ] N *(Brit)* ABBR = **bricklayer**

bricklayer ['brɪkˌleɪəʳ] N maçon *m*

bricklaying ['brɪkˌleɪɪŋ] N *(NonC)* briquetage *m*

brickwork ['brɪkwɜːk] N briquetage *m*, brique *f*

brickworks ['brɪkwɜːks], **brickyard** ['brɪkjɑːd] N briqueterie *f*

bridal ['braɪdl] [1] ADJ [*feast*] de noce(s) ; [*bed*, *chamber*, *procession*] nuptial ; [*bouquet*] de la mariée [2] COMP ► **bridal gown** N robe *f* de mariée ► **bridal party** N famille *f* et amis *mpl* de la mariée ► **bridal shop** N magasin *m* de robes de mariées ► **bridal shower** N *(US)* fête en l'honneur de la future mariée ► **bridal suite** N suite *f* nuptiale ► **bridal veil** N voile *m* de mariée ► **bridal wear** N *(NonC)* vêtements *mpl* de mariée

bride [braɪd] [1] N *(about to be married)* (future) mariée *f* ; *(just married)* (jeune) mariée *f* ; **the ~ and (~)groom** les jeunes mariés *mpl* ; *(Rel)* **the ~ of Christ** l'épouse *f* du Christ [2] COMP ► **bride-to-be** N future mariée *f* ; **his ~-to-be** sa future femme, sa promise *(hum)*

bridegroom ['braɪdgruːm] N *(about to be married)* (futur) marié *m* ; *(just married)* (jeune) marié *m*

bridesmaid ['braɪdzmeɪd] N demoiselle *f* d'honneur

bridge¹ [brɪdʒ] [1] N [a] pont *m* ; **to build/throw a ~ across a river** construire/jeter un pont sur un fleuve ; **to build ~s between two communities/organizations** jeter un pont entre deux communautés/organisations ■ *(PROV)* **don't cross your ~s before you come to them** chaque chose en son temps *(PROV)* ; **let's cross that ~ when we come to it** on s'occupera de ce problème-là en temps et en heure → **burn¹**, **drawbridge**, **footbridge** [b] *(Naut)* passerelle *f* (de commandement) [c] [*of nose*] arête *f*, dos *m* ; [*of spectacles*] arcade *f* ; [*of violin*] chevalet *m* [d] *(Dentistry)* bridge *m* [2] VT [+ *river*] construire *or* jeter un pont sur ; *(fig)* **to ~ a gap** *(in knowledge, facts)* combler une lacune (**in** dans) ; *(in budget)* combler un trou (**in** dans) ; **to ~ the gap** *or* **divide** *(between people)* combler le fossé (**between** entre) [3] COMP ► **bridge-builder** N *(fig)* médiateur *m*, -trice *f* ► **bridge-building** N *(Mil)* pontage *m* ; *(fig)* efforts *mpl* de rapprochement

bridge² [brɪdʒ] [1] N *(Cards)* bridge *m* ; **to play ~** bridger, jouer au bridge → **auction**, **contract** [2] COMP ► **bridge party** N soirée *f* or réunion *f* de bridge ► **bridge player** N bridgeur *m*, -euse *f* ► **bridge roll** N petit pain *m* (brioché)

bridgehead ['brɪdʒhed] N *(Mil)* tête *f* de pont

bridgework ['brɪdʒwɜːk] N *(esp US Dentistry)* bridge *m*

bridging ['brɪdʒɪŋ] [1] N *(Climbing)* opposition *f* [2] COMP ► **bridging loan** N *(Brit Fin)* prêt-relais *m*

bridle ['braɪdl] [1] N [*of horse*] bride *f* ; *(fig)* frein *m*, contrainte *f* [2] VT [+ *horse*] brider ; [+ *one's emotions*] refréner, tenir en bride ; **to ~**

one's tongue se taire, tenir sa langue [3] VI *(in anger)* regimber, se rebiffer ; *(in scorn)* lever le menton *(en signe de mépris)* [4] COMP
► **bridle path** N sentier *m*, piste *f* cavalière

brief [briːf] [1] ADJ [a] (= *short*) [*period*, *career*, *visit*, *glimpse*, *moment*, *interval*] bref [b] (= *concise*) [*description*, *statement*] bref ; **I shall be ~** je serai bref ; **to be ~, the same thing happened again** bref or en deux mots, il s'est passé la même chose [c] (= *curt*) [*person*] sec (sèche *f*) [d] (= *skimpy*) [*skirt*, *shorts*] très court [2] N [a] *(Jur)* dossier *m*, cause *f*, affaire *f* ; *(Jur)* **to hold a ~ for sb** représenter qn en justice ; *(fig)* **I hold no ~ for those who ...** je ne me fais pas l'avocat *or* le défenseur de ceux qui ... ; *(fig)* **I hold no ~ for him** je ne prends pas sa défense ; **to have a watching ~ for ...** veiller aux intérêts de ... ; *(Jur)* **to take a ~** accepter de plaider une cause ; **in ~** en bref ; **in ~ then, do you agree?** en bref, vous êtes d'accord ? ; **the news in ~** les actualités en bref [b] *(Mil = instructions)* briefing *m* ; *(fig)* **his ~ is to ...** la tâche qui lui a été assignée consiste à ... [c] *(Brit* = lawyer)* avocat *m* [3] **briefs** NPL *(Dress)* slip *m* [4] VT [a] *(Jur)* [+ *barrister*] confier une cause à [b] *(Mil)* [+ *pilots*, *soldiers*] briefer, donner des instructions à ; *(gen)* [+ *person*] (= *give order to*) briefer, donner des instructions à ; *(bring up to date)* mettre au courant (**on sth** de qch) ; *(Mil)* **the pilots were ~ed** les pilotes ont reçu leur briefing *or* bref [c] *(Comm)* [+ *salesman*] briefer, donner des instructions à ; **we ~ our salesmen once a week** nous faisons un briefing hebdomadaire à l'intention de nos vendeurs

briefcase ['briːfkeɪs] N serviette *f* ; *(handleless)* porte-documents *m inv*

briefer ['briːfəʳ] N (= *spokesperson*) porte-parole *m inv*

briefing ['briːfɪŋ] N *(Aviat, Mil)* briefing *m*, dernières instructions *fpl* ; *(gen)* briefing *m* ; (= *notes*) notes *fpl*

briefly ['briːflɪ] ADV [a] (= *for short time*) [*smile*, *glance*, *pause*] un bref instant ; [*speak*, *visit*] brièvement [b] (= *concisely*) [*tell*, *reply*, *describe*] en peu de mots ; **put ~, his argument was this** en deux mots *or* en bref, voici quel était son argument ; **the briefest, ~, are these** en deux mots *or* en bref, les faits sont les suivants

briefness ['briːfnɪs] N *(NonC)* [a] (= *shortness*) [*of visit*, *career*] brièveté *f* ; [*of interval*] courte durée *f* [b] (= *conciseness*) [*of description*, *statement*] brièveté *f*

brier ['braɪəʳ] [1] N [a] (= *wood*) (racine *f* de) bruyère *f* ; *(also* ► **pipe**) pipe *f* de bruyère [b] (= *wild rose*) églantier *m* ; (= *thorny bush*) ronces *fpl* ; (= *thorn*) épine *f* [2] COMP ► **brier rose** N églantine *f*

brig [brɪg] N *(Naut)* brick *m*

Brig. (ABBR = **brigadier**) **~ A. Robert** le général A. Robert

brigade [brɪˈgeɪd] N *(Mil, fig)* brigade *f* ; *(fig)* **one of the old ~** un vétéran, un vieux de la vieille → **blue**, **fire**, **green**

brigadier [ˌbrɪgəˈdɪəʳ] [1] N *(Brit)* général *m* de brigade [2] COMP ► **brigadier general** N *(pl* **brigadier generals**) *(US)* *(Mil)* général *m* de brigade ; *(Aviat)* général *m* de brigade aérienne

brigand ['brɪgənd] N brigand *m*, bandit *m*

brigandage ['brɪgəndɪdʒ] N brigandage *m*

bright [braɪt] [1] ADJ [a] (= *vivid*, *shining*) [*colour*, *light*] vif ; [*room*, *water*] clair ; [*clothes*, *bird*, *flower*] (one colour) d'une couleur vive ; (two or more colours) aux couleurs vives ; [*star*, *eyes*] brillant ; [*metal*] luisant ; **~ red/yellow/blue** rouge/jaune/bleu vif *inv* ; **her eyes ~ with excitement, she ...** les yeux brillants d'excitation, elle ... [b] [*day*, *weather*] radieux ; [*sunshine*, *sun*] écla-

tant ; **to become ~er** [*weather*] s'éclaircir ; **~ intervals** *or* **periods** éclaircies *fpl* ; **the outlook is ~er** on prévoit une amélioration (du temps) → **1e** [c] (= *clever*) [*person*] intelligent ; [*child*] éveillé, intelligent ; **she's as ~ as a button** elle est très vive d'esprit ; **full of ~ ideas** plein de bonnes idées ; **to have the ~ idea of doing sth** avoir la bonne idée de faire qch [d] (= *cheerful*) [*person*, *smile*, *voice*] jovial ; **~ and breezy** [*person*, *manner*] décontracté et jovial [e] (= *promising*) [*future*, *outlook*, *prospects*, *start*] brillant ; (= *positive*) [*moment*] bon ; **the future looks ~ (for him)** l'avenir s'annonce bien (pour lui) ; **the outlook is ~er** les perspectives d'avenir sont plus prometteuses ; **~er days** des jours plus heureux ; **~ spot** lueur *f* d'espoir ; **to look on the ~ side** prendre les choses du bon côté ; **(looking) on the ~ side**, ... si l'on prend les choses du bon côté, ... → **1b** [f] **to be (up) ~ and early** se lever de bon matin ; **to arrive ~ and early** arriver de bon matin [2] ADV *(liter)* **to shine ~** briller [3] COMP ► **bright-eyed** ADJ [*person*] aux yeux brillants ; *(fig)* **~-eyed idealism** idéalisme *m* fervent ; **~-eyed and bushy-tailed*** en pleine forme ► **the bright lights** NPL les lumières *fpl* de la grande ville ; **the ~ lights of New York** les lumières *fpl* de New York ► **bright spark*** N petit(e) futé(e)* *m(f)* ► **bright young things** NPL la génération qui monte

brighten ['braɪtn] *(also* **~ up**) [1] VT [a] (= *make cheerful*) [+ *room*, *spirits*, *person*] égayer ; [+ *conversation*] égayer, animer ; [+ *prospects*, *situation*, *future*] améliorer [b] (= *make shine*) faire briller, rendre (plus) brillant ; [+ *metal*] faire reluire ; [+ *colour*] aviver [2] VI [a] [*weather*, *sky*] s'éclaircir, se dégager [b] [*eyes*] s'éclairer, s'allumer ; [*expression*] s'éclairer, s'épanouir ; [*person*] s'égayer, s'animer ; [*prospects*, *future*] s'améliorer, se présenter sous un meilleur jour [3] COMP ► **brightening agent** N [*of washing powder*] agent *m* blanchissant

brightly ['braɪtlɪ] ADV [a] *(with light)* [*sparkle*] de mille feux ; **to burn ~** [*fire*, *substance*] flamber ; [*light*] étinceler ; **~ lit** bien éclairé [b] **the stars were shining ~** les étoiles brillaient ; (= *vividly*) **~ coloured** (one colour) d'une couleur vive ; (two or more colours) aux couleurs vives ; **~ painted** (one colour) peint d'une couleur vive ; (two or more colours) peint avec des couleurs vives ; **~ patterned** (one colour) avec des motifs d'une couleur vive ; (two or more colours) avec des motifs aux couleurs vives [c] (= *cheerfully*) [*say*, *answer*, *smile*] jovialement

brightness ['braɪtnɪs] [1] N *(NonC)* [a] (= *vividness*) [*of colour*] vivacité *f* ; [*of clothes*, *fire*, *sunshine*, *eyes*] éclat *m* ; [*of star*, *daylight*, *room*] luminosité *f* ; [*of light*] intensité *f* ; [*of metal*] brillant *m* ; *(TV, Comput)* [*of screen*] luminosité *f* [b] (= *light*) lumière *f* [c] (= *cheerfulness*) [*of person*, *expression*, *tone*] vivacité *f*, jovialité *f* ; [*of smile*] éclat *m*, jovialité *f* [d] (= *intelligence*) intelligence *f* [e] (= *promise*) [*of prospects*, *future*] caractère *m* prometteur [2] COMP ► **brightness control** N réglage *m* de la luminosité

Bright's disease ['braɪtsdɪˌziːz] N mal *m* de Bright, néphrite *f* chronique

brill¹ [brɪl] N *(pl* **brill** *or* **brills**) barbue *f*

brill²* [brɪl] ADJ *(Brit)* (ABBR = **brilliant**) sensass* *inv*, super* *inv*

brilliance ['brɪljəns], **brilliancy** ['brɪljənsɪ] N [a] (= *splendour: lit, fig*) éclat *m*, brillant *m* [b] (= *great intelligence*) intelligence *f* supérieure

brilliant ['brɪljənt] ADJ [a] (= *clever*) [*person*, *mind*, *book*, *performance*] brillant ; [*idea*] génial [b] (= *successful*) [*career*] brillant ; [*future*] radieux ; [*success*] éclatant ; [*victory*] brillant, éclatant [c] (= *bright*) [*light, sunshine, colour, smile*] éclatant [d] (*Brit* = *excellent*) génial*, super* *inv*; **I'll help — ~!** je vais aider — super !*; **she's ~ with children** elle est super* avec les enfants; **~ at sth** super bon* (bonne* *f*) en qch; **to be ~ at doing sth** être drôlement* doué pour faire qch; **yoga is ~ for stress reduction** *or* **for reducing stress** le yoga est génial* *or* super* pour combattre le stress

brilliantine ['brɪljən,tiːn] N brillantine *f*

brilliantly ['brɪljəntlɪ] ADV [a] (= *cleverly*) [*write, play, perform*] brillamment; [*simple, funny*] remarquablement [b] (= *superbly*) [*succeed, work*] magnifiquement; **he was ~ successful** il a magnifiquement réussi [c] (= *brightly*) [*lit, illuminated*] bien; [*shine*] d'un vif éclat; **to smile ~** sourire de toutes ses dents; **~ coloured** (*one colour*) d'une couleur vive; (*two or more colours*) aux couleurs vives; **a ~ sunny day** une journée radieuse [d] (*Brit* = *excellently*) **she played/drove ~** elle a super bien* joué/conduit

Brillo® ['brɪləʊ] N (*also* **~ pad**) tampon *m* Jex®

brim [brɪm] [1] N [*of cup, hat, lake*] bord *m*; **to be full to the ~ with sth** (*lit*) être plein à ras bord de qch; (*fig*) déborder de qch [2] VI déborder (**with** de); **~ming with** (*lit*) plein à ras de; (*fig*) débordant de
► **brim over** VI (*lit, fig*) déborder (**with** de)

brimful ['brɪm'fʊl] ADJ (*lit*) plein à ras bord; (*fig*) débordant (**with** de)

brimstone ['brɪmstəʊn] N soufre *m* → **fire**

brindle(d) ['brɪndl(d)] ADJ moucheté, tavelé

brine [braɪn] N [a] (= *salt water*) eau *f* salée; (*Culin*) saumure *f* [b] (*liter*) (= *sea*) mer *f*, océan *m*; (= *sea water*) eau *f* de mer

▼ **bring** [brɪŋ] (*pret, ptp* **brought**) [1] VT [a] [+ *person, animal, vehicle*] amener; [+ *object, news, information*] apporter; **to ~ sb up/down/across** *etc* faire monter/faire descendre/faire traverser *etc* qn (**avec soi**); **to ~ sth up/down** monter/descendre qch; **I brought him up his breakfast** je lui ai monté son petit déjeuner → **bacon, bed** [b] (= *cause*) amener; **the hot weather ~s storms** le temps chaud provoque *or* amène des orages; **his books brought him a good income** ses livres lui rapportaient bien *or* lui étaient d'un bon rapport; **to ~ good/bad luck** porter bonheur/malheur; **to ~ a blush to sb's cheeks** faire rougir qn, faire monter le rouge aux joues de qn; **to ~ tears to sb's eyes** faire venir les larmes aux yeux de qn; **that brought him to the verge of insanity** cela l'a mené *or* amené au bord de la folie; **to ~ sth (up)on o.s.** s'attirer qch; **to ~ sb to a close or an end** mettre fin à qch; **to ~ sb to his feet** faire lever qn; **to ~ sb to justice** traduire qn en justice; **to ~ sb low** abaisser qn; **to ~ sth to sb's knowledge** signaler qch à qn, porter qch à la connaissance de qn; **to ~ sth to mind** rappeler qch, évoquer qch; **to ~ sth into question** (= *throw doubt on*) remettre qch en question; (= *make one think about*) faire s'interroger sur qch; **to ~ to nothing** faire échouer, faire avorter; (*liter*) **to ~ sth to pass** causer qch; **to ~ sth to perfection** porter qch à la perfection; **to ~ sth into play** *or* **line** faire jouer qch, faire entrer qch en ligne de compte; **to ~ sb to his senses** ramener qn à la raison; **to ~ into the world** mettre au monde → **bear¹, head, light¹** [c] (+ *infin* = *persuade*) amener (**sb to do** qn à faire); **he brought him to understand that ...** il l'a amené à comprendre que ...; **I cannot ~ myself to speak to him** je ne peux me résoudre à lui parler [d] (*Jur*) **to ~ an action against sb** intenter un procès à qn; **to ~ a charge against sb** inculper qn; **the case was brought before Lord MacLeod** la cause fut entendue par Lord MacLeod; **to ~ evidence** fournir des preuves

[2] COMP ► **bring-and-buy sale** N (*Brit*) vente *f* de charité *or* de bienfaisance
► **bring about** VT SEP [a] [+ *reforms, review*] amener, provoquer; [+ *war*] causer, provoquer; [+ *accident*] provoquer, occasionner; [+ *sb's ruin*] entraîner, amener [b] [+ *boat*] faire virer de bord
► **bring along** VT SEP **to ~ sth along (with one)** apporter qch (avec soi); **to ~ sb along (with one)** amener qn (avec soi); **may I ~ along a friend?** est-ce que je peux amener un ami ?
► **bring back** VT SEP [a] [+ *person*] ramener; [+ *object*] rapporter; **to ~ a spacecraft back to earth** récupérer un vaisseau spatial; **her holiday brought back her health** ses vacances lui ont rendu la santé; **a rest will ~ him back to normal** du repos le remettra d'aplomb [b] (= *call to mind*) rappeler (à la mémoire)
► **bring down** VT SEP [a] (= *cause to fall*) abattre; (= *cause to land*) [+ *kite etc*] ramener au sol; [+ *plane*] faire atterrir; (= *shoot down*) [+ *animal, bird, plane*] abattre [b] [+ *dictator, government*] faire tomber; [+ *temperature, prices, cost of living*] faire baisser; [+ *swelling*] réduire; (*Math*) [+ *figure*] abaisser; **his action brought down everyone's wrath upon him** son action lui a attiré *or* lui a valu la colère de tout le monde → **house**
► **bring forth** VT SEP (*liter*) [+ *fruit*] produire; [+ *child*] mettre au monde; [+ *animal*] mettre bas; (*fig*) [+ *protests, criticism*] attirer
► **bring forward** VT SEP [a] [+ *person*] faire avancer; [+ *chair etc*] avancer; [+ *witness*] produire; [+ *evidence, proof, argument*] avancer [b] (= *advance time of*) [+ *meeting*] avancer [c] (*Accounts*) [+ *figure, amount*] reporter
► **bring in** VT SEP [a] [+ *person*] faire entrer; [+ *object*] rentrer [b] (= *introduce*) [+ *fashion*] lancer; [+ *custom, legislation*] introduire; **to ~ in the police/the troops** faire intervenir la police/l'armée; (*Parl*) **to ~ in a bill** présenter *or* déposer un projet de loi [c] (*Fin*) [+ *income*] rapporter; **to ~ in interest** rapporter des intérêts [d] (*Jur*) **to ~ in a verdict** [*jury*] rendre un verdict; **to ~ in a verdict of guilty** déclarer qn coupable
► **bring off** VT SEP [a] [+ *people from wreck*] sauver [b] [+ *plan, aim, deal*] mener à bien; [+ *attack, hope*] réussir; **he didn't manage to ~ it off** il n'a pas réussi son coup
► **bring on** VT SEP [a] (= *cause*) [+ *illness, quarrel*] provoquer, causer; **to ~ on sb's cold** enrhumer qn [b] (*Agr etc*) [+ *crops, flowers*] faire pousser [c] (*Theat*) [+ *person*] amener; [+ *thing*] apporter sur (la) scène
► **bring out** VT SEP [a] [+ *person*] faire sortir; [+ *object*] sortir; (*fig*) [+ *meaning*] mettre en évidence; [+ *colour*] faire ressortir; [+ *qualities*] faire valoir, mettre en valeur; **it ~s out the best in him** c'est dans des cas comme celui-là qu'il se montre sous son meilleur jour [b] [+ *book*] publier, faire paraître; [+ *actress, new product*] lancer
► **bring over** VT SEP [a] [+ *person*] amener; [+ *object*] apporter [b] (= *convert*) [+ *person*] convertir, gagner (**to** à)
► **bring round** VT SEP [a] (*to one's house etc*) [+ *person*] amener, faire venir; [+ *object*] apporter; **to ~ the conversation round to football** amener la conversation sur le football [b] [+ *unconscious person*] ranimer [c] (= *convert*) [+ *person*] convertir, gagner (**to** à)
► **bring through** VT SEP [+ *sick person*] sauver
► **bring to** VT SEP [a] (*Naut*) arrêter, mettre en panne [b] [+ *unconscious person*] ranimer
► **bring together** VT SEP [a] (= *put in touch*) [+ *people*] mettre en contact, faire se rencontrer [b] (= *end quarrel between*) réconcilier [c] [+ *facts etc*] rassembler
► **bring under** VT SEP (*fig*) assujettir, soumettre
► **bring up** VT SEP [a] [+ *person*] faire monter; [+ *object*] monter [b] [+ *child, animal*] élever; **well/badly brought-up child** enfant *m* bien/mal élevé [c] (= *vomit*) vomir, rendre [d] (=

call attention to) [+ *fact, allegation, problem*] mentionner; [+ *question*] soulever; **we shan't ~ it up again** nous n'en reparlerons plus [e] (= *stop*) [+ *person, vehicle*] (faire) arrêter; **the question brought him up short** la question l'a arrêté net [f] (*Jur*) **to ~ sb up before a court** citer *or* faire comparaître qn devant un tribunal [g] **to ~ up to date** [+ *accounts, correspondence etc*] mettre à jour; [+ *method etc*] moderniser; **to ~ sb up to date on sth** mettre qn au courant (des derniers développements) de qch

brink [brɪŋk] N (*lit, fig*) bord *m*; **on the ~ of sth** à deux doigts de qch, au bord de qch; **on the ~ of doing sth** à deux doigts de faire qch, sur le point de faire qch

brinkmanship ['brɪŋkmənʃɪp] N stratégie *f* de la corde raide

briny ['braɪnɪ] [1] ADJ saumâtre, salé; (*liter*) **the ~ deep** la grande bleue [2] N **the ~**†* la grande bleue

briquet(te) [brɪ'ket] N briquette *f*, aggloméré *m*

brisk [brɪsk] ADJ [a] [*person*] (= *lively*) vif, animé; (= *abrupt in manner*) brusque [*movement*] vif, rapide; **~ pace** allure *f* (très) vive; **to take a ~ walk** marcher *or* se promener d'un bon pas; **at a ~ trot** au grand trot → **start** [c] [*attack*] vigoureux, vivement mené; [*trade*] actif, florissant; [*demand*] important; **business is ~** les affaires marchent (bien); (*St Ex*) **trading was ~** le marché était actif; **the betting was ~** les paris allaient bon train [d] [*beer*] mousseux; [*champagne, cider*] pétillant [e] [*air, weather, day*] frais et vivifiant

brisket ['brɪskɪt] N poitrine *f* de bœuf

briskly ['brɪsklɪ] ADV [*move*] vivement; [*walk*] d'un bon pas; [*speak*] brusquement; [*act*] sans tarder; (*Comm etc*) **these goods are selling ~** ces articles se vendent (très) bien

briskness ['brɪsknɪs] N [a] (= *liveliness*) [*of walk, movement*] vivacité *f*; [*of trade*] dynamisme *m* [b] (= *abruptness*) brusquerie *f*

brisling ['brɪzlɪŋ] N sprat *m*

bristle ['brɪsl] [1] N [*of beard, brush*] poil *m*; [*of boar*] soie *f*; [*of plant*] poil *m*; **a brush with nylon ~s** une brosse en nylon® [2] VI [a] [*animal hair*] se hérisser; (*fig*) **a shirt bristling with pins** une chemise hérissée d'épingles; **bristling with difficulties** hérissé de difficultés; **a town bristling with police** une ville grouillante de policiers [b] (*fig*) [*person*] s'irriter (**at** de), se hérisser; **he ~d at the suggestion** il s'est hérissé à cette suggestion [3] COMP ► **bristle brush** N brosse *f* en soie de sanglier

bristly ['brɪslɪ] ADJ [*animal*] au(x) poil(s) raide(s) *or* dur(s); [*moustache, beard*] aux poils raides; [*hair*] raide; [*chin, cheek*] mal rasé; **you're very ~ today** tu piques drôlement aujourd'hui*

Bristol ['brɪstəl] N **~ Channel** canal *m* de Bristol; (*Art, Comm*) **~ board** bristol *m* → **shipshape**

bristols: ['brɪstəlz] NPL roberts: *mpl*

Brit* [brɪt] N Britannique *mf*

Britain ['brɪtən] N (*also* **Great ~**) la Grande-Bretagne → GREAT BRITAIN, UNITED KINGDOM

Britannia [brɪ'tænɪə] [1] N Britannia *f* [2] COMP ► **Britannia metal** N métal *m* anglais

Britannic [brɪ'tænɪk] ADJ **His** *or* **Her ~ Majesty** sa Majesté britannique

britches ['brɪtʃəz] NPL = **breeches**

Briticism ['brɪtɪsɪzəm] N briticisme *m*

British ['brɪtɪʃ] [1] ADJ britannique; (*loosely*) anglais; [*ambassador, embassy*] de Grande-Bretagne; **~ English** l'anglais *m* britannique [2] **the British** NPL les Britanniques *mpl*; (*loosely*) les Anglais *mpl*

[3] COMP ► **British Airports Authority** N administration *f* des aéroports britanniques ► **British Antarctic Territory** N Territoire *m*

► LANGUAGE IN USE: **bring** 17.1, 26.3

britannique de l'Antarctique ► **British Asian** ADJ *britannique originaire du sous-continent indien* ♦ N *Britannique originaire du sous-continent indien* ► **the British Broadcasting Corporation** N *la BBC* ► **British Columbia** N *la Colombie britannique* ► **British Columbian** ADJ *de la Colombie britannique* ♦ N *habitant(e) m(f) de la Colombie britannique* ► **the British Commonwealth** N *le Commonwealth* ► **British Council** N *British Council m (organisme chargé de promouvoir la langue et la culture britanniques dans le monde)* ► **British Honduras** N *le Honduras britannique* ► **the British Isles** NPL *les îles fpl Britanniques* → [GREAT BRITAIN, UNITED KINGDOM] ► **British Legion** N *organisme d'aide aux anciens combattants* → [LEGION] ► **the British Library** N *la bibliothèque nationale de Grande-Bretagne* ► **British Rail** N *(formerly) chemins de fer britanniques* ► **British Red Cross Society** N *Croix f Rouge britannique* ► **British Summer Time** N *l'heure f d'été britannique* ► **British Telecom** N *société britannique de télécommunications*

Britisher* ['brɪtɪʃəʳ] N *(US)* Britannique *mf*; *(loosely)* Anglais(e) *m(f)*

Briton ['brɪtən] N [a] Britannique *mf* [b] *(Hist)* Breton(ne) *m(f) (de Grande-Bretagne)*

Britpop ['brɪtpɒp] N *musique pop britannique des années 90*

Brittany ['brɪtənɪ] N *la Bretagne*

brittle ['brɪtl] [1] ADJ [a] *(= breakable)* [*twig, hair, nails*] cassant [b] *(= fragile)* [*agreement, peace*] fragile ; [*person, personality*] sec *(sèche f)* ; [*laugh, voice*] crispé [2] COMP ► **brittle-bone disease** N ostéoporose *f*

Brittonic [brɪ'tɒnɪk] ADJ brittonique

bro: [brəʊ] N *(US)* [a] *(= friend)* pote* *m* ; **hi, ~!** salut, vieux* *or* mon pote*! [b] *(= brother)* frangin* *m*

Bro. *(Rel)* ABBR = **Brother**

broach [brəʊtʃ] [1] VT [+ *barrel*] mettre en perce ; [+ *box, supplies*] entamer ; [+ *subject, topic*] entamer, aborder [2] N *(Culin)* broche *f* ; *(= tool)* perçoir *m*, foret *m*

broad [brɔːd] [1] ADJ [a] *(= wide)* [*road, shoulders, smile*] large ; **the lake is 200 metres ~** le lac a 200 mètres de large *or* de largeur ; **a garden about 6 metres long and 3 metres ~** un jardin d'environ 6 mètres de long et 3 mètres de large ; **to grow ~er** s'élargir ; **to make ~er** élargir ; **~ in the shoulder** [*person*] large d'épaules ; [*garment*] un peu large aux épaules → 3 ; **~ in the beam** [*ship*] ventru ; **(*: pej)** [*person*] fort de l'arrière-train* ; *(fig)* **he's got a ~ back** il a bon dos ; *(fig)* **it's as ~ as it's long*** c'est du pareil au même* ; **a ~ expanse of lawn** une vaste étendue de pelouse →-**gauge** [b] *(= approximate, general)* [*aims, objectives, term*] général ; [*phonetic transcription*] large ; **the ~ outlines** les grandes lignes *fpl* ; **in the ~est sense of the word** au sens (le plus) large du terme ; **in ~ terms** grosso modo ; **to be in ~ agreement** être d'accord sur l'essentiel ; **he distinguished three ~ possibilities** il a distingué trois grandes possibilités ; *(fig)* **to paint sth with a ~ brush** décrire qch à grands traits → 3 ; *(US Jur)* **~ construction** interprétation *f* large [c] *(= wide-ranging)* [*category, range*] large ; [*coalition*] vaste ; [*education*] diversifié ; [*syllabus*] étendu ; **a ~ spectrum of opinion** un large éventail d'opinions ; **a film with ~ appeal** un film grand public ; **the agreement won ~ support in Congress** cet accord a été largement soutenu par le Congrès ; **to have ~ implications** avoir de vastes implications [d] *(= unsubtle)* [*hint*] à peine voilé ; [*humour*] grivois ; [*comedy*] grossier ; [*joke*] gras (grasse *f*) [e] *(Ling)* [*accent*] prononcé ; **to speak ~ Scots** *(accent)* parler avec un fort accent écossais ; *(dialect)* s'exprimer en dialecte écossais ; **to**

say sth in ~ Yorkshire dire qch en dialecte du Yorkshire [f] *(= full)* **in ~ daylight** en plein jour ; **it was ~ daylight** il faisait grand jour [g] *(= liberal)* [*mind, ideas*] large, libéral [2] N [a] *(= widest part)* **the ~ of the back** le milieu du dos ; **the (Norfolk) Broads** *les lacs et estuaires du Norfolk* [b] *(US: pej)* *(= woman)* nana* *f* ; *(= prostitute)* putain: *f* [3] COMP ► **broad-based** ADJ [*support, government*] réunissant des tendances très variées, large ► **broad bean** N *(esp Brit)* fève *f* ► **broad-brimmed** ADJ [*hat*] à larges bords ► **broad-brush** ADJ *(fig)* [*analysis, report*] schématique, sommaire ► **Broad Church** N *(Rel)* groupe libéral au sein de l'Église anglicane ; *(fig)* **the Labour Party is a ~ church** le parti travailliste accueille des courants très divers ► **broad jump** N *(US Sport)* saut *m* en longueur ► **broad-minded** ADJ **he is ~-minded** il a les idées larges ► **broadmindedness** N largeur *f* d'esprit ► **broadshouldered** ADJ large d'épaules

broadband ['brɔːdbænd] *(Telec)* [1] N transmission *f* à large bande [2] ADJ à large bande

broadcast ['brɔːdkɑːst] *(pret, ptp* **broadcast)** [1] VT [a] [+ *news, speech, programme*] *(Rad)* (radio)diffuser, émettre ; *(TV)* téléviser, émettre ; [+ *news, rumour etc*] répandre ; *(fig)* **don't ~ it!*** ne va pas le crier sur les toits ! [b] *(Agr)* [+ *seed*] semer à la volée) [2] VI *(Rad, TV)* [*station*] émettre ; [*actor, interviewee etc*] participer à une émission ; [*interviewer*] faire une émission [3] N *(Rad, TV)* émission *f* ; **live/recorded ~** émission *f* en direct/en différé ; **repeat ~** reprise *f*, rediffusion *f* [4] ADJ *(Rad)* (radio)diffusé ; *(TV)* télévisé ; **~ account of a match** *(Rad)* reportage *m* radiodiffusé d'un match ; *(TV)* reportage *m* télévisé d'un match ; **~ journalism** *(TV)* journalisme *m* télévisé ; *(Rad)* journalisme *m* radio ; **~ satellite** satellite *m* de radiodiffusion [5] ADV [*sow*] à la volée

broadcaster ['brɔːdkɑːstəʳ] N *(Rad, TV)* personnalité *f* de la radio *or* de la télévision

broadcasting ['brɔːdkɑːstɪŋ] [1] N *(Rad)* radiodiffusion *f* ; *(TV)* télévision *f* ; **that is the end of ~ for tonight** ainsi prennent fin nos émissions de la journée ; **~ was interrupted** les émissions ont été interrompues ; **a career in ~** une carrière à la radio *(or* à la télévision*)* [2] COMP ► **Broadcasting Standards Council** N *(Brit)* ≈ Conseil *m* supérieur de l'audiovisuel ► **broadcasting station** N station *f* de radio, poste *m* émetteur → **British**

broadcloth ['brɔːdklɒθ] N drap *m* fin *(en grande largeur)*

broaden ['brɔːdn] *(also* **~ out**: *lit, fig)* [1] VT élargir ; **to ~ one's outlook** élargir ses horizons [2] VI s'élargir

broadleaved tree [ˌbrɔːdliːvd'triː] N *(arbre m)* feuillu *m*

broadloom ['brɔːdluːm] ADJ [*carpet*] en grande largeur

broadly ['brɔːdlɪ] ADV [a] *(= generally)* [*agree, accept, define*] dans les grandes lignes, d'une manière générale ; [*welcome*] généralement ; [*support*] largement ; **this is ~ true** c'est vrai, grosso modo ; **~ similar** à peu près semblable ; **~-based** large ; **~ speaking** en gros, généralement parlant [b] [*hint*] fortement [c] **to smile ~** avoir un large sourire

broadness ['brɔːdnɪs] N [of *road*] largeur *f* ; [of *joke, story*] grossièreté *f*, vulgarité *f* ; [of *accent*] caractère *m* prononcé

broadsheet ['brɔːdʃiːt] N *(Hist, Typ)* placard *m* ; *(Press)* [*= large-format newspaper*] journal *m* grand format ; *(= serious newspaper)* journal *m* de qualité → [TABLOIDS, BROADSHEETS]

broadside ['brɔːdsaɪd] [1] N [a] *(Naut = side)* [of *ship*] flanc *m* [b] *(Naut = discharge of guns)*

bordée *f* ; **to fire a ~** lâcher une bordée [c] *(= criticism)* attaque *f* cinglante ; *(= insults)* bordée *f* d'injures *or* d'invectives ; **he let him have a ~** il l'a incendié*, il lui a descendu en flammes* [2] ADV [a] *(Naut)* **to turn ~ (on)** virer en présentant le flanc ; **to hit sth ~ (on)** heurter qch par le travers ; **to be moored ~ to sth** être amarré le long de qch [b] *(Aut)* **he** *or* **his car hit me ~ (on)** il m'a heurté de côté

broadsword ['brɔːdsɔːd] N épée *f* à deux tranchants, glaive† *m*

broadways ['brɔːdweɪz], **broadwise** ['brɔːdwaɪz] ADV en largeur, dans le sens de la largeur

brocade [brəʊ'keɪd] [1] N brocart *m* [2] COMP de brocart

broccoli ['brɒkəlɪ] N brocoli *m*

brochure ['brəʊʃʊəʳ] N [of *college, vacation course*] prospectus *m* ; [of *hotel, travel agent*] brochure *f*, dépliant *m* (touristique)

brock [brɒk] N *(Brit: Zool, rare)* blaireau *m*

brogue¹ [brəʊg] N *(= shoe)* chaussure *f* de marche, richelieu *m*

brogue² [brəʊg] N *(= accent)* *(Irish)* accent *m* irlandais ; *(gen)* accent *m* du terroir

broil [brɔɪl] [1] VT *(US Culin)* griller, faire cuire sur le gril ; *(fig)* griller* ; **~ing sun** soleil *m* brûlant [2] VI *(also fig)* griller

broiler ['brɔɪləʳ] [1] N [a] *(= fowl)* poulet *m* (à rôtir) [b] *(US = grill)* rôtisserie *f*, gril *m* [2] COMP ► **broiler house** N éleveuse *f* ► **broiler pan** N *(US)* plateau *m* à grillades *(avec poignée)*

broiling ['brɔɪlɪŋ] ADJ *(esp US)* [*sun*] brûlant ; [*summer*] torride

broke [brəʊk] [1] VB *pt* of **break** [2] ADJ [a] *(= broken)* **if it ain't ~, don't fix it** s'il n'y a pas de gros problèmes, il ne faut rien changer [b] *(* = penniless)* à sec*, fauché* ; **to be dead** *or* **stony ~** être fauché (comme les blés)*, être (complètement) à sec* ; **to go ~** faire faillite ; **to go for ~** jouer le tout pour le tout, jouer le grand jeu *or* son va-tout

broken ['brəʊkən] [1] VB *ptp* of **break**

[2] ADJ [a] *(= cracked, smashed)* [*cup, window, branch, biscuits etc*] cassé ; *(= uneven, rugged)* [*ground*] accidenté ; [*road*] défoncé ; [*surface*] raboteux ; [*coastline*] dentelé ; **pieces of ~ glass** des éclats *mpl* de verre ; **pieces of ~ crockery** des morceaux *mpl* de vaisselle [b] *(Med = fractured)* [*neck, leg, rib, tooth, nail*] cassé ; [*bone, hand, foot*] fracturé ; **~ bones** fractures *fpl* ; **"do not use on ~ skin"** « ne pas utiliser sur plaie ouverte » [c] *(= not working)* [*machine, phone*] détraqué ; **the coffee machine is ~** la machine à café est détraquée ; **he sounds like a ~ record** on dirait un disque rayé [d] *(fig = ruined)* [*body, mind*] brisé ; [*health*] délabré ; [*spirit*] abattu ; **to be ~ in body and mind** avoir le corps et le cœur brisés ; **the scandal left him a ~ man** ce scandale l'a brisé *or* a fait de lui un homme brisé ; **to have a ~ heart** avoir le cœur brisé ; **she died of a ~ heart** elle est morte de chagrin, elle est morte le cœur brisé ; **he is a ~ reed** on ne peut pas compter sur lui [e] *(= interrupted)* [*journey*] interrompu ; [*sleep*] (= disturbed) interrompu ; *(= restless)* agité ; [*voice, line*] brisé ; **I've had several ~ nights** j'ai eu plusieurs mauvaises nuits ; **a spell of ~ weather** un temps variable ; **~ cloud** ciel *m* couvert avec des éclaircies ; **~ sunshine** soleil *m* intermittent ; **(to speak in) ~ English/French** (parler un) mauvais anglais/français [f] *(= violated)* [*promise, contract, engagement*] rompu ; [*appointment*] manqué [g] *(by divorce)* [*marriage*] brisé ; **he comes from a ~ home** il vient d'un foyer désuni

[3] COMP ► **broken chord** N *(Mus)* arpège *m* ► **broken-down** ADJ *(= out of order)* [*car*] en panne ; [*machine*] détraqué ; *(= dilapidated)*

[*house*] délabré ► **broken-hearted** ADJ au cœur brisé ► **broken lots** NPL (*Comm*) articles *mpl* dépareillés ► **broken numbers** NPL (*Math*) fractions *fpl* ► **broken veins** NPL couperose *f* ► **broken white line** N ligne *f* blanche discontinue ► **broken-winded** ADJ poussif

brokenly ['brəʊkənlɪ] ADV [*say*] d'une voix entrecoupée ; [*sob*] par à-coups

broker ['brəʊkər] **1** N **a** (*St Ex*) ≈ courtier *m* (en bourse), ≈ agent *m* de change **b** (*Comm*) courtier *m* ; (*Naut*) courtier *m* maritime ; **wine ~** courtier *m* en vins **c** (= *secondhand dealer*) brocanteur *m* → **pawnbroker** **2** VT [+ *deal, agreement*] négocier

brokerage ['brəʊkərɪdʒ], **broking** ['brəʊkɪŋ] N (= *trade, commission*) courtage *m*

brolly* ['brɒlɪ] N (*Brit*) pépin* *m*, parapluie *m*

bromide ['brəʊmaɪd] N **a** (*Chem, Typ*) bromure *m* ; (*Med**) bromure *m* (de potassium) ; **~ paper** papier *m* au (gelatino-)bromure d'argent **b** (*fig*) banalité *f* or platitude *f* euphorisante

bromine ['brəʊmiːn] N brome *m*

bronchi ['brɒŋkaɪ] NPL of **bronchus**

bronchial ['brɒŋkɪəl] ADJ [*infection*] des bronches, bronchique ; **~ tubes** bronches *fpl*

bronchiole ['brɒŋkɪəʊl] N bronchiole *f*

bronchitic [brɒŋ'kɪtɪk] ADJ bronchitique

bronchitis [brɒŋ'kaɪtɪs] N (*NonC*) bronchite *f* ; **to have ~** avoir or faire une bronchite

bronchopneumonia [ˌbrɒŋkəʊnjuː'məʊnɪə] N (*NonC*) bronchopneumonie *f*

bronchus ['brɒŋkəs] N (*pl* **bronchi**) bronche *f*

bronco ['brɒŋkəʊ] N cheval *m* semi-sauvage (de l'Ouest américain), bronco *m*

broncobuster* ['brɒŋkəʊbʌstər] N (*US*) cowboy *m* (qui dompte les chevaux sauvages)

brontosaurus [ˌbrɒntə'sɔːrəs] N (*pl* **brontosauruses** or **brontosauri** [ˌbrɒntə'sɔːraɪ]) brontosaure *m*

Bronx [brɒŋks] N **the ~** le Bronx ; (*US fig*) **~ cheer** bruit de dérision

bronze [brɒnz] **1** N (= *metal, colour, work of art*) bronze *m* **2** VI se bronzer, brunir **3** VT [+ *metal*] bronzer ; [+ *skin*] brunir, faire bronzer **4** COMP en bronze ; (= *colour*) (couleur *f* de) bronze ► **the Bronze Age** N l'âge *m* du bronze ► **bronze medal** N médaille *f* de bronze

bronzed [brɒnzd] ADJ [*skin, person*] bronzé

bronzer ['brɒnzər] N autobronzant *m*

bronzing powder ['brɒnzɪŋˌpaʊdər] N poudre *f* de soleil

brooch [brəʊtʃ] N broche *f*

brood [bruːd] **1** N [*of birds*] couvée *f*, nichée *f* ; [*of mice*] nichée *f* ; [*of children*] progéniture *f*, nichée *f* (*hum*) ; [*of vipers, scoundrels*] engeance *f* ; **she has a great ~ of children** elle a une nombreuse progéniture ; **I'm going to take my ~ home*** je vais remmener ma progéniture à la maison **2** VI [*bird*] couver ; [*storm, danger*] couver, menacer ; [*person*] broyer du noir, ruminer ; [*person*] **to ~ on** [+ *misfortune*] remâcher ; [+ *plan*] ruminer ; [+ *the past*] ressasser ; **to ~ over sth** [*night etc*] planer sur qch ; [*storm*] couver sur qch ; (*oppressively*) peser sur qch **3** COMP ► **brood hen** N (*Zool*) couveuse *f* ► **brood mare** N (jument *f*) poulinière *f*

brooding ['bruːdɪŋ] **1** ADJ **a** (= *disturbing*) troublant **b** (= *reflective*) rêveur, songeur ; (= *gloomy*) maussade, soucieux **2** N rumination *f*

broody ['bruːdɪ] ADJ **a** [*hen*] (= *ready to lay eggs*) prêt à pondre ; (= *ready to sit on eggs*) prêt à couver **b** (* *hum*) **to be feeling ~** [*person*] avoir envie d'avoir un enfant **c** (= *pensive*) mélancolique

brook¹ [brʊk] N ruisseau *m*

brook² [brʊk] VT (*liter*) [+ *contradiction, delay, reply*] souffrir ; (*liter*) admettre

brooklet ['brʊklɪt] N ruisselet *m*, petit ruisseau *m*

broom [bruːm] **1** N **a** (*Bot*) genêt *m* **b** (= *brush*) balai *m* ■ (*PROV*) **a new ~ sweeps clean** tout nouveau, tout beau (*PROV*) ; **this firm needs a new ~** cette compagnie a besoin d'un bon coup de balai or a besoin de sang neuf **2** COMP ► **broom closet** N (*US*) = **broom cupboard** ► **broom cupboard** N (*Brit*) placard *m* à balais

broomstick ['bruːmstɪk] N manche à balai

Bros. (*Comm*) (ABBR = **Brothers**) Martin **~** Martin Frères

broth [brɒθ] N bouillon *m*

brothel ['brɒθl] **1** N maison *f* close or de passe **2** COMP ► **brothel-creepers*** NPL (*Brit*) chaussures *f* d'homme en daim à semelles de crêpe

brother ['brʌðər] **1** N **a** (*gen, Rel*) frère *m* ; **older/younger ~** frère *m* aîné/cadet ; **Brother Paul** Frère Paul → **lay⁴** **b** (*in trade unions etc*) camarade *m* ; (*US: also* **soul ~**) frère *m* (de couleur) **2** ADJ **his ~ prisoners** *etc* ceux qui sont (or étaient) prisonniers *etc* comme lui, les autres prisonniers *mpl etc* ; **his ~ officers** ses compagnons *mpl* d'armes **3** COMP ► **brother-in-arms** N (*pl* **brothers-in-arms**) (*liter*) frère *m* d'armes ► **brother-in-law** N (*pl* **brothers-in-law**) beau-frère *m*

brotherhood ['brʌðəhʊd] N **a** (*NonC*) (*lit*) fraternité *f* ; (*fig*) fraternité, confraternité *f* ; **~ of man** fraternité *f* des hommes **b** (= *association: esp Rel*) confrérie *f* ; (*US*) corporation *f* ; (*Freemasonry*) **the Brotherhood** la franc-maçonnerie

brotherly ['brʌðəlɪ] ADJ fraternel ; **~ love** l'amour *m* fraternel

brougham ['bruːəm] N coupé *m* de ville

brought [brɔːt] VB *pret, ptp* of **bring**

brouhaha* ['bruːhɑːhɑː] N histoires* *fpl*

brow [braʊ] N **a** (= *forehead*) front *m* ; (= *arch above eye*) arcade *f* sourcilière ; (*also* **eyebrow**) sourcil *m* → **beetle-browed, highbrow, knit, sweat** **b** [*of hill*] sommet *m* ; [*of cliff*] bord *m* ; (*Min*) tour *f* d'extraction

browbeat ['braʊbiːt] (*pret* **browbeat**, *ptp* **browbeaten**) VT intimider, persécuter ; **to ~ sb into doing sth** forcer qn à faire qch

brown [braʊn] **1** ADJ **a** brun, marron *inv* ; [*hair*] châtain ; [*boots, shoes, leather*] marron ; **light ~ hair** cheveux *mpl* châtain clair *inv* ; **light ~ material** étoffe *f* marron clair ; (*fig*) **in a ~ study†** plongé dans ses pensées or méditations ; **to go ~** [*leaves*] roussir → **nut** **b** (= *tanned*) [*person, skin*] bronzé ; **to go ~** bronzer ; **as ~ as a berry** tout bronzé **c** (= *dusky-skinned*) basané **d** (*US fig*) **to do sth up ~*** soigner qch dans les moindres détails **2** N brun *m*, marron *m* ; **her hair was a rich, deep ~** ses cheveux étaient d'un beau brun foncé **3** VT **a** [*sun*] [+ *skin, person*] bronzer, hâler **b** (*Culin*) [+ *meat, fish, potatoes, onions*] faire dorer ; [+ *sauce*] faire roussir **c** (*Brit*) **he is ~ed off*†** il en a marre* or ras le bol* **4** VI **a** [*leaves*] roussir **b** [*person, skin*] brunir **c** (*Culin*) dorer **5** COMP ► **brown ale** N sorte de bière brune ► **brown bear** N ours *m* brun ► **brown belt** N (*Judo etc*) ceinture *f* marron ► **brown bread** N pain *m* bis ► **brown coal** N lignite *m* ► **brown flour** N farine *f* complète ► **brown-nose** N lèche-cul** *m inv*, lèche-bottes* *mf* ♦ VT lécher le cul à or de**, lécher les bottes de* ► **brown owl** N (*Orn*) chat-huant *m* ; (*in Brownie Guides*) cheftaine *f*

► **brown paper** N papier *m* d'emballage, papier *m* Kraft ► **brown rice** N riz *m* complet ► **brown sauce** N (*Brit Culin*) sauce brune relevée ► **Brown Shirt** N (*Hist*) Chemise *f* brune ► **brown sugar** N cassonade *f*, sucre *m* brun

brownbag* ['braʊnbæg] VT (*US*) **to ~ it ◊ to ~ one's lunch** apporter son repas (dans un sac en papier)

brownie ['braʊnɪ] N **a** (= *fairy*) lutin *m*, farfadet *m* **b** **Brownie (Guide)** jeannette *f* ; (*fig hum*) **to win** or **get** or **earn Brownie points*** obtenir des bons points **c** **Brownie®** (= *camera*) brownie *m* kodak® **d** (*esp US* = *cake*) brownie *m* (*petit gâteau au chocolat*)

browning ['braʊnɪŋ] N (*Brit Culin*) produit préparé pour roux brun

brownish ['braʊnɪʃ] ADJ tirant sur le brun

brownout ['braʊnaʊt] N (*US*) (*Mil*) camouflage *m* partiel des lumières ; (*Elec*) panne *f* partielle

brownstone ['braʊnstəʊn] N (*US*) (= *material*) grès *m* brun ; (= *house*) bâtiment *m* de grès brun

browse [braʊz] **1** VI **a** (*in bookshop, library*) feuilleter les livres ; (*in other shops*) regarder sans acheter ; (*fig*) **to ~ through a book** feuilleter or parcourir un livre ; (*in shop*) **I'm just browsing** je regarde seulement, merci **b** (*Comput*) parcourir le net **c** [*animal*] brouter, paître **2** VT [+ *animals*] brouter, paître **3** N **to have a ~ = to browse** ; → **browse 1a**

browser ['braʊzər] N (*Comput*) navigateur *m*

brucellosis [ˌbruːsɪ'ləʊsɪs] N brucellose *f*

bruise [bruːz] **1** VT **a** [+ *person, part of body*] faire un bleu à, contusionner ; [+ *finger*] faire un pinçon à ; [+ *fruit*] abîmer, taler ; [+ *lettuce*] froisser ; **to ~ one's foot** se faire un bleu au pied ; **to be ~d all over** avoir le corps or être couvert de bleus, être tout contusionné **b** (= *crush*) (*lit*) écraser, piler ; (*fig*) [+ *ego, feelings, pride*] blesser ; (*liter*) **~d heart** cœur *m* meurtri or blessé ; (*liter*) **~d spirit** esprit *m* meurtri ; **to feel ~d** se sentir secoué **2** VI [*fruit*] se taler, s'abîmer ; **peaches ~ easily** les pêches se talent facilement ; **he ~s easily** il se fait facilement des bleus **3** N (*on person*) bleu *m*, ecchymose *f* ; (*on fruit*) meurtrissure *f*, talure *f* ; **body covered with ~s** corps *m* couvert d'ecchymoses or de bleus

bruised [bruːzd] ADJ **a** [*person, body, skin, elbow etc*] contusionné ; **~ all over** couvert de bleus, tout contusionné **b** [*fruit*] meurtri, talé ; [*vegetables*] abîmé, meurtri **c** [*ego, feelings, pride*] blessé ; **to feel ~** [*person*] être blessé

bruiser* ['bruːzər] N malabar* *m*, cogneur* *m*

bruising ['bruːzɪŋ] **1** N bleus *mpl*, contusions *fpl* ; **light** or **minor/heavy** or **severe ~** contusions *fpl* légères/graves **2** ADJ éprouvant

Brum* [brʌm] N (*Brit*) Birmingham

brum* [brʌm] EXCL (*baby talk*) **~, ~!** broum, broum !

Brummie* ['brʌmɪ] N (*Brit*) **he's a ~** il est de Birmingham

brunch [brʌntʃ] N brunch *m*

Brunei [bruː'naɪ] N Brunei, le Brunei

brunette [bruː'net] **1** N (femme *f*) brune *f*, brunette *f* **2** ADJ [*person, skin*] brun ; [*eyes*] marron *inv* ; [*hair*] châtain

brunt [brʌnt] N **the ~** [*of attack, blow*] le (plus gros du) choc ; [*of argument, displeasure*] le poids ; **to bear the ~ of the assault** soutenir or essuyer le plus fort de l'attaque ; **to bear the ~ of the work** faire le (plus) gros du travail ; **to bear the ~ of the expense** payer le (plus) gros des frais ; **he bore the ~ of it all** c'est lui qui a porté le poids de l'affaire

brush [brʌʃ] **1** N **a** brosse *f* ; (*also* **paint ~**) pinceau *m*, brosse *f* ; (= *broom*) balai *m* ; (*short-handled* = *hearth brush etc*) balayette *f* ; (*also* **scrubbing ~**) brosse *f* (dure) ; (*also* **bottle**

~) goupillon *m*, rince-bouteilles *m inv*; (*also* **shaving ~**) blaireau *m*; **nail/clothes/hat ~** brosse *f* à ongles/à habits/à chapeau → **pastry, tar¹**

b (= *act of brushing*) coup *m* de brosse; **give your coat a ~** donne un coup de brosse à ton manteau; **to give one's hair a ~** donner un coup de brosse à ses cheveux, se brosser les cheveux

c (= *light touch*) effleurement *m*

d (= *tail*) [*of fox*] queue *f*

e (*NonC* = *undergrowth*) broussailles *fpl*, taillis *m*

f (= *skirmish*) accrochage *m*, escarmouche *f*; **to have a ~ with the law** avoir des démêlés *mpl* avec la justice, avoir maille à partir avec la justice; (= *quarrel*) **to have a ~ with sb** avoir un accrochage *or* une prise de bec* avec qn

g (*Elec*) [*of commutator*] balai *m*; [*of dynamo*] frottoir *m*; (= *discharge*) décharge *f*

2 VT **a** [+ *carpet*] balayer; [+ *clothes, hair etc*] brosser, donner un coup de brosse à; **to ~ one's teeth** se brosser *or* se laver les dents; **to ~ one's hair** se brosser les cheveux; **hair ~ed back** ◊ **~ed-back hair** cheveux ramenés *or* rejetés en arrière; **he ~ed the chalk off his coat** il a enlevé (à la main *or* à la brosse) les traces de craie qui étaient sur son manteau

b (= *touch lightly*) frôler, effleurer

c (*Tech*) [+ *wool*] gratter; (*Tex*) **~ed cotton** pilou *m*, finette *f*; **~ed nylon** nylon® *m* gratté

3 VI **to ~ against sb/sth** effleurer *or* frôler qn/qch; **to ~ past sb/sth** frôler qn/qch en passant

4 COMP ► **brush maker** N (= *manufacturer*) fabricant *m* de brosses; (= *employee*) brossier *m*, -ière *f* ► **brush-off*** N **to give sb the ~-off** envoyer balader* qn; **to get the ~-off** se faire envoyer sur les roses* ► **brush-stroke** N coup *m or* trait *m* de pinceau ► **brush-up** N coup *m* de brosse; **to give one's German a ~-up*** rafraîchir ses notions d'allemand → **wash**

► **brush aside** VT SEP [+ *argument, objections*] balayer (d'un geste); [+ *protester, objector*] repousser

► **brush away** VT SEP [+ *tears*] essuyer; [+ *mud, dust*] (*on clothes*) enlever à la brosse *or* à la main; (*on floor*) balayer; [+ *insects*] chasser

► **brush down** VT SEP [+ *person, garment*] donner un coup de brosse à; [+ *horse*] brosser

► **brush off** **1** VI **the mud ~es off easily** avec un coup de brosse la boue s'enlève facilement **2** VT SEP **a** [+ *mud, snow*] enlever (à la brosse *or* à coups de balai); [+ *insect*] balayer, écarter d'un geste; [+ *fluff on coat*] enlever (à la brosse *or* à la main) **b** (= *dismiss*) [+ *offer, challenge, threat etc*] repousser **3** **~-off*** N → **brush**

► **brush up** **1** VT SEP **a** [+ *crumbs, dirt*] ramasser avec une brosse *or* à la balayette **b** [+ *wool*] gratter **c** (* = *revise, improve*) rafraîchir (ses notions de); **to ~ up (on) one's English** rafraîchir son anglais *or* ses notions d'anglais **2** **~-up** N → **brush**

brushwood ['brʌʃwʊd] N (= *undergrowth*) broussailles *fpl*, taillis *m*; (= *cuttings*) menu bois *m*, brindilles *fpl*

brushwork ['brʌʃwɜːk] N (*Art*) facture *f*

brusque [bruːsk] ADJ brusque

brusquely ['bruːsklɪ] ADV [*behave, speak*] avec brusquerie, avec rudesse

brusqueness ['bruːsknɪs] N brusquerie *f*, rudesse *f*

Brussels ['brʌslz] **1** N Bruxelles **2** COMP [*lace*] de Bruxelles ► **Brussels sprouts** NPL (*also* **Brussel sprouts**) choux *mpl* de Bruxelles

brutal ['bruːtl] ADJ **a** (= *cruel, violent*) [*person, treatment, attack, régime*] brutal; [*film, scene*] violent **b** (= *unmitigated*) [*frankness, reality, change, reply*] brutal **c** (= *harsh*) [*winter, climate*] rude **d** (*liter* = *animal-like*) [*instincts*] animal

brutality [bruːˈtælɪtɪ] N brutalité *f*

brutalize ['bruːtəlaɪz] VT **a** (= *ill-treat*) brutaliser **b** (= *make brutal*) rendre brutal

brutally ['bruːtəlɪ] ADV [*murder, suppress, say*] brutalement; **to put it ~, ...** pour dire les choses de façon brutale, ...; **~ frank** d'une franchise brutale; **in a ~ competitive world** dans un monde livré à une concurrence sans merci

brute [bruːt] **1** N (= *animal*) brute *f*, bête *f*; (= *person*) (*cruel*) brute *f*, brutal *m*; (*coarse*) brute *f* (épaisse); **this machine is a ~!*** quelle vacherie de machine !* **2** ADJ **a** (= *animal-like*) animal **b** [*strength, passion*] brutal; **by (sheer) ~ force** par la force

brutish ['bruːtɪʃ] ADJ (= *animal-like*) brutal

BS [biːˈes] **a** (ABBR = **British Standard**) norme *f* britannique **b** (*US Univ*) (ABBR = **Bachelor of Science**) **to have a BS in biology** avoir une licence de biologie → **bachelor**; → DEGREE **c** (*esp US*:) = **bullshit**

BSA [ˌbiːesˈeɪ] N (*US*) (ABBR = **Boy Scouts of America**) *scouts américains*

BSC [ˌbiːesˈsiː] N (*Brit*) (ABBR = **Broadcasting Standards Council**) ≈ CSA *m*

BSc [ˌbiːesˈsiː] N (*Univ*) (ABBR = **Bachelor of Science**) **to have a ~ in biology** avoir une licence de biologie → **bachelor**; → DEGREE

BSE [ˌbiːesˈiː] (ABBR = **bovine spongiform encephalopathy**) ESB *f*

BSI [ˌbiːesˈaɪ] N (*Brit*) (ABBR = **British Standards Institution**) ≈ AFNOR *f*

BST [ˌbiːesˈtiː] N (ABBR = **British Summer Time**) → **British**

BT [biːˈtiː] N (ABBR = **British Telecom**) → **British**

Bt ABBR = **Baronet**

BTEC ['biːtek] N (*Brit*) ABBR = **Business and Technology Education Council** **a** (= *organization*) → **business** **b** (= *diploma*) diplôme *m* en gestion, sciences et techniques etc

btu [ˌbiːtiːˈjuː] N (ABBR = **British thermal unit**) → **thermal**

bub* [bʌb] N (*US*) mec* *m*

bubble ['bʌbl] **1** N **a** (*gen: also* **air ~**) bulle *f*; (*in glass*) bulle *f*, soufflure *f*; (*in paint*) boursouflure *f*; (*in metal*) soufflure *f*, boursouflement *m*; **to blow ~s** faire des bulles; **soap ~** bulle *f* de savon; (*fig*) **the ~ burst** (*gen*) le rêve s'est envolé; (*fig*) la chance a tourné; (*fig*) **to burst sb's ~** faire revenir *or* redescendre qn (brutalement) sur terre

b (*Med* = *sterile chamber*) bulle *f*

c (= *sound*) glouglou *m*

2 VI [*liquid*] bouillonner, dégager des bulles; [*champagne*] pétiller; [*gas*] barboter; (= *gurgle*) faire glouglou, glouglouter

3 COMP ► **bubble and squeak** N (*Brit*) purée aux choux et à la viande hachée ► **bubble bath** N bain *m* moussant ► **bubble-car** N (*Brit*) petite voiture *f* (*à toit transparent*) ► **bubble company** N (*Comm, Fin*) compagnie *f* véreuse ► **bubble-jet printer** N imprimante *f* à bulles d'encre ► **bubble memory** N (*Comput*) mémoire *f* à bulles ► **bubble pack** N (*for pills etc*) plaquette *f*; (*in shop: for pens, plugs etc*) blister *m* ► **bubble wrap** N emballage *m* à bulles

► **bubble out** VI [*liquid*] sortir à gros bouillons

► **bubble over** VI (*lit, fig*) déborder; **to ~ over with joy** déborder de joie

► **bubble up** VI (*lit*) [*liquid*] monter en bouillonnant; (*fig*) [*excitement etc*] monter

bubble-gum ['bʌblgʌm] N chewing-gum *m*

bubblehead* ['bʌblhed] N (*esp US: pej*) andouille* *f*, crétin(e)* *m(f)*

bubbly ['bʌblɪ] **1** ADJ (*lit, fig*) pétillant **2** N* (= *champagne*) champagne *m*, champ* *m*; (= *sparkling wine*) mousseux *m*

bubonic [bjuːˈbɒnɪk] ADJ bubonique; **~ plague** peste *f* bubonique

buccaneer [ˌbʌkəˈnɪə*] N (*Hist*) boucanier *m*; (*fig*) flibustier *m*, pirate *m*

buccaneering [ˌbʌkəˈnɪərɪŋ] ADJ (*pej, fig*) aventurier, intrigant

Bucharest [ˌbuːkəˈrest] N Bucarest

buck [bʌk] **1** N **a** (= *male deer, rabbit, hare etc*) mâle *m*

b († = *dandy*) élégant *m*, dandy *m*

c (*US** = *dollar*) dollar *m*; **to be down to one's last ~** être sur la paille; **to make a ~** se faire du fric*; **to make a few ~s on the side** se faire un peu de pognon* à côté, se faire un petit à-côté*; (*at sb's expense*) se sucrer en douce*; **to make a fast** *or* **quick ~** gagner du fric* facile; **to get more bang for the** *or* **one's ~** tirer le maximum de profit de son argent

d (* = *responsibility*) **to pass the ~** refiler* la responsabilité aux autres; **the ~ stops here** la responsabilité commence ici

e (= *sawhorse*) chevalet *m*, baudet *m*; (*Gym*) cheval *m* d'arçons

f the horse gave a ~ le cheval a lancé une ruade

2 VI **a** [*horse*] lancer *or* décocher une ruade **b** (= *object to*) **to ~ at sth** regimber devant qch **c** (*US*) **to ~ for sth*** rechercher qch

3 VT **to ~ the trend/system** se rebiffer contre la tendance/le système

4 COMP ► **buck-naked*** (*esp US*) ADJ à poil*, nu comme un ver ► **buck private** N (*US Mil*) deuxième classe *m inv* ► **buck rabbit** N lapin *m* mâle ► **buck sergeant** N (*US Mil*) simple sergent *m* ► **buck's fizz** N (*Culin*) mimosa *m* ► **buck teeth** N **to have ~ teeth** avoir les dents en avant ► **buck-toothed** ADJ qui a les dents en avant

► **buck up** **1** VI **a** (= *hurry up*) se grouiller*, se magner*; (= *exert o.s.*) se remuer*, se magner*; **~ up!** remue-toi !*, grouille-toi !*, active un peu !* **b** (= *cheer up*) se secouer*; **~ up!** courage ! **2** VT SEP **a** (= *cheer up*) [+ *person*] remonter le moral de, ravigoter* **b** **you'll have to ~ up your ideas** il va falloir que tu te secoues (*subj*) un peu*

bucked* [bʌkt] ADJ tout content

bucket ['bʌkɪt] **1** N **a** seau *m*; **~ of water** seau *m* d'eau; **to weep ~s*** pleurer toutes les larmes de son corps; **chain of ~s** chaîne *f* de seaux; **they made a chain of ~s to fight the fire** ils ont fait la chaîne pour combattre l'incendie → **kick, rain** **b** (*Tech*) [*of dredger, grain elevator*] godet *m*; [*of pump*] piston *m*; [*of wheel*] auget *m* **2** VI **a** [*rain*] **it's ~ing (down)*** ◊ **the rain is ~ing down*** il pleut à seaux, il tombe des cordes **b** (= *hurtle*) aller à fond de train **3** COMP ► **bucket elevator** N (*Tech*) noria *f*, élévateur *m* à godets ► **bucket seat** N (*siège-*)baquet *m* ► **bucket shop** N (*Fin*) bureau *m or* maison *f* de contrepartie, bureau *m* de courtier marron; (*for air tickets*) organisme de vente de billets d'avion à prix réduit

bucketful ['bʌkɪtfʊl] N plein seau *m*; **to produce/get sth by the ~*** produire/obtenir des masses* de qch

Buckeye State ['bʌkaɪ'steɪt] N (*US*) **the ~** N l'Ohio *m*

Buck House* ['bʌk.haʊs] N (*Brit*) = **Buckingham Palace**

Buckingham Palace ['bʌkɪŋəm'pælɪs] N le palais de Buckingham

buckle ['bʌkl] **1** N **a** [*of shoe, belt*] boucle *f* **b** (= *distortion*) [*of wheel*] voilure *f*; [*of metal*] gauchissement *m*, flambage *m* **2** VT **a** [+ *belt, shoe etc*] boucler, attacher **b** [+ *wheel*] voiler; [+ *metal*] gauchir, fausser **3** VI **a** [*belt, shoe*] se boucler, s'attacher **b** [*metal*] gauchir, se déformer; [*wheel*] se voiler

► **buckle down*** VI se coller au boulot*; **to ~ down to a job** s'atteler à un boulot*; **~ down to it!** au boulot !*

► **buckle in** VT SEP (*into seat*) attacher

► **buckle on** VT SEP [+ *armour*] revêtir,

endosser; [+ *sword*] ceindre

► **buckle to*** VI s'y mettre, s'y coller*

buckra: ['bʌkrə] N (*US pej*) Blanc *m*

buckram ['bʌkrəm] N bougran *m*

Bucks N ABBR = **Buckinghamshire**

bucksaw ['bʌksɔ:] N scie *f* à refendre

buckshee: [bʌk'fi:] ADJ, ADV (*Brit*) gratis *inv*, à l'œil*

buckshot ['bʌkʃɒt] N chevrotine(s) *f(pl)*

buckskin ['bʌkskɪn] N peau *f* de daim

buckthorn ['bʌkθɔ:n] N nerprun *m*, bourdaine *f*

buckwheat ['bʌkwi:t] N sarrasin *m*, blé *m* noir

bucolic [bju:'kɒlɪk] 1 ADJ bucolique, pastoral 2 N (*Literat*) **the Bucolics** les Bucoliques *fpl*

bud¹ [bʌd] 1 N a [*of tree, plant*] bourgeon *m*, œil *m*; [*of grafting*] écusson *m*; **to be in ~** bourgeonner; (*fig*) **a poet** *etc* **in the ~** un poète *etc* en herbe → **nip**¹ b [*of flower*] bouton *m*; **in ~** en bouton → **rosebud** c (*Anat*) papille *f* → **taste** 2 VI [*tree, plant*] bourgeonner, se couvrir de bourgeons; [*flower*] former des boutons; [*horns*] (commencer à) poindre or percer; [*talent etc*] (commencer à) percer 3 VT (*Hort*) [+ *tree*] greffer, écussonner

bud²* [bʌd] N (*esp US*) = **buddy**

Budapest [,bju:də'pest] N Budapest

Buddha ['budə] N Bouddha *m*

Buddhism ['budɪzəm] N bouddhisme *m*

Buddhist ['budɪst] 1 N bouddhiste *mf* 2 ADJ [*monk, nation*] bouddhiste; [*religion, art, dogma*] bouddhique

budding ['bʌdɪŋ] ADJ [*plant*] bourgeonnant; [*flower*] en bouton; (*fig*) [*poet etc*] en herbe; [*passion*] naissant

buddleia ['bʌdlɪə] N buddleia *m*, lilas *m* de Chine

buddy* ['bʌdɪ] 1 N (*US*) copain *m*, pote: *m*; **hi there, ~!** salut, mon pote !: ; **~ movie** or **film** film qui raconte l'histoire de deux amis; **they use the ~ system** ils travaillent en équipe de deux 2 COMP ► **buddy-buddy*** ADJ (*esp US*) **Paul and Mark are very ~~** ◊ **Paul is very ~~ with Mark** Paul et Mark sont très copains or copains comme cochons

budge [bʌdʒ] 1 VI (= *move*) bouger; (*fig*) changer d'avis; **I will not ~ an inch** (= *move from here*) je ne bougerai pas d'ici; (= *change my mind*) rien ne me fera changer d'avis 2 VT faire bouger; (*fig*) **you can't ~ him** il reste inébranlable, vous ne le ferez pas changer d'avis

► **budge over***, **budge up*** VI se pousser

budgerigar ['bʌdʒərɪgɑ:*] N perruche *f*

budget ['bʌdʒɪt] 1 N (*gen, Fin*) budget *m*; (*Parl*) budget *m*, loi *f* de finances; **my ~ won't stretch** or **run to steak nowadays** mon budget ne me permet plus d'acheter de bifteck; **to be on a tight ~** disposer d'un budget modeste

2 ADJ a (*Econ, Fin*) [*spending, credit*] budgétaire; (*Comm*) **~ account** compte-crédit *m*; (*Econ*) **~ cuts** compressions *fpl* budgétaires; (*Parl*) **~ day** jour *m* de la présentation du budget; (*Econ*) **~ deficit** découvert *m* budgétaire; (*Econ, Comm*) **~ heading** poste *m* budgétaire; (*US Comm*) **~ plan** système *m* de crédit; (*Parl*) **~ speech** discours *m* de présentation du budget; (*Econ*) **~ surplus** excédent *m* budgétaire b (= *cut-price*) [*tour, holiday, price*] pour petits budgets, économique

3 VI dresser or préparer un budget; **to ~ for sth** (*Econ*) inscrire or porter qch au budget, budgétiser qch; (*gen*) inscrire qch à son budget, prévoir des frais de qch

4 VT budgétiser, budgéter; **to ~ one's time** planifier son temps; **~ed balance sheet** bilan

m provisionnel; **a ~ed expense** une dépense budgétée

┌─────────┐
│ **BUDGET** │
└─────────┘

Le **budget** *de la nation est présenté au Parlement britannique au printemps par le chancelier de l'Échiquier qui rend publiques les prévisions du gouvernement pour l'année à venir et précise en particulier les modifications apportées à la fiscalité et au régime des prestations sociales. L'intervention du ministre est diffusée intégralement à la télévision, et les contribuables peuvent donc prendre connaissance « en direct » des augmentations frappant certains produits, essence, alcool et tabac notamment.*

-budget ['bʌdʒɪt] ADJ (*in compounds*) **big-budget** à gros budget → **low**¹

budgetary ['bʌdʒɪtrɪ] 1 ADJ budgétaire 2 COMP ► **budgetary deficit** N déficit *m* budgétaire ► **budgetary year** N exercice *m* budgétaire

budgeting ['bʌdʒɪtɪŋ] N [*of company, institution*] prévisions *fpl* budgétaires; **with careful ~ ...** si l'on équilibre soigneusement le budget ...

budgie* ['bʌdʒɪ] N ABBR = **budgerigar**

Buenos Aires ['bweɪnɒs'aɪrɪz] N Buenos Aires

buff¹ [bʌf] 1 N a (= *leather*) (peau *f* de) buffle *m*; (= *colour*) (couleur *f*) chamois *m*; **in the ~:** à poil: b [*polishing disc*] polissoir *m* 2 ADJ a (en peau) de buffle, en buffle b (*also* **~-coloured**) (couleur) chamois *inv*; **~ envelope** enveloppe *f* (en papier) bulle 3 VT (= *polish*) polir

buff²* [bʌf] N (= *enthusiast*) mordu(e)* *m(f)*; **a film ~** un(e) mordu(e)* du cinéma

buffalo ['bʌfələu] N (*pl* buffalo or buffaloes) (= *wild ox*) buffle *m*, bufflesse *f*; (*esp in US*) bison *m* → **water**

buffer¹ ['bʌfə*] 1 N (*lit, fig*) tampon *m*; (*Brit Rail*) (*on train*) tampon *m*; (*at terminus*) butoir *m*; (*US Aut*) pare-chocs *m inv*; (*Comput*) mémoire *f* tampon 2 VT [+ *shocks*] amortir; (*Chem*) tamponner 3 COMP ► **buffer fund** N (*Fin, Econ*) fonds *m* régulateur ► **buffer memory** N (*Comput*) mémoire *f* tampon ► **buffer solution** N (*Chem*) solution *f* tampon ► **buffer state** N (*Pol*) état *m* tampon ► **buffer stock** N (*Comm*) stock *m* de sécurité or de régularisation ► **buffer zone** N zone *f* tampon

buffer² ['bʌfə*] N (*for polishing*) polissoir *m*

buffer³: ['bʌfə*] N (*Brit*) (*old*) **~** vieux fossile* *m*

buffet¹ ['bʌfɪt] 1 N (= *blow*) (*with hand*) gifle *f*, soufflet *m*; (*with fist*) coup *m* de poing; (*fig*) **the ~s of fate** les coups *mpl* du sort 2 VT (*with hand*) frapper, souffleter; (*with fist*) donner un coup de poing à; **~ed by the waves** battu or ballotté par les vagues; **~ed by the wind** secoué or ballotté par le vent; (*fig*) **~ed by events** secoué par les événements

buffet² ['bufeɪ] 1 N (= *refreshment bar, sideboard*) buffet *m*; (*in menu*) **cold ~** viandes *fpl* froides 2 COMP ► **buffet car** N (*Brit Rail*) voiture-buffet *f*, buffet *m* ► **buffet lunch** N lunch *m* ► **buffet supper** N buffet *m* dînatoire

buffeting ['bʌfɪtɪŋ] 1 N [*of person, object*] bourrades *fpl*, coups *mpl*; [*of wind, rain etc*] assaut *m*; **to take a ~ from the waves** être ballotté (de tous côtés) par les vagues 2 ADJ [*wind*] violent

buffing ['bʌfɪŋ] N polissage *m*

buffoon [bə'fu:n] N bouffon *m*, pitre *m*

buffoonery [bə'fu:nərɪ] N (*NonC*) bouffonnerie(s) *f(pl)*

bug [bʌg] 1 N a (= *bedbug etc*) punaise *f*; (*esp US* = *any insect*) insecte *m*, bestiole* *f*; **big ~:** (= *important person*) grosse légume* *f*, huile* *f* → **firebug** b (* = *germ*) microbe *m*; **he picked up a ~ on holiday** il a attrapé un mi-

crobe pendant ses vacances; **the flu ~** le virus de la grippe c (= *defect, snag*) défaut *m*, inconvénient *m*; (*Comput*) erreur *f*, bogue *m* or *f* d (* = *hidden microphone*) micro *m* (caché) e (*US** = *car*) petite voiture *f*, coccinelle* *f* f (= *enthusiasm*) **to be bitten by** or **get the jogging ~*** attraper le virus du jogging g (*US* = *enthusiast*) **a basketball ~:** un(e) mordu(e)* du basket 2 VT a* [+ *phone etc*] brancher sur table d'écoute; [+ *room etc*] poser or installer des micros (cachés) dans b (* = *annoy*) embêter*, casser les pieds à* 3 COMP ► **bug-eyed** ADJ aux yeux exorbités ► **bug-hunter*** N entomologiste *mf*, chasseur *m* de petites bestioles* ► **bug-ridden** ADJ infesté de punaises

► **bug out:** VI (*US*) foutre le camp:

bugaboo ['bʌgəbu:] N croquemitaine *m*, loup-garou *m*

bugbear ['bʌgbɛə*] N (= *obsession*) bête *f* noire; (= *ogre*) croquemitaine *m*, ogre *m*

bugger ['bʌgə*] 1 N a († *or Jur* = *sodomite*) pédéraste *m* b (*Brit***) salaud: *m*; **silly ~** pauvre con: *m*; **to play silly ~s** déconner: ; **lucky ~** veinard: *m*; **poor little ~** pauvre petit bonhomme *m* c (*Brit* = *difficulty, annoyance*) **it's a ~:*** c'est casse-couilles** or casse-pieds* 2 EXCL **~ (it** or **me)!:** merde !: 3 VT a (*Jur*) se livrer à la pédérastie avec b (*Brit**) **well, I'm ~ed!** merde alors !: ; **I'll be** or **I'm ~ed if I'm going to do that!** je préfère plutôt crever (que de faire ça !) c **~ all** que dalle: ; **~ him!** il peut aller se faire foutre !*; **~ the consequences!** je me fous des conséquences !:

► **bugger about:***, **bugger around:*** (*Brit*) 1 VI glandouiller: ; (= *play around with*) **to ~ around with sth** faire le con avec qch** 2 VT SEP emmerder:, faire chier:

► **bugger off:*** VI (*Brit*) foutre le camp:

► **bugger up:*** VT SEP (*Brit*) foutre en l'air:

buggered:* ['bʌgəd] (*Brit*) 1 VB *pt, ptp* of **bugger** 2 ADJ a (= *ruined*) [*machine*] foutu:, nase* ; (= *exhausted*) [*person*] nase*

buggery ['bʌgərɪ] N sodomie *f*

bugging ['bʌgɪŋ] N utilisation *f* d'appareils d'écoute; **~ device** appareil *m* d'écoute (clandestine)

buggy ['bʌgɪ] N (*horse-drawn*) boghei *m*; (*also* **beach ~**) buggy *m*; (*also* **moon ~**) jeep® *f* lunaire; (*US** = *car*) bagnole* *f*; (*also* **baby ~**) (*Brit* = *pushchair*) poussette(-canne) *f*; (*US* = *pram*) voiture *f* d'enfant

bughouse:* ['bʌghaus] N (*US* = *asylum*) asile *m*, maison *f* de dingues:

bugle ['bju:gl] N clairon *m*; **~ call** sonnerie *f* de clairon

bugler ['bju:glə*] N (joueur *m* de) clairon *m*

bugs:* [bʌgz] ADJ (*US*) cinglé*, dingue*

build [bɪld] (*vb*: *pret, ptp* built) 1 N (= *physique*) carrure *f*, charpente *f*; **man of strong ~** homme *m* solidement bâti or charpenté; **of medium ~** de corpulence moyenne; **of slim ~** fluet; **he's got the ~ of a wrestler** il a une carrure de catcheur, il est bâti comme un catcheur; **of the same ~ as ...** de même carrure que ...

2 VT [+ *house, town*] bâtir, construire; [+ *bridge, ship, machine*] construire; [+ *temple*] bâtir, édifier; [+ *nest*] faire, bâtir; (*fig*) [+ *theory, plan*] bâtir, construire; [+ *empire, company*] fonder, bâtir; (*in games*) [+ *words, sequence*] former; **the house is being built** la maison se bâtit; **the architect who built the palace** l'architecte qui a bâti or qui a fait bâtir le palais; **this car was not built for speed** cette voiture n'était pas conçue pour la vitesse; (*fig*) **to ~ castles in the air** or **in Spain** faire des châteaux en Espagne; **to ~ a mirror into a wall** encastrer un miroir dans un mur; **house built into the hillside** maison *f* bâtie à flanc de colline; (*fig*) **his theory is not built on facts** sa théorie n'est pas basée or construite sur des faits

3 VI bâtir ; [*edifice*] se bâtir ; **to ~ (up)on a piece of land** bâtir sur un terrain ; (*lit, fig*) **to ~ upon sand** bâtir sur le sable ; (*fig*) **it's a good start, something to ~ on** c'est une base solide sur laquelle on peut bâtir ; (†, *frm*) **to ~ upon sb/a promise** faire fond sur qn/une promesse

► **build in** **1** VT SEP [+ *wardrobe etc*] encastrer (**into** dans) ; (*fig*) [+ *safeguards*] intégrer (**into** à) → **build 2** **2** **built-in** ADJ → **built**

► **build on** VT SEP [+ *room, annex*] ajouter (**to** à)

► **build up** **1** VI [*business connection etc*] se développer ; [*pressure*] s'accumuler ; [*tension, excitement*] monter, augmenter **2** VT SEP **a** (= *establish*) [+ *reputation*] édifier, bâtir ; [+ *business*] créer, monter ; [+ *theory*] échafauder ; (= *increase*) [+ *production, forces*] accroître, augmenter ; [+ *pressure*] accumuler ; [+ *tension, excitement*] augmenter, faire monter ; **to ~ up one's strength** prendre des forces **b** (= *cover with houses*) [+ *area, land*] urbaniser **c** (*fig* = *publicize*) [+ *person, reputation*] faire de la publicité pour, faire du battage* autour de **3** **~-up** → **build-up** **4** **built-up** ADJ → **built**

builder ['bɪldə'] N **a** [*of houses etc*] (= *owner of firm*) entrepreneur *m* ; (= *worker*) maçon *m* ; [*of ships, machines*] constructeur *m* ; **~'s labourer** ouvrier *m* du bâtiment → **organ** **b** (*fig*) fondateur *m*, -trice *f*, créateur *m*, -trice *f* → **empire**

building ['bɪldɪŋ] **1** N **a** (= *edifice*) bâtiment *m*, construction *f* ; (*imposing*) édifice *m* ; (= *habitation or offices*) immeuble *m* ; (*Jur, Insurance: in contract etc*) immeuble *m* → **public** **b** (*NonC*) construction *f* ; **the ~ of the church took seven years** il a fallu sept ans pour construire l'église → **body, empire**

2 COMP ► **building block** N (= *toy*) cube *m* ; (*fig*) composante *f* ► **building contractor** N entrepreneur *m* (en bâtiment) ► **building industry** N (industrie *f* du) bâtiment *m* ► **building labourer** N ouvrier *m* du bâtiment ► **building land** N terrain *m* à bâtir ► **building materials** NPL matériaux *mpl* de construction ► **building permit** N permis *m* de construire ► **building plot** N (petit) terrain *m* à bâtir ► **buildings insurance** N (*NonC*) assurance *f* sur le capital immobilier ► **building site** N chantier *m* (de construction) ► **building society** N (*Brit*) ≈ société *f* de crédit immobilier ► **building trade** N = **building industry** ► **the building trades** NPL les métiers *mpl* du bâtiment ► **building workers** NPL ouvriers *mpl* du bâtiment ► **building works** NPL travaux *mpl* de construction

build-up ['bɪldʌp] N **a** (= *increase*) [*of pressure*] intensification *f* ; [*of gas*] accumulation *f* ; (*Mil*) [*of troops*] rassemblement *m* ; [*of production*] accroissement *m* ; (*Comm*) [*of stock etc*] accumulation *f* ; [*of tension, excitement*] montée *f* ; (*Mil*) **arms ~** accumulation *f* des armements **b** (= *presentation*) présentation *f* publicitaire, battage* *m* ; **to give sb/sth a good ~** faire une bonne publicité pour qn/qch, faire beaucoup de battage* autour de qn/qch

built [bɪlt] **1** VB *pt, ptp of* **build** **2** ADJ **a** (*Constr*) **~ of brick/stone** (construit) en briques/pierres ; **~ to last** fait pour durer ; **a car ~ for speed** une voiture conçue pour faire de la vitesse ; (*hum*) **Anne isn't exactly ~ for speed*** Anne n'est pas vraiment du genre rapide* (*hum*) **b** [*person*] **heavily** *or* **solidly ~** costaud, solidement bâti ; **powerfully ~** puissamment charpenté ; **slightly ~** fluet ; (*Brit*) **to be ~ like a tank** [*machine etc*] être tout ce qu'il y a de plus solide ; (*Brit*) **he's ~ like a tank** *or* **like a brick shithouse**✹ c'est une véritable armoire à glace, il est superbaraqué → **well² 3** COMP ► **built-in** ADJ [*oven, wardrobe, mirror, beam*] encastré ; (*fig*) [*desire etc*] inné → **obsolescence** ; **~-in cupboard** placard *m* (encastré) ► **built-up** ADJ (*Dress*) [*shoulders*]

rehaussé ; [*shoes*] à semelle compensée ; **~-up area** agglomération *f* (urbaine)

-built [bɪlt] ADJ (*in compounds*) **pine-built house** maison *f* (construite) en bois de pin ; **French-built ship** navire *m* de construction française → **clinker**

Bukhara [bʊˈkɑːrə] N (*Geog*) Boukhara

bulb [bʌlb] N **a** [*of plant*] bulbe *m*, oignon *m* ; **~ of garlic** tête *f* d'ail ; **tulip ~** bulbe *m* or oignon *m* de tulipe ; **~ fibre** terreau *m* enrichi (pour bulbes) **b** (*Elec*) ampoule *f* **c** (*Chem*) ballon *m* ; [*of thermometer*] cuvette *f*

bulbous ['bʌlbəs] ADJ [*plant*] bulbeux ; [*nose*] gros (grosse *f*), bulbeux

Bulgar† ['bʌlgɑː'] N Bulgare *mf*

Bulgaria [bʌlˈgɛərɪə] N la Bulgarie

Bulgarian [bʌlˈgɛərɪən] **1** ADJ bulgare **2** N **a** (= *person*) Bulgare *mf* **b** (*Ling*) bulgare *m*

bulge [bʌldʒ] **1** N **a** (*in surface, metal*) bombement *m* ; (*in cheek*) gonflement *m* ; (*in column*) renflement *m* ; (*in jug, bottle*) panse *f*, ventre *m* ; (*in plaster*) bosse *f* ; (*in tyre*) soufflure *f*, hernie *f* ; (*in pocket, jacket*) renflement *m* ; (*Brit Mil*) saillant *m* ; (*Hist*) **the Battle of the Bulge** la bataille des Ardennes **b** (= *increase*) [*of numbers*] augmentation *f* temporaire ; [*of sales, prices, rate*] hausse *f*, poussée *f* ; [*of birth rate*] poussée *f* ; **the postwar ~** l'explosion *f* démographique de l'après-guerre **2** VI (*also* **~ out**) se renfler, bomber ; (= *stick out*) faire *or* former saillie ; [*plaster*] être bosselé ; [*pocket, sack, cheek*] être gonflé (**with** de) ; (*fig*) **my address book is bulging with new numbers** mon carnet d'adresses est bourré de nouveaux numéros

bulging ['bʌldʒɪŋ] ADJ **a** (= *protruding*) [*eyes*] globuleux ; [*muscles*] saillant ; [*stomach*] protubérant ; [*forehead, wall*] bombé **b** (= *full*) [*pockets, suitcase*] bourré (**with** de) ; [*wallet*] bien garni

bulgur ['bʌlgə'] N (*also* **~ wheat**) boulgour *m*

bulimia [bəˈlɪmɪə] N (*also* **~ nervosa**) boulimie *f*

bulimic [bəˈlɪmɪk] ADJ boulimique

bulk [bʌlk] **1** N **a** (= *great size*) [*of thing*] grosseur *f*, grandeur *f* ; [*of person*] corpulence *f* ; (= *large volume*) masse *f*, volume *m* **b** (= *main part*) **the ~** la majeure partie, la plus grande partie, le (plus) gros (**of** de) ; **the ~ of the working community** la plus grande partie *or* l'ensemble *m* de la population ouvrière ; **the ~ of the work is done** le plus gros du travail est fait **c** (*Comm*) **in ~** (= *in large quantities*) en gros ; (*not prepacked*) en vrac **d** (*in food*) fibre *f* (végétale) **e** (*Naut*) cargaison *f* (en cale) **2** ADJ [*order, supplies etc*] en gros ; **~ mailing** mailing *m* à grande diffusion ; **~ mail** envois *mpl* en nombre **3** VI **to ~ large** (**in sb's life/thoughts**) occuper une place importante (dans la vie/les pensées de qn) **4** VT (*Customs*) estimer ; **to ~ a container** estimer le contenu d'un conteneur **5** COMP ► **bulk-buy** VI [*trader*] acheter en gros ; [*individual*] acheter par *or* en grosses quantités ► **bulk-buying** N [*of trader*] achat *m* en gros ; [*of individual*] achat *m* par *or* en grosses quantités ► **bulk carrier** N transporteur *m* de vrac ► **bulk transport** N transport *m* en vrac

bulkhead ['bʌlkhed] N (*Brit Naut*) cloison *f*

bulkiness ['bʌlkɪnɪs] N [*of parcel, luggage*] grosseur *f*, volume *m* ; [*of person*] corpulence *f*

bulky ['bʌlkɪ] ADJ [*parcel, suitcase*] volumineux, encombrant ; [*book*] épais (-aisse *f*) ; [*person*] gros (grosse *f*), corpulent

bull¹ [bʊl] **1** N **a** taureau *m* ; (*fig*) **to take** *or* **seize** *or* **grasp the ~ by the horns** prendre *or* saisir le taureau par les cornes ; **like a ~ in a china shop** comme un éléphant dans un magasin de porcelaine ; **to go at it like a ~ at a gate*** foncer tête baissée ; (*Astron*) **the Bull** le Taureau → **bull's-eye, cock, John, strong** **b** (= *male of elephant, whale etc*) mâle *m* **c** (*St Ex*) haussier *m* ; **the market is all ~s** le marché est à la hausse **d** (*Mil** = *cleaning, polishing*) fourbissage *m* **e** (✹ = *claptrap*) = **bullshit 1** **2** VT (*St Ex*) [+ *stocks, shares*] pousser à la hausse ; **to ~ the market** pousser les cours à la hausse **3** COMP [*elephant, whale etc*] mâle ; (*St Ex*) à la hausse ► **bull bars** NPL (*Brit Aut*) barres *fpl* antibuffles ► **bull calf** N jeune taureau *m*, taurillon *m* ► **bull-dyke**✹ N (*pej*) gouine* *f* (*pej*) aux allures de camionneur ► **bull market** N (*St Ex*) marché *m* haussier *or* à la hausse ► **bull neck** N cou *m* de taureau ► **bull-necked** ADJ au cou de taureau, épais (épaisse *f*) d'encolure ► **bull session*** N (*US*) discussion *f* entre hommes ► **bull terrier** N bull-terrier *m*

bull² [bʊl] N (*Rel*) bulle *f*

bulldog ['bʊldɒg] **1** N bouledogue *m* **2** COMP [*tenacity*] à toute épreuve ► **bulldog breed** N (*fig*) **he is one of the ~ breed** il est d'une ténacité à toute épreuve ► **bulldog clip** N (*Brit*) pince *f* à dessin

bulldoze ['bʊldəʊz] VT (*lit*) passer au bulldozer ; (*fig*) **to ~ sb into doing sth*** forcer qn à faire qch, faire pression sur qn pour qu'il fasse qch ; **he ~d his way into the meeting*** (= *forced his way in*) il a réussi à pénétrer dans la salle où avait lieu la réunion ; (= *managed to contribute*) il a fait du forcing* pour participer à cette réunion ; **the government ~d the bill through parliament** le gouvernement a fait du forcing* pour que le parlement adopte (*subj*) le projet de loi

bulldozer ['bʊldəʊzə'] N bulldozer *m*

bullet ['bʊlɪt] **1** N balle *f* (*projectile*) ; (*Brit*) **to get** *or* **to be given the ~*** se faire virer* **2** COMP ► **bullet-headed** ADJ à (la) tête ronde ► **bullet hole** N trou *m* de balle ► **bullet train** N train *m* à grande vitesse (*japonais*) ► **bullet wound** N blessure *f* par balle

bulletin ['bʊlɪtɪn] **1** N bulletin *m*, communiqué *m* ; **health ~** bulletin *m* de santé → **news 2** COMP ► **bulletin board** N (*gen*) tableau *m* d'affichage ; (*Comput*) panneau *m* d'affichage (électronique)

bulletproof ['bʊlɪtpruːf] **1** ADJ [*garment*] pare-balles *inv* ; [*car, glass*] blindé **2** VT blinder

bullfinch ['bʊlfɪntʃ] N bouvreuil *m*

bullfrog ['bʊlfrɒg] N grenouille-taureau *f*, ouaouaron *m* (*Can*)

bullhorn ['bʊlhɔːn] N (*US*) porte-voix *m inv*, mégaphone *m*

bullion¹ ['bʊljən] N (*NonC*) encaisse-or *f* ; (*also* **gold ~**) or *m* en barre *or* en lingot(s) ; (*also* **silver ~**) argent *m* en lingot(s)

bullion² ['bʊljən] N (= *fringe*) frange *f* de cannetille

bullish ['bʊlɪʃ] ADJ (*St Ex*) haussier

bullock ['bʊlək] **1** N bœuf *m* ; (*young*) bouvillon *m* **2** COMP ► **bullock cart** N char *m* à bœufs

bullpen* ['bʊlpen] N (*US*) **a** (*Baseball*) (= *area*) zone *f* d'entraînement des lanceurs ; (= *players*) lanceurs *mpl* à l'entraînement **b** (= *office*) bureau *m* paysagé *or* sans cloisons **c** (= *cell*) local *m* de garde à vue

bullring ['bʊlrɪŋ] N arène *f* (pour courses de taureaux)

bull's-eye ['bʊlzaɪ] N **a** [*of target*] mille *m*, centre *m* ; (*lit, fig*) **to get a ~** *or* ◊ **to hit the ~** faire mouche, mettre dans le mille **b** (= *sweet*) gros bonbon *m* à la menthe **c** (= *window*) œuf *m*, oculus *m* ; (*in glass*) boudine *f*

bullshit‡ ['bʊl.ʃɪt] **1** N connerie(s)‡ f(pl), foutaise(s)‡ f(pl); **(that's)** ~! c'est des conneries or de la foutaise!‡ **2** VI déconner‡, dire des conneries‡ **3** VT raconter des conneries à‡

bullshitter‡ ['bʊl.ʃɪtəʳ] N **to be a** ~ raconter des conneries‡

bullwhip ['bʊlwɪp] **1** N fouet m (à longue mèche tressée) **2** VT fouetter

bully¹ ['bʊlɪ] **1** N **a** tyran m; (esp Scol) petit(e) dur(e) m(f), (petite) brute f **b** (Brit Hockey: also ~**-off**) engagement m (du jeu) **2** VT (= persecute) tyranniser, persécuter; (= treat cruelly) malmener, brutaliser; (= frighten) intimider; (Scol) brutaliser, brimer; **to** ~ **sb into doing sth** contraindre qn par la menace à faire qch **3** VI être une brute **4** COMP ► **bully boy**‡ N dur m, brute f ► **bully-boy** ADJ ~**-boy tactics/politics** manœuvres fpl/politique f d'intimidation

► **bully off 1** VI (Brit) mettre la balle en jeu, engager (le jeu) **2** ~**-off** N → **bully¹**

bully²‡ ['bʊlɪ] **1** ADJ† épatant† **2** EXCL ~ **for you!** t'es un chef!‡

bully³‡ ['bʊlɪ] N (Mil: also ~ **beef**) corned-beef m, singe‡ m

bullying ['bʊlɪɪŋ] **1** ADJ [person, manner] tyrannique, brutal **2** N brimade(s) f(pl), brutalité(s) f(pl)

bulrush ['bʊlrʌʃ] N jonc m

bulwark ['bʊlwək] N (= rampart) rempart m, fortification f; (= breakwater) brise-lames m inv; (fig = defence) rempart m; (Naut) bastingage m

bum¹‡ [bʌm] (esp US) **1** N (= vagrant) clodo‡ m, clochard m; (= good-for-nothing) bon à rien m; **to get** or **be given the** ~**'s rush**‡ mettre qn en quarantaine or à l'index; **to live on the** ~ vivre en clochard **2** ADJ (= bad) minable‡, de camelote‡; (= false) faux (fausse f); **a** ~ **rap**‡ une accusation bidon‡, une fausse accusation; **a** ~ **steer** un mauvais tuyau‡, un tuyau crevé‡; **to give sb a** ~ **steer** refiler un mauvais tuyau or un tuyau crevé à qn‡ **3** VI **a** (= scrounge) taper‡ les autres **b** (= loaf: also ~ **about** or **around**) vadrouiller‡ **4** VT [+ money, food] taper‡; **to** ~ **a meal/cigarette off sb** taper‡ qn d'un repas/d'une cigarette

bum²‡ [bʌm] (Brit) **1** N (= bottom) derrière m, arrière-train‡ m; **to put** ~**s on seats** remplir les salles **2** COMP ► **bum boy**‡ N (pej) pédale‡ f

bumbag ['bʌmbæg] N (sac m) banane f

bumbershoot†‡ ['bʌmbəʃu:t] N (US) pépin‡ m, parapluie m

bumble ['bʌmbl] VI **a** (= walk) marcher en titubant or d'un pas chancelant; **to** ~ **about** or **around (a place)** s'affairer d'une façon désordonnée (dans un endroit); **we** ~**d about on the computer** nous tapotions sur l'ordinateur **b** (= speak) bafouiller; **to** ~ **on about sth** bafouiller or rabâcher qch

bumblebee ['bʌmblbi:] N bourdon m

bumbling ['bʌmblɪŋ] ADJ (= inept) empoté; (= muttering) rabâcheur

bumboat ['bʌmbəʊt] N canot m d'approvisionnement

bumf‡ [bʌmf] N (Brit) (pej = forms etc) paperasses fpl, paperasserie f; (= toilet paper) PQ‡ m

bumfreezer†‡ ['bʌmfri:zəʳ] N blouson m court

bummer‡ ['bʌməʳ] **1** N **a** (Drugs) mauvais trip‡ m **b** (annoying) **you're working on Sunday? what a** ~! tu travailles dimanche? quelle poisse!‡; **I had a** ~ **of a day** j'ai eu une journée vraiment pourrie‡

bump [bʌmp] **1** N **a** (= blow) choc m, coup m; (= jolt) cahot m, secousse f; **he sat down with a** ~ il s'est assis lourdement; **he came down to earth with a** ~‡ le retour à la réalité a

été brutal pour lui; **the news brought us back to earth with a** ~‡ la nouvelle nous a brutalement rappelés à la réalité **b** (= lump on head, in road, Ski) bosse f; ~ **of locality**‡ sens m de l'orientation **c** (Aviat = rising air current) (soudain) courant m ascendant **d** (Rowing) heurt m **2** VT [car] [+ another car] heurter, tamponner; [+ boat] heurter; **to** ~ **one's head/knee** se cogner la tête/le genou (**against** contre) **3** VI **to** ~ **along** cahoter, bringuebaler; **to** ~ **down** (= sit) s'asseoir brusquement; (Brit) **the economy continues to** ~ **along the bottom** l'économie est toujours au creux de la vague **4** EXCL boum!, pan! **5** COMP ► **bump-start** VT [+ car] (by pushing) démarrer en poussant; (by running down a hill) démarrer dans une descente ♦ N **to give a car a** ~**-start** démarrer une voiture en la poussant

► **bump into** VT FUS **a** [person] butter contre, se cogner contre; [vehicle] entrer en collision avec, rentrer dans‡ **b** (* = meet) rencontrer par hasard, tomber sur‡

► **bump off**‡ VT SEP liquider‡, supprimer‡; (with gun) descendre‡

► **bump up** **1** VI **the car** ~**ed up onto the pavement** la voiture a grimpé sur le trottoir **2** VT SEP ‡ **a** (= increase sharply) [+ prices, sales, points, profits] faire grimper **b** **he was** ~**ed up to first class on his flight home** au retour, il a eu droit à un surclassement à une place en première

► **bump up against** VT FUS = **bump into**

bumper ['bʌmpəʳ] **1** N **a** [of car] pare-chocs m inv; **to be** ~**-to-**~ être pare-chocs contre pare-chocs, être à touche-touche‡ **b** (= full glass) rasade f, plein verre m **2** ADJ [crop, issue] exceptionnel, sensationnel **3** COMP ► **bumper car** N auto f tamponneuse ► **bumper sticker, bumper strip** N autocollant m (pour voiture)

bumph‡ [bʌmf] N = **bumf**

bumpkin ['bʌmpkɪn] N (pej: also **country** ~) plouc‡ mf, péquenaud‡ m

bumptious ['bʌmpʃəs] ADJ suffisant, prétentieux

bumpy ['bʌmpɪ] ADJ [road] bosselé, cahoteux; [forehead] couvert de bosses; [ride] cahoteux; [crossing] agité; **we had a** ~ **flight/drive/crossing** nous avons été très secoués or chahutés‡ pendant le vol/sur la route/pendant la traversée

bun [bʌn] **1** N **a** (Culin) (also **bread** ~) petit pain m au lait; (= cake) petit gâteau m; **to have a** ~ **in the oven**‡ avoir un polichinelle dans le tiroir‡, être en cloque‡ **b** (= hairstyle) chignon m **c** (US‡) **to get a** ~ **on** (= get drunk) prendre une biture‡; **he had a** ~ **on** il tenait une de ces bitures‡‡ **2** COMP ► **bun-fight**‡ N thé m (servi pour un grand nombre de personnes)

bunch [bʌntʃ] **1** N **a** [of flowers] bouquet m; [of feathers] touffe f; [of hair] touffe f, houppe f; [of bananas] régime m; [of radishes, asparagus] botte f; [of twigs] poignée f, paquet m; [of keys] trousseau m; [of ribbons] nœud m, flot m; ~ **of flowers** bouquet m (de fleurs); ~ **of grapes** grappe f de raisins; (Brit) **to wear one's hair in** ~**es** porter des couettes; (fig) **the pick of the** ~ le dessus du panier **b**‡ [of people] groupe m, bande f; **the best of the** ~ le meilleur or la bande or de l'équipe‡; **the best of a bad** ~‡ le or les moins médiocre(s); **what a** ~! quelle équipe!‡ **c** (Sport) [of runners, cyclists] peloton m **2** VT [+ flowers] mettre en bouquets; [+ vegetables, straw] botteler, mettre en bottes

► **bunch together 1** VI se serrer (en foule), se grouper **2** VT SEP [+ people, things] grouper, concentrer

► **bunch up 1** VI **don't** ~ **up so much, space out!** ne vous entassez pas les uns sur les autres, écartez-vous! **2** VT SEP **a** [+ dress, skirt] retrousser, trousser **b** **they sat** ~**ed up on the bench** ils étaient (assis) serrés sur le banc

bunco‡ ['bʌŋkəʊ] (US) **1** N (= swindle) arnaque‡ f, escroquerie f **2** VT arnaquer‡, escroquer **3** COMP ► **bunco squad** N ≈ brigade f de répression des fraudes

buncombe‡ ['bʌŋkəm] N (US) = **bunkum**

bundle ['bʌndl] **1** N **a** [of clothes, goods] paquet m, ballot m; [of hay] botte f; [of letters, papers] liasse f; [of linen] paquet m; [of firewood] fagot m; [of rods, sticks] faisceau m, poignée f; **he's a** ~ **of nerves** c'est un paquet de nerfs; (iro) **he's a** ~ **of laughs**‡ il n'est vraiment pas marrant‡; (Austral fig) **to drop one's** ~‡ baisser les bras; ~ **(of joy)** (= baby) (petit) bout m de chou‡; **that child is a** ~ **of mischief**‡ cet enfant est un petit coquin **b** (‡ = money) **a** ~ beaucoup de fric‡; **to make a** ~ faire son beurre‡; **it cost a** ~‡ ça a coûté bonbon‡, ça a coûté beaucoup de fric‡ **c** (= great deal) beaucoup; **we've learned a** ~ **of lessons** nous avons beaucoup appris; **I don't go a** ~ **on it**‡ ça ne me botte‡ pas, ça ne m'emballe pas beaucoup; **I don't go a** ~ **on him**‡ il ne me branche pas ce type-là‡ **d** (Comput) lot m **2** VT (also ~ **up**) empaqueter, mettre en paquet; [+ clothes] faire un paquet or ballot de; [+ hay] botteler; [+ papers, banknotes] mettre en liasse; [+ letters] mettre en paquet; [+ sticks] mettre en faisceau **b** (= put hastily) **to** ~ **sth into a corner** fourrer‡ or entasser qch dans un coin; (fig) **to** ~ **into the house** pousser or faire entrer qn dans la maison à la hâte or sans ménagement; **to** ~ **sb into a car** pousser qn dans une voiture (sans ménagement) **3** COMP ► **bundled software** N (NonC: Comput) progiciel m

► **bundle off** VT SEP [+ person] faire sortir (en toute hâte), pousser dehors (sans façons); **he was** ~**d off to Australia** on l'a expédié en Australie

► **bundle out** VT SEP pousser dehors (sans façons), faire sortir (en toute hâte)

► **bundle up** VT SEP **a** = **bundle 2a** **b** emmitoufler

bung [bʌŋ] **1** N **a** [of cask] bondon m, bonde f **b** (‡ = bribe) dessous-de-table m **2** VT **a** (esp Brit: also ~ **up**) [+ cask] boucher **b** (Brit‡ = throw) envoyer‡, balancer‡

► **bung in**‡ VT SEP (= include) rajouter (par-dessus le marché)

► **bung out**‡ VT SEP flanquer‡ à la porte; [+ rubbish] jeter

► **bung up** VT SEP **a** (= block up) [+ pipe etc] boucher, obstruer; **my eyes were/his nose was** ~**ed up**‡ il avait les yeux bouffis/le nez bouché or pris; **I'm all** ~**ed up**‡ j'ai un gros rhume (de cerveau) **b** = **bung 2a**

bungaloid‡ ['bʌŋgəlɔɪd] ADJ (pej) de bungalow, genre or style bungalow; ~ **growth** extension f pavillonnaire

bungalow ['bʌŋgələʊ] N (petit) pavillon m (en rez-de-chaussée); (in East) bungalow m

bungee jumping ['bʌndʒi:'dʒʌmpɪŋ] N (NonC) saut m à l'élastique

bunghole ['bʌŋhəʊl] N bonde f

bungle ['bʌŋgl] **1** VT [+ attempt, robbery] rater; [+ piece of work] gâcher, bousiller‡; **he** ~**d it** il s'y est mal pris, il a tout bousillé‡; **it was a** ~**d job** c'était fait n'importe comment **2** VI s'y prendre mal, faire les choses n'importe comment **3** N fiasco m, ratage m

bungler ['bʌŋgləʳ] N bousilleur‡ m, -euse‡ f; **he's a** ~ il bousille‡ tout, il est incompétent

bungling ['bʌŋglɪŋ] **1** ADJ [person] maladroit,

incompétent ; [attempt] maladroit, gauche [2] N (NonC) gâchis m, bousillage*

bunion ['bʌnjən] N (Med) oignon m

bunk [bʌŋk] [1] N [a] (Naut, Rail etc = bed) couchette f [b] (Brit) **to do a ~:** mettre les bouts:̣ or les voiles* [c] ABBR = **bunkum** [2] VI [a] (*: also ~ **down**) coucher, camper (dans un lit de fortune) [b] (Brit: also ~ **off**) mettre les bouts:̣ or les voiles* [3] COMP ► **bunk beds** NPL lits mpl superposés ► **bunk-up*** **to give sb a ~- up** soulever qn par derrière or par en dessous

bunker ['bʌŋkər] [1] N [a] (for coal) coffre m ; (Naut) soute f (à charbon or à mazout) [b] (Golf) bunker m ; (fig) obstacle m [c] (Mil) blockhaus m, bunker m ; (nuclear) ~ bunker m or abri m antinucléaire [2] VT [a] (Naut) [+ coal, oil] mettre en soute ; (Naut) **to ~ a ship** mettre du charbon or du mazout en soute [b] (Golf) **to ~ one's shot** envoyer la balle dans un bunker ; **to be ~ed** (Golf) se trouver dans un bunker ; (:̣ fig) se trouver face à un obstacle, se trouver dans une impasse [3] VI (Naut) charbonner, mazouter

bunkhouse ['bʌŋkhaʊs] N (esp US) bâtiment-dortoir m

bunkum: ['bʌŋkəm] N foutaise(s):̣ f(pl) ; **to talk ~** débiter des balivernes or des foutaises:̣ ; **that's all ~** tout ça c'est des foutaises:̣, tout ça c'est de la blague !*

bunny ['bʌnɪ] N [a] (also ~ **rabbit**) lapin m [b] (US* = pretty girl) jolie fille f or nana* f ; (also ~ **girl**) hôtesse f (dans un club Playboy) → **ski, snow**

Bunsen burner ['bʌnsn'bɜːnər] N bec m Bunsen

bunting[1] ['bʌntɪŋ] N (= bird) bruant m → **reed**

bunting[2] ['bʌntɪŋ] N (NonC) (= material) étamine f (à pavillon) ; (= flags etc) drapeaux mpl, banderoles fpl

buoy [bɔɪ] [1] N bouée f, balise f flottante ; **to put down a ~** mouiller une bouée → **lifebuoy, mooring** [2] VT [+ waterway] baliser ; [+ net] liéger [3] COMP ► **buoy rope** N orin m
► **buoy up** VT SEP (lit) maintenir à flot ; (fig) soutenir ; **they felt ~ed up by their recent successes** leurs récents succès les avaient regonflés*

buoyancy ['bɔɪənsɪ] [1] N [a] [of ship, object] flottabilité f ; [of liquid] poussée f [b] (= lightheartedness) gaieté f, entrain m [c] (Fin) **the ~ of the markets** la fermeté des marchés [2] COMP ► **buoyancy aid** N gilet m de sauvetage ► **buoyancy chamber, buoyancy tank** N (Naut) caisson m étanche

buoyant ['bɔɪənt] ADJ [a] [ship, object] capable de flotter, flottable ; [liquid] dans lequel les objets flottent ; **fresh water is not so ~ as salt water** l'eau douce ne porte pas si bien que l'eau salée [b] (= lighthearted) [person] enjoué, plein d'entrain or d'allant ; [mood] gai, optimiste ; [step] léger, élastique [c] (Fin) [market] soutenu, actif

buoyantly ['bɔɪəntlɪ] ADV [walk, float] légèrement ; (fig) avec entrain

BUPA ['buːpə] N (ABBR = **British United Provident Association**) association britannique d'assurance-maladie privée

buppie* ['bʌpɪ] N yuppie mf noir(e)

bur[1] [bɜːr] N (Bot) bardane f ; (:̣ pej = person) pot m de colle (pej) ; **chestnut ~** bogue f

bur[2] [bɜːr] [1] N (Ling) grasseyement m ; **to speak with a ~** grasseyer [2] VTI **to ~ (one's Rs)** prononcer les R grasseyés

Burberry® ['bɜːbərɪ] N imperméable m (de la marque Burberry)

burble ['bɜːbl] [1] VI [a] [stream] murmurer [b] (pej) [person] marmonner ; **what's he burbling (on) about?** qu'est-ce qu'il est encore en train de raconter ? ; **he ~d on about freedom** il radotait sur le thème de la liberté [2] VT marmonner [3] N [of stream] murmure m

burbling ['bɜːblɪŋ] [1] N (NonC) [a] [of stream] murmure m [b] [of person] jacassements mpl [2] ADJ [person] qui n'arrête pas de jacasser

burbot ['bɜːbət] N (pl **burbot** or **burbots**) lotte f (de rivière)

burbs*, **'burbs*** [bɜːbz] NPL (US) (ABBR = **suburbs**) **the ~** la banlieue

burden ['bɜːdn] [1] N [a] (lit) fardeau m, charge f → **beast** [b] (fig) fardeau m, charge f ; [of taxes, years] poids m ; [of debts] fardeau m ; (Fin, Jur = debt weighing on company's balance sheet or on an estate) encombrement m ; **to be a ~ to** être un fardeau pour ... ; **the ~ of the expense** les frais mpl à charge ; (Jur) **~ of proof** charge f de la preuve ; **the ~ of proof lies** or **rests with him** la charge de la preuve lui incombe, il lui incombe d'en fournir la preuve → **tax** [c] (Naut) jauge f, tonnage m ; **ship of 4,000 tons' ~** navire m qui jauge 4 000 tonneaux [d] (= chorus) refrain m [e] (= chief theme) substance f, fond m ; **the ~ of their complaint** leur principal grief or sujet de plainte
[2] VT (= place burden on) charger (**with** de) ; (= oppress) accabler (**with** de) ; **to ~ the people with taxes** accabler le peuple d'impôts ; **to ~ one's memory with facts** se charger la mémoire or surcharger sa mémoire de faits ; **to be ~ed by guilt** être tenaillé par la culpabilité, être rongé de remords ; **to be ~ed by regret** être accablé de regrets

burdensome ['bɜːdnsəm] ADJ [load] lourd, pesant ; [task, restriction] pénible

burdock ['bɜːdɒk] N bardane f

bureau ['bjʊərəʊ] [1] N (pl **bureaus** or **bureaux**) [a] (esp Brit = writing desk) bureau m, secrétaire m [b] (US = chest of drawers) commode f (souvent à miroir) [c] (= office) bureau m → **information, travel** [d] (esp US = government department) service m (gouvernemental) ; (US) **federal ~** bureau m fédéral [2] COMP ► **Bureau of Indian Affairs** N (US) organisme responsable des affaires amérindiennes ► **Bureau of Prisons** N (US) administration f pénitentiaire

BUREAU OF INDIAN AFFAIRS

Organisme américain responsable des affaires amérindiennes. D'abord rattaché au ministère de la Guerre à sa création en 1824, il était responsable de l'administration des réserves. Aujourd'hui, il relève du ministère de l'Intérieur et a pour mission d'améliorer les conditions de vie des populations autochtones, et en particulier de leur apporter formation et assistance technique pour la gestion de leurs ressources.

bureaucracy [bjʊəˈrɒkrəsɪ] N bureaucratie f

bureaucrat ['bjʊərəʊkræt] N bureaucrate mf

bureaucratese* [ˌbjʊərəʊkræˈtiːz] N jargon m administratif

bureaucratic [ˌbjʊərəʊˈkrætɪk] ADJ bureaucratique

bureaux ['bjʊərəʊz] NPL of **bureau**

burette [bjʊəˈret] N éprouvette f graduée

burg* [bɜːg] N (US pej = town) bled* m, patelin* m

burgeon ['bɜːdʒən] VI (liter) [flower] (commencer à) éclore ; [plant] bourgeonner, se couvrir de bourgeons ; [talent] naître ; [population] être en pleine croissance ; [trade, industry] être en plein essor

burgeoning ['bɜːdʒənɪŋ] ADJ [industry, market, demand, growth, career, popularity] en plein essor ; [population] en pleine croissance ; [numbers, costs, debt] croissant ; **the ~ pacifist movement** le mouvement pacifiste en plein essor ; **a young man with ~ talent** un jeune homme dont le talent grandit de jour en jour

burger ['bɜːgər] [1] N hamburger m [2] COMP ► **burger bar** N fast-food m (où l'on sert des hamburgers)

burgess ['bɜːdʒɪs] N [a] (Brit Hist) (= citizen) bourgeois m, citoyen m ; (Parl) député m (représentant au Parlement d'un bourg ou d'une circonscription universitaire) [b] (US Hist) député m

burgh [bʌrə] N (Scot) ville f (possédant une charte)

burgher ['bɜːgər] N (†† or liter) citoyen(ne) m(f)

burglar ['bɜːglər] [1] N cambrioleur m, -euse f → **cat** [2] COMP ► **burglar alarm** N (système m d')alarme f ► **burglar-proof** ADJ [house] muni d'un système d'alarme ; [lock] incrochetable

burglarize ['bɜːgləraɪz] VT (US) cambrioler

burglary ['bɜːglərɪ] N cambriolage m

burgle ['bɜːgl] [1] VT cambrioler, dévaliser [2] VI cambrioler

burgomaster ['bɜːgəˌmɑːstər] N bourgmestre m

Burgundian [bɜːˈgʌndɪən] [1] ADJ bourguignon, de Bourgogne [2] N Bourguignon(ne) m(f)

Burgundy ['bɜːgəndɪ] N [a] (Geog) la Bourgogne [b] (= wine) **burgundy** bourgogne m

burial ['berɪəl] [1] N (= interment) enterrement m, inhumation f ; (religious) sépulture f ; (= ceremony) funérailles fpl, obsèques fpl ; [of hopes etc] mort f, fin f ; **Christian ~** sépulture f chrétienne ; **~ at sea** funérailles fpl en mer [2] COMP ► **burial ground** N cimetière m ► **burial mound** N tumulus m ► **burial place** N lieu m de sépulture ► **burial service** N office m des morts, service m funèbre ► **burial vault** N tombeau m

burin ['bjʊərɪn] N burin m (à graver)

burk: [bɜːk] N (Brit) = **berk**

burke [bɜːk] VT (= suppress) [+ scandal] étouffer ; (= shelve) [+ question] escamoter

Burkina-Faso [bɜːˈkiːnəˈfæsəʊ] N le Burkina-Faso

burlap ['bɜːlæp] N (esp US) toile f d'emballage, toile f à sac

burlesque [bɜːˈlesk] [1] N [a] (= parody) [of book, poem etc] parodie f ; [of society, way of life] caricature f [b] (NonC: Literat) (genre m) burlesque m [c] (US = striptease) revue f déshabillée (souvent vulgaire) [2] ADJ [poem etc] burlesque ; [description] caricatural [3] VT (= make ridiculous) tourner en ridicule ; (= parody) [+ book, author] parodier

burly ['bɜːlɪ] ADJ de forte carrure, solidement charpenté ; **a big ~ fellow*** un grand costaud* ; **a ~ policeman** un grand gaillard d'agent

Burma ['bɜːmə] N la Birmanie

Burmese [bɜːˈmiːz] [1] ADJ birman, de Birmanie ; **the ~ Empire** l'Empire m birman [2] N [a] (pl inv) Birman(e) m(f) [b] (Ling) birman m [3] COMP ► **Burmese cat** N (chat m) birman m

burn[1] [bɜːn] (vb: pret, ptp **burned** or (Brit) **burnt**) [1] N [a] (Med) brûlure f ; **cigarette ~** brûlure f de cigarette → **degree** [b] (Space) [of rocket] (durée f de) combustion f [2] VT [a] (gen) brûler ; [+ town, building] incendier, mettre le feu à ; **to ~ to a cinder** or **crisp** carboniser, calciner ; **to be ~t to death** être brûlé vif, mourir carbonisé ; **to be ~t alive** être brûlé vif ; **to be ~t at the stake** être brûlé sur le bûcher ; **to ~ o.s.** se brûler ; **to ~ one's finger** se brûler le doigt ; **he ~ed a hole in his coat with a cigarette** il a fait un trou à son manteau avec une cigarette ; (fig) **you could ~ your fingers over this** vous risquez de vous brûler les doigts dans cette affaire ; (fig) **to get ~ed** se brûler les doigts ; (fig) **money ~s a hole in my pocket** l'argent me fond dans les mains ; (fig) **to ~ one's boats/one's bridges**

brûler ses vaisseaux/les ponts; (fig) **to ~ the candle at both ends** brûler la chandelle par les deux bouts → **midnight**

[b] (Culin) [+ meat, toast, cakes] laisser brûler; [+ sauce, milk] laisser attacher

[c] [acid] brûler, ronger; [sun] [+ person, skin] brûler; **delicious curries which won't ~ your throat** de délicieux currys qui ne vous emporteront pas la bouche

[3] VI [a] [wood, meat, cakes etc] brûler; [milk, sauce] attacher; **you left all the lights ~ing** vous avez laissé toutes les lumières allumées; **her skin ~s easily** elle a la peau facilement brûlée par le soleil, elle attrape facilement des coups de soleil; **my head is ~ing** j'ai la tête brûlante; **his wound was ~ing** la blessure le cuisait; **his face was ~ing with cold** le froid lui brûlait le visage; (from heat, embarrassment) **her face was ~ing** elle était cramoisie

[b] [person] (lit) être brûlé vif; (fig) brûler (**with** de); **he was ~ing to get his revenge** or **~ing for revenge** il brûlait (du désir) de se venger; **he was ~ing with ambition** il brûlait d'ambition

[c] **acid ~s into metal** l'acide ronge le métal; (fig) **the date ~ed into his memory** la date grava dans sa mémoire

[d] (Space) [rocket] brûler

[4] COMP ► **burns unit** N (Med) service m des grands brûlés

► **burn away** [1] VI [a] (= go on burning) **the fire was ~ing away** le feu flambait or brûlait bien [b] (= be consumed) se consumer [2] VT SEP détruire (par le feu); [+ paint] brûler (au chalumeau)

► **burn down** [1] VI [a] [house etc] brûler complètement, être réduit en cendres [b] [fire, candle] baisser [2] VT SEP [+ building] incendier; **the house was ~t down** la maison a été réduite en cendres or calcinée

► **burn off** VT SEP [+ paint etc] brûler (au chalumeau)

► **burn out** [1] VI [fire, candle] s'éteindre; [light bulb] griller, sauter [2] VT SEP [a] [+ candle] laisser brûler jusqu'au bout; [+ lamp] griller; **the candle ~t itself out** la bougie est morte; (fig) **he ~t himself out** il s'est usé (à force de travail) [b] (= force out by fire) [+ enemy troops etc] forcer à sortir en mettant le feu; **they were ~t out of house and home** un incendie a détruit leur maison avec tout ce qu'ils possédaient [3] **~out** N → **burnout**

► **burn up** [1] VI [a] [fire etc] flamber, monter [b] [rocket etc in atmosphere] se volatiliser, se désintégrer [2] VT SEP [a] [+ rubbish] brûler [b] **~ed up with envy** mort de jalousie [c] (US* = make angry) foutre en rogne*

burn² [bɜːn] N (Scot) ruisseau m

burner ['bɜːnəʳ] N [of gas cooker] brûleur m; [of lamp] bec m (de gaz) → **back, Bunsen burner, charcoal, front**

Burnham scale ['bɜːnəm,skeɪl] N (Brit Scol Admin) grille f indiciaire des enseignants

burning ['bɜːnɪŋ] [1] ADJ [a] (= on fire) [town, forest] en flammes; [fire, candle] allumé; [coals] ardent; [feeling] cuisant; **the ~ bush** le buisson ardent; **with a ~ face** (from shame) le rouge au front; (from embarrassment) le rouge aux joues [b] (fig) [thirst, fever] brûlant; [faith] ardent, intense; [indignation] violent; [words] véhément, passionné; [topic] brûlant, passionnant; **a ~ question** une question brûlante; **it's a ~* shame that ...** c'est une honte or un scandale que ... (+ subj) [2] N [a] **there is a smell of ~** ça sent le brûlé or le roussi; **I could smell ~** je sentais une odeur de brûlé [b] (= setting on fire) incendie m, embrasement m; **they ordered the ~ of the town** ils ont ordonné l'incendie de la ville, ils ont ordonné qu'on mette le feu à la ville

burnish ['bɜːnɪʃ] VT [+ metal] brunir, polir; **~ed hair** (beaux) cheveux mpl brillants; **~ed skin** (belle) peau f dorée; **~ed leaves** feuilles

---

fpl aux reflets dorés; (fig) **to ~ sb's image** redorer le blason de qn, rehausser l'image de qn

burnisher ['bɜːnɪʃəʳ] N (= person) brunisseur m, -euse f; (= tool) brunissoir m

burnous(e), burnoos (US) [bɜː'nuːs] N burnous m

burnout ['bɜːnaʊt] N [a] (Elec) **there's been a ~** les circuits sont grillés [b] (fig) épuisement m

Burns' Night ['bɜːnz,naɪt] N (Brit) fête écossaise à la gloire du poète Robert Burns

┌─────────────────┐
│ **BURNS' NIGHT** │
└─────────────────┘

Fête écossaise commémorant l'anniversaire de la naissance du poète national écossais Robert Burns (1759-1796). À cette occasion, les Écossais se réunissent pour un dîner (Burns' supper) qui comprend traditionnellement du haggis, apporté au son de la cornemuse, et qui se mange accompagné d'une purée de rutabagas et de pommes de terre (neeps and tatties). Après les toasts d'usage, l'assistance lit des poèmes et chante des chansons de Burns.

burnt [bɜːnt] [1] VB pt, ptp of **burn¹** [2] ADJ brûlé, carbonisé ■ (PROV) **a ~ child dreads the fire** chat échaudé craint l'eau froide (PROV); ~ **smell/taste** odeur f/goût m de brûlé [3] COMP ► **burnt almond** N amande f grillée, praline f ► **burnt lime** N chaux f vive ► **burnt offering** N holocauste m ► **burnt orange** ADJ orange foncé inv ► **burnt sacrifice** N = **burnt offering** ► **burnt sienna** N terre f de sienne or d'ombre brûlée ► **burnt sugar** N caramel m ► **burnt umber** N = **burnt sienna**

burp* [bɜːp] [1] VI roter*, faire un renvoi [2] VT **to ~ a baby** faire faire son rot* or son renvoi à un bébé [3] N rot* m, renvoi m [4] COMP ► **burp gun** N (US) (= pistol) pistolet m automatique; (= submachine gun) sulfateuse* f (Mil), mitraillette f

burr [bɜːʳ] N = **bur**

burrow ['bʌrəʊ] [1] N terrier m [2] VI [rabbit] creuser un terrier; [dog] creuser (la terre); **to ~ under** [person] (in earth) se creuser un chemin sous; (under blanket) se réfugier sous; (= feel around in) fouiller sous; (fig) **to ~ into the past** fouiller dans le passé [3] VT creuser; **to ~ one's way underground** (se) creuser (un chemin) sous terre

bursa ['bɜːsə] N (pl **bursas** or **bursae** ['bɜːsiː]) (Anat) bourse f

bursar ['bɜːsəʳ] N [a] (= administrator: gen) intendant(e) m(f); (in private school, hospital) économe mf [b] (Brit = student) (élève mf) boursier m, -ière f

bursary ['bɜːsərɪ] N (Brit) bourse f (d'études)

bursitis [bɜː'saɪtɪs] N hygroma m

burst [bɜːst] (vb: pret, ptp **burst**) [1] N [of shell, bomb] explosion f, éclatement m; [of anger, indignation] explosion f; [of anger, laughter] éclat m; [of affection, eloquence] élan m, transport m; [of activity] vague f; [of enthusiasm] accès m, montée f; [of thunder] coup m; [of applause] salve f; [of flames] jaillissement m, jet m; **to put on a ~ of speed** faire une pointe de vitesse; **a ~ of gunfire** une rafale (de balles); **a ~ of weeping** une crise de larmes [2] ADJ (Med) **blood vessel** vaisseau m éclaté; (Plumbing) **~ pipe** tuyau m éclaté [3] VI [a] [bomb, shell] éclater, faire explosion; [boiler, pipe] éclater, sauter; [bubble, balloon, abscess] crever; [tyre] (= blow out) éclater; (= puncture) crever; [bud] éclore; **to ~ open** [door] s'ouvrir violemment; [container] s'éventrer [b] **to be ~ing (at the seams*)** [bag, room] être plein à craquer (**with** de); **to fill a sack to ~ing point** remplir un sac à craquer; (fig) **to be ~ing with health** déborder de santé; **to be ~ing with impatience** brûler d'impatience; **to be ~ing with pride** éclater d'orgueil; **to be ~ing with joy** déborder de joie; **I was ~ing to**

---

tell you* je mourais d'envie de vous le dire; **to be ~ing*** [person] avoir une envie pressante [c] (= move etc suddenly) se précipiter, se jeter (**into** dans, **out of** hors de) [d] (= begin etc suddenly) **the horse ~ into a gallop** le cheval a pris le galop; **he suddenly ~ into speech/song** il s'est mis tout d'un coup à parler/chanter; **the truth ~ (in) upon him** la vérité lui a soudain sauté aux yeux; **the applause ~ upon our ears** les applaudissements ont éclaté à nos oreilles; **to ~ into tears** fondre en larmes; **to ~ into bloom** [flower] s'épanouir (soudain); **to ~ into flames** prendre feu (soudain); **the sun ~ through the clouds** le soleil a percé les nuages; **the oil ~ from the well** le pétrole a jailli du puits

[4] VT [+ balloon, bubble] crever; [+ tyre] (= blow out) faire éclater; (= puncture) crever; [+ boiler, pipe] faire sauter; **to ~ open** [+ door] ouvrir violemment; [+ container] éventrer; **the river has ~ its banks** le fleuve a rompu ses digues; **to ~ one's sides with laughter*** se tordre de rire; (Med) **to ~ a blood vessel** (se) faire éclater une veine, (se) rompre un vaisseau; (with anger etc) **he almost ~ a blood vessel*** il a failli prendre un coup de sang* or avoir une attaque*

► **burst forth** VI (liter) [person] sortir précipitamment; [sun] surgir

► **burst in** [1] VI entrer en trombe or en coup de vent, faire irruption; **he ~ in (on us/them etc)** il a fait irruption (chez nous/eux etc); **to ~ in on a conversation** interrompre brutalement une conversation [2] VT SEP [+ door] enfoncer

► **burst out** VI [a] **to ~ out of a room** se précipiter hors d'une pièce, sortir d'une pièce en trombe [b] **she's ~ing out of that dress** elle éclate de partout or elle est très boudinée* dans cette robe [c] (in speech) s'exclamer, s'écrier; **to ~ out into explanations/threats** etc se répandre en explications/menaces etc [d] **to ~ out laughing** éclater de rire; **to ~ out crying** fondre en larmes; **to ~ out singing** se mettre tout d'un coup à chanter

bursting ['bɜːstɪŋ] N (Comput) déliassage m

burthen †† ['bɜːðən] = **burden**

burton ['bɜːtn] N (Brit) **he's gone for a ~** il a eu son compte*, il est fichu* or foutu; **it's gone for a ~*** (= broken) c'est fichu* or foutu; (= lost) ça a disparu

Burundi [bə'rʊndɪ] N le Burundi

Burundian [bə'rʊndʌən] [1] ADJ burundais [2] N Burundais(e) m(f)

bury ['berɪ] VT [a] (gen) enterrer; (at funeral) enterrer, inhumer; **to ~ sb alive** enterrer qn vivant; **he was buried at sea** son corps fut immergé (en haute mer); **buried by an avalanche** enseveli par une avalanche → **dead** [b] [+ treasure] enterrer, enfouir; (fig) [+ quarrel] enterrer, oublier; **the dog buried a bone** le chien a enterré un os; (fig) **to ~ one's head in the sand** pratiquer la politique de l'autruche; (fig) **to ~ the hatchet** or (US) **the tomahawk** enterrer la hache de guerre [c] (= conceal) enfouir, cacher; **to ~ o.s. under the blankets** s'enfouir sous les couvertures; **to ~ one's face in one's hands** se couvrir or se cacher la figure de ses mains; **the bullet was buried deep in the woodwork** la balle était fichée profondément dans le bois; **a village buried in the country** un village enfoui or caché or perdu en pleine campagne; **she buried herself in the country** elle est allée s'enterrer à la campagne [d] (= engross) plonger; **to ~ one's head** or **o.s. in a book** se plonger dans un livre; **to ~ o.s. in one's studies** se plonger dans ses études; **buried in one's work** plongé or absorbé dans son travail; **buried in thought** plongé dans une rêverie or dans ses pensées [e] (= plunge) [+ hands, knife] enfoncer, plonger (**in** dans)

►**bury away** VT SEP **to be buried away** être enterré (fig)

bus [bʌs] **1** N (pl **buses**, (US) **buses** or **busses**) **a** bus m, autobus m; (long-distance) autocar m, car m; **all ~es stop here** arrêt m fixe or obligatoire → **double**, **miss¹**, **trolley** **b** ▪ (= car) bagnole* f; (= plane) (vieux) coucou* m **c** (Comput) bus m **2** VI **a** (* = go by bus) prendre l'autobus (or le car) **b** (US*: in café) travailler comme aide-serveur, desservir **3** VT **to ~ children to school** transporter des enfants à l'école en car → **bussing** **4** COMP ► **bus conductor** N receveur m, -euse f d'autobus or de bus ► **bus depot** N dépôt m d'autobus or de bus ► **bus driver** N conducteur m, -trice f d'autobus or de bus ► **bus lane** N (Brit) voie f réservée aux autobus or bus ► **bus pass** N (Brit) carte f d'autobus or de bus ► **bus route** N **the house is/is not on a ~ route** la maison est/n'est pas sur un trajet d'autobus or de bus ► **bus service** N réseau m or service m d'autobus or d'autobus ► **bus shelter** N Abribus® m ► **bus station** N gare f d'autobus; (for coaches) gare f routière ► **bus stop** N arrêt m d'autobus or de bus ► **bus ticket** N ticket m d'autobus or de bus

busbar ['bʌsbɑːʳ] N (Comput) bus m

busboy ['bʌsbɔɪ] N (US) aide-serveur m

busby ['bʌzbɪ] N (Brit) bonnet m à poil (de soldat)

bush¹ [bʊʃ] **1** N **a** (= shrub) buisson m; (fig) **he had a great ~ of hair** il avait une épaisse tignasse → **beat**, **burning**, **rosebush** **b** (= thicket) taillis m, fourré m; (NonC = brushwood) broussailles fpl; (in Africa, Austral) **the ~** le bush; **to take to the ~** partir or se réfugier dans la brousse **2** COMP ► **bush baby** N (Zool) galago m ► **bush jacket** N saharienne f ► **bush-league** ADJ (US Baseball) de catégorie médiocre ► **bush leaguer** N (US Baseball) joueur m de catégorie médiocre; (fig) minus mf ► **bush telegraph** N (lit) téléphone m de brousse; (* fig) téléphone m arabe

bush² [bʊʃ] N (Tech) bague f

bushed [bʊʃt] ADJ **a** * (= exhausted) flapi*, claqué*; (= puzzled) ahuri **b** (Austral) perdu en brousse

bushel ['bʊʃl] N (Brit = measure) boisseau m → **hide¹**

bushfighting ['bʊʃfaɪtɪŋ] N guérilla f

bushfire ['bʊʃfaɪəʳ] N feu m de brousse

bushing ['bʊʃɪŋ] N (esp US: Tech) bague f

Bushman ['bʊʃmən] N (pl **-men**) (in South Africa) Bochiman m, Bushman m

bushman ['bʊʃmən] N (pl **-men**) (in Austral) broussard* m

bushranger ['bʊʃreɪndʒəʳ] N (in Austral) forçat m réfugié dans la brousse, broussard* m; (in Canada, US) trappeur m

bushwhack ['bʊʃwæk] (US) **1** VI se frayer un chemin à travers la brousse **2** VT (= ambush) tendre une embuscade à

bushwhacker ['bʊʃwækəʳ] N (= frontiersman) colon m de la brousse; (= guerilla soldier) guérillero m; (= bandit) bandit m de la brousse; (in Austral = lumberjack) bûcheron m

bushwhacking ['bʊʃwækɪŋ] N (US) = **bushfighting**

bushy ['bʊʃɪ] ADJ [land, ground] broussailleux, couvert de buissons; [shrub] épais (épaisse f); [tree] touffu; [beard, eyebrows, hair] touffu, broussailleux

busily ['bɪzɪlɪ] ADV (= actively, eagerly) activement; (pej = officiously) avec trop de zèle; **to be ~ engaged in sth/in doing** être très occupé or activement occupé à qch/à faire

business ['bɪznɪs] **1** N **a** (NonC = commerce) affaires fpl; **it's good for ~** ça fait marcher les affaires; **to be in ~** être dans les affaires; **to be in the grocery ~** être dans l'alimentation; **to be in ~ for o.s.** travailler pour son propre compte, être à son compte; **to set up in ~ as a butcher** etc s'établir (comme) boucher etc; **to go out of ~** [businessman] fermer; [company] cesser ses activités, fermer; **to put out of ~** [+ company, businessman] faire fermer; **to do ~ with sb** faire des affaires avec qn; **~ is ~** les affaires sont les affaires; **to go to Paris on ~** aller à Paris pour affaires; **to be away on ~** être en déplacement pour affaires; **his ~ is cattle rearing** il a une affaire d'élevage de bestiaux; **his line of ~** sa partie; **what's his line of ~?** ◊ **what line of ~ is he in?*** qu'est-ce qu'il fait (dans la vie)?; **she's in the publishing ~** elle travaille dans l'édition; **to know one's ~** connaître son affaire, s'y connaître; (fig) **to get down to ~** passer aux choses sérieuses; (fig) **now we're in ~!*** maintenant nous sommes prêts!; **all we need is a microphone and we're in ~*** tout ce qu'il nous faut c'est un micro et le tour est joué; **he means ~*** il ne plaisante pas; (lit) **"~ as usual"** « nous restons ouverts pendant les travaux »; (fig) **it's ~ as usual, despite the bomb** la vie continue, en dépit de l'attentat; **it's the ~!*** c'est super!*; **she's the ~!*** elle est vraiment géniale!* → **mix**, **nobody**

b (NonC = volume of trade) **our ~ has doubled in the last year** notre chiffre d'affaires a doublé par rapport à l'année dernière; **most of the shop's ~ comes from women** la clientèle de la boutique est essentiellement féminine; **he gets a lot of ~ from the Americans** il travaille beaucoup avec les Américains; **during the ten days of the fair, ~ was excellent** pendant les dix jours de la foire, les affaires ont très bien marché; **~ is good/booming** les affaires marchent bien/sont prospères; **to lose ~** perdre des clients

c (= commercial enterprise) commerce m, affaire f; **he has a little ~ in the country** il tient un petit commerce or il a une petite affaire à la campagne; **he owns a grocery ~** il a un commerce d'alimentation; **a small ~** une petite entreprise; **a family ~** une entreprise familiale

d (= task, duty) affaire f, devoir m; **the ~ of the day** les affaires courantes; **it's all part of the day's ~** cela fait partie de la routine journalière; (Admin) **the ~ before the meeting** l'ordre m du jour de l'assemblée; **we're not in the ~ of misleading the public** notre propos n'est pas de tromper le public; **it's time the government got on with the ~ of dealing with this nation's problems** il est temps que le gouvernement s'occupe sérieusement des problèmes de la nation; **to make it one's ~ to do sth** se charger de faire qch; **that's none of his ~** cela ne le regarde pas, ce n'est pas ses affaires; **it's your ~ to do it** c'est à vous de le faire; **you've no ~ to do that** ce n'est pas à vous de faire cela; **I really had no ~ being there** or **to be there** je n'avais rien à faire dans cet endroit; **that's my ~ and none of yours** c'est mon affaire et non la vôtre; **my private life is my own ~** je ne veux pas que l'on se mêle de ma vie privée, ma vie privée ne regarde que moi; **mind your own ~!*** mêlez-vous de vos affaires or de ce qui vous regarde!; **I know my own ~** je ne veux pas me mêler de ce qui ne me regarde pas; **to go about one's ~** s'occuper de ses propres affaires; **to send sb about his ~** envoyer promener* qn

e (= difficult job) **finding a flat is quite a ~** c'est toute une affaire de trouver un appartement; **she made a (real) ~ of helping him** elle a fait toute une histoire* pour l'aider; **moving house is a costly ~** cela coûte cher de déménager, les déménagements sont coûteux; **parenting can be a stressful ~** cela peut être stressant d'élever des enfants

f (pej) affaire f, histoire f; (pej) **I'm tired of this protest ~** j'en ai assez de cette histoire de

contestation; **there's some funny ~ going on** il se passe quelque chose de louche or de pas catholique* → **bad**

g **to do its ~*** [animal] faire ses besoins

2 COMP [lunch, meeting, trip] d'affaires ► **business accounting** N comptabilité f d'entreprise ► **business activity** N activité f industrielle et commerciale ► **business address** N [of individual] adresse f professionnelle; [of company] adresse f du siège social ► **Business and Technology Education Council** N (Brit) organisme habilité à conférer des diplômes en gestion, sciences et techniques etc ► **business associate** N associé(e) m(f); **Jones & Co are ~ associates of ours** nous sommes en relations commerciales avec Jones & Cie ► **business card** N carte f de visite (professionnelle) ► **business centre** N centre m des affaires ► **business class** N classe f affaires ► **business college** N école f de commerce ► **business contact** N relation f de travail ► **business cycle** N cycle m économique ► **business day** N jour m ouvrable ► **business deal** N affaire f ► **business district** N centre m d'affaires ► **business end** N (fig) **the ~ end of a knife** le côté opérant or la partie coupante d'un couteau ► **business expenses** NPL frais mpl généraux ► **business girl** N jeune femme f d'affaires ► **business hours** NPL [of shops etc] heures fpl d'ouverture, heures fpl d'ouverture (Can); [of offices] heures fpl de bureau, heures fpl d'ouverture (Can) ► **business letter** N lettre f commerciale ► **business manager** N (Comm, Ind) directeur m, -trice f commercial(e); (Sport) manager m; (Theat) directeur m, -trice f ► **business park** N parc m d'activités ► **business people** NPL hommes mpl et femmes fpl d'affaires ► **business plan** N [of company] plan m de développement ► **business proposition** N proposition f ► **business reply service** N (on envelope) enveloppe f pré-affranchie ► **business school** N = **business college** ► **business sense** N **to have ~ sense** avoir le sens des affaires ► **business studies** NPL (Univ etc) études fpl commerciales or de commerce ► **business suit** N complet m, complet-veston m

businesslike ['bɪznɪslaɪk] ADJ [person] qui agit en professionnel; [firm, transaction] sérieux; [manner, method, style] de professionnel; [appearance] sérieux; **this is a very ~ knife!*** ça c'est un couteau (sérieux)!*

businessman ['bɪznɪsmæn] N (pl **-men**) homme m d'affaires; **big ~** brasseur m d'affaires; **he's a good ~** il a le sens des affaires

businesswoman ['bɪznɪs,wʊmən] N (pl **-women**) femme f d'affaires; **she's a good ~** elle a le sens des affaires

busing ['bʌsɪŋ] N = **bussing**

busk [bʌsk] VI (Brit) jouer (or chanter) dans la rue

busker ['bʌskəʳ] N (Brit) musicien(ne) m(f) ambulant or des rues

busload ['bʌsləʊd] N **a ~ of children** un autobus or un autocar plein d'enfants; **they came by the ~** or **in ~s** ils sont venus par cars entiers

busman ['bʌsmən] N (pl **-men**) (= driver) conducteur m d'autobus; (= conductor) receveur m; (fig) **to take a ~'s holiday** se servir de ses compétences professionnelles en vacances

bussing ['bʌsɪŋ] N ramassage m scolaire (surtout aux USA comme mesure de déségrégation)

bust¹ [bʌst] **1** N **a** (Sculp) buste m **b** (Anat) buste m, poitrine f **2** COMP ► **bust measurement** N tour m de poitrine

bust² [bʌst] **1** ADJ **a** (* = broken) fichu*, foutu* **b** (* = bankrupt) **to go ~** faire faillite; **to be ~** être fauché*, être à sec* **2** N **a** (* = spree) bombe* f, bringue* f; **to go on the**

~ ◊ to have a ~ faire la bombe* *or* la bringue* **b** (*US** = *failure*) fiasco *m* **3** VT **a*** = **burst 4**; **to ~ a gut** (*lit*) attraper une hernie; (*fig*) se donner un mal de chien* (**to do, doing** pour faire); (*US*) **to ~ one's ass** s'éreinter*, se crever le cul‡ (**to do** pour faire) **b*** [*police*] (= *break up*) [+ *crime ring etc*] démanteler; (= *arrest*) [+ *person*] choper*, arrêter; (= *raid*) [+ *place*] perquisitioner; (*esp US* = *demote*) [+ *police officer*] rétrograder **c** (*US**) [+ *horse*] dresser **4** VI* = **burst 3**; **New York or ~!** New York ou la mort! **5** COMP ► **bust-up** N engueulade* *f*; **to have a ~-up with sb** s'engueuler avec qn*
► **bust out*** VI (= *escape*) **to ~ out (of jail)** il s'est fait la malle (de la prison)*
► **bust up*** **1** VI [*friends*] se brouiller, rompre après une engueulade* (**with sb** avec qn) **2** VT SEP (*fig*) [+ *marriage, friendship*] flanquer en l'air* **3** **~-up** N → **bust²**

bustard ['bʌstəd] N outarde *f*

buster‡ ['bʌstər] N **hi, ~!** salut mon pote!*

bustier [buːstɪeɪ] N bustier *m*

bustle¹ ['bʌsl] **1** VI s'affairer, s'agiter; **to ~ about** s'affairer; **to ~ in/out** *etc* entrer/sortir *etc* d'un air affairé; (*fig*) **to be bustling with** [*place, streets etc*] grouiller de ► **bustling 2** N affairement *m*, remue-ménage *m*

bustle² ['bʌsl] N (*Dress*) tournure *f*

bustling ['bʌslɪŋ] **1** ADJ [*person*] affairé; [*place*] bruyant, agité; **~ with life** plein de vie, plein d'animation, trépidant **2** N = **bustle¹ 2**

busty* ['bʌstɪ] ADJ [*woman*] qui a une forte poitrine; **she's rather ~** elle a beaucoup de poitrine, il y a du monde au balcon*

▼ **busy** ['bɪzɪ] **1** ADJ **a** [*person*] (= *occupied*) occupé (**doing** à faire, **with sth** à qch); (= *active*) énergique; **he's ~ cooking** il est en train de faire la cuisine; **he's ~ playing with the children** il est occupé à jouer avec les enfants; **too ~ to do sth** trop occupé pour faire qch; **he was ~ at work** il était tout entier à *or* absorbé dans son travail; **she's always ~** (= *active*) elle n'arrête pas; (= *not free*) elle est toujours prise *or* occupée; **as ~ as a bee** très occupé; **she's a real ~ bee*** elle est toujours à s'activer, elle est débordante d'activité; **to keep o.s. ~** trouver à s'occuper; **to get ~*** s'y mettre **b** [*day*] chargé; [*period*] de grande activité; [*place*] plein de mouvement *or* d'animation; [*street*] passant, animé; [*town*] animé, grouillant d'activité; **a ~ time** une période de grande activité; **to keep a factory ~** fournir du travail à une usine; **the shop is at its busiest in summer** c'est en été qu'il y a le plus d'affluence dans le magasin **c** [*telephone line, room etc*] occupé **2** VT **to ~ o.s.** s'appliquer, s'occuper (**doing** à faire, **with sth** à qch) **3** N (‡ = *detective*) flic* *m* **4** COMP ► **Busy Lizzie** N impatiente *f*, impatiens *f* ► **busy signal** N (*US*) tonalité *f* occupé *inv*

busybody ['bɪzɪˌbɒdɪ] N fouineur *m*, -euse *f*

but [bʌt] **1** CONJ **a** (*coordinating*) mais; **I would like to do it ~ I have no money** j'aimerais le faire, mais je n'ai pas d'argent; **she was poor ~ she was honest** elle était pauvre, mais honnête **b** (*contradicting*) mais; **he's not English ~ Irish** il n'est pas anglais, mais irlandais; **he wasn't singing, ~ he was shouting** il ne chantait pas, plutôt il criait; **poor, ~ happy** pauvre, mais heureux; **she's like her sister, ~ thinner** elle ressemble à sa sœur, mais en plus mince; **not once, ~ twice** pas une fois mais deux **c** (*subordinating*) **I never eat asparagus ~ I remember that evening** je ne mange jamais d'asperges sans me souvenir de cette soirée; **never a week passes ~ she is ill** il ne se passe jamais une semaine qu'elle ne soit malade, il ne se passe jamais une semaine sans qu'elle

soit malade; (*fig*) **it never rains ~ it pours** un malheur n'arrive jamais seul **d** (*emphatic*) **~ that's crazy!** mais c'est insensé!

2 ADV seulement, ne ... que; (*liter*) **she's ~ a child** ce n'est qu'une enfant; **I cannot (help) ~ think** je suis bien obligé de penser, je ne peux m'empêcher de penser; **you can ~ try** (*to sb trying sth*) vous pouvez toujours essayer; (*after sth has gone wrong*) ça valait quand même la peine d'essayer; (*liter*) **if I could ~ tell you why** si je pouvais seulement vous dire pourquoi; (*liter*) **she left ~ a few minutes ago** il n'y a que quelques minutes qu'elle est partie; **Napoleon, ~ to name ~ one, stayed here** Napoléon, pour n'en citer qu'un, a séjourné ici

3 PREP sauf, excepté; **no one ~ me could do it** personne sauf moi ne pourrait le faire, je suis le seul à pouvoir *or* qui puisse le faire; **they've all gone ~ me** ils sont tous partis sauf moi; **who could do it ~ me?** qui pourrait le faire sinon moi?; **he ~ him** personne d'autre que lui; **France won all ~ two of its matches** la France a gagné tous ses matchs sauf deux; **anything ~ that** tout mais pas ça; **they gave us nothing ~ bread to eat** ils ne nous ont donné que du pain à manger; **he's nothing ~ a thief** ce n'est qu'un voleur; **there was nothing for it ~ to jump** il n'y avait plus qu'à sauter; **the last house ~ one** l'avant-dernière maison; **the next house ~ one** la deuxième maison (à partir d'ici), pas la maison voisine mais la suivante; **~ for you/that I would be dead** sans vous/cela je serais mort; **~ for his illness, we'd have gone on holiday** s'il n'avait pas été malade, nous serions partis en vacances; **I could definitely live in Scotland, ~ for the weather** je pourrais tout à fait vivre en Écosse si le temps n'était pas si mauvais

4 N **no ~s about it!** il n'y a pas de mais (qui tienne)! → **if**

butane ['bjuːteɪn] **1** N butane *m*; (*US: for camping*) Butagaz® *m* **2** COMP ► **butane gas** N gaz *m* butane, Butagaz® *m*

butch* [bʊtʃ] **1** ADJ hommasse **2** N gouine* *f* (*hommasse*)

butcher ['bʊtʃər] **1** N **a** (*for meat*) boucher *m*; **at the ~'s** chez le boucher; (*Brit*) **to have a ~'s** (*hook*) jeter un coup d'œil *‡ ── RHYMING SLANG ── **b** (*US* = *candy etc seller*) vendeur *m* ambulant **2** VT [+ *animal*] tuer, abattre; [+ *person*] égorger; (*fig*) massacrer **3** COMP ► **butcher meat** N viande *f* de boucherie ► **butcher's boy** N garçon *m* boucher, livreur *m* (*du boucher*) ► **butcher's shop** N boucherie *f* (*magasin*) ► **butcher's wife** N (*pl* butchers' wives) bouchère *f*, femme *f* du (*or* de) boucher

butchery ['bʊtʃərɪ] N **a** (*NonC*) (*lit*) abattage *m*; (*fig*) boucherie *f*, massacre *m* **b** (= *slaughterhouse*) abattoir *m*

butler ['bʌtlər] **1** N maître *m* d'hôtel, majordome *m* **2** COMP ► **butler's pantry** N office *m* ► **butler's tray** N (petit) plateau *m* (*de service*)

Butlins® ['bʌtlɪnz] N (*Brit*) chaîne de villages de vacances

──── **BUTLINS** ────
Chaîne de villages de vacances proposant logement, restauration et activités de loisirs pour tous les âges et toutes les bourses. Les distractions sont organisées par des animateurs vêtus d'un costume rouge et qui, pour cette raison, sont surnommés « redcoats ».

butt¹ [bʌt] N (*for wine, rainwater etc*) (gros) tonneau *m*

butt² [bʌt] N (= *end*) bout *m*; [*of rifle*] crosse *f*; [*of cigarette*] mégot *m*; (*US** = *cigarette*) clope* *f*; (*US**) (= *bottom*) cul** *m*, arrière-train* *m*

butt³ [bʌt] N (= *target*) cible *f*; (= *earth mound*) butte *f* (de tir); **the ~s** le champ de tir, le polygone (de tir); (*fig*) **to be a ~ for ridicule** être un objet de risée, être en butte au ridicule; **the ~ of a practical joker** la victime d'un farceur

butt⁴ [bʌt] **1** N coup *m* de tête; [*of goat etc*] coup *m* de corne **2** VT **a** [*goat*] donner un coup de corne à; [*person*] donner un coup de tête à **b** (*Tech*) abouter
► **butt in** VI (*fig*) s'immiscer dans les affaires des autres, intervenir; (*speaking*) dire son mot, mettre son grain de sel*; **I don't want to ~ in** je ne veux pas m'immiscer dans la conversation *or* déranger
► **butt into** VT FUS [+ *meeting, conversation*] intervenir dans, s'immiscer dans
► **butt out** VI (*US*) **to ~ out of sth** ne pas se mêler de qch; **~ out!** mêle-toi de ce qui te regarde!*

butter ['bʌtər] **1** N beurre *m*; **he looks as if ~ wouldn't melt in his mouth** on lui donnerait le bon Dieu sans confession → **bread, peanut** **2** VT [+ *bread etc*] beurrer; [+ *vegetables*] mettre du beurre sur **3** COMP ► **butter bean** N (*Brit*) (gros) haricot *m* blanc ► **butter cloth** N mousseline *f* à beurre, étamine *f* ► **butter cooler** N pot *m* à (rafraîchir le) beurre ► **butter dish** N beurrier *m* ► **butter icing** N glaçage *m* au beurre ► **butter knife** N (*pl* butter knives) couteau *m* à beurre ► **butter muslin** N mousseline *f* à beurre, étamine *f*; (= *dress material*) mousseline *f* ► **butter paper** N papier *m* à beurre, papier *m* sulfurisé
► **butter up*** VT SEP (*esp Brit fig*) passer de la pommade* à

butterball* ['bʌtəbɔːl] N (*US*) patapouf* *m*, rondouillard(e) *m(f)*

buttercup ['bʌtəkʌp] N (*Bot*) bouton *m* d'or, renoncule *f* des champs

buttered ['bʌtəd] ADJ [*potatoes*] au beurre

butterfingers ['bʌtəˌfɪŋgəz] N maladroit(e) *m(f)*, manche* *m*; **~!** quel empoté tu fais!*

butterfly ['bʌtəflaɪ] **1** N (*Zool, fig*) papillon *m*; **to have butterflies in one's stomach*** avoir le trac*; (*Brit fig*) **to break a ~ on a wheel** ne pas y aller avec le dos de la cuillère* **2** COMP ► **butterfly bush** N buddleia *m* ► **butterfly effect** N effet *m* papillon ► **butterfly knot** N nœud *m* papillon ► **butterfly net** N filet *m* à papillons ► **butterfly nut** N papillon *m*, écrou *m* à ailettes ► **butterfly stroke** N brasse *f* papillon *inv*

buttermilk ['bʌtəmɪlk] N babeurre *m*

butterscotch ['bʌtəskɒtʃ] N caramel *m* dur (au beurre)

buttery ['bʌtərɪ] **1** ADJ [*taste*] de beurre; (= *spread with butter*) [*bread*] beurré; [*fingers*] couvert de beurre **2** N [*of college, school*] dépense *f*, office *f*

buttock ['bʌtək] N fesse *f*; **~s** [*of person*] fesses *fpl*; [*of animal*] croupe *f*

button ['bʌtn] **1** N **a** [*of garment, door, bell, lamp, fencing foil*] bouton *m*; **chocolate ~s** pastilles *fpl* de chocolat; (*esp Brit*) **Buttons** (*in hotel*) groom *m*, chasseur *m*; **she knew which ~s to press*** **to get what she wanted** elle savait s'y prendre pour obtenir ce qu'elle voulait; **to be (right) on the ~*** avoir (tout à fait) raison **b** (*Bot*) bouton *m* **c** (*US** = *tip of chin*) pointe *f* de menton **2** VT **a** (*also* **~ up**) [+ *garment*] boutonner **b** **to ~ one's lip*** la fermer‡; **~ your lip!** ◊ **~ it!** boucle-la!‡, la ferme!‡ **3** VI [*garment*] se boutonner **4** COMP ► **button-down** ADJ (*lit*) [*collar*] boutonné; (*fig* = *square*) conformiste ► **button lift** N (*Ski*) téléski *m* à perche ► **button mushroom** N (petit) champignon *m* de couche *or* de Paris ► **button-through** ADJ [*skirt*] boutonné tout du long; **~-through dress** robe *f* chemisier

buttoned-up* ['bʌtnd‚ʌp] ADJ [person] coincé*

buttonhole ['bʌtnhəʊl] **1** N **a** [of garment] boutonnière **b** (Brit = flower) fleur f (portée à la boutonnière) ; **to wear a ~** avoir or porter une fleur à sa boutonnière **2** VT **a** (fig) [+ person] accrocher* **b** (Sewing) faire du point de boutonnière sur **3** COMP ► **buttonhole stitch** N (Sewing) point m de boutonnière

buttonhook ['bʌtnhʊk] N tire-bouton m

buttress ['bʌtrɪs] **1** N **a** (Archit) contrefort m, éperon m ; (also **flying ~**) arc-boutant m ; (fig) (= defence) défense f, rempart m (**against** contre) ; (= support) pilier m (**of** de) **2** VT (Archit) arc-bouter, étayer ; (fig) [+ argument] étayer, soutenir

butty* ['bʌtɪ] N (Brit dial) sandwich m

buxom ['bʌksəm] ADJ bien en chair, aux formes généreuses

buy [baɪ] (pret, ptp **bought**) **1** VT **a** (= purchase) acheter (**sth from sb** qch à qn, **sth for sb** qch pour or à qn) ; **to ~ sth** s'acheter qch ; **the things that money cannot ~** les choses qui ne s'achètent pas ; **to ~ petrol** prendre de l'essence ; **to ~ a train ticket** prendre un billet de train ; **to ~ a theatre ticket** louer or retenir or prendre une place de théâtre ; **to ~ and sell goods** acheter et revendre des marchandises ; **to ~ a pig in a poke** acheter chat en poche ; **to ~ sth cheap** acheter qch bon marché or pour une bouchée de pain ; (Comm) **to ~ (one's way) into a company** prendre une participation dans une entreprise ; (fig) **the victory was dearly bought** la victoire fut chèrement payée **b** (= bribe) [+ person] acheter, corrompre ; **to ~ one's way into a business** avoir recours à la corruption pour entrer dans une affaire **c** (* = believe) croire ; **he won't ~ that explanation** il n'est pas question qu'il avale* (subj) cette explication ; **they bought the whole story** ils ont avalé* or gobé* toute l'histoire ; **all right, I'll ~ it** (bon,) d'accord or je marche* **d** (= die) **to ~ it*** or **~ the farm*** casser sa pipe* **2** N affaire f ; **that house is a good/bad ~** cette maison est une bonne/mauvaise affaire **3** COMP ► **buy-back** ADJ [price, clause] de rachat ► **buy-back option** N option f or possibilité f de rachat

► **buy back 1** VT SEP racheter **2** **~-back** ADJ → **buy-back**

► **buy in** VT SEP (Brit) [+ goods] s'approvisionner en, stocker ; (St Ex) acquérir, acheter

► **buy into** VT FUS **a** (Comm) [+ business, organization] acheter des parts de ; [+ industry] investir dans **b** (* = believe) [+ set of beliefs, ideas] croire

► **buy off** VT SEP (= bribe) [+ person, group] acheter (le silence de)

► **buy out** VT SEP **1** (Fin) [+ business partner] désintéresser, racheter la part de ; (Mil) **to ~ o.s. out** se racheter (d'un engagement dans l'armée) **2** **~out** N → **buyout**

► **buy over** VT SEP (= bribe) corrompre, acheter

► **buy up** VT SEP acheter tout ce qu'il y a de, rafler*

buyer ['baɪər] **1** N **a** (gen) acheteur m, -euse f, acquéreur m ; **house-/car-~s** les gens mpl qui achètent un logement/une voiture **b** (for business, firm, shop etc) acheteur m, -euse f (professionnel(le)) **2** COMP ► **buyer's market** N marché m acheteur or à la hausse

buying ['baɪɪŋ] **1** N achat m **2** COMP ► **buying group** N centrale f d'achat ► **buying power** N pouvoir m d'achat ► **buying spree** N **to go on a ~ spree** se mettre à dépenser sans compter, faire des folies or de folles dépenses

buyout ['baɪaʊt] N rachat m (d'entreprise) ; **leveraged ~** rachat m d'entreprise financé par l'endettement → **management**

buzz [bʌz] **1** N **a** [of insect] bourdonnement m, vrombissement m

b [of conversation] bourdonnement m, brouhaha m ; **a ~ of approval** un murmure d'approbation **c** (* = telephone call) coup m de fil* ; **to give sb a ~** donner or passer un coup de fil* à qn **d** (Rad, Telec etc = extraneous noise) friture f **e** (* = sensation) **driving fast gives me a ~** ◊ **I get a ~ from driving fast** je prends mon pied quand je conduis vite* ; **it gives you a ~** ◊ **you get a ~ from it** [drug] tu t'éclates quand tu prends ça* **2** ADJ (= trendy) en vogue, dernier cri **3** VI **a** [insect] bourdonner, vrombir **b** [ears] tinter, bourdonner ; **my head is ~ing** j'ai des bourdonnements (dans la tête) **c** [hall, town] être (tout) bourdonnant (**with** de) **4** VT **a** (= call by buzzer) [+ person] appeler (par interphone) ; (US* = telephone) donner or passer un coup de fil* à **b** (Aviat) [+ building] raser ; [+ plane] frôler **5** COMP ► **buzz bomb** N V1 m inv ► **buzz saw** N scie f mécanique or circulaire ► **buzz word*** N mot m à la mode

► **buzz about***, **buzz around*** VI s'affairer

► **buzz off*** VI décamper*, foutre le camp*‡

buzzard ['bʌzəd] N **a** (= falcon) buse f ; (= vulture) urubu m **b** (pej) **old ~** (= man) vieux schnock* ; (= woman) vieille bique‡ f

buzzer ['bʌzər] N **a** (= intercom) interphone m **b** (= factory hooter) sirène f, sifflet m **c** (electronic: on cooker, timer etc) sonnerie f

buzzing ['bʌzɪŋ] **1** N **a** = **buzz 1a, 1b** **b** [in ears] tintement m, bourdonnement m **2** ADJ [insect] bourdonnant, vrombissant ; [sound] confus, sourd

BVDs® [‚biːviːˈdiːz] NPL (US) sous-vêtements mpl (d'homme)

b/w (ABBR = **black and white**) NB

by [baɪ]

1 PREPOSITION	**3** COMPOUNDS
2 ADVERB	

When by is the second element in a phrasal verb, eg go by, put by, stand by, look up the verb. When it is part of a set combination, eg by myself, by the sea, by degrees, by night, surrounded by, look up the other word.

1 PREPOSITION

a = close to à côté de, près de ; **come and sit by me** viens t'asseoir à côté de or près de moi ; **the house by the church** la maison à côté de l'église ; **her cousins are over there, and she's sitting by them** ses cousins sont là-bas et elle est assise à côté (d'eux) ; BUT **sitting by the fire** assis auprès or au coin du feu ; **I've got it by me** je l'ai sous la main

by it and by them, when them refers to things, are translated by à côté alone:
her bag was on the table and her keys right by it son sac était sur la table et ses clés juste à côté

b = past à côté de ; **he rushed by me without seeing me** dans sa précipitation il est passé à côté de moi sans me voir

c = via par ; **which route did you come by?** par où êtes-vous passés ? ; **I went by Dover** je suis passé par Douvres ; **by land and (by) sea** par terre et par mer ; **he came in by the window** il est entré par la fenêtre

d = not later than pour ; **I'll be back by midnight** je serai de retour pour minuit ; **can you do it by tomorrow?** pouvez-vous le faire pour demain ? ; **applications must be submitted by 21 April** les candidatures doivent nous parvenir pour le 21 avril

e in year, on date, on day **by 1990 the figure had reached ...** en 1990, ce chiffre avait atteint ... ; **by 2010 the figure will have reached ...** en 2010, cette somme aura atteint ... ; **by 30 September we had paid out £500** au 30

septembre nous avions payé 500 livres ; **by yesterday it was clear that ...** dès hier on savait que ..., il était déjà clair hier que ... ; **by tomorrow/Tuesday, I'll be in France** demain/mardi, je serai en France → **now, then, time**

f = according to **by my calculations** d'après mes calculs ; **by my watch it is 9 o'clock** il est 9 heures à ma montre ; **by the terms of Article 1** aux termes de l'article 1

g * = for **it's fine** or **all right by me** je n'ai rien contre* ; **if that's okay by you** si ça vous va

h margin of difference de ; **wider by a metre** plus large d'un mètre ; **the bullet missed me by inches** la balle m'a raté de quelques centimètres → **far, half**

i dimensions **a room three metres by four** une pièce de trois mètres sur quatre

j points of compass **south by south west** sud quart sud-ouest ; **south-west by south** sud-ouest quart sud

k in oaths **"I swear by Almighty God to ..."** « je jure devant Dieu de ... » ; **by heck***, **there's money to be made in this business!** fichtre* ! il y a vraiment de l'argent à gagner dans cette affaire !

l method, means, manner à ; **to do sth by hand/by machine** faire qch à la main/à la machine ; **to sell by the metre/the kilo** vendre au mètre/au kilo ; **to pay by the hour** payer à l'heure ; **to rent a house by the month** louer une maison au mois

♦ **by** + -ing en ; **by leaving early he missed the rush** en partant de bonne heure il a évité la foule ; **by saving hard he managed to buy a small flat** en économisant beaucoup, il a réussi à s'acheter un petit appartement

m with means of transport en ; **by bus/car/taxi** en bus/voiture/taxi ; **by plane/rail/train** en avion/train ; **by bicycle** à bicyclette, à vélo

n with agent par ; **he was killed by lightning** il a été tué par la foudre ; **he had been warned by his neighbour** il avait été prévenu par son voisin ; **I was surprised by their reaction** j'ai été surpris par leur réaction ; BUT **he had a daughter by his first wife** il a eu une fille de sa première femme

When there is no clear agent, the active is more natural in French:
he was disappointed by it ça l'a déçu

o = created, written by de ; **a painting by Van Gogh** un tableau de Van Gogh ; **who's it by? c'est de qui ?**

p SET STRUCTURES

♦ **by and by** (= in a minute) dans un instant ; (= soon) bientôt ; **I'll be with you by and by** je suis à vous dans un instant ; **you'll be sorry by and by** tu vas bientôt le regretter, tu ne seras pas long à le regretter ; **by and by we heard voices** au bout d'un certain temps, nous avons entendu des voix → **3**

♦ **by and large** globalement ; **by and large, I still think this is true** globalement, je crois toujours que c'est vrai

♦ **by the way** au fait, à propos ; **by the way, did you know it was Ann's birthday?** au fait or à propos, tu savais que c'était l'anniversaire d'Ann ?

2 ADVERB

a = along, past **he'll be by any minute** il sera là dans un instant ; **a train hurtled by** un train passa à toute allure

3 COMPOUNDS

► **by-and-by*** N (hum) **in the sweet by-and-by** un de ces jours ► **by-election** N élection f (législative) partielle ► **by-law** N (Brit) arrêté m (municipal) ► **by-line** N (Press) signature f (en tête d'un article) ► **by-play** N (Theat) jeu m de scène secondaire ► **by-product** N (Ind etc) sous-produit m, dérivé m ; (fig) sous-produit m, conséquence f (indirecte) ► **by-road** N chemin m détourné, chemin m de traverse ► **by-your-leave** N **without so much** as a **by-your-leave** sans même demander la permission

bye¹ [baɪ] **1** N by the ~ à propos, au fait **2** COMP ► **bye-election** N = by-election → by ► **bye-law** N = by-law → by

bye²* [baɪ] EXCL (ABBR = **goodbye**) au revoir! ; ~ **for now!** à tout à l'heure !

bye-bye* [ˈbaɪˈbaɪ] **1** EXCL au revoir! **2** N (*baby talk*) **to go to ~s** aller au dodo*, aller faire dodo*

Byelorussia [ˌbjeləʊˈrʌʃə] N la Biélorussie

Byelorussian [ˌbjeləʊˈrʌʃən] **1** ADJ biélorusse **2** N Biélorusse mf

bygone [ˈbaɪɡɒn] **1** ADJ passé, d'autrefois ; **in ~ days** dans l'ancien temps, jadis **2** N **let ~s be ~s** oublions le passé, passons l'éponge (là-dessus)

BYO [ˌbiːwaɪˈəʊ] N (*Austral*) (ABBR = **bring your own**) *restaurant non autorisé à vendre de l'alcool où l'on peut apporter son propre vin, etc*

BYOB [ˌbiːwaɪəʊˈbiː] (ABBR = **bring your own bottle** or **beer** or **booze**) apportez à boire

bypass [ˈbaɪpɑːs] **1** N **a** (= *road*) route f or bretelle f de contournement ; **the Carlisle ~** la route qui contourne Carlisle **b** (*Tech = pipe etc*) conduit m de dérivation, by-pass m inv **c** (*Elec*) dérivation f, by-pass m inv **d** (*Med*) pontage m ; (*fig*) **he's had a charisma ~*** il est totalement dépourvu de charme ; **he's had a humour ~*** il n'a pas le sens de l'humour **2** VT **a** [+ *town, village*] contourner, éviter **b** [+ *source of supply, material*] éviter d'utiliser, se passer de ; [+ *part of programme, method*] omettre ; [+ *regulations*] contourner ; (*fig*) **he ~ed his foreman and went straight to see**

the manager il est allé trouver le directeur sans passer par le contremaître **3** COMP ► **bypass operation** N (*Med*) pontage m ► **bypass surgery** N (*NonC*) = bypass operation

byre [ˈbaɪəʳ] N (*dial*) étable f

bystander [ˈbaɪˌstændəʳ] N spectateur m, -trice f

byte [baɪt] N (*Comput*) octet m

byway [ˈbaɪweɪ] N chemin m (écarté) ; (*fig*) [*of subject*] élément m annexe → highway

byword [ˈbaɪwɜːd] N (*Brit*) **he** or **his name was a ~ for meanness** son nom était devenu synonyme d'avarice

Byzantine [baɪˈzæntaɪn] ADJ byzantin, de Byzance

Byzantium [baɪˈzæntɪəm] N Byzance

C

C, c [si:] **1** N **a** (= letter) C, c m; **C for Charlie** ≈ C comme Camille **b** (Mus) do m, ut m → **key, middle c** (Comput) C m **d** (Scol = mark) assez bien (12 sur 20) **2 a** (ABBR = **Celsius, Centigrade**) C **b** (US etc) ABBR = **cent c** ABBR = **century d** (ABBR = **circa**) vers **e** ABBR = **centime f** ABBR = **cubic**

CA ABBR = **California**

CA [si:'eɪ] N **a** (ABBR = **chartered accountant**) → **chartered b** (ABBR = **Central America**) → **central**

C/A (Fin) **a** (ABBR = **capital account**) → **capital b** (ABBR = **current account**) → **current c** (ABBR = **credit account**) → **credit**

CAA [,si:eɪ'eɪ] **a** (Brit) (ABBR = **Civil Aviation Authority**) → **civil b** (US) ABBR = **Civil Aeronautics Authority**

CAB [,si:eɪ'bi:] (Brit) (ABBR = **Citizens' Advice Bureau**) → **citizen**

cab [kæb] **1** N **a** (= taxi) taxi m; (horse-drawn) fiacre m; **by ~** en taxi, en fiacre **b** [of lorry, train] (= driver's cab) cabine f **2** COMP ► **cab rank, cab stand** N station f de taxis

cabal [kə'bæl] N cabale f

cabala [kə'bɑːlə] N = **cabbala**

cabalistic [,kæbə'lɪstɪk] ADJ = **cabbalistic**

cabana [kə'bɑːnə] N (US) cabine f (de plage)

cabaret ['kæbəreɪ] N cabaret m; (= floor show) spectacle m (de cabaret)

cabbage ['kæbɪdʒ] **1** N chou m; (fig) **he was little more than a ~: after the accident** il n'était plus qu'un légume* après l'accident **2** COMP ► **cabbage lettuce** N laitue f pommée ► **cabbage rose** N rose f cent-feuilles ► **cabbage tree** N palmiste m ► **cabbage white (butterfly)** N piéride f du chou

cabbala [kə'bɑːlə] N cabale f (juive)

cabbalistic [,kæbə'lɪstɪk] ADJ cabalistique

cabbie*, cabby* ['kæbɪ], **cabdriver** ['kæb,draɪvə'] N [of taxi] chauffeur m (de taxi), taxi* m; [of horse-drawn cab] cocher m

caber ['keɪbə'] N (Scot Sport) tronc m; **to toss the ~** lancer le tronc; **tossing the ~** le lancement du tronc

cabin ['kæbɪn] **1** N (= hut) cabane f, hutte f; [of boat] cabine f; (Rail = signal box) cabine f d'aiguillage; [of lorry, train] (= driver's cabin) cabine f → **log¹ 2** COMP ► **cabin boy** N (Naut) mousse m ► **cabin class** N (Naut) deuxième classe f ► **cabin crew** N (Aviat) équipage m ► **cabin cruiser** N cruiser m ► **cabin trunk** N malle-cabine f

cabinet ['kæbɪnɪt] **1** N **a** (= furniture) meuble m (de rangement); (glass-fronted) vitrine f; (= filing cabinet) classeur m → **medicine b** (Brit Parl) cabinet m, ≈ Conseil m des ministres; **to form a ~** former un gouvernement **c** (US Pol) organe qui conseille le Président **2** COMP (Parl) [crisis, decision, post] ministériel ► **Cabinet meeting** N (Parl) réunion f du Cabinet or du Conseil des ministres ► **Cabinet minister** N membre m du Conseil des ministres → **reshuffle**

cabinetmaker ['kæbɪnɪt,meɪkə'] N ébéniste m

cabinetmaking ['kæbɪnɪt,meɪkɪŋ] N ébénisterie f

cable ['keɪbl] **1** N (Elec, Telec, gen) câble m; (Naut = measure) encablure f; (Telec) **by ~** par câble → **overhead 2** VT [+ news] câbler, télégraphier; [sth to sb] qch à qn); [+ city, homes] câbler; **by ~** to sb câbler à qn **3** COMP ► **cable car** N téléphérique m; (on rail) funiculaire m ► **cable-knit** ADJ [sweater] à torsades ► **cable-laying** N pose f de câbles; **~-laying ship** câblier m ► **cable railway** N funiculaire m ► **cable release** N (Phot) déclencheur m souple ► **cable stitch** N (Knitting) point m de torsade ► **cable television** N télévision f par câble

cablecast ['keɪblkɑːst] (TV) **1** N émission f de télévision par câble **2** VT transmettre par câble

cablegram† ['keɪblgræm] N câblogramme† m

cablevision ['keɪbl,vɪʒən] N = **cable television**; → **cable**

cableway ['keɪblweɪ] N benne f suspendue

cabling ['keɪblɪŋ] N (NonC) (= cables) câbles mpl; (= process) câblage m

caboodle: [kə'buːdl] N **the whole ~** tout le bazar*, tout le tintouin*

caboose [kə'buːs] N (Brit Naut) coquerie f; (US Rail) fourgon m de queue

cabotage [,kæbə'tɑːʒ] N fait de réserver le trafic intérieur aux transporteurs d'un pays

ca' canny* ['kɔː'kænɪ] EXCL (Scot) doucement!

cacao [kə'kɑːəʊ] N (= bean) cacao m; (= tree) cacaoyer m

cache [kæʃ] **1** N **a** (= place) cachette f; **a ~ of weapons** une cache d'armes **b** (Comput) mémoire f tampon **2** VT mettre dans une cachette **3** COMP ► **cache memory** N (Comput) mémoire f tampon

cachepot ['kæʃ,pɒt, kæʃ'pəʊ] N cache-pot m

cachet ['kæʃeɪ] N (all senses) cachet m

cack: [kæk] N (Brit lit, fig) merde‡ f

cack-handed* [,kæk'hændɪd] ADJ (Brit) maladroit

cackle ['kækl] **1** N [of hen] caquet m; [of people] (= laugh) gloussement m; (= talking) caquetage m, jacasserie f **2** VI [hens] caqueter; [people] (= laugh) glousser; (= talk) caqueter, jacasser

cacophonous [kæ'kɒfənəs] ADJ cacophonique, discordant

cacophony [kæ'kɒfənɪ] N cacophonie f

cactus ['kæktəs] N (pl **cactuses** or **cacti** ['kæktaɪ]) cactus m

CAD [kæd] N (ABBR = **computer-aided design**) CAO f

cad†* [kæd] N goujat m, mufle m

cadaver [kə'deɪvə', kə'dɑːvə'] N cadavre m

cadaverous [kə'dævərəs] ADJ (lit, fig) [complexion] cadavéreux; [appearance] cadavérique

CADCAM [kæd,kæm] N (ABBR = **computer-aided design and manufacture**) CFAO f

caddie ['kædɪ] **1** N (Golf) caddie or caddy m **2** VI **to ~ for sb** être le caddie de qn **3** COMP ► **caddie car, caddie cart** N (= trolley) chariot m; (motorized) chariot m électrique, golfette f

caddish†* ['kædɪʃ] ADJ [person] grossier, mufle; **a ~ thing to do** une muflerie

caddy¹ ['kædɪ] N **a** (also **tea ~**) boîte f à thé **b** (US = shopping trolley) chariot m, caddie® m

caddy² ['kædɪ] N = **caddie**

cadence ['keɪdəns] N (= intonation) modulation f (de la voix); (= rhythm) cadence f, rythme m; (Mus) cadence f

cadenza [kə'denzə] N (Mus) cadence f

cadet [kə'det] **1** N **a** (Mil etc) élève m officier (d'une école militaire ou navale); (Police) élève mf agent de police; (Scol) collégien qui poursuit une préparation militaire **b** (= younger son) cadet m **2** ADJ cadet **3** COMP ► **cadet corps** N (in school) peloton m de préparation militaire; (Police) corps m d'élèves policiers (de moins de 18 ans) ► **cadet school** N école f militaire

cadge* [kædʒ] (Brit) VT **to ~ £10 from** or **off sb** taper* qn de 10 livres; **to ~ a meal from** or **off sb** se faire payer* un repas par qn; **to ~ a lift from** or **off sb** se faire emmener en voiture par qn

cadger ['kædʒə'] N (Brit) parasite m; [of money] tapeur* m, -euse* f; [of meals] pique-assiette mf inv

Cadiz [kə'dɪz] N Cadix

cadmium ['kædmɪəm] N cadmium m

cadre ['kædrɪ] N (Mil, Pol, fig) cadre m

CAE [,si:eɪ'i:] N (ABBR = **computer-aided engineering**) IAO f

caecum, cecum (US) ['si:kəm] N (pl **caeca** ['si:kə]) caecum m

Caesar ['si:zə'] N César m; **Julius ~** Jules César m

Caesarea [,si:zə'rɪə] N Césarée

Caesarean, Caesarian [si:'zɛərɪən] ADJ césarien; (Med) **~ (operation** or **section)** césarienne f

caesium, cesium (US) ['si:zɪəm] N cæsium m

caesura [sɪ'zjʊərə] N (pl **caesuras** or **caesurae** [sɪ'zjʊəriː]) césure f

CAF [,siː'eɪ'ef] (ABBR = **cost and freight**) → **cost**

café ['kæfeɪ] **1** N (Brit) snack(-bar) m **2** COMP ► **café society** N (NonC) le beau monde

cafeteria [,kæfɪ'tɪərɪə] N (gen) cafétéria f; (US Scol) cantine f; (US Univ) restaurant m universitaire

cafetière [,kæfə'tjeər] N cafetière f à piston

caff: [kæf] N = **café**

caffein(e) ['kæfiːn] N caféine f; **~-free** décaféiné

caftan ['kæftæn] N caf(e)tan m

cage [keɪdʒ] **1** N cage f; [of elevator] cabine f; (Min) cage f **2** VT (also ~ **up**) mettre en cage, encager **3** COMP ► **cage(d) bird** N oiseau m en cage or captif

cagey* ['keɪdʒɪ] ADJ [person] (= discreet) cachottier; (= suspicious) méfiant; **she is ~ about her age** elle n'aime pas avouer son âge; **the company was ~ about releasing its results** la compagnie était réticente à divulguer ses résultats

cagily* ['keɪdʒɪlɪ] ADV avec méfiance

cagoule [kə'guːl] N anorak m, K-way® m

cahoots* [kə'huːts] N **to be in ~ (with)** être de mèche (avec)*

CAI [,siː'eɪ'aɪ] N (ABBR = **computer-aided instruction**) EAO m

caiman ['keɪmən] N (pl **-mans**) caïman m

Cain [keɪn] N Caïn m; **to raise ~*** (= make a noise) faire un boucan de tous les diables*; (= make a fuss) faire tout un scandale (**about** à propos de)

cairn [kɛən] N **a** (= pile of stones) cairn m **b** (also ~ **terrier**) cairn m

cairngorm ['kɛəŋɔːm] N **a** (= stone) quartz m fumé **b Cairngorm Mountains** ◊ **Cairngorms** monts mpl Cairngorm

Cairo ['kaɪərəʊ] N Le Caire

caisson ['keɪsən] N (Mil, Naut) caisson m

cajole [kə'dʒəʊl] VT cajoler; **to ~ sb into doing sth** faire faire qch à qn à force de cajoleries

cajolery [kə'dʒəʊlərɪ] N cajoleries fpl

Cajun ['keɪdʒən] (US) **1** ADJ cajun **2** N Cajun mf

cake [keɪk] **1** N **a** gâteau m; (= fruit cake) cake m; (= sponge cake) génoise f, gâteau m de Savoie; (fig) **~s and ale** plaisirs mpl; **it's selling** or **going like hot ~s*** cela se vend comme des petits pains; **it's a piece of ~*** c'est du gâteau*; **he takes the ~*** à lui le pompon*; **that takes the ~!*** ça, c'est le bouquet* or le comble!; **they want a slice of the ~** ◊ **they want a fair share of the ~** ils veulent leur part du gâteau; **you can't have your ~ and eat it** on ne peut pas avoir le beurre et l'argent du beurre → **Christmas, fish**
b [of chocolate] tablette f; [of wax, tobacco] pain m; **~ of soap** savonnette f, (pain m de) savon m
2 VI [mud] sécher, former une croûte; [blood] (se) coaguler
3 VT **mud ~d his forehead** la boue formait une croûte sur son front → **caked**
4 COMP ► **cake mix** N préparation f pour gâteaux ► **cake pan** N (US) moule m à gâteau ► **cake shop** N pâtisserie f ► **cake stand** N assiette f montée or à pied; (tiered) serviteur m; (in shop) présentoir m (à gâteaux) ► **cake tin** N (for storing) boîte f à gâteaux; (Brit: for baking) moule m à gâteaux

caked [keɪkt] ADJ [blood] coagulé; [mud] séché; **his clothes were ~ with** or **in blood/mud** ses vêtements étaient maculés de sang séché/crottés

cakewalk ['keɪkwɔːk] N (Mus) cake-walk m

CAL [,siː'eɪ'el] N (ABBR = **computer-aided learning**) EAO m

Cal. ABBR = **California**

calabash ['kæləbæʃ] N (= fruit) calebasse f, gourde f; (= tree) calebassier m; (Mus) calebasse f (utilisée comme bongo ou maraca)

calaboose* ['kæləbuːs] N (US) taule* f

calabrese [,kælə'breɪzɪ] N brocoli m

Calabria [kə'læbrɪə] N la Calabre

Calabrian [kə'læbrɪən] **1** ADJ calabrais **2** N Calabrais(e) m(f)

calamine ['kæləmaɪn] **1** N calamine f **2** COMP ► **calamine lotion** N lotion f calmante à la calamine

calamitous [kə'læmɪtəs] ADJ [event, decision] calamiteux; [person] infortuné

calamity [kə'læmɪtɪ] N calamité f

calcareous [kæl'kɛərɪəs] **1** ADJ calcaire **2** COMP ► **calcareous clay** N marne f

calcification [,kælsɪfɪ'keɪʃən] N calcification f

calcify ['kælsɪfaɪ] **1** VT calcifier **2** VI se calcifier

calcination [,kælsɪ'neɪʃən] N calcination f

calcine ['kælsaɪn] **1** VT (Ind) calciner **2** VI (Ind) se calciner

calcium ['kælsɪəm] **1** N calcium m **2** COMP ► **calcium chloride** N chlorure m de calcium ► **calcium oxide** N oxyde m de calcium

calculable ['kælkjʊləbl] ADJ calculable

calculate ['kælkjʊleɪt] **1** VT **a** [+ speed, weight, distance, numbers] calculer (also Math); **to ~ the cost of sth** calculer le prix de qch; **he ~d that he would have enough money to do it** il a calculé qu'il aurait assez d'argent pour le faire
b (= reckon, judge) [+ probability, consequence, risk] évaluer; **to ~ one's chances of escape** évaluer les chances qu'on a de s'évader
c (US = suppose) supposer, estimer
d (fig) **it is ~d to do ...** (= intended) c'est destiné à faire ...; **their actions were ~d to terrify farmers into abandoning their land** leurs actions étaient destinées à terrifier les fermiers afin qu'ils abandonnent leurs terres; **this was not ~d to reassure me** (= didn't have the effect of) cela n'était pas fait pour me rassurer; **their statement was hardly ~d to deter future immigrants** leur déclaration n'était certes pas faite pour dissuader de futurs immigrants
2 VI (Math) calculer, faire des calculs; (fig) **to ~ on doing sth** avoir l'intention de faire qch; **he is calculating on delaying the elections until spring** il a l'intention de repousser les élections jusqu'au printemps

► **calculate (up)on** VT FUS (= count on) compter sur; **to ~ (up)on having good weather** compter sur le beau temps

calculated ['kælkjʊleɪtɪd] ADJ [action, decision, insult] délibéré; [gamble, risk] pris en toute connaissance de cause → **calculate**

calculating ['kælkjʊleɪtɪŋ] ADJ **a** (= scheming, unemotional) [person] calculateur (-trice f); **to give sb a ~ look** regarder qn d'un air calculateur; **his eyes were ~ and calm** son regard était calme et calculateur; **a cold and ~ criminal** un criminel froid et calculateur **b** (= cautious) prudent, prévoyant **c** **~ machine** = **calculator a**

calculation [,kælkjʊ'leɪʃən] N **a** (Math, fig) calcul m; **to make a ~** faire or effectuer un calcul; **by my ~s** d'après mes calculs; **after much ~ they decided ...** après avoir fait beaucoup de calculs ils ont décidé ...; **it upset his ~s** cela a déjoué ses calculs **b** (NonC = scheming) attitude f calculatrice; **cold, cruel ~** une attitude calculatrice, froide et cruelle

calculator ['kælkjʊleɪtər] N **a** (= machine) machine f à calculer, calculatrice f; (pocket) calculatrice f (de poche), calculette f **b** (= table of figures) table f

calculus ['kælkjʊləs] N (pl **calculuses** or **calculi**

'kælkjʊlaɪ]) (Math, Med) calcul m → **differential, integral

Calcutta [kæl'kʌtə] N Calcutta

caldron ['kɔːldrən] N = **cauldron**

Caledonia [,kælɪ'dəʊnɪə] N la Calédonie

Caledonian [,kælɪ'dəʊnɪən] **1** ADJ calédonien **2** N (liter) Calédonien(ne) m(f)

calendar ['kæləndər] **1** N **a** calendrier m **b** (= directory) annuaire m; (Brit) **university ~** = livret m de l'étudiant **c** (Jur) rôle m **2** VT (= index) classer (par ordre de date); (= record) inscrire sur un calendrier **3** COMP ► **calendar month** N mois m calendaire ► **calendar year** N année f calendaire

calends ['kæləndz] NPL calendes fpl; (fig) **at the Greek ~** aux calendes grecques

calf[1] [kɑːf] **1** N (pl **calves**) **a** (= young cow or bull) veau m; **a cow in** or **with ~** une vache pleine → **fat b** (also **~skin**) (cuir m de) veau m, vachette f; (for shoes, bags) box(-calf) m **c** [of elephant] éléphanteau m; [of deer] faon m; [of whale] baleineau m; [of buffalo] buffletin m **2** COMP ► **calf love** N amour m juvénile

calf[2] [kɑːf] N (pl **calves**) (Anat) mollet m

caliber ['kælɪbər] N (US) = **calibre**

calibrate ['kælɪbreɪt] VT [+ instrument, tool] étalonner, calibrer; [+ level, amount] calibrer

calibration [,kælɪ'breɪʃən] N étalonnage m, calibrage m

calibre, caliber (US) ['kælɪbər] N (lit, fig) calibre m; **a man of his ~** un homme de cette envergure or de ce calibre

calico ['kælɪkəʊ] N (pl **calicoes** or **calicos**) calicot m; (US) indienne f

Calif. ABBR = **California**

California [,kælɪ'fɔːnɪə] N la Californie

Californian [,kælɪ'fɔːnɪən] **1** ADJ californien **2** N Californien(ne) m(f)

californium [,kælɪ'fɔːnɪəm] N californium m

calipers ['kælɪpəz] NPL (US) = **callipers**

caliph ['keɪlɪf] N calife m

calisthenics [,kælɪs'θenɪks] N (NonC) gymnastique f suédoise

calk[1] [kɔːk] **1** VT [+ shoe, horseshoe] munir de crampons **2** N [of shoe, horseshoe] crampon m

calk[2] [kɔːk] VT [+ drawing, design] décalquer, calquer

▼ **call** [kɔːl] **1** N **a** (= shout) appel m, cri m; **within ~** à portée de (la) voix; **a ~ for help** un appel au secours → **roll**
b [of bird] cri m; [of bugle, trumpet] sonnerie f; [of drum] batterie f
c (also **telephone ~**) coup m de téléphone, coup m de fil*; **to make a ~** téléphoner, donner or passer un coup de téléphone or de fil*; **there's a ~ for you** on te demande au téléphone, il y a un appel pour toi; **I have a ~ for you from London** [operator] on vous appelle de Londres, j'ai un appel pour vous de Londres; **I'm putting your ~ through** [operator] je vous mets en communication; **I want to pay for the three ~s I made** je voudrais régler mes trois communications (téléphoniques) → **local, long**[1], **trunk**
d (= summons, invitation) (also Comput) appel m; [of justice] exigence f; [of conscience] voix f; (Theat = actor's reminder) appel m; (also **curtain ~**) rappel m; (= vocation) vocation f; (Rel: in Presbyterian church) nomination f; (Rel) **to have** or **receive a ~ to ...** être nommé pasteur de ...; **to be on ~** [doctor etc] être de garde; **to give sb an early morning ~** réveiller qn de bonne heure; **I'd like a ~ at 7am** j'aimerais qu'on me réveille (subj) à 7 heures; (Telec, Rad etc) **they put out a ~ for him** on l'a fait appeler, on a lancé un appel à son intention; (Fin) **~ for capital** appel m de fonds; **the ~ of the unknown** l'attrait m de l'inconnu; **the ~ of the sea** l'appel m du large; **the ~ of duty** l'appel m

► LANGUAGE IN USE: **call** 26.3, 27

du devoir; (*euph*) **a ~ of nature** un besoin naturel

[e] (= *short visit: also Med*) visite *f*; **to make** or **pay a ~ on sb** rendre visite à qn, aller voir qn; **I have several ~s to make** (*gen*) j'ai plusieurs choses à faire; (*doctor*) j'ai plusieurs visites à faire; (*Naut*) **place** or **port of ~** (port *m* d')escale *f* → **pay**

[f] (= *demand*) **there have been ~s for new security measures** on a demandé de nouvelles mesures de sécurité; **there's not much ~ for these articles** ces articles ne sont pas très demandés; (*Fin*) **money repayable at** or **on ~/at three months' ~** argent *m* remboursable sur demande/à trois mois; **I have many ~s on my time** je suis très pris or très occupé; **the UN has too many ~s on its resources** on fait trop appel aux ressources de l'ONU; **I have many ~s on my purse** j'ai beaucoup de dépenses or de frais; **to have first ~ on sb's time** avoir la priorité dans l'emploi du temps de qn

[g] (= *need*) **there is no ~ for you to worry** il n'y a pas lieu de vous inquiéter; **there was** or **you had no ~ to say that** vous n'aviez aucune raison de dire cela, vous n'aviez pas à dire cela

[h] (*Bridge*) annonce *f*; (*Cards*) demande *f*; **whose ~ is it?** à qui de parler or d'annoncer?

[2] **VT** [a] [+ *person*] appeler; (*from afar*) héler; [+ *sb's name*] appeler, crier; **to ~ sb in/out/up** *etc* crier à qn d'entrer/de sortir/de monter *etc*; **"hello!" he ~ed** «bonjour!» cria-t-il; **let's ~ it a day!*** ça suffira pour aujourd'hui!; **we ~ed it a day*** at 3 o'clock à 3 heures, on a décidé d'arrêter → **shot, tune**

[b] (= *give name to*) appeler; **to be ~ed** s'appeler; **what are you ~ed?** comment vous appelez-vous?; **they ~ each other by their surnames** ils s'appellent par leur nom de famille; **to ~ sb by its proper name** désigner qch par son vrai nom; **he is ~ed after his father** on lui a donné or il porte le nom de son père; **he ~s himself a colonel** il se prétend colonel; **are you ~ing me a liar?** dites tout de suite que je suis un menteur; **he ~ed her a liar** il l'a traitée de menteuse; **she ~s me lazy and selfish** elle dit que je suis fainéant et égoïste, elle me traite de fainéant et d'égoïste → **name, so, spade**

[c] (= *consider*) trouver, considérer; **would you ~ French a difficult language?** diriez-vous que le français est une langue difficile?; **I ~ that a shame** je trouve que c'est (vraiment) dommage; **that's what I ~ rudeness** c'est ce que j'appelle de la grossièreté; (*agreeing on price*) **shall we ~ it £10?** disons 10 livres?

[d] (= *summon*) appeler, convoquer; (= *waken*) réveiller; **to ~ a doctor** appeler or faire venir un médecin; **~ me at eight** réveillez-moi à huit heures; (*Rad*) **London ~ing** ici Londres; **to ~ the police/an ambulance** appeler la police/une ambulance; **the fire brigade was ~ed** on a appelé les pompiers; **~ me a taxi!** appelez-moi un taxi!; **to ~ a meeting** convoquer une assemblée; **a meeting has been ~ed for Monday** une réunion est prévue lundi; **he felt ~ed to be a teacher** sa vocation était d'enseigner → **case, duty, evidence, witness**

[e] (= *telephone*) appeler; **don't ~ us, we'll ~ you** ce n'est pas la peine de nous appeler, on vous appellera

[f] (*Bridge*) **to ~ three spades** annoncer or demander trois piques; **to ~ game** demander la sortie

[g] (*US Sport*) [+ *game*] arrêter, suspendre

[h] (*phrases*) → **account, arm, banns, bar, being, bluff**

[3] **VI** [a] [*person*] appeler, crier; [*bird*] pousser un cri; **I have been ~ing for five minutes** cela fait cinq minutes que j'appelle; **to ~ (out) to sb** appeler qn; (*from afar*) héler qn

[b] (= *visit: also ~ in*) passer; **she ~ed (in) to see her mother** elle est passée voir sa mère; **he was out when I ~ed (in)** il n'était pas là quand je suis passé chez lui; **will you ~ (in) at**

---

the grocer's? voulez-vous passer or vous arrêter chez l'épicier?; (*Naut*) **to ~ (in) at a port/at Dover** faire escale dans un port/à Douvres

[c] (= *telephone*) appeler; **who's ~ing?** c'est de la part de qui?; **to ~ in sick** téléphoner pour dire qu'on est malade

[4] **COMP** ► **call girl** N call-girl *f* ► **call-in, call-in program** N (*US Rad*) émission *f* à lignes ouvertes ► **call letters** NPL (*US Telec*) indicatif *m* (d'appel) ► **call loan** N (*Fin*) prêt *m* exigible ► **call money** N (*NonC: Fin*) taux *m* de l'argent au jour le jour ► **call number** N (*US*) [*of library book*] cote *f* ► **call option** N (*St Ex*) option *f* d'achat ► **call-out charge, call-out fee** N frais *mpl* de déplacement ► **call-over** N appel *m* nominal; (*Mil*) appel *m* ► **call sign, call signal** N (*Telec*) indicatif *m* (d'appel) ► **call slip** N (*in library*) fiche *f* de prêt ► **call-up** N (*Mil*) (= *military service*) appel *m* (sous les drapeaux), convocation *f*; [*of reservists*] rappel *m*; (*in wartime*) **general ~-up** mobilisation *f* générale, levée *f* en masse; (*Sport*) **to get a ~-up into a squad** être sélectionné pour jouer dans une équipe ► **call-up papers** NPL papiers *mpl* militaires

► **call aside** VT SEP [+ *person*] prendre à part

► **call away** VT SEP **to be ~ed away on business** être obligé de s'absenter pour affaires; **to be ~ed away from a meeting** devoir quitter une réunion

► **call back** (*Telec*) [1] VI rappeler [2] VT SEP rappeler

► **call down** VT SEP [a] [+ *curses*] appeler (**on sb** sur la tête de qn) [b] (*US** = *scold*) enguirlander*, attraper

► **call for** VT FUS [a] (= *summon*) [+ *person*] appeler; [+ *food, drink*] demander, commander; (*fig*) [+ *courage*] exiger, nécessiter; **to ~ for measures against** demander que des mesures soient prises contre; **the situation ~s for a new approach** la situation nécessite or exige une nouvelle approche; **this contract ~s for the development of ...** ce contrat prévoit le développement de ...; **strict measures are ~ed for** des mesures strictes sont nécessaires, il est nécessaire de prendre des mesures strictes; **such rudeness was not ~ed for** une telle grossièreté n'était pas justifiée; **to ~ for sb's resignation** réclamer la démission de qn [b] (= *collect*) **I'll ~ for you at 6 o'clock** je passerai vous prendre à 6 heures; **he ~ed for the books** il est passé chercher les livres

► **call forth** VT SEP (*liter*) [+ *protest*] soulever, provoquer; [+ *remark*] provoquer

► **call in** [1] VI → **call 3b, 3c** [2] VT SEP [a] [+ *doctor*] faire venir, appeler; [+ *police*] appeler; **he was ~ed in to lead the inquiry** on a fait appel à lui pour mener l'enquête [b] [+ *money, library books*] faire rentrer; [+ *banknotes*] retirer de la circulation; [+ *faulty machines etc*] rappeler; **the bank ~ed in his overdraft** la banque l'a obligé à couvrir son découvert or à approvisionner son compte; (*esp Brit fig*) **to ~ in one's chips*** utiliser son influence

► **call off** [1] VI se décommander [2] VT SEP [a] [+ *appointment, trip, wedding*] annuler; [+ *agreement*] rompre, résilier; [+ *match*] (= *cancel*) annuler; (= *cut short*) interrompre; **to ~ off a deal** résilier or annuler un marché; **to ~ off a strike** (*before it starts*) annuler une grève; (*after it starts*) mettre fin à une grève; **they ~ed off their engagement** ils ont rompu leurs fiançailles; **he ~ed off their engagement** il a rompu ses fiançailles [b] [+ *dog*] rappeler; (*fig*) **to ~ off the dogs** cesser ses attaques

► **call on** VT FUS [a] (= *visit person*) rendre visite à, aller or passer voir; (*Comm*) **our representative will ~ on you** notre représentant passera vous voir [b] (= *invoke*) [+ *upon*] **to ~ on sb to do** (= *invite*) prier qn de faire; (= *order*) mettre qn en demeure de faire; **I now ~ on Mr Austin to speak** je laisse maintenant la parole à M. Austin; **to ~ on sb for sth** demander or récla-

---

mer qch à qn; **to ~ on God** invoquer le nom de Dieu

► **call out** [1] VI pousser un or des cri(s); **to ~ out for sth** demander qch à haute voix; **to ~ out to sb** héler qn [2] VT SEP [a] [+ *doctor*] appeler; [+ *troops, fire brigade, police*] faire appel à; **to ~ workers out (on strike)** lancer un ordre de grève [b] (*for duel*) appeler sur le terrain

► **call over** [1] VT SEP appeler; **he ~ed me over to see the book** il m'a appelé pour que je vienne voir le livre [2] **~-over** N → **call**

► **call round** VI **to ~ round to see sb** passer voir qn; **I'll ~ round in the morning** je passerai dans la matinée

► **call up** [1] VT SEP [a] (*Mil*) [+ *reinforcements*] appeler; [+ *troops*] mobiliser; [+ *reservists*] rappeler [b] (*esp US Telec*) appeler (au téléphone), téléphoner à [c] (= *recall*) [+ *memories*] évoquer [d] (*Comput*) **to ~ up a file** ouvrir un fichier [2] **~-up** N → **call**

► **call upon** VT FUS = **call on b**

Callanetics® [ˌkælə'netɪks] N (*NonC*) gymnastique douce caractérisée par la répétition fréquente de légers exercices musculaires

callbox ['kɔːlbɒks] N (*Brit*) cabine *f* (téléphonique); (*US*) ≈ dispositif *m* or borne *f* d'urgence

callboy ['kɔːlbɔɪ] N (*Theat*) avertisseur *m*; [*of hotel*] chasseur *m*, groom *m*

▼ **caller** ['kɔːlə^r] N (= *visitor*) visiteur *m*, -euse *f*; (*Brit Telec*) demandeur *m*, -euse *f*

calligramme, calligram (*US*) ['kælɪɡræm] N calligramme *m*

calligrapher [kə'lɪɡrəfə^r] N calligraphe *mf*

calligraphic [ˌkælɪ'ɡræfɪk] ADJ calligraphique

calligraphy [kə'lɪɡrəfɪ] N calligraphie *f*

calling ['kɔːlɪŋ] N (= *occupation*) métier *m*, état† *m*; (= *vocation*) vocation *f*; **by ~** de son état; **a man dedicated to his ~** un homme qui se consacre entièrement à son métier [b] (*NonC*) [*of meeting etc*] convocation *f* [2] **COMP** ► **calling card** N carte *f* de visite

calliope [kə'laɪəpɪ] N orgue *m* à vapeur

callipers ['kælɪpəz] NPL (*Brit*) [a] (*Math*) compas *m* [b] (*Med*) (*for limb*) gouttière *f*; (*for foot*) étrier *m*; (= *leg-irons*) appareil *m* orthopédique

callisthenics [ˌkælɪs'θenɪks] N (*NonC*) = **calisthenics**

callosity [kæ'lɒsɪtɪ] N callosité *f*

callous ['kæləs] ADJ [a] (*fig*) dur, sans cœur; **~ to** insensible à [b] (*Med*) calleux

calloused ['kæləst] ADJ calleux

callously ['kæləslɪ] ADV [*treat, behave, act, speak*] avec dureté, durement; [*decide, suggest*] cyniquement

callousness ['kæləsnɪs] N [*of person*] dureté *f*; [*of statement*] dureté *f*; [*of behaviour*] froideur *f*, insensibilité *f*; [*of crime*] inhumanité *f*

callow ['kæləʊ] ADJ inexpérimenté, novice; **a ~ youth** un blanc-bec*; **~ youth** la folle jeunesse

callus ['kæləs] N (*pl* **calluses**) cal *m*, durillon *m*

callused ['kæləst] ADJ = **calloused**

calm [kɑːm] [1] ADJ calme; **the weather is ~** le temps est au calme; **the sea was dead ~** la mer était d'huile; **to grow ~** se calmer; **to keep** or **remain ~** garder son calme or sang-froid; **keep ~!** du calme!; **(cool,) ~ and collected** maître (maîtresse *f*) de soi(-même); **on ~ reflection** après avoir réfléchi calmement; (*lit, fig*) **~(er) waters** eaux *fpl* (plus) calmes [2] N (= *calm period*) période *f* de calme or de tranquillité; (*after movement, agitation*) accalmie *f*; (*Naut*) **a dead ~** un calme plat; (*lit, fig*) **the ~ before the storm** le calme qui précède la tempête; (= *calmness*) calme *m*; (*under stress*) calme *m*, sang-froid *m* [3] VT calmer [4] VI [*sea, wind*] calmir (*liter*), se calmer

► **calm down** [1] VI se calmer, s'apaiser; **~ down!** du calme!, calmez-vous! [2] VT SEP [+ *person*] calmer, apaiser

calming ['kɑːmɪŋ] ADJ calmant, apaisant

calmly ['kɑːmlɪ] ADV calmement

calmness ['kɑːmnɪs] N (*of person*) calme *m*; (*under stress*) sang-froid *m*; (*of sea, elements*) calme

Calor gas® ['kæləgæs] N (*Brit*) butane *m*, Butagaz® *m*

caloric ['kælərɪk] [1] ADJ thermique [2] N chaleur *f* [3] COMP ► **caloric energy** N énergie *f* thermique

calorie ['kælərɪ] [1] N calorie *f* [2] COMP ► **calorie-conscious*** ADJ **she's too ~conscious** elle pense trop aux calories ► **calorie-controlled diet** N **to be on a ~controlled diet** suivre un régime basses calories → **low**[1]

calorific [,kælə'rɪfɪk] [1] ADJ calorifique [2] COMP ► **calorific value** N valeur *f* calorifique

calque [kælk] N (*also Ling*) calque *m* (**on** de)

calumniate [kə'lʌmnɪeɪt] VT calomnier

calumny ['kæləmnɪ] N calomnie *f*; (*Jur*) diffamation *f*

calvary ['kælvərɪ] N (= *monument*) calvaire *m*; **Calvary** le Calvaire

calve [kɑːv] VI vêler, mettre bas

calves [kɑːvz] NPL *of* **calf**

Calvinism ['kælvɪnɪzəm] N calvinisme *m*

Calvinist ['kælvɪnɪst] ADJ, N calviniste *mf*

Calvinistic [,kælvɪ'nɪstɪk] ADJ calviniste

calyces ['keɪlɪsiːz] NPL *of* **calyx**

calypso [kə'lɪpsəʊ] N calypso *m*

calyx ['keɪlɪks] N (*pl* **calyxes** *or* **calyces**) (*Bot*) calice *m*

calzone [kæl'tsəʊnɪ] N calzone *f or* pizza *f* soufflée

CAM [kæm] N (ABBR = **computer-aided manufacture**) FAO *f*

cam [kæm] N came *f*

camaraderie [,kæmə'rɑːdərɪ] N camaraderie *f*

camber ['kæmbəʳ] [1] N (*of road*) profil *m*, pente *f* transversale; (*Archit*) courbure *f*, courbure *f*; (*Aviat*) courbure *f*; (*Naut*) (*of deck*) tonture *f* [2] VT [+ *road*] bomber; [+ *beam*] cambrer; (*Naut*) [+ *deck*] donner une tonture à [3] VI [*beam*] être cambré; [*road*] bomber, être bombé

Cambodia [kæm'bəʊdɪə] N le Cambodge

Cambodian [kæm'bəʊdɪən] [1] ADJ cambodgien [2] N [a] Cambodgien(ne) *m(f)* [b] (*Ling*) khmer *m*

Cambrian ['kæmbrɪən] [1] ADJ (*Geol*) [*period*] cambrien [2] COMP ► **Cambrian Mountains** NPL monts *mpl* Cambriens

cambric ['keɪmbrɪk] N batiste *f*

Cambs ABBR = **Cambridgeshire**

camcorder ['kæm,kɔːdəʳ] N caméscope *m*

came [keɪm] VB *pt of* **come**

camel ['kæməl] [1] N (*gen*) chameau *m*; (*also* **she-~**) chamelle *f*; (= *dromedary*) dromadaire *m*; (*also racing ~*) méhari *m* → **straw** [2] COMP (*in colour*) [*coat*] (de couleur) fauve *inv* ► **the Camel Corps** (*Mil*) les méharistes *mpl* ► **camel hair**, **camel's hair** N poil *m* de chameau ♦ ADJ [*brush, coat*] en poil de chameau ► **camel train** N caravane *f* de chameaux

camellia [kə'miːlɪə] N camélia *m*

cameo ['kæmɪəʊ] N [a] camée *m* [b] (*Cine*) ~ (**part** *or* **appearance**) brève apparition *f* (*d'une grande vedette*)

camera ['kæmərə] [1] N [a] appareil *m* (photographique), appareil-photo *m*; (= *movie camera*) caméra *f*; **on ~** filmé, enregistré → **aerial**, **capture**, **colour**, **film** [b] (*Jur*) **in ~** à huis clos [2] COMP ► **camera crew** N (*Cine, TV*) équipe *f* de prise de vues ► **camera obscura** N chambre *f* noire (*appareil*) ► **camera operator** N caméraman *m* (caméramans *pl*), cameraman *m* (cameramen *pl*), cadreur *m*

► **camera-ready copy** N (*Typ*) copie *f* prête à la reproduction ► **camera-shy** ADJ qui déteste être pris en photo

cameraman ['kæmərəmən] N (*pl* **-men**) (*Cine, TV*) caméraman *m* (caméramans *pl*), cadreur *m*; (*on credits*) « prise de vue(s) »

camerawork ['kæmərəwɜːk] N (*NonC: Cine*) prise *f* de vue(s)

Cameroon [,kæmə'ruːn] N le Cameroun

Cameroonian [,kæmə'ruːnɪən] [1] ADJ camerounais [2] N Camerounais(e) *m(f)*

camiknickers ['kæmɪ,nɪkəz] NPL chemise-culotte *f*; (*modern*) teddy *m*

camisole ['kæmɪsəʊl] N caraco *m*

camomile ['kæməʊmaɪl] [1] N camomille *f* [2] COMP ► **camomile shampoo** N shampoing *m* à la camomille ► **camomile tea** N (infusion *f* de) camomille *f*

camouflage ['kæməflɑːʒ] (*Mil, fig*) [1] N camouflage *m* [2] VT camoufler

camp[1] [kæmp] [1] N camp *m*; (*less permanent*) campement *m*; (*fig*) camp *m*, parti *m*; **to be in ~ camper**; **to go to ~ partir camper**; (*fig*) **in the same ~** dans le même camp, du même bord; **to break ~** lever le camp; **to set up ~** installer son camp; (*fig*) s'installer → **concentration, foot, holiday, pitch**[1] [2] VI camper; **to go ~ing** partir camper [3] COMP ► **camp chair** N = **camping chair**; → **camping** ► **camp counsellor** N (*US Scol*) animateur *m*, -trice *f* (*de camp de vacances*) ► **camp follower** N (*fig*) sympathisant(e) *m(f)*; (*Mil*† = *prostitute*) prostituée *f*, fille *f* à soldats*; (*Mil*† = *civilian worker*) civil accompagnant une armée ► **camp ground** N = **camping ground** → **camping** ► **camp meeting** N (*US Rel*) rassemblement *m* religieux (*en campement ou sous un chapiteau*) ► **camp site** N = **camping site** → **camping** ► **camp stool** N = **camping stool** → **camping** ► **camp stove** N = **camping stove** → **camping**

► **camp out** VI camper, vivre sous la tente; (*fig*) **we'll have to ~ out in the kitchen*** nous allons devoir camper or il va falloir que nous campions (*subj*) dans la cuisine

camp[2]* [kæmp] [1] ADJ [a] (= *affected*) [*person, behaviour, talk*] affecté, maniéré; (= *overdramatic*) [*person*] cabotin; [*gestures*] théâtral; (= *affecting delight in bad taste*) qui aime le kitsch, qui fait parade de mauvais goût; (= *fashionable because of poor taste*) kitsch [b] (= *effeminate*) efféminé; (= *homosexual*) [*man*] qui fait pédé‡ or tapette‡; [*manners, clothes*] de pédé‡, de tapette‡; **to be as ~ as a row of tents*** être pédé comme un phoque‡ [2] N (*also* **high ~**) (*of manners*) affectation *f*; (*effeminate*) manières *fpl* efféminées [3] VT **to ~ it up** cabotiner

campaign [kæm'peɪn] [1] N (*Mil, fig*) campagne *f*; **to lead** *or* **conduct** *or* **run a ~ for/against** mener une campagne *or* faire campagne pour/contre → **advertising, election, publicity** [2] VI (*Mil*) faire campagne; (*fig*) mener une *or* faire campagne (**for** pour, **against** contre) [3] COMP ► **campaign worker** N (*Pol*) membre *m* de l'état-major (*d'un candidat*)

campaigner [kæm'peɪnəʳ] N (*Mil*) **old ~** vétéran *m*; (*fig*) **a ~ for/against electoral reform** un(e) militant(e) pour/contre la réforme électorale; **a human rights/peace/ environmental ~** un(e) militant(e) des droits de l'homme/de la paix/de la protection de l'environnement; (*Pol*) **his qualities as a ~** ses qualités en tant que candidat en campagne (électorale)

Campania [kæm'peɪnɪə] N la Campanie

campanile [,kæmpə'niːlɪ] N campanile *m*

campanology [,kæmpə'nɒlədʒɪ] N (*NonC*) art *m* du carillonnement

campbed [kæmp'bed] N (*Brit*) lit *m* de camp

camper ['kæmpəʳ] N (= *person*) campeur *m*,

-euse *f*; (= *van*) camping-car *m*; (*US*) caravane *f* pliante

campfire ['kæmpfaɪəʳ] N feu *m* de camp

camphor ['kæmfəʳ] N camphre *m*

camphorated ['kæmfəreɪtɪd] [1] ADJ camphré [2] COMP ► **camphorated oil** N huile *f* camphrée

camping ['kæmpɪŋ] [1] N camping *m* (*activité*) [2] COMP ► **camping chair** N chaise *f* de camping, chaise *f* pliante ► **Camping gas** N (*Brit* = *gas*) butane *m*; (*US* = *stove*) camping-gaz® *m inv* ► **camping ground**, **camping site** N (*commercialized*) (terrain *m* de) camping *m*; (*clearing etc*) endroit *m* où camper ► **camping stool** N pliant *m* ► **camping stove** N réchaud *m* de camping, camping-gaz® *m inv* ► **camping van** N camping-car *m*, autocaravane *f* → **camp**[1]

campion ['kæmpɪən] N (*Bot*) lychnis *m*

campus ['kæmpəs] [1] N (*pl* **campuses**) (*Univ*) (*gen*) campus *m*; (= *building complex*) campus *m*, complexe *m* universitaire; (*fig*) monde *m* universitaire → **off, on** [2] COMP ► **campus police** N (*US Univ*) vigiles *mpl*

campy‡ ['kæmpɪ] ADJ = **camp**[2] 1

CAMRA ['kæmrə] (*Brit*) (ABBR = **Campaign for Real Ale**) association qui cherche à améliorer la qualité de la bière

camshaft ['kæmʃɑːft] N (*Aut*) arbre *m* à cames

▼**can**[1] [kæn] [1] MODAL AUX VB (*neg* **cannot**, *cond, pret* **could**) [a] (*indicating possibility: in neg improbability*) **the situation ~ change from day to day** la situation peut changer d'un jour à l'autre; **it could be true** cela pourrait être vrai, il se peut que cela soit vrai; **she could still decide to go** elle pourrait encore décider d'y aller; **you could be making a big mistake** tu fais peut-être *or* tu es peut-être en train de faire une grosse erreur; **~ he have done it already?** est-il possible qu'il l'ait déjà fait?; **could he have done it without being seen?** est-ce qu'il aurait pu le faire *or* lui aurait-il été possible de le faire sans être vu?; **~ or could you be hiding something from us?** est-il possible *or* se peut-il que vous nous cachiez (*subj*) quelque chose?; **he could have changed his mind without telling you** il aurait pu changer d'avis sans vous le dire; (**perhaps**) **he could have forgotten** il a peut-être oublié; **it could have been you who got hurt** cela aurait aussi bien pu être vous le blessé; **you can't be serious!** (ce n'est pas possible,) vous ne parlez pas sérieusement!; **that cannot be!**† c'est impossible!; **as big/pretty** *etc* **as ~** *or* **could be** aussi grand/joli *etc* qu'il est possible de l'être; **as soon as ~** *or* **could be** aussitôt *or* dès que possible, le plus vite possible; **he can't have known about it until you told him** (il est) impossible qu'il l'ait su avant que vous (ne) lui en ayez parlé; **she can't be very clever if she failed this exam** elle ne doit pas être très intelligente pour avoir été recalée à cet examen; **things can't be as bad as you say they are** la situation n'est sûrement pas aussi mauvaise que tu le dis

[b] (*stressed, expressing astonishment*) **he CAN'T be dead!** ce n'est pas possible, il n'est pas mort!; **how CAN you say that?** comment pouvez-vous *or* osez-vous dire ça?; **where CAN he be?** où peut-il bien être?; **what CAN it be?** qu'est-ce que cela peut bien être?; **what COULD she have done with it?** qu'est-ce qu'elle a bien pu en faire?

[c] (= *am etc able to*) (je) peux *etc*; **he ~ lift the suitcase if he tries hard** il peut soulever la valise s'il fait l'effort nécessaire; **help me if you ~** aidez-moi si vous (le) pouvez; **more cake? — no, I really couldn't** encore du gâteau? — non, je n'ai vraiment plus faim; **he will do what he ~** il fera ce qu'il pourra, il fera son possible; **he will help you all he ~** il vous aidera de son mieux; **~ you come tomorrow?** pouvez-vous venir demain?; **he couldn't**

► **LANGUAGE IN USE:** **can** 3.1, 3.3, 4, 9.2, 15.4

speak because he had a bad cold il ne pouvait pas parler parce qu'il avait un mauvais rhume; **I could have done that 20 years ago but can't now** il y a 20 ans j'aurais pu le faire mais (je ne peux) plus maintenant; **he could have helped us if he'd wanted to** il aurait pu nous aider s'il l'avait voulu; **he could have described it but he refused to do so** il aurait pu or su le décrire mais il a refusé (de le faire)

[d] (= know how to) (je) sais etc; **he ~ read and write** il sait lire et écrire; **he ~ speak Italian** il parle parler (l')italien; **she could not swim** elle ne savait pas nager

[e] (with verbs of perception) **I ~ see you** je vous vois; **they could hear him speak** ils l'entendaient parler; **~ you smell it?** tu le sens?; **I could see them coming in** je les voyais entrer or qui entraient; **he could hear her shouting** il l'entendait crier

[f] (= have the right to, have permission to) (je) peux etc; **you ~ go** vous pouvez partir; **~ I have some milk?** — **yes, you ~** puis-je avoir du lait? — mais oui, bien sûr; **could I have a word with you?** — **yes, of course you could** est-ce que je pourrais vous parler un instant (s'il vous plaît)? — oui bien sûr; **I could have left earlier but decided to stay** j'aurais pu partir plus tôt, mais j'ai décidé de rester; **I can't go out** je ne peux pas sortir, je n'ai pas le droit de sortir; **I couldn't leave until the meeting ended** il m'était impossible de partir or je ne pouvais pas partir avant la fin de la réunion

[g] (indicating suggestion) **you could try telephoning him** tu pourrais (toujours) lui téléphoner; (indicating reproach) **you could have been a little more polite** tu aurais pu être un peu plus poli; **you could have told me before** tu aurais pu me le dire avant or plus tôt

[h] (= be occasionally capable of) **she ~ be very unpleasant** elle peut (parfois) être très désagréable; **it ~ be very cold here** il peut faire très froid ici, il arrive qu'il fasse très froid ici

[i] (*: "want to) **I could smack him!** je le giflerais!, je pourrais le gifler!; **I could have smacked him** je l'aurais giflé; **I could have wept** j'en aurais pleuré

[2] COMP ► **can-do*** ADJ (US) [person, organization] dynamique

can² [kæn] [1] N [a] (for milk, oil, water, petrol) bidon m; (for garbage) boîte f à ordures, poubelle f; (Brit fig) **(to be left) to carry the ~*** payer les pots cassés

[b] (of preserved food) boîte f (de conserve); [of hair spray, deodorant] bombe f, aérosol m; **a ~ of fruit** une boîte de fruits (en conserve); **a ~ of beer** une boîte de bière; **meat in ~s** de la viande en boîte or en conserve; **a ~ of worms*** un sac de nœuds*; **to open a ~ of worms** ouvrir la boîte de Pandore (liter), déclencher un sac de nœuds*

[c] (Cine) [of film] boîte f; **it's in the ~*** c'est dans la boîte

[d] (US*) (= lavatory) waters mpl, chiottes* fpl; (= buttocks) postérieur* m

[e] (US* = jail) taule* f, prison f

[2] VT [a] [+ food] mettre en boîte(s) or en conserve; **~ned fruit/salmon** fruits mpl/saumon m en boîte or en conserve; **~ned food** ◊ **~ned goods** conserves fpl; (US) **~ned heat** méta® m; (fig) **~ned music*** musique f en conserve* or enregistrée; (Rad, TV) **~ned laughter** rires mpl en conserve or préenregistrés; (fig) **to be ~ned*** (= drunk) être rétamé* or rond*; (US*) **~ it!** ferme-la!*, la ferme!*

[b] (US* = dismiss from job) virer*, renvoyer

[3] COMP ► **can opener** N ouvre-boîtes m inv

Canaan ['keɪnən] N terre f or pays m de C(h)anaan

Canaanite ['keɪnənaɪt] N C(h)ananéen(ne) m(f)

Canada ['kænədə] N le Canada

► LANGUAGE IN USE: cancel 21.4

Canadian [kə'neɪdɪən] [1] ADJ (gen) canadien; [ambassador, embassy] du Canada, canadien [2] N Canadien(ne) m(f) → **French** [3] COMP ► **Canadian elk** N original m ► **Canadian English** N (Ling) anglo-canadien m, anglais m du Canada ► **Canadian French** N (Ling) franco-canadien m, français m du Canada

canal [kə'næl] [1] N [a] canal m [b] (Anat) conduit m, canal m → **alimentary** [2] COMP ► **canal barge**, **canal boat** N chaland m, péniche f ► **the Canal Zone** N (Geog) (Brit: Suez) la zone du canal de Suez; (US: Panama) la zone du canal de Panama

canalization [ˌkænəlaɪ'zeɪʃən] N canalisation f

canalize ['kænəlaɪz] VT canaliser

canapé ['kænəpeɪ] N (Culin) canapé m

canard [kæ'nɑːd] N canard* m, bobard* m

Canaries [kə'nɛərɪz] NPL = **Canary Islands**; → **canary**

canary [kə'nɛərɪ] [1] N [a] (= bird) canari m, serin m [b] (= wine) vin m des Canaries [2] COMP (also = **yellow**) (= couleur) jaune serin inv, jaune canari inv ► **canary grass** N (Bot) alpiste m ► **the Canary Islands**, **the Canary Isles** NPL (Geog) les (îles fpl) Canaries fpl ► **canary seed** N (Bot) millet m

canasta [kə'næstə] N canasta f

Canberra ['kænbərə] N Canberra

cancan ['kænkæn] N (also **French ~**) cancan m

▼**cancel** ['kænsəl] [1] VT [a] [+ reservation, room booked, travel tickets, plans] annuler; (= annul, revoke) [+ agreement, contract] résilier, annuler; [+ order, arrangement, meeting, performance, debt] annuler; [+ cheque] faire opposition à; [+ taxi, coach or car ordered, appointment, party] décommander, annuler; [+ stamp] oblitérer; [+ mortgage] lever; [+ decree, will] révoquer; [+ application] retirer; [+ ticket] (= punch) poinçonner; (= stamp) oblitérer [b] [+ flight, train etc] annuler; (= withdraw permanently) supprimer [c] (Math) [+ figures, amounts] éliminer [d] (= cross out, delete) barrer, rayer [2] VI [tourist etc] se décommander

►**cancel out** VT SEP (Math) [+ noughts] barrer; [+ amounts] annuler, éliminer; (fig) neutraliser; **they ~ each other out** (Math) ils s'annulent; (fig) ils se neutralisent

cancellation [ˌkænsə'leɪʃən] N [of event, order, debt, flight, train, reservation, hotel room] annulation f; [of agreement, contract] annulation f, résiliation f (Jur); [of mortgage] levée f; [of decree, will] révocation f; [of stamp] oblitération f; [of writing, numbers] biffage m; (Math) élimination f; **~ of a cheque** opposition f à un chèque; **~ fee** taxe f d'annulation; **~s will not be accepted after ...** (for travel, hotel) les réservations ne peuvent être annulées après ...; (Theat) les locations ne peuvent être annulées après ...

cancer ['kænsə*] [1] N [a] (Med) cancer m; **she has ~** elle a un cancer; **lung/breast ~** cancer m du poumon/du sein; **his battle against ~** sa bataille contre le cancer [b] (Astron) **Cancer** le Cancer; (Astrol) **I'm (a) Cancer** je suis (du) Cancer → **tropic** [2] COMP ► **cancer-causing** ADJ cancérigène ► **cancer patient** N cancéreux m, -euse f ► **cancer-producing** ADJ = **cancer-causing** ► **cancer research** N cancérologie f; (in appeals, funds, charities) recherche f sur or contre le cancer ► **cancer specialist** N cancérologue mf ► **cancer stick**: N (Brit pej) cigarette f, clope* f

Cancerian [kæn'sɪərɪən] N **to be a ~** être (du) Cancer

cancerous ['kænsərəs] ADJ cancéreux

candelabra [ˌkændɪ'lɑːbrə] N (pl **candelabra** or **candelabras**) candélabre m

candelabrum [ˌkændɪ'lɑːbrəm] N (pl **candelabrums** or **candelabra**) = **candelabra**

candid ['kændɪd] [1] ADJ [person, smile, criticism] franc (franche f), sincère; [report, biography] qui ne cache rien; **he gave me his ~ opinion**

of it il m'a dit franchement ce qu'il en pensait [2] COMP ► **candid camera** N (Phot) appareil m photo à instantanés; (= TV game) la Caméra invisible; (Phot) **a ~ camera shot** un instantané

candida ['kændɪdə] N (Med) candidose f

candidacy ['kændɪdəsɪ] N (esp US) candidature f

candidate ['kændɪdeɪt] N candidat(e) m(f); **to stand as/be a ~** se porter/être candidat; **a ~ for president** un candidat à la présidence; (Ftbl) **they are ~s for relegation** ils risquent la relégation; **the obese are prime ~s for heart disease** les obèses sont particulièrement exposés aux maladies cardiaques; **A-level ~s** ≈ candidats mpl au baccalauréat

candidature ['kændɪdətʃə*] N (Brit) candidature f

candidly ['kændɪdlɪ] ADV [admit, confess] avec franchise; [say, reply] avec franchise, franchement

candidness ['kændɪdnɪs] N franchise f, sincérité f

candied ['kændɪd] [1] ADJ (Culin) [whole fruit] glacé, confit; [cherries, angelica etc] confit [2] COMP ► **candied peel** N écorce f d'orange (or de citron etc) confite

candle ['kændl] [1] N (wax: household, on cakes etc) bougie f; (tallow: tall, decorative) chandelle f; [of church] cierge m; **the game isn't worth the ~** le jeu n'en vaut pas la chandelle; **he can't hold a ~ to his brother** il n'arrive pas à la cheville de son frère → **burn¹**, **Roman** [b] = **candle-power** [2] COMP ► **candle grease** N (from household candle) suif m; (from others) cire f ► **candle pin** N (US) quille f ► **candle-power** (Elec) **a 20 ~-power lamp** une (lampe de) 20 bougies

candlelight ['kændllaɪt] [1] N **by ~** à la lueur d'une bougie [2] COMP ► **candlelight dinner** N = **candlelit dinner**; → **candlelit**

candlelit ['kændllɪt] [1] ADJ [room, restaurant] éclairé à la bougie or aux chandelles [2] COMP ► **candlelit dinner** N dîner m aux chandelles

Candlemas ['kændlmæs] N la Chandeleur

candlestick ['kændlstɪk] N (flat) bougeoir m; (tall) chandelier m

candlewick ['kændlwɪk] N chenille f (de coton)

candour, **candor** (US) ['kændə*] N franchise f, sincérité f

C & W [ˌsiːən'dʌbljuː] (ABBR = **country-and-western**) → **country**

candy ['kændɪ] [1] N sucre m candi; (US) bonbon(s) m(pl); **it's like taking ~ from a baby** c'est simple comme bonjour [2] VT [+ sugar] faire candir; [+ fruit] glacer, confire [3] VI se candir, se cristalliser [4] COMP ► **candy-ass**: N (US) couille molle*: f ► **candy bar** N (US) confiserie f en barre ► **candy-floss** N (Brit) barbe f à papa ► **candy store** N (US) confiserie f (souvent avec papeterie et tabac) ► **candy-striped** ADJ à rayures multicolores ► **candy striper** N (US) jeune fille s'occupant d'œuvres de bienfaisance dans un hôpital

cane [keɪn] [1] N [a] [of bamboo etc] canne f; (for plants) tuteur m; (in basket- and furniture-making) rotin m, jonc m → **sugar** [b] (= walking stick) canne f; [of officer, rider] badine f, jonc m; (for punishment) trique f, bâton m; (Scol) verge f, baguette f; **the schoolboy got the ~** l'écolier a été fouetté or a reçu le fouet [2] VT administer or donner des coups de trique or de bâton à; (Scol) fouetter; (* fig) administrer une bonne volée à [3] COMP canné; [chair, furniture] en rotin ► **cane sugar** N (NonC) sucre m de canne

canine ['kænaɪn] [1] ADJ canin; (Anat) (tooth) canine f [2] COMP ► **canine corps** N (US Police) corps m des maîtres-chiens

caning ['keɪnɪŋ] N **to get a ~** (lit) recevoir la trique ; (Scol) recevoir le fouet, être fouetté ; (* fig) recevoir une bonne volée ; **to give sb a ~ = to cane sb** ; → **cane 2**

canister ['kænɪstəʳ] N boîte f ; **a ~ of teargas** une bombe lacrymogène

canker ['kæŋkəʳ] **1** N (Med) ulcère m ; (gen syphilitic) chancre m ; (Bot, fig) chancre m **2** VT (Med) ronger **3** COMP ► **cankerworm** N ver m

cankerous ['kæŋkərəs] ADJ [sore] rongeur ; [tissue] chancreux

cannabis ['kænəbɪs] N **a** (= plant) chanvre m indien **b** (= resin) cannabine f **c** (= drug) cannabis m

cannel(l)oni [,kænɪ'ləʊnɪ] N (NonC) cannelloni mpl

cannery ['kænərɪ] N (US) fabrique f de conserves, conserverie f

cannibal ['kænɪbəl] ADJ, N cannibale mf, anthropophage mf

cannibalism ['kænɪbəlɪzəm] N cannibalisme m, anthropophagie f

cannibalistic [,kænɪbə'lɪstɪk] ADJ [person, tribe] cannibale ; [practices] de cannibale

cannibalization [,kænɪbəlaɪ'zeɪʃən] N [of machine, product] cannibalisation f

cannibalize ['kænɪbəlaɪz] VT (Tech) [+ machine, car] démonter pour en réutiliser les pièces ; **~d parts** pièces fpl récupérées

cannily ['kænɪlɪ] ADV astucieusement

canning ['kænɪŋ] **1** N mise f en conserve or en boîte **2** COMP ► **canning factory** N fabrique f de conserves, conserverie f ► **canning industry** N industrie f de la conserve, conserverie f

cannon ['kænən] **1** (pl **cannon** or **cannons**) **a** (Mil) canon m → **water b** (Tech) canon m **c** (Brit Billiards) carambolage m **2** VI (Brit Billiards) caramboler ; **to ~ off the red** carambolage la rouge ; (fig) **to ~ into** or **against sth** percuter qch ; (fig) **to ~ into** or **against sb** se heurter à qn **3** COMP ► **cannon fodder** N chair f à canon* ► **cannon-shot** N within **~-shot** à portée de canon

cannonade [,kænə'neɪd] N cannonnade f

cannonball ['kænənbɔːl] **1** N boulet m de canon **2** COMP ► **cannonball serve** N (Tennis) service m boulet de canon

▼ **cannot** ['kænɒt] NEG of **can¹**

canny ['kænɪ] ADJ (= cautious) prudent, circonspect ; (= shrewd) malin (-igne f), futé ; (= careful with money) regardant* (pej), économe ; **~ answer** réponse f de Normand → **ca' canny**

canoe [kə'nuː] **1** N (gen) canoë m ; (= dugout) pirogue f ; (Sport) kayak m → **paddle 2** VI (Sport) faire du canoë-kayak ; (in dug-out) aller en pirogue

canoeing [kə'nuːɪŋ] N (Sport) canoë-kayak m

canoeist [kə'nuːɪst] N canoéiste mf

canon ['kænən] **1** N **a** (Mus, Rel, Tech) canon m ; (fig) canon m, critère m ; **~ of the mass** canon m de la messe **b** (Rel = chapter member) chanoine m **2** COMP ► **canon law** N (Rel) droit m canon

cañon ['kænjən] N (US) = **canyon**

canonical [kə'nɒnɪkəl] ADJ (Rel) canonique, conforme aux canons de l'église ; (Mus) en canon ; (fig) autorisé, qui fait autorité ; (Rel) **~ dress** vêtements mpl sacerdotaux

canonization [,kænənaɪ'zeɪʃən] N (Rel) canonisation f

canonize ['kænənaɪz] VT (Rel, fig) canoniser

canoodle† [kə'nuːdl] VI se faire des mamours*

canopied ['kænəpɪd] ADJ [bed] à baldaquin

canopy ['kænəpɪ] N [of bed] baldaquin m, ciel m de lit ; [of throne etc] dais m ; [of tent etc] marquise f ; (Archit) baldaquin m ; (Aviat) [of

parachute] voilure f ; [of cockpit] verrière f ; (fig) [of sky, heavens, foliage] voûte f

cant¹ [kænt] **1** N **a** (= insincere talk) paroles fpl hypocrites ; (= stock phrases) phrases fpl toutes faites, clichés mpl **b** (= jargon) jargon m, argot m de métier ; **lawyers' ~** jargon m juridique → **thief 2** VI parler avec hypocrisie or affectation

cant² [kænt] **1** N **a** (= slope, steepness) pente f, déclivité f ; (= sloping surface) plan m incliné ; **this wall has a definite ~** ce mur penche très nettement **b** (= jolt) secousse f, à-coup m **2** VI (= tilt) pencher, s'incliner **3** VT (= tilt) incliner, pencher ; (= overturn) retourner d'un coup sec

can't [kɑːnt] (ABBR = **cannot**) → **can¹**

Cantab. (ABBR = **Cantabrigiensis**) de Cambridge

Cantabrian [kæn'teɪbrɪən] ADJ ; **the ~s** ◊ **the ~ Mountains** les (monts mpl) Cantabriques mpl

cantaloup(e) ['kæntəluːp] N cantaloup m

cantankerous [kæn'tæŋkərəs] ADJ irascible

cantata [kæn'tɑːtə] N cantate f

canteen [kæn'tiːn] **1** N **a** (= restaurant) cantine f **b** (Mil) (= flask) bidon m ; (= mess tin) gamelle f **c** **a ~ of cutlery** une ménagère

canter ['kæntəʳ] **1** N petit galop m ; **to go for a ~** aller faire une promenade à cheval (au petit galop) ; (Brit fig) **to win in** or **at a ~*** gagner haut la main, arriver dans un fauteuil* **2** VI aller au petit galop **3** VT mener or faire aller au petit galop

Canterbury ['kæntəbərɪ] **1** N Cantorbéry **2** COMP ► **Canterbury bell** N (Bot) campanule f ► **Canterbury Tales** NPL (Literat) Contes mpl de Cantorbéry

canticle ['kæntɪkl] N cantique m, hymne m ; **the Canticles** le cantique des cantiques

cantilever ['kæntɪliːvəʳ] **1** N (Tech) cantilever m ; (Archit) corbeau m, console f **2** COMP ► **cantilever beam** N poutre f en console ► **cantilever bridge** N pont m cantilever inv

canting ['kæntɪŋ] ADJ (= hypocritical) hypocrite, tartufe

cantle ['kæntl] N troussequin m

canto ['kæntəʊ] N chant m (d'un poème)

canton ['kæntɒn] **1** N (Admin) canton m **2** VT **a** [+ land] diviser en cantons **b** (Mil) [+ soldiers] cantonner

cantonal ['kæntənəl] ADJ cantonal

Cantonese [,kæntə'niːz] **1** ADJ cantonais **2** N **a** (pl inv = person) Cantonais(e) m(f) **b** (Ling) cantonais m **3** **the Cantonese** NPL les Cantonais mpl

cantonment [kən'tuːnmənt] N cantonnement m

cantor ['kæntɔːʳ] N (Rel) chantre m

Cantuar. (Brit Rel) (ABBR = **Cantuariensis**) de Cantorbéry

Canuck* [kə'nʌk] N (often pej) Canadien(ne) m(f) français(e)

Canute [kə'njuːt] N Canut m

canvas¹ [kænvəs] **1** N **a** (Art, Naut, also of tent) toile f ; (Sewing) canevas m ; **under ~** (= in a tent) sous la tente ; (Naut) sous voiles **b** (= painting) toile f, tableau m **2** COMP en or de toile ► **canvas chair** N chaise f pliante (en toile) ► **canvas shoes** NPL (gen) chaussures fpl en toile ; (rope-soled) espadrilles fpl

canvas² ['kænvəs] N = **canvass**

canvaser ['kænvəsəʳ] N (US) = **canvasser**

canvass ['kænvəs] **1** VT **a** (Pol) [+ district] faire du démarchage électoral dans ; [+ person] solliciter la voix or le suffrage de ; (US = scrutinize votes) pointer **b** (Comm) [+ district, customers] prospecter **c** (= seek support of) [+ influential person] solliciter le soutien de ; (= seek opinion of) [+ person] sonder (**on** à propos de) ; **to ~ opinions** (**on sth**) sonder l'opinion

or faire un sondage d'opinion (sur qch) **e** (= discuss) [+ matter, question] débattre, examiner à fond **2** VI **a** (Pol) [candidate] faire campagne ; **to ~ for sb** (Pol) solliciter des voix pour qn ; (gen) faire campagne pour qn **b** (Comm) visiter la clientèle ; (door to door) faire du démarchage **3** N = **canvassing**

canvasser, canvaser (US) ['kænvəsəʳ] N **a** (esp Brit Pol: for support) agent m électoral (qui sollicite les voix des électeurs) ; (US: checking votes) scrutateur m, -trice f **b** (Comm) placier m ; (door to door) démarcheur m ; **"no ~s"** « accès interdit aux colporteurs »

canvassing ['kænvəsɪŋ] N (Pol) démarchage m électoral ; (when applying for job, membership etc) visites fpl de candidature ; (US = inspection of votes) vérification f des votes

canyon ['kænjən] N canyon m, cañon m, gorge f

CAP [,siː'eɪ'piː] N (Pol) (ABBR = **Common Agricultural Policy**) PAC f

cap [kæp] **1** N **a** (= headgear) [of man, woman, boy] casquette f ; [of jockey, judge] toque f ; [of soldier] calot m ; [of sailor] bonnet m ; [of gendarme] képi m ; (= skullcap) calotte f ; [of cardinal] barrette f ; (Univ) **~ and gown** costume m universitaire ; **(fig) ~ in hand to sb** aller quémander qch (auprès) de qn ; (fig) **if the ~ fits(, wear it)** il n'y a que la vérité qui blesse, qui se sent morveux (qu'il) se mouche ; **to set one's ~ at sb†** [woman] jeter son dévolu sur qn ; **~ and bells** marotte f (de bouffon) → **black, feather, nightcap, thinking b** (Brit Sport) **he won his first England ~ against France** il a été sélectionné pour la première fois dans l'équipe d'Angleterre à l'occasion de son match contre la France ; **Davis has won 50 ~s for Wales** Davis compte 50 sélections dans l'équipe du pays de Galles ; **Elwood is the team's only new ~** Elwood est le seul nouveau joueur sélectionné dans l'équipe **c** (= lid, cover) [of bottle] capsule f ; [of pen] capuchon m ; [of tooth] couronne f ; (Aut) [of radiator, tyre-valve] bouchon m ; (Med = contraceptive) diaphragme m ; (Archit) chapiteau m, couronnement m ; [of mushroom] chapeau m → **axle, kneecap, toecap d** (= percussion cap) capsule f fulminante ; (for toy gun) amorce f

2 VT **a** (= put cover on) (gen) couvrir d'une capsule, d'un capuchon etc ; [+ bottle etc] capsuler ; (Mil) [+ shell] visser la fusée de ; (Dentistry) [+ tooth] couronner → **snow b** [+ person] coiffer ; (Univ) conférer un grade universitaire à ; (Brit Sport) **he was ~ped four times for England** il a joué quatre fois dans l'équipe d'Angleterre **c** (= surpass, improve on) [+ sb's words] renchérir sur ; [+ achievements] surpasser ; **he ~ped this story/quotation** il a trouvé une histoire/une citation encore meilleure que celle-ci ; **to ~ it all** pour couronner le tout ; **that ~s it all!*** ça, c'est le bouquet* or le comble ! **d** (= limit) [+ spending, taxes etc] imposer un plafond à, plafonner ; **he has the power to ~ city councils that spend excessively** il a le pouvoir d'imposer des restrictions budgétaires aux conseils municipaux qui dépensent trop → **charge, rate**

cap.* [kæp] N (ABBR = **capital letter**) → **capital**

capability [,keɪpə'bɪlɪtɪ] N **a** aptitude f (**to do, of doing** à faire), capacité f (**to do, of doing** de or à faire) ; **mental ~** aptitudes fpl or capacités fpl intellectuelles ; **within/beyond one's capabilities** dans ses/au-dessus de ses capacités **b** [of machine] potentiel m ; (Mil = range of weapons etc) capacité f ; **NATO's nuclear capabilities** le potentiel or la capacité nucléaire de l'OTAN ; **we have the military ~ to defend the area** nous avons le potentiel or la capacité militaire nécessaire pour défendre cette région ;

► **LANGUAGE IN USE:** **cannot** 16.3, 16.4

they have the ~ to produce their own nuclear weapons ils sont en mesure de produire leurs propres armements nucléaires

▼ **capable** ['keɪpəbl] ADJ [a] [*person*] capable (**of** de) ; [*event, situation*] susceptible (**of** de) ; **he is ~ of great warmth/tenderness** il est capable de (montrer) beaucoup de chaleur/de tendresse ; **he was ~ of murder** il était capable de commettre un meurtre ; **sports cars ~ of 150mph** des voitures fpl de sport pouvant atteindre les 240 km/h ; **a ship ~ of carrying 650 people** un bateau pouvant transporter 650 personnes [b] (= *competent*) capable

capably ['keɪpəblɪ] ADV avec compétence

capacious [kə'peɪʃəs] ADJ [*hall, hotel*] vaste, d'une grande capacité ; [*container*] d'une grande contenance *or* capacité

capacitance [kə'pæsɪtəns] N (*Elec*) capacitance f

capacitor [kə'pæsɪtə²] N (*Elec*) condensateur m

capacity [kə'pæsɪtɪ] [1] N [a] (= *ability to hold, cubic content etc*) [*of container*] contenance f, capacité f ; [*of hall, hotel*] capacité f ; **filled to ~** [*jug*] plein à ras bord(s) ; [*box, suitcase*] bourré ; [*hall, bus etc*] comble, bondé ; **the hall has a seating ~ of 400** la salle a 400 places assises ; **the tank has a ~ of 100 litres** le réservoir a une capacité *or* une contenance de 100 litres [b] (*Elec, Phys*) capacité f [c] (*Ind*) (= *production potential*) capacité f de production *or* productrice ; (= *output, production*) rendement m ; **to work at (full) ~** [*factory*] fonctionner à plein rendement ; (*hum*) **I'm not working at (full) ~ today** je ne suis pas très productif aujourd'hui ; **we are increasing (our) ~** nous augmentons notre capacité de production ; **we haven't yet reached (full) ~** nous n'avons pas encore atteint notre rendement maximum ; **the region's electricity-generating ~** le potentiel de production d'électricité de la région [d] (= *mental ability: also* **capacities**) aptitude f, capacité(s) f(pl) ; **her mental capacities** ses aptitudes *or* capacités intellectuelles ; **~ to do** *or* **for doing sth** aptitude f à faire qch ; **this book is within the ~ of children** ce livre est à la portée des enfants ; **he had lost all ~ for happiness** il avait perdu toute aptitude au bonheur *or* à être heureux ; **his ~ for hard work** sa grande aptitude au travail [e] (*frm* = *position, status*) qualité f, titre m ; **in my ~ as a doctor** en ma qualité de médecin ; **in his official ~** à titre officiel ; **in a personal ~** à titre personnel ; **in an advisory ~** à titre consultatif ; **we must not employ him in any ~ whatsoever** il ne faut pas l'employer à quelque titre que ce soit [f] (= *legal power*) pouvoir m légal (**to do** de faire) ; **to have the ~ to do sth** avoir qualité pour faire qch

[2] COMP ► **capacity attendance** N **there was a ~ attendance** c'était plein *or* bondé ► **capacity audience** N **they were hoping for a ~ audience** ils espéraient faire salle comble ► **capacity booking** N **there was a ~ booking** toutes les places étaient louées *or* retenues, on jouait à guichets fermés ► **capacity crowd** N **there was a ~ crowd** il n'y avait plus une place (de) libre ; (*Sport*) le stade était comble

caparison [kə'pærɪsn] (*liter*) [1] N caparaçon m [2] VT [+ *horse*] caparaçonner

cape¹ [keɪp] N (*full length*) cape f ; (*half length*) pèlerine f ; [*of policeman, cyclist*] pèlerine f

cape² [keɪp] [1] N (*Geog*) cap m ; (= *high cape*) promontoire m [2] COMP ► **Cape Canaveral** N le Cap Canaveral ► **Cape Cod** N le cap Cod ► **Cape Coloureds** NPL (*in South Africa*) métis mpl sud-africains ► **Cape Horn** N le cap Horn ► **Cape of Good Hope** N le cap de Bonne-Espérance ► **Cape Province** N province f du Cap ► **Cape Town** N Le Cap

► **Cape Verde** N le Cap-Vert ; **the Cape Verde Islands** N les îles fpl du Cap-Vert

caped [keɪpt] ADJ portant une cape

caper¹ ['keɪpə²] [1] VI (*also* ~ **about**) [*child, elf*] gambader (de joie) [2] N [a] (= *leap, jump*) cabriole f, gambade f [b] (*fig*) **~s** (= *pranks*) farces fpl ; **that was quite a ~*** ça a été une vraie partie de rigolade* ; (= *fuss*) **what a ~!*** quelle histoire ! ; **she served six months in prison for the helicopter ~*** elle a fait six mois de prison pour le coup de l'hélicoptère

caper² ['keɪpə²] [1] N (*Culin*) câpre f ; (= *shrub*) câprier m [2] COMP ► **caper sauce** N sauce f aux câpres

capercaillie, capercailzie [kæpə'keɪlɪ] N grand tétras m, grand coq m de bruyère

Capernaum [kə'pɜːnɪəm] N Capharnaüm

capeskin ['keɪpskɪn] N (*US*) peau f souple pour ganterie

capful ['kæpfʊl] N (= *measure of liquid*) **one ~ to four litres of water** un bouchon (plein) pour quatre litres d'eau

capillary [kə'pɪlərɪ] ADJ, N (*Bio, Bot*) capillaire m

capital ['kæpɪtl] [1] ADJ [a] (*Jur*) capital [b] (= *essential, important*) capital, fondamental, essentiel ; **of ~ importance** d'une importance capitale [c] (= *chief, principal*) capital, principal [d] ~ **letter** majuscule f, capitale f ; ~ **A, B etc** A, B etc majuscule ; **Art/Life with a ~ A/L** l'Art/ la Vie avec un grand A/V [e] († * = *splendid*) épatant*, fameux* [2] N [a] (*also* ~ **city**) capitale f [b] (*Typ: also* ~ **letter**) majuscule f, capitale f [c] (*NonC: Comm, Fin*) (= *money and property*) capital m (en espèces et en nature) ; (= *money only*) capital m, capitaux mpl ; ~ **invested** mise f de fonds ; ~ **and labour** le capital et la main d'œuvre ; (*fig*) **to make ~ out of** tirer parti *or* profit de → **working** [d] (*Archit*) chapiteau m

[3] COMP ► **capital account** N (*Fin, Econ etc*) compte m capital ► **capital allowances** NPL déductions fpl fiscales pour investissements ► **capital assets** NPL actif m immobilisé ► **capital city** N capitale f ► **capital cost** N coût m d'investissement ► **capital equipment** N (*NonC*) biens mpl d'équipement *or* de capital ► **capital expenditure** N dépenses fpl d'investissement ► **capital gains** NPL augmentation f de capital, plus-values fpl (en capital) ; ~ **gains tax** impôt m sur les plus-values (en capital) ► **capital goods** NPL biens mpl d'équipement ► **capital intensive** ADJ [*industry etc*] (à forte intensité) capitalistique ► **capital levy** N prélèvement m *or* impôt m sur le capital ► **capital offence** N crime m capital ► **capital punishment** N peine f capitale, peine f de mort ► **capital reserves** NPL réserves fpl et provisions fpl ► **capital sentence** N condamnation f à mort ► **capital ship** N (*Naut*) grosse unité f de guerre ► **capital stock** N capital m social ► **capital sum** N capital m ► **capital transactions** NPL transactions fpl en capital ► **capital transfer tax** N (*Brit*) impôt m sur le transfert des capitaux

capitalism ['kæpɪtəlɪzəm] N capitalisme m

capitalist ['kæpɪtəlɪst] ADJ, N capitaliste mf

capitalistic [kæpɪtə'lɪstɪk] ADJ capitaliste

capitalization [kə,pɪtəlaɪ'zeɪʃən] N capitalisation f

capitalize [kə'pɪtəlaɪz] [1] VT [a] (*Fin*) [+ *property, plant*] capitaliser ; [+ *company*] constituer le capital social de (*par émission d'actions*) ; (*fig*) capitaliser sur, tirer profit *or* parti de ; (*Fin*) **over-/under-~d** sur-/sous-capitalisé [b] (*Typ* = *put into capitals*) mettre en majuscule(s) [2] VI (*fig*) **to ~ on** (= *circumstances, information*) exploiter, tirer profit *or* parti de ; [+ *talents*] tirer parti de ; (*financially*) monnayer

capitation [kæpɪ'teɪʃən] [1] N (*Fin: also* ~ **tax**) capitation f [2] COMP ► **capitation allowance** N (*Brit Scol*) dotation f forfaitaire par élève (*accordée à un établissement*)

Capitol ['kæpɪtl] N **the ~** (*US*) le Capitole (*siège du Congrès américain*) ; (*Roman Hist*) le Capitole

capitulate [kə'pɪtjʊleɪt] VI (*Mil, fig*) capituler

capitulation [kə,pɪtjʊ'leɪʃən] N [a] (*Mil, fig*) capitulation f [b] (= *summary*) récapitulation f, sommaire m [c] (*Jur*) ~**s** capitulation f

capo ['kæpəʊ] N (*US*) capo m

capon ['keɪpən] N chapon m

cappuccino [kæpʊ'tʃiːnəʊ] N cappuccino m

Capri [kə'priː] N Capri f ; **in ~** à Capri

caprice [kə'priːs] N [a] (= *change of mood*) saute f d'humeur ; (= *whim*) caprice m [b] (*Mus*) capriccio m

capricious [kə'prɪʃəs] ADJ capricieux, fantasque

capriciously [kə'prɪʃəslɪ] ADV capricieusement

Capricorn ['kæprɪkɔːn] N (*Astron, Geog*) le Capricorne ; (*Astrol*) **I'm (a)** ~ je suis (du) Capricorne → **tropic**

caps [kæps] NPL (ABBR = **capital letters**) → **capital**

capsicum ['kæpsɪkəm] N poivron m

capsize [kæp'saɪz] [1] VI se renverser ; (*Naut*) chavirer [2] VT renverser ; (*Naut*) faire chavirer

capstan ['kæpstən] [1] N (*Naut*) cabestan m [2] COMP ► **capstan lathe** N (*Brit*) tour m revolver

capsule ['kæpsjuːl] [1] N (*all senses*) capsule f [2] ADJ [*description, résumé*] succinct

Capt. N (*Mil*) (ABBR = **Captain**) (*on envelope*) ~ **P. Martin** le Capitaine P. Martin

captain ['kæptɪn] [1] N (*Army, US Aviat*) capitaine m ; (*Navy*) capitaine m (de vaisseau) ; [*of Merchant Navy*] capitaine m ; (*Sport*) capitaine m (d'équipe) ; (*US Police: also* **precinct** ~) ≈ commissaire m (de police) de quartier ; (*Brit*) **school** ~ élève (*des classes terminales*) chargé d'un certain nombre de responsabilités ; ~ **of industry** capitaine m d'industrie [2] VT (*Sport*) [+ *team*] être le capitaine de ; (*Mil, Naut*) commander ; (*fig*) diriger

captaincy ['kæptənsɪ] N (*Mil*) grade m de capitaine ; (*Sport*) capitanat m ; (*Mil*) **to get one's** ~ être promu *or* passer capitaine ; (*Sport*) **during his** ~ (**of the team**) quand il était capitaine (de l'équipe)

caption ['kæpʃən] [1] N [a] (*Press*) (= *heading*) sous-titre m ; (*under illustration*) légende f [b] (*Cine*) sous-titre m [2] VT [+ *illustration*] légender, mettre une légende à ; (*Cine*) sous-titrer

captious ['kæpʃəs] ADJ (*liter*) [*person*] chicanier, vétilleux (*liter*) ; [*remark*] critique

captivate ['kæptɪveɪt] VT captiver, fasciner

captivating ['kæptɪveɪtɪŋ] ADJ captivant

captive ['kæptɪv] [1] N captif m, -ive f ; **to take sb** ~ faire qn prisonnier ; **to hold sb** ~ garder qn en captivité ; (*fig*) captiver qn, tenir qn sous le charme [2] ADJ [*person*] prisonnier ; [*animal, bird, balloon, customer*] captif ; **a ~ audience** un public captif ; (*fig*) **to be** ~ **to sth** être prisonnier de qch [3] COMP ► **captive market** N (*Comm*) marché m captif

captivity [kæp'tɪvɪtɪ] N captivité f ; **in** ~ en captivité

captor ['kæptə²] N (*unlawful*) ravisseur m ; (*lawful*) personne f qui capture

capture ['kæptʃə²] [1] VT [+ *animal, soldier*] capturer ; [+ *escapee*] reprendre ; [+ *city*] prendre, s'emparer de ; (*fig*) [+ *attention*] capter ; [+ *interest*] gagner ; (*Art*) reproduire, rendre ; **they have ~d a large part of that market** ils ont conquis une grande partie de ce marché ; **to ~ sth on camera/film** photographier/filmer qch [2] N [*of town, treasure, escapee*] capture f

capuchin [ˈkæpjʊʃɪn] N **a** cape f (avec capuchon) **b** (Rel) **Capuchin** capucin(e) m(f)

car [kɑ:ʳ] **1** N **a** (Aut) voiture f → **racing**, **saloon**, **sports**
b (US Rail) wagon m, voiture f → **dining**, **freight**
c (also **tramcar**) (voiture f de) tramway m, tram m
d [of lift, elevator] cabine f (d'ascenseur)
e (Aviat) nacelle f (de dirigeable)
2 COMP [wheel, door, seat, tyre etc] de voiture; [travel etc] en voiture ► **car alarm** N alarme f de voiture, alarme f auto ► **car allowance** N indemnité f de déplacement (en voiture) ► **car bomb** N voiture f piégée ► **car bombing** N attentat m à la voiture piégée ► **car-boot sale** N (Brit) brocante f, vide-grenier m ► **car chase** N course-poursuite f (en voiture) ► **car coat** N manteau m court ► **car expenses** NPL frais mpl de déplacement (en voiture) ► **car-fare** N (US) prix m du trajet (en bus) ► **car-ferry** N [of sea] ferry(-boat) m; [of river, small channel] bac m (pour voitures) ► **car hire** N location f de voitures; **~ hire company** société f de location de voitures ► **car industry** N industrie f automobile ► **car journey** N voyage m en voiture; (shorter) trajet m en voiture ► **car keys** NPL clés fpl de voiture ► **car licence** N vignette f (auto) ► **car maintenance** N mécanique f auto; **~ maintenance classes** cours fpl de mécanique auto ► **car park** N (Brit) parking m, parc m de stationnement ► **car phone** N téléphone m de voiture ► **car-pool** N groupe de personnes qui partagent une voiture pour se rendre à leur travail ► **car radio** N autoradio m ► **car rental** N location f de voitures ► **car-sharing** N covoiturage m ► **car sick** ADJ **to be ~ sick** être malade en voiture, avoir le mal de la route ► **car sickness** N mal m des transports ► **car sleeper** N (Rail) train m autos-couchettes ► **car stereo** N autoradio m ► **car transporter** N (Aut) camion m transporteur des automobiles; (Rail) wagon m transportant des automobiles ► **car wash** N (= action) lavage m de voitures; (= place) portique m de lavage automatique ► **car-worker** N (Ind) ouvrier m, -ière f de l'industrie automobile

---
CAR-BOOT SALE, GARAGE SALE

Type de brocante très populaire en Grande-Bretagne, où chacun vide sa cave ou son grenier. Les articles sont présentés dans des coffres de voitures et la vente a souvent lieu sur un parking ou dans un champ. Les brocanteurs d'un jour doivent s'acquitter d'une petite contribution pour participer à la vente.
　　Aux États-Unis et en Australie, les ventes de ce genre s'appellent **garage sales** ou **yard sales**.

Caracas [kəˈrækəs] N Caracas

carafe [kəˈræf] N carafe f; (small) carafon m

caramel [ˈkærəməl] N caramel m; **~ custard** or **cream** crème f(au) caramel

caramelize [ˈkærəməlaɪz] **1** VT caraméliser **2** VI se caraméliser

carapace [ˈkærəpeɪs] N carapace f

carat [ˈkærət] N carat m; **22 ~ gold** or m à 22 carats

caravan [ˈkærəvæn] **1** N (Brit Aut) caravane f; [of gipsy] roulotte f; (= group: in desert etc) caravane f **2** VI **to go ~ning** faire du caravaning **3** COMP ► **caravan site** N [of tourists] camping m pour caravanes; [of gipsies] campement m

caravanette [ˌkærəvəˈnet] N (Brit) auto-camping f, voiture-camping f

caravanserai [ˌkærəˈvænsəraɪ], **caravansary** [ˌkærəˈvænsərɪ] N caravansérail m

caravel [ˈkærəvel] N (Naut) caravelle f

caraway [ˈkærəweɪ] **1** N graines fpl de carvi, cumin m des prés **2** COMP ► **caraway seeds** NPL graines fpl de carvi, cumin m

carbide [ˈkɑ:baɪd] N carbure m

carbine [ˈkɑ:baɪn] N carabine f

carbohydrate [ˌkɑ:bəˈhaɪdreɪt] N hydrate m de carbone; (in diets etc) **~s** farineux mpl, féculents mpl

carbolic [kɑ:ˈbɒlɪk] **1** ADJ phéniqué **2** COMP ► **carbolic acid** N phénol m ► **carbolic soap** N savon m au crésol, crésyl® m

carbon [ˈkɑ:bən] **1** N (Chem) carbone m; (Art, Elec) charbon m; (= paper, copy) carbone m **2** COMP ► **carbon-14 dating** N = **carbon dating** ► **carbon copy** N [of typing etc] carbone m; (fig) réplique f ◆ ADJ (fig) identique ► **carbon-date** VT (Archeol) dater au carbone 14 ► **carbon dating** N datation f au carbone 14 ► **carbon dioxide** N gaz m carbonique ► **carbon fibre** N fibre f de carbone ► **carbon microphone** N microphone m à charbon ► **carbon monoxide** N oxyde m de carbone ► **carbon paper** N (Typ) (papier m) carbone m ► **carbon ribbon** N (Typ) ruban m de machine à écrire ► **carbon tissue** N (Phot) = **carbon paper**

carbonaceous [ˌkɑ:bəˈneɪʃəs] ADJ charbonneux; (Chem) carboné

carbonate [ˈkɑ:bənɪt] N carbonate m

carbonated [ˈkɑ:bəneɪtɪd] ADJ [water, drink] gazeux

carbonic [kɑ:ˈbɒnɪk] ADJ carbonique

carboniferous [ˌkɑ:bəˈnɪfərəs] ADJ carbonifère

carbonization [ˌkɑ:bənaɪˈzeɪʃən] N carbonisation f

carbonize [ˈkɑ:bənaɪz] VT carboniser

carbonless paper [ˌkɑ:bənlɪsˈpeɪpəʳ] N papier m autocopiant

carborne [ˈkɑ:bɔ:n] ADJ (US) transporté en voiture

Carborundum® [ˌkɑ:bəˈrʌndəm] N carborundum® m, siliciure m de carbone

carboy [ˈkɑ:bɔɪ] N bonbonne f

carbuncle [ˈkɑ:bʌŋkl] N **a** (= jewel) escarboucle f **b** (Med) furoncle m

carburation [ˌkɑ:bjuˈreɪʃən] N carburation f

carburettor, **carburetor** (US) [ˌkɑ:bjuˈretəʳ] N carburateur m

carcass [ˈkɑ:kəs] N **a** [of animal] carcasse f, cadavre m; (Butchery) carcasse f; (= human corpse) cadavre m; (hum, iro = body) carcasse f; (Culin) **chicken ~** os mpl or carcasse f de poulet **b** (Aut, Naut, Tech) charpente f, carcasse f

carcinogen [kɑ:ˈsɪnədʒen] N substance f cancérigène or cancérogène

carcinogenic [ˌkɑ:sɪnəˈdʒenɪk] **1** N = **carcinogen 2** ADJ cancérigène or cancérogène

carcinoma [ˌkɑ:sɪˈnəʊmə] N (pl **carcinomas** or **carcinomata** [ˌkɑ:sɪˈnəʊmətə]) carcinome m

card¹ [kɑ:d] **1** N **a** (gen) carte f; (also **playing ~**) carte f (à jouer); (also **visiting ~**) carte f (de visite); (also **invitation ~**) carton m or carte f d'invitation; (also **postcard**) carte f (postale); (also **index ~**) fiche f; (also **member's ~**) carte f de membre or d'adhérent; (also **press ~**) carte f de presse; (at dance, races) programme m; (= piece of cardboard) (morceau m de) carton m; **identity ~** carte f d'identité; **game of ~s** partie f de cartes; **to play ~s** jouer aux cartes; **high/low ~** haute/basse carte f → **court**, **face**, **scorecard**, **trump**
b (fig phrases) **to hold all the ~s** avoir tous les atouts (dans son jeu or en main); **to put** or **lay one's ~s on the table** jouer cartes sur table; **to have a ~ up one's sleeve** avoir un atout dans sa manche; **to play** or **keep one's ~s close to one's chest** ◊ or **keep one's ~s close to the vest** (US) cacher son jeu; **to throw in the ~s** abandonner la partie; **it's on the ~s** or (US) **in the ~s that ...*** il y a de grandes chances

(pour) que ... (+ subj); (Brit Ind etc) **to get one's ~s†*** être mis à la porte, être licencié; (Brit Ind etc) **to ask for one's ~s** demander son compte; **he's (quite) a ~!†*** c'est un rigolo!* → **play**
2 VT **a** (= put on cards) ficher, mettre sur fiches
b (US = check sb's identity) **to ~ sb*** contrôler l'identité de qn
3 COMP ► **card-carrying member** N membre m, adhérent(e) m(f) ► **card catalogue** N catalogue m, fichier m (de bibliothèque etc) ► **card game** N (= bridge, whist etc) jeu m de cartes; (= game of cards) partie f de cartes ► **card-holder** N [of political party, organization etc] membre m, adhérent(e) m(f); [of library] lecteur m, -trice f; [of restaurant etc] détenteur m, -trice f de carte de fidélité; [of credit cards] titulaire mf d'une carte (or de cartes) de crédit ► **card hopper** N (Comput) magasin m d'alimentation ► **card index** N fichier m ► **card-index** VT ficher, mettre sur fiches ► **card player** N joueur m, -euse f de cartes ► **card punch** N perforatrice f de cartes ► **card reader** N (Comput) lecteur m de cartes perforées ► **card stacker** N (Comput) case f de réception ► **card table** N table f de jeu or à jouer ► **card trick** N tour m de cartes ► **card vote** N (Ind) vote m sur carte (même nombre de voix que d'adhérents représentés)

card² [kɑ:d] (Tech) **1** N carde f **2** VT [+ wool, cotton] carder

cardamom [ˈkɑ:dəməm] N cardamome f

cardboard [ˈkɑ:dbɔ:d] **1** N carton m (NonC) **2** ADJ [bookcover] cartonné; [doll] de or en carton; **~ box** (boîte f en) carton m; **~ cutout** (lit) figurine f de carton à découper; (fig) homme m de paille; **~ city*** endroit de la ville où dorment les sans-abri; **he sleeps in ~ city*** il dort sous les ponts, c'est un SDF

carder [ˈkɑ:dəʳ] N (Tech) cardeuse f

cardiac [ˈkɑ:dɪæk] **1** ADJ cardiaque **2** COMP ► **cardiac arrest** N arrêt m du cœur

cardie* [ˈkɑ:dɪ] N ABBR = **cardigan**

cardigan [ˈkɑ:dɪgən] N cardigan m, gilet m (de laine)

cardinal [ˈkɑ:dɪnl] **1** ADJ [number, point] (Ling) [vowel] cardinal; **the four ~ virtues** les quatre vertus fpl cardinales; **of ~ importance/significance** d'une importance/portée capitale **2** N (Rel) cardinal m → **college 3** COMP ► **cardinal red** N, ADJ rouge cardinal inv, pourpre m ► **cardinal sin** N (Rel, fig) péché m capital

cardio... [ˈkɑ:dɪəʊ] PREF cardio-; **~vascular** cardio-vasculaire

cardiogram [ˈkɑ:dɪəgræm] N cardiogramme m

cardiograph [ˈkɑ:dɪəgræf] N cardiographe m

cardiography [ˌkɑ:dɪˈɒgrəfɪ] N cardiographie f

cardiological [ˌkɑ:dɪəˈlɒdʒɪkəl] ADJ cardiologique

cardiologist [ˌkɑ:dɪˈɒlədʒɪst] N cardiologue mf

cardiology [ˌkɑ:dɪˈɒlədʒɪ] N cardiologie f

cardphone [ˈkɑ:dfəʊn] N (Brit Telec) téléphone m à carte

cardsharp [ˈkɑ:dʃɑ:p], **cardsharper** [ˈkɑ:dˌʃɑ:pəʳ] N tricheur m, -euse f (professionnel)

cardy* [ˈkɑ:dɪ] N ABBR = **cardigan**

care [kɛəʳ] **1** N **a** (= attention, heed) attention f, soin m; **with the greatest ~** avec le plus grand soin; (on parcels) **"with ~"** « fragile »; **to take ~** faire attention; **it got broken despite all our ~** ça s'est cassé bien que nous y ayons fait très attention; **take ~ not to catch cold** or **that you don't catch cold** faites attention de or à ne pas prendre froid; **take ~ (fais) attention;** (as good wishes) fais bien attention (à toi); **have a ~!†** prenez garde!;

you should take more ~ with or give more ~ to your work vous devriez apporter plus d'attention or plus de soin à votre travail; you should take more or better ~ of yourself tu devrais faire plus attention (à ta santé); he took ~ to explain why ... il a pris soin d'expliquer pourquoi ...; to take ~ of [+ book, details, arrangements] s'occuper de, se charger de; [+ valuables] garder; [+ person, animal] prendre soin de, s'occuper de; to take good ~ of sb bien s'occuper de qn; to take good ~ of sth prendre grand soin de qch; (threateningly) I'll take ~ of him! je vais m'occuper de lui!; I'll take ~ of that je vais m'en occuper; he can take ~ of himself* il peut or sait se débrouiller* tout seul; that can take ~ of itself* cela s'arrangera tout seul; let the car take ~ of itself for a moment!* laisse la voiture tranquille cinq minutes!; (Aut, Jur) convicted of driving without due ~ and attention condamné pour conduite dangereuse; I leave or put it in your ~ je vous le confie; (on letters) ~ of (abbr: c/o) aux bons soins de, chez; he was left in his aunt's ~ on l'a laissé à la garde de sa tante; (frm) to be in ~ of sb être sous la garde or la surveillance de qn; the four children in her ~ les quatre enfants dont elle a la responsabilité; he is in the ~ of Dr Harrison c'est le docteur Harrison qui le soigne; children placed in the ~ of the council des enfants mpl confiés à l'assistance publique

[b] (= anxiety) souci m; he hasn't a ~ in the world il n'a pas le moindre souci; full of ~s◊ full of ~† accablé de soucis; the ~s of State les responsabilités fpl de l'État

[c] (Admin, Social Work) to put a child in or take a child into ~ mettre un enfant à l'assistance; he's been in ~ since the age of three il est à l'assistance publique depuis l'âge de trois ans

[2] VI [a] (= feel interest, anxiety, sorrow) se soucier (about de), s'intéresser (about à); money is all he ~s about il n'y a que l'argent qui l'intéresse (subj); to ~ deeply about sth être profondément concerné par qch; to ~ deeply about sb être profondément attaché à qn; not to ~ about se moquer de, se ficher de; he really ~s (about this) c'est vraiment important pour lui; I don't ~! ◊ as if I ~d!* ça m'est égal!, je m'en moque!, je m'en fiche!*; what do I ~?* qu'est-ce que ça peut me faire?; for all I ~* pour ce que cela me fait; I couldn't ~ less* what people say je me fiche pas mal* de ce que les gens peuvent dire; he doesn't ~ a (brass) farthing* or a hang* or two hoots* or a damn* il s'en fiche* comme de l'an quarante or de sa première chemise; who ~s! qu'est-ce que cela peut bien faire!, on s'en moque!, on s'en fiche!* → naught

[b] (= like) aimer; would you ~ to take off your coat? voulez-vous retirer votre manteau?; I shouldn't ~ to meet him je n'aimerais pas le rencontrer, ça ne me dirait rien de le rencontrer; I don't much ~ for it cela ne me dit rien; I don't ~ for him il ne me plaît pas tellement or beaucoup; would you ~ for a cup of tea? voulez-vous (prendre) une tasse de thé?; thank you, I don't ~ for tea merci, je n'aime pas le thé; would you ~ for a walk? voulez-vous faire une promenade?

[3] COMP ► care assistant N (Brit) aide-soignant(e) m(f) ► care label N (on garment) instructions fpl de lavage ► care order N (Brit Jur, Social Work) ordre m de placement à l'assistance publique ► care-worker N travailleur m, -euse f social(e) → child, health

► **care for** VT FUS [+ invalid] soigner; [+ child] s'occuper de; **well-~d for** [invalid] qu'on soigne bien; [child] dont on s'occupe bien; [hands, hair] soigné; [garden] bien entretenu; [house] bien tenu

careen [kə'riːn] [1] VT (Naut) [+ ship] caréner,

mettre or abattre en carène [2] VI (Naut) donner de la bande (de façon dangereuse)

career [kə'rɪə'] [1] N [a] (= profession, occupation) carrière f, profession f; journalism is his ~ il fait carrière dans le journalisme; he is making a ~ (for himself) in advertising il est en train de faire carrière dans la publicité

[b] (= life, development, progress) vie f, carrière f; he studied the ~s of the great il a étudié la vie des grands hommes; his university ~ sa carrière universitaire

[c] (= movement) in full ~ en pleine course

[2] VI (also ~ along) aller à toute vitesse or à toute allure; to ~ up/down etc monter/descendre etc à toute allure

[3] COMP [soldier, diplomat] de carrière ► career break N (to look after one's children) congé m parental; (for further education) congé m de formation ► career girl N jeune femme f ambitieuse; she's a ~ girl elle s'intéresse avant tout à sa carrière, elle est très ambitieuse ► career move N changement m d'emploi, étape f dans un plan de carrière; (= decision: also hum) a good/bad ~ move une bonne/mauvaise décision sur le plan professionnel ► career prospects NPL possibilités fpl d'avancement, débouchés mpl ► careers advisor, careers counselor (US) N conseiller m, -ère f d'orientation professionnelle ► careers guidance N (Brit) orientation f professionnelle ► careers office N centre m d'orientation professionnelle ► careers officer, careers teacher N (Brit Scol) = careers advisor ► career woman N femme f qui s'intéresse avant tout à sa carrière

careerism [kə'rɪərɪzəm] N carriérisme m

careerist [kə'rɪərɪst] N (pej) carriériste mf (pej)

carefree ['kɛəfriː] ADJ sans souci, insouciant

careful ['kɛəfʊl] ADJ [a] (= painstaking) [writer, worker] consciencieux, soigneux; [work] soigné; [planning, study, examination] minutieux; managing your workload takes ~ planning gérer sa charge de travail demande une organisation minutieuse; we have made a ~ study of the report nous avons étudié le rapport soigneusement, nous avons procédé à une étude minutieuse du rapport; after giving this problem ~ thought, I believe ... après avoir longuement réfléchi à ce problème, je pense que ...; long hair needs ~ attention les cheveux longs demandent beaucoup de soin; after ~ consideration of the facts ... après avoir soigneusement examiné les faits ..., après un examen minutieux des faits ...; ~ over detail attentif aux détails

[b] (= cautious) prudent; (= acting with care) soigneux; (be) ~! (fais) attention!; she's very ~ about what she eats elle fait très attention à ce qu'elle mange; be ~ with the glasses fais attention aux verres; be ~ of the dog (faites) attention au chien; be ~ what you do/say to him faites attention à ce que vous faites/vous lui dites; ~ on those stairs! faites attention à ces escaliers!; be ~ (that) he doesn't hear you faites attention à ce qu'il ne vous entende pas; be ~ to shut the door n'oubliez pas de fermer la porte; he was ~ to point out that ... il a pris soin de faire remarquer que ...; be ~ not to drop it ◊ be ~ (that) you don't drop it faites attention à ne pas le laisser tomber; he was ~ not to offend them il a pris soin de ne pas les offenser; we have to be very ~ not to be seen nous devons faire bien attention de ne pas être vus; (gen) you can't be too ~ on n'est jamais trop prudent

[c] (= rather miserly) économe; (pej) regardant; he is very ~ with (his) money il est très regardant

carefully ['kɛəfʊlɪ] ADV [a] (= painstakingly) [look at, consider, plan, write, place, explain] soigneusement, avec soin; [listen, read] attentivement [b] (= cautiously) [drive, choose] pru-

demment, avec précaution; [reply] avec circonspection; (fig) we must go ~ here il faut nous montrer prudents

carefulness ['kɛəfʊlnɪs] N soin m, attention f

caregiver ['kɛə,gɪvə'] N = carer

careless ['kɛəlɪs] ADJ [a] (= taking little care) négligent, insouciant (of de); (= done without care) [action] inconsidéré, irréfléchi; [work] bâclé; to be ~ in sth se montrer négligent dans qch; it was ~ of her to do that elle a fait preuve de négligence en faisant cela; how ~ of me! comme j'ai été négligent!; ~ driver conducteur m négligent; convicted of ~ driving condamné pour conduite dangereuse; ~ mistake faute f d'inattention; his spelling is ~ il ne fait pas attention à son orthographe [b] (= carefree) sans souci, insouciant

carelessly ['kɛəlɪslɪ] ADV [a] (= inattentively, thoughtlessly) [leave, discard, place, handle, allow] négligemment [b] (= casually) [say] avec insouciance; [throw, toss] négligemment; a shirt ~ open at the neck une chemise au col négligemment ouvert

carelessness ['kɛəlɪsnɪs] N (NonC) négligence f; the ~ of his work le peu de soin qu'il apporte (or a apporté) à son travail

carer ['kɛərə'] N (professional) travailleur m social; (Brit = relative, friend) personne qui s'occupe d'un proche dépendant

caress [kə'res] [1] N caresse f [2] VT caresser

caret ['kærət] N (Typ) lambda m (signe d'insertion)

caretaker ['kɛə,teɪkə'] N (Brit) gardien(ne) m(f) (d'immeuble), concierge mf; (Pol) ~ government/president gouvernement m/président(e) m(f) intérimaire

careworn ['kɛəwɔːn] ADJ rongé par les soucis

cargo ['kɑːgəʊ] [1] N (pl cargoes or cargos) cargaison f, chargement m [2] COMP ► cargo boat N cargo m ► cargo plane N avion-cargo m

carhop ['kɑːhɒp] N (US) (serving food) serveur m, -euse f (dans un restaurant drive-in); (parking cars) gardien m de parking (qui gare les voitures)

Carib ['kærɪb] [1] ADJ caraïbe [2] N Caraïbe mf

Caribbean [,kærɪ'biːən, (esp US) kə'rɪbɪən] ADJ caribéen, des Caraïbes; a ~ island une île des Caraïbes; the ~ (Sea) la mer des Antilles or des Caraïbes; the ~ Islands les petites Antilles fpl

caribou ['kærɪbuː] N (pl caribous or caribou) caribou m

caricature ['kærɪkətjʊə'] [1] N [a] (Art, fig) caricature f [b] (NonC) (art m de la) caricature f [2] VT (Art, fig) caricaturer

caricaturist [,kærɪkə'tjʊərɪst] N caricaturiste mf

CARICOM ['kærɪ,kɒm] N ABBR = Caribbean Community and Common Market

caries ['kɛəriːz] N (pl inv) carie f

carillon [kə'rɪljən] N carillon m

caring ['kɛərɪŋ] ADJ [parent] aimant; [teacher] bienveillant; we want a ~ society nous voulons une société à visage humain; the ~ professions les professions fpl à vocation sociale; a child needs a ~ environment un enfant a besoin d'être entouré d'affection

carious ['kɛərɪəs] ADJ carié, gâté

carjacker ['kɑː,dʒækə'] N pirate m de la route

carjacking ['kɑː,dʒækɪŋ] N piraterie f sur la route

carload ['kɑːləʊd] N [of books etc] voiturée f; a ~ of people une voiture pleine de gens

Carmelite ['kɑːməlaɪt] ADJ, N carmélite f

carminative ['kɑːmɪnətɪv] ADJ (Med) carminatif

carmine ['kɑːmaɪn] ADJ, N carmin m

carnage ['kɑːnɪdʒ] N carnage m

carnal ['kɑːnl] [1] ADJ (liter) charnel† [2] COMP ► carnal knowledge N (Jur) acte m or union *f* charnel(le); **to have ~ knowledge of sb** connaître qn charnellement

carnally ['kɑːnlɪ] ADV [*desire*] charnellement

carnation [kɑːˈneɪʃən] ① N (*Bot*) œillet *m* ② ADJ (= *pink*) rose; (= *red*) incarnat

carnet ['kɑːneɪ] N (*Jur, Comm*) passavant *m*

carnival ['kɑːnɪvəl] ① N carnaval *m*; (*US* = *fair*) fête *f* foraine ② COMP [*hat, procession*] de carnaval

carnivora [kɑːˈnɪvərə] NPL (*Zool*) carnivores *mpl*

carnivore ['kɑːnɪvɔːʳ] N a carnivore *m* b (*: hum = non-vegetarian*) carnivore *m*, amateur *m* de viande

carnivorous [kɑːˈnɪvərəs] ADJ [*animal, plant*] carnivore; **~ guests will enjoy the excellent game** les amateurs de viande ne seront pas déçus par le gibier

carny: ['kɑːnɪ] N (*US*) (= *carnival*) foire *f*, fête *f* foraine; (= *person*) forain *m*

carob ['kærəb] ① N ~ (**powder**) (poudre *f* de) caroube *f* ② COMP ► **carob tree** N caroubier *m*

carol ['kærəl] ① N (= *song*) chant *m* joyeux; (*also* **Christmas ~**) chant *m* de Noël; **~-singers** groupe de gens qui chantent des chants de Noël ② VI (*liter*) chanter joyeusement; [*birds*] chanter; [*small birds*] gazouiller

caroller ['kærələʳ] N chanteur *m*, -euse *f*

carom ['kærəm] (*Billiards*) ① N carambolage *m* ② VI caramboler

carotene ['kærətiːn] N carotène *m*

carotid [kəˈrɒtɪd] ① N carotide *f* ② ADJ carotidien ③ COMP ► **carotid artery** N carotide *f*

carousal [kəˈrauzəl] N beuverie *f*, ribote† *f*

carouse [kəˈrauz] VI faire ribote†

carousel [ˌkærʊˈsel] N a (*esp US* = *merry-go-round*) manège *m* (*de chevaux de bois etc*) b [*Phot: for slides*] magasin *m* or panier *m* circulaire (*pour diapositives*) c (*at airport: for luggage*) carrousel *m*, tapis *m* roulant à bagages

carp¹ [kɑːp] N (*pl* **carp** *or* **carps**) (= *fish*) carpe *f*

carp² [kɑːp] VI critiquer; **to ~ at** [+ *person*] critiquer, blâmer; [+ *thing, action*] trouver à redire à

carpal ['kɑːpl] ① ADJ (*Anat*) carpien ② COMP ► **carpal tunnel syndrome** N (*Med*) syndrome *m* du canal carpien

Carpathians [kɑːˈpeɪθɪənz] NPL **the ~** les Carpates *fpl*

carpel ['kɑːpl] N (*Bot*) carpelle *m*

Carpentaria [ˌkɑːpənˈtɛərɪə] N **Gulf of ~** golfe *m* de Carpentarie

carpenter ['kɑːpɪntəʳ] ① N charpentier *m*; (= *joiner*) menuisier *m* ② VI (*in building*) faire de la charpenterie; [*joiner*] faire de la menuiserie

carpentry ['kɑːpɪntrɪ] N (*NonC*) charpenterie *f*; (= *joinery*) menuiserie *f*

carpet ['kɑːpɪt] ① N tapis *m*; (*fitted*) moquette *f*; (*fig*) **to be on the ~*** [*subject*] être sur le tapis; [*person scolded*] être sur la sellette → **fitted, red, sweep** ② VT a [+ *floor*] recouvrir d'un tapis; (*with fitted carpet*) recouvrir d'une moquette, moquetter; (*fig*) **a garden ~ed with flowers** un jardin tapissé de fleurs b (†* = *scold*) [+ *person*] houspiller ③ COMP ► **carpet bombing** N (*Mil*) bombardement *m* intensif ► **carpet slippers** NPL pantoufles *fpl* ► **carpet sweeper** N balai *m* mécanique ► **carpet tile** N dalle *f* de moquette

carpetbagger* ['kɑːpɪtbægəʳ] N (*US*) (*Pol*) candidat(e) *m(f)* parachuté(e); (*Fin*) opportuniste *mf* (*qui cherche à profiter financièrement du changement de statut d'une société de crédit immobilier*); (*Hist*) carpetbagger *m*

carpeting ['kɑːpɪtɪŋ] N (*NonC*) moquette *f* → **wall**

carpi ['kɑːpaɪ] NPL *of* **carpus**

carping ['kɑːpɪŋ] ① ADJ [*person*] chicanier, qui trouve à redire à tout; [*manner*] chicanier; [*criticism*] mesquin; [*voice*] malveillant ② N chicanerie *f*, critique *f* (*malveillant*)

carport ['kɑːpɔːt] N auvent *m* (*pour voiture*)

carpus ['kɑːpəs] N (*pl* **carpi**) (*Anat*) carpe *m*

carrel(l) ['kærəl] N box *m* (*dans une bibliothèque*)

carriage ['kærɪdʒ] ① N a (*horse-drawn*) voiture *f* (*de maître*), équipage *m*; **~ and pair/four** voiture *f or* équipage *m or* attelage *m* à deux/quatre chevaux b (*Brit Rail*) voiture *f*, wagon *m* (*de voyageurs*) c (*NonC: Brit Comm = conveyance of goods*) transport *m*, factage *m*; **~ forward** (en) port dû; **~ free** franco de port; **~ paid** (en) port payé d [*of typewriter*] chariot *m*; [*of printing press*] train *m* e [*of person*] (= *bearing*) maintien *m*, port *m* ② COMP ► **carriage clock** N pendulette *f* ► **carriage drive** N allée *f* (*pour voitures*), grande allée *f* ► **carriage return** N (*Typ*) retour *m* du chariot ► **carriage trade** N (*Comm*) clientèle *f* riche, grosse clientèle *f*

carriageway ['kærɪdʒweɪ] N (*Brit*) chaussée *f* → **dual**

carrier ['kærɪəʳ] ① N a (*Comm*) (= *company*) entreprise *f* de transports; (= *passenger airline*) compagnie *f* aérienne; (= *truck owner etc*) entrepreneur *m* de transports, transporteur *m*, camionneur *m*; **by ~** (*Aut*) par la route, par camion; (*Rail*) par chemin de fer; **express ~** messageries *fpl* b (*for luggage: on car, cycle etc*) porte-bagages *m inv*; (= *bag*) sac *m* (en plastique) c (*Med* = *person*) porteur *m*, -euse *f* d (*also* **aircraft ~**) porte-avions *m inv*; (*also* **troop ~**) (= *plane*) appareil *m* transporteur (de troupes); (= *ship*) transport *m* ② COMP ► **carrier bag** N (*Brit*) sac *m* (en plastique) ► **carrier pigeon** N pigeon *m* voyageur

carrion ['kærɪən] ① N (*NonC*) charogne *f* ② COMP ► **carrion crow** N corneille *f* noire ► **carrion feeder** N charognard *m* ► **carrion flesh** N charogne *f*

carrot ['kærət] ① N (*lit, fig*) carotte *f*; (*fig*) **to dangle a ~ in front of sb** ◊ **to offer sb a ~** essayer d'appâter qn ② COMP ► **carrot and stick** ADJ (*fig*) alternant la carotte et le bâton ► **carrot cake** N gâteau *m* à la carotte ► **carrot-top** N (**: hum = redhead*) rouquin(e)* *m(f)*; (*Culin*) **~-tops** fanes *fpl*

carroty ['kærətɪ] ADJ [*hair*] carotte *inv*, roux (rousse *f*)

carrousel [ˌkærəˈsel] N (*US*) = **carousel**

carry ['kærɪ] ① VT a (= *bear, transport*) [*person*] porter; [*vehicle*] transporter; [+ *goods, heavy loads*] transporter; [+ *message, news*] porter; **she was ~ing the child in her arms** elle portait l'enfant dans ses bras; **this ship carries coal/passengers** ce bateau transporte du charbon/des passagers; **this coach carries 30 people** ce car peut transporter 30 personnes; **he carried the plates through to the kitchen** il a emporté les assiettes à la cuisine; **as fast as his legs could ~ him** à toutes jambes; **the sea carried the boat westward** la mer a emporté le bateau vers l'ouest; **to ~ sth in one's head** connaître qch par cœur; (*fig*) **he carried his audience with him** il a enthousiasmé son auditoire, il a emporté la conviction de son auditoire; **enough food to ~ us through the winter** assez de provisions pour nous durer or nous faire* tout l'hiver; **he's had one or two drinks more than he can ~*** il a bu un ou deux verres de trop → **can², coal, torch** b (= *have on one's person*) [+ *identity card, documents*] porter or avoir (sur soi); [+ *matches, cigarettes, money*] avoir (sur soi); [+ *umbrella, gun, sword*] porter c (*Med*) [+ *disease*] être porteur de; **people ~ing the AIDS virus** des porteurs *mpl* du virus du sida d (= *have, be provided with*) [+ *label, tag*] porter, être muni de; [+ *warning, notice*]

comporter; (*Comm*) **it carries a five-year guarantee** c'est garanti cinq ans e (= *involve, lead to, entail*) avoir comme conséquence(s), produire; [+ *consequences*] entraîner; [+ *risk*] comporter; **this job carries a lot of responsibility** ce travail comporte beaucoup de responsabilités; **it also carries extra pay** cela comporte aussi un supplément de salaire; **this offence carries a penalty of £100** ce délit est passible d'une amende de 100 livres; **a crime which carries the death penalty** un crime passible de la peine de mort; **to ~ a crop** donner or produire une récolte; (*fig*) **to ~ authority** faire autorité → **conviction, interest, mortgage, weight** f (= *support*) [*pillar etc*] supporter, soutenir, porter; **the ship was ~ing too much canvas** or **sail** le navire portait trop de toile g (*Comm*) [+ *goods, stock*] stocker, vendre; **we don't ~ that article** nous ne faisons pas cet article h (*Tech*) [*pipe*] [+ *water, oil*] amener; [*wire*] [+ *sound*] conduire i (= *extend*) faire passer; **they carried the pipes under the street** ils ont fait passer les tuyaux sous la rue; (*fig*) **to ~ sth too far** or **to excess** pousser qch trop loin; **this basic theme is carried through the book** ce thème fondamental se retrouve tout au long du livre j (= *win*) gagner, remporter; [+ *fortress*] enlever; [+ *enemy's position*] emporter d'assaut; **to ~ the day** (*fig*) gagner (la partie), l'emporter; (*Mil*) être vainqueur; **to ~ all** or **everything before one** marcher en vainqueur, l'emporter sur tous les tableaux; **he carried his point** il a eu gain de cause; **the motion/bill was carried (by 302 votes to 197)** la motion/le projet de loi a été voté(e) (par 302 voix contre 197); (*US Pol*) **he will ~ Ohio** [*presidential candidate*] il va l'emporter dans l'Ohio k **to ~ o.s.** (*physical*) se tenir; (*behaviour*) se comporter, se conduire; **she carries herself very well** elle se tient très bien; **he carries himself like a soldier** il a le port d'un militaire; **he carries himself with dignity** il a un maintien fort digne; **he carried his head erect** il tenait la tête bien droite l [*newspaper etc*] [+ *story, details*] rapporter; **all the papers carried (the story of) the murder** l'histoire du meurtre était dans tous les journaux, tous les journaux ont parlé du meurtre; **the papers all carried a photograph of the explosion** dans tous les journaux on trouvait une photo de l'explosion m (*Math*) retenir; **... and ~ three** ... et je retiens trois n (*Med*) [+ *child*] attendre; **when she was ~ing her third son** quand elle était enceinte de or quand elle attendait son troisième fils

② VI [*voice, sound*] porter

③ COMP ► **carry-on*** N (*pej*) histoires* *fpl*; **what a ~-on (about nothing)!*** que d'histoires (pour rien)!* ► **carry-out** ADJ [*meal etc*] à emporter ◆ N (= *food*) snack *m* à emporter; (= *drink*) boisson *f* à emporter

► **carry away** VT SEP a (*lit*) [+ *sick or injured person*] emporter; [+ *thing*] emporter, enlever; [*tide, wind*] emporter b (*fig*) transporter; **he was carried away by his friend's enthusiasm** il a été transporté par l'enthousiasme de son ami; **to get carried away by sth*** s'emballer* pour qch; **don't get carried away!*** ne t'emballe pas!*, du calme!*; **I got carried away*** (*with excitement etc*) je me suis laissé emporter (**by** par); (*forgetting time*) je n'ai pas vu passer l'heure

► **carry back** VT SEP (*lit*) [+ *things*] rapporter; (*fig*) reporter; (*Fin*) reporter (*sur comptes antérieurs*); (*fig*) **the music carried me back to my youth** la musique m'a reporté à l'époque de ma jeunesse

► **carry forward** VT SEP (*Accounts, gen*) reporter (**to** à); **carried forward** à reporter

► **carry off** VT SEP ⓐ (lit) [+ thing] emporter, enlever; (= kidnap) enlever, ravir ⓑ (fig) [+ prizes, honours] remporter; **to ~ it off well** bien s'en tirer; **to ~ it off*** réussir (son coup) ⓒ (euph) **he was carried off by pneumonia** il a été emporté par une pneumonie

► **carry on** ⓵ VI ⓐ (= continue) continuer (**doing** à or de faire); **~ on!** continuez!; **~ on with your work!** continuez votre travail!; **if you ~ on like that ...** si tu continues comme ça ... ⓑ (* = make a scene) faire une scène, faire des histoires; **you do ~ on!** tu en fais des histoires!; **don't ~ on so!** ne fais (donc) pas tant d'histoires or toute une scène!* ⓒ (= have an affair) **to be ~ing on with sb*** avoir une liaison avec qn ⓶ VT SEP ⓐ (= conduct) [+ business, trade] faire marcher, diriger; [+ correspondence] entretenir; [+ conversation] soutenir; [+ negotiations] mener ⓑ (= continue) [+ business, conversation] continuer, poursuivre; [+ tradition] entretenir, continuer ⓷ VT FUS **he carried on a passionate affair with Mrs Gilbert** il avait liaison passionnée avec Mme Gilbert ⓸ **~-on*** N → **carry** ⓹ **~ing-on** N → **carrying-on**

► **carry out** VT SEP ⓐ (lit) [+ thing, sick or injured person, meal] emporter; **the current carried him out (to sea)** le courant l'a entraîné vers le large ⓑ (fig = put into action) [+ plan] exécuter, mener à bonne fin; [+ order] exécuter; [+ idea] mettre à exécution, donner suite à; [+ obligation] s'acquitter de; [+ experiment] se livrer à, effectuer; [+ search, investigation, inquiry] mener, procéder à, conduire; [+ reform] effectuer; [+ the law, regulations] appliquer; **to ~ out one's duty** faire son devoir; **to ~ out one's duties** s'acquitter de ses fonctions; **to ~ out a promise** respecter or tenir une promesse

► **carry over** VT SEP ⓐ (lit) faire passer du côté opposé, faire traverser ⓑ (from one page to the other) reporter; (Accounts, St Ex) reporter; (Comm) **to ~ over stock from one season to the next** stocker des marchandises d'une saison à l'autre

► **carry through** VT SEP [+ plan] mener or conduire à bonne fin, exécuter; [+ person] soutenir dans l'épreuve; **his courage carried him through** son courage lui a permis de surmonter l'épreuve

► **carry up** VT SEP monter

carryall ['kærɪɔːl] N (US) (sac m) fourre-tout m inv

carrycot ['kærɪkɒt] N (Brit) (gen) porte-bébé m; (wicker) moïse m

carrying-on ['kærɪŋ'ɒn] ⓵ N ⓐ (NonC) [of work, business etc] continuation f ⓑ (often pl: pej) **carryings-on*** façons fpl de se conduire or de faire

cart [kɑːt] ⓵ N (horse-drawn) charrette f; (also **tip-~**) tombereau m; (also **hand ~**) voiture f à bras; (US: for luggage, shopping) chariot m; (fig) **to put the ~ before the horse** mettre la charrue avant les bœufs ⓶ VT [+ goods] (in van, truck) transporter (par camion), camionner; (in cart) charroyer, charrier; (*: also **~ about, ~ around**) [+ shopping, books] trimballer*, coltiner ⓷ COMP ► **cart horse** N cheval m de trait ► **cart track** N chemin m rural or de terre

► **cart away, cart off** VT SEP [+ goods] emporter; [+ garbage] ramasser

cartage ['kɑːtɪdʒ] N (in van, truck) camionnage m, transport m; (in cart) charroi m

carte blanche [,kɑːt'blɑːnʃ] N (NonC) carte f blanche; **to give sb ~ to do sth** donner carte blanche à qn pour faire qch

cartel [kɑː'tel] N (Comm) cartel m

carter ['kɑːtəʳ] N charretier m

Cartesian [kɑː'tiːzɪən] ADJ, N cartésien(ne) m(f)

Cartesianism [kɑː'tiːzɪənɪzəm] N cartésianisme m

Carthage ['kɑːθɪdʒ] N Carthage

Carthaginian [,kɑːθə'dʒɪnɪən] ⓵ N (Rel) Carthaginois m ⓶ ADJ carthaginois

Carthusian [kɑː'θjuːzɪən] ⓵ ADJ de(s) chartreux; **a ~ monk** un chartreux ⓶ N chartreux m, -euse f

cartilage ['kɑːtɪlɪdʒ] N cartilage m

cartload ['kɑːtləʊd] N charretée f

cartographer [kɑː'tɒgrəfəʳ] N cartographe mf

cartographic(al) [,kɑːtə'græfɪk(l)] ADJ cartographique

cartography [kɑː'tɒgrəfɪ] N cartographie f

cartomancy ['kɑːtəmænsɪ] N cartomancie f

carton ['kɑːtən] N (for yogurt, cream) pot m (en carton); (for milk, squash) carton m, brick m; (for ice cream) boîte f (en carton); (for cigarettes) cartouche f

cartoon [kɑː'tuːn] ⓵ N [of newspaper etc] dessin m (humoristique); (Cine, TV) dessin m animé; (Art = sketch) carton m ⓶ VT caricaturer, ridiculiser (par un dessin humoristique)

cartoonist [kɑː'tuːnɪst] N [of newspaper etc] caricaturiste mf, dessinateur m, -trice f humoristique; (Cine, TV) dessinateur m, -trice f de dessins animés, animateur m, -trice f

cartridge ['kɑːtrɪdʒ] ⓵ N [of rifle etc] cartouche f; [of cannon] gargousse f; [of stylus] cellule f; [of recording tape, typewriter or printer ribbon, pen] cartouche f; [of camera] chargeur m; (Comput) chargeur m, cartouche f ⓶ COMP ► **cartridge belt** N (= belt) cartouchière f; (= strip) bande f (de mitrailleuse) ► **cartridge case** N [of rifle] douille f, étui m (de cartouche); [of cannon] douille f ► **cartridge clip** N chargeur m (d'arme à feu) ► **cartridge paper** N papier m à cartouche, papier m fort ► **cartridge player** N lecteur m de cartouche

cartwheel ['kɑːtwiːl] N (lit) roue f de charrette; (fig) **to do** or **turn a ~** faire la roue

cartwright ['kɑːtraɪt] N charron m

carve [kɑːv] ⓵ VT tailler; (= sculpt) sculpter; (= chisel) ciseler; (Culin) découper; **~d out of** or **in wood/ivory** en bois/ivoire sculpté; **~d in(to) the wood/the stone** sculpté dans le bois/la pierre; **to ~ one's initials on** or **in sth** graver ses initiales sur qch; **to ~ one's way through sth** se frayer un chemin à travers qch à coups de hache (or d'épée etc); **to ~ a road through the jungle** percer une route à travers la jungle; **to ~ a niche for o.s.** ◊ **to ~ o.s. a niche** se faire une place; **to ~ o.s. a career (as)** faire carrière (comme) → **stone** ⓶ COMP ► **carve-up*** N (fig) [of inheritance] partage m; [of estate, country] morcellement m

► **carve out** VT SEP [+ piece of wood] découper (**from** dans); [+ piece of land] prendre (**from** à); [+ statue, figure] sculpter, tailler; (fig) [+ reputation, market share, role] se tailler; **to ~ out a career (for o.s.) (as)** faire carrière (comme)

► **carve up** ⓵ VT SEP ⓐ [+ meat] découper; (fig) [+ country] morceler ⓑ (* = disfigure) [+ person] amocher à coups de couteau*; [+ sb's face] taillader, balafrer ⓒ (‡ fig) [+ play, performer] massacrer*, éreinter; [+ candidate, opponent] tailler en pièces ⓶ **~-up*** N → **carve**

carver ['kɑːvəʳ] N ⓐ (Culin = knife) couteau m à découper; **~s** service m à découper ⓑ (= person) personne f qui découpe ⓒ (Brit = chair) chaise f de salle à manger avec accoudoirs

carvery ['kɑːvərɪ] N grill m

carving ['kɑːvɪŋ] ⓵ N ⓐ (Art) sculpture f ⓑ (NonC: Culin) découpage m ⓶ COMP ► **carving knife** N (pl carving knives) couteau m à découper

caryatid [,kærɪ'ætɪd] N (pl caryatids or caryatides [,kærɪ'ætɪ,diːz]) cariatide f

Casablanca [,kæsə'blæŋkə] N Casablanca

Casanova [,kæsə'nəʊvə] N (also fig) Casanova m

cascade [kæs'keɪd] ⓵ N cascade f; (fig) [of ribbons, silks, lace] flot m; [of sparks] pluie f ⓶ VI tomber en cascade

cascara [kæs'kɑːrə] N (Pharm) cascara sagrada f

▼**case¹** [keɪs] ⓵ N ⓐ (= fact, eventuality, example) cas m; **is it the ~ that ...?** est-il vrai que ...?; **that's not the ~** ce n'est pas le cas; **if that's the ~** en ce cas, dans ce cas-là; **as is the ~ here** comme c'est le cas ici; **that** or **such being the ~** par conséquent; **in such a ~** en pareil cas; **if such is the ~** (now) si tel est le cas; (= if it happens) le cas échéant, en pareil cas; **put the ~ that ...** admettons que ... (+ subj); **as the ~ may be** selon le cas; **it's a clear ~ of sexual harassment** c'est un cas flagrant de harcèlement sexuel; **in ~ he comes** au cas où or pour le cas où il viendrait; **I'm supposed to be in charge here, in ~ you've forgotten!*** je suis censé commander ici, au cas où vous l'auriez oublié!; **she's nervous about something, in ~ you didn't notice** il y a quelque chose qui la rend nerveuse, au cas où vous ne l'auriez pas remarqué; **in ~ of** en cas de; (just) **in ~** à tout hasard, au cas où*; **in any ~** en tout cas, de toute façon; **in this ~** dans ce cas; **in that ~** dans ce cas-là; **in no ~** en aucun cas; **in the present ~** dans le cas présent; **as in the ~ of ...** comme dans le cas de ...; **in the ~ in point** en l'occurrence; **here is a ~ in point** en voici un bon exemple, en voici un exemple typique; **in your ~** dans votre cas; **in most ~s** dans la plupart des cas; **in nine ~s out of ten** neuf fois sur dix; **that alters the (whole) ~** cela change tout; **a difficult ~** un cas difficile ⓑ (Med, also gen) cas m; **six ~s of pneumonia** six cas de pneumonie; **the most serious ~s were sent to hospital** les cas les plus graves or les malades les plus atteints ont été envoyés à l'hôpital; **it's a hopeless ~** c'est un cas désespéré; (fig) **he's a hopeless ~** c'est un cas pathologique*; **he's a hard ~*** c'est un dur*; **she's a real ~!*** c'est un cas* or un sacré numéro* (celle-là)!; **to be on sb's ~*** enquiquiner qn; **to get on sb's ~*** prendre la tête à qn*; **get off my ~!*** lâche-moi les baskets!*, ne me prends pas la tête!* ⓒ (Jur) affaire f, procès m; **he's a suspect in the ~** c'est un suspect dans cette affaire or ce procès; **to try a ~** (Jur) juger une affaire; **to win one's ~** (Jur) gagner son procès; (fig) avoir gain de cause; **the ~ for the defendant** or **defence** les arguments mpl en faveur de l'accusé, les arguments mpl de la défense; **the ~ for the prosecution** les arguments mpl contre l'accusé, les arguments mpl de l'accusation; **there is no ~ against ...** il n'y a pas lieu de poursuites contre ...; **he's working on the Gibson ~** il s'occupe de l'affaire Gibson; **~ before the Court** affaire f portée devant le tribunal; (Jur) **his ~ was called today** son affaire est venue aujourd'hui devant le tribunal; **to take a ~ to the High Court** en appeler à la Cour suprême ⓓ (argument, reasoning) arguments mpl; **to make out one's ~** présenter ses arguments; **to make a ~ for sth** plaider en faveur de qch; **to make (out) a good ~ for sth** réunir or présenter de bons arguments en faveur de qch; **to make out a good ~ for doing sth** bien expliquer pourquoi il faudrait faire qch; **there is a strong ~ for/against compulsory vaccination** il y a or aurait beaucoup à dire en faveur de la/contre la vaccination obligatoire; **that is my ~** voilà mes arguments; **a ~ of conscience** un cas de conscience; **to have a good/strong ~** avoir de bons/solides arguments ⓔ (Gram) cas m; **the nominative ~** le nominatif; **the accusative ~** l'accusatif m

⓶ COMP ► **case conference** N (Med, Social Work) réunion de spécialistes pour parler d'un patient ou d'un cas social ► **case file** N (Jur, Med, Social Work) dossier m ► **case grammar** N (Gram) grammaire f des cas ► **case history**

N (*Social Work*) passé *m* du (*or* d'un) cas social ; (*Med*) (= *past facts*) antécédents *mpl* médicaux ; (= *past and present development*) évolution *f* de la maladie ► **case law** N (*NonC*: *Jur*) droit *m* jurisprudentiel ► **case load** N (*Social Work*) dossiers *mpl* (confiés à un assistant social) ; **to have a heavy ~ load** avoir beaucoup de dossiers à traiter ► **case notes** NPL (*Jur, Med, Social Work*) (notes *fpl* pour l'établissement d'un) dossier *m* ► **case papers** NPL (*Jur, Med, Social Work*) pièces *fpl* du dossier ► **case study** N étude *f* de cas ; (*US Univ*) ~ **study method** méthode *f* d'études de cas ► **case system** N (*Gram*) système *m* casuel ► **case work** N (*Social Work*) travail *m* avec des cas (sociaux) individuels ► **case worker** N (*Social Work*) ≈ assistant(e) social(e)

case² [keɪs] **1** N **a** (*Brit* = *suitcase*) valise *f* ; (= *packing case*) caisse *f* ; (= *crate: for bottles etc*) caisse *f* ; (*for peaches, lettuce, oysters etc*) cageot *m* ; (= *box*) boîte *f* ; (= *chest*) coffre *m* ; (*for goods on display*) vitrine *f* ; (*for jewels*) coffret *m* ; (*for watch, pen, necklace etc*) écrin *m* ; (*for camera, binoculars etc*) étui *m* ; (= *covering*) enveloppe *f* ; (*Bookbinding*) couverture *f* ; (*Tech*) carter *m* ; (*Aut*) carter *m* ; **violin/umbrella** *etc* ~ étui *m* à violon/parapluie *etc* → **bookcase, pillowcase**

b (*Typ*) casse *f* → **lower¹, upper**

2 VT **a** = **1a** ; mettre dans une caisse *or* un cageot *etc*, mettre en boîte

b **to ~ the joint*** [*burglars etc*] surveiller la maison *etc* (*avant un mauvais coup*)

3 COMP ► **cased edition** N (*of book*) édition *f* cartonnée ► **case-harden** VT (*Metal*) cémenter ; (*fig*) endurcir ► **case knife** N (*pl* **case knives**) (*US*) couteau *m* à gaine

casebook [ˈkeɪsbʊk] N (*Social Work*) comptes rendus *mpl or* rapports *mpl* de cas sociaux (*réunis dans un registre*)

casement [ˈkeɪsmənt] N (= *window*) fenêtre *f* (à battants), croisée *f* ; (= *frame*) battant *m* de fenêtre ; (*liter*) fenêtre *f*

cash [kæʃ] **1** N (*NonC*) **a** (= *notes and coins*) espèces *fpl*, argent *m* ; **how much ~ is there in the till?** combien d'argent y a-t-il dans la caisse ? ; **I want to be paid in ~ and not by cheque** je veux être payé en espèces et non par chèque ; **to pay in ~** payer en argent comptant *or* en espèces ; (*esp US: in shop*) ~ **or charge?** vous payez en espèces ou par carte ? ; **to take the ~ to the bank** porter l'argent à la banque ; **ready ~** (argent *m*) liquide *m* ; **how much do you have in (ready) ~?** combien avez-vous en liquide ? → **hard, petty, spot**

b ~ **down** (= *immediate payment*) argent *m* comptant ; **to pay ~ (down)** payer comptant *or* cash* ; **discount for ~** escompte *m or* remise *f* au comptant ; ~ **with order** payable à la commande ; ~ **on delivery** paiement *m* à la livraison, livraison *f* contre espèces *or* contre remboursement ; ~ **on shipment** comptant *m* à l'expédition

c (* = *money in general*) argent *m*, sous* *mpl* ; **how much ~ have you got?** combien d'argent as-tu ?, qu'est-ce que tu as comme argent ? ; **I have no ~** je n'ai pas un sou *or* un rond* ; **to be short of ~** être à court d'argent ; **I am out of ~** je suis à sec*, je n'ai plus de sous*

2 VT [+ *cheque*] encaisser, toucher ; [+ *banknote*] changer, faire la monnaie de ; **to ~ sb a cheque** donner à qn de l'argent contre un chèque ; [*bank*] payer un chèque à qn ; **to ~ a bill** encaisser une facture

3 COMP (*gen*) [*problems, calculations etc*] d'argent ► **cash account** N compte *m* de caisse ► **cash advance** N (*Fin*) crédit *m* de caisse ► **cash-and-carry** N libre-service *m* de gros, cash and carry *m inv* ♦ ADJ [*goods, business*] de gros, de cash and carry ► **cash bar** N bar *m* payant (*à une réception*) ► **cash card** N carte *f* bancaire (*permettant le retrait d'argent aux distributeurs de billets*) ► **cash cow*** N

(*Comm*) mine *f* d'or (*fig*) ► **cash crop** N culture *f* de rapport *or* commerciale ► **cash dealings** NPL transactions *fpl* immédiates ► **cash deficit** N déficit *m or* découvert *m* de trésorerie ► **cash desk** N [*of shop, restaurant*] caisse *f* ; [*of cinema, theatre*] guichet *m* ► **cash discount** N escompte *m or* remise *f* au comptant ► **cash dispenser** N distributeur *m* (automatique) de billets ► **cash economy** N économie *f* monétaire ► **cash flow** N marge *f* brute d'autofinancement, cash-flow *m* ; ~ **flow problems** difficultés *fpl* de trésorerie ► **cash holdings** NPL avoirs *mpl* en caisse *or* en numéraire ► **cash income** N revenu *m* monétaire ► **cash in hand** N espèces *fpl* en caisse, encaisse *f* ♦ ADV **$100, ~ in hand** 100 dollars, de la main à la main ► **cash machine** N (*US*) = **cash dispenser** ► **cash offer** N offre *f* d'achat avec paiement comptant ; **he made me a ~ offer** il m'a offert de l'argent ► **cash payment** N paiement *m* comptant, versement *m* en espèces ► **cash point** N (*in shop*) caisse *f* ; (*Brit* = *cash dispenser*) distributeur *m* (automatique) de billets ► **cash price** N prix *m* au comptant ► **cash prize** N prix *m* en espèces ► **cash receipts** NPL recettes *fpl* de caisse ► **cash reduction** N = **cash discount** ► **cash register** N caisse *f* (enregistreuse) ► **cash reserves** NPL liquidités *fpl* ► **cash sale** N vente *f* (au) comptant ► **cash squeeze** N (*Econ*) restrictions *fpl* de crédit ► **cash terms** NPL conditions *fpl* au comptant ► **cash transaction** N affaire *f or* opération *f* au comptant

► **cash in** VT SEP [+ *bonds, savings certificates*] réaliser, se faire rembourser

► **cash in on*** VT FUS tirer profit de

► **cash up** VI (*Brit*) faire sa caisse

cashback [ˈkæʃbæk] N **a** (= *discount*) remise *f* **b** (*at supermarket etc*) retrait d'espèces à la caisse d'un magasin

cashbook [ˈkæʃbʊk] N livre *m* de caisse

cashbox [ˈkæʃbɒks] N caisse *f*

cashew [kæˈʃuː] N anacardier *m* ; (*also* ~ **nut**) noix *f* de cajou

cashier¹ [kæˈʃɪəʳ] **1** N (*Comm, Banking*) caissier *m*, -ière *f* **2** COMP ► **cashier's check** N (*US*) chèque *m* de banque

cashier² [kæˈʃɪəʳ] VT (*Mil*) casser ; (*gen*) renvoyer, congédier

cashless [ˈkæʃlɪs] ADJ **the ~ society** *or* **economy** la société sans argent (*où l'on ne paie plus qu'en argent électronique*)

cashmere [kæʃˈmɪəʳ] **1** N (*Tex*) cachemire *m* **2** COMP de *or* en cachemire

casing [ˈkeɪsɪŋ] N (*gen*) revêtement *m*, enveloppe *f* ; [*of door, window*] chambranle *m* ; [*of tyre*] chape *f* ; [*of oil well*] cuvelage *m*

casino [kəˈsiːnəʊ] N casino *m*

cask [kɑːsk] N (*gen*) tonneau *m*, fût *m* ; (*large*) pièce *f*, barrique *f* ; (*small*) baril *m* ; **wine in ~** vin *m* en fût

casket [ˈkɑːskɪt] N [*of jewels etc*] coffret *m*, boîte *f* ; (*esp US* = *coffin*) cercueil *m*

Caspian [ˈkæspɪən] ADJ **the ~ Sea** la mer Caspienne

Cassandra [kəˈsændrə] N (*Myth, fig*) Cassandre *f*

cassava [kəˈsɑːvə] N (*Bot*) manioc *m* ; (*Culin*) farine *f* de manioc

casserole [ˈkæsərəʊl] **1** N (*Brit Culin* = *utensil*) cocotte *f* ; (= *food*) ragoût *m* en cocotte **2** VT [+ *meat*] (faire) cuire en *or* à la cocotte

cassette [kæˈset] **1** N (*Recording*) cassette *f* ; (*Phot*) recharge *f* **2** COMP ► **cassette deck** N platine *f* (à) cassettes ► **cassette player** N lecteur *m* de cassettes ► **cassette recorder** N magnétophone *m* à cassettes

cassis [kæˈsiːs] N cassis *m*

cassock [ˈkæsək] N soutane *f*

cassowary [ˈkæsəwɛərɪ] N casoar *m*

cast [kɑːst] (*vb: pret, ptp* **cast**) **1** N **a** (= *throw*) [*of dice, net*] coup *m* ; (*Fishing*) lancer *m* **b** (*Art, Tech* = *act of casting metal*) coulage *m*, coulée *f* **c** (= *mould*) moule *m* ; (*in plaster, metal etc*) moulage *m* ; [*of medallion etc*] empreinte *f* ; (*Med*) **to have one's leg in a ~** avoir une jambe dans le plâtre ; (*fig*) ~ **of features** traits *mpl* (du visage) ; ~ **of mind** *or* **thought** mentalité *f*, tournure *f* d'esprit ; **a man of quite a different ~** un homme d'une tout autre trempe → **plaster** **d** (*Theat*) (= *allocation of parts*) distribution *f* ; (= *actors collectively*) acteurs *mpl* ; (*Cine, TV*) ~ **(and credits)** générique *m* ; (*Theat etc*) ~ **list** distribution *f* ; **he was in the ~ of Evita** il a joué dans Evita **e** [*of snake*] dépouille *f* ; [*of worm*] déjections *fpl* **f** (*Med* = *squint*) strabisme *m* ; **to have a ~ in one eye** avoir un œil qui louche, loucher d'un œil

2 VT **a** (= *throw*) [+ *dice*] jeter ; [+ *net, fishing line, stone*] lancer, jeter ; (*Naut*) **to ~ anchor** jeter l'ancre, mouiller (l'ancre) ; **to ~ sb into jail** jeter qn en prison ; **to ~ sb's horoscope** tirer *or* dresser l'horoscope de qn ; (*liter*) **to ~ o.s. on sb's mercy** s'en remettre à la clémence (*liter*) de qn, remettre son sort entre les mains de qn ; **to ~ a vote** voter ; **to ~ aspersions on sth/sb** dénigrer qch/qn ; **to ~ the blame on sb** rejeter la responsabilité sur qn ; **to ~ doubt on sth** jeter un doute sur qch ; **to ~ a look at sth** jeter un regard sur qch ; **to ~ a shadow on** *or* **over sb/sth** (*lit*) projeter une ombre sur qn/qch ; (*fig*) jeter une ombre sur qn/qch ; (*lit*) **to ~ a light on sth** éclairer qch ; **to ~ one's eye(s) round a room** promener ses regards sur une pièce, balayer une pièce du regard ; **to ~ one's eye(s) in the direction of ...** porter les yeux *or* son regard du côté de ... ; **to ~ a critical eye on sth** considérer qch d'un œil critique ; **to ~ a greedy eye** *or* **greedy eyes on sth** dévorer qch des yeux → **die², light, lot, spell¹** **b** (= *shed*) **to ~ its skin** [*snake*] muer ; **to ~ a shoe** [*horse*] perdre un fer **c** (*Art, Tech*) [+ *plaster*] couler ; [+ *metal*] couler, fondre ; [+ *statue*] mouler → **mould¹, stone** **d** (*Theat*) [+ *play, film*] distribuer les rôles de ; **he was ~ as Hamlet** *or* **for the part of Hamlet** on lui a donné le rôle de Hamlet **e** (= *describe*) étiqueter, cataloguer ; **to ~ o.s. as** se présenter comme

3 VI (*Fishing*) lancer sa ligne

4 COMP ► **cast-iron** N fonte *f* ♦ ADJ de *or* en fonte ; (*fig*) [*will, constitution*] de fer ; [*excuse, alibi*] inattaquable, (en) béton* ; [*case*] solide ► **cast-off clothes, cast-offs** NPL vêtements *mpl* dont on ne veut plus ; (*pej*) vieilles nippes* *fpl or* frusques* *fpl* ; (*fig*) **the ~-offs from society** les laissés *mpl* pour compte (de la société)

► **cast about, cast around** VI **to ~ about for sth** chercher qch ; **she has been ~ing around for a good excuse to ...** elle cherche une bonne excuse pour ... ; **to ~ about for how to do/how to reply** chercher le moyen de faire/la façon de répondre

► **cast aside** VT SEP rejeter, mettre de côté ; (*fig*) [+ *person*] rejeter, abandonner ; [+ *object*] abandonner, se défaire de

► **cast away** **1** VT SEP rejeter ; (*fig*) se défaire de ; (*Naut*) **to be ~ away** être naufragé **2** ~**away** N → **castaway**

► **cast back** **1** VI (*fig, liter*) revenir (**to** à) **2** VT SEP **to ~ one's thoughts back** se reporter en arrière

► **cast down** VT SEP [+ *object*] jeter par terre ; [+ *eyes*] baisser ; [+ *weapons*] déposer, mettre bas ; (*fig, liter*) **to be ~ down** être abattu *or* découragé *or* démoralisé

► **cast in** VI, VT SEP **to ~ in (one's lot) with sb** partager le sort de qn

► **cast off** **1** VI (*Naut*) larguer les amarres,

appareiller; (*Knitting*) arrêter les mailles **2** VT SEP (*Naut*) larguer les amarres de; (*Knitting*) arrêter; [+ *bonds, chains*] (*lit*) se défaire de, se libérer de; (*fig*) s'affranchir de; (*Knitting*) **~ off eight stitches at the beginning of the next row** rabattez huit mailles au début du prochain rang **3** **~-off** N, ADJ → **cast**

► **cast on** (*Knitting*) **1** VI monter les mailles **2** VT SEP [+ *stitch, sleeve*] monter; **~ on 159 stitches** montez 159 mailles

► **cast out** VT SEP (*liter*) chasser

► **cast up** VT SEP **a** (*lit*) lancer en l'air; (*fig*) **to ~ one's eyes up** lever les yeux au ciel **b** (*Math*) calculer **c** (*fig = reproach*) **to ~ sth up to** or **at sb** reprocher qch à qn

castanets [ˌkæstə'nets] NPL castagnettes *fpl*

castaway ['kɑːstəweɪ] N naufragé(e) *m(f)*; (*fig: from society etc*) réprouvé(e) *m(f)*, paria *m*

caste [kɑːst] **1** N caste *f*, classe *f* sociale; **to lose** ~ déroger, déchoir **2** COMP ► **caste mark** N (*in India*) signe *m* de (la) caste; (*fig*) signe *m* distinctif (d'un groupe) ► **caste system** N système *m* des castes

castellated ['kæstəleɪtɪd] **1** ADJ (*Archit*) crénelé, de style féodal **2** COMP ► **castellated nut** N (*Tech*) écrou *m* crénelé

caster ['kɑːstə'] **1** N **a** (= *sifter*) saupoudroir *m* **b** (= *wheel*) roulette *f* **2** COMP ► **caster angle** N (*Aut*) angle *m* de chasse ► **caster sugar** N (*Brit*) sucre *m* en poudre

castigate ['kæstɪgeɪt] VT [+ *person*] châtier (*liter*), corriger; [+ *book etc*] éreinter; [+ *theory, vice*] fustiger (*liter*)

castigation [ˌkæstɪ'geɪʃən] N [*of person*] châtiment *m*, correction *f*; [*of book etc*] éreintement *m*

Castile [kæ'stiːl] N Castille *f*

Castilian [kæs'tɪlɪən] **1** ADJ castillan **2** N **a** Castillan(e) *m(f)* **b** (*Ling*) espagnol *m*, castillan *m*

casting ['kɑːstɪŋ] **1** N (*NonC* = *act of throwing*) lancer *m*, lancement *m*; (*Tech*) (= *act*) fonte *f*, coulée *f*; (= *object*) pièce *f* fondue; (*Art*) moulage *m*; (*Theat*) distribution *f*; (*Cine*) casting *m* **2** COMP ► **casting couch** N **she got the role on the ~ couch** elle a couché pour avoir ce rôle ► **casting director** N (*Theat*) responsable *mf* de la distribution; (*Cine*) directeur *m*, -trice *f* du casting ► **casting vote** N voix *f* prépondérante; **to have a** or **the ~ vote** avoir voix prépondérante

castle ['kɑːsl] **1** N **a** château *m* (fort) → **build b** (*Chess*) tour *f* **2** VI (*Chess*) roquer

castling ['kɑːslɪŋ] N (*Chess*) roque *f*

castor¹ ['kɑːstə'] N = **caster**

castor² ['kɑːstə'] **1** N **a** (= *beaver*) castor *m* **b** (*Med*) castoréum *m* **2** COMP ► **castor oil** N huile *f* de ricin ► **castor oil plant** N ricin *m*

castrate [kæs'treɪt] VT [+ *animal, man*] châtrer, castrer; (*fig*) [+ *personality*] émasculer; [+ *text, film, book*] expurger

castration [kæs'treɪʃən] N castration *f*

castrato [kæs'trɑːtəʊ] N (*pl* **castrato** or **castrati** [kæs'trɑːtiː]) castrat *m*

Castroism ['kæstrəʊɪzəm] N (*Pol*) castrisme *m*

Castroist ['kæstrəʊɪst] ADJ, N (*Pol*) castriste *mf*

casual ['kæʒjʊl] **1** ADJ **a** (= *nonchalant*) [*person, manner, attitude, tone, glance, wave*] désinvolte; [*chat, conversation*] informel; **he tried to sound ~** il a essayé de parler avec désinvolture; **to the ~ eye** or **observer** pour le simple observateur; **he ran a ~ eye down the page** il a négligemment parcouru la page; (*pej*) **to be ~ about sth** prendre qch à la légère or avec désinvolture; **her ~ attitude (to safety/discipline)** la désinvolture dont elle fait preuve (en matière de sécurité/discipline) **b** (= *occasional*) [*drinker, drug use, relationship*] occasionnel; [*sexual partner*] occasionnel; **a ~ acquaintance** une (simple) connaissance; **a ~**

affair une passade, une aventure; **~ contact** contacts *mpl* ordinaires; **~ drug users** les consommateurs *mpl* (de drogue) occasionnels; **~ sex** rapports *mpl* sexuels occasionnels; **to have ~ sex** faire l'amour au hasard d'une rencontre

c (= *by chance*) [*remark, comment*] fait en passant; [*meeting, encounter*] fortuit; [*spark*] accidentel; [*visitor, caller*] de passage

d (= *informal*) [*clothes, shoes*] sport *inv*, décontracté; **~ wear** vêtements *mpl* sport *inv*, tenue *f* décontractée

e (= *temporary*) [*work, employment, job, labour*] temporaire; [*farm worker*] (*daily*) journalier; (*seasonally*) saisonnier; **~ labourer** (*on building site*) ouvrier *m* sans travail fixe; (*on farm*) (*daily*) journalier *m*, -ière *f*; (*seasonally*) saisonnier *m*, -ière *f*; **on a ~ basis** à titre temporaire

2 N **a** **~s** (= *shoes*) chaussures *fpl* sport *inv*; (= *clothes*) vêtements *mpl* sport *inv*

b (= *worker*) (*in office*) employé(e) *m(f)* temporaire; (*in factory*) ouvrier *m*, -ière *f* temporaire

casually ['kæʒjʊlɪ] ADV **a** (= *nonchalantly*) [*mention, say, ask, walk, lean*] avec désinvolture, nonchalamment **b** (= *accidentally*) par hasard **c** (= *informally*) [*dress*] de façon contractée, décontracté* *inv*

casualness ['kæʒjʊlnɪs] N [*of speech, manner*] désinvolture *f*; [*of dress*] style *m* décontracté

casualty ['kæʒjʊltɪ] **1** N **a** (*Mil*) (= *dead*) mort(e) *m(f)*; (= *wounded*) blessé(e) *m(f)*; **casualties** les morts *mpl* et blessés *mpl*; (= *dead*) les pertes *fpl* **b** (= *accident victim*) accidenté(e) *m(f)*, victime *f*; (= *accident*) accident *m* **2** COMP ► **casualty department** N service *m* des urgences ► **casualty list** N (*Mil*) état *m* des pertes; (*Aviat, gen*) liste *f* des victimes ► **casualty ward** N salle *f* des urgences

casuist ['kæzjʊɪst] N casuiste *mf*

casuistry ['kæzjʊɪstrɪ] N (*NonC*) casuistique *f*; (*instance of this*) arguments *mpl* de casuiste

CAT **1** N **a** [ˌsiːeɪ'tiː] (ABBR = **computer-aided teaching**) EAO *m* **b** [kæt] (ABBR = **computerized axial tomography**) scanographie *f*, tomodensitométrie *f*, scanner* *m* **2** COMP ► **CAT scan** N scanographie *f*, tomodensitométrie *f*, scanner* *m*; **to have a ~ scan** se faire faire une scanographie or un scanner* ► **CAT scanner** N tomodensitomètre *m*, scanner* *m*

cat [kæt] N chat(te) *m(f)*; (= *species*) félin *m*; (* *pej* = *woman*) mégère *f*; (*Zool*) **the big ~s** les fauves *mpl* → **tabby**, **tom**

b = **cat-o'-nine-tails**

c (*phrases*) **to let the ~ out of the bag** vendre la mèche; **the ~'s out of the bag** ce n'est plus un secret maintenant; **to look like the ~ that got the cream** (*esp Brit*) or **that ate the canary** avoir l'air content de soi; **to wait for the ~ to jump** ◊ **to wait to see which way the ~ jumps** attendre pour voir d'où vient le vent; (**has the**) **~ got your tongue?*** tu as perdu ta langue?; **to fight** or **be at each other like ~ and dog** (*lit*) se battre comme des chiffonniers; (*fig*) être or s'entendre comme chien et chat; (*Brit*) **to fight like Kilkenny ~s†** se battre comme des chiffonniers; **he doesn't have a ~ in hell's chance of winning** il n'a pas l'ombre d'une chance de gagner ■ (*PROV*) **a ~ may look at a king** un chien regarde bien un évêque (*PROV*); **to be like a ~ on a hot tin roof** or **a ~ on hot bricks** être sur des charbons ardents ■ (*PROV*) **when** or **while the ~'s away the mice will play** quand le chat n'est pas là, les souris dansent; **that set the ~ among the pigeons** ça a été le pavé dans la mare; **he thinks he's the ~'s whiskers** or **the ~'s miaow*** il se prend pour le nombril du monde*; (*Ir fig*) **to be a bag of ~s** être d'une humeur massacrante or de chien (*pej*); (*pej*) **look what the ~ dragged in** or **brought in!*** regarde donc un peu qui pointe son nez!; (*pej*) **you look like something the ~ dragged in** or **brought in!***

non mais regarde à quoi tu ressembles! → **2**; → **bell¹**, **grin**, **rain**, **room**, **skin**

d (*US‡*) (= *man*) gars* *m*, type* *m*; (= *woman*) gonzesse‡ *f*, nana* *f*; **cool ~** type *m* (or nana *f*) cool*

e **~s and dogs** (*St Ex*) actions *fpl* et obligations *fpl* de valeur douteuse; (*Comm*) articles *mpl* peu demandés

f (* = *catalytic converter*) pot *m* catalytique

2 COMP ► **cat-and-mouse** N, ADJ (*fig*) **to play (at) ~-and-mouse with sb** ◊ **to play a ~-and-mouse game with sb** jouer au chat et à la souris avec qn ► **cat-basket** N (*for carrying*) panier *m* pour chat; (*for sleeping*) corbeille *f* pour chat ► **cat burglar** N monte-en-l'air* *m inv* ► **cat door** N chatière *f* ► **cat fight** N (*esp US: between women*) crêpage *m* de chignon* ► **cat flap** N = **cat door** ► **cat-lick*** N toilette *f* de chat, brin *m* de toilette; **to give o.s. a ~-lick** faire une toilette de chat or un brin de toilette ► **cat litter** N litière *f* (pour chats) ► **cat-o'-nine-tails** N (*pl inv*) martinet *m*, chat-à-neuf-queues ► **cat's-cradle** N (*jeu m des*) figures *fpl* (*que l'on forme entre ses doigts avec de la ficelle*) ► **cat's-eye** N (= *gemstone*) œil-de-chat *m*; (*Brit Aut*) (clou *m* à) catadioptre *m*, cataphote® *m* ► **cat's-paw** N dupe *f* (*qui tire les marrons du feu*) ► **cat's-whisker** N (*Rad*) chercheur *m* (du détecteur à galène)

cataclysm ['kætəklɪzəm] N cataclysme *m*

cataclysmic [ˌkætə'klɪzmɪk] ADJ cataclysmique

catacombs ['kætəkuːmz] NPL catacombes *fpl*

catafalque ['kætəfælk] N catafalque *m*

Catalan ['kætəˌlæn] **1** N Catalan(e) *m(f)*; (*Ling*) catalan *m* **2** ADJ catalan

catalepsy ['kætəlepsɪ] N catalepsie *f*

cataleptic [ˌkætə'leptɪk] ADJ cataleptique

catalogue, catalog (*US*) ['kætəlɒg] **1** N (*gen*) catalogue *m*; (*in library*) fichier *m*; (*US Univ etc* = *brochure*) brochure *f* (*d'un établissement d'enseignement supérieur*) **2** VT cataloguer

Catalonia [ˌkætə'ləʊnɪə] N la Catalogne

catalysis [kə'tæləsɪs] N (*pl* **catalyses** [kə'tælə,siːz]) catalyse *f*

catalyst ['kætəlɪst] N (*Chem, fig*) catalyseur *m*

catalytic [ˌkætə'lɪtɪk] **1** ADJ (*Tech*) catalytique; (*fig*) [*person*] qui agit comme un catalyseur; [*role*] de catalyseur **2** COMP ► **catalytic converter** N (*Aut*) pot *m* catalytique

catalyze ['kætəlaɪz] VT (*US Chem, fig*) catalyser

catamaran [ˌkætəmə'ræn] N catamaran *m*

cataphoric [ˌkætə'fɒrɪk] ADJ (*Ling*) cataphorique

catapult ['kætəpʌlt] **1** N (*Brit* = *slingshot*) lance-pierre(s) *m inv*; (*Aviat, Mil*) catapulte *f* **2** VT (*gen, Aviat, fig*) catapulter **3** COMP ► **catapult-launched** ADJ (*Aviat*) catapulté ► **catapult launching** N (*Aviat*) catapultage *m*

cataract ['kætərækt] N **a** (= *waterfall*) cataracte *f* **b** (*Med*) cataracte *f*

catarrh [kə'tɑːʳ] N rhume *m* (chronique), catarrhe *m*

catarrhal [kə'tɑːrəl] ADJ catarrheux

catastrophe [kə'tæstrəfɪ] N catastrophe *f*

catastrophic [ˌkætə'strɒfɪk] ADJ catastrophique

catastrophically [ˌkætə'strɒfɪklɪ] ADV [*fail*] de façon catastrophique; **~ inept** d'une ineptie catastrophique; **to go ~ wrong** tourner à la catastrophe; **supplies were at ~ low levels** les vivres étaient tombés à un niveau catastrophique

catatonia [ˌkætə'təʊnɪə] N (*NonC*) catatonie *f*

catatonic [ˌkætə'tɒnɪk] ADJ catatonique

catbird ['kætbɜːd] N (*US*) **to be (sitting) in the ~ seat*** être en position de force

catcall ['kætkɔ:l] (*Theat*) [1] N sifflet *m* [2] VI siffler

catch [kætʃ] (*vb: pret, ptp* **caught**) [1] N [a] (= *act, thing caught*) prise *f*, capture *f*; (*Fishing*) (= *several fish*) pêche *f*; (= *one fish*) prise *f*; (*Sport*) **good ~!** bien rattrapé!; **the fisherman lost his whole ~** le pêcheur a perdu toute sa pêche; (*as husband*) **he's a good ~*** c'est un beau parti

[b] (* = *concealed drawback*) attrape *f*, entourloupette* *f*; **there must be a ~ (in it)** il y a anguille sous roche; **where's the ~?** qu'est-ce qui se cache là-dessous?

[c] [*of buckle*] ardillon *m*; (*Brit: on door*) loquet *m*; [*of latch*] loquet *m*; [*of wheel*] cliquet *m*; (*Brit: on window*) loqueteau *m*

[d] (*fig*) **with a ~ in one's voice** d'une voix entrecoupée

[e] (*Mus*) canon *m*

[f] (= *ballgame*) jeu *m* de balle; (= *tag*) (jeu *m* du) chat *m*

[2] VT [a] [+ *ball*] attraper; [+ *object*] attraper, saisir; [+ *fish, mice, thief*] attraper; **to ~ an animal in a trap** prendre un animal dans un piège *or* au piège; **to ~ sb by the arm** ◊ **to ~ sb's arm** prendre qn par le bras; **to be caught between two people/alternatives** être pris entre deux personnes/possibilités; **a toaster with a tray to ~ the breadcrumbs** un grille-pain avec un plateau pour ramasser les miettes de pain; **you can usually ~ me (in) around noon*** en général on peut me trouver vers midi; **I dialled her number hoping to ~ her before she went to work** je lui ai téléphoné en espérant l'avoir* *or* la joindre avant qu'elle (ne) parte au travail; **hello Adrienne, glad I caught you*** bonjour Adrienne, je suis content de te trouver *or* que tu sois là; **can I ring you back? you've caught me at a bad time** je peux vous rappeler? je suis occupé en ce moment; **(I'll) ~ you later!*** à plus!*, à plus tard! → **crab, sun**

[b] (= *take by surprise*) surprendre; **to ~ sb doing sth** surprendre qn à faire qch; **to be caught unprepared** être pris au dépourvu; **to ~ sb by surprise** prendre qn à l'improviste; (*esp Brit Sport*) **to be caught cold** être pris au dépourvu; **she caught herself dreaming of Spain** elle se surprit à rêver de l'Espagne; **I caught myself feeling sorry for them** je me suis surpris à les plaindre; **if I ~ them at it!*** si je les y prends!; **if I ~ you at it again!*** que je t'y reprenne!; **(you won't) ~ me doing that again!*** (il n'y a) pas de danger que je recommence (*subj*)!, c'est bien la dernière fois que je le fais!; **to ~ sb in the act** prendre qn sur le fait *or* en flagrant délit; **we were caught in a storm** nous avons été pris dans *or* surpris par un orage; **to get caught by sb** se faire *or* se laisser attraper par qn

[c] [+ *bus, train etc*] (= *be in time for*) attraper; (= *get on board*) prendre; **he didn't ~ his train** il a manqué son train; **to ~ the post** arriver à temps pour la levée; (= *go by*) **he caught the ferry to France** il a pris le ferry pour aller en France; (*TV*) **did you ~ the news/that film last night?** tu as vu *ou* pu voir les informations/ce film hier soir?

[d] (= *trap*) **the branch caught my skirt** ◊ **I caught my skirt on the branch** ma jupe s'est accrochée à la branche; **the door caught my skirt** ◊ **I caught my skirt in the door** ma jupe s'est prise dans la porte; **the top of the lorry caught the bridge** le haut du camion a accroché le pont; **she caught him with her elbow** elle lui a donné un coup de coude (sans le faire exprès); **to ~ one's foot in sth** se prendre le pied dans qch

[e] (= *understand, hear*) saisir, comprendre; **to ~ the meaning of sth** saisir le sens de qch; **I didn't ~ what he said** je n'ai pas saisi ce qu'il a dit

[f] [+ *flavour*] sentir, discerner; **to ~ the sound of sth** percevoir le bruit de qch

[g] (*Med*) [+ *disease*] attraper; **to ~ a cold** attraper un rhume; **to ~ cold** attraper *or* prendre froid; **to ~ one's death of cold*** ◊ **to ~ one's death*** attraper la crève*

[h] (*phrases*) **to ~ sb's attention** *or* **eye** attirer l'attention de qn; **to ~ the chairman's eye** obtenir la parole; (*Brit Parl*) **to ~ the Speaker's eye** obtenir la parole (*à la Chambre des communes*); **to be caught between envy and admiration** osciller entre l'envie et l'admiration; **to ~ sb a blow** donner un coup à qn; **she caught him one on the nose*** elle lui a flanqué* un coup sur le nez; **to ~ the light** accrocher la lumière; **his speech caught the mood of the assembly** son discours traduisait *or* reflétait l'humeur de l'assemblée; (*fig*) **to ~ sb with his (or her etc) pants or trousers down** surprendre qn dans une situation embarrassante; **you'll ~ it!*** tu vas écoper!*; **he caught it all right!*** qu'est-ce qu'il a pris!*; **to ~ sb on the wrong foot** ◊ **to ~ sb off balance** (*lit*) prendre qn à contre-pied; (*fig*) prendre qn au dépourvu → **breath, fire, glimpse, likeness, nap, sight**

[3] VI [a] [*fire, wood, ice*] prendre; (*Culin*) attacher

[b] [*lock*] fermer

[c] **her dress caught in the door/on a nail** sa robe s'est prise dans la porte/s'est accrochée à un clou

[4] COMP ► **catch 22*** N **it's a ~ 22 situation** il n'y a pas moyen de s'en sortir, c'est une situation inextricable ► **catch-all** N fourre-tout *m inv* (*fig*) ◆ ADJ [*regulation, clause etc*] général, fourre-tout *inv*; **~-all phrase** expression *f* passe-partout *inv* ► **catch-as-catch-can** N catch *m* ► **catch phrase** N (*constantly repeated*) rengaine *f*; (= *vivid, striking phrase*) accroche *f*, slogan *m* accrocheur ► **catch question** N colle* *f*

► **catch at** VT FUS [+ *object*] (*essayer d'*)attraper; **to ~ at an opportunity** sauter sur une occasion

► **catch on** VI [a] (= *become popular*) [*fashion*] prendre; [*song*] devenir populaire, marcher [b] (= *understand*) saisir, comprendre (**to sth** qch)

► **catch out** VT SEP (*esp Brit*) (= *catch napping*) prendre en défaut; (= *catch in the act*) prendre sur le fait; **to ~ sb out in a lie** surprendre qn en train de mentir, prendre qn à mentir; **to be caught out (by sth)** être pris par surprise (par qch); **he'll get caught out some day** un beau jour il se fera prendre

► **catch up** [1] VI [a] se rattraper, combler son retard; (*with studies*) se rattraper, se remettre au niveau; (*with news, gossip*) se remettre au courant; **to ~ up on** *or* **with one's work** (re)mettre à jour dans son travail; **to ~ up on one's sleep** rattraper *or* combler son retard de sommeil; **to ~ up on** *or* **with sb** (*going in the same direction*) rattraper qn, rejoindre qn; (*in work etc*) rattraper qn; **the police caught up with him in Vienna** la police l'a attrapé à Vienne; **the truth/illness has finally caught up with him** la vérité/la maladie a fini par le rattraper

[b] **to be** *or* **get caught up in sth** (*in net etc*) être pris dans qch; (*fig*) (*in activity, campaign etc*) être pris dans qch; (*in sb's enthusiasm etc*) être gagné par qch; (*in sb's ideas etc*) être emballé par qch; (*in circumstances etc*) être prisonnier de qch; (*in scandal*) être mêlé à qch

[2] VT SEP [a] [+ *person*] rattraper [b] (= *interrupt*) [+ *person*] interrompre, couper la parole à [c] (= *pick up quickly*) ramasser vivement [d] [+ *hair*] relever; [+ *curtain*] retenir

catcher ['kætʃə'] [1] N [a] (*Baseball*) attrapeur *m* [b] → **mole¹, rat** [2] COMP ► **catcher's mitt** N gant *m* de baseball

catching* ['kætʃɪŋ] ADJ (*Med*) contagieux; (*fig*) [*laughter, enthusiasm*] contagieux, communicatif; [*habit, mannerism*] contagieux

catchment ['kætʃmənt] [1] N captage *m* [2] COMP ► **catchment area** N (*Brit Geog: also ~ basin*) bassin *m* hydrographique; [*of hospital*] circonscription *f* hospitalière; [*of school*] secteur *m* de recrutement scolaire

catchpenny ['kætʃpenɪ] (*pej*) [1] ADJ clinquant, accrocheur [2] **it's a ~** c'est de la pacotille

catchup ['kætʃəp] N (*US*) = **ketchup**

catchword ['kætʃwɜ:d] N (= *slogan*) slogan *m*; (*Pol*) mot *m* d'ordre, slogan *m*; (*Printing*) [*of foot of page*] réclame *f*; [*of top of page*] mot-vedette *f*; (*Theat* = *cue*) réplique *f*

catchy* ['kætʃɪ] ADJ [*tune*] entraînant; [*title, name, slogan*] accrocheur

catechism ['kætɪkɪzm] N catéchisme *m*

catechist ['kætɪkɪst] N catéchiste *mf*

catechize ['kætɪkaɪz] VT (*Rel*) catéchiser; (*fig*) (= *teach*) instruire (*par questions et réponses*); (= *examine*) interroger, questionner

categoric(al) [,kætɪ'gɒrɪk(əl)] ADJ catégorique

categorically [,kætɪ'gɒrɪkəlɪ] ADV catégoriquement

categorization [,kætɪgəraɪ'zeɪʃən] N catégorisation *f*

categorize ['kætɪgəraɪz] VT classer par catégories

category ['kætɪgərɪ] [1] N catégorie *f* [2] COMP ► **Category A prisoner** N (*Brit*) détenu *condamné pour meurtre, vol à main armée ou terrorisme*

cater ['keɪtə'] VI (= *provide food*) s'occuper de la nourriture, préparer un *or* des repas (**for** pour); (*fig*) **to ~ for** (*sb's needs*) pourvoir à; (*sb's tastes*) satisfaire; **this magazine ~s for all ages** ce magazine s'adresse à tous les âges; (= *expect*) **I didn't ~ for that*** je n'avais pas prévu cela

cater-corner(ed) [,keɪtə'kɔ:nə'(-əd)] ADV (*US*) en diagonale (**from, to** par rapport à)

caterer ['keɪtərə'] N (*providing meals*) traiteur *m*; (*providing supplies*) fournisseur *m* (*en alimentation*)

catering ['keɪtərɪŋ] [1] N (*providing meals*) restauration *f*; (*providing supplies*) approvisionnement *m*, ravitaillement *m*; **the ~ for our reception was done by Smith and Lee** nous avons pris Smith and Lee comme traiteur pour notre réception [2] COMP ► **catering industry** N industrie *f* de la restauration ► **catering manager** N intendant(e) *m(f)* ► **catering trade** N restauration *f*

caterpillar ['kætəpɪlə'] [1] N (*Tech, Zool*) chenille *f* [2] COMP [*vehicle, wheel*] à chenilles ► **Caterpillar track®** N (*Tech*) chenille *f* ► **Caterpillar tractor®** N autochenille *f*

caterwaul ['kætəwɔ:l] [1] VI [a] (*lit*) [*cat*] miauler [b] (* *fig*) [*person*] brailler, pousser des braillements [2] N [a] (*lit*) [*of cat*] miaulement *m* [b] (*fig*) [*of person*] braillements *mpl*, hurlements *mpl*

caterwauling ['kætəwɔ:lɪŋ] N [*of cat*] miaulement *m*; [*of music*] cacophonie *f*; [*of person*] braillements *mpl*, hurlements *mpl*

catfish ['kætfɪʃ] N (*pl* **catfish** *or* **catfishes**) poisson-chat *m*

catfood ['kætfu:d] N nourriture *f* pour chats

catgut ['kætgʌt] N (*Mus, Sport*) boyau *m* (de chat); (*Med*) catgut *m*

Cath. [a] ABBR = **Cathedral** [b] ABBR = **Catholic**

Cathar ['kæθə'] [1] N (*pl* **Cathars** *or* **Cathari** ['kæθəri]) Cathare *mf* [2] ADJ cathare

catharsis [kə'θɑ:sɪs] N (*pl* **catharses** [kə'θɑ:si:z]) (*Literat, Psych*) catharsis *f*

cathartic [kə'θɑ:tɪk] [1] ADJ (*Literat, Med, Psych*) cathartique [2] N (*Med*) purgatif *m*, cathartique *m*

Cathay [kæ'θeɪ] N le Cathay

cathedral [kə'θi:drəl] [1] N cathédrale f [2] COMP ► **cathedral church** N cathédrale f ► **cathedral city** N évêché m, ville f épiscopale

Catherine ['kæθərɪn] [1] N Catherine f; (Hist) ~ **the Great** la Grande Catherine, Catherine la Grande [2] COMP ► **Catherine wheel** N (= firework) soleil m

catheter ['kæθɪtə'] N cathéter m

catheterize ['kæθɪtə,raɪz] VT [+ bladder, person] sonder

cathiodermie [,kæθɪəʊ'dɜːmɪ] N ionophorèse f

cathode ['kæθəʊd] [1] N cathode f [2] COMP [ray] cathodique ► **cathode ray tube** N tube m cathodique

catholic ['kæθəlɪk] [1] ADJ [a] (Rel) **Catholic** catholique [b] (= varied, all-embracing) [tastes, person] éclectique; (= universal) universel; **to be ~ in one's tastes** avoir des goûts éclectiques [2] N **Catholic** catholique mf [3] COMP ► **the Catholic Church** N l'Église f catholique ► **Catholic school** N école f catholique

Catholicism [kə'θɒlɪsɪzəm] N catholicisme m

cathouse ['kæthaʊs] N (US) bordel• m

cation ['kætaɪən] N (Chem) cation m

catkin ['kætkɪn] N (Bot) chaton m

catlike ['kætlaɪk] [1] ADJ félin [2] ADV comme un chat

catmint ['kætmɪnt] N herbe f aux chats

catnap• ['kætnæp] [1] VI sommeiller, faire un (petit) somme [2] N (petit) somme m; **to take a ~** sommeiller, faire un (petit) somme

catnip ['kætnɪp] N (US) = **catmint**

Cato ['keɪtəʊ] N Caton m

catsuit ['kætsuːt] N combinaison-pantalon f

catsup ['kætsəp] N (US) = **ketchup**

cattery ['kætərɪ] N pension f pour chats

cattiness• ['kætɪnɪs] N méchanceté f, rosserie• f

cattle ['kætl] [1] N bovins mpl; **the prisoners were treated like ~** les prisonniers étaient traités comme du bétail; "~ crossing" «passage m de troupeaux» ► ~ **head** [2] COMP ► **cattle breeder** N éleveur m (de bétail) ► **cattle breeding** N élevage m (de bétail) ► **cattle drive** N (US) déplacement m de bétail ► **cattle grid** N (Brit) grille à même la route permettant aux voitures mais non au bétail de passer ► **cattle market** N foire f or marché m aux bestiaux ► **cattle plague** N peste f bovine ► **cattle raising** N = **cattle breeding** ► **cattle shed** N étable f ► **cattle show** N concours m agricole ► **cattle truck** N (Aut) fourgon m à bestiaux; (Brit Rail) fourgon m or wagon m à bestiaux

cattleman ['kætlmən] N (pl **-men**) vacher m, bouvier m

catty• ['kætɪ] ADJ (pej) [person, gossip, criticism] rosse•, vache•; ~ **remark** vacherie• f; **to be ~ about sb/sth** dire des vacheries• sur qn/qch

catty-corner(ed) [,kætɪ'kɔːnə'(-əd)] ADV (US) = **cater-corner(ed)**, **cater-corner(ed)**

Catullus [kə'tʌləs] N Catulle m

CATV [,siːeɪtiː'viː] (ABBR = **community antenna television**) → **community**

catwalk ['kætwɔːk] N (Constr, Theat) passerelle f; (Fashion) podium m; **the models on the ~** les mannequins mpl du défilé

Caucasia [kɔː'keɪzɪə] N le Caucase

Caucasian [kɔː'keɪzɪən] [1] ADJ (Geog, Ling) caucasien; (Ethnology) de race blanche or caucasique [2] N (= person) (Geog) Caucasien(ne) m(f); (Ethnology) Blanc m, Blanche f

caucasoid ['kɔːkəsɔɪd] [1] ADJ de race blanche or caucasique [2] N Blanc m, Blanche f

Caucasus ['kɔːkəsəs] N **the ~** le Caucase

caucus ['kɔːkəs] N (pl **caucuses**) (US) (= committee) comité m électoral; (= meeting)

► LANGUAGE IN USE: **cause** 16.1

réunion f du comité électoral; (Brit pej) coterie f politique

caudal ['kɔːdl] ADJ caudal

caught [kɔːt] VB pt, ptp of **catch**

caul [kɔːl] N (Anat) coiffe f

cauldron ['kɔːldrən] N chaudron m; (fig) **a ~ of intrigue/ethnic strife** un foyer d'intrigues/ de conflit ethnique

cauliflower ['kɒlɪflaʊə'] [1] N chou-fleur m [2] COMP ► **cauliflower cheese** N (Culin) chou-fleur m au gratin ► **cauliflower ear•** N oreille f en feuille de chou

caulk [kɔːk] VT (Naut) calfater

causal ['kɔːzəl] ADJ causal; (Gram) causal, causatif; ~ **link** lien m causal

causality [kɔː'zælɪtɪ] N causalité f

causally ['kɔːzəlɪ] ADV causalement; **to be ~ related** avoir un lien or une relation de cause à effet

causation [kɔː'zeɪʃən] N [a] (= causing) causalité f [b] (= cause-effect relation) relation f de cause à effet

causative ['kɔːzətɪv] [1] ADJ causal; (Gram) causal, causatif; (frm) ~ **of** (qui est) cause de [2] N (Gram) mot m causal or causatif

▼ cause [kɔːz] [1] N [a] (gen, also Philos) cause f; (= reason) cause f, raison f, motif m; ~ **and effect** la cause et l'effet m; **the relation of ~ and effect** la relation de cause à effet; **the ~ of his failure** la cause de son échec; **to be the ~ of sth** être cause de qch, causer qch; (Jur) ~ **of action** fondement m (d'une action en justice); (Jur) ~ **of loss** fait m générateur du sinistre; **she has no ~ to be angry** elle n'a aucune raison de se fâcher; **there's no ~ for anxiety** il n'y a pas lieu de s'inquiéter or de raison de s'inquiéter or de quoi s'inquiéter; **with (good) ~** à juste titre; **not without ~** non sans raison; **without ~** sans cause or raison or motif; **without good ~** sans raison or cause or motif valable; ~ **for complaint** sujet m de plainte [b] (= purpose) cause f, parti m; (frm) **to make common ~ with sb** faire cause commune avec qn; **to work in a good ~** travailler pour la or une bonne cause; **it's all in a good ~•** c'est pour une bonne cause → **lost** [c] (Jur) cause f; **to plead sb's ~** plaider la cause de qn; ~ **list** rôle m des audiences [2] VT causer, occasionner; **to ~ damage/an accident** causer des dégâts/un accident; **to ~ grief to sb** causer du chagrin à qn; **to ~ trouble** causer des ennuis; **to ~ trouble to sb** causer des ennuis à qn; **I don't want to ~ you any trouble** je ne veux pas vous déranger; **to ~ sb to do sth** faire faire qch à qn; **to ~ sth to be done** faire faire qch

causeway ['kɔːzweɪ] N chaussée f

caustic ['kɔːstɪk] [1] ADJ (Chem, fig) caustique; ~ **remark** remarque f caustique [2] N substance f caustique, caustique m [3] COMP ► **caustic soda** N soude f caustique

caustically ['kɔːstɪklɪ] ADV [say, describe] de façon caustique; **to be ~ funny** [person] avoir un humour caustique; [book] être d'un humour caustique

cauterize ['kɔːtəraɪz] VT cautériser

cautery ['kɔːtərɪ] N cautère m

caution ['kɔːʃən] [1] N [a] (NonC = circumspection) prudence f, circonspection f; **proceed with ~** (gen) agissez avec prudence or circonspection; (Aut) avancez lentement [b] (= warning) avertissement m; (= rebuke) réprimande f; (on label) "~" «attention»; **he got off with a ~** il s'en est tiré avec une réprimande [c] (†* = rascal) numéro• m, phénomène• m [2] VT avertir, donner un avertissement à; (Brit Police: on charging suspect) mettre en garde (un suspect que toute déclaration de sa part peut être retenue contre lui); **to ~ sb against sth** mettre qn en garde contre qch; **to ~ sb against doing sth** déconseiller à qn de faire

qch [3] COMP ► **caution money** N (Jur) cautionnement m

cautionary ['kɔːʃənərɪ] ADJ (servant) d'avertissement; (Jur) donné en garantie; **a ~ tale** un récit édifiant

cautious ['kɔːʃəs] ADJ [person, welcome, response, optimism] prudent, circonspect

cautiously ['kɔːʃəslɪ] ADV [move] avec précaution; [say, react] prudemment, avec prudence; [welcome, accept] avec circonspection; ~ **optimistic** d'un optimisme prudent

cautiousness ['kɔːʃəsnɪs] N circonspection f

cavalcade [,kævəl'keɪd] [1] N cavalcade f [2] VI cavalcader

cavalier [,kævə'lɪə'] [1] N (gen, Mil) cavalier m; (Brit Hist) royaliste m (partisan de Charles Ier et de Charles II) [2] ADJ [a] (Brit Hist) royaliste [b] [person, behaviour, attitude] cavalier

cavalierly [,kævə'lɪəlɪ] ADV cavalièrement

cavalry ['kævəlrɪ] [1] N cavalerie f [2] COMP ► **cavalry charge** N charge f de cavalerie ► **cavalry officer** N officier m de cavalerie ► **cavalry twill** N (Tex) drap m sergé pour culotte de cheval, tricotine f

cavalryman ['kævəlrɪmən] N (pl **-men**) cavalier m

cave¹ [keɪv] [1] N caverne f, grotte f [2] VI **to go caving** faire de la spéléologie [3] COMP ► **cave dweller** N (Hist: in prehistory) homme m des cavernes; [of primitive tribes] troglodyte mf ► **cave-in** N [of floor, building] effondrement m, affaissement m; (* = defeat, surrender) effondrement m ► **cave painting** N peinture f rupestre ► **caving-in** N = **cave-in**

► **cave in** [1] VI [a] [floor, building] s'effondrer, s'affaisser; [wall, beam] céder [b] (* = yield) se dégonfler•, caner• [2] ~**in** ◊ **caving-in** N → **cave**

cave² †* ['keɪvɪ] EXCL (Brit Scol) ~**!** pet pet!•, vingt-deux!•; **to keep ~** faire le guet

caveat ['kævɪæt] N (gen) avertissement m; (Jur) notification f d'opposition; ~ **emptor** sans garantie du fournisseur, aux risques de l'acheteur

caveman ['keɪvmæn] N (pl **-men**) homme m des cavernes

caver ['keɪvə'] N spéléologue mf

cavern ['kævən] N caverne f

cavernous ['kævənəs] ADJ [room, building, space etc] énorme; [eyes] cave (liter), enfoncé; [mouth] immense; [voice, laugh] caverneux; [yawn] profond

caviar(e) ['kævɪɑː'] N caviar m

cavil ['kævɪl] VI ergoter, chicaner (**about, at** sur)

caving ['keɪvɪŋ] N spéléologie f

cavity ['kævɪtɪ] [1] N (gen) cavité f; (Med) (in rotten tooth) carie f; (Phon) orifice m; **to have cavities (in one's teeth)** avoir des caries [2] COMP ► **cavity wall** N mur m creux; ~ **wall insulation** isolation f des murs creux

cavort• [kə'vɔːt] VI (= jump about) [children] s'ébattre; (fig) **while you were ~ing (around) in Paris ...** pendant que tu prenais du bon temps à Paris ...; **they were ~ing (around) in the Jacuzzi®** ils faisaient les fous dans le jacuzzi®

cavortings [kə'vɔːtɪŋz] NPL ébats mpl

cavy ['keɪvɪ] N (Zool) cobaye m, cochon m d'Inde

caw [kɔː] [1] VI croasser [2] N croassement m

cawing ['kɔːɪŋ] N (NonC) croassement m

cay [keɪ] N (= sandbank) banc m de sable; (= coral reef) récif m or banc m de corail

Cayenne [keɪen] N (also ~ **pepper**) (poivre m de) Cayenne f

cayman ['keɪmən] N (pl **-mans**) [a] caïman m [b] **the Cayman Islands** les îles fpl Caïmans

CB [siː'biː] [1] [a] (ABBR = **Citizens' Band Radio**) (= activity) CB f; (= set) poste m de CB [b] (Mil)

CBE (ABBR = **confined to barracks**) → **confined** [c] (ABBR = **Companion (of the Order) of the Bath**) titre honorifique [2] COMP ► **CB user** N cibiste mf

CBE [ˌsiːbiː'iː] N (ABBR = **Companion (of the Order) of the British Empire**) titre honorifique

CBI [ˌsiːbiː'aɪ] N (ABBR = **Confederation of British Industry**) conseil du patronat en Grande-Bretagne

CBS [ˌsiːbiː'es] N ABBR = **Columbia Broadcasting System**

CC [siː'siː] (in Brit: formerly) (ABBR = **County Council**) → **county**

cc [siː'siː] [a] (ABBR = **cubic centimetre(s)**) cm³ [b] (ABBR = **carbon copy, carbon copies**) → **carbon**

CCTV [ˌsiːsiːtiːˈviː] N (ABBR = **closed-circuit television**) → **closed**

CD [siːˈdiː] [1] N [a] (ABBR = **compact disc**) CD m [b] (ABBR = **Corps Diplomatique**) CD m [c] (ABBR = **Civil Defence**) → **civil** [d] (US) (ABBR = **Congressional District**) → **congressional** [2] COMP ► **CD player** N platine f laser

CDC [ˌsiːdiː'siː] N (US) (ABBR = **Center for Disease Control and Prevention**) → **centre**; → CENTERS FOR DISEASE CONTROL

CD-I® [ˌsiːdiː'aɪ] N (ABBR = **compact disc interactive**) CD-I m, disque m compact interactif

Cdr. (Mil) (ABBR = **Commander**) (on envelope) ~ J. Thomas le commandant J. Thomas

CD-ROM [ˌsiːdiː'rɒm] (ABBR = **compact disc read-only memory**) CD-ROM m [2] COMP ► **CD-ROM drive** N lecteur m (de) CD-ROM

CDT [ˌsiːdiː'tiː] (US) (ABBR = **Central Daylight Time**) → **central**

CDTV [ˌsiːdiːtiːˈviː] N (NonC) (ABBR = **compact disc television**) télévision f interactive

CDV [ˌsiːdiːˈviː], **CD-video** [ˌsiːdiːˈvɪdɪəʊ] N (ABBR = **compact disc video**) CD-V m, vidéodisque m compact

CE [siː'iː] N (ABBR = **Church of England**) → **church**

cease [siːs] [1] VI [activity, noise etc] cesser, s'arrêter; **to ~ from work** cesser le travail; **to ~ from doing sth** cesser or s'arrêter de faire qch [2] VT [+ work, activity] cesser, arrêter; **to ~ doing sth** cesser or arrêter de faire sth; (Mil) **to ~ fire** cesser le feu; (Comm) **to ~ trading** fermer, cesser ses activités [3] N **without ~** sans cesse

ceasefire [ˈsiːsfaɪər] N (Mil) cessez-le-feu m inv

ceaseless [ˈsiːslɪs] ADJ incessant, continuel

ceaselessly [ˈsiːslɪslɪ] ADV sans arrêt, sans cesse

cecum [ˈsiːkəm] N (pl ceca) (US) = **caecum**

cedar [ˈsiːdər] [1] N cèdre m; **~ of Lebanon** cèdre m du Liban [2] COMP de or en cèdre ► **cedar wood** N (bois m de) cèdre m

cede [siːd] VT céder

cedilla [sɪˈdɪlə] N cédille f; **"c"** « c » cédille

Ceefax® [ˈsiːfæks] N télétexte® m (de la BBC)

ceilidh [ˈkeɪlɪ] N bal m folklorique écossais (or irlandais)

ceiling [ˈsiːlɪŋ] [1] N (gen, Aviat, fig) plafond m; **to fix a ~ for** or **put a ~ on prices/wages** fixer un plafond pour les prix/salaires; **to hit the ~**: (= get angry) sortir de ses gonds, piquer une crise*; [prices] crever le plafond; **prices have reached their ~ at 160 pence** les prix plafonnent à 160 pence [2] COMP [lamp, covering] de plafond; (fig) [rate, charge] plafond inv ► **ceiling decoration** N décoration f de plafond ► **ceiling price** N prix m plafond inv

celadon [ˈseləˌdɒn] N (= porcelaine) céladon m

celandine [ˈseləndaɪn] N chélidoine f

celeb: [səˈleb] N célébrité f, vedette f

celebrant [ˈselɪbrənt] N célébrant m, officiant m

▼ **celebrate** [ˈselɪbreɪt] [1] VT [+ person] célébrer, glorifier; [+ event] célébrer, fêter; **to ~ the anniversary of sth** commémorer qch; (Rel) **to ~ mass** célébrer la messe [2] VI [a] (Rel) célébrer

(l'office) [b] faire la fête; **let's ~!** il faut fêter ça!; (with drink) il faut arroser ça!*

celebrated [ˈselɪbreɪtɪd] ADJ (= famous) célèbre

celebration [ˌselɪˈbreɪʃən] [1] N [a] (also ~s) fête(s) f(pl); (at Christmas) (for family event etc) fête f, festivités fpl; (public event) cérémonies fpl, fête(s) f(pl); **we must have a ~!** il faut fêter ça!; **to join in the ~s** participer à la fête or aux festivités; **the victory ~s** les cérémonies marquant la victoire [b] (NonC = act of celebrating) [of event] (also Rel) célébration f; [of past event] commémoration f; [of sb's virtues etc] éloge m, louange f; **in ~ of** (victory etc) pour fêter or célébrer; (past victory etc) pour commémorer; (sb's achievements) pour célébrer [2] COMP [dinner, outing etc] de fête; (for past event) commémoratif

celebratory [ˌselɪˈbreɪtərɪ] ADJ de célébration; **how about a ~ drink?** et si on prenait un verre pour fêter ça?

celebrity [sɪˈlebrɪtɪ] N (= famous person) célébrité f

celeriac [səˈlerɪæk] N céleri(-rave) m

celerity [sɪˈlerɪtɪ] N (liter) célérité f

celery [ˈselərɪ] [1] N céleri m (ordinaire or à côtes); **a bunch** or **head of ~** un pied de céleri; **a stick of ~** une côte de céleri [2] COMP [seeds, salt] de céleri

celesta [sɪˈlestə] N célesta m

celestial [sɪˈlestɪəl] ADJ (lit, fig) céleste

celiac [ˈsiːlɪˌæk] ADJ (esp US) = **coeliac**

celibacy [ˈselɪbəsɪ] N célibat m

celibate [ˈselɪbɪt] ADJ, N (= unmarried) [priest, nun] célibataire mf; (= sexually inactive) chaste

cell [sel] [1] N [a] (gen, Bot, Bot, Phot, Telec) cellule f; (Elec) élément m (de pile); (Pol) **to form a ~** créer une cellule [b] (Police etc) cellule f; **he spent the night in the ~s** il a passé la nuit au poste or en cellule → **condemn** [2] COMP ► **cell culture** N (Bio) culture f de cellules ► **cell wall** N (Bio) paroi f cellulaire

cellar [ˈselər] N [a] (for wine, coal) cave f; (for food etc) cellier m; **in the ~** à la cave [b] (= store for wine) cave f (à vins); **he keeps an excellent ~** il a une excellente cave → **coal**, **saltcellar**

cellist [ˈtʃelɪst] N violoncelliste mf

cellmate [ˈselmeɪt] N compagnon m, compagne f de cellule

cello [ˈtʃeləʊ] [1] N violoncelle m [2] COMP de violoncelle

Cellophane® [ˈseləfeɪn] N cellophane® f

cellphone [ˈselfəʊn] N téléphone m cellulaire

cellular [ˈseljʊlər] [1] ADJ [a] (Anat, Bio etc) cellulaire [b] (Tex) [blanket] en cellular [2] COMP ► **cellular phone** N = **cellular telephone** ► **cellular radio** N (Rad) radio f cellulaire ► **cellular telephone** N téléphone m cellulaire

cellulite [ˈseljʊˌlaɪt] N cellulite f (gonflement)

cellulitis [ˌseljʊˈlaɪtɪs] N cellulite f (inflammation)

Celluloid® [ˈseljʊlɔɪd] [1] N celluloïd m [2] COMP en celluloïd

cellulose [ˈseljʊləʊs] [1] N cellulose f [2] COMP cellulosique, en or de cellulose ► **cellulose acetate** N acétate m de cellulose ► **cellulose varnish** N vernis m cellulosique

Celsius [ˈselsɪəs] ADJ Celsius inv; **degrees ~** degrés mpl Celsius

Celt [kelt, selt] N Celte mf

Celtic [ˈkeltɪk, ˈseltɪk] [1] ADJ celtique, celte [2] N (Ling) celtique m

cembalo [ˈtʃembələʊ] N (pl cembalos or cembali [ˈtʃembəliː]) (Mus) clavecin m

cement [səˈment] [1] N [a] (Constr, fig) ciment m [b] (Chem, Dentistry) amalgame m [c] = **cementum** [2] VT (Constr, fig) cimenter; (Chem) cémenter; (Dentistry) obturer [3] COMP

► **cement mixer** N bétonnière f, bétonneuse f

cementation [ˌsiːmenˈteɪʃən] N (Constr, fig) cimentation f; (Tech) cémentation f

cementum [sɪˈmentəm] N (Anat) cément m

cemetery [ˈsemɪtrɪ] N cimetière m

cenotaph [ˈsenətɑːf] N cénotaphe m

censer [ˈsensər] N encensoir m

censor [ˈsensər] [1] N censeur m [2] VT censurer

censorious [senˈsɔːrɪəs] ADJ [person, comments] critique, sévère

censorship [ˈsensəʃɪp] N (NonC) (= censoring) censure f; (= function of censor) censorat m

censurable [ˈsenʃərəbl] ADJ blâmable, critiquable

censure [ˈsenʃər] [1] VT blâmer, critiquer [2] N critique f, blâme m → **vote**

census [ˈsensəs] [1] N (pl censuses) recensement m; **to take a ~ of the population** faire le recensement de la population; **the increase between ~s** l'augmentation f intercensitaire [2] COMP ► **census enumerator**, **census taker** (US) N agent m recenseur

cent [sent] N [a] **per ~** pour cent [b] (Can, US = coin) cent m; **I haven't a ~*** je n'ai pas un centime or rond*

cent. [a] ABBR = **centigrade** [b] ABBR = **central** [c] ABBR = **century**

centaur [ˈsentɔːr] N centaure m

centenarian [ˌsentɪˈnɛərɪən] ADJ, N centenaire mf

centenary [senˈtiːnərɪ] (esp Brit) [1] ADJ centenaire [2] N (= anniversary) centenaire m; (= century) siècle m; **he has just passed his ~** il vient de fêter son centième anniversaire or son centenaire [3] COMP ► **centenary celebrations** NPL fêtes fpl du centenaire

centennial [senˈtenɪəl] (esp US) [1] ADJ (= 100 years old) centenaire, séculaire; (= every 100 years) séculaire (frm) [2] N centenaire m, centième anniversaire m [3] COMP ► **the Centennial State** N (US) le Colorado

center [ˈsentər] (US) = **centre**

centesimal [senˈtesɪməl] ADJ centésimal

centigrade [ˈsentɪɡreɪd] ADJ [thermometer, scale] centigrade; [degree] centigrade, Celsius inv

centigramme, **centigram** (US) [ˈsentɪɡræm] N centigramme m

centilitre, **centiliter** (US) [ˈsentɪˌliːtər] N centilitre m

centimetre, **centimeter** (US) [ˈsentɪˌmiːtər] N centimètre m

centipede [ˈsentɪpiːd] N mille-pattes m inv

CENTO [ˈsentəʊ] N (Pol) (ABBR = **Central Treaty Organization**) CENTO m

central [ˈsentrəl] [1] ADJ [courtyard, committee, control, command, idea, character] central; [location] central, proche du centre; [flat, house, office] proche du centre; [planning] centralisé; [aim, fact, role] essentiel; **~ London/Poland** le centre de Londres/de la Pologne; **of ~ importance** d'une importance capitale; **to be ~ to sth** jouer un rôle essentiel dans qch, être au centre de qch [2] N (US) central m téléphonique [3] COMP ► **Central African** ADJ centrafricain ► **Central African Republic** N République f centrafricaine ► **Central America** N l'Amérique f centrale ► **Central American** ADJ d'Amérique centrale ♦ N habitant(e) m(f) d'Amérique centrale ► **Central Asia** N l'Asie f centrale ► **Central Asian** ADJ d'Asie centrale ► **central bank** N banque f centrale ► **central casting** N (NonC: esp US Cine) service m du casting (d'un studio de cinéma); (fig) **straight out of ~ casting** caricatural ► **Central Committee** N (Pol) comité m central ► **Central Daylight Time** N (US) heure f d'été du Centre (des États-Unis) ► **Central Europe** N l'Europe f centrale ► **Central European** ADJ d'Europe centrale ♦ N habitant(e) m(f) d'Europe centrale ► **Central European Time** N (Geog) heure f d'Europe centrale ► **central government** N gouvernement m central ► **central heating** N chauffage m central ► **central locking** N (Aut) verrouillage m central or centralisé ► **central locking device** N (Aut) condamnation f électromagnétique des serrures ► **central nervous system** N système m nerveux central ► **central processing unit** N (Comput) unité centrale ► **central reservation** N (Brit) [of road, motorway] terre-plein m central ► **Central Standard Time** N (US) heure f normale du Centre (des États-Unis)

centralism ['sentrəlɪzəm] N (Pol) centralisme m

centralist ['sentrəlɪst] ADJ, N (Pol) centraliste mf

centrality [sen'trælɪtɪ] N (= central role) rôle m central; **the ~ of rice to their economy** le rôle central du riz dans leur économie; (= central location) **the ~ of the hotel's location is ideal** ce qui est idéal, c'est que l'hôtel est situé dans le centre-ville

centralization [ˌsentrəlaɪ'zeɪʃən] N centralisation f

centralize ['sentrəlaɪz] [1] VT centraliser [2] VI se centraliser, être centralisé

centrally ['sentrəlɪ] [1] ADV [a] (= in middle) [positioned, placed] au centre [b] (= near city centre) [located, situated] dans le centre; **very ~ situated** situé tout près du centre; **he lives ~** il habite dans le centre or près du centre [c] (= primarily) **to be ~ important** être d'une importance capitale, occuper une place centrale; **the novel is ~ concerned with the subject of unhappiness** la tristesse est le motif central de ce roman [d] (Admin, Pol) [organize] de façon centralisée; **~ based** centralisé; **~ planned economy** économie f dirigée or centralisée [2] COMP ► **centrally heated** ADJ équipé du chauffage central; **the house is ~ heated** la maison a le chauffage central

centre, center (US) ['sentə] [1] N [a] (gen, Comput) centre m; **the ~ of the target** le centre de la cible, le mille; **in the ~** au centre; **~ of attraction** (lit) centre m d'attraction; (fig) point m de mire; **she was the ~ of attention** or **interest** elle a été le centre d'attention or d'intérêt; **she likes to be the ~ of attention** elle aime être le point de mire; **the man at the ~ of the controversy** l'homme au cœur de la controverse; **~ of industry/commerce** un centre industriel/commercial; (Pol) **a party of the ~** un parti du centre → **city, nerve, town** [b] (= place for specific activity) centre m; **adult education ~** centre m d'enseignement (postscolaire) pour adultes; **law/business consultancy ~** boutique f de droit/de gestion → **civic, community, job** [2] VT (gen, Comput) centrer; (Ftbl) **to ~ the ball** centrer; **the fighting has been ~d around the capital** les combats se sont concentrés autour de la capitale; **the silk industry was ~d in Valencia** l'industrie de la soie était concentrée à Valence; (mentally) **to be ~d** être équilibré [3] VI [a] [thoughts, hatred] se concentrer (**on, in** sur); [problem, discussion] tourner (**on** autour de) [b] (Archery) frapper au centre [4] COMP [row etc] central ► **Center for Disease Control and Prevention** N (US) organisme de santé publique ► **centre armrest** N (in car, bus, train) accoudoir m central ► **centre bit** N (Tech) mèche f, foret m, mèche f anglaise ► **centre court** N (Tennis) court m central ► **centre-forward** N (Sport) avant-centre m ► **centre-half** N (Sport) demi-centre m ► **centre of gravity** N centre m de gravité ► **centre parties** NPL (Pol)

partis mpl du centre ► **centre-piece** N [of table] milieu m de table ► **centre spread** N (Advertising) pages fpl centrales ► **centre-stage** N (lit, fig) **to take ~-stage** occuper le devant de la scène ► **centre three-quarter** N (Sport) trois-quarts m centre ► **centre vowel** N (Phon) voyelle f centrale

---

| **CENTERS FOR DISEASE CONTROL** |

Les Centers for Disease Control and Prevention (ou CDC) sont un organisme américain de santé publique dont le siège se trouve à Atlanta, en Géorgie. Le rôle de cet organisme est d'élaborer des règlements sanitaires et des normes de sécurité, de collecter et d'analyser les informations relatives à la santé publique et d'organiser la prévention des maladies transmissibles. Il doit son renom international au rôle de pionnier qu'il a joué dans la détection du virus HIV et dans l'identification de ses modes de transmission.

---

centreboard ['sentəbɔ:d] N (Naut) dérive f

-centred ['sentəd] ADJ (in compounds) basé sur

centrefold ['sentəfəʊld] N (Press) double page f (détachable); (= pin-up picture) photo f de pin up (au milieu d'un magazine)

centrifugal [sentrɪ'fju:gəl] [1] ADJ centrifuge [2] COMP ► **centrifugal force** N force f centrifuge

centrifuge ['sentrɪfju:ʒ] [1] N (Tech) centrifugeur m, centrifugeuse f [2] VT centrifuger

centripetal [sen'trɪpɪtl] [1] ADJ centripète [2] COMP ► **centripetal force** N force f centripète

centrism ['sentrɪzəm] N (Pol) centrisme m

centrist ['sentrɪst] ADJ, N (Pol) centriste mf

centurion [sen'tjʊərɪən] N centurion m

century ['sentjʊrɪ] [1] N [a] siècle m; **several centuries ago** il y a plusieurs siècles; **in the twentieth ~** au vingtième siècle [b] (Mil Hist) centurie f [c] (Cricket) cent courses fpl [2] COMP ► **centuries-old** ADJ séculaire, vieux (vieille f) de plusieurs siècles ► **century note*** N (US) billet m de cent dollars

CEO [ˌsi:i:'əʊ] (ABBR = **chief executive officer**) → **chief**

cephalic [sɪ'fælɪk] ADJ céphalique

ceramic [sɪ'ræmɪk] [1] ADJ [art] céramique; [cup, vase] en céramique [2] N [a] (NonC) céramique f [b] (objet m en) céramique f [3] COMP ► **ceramic hob** N table f de cuisson en vitrocéramique

Cerberus ['sɜ:bərəs] N Cerbère m

cereal ['sɪərɪəl] [1] N (= plant) céréale f; (= grain) grain m (de céréale); **baby ~** Blédine® f; **breakfast ~** céréale f [2] ADJ de céréale(s)

cerebellum [ˌserɪ'beləm] N (pl **cerebellums** or **cerebella** [ˌserɪ'belə]) cervelet m

cerebra ['serɪbrə] NPL of **cerebrum**

cerebral ['serɪbrəl] [1] ADJ cérébral [2] COMP ► **cerebral death** N mort f cérébrale ► **cerebral palsy** N paralysie f cérébrale

cerebration [ˌserɪ'breɪʃən] N (frm) cogitation f

cerebrum ['serɪbrəm] N (pl **cerebrums** or **cerebra** ['serɪbrə]) (Anat) cerveau m

ceremonial [ˌserɪ'məʊnɪəl] [1] ADJ [rite] cérémoniel; [dress] de cérémonie; (US) [office, post] honorifique [2] N cérémonial m (NonC); (Rel) cérémonial m, rituel m

ceremonially [ˌserɪ'məʊnɪəlɪ] ADV selon le cérémonial d'usage

ceremonious [ˌserɪ'məʊnɪəs] ADJ solennel; (slightly pej) cérémonieux

ceremoniously [ˌserɪ'məʊnɪəslɪ] ADV solennellement, avec cérémonie; (slightly pej) cérémonieusement

ceremony ['serɪmənɪ] N [a] (= event) cérémonie f → **master** [b] (NonC) cérémonies fpl, façons fpl; **to stand on ~** faire des cérémonies,

faire des manières; **with ~** cérémonieusement; **without ~** sans cérémonie(s)

cerise [sə'ri:z] ADJ (de) couleur cerise, cerise inv

cerium ['sɪərɪəm] N cérium m

cert* [sɜ:t] N (Brit) certitude f; **it's a dead ~** ça ne fait pas un pli*, c'est couru*; **he's a (dead) ~ for the job** il est sûr et certain de décrocher le poste*

cert. [a] ABBR = **certificate** [b] ABBR = **certified**

▼ **certain** ['sɜ:tən] [1] ADJ [a] (= sure) certain; **to be** or **feel ~ (about** or **of sth)** être certain (de qch); **are you absolutely ~ (about** or **of that)?** en es-tu absolument certain?; **you don't sound very ~** tu n'en as pas l'air très sûr; **~ of oneself** sûr de soi; **to be ~ that ...** être certain que ...; **be ~ to go!** allez-y sans faute!; **I am not ~ who/why/when/how ...** je ne sais pas avec certitude qui/pourquoi/quand/comment ...; **we are not ~ what is happening** nous ne sommes pas certains de or nous ne savons pas au juste ce qui se passe [b] **to make ~ that ...** (= check, ensure) s'assurer que ...; **to make ~ of sth** (= get facts about) s'assurer de qch; (= be sure of getting) s'assurer qch [c] **for ~** (= definitely): **he's up to something, that's for ~** il manigance quelque chose, c'est une certitude or c'est sûr et certain; **he'll do it for ~** il le fera, c'est certain; **to know sth for ~** savoir qch avec certitude; **to know for ~ that ...** avoir la certitude que ...; **to know for ~ what/where ...** savoir avec certitude ce qui or que/où ...; **we know for ~ of ten fatalities** nous savons avec certitude qu'il y a au moins dix victimes; **I don't know for ~ ◊ I can't say for ~** je n'en suis pas certain or sûr; **I can't say for ~ that ...** je ne peux pas affirmer que ... [d] (= assured, guaranteed) [defeat, success, victory, death] certain (after n); **nothing's ~ in this world** il n'y a rien de certain dans ce monde; **one thing is ~ ...** une chose est certaine ...; **he's a ~ winner/loser** il est sûr de gagner/perdre; **there's ~ to be strong opposition to these proposals** ces propositions se heurteront certainement à une forte opposition; **he is ~ to come** il viendra sans aucun doute; **it is ~ that ...** il est certain que ...; **he was 99% ~ of winning** il était à 99 % certain de gagner; **to my ~ knowledge, she has never been there** je sais pertinemment qu'elle n'y est jamais allée [e] (= particular) [person, matter, place, manner, type] certain (before n); **of a ~ age** d'un certain âge; **in ~ circumstances** dans certaines circonstances; **on a ~ day in spring** un certain jour de printemps; **there is a ~ knack to doing it** il faut un certain coup de main pour le faire; **a ~ Mrs Wendy Smith** une certaine Mme Wendy Smith; **a ~ number of people** un certain nombre de personnes; **at ~ times** à certains moments [f] (= slight) [impatience, bitterness, courage] certain (before n); **to a ~ extent** or **degree** dans une certaine mesure [2] PRON certains; **~ of our members have not paid** certains or quelques uns de nos membres n'ont pas payé

▼ **certainly** ['sɜ:tənlɪ] ADV [a] (= undoubtedly) certainement, assurément; **it is ~ true that ...** on ne peut pas nier que ... (+ subj or indic); **your answer is almost ~ right** il est presque certain que votre réponse est juste [b] (= definitely) **it ~ impressed me** cela m'a vraiment impressionné; **I shall ~ be there** j'y serai sans faute, je ne manquerai pas d'y être; **such groups most ~ exist** il est absolument certain que de tels groupes existent, de tels groupes existent, c'est une certitude [c] (expressing agreement) certainement; **wouldn't you agree? — oh, ~** vous ne croyez pas? — oh si, bien sûr; **had you forgotten? — ~ not** vous aviez oublié? — certainement pas

---

[d] (*expressing willingness*) certainement, bien sûr ; **could you help me? — ~** pourriez-vous m'aider ? — certainement *or* bien sûr [e] (= *granted*) certes ; **~, she has potential, but ...** certes, elle a des capacités mais ...

certainty ['sɜːtəntɪ] N [a] (= *fact, quality*) certitude *f* ; **for a ~** à coup sûr, sans aucun doute ; **to bet on a ~** parier en étant sûr de gagner ; **his success is a ~** son succès est certain *or* ne fait aucun doute ; **that reunification will eventually happen is a ~** il ne fait aucun doute que la réunification finira par se faire ; **it is a moral ~** c'est une certitude morale ; **faced with the ~ of disaster ...** face à un désastre inévitable ... ; **there are no certainties in modern Europe** il n'y a aucune certitude dans l'Europe moderne ; **there is too little ~ about the future** l'avenir est trop incertain [b] (*NonC* = *conviction*) certitude *f*, conviction *f*

certifiable [ˌsɜːtɪ'faɪəbl] ADJ [a] [*fact, statement*] qu'on peut certifier [b] (* = *mad*) bon à enfermer

certificate [sə'tɪfɪkɪt] N [a] (= *legal document*) certificat *m*, acte *m* ; **~ of airworthiness ◊ ~ of seaworthiness** certificat *m* de navigabilité ; (*Comm*) **~ of origin/value** certificat *m* d'origine/de valeur ; **~ of posting** récépissé *m* ; **birth ~** acte *m* or extrait *m* de naissance → **death, marriage** [b] (= *academic document*) diplôme *m* ; (*for skilled or semi-skilled work*) qualification *f* professionnelle ; (*Brit Scol: formerly*) **Certificate of Secondary Education** ≈ brevet *m* (d'études du premier cycle) (*dans une seule matière*) → **teacher**

certificated [sə'tɪfɪkeɪtɪd] ADJ diplômé

certification [ˌsɜːtɪfɪ'keɪʃən] N [a] (*NonC*) certification *f*, authentification *f* [b] (= *document*) certificat *m*

certify ['sɜːtɪfaɪ] [1] VT [a] certifier, attester (**that** que) ; (*Jur*) **certified as a true copy** certifié conforme ; (*Psych*) **to ~ sb (insane)** déclarer qn atteint d'aliénation mentale ; **she was certified dead** elle a été déclarée morte ; **the painting has been certified (as) genuine** le tableau a été authentifié [b] (*Fin*) [+ *cheque*] certifier [c] (*Comm*) [+ *goods*] garantir ; (*US Post*) **to send by certified mail** ≈ envoyer avec accusé de réception [2] VI **to ~ to sth** attester qch [3] COMP ► **certified milk** N (*US*) lait soumis aux contrôles d'hygiène réglementaires ► **certified public accountant** N (*US*) expert-comptable *mf*, comptable *mf* agréé(e) (*Can*) ► **certified teacher** N (*US Scol*) professeur *m* diplômé

certitude ['sɜːtɪtjuːd] N certitude *f*, conviction *f* absolue

cerulean [sɪ'ruːlɪən] ADJ (*liter*) bleu ciel *inv*, azuré

cerumen [sɪ'ruːmen] N cérumen *m*

ceruminous [sɪ'ruːmɪnəs] ADJ cérumineux

cervical ['sɜːvɪkl] [1] ADJ cervical [2] COMP ► **cervical cancer** N cancer *m* du col de l'utérus ► **cervical smear** N frottis *m* vaginal

cervix ['sɜːvɪks] N (*pl* **cervixes** *or* **cervices** [sə'vaɪsiːz]) col *m* de l'utérus

cesium ['siːzɪəm] N (*esp US*) = **caesium**

cessation [se'seɪʃən] N cessation *f* ; **~ of hostilities** cessation *f* des hostilités

cession ['seʃən] N cession *f* ; **act of ~** acte *m* de cession

cesspit ['sespɪt] N fosse *f* d'aisance ; (*fig*) cloaque *m*

cesspool ['sespuːl] N = **cesspit**

CET [ˌsiːiː'tiː] (ABBR = **Central European Time**) → **central**

cetacean [sɪ'teɪʃən] ADJ, N cétacé *m*

Ceylon [sɪ'lɒn] N (*formerly*) (= *island*) Ceylan *f* ; (= *state*) Ceylan *m* → **à** Ceylan

Ceylonese [ˌsɪlɒ'niːz] (*formerly*) [1] ADJ ceylanais [2] N Ceylanais(e) *m(f)*

cf (ABBR = **confer**) cf

---

c/f (*Fin*) (ABBR = **carried forward**) → **carry forward**

CFC [ˌsiːef'siː] N (ABBR = **chlorofluorocarbon**) CFC *m*

CFE [ˌsiːef'iː] [1] N (*Brit*) (ABBR = **college of further education**) → **college** [2] NPL (ABBR = **Conventional Forces in Europe**) FCE *fpl*

CG [siː'dʒiː] ABBR = **coastguard**

cg (ABBR = **centigram(me)(s)**) cg

CGA [ˌsiːdʒiː'eɪ] [1] N (ABBR = **colour graphics adaptor**) → **colour** [2] COMP ► **CGA card** N carte *f* graphique CGA ► **CGA monitor** N moniteur *m* CGA

CH (ABBR = **Companion of Honour**) *titre honorifique*

Ch. ABBR = **chapter**

c.h. (ABBR = **central heating**) → **central**

cha-cha ['tʃɑːtʃɑː] N (*Mus*) cha-cha-cha *m*

Chad [tʃæd] [1] N le Tchad ; **Lake ~** le lac Tchad [2] ADJ tchadien

chafe [tʃeɪf] [1] VT [a] (= *rub*) frotter, frictionner ; **she ~d the child's hands to warm them** elle a frotté *or* frictionné les mains de l'enfant pour les réchauffer [b] (= *rub against*) frotter contre ; (= *irritate*) irriter ; **his shirt ~d his neck** sa chemise frottait contre son cou *or* lui irritait le cou ; **his neck was ~d** il avait le cou irrité [c] (= *wear out*) [+ *collar, cuffs, rope*] user (en frottant) ; (*Naut*) raguer [2] VI s'user ; [*rope*] raguer ; **his wrists ~d against the ropes binding them** ses poignets frottaient contre les cordes qui les entravaient ; (*fig*) **to ~ at sth** s'irriter de qch ; **he ~d at having to take orders from her** cela l'irritait de recevoir des ordres d'elle ; **to ~ at the bit** ronger son frein ; **he ~d against these restrictions** ces restrictions l'irritaient ; (*liter*) **they ~d under the yoke of tyranny** ils rongeaient leur frein sous la tyrannie

chaff¹ [tʃɑːf] [1] N (*NonC: Agr*) [*of grain*] balle *f* ; (= *cut straw*) menue paille *f* → **wheat** [2] VT [+ *straw*] hacher

chaff² [tʃɑːf] [1] N (*NonC* = *banter*) taquinerie *f* [2] VT taquiner

chaffinch ['tʃæfɪntʃ] N pinson *m*

chafing dish ['tʃeɪfɪŋdɪʃ] N poêlon *m* (de table)

chagrin ['ʃægrɪn] [1] N (= *deception*) déception *f*, dépit *m* ; (= *annoyance*) contrariété *f* ; **much to my ~** à ma grande déception [2] VT (*frm*) (= *deceive*) dépiter, décevoir ; (= *annoy*) contrarier

chain [tʃeɪn] [1] N [a] (*gen, also ornamental*) chaîne *f* ; **~s** (= *fetters*) chaînes *fpl* ; **~ of office** [*of mayor*] chaîne *f* (*insigne de la fonction de maire*) ; **to keep a dog on a ~** tenir un chien à l'attache ; **in ~s** enchaîné ; (*for car*) **(snow) ~s** chaînes *fpl* (à neige) ; **to pull the ~** [*of lavatory*] tirer la chasse (d'eau) *or* la chaîne → **ball, bicycle** [b] [*of mountains, atoms etc*] chaîne *f* ; (*fig*) [*of ideas*] enchaînement *m* ; [*of events*] série *f*, suite *f* ; (*Comm*) **~ of shops** chaîne *f* de magasins ; **to make a ~** [*people*] faire la chaîne → **bucket** [c] (*Tech*) (*for measuring*) chaîne *f* d'arpenteur ; (= *measure*) chaînée *f* [2] VT (*lit, fig*) enchaîner ; [+ *door*] mettre la chaîne à ; **he was ~ed to the wall** il était enchaîné au mur [3] COMP ► **chain gang** N chaîne *f* de forçats ► **chain letter** N lettre *f* faisant partie d'une chaîne ; **~ letters** chaîne *f* (de lettres) ► **chain lightning** N éclairs *mpl* en zigzag ► **chain-link fence** N grillage *m* ► **chain mail** N (*NonC*) cotte *f* de mailles ► **chain of command** N (*Mil*) voies *fpl* hiérarchiques ► **chain reaction** N (*Phys, fig*) réaction *f* en chaîne ► **chain saw** N tronçonneuse *f* ► **chain-smoke** VI fumer cigarette sur cigarette ► **chain smoker** N grand(e) *or* gros(se) fumeur *m*, -euse *f* ► **chain stitch** N (*Sewing*) (point *m* de) chaînette *f* ► **chain store** N

---

grand magasin *m* à succursales multiples ► **chain down** VT SEP enchaîner ► **chain up** VT SEP [+ *animal*] mettre à l'attache

chair [tʃeər] [1] N [a] chaise *f* ; (= *armchair*) fauteuil *m* ; (= *seat*) siège *m* ; (*Univ*) chaire *f* ; (= *wheelchair*) fauteuil *m* roulant ; (*US* = *electric chair*) chaise *f* (électrique) ; **to take a ~** s'asseoir ; **dentist's ~** fauteuil *m* de dentiste ; (*Univ*) **to hold the ~ of French** être titulaire de *or* avoir la chaire de français ; (*US*) **to go to the ~** passer à la chaise (électrique) → **deck, easy, highchair** [b] (*at meeting etc* = *function*) fauteuil *m* présidentiel, présidence *f* ; **to take the ~ ◊ to be in the ~** présider ; **to address the ~** s'adresser au président ; **~! ~!** à l'ordre ! [c] (*Admin*) = **chairman, chairwoman** [2] VT [a] (*Admin*) [+ *meeting*] présider [b] [+ *hero*] porter en triomphe [3] COMP ► **chair back** N dossier *m* (de chaise)

chairlift ['tʃeəlɪft] N télésiège *m*

chairman ['tʃeəmən] N (*pl* **-men**) président *m* (*d'un comité etc*) ; **Mr Chairman** Monsieur le Président ; **Madam Chairman** Madame la Présidente ; **~ and chief executive officer** président-directeur *m* général, P.D.G. *m* ; **Chairman Mao** le président Mao

chairmanship ['tʃeəmənʃɪp] N présidence *f* (*d'un comité etc*) ; **under the ~ of ...** sous la présidence de ...

chairperson ['tʃeəˌpɜːsn] N président(e) *m(f)*

chairwarmer ['tʃeəˌwɔːmər] N (*US*) rond-de-cuir *m* (paresseux)

chairwoman ['tʃeəwʊmən] N (*pl* **-women**) présidente *f*

chaise [ʃeɪz] N cabriolet *m*

chaise longue ['ʃeɪz'lɒŋ] N (*pl* **chaise longues**) méridienne *f*

chakra ['tʃækrə] N (*Rel*) chakra *m*

chalet ['ʃæleɪ] N (*gen*) chalet *m* ; [*of motel*] bungalow *m*

chalice ['tʃælɪs] N (*Rel*) calice *m* ; (*liter* = *wine cup*) coupe *f*

chalk [tʃɔːk] [1] N (*NonC*) craie *f* ; **a piece of ~** une craie, un morceau de craie ; (*Brit*) **they're as different as ~ and cheese** c'est le jour et la nuit ; (*Brit fig*) **by a long ~** de loin ; **the biggest by a long ~** de loin le plus grand ; **did he win? — not by a long ~** est-ce qu'il a gagné ? — non, loin de là *or* loin s'en faut → **French** [2] VT (= *write with chalk*) écrire à la craie ; (= *rub with chalk*) frotter de craie ; [+ *billiard cue*] mettre du bleu sur ; [+ *luggage*] marquer à la craie [3] COMP ► **chalk board** N (*US*) tableau *m* (noir) ► **chalk dust** N poussière *f* de craie ► **chalk talk** N (*US*) conférence *f* illustrée au tableau noir ► **chalk out** VT SEP (*lit*) [+ *pattern*] esquisser, tracer (à la craie) ; (*fig*) [+ *project*] esquisser ; [+ *plan of action*] tracer ► **chalk up** VT SEP [a] **~ it up** mettez-le sur mon ardoise *or* compte ; **he ~ed it up to experience** il l'a mis au compte de l'expérience [b] [+ *achievement, victory*] remporter

chalkface ['tʃɔːkfeɪs] N (*NonC: Brit Scol: hum*) **at the ~** en classe

chalkpit ['tʃɔːkpɪt] N carrière *f* de craie

chalky ['tʃɔːkɪ] ADJ [*soil*] crayeux, calcaire ; [*water*] calcaire ; [*complexion*] crayeux, blafard

challenge ['tʃælɪndʒ] [1] N [a] défi *m* ; **to issue or put out a ~** lancer un défi ; **to rise to the ~** se montrer à la hauteur ; **to take up the ~** relever le défi ; **the ~ of new ideas** la stimulation qu'offrent de nouvelles idées ; **the ~ of the 20th century** le défi du 20ᵉ siècle ; **Hunter's ~ for the party leadership** la tentative de Hunter pour prendre la tête du parti ; **this is a ~ to us all** c'est un défi pour nous tous ; **the job was a great ~ to him** cette tâche était une gageure pour lui ; **action that is a ~ to authority** acte *m* qui défie l'autorité ; **it was a ~ to his skill** c'était un défi à son savoir-faire

ⓑ (*Mil: by sentry*) sommation *f* ⓒ (*Jur*) [*of juror, jury*] récusation *f* ② VT ⓐ (= *summon, call*) défier ; (*Sport*) inviter ; **to ~ sb to do sth** défier qn de faire qch ; **to ~ sb to a game** proposer à qn de faire une partie ; **to ~ sb to a duel** provoquer qn en duel ⓑ (= *call into question*) [+ *statement*] mettre en question, contester ; **to ~ sb's authority to do sth** contester à qn le droit de faire qch ; **to ~ the wisdom of a plan** mettre en question la sagesse d'un projet ; (*Jur*) **to ~ a measure** attaquer une mesure ⓒ (*Mil*) [*sentry*] faire une sommation à ⓓ [+ *juror, jury*] récuser

-challenged ['tʃælɪndʒd] ADJ ⓐ (*esp US euph*) **visually-challenged** malvoyant ; **physically-challenged** handicapé ⓑ (*hum*) **vertically-challenged** de petite taille ; **intellectually-challenged** limité intellectuellement

challenger ['tʃælɪndʒəʳ] N (*Sport, Pol, also fig*) challenger *m*

challenging ['tʃælɪndʒɪŋ] ADJ [*look, tone*] de défi ; [*remark, speech*] provocateur (-trice *f*) ; [*job, work*] difficile, qui représente un challenge ; [*job*] stimulant ; **he found himself in a ~ situation** il s'est trouvé là devant une gageure ; **this is a very ~ situation** cette situation est une véritable gageure

challengingly ['tʃælɪndʒɪŋlɪ] ADV ⓐ (= *defiantly*) [*say, announce*] avec un air de défi ; **to look ~ at sb** lancer un regard de défi à qn ⓑ (= *demandingly*) **~ difficult** difficile mais stimulant

chamber ['tʃeɪmbəʳ] ① N ⓐ (†, *frm* = *room*) salle *f*, pièce *f* ; (*also* **bedchamber**) chambre *f* ⓑ (= *hall*) chambre *f* ; (*Parl*) **the Upper/Lower Chamber** la Chambre haute/basse → **audience, second¹** ⓒ [*of revolver*] chambre *f* ; (*Anat*) cavité *f* ; **the ~s of the eye** les chambres *fpl* de l'œil ② **chambers** NPL (*Brit*) ⓐ († = *lodgings*) logement *m*, appartement *m* ; [*of bachelor*] garçonnière† *f* ⓑ [*of barrister, judge, magistrate*] cabinet *m* ; [*of solicitor*] étude *f* ; (*Jur*) **to hear a case in ~s** ≈ juger un cas en référé ③ COMP ► **chamber concert** N concert *m* de musique de chambre ► **chamber music** N musique *f* de chambre ► **Chamber of Commerce** N Chambre *f* de commerce ► **the Chamber of Deputies** N la Chambre des députés ► **Chamber of Horrors** N cabinet *m* des horreurs ► **Chamber of Trade** N Chambre *f* des métiers ► **chamber orchestra** N orchestre *m* (de musique) de chambre ► **chamber pot** N pot *m* de chambre, vase *m* de nuit†

chamberlain ['tʃeɪmbəlɪn] N chambellan *m* → **lord**

chambermaid ['tʃeɪmbəmeɪd] N femme *f* de chambre

chambray ['tʃæmbreɪ] N (*US*) = **cambric**

chameleon [kə'miːlɪən] N (*Zool, fig*) caméléon *m*

chamfer ['tʃæmfəʳ] (*Tech*) ① N (= *bevel*) chanfrein *m* ; (= *groove*) cannelure *f* ② VT chanfreiner, canneler

chammy* ['ʃæmɪ] N = **chamois b**

chamois ['ʃæmwɑː] ① N (*pl inv*) ⓐ (*Zool*) chamois *m* ⓑ ['ʃæmɪ] (*also* **~ cloth**) chamois *m* ② COMP ► **chamois leather** N peau *f* de chamois

chamomile ['kæməʊmaɪl] N = **camomile**

champ¹ ['tʃæmp] ① VI mâchonner ; (*lit, fig*) **to ~ at the bit** ronger son frein ② VT mâchonner

champ²* ['tʃæmp] N ABBR = **champion 1b**

champagne [ʃæm'peɪn] ① N ⓐ (= *wine*) champagne *m* ⓑ (*Geog*) **Champagne** la Champagne ② COMP (*also* **~-coloured**)

champagne *inv* ► **champagne cup** N cocktail *m* au champagne ► **champagne glass** N (*wide*) coupe *f* à champagne ; (*tall and narrow*) flûte *f* à champagne ► **champagne lifestyle** N grand train *m* de vie ► **champagne socialist** N to be a ~ socialist appartenir à la gauche caviar

champers* ['ʃæmpəz] N (*NonC*) champ* *m*, champagne *m*

champion ['tʃæmpjən] ① N ⓐ champion(ne) *m(f)* ; **the ~ of free speech** le champion de la liberté d'expression ⓑ (*Sport* = *person, animal*) champion(ne) *m(f)* ; **world ~** champion(ne) *m(f)* du monde ; **boxing ~** champion *m* de boxe ; **skiing ~** champion(ne) *m(f)* de ski ② ADJ [*show animal*] champion ; **~ swimmer/skier** *etc* champion(ne) *m(f)* de natation/de ski *etc* ⓑ (*dial* = *excellent*) [*meal, holiday, film*] du tonnerre* ; **that's ~!** c'est super!*, c'est champion!* ③ VT [+ *person*] prendre fait et cause pour ; [+ *action, cause, sb's decision*] se faire le champion de, défendre

championship ['tʃæmpjənʃɪp] N ⓐ (*Sport*) championnat *m* ; **world ~** championnat *m* du monde ; **boxing ~** championnat *m* de boxe ; **world boxing ~** championnat *m* du monde de boxe ⓑ (*NonC*) [*of cause etc*] défense *f*

▼ **chance** [tʃɑːns] ① N ⓐ (= *luck*) hasard *m* ; **(totally) by ~** ◊ **by (sheer) ~** (*tout à fait*) par hasard, par (pur) hasard ; (= *fortunately*) par chance ; **have you a pen on you by (any) ~?** auriez-vous par hasard un stylo sur vous ? ; **it was not (by) ~ that he came** ce n'est pas par hasard qu'il est venu, ce n'est pas un hasard s'il est venu ; **to trust (o.s.) to ~** s'en remettre au hasard ; **a game of ~** un jeu de hasard ; **to leave things to ~** laisser faire le hasard ; **he left nothing to ~** il n'a rien laissé au hasard ⓑ (= *possibility*) chance(s) *f(pl)*, possibilité *f* ; **to stand a ~ (of doing)** avoir une bonne chance (de faire) ; **to stand no ~ (of doing)** ne pas avoir la moindre chance (de faire) ; **he hasn't much ~ or doesn't stand much ~ of winning** il n'a pas beaucoup de chances de gagner ; **he's still in with a ~** il a encore une petite chance ; **on the ~ of your returning** dans le cas où vous reviendriez ; **I went there on the ~ of seeing him** j'y suis allé dans l'espoir de le voir ; **the ~s are that ...** il y a de grandes chances que ... (+ *subj*), il est très possible que ... (+ *subj*) ; **the ~s are against that happening** il y a peu de chances pour que cela arrive (*subj*) ; **the ~s are against him** il y a peu de chances pour qu'il réussisse ; **there is little ~ of his coming** il est peu probable qu'il vienne ; **you'll have to take a ~ on his coming** tu verras bien s'il vient ou non ; **he's taking no ~s** il ne veut rien laisser au hasard, il ne veut prendre aucun risque ; **that's a ~ we'll have to take** c'est un risque que nous allons devoir prendre *or* que nous devons courir ; **no ~!** ◊ **not a ~!** pas de danger!*, jamais! → **off** ⓒ (= *opportunity*) occasion *f* ; **I had the ~ to go** *or* **of going** j'ai eu l'occasion d'y aller, l'occasion m'a été donnée d'y aller ; **if there's a ~ of buying it** s'il y a une possibilité d'achat ; **to lose a ~** laisser passer une occasion ; **she was waiting for her ~** elle attendait son heure ; **she was waiting for her ~ to speak** elle attendait *or* guettait l'occasion de parler ; **now's your ~!** (*in conversation, traffic etc*) vas-y! ; (*in career etc*) saute sur l'occasion!, à toi de jouer! ; **this is his big ~** c'est le grand moment pour lui ; **give him another ~** laisse-lui encore une chance ; **he has had every ~** il a eu toutes les chances ; **he never had a ~ in life** il n'a jamais eu sa chance dans la vie ; **give me a ~ to show you what I can do** donnez-moi la possibilité de vous montrer ce que je sais faire ; **you'll have your ~** (= *your turn will come*) votre tour viendra

② ADJ de hasard, accidentel ; **a ~ companion** un compagnon rencontré par hasard ; **a ~ dis-**

covery une découverte accidentelle ; **a ~ meeting** une rencontre de hasard *or* fortuite ③ VT (*frm* = *happen*) **to ~ to do** for hasard ; **I ~d to hear his name** j'ai entendu son nom par hasard, il s'est trouvé que j'ai entendu son nom ; **it ~d that I was there** il s'est trouvé que j'étais là ⓑ (= *risk*) [+ *rejection, fine*] risquer, courir le risque de ; **to ~ doing sth** se risquer à faire qch, prendre le risque de faire qch ; **I'll go round without phoning and ~ finding him there** je vais passer chez lui sans téléphoner en espérant l'y trouver *or* avec l'espoir de l'y trouver ; **I want to see her alone but I'll have to ~ finding her husband there** je voudrais la voir seule, mais il faut que je prenne le risque d'y trouver son mari ; **I'll ~ it!*** je vais risquer le coup!* ; **to ~ one's arm*** risquer le tout (pour le tout) ; **to ~ one's luck** tenter *or* courir sa chance

► **chance upon** VT FUS (*frm*) [+ *person*] rencontrer par hasard ; [+ *thing*] trouver par hasard

chancel ['tʃɑːnsəl] ① N chœur *m* (*d'une église*) ② COMP ► **chancel screen** N clôture *f* du chœur, jubé *m*

chancellery ['tʃɑːnsələrɪ] N chancellerie *f*

chancellor ['tʃɑːnsələʳ] ① N (*Hist, Jur, Pol*) chancelier *m* ; (*Brit Univ*) président(e) *m(f)* honoraire ; (*US Univ*) président(e) *m(f)* d'université ② COMP ► **Chancellor of the Exchequer** N (*Brit*) chancelier *m* de l'Échiquier, ≈ ministre *m* des Finances → **lord** ; → *TREASURY*

chancellorship ['tʃɑːnsələʃɪp] N fonctions *fpl* de chancelier

chancer* ['tʃɑːnsəʳ] N arnaqueur* *m*, -euse* *f* ; (= *child*) loustic* *m*

chancery ['tʃɑːnsərɪ] N ⓐ (*Brit, Jur*) cour *f* de la chancellerie (*une des cinq divisions de la Haute Cour de justice anglaise*) ; **ward in ~** pupille *mf* (*sous tutelle judiciaire*) ⓑ (*US*) = **chancellery** ⓒ (*US: also* **court of ~**) ≈ cour *f* d'équité *or* de la chancellerie

chancre ['ʃæŋkəʳ] N (*Med*) chancre *m*

chancy* ['tʃɑːnsɪ] ADJ (= *risky*) risqué, hasardeux ; (= *doubtful*) aléatoire, problématique

chandelier [ˌʃændə'lɪəʳ] N lustre *m*

chandler ['tʃɑːndləʳ] N (**ship's**) **~** shipchandler *m*, marchand *m* de fournitures pour bateaux

▼ **change** [tʃeɪndʒ] ① N ⓐ (= *alteration*) changement *m* (**from, in** de, **into** en) ; **a ~ for the better** un changement en mieux, une amélioration ; **a ~ for the worse** un changement en mal ; **~ in the weather** changement *m* de temps ; **~ in public opinion** revirement *m* de l'opinion publique ; **~ in attitudes** changement *m* d'attitude, évolution *f* des attitudes ; **a ~ in government policy** un changement dans la politique du gouvernement ; **(just) for a ~** pour changer un peu ; **by way of a ~** histoire de changer* ; **to make a ~ in sth** changer qch ; (*fig*) **to make a ~ of direction** changer son fusil d'épaule (*fig*) ; (*fig*) **to have a ~ of heart** changer d'avis ; **it makes a ~** ça change un peu ; **it will be a nice ~** cela nous fera un changement, voilà qui nous changera agréablement! ; (*iro*) ça nous changera! (*iro*) ; **a picnic will be** *or* **make a nice ~ from being stuck indoors** un pique-nique nous changera de rester toujours enfermé à l'intérieur ; **the ~ of life** le retour d'âge ⓑ (= *substitution*) changement *m* ; **~ of address** changement *m* d'adresse ; **~ of air** changement *m* d'air ; **a ~ of air will do us good** un changement d'air *or* changer d'air nous fera du bien ; **he brought a ~ of clothes** il a apporté des vêtements de rechange ; **I need a ~ of clothes** il faut que je me change (*subj*) ; (*Theat, fig*) **~ of scene** changement *m* de décor ; **~ of horses** relais *m* ; **~ of job** changement *m* de travail *or* de poste ⓒ (*NonC*) changement *m*, variété *f* ; **she likes**

~ elle aime le changement *or* la variété ; **political ~** changement *m* politique

d (*NonC* = *money*) monnaie *f* ; **small ~** petite monnaie *f* ; **can you give me ~ for this note/of £5?** pouvez-vous me faire la monnaie de ce billet/de 5 livres ? ; **keep the ~** gardez la monnaie ; **"no ~ given"** «faites l'appoint» ; **you don't get much ~ from a fiver these days** aujourd'hui il ne reste jamais grand-chose d'un billet de cinq livres ; **you won't get much ~ out of him*** tu perds ton temps avec lui

e (*St Ex*) **the Change** la Bourse ; **on the Change** en Bourse

2 VT **a** (*by substitution*) changer de ; **to ~ (one's) clothes** changer de vêtements, se changer ; **to ~ one's shirt/skirt** *etc* changer de chemise/jupe *etc* ; **to ~ one's address** changer d'adresse ; **to ~ the baby/his nappy** changer le bébé/ses couches ; **to ~ hands** (= *one's grip*) changer de main ; [*goods, property, money*] changer de mains ; (*Theat*) **to ~ the scene** changer le décor ; **to ~ trains/stations/buses** changer de train/de gare/d'autobus ; **to ~ one's name/seat** changer de nom/place ; **to ~ one's opinion** *or* **mind** changer d'avis ; **to ~ sb's mind (about sth)** faire changer qn d'avis (à propos de qch) → **bed, colour, gear, guard, subject, track, tune, wheel**

b (= *exchange*) échanger (**X for Y** X contre Y) ; (*lit*) **to ~ places (with sb)** changer de place (avec qn) ; (*fig*) **I wouldn't like to ~ places with you** je n'aimerais pas être à votre place ; **to ~ sides** *or* **ends** (*Tennis*) changer de côté ; (*Ftbl etc*) changer de camp ; (*fig: in argument etc*) **to ~ sides** changer de camp

c [+ *banknote, coin*] faire la monnaie de, changer ; [+ *foreign currency*] changer (**into** en)

d (= *alter, modify, transform*) changer, transformer (**X into Y** X en Y) ; **the witch ~d him into a cat** la sorcière l'a changé en chat ; **drugs ~d him into a person we didn't recognize** les drogues l'ont changé au point qu'on ne le reconnaissait plus ; **this has ~d my ideas** cela m'a fait changer d'idée ; **success has greatly ~d her** la réussite l'a complètement transformée

3 VI **a** (= *become different*) changer, se transformer ; **you've ~d a lot!** tu as beaucoup changé! ; **he will never ~** il ne changera jamais, on ne le changera pas ; **his mood ~d from resignation to rage** il est passé de la résignation à la fureur ; **the prince ~d into a swan** le prince s'est changé en cygne ; **the water had ~d to ice** l'eau s'était changée en glace

b (= *change clothes*) se changer ; **I must ~ at once** je dois me changer tout de suite, il faut que je me change (*subj*) tout de suite ; **she ~d into an old skirt** elle s'est changée et a mis une vieille jupe

c (*on bus, plane, train journey*) changer ; **you must ~ at Edinburgh** vous devez changer à Édimbourg ; **all ~!** tout le monde descend!

d [*moon*] entrer dans une nouvelle phase

4 COMP ► **change machine** N distributeur *m* de monnaie ► **change purse** N (*US*) porte-monnaie *m inv*

►**change around** VT SEP changer de place

►**change down** VI (*Brit: in car gears*) rétrograder

►**change over** **1** VI (*gen*) passer (**from** de, **to** à) ; [*two people*] faire l'échange ; (*Sport* = *change ends*) (*Tennis*) changer de côté ; (*Ftbl etc*) changer de camp **2** **~over** N → **change-over**

►**change round** VT SEP = **change around**

►**change up** VI (*Brit: in car gears*) passer la vitesse supérieure

changeability [ˌtʃeɪndʒəˈbɪlɪtɪ] N [*of circumstances, weather*] variabilité *f*

changeable [ˈtʃeɪndʒəbl] ADJ [*person*] changeant, inconstant ; [*character*] versatile, changeant ; [*colour*] changeant ; [*weather, wind, circumstances*] variable

changeless [ˈtʃeɪndʒlɪs] ADJ [*rite*] immuable, invariable ; [*person*] constant ; [*character*] inaltérable

changeling [ˈtʃeɪndʒlɪŋ] N enfant *mf* changé(e) (*substitué à un enfant volé*)

changeover [ˈtʃeɪndʒəʊvər] N changement *m*, passage *m* ; (*NonC: Mil*) [*of guard*] relève *f* ; **the ~ from dictatorship to democracy** le passage de la dictature à la démocratie

changing [ˈtʃeɪndʒɪŋ] **1** ADJ [*wind, prices, interest rates*] variable, changeant ; [*expression*] mobile ; [*social attitudes, principles*] qui change, qui évolue ; **a ~ society** une société en mutation **2** N (*NonC*) acte *m* de (se) changer, changement *m* ; **the ~ of the guard** la relève de la garde **3** COMP ► **changing-room** N (*Brit Sport*) vestiaire *m*

channel [ˈtʃænl] **1** N **a** (= *bed of river etc*) lit *m* ; (= *navigable passage*) chenal *m* ; (*between two land masses*) bras *m* de mer ; (*for irrigation*) (*small*) rigole *f* ; (*wider*) canal *m* ; (*in street*) caniveau *m* ; (= *duct*) conduit *m* ; (*Geog*) **the (English) Channel** la Manche **b** (= *groove in surface*) rainure *f* ; (*Archit*) cannelure *f* **c** (*TV*) chaîne *f* **d** (*Customs*) **red/green ~** file *f* marchandises à déclarer/rien à déclarer **e** (*fig*) direction *f* ; **he directed the conversation into a new ~** il a orienté la conversation dans une nouvelle direction ; **~ of communication** voie *f* de communication ; **the government used all the diplomatic ~s available** le gouvernement a utilisé toutes les voies diplomatiques possibles ; **they applied for asylum through the official ~s** ils ont fait une demande d'asile par voie officielle ; (*Admin*) **to go through the usual ~s** suivre la filière (habituelle) **f** (*Comput*) canal *m*

2 VT **a** (= *make channels in: for irrigation*) creuser des rigoles (*or* des canaux) dans ; [+ *street*] pourvoir d'un *or* de caniveau(x) ; **the river ~led its way towards ...** la rivière a creusé son lit vers ... **b** (*fig*) [+ *crowd*] canaliser (**into** vers) ; [+ *energies, efforts, resources*] canaliser, diriger (**towards, into** vers) ; [+ *information*] canaliser (**into, towards** vers), concentrer (**into, towards** dans) **c** (*Archit*) canneler

3 COMP ► **Channel ferry** N (*Brit*) ferry *m* transmanche *inv* ► **channel-hop** VI (*Brit TV*) zapper* ► **channel-hopping** N (*Brit TV*) zapping* *m* ► **Channel Islander** N habitant(e) *m(f)* des îles Anglo-Normandes ► **the Channel Islands, the Channel Isles** NPL (*Geog*) les îles *fpl* Anglo-Normandes ► **channel-surf** VI (*US*) = **channel-hop** ► **channel-surfing** N (*US*) = **channel-hopping** ► **the Channel tunnel** N le tunnel sous la Manche

►**channel off** VT SEP (*lit*) [+ *water*] capter ; (*fig*) [+ *energy, resources*] canaliser

chant [tʃɑːnt] **1** N (*Mus*) chant *m* (lent), mélopée *f* ; (*Rel Mus*) psalmodie *f* ; [*of crowd, demonstrators, audience etc*] chant *m* scandé **2** VT (= *sing*) chanter lentement ; (= *recite*) réciter ; (*Rel*) psalmodier ; [*crowd, demonstrators etc*] scander, crier sur l'air des lampions **3** VI chanter ; (*Rel*) psalmodier ; [*crowd, demonstrators etc*] scander des slogans

chantey [ˈʃæntɪ] N (*US*) chanson *f* de marin

Chanukah [ˈhɑːnəkə] N Hanoukka *f*

chaos [ˈkeɪɒs] **1** N (*lit, fig*) chaos *m* **2** COMP ► **chaos theory** N théorie *f* du chaos

chaotic [keɪˈɒtɪk] ADJ chaotique

chaotically [keɪˈɒtɪklɪ] ADV de façon chaotique ; **he's ~ untidy/disorganized** il est effroyablement désordonné/désorganisé

chap¹ [tʃæp] **1** N (*Med*) gerçure *f*, crevasse *f* **2** VI se gercer, se crevasser **3** VT gercer, cre-

vasser **4** COMP ► **Chap Stick**® N pommade *f* rosat *or* pour les lèvres

chap² [tʃæp] N = **chop²**

chap³* [tʃæp] N (= *man*) gars* *m* ; (*term of address*) **old ~** mon vieux* ; **he was a young ~** c'était un jeune gars* ; **a nice ~** un chic type*, un bon gars* ; **the poor old ~** le pauvre vieux* ; **poor little ~** pauvre petit *m* ; **he's very deaf, poor ~** il est très sourd, le pauvre garçon *or* le pauvre vieux* ; **be a good ~ and say nothing** sois gentil (et) ne dis rien

chapat(t)i [tʃəˈpætɪ, tʃəˈpɑːtɪ] N (*pl* **chapat(t)i** *or* **chapat(t)is** *or* **chapat(t)ies**) chapati *m*

chapel [ˈtʃæpəl] **1** N **a** chapelle *f* → **lady** **b** (= *nonconformist church*) église *f* (non conformiste) ; **a ~ family** une famille non conformiste **c** (*Ind*) [*of print union*] section *f* syndicale (*dans l'édition*) **2** COMP ► **chapel of ease** N (*église f*) succursale *f* ► **chapel of rest** N chapelle *f* ardente

chaperon(e) [ˈʃæpərəʊn] **1** N chaperon *m* ; **she was the ~** elle faisait office de chaperon **2** VT chaperonner

chaplain [ˈtʃæplɪn] N (*in armed forces, prison, school, hospital*) aumônier *m* ; (*to nobleman*) chapelain *m*

chaplaincy [ˈtʃæplɪnsɪ] N **a** (= *building, room*) aumônerie *f* **b** (*NonC* = *work*) (*in armed forces, prison, school, hospital*) aumônerie *f* ; (*for nobleman*) chapellenie *f*

chaplet [ˈtʃæplɪt] N [*of flowers*] guirlande *f*, chapelet *m* ; (*Archit, Rel*) chapelet *m*

chappy* [ˈtʃæpɪ] N = **chap³**

chaps [tʃæps] NPL (*US*) jambières *fpl* de cuir (*portées par les cow-boys*)

chapter [ˈtʃæptər] **1** N **a** [*of book*] chapitre *m* ; **in ~ four** au chapitre quatre ; (*fig*) **to give** *or* **quote ~ and verse** citer ses références *or* ses autorités **b** (*Rel*) chapitre *m* **c** (*fig* = *period*) chapitre *m*, épisode *m* ; **a ~ of accidents** une succession de mésaventures, une kyrielle de malheurs ; **this ~ is now closed** ce chapitre est maintenant clos **d** (= *branch of society, club, organization etc*) branche *f*, section *f* **2** COMP ► **chapter room** N (*Rel*) salle *f* capitulaire *or* du chapitre

chapterhouse [ˈtʃæptəhaʊs] N (*Rel*) chapitre *m* (*lieu*)

char¹ [tʃɑːʳ] **1** VT (= *burn black*) carboniser **2** VI être carbonisé

char²†* [tʃɑːʳ] (*Brit*) **1** N (= *charwoman*) femme *f* de ménage **2** VI (*also* **go out ~ring**) faire des ménages

char³†* [tʃɑːʳ] N (*Brit* = *tea*) thé *m*

char⁴ [tʃɑːʳ] N (*Zool*) omble *m*

char-à-banc† [ˈʃærəbæŋ] N (*Brit*) (auto)car *m* (*décapotable*)

character [ˈkærɪktəʳ] **1** N **a** (= *temperament, disposition*) [*of person*] caractère *m*, tempérament *m* ; **he has the same ~ as his brother** il a le même caractère que son frère ; **it's very much in ~ (for him)** cela est bien de lui, cela lui ressemble tout à fait ; **that was not in ~ (for him)** cela ne lui ressemblait pas, ce n'était pas dans son caractère **b** (*NonC*) [*of country, village*] caractère *m* ; [*of book, film*] caractère *m*, nature *f* **c** (*NonC* = *strength, energy, determination etc*) caractère *m* ; **to have ~** avoir du caractère ; **it takes ~ to say such a thing** il faut avoir du caractère pour dire une chose pareille → **strength d** (= *outstanding individual*) personnage *m* ; (* = *original person*) numéro* *m*, phénomène* *m* ; **he's quite a ~!** c'est un sacré numéro* *or* un phénomène!* ; **he's a queer** *or* **an odd ~** c'est un curieux personnage **e** réputation *f* ; **of good/bad ~** de bonne/mauvaise réputation, qui a une bonne/qui a mauvaise réputation ; (*Jur*) **evidence of good ~** preuve *f* d'honorabilité **f** (= *testimonial*) références *fpl*

g (*Literat*) personnage *m*; (*Theat*) personnage *m*, rôle *m*; **one of Shakespeare's ~s** un des personnages de Shakespeare; **he played the ~ of Hamlet** il a joué (le rôle de) Hamlet **h** (*Typ*) caractère *m*, signe *m*; **Gothic ~s** caractères *mpl* gothiques **i** (*Comput*) caractère *m*; **~s per inch** caractères *mpl* par pouce; **~s per second** caractères/seconde *mpl*

2 COMP ► **character actor** N acteur *m* de genre ► **character actress** N actrice *f* de genre ► **character assassination** N diffamation *f* ► **character-building** ADJ qui forme le caractère ► **character comedy** N comédie *f* de caractère ► **character part** N rôle *m* de composition ► **character reference** N certificat *m* de (bonne) moralité ► **character set** N (*Typ*) chasse *f* (de caractères); (*Comput*) jeu *m* de caractères ► **character sketch** N portrait *m* or description *f* rapide ► **character space** N (*Typ*) espace *m* ► **character string** N (*Comput*) chaîne *f* de caractères ► **character witness** N (*Jur*) témoin *m* de moralité

characterful [ˈkærɪktəfʊl] ADJ [*place, building*] de caractère, qui a du cachet

characteristic [ˌkærɪktəˈrɪstɪk] **1** ADJ caractéristique; **with (his) ~ enthusiasm** avec l'enthousiasme qui le caractérise **2** N (*gen, Math*) caractéristique *f*

characteristically [ˌkærɪktəˈrɪstɪkəlɪ] ADV **he was ~ laconic** comme à son habitude, il a été laconique; **she proposed a ~ brilliant solution** elle a proposé une excellente solution, comme à son habitude; **he replied in ~ robust style** il a répondu dans ce style robuste qui le caractérise; **~, she refused** comme on pouvait s'y attendre, elle a refusé

characterization [ˌkærɪktəraɪˈzeɪʃən] N (*gen*) caractérisation *f*; (*by playwright, novelist etc*) manière *f* de camper les personnages; (*by actor*) interprétation *f*; **~ in Dickens** la manière dont Dickens campe ses personnages

characterize [ˈkærɪktəraɪz] VT caractériser, être caractéristique de; (*Literat*) camper un (or des) personnage(s)

characterless [ˈkærɪktəlɪs] ADJ sans caractère, fade

charade [ʃəˈrɑːd] N **a** (*fig*) comédie *f* **b** (= *game*) **~s** charades *fpl* en action

charbroiled [ˈtʃɑːˌbrɔɪld] ADJ (*US*) = **chargrilled**

charcoal [ˈtʃɑːkəʊl] **1** N charbon *m* de bois **2** COMP [*drawing, sketch*] au charbon; (= *colour: also* **~-grey**) gris foncé *inv*, (gris) anthracite *inv* ► **charcoal burner** N (= *person*) charbonnier *m*; (= *stove*) réchaud *m* à charbon de bois

chard [tʃɑːd] N (*also* **Swiss ~**) bettes *fpl*, blettes *fpl*

charge [tʃɑːdʒ]

1	NOUN	**4**	COMPOUNDS
2	TRANSITIVE VERB	**5**	PHRASAL VERBS
3	INTRANSITIVE VERB		

1 NOUN **a** Jur inculpation *f*, chef *m* d'accusation; **what is the ~?** quelle est le chef d'accusation?; **the ~ was murder** il était (or j'étais *etc*) inculpé de meurtre; **the ~ was read** on a lu l'acte *m* d'accusation; **no ~ was brought against him** il n'y a pas eu de poursuites (judiciaires), il n'a pas été poursuivi or inculpé; **the ~ was dropped** l'inculpation a été retirée, on a cessé les poursuites; **to press ~s (against sb)** engager des poursuites (contre qn); **to bring** or **lay a ~ against sb** porter plainte or déposer une plainte contre qn; **to give sb in ~** remettre qn à la police; **they were convicted on all three ~s** ils ont été reconnus coupables pour les trois chefs d'accusation; **to be on a murder ~** être inculpé de meurtre; **he was arrested on a ~ of murder** il a été arrêté sous

l'inculpation de meurtre; **to be on a ~** [*soldier*] être aux arrêts

b = **accusation** accusation *f* (**of** de); **he denied** or **repudiated these ~s** il a repoussé or rejeté ces accusations; **there were many ~s of cruelty** on les (*or* nous *etc*) a fréquemment accusés de cruauté; **the ~s made against him** les accusations *fpl* or les charges *fpl* portées contre lui; **~s that he had betrayed his friends** des accusations selon lesquelles il aurait trahi ses amis

c = **attack** (*esp Mil*) charge *f*, attaque *f*; [*of police, bull*] charge *f*; **the police made three ~s into the crowd** la police a chargé la foule par trois fois; (*Mil*) **to sound the ~** sonner la charge → **baton, bayonet**

d = **fee** prix *m*; **what's the ~?** ça coûte combien?, ça revient à combien?; **is there a ~?** faut-il payer?, y a-t-il quelque chose à payer?; **at a ~ of ...** pour ..., moyennant ...; **for a small ~, we can supply ...** pour un prix modique, nous pouvons fournir ...; **there's no ~ for this** ◊ no ~ is made for this c'est gratuit; **there is an extra** or **additional ~ for ...** il y a un supplément (à payer) pour ...; **to make a ~ for sth** facturer qch; **he made no ~ for mending it** il n'a pas facturé la réparation, il n'a rien pris pour la réparation; **he made a ~ of £20 for doing it** il a facturé 20 livres pour le faire; **~ for admission** droit *m* d'entrée; **"no ~ for admission"** « entrée libre »; (*Comm*) **~ for delivery** frais *mpl* de port → **bank, delivery, free, reverse**

e = **responsibility** **I've been given ~ of this class** on m'a donné la responsabilité or la charge de cette classe; **the patients in** or **under her ~** les malades *mpl* dont elle a la charge

◆ **in charge: who's in ~ here?** qui est le or la responsable?; **look, I'm in ~ here!** c'est moi qui commande ici!; **the person in ~** le or la responsable; **I left him in ~** je lui ai laissé la charge de tout

◆ **in charge of: to be in ~ of** [+ *firm, department*] diriger, être à la tête de; [+ *ship, plane*] commander; [+ *operation, project*] diriger, être responsable de; [+ *children, animals*] s'occuper de, avoir la charge de; **a few months later, he was in ~ of the shop** au bout de quelques mois, il dirigeait le magasin; **he's in ~ of the shop when I'm out** c'est lui qui s'occupe du magasin or qui surveille le magasin lorsque je m'absente; **while in ~ of a motor vehicle, he ...** alors qu'il était au volant d'un véhicule, il ...; **to put sb in ~ of** [+ *firm, department, operation, project*] confier à qn la direction de; [+ *ship, plane*] confier à qn le commandement de; [+ *children, animals*] confier aux soins or à la garde de qn; **to put sb in ~ of doing sth** charger qn de faire qch

◆ **to take charge** (*in firm, project etc*) prendre or assurer la direction (**of** de); (*in ship, plane*) prendre or assurer le commandement (**of** de); **he took ~ of the situation at once** il a immédiatement pris la situation en main; **will you take ~ of the children while I'm away?** est-ce que tu veux bien te charger des enfants pendant mon absence?

f = **person or thing cared for** **she took her ~s for a walk** elle a emmené les personnes dont elle avait la charge en promenade

g Rel (= *priest's parish*) cure *f*; (= *parishioners*) **the priest's ~s** les ouailles *fpl* du curé

h = **financial burden** charge *f*, fardeau *m* (**on** pour); **to be a ~ on ...** constituer une charge or un fardeau pour ...

i = **instructions**: *frm* recommandation *f*, instruction *f*; **to have strict ~ to do sth** avoir reçu l'ordre formel de faire qch; (*Jur*) **the judge's ~ to the jury** les recommandations données aux jurés par le juge

j Elec, Phys charge *f*; **to put a battery on ~** mettre une batterie en charge; **there is no ~ left in the battery** la batterie est déchargée or à plat; **an electrical ~** une charge électrique;

(*fig*) **it still gives me a ~*** ça me fait toujours de l'effet

k of firearm, rocket charge *f* → **depth** **l** Her meuble *m*

2 TRANSITIVE VERB **a** = **accuse** (*gen*) accuser; (*Jur*) inculper; **to find sb guilty/not guilty as ~d** déclarer qn coupable/non coupable; (*US*) **he ~d that some companies had infringed the regulations** il a allégué que certaines compagnies avaient enfreint le règlement

◆ **to charge sb with** (*gen*) accuser qn de; (*Jur*) inculper qn de; **to ~ sb with doing** or **having done sth** accuser qn d'avoir fait qch; (*Jur*) **he was ~d with murder/with stealing a car** il a été inculpé de meurtre/de vol de voiture → **2f**

b = **attack** [*troops*] charger, attaquer; [*police, bull*] charger

c in payment [+ *person*] facturer à; [+ *amount*] facturer (**for** pour); **to ~ a commission** facturer une commission; **to ~ £100 a day** facturer 100 livres par jour; **to ~ a fair price** facturer or prendre un prix raisonnable; **to ~ sb a fee of £200** facturer 200 livres à qn

◆ **to charge sb for: I ~d him £20 for this table** je lui ai facturé 20 livres pour cette table, je lui ai fait payer cette table 20 livres; **how much do you ~ for mending shoes?** combien prenez-vous pour réparer des chaussures?; **to ~ sb too much for sth** faire payer qch trop cher à qn; **I won't ~ you for that** je ne vous facturerai or compterai rien pour cela

d = **record as debt**: *also* ~ **up** mettre sur le compte, porter au compte or au débit (**to sb** de qn); (*US: in library*) **to ~ a book** inscrire un livre au registre du prêt → **cash**

◆ **to charge sth to sb: ~ all these purchases (up) to my account** mettez tous ces achats sur mon compte; **I can ~ it to the company** je peux le faire payer or rembourser par la société

e + firearm, battery (*also Phys*) charger

f = **command**: *frm* **to ~ sb to do sth** ordonner à qn or sommer qn de faire qch; **to ~ sb with sth** confier qch à qn

3 INTRANSITIVE VERB **a** = **rush** se précipiter, foncer; **to ~ in/out** entrer/sortir en coup de vent; **to ~ up/down** grimper/descendre à toute vitesse; **to ~ through** passer en coup de vent → **charge off**

b Mil **to ~ (down) on the enemy** fondre or foncer sur l'ennemi

c battery se (re)charger, être en charge

4 COMPOUNDS ► **charge account** N (*Comm*) compte *m* ► **charge-cap** VT (*Brit*) fixer un plafond aux impôts locaux à ► **charge capping** N (*Brit*) plafonnement *m* des impôts locaux ► **charge card** N (*Brit Comm*) carte *f* de paiement ► **charge hand** N (*Brit*) sous-chef *m* d'équipe ► **charge nurse** N (*Brit*) infirmier *m*, -ière *f* en chef (*responsable d'une salle ou d'un pavillon*) ► **charge sheet** N (*Brit Police*) ≈ procès-verbal *m*

5 PHRASAL VERBS ► **charge down** VT SEP (*Rugby*) **to ~ a kick down** contrer un coup de pied → **charge 3** ► **charge off 1** VI partir en courant **2** VT SEP (*Comm*) [+ *machine*] amortir; **they ~d off drilling costs as business expenses** ils ont imputé les coûts de forage à l'exploitation; **to ~ off an expense** passer une dépense en charge ► **charge up 1** VI = **charge 3c** **2** VT SEP = **charge 2e**

chargeable [ˈtʃɑːdʒəbl] ADJ **a** (*Jur*) [*crime, offence*] passible de poursuites; **~ with sth** [*person*] passible de poursuites pour qch **b** (= *payable*) [*fee*] chargé; **a late entry fee of $20 is ~** il y a un supplément de 20 dollars à payer pour les inscriptions en retard; **fees ~ by the solicitor** honoraires *mpl* qu'il faut payer à l'avocat; **the lowest lending rates ~ by UK banks** les taux les plus bas pratiqués par les banques du Royaume-Uni [c] (= *assignable*) [*expenses*] (*to tax office*) déductible; (*to employer*) à la charge de l'employeur; **~ to sb** à facturer à qn, à porter au compte de qn; **~ to an account** imputable sur un compte [d] (= *taxable*) [*asset*] imposable

charged ['tʃɑːdʒd] ADJ [a] (*Elec*) [*particles*] chargé [b] (*fig*) **~ with emotion** ◊ **emotionally ~** plein d'émotion; **a highly ~ atmosphere** une atmosphère très tendue

chargé d'affaires [,ʃɑːʒeɪdæ'feə] N (*pl* **chargés d'affaires**) chargé *m* d'affaires

charger ['tʃɑːdʒəʳ] N [a] [*of battery, firearm*] chargeur *m* [b] (*Mil* = *horse*) cheval *m* (de combat)

chargrilled ['tʃɑːˌgrɪld] ADJ (*Brit Culin*) grillé au feu de bois

charily ['tʃɛərɪlɪ] ADV prudemment, avec prudence *or* circonspection

chariot ['tʃærɪət] N char *m*

charioteer [,tʃærɪə'tɪəʳ] N conducteur *m* de char, aurige *m*

charisma [kæ'rɪzmə] N (*Rel, fig*) charisme *m*

charismatic [,kærɪz'mætɪk] ADJ [a] (= *fascinating*) [*person, personality, charm*] charismatique [b] [*church, movement*] charismatique; **~ Christian** charismatique *mf*

charitable ['tʃærɪtəbl] ADJ [a] (= *helping the needy*) [*organization, foundation, institution*] caritatif; [*donation*] à une œuvre d'intérêt public; **~ work** bonnes œuvres *fpl*; **to have ~ status** avoir le statut d'organisation caritative [b] (*kindly*) [*person, thought, deed, gesture*] charitable (**to sb** envers qn); **to take a ~ view of sth** être indulgent pour qch

charitably ['tʃærɪtəblɪ] ADV charitablement

charity ['tʃærɪtɪ] [1] N [a] (*NonC*) charité *f*; **for ~'s sake** ◊ **out of ~** par (pure) charité ▪ (*PROV*) **~ begins at home** charité bien ordonnée commence par soi-même (*PROV*); (*Rel*) **sister of Charity** sœur *f* de charité → **cold, faith** [b] (= *charitable action*) acte *m* de charité, action *f* charitable [c] (*NonC* = *alms*) charité *f*, aumône *f*; **to live on ~** vivre d'aumônes; **to collect for ~** faire une collecte pour une œuvre (charitable); **the proceeds go to ~** les fonds recueillis sont versés à des œuvres [d] (= *charitable society*) fondation *f or* institution *f* caritative, œuvre *f* de bienfaisance [2] COMP ► **charity sale** N vente *f* de charité *or* de bienfaisance ► **charity shop** N boutique *f* vendant des articles d'occasion au profit d'une organisation caritative ► **charity toss** N (*Basketball*) lancer *m* franc

charlady ['tʃɑːleɪdɪ] N (*Brit*) femme *f* de ménage

charlatan ['ʃɑːlətən] [1] N charlatan *m* [2] ADJ charlatanesque

Charlemagne ['ʃɑːləmeɪn] N Charlemagne *m*

Charles ['tʃɑːlz] N Charles *m*

charleston ['tʃɑːlstən] N charleston *m*

charley horse* ['tʃɑːlɪhɔːs] N (*US*) crampe *f*, spasme *m*

Charlie ['tʃɑːlɪ] N Charlot *m*; (*Brit*) **he must have looked a proper ~!** il a dû avoir l'air fin *or* malin!*; (*Brit*) **I felt a right ~!** j'ai vraiment eu l'air idiot!*

charlotte ['ʃɑːlət] N (*Culin*) charlotte *f*; **apple ~** charlotte *f* aux pommes

charm [tʃɑːm] [1] N [a] (= *attractiveness*) charme *m*, attrait *m*; **a lady's ~s** les charmes d'une dame; **to have a lot of ~** avoir beaucoup de charme; **to fall victim to sb's ~s** succomber aux charmes de qn [b] (= *spell*) charme *m*, enchantement *m*; **to hold sb under a ~** tenir qn sous le charme; **it works like a ~*** ça marche à merveille; **the plan worked like a ~*** tout s'est déroulé exactement comme prévu

[c] (*for bracelet*) breloque *f*; (= *amulet*) charme *m*, amulette *f*
[2] VT (= *attract, please*) charmer, enchanter; (= *cast spell on*) enchanter, ensorceler; [+ *snakes*] charmer; **to have** *or* **lead a ~ed life** être béni des dieux; **to ~ sth out of sb** obtenir qch de qn par le charme *or* en lui faisant du charme; **to ~ one's way somewhere** s'introduire quelque part grâce à son charme; **to ~ one's way out of a situation** se sortir d'une situation grâce à son charme; **he could ~ the birds off** *or* **out of the trees** il sait vraiment y faire
[3] COMP ► **charm bracelet** N bracelet *m* à breloques ► **charmed circle** N **they seemed part of a ~ed circle** ils semblaient comme protégés par un enchantement ► **charm offensive** N (*hum*) offensive *f* de charme ► **charm price** N prix *m* psychologique ► **charm school** N cours *m* de maintien
► **charm away** VT SEP faire disparaître comme par enchantement *or* par magie; **to ~ away sb's cares** dissiper les soucis de qn comme par enchantement *or* par magie

charmer ['tʃɑːməʳ] N charmeur *m*, -euse *f* → **snake**

charming ['tʃɑːmɪŋ] ADJ (*also iro*) charmant

charmingly ['tʃɑːmɪŋlɪ] ADV [*behave, smile*] d'une façon charmante; **~ naïve/simple** d'une naïveté/simplicité charmante

charmless ['tʃɑːmlɪs] ADJ dénué de charme

charnel-house† ['tʃɑːnlhaʊs] N ossuaire *m*, charnier *m*

charr [tʃɑːʳ] N = **char⁴**

chart [tʃɑːt] [1] N [a] (= *map*) carte *f* (marine) [b] (= *graph*) graphique *m*; (= *diagram*) diagramme *m*; (= *table*) tableau *m*; (*Med*) courbe *f*; **temperature ~** (= *sheet*) feuille *f* de température; (= *line*) courbe *f* de température [c] (*Mus*) **the ~s** le Top 50, le hit-parade, le palmarès de la chanson; **in the ~s** au Top 50 *or* au hit-parade; **to reach the ~s** figurer au Top 50 *or* au hit-parade; **to top the ~s** être en tête des meilleures ventes *or* du Top 50 *or* du hit-parade
[2] VT [a] (= *draw on map*) [+ *route, journey*] porter sur la carte [b] (*on graph*) [+ *sales, profits, results*] faire le graphique *or* la courbe de; **this graph ~s the progress made last year** ce graphique montre les progrès accomplis l'an dernier [c] (*fig* = *plan*) organiser, planifier
[3] COMP ► **chart topper** N (*Mus*) ≈ numéro *m* 1 du Top 50 ► **chart-topping** ADJ qui vient en tête des meilleures ventes *or* du Top 50

charter ['tʃɑːtəʳ] [1] N [a] (= *document*) charte *f*; [*of society, organization*] statuts *mpl*, acte *m* constitutif; **the Charter of the United Nations** la Charte des Nations unies → **citizen** [b] (*NonC*) [*of boat, plane, coach, train etc*] affrètement *m*; **on ~** sous contrat d'affrètement [c] (*also ~ flight*) (vol *m*) charter *m*
[2] VT [a] accorder une charte à, accorder un privilège (par une charte) à [b] [+ *plane etc*] affréter
[3] COMP ► **chartered accountant** N (*Brit, Can*) expert-comptable *mf*, comptable *mf* agréé(e) (*Can*) ► **chartered company** N société *f* privilégiée ► **chartered society** N compagnie *f* à charte ► **chartered surveyor** N expert *m* immobilier ► **charter flight** N (vol *m*) charter *m*; **to take a ~ flight to Rome** aller à Rome en charter ► **charter member** N (*US*) membre *m* fondateur ► **charter party** N (*Jur*) charte-partie *f* ► **charter plane** N (avion *m*) charter *m* ► **charter train** N train *m* charter

charterer ['tʃɑːtərəʳ] N affréteur *m*

Chartist ['tʃɑːtɪst] N (*Hist*) **the ~s** les chartistes *mpl*

charwoman† ['tʃɑːˌwʊmən] N (*pl* **-women**) femme *f* de ménage

chary ['tʃɛərɪ] ADJ [a] (= *cautious*) prudent, circonspect; **to be ~ of doing** hésiter à faire [b] (= *stingy*) pingre, ladre† (*also liter*) (**of** de); **he is ~ of praise** il est avare de compliments

chase¹ [tʃeɪs] [1] N (= *action*) chasse *f*, poursuite *f*; (*Racing* = *steeple-chase*) steeple *m*; **a high-speed car ~** une course-poursuite en voiture; (*Sport*) **the ~ for the championship** la course au titre (de champion); **to give ~ (to sb)** donner la chasse (à qn), se lancer à la poursuite (de qn); **US fighters gave ~ to two enemy planes** des chasseurs américains ont donné la chasse à *or* se sont lancés à la poursuite de deux avions ennemis; **they ran out and the police gave ~** ils sont sortis en courant et la police leur a donné la chasse *or* s'est lancée à leur poursuite; **in ~ of** à la poursuite de; **the ~** (*Sport*) la chasse (à courre); (= *huntsmen*) la chasse, les chasseurs *mpl* → **paper, steeplechase, wild**
[2] VT poursuivre, donner la chasse à; [+ *success, women, job etc*] courir après; **he ~d him down the hill** il l'a poursuivi jusqu'au bas de la colline; **she ~d the thief for 100 metres** elle a poursuivi le voleur sur 100 mètres; **2,000 unemployed people chasing five jobs** 2000 chômeurs qui se disputent cinq emplois; (*Drugs*) **to ~ the dragon:** fumer de l'héroïne
[3] VI [a] (*lit, fig*) **to ~ after sb** courir après qn [b] (= *rush*) **to ~ up/down/out** *etc* monter/descendre/sortir *etc* au grand galop; (*Brit*) **to ~ about** ◊ **to ~ here and there** courir à droite et à gauche
► **chase away** [1] VI* filer*, se tirer:* [2] VT SEP [+ *person, animal*] chasser, faire partir
► **chase down** VT SEP (= *track down*) retrouver [b] (*US* = *catch*) rattraper
► **chase off** = **chase away**
► **chase up*** VT SEP [+ *information*] rechercher; [+ *sth already asked for*] réclamer; **to ~ sb up for sth** relancer qn pour qch; (= *hurry things along*) **I'll ~ it up for you** je vais essayer d'activer les choses

chase² [tʃeɪs] VT (*Tech*) [+ *diamond*] sertir, enchâsser (**in** dans); [+ *silver*] ciseler; [+ *metal*] repousser; [+ *screw*] fileter

chaser ['tʃeɪsəʳ] N [a] (= *pursuer*) poursuivant *m* [b] (*Tech*) graveur *m* sur métaux; [*of screw*] peigne *m* (à fileter) [c] (* = *drink*) verre pris pour en faire descendre un autre

chasm ['kæzəm] N (*lit, fig*) gouffre *m*, abîme *m*

chassis ['ʃæsɪ] N (*pl* **chassis** ['ʃæsɪz]) (*Aut*) châssis *m*; (*Aviat*) train *m* d'atterrissage; (*US* = *body*) châssis* *m*

chaste [tʃeɪst] ADJ [*person*] chaste, pur; [*style*] sobre

chastely ['tʃeɪstlɪ] ADV [*behave*] chastement; [*dress*] avec sobriété, simplement

chasten ['tʃeɪsn] VT (= *punish*) châtier, corriger; (= *subdue*) assagir, calmer; (= *rebuke*) réprimander

chastened ['tʃeɪsnd] ADJ [*person*] assagi, calmé; [*style*] châtié

chasteness ['tʃeɪstnɪs] N (*NonC*) [a] (*sexual*) [*of person, relationship*] chasteté *f* [b] (*frm* = *simplicity*) [*of style*] sobriété *f*

chastening ['tʃeɪsnɪŋ] ADJ [*thought*] qui fait réfléchir (à deux fois); **the accident had a ~ effect on him** l'accident l'a fait réfléchir

chastise [tʃæs'taɪz] VT (= *scold*) réprimander; (= *punish*) punir, châtier; (= *beat*) battre, corriger

chastisement ['tʃæstɪzmənt] N (*NonC*) [a] (= *criticism*) condamnation *f*, fustigation *f* (*liter*) [b] († = *punishment*) châtiment *m*

chastity ['tʃæstɪtɪ] [1] N chasteté *f* [2] COMP ► **chastity belt** N ceinture *f* de chasteté

chasuble ['tʃæzjʊbl] N chasuble *f*

chat [tʃæt] **1** N (NonC) bavardage m; (= casual conversation) brin m de conversation or de causette*; **to have a ~** bavarder un peu, faire un brin de conversation or de causette*; **I must have a ~ with him about this** il faut que je lui en parle or que je lui en touche un mot **2** VI bavarder, causer (**with, to** avec) **3** COMP ► **chat show** N (Brit TV) causerie f télévisée ► **chat-up line** N (Brit) **that's his usual ~-up line** c'est son entrée en matière habituelle pour draguer*

►**chat up*** VT SEP (Brit) baratiner*, faire du plat* à

chatline [ˈtʃætlaɪn] N (for dating) ≈ téléphone m rose

chattel [ˈtʃætl] **1 chattels** NPL (gen) biens mpl, possessions fpl; (Jur) biens meubles mpl; **with all his goods and ~s** avec tout ce qu'il possède (or possédait etc) **2** COMP ► **chattel mortgage** N (Jur, Fin) nantissement m de biens meubles

chatter [ˈtʃætər] **1** VI bavarder, jacasser (pej); [children, monkeys] jacasser; [birds] jacasser, jaser; **his teeth were ~ing** il claquait des dents **2** N [of person] bavardage m; [of birds, children, monkeys] jacassement m; [of teeth] claquement m

chatterbox* [ˈtʃætəbɒks], **chatterer** [ˈtʃætərər] N moulin m à paroles*, bavard(e) m(f); **to be a ~** être bavard comme une pie

chattering [ˈtʃætərɪŋ] **1** N bavardage m **2** COMP ► **the chattering classes*** NPL (Brit esp pej) les intellos* mpl

chatty* [ˈtʃætɪ] ADJ [person] bavard; [style] familier, qui reste au niveau du bavardage; [letter] plein de bavardages

Chaucerian [tʃɔːˈsɪərɪən] ADJ de Chaucer, chaucérien

chauffeur [ˈʃəʊfər] **1** N chauffeur m (de maître) **2** VT **to ~ sb around** or **about** servir de chauffeur à qn **3** COMP ► **chauffeur-driven car** N voiture f avec chauffeur

chauvinism [ˈʃəʊvɪnɪzəm] N (gen) chauvinisme m; (= male chauvinism) machisme m, phallocratie f

chauvinist [ˈʃəʊvɪnɪst] **1** N (gen) chauvin(e) m(f); (= male chauvinist) phallocrate m **2** ADJ (gen) chauvin; (= male chauvinist) machiste, phallocrate; **male ~ pig** phallocrate m

chauvinistic [ˌʃəʊvɪˈnɪstɪk] ADJ (gen) chauvin; (= male chauvinistic) machiste, phallocrate

chaw [tʃɔː] (dial) = **chew**

CHE [ˌsiːeɪtʃˈiː] (ABBR = **Campaign for Homosexual Equality**) campagne f pour l'égalité des homosexuels

cheap [tʃiːp] **1** ADJ **a** (= inexpensive) [goods, services, housing, café, price, labour] bon marché inv; [rate, fare] réduit; [loan, credit] à faible taux d'intérêt; [currency, pound, dollar] déprécié; **~er** meilleur marché inv, moins cher (chère f); **it's 10 pence ~er** ça coûte 10 pence de moins; **an electrician** un électricien pas cher; **the ~est seats are around £15** les places les moins chères sont autour de 15 livres; (Telec) **calls cost 36p per minute ~ rate** les appels coûtent 36 pence la minute en tarif réduit; (Printing) **~ edition** édition f populaire or bon marché; **it was going ~** cela se vendait à bas prix; **it is ~er to buy than to rent** cela revient moins cher d'acheter que de louer; **to be ~ to run** ne pas revenir cher à l'emploi; **these cars are very ~ to produce** la production de ces voitures est très bon marché; **quality doesn't come ~** la qualité se paie; **it's ~ at the price*** [goods, services] sa ce prix-là, c'est bon marché; [freedom] ce n'est pas cher payé; **~ and cheerful*** pas cher et sans prétentions; **human life is ~ in wartime** la vie humaine ne vaut pas grand-chose en temps de guerre → **dirt**

b (pej = poor-quality) [wine, material, brand, copy, imitation, perfume, seat] bon marché; [cut of meat] de qualité inférieure; [jewellery] de pacotille; [hotel, café] de second ordre; **~ and nasty*** [wine, plastic] minable et bon marché **c** (pej) **on the ~*** [buy, employ] au rabais; [decorate] à bas prix; **it was a bad idea, done on the ~** c'était une mauvaise idée, réalisée avec de petits moyens **d** (pej = unworthy) [remark, question, opportunism, sensationalism] de bas étage; [joke, jibe, trick, ploy, gimmick, woman] facile; [behaviour, attitude] minable; **to feel ~** se sentir minable; **to look ~** [person] avoir l'air minable; [clothes, make-up] faire bon marché; **to make o.s. ~** s'avilir; **~ thrills** sensations fpl fortes **2** ADV [buy] (= inexpensively) bon marché; (= cut-price) au rabais **3** COMP ► **cheap shot** N coup m bas

cheapen [ˈtʃiːpən] **1** VT baisser le prix de; (fig) déprécier; **to ~ o.s.** se déprécier, s'abaisser **2** VI baisser, devenir moins cher

cheapie* [ˈtʃiːpɪ] **1** ADJ pas cher **2** N (= ticket/meal etc) billet m/repas m etc pas cher

cheapjack [ˈtʃiːpdʒæk] ADJ de mauvaise qualité

cheaply [ˈtʃiːplɪ] ADV [buy, sell] bon marché; [borrow, produce, decorate, furnish, eat] à bon marché; [live] à peu de frais; [available] à moindre prix ■ (PROV) **two can live as ~ as one** ≈ quand il y en a pour l'un, il y en a pour l'autre

cheapness [ˈtʃiːpnɪs] N (lit) bas prix m

cheapo* [ˈtʃiːpəʊ] ADJ bon marché

cheapshot [ˈtʃiːpʃɒt] VT (US) débiner*, dénigrer

cheapskate* [ˈtʃiːpskeɪt] N radin* mf, avare mf

cheat [tʃiːt] **1** VT (= deceive) tromper, duper; (= defraud) frauder; (= swindle) escroquer; (fig) [+ time etc] tromper; **to ~ sb at cards** tricher aux cartes en jouant avec qn; **to ~ sb out of sth** escroquer qch à qn; **to ~ sb into doing sth** faire faire qch à qn en le trompant; **to feel ~ed** (= swindled) se sentir floué; (= betrayed) se sentir trahi **2** VI (at cards, games) tricher (**at** à); (= defraud) frauder; **to ~ on sb*** (= be unfaithful to) tromper qn **3** N (also **~er**: US) **a** (= person) tricheur m, -euse f **b** (= deception) tricherie f, triche* f; **it's a bit of a ~ to use ready-prepared meals** c'est un peu de la triche d'utiliser des plats cuisinés

cheater [ˈtʃiːtər] N (US) = **cheat**

cheating [ˈtʃiːtɪŋ] **1** N (NonC) (at cards, games) tricherie f; (= deceit) tromperie f; (= fraud) fraude f; (= swindle) escroquerie f **2** ADJ tricheur

Chechen [ˈtʃetʃən] **1** N (pl **Chechen** or **Chechens**) (= person) Tchétchène mf **2** ADJ tchétchène

Chechnya [ˈtʃetʃnɪə] N la Tchétchénie

check¹ [tʃek] N (US) = **cheque**

check² [tʃek] **1** N **a** (= setback) [of movement] arrêt m brusque; [of machine etc] recul m; **to hold** or **keep in ~** (gen) [+ emotions etc] contenir, maîtriser; (Mil) tenir en échec; **to put a ~ on** mettre un frein à; **to act as a ~ upon** constituer un frein à; (Pol) **~s and balances** freins mpl et contrepoids mpl **b** (= examination) [of papers, passport, ticket] contrôle m; [of luggage] vérification f; (at factory door) pointage m; **to make a ~ on** contrôler; **to keep a ~ on** surveiller; (US) **~!*** (= OK) d'accord!, OK!* **c** (Chess) échec m; **in ~** en échec; **~!** échec au roi! **d** (US) [of left luggage] ticket m de consigne; (Theat) ticket m de vestiaire; [of restaurant] addition f

2 VT **a** (also **~ out**) (= examine, verify) [+ accounts, figures, statement, quality etc] vérifier; [+ tickets, passports] contrôler; (= mark off) pointer, faire le pointage de; (= tick off) cocher; **to ~ a copy against the original** compa-

rer une copie à l'original, collationner une copie avec l'original; **I'll have to ~ whether** or **if there's an age limit** il faudra que je vérifie s'il y a une limite d'âge **b** [+ baggage to be loaded] enregistrer **c** (*: also **~ out** = look at) mater*, viser*; **~ his shoes!** vise (un peu) or mate un peu ses chaussures! **d** (= stop) [+ enemy] arrêter; [+ advance] enrayer; (= restrain) [+ excitement] refréner, contenir; [+ anger] maîtriser, réprimer; **he was going to protest, but she ~ed him** il allait protester, mais elle l'a retenu; **to ~ o.s.** se contrôler, se retenir; **it is hoped that sex education will help ~ the spread of AIDS** on espère que l'éducation sexuelle aidera à enrayer la progression du sida **e** (= rebuke) réprimander **f** (Chess) faire échec à **g** (US) [+ coats] (in cloakroom) mettre au vestiaire; (Rail) [+ luggage] (= register) faire enregistrer; [+ left luggage] mettre à la consigne

3 VI **a** **is Matthew there? — hold on, I'll just ~** est-ce que Matthew est là? — attends, je vais voir **b** (= pause) s'arrêter (momentanément) **c** (also **~ out** = confirm each other) [figures, stories] correspondre, s'accorder

4 COMP ► **check-in** N (at airport) enregistrement m (des bagages); **your ~-in time is half-an-hour before departure** présentez-vous à l'enregistrement des bagages une demi-heure avant le départ ► **check-out** N (Comm) caisse f (dans un libre-service) ► **check-out time** N (in hotel) heure f limite d'occupation

►**check in** **1** VI (in hotel) (= arrive) arriver; (= register) remplir une fiche (d'hôtel); (at airport) se présenter à l'enregistrement **2** VT SEP faire remplir une fiche (d'hôtel) à; (at airport) enregistrer **3** **~-in** → **check²**

►**check off** VT SEP pointer, cocher

►**check on** VT FUS [+ information, time etc] vérifier; **to ~ on sb** voir ce que fait qn; **just go and ~ on the baby** va jeter un coup d'œil sur le bébé

►**check out** **1** VI **a** (from hotel) régler sa note **b** → **check² 3c** **c** (* euph = die) passer l'arme à gauche*, mourir **2** VT SEP **a** → **check² 2a** **b** (* = look at) jeter un œil à* **c** [+ luggage] enregistrer; [+ person] contrôler la sortie de; [+ hotel guest] faire payer sa note à **3** **~-out** N → **check²**

►**check over** VT SEP examiner, vérifier

►**check up** **1** VI se renseigner, vérifier; **to ~ up on sth** vérifier qch; **to ~ up on sb** se renseigner sur qn **2** **~up** N → **checkup**

Dans le système politique américain, les « freins et contrepoids » sont des mécanismes qui tendent à garantir l'équilibre des pouvoirs par une stricte séparation entre l'exécutif, le législatif et le judiciaire, et à empêcher la domination d'un de ces pouvoirs sur les autres. Dans l'esprit des auteurs de la Constitution, la liberté est assurée par le fait qu'il est toujours possible de contester les pouvoirs du Président, du Congrès, des tribunaux ou de l'administration des États.

check³ [tʃek] **1** N (gen pl) **~s** (= pattern) carreaux mpl, damier m; (= cloth) tissu m à carreaux; **broken ~** pied-de-poule m **2** COMP = **checked**

checkbook [ˈtʃekbʊk] N (US) carnet m de chèques, chéquier m

checked [tʃekt] ADJ **a** [tablecloth, suit, pattern] à carreaux **b** (Phon) [vowel] entravé

checker [ˈtʃekər] **1** N **a** (= examiner) fact ~ vérificateur m, -trice f; **work ~** contrôleur m, -euse f du travail → **grammar, spellchecker** **b** (US) (in supermarket) caissier m, -ière f; (in cloakroom) préposé(e) m(f) au vestiaire

checkerboard ['tʃekəbɔːd] **1** N (US) (Chess) échiquier m; (Checkers) damier m **2** COMP ▶ **checkerboard pattern** N motif m à damiers

Checker cab® ['tʃekə‚kæb] N (US Aut) ancien modèle de taxi américain à damier

checkered ['tʃekəd] (US) = **chequered**

checkers ['tʃekəz] NPL (US) jeu m de dames

checking ['tʃekɪŋ] **1** N (NonC) [of equipment, system, facts, exam paper, document] vérification f; [of ticket, passport] contrôle m; (Med) examen m médical; **to do some ~ on sb/sth** effectuer des vérifications sur qn/qch **2** COMP ▶ **checking account** N (US Fin) compte m courant ▶ **checking deposit** N dépôt m à vue

checklist ['tʃeklɪst] N (gen, Aviat) check-list f, liste f de contrôle

checkmate ['tʃekmeɪt] **1** N (Chess) (échec m et) mat m; (fig) échec m total, fiasco m **2** VT (Chess) mettre (échec et) mat; (fig) [+ person] coincer*, faire échec à; [+ plans etc] déjouer

checkpoint ['tʃekpɔɪnt] **1** N (Aut, Mil, Sport) (poste m de) contrôle m **2** COMP ▶ **Checkpoint Charlie** N (Mil) Checkpoint m Charlie

checkroom ['tʃekrʊm] N (US = cloakroom) vestiaire m

checkup ['tʃekʌp] N (gen) contrôle m, vérification f; (Med) bilan m de santé, check-up m; (Med) **to go for** or **have a ~** se faire faire un bilan (de santé)

cheddar ['tʃedə'] N (fromage m de) cheddar m

cheek [tʃiːk] **1** N **a** (Anat) joue f; **by jowl** côte à côte; **~ by jowl with** tout près de; **to dance ~ to ~** danser joue contre joue; (fig) **to turn the other ~** tendre l'autre joue → **tongue** **b** (= buttock) fesse f **c** (= impudence) effronterie f, toupet* m, culot* m; **to have the ~ to do sth*** avoir le toupet* or le culot* de faire qch; **what (a) ~!*** ◊ **of all the ~!*** quel culot !*, quel toupet !*; **the ~ of it!*** ce toupet !* **2** VT (Brit*) [+ person] être insolent avec, narguer

cheekbone ['tʃiːkbəʊn] N pommette f

cheekily ['tʃiːkɪlɪ] ADV (Brit) [say] avec insolence; [grin] d'un air effronté

cheekiness ['tʃiːkɪnɪs] N effronterie f, toupet* m, culot* m

cheeky ['tʃiːkɪ] ADJ [child] effronté, insolent; [remark] impertinent; **~ child** petit(e) effronté(e) m(f); **(you) ~ monkey!*** quel toupet !*

cheep [tʃiːp] **1** N [of bird] piaulement m; [of mouse] couinement m; **~, ~!** cui-cui ! **2** VI [bird] piauler; [mouse] couiner

cheer [tʃɪə'] **1** N **a** **~s** acclamations fpl, applaudissements mpl, hourras mpl, bravos mpl; **to give three ~s for** acclamer; **three ~s for ...!** un ban pour ...!, hourra pour ...!; **three ~s!** hourra !; **the children gave a loud ~** les enfants ont poussé des acclamations; (esp Brit) **~s!*** (= your health!) à la vôtre !* (or à la tienne !*); (= goodbye) salut!, tchao !*; (= thanks) merci ! **b** († = cheerfulness) gaieté f, joie f; **words of ~** paroles fpl d'encouragement; **be of good ~!** prenez courage ! **c** († = food etc) chère† f; **good ~** bonne chère **2** VT **a** (also **~ up**) [+ person] remonter le moral à, réconforter; [+ room] égayer **b** (= applaud) acclamer, applaudir **3** VI applaudir, pousser des vivats or des hourras

▶ **cheer on** VT SEP [+ person, team] encourager

▶ **cheer up** **1** VI (= be gladdened) s'égayer, se dérider; (= be comforted) prendre courage, prendre espoir; **~ up!** courage ! **2** VT SEP → **cheer 2a**

cheerful ['tʃɪəfʊl] ADJ [person] joyeux, gai; [mood, colour, occasion, place, atmosphere] gai; [smile, expression, voice, conversation] enjoué; [news, prospect, outlook, belief] réjouissant; **to be ~ about sth** se réjouir de qch; **to sound ~** avoir l'air réjoui → **cheap**

cheerfully ['tʃɪəfʊlɪ] ADV **a** (= happily) [smile, say, greet] joyeusement, gaiement **b** (= enthusiastically) [work] avec enthousiasme; **she went ~ off to work** elle partit gaiement au travail **c** (= blithely) [ignore] allègrement **d** (= gladly) **I could ~ strangle him*** je l'étranglerais avec joie

cheerfulness ['tʃɪəfʊlnɪs] N [of person] bonne humeur f, gaieté f; [of smile, conversation, place] gaieté f

cheerily ['tʃɪərɪlɪ] ADV gaiement, avec entrain

cheering ['tʃɪərɪŋ] **1** N (NonC) acclamations fpl, hourras mpl **2** ADJ [news, sight] réconfortant, réjouissant

cheerio ['tʃɪərɪ'əʊ] EXCL (esp Brit) **a** (= goodbye) salut !*, tchao !* **b** † (= your health) à la vôtre (or à la tienne) !

cheerleader ['tʃɪəliːdə'] N (Sport) pom-pom girl f; (fig) meneur m, -euse f (qui œuvre pour une cause, une personnalité politique)

cheerless ['tʃɪəlɪs] ADJ [person, thing] morne, triste

cheery ['tʃɪərɪ] ADJ gai, joyeux

cheese [tʃiːz] **1** N fromage m; **Dutch ~** fromage m de Hollande; (for photograph) **"say ~!"** « un petit sourire ! »; **big ~*** gros bonnet m → **cottage**, **cream**, **lemon** **2** VT **a** (Brit*) **to be ~d (off)** en avoir marre*; **to be ~d off with sth** en avoir marre de qch* **b** (Brit*) **~ it!*** (= look out) vingt-deux !*; (= run away) tire-toi !* **3** COMP [sandwich] au fromage ▶ **cheese and wine (party)** N ≈ buffet m campagnard ▶ **cheese dip** N sauce f au fromage dans laquelle on trempe des légumes etc en bâtonnets ▶ **cheese dish** N = **cheeseboard** ▶ **cheese straw** N allumette f au fromage ▶ **cheese wire** N fil m à couper le beurre

cheeseboard ['tʃiːzbɔːd] N (= dish) plateau m à fromage(s); (with cheeses on it) plateau m de fromages

cheeseburger ['tʃiːz‚bɜːgə'] N hamburger m au fromage, cheeseburger m

cheesecake ['tʃiːzkeɪk] N (NonC) (Culin) cheesecake m, ≈ gâteau m au fromage blanc; (* fig) photo f (de fille) déshabillée

cheesecloth ['tʃiːzklɒθ] N (for cheese) étamine f, mousseline f à fromage; (for clothes) toile f à beurre

cheeseparing ['tʃiːz‚pɛərɪŋ] **1** N économie(s) f(pl) de bouts de chandelles **2** ADJ [person] pingre, qui fait des économies de bouts de chandelles; [attitude, action] mesquin

cheesy ['tʃiːzɪ] ADJ **a** (lit) qui a un goût de fromage, qui sent le fromage **b** (* = naff) moche*, ringard* **c*** [grin] large **d** (* = banal) rebattu

cheetah ['tʃiːtə] N guépard m

chef [ʃef] N chef m (de cuisine)

chef d'œuvre [‚ʃeɪ'dɜːvrə] N (pl chefs d'œuvre) chef-d'œuvre m

cheiromancer ['kaɪərəmænsə'] N = **chiromancer**

cheiromancy ['kaɪərəmænsɪ] N = **chiromancy**

Chekhov ['tʃekɒf] N Tchekhov m

Chelsea Pensioner [‚tʃelsɪ'penʃənə'] N (Brit) ancien combattant résidant au « Chelsea Royal Hospital »

chemical ['kemɪkəl] **1** ADJ chimique **2** N (gen pl) produit m chimique **3** COMP ▶ **chemical agent** N agent m chimique ▶ **chemical castration** N castration f chimique ▶ **chemical engineer** N ingénieur m chimiste ▶ **chemical engineering** N génie m chimique ▶ **chemical toilet** N toilettes fpl chimiques ▶ **chemical warfare** N guerre f chimique ▶ **chemical weapons** NPL armes fpl chimiques

chemically ['kemɪkəlɪ] ADV chimiquement

chemise [ʃə'miːz] N (= undergarment) chemise f (de femme); (= dress) robe-chemisier f

chemist ['kemɪst] N **a** (= researcher etc) chimiste mf **b** (Brit = pharmacist) pharmacien(ne) m(f); **~'s (shop)** pharmacie f

chemistry ['kemɪstrɪ] **1** N chimie f; (fig) **they work so well together because the ~ is right** ils travaillent très bien ensemble parce que le courant passe **2** COMP [laboratory, lesson, teacher] de chimie ▶ **chemistry set** N panoplie f de chimiste

chemotherapy [‚kemoʊ'θerəpɪ] N chimiothérapie f

chenille [ʃə'niːl] N (Tex) chenille f

cheque, check (US) [tʃek] **1** N chèque m; **~ for £10** chèque m de 10 livres; **~ in the amount of $10** chèque m de 10 dollars; **to pay by ~** payer par chèque; (Brit) **to cross a ~** barrer un chèque; **bad** or **dud*** or **rubber*** ~ chèque m sans provision or en bois* **2** COMP ▶ **cheque account** N compte-chèque m ▶ **cheque card** N (Brit) carte f d'identité bancaire → **traveller**

chequebook ['tʃekbʊk] **1** N carnet m de chèques, chéquier m **2** COMP ▶ **chequebook journalism** N (pej) pratique qui consiste à payer des sommes considérables pour obtenir les confidences exclusives de personnes impliquées dans une affaire

chequered, checkered (US) ['tʃekəd] **1** ADJ **a** (= varied) [history, career, past] en dents de scie **b** (= checked) [tablecloth, dress, shirt, pattern] à carreaux; **~ floor** or **tiles** carrelage m **2** COMP ▶ **chequered flag** N (Motor Racing) drapeau m à damier

chequers ['tʃekəz] N jeu m de dames

cherish ['tʃerɪʃ] VT [+ person] chérir, aimer; [+ feelings, opinion] entretenir; [+ hope, illusions] nourrir, caresser; [+ memory] chérir

cherished ['tʃerɪʃt] ADJ [dream, belief, ambition, memory] cher; **a ~ memory of mine** un souvenir qui m'est cher

Chernobyl [tʃɜː'nəʊbl] N Tchernobyl

Cherokee ['tʃerəkiː] N (= person) Cherokee mf

cheroot [ʃə'ruːt] N petit cigare m (à bouts coupés), cigarillo m

cherry ['tʃerɪ] **1** N **a** (= fruit) cerise f; (also ~ **tree**) cerisier m; **wild ~** (= fruit) merise f; (= tree) merisier m → **bite** (‡ = virginity) **to take sb's ~** dépuceler qn; **to lose one's ~** se faire dépuceler* **b** (= colour) (rouge) cerise inv; (liter) [lips] vermeil; (Culin) [pie, tart] aux cerises ▶ **cherry blossom** N (NonC) fleurs fpl de cerisier ▶ **cherry bomb** N (US) pétard m (rond et rouge) ▶ **cherry brandy** N cherry m, liqueur f de cerise ▶ **cherry orchard** N cerisaie f ▶ **cherry picker** N (= vehicle) grue f à nacelle ▶ **cherry-red** ADJ (rouge) cerise inv ▶ **cherry tomato** N tomate f cerise

cherub ['tʃerəb] N **a** (pl **cherubs**) chérubin m, petit ange m **b** (pl **cherubim** ['tʃerəbɪm]) (Rel) chérubin m

cherubic [tʃe'ruːbɪk] ADJ [child, face, smile] angélique

chervil ['tʃɜːvɪl] N cerfeuil m

Ches. ABBR = **Cheshire**

Cheshire cat [‚tʃeʃə'kæt] N **to grin like a ~** avoir un sourire jusqu'aux oreilles

chess [tʃes] **1** N échecs mpl **2** COMP ▶ **chess piece** N = **chessman** ▶ **chess set** N jeu m d'échecs

chessboard ['tʃesbɔːd] N échiquier m

chessman ['tʃesmæn] N (pl **-men**) pièce f (de jeu d'échecs)

chessplayer ['tʃes‚pleɪə'] N joueur m, -euse f d'échecs

chest¹ [tʃest] **1** N (= box) coffre m, caisse f; (= tea chest) caisse f → **medicine**, **toolchest** **2** COMP ▶ **chest freezer** N congélateur-bahut m ▶ **chest of drawers** N commode f

chest² [tʃest] **1** N (Anat) poitrine f, cage f thoracique (Med frm); **to have a weak ~** être faible des bronches; **to get something off one's ~***

dire ce que l'on a sur le cœur [2] COMP ► **chest cold** N inflammation f des voies respiratoires ► **chest expander** N extenseur m (pour développer les pectoraux) ► **chest infection** N infection f des voies respiratoires ► **chest pain** N (NonC) = **chest pains** ► **chest pains** NPL douleurs fpl de poitrine ► **chest specialist** N spécialiste mf des voies respiratoires

chesterfield ['tʃestəfiːld] N canapé m, chesterfield m

chestnut ['tʃesnʌt] [1] N [a] (= fruit) châtaigne f; (Culin) châtaigne f, marron m; (fig) **to pull sb's ~s out of the fire** tirer les marrons du feu pour qn → **horse, Spanish, sweet** [b] (also ~ **tree**) châtaignier m, marronnier m [c] (= horse) alezan m [d] (pej) (**old**) **~*** (= story) vieille histoire f rabâchée; (= joke) vieille blague* f usée [2] ADJ (also **~-brown**) châtain ; ~ **hair** cheveux mpl châtains [3] COMP ► **chestnut horse** N (cheval m) alezan m

chesty ['tʃestɪ] ADJ [illness] [person] fragile de la poitrine ; [cough] de poitrine

Chetnik ['tʃetnɪk] N (Pol, Hist) tchetnik m

cheval glass [ʃə'vælglɑːs] N psyché f (glace)

chevron ['ʃevrən] N chevron m

chew [tʃuː] [1] VT [+ food] mâcher, mastiquer ; [+ betel, coca etc] chiquer ; [+ pencil] mâchonner, mordiller ; [+ lip] mordiller ; **to ~ tobacco** chiquer ; (lit, fig) **to ~ the cud** ruminer ; **to ~ the fat*** or **the rag*** tailler le bout de gras*, tailler une bavette* [2] N [a] (= action) mastication f [b] (Brit = sweet) bonbon m ; [of tobacco] chique f [3] COMP ► **chewing gum** N chewing-gum m
► **chew on** VT FUS (fig) [+ facts, problem] tourner et retourner
► **chew out** VT SEP engueuler
► **chew over** VT SEP [+ problem etc] (= think over) tourner et retourner ; (= discuss) discuter de
► **chew up** VT SEP mâchonner, mâchouiller*

chewy ['tʃuːɪ] [1] ADJ (pej) difficile à mâcher [2] COMP ► **chewy toffee** N caramel m mou

Cheyenne [ʃaɪ'æn] N (= person) Cheyenne mf

chi [kaɪ] N (= letter) chi m

chiaroscuro [kɪˌɑːrəs'kʊərəʊ] N clair-obscur m

chiasma [kaɪ'æzmə] N (pl **chiasmas** or **chiasmata** [kaɪ'æzmətə]) chiasma m, chiasme m

chic [ʃiːk] [1] ADJ chic inv, élégant [2] N chic m, élégance f

chicanery [ʃɪ'keɪnərɪ] N (= legal trickery) chicane f ; (= false argument) chicane f, chicanerie f

Chicano [tʃɪ'kɑːnəʊ] N (US) Mexicain(e) m(f) américain(e), Chicano mf

chichi* ['ʃiː.ʃiː] ADJ trop recherché

chick [tʃɪk] [1] N [a] (= chicken) poussin m ; (= nestling) oisillon m → **day** [b] (= child) poulet* m, coco* m ; **come here ~!** viens ici mon coco or mon petit poulet ! [c] (* = girl) pépée* f, poulette* f

chickadee ['tʃɪkə,diː] N mésange f à tête noire

chicken ['tʃɪkɪn] [1] N poulet(te) m(f) ; (very young) poussin m ; (Culin) poulet m ; (pej) **she's no** (spring) **~*** elle n'est plus toute jeune or de la première jeunesse ; (pej) **you're a big ~ at times!** quelle poule mouillée tu fais parfois !* ; **to run around like a headless ~** or **a ~ with its head cut off** courir dans tous les sens, ne pas savoir où donner de la tête ; **which came first, the ~ or the egg?** qui vient en premier, l'œuf ou la poule ? ; **it's a ~ and egg situation*** c'est la vieille histoire de l'œuf et de la poule ; **don't count your ~s (before they're hatched)** il ne faut pas vendre la peau de l'ours (avant de l'avoir tué) [2] ADJ (* pej = cowardly) froussard* ; **to play ~** jouer au premier qui se dégonfle* [3] COMP ► **chicken farmer** N éleveur m de poules or de volailles, volailleur m ► **chicken farming** N élevage m avicole or de volailles or de poules ► **chicken-hearted**

ADJ peureux ► **chicken liver** N foie(s) m(pl) de volaille ► **chicken run** N poulailler m ► **chicken wire** N grillage m
► **chicken out:** VI se dégonfler* ; **he ~ed out of his exams** au moment de ses examens, il s'est dégonflé* ; **he ~ed out of asking her to dinner** il s'est dégonflé* au moment de l'inviter à dîner

chickenfeed ['tʃɪkɪnfiːd] N [a] (lit) nourriture f pour volaille [b] (esp US* = insignificant sum) somme f dérisoire, bagatelle f

chickenpox ['tʃɪkɪnpɒks] N varicelle f

chickenshit** ['tʃɪkɪnʃɪt] (US) [1] N [a] (= coward) dégonflé(e)* m(f) [b] (NonC) **to be ~** (= be worthless) être de la merde** [2] ADJ [a] (= cowardly) dégonflé* [b] (= worthless) de merde**

chickpea ['tʃɪkpiː] N pois m chiche

chickweed ['tʃɪkwiːd] N mouron m blanc or des oiseaux

chicory ['tʃɪkərɪ] N (for coffee) chicorée f ; (= endive) endive f ; (= frisée) chicorée f frisée

chide [tʃaɪd] (pret **chided** or **chid** [tʃɪd], ptp **chided** or **chidden** ['tʃɪdn]) VT gronder, réprimander

chief [tʃiːf] [1] N [a] (gen) chef m ; **in ~** (= principally) principalement, surtout → **commander, lord** [b] (* = boss) patron m ; **yes, ~!** oui, chef or patron ! ; (fig) **too many ~s and not enough Indians*** trop de chefs et pas assez d'exécutants [c] (Her) chef m [2] ADJ principal, en chef [3] COMP ► **chief assistant** N premier assistant m ► **chief constable** N (Brit Police) ≈ directeur m (de police) ► **chief education officer** N (Scol) ≈ recteur m d'académie ► **chief engineer** N (Naut) ingénieur m en chef ► **Chief Executive** N (Brit: in local government) directeur m ; (US Pol) chef m de l'Exécutif, président m des États-Unis ► **chief executive officer** N (Ind, Comm) directeur m général ► **chief inspector** N (gen) inspecteur m principal or en chef ; (Brit Police) commandant m (des gardiens de la paix) ► **chief inspector of schools** N (Brit Scol) ≈ inspecteur m général ► **chief master sergeant** N (US Aviat) major m → **chief of police** N ≈ préfet m de police ► **chief of staff** N (Mil) chef m d'état-major ; (US) (**White House**) **Chief of Staff** secrétaire mf général (de la Maison-Blanche) ► **chief of state** N chef m d'État ► **chief petty officer** N (Naut) ≈ maître m → **chief priest** N archiprêtre m ► **chief rabbi** N grand rabbin m ► **Chief Secretary (to the Treasury)** N (Brit Pol) ≈ ministre m délégué au budget ► **chief state school officer** N (US Scol) ≈ recteur m d'académie ► **chief superintendent** N (Brit Police) ≈ commissaire m divisionnaire ► **chief technician** N (gen) technicien m en chef ; (Mil) sergent m (de l'armée de l'air) ► **chief town** N chef-lieu m ► **chief warrant officer** N (Mil) adjudant m chef ► **chief whip** N (Brit Parl) chef des parlementaires responsable de la discipline de vote → **lord**

┌─── **CHIEF WHIP** ───┐

Le parti gouvernemental et celui de l'opposition britanniques ont chacun leur **Chief Whip**, qui est le responsable de la discipline du parti à la Chambre des communes. Il tient les députés informés des activités parlementaires et fait remonter l'opinion des députés jusqu'à la direction du parti. Il veille également à ce que les députés participent aux scrutins importants ; son rôle est donc particulièrement décisif lorsque le gouvernement ne dispose que d'une faible majorité aux Communes.

chiefly ['tʃiːflɪ] ADV principalement, surtout

chieftain ['tʃiːftən] N chef m (de clan, de tribu)

chiffchaff ['tʃɪf,tʃæf] N pouillot m véloce

chiffon ['ʃɪfɒn] [1] N mousseline f de soie [2] ADJ [dress] en mousseline (de soie)

chignon ['ʃiːnjɔ̃:ŋ] N chignon m

chihuahua [tʃɪ'wɑːwɑː] N chihuahua m

chilblain ['tʃɪlbleɪn] N engelure f

child [tʃaɪld] (pl **children**) [1] N [a] enfant mf ; **when still a ~, he ...** tout enfant, il ... ; **don't be such a ~** ne fais pas l'enfant ; **she has three children** elle a trois enfants ; **to be with ~†** être enceinte
[b] (fig) produit m, fruit m ; **the ~ of his imagination** le produit or le fruit de son imagination → **brain**
[2] COMP [labour] des enfants ; [psychology, psychiatry] de l'enfant, infantile ; [psychologist, psychiatrist] pour enfants ► **child abduction** N (Jur) enlèvement m d'enfant ► **child abuse** N (gen) maltraitance f d'enfant(s) ; (sexual) abus m sexuel sur enfant, sévices mpl sexuels infligés à enfant ► **child abuser** N (gen) auteur m de sévices sur enfant(s) ; (sexual) auteur m de sévices sexuels or d'abus sexuels sur enfant(s) ► **child battering** N mauvais traitements mpl à enfant, maltraitance f d'enfant(s) ► **child benefit** N (Brit) ≈ allocations fpl familiales ► **child care** N protection f infantile or de l'enfance, assistance f à l'enfance ► **child-care center** N (US) crèche f, garderie f ► **child-care worker** N travailleur m, -euse f social(e) (s'occupant d'enfants) ► **child guidance** N soutien m psychopédagogique ; **~ guidance centre** or **clinic** centre m psychopédagogique ► **child lock** N [of door] (serrure f de) sécurité f enfants ► **child molester†** N auteur m de sévices sexuels or d'abus sexuels sur enfant(s) ► **child prodigy** N enfant mf prodige ► **Child Protection Register** N (Brit) registre des enfants en danger selon les services locaux de la protection de l'enfance ► **child's play** N (fig) **it's ~'s play** c'est enfantin, c'est un jeu d'enfant (**to sb** pour qn) ► **child sex abuser** N (gen) auteur m de sévices sexuels or abus sexuels sur enfants ► **Child Support Agency** N (Brit) organisme chargé de faire respecter le paiement des pensions alimentaires chez les couples divorcés → DSS ► **child welfare** N protection f de l'enfance ; **Child Welfare Centre** centre m or service m de protection de l'enfance

childbearing ['tʃaɪld,bɛərɪŋ] N (NonC) maternité f ; constant **~s** grossesses fpl répétées ; **of ~ age** en âge d'avoir des enfants

childbed ['tʃaɪldbɛd] N **in ~** en couches

childbirth ['tʃaɪldbɜː:θ] N accouchement m ; **in ~** en couches

childhood ['tʃaɪldhʊd] N enfance f ; **in his ~ he ...** tout enfant il ... → **second**

childish ['tʃaɪldɪʃ] ADJ [a] [behaviour] puéril (puérile f) ; **~ reaction** réaction f puérile ; **don't be so ~** ne fais pas l'enfant ; **he was very ~ about it** il s'est montré très puéril à ce sujet [b] [ailment, disease] infantile ; **~ games** jeux mpl d'enfant

childishly ['tʃaɪldɪʃlɪ] ADV (pej) [say, behave, act] puérilement, d'une manière puérile ; **~ simple** simple comme bonjour, d'une simplicité enfantine

childishness ['tʃaɪldɪʃnɪs] N (slightly pej) puérilité f, enfantillage m

childless ['tʃaɪldlɪs] ADJ sans enfants

childlike ['tʃaɪldlaɪk] ADJ d'enfant, enfantin

childminder ['tʃaɪld,maɪndə²] N (Brit) assistante f maternelle, nourrice f

childminding ['tʃaɪld,maɪndɪŋ] N (Brit) garde f d'enfants (en bas âge)

childproof ['tʃaɪldpruːf] ADJ [door etc] sans danger pour les enfants ; **~ (door) lock** (serrure f de) sécurité f enfants ; **the house is ~*** (=

safe) la maison est sans danger pour les enfants; (= *cannot be damaged*) les enfants ne peuvent rien abîmer dans la maison

children ['tʃɪldrən] NPL *of* **child**; → **home**

Chile ['tʃɪlɪ] N le Chili

Chilean ['tʃɪlɪən] **1** ADJ chilien **2** N Chilien(ne) *m(f)*

chili ['tʃɪlɪ] **1** N (*pl* **chilies**) piment *m* (rouge); **~ con carne** chili con carne *m* **2** COMP ► **chili powder** N piment *m* (rouge) en poudre, poudre *f* de piment (rouge)

chill [tʃɪl] **1** N **a** (*lit*) fraîcheur *f*, froid *m*; **there's a ~ in the air** il fait assez frais *or* un peu froid; **to take the ~ off** [+ *wine*] chambrer; [+ *water, room*] réchauffer un peu **b** (*fig*) froid *m*, froideur *f*; **to cast a ~ over** jeter un froid sur; **there was a certain ~ in the way she looked at me** il y avait une certaine froideur dans sa façon de me regarder; **it sent a ~ down my spine** j'en ai eu un frisson dans le dos; **he felt a certain ~ as he remembered ...** il a eu un *or* le frisson en se rappelant ... **c** (*Med*) refroidissement *m*; **to catch a ~** prendre froid, attraper un refroidissement **2** ADJ (*liter*) frais (fraîche *f*), froid; (*fig*) froid, glacial **3** VT **a** (*lit*) [+ *person*] faire frissonner, donner froid à; [+ *wine, melon*] rafraîchir; [+ *champagne*] frapper; [+ *meat*] réfrigérer; [+ *dessert*] mettre au frais; [+ *plant*] geler; (*Tech*) tremper en coquille; **to be ~ed to the bone** *or* **marrow** être transi **b** (*fig*) [+ *enthusiasm*] refroidir; **to ~ sb's blood** glacer le sang de qn → **spine 4** VI [*wine*] rafraîchir **5** COMP ► **chill cabinet** N (*Brit*) vitrine *f* réfrigérante ► **chill-out** ADJ [*music*] relaxant; (*in rave club*) **~-out room** salle *f* de repos (*dans une boîte de nuit*)

► **chill out*** VI se relaxer, décompresser*; **~ out relax!***

chiller* ['tʃɪlər] N (= *film*) film *m* d'épouvante; (= *book*) roman *m* d'épouvante

chilli ['tʃɪlɪ] N = **chili**

chill(i)ness ['tʃɪl(ɪ)nɪs] N (= *cold*) froid *m*; (= *coolness*) fraîcheur *f*; (*fig*) froideur *f*

chilling ['tʃɪlɪŋ] ADJ **a** (= *frightening*) [*effect, reminder, story, sight, prospect, sound, look, thought*] effrayant, qui fait froid dans le dos → **bone, spine b** (= *freezing*) [*wind*] glacial

chillingly ['tʃɪlɪŋlɪ] ADV [*say, describe*] d'une façon qui fait froid dans le dos; **the voice was ~ familiar** la voix était familière et cela faisait froid dans le dos

chilly ['tʃɪlɪ] ADJ **a*** (*Met*) [*weather, wind, air, water, room*] froid; [*day, afternoon*] frais (fraîche *f*); **to be** *or* **feel ~** [*person*] avoir froid; **it's ~ today** il fait frais aujourd'hui **b** (= *unfriendly*) [*person, manner, look, smile, response, reception*] froid; [*relationship*] distant

chime [tʃaɪm] **1** N carillon *m*; **to ring the ~s** carillonner; **~ of bells** un carillon; **door ~s** carillon *m* de porte **2** VI [*bells, voices*] carillonner; [*clock*] sonner **3** VT [+ *bells, hours*] sonner

► **chime in** VI (*fig*) [*person*] (*in agreement, approval*) faire chorus; **he ~d in with another complaint** il a fait chorus pour se plaindre à son tour

chimera [kaɪˈmɪərə] N (*liter*) chimère *f*

chimerical [kaɪˈmerɪkəl] ADJ chimérique

chimney ['tʃɪmnɪ] **1** N (*Archit, Geog, Naut, Sport*) cheminée *f*; [*of lamp*] verre *m* **2** COMP ► **chimney breast** N (*Brit*) manteau *m* de (la) cheminée ► **chimney-climbing** N (*Climbing*) ramonage *m* ► **chimney corner** N coin *m* du feu ► **chimney pot** N tuyau *m* de cheminée ► **chimney-pot hat*** N (chapeau *m*) tuyau *m* de poêle* ► **chimney stack** N (*Brit* = *group of chimneys*) souche *f* de cheminée; [*of factory*]

tuyau *m* de cheminée ► **chimney sweep** N ramoneur *m*

chimneypiece ['tʃɪmnɪpiːs] N (*Brit*) (dessus *m* or tablette *f* de) cheminée *f*

chimp* [tʃɪmp] N = **chimpanzee**

chimpanzee [,tʃɪmpænˈziː] N chimpanzé *m*

chin [tʃɪn] N menton *m*; **to keep one's ~ up*** tenir bon, tenir le coup*; (**keep your**) **~ up!*** courage!, du cran!*; (*fig*) **to take it on the ~*** encaisser*; **double 2** VI (*US**) bavarder **3** COMP ► **chin-chin!**† ! EXCL tchintchin!* ► **chin job*** N lifting *m* du menton; **to have a ~ job** se faire rectifier le menton ► **chin-up** N (*Sport*) **to do ~-ups** faire des tractions à la barre fixe

China ['tʃaɪnə] **1** N la Chine **2** COMP ► **China Sea** N mer *f* de Chine ► **China tea** N thé *m* de Chine

china ['tʃaɪnə] **1** N **a** (*NonC* = *material, dishes*) porcelaine *f*; **a piece of ~** une porcelaine → **bone b** (‡ = *friend*) poteau* *m* **2** COMP [*cup, plate, figure etc*] de *or* en porcelaine ► **china cabinet** N dressoir *m* ► **china clay** N kaolin *m* ► **china industry** N industrie *f* de la porcelaine

Chinaman† ['tʃaɪnəmən] N (*pl* **-men**) Chinois *m*

Chinatown ['tʃaɪnətaʊn] N quartier *m* chinois

chinaware ['tʃaɪnəweər] N (*NonC*) (objets *mpl* de) porcelaine *f*

chinchilla [tʃɪnˈtʃɪlə] **1** N chinchilla *m* **2** COMP ► **chinchilla coat** N manteau *m* de chinchilla

Chinese [tʃaɪˈniːz] **1** ADJ (*gen*) chinois; [*ambassador, embassy*] de Chine; [*teacher*] de chinois **2** N **a** (*pl inv*) Chinois(e) *m(f)* **b** (*Ling*) chinois *m* **c** (*: also* = **meal**) (repas *m*) chinois *m*; (*: also* = **restaurant**) (restaurant *m*) chinois *m* **3** the Chinese NPL les Chinois *mpl* **4** COMP ► **Chinese cabbage** N = **Chinese leaves** ► **Chinese gooseberry**† N kiwi *m* ► **Chinese lantern** N lanterne *f* vénitienne ► **Chinese leaves** NPL chou *m* chinois ► **Chinese puzzle** N casse-tête *m inv* chinois ► **Chinese whispers** NPL (*Brit*) (= *game*) jeu *m* du téléphone; (*fig* = *garbled messages*) téléphone *m* arabe ► **Chinese white** N, ADJ blanc *m* de zinc

Chink‡ [tʃɪŋk] N (*pej*) Chin(e)toque‡ *mf* (*pej*)

chink[1] [tʃɪŋk] N (= *slit, hole*) [*of wall*] fente *f*, fissure *f*; [*of door*] entrebâillement *m*; (*fig*) **the ~ in the armour** le défaut de la cuirasse

chink[2] [tʃɪŋk] **1** N (= *sound*) tintement *m* (*de verres, de pièces de monnaie*) **2** VT faire tinter **3** VI tinter

chinless ['tʃɪnlɪs] **1** ADJ (*lit*) qui a le menton fuyant; (*fig* = *feeble*) mou (molle *f*) **2** COMP ► **chinless wonder*** N (*Brit*) (aristo *m*) chiffe *f* molle*

chinning bar ['tʃɪnɪŋˌbɑːr] N (*Sport*) barre *f* fixe

chinos ['tʃiːnəʊz] NPL chinos *mpl*

chinstrap ['tʃɪnstræp] N [*of helmet etc*] jugulaire *f*

chintz [tʃɪnts] **1** N (*Tex*) chintz *m* **2** COMP ► **chintz curtains** NPL rideaux *mpl* de chintz

chintzy ['tʃɪntsɪ] ADJ **a** [*style*] rustique **b** (*US‡* = *mean*) moche*, mesquin

chinwag‡ ['tʃɪnwæg] N causerie *f*; **to have a ~ (with sb)** tailler une bavette* *or* papoter (avec qn)

chip [tʃɪp] **1** N **a** (*gen*) fragment *m*; [*of wood*] copeau *m*, éclat *m*; [*of glass, stone*] éclat *m*; (*Elec*) microplaquette *f*; **he's/she's a ~ off the old block*** c'est bien le fils/la fille de son père; **to have a ~ on one's shoulder** être aigri; **to have a ~ on one's shoulder because ...** n'avoir jamais digéré* le fait que ...; **Chips** charpentier *m* → **polystyrene b** (*Culin*) **~s** (*Brit*) (pommes *fpl* de terre) frites *fpl*; (*US*) chips *mpl*

c (*Comput*) puce *f*, pastille *f* **d** (= *break*) [*of stone, crockery, glass*] ébréchure *f*; [*of furniture*] écornure *f*; **this cup has a ~** cette tasse est ébréchée **e** (*Poker etc*) jeton *m*, fiche *f*; (*fig*) **to pass in** *or* **hand in** *or* **cash in one's ~s** passer l'arme à gauche*; **he's had his ~s!** il est cuit* *or* fichu*; **when the ~s are down*** dans les moments cruciaux; (*US*) **in the ~s** plein aux as* **f** (*Golf: also* **~ shot**) coup *m* coché **2** VT **a** (= *damage*) [+ *cup, plate*] ébrécher; [+ *furniture*] écorner; [+ *varnish, paint*] écailler; [+ *stone*] écorner, enlever un éclat de; **to ~ wood** faire des copeaux; **the chicken ~ped the shell open** le poussin a cassé sa coquille **b** (*Brit*) [+ *vegetables*] couper en lamelles **c** (= *cut deliberately*) tailler **d** (*Golf*) **to ~ the ball** cocher **3** VI [*cup, plate*] s'ébrécher; [*furniture*] s'écorner; [*varnish, paint*] s'écailler **4** COMP ► **chip basket** N (*Brit*) panier *m* à frites ► **chip pan** N (*Brit*) friteuse *f* ► **chip shop** N (*Brit*) friterie *f*

► **chip at** VT FUS **a** [+ *stone etc*] enlever des éclats de **b** (* = *make fun of*) se ficher de*

► **chip away** **1** VI [*paint etc*] s'écailler; (*fig*) **to ~ away at** [+ *sb's authority, lands*] grignoter, réduire petit à petit; [+ *law, decision*] réduire petit à petit la portée de **2** VT SEP [+ *paint etc*] enlever *or* décaper petit à petit (*au couteau etc*)

► **chip in** VI **a** (= *interrupt*) dire son mot, mettre son grain de sel* **b** (* = *contribute*) contribuer, souscrire (*à une collecte etc*); **he ~ped in with 10 francs** il y est allé de (ses) 10 F*

► **chip off** = **chip away**

chipboard ['tʃɪpbɔːd] N (*US*) carton *m*; (*Brit*) panneau *m* de particules, aggloméré *m*

chipmunk ['tʃɪpmʌŋk] N tamia *m*, suisse *m* (*Can*)

chipolata [tʃɪpəˈlɑːtə] N (*Brit*) chipolata *f*

chipped [tʃɪpt] ADJ [*cup, bone, tooth*] ébréché; [*enamel, step, windowsill*] abîmé; [*paint, nail varnish*] écaillé **2** COMP ► **chipped potatoes** N (pommes *fpl* de terre) frites *fpl*

Chippendale ['tʃɪpəndeɪl] ADJ [*chair*] chippendale *inv*

chipper* ['tʃɪpər] ADJ (= *happy*) joyeux, gai; N (= *smart*) chic *inv*

chippings ['tʃɪpɪŋz] NPL gravillons *mpl*; **"loose ~"** « attention gravillons »

chippy* ['tʃɪpɪ] **1** N **a** (*Brit*) friterie *f* **b** (*Brit* = *carpenter*) charpentier *m* **2** ADJ aigri

chiromancer ['kaɪərəmænsər] N chiromancien(ne) *m(f)*

chiromancy ['kaɪərəmænsɪ] N chiromancie *f*

chiropodist [kɪˈrɒpədɪst] N (*Brit*) pédicure *mf*

chiropody [kɪˈrɒpədɪ] N (*Brit*) (= *science*) podologie *f*; (= *treatment*) soins *mpl* du pied, traitement *m* des maladies des pieds

chiropractic ['kaɪərəpræktɪk] N (*NonC*) chiropraxie *or* chiropractie *f*

chiropractor ['kaɪərəpræktər] N chiropracteur *m*

chirp [tʃɜːp] **1** VI [*birds*] pépier, gazouiller; [*crickets*] chanter, striduler (*liter*); (* *fig*) [*person*] pépier, couiner* (*pej*) **2** N [*of birds*] pépiement *m*, gazouillis *m*; [*of crickets*] chant *m*, stridulation *f*

chirpy* ['tʃɜːpɪ] ADJ [*person*] gai, de bonne humeur; [*voice, mood*] gai

chirrup ['tʃɪrəp] N = **chirp**

chisel ['tʃɪzl] **1** N [*of carpenter, sculptor, silversmith*] ciseau *m*; [*of stonemason*] burin *m*; (= *blunt chisel*) matoir *m*; (= *hollow chisel*) gouge *f*; (= *mortise chisel*) bédane *m*; (= *roughing-out chisel*) ébauchoir *m* → **cold 2** VT **a** (*Engraving*) buriner **b** (* = *swindle*) [+ *thing*] resquiller; [+ *person*] rouler*, posséder‡; **to ~ sb out of sth** carotter* qch à qn

chiselled ['tʃɪzld] ADJ [*features*] buriné; **finely ~ features** traits *mpl* finement ciselés

chiseller⁎, chiseler⁎ (US) ['tʃɪzlər] N (= crook) escroc m, filou m; (= scrounger) resquilleur m, -euse f

chit[1] [tʃɪt] N **she's a mere ~ of a girl** ce n'est qu'une gosse⁎ or une gamine⁎

chit[2] [tʃɪt] N (gen) bulletin m de livraison; (= receipt) reçu m; (= note) note f

chitchat ['tʃɪttʃæt] N bavardage m

chitterlings ['tʃɪtəlɪŋz] NPL tripes fpl (de porc)

chitty ['tʃɪtɪ] N = **chit**[2]

chiv⁎ [tʃɪv] N surin⁎ m, couteau m

chivalresque [ʃɪvəl'resk], **chivalric** [ʃɪ'vælrɪk] ADJ chevaleresque

chivalrous ['ʃɪvəlrəs] ADJ (= courteous) chevaleresque; (= gallant) galant

chivalrously ['ʃɪvəlrəslɪ] ADV de façon chevaleresque

chivalry ['ʃɪvəlrɪ] [1] N [a] chevalerie f; **the rules/the age of ~** les règles fpl/l'âge m de la chevalerie; (hum) **the age of ~ is not dead** on sait encore être galant aujourd'hui [b] (= quality) qualités fpl chevaleresques; (= gallantry) galanterie f [c] (collective: Hist = knights) chevalerie f

chives [tʃaɪvz] NPL ciboulette f, civette f

chiv(v)y⁎ ['tʃɪvɪ] VT (Brit) [a] (also ~ **along**) [+ person, animal] chasser, pourchasser [b] (= pester) ne pas laisser la paix à; **she chiv(v)ied him into writing the letter** elle l'a harcelé jusqu'à ce qu'il écrive la lettre

► **chiv(v)y about⁎** VT SEP (Brit) [person] harceler, tarabuster

► **chivvy up⁎** VT SEP [+ person] faire activer

chlamydia [klə'mɪdɪə] N (Med) chlamydia f

chloral ['klɔːrəl] N chloral m

chlorate ['klɔːreɪt] N chlorate m

chloric ['klɔːrɪk] [1] ADJ chlorique [2] COMP ► **chloric acid** N acide m chlorique

chloride ['klɔːraɪd] [1] N chlorure m [2] COMP ► **chloride of lime** N chlorure m de chaux

chlorinate ['klɒrɪneɪt] VT [+ water] chlorer; (Chem) chlorurer

chlorination [klɒrɪ'neɪʃən] N [of water] javellisation f

chlorine ['klɔːriːn] N chlore m

chlorofluorocarbon [ˌklɔːrəˌfluərəʊ'kɑːbən] N (Chem) chlorofluorocarbone m

chloroform ['klɒrəfɔːm] [1] N chloroforme m [2] VT chloroformer

chlorophyll ['klɒrəfɪl] N chlorophylle f

chloroplast ['klɔːrəʊ,plæst] N chloroplaste m

choc⁎ [tʃɒk] [1] N ABBR = **chocolate** [2] COMP ► **choc-ice** N esquimau® m

chock [tʃɒk] [1] N [of wheel] cale f; [of barrel] cale f, chantier m; (Naut) chantier m, cale f [2] VT [+ wheel] caler; (Naut) mettre sur le chantier or sur cales [3] COMP ► **chock-a-block⁎**, **chock-full⁎** ADJ [basket, pan, box] plein à ras bord (**with, of** de); [room] plein à craquer (**with, of** de), comble

chocolate ['tʃɒklɪt] [1] N chocolat m; (drinking) ~ chocolat m; **a ~** un chocolat, une crotte de chocolat → **dessert**, **milk**, **plain** [2] COMP (= made of chocolate) en chocolat; (= containing, flavoured with chocolate) (au) chocolat, chocolaté; (= colour: also ~ **brown**) chocolat inv ► **chocolate bar** N barre f de chocolat ► **chocolate biscuit** N biscuit m au chocolat ► **chocolate-box** ADJ trop joli or mignon ► **chocolate chip cookie** N biscuit m aux pépites de chocolat ► **chocolate drop** N pastille f au chocolat ► **chocolate eclair** N éclair m au chocolat

▼ **choice** [tʃɔɪs] [1] N [a] (= act or possibility of choosing) choix m; **to make a ~** faire un choix, choisir; **to make** or **take one's ~** faire son choix; **to have no ~** ne pas avoir le choix; **be careful in your ~** faites attention en choi-

sissant; **he didn't have a free ~** il n'a pas été libre de choisir; **to have a very wide ~** avoir l'embarras du choix; **he had no ~ but to obey** il ne pouvait qu'obéir; **from** or **for ~** de or par préférence; **he did it from ~** il l'a fait de son plein gré, il a choisi de le faire; **the house/girl of his (own)** ~ la maison/fille de son choix; **it's your ~!⁎** c'est ton problème!⁎ → Hobson's choice

[b] (= thing or person chosen) choix m; **this book would be my ~** c'est ce livre que je choisirais

[c] (Comm etc = variety to choose from) choix m, variété f; **a wide ~ of dresses** un grand choix de robes

[2] ADJ [a] (Comm) [goods, fruit] de choix; **choicest** de premier choix [b] [word, phrase] (= well-chosen) bien choisi

choir [kwaɪər] [1] N [a] (Mus) chœur m, chorale f; (Rel) chœur m, maîtrise f; **to sing in the ~** faire partie du chœur or de la chorale, chanter dans la maîtrise [b] (Archit, Rel) chœur m [2] VTI chanter en chœur [3] COMP ► **choir organ** N petit orgue m; (= keyboard) positif m ► **choir practice** N **to go to ~ practice** aller à la chorale ► **choir school** N maîtrise f, manécanterie f (rattachée à une cathédrale) ► **choir-stall** N stalle f (du chœur)

choirboy ['kwaɪəbɔɪ] N (Rel) enfant m de chœur

choirgirl ['kwaɪəgɜːl] N (Rel) enfant f de chœur

choirmaster ['kwaɪəˌmɑːstər] N (Mus) chef m de(s) chœur(s); (Rel) maître m de chapelle

choke [tʃəʊk] [1] VT [a] [+ person, voice, breathing] étrangler; **fumes ~d her** la fumée l'a fait suffoquer; **to ~ the life out of sb** étrangler qn; **in a voice ~d with sobs** d'une voix étranglée par les sanglots [b] (fig) [+ fire] étouffer; [+ pipe, tube] boucher, engorger; **flowers ~d by weeds** fleurs fpl étouffées par les mauvaises herbes; **street ~d with traffic** rue f engorgée or embouteillée

[2] VI étouffer, s'étrangler; **to ~ to death** mourir étouffé; **he ~d on some bread** il s'est étranglé en avalant un morceau de pain de travers; **she ~d on a fish bone** elle s'est étranglée avec une arête; **she ~d with anger** la rage l'étouffait, elle étouffait de rage; **he was choking with laughter** il s'étranglait de rire

[3] N (Aut) starter m; (Rad) bobine f de réactance, inductance f de protection

[4] COMP ► **choke chain** N collier m étrangleur

► **choke back** VT SEP [+ feelings] réprimer, contenir; [+ tears] refouler; [+ words] ravaler

► **choke down** VT SEP [+ rage] contenir; [+ sobs] ravaler, étouffer

► **choke off⁎** VT SEP (fig) [+ suggestions etc] étouffer (dans l'œuf); [+ discussion] empêcher; **raising taxes could ~ off the recovery** une augmentation des impôts pourrait empêcher la reprise

► **choke up** [1] VI s'engorger, se boucher [2] VT SEP [+ pipe, drain] engorger, boucher

choked [tʃəʊkt] ADJ [a] (= strangled) étranglé; **in a ~ voice** d'une voix étranglée; ~ **with emotion** d'une voix étranglée par l'émotion [b] (Brit⁎) (= moved) (très) ému; (= angry) (très) vexé or contrarié; **I still feel ~ about him leaving** je n'ai pas encore encaissé⁎ or digéré⁎ qu'il soit parti

choker ['tʃəʊkər] N [a] (= scarf) foulard m, écharpe f; (= collar) col m droit; (= necklace) collier m (de chien) [b]⁎ **what a ~!** c'est difficile à encaisser⁎ or digérer⁎!; **losing at Wembley was a ~!** on n'a pas encaissé⁎ or digéré⁎ d'avoir perdu à Wembley!

choking ['tʃəʊkɪŋ] N (Med) suffocation f

cholera ['kɒlərə] [1] N choléra m [2] COMP [epidemic] de choléra; [victim, symptoms] du choléra

choleric ['kɒlərɪk] ADJ colérique, coléreux

cholesterol [kə'lestərɒl] N cholestérol m

chomp⁎ [tʃɒmp] VTI mâcher bruyamment; **to ~ (away) on** or **at sth** dévorer qch à belles dents

Chomskyan ['tʃɒmskɪən] ADJ chomskien, de Chomsky

choo-choo ['tʃuː,tʃuː] N (baby talk) train m, tchou-tchou m (baby talk)

choose [tʃuːz] (pret chose, ptp chosen) [1] VT [a] (= select; = elect) élire; **which will you ~?** lequel choisirez-vous?; **they chose a president** ils ont élu un président; **he was chosen (as) leader** c'est lui qui fut pris pour chef; **the Chosen (People)** le peuple élu; **the chosen (few)** les (quelques) élus mpl; **there is little** or **not much to ~ between them** il n'y a guère de différence entre eux; **there is nothing to ~ between them** ils se valent; (pej) ils ne valent pas mieux l'un que l'autre; **in a few (well-)chosen words** en quelques mots choisis

[b] (= opt) décider, juger bon (**to do** de faire), vouloir (**to do** faire); **he chose not to speak** il a jugé bon de se taire; **I didn't ~ to do so** (= decided not to) j'ai décidé de ne pas le faire; (= did it unwillingly) je ne l'ai pas fait de mon propre gré

[2] VI choisir; **as you ~** comme vous voulez or l'entendez, à votre gré; **if you ~** si cela vous dit, il le fera quand il voudra or quand ça lui plaira; **to ~ between/among** faire un choix entre/parmi; **there's not much to ~ from** il n'y a pas tellement de choix

choos(e)y⁎ ['tʃuːzɪ] ADJ [person] difficile (à satisfaire); **I'm not ~** je ne suis pas difficile; **you can't be ~ in your position** votre situation ne vous permet pas de faire la fine bouche; **I'm ~ about the people I go out with** je ne sors pas avec n'importe qui

chop[1] [tʃɒp] [1] N [a] (Culin) côtelette f; **mutton/pork ~** côtelette f de mouton/de porc → **loin** [b] (= blow) coup m (de hache etc); (Brit) **you're (the) next for the ~⁎** tu es le prochain à y passer⁎; (Brit) **to get the ~⁎** [employee] se faire sacquer⁎ or virer⁎; [project] être annulé [c] (Tennis) volée f coupée or arrêtée [2] VT [a] couper; **to ~ wood** couper du bois; **to ~ one's way through sth** se frayer un chemin (à coups de hache) à travers qch; (fig) **to ~ a project⁎** (= cancel) annuler un projet; (= reduce costs, bills) faire des coupes sombres dans, sabrer dans [b] (Culin) [+ meat, vegetables] hacher [c] (Sport) [+ ball] couper [3] COMP ► **chop-chop⁎** EXCL au trot!⁎, et que ça saute!⁎ ♦ ADV fissa⁎ ► **chopping block** N billot m ► **chopping board** N planche f à hacher ► **chopping knife** N (pl chopping knives) hachoir m (couteau)

► **chop at** VT FUS [+ person etc] essayer de frapper; (with axe) [+ wood] taillader

► **chop down** VT SEP [+ tree] abattre

► **chop off** VT SEP trancher, couper; **they ~ped off his head** on lui a tranché la tête

► **chop up** VT SEP hacher, couper en morceaux

chop[2] [tʃɒp] [1] N (Culin) [of pork] joue f [2] **chops** NPL (= jaws) [of animal] mâchoires fpl; (= cheeks) joues fpl; [of animals] bajoues fpl; (Tech) [of vice] mâchoires fpl → **lick**

chop[3] [tʃɒp] [1] VI [a] (Naut) [wind] varier; [waves] clapoter [b] (Brit fig) **to ~ and change** changer constamment d'avis; **he's always ~ping and changing** c'est une vraie girouette, il ne sait pas ce qu'il veut [2] VT (pej) **to ~ logic** ergoter, discutailler

chop[4]⁎ [tʃɒp] N (= food) bouffe⁎ f

chophouse ['tʃɒphaʊs] N (petit) restaurant m, gargote f (US)

chopper ['tʃɒpər] [1] N [a] (for cutting) couperet m, hachoir m; (Agr) coupe-racines m inv [b] (⁎ = helicopter) hélico⁎ m, hélicoptère m; (US⁎ = motorcycle) chopper m; (Brit = cycle) vélo *m* à haut guidon [2] VI (*US* = *go by helicopter*) se rendre en hélicoptère (**to** à)

choppers‡ ['tʃɒpəz] NPL (= *teeth*) ratiches‡ *fpl*; (= *false teeth*) râtelier* *m*

choppy ['tʃɒpɪ] ADJ [*lake*] clapoteux; [*sea*] agité; [*wind*] variable

chopsticks ['tʃɒpstɪks] NPL baguettes *fpl* (*pour manger*)

chop suey [tʃɒp'su:ɪ] N chop suey *m*

choral ['kɔ:rəl] [1] ADJ choral, chanté en chœur [2] COMP ► **choral society** N chorale *f*

chorale [kɒ'rɑ:l] N choral *m*

chord [kɔ:d] N (*Anat, Geom: also of harp etc*) corde *f*; (*Mus*) accord *m*; (*fig*) **to strike** *or* **touch a ~** ◊ **to touch the right ~** toucher la corde sensible → **vocal** [2] COMP ► **chord change** N changement *m* d'accord ► **chord progression** N suite *f* d'accords

chore [tʃɔ:ʳ] N (*everyday*) travail *m* de routine; (*unpleasant*) corvée *f*; **the ~s** les tâches *fpl* ménagères; **to do the ~s** faire le ménage

choreograph ['kɒrɪə‚grɑ:f] VT [a] chorégraphier [b] (*fig* = *stage*) monter, mettre en scène (*fig*)

choreographer [‚kɒrɪ'ɒgrəfəʳ] N chorégraphe *mf*

choreographic [‚kɒrɪəʊ'græfɪk] ADJ chorégraphique

choreography [‚kɒrɪ'ɒgrəfɪ] N chorégraphie *f*

chorister ['kɒrɪstəʳ] N (*Rel*) choriste *mf*

chortle ['tʃɔ:tl] [1] VI rire (**about, at, over** de), glousser; **he was chortling over the newspaper** la lecture du journal le faisait glousser [2] N gloussement *m*

chorus ['kɔ:rəs] [1] N (*pl* **choruses**) [a] (*Mus, Theat* = *song, singers, speakers*) chœur *m*; **in ~** en chœur; **she's in the ~** (*at concert*) elle chante dans le chœur; (*Theat*) elle fait partie de la troupe; (*fig*) **a ~ of praise/objections** un concert de louanges/protestations [b] (= *part of song*) refrain *m*; **to join in the ~** [*one person*] reprendre le refrain; [*several people*] reprendre le refrain en chœur [2] VT [+ *song*] chanter *or* réciter en chœur; [+ *verse*] réciter en chœur; **"yes", they ~ed** «oui», répondirent-ils en chœur [3] COMP ► **chorus girl** N (*Theat*) girl *f* ► **chorus line** N (*Theat: in musical*) chœurs *mpl*

chose [tʃəʊz] VB *pt of* **choose**

chosen ['tʃəʊzn] VB *ptp of* **choose**; → **choose 1a**

chough [tʃʌf] N crave *m* à bec rouge

choux [ʃu:] N (*Culin: also* ~ **pastry**) pâte *f* à choux

chow¹ [tʃaʊ] N (= *dog*) chow-chow *m*

chow² [tʃaʊ] N (*esp US* = *food*) bouffe‡ *f*, boustifaille‡ *f*

chowder ['tʃaʊdəʳ] N soupe *f* épaisse de palourdes → **clam**

chow mein [tʃaʊ'meɪn] N chow mein *m*, nouilles *fpl* sautées

Christ [kraɪst] [1] N le Christ, Jésus-Christ [2] EXCL ~!‡ nom de Dieu!‡, Bon Dieu (de Bon Dieu)!‡; ~ (**only) knows!** Dieu seul le sait!* [3] COMP ► **the Christ Child** N l'enfant *m* Jésus

Christadelphian [‚krɪstə'delfɪən] ADJ, N christadelphe *mf*

christen ['krɪsn] VT (*Rel, also Naut*) baptiser; (*gen*) (= *name*) appeler, nommer; (= *nickname*) surnommer; (= *use for first time*) étrenner; **to ~ sb after** ... donner à qn le nom de ...; **he was ~ed Robert but everyone calls him Bob** son nom de baptême est Robert mais tout le monde l'appelle Bob

Christendom ['krɪsndəm] N chrétienté *f*

christening ['krɪsnɪŋ] [1] N baptême *m* [2] COMP ► **christening robe** N robe *f* de baptême

Christian ['krɪstɪən] [1] ADJ (*lit*) chrétien; (*fig*) charitable, compatissant; **the ~ era** l'ère *f* chrétienne; **early ~** paléochrétien [2] N chrétien(ne) *m(f)*; **to become a ~** se faire chrétien [3] COMP ► **Christian Democrat** N chrétien-démocrate *m* ► **Christian Democratic** ADJ chrétien-démocrate ► **Christian name** N prénom *m*, nom *m* de baptême; **my ~ name is Julie** je m'appelle Julie, mon prénom est Julie ► **Christian Science** N science *f* chrétienne ► **Christian Scientist** N scientiste *mf* chrétien(ne)

christiania [‚krɪstɪ'ɑ:nɪə] N (*Ski*) christiania *m*

Christianity [‚krɪstɪ'ænɪtɪ] N (= *faith, religion*) christianisme *m*; (= *character*) caractère *m or* qualité *f* du chrétien; **his ~ did not prevent him from ...** le fait d'être chrétien ne l'a pas empêché de ...

Christianize ['krɪstɪənaɪz] VT christianiser

christie ['krɪstɪ] N (*Ski*) christiania *m*

Christlike ['kraɪstlaɪk] ADJ qui ressemble *or* semblable au Christ; **he had a ~ forbearance** il avait une patience d'ange

▼ **Christmas** ['krɪsməs] [1] N Noël *m*; **at ~** à Noël; **the week before ~** la semaine précédant Noël; **for ~** pour Noël; **they spent ~ with us** elle a passé (la) Noël chez nous; (*fig*) **it's as if ~ had come early!** c'est comme si c'était Noël!; **I thought all my ~es had come at once** pour moi c'était Noël avant l'heure!, c'est comme si tous mes vœux étaient exaucés! → **father, happy, merry** [2] COMP [*visit, gift*] de Noël ► **Christmas box** N (*Brit*) étrennes *fpl* (*offertes à Noël*) ► **Christmas cake** N gâteau *m* de Noël (*gros cake décoré au sucre glace*) ► **Christmas card** N carte *f* de Noël ► **Christmas carol** N chant *m* de Noël, noël *m*; (*Rel*) cantique *m* de Noël ► **Christmas Day** N le jour de Noël ► **Christmas Eve** N la veille de Noël ► **Christmas Island** N l'île *f* Christmas ► **Christmas party** N fête *f* de Noël ► **Christmas present** N cadeau *m* de Noël ► **Christmas pudding** N (*esp Brit*) (plum-)pudding *m* (*pudding traditionnel de Noël*) ► **Christmas rose** N rose *f* de Noël ► **Christmas stocking** N **I got it in my ~ stocking** ≈ je l'ai trouvé dans mon soulier *or* dans la cheminée *or* sous l'arbre (de Noël) ► **Christmas time** N la période de Noël *or* des fêtes; **at ~ time** à Noël ► **Christmas tree** N arbre *m* de Noël

Christmassy* ['krɪsməsɪ] ADJ [*atmosphere*] de Noël; **the town is looking very ~** la ville a un air de fête pour Noël

Christopher ['krɪstəfəʳ] N Christophe *m*

christy ['krɪstɪ] N (*Ski*) = **christie**

chromatic [krə'mætɪk] [1] ADJ (*Art, Mus*) chromatique [2] COMP ► **chromatic printing** N impression *f* polychrome ► **chromatic scale** N gamme *f* chromatique

chromatics [krə'mætɪks] N (*NonC*) science *f* des couleurs

chromatography [‚krəʊmə'tɒgrəfɪ] N chromatographie *f*

chrome [krəʊm] [1] N chrome *m* [2] COMP [*fittings etc*] chromé ► **chrome dioxide** N dioxyde *m* de chrome ► **chrome lacquer** N laque *f or* peinture *f* laquée (à base de chrome) ► **chrome steel** N acier *m* chromé ► **chrome yellow** N jaune *m* de chrome

chromium ['krəʊmɪəm] [1] N chrome *m* [2] COMP ► **chromium-plated** ADJ chromé ► **chromium-plating** N chromage *m*

chromosomal [‚krəʊmə'səʊml] ADJ chromosomique

chromosome ['krəʊməsəʊm] N chromosome *m*

chronic ['krɒnɪk] ADJ [a] (= *lasting, severe*) [*illness, depression, pain, problem, shortage, unemployment*] chronique [b] (= *inveterate*) [*smoker, liar, alcoholism, alcoholic*] invétéré,

incorrigible; [*worrier, idealist*] incorrigible [c] (*Brit** = *terrible*) [*film, singing, food*] nul; [*weather*] dégueulasse*, pourri*

chronically ['krɒnɪkəlɪ] ADV [a] (*Med*) **to be ~ sick/depressed** souffrir de maladie/dépression chronique; **the ~ ill** *or* **sick** les malades *mpl* chroniques [b] (= *extremely*) [*tired, overworked, overloaded, underfunded*] terriblement; **~ jealous** en proie à une jalousie chronique; **~ overcrowded** (extrêmement) surpeuplé

chronicle ['krɒnɪkl] [1] N chronique *f*; (*Bible*) **(the Book of) Chronicles** le livre des Chroniques; (*fig*) **a ~ of disasters** une succession de catastrophes [2] VT faire la chronique de, enregistrer au jour le jour

chronicler ['krɒnɪkləʳ] N chroniqueur *m*

chronological [‚krɒnə'lɒdʒɪkəl] ADJ chronologique; **~ age** âge *m* réel; **in ~ order** par ordre chronologique

chronologically [‚krɒnə'lɒdʒɪkəlɪ] ADV chronologiquement

chronology [krə'nɒlədʒɪ] N chronologie *f*

chronometer [krə'nɒmɪtəʳ] N chronomètre *m*

chrysalis ['krɪsəlɪs] N (*pl* **chrysalises** ['krɪsəlɪsɪz]) chrysalide *f*

chrysanthemum [krɪ'sænθəməm], **chrysanth*** [krɪ'sænθ] N chrysanthème *m*

chub [tʃʌb] N (*pl* **chub** *or* **chubs**) chevesne *m*, chevaine *m*

Chubb lock® ['tʃʌblɒk] N (*Brit*) serrure incrochetable

chubby ['tʃʌbɪ] ADJ [*person, arm*] potelé; **~-cheeked** ◊ **~-faced** joufflu

chuck¹ [tʃʌk] [1] VT [a] (* = *throw*) lancer, jeter; (*in bin*) balancer* [b] (‡ = *give up*) [+ *job, hobby*] lâcher, laisser tomber*; [+ *boyfriend, girlfriend*] plaquer‡, laisser tomber*; **~ it!** assez!*, ça va!*, laisse tomber!* [c] **he ~ed her under the chin** il lui a pris *or* caressé le menton [2] N [a] **to give sb a ~ under the chin** prendre *or* caresser le menton à qn [b] **to give sb the ~** balancer qn*; (*from job*) **he got the ~‡** il s'est fait virer*; (*from relationship*) **she gave him the ~‡** elle l'a plaqué*
► **chuck away*** VT SEP (= *throw out*) [+ *old clothes, books*] balancer*; (= *waste*) [+ *money*] jeter par les fenêtres; [+ *opportunity*] laisser passer
► **chuck in‡** VT SEP = **chuck up a**
► **chuck out*** VT SEP [+ *useless article, old clothes, books*] balancer*; [+ *person*] vider*, sortir*
► **chuck up‡** VT SEP [a] [+ *job, hobby*] lâcher, laisser tomber* [b] (= *vomit*) dégueuler‡, vomir

chuck² [tʃʌk] [1] N (*Tech*) mandrin *m* [2] VT (*Tech*) fixer sur un mandrin

chuck³ [tʃʌk] N (*also* ~ **steak**) morceau *m* dans le paleron

chucker-out ['tʃʌkər'aʊt] N (*Brit*) videur* *m*

chuckle ['tʃʌkl] [1] N gloussement *m*, petit rire *m*; **we had a good ~ over it** ça nous a bien fait rire [2] VI rire (**over, at** de), glousser

chuffed‡ [tʃʌft] ADJ (*Brit*) vachement‡ content (**about** de); **he was quite ~ about it** il était vachement‡ content

chug [tʃʌg] [1] N [*of machine*] souffle *m*; [*of car, railway engine*] teuf-teuf *m* [2] VI [*machine*] souffler; [*car*] haleter, faire teuf-teuf
► **chug along** VI [*car, train*] avancer en haletant *or* en faisant teuf-teuf

chug-a-lug‡ ['tʃʌgəlʌg] VT (*US*) boire d'un trait

chukka, chukker ['tʃʌkəʳ] N (*Polo*) période *f* (de 7,5 minutes)

chum†* [tʃʌm] [1] N copain* *m*, copine* *f* [2] VI (= *share lodgings*) crécher ensemble‡
► **chum up*** VI fraterniser (**with** avec)

chummy* ['tʃʌmɪ] ADJ sociable, (très) liant; **she is very ~ with him** elle est très copine avec lui*

► LANGUAGE IN USE: Christmas 23.2

chump [tʃʌmp] N [a]* ballot* m, crétin(e)* m(f) [b] (: = head) citron* m, caboche* f ; **he's off his ~** il est timbré* or toqué*, il a perdu la boule* [c] (Culin) **~ chop** côte f de mouton

chunder: ['tʃʌndər] VI (esp Austral) dégueuler:

chunk [tʃʌŋk] N [of wood, metal, dough] gros morceau m ; [of bread] quignon m

chunky ['tʃʌŋkɪ] ADJ [person] trapu ; [jumper, cardigan, shoes, jewellery] gros (grosse f) ; **~ pieces of meat** de gros morceaux de viande

Chunnel* ['tʃʌnəl] N (ABBR = **Channel Tunnel**) → channel

church [tʃɜːtʃ] [1] N [a] (= building) église f ; [of French Protestants] église f, temple m ; **he is inside the ~ now** il est maintenant dans l'église or dans le temple
[b] (NonC) **to go to ~** (= to church service) (gen) aller à l'église f ; [Catholic] aller à la messe ; **he doesn't go to ~ any more** il n'est plus pratiquant, il ne va plus à l'église or à la messe ; **to be in ~** être à l'église or à la messe ; **after ~** après l'office, (for Catholics) après la messe
[c] (= whole body of Christians) **the Church** l'Église f ; **the Church Militant** l'Église f militante
[d] (= denomination) **the Church of England** l'Église f anglicane ; **the Church of Rome** l'Église f catholique ; **the Church of Scotland/Ireland** l'Église f d'Écosse/d'Irlande → high
[e] (= religious orders) **Church** ordres mpl ; **he has gone into the Church** il est entré dans les ordres
[2] VT (Rel) faire assister à une messe
[3] COMP **► Church Fathers** NPL Pères mpl de l'Église **► church hall** N salle f paroissiale **► church owl** N chouette f des clochers, effraie f **► church school** N (Brit) école f confessionnelle **► church service** N office m **► church wedding** N **they want a ~ wedding** ils veulent se marier à l'église

churchgoer ['tʃɜːtʃgəʊər] N pratiquant(e) m(f)

Churchillian [tʃɜː'tʃɪlɪən] ADJ churchillien

churching ['tʃɜːtʃɪŋ] N (Rel) **the ~ of women** la messe de relevailles

churchman ['tʃɜːtʃmən] N (pl -men) (= clergy) ecclésiastique m ; (= churchgoer) **he is/is not a good ~** il est/n'est pas pratiquant

churchwarden [,tʃɜː'tʃwɔːdn] N [a] (= person) bedeau m, marguillier m [b] (= pipe) longue pipe en terre

churchy* ['tʃɜːtʃɪ] ADJ (pej) [person] bigot, calotin* (pej) ; **a ~ person** une grenouille de bénitier* (pej)

churchyard ['tʃɜːtʃjaːd] N cimetière m (autour d'une église)

churl [tʃɜːl] N [a]† (= ill-mannered person) rustre m, malotru m ; (= bad-tempered person) ronchon m, personne f revêche [b] (Hist) manant† m

churlish ['tʃɜːlɪʃ] ADJ [person, behaviour] (= rude) grossier ; (= surly) revêche ; **it would be ~ to complain** il serait malvenu de se plaindre

churlishly ['tʃɜːlɪʃlɪ] ADV [say, refuse] (= rudely) grossièrement ; (= surlily) d'un ton revêche

churlishness ['tʃɜːlɪʃnɪs] N (= bad manners) grossièreté f ; (= bad temper) mauvaise humeur f

churn [tʃɜːn] [1] N baratte f ; (Brit = milk can) bidon m [2] VT [a] (Culin) [+ butter] baratter [b] (also **~ up**) [+ water] faire bouillonner ; (fig) **to ~ sb up** retourner* qn [c] (Aut) [+ engine] faire tourner [3] VI [water, sea] bouillonner ; **his stomach was ~ing** (feeling sick) il avait l'estomac barbouillé ; (from nerves) son cœur se serra
► churn out VT SEP [+ objects] débiter ; [+ essays, letters, books] produire à la chaîne, pondre en série*
► churn up VT SEP = churn 2b

chute [ʃuːt] N [a] glissière f **► coal, refuse²** [b] (in river) rapide m [c]* **► parachute**

---

[d] (Sport, for toboggans) piste f ; (Brit = children's slide) toboggan m

chutney ['tʃʌtnɪ] N condiment m (à base de fruits) ; **apple/tomato ~** condiment m à la pomme/à la tomate

chutzpa(h): ['xʊtspə] N (US) culot* m

chyme [kaɪm] N chyme m

CI (ABBR = **Channel Islands**) → channel

CIA [,siːaɪ'eɪ] (US) (ABBR = **Central Intelligence Agency**) CIA f

ciao [tʃaʊ] INTERJ tchao !, salut !*

cicada [sɪ'kaːdə] N (pl **cicadas** or **cicadae** [sɪ'kaːdiː]) cigale f

cicatrix ['sɪkətrɪks] N (pl **cicatrices** [,sɪkə'traɪsɪːz]) (Med) cicatrice f

cicatrize ['sɪkə,traɪz] VI (Med) (se) cicatriser

Cicero ['sɪsərəʊ] N Cicéron m

cicerone [,tʃɪtʃə'rəʊnɪ] N (pl **cicerones** or **ciceroni** [,tʃɪtʃə'rəʊnɪ]) cicérone m

Ciceronian [,sɪsə'rəʊnɪən] ADJ cicéronien

CID [,siːaɪ'diː] [1] (Brit) (ABBR = **Criminal Investigation Department**) ≈ PJ f, ≈ police f judiciaire [2] COMP (operation, team etc) ► **CID man** (pl CID men), **CID officer** N ≈ inspecteur m de police judiciaire or de la PJ

cider ['saɪdər] [1] N cidre m [2] COMP **► cider-apple** N pomme f à cidre **► cider-press** N pressoir m à cidre **► cider vinegar** N vinaigre m de cidre

CIF, **c.i.f.** [,siːaɪ'ef] (ABBR = **cost, insurance, freight**) CAF

cig* [sɪg] N (esp Brit) = **ciggy**

cigar [sɪ'gaːr] [1] N cigare m [2] COMP (box etc) à cigares **► cigar case** N à cigares, porte-cigares m inv **► cigar holder** N fume-cigare m inv **► cigar lighter** N (in car) allume-cigare m inv **► cigar-shaped** ADJ en forme de cigare

cigarette [,sɪgə'ret] [1] N cigarette f [2] COMP (box etc) à cigarettes **► cigarette ash** N cendre f de cigarette **► cigarette butt** = **cigarette end ► cigarette card** N carte avec des publicités ou des jeux, dans les paquets de cigarettes **► cigarette case** N étui m à cigarettes, porte-cigarettes m inv **► cigarette end** N mégot m **► cigarette holder** N fume-cigarette m inv **► cigarette lighter** N (gen) briquet m ; (in car) allume-cigare m inv **► cigarette machine** N distributeur m de paquets de cigarettes **► cigarette paper** N papier m à cigarettes

ciggy* ['sɪgɪ] N (Brit) clope f, tige* f

ciliary ['sɪlɪərɪ] ADJ ciliaire

CIM [,siːaɪ'em] N (Comput) (ABBR = **computer-integrated manufacturing**) FIO f

C.-in-C. (ABBR = **Commander-in-Chief**) → **commander**

cinch [sɪntʃ] [1] N [a] (US = saddle girth) sous-ventrière f, sangle f (de selle) [b] **it's a ~:** (= certain) c'est du tout cuit*, c'est du gâteau* ; (= easy) c'est l'enfance de l'art [2] VT [a] [+ horse] sangler ; [+ saddle] attacher par une sangle (de selle) [b] (fig) [+ success] rendre sûr, assurer

cinder ['sɪndər] [1] N cendre f ; **~s** (= burnt coal) cendres fpl (de charbon) ; [of furnace, volcano] scories fpl ; **to rake out the ~s** racler les cendres (du foyer) ; **burnt to a ~** réduit en cendres [2] COMP **► cinder block** N (US) parpaing m **► cinder track** N (piste f) cendrée f

Cinderella [,sɪndə'relə] N Cendrillon f

cineaste ['sɪnɪæst] N cinéphile mf

cine-camera ['sɪnɪ,kæmərə] N (Brit) caméra f

cine-film ['sɪnɪ,fɪlm] N (Brit) film m

cinema ['sɪnəmə] (esp Brit) [1] N cinéma m ; **to go to the ~** aller au cinéma [2] COMP **► cinema complex** N complexe m or cinéma m multisalle(s) **► cinema-going** N fré-

---

quentation f des cinémas **◆** ADJ **the ~-going public** le public qui fréquente les cinémas

Cinemascope® ['sɪnəməskəʊp] N cinémascope® m

cinematic [,sɪnɪ'mætɪk] ADJ filmique

cinematograph [,sɪnɪ'mætəgraːf] N (Brit) cinématographe m

cinematographer [,sɪnɪmə'tɒgrəfər] N directeur m de la photo

cinematography [,sɪnɪmə'tɒgrəfɪ] N cinématographie f

cine projector ['sɪnɪprə,dʒektər] N (Brit) projecteur m de cinéma

Cinerama® [,sɪnə'raːmə] N Cinérama® m

cinerary ['sɪnərərɪ] ADJ cinéraire

cinnabar ['sɪnəbaːr] N cinabre m

cinnamon ['sɪnəmən] [1] N cannelle f [2] COMP (cake, biscuit) à la cannelle ; (in colour) cannelle inv

Cinque [sɪŋk] ADJ (Brit Hist) **the ~ Ports** les Cinq Ports mpl (ancienne confédération des cinq ports du Kent et du Sussex)

cipher ['saɪfər] [1] N [a] (= Arabic numeral) chiffre m (arabe) ; (= zero) zéro m ; (fig) **he's a mere ~** c'est un zéro ou une nullité [b] (= secret writing) chiffre m, code m secret ; **in ~** en chiffre, en code [c] (= message) message m chiffré or codé [d] (= monogram) chiffre m, monogramme m [2] VT [+ calculations, communications] chiffrer

circa ['sɜːkə] PREP circa, environ

circadian [sɜː'keɪdɪən] ADJ circadien

circle ['sɜːkl] [1] N (= shape) cercle m ; [of hills, houses, vehicles] cercle m ; [of mountains] cirque m ; (round eyes) cerne m ; (Gym) soleil m ; (Astron = orbit) orbite f ; (Brit Theat) balcon m ; [of knowledge] cercle m, sphère f ; (= group of persons) cercle m, groupe m ; [of underground railway] ligne f de ceinture ; **to stand in a ~** faire (un) cercle, se tenir en cercle ; **to draw a ~** tracer un cercle ; **an inner ~ of advisers** un groupe de proches conseillers ; **in political ~s** dans les milieux mpl politiques ; **to come full ~** revenir à son point de départ ; (fig) **they were going** or **running round in ~s** ils tournaient en rond → wheel
[2] VT [a] (= go round outside of sth) contourner ; (= keep moving round sth) tourner autour de ; (liter = encircle) entourer, encercler [b] (= draw circle round) entourer
[3] VI [birds] faire or décrire des cercles ; [aircraft] tourner (en rond) ; **the cyclists ~d round him** les cyclistes ont tourné autour de lui
► circle about, **circle (a)round** VI faire or décrire des cercles, tourner

circlet ['sɜːklɪt] N petit cercle m ; [of hair] bandeau m ; [of arm] brassard m ; [of finger] anneau m

circuit ['sɜːkɪt] [1] N [a] (= journey around) tour m, circuit m ; **to make the tour or ~ of ...** faire le tour de ... ; **to make a wide ~ round a town** faire un grand détour or circuit autour d'une ville [b] (Brit Jur = journey) tournée f (des juges d'assises) ; (= district) circonscription f (judiciaire) ; **he is on the eastern ~** il fait la tournée de l'est [c] (Cine, Theat: houses visited by same company) tournée f ; (houses owned by same owner) groupe m [d] (Sport = series of races, matches etc) circuit m ; (Tourism) **the Scottish cathedrals ~** le circuit des cathédrales d'Écosse [e] (Elec) circuit m → **closed**, **short** [f] (esp Brit Sport = track) circuit m, parcours m
[2] COMP **► circuit board** N (Comput) circuit m imprimé **► circuit breaker** N (Elec) disjoncteur m **► circuit court** N (Jur) tribunal m itinérant **► circuit judge** N (Jur) juge m en tournée **► circuit training** N (Sport) entraînement m (selon un programme préétabli)

circuitous [sɜː'kjuːɪtəs] ADJ [route, road] tortueux; [journey] plein de détours; [means] détourné; [method] indirect, détourné

circuitously [sɜː'kjuːɪtəslɪ] ADV (lit) [approach, reach] en faisant des détours; (fig) [speak] de façon contournée

circuitry ['sɜːkɪtrɪ] N (Elec) circuit m

circular ['sɜːkjʊləʳ] **1** ADJ [outline, saw, ticket] circulaire; **~ letter** circulaire f; **~ tour** voyage m circulaire, circuit m **2** N (= letter) circulaire f; (= printed advertisement etc) prospectus m

circularity [sɜːkjʊ'lærɪtɪ] N circularité f

circularize ['sɜːkjʊləraɪz] VT [+ person, firm] envoyer des circulaires or des prospectus à

circulate ['sɜːkjʊleɪt] **1** VI (gen) circuler; (at party etc) se mêler aux invités or à la fête **2** VT [+ object, bottle] faire circuler; [+ news, rumour] propager; [+ document] (from person to person) faire circuler; (= send out) diffuser **3** COMP ► **circulating decimal** N (Math) fraction f périodique ► **circulating library** N bibliobus m ► **circulating medium** N (Fin) monnaie f d'échange

circulation [sɜːkjʊ'leɪʃən] **1** N (NonC) (Anat, Bot, Fin, Med) circulation f; [of news, rumour] propagation f; [of newspaper etc] tirage m; **a magazine with a ~ of 10,000** un magazine qui tire à 10000 exemplaires; (Med) **he has poor ~** il a une mauvaise circulation; (Fin) **in ~** en circulation; (Fin) **to put into ~** mettre en circulation; (Fin) **to take out of** or **withdraw from ~** retirer de la circulation; **he's now back in ~*** il est à nouveau dans le circuit*; **to be out of ~*** [person] avoir disparu de la circulation* → **drop out 2** COMP ► **circulation manager** N (Press) directeur m du service de la diffusion

circulatory [sɜːkjʊ'leɪtərɪ] ADJ circulatoire

circum... ['sɜːkəm] PREF circon...

circumcise ['sɜːkəmsaɪz] VT [+ male] circoncire; [+ female] exciser

circumcision [sɜːkəm'sɪʒən] N [of male] circoncision f; [of female] excision f; (Rel) **the Circumcision** (la fête de) la Circoncision

circumference [sə'kʌmfərəns] N circonférence f

circumflex ['sɜːkəmfleks] **1** ADJ circonflexe **2** N accent m circonflexe

circumlocution [sɜːkəmlə'kjuːʃən] N circonlocution f

circumlunar [sɜːkəm'luːnəʳ] ADJ autour de la lune; **~ flight** vol m autour de la lune

circumnavigate [sɜːkəm'nævɪgeɪt] VT [+ cape] doubler, contourner; **to ~ the globe** faire le tour du monde en bateau

circumnavigation ['sɜːkəmˌnævɪ'geɪʃən] N circumnavigation f

circumscribe ['sɜːkəmskraɪb] VT (gen) circonscrire; [+ powers] limiter

circumspect ['sɜːkəmspekt] ADJ circonspect (about sth à l'égard de qch or sur qch); **to be ~ in one's behaviour** faire preuve de circonspection; **to be ~ in one's language** s'exprimer avec circonspection

circumspection [sɜːkəm'spekʃən] N circonspection f

circumspectly ['sɜːkəmspektlɪ] ADV avec circonspection

circumstance ['sɜːkəmstəns] N **a** circonstance f; (= fact, detail) circonstance f, détail m; **in** or **under the present ~s** dans les circonstances actuelles, vu l'état des choses; **in** or **under no ~s** en aucun cas or en aucune circonstance; **under similar ~s** en pareil cas, en or dans de pareilles circonstances; **to take the ~s into account** tenir compte des circonstances; **a victim of ~** une victime des circonstances → **attenuate**, **extenuate**, **pomp b** (= financial condition) **~s** situation f financière or pécuniaire; **in easy ~s** dans l'aisance, à l'aise; **in poor ~s** gêné, dans la gêne;

what are his ~s? quelle est sa situation financière or pécuniaire?; **if our ~s allow it** si nos moyens nous le permettent

circumstantial [sɜːkəm'stænʃəl] ADJ **a** (Jur) [case] fondé sur des présomptions; **~ evidence** présomptions fpl, preuves fpl indirectes; **much of the evidence is ~** il s'agit surtout de présomptions **b** (= detailed) [account, report, description] détaillé, circonstancié **c** (= anecdotal) [reasons, factors, detail] anecdotique

circumstantiate [sɜːkəm'stænʃɪeɪt] VT (frm) [+ evidence] confirmer en donnant des détails sur; [+ event] donner des détails circonstanciés sur

circumvent [sɜːkəm'vent] VT [+ person] circonvenir; [+ law, regulations, rule] tourner; [+ sb's plan, project] faire échouer

circumvention [sɜːkəm'venʃən] N [of plan, project] mise f en échec; **the ~ of the guard/rule proved easy** circonvenir le garde/tourner le règlement s'avéra facile

circus ['sɜːkəs] **1** N (pl **circuses**) **a** (Hist, Theat) cirque m **b** (in town) rond-point m **2** COMP [animal, clown] de cirque

cirrhosis [sɪ'rəʊsɪs] N cirrhose f

cirrus ['sɪrəs] N (pl **cirri** ['sɪraɪ]) **a** (= cloud) cirrus m **b** (Bot) vrille f

CIS [siːaɪ'es] N (ABBR = **Commonwealth of Independent States**) CEI f

cissy ['sɪsɪ] N = **sissy**

Cistercian [sɪs'tɜːʃən] **1** N cistercien(ne) m(f) **2** ADJ cistercien; **~ Order** ordre m de Cîteaux; **a ~ monk** un cistercien

cistern ['sɪstən] N citerne f; [of lavatory] réservoir m de la chasse d'eau; [of barometer] cuvette f

citadel ['sɪtədl] N citadelle f

citation [saɪ'teɪʃən] N (gen, US Jur, Mil) citation f

cite [saɪt] VT (gen, Jur, Mil) citer; (Sport = sanction) sanctionner; **as an example** citer en exemple; (Jur) **to ~ sb to appear** citer qn → **dispatch**

citified ['sɪtɪˌfaɪd] ADJ (pej) qui a pris les manières de la ville

citizen ['sɪtɪzn] **1** N [of town] habitant(e) m(f); [of state] citoyen(ne) m(f); (Admin) ressortissant(e) m(f); (Hist) bourgeois(e) m(f); (= townsman) citadin(e) m(f); **the ~s of Paris** les habitants mpl de Paris, les Parisiens mpl; **French ~** citoyen(ne) m(f) français(e); (when abroad) ressortissant m français; **~ of the world** citoyen m du monde → **fellow** **2** COMP ► **Citizens' Advice Bureau** N centre m d'information sur les droits des citoyens ► **citizen's arrest** N arrestation effectuée par un simple citoyen conformément au droit coutumier; **to make a ~'s arrest** effectuer une arrestation, en tant que simple citoyen, conformément au droit coutumier ► **Citizen's Band Radio** N CB f, bande f de fréquences publique ► **Citizen's Charter** N (Brit) charte mise en place par le gouvernement britannique en 1991 et visant à améliorer la qualité des services publics

Les **Citizens' Advice Bureaux** ont été créés en 1939 pour diffuser auprès de la population britannique la réglementation applicable en temps de guerre. Transformés par la suite en organismes d'assistance gratuite, ils dispensent des conseils sur tout problème concernant l'endettement des ménages, le logement, l'assurance maladie, les services sociaux ou les droits du consommateur. Le service, financé par des fonds publics, emploie dans ses nombreuses antennes locales des cadres salariés qui forment et gèrent un volant de personnels bénévoles.

citizenry ['sɪtɪznrɪ] N (esp US) **the ~** l'ensemble m des citoyens

citizenship ['sɪtɪznʃɪp] N citoyenneté f; (US) **~ papers** déclaration f de naturalisation

citrate ['sɪtreɪt] N citrate m

citric ['sɪtrɪk] **1** ADJ citrique **2** COMP ► **citric acid** N acide m citrique

citron ['sɪtrən] N (= fruit) cédrat m; (= tree) cédratier m

citronella [sɪtrə'nelə] N (= grass) citronnelle f; (= oil) (huile f de) citronnelle f

citrus ['sɪtrəs] N (pl **citruses**) (= tree) citrus m; (= fruit) agrume m

city ['sɪtɪ] **1** N **a** (gen) (grande) ville f; (= population) **the ~** la ville; **large cities like Leeds** les grandes villes comme Leeds; **life in the modern ~** la vie dans la cité or la ville moderne **b** (Brit) **the City** la City (centre des affaires à Londres); **he's (something) in the City*** il est dans les affaires, il travaille dans la City **2** COMP [streets] de la ville; [offices, authorities] municipal; (Brit Press) [editor, page, news] financier ► **City and Guilds (examination)** N (Brit) ≈ CAP m, ≈ certificat m d'aptitude professionnelle ► **city centre** N centre m de la ville, centre-ville m ► **city college** N (US Univ) université f (financée par la ville) ► **city councilman** N (US) (pl **city councilmen**) conseiller m municipal ► **city desk** N (Brit) antenne f financière; (US) antenne f locale ► **city dweller** N citadin(e) m(f) ► **city editor** N (Brit) responsable mf de la rubrique financière (dans un journal); (US) rédacteur m en chef (pour les nouvelles locales) ► **city fathers** NPL édiles mpl ► **city hall** N (lit) mairie f; (in large towns) hôtel m de ville; (US fig = city authorities) administration f municipale ► **city manager** N (US) administrateur m communal (payé par une municipalité et faisant fonction de maire) ► **city planner** N (US) urbaniste mf ► **city planning** N (US) urbanisme m ► **city police** N (US) police f municipale ► **city slicker*** N (pej) citadin(e) m(f) sophistiqué(e), rat m des villes ► **city-state** N cité f ► **city technology college** N (Brit) établissement m d'enseignement technologique

Si l'on sait que « The Big Apple » désigne la ville de New York (« apple » est en réalité un terme d'argot signifiant « grande ville »), on connaît moins les surnoms donnés aux autres grandes villes américaines. Chicago est surnommée « Windy City » à cause des rafales soufflant du lac Michigan, La Nouvelle-Orléans doit son sobriquet de « Big Easy » à son style de vie décontracté, et l'industrie automobile a donné à Detroit son surnom de « Motown ».

D'autres villes sont familièrement désignées par leurs initiales : « LA » pour Los Angeles, « Big D » pour Dallas, ou par des diminutifs : « Vegas » pour Las Vegas, « Frisco » pour San Francisco, « Philly » pour Philadelphie.

cityfied ['sɪtɪˌfaɪd] ADJ (pej) = **citified**

cityscape ['sɪtɪskeɪp] N paysage m or panorama m urbain

civet ['sɪvɪt] N (= cat, substance) civette f

civic ['sɪvɪk] **1** ADJ [duty, rights, pride, virtue, movement] civique; [life] des citoyens; [authorities, administration, building] municipal; **~ event/reception** cérémonie f/réception f officielle locale; **~ leader** notable m **2** COMP ► **civic centre** N (Brit) centre m administratif (municipal) ► **civic hall** N salle f municipale

civics ['sɪvɪks] N instruction f civique

civies* ['sɪvɪz] NPL (US) = **civvies**; → **civvy**

civil ['sɪvl] **1** ADJ **a** (= civic or non-military) civil; **~ commotion** émeute f; **~ divorce** divorce non reconnu par l'église; **~ marriage** mariage m

civil ; **~ wedding** mariage *m* civil ; **to have a ~ wedding** se marier civilement
[b] (= *polite*) civil, poli ; **that's very ~ of you** vous êtes bien aimable → **tongue**
[2] COMP ► **Civil Aviation Authority** N (*Brit*) ≈ Direction *f* générale de l'aviation civile ► **civil defence** N défense *f* passive ► **civil disobedience** N désobéissance *f* civile ; **~ disobedience campaign** campagne *f* de désobéissance civile ► **civil engineer** N ingénieur *m* civil ► **civil engineering** N génie *m* civil ► **civil law** N (= *system*) code *m* civil ; (= *study*) droit *m* civil ► **civil liberties** NPL libertés *fpl* civiques ► **civil list** N (*Brit*) liste *f* civile (allouée à la famille royale) ► **civil rights** NPL droits *mpl* civils ; **~ rights movement** mouvement *m* pour les droits civils ► **civil servant** N fonctionnaire *mf* ► **civil service** N fonction *f* publique, administration *f* ; **~ service examination** concours *m* d'entrée dans la fonction publique ; **~ service recruitment** recrutement *m* de(s) fonctionnaires ► **Civil Service Commission** N commission *f* de recrutement dans la fonction publique ► **civil war** N guerre *f* civile ; **the (American) Civil War** la guerre de Sécession

civilian [sɪ'vɪlɪən] [1] N civil(e) *m(f)* (*opposé à militaire*) [2] ADJ civil

civility [sɪ'vɪlɪtɪ] N courtoisie *f*, civilité† *f* ; **civilities** civilités *fpl*

civilization [ˌsɪvɪlaɪˈzeɪʃən] N civilisation *f*

civilize [ˈsɪvɪlaɪz] VT civiliser

civilized [ˈsɪvɪlaɪzd] ADJ [a] (= *socially advanced*) [*society, country, world, people*] civilisé ; [*values*] de civilisation ; **to become ~** se civiliser [b] (= *refined*) [*person, behaviour, conversation, place, meal*] raffiné ; [*time of day*] (tout à fait) convenable ; **let's try and be ~ about this** essayons d'être conciliants ; **I know we disagree, but we could at least be ~ about it** je sais que nous ne sommes pas d'accord, mais nous pourrions au moins essayer de rester aimables

civilizing [ˈsɪvɪlaɪzɪŋ] ADJ civilisateur (-trice *f*)

civilly [ˈsɪvɪlɪ] ADV poliment

civism [ˈsɪvɪzəm] N civisme *m*

civvy [ˈsɪvɪ] ABBR = **civilian** [1] **civvies** NPL vêtements *mpl* civils (habillé) en civil or en bourgeois* [2] COMP ► **civvy street** N (*Brit*) vie *f* civile ; **to be in ~ street** être civil or pékin*

CJD [ˌsiːdʒeɪ'diː] N (ABBR = **Creutzfeldt-Jakob disease**) MCJ *f*

cl (ABBR = **centilitre(s)**) cl

clack [klæk] [1] N claquement *m* ; [*of pump etc*] clapet *m* ; (*fig = talk*) jacasserie *f*, caquet *m* [2] VI claquer ; (*fig*) jacasser ; **this will set tongues ~ing** cela va faire jaser

clad [klæd] ADJ habillé, vêtu (**in** de) ; (*liter*) **~ with** (= *covered with*) revêtu de

cladding [ˈklædɪŋ] N [*of building*] revêtement *m* ; [*of nuclear reactor*] gainage *m*

▼ **claim** [kleɪm] [1] VT [a] (= *demand as one's due*) réclamer (**from sb** à qn), revendiquer ; [+ *property, prize, right*] revendiquer ; **to ~ diplomatic immunity** invoquer l'immunité diplomatique ; **to ~ the right to decide** revendiquer le droit de décider ; **the group which ~ed responsibility for the attack** le groupe qui a revendiqué l'attentat ; **no one has yet ~ed responsibility for the explosion** l'explosion n'a pas encore été revendiquée ; **to ~ damages** réclamer des dommages et intérêts ; (*fig*) **the epidemic has ~ed 100 victims** l'épidémie a fait 100 victimes ; **the fighting ~ed many lives** les combats ont fait de nombreuses victimes → **credit**
[b] (= *profess, contend, maintain*) prétendre, déclarer ; **to ~ acquaintance with sb** prétendre connaître qn ; **he ~s to have seen you** *or* (*that*) **he's seen you** il prétend *or* déclare vous avoir vu, il déclare qu'il vous a vu ; **both armies ~ed**

the victory les deux armées ont revendiqué la victoire
[c] (= *demand*) [+ *sb's attention*] demander, solliciter ; [+ *sb's sympathy*] solliciter
[2] N [a] (= *act of claiming*) revendication *f*, réclamation *f* ; (*Insurance*) ≈ déclaration *f* de sinistre, ≈ demande *f* d'indemnité ; **to lay ~ to** prétendre à, avoir des prétentions à ; **there are many ~s on my time** je suis très pris ; **there are many ~s on my purse** j'ai beaucoup de frais, mes moyens sont fortement mis à contribution ; **that's a big ~ to make!** la *or* cette prétention est de taille! ; **his ~ that he acted legally** son affirmation selon laquelle il aurait agi dans les limites de la loi ; **to put in a ~** (*gen*) faire une réclamation ; (*Insurance*) faire une déclaration de sinistre *or* une demande d'indemnité ; (*Ind*) **they put in a ~ for a 3% pay rise** ils ont demandé une augmentation de 3% ; (*Ind*) **a ~ for an extra 3%** une demande d'augmentation de 3% ; (*Insurance*) **the ~s were all paid** les dommages ont été intégralement payés *or* réglés → **outstanding**
[b] (= *right*) droit *m*, titre *m* ; **~ to ownership** titre *m* de propriété ; **he renounced his ~ to the throne** il a renoncé à toute prétention à la couronne *or* à faire valoir ses droits à la couronne ; **~s to sb's friendship** droits *mpl* à l'amitié de qn
[c] (*Min etc*) concession *f* → **stake**
[3] COMP ► **claim form** N (*Admin*) (*for benefit*) (formulaire *m* de) demande *f* ; (*for expenses*) (feuille *f* pour) note *f* de frais ► **claims adjuster** N (*Insurance*) agent *m* général d'assurances

claimant [ˈkleɪmənt] N [*of throne*] prétendant(e) *m(f)* (**to** à) ; (*Brit*) [*of social benefits*] demandeur *m*, -euse *f* ; (*Jur, Insurance*) requérant(e) *m(f)*

clairvoyance [klɛəˈvɔɪəns] N voyance *f*, (don *m* de) double vue *f*

clairvoyant(e) [klɛəˈvɔɪənt] [1] N voyant(e) *m(f)*, extralucide *mf* [2] ADJ doué de double vue

clam [klæm] [1] N [a] (*Zool*) palourde *f*, clam *m* [b] (*US*‡) dollar *m* [2] COMP ► **clam chowder** N (*Culin*) soupe *f* épaisse de palourdes
► **clam up*** VI la boucler*, la fermer‡ ; **to ~ up like an oyster** se fermer comme une huître ; **he ~med up on me** il l'a bouclée‡, il ne m'a plus dit un mot là-dessus

clambake [ˈklæmbeɪk] N (*US*) [a] (*Culin*) barbecue *m* de fruits de mer [b] (= *party*) réunion *f* à la bonne franquette

clamber [ˈklæmbə‹r›] [1] VI grimper (*en s'aidant des mains ou en rampant*), se hisser (*avec difficulté*) ; **to ~ up a hill** gravir péniblement une colline ; **to ~ over a wall** escalader un mur [2] N escalade *f*

clammy [ˈklæmɪ] ADJ [*skin, hands, handshake, clothes, sheets*] moite ; [*weather*] lourd ; **~ with sweat/fear** moite de sueur/peur

clamor [ˈklæmə‹r›] (*US*) = **clamour**

clamorous [ˈklæmərəs] ADJ [a] (= *noisy*) [*voice, noise*] tonitruant ; [*crowd*] bruyant ; **~ applause** tonnerre *m* d'applaudissements [b] (= *vehement*) [*demand, campaign*] véhément

clamour, clamor (*US*) [ˈklæmə‹r›] [1] N [a] (= *shouts*) clameur *f*, cris *mpl* ; (= *angry cries*) vociférations *fpl* ; (= *demands*) revendications *fpl* *or* réclamations *fpl* bruyantes [2] VI pousser des cris ; **to ~ against sth/sb** vociférer contre qch/qn ; **to ~ for sth/sb** demander qch/qn à grands cris ; (= *demand*) réclamer qch/qn à cor et à cri

clamp¹ [klæmp] [1] N (*gen*) attache *f*, pince *f* ; (*bigger*) crampon *m* ; (*Med*) clamp *m* ; (*also* **ring ~**) collier *m* de serrage ; (*Carpentry*) valet *m* (d'établi) ; (*Archit*) agrafe *f* ; [*of china*] agrafe *f* ; (*Aut*) sabot *m* de Denver ; (*Elec*) serre-fils *m inv* ; (*Naut*) serre-câbles *m inv* [2] VT [a] (= *put clamp on*) serrer, attacher ; [+ *stones, china*]

agrafer ; [+ *car, car wheels*] mettre un sabot à ; **to ~ sth to sth** fixer qch à qch [b] **to ~ shut** *or* **together** [+ *teeth*] serrer [c]* [+ *embargo, curfew*] imposer (**on** sur)
► **clamp down on*** [1] VT FUS [+ *person*] prendre des mesures autoritaires contre ; [+ *inflation, expenditure*] mettre un frein à ; [+ *the press, the opposition*] bâillonner [2] **~down** N → **clampdown**
► **clamp together** VT SEP serrer ensemble

clamp² [klæmp] [1] N [*of bricks*] tas *m*, pile *f* ; [*of potatoes*] silo *m* [2] VT entasser

clampdown [ˈklæmpdaʊn] N (*gen*) répression *f* (**on sth** de qch, **on sb** contre qn) ; **a ~ on terrorists** la répression *or* des mesures répressives contre les terroristes ; **a ~ on arms sales** un renforcement des restrictions sur la vente d'armes

clan [klæn] N clan *m* (*écossais*) ; (*fig*) famille *f*

clandestine [klæn'destɪn] ADJ clandestin

clang [klæŋ] [1] N bruit *m* *or* son *m* métallique ; (*louder*) fracas *m* métallique [2] VI émettre un son métallique ; **the gate ~ed shut** la grille s'est refermée bruyamment *or* avec un bruit métallique

clanger* [ˈklæŋə‹r›] N (*Brit*) gaffe *f* ; **to drop a ~** faire une gaffe, gaffer lourdement

clangor [ˈklæŋə‹r›] N (*US*) = **clangour**

clangorous [ˈklæŋərəs] ADJ [*noise*] métallique

clangour, clangor (*US*) [ˈklæŋgə‹r›] N son *m* *or* bruit *m* *or* fracas *m* métallique

clank [klæŋk] [1] N cliquetis *m*, bruit *m* métallique (*de chaînes etc*) [2] VI cliqueter, émettre un son métallique [3] VT faire cliqueter

clankpin [ˈklæŋkpɪn] N (*Aut*) maneton *m*

clannish [ˈklænɪʃ] ADJ (*slightly pej = exclusive, unwelcoming*) [*group*] fermé ; [*person*] qui a l'esprit de clan *or* de clique

clansman [ˈklænzmən] (*pl* **-men**), **clanswoman** [ˈklænz,wʊmən] (*pl* **-women**) N (*in Scotland*) membre *m* d'un clan (*écossais*)

clap¹ [klæp] [1] N (= *sound*) claquement *m*, bruit *m* sec ; [*of hands*] battement *m* ; (= *action*) tape *f* ; (= *applause*) applaudissements *mpl* ; **a ~ on the back** une tape dans le dos ; (*Scot* = *stroke*) **to give the dog a ~** caresser le chien ; **a ~ of thunder** un coup de tonnerre ; **he got a good ~** il a été très applaudi [2] VT [a] (= *applaud*) applaudir ; **to ~ one's hands** battre des mains ; **to ~ sb on the back/the shoulder** donner à qn une tape dans le dos/sur l'épaule ; (*Scot* = *stroke*) **to ~ a dog** caresser un chien ; **he ~ped his hand over my mouth** il a mis *or* plaqué sa main sur ma bouche [b] (= *put, set*) **to ~ sb in irons** jeter qn aux fers ; **to ~ sb into prison** jeter qn en prison ; **to ~ eyes on** voir ; **to ~ hands on sb** prendre qn sur le fait [3] VI taper *or* frapper dans ses mains ; (= *applaud*) applaudir
► **clap on** VT SEP **to ~ on one's hat** enfoncer son chapeau sur sa tête ; (*Naut*) **to ~ on sail** mettre toutes voiles dehors
► **clap to** VTI claquer

clap²‡* [klæp] N (= *disease*) **the ~** la chtouille‡, la chaude-pisse‡

clapboard [ˈklæpbɔːd] N bardeau *m*

clapped-out* [ˈklæptaʊt] ADJ (*Brit*) [*person, horse*] au bout du rouleau* ; [*car, train*] pourri* ; [*TV, washing machine*] fichu*, nase*

clapper [ˈklæpə‹r›] N [*of bell*] battant *m* ; (*Brit*) **to go like the ~s**‡ aller à toute blinde*

clapperboard [ˈklæpə,bɔːd] N clap *m*, claquette *f*

clapping [ˈklæpɪŋ] N applaudissements *mpl*

claptrap* [ˈklæptræp] N boniment* *m*, baratin* *m*

claque [klæk] N (*Theat*) claque *f*

Clare [klɛə‹r›] N Claire *f* ; (*Rel*) **the Poor ~s** clarisses *fpl*, Pauvres Dames *fpl*

claret [ˈklærət] [1] N (vin *m* de) bordeaux *m* (rouge) [2] ADJ (*also* **~-coloured**) bordeaux *inv*

clarification [ˌklærɪfɪˈkeɪʃən] N (gen) clarification f, éclaircissement m; [of wine] collage m; (Jur) **request for ~** demande f d'éclaircissement

clarified [ˈklærɪfaɪd] ADJ [butter, stock, wine, sugar] clarifié

clarify [ˈklærɪfaɪ] [1] VT [+ sugar, butter, wine] clarifier; [fig] [+ situation] éclaircir, clarifier [2] VI se clarifier; (fig) s'éclaircir

clarinet [ˌklærɪˈnet] N clarinette f

clarinettist [ˌklærɪˈnetɪst] N clarinettiste mf

clarion [ˈklærɪən] (liter) [1] N clairon m [2] VT (frm) **to ~ (forth)** claironner [3] COMP ► **clarion call** N appel m de clairon

clarity [ˈklærɪtɪ] N clarté f, précision f

clash [klæʃ] [1] VI [a] (= bang noisily) [swords, metallic objects] s'entrechoquer; [cymbals] résonner [b] (= be in dispute) [armies] se heurter; **the two parties ~ over …** les deux partis sont en désaccord total à propos de … [c] (= conflict) [interests] se heurter, être incompatible (with avec); [personalities] être incompatible (with avec); [colours] jurer, détonner (with avec) [d] (= coincide) [two events, invitations etc] tomber en même temps (or le même jour etc); **the dates ~** les deux événements (or rencontres etc) tombent le même jour [2] VT [+ metallic objects] entrechoquer bruyamment; [+ cymbals] faire résonner; (Aut) **to ~ the gears** faire grincer les vitesses [3] N [a] (= sound) choc m or fracas m métallique [b] [of armies, weapons] choc m, heurt m; (between people, parties) désaccord m; (with police, troops) affrontement m, échauffourée f; **during a ~ with the police** au cours d'un affrontement or d'une échauffourée avec la police; **~es between police and demonstrators** des heurts mpl entre la police et les manifestants; **I don't want a ~ with him about it** je ne veux pas me disputer avec lui à ce sujet; **to have a (verbal) ~ with sb** avoir un accrochage* or une algarade avec qn [c] [of interests] conflit m; **a ~ of personalities** une incompatibilité de caractères [d] **a ~ of colours** des couleurs qui détonnent [e] [of dates, events, invitations] coïncidence f fâcheuse

clasp [klɑːsp] [1] N [a] [of brooch, necklace, purse] fermoir m; [of belt] boucle f [b] (NonC: in one's arms, of a hand) étreinte f [2] VT étreindre, serrer; **to ~ sb's hand** serrer la main de qn; **to ~ one's hands (together)** joindre les mains; **with ~ed hands** les mains jointes; **to ~ sb in one's arms/to one's heart** serrer qn dans ses bras/sur son cœur [3] COMP ► **clasp knife** N (pl **clasp knives**) grand couteau m pliant

class [klɑːs] [1] N [a] (= group, division) classe f, catégorie f; (Bot, Ling, Mil, Sociol, Zool etc) classe f; (Naut) [of ship] type m; (in Lloyd's Register) cote f; (fig) **he's not in the same ~ as his brother** il n'arrive pas à la cheville de son frère; **these books are just not in the same ~** il n'y a pas de comparaison (possible) entre ces livres; **in a ~ by itself** ◊ **in a ~ of its own** hors concours, unique; **they are in a ~ apart** ils sont tout à fait à part; **a good ~ (of) hotel** un très bon hôtel, un hôtel de très bonne classe; **the ruling ~** la classe dirigeante; (Brit Univ) **what ~ of degree did he get?** quelle mention a-t-il obtenue (à sa licence)?; **first ~ honours in history** ≈ licence f d'histoire avec mention très bien → **middle, working** [b] (Scol, Univ, gen) (= lesson) classe f, cours m; (= students) classe f; (US = year) promotion f scolaire; **to give** or **take a ~** faire un cours; **to attend a ~** suivre un cours; **the French ~** la classe or le cours de français; **an evening ~** un cours du soir; (US) **the ~ of 1970** la promotion or la promo* de 1970

[c] (NonC: *) classe f, distinction f; **to have ~** avoir de la classe [2] VT classer, classifier; (Naut Insurance) coter; **he was ~ed with the servants** il était assimilé aux domestiques [3] ADJ (= classy) de grande classe [4] COMP ► **class action** N (Jur) **~ actions** actions fpl de groupe; **~ action suit** recours m collectif en justice ► **class bias** N (Sociol) préjugés mpl de classe ► **class-conscious** ADJ [person] conscient des distinctions sociales; (pej = snobbish) [person, attitude] snob inv ► **class consciousness** N conscience f de classe ► **class distinction** N distinction f sociale ► **class list** N (Scol) liste f des élèves ► **class number** N (Brit: in library) cote f ► **class president** N (US) ≈ chef m de classe ► **class rank** N (US Scol, Univ) numéro m de sortie ► **class roll** N = **class list** ► **class society** N (Pol) société f de classes ► **class struggle** N lutte f des classes ► **class system** N système m de classes ► **class teacher** N (Brit Scol) professeur m principal ► **class war(fare)** N = **class struggle**

classic [ˈklæsɪk] [1] ADJ (gen) classique; **it was ~** c'était le coup classique* [2] N (= author, work) classique m; (Racing) classique f; (fig) **it is a ~ of its kind** c'est un classique du genre [3] COMP ► **classic car** N voiture f ancienne

classical [ˈklæsɪkəl] [1] ADJ [pianist, economist, Greece, Latin] classique; [Greek] de l'époque classique; [album, CD] de musique classique; **~ times** antiquité f gréco-latine; **~ scholar** spécialiste mf en lettres classiques [2] COMP ► **classical music** N (NonC) musique f classique, classique m

classically [ˈklæsɪkəlɪ] ADV [a] (Mus, Dancing) **to be ~ trained** avoir reçu une formation classique; **a ~ trained pianist/dancer** un pianiste/danseur de formation classique [b] (Hist, Art) **a ~ proportioned building** un bâtiment aux proportions classiques; **a ~ inspired church** une église d'inspiration classique; **a ~ shaped vase** un vase de forme classique or aux formes classiques [c] (= traditionally) ~ **beautiful/elegant** d'une beauté/élégance classique [d] (= typically) typiquement; ~ **English** typiquement anglais; **~, overweight people underestimate how much they eat** on constate généralement que les personnes qui ont des kilos en trop sousestiment la quantité de nourriture qu'elles absorbent

classicism [ˈklæsɪsɪzəm] N classicisme m

classicist [ˈklæsɪsɪst] N spécialiste mf de lettres classiques; (esp Archit) partisan(e) m(f) du classicisme

classics [ˈklæsɪks] N lettres fpl classiques; **to study ~** faire des études de lettres classiques

classifiable [ˈklæsɪfaɪəbl] ADJ qu'on peut classifier

classification [ˌklæsɪfɪˈkeɪʃən] N classification f

classified [ˈklæsɪfaɪd] [1] ADJ [a] classifié [b] (Admin = secret etc) [document] classé secret (classée secrète f); **~ information** renseignements mpl (classés) secrets [2] COMP ► **classified advertisement** N (Press) petite annonce f ► **classified results** NPL (Brit Sport) résultats mpl sportifs complets ► **classified section** N (Press) (rubrique f des) petites annonces fpl

classify [ˈklæsɪfaɪ] VT [a] classer, classifier [b] (Admin = restrict circulation) classer secret

classism [ˈklɑːsɪzəm] N (NonC) discrimination f sociale or de classe

classless [ˈklɑːslɪs] ADJ [society] sans classes; [person] qui n'appartient à aucune classe; [accent] standard

classmate [ˈklɑːsmeɪt] N (Brit) camarade mf de classe; (US) camarade mf de promotion (or de classe)

classroom [ˈklɑːsrʊm] N (salle f de) classe f

classy* [ˈklɑːsɪ] ADJ [person] classe inv*; [hotel, restaurant] classe inv*, chic inv; [area, neighbourhood, clothes, car] chic inv; [watch, image] de luxe; [performance, album, film] de grande classe; **her flat looks very ~** son appartement fait très classe* or très chic

clatter [ˈklætəʳ] [1] N (= noise) cliquetis m; (louder) fracas m; **the ~ of cutlery** le bruit or cliquetis de couverts entrechoqués [2] VI (= rattle) [heels, keys, typewriter, chains] cliqueter; (= bang) [large falling object, cymbals] résonner; **to ~ in/out/away** etc entrer/sortir/partir etc bruyamment [3] VT choquer or entrechoquer bruyamment

clause [klɔːz] N [a] (Gram) membre m de phrase, proposition f; **principal/subordinate ~** proposition f principale/subordonnée [b] (Jur) [of contract, law, treaty] clause f; [of will] disposition f → **saving**

claustrophobia [ˌklɔːstrəˈfəʊbɪə] N claustrophobie f; (fig) atmosphère f oppressante

claustrophobic [ˌklɔːstrəˈfəʊbɪk] [1] ADJ [person] claustrophobe; [feeling] de claustrophobie; [room] où l'on se sent claustrophobe; [atmosphere] oppressant; [film, thriller] à l'atmosphère oppressante; **to feel ~** [person] avoir une sensation de claustrophobie; **the house felt too ~** on se sentait trop à l'étroit dans la maison [2] N claustrophobe mf

clavichord [ˈklævɪkɔːd] N clavicorde m

clavicle [ˈklævɪkl] N clavicule f

claw [klɔː] [1] N [a] [of cat, lion, small bird etc] griffe f; [of bird of prey] serre f; [of lobster etc] pince f; **to get one's ~s into sb*** tenir qn entre ses griffes; **to get one's ~s on sth*** mettre le grappin sur qch*; **get your ~s off (that)!**ǂ bas les pattes!* [b] (Tech) [of bench] valet m; [of hammer] pied-de-biche m [2] VT (= scratch) griffer; (= rip) déchirer or labourer avec ses griffes or ses serres; (= clutch) agripper, serrer; (fig) **to ~ one's way to the top** se hisser en haut de l'échelle [3] COMP ► **claw hammer** N marteau m fendu, marteau m à pied-de-biche ► **claw at** VT FUS [+ object] essayer de s'agripper à; [+ person] essayer de griffer ► **claw back** [1] VT SEP (Econ) récupérer [2] **~back** N → **clawback**

clawback [ˈklɔːbæk] N (Econ) récupération f

clay [kleɪ] [1] N argile f, (terre f) glaise f; (Tennis) terre f battue; **potter's ~** argile f (à potier); (Tennis) **to play on ~** jouer sur terre battue → **china** [2] COMP ► **clay court** N (Tennis) court m de terre battue ► **clay pigeon** N pigeon m d'argile or de ball-trap; (US fig) victime f or cible f facile; **~ pigeon shooting** ball-trap m ► **clay pipe** N pipe f en terre ► **clay pit** N argilière f, glaisière f ► **clay-with-flints** N (Geol) argile f à silex

clayey [ˈkleɪɪ] ADJ argileux, glaiseux

claymore [ˈkleɪmɔːʳ] N claymore f

clean [kliːn] [1] ADJ [a] (= not dirty, having clean habits) propre; **to keep sth ~** tenir qch propre, ne pas salir qch; **he washed the floor ~** il a bien nettoyé or lavé le sol; **the rain washed it ~** la pluie l'a entièrement nettoyé; **the rain washed the car ~ of mud** la pluie a fait partir or a lavé toute la boue de la voiture; **to wipe sth ~** bien essuyer qch; (lit, fig) **to have ~ hands** avoir les mains propres; **to be washed ~ of sin** être lavé de tout péché; **as ~ as a new pin** or **as a whistle** propre comme un sou neuf; **it broke off as ~ as a whistle** ça a cassé net → **2** [b] (= respectable) [joke, story, film] décent; **it's all good ~ fun*** ce sont des plaisirs honnêtes; **~ living** vie f saine; **to lead a good ~ life** mener une vie bien honnête; **keep it ~!*** restons décents!; (fig) **let's keep the party ~!*** pas d'inconvenances!, un peu de tenue! [c] (= fair) [game, match, player] fair-play inv; (Boxing, fig) **a ~ fight** un combat dans les règles, un combat loyal

d (= *blank*) [*sheet of paper*] vierge; **the doctor gave him a ~ bill of health** le médecin l'a trouvé en parfait état de santé; (*Comm*) **~ bill of lading** connaissement *m* net *or* sans réserves; (*Jur*) **~ record** casier *m* (judiciaire) vierge; (*Ftbl*) **to have a ~ sheet** n'avoir encaissé aucun but

e (= *corrected*) **let me have a ~ copy of your report** donnez-moi une copie propre de votre rapport

f (= *untarnished*) [*image, reputation*] sans tache

g (= *pure, smooth*) [*smell, taste, profile*] pur; [*look, sound, edge, stroke, shape*] net; [*curve*] élégant; **this car has very ~ lines** cette voiture a une belle ligne; **a ~ cut** une coupure nette *or* franche

h (= *ritually pure*) [*animal*] pur

i (*Nucl Phys*) [*bomb, area, person, object*] propre

j (= *uninterrupted*) [*shot*] direct; **~ leap** saut *m* sans toucher (l'obstacle); (*Tennis*) **a ~ ace** un as

k (= *trouble-free*) [*operation, job*] sans bavures; **~ getaway** fuite *f* sans encombre

l (* = *innocent of wrongdoing*) **to be ~** (*gen*) n'avoir rien à se reprocher; **he's been ~ for six months** [*criminal*] ça fait six mois qu'il se tient à carreau*

m * **to be ~** (= *not in possession of drugs, weapon, stolen property*) n'avoir rien sur soi; **his room was ~** il n'y avait rien dans sa chambre, on n'a rien trouvé dans sa chambre

n * (= *off drugs*) clean *inv*; (= *off alcohol*) qui ne touche plus à l'alcool

o **~ break** (*Med*) fracture *f* simple; (*fig*) rupture *f* définitive; (*fig*) **to make a ~ break** tourner la page; **to make a ~ break with the past** rompre définitivement avec le passé; (*Jur*) **~ break divorce** divorce à la suite duquel les époux, grâce à un versement unique, ne se doivent plus rien

p (*fig*) **to make a ~ breast of it** décharger sa conscience, dire ce qu'on a sur la conscience

q **~ sweep** grand chelem *m* (*fig*); **to make a ~ sweep** réussir le grand chelem; **the first club to make a ~ sweep of all three trophies** le premier club à remporter les trois trophées

2 ADV* **a** (= *completely*) **to cut ~ through sth** couper qch de part en part; **the chain saw cut his fingers ~ off** la tronçonneuse lui a coupé les doigts tout net; **it broke off ~ ◊ it broke off as ~ as a whistle** ça a cassé net; **the bullet went ~ through his forehead** la balle lui a transpercé le front tout net; **the car went ~ through the hedge** la voiture est carrément passée à travers la haie; **the fish jumped ~ out of the net** le poisson a sauté carrément hors du filet; **he jumped ~ over the fence** il a sauté la barrière sans la toucher; **the thief got ~ away** le voleur s'est enfui sans encombre; **I forgot** j'ai bel et bien oublié

b **to come ~** (= *confess: gen*) tout déballer*; [*criminal*] se mettre à table*; **to come ~ about sth** tout déballer* sur qch; **he came ~ about it** il a lâché le morceau*, il a tout déballé*

3 N **to give sth a good ~(up)** bien nettoyer qch

4 VT [+ *clothes, room, fish*] nettoyer; [+ *vegetables*] laver; [+ *blackboard*] essuyer; **to ~ one's teeth** se laver les dents; **to ~ one's nails** se nettoyer les ongles; **to ~ one's face** se débarbouiller, se laver la figure; **to ~ the windows** faire les vitres → **dry**

5 VI **a** (= *do housework*) faire le ménage **b** (= *be cleaned*) se nettoyer; **that floor ~s easily** ce plancher se nettoie facilement *or* est facile à nettoyer

6 COMP ► **clean-and-jerk** N (*Weight Lifting*) épaulé-jeté *m* ► **clean-cut** ADJ bien délimité,

net, clair; [*person*] à l'allure soignée ► **clean-limbed** ADJ bien proportionné, bien découplé ► **clean-living** ADJ décent, honnête ► **clean-out** N nettoyage *m* à fond ► **clean room** N (*Ind*) salle *f* blanche ► **clean-shaven** ADJ sans barbe ni moustache; (= *close-shaven*) rasé de près

► **clean off** VT SEP [+ *writing*] (*from blackboard*) essuyer; (*from wall*) enlever

► **clean out** **1** VT SEP [+ *drawer, box*] nettoyer à fond; [+ *cupboard, room*] nettoyer *or* faire à fond; (* *fig* = *leave penniless etc*) [+ *person*] nettoyer*; **the hotel bill ~ed me out*** la note de l'hôtel m'a nettoyé* *or* m'a mis à sec*; **he was ~ed out*** il était fauché *or* à sec*; **the burglars had ~ed out the whole house*** les cambrioleurs avaient complètement vidé la maison **2** **~-out** N → **clean**

► **clean up** **1** VI **a** tout nettoyer, mettre de l'ordre; **she had to ~ up after the children's visit** elle a dû tout remettre en ordre après la visite des enfants; **to ~ up after sb** nettoyer après qn **b** (* *fig* = *make profit*) faire son beurre*; **he ~ed up on that sale*** cette vente lui a rapporté gros, il a touché un joli paquet* sur cette vente **2** VT **a** [+ *room, mess, person*] nettoyer; **to ~ o.s. up** se laver, se débarbouiller **b** (*fig*) remettre de l'ordre dans les affaires de, épurer; **to ~ up one's act*** acheter une conduite*, s'amender; **the new mayor ~ed up the city** le nouveau maire a épuré la ville *or* a remis de l'ordre dans la ville; **they are trying to ~ up television** ils essaient d'épurer la télévision **3** **~up** N → **cleanup**

cleaner ['kliːnəʳ] N **a** (= *woman*) (*in home*) femme *f* de ménage; (*in office, school*) femme *f* de service; (*in hospital*) fille *f* de salle; (= *man*) agent *m* de service, ouvrier *m* nettoyeur **b** (*Comm*) teinturier *m*, -ière *f*; (= *device*) appareil *m* de nettoyage; (= *household cleaner*) produit *m* d'entretien; (= *stain-remover*) détachant *m*; **the ~'s shop** la teinturerie; **he took his coat to the ~'s** il a donné son pardessus à nettoyer *or* au teinturier; (*fig*) **to take sb to the ~'s** plumer* qn → **dry, vacuum**

cleaning ['kliːnɪŋ] **1** N nettoyage *m*; (= *housework*) ménage *m* → **spring 2** COMP ► **cleaning fluid** N (*for stains*) détachant *m* (liquide) ► **cleaning lady, cleaning woman** N femme *f* de ménage

cleanliness ['klenlɪnɪs] N propreté *f*, habitude *f* de la propreté; (*PROV*) **~ is next to godliness** la propreté du corps est parente de la propreté de l'âme

cleanly¹ ['kliːnlɪ] ADV **a** (= *smoothly*) [*cut*] de façon bien nette **b** (= *fairly*) [*play, fight*] (*Sport*) dans les règles; (*fig*) loyalement **c** (= *skilfully*) [*strike, hit, catch*] avec précision **d** (= *without polluting*) [*burn*] proprement

cleanly² ['klenlɪ] (*liter*) ADJ [*person, animal*] propre

cleanness ['kliːnnɪs] N propreté *f*

cleanse [klenz] VT nettoyer; [+ *ditch, drain etc*] curer; (*Bible* = *cure*) guérir; (*fig*) [+ *person*] laver (**of** de); (*Rel*) [+ *soul etc*] purifier; (*Med*) **to ~ the blood** dépurer le sang

cleanser ['klenzəʳ] N (= *detergent*) détersif *m*, détergent *m*; (*for complexion*) démaquillant *m*

cleansing ['klenzɪŋ] **1** ADJ (*for complexion*) démaquillant; (*fig*) purifiant; **~ cream/lotion** crème *f*/lotion *f* démaquillante; **~ milk** lait *m* démaquillant; **~ department** service *m* de voirie **2** N nettoyage *m*

cleanup ['kliːnʌp] N **a** [*of room*] nettoyage *m*; [*of person*] débarbouillage *m*; (*fig*) épuration *f*, assainissement *m*; **to give o.s. a ~** se laver, se débarbouiller → **clean 3 b** (* *fig*) profit *m*; **he made a good ~ from that business** il a fait son beurre dans cette affaire*, cette affaire lui a rapporté gros

clear [klɪəʳ]

1 ADJECTIVE		**5** INTRANSITIVE VERB
2 NOUN		**6** COMPOUNDS
3 ADVERB		**7** PHRASAL VERBS
4 TRANSITIVE VERB		

1 ADJECTIVE

a = **lucid, definite** [*message, motive, proof, explanation, reasoning, style*] clair; [*commitment*] évident; [*mind, thought, thinking*] lucide; **they are faced with ~ alternatives** ils sont confrontés à des possibilités *or* solutions bien distinctes; **a ~ case of homicide** un cas évident d'homicide; **~ indication** signe *m* manifeste *or* certain; **to have a ~ head** avoir les idées claires; **to be a ~ thinker** être un esprit lucide; **you'll do as I say, is that ~?** tu vas faire ce que je te dis, c'est clair?; **as ~ as** day clair comme le jour *or* comme de l'eau de roche; (*iro*) **as ~ as mud*** clair comme de l'encre → **crystal**

♦ **to get sth clear** bien comprendre qch; **I think I've got it pretty ~** ça me paraît tout à fait clair; **now let's get this ~ ...** maintenant, que les choses soient bien claires ...

♦ **to make sth clear** bien faire comprendre qch; **to make it ~ (to sb) that ...** bien faire comprendre (à qn) que ...; **I wish to make it ~ that ...** je tiens à préciser que ...

♦ **to be/seem clear (to sb)**: it's ~ to me that ... pour moi, il est clair que ...; **it was ~ that ...** il était clair que ...; **the matter is ~ to me** pour moi, l'affaire est claire; **it's not ~ whether ...** on ne sait pas avec certitude si ...; **it all seems ~ enough to me** tout cela me semble *or* paraît assez clair

♦ **to become clear (to sb)**: now it becomes ~ to me maintenant, j'y vois (plus) clair; **the matter became ~ to me** l'affaire m'a semblé *or* m'est apparue plus claire; **it became ~ that ...** il devint de plus en plus clair *or* évident que ...; **it becomes ~ to me that ...** il me semble *or* paraît de plus en plus clair que ...; **it became ~ to me that ...** il m'est apparu clairement que ...

b = **understandable** [*person*] clair

♦ **to make o.s. clear** se faire bien comprendre; **do I make myself ~?** me suis-je bien fait comprendre?

c = **sure** [*person*] if you are not ~ about anything, ask me s'il y a quelque chose qui ne vous paraît *or* semble pas clair, dites-le-moi; **he is not quite ~ about what he must do** il n'a pas bien compris ce qu'il doit faire; **it is important to be ~ about what the author is saying here** il est important de bien comprendre ce que l'auteur dit ici; **I want to be quite ~ on this point** je veux que les choses soient bien claires; **I'm not ~ whether you agree or not** je ne suis pas sûr de comprendre si vous êtes d'accord ou pas

d = **distinct** [*handwriting, footprint, picture, voice, tone, majority*] net; **as ~ as a bell** [*sound*] parfaitement clair; [*voice*] limpide

e = **transparent** [*plastic, glass, gel*] transparent; [*honey*] liquide; [*water, air*] limpide; **a ~ soup** un bouillon

f = **pure in sound** [*voice, tone*] clair

g = **bright** [*light, colour*] vif; **~ blue eyes** des yeux *mpl* bleus limpides; **her eyes were ~ and steady** ses yeux étaient clairs et ne cillaient pas

h = **unobstructed** [*road, runway*] dégagé, libre; [*area, view*] dégagé; [*space*] libre; [*route*] sans obstacles; **all exits must be kept ~** toutes les sorties doivent rester dégagées; **she keeps her desk ~ of clutter** son bureau n'est jamais en désordre; **to get a ~ look at sb/sth** apercevoir qn/qch distinctement → **all, coast**

i (*Met*) [*weather*] clair; [*sky*] dégagé; **on a ~ day** par temps clair; **the days were warm and ~** les journées étaient chaudes et le ciel dégagé

j = **unblemished** [*skin*] sans taches, immaculé; [*complexion*] frais (fraîche *f*)

k = not guilty [conscience] tranquille; **my conscience is ~** ◊ **I have a ~ conscience** j'ai la conscience tranquille; **he left with a ~ conscience** il est parti la conscience tranquille

l = without commitments [afternoon, morning, diary] libre

m = complete [day, week] plein; **that gives us four ~ days to finish the job** ça nous donne quatre jours pleins pour finir le travail

n = after deductions net inv; **I'll make a ~ hundred from the deal** je tirerai cent livres net de la transaction; **a ~ profit** un bénéfice net

o = away from **raise the jack until the wheel is ~ of the ground** actionnez le cric jusqu'à ce que la roue ne touche plus le sol; **as soon as he was ~ of the terminal building** ... dès qu'il fut sorti de l'aérogare ...

p Brit Sport **to be 7 metres/seconds/points ~ of sb** (= ahead of) avoir 7 mètres/secondes/points d'avance sur qn

q Phon [vowel] clair

2 NOUN
♦ **in clear** en clair; **to send a message in ~** envoyer un message en clair
♦ **to be in the clear*** (= above suspicion) être au-dessus de tout soupçon; (= no longer suspected) être blanchi de tout soupçon; (= out of debt) être libre de toutes dettes; (= out of danger) être hors de danger

3 ADVERB
a = distinctly → loud 2
b = completely **the thief got ~ away** le voleur s'est enfui sans encombre
c = away **to steer or keep or stay ~ of sb/sth** éviter qn/qch → jump, pull, stand, steer
♦ **to get clear of sth** (= go away from) s'éloigner or s'écarter de qch; (= rid o.s. of) se débarrasser de qch; **it will be easier once we get ~ of winter** cela sera plus facile une fois l'hiver passé
d = net **he'll get £250 ~** il aura 250 livres net
e esp US **~ to sth** (= as far as) jusqu'à qch; **they went ~ to Mexico** ils sont allés jusqu'au Mexique

4 TRANSITIVE VERB
a = clarify [+ liquid] clarifier; [+ wine] coller, clarifier; [+ skin] purifier; [+ complexion] éclaircir; (Med) [+ blood] dépurer, purifier; (fig) [+ situation, account] éclaircir, clarifier; **to ~ the air** aérer; (fig) détendre l'atmosphère; **to ~ one's head** s'éclaircir les idées
b = remove obstacles etc from [+ canal, path, road, railway line] dégager, déblayer; [+ lungs, chest, airway] dégager; [+ pipe] déboucher; [+ land] défricher; [+ computer screen] effacer; (fig) [+ one's conscience] décharger; [+ doubts] dissiper; **to ~ sth of rubbish** déblayer qch; **to ~ one's throat** s'éclaircir la voix; **to ~ a room** (of people) faire évacuer une salle; (of things) débarrasser une salle; (Post) **the box is ~ed twice a day** la levée a lieu deux fois par jour; **to ~ a way** or **a path through** (se) frayer un passage à travers; **~ the way!** circulez!, dégagez!*; (lit) **to ~ the way for** ... faire place à ..., libérer le passage pour ...; (fig) **to ~ the way for further discussions** préparer or déblayer le terrain pour des négociations ultérieures; (Ftbl) **to ~ the ball** dégager le ballon → court, deck, ground, table
c = find innocent [+ person] innocenter, disculper (of de); **he was ~ed of the murder charge** il a été disculpé du meurtre dont on l'accusait; **he will easily ~ himself** il se disculpera facilement, il prouvera facilement son innocence; **to ~ sb of suspicion** laver qn de tout soupçon
d = authorize **you will have to be ~ed by our security department** il faudra que nos services de sécurité donnent leur feu vert
♦ **to clear sth with sb**: **we've ~ed it with him before beginning** nous avons obtenu son accord avant de commencer; **you must ~ the**

project with the manager il faut que le directeur donne (subj) le feu vert à votre projet
e = get past or over sauter par-dessus, franchir; [+ obstacle, rocks] éviter; [+ harbour] quitter; **the horse ~ed the gate by 10cm** le cheval a sauté or a franchi la barrière avec 10 cm de marge; **the car just ~ed the lamppost** la voiture a évité le réverbère de justesse; **raise the car till the wheel ~s the ground** soulevez la voiture jusqu'à ce que la roue ne touche (subj) plus le sol; **the boat just ~ed the bottom** le bateau a tout juste réussi à passer sans toucher le fond
f Fin, Comm [+ cheque] compenser; [+ account] solder, liquider; [+ debt] s'acquitter de; [+ profit] gagner net; (Comm) [+ goods] liquider; (Customs) [+ goods] dédouaner; [+ port dues] acquitter; [+ ship] expédier; (Comm) **"half price to ~"** « soldé à moitié prix pour liquider »; **I've ~ed £100 on this business** cette affaire m'a rapporté 100 livres net or tous frais payés

5 INTRANSITIVE VERB
a = brighten, improve [weather] s'éclaircir; [sky] se dégager; [fog] se dissiper; [face, expression] s'éclairer; [complexion] s'éclaircir; [skin] devenir plus sain; **his brow ~ed** son visage s'est éclairé
b Naut [ship] prendre la mer

6 COMPOUNDS
► **clear-cut** ADJ [outline, shape] net, précis, nettement défini; [attitude, proposal, situation] précis, clair; [problem, division] précis; **~-cut features** traits mpl nets or bien dessinés ► **clear-headed** ADJ lucide ► **clear-headedness** N lucidité f ► **clear-out** N rangement m complet ► **clear round** N (Horse-riding) parcours m sans faute, sans faute m inv; **to do a ~ round** faire un sans-faute ► **clear-sighted** ADJ [person] clairvoyant, lucide; [plan] lucide ► **clear-sightedness** N [of person] clairvoyance f; [of plan] réalisme m ► **clear-up rate** N **the ~-up rate for murders** le taux de meurtres résolus

7 PHRASAL VERBS
► **clear away** **1** VI **a** [mist etc] se dissiper
b (= clear the table) débarrasser, desservir
2 VT SEP enlever, retirer; **to ~ away the dishes** desservir, débarrasser (la table)
► **clear off** **1** VI* filer*, décamper; **~ off!** fichez le camp!*, filez!*
2 VT SEP **a** (= get rid of) se débarrasser de; [+ debts] s'acquitter de; (Comm) [+ stock] liquider; [+ goods] solder; **to ~ off arrears of work** rattraper le retard dans son travail
b (= remove) [+ things on table etc] enlever
► **clear out** **1** VI* = clear off 1
2 VT SEP [+ cupboard] vider; [+ room] nettoyer, débarrasser; [+ unwanted objects] enlever, jeter; **he ~ed everyone out of the room** il a fait évacuer la pièce; **he ~ed everything out of the room** il a débarrassé la pièce
► **clear up** **1** VI **a** [weather] s'éclaircir, se lever; **I think it will ~ up** je pense que ça va se lever
b [illness, spots] disparaître; **his skin has ~ed up** sa peau est devenue nette
c (= tidy) ranger, faire des rangements
2 VT SEP **a** [+ mystery] éclaircir, résoudre; [+ matter, subject] éclaircir, tirer au clair
b (= tidy) [+ room] ranger, mettre en ordre; [+ books, toys] ranger

clearance ['klɪərəns] **1** N **a** (NonC) [of road, path] déblaiement m, dégagement m; [of land, bomb site] déblaiement m; [of room, court] évacuation f; [of litter, objects, rubbish] enlèvement m; (Comm) soldes mpl, liquidation f (du stock)
b [of boat, car etc] dégagement m, espace m libre; **2 metre ~** espace m de 2 mètres; **how much ~ is there between my car and yours?** je suis à combien de votre voiture?

c [of cheque] compensation f; (Customs) dédouanement m; (= permission etc) autorisation f, permis m (de publier etc); (Naut) **~ outwards/inwards** permis m de sortie/d'entrée; **the dispatch was sent to the Foreign Office for ~** la dépêche a été soumise au ministère des Affaires étrangères pour contrôle; (Aviat) **to give (sb) ~ for takeoff** donner (à qn) l'autorisation de décoller
d (Ftbl) dégagement m
2 COMP ► **clearance certificate** N (Naut) congé m de navigation, lettre f de mer ► **clearance sale** N (Comm) liquidation f

clearing ['klɪərɪŋ] **1** N **a** (in forest) clairière f
b (NonC) [of liquid] clarification f; [of wine] collage m; (Med) [of bowels] purge f; [of blood] dépuration f **c** (NonC = tidying, unblocking) [of room, cupboard, passage] dégagement m, désencombrement m; [of litter, objects, rubbish] enlèvement m; [of land] défrichement m; [of pipe etc] débouchage m; [of road] dégagement m, déblaiement m; [of room, court] évacuation f **d** (Jur) [of accused] disculpation f **e** (Fin) [of cheque] compensation f; [of account] liquidation f; [of debt] acquittement m **2** COMP ► **clearing bank** N (Brit) banque f (appartenant à une chambre de compensation) ► **clearing house** N (Banking) chambre f de compensation; (fig: for documents etc) bureau m central

▼ **clearly** ['klɪəlɪ] ADV **a** (= lucidly) [define, explain, express o.s., think, remember, understand] clairement **b** (= explicitly) [forbidden] explicitement **c** (= distinctly) [see] clairement, nettement; [speak] distinctement; [hear] distinctement, nettement; [label, write] clairement, lisiblement; [visible] bien, nettement; [audible] nettement **d** (= obviously) [intelligent, worried, upset, overjoyed] manifestement; **he ~ believes that ...** il croit manifestement que ...; **he was ~ not expecting us** manifestement, il ne nous attendait pas; **~, we must find a solution quickly** il est évident que nous devons trouver une solution rapidement

clearness ['klɪənɪs] N **a** [of air, liquid] transparence f, limpidité f; [of glass] transparence f **b** [of sound, sight, print, thought etc] clarté f, netteté f

clearway ['klɪəweɪ] N (Brit) route f à stationnement interdit

cleat [kli:t] N (Carpentry) tasseau m; (Naut) taquet m; (on shoe) clou m

cleavage ['kli:vɪdʒ] N (lit) (Chem, Geol) clivage m; (Bio) [of cell] division f; (between breasts) décolleté m; (fig) [of opinion] division f, clivage m

cleave¹ [kli:v] (pret **cleft** or **clove**, ptp **cleft** or **cloven**) **1** VT (gen liter) fendre; (Chem, Geol) cliver; (Bio, also fig) diviser **2** VI se fendre; (Chem, Geol) se cliver; (Bio) se diviser; **to ~ through the waves** fendre les vagues

cleave² [kli:v] (pret, ptp **cleaved**) VI (liter) (= stick) coller, adhérer (**to** à); (fig) s'attacher, rester attaché or fidèle (**to** à)

cleaver ['kli:vər] N fendoir m, couperet m

clef [klef] N (Mus) clé or clef f (signe) → bass¹, treble

cleft [kleft] **1** VB pt, ptp of **cleave¹** **2** ADJ fendu; [stick] fourchu; (fig) **to be in a ~ stick** se trouver or être dans une impasse; (Anat) **~ palate** palais m fendu; **a ~ chin** un menton creusé d'un sillon vertical; (Gram) **~ sentence** phrase f clivée **3** N (in rock) crevasse f, fissure f; (in chin) sillon m

cleg [kleg] N taon m

clematis ['klemətɪs] N clématite f

clemency ['klemənsɪ] N [of person] clémence f (**towards** envers); [of weather etc] douceur f, clémence f

clement ['klemənt] ADJ [person] clément (**towards** envers); [weather] doux (douce f), clément

► LANGUAGE IN USE: **clearly** 26.3

clementine ['klemǝntaɪn] N clémentine f

clench [klenʃ] 1 VT a to ~ sth (in one's hands) empoigner or serrer qch dans ses mains; to ~ one's fists/teeth serrer les poings/les dents b = clinch 1 2 N = clinch 3a

Cleopatra [,kliːǝ'pætrǝ] 1 N Cléopâtre f 2 COMP ► **Cleopatra's needle** N l'obélisque m de Cléopâtre

clerestory ['klɪǝstɔːrɪ] N (Archit) claire-voie f, clair-étage m

clergy ['klɜːdʒɪ] COLLECTIVE N (membres mpl du) clergé m

clergyman ['klɜːdʒɪmǝn] N ecclésiastique m; (Protestant) pasteur m; (Roman Catholic) prêtre m, curé m

clergywoman ['klɜːdʒɪ,wumǝn] N (pl **-women**) femme f pasteur

cleric ['klerɪk] N ecclésiastique m

clerical ['klerɪkǝl] 1 ADJ a (Comm, Fin, Jur) [job, work, staff] de bureau; [position, skills] administratif; ~ **error** (in book-keeping) erreur f d'écriture; (in documentation) erreur f administrative; ~ **worker** employé(e) m(f) de bureau b (Rel) [life, training] clérical 2 COMP ► **clerical collar** N col m d'ecclésiastique

clericalism ['klerɪkǝlɪzǝm] N cléricalisme m

clerihew ['klerɪhjuː] N petit poème m humoristique (pseudo-biographique)

clerk [klɑːk, (US) klɜːk] 1 N a (in office) employé(e) m(f) de bureau; (Jur) clerc m; **bank ~** employé(e) m(f) de banque; (in hotel) **desk ~** réceptionniste m(f); (Jur) **Clerk of the Court** greffier m (du tribunal) → **head, town** b †† (Rel) ecclésiastique m; (= scholar) clerc† m, savant m c (US = shop assistant) vendeur m, -euse f d (Brit Constr) ~ **of works** conducteur m de travaux 2 VI a (US Jur) **to ~ for a judge** être assistant(e) m(f) stagiaire d'un juge b (US Comm) travailler comme vendeur/vendeuse

clerkship ['klɑːkʃɪp, (US) 'klɜːrkʃɪp] N fonctions fpl d'employé de bureau; (Med) stage m

clever ['klevǝr] 1 ADJ a (= intelligent) [person, face, eyes] intelligent; ~ **girl!** quelle fille intelligente tu fais! b (= skilful) [craftsman] habile, adroit; [sportsman] habile; [piece of work] astucieux, ingénieux; (Sport) [shot, pass, header] bien pensé; ~ **at doing sth** habile à faire qch, doué pour faire qch; ~ **with one's hands** habile or adroit de ses mains c (= astute) [plan, trick, idea, accounting, advertising, explanation] astucieux; [technique] astucieux, ingénieux; [invention, gadget, design, approach] ingénieux; [person] malin (-igne f); [book, film] astucieusement construit; [joke] fin; (Brit pej) ~ **clogs** or **Dick*** petit malin, petite maligne; **don't be** or **get ~ with me!** ne fais pas le malin avec moi! → **half** 2 COMP ► **clever-clever*** ADJ (pej) un peu trop futé

cleverly ['klevǝlɪ] ADV (with vb) a (= intelligently) intelligemment b (= skilfully) ingénieusement; ~ **designed** d'une conception ingénieuse c (often pej = astutely) [plan, disguise] astucieusement; [construct] d'une façon ingénieuse

cleverness ['klevǝnɪs] N (NonC) a (= intelligence) [of person, face, eyes] intelligence f b (= skill) [of craftsman] habileté f, adresse f (at sth à qch); [of sportsman] habileté f; [of piece of work] ingéniosité f; (Sport) [of shot, pass, header] intelligence f c (= astuteness) [of person, plan, trick, accounting, advertising] astuce f; [of technique, idea, invention, design, solution, scheme, script] ingéniosité f; [of book, film, argument, story] construction f astucieuse; [of joke] finesse f

clew [kluː] N (US) = **clue**

cliché ['kliːʃeɪ] N cliché m, expression f or phrase f toute faite

clichéd ['kliːʃeɪd] ADJ rebattu, galvaudé

click [klɪk] 1 N déclic m, petit bruit m sec; [of tongue] claquement m; [of wheel] cliquet m; (Phon) clic m 2 VI a faire un bruit sec, cliqueter; **the door ~ed shut** la porte s'est refermée avec un déclic; **the part ~ed into place** la pièce s'est mise en place or s'est enclenchée avec un déclic; (fig) **suddenly it ~ed*** tout à coup ça a fait tilt*; (fig) **to ~ with sb*** (= hit it off) se découvrir des atomes crochus* avec qn b (* = be successful) [product, invention] bien marcher 3 VT **to ~ one's heels** claquer des talons; **to ~ one's tongue** faire claquer sa langue; **she ~ed the shelf back into place** elle a remis l'étagère en place avec un déclic

► **click on** VT FUS (Comput) cliquer sur

clicking ['klɪkɪŋ] N cliquetis m

client ['klaɪǝnt] 1 N client(e) m(f) 2 COMP ► **client state** N (Pol) pays m satellite

clientele [,kliːɑːn'tel] N (Comm) clientèle f; (Theat) habitués mpl

cliff [klɪf] 1 N [of seashore] falaise f; [of mountains] escarpement m; (Climbing) à-pic m 2 COMP ► **cliff-dweller** N (lit) troglodyte mf; (US) habitant(e) m(f) de gratte-ciel

cliffhanger* ['klɪf,hæŋǝr] N récit m (or situation f etc) à suspense; (= moment of suspense) moment m d'angoisse

cliffhanging* ['klɪf,hæŋɪŋ] ADJ tendu, à suspense; ~ **vote*** vote m à suspense

clifftop ['klɪftɒp] 1 N **a ~** le sommet d'une falaise 2 ADJ [walk, setting] sur le sommet d'une falaise

climacteric [klaɪ'mæktǝrɪk] 1 N climatère m; (esp US Med) ménopause f 2 ADJ climatérique; (fig) crucial, dangereux

climactic [klaɪ'mæktɪk] ADJ à son or au point culminant, à son apogée

climate ['klaɪmɪt] N (Met, fig) climat m; **the ~ of opinion** (les courants mpl de) l'opinion f

climatic [klaɪ'mætɪk] ADJ climatique

climatologist [,klaɪmǝ'tɒlǝdʒɪst] N climatologue mf, climatologiste mf

climatology [,klaɪmǝ'tɒlǝdʒɪ] N climatologie f

climax ['klaɪmæks] 1 N point m culminant, apogée m, paroxysme m; (= orgasm) orgasme m; (Rhetoric) gradation f; **the ~ of his political career** l'apogée m de sa vie politique; **this brought matters to a ~** cela a porté l'affaire à son paroxysme; **to come to a ~** atteindre son paroxysme; **to work up to a ~** [story, events] atteindre un paroxysme; [orator] parachever son discours 2 VT pousser or porter à son paroxysme or au paroxysme 3 VI atteindre son or le paroxysme; (= orgasm) jouir

climb [klaɪm] 1 VT (also ~ **up**) [+ stairs, steps, slope] monter, grimper; [+ hill] grimper, escalader; [+ tree] grimper dans or sur; [+ ladder] grimper or monter sur or à; [+ rope] monter à; [+ cliff, wall] escalader; [+ mountain] gravir, faire l'ascension de; (fig) **the record ~ed three places** le disque a gagné trois places au hitparade); (St Ex) **shares ~ed three points** les actions ont augmenté de trois points; (fig) **to be ~ing the wall** être dingue

2 VI a (lit, fig: also ~ **up**) monter, grimper; [aircraft, rocket] monter, prendre de l'altitude; [sun] monter; [prices, shares, costs] augmenter; (Sport) escalader, grimper; (also **rock-~**) varapper

b **to ~ down a tree** descendre d'un arbre; **to ~ down a mountain** descendre d'une montagne, effectuer la descente d'une montagne; **to ~ over a wall/an obstacle** escalader un mur/un obstacle; **to ~ into an aircraft/a boat** monter or grimper à bord d'un avion/bateau; **to ~ out of a hole** se hisser hors d'un trou; (fig) **to ~ to power** s'élever (jusqu')au pouvoir

3 N [of hill] montée f, côte f; (Climbing) ascension f; [of aircraft] montée f, ascension f

4 COMP ► **climb-down*** N reculade f, dérobade f

► **climb down** 1 VI a (lit: from tree, wall) descendre; (Climbing) descendre, effectuer une descente b (* = abandon one's position) en rabattre 2 ~**-down*** N → **climb**

► **climb up** → **climb** 1, 2a

climber ['klaɪmǝr] N (= person) grimpeur m, -euse f; (= mountaineer) alpiniste mf, ascensionniste mf; (fig pej: also **social ~**) arriviste mf (pej); (= plant) plante f grimpante; (also **rock-~**) varappeur m, -euse f

climbing ['klaɪmɪŋ] 1 ADJ [person, bird] grimpeur; (Bot) grimpant; (Astron, Aviat) ascendant 2 N montée f, escalade f; (Sport) alpinisme m; (also **rock-~**) varappe f; (fig pej: also **social ~**) arrivisme m (pej); **to go ~** (= mountaineering) faire de l'alpinisme; (= rock-climbing) faire de la varappe 3 COMP ► **climbing boot** N chaussure f de montagne ► **climbing frame** N cage f à poules ► **climbing irons** NPL crampons mpl ► **climbing speed** N (Aviat) vitesse f ascensionnelle

clime [klaɪm] N (liter) (= climate) climat m; (= country) contrée f; **a summer ~** ◊ **summer ~s** un climat plus ensoleillé

clinch [klɪntʃ] 1 VT (also **clench**) (Tech) [+ nail, rivet] river; (Naut) étalinguer; (fig) [+ argument] mettre un point final à; [+ bargain] conclure; **to ~ the deal** conclure l'affaire; **to ~ an agreement** sceller un pacte; **that ~es it** comme ça c'est réglé, ça coupe court à tout* 2 VI (Boxing) combattre corps à corps 3 N a (Tech) rivetage m; (Naut) étalingure f b (Boxing) corps-à-corps m; **to get into a ~** s'accrocher* c (* = embrace) étreinte f; **in a ~** enlacés

clincher* ['klɪntʃǝr] ADJ argument m décisif

clinching ['klɪntʃɪŋ] ADJ convaincant, concluant

cline [klaɪn] N cline m

cling [klɪŋ] (pret, ptp **clung**) VI a (= hold tight) se cramponner, s'accrocher (**to** à); **to ~ together** ◊ **to ~ to one another** se tenir étroitement enlacés, se cramponner l'un à l'autre; (fig) **despite the opposition of all he clung to his opinion** il s'est cramponné à or a maintenu son opinion envers et contre tous; (fig) **to ~ to a belief** se raccrocher à une croyance; **to ~ to the belief that ...** se raccrocher à la notion que ... b (= stick) adhérer, (se) coller (**to** à); [clothes] coller; **to ~ together** ◊ **to ~ to one another** rester or être collés l'un à l'autre

Clingfilm®, **clingfilm** ['klɪŋfɪlm] N film m alimentaire (transparent), Scellofrais® m

clinging ['klɪŋɪŋ] 1 ADJ a (pej = overdependent) [person] collant, crampon inv* b [material, garment] collant, moulant c [smell] tenace 2 COMP ► **clinging vine** N (US) pot m de colle*

clingwrap ['klɪŋræp] N = **Clingfilm**

clingy* ['klɪŋɪ] ADJ a (pej = overdependent) [person] collant, crampon inv* b [material, garment] collant, moulant

clinic ['klɪnɪk] N (= private nursing home, consultant's teaching session) clinique f; (= health centre) centre m médicosocial or d'hygiène sociale; (also **outpatients' ~**) service m de consultation (externe), dispensaire m (municipal)

clinical ['klɪnɪkǝl] 1 ADJ a (Med) [test, research, practice, medicine] clinique; [waste] médical b (fig pej = dispassionate) [person, attitude, tone, term] froidement objectif; [detachment] froid c (pej = austere) [room, building, decor, style] austère, froid; [colour] froid 2 COMP ► **clinical depression** N dépression f (nerveuse) ► **clinical psychologist** N psychologue mf clinicien(ne) ► **clinical psychology** N psychologie f clinique ► **clinical thermometer** N thermomètre m médical

clinically ['klɪnɪkəlɪ] ADV [a] (Med) [prove] cliniquement; **~ dead** cliniquement mort; **to be ~ insane** être fou au sens médical du terme, être un malade mental; **to be ~ depressed** souffrir de dépression (nerveuse), faire de la dépression (nerveuse) [b] (= dispassionately) [say] d'un ton froidement objectif, avec une froide objectivité

clinician [klɪ'nɪʃən] N clinicien(ne) m(f)

clink[1] [klɪŋk] [1] VT faire tinter or résonner or sonner; **to ~ glasses with sb** trinquer avec qn [2] VI tinter, résonner [3] N tintement m (de verres etc)

clink[2]*: [klɪŋk] N taule*: f, bloc* m; **in ~** en taule*:

clinker ['klɪŋkəʳ] [1] N [a] (= burnt out coal) mâchefer m, scories fpl [b] (= paving material) brique f vitrifiée [c] (US*: = mistake) (Mus) pavé m; (gen) couac m; (= failed film, play etc) four* m, bide* m [2] COMP ▸ **clinker-built** ADJ (Naut) (bordé) à clins

clip[1] [klɪp] [1] N (for papers) trombone m; (for tube) collier m, bague f; (also **cartridge ~**) chargeur m; (= brooch) clip m [2] VT [a] [+ papers] attacher (avec un trombone); **to ~ a brooch on one's dress** fixer une broche sur sa robe [b] (US fig) **to ~* the customers** estamper* les clients [3] COMP ▸ **clip art** N (NonC: Comput) images fpl numériques insérables ▸ **clip-clop** N the **~-clop of hooves** les claquements mpl de sabots ▸ **clip frame** N sous-verre m ▸ **clip-on** ADJ avec clip; **~-on sunglasses** lunettes de soleil que l'on fixe sur ses lunettes de vue

▸**clip on** [1] VT SEP [+ brooch] fixer; [+ document etc] attacher (avec un trombone) [2] **~-on** ADJ → **clip**[1]

▸**clip together** VT SEP attacher

clip[2] [klɪp] [1] VT [a] (= cut, snip) couper (avec des ciseaux); [+ hedge] tailler; [+ sheep, dog] tondre; [+ ticket] poinçonner; [+ article from newspaper] découper; [+ hair] couper; [+ wings] rogner, couper; (fig) **to ~ sb's wings** rogner les ailes à qn [b] (* = hit) donner une baffe à*; (= collide with) accrocher; **I ~ped him on the jaw*** je lui ai envoyé le poing dans la mâchoire*; **to ~ sb's heels** cogner dans les pieds de qn [c] (= reduce time) **to ~ a few seconds off a record** améliorer un record de quelques secondes [2] N [a] **to give sth a ~ to clip sth**; → **1a** [b] (Cine, Rad) court extrait m; (TV) clip m [c] (* = blow) taloche* f, marron*: m; **to give sb a ~ round the ear** filer une claque à qn*; [d] (US) **at a ~** à toute vitesse [3] COMP ▸ **clip joint*** N (pej) boîte f où l'on se fait tondre or fusiller*; **that's a real ~ joint** c'est vraiment le coup de fusil dans cette boîte*

clipboard ['klɪpbɔːd] N (gen) écritoire f à pince, clipboard m; (Comput) bloc-notes m

clipped [klɪpt] ADJ [tone, voice] sec (sèche f); **he has a ~ way of speaking** il avale ses mots or les syllabes (en parlant); (fig) **in a ~ voice** d'un ton sec

clipper ['klɪpəʳ] [1] N (Aviat, Naut) clipper m [2] **clippers** NPL (= tool) tondeuse f → **hair, hedge, nail**

clippie *[: ['klɪpɪ] N (Brit = conductress) receveuse f

clipping ['klɪpɪŋ] N [a] [of newspaper etc] coupure f de presse or de journal [b] **~s** [of grass, hedge] chutes fpl; [of nails] bouts mpl d'ongles (qu'on a coupés)

clique [kliːk] N (pej) coterie f (pej), clique* f

cliquey ['kliːkɪ], **cliquish** ['kliːkɪʃ] ADJ (pej) exclusif, qui a l'esprit de clique or de chapelle

cliquishness ['kliːkɪʃnɪs] N (pej) esprit m de clique or de chapelle

clitoral ['klɪtərəl] ADJ clitoridien

clitoridectomy [ˌklɪtərɪ'dektəmɪ] N clitoridectomie f

clitoris ['klɪtərɪs] N clitoris m

Cllr N (Brit) ABBR = **Councillor**

cloak [kləʊk] [1] N grande cape f; [of shepherd etc] houppelande f; (fig) **as a ~ for sth** pour cacher or masquer qch; **a ~ of mist** une nappe de brouillard; **under the ~ of darkness** sous le manteau or le voile de la nuit [2] VT (fig) masquer, cacher; (= dress) revêtir d'un manteau; (fig) **~ed with respectability/mystery** empreint de respectabilité/de mystère [3] COMP ▸ **cloak-and-dagger** ADJ clandestin; **the ~-and-dagger boys*** les membres mpl du service secret, les barbouzes*: fpl; **a ~-and-dagger story** un roman d'espionnage

cloakroom ['kləʊkrʊm] [1] N [a] [of coats etc] vestiaire m; (Brit = left luggage) consigne f; **to put** or **leave in the ~** [+ clothes] mettre au or déposer au vestiaire; [+ luggage] mettre à la consigne [b] (Brit = toilet) (public) toilettes fpl; (in house) cabinets mpl [2] COMP ▸ **cloakroom attendant** N (in theatre) préposé(e) m(f) au vestiaire ▸ **cloakroom ticket** N (for clothes) numéro m de vestiaire; (for luggage) bulletin m de consigne

clobber* ['klɒbəʳ] [1] N (NonC: Brit = belongings) barda* m [2] VT (= hit) tabasser*: ; (fig) frapper de plein fouet; (fig) **to be ~ed by the rise in interest rates** être mis à mal par la hausse des taux d'intérêt

cloche [klɒʃ] N (Agr, Dress) cloche f

clock [klɒk] [1] N [a] (large) horloge f; (smaller) pendule f; **it's midday by the church ~** il est midi à l'horloge de or au clocher de l'église; **it lasted two hours by the ~** cela a duré deux heures d'horloge; **to keep one's eyes on the ~** surveiller l'heure; **they're watching the premises round the ~** ils surveillent les locaux vingt-quatre heures sur vingt-quatre; **to work round the ~** travailler vingt-quatre heures d'affilée; (fig) travailler sans relâche; **to work against the ~** travailler contre la montre; **to do sth by the ~** or **according to the ~** faire qch en respectant l'horaire; **to put the ~(s) back/forward** retarder/avancer l'horloge; (fig) **to put** or **turn the ~ back** revenir en arrière; **you can't put the ~ back** ce qui est fait est fait; **this decision will put the ~ back 50 years** cette décision va nous ramener 50 ans en arrière → **grandfather, o'clock, sleep** [b] (* = meter) [of taxi] compteur m, taximètre m; (= milometer) ≈ compteur m (kilométrique); (Aut) **there were 50,000 miles on the ~** la voiture avait 80 000 kilomètres au compteur [c] (Comput) horloge f, base f de temps [2] VT [a] (Sport) [+ runner] chronométrer; **he ~ed four minutes for the 1500 metres** il a fait le 1500 mètres en quatre minutes [b] (Brit = hit) **he ~ed him one*** il lui a collé un pain*: or un marron*: [c] (Brit* = notice) voir [d] (Aut) **to ~ a car*** trafiquer* le compteur d'une voiture [3] COMP ▸ **clock card** N (Ind) carte f de pointage ▸ **clock-golf** N jeu m de l'horloge ▸ **clock-radio** N radio-réveil m ▸ **clock repairer** N horloger m réparateur ▸ **clock-tower** N clocher m ▸ **clock-watcher** N (pej) **he's a terrible ~-watcher** il ne fait que guetter l'heure de sortie, il a les yeux fixés sur la pendule ▸ **clock-watching** N **to be guilty of ~-watching** passer son temps à surveiller les aiguilles de la pendule

▸**clock in** [1] VI (Ind) pointer (à l'arrivée) [2] VT SEP **he ~ed in three hours' work** il a fait trois heures de travail

▸**clock off** VI (Ind) pointer (à la sortie)

▸**clock on** VI = **clock in 1**

▸**clock out** VI = **clock off**

▸**clock up** VT SEP [a] = **clock in 2** [b] (Aut) **he ~ed up 250 miles** il a fait 250 milles au compteur

clockface ['klɒkfeɪs] N cadran m (d'une horloge)

---

clockmaker ['klɒk,meɪkəʳ] N horloger m, -ère f

clockwise ['klɒkwaɪz] ADV, ADJ dans le sens des aiguilles d'une montre

clockwork ['klɒkwɜːk] [1] N (= mechanism) [of clock] mouvement m (d'horloge); [of toy etc] mécanisme m, rouages mpl; (fig) **to go** or **run like ~** aller comme sur des roulettes → **regular** [2] COMP [toy, train, car] mécanique; (fig) précis, régulier ▸ **clockwork precision** N with **~ precision** avec la précision d'une horloge

clod [klɒd] N [a] [of earth etc] motte f (de terre etc) [b] (* pej) balourd(e)* m(f)

clodhopper* ['klɒd,hɒpəʳ] N (pej) (= person) lourdingue* m; (= shoe) godillot* m, croquenot* m

clodhopping* ['klɒd,hɒpɪŋ] ADJ [person] lourdingue*; **~ shoes/boots** godillots* mpl, croquenots* mpl

clog [klɒg] [1] N (= shoe) (wooden) sabot m; (with wooden soles) socque m, galoche†f [2] VT (also **~ up**) [+ pores, arteries, lungs] obstruer; [+ pipe] boucher, encrasser; [+ streets, system] congestionner; **~ged with traffic** congestionné, embouteillé [3] VI (also **~ up**) [pipe etc] se boucher, s'encrasser

cloister ['klɔɪstəʳ] [1] N (Archit, Rel) cloître m [2] VT (Rel) cloîtrer; (fig) **to lead a ~ed life** mener une vie monacale or de cloître

clone [kləʊn] [1] N (also Comput) clone m [2] VT cloner

cloning ['kləʊnɪŋ] N clonage m

clonk [klɒnk] [1] N (= sound) bruit m sourd [2] VI (= make sound) émettre un bruit sourd

close[1] [kləʊs] [1] ADJ [a] (= near) proche; **an agreement seems ~** il semble qu'on s'approche d'un accord; **in ~ proximity to sb/sth** dans le voisinage immédiat de qn/qch; **at ~ quarters** très près; **to shoot sb at ~ range** tirer sur qn à bout portant; (lit) **to have a ~ shave** se (faire) raser de près; (fig) **it was a ~ shave*** or **thing*** or **call*** je l'ai (or il l'a etc) échappé belle; **the house is ~ to the shops** la maison est près or proche des magasins; **his birthday is ~ to mine** son anniversaire est proche du mien; **she was very ~ to her brother** (in age) il y avait très peu de différence d'âge entre son frère et elle; (in friendship) elle était très proche de son frère → **c**; **to be ~ to success** être près de réussir; **to be very ~ to success** être à deux doigts de réussir; **to be ~ to starvation** être au bord de la famine; **to be ~ to tears** être au bord des larmes; **to be ~ to doing sth** être à deux doigts de faire qch → **bone, comfort, home** [b] (= similar) **~ to** proche de; **it was something ~ to obsession** cela tenait de l'obsession; **she felt something ~ to loathing for the man** elle éprouvait un sentiment proche de la haine pour cet homme; **she regarded him with something that was ~ to fear** elle le regardait avec une sorte de peur; **her desire was ~r to passion than love** son désir tenait plus de la passion que de l'amour [c] (= intimate) [friend, relative, partner, adviser] proche; [relationship] profond; [cooperation, ties, links, connection] étroit; [friendship] intime; [resemblance] fort; **she is very ~ to her brother** elle est très proche de son frère; **we are very ~** nous sommes très proches; **a ~ circle of friends** un cercle d'amis proches; **to be in/keep in ~ contact with sb** être/rester en contact étroit avec qn; **to be/feel ~ to sb** être/se sentir proche de qn; **a source ~ to the president** une source proche du président [d] (= careful) [examination, inspection, study] attentif; [questioning, reasoning] serré; [investigation, enquiry, checking] minutieux; [translation] fidèle; [account] détaillé; [argument] précis; **to pay ~ attention to sth** faire bien attention à qch; **the children were paying ~ attention to the teacher** les enfants écoutaient le professeur avec beaucoup

d'attention; **to be (kept) in ~ confinement** être sous bonne garde; **(up)on ~r inspection** *or* **examination** après un examen plus minutieux; **to have a ~r look at sth** regarder qch de plus près; **to keep sb/sth under ~ surveillance** ◊ **to keep a ~ eye** *or* **watch on sb/sth** surveiller qn/qch de près
e (= *dense*) [*handwriting, ranks*] serré; [*grain, texture*] fin; **I find it difficult to read such ~ print** j'ai du mal à lire un texte si serré; (*esp Aviat, Mil*) **in ~ formation** *or* **order** en formation serrée
f (= *decided by a small amount*) [*election, contest, race, finish*] serré
g (= *stuffy*) [*room*] mal aéré; [*atmosphere, air*] lourd; **it's very ~ in here** ça manque d'air ici; (*Met*) **it's very ~ today** il fait très lourd aujourd'hui
h (= *secretive*) **to be ~ (about sth)** [*person*] rester secret (quant à qch)
i (*Ling*) [*vowel*] fermé
2 ADV **a** **~ to sb/sth** près de qn/qch; **sit ~ up to me** assieds-toi tout près de moi; **~ against the wall** tout contre le mur; **~ behind (sb/sth)** juste derrière (qn/qch); **~ behind me** il me suivait de près; **~ by (sb/sth)** tout près (de qn/qch); **to get ~ (to sb/sth)** s'approcher (de qn/qch); **to get ~r (to sb/sth)** se rapprocher (de qn/qch); **to be ~ at hand** *or* **to hand** [*object*] être à portée de main; [*place*] être à proximité; [*date, event*] être très proche; **to hold sb ~** serrer qn dans ses bras; **shut ~** ◊ **~ shut** hermétiquement fermé *or* clos; **their two heads were ~ together** leurs deux têtes étaient tout près l'une de l'autre; **the tables were pushed ~ together** on a rapproché les tables; **to come ~r together** se rapprocher; **to look at sth ~ to/up** regarder qch de très près
b **~ to** *or* **on** (= *almost*) près de; **~ to** *or* **on ten thousand pounds** près de dix mille livres; **he is ~ on 60** il a près de 60 ans; **it's ~ on midnight** il est près de minuit
3 N (= *enclosure*) clos *m*; [*of cathedral*] enceinte *f*; (*Scot* = *alleyway*) passage *m*, couloir *m*
4 COMP ► **close combat** N (*gen*) corps à corps *m*, close-combat *m* (*SPEC*) ► **close company** N (*Brit Fin*) société dont le nombre d'actionnaires est limité ► **close-cropped** ADJ [*hair*] (coupé) ras; [*grass*] ras ► **close-fisted** ADJ avare, grippe-sou *inv*, pingre ► **close-fitting** ADJ [*clothes*] ajusté, près du corps ► **close-grained** ADJ [*wood*] au grain serré ► **close-harmony singing** N chant *m* dans une tessiture restreinte *or* rapprochée *or* réduite ► **close-knit** ADJ (*fig*) très uni ► **close-mouthed** ADJ (*fig*) taciturne, peu bavard ► **close-run** ADJ **~-run race** course *f* très serrée; (*fig*) **it was a ~-run thing** ils sont arrivés dans un mouchoir ► **close-set** ADJ [*eyes*] rapprochés ► **close-shaven** ADJ [*person, head*] rasé de près ► **close-up** N (*Cine, TV* = *photo, shot*) gros plan *m*; **in ~-up** en gros plan

close² [kləʊz] **1** N (= *end*) fin *f*, conclusion *f*; **to come to a ~** se terminer, prendre fin; **to draw to a ~** tirer à sa fin; **to draw sth** *or* **bring sth to a ~** mettre fin à qch; (*liter*) **the ~ of (the) day** la tombée du jour; **towards the ~ of the century** vers la fin du siècle
2 VT **a** (= *shut*) fermer; [+ *eyes, door, factory, shop*] fermer; [+ *pipe, tube, opening*] boucher; [+ *road*] barrer; **road ~d to traffic** route *f* interdite à la circulation; (*fig*) **to ~ one's mind to new ideas** fermer son esprit à toute idée nouvelle → **ear¹, eye**
b (= *bring to an end*) [+ *proceedings, discussion*] mettre fin à, clore; (*Fin*) [+ *account*] arrêter, clore; [+ *bargain*] conclure; **to ~ the meeting** lever la séance
c (= *bring together*) serrer, rapprocher; **to ~ the gap between two objects** réduire l'intervalle entre deux objets; (*fig*) **to ~ the gap between ...** combler le fossé entre ...; **Brit-**

ain is closing the gap on *or* with Japan la Grande-Bretagne comble son retard sur le Japon; (*Mil, also fig*) **to ~ ranks** serrer les rangs
d (*Elec*) [+ *circuit*] fermer
3 VI **a** [*door, box, lid, drawer*] fermer, se fermer; [*museum, theatre, shop*] fermer; **the door ~d** la porte s'est fermée; **the door/box ~s badly** la porte/la boîte ferme mal; **the shop ~s 6 o'clock** le magasin ferme à 18 heures; **the shop ~s on Sundays** le magasin est fermé le dimanche; **his eyes ~d** ses yeux se fermèrent; **his fingers ~d around the pencil** ses doigts se sont refermés sur le crayon
b (= *end*) [*session*] se terminer, prendre fin; [*speaker*] terminer, finir; **the meeting ~d abruptly** la séance a pris fin *or* s'est terminée brusquement; **he ~d with an appeal to their generosity** il a terminé par un appel à leur générosité; (*St Ex*) **shares ~d at 120p** les actions étaient cotées à *or* valaient 120 pence en clôture
4 COMP ► **close-down** N [*of shop, business etc*] fermeture *f* (définitive); (*Brit Rad, TV*) fin *f* des émissions ► **close-out sale** N (*US*) liquidation *f* avant fermeture ► **close season** N (*Brit*) (*Hunting*) période *f* de fermeture de la chasse; (*Fishing*) période *f* de fermeture de la pêche; (*Ftbl*) intersaison *f*
► **close down 1** VI [*business, shop*] fermer (définitivement); (*Brit Rad, TV*) terminer les émissions **2** VT SEP [+ *shop, business*] fermer (définitivement) **3** **~-down** N → **close²**
► **close in 1** VI [*hunters etc*] se rapprocher, approcher; [*evening, darkness, night*] tomber; [*fog*] descendre; **the days are closing in** les jours raccourcissent (de plus en plus); **to ~ in on sb** (= *approach*) s'approcher *or* se rapprocher de qn; (*in race, pursuit*) rattraper; **the police are closing in on the killer** (= *approaching*) la police resserre son étau autour du meurtrier; (*fig* = *nearer to finding*) le filet de la police se resserre autour du meurtrier **2** VT SEP clôturer, enclore
► **close off** VT SEP [+ *room*] condamner; [+ *road etc*] barrer
► **close on** VT FUS **a** (= *get nearer to: in race, achievement etc*) rattraper **b** (*US*) = **close in on**; → **close in 1**
► **close out** VT SEP (*US Comm*) [+ *stock*] liquider (avant fermeture)
► **close up 1** VI [*people in line etc*] se rapprocher, se serrer; (*Mil*) serrer les rangs; [*wound*] se refermer **2** VT SEP [+ *house, shop*] fermer (complètement); [+ *pipe, tube, opening*] fermer, obturer, boucher; [+ *wound*] refermer, recoudre
► **close with** VT FUS **a** (= *strike bargain with*) conclure un marché avec, tomber d'accord avec **b** (= *agree to*) [+ *offer, conditions*] accepter

closed [kləʊzd] **1** ADJ [*door, eyes*] fermé, clos; [*road*] barré; [*pipe, opening etc*] bouché, obturé; [*class, economy*] fermé; (*Ling*) [*syllable*] couvert; (*notice*) "**~**" (*gen*) « fermé »; (*Theat*) « relâche »; **the shop is ~ (now)** le magasin est fermé (maintenant); **the shop is ~ on Sundays** le magasin ferme le dimanche; (*lit, fig*) **to find the door ~** trouver porte close; **to have a ~ mind** avoir l'esprit étroit; (*Jur*) **~ session** huis *m* clos; **maths is a ~ book to me*** je ne comprends rien aux maths; (*fig*) **behind ~ doors** à l'abri des indiscrets; (*US*) **~ staff hospital** hôpital où des médecins agréés peuvent traiter leurs propres malades
2 COMP ► **closed-circuit television** N télévision *f* en circuit fermé ► **closed company** N (*Brit Fin*) société dont le nombre d'actionnaires est limité ► **closed-door** ADJ [*meeting, session*] à huis clos ► **closed primary** N (*US Pol*) élection primaire réservée aux membres d'un parti ► **closed season** N (*US*) (*Hunting*) période *f* de fermeture de la chasse; (*Fishing*) période *f* de fermeture de la pêche ► **closed set** N (*Math*) ensemble *m* fermé

► **closed shop** N *atelier or organisation qui n'admet que des travailleurs syndiqués*; (*Ind*) **the unions insisted on a ~-shop policy** les syndicats ont exigé l'exclusion des travailleurs non syndiqués

closely ['kləʊslɪ] ADV **a** (= *strongly*) [*linked, connected, associated*] étroitement; [*resemble*] beaucoup; **we are ~ related** nous sommes proches parents; **fruits ~ related to the orange** des fruits *mpl* très proches de l'orange; **~ identified with sth** étroitement associé à qch; **~ involved with a campaign/project** étroitement associé à une campagne/un projet; (*romantically*) **to become ~ involved with sb** se lier intimement à qn; **a ~ knit community** une communauté très unie
b (= *carefully*) [*look at, study*] de près; [*listen*] attentivement; **to monitor sth ~** suivre qch de près; **to question sb ~** presser qn de questions; **a ~ guarded secret/prisoner** un secret/prisonnier bien gardé
c (= *tightly*) **he held her ~ to him** il la serrait *or* la tenait serrée (tout) contre lui; **they crowded more ~ around the television** ils se sont pressés davantage autour de la télévision; **~ followed by sb/sth** suivi de près par qn/qch; **to stick ~ to the subject** rester près du sujet
d (= *densely*) **~ typed** aux caractères serrés; **~ written** à l'écriture serrée
e (= *intimately*) **to work ~ with sb** travailler en étroite collaboration avec qn
f (= *keenly*) [*fought, contested*] âprement

closeness ['kləʊsnɪs] N **a** [*of cloth, weave*] texture *f* or contexture *f* serrée; [*of friendship*] solidité *f*; [*of translation, reproduction*] fidélité *f*; [*of examination, interrogation, study*] minutie *f*, rigueur *f*; [*of reasoning*] logique *f*; [*of pursuit*] vigueur *f*; [*of pursuers*] proximité *f*; **~ of blood relationship** proche degré *m* de parenté; **the ~ of the resemblance** la grande ressemblance
b (= *proximity*) proximité *f* **c** [*of weather, atmosphere*] lourdeur *f*; [*of room*] manque *m* d'air **d** (= *stinginess*) avarice *f*

closet ['klɒzɪt] **1** N **a** (*US* = *cupboard*) armoire *f*, placard *m*; (*for hanging clothes*) penderie *f*
b (*esp US* = *small room*) cabinet *m* (de travail), (*petit*) bureau *m* **c** (*also* **water ~**) cabinets *mpl*, waters *mpl* **d** (*fig*) **to come out of the ~*** se montrer au grand jour **2** VT (*gen pass*) enfermer (*dans un cabinet de travail etc*); **he was ~ed with his father for several hours** son père et lui sont restés enfermés plusieurs heures à discuter; **she ~ed herself (away) in her bedroom** elle s'est cloîtrée dans sa chambre **3** ADJ (* *fig* = *secret*) honteux, qui n'ose pas s'avouer; **a ~ homosexual** un(e) homosexuel(le) refoulé(e) *or* qui ne s'assume pas; **he's a ~ fascist** c'est un fasciste refoulé *or* un crypto-fasciste

closing ['kləʊzɪŋ] **1** N (*NonC*) [*of factory, house, shop*] fermeture *f*; [*of meeting*] clôture *f*; (*Fin*) clôture *f* **2** ADJ **a** (= *final*) final, dernier; **~ remarks** observations *fpl* finales; **~ speech** discours *m* de clôture; (*St Ex*) **~ price** cours *m* en clôture **b** (= *concluding*) [*speech, ceremony*] de clôture; **~ date** (*for applications*) date *f* limite de dépôt; (*Fin, Jur*) date de réalisation (*d'une opération*); (*Brit*) **~ time** heure *f* de fermeture (*d'un magasin, d'un café etc*); **when is ~ time?** à quelle heure fermez-vous?; **"~ time!"** « on ferme! » → **early 3** COMP ► **closing-down sale** N (*Brit Comm*) liquidation *f* totale (*avant fermeture définitive*) ► **closing-out sale** N (*US*) = **close-out sale**; →**close²**

closure ['kləʊʒə²] N (*NonC: = act, condition*) [*of factory, business*] fermeture *f*; (*Parl*) clôture *f*; (*Parl*) **to demand the ~** demander la clôture; (*US Pol*) **~ rule** règlement *m* limitant le temps de parole → **lane**

clot [klɒt] **1** N **a** [*of blood, milk*] caillot *m*; **a ~ in the lung/on the brain** une embolie pulmonaire/cérébrale; **a ~ in the leg** une thrombose à la jambe **b** (*Brit: pej* = *person*) ballot* *m*, cruche* *f* **2** VT [+ *blood*] coaguler **3** VI [*blood*] (se) coaguler **4** COMP ► **clotted cream** N (*Brit*) sorte de crème fraîche épaisse

cloth [klɒθ] **1** **a** (*NonC*) tissu *m*, étoffe *f*; [*of linen, cotton*] toile *f*; [*of wool*] drap *m*; (*Bookbinding*) toile *f*; (*Naut*) toile *f*, voile *f*; **bound in ~** [*book*] relié (en) toile; **~ of gold** drap *m* d'or → **oilcloth** **b** (= *tablecloth*) nappe *f*; (= *duster*) chiffon *m*, linge *m* → **dishcloth**, **tea** **c** (*Rel: collective*) **the ~** le clergé; **out of respect for his ~** par respect pour son sacerdoce **2** COMP (= *made of cloth*) de or en tissu, de *or* en étoffe ► **cloth-binding** N [*of books*] reliure *f* (en) toile ► **cloth-bound** ADJ [*book*] relié (en) toile ► **cloth cap** N (*Brit*) casquette *f* (d'ouvrier) ► **cloth-eared**‡ ADJ (= *deaf*) sourdingue‡, dur de la feuille‡ ► **cloth ears**‡ N **wake up ~ ears!** hé! tu es sourd ou quoi?*

clothe [kləʊð] VT habiller, vêtir (**in, with** de); (*fig*) revêtir, couvrir (**in, with** de)

clothes [kləʊðz] **1** NPL **a** vêtements *mpl*, habits *mpl*; **with one's ~ on** (tout) habillé; **with one's ~ off** déshabillé; **to put on one's ~** s'habiller; **to take off one's ~** se déshabiller → **plain** **b** (*also* **bedclothes**) draps *mpl* et couvertures *fpl* **2** COMP ► **clothes basket** N panier *m* à linge ► **clothes brush** N brosse *f* à habits ► **clothes drier, clothes dryer** N séchoir *m* (à linge), sèche-linge *m* ► **clothes hanger** N cintre *m* ► **clothes horse** N séchoir *m* (à linge); (*fig*) mannequin *m*; (*US* = *clothes-conscious*) **she's just a ~ horse*** à part la mode, rien ne l'intéresse ► **clothes line** N corde *f* (à linge) ► **clothes moth** N mite *f* ► **clothes peg** N (*Brit*) pince *f* à linge ► **clothes pole, clothes prop** N perche *f or* support *m* pour corde à linge ► **clothes rack** N (*in shop*) portant *m* de vêtements ► **clothes rope** N clothes line ► **clothes shop** N magasin *m* de vêtements ► **clothes tree** N (*US*) portemanteau *m*

clothespin [ˈkləʊðzpɪn] N (*US, Scot*) = clothes peg; → clothesline

clothier [ˈkləʊðɪəʳ] N (= *clothes seller*) marchand *m* (de vêtements) de confection; (= *cloth dealer, maker*) drapier *m*

clothing [ˈkləʊðɪŋ] **1** N (*NonC*) **a** (= *clothes*) vêtements *mpl*; **an article of ~** un vêtement, une pièce d'habillement **b** (= *act of clothing*) habillage *f*; [*of monks, nuns*] prise *f* d'habit; (= *providing with clothes*) habillement *m* **2** COMP ► **clothing allowance** N indemnité *f* vestimentaire

cloture [ˈkləʊtʃəʳ] (*US Pol*) **1** N clôture *f* **2** COMP ► **cloture rule** N règlement *m* limitant le temps de parole

cloud [klaʊd] **1** N **a** (*in sky*) nuage *m*, nuée *f* (*liter*); [*of smoke, dust etc*] nuage *m*; [*of insects, arrows etc*] nuée *f*; [*of gas*] nappe *f*; **to have one's head in the ~s** être dans les nuages *or* dans la lune; **to be on ~ nine*** être aux anges *or* au septième ciel* ▪ (*PROV*) **every ~ has a silver lining** à quelque chose malheur est bon (*PROV*); (*fig*) **under a ~** (= *under suspicion*) en butte aux soupçons; (= *in disgrace*) en disgrâce **b** (= *cloudiness*) [*of liquid*] nuage *m*; [*of mirror*] buée *f*; [*of marble*] tache *f* noire **2** VT [+ *liquid*] rendre trouble; [+ *mirror*] embuer; [+ *prospects, career*] assombrir; [+ *reputation*] ternir; **a ~ed sky** un ciel couvert *or* nuageux; **a ~ed expression** *or* **face** un air sombre *or* attristé; **a ~ed mind** un esprit obscurci; **to ~ the issue** embrouiller les choses **3** VI (*also* **~ over**) [*sky*] se couvrir (de nuages), s'obscurcir; (*fig*) [*face, expression*] s'assombrir, se rembrunir

4 COMP ► **cloud cover** N (*Aviat, Met*) couche *f* de nuages ► **cloud-cuckoo-land** N **she lives in ~-cuckoo-land** elle plane complètement, elle n'a pas les pieds sur terre

cloudberry [ˈklaʊdbərɪ] N (= *fruit*) baie jaune, de la famille de la framboise

cloudburst [ˈklaʊdbɜːst] N grosse averse *f*

cloudiness [ˈklaʊdɪnɪs] N [*of sky*] état *m or* aspect *m* nuageux; [*of liquid*] aspect *m* trouble; [*of mirror*] buée *f*

cloudless [ˈklaʊdlɪs] ADJ (*lit, fig*) sans nuages

cloudy [ˈklaʊdɪ] ADJ [*sky*] nuageux, couvert; [*liquid*] trouble; [*diamond etc*] taché, nuageux; [*leather*] marbré; (*fig*) [*ideas*] nébuleux, embrumé (*fig*); **it was a ◊ it was a ~ day** le temps était couvert

clout [klaʊt] **1** N **a** (= *blow*) coup *m* de poing (*or* de canne *etc*) **b** (* *fig* = *influence*) influence *f*, poids *m*; **he's got** *or* **he carries** *or* **he wields a lot of ~** c'est un homme de poids **c** (*dial*) (= *cloth*) chiffon *m*; (= *garment*) vêtement *m* **2** VT [+ *object*] frapper; [+ *person*] donner un coup de poing (*or* de canne *etc*) à

clove[1] [kləʊv] N clou *m* de girofle; **oil of ~s** essence *f* de girofle; **~ of garlic** gousse *f* d'ail

clove[2] [kləʊv] **1** VB *pt of* **cleave**[1] **2** COMP ► **clove hitch** N (= *knot*) demi-clé *f*

cloven [ˈkləʊvn] **1** VB *ptp of* **cleave**[1] **2** COMP ► **cloven-footed** ADJ [*animal*] aux sabots fendus; [*devil*] aux pieds fourchus ► **cloven hoof** N [*of animal*] sabot *m* fendu; [*of devil*] pied *m* fourchu

clover [ˈkləʊvəʳ] N trèfle *m*; (*fig*) **to be in ~** être *or* vivre comme un coq en pâte → **four**

cloverleaf [ˈkləʊvəliːf] N (*Bot*) feuille *f* de trèfle; (= *road intersection*) (croisement *m* en) trèfle *m*

clown [klaʊn] **1** N [*of circus etc*] clown *m*; (*Theat*) bouffon *m*; (*fig*) (= *funny person*) clown *m*, pitre *m*; (= *idiot*) imbécile *m* **2** VI (*fig: also* **~ about, ~ around**) faire le clown *or* le pitre *or* le singe

clowning [ˈklaʊnɪŋ] N (*NonC*) pitreries *fpl*, singeries *fpl*

clownish [ˈklaʊnɪʃ] ADJ [*person, behaviour, sense of humour*] de clown

cloy [klɔɪ] **1** VT écœurer (**with** de) **2** VI perdre son charme

cloying [ˈklɔɪɪŋ] ADJ (*lit*) écœurant; (*fig*) sirupeux

cloyingly [ˈklɔɪɪŋlɪ] ADV **~ sentimental** d'une sentimentalité écœurante, dégoulinant de sentimentalité

cloze test [ˈkləʊz ˌtest] N texte *m* à trous *or* blancs

club [klʌb] **1** N **a** (*social, sports*) club *m*; **tennis ~** club *m* de tennis; **sports/drama ~** club *m* sportif/de théâtre; **yacht ~** yacht-club *m*, club *m* nautique; **literary ~** cercle *m* littéraire; **he is dining at his ~** il dîne à son club *or* à son cercle; (*fig*) **join the ~!*** tu n'es pas le *or* la seul(e)!; (*Brit*) **to be in the ~**‡ (= *pregnant*) être en cloque‡ → **benefit, youth** **b** (*also* **night ~**) boîte *f* de nuit, boîte* *f*; **the ~ scene** le monde des boîtes de nuit; **London's ~ scene** la nuit londonienne **c** (= *weapon*) (*gen*) massue *f*, gourdin *m*; (= *truncheon*) matraque *f*; (*also* **golf ~**) club *m* → **Indian** **d** (*Cards*) trèfle *m*; **~s** trèfles *mpl*; **the ace of ~s** l'as *m* de trèfle; **the six of ~s** le six de trèfle; **he played a ~** il a joué (un *or* du) trèfle; **~s are trumps** atout trèfle; **a low/high ~** un petit/gros trèfle; **have you any ~s?** avez-vous du trèfle?; **I haven't any ~s** je n'ai pas de trèfle; **three tricks in ~s** trois levées à trèfle **2** VT [+ *person*] frapper avec un gourdin *or* une massue; (*with truncheon*) matraquer; **to ~ sb with a rifle** frapper qn à coups de crosse; **they ~ the baby seals to death** ils tuent les bébés phoques à coups de massue *or* gourdin

3 VI **to go ~bing** sortir en boîte* **4** COMP [*premises, secretary etc*] du club ► **club car** N (*US Rail*) wagon-restaurant *m* ► **club chair** N fauteuil *m* club *inv* ► **club class** N classe *f* club ► **club foot** N (*pl* **club feet**) pied-bot *m* ► **club-footed** ADJ pied bot *inv* ► **club member** N membre *m* d'un club ► **club sandwich** N club sandwich *m*, ~ sandwich *m* mixte ► **club soda** N (*US*) eau *f* de seltz ► **club steak** N (*US*) (bifteck *m* pris dans la) queue *f* de filet ► **club subscription** N cotisation *f* (à un club) ► **club together** VI (*esp Brit*) se cotiser; **to ~ together to buy sth** se cotiser pour acheter qch

clubbable* [ˈklʌbəbl] ADJ sociable

clubber* [ˈklʌbəʳ] N (*Brit*) noctambule *mf*, habitué(e) *m(f)* des boîtes de nuit

clubbing* [ˈklʌbɪŋ] N (*Brit*) sorties *fpl* en boîte*

clubhouse [ˈklʌbhaʊs] N (*Sport*) pavillon *m*, club-house *m*

clubland [ˈklʌblænd] N (*NonC*) **a** (*esp Brit: for nightclubs*) le monde des boîtes de nuit **b** (*Brit: for gentlemen's clubs*) quartier des clubs chics à Londres

clubman [ˈklʌbmən] N (*pl* **-men**) membre *m* d'un club; (= *man about town*) homme *m* du monde, mondain *m*; **he is not a ~** il n'est pas homme à fréquenter les clubs *or* les cercles

clubroom [ˈklʌbruːm] N salle *f* de club *or* de réunion

cluck [klʌk] **1** VI [*hens, people*] glousser **2** N gloussement *m*

clue, clew (*US*) [kluː] N (*gen*) indication *f*, indice *m*; (*in crime*) indice *m*; (*in crossword*) définition *f*; **the killer left behind few ~s to his identity** le meurtrier n'a laissé que peu d'indices sur son identité; **he gave few ~s about when he intends to leave** il n'a pas donné beaucoup d'indications sur la date/l'heure de son départ; **have the police found any ~s as to who killed him?** la police a-t-elle trouvé des indices quant à l'identité du meurtrier?; **to find the ~ to sth** découvrir *or* trouver la clef de qch; **they may have found the ~ to the cause of this disease** ils ont peut-être découvert *or* trouvé la cause de cette maladie; **the condition of your cat's fur can be a ~ to his state of health** l'aspect du pelage de votre chat peut être une indication de son état de santé; **a person's record collection is often a big ~ to their character** la collection de disques d'une personne en dit souvent long sur son caractère; **my hesitation gave her the ~ to what I was thinking about** mon hésitation lui a permis de deviner à quoi je pensais; **the outside of the building gives little ~ to what goes on inside** il est difficile de deviner, quand on voit l'extérieur du bâtiment, ce qui s'y passe à l'intérieur; **give me a ~!** mets-moi sur la voie!; **I'll give you a ~** je vais te mettre sur la voie, je vais te donner un indice; (*fig*) **I haven't a ~!** je n'en ai pas la moindre idée!, aucune idée!*; **he hasn't a ~ what he's going to do about it*** il n'a pas la moindre idée de ce qu'il va faire à ce sujet; **you haven't got a ~ what I'm talking about, have you?*** tu n'as pas la moindre idée de ce que je raconte, n'est-ce pas?; **I haven't got a ~ where she's gone*** je n'ai pas la moindre idée de l'endroit où elle est allée, je ne sais pas du tout où elle est allée ► **clue in**‡ VT SEP mettre au courant *or* au parfum* (**on** *or* **about sth** à propos de qch) ► **clue up*** VT SEP mettre au parfum* (**on** de); **to be ~d up** être au parfum*; **to get ~d up about** *or* **on sth** se renseigner sur qch; **he's pretty ~d up on the current political situation** il est assez au courant de la situation politique actuelle

clueless* [ˈkluːlɪs] ADJ **he's ~** il ne sait rien de rien*

clump¹ [klʌmp] **1** N [of shrubs] massif m; [of trees] bouquet m; [of flowers] touffe f; (larger) massif m; [of grass] touffe f **2** VT **~ (together)** rassembler

clump² [klʌmp] **1** N (= noise) bruit m de pas lourd(s) or pesant(s) **2** VI (also **~ about**) marcher d'un pas lourd or pesant

clumpy [ˈklʌmpɪ] ADJ **~ shoes** godillots* mpl, croquenots* mpl

clumsily [ˈklʌmzɪlɪ] ADV (= inelegantly) gauchement, maladroitement; (= tactlessly) sans tact

clumsiness [ˈklʌmzɪnɪs] N [of person, action] gaucherie f, maladresse f; [of tool etc] incommodité f, caractère m peu pratique; [of shape, form] lourdeur f; (fig = tactlessness) [of person, remark] maladresse f, manque m de tact or de discrétion

clumsy [ˈklʌmzɪ] ADJ [person, action] gauche, maladroit; [tool etc] incommode, peu pratique; [shape, form] lourd, disgracieux; [painting, forgery] maladroit; (fig = tactless) [person, apology, remark] maladroit; [style] gauche, lourd

clung [klʌŋ] VB pt, ptp of **cling**

Cluniac [ˈkluːnɪæk] ADJ, N clunisien m

clunk [klʌŋk] **1** N **a** (= sound) bruit m sourd **b** (US: = stupid person) pauvre imbécile mf **2** VI (= make sound) faire un bruit sourd

clunker: [ˈklʌŋkər] N (US = old car) guimbarde* f

clunky [ˈklʌŋkɪ] ADJ [vehicle] bringuebalant; **a ~ old car** une vieille guimbarde; **~ shoes** godillots* mpl

cluster [ˈklʌstər] **1** N [of flowers, blossom, fruit] grappe f; [of bananas] régime m; [of trees] bouquet m; [of bees] essaim m; [of people] (petit) groupe m, rassemblement m; [of houses, islands] groupe m; [of stars] amas m; (Ling) groupe m, agglomérat m; **a sapphire set in a ~ of diamonds** un saphir entouré de brillants **2** VI [people] se rassembler, se grouper (**around** autour de); [flowers, blossom, fruit] être rassemblé (en grappe or en bouquet) (**around** autour de) **3** COMP ► **cluster bomb** N bombe f à fragmentation ► **cluster pack** N (Comm) emballage m groupé, pack m

clutch [klʌtʃ] **1** N **a** (= action) étreinte f, prise f **b** (Aut) embrayage m; (also **~ pedal**) pédale f d'embrayage; **to let in the ~** embrayer; **to let out the ~** débrayer; **~ (linkage or pedal) play** garde f d'embrayage **c** [of chickens, eggs] couvée f; (fig) **a ~ of** [+ prizes etc] un lot de **d** (fig) **to fall into sb's/sth's ~es** tomber sous la griffe or sous la patte or sous les pattes de qn/qch; **to get out of sb's/sth's ~es** se tirer des griffes or des pattes de qn/qch **e** (US: = crisis) crise f **2** VT (= grasp) empoigner, saisir; (= hold tightly) étreindre, serrer fort; (= hold on to) se cramponner à **3** VI **a** (= cling) **to ~ at** (lit) se cramponner à, s'agripper à; (fig) [+ hope, idea, chance] se cramponner à, se raccrocher à; (fig) **to ~ at a straw** or **at straws** se raccrocher à n'importe quoi **b** (US) embrayer **4** COMP ► **clutch bag** N pochette f ► **clutch plate** N disque m d'embrayage

clutter [ˈklʌtər] **1** N **a** (NonC = disorder, confusion) désordre m, pagaïe* f; **in a ~** en désordre **b** (= objects lying about) fouillis m, pagaille* f, pagaïe* f; **the ~ of bottles and crockery in the kitchen** le fouillis de bouteilles et de vaisselle dans la cuisine **2** VT (also **~ up**: lit, fig) encombrer (**with** de)

Clytemnestra [ˌklaɪtɪmˈnɛstrə] N Clytemnestre f

cm ABBR = **centimetre(s)**

Cmdr N (Mil) ABBR = **Commander**

CNAA [ˌsiːeneɪˈeɪ] (Brit Educ) (ABBR = **Council for National Academic Awards**) organisme qui valide les diplômes de l'enseignement supérieur décernés en dehors des universités

CND [ˌsiːenˈdiː] (in Brit) (ABBR = **Campaign for Nuclear Disarmament**) mouvement pour le désarmement nucléaire

CNN [ˌsiːenˈen] (ABBR = **Cable News Network**) CNN f (chaîne de télévision américaine émettant sur le réseau câblé)

CO [siːˈəʊ] **a** (Mil) (ABBR = **Commanding Officer**) → **commanding b** (Brit Admin) (ABBR = **Commonwealth Office**) ministère m des Affaires étrangères et du Commonwealth **c** (ABBR = **conscientious objector**) → **conscientious d** ABBR = **Colorado**

Co. **a** (Comm) (ABBR = **company**) Cie; **Joe and ~* are coming** Joe et compagnie or et sa bande* vont venir **b** ABBR = **County**

co..., co- [kəʊ] PREF co..., co-; **co-organizer** co-organisateur m → **co-driver**, **co(-)partner**

c/o [ˈkeərəv] (ABBR = **care of**) chez, aux bons soins de

coach [kəʊtʃ] **1** N **a** (horse-drawn) carrosse m; (= stagecoach) diligence f, coche m; (Brit = bus) autocar m; (Brit = of train) voiture f, wagon m; **~ and four** carrosse m à quatre chevaux **b** (= tutor) répétiteur m, -trice f; (Sport: gen) entraîneur m; (Ski) moniteur m, -trice f **2** VT donner des leçons particulières à; (Sport) entraîner; **to ~ sb for an exam** préparer qn à un examen; **he had been ~ed in what to say** on lui avait fait répéter ce qu'il aurait à dire **3** COMP ► **coach building** N (Brit) carrosserie f (construction) ► **coach driver** N (Brit) chauffeur m d'autocar ► **coach operator** N (Brit) compagnie f d'autocars ► **coach park** N (Brit) parking m pour autocars ► **coach party** N groupe m voyageant en car ► **coach station** N (Brit) gare f routière ► **coach trip** N (Brit) excursion f en car

coachbuilder [ˈkəʊtʃˌbɪldər] N (Brit Aut) carrossier m

coaching [ˈkəʊtʃɪŋ] N (Sport) entraînement m; (Scol) soutien m (scolaire)

coachload [ˈkəʊtʃləʊd] N (Brit) **a ~ of tourists** un car plein de touristes

coachman [ˈkəʊtʃmən] N (pl **-men**) cocher m

coachwork [ˈkəʊtʃwɜːk] N (NonC: Brit Aut) carrosserie f

coadjutant [kəʊˈædʒʊtənt] N assistant(e) m(f), aide mf

coagulant [kəʊˈægjʊlənt] N coagulant m

coagulate [kəʊˈægjʊleɪt] **1** VT coaguler **2** VI se coaguler

coagulation [kəʊˌægjʊˈleɪʃən] N coagulation f

coal [kəʊl] **1** N charbon m; (Ind) houille f; **a piece of ~** un morceau de charbon; **as black as ~** noir comme du charbon; (fig) **to be on hot ~s** être sur des charbons ardents; **it's like carrying** or **taking ~s to Newcastle** c'est comme porter de l'eau à la rivière† → **heap, soft** **2** VT fournir or ravitailler en charbon; (Naut) **to ~ ship** charbonner **3** VI (Naut) charbonner **4** COMP [fire, dealer; box, shed] à charbon ► **coal basin** N bassin m houiller ► **coal-black** ADJ noir comme du charbon ► **Coal Board** N (Brit: formerly) ≈ Charbonnages mpl ► **coal-burning** ADJ à charbon, qui marche au charbon ► **coal cellar** N cave f à charbon ► **coal chute** N goulotte f à charbon ► **coal cutter** N haveur m ► **coal depot** N dépôt m de charbon ► **coal face** N front m de taille ► **coal fire** N feu m de charbon or de cheminée ► **coal-fired power station** N centrale f thermique or électrique au charbon ► **coal gas** N gaz m (de houille) ► **coal hod** N seau m à charbon ► **coal hole** N petite cave f à charbon

► **coal industry** N industrie f houillère or charbonnière, charbonnages mpl ► **coaling station** N dépôt m de charbon ► **coal measures** NPL (Geol) gisements mpl houillers ► **coal merchant** N = **coalman** a ► **coal mine** N houillère f, mine f de charbon ► **coal miner** N mineur m ► **coal mining** N charbonnage m ► **coal oil** N (US) pétrole m lampant, kérosène m ► **coal pit** N = **coal mine** ► **coal scuttle** N seau m à charbon ► **coal strike** N (Ind) grève f des mineurs ► **coal tar** N coaltar m, goudron m de houille ► **coal tit** N (= bird) mésange f noire ► **coal yard** N dépôt m de charbon

coaldust [ˈkəʊldʌst] N poussier m, poussière f de charbon

coalesce [ˌkəʊəˈles] VI (lit, fig) s'unir, se fondre

coalescence [ˌkəʊəˈlesəns] N (lit, fig) fusion f, union f

coalfield [ˈkəʊlfiːld] N gisement m de houille

coalfish [ˈkəʊlfɪʃ] N (pl **coalfish** or **coalfishes**) lieu m noir, colin m

coalition [ˌkəʊəˈlɪʃən] **1** N coalition f **2** COMP ► **coalition government** N (Pol) gouvernement m de coalition

coalman [ˈkəʊlmən] N (pl **-men**) **a** (= merchant) charbonnier m, marchand m de charbon **b** (= delivery man) charbonnier m

coarse [kɔːs] **1** ADJ **a** (in texture) [fabric, feathers, fur, features, grass, gravel, powder] grossier; [face] aux traits grossiers; **~ cloth** drap m grossier; **~ linen** grosse toile f; **~ salt** gros sel m; **~ sand** sable m à gros grains, gros sable m; **~ sandpaper** papier m de verre à gros grain; **~ skin** peau f rêche; **~ weave** texture f grossière **b** (= common) ordinaire, grossier; **~ red wine** gros rouge m; (pej) (= uncouth) [person] grossier; [manners] grossier, vulgaire; (= indecent) [language, joke] grossier, cru; [laugh] gros (grosse f), gras (grasse f); [accent] commun, vulgaire **2** COMP ► **coarse fishing** N pêche f à la ligne (pour poissons autres que le saumon et la truite) ► **coarse-grained** ADJ à gros grain ► **coarse-grain salt** N sel m

coarsely [ˈkɔːslɪ] ADV **a** (= in large pieces) [chop, grate, grind] grossièrement; **~ woven cloth** tissu m de texture grossière **b** (= uncouthly, vulgarly) [speak] d'une voix or d'un ton vulgaire; [laugh] grassement, vulgairement; [say] grossièrement, vulgairement; [behave] vulgairement

coarsen [ˈkɔːsn] **1** VI [voice] s'érailler; [features] s'épaissir; [laugh, language] devenir vulgaire **2** VT [+ voice] érailler; [+ features] épaissir

coarseness [ˈkɔːsnɪs] N (NonC) **a** (in texture) [of grain, sand] grossièreté f; [of material] grossièreté f, rudesse f; [of skin] rugosité f; [of grass] rigidité f **b** (= vulgarity) [of person, behaviour, language, laugh, accent] vulgarité f

coast [kəʊst] **1** N côte f; (= coastline) littoral m; **from ~ to ~** du nord au sud; (fig) **the ~ is clear** la voie or le champ est libre **2** VI **a** (to ~ along/down** [motorist, cyclist] avancer/descendre en roue libre; (fig) **to ~ along** (= encounter few problems) avancer (sans problèmes); (= take things easy) se la couler douce*; (fig) **to ~ through** passer sans difficultés **b** (Naut) caboter

coastal [ˈkəʊstəl] ADJ [defence, state] côtier; **~ navigation** navigation f côtière; **~ traffic** navigation f côtière, cabotage m

coaster [ˈkəʊstər] **1** N **a** (Naut) caboteur m **b** (= drip mat) dessous m de verre or de bouteille; (= wine tray) présentoir m à bouteilles → **roller** **2** COMP ► **coaster brake** N (US) [of cycle] frein m à rétropédalage

coastguard [ˈkəʊstˌgɑːd] **1** N **a** (= service) ≈ gendarmerie f maritime **b** (= person) membre m de la gendarmerie maritime; (Hist) garde-côte m **2** COMP ► **coastguard sta-**

tion N (bureau *m* de la) gendarmerie *f* maritime → **coastguard vessel** N (vedette *f*) garde-côte *m*

coastguard(s)man ['kəʊst,gɑːd(z)mən] N (*pl* **-men**) (*esp US*) = **coastguard 1b**

coastline ['kəʊstlaɪn] N littoral *m*

coat [kəʊt] **1** N **a** (*gen*) manteau *m*; (*also* **overcoat, topcoat**) pardessus *m*; **winter ~** manteau *m* d'hiver *or* pour l'hiver; (*fig*) **to cut one's ~ according to one's cloth** vivre selon ses moyens → **housecoat, morning, sport** **b** [*of animal*] pelage *m*, livrée *f*; [*of horse*] robe *f*; **winter ~** pelage *m* d'hiver **c** (= *covering*) [*of paint, tar etc*] couche *f*; [*of plastic*] enveloppe *f* → **base¹, topcoat** **2** VT [*dust, frost, conditioner, plastic*] (re)couvrir; [*person*] (*with glue, paste, ointment*) enduire; (*with chocolate*) enrober; (*with breadcrumbs etc*) paner; (*with egg, batter*) tremper (**with** dans); **to ~ the wall with paint** passer une couche de peinture sur le mur, enduire le mur de peinture; (*Med*) **his tongue was ~ed** il avait la langue chargée; (*Phot*) **~ed lens** objectif *m* traité **3** COMP ► **coat hanger** N cintre *m* ► **coat of arms** N (*Her*) blason *m*, armoiries *fpl*, écu *m* ► **coat of mail** N cotte *f* de mailles ► **coat rack** N = **coatstand** ► **coat-tails** NPL queue *f* de pie (*habit*); (*fig*) **to be hanging on sb's ~-tails** être pendu aux basques de qn; (*US Pol*) **to ride on sb's ~-tails** se faire élire dans le sillage de qn

-coated ['kəʊtɪd] ADJ (*in compounds*) recouvert de; **chocolate-coated** enrobé de chocolat

coating ['kəʊtɪŋ] N (*gen*) couche *f*; (*on saucepan etc*) revêtement *m*

coatstand ['kəʊtstænd] N portemanteau *m*

co-author ['kəʊ,ɔːθəʳ] **1** N coauteur *m* **2** VT [*+ book, play, report*] cosigner

coax [kəʊks] VT amadouer; **to ~ sb into/out of doing** amener qn à faire/à ne pas faire à force de cajoleries *or* de câlineries; **to ~ sth out of sb** obtenir *or* tirer qch de qn par des cajoleries ỏr des câlineries

coaxial [kəʊ'æksɪəl] **1** ADJ (*gen, Geom, Elec*) coaxial **2** COMP ► **coaxial cable** N (*TV*) câble *m* coaxial

coaxing ['kəʊksɪŋ] **1** N câlineries *fpl*, cajolerie(s) *f(pl)* **2** ADJ enjôleur, câlin

coaxingly ['kəʊksɪŋlɪ] ADV [*speak, ask*] d'une manière câline, d'un ton enjôleur; [*look*] d'un air câlin *or* enjôleur

cob [kɒb] N (= *swan*) cygne *m* mâle; (= *horse*) cob *m*; (*also* **~-nut**) grosse noisette *f*; (*Brit: also* **~ loaf**) miche *f* de pain; [*of maize*] épi *m* (de maïs) → **corn¹**

cobalt ['kəʊbɔːlt] N cobalt *m*; **~ 60** cobalt 60, cobalt *m* radioactif; **~ blue** bleu *m* de cobalt; **~ bomb** bombe *f* au cobalt

cobber ['kɒbəʳ] N (*Austral*) pote* *m*

cobble ['kɒbl] **1** VT **to ~ together** [*+ object, figures*] bricoler*; [*+ solution, agreement*] bricoler*, concocter* **2** N = **cobblestone**

cobbled ['kɒbld] ADJ **~ street** rue *f* pavée

cobbler ['kɒbləʳ] N **a** cordonnier *m*; **~'s wax** poix *f* de cordonnier **b** (*US Culin*) tourte *f* aux fruits **c** (*US* = *drink*) (sorte *f* de) punch *m* (glacé) **d** (*Brit* = *nonsense*) **that's a load of ~s!** c'est de la connerie!

cobblestone ['kɒblstəʊn] N pavé *m* rond

COBOL, Cobol ['kəʊbɒl] N (*Comput*) COBOL *m*

cobra ['kəʊbrə] N cobra *m*

cobweb ['kɒbweb] N toile *f* d'araignée; (*fig*) **to blow** *or* **clear away the ~s** remettre les idées en place

cobwebbed ['kɒbwebd] ADJ couvert de toiles d'araignée

coca ['kəʊkə] N **a** (= *shrub*) coca *m or f* **b** (*NonC* = *dried leaves*) coca *f*

cocaine [kə'keɪn] N cocaïne *f*; **~ addict** cocaïnomane *mf*; **~ addiction** cocaïnomanie *f*

coccus ['kɒkəs] N (*pl* **cocci** ['kɒksaɪ]) coccidie *f*

coccyx ['kɒksɪks] N (*pl* **coccyges** [kɒk'saɪdʒiːz]) coccyx *m*

co-chairman [kəʊ,tʃɛəmən] N (*pl* **-men**) coprésident(e) *m(f)*

co-chairmanship [kəʊ'tʃɛəmənˌʃɪp] N coprésidence *f*

Cochin China [ˌkəʊtʃɪn'tʃaɪnə] N la Cochinchine

cochineal ['kɒtʃɪniːl] N (= *insect*) cochenille *f*; (= *colouring*) colorant *m* rouge

cochlea ['kɒklɪə] N (*pl* **cochleae** ['kɒklɪˌiː]) (*Anat*) limaçon *m*

cochlear ['kɒklɪəʳ] ADJ cochléaire

cock [kɒk] **1** N **a** (*esp Brit* = *rooster*) coq *m*; (= *male bird*) (oiseau *m*) mâle *m*; (*fig*) **he thinks he's the ~ of the walk** il est vaniteux comme un paon → **fighting, gamecock, weather** **b** (= *tap*) robinet *m* **c** [*of rifle*] chien *m*; **at full ~** armé; **at half ~** au cran de repos → **half** **d** [*of hay*] meulon *m*; [*of corn, oats*] moyette *f* **e** (✱✱ = *penis*) bite✱✱ *f* **2** VT **a** [+ *gun*] armer **b** **to ~ one's ears** (*lit*) dresser les oreilles; (*fig*) dresser l'oreille; **to ~ one's eye at ...** glisser un coup d'œil à ...; (*Brit fig*) **to ~ a snook at ...**✱ faire la nique à ... **3** COMP [*bird*] mâle ► **cock-a-doodle-doo** EXCL cocorico! ► **cock-a-hoop** ADJ fier comme Artaban ♦ ADV d'un air triomphant ► **cock-a-leekie soup** N (*Scot*) potage à la volaille *et* aux poireaux ► **cock-and-bull story** N (*pej*) histoire *f* à dormir debout ► **cock lobster** N homard *m* (mâle) ► **cock sparrow** N moineau *m* (mâle) ► **cock-teaser**✱✱ N allumeuse✱ *f* ► **cock-up**✱✱ N (*Brit*) foirade* *f*, couille✱ *f*; **there's been a ~-up** il y a eu une couille✱; **he made a ~-up of the job** il a salopé le boulot✱; **the meeting was a ~-up** la réunion a complètement foiré*

► **cock up**✱✱ (*Brit*) **1** VT SEP saloper✱; [+ *exam*] foirer✱ **2** VI merder✱, foirer✱ **3** **~-up** N → **cock**

cockade [kɒ'keɪd] N cocarde *f*

Cockaigne [kɒ'keɪn] N **(the land of) ~** le pays de Cocagne

cockamamie [ˌkɒkə'meɪmɪ] ADJ (*US*) farfelu

cockatoo [ˌkɒkə'tuː] N cacatoès *m*

cockchafer ['kɒk,tʃeɪfəʳ] N hanneton *m*

cockcrow ['kɒkkrəʊ] N **at ~** au chant du coq, à l'aube

cocked [kɒkt] ADJ **~ hat** chapeau *m* à cornes; (*two points*) bicorne *m*; (*three points*) tricorne *m*; **to knock** *or* **beat sb into a ~ hat** battre qn à plate(s) couture(s)

cocker ['kɒkəʳ] N (*also* **~ spaniel**) cocker *m*

cockerel ['kɒkərəl] N jeune coq *m*

cockeyed✱ ['kɒk'aɪd] ADJ **a** (= *cross-eyed*) qui louche; (= *crooked*) de travers, de traviole*; (= *mad, absurd*) qui ne tient pas debout, dingue*; (= *drunk*) soûl*, schlass✱ *inv*

cockfight ['kɒkfaɪt] N combat *m* de coqs

cockfighting ['kɒk,faɪtɪŋ] N combats *mpl* de coqs

cockieleekie soup [ˌkɒkɪliːkɪ'suːp] N = **cock-a-leekie soup** → **cock**

cockily ['kɒkɪlɪ] ADV avec impudence *or* effronterie

cockiness ['kɒkɪnɪs] N impudence *f*, effronterie *f*

cockle ['kɒkl] N (= *shellfish*) coque *f*; († *or hum*) **it warmed the ~s of his heart** cela lui a réchauffé le cœur

cockleshell ['kɒklʃel] N (*Zool*) coquille *f* (de coque *f*); (= *boat*) petit canot *m*, coquille *f* de noix

cockney ['kɒknɪ] **1** N **a** (= *person*) cockney *mf* → RHYMING SLANG **b** (*Ling*) cockney *m* **2** ADJ cockney, londonien

COCKNEY

Les véritables **cockneys** *sont les personnes nées à portée du son des Bow Bells, c'est-à-dire des cloches de l'église de St Mary-le-Bow dans la City, mais on y inclut tous les habitants de l'est londonien. Le mot désigne aussi le parler des habitants de ces quartiers et, par extension, n'importe quel accent, argot ou parler populaire londonien.* → RHYMING SLANG

cockpit ['kɒkpɪt] N [*of aircraft*] poste *m* de pilotage, cockpit *m*; [*of yacht, racing car*] cockpit *m*; (*for cockfighting*) arène *f*; (*fig*) arènes *fpl*

cockroach ['kɒkrəʊtʃ] N cafard *m*, blatte *f*

cockscomb ['kɒkskəʊm] N **a** (*Orn*) crête *f* (de coq) **b** (*Bot*) crête-de-coq *f* **c** († = *dandy*) fat *m*, poseur *m*, muscadin† *m*

cocksucker✱✱ ['kɒk,sʌkəʳ] N enfoiré✱✱ *m*, enculé✱✱ *m*

cocksure ['kɒkʃʊəʳ] ADJ (*pej*) (trop) sûr de soi, outrecuidant

cocktail ['kɒkteɪl] **1** N (*lit, fig*) cocktail *m* (boisson); **fruit ~** salade *f* de fruits; **prawn ~** (*Brit*) ◊ **shrimp ~** (*US*) coupe *f* or cocktail de crevettes → **Molotov** **2** COMP ► **cocktail bar** N bar *m* américain, cocktail-bar *m* ► **cocktail cabinet** N meuble *m* bar ► **cocktail dress** N robe *f* de cocktail ► **cocktail lounge** N bar *m* (de luxe, dans un hôtel) ► **cocktail onion** N petit oignon *m* (au vinaigre) ► **cocktail party** N cocktail *m* ► **cocktail sausage** N petite saucisse *f* (pour l'apéritif) ► **cocktail shaker** N shaker *m* ► **cocktail stick** N pique *f* (à apéritif) ► **cocktail waitress** N (*US*) serveuse *f* (de bar)

cocky✱ ['kɒkɪ] ADJ (*pej*) effronté, impudent

cocoa ['kəʊkəʊ] **1** N (= *drink, powder*) cacao *m* **2** COMP ► **cocoa bean** N fève *f* de cacao ► **cocoa butter** N beurre *m* de cacao

coconut ['kəʊkənʌt] **1** N noix *f* de coco **2** COMP ► **coconut ice** N (*NonC*) confiserie *f* à la noix de coco ► **coconut matting** N tapis *m* de fibre de noix de coco ► **coconut oil** N huile *f* (de noix de) coco ► **coconut palm** N cocotier *m* ► **coconut shy** N jeu *m* de massacre ► **coconut tree** N cocotier *m*

cocoon [kə'kuːn] **1** N cocon *m*; (*fig*) **wrapped in a ~ of blankets** emmitouflé dans des couvertures **2** VT (*fig*) [+ *object*] envelopper avec soin; [+ *child*] couver; (*fig*) **~ed from** à l'abri de; **~ed in the bosom of one's family** bien à l'abri au sein de sa famille

COD [ˌsiːəʊ'diː] **a** (*Brit*) (ABBR = **cash on delivery**) → **cash** **b** (*US*) (ABBR = **collect on delivery**) → **collect**

cod [kɒd] **1** N (*pl* **cod** *or* **cods**) (*Zool*) morue *f*; (*Culin: fresh*) morue *f* fraîche, cabillaud *m*; **dried ~** merluche *f* **2** ADJ (*Brit*) (= *not genuine*) faux (fausse *f*), prétendu; (= *assumed*) [*accent*] faux (fausse *f*) **3** COMP ► **cod-liver oil** N huile *f* de foie de morue ► **the Cod War** N (*Brit*) la guerre de la morue

coda ['kəʊdə] N (*Mus*) coda *f*

coddle ['kɒdl] VT **a** [+ *child, invalid*] dorloter, choyer **b** (*Culin*) [+ *eggs*] cuire à feu doux au bain-marie

▼ **code** [kəʊd] **1** N **a** (*Admin, Comput, Jur, Ling, fig*) code *m*; **~ of behaviour/of honour** code *m* de conduite/de l'honneur → **highway, penal** **b** (= *cipher*) code *m*, chiffre *m*; (*Bio, Comput, Post etc*) code *m*; **in ~** en code, chiffré; (*Mil*) **to break a secret ~** déchiffrer *or* décrypter un code secret → **Morse, zip** **2** VT [+ *letter, dispatch*] chiffrer, coder; (*Comput*) programmer **3** COMP ► **code dating** N (*Comm*) inscription *f* de date codée (*sur les denrées périssa-*

bles) ► **code letter** N chiffre *m* ► **code name** N nom *m* de code ► **code-name** VT **an operation ~-named "Condor"** une opération qui a pour nom de code «Condor» ► **code number** N (= *access code*) code *m* d'accès ; (*Telec* = *dialling code*) indicatif *m* ; (*Tax*) *code numérique désignant chaque tranche d'imposition* ► **code of conduct** N code *m* de conduite ► **code of ethics** N (*gen*) code *m* (d')éthique ; [*of profession*] (code *m* de) déontologie *f* ► **code of practice** N (*gen*) déontologie *f* ; (= *set of rules*) règlements *mpl* et usages *mpl* ► **code word** N (*lit*) mot *m* de passe ; (*fig: Pol*) mot *m* codé

coded ['kəʊdɪd] ADJ a (= *in code*) [*message, instructions*] codé ; **in ~ form** codé, sous forme de code ; **a ~ telephone warning** un avertissement téléphonique codé b (= *indirect*) [*criticism, attack, reference*] voilé ; **in ~ language** en termes voilés, à mots couverts c (*Telec*) [*signal*] codé

codeine ['kəʊdiːn] N codéine *f*

co-dependent [,kəʊdɪ'pendənt] (*esp US Psych*) 1 N codépendant(e) *m(f)* 2 ADJ codépendant

codex ['kəʊdeks] N (*pl* **codices**) manuscrit *m* (ancien)

codfish ['kɒdfɪʃ] N (*pl* **codfish** or **codfishes**) morue *f*

codger: ['kɒdʒəʳ] N **old ~** drôle de vieux bonhomme *m*

codices ['kɒdɪsiːz] NPL of **codex**

codicil ['kɒdɪsɪl] N codicille *m*

codify ['kəʊdɪfaɪ] VT codifier

coding ['kəʊdɪŋ] 1 N (*NonC*) [*of telegram, message*] encodage *m* ; (*Comput*) codage *m* → **tax** 2 COMP ► **coding sheet** N (*Comput*) feuille *f* de programmation

codpiece ['kɒd.piːs] N braguette *f* (*portée aux* 15ᵉ *et* 16ᵉ *siècles*)

co-driver ['kəʊdraɪvəʳ] N (*in race*) copilote *m* ; [*of lorry, bus*] deuxième chauffeur *m*

codswallop: ['kɒdzwɒləp] N (*NonC: Brit*) bobards* *mpl*, foutaises: *fpl*

coed· ['kəʊ'ed] 1 ADJ ABBR = **coeducational** 2 N (*US*) étudiante *f* (*dans un établissement mixte*)

co-edit [,kəʊ'edɪt] VT [+ *book*] coéditer

co-edition [,kəʊɪ'dɪʃən] N coédition *f*

coeducation ['kəʊ,edjʊ'keɪʃən] N éducation *f* mixte

coeducational ['kəʊ,edjʊ'keɪʃənl] ADJ [*school, teaching*] mixte

coefficient [,kəʊɪ'fɪʃənt] N coefficient *m*

coeliac ['siːlɪˌæk] ADJ cœliaque ; **~ disease** cœlialgie *f*

coequal [,kəʊ'iːkwəl] ADJ, N égal(e) *m(f)*

coerce [kəʊ'ɜːs] VT contraindre ; **to ~ sb into doing sth** contraindre qn à faire qch

coercion [kəʊ'ɜːʃən] N contrainte *f*, coercition *f*

coercive [kəʊ'ɜːsɪv] ADJ coercitif

coeval [kəʊ'iːvəl] 1 ADJ contemporain (**with** de), du même âge (**with** que) 2 N contemporain(e) *m(f)*

coexist [,kəʊɪg'zɪst] VI coexister (**with** avec)

coexistence [,kəʊɪg'zɪstəns] N coexistence *f* → **peaceful**

coexistent ['kəʊɪg'zɪstənt] ADJ coexistant (**with** avec)

coextensive ['kəʊɪk'stensɪv] ADV **~ with** (*in space*) de même étendue que ; (*in time*) de même durée que

C of C (ABBR = **Chamber of Commerce**) → **chamber**

C of E [,siː'viː] N (*Brit*) (ABBR = **Church of England**) → **church**

coffee ['kɒfɪ] 1 N café *m* ; **a cup of ~** une tasse de café ; **one** or **a ~** un café ; **black ~** café *m* noir ; **white ~** (*Brit*) ◊ **~ with milk** (*US*) (*gen*)

---

café *m* au lait ; (*in café: when ordering*) **a white ~** (*Brit*) ◊ **a ~ with milk** (*US*) un café-crème 2 COMP (= *coffee flavoured*) au café ; (= *coffee coloured*) (*dark*) couleur café *inv* ; (*light*) café au lait *inv* ► **coffee bar** N (*Brit*) café *m*, cafétéria *f* ► **coffee bean** N grain *m* de café ► **coffee break** N pause-café *f* ► **coffee cake** N (*Brit: coffee-flavoured*) moka *m* (*au café*) ; (*US: served with coffee*) gâteau *m* (*que l'on sert avec le café*) ► **coffee-coloured** ADJ (*dark*) couleur café *inv* ; (*light*) couleur café au lait *inv* ► **coffee cup** N tasse *f* à café ► **coffee filter** N filtre *m* à café ► **coffee grounds** NPL marc *m* de café ► **coffee house** N (*Hist*) café *m* (*au 18ᵉ siècle*) ► **coffee machine** N (*in café etc*) percolateur *m* ; (= *vending machine*) machine *f* à café ► **coffee-maker** N (*electric*) cafetière *f* électrique ; (*non-electric*) cafetière *f* ► **coffee mill** N moulin *m* à café ► **coffee morning** N (*gen*) réunion de femmes qui se retrouvent pour bavarder autour d'une tasse de café ; (*for fund-raising*) vente *f* de charité (*où l'on sert le café*) ► **coffee percolator** N = **coffee-maker** ► **coffee service**, **coffee set** N service *m* à café ► **coffee shop** N (= *restaurant*) cafétéria *f* ; (= *shop*) brûlerie *f* ► **coffee spoon** N cuiller *f* à café ► **coffee table** N table *f* basse ► **coffee table book** N beau livre *m* (*grand format*) ► **coffee tree** N caféier *m* ► **coffee whitener** N succédané *m* de lait

coffeepot ['kɒfɪpɒt] N cafetière *f*

coffer ['kɒfəʳ] N a coffre *m*, caisse *f* ; (*fig* = *funds*) **~s** coffres *mpl* ; **the ~s (of State)** les coffres *mpl* de l'État b (*Hydraulics*) caisson *m* c (*also* **~ dam**) batardeau *m*

coffin ['kɒfɪn] 1 N cercueil *m*, bière *f* ; **~ nail**†: (= *cigarette*) sèche: *f* 2 COMP ► **coffin dodger·** N (*hum*) vieux débris *m*

C of I [,siː'aɪ] (*Brit*) (ABBR = **Church of Ireland**) → **church**

C of S [,siː'es] a (*Brit*) (ABBR = **Church of Scotland**) → **church** b (*Mil*) (ABBR = **Chief of Staff**) → **chief**

cog [kɒg] N (*Tech*) dent *f* (*d'engrenage*) ; (*fig*) **he's only a ~ in the wheel** or **machine** il n'est qu'un simple rouage (*de or dans la machine*)

cogency ['kəʊdʒənsɪ] N [*of argument etc*] puissance *f*, force *f*

cogent ['kəʊdʒənt] ADJ (= *compelling*) irrésistible ; (= *convincing*) puissant, convaincant ; (= *relevant*) pertinent, (fait) à-propos

cogently ['kəʊdʒəntlɪ] ADV (*frm*) [*argue, speak, express*] de façon convaincante

cogitate ['kɒdʒɪteɪt] 1 VI méditer, réfléchir ((up)on sur) ; (*hum*) cogiter ((up)on sur) 2 VT [+ *scheme*] méditer

cogitation [,kɒdʒɪ'teɪʃən] N (*NonC*) réflexion *f* ; (*hum*) cogitations *fpl*

cognac ['kɒnjæk] N cognac *m*

cognate ['kɒgneɪt] 1 ADJ apparenté, analogue (**with** à), de même origine or source (**with** que) ; (*Ling*) [*word, language*] apparenté (**with** que) 2 N (*Ling*) mot *m* apparenté ; (*Jur*) cognat *m*, parent *m* proche

cognition [kɒg'nɪʃən] N (*NonC*) connaissance *f* ; (*Philos*) cognition *f*

cognitive ['kɒgnɪtɪv] 1 ADJ cognitif 2 COMP ► **cognitive meaning** N (*Ling*) sens *m* cognitif ► **cognitive psychology** N psychologie *f* cognitive ► **cognitive therapy** N thérapie *f* cognitive

cognizance ['kɒgnɪzəns] N a (*Jur, gen: frm*) connaissance *f* ; **to take/have ~ of ...** prendre/ avoir connaissance de ... ; **this is outside his ~** ceci n'est pas de sa compétence ; (*Jur*) **this case falls within the ~ of the court** cette affaire est de la compétence du tribunal b (*Her*) emblème *m*

cognizant ['kɒgnɪzənt] ADJ (*frm*) instruit, ayant connaissance (**of** de) ; (*Jur*) compétent (**of** pour)

---

cognomen [kɒg'nəʊmen] N (*pl* **cognomens** or **cognomina** [kɒg'nɒmɪnə]) (= *surname*) nom *m* de famille ; (= *nickname*) surnom *m*

cognoscenti [,kɒgnəʊ'ʃentɪ, kɒnjəʊ'ʃentɪ] NPL **the ~** les spécialistes, les connaisseurs

cogwheel ['kɒgwiːl] N roue *f* dentée

cohabit [kəʊ'hæbɪt] VI cohabiter (**with** avec)

cohabitant [kəʊ'hæbɪtənt] N = **cohabitee**

cohabitation [,kəʊhæbɪ'teɪʃən] N cohabitation *f*

cohabitee [,kəʊhæbɪ'tiː], **cohabiter** [kəʊ'hæbɪtəʳ] N (*Admin*) concubin(e) *m(f)*

coheir ['kəʊ'ɛəʳ] N cohéritier *m*

coheiress ['kəʊ'ɛərɪs] N cohéritière *f*

cohere [kəʊ'hɪəʳ] VI a (*fig*) être cohérent, se tenir b (*lit* = *stick*) adhérer

coherence [kəʊ'hɪərəns] N a (*fig*) cohérence *f* b (*lit*) adhérence *f*

coherent [kəʊ'hɪərənt] ADJ cohérent ; **incapable of ~ speech** incapable de s'exprimer de façon cohérente

coherently [kəʊ'hɪərəntlɪ] ADV de façon cohérente

cohesion [kəʊ'hiːʒən] N cohésion *f*

cohesive [kəʊ'hiːsɪv] ADJ cohésif

cohort ['kəʊhɔːt] N (*gen, Mil*) cohorte *f* ; (*pej* = *supporter*) acolyte *m*

COHSE ['kəʊzɪ] (*Brit: formerly*) (ABBR = **Confederation of Health Service Employees**) *ancien syndicat*

COI [,siːəʊ'aɪ] (*Brit*) (ABBR = **Central Office of Information**) *service d'information gouvernemental*

coif [kɔɪf] N (= *headdress*) coiffe *f* ; (= *skullcap*) calotte *f*

coiffed [kɔɪfd] ADJ (*frm*) coiffé

coiffure [kwɒ'fjʊəʳ] N (*frm*) coiffure *f*

coiffured [kwɒ'fjʊəd] ADJ (*frm*) = **coiffed**

coil [kɔɪl] 1 VT [+ *rope*] enrouler ; [+ *hair*] enrouler, torsader ; (*Elec*) [+ *wire*] embobiner ; (*Naut*) gléner ; **the snake ~ed itself (up)** le serpent s'est lové 2 VI [*river*] onduler, serpenter ; [*rope*] s'enrouler (**round, about** autour de) ; [*snake*] se lover 3 N a (= *loops, roll*) [*of rope, wire*] rouleau *m* ; (*Naut*) glène *f* ; [*of hair*] rouleau *m* ; (*at back of head*) chignon *m* ; (*over ears*) macaron *m* b (*one loop*) spire *f* ; [*of cable*] tour *m* ; [*of hair*] boucle *f* ; [*of snake, smoke*] anneau *m* c (*Elec*) bobine *f* ; (*one loop*) spire *f* d (*Med* = *contraceptive*) **the ~·** le stérilet 2 COMP ► **coil spring** N ressort *m* hélicoïdal

coin [kɔɪn] 1 N a pièce *f* de monnaie ; **a 10p ~** une pièce de 10 pence → **toss** b (*NonC*) monnaie *f* ; **current ~** monnaie *f* courante ; **in (the) ~ of the realm** en espèces (sonnantes et trébuchantes) ; (*fig*) **to pay sb back in his own ~** rendre à qn la monnaie de sa pièce 2 VT a [+ *money, medal*] frapper ; (*fig*) **he is ~ing money** or **it (in)** il fait des affaires en or b (*fig*) [+ *word, phrase*] inventer ; (*hum iro*) **to ~ a phrase ...** si je peux m'exprimer ainsi ... 3 COMP ► **coin box** N (= *phone box*) cabine *f* téléphonique (à pièces) ; (= *part of vending machine*) caisse *f* ► **coin-operated** ADJ automatique ; **~-operated laundry** (*abbr: coin-op*) laverie *f* automatique

coinage ['kɔɪnɪdʒ] N (*NonC*) a (= *coins*) monnaie *f* ; (= *system*) système *m* monétaire b (= *act*) [*of money*] frappe *f* ; (*fig*) [*of word etc*] création *f*, invention *f*

coincide [,kəʊɪn'saɪd] VI coïncider (**with** avec)

coincidence [kəʊ'ɪnsɪdəns] N coïncidence *f*

coincident [kəʊ'ɪnsɪdənt] ADJ (*frm*) identique (**with** à)

coincidental [kəʊ,ɪnsɪ'dentl] ADJ de coïncidence ; **it's entirely ~** c'est une pure coïncidence

coincidentally [kəʊ,ɪnsɪ'dentlɪ] ADV par

coïncidence; **quite** or **purely** ~ par pure coïncidence

coinsurance [ˌkəʊɪnˈʃʊərəns] N (US Med) assu- rance dont les cotisations sont payées pour moi- tié par l'entreprise

coir [kɔɪr] ① N coco m, coir m ② COMP ► **coir matting** N (NonC) tapis m de coco

coital [ˈkɔɪtəl] ADJ coïtal

coitus [ˈkɔɪtəs] ① N coït m ② COMP ► **coitus interruptus** coït m interrompu; **to practise ~ interruptus** pratiquer le coït interrompu

Coke® [kəʊk] N coca® m

coke[1] [kəʊk] ① N coke m ② COMP ► **coke oven** N four m à coke

coke[2]: [kəʊk] N (= drug) coco f, coke f

Col. (Mil) (ABBR = **Colonel**) (on envelope) ~ **T. Richard** le Colonel T. Richard

col. [a] ABBR = **column** [b] ABBR = **colour**

COLA [ˈkəʊlə] N (US Fin) (ABBR = **cost-of-living adjustment**) → **cost**

cola[1] [ˈkəʊlə] ① N cola or kola m ② COMP ► **cola nut** N noix f de cola

cola[2] [ˈkəʊlə] NPL of **colon**

colander [ˈkʌləndər] N passoire f

▼ **cold** [kəʊld] ① ADJ [a] [day, drink, meal, meat, metal, water] froid; **to be as ~ as ice** [object] être froid comme de la glace; [room] être gla- cial; [person] être glacé jusqu'aux os; **it's a ~ morning/day** il fait froid ce matin/ aujourd'hui; **it's as ~ as charity** il fait un froid de canard* or un froid sibérien; **I am ~** j'ai froid; **my feet are ~** j'ai froid aux pieds; (fig) **to have** or **get ~ feet (about doing sth)** hésiter (à faire qch); **to get** ~ [weather, room] se re- froidir; [food] refroidir; [person] commencer à avoir froid; (in guessing games) **you're getting ~(er)!** tu refroidis!; **a ~ colour** une couleur froide; **~ steel** arme f blanche; **the scent is ~** la piste a disparu (also fig); **that's ~ comfort** ce n'est pas tellement réconfortant or rassurant, c'est une maigre consolation; **to be in a ~ sweat (about)*** avoir des sueurs froides (au su- jet de); **that brought him out in a ~ sweat** cela lui a donné des sueurs froides; (fig) **to pour** or **throw ~ water on** [+ optimism, hopes] refroidir; **he poured ~ water on my idea** sa réaction de- vant mon idée m'a refroidi → **4**, **blow**[1], **icy** [b] (fig) froid; **a ~ reception** un accueil froid; **to be ~ to sb** se montrer froid envers qn; **that leaves me ~*** ça ne me fait ni chaud ni froid; **in ~ blood** de sang-froid; **he's a ~ fish!*** qu'est-ce qu'il est froid! [c] (* = unconscious) **to be out** = être dans les pommes*; (lit, fig) **it knocked him (out) ~** ça l'a mis KO

② N [a] (in temperature) froid m; **don't go out in this ~!** ne sors pas par ce froid!; **to come in out of** or **from the ~** se mettre à l'abri; (fig) rentrer en grâce; (fig) **to be left out in the ~** rester en plan* → **feel** [b] (Med) rhume m; **~ in the head/on the chest** rhume de cerveau/de poitrine; **a heavy** or **bad ~** un gros or mauvais rhume; **to have a ~** être enrhumé; **to get a ~** s'enrhumer, attra- per un rhume; **to take ~** prendre froid

③ ADV (US*) (= completely) absolument; (= unexpectedly) de façon totalement inattendue; **to know sth ~** connaître qch à fond or sur le bout des doigts

④ COMP ► **cold-blooded** ADJ [animal] à sang froid; (fig) [person] insensible, sans pitié; [murder, attack] commis de sang-froid; (fig) **to be ~-blooded about sth** faire qch sans aucune pitié ► **cold-bloodedly** ADV de sang- froid ► **cold call** N (Comm) (on phone) appel m de démarchage; (= visit) démarchage m (à domicile) ► **cold chisel** N ciseau m à froid ► **cold cream** N crème f de beauté ► **cold cuts** NPL (Culin) ≈ assiette f anglaise ► **cold frame** N châssis m de couches ► **cold front** N (Met) front m froid ► **cold fusion** N (Phys) fusion f froide ► **cold-hearted** ADJ

impitoyable, sans pitié ► **cold room** N chambre f froide or frigorifique ► **cold shoulder*** N (fig) **to give sb the ~ shoulder** ◊ **to turn a ~ shoulder on** or **to sb** (US) snober qn, battre froid à qn ► **cold-shoulder** VT to **~-shoulder sb** = **to give sb the cold shoulder** ► **cold snap** N (Met) coup m de froid, vague f de froid de courte durée ► **cold sore** N (Med) bouton m de fièvre ► **cold start, cold starting** (US) N (Aut) démarrage m à froid ► **cold storage** N conservation f par le froid; **to put into ~ storage** [+ food] mettre en chambre froide; [+ fur coat] mettre en garde; (fig) [+ idea, book, scheme] mettre de côté or en attente ► **cold store** N entrepôt m frigo- rifique ► **cold turkey*** N (Drugs) manque m ♦ ADJ **to go ~ turkey** (= stop) arrêter la drogue d'un seul coup; (= suffer withdrawal symptoms) être en manque* ► **the cold war** N (Pol) la guerre froide ► **cold warrior** N (Pol) parti- san(e) m(f) de la guerre froide ► **cold wave** N (Met) vague f de froid; (Hairdressing) miniva- gue f ► **cold-weather payment** N (Brit) allo- cation supplémentaire aux retraités et personnes à faibles revenus en période de grand froid

coldly [ˈkəʊldlɪ] ADV [look, say] froidement; [behave] avec froideur

coldness [ˈkəʊldnɪs] N (lit, fig) froideur f

coleslaw [ˈkəʊlslɔː] N salade f de chou cru

coley [ˈkəʊlɪ] N lieu noir m, colin m

colic [ˈkɒlɪk] N coliques fpl

colicky [ˈkɒlɪkɪ] ADJ [baby] qui souffre de coli- ques; [pain] dû à des coliques; (fig) [disposi- tion] grincheux

Coliseum [ˌkɒlɪˈsiːəm] N Colisée m

colitis [kɒˈlaɪtɪs] N colite f

collaborate [kəˈlæbəreɪt] VI (also pej) collabo- rer; **to ~ with sb on** or **in sth** collaborer avec qn à qch

collaboration [kəˌlæbəˈreɪʃən] N (also pej) collaboration f (**in** à); (= piece of work) œuvre f produite en commun

collaborationist [kəˌlæbəˈreɪʃənɪst] N colla- borationniste mf

collaborative [kəˈlæbərətɪv] ADJ fait en colla- boration, commun

collaboratively [kəˈlæbərətɪvlɪ] ADV [work] en collaboration (**with** avec)

collaborator [kəˈlæbəreɪtər] N (gen) collabora- teur m, -trice f; (pej: in World War II) collabora- teur m, -trice f, collabo* mf

collage [kɒˈlɑːʒ] N (Art) collage m

collagen [ˈkɒlədʒən] N (Bio) collagène m

collapsar [kəˈlæpsər] N (Astron) trou m noir

collapse [kəˈlæps] ① VI [a] [person, building, roof, floor, bridge, scaffolding] s'écrouler, s'effondrer; [balloon] se dégonfler; [beam] s'affaisser; (fig) [one's health] se délabrer; [government] s'écrouler; [coalition] se dislo- quer; [business, communism, defences, market, prices, system] s'effondrer; [civilization, society, institution] s'effondrer; s'écrouler; [plan, scheme] s'écrouler, tomber à l'eau; [company] faire faillite; [talks, legal case, trial] échouer; [agreement] tomber à l'eau; [marriage] se solder par un échec; (*: with laughter) être écroulé de rire; **he ~d at work and was taken to hospital** il a eu un grave malaise à son tra- vail et on l'a emmené à l'hôpital; **she ~d onto her bed, exhausted** elle s'est écroulée or effondrée sur son lit, épuisée; (Med) **his lung ~d** il a fait un collapsus pulmonaire; (Med) **~d lung** collapsus m pulmonaire [b] (lit: fold for storage etc) [table, chairs] se plier ② VT [a] [+ table, chair] plier [b] (fig) [+ paragraphs, items] réduire, compri- mer

③ N [of person, building, roof, bridge, scaffolding] écroulement m, effondrement m; [of beam] affaissement m; [of lung] collapsus m; [of health] délabrement m; [of government] chute

f; [of coalition] dislocation f; [of company] faillite f; [of business, communism, defences, market, prices, system] effondrement m; [of talks, agreement, marriage, legal case, trial] échec m; [of civilization, empire, plan, scheme] effondrement m, écroulement m; **the country faces economic ~** le pays risque l'effondre- ment de son économie; **a 90% ~ in profits** une chute des profits de 90%; **this led to a ~ in confidence in the economy** cela a eu pour effet de détruire la confiance dans l'écono- mie; **the ~ in demand for cars** l'effondrement de la demande de voitures

collapsible [kəˈlæpsəbl] ADJ [table, chair, um- brella] pliant

collar [ˈkɒlər] ① N (attached: on garment) col m; (separate) (for men) faux-col m; (for women) col m, collerette f; (for dogs, horses etc) collier m; (= part of animal's neck) collier m; (Culin) [of beef, mutton etc] collier m; (Tech: on pipe etc) bague f; **to get hold of sb by the ~** saisir qn au collet → **white** ② VT [a]* [+ person] (lit, fig) mettre la main au collet de; [+ book, object] faire main basse sur [b] (Tech) baguer ③ COMP ► **collar button** N (US) = **collarstud**

collarbone [ˈkɒləbəʊn] N clavicule f

collarstud [ˈkɒləstʌd] N (Brit) bouton m de col

collate [kɒˈleɪt] VT [a] collationner (**with** avec) [b] (Rel) nommer (**to** à)

collateral [kɒˈlætərəl] ① ADJ [a] (= parallel) parallèle; [fact, phenomenon] concomitant; (Jur, Med) collatéral [b] (= subordinate) se- condaire, accessoire; (Fin) subsidiaire; (Fin) ~ **security** nantissement m [c] (Mil) ~ **damage** dommages mpl de guerre ② N [a] (Fin) nantissement m; **securities lodged as ~** titres mpl remis en nantissement [b] (Jur) collaté- ral(e) m(f)

collateralize [kɒˈlætərəlaɪz] VT garantir par nantissement

collation [kəˈleɪʃən] N collation f

colleague [ˈkɒliːg] N collègue mf

collect[1] [ˈkɒlekt] N (Rel) collecte f (prière)

collect[2] [kəˈlekt] ① VT [a] (= gather together, assemble) [+ valuables, wealth] accumuler, amasser; [+ facts, information, documents] rassembler, recueillir; [+ evidence, proof] rassembler; **the ~ed works of Shakespeare** les œuvres fpl complètes de Shakespeare; **she ~ed (together) a group of volunteers** elle a réuni un groupe de volontaires; **the dam ~s the water from the mountains** le barrage re- tient l'eau des montagnes; (fig) **to ~ one's wits** rassembler ses esprits; (fig) **to ~ o.s.** (= re- gain control of o.s.) se reprendre; (= reflect quietly) se recueillir; (fig) **to ~ one's thoughts** se recueillir, se concentrer [b] (= pick up) ramasser; **the children ~ed (up) the books for the teacher** les enfants ont ra- massé les livres pour le professeur; **these vases ~ the dust** ces vases attirent la poussière [c] (= obtain) [+ money, subscriptions, signatures] recueillir; [+ taxes, dues, fines] percevoir; [+ rents] encaisser, toucher; (US) ~ **on delivery** paiement m à la livraison, livraison f contre remboursement; **she ~ed the prize for best writer** elle a reçu le prix du meilleur écrivain [d] (= take official possession of) [bus or railway company] [+ luggage etc] venir chercher (à do- micile); [ticket collector] [+ tickets] ramasser; (Brit Post) ~ **to ~ letters** faire la levée du courrier; **the rubbish is ~ed twice a week** les ordures sont ramassées deux fois par semai- ne; **the firm ~s the empty bottles** la compa- gnie récupère les bouteilles vides; (Comm) **to ~ goods/an order** retirer des marchandises/ une commande [e] (as hobby) [+ stamps, antiques, coins] collectionner, faire collection de; (fig) **she ~s* poets/lame ducks** etc elle collectionne* les poètes/canards boiteux etc [f] (= call for) [+ person] aller chercher, (passer) prendre; **I'll ~ you in the car/at 8 o'clock** j'irai

| ► LANGUAGE IN USE: | **cold** | 7.5 |

vous chercher *or* je passerai vous prendre en voiture/à 8 heures ; **to ~ one's mail/one's keys** *etc* (*passer*) prendre son courrier/ses clefs *etc* ; **I'll come and ~ the book this evening** je passerai prendre le livre ce soir ; **the bus ~s the children each morning** l'autobus ramasse les enfants tous les matins

2 VI a [*people*] se rassembler, se réunir ; [*things*] s'amasser, s'entasser ; [*dust, water*] s'accumuler ; **a crowd had ~ed outside the building** une foule s'était rassemblée devant le bâtiment
b (*for charity*) **to ~ for the injured** faire la quête *or* quêter pour les blessés
3 ADV (*US Telec*) **to call ~** téléphoner en PCV
4 COMP ► **collect call** N (*US Telec*) communication *f* en PCV

collectable [kəˈlektɪd] ADJ **a ~ antique** *or* **item** une pièce de collection
collected [kəˈlektɪd] ADJ serein
collection [kəˈlekʃən] 1 N a (*= group*) [*of records, coins, stamps, paintings*] collection *f* ; (*Fashion*) **winter/summer ~** collection *f* d'hiver/d'été
b (*= anthology*) [*of stories, essays, songs*] recueil *m*
c **a ~ of buildings/people** (*= a number of*) un ensemble de bâtiments/personnes ; **there was a ~ of books on the table** il y avait un assortiment de livres sur la table
d (*= pick-up*) [*of goods, refuse*] ramassage *m* ; **your curtains are ready for ~** vos rideaux sont prêts, vous pouvez venir les chercher
e (*Brit Post*) [*of mail*] levée *f*
f [*of money*] (*for charity*) collecte *f* ; (*in church*) quête *f* ; **to take the ~** faire la quête ; **to take a ~ (for sb/sth)** faire une collecte (au profit de qn/qch *or* pour qn/qch)
g (*NonC = act of gathering*) [*of taxes*] perception *f*, collecte *f* ; levée *f* ; [*of rents*] encaissement *m* ; [*of information, signatures*] collecte *f*
2 COMP ► **collection box** N (*Rel*) tronc *m* ► **collection charges** NPL (*Fin, Comm*) frais *mpl* d'encaissement ► **collection plate** N (*Rel*) plateau *m* pour la quête ► **collection tin** N = **collection box**

collective [kəˈlektɪv] 1 ADJ collectif 2 N coopérative *f* 3 COMP ► **collective bargaining** N (*négociations fpl* pour une) convention *f* collective de travail ► **collective noun** N (*Ling*) collectif *m* ► **collective unconscious** N (*Psych*) inconscient *m* collectif
collectively [kəˈlektɪvlɪ] ADV collectivement
collectivism [kəˈlektɪvɪzəm] N collectivisme *m*
collectivist [kəˈlektɪvɪst] ADJ collectiviste *mf*
collectivization [kəˌlektɪvaɪˈzeɪʃən] N collectivisation *f*
collectivize [kəˈlektɪvaɪz] VT collectiviser
collector [kəˈlektə*r*] 1 N [*of taxes*] percepteur *m* ; [*of dues*] receveur *m* ; [*of rent, cash*] encaisseur *m* ; [*of stamps, coins etc*] collectionneur *m*, -euse *f* ; (*also* **ticket ~**) contrôleur *m*, -euse *f* 2 COMP ► **collector's item** N pièce *f* de collection
colleen [kɒˈliːn] N jeune Irlandaise *f* ; (*in Ireland*) jeune fille *f*
college [ˈkɒlɪdʒ] 1 N a (*= institution for higher education*) établissement *m* d'enseignement supérieur ; (*for professional training*) école *f* professionnelle, collège *m* technique ; (*Brit*) **College of Advanced Technology** ≈ IUT *m*, ≈ Institut *m* universitaire de technologie ; ~ **of agriculture** institut *m* agronomique ; ~ **of art** école *f* des beaux-arts ; ~ **of domestic science** école *f* or centre *m* d'enseignement ménager ; (*Brit*) **College of Education** ≈ IUFM *m*, ≈ institut *m* universitaire de formation des maîtres ; (*Brit*) **College of Further Education** centre *m* de

formation continue ; ~ **of music** conservatoire *m* de musique ; **to go to ~** faire des études supérieures ; (*US Univ*) ~ **catalog(ue)** livret *m* de l'étudiant ; ~ **staff** corps *m* enseignant → **naval, teacher**
b (*within a university*) (*Brit*) collège *m* ; (*US*) faculté *f*
c (*= club*) société *f* ; (*= learned society*) académie *f* ; **College of Physicians/Surgeons** Académie *f* de médecine/de chirurgie ; **the College of Cardinals** le Sacré Collège → **electoral**
2 COMP ► **college-bound** ADJ (*US Scol*) **~-bound student** élève *mf* qui se destine aux études universitaires ; **~-bound program** programme *m* de préparation aux études universitaires

---

COLLEGE

Terme très général désignant un établissement d'enseignement supérieur. En Grande-Bretagne, un **college** *peut aussi bien enseigner les arts plastiques ou la musique que préparer des brevets de technicien supérieur en coiffure ou en secrétariat. Certaines universités, dont Oxford et Cambridge, sont organisées en* **colleges***, qui, dans ces universités dites « collégiales », sont responsables de l'organisation de l'enseignement ; la délivrance des diplômes reste la prérogative des universités.*

Aux États-Unis, les universités sont administrativement divisées en **colleges***, qui correspondent à des facultés, par exemple «* **College of Arts and Sciences** *» et «* **College of Medicine** *». Les « junior* **colleges** *» ou « community* **colleges** *» sont des établissements de premier cycle universitaire, qui assurent également la formation continue des adultes salariés. Les diplômes de troisième cycle universitaire sont décernés par une « graduate school ». →* DEGREE ; OXBRIDGE

---

collegiate [kəˈliːdʒɪt] 1 ADJ [*life*] de collège ; (*Can*) [*studies*] secondaire 2 COMP ► **collegiate church** N collégiale *f*
collide [kəˈlaɪd] VI a (*lit*) [*vehicles, trains, planes*] entrer en collision, se heurter ; [*people*] se heurter ; **to ~ with** [*vehicle, train, plane*] entrer en collision avec, heurter ; [*person*] heurter ; (*Naut*) aborder b (*fig*) se heurter (**with** à), entrer en conflit (**with** avec)
collie [ˈkɒlɪ] N colley *m*
collier [ˈkɒlɪə*r*] N a (*= miner*) mineur *m* b (*= ship*) charbonnier *m*
colliery [ˈkɒlɪərɪ] N (*Brit*) houillère *f*, mine *f* (de charbon)
collimator [ˈkɒlɪˌmeɪtə*r*] 1 N collimateur *m* 2 COMP ► **collimator viewfinder** N (*Phot*) viseur *m* à cadre lumineux
collision [kəˈlɪʒən] 1 N a (*lit*) collision *f*, heurt *m* ; (*Rail*) collision *f* ; (*Naut*) abordage *m* ; **to come into ~ with** [+ *car, train*] entrer en collision avec, heurter ; [+ *boat*] aborder b (*fig*) conflit *m*, opposition *f* 2 COMP ► **collision course** N **to be on a ~ course** (*Naut etc*) être sur une route de collision ; (*fig*) aller au-devant de l'affrontement (**with** avec) ► **collision damage waiver** N (*Insurance*) clause d'exclusion des dommages dus à une collision, donnant droit à une réduction des frais de contrat
collocate [ˈkɒləkət] (*Ling*) 1 N cooccurrent *m* 2 [ˈkɒləkeɪt] VI [*words*] être cooccurrents ; **to ~ with ...** être le cooccurrent de ...
collocation [ˌkɒləˈkeɪʃən] N (*Ling*) collocation *f*
colloquial [kəˈləʊkwɪəl] ADJ familier
colloquialism [kəˈləʊkwɪəlɪzəm] N (*Ling*) expression *f* familière
colloquially [kəˈləʊkwɪəlɪ] ADV familièrement, dans le langage parlé
colloquium [kəˈləʊkwɪəm] N (*pl* **colloquiums** *or* **colloquia** [kəˈləʊkwɪə]) colloque *m*
colloquy [ˈkɒləkwɪ] N colloque *m*, conversation *f*

collude [kəˈluːd] VI s'associer (*dans une affaire louche*)
collusion [kəˈluːʒən] N collusion *f* ; **in ~ with ...** en complicité avec ..., de connivence avec ...
collusive [kəˈluːsɪv] ADJ (*frm pej*) collusoire (*frm*)
collywobbles: [ˈkɒlɪˌwɒblz] NPL **to have the ~** (*= be scared*) avoir la frousse* *or* la trouille* ; (*= have stomach trouble*) avoir la chiasse‡
Colo. ABBR = **Colorado**
Cologne [kəˈləʊn] N a Cologne b (**eau de**) ~ eau *f* de Cologne
Colombia [kəˈlɒmbɪə] N la Colombie
Colombian [kəˈlɒmbɪən] 1 ADJ colombien 2 N Colombien(ne) *m(f)*
colon[1] [ˈkəʊlən] N (*pl* **colons** *or* **cola**) (*Anat*) côlon *m*
colon[2] [ˈkəʊlən] N (*pl* **colons**) (*Gram*) deux-points *m inv*
colonel [ˈkɜːnl] N colonel *m* ; **Colonel Smith** le colonel Smith ; (*on envelope*) le Colonel Smith
colonial [kəˈləʊnɪəl] 1 ADJ a colonial b (*US*) [*house*] en style du 18ᵉ siècle, style 18ᵉ → HOUSE 2 N colonial(e) *m(f)* 3 COMP ► **Colonial Office** N ministère *m* des Colonies
colonialism [kəˈləʊnɪəlɪzəm] N colonialisme *m*
colonialist [kəˈləʊnɪəlɪst] ADJ, N colonialiste *mf*
colonic [kəʊˈlɒnɪk] 1 ADJ du côlon 2 COMP ► **colonic irrigation** N lavement *m*
colonist [ˈkɒlənɪst] N colon *m* (*habitant etc d'une colonie*)
colonization [ˌkɒlənaɪˈzeɪʃən] N colonisation *f*
colonize [ˈkɒlənaɪz] VT coloniser
colonized [ˈkɒlənaɪzd] ADJ colonisé
colonnade [ˌkɒləˈneɪd] N colonnade *f*
colony [ˈkɒlənɪ] N (*all senses*) colonie *f* → **leper**
colophon [ˈkɒləfən] N (*= emblem*) logotype *m*, colophon *m* ; (*= end text in book*) achevé *m* d'imprimer ; (*= end text in manuscript*) colophon *m*
color *etc* [ˈkʌlə*r*] (*US*) = **colour**
Colorado [ˌkɒləˈrɑːdəʊ] 1 N (*= state*) le Colorado ; **in ~** dans le Colorado 2 COMP ► **Colorado beetle** N doryphore *m*
colorant [ˈkʌlərənt] N (*US*) = **colourant**
coloration [ˌkʌləˈreɪʃən] N coloration *f*, coloris *m* → **protective**
coloratura [ˌkɒlərəˈtʊərə] 1 N coloratura *f* 2 ADJ [*voice, part*] de coloratura
colorcast [ˈkʌləkɑːst] 1 N émission *f* en couleurs 2 VT retransmettre en couleurs
colossal [kəˈlɒsl] ADJ (*lit, fig*) colossal
colossally [kəˈlɒsəlɪ] ADV [*expensive, destructive*] effroyablement ; [*improve, increase*] de façon phénoménale ; ~ **powerful** d'une puissance colossale
colossi [kəˈlɒsaɪ] NPL of **colossus**
Colossians [kəˈlɒʃənz] N Colossiens *mpl*
colossus [kəˈlɒsəs] N (*pl* **colossi** *or* **colossuses**) colosse *m*
colostomy [kəˈlɒstəmɪ] 1 N colostomie *f* 2 COMP ► **colostomy bag** N poche *f* pour colostomie
colostrum [kəˈlɒstrəm] N colostrum *m*
colour, color (*US*) [ˈkʌlə*r*] 1 N a (*= hue*) couleur *f* ; **what ~ is it?** de quelle couleur est-ce ? ; **there is not enough ~ in it** cela manque de couleur ; **to change ~** changer de couleur ; **to take the ~ out of sth** décolorer qch → **primary**
b (*fig*) **the ~ of a newspaper** la couleur *or* les opinions *fpl* d'un journal ; **let's see the ~ of your money*** fais voir la couleur de ton fric* ; **a symphony/a poem full of ~** une symphonie

pleine/un poème plein de couleur; **to give** or **lend ~ to a tale** colorer un récit; **to give a false ~ to sth** présenter qch sous un faux jour, dénaturer qch; **under (the) ~ of ...** sous prétexte or couleur de ...

c (= *complexion*) teint *m*, couleur *f* (*du visage*); **to change ~** changer de couleur or de visage; **to lose (one's)** pâlir, perdre ses couleurs; **to get one's ~ back** reprendre des couleurs; **he looks an unhealthy ~** il a très mauvaise mine; **he had gone a funny ~** il avait pris une couleur bizarre; **to have a high ~** être haut en couleur → **off**

d (*Art*) (= *pigment*) matière *f* colorante, couleur *f*; (= *paint*) peinture *f*; (= *dye*) teinture *f*; (= *shades, tones*) coloris *m*, couleur *f*; **to paint sth in bright/dark ~s** (*lit*) peindre qch de couleurs vives/sombres; (*fig*) peindre qch sous de belles couleurs/sous de couleurs sombres; (*fig*) **to see sth in its true ~s** voir qch sous son vrai jour → **2**; → **local, watercolour**

e (*of race*) couleur *f*; **his ~ counted against him** sa couleur jouait contre lui; **it is not a question of ~** ce n'est pas une question de race; **people of ~†** gens *mpl* de couleur

2 colours NPL (= *symbol of allegiance*) couleurs *fpl* (*d'un club, d'un parti etc*); (*Mil*) couleurs *fpl*, drapeau *m*; (*Naut*) couleurs *fpl*, pavillon *m*; (*Sport*) **to get** or **win one's ~s** être sélectionné pour (faire partie de) l'équipe; **to salute the ~s** saluer le drapeau; **to fight with the ~s** combattre sous les drapeaux; (*fig*) **to stick to one's ~s** rester fidèle à ses principes or à ce qu'on a dit; (*fig*) **he showed his true ~s when he said ...** il s'est révélé tel qu'il est vraiment quand il a dit ... → **flying, nail, troop**

3 VT **a** (*lit*) (= *give colour to*) colorer, donner de la couleur à; (*with paint*) peindre; (*with crayons etc*) colorier; (= *dye*) teindre; (= *tint*) teinter; **to ~ sth red** colorer (or colorier etc) qch en rouge; **to ~ (in) a picture** colorier une image **b** (*fig*) [+ *story, description*] colorer; [+ *facts*] (= *misrepresent*) fausser; (= *exaggerate*) exagérer → **coloured 1b**

4 VI [*thing*] se colorer; [*person*] rougir

5 COMP ► **color line** N (*US*) = **colour bar** ► **colour bar** N (*Brit*) discrimination *f* raciale ► **colour-blind** ADJ daltonien; (*fig = non-discriminatory*) sans discrimination raciale ► **colour blindness** N daltonisme *m*, achromatopsie *f* ► **colour camera** N (*TV*) caméra *f* couleur *inv* ► **colour code** N code *m* couleurs ► **colour-code** VT codifier par couleurs ► **colour film** N (*for camera*) pellicule *f* couleur(s); (*for movie camera; in cinema*) film *m* en couleur(s) ► **colour filter** N (*Phot*) filtre *m* coloré ► **colour photograph** N photo *f* en couleur(s) ► **colour photography** N photographie *f* en couleur(s) ► **colour scheme** N combinaison *f* de(s) couleurs; **to choose a ~ scheme** assortir les couleurs or les tons ► **colour sergeant** N (*Brit Mil*) ≈ sergent-chef *m* ► **colour slide** N diapositive *f* en couleur(s) ► **colour supplement** N (*Brit Press*) supplément *m* illustré ► **colour television** N télévision *f* en couleur(s)

colourant ['kʌlərənt] N (*Brit*) colorant *m*

coloured, colored (*US*) ['kʌləd] **1** ADJ **a** (= *not black or white*) [*glass, water*] coloré; [*chalk, pencil, bead*] de couleur; [*picture, photo, television*] en couleur(s); [*fabric, garment*] de couleur; [*drawing*] colorié; **to be ~ pink/blue** être coloré en rose/en bleu; **brightly ~** aux couleurs vives; **coffee-~** couleur café *inv*; **gold-~** doré; **mauve-~** (de couleur) mauve; **muddy-~** couleur de boue; **a straw-~ hat** un chapeau couleur paille **b** (= *exaggerated*) **a highly ~ tale** un récit enjolivé **c†** [*person*] de couleur **d** (*in South Africa*) [*person*] métis (métisse *f*) **2 coloureds†** NPL (*US, Brit*) personnes *fpl* de couleur; (*in South Africa*) métis *mpl* → **cape²**

---

colourfast, colorfast (*US*) ['kʌlərfɑːst] ADJ grand teint *inv*

colourful, colorful (*US*) ['kʌləfʊl] ADJ **a** (= *bright*) [*flowers, clothes, poster, design*] aux couleurs vives **b** (= *exciting*) [*story, account, history, character, figure*] pittoresque, haut en couleur **c** (*euph = immoral*) [*past, career, background*] mouvementé **d** (*euph = vulgar*) [*language*] très libre

colourfully, colorfully (*US*) ['kʌləfʊlɪ] ADV **a** (= *brightly*) [*dressed, painted, decorated*] de couleurs vives **b** (= *excitingly*) [*describe*] dans un style pittoresque or haut en couleur **c** (*euph = vulgarly*) [*swear, call*] d'une manière expressive

colouring, coloring (*US*) ['kʌlərɪŋ] **1** N **a** (= *complexion*) teint *m*; **high ~** teint m coloré **b** (*NonC*) coloration *f*; [*of drawings etc*] coloriage *m*; (*fig*) [*of news, facts etc*] travestissement *m*, dénaturation *f* **c** (= *hue*) coloris *m*, coloration *f* **d** (*in food*) colorant *m* (alimentaire) **2** COMP ► **colouring book** N album *m* à colorier

colourist, colorist (*US*) ['kʌlərɪst] N (*Phot*) chromiste *mf*

colourization, colorization (*US*) [ˌkʌləraɪˈzeɪʃən] N (*Cine*) colorisation *f*

colourize, colorize (*US*) ['kʌləraɪz] VT (*Cine*) coloriser

colourless, colorless (*US*) ['kʌləlɪs] ADJ (*lit*) sans couleur, incolore; (*fig*) terne, fade

colourway ['kʌləweɪ] N (*Brit*) coloris *m*

colt [kəʊlt] N **a** (*Zool*) poulain *m*; (*fig = a youth*) petit jeune *m* (*pej*), novice *m* **b** **Colt®** (= *pistol*) colt *m*

coltish ['kəʊltɪʃ] ADJ (= *frisky*) guilleret, folâtre; (= *inexperienced*) jeunet, inexpérimenté

coltsfoot ['kəʊltsfʊt] N (*pl* **coltsfoots**) (*Bot*) pas-d'âne *m inv*, tussilage *m*

Columbia [kəˈlʌmbɪə] N (*US*) **(District of) ~** (le district fédéral de) Columbia → **British**

Columbine ['kɒləmbaɪn] N (*Theat*) Colombine *f*

columbine ['kɒləmbaɪn] N ancolie *f*

Columbus [kəˈlʌmbəs] **1** N **(Christopher) ~** Christophe Colomb *m* **2** COMP ► **Columbus Day** N (*US*) jour férié le deuxième lundi d'octobre, commémorant la découverte de l'Amérique par Christophe Colomb

column ['kɒləm] **1** N (*all senses*) colonne *f* → **fifth 2** COMP ► **column inch** N *dans un journal*, espace de 2,5 centimètres sur la largeur d'une colonne

columnist ['kɒləmnɪst] N (*Press*) chroniqueur *m*, échotier *m*, -ière *f*

coma ['kəʊmə] N coma *m*; **in a ~** dans le coma

comatose ['kəʊmətəʊs] ADJ comateux

comb [kəʊm] **1** N **a** peigne *m*; (*large-toothed*) démêloir *m*; **to run a ~ through one's hair ◊ to give one's hair a ~** se donner un coup de peigne, se peigner **b** (*for horse*) étrille *f*; (*Tech: for wool etc*) peigne *m*, carde *f*; (*Elec*) balai *m* **c** [*of fowl*] crête *f*; [*of helmet*] cimier *m* **d** (= *honeycomb*) rayon *m* de miel **2** VT **a** peigner; (*Tech*) peigner, carder; [+ *horse*] étriller; **to ~ one's hair** se peigner; **to ~ sb's hair** peigner qn **b** (*fig = search*) [+ *area, hills, town*] fouiller, ratisser; **he ~ed (through) the papers looking for evidence** il a dépouillé le dossier à la recherche d'une preuve

► **comb out** VT SEP [+ *hair*] peigner, démêler; **they ~ed out the useless members of the staff** on a passé le personnel au peigne fin et éliminé les incapables

combat ['kɒmbæt] **1** N combat *m* → **close¹, fatigue, unarmed 2** VT (*lit, fig*) combattre, lutter contre **3** VI combattre, lutter (**for** pour, **with, against** contre) **4** COMP ► **combat car** N (*véhicule m*) blindé *m* léger de campagne ► **combat duty** N **on ~ duty** en service commandé ► **combat fatigue** N psychose *f*

---

traumatique (*du soldat*) ► **combat jacket** N veste *f* de treillis ► **combat knife** N (*pl* **combat knives**) poignard *m* ► **combat neurosis** N = **combat fatigue** ► **combat troops** NPL troupes *fpl* de combat ► **combat zone** N zone *f* de combat

combatant ['kɒmbətənt] ADJ, N combattant(e) *m(f)*

combative ['kɒmbətɪv] ADJ combatif

combe [kuːm] N = **coomb**

combination [ˌkɒmbɪˈneɪʃən] **1** N (*gen, Chem, Math: also of lock*) combinaison *f*; [*of people*] association *f*, coalition *f*; [*of events*] concours *m*; [*of interests*] coalition *f*; (*Brit Aut*) **(motorcycle) ~** side-car *m* **2 combinations** NPL (= *undergarment*) combinaison-culotte *f* (*de femme*) **3** COMP ► **combination lock** N serrure *f* à combinaison ► **combination sandwich** N (*US*) gros sandwich *m* mixte ► **combination therapy** N thérapie *f* combinée

combine [kəmˈbaɪn] **1** VT combiner (**with** avec), joindre (**with** à); (*Chem*) combiner; **he ~d generosity with discretion** il alliait la générosité à la discrétion; **they ~d forces/efforts** ils ont uni or joint leurs forces/efforts; **to ~ business with pleasure** mélanger le travail et l'agrément, joindre l'utile à l'agréable **2** VI s'unir, s'associer; [*parties*] fusionner; [*workers*] s'associer; (*Chem*) se combiner; (*fig*) se liguer (**against** contre); [*events*] concourir (**to do** à faire) **3** ['kɒmbaɪn] N **a** association *f*; (*Comm, Fin*) trust *m*, cartel *m*; (*Jur*) corporation *f* **b** (*also* ~ **harvester**) moissonneuse-batteuse *f* **4** COMP ► **combining form** N (*Ling*) élément *m* de mot

combined [kəmˈbaɪnd] **1** ADJ **a** (= *mixed*) **~ with** conjugué à or avec **b** (= *joint*) [*efforts*] conjugué, combiné **c** (= *total*) [*salaries*] joint; **~ assets** capital *m* commun; **their ~ wealth** leurs fortunes réunies **d** **~ clock and radio** radio-réveil *m* **2** COMP ► **combined forces** NPL (*Mil*) forces *f* alliées ► **combined honours** N (*Brit Univ*) **to do ~ honours** faire un double cursus ► **combined operation** N (*Mil*) opération *f* combinée

combo: ['kɒmbəʊ] N (*Mus*) petite formation *f* musicale

combustible [kəmˈbʌstɪbl] ADJ [*material*] combustible; (*fig*) [*situation, atmosphere*] explosif, critique

combustion [kəmˈbʌstʃən] **1** N combustion *f* → **internal, spontaneous 2** COMP ► **combustion chamber** N (*Aut*) chambre *f* d'explosion

---

come [kʌm]

vb: pret **came**, *ptp* **come**

1 INTRANSITIVE VERB	**4** COMPOUNDS
2 TRANSITIVE VERB	**5** PHRASAL VERBS
3 NOUN	

1 INTRANSITIVE VERB

a venir; (= *arrive*) venir, arriver; **~ here** venez ici; **no one has ~** personne n'est venu; **~ and see me soon ◊ ~ see me soon** (*US*) venez me voir bientôt; **he has ~ to mend the television** il est venu réparer la télévision; **the time will ~ when ...** un jour viendra où ..., il viendra un temps où ...; **he has ~ a long way** (*lit*) il est venu de loin; (*fig = made great progress*) il a fait du chemin; **help came in time** les secours sont arrivés à temps; **when did he ~?** quand est-il arrivé?; **to ~ home** rentrer (chez soi or à la maison); **coming!** j'arrive!; **~, ~!** ◊ now! allons!, voyons!; **when your turn ~s** quand ce sera (à) votre tour, quand votre tour viendra; **she is coming* six** elle va sur ses six ans, elle va avoir six ans; **she had it coming to her*** elle l'a or l'avait (bien) cherché; **he got what was coming to him** il n'a eu que ce qu'il méritait; **~ again?:** comment?, pardon?; **I don't know whether I'm coming or going** je ne sais plus où donner de la tête

♦ **to come** + *preposition*: you go on, I'll ~ **after** (you) allez-y, je vous suis; **the rain came closely after the thunderclap** la pluie a suivi de près le coup de tonnerre; **it came as a shock to him** cela lui a fait un choc; **it came as a surprise to him** cela l'a (beaucoup) surpris; **to ~ before** sb/sth venir avant qn/qch; (*Jur*) **to ~ before a judge** [*accused*] comparaître devant un juge; [*case*] être entendu par un juge; **to ~ behind sb/sth** suivre qn/qch; (*fig*) **to ~ between two people** (= *cause trouble*) (venir) se mettre entre deux personnes; **to ~ for sb/sth** venir chercher *or* venir prendre qn/qch; **he has ~ from Edinburgh** il vient d'Édimbourg; **he has just ~ from Edinburgh** il arrive d'Édimbourg; (*fig*) **to ~ from** (= *originate from*) [*person*] venir de, être originaire *or* natif de; [*object, commodity*] provenir *or* venir de; **he ~s from a very poor family** il vient *or* il est issu d'une famille très pauvre; **it came into my head that ...** il m'est venu à l'esprit que ...; **to ~ into sight** apparaître, devenir visible; **they came to a town** ils sont arrivés à une ville, ils ont atteint une ville; **so it has ~ to this!** nous en sommes donc là!; **if it ~s to that, you shouldn't have done it either** à ce compte-là *or* à ce moment-là* tu n'aurais pas dû le faire non plus; **if it ~s to that, why did you go?** dans ce cas-là *or* à ce moment-là, pourquoi y es-tu allé?; **when it ~s to mathematics, no one can beat her** pour ce qui est des mathématiques, elle est imbattable; **~ with me** venez avec moi → **agreement, bloom, blossom, blow², effect, grief**

♦ **to come** + *-ing*: **to ~ running/shouting** *etc* arriver en courant/en criant *etc*; **to ~ hurrying** arriver en toute hâte

♦ **to come** + *infinitive* (= *be finally in a position to*) en venir à, finir par; **I have ~ to believe him** j'en suis venu à le croire; **he came to admit he was wrong** il a fini par reconnaître qu'il avait tort; **now I ~ to think of it** réflexion faite, quand j'y songe; (*liter*) **it came to pass that ...** il advint que ... (*liter*)

♦ **to come** + *adverb/adjective*: **to ~ apart** (= *come off*) se détacher; (= *come unstuck*) se décoller; (= *fall to pieces*) tomber en morceaux; **it came apart in my hands** ça s'est cassé tout seul; **all the other candidates came far behind** tous les autres candidats sont arrivés loin derrière; **everything came right in the end** tout s'est arrangé à la fin; **his dreams came true** ses rêves se sont réalisés; **to ~ undone** se défaire, se dénouer → **clean, loose, naturally, unstick**

♦ **to come and go** aller et venir; **they were coming and going all day** ils n'ont fait qu'aller et venir toute la journée; **the pain ~s and goes** la douleur est intermittente

♦ **... to come**: **the life to ~** la vie future; **the years to ~** les années *fpl* à venir; **in time to ~** à l'avenir

♦ **come** + *day, month*: **I've known him for three years** – **January** cela fera trois ans en janvier que je le connais; **she will be six ~ August** elle aura six ans au mois d'août *or* en août; **a week ~ Monday** il y aura huit jours lundi

[b] **= have one's place** venir, se trouver, être placé; **May ~s before June** mai vient avant *or* précède juin; **July ~s after June** juillet vient après *or* suit juin; **this passage ~s on page 10** ce passage se trouve à la page 10; **the adjective must ~ before the noun** l'adjectif doit être placé devant *or* précéder le substantif; **a princess ~s before a duchess** une princesse prend le pas *or* a la préséance sur une duchesse

[c] **= happen** arriver (**to** à), se produire; **no harm will ~ to him** il ne lui arrivera rien de mal; **economic recovery came slowly** la reprise économique a été lente; **how do you ~ to be so late?** comment se fait-il que vous soyez si en retard?; **~ what may** quoi qu'il arrive (*subj*)

♦ **to come of sth**: **nothing came of it** il n'en est rien résulté; **that's what ~s of not doing as you're told!** voilà ce que c'est que de dé-

sobéir!, voilà ce qui arrive quand on désobéit!; **no good will ~ of it** ça ne mènera à rien de bon, il n'en sortira rien de bon

♦ **how come?** * comment ça se fait?*; **how ~ you can't find it?** * comment se fait-il que tu n'arrives pas à le trouver?

[d] **= be available** **this dress ~s in three sizes** cette robe existe *or* se fait en trois tailles; **she's as clever as they ~** * elle est futée comme pas une*; **how do you like your tea? — as it ~s** comment voulez-vous votre thé? — peu importe *or* ça m'est égal

[e] ⁂ **= reach orgasm** jouir

[2] TRANSITIVE VERB
⁂ **that's coming it a bit strong!** faut pas pousser!*, ça, c'est un peu fort! → **game, innocent**

[3] NOUN
⁂ **= semen** foutre⁂ *m*

[4] COMPOUNDS
▸ **come-at-able** * ADJ accessible ▸ **come-hither** * ADJ **she gave him a ~-hither look** elle lui a lancé un regard aguichant ▸ **come-on** * N (*gen* = *lure*) attrape-nigaud *m*, truc* *m*; (*sexual*) **to give sb the ~-on** provoquer qn, allumer* qn ▸ **come-to-bed eyes** * NPL **she has ~-to-bed eyes** elle a un regard provocant *or* aguicheur

[5] PHRASAL VERBS
▸ **come about** VI [a] (*impers* = *happen*) se faire (*impers* + *que* + *subj*), arriver, se produire; **how does it ~ about that you are here?** comment se fait-il que vous soyez ici?; **this is why it came about** voilà pourquoi c'est arrivé *or* cela s'est produit
[b] (*Naut*) [*wind*] tourner, changer de direction

▸ **come across** [1] VI [a] (= *cross*) traverser
[b] **he ~s across as an honest man** il donne l'impression d'être un honnête homme; **his speech came across very well** son discours a fait bonne impression; **his speech came across very badly** son discours n'a pas fait d'effet *or* n'a pas passé la rampe; **despite his attempts to hide them, his true feelings came across quite clearly** malgré ses efforts pour les cacher, ses vrais sentiments se faisaient sentir clairement
[c] (*US** = *keep promise etc*) s'exécuter, tenir parole

[2] VT FUS (= *find or meet by chance*) [+ *thing*] trouver par hasard, tomber sur; [+ *person*] rencontrer par hasard, tomber sur; **if you ~ across my watch ...** si vous tombez sur ma montre ...

▸ **come across with** * VT FUS [+ *money*] se fendre de*, y aller de*; [+ *information*] donner, vendre; **he came across with £10** il s'est fendu* de 10 livres; **the criminal came across with the names of his accomplices** le criminel a donné* ses complices

▸ **come along** VI [a] (*imper only*) **~ along!** (*impatiently*) allons *or* voyons, dépêchez-vous!; (*in friendly tone*) (allez,) venez!
[b] (= *accompany*) venir, suivre; **could my sister ~ along as well?** est-ce que ma sœur peut venir aussi?; **why don't you ~ along?** pourquoi ne viendrais-tu pas?; **~ along with me** venez avec moi, suivez-moi
[c] (= *arrive by chance*) **it was lucky you came along** c'est une chance que vous soyiez venu; **he waited a long time for the perfect job to ~ along** il a attendu longtemps avant que l'emploi idéal ne se présente (*subj*)
[d] (= *progress*) avancer, faire des progrès; [*plants, children*] pousser; [*plans*] avancer; **he's coming along in French** il fait des progrès en français; **how is your broken arm? — it's coming along quite well** comment va votre bras cassé? — il va *or* ça se remet bien; **my book isn't coming along at all well** mon livre n'avance pas bien

▸ **come around** VI = **come round**
▸ **come at** VT FUS attaquer; **he came at me with an axe** il s'est jeté sur moi en brandissant une

hache

▸ **come away** VI [a] (= *leave*) partir, s'en aller; **she had to ~ away before the end** elle a dû partir avant la fin; **~ away from there!** sors de là!, écarte-toi de là!
[b] (= *become detached*) [*button etc*] se détacher, partir; **it came away in my hands** cela m'est resté dans les mains

▸ **come back** VI [*person*] revenir; [*fashion*] revenir à la mode; **he came back two hours later** il est revenu deux heures plus tard; (*Sport*) **he came back strongly into the game** il est revenu en force dans le jeu; **I asked her to ~ back with me** je lui ai demandé de me raccompagner; **to ~ back to what I was saying ...** pour en revenir à ce que je disais ...; **I'll ~ back to you on that one** * nous en reparlerons (plus tard); **his face/name is coming back to me** son visage/son nom me revient (à la mémoire *or* à l'esprit)

▸ **come back with** VT FUS répondre par; **when accused, he came back with a counteraccusation** quand on l'a accusé, il a répondu par une contre-accusation

▸ **come by** [1] VI passer (par là); **he came by yesterday and told us** il est venu *or* passé (par là) hier et nous l'a raconté
[2] VT FUS (= *obtain*) [+ *object*] obtenir, se procurer; [+ *idea, opinion*] se faire; **how did you ~ by that book?** comment vous êtes-vous procuré ce livre?

▸ **come down** VI [a] (*from ladder, stairs*) descendre (**from** de); (*from mountain*) descendre, faire la descente (**from** de); [*aircraft*] descendre; **~ down from there at once!** descends de là tout de suite!; (*fig*) **to ~ down in the world** descendre dans l'échelle sociale, déchoir; **her hair ~s down to her shoulders** ses cheveux lui descendent jusqu'aux épaules *or* lui tombent sur les épaules; (*fig*) **to ~ down (strongly) for or in favour of or on the side of sth** prendre (fermement) position en faveur de qch; **he came down on the side of the President** il s'est rangé du côté du président, il a pris parti pour le président
[b] (*the problem ~s down to money*) le problème se résume à *or* se réduit à une question d'argent; **it all ~s down to the fact that people are very dependent on their cars** tout le problème réside dans le fait que les gens ne peuvent pas se passer de leurs voitures; **when it ~s down to it, are we really free to speak our mind?** au fond, sommes-nous vraiment libres de dire ce que nous pensons?
[c] [*buildings etc*] (= *be demolished*) être démoli, être abattu; (= *fall down*) s'écrouler
[d] (= *drop*) [*prices*] baisser; **if you buy three, the price ~s down to £2** si vous en achetez trois, le prix est ramené à 2 livres
[e] (= *be transmitted*) [*tradition etc*] être transmis (de père en fils)

▸ **come down on** VT FUS [a] (= *punish*) punir; (= *rebuke*) s'en prendre à; **he came down on me like a ton of bricks** * il m'est tombé dessus à bras raccourcis
[b] **they came down on me** * **for a subscription** ils m'ont mis le grappin dessus* pour que je souscrive

▸ **come down with** VT FUS [a] (= *become ill from*) attraper; **to ~ down with flu** attraper une grippe
[b] (* = *pay out*) allonger⁂

▸ **come forward** VI se présenter (**as** comme); **several witnesses have ~ forward** plusieurs personnes se sont présentées comme témoins; **who will ~ forward as a candidate?** qui va se présenter comme candidat *or* se porter candidat?; **after the burglary, her neighbours came forward with help/money** après le cambriolage, ses voisins ont offert de l'aider/lui ont offert de l'argent; **to ~ forward with a suggestion** faire une suggestion; **to ~ forward with an answer** suggérer une réponse

▸ **come in** VI [a] [*person*] entrer; [*train, plane etc*] arriver; [*tide*] monter; **reports are now** coming in of a terrorist attack des informations nous parviennent selon lesquelles il y aurait eu un attentat terroriste; *(fig)* **when** *or* **where do I ~ in?** quand est-ce que j'entre en jeu, moi?; *(fig)* **where does your brother ~ in?** *(= how is he involved?)* qu'est-ce que ton frère a à voir là-dedans?; *(= what's to be done with him?)* qu'est-ce qu'on fait de ton frère là-dedans?, qu'est-ce que ton frère devient là-dedans?; *(fig)* **this is where we came in!** nous sommes revenus à la case départ!

b *[fashion]* devenir à la mode

c *(in a race)* arriver; **he came in fourth** il est arrivé quatrième; *(Scol)* **he came in first in geography** il a eu la meilleure note en géographie, il a été premier en géographie

d *(Pol = be elected to power)* être élu, arriver au pouvoir; **the socialists came in at the last election** les socialistes sont arrivés au pouvoir aux dernières élections

e **he has £20,000 coming in every year** il touche *or* encaisse 20 000 livres chaque année; **if I'm not working my pay won't be coming in** si je ne travaille pas, je ne toucherai pas ma paie; **we have no money coming in at the moment** nous n'avons aucune rentrée d'argent en ce moment

f **to ~ in handy** *or* **useful** avoir son utilité, venir à propos; **to ~ in handy** *or* **useful for sth** servir à qch, être commode pour qch

► **come in for** VT FUS *(= receive)* *[+ criticism]* être l'objet de, subir, être en butte à; *[+ reproach]* subir; *[+ praise]* recevoir

► **come into** VT FUS a *(= inherit)* hériter de, entrer en possession de; **to ~ into some money** *(gen)* recevoir une somme d'argent; *(by inheritance)* hériter (d'une somme d'argent); *(fig)* **to ~ into one's own** se réaliser, trouver sa voie

b *(= play a role)* **logic doesn't really ~ into it** la logique n'a pas grand-chose à voir là-dedans

► **come near to** VT FUS **to ~ near to doing** faillir faire, être à deux doigts de faire; **I came near to telling her everything** pour un peu je lui aurais tout dit, j'étais à deux doigts de tout lui dire; **he came near to (committing) suicide** il a été à deux doigts de se suicider

► **come off** 1 VI a *[button]* se détacher, se découdre; *[stains, marks]* s'enlever, partir

b *(= take place)* avoir lieu, se produire; **her wedding did not ~ off after all** son mariage n'a finalement pas eu lieu

c *(= succeed)* *[plan]* se réaliser; *[attempt, experiment]* réussir

d *(= acquit o.s.)* s'en tirer, s'en sortir; **he came off well by comparison with his brother** il s'en est très bien tiré en comparaison de son frère; **to ~ off best** gagner

e *(Theat)* *[actor]* sortir de scène; *[play]* s'arrêter, cesser d'être donné

f *(‡ = reach orgasm)* venir‡, jouir

2 VT FUS a **a button came off his coat** un bouton s'est détaché *or* décousu de son manteau; **he came off his bike** il est tombé de son vélo; *(Fin)* **to ~ off the gold standard** abandonner l'étalon-or

b *[+ drugs, medication]* arrêter

c **~ off it!‡** et puis quoi encore?, à d'autres!

► **come on** 1 VI a *(= follow)* suivre; *(= continue to advance)* continuer d'avancer

b *(imper only)* **~ on, try again!** allons *or* allez, encore un effort!

c *(= progress, develop)* faire des progrès, avancer; **how are your lettuces/plans coming on?** où en sont vos laitues/vos projets?; **my lettuces are coming on nicely** mes laitues poussent bien; **my plans are coming on nicely** mes plans avancent; **how are the children?** — **they are coming on** comment vont les enfants? — ils poussent bien *or* ça pousse!*

d *(= start)* *[night]* tomber; *[illness]* se déclarer; *[storm]* survenir, éclater; *[seasons]* arriver; **it came on to rain** ◊ **the rain came on** il s'est mis

à pleuvoir; **I feel a cold coming on** je sens que je m'enrhume

e *(= arise for discussion or judgement)* *[subject]* être soulevé, être mis sur le tapis; *[question]* être posé; *(Jur)* **his case ~s on this afternoon** son affaire viendra devant le juge cet après-midi

f *(Theat)* *[actor]* entrer en scène; *[play]* être joué *or* représenté *or* donné; **"Hamlet" is coming on next week** on donne « Hamlet » la semaine prochaine

g *(US fig)* **he came on quite sincere** il a donné l'impression d'être tout à fait sincère; **he came on as a fine man** il a fait l'effet d'être un homme bien

2 VT FUS = **come upon**

► **come on to** VT FUS a *(= start discussing)* *[+ question, topic, issue]* aborder; **I'll ~ on to that in a moment** j'aborderai cela dans un moment

b *(sexually)* **to ~ on to sb*** draguer qn*

► **come out** VI a *(gen)* sortir *(of* de); *[sun, stars]* paraître, se montrer; *[flower]* pousser, sortir; *[spots, rash]* sortir; *[secret, news]* être divulgué *or* révélé; *[truth]* se faire jour; *[book, magazine]* paraître, sortir, être publié; *[film]* sortir; *(Scol etc: in exams)* se classer; *[qualities]* se manifester, se révéler, se faire remarquer; *[stain]* s'en aller, partir; *[dye, colour]* *(= run)* déteindre; *(= fade)* passer, se faner; *[Math]* *[problem]* se résoudre; *[division etc]* tomber juste; **he came out third in French** il s'est classé *or* il est troisième en français

b **to ~ out well** être réussi; **this photo didn't ~ out well** cette photo n'a rien donné *or* n'est pas réussie; **the photo came out well** la photo est réussie *or* est très bonne; **you always ~ out well in photos** tu es toujours très bien sur les photos, tu es très photogénique

c *(with preposition)* **the total ~s out at** *or* **to 500** le total s'élève à 500; *(Med)* **to ~ out in a rash** avoir une éruption; *(fig)* **to ~ out for/against sth** se déclarer ouvertement pour/contre qch, prendre position pour/contre qch; *(fig)* **to ~ out of o.s.** *or* **one's shell** sortir de sa coquille *or* réserve *(fig)*

d *(Brit Ind: also* **to ~ out on strike***)* se mettre en grève, faire grève

e *(also* **to ~ out of the closet***)* *[homosexual]* se déclarer ouvertement homosexuel; **she came out as a lesbian** elle s'est ouvertement déclarée lesbienne

f *(= go into society)* faire ses débuts dans le monde

g *(= result from)* **~ out of** être né de

► **come out with** VT FUS* *(= say)* sortir*, dire; **you never know what she's going to ~ out with next** on ne sait jamais ce qu'elle va sortir* *or* dire; **~ out with it!** dis ce que tu as à dire!, accouche!‡

► **come over** 1 VI a *(lit)* venir; **he came over to England for a few months** il est venu passer quelques mois en Angleterre; **his family came over with the Normans** sa famille s'est installée ici du temps des Normands; *(fig)* **he came over to our side** il est passé de notre côté; **he came over to our way of thinking** il s'est rangé à notre avis

b *(* *= feel suddenly)* **to ~ over giddy** *or* **funny** se sentir mal tout d'un coup, se sentir tout chose*; **she came over faint** elle a failli s'évanouir *or* tourner de l'œil*; **she came over all shy** tout à coup la timidité la saisit *or* elle fut prise de timidité

c *(= make impression)* **he came over well in his speech** son discours l'a bien mis en valeur; **his speech came over well** son discours a fait bonne impression; **he came over as a fine politician** il a donné l'impression d'être un bon homme politique

2 VT FUS *[influences, feelings]* *[+ person]* saisir, s'emparer de; **a feeling of shyness came over her** la timidité la saisit, elle fut saisie de timidité; **a sudden change came over him** un changement soudain s'est fait jour en lui; **I**

don't know what came over her to speak like that! je ne sais pas ce qui lui a pris de parler comme ça!; **what's ~ over you?** qu'est-ce qui vous prend?

► **come round** VI a faire le tour *or* un détour; **the road was blocked and we had to ~ round by the farm** la route était bloquée et nous avons dû faire un détour par la ferme

b *(= drop in)* venir, passer; **do ~ round and see me one evening** passez me voir un de ces soirs

c *(= recur regularly)* revenir périodiquement; **your birthday will soon ~ round again** ce sera bientôt à nouveau ton anniversaire

d *(= change one's mind)* changer d'avis; **perhaps in time she will ~ round** peut-être qu'elle changera d'avis avec le temps; **he came round to our way of thinking in the end** il a fini par se ranger à notre avis

e *(= regain consciousness)* revenir à soi, reprendre connaissance; *(= get better)* se rétablir, se remettre **(after** de)

f *(= throw off bad mood etc)* se radoucir, redevenir aimable; **leave her alone, she'll soon ~ round** laissez-la tranquille, elle reviendra bientôt à d'autres sentiments

g *[boat]* venir au vent

► **come through** 1 VI a *(= cope)* s'en tirer, s'en sortir

b *(= arrive)* **reports of fighting are coming through** on raconte qu'il y a des combats; **his divorce has ~ through** son divorce a été prononcé; *(Telec)* **the call came through** on a reçu *or* eu la communication

c **what came through most was her enthusiasm for the project** ce qui ressortait surtout *or* ce qui était frappant, c'était son enthousiasme pour le projet

d **she came through for us** elle nous a donné satisfaction; **they came through on their promises** ils ont respecté leurs promesses, ils ont tenu parole

2 VT FUS *(= survive)* *[+ illness, danger, war]* survivre à

► **come through with** VT FUS *(US)* = **come up with**

► **come to** 1 VI a *(= regain consciousness)* revenir à soi, reprendre connaissance

b *(Naut = stop)* s'arrêter

2 VT FUS *[cost, sum]* revenir à, se monter à; **how much does it ~ to?** cela fait combien?, cela se monte à combien?; **it ~s to £20** ça fait 20 livres en tout; **it ~s to much less per metre if you buy a lot** cela revient beaucoup moins cher le mètre si vous en achetez beaucoup; *(fig)* **it ~s to the same thing** ça revient au même *or* à la même chose; *(fig)* **he will never ~ to much** il ne sera *or* fera jamais grand-chose

► **come together** VI *(= assemble)* se rassembler; *(= meet)* se rencontrer; *(fig)* **to ~ together again** se réconcilier

► **come under** VT FUS a *(= be subjected to)* *[+ sb's influence, domination]* tomber sous, subir; *[+ attack, criticism]* être l'objet de, essuyer

b *(= be classified under)* être classé sous; **that ~s under "towns"** c'est classé *or* cela se trouve sous la rubrique « villes »; *(Admin, Comm)* **this ~s under another department** c'est du ressort *or* de la compétence d'un autre service

► **come up** VI a monter; **do you ~ up to York often?** est-ce que vous venez *or* montez souvent à York?; **he came up to me** il s'est approché de moi, il est venu vers moi; **he came up to me with a smile** il m'a abordé en souriant; *(Brit)* **he came up to Oxford last year** il est entré à (l'université d')Oxford l'année dernière; *(in restaurant)* **"coming up!"** « ça marche! »*; *(fig)* **he has ~ up in the world** il a grimpé les échelons

b *(Jur)* *[accused]* comparaître **(before** devant); *[case]* être entendu **(before** par)

c *[plant]* sortir, pointer; **the tulips haven't ~ up yet** les tulipes ne sont pas encore sorties

d [sun] se lever
e (= arise) [matter for discussion] être soulevé, être mis sur le tapis; [question] se poser, être soulevé; **the question of a subsidy came up** la question d'une subvention s'est posée or a été soulevée; **I'm afraid something's ~ up** malheureusement j'ai un empêchement
f [job, vacancy] se présenter
► **come up against** VT FUS se heurter (fig) à or contre; **he came up against total opposition to his plans** il s'est heurté à une opposition radicale à ses projets; **to ~ up against sb** entrer en conflit avec qn
► **come upon** VT FUS (= find or meet by chance) [+ object] trouver par hasard, tomber sur; [+ person] rencontrer par hasard, tomber sur
► **come up to** VT FUS **a** (= reach up to) s'élever jusqu'à, arriver à; **the water came up to his knees** l'eau lui montait or arrivait jusqu'aux genoux; **my son ~s up to my shoulder** mon fils m'arrive à l'épaule; **it's just coming up to five minutes to six** il est presque six heures moins cinq
b (= equal) répondre à; **to ~ up to sb's hopes** réaliser les or répondre aux espoirs de qn; **his work has not ~ up to our expectations** son travail n'a pas répondu à notre attente
► **come up with** VT FUS [+ object, money, funds] fournir; [+ idea, plan] proposer, suggérer; **she ~s up with some good ideas** elle propose or suggère de bonnes idées

comeback ['kʌmbæk] N (Theat etc) retour m, rentrée f; (= response) réplique f; (= redress) recours m; **to make** or **stage a ~** (Theat) faire une rentrée; (fig) faire un come-back

Comecon ['kɒmɪˌkɒn] N (formerly) (ABBR = Council for Mutual Economic Aid) COMECON m

comedian [kə'miːdɪən] N **a** (Theat) [of variety] comique m; [of plays] comédien m; (fig) comique m **b** (†† = author) auteur m de comédies

comedic [kə'miːdɪk] ADJ (frm) [moment, incident, performer] de comédie

comedienne [kəˌmiːdɪ'en] N **a** (Theat) [of variety] actrice f comique; [of plays] comédienne f

comedown [ˈkʌmdaʊn] N dégringolade* f, déchéance f; **it was rather a ~ for him to have to work for his brother** c'était assez humiliant pour lui de devoir travailler pour son frère

comedy ['kɒmɪdɪ] N (= play: also fig) comédie f; (NonC = style of play) la comédie, le genre comique; **"The Comedy of Errors"** «La Comédie des Méprises»; **~ of manners** comédie f de mœurs; **high ~** haute comédie f; **low ~** farce f; (fig) **cut (out) the ~!*** pas de comédie! → **musical**

comeliness ['kʌmlɪnɪs] N (liter) beauté f

comely ['kʌmlɪ] ADJ (liter = beautiful) beau (belle f); (†† = proper) bienséant

comer ['kʌmə'] N (gen in compounds) arrivant(e) m(f); **open to all ~s** ouvert à tout venant; **the first ~** le premier venu, le premier arrivant → **latecomer**, **newcomer**

comestible† [kə'mestɪbl] **1** ADJ comestible **2** N (gen pl) **~s** denrées fpl comestibles, comestibles mpl

comet ['kɒmɪt] N comète f

comeuppance* [ˌkʌm'ʌpəns] N **to get one's ~** recevoir ce qu'on mérite; **he got his ~** il a échoué (or perdu etc) et il ne l'a pas volé* or et il l'a bien cherché

comfit ['kʌmfɪt] N dragée f

comfort ['kʌmfət] **1** N **a** (= well-being) confort m, bien-être m; **he has always been used to ~** il a toujours eu tout le or son confort; **to live in ~** vivre dans l'aisance or à l'aise; **~s** (= material goods) **~s** aises fpl, commodités fpl (de la vie); **every (modern) ~** tout le confort moderne; **he likes his ~s** il aime ses aises; **he has never lacked ~s** il n'a jamais

manqué des choses matérielles
b (= consolation) consolation f, réconfort m; **to take ~ from sth** trouver du réconfort or une consolation à or dans qch; **your presence is/you are a great ~ to me** votre présence est/vous êtes pour moi d'un grand réconfort; **if it's any ~ to you** si ça peut te consoler; **it is a ~ to know that ...** c'est un soulagement or c'est consolant de savoir que ...; **to take ~ from the fact that/from the knowledge that ...** trouver rassurant le fait que/de savoir que ... → **cold**
c (= peace of mind) **the fighting was too close for (my) ~** les combats étaient trop près pour ma tranquillité (d'esprit) or mon goût
2 VT (= console) consoler; (bring relief to) soulager; (†† = hearten) réconforter, encourager
3 COMP ► **comfort eating** N suralimentation f par compensation ► **comfort station** N (US euph) toilette(s) f(pl) ► **comfort zone** N zone f de confort

comfortable ['kʌmfətəbl] ADJ **a** [chair, clothes, room, journey, life, position, majority] confortable; [temperature] agréable; **to be a ~ winner of sth** remporter qch haut la main
b (= physically at ease) **are you ~ there?** vous êtes bien?; **would you prefer to sit here? — no thanks, I'm quite ~ where I am** préféreriez-vous vous asseoir là? — non merci, je me trouve très bien ici; **to feel ~** se sentir bien; **you don't look very ~** vous n'avez pas l'air bien installé; **to make o.s. ~** (= make o.s. at home) s'installer confortablement; (= make o.s. at home) se mettre à l'aise; (Med) **to be ~** être dans un état satisfaisant
c (= mentally at ease) [person] à l'aise; **I'm not ~ at formal dinners** je ne suis pas à l'aise dans les dîners protocolaires; **to be** or **feel ~ doing sth** être à l'aise pour faire qch; **to feel ~ with sb/sth** se sentir à l'aise avec qn/qch; **I am not very ~ about it** cela me met mal à l'aise
d (financially) [person, family] aisé; **to have a ~ income** avoir des revenus confortables; **he is in ~ circumstances** il est (financièrement) à l'aise
e (= undemanding) [job] de tout repos
f (= kindly) **she was a ~ grandmotherly woman** c'était une femme avec qui on se sentait à l'aise, comme on peut l'être avec une grand-mère
g (= comforting) [belief] rassurant

comfortably ['kʌmfətəblɪ] ADV **a** (physically) [sit, settle, sleep] confortablement; **~ furnished** confortablement meublé **b** (financially) [live] à l'aise, confortablement; **to be ~ off** être (financièrement) à l'aise **c** (= easily) [manage, win, fit, afford] sans difficulté

comforter ['kʌmfətə'] N **a** (= person) consolateur m, -trice f **b** (= scarf) cache-nez m inv; (= dummy-teat) tétine f, sucette f **c** (US = quilt) édredon m

comforting ['kʌmfətɪŋ] ADJ [words, thoughts, feeling] réconfortant; [voice] apaisant; **it is ~ to think that ...** il est réconfortant de penser que ...

comfortless ['kʌmfətlɪs] ADJ [room] sans confort; [person] désolé, triste; [thought, prospect] peu réconfortant, triste

comfrey ['kʌmfrɪ] N (Bot) consoude f

comfy* ['kʌmfɪ] ADJ [chair, room etc] confortable; **are you ~?** êtes-vous bien?

comic ['kɒmɪk] **1** ADJ comique, amusant; (Theat) comique, de la comédie **2** N **a** (= person) (acteur m) comique m, actrice f comique **b** (esp Brit = magazine) comic m; (within newspaper etc) **the ~s** les bandes fpl dessinées **3** COMP ► **comic book** N (esp US) magazine m de bandes dessinées or de BD* ► **comic opera** N opéra m comique ► **comic relief** N (Theat) intervalle m comique; (fig) moment m de détente (comique) ► **comic strip** N bande f dessinée, BD* f ► **comic verse** N poésie f humoristique

comical ['kɒmɪkəl] ADJ cocasse, comique

comically ['kɒmɪkəlɪ] ADV [say, behave] comiquement, de façon comique; **~ naive** d'une naïveté comique

coming ['kʌmɪŋ] **1** N **a** arrivée f, venue f; **~ and going** va-et-vient m; **~s and goings** allées fpl et venues fpl; **~ away/back/down/in/out** etc départ m/retour m/descente f/entrée f/sortie f etc **b** (Rel) avènement m → **second¹ 2** ADJ **a** (= approaching) [weeks, months, years] à venir, prochain (before n); [election, battle] prochain (before n), futur (after n); [revolution] prochain (before n), futur (after n), qui se prépare (or préparait); **the ~ year** l'année f à venir, l'année f prochaine; **~ generations** les générations fpl à venir or futures **b** (= promising) **a ~ politician** un homme politique d'avenir → **up c** (= becoming significant) **it's the ~ thing*** c'est le truc* qui devient à la mode **3** COMP ► **coming of age** N passage m à l'âge adulte

Comintern ['kɒmɪnˌtɜːn] N Komintern m

comity ['kɒmɪtɪ] N courtoisie f; (Jur) **~ of nations** courtoisie f internationale

comm. **a** ABBR = **commerce** **b** ABBR = **commercial** **c** ABBR = **committee**

comma ['kɒmə] N **a** (Gram) virgule f → **invert b** (Mus) comma m

command [kə'mɑːnd] **1** VT **a** (= order) ordonner, donner l'ordre (**sb to do** à qn de faire); **to ~ that ...** ordonner or donner l'ordre que ... (+ subj); **to ~ sth to be done** donner l'ordre de (faire) faire qch
b (= be in control of) [+ army, ship] commander; [+ passions, instincts] maîtriser, dominer
c (= be in position to use) [+ money, services, resources] disposer de, avoir à sa disposition
d (= deserve and get) [+ respect etc] imposer, exiger; **that ~s a high price** cela se vend très cher
e [place, building] (= overlook) avoir vue sur, donner sur; (= overlook and control) commander, dominer
2 VI (= be in command) (Mil, Naut) commander, avoir le commandement; (gen) commander; (= order) commander, donner un ordre
3 N **a** (= order) ordre m; (Mil) commandement m; (Comput) commande f; **at** or **by the ~ of ...** sur l'ordre de ...; **at the word of ~** au commandement
b (NonC: Mil = power, authority) commandement m; **to be ~ of ...** être à la tête de ..., avoir sous ses ordres ...; **to have/take ~ of ...** avoir/prendre le commandement de ...; **under the ~ of ...** sous le commandement or les ordres de ...; (gen) **who's in ~ here?** qui est-ce qui commande ici? → **second¹**
c (Mil) (= troops) troupes fpl; (= district) région f militaire; (= military authority) commandement m → **high**
d (fig = possession, mastery) maîtrise f, possession f; **~ of the seas** maîtrise f des mers; **he has a ~ of three foreign languages** il possède trois langues étrangères; **his ~ of English** sa maîtrise de l'anglais; **to have sth at one's ~** avoir qch à sa disposition; **all the money at my ~** tout l'argent à ma disposition or dont je peux disposer; **to be at sb's ~** être à la disposition de qn, être prêt à obéir à qn; **to be in full ~ of one's faculties** être en pleine possession de ses moyens
4 COMP ► **command economy** N économie f planifiée ► **command key** N (Comput) touche f de commande ► **command language** N (Comput) ordres mpl de gestion ► **command line** N (Comput) ligne f de commande ► **command module** N (Space) module m de commande ► **command performance** N (Theat) ≈ représentation f de gala (à la requête du souverain) ► **command post** N (Mil) poste m de commandement

commandant ['kɒmən‚dænt] N (Mil) commandant m (d'un camp militaire, d'une place forte etc)

commandeer [‚kɒmən'dɪəʳ] VT réquisitionner

commander [kə'mɑːndəʳ] [1] N [a] (gen) chef m; (Mil) commandant m; (Naut) capitaine de frégate; (Brit Police) ≈ commissaire m (de police) divisionnaire, ≈ divisionnaire m → **lieutenant**, **wing** [b] [of order of chivalry] commandeur m [2] COMP ▸ **commander in chief** N (pl **commanders in chief**) (Mil) commandant m en chef, généralissime m

commanding [kə'mɑːndɪŋ] [1] ADJ [a] (= powerful) **to be in a ~ position** être en position de force; **to have a ~ lead** avoir une avance respectable [b] (= authoritative) [person, voice, manner, look, air] plein d'autorité; [tone] de commandement, plein d'autorité [c] (= overlooking) **the house offers a ~ view of the capital** depuis la maison, on domine la capitale; **the castle stands in a ~ position overlooking the lake** le château domine le lac [2] COMP ▸ **commanding officer** N (Mil) commandant m

commandingly [kə'mɑːndɪŋlɪ] ADV [behave] de manière imposante; [speak] d'un ton imposant

commandment [kə'mɑːndmənt] N commandement m (de Dieu ou de l'Église); **the Ten Commandments** les dix commandements mpl, le décalogue (frm)

commando [kə'mɑːndəʊ] N (pl **commandos** or **commandoes**) (all senses) commando m

commemorate [kə'meməreɪt] VT commémorer

commemoration [kə‚memə'reɪʃən] N commémoration f

commemorative [kə'memərətɪv] ADJ commémoratif

commence [kə'mens] VTI commencer (**to do, doing** à faire); (Jur) **to ~ proceedings against ...** former un recours contre ... (devant une juridiction)

commencement [kə'mensmənt] N [a] commencement m, début m; [of law] date f d'entrée en vigueur [b] (Univ: Cambridge, Dublin, US) remise f des diplômes

commend [kə'mend] VT (= praise) louer, faire l'éloge de; (= recommend) recommander, conseiller; (= entrust) confier (**to** à), remettre (**to** aux soins de); (= entrust) **to ~ o.s. to** [person] se recommander à; [idea, project] être du goût de; **his scheme did not ~ itself to the public** son projet n'a pas été du goût du public; **his scheme has little to ~ it** son projet n'a pas grand-chose qui le fasse recommander; (†, frm) **~ me to Mr White** présentez mes respects à M. White (frm), rappelez-moi au bon souvenir de M. White; **to ~ one's soul to God** recommander son âme à Dieu

commendable [kə'mendəbl] ADJ louable

commendably [kə'mendəblɪ] ADV [behave] de façon louable; **~ restrained** d'une retenue louable; **his speech was ~ short** son discours avait le mérite d'être bref

commendation [‚kɒmen'deɪʃən] N [a] (= praise) éloges mpl (**for sth** pour qch) [b] (= recommendation) recommandation f [c] (= award) récompense f (**for sth** pour qch) [d] (NonC: † = entrusting) remise f (**to sb** à qn, aux soins de qn)

commensurable [kə'menʃərəbl] ADJ commensurable (**with, to** avec)

commensurate [kə'menʃərɪt] ADJ (= of equal extent) de même mesure (**with** que); (Math) coétendu (**with** à), de même mesure (**with** que); (= proportionate) proportionné (**with, to** à)

▾ **comment** ['kɒment] [1] N (spoken, written) commentaire m, remarque f; (written) annotation f; **his action went** or **passed without ~** son action n'a donné lieu à aucun commentaire; **he let it pass without ~** il ne l'a pas relevé; (Press) **"no ~"** « je n'ai rien à dire »; **he passed a sarcastic ~** il a fait une observation or une remarque sarcastique; **put your ~s in the margin** inscrivez vos commentaires dans la marge; (Scol: on report) **teacher's ~s** appréciations fpl du professeur [2] VT [+ text] commenter; **he ~ed that ...** il a remarqué que ..., il a fait la remarque que ... [3] VI faire des remarques or des observations or des commentaires; **to ~ on sth** commenter qch, faire des remarques or des observations sur qch

commentary ['kɒməntərɪ] [1] N (= remarks) commentaire m, observation f; (Rad, TV: on news, events) commentaire m; (Sport) reportage m → **running** [2] COMP ▸ **commentary box** N (Sport) cabine f de reportage

commentate ['kɒmenteɪt] [1] VI (Rad, TV) faire un reportage (**on** sur) [2] VT (Rad, TV) [+ match] commenter

commentator ['kɒmenteɪtəʳ] N [a] (Rad, TV) reporter m [b] (on texts etc) commentateur m, -trice f

commerce ['kɒmɜːs] N [a] (Comm) commerce m, affaires fpl; **he is in ~** il est dans le commerce or dans les affaires; (US) **Secretary/Department of Commerce** ≈ ministre m/ministère m du Commerce → **chamber** [b] (fig = intercourse, dealings) relations fpl, rapports mpl

commercial [kə'mɜːʃəl] [1] ADJ (Admin, Comm, Fin, Jur) [dealings, art, attaché, radio, TV] commercial; [world] du commerce; [value] marchand, commercial; [district] commerçant; **to produce sth on a ~ scale** fabriquer or produire qch à une échelle industrielle; **Christmas has become very ~** les fêtes de Noël sont devenues une affaire commerciale → **establishment** [2] N (Rad, TV) publicité f, spot m publicitaire [3] COMP ▸ **commercial artist** N dessinateur m de publicité, créateur m, -trice f publicitaire ▸ **commercial bank** N banque f commerciale or de commerce ▸ **commercial break** N (TV, Rad) page f de publicité ▸ **commercial college** N école f de commerce ▸ **commercial law** N droit m commercial ▸ **commercial traveller** N voyageur m or représentant m de commerce, commis-voyageur† m ▸ **commercial vehicle** N véhicule m utilitaire

commercialese [kə‚mɜːʃə'liːz] N jargon m commercial

commercialism [kə'mɜːʃəlɪzəm] N (NonC) (attitude) mercantilisme m (pej), esprit m commerçant; (on large scale) affairisme m (pej); (= business practice) (pratique f du) commerce m, (pratique f des) affaires fpl

commercialization [kə‚mɜːʃəlaɪ'zeɪʃən] N commercialisation f

commercialize [kə'mɜːʃəlaɪz] VT commercialiser

commercialized [kə'mɜːʃəlaɪzd] ADJ (pej) commercial

commercially [kə'mɜːʃəlɪ] ADV [a] (= financially) [viable, competitive] commercialement; **to be ~ minded** avoir le sens des affaires [b] (= on a large scale) [produce] à échelle commerciale [c] (= publicly) [available] dans le commerce

commie* ['kɒmɪ] ADJ, N (pej) (ABBR = **communist**) coco‡ mf (pej)

commis chef ['kɒmɪʃef] N commis m de cuisine

commiserate [kə'mɪzəreɪt] VI (= show commiseration) témoigner de la sympathie (**with** à); (= feel commiseration) éprouver de la commisération (**with** pour); **I do ~ with you** je compatis; **I went to ~ with him on his exam results** je suis allé m'apitoyer avec lui sur ses résultats d'examen

commiseration [kə‚mɪzə'reɪʃən] N commisération f

commissar† ['kɒmɪsɑːʳ] N commissaire m du peuple (en URSS etc)

commissariat [‚kɒmɪ'sɛərɪət] N (Mil) intendance f; (Admin, Pol) commissariat m; (= food supply) ravitaillement m

commissary ['kɒmɪsərɪ] N [a] (US Mil etc = shop) intendance f [b] (US Mil = officer) intendant m [c] (US Cine) restaurant m du studio [d] (= representative) représentant m; (Rel) [of bishop] délégué m (d'un évêque)

commission [kə'mɪʃən] [1] N [a] (gen) ordres mpl, instructions fpl; (to artist etc) commande f; **he gave the artist a ~** il a passé une commande à l'artiste [b] (Comm) commission f, courtage m; **on a ~ basis** à la commission; **he gets 10% ~** il reçoit une commission de 10 % [c] (= errand) commission f [d] (NonC) [of crime etc] perpétration f (Jur, liter) [e] (= official warrant) pouvoir m, mandat m; (Mil) brevet m; **to get one's ~** être nommé officier; **to give up one's ~** démissionner [f] (NonC = delegation of authority etc) délégation f de pouvoir or d'autorité, mandat m [g] (= body of people) commission f, comité m → **royal** [h] (NonC: Naut) armement m (d'un navire); **to put in ~** armer; **to take out of ~** désarmer; **in ~** en armement, en service; **out of ~** (Naut) hors de service; (Naut = in reserve) en réserve; (gen = not in working order) hors service [2] VT [a] donner pouvoir or mission à, déléguer; **he was ~ed to inquire into ...** il a été chargé de faire une enquête sur ... [b] [+ artist] passer une commande à; [+ book, painting, article] commander, commanditer; **this work was ~ed by the town council** cette œuvre a été commandée or commanditée par le conseil municipal [c] (Mil etc) [+ officer] nommer à un commandement; **he was ~ed in 1990** il a été nommé officier en 1990; **he was ~ed sub-lieutenant** il a été nommé or promu au grade de sous-lieutenant [d] (Naut) [+ ship] mettre en service, armer [3] COMP ▸ **commission agent** N (= bookmaker) bookmaker m; (Comm) courtier m ▸ **commissioned officer** N (Mil etc) officier m ▸ **Commission for Racial Equality** N (Brit) commission f pour l'égalité des races → EOC, EEOC ▸ **commissioning editor** N responsable mf de publication ▸ **commission of inquiry** N commission f d'enquête

commissionaire [kə‚mɪʃə'nɛəʳ] N (Brit, Can) commissionnaire m (d'un hôtel etc), coursier m

commissioner [kə'mɪʃənəʳ] [1] N membre m d'une commission, commissaire m; (Brit Police) ≈ préfet m de police; (US Police) (commissaire m) divisionnaire m → **high, lord** [2] COMP ▸ **commissioner for oaths** N (Jur) officier ayant qualité pour recevoir les déclarations sous serment ▸ **commissioner of education** N (US Scol, Univ) ≈ recteur m, ≈ doyen m ▸ **Commissioner of Official Languages** N (Can) Commissaire m aux langues officielles

commit [kə'mɪt] [1] VT [a] [+ crime, sacrilege] commettre; [+ mistake] commettre, faire; **to ~ hara-kiri** faire hara-kiri; **to ~ perjury** se parjurer; (Jur) faire un faux serment; **to ~ suicide** se suicider [b] (= consign) [+ letter etc] confier (**to** à), remettre (**to** à la garde de, aux soins de); [+ person] (gen) confier (**to** à); (for mental health reasons) faire interner; **to ~ sb to sb's care** confier qn à la garde de qn; (Jur) **to ~ sb (to prison)** faire incarcérer qn; (Jur) **to ~ sb for trial** mettre qn en accusation; **to ~ sth to writing** or **to paper** consigner or coucher qch par écrit; (liter) **to ~ sth to the flames** livrer qch

▸ **LANGUAGE IN USE:** comment 6.3

aux flammes ; **to ~ sth to memory** apprendre qch par cœur
[c] (*Parl*) [+ *bill*] renvoyer à une commission
[d] **to ~ o.s.** s'engager (**to sth** à qch, **to doing** à faire) ; **to be ~ted to a policy** s'être engagé à poursuivre une politique ; **I'm afraid I'm ~ted** je regrette, je me suis déjà engagé
[2] VI **to ~ to sth/sb** s'engager à qch/envers qn
[3] COMP ► **committing magistrate** N (*US Jur*) juge *m* d'instruction

commitment [kə'mɪtmənt] [1] N [a] (*gen*) engagement *m* ; (= *responsibility, obligation*) charges *fpl*, responsabilité(s) *f(pl)* ; (*Comm, Fin*) engagement *m* financier ; (*Comm*) **"without ~"** « sans obligation d'achat » ; **teaching ~s** (heures *fpl* d')enseignement *m* ; **he has heavy teaching ~s** il a un enseignement chargé ; (*Comm etc*) **to have a ~ to another firm** avoir des obligations envers une autre société [b] (*Jur: also* = **order**) mandat *m* de dépôt [c] (*Parl*) [*of bill*] renvoi *m* à une commission [2] COMP ► **commitment fee** N (*Fin*) commission *f* d'engagement

committal [kə'mɪtl] [1] N [a] (*NonC*) remise *f* (**to** à, aux soins de) ; (*to prison*) incarcération *f*, emprisonnement *m* ; (*for mental health reasons*) internement *m* ; (= *burial*) mise *f* en terre ; ~ **for trial** mise *f* en accusation [b] (*NonC*) [*of crime etc*] perpétration *f* (*Jur, liter*) [c] (*Parl*) = **commitment** c [2] COMP ► **committal order** N (*Jur*) mandat *m* de dépôt ► **committal proceedings** NPL ≈ mise *f* en accusation

committed [kə'mɪtɪd] ADJ [*writer*] engagé ; [*Christian etc*] convaincu ; [*parent*] dévoué, attentif ; **a ~ supporter** un ardent défenseur, un adepte convaincu

committee [kə'mɪtɪ] [1] N commission *f*, comité *m* ; (*Parl*) commission *f* ; **to be** *or* **sit on a ~** faire partie d'une commission *or* d'un comité → **management** [2] COMP ► **committee meeting** N réunion *f* de commission *or* de comité ► **committee member** N membre *m* d'une commission *or* d'un comité ► **committee of inquiry** N (*Parl*) commission *f* d'enquête ► **Committee of the Whole** N (*US Pol*) séance de commission étendue à la chambre entière ; ► **committee stage** N (*Brit Parl*) étape de discussion d'un projet de loi en commission

committeeman [kə'mɪtɪmæn] N (*pl* **-men**) (*esp US*) (= *member of committee*) membre *m* d'un comité [b] (*Pol*) responsable d'un parti pour une circonscription électorale

committeewoman [kə'mɪtɪwʊmən] N (*pl* **-women**) (*esp US*) [a] (= *member of committee*) membre *m* d'un comité [b] (*Pol*) responsable d'un parti pour une circonscription électorale

commode [kə'məʊd] N [a] (= *chest of drawers*) commode *f* [b] (*also* **night-~**) chaise *f* percée

commodious [kə'məʊdɪəs] ADJ spacieux, vaste

commodity [kə'mɒdɪtɪ] [1] N produit *m* de base, matière *f* première ; (= *consumer goods*) produit *m*, article *m* ; (= *food*) denrée *f* ; **staple commodities** produits *mpl* de base ; **household commodities** articles *mpl* de ménage ; **dollar commodities** matières *fpl* premières négociées en dollars [2] COMP ► **commodity exchange** N bourse *f* du commerce *or* des marchandises ► **commodity loan** N financement *m* de marchandises gagées ► **commodity markets** NPL bourse *f* de marchandises ► **commodity-producing countries** NPL pays *mpl* de production primaire ► **commodity trade** N négoce *m* de matières premières

commodore [kə'mədɔːr] N (*Mil*) contre-amiral *m* ; (*Naut*) commodore *m* ; [*of yacht club*] président *m* ; [*of shipping line*] doyen *m* (*des capitaines*)

▼ **common** ['kɒmən] [1] ADJ [a] (= *used by or affecting many*) [*interest, cause, language*] commun ; **to make ~ cause with sb** faire cause commune avec qn ; **by ~ consent** d'un commun accord ; (*fig*) ~ **ground** point *m* commun, terrain *m* d'entente ; **there is no ~ ground for negotiations** il n'y a aucun terrain d'entente pour (entreprendre) des négociations ; **it's ~ knowledge** *or* **property that ...** chacun sait que ..., il est de notoriété publique que ... ; ~ **land** terrain *m* communal *or* banal ; ~ **lodging house** hospice *m*, asile *m* de nuit ; ~ **ownership** copropriété *f* ; (*Admin, Jur*) ~ **prostitute** prostituée *f* ; ~ **wall** mur *m* mitoyen → **talk**
[b] (= *usual, ordinary*) commun, ordinaire ; [*plant*] commun ; (= *universal*) général, universel ; (= *not outstanding*) moyen, ordinaire ; **it's quite ~** c'est très courant, ça n'a rien d'extraordinaire ; ~ **belief** croyance *f* universelle ; (*Med*) **the ~ cold** le rhume de cerveau ; **it's a ~ experience** cela arrive à tout le monde, c'est une chose qui arrive à tout le monde ; **it is only ~ courtesy to apologise** la politesse la plus élémentaire veut qu'on s'excuse (*subj*) ; (*pej*) **the ~ herd** la plèbe, la populace (*pej*) ; ~ **honesty** la simple honnêteté ; **the ~ man** l'homme *m* du commun *or* du peuple ; **the ~ people** le peuple, les gens *mpl* du commun (*pej*) ; **a ~ occurrence** une chose fréquente *or* répandue ; **in ~ parlance** dans le langage courant ; (*Rel*) **the Book of Common Prayer** le livre du rituel anglican ; **the ~ run of mankind** le commun des hommes *or* des mortels ; **out of the ~ run** hors du commun, exceptionnel ; **a ~ sight** un spectacle familier ; **a ~ soldier** un simple soldat ; (*esp Brit*) ~ **or garden** [*plant*] commun ; (*hum*) **he's just a ~ or garden office boy** il n'est qu'un vulgaire *or* simple garçon de bureau ; (*hum*) **the ~ or garden variety** le modèle standard *or* ordinaire
[c] (= *vulgar*) [*accent, clothes, person*] commun, vulgaire
[d] (*Math*) ~ **denominator/factor** dénominateur *m*/facteur *m* commun ; ~ **multiple** commun multiple *m* → **low**
[e] (*Gram*) [*gender*] non marqué ; [*noun*] commun
[f] (*Mus*) ~ **time** *or* **measure** (= *duple*) mesure *f* à deux temps ; (= *quadruple*) mesure *f* à quatre temps ; ~ **chord** accord *m* parfait
[2] N [a] (*land*) terrain *m* communal ; (*Jur*) **right of ~** [*of land*] communauté *f* de jouissance ; [*of property*] droit *m* de servitude
[b] **in ~** commun ; **to hold in ~** partager ; (*fig*) **they have nothing in ~** ils n'ont rien de commun ; **in ~ with** en commun avec ; (= *by agreement with*) en accord avec
[3] COMP ► **Common Agricultural Policy** N politique *f* agricole commune ► **common area charges** NPL (*US*) charges *fpl* locatives ► **common assault** N (*Jur*) voie *f* de fait simple ► **common carrier** N transporteur *m* (public), entreprise *f* de transport public ► **common core, common-core syllabus** N (*Educ*) tronc *m* commun ► **common crab** N dormeur *m*, tourteau *m* ► **common currency** N (*NonC*) **to be ~ currency** [*idea, story*] être généralement admis ; **to become ~ currency** se répandre ► **Common Entrance** N (*Brit Scol*) examen d'entrée dans l'enseignement privé ► **common gull** N goéland *m* cendré ► **common law** N le droit coutumier ► **common-law** ADJ ~**-law wife** concubine *f* ; ~**-law marriage** concubinage *m* ► **the Common Market** N le Marché commun ► **common market** N (= *free trade organization*) organisation *f* de libre-échange, marché *m* commun (*entre pays quelconques*) ► **common room** N (*Brit*) salle *f* commune ; (= *staffroom*) salle *f* des professeurs ► **common salt** N sel *m* (ordinaire) ► **common stock** N (*US St Ex*) actions *fpl* cotées en Bourse

► LANGUAGE IN USE : **common** 5.4

---

commonality [,kɒmə'nælɪtɪ] N (*Ind*) standardisation *f* ; **we are looking for commonalities** nous cherchons à utiliser des composants communs à plusieurs produits

commoner ['kɒmənər] N (= *not noble*) roturier *m*, -ière *f* ; (*at Oxford Univ etc*) étudiant(e) *m(f)* non boursier (-ière) ; (*Brit Jur: with common land rights*) personne *f* qui a droit de vaine pâture

commonly ['kɒmənlɪ] ADV [a] (= *frequently*) [*use, occur, prescribe*] fréquemment ; [*called*] couramment ; **more ~ known as ...** plus connu sous le nom de ... ; **eating disorders are more ~ found among women students** on constate que les troubles alimentaires sont plus fréquents chez les étudiantes ; **such a shrub is not ~ found in this country** cet arbuste n'est pas commun dans ce pays ; **it is ~ the case that ...** il est fréquent que ... (+ *subj*) [b] (= *generally*) [*accept, associate, think, believe*] généralement ; **it is ~ believed that ...** on croit généralement que ... ; **the ~ held view** l'opinion *f* généralement répandue [c] (*pej* = *vulgarly*) [*behave, speak, dress*] vulgairement, d'une façon vulgaire *or* commune

commonness ['kɒmənnɪs] N (*NonC*) (= *frequency*) fréquence *f* ; (= *ordinariness*) caractère *m* commun *or* ordinaire, banalité *f* (*pej*) ; (= *universality*) caractère *m* général *or* universel ; (= *vulgarity*) vulgarité *f*

commonplace ['kɒmənpleɪs] [1] ADJ banal, commun, ordinaire ; **such things are ~** de telles choses sont courantes *or* sont monnaie courante [2] N lieu *m* commun, banalité *f*

commons ['kɒmənz] NPL [a] **the ~** le peuple, le tiers état ; (*Parl*) **the Commons** les Communes *fpl* → **house** [b] (= *food*) nourriture *f* (partagée en communauté) ; **to be on short ~** faire maigre chère, être réduit à la portion congrue

commonsense ['kɒmən'sens] [1] N sens *m* commun, bon sens *m* [2] ADJ [*approach, view, precaution, solution*] plein de bon sens

commonweal ['kɒmən,wiːl] N (= *general good*) bien *m* public ; (= *the people*) l'État *m*

commonwealth ['kɒmənwelθ] [1] N [a] **the (British) Commonwealth (of Nations)** le Commonwealth ; (*Brit*) **Minister** *or* **Secretary of State for Commonwealth Affairs** ministre *m* du Commonwealth [b] (*Brit Hist*) **the Commonwealth** la république de Cromwell [c]†† = **commonweal** [d] **the Commonwealth of Australia/Puerto Rico** *etc* le Commonwealth d'Australie/de Porto-Rico *etc* ; **Commonwealth of Independent States** Communauté *f* des États indépendants [2] COMP ► **Commonwealth Games** NPL Jeux *mpl* du Commonwealth

> **COMMONWEALTH**
>
> Le **Commonwealth**, ou **Commonwealth of Nations**, est une communauté d'États souverains (en général d'anciens territoires britanniques) qui compte une cinquantaine de membres, parmi lesquels le Royaume-Uni, l'Australie, le Canada, l'Inde, la Jamaïque, le Kenya, la Nouvelle-Zélande et la République sud-africaine. Tous ces pays reconnaissent le souverain britannique comme chef du **Commonwealth** et se réunissent lors de conférences annuelles pour débattre de questions d'ordre politique ou économique. Chaque État membre est représenté dans les autres pays du **Commonwealth** par un Haut-Commissariat (High Commission) qui fait fonction d'ambassade.

commotion [kə'məʊʃən] N [a] (= *noise*) **to make a ~** faire du tapage ; **what a ~!** quel brouhaha *or* vacarme ! [b] (= *upheaval*) **to cause a ~** semer la perturbation ; **what a ~!** quel cirque ! ; **to be in a state of ~** [*crowd*] être agité ; [*town*] être en émoi [c] (*Pol* = *uprising*) insurrection *f*, troubles *mpl* → **civil**

communal ['kɒmjuːnl] ADJ (= of whole community) [profit, good] communautaire, de la communauté; (= shared) commun; **a ~ bathroom** une salle de bains commune; **~ life** la vie collective

communally ['kɒmjuːnəlɪ] ADV en commun; [agree, decide] en commun, collectivement; [live] en communauté

commune [kə'mjuːn] **1** VI **a** converser intimement, avoir un entretien à cœur ouvert (**with** avec); **to ~ with nature** communier avec la nature **b** (US Rel) communier **2** ['kɒmjuːn] N **a** (= group of people living together) communauté f; **to live in a ~** vivre en communauté **b** (= administrative division) commune f **c** (French Hist) **the Commune** la Commune

communicable [kə'mjuːnɪkəbl] ADJ communicable; (Med) transmissible

communicant [kə'mjuːnɪkənt] **1** N **a** (Rel) communiant(e) m(f) **b** (= informant) informateur m, -trice f **2** ADJ **a** qui communique (avec), communicant **b** (Rel) **~ member** fidèle mf, pratiquant(e) m(f)

communicate [kə'mjuːnɪkeɪt] **1** VT **a** [+ news etc] communiquer, transmettre; [+ illness] transmettre (**to** à); [+ feelings, enthusiasm] communiquer, faire partager **b** (Rel) donner la communion à **2** VI **a** communiquer (**with** avec); **to ~ with sb by letter/by telephone** communiquer avec qn par lettre/ par téléphone; **I no longer ~ with him** je n'ai plus aucun contact avec lui; [rooms] communiquer; **communicating rooms** des pièces fpl qui communiquent or communicantes **c** (Rel) communier, recevoir la communion

communication [kə,mjuːnɪ'keɪʃən] **1** N **a** (NonC) communication f; **to be in ~ with sb** être en contact or relations avec qn; **to be in radio ~ with sb** communiquer avec qn par radio; **to get into ~ with sb** se mettre or entrer en contact or rapport avec qn; **there is/has been no ~ between them** il n'y a/n'y a eu aucun contact entre eux **b** (= message transmitted) communication f **c** (= roads, railways, telegraph lines etc) **~s** communications fpl; (Mil) liaison f, communications fpl

2 COMP ► **communication cord** N (Brit Rail) sonnette f d'alarme ► **communication gap** N manque m or absence f de communication ► **communication line** N (Mil etc) ligne f de communication ► **communication science** N sciences fpl de la communication ► **communication skills** NPL techniques fpl de communication ► **communications satellite** N satellite m de communication ► **communications zone** N (zone f des) arrières mpl

communicative [kə'mjuːnɪkətɪv] ADJ **a** [person] talkative) communicatif, expansif **b** [difficulties etc] de communication; **~ competence** compétence f à la communication

communicator [kə'mjuːnɪkeɪtə'] N communicateur m, -trice f

communion [kə'mjuːnɪən] **1** N (gen) communion f; (Rel) (= religious group) communion f; (= denomination) confession f; (also **Holy Communion**) communion f; **a ~ of interests** des intérêts mpl en commun; **to make one's ~** communier; **to make one's Easter ~** faire ses pâques; **to take ~** recevoir la communion **2** COMP ► **communion rail** N (Rel) balustre m du chœur (où l'on vient communier) ► **communion service** N office m de communion ► **communion table** N sainte table f

communiqué [kə'mjuːnɪkeɪ] N communiqué m

communism ['kɒmjʊnɪzəm] N communisme m

communist ['kɒmjʊnɪst] ADJ, N communiste mf; **the Communist Manifesto** le Manifeste communiste

communistic [,kɒmjʊ'nɪstɪk] ADJ communisant

community [kə'mjuːnɪtɪ] **1** N **a** (= group of people) communauté f, groupement m; [of monks, nuns] communauté f; **the French ~ in Edinburgh** la colonie française d'Édimbourg; **the student ~** les étudiants mpl, le monde étudiant; **to belong to the same ~** appartenir à la même communauté; **the ~** (= the public) le public, la communauté; **for the good of the ~** pour le bien de la communauté **b** (= common ownership) propriété f collective; (Jur) communauté f; **~ of goods/interests** communauté f de biens/d'intérêts **c** (Pol = EU) **the Community** la Communauté

2 COMP ► **community antenna distribution** N câblodistribution f ► **community antenna television** N télévision f par câble ► **community association** N (Brit) association f de quartier (reconnue d'utilité publique) ► **Community bodies** NPL (Pol) instances fpl communautaires ► **Community budget** N (Pol) budget m communautaire ► **community care** N (NonC: Brit Social Work) (= home care) soins mpl à domicile; (also **~ care programme**) programme visant à déléguer la responsabilité de l'État aux collectivités locales en matière d'aide sociale ► **community centre** N foyer m municipal, ≈ MJC f ► **community charge** N (Brit Pol: formerly) ancien impôt local, fondé sur le principe de la capitation ► **community chest** N (US) fonds m commun ► **community college** N (US Univ) centre m universitaire (de premier cycle) ► **community correctional center** N (US) centre m de détention ► **community education** N (Brit) cours mpl organisés par les municipalités ► **community health centre** N centre m médico-social ► **community home** N (Brit) **a** (children's home) ≈ foyer m de la DDASS; **he grew up in a ~ home** il a grandi à la DDASS **b** (for young offenders) centre m d'éducation surveillée ► **community hospital** N (US Med) hôpital m communal ► **community life** N (Social Work) vie f associative ► **community medicine** N médecine f générale ► **community policeman** N (pl **community policemen**) (Brit) ≈ îlotier m ► **community policing** N ≈ îlotage m ► **community property** N (US Jur) communauté f des biens entre époux ► **Community regulations** NPL (Pol) règlements mpl communautaires ► **community school** N (Brit) école servant de maison de la culture ► **community service** N (Jur) travaux mpl d'intérêt général ► **community singing** N chants mpl en chœur (improvisés) ► **community spirit** N sens m or esprit m communautaire ► **community worker** N animateur m, -trice f socioculturel(le)

communize ['kɒmjuːnaɪz] VT **a** (= impose communism on) imposer le communisme à **b** [+ land, factories, peoples] collectiviser

commutability [kə,mjuːtə'bɪlɪtɪ] N interchangeabilité f, permutabilité f; (Jur) commuabilité f

commutable [kə'mjuːtəbl] ADJ **a** (= exchangeable) interchangeable, permutable **b** (Jur) [sentence] commuable (**to** en) **c** **within ~ distance** à un distance que l'on peut facilement parcourir tous les jours

commutation [,kɒmjuː'teɪʃən] **1** N **a** (= exchange) échange m, substitution f; (Fin) échange m; (Elec, Jur) commutation f **b** (Jur) **~ of punishment** commutation f de peine **c** (US) trajet m journalier **2** COMP ► **commutation ticket** N carte f d'abonnement

commutative [kə'mjuːtətɪv] ADJ (Math) **~ laws** lois fpl commutatives

commutator ['kɒmjʊ,teɪtə] N commutateur m

commute [kə'mjuːt] **1** VT **a** (= exchange) substituer (**into** à), échanger (**for**, **into** pour, contre, avec); (Elec) commuer **b** (Jur) commuer (**into** en); (Jur) **~d sentence** sentence f commuée **2** VI faire un or le trajet régulier, faire la navette (**between** entre, **from** de)

commuter [kə'mjuːtə'] **1** N banlieusard(e) m(f) (qui fait un trajet régulier pour se rendre à son travail), navetteur m, -euse f; **I work in London but I'm a ~** je travaille à Londres mais je fais la navette tous les jours **2** COMP ► **the commuter belt** N (Brit) la grande banlieue ► **commuter train** N train m de banlieue

commuting [kə'mjuːtɪŋ] N (NonC) migrations fpl quotidiennes, trajets mpl réguliers, migrations fpl pendulaires (SPEC); **~ every day is hell!** faire la navette tous les jours, c'est l'enfer!

Comoro ['kɒmə,rəʊ] N **the ~ Islands** ◊ **the ~s** les Comores fpl

compact [kəm'pækt] **1** ADJ (lit) (in size) compact; (fig = concise) [style] concis, condensé; **a ~ mass** une masse compacte; **the house is very ~** la maison n'a pas de place perdue **2** VT (gen pass) (lit) rendre compact, resserrer; (fig) condenser; **~ed of**†† composé de **3** ['kɒmpækt] N **a** (= agreement) contrat m, convention f; (informal) entente f **b** (also **powder ~**) poudrier m **c** (US: also **~ car**) (voiture f) compacte f, voiture f de faible encombrement **d** (also **~ camera**) (appareil-photo m) compact m **4** COMP ► **compact disc** N disque m compact ► **compact disc player** N lecteur m de CD, platine f laser ► **compact video disc** N compact-disc m vidéo

compactly [kəm'pæktlɪ] ADV (lit) [store, fold up] de façon compacte; (fig) [write] dans un style concis, d'une manière concise; **~ built** [car] d'une facture compacte, compact; [person] trapu

compactness [kəm'pæktnɪs] N (NonC) (lit: in size) [of room, building, computer, equipment] compacité f; (fig = conciseness) [of style, writing] concision f

companion [kəm'pænjən] **1** N **a** compagnon m, compagne f; (also **lady ~**) dame f de compagnie; (in order of knighthood) compagnon m; **travelling ~s** compagnons mpl de voyage; **~s in arms/in misfortune** compagnons mpl d'armes/d'infortune **b** (= one of pair of objects) pendant m (**to** à) **c** (= handbook) manuel m **2** COMP ► **companion hatch** N = **companionway** ► **companion ladder** N (Navy) échelle f; (Merchant Navy) escalier m ► **companion piece** N pendant m (**to** à) ► **companion volume** N volume m qui va de pair (**to** avec), autre volume m

companionable [kəm'pænjənəbl] ADJ [person] de compagnie agréable; [evening, group] sympathique; **to sit in ~ silence** être assis dans un silence complice

companionship [kəm'pænjənʃɪp] N (NonC) **a** (= friendliness) **I enjoy the ~ at the club** j'apprécie la camaraderie or l'esprit cordial du cercle **b** (= company) compagnie f; **she keeps a cat for ~** elle a un chat, ça lui fait une compagnie

companionway [kəm'pænjənweɪ] N (Naut) escalier m menant aux cabines; [of small vessel] escalier m; (in yacht: also **companion hatch**) capot m (d'escalier)

▼**company** ['kʌmpənɪ] **1** N **a** compagnie f; **to keep sb ~** tenir compagnie à qn; **to keep ~ with** fréquenter; **to part ~ with** se séparer de; **in ~** en public or société; **in ~ with** en compagnie de; **he's good ~** on ne s'ennuie pas avec lui; **he's bad ~** il n'est pas d'une compagnie très agréable; **she keeps a cat, it's ~ for her** elle a un chat, ça lui fait une compa-

► LANGUAGE IN USE: **company** 25.1

gnie → **two**

[b] (= *guests*) compagnie *f*; **we are expecting ~** nous attendons des visites *or* des invités; **we've got ~** nous avons de la visite*; (*lit*, *fig*) **to be in good ~** être en bonne compagnie → **present**

[c] (= *companions*) compagnie *f*, fréquentation *f*; **to keep** *or* **get into good/bad ~** avoir de bonnes/mauvaises fréquentations; **she is no(t) fit ~ for your sister** ce n'est pas une compagnie *or* une fréquentation pour votre sœur ■ (*PROV*) **a man is known by the ~ he keeps** dis-moi qui tu hantes, je te dirai qui tu es (*PROV*)

[d] (*Comm*, *Fin*) entreprise *f*, société *f*, compagnie *f*; **Smith & Company** Smith et Compagnie; **shipping ~** compagnie *f* de navigation; (*US = CIA*) **the Company*** la CIA; (*also pej*) **... and ~*** ... et compagnie → **affiliate**, **holding**

[e] (= *group*) compagnie *f*; [*of actors*] troupe *f*, compagnie *f*; **National Theatre Company** la troupe du Théâtre National; (*Naut*) **ship's ~** équipage *m*

[f] (*Mil*) compagnie *f*

[2] COMP ► **Companies Act** N (*Jur*) loi *f* sur les sociétés ► **company car** N voiture *f* de fonction ► **company commander** N (*Mil*) capitaine *m* (de compagnie) ► **company director** N directeur *m* général ► **company doctor** N médecin *m* du travail ► **company law** N droit *m* des sociétés ► **company lawyer** N (*Jur*) avocat *m* d'entreprise; (*working within company*) juriste *m* ► **company man** N (*pl* **company men**) employé *m* dévoué; **he's a real ~ man** il a vraiment l'esprit maison ► **company manners*** NPL (*Brit*) belles manières *fpl* ► **company policy** N politique *f* de l'entreprise ► **company secretary** N (*Brit Comm*) secrétaire *m* général ► **company sergeant-major** N (*Mil*) adjudant *m* ► **company time** N temps *m* de travail ► **company union** N (*US*) syndicat *m* maison

comparability [ˌkɒmpərəˈbɪlətɪ] N comparabilité *f*; **pay ~** alignement *m* des salaires (*sur ceux d'autres secteurs industriels*)

▼ **comparable** [ˈkɒmpərəbl] ADJ comparable (**with, to** à); **the two things are not ~** il n'y a pas de comparaison possible entre ces deux choses

comparably [ˈkɒmpərəblɪ] ADV **~ sized buildings** des bâtiments ayant des dimensions comparables; **~ qualified students** des étudiants possédant des qualifications comparables

comparative [kəmˈpærətɪv] [1] ADJ [a] (= *relative*) [*ease, safety, peace, silence, freedom, cost*] relatif; **he's a ~ stranger (to me)** je le connais relativement peu; **to be a ~ newcomer/beginner** être relativement nouveau/débutant [b] (*involving comparison*) [*study, analysis, method*] comparatif; [*literature, religion, linguistics, law, data*] comparé; **~ form** (*Gram*) comparatif *m*; **~ mythologist** spécialiste *mf* de mythologie comparée [2] N (*Gram*) comparatif *m*; **in the ~** au comparatif

▼ **comparatively** [kəmˈpærətɪvlɪ] ADV [a] (= *relatively*) relativement [b] (*involving comparison*) comparativement

▼ **compare** [kəmˈpɛəʳ] [1] VT [a] comparer (**with** à, avec), mettre en comparaison (**with** avec); **~ the first letter with the second** comparez la première lettre à *or* avec la seconde; **~d to** *or* **with ...** par comparaison avec ..., par rapport à ...; (*fig*) **to ~ notes with sb** échanger ses impressions *or* ses vues avec qn [b] comparer, assimiler (**to** à); **the poet ~d her eyes to stars** le poète compara ses yeux à des étoiles [c] (*Gram*) [+ *adjective, adverb*] former les degrés de comparaison de [2] VI être comparable (**with** à); **how do the cars ~ for speed?** quelles sont les vitesses

respectives des voitures?; **how do the prices ~?** est-ce que les prix sont comparables?; **it doesn't** *or* **can't ~ with the previous one** il n'y a aucune comparaison avec le précédent; **he can't ~ with you** il n'y a pas de comparaison (possible) entre vous et lui; **it ~s very favourably** cela soutient la comparaison

[3] N **beyond** *or* **without** *or* **past ~** ADV incomparablement ADJ sans comparaison possible

▼ **comparison** [kəmˈpærɪsn] [1] N [a] comparaison *f* (**with** avec, **to** à); **in ~ with** *or* **to ...** ◊ **by ~ with ...** par comparaison avec ..., par rapport à ...; **by** *or* **in ~** par comparaison; **for ~** pour comparaison; **to make a ~** faire une comparaison; **to stand** *or* **bear ~ (with)** soutenir la comparaison (avec); **there's no ~** ça ne se compare pas [b] (*Gram*) comparaison *f*; **degrees of ~** degrés *mpl* de comparaison [2] COMP ► **comparison test** N essai *m* comparatif

compartment [kəmˈpɑːtmənt] N compartiment *m* → **freezer**, **glove**

compartmentalize [ˌkɒmpɑːˈtmentəlaɪz] VT compartimenter

compass [ˈkʌmpəs] [1] N [a] boussole *f*; (*Naut*) compas *m* → **point** [b] (*Math*) **~es** ◊ **a pair of ~es** compas *m* [c] (*fig*) (= *extent*) étendue *f*; (= *reach*) portée *f*; (= *scope*) rayon *m*, champ *m*; (*Mus*) [*of voice*] étendue *f*, portée *f*; **within the ~ of sth** dans les limites de qch; **within the ~ of sb** dans les possibilités de qn; **to be within the ~ of a committee** relever des compétences d'un comité [2] VT (= *go round*) faire le tour de; (= *surround*) encercler, entourer [3] COMP ► **compass card** N (*Naut*) rose *f* des vents ► **compass course** N route *f* magnétique ► **compass rose** N = **compass card**

compassion [kəmˈpæʃən] N compassion *f*

compassionate [kəmˈpæʃənət] [1] ADJ compatissant; **on ~ grounds** pour raisons de convenance personnelle *or* de famille [2] COMP ► **compassionate leave** N (*Mil*) permission *f* exceptionnelle (*pour raisons de famille*)

compassionately [kəmˈpæʃənətlɪ] ADV [*look, say*] avec compassion; [*release*] par compassion

compatibility [kəmˌpætəˈbɪlɪtɪ] N compatibilité *f* (**with** avec)

compatible [kəmˈpætɪbl] [1] ADJ [a] [*people*] fait pour s'entendre; **a ~ board of directors** un conseil d'administration sans problèmes de compatibilité d'humeur; **with sb** bien s'entendre avec qn [b] (= *reconcilable*) [*ideas, aims, interests*] (*also Comput, Telec*) compatible (**with sth** avec qch); **an IBM-~ computer** un ordinateur compatible IBM [2] N (*Comput*) compatible *m*; **an IBM-~** un compatible IBM

compatibly [kəmˈpætɪblɪ] ADV de façon compatible

compatriot [kəmˈpætrɪət] N compatriote *mf*

▼ **compel** [kəmˈpel] VT [a] [+ *person*] (*physically*) contraindre, obliger; (*legally, morally*) obliger; (*psychologically*) pousser; **to be ~led to do sth** (*physically*) être contraint *or* obligé de faire qch; (*psychologically*) se sentir poussé à faire qch, éprouver l'envie profonde *or* irrésistible de faire qch; **to feel morally ~led to do sth** se sentir moralement obligé *or* tenu de faire qch [b] [+ *admiration etc*] imposer, forcer; **to ~ obedience/respect from sb** imposer l'obéissance/le respect à qn

compelling [kəmˈpelɪŋ] ADJ [a] (= *convincing*) [*reason, argument*] irréfutable; [*evidence*] incontestable; **to make a ~ case for sth** réunir des arguments irréfutables en faveur de qch; **to have a ~ interest in doing sth** avoir le plus grand intérêt à faire qch [b] (= *riveting*) [*story, account, film, book*] fascinant; **his new novel**

makes ~ reading son nouveau roman est fascinant (à lire)

compellingly [kəmˈpelɪŋlɪ] ADV [*write, tell*] d'une manière fascinante; [*persuasive, attractive*] irrésistiblement

compendia [kəmˈpendɪə] NPL of **compendium**

compendious [kəmˈpendɪəs] ADJ compendieux, concis

compendium [kəmˈpendɪəm] N (*pl* **compendiums** *or* **compendia**) [a] (= *summary*) abrégé *m*, compendium *m* [b] (*Brit*) **~ of games** boîte *f* de jeux

compensate [ˈkɒmpənseɪt] [1] VI compenser (**by** en); **to ~ for sth** compenser qch [2] VT (= *indemnify*) dédommager, indemniser (**for** de); (= *pay*) rémunérer (**for** pour); (*in weight, strength etc*) compenser, contrebalancer; (*Tech*) compenser, neutraliser

compensation [ˌkɒmpənˈseɪʃən] [1] N (= *indemnity*) (*gen, Psych*) compensation *f*; (*financial*) dédommagement *m*, indemnisation *f*; (= *payment*) rémunération *f*; (*in weight, strength etc*) contrepoids *m*; (*Tech*) compensation *f*, neutralisation *f*; **in ~** (*financial*) en dédommagement [2] COMP ► **Compensation Fund** N (*St Ex*) caisse *f* de garantie

compensatory [ˌkɒmpənˈseɪtərɪ] ADJ (*gen*) compensateur (-trice *f*); (*Econ: of EU*) **~ levy** prélèvement *m* compensatoire

compère [ˈkɒmpɛəʳ] (*Brit Rad, Theat, TV*) [1] N animateur *m*, -trice *f*, meneur *m*, -euse *f* de jeu [2] VT [+ *show*] animer, présenter

compete [kəmˈpiːt] VI [a] (*gen*) rivaliser (**with sb** avec qn, **for sth** pour obtenir qch, **to do** pour faire); **there were ten students competing for six places on the course** dix étudiants se disputaient les six places disponibles pour cette option, il y avait dix concurrents pour les six places disponibles de l'option; **there were only four people competing** il n'y avait que quatre concurrents; **they are competing for the history prize** ils se disputent le prix d'histoire, ils sont rivaux pour le prix d'histoire; **to ~ with sb for a prize** disputer un prix à qn; (*fig*) **his poetry can't ~ with Eliot's** sa poésie ne peut pas rivaliser avec celle d'Eliot; (*fig*) **we can't ~ with their financial resources** vu leurs ressources financières, il nous est impossible de rivaliser avec eux; (*fig*) **he can't ~ any more** il est à bout de course maintenant [b] (*Comm*) faire concurrence (**with sb** à qn, **for sth** pour (obtenir) qch); **there are six firms competing for a share in the market** six entreprises se font concurrence pour une part du marché; **they are forced to ~ with the multinationals** ils sont obligés d'entrer en concurrence *or* en compétition avec les multinationales [c] (*Sport*) concourir (**against sb** avec qn, **for sth** pour (obtenir) qch, **to do** pour faire); **to ~ in a race** participer à une course; **he's competing against world-class athletes** il concourt avec *or* il est en compétition avec des athlètes de réputation mondiale; **there were only four horses/teams/runners competing** il n'y avait que quatre chevaux/équipes/coureurs sur les rangs

competence [ˈkɒmpɪtəns] N [a] (*gen, Ling*) compétence *f* (**for** pour, **in** en) [b] (*Jur*) compétence *f*; **within the ~ of the court** de la compétence du tribunal

competency [ˈkɒmpɪtənsɪ] N [a] = **competence** [b] (= *money, means*) aisance *f*, moyens *mpl*

competent [ˈkɒmpɪtənt] ADJ [a] (= *proficient*) [*person*] compétent (**at sth** dans qch, **to do sth** pour faire qch); **to be ~ at** *or* **in maths** être compétent en mathématiques; **to feel ~ to do sth** se sentir compétent pour *or* capable de faire qch [b] (= *satisfactory*) [*work, performance*] satisfaisant; **to do a ~ job** faire un travail satisfaisant; **a ~ knowledge of the language** une connaissance suffisante de la langue [c] (*Jur*) [*court*] compétent ; [*evidence*] admissible, recevable ; [*person*] habile → **court**

competently ['kɒmpɪtəntlɪ] ADV [*handle, perform, play*] (= *proficiently*) avec compétence, de façon compétente ; (= *satisfactorily*) suffisamment bien, assez bien

competing [kəm'piːtɪŋ] ADJ concurrent

competition [ˌkɒmpɪ'tɪʃən] [1] N [a] (*NonC*) compétition *f*, rivalité *f* (**for** pour) ; (*Comm*) concurrence *f* ; **unfair ~** concurrence *f* or compétition *f* déloyale ; **there was keen ~ for it** on se l'est âprement disputé, il y a eu beaucoup de concurrence pour l'avoir ; **in ~ with** en concurrence avec [b] concours *m* (**for** pour) ; (*Sport*) compétition *f* ; (*Aut*) course *f* ; **to go in for a ~** se présenter à un concours ; **beauty/swimming ~** concours *m* de beauté/de natation ; **I won it in a newspaper ~** je l'ai gagné en faisant un concours dans le journal ; **to choose by ~** choisir au concours [c] (*NonC* = *competitors*) (*gen*) concurrence *f* ; (*Sport*) autres concurrents *mpl* ; **he was waiting to see what the ~ would be like** il attendait de voir qui lui ferait concurrence or qui seraient ses rivaux [2] COMP ► **competition car** N voiture *f* de compétition

competitive [kəm'petɪtɪv] [1] ADJ [a] (*Comm*) [*society, system*] compétitif ; [*market, prices, rates*] compétitif, concurrentiel ; [*product*] concurrentiel ; **to gain a ~ advantage** or **edge (over sb)** obtenir un avantage concurrentiel (sur qn) [b] (= *ambitious*) [*person*] qui a (or avait) l'esprit de compétition ; **I'm a very ~ person** j'ai un esprit de compétition très développé [c] (*Sport*) [*spirit, tennis, match*] de compétition ; **his ~ ability** sa capacité à être compétitif ; **to gain a ~ advantage** or **edge (over sb)** avoir un avantage dans la compétition (sur qn) [d] (*Educ*) [*entry, selection*] par concours ; **~ examination** concours *m* [2] COMP ► **competitive bidding, competitive tendering** N appel *m* d'offres

competitively [kəm'petɪtɪvlɪ] ADV [a] (*Comm*) **both models are ~ priced** les deux modèles sont à des prix compétitifs ; **a very ~ priced car** une voiture à prix très compétitif [b] (*in competitions*) en compétition, en lice ; **I stopped playing ~ in 1995** j'ai arrêté la compétition en 1995

competitiveness [kəm'petɪtɪvnɪs] N compétitivité *f*

competitor [kəm'petɪtəʳ] N (*also Comm*) concurrent(e) *m(f)*

compilation [ˌkɒmpɪ'leɪʃən] N compilation *f*

compile [kəm'paɪl] VT (*gen, Comput*) compiler ; [+ *dictionary*] élaborer ; [+ *list, catalogue, inventory*] dresser

compiler [kəm'paɪləʳ] N (*gen*) compilateur *m*, -trice *f* ; [*of dictionary*] rédacteur *m*, -trice *f* ; (*Comput*) compilateur *m*

complacence [kəm'pleɪsəns], **complacency** [kəm'pleɪsnsɪ] N contentement *m* de soi, suffisance *f*

complacent [kəm'pleɪsənt] ADJ content or satisfait de soi, suffisant ; **to be ~ about ...** ne pas être mécontent de ... ; **we can't afford to be ~** nous n'avons pas tellement de raisons de nous laisser aller

complacently [kəm'pleɪsəntlɪ] ADV avec suffisance

complain [kəm'pleɪn] VI [a] se plaindre (**of, about** de) ; **to ~ that ...** se plaindre que ... (+ *subj or indic*) or de ce que ... (+ *indic*) ; **how are you? — I can't ~*** comment vas-tu ? — je ne peux pas me plaindre [b] (= *make a complaint*) formuler une plainte or une réclamation (**against** contre), se plaindre ; **you should ~ to the manager** vous devriez vous plaindre au directeur ; (*Jur*) **to ~ to the court of justice** saisir la Cour de justice

complainant [kəm'pleɪnənt] N (*Jur*) plaignant(e) *m(f)*, demandeur *m*, -deresse *f*

complaint [kəm'pleɪnt] N [a] (= *expression of discontent*) plainte *f* ; (= *reason for complaint*) grief *m*, sujet *m* de plainte ; (*Jur*) plainte *f* ; (*Comm*) réclamation *f* ; (*Comm*) **~s department** service *m* des réclamations ; **don't listen to his ~s** n'écoutez pas ses plaintes or ses récriminations ; **I have no ~(s) ◊ I have no cause for ~** je n'ai aucun sujet or motif de plainte, je n'ai pas lieu de me plaindre ; (*Comm*) **to make a ~** se plaindre (**about** de), faire une réclamation ; (*Jur*) **to lodge** or **lay a ~ against ...** porter plainte contre ... → **police** [b] (*Med*) maladie *f*, affection *f* ; **what is his ~?** de quoi souffre-t-il ?, de quoi se plaint-il ? ; **a heart ~** une maladie de cœur ; **bowel ~** affection *f* intestinale

complaisance [kəm'pleɪzəns] N complaisance *f*, obligeance *f*

complaisant [kəm'pleɪzənt] ADJ complaisant, obligeant

-complected [kəm'plektɪd] ADJ (*in compounds: US*) = **-complexioned**

complement ['kɒmplɪmənt] [1] N (*gen, Gram, Math*) complément *m* ; [*of staff etc*] personnel *m*, effectif *m* ; **with full ~** au grand complet [2] ['kɒmplɪment] VT compléter, être le complément de

complementary [ˌkɒmplɪ'mentərɪ] [1] ADJ (*gen, Math*) complémentaire [2] COMP ► **complementary medicine** N médecine *f* parallèle or douce

complete [kəm'pliːt] [1] ADJ [a] (= *whole*) [*list, set*] complet (-ète *f*) ; **the ~ works of Shakespeare** les œuvres *fpl* complètes de Shakespeare ; **no garden is ~ without a bed of roses** sans un parterre de rosiers, un jardin est incomplet [b] **~ with sth** (= *also having*) avec qch ; **a large hotel ~ with swimming pool** un grand hôtel avec piscine ; **a house ~ with furniture** une maison meublée ; **to come ~ with sth** être pourvu de qch [c] (= *entire*) [*office block, city, roof, book*] tout *inv* entier [d] (= *finished*) [*work*] achevé ; **the task is now ~** la tâche est accomplie [e] (= *total, full*) [*change, surprise, disaster, failure*] complet (-ète *f*) ; [*lack*] total ; [*approval*] entier ; [*idiot, liar*] fini ; **in ~ agreement** en parfait accord ; **in ~ contrast to sb/sth** en contraste absolu avec qn/qch ; **to take ~ control of sth** prendre le contrôle complet de qch ; **at last her happiness was ~** enfin son bonheur était complet ; **he is the ~ opposite of me** il est tout le contraire de moi ; **to my ~ satisfaction** à mon entière satisfaction ; **she's a ~ bitch**‡ c'est une vraie peau de vache‡ [f] (= *accomplished*) **he is the ~ film-maker/footballer**† c'est le parfait cinéaste/footballeur [2] VT [a] (= *finish*) [+ *collection*] compléter ; [+ *piece of work*] achever, terminer ; **and to ~ his happiness/misfortune** et pour comble de bonheur/d'infortune ; **and just to ~ things** et pour couronner le tout ; **to ~ an order** exécuter une commande [b] (= *fill in*) [+ *form, questionnaire*] remplir

completely [kəm'pliːtlɪ] ADV totalement, complètement ; **~ and utterly** totalement ; **almost ~** presque entièrement

completeness [kəm'pliːtnɪs] N caractère *m* complet ; [*of report, study*] exhaustivité *f* ; **at varying stages of ~** à différents stades d'achèvement

completion [kəm'pliːʃən] [1] N [*of work*] achèvement *m* ; [*of happiness, misfortune*] comble *m* ; (*Jur*) [*of contract, sale*] exécution *f* ; **near ~** près d'être achevé ; **payment on ~ of contract** paiement *m* à la signature du contrat [2] COMP ► **completion date** N (*Jur*) (*for work*) date *f* d'achèvement (des travaux) ; (*in house-buying*) date *f* d'exécution du contrat

complex ['kɒmpleks] [1] ADJ complexe [2] N [a] complexe *m* ; **industrial/mining ~** complexe *m* industriel/minier ; **housing ~** (ensemble *m* de) résidences *fpl* ; (*high rise*) grand ensemble *m* → **cinema** [b] (*Psych*) complexe *m* ; **he's got a ~ about it** ça lui a donné un complexe, il en fait (tout) un complexe → **guilt, inferiority**

complexion [kəm'plekʃən] N [*of face*] teint *m* ; (*fig*) caractère *m*, aspect *m* ; **that puts a new or different ~ on the whole affair** l'affaire se présente maintenant sous un tout autre aspect or jour

-complexioned [kəm'plekʃənd] ADJ (*in compounds*) **dark-complexioned** de or au teint mat, mat de teint ; **fair-complexioned** de or au teint clair, clair de teint

complexity [kəm'pleksɪtɪ] N complexité *f*

compliance [kəm'plaɪəns] [1] N (*NonC*) [a] (= *acceptance*) acquiescement *m* (**with** à) ; (= *conformity*) conformité *f* (**with** avec) ; **in ~ with ...** conformément à ..., en accord avec ... [b] (= *submission*) basse complaisance *f*, servilité *f* [2] COMP ► **compliance lawyer, compliance officer** N conseiller *m* fiscal

compliant [kəm'plaɪənt] ADJ [*person*] accommodant ; [*child*] docile ; **to be ~ with** être conforme à ; [*person*] se conformer à

complicate ['kɒmplɪkeɪt] VT compliquer (**with** de) ; (= *muddle*) embrouiller ; **that ~s matters** cela complique les choses ; **she always ~s things** elle complique toujours tout, elle se crée des problèmes

complicated ['kɒmplɪkeɪtɪd] ADJ (= *involved*) compliqué, complexe ; (= *muddled*) embrouillé

complication [ˌkɒmplɪ'keɪʃən] N (*gen, Med*) complication *f*

complicit [kəm'plɪsɪt] ADJ [a] (= *knowing*) [*look, wink, silence*] complice [b] (= *involved*) **~ in sth** complice de qch ; **he was ~ in allowing it to happen** il a été complice en laissant la chose se produire

complicity [kəm'plɪsɪtɪ] N complicité *f* (**in** dans)

compliment ['kɒmplɪmənt] [1] N [a] compliment *m* ; **to pay sb a ~** faire or adresser un compliment à qn ; (*fig*) **to return the ~** retourner le compliment, renvoyer l'ascenseur [b] (*frm*) **~s** compliments *mpl*, respects *mpl*, hommages *mpl* (*frm*) ; **give him my ~s** faites-lui mes compliments ; **(I wish you) the ~s of the season** (je vous présente) tous les vœux ; **with the ~s of Mr Green** avec les hommages or les compliments de M. Green ; **"with ~s"** « avec nos compliments » [2] ['kɒmplɪment] VT complimenter, féliciter (**on** de), faire des compliments à (**on** de, **sur**) [3] COMP ► **compliments slip** N (*Comm*) ≈ papillon *m* (avec les bons compliments de l'expéditeur)

complimentary [ˌkɒmplɪ'mentərɪ] ADJ [a] (= *flattering*) [*person*] élogieux ; [*remark*] élogieux, flatteur ; **to be ~ about sb/sth** faire des compliments sur qn/qch [b] (= *free*) [*ticket, drink*] gratuit ; **~ copy** exemplaire *m* offert à titre gracieux

complin(e) ['kɒmplɪn] N (*Rel*) complies *fpl*

comply [kəm'plaɪ] VI [a] [*person*] se soumettre (**with** à) ; **to ~ with the rules** observer or respecter le règlement ; **to ~ with sb's wishes** se conformer aux désirs de qn ; **to ~ with a request** faire droit à une requête, accéder à une demande ; (*Admin, Jur*) **to ~ with a clause** observer or respecter une disposition [b] [*equipment, object*] (*to specifications etc*) être conforme (**with** à)

component [kəm'pəʊnənt] [1] ADJ composant, constituant ; **the ~ parts** les parties *fpl* constituantes [2] N (*gen, also Econ*) élément *m* ; (*Chem*) composant *m* ; (*Aut, Tech*) pièce *f* ; **~s factory** usine *f* de pièces détachées

componential [ˌkɒmpə'nenʃəl] ADJ componentiel ; (*Ling*) ~ **analysis** analyse *f* componentielle

comport [kəm'pɔːt] ① VT **to ~ o.s.** se comporter, se conduire ② VI convenir (**with** à), s'accorder (**with** avec)

comportment [kəm'pɔːtmənt] N comportement *m*, conduite *f*

compose [kəm'pəʊz] VT (*Literat, Mus, Typ*) composer ; (*gen, Chem, Tech*) composer, constituer ; **to be ~d of ...** se composer de ... ; **to ~ o.s.** se calmer ; **to ~ one's features** composer son visage ; **to ~ one's thoughts** mettre de l'ordre dans ses pensées

composed [kəm'pəʊzd] ADJ calme, posé

composedly [kəm'pəʊzɪdlɪ] ADV calmement, posément

composer [kəm'pəʊzəʳ] N (*Mus*) compositeur *m*, -trice *f*

composite ['kɒmpəzɪt] ① ADJ (*gen, Archit, Phot*) composite ; (*Bot, Math*) composé ② N (*Archit*) (ordre *m*) composite *m* ; (*Bot*) composée *f*, composacée *f* ③ COMP ► **composite school** N (*Can*) école *f* polyvalente ► **composite vote** N vote *m* groupé

composition [ˌkɒmpə'zɪʃən] ① N ⓐ (*NonC: gen, Art, Mus, Typ*) composition *f* ; **music/verse of her own ~** de la musique/des vers de sa composition ⓑ (= *thing composed*) composition *f*, œuvre *f* ; (*Scol* = *essay*) rédaction *f* ; **one of her most famous ~s** une de ses œuvres les plus célèbres ⓒ (*gen, Chem, Tech* = *parts composing whole*) composition *f*, constitution *f* ; (= *mixture of substances*) composition *f* (**of** de) ; (*Archit*) stuc *m* ; **to study the ~ of a substance** étudier la constitution d'une substance ⓓ (*Gram*) [*of sentence*] construction *f* ; [*of word*] composition *f* ⓔ (= *temperament, make-up*) nature *f*, constitution *f* intellectuelle (*or* morale) ⓕ (*Jur*) accommodement *m*, compromis *m*, arrangement *m* (*avec un créancier*) ; (*frm*) **to come to a ~** venir à composition (*frm*), arriver à une entente *or* un accord ② COMP [*substance*] synthétique ► **composition rubber** N caoutchouc *m* synthétique

compositional [ˌkɒmpə'zɪʃənl] ADJ [*style*] de composition ; [*skills, tools*] de compositeur

compositor [kəm'pɒzɪtəʳ] N (*Typ*) compositeur *m*, -trice *f*

compos mentis ['kɒmpɒs'mentɪs] ADJ sain d'esprit

compost ['kɒmpɒst] ① N compost *m* ② VT composter ③ COMP ► **compost heap** N tas *m* de compost

composure [kəm'pəʊʒəʳ] N calme *m*, sang-froid *m* ; **to lose (one's) ~** (*gen*) perdre contenance ; (= *get angry*) perdre son sang-froid

compote ['kɒmpəʊt] N compote *f* ; (*US* = *dish*) compotier *m*

compound ['kɒmpaʊnd] ① N ⓐ (*Chem*) composé *m* (**of** de) ; (*Gram*) (mot *m*) composé *m* ; (*Tech*) compound *f* ⓑ (= *enclosed area*) enclos *m*, enceinte *f* ② ADJ (*Chem*) composé, combiné ; (*Math*) [*number, fraction*] complexe ; (*Fin*) [*interest*] composé ; (*Med*) [*fracture*] compliqué ; (*Tech*) [*engine*] compound *inv* ; (*Gram*) [*tense, word*] composé ; [*sentence*] complexe ; (*Mus*) ~ **time** la mesure composée ③ [kəm'paʊnd] VT ⓐ (*Chem, Pharm*) [+ *mixture*] composer (**of** de) ; [+ *ingredients*] combiner, mélanger ; (*fig*) [+ *problem, difficulties*] aggraver ⓑ (*Jur etc*) [+ *debt, quarrel*] régler à l'amiable, arranger par des concessions mutuelles ; **to ~ a felony** composer *or* pactiser (avec un criminel) ④ [kəm'paʊnd] VI (*Jur etc*) composer, transiger (**with** avec, **for** au sujet de, pour), s'arranger à l'amiable (**with** avec, **for** au sujet

de) ; **to ~ with one's creditors** s'arranger à l'amiable *or* composer avec ses créanciers

compounding ['kɒmpaʊndɪŋ] N (*Ling*) composition *f*

comprehend [ˌkɒmprɪ'hend] ① VT ⓐ (= *understand*) comprendre, saisir ⓑ (= *include*) comprendre, englober ② VI comprendre

comprehending [ˌkɒmprɪ'hendɪŋ] ADJ compréhensif

comprehensibility [ˌkɒmprɪhensə'bɪlətɪ] N intelligibilité *f*

comprehensible [ˌkɒmprɪ'hensəbl] ADJ compréhensible

comprehensibly [ˌkɒmprɪ'hensəblɪ] ADV de façon compréhensible *or* intelligible

comprehension [ˌkɒmprɪ'henʃn] N ⓐ (= *understanding*) compréhension *f*, entendement *m* ; **that is beyond my ~** cela dépasse ma compréhension *or* mon entendement ⓑ (*Scol*) exercice *m* de compréhension ⓒ (= *inclusion*) inclusion *f*

comprehensive [ˌkɒmprɪ'hensɪv] ① ADJ ⓐ (= *broad, inclusive*) [*description, report, review, survey*] détaillé, complet (-ète *f*) ; [*knowledge*] vaste, étendu ; [*planning*] global ; [*label, rule*] compréhensif ; **~ measures** mesures *fpl* d'ensemble ; (*Insurance*) **~ insurance (policy)** assurance *f* tous risques ⓑ (*Brit Scol*) [*education, system*] polyvalent ; **~ school** établissement *m* polyvalent d'enseignement secondaire ; **to go ~** abandonner les critères sélectifs d'entrée ② N = **comprehensive school**

COMPREHENSIVE SCHOOL

Créées dans les années 60 par le gouvernement travailliste de l'époque, les **comprehensive schools** *sont des établissements polyvalents d'enseignement secondaire conçus pour accueillir tous les élèves sans distinction et leur offrir des chances égales, par opposition au système sélectif des « grammar schools ». La majorité des enfants britanniques fréquentent aujourd'hui une* **comprehensive school**, *mais les « grammar schools » n'ont pas toutes disparu.*

---

comprehensively [ˌkɒmprɪ'hensɪvlɪ] ADV complètement ; **we were ~ beaten** nous avons été battus à plate couture ; **to be ~ insured** avoir une assurance tous risques

compress [kəm'pres] ① VT [+ *substance*] comprimer ; [+ *essay, facts*] condenser, concentrer ; (*Comput*) [+ *data*] compresser ; **~ed air** air *m* comprimé ② VI (*gen*) se comprimer ; [*gas*] se condenser ③ ['kɒmpres] N compresse *f*

compression [kəm'preʃən] ① N (*gen, Comput*) compression *f* ② COMP ► **compression pistol** N ensemble *m* pistolet compresseur ► **compression ratio** N (*Aut*) taux *m* de compression

compressor [kəm'presəʳ] ① N compresseur *m* ② COMP ► **compressor program** N (*Comput*) programme *m* de compression ► **compressor unit** N groupe *m* compresseur

comprise [kəm'praɪz] VT ⓐ (= *include*) comprendre, être composé de ; **to be ~d of** se composer de ⓑ (= *make up*) constituer ; **women ~ 80% of the workforce** les femmes constituent 80 % de l'effectif

compromise ['kɒmprəmaɪz] ① N compromis *m* ; **to come to** *or* **reach a ~** aboutir à un compromis ; **to agree to a ~** accepter un compromis ② VI transiger (**over** sur), aboutir à *or* accepter un compromis ③ VT [+ *reputation, safety, security, plan*] compromettre ; **to ~ o.s.** se compromettre ④ COMP ► **compromise decision** N décision *f* de compromis ► **compromise solution** N solution *f* de compromis

compromising ['kɒmprəmaɪzɪŋ] ADJ compromettant

Comptometer® [kɒmp'tɒmɪtəʳ] ① N machine *f* comptable ② COMP ► **Comptometer operator** N mécanographe *mf*

comptroller [kən'trəʊləʳ] ① N (*Admin, Fin*) contrôleur *m*, -euse *f* (des finances) ② COMP ► **Comptroller General** N (*US Jur, Pol*) ≈ président *m* de la Cour des comptes

compulsion [kəm'pʌlʃən] N contrainte *f* ; **under ~** de force, sous la contrainte ; **you are under no ~** vous n'êtes nullement obligé, rien ne vous force

compulsive [kəm'pʌlsɪv] ADJ ⓐ (= *habitual*) **to be a ~ gambler/liar** être un joueur/menteur invétéré ; **to be a ~ eater** ne pas pouvoir s'empêcher de manger, être boulimique ⓑ (*Psych*) [*behaviour, desire, need*] compulsif → **obsessive** ⓒ (= *irresistible*) [*reading*] fascinant ; **the programme was ~ viewing** l'émission était fascinante

compulsively [kəm'pʌlsɪvlɪ] ADV ⓐ [*lie*] compulsivement ; [*behave, gamble, talk*] d'une façon compulsive ; **to eat ~** être boulimique ; **she is ~ tidy** elle est tellement ordonnée que cela tourne à l'obsession ⓑ (= *irresistibly*) **~ readable** d'une lecture fascinante ; **the series is ~ watchable** le feuilleton est fascinant, on n'arrive pas à décrocher de ce feuilleton

compulsorily [kəm'pʌlsərɪlɪ] ADV [*purchased, retired*] d'office

▼ **compulsory** [kəm'pʌlsərɪ] ① ADJ ⓐ (= *obligatory*) [*education, test, school subject, military service*] obligatoire ; [*retirement*] obligatoire, d'office ; [*redundancies*] d'office ⓑ (= *compelling*) [*powers*] coercitif ② N **the compulsories** NPL (*Skating*) les figures *fpl* imposées ③ COMP ► **compulsory liquidation** N (*Fin*) liquidation *f* forcée ► **compulsory purchase (order)** N (*Brit*) (ordre *m* d')expropriation *f* (*pour cause d'utilité publique*)

compunction [kəm'pʌŋkʃən] N remords *m*, scrupule *m* ; (*Rel*) componction *f* ; **without the slightest** *or* **the least ~** sans le moindre scrupule *or* remords ; **he had no ~ about doing it** il n'a eu aucun scrupule à le faire

computation [ˌkɒmpjʊ'teɪʃən] N ⓐ (*gen*) calcul *m* ⓑ (*NonC*) estimation *f*, évaluation *f* (**of** de)

computational [ˌkɒmpjʊ'teɪʃənl] ① ADJ statistique, quantitatif ② COMP ► **computational linguistics** N (*NonC*) linguistique *f* computationnelle

compute [kəm'pjuːt] VT calculer ; **to ~ sth at ...** évaluer *or* estimer qch à ...

computer [kəm'pjuːtəʳ] ① N ⓐ (*electronic*) ordinateur *m* ; (*mechanical*) calculatrice *f* ; **he is in ~s** il est dans l'informatique ; **on ~** sur ordinateur ; **to do sth by ~** faire qch sur ordinateur → **digital, personal** ⓑ (= *person*) calculateur *m*, -trice *f* ② COMP ► **the computer age** N l'ère *f* informatique *or* de l'ordinateur ► **computer agency** N bureau *m* d'informatique ► **computer-aided** ADJ assisté par ordinateur ► **computer-aided design** N conception *f* assistée par ordinateur ► **computer-assisted** ADJ = **computer-aided** ► **computer code** N code *m* machine ► **computer crime** N (= *illegal activities*) criminalité *f* informatique ; (= *illegal act*) délit *m* informatique ► **computer dating service** N club *m* de rencontres sélectionnées par ordinateur ► **computer error** N erreur *f* informatique ► **computer game** N jeu *m* électronique ► **computer-generated** ADJ [*graphics*] généré par ordinateur ; [*image*] de synthèse ► **computer graphics** N (*NonC*) (= *field*) infographie *f* ; (= *pictures*) images *fpl* de synthèse ► **computer-integrated manufacturing** N fabrication *f* assistée par ordinateur ► **computer language** N langage *m* de programmation, langage *m* machine

► **computer literacy** N compétence *f* (en) informatique ► **computer-literate** ADJ initié à l'informatique ► **computer model** N modèle *m* informatique ► **computer nerd** N *(pej)* cinglé(e)* *m(f)* d'informatique ► **computer operator** N opérateur *m*, -trice *f* ► **computer peripheral** N périphérique *m* d'ordinateur ► **computer printout** N listage *m or* listing *m* d'ordinateur ► **computer program** N programme *m* informatique ► **computer programmer** N programmeur *m*, -euse *f* ► **computer programming** N programmation *f* ► **computer science** N informatique *f* ► **computer scientist** N informaticien(ne) *m(f)* ► **computer studies** NPL l'informatique *f* ► **computer system** N système *m* informatique ► **computer typesetting** N composition *f* informatique ► **computer virus** N virus *m* informatique

computerese* [kəm,pjuːtəˈriːz] N jargon *m* informatique

computerist [kəmˈpjuːtərɪst] N *(US)* informaticien(ne) *m(f)*

computerization [kəm,pjuːtəraɪˈzeɪʃən] N informatisation *f*

computerize [kəmˈpjuːtəraɪz] **1** VT informatiser **2** COMP ► **computerized axial tomography** N scanographie *f*, tomodensitométrie *f*

computing [kəmˈpjuːtɪŋ] **1** N informatique *f* **2** COMP [*service, facility, problem*] informatique ; [*course, department*] d'informatique

comrade [ˈkɒmreɪd] **1** N camarade *mf* **2** COMP ► **comrade-in-arms** N compagnon *m* d'armes

comradely [ˈkɒmreɪdlɪ] ADJ amical

comradeship [ˈkɒmreɪdʃɪp] N camaraderie *f*

Comsat® [ˈkɒmsæt] N *(US)* ABBR = **Communications Satellite Corporation**

con¹ [kɒn] VT **a** († = *study*) apprendre par cœur **b** *(Naut)* gouverner ; *(US Naut)* piloter

con² [kɒn] PREP, N contre *m* → **pro¹**

con³* [kɒn] **1** VT arnaquer*, escroquer ; **to ~ sb into doing** amener qn à faire en l'abusant *or* en le dupant ; **I've been ~ned!** on m'a eu !*, je me suis fait avoir !* ; **he ~ned his way into the building** il est entré dans l'immeuble par ruse **2** N **it was all a big ~** (= *empty boasting etc*) tout ça c'était de la frime* ; (= *swindle*) c'était une vaste escroquerie *or* arnaque* **b*** (ABBR = **convict**) taulard* *m* **3** COMP ► **con artist*** N arnaqueur* *m* ► **con game*** N (= **con trick**) ► **con man*** N (*pl* **con men**) escroc *m* ► **con trick*** N escroquerie *f*

Con. N *(Brit)* **a** ABBR = **Conservative b** ABBR = **constable**

conc. N (ABBR = **concessions**) admission £5 (~ £4) entrée 5 livres (tarif réduit 4 livres)

concatenate [kɒnˈkætɪˌneɪt] VT enchaîner

concatenation [kɒn,kætɪˈneɪʃən] N [*of circumstances*] enchaînement *m* ; *(Ling, Comput)* concaténation *f*

concave [kɒnˈkeɪv] ADJ concave

concavity [kɒnˈkævɪtɪ] N concavité *f*

conceal [kənˈsiːl] VT (= *hide*) [+ *object*] cacher, dissimuler ; (= *keep secret*) [+ *news, event*] garder *or* tenir secret ; [+ *emotions, thoughts*] dissimuler ; **to ~ sth from sb** cacher qch à qn ; **to ~ the fact that ...** dissimuler le fait que ... ; **~ed lighting** éclairage *m* indirect ; *(Aut)* **~ed turning** *or* **road** intersection *f* cachée

concealment [kənˈsiːlmənt] N *(NonC)* dissimulation *f* ; *(Jur)* [*of criminal*] recel *m* ; [*of background, knowledge, truth, facts*] occultation *f* ; (= *place of concealment*) cachette *f*

▼ **concede** [kənˈsiːd] **1** VT [+ *privilege*] concéder, accorder ; [+ *point*] concéder ; *(Sport)* [+ *match*] concéder ; **to ~ that ...** concéder *or* reconnaître que ... ; **to ~ victory** s'avouer vaincu **2** VI céder

conceit [kənˈsiːt] N **a** *(NonC = pride)* vanité *f*, suffisance *f* **b** (= *witty expression*) trait *m* d'esprit, expression *f* brillante ; *(liter)* **he is wise in his own ~** il se croit très sage ; *(Literat)* **~s** concetti *mpl*

conceited [kənˈsiːtɪd] ADJ vaniteux, suffisant

conceitedly [kənˈsiːtɪdlɪ] ADV [*say*] avec suffisance ; **I don't mean that ~** je ne dis pas cela par vanité

conceivable [kənˈsiːvəbl] ADJ concevable, imaginable ; **it is hardly ~ that ...** il est à peine concevable que ... (+ *subj*)

conceivably [kənˈsiːvəblɪ] ADV de façon concevable, en théorie ; **she may ~ be right** il est concevable *or* il se peut bien qu'elle ait raison

conceive [kənˈsiːv] **1** VT [+ *child, idea, plan*] concevoir ; **to ~ a hatred/love for sb/sth** concevoir de la haine/de l'amour pour qn/qch ; **I cannot ~ why he wants to do it** je ne comprends vraiment pas pourquoi il veut le faire **2** VI [*woman*] **unable to ~** qui ne peut pas avoir d'enfants ; **to ~ of** concevoir, avoir le concept de ; **I cannot ~ of anything better** je ne conçois rien de mieux ; **I cannot ~ of a better way to do it** je ne conçois pas de meilleur moyen de le faire

concelebrant [kɒnˈselɪˌbrənt] N *(Rel)* concélébrant *m*

concentrate [ˈkɒnsəntreɪt] **1** VT [+ *attention*] concentrer (**on** sur) ; [+ *hopes*] reporter (**on** sur) ; [+ *supplies*] concentrer, rassembler ; *(Chem, Mil)* concentrer ; **it ~s the mind** cela fait réfléchir

2 VI **a** (= *direct thoughts, efforts etc*) se concentrer, concentrer *or* fixer son attention (**on** sur) ; **to ~ on doing** s'appliquer à faire ; **I just can't ~!** je n'arrive pas à me concentrer ! ; **try to ~ a little more** essaie de te concentrer un peu plus *or* de faire un peu plus attention ; **~ on getting yourself a job** essaie avant tout de *or* occupe-toi d'abord de te trouver du travail ; **~ on getting well** occupe-toi d'abord de ta santé ; **the terrorists ~d on the outlying farms** les terroristes ont concentré leurs attaques sur les fermes isolées ; *(giving speech etc)* **today I shall ~ on the 16th century** aujourd'hui je traiterai en particulier le 16ᵉ siècle *or* m'occuperai en particulier du 16ᵉ siècle **b** (= *converge*) [*troops, people*] se concentrer, converger ; **the crowds began to ~ round the palace** la foule a commencé à se concentrer *or* à se rassembler autour du palais

3 ADJ, N *(Chem)* concentré *m*

concentrated [ˈkɒnsəntreɪtɪd] ADJ **a** [*liquid, substance*] concentré ; **in a ~ form** sous une forme concentrée **b** (= *focused*) [*effort*] intense ; [*attack*] en règle

concentration [,kɒnsənˈtreɪʃən] **1** N concentration *f* **2** COMP ► **concentration camp** N camp *m* de concentration

concentric [kənˈsentrɪk] ADJ concentrique

concept [ˈkɒnsept] **1** N notion *f*, idée *f* ; *(Philos, Marketing etc)* concept *m* **2** COMP ► **concept album** N *(Mus)* album *m* concept

conception [kənˈsepʃən] N idée *f*, conception *f* ; *(Med)* conception *f* ; **he has not the slightest ~ of teamwork** il n'a pas la moindre idée de ce qu'est le travail en équipe ; **a new ~ of democracy** une nouvelle conception de la démocratie → **immaculate**

conceptual [kənˈseptjuəl] **1** ADJ conceptuel **2** COMP ► **conceptual art** N art *m* conceptuel

conceptualize [kənˈseptjuəˌlaɪz] VT concevoir, conceptualiser

conceptually [kənˈseptjuəlɪ] ADV du point de vue conceptuel

▼ **concern** [kənˈsɜːn] **1** VT **a** (= *affect*) concerner ; (= *be of importance to*) intéresser, importer à ; (= *be the business of*) regarder, être

l'affaire de ; (= *be about*) [*report etc*] se rapporter à ; **that doesn't ~ you** cela ne vous regarde pas, ce n'est pas votre affaire ; *(frm)* **to whom it may ~** à qui de droit ; **as ~s** en ce qui concerne, à propos de ; **as far as** *or* **so far as he is ~ed** en ce qui le concerne, quant à lui ; **where we are ~ed** en ce qui nous concerne ; **the persons ~ed** les intéressés *mpl* ; **the department ~ed** (= *under discussion*) le service en question *or* dont il s'agit ; (= *relevant*) le service compétent ; **my brother is the most closely ~ed** le premier intéressé c'est mon frère ; **to be ~ed in ...** avoir un intérêt dans ... ; **to ~ o.s. in** *or* **with** s'occuper de, s'intéresser à ; **we are ~ed only with facts** nous ne nous occupons que des faits

b (= *trouble, worry*) inquiéter ; **to be ~ed by sth** s'inquiéter de qch, être inquiet de qch ; **what ~s me is that ...** ce qui me préoccupe, c'est que ... → **concerned**

2 N **a** (= *relation, connexion*) rapport *m* (**with** avec), relation *f* (**with** avec) ; **to have no ~ with** n'avoir rien à voir avec, être sans rapport avec

b (= *interest, business*) affaire *f* ; (= *responsibility*) responsabilité *f* ; **it's no ~ of his** ◊ **it's none of his ~** ce n'est pas son affaire, cela ne le regarde pas ; **it is of no ~ to him** cela n'a aucun intérêt pour lui ; **what ~ is it of yours?** en quoi est-ce que cela vous regarde ?

c *(Comm: also* **business ~**) entreprise *f*, affaire *f* → **going**

d (= *interest, share*) intérêt(s) *m(pl)* (**in** dans) ; **he has a ~ in the business** il a des intérêts dans l'affaire

e (= *anxiety*) inquiétude *f*, préoccupation *f* ; *(stronger)* anxiété *f* ; **he was filled with ~** il était très soucieux *or* préoccupé ; **a look of ~** un regard inquiet ; **it is of great ~ to us (that)** c'est un grand souci pour nous (que) ; **this is a matter of great ~ to us** c'est un sujet de grande inquiétude pour nous

f (* = *object, contrivance*) truc* *m*, bidule* *m*

concerned [kənˈsɜːnd] ADJ **a** (= *worried*) [*parent, neighbour, look*] préoccupé, inquiet (-ète *f*) (**for sb/sth** pour qn/qch) ; **to be ~ about sb** se faire du souci pour qn ; **to be ~ about sth** être inquiet de qch ; **to be ~ that ...** être inquiet que ... (+ *subj*) ; **I am ~ to hear that ...** j'apprends avec inquiétude que ... → **concern** **b** (= *keen*) **to be ~ to do sth** tenir à faire qch ; **they are more ~ to save face than to ...** ils se soucient davantage de ne pas perdre la face que de ...

concerning [kənˈsɜːnɪŋ] PREP concernant, en ce qui concerne

concert [ˈkɒnsət] **1** N **a** *(Mus)* concert *m* ; **in ~** en concert **b** [*of voices etc*] unisson *m*, chœur *m* ; **in ~** à l'unisson, en chœur **c** *(fig)* **a ~ of colours** une harmonie de couleurs ; **in ~ with** de concert avec **2** [kənˈsɜːt] VT concerter, arranger (ensemble) **3** COMP [*ticket, hall*] de concert ► **concert grand** N piano *m* de concert ► **concert party** N *(Mus)* concert *m* populaire *(donné en plein air ou dans une salle des fêtes)* ► **concert performer** N concertiste *mf* ► **concert pianist** N pianiste *mf* de concert ► **concert pitch** N *(Mus)* diapason *m* (de concert) ; *(fig)* **at ~ pitch** (= *on top form*) au maximum *or* à l'apogée de sa forme ► **concert tour** N tournée *f* de concerts

concerted [kənˈsɜːtɪd] ADJ concerté

concertgoer [ˈkɒnsətgəʊə^r] N amateur *m* de concerts, personne *f* allant régulièrement au concert

concertina [,kɒnsəˈtiːnə] **1** N concertina *m* **2** VI **the vehicles ~ed into each other** les véhicules se sont emboutis *or* télescopés (les uns les autres) **3** COMP ► **concertina crash** N *(Aut)* carambolage *m*

concertmaster [ˈkɒnsət'mɑːstə^r] N *(US)* premier violon *m*

► LANGUAGE IN USE: concede 11.1   concern 6.2, 26.2

concerto [kən'tʃeətəʊ] N (pl **concertos** or **concerti** [kən'tʃeəti:]) concerto m (**for** pour)

concession [kən'seʃən] N (gen, Jur) concession f; (Comm) réduction f

concessionaire [kən,seʃə'neəʳ] N (esp Brit) concessionnaire mf

concessionary [kən'seʃənərɪ] **1** ADJ (Fin, Jur etc) concessionnaire; (Comm) [ticket, fare] à prix réduit; ~ **aid** aide f libérale **2** N concessionnaire mf

conch [kɒntʃ] N (pl **conchs** or **conches**) (= shell, Anat) conque f; (Archit) voûte f semi-circulaire, (voûte f d')abside f

concha [ˈkɒŋkə] N (pl **conchae** [ˈkɒŋkiː]) (Anat) conque f

conchology [kɒŋˈkɒlədʒɪ] N conchyliologie f

conciliate [kən'sɪlɪeɪt] VT **a** (= appease) apaiser; (= win over) se concilier (l'appui de) **b** (= reconcile) [+ opposing views or factions, extremes] concilier

conciliation [kən,sɪlɪ'eɪʃən] **1** N (NonC) **a** (Pol, Ind) conciliation f **b** (= appeasement) [of person] apaisement m **c** (= resolution) [of dispute, differences] règlement m **2** COMP ► **conciliation board** N (Ind) conseil m d'arbitrage ► **conciliation service** N (gen) service m de conciliation; (Ind) service m de règlement amiable

conciliator [kən'sɪlɪ,eɪtəʳ] N conciliateur m, -trice f; (Ind) médiateur m

conciliatory [kən'sɪlɪətərɪ] ADJ [person, tone, gesture, mood, statement] conciliant; [spirit] de conciliation; (Pol, Ind) [procedure] conciliatoire

concise [kən'saɪs] ADJ (= short) concis; (= shortened) abrégé

concisely [kən'saɪslɪ] ADV de façon concise

conciseness [kən'saɪsnɪs], **concision** [kən'sɪʒən] N concision f

conclave [ˈkɒnkleɪv] N (Rel) conclave m; (fig) assemblée f (secrète), réunion f (privée); (fig) **in** ~ en réunion privée

conclude [kən'kluːd] **1** VT **a** (= end) [+ business, agenda] conclure, terminer; "**to be ~d**" (in magazine) «suite et fin au prochain numéro»; (in TV programme) «suite et fin au prochain épisode» **b** (= arrange) [+ treaty] conclure, aboutir à **c** (= infer) conclure, déduire (**from** de, **that** que) **d** (US = decide) décider (**to do** de faire) **2** VI (= end) [things, events] se terminer, s'achever (**with** par, sur); [person] conclure; **to** ~ **I must say ...** pour conclure or en conclusion je dois dire ...

concluding [kən'kluːdɪŋ] ADJ final

▼**conclusion** [kən'kluːʒən] **1** N **a** (= end) conclusion f, fin f; **in** ~ pour conclure, finalement, en conclusion; **to bring to a** ~ mener à sa conclusion or à terme **b** (= settling) [of treaty etc] conclusion f **c** (= opinion, decision) conclusion f, déduction f; **to come to the** ~ **that ...** conclure que ...; **to draw a** ~ **from ...** tirer une conclusion de ...; **this leads one to the** ~ **that ...** ceci amène à conclure que ... → **foregone**, **jump d** (Philos) conclusion f **e to try** ~**s with sb** se mesurer avec or contre qn

conclusive [kən'kluːsɪv] ADJ concluant, probant

conclusively [kən'kluːsɪvlɪ] ADV de façon concluante or probante

concoct [kən'kɒkt] VT (lit, fig) concocter

concoction [kən'kɒkʃən] N mélange m, préparation f

concomitant [kən'kɒmɪtənt] **1** ADJ concomitant **2** N événement m concomitant

concord [ˈkɒŋkɔːd] N **a** concorde f, harmonie f; **in complete** ~ en parfaite harmonie **b** (Gram) accord m; **to be in** ~ **with ...** s'accorder avec ... **c** (Mus) accord m

concordance [kən'kɔːdəns] N **a** (= agreement) accord m **b** (= index) index m; (Bible, Ling) concordance f

concordant [kən'kɔːdənt] ADJ concordant, s'accordant (**with** avec)

concordat [kɒn'kɔːdæt] N concordat m

Concorde [ˈkɒŋkɔːd] N (Aviat) Concorde m; **in** ~ en Concorde

concourse [ˈkɒŋkɔːs] N **a** (in building, station) hall m; (in pedestrian precinct) parvis m, piazza f; (US: in a park) carrefour m; (US = street) cours m, boulevard m **b** [of people, vehicles] affluence f

concrete [ˈkɒŋkriːt] **1** ADJ **a** [floor, wall, steps] en béton; [block] de béton **b** (= definite, not abstract) concret (-ète f) **2** N **a** béton m; **nothing is yet set** or **embedded in** ~ rien n'est encore arrêté or décidé → **prestressed**, **reinforce b** (Philos) **the** ~ le concret **3** VT bétonner **4** COMP ► **concrete jungle** N jungle f de béton ► **concrete mixer** N bétonneuse f

concretion [kən'kriːʃən] N concrétion f

concubine [ˈkɒŋkjʊbaɪn] N concubine f

concupiscence [kən'kjuːpɪsəns] N (frm) concupiscence f

concupiscent [kən'kjuːpɪsənt] ADJ (frm) concupiscent

concur [kən'kɜːʳ] VI **a** (= agree) [person] être d'accord, s'entendre (**with sb** avec qn, **in sth** sur or au sujet de qch); [opinions] converger **b** (= happen together) coïncider, arriver en même temps; (= contribute) concourir (**to** à); **everything** ~**red to bring about this result** tout a concouru à produire ce résultat

concurrence [kən'kʌrəns] N (frm) **a** (= consent) accord m **b** (= coincidence) coïncidence f; **a** ~ **of events** une coïncidence, un concours de circonstances **c** (= consensus) **a** ~ **of opinion** une convergence de vues

concurrent [kən'kʌrənt] ADJ **a** (= occurring at same time) concomitant, simultané; ~ **with her acting career, she managed to ...** parallèlement à sa carrière d'actrice, elle a réussi à ...; ~ **with** en même temps que; **he was given** ~ **sentences totalling 24 years** il a été condamné à 24 ans de prison par confusion des peines **b** (frm = acting together) concerté **c** (= in agreement) [views etc] concordant **d** (Math, Tech) concourant

concurrently [kən'kʌrəntlɪ] ADV simultanément

concuss [kən'kʌs] VT **a** (Med: gen pass) commotionner; **to be** ~**ed** être commotionné **b** (= shake) secouer violemment, ébranler

concussion [kən'kʌʃən] N **a** (Med) commotion f (cérébrale) **b** (= shaking) ébranlement m, secousse f

▼**condemn** [kən'dem] VT **a** (gen, Jur, Med, fig) condamner (**to** à); (Jur) ~ **sb to death** condamner qn à mort; **the** ~**ed man** le condamné; **the** ~**ed cell** la cellule des condamnés **b** (Tech) [+ building] déclarer inhabitable, condamner; (Mil, Tech) [+ materials] réformer, déclarer inutilisable

condemnation [,kɒndem'neɪʃən] N (gen, Jur, fig) condamnation f; (US Jur) [of property] expropriation f pour cause d'utilité publique; **the murder drew unanimous** ~ **from the press** l'assassinat a été unanimement condamné par la presse

condemnatory [kəndem'neɪtərɪ] ADJ réprobateur (-trice f)

condensation [,kɒnden'seɪʃən] N condensation f

condense [kən'dens] **1** VT condenser, concentrer; (Phys) [+ gas] condenser; [+ rays] concentrer; (fig) condenser, résumer; ~**d book** livre m condensé **2** VI se condenser, se concentrer **3** COMP ► **condensed milk** N lait m concentré

condenser [kən'densəʳ] N (Elec, Tech)

condensateur m; (Phys) [of gas] condenseur m; [of light] condensateur m

condescend [,kɒndɪ'send] VI **a** condescendre (**to do** à faire), daigner (**to do** faire); **to** ~ **to sb** se montrer condescendant envers or à l'égard de qn **b** (= stoop to) s'abaisser (**to** à), descendre (**to** à, jusqu'à)

condescending [,kɒndɪ'sendɪŋ] ADJ condescendant (**to** or **towards sb** avec qn); **in a** ~ **way** avec condescendance

condescendingly [,kɒndɪ'sendɪŋlɪ] ADV avec condescendance

condescension [,kɒndɪ'senʃən] N condescendance f

condign [kən'daɪn] ADJ (= fitting) adéquat, proportionné; (= deserved) mérité

condiment [ˈkɒndɪmənt] N condiment m

condition [kən'dɪʃən] **1** N **a** (= determining factor) condition f; (Comm) ~ **of sale** condition f de vente; (Jur) ~ **of a contract** condition f d'un contrat; **he made the** ~ **that no one should accompany him** il a stipulé que personne ne devait l'accompagner; **on this** ~ à cette condition; **I'll lend you my car on** ~ **that** or (US) **on the** ~ **that you don't damage it** je vous prête ma voiture à condition que vous ne l'abîmiez (subj) pas; **you can go on holiday on** ~ **that** or (US) **on the** ~ **that you pass your exam** tu partiras en vacances à condition de réussir ton examen → **term b** (= circumstance) condition f; **under** or **in the present** ~**s** dans les conditions or circonstances actuelles; **working/living** ~**s** conditions fpl de travail/de vie; **weather** ~**s** conditions fpl météorologiques; **the human** ~ la condition humaine **c** (NonC = state, nature) état m, condition f; **physical/mental** ~ état m physique/mental; **in** ~ [thing] en bon état; [person] en forme, en bonne condition physique; (Comm etc) **in good** ~ en bon état; **it's out of** ~ c'est en mauvais état; **he's out of** ~ il n'est pas en forme; **she was in no** ~ or **was not in a** ~ or **not in any** ~ **to go out** elle n'était pas en état de sortir; (euph) **she is in an interesting** ~* elle est dans une position intéressante† **d** (NonC: frm = social position) position f, situation f **2** VT **a** (= determine) déterminer, conditionner; **his standard of living is** ~**ed by his income** son niveau de vie dépend de ses revenus **b** (= bring into good condition) [+ animal] mettre en forme; [+ thing] remettre en bon état; [+ hair, skin] traiter → **air c** (Psych, fig) [+ person, animal] provoquer un réflexe conditionné chez, conditionner; (by propaganda) [+ person] conditionner; **he was** ~**ed into believing that ...** il a été conditionné à croire que ...; ~**ed reflex** réflexe m conditionné; ~**ed response** réaction f conditionnée

conditional [kən'dɪʃənl] **1** ADJ **a** (gen) [offer, acceptance, support, ceasefire] conditionnel; **to be** ~ **(up)on sth** dépendre de qch; **his appointment is** ~ **(up)on his passing his exams** il sera nommé à condition qu'il soit reçu à ses examens **b** (Gram) conditionnel **2** N (Gram) conditionnel m; **in the** ~ au conditionnel **3** COMP ► **conditional access** N (TV) accès m limité aux abonnés ► **conditional discharge** N (Brit Jur) condamnation f avec sursis; **a one-year** ~ **discharge** un an de prison avec sursis

conditionally [kən'dɪʃnəlɪ] ADV [agree] sous condition, à certaines conditions; **she said yes,** ~ elle a dit oui, mais à certaines conditions

conditioner [kən'dɪʃənəʳ] N (for hair) après-shampooing m; (for skin) crème f traitante → **fabric**

conditioning [kən'dɪʃənɪŋ] **1** N (Psych) conditionnement m; [of hair] traitement m **2** ADJ traitant

► LANGUAGE IN USE: **conclusion** 26.1, 26.2 **condemn** 14, 26.3

condo ['kɒn,dəʊ] N (US) (ABBR = **condominium unit**) → **condominium**

condole [kən'dəʊl] VI exprimer or présenter ses condoléances (**with sb** à qn)

▼ **condolence** [kən'dəʊləns] N ~**s** condoléances *fpl*; **message/letter of** ~ message *m*/lettre *f* de condoléances; **book of** ~**(s)** registre *m* de condoléances

condom ['kɒndəm] N préservatif *m*

condominium [,kɒndə'mɪnɪəm] 1 N (*pl* **condominiums**) a condominium *m* b (US) (= *ownership*) copropriété *f*; (= *building*) immeuble *m* (en copropriété); (= *rooms*) appartement *m* (dans un immeuble en copropriété) 2 COMP ► **condominium unit** N appartement *m* en copropriété → HOUSE

condonation [,kɒndəʊ'neɪʃən] N (*Fin*) remise *f* d'une dette

condone [kən'dəʊn] VT (= *tolerate*) admettre, laisser faire; (= *overlook*) fermer les yeux sur; (= *forgive*) pardonner; **we cannot** ~ **that kind of behaviour** nous ne pouvons pas admettre ce genre de comportement, nous ne pouvons pas laisser faire cela; (*Jur*) **to** ~ **adultery** ≈ pardonner un adultère; (*Educ*) **to** ~ **a student** repêcher un étudiant; **to** ~ **a student's exam results** remonter les notes d'un étudiant

condor ['kɒndɔːr] N condor *m*

conduce [kən'djuːs] VI **to** ~ **to** conduire à, provoquer

conducive [kən'djuːsɪv] ADJ **to be** ~ **to** être propice à or favorable à

conduct ['kɒndʌkt] 1 N a (= *behaviour*) conduite *f*, comportement *m*; **good/bad** ~ bonne/mauvaise conduite *f* or tenue *f*; **his** ~ **towards me** sa conduite or son comportement à mon égard or envers moi → **disorderly** b (= *leading*) conduite *f* → **safe** 2 [kən'dʌkt] VT a (= *lead*) conduire, mener; **he** ~**ed me round the gardens** il m'a fait faire le tour des jardins; ~**ed visit** visite *f* guidée b (= *direct, manage*) diriger; **to** ~ **one's business** diriger ses affaires; **to** ~ **an orchestra** diriger un orchestre; (*Jur*) **to** ~ **an inquiry** conduire or mener une enquête; (*Jur*) **to** ~ **sb's case** assurer la défense de qn c **to** ~ **o.s.** se conduire, se comporter d (*Elec, Phys*) [+ *heat etc*] conduire, être conducteur de *f* de 3 COMP ► **conducted tour** N (*Brit*) excursion *f* accompagnée, voyage *m* organisé; [*of building*] visite *f* guidée ► **conduct mark** N (*Scol*) avertissement *m* ► **conduct report** N (*Scol*) rapport *m* (*sur la conduite d'un élève*) ► **conduct sheet** N (*Mil*) feuille *f* or certificat *m* de conduite

conductance [kən'dʌktəns] N (*Elec, Phys*) conductance *f*

conduction [kən'dʌkʃən] N (*Elec, Phys*) conduction *f*

conductive [kən'dʌktɪv] ADJ (*Elec, Phys*) conducteur (-trice *f*)

conductivity [,kɒndʌk'tɪvɪtɪ] N (*Elec, Phys*) conductivité *f*

conductor [kən'dʌktər] N a (= *leader*) conducteur *m*, chef *m*; (*Mus*) [*of orchestra*] chef *m* d'orchestre; [*of choir*] chef *m* de chœur b [*of bus*] receveur *m*; (US *Rail*) chef *m* de train c (*Phys*) (corps *m*) conducteur *m* → **lightning**

conductress [kən'dʌktrɪs] N receveuse *f*

conduit ['kɒndɪt] N a (*Tech*) conduite *f* d'eau, canalisation *f*; (*Elec*) gaine *f* b (= *person*) intermédiaire *mf*

condyle ['kɒndɪl] N (*Anat*) condyle *m*

cone [kəʊn] N (*Astron, Geol, Math, Mil, Naut, Opt, Rad, Tech*) cône *m*; (*Aut*) cône *m* de signalisation; [*of tree*] cône *m*; [*of pine tree*] pomme *f*; (*Culin*) [*of ice cream*] cornet *m*

► **cone off** VT SEP [+ *road*] placer des cônes de signalisation sur

coney ['kəʊnɪ] N = **cony**

confab* ['kɒnfæb] N (brin *m* de) causette* *f*

confabulate [kən'fæbjʊleɪt] VI s'entretenir, deviser

confabulation [kən,fæbjʊ'leɪʃən] N conciliabule *m*, conversation *f*

confection [kən'fekʃən] N a (*Culin*) (= *sweet*) sucrerie *f*, friandise *f*; (= *cake*) gâteau *m*, pâtisserie *f*; (= *dessert*) dessert *m* (sucré); (*Dress*) vêtement *m* de confection b (= *action, process*) confection *f*

confectioner [kən'fekʃənər] 1 N (= *sweet-maker*) confiseur *m*, -euse *f*; (= *cakemaker*) pâtissier *m*, -ière *f*; ~**'s (shop)** confiserie *f* (-pâtisserie *f*) 2 COMP ► **confectioner's sugar** N (US) sucre *m* glace

confectionery [kən'fekʃənərɪ] 1 N (= *sweets*) confiserie *f*; (*Brit* = *cakes etc*) pâtisserie *f* 2 COMP ► **confectionery sugar** N (US) sucre *m* glace

confederacy [kən'fedərəsɪ] N a (*Pol* = *group of states*) confédération *f*; (US *Hist*) **the Confederacy** les États *mpl* confédérés b (= *conspiracy*) conspiration *f*

confederate [kən'fedərɪt] 1 ADJ a confédéré *b* (US *Hist*) **Confederate** Confédéré 2 a confédéré(e) *m(f)*; (*in criminal act*) complice *mf* b (US *Hist*) **Confederate** Confédéré *m* 3 [kən'fedəreɪt] VT confédérer 4 VI se confédérer

confederation [kən,fedə'reɪʃən] N confédération *f*

confer [kən'fɜːr] 1 VT conférer, accorder (**on** à); **to** ~ **a title** conférer un titre; (*at ceremony*) **to** ~ **a degree (on)** remettre un diplôme (à) 2 VI s'entretenir (**with sb** avec qn, **on** or **about sth** de qch)

conferee [,kɒnfɜː'riː] N (*at congress*) congressiste *mf*

conference ['kɒnfərəns] 1 N (= *meeting, Pol*) conférence *f*, congrès *m*; (*especially academic*) congrès *m*, colloque *m* (**on** sur); (= *discussion*) conférence *f*, consultation *f*; **to be in** ~ être en conférence; (**the**) ~ **decided ...** les participants à la conférence or les congressistes ont décidé ... → **press** 2 COMP ► **conference call** N (*Telec*) audioconférence *f*, téléconférence *f* ► **conference centre** N (= *town*) ville *f* de congrès; (= *building*) palais *m* des congrès; (*in institution*) centre *m* de conférences ► **conference committee** N (US *Pol*) commission interparlementaire de compromis sur les projets de loi ► **conference member** N congressiste *mf* ► **conference room** N salle *f* de conférences ► **conference table** N (*lit, fig*) table *f* de conférence

conferencing ['kɒnfərənsɪŋ] N (*Telec*) ~ (**facility**) possibilité *f* de réunion-téléphone

conferment [kən'fɜːmənt] N (*Univ*) [*of degree*] remise *f* (de diplômes); [*of title, favour*] octroi *m*

confess [kən'fes] 1 VT a [+ *crime*] avouer, confesser; [+ *mistake*] reconnaître, avouer; **he** ~**ed that he had stolen the money/to having stolen the money** il a avoué or reconnu or confessé qu'il avait volé l'argent/avoir volé l'argent; **to** ~ **(to) a liking for sth** reconnaître qu'on aime qch; **she** ~**ed herself guilty/ ignorant of ...** elle a confessé qu'elle était coupable/ignorante de ... b (*Rel*) [+ *faith*] confesser, proclamer; [+ *sins*] confesser, se confesser de; [+ *penitent*] confesser 2 VI a avouer, passer aux aveux; **to** ~ **to** [+ *crime*] avouer, confesser; [+ *mistake*] reconnaître, avouer; **to** ~ **to having done** avouer or reconnaître or confesser avoir fait → **1** b (*Rel*) se confesser

confessedly [kən'fesɪdlɪ] ADV (= *generally admitted*) de l'aveu de tous; (= *on one's own admission*) de son propre aveu; **a** ~ **terrorist**

group un groupe terroriste qui se revendique comme tel

confession [kən'feʃən] N a (= *admission of guilt*) [*of mistake, crime*] aveu *m*; (*Jur*) aveux *mpl*; **to make a full** ~ faire des aveux complets b (*Rel*) confession *f*; **to go to** ~ aller se confesser; **to hear sb's** ~ confesser qn; **to make one's** ~ se confesser; **to make a** ~ (**of faith**) faire une confession (de foi); **general** ~ confession *f* générale; **to be of the Protestant** ~ (= *denomination*) être de confession protestante; (*as title of book, article etc*) **"Confessions of a Taxi Driver"** « les Confessions d'un chauffeur de taxi »

confessional [kən'feʃənl] (*Rel*) 1 N confessionnal *m*; **under the seal of the** ~ sous le secret de la confession 2 ADJ confessionnel

confessor [kən'fesər] N (*Rel*) confesseur *m*; (= *confidant*) confident(e) *m(f)*

confetti [kən'fetɪ] N (*NonC*) confettis *mpl*

confidant [,kɒnfɪ'dænt] N confident *m*

confidante [,kɒnfɪ'dænt] N confidente *f*

confide [kən'faɪd] VT a [+ *object, person, job, secret*] confier (**to sb** à qn); **to** ~ **sth to sb's care** confier qch à la garde or aux soins de qn; **to** ~ **secrets to sb** confier des secrets à qn b avouer en confidence; **she** ~**d to me that ...** elle m'a avoué en confidence que ..., elle m'a confié que ...

► **confide in** VT FUS a (= *tell secrets to*) s'ouvrir à, se confier à; **to** ~ **in sb about sth** confier qch à qn; **to** ~ **in sb about what one is going to do** révéler à qn ce qu'on va faire b (= *have confidence in*) [+ *sb's ability*] se fier à, avoir confiance en; **you can** ~ **in me** vous pouvez me faire confiance

▼ **confidence** ['kɒnfɪdəns] 1 N a (= *trust, hope*) confiance *f*; **to have** ~ **in sb/sth** avoir confiance en qn/qch, faire confiance à qn/qch; **to put one's** ~ **in sb/sth** mettre sa confiance en qn/qch; **to have every** ~ **in sb/sth** faire totalement confiance à qn/qch, avoir pleine confiance en qn/en or dans qch; **to have** ~ **in the future** faire confiance à l'avenir; **I have every** ~ **that he will come back** je suis sûr or certain qu'il reviendra; (*Pol etc*) **motion of no** ~ motion *f* de censure → **vote** b (= *self-confidence*) confiance *f* en soi, assurance *f*; **he lacks** ~ il manque d'assurance c (*NonC*) confidence *f*; **to take sb into one's** ~ faire des confidences à qn, se confier à qn; **he told me that in** ~ il me l'a dit en confidence or confidentiellement → **strict** d (= *private communication*) confidence *f*; **they exchanged** ~**s** ils ont échangé des confidences 2 COMP ► **confidence game** N abus *m* de confiance, escroquerie *f* ► **confidence man** N (*pl* **confidence men**) escroc *m* ► **confidence trick** N = **confidence game** ► **confidence trickster** N = **confidence man**

confident ['kɒnfɪdənt] ADJ a (= *self-assured*) [*person*] sûr de soi, assuré; [*manner, smile, prediction*] confiant; [*performance*] plein d'assurance; [*reply*] assuré; **to be in (a)** ~ **mood** être confiant b (= *sure*) **to be** ~ **of sth** [*person*] être sûr de qch; **to be** ~ **of success** être sûr de réussir; **to be** or **feel** ~ **about sth** avoir confiance en qch; **to be** ~ **that ...** être sûr que ...

confidential [,kɒnfɪ'denʃəl] 1 ADJ a (= *secret*) [*information, document, advice, discussion, tone*] confidentiel; **he became very** ~ il a pris un ton très confidentiel; **to say sth in a** ~ **whisper** chuchoter qch d'un ton confidentiel; **in a** ~ **tone** sur le ton de la confidence b (= *trusted*) [*servant, clerk*] de confiance 2 COMP ► **confidential secretary** N secrétaire *mf* particulier (-ière *f*)

confidentiality [,kɒnfɪ,denʃɪ'ælɪtɪ] N confidentialité *f*

confidentially [ˌkɒnfɪˈdənʃəlɪ] ADV [a] (= privately) [discuss] confidentiellement; **to write ~ to sb** envoyer une lettre confidentielle à qn; **all information will be treated ~** tous les renseignements resteront confidentiels [b] (= confidingly) [speak, whisper] sur le ton de la confidence; (= between ourselves) **~, I don't like him at all** tout à fait entre nous, je ne l'aime pas du tout

confidently [ˈkɒnfɪdəntlɪ] ADV [predict, assert] avec beaucoup d'assurance; [stride, walk] d'un pas assuré; [smile] d'un air assuré; [speak] avec assurance

confiding [kənˈfaɪdɪŋ] ADJ confiant

confidingly [kənˈfaɪdɪŋlɪ] ADV [say, speak] sur un ton de confidence; **he leaned towards her ~** il s'est penché vers elle comme pour lui faire une confidence

configuration [kənˌfɪgjʊˈreɪʃən] N (gen, Ling, Comput) configuration f

configure [kənˈfɪgə] VT (gen, Comput) configurer

confine [kənˈfaɪn] [1] VT [a] (= imprison) emprisonner, enfermer; (= shut up) confiner, enfermer (**in** dans); **to ~ a bird in a cage** enfermer un oiseau dans une cage; **to be ~d to the house/to one's room/to bed** être obligé de rester chez soi/de garder la chambre/de garder le lit; **to ~ sb to barracks** consigner qn [b] (= limit) [+ remarks] limiter; **to ~ o.s. to doing sth** se borner à faire qch; **to ~ o.s. to generalities** s'en tenir à des généralités; **the damage is ~d to the back of the car** seul l'arrière de la voiture est endommagé [2] **confines** [ˈkɒnfaɪnz] NPL (lit, fig) limites fpl; **within the ~s of ...** dans les limites de ...

confined [kənˈfaɪnd] ADJ [atmosphere, air] confiné; **in a ~ space** dans un espace restreint or réduit; (Mil) **~ to barracks/base** consigné; (in childbirth) **to be ~†** accoucher, être en couches

confinement [kənˈfaɪnmənt] N (Med†) couches fpl; (= imprisonment) détention f, incarcération f (Jur); (Mil) **~ to barracks** consigne f au quartier; (Mil) **to get ten days' ~ to barracks** attraper dix jours de consigne; **~ to bed** alitement m; **~ to one's room/the house** obligation f de garder la chambre/de rester chez soi → **close¹**

▼ **confirm** [kənˈfɜːm] VT [a] [+ statement, claim, theory, report, news, suspicion] confirmer, corroborer; [+ arrangement, reservation] confirmer (**with** auprès de qn); [+ authority] (r)affermir, consolider; [+ one's resolve] fortifier, raffermir; [+ treaty, appointment] ratifier; (Jur) [+ decision] entériner, homologuer; [+ election] valider; **to ~ sth to sb** confirmer qch à qn; **to ~ sb in an opinion** confirmer or fortifier qn dans une opinion; **to be ~ed in one's opinion** voir son opinion confirmée; **his new play ~s him as a leading playwright** sa nouvelle pièce le confirme dans sa position de grand auteur dramatique; **we ~ receipt of your letter** nous avons bien reçu votre courrier, nous accusons réception de votre courrier [b] (Rel) confirmer

confirmation [ˌkɒnfəˈmeɪʃən] N [a] [of statement, claim, theory, suspicion, arrangement, appointment] confirmation f; [of treaty] ratification f; (Jur) entérinement m; **she looked at me for ~** (confidently) elle m'interrogea du regard pour (avoir) confirmation; **the ~ of** or **for a booking** la confirmation d'une réservation; **"subject to ~"** « à confirmer »; **that's subject to ~** cela reste à confirmer; **all timings are subject to ~ when booking** tous les horaires doivent être confirmés lors des réservations [b] (Rel) confirmation f

confirmed [kənˈfɜːmd] [1] ADJ [a] (= inveterate) [non-smoker, meat-eater, atheist] convaincu; [bachelor] endurci; **I am a ~ admirer of ...** je suis un fervent admirateur de ... [b] (= definite) [booking, reservation] confirmé [2] COMP

▸ **confirmed credit** N crédit m confirmé
▸ **confirmed letter of credit** N lettre f de crédit confirmée

confiscate [ˈkɒnfɪskeɪt] VT confisquer (**sth from sb** qch à qn)

confiscation [ˌkɒnfɪsˈkeɪʃən] N confiscation f

conflagration [ˌkɒnfləˈgreɪʃən] N incendie m, sinistre m; (fig) conflagration f

conflate [kənˈfleɪt] VT assembler, réunir

conflation [kənˈfleɪʃən] N assemblage m, réunion f

conflict [ˈkɒnflɪkt] [1] N conflit m, lutte f; (= quarrel) dispute f; (Mil) conflit m, combat m; (Jur) conflit m; (fig) [of interests, ideas, opinions] conflit m; (Mil) **armed ~** conflit m armé; **to be in ~ (with)** être en conflit (avec); **to come into ~ with ...** entrer en conflit or en lutte avec ...; **a great deal of ~** un conflit considérable [2] [kənˈflɪkt] VI [a] être or entrer en conflit or en lutte (**with** avec); [b] [opinions, ideas] s'opposer, se heurter; [dates] coïncider; **that ~s with what he told me** ceci est en contradiction avec or contredit ce qu'il m'a raconté

conflicting [kənˈflɪktɪŋ] ADJ (= incompatible) [views, opinions, demands, evidence] contradictoire; (= divided) [emotions, loyalties] conflictuel

confluence [ˈkɒnfluəns] N [of rivers] (= place) confluent m; (= act) confluence f; (fig = crowd) foule f, assemblée f

conform [kənˈfɔːm] VI [a] se conformer (**to, with** à); [actions, sayings] être en conformité (**to** avec); [b] (gen, Rel) être conformiste mf

conformable [kənˈfɔːməbl] ADJ [a] conforme (**to** à); [b] (= in agreement with) en conformité, en accord (**to** avec); [c] (= submissive) docile, accommodant

conformation [ˌkɒnfəˈmeɪʃən] N conformation f, structure f

conformism [kənˈfɔːmɪzəm] N conformisme m

conformist [kənˈfɔːmɪst] ADJ, N (gen, Rel) conformiste mf

conformity [kənˈfɔːmɪtɪ] N (= likeness) conformité f; (= conformism) conformisme m; (Rel) adhésion à la religion conformiste; **in ~ with** conformément à

confound [kənˈfaʊnd] VT (= perplex) déconcerter; (frm = defeat) [+ enemy, plans] confondre (frm); (= mix up) confondre (**A with B** A avec B), prendre (**A with B** A pour B); **~ it!**⁣* la barbe!*; **~ him!*** qu'il aille au diable!, (que) le diable l'emporte!†; **it's a ~ed nuisance!*** c'est la barbe!*, quelle barbe!*

confront [kənˈfrʌnt] VT [a] (= bring face to face) confronter (**with** avec), mettre en présence (**with** de); **the police ~ed the accused with the witnesses** la police a confronté l'accusé avec les témoins; **the police ~ed the accused with the evidence** la police a mis l'accusé en présence des témoignages; **to ~ two witnesses** confronter deux témoins (entre eux) [b] [+ enemy, danger] affronter, faire face à; (= defy) affronter, défier; **the problems which ~ us** les problèmes auxquels nous devons faire face

confrontation [ˌkɒnfrʌnˈteɪʃən] N [a] (military) affrontement m; (in human relationships) conflit m, affrontement m [b] (= act of confronting) confrontation f (**of sb with sth** de qn à or avec qch)

confrontational [ˌkɒnfrʌnˈteɪʃənəl] ADJ (gen) conflictuel; **to be ~** [person] être agressif, rechercher la confrontation

Confucian [kənˈfjuːʃən] [1] ADJ confucéen [2] N confucianiste mf

Confucianism [kənˈfjuːʃənɪzəm] N confucianisme m

Confucius [kənˈfjuːʃəs] N Confucius m

confuse [kənˈfjuːz] VT [a] (= throw into disorder) [+ opponent] confondre; [+ plans] semer le désordre dans, bouleverser; (= perplex) jeter dans la perplexité; (= embarrass) embarrasser; (= disconcert) troubler; (= mix up) [+ person] embrouiller; [+ ideas] embrouiller, brouiller; [+ memory] brouiller; **you're just confusing me** tu ne fais que m'embrouiller (les idées); **to ~ the issue** compliquer or embrouiller les choses [b] **to ~ A with B** confondre A avec B, prendre A pour B; **to ~ two problems** confondre deux problèmes

confused [kənˈfjuːzd] ADJ [person] (= muddled) désorienté; (= perplexed) déconcerté; (= embarrassed) confus, embarrassé; [opponent] confondu; [mind] embrouillé, confus; [sounds, voices] confus, indistinct; [memories] confus, vague; [ideas, situation] confus, embrouillé; **to have a ~ idea** avoir une vague idée; **to get ~** (= muddled up) ne plus savoir où on en est, s'y perdre; (= embarrassed) se troubler

confusedly [kənˈfjuːzɪdlɪ] ADV [a] (= in bewilderment) [shake one's head] avec perplexité [b] (= in disorder) confusément

confusing [kənˈfjuːzɪŋ] ADJ déroutant; **it's all very ~** on ne s'y retrouve plus, on s'y perd

confusingly [kənˈfjuːzɪŋlɪ] ADV [do, write, say] d'une manière qui prête à confusion; **the two names are ~ similar** la similitude des deux noms prête à confusion

confusion [kənˈfjuːʒən] N (= disorder, muddle) confusion f, désordre m; (= embarrassment) confusion f, trouble m; (= mixing up) confusion f (**of X with Y** de X avec Y); **he was in a state of ~** la confusion régnait dans son esprit, il avait l'esprit troublé; **the books lay about in ~** les livres étaient en désordre or pêle-mêle → **throw**

confute [kənˈfjuːt] VT [+ person] démontrer l'erreur de; [+ notion] réfuter

conga [ˈkɒŋgə] N [a] (= dance) conga f [b] (also **~ drum**) conga f

congeal [kənˈdʒiːl] [1] VI [fat, grease, oil] (se) figer; [milk] (se) cailler; [blood] se coaguler; [paint] sécher [2] VT [+ fat, grease, oil] faire figer; [+ milk] faire cailler; [+ blood] coaguler

congenial [kənˈdʒiːnɪəl] ADJ (frm) [atmosphere, environment, work, place] agréable (**to sb** pour qn); [person] sympathique, agréable; **to be in ~ company** être en agréable compagnie; **he found few people ~ to him** il trouvait peu de gens à son goût

congenital [kənˈdʒenɪtl] ADJ [dislike, aversion, mistrust] (also Med) congénital; [liar] de naissance

congenitally [kənˈdʒenɪtəlɪ] ADV [lazy, suspicious etc] (also Med) de naissance

conger [ˈkɒŋgə] N (also **~ eel**) congre m, anguille f de roche

congested [kənˈdʒestɪd] ADJ [a] (= busy) [place] congestionné; [telephone lines] surchargé; **~ traffic** encombrements mpl; **~ with traffic** embouteillé [b] (Med = blocked) [nose] bouché; [lungs] congestionné; **I feel very ~** j'ai vraiment les bronches prises

congestion [kənˈdʒestʃən] N [of town, countryside] surpeuplement m; [of street, traffic] encombrement m, embouteillage m; (Med) congestion f

congestive [kənˈdʒestɪv] ADJ (Med) congestif

conglomerate [kənˈglɒmərɪt] [1] VT conglomérer (frm), agglomérer [2] VI s'agglomérer [3] [kənˈglɒmərɪt] ADJ congloméré (also Geol), aggloméré [4] N (gen, Econ, Geol) conglomérat m

conglomeration [kənˌglɒməˈreɪʃən] N (= group) [of objects] assemblage m (hétéroclite); [of houses] agglomération f

Congo [ˈkɒŋgəʊ] N [a] (= country) le Congo; **the Democratic/People's Republic of the ~** la République démocratique/populaire du Congo; **~-Kinshasa** le Congo-Kinshasa; **~-Brazzaville** le Congo-Brazzaville [b] (= river) Congo m

---

▸ **LANGUAGE IN USE:** confirm 19.5, 21.3, 21.4

Congolese [ˌkɒŋgəʊˈliːz] [1] ADJ congolais [2] N (pl inv) Congolais(e) m(f)

congrats* [kənˈgræts] EXCL bravo !

▼ **congratulate** [kənˈgrætjʊleɪt] VT féliciter, complimenter (**sb on sth** qn de qch, **sb on doing** qn d'avoir fait); **to ~ o.s. on sth/on doing sth** se féliciter de qch/d'avoir fait qch; **we would like to ~ you on your engagement** nous vous présentons toutes nos félicitations à l'occasion de vos fiançailles

▼ **congratulations** [kənˌgrætjʊˈleɪʃənz] NPL félicitations fpl, compliments mpl; **~!** toutes mes félicitations!; **~ on your success/engagement** (toutes mes) félicitations pour votre succès/à l'occasion de vos fiançailles

congratulatory [kənˈgrætjʊlətərɪ] ADJ [telegram, letter, message, speech] de félicitations; **to give sb a ~ handshake** féliciter qn en lui serrant la main

congregate [ˈkɒŋgrɪgeɪt] [1] VI se rassembler, se réunir (**round autour de, at** à) [2] VT rassembler, réunir

congregation [ˌkɒŋgrɪˈgeɪʃən] N rassemblement m, assemblée f; (Rel) [of worshippers] assemblée f (des fidèles), assistance f; [of cardinals, monks etc] congrégation f; (Univ) [of professors] assemblée f générale

congregational [ˌkɒŋgrɪˈgeɪʃnl] ADJ [minister] de l'Église congrégationaliste; [prayer] prononcé par l'ensemble des fidèles; **the Congregational Church** l'Église f congrégationaliste

Congregationalist [ˌkɒŋgrɪˈgeɪʃənəˌlɪst] ADJ, N congrégationaliste mf

congress [ˈkɒŋgres] [1] N [a] congrès m; **education** ~ congrès m de l'enseignement or **trade** [b] (US Pol) **Congress** Congrès m; (= session) session f du Congrès [2] COMP ► **congress member** N congressiste mf

congressional [kɒŋˈgreʃənl] ADJ [a] d'un congrès [b] (Pol: in US, India) **Congressional** du Congrès; **Congressional Directory** annuaire m du Congrès; **Congressional district** circonscription f d'un Représentant; **Congressional Record** Journal m Officiel du Congrès

congressman [ˈkɒŋgresmən] (US Pol) [1] N (pl **-men**) membre m du Congrès, ≈ député m; **Congressman J. Smith said that ...** le député J. Smith a dit que ... [2] COMP ► **congressman-at-large** N représentant non attaché à une circonscription électorale

congressperson [ˈkɒŋgres,pɜːsən] N (US Pol) membre m du Congrès, ≈ député m

congresswoman [ˈkɒŋgres,wʊmən] N (pl **-women**) (US Pol) membre m du Congrès, député m

congruence [ˈkɒŋgrʊəns] N (Math) congruence f; (fig) conformité f

congruent [ˈkɒŋgrʊənt] ADJ en accord or harmonie (**with** avec); (Math) [number] congru (**with** à); [triangle] isométrique

congruity [kɒŋˈgruːɪtɪ] N convenance f, congruité f

congruous [ˈkɒŋgrʊəs] ADJ qui s'accorde, en harmonie (**to, with** avec); (Rel) congru

conic(al) [ˈkɒnɪk(əl)] ADJ (de forme) conique

conifer [ˈkɒnɪfə*] N conifère m

coniferous [kəˈnɪfərəs] ADJ [tree] conifère; [forest] de conifères

conjectural [kənˈdʒektʃərəl] ADJ conjectural

conjecture [kənˈdʒektʃə*] [1] VT conjecturer [2] VI conjecturer, faire des conjectures [3] N conjecture f

conjoin [kənˈdʒɔɪn] (frm) [1] VT lier, unir [2] VI s'unir

conjoint [ˈkɒndʒɔɪnt] ADJ (frm) [therapy, counselling] de couple

conjointly [ˈkɒndʒɔɪntlɪ] ADV conjointement

conjugal [ˈkɒndʒʊgəl] ADJ [state, rights, happiness] conjugal

conjugate [ˈkɒndʒʊgeɪt] (Bio, Gram) [1] VT conjuguer [2] VI se conjuguer

conjugation [ˌkɒndʒʊˈgeɪʃən] N conjugaison f

conjunct [kənˈdʒʌŋkt] ADJ conjoint

conjunction [kənˈdʒʌŋkʃən] N (Astron, Gram) conjonction f; **in ~ with** conjointement avec

conjunctiva [ˌkɒndʒʌŋkˈtaɪvə] N (pl **conjunctivas** or **conjunctivae** [ˌkɒndʒʌŋkˈtaɪviː]) (Anat) conjonctive f

conjunctive [kənˈdʒʌŋktɪv] ADJ (Anat, Gram) conjonctif

conjunctivitis [kənˌdʒʌŋktɪˈvaɪtɪs] N conjonctivite f; **to have ~** avoir de la conjonctivite

conjuncture [kənˈdʒʌŋktʃə*] N conjoncture f

conjure [kənˈdʒʊə*] [1] VT [a] (= appeal to) conjurer (liter) (**sb to do** qn de faire) [b] [ˈkʌndʒə*] faire apparaître (par la prestidigitation); **he ~d a rabbit from his hat** il a fait sortir un lapin de son chapeau [2] [ˈkʌndʒə*] VI faire des tours de passe-passe; (= juggle) jongler (**with** avec); (fig) jongler (**with** avec); (fig) **a name to ~ with** un nom prestigieux

► **conjure away** VT SEP faire disparaître (comme par magie)

► **conjure up** VT SEP [+ ghosts, spirits] faire apparaître; [+ memories] évoquer, rappeler; [+ meal] préparer à partir de (trois fois) rien; **to ~ up visions of ...** évoquer ...

conjurer [ˈkʌndʒərə*] N prestidigitateur m, -trice f

conjuring [ˈkʌndʒərɪŋ] [1] N prestidigitation f [2] COMP ► **conjuring trick** N tour m de passe-passe or de prestidigitation

conjuror [ˈkʌndʒərə*] N = **conjurer**

conk* [kɒŋk] [1] N (Brit = nose) pif* m, blair* m; (US = head) caboche* f [2] VT (US) frapper sur la caboche* [3] COMP ► **conk-out*** N (US) panne f mécanique

► **conk out*** [1] VI [person] (= faint) tomber dans les pommes*; (= tire) s'écrouler de fatigue; [engine, machine] tomber or rester en rade; **her car ~ed out** sa voiture est restée en carafe* [2] **~-out*** N → **conk**

conker* [ˈkɒŋkə*] N (Brit) marron m

Conn. ABBR = **Connecticut**

▼ **connect** [kəˈnekt] [1] VT [a] (= join: gen) [person] [+ machine] connecter (**to** à); [+ plug] brancher (**to** sur); (Tech) [+ pinions] embrayer; [+ wheels] engrener; [+ pipes, drains] raccorder (**to** à); [+ shafts etc] articuler, conjuguer; (Elec) [+ two objects] raccorder, connecter; (Elec) **to ~ sth to the mains** brancher qch sur le secteur; (Elec) **to ~ sth to earth** mettre qch à la terre or à la masse; (to water, electricity etc services) **we haven't been ~ed yet** nous ne sommes pas encore reliés or branchés, nous n'avons pas encore l'eau (or l'électricité etc) [b] (Telec) [+ caller] mettre en communication (**with** avec qn); [+ telephone] brancher; **we're trying to ~ you** nous essayons d'obtenir votre communication; **I'm ~ing you now** vous êtes en ligne, vous avez votre communication; **~ed by telephone** [person, place] relié par téléphone (**to, with** à) [c] (= associate) associer (**with, to** à); **I always ~ Paris with springtime** j'associe toujours Paris au printemps; **I'd never have ~ed them** je n'aurais jamais fait le rapport entre eux → **connected** [d] (= form link between) [road, railway] relier (**with, to** à); [rope etc] relier, rattacher (**with, to** à); **the city is ~ed to the sea by a canal** la ville est reliée à la mer par un canal

[2] VI [a] (= be joined) [two rooms] être relié, communiquer; [two parts, wires etc] être connectés or raccordés [b] [coach, train, plane] assurer la correspondance (**with** avec); **this train ~s with the Rome express** ce train assure la correspondance avec l'express de Rome [c] (* = hit) **to ~ with the ball** [golf club etc]

frapper la balle; **my fist ~ed with his jaw*** je l'ai touché à la mâchoire, mon poing l'a cueilli à la mâchoire

[d] (two people) se comprendre; **to ~ with sb** communiquer avec qn

connected [kəˈnektɪd] ADJ [a] [languages] affin (frm), connexe; (Bot, Jur) connexe; (fig) [argument] logique; [talk, oration] suivi; **(closely) ~ professions** des professions fpl connexes; **a (properly) ~ sentence** une phrase correctement construite; (Ling) **~ speech** la chaîne parlée

[b] **these matters are not ~ at all** ces affaires n'ont aucun lien or rapport entre elles; **these two things are ~ in my mind** les deux sont liés dans mon esprit; **to be ~ with** (= be related to) être allié à, être parent de; (= have dealings with) être en contact or en relation avec; (= have a bearing on) se rattacher à, avoir rapport à; **people ~ with education** ceux qui ont quelque chose à voir avec le monde de l'éducation; **he is ~ with many big firms** il a des contacts avec beaucoup de grandes entreprises, il est en relation avec beaucoup de grandes entreprises; **his departure is not ~ with the murder** son départ n'a aucun rapport or n'a rien à voir avec le meurtre; **he's very well ~** (= of good family) il est de très bonne famille, il est très bien apparenté; (= of influential family) sa famille a des relations → **connect**

Connecticut [kəˈnektɪkət] N le Connecticut; **in ~** dans le Connecticut

connecting [kəˈnektɪŋ] [1] ADJ [rooms] communicant; [parts, wires] connecté; **bedroom with ~ bathroom** chambre f avec salle de bains attenante [2] COMP ► **connecting flight** N (vol m de) correspondance f ► **connecting rod** N (US Aut) bielle f

▼ **connection** [kəˈnekʃən] [1] N [a] (= association) rapport m, lien m (**with** or **to** avec, **between** entre); (= relationship) rapports mpl, relations fpl (**with** or **to** avec, **between** entre); **this has no ~ with what he did** ceci n'a aucun rapport avec ce qu'il a fait; **to form a ~ with sb** établir des relations or des rapports avec qn; **to break off a ~ (with sb)** rompre les relations or les rapports (avec qn); **to build up a ~ with a firm** établir des relations d'affaires avec une entreprise; **to have no further ~ with sb/sth** ne plus avoir aucun contact avec qn/qch; **in ~ with sth** à propos de qch; (frm) **in this** or **that ~** à ce sujet, à ce propos; (frm) **in another ~** dans un autre contexte

[b] (= associate) **a business ~ of mine** ◊ one of my business ~s une de mes relations d'affaires; **to have important ~s** avoir des relations (importantes); **to have criminal ~s** avoir des relations or des contacts dans le milieu

[c] (= kinship) parenté f; (= relative) parent(e) m(f); **~s** famille f; **there is some family ~ between them** ils ont un lien de parenté; **he is a distant ~** c'est un parent éloigné; **she is a ~ of mine** c'est une de mes parentes

[d] (Transport) (= link) liaison f; (= train, bus, plane) correspondance f (**with** avec); **to miss one's ~** rater la correspondance

[e] (Elec) raccordement m, branchement m → **loose**

[f] (Telec) (= link) liaison f; (= act of connecting) (for call) branchement m; (= installing) raccordement m; **a telephone/radio/satellite ~** une liaison téléphonique/radio/par satellite; **to break the ~** couper la communication

[g] (Tech = joint) raccord m

[h] (Drugs*) filière f

[2] COMP ► **connection charge**, **connection fee** N (Telec) frais mpl de raccordement

▼ **connective** [kəˈnektɪv] [1] ADJ (gen, Gram, Anat) conjonctif [2] N (Gram, Logic) conjonction f [3] COMP ► **connective tissue** N (Bio) tissu m conjonctif

► LANGUAGE IN USE: **congratulate** 24.3   **congratulations** 23.6, 24.1, 24.3   **connect** 27.4   **connection** 5.3

connector [kəˈnektər] N (gen) raccord m, connecteur m; (Elec) pince f de bout, pince f de courant

connexion [kəˈnekʃən] = **connection**

conning tower [ˈkɒnɪŋˌtaʊər] N [of submarine] kiosque m; [of warship] centre m opérationnel

conniption* [kəˈnɪpʃən] N (US: also **~s**) accès m de colère or de rage

connivance [kəˈnaɪvəns] N connivence f, accord m tacite; **this was done with her ~/in ~ with her** cela s'est fait avec sa connivence or son accord tacite/de connivence avec elle

connive [kəˈnaɪv] VI **to ~ at** (= pretend not to notice) fermer les yeux sur; (= aid and abet) être de connivence dans, être complice de; **to ~ (with sb) in sth/in doing** être de connivence (avec qn) dans qch/pour faire

conniving [kəˈnaɪvɪŋ] (pej) [1] ADJ intrigant [2] N (NonC) machinations fpl, intrigues fpl

connoisseur [ˌkɒnəˈsɜːr] N connaisseur m, -euse f (**of** de, en)

connotation [ˌkɒnəʊˈteɪʃən] N (Ling, Philos) connotation f; (Logic) implication f

connotative [ˈkɒnəˌteɪtɪv] ADJ [meaning] connotatif

connote [kɒˈnəʊt] VT évoquer, suggérer; (Ling, Philos) connoter

connubial [kəˈnjuːbɪəl] ADJ conjugal

conquer [ˈkɒŋkər] VT [+ enemy, mountain, illness] vaincre; [+ nation, country] conquérir; [+ fear, obsession] surmonter, vaincre; [+ one's feelings] dominer; [+ one's audience] subjuguer

conquering [ˈkɒŋkərɪŋ] ADJ victorieux

conqueror [ˈkɒŋkərər] N (Mil) conquérant m; [of mountain etc] vainqueur m → **William**

conquest [ˈkɒŋkwest] N conquête f; **to make a ~*** faire une conquête; **she's his latest ~*** c'est sa dernière conquête*

conquistador [kɒnˈkwɪstədɔːr] N (Hist) conquistador m

Cons. (Brit) ABBR = **Conservative**

consanguinity [ˌkɒnsæŋˈgwɪnɪtɪ] N consanguinité f

conscience [ˈkɒnʃəns] [1] N conscience f; **to have a clear** or **an easy ~** avoir bonne conscience, avoir la conscience tranquille; **he left with a clear ~** il est parti la conscience tranquille; **he has a bad** or **guilty ~** il a mauvaise conscience, il n'a pas la conscience tranquille; **to have sth on one's ~** avoir qch sur la conscience; **in (all) ~** en conscience; **for ~' sake** par acquit de conscience; (frm) **upon my ~, I swear ...** en mon âme et conscience, je jure ...; **to make sth a matter of ~** faire de qch un cas de conscience [2] COMP ► **conscience clause** N (Jur) clause f de conscience ► **conscience money** N don m d'argent (pour racheter une faute) ► **conscience-stricken** ADJ pris de remords

conscientious [ˌkɒnʃɪˈenʃəs] ADJ [a] [person, worker, piece of work] consciencieux [b] [scruple, objection] de conscience; **~ objector** objecteur m de conscience

conscientiously [ˌkɒnʃɪˈenʃəslɪ] ADV consciencieusement

conscientiousness [ˌkɒnʃɪˈenʃəsnɪs] N conscience f

conscious [ˈkɒnʃəs] [1] ADJ [a] (Med, Psych, Philos) [person, memory, mind, thought, prejudice] conscient; **to become ~** [person] revenir à soi, reprendre connaissance; **below the level of ~ awareness** au-dessous du seuil de conscience; **on a ~ level** à un niveau conscient [b] (= aware) **~ of sth** conscient de qch; **to become ~ of sth** prendre conscience de qch, se rendre compte de qch; **she became ~ of him looking at her** elle prit conscience du fait qu'il la regardait, elle se rendit compte qu'il la regardait; **to be ~ of doing sth** avoir

conscience de faire qch; **to be ~ that ...** être conscient du fait que ...; **to become ~ that ...** se rendre compte que ...
[c] (after adv) **politically ~** politisé; **environmentally ~** sensibilisé aux problèmes de l'environnement → **-conscious**
[d] (= deliberate) [effort, choice, insult] délibéré; **to make a ~ decision to do sth** prendre délibérément la décision de faire qch; **~ humour** humour m voulu
[e] (= clearly felt) **... he said, with ~ guilt/superiority** ... dit-il, conscient de sa culpabilité/supériorité
[2] N (Psych) conscient m

-conscious [ˈkɒnʃəs] SUF **to be image-conscious** être conscient de son image; **to be health-/price-conscious** faire attention à sa santé/aux prix des choses; **to be security-conscious** être sensibilisé aux problèmes de sécurité

consciously [ˈkɒnʃəslɪ] ADV [a] (= with full awareness) [remember, think] consciemment; **to be ~ aware of sth** avoir pleinement conscience de qch [b] (= deliberately) [hurt, mislead, deceive] sciemment

consciousness [ˈkɒnʃəsnɪs] [1] N [a] (Med) connaissance f; **to lose ~** perdre connaissance; **to regain ~** revenir à soi, reprendre connaissance [b] (Philos) conscience f [c] (= awareness) conscience f (**of** de), sentiment m (**of** de); **the ~ that he was being watched prevented him from ...** le sentiment qu'on le regardait l'empêchait de ... [2] COMP ► **consciousness-raising** N sensibilisation f; **~-raising is a priority** il nous faut d'abord faire prendre conscience aux gens

conscript [kənˈskrɪpt] [1] VT [+ troops] enrôler, appeler sous les drapeaux; (fig, hum) **we were ~ed to help with the dishes** nous avons été embauchés pour aider à faire la vaisselle → **conscripted** [2] [ˈkɒnskrɪpt] N (Brit) conscrit m, appelé m [3] ADJ [army] d'appelés

conscripted [kənˈskrɪptɪd] ADJ [troops] enrôlé; [workers, labourers] enrôlé de force

conscription [kənˈskrɪpʃən] N conscription f

consecrate [ˈkɒnsɪkreɪt] VT [+ church, ground] consacrer; [+ bishop] consacrer, sacrer; (fig) [+ custom, one's life] consacrer (**to** à); **he was ~d bishop** il a été sacré or consacré évêque

consecration [ˌkɒnsɪˈkreɪʃən] N (NonC) [of church, cathedral, one's life] consécration f (**to** sth à qch); [of bishop, pope] consécration f, sacre m

consecutive [kənˈsekjʊtɪv] ADJ [a] consécutif; **on four ~ days** pendant quatre jours consécutifs or de suite [b] (Gram) [clause] consécutif

consecutively [kənˈsekjʊtɪvlɪ] ADV consécutivement; **he won two prizes ~** il a gagné consécutivement or coup sur coup deux prix; (Jur) **... the sentences to be served ~** ... avec cumul de peines

consensual [kənˈsensjʊəl] ADJ (Jur, Physiol) consensuel

consensus [kənˈsensəs] [1] N consensus m, accord m général; **~ of opinion** consensus m d'opinion; **what is the ~?** quelle est l'opinion générale? [2] ADJ [decision, view] collectif

▼**consent** [kənˈsent] [1] VI consentir (**to sth** à qch, **to do** à faire); (= to request) accéder (**to sth** à qch); (Jur) **between ~ing adults** entre adultes consentants [2] N consentement m, assentiment m; **to refuse one's ~ to sth** refuser son consentement or assentiment à qch; **by common ~** de l'aveu de tous or de tout le monde, de l'opinion de tous; **by mutual ~** (= general agreement) d'un commun accord; (= private arrangement) de gré à gré, à l'amiable; **divorce by (mutual) ~** divorce m par consentement mutuel; (Jur) **age of ~** âge m légal (pour avoir des relations sexuelles) → **silence** [3] COMP ► **consent form** N (Med) autorisation f d'opérer

consentient [kənˈsenʃɪənt] ADJ (frm) d'accord, en accord (**with** avec)

▼**consequence** [ˈkɒnsɪkwəns] N [a] (= result, effect) conséquence f, suites fpl; **in ~** par conséquent; **in ~ of which** par suite de quoi; **as a ~ of sth** en conséquence de qch; **to take** or **face** or **suffer the ~s** accepter or supporter les conséquences (**of** de) [b] (NonC = importance) importance f, conséquence f; **it's of no ~** cela ne tire à conséquence, cela n'a aucune importance; **a man of no ~** un homme de peu d'importance or de peu de poids; **he's of no ~** lui, il ne compte pas

consequent [ˈkɒnsɪkwənt] ADJ (= following) consécutif (**on** à); (= resulting) résultant (**on** de); **the loss of harvest ~ upon the flooding** la perte de la moisson résultant des or causée par les inondations

consequential [ˌkɒnsɪˈkwenʃəl] ADJ [a] consécutif, conséquent (**to** à); (Jur) **~ damages** dommages-intérêts mpl indirects [b] (pej) [person] suffisant, arrogant

▼**consequently** [ˈkɒnsɪkwəntlɪ] ADV **~, he has been able to ...** c'est pourquoi il a pu ...; **he has ~ been able to ...** il a donc pu ...; **he didn't have enough money: ~, he was unable to ...** il n'avait pas assez d'argent: par conséquent, il n'a pas pu ...; **who, ~, did as little as possible** qui, en conséquence, en a fait le moins possible

conservancy [kənˈsɜːvənsɪ] N [a] (Brit) commission controlling forests, ports etc) ≈ Office m des eaux et forêts [b] = **conservation**

conservation [ˌkɒnsəˈveɪʃən] [1] N sauvegarde f, protection f; (Phys) conservation f; **energy ~** économies fpl d'énergie [2] COMP ► **conservation area** N (Brit) secteur m sauvegardé

conservationist [ˌkɒnsəˈveɪʃənɪst] N défenseur m de l'environnement, écologiste mf

conservatism [kənˈsɜːvətɪzəm] N conservatisme m

conservative [kənˈsɜːvətɪv] [1] ADJ [a] conservateur (-trice f); (Pol) **the Conservative Party** le parti conservateur; **Conservative and Unionist Party** parti m conservateur et unioniste [b] (= moderate) [assessment] modeste; (= conventional) [clothes, appearance, style, behaviour] classique, conventionnel; **at a ~ estimate** au bas mot [2] N (Pol) conservateur m, -trice f

conservatively [kənˈsɜːvətɪvlɪ] ADV [dressed] classique inv, d'une manière conventionnelle; **the cost of the operation was ~ estimated at £500** le coût de l'opération est estimé au bas mot à 500 livres

conservatoire [kənˈsɜːvətwɑːr] N (Mus) conservatoire m

conservator [ˈkɒnsəˌveɪtər] N (gen) conservateur m; (US Jur) tuteur m (d'un incapable)

conservatorship [ˈkɒnsəveɪtəˌʃɪp] N (US Jur) tutelle f

conservatory [kənˈsɜːvətrɪ] N [a] (= greenhouse) jardin m d'hiver (attenante à une maison) [b] (Art, Mus, Theat) conservatoire m

conserve [kənˈsɜːv] [1] VT conserver, préserver; [+ one's resources, one's strength] ménager; [+ energy, electricity, supplies] économiser [2] N (Culin) confiture f, conserve f (de fruits)

▼**consider** [kənˈsɪdər] VT [a] (= think about) [+ problem, possibility] considérer, examiner; [+ question, matter, subject] réfléchir à; **I had not ~ed taking it with me** je n'avais pas envisagé de l'emporter; **everything** or **all things ~ed** tout bien considéré, tout compte fait; **it is my ~ed opinion that ...** après avoir mûrement réfléchi je pense que ...; **he is being ~ed for the post** on songe à lui pour le poste [b] (= take into account) [+ facts] prendre en considération; [+ person's feelings] avoir égard à, ménager; [+ cost, difficulties, dangers] tenir compte de, considérer; **when one ~s that ...**

quand on considère *or* pense que ...
[c] (= *be of the opinion*) considérer, tenir; **she ~s him very mean** elle le considère comme très avare; **to ~ sb responsible** tenir qn pour responsable; **to ~ o.s. happy** s'estimer heureux; **~ yourself lucky*** estimez-vous heureux; **~ yourself dismissed** considérez-vous comme renvoyé; **I ~ that we should have done it** je considère que *or* à mon avis nous aurions dû le faire; **~ it (as) done** considérez que c'est chose faite; **I ~ it an honour to help you** je m'estime honoré de (pouvoir) vous aider

considerable [kənˈsɪdərəbl] ADJ [*number, size, amount, influence, success, damage*] considérable; **to face ~ difficulties** être confronté à des difficultés considérables *or* à de grosses difficultés; **we had ~ difficulty in finding you** nous avons eu beaucoup de mal à vous trouver; **to a ~ extent** dans une large mesure; **I've been living in England for a ~ time** je vis en Angleterre depuis longtemps

considerably [kənˈsɪdərəblɪ] ADV considérablement

considerate [kənˈsɪdərɪt] ADJ prévenant (**towards** envers), attentionné

considerately [kənˈsɪdərɪtlɪ] ADV [*behave, say*] gentiment

▼ **consideration** [kənˌsɪdəˈreɪʃən] N [a] (*NonC* = *thoughtfulness*) considération *f*, égard *m*; **out of ~ for ...** par égard pour ...; **to show ~ for sb's feelings** ménager les susceptibilités de qn [b] (*NonC* = *careful thought*) considération *f*; **to take sth into ~** prendre qch en considération, tenir compte de qch; **taking everything into ~ ...** tout bien considéré *or* pesé ...; **he left it out of ~** il n'en a pas tenu compte, il n'a pas pris cela en considération; **the matter is under ~** l'affaire est à l'examen *or* à l'étude; **in ~ of** en considération de, eu égard à; **after due ~** après mûre réflexion; **please give my suggestion your careful ~** je vous prie d'apporter toute votre attention à ma suggestion [c] (= *factor to be taken into account*) préoccupation *f*, considération *f*; (= *motive*) motif *m*; **money is the first ~** il faut considérer d'abord *or* en premier lieu la question d'argent; **many ~s have made me decide that ...** plusieurs considérations m'ont amené à décider que ...; **it's of no ~** cela n'a aucune importance; **money is no ~** l'argent n'entre pas en ligne de compte; **his age was an important ~** son âge constituait un facteur important [d] (= *reward, payment*) rétribution *f*, rémunération *f*; **to do sth for a ~** faire qch moyennant finance *or* contre espèces; (*Jur, Fin*) **for a good and valuable ~** ≈ moyennant contrepartie valable

considering [kənˈsɪdərɪŋ] [1] PREP vu, étant donné; **~ the circumstances** vu *or* étant donné les circonstances [2] CONJ vu que, étant donné que; **~ she has no money** vu *or* étant donné qu'elle n'a pas d'argent [3] ADV tout compte fait, en fin de compte; **he played very well, ~** il a très bien joué, tout compte fait *or* en fin de compte

consign [kənˈsaɪn] VT [a] (= *hand over*) [+ *person, thing*] confier, remettre; **to ~ a child to sb's care** confier un enfant aux soins de qn [b] (= *send*) [+ *goods*] expédier (**to sb** à qn, à l'adresse de qn)

consignee [ˌkɒnsaɪˈniː] N consignataire *mf*

consigner [kənˈsaɪnəʳ] N = **consignor**

consignment [kənˈsaɪnmənt] [1] N [a] (*NonC*) envoi *m*, expédition *f*; **goods for ~ abroad** marchandises *fpl* à destination de l'étranger [b] (= *quantity of goods*) (*incoming*) arrivage *m*; (*outgoing*) envoi *m* [2] COMP ► **consignment note** N (*Brit Comm*) bordereau *m* d'expédition

consignor [kənˈsaɪnəʳ] N expéditeur *m*, -trice *f* (*de marchandises*), consignateur *m*, -trice *f*

consist [kənˈsɪst] VI [a] (= *be composed*) se composer (**of** de), consister (**of** en); **what does the house ~ of?** en quoi consiste la maison?, de quoi la maison est-elle composée? [b] (= *have as its essence*) consister (**in doing** à faire, **in sth** dans qch); **his happiness ~s in helping others** son bonheur consiste à aider autrui

consistency [kənˈsɪstənsɪ] N [a] (= *texture*) consistance *f* [b] (*fig*) [*of actions, argument, behaviour*] cohérence *f*, uniformité *f*; (*fig*) **to lack ~** manquer de logique

consistent [kənˈsɪstənt] ADJ [*person, behaviour*] cohérent, conséquent; **his arguments are not ~ ses arguments ne se tiennent pas *or* ne sont pas cohérents; **to be ~ with** (= *in agreement with*) être compatible *or* en accord avec; (= *compatible with*) [*injury etc*] correspondre à

consistently [kənˈsɪstəntlɪ] ADV [a] (= *unfailingly*) [*good, bad*] invariablement; **to be ~ successful** réussir invariablement; **you have ~ failed to meet the deadlines** vous avez constamment dépassé les délais [b] (= *logically*) avec logique [c] (= *in agreement*) conformément (**with sth** à qch)

consolation [ˌkɒnsəˈleɪʃən] [1] N consolation *f*, réconfort *m* [2] COMP [*prize*] de consolation

consolatory [kənˈsɒlətərɪ] ADJ consolant, réconfortant

console¹ [kənˈsəʊl] VT consoler (**sb for sth** qn de qch)

console² [ˈkɒnsəʊ] N [a] [*of organ, language lab*] console *f*; (*Comput*) console *f*, pupitre *m*; [*of aircraft*] tableau *m* de bord, commandes *fpl* [b] (= *radio cabinet*) meuble *m* de hi-fi [c] (*Archit*) console *f*

consolidate [kənˈsɒlɪdeɪt] [1] VT [a] (= *make strong*) [+ *one's position*] consolider, raffermir [b] (*Comm, Fin* = *unite*) [+ *businesses*] réunir; [+ *loan, funds, annuities*] consolider [2] VI se consolider, s'affermir [3] COMP ► **consolidated balance sheet** N bilan *m* consolidé ► **consolidated deliveries** NPL livraisons *fpl* groupées ► **consolidated fund** N ≈ fonds *mpl* consolidés ► **consolidated laws** NPL (*Jur*) codification *f* (*des lois*) ► **consolidated school district** N (*US Scol*) secteur *m* scolaire élargi

consolidation [kənˌsɒlɪˈdeɪʃən] [1] N (*NonC*) [a] (= *strengthening*) [*of power, democracy, nation, one's position*] consolidation *f* [b] (*Comm* = *amalgamation*) [*of companies, divisions*] fusion *f* [c] (*Fin*) [*of balance sheet*] consolidation *f* [2] COMP ► **Consolidation Act** N (*Jur*) codification *f*

consoling [kənˈsəʊlɪŋ] ADJ consolant

consols [ˈkɒnsɒlz] NPL (*Brit Fin*) consolidés *mpl*

consonance [ˈkɒnsənəns] N [*of sounds*] consonance *f*, accord *m*; [*of ideas*] accord *m*, communion *f*

consonant [ˈkɒnsənənt] [1] N (*Ling*) consonne *f* [2] ADJ (*frm*) en accord (**with** avec); **behaviour ~ with one's beliefs** comportement *m* qui s'accorde avec ses croyances [3] COMP (*Ling*) ► **consonant cluster** N groupe *m* consonantique ► **consonant shift** N mutation *f* consonantique

consonantal [ˌkɒnsəˈnæntl] ADJ consonantique

consort [ˈkɒnsɔːt] [1] N [a] (†† = *spouse*) époux *m*, épouse *f* [b] (*also* **prince ~**) (prince *m*) consort *m* [c] [*of musicians, instruments*] ensemble *m* [d] (*Naut*) conserve *f*; **in ~** de conserve [2] [kənˈsɔːt] VI (*frm*) [a] (= *associate*) **to ~ with sb** fréquenter qn, frayer avec qn [b] (= *be consistent*) [*behaviour*] s'accorder (**with** avec)

consortium [kənˈsɔːtɪəm] N (*pl* **consortia** [kənˈsɔːtɪə]) consortium *m*

conspectus [kənˈspektəs] N vue *f* générale

conspicuous [kənˈspɪkjʊəs] [1] ADJ [a] (= *attracting attention*) [*person, behaviour, clothes*]

peu discret (-ète *f*), que l'on remarque; **to be ~ se remarquer; **to be ~ for sth** se faire remarquer par qch; **to feel ~** sentir que l'on attire les regards; **to look ~** ◊ **to make o.s. ~** se faire remarquer; **to be ~ by one's absence** briller par son absence [b] (= *noticeable*) [*success, failure*] manifeste, flagrant; [*absence, lack*] manifeste, notable; [*change*] visible, évident; [*gallantry, bravery*] remarquable [2] COMP ► **conspicuous consumption** N (*Sociol*) consommation *f* ostentatoire

conspicuously [kənˈspɪkjʊəslɪ] ADV [a] (= *so as to attract attention*) [*behave*] avec ostentation [b] (= *noticeably*) [*silent*] ostensiblement; [*uneasy*] visiblement, manifestement; **to be ~ successful** réussir visiblement *or* manifestement; **to be ~ lacking in sth** manquer visiblement *or* manifestement de qch; **to be ~ absent** briller par son absence; **the government has ~ failed to intervene** la non-intervention du gouvernement a été remarquée

conspiracy [kənˈspɪrəsɪ] [1] N [a] (= *plot*) conspiration *f*, complot *m*; **a ~ of silence** une conspiration du silence [b] (*NonC: Jur: also* **criminal ~**) ≈ association *f* de malfaiteurs; **~ to defraud** *etc* complot *m* d'escroquerie *etc* [2] COMP ► **conspiracy theory** N thèse *f* du complot

conspirator [kənˈspɪrətəʳ] N conspirateur *m*, -trice *f*, conjuré(e) *m(f)*

conspiratorial [kənˌspɪrəˈtɔːrɪəl] ADJ [*whisper, smile, wink, nod, activity*] de conspirateur; [*group, meeting*] de conspirateurs; **in a ~ manner** *or* **way** avec un air de conspirateur; **to be ~ about sth** avoir l'air de conspirer *or* comploter; **they were ~ about getting her birthday present** complotaient pour lui faire un cadeau d'anniversaire

conspiratorially [kənˌspɪrəˈtɔːrɪəlɪ] ADV [*behave, smile*] d'un air conspirateur; [*say, whisper*] sur le ton de la conspiration, avec un air de conspirateur

conspire [kənˈspaɪəʳ] [1] VI [a] [*people*] conspirer (**against** contre); **to ~ to do sth** comploter de *or* se mettre d'accord pour faire qch [b] [*events*] conspirer, concourir (**to do** à faire) [2] VT† comploter, méditer

constable [ˈkʌnstəbl] N (*Brit: also* **police ~**) (*in town*) agent *m* de police, gardien *m* de la paix; (*in country*) gendarme *m*; **"yes, Constable"** «oui, monsieur l'agent» → **chief**, **special**

constabulary [kənˈstæbjʊlərɪ] COLLECTIVE N (*Brit*) (*in town*) (la) police en uniforme; (*in country*) (la) gendarmerie → **royal**

Constance [ˈkɒnstəns] N **Lake ~** le lac de Constance

constancy [ˈkɒnstənsɪ] N (= *firmness*) constance *f*, fermeté *f*; [*of feelings, love*] constance *f*; [*of temperature etc*] invariabilité *f*, constance *f*

constant [ˈkɒnstənt] [1] ADJ [a] (= *occurring often*) [*quarrels, interruptions*] incessant, continuel, perpétuel [b] (= *unchanging*) [*love*] constant; [*friend*] fidèle, loyal [2] N (*Math, Phys*) constante *f*

Constantine [ˈkɒnstəntaɪn] N Constantin *m*

Constantinople [ˌkɒnstæntɪˈnəʊpl] N Constantinople

constantly [ˈkɒnstəntlɪ] ADV constamment, continuellement; **~ evolving** en évolution constante

constellation [ˌkɒnstəˈleɪʃən] N constellation *f*

consternation [ˌkɒnstəˈneɪʃən] N consternation *f*; **filled with ~** frappé de consternation, consterné; **there was general ~** la consternation était générale

constipate [ˈkɒnstɪpeɪt] VT constiper

constipated [ˈkɒnstɪpeɪtɪd] ADJ (*lit, fig*) constipé

constipation [ˌkɒnstɪˈpeɪʃən] N constipation *f*

► **LANGUAGE IN USE:** **consideration** 19.5

constituency [kən'stɪtjʊənsɪ] ① N (Pol) (= place) circonscription f électorale; (= people) électeurs mpl (d'une circonscription) ② COMP ► **constituency party** N section f locale (du parti)

constituent [kən'stɪtjʊənt] ① ADJ [part, element] constituant, constitutif; (Pol) ~ **assembly** assemblée f constituante; ~ **power** pouvoir m constituant ② N ⓐ (Pol) électeur m, -trice f (de la circonscription d'un député); **one of my ~s wrote to me** ... quelqu'un dans ma circonscription m'a écrit ...; **he was talking to one of his ~s** il parlait à un habitant or un électeur de sa circonscription ⓑ (= part, element) élément m constitutif; (Ling) constituant m; (Ling) ~ **analysis** analyse f en constituants immédiats

constitute ['kɒnstɪtjuːt] VT ⓐ (= appoint) [+ government, assembly] constituer; [+ people] désigner; **to be ~d** être constitué; **to ~ sb leader of the group** désigner qn (comme) chef du groupe ⓑ (= establish) [+ organization] monter, établir; [+ committee] constituer ⓒ (= amount to, make up) faire, constituer; **these parts ~ a whole** toutes ces parties font or constituent un tout; **that ~s a lie** cela constitue un mensonge; **it ~s a threat to our sales** ceci représente une menace pour nos ventes; **so ~d that** ... fait de telle façon que ..., ainsi fait que ...

constitution [ˌkɒnstɪ'tjuːʃən] N ⓐ (Pol) constitution f; **under the French ~** selon or d'après la constitution française; **the Constitution State** le Connecticut ⓑ [of person] constitution f; **to have a strong/weak** or **poor ~** avoir une robuste/chétive constitution; **iron ~** santé f de fer ⓒ (= structure) composition f, constitution f (of de)

┌─────────────────┐
│ **CONSTITUTION** │
└─────────────────┘

Contrairement à la France ou aux États-Unis, la Grande-Bretagne n'a pas de constitution écrite à proprement parler. Le droit constitutionnel britannique se compose donc d'un ensemble de textes épars qui peut être amendé ou complété par le Parlement.

constitutional [ˌkɒnstɪ'tjuːʃənl] ① ADJ ⓐ (Pol, Univ) [reform, amendment] de la constitution; [change, crisis, law] constitutionnel; [monarch] soumis à une constitution; ~ **lawyer** spécialiste mf du droit constitutionnel; **we have a ~ right to demonstrate** de par la constitution, nous avons le droit de manifester; **the ~ head of state is the Queen** le chef de l'État est, de par la constitution, la reine ⓑ [weakness, tendency] constitutionnel ⓒ (frm = inherent) [optimism, envy] inhérent ② N (hum) **to go for a ~*** faire sa petite promenade or son petit tour ③ COMP ► **constitutional monarch** N souverain(e) m(f) d'une monarchie constitutionnelle ► **constitutional monarchy** N monarchie f constitutionnelle

constitutionality [ˌkɒnstɪtjuːʃə'nælɪtɪ] N constitutionnalité f

constitutionally [ˌkɒnstɪ'tjuːʃənəlɪ] ADV ⓐ (Pol, Univ = legally) [act] conformément à la constitution; [protected, guaranteed] par la constitution ⓑ (= physically) ~ **frail** de faible constitution ⓒ (= inherently) [incapable, reserved] par nature, de nature

constitutive ['kɒnstɪtjuːtɪv] ADJ constitutif

constrain [kən'streɪn] VT ⓐ (= compel) contraindre (**sb to do** qn à faire); **I find myself ~ed to write to you** je me vois dans la nécessité de vous écrire; **to be/feel ~ed to do** être/se sentir contraint or obligé de faire ⓑ (= limit) limiter ⓒ (= restrict) [work, person] contraindre; **women often feel ~ed by family commitments** les femmes trouvent souvent contraignantes les responsabilités familiales

constrained [kən'streɪnd] ADJ ⓐ (= awkward) [smile, expression] contraint; [voice, silence] gêné; [atmosphere] de gêne ⓑ (= limited) [resources, budget] limité

constraint [kən'streɪnt] N contrainte f; **to act under ~** agir sous la contrainte; **to speak freely and without ~** parler librement et sans contrainte; **the ~s placed upon us** les contraintes auxquelles nous sommes soumis

constrict [kən'strɪkt] VT (gen) resserrer; (= tighten) [+ muscle etc] serrer; (= hamper) [+ movements] gêner; (fig) [convention etc] limiter

constricted [kən'strɪktɪd] ADJ ⓐ (= narrow, limited) [artery] rétréci; [throat] serré; [breathing] gêné; [space] réduit, restreint; [freedom] restreint; [movement] limité; **to feel ~ (by sth)** (lit) se sentir à l'étroit (dans qch); (fig: by convention etc) se sentir limité (par qch) ⓑ (Phon) constrictif

constricting [kən'strɪktɪŋ] ADJ [garment] gênant, étriqué; [ideology] étroit; (fig) restreignant

constriction [kən'strɪkʃən] N (esp Med) constriction f, resserrement m, étranglement m

constrictive [kən'strɪktɪv] ADJ = **constricting**

construct [kən'strʌkt] ① VT [+ building, model] construire; [+ novel, play] construire, composer; [+ theory] bâtir, élaborer; (Ling, Psych) construire; [+ model] élaborer ② ['kɒnstrʌkt] N (Philos, Psych) construction f mentale; (= machine etc) construction f

construction [kən'strʌkʃən] ① N ⓐ [of roads, buildings] construction f, édification f; **in course of ~** ◊ **under ~** en construction ⓑ (= building, structure) construction f, bâtiment m ⓒ (= interpretation) interprétation f; **to put a wrong ~ on sb's words** mal interpréter or interpréter à contresens les paroles de qn ⓓ (Gram) construction f ② COMP ► **construction engineer** N ingénieur m des travaux publics et des bâtiments ► **construction site** N chantier m ► **construction worker** N ouvrier m du bâtiment

constructional [kən'strʌkʃənl] ADJ de construction; ~ **engineering** construction f mécanique

constructive [kən'strʌktɪv] ① ADJ constructif ② COMP ► **constructive dismissal** N démission f forcée

constructively [kən'strʌktɪvlɪ] ADV d'une manière constructive

constructivism [kən'strʌktɪvɪzəm] N constructivisme m

constructivist [kən'strʌktɪvɪst] ① ADJ constructiviste ② N constructiviste mf

constructor [kən'strʌktəʳ] N constructeur m, -trice f; (Naut) ingénieur m des constructions navales

construe [kən'struː] ① VT ⓐ (gen = interpret meaning of) interpréter; **you can ~ that in different ways** vous pouvez interpréter cela de différentes manières; **her silence was ~d as consent** son silence a été interprété comme or pris pour un assentiment; **this was ~d as a step forward in the negotiations** cela a été interprété comme un pas en avant dans les négociations; **his words were wrongly ~d** ses paroles ont été mal comprises, on a interprété ses paroles à contresens ⓑ (Gram = parse etc) [+ sentence] analyser, décomposer; [+ Latin etc text] analyser ⓒ (= explain) [+ poem, passage] expliquer ② VI (Gram) s'analyser grammaticalement; **the sentence will not ~** la phrase n'a pas de construction

consul ['kɒnsəl] ① N consul m ② COMP ► **consul general** N (pl **consuls general**) consul m général

consular ['kɒnsjʊləʳ] ADJ consulaire; ~ **section** service m consulaire

consulate ['kɒnsjʊlɪt] ① N consulat m ② COMP ► **consulate general** N consulat m général

consulship ['kɒnsəlʃɪp] N poste m or charge f de consul

consult [kən'sʌlt] ① VT ⓐ [+ book, person, doctor] consulter (**about** sur, au sujet de) ⓑ (= show consideration for) [+ person's feelings] avoir égard à, prendre en considération; [+ one's own interests] consulter ② VI consulter, être en consultation (**with** avec); **to ~ together** se consulter sur or au sujet de qch ③ COMP ► **consulting engineer** N ingénieur-conseil m ► **consulting hours** NPL (Brit Med) heures fpl de consultation ► **consulting room** N (Brit esp Med) cabinet m de consultation

consultancy [kən'sʌltənsɪ] N (= company, group) cabinet-conseil m; ~ **(service)** service m d'expertise or de consultants

consultant [kən'sʌltənt] ① N (gen) consultant m, expert-conseil m; (Brit Med) médecin m consultant, spécialiste m; **he acts as ~ to the firm** il est expert-conseil auprès de la compagnie → **management** ② COMP ► **consultant engineer** N ingénieur-conseil m, ingénieur m consultant ► **consultant physician** N médecin-chef m, chef m de service ► **consultant psychiatrist** N (médecin-)chef m de service psychiatrique

consultation [ˌkɒnsəl'teɪʃən] N ⓐ (NonC) consultation f; **in ~ with** en consultation avec ⓑ (= meeting) consultation f; **to hold a ~** conférer (**about** de), délibérer (**about** sur)

consultative [kən'sʌltətɪv] ADJ consultatif; **in a ~ capacity** dans un rôle consultatif

consumable [kən'sjuːməbl] ADJ (Econ etc) de consommation; ~ **goods** biens mpl or produits mpl de consommation

consumables [kən'sjuːməblz] NPL (Econ etc) produits mpl de consommation; (Comput) consommables mpl

consume [kən'sjuːm] VT [+ food, drink] consommer; [+ supplies, resources] consommer, dissiper; [engine fuel] brûler, consommer; [fire] [+ buildings] consumer, dévorer; (fig) **to be ~d with grief** se consumer de chagrin; **to be ~d with desire** brûler de désir; **to be ~d with jealousy** être rongé par la jalousie

consumer [kən'sjuːməʳ] ① N (gen) consommateur m, -trice f; (= user) abonné(e) m(f); **gas etc ~** abonné(e) m(f) au gaz etc ② COMP ► **consumer behaviour** N comportement m du consommateur ► **consumer credit** N crédit m à la consommation ► **consumer demand** N demande f de consommation or des consommateurs ► **consumer durables** NPL biens mpl durables ► **consumer electronics** N (NonC) électronique f grand public ► **consumer goods** NPL biens mpl de consommation ► **consumer group** N association f de consommateurs ► **consumer price index** N (US) indice m des prix à la consommation, indice m des prix de détail ► **consumer protection** N défense f du consommateur; (Brit) **Secretary of State for** or **Minister of Consumer Protection** ministre m chargé de la Défense des consommateurs, ≈ secrétaire m d'État à la Consommation; **Department** or **Ministry of Consumer Protection** ministère m chargé de la Défense des consommateurs, ≈ secrétariat m d'État à la Consommation ► **consumer research** N études fpl de marchés ► **consumer resistance** N résistance f du consommateur ► **consumer sampling** N enquête f auprès des consommateurs ► **the Consumers' Association** N (in Brit) association britannique des consommateurs ► **consumer society** N société f de consommation ► **consumer spending** N (NonC) dépenses fpl de consommation ► **consumer watchdog** N organisme *m* de protection des consommateurs

consumerism [kən'sjuːməˌrɪzəm] N [a] (= *consumer protection*) défense *f* du consommateur, consumérisme *m* [b] (*Econ* = *policy*) consumérisme *m*

consumerist [kən'sjuːməˌrɪst] N consumériste *mf*, défenseur *m* des consommateurs

consuming [kən'sjuːmɪŋ] ADJ [*desire, passion*] dévorant, brûlant

consummate [kən'sʌmɪt] [1] ADJ consommé, achevé [2] ['kɒnsəmeɪt] VT consommer

consummately [kən'sʌmɪtlɪ] ADV [*acted, executed*] à la perfection; [*professional, skilful*] éminemment

consummation [ˌkɒnsʌ'meɪʃən] N [*of union, esp marriage*] consommation *f*; [*of art form*] perfection *f*; [*of one's desires, ambitions*] couronnement *m*, apogée *m*

consumption [kən'sʌmpʃən] N (*NonC*) [a] [*of food, fuel*] consommation *f*; **not fit for human ~** (*lit*) non comestible; (* *pej*) pas mangeable, immangeable [b] (*Med* † = *tuberculosis*) consomption *f* (pulmonaire)†, phtisie† *f*

consumptive† [kən'sʌmptɪv] ADJ, N phtisique† *mf*, tuberculeux *m*, -euse *f*

cont. ABBR = **continued**

contact ['kɒntækt] [1] N [a] (*communicating*) contact *m*; **to be in/come into/get into ~ with sb** être/entrer/se mettre en contact *or* rapport avec qn; **to make ~ (with sb)** prendre contact (avec qn); **we've lost ~ (with him)** nous avons perdu contact (avec lui); **we have had no ~ with him for six months** nous sommes sans contact avec lui depuis six mois; **I seem to make no ~ with him** je n'arrive pas à communiquer avec lui; (*Volleyball*) **~ with the net** faute *f* de filet [b] (= *touching*) (*Elec*) contact *m*; **point of ~** point *m* de contact *or* de tangence; **to make/break the ~** établir/couper le contact; (*Aviat*) **~!** contact! [c] (= *person in secret service etc*) agent *m* de liaison; (= *acquaintance*) connaissance *f*, relation *f*; **he has some ~s in Paris** il a des relations à Paris, il connaît des gens *or* il est en relation avec des gens à Paris; **a business ~** une relation de travail [d] (*Med*) contaminateur *m* possible, contact *m* [e] = **contact lens** [2] VT [+ *person*] se mettre en contact *or* en rapport avec, contacter; **we'll ~ you soon** nous nous mettrons en rapport avec vous sous peu [3] COMP [*adhesive etc*] de contact ► **contact breaker** N (*Elec*) interrupteur *m*, rupteur *m* ► **contact cement** N ciment *m* de contact ► **contact lens** N verre *m* de contact, lentille *f* (cornéenne) ► **contact man** N (*pl* **contact men**) (*Comm*) agent *m* de liaison ► **contact print** N (*Phot*) (épreuve *f* par) contact *m* ► **contact sport** N sport *m* de contact

contagion [kən'teɪdʒən] N contagion *f*

contagious [kən'teɪdʒəs] ADJ [*disease, person, sense of humour, enthusiasm, laugh*] contagieux

contain [kən'teɪn] VT [a] (= *hold*) [*box, bottle, envelope etc*] contenir; [*book, letter, newspaper*] contenir, renfermer; **sea water ~s a lot of salt** l'eau de mer contient beaucoup de sel *or* a une forte teneur en sel; **the room will ~ 70 people** la salle peut contenir 70 personnes → **self** [b] (= *hold back, control*) [+ *one's emotions, anger*] contenir, maîtriser; **he couldn't ~ himself for joy** il ne se sentait pas de joie; (*Mil*) **to ~ the enemy forces** contenir les troupes ennemies [c] (*Math*) être divisible par

contained [kən'teɪnd] ADJ (*emotionally*) réservé

container [kən'teɪnər] [1] N [a] (= *goods transport*) conteneur *m* [b] (= *jug, box etc*) récipient *m*; (*for plants*) godet *m*; (*for food*) barquette *f* [2] COMP [*of train, ship*] porteconteneurs *inv* ► **container dock** N dock *m* pour la manutention de conteneurs ► **container line** N (*Naut*) ligne *f* transconteneurs ► **container port** N port *m* à conteneurs ► **container terminal** N terminal *m* (à conteneurs) ► **container transport** N transport *m* par conteneurs

containerization [kənˌteɪnəraɪ'zeɪʃən] N conteneurisation *f*

containerize [kən'teɪnəraɪz] VT mettre en conteneurs, conteneuriser

containment [kən'teɪnmənt] N (*Pol*) endiguement *m*

contaminant [kən'tæmɪnənt] N polluant *m*

contaminate [kən'tæmɪneɪt] VT (*lit, fig*) contaminer, souiller; [*radioactivity*] contaminer; **~d air** air *m* vicié *or* contaminé

contamination [kənˌtæmɪ'neɪʃən] N (*NonC*) contamination *f*

contango [kən'tæŋɡəʊ] N (*Brit*) report *m*

contd. ABBR = **continued**

contemplate ['kɒntempleɪt] VT [a] (= *plan, consider*) [+ *action, purchase*] envisager; **to ~ doing** envisager de *or* se proposer de faire; **I don't ~ a refusal from him** je ne m'attends pas à *or* je n'envisage pas un refus de sa part [b] (= *look at*) contempler, considérer avec attention

contemplation [ˌkɒntem'pleɪʃən] N (*NonC*) [a] (= *deep thought*) contemplation *f*, méditation *f*; **deep in ~** plongé dans de profondes méditations [b] (= *act of looking*) contemplation *f* [c] (= *expectation*) prévision *f*; **in ~ of their arrival** en prévision de leur arrivée

contemplative [kən'templətɪv] [1] ADJ [a] (= *thoughtful*) [*person*] songeur, pensif; [*mood*] contemplatif; [*walk*] méditatif [b] (*Rel*) [*life, order, prayer*] contemplatif [2] N (*Rel*) contemplatif *m*, -ive *f*

contemplatively [kən'templətɪvlɪ] ADV [*look, stare, say*] d'un air pensif

contemporaneous [kənˌtempə'reɪnɪəs] ADJ contemporain (**with** de)

contemporaneously [kənˌtempə'reɪnɪəslɪ] ADV à la même époque (**with** que)

contemporary [kən'tempərərɪ] [1] ADJ (= *of the same period*) contemporain (**with** de), de la même époque (**with** que); (= *modern*) contemporain, moderne; **Dickens and ~ writers** Dickens et les écrivains contemporains *or* de son époque; **he's bought an 18th century house and is looking for ~ furniture** il a acheté une maison du 18ᵉ siècle et il cherche des meubles d'époque; **a ~ narrative** un récit de l'époque; **I like ~ art** j'aime l'art contemporain *or* moderne; **it's all very ~** c'est tout ce qu'il y a de plus moderne [2] N contemporain(e) *m(f)*

contempt [kən'tempt] N mépris *m*; **to hold in ~** mépriser, avoir du mépris pour; **in ~ of danger** au mépris *or* en dépit du danger; **it's beneath ~** c'est tout ce qu'il y a de plus méprisable, c'est au-dessous de tout; (*Jur*) **~ of court** outrage *m* à la Cour

contemptible [kən'temptəbl] ADJ méprisable, indigne

contemptuous [kən'temptjʊəs] ADJ [*person, manner*] dédaigneux, méprisant; [*dismissal, disregard, look, laugh, remark*] méprisant; [*gesture*] de mépris; **to be ~ of sb/sth** avoir du mépris pour qn/qch

contemptuously [kən'temptjʊəslɪ] ADV avec mépris, dédaigneusement

contend [kən'tend] VI [a] (= *assert*) prétendre (**that** que) [b] **to ~ with** combattre, lutter contre; **to ~ with sb for sth** disputer qch à qn; **to ~ with sb over sth** se disputer *or* se

battre avec qn au sujet de qch; **they had to ~ with very bad weather conditions** ils ont dû faire face à des conditions météorologiques déplorables; **we have many problems to ~ with** nous sommes aux prises avec de nombreux problèmes; **he has a lot to ~ with** il a pas mal de problèmes à résoudre; **I should not like to have to ~ with him** je ne voudrais pas avoir affaire à lui; **you'll have me to ~ with** vous aurez affaire à moi [c] **to ~ for** [+ *title, medal, prize*] se battre pour; [+ *support, supremacy*] lutter pour

contender [kən'tendər] N prétendant(e) *m(f)* (**for** à); (*in contest, competition, race*) concurrent(e) *m(f)*; (*in election, for a job*) candidat *m*; **presidential ~** candidat *m* à l'élection présidentielle

contending [kən'tendɪŋ] ADJ opposé, ennemi

content¹ [kən'tent] [1] ADJ content, satisfait; **to be ~ with sth** se contenter *or* s'accommoder de qch; **she is quite ~ to stay there** elle ne demande pas mieux que de rester là [2] N contentement *m*, satisfaction *f* → **heart** [3] VT [+ *person*] contenter, satisfaire; **to ~ o.s. with doing** se contenter de *or* se borner à faire

content² ['kɒntent] [1] N [a] **~s** (= *thing contained*) contenu *m*; (= *amount contained*) contenu *m*, contenance *f*; [*of house etc*] (*gen*) contenu *m*; (*Insurance*) biens *mpl* mobiliers; **(table of) ~s** [*of book*] table *f* des matières [b] (*NonC*) [*of book, play, film*] contenu *m* (*also Ling*); [*of official document*] teneur *f*; [*of metal*] teneur *f*, titre *m*; **what do you think of the ~ of the article?** que pensez-vous du contenu *or* du fond de l'article?; **oranges have a high vitamin C ~** les oranges sont riches en vitamine C *or* ont une haute teneur en vitamine C; **gold ~** teneur *f* en or; **the play lacks ~** la pièce est mince *or* manque de profondeur [2] COMP ► **contents insurance** N (*NonC*) assurance *f* sur le contenu de l'habitation

contented [kən'tentɪd] ADJ content, satisfait (**with** de)

contentedly [kən'tentɪdlɪ] ADV avec contentement; **to smile ~** avoir un sourire de contentement

contentedness [kən'tentɪdnɪs] N contentement *m*, satisfaction *f*

contention [kən'tenʃən] N [a] (= *dispute*) dispute *f* → **bone** [b] (= *argument, point argued*) assertion *f*, affirmation *f*; **it is my ~ that ...** je soutiens que ...

contentious [kən'tenʃəs] ADJ [a] (= *controversial*) [*issue, question*] controversé, litigieux; [*view, proposal*] controversé [b] (= *argumentative*) [*person*] querelleur

contentment [kən'tentmənt] N contentement *m*, satisfaction *f*

conterminous [ˌkɒn'tɜːmɪnəs] ADJ (*frm* = *contiguous*) [*county, country*] limitrophe (**with, to** de); [*estate, house, garden*] adjacent, attenant (**with, to** à)

contest [kən'test] [1] VT [a] (= *argue, debate*) [+ *question, matter, result*] contester, discuter; (*Jur*) [+ *judgement*] contester; **to ~ sb's right to do** contester à qn le droit de faire; (*Jur*) **to ~ a will** attaquer *or* contester un testament [b] (= *compete for*) disputer; (*Parl*) **to ~ a seat** disputer un siège; (*Pol*) **to ~ an election** disputer une élection, contester [3] ['kɒntest] N (= *struggle*) (*lit, fig*) combat *m*, lutte *f* (**with** avec, contre, **between** entre); (*Sport*) lutte *f*; (*Boxing, Wrestling*) combat *m*, rencontre *f*; (= *competition*) concours *m*; **~ of beauty** concours *m* de beauté; **~ of skill** lutte *f* d'adresse; **the mayoral ~** (la lutte pour) l'élection du maire

contestant [kən'testənt] N [a] (*for prize, reward*) concurrent(e) *m(f)* [b] (*in fight*) adversaire *mf*

contestation [ˌkɒntes'teɪʃən] N contestation *f*

context ['kɒntekst] [1] N contexte *m* ; **in/out of ~** dans le/hors contexte ; **to put sth in(to) ~** mettre qch en contexte ; **to see sth in ~** regarder qch dans son contexte ; (*Ling*) **~ of situation** situation *f* de discours [2] COMP ► **context-sensitive** ADJ (*Comput*) contextuel

contextual [kɒn'tekstjʊəl] ADJ contextuel, d'après le contexte

contextualize [kɒn'tekstjʊəlaɪz] VT remettre *or* replacer dans son contexte

contiguity [ˌkɒntɪ'gjuːɪtɪ] N contiguïté *f*

contiguous [kən'tɪgjʊəs] ADJ contigu (-guë *f*) ; **~ to** contigu à *or* avec, attenant à ; **the two fields are ~** les deux champs se touchent *or* sont contigus

continence ['kɒntɪnəns] N continence *f*

continent¹ ['kɒntɪnənt] ADJ (= *chaste*) chaste ; (= *self-controlled*) continent† ; (*Med*) qui n'est pas incontinent

continent² ['kɒntɪnənt] N (*Geog*) continent *m* ; (*Brit*) **the Continent** l'Europe *f* continentale ; **the Continent of Europe** le continent européen ; (*Brit*) **on the Continent** en Europe (*continentale*)

continental [ˌkɒntɪ'nentl] [1] ADJ continental ; **~ climate** climat *m* continental [2] N (*Brit*) Européen(ne) *m(f)* (continental(e)) [3] COMP ► **continental breakfast** N petit déjeuner *m* continental ► **continental crust** N croûte *f* continentale ► **continental drift** N dérive *f* des continents ► **continental quilt** N (*Brit*) couette *f* ► **continental shelf** N plate-forme *f* continentale, plateau *m* continental ► **continental shields** NPL aires *fpl* continentales

contingency [kən'tɪndʒənsɪ] [1] N [a] éventualité *f*, événement *m* imprévu *or* inattendu ; **in a ~** ◊ **should a ~ arise** en cas d'imprévu ; **to provide for all contingencies** parer à toute éventualité [b] (*Stat*) contingence *f* [2] COMP ► **contingency fee** N (*US Jur*) honoraires *versés par un client à son avocat seulement s'il gagne son procès* ► **contingency fund** N caisse *f* de prévoyance ► **contingency planning** N mise *f* sur pied de plans d'urgence ► **contingency plans** NPL plans *mpl* d'urgence ► **contingency reserve** N (*Fin*) fonds *mpl* de prévoyance ► **contingency sample** N (*Space*) échantillon *m* lunaire (*prélevé dès l'alunissage*)

contingent [kən'tɪndʒənt] [1] ADJ contingent ; **to be ~ upon sth** dépendre de qch, être subordonné à qch [2] N (*gen, also Mil*) contingent *m*

continua [kən'tɪnjʊə] NPL of **continuum**

continual [kən'tɪnjʊəl] ADJ continuel

continually [kən'tɪnjʊəlɪ] ADV continuellement, sans cesse

continuance [kən'tɪnjʊəns] N (= *duration*) durée *f* ; (= *continuation*) continuation *f* ; [*of human race etc*] perpétuation *f*, continuité *f*

continuant [kən'tɪnjʊənt] N (*Phon*) continue *f*

continuation [kən,tɪnjʊ'eɪʃən] N [a] (*no interruption*) continuation *f* [b] (*after interruption*) reprise *f* ; **the ~ of work after the holidays** la reprise du travail après les vacances [c] [*of serial story*] suite *f*

continue [kən'tɪnjuː] [1] VT continuer (**to do** à *or* de faire) ; [+ *piece of work*] continuer, poursuivre ; [+ *tradition*] perpétuer, maintenir ; [+ *policy*] maintenir ; (*after interruption*) reprendre ; [+ *conversation, work*] reprendre ; **to be ~d** [*serial story etc*] à suivre ; **~d on page 10** suite page 10 ; **to ~ (on) one's way** continuer *or* poursuivre son chemin ; (*after pause*) se remettre en marche ; **"and so", he ~d** « et ainsi », reprit-il *or* poursuivit-il
[2] VI [a] (= *go on*) [*road, weather, celebrations*] continuer ; (*after interruption*) reprendre ; **the forest ~s to the sea** la forêt s'étend jusqu'à la mer ; **his speech ~d until 3am** son discours s'est prolongé jusqu'à 3 heures du matin [b] (= *remain*) rester ; **to ~ in one's job** garder *or* conserver son poste ; **he ~d with his voluntary work** il a poursuivi son travail bénévole ; **she ~d as his secretary** elle est restée sa secrétaire

continuing [kən'tɪnjʊɪŋ] ADJ [*argument*] ininterrompu ; [*correspondence*] soutenu ; **~ education** formation *f* permanente *or* continue

continuity [ˌkɒntɪ'njuːɪtɪ] [1] N (*gen, Cine, Rad*) continuité *f* [2] COMP ► **continuity announcer** N (*TV, Rad*) speaker(ine) *m(f)* annonçant la suite des émissions ► **continuity girl** N (*Cine, TV*) script-girl *f*, script *f*

continuo [kən'tɪnjʊ,əʊ] N (*Mus*) basse *f* continue

continuous [kən'tɪnjʊəs] ADJ [a] continu ; (*Scol, Univ*) **~ assessment** contrôle *m* continu des connaissances ; (*Cine*) **~ performance** spectacle *m* permanent ; (*Comput*) **~ paper** *or* **stationery** papier *m* en continu [b] (*Gram*) [*aspect*] imperfectif ; [*tense*] progressif ; **in the present/past ~** à la forme progressive du présent/du passé

continuously [kən'tɪnjʊəslɪ] ADV [a] (= *uninterruptedly*) sans interruption [b] (= *repeatedly*) continuellement, sans arrêt

continuum [kən'tɪnjʊəm] N (*pl* **continuums** *or* **continua**) continuum *m*

contort [kən'tɔːt] VT [a] [+ *one's features, limbs*] tordre, contorsionner ; **a face ~ed by pain** un visage tordu *or* contorsionné par la douleur [b] (*fig*) [+ *sb's words, story*] déformer, fausser

contortion [kən'tɔːʃən] N [*of esp acrobat*] contorsion *f* ; [*of features*] torsion *f*, crispation *f*

contortionist [kən'tɔːʃənɪst] N contorsionniste *mf*

contour ['kɒntʊə] [1] N contour *m*, profil *m* [2] VT **to ~ a map** tracer les courbes de niveau sur une carte [3] COMP ► **contour flying** N vol *m* à très basse altitude ► **contour line** N courbe *f* de niveau ► **contour map** N carte *f* avec courbes de niveau

contoured ['kɒntʊəd] ADJ [*shape, lines*] sinueux ; **a comfortably ~ seat** un siège bien galbé

contra ['kɒntrə] N (*Pol*) contra *f*

contra... ['kɒntrə] PREF contre-, contra...

contraband ['kɒntrəbænd] [1] N contrebande *f* [2] COMP [*goods*] de contrebande

contrabass [ˌkɒntrə'beɪs] N contrebasse *f*

contrabassoon [ˌkɒntrəbə'suːn] N contrebasson *m*

contraception [ˌkɒntrə'sepʃən] N contraception *f*

contraceptive [ˌkɒntrə'septɪv] [1] N contraceptif *m* [2] ADJ [*device, measures*] contraceptif, anticonceptionnel

contract ['kɒntrækt] [1] N [a] (= *agreement*) contrat *m* ; (*US Comm* = *tender*) adjudication *f* ; **marriage ~** contrat *m* de mariage ; **to enter into a ~ with sb for sth** passer un contrat avec qn pour qch ; **to put work out to ~** mettre *or* donner du travail en adjudication *or* à l'entreprise ; **by ~** par *or* sur contrat ; **under ~ (to)** sous contrat (avec) ; (*Jur*) **~ for services** contrat *m* de louage d'ouvrage ; (*fig: by killer*) **there's a ~ out on** *or* **for him*** on a engagé un tueur pour le descendre* → **breach** [b] (*also ~* **bridge**) (bridge *m*) contrat *m*
[2] [kən'trækt] VT [a] [+ *debts, illness*] contracter ; [+ *habits, vices*] prendre, contracter [b] [+ *alliance*] contracter [c] (= *commit*) **to ~ to do** s'engager (par contrat) à faire ; **to ~ with sb to do** passer un contrat avec qn pour faire [d] [+ *metal, muscle etc*] contracter [e] (*Ling*) [+ *word, phrase*] contracter (**to** en) ; **~ed form** forme *f* contractée
[3] [kən'trækt] VI [a] [*metal, muscles*] se contracter [b] (*Comm*) s'engager (par contrat) ; **he has ~ed for the building of the motorway** il a un contrat pour la construction de l'autoroute
[4] COMP ► **contract bargaining** N (*Jur*) négociations *fpl* salariales ► **contracting parties** NPL contractants *mpl* ► **contracting party** N partie *f* contractante ► **contract killer** N tueur *m* à gages ► **contract killing** N meurtre *m* commis par un tueur à gages ► **contract law** N (*NonC*) droit *m* des contrats ► **contract price** N prix *m* forfaitaire ► **contract work** N travail *m* à forfait
► **contract in** VI s'engager (par contrat)
► **contract out** [1] VI (*Brit*) se dégager (**of** de), se soustraire (**of** à) ; **~ out of a pension scheme** cesser de cotiser à une caisse de retraite [2] VT SEP [+ *work etc*] sous-traiter (**to sb** à qn)

contractile [kən'træktaɪl] ADJ contractile

contraction [kən'trækʃən] N [a] (*NonC*) [*of metal etc*] contraction *f* [b] (*Med*) contraction *f* [c] (*Ling*) forme *f* contractée, contraction *f* ; **"can't" is a ~ of "cannot"** « can't » est une forme contractée *or* une contraction de « cannot » [d] (= *acquiring*) **~ of debts** endettement *m*

contractionary [kən'trækʃənərɪ] ADJ (*Econ*) **~ pressure** poussée *f* récessionniste ; **~ policy** politique *f* d'austérité

contractor [kən'træktə] N [a] (*Comm*) entrepreneur *m* ; **army ~** fournisseur *m* de l'armée → **building** [b] (*Jur*) partie *f* contractante

contractual [kən'træktʃʊəl] ADJ contractuel

contractually [kən'træktʃʊəlɪ] ADV par contrat ; **~, we have to ...** d'après le contrat, nous devons ...

▼ contradict [ˌkɒntrə'dɪkt] VT [a] (= *deny truth of*) [+ *person, statement*] contredire ; **don't ~!** ne (me) contredis pas ! [b] (= *be contrary to*) [+ *statement, event*] contredire, démentir ; **his actions ~ed his words** ses actions démentaient ses paroles

contradiction [ˌkɒntrə'dɪkʃən] N contradiction *f*, démenti *m* ; **to be in ~ with ...** être en contradiction avec ..., donner un démenti à ... ; **a ~ in terms** une contradiction dans les termes

contradictory [ˌkɒntrə'dɪktərɪ] ADJ contradictoire, opposé (**to** à)

contradistinction [ˌkɒntrədɪs'tɪŋkʃən] N contraste *m*, opposition *f* ; **in ~ to ...** en contraste avec ..., par opposition à ...

contraflow ['kɒntrə,fləʊ] ADJ (*Brit Aut*) **~ lane** voie *f* à contresens ; **there is a ~ system in operation on ...** une voie a été mise en sens inverse sur ... ; **~ (bus) lane** couloir *m* (d'autobus) à contre-courant

contraindicated [ˌkɒntrə'ɪndɪ,keɪtɪd] ADJ (*Med*) contre-indiqué

contraindication [ˌkɒntrə,ɪndɪ'keɪʃən] N (*Med*) contre-indication *f*

contralto [kən'træltəʊ] [1] N (*pl* **contraltos** *or* **contralti** [kən'træltɪ]) (= *voice, person*) contralto *m* [2] ADJ [*voice, part*] de contralto ; [*aria*] pour contralto

contraption* [kən'træpʃən] N bidule* *m*, truc* *m*

contrapuntal [ˌkɒntrə'pʌntl] ADJ en contrepoint, contrapuntique

contrarian [kən'treərɪən] ADJ, N anticonformiste *mf*

contrarily [kən'treərɪlɪ] ADV [a] (= *from contrariness*) par esprit de contradiction [b] (= *on the contrary*) au contraire

contrariness [kən'treərɪnɪs] N esprit *m* de contradiction, esprit *m* contrariant

contrariwise ['kɒntrərɪ,waɪz] ADV [a] (= *on the contrary*) au contraire, par contre [b] (= *in opposite direction*) en sens opposé

contrary ['kɒntrərɪ] [1] ADJ [a] (= *opposing*) [*idea, opinion, evidence, information, wind*] contraire (**to sth** à qch); [*direction*] opposé (**to sth** à qch); ~ **to public interest** contraire à l'intérêt du public; ~ **to nature** contre nature; **to run ~ to sth** aller à l'encontre de qch [b] [kən'treərɪ] (*pej = unreasonable*) [*person, attitude*] contrariant [2] ADV ~ **to sth** contrairement à qch [3] N **the ~** le contraire; **I think the ~ is true** je pense que c'est le contraire; **on the ~** au contraire; **quite the ~!** bien au contraire!; **come tomorrow unless you hear to the ~** venez demain sauf avis contraire *or* sauf contrordre; **I have nothing to say to the ~** je n'ai rien à redire; **a statement to the ~** une déclaration affirmant le contraire; **there is considerable evidence to the ~** il y a énormément de preuves du contraire

▼ **contrast** [kən'trɑːst] [1] VT mettre en contraste, contraster (**X with Y** X avec Y) [2] VI contraster, faire contraste (**with** avec); **to ~ strongly** [*colour*] contraster fortement (**with** avec), trancher (**with** sur) [3] ['kɒntrɑːst] N (*gen, TV*) contraste *m* (**between** entre); **in** *or* **by ~** par contraste; **in ~ to ...** en opposition à ..., par contraste avec ...; **to stand out in ~** (*in landscapes, photographs*) se détacher (**to** de, sur), ressortir (**to** sur, contre); [*colours*] contraster (**to** avec), trancher (**to** sur)

contrasting [kən'trɑːstɪŋ] ADJ très différent, contrasté

contrastive [kən'trɑːstɪv] ADJ contrastif

contravene [,kɒntrə'viːn] VT [a] [+ *law*] enfreindre, contrevenir à (*frm*) [b] [+ *sb's freedom*] nier, s'opposer à; [+ *myth*] contredire

contravention [,kɒntrə'venʃən] N infraction *f* (**of** à); **in ~ of the rules** en violation des règles, en dérogation aux règles

contretemps ['kɒntrətɒm] N (*pl inv*) [a] (= *mishap*) contretemps *m* [b] (= *disagreement*) malentendu *m*

contribute [kən'trɪbjuːt] [1] VT [+ *money*] contribuer, cotiser; **he has ~d £5** il a offert *or* donné 5 livres; **to ~ an article to a newspaper** écrire un article pour un journal; **his presence didn't ~ much to the success of the evening** sa présence n'a guère contribué au succès de la soirée [2] VI **to ~ to** contribuer à; **he ~d to the success of the venture** il a contribué à assurer le succès de l'affaire; **to ~ to a discussion** prendre part *or* participer à une discussion; **to ~ to a newspaper** collaborer à un journal; **it all ~d to the muddle** tout cela a contribué au désordre

contribution [,kɒntrɪ'bjuːʃən] N [*of money, goods etc*] contribution *f*; (*Admin*) cotisation *f*; (*to publication*) article *m*; → DSS

contributor [kən'trɪbjʊtə'] N (*to publication*) collaborateur *m*, -trice *f*; [*of money, goods*] donateur *m*, -trice *f*

contributory [kən'trɪbjʊtərɪ] [1] ADJ [a] (= *partly responsible*) [*cause, reason*] accessoire; **a ~ factor in sth** un des facteurs responsables de qch; **to be ~ to sth** contribuer à qch [b] (*Fin*) [*pension scheme, fund*] contributif [2] COMP ▸ **contributory negligence** N (*Jur*) faute *f* de la victime

contrite ['kɒntraɪt] ADJ penaud, contrit

contritely [kən'traɪtlɪ] ADV d'un air penaud *or* contrit

contrition [kən'trɪʃən] N contrition *f*

contrivance [kən'traɪvəns] N (= *tool, machine etc*) appareil *m*, machine *f*; (= *scheme*) invention *f*, combinaison *f*; **it is beyond his ~** il n'en est pas capable

contrive [kən'traɪv] VT [a] (= *invent, design*) [+ *plan, scheme*] combiner, inventer; **to ~ a means of doing** trouver un moyen pour faire [b] (= *manage*) **to ~ to do** s'arranger pour faire, trouver (le) moyen de faire; **can you ~ to be here at 3 o'clock?** est-ce que vous pouvez vous arranger pour être ici à 3 heures?; **he ~d to make matters worse** il a trouvé moyen d'aggraver les choses

contrived [kən'traɪvd] ADJ forcé, qui manque de naturel

control [kən'trəʊl] [1] N [a] (*NonC*) (= *authority, power to restrain*) autorité *f*; (= *regulating*) [*of traffic*] réglementation *f*; [*of aircraft*] contrôle *m*; [*of pests*] élimination *f*, suppression *f*; **the ~ of disease/forest fires** la lutte contre la maladie/les incendies de forêt; (*Pol*) ~ **of the seas** maîtrise *f* des mers; **he has no ~ over his children** il n'a aucune autorité sur ses enfants; **to keep a dog under ~** se faire obéir d'un chien; **to have a horse under ~** (savoir) maîtriser un cheval; **to keep ~ (of o.s.)** se contrôler; **to lose ~ (of o.s.)** perdre le contrôle de soi; **to lose ~ of a vehicle/situation** perdre le contrôle d'un véhicule/d'une situation, ne plus être maître d'un véhicule/d'une situation; **to be in ~ of a vehicle/situation** ◊ **to have a vehicle/situation under ~** être maître d'un véhicule/d'une situation; **to bring** *or* **get under ~** [+ *fire*] maîtriser; [+ *situation*] dominer; [+ *gangsters, terrorists, children, dog*] maîtriser; [+ *inflation*] maîtriser, juguler; **the situation is under ~** on a *or* on tient la situation bien en main; **everything's under ~** tout est en ordre; **his car got out of ~** il a perdu le contrôle *or* la maîtrise de sa voiture; **the children are quite out of ~** les enfants sont déchaînés; **under French ~** sous contrôle français; **under government ~** sous contrôle gouvernemental; **circumstances beyond our ~** circonstances *fpl* indépendantes de notre volonté; **who is in here?** qui *or* quel est le responsable ici?; (*Sport*) **his ~ of the ball is not very good** il ne contrôle pas très bien le ballon → **birth, self** [b] ~**s** [*of train, car, ship, aircraft*] commandes *fpl*; [*of radio, TV*] boutons *mpl* de commande; (*Rail etc*) **to be at the ~s** être aux commandes; (*Rad, TV*) **volume/tone ~** réglage *m* de volume/de sonorité [c] **price ~s** le contrôle des prix [d] (*Phys, Psych etc = standard of comparison*) cas *m* témoin [e] (*Comput*) "**~ W**" «contrôle W» [2] VT (= *regulate, restrain*) [+ *emotions*] maîtriser, dominer; [+ *child, animal*] se faire obéir de; [+ *car*] avoir *or* garder la maîtrise de; [+ *crowd*] contenir; [+ *organization, business*] diriger, être à la tête de; [+ *expenditure*] régler; [+ *prices, wages*] juguler; [+ *immigration*] contrôler; [+ *inflation, unemployment*] maîtriser, juguler; [+ *a market*] dominer; **to ~ o.s.** se contrôler, se maîtriser, rester maître de soi; ~ **yourself!** maîtrisez-vous!; **she can't ~ the children** elle n'a aucune autorité sur les enfants; **to ~ traffic** régler la circulation; **to ~ a disease** enrayer une maladie; (*Sport*) **to ~ the ball** contrôler le ballon → **controlled** [3] COMP ▸ **control case** N (*Med, Psych etc*) cas *m* témoin ▸ **control column** N (*Aviat*) manche *m* à balai ▸ **control experiment** N (*Sci, Med, Psych etc*) expérience *f* de contrôle ▸ **control freak** N (*pej*) personne *f* qui veut tout régenter ▸ **control group** N (*Med, Psych etc*) groupe *m* témoin ▸ **control key** N (*Comput*) touche *f* contrôle ▸ **control knob** N bouton *m* de commande *or* de réglage ▸ **control panel** N [*of aircraft, ship*] tableau *m* de bord; [*of TV, computer*] pupitre *m* de commande ▸ **control point** N poste *m* de contrôle ▸ **control room** N (*Naut*) poste *m* de commande; (*Mil*) salle *f* de commande; (*Rad, TV*) régie *f* ▸ **control tower** N (*Aviat*) tour *f* de contrôle ▸ **control unit** N (*Comput*) unité *f* de commande

controllable [kən'trəʊləbl] ADJ [*child, animal*] discipliné; [*expenditure, inflation, imports, immigration*] maîtrisable; [*disease*] qui peut être enrayé

controlled [kən'trəʊld] [1] ADJ [*emotion*] contenu; **he was very ~** il se dominait très bien; **... he said in a ~ voice** ... dit-il en se contrôlant *or* en se dominant; (*Econ*) ~ **economy** économie *f* dirigée *or* planifiée [2] COMP ▸ **controlled drug, controlled substance** N substance *f* inscrite au tableau

-controlled [kən,trəʊld] ADJ (*in compounds*) **a Labour-controlled council** un conseil municipal à majorité travailliste; **a government-controlled organisation** une organisation sous contrôle gouvernemental; **computer-controlled equipment** outillage *m* commandé par ordinateur; **radio-controlled car** voiture *f* télécommandée

controller [kən'trəʊlə'] N [a] [*of accounts etc*] contrôleur *m*, vérificateur *m* [b] (*Admin, Ind etc* = *manager*) contrôleur *m* [c] (*Tech = device*) appareil *m* de contrôle

controlling [kən'trəʊlɪŋ] ADJ [*factor*] déterminant; (*Fin*) ~ **interest** participation *f* majoritaire

controversial [,kɒntrə'vɜːʃəl] ADJ [*person, theory, decision, proposal, speech*] controversé; [*issue*] controversé, sujet à controverse; [*action*] sujet à controverse

controversially [,kɒntrə'vɜːʃəlɪ] ADV de façon controversée

controversy [kən'trɒvəsɪ] N controverse *f*, polémique *f*; (*Jur, Fin*) différend *m*; **there was a lot of ~ about it** ça a provoqué *or* soulevé beaucoup de controverses, ça a été très contesté *or* discuté; **to cause ~** provoquer *or* soulever une controverse; **they were having a great ~** ils étaient au milieu d'une grande polémique

controvert ['kɒntrəvɜːt] VT disputer, controverser

contumacious [,kɒntjʊ'meɪʃəs] ADJ rebelle, insoumis, récalcitrant

contumacy ['kɒntjʊməsɪ] N (= *resistance*) résistance *f*, opposition *f*; (= *rebelliousness*) désobéissance *f*, insoumission *f*; (*Jur*) contumace *f*

contumelious [,kɒntjʊ'miːlɪəs] ADJ (*liter*) insolent, méprisant

contumely ['kɒntjʊ(ː)mlɪ] N (*liter*) mépris *m*

contusion [kən'tjuːʒən] N contusion *f*

conundrum [kə'nʌndrəm] N devinette *f*, énigme *f*; (*fig*) énigme *f*

conurbation [,kɒnɜː'beɪʃən] N (*Brit*) conurbation *f*

convalesce [,kɒnvə'les] VI relever de maladie, se remettre (d'une maladie); **to be convalescing** être en convalescence

convalescence [,kɒnvə'lesəns] N convalescence *f*

convalescent [,kɒnvə'lesənt] [1] N convalescent(e) *m(f)* [2] ADJ convalescent; ~ **home** maison *f* de convalescence *or* de repos

convection [kən'vekʃən] [1] N convection *f* [2] COMP [*heating*] à convection

convector [kən'vektə'] N (*also* ~ **heater**) radiateur *m* (à convection)

convene [kən'viːn] [1] VT convoquer [2] VI se réunir, s'assembler → **convening**

convener [kən'viːnə'] N (*Brit Ind*) [*of union*] responsable *mf* des délégués syndicaux; [*of other committee*] président(e) *m(f)*

convenience [kən'viːnɪəns] [1] N (*NonC*) (= *suitability, comfort*) commodité *f*; **the ~ of a modern flat** la commodité d'un appartement moderne; **I doubt the ~ of an office in the suburbs** je ne suis pas sûr qu'un bureau en banlieue soit pratique; **for ~('s) sake** par souci de commodité; (*Comm*) **at your earliest ~** dans les meilleurs délais; **to find sth to one's**

~ trouver qch à sa convenance ; **do it at your own** ~ faites-le quand cela vous conviendra → **marriage**

[b] **~s** commodités *fpl* ; **the house has all modern ~s** la maison a tout le confort moderne [c] (*Brit euph*) toilettes *fpl*, W.-C. *mpl* → **public** [2] COMP ► **convenience foods** NPL aliments *mpl* tout préparés ; (*complete dishes*) plats *mpl* cuisinés ► **convenience goods** NPL produits *mpl* de grande consommation *or* de consommation courante ► **convenience market**, **convenience store** N (*US*) commerce *m* de proximité, dépanneur *m* (*Can*)

convenient [kən'vi:nɪənt] ADJ [*tool, place*] commode ; **if it is ~ (to you)** si vous n'y voyez pas d'inconvénient, si cela ne vous dérange pas ; **will it be ~ for you to come tomorrow?** est-ce que cela vous arrange *or* vous convient de venir demain ? ; **what would be a ~ time for you?** quelle heure vous conviendrait ? ; **is it ~ to see him now?** est-il possible de le voir tout de suite ? ; **it is not a very ~ time** le moment n'est pas très bien choisi ; **we were looking for a ~ place to stop** nous cherchions un endroit convenable *or* un bon endroit où nous arrêter ; **his cousin's death was very ~ for him** la mort de son cousin l'a bien arrangé *or* est tombée au bon moment pour lui ; **the house is ~ for** *or* **to shops and buses** la maison est bien située, à proximité des magasins et des lignes d'autobus ; **he put it down on a ~ chair** il l'a posé sur une chaise qui se trouvait (là) à portée

conveniently [kən'vi:nɪəntlɪ] ADV [a] (= *handily*) [*located, situated*] de façon pratique, de façon commode ; **~ situated for the shops** bien situé pour les magasins ; **to be ~ close** *or* **near to sth** être commodément situé à proximité de qch [b] (*iro* = *deliberately*) [*forget, ignore, overlook*] fort à propos ; **he ~ forgot to post the letter** comme par hasard, il a oublié de poster la lettre

convening [kən'vi:nɪŋ] [1] ADJ **~ authority** autorité *f* habilitée à *or* chargée de convoquer ; **~ country** pays *m* hôte [2] N convocation *f*

convenor [kən'vi:nər] N = **convener**

convent ['kɒnvənt] [1] N couvent *m* ; **to go into a ~** entrer au couvent [2] COMP ► **convent school** N couvent *m*

conventicle [kən'ventɪkl] N conventicule *m*

convention [kən'venʃən] [1] N (= *meeting, agreement, rule*) convention *f* ; (= *accepted behaviour*) usage *m*, convenances *fpl* ; (= *conference, fair*) salon *m* ; **according to ~** selon l'usage, selon les convenances ; **there is a ~ that ladies do not dine here** l'usage veut que les dames ne dînent pas ici ; **stamp collectors' ~** salon *m* de la philatélie [2] COMP ► **convention centre** N palais *m* des congrès

conventional [kən'venʃənl] [1] ADJ [a] (= *unoriginal*) [*person, organization, life, clothes*] conformiste ; [*behaviour, tastes, opinions, expression*] conventionnel [b] (= *traditional*) [*method, approach*] conventionnel ; [*argument, belief, product, values*] traditionnel, classique ; **in the ~ sense** au sens classique du terme [c] (= *not nuclear*) [*war, weapon*] conventionnel [2] COMP ► **Conventional Forces in Europe** NPL Forces *fpl* conventionnelles en Europe ► **conventional medicine** N médecine *f* traditionnelle ► **conventional wisdom** N sagesse *f* populaire ; **~ wisdom has it that ...** selon la sagesse populaire, ...

conventionality [kən,venʃə'nælɪtɪ] N [*of person, clothes*] conformisme *m* ; [*of behaviour, remarks*] banalité *f*

conventionally [kən'venʃənəlɪ] ADV (= *according to accepted norms*) d'une manière conventionnelle, conventionnellement ; (= *by agreement*) par convention, conven-

tionnellement ; **~ armed** doté d'armes conventionnelles

conventioneer [kən,venʃə'nɪər] N (*esp US Pol*) délégué(e) *m(f)* à la convention d'un parti

converge [kən'vɜ:dʒ] VI converger (**on** sur)

convergence [kən'vɜ:dʒəns] N convergence *f*

convergent [kən'vɜ:dʒənt], **converging** [kən'vɜ:dʒɪŋ] ADJ convergent ; **~ thinking** raisonnement *m* convergent

conversant [kən'vɜ:sənt] ADJ **to be ~ with** [+ *car, machinery*] s'y connaître en ; [+ *language, science, laws, customs*] connaître ; [+ *facts*] être au courant de ; **I am ~ with what he said** je suis au courant de ce qu'il a dit ; **I am not ~ with nuclear physics** je ne comprends rien à la physique nucléaire ; **I am not ~ with sports cars** je ne m'y connais pas en voitures de sport

conversation [,kɒnvə'seɪʃən] [1] N conversation *f*, entretien *m* ; **to have a ~ with sb** avoir une conversation *or* un entretien avec qn, s'entretenir avec qn ; **I have had several ~s with him** j'ai eu plusieurs entretiens *or* conversations avec lui ; **to be in ~ with ...** s'entretenir avec ..., être en conversation avec ... ; **they were deep in ~** ils étaient en grande conversation ; **what was your ~ about?** de quoi parliez-vous ? ; **she has no ~** elle n'a aucune conversation ; **to make ~** faire (la) conversation [2] COMP ► **conversation piece** N [a] (*something interesting*) **her hat was a real ~ piece** son chapeau a fait beaucoup jaser [b] (*Art*) tableau *m* de genre, scène *f* d'intérieur ► **conversation stopper** N **that was a (real) ~ stopper** cela a arrêté net la conversation, cela a jeté un froid

conversational [,kɒnvə'seɪʃənl] ADJ [a] [*style*] de conversation ; [*person*] qui a la conversation facile ; **his tone was ~ ◊ he spoke in a ~ tone** *or* **voice** il parlait sur le ton de la conversation ; **to adopt a ~ manner** se mettre à parler sur le ton de la conversation ; **a ~ gambit** (*starting*) une astuce pour engager la conversation ; (*continuing*) une astuce pour alimenter la conversation ; **her ~ skills are limited to the weather** ses talents en matière de conversation se limitent à parler du temps ; **his ~ ability** *or* **powers** son don de la conversation ; **to learn ~ German** apprendre l'allemand de la conversation courante ; **classes in ~ German** des cours *mpl* de conversation allemande [b] (*Comput*) conversationnel

conversationalist [,kɒnvə'seɪʃnəlɪst] N causeur *m*, -euse *f* ; **she's a great ~** elle a de la conversation, elle brille dans la conversation

conversationally [,kɒnvə'seɪʃnəlɪ] ADV [*speak, write, describe*] sur le ton de la conversation ; **"nice day" she said ~** « il fait beau » dit-elle en cherchant à engager la conversation

converse¹ [kən'vɜ:s] VI converser ; **to ~ with sb about sth** s'entretenir avec qn de qch

converse² ['kɒnvɜ:s] [1] ADJ (= *opposite, contrary*) [*statement*] contraire, inverse ; (*Math, Philos*) inverse ; [*proposition*] inverse, réciproque [2] N [*of statement*] contraire *m*, inverse *m* ; (*Math, Philos*) inverse *m*

▼ **conversely** [kən'vɜ:slɪ] ADV inversement

conversion [kən'vɜ:ʃən] [1] N (*NonC: gen, Fin, Math, Philos, Rel*) conversion *f* ; (*Rugby*) transformation *f* ; **the ~ of salt water into drinking water** la conversion *or* la transformation d'eau salée en eau potable ; **the ~ of an old house into flats** l'aménagement *m* *or* l'agencement *m* d'une vieille maison en appartements ; **improper ~ of funds** détournement *m* de fonds, malversations *fpl* ; **his ~ to Catholicism** sa conversion au catholicisme [2] COMP ► **conversion table** N table *f* de conversion

convert ['kɒnvɜ:t] [1] N converti(e) *m(f)* ; **to become a ~ to ...** se convertir à ... [2] [kən'vɜ:t] VT [a] (= *transform*) transformer

(**into** en) ; (*Rel etc*) convertir (**to** à) ; **to ~ pounds into francs** convertir des livres en francs ; (*Rugby*) **to ~ a try** transformer un essai ; **he has ~ed me to his way of thinking** il m'a converti *or* amené à sa façon de penser [b] (= *make alterations to*) [+ *house*] aménager, agencer (**into** en) ; **they have ~ed one of the rooms into a bathroom** ils ont aménagé une des pièces en salle de bains

converted [kən'vɜ:tɪd] ADJ [*barn, chapel, loft*] aménagé → **preach**

converter [kən'vɜ:tər] N (*Elec, Metal*) convertisseur *m* ; (*Rad*) changeur *m* de fréquence

convertibility [kən,vɜ:tə'bɪlɪtɪ] N convertibilité *f*

convertible [kən'vɜ:təbl] [1] ADJ (*gen*) convertible (**into** en) ; (*room, building*) **~ into ...** aménageable en ... [2] N (*Aut*) (voiture *f*) décapotable *f*

convertor [kən'vɜ:tər] N = **converter**

convex ['kɒn'veks] ADJ convexe

convexity [kɒn'veksɪtɪ] N convexité *f*

convey [kən'veɪ] VT [+ *goods, passengers*] transporter ; [*pipeline etc*] amener ; [+ *sound*] transmettre ; (*Jur*) [+ *property*] transférer, transmettre (**to** à) ; [+ *message, opinion, idea*] communiquer (**to** à) ; [+ *order, thanks*] transmettre (**to** à) ; **to ~ to sb that ...** faire savoir à qn que ... ; **I couldn't ~ my meaning to him** je n'ai pas pu lui communiquer ma pensée *or* me faire comprendre de lui ; **would you ~ my congratulations to him?** voudriez-vous lui transmettre mes félicitations ? ; **words cannot ~ how I feel** les paroles ne peuvent traduire ce que je ressens ; **the name ~s nothing to me** le nom ne me dit rien ; **what does this music ~ to you?** qu'est-ce que cette musique évoque pour vous ?

conveyance [kən'veɪəns] N [a] (*NonC*) transport *m* ; **~ of goods** transport *m* de marchandises ; **means of ~** moyens *mpl* de transport [b] (= *vehicle*) voiture *f*, véhicule *m* [c] (*Jur*) [*of property*] transmission *f*, transfert *m*, cession *f* ; (= *document*) acte *m* translatif (*de propriété*), acte *m* de cession

conveyancer [kən'veɪənsər] N rédacteur *m* d'actes translatifs de propriété

conveyancing [kən'veɪənsɪŋ] N (*Jur*) (= *procedure*) procédure *f* translative (*de propriété*) ; (= *operation*) rédaction *f* d'actes translatifs

conveyor [kən'veɪər] [1] N transporteur *m*, convoyeur *m* [2] COMP ► **conveyor belt** N (*Tech*) convoyeur *m*, tapis *m* roulant

convict ['kɒnvɪkt] [1] N prisonnier *m*, détenu *m* [2] [kən'vɪkt] VT (*Jur*) [+ *person*] déclarer *or* reconnaître coupable ; **he was ~ed** il a été déclaré *or* reconnu coupable ; **to ~ sb of a crime** reconnaître qn coupable d'un crime ; **he is a ~ed criminal/murderer** il a été jugé *or* reconnu (*frm*) coupable de crime/meurtre [3] [kən'vɪkt] VI [*jury*] rendre un verdict de culpabilité

conviction [kən'vɪkʃən] N [a] (*Jur*) condamnation *f* ; **there were 12 ~s for drunkenness** 12 personnes ont été condamnées pour ivresse → **previous**, **record** [b] (*NonC* = *persuasion, belief*) persuasion *f*, conviction *f* ; **to be open to ~** être ouvert à la persuasion ; **to carry ~** être convaincant ; **his explanation lacked ~** son explication manquait de conviction *or* n'était pas très convaincante [c] (= *belief*) conviction *f* ; **the ~ that ...** la conviction selon laquelle ... → **courage**

▼ **convince** [kən'vɪns] VT convaincre, persuader (**sb of sth** qn de qch) ; **he ~d her that she should leave** il l'a persuadée de partir, il l'a convaincue qu'elle devait partir ; **I am ~d he won't do it** je suis persuadé *or* convaincu qu'il ne le fera pas ; **a ~d Christian** un chrétien convaincu

▼ **convincing** [kən'vɪnsɪŋ] ADJ [a] (= *persuasive*) [*argument, evidence, performance, picture*]

convaincant; [*person*] convaincant, persuasif ; **he was ~ as Richard III** il était convaincant dans le rôle de Richard III **b** (= *decisive*) [*win, victory, lead*] net ; **to be a ~ winner of a race** gagner une course haut la main

convincingly [kənˈvɪnsɪŋlɪ] ADV **a** (= *persuasively*) [*speak, argue, demonstrate*] de façon convaincante **b** (= *decisively*) [*win, beat*] haut la main

convivial [kənˈvɪvɪəl] ADJ [*person*] de bonne compagnie ; [*mood, atmosphere, occasion*] convivial ; **in ~ company** en agréable compagnie

conviviality [kən,vɪvɪˈælɪtɪ] N convivialité *f*

convocation [,kɒnvəˈkeɪʃən] N (= *act*) convocation *f* ; (= *assembly*) assemblée *f*, réunion *f* ; (*Rel*) assemblée *f*, synode *m* ; (*US Educ*) cérémonie *f* de remise des diplômes

convoke [kənˈvəʊk] VT convoquer

convoluted [ˈkɒnvəluːtɪd] ADJ **a** (*pej* = *tortuous*) [*argument, reasoning, sentence, plot*] alambiqué **b** (= *coiling*) [*pattern*] en volutes ; [*shape, object*] enroulé

convolution [,kɒnvəˈluːʃən] **1** N circonvolution *f* **2 convolutions** NPL [*of plot*] méandres *mpl* ; **the ~s of this theory** la complexité infinie de cette théorie

convolvulus [kənˈvɒlvjʊləs] N (*pl* **convolvuluses** or **convolvuli** [kənˈvɒlvjʊˌlaɪ]) (= *flower*) volubilis *m* ; (= *weed*) liseron *m*

convoy [ˈkɒnvɔɪ] **1** N [*of ships, vehicles*] convoi *m* ; **in ~** en convoi **2** VT convoyer, escorter (**to** à)

convulse [kənˈvʌls] VT ébranler, bouleverser ; **a land ~d by war** un pays bouleversé par la guerre ; **a land ~d by earthquakes** un pays ébranlé par des tremblements de terre ; (*fig*) **to be ~d (with laughter)** se tordre de rire ; **a face ~d with pain** un visage décomposé or contracté par la douleur

convulsion [kənˈvʌlʃən] N **a** (*Med*) convulsion *f* ; **to have ~s** avoir des convulsions ; (*fig*) **to go into ~s of laughter** se tordre de rire **b** (= *violent disturbance*) [*of land*] bouleversement *m*, convulsion *f* ; [*of sea*] violente agitation *f*

convulsive [kənˈvʌlsɪv] ADJ convulsif

convulsively [kənˈvʌlsɪvlɪ] ADV convulsivement

cony [ˈkəʊnɪ] N (*US*) lapin *m* ; (*also* **~ skin**) peau *f* de lapin

coo[1] [kuː] **1** VTI [*doves etc*] roucouler ; [*baby*] gazouiller → **bill**[2] **2** N roucoulement *m*, roucoulade *f*

coo[2]* [kuː] EXCL (*Brit*) ça alors !*

co-occur [,kəʊəˈkɜːr] VI figurer simultanément, être cooccurrent(s) (**with** avec)

co-occurrence [,kəʊəˈkʌrəns] N cooccurrence *f*

cooing [ˈkuːɪŋ] N [*of doves*] roucoulement *m*, roucoulade *f* ; [*of baby*] gazouillement *m*

cook [kʊk] **1** N cuisinier *m*, -ière *f* ; **she is a good ~** elle est bonne cuisinière ; **to be head or chief ~ and bottle-washer** servir de bonne à tout faire, être le factotum **2** VT **a** [+ *food*] (faire) cuire ; **~ed breakfast** petit déjeuner *m* complet à l'anglaise ; **~ed meat** viande *f* froide ; (*Comm*) **~ed meat(s)** ≈ charcuterie *f* ; (*fig*) **to ~ sb's goose** mettre qn dans le pétrin* **b** (*Brit** = *falsify*) [+ *accounts*] truquer, maquiller ; **to ~ the books** truquer les comptes **3** VI [*food*] cuire ; [*person*] faire la cuisine, cuisiner ; **she ~s well** elle fait bien la cuisine, elle cuisine bien ; (*fig*) **what's ~ing?** qu'est-ce qui se passe ? **4** COMP ► **cook-chill foods** NPL plats *mpl* cuisinés ► **cook-off** N (*US*) concours *m* de cuisine

► **cook up*** VT SEP [+ *story, excuse*] inventer, fabriquer

cookbook [ˈkʊkbʊk] N livre *m* de cuisine

cooker [ˈkʊkər] N **a** (*Brit*) cuisinière *f* (*fourneau*) → **gas b** (= *apple*) pomme *f* à cuire

cookery [ˈkʊkərɪ] N (*gen, also school etc subject*) cuisine *f* (*activité*) ; (*Brit*) **~ book** livre *m* de cuisine ; **~ teacher** professeur *m* d'enseignement ménager

cookhouse [ˈkʊkhaʊs] N (*Mil, Naut*) cuisine *f*

cookie [ˈkʊkɪ] **1** N **a** (*Culin*) (*US*) petit gâteau *m* (sec) ; (*Brit*) cookie *m* ; **that's the way the ~ crumbles!*** c'est la vie ! ; (*esp US*) **to be caught with one's hand in the ~ jar** être pris sur le fait **b** (* = *person*) type* *m* ; (*US* = *girl*) jolie fille *f* ; **a smart ~** un petit malin, une petite maligne ; **tough ~** dur(e) *m(f)* à cuire **2** ADJ (* *fig*) sans originalité **3** COMP ► **cookie cutter** N (*US*) forme *f* à biscuits

cooking [ˈkʊkɪŋ] **1** N cuisine *f* (*activité*) ; **plain/French ~** cuisine *f* bourgeoise/française **2** COMP [*utensils*] de cuisine ; [*apples, chocolate*] à cuire ► **cooking film** N matériel alimentaire ► **cooking foil** N papier *m* d'aluminium, papier *m* alu* ► **cooking salt** N (*NonC*) gros sel *m*, sel *m* de cuisine ► **cooking time** N temps *m* de cuisson

cookout [ˈkʊkaʊt] N (*US*) barbecue *m*

cookware [ˈkʊkwɛər] N batterie *f* de cuisine

cool [kuːl] **1** ADJ **a** (*in temperature*) frais (fraîche *f*) ; (*Met*) **it is ~** il fait frais ; (*Met*) **it's getting** or **turning ~(er)** il commence à faire frais, ça se rafraîchit ; **to get ~** [*person*] se rafraîchir ; **to feel ~** [*person*] ne pas avoir trop chaud ; **I feel quite ~ now** j'ai bien moins chaud maintenant ; **to keep ~** [*person*] éviter d'avoir chaud ; **it helps you (to) keep ~** ça vous empêche d'avoir chaud ; **to keep sth ~** tenir qch au frais ; **"keep in a ~ place"** « tenir au frais », « conserver dans un endroit frais » ; **"store in a ~, dark place"** « conserver au frais et à l'abri de la lumière » ; **"serve ~, not cold"** « servir frais mais non glacé » ; **his forehead is much ~er now** il a le front beaucoup moins chaud maintenant

b (= *light*) [*clothing, shirt, dress*] léger ; **to slip into something ~** passer quelque chose de plus léger

c (= *pale*) [*colour, blue, green*] rafraîchissant

d (= *calm*) [*person, manner, composure, action, tone, voice*] calme ; **the police's ~ handling of the riots** le calme avec lequel la police a fait face aux émeutes ; **to keep a ~ head** garder la tête froide ; **to keep** or **stay ~** garder son calme ; **keep** or **stay ~!** du calme !

e (= *audacious*) [*behaviour*] d'une décontraction insolente ; **to be a ~ customer*** ne pas avoir froid aux yeux ; **as ~ as you please** [*person*] parfaitement décontracté

f (= *unfriendly*) [*person, relations*] froid (**with** or **towards sb** avec qn) ; **~ and calculating** froid et calculateur ; **to get a ~ welcome/reception** être fraîchement accueilli/reçu ; **the idea met with a ~ response** cette idée a été accueillie avec indifférence or n'a guère suscité d'enthousiasme

g **to be (as) ~ as a cucumber** (= *calm, audacious*) être d'un calme olympien

h (* = *trendy*) **computers are ~** les ordinateurs, c'est cool* ; **he acts ~, but he's really very insecure** il agit de façon calme et détendue mais en fait il n'est pas du tout sûr de lui ; **to look ~** avoir l'air cool*

i (* = *excellent*) super* *inv*, génial*

j (* = *acceptable*) **that's ~!** ça c'est cool !* ; **don't worry: it's ~** t'inquiète pas : c'est cool*

k (= *not upset*) **to be ~ (about sth)*** [*person*] rester cool* (à propos de qch)

l (= *full*) **he earns a ~ £40,000 a year*** il se fait* la coquette somme de 40 000 livres par an

m (*Mus*) [*jazz*] cool* *inv*

2 ADV ► **play**

3 N **a** fraîcheur *f*, frais *m* ; **in the ~ of the evening** dans la fraîcheur du soir ; **to keep sth in the ~** tenir qch au frais

b * **keep your ~!** t'énerve pas !* ; **he lost his ~** (= *panicked*) il a paniqué* ; (= *got angry*) il s'est fichu en rogne*

4 VT **a** [+ *air*] rafraîchir, refroidir ; (*fig*) **to ~ one's heels** faire le pied de grue, poireauter* ; **to leave sb to ~ his heels** faire attendre qn, faire poireauter* qn

b ~ **it!*** t'énerve pas !*, panique pas !*

5 VI (*also* **~ down**) [*air, liquid*] (se) rafraîchir, refroidir

6 COMP ► **cool bag** N sac *m* isotherme ► **cool box** N glacière *f* ► **cool-headed** ADJ calme, imperturbable

► **cool down 1** VI (*lit*) refroidir ; (*fig*) [*anger*] se calmer, s'apaiser ; [*critical situation*] se détendre ; * [*person*] se calmer ; **let the situation ~ down!** attendez que la situation se détende or que les choses se calment (*subj*) ! **2** VT SEP (= *make colder*) faire refroidir ; (= *make calmer*) calmer

► **cool off** VI (= *lose enthusiasm*) perdre son enthousiasme, se calmer ; (= *change one's affections*) se refroidir (**towards sb** à l'égard de qn, envers qn) ; (= *become less angry*) se calmer, s'apaiser

coolant [ˈkuːlənt] N liquide *m* de refroidissement

cooler [ˈkuːlər] N **a** (*for food*) glacière *f* **b** [*prison**] taule* *f* ; **in the ~** en taule* ; **to get put in the ~** se faire mettre au frais* or à l'ombre* **c** (= *drink*) boisson *f* à base de vin, de jus de fruit et d'eau gazeuse

coolie [ˈkuːlɪ] N coolie *m*

cooling [ˈkuːlɪŋ] **1** ADJ [*drink, swim, breeze*] rafraîchissant **2** N (*Aut*) refroidissement *m* **3** COMP ► **cooling fan** N (*Aut*) ventilateur *m* ► **cooling-off period** N (*Comm, Ind*) délai *m* de réflexion ► **cooling process** N refroidissement *m* ► **cooling rack** N grille *f* à gâteaux ► **cooling system** N circuit *m* de refroidissement ► **cooling tower** N (*Tech*) tour *f* de refroidissement

coolly [ˈkuːlɪ] ADV **a** (= *calmly*) calmement **b** (= *in unfriendly way*) froidement **c** (= *unenthusiastically*) froidement, fraîchement **d** (= *audaciously*) avec une décontraction insolente

coolness [ˈkuːlnɪs] N [*of water, air, weather*] fraîcheur *f* ; [*of welcome*] froideur *f* ; (= *calmness*) sang-froid *m*, impassibilité *f*, flegme *m* ; (= *impudence*) toupet* *m*, culot* *m*

coomb [kuːm] N petite vallée *f*, combe *f*

coon [kuːn] N **a** (*Zool*) ABBR = **raccoon b** (** *pej = Negro*) nègre** *m*, négresse** *f*

coop [kuːp] **1** N (*also* **hen ~**) poulailler *m*, cage *f* à poules ; (*fig*) **to fly the ~*** se défiler* **2** VT [+ *hens*] faire rentrer dans le poulailler

► **coop up** VT SEP [+ *person*] claquemurer, cloîtrer, enfermer

co-op [ˈkəʊɒp] N **a** (= *shop*) (ABBR = **cooperative**) coopérative *f*, coop* *f* **b** (*US*) (ABBR = **cooperative apartment**) → **cooperative c** (*US Univ*) (ABBR = **cooperative**) coopérative *f* étudiante

cooper [ˈkuːpər] N tonnelier *m*

cooperage [ˈkuːpərɪdʒ] N tonnellerie *f*

cooperate [kəʊˈɒpəreɪt] VI collaborer (**with sb** avec qn, **in sth** à qch, **to do** pour faire), coopérer ; **I hope he'll ~** j'espère qu'il va se montrer coopératif or qu'il va coopérer

cooperation [kəʊˌɒpəˈreɪʃən] N coopération *f* ; **in ~ with the ~ of ...** ◊ en coopération avec ..., avec la coopération or le concours de ... ; (*Jur*) **international judicial ~** entraide *f* judiciaire internationale

cooperative [kəʊˈɒpərətɪv] **1** ADJ [*person, firm, attitude*] coopératif ; (*US*) **~ apartment** appartement *m* en copropriété ; (*Brit Comm etc*) **~ society** coopérative *f*, société *f* coopérative or mutuelle ; (*Can Pol*) **Cooperative Commonwealth Federation** parti *m* social démocratique (*Can*) **2** N coopérative *f*

cooperatively [kəʊ'ɒpərətɪvlɪ] ADV (= *jointly*) en coopération ; (= *obligingly*) obligeamment

coopt [kəʊ'ɒpt] VT [+ *person*] (= *get help of*) s'assurer les services de ; (= *cause to join sth*) coopter (**on to** à) ; [+ *slogan, policy*] récupérer ; **~ed member** membre *m* coopté

cooption [kəʊ'ɒpʃən] N cooptation *f*

coordinate [kəʊ'ɔːdɪnɪt] **1** ADJ (*gen, Gram, Math*) coordonné ; **~ geometry** géométrie *f* analytique **2** N (*gen, Math, on map*) coordonnée *f* **3** **coordinates** NPL (*Dress*) ensemble *m* (coordonné), coordonnés *mpl* **4** [kəʊ'ɔːdɪneɪt] VT coordonner (**X with Y** X à Y) ; **coordinating committee** comité *m* de coordination ; (*Ling*) **coordinating conjunction** conjonction *f* de coordination

coordinated [kəʊ'ɔːdɪneɪtɪd] ADJ **a** (= *organized*) [*action, effort, approach, operation*] coordonné, concerté **b** (*physically*) [*person*] qui a une bonne coordination ; [*hands, limbs*] coordonné ; [*movements*] coordonné ; **to be badly ~** [*person*] avoir une mauvaise coordination **c** (= *matching*) [*clothes, designs*] coordonné ; **colour ~** [*clothes*] aux couleurs assorties

coordination [kəʊ'ɔːdɪ'neɪʃən] N coordination *f* ; **in ~ with ...** en coordination avec ...

coordinator [kəʊ'ɔːdɪneɪtə'] N coordinateur *m*, -trice *f*

coot [kuːt] N **a** (*Orn*) foulque *f* → **bald** **b** (= *fool*) **old ~:** vieux chnoque* *m*

co-owner ['kəʊ'əʊnə'] N copropriétaire *mf*

co-ownership [,kəʊ'əʊnəʃɪp] N copropriété *f*

cop* [kɒp] **1** N **a** (= *policeman*) flic* *m*, poulet* *m* ; **to play at ~s and robbers** jouer aux gendarmes et aux voleurs ; (*Brit*) **it's not much ~** ◊ **it's no great ~** ça ne vaut pas grand-chose *or* tripette **2** VT (*Brit* = *arrest, catch*) pincer*, piquer* ; (= *steal*) piquer*, faucher ; (= *obtain*) obtenir ; (*Brit*) **to ~ hold of** prendre ; (*Brit*) **to ~ it** écoper*, trinquer* ; (*US*) **to ~ a plea:** plaider coupable (*pour une charge mineure, afin d'en éviter une plus grave*) **3** COMP ► **cop-out:** N (= *excuse*) excuse *f* bidon* ; (= *act*) échappatoire *f* ► **cop-shop*** N (*Brit*) maison *f* Poulaga*, poste *m* (de police)

► **cop out** **1** VI se défiler* **2** **~-out** N → **cop**

copacetic* [,kəʊpə'setɪk] ADJ (*US*) formidable

copartner ['kəʊ'pɑːtnə'] N coassocié(e) *m(f)*, coparticipant(e) *m(f)*

copartnership ['kəʊ'pɑːtnəʃɪp] N (*Fin*) société *f* en nom collectif ; (*gen*) coassociation *f*, co-participation *f* ; **to go into ~ with ...** entrer en coassociation avec ...

cope¹ [kəʊp] N (*Dress Rel*) chape *f*

cope² [kəʊp] VI se débrouiller, s'en sortir ; **can you ~?** vous vous en sortirez ?, vous vous débrouillerez ? ; **how are you coping without a secretary?** comment vous débrouillez-vous sans secrétaire ? ; **he's coping pretty well** il s'en tire *or* se débrouille pas mal ; **I can ~ in Spanish** je me débrouille en espagnol ; **she just can't ~ any more** (= *she's overworked etc*) elle ne s'en sort plus ; (= *work is too difficult for her*) elle n'est plus du tout dans la course*, elle est complètement dépassée

► **cope with** VT FUS **a** (= *deal with, handle*) [+ *task, person*] se charger de, s'occuper de ; [+ *situation*] faire face à ; [+ *difficulties, problems*] (= *tackle*) affronter ; (= *solve*) venir à bout de ; **they ~ with 500 applications a day** 500 formulaires leur passent entre les mains chaque jour ; **you get the tickets, I'll ~ with the luggage** toi tu vas chercher les billets, moi je m'occupe *or* je me charge des bagages ; **I'll ~ with him** je m'occupe *or* je me charge de lui ; **he's got a lot to ~ with** (*work*) il a du pain sur la planche ; (*problems*) il a pas mal de problèmes à résoudre **b** (= *manage*) [+ *child, work*] s'en sortir avec ; **I just can't ~ with my son** je ne sais plus quoi faire avec mon fils, je ne m'en sors plus avec mon fils ; **we can't ~ with**

all this work avec tout ce travail nous ne pouvons plus en sortir

Copenhagen [,kəʊpn'heɪgən] N Copenhague

Copernican [kəʊ'pɜːnɪkən] ADJ copernicien

Copernicus [kə'pɜːnɪkəs] N Copernic *m*

copestone ['kəʊpstəʊn] N (*Archit*) couronnement *m* ; [*of wall*] chaperon *m* ; (*fig*) [*of career etc*] couronnement *m*, point *m* culminant

copier ['kɒpɪə'] N machine *f* à photocopier

co-pilot ['kəʊ'paɪlət] N (*Aviat*) copilote *m*, pilote *m* auxiliaire

coping ['kəʊpɪŋ] **1** N chaperon *m* **2** COMP ► **coping stone** N = **copestone**

copious ['kəʊpɪəs] ADJ [*quantities*] grand ; [*amount*] ample, abondant ; [*notes*] abondant ; [*writer, letter*] prolixe

copiously ['kəʊpɪəslɪ] ADV [*bleed, sweat*] abondamment ; [*write*] longuement ; [*cry*] à chaudes larmes ; **to water a plant ~** arroser une plante copieusement *or* abondamment ; **~ illustrated** abondamment illustré

copper ['kɒpə'] **1** N **a** (*NonC*) cuivre *m* **b** (*Brit* = *money*) **~s** la petite monnaie ; **I gave the beggar a ~** j'ai donné une petite pièce au mendiant **c** (*St Ex*) **~s** les cuprifères *mpl* **d** (= *washtub*) lessiveuse *f* **e** (*Brit** = *policeman*) flic: *m*, poulet: *m* ; **~'s nark** indic* *m*, mouchard *m* **2** COMP [*mine*] de cuivre ; [*bracelet*] de *or* en cuivre ► **copper beech** N hêtre *m* pourpre ► **copper-bottomed** ADJ [*saucepan*] avec un fond en cuivre ; [*investment*] sûr ► **copper-coloured** ADJ cuivré ► **copper sulphate** N sulfate *m* de cuivre ► **copper wire** N fil *m* de cuivre

copperhead ['kɒpəhed] N (*US* = *snake*) vipère *f* cuivrée

copperplate ['kɒpəpleɪt] (*in engraving*) **1** N planche *f* (de cuivre) gravée **2** ADJ sur cuivre, en taille-douce ; **~ handwriting** écriture *f* moulée, belle ronde *f*

coppersmith ['kɒpəsmɪθ] N artisan *m* en chaudronnerie d'art

coppery ['kɒpərɪ] ADJ cuivré

coppice ['kɒpɪs] **1** N taillis *m*, boqueteau *m* **2** VT [+ *tree*] élaguer, émonder

copra ['kɒprə] N copra *m*

co-presidency [kəʊ'prezɪdənsɪ] N coprésidence *f*

co-president [kəʊ'prezɪdənt] N coprésident(e) *m(f)*

co-processor [kəʊ'prəʊsesə'] N (*Comput*) co-processeur *m*

co-produce [,kəʊprə'djuːs] VT [+ *film, album*] coproduire

co-production [,kəʊprə'dʌkʃən] N coproduction *f*

copse [kɒps] N = **coppice**

Copt [kɒpt] N Copte *mf*

'copter* ['kɒptə'] N (ABBR = **helicopter**) hélico* *m*

coptic ['kɒptɪk] ADJ copte ; **the Coptic Church** l'Église *f* copte

copula ['kɒpjʊlə] N (*pl* **copulas** *or* **copulae** ['kɒpjʊ,liː]) (*Gram*) copule *f*

copulate ['kɒpjʊleɪt] VI copuler

copulation [,kɒpjʊ'leɪʃən] N copulation *f*

copulative ['kɒpjʊlətɪv] ADJ (*Gram*) copulatif

copy ['kɒpɪ] **1** N **a** (= *duplicate*) [*of painting etc*] copie *f*, reproduction *f* ; [*of letter, document, memo*] copie *f* ; (*Phot*) [*of print*] épreuve *f* ; **to take** *or* **make a ~ of sth** faire une copie de qch → **carbon, fair¹** **b** (= *one of series*) [*of book*] exemplaire *m* ; [*of magazine, newspaper*] exemplaire *m*, numéro *m* → **author, presentation** **c** (*NonC* = *text written*) (*Press*) copie *f* ; (*for advertisement*) message *m*, texte *m* ; **it gave him ~ for several articles** cela lui a fourni la matière de *or* un sujet pour plusieurs articles ; **that's always good ~** ça fait toujours de la très

bonne copie ; **the murder will make good ~** le meurtre fera de l'excellente copie ; **the journalist handed in his ~** le journaliste a remis son article *or* papier* ; **they are short of ~** ils sont en mal de copie* **d** (*Comput*) copie *f* **2** VT **a** (*also* **~ down, ~ out**) [+ *letter, passage from book*] copier **b** (= *imitate*) [+ *person, gestures*] imiter **c** (*Scol etc*) copier ; **to ~ sb's work** copier sur qn ; **he copied in the exam** il a copié à l'examen **d** (*Comput*) copier ; **to ~ sth to a disk** copier qch sur une disquette **e** (*Rad, Telec**) copier **f** (= *send a copy to*) envoyer une copie à **3** COMP ► **copy and paste** (*Comput*) N copier-coller *m* ♦ VT copier-coller ► **copy-edit** VT corriger ► **copy editor** N (*Press*) secrétaire *mf* de rédaction ; [*of book*] secrétaire *mf* d'édition ► **copy machine** N photocopieuse *f* ► **copy press** N presse *f* à copier

copybook ['kɒpɪbʊk] **1** N cahier *m* → **blot** **2** ADJ (= *trite*) banal ; (= *ideal, excellent*) modèle

copyboy ['kɒpɪbɔɪ] N (*Press*) grouillot *m* de rédaction

copycat* ['kɒpɪkæt] **1** N copieur *m*, -ieuse *f* **2** ADJ [*crime*] inspiré par un autre

copying ['kɒpɪɪŋ] **1** N **he was disqualified from the exam for ~** il a été recalé à l'examen pour avoir copié **2** COMP ► **copying ink** N encre *f* à copier

copyist ['kɒpɪɪst] N copiste *mf*, scribe *m*

copyreader ['kɒpɪ,riːdə'] N correcteur-rédacteur *m*, correctrice-rédactrice *f*

copyright ['kɒpɪraɪt] **1** N droit *m* d'auteur, copyright *m* ; **~ reserved** tous droits (de reproduction) réservés ; **out of ~** dans le domaine public **2** VT [+ *book*] obtenir les droits exclusifs sur *or* le copyright de

copywriter ['kɒpɪraɪtə'] N rédacteur *m*, -trice *f* publicitaire

coquetry ['kɒkɪtrɪ] N coquetterie *f*

coquette [kə'ket] N coquette *f*

coquettish [kə'ketɪʃ] ADJ [*woman*] coquet ; [*look, smile, behaviour*] plein de coquetterie

coquettishly [kə'ketɪʃlɪ] ADV avec coquetterie

cor: [kɔː] EXCL (*Brit: also* **~ blimey**) mince alors !*

coracle ['kɒrəkl] N coracle *m*, canot *m* (d'osier)

coral ['kɒrəl] **1** N corail *m* **2** COMP [*necklace*] de corail ; [*island*] corallien ; (*also* **~-coloured**) (couleur) corail *inv* ► **coral lips** NPL (*liter*) **her ~ lips** ses lèvres de corail ► **coral reef** N récif *m* corallien ► **Coral Sea** N mer *f* de Corail

cor anglais ['kɔːr'ɑːŋgleɪ] N (*pl* **cors anglais** ['kɔːz'ɑːŋgleɪ]) cor *m* anglais

corbel ['kɔːbəl] N corbeau *m*

cord [kɔːd] **1** N **a** [*of curtains, pyjamas*] cordon *m* ; [*of windows*] corde *f* ; [*of parcel*] ficelle *f* ; (*also* **umbilical ~**) cordon *m* ombilical → **communication, sash², spinal, vocal** **b** (*NonC: Tex*) = **corduroy** ; (*Elec*) cordon *m* **2** **cords** NPL pantalon *m* en velours côtelé **3** VT (= *tie*) corder **4** COMP [*trousers, skirt, jacket*] en velours côtelé ► **cord carpet** N tapis *m* de corde

cordage ['kɔːdɪdʒ] N (*NonC*) cordages *mpl*

corded ['kɔːdɪd] ADJ [*fabric*] côtelé

cordial ['kɔːdɪəl] **1** ADJ **a** (= *friendly*) [*person, tone, relationship, atmosphere, visit*] cordial **b** (= *strong*) **to have a ~ dislike for sb/sth** détester qn/qch cordialement **2** N (*Brit*) cordial *m*

cordiality [,kɔːdɪ'ælɪtɪ] N cordialité *f*

cordially ['kɔːdɪəlɪ] ADV cordialement ; **I ~ detest him** je le déteste cordialement

cordite ['kɔːdaɪt] N cordite *f*

cordless ['kɔːdlɪs] ADJ à piles, fonctionnant sur piles ; ~ **phone** téléphone *m* sans fil

cordon ['kɔːdn] **1** N (*all senses*) cordon *m* **2** VT (*also* ~ **off**) [+ *crowd*] contenir (*au moyen d'un cordon de sécurité*) ; [+ *area*] mettre en place un cordon de sécurité autour de **3** COMP ► **cordon bleu** ADJ cordon bleu ► **cordon sanitaire** N (*Med, Pol*) cordon *m* sanitaire

corduroy ['kɔːdərɔɪ] **1** N (*Tex*) velours *m* côtelé **2** **corduroys** NPL pantalon *m* en velours côtelé **3** COMP [*trousers, jacket*] en velours côtelé ; (*US*) [*road*] de rondins

CORE [kɔːʳ] N (*US*) (ABBR = **Congress of Racial Equality**) *défense des droits des Noirs*

core [kɔːʳ] **1** N [*of fruit*] trognon *m* ; [*of magnet, earth*] noyau *m* ; [*of cable*] âme *f*, noyau *m* ; (*Chem*) [*of atom*] noyau *m* ; [*of nuclear reactor*] cœur *m* ; (*Comput: also* ~ **memory**) mémoire *f* centrale ; [*of problem etc*] (*fig*) [*of person*] centre *m*, essentiel *m* ; **apple** ~ trognon *m* de pomme ; **the earth's** ~ le noyau terrestre ; (*Geol*) ~ **sample** carotte *f* ; (*fig*) **he is rotten to the** ~ il est pourri jusqu'à la moelle ; **English to the** ~ anglais jusqu'au bout des ongles → **hard 2** VT [+ *fruit*] enlever le trognon or le cœur de **3** COMP [*issue, assumption, subject*] fondamental ► **core curriculum** N (*Scol, Univ*) tronc *m* commun ► **core subject** N (*Scol, Univ*) matière *f* principale ► **core time** N plage *f* fixe

co-religionist ['kəʊrɪ'lɪdʒənɪst] N coreligionnaire *mf*

corer ['kɔːrəʳ] N (*Culin*) vide-pomme *m*

co-respondent ['kəʊrɪs'pɒndənt] N (*Jur*) co-défendeur *m*, -deresse *f* (*dans une affaire d'adultère*)

Corfu [kɔː'fuː] N Corfou *f*

corgi ['kɔːgɪ] N corgi *m*

coriander [ˌkɒrɪ'ændəʳ] N coriandre *f*

Corinth ['kɒrɪnθ] **1** N Corinthe **2** COMP ► **Corinth Canal** N le canal de Corinthe

Corinthian [kə'rɪnθɪən] **1** ADJ corinthien **2** N Corinthien(ne) *m(f)*

Coriolanus [ˌkɒrɪə'leɪnəs] N Coriolan *m*

cork [kɔːk] **1** N **a** (*NonC*) liège *m* **b** (*in bottle etc*) bouchon *m* ; **to pull the** ~ **out of a bottle** déboucher une bouteille **c** (*Fishing: also* ~ **float**) bouchon *m* flotteur **2** VT (*also* ~ **up**) [+ *bottle*] boucher **3** COMP [*mat, tiles, flooring*] de liège ► **cork oak** N = **cork tree** ► **cork-tipped** ADJ à bout de liège ► **cork tree** N chêne-liège *m*

corkage ['kɔːkɪdʒ] N droit *m* de bouchon (*payé par le client qui apporte dans un restaurant une bouteille achetée ailleurs*)

corked [kɔːkt] ADJ [*wine*] qui sent le bouchon

corker† * ['kɔːkəʳ] N (= *lie*) mensonge *m* de taille, gros mensonge *m* ; (= *story*) histoire *f* fumante* ; (*Sport*) (= *shot, stroke*) coup *m* fumant* ; (= *player*) crack* *m* ; (= *girl*) beau brin* *m* (de fille)

corking† * ['kɔːkɪŋ] ADJ (*Brit*) épatant† *, fameux*

corkscrew ['kɔːkskruː] **1** N tire-bouchon *m* **2** COMP ► **corkscrew curls** NPL anglaises *fpl* (boucles)

corm [kɔːm] N bulbe *m* (*de crocus etc*)

cormorant ['kɔːmərənt] N cormoran *m*

Corn (*Brit*) = **Cornwall**

corn¹ [kɔːn] **1** N **a** (= *seed*) grain *m* (*de céréale*) **b** (*Brit*) blé *m* ; (*US*) maïs *m* ; ~ **on the cob** épis *mpl* de maïs **c** (*US* = *whiskey*) bourbon *m* **d** * (= *sentimentality*) sentimentalité *f* vieillotte or bébête ; (= *humour*) humour *m* bébête **2** COMP ► **corn bread** N (*US*) pain *m* de maïs ► **corn crops** NPL céréales *fpl* ► **corn dog** N (*US Culin*) saucisse *f* en beignet ► **corn dolly** N (*Brit*) poupée *f* de paille ► **corn exchange** N halle *f* au blé ► **corn-**

fed ADJ [*chicken*] de grain ► **corn liquor** N (*US*) eau-de-vie *f* à base de maïs (*de fabrication artisanale*) ► **corn meal** N farine *f* de maïs ► **corn oil** N huile *f* de maïs ► **corn pone** N (*NonC: US*) pain *m* de maïs ► **corn poppy** N coquelicot *m* ► **corn salad** N doucette *f* ► **corn whiskey** N (*US*) whisky *m* de maïs, bourbon *m*

corn² [kɔːn] N (*Med*) cor *m* ; (*Brit fig*) **to tread on sb's** ~**s** toucher qn à l'endroit sensible, blesser qn dans son amour-propre ; (*Med*) ~ **plaster** pansement *m* pour cor

cornball: ** ['kɔːnbɔːl] (*US*) **1 N **to be a** ~ [*person*] être très fleur bleue **2** ADJ cucul (la praline)*

corncob ['kɔːnkɒb] N (*US*) épi *m* de maïs

Corncracker State [ˌkɔːnkrækə'steɪt] N **the** ~ le Kentucky

corncrake ['kɔːnkreɪk] N (*Orn*) râle *m* des genêts

corncrib ['kɔːnkrɪb] N (*US Agr*) séchoir *m* à maïs

cornea ['kɔːnɪə] N (*pl* **corneas** or **corneae** ['kɔːnɪiː]) cornée *f*

corneal ['kɔːnɪəl] ADJ cornéen ; ~ **lenses** lentilles *fpl* cornéennes, verres *mpl* cornéens

corned beef [kɔːnd'biːf] N corned-beef *m*

cornelian [kɔː'niːlɪən] N cornaline *f*

corner ['kɔːnəʳ] **1** N **a** (= *angle*) [*of page, field, eye, mouth, room, boxing ring*] coin *m* ; [*of street, box, table*] coin *m*, angle *m* ; [*of road*] tournant *m*, virage *m* ; (*Climbing*) dièdre *m* ; (*Ftbl*) corner *m*, coup *m* de pied de coin ; **to look at sb out of the** ~ **of one's eye** regarder qn du coin de l'œil ; **to put a child in the** ~ mettre un enfant au coin ; **to drive** or **force sb into a** ~ (*lit*) pousser qn dans un coin ; (*fig*) acculer qn ; (*fig*) **to be in a (tight)** ~ être dans le pétrin, être dans une situation difficile ; **you'll find the church round the** ~ vous trouverez l'église juste après le coin ; **the little shop around the** ~ la petite boutique du coin ; **it's just round the** ~ (= *very near*) c'est à deux pas d'ici ; **Christmas is just around the** ~ Noël n'est pas loin ; **the domestic robot is just around the** ~ le robot domestique, c'est pour demain ; **to take a** ~ (*Aut*) prendre un tournant ; (*Ftbl*) faire un corner ; (*Aut*) **to cut a** ~ prendre un virage à la corde ; (*fig*) **to cut** ~**s** prendre des raccourcis (*fig*) ; (*financially*) **to cut** ~**s (on sth)** rogner sur les coûts (*de qch*) ; **to turn the** ~ (*lit*) tourner au or le coin de la rue ; (*fig*) passer le moment critique ; [*patient*] passer le cap

b (= *cranny, place*) **in every** ~ **of the garden** dans tout le jardin ; **treasures hidden in odd** ~**s** des trésors *mpl* cachés dans des recoins ; **in every** ~ **of the house** dans tous les recoins de la maison ; (*fig*) **in every** ~ **of Europe** dans toute l'Europe ; **in (all) the four** ~**s of the earth** aux quatre coins du monde

c (*fig* = *position*) **to fight one's** ~ défendre sa position or son point de vue

d (*Econ*) **to make a** ~ **in wheat** accaparer le marché du blé

e (*Boxing* = *person*) soigneur *m*

2 VT [+ *hunted animal*] acculer ; (*fig* = *catch to speak to etc*) coincer* ; **she** ~**ed me in the hall** elle m'a coincé* dans l'entrée ; (*fig*) **he's got you** ~**ed** il t'a coincé*, il t'a mis au pied du mur ; (*Econ*) **to** ~ **the market** accaparer le marché

3 VI (*Aut*) prendre un virage

4 COMP ► **corner cupboard** N placard *m* d'angle ► **corner flag** N (*Ftbl*) piquet *m* de corner ; (*in roadway*) dalle *f* de coin ► **the corner house** N la maison du coin, la maison qui fait l'angle (de la rue) ► **corner kick** N (*Ftbl*) corner *m* ► **corner seat** N (*Rail*) (place *f* de) coin *m* ► **corner shop** N (*Brit*) magasin *m* or boutique *f* du coin ► **corner situation** N **the house has a** ~ **situation** la maison

fait l'angle ► **corner store** N (*US*) = **corner shop**

cornering ['kɔːnərɪŋ] N **a** (*Aut*) amorce *f* du virage **b** (*Econ*) accaparement *m*, monopolisation *f*

cornerstone ['kɔːnəstəʊn] N (*lit, fig*) pierre *f* angulaire ; (= *foundation stone*) première pierre *f*

cornerways fold ['kɔːnəweɪz'fəʊld] N pli *m* en triangle

cornet ['kɔːnɪt] N **a** (*Mus*) cornet *m* (à pistons) ; ~ **player** cornettiste *mf* **b** (*Brit*) [*of sweets etc*] cornet *m* ; [*of ice cream*] cornet *m* (de glace)

cornfield ['kɔːnfiːld] N (*Brit*) champ *m* de blé ; (*US*) champ *m* de maïs

cornflakes ['kɔːnfleɪks] NPL pétales *mpl* de maïs, corn-flakes *mpl*

cornflour ['kɔːnflaʊəʳ] N (*Brit*) farine *f* de maïs, maïzena® *f*

cornflower ['kɔːnflaʊəʳ] **1** N bleuet *m*, barbeau *m* **2** ADJ (*also* ~ **blue**) bleu vif *inv*, bleu barbeau *inv*

cornice ['kɔːnɪs] N corniche *f*

corniche [kɔː'niːʃ, kɔː'nɪʃ] N (*also* ~ **road**) corniche *f*

Cornish ['kɔːnɪʃ] **1** ADJ de Cornouailles, cornouaillais **2** COMP ► **Cornish pasty** N *chausson à la viande avec des pommes de terre et des carottes*

Cornishman ['kɔːnɪʃmən] N (*pl* -**men**) natif *m* de Cornouailles

Cornishwoman ['kɔːnɪʃwʊmən] N (*pl* -**women**) native *f* de Cornouailles

cornstarch ['kɔːnstaːtʃ] N (*US*) farine *f* de maïs, maïzena® *f*

cornucopia [ˌkɔːnjʊ'kəʊpɪə] N corne *f* d'abondance

Cornwall ['kɔːnwəl] N la Cornouailles ; **in** ~ en Cornouailles

corny * ['kɔːnɪ] ADJ [*joke*] rebattu, éculé ; [*film, novel*] (*sentimental*) à l'eau de rose ; (*obvious*) bateau* *inv* ; [*song*] sentimental ; **the** ~ **line "do you come here often?"** la phrase bateau* « vous venez souvent ici ? » ; **I know it sounds** ~, **but ...** je sais que ça a l'air idiot mais ...

corolla [kə'rɒlə] N corolle *f*

corollary [kə'rɒlərɪ] N corollaire *m*

corona [kə'rəʊnə] N (*pl* **coronas** or **coronae** [kə'rəʊniː]) (*Anat, Astron*) couronne *f* ; (*Elec*) couronne *f* électrique ; (*Archit*) larmier *m*

coronary ['kɒrənərɪ] **1** ADJ (*Anat*) coronaire ; ~ **bypass** pontage *m* coronarien ; ~ **care unit** unité *f* de soins coronariens ; ~ **heart disease** maladie *f* coronarienne ; ~ **thrombosis** infarctus *m* du myocarde, thrombose *f* coronarienne **2** N (*Med**) infarctus *m*

coronation [ˌkɒrə'neɪʃən] **1** N (= *ceremony*) couronnement *m* ; (= *actual crowning*) sacre *m* **2** COMP [*ceremony, oath, robe*] du sacre ; [*day*] du couronnement

coroner ['kɒrənəʳ] N coroner *m* (*officiel chargé de déterminer les causes d'un décès*) ; ~**'s inquest** enquête *f* judiciaire (*menée par le coroner*) ; ~**'s jury** jury *m* (*siégeant avec le coroner*)

coronet ['kɒrənɪt] N [*of duke etc*] couronne *f* ; [*of lady*] diadème *m*

Corp, corp ABBR = **corporation**

corpora ['kɔːpərə] NPL of **corpus**

corporal¹ ['kɔːpərəl] N [*of infantry, RAF*] caporal-chef *m* ; [*of cavalry etc*] brigadier-chef *m* ; (*on envelope etc*) **Corporal Smith** le Caporal-Chef Smith

corporal² ['kɔːpərəl] ADJ corporel ; ~ **punishment** châtiment *m* corporel

corporate ['kɔːpərɪt] **1** ADJ **a** (*Comm*) (= *of a business*) [*executive, culture, restructuring, sponsorship, planning etc*] d'entreprise ; [*finance, image, identity, logo, jet*] de l'entreprise ; (= *of business in general*) [*affairs, debt, earnings etc*]

des entreprises ; **~ America** l'Amérique f des entreprises ; **~ clients** or **customers** entreprises fpl clientes ; **the ~ world** le monde de l'entreprise
[b] (= joint) [decision, responsibility] collectif ; [objective] commun ; [action, ownership] en commun
[2] COMP ► **corporate body** N personne f morale ► **corporate bond** N (US) (local) obligation f municipale ; (private) obligation f émise par une société privée ► **corporate headquarters** NPL siège m social ► **corporate hospitality** N soirées aux frais d'une entreprise ► **corporate institution** N institution fonctionnant comme une entreprise ► **corporate ladder** N **to move up the ~ ladder** monter dans la hiérarchie d'une entreprise ► **corporate law** N droit m des entreprises ► **corporate lawyer** N juriste mf spécialisé(e) dans le droit des entreprises ; (working for corporation) avocat(e) m(f) d'entreprise ; (= specialist in corporate law) juriste mf d'entreprise ► **corporate name** N raison f sociale ► **corporate property** N biens mpl sociaux ► **corporate raider** N raider m ► **corporate sponsor** N gros sponsor m ► **corporate stock** N actions fpl ► **corporate takeover** N OPA f ► **corporate tax** N impôt m sur les sociétés

corporately ['kɔːpərɪtlɪ] ADV **to be ~ owned** appartenir à une entreprise (or des entreprises)

corporation [ˌkɔːpə'reɪʃən] [1] N [a] (Brit) (of town) conseil m municipal ; **the Mayor and Corporation** le corps municipal, la municipalité [b] (Comm, Fin) société f commerciale ; (US) société f à responsabilité limitée, compagnie f commerciale [c] (Brit*) bedaine* f, brioche* f ; **he's developed quite a ~** il a pris une sacrée brioche* [2] COMP (Brit) [school, property] de la ville, municipal ► **corporation lawyer** N (working for corporation) avocat(e) m(f) d'entreprise ; (= specialist in corporation law) juriste mf d'entreprise ► **corporation tax** N (Brit) impôt m sur les sociétés

corporatism ['kɔːpərətɪzəm] N corporatisme m

corporatist ['kɔːpərətɪst] ADJ corporatiste

corporeal [kɔː'pɔːrɪəl] ADJ corporel, physique

corps [kɔːʳ] [1] N (pl **corps** [kɔːz]) corps m → **army**, **diplomatic** [2] COMP ► **corps de ballet** N corps m de ballet

corpse [kɔːps] N cadavre m, corps m

corpulence ['kɔːpjʊləns] N corpulence f, embonpoint m

corpulent ['kɔːpjʊlənt] ADJ corpulent

corpus ['kɔːpəs] N (pl **corpuses** or **corpora** ['kɔːpərə]) (Literat) corpus m, recueil m ; (Ling) corpus m ; (Fin) capital m ; (Rel) **Corpus Christi** la Fête-Dieu

corpuscle ['kɔːpʌsl] N [a] (Anat, Bio) corpuscule m ; **(blood) ~** globule m sanguin ; **red/white ~s** globules mpl rouges/blancs [b] (Phys) électron m

corral [kə'rɑːl] (US) [1] N corral m [2] VT [+ cattle] enfermer dans un corral ; (* fig) [+ people, support] réunir

correct [kə'rekt] [1] ADJ [a] (= right) [answer, number, term, estimate, information] correct ; [suspicions] bien fondé ; **that's ~!** (confirming guess) exactement! ; (confirming right answer) c'est juste or exact! ; (in buses etc) **"~ money or change only"** «vous êtes prié de faire l'appoint » ; **in the ~ order** dans le bon ordre ; **to prove ~** s'avérer juste ; **have you the ~ time?** avez-vous l'heure exacte? ; **at the ~ time** au bon moment ; **it is ~ to say that ...** il est juste de dire que ... ; **it is not ~ to say that ...** (rationally) il est inexact de dire que ... ; (fair) il n'est pas juste de dire que ... ; (morally) il n'est pas correct de dire que ...

[b] **to be ~** [person] avoir raison ; **you are quite ~** vous avez parfaitement raison ; **he was ~ in his estimates** ses estimations étaient justes ; **he is ~ in his assessment of the situation** son évaluation de la situation est juste ; **to be ~ in doing sth** avoir raison de faire qch ; **to be ~ to do sth** avoir raison de faire qch ; **he was quite ~ to do it** il a eu tout à fait raison de le faire
[c] (= appropriate) [object, method, decision, size, speed, temperature] bon ; **in the ~ place** au bon endroit ; **the ~ use of sth** le bon usage de qch ; **the ~ weight for your height and build** le bon poids pour votre taille et votre corpulence
[d] (= proper) [behaviour] correct ; [manners] correct, convenable ; [etiquette, form of address] convenable ; [person] comme il faut ; **~ dress must be worn** une tenue correcte est exigée ; **it's the ~ thing to do** c'est l'usage, c'est ce qui se fait ; **socially ~** admis en société
[2] VT [a] [+ piece of work, text, error] corriger ; (Typ) [+ proofs] corriger ; **to ~ sb's punctuation/spelling** corriger la ponctuation/ l'orthographe de qn ; **he asked her to ~ his English** il lui a demandé de corriger son anglais
[b] [+ person] reprendre, corriger ; **to ~ o.s.** se reprendre, se corriger ; **~ me if I'm wrong** reprenez-moi or corrigez-moi si je me trompe ; **I stand ~ed** je reconnais mon erreur
[c] (= rectify) [+ problem] arranger ; [+ eyesight] corriger ; [+ imbalance] redresser
[d] (†† = punish) réprimander, reprendre
[3] COMP ► **correcting fluid** N liquide m correcteur

correction [kə'rekʃən] [1] N [a] (NonC) [of proofs, essay] correction f ; [of error] correction f, rectification f ; **I am open to ~, but ...** corrigez-moi si je me trompe, mais ... [b] [of school work, proof, text, manuscript] correction f ; **a page covered with ~s** une page couverte de corrections [c] (†† = punishment) correction f, châtiment m ; **house of ~** maison f de correction† [2] COMP ► **correction fluid** N liquide m correcteur ► **correction tape** N ruban m correcteur

correctional [kə'rekʃənəl] (US) [1] ADJ [system] pénitentiaire [2] COMP ► **correctional facility** N établissement m pénitentiaire ► **correctional officer** N gardien(ne) m(f) de prison

corrective [kə'rektɪv] [1] ADJ [action] rectificatif ; (Jur, Med) [measures, training] de rééducation, correctif ; (Med) **~ surgery** chirurgie f réparatrice [2] N correctif m

correctly [kə'rektlɪ] ADV [a] (= accurately, in right way) [predict] avec justesse, correctement ; [answer, respond, cook, perform] correctement ; **if I understand you ~** si je vous ai bien compris ; **if I remember ~** si je me souviens bien [b] (= respectably, decently) [behave] convenablement

correctness [kə'rektnɪs] N (NonC) [a] (= rightness, appropriateness) [of decision, action, statement, calculation, spelling] justesse f [b] (= propriety) [of person, behaviour, manners, dress] correction f ; **to treat sb with polite ~** traiter qn avec une correction polie

Correggio [kə'redʒəʊ] N le Corrège

correlate ['kɒrɪleɪt] [1] VI correspondre (with à), être en corrélation (with avec) [2] VT mettre en corrélation, corréler (with avec)

correlation [ˌkɒrɪ'leɪʃən] N corrélation f

correlative [kɒ'relətɪv] [1] N corrélatif m [2] ADJ corrélatif

▼ **correspond** [ˌkɒrɪs'pɒnd] VI [a] (= agree) correspondre (with à), s'accorder (with avec) ; **that does not ~ with what he said** cela ne correspond pas à ce qu'il a dit [b] (= be similar, equivalent) correspondre (to à), être l'équivalent (to de) ; **this ~s to what she was doing last year** ceci est semblable or correspond à ce qu'elle faisait l'année dernière ; **his job ~s**

roughly to mine son poste équivaut à peu près au mien or est à peu près l'équivalent du mien [c] (= exchange letters) correspondre (with avec) ; **they ~** ils s'écrivent, ils correspondent

correspondence [ˌkɒrɪs'pɒndəns] [1] N [a] (= similarity, agreement) correspondance f (between entre, with avec) [b] (= letter-writing) correspondance f ; **to be in ~ with sb** entretenir une or être en correspondance avec qn ; **to read one's ~** lire son courrier or sa correspondance [2] COMP ► **correspondence card** N carte-lettre f ► **correspondence college** N établissement m d'enseignement par correspondance ► **correspondence column** N (Press) courrier m des lecteurs ► **correspondence course** N cours m par correspondance

correspondent [ˌkɒrɪs'pɒndənt] N (gen, Comm, Press, Banking) correspondant(e) m(f) ; **foreign/sports ~** correspondant m étranger/ sportif → **special**

corresponding [ˌkɒrɪs'pɒndɪŋ] ADJ correspondant ; **~ to ...** conforme à ... ; **a ~ period** une période analogue ; **the ~ period** la période de correspondance

correspondingly [ˌkɒrɪs'pɒndɪŋlɪ] ADV [a] (= proportionately) proportionnellement [b] (= as a result) en conséquence

corridor ['kɒrɪdɔː] N couloir m, corridor m ; (Brit) **~ train** train m à couloir ; (fig) **the ~s of power** les allées fpl du pouvoir

corroborate [kə'rɒbəreɪt] VT corroborer, confirmer

corroboration [kəˌrɒbə'reɪʃən] N confirmation f, corroboration f ; **in ~ of ...** à l'appui de ..., en confirmation de ...

corroborative [kə'rɒbərətɪv] ADJ qui corrobore (or corroborait etc)

corrode [kə'rəʊd] [1] VT (lit, fig) corroder, ronger [2] VI [metals] se corroder

corroded [kə'rəʊdɪd] ADJ corrodé

corrosion [kə'rəʊʒən] N corrosion f

corrosive [kə'rəʊzɪv] [1] ADJ (Chem) corrosif ; (fig = harmful) [effect, influence, power, emotion] destructeur (-trice f) [2] N corrosif m

corrugated ['kɒrəgeɪtɪd] [1] ADJ [tin, steel, surface] ondulé ; [roof] en tôle ondulée ; [brow, face] ridé [2] COMP ► **corrugated cardboard** N carton m ondulé ► **corrugated iron** N tôle f ondulée ► **corrugated paper** N papier m ondulé

corrupt [kə'rʌpt] [1] ADJ [a] (= dishonest) corrompu ; (= depraved) dépravé ; [practice] malhonnête ; **~ practices** (= dishonesty) tractations fpl malhonnêtes ; (= bribery etc) trafic m d'influence, malversations fpl [b] (Comput, Ling) [data, text] altéré ; [language] corrompu [c] (liter = putrid) [flesh, corpse] putride [2] VT (dishonesty) corrompre ; (immorality) dépraver ; (Comput) altérer [3] VI corrompre

corruptible [kə'rʌptəbəl] ADJ corruptible

corruption [kə'rʌpʃən] [1] N [a] (NonC: moral) [of person, morals] corruption f ; **police ~** corruption f de la police [b] (Ling) **"jean" is a ~ of "Genoa"** « jean » est une déformation de « Gênes » [c] (NonC: liter = putrefaction) décomposition f, putréfaction f [2] COMP ► **the corruption of minors** N (Jur) le détournement de mineur(s)

corsage [kɔː'sɑːʒ] N (= bodice) corsage m ; (= flowers) petit bouquet m (de fleurs porté au corsage)

corsair ['kɔːsɛəʳ] N (= ship, pirate) corsaire m, pirate m

cors anglais ['kɔː'zɑːŋgleɪ] NPL of **cor anglais**

corset ['kɔːsɪt] N (Dress: also **~s**) corset m ; (lightweight) gaine f ; (Med) corset m

corseted ['kɔːsɪtɪd] ADJ corseté

Corsica ['kɔːsɪkə] N la Corse

► LANGUAGE IN USE: **correspond** 5.3

Corsican ['kɔːsɪkən] ① ADJ corse ② N Corse *mf*

cortège [kɔː'teːʒ] N cortège *m*

cortex ['kɔːteks] N (*pl* **cortices** ['kɔːtɪsiːz]) (*Bot*) cortex *m*, écorce *f*; (*Anat*) cortex *m*

corticoids ['kɔːtɪkɔɪdz], **corticosteroids** [ˌkɔːtɪkəʊ'stɪərɔɪdz] NPL corticoïdes *mpl*

cortisone ['kɔːtɪzəʊn] N cortisone *f*

corundum [kə'rʌndəm] N corindon *m*

coruscate ['kɒrəskeɪt] VI briller, scintiller

coruscating ['kɒrəskeɪtɪŋ] ADJ brillant, scintillant

corvette [kɔː'vet] N (*Naut*) corvette *f*

COS [ˌsiːəʊ'es] (ABBR = **cash on shipment**) → **cash**

cos¹ [kɒs] N (*Brit: also* ~ **lettuce**) (laitue *f*) romaine *f*

cos² [kɒs] N ABBR = **cosine**

cos³ [kɒz] CONJ parce que

cosh [kɒʃ] (*Brit*) ① VT* taper sur, cogner* sur ② N gourdin *m*, matraque *f*

cosignatory ['kəʊ'sɪgnətərɪ] N cosignataire *mf*

cosily, cozily (*US*) ['kəʊzɪlɪ] ADV [*furnished*] confortablement; [*settled*] douillettement

cosine ['kəʊsaɪn] N cosinus *m*

cosiness ['kəʊzɪnɪs] N (*NonC*) ⓐ (= *warmth*) [*of room, pub*] atmosphère *f* douillette ⓑ (= *intimacy*) [*of evening, chat, dinner*] intimité *f*; **the ~ of the atmosphere** l'atmosphère *f* douillette ⓒ (*pej = convenience*) [*of relationship*] complicité *f*, connivence *f*

cosmetic [kɒz'metɪk] ① ADJ [*surgery*] plastique, esthétique; [*preparation*] cosmétique; (*fig*) superficiel, symbolique ② N cosmétique *m*, produit *m* de beauté

cosmetician [kɒzme'tɪʃən] N cosmétologue *mf*

cosmic ['kɒzmɪk] ADJ (*lit*) cosmique; (*fig*) immense, incommensurable; ~ **dust/rays** poussière *f*/rayons *mpl* cosmique(s)

cosmogony [kɒz'mɒgənɪ] N cosmogonie *f*

cosmographer [kɒz'mɒgrəfəʳ] N cosmographe *mf*

cosmography [kɒz'mɒgrəfɪ] N cosmographie *f*

cosmological [ˌkɒzməʊ'lɒdʒɪkəl] ADJ cosmologique

cosmology [kɒz'mɒlədʒɪ] N cosmologie *f*

cosmonaut ['kɒzmənɔːt] N cosmonaute *mf*

cosmopolitan [ˌkɒzmə'pɒlɪtən] ADJ, N cosmopolite *mf*

cosmos ['kɒzmɒs] N cosmos *m*

co-sponsor ['kəʊ'spɒnsəʳ] N (*Advertising*) commanditaire *m* associé

Cossack ['kɒsæk] N cosaque *m*

cosset ['kɒsɪt] VT dorloter, choyer

cossie* ['kɒzɪ] N (*Brit, Austral*) maillot *m* (de bain)

▼ **cost** [kɒst] ① VT (*pret, ptp* **cost**) ⓐ (*lit, fig*) coûter; **how much** *or* **what does the dress ~?** combien coûte *or* vaut la robe?; **how much** *or* **what will it ~ to have it repaired?** combien est-ce que cela coûtera de le faire réparer?; **what does it ~ to get in?** quel est le prix d'entrée?; **it ~ him a lot of money** cela lui a coûté cher; **it ~s him £22 a week** cela lui revient à *or* lui coûte 22 livres par semaine, il en a pour 22 livres par semaine; **it ~s too much** cela coûte trop cher, c'est trop cher; **it ~s the earth*** cela coûte les yeux de la tête; **it ~ (him) an arm and a leg*** ça lui a coûté les yeux de la tête; **I know what it ~ him to apologize** je sais ce qu'il lui en a coûté de s'excuser; **it ~ her dear/her job** cela lui a coûté cher/son emploi; **it ~ him a great effort** cela lui a coûté *or* demandé un gros effort; **it ~ him a lot of trouble** cela lui a causé beaucoup d'ennuis; **it will ~ you your life** il vous en coûtera la vie; **it'll *or* that'll ~ you!*** tu vas le sentir passer!; **it will ~**

you a present! vous en serez quitte pour lui (*or me etc*) faire un cadeau!; **politeness ~s very little** il ne coûte rien d'être poli; (*fig*) **what it may ◊ whatever it ~s** coûte que coûte ⓑ (*pret, ptp* **costed**) (*Comm = set price for*) [+ *article*] établir le prix de revient de; [+ *piece of work*] évaluer le coût de; **the job was ~ed at £2,000** le devis pour (l'exécution de) ces travaux s'est monté à 2 000 livres

② N coût *m*; ~ **insurance and freight** coût *m* assurance *f* et fret *m*; **the ~ of these apples** le coût *or* le prix de ces pommes; (*Fin*) **to cut the ~ of loans** réduire le loyer de l'argent; **to bear the ~ of ...** (*lit*) faire face aux frais *mpl* *or* aux dépenses *fpl* de ...; (*fig*) faire les frais de ...; (*lit, fig*) **at great ~** à grands frais; **at little ~** à peu de frais; (*fig*) **at little ~ to himself** sans que cela lui coûte (*subj*) beaucoup; **at ~ (price)** au prix coûtant; **at the ~ of his life/health** au prix de sa vie/santé; (*fig*) **to my ~** à mes dépens; (*Jur*) ~**s** dépens *mpl*, frais *mpl* judiciaires; (*Jur*) **to be ordered to pay ~s** être condamné aux dépens; (*fig*) **at all ~s** ◊ **at any ~** coûte que coûte, à tout prix → **count¹**

③ COMP ► **cost accountant** N analyste *mf* de coûts ► **cost accounting** N (*NonC*) comptabilité *f* analytique *or* d'exploitation ► **cost analysis** N analyse *f* des coûts ► **cost-benefit analysis** N analyse *f* coûts-bénéfices ► **cost centre** N centre *m* de coût(s) ► **cost conscious** ADJ qui fait attention à ses dépenses ► **cost control** N contrôle *m* des dépenses ► **cost-cutting** N compression *f* *or* réduction *f* des coûts; ~-**cutting plan** *etc* plan *m etc* de réduction des coûts ► **cost-effective** ADJ rentable, d'un bon rapport coût-performance *or* coût-efficacité *f*, rapport *m* coût-performance *or* coût-efficacité N rentabilité *f* ► **cost estimate** N devis *m*, estimation *f* des coûts ► **cost-in-use** N coûts *mpl* d'utilisation ► **cost of living** N coût *m* de la vie, ~-**of-living adjustment** augmentation *f* indexée sur le coût de la vie; ~-**of-living allowance** indemnité *f* de vie chère; ~-**of-living increase** rattrapage *m* pour cherté de la vie; ~-**of-living index** index *m* du coût de la vie ► **cost-plus** N prix *m* de revient majoré du pourcentage contractuel; **on a ~-plus basis** à des coûts majorés ► **cost price** N (*Brit*) prix *m* coûtant *or* de revient

► **cost out** VT SEP [+ *project*] évaluer le coût de

co-star ['kəʊstɑːʳ] (*Cine, Theat*) ① N partenaire *mf* ② VI partager l'affiche (**with** avec); **"~-ring X"** « avec X »

Costa Rica ['kɒstə'riːkə] N le Costa Rica

Costa Rican ['kɒstə'riːkən] ① ADJ costaricain(e), costaricien ② N Costaricain(ne) *m(f)*, Costaricien(ne) *m(f)*

coster ['kɒstəʳ] N, **costermonger** ['kɒstə,mʌŋgəʳ] N (*Brit*) marchand(e) *m(f)* des quatre saisons

costing ['kɒstɪŋ] N estimation *f* du prix de revient

costive ['kɒstɪv] ADJ constipé

costliness ['kɒstlɪnɪs] N (= *value*) (grande) valeur *f*; (= *high price*) cherté *f*

costly ['kɒstlɪ] ADJ (*gen*) coûteux; [*furs, jewels*] de grande valeur, précieux; **a ~ business** une affaire coûteuse

costume ['kɒstjuːm] ① N ⓐ (*gen*) costume *m*; **national ~** costume *m* national; (= *fancy dress*) **in ~** déguisé ⓑ (†= *lady's suit*) tailleur *m* ② COMP ► **costume ball** N bal *m* masqué ► **costume drama** N (= *film/play etc*) pièce *f*/ film *m etc* en costume d'époque; (*genre: Theat/Cine etc*) théâtre *m*/cinéma *m* en costume d'époque ► **costume jewellery** N bijoux *mpl* (de) fantaisie ► **costume piece** N = **costume drama;**, **costume play** ♦ N pièce *f* en costume d'époque

costumier [kɒs'tjuːmɪəʳ], **costumer** (*esp US*) [kɒs'tjuːməʳ] N costumier *m*, -ière *f*

cosy, cozy (*US*) ['kəʊzɪ] ① ADJ ⓐ (= *warm*) [*flat, home, room*] douillet, cosy; [*restaurant*] confortable; **nights in front of a ~ fire** des soirées agréables au coin du feu; **to be ~** [*person*] être bien; **in here** on est bien ici ⓑ (= *friendly*) [*atmosphere, evening, chat, dinner*] intime ⓒ (*pej = convenient*) [*arrangement, deal, relationship*] commode ② N (= *tea cosy*) couvre-théière *m*; (= *egg cosy*) couvre-œuf *m* ③ **to ~ up to sb** caresser qn dans le sens du poil*

cot [kɒt] N (*Brit: child's*) lit *m* d'enfant, petit lit *m*; (*US = folding bed*) lit *m* de camp; (*Brit*) ~-**death** mort *f* subite du nourrisson

Côte d'Ivoire [ˌkəʊtdɪ'vwɑːr] N (**the**) ~ la Côte-d'Ivoire

coterie ['kəʊtərɪ] N coterie *f*, cénacle *m*

cotillion [kə'tɪljən] N cotillon *m*, quadrille *m*

cottage ['kɒtɪdʒ] ① N petite maison *f* (à la campagne), cottage *m*; (*thatched*) chaumière *f*; (*holiday home*) villa *f* ② COMP ► **cottage cheese** N fromage *m* blanc (égoutté), cottage *m* (cheese) ► **cottage flat** N (*Brit*) appartement dans une maison en regroupant quatre en copropriété ► **cottage hospital** N (*Brit*) petit hôpital ► **cottage industry** N (*working at home*) industrie *f* familiale; (= *informally organized industry*) industrie *f* artisanale ► **cottage loaf** N (*Brit*) miche *f* de pain ► **cottage pie** N (*Brit*) ≈ hachis *m* Parmentier

cottager ['kɒtɪdʒəʳ] N (*Brit*) paysan(ne) *m(f)*; (*US*) propriétaire *mf* de maison de vacances

cottaging* ['kɒtɪdʒɪŋ] N (*Brit*) rencontres homosexuelles dans des toilettes publiques

cottar, cotter ['kɒtəʳ] N (*Scot*) paysan(ne) *m(f)*

cotton ['kɒtn] ① N (*NonC*) (*Bot, Tex*) coton *m*; (*Brit = sewing thread*) fil *m* (de coton) → **absorbent, gin**

② COMP [*shirt, dress*] de coton ► **cotton batting** N (*US*) ouate *f* ► **the cotton belt** N (*Agr*) le Sud cotonnier (*Alabama, Géorgie, Mississippi*) ► **cotton bud** N (*Brit*) cotontige® *m* ► **cotton cake** N tourteau *m* de coton ► **cotton candy** N (*US*) barbe *f* à papa ► **cotton goods** NPL cotonnades *fpl* ► **cotton grass** N linaigrette *f*, lin *m* des marais ► **cotton industry** N industrie *f* cotonnière *or* du coton ► **cotton lace** N dentelle *f* de coton ► **cotton mill** N filature *f* de coton ► **cotton-picking** ADJ (*US pej*) sale* (*before n*), sacré (*before n*) ► **the Cotton State** N l'Alabama *m* ► **cotton waste** N déchets *mpl* de coton, coton *m* d'essuyage ► **cotton wool** N (*Brit*) ouate *f*; absorbent ~ **wool** ouate *f or* coton *m* hydrophile; (*fig*) **to bring up a child in ~ wool** élever un enfant dans du coton; **my legs felt like ~ wool*** j'avais les jambes en coton ► **cotton yarn** N fil *m* de coton

► **cotton on*** VI (*Brit*) piger*; **to ~ on to sth** piger* qch, saisir qch

► **cotton to*** VT FUS [+ *person*] avoir à la bonne*; [+ *plan, suggestion*] apprécier, approuver; **I don't ~ to it much** je ne suis pas tellement pour*, ça ne me botte pas tellement*

cottonseed oil ['kɒtnsiːd'ɔɪl] N huile *f* de coton

cottontail ['kɒtnteɪl] N (*US*) lapin *m*

cottonwood ['kɒtnwʊd] N (*US*) peuplier *m* de Virginie

cotyledon [ˌkɒtɪ'liːdən] N cotylédon *m*

couch [kaʊtʃ] ① N ⓐ (= *settee*) canapé *m*, divan *m*, sofa *m*; [*of doctor*] lit *m*; [*of psychoanalyst*] divan *m*; (*liter = bed*) couche *f* (*liter*); (*US fig*) **to be on the ~*** être en analyse ⓑ (*Bot*) chiendent *m* ② VT formuler, exprimer; **request ~ed in insolent language** requête *f* formulée *or* exprimée en des termes insolents; **request ~ed in the following terms** demande *f* ainsi rédigée ③ VI [*animal*] (= *lie* *asleep*) être allongé *or* couché; (= *ready to spring*) s'embusquer [4] COMP ► **couch grass** N chiendent *m* ► **couch potato*** N mollasson *m* (*qui passe son temps devant la télé*)

couchette [kuːˈʃet] N (*Rail etc*) couchette *f*

cougar [ˈkuːgəʳ] N couguar *m*

cough [kɒf] [1] N toux *f*; **he has a bad ~** il a une mauvaise toux, il tousse beaucoup; **he has a bit of a ~** il tousse un peu; **to give a warning ~** tousser en guise d'avertissement [2] VI tousser [3] COMP ► **cough drop** N pastille *f* pour la toux ► **cough mixture** N sirop *m* pour la toux, (sirop *m*) antitussif *m* ► **cough sweet** N pastille *f* pour la toux ► **cough syrup** N = cough mixture

►**cough up** VT SEP [a] (*lit*) expectorer, cracher en toussant [b] (** fig*) [+ *money*] cracher*

coughing [ˈkɒfɪŋ] N toux *f*; **to hear ~** entendre tousser; **~ fit** quinte *f* de toux

▼**could** [kʊd] VB *pt, cond of* **can¹**

couldn't [ˈkʊdnt] = could not; → **can¹**

could've [ˈkʊdəv] = could have; → **can¹**

coulee [ˈkuːleɪ] N (*US*) ravine *f*

couloir [ˈkuːlwaːʳ] N (*Climbing*) couloir *m*

coulomb [ˈkuːlɒm] N coulomb *m*

council [ˈkaʊnsl] [1] N conseil *m*, assemblée *f*; **~ of war** conseil *m* de guerre; **city** *or* **town ~** conseil *m* municipal; **they decided in ~ that ...** l'assemblée a décidé que ...; **the Security Council of the UN** le conseil de Sécurité des Nations Unies → **lord, parish, privy** [2] COMP ► **council chamber** N (*Brit*) salle *f* du conseil municipal ► **council estate** N (*Brit*) cité *f* (de logements sociaux *or* de HLM) ► **council flat** N (*Brit*) appartement *m/* maison *f* loué(e) à la municipalité, ≈ HLM *m or f* ► **council house** N (*Brit*) maison *f* louée à la municipalité, ≈ HLM *m or f* ► **council housing** N (*Brit*) logements *mpl* sociaux ► **council housing estate** N = council estate ► **the Council of Economic Advisors** N (*US*) les Conseillers *mpl* économiques (du Président) ► **Council of Europe** N Conseil *m* de l'Europe ► **Council of Ministers** (*Pol*) Conseil *m* des ministres ► **council school** N (*Brit*) école *f* publique ► **council tax** N (*Brit*) impôts *mpl* locaux ► **council tenant** N (*Brit*) locataire *mf* d'un logement social

councillor [ˈkaʊnslər] N conseiller *m*, -ère *f*, membre *m* d'un conseil; (*form of address*) **Councillor X** Monsieur le conseiller municipal X, Madame la conseillère municipale X → **privy, town**

councilman [ˈkaʊnslmæn] N (*pl* -men) (*US*) conseiller *m*

councilwoman [ˈkaʊnslwʊmən] N (*pl* -women) (*US*) conseillère *f*

counsel [ˈkaʊnsl] [1] N [a] (*NonC*) conseil *m*; **to take ~ with sb** prendre conseil de qn, consulter qn; **to keep one's own ~** garder ses intentions (*or ses projets or ses opinions*) pour soi [b] (*pl inv: Jur*) avocat(e) *m(f)*; (*Brit*) ► **for the defence** (avocat *m* de la) défense *f*; (*Brit*) **~ for the prosecution** avocat *m* du ministère public; **King's** *or* **Queen's Counsel** avocat *m* de la couronne (*qui peut néanmoins plaider pour des particuliers*) → **defending, prosecuting** [2] VT (*frm, liter*) recommander, conseiller (**sb to do** à qn de faire); **to ~ caution** recommander *or* conseiller la prudence

counselling, counseling (*US*) [ˈkaʊnsəlɪŋ] [1] N (*gen = advice*) conseils *mpl*; (*Psych, Social Work*) assistance *f* socio-psychologique; (*Brit Scol*) aide *f* psychopédagogique [2] COMP ► **counseling service** N (*US Univ*) service *m* d'orientation et d'assistance universitaire

counsellor, counselor (*US*) [ˈkaʊnsələr] [a] (*gen*) conseiller *m*, -ère *f*; (*Psych, Social Work*) conseiller *m*, -ère *f* socio-psychologique; (*US Educ*) conseiller *m*

d'orientation [b] (*Ir, US: also* **~-at-law**) avocat *m*

▼**count¹** [kaʊnt] [1] N [a] compte *m*; [*of votes at election*] dépouillement *m*; **to make a ~** faire un compte; **at the last ~** (*gen*) la dernière fois qu'on a compté; (*Admin*) au dernier recensement; (*Boxing*) **to be out for the ~ ◊ to take the ~** être (mis) knock-out, aller au tapis pour le compte; (*fig*) **to be out for the ~*** (= *unconscious*) être KO*, avoir son compte*; (= *asleep*) avoir son compte*; **I'll come and look for you after a ~ of ten** je compte jusqu'à dix et je viens te chercher; **to keep (a) ~ of ...** tenir le compte de ...; (*fig*) **to take no ~ of ...** ne pas tenir compte de ...; **every time you interrupt you make me lose ~** chaque fois que tu m'interromps je perds le fil; **I've lost ~** je ne sais plus où j'en suis; **I've lost ~ of the number of times I've told you** je ne sais plus combien de fois je te l'ai dit; **he lost ~ of the tickets he had sold** il ne savait plus combien de billets il avait vendus [b] (*Jur*) chef *m* d'accusation; **guilty on three ~s** reconnu coupable pour trois chefs d'accusation

[2] VT [a] (= *add up*) compter; [+ *inhabitants, injured, causes*] dénombrer, compter; **to ~ the eggs in the basket** compter les œufs dans le panier; (*Admin, Pol*) **to ~ the votes** dépouiller le scrutin ■ (*PROV*) **don't ~ your chickens (before they're hatched)** il ne faut pas vendre la peau de l'ours (avant de l'avoir tué) (*PROV*); (*US fig*) **to ~ noses*** compter les présents; (*fig*) **to ~ sheep** compter les moutons; **to ~ the cost** (*lit*) calculer la dépense; (*fig*) faire le bilan; (*lit, fig*) **without ~ing the cost** sans compter; **(you must) ~ your blessings** estimez-vous heureux → **stand** [b] (= *include*) compter; **ten people not ~ing the children** dix personnes sans compter les enfants; **three more ~ing Charles** trois de plus, en comptant Charles; **to ~ sb among one's friends** compter qn parmi ses amis; **don't ~ his youth against him** ne lui faites pas grief de sa jeunesse; **will you ~ it against me if I refuse?** m'en tiendrez-vous rigueur *or* m'en voudrez-vous si je refuse? [c] (= *consider*) tenir, estimer; **to ~ sb as dead** tenir qn pour mort; **we must ~ ourselves fortunate** *or* **lucky (men)** nous devons nous estimer heureux; **I ~ it an honour to (be able to) help you** je m'estime honoré de pouvoir vous aider

[3] VI [a] compter; **can he ~?** est-ce qu'il sait compter?; **~ing from tonight** à compter de ce soir; **~ing from the left** à partir de la gauche [b] (= *be considered*) compter; **you ~ among my best friends** vous comptez parmi *or* au nombre de mes meilleurs amis; **two children ~ as one adult** deux enfants comptent pour un adulte; **that doesn't ~** cela ne compte pas [c] (= *have importance*) compter; **every minute ~s** chaque minute compte; **to ~ against sb** desservir qn; **his lack of experience ~s against him** son inexpérience le dessert *or* joue contre lui; **that ~s for nothing** cela ne compte pas, cela compte pour du beurre*; **he ~s for a lot in that firm** il joue un rôle important dans cette compagnie; **a university degree ~s for very little nowadays** de nos jours un diplôme universitaire n'a pas beaucoup de valeur *or* ne pèse pas lourd*

[4] COMP ► **count noun** N nom *m* comptable

►**count down** [1] VI faire le compte à rebours [2] **~down** N → **countdown**

►**count in*** VT SEP compter; **to ~ sb in on a plan** compter qn dans un projet; **you can ~ me in!** je suis de la partie!

►**count on** VT FUS = count upon

►**count out** VT SEP [a] (*Boxing*) **to be ~ed out** être mis knock-out, être envoyé *or* aller au tapis pour le compte [b] [+ *money*] compter pièce par pièce; [+ *small objects*] compter, dé-

nombrer [c] **you can ~ me out of* this business** ne comptez pas sur moi dans cette affaire [d] (*Parl etc*) **to ~ out a meeting** ajourner une séance (*le quorum n'étant pas atteint*); (*Brit*) **to ~ out the House** ajourner la séance (*du Parlement*)

►**count towards** VT FUS **these contributions will ~ towards your pension** ces cotisations compteront pour *or* seront prises en compte *or* en considération pour votre retraite

►**count up** VT SEP compter

►**count upon** VT FUS compter (sur); **I'm ~ing upon you** je compte sur vous; **to ~ upon doing** compter faire

count² [kaʊnt] N (= *nobleman*) comte *m*

countability [ˌkaʊntəˈbɪlɪtɪ] N (*Ling* = *fact of being countable*) fait *m* d'être comptable; **the problem of ~** le problème de savoir si un (*or* le *etc*) substantif est comptable ou non

countable [ˈkaʊntəbl] ADJ (*Gram*) **~ noun** nom *m* comptable

countdown [ˈkaʊntdaʊn] N compte *m* à rebours

countenance [ˈkaʊntɪnəns] [1] N [a] (*liter* = *face*) (expression *f* du) visage *m*, figure *f*; (= *expression*) mine *f*; (= *composure*) contenance *f*; **out of ~** décontenancé; **to keep one's ~** faire bonne contenance, ne pas se laisser décontenancer [b] (*frm* = *approval*) **to give ~ to** [+ *person*] encourager; [+ *plan*] favoriser; [+ *rumour, piece of news*] accréditer [2] VT approuver, admettre (**sth** qch, **sb's doing** que qn fasse)

counter¹ [ˈkaʊntər] [1] N [a] (*in shop, canteen*) comptoir *m*; (= *position: in bank, post office etc*) guichet *m*; (*in pub*) comptoir *m*, zinc* *m*; **the girl behind the ~** (*in shop*) la vendeuse; (*in pub*) la serveuse; (*St Ex*) **over the ~** hors cote; (*Pharm*) **available over the ~** vendu sans ordonnance; **to buy/sell medicines over the ~** acheter/vendre des médicaments sans ordonnance → **over-the-counter; to buy/sell sth under the ~** acheter/vendre qch sous le manteau → **under-the-counter** [b] (= *disc*) jeton *m* [c] (*Tech*) compteur *m* → **Geiger counter**

[2] COMP ► **counter hand** N (*in shop*) vendeur *m*, -euse *f*; (*in snack bar*) serveur *m*, -euse *f* ► **counter staff** N (*NonC*) (*in bank*) caissiers *mpl*, -ières *fpl*, guichetiers *mpl*; (*in shop*) vendeurs *mpl*, -euses *fpl*

counter² [ˈkaʊntər] [1] ADV **~ to sb's wishes** à l'encontre des *or* contrairement aux souhaits de qn; **~ to sb's orders** contrairement aux ordres de qn; **to run ~ to sth** aller à l'encontre de qch [2] ADJ **~ to sth** contraire à qch [3] N **to be a ~ to sth** contrebalancer qch [4] VT [+ *remark*] répliquer à (**by, with** par); [+ *decision, order*] aller à l'encontre de, s'opposer à; [+ *plan*] contrecarrer, contrarier; [+ *blow*] parer [5] VI (*fig*) riposter, répliquer; (*Boxing, Fencing etc*) contrer; **he ~ed with a right** il a contré d'une droite

counter... [ˈkaʊntər] PREF contre...

counteract [ˌkaʊntərˈækt] VT neutraliser, contrebalancer

counter-argument [ˈkaʊntərˌɑːgjʊmənt] N contre-argument *m*

counterattack [ˈkaʊntərəˌtæk] (*Mil, fig*) [1] N contre-attaque *f* [2] VTI contre-attaquer

counterattraction [ˈkaʊntərəˌtrækʃən] N attraction *f* concurrente, spectacle *m* rival

counterbalance [ˈkaʊntəˌbæləns] [1] N contrepoids *m* [2] VT contrebalancer, faire contrepoids à

counterbid [ˈkaʊntəˌbɪd] N surenchère *f*, suroffre *f*

counterblast [ˈkaʊntəblɑːst] N réfutation *f* or démenti *m* énergique

countercharge [ˈkaʊntətʃɑːdʒ] N (*Jur*) contre-accusation *f*

countercheck ['kaʊntətʃek] 1 N deuxième contrôle m or vérification f 2 VT revérifier

counterclaim ['kaʊntəkleɪm] N (Jur) demande f reconventionnelle ; **to bring a ~** introduire une demande reconventionnelle

counterclockwise [,kaʊntə'klɒk,waɪz] ADV, ADJ (US) dans le sens inverse des aiguilles d'une montre

counterculture ['kaʊntə,kʌltʃə] N contre-culture f

counterespionage [,kaʊntər'espɪə,nɑːʒ] N contre-espionnage m

counterexample ['kaʊntərɪg,zɑːmpəl] N contre-exemple m

counterfeit ['kaʊntəfiːt] 1 ADJ faux (fausse f) ; **~ coin/money** fausse pièce f/monnaie f 2 N faux m, contrefaçon f 3 VT [+ banknote, signature] contrefaire ; **to ~ money** fabriquer de la fausse monnaie

counterfoil ['kaʊntəfɔɪl] N (Brit) [of cheque etc] talon m, souche f

counter-gambit ['kaʊntəgæmbɪt] N contre-gambit m

counter-inflationary [,kaʊntərɪn'fleɪʃənrɪ] ADJ (Brit Econ) anti-inflationniste

counterinsurgency [,kaʊntərɪn'sɜːdʒənsɪ] N contre-insurrection f

counterinsurgent [,kaʊntərɪn'sɜːdʒənt] N contre-insurgé(e) m(f)

counterintelligence [,kaʊntərɪn'telɪdʒəns] N contre-espionnage m

counterintuitive [,kaʊntərɪn'tjuːɪtɪv] ADJ contraire à l'intuition

counterirritant [,kaʊntər'ɪrɪtənt] N (Med) révulsif m

counterman ['kaʊntəmæn] N (pl **-men**) (US) serveur m

countermand ['kaʊntəmɑːnd] VT [+ order] annuler ; **unless ~ed** sauf contrordre

countermeasure ['kaʊntəmeʒə] N contre-mesure f

countermove ['kaʊntəmuːv] N (Mil) contre-attaque f, riposte f

counteroffensive ['kaʊntərəfensɪv] N (Mil) contre-offensive f

counteroffer ['kaʊntər,ɒfə] N contre-offre f, contre-proposition f

counter-order ['kaʊntə,rɔːdə] N contrordre m

counterpane ['kaʊntəpeɪn] N dessus-de-lit m inv, couvre-lit m ; (quilted) courtepointe f

counterpart ['kaʊntəpɑːt] N [of document etc] (= duplicate) double m, contrepartie f ; (= equivalent) équivalent m ; [of person] homologue mf

counterplea ['kaʊntəpliː] N réplique f

counterpoint ['kaʊntəpɔɪnt] 1 N (Mus) contrepoint m 2 VT (fig) contraster avec

counterpoise ['kaʊntəpɔɪz] 1 N (= weight, force) contrepoids m ; (= equilibrium) équilibre m ; **in ~** en équilibre 2 VT contrebalancer, faire contrepoids à

counterproductive [,kaʊntəprə'dʌktɪv] ADJ contre-productif

counter-proposal [,kaʊntəprə'pəʊzəl] N contre-proposition f

Counter-Reformation [,kaʊntə,refə'meɪʃən] N (Hist) Contre-Réforme f

counter-revolution [,kaʊntə,revə'luːʃən] N contre-révolution f

counter-revolutionary [,kaʊntə,revə'luːʃənrɪ] ADJ, N contre-révolutionnaire mf

counter-shot ['kaʊntəʃɒt] N (Cine) contre-champ m

countersign ['kaʊntəsaɪn] 1 VT contresigner 2 N mot de passe or d'ordre

countersink ['kaʊntəsɪŋk] VT [+ hole] fraiser ; [+ screw] noyer

counter-stroke ['kaʊntəstrəʊk] N (lit, fig) retour m

countersunk [,kaʊntəsʌŋk] ADJ fraisé

countertenor [,kaʊntə'tenə] N (Mus) (= singer) haute-contre m ; (= voice) haute-contre f

counter-turn ['kaʊntətɜːn] N (Ski) contre-virage m

countervailing ['kaʊntəveɪlɪŋ] ADJ (Fin) **~ duties** droits mpl compensatoires

counterweight ['kaʊntəweɪt] N contrepoids m

countess ['kaʊntɪs] N comtesse f

counting ['kaʊntɪŋ] 1 N (= school subject) calcul m 2 COMP ► **counting house**† N (Brit) salle f or immeuble m des comptables

countless ['kaʊntlɪs] ADJ innombrable, sans nombre ; **on ~ occasions** en d'innombrables occasions ; **~ millions of ...** des millions et des millions de ...

countrified ['kʌntrɪfaɪd] ADJ rustique, campagnard

country ['kʌntrɪ] 1 N a pays m ; **the different countries of the world** les divers pays mpl du monde ; **the ~ wants peace** le pays désire la paix ; (Brit Pol) **to go to the ~** appeler le pays aux urnes b (= native land) patrie f, pays m ; **to die for one's ~** mourir pour son pays → **old** c (NonC: as opposed to town) campagne f ; **in the ~** à la campagne ; **the ~ round the town** les environs mpl de la ville ; **the surrounding ~** la campagne environnante ; **to live off the ~** (gen) vivre de la terre ; (Mil) vivre sur le pays d (NonC = region) pays m, région f ; **there is some lovely ~ to the north** il y a de beaux paysages mpl dans le nord ; **this is good fishing ~** c'est une bonne région pour la pêche ; **this is unknown ~ to me** (lit) je ne connais pas la région ; (fig) je suis en terrain inconnu → **open** 2 COMP [lifestyle] campagnard, de (la) campagne ► **country-and-western** N (Mus) musique f country (and western) ► **country-born** ADJ né à la campagne ► **country-bred** ADJ élevé à la campagne ► **country bumpkin** N (pej) péquenaud(e) m(f) (pej), cul-terreux* m (pej) ► **country club** N club m de loisirs (à la campagne) ► **the country code** N (Brit) les us mpl et coutumes fpl de la campagne ► **country cottage** N cottage m, petite maison f (à la campagne) ; [of weekenders] maison f de campagne ► **country cousin** N (fig) cousin(e) m(f) de province ► **country dance** N (NonC), **country dancing** N danse f folklorique ; **to go ~ dancing** danser (des danses folkloriques) ► **country dweller** N campagnard(e) m(f), habitant(e) m(f) de la campagne ► **country folk** NPL gens mpl de la campagne, campagnards mpl ► **country gentleman** N (pl **country gentlemen**) gentilhomme m campagnard ► **country house** N manoir m, (petit) château m ► **country life** N vie f à la campagne, vie f campagnarde ► **country mile*** N (US) **to miss sth by a ~ mile** manquer qch de beaucoup ► **country music** N (NonC) (musique f) country m ► **country park** N (Brit) parc m naturel ► **country people** N (NonC) campagnards mpl, gens mpl de la campagne ► **country road** N petite route f (de campagne) ► **country seat** N manoir m, gentilhommière f

countryman ['kʌntrɪmæn] N (pl **-men**) (also **fellow ~**) compatriote m, concitoyen m ; (opposed to town dweller) habitant m de la campagne, campagnard m

countryside ['kʌntrɪsaɪd] 1 N **the ~** la campagne 2 COMP ► **the Countryside Commission** N (Brit) organisme chargé de la protection du milieu rural

countrywide ['kʌntrɪwaɪd] ADJ à l'échelle nationale

countrywoman ['kʌntrɪwʊmən] N (pl **-women**) (also **fellow ~**) compatriote f, concitoyenne f ; (opposed to town dweller) habitante f de la campagne, campagnarde f

county ['kaʊntɪ] 1 N a comté m (division administrative), ≈ département m → **home** b (= people) habitants mpl d'un comté ; (Brit) **the ~** (= nobility etc) l'aristocratie f terrienne (du comté) 2 ADJ (Brit) [voice, accent] aristocratique ; **he's very ~** il est or fait très aristocratie terrienne 3 COMP ► **county agent** N (US) ingénieur-agronome m ► **county clerk** N (US Admin) ≈ sous-préfet m ► **county council** N (in Brit: formerly) ≈ conseil m régional ► **county court** N ≈ tribunal m de grande instance ► **county cricket** N (Brit) le cricket disputé entre les comtés ► **county family** N (Brit) vieille famille f ► **county jail** N (US) → **county prison** ► **county police** N (US) police f régionale, ≈ gendarmerie f ► **county prison** N centrale f ► **county seat** N (US) = county town ► **county town** N chef-lieu m

coup [kuː] N (beau) coup m (fig) ; (Pol) coup m d'Etat

coupé ['kuːpeɪ] N (= car) coupé m

couple ['kʌpl] 1 N couple m ; **the young (married) ~** les jeunes mariés, le jeune couple ; **a ~ of deux** ; **I've seen a ~ of times** je l'ai vu deux ou trois fois ; **I did it in a ~ of hours** je l'ai fait en deux heures environ ; **we had a ~* in the bar** nous avons pris un verre ou deux au bar ; **when he's had a ~* he begins to sing** après un ou deux verres, il se met à chanter → **first** 2 VT a (also **~ up**) [+ railway carriages] atteler, (ac)coupler ; [+ ideas, names] associer b **~d with** ajouté à ; **~d with the fact that ...** venant en plus du fait que ... 3 VI (= mate) s'accoupler

coupledom ['kʌpldəm] N la vie de couple

coupler ['kʌplə] N (Comput) coupleur m ; (US Rail) attelage m ; (Comput) **acoustic ~** coupleur m acoustique

couplet ['kʌplɪt] N distique m

coupling ['kʌplɪŋ] N a (NonC = combination) association f b (= device) (Rail) attelage m ; (Elec) couplage m c (= sexual intercourse) accouplement m

coupon ['kuːpɒn] N (= money-off voucher) bon m de réduction ; (= form in newspaper, magazine) bulletin-réponse m ; (for rationed product) ticket m or carte f de rationnement ; [of cigarette packets etc] bon m, vignette f → **international**

courage ['kʌrɪdʒ] N courage m ; **I haven't the ~ to refuse** je n'ai pas le courage de refuser ; **to take/lose ~** prendre/perdre courage ; **to take ~ from sth** être encouragé par qch ; **to have the ~ of one's convictions** avoir le courage de ses opinions ; **to take one's ~ in both hands** prendre son courage à deux mains → **Dutch**, **pluck up**

courageous [kə'reɪdʒəs] ADJ courageux

courageously [kə'reɪdʒəslɪ] ADV courageusement

courgette [kʊə'ʒet] N (Brit) courgette f

courier ['kʊrɪə] N (= messenger) (gen) messager m ; (Mil) courrier m ; [of urgent mail] coursier m, -ière f ; (= tourist guide) guide m, cicérone m

course [kɔːs] 1 N a **of ~** bien sûr, bien entendu ; **did he do it? — of ~!/of ~ not!** est-ce qu'il l'a fait ? — bien sûr or bien entendu !/bien sûr que non ! ; **may I take it? — of ~!/of ~ not!** est-ce que je peux le prendre ? — mais oui !/certainement pas ! ; **do you love him? — of ~ I do!/of ~ I don't!** tu l'aimes ? — bien sûr (que je l'aime) !/bien sûr que non ! ; **of ~ I won't do it!** je ne vais pas faire ça, bien sûr ! ; **he denied it ; nobody believed him of ~** il l'a nié ; évidemment, personne ne l'a cru ; **you'll come**

on Saturday of ~ vous viendrez samedi bien sûr
[b] (= *duration, process*) [*of life, events, time, disease*] cours *m*; **in the normal/ordinary** ~ **of things** *or* **events** en temps normal/ordinaire; **in the** ~ **of the conversation** au cours de la conversation; **a house in (the)** ~ **of construction** une maison en cours de construction; **it is in (the)** ~ **of being investigated** c'est en cours d'investigation; **in the** ~ **of centuries** au cours des siècles; **in the** ~ **of the next few months** au cours des prochains mois; **in the** ~ **of time** avec le temps; **in the** ~ **of the week** dans le courant de la semaine → **due, matter**
[c] (= *direction, way, route*) [*of river, war*] cours *m*; [*of ship*] route *f*; [*of planet*] trajectoire *f*, orbite *f*; **to keep** *or* **hold (one's)** ~ poursuivre sa route; (*Naut*) **to hold (one's)** ~ garder le cap; **on** ~ [*rocket*] sur la bonne trajectoire; **on** ~ **for** (*lit*) en route pour; (*fig*) sur la voie de; (*Naut*) **to set** ~ **for** mettre le cap sur; (*Naut, fig*) **to change** ~ changer de cap; **to change the** ~ **of history** changer le cours de l'histoire; **to get back on** ~ [*ship*] reprendre son cap; **to go off** ~ (*Naut, Aviat, Space*) dévier de son cap; (*fig*) faire fausse route; **to take a certain** ~ **of action** adopter une certaine ligne de conduite; **we have no other** ~ **but to ...** nous n'avons d'autre moyen que de ...; **there are several** ~**s open to us** plusieurs possibilités s'offrent à nous; **what** ~ **do you suggest?** quel parti (nous) conseillez-vous de prendre?; **let him take his own** ~ laissez-le agir à sa guise *or* comme bon lui semble; **the best** ~ **would be to leave at once** la meilleure chose *or* le mieux à faire serait de partir immédiatement; **to let sth take its** ~ laisser qch suivre son cours; **to let events run their** ~ laisser les événements suivre leur cours; **the affair/the illness has run its** ~ l'affaire/la maladie a suivi son cours → **middle**
[d] (*Scol, Univ*) cours *m*; **to go to a French** ~ suivre un cours *or* des cours de français; **a** ~ **in novel writing** ◊ **a novel-writing** ~ un cours sur l'écriture romanesque; **the people on the** ~ **are really nice** les gens du cours sont vraiment bien; **he gave a** ~ **of lectures on Proust** il a donné une série de conférences sur Proust; **I have bought part two of the German** ~ j'ai acheté la deuxième partie de la méthode *or* du cours d'allemand → **correspondence, foundation, refresher, sandwich**
[e] (*Sport*) (*gen*) parcours *m*; (*Golf etc*) terrain *m* → **assault, golf, racecourse, stay¹**
[f] [*of meal*] plat *m*; **first** ~ entrée *f*; **three-/four-** ~ **meal** repas *m* de trois/quatre plats → **main**
[g] (*Med*) [*of injections*] série *f*; ~ **of pills** traitement *m* à base de comprimés; ~ **of treatment** traitement *m*
[h] (*Constr*) assise *f* (*de briques etc*) → **damp**
[2] **courses** NPL (*Naut*) basses voiles *fpl*
[3] VI [a] [*water*] couler à flots; **tears** ~**d down her cheeks** les larmes ruisselaient sur ses joues; **it sent the blood coursing through his veins** cela lui fouetta le sang
[b] (*Sport*) chasser (le lièvre)
[4] VT (*Sport*) [+ *hare*] courir, chasser
[5] COMP ► **course of study** N (*Scol*) programme *m* scolaire; (*Univ*) cursus *m* universitaire ► **course work** N (*NonC: Univ*) contrôle *m* continu

coursebook ['kɔːsbʊk] N (*Scol*) manuel *m*

courser ['kɔːsəʳ] N (= *person*) chasseur *m* (*gén de lièvres*); (= *dog*) chien *m* courant; (*liter = horse*) coursier *m* (*liter*)

coursing ['kɔːsɪŋ] N (*Sport*) chasse *f* au lièvre

court [kɔːt] [1] N [a] (*Jur*) cour *f*, tribunal *m*; **to settle a case out of** ~ arranger une affaire à l'amiable; **to rule sth out of** ~ déclarer qch inadmissible; **to take sb to** ~ **over** *or* **about sth** poursuivre qn en justice pour qch, intenter un procès contre qn pour qch; **he**

was brought before the ~**s several times** il est passé plusieurs fois en jugement; **to clear the** ~ faire évacuer la salle; (*esp US fig*) **to give sb a day in** ~* donner à qn l'occasion de s'expliquer *or* de se faire entendre → **high, law**
[b] [*of monarch*] cour *f* (royale); **the Court of St James** la cour de Saint-James; **to be at** ~ (*for short time*) être à la cour; (*for long time*) faire partie de la cour; (*fig*) **to hold** ~ être entouré de sa cour
[c] **to pay** ~ **to a woman**† faire sa *or* la cour à une femme
[d] (*Tennis*) court *m*; (*Basketball*) terrain *m*; (*Tennis*) **they've been on** ~ **for two hours** cela fait deux heures qu'ils sont sur le court *or* qu'ils jouent
[e] (*also* ~**yard**) cour *f*; (= *passage between houses*) ruelle *f*, venelle *f*
[2] VT [+ *woman*] faire la *or* sa cour à, courtiser; [+ *sb's favour*] solliciter, rechercher; [+ *danger, defeat*] aller au-devant de, s'exposer à
[3] VI **they are** ~**ing**† ils sortent ensemble; **are you** ~**ing?**† tu as un petit copain* (*or* une petite amie*)?
[4] COMP ► **court card** N (*esp Brit*) figure *f* (*de jeu de cartes*) ► **court case** N procès *m*, affaire *f* ► **court circular** N bulletin *m* quotidien de la cour ► **court correspondent** N (*Brit Press*) correspondant(e) *m(f)* chargé(e) des affaires royales ► **courting couple**† N couple *m* d'amoureux ► **court of appeal** (*Brit*), **court of appeals** (*US*) N cour *f* d'appel ► **Court of Claims** N (*US*) tribunal *fédéral* chargé de régler les réclamations contre l'État ► **court of competent jurisdiction** N tribunal *m* compétent ► **court of inquiry** N commission *f* d'enquête ► **Court of International Trade** N (*US*) tribunal de commerce international ► **court of justice** N cour *f* de justice ► **court of last resort** N (*US*) tribunal *m* jugeant en dernier ressort ► **Court of Session** N (*Scot*) cour *f* de cassation ► **court order** N (*Jur*) ordonnance *f* du (*or* d'un) tribunal ► **court record** N (*US Jur*) compte rendu *m* d'audience ► **court reporter** N (*Jur*) greffier *m*, -ière *f*; (*Brit Press*) = court correspondent ► **court room** N (*Jur*) salle *f* d'audience ► **court shoe** N (*Brit*) escarpin *m*

Courtelle® [kɔːˈtel] N Courtelle® *m*

courteous ['kɜːtɪəs] ADJ courtois (**towards** envers)

courteously ['kɜːtɪəslɪ] ADV courtoisement

courtesan [ˌkɔːtɪˈzæn] N courtisane *f*

courtesy ['kɜːtɪsɪ] [1] N courtoisie *f*; **you might have had the** ~ **to explain yourself** vous auriez pu avoir la courtoisie de vous expliquer; **will you do me the** ~ **of reading it?** auriez-vous l'obligeance de me lire?; **an exchange of courtesies** un échange de politesses; **by** ~ **of** avec la permission de [2] COMP ► **courtesy bus** N navette *f* gratuite ► **courtesy call** N visite *f* de politesse ► **courtesy car** N *voiture gracieusement mise à la disposition d'un client*; (*provided by insurance company, garage etc*) véhicule *m* de remplacement ► **courtesy card** N (*US*) carte *f* privilège (*utilisable dans les hôtels, banques etc*) ► **courtesy coach** N (*Brit*) = courtesy bus ► **courtesy light** N (*Aut*) plafonnier *m* ► **courtesy title** N titre *m* de courtoisie ► **courtesy visit** N = courtesy call

courthouse ['kɔːthaʊs] N palais *m* de justice, tribunal *m*

courtier ['kɔːtɪəʳ] N courtisan *m*, dame *f* de la cour

courtly ['kɔːtlɪ] [1] ADJ élégant, raffiné [2] COMP ► **courtly love** N (*Hist, Literat*) amour *m* courtois

court martial ['kɔːtˈmɑːʃəl] [1] N (*pl* **courts martial** *or* **court martials**) (*Mil*) cour *f* martiale; **to be tried by** ~ passer en cour *f* martiale [2] VT **court-martial** traduire *or* faire passer en conseil de guerre

courtship ['kɔːtʃɪp] [1] N **his** ~ **of her** la cour qu'il lui fait (*or* faisait *etc*); **during their** ~ au temps où ils sortaient ensemble [2] COMP ► **courtship display** N [*of birds, animals*] parade *f* nuptiale

courtyard ['kɔːtjɑːd] N cour *f* (*de maison, de château*)

couscous ['kuːskuːs] N couscous *m*

cousin ['kʌzn] N cousin(e) *m(f)* → **country, first**

couth [kuːθ] [1] ADJ raffiné [2] N bonnes manières *fpl*

couture [kuːˈtjʊə] N (*NonC*) haute couture *f*

couturier [kuːˈtʊərɪeɪ] N grand couturier *m*

cove¹ [kəʊv] N (*Geog*) crique *f*, anse *f*; (= *cavern*) caverne *f* naturelle; (*US*) vallon *m* encaissé

cove²‡ [kəʊv] N (*Brit* = *fellow*) mec‡ *m*

coven ['kʌvən] N assemblée *f* de sorcières

covenant ['kʌvɪnənt] [1] N (*gen*) convention *f*, engagement *m* formel; (*Brit Fin*) engagement *m* contractuel; (*Jewish Hist*) alliance *f*; (*Scot Hist*) **the Covenant** le Covenant (*de 1638*) → **deed** [2] VT s'engager (**to do** à faire), convenir (**to do** de faire); (*Fin*) **to** ~ (**to pay**) **£100 per annum to a charity** s'engager par contrat à verser 100 livres par an à une œuvre [3] VI convenir (**with sb for sth** de qch avec qn)

covenanter ['kʌvɪnəntəʳ] N (*Scot Hist*) covenantaire *mf* (*adhérent au Covenant de 1638*)

Coventry ['kɒvəntrɪ] N Coventry *m*; (*Brit fig*) **to send sb to** ~ mettre qn en quarantaine

cover ['kʌvəʳ]

[1] NOUN	[3] COMPOUNDS
[2] TRANSITIVE VERB	[4] PHRASAL VERBS

[1] NOUN
[a] for protection [*of table*] nappe *f*; [*of umbrella*] fourreau *m*, étui *m*; (*over furniture, typewriter*) housse *f*; (*over merchandise, vehicle etc*) bâche *f*; [*of lens*] bouchon *m*; [*of book*] couverture *f*; (= *lid*) couvercle *m*; (= *envelope*) enveloppe *f*; **to read a book from** ~ **to** ~ lire un livre de la première à la dernière page; (*Comm*) **under separate** ~ sous pli séparé → **first, loose, plain**
[b] = for bed (= *bedcover*) dessus-de-lit *m inv*; (= *bedclothes*) **the** ~**s** les couvertures *fpl*
[c] = shelter abri *m*; (*Hunting: for game*) fourré *m*, abri *m*; (*Mil etc* = *covering fire*) feu *m* de couverture *or* de protection; (*Mil, gen*) **there was no** ~ **for miles around** il n'y avait aucun abri à des kilomètres à la ronde; **he was looking for some** ~ il cherchait un abri
♦ **to break cover** [*animal*] débusquer; [*hunted person*] sortir à découvert
♦ **to give sb cover**: **the trees gave him** ~ (= *hid him*) les arbres le cachaient; (= *sheltered him*) les arbres l'abritaient; (*to soldier etc*) **give me** ~! couvrez-moi!
♦ **to run for cover** courir se mettre à l'abri; (*fig*) **critics within his own party are already running for** ~ c'est déjà le sauve-qui-peut général parmi ses détracteurs à l'intérieur de son propre parti
♦ **to take cover** (= *hide*) se cacher; (*Mil*) se mettre à couvert; (= *shelter*) s'abriter, se mettre à l'abri; **to take** ~ **from the rain/the bombing** se mettre à l'abri *or* s'abriter de la pluie/des bombes; (*Mil*) **to take** ~ **from enemy fire** se mettre à l'abri du feu ennemi
♦ **under cover** à l'abri, à couvert; **to get under** ~ se mettre à l'abri *or* à couvert; **under** ~ **of darkness** à la faveur de la nuit; **under** ~ **of diplomacy** sous couvert de diplomatie → **undercover**
[d] Fin couverture *f*, provision *f*; **to operate without** ~ opérer à découvert
[e] Brit Insurance: *gen* couverture *f*, garantie *f* (d'assurances) (**against** contre); ~ **for a building**

against fire *etc* couverture *f or* garantie *f* d'un immeuble contre l'incendie *etc*; **full ~** garantie *f* totale *or* tous risques; **fire ~** assurance-incendie *f*; **they've got no (insurance) ~ for** *or* **on this** ils ne sont pas assurés pour *or* contre cela; **we must extend our (insurance) ~** nous devons augmenter le montant de notre garantie (d'assurances); **the (insurance) ~ ends on 5 July** le contrat d'assurances *or* la police d'assurances expire le 5 juillet

[f] **in espionage** *etc* fausse identité *f*, couverture *f*; **what's your ~?** quelle est votre couverture?; **to blow sb's ~** démasquer qn; **the conference was merely a ~ for an illegal political gathering** en fait, la conférence servait de couverture à un rassemblement politique illégal

[g] **for meal** couvert *m*; **~s laid for six** une table de six couverts

[h] = cover version; → 3

[2] TRANSITIVE VERB

[a] [gen] [+ *object, person*] couvrir (**with** de); **snow ~s the ground** la neige recouvre le sol; **ground ~ed with leaves** sol *m* couvert de feuilles; **he ~ed the paper with scribbles** il a couvert la page de gribouillages; **the car ~ed us in mud** la voiture nous a couverts de boue; **to ~ one's eyes** (*when crying*) se couvrir les yeux; (*against sun etc*) se protéger les yeux; **to ~ one's face with one's hands** se couvrir le visage de ses mains; **to be ~ed in** *or* **with snow/dust/chocolate** être couvert de neige/de poussière/de chocolat; **~ed with confusion** confus *or* ∼; **to o.s. with ridicule** se couvrir de ridicule; **to ~ o.s. with glory** se couvrir de gloire

[b] [+ *book, chair*] recouvrir, couvrir (**with** de)

[c] = hide [+ *feelings, facts*] dissimuler, cacher; [+ *noise*] couvrir; **to ~ (up) one's tracks** (*lit*) effacer ses traces; (*fig*) brouiller les pistes *or* les cartes

[d] = protect [+ *person*] couvrir, protéger; **the soldiers ~ed our retreat** les soldats ont couvert notre retraite; (*fig*) **he only said that to ~ himself** il n'a dit cela que pour se couvrir

[e] Insurance couvrir; **the house is ~ed against fire** *etc* l'immeuble est couvert contre l'incendie *etc*; **it doesn't ~ you for** *or* **against flood damage** vous n'êtes pas couvert contre les dégâts des eaux; **it ~s (for) fire only** cela ne couvre que l'incendie; **what does your travel insurance ~ you for?** contre quoi êtes-vous couvert avec votre assurance voyage?

[f] = point gun at [+ *person*] braquer un revolver sur, braquer*; **to keep sb ~ed** tenir qn sous la menace d'un revolver; **I've got you ~ed!** ne bougez pas ou je tire!

[g] Sport [+ *opponent*] marquer

[h] [+ *distance*] parcourir, couvrir; **we ~ed 8km in two hours** nous avons parcouru *or* couvert 8 km en deux heures; **we ~ed 300 miles on just one tank of petrol** nous avons fait 300 miles avec un seul plein d'essence; **to ~ a lot of ground** (*travelling*) faire beaucoup de chemin; (= *deal with many subjects*) traiter un large éventail de questions; (= *do large amount of work*) faire du bon travail

[i] = be sufficient for couvrir; **£50 will ~ everything** 50 livres suffiront (à couvrir toutes les dépenses); **in order to ~ the monthly payments** pour faire face aux mensualités; **to ~ one's costs** *or* **expenses** rentrer dans ses frais; **to ~ a deficit/a loss** combler un déficit/une perte

[j] = take in, include englober, comprendre; **his work ~s many different fields** son travail englobe de nombreux domaines; **goods ~ed by this invoice** les marchandises faisant l'objet de cette facture; **in order to ~ all possibilities** pour parer à toute éventualité

[k] = deal with traiter; **the book ~s the subject thoroughly** le livre traite le sujet à fond; **the article ~s the 18th century** l'article traite tout le 18ᵉ siècle; **his speech ~ed most of the points raised** dans son discours il a traité la plupart

des points en question; **such factories will not be ~ed by this report** ce rapport ne traitera pas de ces usines; **no law ~s a situation like that** aucune loi ne prévoit une telle situation

[l] Press *etc* [+ *news, story, scandal*] assurer la couverture de; [+ *lawsuit*] faire le compte rendu de; **he was sent to ~ the riots** on l'a envoyé assurer le reportage des émeutes; **all the newspapers ~ed the story** les journaux ont tous parlé de l'affaire

[m] Mus reprendre; **to ~ a song** reprendre une chanson

[n] = inseminate [*animal*] couvrir

[3] COMPOUNDS

► **cover charge** N (*in restaurant*) couvert *m* ► **covered market** N marché *m* couvert ► **covered wagon** N chariot *m* couvert *or* bâché ► **cover letter** N (*US*) = covering letter; → covering ► **cover note** N (*Brit Insurance*) attestation *f* provisoire d'assurance ► **cover price** N [*of newspaper, magazine*] prix *m* de vente (au numéro); [*of book*] prix *m* conseillé ► **cover story** N (*Press*) article *m* principal; (*in espionage etc*) couverture *f*; **our ~ story this week** en couverture cette semaine ► **cover-up** N **there's been a ~-up** on a tenté d'étouffer l'affaire ► **cover version** N (*Mus*) reprise *f*

[4] PHRASAL VERBS

► **cover for** VT FUS [a] (= *protect*) [+ *person*] couvrir, protéger; (*Insurance*) [+ *risk*] couvrir; **why would she ~ for him if he's trying to kill her?** pourquoi voudrait-elle le couvrir *or* le protéger s'il cherche à la tuer? [b] (= *stand in for*) remplacer

► **cover in** VT SEP [+ *trench, grave*] remplir

► **cover over** VT SEP recouvrir

► **cover up** [1] VI [a] (= *protect*) **it's cold, ~ up warmly** il fait froid, couvre-toi chaudement [b] **to ~ up for sb** couvrir qn, protéger qn [2] VT SEP [a] [+ *object*] recouvrir, envelopper; [+ *child*] couvrir [b] = hide [+ *truth, facts*] dissimuler, cacher; [+ *affair*] étouffer → cover 2c

coverage ['kʌvərɪdʒ] N [a] (*Press, Rad, TV*) reportage *m*; **to give full ~ to an event** assurer la couverture complète d'un événement, traiter à fond un événement; **the match got nationwide ~** le match a été retransmis *or* diffusé dans tout le pays; (*Press*) **it got full-page ~ in the main dailies** les principaux quotidiens y ont consacré une page entière [b] (*Insurance*) couverture *f*

coveralls ['kʌvərɔːlz] NPL bleu(s) *m(pl)* de travail, salopette *f*

covergirl ['kʌvəgɜːl] N cover-girl *f*

covering ['kʌvərɪŋ] [1] N (= *wrapping etc*) couverture *f*, enveloppe *f*; (= *layer*) [*of snow, dust etc*] couche *f* [2] COMP ► **covering fire** N (*Mil*) feu *m* de protection *or* de couverture ► **covering letter** N (*Brit*) lettre *f* explicative

coverlet ['kʌvəlɪt] N dessus-de-lit *m inv*, couvre-lit *m*; (*quilted*) courtepointe *f*

covert ['kʌvət] [1] [*threat*] voilé, caché; [*attack*] indirect; [*glance*] furtif, dérobé; [*operation, action, surveillance*] clandestin; [*homosexuality*] refoulé [2] N (*Hunting*) fourré *m*, couvert *m*; (= *animal's hiding place*) gîte *m*, terrier *m*

covertly ['kʌvətlɪ] ADV (*gen*) en secret; [*watch*] à la dérobée; **to film sb ~** filmer qn à son insu

covet ['kʌvɪt] VT (*frm*) convoiter

covetous ['kʌvɪtəs] ADJ (*frm*) [*person, attitude, nature*] avide; [*look*] de convoitise; **to cast ~ eyes on sth** regarder qch avec convoitise

covetously ['kʌvɪtəslɪ] ADV (*frm*) avec convoitise

covetousness ['kʌvɪtəsnɪs] N (*frm*) convoitise *f*

covey ['kʌvɪ] N compagnie *f* (*de perdrix*)

cow[1] [kaʊ] [1] N [a] vache *f*; (= *female*) [*of elephant etc*] femelle *f*; (= *female buffalo etc*) buffle *m etc* femelle; (*fig*) **till the ~s come home*** jusqu'à la saint-glinglin* *or* jusqu'à perpète* [b] (‡ *pej = woman*) vache* *f*, chameau* *m*; **she's a cheeky ~** elle est sacrément* culottée; **you're a lazy ~!** tu es une sacrée* fainéante!; **that nosey ~** cette sacrée* fouineuse; **silly** *or* **stupid ~!** pauvre conne!‡ [2] COMP ► **cow college** N (*US Scol*) (= *provincial college*) boîte *f* dans un trou perdu*; (= *agricultural college*) école *f* d'agriculture ► **cow parsley** N (*Bot*) cerfeuil *m* sauvage

cow[2] [kaʊ] VT [+ *person*] effrayer, intimider; **a ~ed look** un air de chien battu

coward ['kaʊəd] N lâche *mf*, poltron(ne) *m(f)*

cowardice ['kaʊədɪs], **cowardliness** ['kaʊədlɪnɪs] N lâcheté *f*

cowardly ['kaʊədlɪ] ADJ [*person*] lâche, poltron; [*action, words*] lâche

cowbell ['kaʊbel] N cloche *f* de *or* à vache

cowboy ['kaʊbɔɪ] [1] N cow-boy *m*; (*Brit* pej) fumiste *m*; **to play ~s and Indians** jouer aux cow-boys et aux Indiens [2] ADJ (*Brit* pej) pas sérieux, fumiste [3] COMP ► **cowboy boots** NPL santiags* *mpl* ► **cowboy hat** N chapeau *m* de cow-boy, feutre *m* à larges bords

cowcatcher ['kaʊkætʃəʳ] N (*Rail*) chasse-pierres *m inv*

cower ['kaʊəʳ] VI (*also* ~ **down**) se tapir, se recroqueviller; (*fig*) **to ~ before sb** trembler devant qn

cowgirl ['kaʊgɜːl] N vachère *f* à cheval

cowherd ['kaʊhɜːd] N vacher *m*, -ère *f*, bouvier *m*, -ière *f*

cowhide ['kaʊhaɪd] [1] N (= *skin*) peau *f* or cuir *m* de vache; (*US* = *whip*) fouet *m* (à lanière de cuir) [2] VT (*US*) fouetter (avec une lanière de cuir)

cowl [kaʊl] N [a] (= *hood*) capuchon *m* (*de moine*); **~ neck(line)** col *m* boule [b] [*of chimney*] capuchon *m*

cowlick ['kaʊlɪk] N épi *m*

cowling ['kaʊlɪŋ] N capotage *m*

cowman ['kaʊmən] N (*pl* -men) (*Brit*) = cowherd

co-worker ['kəʊ'wɜːkəʳ] N collègue *mf*, camarade *mf* (de travail)

cowpat ['kaʊpæt] N bouse *f* (de vache)

cowpea ['kaʊpiː] N (*US*) dolique *m or* dolic *m*

cowpoke ['kaʊpəʊk] N (*US*) cowboy *m*

cowpox ['kaʊpɒks] N (*Vet*) vaccine *f*, cow-pox *m*; **~ vaccine** vaccin *m* antivariolique

cowpuncher* ['kaʊpʌntʃəʳ] N (*US*) = cowboy

cowrie, cowry ['kaʊrɪ] N cauri *m*

cowshed ['kaʊʃed] N étable *f*

cowslip ['kaʊslɪp] N (*Bot*) coucou *m*, primevère *f*; (*US* = *marsh marigold*) populage *m*

cowtown ['kaʊtaʊn] N (*US* pej) bled* *m*, patelin* *m*

cox [kɒks] [1] N (*Rowing*) barreur *m* [2] VT (*Rowing*) [+ *boat*] barrer, gouverner; **~ed four** quatre *m* barré, quatre *m* avec barreur [3] VI (*Rowing*) barrer

coxcomb† ['kɒkskəʊm] N fat† *m*

coxless ['kɒkslɪs] ADJ (*Rowing*) ► **four** quatre *m* sans barreur

coxswain ['kɒksn] N (*Rowing*) barreur *m*; (*Naut*) patron *m*

coy [kɔɪ] ADJ [a] (= *demure*) [*person, look, smile*] faussement timide; **to go (all) ~*** faire la sainte nitouche (*pej*) [b] (= *evasive*) évasif (**about sth** à propos de qch); **they maintained a ~ refusal to disclose his name** ils ont continué à se montrer évasifs lorsqu'on leur demandait de révéler son nom [c] (= *twee*) [*picture, rhyme*] mièvre

coyly ['kɔɪlɪ] ADV [a] (= *demurely*) [*describe*] par euphémisme; **to look at/smile ~** regarder/sourire avec une fausse timidité, regarder/sourire avec un air de sainte nitouche (*pej*)

b (= *evasively*) [*say, answer, refuse*] évasivement

coyness ['kɔɪnɪs] N (*NonC*) **a** (= *demureness*) [*of person*] fausse timidité *f* **b** (= *evasiveness*) [*of person, film, book*] réserve *f* (**about sth** quant à qch) **c** (= *tweeness*) [*of picture, rhyme*] mièvrerie *f*

coyote [kɔɪˈəʊtɪ] N coyote *m*; **the Coyote State** le Dakota du Sud

coypu ['kɔɪpu:] N (*pl* **coypus** or **coypu**) (*Zool*) coypou *m*, ragondin *m*

cozily ['kəʊzɪlɪ] ADV (*US*) = **cosily**

cozy ['kəʊzɪ] (*US*) = **cosy**

cozzie* ['kɒzɪ] N (*Brit, Austral*) = **cossie**

CP [si:'pi:] N **a** ABBR = **Cape Province** **b** ABBR = **Communist Party**

cp ABBR = **compare**

c/p (ABBR = **carriage paid**) → **carriage**

CPA [ˌsi:pi:'eɪ] N (*US Fin*) (ABBR = **certified public accountant**) → **certify**

CPI [ˌsi:pi:'aɪ] N (*US*) (ABBR = **Consumer Price Index**) → **consumer**

cpi [ˌsi:pi:'aɪ] N (*Comput*) (ABBR = **characters per inch**) CCPP *mpl*

Cpl (*Mil*) ABBR = **corporal**

CP/M [ˌsi:pi:'em] (ABBR = **Control Program for Microprocessors**) CP/M *m*

CPO [ˌsi:pi:'əʊ] N (*Naut*) (ABBR = **chief petty officer**) → **chief**

cps [ˌsi:pi:'es] (*Comput*) ABBR = **a** = **characters per second**; **b** ABBR = **cycles per second**) cycles *mpl* par seconde

CPU [ˌsi:pi:'ju:] N (*Comput*) (ABBR = **central processing unit**) UC *f*

CPVE [ˌsi:pi:vi:'i:] N (*Brit*) (ABBR = **Certificate of Pre-vocational Education**) *brevet technique*

cr. **a** ABBR = **credit** **b** ABBR = **creditor**

crab¹ [kræb] N **a** (*Zool*) crabe *m*; (*Rowing*) **to catch a ~** plonger la rame trop profond **b** (*Tech*) [*of crane*] chariot *m* **c** (*Med: also ~ louse*) morpion *m* **d** (*Climbing*) mousqueton *m*

crab² [kræb] N (*also* **~apple**) pomme *f* sauvage; (*also* **~(apple) tree**) pommier *m* sauvage

crab³ [kræb] **1** VT (*US*‡ = *spoil*) gâcher; **to ~ sb's act** gâcher les effets de qn; **to ~ a deal** faire rater* une affaire **2** VI (*US*‡ = *complain*) rouspéter* (**about** à cause de)

crabbed ['kræbd] ADJ [*person*] revêche, grincheux; **in a ~ hand** ◊ **in ~ writing** en pattes de mouche

crabby ['kræbɪ] ADJ [*person*] revêche, grincheux

crabmeat ['kræbmi:t] N chair *f* de crabe

crabwise ['kræb,waɪz] ADV en crabe

crack [kræk] **1** N **a** (= *split, slit*) fente *f*, fissure *f*; (*in glass, mirror, pottery, bone etc*) fêlure *f*; (*in wall*) lézarde *f*, crevasse *f*; (*in ground, skin*) crevasse *f*; (*Climbing*) fissure *f*; (*in paint, varnish*) craquelure *f*; (= *slight opening*) **through the ~ in the door** par l'entrebâillement de la porte; **leave the window open a ~** laissez la fenêtre entrouverte; **at the ~ of dawn** au point du jour, aux aurores* **b** (= *noise*) [*of twigs*] craquement *m*; [*of whip*] claquement *m*; [*of rifle*] coup *m* (sec), détonation *f*; **a ~ of thunder** un coup de tonnerre; **the ~ of doom** la trompette du Jugement dernier **c** (= *sharp blow*) **to give sb a ~ on the head** asséner à qn un grand coup sur la tête **d** (* = *joke etc*) plaisanterie *f*; **that was a ~ at your brother** ça, c'était pour votre frère; **that was a nasty** or **mean ~ he made** c'est une vacherie‡ ce qu'il a dit là, c'était vache* or rosse* de dire ça **e** (* = *try*) **to have a ~ at doing** essayer (un coup*) de faire; **to have a ~ at sth** se lancer dans qch, tenter le coup* sur qch; **I'll have a ~ at it** je vais essayer (un coup*) → **fair**

f (*esp Ir*) ambiance *f*; **tourists come to Ireland for the ~** les touristes viennent en Irlande pour l'ambiance

g (= *drug*) = **crack cocaine**

2 VT **a** [+ *pottery, glass, bone*] fêler; [+ *wall*] lézarder, crevasser; [+ *ground*] crevasser; [+ *nut etc*] casser; **to ~ one's skull** se fendre le crâne; **to ~ sb over the head** assommer qn; **to ~ a safe*** percer un coffre-fort; (*US Comm*) **to ~ a market*** réussir à s'implanter sur un marché; **to ~ (open) a bottle*** ouvrir or déboucher une bouteille; (*US*) **to ~ a book*** ouvrir un livre (pour l'étudier) **b** [+ *petroleum etc*] craquer, traiter par craquage **c** [+ *whip*] faire claquer; **to ~ one's finger joints** faire craquer ses doigts **d** **to ~ a joke** raconter une blague; **to ~ jokes** blaguer* **e** [+ *code etc*] déchiffrer; [+ *spy network*] démanteler; **to ~ a case** [*detective, police*] résoudre une affaire

3 VI **a** [*pottery, glass*] se fêler; [*ground*] se crevasser, se craqueler; [*wall*] se fendiller, se lézarder; [*skin*] se crevasser; (*from cold*) se gercer; [*ice*] se craqueler **b** [*whip*] claquer; [*dry wood*] craquer; **we heard the pistol ~** nous avons entendu le coup de pistolet **c** [*voice*] se casser; [*boy's voice*] muer **d** (*Brit**) **to get ~ing** s'y mettre, se mettre au boulot*; **let's get ~ing!** allons-y!, au boulot!*; **get ~ing!** magne-toi!‡, grouille-toi!‡ **e** [*person*] (*from overwork, pressure etc*) craquer*

4 ADJ [*sportsman, sportswoman*] de première classe, fameux*; **a ~ tennis player/skier** un as or un crack du tennis/du ski; **a ~ shot** un bon or excellent fusil; (*Mil, Police etc*) un tireur d'élite

5 COMP ► **crack-brained** ADJ (*pej*) [*person, plan*] cinglé*; **a ~-brained idea** une idée saugrenue or loufoque* ► **crack cocaine** N crack *m* ► **crack house** N crack-house *f* ► **crack-jaw*** ADJ impossible à prononcer, imprononçable; **~-jaw name** nom *m* à coucher dehors* ► **crack-up*** N [*of plan, organization*] effondrement *m*, écroulement *m*; [*of person*] (*physical*) effondrement *m*; (*mental*) dépression *f* nerveuse; (*US = accident*) [*of vehicle*] collision *f*, accident *m*; [*of plane*] accident *m* (d'avion)

► **crack down on** **1** VT FUS [+ *person*] sévir contre; [+ *expenditure, sb's actions*] mettre un frein à **2** **~down on** → **crackdown**

► **crack up*** **1** VI **a** (*physically*) ne pas tenir le coup; (*mentally*) craquer*; (*hum*) **I must be ~ing up!** ça ne tourne plus rond chez moi!* **b** (*US*) [*vehicle*] s'écraser; [*plane*] s'écraser (au sol) **c** [*person*] (*with laughter*) se tordre de rire, éclater de rire **2** VT SEP **a** (= *praise*) [+ *person, quality, action, thing*] vanter, louer; [+ *method*] prôner; **he's not all he's ~ed up to be*** il n'est pas aussi sensationnel qu'on le dit or prétend **b** (*US = crash*) [+ *vehicle*] emboutir; [+ *plane*] faire s'écraser **3** **~-up** N → **crack**

crackdown ['krækdaʊn] N **~ on** mesures *fpl* énergiques contre, mesures *fpl* de répression contre

cracked [krækt] **1** ADJ **a** (= *damaged*) [*cup, window, mirror, tooth, bone, rib*] fêlé; [*sink, plaster, paintwork, glaze, rubber*] craquelé; [*wall, ceiling*] lézardé, fissuré; [*lips, skin*] gercé; (*stronger*) crevassé **b** (= *unsteady*) [*voice*] cassé; (*Mus*) **~ note** couac *m* **c** (* = *mad*) [*person*] toqué*, timbré* **2** COMP ► **cracked wheat** N blé *m* concassé

cracker ['krækəʳ] **1** N **a** (= *biscuit*) cracker *m*, biscuit *m* salé **b** (= *firework*) pétard *m* **c** (*Brit: at parties etc: also* **Christmas ~**) diablotin *m* **d** (*Brit*) **to be a ~*** (= *excellent*) être super*; (= *very funny*) être impayable* **e** (*US*) pauvre blanc *m* (du Sud) **2** COMP ► **cracker-barrel**

ADJ (*US*) ≈ du café du commerce ► **the Cracker State** N la Géorgie

crackers‡ ['krækəz] ADJ (*Brit*) cinglé*, dingue‡

crackhead‡ ['krækhed] N accro‡ *mf* du crack

cracking ['krækɪŋ] **1** N (*NonC*) **a** [*of petroleum*] craquage *m*, cracking *m*; **b** (= *cracks: in paint, varnish etc*) craquelure *f* **2** ADJ **a** (*Brit*) **a ~ speed** or **pace** un train d'enfer* **b** (*Brit**) = **cracking good** **3** ADV (*Brit**) **~ good** vachement* bon; **his book's a ~ good read** son livre est vachement* bon; **he tells a ~ good yarn** il en raconte de vachement* bonnes

crackle ['krækl] **1** VI [*twigs burning*] crépiter; [*sth frying*] grésiller **2** N **a** (= *noise*) [*of wood*] crépitement *m*, craquement *m*; [*of food*] grésillement *m*; (*on telephone etc*) crépitement(s) *m(pl)*, friture* *f* **b** [*of china, porcelain etc*] craquelure *f* **3** COMP ► **crackle china** N porcelaine *f* craquelée

crackling ['kræklɪŋ] N **a** (= *sound*) crépitement *m*; (*Rad*) friture* *f* (*NonC*) **b** (*Culin*) couenne *f* rissolée (*de rôti de porc*)

crackly ['kræklɪ] ADJ **a ~ sound** un crépitement, un grésillement; **the line is ~** il y a de la friture* sur la ligne

cracknel ['kræknl] N (= *biscuit*) craquelin *m*; (= *toffee*) nougatine *f*

crackpot ['krækpɒt] (*pej*) **1** N (= *person*) tordu(e)* *m(f)*, cinglé(e)* *m(f)* **2** ADJ [*idea*] tordu

cracksman ['kræksmən] N (*pl* **-men**) (= *burglar*) cambrioleur *m*, casseur* *m*

Cracow ['krækaʊ] N Cracovie

cradle ['kreɪdl] **1** N **a** (*lit, fig*) berceau *m*; **from the ~ to the grave** du berceau à la tombe; **the ~ of civilization** le berceau de la civilisation; (*fig*) **to rob the ~*** les prendre au berceau* **b** (*Naut = framework*) ber *m*; (*Constr*) nacelle *f*, pont *m* volant; (*of telephone*) support *m*; (*Med*) arceau *m* **2** VT **to ~ a child (in one's arms)** bercer un enfant (dans ses bras); **she ~d the vase in her hands** elle tenait délicatement le vase entre ses mains; **he ~d the telephone under his chin** il maintenait le téléphone sous son menton **3** COMP ► **cradle cap** N (*Med*) croûte *f* de lait ► **cradle snatcher*** N (*pej*) **she's a ~ snatcher** elle les prend au berceau*

cradlesong ['kreɪdlsɒŋ] N berceuse *f*

craft [krɑ:ft] **1** N **a** (= *skill*) art *m*, métier *m*; (= *job, occupation*) métier *m*, profession *f* (*généralement de type artisanal*); (*NonC: Scol = subject*) travaux *mpl* manuels → **art¹**, **needlecraft** **b** (= *tradesmen's guild*) corps *m* de métier, corporation *f* **c** (*pl inv*) (= *boat*) embarcation *f*, petit bateau *m*; (= *plane*) appareil *m* → **aircraft, spacecraft** **d** (*NonC = cunning*) astuce *f*, ruse *f* (*pej*); **by ~** par ruse; **his ~ in doing that** l'astuce dont il a fait preuve en le faisant **2** VT **beautifully ~ed** [*vase, poem*] réalisé avec art **3** COMP ► **craft fair** N exposition-vente *f* d'artisanat ► **craft union** N fédération *f*

craftily ['krɑ:ftɪlɪ] ADV avec ruse

craftiness ['krɑ:ftɪnɪs] N astuce *f*, finesse *f*, ruse *f* (*pej*)

craftsman ['krɑ:ftsmən] N (*pl* **-men**) artisan *m*; (*fig = musician etc*) artiste *m*

craftsmanship ['krɑ:ftsmənʃɪp] N (*NonC*) connaissance *f* d'un métier; (= *artistry*) art *m*; **what ~!** quel travail!; **a superb piece of ~** un or du travail superbe

craftsperson ['krɑ:ftspɜːsən] N (*pl* **-people**) artisan(e) *m(f)*; (*fig = musician etc*) artiste *mf*

craftswoman ['krɑ:ftswʊmən] N (*pl* **-women**) artisane *f*; (*fig = musician etc*) artiste *f*

crafty ['krɑ:ftɪ] ADJ malin (-igne *f*), rusé (*pej*); **he's a ~ one*** c'est un malin; **a ~ little gadget*** un petit gadget astucieux; **that was a ~ move*** or **a ~ thing to do** c'était un coup très astucieux

crag [kræg] N rocher m escarpé or à pic; (*Climbing*) école f d'escalade

craggy ['krægɪ] ADJ [*Geog*] [*mountain*] escarpé, à pic; [*cliff, outcrop*] à pic **[b]** (= *strong-featured*) [*face, features*] taillé à la serpe

cram [kræm] **1** VT **[a]** [+ *object*] fourrer (**into** dans); **to ~ books into a case** fourrer des livres dans une valise, bourrer une valise de livres; **we can ~ in another book** nous pouvons encore faire de la place pour un autre livre or y faire tenir un autre livre; **to ~ food into one's mouth** enfourner* de la nourriture; **we can't ~ any more people into the hall/the bus** on ne peut plus faire entrer personne dans la salle/l'autobus; **we were all ~med into one room** nous étions tous entassés dans une seule pièce; **he ~med his hat (down) over his eyes** il a enfoncé son chapeau sur ses yeux **[b]** [+ *place*] bourrer (**with** de); **a shop ~med with good things** un magasin qui regorge de bonnes choses; **a drawer ~med with letters** un tiroir bourré de lettres; **to ~ sb with food** bourrer or gaver qn de nourriture; **to ~ o.s. with food** se bourrer or se gaver de nourriture; (*fig*) **he has his head ~med with odd ideas** il a la tête bourrée or farcie d'idées bizarres **[c]** [*Scol*] [+ *pupil*] chauffer*, faire bachoter **2** VI **[a]** [*people*] s'entasser; **they all ~med into the kitchen** tout le monde s'est entassé dans la cuisine **[b]** **to ~ for an exam** bachoter, préparer un examen **3** COMP ► **cram-full** ADJ [*room, bus*] bondé; [*case*] bourré (**of** de)

crammer ['kræmə'] N (*slightly pej*) (= *tutor*) répétiteur m, -trice f (*qui fait faire du bachotage*); (= *student*) bachoteur m, -euse f; (= *book*) précis m, aide-mémoire m inv; (*also* **~'s** = *school*) boîte f à bac or à bachot*

cramp¹ [kræmp] **1** N (*Med*) crampe f; **to have ~ in one's leg** avoir une crampe à la jambe → **writer 2** VT (= *hinder*) [+ *person*] gêner, entraver; **to ~ sb's progress** gêner or entraver les progrès de qn; (*fig*) **to ~ sb's style*** priver qn de ses moyens; (*fig*) **your presence is ~ing my style*** tu me fais perdre mes moyens

cramp² [kræmp] **1** N (*Constr, Tech*) agrafe f, crampon m, happe f **2** VT [+ *stones*] cramponner

cramped [kræmpt] ADJ **[a]** (= *not spacious*) [*flat, room, accommodation*] exigu (-guë f); [*coach, train, plane*] où l'on est (or était) à l'étroit; [*space*] restreint; **to live in ~ quarters** or **conditions** être logé à l'étroit; **it was ~ in the cockpit** on était à l'étroit dans le cockpit; **to be ~ (for space)** [*people*] être à l'étroit; **the museum is ~ for space** le musée manque de place **[b]** (= *squashed*) [*handwriting*] en pattes de mouche **[c]** (= *stiff*) [*muscle, limb*] raide

crampon ['kræmpən] **1** N (*Climbing, Constr*) crampon m **2** COMP ► **crampon technique** N (*Climbing*) cramponnage m

cramponning ['kræmpənɪŋ] N (*Climbing*) cramponnage m

cranberry ['krænbərɪ] **1** N (*Bot*) canneberge f **2** COMP ► **cranberry sauce** N **turkey with ~ sauce** dinde f aux canneberges

crane [kreɪn] **1** N (*Orn, Tech*) grue f **2** VT **to ~ one's neck** tendre le cou **3** COMP ► **crane driver, crane operator** N grutier m, -ière f ► **crane forward** VI tendre le cou (*pour voir etc*)

cranefly ['kreɪnflaɪ] N tipule f

cranesbill ['kreɪnzbɪl] N (*Bot*) géranium m

crania ['kreɪnɪə] NPL of **cranium**

cranial ['kreɪnɪəl] ADJ crânien

cranium ['kreɪnɪəm] N (*pl* **craniums** or **crania**) crâne m, boîte f crânienne

crank¹* [kræŋk] N (*Brit* = *person*) excentrique mf, loufoque* mf; **a religious ~** un fanatique religieux

crank² [kræŋk] **1** N (*Tech*) manivelle f **2** VT (*also* ~ **up**) [+ *car*] faire partir à la manivelle; [+ *cine-camera, gramophone etc*] remonter (à la manivelle); [+ *barrel organ*] tourner la manivelle de ► **crank out** VT produire (avec effort)

crankcase ['kræŋkkeɪs] N (*Aut*) carter m

crankshaft ['kræŋkʃɑːft] N (*Aut*) vilebrequin m

cranky* ['kræŋkɪ] ADJ (= *eccentric*) excentrique, loufoque*; (*US* = *bad-tempered*) revêche, grincheux

cranny ['krænɪ] N (petite) faille f, fissure f, fente f → **nook**

crap: [kræp] **1** N (= *excrement*) merde:: f; (= *nonsense*) conneries fpl; (= *junk*) merde:: f, saloperie: f; **the film was ~** le film était merdique:: **2** ADJ = **crappy 3** VI chier::
► **crap out:** VI (*US* = *chicken out*) se dégonfler*

crape [kreɪp] **1** N **[a]** = **crêpe [b]** (*for mourning*) crêpe m (de deuil); ~ **band** brassard m (de deuil)

crapehanger: ['kreɪp,hæŋə'] N (*US*) rabat-joie m inv

crappy: ['kræpɪ] ADJ merdique::

craps [kræps] N (*US*) jeu m de dés (*sorte de zanzi ou de passe anglaise*); **to shoot ~** jouer aux dés

crapshooter ['kræpʃuːtə'] N joueur m, -euse f de dés

crapulous ['kræpjʊləs] ADJ crapuleux

crash¹ [kræʃ] **1** N **[a]** (= *noise*) fracas m; **a ~ of thunder** un coup de tonnerre; **a sudden ~ of dishes** un soudain fracas d'assiettes cassées; ~, **bang, wallop!*** badaboum!, patatras! **[b]** (= *accident*) [*of car*] collision f, accident m; [*of aeroplane*] accident m (d'avion); **in a car/plane ~** dans un accident de voiture/d'avion; **we had a ~ on the way here** nous avons eu un accident en venant ici **[c]** (*Fin*) [*of company, firm*] faillite f; (*St Ex*) krach m **2** ADV **he went ~ into the tree** il est allé je-ter or se fracasser contre l'arbre **3** VI **[a]** [*aeroplane*] s'écraser (au sol); [*vehicle*] avoir un accident; [*two vehicles*] se percuter, entrer en collision dedans*; **the cars ~ed at the junction** les voitures se sont percutées or sont entrées en collision au croisement; **to ~ into sth** rentrer dans qch*, percuter qch; **the plate ~ed to the ground** l'assiette s'est fracassée par terre; **the car ~ed through the gate** la voiture a enfoncé la barrière **[b]** (*Comm, Fin*) [*bank, firm*] faire faillite; **the stock market ~ed** les cours de la Bourse se sont effondrés **[c]** (:: = *sleep*) pieuter::, crécher::; **can I ~ at your place for a few days?** est-ce que je peux pieuter: chez toi pendant quelques jours?; **to ~ at sb's place** pieuter:: or crécher:: chez qn **[d]** (*Comput*) tomber en panne **4** VT **[a]** [+ *car*] avoir une collision or un accident avec; **he ~ed the car through the barrier** il a enfoncé la barrière (avec la voiture); **he ~ed the car into a tree** il a percuté un arbre (avec la voiture); **he ~ed the plane** il s'est écrasé (au sol); **to ~ the gears** faire grincer le changement de vitesse **[b]:** **to ~ a party** s'incruster dans une fête; (*US Comm*) **to ~ a market** pénétrer en force sur un marché **5** COMP ► **crash barrier** N (*Brit*) glissière f de sécurité ► **crash course** N cours m intensif ► **crash diet** N régime m draconien ► **crash helmet** N casque m de protection ► **crash-land** VI faire un atterrissage forcé ♦ VT poser en catastrophe ► **crash landing** N atterrissage m forcé ► **crash programme, crash programme** m intensif
► **crash down, crash in** VI [*roof etc*] s'effondrer (avec fracas)
► **crash out:** **1** VI (= *fall asleep etc*) tomber rai-

de **2** VT SEP **to be ~ed out** être raide* or pété:: or fait::

crash² [kræʃ] N (*Tex*) grosse toile f

crashing † ['kræʃɪŋ] ADJ **a ~ bore** un raseur de première

crashingly † ['kræʃɪŋlɪ] ADV [*boring*] terriblement

crashpad: ['kræʃpæd] N piaule: f de dépannage

crass [kræs] ADJ [*comment, behaviour, mistake, film, person*] grossier; [*joke*] lourd; [*stupidity, ignorance*] crasse

crassly ['kræslɪ] ADV grossièrement

crassness ['kræsnɪs] N grossièreté f

crate [kreɪt] **1** N **[a]** [*of fruit*] cageot m; [*of bottles*] caisse f (à claire-voie); (*esp Naut*) caisse f **[b]** (:: = *aeroplane*) zinc* m; (:: = *car*) bagnole* f **2** VT (*also* ~ **up**: *goods*) mettre en cageot(s) or en caisse(s)

crater ['kreɪtə'] N [*of volcano, moon*] cratère m; **bomb ~** entonnoir m; **shell ~** trou m d'obus, entonnoir

cravat(e) [krə'væt] N cravate f, foulard m (noué autour du cou)

crave [kreɪv] **1** VT **[a]** (*also* ~ **for**) [+ *drink, tobacco etc*] avoir un besoin maladif or physiologique de; **to ~ (for) affection** avoir soif or avoir grand besoin d'affection **[b]** (*frm*) [+ *attention*] solliciter; **to ~ permission** solliciter humblement l'autorisation; **he ~d permission to leave** il supplia qu'on lui accordât la permission de partir; **may I ~ leave to ...?** je sollicite humblement l'autorisation de ...; **to ~ sb's pardon** implorer le pardon de qn **2** VI ~ **for** → **1a**

craven ['kreɪvən] ADJ, N (*liter*) lâche mf, poltron(ne) m(f)

cravenly ['kreɪvənlɪ] ADV (*liter*) lâchement

craving ['kreɪvɪŋ] N (*for drink, drugs, tobacco*) besoin m (maladif or physiologique) (**for** de); (*for affection*) grand besoin m, soif f (**for** de); (*for freedom*) désir m insatiable (**for** de)

craw [krɔː] N [*of bird*] jabot m; [*of animal*] estomac m; (*fig*) **it sticks in my ~** cela me reste en travers de la gorge

crawfish ['krɔːfɪʃ] **1** N (*pl* **crawfish** or **crawfishes**) (*esp US*) = **crayfish 2** VI (*US*: *fig*) se défiler*, faire marche arrière

crawl [krɔːl] **1** N [*of vehicle*] allure f très ralentie; **we had to go at a ~ through the main streets** nous avons dû avancer au pas dans les rues principales **[b]** (*Swimming*) crawl m; **to do the ~** nager le crawl, crawler **2** VI **[a]** [*animals*] ramper, se glisser; [*person*] se traîner, ramper; **to ~ in/out** etc entrer/sortir etc en rampant or à quatre pattes; **to ~ on one's hands and knees** aller à quatre pattes; **the child has begun to ~ (around)** l'enfant commence à ramper; (*fig*) **to ~ to sb** s'aplatir devant qn*, lécher les bottes de or à qn*; **the fly ~ed up the wall/along the table** la mouche a grimpé le long du mur/a avancé sur la table; **to make sb's skin ~** donner la chair de poule à qn; **to ~ with vermin** grouiller de vermine; **the street is ~ing* with policemen** la rue grouille d'agents de police → **crawling [b]** [*vehicle*] avancer au pas or pare-chocs contre pare-chocs **3** COMP ► **crawl space** N (*US*) (*under ground floor*) vide m sanitaire; (*under roof*) vide m de comble

crawler ['krɔːlə'] **1** N **[a]** (* = *person*) lécheur* m, -euse* f, lèche-bottes* mf inv **[b]** (= *vehicle*) véhicule m lent **2** COMP ► **crawler lane** N (*Brit Aut*) file f or voie f pour véhicules lents

crawling ['krɔːlɪŋ] ADJ [*insect, movement*] rampant; **a baby at the ~ stage** un bébé qui rampe → **crawl**

crayfish ['kreɪfɪʃ] N (*pl* **crayfish** or **crayfishes**) (*freshwater*) écrevisse *f*; (*saltwater*) (*large*) langouste *f*; (*small*) langoustine *f*

crayon ['kreɪən] **1** N (= *coloured pencil*) crayon *m* (de couleur); (*Art* = *pencil, chalk etc*) pastel *m*; (*Art* = *drawing*) crayon *m*, pastel *m* **2** VT crayonner, dessiner au crayon; (*Art*) colorier au crayon *or* au pastel

craze [kreɪz] **1** N engouement *m* (**for** pour) **2** VT **a** (= *make mad*) rendre fou **b** [+ *glaze, pottery*] craqueler; [+ *windscreen*] étoiler **3** VI [*glaze, pottery*] craqueler; [*windscreen*] s'étoiler

crazed [kreɪzd] ADJ **a** (= *mad*) affolé, rendu fou (folle *f*) (**with** de) **b** [*glaze, pottery*] craquelé; [*windscreen*] étoilé

crazily ['kreɪzɪlɪ] ADV [*shout, gesticulate*] comme un fou; [*skid, bounce, whirl, tilt*] follement; ~ **jealous/extravagant** follement jaloux/extravagant

craziness ['kreɪzɪnɪs] N folie *f*

crazy ['kreɪzɪ] **1** ADJ **a** (= *mad*) fou (folle *f*); **to go ~** devenir fou *or* cinglé* *or* dingue*; **to be ~ with worry** être fou d'inquiétude; **it's enough to drive you ~** c'est à vous rendre fou *or* dingue*; **what a ~ idea** quelle idée folle; **you were ~ to want to go there** tu étais fou *or* dingue* de vouloir y aller, c'était de la folie de vouloir y aller **b** (* = *enthusiastic*) fou (folle *f*), fana* (*f inv*) (**about sb/sth** de qn/qch); **I'm not ~ about it** ça ne m'emballe* pas; **he's ~ about her** il est fou d'elle **c** (*fig*) [*price, height etc*] incroyable; (*US* = *excellent*) terrible*, formidable; **the tower leant at a ~ angle** la tour penchait d'une façon menaçante *or* inquiétante **d** like ~* comme un fou *or* une folle **2** COMP ► **crazy bone** N (*US*) petit juif* *m* (*partie du coude*) ► **crazy golf** N (*NonC: Brit*) minigolf *m* ► **crazy house** N (*US*) cabanon* *m*, asile *m* d'aliénés ► **crazy paving** N dallage *m* irrégulier (*en pierres plates*) ► **crazy quilt** N (*US*) édredon *m* (piqué) en patchwork, courtepointe *f* en patchwork

CRE [,si:ɑ:'ri:] N (*Brit*) (ABBR = **Commission for Racial Equality**) → **commission**; → *EOC, EEOC*

creak [kri:k] **1** VI [*door hinge, floorboard, bed, bedsprings*] grincer; [*shoes, joints*] craquer **2** N [*of floorboard, door, hinge, bedsprings*] grincement *m*; [*of shoes, leather, wood, bones*] crissement *m*; **the door opened with a ~** la porte s'ouvrit en grinçant

creaky ['kri:kɪ] ADJ **a** (= *noisy*) [*floorboard, stair, door, hinge*] grinçant; [*shoes*] qui crisse **b** (= *old*) [*system, film, play, equipment*] vieillot; [*body, legs*] usé

cream [kri:m] **1** N **a** crème *f*; (*Brit*) **single/double ~** crème *f* fraîche liquide/épaisse; **to take the ~ off the milk** écrémer le lait; (*fig*) **the ~ of the crop** (= *people*) le dessus du panier; (= *things*) le nec plus ultra; **the ~ of society** la crème *or* la fine fleur de la société; **chocolate ~** chocolat *m* fourré (à la crème); **vanilla ~** (= *dessert*) crème *f* à la vanille; (*biscuit*) biscuit *m* fourré à la vanille → **clot** **b** (= *face cream, shoe cream*) crème *f* → **cold, foundation** **2** ADJ (= *cream-coloured*) crème *inv*; (= *made with cream*) [*cake*] à la crème **3** VT **a** [+ *milk*] écrémer **b** (*Culin*) [+ *butter*] battre; **to ~ (together) sugar and butter** travailler le beurre en crème avec le sucre **c** (*US*, *fig*) [+ *enemy, opposing team*] rosser*, rétamer*; [+ *car*] bousiller* **4** COMP ► **cream cheese** N fromage *m* frais à tartiner ► **cream cracker** N (*Brit Culin*) cracker *m* ► **creamed potatoes** N purée *f* de pommes de terre ► **cream jug** N (*Brit*) pot *m* à crème ► **cream of tartar** N crème *f* de tartre ► **cream of tomato soup** N crème *f* de tomates ► **cream puff** N chou *m* à la crème ► **cream soda** N boisson *f* gazeuse à la

vanille ► **cream tea** N (*Brit*) goûter où l'on sert du thé et des scones avec de la crème et de la confiture

► **cream off** VT SEP (*fig*) [+ *best talents, part of profits*] prélever, écrémer

creamer ['kri:mər] N **a** (= *to separate cream*) écrémeuse *f* **b** (= *milk substitute*) succédané *m* de lait **c** (= *pitcher*) pot *m* à crème

creamery ['kri:mərɪ] N **a** (*on farm*) laiterie *f*; (= *butter factory*) laiterie *f*, coopérative *f* laitière **b** (= *small shop*) crémerie *f*

creamy ['kri:mɪ] ADJ crémeux; [*complexion*] crème *inv*, crémeux; ~ **white/yellow** blanc/jaune crème *inv*

crease [kri:s] **1** N (*made intentionally*) (*in material, paper*) pli *m*, pliure *f*; (*in trouser legs, skirt etc*) pli *m*; (*made accidentally*) faux pli *m*, pli *m*; (*on face*) ride *f* **2** VT (= *crumple*) (*accidentally*) froisser, chiffonner; (*intentionally*) plisser **3** VI se froisser, se chiffonner; (*fig*) **his face ~d with laughter** le rire a plissé son visage **4** COMP ► **crease-resistant** ADJ infroissable

► **crease up** **1** VT SEP **a** (= *crumple*) froisser, chiffonner **b** (*Brit** = *amuse*) faire mourir de rire **2** VI **a** (= *crumple*) se froisser, se chiffonner **b** (*Brit** = *laugh*) être plié en quatre

create [kri:'eɪt] **1** VT (*gen*) créer; [+ *new fashion*] lancer, créer; [+ *work of art, character, role*] créer; [+ *impression*] produire, faire; (*Comput*) [+ *file*] créer; [+ *problem, difficulty*] créer, susciter; [+ *noise, din*] faire; **to ~ a sensation** faire sensation; **two posts have been ~d** il y a eu deux créations de poste, deux postes ont été créés; **he was ~d baron** il a été fait baron **2** VI (*Brit* = *fuss*) faire une scène, faire un foin*

creation [kri:'eɪʃən] N **a** (*NonC*) création *f*; **since the ~** *or* **the Creation** depuis la création du monde **b** (*Art, Dress*) création *f*; **the latest ~s from Paris** les toutes dernières créations de Paris

creationism [kri:'eɪʃənɪzəm] N créationnisme *m*

creationist [kri:'eɪʃənɪst] ADJ, N créationniste *mf*

creative [kri:'eɪtɪv] **1** ADJ **a** (= *imaginative*) [*person, talent, skill, activity, atmosphere*] créatif; [*mind*] créatif, créateur (-trice *f*); [*energy, power*] créateur (-trice *f*); [*process*] de création; (*Educ*) ~ **toys** jouets *mpl* créatifs *or* d'éveil **b** (= *original*) [*person*] inventif; [*solution*] ingénieux; [*design*] novateur (-trice *f*); **the ~ use of language** l'utilisation créative du langage; **with a little ~ thinking you can find a solution** avec un peu d'imagination, vous trouverez une solution **2** COMP ► **creative accounting** N (*pej*) manipulations *fpl* comptables ► **creative writing** N création *f* littéraire

creatively [kri:'eɪtɪvlɪ] ADV de façon créative

creativity [,kri:eɪ'tɪvɪtɪ] N créativité *f*

creator [kri:'eɪtər] N créateur *m*, -trice *f*

creature ['kri:tʃər] **1** N (*gen, also fig*) créature *f*; (= *animal*) bête *f*, animal *m*; (= *human*) être *m*, créature *f*; **dumb ~s** les bêtes *fpl*; **the ~s of the deep** les animaux *mpl* marins; **she's a poor/lovely ~** c'est une pauvre/ravissante créature; (*fig*) **to be a ~ of habit** avoir ses (petites) habitudes; (*fig pej*) **they were all his ~s** tous étaient ses créatures → **habit** **2** COMP ► **creature comforts** NPL confort *m* matériel; **he likes his ~ comforts** il aime son petit confort

crèche [kreɪʃ] N (*Brit*) (*up to 3 years old*) crèche *f*; (*after 3 years old*) (halte-)garderie *f*

cred* [kred] N (*NonC*) crédibilité *f* → **street cred**

credence ['kri:dəns] N croyance *f*, foi *f*; **to give** *or* **lend ~ to** ajouter foi à

credentials [krɪ'denʃəlz] NPL (= *identifying papers*) pièce *f* d'identité; [*of diplomat*] lettres *fpl*

de créance; (= *references*) références *fpl*; **to have good ~** avoir de bonnes références

credibility [,kredə'bɪlɪtɪ] **1** N crédibilité *f*; **to lose ~** perdre sa crédibilité **2** COMP ► **credibility gap** N manque *m* de crédibilité ► **credibility rating** N his ~ **rating is not very high** sa crédibilité est très entamée

credible ['kredɪbl] ADJ crédible; **it is scarcely ~ that ...** on a du mal à croire que ...

credibly ['kredɪblɪ] ADV de façon crédible

credit ['kredɪt] **1** N **a** (*Banking, Comm, Fin*) crédit *m*; (*Accounts*) crédit *m*, avoir *m*; **to give sb ~** faire crédit à qn; **"no ~"** « la maison ne fait pas crédit »; **to buy/sell on ~** acheter/vendre à crédit; **you have £10 to your ~** vous avez un crédit de 10 livres; (*account*) **in ~** approvisionné; **am I in ~?** est-ce que mon compte est approvisionné? **b** (= *belief, acceptance*) **to give ~ to** [+ *person*] ajouter foi à; [+ *event*] donner foi à, accréditer; **I gave him ~ for more sense** je lui supposais *or* croyais plus de bon sens; **to gain ~ with** s'accréditer auprès de; **his ~ with the electorate** son crédit auprès des électeurs **c** honneur *m*; **to his ~ we must point out that ...** il faut faire remarquer à son honneur *or* à son crédit que ...; **it is to his ~** c'est tout à son honneur; **he is a ~ to his family** il fait honneur à sa famille, il est l'honneur de sa famille; **the only people to emerge with any ~** les seuls à s'en sortir à leur honneur; **to give sb ~ for his generosity** reconnaître la générosité de qn à fait qch; **to claim** *or* **take (the) ~ for sth** s'attribuer le mérite de qch; **it does you (great) ~** cela est tout à votre honneur, cela vous fait grand honneur; ~ **where ~'s due** il faut rendre à César ce qui appartient à César **d** (*Scol*) unité *f* d'enseignement *or* de valeur, UV *f*

2 **credits** NPL (*Cine*) générique *m*

3 VT **a** (= *believe*) [+ *rumour, news*] croire; **I could hardly ~ it** je n'arrivais pas à le croire; **you wouldn't ~ it** vous ne le croiriez pas **b** (*gen*) **to ~ sb/sth with (having) certain powers/qualities** reconnaître à qn/qch certains pouvoirs/certaines qualités; **to be ~ed with having done ...** passer pour avoir fait ...; **I ~ed him with more sense** je lui croyais *or* supposais plus de bon sens; **it is ~ed with (having) magical powers** on lui attribue des pouvoirs magiques **c** (*Banking*) **to ~ £50 to sb** *or* **to sb's account** ◊ **to ~ sb** *or* **sb's account with £50** créditer (le compte de) qn de 50 livres, porter 50 livres au crédit de qn

4 COMP ► **credit account** N compte *m* créditeur ► **credit agency** N établissement *m* *or* agence *f* de crédit ► **credit arrangements** NPL accords *mpl* de crédit ► **credit balance** N (*Banking*) solde *m* créditeur ► **credit bureau** N (*US*) = **credit agency** ► **credit card** N carte *f* de crédit ► **credit charges** NPL coût *m* du crédit ► **credit check** N vérification *f* de solvabilité; **to run a ~ check on sb** vérifier la solvabilité de qn ► **credit control** N (= *action*) encadrement *m* de crédit; (= *department*) (service *m* de l')encadrement *m* du crédit ► **credit entry** N (*Fin*) inscription *f* *or* écriture *f* au crédit ► **credit facilities** NPL (*Banking*) ligne *f* de crédit; (*Comm: to buyer*) facilités *fpl* de paiement *or* de crédit ► **credit hour** N (*US Scol, Univ*) ≈ unité *f* de valeur ► **credit limit** N limite *f* *or* plafond *m* de crédit ► **credit line** N (*Banking*) ligne *f* de crédit; (*Cine*) mention *f* au générique; (*in book*) mention *f* de la source ► **credit note** N (*Brit*) avoir *m* ► **credit rating** N indice *m* de solvabilité ► **credit reference agency** N agence *f* de notation financière *or* de rating ► **credit risk** N **to be a good/poor ~ risk** présenter peu de risques de crédit/un certain risque de crédit ► **credit sales** NPL ventes *fpl* à crédit ► **credit side** N (*Accounts, also fig*) **on the ~ side** à l'actif ► **credit squeeze** N (*Econ*) restrictions *fpl* de crédit ► **credit terms** NPL conditions *fpl* de crédit ► **credit titles** NPL (*Cine*) générique *m* ► **credit transfer** N transfert *m*, virement *m* ► **credit union** N (*US*) société *f* de crédit mutuel

creditable ['krɛdɪtəbl] ADJ honorable

creditably ['krɛdɪtəblɪ] ADV [*behave, perform, play*] honorablement

creditor ['krɛdɪtəʳ] [1] N créancier *m*, -ière *f* [2] COMP ► **creditor nation** N (*Econ*) pays *m* créditeur

creditworthiness ['krɛdɪtwɜːðɪnɪs] N solvabilité *f*, capacité *f* d'emprunt

creditworthy ['krɛdɪtwɜːðɪ] ADJ solvable

credo ['kreɪdəʊ] N credo *m*

credulity [krɪ'djuːlɪtɪ] N crédulité *f*

credulous ['krɛdjʊləs] ADJ crédule, naïf (naïve *f*)

credulously ['krɛdjʊləslɪ] ADV avec crédulité, naïvement

creed [kriːd] N credo *m*; (*Rel*) **the Creed** le Credo

creek [kriːk] N [a] (*esp Brit* = *inlet*) crique *f*, anse *f*; **to be up the ~ (without a paddle)**‡ (= *be wrong*) se fourrer le doigt dans l'œil (jusqu'au coude)*; (= *be in trouble*) être dans le pétrin [b] (*US* = *stream*) ruisseau *m*, petit cours *m* d'eau

creel [kriːl] N panier *m* de pêche

creep [kriːp] (*pret, ptp* **crept**) [1] VI [*animal, person, plant*] ramper; (= *move silently*) se glisser; **to ~ between** se faufiler entre; **to ~ in/out/away** [*person*] entrer/sortir/s'éloigner à pas de loup; [*animal*] entrer/sortir/s'éloigner sans un bruit; **to ~ about/along** on tiptoe marcher/avancer sur la pointe des pieds; **to ~ up on sb** [*person*] s'approcher de qn à pas de loup; [*old age etc*] prendre qn par surprise; **old age is ~ing on** on se fait vieux*; **the traffic crept along** les voitures avançaient au pas; (*fig*) **an error crept into it** une erreur s'y est glissée; **a feeling of peace crept over me** un sentiment de paix me gagnait peu à peu et commençait à me gagner [2] N [a] **it gives me the ~s*** cela me donne la chair de poule, cela me fait froid dans le dos [b] (*pej* = *person*) sale type* *m*

creeper ['kriːpəʳ] N [a] (*Bot*) plante *f* rampante → **Virginia** [b] (*US*) **~s** barboteuse *f* [c] (* = *person*) lécheur* *m*, -euse* *f*, lèche-bottes* *mf inv*

creeping ['kriːpɪŋ] [1] ADJ [a] (*Bot*) [*plant*] rampant [b] (= *gradual*) [*process, inflation, privatization*] rampant; [*change*] larvé [2] COMP ► **creeping paralysis** N (*Med*) paralysie *f* progressive

creepy ['kriːpɪ] [1] ADJ [*story, place, feeling*] qui donne la chair de poule [2] COMP ► **creepy-crawly*** ADJ qui donne la chair de poule ♦ N (*pl* **creepy-crawlies**) petite bestiole *f*

cremate [krɪ'meɪt] VT incinérer

cremation [krɪ'meɪʃən] N crémation *f*, incinération *f*

crematorium [ˌkrɛmə'tɔːrɪəm] (*pl* **crematoriums** *or* **crematoria** [ˌkrɛmə'tɔːrɪə]), **crematory** (*US*) ['krɛmə,tɔːrɪ] N (= *place*) crématorium *m*, crématoire *m*; (= *furnace*) four *m* crématoire

crème de la crème ['krɛmdəlaː'krɛm] N **the ~** le dessus du panier, le gratin*

crenellated ['krɛnɪleɪtɪd] ADJ crénelé, à créneaux

crenellations [ˌkrɛnɪ'leɪʃənz] NPL créneaux *mpl*

creole ['kriːəʊl] [1] ADJ créole [2] N **Creole** Créole *mf* [3] COMP ► **the Creole State** N la Louisiane

creosote ['krɪəsəʊt] [1] N créosote *f* [2] VT créosoter

---

crêpe [kreɪp] [1] N [a] (*Tex*) crêpe *m* [b] (*Culin*) crêpe *f* [2] COMP ► **crêpe bandage** N bande *f* Velpeau® ► **crêpe paper** N papier *m* crépon ► **crêpe shoes, crêpe-soled shoes** NPL chaussures *fpl* à semelles de crêpe

crept [krɛpt] VB *pt, ptp of* **creep**

crepuscular [krɪ'pʌskjʊləʳ] ADJ crépusculaire

crescendo [krɪ'ʃɛndəʊ] [1] N (*pl* **crescendos** *or* **crescendi** [krɪ'ʃɛndiː]) (*Mus, fig*) crescendo *m inv* [2] VI (*Mus*) faire un crescendo

crescent ['krɛsnt] [1] N [a] croissant *m*; (*Islamic faith etc*) **the Crescent** le Croissant [b] (= *street*) rue *f* (*en arc de cercle*) [2] COMP ► **crescent moon** N croissant *m* de lune ► **crescent roll** N (*Culin*) croissant *m* ► **crescent-shaped** ADJ en (forme de) croissant

cress [krɛs] N cresson *m* → **mustard, watercress**

crest [krɛst] [1] N [*of bird, wave, mountain*] crête *f*; [*of helmet*] cimier *m*; (= *long ridge*) arête *f*; [*of road*] haut *m* de côte, sommet *m* de côte; (*above coat of arms, shield*) timbre *m*; (*on seal etc*) armoiries *fpl*; **the family ~** les armoiries *fpl* familiales; (*fig*) **he is on the ~ of the wave** tout lui réussit en ce moment [2] VT [+ *wave, hill*] franchir la crête de; **~ed notepaper** papier *m* à lettres armorié; **~ed tit** mésange *f* huppée

crestfallen ['krɛst,fɔːlən] ADJ [*person*] déconfit; **to look ~** avoir l'air penaud

cretaceous [krɪ'teɪʃəs] ADJ crétacé; (*Geol*) **the Cretaceous (period)** le crétacé

Cretan ['kriːtən] [1] ADJ crétois [2] N Crétois(e) *m(f)*

Crete [kriːt] N la Crète; **in ~** en Crète

cretin ['krɛtɪn] N crétin(e) *m(f)*

cretinism ['krɛtɪnɪzəm] N (*Med*) crétinisme *m*

cretinous* ['krɛtɪnəs] ADJ (*Med pej*) crétin

cretonne [krɛ'tɒn] N cretonne *f*

Creutzfeldt-Jakob disease [ˌkrɔɪtsfɛlt-'jækɒbdɪˌziːz] N (*NonC*) maladie *f* de Creutzfeldt-Jakob

crevasse [krɪ'væs] N (*Geol, Climbing*) crevasse *f*

crevice ['krɛvɪs] N (*in rock*) fissure *f*; (*in wall*) lézarde *f*

crew¹ [kruː] [1] N (*Aviat, Naut*) équipage *m*; (*Cine, Rowing etc*) équipe *f*; (= *group, gang*) bande *f*, équipe *f*; (*pej*) **what a ~!*** tu parles d'une équipe!*, quelle engeance! [2] VI (*Sailing*) **to ~ for sb** être l'équipier de qn; **would you like me to ~ for you?** voulez-vous de moi comme équipier? [3] VT [+ *yacht*] armer [4] COMP ► **crew cut** N **to have a ~ cut** avoir les cheveux en brosse ► **crew-neck sweater** N pull *m* ras du cou, ras-du-cou *m inv*

crew² [kruː] VB *pt of* **crow**²

crewel ['kruːɪl] N (= *yarn*) laine *f* à tapisserie; (= *work*) tapisserie *f* sur canevas

crewman ['kruːmən] N (*pl* **-men**) (*TV etc*) équipier *m*

crib [krɪb] [1] N [a] (*Brit: for infant*) berceau *m*; (*US: for toddler*) lit *m* d'enfant; (*Rel*) crèche *f* [b] (= *manger*) mangeoire *f*, râtelier *m* [c] (= *plagiarism*) plagiat *m*, copiage *m*; (*Scol*) antisèche* *f* [2] VT (*Scol*) copier, pomper*; **to ~ sb's work** copier le travail de qn, copier *or* pomper* sur qn [3] VI copier; **to ~ from a friend** copier sur un camarade; **he had ~bed from Shakespeare** il avait plagié Shakespeare [4] COMP ► **crib death** N (*US*) mort *f* subite du nourrisson

cribbage ['krɪbɪdʒ] N jeu *m* de cartes

crick [krɪk] [1] N crampe *f*; **~ in the neck** torticolis *m*; **~ in the back** tour *m* de reins [2] VT **to ~ one's neck** attraper un torticolis; **to ~ one's back** se faire un tour de reins

cricket¹ ['krɪkɪt] N (= *insect*) grillon *m*, cricri* *m inv*

cricket² ['krɪkɪt] [1] N (*Sport*) cricket *m*; (*fig*) **that's not ~** cela ne se fait pas, ce n'est pas

---

correct [2] COMP [*ball, bat, match, pitch*] de cricket

> ┌─ CRICKET ─┐
>
> Le cricket est souvent considéré comme un sport typiquement anglais, bien qu'il soit pratiqué dans toute la Grande-Bretagne et dans beaucoup de pays du Commonwealth. C'est surtout un sport d'été, dans lequel deux équipes de onze joueurs s'affrontent selon des règles assez complexes.
>
> Comme le base-ball aux États-Unis, ce sport a fourni à la langue courante un certain nombre d'expressions imagées, parmi lesquelles « a sticky wicket » (une situation difficile); « to knock someone for six » (démolir qn); « to be stumped » (sécher) et le fameux « it's not cricket » (cela ne se fait pas, ce n'est pas correct).

cricketer ['krɪkɪtəʳ] N joueur *m* de cricket

cricketing ['krɪkɪtɪŋ] ADJ **England's ~ heroes** les héros du cricket anglais; **his ~ career** sa carrière de joueur de cricket

crier ['kraɪəʳ] N crieur *m*; [*of law courts*] huissier *m* → **town**

crikey* ['kraɪkɪ] EXCL (*Brit*) mince (alors)!

crime [kraɪm] [1] N (*gen*) crime *m*; (*Mil*) manquement *m* à la discipline, infraction *f*; **minor ~** délit *m*; **~ and punishment** le crime et le châtiment; **a life of ~** une vie de criminel *or* de crime; **~ is on the increase/decrease** il y a un accroissement/une régression de la criminalité; **~ doesn't pay** le crime ne paye pas; **it's a ~ to make him do it*** c'est un crime de le forcer à le faire → **organized** [2] COMP ► **crime fighting** N (*NonC*) lutte *f* contre la criminalité ► **crime-fighting** ADJ [*plan, strategy, group*] de lutte contre la criminalité ► **crime of passion** N crime *m* passionnel ► **crime prevention** N prévention *f* de la criminalité ► **crime prevention officer** N policier *m* chargé de la prévention de la criminalité ► **crime spree** N série *f* de délits; **to go on a ~ spree** multiplier les délits ► **Crime Squad** N brigade *f* criminelle ► **crime wave** N vague *f* de criminalité ► **crime writer** N auteur *m* de romans policiers

Crimea [kraɪ'mɪə] N **the ~** la Crimée

Crimean [kraɪ'mɪən] ADJ, N **the ~ (War)** la guerre de Crimée

criminal ['krɪmɪnl] [1] N criminel *m*, -elle *f* [2] ADJ [*action, motive, law*] criminel; **a ~ waste of resources** un gaspillage criminel (des ressources); (*fig*) **it's ~ to stay indoors today** c'est un crime de rester enfermé aujourd'hui → **conspiracy** [3] COMP ► **criminal assault** N (*Jur*) agression *f* criminelle, voie *f* de fait ► **criminal code** N code *m* pénal ► **criminal conversation** N (*US Jur*) adultère *m* (*de la femme*) ► **criminal court** N cour *f* d'assises ► **criminal damage** N (*NonC: Jur*) dégradations *fpl* volontaires ► **criminal investigation** N enquête *f* criminelle ► **the Criminal Investigation Department** N (*in Brit*) la police judiciaire, la PJ ► **criminal law** N droit *m* pénal *or* criminel ► **criminal lawyer** N pénaliste *m*, avocat *m* au criminel ► **criminal negligence** N (*NonC: Jur*) négligence *f* coupable *or* criminelle ► **criminal offence** N délit *m*; **it's a ~ offence to do that** c'est un crime puni par la loi de faire cela ► **criminal proceedings** NPL (*Jur*) **to take ~ proceedings against sb** poursuivre qn au pénal ► **criminal record** N casier *m* judiciaire; **he hasn't got a ~ record** il a un casier judiciaire vierge ► **the Criminal Records Office** N (*in Brit*) l'identité *f* judiciaire

criminality [ˌkrɪmɪ'nælɪtɪ] N criminalité *f*

criminalization [ˌkrɪmɪnəlaɪ'zeɪʃən] N criminalisation *f*

criminalize ['krɪmɪnəlaɪz] VT criminaliser

criminally ['krɪmɪnəlɪ] ADV a (Jur) [liable, responsible] pénalement ; **to be ~ negligent** faire preuve de négligence coupable or criminelle ; **the ~ insane** les psychopathes mpl b (= scandalously) [underpaid] scandaleusement ; **~ irresponsible** d'une irresponsabilité criminelle ; **a ~ wasteful use of resources** un gaspillage criminel (des ressources)

criminologist [,krɪmɪ'nɒlədʒɪst] N criminologiste mf, criminologue mf

criminology [,krɪmɪ'nɒlədʒɪ] N criminologie f

crimp [krɪmp] 1 VT a [+ hair] crêper, friser ; [+ pastry] pincer b (US = hinder) gêner, entraver 2 N (US = person) raseur m, -euse f ; **to put a ~ in ...** mettre obstacle à ..., mettre des bâtons dans les roues de ...

crimped [krɪmpt] ADJ [fabric etc] plissé, froncé ; [hair] crêpé

Crimplene® ['krɪmpliːn] N ≈ crêpe m polyester

crimson ['krɪmzn] ADJ, N cramoisi m

cringe [krɪndʒ] 1 VI (= shrink back) avoir un mouvement de recul, reculer (**from** devant) ; (fig = humble o.s.) ramper, s'humilier (**before** devant) ; (fig) **the very thought of it makes me ~** rien que d'y penser j'ai envie de rentrer sous terre 2 COMP ► **cringe-making** ADJ (Brit) qui donne des boutons, qui fait grincer les dents

cringing ['krɪndʒɪŋ] ADJ [bow, attitude, person] servile

crinkle ['krɪŋkl] 1 VT [+ paper] froisser, chiffonner 2 VI se froisser 3 N fronce f, pli m 4 COMP ► **crinkle-cut** ADJ (Brit) [chips, crisps] dentelé

crinkled ['krɪŋkld] ADJ [leaf, paper, clothes] froissé ; [face, head] plein de rides

crinkly ['krɪŋklɪ] ADJ [hair] crépu, crêpelé ; [skin, face, eyes] plissé ; [paper] gaufré

crinoline ['krɪnəlɪn] N crinoline f

cripple ['krɪpl] 1 N (= lame) estropié(e) m(f), boiteux m, -euse f ; (= disabled) infirme mf, invalide mf ; (from accident, war) invalide mf ; (= maimed) mutilé(e) m(f) ; **he's an emotional ~** il est complètement bloqué sur le plan affectif 2 VT a estropier b (fig) [+ ship, plane] désemparer ; (Ind) [strikes etc] [+ production, exports etc] paralyser ; [+ person] inhiber, bloquer ; **activities ~d by lack of funds** activités paralysées par le manque de fonds

crippled ['krɪpld] 1 ADJ a (= physically disabled) [person] (gen) infirme ; (through mutilation) estropié ; [leg, hand] estropié ; **the bomb blast left her ~** l'explosion l'a rendue infirme ; **~ for life** handicapé à vie ; **~ with arthritis** perclus d'arthrite b (psychologically) **~ with shyness** perclus de timidité ; **emotionally ~** bloqué sur le plan affectif c (= stricken) [aircraft, ship] désemparé d (= dysfunctional) [society, economy, organization] handicapé ; **~ with debt** écrasé de dettes 2 **the crippled** NPL les estropiés mpl

crippling ['krɪplɪŋ] ADJ a [disease, illness, injury] invalidant b (fig) [pain, inflation, strike, effect] paralysant ; [guilt, depression] qui paralyse ; [tax, debt, cost] écrasant ; **a ~ blow** un coup dur

crisis ['kraɪsɪs] 1 N (pl crises ['kraɪsiːz]) crise f ; **to come to a ◊ to reach ~ point** or **a ~** atteindre un point critique ; **to solve a ~** dénouer or résoudre une crise ; **we've got a ~ on our hands** nous avons un problème urgent, nous sommes dans une situation critique ; **the first oil ~** le premier choc pétrolier, la première crise du pétrole 2 COMP ► **crisis centre** N (for large-scale disaster) cellule f de crise ; (for personal help) centre m d'aide ; (for battered women) association f d'urgence ► **crisis management** N (NonC) gestion f de crise

crisp [krɪsp] 1 ADJ a (= crunchy) [apple, salad] croquant ; [biscuit, pastry, bacon] croustillant ;

[snow] qui crisse ; [leaves] craquant b [shirt, suit, cotton, linen] tout propre, impeccable c (= refreshing) [air] vif, piquant ; [weather] tonifiant ; [day, morning] frais (fraîche f) et piquant(e) ; [wine, sherry] gouleyant, coulant d (= clear) [picture, image] net et précis ; [shape] épuré ; [voice, sound] clair ; [style] précis e (= succinct) [writing, style] épuré ; [phrase] vif ; [statement, speech] concis f (= brisk) [tone, voice, comment] sec (sèche f) g (= tight) [curls] serré 2 N (Brit) (potato) **~s** (pommes) chips fpl ; **packet of ~s** sachet m or paquet m de chips 3 VT (Culin: also **~ up**: with crispy topping) faire gratiner ; [+ chicken etc] faire dorer

crispbread ['krɪspbred] N pain m scandinave

crisper ['krɪspə'] N (= salad crisper) bac m à légumes

Crispin ['krɪspɪn] N Crépin f

crisply ['krɪsplɪ] ADV a (Culin) **~ fried** or **grilled** croustillant b (= stiffly) **~ pressed** or **ironed** parfaitement repassé c (= briskly) [say, reply] sèchement

crispness ['krɪspnɪs] N a (= crunchiness) [of biscuit etc] craquant m b (= freshness) [of air, weather] fraîcheur f, piquant m c (= succinctness) [of style] précision f, tranchant m

crispy ['krɪspɪ] ADJ croquant, croustillant ; **~ noodles** nouilles fpl sautées ; **~ pancakes** crêpes fpl croustillantes

criss-cross ['krɪskrɒs] 1 ADJ [lines] entrecroisés ; (in muddle) enchevêtré ; **in a ~ pattern** en croisillons 2 N entrecroisement m, enchevêtrement m 3 VT entrecroiser (**by** de) 4 VI [lines] s'entrecroiser 5 ADV formant (un) réseau

crit* [krɪt] N [of play, book etc] papier* m, critique f

criterion [kraɪ'tɪərɪən] N (pl **criterions** or **criteria** [kraɪ'tɪərɪə]) critère m

critic ['krɪtɪk] N [of books, painting, music, films etc] critique m ; (= faultfinder) critique m, détracteur m, -trice f ; (Press) **film ~** critique m de cinéma ; **he's a strong ~ of the government** il est très critique à l'égard du gouvernement ; **he is a constant ~ of the government** il ne cesse de critiquer le gouvernement ; **his wife is his most severe ~** sa femme est son plus sévère critique

critical ['krɪtɪkəl] 1 ADJ a (= important) [factor, element, issue] crucial (**for** or **to** pour) ; **it was ~ for him to gain their support** il était crucial pour lui d'obtenir leur soutien b (= decisive) [moment, point, time] critique, crucial ; [situation, state] critique ; **at a ~ stage** dans une phase critique ; **of ~ importance** d'une importance décisive c (Med) [patient] dans un état critique ; **in a ~ condition** ◊ **on the ~ list** dans un état critique ; **to be off the ~ list** être dans un état stable d (= censorious) [person, attitude, speech, report] critique (**of sb/sth** à l'égard de qn/qch) ; **~ remark** critique f e (Art, Literat, Mus, Theat) [study, writings, edition] critique ; **to meet with ~ acclaim** or **praise** être salué par la critique ; **to be a ~ success** connaître un succès critique f (Phys) **to go ~** atteindre le seuil or l'état or la valeur critique 2 COMP ► **critical angle** N (Aviat, Opt) angle m critique ► **critical mass** N (Phys) masse f critique ; (fig) point m critique ; **to reach (a) ~ mass** (Phys) atteindre une masse critique ; (fig) atteindre un point critique ► **critical path** N chemin m critique ► **critical path analysis** N analyse f du chemin critique ► **critical path method** N méthode f du chemin critique ► **critical temperature** N (Phys) température f critique

critically ['krɪtɪkəlɪ] ADV a (= crucially) **to be ~ important** être d'une importance capitale ; **a ~**

important moment un moment critique ; **the success of the project is ~ dependent on his contribution** sa contribution est d'une importance capitale pour la réussite du projet ; **to be (running) ~ low on sth** manquer sérieusement de qch ; **books are in ~ short supply** on manque sérieusement de livres b (Med) [ill, injured] gravement c (= censoriously) [speak, say] sévèrement d (= analytically) [study, examine, watch] d'un œil critique e (Art, Literat, Mus, Theat) **~ acclaimed** salué par la critique

criticism ['krɪtɪsɪzəm] N critique f ; **the decision is open to ~** cette décision prête le flanc à la critique or est critiquable

▼ **criticize** ['krɪtɪsaɪz] VT a (= assess) [+ book etc] critiquer, faire la critique de b (= find fault with) [+ behaviour, person] critiquer ; **I don't want to ~, but ...** je ne veux pas avoir l'air de critiquer, mais ...

critique [krɪ'tiːk] N critique f

critter* ['krɪtə'] N (US) créature f ; (= animal) bête f, bestiole f

croak [krəʊk] 1 VI a [frog] coasser ; [raven] croasser ; [person] (gen) parler d'une voix rauque ; (due to sore throat) parler d'une voix enrouée ; (* = grumble) maugréer, ronchonner b (‡ = die) claquer*, crever* 2 VT (gen) dire d'une voix rauque ; (due to sore throat) dire d'une voix enrouée ; **"help" he ~ed feebly** « au secours » appela-t-il d'une voix rauque 3 N [of frog] coassement m ; [of raven] croassement m ; **his voice was a mere ~** il ne proférait que des sons rauques

croaky ['krəʊkɪ] ADJ [voice] (gen) rauque ; (due to sore throat) enroué

Croat ['krəʊæt] N Croate mf

Croatia [krəʊ'eɪʃə] N la Croatie

Croatian [krəʊ'eɪʃən] ADJ croate

crochet ['krəʊʃeɪ] 1 N (NonC: also **~ work**) (travail m au) crochet m 2 VT [+ garment] faire au crochet 3 VI faire du crochet 4 COMP ► **crochet hook** N crochet m

crock [krɒk] N a (= pot) cruche f, pot m de terre ; **~s** (= broken pieces) débris mpl de faïence ; **the ~s*** la vaisselle b* (= horse) vieille rosse f, cheval m fourbu ; (esp Brit = car) vieille bagnole* f, vieux clou* m ; (Sport = injured player) joueur m, -euse f amoché(e)* ; **he's an old ~** c'est un croulant*

crocked‡ [krɒkt] ADJ (US) bourré*

crockery ['krɒkərɪ] N (NonC: Brit) (= cups, saucers, plates) vaisselle f ; (= earthenware) poterie f, faïence f

crocodile ['krɒkədaɪl] 1 N a crocodile m b (Brit Scol) cortège m en rangs (par deux) ; **to walk in a ~** aller deux par deux 2 COMP [shoes, handbag] en crocodile, en croco* ► **crocodile clip** N pince f crocodile ► **crocodile tears** NPL larmes fpl de crocodile

crocus ['krəʊkəs] N (pl **crocuses**) crocus m

Croesus ['kriːsəs] N Crésus m ; **as rich as ~** riche comme Crésus

croft [krɒft] N petite exploitation f agricole

crofter ['krɒftə'] N petit exploitant m agricole

crofting ['krɒftɪŋ] N organisation f de l'agriculture en petites exploitations

croissant ['kwæsɒŋ] N croissant m

Cromwellian [krɒm'welɪən] ADJ de Cromwell

crone [krəʊn] N vieille ratatinée* f, vieille bique f

crony* ['krəʊnɪ] N copain* m, copine* f

cronyism* ['krəʊnɪɪzəm] N copinage* m

crook [krʊk] 1 N a [of shepherd] houlette f ; [of bishop] crosse f ; (Mus) [of brass instrument] ton m de rechange ; [of road] angle m ; [of river] coude m ; (* = thief) escroc m, filou m 2 VT [+ one's finger] courber, recourber ; [+ one's arm] plier

crooked ['krʊkɪd] [1] ADJ [a] (= *bent, askew*) [*line, stick, back*] tordu; [*nose, tooth, picture, tie*] de travers; [*street*] tortueux; **to give a ~ smile** sourire du coin des lèvres; **a ~ old man** un vieillard tout tordu [b] (* = *dishonest*) [*person, business*] véreux; [*deal, method*] malhonnête [2] ADV* de travers, de traviole*

crookedly ['krʊkɪdlɪ] ADV [*smile, grin*] du coin des lèvres; [*hang*] de travers

crookedness ['krʊkɪdnɪs] N (= *dishonesty*) malhonnêteté *f*; [*of features*] manque *m* de symétrie

croon [kruːn] VTI (= *sing softly*) chantonner, fredonner; (*in show business*) chanter (*en crooner*)

crooner ['kruːnəʳ] N chanteur *m*, -euse *f* de charme, crooner *m*

crooning ['kruːnɪŋ] N (*NonC*) la chanson de charme

crop [krɒp] [1] N [a] (= *produce*) produit *m* agricole, culture *f*; (= *amount produced*) récolte *f*; (*of fruit etc*) récolte *f*, cueillette *f*; (*of cereals*) moisson *f*; (*fig*) [*of problems, questions*] série *f*; [*of people*] fournée *f*; (*at harvest time*) **the ~s** la récolte; **one of the basic ~s** l'une des cultures de base; **we had a good ~ of strawberries** la récolte or la cueillette des fraises a été bonne; **to get the ~s in** faire la récolte or la cueillette or la moisson, rentrer les récoltes or la moisson [b] [*of bird*] jabot *m* [c] [*of whip*] manche *m*; (*also* **riding ~**) cravache *f* [d] (*Hairdressing*) **to give sb a (close) ~** couper ras les cheveux de qn; **Eton ~** cheveux *mpl* à la garçonne [2] VT [a] [*animals grass*] brouter, paître [b] [+ *tail*] écourter; [+ *hair*] tondre; **~ped hair** cheveux *mpl* coupés ras [c] (*Phot*) recadrer [3] VI [*land*] donner or fournir une récolte [4] COMP ► **crop circle** N cercle *m* dans les blés ► **crop dusting** N = **crop spraying** ► **crop rotation** N assolement *m*, rotation *f* des cultures ► **crop sprayer** N (= *device*) pulvérisateur *m*; (= *plane*) avion-pulvérisateur *m* ► **crop spraying** N (*NonC*) pulvérisation *f* des cultures

► **crop out** VI (*Geol*) affleurer

► **crop up** VI [a] [*questions, problems*] survenir, se présenter; **the subject ~ped up during the conversation** le sujet a été amené or mis sur le tapis au cours de la conversation; **something's ~ped up and I can't come** j'ai un contretemps, je ne pourrai pas venir; **he was ready for anything that might ~ up** il était prêt à toute éventualité [b] (*Geol*) affleurer

cropper * ['krɒpəʳ] N (*lit, fig*) **to come a ~** (= *fall*) se casser la figure*; (= *fail in attempt*) se planter*; (*in exam*) se faire coller* or étendre

cropping ['krɒpɪŋ] N (*Phot*) recadrage *m*

croquet ['krəʊkeɪ] [1] N croquet *m* [2] COMP ► **croquet hoop** N arceau *m* de croquet ► **croquet mallet** N maillet *m* de croquet

croquette [krəʊ'ket] N croquette *f*; **potato ~** croquette *f* de pommes de terre

crosier ['krəʊʒəʳ] N [*of bishop*] crosse *f*

▼ **cross** [krɒs] [1] N [a] (= *mark, emblem*) croix *f*; **to mark/sign with a ~** marquer/signer d'une croix; **the iron ~** la croix de fer; (*Rel*) **the Cross** la Croix → **bear¹, market, red, sign** [b] (*Bio, Zool*) hybride *m*; **~ between two different breeds** mélange *m* or croisement *m* de deux races différentes, hybride *m*; (*fig*) **it's a ~ between a novel and a poem** cela tient du roman et du poème; **a ~ between a laugh and a bark** un bruit qui tient du rire et de l'aboiement [c] (*NonC*) [*of material*] biais *m*; (*Sewing*) **to cut material on the ~** couper du tissu dans le biais; **a skirt cut on the ~** une jupe en biais; **line drawn on the ~** ligne tracée en biais or en

diagonale [d] (*Sport*) centre *m*; **to hit a ~ to sb** centrer sur qn, envoyer un centre sur qn [2] ADJ [a] (= *angry*) [*person*] en colère; **to be ~ with sb** être fâché or en colère contre qn; **it makes me ~ when ...** cela me met en colère quand ...; **to get ~ with sb** se mettre en colère or se fâcher contre qn; **don't be ~ with me** ne m'en veuillez pas, il ne faut pas m'en vouloir; **they haven't had a ~ word in ten years** ils ne se sont pas disputés une seule fois en dix ans [b] (= *traverse, diagonal*) transversal, diagonal [3] VT [a] [+ *room, street, sea, continent, river, bridge*] traverser; [+ *threshold, fence, ditch*] franchir; **the bridge ~es the river here** c'est ici que le pont franchit or enjambe la rivière; **it ~ed my mind that ...** il m'est venu à l'esprit que ...; **they have clearly ~ed the boundary into terrorism** ils ont manifestement basculé dans le terrorisme; **a smile ~ed her lips** un sourire se dessina sur ses lèvres → **bridge, floor, line, path** [b] **to ~ one's arms/legs** croiser les bras/les jambes; (*Brit Telec*) **the lines are ~ed ◊ we've got a ~ed line** il y a un problème sur la ligne; (*fig*) **they've got their lines ~ed** il y a un malentendu quelque part → **finger, sword** [c] (*Rel*) **to ~ o.s.** se signer, faire le signe de la croix; (*fig*) **my heart (and hope to die)!*** croix de bois, croix de fer(, si je mens je vais en enfer)!* [d] **to ~ a "t"** barrer un « t » → **cheque, palm** [e] [+ *person*] (= *anger*) contrarier; (= *thwart*) contrecarrer les projets de; [+ *plans*] contrecarrer; **~ed in love** malheureux en amour [f] [+ *animals, plants*] croiser (**with** avec); **to ~ two animals/plants** croiser or métisser deux animaux/plantes [4] VI [a] (*also* **~ over**) **he ~ed from one side of the room to the other to speak to me** il a traversé la pièce pour venir me parler; **to ~ from one place to another** passer d'un endroit à un autre; **to ~ from Newhaven to Dieppe** faire la traversée de Newhaven à Dieppe [b] [*roads, paths*] se croiser, se rencontrer; [*letters, people*] se croiser [5] COMP ► **cross-border** ADJ transfrontalier ► **cross-Channel ferry** N ferry *m* qui traverse la Manche ► **cross-check** N contre-épreuve *f*, recoupement *m* ♦ VT [+ *facts*] vérifier par recoupement or contre-épreuve ♦ VI vérifier par recoupement ► **cross-compiler** N (*Comput*) compilateur *m* croisé ► **cross-country** ADJ à travers champs; **~-country race** or **running** cross(-country) *m*; **~-country skier** skieur *m* de fond or de randonnée; **~-country skiing** ski *m* de fond or de randonnée ► **cross-court** ADJ (*Tennis*) [*drive, shot, forehand*] croisé ► **cross-cultural** ADJ interculturel ► **cross-current** N contre-courant *m* ► **cross-curricular** ADJ [*approach etc*] pluridisciplinaire ► **cross-cut chisel** N bédane *m* ► **cross-disciplinary** ADJ interdisciplinaire ► **cross-dress** VI se travestir ► **cross-dresser** N travesti(e) *m(f)* ► **cross-dressing** N (*NonC* = *transvestism*) transvestisme *m*, travestisme *m* ► **cross-examination** N (*esp Jur*) contre-interrogatoire *m* ► **cross-examine** VT (*Jur*) faire subir un contre-interrogatoire à; (*gen*) interroger or questionner (*de façon serrée*) ► **cross-eyed** ADJ qui louche, bigleux*; **to be ~-eyed** loucher, avoir un œil qui dit zut* or merde* à l'autre ► **cross-fertilize** VT (*Bot*) croiser, faire un croisement de ► **cross-grained** ADJ [*wood*] à fibres irrégulières; [*person*] acariâtre, atrabilaire ► **cross hairs** NPL [*of telescope, gun*] réticule *m* ► **cross holdings** NPL (*St Ex*) participations *fpl* croisées ► **cross-legged** ADV [*sit*] en tailleur ► **cross-match** VT [+ *blood*] tester la compatibilité de ► **cross-party** ADJ (*Brit Pol*) [*talks*] entre partis, interpartis; [*support*] de plusieurs partis; [*committee*] composé de

membres de différents partis ► **cross-ply** ADJ (*Aut*) à carcasse diagonale ► **cross-pollination** N pollinisation *f* croisée ► **cross-purposes** NPL **to be at ~-purposes with sb** (= *misunderstand*) comprendre de travers; (= *disagree*) être en désaccord avec qn; **I think we are at ~-purposes** je crois qu'il y a malentendu, nous nous sommes mal compris; **we were talking at ~-purposes** notre conversation tournait autour d'un quiproquo ► **cross-question** VT faire subir un interrogatoire à ► **cross-refer** VT renvoyer (**to** à) ► **cross-reference** N renvoi *m*, référence *f* (**to** à) ♦ VT renvoyer ► **cross section** N (*Bio etc*) coupe *f* transversale; [*population etc*] échantillon *m* ► **cross-stitch** N point *m* de croix ♦ VT coudre or broder au point de croix ► **cross swell** N houle *f* traversière ► **cross-town** ADJ (*US*) [*bus*] qui traverse la ville ► **cross volley** N (*Tennis*) volée *f* croisée ► **cross-vote** VI (*Pol*) voter contre son parti

► **cross off** VT SEP [+ *item on list*] barrer, rayer; [+ *person*] radier (**from** de); **to ~ sb off a list** radier qn d'une liste

► **cross out** VT SEP [+ *word*] barrer, rayer

► **cross over** [1] VI traverser → **cross 4a** [2] **~over** N, ADJ → **crossover**

crossbar ['krɒsbɑːʳ] N (*Rugby etc*) barre *f* transversale; [*of bicycle*] barre *f*

crossbeam ['krɒsbiːm] N traverse *f*

crossbencher ['krɒsˌbentʃəʳ] N (*Parl*) député *m* non inscrit

crossbill ['krɒsbɪl] N (*Orn*) bec-croisé *m*

crossbones ['krɒsbəʊnz] NPL → **skull**

crossbow ['krɒsbəʊ] [1] N arbalète *f* [2] COMP ► **crossbow archery** N tir *m* à l'arbalète

crossbred ['krɒsbred] [1] VB *pt, ptp of* **crossbreed** [2] ADJ, N métis(se) *m(f)*

crossbreed ['krɒsbriːd] [1] N (= *animal*) hybride *m*, métis(se) *m(f)*; (* *pej* = *person*) sang-mêlé *mf inv*, métis(se) *m(f)* [2] VT (*pret, ptp* **crossbred**) croiser, métisser

crosse [krɒs] N (*in lacrosse*) crosse *f*

crossfire ['krɒsfaɪəʳ] N (*Mil*) feux *mpl* croisés; (*Mil*) **exposed to ~** pris entre deux feux; (*fig*) **caught in a ~ of questions** pris dans un feu roulant de questions

crosshatch ['krɒshætʃ] VT hachurer

crosshatching ['krɒsˌhætʃɪŋ] N hachures *fpl*

crossing ['krɒsɪŋ] [1] N [a] (*esp by sea*) traversée *f*; **the ~ of the line** le passage de l'équateur or de la ligne [b] (= *road junction*) croisement *m*, carrefour *m*; (*also* **pedestrian ~**) passage *m* clouté; (*Rail: also* **level ~**) passage *m* à niveau; (*on road*) **green at the ~** traversez sur le passage clouté or dans les clous* → **zebra** [2] COMP ► **crossing guard** N (*US*) = **crossing patrol** ► **crossing patrol** N (*Brit: also* **school ~ patrol**) contractuel(le) *m(f)* (*chargé(e) de faire traverser la rue aux enfants*) ► **crossing point** N point *m* de passage; [*of river*] gué *m*

crossly ['krɒslɪ] ADV avec (mauvaise) humeur

crossover ['krɒsəʊvəʳ] [1] N [*of roads*] (croisement *m* par) pont *m* routier; (*Rail*) voie *f* de croisement; (*Mus, Literat, Art*) mélange *m* de genres; **a jazz-rap ~** un mélange de jazz et de rap [2] COMP ► **crossover bodice** N (*Dress*) corsage *m* croisé

crosspatch* ['krɒspætʃ] N grincheux *m*, -euse *f*, grognon(ne) *m(f)*

crosspiece ['krɒspiːs] N traverse *f*

crossroads ['krɒsrəʊdz] NPL (*lit*) croisement *m*, carrefour *m*; (*fig*) carrefour *m*

crosstalk ['krɒstɔːk] N (*Rad, Telec*) diaphonie *f*; (*Brit* = *conversation*) joutes *fpl* oratoires

crosstie ['krɒstaɪ] N (*US*) traverse *f* (*de voie ferrée*)

crosswalk ['krɒswɔːk] N (*US*) passage *m* clouté

crossway ['krɒsweɪ] N (*US*) croisement *m*

crosswind ['krɒswɪnd] N vent *m* de travers

crosswise ['krɒswaɪz] ADV (= in shape of cross) en croix ; (= across) en travers ; (= diagonally) en diagonale

crossword ['krɒswɜːd] N (also ~ puzzle) mots mpl croisés

crotch [krɒtʃ] N [of body, tree] fourche f ; [of garment] entrejambes m inv ; **a kick in the ~** un coup de pied entre les jambes

crotchet ['krɒtʃɪt] N (Brit Mus) noire f

crotchety ['krɒtʃɪtɪ] ADJ grognon, grincheux

crouch [krautʃ] 1 VI (also ~ down) [person, animal] (gen) s'accroupir ; (= snuggle) se tapir ; (before springing) se ramasser 2 N position f accroupie

croup[1] [kruːp] N (Med) croup m

croup[2] [kruːp] N [of horse] croupe f

croupier ['kruːpɪeɪ] N croupier m

crouton ['kruːtɒn] N croûton m

crow[1] [krəʊ] 1 N (Orn) corneille f ; (generic term) corbeau m ; **as the ~ flies** à vol d'oiseau, en ligne droite ; (US) **to make sb eat ~** faire rentrer les paroles dans la gorge à qn ; (US) **to eat ~** faire de plates excuses → **carrion** 2 COMP ► **Crow Jim** N racisme m contre les Blancs, racisme m inversé ► **crow's feet** NPL pattes fpl d'oie (rides) ► **crow's-nest** N (Naut) nid m de pie

crow[2] [krəʊ] 1 N [of cock] chant m (du or d'un coq), cocorico m ; [of baby] gazouillis m ; (= triumphant cry) cri m de triomphe 2 VI [a] (pret **crowed** or **crew**, ptp **crowed**) [cock] chanter [b] (pret, ptp **crowed**) [baby] gazouiller ; [victor] chanter victoire ; **he ~ed with delight** il poussait des cris de triomphe ; **it's nothing to ~ about** il n'y a pas de quoi pavoiser

► **crow over** VT FUS **to ~ over sb** se vanter d'avoir triomphé de qn, chanter sa victoire sur qn

crowbar ['krəʊbɑː'] N (pince f à) levier m

crowd [kraʊd] 1 N [a] foule f ; (disorderly) cohue f ; **in ~s** se perdre dans la foule ; **a large ~** or **large ~s had gathered** une foule immense s'était assemblée ; **there was quite a ~** il y avait beaucoup de monde, il y avait foule ; **how big was the ~?** est-ce qu'il y avait beaucoup de monde ? ; **there was quite a ~ at the concert/at the match** il y avait du monde au concert/au match ; (Cine, Theat = actors) **the ~** les figurants mpl ; (fig) **that would pass in a ~*** ça peut passer si on n'y regarde pas de trop près, en courant vite on n'y verrait que du feu* ; **~s** or **a whole ~ of books/people** des masses* de livres/de gens [b] (NonC = people in general) **the ~** la foule, la masse du peuple ; **to follow** or **go with the ~** suivre la foule or le mouvement [c] (* = group, circle) bande f, clique f ; **I don't like that ~ at all** je n'aime pas du tout cette bande ; **he's one of our ~** il fait partie de notre groupe or bande ; **the usual ~** la bande habituelle

2 VI **they ~ed into the small room** ils se sont entassés dans la petite pièce ; **don't all ~ together** ne vous serrez donc pas comme ça ; **to ~ through the gates** passer en foule par le portail ; **they ~ed round to see ...** ils ont fait cercle or se sont attroupés pour voir ... ; **they ~ed round him** ils se pressaient autour de lui ; **they ~ed up against him** ils l'ont bousculé ; **to ~ down/in/up** etc descendre/entrer/monter etc en foule

3 VT (= push) [+ objects] entasser (**into** dans) ; (= jostle) [+ person] bousculer ; **pedestrians ~ed the streets** les piétons se pressaient dans les rues ; **he was ~ed off the pavement** la cohue l'a forcé à descendre du trottoir ; **don't ~ me** ne poussez pas, arrêtez de me bousculer ; **the houses are ~ed together** les maisons sont les unes sur les autres ; **a room ~ed with children** une pièce pleine d'enfants ; **house ~ed with**

furniture maison f encombrée de meubles ; **a house ~ed with guests** une maison pleine d'invités ; **a week ~ed with incidents** une semaine riche en incidents ; **memory ~ed with facts** mémoire f bourrée de faits ; (Naut) **to ~ on sail** mettre toutes voiles dehors → **crowded**

4 COMP ► **crowd control** N (NonC) ~ **control was becoming difficult** il devenait difficile de contenir or contrôler la foule ; **expert in ~ control** spécialiste mf du service d'ordre ► **crowd-pleaser** N **to be a ~-pleaser** plaire aux foules ► **crowd-puller*** N grosse attraction f ; **to be a real ~-puller** attirer les foules ► **crowd scene** N (Cine, Theat) scène f de foule ► **crowd trouble** N (NonC) mouvements mpl de foule

► **crowd out** VT SEP **the place was ~ed out** l'endroit était bondé ; **we shall be ~ed out** la cohue nous empêchera d'entrer ; **this article was ~ed out of yesterday's edition** cet article n'a pas pu être inséré dans l'édition d'hier faute de place ; **he's really ~ing me out*** il me colle aux fesses*

crowded ['kraʊdɪd] ADJ [a] (= filled with people) [room, street, train, beach] plein de monde, bondé ; **the shops are too ~** il y a trop de monde dans les magasins ; **it's getting ~ in there ◊ the place is getting ~** il commence à y avoir trop de monde ; **the people live ~ together in insanitary conditions** les gens vivent les uns sur les autres dans des conditions insalubres ; **~ with people** plein de monde [b] (= overpopulated) [city, area] surpeuplé ; [conditions] de surpeuplement ; **it is a very ~ profession** c'est une filière très encombrée [c] (= packed with things) [place] plein à craquer ; **a room ~ with furniture** une pièce pleine de meubles [d] (= busy) [agenda, day] chargé ; [life] bien rempli

crowfoot ['krəʊfʊt] N (pl **crowfoots**) (Bot) renoncule f ; (Naut) araignée f ; (Mil) chausse-trappe f

crowing ['krəʊɪŋ] N [of cockerel] chant m (du coq), cocorico m ; (fig = boasting) vantardise f

crown [kraʊn] 1 N [a] (lit, fig) couronne f ; **~ of roses/thorns** couronne f de roses/d'épines ; (fig) **to wear the ~** porter la couronne ; **to succeed to the ~** monter sur le trône ; (Jur) **the Crown** la Couronne, ≈ le ministère public ; **the law officers of the Crown** les conseillers mpl juridiques de la Couronne [b] (= coin) couronne f (ancienne pièce valant cinq shillings) [c] (= top part) [of hill] sommet m, faîte m ; [of tree] cime f ; [of roof] faîte m ; [of arch] clef f ; [of tooth] couronne f ; [of hat] fond m ; [of anchor] diamant m ; (fig = climax, completion) couronnement m ; **the ~ (of the head)** le sommet de la tête ; **the ~ of the road** le milieu de la route [d] (= size of paper) couronne f (format 0,37 sur 0,47 m)

2 VT couronner (**with** de) ; [draughts] damer ; [+ tooth] couronner ; (* = hit) flanquer* un coup sur la tête à ; **he was ~ed king** il fut couronné roi ; (fig) **all the ~ed heads of Europe** toutes les têtes couronnées d'Europe ; **work ~ed with success** travail m couronné de succès ; **the hill is ~ed with trees** la colline est couronnée d'arbres ; (fig) **to ~ it all*** it began **to snow** pour comble (de malheur) or pour couronner le tout il s'est mis à neiger ; **that ~s it all!*** il ne manquait plus que ça !

3 COMP (Brit Jur) [witness, evidence etc] à charge ► **Crown Agent** N (Brit Pol) ≈ délégué(e) m(f) du ministère de la Coopération ► **crown colony** N (Brit) colonie f de la couronne ► **Crown court** N (Jur) Cour f d'assises (en Angleterre et au Pays de Galles) ► **crown estate** N domaine m de la couronne ► **crown green bowling** N (NonC: Brit) jeu de boules sur un terrain légèrement surélevé en son

milieu ► **crown jewels** NPL joyaux mpl de la couronne ; (‡ hum = male genitals) bijoux mpl de famille* (hum) ► **crown lands** NPL terres fpl domaniales ► **crown law** N droit m pénal ► **crown prince** N prince m héritier ► **crown princess** N princesse f héritière ► **Crown Prosecution Service** N (Brit) ≈ Ministère m public (qui décide si les affaires doivent être portées devant les tribunaux) ► **crown wheel** N (Brit Aut) grande couronne f ; **~ wheel and pinion** couple m conique

crowning ['kraʊnɪŋ] 1 N (= ceremony) couronnement m 2 ADJ [achievement, moment] suprême ; critique ; **his ~ glory** son plus grand triomphe ; **her hair was her ~ glory** sa chevelure faisait sa fierté

cruces ['kruːsiːz] NPL of **crux**

crucial ['kruːʃəl] ADJ [issue, factor, decision, vote, difference] crucial ; [moment, stage, time] crucial, critique ; **~ to** or **for sb/sth** crucial pour qn/qch ; **it is ~ that ...** il est essentiel or capital que ... (+ subj) ; **to play a ~ role in sth** jouer un rôle capital dans qch

crucially ['kruːʃəlɪ] ADV [influence, affect] d'une manière décisive ; **~ important** d'une importance cruciale ; **the success of the project is ~ dependent on** or **depends ~ on his contribution** sa contribution est d'une importance capitale pour la réussite du projet

crucible ['kruːsɪbl] N [a] (lit) creuset m [b] (fig) (= melting pot) creuset m ; (= test) (dure) épreuve f

crucifix ['kruːsɪfɪks] N crucifix m ; (at roadside) calvaire m

crucifixion [ˌkruːsɪ'fɪkʃən] N crucifiement m ; (Rel) **the Crucifixion** la crucifixion, la mise en croix

cruciform ['kruːsɪfɔːm] ADJ cruciforme

crucify ['kruːsɪfaɪ] VT (lit) crucifier, mettre en croix ; (fig) crucifier, mettre au pilori ; (Rel) **to ~ the flesh** mortifier la chair ; **he'll ~ me*** when **he finds out!** il va m'étrangler quand il le saura !

crud: [krʌd] N [a] (= filth) saloperies: fpl, saletés fpl ; (= person) salaud: m, ordure: f ; (= illness) **the ~** la crève: [b] (= residue) résidu m

cruddy: ['krʌdɪ] ADJ dégueulasse:

crude [kruːd] 1 ADJ [a] (= vulgar) [person, behaviour, language, joke, attempt] grossier [b] (= rudimentary) [device, weapon, hut] rudimentaire ; [furniture, shelter, housing] rudimentaire, sommaire ; [drawing] schématique ; **a ~ form or kind of ...** une forme grossière de ... ; **a ~ method of doing sth** un moyen rudimentaire de faire qch [c] (= garish) [light, colour] cru [d] (= not refined) [materials] brut ; [sugar] non raffiné 2 N (also ~ oil) brut m → **heavy** 3 COMP ► **crude oil** N (pétrole m) brut m ► **crude steel** N acier m brut

crudely ['kruːdlɪ] ADV [a] (= approximately) [divide, express, explain] sommairement [b] (= primitively) [carved, constructed, drawn] grossièrement, de façon rudimentaire [c] (= coarsely) [speak, behave] grossièrement ; **to put it ~** pour dire les choses crûment

crudeness ['kruːdnɪs] N [of system, method] caractère m rudimentaire ; (= vulgarity) vulgarité f, grossièreté f

crudités ['kruːdɪteɪz] NPL crudités fpl

crudity ['kruːdɪtɪ] N = **crudeness**

cruel ['krʊəl] ADJ cruel (**to sb** avec qn) ; **it was a ~ blow to his pride** sa fierté en a pris un coup*, cela a porté un coup sévère à son orgueil ■ (PROV) **you have to be ~ to be kind** qui aime bien châtie bien (PROV)

cruelly ['krʊəlɪ] ADV cruellement

cruelty ['krʊəltɪ] 1 N cruauté f (**to** envers) ; (Jur) sévices mpl ; **prosecuted for ~ to his wife** poursuivi pour sévices sur sa femme ; **divorce on the grounds of ~** divorce m pour sévices ; **mental ~** cruauté f mentale → **prevention**

2 COMP ► **cruelty-free** ADJ non testé sur les animaux

cruet ['kruːɪt] N (Brit: also ~ **set**, ~ **stand**) service m à condiments, garniture f de table (pour condiments) b (US = small bottle) petit flacon m (pour l'huile ou le vinaigre) c (Rel) burette f

cruise [kruːz] 1 VI a [fleet, ship] croiser ; **they are cruising in the Pacific** (Naut) ils croisent dans le Pacifique ; [tourists] ils sont en croisière dans le Pacifique
b [cars] rouler ; [aircraft] voler ; **the car was cruising (along) at 80km/h** la voiture faisait 80 km/h sans effort ; **we were cruising along the road when suddenly ...** nous roulions tranquillement quand tout à coup ... ; **to ~ to victory** remporter la victoire haut la main
c [taxi, patrol car] marauder, faire la maraude ; **a cruising taxi** un taxi en maraude
d (* = look for pick-up) draguer*
2 N a (Naut) croisière f ; **to go on a ~** partir en croisière, faire une croisière
b (also ~ **missile**) missile m de croisière ; **a campaign against** ~ une campagne contre les missiles de croisière
3 COMP ► **cruise control** N contrôle m (de vitesse) ► **cruise missile** N missile m de croisière ► **cruising range** N (Aviat) autonomie f de vol ► **cruising speed** N vitesse f or régime m de croisière ► **cruising yacht** N yacht m de croisière

cruiser ['kruːzə'] 1 N (= warship) croiseur m ; (= cabin cruiser) yacht m de croisière → **battle**
2 COMP ► **cruiser weight** N (Boxing) poids m mi-lourd

cruller ['krʌlə'] N (US) beignet m

crumb [krʌm] N miette f ; (NonC: inside of loaf) mie f ; (fig) miette f, brin m ; [of information] miettes fpl, fragments mpl ; **a ~ of comfort** un brin de réconfort ; **~s!** ça alors !, zut !*

crumble ['krʌmbl] 1 VT [+ bread] émietter ; [+ plaster] effriter ; [+ earth, rocks] (faire) s'ébouler 2 VI [buildings etc] tomber en ruines, se désagréger ; [plaster] s'effriter ; [earth, rocks] s'ébouler ; [bread] s'émietter ; (fig) [hopes, economy etc] s'effondrer, s'écrouler ; (fig) [person] se laisser abattre → **cookie** 3 N (Brit Culin) crumble m

crumbly ['krʌmblɪ] 1 ADJ friable 2 N (* = old person) vieux croulant* m

crummy*, **crumby*** ['krʌmɪ] ADJ a [hotel, town, job, film] minable* ; **what a ~ thing to do!** c'est un coup minable !*, c'est vraiment mesquin de faire ça ! b (= ill) **to feel ~** ne pas avoir la pêche*, être patraque* c (= guilty) **to feel ~ about doing sth** se sentir minable* de faire qch

crump [krʌmp] N éclatement m (d'un obus) ; (Mil * = shell) obus m

crumpet ['krʌmpɪt] N (esp Brit Culin) petite crêpe f épaisse ; (Brit fig) **a bit of ~*** une belle nana*

crumple ['krʌmpl] 1 VT froisser, friper ; (also ~ **up**) chiffonner ; **he ~d the paper (up) into a ball** il a fait une boule de la feuille de papier 2 VI se froisser, se chiffonner, se friper ; (fig) **her features ~d when she heard the bad news** son visage s'est décomposé quand elle a appris la mauvaise nouvelle 3 COMP ► **crumple zone** N (Aut) structure f déformable

crunch [krʌntʃ] 1 VT a (with teeth) croquer ; **to ~ an apple/a biscuit** croquer une pomme/ un biscuit b (underfoot) écraser, faire craquer c **to ~ numbers** [computer] traiter des chiffres à grande vitesse ; **he doesn't want to spend his life ~ing numbers** il ne veut pas passer le reste de sa vie penché sur des chiffres 2 VI **he ~ed across the gravel** il a traversé en faisant craquer le gravier sous ses pas 3 N a (= sound of teeth) coup m de dents ; [of broken glass, gravel etc] craquement m, crissement m

b (*: fig) (= moment of reckoning) **the ~** l'instant m critique ; **here's the ~** c'est le moment crucial ; **when it comes to the ~ he ...** dans une situation critique or au moment crucial, il ...
► **crunch up** VT SEP broyer

crunchy ['krʌntʃɪ] ADJ [foods, peanut butter, texture] croquant ; [gravel, snow] qui crisse

crupper ['krʌpə'] N [of harness] croupière f ; (= hindquarters) croupe f

crusade [kruː'seɪd] 1 N (Hist, also fig) croisade f 2 VI (fig) partir en croisade (**against** contre, **for** pour) ; (Hist) partir pour la or en croisade

crusader [kruː'seɪdə'] N (Hist) croisé m ; (fig) champion m (**for** de, **against** en guerre contre), militant(e) m(f) (**for** en faveur de, **against** en guerre contre) ; **the ~s for peace/ against the bomb** ceux qui militent pour la paix/contre la bombe

crush [krʌʃ] 1 N a (= crowd) foule f, cohue f ; **there was a great ~ to get in** c'était une bousculade pour entrer ; **there was a terrible ~ at the concert** il y avait une vraie cohue au concert ; **he was lost in the ~** il était perdu dans la foule or la cohue
b **to have a ~ on sb*** avoir le béguin* pour qn
c (Brit = drink) jus m de fruit ; **orange ~** orange f pressée
2 VT a (= compress) [+ stones, old cars] écraser, broyer ; [+ ice] piler ; [+ grapes] écraser, presser ; [+ ore] bocarder ; **to ~ to a pulp** réduire en pulpe
b (= crumple) [+ clothes] froisser ; **to ~ clothes into a bag** fourrer or bourrer des vêtements dans une valise ; **to ~ objects into a suitcase** tasser or entasser des objets dans une valise ; **we were very ~ed in the car** nous étions très tassés dans la voiture
c (= overwhelm) [+ enemy] écraser, accabler ; [+ opponent in argument, country] écraser ; [+ revolution] écraser, réprimer ; [+ hope] détruire ; (= snub) remettre à sa place, rabrouer
3 VI a se presser, se serrer ; **they ~ed round him** ils se pressaient autour de lui ; **they ~ed into the car** ils se sont entassés or tassés dans la voiture ; **to ~ (one's way) into/through** etc se frayer un chemin dans/à travers etc
b [clothes] se froisser
4 COMP ► **crush bar** N [of theatre] bar m du foyer ► **crush barrier** N (Brit) barrière f de sécurité ► **crushed velvet** N panne f de velours ► **crush-resistant** ADJ infroissable
► **crush out** VT SEP [+ juice etc] presser, exprimer ; [+ cigarette end] écraser, éteindre

crusher ['krʌʃə'] N (= machine) broyeur m, concasseur m

crushing ['krʌʃɪŋ] ADJ [defeat, victory] écrasant ; [news] accablant ; [blow, disappointment] terrible ; [remark, reply] cinglant ; **a ~ burden of debt** des dettes fpl écrasantes

crushingly ['krʌʃɪŋlɪ] ADV (= humiliatingly) [say] d'un ton cinglant ; (= extremely) [bad, dull, boring] terriblement

crust [krʌst] 1 N (on bread, pie, snow) croûte f ; (= piece of crust) croûton m, croûte f ; (Med: on wound, sore) croûte f, escarre f ; [of wine] dépôt m (de tanin) ; **there were only a few ~s to eat** pour toute nourriture il n'y avait que quelques croûtes de pain ; **a thin ~ of ice** une fine couche de glace ; (Geol) **the earth's ~** la croûte terrestre → **earn**, **upper** 2 VT **frost ~ing the windscreen** le givre recouvrant le pare-brise ; **~ed snow** neige f croûtée ; **~ed with mud** etc couvert d'une croûte de boue etc

crustacean [krʌs'teɪʃən] N, ADJ, N crustacé m

crusty ['krʌstɪ] 1 ADJ [loaf, roll] croustillant ; (* fig) [old man] hargneux, bourru 2 N (* = scruffy youth) jeune mf crado*

crutch [krʌtʃ] N a (= support) soutien m, support m ; (Med) béquille f ; (Archit) étançon m ; (Naut) support m (de gui) ; **he gets about**

on ~es il marche avec des béquilles ; (fig) **alcohol is a ~ for him** l'alcool lui sert de soutien b (Anat = crotch) fourche f ; [of trousers etc] entre-jambes m inv

crux [krʌks] N (pl **cruxes** or **cruces** ['kruːsiːz]) a point m crucial ; [of problem] cœur m, centre m ; **the ~ of the matter** le cœur du sujet, l'essentiel m b (Climbing) passage-clé m

cry [kraɪ] 1 N a (= loud shout) cri m ; [of hounds] aboiements mpl, voix f ; **to give a ~** pousser un cri ; **he gave a ~ for help** il a crié or appelé au secours ; **he heard a ~ for help** il a entendu crier au secours ; **the cries of the victims** les cris mpl des victimes ; (fig) **there was a great ~ against the rise in prices** la hausse des prix a déclenché un tollé ; (Hunting) **the pack was in full ~** toute la meute donnait de la voix ; **the crowd was in full ~ after the thief** la foule poursuivait le voleur en criant à pleine voix ; **they are in full ~ against the Prime Minister** ils s'acharnent sur or contre le Premier ministre ; **the newspapers are in full ~ over the scandal** les journaux font des gorges chaudes de ce scandale → **far**
b (= watchword) slogan m ; **"votes for women" was their ~** leur slogan or leur cri de guerre était « le vote pour les femmes » → **battle**, **war**
c (= weep) **she had a good ~*** elle a pleuré un bon coup*
2 VT a (= shout out) crier ; **"here I am" he cried** « me voici » s'écria-t-il or cria-t-il ; **"go away", he cried to me** « allez-vous-en », me cria-t-il ; **to ~ mercy** crier grâce ; **to ~ shame** crier au scandale ; **to ~ shame on sb/sth** crier haro sur qn/qch ; (fig) **to ~ wolf** crier au loup
b **to ~ o.s. to sleep** s'endormir à force de pleurer ; **to ~ one's eyes out** or **one's heart out** pleurer toutes les larmes de son corps
3 VI a (= weep) pleurer (**about, for, over** sur) ; **to ~ with rage** pleurer de rage ; **to laugh till one cries** pleurer de rire, rire aux larmes ; **to ~ for sth** pleurer pour avoir qch ; (fig) **I'll give him something to ~ for!*** je vais lui apprendre à pleurnicher ! ■ (PROV) **it's no use ~ing over spilt milk** ce qui est fait est fait → **shoulder**
b (= call out) [person, animal, bird] pousser un cri or des cris ; **the baby cried at birth** l'enfant a poussé un cri or a crié en naissant ; **he cried (out) with pain** il a poussé un cri de douleur ; **to ~ for help** appeler à l'aide, crier au secours ; **to ~ for mercy** demander miséricorde, implorer la pitié ; **the starving crowd cried for bread** la foule affamée réclama du pain ; **to ~ foul** crier à l'injustice, crier au scandale
c [hunting dogs] donner de la voix, aboyer
► **cry down** VT SEP (= decry) décrier
► **cry off** (Brit) 1 VI (from meeting) se décommander ; (from promise) se dédire ; **I'm ~ing off!** je ne veux plus rien savoir ! 2 VT FUS (= cancel) [+ arrangement, deal] annuler ; (= withdraw from) [+ meeting] décommander
► **cry out** VI (inadvertently) pousser un cri ; (deliberately) s'écrier ; **he cried out with joy** il a poussé un cri de joie ; **to ~ out to sb** appeler qn en criant, crier pour appeler qn ; **to ~ out for sth** demander qch à grands cris ; **for ~ing out loud!*** pour l'amour de Dieu ! ; (fig) **that floor is just ~ing out to be washed*** ce plancher a vraiment besoin d'être lavé ; (fig) **the door is ~ing out for a coat of paint*** la porte a bien besoin d'une couche de peinture
► **cry out against** VT FUS protester contre
► **cry up*** VT SEP (= praise) vanter, exalter ; **he's not all he's cried up to be** il n'est pas à la hauteur de sa réputation, il n'est pas aussi formidable* qu'on le dit

crybaby ['kraɪbeɪbɪ] N (pej) pleurnicheur m, -euse f

crying ['kraɪɪŋ] 1 ADJ (lit) pleurant, qui pleure ; (fig) criant, flagrant ; **~ injustice** injustice f criante or flagrante ; **~ need for sth** besoin pressant *or* urgent de qch; **it's a ~ shame** c'est une honte, c'est honteux **2** N (= *shouts*) cris *mpl*; (= *weeping*) larmes *fpl*, pleurs *mpl*

cryobiology [ˌkraɪəʊbaɪˈɒlədʒɪ] N cryobiologie *f*

cryogenic [ˌkraɪəˈdʒenɪk] ADJ cryogénique

cryogenics [ˌkraɪəˈdʒenɪks] N (*NonC*) cryogénie *f*

cryonic [kraɪˈɒnɪk] ADJ cryonique

cryonics [kraɪˈɒnɪks] N (*NonC*) cryonique *f*

cryosurgery [ˌkraɪəʊˈsɜːdʒərɪ] N cryochirurgie *f*

crypt [krɪpt] N crypte *f*

cryptic [ˈkrɪptɪk] ADJ (= *secret*) secret (-ète *f*); (= *mysterious*) sibyllin, énigmatique; (= *terse*) laconique

cryptically [ˈkrɪptɪkəlɪ] ADV (= *mysteriously*) énigmatiquement; (= *tersely*) laconiquement

crypto- [krɪptəʊ] PREF crypto-; **~communist** *etc* cryptocommuniste *etc*

cryptogram [ˈkrɪptəʊɡræm] N cryptogramme *m*

cryptographer [krɪpˈtɒɡrəfəʳ] N cryptographe *mf*

cryptographic(al) [ˌkrɪptəʊˈɡræfɪk(əl)] ADJ cryptographique

cryptography [krɪpˈtɒɡrəfɪ] N cryptographie *f*

crystal [ˈkrɪstl] **1** N **a** (*NonC*) cristal *m* → **rock²** **b** (*Chem, Min*) cristal *m*; **salt ~s** cristaux *mpl* de sel **c** (*US* = *watch glass*) verre *m* de montre **d** (*Rad*) galène *f* **2** COMP (*lit*) [*vase*] de cristal; (*fig*) [*waters, lake*] cristallin, de cristal (*fig, liter*) ► **crystal ball** N boule *f* de cristal ► **crystal-clear** ADJ clair comme le jour *or* comme de l'eau de roche ► **crystal-gazer** N voyant(e) *m(f)* (*qui lit dans une boule de cristal*) ► **crystal-gazing** N (l'art *m* de la) voyance *f*; (*fig*) prédictions *fpl*, prophéties *fpl* ► **crystal set** N (*Rad*) poste *m* à galène

crystalline [ˈkrɪstəlaɪn] ADJ cristallin, clair *or* pur comme le cristal; (*Opt*) ~ **lens** cristallin *m*

crystallize [ˈkrɪstəlaɪz] **1** VI (*lit, fig*) se cristalliser **2** VT cristalliser; [+ *sugar*] (faire) cuire au cassé **3** COMP ► **crystallized fruits** NPL fruits *mpl* confits *or* candis

crystallography [ˌkrɪstəˈlɒɡrəfɪ] N cristallographie *f*

CSA [ˌsiːesˈeɪ] N (*Brit*) (ABBR = **Child Support Agency**) → **child**

CSC [ˌsiːesˈsiː] N (ABBR = **Civil Service Commission**) → **civil**

CSE [ˌsiːesˈiː] N (*Brit*) (ABBR = **Certificate of Secondary Education**) ≈ BEPC *m*

CSEU [ˌsiːesiːˈjuː] N (*Brit*) (ABBR = **Confederation of Shipbuilding and Engineering Unions**) syndicat

CS gas [ˌsiːesˈɡæs] N (*Brit*) gaz *m* CS

CST [ˌsiːesˈtiː] N (*US*) (ABBR = **Central Standard Time**) → **central**

CSU [ˌsiːesˈjuː] N (*Brit*) (ABBR = **Civil Service Union**) syndicat

CT ABBR = **Connecticut**

ct **a** ABBR = **carat** **b** ABBR = **cent**

CTT [ˌsiːtiːˈtiː] N (*Brit*) (ABBR = **capital transfer tax**) → **capital**

cub [kʌb] **1** N **a** [*of animal*] petit(e) *m(f)*; (* = *youth*) gosse *m*, petit morveux *m* (*pej*) → **bear²**, **fox**, **wolf** **b** (*also* ~ **scout**) louveteau *m* (*scout*) **2** COMP ► **cub master** N (*Scouting*) chef *m* ► **cub mistress** N cheftaine *f* ► **cub reporter** N (*Press*) jeune reporter *m*

Cuba [ˈkjuːbə] N Cuba *f or m*; **in** ~ à Cuba

Cuban [ˈkjuːbən] **1** ADJ cubain **2** N Cubain(e) *m(f)*

cubbyhole [ˈkʌbɪhəʊl] N (= *cupboard*) débarras *m*, cagibi *m*; (= *poky room*) cagibi *m*

cube [kjuːb] **1** N (*gen, Culin, Math*) cube *m* → **soup**, **stock** **2** VT (*Math*) cuber; (*Culin*) cou-

per en cubes *or* en dés **3** COMP ► **cube root** N (*Math*) racine *f* cubique

cubic [ˈkjuːbɪk] ADJ (*of shape, volume*) cubique; (*of measures*) cube; ~ **capacity** volume *m*; ~ **centimetre** centimètre *m* cube; ~ **content** contenance *f* cubique; ~ **measure** mesure *f* de volume; ~ **metre** mètre *m* cube; (*Math*) ~ **equation** équation *f* du troisième degré

cubicle [ˈkjuːbɪkəl] N [*of hospital, dormitory*] box *m*, alcôve *f*; [*of swimming baths*] cabine *f*

cubism [ˈkjuːbɪzəm] N cubisme *m*

cubist [ˈkjuːbɪst] ADJ, N cubiste *mf*

cubit [ˈkjuːbɪt] N (*Bible*) coudée *f*

cuckold† [ˈkʌkəld] **1** N (*mari m*) cocu* *m* **2** VT tromper, cocufier*

cuckoo [ˈkʊkuː] **1** N (*Orn*) coucou *m* **2** ADJ (* = *mad*) piqué*, toqué*; **to go** ~ perdre la boule* **3** COMP ► **cuckoo clock** N coucou *m* (*pendule*) ► **cuckoo spit** N (*Bot*) crachat *m* de coucou

cuckoopint [ˈkʊkuːpaɪnt] N (*Bot*) pied-de-veau *m*

cucumber [ˈkjuːkʌmbəʳ] **1** N concombre *m* → **cool** **2** COMP [*sandwich*] au concombre

cud [kʌd] N → **chew 1**

cuddle [ˈkʌdl] **1** N câlin *m*; **to have a** ~ (se) faire (un) câlin*; **to give sb a** ~ faire un câlin* à qn **2** VT câliner **3** VI s'enlacer
► **cuddle down** VI [*child in bed*] se pelotonner; ~ **down now!** maintenant allonge-toi (et dors)!
► **cuddle up** VI se pelotonner (**to, against** contre)

cuddly [ˈkʌdlɪ] ADJ [*child*] caressant, câlin; [*animal*] qui donne envie de le caresser; [*teddy bear, doll*] doux (douce *f*), qu'on a envie de câliner; ~ **toy** (jouet *m* en) peluche *f*

cudgel [ˈkʌdʒəl] **1** N gourdin *m*, trique *f*; (*fig*) **to take up the ~s for** *or* **on behalf of** ... prendre fait et cause pour ... **2** VT frapper à coups de trique; (*fig*) **to ~ one's brains** se creuser la cervelle *or* la tête (**for** pour)

cue [kjuː] **1** N **a** (*Theat*) (*verbal*) réplique *f* (*indiquant à un acteur qu'il doit parler*); (*action*) signal *m*; (*Mus*) signal *m* d'entrée; (*Rad, TV*) signal *m*; **to give sb his** ~ (*Theat*) donner la réplique à qn; (*fig*) faire un signal à qn; (*Theat*) **to take one's** ~ entamer sa réplique; (*Theat*) **X's exit was the ~ for Y's entrance** la sortie d'X donnait à Y le signal de son entrée; (*fig*) **to take one's ~ from sb** emboîter le pas à qn (*fig*); (*fig*) **that was my ~ to** ... c'était mon signal pour ... **b** (*Billiards etc*) queue *f* de billard **2** VT (*Cine, Rad, Theat etc*) donner la réplique à **3** COMP ► **cue ball** N (*Billiards etc*) bille *f* du joueur
► **cue in** VT SEP (*Rad, TV*) donner le signal à; (*Theat*) donner la réplique à; (*fig*) **to ~ sb in on sth** mettre qn au courant de qch

cuesta [ˈkwestə] N (*Geog, Geol*) cuesta *f*

cuff [kʌf] **1** N **a** (*gen*) poignet *m*; [*of shirt*] manchette *f*; [*of coat*] parement *m*; (*US*) [*of trousers*] revers *m inv*; (*fig*) **off the** ~ à l'improviste, au pied levé; **to speak off the** ~ improviser → **off**; (*US*) **to buy on the ~** acheter à crédit **b** (= *blow*) gifle *f*, calotte* *f* **2** [*cuffs**] NPL (= *handcuffs*) menottes *fpl* **3** VT (= *strike*) gifler, calotter*

cufflink [ˈkʌflɪŋk] N bouton *m* de manchette

cu.in. ABBR = **cubic inch(es)**

cuisine [kwɪˈziːn] N cuisine *f*; **French/oriental** ~ la cuisine française/orientale

cul-de-sac [ˈkʌldəˌsæk] N (*pl* **culs-de-sac** *or* **cul-de-sacs**) (*esp Brit*) cul-de-sac *m*, impasse *f*; (*road sign*) "**~**" « voie sans issue »

culinary [ˈkʌlɪnərɪ] ADJ culinaire

cull [kʌl] **1** VT **a** (= *take samples from*) sélectionner **b** (= *remove inferior items, animals etc*) éliminer, supprimer; [+ *seals, deer etc*] abattre **c** (= *pick*) [+ *flowers, fruit*] cueillir **2** N **a** (= *killing*) abattage *m* → **seal¹** **b** (=

animal) animal *m* à éliminer (dans une portée)

culling [ˈkʌlɪŋ] N (*NonC*) **seal/deer** ~ réduction *f* de la population de phoques/cervidés

culminate [ˈkʌlmɪneɪt] VI **to ~ in sth** (= *end in*) finir *or* se terminer par qch; (= *lead to*) mener à qch; **it ~d in his throwing her out** pour finir, il l'a mise à la porte

culminating [ˈkʌlmɪneɪtɪŋ] ADJ culminant; ~ **point** point *m* culminant, sommet *m*

culmination [ˌkʌlmɪˈneɪʃən] N (*Astron*) culmination *f*; (*fig*) [*of success, career*] apogée *m*; [*of disturbance, quarrel*] point *m* culminant

culotte(s) [kjuːˈlɒt(s)] N(PL) jupe-culotte *f*

culpability [ˌkʌlpəˈbɪlɪtɪ] N culpabilité *f*

culpable [ˈkʌlpəbl] ADJ coupable (**of** de), blâmable; (*Jur*) ~ **homicide** homicide *m* volontaire; (*Scot*) homicide *m* sans préméditation; (*Jur*) ~ **negligence** négligence *f* coupable

culprit [ˈkʌlprɪt] N coupable *mf*

cult [kʌlt] **1** N (*Rel, fig*) culte *m* (**of** de); **he made a ~ of cleanliness** il avait le culte de la propreté **2** COMP ► **cult figure** N objet *m* d'un culte, idole *f*; (*fig*) **he has become a ~ figure** il est devenu l'objet d'un véritable culte *or* une véritable idole ► **cult film** N film-culte *m* ► **cult following** N **a film/book/group with a ~ following** un film-/livre-/groupe-culte ► **cult movie** N = **cult film**

cultivable [ˈkʌltɪvəbl] ADJ cultivable

cultivar [ˈkʌltɪˌvɑːʳ] N variété *f* cultivée

cultivate [ˈkʌltɪveɪt] VT (*lit, fig*) cultiver; **to ~ the mind** se cultiver (l'esprit)

cultivated [ˈkʌltɪveɪtɪd] ADJ [*land, person*] cultivé; [*voice*] distingué; ~ **pearls** perles *fpl* de culture

cultivation [ˌkʌltɪˈveɪʃən] N culture *f*; **fields under ~** cultures *fpl*; **out of ~** en friche, inculte

cultivator [ˈkʌltɪveɪtəʳ] N (= *person*) cultivateur *m*, -trice *f*; (= *machine*) cultivateur *m*; (*power-driven*) motoculteur *m*

cultural [ˈkʌltʃərəl] ADJ **a** [*background, activities*] culturel; ~ **attaché** attaché *m* culturel; ~ **environment** environnement *m or* milieu *m* culturel; ~ **integration** acculturation *f*; **the Cultural Revolution** la Révolution Culturelle **b** (*Agr*) de culture, cultural

culturally [ˈkʌltʃərəlɪ] ADV culturellement

culture [ˈkʌltʃəʳ] **1** N **a** (= *education, refinement*) culture *f*; **physical ~†** la culture physique; **a woman of no ~** une femme sans aucune culture *or* complètement inculte **b** [*of country, society, organization*] culture *f*; **French ~** la culture française; (*Pol*) **a ~ of dependency** ◊ **a dependency ~** une culture fondée sur l'assistanat **c** (*Agr*) culture *f*; [*of bees*] apiculture *f*; [*of fish*] pisciculture *f*; [*of farm animals*] élevage *m* **d** (*Bio, Med*) culture *f* **2** VT (*Bio*) cultiver **3** COMP [*tube*] à culture ► **culture-fair test** N *examen conçu pour ne pas défavoriser les minorités ethniques* ► **culture fluid** N (*Bio*) bouillon *m* de culture ► **culture-free test** N = **culture-fair test** ► **culture gap** N fossé *m* culturel ► **culture medium** N (*Bio*) milieu *m* de culture ► **culture shock** N choc *m* culturel ► **culture vulture*** N (*hum*) fana* *mf* de culture

cultured [ˈkʌltʃəd] ADJ cultivé; ~ **pearl** perle *f* de culture

culvert [ˈkʌlvət] N caniveau *m*

-cum- [kʌm] PREP **a carpenter-cum-painter** un charpentier-peintre; **a secretary-cum-chauffeur** une secrétaire qui fait office de chauffeur; **a dining room-cum-living room** une salle à manger-salon

cumbersome [ˈkʌmbəsəm], **cumbrous** [ˈkʌmbrəs] ADJ (= *bulky*) encombrant, embarrassant; (= *heavy*) lourd, pesant

cumin [ˈkʌmɪn] N cumin *m*

cum laude [kʊm 'laʊdeɪ] ADJ (*Univ*) avec mention (*obtention d'un diplôme, d'un titre*)

cummerbund ['kʌməbʌnd] N ceinture *f* (*de smoking*)

cumulative ['kjuːmjʊlətɪv] ADJ cumulatif; (*Jur*) ~ **evidence** preuve *f* par accumulation de témoignages; (*Fin*) ~ **interest** intérêt *m* cumulatif; ~ **voting** vote *m* plural

cumulatively ['kjuːmjʊlətɪvlɪ] ADV cumulativement

cumuli ['kjuːmjə,laɪ] NPL *of* **cumulus**

cumulonimbus [,kjuːmjələʊ'nɪmbəs] N cumulonimbus *m inv*

cumulus ['kjuːmjələs] N (*pl* **cumuli** ['kjuːmjə,laɪ]) cumulus *m*

cuneiform ['kjuːnɪfɔːm] **1** ADJ cunéiforme **2** N écriture *f* cunéiforme

cunnilingus [,kʌnɪ'lɪŋgəs] N cunnilingus *m*

cunning ['kʌnɪŋ] **1** N finesse *f*, astuce *f*; (*pej*) ruse *f*, fourberie *f*; (†† = *skill*) habileté *f*, adresse *f* **2** ADJ astucieux, malin (-igne *f*); (*pej*) rusé, fourbe; **a ~ little gadget*** un petit truc astucieux*

cunningly ['kʌnɪŋlɪ] ADV **a** (= *cleverly*) [*disguised, camouflaged, concealed*] avec astuce, astucieusement; [*contrived, designed, positioned, placed*] astucieusement **b** (*pej* = *deceitfully*) [*speak*] d'une manière fourbe; [*say*] avec fourberie; [*look at*] d'un air fourbe

cunt** [kʌnt] N **a** (= *genitals*) con** *m*, chatte** *f* **b** (= *person*) salaud* *m*, salope* *f*

cup [kʌp] **1** N **a** tasse *f*; (= *goblet*) coupe *f*; (= *cupful*) tasse *f*, coupe *f*; ~ **of tea** tasse *f* de thé; **he drank four ~s** or **~fuls** il (en) a bu quatre tasses; (*Culin*) **one ~** or **~ful of sugar/flour** etc une tasse de sucre/farine etc; **cider/ champagne ~** cocktail *m* au cidre/au champagne; **he was in his ~s†** il était dans les vignes du Seigneur, il avait un verre dans le nez*; (*fig*) **that's just his ~ of tea*** c'est son truc*; (*fig*) **that's not my ~ of tea*** ce n'est pas ma tasse de thé* or mon truc*; (*fig*) **it isn't everyone's ~ of tea*** ça ne plaît pas à tout le monde; (*liter*) **his ~ of happiness was full** il jouissait d'un bonheur sans mélange or nuage; (*liter*) **to drain the ~ of sorrow** boire le calice jusqu'à la lie → **coffee, slip** **b** (*Tech*) godet *m*; [*of flower*] corolle *f*; (*Rel: also* **communion ~**) calice *m*; (*Brit Sport etc* = *prize competition*) coupe *f*; (*Geog*) cuvette *f*; (*Anat*) [*of bone*] cavité *f* articulaire, glène *f*; (*Med Hist* = *cupping glass*) ventouse *f*; [*of brassière*] bonnet *m* (*de soutien-gorge*) → **world** **2** VT **a** **to ~ one's hands** faire une coupe avec ses deux mains; **to ~ one's hands round sth** mettre ses mains autour de qch; **to ~ one's hands round one's ear/one's mouth** mettre ses mains en cornet/en porte-voix **b** (*Med Hist*) appliquer des ventouses sur **c** (*Golf*) **to ~ the ball** faire un divot **3** COMP ► **cup bearer** N échanson *m* ► **cup final** N (*Brit Ftbl*) finale *f* de la coupe ► **cup size** N [*of bra*] profondeur *f* de bonnet ► **cup-tie** N (*Brit Ftbl*) match *m* de coupe or comptant pour la coupe

cupboard ['kʌbəd] **1** N (*esp Brit*) placard *m* → **skeleton** **2** COMP ► **cupboard love** N (*Brit*) amour *m* intéressé

cupcake ['kʌpkeɪk] N (*Culin*) petit gâteau *m*

cupful ['kʌpfʊl] N (contenu *m* d'une) tasse *f* → **cup**

Cupid ['kjuːpɪd] N (*Myth*) Cupidon *m*; (*Art* = *cherub*) amour *m*; **~'s darts** les flèches *fpl* de Cupidon

cupidity [kjuː'pɪdɪtɪ] N (*frm*) cupidité *f*

cupola ['kjuːpələ] N **a** (*Archit*) (= *dome*) coupole *f*, dôme *m*; (*US* = *lantern, belfry*) belvédère *m* **b** (*Naut*) coupole *f* **c** (*Metal*) cubilot *m*

cuppa ['kʌpə] N (*Brit*) tasse *f* de thé

cupric ['kjuːprɪk] ADJ cuprique; **~ oxide** oxyde *m* de cuivre

---

cur [kɜː'] N **a** (*pej* = *dog*) sale chien *m*, sale cabot* *m* **b** (* *pej* = *man*) malotru *m*, mufle* *m*, rustre *m*

curable ['kjʊərəbl] ADJ guérissable, curable

curacy ['kjʊərəsɪ] N vicariat *m*

curare [kjʊə'rɑːrɪ] N curare *m*

curate¹ ['kjʊərɪt] N vicaire *m*; (*Brit*) **it's like the ~'s egg** il y a du bon et du mauvais

curate² [kjʊə'reɪt] VT (= *organize*) [+ *exhibition*] organiser

curative ['kjʊərətɪv] ADJ curatif

curator [kjʊə'reɪtə'] N **a** [*of museum etc*] conservateur *m* **b** (*Scot Jur*) curateur *m* (*d'un aliéné or d'un mineur*)

curatorial [,kjʊərə'tɔːrɪəl] ADJ [*expertise, career*] de conservateur; [*policy*] en matière de conservation; **the museum's ~ team** l'équipe qui administre le musée

curb [kɜːb] **1** N **a** [*of harness*] gourmette *f*; (*fig*) frein *m*; (*on trade etc*) restriction *f*; (*fig*) **to put a ~ on sth** mettre un frein à qch **b** (*US: at roadside*) bord *m* du trottoir **2** VT **a** (*US*) [+ *horse*] mettre un mors à; (*fig*) [+ *impatience, passion*] refréner, contenir; [+ *expenditure*] réduire, restreindre **b** (*US*) [+ *dog*] promener au caniveau **3** COMP ► **curb bit** N mors *m* ► **curb chain** N gourmette *f* ► **curb crawler** N (*US*) = **kerb crawler** → **kerb** ► **curb crawling** N (*US*) = **kerb crawling** → **kerb** ► **curb market** N (*US St Ex*) = **kerb market** → **kerb** ► **curb reins** NPL rênes *fpl* de filet ► **curb roof** N (*Archit*) comble *m* brisé ► **curb service** N (*US*) service *m* au volant (dans un restaurant drive-in) ► **curb weight** N (*US Aut*) poids *m* à vide

curbstone ['kɜːbstəʊn] **1** N (*US*) pavé *m* (pour bordure de trottoir) **2** COMP ► **curbstone market** N (*US St Ex*) = **kerb market** → **kerb**

curd [kɜːd] **1** N (*gen pl*) ~(**s**) lait *m* caillé → **lemon** **2** COMP ► **curd cheese** N ≈ fromage *m* blanc

curdle ['kɜːdl] **1** VT [+ *milk*] cailler; [+ *mayonnaise*] faire tomber; **it was enough to ~ the blood** c'était à vous glacer le sang **2** VI [*milk*] se cailler; [*mayonnaise*] tomber; (*fig*) **his blood ~d** son sang s'est figé; **it made my blood ~** cela m'a glacé le sang

cure [kjʊə'] **1** VT **a** (*Med*) [+ *disease, patient*] guérir (**of** de); (*fig*) [+ *poverty*] éliminer; [+ *unfairness*] éliminer, remédier à; **to ~ an injustice** réparer une injustice; **to ~ an evil** remédier à un mal; **to ~ sb (of sth)** guérir qn (de qch); **to ~ a child of a bad habit** faire perdre une mauvaise habitude à un enfant; **to ~ o.s. of smoking** se déshabituer du tabac, se guérir de l'habitude de fumer ■ (*PROV*) **what can't be ~d must be endured** il faut savoir accepter l'inévitable **b** [+ *meat, fish*] (= *salt*) saler; (= *smoke*) fumer; (= *dry*) sécher **2** N **a** (*Med*) (= *remedy*) remède *m*; (= *recovery*) guérison *f*; **to take** or **follow a ~** faire une cure; **past** or **beyond** ~ [*person*] inguérissable, incurable; [*state, injustice, evil*] irrémédiable, irréparable → **prevention, rest** **b** (*Rel*) cure *f*; **~ of souls** charge *f* d'âmes **3** COMP ► **cure-all** N panacée *f*

cured [kjʊəd] ADJ (*Culin*) (= *salted*) salé; (= *smoked*) fumé; (= *dried*) séché

curfew ['kɜːfjuː] N couvre-feu *m*; **to impose a/ lift the ~** décréter/lever le couvre-feu

curie ['kjʊərɪ] N (*Phys*) curie *m*

curing ['kjʊərɪŋ] N (*by salting*) salaison *f*; (*by smoking*) fumaison *f*; (*by drying*) séchage *m*

curio ['kjʊərɪəʊ] N bibelot *m*, curiosité *f*

curiosity [,kjʊərɪ'ɒsɪtɪ] **1** N **a** (*NonC* = *inquisitiveness*) curiosité *f* (**about** de); **out of ~** par curiosité ■ (*PROV*) **~ killed the cat** la curiosité est un vilain défaut (*PROV*) **b** (= *rare thing*) curiosité *f*, rareté *f* **2** COMP ► **curiosity shop** N magasin *m* de brocante or de curiosités

---

curious ['kjʊərɪəs] ADJ **a** (*also pej*) curieux (*also pej*); **to know what he did** je suis or serais curieux de savoir ce qu'il a fait; **I'm ~ about him** il m'intrigue; **why do you ask? — I'm just ~** pourquoi vous me demandez ça? — par curiosité, c'est tout **b** (= *strange*) curieux; **it is ~ that .../how ...** c'est curieux que ... (+ *subj*)/comme ...

curiously ['kjʊərɪəslɪ] ADV **a** (= *inquisitively*) [*ask*] d'un ton inquisiteur **b** (= *oddly*) [*silent, reticent*] curieusement; **~ shaped** d'une forme curieuse; **~, he didn't object** curieusement, il n'a pas émis d'objection

curium ['kjʊərɪəm] N curium *m*

curl [kɜːl] **1** N **a** [*of hair*] boucle *f* (de cheveux) **b** (*gen*) courbe *f*; [*of smoke*] spirale *f*, volute *f*; [*of waves*] ondulation *f*; (*fig*) **with a ~ of the lip** avec une moue méprisante **2** VT [+ *hair*] (*loosely*) (faire) boucler; (*tightly*) friser; **she ~s her hair** elle frise or boucle ses cheveux; **he ~ed his lip in disdain** il a eu une moue dédaigneuse; **the dog ~ed its lip menacingly** le chien a retroussé ses babines d'un air menaçant **3** VI **a** [*hair*] (*tightly*) friser; (*loosely*) boucler; (*fig*) **it's enough to make your hair ~** c'est à vous faire dresser les cheveux sur la tête; **his lip ~ed disdainfully** il a eu une moue dédaigneuse; **the dog's lip ~ed menacingly** le chien a retroussé ses babines d'un air menaçant **b** [*person, animal*] = **curl up** **4** COMP ► **curling irons, curling tongs** NPL fer *m* à friser ► **curl paper** N papillote *f*

► **curl up 1** VI s'enrouler; [*person*] se pelotonner; (*: *from shame etc*) rentrer sous terre; [*cat*] se mettre en boule, se pelotonner; [*dog*] se coucher en rond; [*leaves*] se recroqueviller; [*paper*] se recourber, se replier; [*corners*] se corner; [*stale bread*] se racornir; **he lay ~ed up on the floor** il était couché en boule par terre; **to ~ up with laughter** se tordre de rire; **the smoke ~ed up** la fumée montait en volutes or en spirales **2** VT SEP enrouler; **to ~ o.s. up** [*person*] se pelotonner; [*cat*] se mettre en boule, se pelotonner; [*dog*] se coucher en rond

curler ['kɜːlə'] N **a** [*of hair*] rouleau *m*, bigoudi *m* **b** (*Sport*) joueur *m*, -euse *f* de curling

curlew ['kɜːljuː] N courlis *m*

curlicue ['kɜːlɪkjuː] N [*of handwriting*] fioriture *f*; [*of skating*] figure *f* (de patinage)

curling ['kɜːlɪŋ] N (*Sport*) curling *m*

curly ['kɜːlɪ] **1** ADJ [*hair*] (*loosely*) bouclé; (*tightly*) frisé; ~ **eyelashes** cils *mpl* recourbés **2** COMP ► **curly bracket** N accolade *f* ► **curly-haired, curly-headed** ADJ aux cheveux bouclés or frisés ► **curly lettuce** N laitue *f* frisée

curmudgeon [kɜː'mʌdʒən] N (= *miser*) harpagon *m*, grippe-sou* *m*; (= *surly person*) grincheux *m*

curmudgeonly [kɜː'mʌdʒənlɪ] ADJ (= *miserly*) grippe-sou; (= *surly*) grincheux

currant ['kʌrənt] **1** N **a** (*Bot*) (= *fruit*) groseille *f*; (*also* ~ **bush**) groseillier *m* → **blackcurrant, redcurrant b** (= *dried fruit*) raisin *m* de Corinthe **2** COMP ► **currant bun** N petit pain *m* aux raisins ► **currant loaf** N pain *m* aux raisins

currency ['kʌrənsɪ] **1** N **a** (*Fin*) monnaie *f*, devise *f*; (= *money*) argent *m*; **the ~ is threatened** la monnaie est en danger; **this coin is no longer legal ~** cette pièce n'a plus cours (légal); **foreign ~** devise *f* or monnaie *f* étrangère; **I have no French ~** je n'ai pas d'argent français → **hard, paper b** (= *acceptance, prevalence*) cours *m*, circulation *f*; **to gain ~** se répandre, s'accréditer; **to give ~ to** accréditer; **such words have short ~** de tels mots n'ont pas cours longtemps; **this coin is no longer in ~** cette pièce n'est plus en circulation

2 COMP ► **currency exemptions** NPL (*Fin, Jur*) dispenses *fpl* en matière de réglementation des changes ► **currency market** N (*Fin*) place *f* financière ► **currency note** N billet *m* de banque ► **currency rate** N cours *m* des devises ► **currency restrictions** NPL contrôle *m* des changes ► **currency snake** N serpent *m* monétaire ► **currency unit** N unité *f* monétaire

current ['kʌrənt] **1** ADJ [*opinion*] courant, commun; [*word, phrase, price*] courant, en cours; [*fashion, tendency, popularity*] actuel; **to be ~** [*phrase, expression*] être accepté *or* courant; **to be in ~ use** être d'usage courant; **at the ~ rate of exchange** au cours actuel du change; (*Brit Banking*) **~ account** compte *m* courant; **~ affairs** questions *fpl or* problèmes *mpl* d'actualité, actualité *f* (*NonC*); (*Fin*) **~ assets** actif *m* de roulement; (*Fin*) **~ cost accounting** comptabilité *f* en coûts actuels; **~ liabilities** passif *m* exigible *or* dettes *fpl* exigibles à court terme; **~ events** événements *mpl* actuels, actualité *f* (*NonC*); **~ expenditure** dépenses *fpl* courantes; (*Press*) **~ issue** dernier numéro *m*; **~ month/year** mois *m*/année *f* en cours; (*St Ex*) **~ yield** taux *m* de rendement courant, taux *m* actuariel; **~ week** semaine *f* en cours; **his ~ job** le travail qu'il fait *or* le poste qu'il occupe en ce moment; **her ~ boyfriend** son copain* *or* petit ami du moment

2 [*air, water*] courant *m* (*also Elec*); (*fig*) [*of events etc*] cours *m*, tendance *f*; [*of opinions*] tendance *f*; (*lit, fig*) **to go with the ~** suivre le courant; **to drift with the ~** (*lit*) se laisser aller au fil de l'eau; (*fig*) aller selon le vent; **to go against the ~** (*lit*) remonter le courant; (*fig*) aller à contre-courant → **alternating**, **direct**

currently ['kʌrəntlɪ] ADV actuellement, à présent

curriculum [kə'rɪkjʊləm] **1** N (*pl* **curriculums** *or* **curricula** [kə'rɪkjʊlə]) programme *m* scolaire *or* d'études **2** COMP ► **curriculum coordinator** N responsable *mf* des programmes scolaires ► **curriculum council** N (*US Scol*) ≈ service *m* des programmes scolaires ► **curriculum vitae** N (*pl* **curricula vitae**) (*esp Brit Scol*) curriculum vitae *m*, C.V. *m*

curried ['kʌrɪd] ADJ au curry

curry[1] ['kʌrɪ] (*Culin*) **1** N curry *or* cari *m*; **beef ~ curry** *m* de bœuf **2** VT accommoder au curry **3** COMP ► **curry powder** N (poudre *f* de) curry *m*

curry[2] ['kʌrɪ] **1** VT [+ *horse*] étriller; [+ *leather*] corroyer; **to ~ favour with sb** chercher à gagner la faveur de qn **2** COMP ► **curry-comb** N étrille *f* ♦ VT étriller

curse [kɜːs] **1** N **a** (= *malediction, spell*) malédiction *f*; **a ~ on him!**† maudit soit-il!†; **to call down** *or* **put** *or* **lay a ~ on sb** maudire qn **b** (= *swearword*) juron *m*, imprécation *f*; **~s!** zut!* **c** (*fig* = *bane*) fléau *m*, calamité *f*; **the ~ of drunkenness** le fléau de l'ivrognerie; (= *menstruation*) **she has the ~*** elle a ses règles **2** VT maudire; **~ the child!*** maudit enfant!; (*fig*) **to be ~d with** être affligé de **3** VI (= *swear*) jurer, sacrer

cursed* ['kɜːsɪd] ADJ sacré*, maudit, satané (*all before n*)

cursive ['kɜːsɪv] **1** ADJ cursif **2** N (écriture *f*) cursive *f*

cursor ['kɜːsər] N (*Comput*) curseur *m*

cursorily ['kɜːsərɪlɪ] ADV en vitesse, à la hâte (*pej*)

cursory ['kɜːsərɪ] ADJ (= *superficial*) superficiel; (= *hasty*) hâtif; **to give a ~ glance at** [+ *person, object*] jeter un coup d'œil à; [+ *book, essay, letter*] lire en diagonale*

curt [kɜːt] ADJ [*person, manner*] brusque, sec (sèche *f*), cassant; [*explanation, question*] brusque, sec (sèche *f*); **in a ~ voice** d'un ton cassant; **with a ~ nod** avec un bref signe de tête

curtail [kɜː'teɪl] VT [+ *account*] écourter, raccourcir, tronquer; [+ *proceedings, visit*] écourter; [+ *period of time*] écourter, raccourcir; [+ *wages*] rogner, réduire; [+ *expenses*] restreindre, réduire

curtailment [kɜː'teɪlmənt] N (*NonC: frm*) **a** (= *reduction*) [*of money, aid*] réduction *f* **b** (= *restriction*) [*of sb's power, freedom*] limitation *f* **c** (= *shortening*) [*of visit*] raccourcissement *m*

curtain ['kɜːtn] **1** N **a** (*gen*) rideau *m*; (*fig*) rideau *m*, voile *m*; **to draw** *or* **pull the ~s** tirer les rideaux; **to open/close the ~s** ouvrir/fermer les rideaux; (*Mil*) **~ of fire** rideau *m* de feu; (*fig*) **it was ~s for him*** il était fichu* *or* foutu*; → **iron**, **safety**

b (*Theat*) rideau *m*; (= *time when curtain rises or falls*) lever *m or* baisser *m* de rideau; (*also* **~ call**) rappel *m*; **she took three ~s** elle a été rappelée trois fois; **the last** *or* **final ~** le dernier rappel; **to drop the ~** baisser le rideau; **the ~ drops** le rideau tombe

2 VT [+ *window*] garnir de rideaux

3 COMP ► **curtain hook** N crochet *m* de rideau ► **curtain pole** N tringle *f* à rideaux ► **curtain raiser** N (*Theat, also fig*) lever *m* de rideau ► **curtain ring** N anneau *m* de rideau ► **curtain rod** N tringle *f* à rideaux ► **curtain-up** N (*Theat*) lever *m* du rideau ► **curtain wall** N (*Constr*) mur *m*

► **curtain off** VT SEP [+ *room*] diviser par un *or* des rideau(x); [+ *bed, kitchen area*] cacher derrière un *or* des rideau(x)

curtly ['kɜːtlɪ] ADV avec brusquerie, sèchement, d'un ton cassant

curtness ['kɜːtnɪs] N brusquerie *f*, sécheresse *f*

curtsey, curtsy ['kɜːtsɪ] **1** N révérence *f*; **to make** *or* **drop a ~** faire une révérence **2** VI faire une révérence (**to** à)

curvaceous* [kɜː'veɪʃəs] ADJ [*woman*] bien balancée*, bien roulée*

curvature ['kɜːvətʃər] N courbure *f*; (*Med*) déviation *f*; **~ of the spine** déviation *f* de la colonne vertébrale, scoliose *f*; **the ~ of space/the earth** la courbure de l'espace/de la terre

curve [kɜːv] **1** N (*gen*) courbe *f*; [*of arch*] voussure *f*; [*of beam*] cambrure *f*; [*of graph*] courbe *f*; **~ in the road** courbe *f*, tournant *m*, virage *m*; **a woman's ~s*** les rondeurs *fpl* d'une femme **2** VT courber; (*Archit*) [+ *arch, roof*] cintrer **3** VI [*line, surface, beam*] se courber, s'infléchir; [*road etc*] faire une courbe, être en courbe; **the road ~s down into the valley** la route descend en courbe dans la vallée; **the river ~s round the town** la rivière fait un méandre autour de la ville

curveball ['kɜːvbɔːl] N (*US Baseball*) balle *f* à effet

curved [kɜːvd] ADJ (*gen*) courbe; [*edge of table etc*] arrondi; [*road*] en courbe; (= *convex*) convexe

curvet [kɜː'vet] (*Horse-riding*) **1** N courbette *f* **2** VI faire une courbette

curvilinear [ˌkɜːvɪ'lɪnɪər] ADJ curviligne

curvy* ['kɜːvɪ] ADJ [*girl, body*] bien roulé*; (*gen*) courbe

cushion ['kʊʃən] **1** N **a** coussin *m*; **on a ~ of air** sur un coussin d'air → **pincushion b** (*Billiards*) bande *f*; **a stroke off the ~** un doublé **2** VT [+ *sofa*] mettre des coussins à; [+ *seat*] rembourrer; (*Tech*) matelasser; (*fig*) [+ *shock*] amortir; (*Fin*) [+ *losses*] atténuer; **to ~ sb's fall** amortir la chute de qn; (*fig*) **to ~ sb against sth** protéger qn contre qch; **to ~ one's savings against inflation** mettre ses économies à l'abri de l'inflation

cushy* ['kʊʃɪ] ADJ (*Brit*) pépère*, tranquille; **a ~ job** une bonne planque*, un boulot pépère*; **to have a ~ time** se la couler douce* → **billet**[1]

cusp [kʌsp] N (*Bot*) [*of tooth*] cuspide *f*; [*of moon*] corne *f*

cuspidor ['kʌspɪdɔːr] N (*US*) crachoir *m*

cuss* [kʌs] (*US*) = **curse 1** **a** (= *oath*) juron *m*; **he's not worth a tinker's ~** il ne vaut pas un pet de lapin* **b** (*gen pej* = *person*) type* *m*, bonne femme *f* (*gen pej*); **he's a queer ~** c'est un drôle de type* **2** VI jurer

cussed* ['kʌsɪd] ADJ entêté, têtu comme une mule*

cussedness* ['kʌsɪdnɪs] N esprit *m* contrariant *or* de contradiction; **out of sheer ~** par pur esprit de contradiction

cussword* ['kʌswɜːd] N (*US*) gros mot *m*

custard ['kʌstəd] **1** N (*pouring*) crème *f* anglaise; (*set*) crème *f* renversée **2** COMP ► **custard apple** N (*Bot*) pomme *f* cannelle, anone *f* ► **custard cream, custard cream biscuit** N biscuit *m* fourré ► **custard pie** N tarte *f* à la crème ► **custard powder** N crème *f* anglaise en poudre ► **custard tart** N flan *m*

custodial [kʌs'təʊdɪəl] ADJ **a** (*Jur*) [*parent*] à qui est attribué la garde des enfants; **~ sentence** peine *f* privative de liberté **b** [*of museum etc*] **~ staff** personnel *m* de surveillance

custodian [kʌs'təʊdɪən] N [*of building*] concierge *mf*, gardien(ne) *m(f)*; [*of museum*] conservateur *m*, -trice *f*; [*of tradition etc*] gardien(ne) *m(f)*, protecteur *m*, -trice *f*

custody ['kʌstədɪ] **1** N **a** (*Jur etc*) garde *f*; **in safe ~** sous bonne garde; **the child is in the ~ of his aunt** l'enfant est sous la garde de sa tante; (*Jur*) **after the divorce she was given ~ of the children** après le divorce elle a obtenu la garde des enfants **b** (*gen*) garde *f* à vue; (= *imprisonment*) emprisonnement *m*, captivité *f*; (*also* **police ~**) (*for short period*) garde *f* à vue; (*before trial*) détention *f* provisoire; **in ~** en détention provisoire; **to be kept in (police) ~** être mis en garde à vue; **to take sb into ~** mettre qn en état d'arrestation; **to give sb into ~** remettre qn aux mains de la police → **protective**, **remand**

custom ['kʌstəm] **1** N **a** (= *tradition, convention*) coutume *f*, usage *m*; (= *habit*) coutume *f*, habitude *f*; **as ~ has it** selon la coutume, selon les us et coutumes; **it was his ~ to rest each morning** il avait coutume *or* il avait l'habitude de se reposer chaque matin **b** (*NonC: Brit Comm*) clientèle *f*; **the grocer wanted to get her ~** l'épicier voulait la compter parmi ses clients; **he has lost a lot of ~** il a perdu beaucoup de clients; **he took his ~ elsewhere** il est allé se fournir ailleurs **c** (*Jur*) coutume *f*, droit *m* coutumier → **customs** **2** ADJ (= *custom-made*) personnalisé **3** COMP ► **custom-built** ADJ (*Comm*) fait sur commande ► **custom car** N voiture *f* faite sur commande ► **custom-made** ADJ (*Comm*) [*clothes*] (fait) sur mesure; (*other goods*) fait sur commande

customarily ['kʌstəmərɪlɪ] ADV habituellement, ordinairement

customary ['kʌstəmərɪ] **1** ADJ (*gen*) habituel, coutumier; **it is ~ (to do that)** c'est la coutume; **it is ~ to thank the host** la coutume veut que l'on remercie (*subj*) l'hôte; **it is ~ for the children to be present** la coutume veut que les enfants soient présents **2** COMP ► **customary tenant** N (*Jur*) tenancier *m* censitaire

customer ['kʌstəmər] **1** N **a** (*Comm*) client(e) *m(f)* **b** (*esp Brit*) type* *m*, individu *m* (*pej*); **he's an awkward ~** il n'est pas commode; **queer ~** drôle de type* *or* d'individu; **ugly ~** sale type* *m or* individu *m* **2** COMP ► **customer appeal** N facteur *m* de séduction du client ► **customer base** N clientèle *f* ► **customer profile** N profil *m* du consommateur ► **customer services** NPL service *m* clientèle *or* clients

customize ['kʌstəmaɪz] VT fabriquer (*or* construire *or* arranger *etc*) sur commande

customized [ˈkʌstəmaɪzd] ADJ [*software, service*] sur mesure

customs [ˈkʌstəmz] **1** N **a** (*sg or pl = authorities, place*) douane *f*; **to go through (the) ~** passer la douane; **at** *or* **in the ~** à la douane **b** (*pl = duty payable*) droits *mpl* de douane **2** COMP [*regulations, receipt etc*] de la douane ► **Customs and Excise** N (*Brit*) douanes *fpl* ► **customs border patrol** N brigade *f* volante des services de douane ► **customs clearance** N dédouanement *m* ► **customs declaration** N déclaration *f* de douane ► **customs duty** N droit(s) *m(pl)* de douane ► **customs house** N (poste *m* or bureaux *mpl* de) douane *f* ► **customs inspection** N visite *f* douanière *or* de douane ► **customs officer** N douanier *m*, -ière *f* ► **customs post** N = customs house ► **customs service** N service *m* des douanes ► **customs shed** N poste *m* de douane ► **customs union** N union *f* douanière

cut [kʌt] (*vb: pret, ptp* **cut**) **1** N **a** (= *stroke*) coup *m*; (= *mark, slit*) coupure *f*; (= *notch*) entaille *f*; (= *slash*) estafilade *f*; (= *gash*) balafre *f*; (*Med*) incision *f*; **sabre ~** coup *m* de sabre; **saw ~** trait *m* de scie; **a deep ~ in the leg** une profonde coupure à la jambe; **he had a ~ on his chin from shaving** il s'était coupé au menton en se rasant; **he was treated for minor ~s and bruises** on l'a soigné pour des petites coupures et des contusions; **there is a ~ in his jacket** il y a une entaille à sa veste; (*fig*) **the ~ and thrust of modern politics** les estocades *fpl* de la politique contemporaine; (*fig*) **that remark was a ~ at me** cette remarque était une pierre dans mon jardin *or* une pique contre moi; (*fig*) **the unkindest ~ of all** le coup le plus perfide; (*fig*) **he is a ~ above (the others)*** il vaut mieux que les autres, il est supérieur aux autres; (*fig*) **that's a ~ above him*** ça le dépasse → **short b** [*of cards*] coupe *f* **c** (= *reduction: gen, esp Econ*) réduction *f* (**in** de), diminution *f* (**in** de); (*in staff*) compression *f* (**in** de); (*Fin*) **the ~s** les compressions *fpl* budgétaires; (*Econ*) **drastic ~s coupes** *fpl* claires; **power** *or* **electricity ~** coupure *f* de courant; **to make ~s in a book/play** *etc* faire des coupures dans un livre/une pièce *etc*; **a 1% ~ in interest rates** une réduction *or* une diminution de 1% des taux d'intérêt → **tax**; **the ~s in defence** *or* **the defence budget** la diminution *or* la réduction du budget de la défense; **to take a ~ in salary** subir une diminution *or* réduction de salaire **d** [*of meat*] (= *piece*) morceau *m*; (= *slice*) tranche *f*; **a nice ~ of beef** un beau morceau de bœuf; **a ~ off** *or* **from the joint** un morceau de rôti **e** (* = *share*) part *f*; **they all want a ~ in the profits** ils veulent tous leur part du gâteau* (*fig*); **there won't be much left once the lawyers have taken their ~** il ne restera pas grand-chose une fois que les avocats auront pris leur part **f** [*of clothes*] coupe *f*; [*of jewel*] taille *f*; **I like the ~ of this coat** j'aime la coupe de ce manteau → **jib g** (= *haircut*) **~ (and blow-dry)** coupe *f* (et brushing) **h** (*Comput*) **~ and paste** couper-coller *m* **i** (*US Typ = block*) cliché *m* **j** (*Cine, TV*) (= *edit*) coupure *f*; (= *transition*) passage *m* (**from** de, **to** à) **k** (*US*: *from school etc*) absence *f* injustifiée **2** ADJ [*flowers, grass*] coupé; **he had a ~ finger/hand** il avait une coupure au doigt/à la main, il s'était coupé au doigt/à la main; **a ~ lip** une lèvre coupée; **well-~ coat** manteau *m* bien coupé *or* de bonne coupe; (*fig*) **it was all ~ and dried** (= *fixed beforehand*) c'était déjà décidé, tout était déjà arrangé; (= *impossible to adapt*) il n'y avait pas moyen de changer quoi que ce soit; **~ and dried opinions** opinions *fpl* toutes faites

3 VT **a** couper; [+ *joint of meat, tobacco*] découper; (= *slice*) découper en tranches; (= *notch*) encocher; (*Med*) [+ *abscess*] inciser; **to ~ in half/in three** *etc* couper en deux/en trois *etc*; **she ~ the cake in six** elle a coupé le gâteau en six; **to ~ in(to) pieces** (*lit*) couper en morceaux; (*fig*) [+ *army*] tailler en pièces; [+ *reputation*] démolir; **to ~ one's finger** se couper le doigt *or* au doigt; **to ~ o.s. (shaving)** se couper (en se rasant); **to ~ sb's throat** couper la gorge à qn, égorger qn; (*fig*) **he is ~ting his own throat** il prépare sa propre ruine (*fig*); **to ~ sth open** (*with knife*) ouvrir qch au *or* avec un couteau; (*with scissors etc*) ouvrir qch avec des ciseaux *etc*; **he ~ his arm open on a nail** il s'est ouvert le bras sur un clou; **he ~ his head open** il s'est ouvert le crâne; (*fig*) **to ~ sb short** couper la parole à qn; **he came ~ short, he came** bref, il est venu; **to ~ sb free** délivrer qn en coupant ses liens → **corner, dash, figure, fine, Gordian, ground, ice, loss, mustard, tooth b** (*fig = wound, hurt*) [+ *person*] blesser (profondément), affecter; **the wind ~ his face** le vent lui coupait le visage → **heart, quick c** (= *shape*) couper, tailler; [+ *steps*] tailler; [+ *channel*] creuser, percer; [+ *figure, statue*] sculpter (**out of** dans); (= *engrave*) graver; [+ *jewel, key, glass, crystal*] tailler; [+ *screw*] fileter; [+ *dress*] couper; **to ~ a hole in sth** faire un trou dans qch; **to ~ one's way through the crowd/forest** se frayer un chemin à travers la foule/les bois → **coat, record d** (= *mow, clip, trim*) [+ *hedge, trees*] tailler; [+ *corn, hay*] faucher; [+ *lawn*] tondre; **to ~ one's nails/hair** se couper les ongles/les cheveux; **to have** *or* **get one's hair ~** se faire couper les cheveux **e** (*esp US = not to go*) [+ *class, school etc*] manquer, sécher*; [+ *appointment*] manquer exprès → **dead f** (= *cross, intersect*) couper, croiser, traverser; (*Math*) couper; **the path ~s the road here** le sentier coupe la route à cet endroit **g** (= *reduce*) [+ *profits, wages*] réduire, diminuer; [+ *text, book, play*] réduire, faire des coupures dans; **to ~ costs** réduire les coûts; **to ~ prices** réduire les prix, vendre à prix réduit *or* au rabais; **to ~ spending by 35%** réduire *or* diminuer les dépenses de 35%; **we ~ the journey time by half** nous avons réduit de moitié la durée du trajet; (*Sport*) **he ~ 30 seconds off the record** ◊ **he ~ the record by 30 seconds** il a amélioré le record de 30 secondes **h** (= *stop*) couper; **to ~ electricity supplies** couper l'électricité; **to ~ the euphemisms and just tell me what's happened!*** arrête de tourner autour du pot et dis-moi simplement ce qui s'est passé!; (*esp US*) **~ the crap!*** arrête tes conneries!‡, assez bavardé comme ça!* **i** [+ *cards*] couper **j** (*Sport*) **to ~ the ball** couper la balle **k** (*Cine etc* = *edit*) [+ *film*] monter **l** (= *dilute*) [+ *drink*] couper **m** (*Comput*) **~ and paste** [+ *document etc*] couper-coller; **~ and paste these lines of text into your file** coupez-collez ces lignes de texte dans votre fichier **4** VI **a** [*person, knife etc*] couper; **this knife ~s well** ce couteau coupe bien; **he ~ into the cake** il a fait une entaille dans le gâteau, il a entamé le gâteau; **~ along the dotted line** découper suivant le pointillé; **his sword ~ through the air** son épée fendit l'air; **the boat ~ through the waves** le bateau fendait l'eau; (*fig*) **this ~s across all I have learnt** ceci va à l'encontre de tout ce que j'ai appris; **what you say ~s both ways** ce que vous dites est à double tranchant; **that argument ~s both**

ways c'est un argument à double tranchant; **to ~ and run*** mettre les bouts‡, filer* → **loose b** [*material*] se couper; **paper ~s easily** le papier se coupe facilement; **this piece will ~ into four** ce morceau peut se couper en quatre **c** (*Math*) se couper; **lines A and B ~ at point C** les lignes A et B se coupent au point C **d** (= *take short route*) **across the fields and you'll soon be there** coupez à travers champs et vous serez bientôt arrivé; **to ~ across country** couper à travers champs; **if you ~ through the lane you'll save time** si vous coupez *or* passez par la ruelle vous gagnerez du temps **e** (*Cine, TV*) **they ~ from the street to the shop scene** ils passent de la rue à la scène du magasin; **~!** coupez! **f** (*Cards*) couper; **to ~ for deal** tirer pour la donne **5** COMP ► **cut glass** N (*NonC*) cristal *m* taillé ◊ ADJ de *or* en cristal taillé ► **cut-price** ADJ [*goods, ticket*] à prix réduit, au rabais; [*manufacturer, shopkeeper*] qui vend à prix réduits; **~-price shop** *or* **store** magasin *m* à prix réduits ◊ ADV [*buy, get*] à prix réduit ► **cut prices** NPL prix *mpl* réduits ► **cut-rate** ADJ (*Brit*) = **cut-price** ► **cut-throat**† N (= *murderer*) assassin *m* ◊ ADJ **~-throat competition** concurrence *f* acharnée; (*Cards*) **~-throat game** partie *f* à trois; (*Brit*) **~-throat razor** rasoir *m* à main *or* de coiffeur ► **cut tobacco** N tabac *m* découpé ► **cut up*** ADJ (*Brit = upset*) affligé; (*US = funny*) rigolo* (-ote* *f*)

► **cut across** VT FUS [*problem, issue*] toucher; **this problem ~s across all ages** ce problème touche toutes les tranches d'âge

► **cut along** VI s'en aller, filer*

► **cut away 1** VT SEP [+ *branch*] élaguer; [+ *unwanted part*] enlever (en coupant) **2** **~away** N → **cutaway**

► **cut back 1** VT SEP [+ *plants, shrubs*] élaguer, tailler; (*fig: also* **~ back on**) [+ *production, expenditure*] réduire, diminuer **2** VI revenir (sur ses pas); **he ~ back to the village and gave his pursuers the slip** il est revenu au village par un raccourci et a semé ses poursuivants **3** **~back** N → **cutback**

► **cut down** VT SEP **a** [+ *tree*] couper, abattre; [+ *corn*] faucher; [+ *person*] (*by sword etc*) abattre (*d'un coup d'épée etc*); (*fig: through illness etc*) terrasser; **~ down by pneumonia** terrassé par la *or* une pneumonie **b** (= *reduce*) [+ *expenses, pollution*] réduire; [+ *article, essay*] couper; [+ *clothes*] (*gen*) rapetisser, diminuer; (*fig*) **to ~ sb down to size*** remettre qn à sa place

► **cut down on** VT FUS [+ *food*] manger moins de; [+ *alcohol*] boire moins de; [+ *cigarettes*] fumer moins de; [+ *expenditure, costs*] réduire; **you should ~ down on drink** vous devriez boire moins

► **cut in 1** VI (*into conversation*) se mêler à la conversation; (*Aut*) se rabattre; **to ~ in on sb** (*Aut*) faire une queue de poisson à qn; (= *interrupt*) couper la parole à qn; (*Comm, Fin*) **to ~ in on the market** s'infiltrer sur le marché **2** VT SEP **to ~ sb in on** *or* **into a deal*** intéresser qn à une affaire

► **cut off 1** VI (†* = *leave*) filer* **2** VT SEP **a** [+ *piece of cloth, cheese, meat, bread*] couper (**from** dans); [+ *limbs*] amputer, couper; **to ~ off sb's head** trancher la tête de *or* à qn, décapiter qn; **to ~ off one's nose to spite one's face** scier la branche sur laquelle on est assis (*par dépit*) **b** (= *disconnect*) [+ *telephone caller, telephone, car engine, gas, electricity*] couper; **our water supply has been ~ off** on nous a coupé l'eau; (*Telec*) **we were ~ off** nous avons été coupés; **to ~ sb off in the middle of a sentence** interrompre qn au milieu d'une phrase; **to ~ off sb's supplies** (*of food, money etc*) couper les vivres à qn **c** (= *isolate*) isoler (**sb from sth** qn de qch); **to ~ o.s. off from** rompre ses liens avec; **he**

feels very ~ off in the country il se sent très isolé à la campagne; **town ~ off by floods** ville *f* isolée par des inondations; (*Mil*) **to ~ off the enemy's retreat** couper la retraite à l'ennemi; (*fig*) **to ~ sb off with a shilling** déshériter qn

[3] **~off** N → **cutoff**

► **cut out** [1] VI [a] (*Aut, Aviat*) [*engine*] caler [b] (♦ = *leave*) filer*, se tailler* [2] VT SEP [a] [+ *picture, article*] découper (**of, from** de); [+ *statue, figure*] sculpter, tailler (**of** dans); [+ *coat*] couper, tailler (**of, from** dans); (*Phot*) détourer; **to ~ out a path through the jungle** se frayer un chemin à travers la jungle; (*fig*) **to be ~ out for sth** avoir des dispositions pour qch; (*fig*) **he's not ~ out for** or **to be a doctor** il n'est pas fait pour être médecin, il n'a pas l'étoffe d'un médecin; (*fig*) **he had his work ~ out (for him)** (= *plenty to do*) il avait du pain sur la planche; (*fig*) **you'll have your work ~ out to get there on time** vous n'avez pas de temps à perdre si vous voulez y arriver à l'heure; **you'll have your work ~ out to persuade him to come** vous aurez du mal à le persuader de venir [b] (*fig*) [+ *rival*] supplanter [c] (= *remove*) enlever, ôter; [+ *intermediary, middleman*] supprimer; [+ *light*] empêcher de passer; [+ *unnecessary details*] élaguer; **to ~ sb out of one's will** déshériter qn; (*fig*) **~ it out!** ça suffit !*, ça va comme ça !*; (*fig*) **~ out the talking!** assez bavardé !, vous avez fini de bavarder ?; **~ out the noise!** arrêtez ce bruit !, moins de bruit !; (*fig*) **you can ~ out the tears for a start!** et pour commencer, arrête de pleurnicher ! [d] (= *give up*) [+ *tobacco*] supprimer; **to ~ out smoking/drinking** arrêter de fumer/boire [3] **~out** N → **cutout**

► **cut up** [1] VI [a] (*Brit*) **to ~ up rough*** se mettre en rogne* or en boule* [b] (*US* = *clown around*) faire le pitre [2] VT SEP [a] [+ *wood, food*] couper; [+ *meat*] (= *carve*) découper; (= *chop up*) hacher; (*fig*) [+ *enemy, army*] tailler en pièces, anéantir [b] (*Aut**) faire une queue de poisson à; **he was crossing from lane to lane, ~ting everyone up** il passait d'une file à l'autre, faisant des queues de poisson à tout le monde [c] (*Brit*♦: *pass only*) **to be ~ up about sth** (= *hurt*) être affecté or démoralisé par qch; (= *annoyed*) être très embêté par qch*; **he's very ~ up** il n'a plus le moral*; **he was very ~ up by the death of his son** la mort de son fils l'a beaucoup affecté [3] **~-up**♦ ADJ → **cut**

cutaneous [kjuːˈteɪnɪəs] ADJ cutané

cutaway [ˈkʌtəweɪ] N (*also* ~ **drawing** or **sketch**) (dessin *m*) écorché *m*

cutback [ˈkʌtbæk] N (= *reduction*) [*of expenditure, production*] réduction *f*, diminution *f* (**in** de); [*of staff*] compressions *fpl* (**in** de); (*Cine* = *flashback*) flash-back *m* (**to** sur); (*Econ etc*) **drastic ~s** coupes *fpl* claires

cute* [kjuːt] ADJ [a] (= *attractive*) mignon [b] (*esp US* = *clever*) malin (-igne *f*), futé; **don't try and be ~ (with me)!** ne fais pas le malin !

cutely* [ˈkjuːtlɪ] ADV [a] (= *attractively*) [*smile, blush, pose*] avec coquetterie [b] (*US* = *cleverly*) astucieusement

cutesy* [ˈkjuːtsɪ] ADJ (*esp US: pej*) [*person, painting, clothes*] mièvre

cuticle [ˈkjuːtɪkl] [1] N (= *skin*) épiderme *m*; [*of fingernails*] petites peaux *fpl*, envie *f*; (*Bot*) cuticule *f* [2] COMP ► **cuticle remover** N repousse-peaux *m*

cutie* [ˈkjuːtɪ] [1] N (*esp US* = *girl*) jolie fille *f*; (= *boy*) beau mec* *m*; (= *shrewd person*) malin *m*, -igne *f*; (= *shrewd action*) beau coup *m* [2] COMP ► **cutie pie♦** N (*esp US*) mignon(ne) *m(f)*; **she's a real ~ pie** elle est vraiment mignonne

cutlass [ˈkʌtləs] N (*Naut*) coutelas *m*, sabre *m* d'abordage

cutler [ˈkʌtlər] N coutelier *m*

cutlery [ˈkʌtlərɪ] [1] N [a] (*Brit* = *knives, forks, spoons etc*) couverts *mpl* → **canteen** [b] (= *knives, daggers etc: also trade*) coutellerie *f* [2] COMP ► **cutlery drawer** N tiroir *m* des couverts

cutlet [ˈkʌtlɪt] N [a] (*gen*) côtelette *f*; [*of veal*] escalope *f* [b] (*US* = *croquette of meat, chicken etc*) croquette *f*

cutoff [ˈkʌtɒf] [1] N (= *short cut*) raccourci *m*; (*Tech* = *stopping*) arrêt *m* [2] **cutoffs** NPL jeans *mpl* coupés [3] COMP ► **cutoff date** N date *f* limite ► **cutoff device** N (*also* **automatic ~ device**) système *m* d'arrêt (automatique) ► **cutoff point** N (*in age etc*) limite *f*; (*in time*) dernier délai *m* ► **cutoff switch** N interrupteur *m*

cutout [ˈkʌtaʊt] N [a] (*Elec*) disjoncteur *m*, coupe-circuit *m inv*; (*Aut*) échappement *m* libre [b] (= *figure of wood* or *paper*) découpage *m*; (*fig*) **his characters are just cardboard ~s** ses personnages manquent d'épaisseur

cutter [ˈkʌtər] N [a] (= *person*) [*of clothes*] coupeur *m*, -euse *f*; [*of stones, jewels*] tailleur *m*; [*of films*] monteur *m*, -euse *f* [b] (= *tool*) coupoir *m*, couteau *m*; **(pair of) ~s** (*for metal etc*) pinces *fpl* coupantes → **bolt** [c] (= *sailing boat*) cotre *m*, cutter *m*; (= *motor boat*) vedette *f*; [*of coastguards*] garde-côte *m*; [*of warship*] canot *m* [d] (*US* = *sleigh*) traîneau *m*

cutting [ˈkʌtɪŋ] [1] N [a] (*NonC*) coupe *f*; [*of diamond*] taille *f*; [*of film*] montage *m*; [*of trees*] coupe *f*, abattage *m* [b] (*for road, railway*) tranchée *f* [c] (= *piece cut off*) [*of newspaper*] coupure *f*; [*of cloth*] coupon *m*; (*Agr*) bouture *f*; [*of vine*] marcotte *f* [d] (= *reduction*) [*of prices, expenditure*] réduction *f*, diminution *f* [2] ADJ [a] [*knife*] coupant, tranchant; **~ pliers** pinces *fpl* coupantes; (*lit*) **the ~ edge** le tranchant; (*fig*) **to be at the ~ edge of scientific research** être à la pointe de la recherche scientifique [b] (*fig*) [*wind*] glacial, cinglant; [*rain*] cinglant; [*cold*] piquant, glacial; [*words*] blessant, cinglant; [*remark*] mordant, blessant; **~ tongue** langue *f* acérée [3] COMP ► **cutting board** N planche *f* à découper ► **cutting-out scissors** NPL (*Sewing*) ciseaux *mpl* de couturière ► **cutting room** N (*Cine*) salle *f* de montage; (*fig*) **to end up on the ~ room floor** finir au panier

cuttlebone [ˈkʌtlbəʊn] N os *m* de seiche

cuttlefish [ˈkʌtlfɪʃ] N (*pl* **cuttlefish** or **cuttlefishes**) seiche *f*

CV [ˌsiːˈviː] N (ABBR = **curriculum vitae**) → **curriculum**

CWO [ˌsiːdʌbljuːˈəʊ] [a] (ABBR = **cash with order**) → **cash** [b] (*Mil*) (ABBR = **chief warrant officer**) → **chief**

CWS [ˌsiːdʌbljuːˈes] (ABBR = **Cooperative Wholesale Society**) coopérative *f*

cwt ABBR = **hundredweight(s)**

cyanide [ˈsaɪənaɪd] N cyanure *m*; **~ of potassium** cyanure *m* de potassium

cyanose [ˈsaɪənəʊz] N cyanose *f*

cyanosed [ˈsaɪənəʊzd] ADJ (*Med*) cyanosé

cyber... [ˈsaɪbə] PREF cyber...

cybercafé [ˈsaɪbəˌkæfeɪ] N cybercafé *m*

cybernaut [ˈsaɪbənɔːt] N cybernaute *mf*

cybernetic [ˌsaɪbəˈnetɪk] ADJ cybernétique

cybernetics [ˌsaɪbəˈnetɪks] N (*NonC*) cybernétique *f*

cyberpet [ˈsaɪbəpet] N Tamagotchi® *m*

cyberpunk [ˈsaɪbəpʌŋk] N (*Literat*) (= *writing*) cyberpunk *m*; (= *writer*) cyberpunk *m*

cybersex [ˈsaɪbəseks] N (*NonC*) cybersexe *m*

cyberspace [ˈsaɪbəspeɪs] N cyberespace *m*

cyborg [ˈsaɪbɔːg] N cyborg *m*

cyclamate [ˈsaɪkləˌmeɪt, ˈsɪkləˌmeɪt] N cyclamate *m*

cyclamen [ˈsɪkləmən] N cyclamen *m*

cycle [ˈsaɪkl] [1] N [a] vélo *m*, bicyclette *f* [b] (*also* **menstrual ~**) cycle *m* (menstruel) [c] [*of poems, seasons etc*] cycle *m* [2] VI faire du vélo, faire de la bicyclette; **he ~s to school** il va à l'école à bicyclette or à vélo or en vélo [3] COMP [*lamp, chain, wheel*] de vélo or de bicyclette; [*race*] cycliste ► **cycle clip** N pince *f* à vélo ► **cycle lane** N (*Brit*) piste *f* cyclable ► **cycle path** N piste *f* cyclable ► **cycle pump** N pompe *f* à vélo ► **cycle rack** N (*on floor*) râtelier *m* à bicyclettes; (*on car roof*) porte-vélos *m inv* ► **cycle shed** N abri *m* à bicyclettes ► **cycle shop** N magasin *m* de cycles ► **cycle track** N (= *lane*) piste *f* cyclable; (*Sport*) vélodrome *m*

cycler [ˈsaɪklər] N (*US*) = **cyclist**

cycleway [ˈsaɪklweɪ] N (*Brit*) piste *f* cyclable

cyclic(al) [ˈsaɪklɪk(əl)] ADJ cyclique

cycling [ˈsaɪklɪŋ] [1] N cyclisme *m*; **to do a lot of ~** (*gen*) faire beaucoup de bicyclette or de vélo; (*Sport*) faire beaucoup de cyclisme [2] COMP de bicyclette ► **cycling clothes** NPL tenue *f* de cycliste ► **cycling holiday** N **to go on a ~ holiday** faire du cyclotourisme ► **cycling shorts** NPL (*pair of*) ~ **shorts** (short *m* de) cycliste *m* ► **cycling tour** N circuit *m* à bicyclette ► **cycling track** N vélodrome *m*

cyclist [ˈsaɪklɪst] N cycliste *mf* → **racing**

cyclone [ˈsaɪkləʊn] [1] N cyclone *m* [2] COMP ► **cyclone cellar** N (*US*) abri *m* anticyclone

Cyclops [ˈsaɪklɒps] N (*pl* **Cyclopses** or **Cyclopes** [saɪˈkləʊpiːz]) cyclope *m*

cyclorama [ˌsaɪkləˈrɑːmə] N (*also Cine*) cyclorama *m*

cyclostyle [ˈsaɪkləstaɪl] [1] N machine *f* à polycopier (*à stencils*) [2] VT polycopier

cyclothymia [ˌsaɪkləʊˈθaɪmɪə] N cyclothymie *f*

cyclothymic [ˌsaɪkləʊˈθaɪmɪk] ADJ, N cyclothymique *mf*

cyclotron [ˈsaɪklətrɒn] N cyclotron *m*

cygnet [ˈsɪgnɪt] N jeune cygne *m*

cylinder [ˈsɪlɪndər] [1] N [a] (*Aut, Math, Tech*) cylindre *m*; **a six-cylinder** une six-cylindres; **to be firing on all four ~s** marcher or fonctionner à pleins gaz* or tubes*; (*fig*) **he's only firing on two ~s** complètement [b] [*of typewriter*] rouleau *m*; [*of clock, gun*] barillet *m* [2] COMP ► **cylinder block** N (*Aut*) bloc-cylindres *m* ► **cylinder capacity** N cylindrée *f* ► **cylinder head** N culasse *f*; **to take off the ~ head** déculasser ► **cylinder head gasket** N joint *m* de culasse ► **cylinder vacuum cleaner** N aspirateur-traîneau *m*

cylindrical [sɪˈlɪndrɪkəl] ADJ cylindrique

cymbal [ˈsɪmbəl] N cymbale *f*

cynic [ˈsɪnɪk] [1] N (*gen, Philos*) cynique *mf* [2] ADJ = **cynical**

cynical [ˈsɪnɪkəl] ADJ (*gen, Philos*) cynique; (*Sport*) **a ~ foul** de l'antijeu *m* flagrant

cynically [ˈsɪnɪklɪ] ADV cyniquement

cynicism [ˈsɪnɪsɪzəm] N (*gen, Philos*) cynisme *m*; **~s** remarques *fpl* cyniques, sarcasmes *mpl*

cynosure [ˈsɪnəzjʊər] N (*also* ~ **of every eye**) point *m* de mire, centre d'attraction

CYO [ˌsiːwaɪˈəʊ] N (*in US*) (ABBR = **Catholic Youth Organization**) mouvement catholique

cypher [ˈsaɪfər] = **cipher**

cypress [ˈsaɪprɪs] N cyprès *m*

Cypriot [ˈsɪprɪət] [1] ADJ chypriote or cypriote; **Greek/Turkish ~** chypriote grec (grecque *f*)/turc (turque *f*) [2] N Chypriote or Cypriote *mf*; **Greek/Turkish ~** Chypriote *mf* grec (grecque)/turc (turque)

Cyprus [ˈsaɪprəs] N Chypre *f*; **in ~** à Chypre

Cyrillic [sɪ'rɪlɪk] ADJ cyrillique

cyst [sɪst] N (Med) kyste *m*; (Bio) sac *m* (membraneux)

cystic fibrosis ['sɪstɪk,faɪ'brəʊsɪs] N mucoviscidose *f*

cystitis [sɪs'taɪtɪs] N cystite *f*

cytological [,saɪtə'lɒdʒɪkəl] ADJ cytologique

cytology [saɪ'tɒlədʒɪ] N cytologie *f*

CZ [si:'zed] (US Geog) (ABBR = **Canal Zone**) → **canal**

czar [zɑ:ʳ] N = **tsar**

czarevitch ['zɑ:rɪvɪtʃ] N = **tsarevitch**

czarina [zɑ:'ri:nə] N = **tsarina**

czarism ['zɑ:rɪzəm] N = **tsarism**

czarist ['zɑ:rɪst] N, ADJ = **tsarist**

Czech [tʃek] [1] ADJ (gen) tchèque; [ambassador, embassy] de la République tchèque; [teacher] de tchèque [2] N [a] Tchèque *mf* [b] (Ling) tchèque *m* [3] COMP ► **the Czech Republic** N la République tchèque

Czechoslovak [tʃekəʊ'sləʊvæk] [1] ADJ tchécoslovaque [2] N Tchécoslovaque *mf*

Czechoslovakia [tʃekəʊslə'vækɪə] N la Tchécoslovaquie

Czechoslovakian [tʃekəʊslə'vækɪən] = **Chekechoslovak**

D

D, d [di:] ☐1 N a (= *letter*) D, d *m*; **D for dog** ◊ **D for David** (*US*) ≈ D comme Denise; (*Cine etc*) **(in) 3D** (en) 3D b (*Mus*) ré *m* → **key** c (*Scol* = *mark*) passable (*10 sur 20*) d (*Brit* †) ABBR = **penny** e ABBR = **died** f (*US*) ABBR = **Democrat(ic)** ☐2 COMP ► **D and C**∗ N (*Med*) (ABBR = **dilation and curettage**) → **dilation** ► **D-day** N (*Mil, fig hum*) le jour J

DA [di:'eɪ] N (*US Jur*) (ABBR = **District Attorney**) → **district**

dab¹ [dæb] ☐1 N a **a ~ of** un petit peu de; **a ~ of glue** une goutte de colle; **to give sth a ~ of paint** donner un petit coup *or* une petite touche de peinture à qch b (*esp Brit*) **~s**∗ (= *fingerprints*) empreintes *fpl* digitales ☐2 VT tamponner; **to ~ one's eyes** se tamponner les yeux; **to ~ paint on sth** donner un petit coup de peinture à qch, mettre un peu de peinture sur qch; **to ~ iodine on a wound** appliquer de la teinture d'iode à petits coups sur une blessure
► **dab at** VT FUS **to ~ at a stain** tamponner une tache; **to ~ at one's mouth/eyes** se tamponner la bouche/les yeux
► **dab off** VT SEP enlever (en tamponnant)
► **dab on** VT SEP appliquer *or* mettre *or* étaler à petits coups

dab² [dæb] N (= *fish*) limande *f*

dab³ [dæb] ☐1 N a **to be a ~ hand**∗ **at sth/at doing sth** être doué en qch/pour faire qch

dabble ['dæbl] ☐1 VT **to ~ one's hands/feet in the water** tremper ses mains/ses pieds dans l'eau ☐2 VI **to ~ in** *or* **with** [+ *music, theatre, journalism, drugs, cocaine*] tâter de; **to ~ in stocks and shares** *or* **on the Stock Exchange** boursicoter; **to ~ in politics/acting** tâter de la politique/du théâtre (*or* du cinéma); **she ~d with the idea of going into acting** elle a pensé un moment devenir actrice

dabbler ['dæblə'] N (*pej*) amateur *m*

dabchick ['dæbtʃɪk] N petit grèbe *m*

Dacca ['dækə] N Dacca

dace [deɪs] N (*pl* **dace** *or* **daces**) vandoise *f*

dacha ['dætʃə] N datcha *f*

dachshund ['dækshund] N teckel *m*

Dacron® ['dækrɒn] N dacron® *m*

dactyl ['dæktɪl] N dactyle *m*

dactylic [dæk'tɪlɪk] ADJ dactylique

dad [dæd] ☐1 N a∗ papa *m* b (*to old man*) **come on, ~!**∗ allez viens pépé!∗ ☐2 COMP ► **Dad's army** N (*hum*) l'armée *f* de (grand-)papa (*hum*)

Dada ['dɑːdɑː] ☐1 N Dada *m* ☐2 COMP [*school, movement*] dada *inv*, dadaïste

Dadaism ['dɑːdɑːɪzəm] N dadaïsme *m*

Dadaist ['dɑːdɑːɪst] ADJ, N dadaïste *mf*

daddy ['dædɪ] ☐1 N∗ papa *m* ☐2 COMP ► **daddy-longlegs** N (*pl inv*) (*Brit* = *cranefly*) tipule *f*; (*US, Can* = *harvestman*) faucheur *m*, faucheux *m*

dado ['deɪdəʊ] ☐1 N (*pl* **dadoes** *or* **dados**) plinthe *f* ☐2 COMP ► **dado rail** N lambris *m* d'appui

Daedalus ['diːdələs] N Dédale *m*

daemon ['diːmən] N démon *m*

daff∗ [dæf] N (*Brit*) jonquille *f*

daffodil ['dæfədɪl] ☐1 N jonquille *f* ☐2 COMP ► **daffodil yellow** N, ADJ (jaune *m*) jonquille *m inv*

daffy∗ ['dæfɪ] ADJ loufoque∗

daft∗ [dɑːft] ADJ (*esp Brit*) [*person*] dingue∗, cinglé∗; [*idea, behaviour*] loufoque∗; **that was a ~ thing to do** c'était pas très malin∗; **have you gone ~?** ça va pas la tête?∗; **I'll get the bus — don't be ~, I'll give you a lift!** je vais prendre le bus — ne dis pas de bêtises, je te ramène!; **to be ~ about sb/sth**∗ être fou de qn/qch; **he's ~ in the head**∗ il est cinglé∗; **~ as a brush**∗ complètement dingue∗ *or* cinglé∗

dagger ['dægə'] ☐1 N a (*shorter*) dague *f*; (*fig*) **to be at ~s drawn with sb** être à couteaux tirés avec qn; **to look ~s at sb** lancer des regards furieux *or* meurtriers à qn, fusiller *or* foudroyer qn du regard b (*Typ*) croix *f*

dago∗ ['deɪgəʊ] N (*pl* **dagos** *or* **dagoes**) (*pej*) métèque *m* (*pej*)

daguerreotype [də'gerəʊtaɪp] N daguerréotype *m*

dahlia ['deɪlɪə] N dahlia *m*

Dáil Éireann [dɔɪl'ɛərən] N *Chambre des députés de la république d'Irlande*

daily ['deɪlɪ] ☐1 ADV quotidiennement, tous les jours; **the office is open ~** le bureau est ouvert tous les jours; **twice ~** deux fois par jour ☐2 ADJ quotidien; [*wage, charge*] journalier; **~ consumption** consommation *f* quotidienne; **~ life** la vie de tous les jours; (*Rel*) **our ~ bread** notre pain *m* quotidien; **~ paper** quotidien *m* → **3a**; → **recommend** ☐3 N a (= *newspaper*) quotidien *m* b (*Brit*∗: *also* **~ help, ~ woman**) femme *f* de ménage

daimon ['daɪmɒn] N = **daemon**

daintily ['deɪntɪlɪ] ADV [*eat, hold*] délicatement; [*walk*] d'un pas gracieux; **~ served** servi avec raffinement

daintiness ['deɪntɪnɪs] N délicatesse *f*

dainty ['deɪntɪ] ☐1 ADJ a (= *delicate*) [*hands, object, food*] délicat b (= *fussy*) **to be a ~ eater** être difficile sur la nourriture ☐2 N mets *m* délicat

daiquiri ['daɪkərɪ] N daïquiri *m*

dairy ['dɛərɪ] ☐1 N (*on farm*) laiterie *f*; (= *shop*) crémerie *f* ☐2 COMP [*cow, farm*] laitier ► **dairy butter** N beurre *m* fermier ► **dairy farming** N industrie *f* laitière ► **dairy herd** N troupeau *m* de vaches laitières ► **dairy ice cream** N crème *f* glacée ► **dairy produce** N (*NonC*) produits *mpl* laitiers

dairymaid ['dɛərɪmeɪd] N fille *f* de laiterie

dairyman ['dɛərɪmən] N (*pl* **-men**) (*on farm*) employé *m* de laiterie; (*in shop*) crémier *m*

dais ['deɪs] N estrade *f*

daisy ['deɪzɪ] ☐1 N a (= *flower*) pâquerette *f*; (*cultivated*) marguerite *f* → **fresh, push up** b (*US*) = **daisy ham** ☐2 COMP ► **daisy chain** N guirlande *f* *or* collier *m* de pâquerettes; (*fig*) série *f*, chapelet *m* ► **daisy ham** N (*US Culin*) jambon *m* fumé désossé

daisywheel ['deɪzɪwiːl] ☐1 N (*Comput*) marguerite *f* ☐2 COMP ► **daisywheel printer** N imprimante *f* à marguerite

Dakar ['dækə'] N Dakar

Dakota [də'kəʊtə] N le Dakota; **North/South ~** le Dakota du Nord/du Sud

Dalai Lama ['dælaɪ'lɑːmə] N dalaï-lama *m*

dale [deɪl] N a (*N Engl, also liter*) vallée *f*, vallon *m*; (*Brit*) **the (Yorkshire) Dales** le pays vallonné du Yorkshire

dalliance ['dælɪəns] N a (*liter* = *affair*) badinage *m* (*amoureux*) b (= *involvement with sth*) flirt *m*; **his brief ~ with politics** son bref flirt avec la politique

dally ['dælɪ] VI a (= *dawdle*) lambiner∗, lanterner (**over sth** dans *or* sur qch); **to ~ with an idea** caresser une idée; **to ~ with sb**† badiner (*amoureusement*) avec qn

Dalmatian [dæl'meɪʃən] ☐1 N a (*liter* = *dawdle*) lambiner∗, lanterner (*Geog*) Dalmate *mf*; (*also* **dalmatian** = *dog*) dalmatien *m* ☐2 ADJ dalmate

dalmatic [dæl'mætɪk] N dalmatique *f*

daltonism ['dɔːltənɪzəm] N daltonisme *m*

dam¹ [dæm] ☐1 N a (= *wall*) [*of river*] barrage *m* (de retenue), digue *f*; [*of lake*] barrage *m* (de retenue) b (= *water*) réservoir *m*, lac *m* de retenue ☐2 VT a (*also* **~ up**) [+ *river*] endiguer; [+ *lake*] construire un barrage sur; **to ~ the waters of the Nile** faire *or* construire un barrage pour contenir les eaux du Nil b [+ *flow of words, oaths*] endiguer

dam² [dæm] N (= *animal*) mère *f*

dam³∗ [dæm] ADJ, ADV a = **damn 4, 5** b (*US*) ► **Yankee** sale∗ Yankee *or* Nordiste

damage ['dæmɪdʒ] ☐1 N a (*NonC: physical*) dégâts *mpl*, dommage(s) *m(pl)*; **environmental ~** dégâts *mpl* *or* dommages *mpl* causés à l'environnement; **bomb ~** dégâts *mpl* *or* dommages *mpl* causés par une bombe *or* par un bombardement; **earthquake/fire ~** dégâts *mpl* *or* dommages *mpl* causés par un tremblement de terre/un incendie; **water ~** dégâts *mpl* des eaux; **~ to property** dégâts *mpl* matériels; **~ to the building** dégâts *mpl* *or* dommages *mpl* subis par le bâtiment; **~ to the ozone layer** détérioration *f* de la couche d'ozone; **to make good the ~** réparer les dégâts *or* les dommages; (*Med*) **liver/tissue ~** lésions *fpl* au foie/des tissus; **kidney ~** lésions *fpl* rénales; **~ to the heart** lésions *fpl* cardiaques; **~ to your health** effets *mpl* néfastes pour votre santé; **to do** *or* **cause ~** causer *or* provoquer des dégâts *or* dommages; **the storm/vandals caused £50,000 worth of ~** la tempête a provoqué/les vandales ont provoqué des dégâts *or* des dommages s'élevant à 50 000 livres; **the bomb did a lot of ~** la bombe a fait de gros dégâts, la bombe a causé de gros dommages importants; **not much ~ was done to the car/the house** la voiture/la maison n'a pas subi de gros dégâts *or* dommages; **to cause ~ to sth** = **to damage**

sth; → 3; → **brain, structural**
[b] (NonC: fig) préjudice m (**to** à), tort m (**to** à); **there was considerable ~ to the local economy** cela a fait énormément de tort à l'économie locale; **have you thought about the possible ~ to your child's education?** avez-vous pensé aux conséquences négatives que cela pourrait avoir pour l'éducation de votre enfant?; **to do** or **cause ~** [person, gossip, scandal] faire des dégâts; **to do** or **cause ~ to** [+ person] faire du tort à; [+ reputation, relationship, confidence, country, economy] nuire à, porter atteinte à; **that has done ~ to our cause** cela a fait du tort or porté préjudice à notre cause; **there's no ~ done** il n'y a pas de mal; **the ~ is done (now)** le mal est fait; (fig) **what's the ~?*** (= how much is it?) à combien s'élève la douloureuse?* → **storm**
[2] damages NPL (Jur) dommages mpl et intérêts mpl, dommages-intérêts mpl; **liable for ~s** tenu de verser des dommages et intérêts; **war ~s** dommages mpl or indemnités fpl de guerre → **sue**
[3] VT **[a]** (physically) [+ furniture, goods, crops, machine, vehicle] endommager, abîmer; [+ food] abîmer, gâter; [+ eyesight, health] être mauvais pour; [+ environment] porter atteinte à; [+ ozone layer] endommager; **to ~ the kidneys/heart/muscles** provoquer des lésions rénales/cardiaques/musculaires; **to ~ the liver/ligaments** provoquer des lésions au foie/ aux ligaments; **a ~d knee joint/ankle** une lésion au genou/à la cheville; **~d goods** marchandises fpl endommagées; **to ~ property** causer or provoquer des dégâts matériels
[b] (fig) [+ good relations, reputation, relationship, country, economy, confidence, credibility, image] nuire à, porter atteinte à; [+ cause, objectives, person, party] faire du tort à; **to ~ one's chances** compromettre ses chances; (emotionally) **~d children** enfants mpl traumatisés
[4] COMP ► **damage limitation** N (lit, fig) **it's too late for ~ limitation** il est trop tard pour essayer de limiter les dégâts ► **damage-limitation exercise** N (lit, fig) opération f visant à limiter les dégâts ► **damage survey** N (Insurance) expertise f d'avarie

damageable ['dæmidʒəbl] ADJ dommageable
damaging ['dæmidʒɪŋ] ADJ préjudiciable (**to** pour), nuisible (**to** à); (Jur) préjudiciable
Damascus [də'mɑːskəs] N Damas
damask ['dæməsk] **[1]** N **[a]** (= cloth) [of silk] damas m, soie f damassée; [of linen] (linge m) damassé m **[b]** ~ (**steel**) (acier m) damasquiné m **[2]** ADJ [cloth] damassé; (liter) **her ~ cheeks** ses joues fpl vermeilles (liter) **[3]** COMP ► **damask rose** N rose f de Damas
dame [deim] **[1]** N **[a]** (esp Brit:†, liter or hum) dame f; (Brit Theat) **the ~** la vieille dame (rôle féminin de farce bouffonne joué par un homme) **[b]** (Brit: in titles) **Dame** titre porté par une femme décorée d'un ordre de chevalerie **[c]** (US‡) fille f, nana‡ f **[2]** COMP ► **Dame Fortune** N (†, liter) Dame Fortune f ► **dame school** N (Hist) école f enfantine, petit cours m privé
damfool‡ ['dæm'fuːl] ADJ (Brit) crétin, fichu*; **that was a ~ thing to do** c'était vraiment une connerie‡; **you and your ~ questions!** toi et tes fichues* questions!; **that ~ waiter** ce crétin de garçon, ce fichu* garçon
dammit‡ ['dæmɪt] EXCL bon sang!*, merde!‡; (Brit) **it weighs 2 kilos as near as ~** ça pèse 2 kilos à un poil* près
damn [dæm] **[1]** EXCL (‡: also ~ **it!**) bon sang!*, merde!→ **2c**
[2] VT **[a]** (Rel) damner; [+ book] condamner, éreinter; **he has already ~d himself in her eyes** il s'est déjà discrédité à ses yeux; **to ~ sb/sth with faint praise** se montrer peu élogieux envers qn/qch
[b] (= swear at) pester contre, maudire
[c] ~ **him!** qu'il aille au diable!; ~ **you!** va te faire foutre!‡; **shut up and listen to me,** ~

you! tais-toi et écoute-moi, bordel!‡; ~ **it!** merde!‡; **well I'll be** or **I'm ~ed!** ça c'est trop fort!; **I'll be** or **I'm ~ed if ...** je veux bien être pendu si ..., que le diable m'emporte si ...; ~ **this machine!** au diable cette machine!, il y en a marre de cette machine!*
[3] N‡ **I don't care** or **give a ~** je m'en fous‡ pas mal; **he just doesn't give a ~ about anything** il se fout‡ de tout; **he doesn't give a ~ for** or **about anyone** il se fout‡ complètement des autres → **give**
[4] ADJ‡ sacré* (before n), fichu* (before n); **those ~ keys** ces sacrées* clés; **you ~ fool!** espèce de crétin!*; **it's a ~ nuisance!** c'est vachement* embêtant!; **it's one ~ thing after another** ça n'arrête pas!*; **I don't know a ~ thing about it** je n'en sais foutre‡ rien
[5] ADV‡ **[a]** (= extremely) sacrément*, rudement*; **it's a ~ good wine!** il est sacrément* bon, ce vin!; ~ **right!** et comment!
[b] (Brit) sacrément*, rudement*; **you know ~ well** tu sais très bien; **I ~ near died** j'ai failli crever*; ~ **all** que dalle‡; **can you see anything?** — ~ **all!** tu vois quelque chose? — que dalle!‡; ~ **well** carrément; **he ~ well insulted me!** il m'a carrément injurié!; **I should ~ well think so!** j'espère bien!

damnable* ['dæmnəbl] ADJ détestable, fichu*
damnably†* ['dæmnəblɪ] ADV sacrément*
damnation [dæm'neɪʃən] **[1]** N (Rel) damnation f **[2]** EXCL‡ enfer et damnation! (hum), misère!
damned [dæmd] **[1]** ADJ **[a]** [soul] damné, maudit **[b]**‡ → **damn 4 [2]** ADV‡ → **damn 5 [3] the damned** NPL (Rel, liter) les damnés mpl
damnedest* ['dæmdɪst] **[1]** N **to do one's ~ to help** faire son possible or se démener* pour aider **[2]** ADJ **he's the ~†** eccentric il est d'une excentricité folle* or renversante*
damnfool‡ ['dæm'fuːl] ADJ = **damfool**
damning ['dæmɪŋ] ADJ [report, evidence] accablant; **his speech was a ~ indictment of ...** son discours était un réquisitoire accablant contre ...
Damocles ['dæməkliːz] N **the Sword of ~** l'épée f de Damoclès
damp [dæmp] **[1]** ADJ [clothes, cloth, place, weather, heat, skin, hair] humide; (with sweat) [skin, palm] moite; **a ~ patch** une tache d'humidité; (Brit) **a ~ squib** un pétard mouillé **[2]** N **[a]** [of atmosphere, walls] humidité f **[b]** (Min) (also **choke ~**) mofette f; (also **fire ~**) grisou m **[3]** VT **[a]** [+ a cloth, ironing] humecter **[b]** [+ sounds] amortir, étouffer; (Mus) étouffer; [+ fire] couvrir **[c]** [+ enthusiasm, courage, ardour] refroidir; **to ~ sb's spirits** décourager qn; **to ~ sb's appetite** faire passer l'envie de manger à qn **[4]** COMP ► **damp course** N (Brit Constr) couche f d'étanchéité ► **damp-dry** ADJ prêt à repasser (encore humide) ► **damp-proof** ADJ imperméabilisé ► **damp-proof course** N = **damp course**
► **damp down** VT SEP [+ leaves, plant, fabric] humecter; [+ fire] couvrir; (fig) [+ crisis etc] dédramatiser; [+ consumption, demand] freiner, réduire
dampen ['dæmpən] VT = **damp 3a, 3c**
damper ['dæmpə'], **dampener** (US) ['dæmpənə'] N **[a]** [of chimney] registre m **[b]** (* = depressing event) douche f (froide); **his presence put a ~ on things** sa présence a fait l'effet d'une douche froide; **the rain had put a ~ on the demonstrations/their picnic** la pluie avait quelque peu découragé les manifestants/gâché leur pique-nique **[c]** (Mus) étouffoir m **[d]** (Aut, Elec, Tech) amortisseur m **[e]** (for stamps, envelopes) mouilleur m
dampish ['dæmpɪʃ] ADJ un peu humide
damply ['dæmplɪ] ADV **[a]** (= wetly) **his shirt clung ~ to him** sa chemise mouillée lui collait

au corps **[b]** (= unenthusiastically) sans grand enthousiasme
dampness ['dæmpnɪs] N humidité f; (= sweatiness) moiteur f
damsel†† ['dæmzəl] N (liter, also hum) damoiselle f; ~ **in distress** damoiselle f en détresse
damselfly ['dæmzəlflaɪ] N (Zool) demoiselle f, libellule f
damson ['dæmzən] N (= fruit) prune f de Damas; (= tree) prunier m de Damas
dan [dæn] N (Sport) dan m
dance [dɑːns] **[1]** N **[a]** (= movement) danse f; **modern** or **contemporary ~** danse f moderne or contemporaine; **to study ~** étudier la danse; **may I have the next ~?** voudriez-vous m'accorder la prochaine danse?; (Brit) **to lead sb a (merry) ~** donner du fil à retordre à qn; **the Dance of Death** la danse macabre → **folk, sequence**
[b] (= social gathering) bal m, soirée f dansante **[2]** VT [+ waltz, tango etc] danser; **to ~ a step** exécuter un pas de danse; **she ~d (the role of) Coppelia** elle a dansé (le rôle de) Coppélia; **to ~ attendance on sb** être aux petits soins pour qn
[3] VI [person, leaves in wind, boat on waves, eyes] danser; (fig) **to ~ about** ◊ **to ~ up and down** sautiller; **the child ~d away** or **off** l'enfant s'est éloigné en gambadant or en sautillant; **to ~ in/out** etc entrer/sortir etc joyeusement; **to ~ for joy** sauter de joie; **to ~ with rage** trépigner de colère; **to ~ to the music** danser sur la musique; (fig) **to ~ to sb's tune** faire les quatre volontés de qn
[4] COMP [class, teacher, partner] de danse ► **dance band** N orchestre m (de danse) ► **dance floor** N piste f (de danse) ► **dance hall** N dancing m ► **dance hostess** N entraîneuse f ► **dance music** N dance music f ► **dance programme** N carnet m de bal ► **dance studio** N cours m de danse
dancer ['dɑːnsə'] N danseur m, -euse f
dancing ['dɑːnsɪŋ] **[1]** N (NonC) danse f; **there will be ~** on dansera **[2]** COMP [teacher, school] de danse ► **dancing girl** N danseuse f ► **dancing partner** N cavalier m, -ière f, partenaire mf ► **dancing shoes** NPL [of men] escarpins mpl; [of women] souliers mpl de bal; (for ballet) chaussons mpl de danse
dandelion ['dændɪlaɪən] N pissenlit m, dent-de-lion f
dander† ['dændə'] N **to get sb's ~ up** mettre qn en boule*; **to have one's ~ up** être hors de soi or en rogne*
dandified ['dændɪfaɪd] ADJ [arrogance, ways] de dandy; [person] qui a une allure de dandy
dandle ['dændl] VT [+ child] (on knees) faire sauter sur ses genoux; (in arms) bercer dans ses bras, câliner
dandruff ['dændrəf] **[1]** N (NonC) pellicules fpl (du cuir chevelu) **[2]** COMP ► **dandruff shampoo** N shampooing m antipelliculaire
dandy ['dændɪ] **[1]** N dandy m **[2]** ADJ* épatant*
Dane [deɪn] N **[a]** Danois(e) m(f) **[b]** → **great**
dang* [dæŋ] (euph) = **damn 1, 4, 5**
danger ['deɪndʒə'] **[1]** N danger m; **the ~s of smoking/drink-driving** les dangers mpl du tabac/de la conduite en état d'ivresse; **there is a ~** or **some ~ in doing** il est dangereux de faire; **there's no ~ in doing** il n'est pas dangereux de faire; **"~ keep out"** « danger: défense d'entrer »; **in ~** en danger; **to put sb/sth in ~** mettre qn/qch en danger; **your life is in ~** votre vie est en danger; **he was in little ~** il ne courait pas grand risque; **in ~ of invasion/ extinction** menacé d'invasion/de disparition; **he was in ~ of losing his job/falling** il risquait de perdre sa place/de tomber; **there's no ~ of that** (lit) il n'y a pas le moindre danger or risque; (iro) il n'y a pas de danger, aucune

chance; **there is a ~ of fire** il y a un risque d'incendie; (*gen, Med*) **out of ~** hors de danger; (*Rail*) **signal at ~** signal à l'arrêt; **there was no ~ that she would be recognized** *or* **of her being recognized** elle ne courait aucun risque d'être reconnue; **to be a ~ to sb/ sth** être un danger pour qn/qch; **he's a ~ to himself** il risque de se faire du mal

2 COMP ► **danger area** N = danger zone ► **danger list** N (*Med*) **to be on the ~ list** être dans un état critique *or* très grave; **to be off the ~ list** être hors de danger ► **danger money** N prime *f* de risque ► **danger point** N point *m* critique, cote *f* d'alerte; **to reach ~ point** atteindre la cote d'alerte *or* le point critique ► **danger signal** N signal *m* d'alarme ► **danger zone** N zone *f* dangereuse

dangerous ['deɪndʒrəs] **1** ADJ dangereux; (*Med*) [*operation*] risqué (**for, to** pour); **it's ~ to do that** c'est dangereux de faire ça; **the car was ~ to drive** cette voiture était dangereuse à conduire → **ground 2** COMP ► **dangerous driving** N conduite *f* dangereuse

dangerously ['deɪndʒrəslɪ] ADV dangereusement; **~ close to the fire** dangereusement près du feu; **~ ill** gravement malade; **food supplies were ~ low** les vivres commençaient sérieusement à manquer; **he came ~ close to admitting it** il a été à deux doigts de l'admettre; **the date is getting ~ close** la date fatidique approche; **to live ~** vivre dangereusement

dangle ['dæŋgl] **1** VT **a** [+ *object on string*] balancer, suspendre; [+ *arm, leg*] laisser pendre, balancer **b** (*fig*) [+ *prospect, offer*] faire miroiter (**before** sb à qn) **2** VI [*object on string*] pendre, pendiller; [*arms, legs*] pendre, (se) balancer; **with arms dangling** les bras ballants; **with legs dangling** les jambes pendantes

Daniel ['dænjəl] N Daniel *m*

Danish ['deɪnɪʃ] **1** ADJ (*gen*) danois; [*ambassador, embassy*] du Danemark; [*teacher*] de danois **2** N **a** (*Ling*) danois *m* **b** = **Danish pastry 3** **the Danish** NPL les Danois *mpl* **4** COMP ► **Danish blue (cheese)** N bleu *m* (du Danemark) ► **Danish pastry** N feuilleté *m* (fourré aux fruits *etc*); (*with raisins*) pain *m* aux raisins

dank [dæŋk] ADJ [*air, weather, dungeon*] froid et humide

Dante ['dæntɪ] N Dante *m*

Dantean ['dæntɪən], **Dantesque** [dæn'tesk] ADJ dantesque

Danube ['dænjuːb] N Danube *m*

Danzig ['dænsɪg] N Danzig *or* Dantzig

Daphne ['dæfnɪ] N **a** (= *name*) Daphné *f* **b** (= *plant*) daphne lauréole *f*, laurier *m* des bois

daphnia ['dæfnɪə] N daphnie *f*

dapper ['dæpə'] ADJ fringant, sémillant

dapple ['dæpl] **1** VT tacheter **2** COMP ► **dapple grey** (= *colour*) gris *m* pommelé; (= *horse*) cheval *m* pommelé

dappled ['dæpld] ADJ [*surface, horse*] tacheté; [*sky*] pommelé; [*shade*] avec des taches de lumière

DAR [,diː'eɪ'ɑːʳ] (*US*) (ABBR = **Daughters of the American Revolution**) club *de descendantes des combattants de la Révolution américaine*

Darby ['dɑːbɪ] N **~ and Joan** ≈ Philémon et Baucis; (*Brit*) **~ and Joan club** cercle *m* pour couples du troisième âge

Dardanelles [,dɑːdə'nelz] N **the ~** les Dardanelles *fpl*

dare [dɛəʳ] (*pret* **dared** *or* **durst**, *ptp* **dared**) **1** VT, MODAL AUX VB **a** oser (**do, to do** faire); **he ~ not** *or* **daren't climb that tree** il n'ose pas grimper à cet arbre; **he ~d not do it** *◊* **he didn't ~ (to) do it** il n'a pas osé le faire; **~ you do it?** oserez-vous le faire?; **how ~ you say**

such things? comment osez-vous dire des choses pareilles?; **how ~ you!** vous osez!, comment osez-vous?; **don't ~ say that!** je vous défends de dire cela!; **don't you ~!** ne t'avise pas de faire ça!; **I daren't!** je n'ose pas!; **the show was, ~ I say it, dull** le spectacle était, si je puis me permettre, ennuyeux

b **I ~ say he'll come** il viendra sans doute, il est probable qu'il viendra; **I ~ say you're tired after your journey** vous êtes sans doute fatigué *or* j'imagine que vous êtes fatigué après votre voyage; **I ~ say she's 40** je lui donne dans les 40 ans; (*iro*) **he is very sorry — I ~ say!** il le regrette beaucoup — encore heureux *or* j'espère bien!

c (= *face the risk of*) [+ *danger, death*] affronter, braver

d (= *challenge*) **to ~ sb to do** défier qn de faire, mettre qn au défi de faire; **(I) ~ you!** chiche!*

2 N défi *m*; **to do sth for a ~** faire qch pour relever un défi

daredevil ['dɛədevl] **1** N casse-cou *m inv*, tête *f* brûlée **2** ADJ [*behaviour*] de casse-cou; [*adventure*] fou (folle *f*), audacieux

daresay [dɛə'seɪ] (*esp Brit*) **I ~** = **I dare say**; → **dare 1b**

Dar es Salaam [,dɑːressəˈlɑːm] N Dar es Salaam

daring ['dɛərɪŋ] **1** ADJ **a** (= *courageous*) [*person, attempt*] audacieux **b** (= *risqué*) [*dress, opinion, novel*] osé **2** N audace *f*, hardiesse *f*

daringly ['dɛərɪŋlɪ] ADV [*say, suggest*] avec audace; **~, she remarked that ...** elle a observé avec audace que ...; **a ~ low-cut dress** une robe au décolleté audacieux

dark [dɑːk] **1** ADJ **a** (= *lacking light*) [*place, night*] sombre; (= *unlit*) dans l'obscurité; **it's ~** il fait nuit *or* noir; **it's getting ~** il commence à faire nuit; **to grow ~(er)** s'assombrir, s'obscurcir; **the ~ side of the moon** la face cachée de la lune; **it's as ~ as pitch** *or* **night** il fait noir comme dans un four; **the whole house was ~** la maison était plongée dans l'obscurité; **to go ~** être plongé dans l'obscurité

b [*colour, clothes*] foncé, sombre; **~ blue/ green** *etc* bleu/vert *etc* foncé *inv*; **~ brown hair** cheveux *mpl* châtain foncé *inv* → **blue**

c [*complexion*] mat; [*hair*] foncé; [*eyes*] sombre; **she's very ~** elle est très brune; **she has a ~ complexion** elle a le teint mat; **she has ~ hair** elle est brune, elle a les cheveux bruns

d (= *sinister*) [*hint*] sinistre; **~ hints were dropped about a possible prosecution** on a fait planer la menace d'éventuelles poursuites judiciaires; **I got some ~ looks from Janet** Janet m'a jeté un regard noir, Janet me regardait d'un œil noir; **a ~ secret** un lourd secret; **~ threats** de sourdes menaces *fpl*; **deeds** de mauvaises actions *fpl*; **the ~ side of sth** la face cachée de qch

e (= *gloomy, bleak*) [*thoughts, mood*] sombre, noir; **these are ~ days for the steel industry** c'est une époque sombre pour l'industrie sidérurgique; **to think ~ thoughts** broyer du noir; **to look on the ~ side of things** tout voir en noir

f (= *mysterious*) mystérieux; **~est Africa**† le fin fond de l'Afrique; **to keep sth ~*** tenir *or* garder qch secret; **keep it ~!** motus et bouche cousue!

g (*Phon*) sombre

h (*Theat* = *closed*) fermé

2 N **a** (= *absence of light*) obscurité *f*, noir *m*; **after ~** la nuit venue, après la tombée de la nuit; **until ~** jusqu'à (la tombée de) la nuit; **to be afraid of the ~** avoir peur du noir; **she was sitting in the ~** elle était assise dans le noir

b (*fig*) **I am quite in the ~ about it** je suis tout à fait dans le noir là-dessus, j'ignore tout de

cette histoire; **he has kept** *or* **left me in the ~ as to** *or* **about what he wants to do** il m'a laissé dans l'ignorance *or* il ne m'a donné aucun renseignement sur ce qu'il veut faire; **to work in the ~** travailler à l'aveuglette → **shot**

3 COMP ► **dark age** N (*fig*) période *f* sombre ► **the Dark Ages** NPL l'âge *m* des ténèbres ► **dark chocolate** N chocolat *m* noir *or* à croquer ► **dark-complexioned** ADJ brun, basané ► **the Dark Continent** N le continent noir ► **dark-eyed** ADJ aux yeux noirs ► **dark glasses** NPL lunettes *fpl* noires ► **dark-haired** ADJ aux cheveux bruns ► **dark horse** N (*fig*) (*gen*) quantité *f* inconnue; (*US Pol*) candidat *m* inattendu ► **dark-skinned** ADJ [*person*] brun (de peau), à peau brune; [*race*] de couleur

darken ['dɑːkən] **1** VT **a** (*lit: in brightness, colour*) [+ *room, landscape*] obscurcir, assombrir; [+ *sky*] assombrir; [+ *sun*] obscurcir, voiler; [+ *colour*] foncer; [+ *complexion*] brunir; **a ~ed house/room/street** une maison/pièce/rue sombre; **to ~ one's hair** se foncer les cheveux; (*† or hum*) **never ~ my door again!** ne remets plus les pieds chez moi! **b** (*fig*) [+ *future*] assombrir; [+ *prospects, atmosphere*] assombrir **2** VI **a** [*sky*] s'assombrir; [*room*] s'obscurcir; [*colours*] foncer **b** [*atmosphere*] s'assombrir; **his face/features ~ed with annoyance** son visage/sa mine s'est rembruni(e) (sous l'effet de la contrariété); **his eyes ~ed** son regard s'est assombri; **his mood ~ed** il s'est rembruni

darkey, **darkie** ['dɑːkɪ] N (*pej*) moricaud(e) *m(f)* (*pej*), nègre* *m* (*pej*), négresse* *f* (*pej*)

darkish ['dɑːkɪʃ] ADJ [*colour*] assez sombre; [*complexion*] plutôt mat; [*person*] plutôt brun; **a ~ blue/green** *etc* un bleu/vert *etc* plutôt foncé *inv*

darkly ['dɑːklɪ] ADV sinistrement; **"we'll see", he said ~** « on verra », dit-il d'un ton sinistre; **the newspapers hinted ~ at conspiracies** les journaux ont fait des allusions inquiétantes à des complots; **~ comic** plein d'humour noir; **~ handsome** à la beauté ténébreuse; **a ~ handsome man** un beau brun ténébreux

darkness ['dɑːknɪs] N (*NonC*) **a** [*of night, room*] (*also fig*) obscurité *f*, ténèbres *fpl*; **in total** *or* **utter ~** dans une obscurité complète *or* totale; **the house was in ~** la maison était plongée dans l'obscurité; **the powers** *or* **forces of ~** les forces *fpl* des ténèbres ► **prince b** [*of colour*] teinte *f* foncée; [*of face, skin*] couleur *f* basanée

darkroom ['dɑːkrʊm] N (*Phot*) chambre *f* noire

darky ['dɑːkɪ] N (*pej*) = **darkey**

darling ['dɑːlɪŋ] **1** N bien-aimé(e)† *m(f)*, favori(te) *m(f)*; (*fig*) **the ~ of ...** la coqueluche de ...; **a mother's ~** un(e) chouchou(te)*; **she's a little ~** c'est un amour, elle est adorable; **come here, (my) ~** viens (mon) chéri *or* mon amour; (*to child*) viens (mon) chéri *or* mon petit chou; **be a ~* and bring me my glasses** apporte-moi mes lunettes, tu seras un ange; **she was a perfect ~ about it** elle a été un ange *or* vraiment sympa* **2** ADJ [*child*] chéri, bien-aimé†; (*liter*) [*wish*] le plus cher; **a ~ little place*** un petit coin ravissant *or* adorable

darn[1] ['dɑːn] **1** VT [+ *socks*] repriser; [+ *clothes etc*] raccommoder **2** N reprise *f*

darn[2]*, **darned*** ['dɑːn], ['dɑːnd] (*esp US: euph*) = **damn, damned**; → **damn 1, 2c, 3, 4, 5**

darnel ['dɑːnl] N ivraie *f*, ray-grass *m*

darning ['dɑːnɪŋ] **1** N (*NonC*) raccommodage *m*, reprise *f* **b** (= *things to be darned*) raccommodage *m*, linge *m or* vêtements *mpl* à raccommoder **2** COMP ► **darning needle** N aiguille *f* à repriser ► **darning stitch** N point *m* de reprise ► **darning wool** N laine *f* à repriser

dart [dɑːt] **1** N **a** (= *movement*) **to make a sudden ~ at ...** se précipiter sur ...
b (*Sport*) fléchette *f*; **a game of ~s** une partie de fléchettes; **I like (playing) ~s** j'aime jouer aux fléchettes
c (= *weapon*) flèche *f*
d (*fig*) **... he said with a ~ of spite** ... dit-il avec une pointe de malveillance; **a ~ of pain went through him** il ressentit une vive douleur → **Cupid, paper**
e (*Sewing*) pince *f*
2 VI se précipiter, s'élancer (**at** sur); **to ~ in/out** *etc* entrer/sortir *etc* en coup de vent; **the snake's tongue ~ed out** le serpent dardait sa langue; **her eyes ~ed round the room** elle jetait des regards furtifs autour de la pièce; **his eyes ~ed about nervously** il lançait des regards nerveux autour de lui
3 VT **the snake ~ed its tongue out** le serpent dardait sa langue; **she ~ed a glance at him** ◊ **she ~ed him a glance** elle lui décocha un regard, elle darda (*liter*) un regard sur lui; **she ~ed a glance at her watch** elle jeta un coup d'œil (furtif) à sa montre

dartboard ['dɑːtbɔːd] N cible *f* (*de jeu de flé-chettes*)

Darwinian [dɑːˈwɪnɪən] ADJ darwinien

Darwinism ['dɑːwɪnɪzəm] N darwinisme *m*

dash [dæʃ] **1** N **a** (= *sudden rush*) mouvement *m* brusque (*en avant*), élan *m*; [*of crowd*] ruée *f*; **there was a ~ for the door** tout le monde se précipita *or* se rua vers la porte; **there was a mad/last-minute ~ to get the Christmas shopping done** il y a eu une ruée effrénée/de dernière minute dans les magasins pour acheter des cadeaux de Noël; **to make a ~ for/towards ...** se précipiter sur/vers ...; **to make a ~ for freedom** saisir l'occasion de s'enfuir; **he made a ~ for it** il a pris ses jambes à son cou
b (= *small amount*) [*of wine, oil, milk, water*] goutte *f*; [*of spirits*] doigt *m*, goutte *f*; [*of pepper, nutmeg*] pincée *f*; [*of mustard*] pointe *f*; [*of vinegar, lemon*] filet *m*; **a ~ of soda** un peu d'eau de Seltz; **cushions can add a ~ of colour to the room** les coussins peuvent apporter une touche de couleur à la pièce; **her character adds a ~ of glamour to the story** son personnage apporte un peu de glamour à l'histoire
c (= *flair, style*) panache *m*; **to cut a ~** faire de l'effet; **people with more ~ than cash** des gens qui ont plus de goût que de sous
d (= *punctuation mark*) tiret *m*
e (*in Morse code*) trait *m*
f [*of car*] → **dashboard**
g (*Sport*) **the 100 metre ~**† le 100 mètres
2 VT **a** (*liter = throw violently*) jeter *or* lancer violemment; **to ~ sth to pieces** casser qch en mille morceaux; **to ~ sth down** *or* **to the ground** jeter qch par terre; **to ~ one's head against ...** se cogner la tête contre ...; **the ship was ~ed against a rock** le navire a été précipité contre un écueil
b (*fig*) [+ *spirits*] abattre; [+ *person*] démoraliser; **to ~ sb's hopes (to the ground)** anéantir les espoirs de qn
3 VI **a** (= *rush*) se précipiter; **to ~ away/back/up** *etc* s'en aller/revenir/monter *etc* à toute allure *or* en coup de vent; **to ~ into a room** se précipiter dans une pièce; **I have to** *or* **must ~** il faut que je file* (*subj*)
b (= *crash*) **to ~ against sth** [*waves*] se briser contre qch; [*car, bird, object*] se heurter à qch
4 EXCL (†* *euph*) = **damn**; **~ (it)!** ◊ **~ it all!** zut alors!*, flûte!*
► **dash off 1** VI partir précipitamment **2** VT SEP [+ *letter etc*] faire en vitesse

dashboard ['dæʃbɔːd] N [*of car*] tableau *m* de bord

dashed* [dæʃt] ADJ, ADV (*euph*) = **damned**; → **damn 4, 5**

dashiki [dɑːˈʃiːkɪ] N tunique *f* africaine

dashing ['dæʃɪŋ] ADJ fringant; **to cut a ~ figure** avoir fière allure

dashingly ['dæʃɪŋlɪ] ADV [*perform*] avec brio

dastardly ['dæstədlɪ] ADJ († *or liter*) [*person, action*] ignoble

DAT [diːˈeɪˈtiː] N (ABBR = **digital audio tape**) DAT *m*

data ['deɪtə] **1** NPL of **datum** (*often with sg vb*) données *fpl*
2 VT (*US**) [+ *person etc*] ficher
3 COMP (*Comput*) [*input, sorting etc*] de(s) données ► **data bank** N banque *f* de données ► **data capture** N saisie *f* des données ► **data carrier** N support *m* d'informations *or* de données ► **data collection** N collecte *f* de données ► **data dictionary** N dictionnaire *m* de données ► **data directory** N répertoire *m* de données ► **data file** N fichier *m* informatisé *or* de données ► **data link** N liaison *f* de transmission ► **data preparation** N préparation *f* des données ► **data processing** N traitement *m* des données ► **data processor** N (= *machine*) machine *f* de traitement de données; (= *person*) informaticien(ne) *m(f)* ► **data protection act** N ≈ loi *f* informatique et libertés ► **data security** N sécurité *f* des informations ► **data transmission** N transmission *f* de données

database ['deɪtəbeɪs] **1** N (*Comput*) base *f* de données **2** COMP ► **database management** N (*Comput*) gestion *f* de (base de) données ► **database management system** N (*Comput*) système *m* de gestion de (base de) données ► **database manager** N (*Comput*) (= *software*) logiciel *m* de gestion de base de données; (= *person*) gestionnaire *mf* de base de données

Datapost® ['deɪtəpəʊst] N (*Brit Post*) **by ~** en express; ≈ par Chronopost®

datcha ['dætʃə] N = **dacha**

date¹ [deɪt] **1** N **a** (= *time of some event*) date *f*; **what is today's ~?** quelle est la date aujourd'hui?, nous sommes le combien aujourd'hui?; **what ~ is he coming (on)?** quel jour arrive-t-il?; **what ~ is your birthday?** quelle est la date de votre anniversaire?; **what ~ is Easter this year?** quelle est la date de Pâques cette année?; **what is the ~ of this letter?** de quand est cette lettre?; **departure/delivery** *etc* **~** date *f* de départ/de livraison *etc*; **there is speculation about a June election ~** on parle de juin pour les élections; **to fix** *or* **set a ~ (for sth)** fixer une date *or* convenir d'une date (pour qch); (*for wedding*) **have they set a ~ yet?** ont-ils déjà fixé la date du mariage?
b (*Jur*) quantième *m* (du mois)
c [*of coins, medals etc*] millésime *m*
d (*phrases*) **to be out of ~** [*document*] ne plus être applicable; [*person*] ne pas être de son temps *or* à la page; **he's very out of ~** il n'est vraiment pas de son temps *or* à la page; **to be out of ~ in one's ideas** avoir des idées complètement dépassées; **to ~ we have accomplished nothing** à ce jour *or* jusqu'à présent nous n'avons rien accompli; **this is her best novel to ~** c'est le meilleur roman qu'elle ait jamais écrit; **to be up to ~** [*document*] être à jour; [*building*] être moderne, être au goût du jour; [*person*] être moderne *or* à la page; **to be up to ~ in one's work** être à jour dans son travail; **to bring up to ~** [+ *accounts, correspondence etc*] mettre à jour; [+ *method etc*] moderniser; **to bring sb up to ~** mettre qn au courant (**about sth** de qch) → **out, up**
e (= *appointment*) rendez-vous *m*; (= *person*) petit(e) ami(e) *m(f)*; **to have a ~ with sb** (*with boyfriend, girlfriend*) avoir rendez-vous avec qn; **they made a ~ for 8 o'clock** ils ont fixé un rendez-vous pour 8 heures; **I've got a lunch ~ today** je déjeune avec quelqu'un au-jourd'hui; **have you got a ~ for tonight?** (= *appointment*) as-tu (un) rendez-vous ce soir?; (= *person*) tu as quelqu'un avec qui sortir ce soir?; **he's my ~ for this evening** je sors avec lui ce soir → **blind**
f (= *pop concert*) concert *m*; **they're playing three ~s in Britain** ils donnent trois concerts en Grande-Bretagne; **the band's UK tour ~s** les dates de la tournée du groupe au Royaume-Uni
2 VT **a** [+ *letter*] dater; [+ *ticket, voucher*] dater; (*with machine*) composter; **a cheque/letter ~d 7 August** un chèque/une lettre daté(e) du 7 août; **a coin ~d 1390** une pièce datée de 1390
b (= *establish date of*) **the manuscript has been ~d at around 3,000 years old/1,000 BC** on estime que le manuscrit a 3 000 ans/ remonte à 1 000 ans avant Jésus-Christ; **his taste in ties certainly ~s him** son goût en matière de cravates trahit son âge; **the hairstyles really ~ this film** les coupes de cheveux démodées montrent que le film ne date pas d'hier → **carbon**
c (*esp US = go out with*) sortir avec
3 VI **a** **to ~ from** ◊ **to ~ back to** dater de, remonter à
b (= *become old-fashioned*) [*clothes, expressions etc*] dater
c (*esp US = go out with sb*) **they're dating** ils sortent ensemble; **she has started dating** elle commence à sortir avec des garçons
4 COMP ► **date book** N (*US*) agenda *m* ► **date line** N (*Geog*) ligne *f* de changement de date *or* de changement de jour; (*Press*) date *f* (d'une dépêche) ► **date of birth** N date *f* de naissance ► **date rape** N viol commis par une connaissance (lors d'un rendez-vous) ► **date-rape** VT **she was ~-raped** elle a été violée par une connaissance (lors d'un rendez-vous) ► **date stamp** N [*of library etc*] tampon *m* (encreur) (*pour dater un livre etc*), dateur *m*; (*Post*) tampon *m* *or* cachet *m* (de la poste); (*for cancelling*) oblitérateur *m*; (= *postmark*) cachet *m* de la poste ► **date-stamp** VT [+ *library book*] tamponner; [+ *letter, document*] (*gen*) apposer un cachet de la date sur; (*Post*) apposer le cachet de la poste sur; (= *cancel*) [+ *stamp*] oblitérer

date² [deɪt] N (= *fruit*) datte *f*; (= *tree: also* **~ palm**) dattier *m*

dated ['deɪtɪd] ADJ [*book, film etc*] démodé; [*word, language, expression*] vieilli; [*idea, humour*] désuet (-ète *f*)

dateless ['deɪtlɪs] ADJ hors du temps

dating ['deɪtɪŋ] **1** N (*Archeol*) datation *f* **2** COMP ► **dating agency** N agence *f* de rencontres

dative ['deɪtɪv] (*Ling*) **1** N datif *m*; **in the ~** au datif **2** ADJ **~ case** (cas *m*) datif *m*; **~ ending** flexion *f* du datif

datum ['deɪtəm] N (*pl* **data**) donnée *f* → **data**

DATV [diːeɪtiːˈviː] N (= **digitally assisted television**) télévision *f* numérique

daub [dɔːb] **1** VT (*pej*) (*with paint, make-up*) barbouiller (**with** de); (*with clay, grease*) enduire, barbouiller (**with** de) **2** N **a** (*Constr*) enduit *m* **b** (*pej = bad picture*) croûte* *f*, barbouillage *m*

daughter ['dɔːtə] **1** N (*lit, fig*) fille *f* **2** COMP ► **daughter-in-law** N (*pl* **daughters-in-law**) belle-fille *f*, bru *f*

daughterboard ['dɔːtəbɔːd] N (*Comput*) carte *f* fille

daunt [dɔːnt] VT décourager; **nothing ~ed, he continued** il a continué sans se (laisser) démonter

daunting ['dɔːntɪŋ] ADJ intimidant; **it's a ~ prospect** c'est décourageant

dauntless ['dɔːntlɪs] ADJ [*person, courage*] intrépide

dauntlessly ['dɔːntlɪslɪ] ADV avec intrépidité

dauphin ['dɔːfin] N (*Hist*) Dauphin *m*

davenport ['dævnpɔːt] N a (*esp US* = *sofa*) canapé *m* b (*Brit* = *desk*) secrétaire *m*

David ['deɪvɪd] N David *m*

davit ['dævɪt] N (*Naut*) bossoir *m*

Davy ['deɪvɪ] 1 N a *dim of* **David** b (*Naut*) **to go to ~ Jones' locker*** se noyer 2 COMP ► **Davy lamp** N (*Min*) lampe *f* de sécurité

dawdle ['dɔːdl] VI (*also* ~ **about**, ~ **around**) (= *walk slowly, stroll*) flâner; (= *go too slowly*) traîner, lambiner*; **to ~ on the way** s'amuser en chemin; **to ~ over one's work** traînasser sur son travail

dawdler ['dɔːdlə] N traînard(e) *m(f)*, lambin(e) *m(f)*

dawdling ['dɔːdlɪŋ] 1 ADJ traînard 2 N flânerie *f*

dawn [dɔːn] 1 N a aube *f*, aurore *f*; **at ~** à l'aube, au point du jour; **from ~ to dusk** de l'aube au crépuscule, du matin au soir; **it was the ~ of another day** c'était l'aube d'un nouveau jour b (*NonC*) [*of civilization*] aube *f*; [*of an idea, hope*] naissance *f* 2 VI a [*day*] se lever; **the day ~ed bright and clear** l'aube parut, lumineuse et claire; **the day ~ed rainy** le jour s'est levé sous la pluie, il pleuvait au lever du jour; **the day will ~ when ...** un jour viendra où ... b [*hope*] [*era, new society*] naître, se faire jour; [*hope*] luire; **an idea ~ed upon him** une idée lui est venue à l'esprit; **the truth ~ed upon her** elle a commencé à entrevoir la vérité; **it suddenly ~ed on him that no one would know** il lui vint tout à coup à l'esprit que personne ne saurait; **suddenly the light ~ed on him** soudain, ça a fait tilt* 3 COMP ► **dawn chorus** N (*Brit*) concert *m* (matinal) des oiseaux ► **dawn raid** N (*St Ex*) tentative *f* d'OPA surprise, raid *m*; **the police made a ~ raid on his house** la police a fait une descente chez lui à l'aube ► **dawn raider** N (*St Ex*) raider *m*

dawning ['dɔːnɪŋ] 1 ADJ [*day, hope*] naissant, croissant 2 N = **dawn 1b**

day [deɪ] 1 N a (= *unit of time: 24 hours*) jour *m*; **three ~s** il y a trois jours; **to do sth in three ~s** faire qch en trois jours, mettre trois jours à faire qch; **he's coming in three ~s** *or* **three ~s'** time il vient dans trois jours; **twice a ~** deux fois par jour; (*Brit*) **this ~ week** aujourd'hui en huit; **what ~ is it today?** quel jour sommes-nous aujourd'hui?; **what ~ of the month is it?** le combien sommes-nous?; **she arrived (on) the ~ they left** elle est arrivée le jour de leur départ; **on that ~** ce jour-là; **on a ~ like this** un jour comme aujourd'hui; **on the following ~** le lendemain; **two years ago to the ~** il y a deux ans jour pour jour *or* exactement; **to this ~** à ce jour, jusqu'à aujourd'hui; **the ~ before yesterday** avant-hier; **the ~ before/two ~s before her birthday** la veille/l'avant-veille de son anniversaire; **the ~ after ◊ the following ~** le lendemain; **two ~s after her birthday** le surlendemain de son anniversaire; **the ~ after tomorrow** après-demain; **from that ~ onwards** *or* **on** dès lors, à partir de ce jour(-là); (*frm*) **from this ~ forth** désormais, dorénavant; **he will come any ~ now** il va venir d'un jour à l'autre; **every ~** tous les jours; **every other ~** tous les deux jours; **one ~ we saw the king** un (beau) jour, nous avons vu le roi; **one ~ she will come** un jour (ou l'autre) elle viendra; **one of these ~s** un de ces jours; **~ after ~** jour après jour; **for ~s on end** pendant des jours et des jours; **for ~s at a time** pendant des jours entiers; **~ by ~** jour après jour; **~ in ~ out** jour après jour; **the other ~** l'autre jour, il y a quelques jours; **it's been one of those ~s** ça a été une de ces journées où tout va de travers *or* où rien ne va; **this ~ of all ~s** ce jour entre tous; **some ~**

un de ces jours; **I remember it to this (very) ~** je m'en souviens encore aujourd'hui; **he's fifty if he's a ~*** il a cinquante ans bien sonnés*; **as of ~ one* ◊ from ~ one* ◊ on one*** dès le premier jour; **that'll be the ~!** j'aimerais voir ça!; **let's make a ~ of it and ...** profitons de la journée pour ...; **to live from ~ to ~** vivre au jour le jour; **take it one ~ at a time** à chaque jour suffit sa peine → **Christmas, Easter, judg(e)ment, reckoning**

b (= *daylight hours*) jour *m*, journée *f*; **during the ~** pendant la journée; **to work all ~** travailler toute la journée; **to travel by ~** voyager de jour; **to work ~ and night** travailler jour et nuit; (*liter*) **the ~ is done** le jour baisse, le jour tire à sa fin; **one summer's ~** un jour d'été; **on a wet ~** par une journée pluvieuse; **to have a ~ out** faire une sortie; (*Mil, fig*) **to carry** *or* **win the ~** remporter la victoire; (*Mil, fig*) **to lose the ~** perdre la bataille; **(as) clear** *or* **plain as ~** clair comme de l'eau de roche → **break, court, fine, good, late, time**

c (= *working hours*) journée *f*; **paid by the ~** payé à la journée; **I've done a full ~'s work** (*lit*) j'ai fait ma journée (de travail); (*fig*) j'ai eu une journée bien remplie; **it's all in a ~'s work!** ça fait partie de la routine!, ça n'a rien d'extraordinaire!; **to work an eight-hour ~** travailler huit heures par jour; **to take/get a ~ off** prendre/avoir un jour de congé; **it's my ~ off** c'est mon jour de congé → **call, off, rest, working**

d (*period of time: often pl*) époque *f*, temps *m*; **these ~s ◊ at the present ~** à l'heure actuelle, de nos jours; **in this ~ and age** par les temps qui courent; **in ~s to come** à l'avenir; **in his working ~s** au temps *or* à l'époque où il travaillait; **in his younger ~s** quand il était plus jeune; **in the ~s of Queen Victoria ◊ in Queen Victoria's ~** du temps de *or* sous le règne de la reine Victoria; **in Napoleon's ~** à l'époque *or* du temps de Napoléon; **in those ~s** à l'époque; **famous in her ~** célèbre à son époque; **in the good old ~s** au *or* dans le bon vieux temps; **in ~s gone by** autrefois, jadis; **those were the ~s!** c'était le bon vieux temps!; **those were sad ~s** c'était une époque sombre; **the happiest ~s of my life** les jours les plus heureux *or* la période la plus heureuse de ma vie; **to end one's ~s in misery** finir ses jours dans la misère; **that has had its ~** (= *old-fashioned*) cela est passé de mode; (= *worn out*) cela a fait son temps; **his ~ will come** son jour viendra; **during the early ~s of the war** au début de la guerre; **it's early ~s (yet)** (= *too early to say*) c'est un peu tôt pour le dire; (= *there's still time*) on n'en est encore qu'au début → **dog, olden**

2 COMP ► **day bed** N (*US*) banquette-lit *f* ► **day boarder** N (*Brit Scol*) demi-pensionnaire *mf* ► **day boy** N (*Brit Scol*) externe *m* ► **day centre** N (*Brit*) centre *m* d'accueil ► **day girl** N (*Brit Scol*) externe *f* ► **Day-Glo®** ADJ fluorescent ► **day job** N travail *m* principal; (*hum*) **don't give up the ~ job** chacun son métier, les vaches seront bien gardées ► **day labourer** N journalier *m*, ouvrier *m* à la journée ► **day letter** N (*US*) télégramme-lettre *m* ► **day nurse** N infirmier *m*, -ière *f* de jour ► **day nursery** N (*public*) garderie *f*, crèche *f*; (*room in private house*) pièce *f* réservée aux enfants, nursery *f* ► **the Day of Atonement** N (*Jewish Rel*) le Grand pardon, le jour du Pardon ► **the day of judgement** N (*Rel*) le jour du jugement dernier ► **the day of reckoning** N (*Rel*) le jour du jugement dernier; (*fig*) **the ~ of reckoning will come** un jour, il faudra rendre des comptes ► **day-old** ADJ [*bread*] de la veille; (= *yesterday's*) d'hier; **~-old chick** poussin *m* d'un jour ► **day-pass** N (*for library, museum, train etc*) carte *f* d'abonnement valable pour une journée; (*Ski*) forfait *m* d'une journée ► **day pupil** N (*Brit Scol*) externe *mf* ► **day**

release N (*Brit Comm, Ind*) ~ **release course** ≈ cours *m* professionnel à temps partiel; **to be on ~ release** faire un stage (de formation) à temps partiel ► **day return (ticket)** N (*Brit Rail*) (billet *m*) aller et retour *m* (*valable pour la journée*) ► **day room** N (*in hospital etc*) salle *f* de séjour commune ► **day school** N externat *m*; **to go to ~ school** être externe ► **day shift** N (= *workers*) équipe *f* *or* poste *m* de jour; **to be on ~ shift ◊ to work ~ shift** travailler de jour, être de jour ► **day-ticket** N (*Ski*) = **day-pass** ► **day-to-day** ADJ [*occurrence, routine*] quotidien; **on a ~-to-~ basis** au jour le jour ► **day trip** N excursion *f* (*d'une journée*); **to go on a ~ trip to Calais** faire une excursion (d'une journée) à Calais ► **day-tripper** N excursionniste *mf*

daybook ['deɪbuk] N (*Comm*) main *f* courante, brouillard *m*

daybreak ['deɪbreɪk] N point *m* du jour, aube *f*; **at ~** au point du jour, à l'aube

daycare ['deɪkeə] 1 N (*for children*) garderie *f*; (*for old or disabled people*) soins dans des centres d'accueil de jour 2 COMP ► **daycare centre** N (*for children*) ≈ garderie *f*; (*for old or disabled people*) établissement *m* de jour, centre *m* d'accueil de jour ► **daycare worker** N (*US*) animateur *m*, -trice *f*

daydream ['deɪdriːm] 1 N rêverie *f*, rêvasserie *f* 2 VI rêvasser, rêver (tout éveillé)

daylight ['deɪlaɪt] 1 N a = **daybreak** b (*lumière f du*) jour *m*; **in (the) ~** à la lumière du jour, au grand jour; **it's still ~** il fait encore jour; **I'm beginning to see ~*** (= *understand*) je commence à y voir clair; (= *see the end appear*) je commence à voir le bout du tunnel; **to beat** *or* **knock** *or* **thrash the (living) ~s out of sb*** (= *beat up*) rosser* qn, tabasser* qn; (= *knock out*) mettre qn K.-O.; **to scare** *or* **frighten the (living) ~s out of sb*** flanquer une peur bleue *or* la frousse* à qn → **broad** 2 COMP [*attack*] de jour ► **daylight robbery*** N (*Brit*) **it's ~ robbery** c'est de l'arnaque* ► **daylight-saving time** N (*US*) heure *f* d'été

daylong ['deɪlɒŋ] ADJ qui dure toute la journée; **we had a ~ meeting** notre réunion a duré toute la journée

daytime ['deɪtaɪm] 1 N jour *m*, journée *f*; **in the ~** de jour, pendant la journée 2 ADJ de jour

daze [deɪz] 1 N (*after blow*) étourdissement *m*; (*at news*) stupéfaction *f*, ahurissement *m*; (*from drug*) hébétement *m*; **in a ~** (*after blow*) étourdi; (*at news*) stupéfait, médusé; (*from drug*) hébété 2 VT [*drug*] hébéter; [*blow*] étourdir; [*news etc*] abasourdir, méduser

dazed [deɪzd] ADJ hébété; **to feel ~** = **to be in a daze**; → **daze**

dazzle ['dæzl] 1 VT (*lit*) éblouir, aveugler; (*fig*) éblouir; **to ~ sb's eyes** éblouir qn 2 N lumière *f* aveuglante, éclat *m*; **blinded by the ~ of the car's headlights** ébloui par les phares de la voiture

dazzling ['dæzlɪŋ] ADJ (*lit, fig*) éblouissant; **a ~ display of agility** une démonstration d'agilité éblouissante

dazzlingly ['dæzlɪŋlɪ] ADV [*shine*] de manière éblouissante; **~ beautiful** d'une beauté éblouissante

dB (ABBR = **decibel**) dB

DBMS [diːbiːem'es] N (ABBR = **database management system**) → **database**

DBS [diːbiː'es] N a (ABBR = **direct broadcasting by satellite**) → **direct** b (ABBR = **direct broadcasting satellite**) → **direct**

DC [diː'siː] a (ABBR = **direct current**) → **direct** b (ABBR = **District of Columbia**) DC → DISTRICT OF COLUMBIA

DCI [ˌdiːsiː'aɪ] N (*Brit*) (ABBR = **Detective Chief Inspector**) → **detective**

DD [a] (Univ) (ABBR = Doctor of Divinity) docteur en théologie [b] (Comm, Fin) (ABBR = **direct debit**) → **direct** [c] (US Mil) (ABBR = **dishonourable discharge**) → **dishonourable**

dd (Comm) [a] (ABBR = **delivered**) livré [b] (ABBR = **dated**) en date du ... [c] (ABBR = **demand draft**) → **demand**

DDT [di:di:'ti:] N (ABBR = **dichlorodiphenyltrichloroethane**) DDT m

DE¹ [di:'i:] N (ABBR = **Department of Employment**) → **employment**

DE², **De** ABBR = **Delaware**

de... [di] PREF de..., dé..., des..., dés...

DEA [di:i:'eɪ] N (US) (ABBR = **Drug Enforcement Administration**) ≈ Brigade f des stupéfiants

deacon ['di:kən] N diacre m; (US) **~'s bench** siège m à deux places (de style colonial)

deaconess ['di:kənes] N diaconesse f

deactivate [di:'æktɪveɪt] VT désactiver

dead [ded] **1** ADJ [a] [person, animal, plant] mort; **~ or alive** mort ou vif; **more ~ than alive** plus mort que vif; (lit, fig) **~ and buried** or **gone** mort et enterré; **to drop down ~** or **◊ to fall (stone) ~** tomber (raide) mort; **as ~ as a doornail** or **as mutton** or **as a dodo** tout ce qu'il y a de plus mort; **to wait for a ~ man's shoes*** attendre que quelqu'un veuille bien mourir (pour prendre sa place); **will he do it? — over my ~ body!*** il le fera? — il faudra d'abord qu'il me passe (subj) sur le corps!; (fig) **to flog** (Brit) or **beat** (US) **a ~ horse** s'acharner inutilement, perdre sa peine et son temps ■(PROV) **~ men tell no tales** les morts ne parlent pas; **he's/it's a ~ duck**; il/c'est fichu* or foutu;; (fig) **~ in the water*** fichu*; **to leave sb for ~** laisser qn pour mort; (at hospital) **he was found to be ~ on arrival** les médecins n'ont pu que constater le décès; **I wouldn't be seen ~ wearing that hat** or **in that hat!*** je ne porterais ce chapeau pour rien au monde!; **I wouldn't be seen ~ with him!*** pour rien au monde je ne voudrais être vu avec lui!; **I wouldn't be seen ~ in that pub!*** il est hors de question que je mette les pieds* dans ce bar!; (esp US) **you're ~ meat!**; t'es un homme mort!* (fig) → **5**, **drop**; → **strike**
[b] [limbs] engourdi; **my fingers are ~** j'ai les doigts gourds; **he's ~ from the neck up*** il n'a rien dans le ciboulot;; **he was ~ to the world*** (= asleep) il dormait comme une souche; (= drunk) il était ivre mort
[c] (fig) [custom] tombé en désuétude; [fire] mort, éteint; [cigarette] éteint; [battery] à plat; [town] mort, triste; [sound] sourd, feutré; **~ language** langue f morte; (Telec) **the line is ~** il n'y a pas de tonalité; **the line's gone ~** la ligne est coupée; **the engine's ~** le moteur est en panne
[d] (= absolute, exact) **~ calm** calme plat; **to hit sth (in the) ~ centre** frapper qch au beau milieu or en plein milieu; **it's a ~ cert**; that he'll come il viendra à coup sûr, sûr qu'il viendra*; **this horse is a ~ cert**; ce cheval va gagner, c'est sûr; **in ~ earnest** avec le plus grand sérieux, très sérieusement; **he's in ~ earnest** il ne plaisante pas; **on a ~ level with** exactement au même niveau que; **a ~ loss** (Comm) une perte sèche; (* = person) un bon à rien; **that idea was a ~ loss*** cette idée n'a absolument rien donné; **this knife is a ~ loss*** ce couteau ne vaut rien; **I'm a ~ loss at sports*** je suis nul en sport; **to be a ~ shot** être un tireur d'élite; **~ silence** silence m de mort; **he's the ~ spit of his father*** c'est son père tout craché; **to come to a ~ stop** s'arrêter net or pile

2 ADV (Brit = exactly, completely) absolument, complètement; **~ ahead** tout droit; **~ broke*** fauché (comme les blés)*; **to be ~ certain* about sth** être sûr et certain de qch*, être absolument certain or convaincu de qch; **to be ~ against* sth** être farouchement opposé à qch; **your guess was ~ on*** tu as deviné juste;

she was or her shot was **~ on target*** elle a mis dans le mille; **~ drunk*** ivre mort; **it's ~ easy** or **simple*** c'est simple comme bonjour*, il n'y a rien de plus facile or simple; **to be/arrive ~ on time** être/arriver juste à l'heure or à l'heure pile; **it was ~ lucky*** c'était un coup de pot monstre;; **she's ~ right*** elle a tout à fait raison; (as instruction) **~ slow** (Aut) roulez au pas; (Naut) en avant lentement; **to go ~ slow** aller aussi lentement que possible; **to stop ~** s'arrêter or pile; **to cut sb ~** faire semblant de ne pas voir or reconnaître qn; **she cut me ~** elle a fait comme si elle ne me voyait pas; **~ tired** éreinté, crevé*; **he went ~ white** il est devenu pâle comme un mort → **stop**

3 N **at ~ of night** ◊ **in the ~ of night** au cœur de or au plus profond de la nuit; **in the ~ of winter** au plus fort de l'hiver, au cœur de l'hiver; (fig) **to come back** or **rise from the ~** refaire surface

4 **the dead** NPL les morts mpl; (Rel) **office** or **service for the ~** office m des morts or funèbre

5 COMP ► **dead account** N (Fin) compte m dormant or inactif ► **dead-and-alive** ADJ [town] triste, mort; **a ~-and-alive little place** un trou* perdu ► **dead ball** N (Ftbl, Rugby) ballon m mort ► **dead-ball line** N (Rugby) ligne f du ballon mort ► **dead-beat*** N (= lazy person) chiffe f molle; (US) parasite m, pique-assiette mf inv ♦ ADJ crevé*, claqué* ► **dead centre** N (Tech) point m mort ► **dead end** N (lit, fig) impasse f; (fig) **to come to a ~ end** être dans l'impasse ► **dead-end** ADJ **a ~-end job** un travail sans perspective d'avenir ► **dead hand** N **the ~ hand of the state/ bureaucracy** la mainmise or le carcan d'État/ de la bureaucratie; **to shrug off the ~ hand of communism** se débarrasser de ce poids mort qu'est le communisme ► **dead-head** VT enlever les fleurs fanées de → **deadhead** ► **dead heat** N **the race was a ~ heat** ils sont arrivés ex æquo; (Racing) la course s'est terminée par un dead-heat ► **dead leg*** N (Med, Sport) jambe f insensible (à la suite d'un traumatisme musculaire); (= person) poids m mort ► **dead letter** N (Post) lettre f tombée au rebut;* (= useless thing) chose f du passé; **to become a ~ letter** [law, agreement] tomber en désuétude, devenir lettre morte ► **dead-letter office** N (Post) bureau m des rebuts ► **dead march** N marche f funèbre ► **dead matter** N finanimée; (Typ) composition f à distribuer ► **dead men*** NPL (fig = empty bottles) bouteilles fpl vides, cadavres* mpl ► **dead-nettle** N ortie f blanche ► **dead reckoning** N (Naut) estime f; **by ~ reckoning** à l'estime ► **the Dead Sea** N la mer Morte ► **the Dead Sea Scrolls** NPL les manuscrits mpl de la mer Morte ► **dead season** N (Comm, Press) morte-saison f ► **dead set*** N **to make a ~ set at sth** s'acharner comme un beau diable pour avoir qch; **to make a ~ set at sb** chercher à mettre le grappin sur qn* ♦ ADJ **to be ~ set on doing sth** tenir mordicus à faire qch; **to be ~ set against sth** être farouchement opposé à qch ► **dead soldiers*** NPL (US fig) bouteilles fpl vides, cadavres* mpl ► **dead stock** N invendu(s) m(pl), rossignols* mpl ► **dead weight** N poids m mort or inerte; (Naut) charge f or port m en lourd ► **Dead White European Male** N (esp US) homme célèbre qui devrait sa réputation à son appartenance au sexe masculin et à la race blanche ► **dead wire** N (Elec) fil m sans courant

deaden ['dedn] VT [+ shock, blow] amortir; [+ feeling] émousser; [+ sound] assourdir; [+ passions] étouffer; [+ pain] calmer; [+ nerve] endormir

deadening ['dednɪŋ] **1** N [of emotions, spirit] engourdissement m **2** ADJ abrutissant; **it has a ~ effect on creativity** ça tue la créativité

deadhead* ['dedhed] (US) **1** N [a] (= person using free ticket) (on train) personne f possédant un titre de transport gratuit; (at theatre) personne f possédant un billet de faveur [b] (= stupid person) nullité f [c] (= empty truck/train etc) camion m/train m etc roulant à vide **2** ADJ [truck etc] roulant à vide

deadline ['dedlaɪn] N (Press etc) date f (or heure f) butoir or limite, dernière limite f; (US = boundary) limite f (qu'il est interdit de franchir); **to work to a ~** avoir un délai à respecter; **he was working to a 6 o'clock ~** son travail devait être terminé à 6 heures, dernière limite

deadliness ['dedlɪnɪs] N [of poison] caractère m mortel or fatal; [of aim] précision f infaillible

deadlock ['dedlɒk] N impasse f; **to reach (a) ~** aboutir à une impasse; **to be at (a) ~** être dans l'impasse, être au point mort

deadly ['dedlɪ] **1** ADJ [a] (= lethal) [blow, poison, disease, enemy, combination] mortel (**to** pour); [weapon, attack] meurtrier; **to play a ~ game** jouer un jeu dangereux; **the seven ~ sins** les sept péchés capitaux ■(PROV) **the female of the species is deadlier** or **more ~ than the male** la femme est plus dangereuse que l'homme; (US Jur) **assault with a ~ weapon** attaque f à main armée
[b] (= devastating) [accuracy, logic] implacable; [wit] mordant; **a ~ silence** un silence de mort; **in ~ silence** dans un silence de mort; (Police, Mil) **to use ~ force (against sb)** utiliser la force (contre qn); **the police were authorized to use ~ force against the demonstrators** la police a reçu l'autorisation de tirer sur les manifestants; **I am in ~ earnest** je suis on ne peut plus sérieux; **he spoke in ~ earnest** il était on ne peut plus sérieux, il parlait le plus sérieusement du monde
[c] (* = boring) mortel*
2 ADV **~ dull** mortellement ennuyeux; **~ pale** d'une pâleur mortelle, pâle comme la mort; **it's/I'm ~ serious** c'est/je suis on ne peut plus sérieux
3 COMP ► **deadly nightshade** N (Bot) belladone f

deadness ['dednɪs] N [of limbs] engourdissement m; **the ~ of his eyes** son regard vide

deadpan ['dedpæn] ADJ [face] de marbre; (humour) pince-sans-rire inv; **"good heavens" he said, ~** « mon Dieu » dit-il, pince-sans-rire

deadwood ['dedwʊd] N (lit, fig) bois m mort; (fig) **to get rid of the ~** (in office, company etc) élaguer, dégraisser

deaf [def] **1** ADJ [a] (lit) sourd; **~ in one ear** sourd d'une oreille; **~ as a (door)post** or **a stone** sourd comme un pot ■(PROV) **there's** or **there are none so ~ as those who will not hear** il n'est pire sourd que celui qui ne veut pas entendre (PROV) [b] (fig = unwilling to listen) sourd, insensible (**to** à); **to be ~ to sth** rester sourd à qch; **to turn a ~ ear to sth** faire la sourde oreille à qch; **her pleas fell on ~ ears** ses appels n'ont pas été entendus **2** **the deaf** NPL les sourds mpl **3** COMP ► **deaf aid** N appareil m acoustique, audiophone m, sonotone® m ► **deaf-and-dumb** ADJ sourd-muet; **~-and-dumb alphabet** alphabet m des sourds et muets ► **deaf-mute** N sourd(e)-muet(te) m(f)

deafen ['defn] VT (lit) rendre sourd; (fig) assourdir, rendre sourd

deafening ['defnɪŋ] ADJ (lit, fig) assourdissant; **a ~ silence** un silence pesant or assourdissant

deafness ['defnɪs] N surdité f

deal¹ [di:l] (vb: pret, ptp **dealt**) **1** N [a] (NonC) (n phrase) **a good** or **great ~ of** ◊ **a ~ of**† (= large amount) beaucoup de; **to have a great ~ to do** avoir beaucoup à faire, avoir beaucoup de choses à faire; **a good ~ of the work is done** une bonne partie du travail est terminée ; **that's saying a good ~** ce n'est pas peu dire ; **there's a good ~ of truth in what he says** il y a du vrai dans ce qu'il dit ; **to think a great ~ of sb** avoir beaucoup d'estime pour qn ; **to mean a great ~ to sb** compter beaucoup pour qn

[b] (*adv phrases*) **a good ~** (= *significantly*) [*easier, further, longer, higher, older, happier, stronger etc*] beaucoup, nettement ; **she's a good ~ cleverer than her brother** elle est beaucoup *or* nettement plus intelligente que son frère ; **she's a good ~ better today** elle va beaucoup *or* nettement mieux aujourd'hui ; **to learn/change/travel a great ~** beaucoup apprendre/changer/voyager ; **we have discussed this a great ~** nous en avons beaucoup parlé ; **he talks a great ~** il parle beaucoup ; **we have already achieved a great ~** nous avons déjà beaucoup accompli ; **it says a great ~ for him (that ...)** c'est tout à son honneur (que ...)

[c] (= *agreement*) marché *m*, affaire *f* ; (*pej*) coup *m* ; (*Comm, Fin: also* **business ~**) affaire *f*, marché *m* ; (*St Ex*) opération *f*, transaction *f* ; **to do a ~ with sb** (*gen*) conclure un marché avec qn ; (*Comm etc*) faire *or* passer un marché avec qn, faire (une) affaire avec qn ; **we might do a ~?** on pourrait (peut-être) s'arranger ? ; **it's a ~!** d'accord !, marché conclu ! ; (*US*) **a done ~** une affaire réglée ; (= *treatment*) **he got a very bad ~ from them** ils ne l'ont pas bien traité ; (*Comm*) **he got a very bad ~ on that car** il a fait une très mauvaise affaire en achetant cette voiture ; **the agreement is likely to be a bad ~ for consumers** cet accord risque d'être une mauvaise affaire pour les consommateurs ; (*Pol etc*) **a new ~** un programme de réformes → **fair¹, deal**

[d] (* *iro*) **big ~!** la belle affaire !, tu parles !* ; **it's no big ~** qu'est-ce que ça peut faire ? ; **the delay is no big ~** le retard n'a aucune importance ; **don't make such a big ~ out of it!** n'en fais pas toute une histoire *or* tout un plat !*

[e] (*Cards*) donne *f*, distribution *f* ; **it's your ~** à vous la donne, à vous de distribuer *or* donner

[2] VT [a] (*also* **~ out**) [+ *cards*] donner, distribuer

[b] **to ~ sb a blow** (*physically*) porter *or* assener un coup à qn ; **this dealt a blow to individual freedom** cela a porté un coup aux libertés individuelles

[c] * [+ *drugs*] revendre, dealer*

[3] VI [a] (*Comm*) [*business, firm*] **this company has been ~ing for 80 years** cette société est en activité depuis 80 ans ; **to ~ on the Stock Exchange** faire *or* conclure des opérations de bourse ; **to ~ in wood/property** *etc* être dans le commerce du bois/dans l'immobilier *etc*

[b] (*traffic: in drugs*) revendre de la drogue, dealer* ; **the police suspect him of ~ing (in drugs)** la police le soupçonne de revendre de la drogue *or* de dealer* ; **to ~ in stolen property** revendre des objets volés ; **to ~ in pornography** faire le commerce de la pornographie

[c] (*fig*) **they ~ in terror/human misery** leur fonds de commerce, c'est la terreur/la misère humaine ; **drug-pushers* who ~ in death** ces dealers* qui sont des marchands de mort ; **we ~ in facts, not speculation** nous nous intéressons aux faits, pas aux suppositions

[d] (*Cards*) donner, distribuer

► **deal out** VT SEP [+ *gifts, money*] distribuer, répartir (**between** entre) ; **to ~ out justice** rendre (la) justice → **deal¹ 2a**

► **deal with** VT FUS [a] (= *have to do with*) [+ *person*] avoir affaire à ; (*esp Comm*) traiter avec ; **teachers who have to ~ with very young children** les enseignants qui ont affaire à de très jeunes enfants ; **employees ~ing with the public** les employés qui sont en contact avec le public *or* qui ont affaire au public ; **they refused to ~ with him because of this** ils ont refusé de traiter avec lui *or* d'avoir affaire à lui à

cause de cela ; **he's not very easy to ~ with** il n'est pas commode

[b] (= *be responsible for*) [+ *person*] s'occuper de ; [+ *task, problem*] se charger de ; (= *take action as regards*) [+ *person, problem*] s'occuper de, prendre des mesures concernant ; **I'll ~ with it/him** je me charge de cela/lui ; **I can ~ with that alone** je peux m'en occuper tout seul ; **in view of the situation he had to ~ with** vu la situation qu'il avait sur les bras ; **he dealt with the problem very well** il a très bien résolu le problème ; **you naughty boy, I'll ~ with you later!** vilain garçon, tu vas avoir affaire à moi *or* tu vas avoir de mes nouvelles tout à l'heure ! ; **the headmaster dealt with the culprits individually** le directeur s'est occupé des coupables un par un ; **the committee ~s with questions such as ...** le comité s'occupe de questions telles que ... ; **the police officer ~ing with crime prevention** l'agent chargé de la prévention des crimes ; (= *treat*) **to know how to ~ with sb** savoir s'y prendre avec qn ; **they dealt with him very fairly** il n'ont été très corrects avec lui ; **you must ~ with them firmly** il faut vous montrer fermes à leur égard ; **the firm ~s with over 1,000 orders every week** l'entreprise traite plus de 1000 commandes par semaine

[c] (= *be concerned with, cover*) [*book, film etc*] traiter de ; [*speaker*] parler de ; **the next chapter ~s with ...** le chapitre suivant traite de ... ; **I shall now ~ with ...** je vais maintenant vous parler de ...

[d] (= *buy from or sell to*) **a list of the suppliers our company ~s with** une liste des fournisseurs de notre société ; **I won't ~ with that firm again** je ne m'adresserai plus à cette société ; **I always ~ with the same butcher** je me sers *or* me fournis toujours chez le même boucher

deal² [di:l] N bois *m* blanc

dealer ['di:lə'] N [a] (*Comm*) (*gen*) marchand *m* (**in** de), négociant *m* (**in** en) ; (= *wholesaler*) stockiste *m*, fournisseur *m* (en gros) (**in** de) ; (*St Ex*) opérateur *m* ; **arms ~** marchand *m* d'armes ; **Citroën ~** concessionnaire *mf* Citroën → **double, secondhand** [b] (*Cards*) donneur *m* [c] (*Drugs*) dealer* *m*

dealership ['di:ləʃɪp] N (*Comm*) concession *f* ; **~ network** réseau *m* de concessionnaires

dealing ['di:lɪŋ] [1] N [a] (*NonC: also* **~ out**) distribution *f* ; [*of cards*] donne *f* [b] (*St Ex*) opérations *fpl*, transactions *fpl* → **wheel** [2] COMP ► **dealing room** N (*St Ex*) salle *f* des transactions *or* des opérations

dealings ['di:lɪŋz] NPL (*gen*) relations *fpl* (**with sb** avec qn) ; (*Comm, St Ex*) transactions *fpl* (**in sth** en qch) ; (= *trafficking*) trafic *m* (**in sth** de qch)

dealmaker ['di:l,meɪkə'] N (*St Ex*) opérateur *m*, -trice *f*

dealt [delt] VB *pt, ptp* of **deal¹**

dean [di:n] N (*Rel, fig*) doyen *m* ; (*Univ*) doyen *m* ; (*US Univ*) **~'s list** liste *f* des meilleurs étudiants

deanery ['di:nərɪ] N (*Univ*) résidence *f* du doyen ; (*Rel*) doyenné *m*

deanship [di:nʃɪp] N décanat *m*

dear [dɪə'] [1] ADJ [a] (= *loved*) [*person, animal*] cher ; (= *precious*) [*object*] cher, précieux ; (= *lovable*) adorable ; [*child*] mignon, adorable ; **she is very ~ to me** elle m'est très chère ; **a ~ friend of mine** un de mes meilleurs amis, un de mes amis les plus chers ; **to hold sb/sth ~** chérir qn/qch ; **all that he holds ~** tout ce qui lui est cher ; (*liter*) **his ~est wish** son plus cher désir, son souhait le plus cher ; **what a ~ child!** quel amour d'enfant ! ; **what a ~ little dress!**†* quelle ravissante *or* mignonne petite robe ! → **departed**

[b] (*in letter-writing*) cher ; **Dear Daddy** Cher Papa ; **My ~ Anne** Ma chère Anne ; **Dear Alice and Robert** Chère Alice, cher Robert, Chers

Alice et Robert ; **Dearest Paul** Bien cher Paul ; **Dear Mr Smith** Cher Monsieur ; **Dear Mr & Mrs Smith** Cher Monsieur, chère Madame ; **Dear Sir** Monsieur ; **Dear Sirs** Messieurs ; **Dear Sir or Madam** Madame, Monsieur ; (*fig*) **Dear John letter*** lettre *f* de rupture

[c] (= *expensive*) [*prices, goods*] cher, coûteux ; [*price*] élevé ; [*shop*] cher ; **to get ~er** [*goods*] augmenter, renchérir ; [*prices*] augmenter

[2] EXCL (*surprise: also* **~!, ~ me!**) mon Dieu !, vraiment ! ; (*regret: also* **oh ~!**) oh là là !, oh mon Dieu !

[3] N cher *m*, chère *f* ; **my ~** mon ami(e), mon cher ami, ma chère amie ; (*to child*) mon petit ; **poor ~** (*to child*) pauvre petit, pauvre chou* ; (*to woman*) ma pauvre ; **your mother is a ~*** votre mère est un amour ; **give it to me, there's a ~!*** sois gentil, donne-le-moi !, donne-le-moi, tu seras (bien) gentil ! → **dearest**

[4] ADV (*lit, fig*) [*buy, pay, sell*] cher

dearest ['dɪərɪst] N (= *darling*) chéri(e) *m(f)*

dearie†* ['dɪərɪ] (*esp Brit*) [1] N mon petit chéri, ma petite chérie [2] EXCL **~ me!** Grand Dieu !, Dieu du ciel !

dearly ['dɪəlɪ] ADV [a] (= *very much*) [*love*] profondément ; (*Rel*) **"Dearly beloved ..."** « Mes bien chers frères ... » ; **Joan Smith, ~ beloved wife of Peter** Joan Smith, épouse bien-aimée de Peter ; **I would ~ love to marry** j'aimerais tellement me marier ; **I ~ hope I will meet him one day** j'espère vivement le rencontrer un jour → **departed** [b] (*fig = at great cost*) **he paid ~ for his success** il l'a payé cher, son succès, son succès lui a coûté cher ; **~ bought** chèrement payé

dearness ['dɪənɪs] N [a] (= *expensiveness*) cherté *f* [b] (= *lovableness*) **your ~ to me** la tendresse que j'ai pour vous

dearth [dɜ:θ] N [*of food*] disette *f* ; [*of money, resources, water*] pénurie *f* ; [*of ideas etc*] stérilité *f*, pauvreté *f* ; **there is no ~ of young men** les jeunes gens ne manquent pas

deary* ['dɪərɪ] = **dearie**

▼ **death** [deθ] [1] N [a] mort *f*, décès *m* (*Jur, frm*) ; [*of plans, hopes*] effondrement *m*, anéantissement *m* ; **~ by suffocation/drowning/hanging** *etc* mort *f* par suffocation/noyade/pendaison *etc* ; **he jumped/fell to his ~** il a sauté/est tombé et s'est tué ; **at the time of his ~** au moment de sa mort ; (*fig*) **to be in at the ~** assister au dénouement (d'une affaire) ; **to be at ~'s door** être à l'article de) la mort ; **in ~, as in life, he was courageous** devant la mort, comme de son vivant, il s'est montré courageux ; (*lit*) **it will be the ~ of him*** il le paiera de sa vie ; **smoking will be the ~ of him*** le tabac le tuera ; (*fig*) **he'll be the ~ of me!*** il me tuera ! ; (*fig*), **to look/feel like ~ warmed up*** *or* (*US*) **warmed over*** avoir l'air/se sentir complètement nase* → **catch, dance, do¹**

[b] **to ~**: **he was stabbed to ~** il est mort poignardé ; **starved/frozen to ~** mort de faim/de froid ; **to starve/freeze to ~** mourir de faim/de froid ; **to bleed to ~** se vider de son sang ; **to be burnt to ~** mourir carbonisé ; **he drank himself to ~** c'est la boisson qui l'a tué ; (*Jur*) **to sentence sb to ~** condamner qn à mort ; (*Jur*) **to put sb to ~** mettre qn à mort, exécuter qn ; **to fight to the ~** lutter jusqu'à la mort ; **a fight to the ~** une lutte à mort ; **to be bored to ~*** s'ennuyer à mourir ; **you look tired to ~*** tu as l'air crevé* ; **I'm sick to ~*** *or* **tired to ~*** **of all this** j'en ai ras le bol de* *or* j'en ai marre* de tout ça ; **to be scared/worried to ~** être mort de peur/d'inquiétude

[2] COMP ► **death benefit** N (*Insurance*) capital-décès *m* ► **death camp** N camp *m* de la mort ► **death cell** N cellule *f* de condamné à mort ► **death certificate** N certificat *m* or acte *m* de décès ► **death-dealing** ADJ mortel ► **death duties** NPL (*Brit*) = **death duty** ► **death duty** N (*Brit:*

formerly) droits *mpl* de succession ► **death grant** N allocation *f* de décès ► **death house** N (*US: in jail*) = death row ► **death knell** N → **knell** ► **death march** N marche *f* funèbre ► **death mask** N masque *m* mortuaire ► **death metal** N (*Mus*) death metal *m* ► **death penalty** N (*Jur*) peine *f* de mort ► **death rate** N (taux *m* de) mortalité *f* ► **death rattle** N râle *m* (d'agonie) ► **death ray** N rayon *m* de la mort, rayon *m* qui tue ► **death roll** N liste *f* des morts ► **death row** N (*US: in jail*) le couloir de la mort ; **he's on ~ row** il a été condamné à mort ► **death sentence** N (*lit*) condamnation *f* à mort ; (*fig*) arrêt *m* de mort ► **death's-head** N tête *f* de mort ► **death's-head moth** N (sphinx *m*) tête *f* de mort ► **death squad** N escadron *m* de la mort ► **death taxes** NPL (*US*) = **death duty** ► **death threat** N menace *f* de mort ► **death throes** NPL affres *fpl* (*liter*) de la mort, agonie *f* ; (*fig*) agonie *f* ; **in one's ~ throes** dans les affres (*liter*) de la mort, à l'agonie ► **death toll** N nombre *m* des victimes, bilan *m* ► **death warrant** N (*Jur*) ordre *m* d'exécution ; (*fig*) **to sign the ~ warrant of a project** condamner un projet, signer la condamnation d'un projet ; (*fig*) **to sign sb's/ one's own ~ warrant** signer l'arrêt de mort de qn/son propre arrêt de mort ► **death wish** N (*Psych*) désir *m* de mort ; (*fig*) attitude *f* suicidaire

deathbed ['deθbed] [1] N lit *m* de mort ; **to repent on one's ~** se repentir sur son lit de mort [2] COMP ► **deathbed confession** N **he made a ~ confession** il s'est confessé sur son lit de mort ► **deathbed scene** N (*Theat*) **this is a ~ scene** la scène se passe au chevet du mourant

deathblow ['deθbləʊ] N (*lit, fig*) coup *m* mortel *or* fatal

deathless ['deθlɪs] ADJ immortel, éternel ; (*iro, hum*) ► **prose** prose *f* impérissable

deathlike ['deθlaɪk] ADJ semblable à la mort, de mort

deathly ['deθlɪ] [1] ADJ [*pallor*] cadavérique ; **a ~ hush** *or* **silence** un silence de mort [2] ADV ► **pale** pâle comme la mort, d'une pâleur mortelle

deathtrap* ['deθtræp] N (= *vehicle, building etc*) piège *m* à rats (*fig*) ; **that corner is a real ~** cette intersection est extrêmement dangereuse

deathwatch beetle [,deθwɒtʃ'biːtl] N (*Zool*) vrillette *f*, horloge *f* de la mort

deb* [deb] N ABBR = **debutante**

debacle, débâcle [deɪ'bɑːkl] N fiasco *m* ; (*Mil*) débâcle *f*

debag [diː'bæg] VT (*Brit*) déculotter

debar [dɪ'bɑːʳ] VT (*from club, competition*) exclure (**from** de) ; **to ~ sb from doing** interdire *or* défendre à qn de faire

debark [diː'bɑːk] VTI (*US*) débarquer

debarkation [,diːbɑː'keɪʃən] N (*US*) débarquement *m*

debarment [dɪ'bɑːmənt] N exclusion *f* (**from** de)

debase [dɪ'beɪs] VT [a] [+ *person*] avilir, ravaler ; **to ~ o.s.** s'avilir *or* se ravaler (**by doing** en faisant) [b] (= *reduce in value or quality*) [+ *word, object*] dégrader ; [+ *metal*] altérer ; (*Fin*) [+ *coinage*] déprécier, dévaloriser

debasement [dɪ'beɪsmənt] N [*of people*] rabaissement *m* ; [*of language, values*] dégradation *f* ; [*of culture*] dévalorisation *f* ; [*of currency*] dévalorisation *f*, dépréciation *f*

▼ **debatable** [dɪ'beɪtəbl] ADJ discutable, contestable ; **it's a ~ point** c'est discutable *or* contestable ; **it is ~ whether ...** on est en droit de se demander si ...

debate [dɪ'beɪt] [1] VT [+ *question*] discuter, débattre ; **much ~d** [+ *subject, theme etc*] très discuté [2] VI discuter (**with** avec, **about** sur) ; **he was debating with himself whether to re-**

fuse or not il se demandait s'il refuserait ou non, il s'interrogeait pour savoir s'il refuserait ou non [3] N discussion *f*, débat *m* ; (*Parl*) débat(s) *m(pl)* ; (*esp in debating society*) conférence *f* *or* débat *m* contradictoire ; **to hold long ~s** discuter longuement ; **after much ~ about ...** après de longues discussions ; **the ~ was on** *or* **about ...** la discussion portait sur ... ; **the death penalty was under ~** on délibérait sur la peine de mort ; **to be in ~** [*fact, statement*] être controversé

debater [dɪ'beɪtəʳ] N débatteur *m* ; **he is a keen ~** c'est un excellent débatteur

debating [dɪ'beɪtɪŋ] N art *m* de la discussion ; **~ society** société *f* de conférences *or* débats contradictoires

debauch [dɪ'bɔːtʃ] [1] VT [+ *person*] débaucher, corrompre ; [+ *morals*] corrompre ; [+ *woman*] séduire [2] N débauche *f*

debauched [dɪ'bɔːtʃt] ADJ [*person*] débauché ; [*society*] dépravé ; [*lifestyle*] de débauché

debauchee [,debɔː'tʃiː] N débauché(e) *m(f)*

debaucher [dɪ'bɔːtʃəʳ] N [*of person, taste, morals*] corrupteur *m*, -trice *f* ; [*of woman*] séducteur *m*

debauchery [dɪ'bɔːtʃərɪ] N (*NonC*) débauche *f*

debenture [dɪ'bentʃəʳ] [1] N (*Customs*) certificat *m* de drawback ; (*Fin*) obligation *f*, bon *m* ; (*Fin*) **the conversion of ~s into equity** la conversion d'obligations en actions [2] COMP ► **debenture bond** N titre *m* d'obligation ► **debenture holder** N obligataire *mf* ► **debenture stock** N obligations *fpl* sans garantie

debilitate [dɪ'bɪlɪteɪt] VT débiliter

debilitated [dɪ'bɪlɪteɪtɪd] ADJ (*lit, fig*) affaibli

debilitating [dɪ'bɪlɪteɪtɪŋ] ADJ [a] (*Med*) [*disease, climate, atmosphere*] débilitant [b] (*fig*) qui mine, qui sape ; **the country has suffered years of ~ poverty and war** pendant des années, ce pays a été miné par la pauvreté et la guerre

debility [dɪ'bɪlɪtɪ] N (*Med*) débilité *f*, extrême faiblesse *f*

debit ['debɪt] [1] N (*Comm*) débit *m* [2] VT **to ~ sb's account with a sum** *or* **to ~ a sum against sb's account** débiter le compte de qn d'une somme ; **to ~ sb with a sum** ◊ **to ~ a sum to sb** porter une somme au débit de qn, débiter qn d'une somme [3] COMP ► **debit account** N compte *m* débiteur ► **debit balance** N solde *m* débiteur ► **debit card** N carte *f* de paiement ► **debit entry** N inscription *f* *or* écriture *f* au débit ► **debit side** N **on the ~ side** au débit ; (*fig*) **on the ~ side there is the bad weather** parmi les points négatifs, il y a le mauvais temps

debonair [,debə'nɛəʳ] ADJ d'une élégance nonchalante

debone [diː'bəʊn] VT [+ *meat*] désosser ; [+ *fish*] désosser, ôter les arêtes de

debouch [dɪ'baʊtʃ] (*Geog, Mil*) [1] VI déboucher [2] N débouché *m*

debrief [,diː'briːf] VT (*Mil etc*) [+ *patrol, astronaut, spy*] faire faire un compte rendu (*de fin de mission*) à, débriefer ; [+ *freed hostages etc*] recueillir le témoignage de ; (*Mil*) **to be ~ed** faire un compte rendu oral

debriefing [,diː'briːfɪŋ] N [*soldier, diplomat, astronaut*] compte rendu *m* de mission, débriefing *m* ; [*freed hostage*] débriefing *m*

debris ['debriː] N (*gen*) débris *mpl* ; [*of building*] décombres *mpl* ; (*Geol*) roches *fpl* détritiques

debt [det] [1] N [a] (= *payment owed*) dette *f*, créance *f* ; **bad ~s** créances *fpl* irrécouvrables ; **~ of honour** dette *f* d'honneur ; **outstanding ~** créance *f* à recouvrer ; **to be in ~** avoir des dettes, être endetté ; **to be in ~ to sb** devoir de l'argent à qn ; **I am £500 in ~** j'ai 500 livres de dettes ; **to be out of sb's ~** être quitte envers qn ; **to get** *or* **run into ~** faire des

dettes, s'endetter ; **to get out of ~** s'acquitter de ses dettes ; **to be out of ~** ne plus avoir de dettes [b] (= *gratitude owed*) **to be in sb's ~** être redevable à qn ; **I am greatly in your ~** je vous suis très redevable ; **to repay a ~** acquitter une dette → **eye, national** [2] COMP ► **debt collection agency** N agence *f* de recouvrement de créances ► **debt collector** N agent *m* de recouvrement de créances ► **debt consolidation** N consolidation *f* de la dette ► **debt-ridden** ADJ criblé de dettes

debtor ['detəʳ] N débiteur *m*, -trice *f*

debug [diː'bʌg] VT [a] (*Comput*) déboguer [b] (= *remove microphones from*) [+ *room etc*] enlever les micros cachés dans

debugging [diː'bʌgɪŋ] N (*Comput*) suppression *f* des bogues (**of** dans), débogage *m*

debunk* [diː'bʌŋk] VT [+ *hero*] débboulonner* ; [+ *myth, concept*] démythifier ; [+ *system, institution*] discréditer

début ['deɪbjuː] [1] N (*Theat*) début *m* ; (*in society*) entrée *f* dans le monde ; **he made his ~ as a pianist** il a débuté comme pianiste [2] VI faire ses débuts

débutante ['debjuːtɑːnt] N débutante *f*

Dec. ABBR = **December**

dec. ABBR = **deceased**

decade ['dekeɪd] N [a] décennie *f* [b] [*of rosary*] dizaine *f*

decadence ['dekədəns] N décadence *f*

decadent ['dekədənt] [1] ADJ décadent [2] N (*Literat*) décadent *m*

decaf(f)* ['diː'kæf] [1] N déca* *m* [2] ADJ ► **coffee** déca* *m* ; **~ tea** thé *m* déthéiné

decaffeinate [diː'kæfɪneɪt] VT décaféiner

decaffeinated [,diː'kæfɪneɪtɪd] ADJ [*coffee*] décaféiné ; [*tea*] déthéiné

decagramme, decagram (*US*) ['dekəgræm] N décagramme *m*

decal [dɪ'kæl] N (*US*) décalcomanie *f*

decalcification ['diː,kælsɪfɪ'keɪʃən] N décalcification *f*

decalcify [,diː'kælsɪfaɪ] VT décalcifier

decalitre, decaliter (*US*) ['dekə,liːtəʳ] N décalitre *m*

Decalogue ['dekəlɒg] N décalogue *m*

decametre, decameter (*US*) ['dekə,miːtəʳ] N décamètre *m*

decamp [dɪ'kæmp] VI [a]* décamper, ficher le camp* [b] lever le camp

decant [dɪ'kænt] VT [a] [+ *wine*] décanter ; **he ~ed the solution into another container** il a transvasé la solution [b] (*fig* = *rehouse*) reloger

decanter [dɪ'kæntəʳ] N carafe *f* ; (*small*) carafon *m*

decapitate [dɪ'kæpɪteɪt] VT décapiter

decapitation [dɪ,kæpɪ'teɪʃən] N décapitation *f*

decapod ['dekəpɒd] N décapode *m*

decarbonization ['diː,kɑːbənaɪ'zeɪʃən] N (*Aut*) décalaminage *m* ; [*of steel*] décarburation *f*

decarbonize [,diː'kɑːbənaɪz] VT (*Aut*) décalaminer ; [+ *steel*] décarburer

decartelize [dɪ'kɑːtəlaɪz] VT décartelliser

decasualization [,diː,kæʒjʊlaɪ'zeɪʃən] N (*US*) octroi d'un poste fixe au personnel temporaire

decasualize [dɪ'kæʒjʊ,laɪz] VT (*US*) octroyer un poste fixe à

decathlete [dɪ'kæθliːt] N décathlonien *m*

decathlon [dɪ'kæθlən] N décathlon *m*

decay [dɪ'keɪ] [1] VI [a] (= *go bad, rot*) [*food*] pourrir, se gâter ; [*vegetation, wood*] pourrir ; [*corpse, flesh*] se décomposer, pourrir ; [*cloth, fabric*] moisir [b] (= *disintegrate*) [*building*] se délabrer, tomber en ruine ; [*stone*] s'effriter [c] (*Dentistry*) [*tooth*] se carier

|d| (*Phys*) [*radioactive particle*] se désintégrer |e| (*fig*) [*civilization*] décliner ; [*city, district*] se délabrer ; [*infrastructure, system*] tomber en ruine |2| VT |a| [+ *food, wood*] faire pourrir |b| (*Dentistry*) [+ *tooth*] carier |3| N |a| [*of food, vegetation, wood*] pourriture *f* |b| (*Dentistry*: also **tooth** or **dental ~**) carie *f* (dentaire) ; **to have** or **suffer from tooth ~** avoir des caries |c| (*Archit*) [*of building, stone*] délabrement *m* ; **to fall into ~** tomber en ruine, se délabrer |d| (*Phys*) [*of radioactive particle*] désintégration *f* |e| (*fig*) [*of civilization*] décadence *f*, déclin *m* ; [*of infrastructure, system, organization, region, city*] déclin *m* ; **social/industrial/economic ~** déclin *m* social/industriel/économique ; **moral ~** déchéance *f* morale

decayed [dɪˈkeɪd] ADJ |a| (= *rotten*) [*wood*] pourri ; [*tooth*] carié ; [*corpse*] décomposé ; [*building*] délabré |b| (*fig*) [*civilization, nobility*] décadent ; [*health*] chancelant ; [*beauty*] fané |c| (*Phys*) désintégré

decaying [dɪˈkeɪɪŋ] ADJ |a| [*wood, vegetation*] pourrissant ; [*food*] en train de s'avarier ; [*tooth*] qui se carie ; [*corpse, flesh*] en décomposition ; [*building*] en état de délabrement ; [*stone*] qui s'effrite |b| (*fig*) [*civilization, district*] sur le déclin ; [*infrastructure*] qui se dégrade

decease [dɪˈsiːs] (*Admin, frm*) |1| N décès *m* |2| VI décéder

deceased [dɪˈsiːst] (*Admin, frm*) |1| ADJ décédé, défunt ; **John Brown ~** feu John Brown |2| N **the ~** le défunt, la défunte

deceit [dɪˈsiːt] |a| N escroquerie *f*, tromperie *f* |b| (*NonC*) = **deceitfulness**

deceitful [dɪˈsiːtfʊl] ADJ [*person, behaviour, manner*] fourbe, déloyal

deceitfully [dɪˈsiːtfʊlɪ] ADV trompeusement

deceitfulness [dɪˈsiːtfʊlnɪs] N fausseté *f*, duplicité *f*

deceive [dɪˈsiːv] |1| VT tromper, abuser, duper ; [+ *spouse*] tromper ; [+ *hopes*] tromper, décevoir ; **to ~ sb into doing sth** amener qn à faire qch (en le trompant) ; **he ~d me into thinking that he had bought it** il m'a (faussement) fait croire qu'il l'avait acheté ; **I thought my eyes were deceiving me** je n'en croyais pas mes yeux ; **to be ~d by appearances** être trompé par or se tromper sur les apparences ; **to ~ o.s. (about sth)** se faire des illusions (à propos de qch) |2| VI tromper, être trompeur ; **appearances ~** les apparences sont trompeuses

deceiver [dɪˈsiːvəʳ] N escroc *m*, imposteur *m*

decelerate [diːˈseləreɪt] VI décélérer

deceleration [ˈdiːˌseləˈreɪʃən] N décélération *f*

December [dɪˈsembəʳ] N décembre *m* ; *for phrases see* **September**

decency [ˈdiːsənsɪ] N |a| (*NonC*) [*of dress, conversation*] décence *f*, bienséance *f* ; [*of person*] pudeur *f* ; **to have a sense of ~** avoir de la pudeur |b| (= *good manners*) convenances *fpl* ; **to observe the decencies** observer or respecter les convenances ; **common ~** la simple politesse, le simple savoir-vivre ; **for the sake of ~** par convenance, pour garder les convenances ; **to have the ~ to do sth** avoir la décence de faire qch ; **you can't in all ~ do that** tu ne peux pas décemment faire ça ; **sheer human ~ requires that ...** le respect de la personne humaine exige que ... |c| (* = *niceness*) gentillesse *f*

decent [ˈdiːsənt] ADJ |a| (= *respectable*) [*person*] convenable, honnête, bien* *inv* ; [*house, shoes*] convenable ; (= *seemly*) [*language, behaviour, dress*] décent, bienséant ; **no ~ person would do it** jamais une personne convenable ne ferait cela, quelqu'un de bien* ne ferait jamais cela ; **to do the ~ thing (by sb)** agir comme il se doit (à l'égard de qn) ; (= *dressed*) **are you ~?** es-tu présentable ? |b| (* = *good, pleasant*) [*person*] bon, brave ; **a ~ sort of fellow** un bon or brave garçon, un type bien* ; **it was ~ of him** c'était chic* de sa part ; **I've got quite a ~ flat** j'ai un appartement qui n'est pas mal ; **I could do with a ~ meal** un bon repas ne me ferait pas de mal |c| (*US** = *great*) formidable, terrible*

decently [ˈdiːsəntlɪ] ADV |a| (= *properly, honourably*) décemment, convenablement ; **~ paid/housed** correctement or convenablement payé/logé ; **you can't ~ ask him that** vous ne pouvez pas décemment lui demander cela |b| (= *respectably*) [*dress*] convenablement ; [*live, bury sb*] d'une façon décente ; [*behave*] décemment, avec bienséance ; **they married as soon as they ~ could** ils se sont mariés dès que la décence l'a permis |c| (* = *kindly*) gentiment ; **he very ~ lent me some money** il m'a très gentiment prêté de l'argent

decentralization [diːˌsentrəlaɪˈzeɪʃən] N décentralisation *f*

decentralize [diːˈsentrəlaɪz] VT décentraliser

deception [dɪˈsepʃən] N |a| (*NonC*) (= *deceiving*) tromperie *f*, duperie *f* ; (= *being deceived*) illusion *f*, erreur *f* ; **he is incapable of ~** il est incapable de tromperie ; **to obtain money by ~** obtenir de l'argent par des moyens frauduleux |b| (= *deceitful act*) supercherie *f*

deceptive [dɪˈseptɪv] ADJ trompeur → **appearance**

deceptively [dɪˈseptɪvlɪ] ADV **it looks ~ simple** c'est plus compliqué qu'il n'y paraît ; **the wine was ~ strong** le vin était plus fort qu'il n'y paraissait ; **he has a ~ gentle manner** il semble d'un naturel doux mais il ne faut pas s'y fier

deceptiveness [dɪˈseptɪvnɪs] N caractère *m* trompeur or illusoire

decibel [ˈdesɪbel] N décibel *m*

▼**decide** [dɪˈsaɪd] |1| VT |a| (= *make up one's mind*) se décider (**to do** à faire), décider (**to do** de faire), se résoudre (**to do** à faire) ; **I ~d to go** or **that I would go** je me suis décidé à y aller, j'ai décidé d'y aller ; **what made you ~ to go?** qu'est-ce qui vous a décidé à y aller ? ; **it has been ~d that ...** on a décidé or il a été décidé que ... ; **she's ~d she hates golf** elle a décidé qu'elle détestait le golf ; **she's ~d she'd hate golf** elle a décidé qu'elle détesterait le golf |b| (= *settle*) [+ *question*] décider, trancher ; [+ *quarrel*] décider, arbitrer ; [+ *piece of business*] régler ; [+ *difference of opinion*] juger ; [+ *sb's fate, future*] décider de ; (*Jur*) **to ~ a case** statuer sur un cas |c| (= *cause to make up one's mind*) décider, déterminer (**sb to do** qn à faire) |2| VI se décider ; **you must ~** il vous faut prendre une décision, il faut vous décider ; **to ~ for sth** se décider pour qch or en faveur de qch ; **to ~ against sth** se décider contre qch ; [*judge, arbitrator, committee*] **to ~ for/against sb** donner raison/tort à qn ; **to ~ in favour of sb** donner gain de cause à qn

▶**decide (up)on** VT FUS [+ *thing, course of action*] se décider pour, choisir (finalement) ; **to ~ (up)on doing sth** se décider à faire qch

decided [dɪˈsaɪdɪd] ADJ |a| (= *distinct*) [*advantage, improvement*] net ; **a ~ lack of ...** un manque flagrant de ... |b| (= *categorical*) [*opinions*] arrêté ; **he's a man of very ~ opinions** c'est un homme aux opinions très arrêtées, il a des opinions très arrêtées

decidedly [dɪˈsaɪdɪdlɪ] ADV |a| (= *distinctly*) **~ conservative/French** résolument conservateur/français ; **~ odd/unpleasant** franchement bizarre/désagréable ; **~ different** vraiment très différent ; **~ better/more expensive**

decider [dɪˈsaɪdəʳ] N (*esp Brit*) (= *goal*) but *m* décisif ; (= *point*) point *m* décisif ; (= *factor*) facteur *m* décisif ; (= *game*) **the ~** la belle

deciding [dɪˈsaɪdɪŋ] ADJ [*factor, game, point*] décisif

deciduous [dɪˈsɪdjʊəs] ADJ [*tree*] à feuilles caduques ; [*leaves, antlers*] caduc (-uque *f*)

decilitre, deciliter (*US*) [ˈdesɪˌliːtəʳ] N décilitre *m*

decimal [ˈdesɪməl] |1| ADJ [*number, system, coinage*] décimal ; **~ fraction** fraction *f* décimale ; **to three ~ places** (jusqu')à la troisième décimale ; **~ point** virgule *f* (*de fraction décimale*) → **fixed, floating** |2| N décimale *f* ; **~s** le calcul décimal, la notation décimale → **recurring**

decimalization [ˌdesɪməlaɪˈzeɪʃən] N décimalisation *f*

decimalize [ˈdesɪməlaɪz] VT décimaliser

decimate [ˈdesɪmeɪt] VT (*lit, fig*) décimer

decimation [ˌdesɪˈmeɪʃən] N décimation *f*

decimetre, decimeter (*US*) [ˈdesɪˌmiːtəʳ] N décimètre *m*

decipher [dɪˈsaɪfəʳ] VT (*lit, fig*) déchiffrer

decipherable [dɪˈsaɪfərəbl] ADJ déchiffrable

decision [dɪˈsɪʒən] |1| N |a| (= *act of deciding*) décision *f* ; (*Jur*) jugement *m*, arrêt *m* ; **to come to a ~** arriver à or prendre une décision ; **his ~ is final** sa décision est irrévocable or sans appel ; (*Jur*) **to give a ~ on a case** statuer sur un cas |b| (*NonC*) décision *f* ; **with ~** [*act*] d'un air décidé or résolu ; [*say*] d'un ton décidé or résolu ; **a look of ~** un air décidé or résolu |2| COMP ▶ **decision-maker** N décideur *m*, -euse *f*, décisionnaire *mf* ▶ **decision-making** N **he's good at ~-making** il sait prendre des décisions ▶ **decision table** N (*Comput*) table *f* de décision

decisive [dɪˈsaɪsɪv] ADJ |a| (= *conclusive*) [*battle, step, moment, role*] décisif ; **the ~ factor** le facteur décisif |b| (= *resolute*) [*person*] décidé, ferme ; [*manner, attitude*] décidé, résolu ; [*answer*] ferme ; **he's very ~** c'est quelqu'un qui sait prendre des décisions

decisively [dɪˈsaɪsɪvlɪ] ADV |a| (= *conclusively*) [*defeat, reject, influence*] de manière décisive |b| (= *resolutely*) [*speak*] de manière résolue, avec fermeté ; [*act*] avec décision

decisiveness [dɪˈsaɪsɪvnɪs] N (*NonC*) (= *character*) esprit *m* de décision ; (= *manner*) air *m* décidé

deck [dek] |1| N |a| (*Naut*) pont *m* ; **to go up on ~** monter sur le pont ; **below ~s** sous le pont, en bas ; **between ~s** dans l'entrepont ; **to clear the ~s (for action)** se mettre en branle-bas (de combat) ; (*fig*) tout déblayer ; (*US fig*) **on ~** prêt à l'action → **afterdeck, flight¹, hand** |b| [*of vehicle*] plateforme *f* ; **top ~** ◊ **upper ~** [*of bus*] impériale *f* ; [*of jumbo jet*] étage *m* |c| (*US: also* ~ **of cards**) jeu *m* de cartes ; **he's not playing with a full ~*** ◊ **he's playing with a loaded** or **stacked ~*** il ne joue pas franc jeu or cartes sur table ; (*fig*) **he's not playing with a full ~*** (= *not very bright*) il n'est pas très futé |d| (*also* **mixing ~**) table *f* de mixage ; (*also* **cassette ~**) platine *f* cassettes ; (*also* **record ~**) platine *f* disques → **cassette** |2| VT |a| (*also* **~ out**) [+ *person, room etc*] parer (**with** de) ; **she was ~ed out in her Sunday best** elle s'était mise sur son trente et un, elle s'était endimanchée |b| (‡ = *knock down*) flanquer* par terre |3| COMP ▶ **deck cabin** N cabine *f* (de pont) ▶ **deck cargo** N pontée *f* ▶ **deck chair** N chaise *f* longue, transat* *m*, transatlantique *m* ▶ **deck hand** N matelot *m*

-decker ['dekər] N (*in compounds*) **a single-decker** [*bus*] un autobus sans impériale; (*Naut*) **a three-decker** un vaisseau à trois ponts, un trois-ponts → **double**

deckhouse ['dekhaʊs] N rouf *m*

deckle ['dekl] N (*also* **~ edge**) barbes *fpl*

deckle-edged [,dekl'edʒd] ADJ [*paper*] non ébarbé

declaim [dɪ'kleɪm] VTI (*lit, fig*) déclamer (**against** contre)

declamation [,deklə'meɪʃən] N déclamation *f*

declamatory [dɪ'klæmətərɪ] ADJ déclamatoire

declaration [,deklə'reɪʃən] [1] N [*of intentions, taxes, goods at Customs*] déclaration *f*; (*Cards*) annonce *f* [2] COMP ► **Declaration of Independence** N (*US Hist*) Déclaration *f* d'indépendance ► **declaration of love** N déclaration *f* d'amour ► **declaration of war** N déclaration *f* de guerre

declarative [dɪ'klærətɪv] ADJ (*Gram*) déclaratif, assertif

declaratory [dɪ'klærətərɪ] ADJ (*Jur*) **~ judgement** jugement *m* déclaratoire

▼ **declare** [dɪ'klɛər] [1] VT [a] [+ *intentions, love, war, hostilities*] (*also Fin etc*) [+ *income*] déclarer; [+ *results*] proclamer; (*Customs*) **have you anything to ~?** avez-vous quelque chose à déclarer?; **to ~ o.s.** [*suitor*] faire sa déclaration, se déclarer; **to ~ war (on ...)** déclarer la guerre (à ...); **to ~ a state of emergency** déclarer l'état d'urgence [b] (= *assert*) déclarer (**that** que); **to ~ o.s. for** *or* **in favour of/against** se déclarer *or* se prononcer *or* prendre parti en faveur de/contre; **to ~ sb president/bankrupt** déclarer qn président/en faillite [2] VI [a] **well I (do) ~!†** (ça) par exemple! [b] (*US Pol*) [*presidential candidate*] annoncer sa candidature

declared [dɪ'klɛəd] ADJ [*intention*] déclaré, avoué; **he's a ~ homosexual** il ne cache pas son homosexualité

declaredly [dɪ'klɛərɪdlɪ] ADV ouvertement

declarer [dɪ'klɛərər] N (*Cards*) déclarant(e) *m(f)*

declassify [di:'klæsɪfaɪ] VT [+ *information, document*] déclassifier

declension [dɪ'klenʃən] N (*Gram*) déclinaison *f*; **first/second ~** première/deuxième déclinaison *f*

declinable [dɪ'klaɪnəbl] ADJ (*Gram*) déclinable

declination [,deklɪ'neɪʃən] N (*Astron*) déclinaison *f*

▼ **decline** [dɪ'klaɪn] [1] N [*of day, life*] déclin *m*; [*of empire*] déclin *m*, décadence *f*; **~ in price** baisse *f* de prix; **to be on the ~** [*prices*] être en baisse, baisser; [*fame, health*] décliner; **cases of real poverty are on the ~** les cas d'indigence réelle sont de moins en moins fréquents *or* sont en diminution; **to fall** *or* **go into a ~** dépérir

[2] VT [a] (*gen*) refuser (**to do** de faire); [+ *invitation, offer, honour*] décliner; [+ *responsibility*] décliner, rejeter; **he ~d to do it** il a refusé (poliment) de le faire; **he offered me a lift but I ~d** il a proposé de m'emmener mais j'ai refusé; (*Jur*) **to ~ a jurisdiction** se déclarer incompétent [b] (*Gram*) décliner

[3] VI [a] [*health, influence*] décliner; [*empire*] tomber en décadence; [*prices*] baisser, être en baisse; [*business*] péricliter, décliner; **to ~ in importance** perdre de l'importance [b] (= *slope*) s'incliner, descendre [c] [*sun*] décliner, se coucher; [*day*] tirer à sa fin, décliner [d] (*Gram*) se décliner

declining [dɪ'klaɪnɪŋ] [1] ADJ [*sales, standards, popularity*] en baisse; **he's in ~ health** sa santé décline peu à peu; **a ~ industry** une industrie sur le déclin; **in his ~ years** au déclin de sa vie; **she spent her ~ years in Devon** elle a passé ses dernières années dans le Devon

[2] N [a] [*of invitation*] refus *m* [b] [*of empire*] dé-cadence *f* [c] (*Gram*) déclinaison *f*

declivity [dɪ'klɪvɪtɪ] N déclivité *f*, pente *f*

declutch ['di:'klʌtʃ] VI débrayer → **double**

decoction [dɪ'kɒkʃən] N décoction *f*

decode ['di:'kəʊd] VT [a] (*Telec, TV*) décoder, traduire (en clair) [b] (*Comput, Ling*) décoder [c] (*fig* = *understand, explain*) décoder

decoder [di:'kəʊdər] N (*Comput, Telec, TV*) décodeur *m*

decoding [di:'kəʊdɪŋ] N (*Comput, Telec, TV, Ling*) décodage *m*

decoke (*Brit Aut*) [1] VT [di:'kəʊk] décalaminer [2] ['di:kəʊk] N décalaminage *m*

decollate [dɪ'kɒleɪt] VT (*Comput*) déliasser

décolletage [deɪ'kɒltɑːʒ] N décolletage *m*, décolleté *m*

décolleté [deɪ'kɒleɪ] [1] ADJ décolleté [2] N = **décolletage**

decolonization [di:,kɒlənaɪ'zeɪʃən] N décolonisation *f*

decolonize [di:'kɒlə,naɪz] VT décoloniser

decommission [,di:kə'mɪʃən] VT [a] [+ *nuclear power station*] fermer [b] [+ *warship, aircraft*] retirer de la circulation

decompartmentalization [,di:kɒmpɑːt,mentəlaɪ'zeɪʃən] N (*Sociol*) décloisonnement *m*

decompartmentalize [,di:kɒmpɑːt'mentəlaɪz] VT (*Sociol*) décloisonner

decompose [,di:kəm'pəʊz] [1] VT décomposer [2] VI se décomposer

decomposition [,di:kɒmpə'zɪʃən] N décomposition *f*

decompress [,di:kəm'pres] VT décompresser

decompression [,di:kəm'preʃən] [1] N (*Med, Phys, Tech*) décompression *f* [2] COMP ► **decompression chamber** N chambre *f* de décompression ► **decompression illness, decompression sickness** N maladie *f* des caissons

decongestant [,di:kən'dʒestənt] ADJ, N décongestif *m*

deconsecrate [,di:'kɒnsɪkreɪt] VT séculariser

deconstruct [,di:kən'strʌkt] VT (*Literat*) déconstruire

deconstruction [,di:kən'strʌkʃən] N (*Literat*) déconstruction *f*

decontaminate [,di:kən'tæmɪneɪt] VT décontaminer

decontamination [,di:kən,tæmɪ'neɪʃən] N décontamination *f*

decontextualize [,di:kən'tekstjʊəlaɪz] VT isoler de son contexte

decontrol [,di:kən'trəʊl] (*esp US*) [1] VT (*Admin, Comm*) libérer des contrôles gouvernementaux; **to ~ (the price of) butter** libérer le prix du beurre, lever *or* supprimer le contrôle du prix du beurre [2] N [*of price*] libération *f*

décor ['deɪkɔː] N décor *m*

decorate ['dekəreɪt] [1] VT [a] orner, décorer (**with** de); [+ *cake*] décorer; (= *paint etc*) [+ *room*] décorer, peindre (et tapisser); **to ~ with flags** pavoiser [b] [+ *soldier*] décorer, médailler; **he was ~d for gallantry** il a été décoré pour sa bravoure [2] VI (= *paint etc*) peindre (et tapisser)

decorating ['dekəreɪtɪŋ] N [a] (*also* **painting and ~**) décoration *f* intérieure; **they are doing some ~** ils sont en train de refaire les peintures [b] [*of cake etc*] décoration *f*

decoration [,dekə'reɪʃən] N [a] (*NonC*) [*of cake*] décoration *f*; [*of hat*] ornementation *f*; [*of room*] (= *act*) décoration *f* (intérieure); (= *state*) décoration *f*, décor *m*; [*of town*] décoration *f*; (*with flags*) pavoisement *m* [b] (= *ornament*) [*of hat*] ornement *m*; (*in streets*) décoration *f*; **Christmas ~s** décorations *fpl* de Noël [c] (*Mil*) décoration *f*, médaille *f*

decorative ['dekərətɪv] [1] ADJ décoratif [2] COMP ► **decorative art** N arts *mpl* décoratifs

decorator ['dekəreɪtər] N (= *designer*) décorateur *m*, -trice *f*, ensemblier *m*; (*esp Brit also* painter-and-~) peintre *m* décorateur

decorous ['dekərəs] ADJ convenable, bienséant; **try to be ~ at all times** essayez toujours de respecter les convenances

decorously ['dekərəslɪ] ADV de façon convenable

decorum [dɪ'kɔːrəm] N décorum *m*, bienséance *f*; **with ~** avec bienséance, comme il faut; **a breach of ~** une inconvenance; **to have a sense of ~** avoir le sens des convenances

decouple [di:'kʌpl] VT découpler

decoy [1] N (= *bird*) (live) appeau *m*, chanterelle *f*; (*artificial*) leurre *m*; (= *animal*) proie *f* (servant d'appât); (= *person*) compère *m*; **police ~** policier *m* en civil (*servant à attirer un criminel dans une souricière*) [2] [dɪ'kɔɪ] VT attirer avec un appeau *or* une chanterelle *or* un leurre → **1**; (*also fig*) attirer dans un piège; **to ~ sb into doing sth** faire faire qch à qn en le leurrant [3] COMP ► **decoy duck** N (*lit*) appeau *m*, chanterelle *f*; (*fig*) compère *m*

decrease [di:'kri:s] [1] VI [*amount, numbers, supplies, birth rate, population*] diminuer, décroître; [*power*] s'affaiblir; [*strength, intensity*] s'affaiblir, décroître; [*price, value*] baisser; [*enthusiasm*] se calmer, se refroidir; (*Knitting*) diminuer [2] VT diminuer, réduire [3] ['di:kri:s] N [*of amount, supplies*] diminution *f*, amoindrissement *m* (**in** de); [*of numbers*] diminution *f*, décroissance *f* (**in** de); [*of birth rate, population*] diminution *f* (**in** de); [*of power*] affaiblissement *m* (**in** de); [*of strength, intensity*] diminution *f*, décroissance *f* (**in** de); [*of price, value*] baisse *f* (**in** de); [*of enthusiasm*] baisse *f*, refroidissement *m* (**in** de); **~ in speed** ralentissement *m*; **~ in strength** affaiblissement *m*

decreasing [di:'kri:sɪŋ] ADJ [*amount, quantity, value, sales, numbers, statistic*] en baisse; [*intensity*] décroissant; [*strength*] déclinant; **a ~ population** une baisse de la démographie, une population en baisse

decreasingly [di:'kri:sɪŋlɪ] ADV de moins en moins

decree [dɪ'kri:] [1] N (*Pol, Rel*) décret *m*; [*of tribunal*] arrêt *m*, jugement *m*; (*municipal*) arrêté *m*; **by royal/government ~** par décret du roi/du gouvernement; (*divorce*) **~ absolute** jugement *m* définitif (de divorce); **~ nisi** jugement *m* provisoire (de divorce) [2] VT (*gen, also Pol, Rel*) décréter (**that** que + *indic*); (*Jur*) ordonner (**that** que + *subj*); [*mayor, council etc*] arrêter (**that** que + *indic*); (*frm*) **to ~ an end to ...** décréter la fin de ...

decrepit [dɪ'krepɪt] ADJ [*object, building*] délabré;* [*person*] décrépit, décati*

decrepitude [dɪ'krepɪtjuːd] N [a] (= *dilapidation*) [*of building, place*] délabrement *m*; [*of system*] vétusté *f*, décrépitude *f* [b] (= *infirmity*) décrépitude *f*

decretal [dɪ'kri:tl] N décrétale *f*

decriminalization [,di:krɪmɪnəlaɪ'zeɪʃən] N dépénalisation *f*

decriminalize [di:'krɪmɪnəlaɪz] VT dépénaliser

decry [dɪ'kraɪ] VT décrier, dénigrer

decrypt [di:'krɪpt] VT (*Comput, Telec*) décrypter, déchiffrer

decumulation [,dɪkjuːmjʊ'leɪʃən] N [*of capital*] réduction *f*, diminution *f*; [*of stocks*] contraction *f*, réduction *f*; **stock ~** déstockage *m*

dedicate ['dedɪkeɪt] VT [a] (= *devote*) [+ *time, one's life*] consacrer (**to sth** à qch, **to doing** à faire); [+ *resources, money*] allouer (**to sth** à qch, **to doing sth** pour faire qch); **to ~ o.s. to**

► LANGUAGE IN USE: **declare** 26.2 **decline** 12.3, 19.5, 25.2

sth/to doing se consacrer à qch/à faire [b] (*as mark of respect, affection etc*) [+ *building, memorial, book, film, award*] dédier (**to** à); **to ~ a song to sb** [*singer*] dédier une chanson à qn; [*disc jockey*] passer une chanson à la demande de qn; **they ~d the statue to the memory of ...** ils ont dédié cette statue à la mémoire de ...; **"this thesis is ~d to my parents"** « je dédie cette thèse à mes parents » [c] (*Rel = consecrate*) [+ *church, shrine*] consacrer

dedicatee [ˌdedɪkə'tiː] N dédicataire *mf*

dedicated ['dedɪkeɪtɪd] ADJ [a] (= *devoted*) [*person*] dévoué; [*work, attitude*] sérieux; **a ~ traveller** un voyageur enthousiaste; **a ~ socialist** un socialiste convaincu; **a ~ follower of fashion** un fervent adepte de la mode; **to be ~ to sth** [*person*] tenir beaucoup à qch; [*organization*] se consacrer à qch; **as a party we are ~ to social change** notre parti a pour vocation de promouvoir le changement social; **as a party we are ~ to achieving social equality** notre parti œuvre en faveur de l'établissement de l'égalité sociale; **we are ~ to making banking more convenient for our customers** nous faisons tout notre possible pour faciliter les formalités bancaires à nos clients [b] **~ to** (= *given over to*) consacré à; **a museum ~ to Napoleon** un musée consacré à Napoléon; **a charity ~ to famine relief** une association caritative ayant pour but de combattre la famine [c] (= *bearing a dedication*) [*copy of book etc*] dédicacé [d] (= *specialized*) [*word processor*] dédié

dedication [ˌdedɪ'keɪʃən] N [a] [*of church*] dédicace *f*, consécration *f* [b] (*in book, on radio*) dédicace *f*; **to write a ~ in a book** dédicacer un livre; **the ~ reads: "to Emma, with love from Harry"** le livre est dédicacé « à Emma, avec tout mon amour, Harry »; (*Rad*) **if you want a ~ just write in** si vous voulez faire une dédicace, écrivez-nous [c] (*quality = devotion*) dévouement *m*

deduce [dɪ'djuːs] VT déduire, conclure (**from** de, **that** que)

deducible [dɪ'djuːsɪbl] ADJ **~ from** que l'on peut déduire *or* inférer de

deduct [dɪ'dʌkt] VT [+ *amount*] déduire, retrancher (**from** de); [+ *numbers*] retrancher, soustraire (**from** de); [+ *tax*] retenir, prélever (**from** sur); **to ~ something from the price** faire une réduction sur le prix; **to ~ sth for expenses** retenir qch pour les frais; **to ~ 5% from the wages** faire une retenue de *or* prélever 5% sur les salaires; **after ~ing 5%** déduction faite de 5%

deductible [dɪ'dʌktəbl] [1] ADJ à déduire (**from** de); (*Tax*) [*expenses*] déductible [2] N (*US Insurance*) franchise *f*; **a 50 dollar ~** une franchise de 50 dollars

deduction [dɪ'dʌkʃən] N [a] (= *sth deducted*) déduction *f* (**from** de); (*from wage*) retenue *f*, prélèvement *m* (**from** sur) [b] (= *sth deduced*) déduction *f* [c] (*NonC = deductive reasoning*) raisonnement *m* déductif

deductive [dɪ'dʌktɪv] ADJ déductif

deed [diːd] [1] N [a] (= *action*) action *f*, acte *m*; **brave ~** haut fait *m*, exploit *m*; **good ~(s)** bonne(s) action(s) *f(pl)*; (*hum*) **to do one's good ~ for the day** faire sa B.A. quotidienne → **word** [b] **in ~** de fait, en fait; **master in ~ if not in name** maître de *or* en fait sinon de *or* en titre [c] (*Jur*) acte *m* notarié, contrat *m*; **~ of covenant** *or* **gift** acte *m* de donation; **~ of partnership** contrat *m* de société [2] VT (*US Jur*) transférer par acte notarié [3] COMP ► **deed box** N coffre *m* or mallette *f* pour documents (officiels) ► **deed poll** N **to change one's name by ~ poll** ≈ changer de nom officiellement

deejay* ['diːˌdʒeɪ] N disc-jockey *m*, animateur *m*, -trice *f*

deem [diːm] VT **to ~ it prudent to do sth** juger prudent de faire qch; **to be ~ed worthy of (doing) sth** être jugé digne de (faire) qch; **he was ~ed too ill to leave the hospital** on a décidé qu'il était trop malade pour quitter l'hôpital; **military intervention was not ~ed necessary** on a jugé qu'une intervention militaire n'était pas nécessaire

deep [diːp] [1] ADJ [a] (= *extending far down*) [*water, hole, wound, cut, wrinkle*] profond; [*mud, snow, carpet*] épais (-aisse *f*); [*pan, bowl, container*] à hauts bords; **the lake/pond was 4 metres ~** le lac/l'étang avait 4 mètres de profondeur; **the water was 2 metres ~** la profondeur de l'eau était de 2 mètres; **the snow lay ~** il y avait une épaisse couche de neige; **the streets were 2 feet ~ in snow** les rues étaient sous 60 cm *or* étaient recouvertes de 60 cm de neige; **he was ankle-/thigh-~ in water** l'eau lui arrivait aux chevilles/aux cuisses; (*fig*) **to be in ~ water(s)** avoir de gros ennuis, être en mauvaise posture; **the ~ end** [*of swimming pool*] le grand bain; (*fig*) **to go off (at) the ~ end*** (*excited, angry*) se mettre dans tous ses états; (*esp Brit fig*) **to go in** or **jump in at the ~ end** foncer tête baissée; (*fig*) **to throw sb in at the ~ end*** mettre tout de suite qn dans le bain [b] (= *extending far back*) [*edge, border*] large, haut; [*shelf, cupboard*] large, profond; **a plot of ground 15 metres ~** un terrain qui s'étend sur 15 mètres; **the spectators stood ten ~** il y avait dix rangées de spectateurs; **a line of policemen three ~** trois rangées de policiers; **a line of cars parked three ~** des voitures garées sur trois rangées [c] (= *low-pitched*) [*sound, voice, tones*] grave; **the animal gave a ~ growl** l'animal a émis un grognement sourd [d] (= *strong in colour*) [*colour*] profond; [*darkness*] profond, total; **~ blue/green/yellow** *etc* bleu/vert/jaune *etc* profond *inv* [e] [*breath, sigh*] profond; **~ breathing** respiration *f* profonde; (= *exercises*) exercices *mpl* respiratoires; **to take a ~ breath** respirer profondément [f] (= *intense, far-reaching*) [*sorrow, relief*] profond, intense; [*concern, interest*] vif; [*admiration, respect, divisions, differences, sleep, relaxation, recession*] profond; [*mystery*] profond, total; **our ~est feelings** nos sentiments les plus profonds; **to gain a ~er understanding of sth** parvenir à mieux comprendre qch; **to gain a ~er understanding of o.s.** parvenir à mieux se connaître → **breath, mourning** [g] (= *profound*) [*writer, thinker, book*] profond; **the film is not intended to be ~ and meaningful** le film ne cherche pas à être profond; **I'm not looking for a ~ and meaningful relationship** je ne recherche pas une relation sérieuse; (= *crafty*) **he's a ~ one*** il est plus malin qu'il n'en a l'air, il cache bien son jeu [h] (*in location*) **~ in the forest/in enemy territory** au cœur de la forêt/du territoire ennemi [i] (= *absorbed, implicated*) **~ in thought/in a book** plongé *or* absorbé dans ses pensées/dans un livre; **she was ~ in conversation (with him)** elle était en pleine conversation (avec lui); **~ in debt** criblé de dettes; **the country is ~ in recession** le pays est en pleine récession [j] (*Sport*) [*shot, volley, pass, cross*] long (longue *f*) [k] (*Gram*) **~ structure** structure *f* profonde; **~ grammar** grammaire *f* profonde [2] ADV profondément; **to go ~ into the forest** pénétrer profondément *or* très avant dans la forêt; **to bury sth ~ underground** enfouir qch profondément dans le sol; **it makes its burrow ~ underground** il creuse son terrier très profond; **don't go in too ~ if you can't swim** ne va pas trop loin si tu ne sais pas nager; **to thrust one's hands ~ in one's pockets** enfoncer ses mains dans ses poches; **to talk/read** *etc* **~ into the night** parler/lire *etc* jusque

tard dans la nuit; **to drink ~** boire à longs traits; **to breathe ~** respirer profondément; **to gaze ~ into sb's eyes** regarder qn au fond des yeux, plonger son regard dans celui de qn; **to go** *or* **run ~** [*divisions, crisis, tendency*] être profond; [*problems*] être grave, remonter à loin; [*passions, feelings*] être exacerbé; [*racism, prejudice, memories*] être bien enraciné; **the difference between them goes** *or* **runs ~** il y a une profonde différence entre eux; **their family roots run ~** leur famille remonte à loin; **he's in (it) pretty ~*** (*in relationship, plot*) il s'est engagé à fond; (*in conspiracy, illegal activity*) il est dedans jusqu'au cou; **~ down she still mistrusted him** en son for intérieur, elle se méfiait encore de lui; **she seems abrupt, but ~ down she's kind** sous son air *or* son extérieur brusque, c'est quelqu'un de gentil → **dig, knee, skin, still²** [3] N [a] (*liter = sea, ocean*) **the ~** (les grands fonds *mpl* de) l'océan *m*, les grandes profondeurs *fpl* [b] (= *depths*) **in the ~ of winter** au plus fort *or* au cœur de l'hiver [4] COMP ► **deep-chested** ADJ [*person*] large de poitrine; [*animal*] à large poitrail ► **deep-discount bond** N (*Fin*) obligation *f* à forte décote ► **deep-dyed** ADJ (*fig*) invétéré ► **deep-fat fryer** N friteuse *f* ► **deep freezer** N (*US*) congélateur *m* ► **deep-freezing** N congélation *f*, surgélation *f* ► **deep-frozen foods** NPL aliments *mpl* surgelés ► **deep-fry** VT faire frire ► **deep fryer** N → **deep-fat fryer** ► **deep kissing** N (*NonC*) baisers *mpl* profonds ► **deep-pan pizza** N pizza *f* à pâte épaisse ► **deep-rooted** ADJ [*affection, prejudice*] profond, profondément enraciné, vivace; [*habit*] invétéré, ancré; [*tree*] aux racines profondes ► **deep-sea** ADJ [*animal, plant*] pélagique, abyssal; [*current*] pélagique ► **deep-sea diver** N plongeur *m* sous-marin ► **deep-sea diving** N plongée *f* sous-marine ► **deep-sea fisherman** N (*pl* deep-sea fishermen) pêcheur *m* hauturier *or* de haute mer ► **deep-sea fishing** N pêche *f* hauturière ► **deep-seated** ADJ [*prejudice, dislike*] profond, profondément enraciné; [*conviction*] fermement ancré; **~-seated cough** toux *f* bronchique *or* caverneuse ► **deep-set** ADJ [*eyes*] très enfoncé, creux, cave; [*window*] profondément encastré ► **deep-six*** VT (*US*) (= *throw out*) balancer‡; (= *kill*) liquider‡ ► **the Deep South** N (*US Geog*) le Sud profond (des États-Unis) ► **deep space** N espace *m* intersidéral *or* interstellaire

deepen ['diːpən] [1] VT [+ *relationship, knowledge*] approfondir; [+ *gloom, recession*] aggraver [2] VI [*crisis, recession*] s'aggraver; [*voice*] devenir plus grave; [*water*] devenir plus profond; [*snow*] devenir plus épais; [*relationship*] devenir plus profond; [*knowledge*] s'approfondir; [*darkness*] s'épaissir

deepening ['diːpənɪŋ] [1] ADJ [*crisis, gloom, depression*] qui s'aggrave; [*friendship, understanding*] de plus en plus profond; [*wrinkles*] qui se creuse [2] N intensification *f*

deepfreeze [ˌdiːp'friːz] [1] N (*in US: also* **Deepfreeze®**) congélateur *m* [2] VT congeler

deeply ['diːplɪ] ADV [a] [*cut, sleep, breathe, love, think, regret*] profondément; [*dig*] profond; [*drink*] à grands *or* longs traits; **to blush ~** rougir jusqu'aux oreilles; **~ embedded** profondément incrusté; **to sigh ~** pousser un gros soupir; **to look ~ into sb's eyes** regarder qn au fond des yeux, plonger son regard dans celui de qn [b] [*shocked, divided, sceptical, religious, unhappy, hurt*] profondément; [*concerned, troubled, unpopular*] extrêmement; [*grateful*] infiniment; **~ tanned** très bronzé; **~ in debt** criblé de dettes

deer [dɪə'] N (*pl* deer *or* deers) cerf *m*, biche *f*; (*also* **red ~**) cerf *m*; (*also* **fallow ~**) daim *m*;

(*also* roe ~) chevreuil *m*; **certain types of ~** certains types de cervidés; **look at those ~!** regardez ces cerfs (*or* ces biches)!

deerhound ['dɪəhaʊnd] N limier *m*

deerskin ['dɪəskɪn] N peau *f* de daim

deerstalker ['dɪə,stɔːkəʳ] N (= *hat*) casquette *f* à la Sherlock Holmes; (= *hunter*) chasseur *m* de cerfs

deerstalking ['dɪə,stɔːkɪŋ] N chasse *f* au cerf (à pied)

de-escalate [diː'eskə,leɪt] VT [+ *tension*] faire baisser, diminuer; [+ *situation*] détendre, décrisper

de-escalation [diː,eskə'leɪʃən] N (*Mil, Pol*) désescalade *f*; (*in industrial relations*) décrispation *f*

deface [dɪ'feɪs] VT dégrader

de facto [deɪ'fæktəʊ] ① ADJ, ADV de fait, de facto ② N (*Austral*) concubin(e) *m(f)*

defamation [,defə'meɪʃən] N (*also* ~ **of character**) diffamation *f*

defamatory [dɪ'fæmətərɪ] ADJ diffamatoire

defame [dɪ'feɪm] VT diffamer

default [dɪ'fɔːlt] ① N ⓐ (*Jur*) (= *failure to appear*) (*in civil cases*) défaut *m*, non-comparution *f*; (*in criminal cases*) contumace *f*; (= *failure to meet financial obligation*) défaillance *f*, manquement *m*; **judgement by ~** jugement *m or* arrêt *m* par contumace *or* par défaut; **to be in ~ of payment** [*company*] être en (situation de) cessation de paiement ⓑ **by ~: we must not let it go by ~** ne laissons pas échapper l'occasion (faute d'avoir agi); **they won the election by ~** ils ont remporté l'élection en l'absence d'autres candidats sérieux; **he got the job by ~** il a eu le poste en l'absence d'autres candidats (valables); (*Sport*) **match won by ~** match gagné par forfait ⓒ (= *lack, absence*) manque *m*, carence *f*; **in ~ of** à défaut de, faute de ⓓ (*Fin*) cessation *f* de paiements ⓔ (*Comput*) position *f* par défaut; **~ option/value** option *f*/valeur *f* par défaut
② VT (*Jur*) condamner par défaut *or* par contumace, rendre un jugement par défaut contre
③ VI ⓐ (*Jur*) faire défaut, être en état de contumace ⓑ (*gen, Fin*) manquer à ses engagements ⓒ (*Comput*) **to ~ to a value** prendre une valeur par défaut; **it ~s to drive C** ça se positionne par défaut sur le disque C

defaulter [dɪ'fɔːltəʳ] N ⓐ (= *offender*) délinquant(e) *m(f)*; (*Mil, Naut*) soldat *m* (*or* marin *m*) en infraction; (*Mil, Naut: undergoing punishment*) consigné *m* ⓑ (*Fin, St Ex*) défaillant(e) *m(f)*, débiteur *m*, -trice *f* défaillant(e); (= *defaulting tenant*) locataire *mf* qui ne paie pas son loyer

defaulting [dɪ'fɔːltɪŋ] ADJ ⓐ (*St Ex etc*) défaillant, en défaut ⓑ (*Jur*) défaillant, qui n'a pas comparu

defeat [dɪ'fiːt] ① N (= *act, state*) [*of army, team*] défaite *f*; [*of project, ambition*] échec *m*, insuccès *m*; [*of legal case, appeal*] rejet *m* ② VT (= *opponent, army*] vaincre, battre; [+ *team*] battre; [+ *hopes*] frustrer, ruiner; [+ *ambitions, plans, efforts, attempts*] faire échouer; (*Parl*) [+ *government, opposition*] mettre en minorité; [+ *bill, amendment*] rejeter; **~ed in his attempts to ...** n'ayant pas réussi à ...; **to ~ one's own ends** *or* **object** aller à l'encontre du but que l'on s'est (*or* s'était *etc*) proposé; **that plan will ~ its own ends** ce plan sera autodestructeur

defeated [dɪ'fiːtɪd] ADJ [*army*] vaincu; [*team, player*] perdant

defeatism [dɪ'fiːtɪzəm] N défaitisme *m*

defeatist [dɪ'fiːtɪst] ADJ, N défaitiste *mf*

defecate ['defəkeɪt] VTI déféquer

defecation [,defə'keɪʃən] N défécation *f*

defect ['diːfekt] ① N (*gen*) défaut *m*; (*in workmanship*) défaut *m*, malfaçon *f*; **physical ~** défaut *m* physique; **hearing/sight ~** défaut *m* de l'ouïe/de la vue; **speech ~** défaut *m* de prononciation; **mental ~** anomalie *f or* déficience *f* mentale; **moral ~** défaut *m* → **latent** ② [dɪ'fekt] VI faire défection; **to ~ from one country to another** s'enfuir d'un pays pour aller dans un autre (*pour raisons politiques*); **to ~ to the West/to another party/to the enemy** passer à l'Ouest/à un autre parti/à l'ennemi

defection [dɪ'fekʃən] N (*Pol*) défection *f*; (*Rel*) apostasie *f*; **his ~ to the East was in all the papers** quand il est passé à l'Est, tous les journaux en ont parlé; **after his ~ from Russia, he lost contact with his family** quand il s'est enfui de Russie, il a perdu contact avec sa famille

defective [dɪ'fektɪv] ① ADJ [*goods, machine, work, reasoning, sight, hearing, gene*] défectueux; [*chromosome*] anormal; (*Gram*) [*verb*] défectif; **to be born with a ~ heart** naître avec une malformation cardiaque; **~ workmanship** malfaçons *fpl* → **mental, mentally** ② N (*Med*) déficient(e) *m(f)*; (*Gram*) verbe *m* défectif

defector [dɪ'fektəʳ] N (*Pol*) transfuge *mf*; (*Rel*) apostat *m*

defence, defense (*US*) [dɪ'fens] ① N ⓐ (*NonC*) défense *f*; [*of action, belief*] justification *f*; (*Physiol, Psych, Sport*) défense *f*; (*Sport*) **to play in ~** jouer en défense; **in ~ of** à la défense de, pour défendre; **Secretary of State for** *or* **Minister of Defence** (*Brit*) *or* **Secretary of Defense** (*US*) ministre *m* de la Défense; **Department** *or* **Ministry of Defence** (*Brit*) *or* **Department of Defense** (*US*) ministère *m* de la Défense → **civil, self** ⓑ (= *means of defence*) défense *f*; **~s** (*gen, also Mil* = *weapons etc*) moyens *mpl* de défense; (*Mil* = *constructions*) ouvrages *mpl* défensifs; **the body's ~s against disease** les défenses *fpl* de l'organisme contre la maladie; **as a ~ against** pour se défendre contre; **she put up a spirited ~ of her government's policies** elle a défendu la politique de son gouvernement avec fougue; (*Sport*) **Smith made a successful ~ of her title** Smith a réussi à conserver son titre; **to come to sb's ~** défendre qn; **his conduct needs no ~** sa conduite n'a pas à être justifiée; **in his ~ I will say that ...** pour sa défense *or* à sa décharge je dirai que ... ⓒ (*Jur*) défense *f*; **in his ~** pour sa défense, à sa décharge; **witness for the ~** témoin *m* à décharge; **the case for the ~** la défense ⓓ [*of argument, decision*] justification *f*; (*Univ*) [*of thesis*] soutenance *f*
② COMP (*gen*) de défense; [*industry, manufacturer etc*] travaillant pour la défense nationale; [*product, contract*] destiné à la défense nationale ► **defence counsel** N avocat *m* de la défense ► **defence expenditure** N dépenses *fpl* militaires ► **defence forces** NPL (*Mil*) forces *fpl* défensives, défense *f* ► **defence mechanism** N (*Physiol*) système *m* de défense; (*Psych*) défenses *fpl*

defenceless [dɪ'fenslɪs] ADJ (*lit, fig*) sans défense (**against** contre); **he is quite ~** il est incapable de se défendre, il est sans défense

defend [dɪ'fend] ① VT ⓐ (*gen, Sport*) défendre; **to ~ o.s.** se défendre; **to ~ one's (own) interests** défendre ses (propres) intérêts ⓑ (= *justify*) justifier; (= *attempt to justify*) essayer de justifier; **how can he possibly ~ the way he's behaved towards her?** comment peut-il justifier la manière dont il s'est comporté avec elle?; **they ~ed their actions** ils ont justifié leurs actions, ils se sont justifiés; (*Sport*) **Smith successfully ~ed her title** Smith a réussi à conserver son titre; (*Univ*) **to ~ a thesis** soutenir une thèse ② VI (*Sport, gen*) défendre; (=

play in defence) être en défense; **they ~ed very well** ils ont très bien défendu; **to ~ against sb** [*champion*] défendre son titre contre qn, remettre son titre en jeu contre qn → **defending**

defendant [dɪ'fendənt] N (*Jur*) défendeur *m*, -deresse *f*; (*on appeal*) intimé(e) *m(f)*; (*in criminal case*) prévenu(e) *m(f)*; (*in assizes court*) accusé(e) *m(f)*

defender [dɪ'fendəʳ] N (*lit, fig*) défenseur *m*; (*Sport*) [*of record*] détenteur *m*, -trice *f* [*of title*] tenant(e) *m(f)*; (*Brit Hist*) **~ of the faith** défenseur *m* de la foi

defending [dɪ'fendɪŋ] ADJ **the ~ team** ◊ **the ~ champion** le tenant du titre; (*Jur*) **~ counsel** avocat *m* de la défense

defense [dɪ'fens] (*US*) = **defence**

defensible [dɪ'fensɪbl] ADJ (*lit, fig*) défendable

defensive [dɪ'fensɪv] ① ADJ (*Mil, fig*) défensif; **he's so ~!** il est toujours sur la défensive! ② N (*Mil, fig*) défensive *f*; (*lit, fig*) **to be on the ~** être sur la défensive; **to put sb/go on the ~** mettre qn/se mettre sur la défensive

defensively [dɪ'fensɪvlɪ] ADV [*speak*] sur la défensive; [*play*] défensivement

defensiveness [dɪ'fensɪvnɪs] N **his ~ (when we talk about ...)** sa façon d'être sur la défensive (chaque fois que nous parlons de ...)

defer¹ [dɪ'fɜːʳ] ① VT ⓐ [+ *journey, meeting*] remettre à plus tard, reporter; [+ *business*] remettre à plus tard; [+ *payment, decision, judgement*] remettre à plus tard, différer; **our meeting was ~red until 22 May** notre réunion a été reportée au 22 mai; **to ~ making a decision/paying one's taxes** différer une décision/le paiement de ses impôts, remettre une décision/le paiement de ses impôts à plus tard ⓑ (*Mil*) **to ~ sb's call-up** accorder un sursis d'appel *or* d'incorporation à qn; **to ~ sb on medical grounds** accorder un sursis d'appel *or* d'incorporation à qn pour raisons médicales ② COMP ► **deferred annuity** N (*Fin*) rente *f* à paiement différé ► **deferred liabilities** NPL (*Jur, Fin*) dettes *fpl* à moyen et long terme ► **deferred payment** N (*Comm etc*) paiement *m* échelonné

defer² [dɪ'fɜːʳ] VI (= *submit*) **to ~ to sb** déférer (*frm*) à qn, s'incliner devant qn; **to ~ to sb's knowledge** s'en remettre aux connaissances de qn; (*Jur*) **to ~ to California jurisdiction** accepter la compétence des tribunaux californiens

deference ['defərəns] N déférence *f*, égards *mpl* (**to** pour); **in ~ to** ◊ **out of ~ for** par déférence *or* égards pour; **with all due ~ to you** avec tout le respect que je vous dois, sauf votre respect

deferential [,defə'renʃəl] ADJ [*person, attitude*] respectueux, plein de déférence; [*tone*] de déférence; **to be ~ to sb** se montrer plein de déférence pour *or* envers qn

deferentially [,defə'renʃəlɪ] ADV avec déférence

deferment [dɪ'fɜːmənt] N [*of payment, tax*] report *m*; (*Mil*) sursis *m* d'appel *or* d'incorporation; **he was given ~ from military service** on lui a accordé un sursis d'appel *or* d'incorporation; (*US Mil*) **draft ~** sursis *m* d'appel, sursis *m* d'incorporation

deferral [dɪ'fɜːrəl] N = **deferment**

defiance [dɪ'faɪəns] N défi *m*; **a gesture/act of ~** un geste/acte de défi; **a ~ of our authority** un défi à notre autorité; **his ~ of my orders caused an accident** en bravant mes ordres *or* en refusant d'obéir à mes ordres, il a causé un accident; **he will have to answer in court for his ~ of the curfew** il devra comparaître en justice pour n'avoir pas respecté le couvre-feu; **in ~ of** [+ *the law, instructions*] au mépris de; [+ *person*] au mépris des ordres de

defiant [dɪ'faɪənt] ADJ [*reply, statement*] provocant; [*attitude, tone, gesture, look*] de défi;

[person] rebelle ; **the team is in ~ mood** l'équipe est prête à relever le défi ; **to be ~ of sth** défier qch

defiantly [dɪˈfaɪəntlɪ] ADV [speak] d'un ton de défi ; [reply, stare] d'un air de défi ; [behave] avec une attitude de défi

defibrillator [diːˈfɪbrɪleɪtəʳ] N (Med) défibrillateur m

deficiency [dɪˈfɪʃənsɪ] 1 N a (= lack) [of goods] manque m, insuffisance f (**of** de) ; (Med) [of iron, calcium, vitamins etc] carence f [of iron, calcium, vitamins etc] carence f alimentaire or nutritionnelle → **mental, vitamin** b (Med = failure to function properly) [of organ, immune system] insuffisance f c (= flaw) [in character, system] faille f, faiblesse f ; (in construction, machine) imperfection f ; (in service) faiblesse f ; **his deficiencies as an administrator** ses points mpl faibles en tant qu'administrateur d (Fin) déficit m 2 COMP ► **deficiency disease** N (Med) maladie f de carence or carentielle ► **deficiency payment** N (Econ) paiement m différentiel

deficient [dɪˈfɪʃənt] ADJ a (= inadequate, defective) défectueux ; (= insufficient) insuffisant ; **to be ~ in sth** manquer de qch ; **his diet is ~ in fruit and vegetables** il ne mange pas assez de fruits et de légumes

deficit [ˈdefɪsɪt] N (Fin etc) déficit m ; **in ~** en déficit

defile¹ [ˈdiːfaɪl] 1 N (= procession: place) défilé m 2 [dɪˈfaɪl] VI (= march in file) défiler

defile² [ˈdiːfaɪl] VT (lit, fig = pollute) souiller (liter), salir ; (= desecrate) profaner

defilement [dɪˈfaɪlmənt] N (lit, fig = pollution) souillure f (liter) ; (= desecration) profanation f

definable [dɪˈfaɪnəbl] ADJ définissable

define [dɪˈfaɪn] VT a (= describe, characterize) [+ word, feeling, attitude] définir ; [+ responsibilities, conditions] définir, déterminer ; [+ functions] définir ; [+ boundaries, powers, duties] délimiter, définir ; [+ problem] délimiter, cerner ; **an agreement that ~s how much they are paid** un accord qui détermine le niveau des salaires ; **the legislation does not ~ what exactly is meant by the term "depression"** la loi ne précise pas exactement ce que recouvre le terme « dépression » ; **she doesn't ~ herself as a feminist** elle ne se définit pas comme une féministe ; **how would you ~ yourself politically?** comment vous définiriez-vous or où vous situez-vous d'un point de vue politique ? b (= outline) dessiner or dégager (les formes de) ; **the tower was clearly ~d against the sky** la tour se détachait nettement sur le ciel

definite [ˈdefɪnɪt] 1 ADJ a (= fixed, certain) [plan] précis ; [intention, order, sale] ferme ; **is that ~?** c'est certain or sûr ? ; **have you got a ~ date for the wedding?** avez-vous décidé de la date du mariage ? ; **12 August is ~ for the trip** le voyage aura lieu le 12 août, c'est sûr ; **nothing ~** rien de précis b (= distinct, appreciable) [impression, feeling, increase] net ; [advantage] certain ; **a ~ improvement** une nette amélioration ; **it's a ~ possibility** c'est tout à fait possible c (= positive, emphatic) [person, tone] catégorique ; [manner] ferme ; [views] arrêté ; **to be ~ about sth** être catégorique à propos de qch d (Gram) **past ~ (tense)** prétérit m 2 COMP ► **definite article** N (Gram) article m défini ► **definite integral** N (Math) intégrale f définie

definitely [ˈdefɪnɪtlɪ] ADV a (expressing an intention) [decide, agree, say] de manière définitive ; **is he ~ coming?** est-il sûr or certain qu'il va venir ? ; **I'm ~ going to get in touch with them** j'ai la ferme intention de les contacter ; **probably next week, but not ~** sans doute la semaine prochaine, mais rien n'est encore décidé or mais sous toute réserve b (expressing an opinion) vraiment ; **you ~ need a holiday** tu as vraiment besoin de vacances ; **she's ~ more intelligent than her brother** elle

est plus intelligente que son frère, c'est sûr, elle est indéniablement plus intelligente que son frère ; **~ not** certainement pas ; **~!** (= I agree) absolument !, tout à fait ! c (= emphatically) [deny, refuse, say] catégoriquement

definition [ˌdefɪˈnɪʃən] N a [of word, concept] définition f ; **by ~** par définition b [of powers, boundaries, duties] délimitation f c (Phot, TV) définition f

definitive [dɪˈfɪnɪtɪv] ADJ a (= definite) [answer, refusal etc] définitif b (= authoritative) [map, authority etc] de référence, qui fait autorité

definitively [dɪˈfɪnɪtɪvlɪ] ADV définitivement

deflate [diːˈfleɪt] 1 VT a [+ tyre] dégonfler ; **~d tyre** pneu m dégonflé or à plat b (Fin) **to ~ the currency** provoquer une déflation monétaire c* [+ person] démonter, rabattre le caquet à 2 VI se dégonfler

deflated [diːˈfleɪtɪd] ADJ a (= flat) [tyre] dégonflé, à plat b (= downcast) découragé

deflation [diːˈfleɪʃən] N a (Econ) déflation f b [of tyre, ball] dégonflement m

deflationary [diːˈfleɪʃənərɪ] ADJ [measures, policy] déflationniste

deflationist [diːˈfleɪʃənɪst] ADJ déflationniste

deflator [diːˈfleɪtəʳ] N déflateur m, mesure f déflationniste

deflect [dɪˈflekt] 1 VT [+ ball, projectile] faire dévier ; [+ stream] détourner ; [+ light] défléchir, dévier ; [+ person] détourner (**from** de) 2 VI dévier ; [magnetic needle] décliner

deflection [dɪˈflekʃən] N [of projectile] déviation f ; [of light] déflexion f, déviation f ; [of magnetic needle] déclinaison f (magnétique), déviation f

deflector [dɪˈflektəʳ] N déflecteur m

defloration [ˌdiːflɔːˈreɪʃən] N (lit, fig) défloration f

deflower [diːˈflaʊəʳ] VT a (liter) [+ girl] déflorer b (Bot) défleurir

defoliant [diːˈfəʊlɪənt] N défoliant m

defoliate [diːˈfəʊlɪeɪt] VT défolier

defoliation [ˌdiːfəʊlɪˈeɪʃən] N défoliation f

deforest [diːˈfɒrɪst] VT déboiser

deforestation [diːˌfɒrɪsˈteɪʃən] N déboisement m

deform [dɪˈfɔːm] VT déformer ; (Tech) fausser

deformation [ˌdiːfɔːˈmeɪʃən] N déformation f

deformed [dɪˈfɔːmd] ADJ [person, limb, bones, body] difforme ; [mind, structure] déformé, tordu

deformity [dɪˈfɔːmɪtɪ] N [of body] difformité f ; [of mind] déformation f

defraud [dɪˈfrɔːd] VT [+ state] frauder ; [+ person] escroquer ; **to ~ sb of sth** escroquer qch à qn, frustrer qn de qch (Jur) → **conspiracy**

defrauder [dɪˈfrɔːdəʳ] N fraudeur m, -euse f

defray [dɪˈfreɪ] VT [+ expenses] payer, rembourser ; [+ cost] couvrir ; **to ~ sb's expenses** défrayer qn, rembourser ses frais à qn

defrayal [dɪˈfreɪəl], **defrayment** [dɪˈfreɪmənt] N paiement m or remboursement m des frais

defrock [diːˈfrɒk] VT défroquer

defrost [diːˈfrɒst] 1 VT a [+ refrigerator, windscreen] dégivrer ; [+ meat, vegetables] décongeler 2 VI [fridge] se dégivrer ; [frozen food] se décongeler

defroster [diːˈfrɒstəʳ] N a (Aut) dégivreur m ; (US) dispositif m antibuée

deft [deft] ADJ habile, adroit

deftly [ˈdeftlɪ] ADV adroitement

deftness [ˈdeftnɪs] N adresse f, dextérité f

defunct [dɪˈfʌŋkt] 1 ADJ [organization, company, publication] défunt (before n), ancien ; [practice] révolu ; [policy, tradition] dépassé ; [factory] désaffecté ; **the ~ Soviet Union** l'ex-Union soviétique ; **the special relationship**

between Russia and Cuba is now ~ la relation privilégiée entre la Russie et Cuba n'existe plus or est révolue 2 N (frm) **the ~** le défunt, la défunte

defuse [diːˈfjuːz] VT [+ bomb] désamorcer ; (fig) **to ~ the situation** désamorcer la situation

defy [dɪˈfaɪ] VT a (= disobey) [+ law, authority, convention] défier ; [+ person] désobéir à ; [+ orders] désobéir à, braver ; [+ curfew] ne pas respecter ; (= stand up to) [+ person] défier ; **she was bold enough to stand up and ~ him** elle a osé le défier ; **she defied him and spoke publicly about her ordeal** elle lui a désobéi en parlant ouvertement de son épreuve ; **to ~ death** (= face without fear) braver la mort ; (= narrowly escape) frôler or échapper de justesse à la mort ; **the virus has defied all attempts to find a vaccine** jusqu'à maintenant, ce virus a résisté à tous les efforts qu'on a fait pour trouver un vaccin b (= contradict, go beyond) [+ logic] défier ; **to ~ gravity** défier les lois de la gravité ; **it defies description** cela défie toute description ; **that defies belief!** cela dépasse l'entendement !, c'est incroyable ! c (= challenge) **to ~ sb to do** défier qn de faire, mettre qn au défi de faire d (liter) **to ~ one's age** or **the years** ne pas faire son âge

degeneracy [dɪˈdʒenərəsɪ] N dégénérescence f

degenerate 1 [dɪˈdʒenəreɪt] VI [race, people] dégénérer (**into** en), s'abâtardir ; [situation] dégénérer ; **the situation ~d into civil war/rioting/violence** la situation a dégénéré en guerre civile/en émeutes/dans la violence ; **the demonstration ~d into violence** la manifestation a dégénéré (dans la violence) ; **the election campaign has ~d into farce** la campagne électorale a tourné à la farce 2 [dɪˈdʒenərɪt] ADJ dégénéré 3 [dɪˈdʒenərɪt] N dégénéré(e) m(f)

degeneration [dɪˌdʒenəˈreɪʃən] N [of mind, body, morals, race, people] dégénérescence f

degenerative [dɪˈdʒenərɪtɪv] ADJ dégénératif

degradable [dɪˈɡreɪdəbl] ADJ dégradable

degradation [ˌdeɡrəˈdeɪʃən] N a (= process of worsening: Chem, Geol, Mil, Phys) dégradation f ; [of person] déchéance f ; [of character] avilissement m ; **environmental ~** dégradation f de l'environnement b (= debasement) déchéance f, avilissement m ; (= humiliation) humiliation f ; **the moral ~ of our society** la déchéance morale de notre société ; **the ~ of prison life** le caractère dégradant de la vie carcérale ; **sexual ~** avilissement m sexuel ; **the ~ of having to accept charity** l'humiliation d'avoir à accepter la charité ; **the ~s she had been forced to suffer** les humiliations qu'elle avait été obligée de subir

degrade [dɪˈɡreɪd] 1 VT a (= debase) avilir, dégrader (liter) ; **he felt ~d** il se sentait avili or dégradé ; **he ~d himself by accepting it** il s'est avili or dégradé en l'acceptant ; **I wouldn't ~ myself to do that** je n'irais pas m'avilir or m'abaisser à faire cela b (Chem, Geol, Phys) dégrader ; [+ official] dégrader ; (Mil) dégrader, casser 2 VI (= break down) se dégrader

degrading [dɪˈɡreɪdɪŋ] ADJ dégradant (**to** pour)

degree [dɪˈɡriː] 1 N a (Geog, Math) degré m ; **angle of 90 ~s** angle m de 90 degrés ; **40 ~s east of Greenwich** à 40 degrés de longitude est (de Greenwich) ; **20 ~s of latitude** 20 degrés de latitude ; (fig) **a 180-~ turn** un virage à 180 degrés b [of temperature] degré m ; **it was 35 ~s in the shade** il faisait 35 (degrés) à l'ombre ; **he's got a temperature of 39 ~s** il a 39 de fièvre c (= amount) degré m ; **some ~** or **a (certain) ~ of independence/optimism/freedom** un certain degré d'indépendance/d'optimisme/de liberté ; **with varying ~s of success** avec plus ou moins de succès ; **a fairly high ~ of er-**

ror d'assez nombreuses erreurs, un taux d'erreurs assez élevé; **a considerable ~ of doubt** des doutes considérables; **his ~ of commitment was low** il ne se sentait pas vraiment engagé à fond; **I couldn't summon up the least ~ of enthusiasm for his idea** je n'arrivais pas à éprouver le moindre enthousiasme pour son idée; **to do sth by ~s** faire qch petit à petit; **to some ~ ◊ to a (certain) ~** dans une certaine mesure; **he possesses to a high ~ the art of putting people at their ease** il possède au plus haut degré l'art de mettre les gens à l'aise; **the departments are independent to a very high ~** les services sont, dans une large mesure, indépendants; **to such a ~ that ...** à (un) tel point que ...

d (Med) **first-/second-/third-~ burns** brûlures fpl au premier/deuxième/troisième degré → **third**

e (US Jur) **first-~ murder ◊ murder in the first ~** assassinat m, meurtre m avec préméditation; **second-~ murder ◊ murder in the second ~** meurtre m (sans préméditation)

f (Univ) diplôme m (universitaire), titre m universitaire; **first ~** ≈ licence f; **higher ~** (= master's) ≈ maîtrise f; (= doctorate) ≈ doctorat m; **~ in** licence f de; **I'm taking a science ~ or a ~ in science** je fais une licence de sciences; **he got his ~** il a eu son diplôme; **he got his ~ in geography** il a eu sa licence de géographie → **honorary**

g (Gram) degré m; **three ~s of comparison** trois degrés de comparaison

h (liter = position in society) rang m; **of high ~** de haut rang; **of low ~** de rang inférieur

i (in genealogy) **~s of kinship** degrés mpl de parenté

2 COMP ► **degree ceremony** N (Brit Univ) cérémonie f de remise des diplômes ► **degree course** N (Brit Univ) **to do a ~ course (in)** faire une licence (de); **the ~ course consists of ...** le cursus (universitaire) consiste en ... ► **degree mill** N (US pej) usine f à diplômes

---
DEGREE

Dans les systèmes universitaires britannique et américain, le premier titre universitaire (généralement obtenu après trois années d'études supérieures) est le « bachelor's **degree** », qui permet à l'étudiant en lettres de devenir « Bachelor of Arts » (« BA » en Grande-Bretagne, « AB » aux États-Unis) et à l'étudiant en sciences ou en sciences humaines d'être un « Bachelor of Science » (« BSc » en Grande-Bretagne, « BS » aux États-Unis). L'année suivante débouche sur les diplômes de « Master of Arts » (« MA ») et de « Master of Science » (« MSc » en Grande-Bretagne, « MS » aux États-Unis).

---

degressive [dɪ'gresɪv] ADJ [taxation] dégressif

dehumanization [di:ˌhjuːmənaɪ'zeɪʃən] N déshumanisation f

dehumanize [di:'hjuːmənaɪz] VT déshumaniser

dehumanizing [di:'hjuːmənaɪzɪŋ] ADJ déshumanisant

dehydrate [ˌdi:haɪ'dreɪt] VT déshydrater

dehydrated [ˌdi:haɪ'dreɪtɪd] ADJ [person, skin, vegetables] déshydraté; [milk, eggs] en poudre

dehydration [ˌdi:haɪ'dreɪʃən] N déshydratation f

de-ice [di:'aɪs] VT dégivrer

de-icer [di:'aɪsər] N (Aut, Aviat) dégivreur m

de-icing [di:'aɪsɪŋ] **1** N (Aut, Aviat) dégivrage m **2** COMP ► **de-icing fluid** N (Aut) antigel m

deictic [daɪktɪk] N (Ling) déictique m

deification [ˌdi:ɪfɪ'keɪʃən] N déification f

deify [di:'ɪfaɪ] VT déifier, diviniser

deign [deɪn] VT daigner (**to do** faire), condescendre (**to do** à faire)

de-indexation [ˌdi:ɪndek'seɪʃən] N désindexation f

deism [di:'ɪzəm] N déisme m

deist [di:'ɪst] N déiste mf

deity [di:'ɪtɪ] N **a** (Myth, Rel) divinité f, déité f (liter); **the Deity** Dieu m **b** (NonC) divinité f

deixis [daɪksɪs] N (Ling) deixis f

déjà vu [ˌdeɪʒɑ'vu:] N déjà(-)vu m

dejected [dɪ'dʒektɪd] ADJ abattu, découragé; **to become** or **get ~** se décourager, se laisser abattre

dejectedly [dɪ'dʒektɪdlɪ] ADV [say, talk] d'un ton abattu; [look] d'un air abattu

dejection [dɪ'dʒekʃən] N abattement m, découragement m

de jure [ˌdeɪ'dʒʊərɪ] ADJ, ADV de jure

dekko [ˈdekəʊ] N (Brit) petit coup m d'œil; **let's have a ~** fais voir ça, on va (y) jeter un œil*

Del. ABBR = **Delaware**

Delaware ['delə‚wɛər] N le Delaware; **in ~** dans le Delaware

delay [dɪ'leɪ] **1** VT **a** (= postpone) [+ action, event] retarder, différer; [+ payment] différer; **~ed effect** effet m à retardement; **to ~ doing sth** tarder à faire qch, remettre qch à plus tard

b (= keep waiting, hold up) [+ person, traffic] retarder, retenir; [+ train, plane] retarder; **I don't want to ~ you** je ne veux pas vous retenir or retarder

2 VI s'attarder (**in doing** en faisant); **don't ~!** dépêchez-vous!

3 N retard m; **after two or three ~s** après deux ou trois arrêts; **there will be ~s to trains on the London-Brighton line** on prévoit des retards sur la ligne Londres-Brighton; **there will be ~s to traffic** il y aura des ralentissements (de la circulation), la circulation sera ralentie; (on roadsign) **"~s possible (until Dec 1999)"** « ralentissements possibles (jusqu'en décembre 1999) »; **with as little ~ as possible** dans les plus brefs délais; **there's no time for ~** il n'y a pas de temps à perdre; **without ~** sans délai; **without further ~** sans plus tarder or attendre; **they arrived with an hour's ~** ils sont arrivés avec une heure de retard

4 COMP ► **delayed-action** ADJ [bomb, fuse] à retardement ► **delayed-action shutter** N (Phot) obturateur m à retardement

delayering [di:'leɪərɪŋ] N écrasement m des niveaux hiérarchiques

delaying [dɪ'leɪɪŋ] ADJ [action] dilatoire, qui retarde; **~ tactics** moyens mpl dilatoires

delectable [dɪ'lektəbl] ADJ (liter or hum) [food, drink] délectable (liter or hum); **the ~ Miss Campbell** la délicieuse Mlle Campbell

delectation [ˌdi:lek'teɪʃən] N délectation f

delegate ['delɪgeɪt] **1** VT [+ authority, power] déléguer (**to** à); **to ~ responsibility** déléguer les responsabilités; **to ~ sb to do sth** déléguer qn pour faire qch **2** VI déléguer ses responsabilités **3** ['delɪgɪt] N délégué(e) m(f) (**to** à); **~ to a congress** congressiste mf

delegation [ˌdelɪ'geɪʃən] N **a** (NonC) [of power] délégation f; [of person] nomination f, désignation f (**as** comme) **b** (= group of delegates) délégation f

delete [dɪ'li:t] VT (gen) effacer (**from** de); (= score out) barrer, rayer (**from** de); (Gram, Comput) supprimer, effacer; (on forms etc) **"~ where inapplicable"** « rayer les mentions inutiles »

deleterious [ˌdelɪ'tɪərɪəs] ADJ [effect, influence] nuisible, délétère (**to** à); [gas] délétère

deletion [dɪ'li:ʃən] N **a** (NonC) effacement m **b** (= thing deleted) rature f

delft [delft] **1** N faïence f de Delft **2** COMP ► **Delft blue** N (= colour) bleu m (de) faïence

Delhi ['delɪ] **1** N Delhi **2** COMP ► **Delhi belly*** N turista* f, maladie f du touriste

deli* ['delɪ] N (ABBR = **delicatessen**) épicerie f fine, traiteur m

deliberate [dɪ'lɪbərɪt] **1** ADJ **a** (= intentional) [action, insult, lie] délibéré; **it wasn't ~** ce n'était pas fait exprès **b** (= cautious, thoughtful) [action, decision] bien pesé, mûrement réfléchi; [character, judgement] réfléchi, circonspect; (= slow, purposeful) [air, voice] décidé; [manner, walk] mesuré, posé **2** [dɪ'lɪbəreɪt] VI **a** (= think) délibérer, réfléchir (**upon** sur) **b** (= discuss) délibérer, tenir conseil **3** [dɪ'lɪbəreɪt] VT **a** (= study) considérer, examiner **b** (= discuss) délibérer sur, débattre

deliberately [dɪ'lɪbərɪtlɪ] ADV **a** (= on purpose) délibérément; **I didn't do it ~** je ne l'ai pas fait exprès; **~ vague** délibérément vague **b** (= purposefully) posément

deliberation [dɪˌlɪbə'reɪʃən] N **a** (= consideration) délibération f, réflexion f; **after due** or **careful ~** après mûre réflexion **b** (= discussion: gen pl) **~s** débats mpl, délibérations fpl **c** (= slowness) mesure f, manière f posée

deliberative [dɪ'lɪbərətɪv] ADJ **a** (speech) mûrement réfléchi **b** ► **deliberative assembly** assemblée f délibérante

delicacy ['delɪkəsɪ] N **a** (NonC) délicatesse f; (= fragility) fragilité f, délicatesse f; **a matter of some ~** une affaire assez délicate **b** (= special dish) mets m délicat; **a great ~** un mets très délicat

delicate ['delɪkɪt] ADJ **a** (= fine, subtle) [object, movement, colour, flavour, touch] délicat **b** (= easily damaged, not robust) [china, skin, fabric, person, health] fragile, délicat; († euph) **in a ~ condition** dans une position intéressante† (also euph) **c** (= touchy, tricky) [situation, negotiations] délicat **d** (= sensitive) [instrument, sense] délicat; [compass] sensible

delicately ['delɪkɪtlɪ] ADV **a** (= subtly, daintily) délicatement; **~ flavoured** délicatement parfumé **b** (= tactfully) avec tact or délicatesse; **~ worded** formulé avec tact or délicatesse

delicatessen [ˌdelɪkə'tesn] N (= shop) épicerie f fine, traiteur m

delicious [dɪ'lɪʃəs] ADJ (lit, fig) délicieux

deliciously [dɪ'lɪʃəslɪ] ADV (lit, fig) délicieusement; **~ creamy** délicieusement crémeux; **~ ironic** d'une ironie délicieuse

delight [dɪ'laɪt] **1** N **a** (= intense pleasure) grand plaisir m, joie f; **to my ~** à or pour ma plus grande joie; **to take a ~ in sth/in doing** prendre grand plaisir à qch/à faire; **with ~** (gen) avec joie; (more sensual) [taste, smell] avec délices; **to give ~** charmer **b** (= source of pleasure: often pl) délice m, joie f; **she is the ~ of her mother** elle fait la joie de sa mère; **this book is a great ~** ce livre est vraiment merveilleux; **a ~ to the eyes** un régal or un plaisir pour les yeux; **he's a ~ to watch** il fait plaisir à voir; **the ~s of life in the open** les charmes or les délices (liter) de la vie en plein air

2 VT [+ person] enchanter, ravir → **delighted 3** VI prendre plaisir (**in sth** à qch, **in doing** à faire), se délecter, se complaire (**in doing** à faire); **she ~s in him/it** il/cela lui donne beaucoup de joie

▼ **delighted** [dɪ'laɪtɪd] ADJ ravi, enchanté (**with, at, by** de, par, **to do** de faire, **that** que + subj); **absolutely ~!** tout à fait ravi!; **~ to meet you!** enchanté (de faire votre connaissance)!; **will you go? — (I shall be) ~** voulez-vous y aller? — avec grand plaisir or très volontiers

delightedly [dɪ'laɪtɪdlɪ] ADV avec ravissement

delightful [dɪ'laɪtfʊl] ADJ charmant; **it's ~ to ...** c'est merveilleux de ...

delightfully [dɪ'laɪtfʊlɪ] ADV [friendly, vague] délicieusement; [arranged, decorated] d'une

---
► LANGUAGE IN USE: **delighted** 11.3, 23.6, 25.1, 25.2

façon ravissante ; [*smile, behave*] de façon charmante

Delilah [dɪ'laɪlə] N Dalila f

delimit [di:'lɪmɪt] VT délimiter

delimitation [ˌdi:lɪmɪ'teɪʃən] N délimitation f

delineate [dɪ'lɪnɪeɪt] VT **a** (*lit*) [+ *outline etc*] délinéer, tracer ; **mountains clearly ~d** montagnes *fpl* qui se détachent clairement à l'horizon **b** [+ *plan etc*] (= *present*) présenter ; (*in more detail*) énoncer en détail ; (*with diagram etc*) représenter graphiquement **c** (*fig*) [+ *character*] représenter, dépeindre

delineation [dɪˌlɪnɪ'eɪʃən] N [*of outline*] dessin m, tracé m ; [*of plan*] présentation f (détaillée) ; [*of character*] description f, peinture f

delinquency [dɪ'lɪŋkwənsɪ] N **a** (*NonC*) délinquance f → **juvenile b** (= *act of delinquency*) faute f, délit m **c** (*US Fin = failure to pay*) défaillance f, défaut m de paiement

delinquent [dɪ'lɪŋkwənt] **1** ADJ **a** délinquant → **juvenile b** (*US Fin*) [*debtor*] défaillant ; [*payment*] arriéré, impayé, échu **2** **a** délinquant(e) m(f) ; (*fig*) coupable mf, fautif m, -ive f **b** (*US Fin*) défaillant(e) m(f)

deliquescence [ˌdelɪ'kwesəns] N déliquescence f

delirious [dɪ'lɪrɪəs] ADJ **a** (*Med*) délirant ; **to be ~ b** (*fig = ecstatic*) **to be ~ (with joy)** délirer de joie, être ivre de joie ; [*crowd*] être en délire

deliriously [dɪ'lɪrɪəslɪ] ADV **a** (*fig = ecstatically*) avec une joie délirante ; **~ happy** fou de joie **b** (*Med*) **to rave ~ about sth** délirer en parlant de qch

delirium [dɪ'lɪrɪəm] N (*pl* **delirium** *or* **deliria** [dɪ'lɪrɪə]) (*Med, fig*) délire m ; **bout of ~** accès m de délire ; **~ tremens** delirium m tremens

delist [di:'lɪst] VT (*St Ex: security*) radier du registre (des valeurs cotées en Bourse)

▼ **deliver** [dɪ'lɪvər] **1** VT **a** (= *take*) remettre (**to** à) ; [+ *letters etc*] distribuer (*à domicile*) ; [+ *goods*] livrer ; **to ~ a message to sb** remettre un message à qn ; **milk is ~ed each day** le lait est livré tous les jours ; (*Comm*) **"we ~ daily"** « livraisons quotidiennes » ; **"~ed free"** « livraison gratuite » ; **I will ~ the children to school tomorrow** j'emmènerai les enfants à l'école demain ; **to ~ a child (over) into sb's care** confier un enfant aux soins de qn ; (*fig*) **to ~ the goods*** être à la hauteur **b** (= *rescue*) délivrer, sauver (**sb from sth** qn de qch) ; **~ us from evil** délivrez-nous du mal **c** (= *utter*) [+ *speech, sermon*] prononcer ; **to ~ an ultimatum** lancer un ultimatum ; (*frm*) **to ~ o.s. of an opinion** émettre une opinion **d** (*Med*) [+ *baby*] mettre au monde ; [+ *woman*] (faire) accoucher ; (*frm*) **to be ~ed of a son** accoucher d'un fils **e** (= *hand over: also* ~ **over,** ~ **up**) remettre, transmettre ; **to ~ a town (up** *or* **over) into the hands of the enemy** livrer une ville à l'ennemi → **stand f** [+ *blow*] porter, assener **2** VI (* = *do what is expected*) [*person, nation, government etc*] être à la hauteur (**on sth** quant à qch) ; [*machine etc*] faire le travail ; **the match promised great things but didn't ~** le match promettait beaucoup mais n'a pas été à la hauteur (de ce qu'on en attendait)

deliverance [dɪ'lɪvərəns] N **a** (*NonC*) délivrance f, libération f (**from** de) **b** (= *statement of opinion*) déclaration f (formelle) ; (*Jur*) prononcé m (du jugement)

deliverer [dɪ'lɪvərər] N **a** (= *saviour*) sauveur m, libérateur m, -trice f **b** (*Comm*) livreur m

▼ **delivery** [dɪ'lɪvərɪ] **1** N **a** [*of goods*] livraison f ; [*of parcels*] remise f, livraison f ; [*of letters*] distribution f ; **to take ~ of** prendre livraison de ; **to pay on ~** payer à la *or* sur livraison ; **payable on ~** payable à la livraison ; (*Comm*) **price on ~** (*gen*) prix m à la livraison ; (*of car*) prix m clés en main → **charge, free**

b (*Med*) accouchement m
c (*NonC*) [*of speaker*] débit m, élocution f ; [*of speech*] débit m ; **his speech was interesting but his ~ dreary** son discours était intéressant mais son débit monotone
2 COMP ► **delivery charge** N frais *mpl* de port ► **delivery man** N (*pl* **delivery men**) livreur m ► **delivery note** N bulletin m de livraison ► **delivery order** N bon m de livraison ► **delivery room** N (*Med*) salle f d'accouchement ► **delivery service** N service m de livraison ► **delivery time** N délai m de livraison ► **delivery truck** N (*esp US*) ► **delivery van** ► **delivery van** N camionnette f de livraison

dell [del] N vallon m

delouse ['di:'laʊs] VT [+ *person, animal*] épouiller ; [+ *object*] ôter les poux de

Delphi ['delfaɪ] N Delphes f

Delphic ['delfɪk] ADJ [*oracle*] de Delphes ; (*fig liter*) obscur

delphinium [del'fɪnɪəm] N (*pl* **delphiniums** *or* **delphinia** [del'fɪnɪə]) pied-d'alouette m, delphinium m

delta ['deltə] **1** N delta m **2** COMP ► **delta-winged** ADJ (*Aviat*) à ailes (en) delta

deltoid ['deltɔɪd] ADJ, N deltoïde m

delude [dɪ'lu:d] VT tromper, duper (**with** par), induire en erreur (**with** par) ; **to ~ sb into thinking that ...** amener qn à penser que ..., faire croire à qn que ... ; **to ~ o.s.** se faire des illusions, se bercer d'illusions

deluded [dɪ'lu:dɪd] ADJ **to be ~** être victime d'illusions, être bercé d'illusions

deluding [dɪ'lu:dɪŋ] ADJ trompeur, illusoire

deluge ['delju:dʒ] **1** N (*lit*) déluge m, inondation f ; (*fig*) déluge m ; **the Deluge** le Déluge ; **a ~ of rain** une pluie diluvienne ; **a ~ of protests** un déluge de protestations ; **a ~ of letters** une avalanche de lettres **2** VT (*lit, fig*) inonder, submerger (**with** de)

delusion [dɪ'lu:ʒən] N (= *false belief*) illusion f ; (*Psych*) fantasme m, hallucination f, psychose f paranoïaque ; **to suffer from ~s** être en proie à des fantasmes ; **to be (labouring) under a ~** être victime d'une illusion, être le jouet d'une illusion ; **~s of grandeur** folie f des grandeurs ; **happiness is a ~** le bonheur est une illusion

delusive [dɪ'lu:sɪv] ADJ trompeur, illusoire

delusiveness [dɪ'lu:sɪvnɪs] N caractère m trompeur *or* illusoire

delusory [dɪ'lu:sərɪ] ADJ trompeur, illusoire

de luxe [dɪ'lʌks] ADJ (*gen*) de luxe, somptueux ; **a ~ flat** un appartement (de) grand standing ; (*car, machine*) **~ model** modèle m (de) grand luxe

delve [delv] VI **a** (*into book etc*) fouiller (**into** dans) ; **to ~ into a subject** creuser *or* approfondir un sujet, étudier un sujet à fond ; **to ~ (down) into the past** fouiller le passé **b** (*in drawer etc*) fouiller (**into** dans) ; **to ~ into one's pockets** (*lit*) fouiller dans ses poches ; (*fig*) mettre la main au portefeuille **c** (= *dig*) creuser (**into** dans) ; (*with spade*) bêcher

Dem. (*US Pol*) **1** N ABBR = **Democrat 2** ADJ ABBR = **Democratic**

demagnetize [ˌdi:'mægnɪtaɪz] VT démagnétiser

demagog ['demagɒg] N (*US*) = **demagogue**

demagogic [ˌdemə'gɒgɪk] ADJ démagogique

demagogue, demagog (*US*) ['demagɒg] N démagogue mf

demagoguery [ˌdemə'gɒgərɪ] N agissements *mpl* *or* méthodes *fpl* de démagogue, démagogie f

demagogy ['demagɒgɪ] N démagogie f

de-man [ˌdi:'mæn] VT (*Brit Ind = reduce manpower*) réduire *or* dégraisser les effectifs de **b** (= *deprive of virility*) déviriliser

demand [dɪ'mɑ:nd] **1** VT [+ *money, explanation, help*] exiger, réclamer (**from, of** de) ; [+ *higher pay etc*] revendiquer, réclamer ; **to ~ to do** exiger de faire, demander expressément à faire ; **he ~s to be obeyed** il exige qu'on lui obéisse ; **he ~s that you leave at once** il exige que vous partiez (*subj*) tout de suite ; **a question/situation that ~s our attention** une question/une situation qui réclame *or* exige notre attention

2 N **a** [*of person*] exigence(s) f(*pl*), demande f ; [*of duty, problem, situation etc*] exigence(s) *fpl* ; (= *claim*) [*for better pay etc*] revendication f, réclamation f ; (*for help, money*) demande f ; **to feed a baby on ~** allaiter un bébé quand il le demande ; **payable on ~** payable sur demande *or* sur présentation ; **final ~ (for payment)** dernier avertissement m (d'avoir à payer) ; **to make ~s on sb** exiger beaucoup de qn *or* de la part de qn ; **you make too great ~s on my patience** vous abusez de ma patience ; **the ~s of the case** les nécessités *fpl* du cas ; **I have many ~s on my time** je suis très pris, mon temps est très pris **b** (*NonC: Comm, Econ*) demande f ; **the ~ for this product increases** ce produit est de plus en plus demandé ; **to create a ~ for a product** créer la demande pour un produit ; **do you stock suede hats? — no, there's no ~ for them** avez-vous des chapeaux en daim ? — non, il n'y a pas de demande → **supply¹ c** **to be in (great) ~** être très demandé *or* recherché

3 COMP ► **demand bill, demand draft** N (*Fin*) bon m *or* effet m à vue ► **demand feeding** N allaitement m à la demande ► **demand liabilities** NPL engagements *mpl* à vue ► **demand management** N (*Econ*) contrôle m (gouvernemental) de la demande ► **demand note** N = **demand bill**

demanding [dɪ'mɑ:ndɪŋ] ADJ **a** [*person*] exigeant **b** (= *taxing*) astreignant, difficile ; [*schedule*] éprouvant ; **physically ~** physiquement éprouvant, qui demande beaucoup de résistance physique ; **intellectually ~** qui demande un gros effort intellectuel ; **Stravinsky is the most intellectually ~ of all composers** Stravinski est le plus difficile d'accès de tous les compositeurs ; **working with children can be emotionally ~** travailler avec des enfants peut être très éprouvant sur le plan émotionnel

de-manning [ˌdi:'mænɪŋ] N (*Brit Ind*) licenciements *mpl*, réduction f des effectifs

demarcate ['di:mɑ:keɪt] VT délimiter

demarcation [ˌdi:mɑ:'keɪʃən] **1** N démarcation f, délimitation f **2** COMP ► **demarcation dispute** N conflit m d'attributions ► **demarcation line** N ligne f de démarcation

démarche ['deɪmɑ:ʃ] N démarche f, mesure f

dematerialize [ˌdi:mə'tɪərɪəlaɪz] VI se dématérialiser

demean [dɪ'mi:n] VT [+ *person*] rabaisser, humilier ; [+ *thing*] rabaisser ; **to ~ o.s.** s'abaisser (**to do** à faire)

demeaning [dɪ'mi:nɪŋ] ADJ dégradant (**to** pour), humiliant (**to** pour)

demeanour, demeanor (*US*) [dɪ'mi:nər] N (= *behaviour*) comportement m, conduite f ; (= *bearing*) maintien m

demented [dɪ'mentɪd] ADJ **a** (* = *crazy*) fou (folle f) **b** (*Med*) dément ; **to become ~** sombrer dans la démence

dementedly [dɪ'mentɪdlɪ] ADV comme un fou (*or* une folle)

dementia [dɪ'menʃɪə] **1** N démence f → **senile 2** COMP ► **dementia praecox** N démence f précoce

demerara [ˌdemə'rɛərə] N (*Brit: also* ~ **sugar**) sucre m roux (cristallisé), cassonade f

demerge [ˌdiːˈmɜːdʒ] VT (Brit) [+ company] défusionner

demerger [ˌdiːˈmɜːdʒəʳ] N (Brit) scission f

demerit [diːˈmerɪt] N démérite m; (US Scol) ~ **(point)** avertissement m, blâme m

demesne [dɪˈmeɪn] N domaine m, terre f; (Jur) possession f; (Jur) **to hold sth in** ~ posséder qch en toute propriété

demi... [ˈdemɪ] PREF demi-; ~**god** demi-dieu m

demijohn [ˈdemɪdʒɒn] N dame-jeanne f, bonbonne f

demilitarization [ˈdiːˌmɪlɪtəraɪˈzeɪʃən] N démilitarisation f

demilitarize [diːˈmɪlɪtəraɪz] 1 VT démilitariser 2 COMP ► **demilitarized zone** N zone f démilitarisée

demise [dɪˈmaɪz] 1 N a (frm, hum = death) décès m, mort f; (fig) [of institution, custom etc] mort f, fin f b (Jur) (by legacy) cession f or transfert m par legs, transfert m par testament; (by lease) transfert m par bail; ~ **of the Crown** transmission f de la Couronne (par décès ou abdication) 2 VT (Jur) [+ estate] léguer; [+ the Crown, sovereignty] transmettre

demisemiquaver [ˈdemɪsemɪˌkweɪvəʳ] N (Brit) triple croche f

demist [diːˈmɪst] VT désembuer

demister [diːˈmɪstəʳ] N (Brit Aut) dispositif m antibuée

demisting [diːˈmɪstɪŋ] N désembuage m

demitasse [ˈdemɪtæs] N (US) (= cup) tasse f (à moka), (= drink) (tasse f de) café m noir

demi-vegetarian [ˌdemɪvedʒɪˈteərɪən] N personne qui ne mange pas de viande rouge

demo* [ˈdeməʊ] N a (Brit) (ABBR = **demonstration**) manif* f b (US) = **demonstration model**; → **demonstration** c (US) = **demolition worker**; → **demolition** d = **demonstration record**; → **demonstration**

demob* [ˈdiːˈmɒb] VT, N (Brit) ABBR = **demobilize, demobilization**

demobilization [ˈdiːˌməʊbɪlaɪˈzeɪʃən] N démobilisation f

demobilize [diːˈməʊbɪlaɪz] VT démobiliser

democracy [dɪˈmɒkrəsɪ] N démocratie f; **they are working towards** ~ ils sont en train de se démocratiser → **people**

Democrat [ˈdeməkræt] N a (Brit Pol) (libéral) démocrate mf b (US Pol) démocrate mf

democrat [ˈdeməkræt] N démocrate mf

democratic [ˌdeməˈkrætɪk] ADJ a (Pol) [institution, organization, spirit] démocratique b (US Pol) **Democratic** démocrate; **the Democratic Party** le parti démocrate; **the Democratic Republic of ...** la République démocratique de ... → **Christian, liberal, social** c (= egalitarian) [boss, management style, atmosphere] démocratique, non directif

democratically [ˌdeməˈkrætɪkəlɪ] ADV démocratiquement; ~ **elected** démocratiquement élu; **to be** ~ **minded** être démocratique

democratization [dɪˌmɒkrətaɪˈzeɪʃən] N démocratisation f

democratize [dɪˈmɒkrətaɪz] 1 VT démocratiser 2 VI se démocratiser

demographer [dɪˈmɒɡrəfəʳ] N démographe mf

demographic [ˌdeməˈɡræfɪk] ADJ démographique

demographics [ˌdeməˈɡræfɪks] NPL données fpl démographiques; [of market] profil m démographique; **the** ~ **of housing demand** les données démographiques concernant la demande de logement

demography [dɪˈmɒɡrəfɪ] N démographie f

demolish [dɪˈmɒlɪʃ] VT [+ building] démolir, abattre; [+ fortifications] démanteler; (fig) [+ theory] démolir, détruire;* [+ cake] liquider*, dire deux mots à*

demolisher [dɪˈmɒlɪʃəʳ] N (lit, fig) démolisseur m

demolition [ˌdeməˈlɪʃən] 1 N démolition f 2 COMP ► **demolition area** N = **demolition zone** ► **demolition squad** N équipe f de démolition ► **demolition work** N (travail m de) démolition ► **demolition worker** N démolisseur m ► **demolition zone** N zone f de démolition

demon [ˈdiːmən] N (all senses) démon m; **the Demon** le Démon; **the Demon drink** le démon de la boisson; **that child's a ~!*** cet enfant est un petit démon!; **to be a ~ for work** être un bourreau de travail; **a ~ driver** (skilful) un as* du volant; (dangerous) un conducteur pris de folie; **he's a ~ squash player** etc il joue au squash etc comme un dieu

demonetization [diːˌmʌnɪtaɪˈzeɪʃən] N démonétisation f

demonetize [diːˈmʌnɪtaɪz] VT démonétiser

demoniac [dɪˈməʊnɪæk] ADJ, N démoniaque mf

demoniacal [ˌdiːməʊˈnaɪəkəl] ADJ démoniaque, diabolique; ~ **possession** possession f diabolique

demonic [diːˈmɒnɪk, dɪˈmɒnɪk] ADJ démoniaque, diabolique

demonize [ˈdiːmənaɪz] VT diaboliser

demonology [ˌdiːməˈnɒlədʒɪ] N démonologie f

demonstrable [ˈdemənstrəbl] ADJ démontrable

demonstrably [ˈdemənstrəblɪ] ADV manifestement

▼ **demonstrate** [ˈdemənstreɪt] 1 VT a [+ truth, need] démontrer, prouver; **to ~ that ...** démontrer or prouver que ... b [+ appliance] faire une démonstration de; [+ system] expliquer, décrire; **to ~ how sth works** montrer le fonctionnement de qch, faire une démonstration de qch; **to ~ how to do sth** montrer comment faire qch 2 VI (Pol etc) manifester, faire or organiser une manifestation (**for** pour, **in favour of** en faveur de, **against** contre)

demonstration [ˌdemənˈstreɪʃən] 1 N a (NonC) [of truth etc] démonstration f b (Comm) démonstration f; **to give a ~ (of)** faire une démonstration (de) c (Pol etc) manifestation f; **to hold a ~** manifester, faire or organiser une manifestation d [of love, affection] manifestations fpl, témoignage(s) m(pl) 2 COMP [car, lecture, tape, diskette] de démonstration ► **demonstration model** N modèle m de démonstration

demonstrative [dɪˈmɒnstrətɪv] ADJ [behaviour, person] démonstratif, expansif; (Gram, Math, Philos) démonstratif

demonstrator [ˈdemənstreɪtəʳ] N a (= person) (Comm) démonstrateur m, -trice f; (Educ) préparateur m, -trice f; (Pol) manifestant(e) m(f) b (= appliance) appareil m (or article m) de démonstration; (= car) voiture f de démonstration

demoralization [dɪˌmɒrəlaɪˈzeɪʃən] N démoralisation f

demoralize [dɪˈmɒrəlaɪz] VT démoraliser; **to become ~d** perdre courage, être démoralisé

demoralizing [dɪˈmɒrəlaɪzɪŋ] ADJ démoralisant

demote [dɪˈməʊt] VT (also Mil) rétrograder

demotic [dɪˈmɒtɪk] 1 ADJ a (= of the people) populaire b (Ling) démotique 2 N démotique f

demotion [dɪˈməʊʃən] N rétrogradation f

demotivate [ˌdiːˈməʊtɪveɪt] VT démotiver

demulcent [dɪˈmʌlsənt] ADJ, N (Med) émollient m, adoucissant m

demur [dɪˈmɜːʳ] 1 VI rechigner (**at sth** devant qch, **at doing** à faire); (Jur) opposer une ex-

ception 2 N réserve f, objection f; **without** ~ sans hésiter, sans faire de difficultés

demure [dɪˈmjʊəʳ] ADJ [smile, look, girl] modeste, sage; [child] très sage; **a ~ hat** un petit chapeau bien sage

demurely [dɪˈmjʊəlɪ] ADV (= modestly) [smile, move] d'un air modeste or sage; [speak] d'un ton modeste; [behave] sagement, de façon modeste; ~ **dressed (in)** sagement habillé (de)

demureness [dɪˈmjʊənɪs] N (= modesty) [of person] air m sage; [of clothes] allure f sage; (pej = coyness) modestie f affectée

demurrage [dɪˈmʌrɪdʒ] N (Jur) surestarie f; **goods in** ~ marchandises fpl en souffrance (sur le quai)

demurrer [dɪˈmʌrəʳ] N (Jur) ≈ exception f péremptoire

demystification [diːˌmɪstɪfɪˈkeɪʃən] N démystification f

demystify [diːˈmɪstɪˌfaɪ] VT démystifier

demythification [diːˌmɪθɪfɪˈkeɪʃən] N démythification f

demythify [diːˈmɪθɪˌfaɪ] VT démythifier

den [den] N a [of lion, tiger] tanière f, antre m; [of thieves] repaire m, antre m; (lit, fig) **the lion's** ~ l'antre m du lion; ~ **of iniquity** or **vice** lieu m de perdition or de débauche → **gambling, opium** b (= room, study) antre m ► **den up*** VI (US) se retirer dans sa piaule*

denationalization [ˈdiːˌnæʃnələʳˈzeɪʃən] N dénationalisation f

denationalize [diːˈnæʃnəlaɪz] VT dénationaliser

denature [ˌdiːˈneɪtʃəʳ] VT dénaturer

dengue [ˈdeŋɡɪ] N dengue f

deniability [dɪˌnaɪəˈbɪlɪtɪ] N (NonC) possibilité f de démenti

deniable [dɪˈnaɪəbl] ADJ (Pol) ~ **operation** opération confidentielle dont les commanditaires déclineront toute responsabilité

denial [dɪˈnaɪəl] N a [of rights, truth] dénégation f; [of report, accusation] démenti m; [of guilt] dénégation f; [of authority] rejet m; ~ **of justice** déni m (de justice); ~ **of self** abnégation f; **he met the accusation with a flat** ~ il a nié catégoriquement l'accusation; **to issue a** ~ publier un démenti b (Psych) dénégation f, déni m; (fig) **AIDS will not be stopped by inertia and** ~ on n'arrêtera pas le sida par l'immobilisme et la négation des faits; **to be in** ~ **about sth** refuser d'admettre qch c **Peter's** ~ **of Christ** le reniement du Christ par Pierre

denier [ˈdenɪəʳ] N a (= weight) denier m; **25 ~ stockings** bas mpl 25 deniers b (= coin) denier m

denigrate [ˈdenɪɡreɪt] VT dénigrer, discréditer

denigration [ˌdenɪˈɡreɪʃən] N dénigrement m

denim [ˈdenɪm] 1 N (for jeans, skirts etc) (toile f de) jean m; (heavier: for uniforms, overalls etc) treillis m 2 **denims** NPL (= jeans) blue-jean m, jean m; (= workman's overalls) bleus mpl de travail

denizen [ˈdenɪzn] N a (= inhabitant) habitant(e) m(f); ~**s of the forest** habitants mpl or hôtes mpl (liter) des forêts b (Brit Jur) étranger m, -ère f (ayant droit de cité) c (= naturalized plant/animal) plante f/animal m acclimaté(e)

Denmark [ˈdenmɑːk] N le Danemark

denominate [dɪˈnɒmɪneɪt] VT dénommer

denomination [dɪˌnɒmɪˈneɪʃən] N a (= group) groupe m, catégorie f; (Rel) confession f; [of money] valeur f; [of weight, measure] unité f b (NonC) dénomination f, appellation f

denominational [dɪˌnɒmɪˈneɪʃənl] 1 ADJ (Rel) confessionnel, appartenant à une confession 2 COMP ► **denominational college** N (US) université f confessionnelle ► **denominational school** N (US) école f libre or confessionnelle

---

► LANGUAGE IN USE: **demonstrate** 26.1

denominative [dɪˈnɒmɪnətɪv] ADJ, N dénominatif *m*

denominator [dɪˈnɒmɪneɪtəʳ] N dénominateur *m* → **common**

denotation [ˌdiːnəʊˈteɪʃən] N **a** (NonC) (gen, also Ling, Philos) dénotation *f*; (= meaning) signification *f* **b** (= symbol) indices *mpl*, signes *mpl*

denotative [dɪˈnəʊtətɪv] ADJ (Ling) dénotatif *m*

denote [dɪˈnəʊt] VT (= indicate) dénoter, indiquer; (= mean) signifier; (Ling, Philos) dénoter

denouement, dénouement [deɪˈnuːmɑ̃] N dénouement *m*

denounce [dɪˈnaʊns] VT [+ person, treaty, act] dénoncer (to à); **to ~ sb as an impostor** accuser publiquement qn d'imposture

denouncement [dɪˈnaʊnsmənt] N = **denunciation**

denouncer [dɪˈnaʊnsəʳ] N dénonciateur *m*, -trice *f*

dense [dens] ADJ **a** (lit, fig: also Phys) [fog, crowd, vegetation, prose etc] dense **b** (* = stupid) bouché*

densely [ˈdensli] ADV ~ **populated** densément peuplé, à forte densité démographique; ~ **packed** plein à craquer; ~ **wooded** très boisé

denseness [ˈdensnɪs] N **a** (gen) densité *f* **b** (* = stupidity) stupidité *f*

densitometer [ˌdensɪˈtɒmɪtəʳ] N densimètre *m*

density [ˈdensɪtɪ] N densité *f*; **double/high/single ~ diskette** disquette *f* double/haute/simple densité

dent [dent] **1** N (in wood) entaille *f*; (in metal) bosse *f*, bosselure *f*; (Aut) **to have a ~ in the bumper** avoir le parechoc bosselé or cabossé; (fig) **to make a ~ in** [+ savings, budget] faire un trou dans; [+ sb's enthusiasm, confidence] ébranler **2** VT [+ hat] cabosser; [+ car] bosseler, cabosser; [+ wood] entailler

dental [ˈdentl] **1** ADJ **a** [treatment, school] dentaire **b** (Ling) dental **2** N (Ling) dentale *f* **3** COMP ► **dental floss** N fil *m* dentaire ► **dental hygiene** N hygiène *f* dentaire ► **dental hygienist** N hygiéniste *mf* dentaire ► **dental nurse** N assistant(e) *m(f)* de dentiste ► **dental receptionist** N réceptionniste *mf* dans un cabinet dentaire ► **dental surgeon** N chirurgien *m* dentiste ► **dental surgery** N cabinet *m* dentaire or de dentiste ► **dental technician** N mécanicien(ne) *m(f)* dentiste

dentifrice [ˈdentɪfrɪs] N dentifrice *m*

dentine [ˈdentiːn] N dentine *f*

dentist [ˈdentɪst] N dentiste *mf*; ~**'s chair** fauteuil *m* de dentiste; ~**'s surgery** cabinet *m* dentaire or de dentiste; **to go to the ~('s)** aller chez le dentiste

dentistry [ˈdentɪstrɪ] N dentisterie *f*; **to study ~** faire des études dentaires, faire l'école dentaire

dentition [denˈtɪʃən] N dentition *f*

denture(s) [ˈdentʃə(ʳ-ʃəz)] N(PL) dentier *m*, râtelier† *m* (hum)

denude [dɪˈnjuːd] VT (lit, fig) dénuder, dépouiller; ~**d landscape** paysage *m* nu or dépouillé; **area ~d of trees** région *f* dépouillée d'arbres

denunciation [dɪˌnʌnsɪˈeɪʃən] N [of person] dénonciation *f*; (in public) accusation *f* publique, condamnation *f*; [of action] dénonciation *f*; [of treaty] dénonciation *f*

denunciator [dɪˈnʌnsɪeɪtəʳ] N dénonciateur *m*, -trice *f*

▼**deny** [dɪˈnaɪ] VT **a** (= repudiate) nier (**having done** avoir fait, **that** que + indic or subj); [+ fact, accusation] nier, refuser d'admettre; [+ sb's authority] rejeter; **there is no ~ing it** c'est indéniable; **I'm not ~ing the truth of it** je ne nie pas que ce soit vrai **b** (= refuse) **to ~ sb sth** refuser qch à qn, priver qn de qch; **he**

was **denied admittance** on lui a refusé l'entrée; **to ~ o.s. cigarettes** se priver de cigarettes; **to ~ sb the right to do** refuser or dénier à qn le droit de faire **c** (= disown) [+ leader, religion] renier

deodorant [diːˈəʊdərənt] ADJ, N (gen) déodorant *m*; (= air-freshener) désodorisant *m*

deodorize [diːˈəʊdəraɪz] VT désodoriser

deontology [ˌdiːɒnˈtɒlədʒɪ] N déontologie *f*

deoxidize [diːˈɒksɪdaɪz] VT désoxyder

deoxygenate [diːˈɒksɪdʒəneɪt] VT désoxygéner

deoxyribonucleic [diːˌɒksɪˌraɪbəʊnjuːˈkleɪɪk] ADJ ~ **acid** acide *m* désoxyribonucléique

dep. (ABBR = **departs, departure**) (on timetable) dép., départ

depart [dɪˈpɑːt] **1** VI **a** (= go away) [person] partir, s'en aller; [bus, plane, train etc] partir; **to ~ from a city** quitter une ville, partir or s'en aller d'une ville; **to be about to ~** être sur le or son départ **b** (fig) **to ~ from** (gen) s'écarter de; [+ habit, principle, the truth] faire une entorse à **2** VT (esp Rail, Aviat etc) partir de, quitter; (on timetable etc) **"~ing London at 12.40"** « départ de Londres (à) 12.40 »; (liter) **to ~ this world** or **this life** quitter ce monde, trépasser (liter)

departed [dɪˈpɑːtɪd] **1** ADJ **a** (liter = dead) défunt; **the ~ leader** le chef défunt, le défunt chef **b** (= bygone) [glory, happiness] passé; [friends] disparu **2** N (liter) **the ~** le défunt, la défunte, les défunts *mpl*; **the dear(ly) ~** le cher disparu, la chère disparue, les chers disparus *mpl*

department [dɪˈpɑːtmənt] **1** N (in office, firm) service *m*; [of shop, store] rayon *m*; [of smaller shop] comptoir *m*; (Scol) section *f*; (Univ) ≈ UFR *f* (unité de formation et de recherche), ≈ département *m*; (also **government ~**) ministère *m*, département *m*; (French Admin, Geog) département *m*; (fig = field of activity) domaine *m*, rayon *m*; (Comm) **he works in the sales ~** il travaille au service des ventes; **in all the ~s of public service** dans tous les services publics; (Comm) **the shoe ~** le rayon des chaussures; **the French Department** (Scol) la section de français; (Univ) l'UFR *f* or le département de français; **gardening is my wife's ~*** le jardinage, c'est le rayon de ma femme → **head, state 2** COMP ► **department chairman** N (pl **department chairmen**) (Univ) ≈ directeur *m*, -trice *f* d'UFR ► **department head** = **department chairman** ► **Department of Health** N (Brit) ministère *m* de la Santé ► **Department of Social Security** N (Brit) ≈ Sécurité *f* sociale; → DSS; → **education, trade** ► **department store** N grand magasin *m*

departmental [ˌdiːpɑːtˈmentl] ADJ **a** (gen) du département; (in office, firm) du service; **a ~ meeting** une réunion du département (or du service); **the ~ budget** le budget du département (or du service); **~ manager** or **head** chef *m* de service **b** (= of a French area) départemental

departmentalization [ˌdiːpɑːtˌmentəlaɪˈzeɪʃən] N organisation *f* en départements

departmentalize [ˌdiːpɑːtˈmentəlaɪz] VT organiser en départements

departure [dɪˈpɑːtʃəʳ] **1** N **a** (from place) [of person, vehicle] départ *m*; (from job) départ *m*, démission *f*; **on the point of ~** sur le point de partir, sur le départ → **arrival b** (from custom, principle) dérogation *f*, entorse *f* (**from** à); (from law) manquement *m* (**from** à); **a ~ from the norm** une exception; **a ~ from the truth** une entorse à la vérité **c** (= change of course, action) nouvelle voie *f* or orientation *f* or direction *f*; (Comm = new type of goods) nouveauté *f*, innovation *f*; **it's a new ~ in biochemistry** c'est une nouvelle voie qui s'ouvre en or pour la biochimie **d** (liter = death) trépas *m* (liter)

2 COMP [preparations etc] de départ ► **departure board** N (Aviat, Rail) tableau *m* des départs ► **departure gate** N (Aviat) porte *f* d'embarquement ► **departure lounge** N (Aviat) salle *f* d'embarquement ► **departure platform** N (Rail) quai *m* (de départ) ► **departure signal** N (Rail) signal *m* de départ ► **departure time** N heure *f* de départ

▼**depend** [dɪˈpend] IMPERS VI dépendre (**on sb/sth** de qn/qch); **it all ~s** ◊ **that ~s** cela dépend, c'est selon*; **it ~s on you whether he comes or not** cela dépend de vous or il ne tient qu'à vous qu'il vienne ou non; **it ~s (on) whether he will do it or not** cela dépend s'il veut le faire ou non; **it ~s (on) what you mean** cela dépend de ce que vous voulez dire; ~**ing on the weather** selon le temps; ~**ing on what happens tomorrow ...** selon ce qui se passera demain ...

► **depend (up)on** VT FUS **a** (= count on) compter sur; (= be completely reliant on) se reposer sur; **you can always ~ (up)on him** on peut toujours compter sur lui; **he ~s (up)on her for everything** il se repose sur elle pour tout; **you may ~ (up)on his coming** vous pouvez compter qu'il viendra or compter sur sa venue; **I'm ~ing (up)on you to tell me what he wants** je compte sur vous pour savoir ce qu'il veut; **you can ~ (up)on it** soyez-en sûr, je vous le promets or garantis; **you can ~ (up)on it that he'll forget again** tu peux être sûr (et certain) qu'il va encore oublier **b** (= need support or help from) dépendre de; **he ~s (up)on his father for pocket money** il dépend de son père pour son argent de poche; **I'm ~ing (up)on you for moral support** votre appui moral m'est indispensable; **your success ~s (up)on your efforts** votre succès dépendra de vos efforts

dependability [dɪˌpendəˈbɪlɪtɪ] N [of machine] sécurité *f* de fonctionnement; [of person] sérieux *m*; **his ~ is well-known** tout le monde sait que l'on peut compter sur lui

dependable [dɪˈpendəbl] ADJ [person] sûr, sur qui on peut compter; [mechanism, machine, car] fiable; [information] sûr; **he is not ~** on ne peut pas compter sur lui

dependably [dɪˈpendəblɪ] ADV de façon fiable

dependance [dɪˈpendəns] N = **dependence**

dependant [dɪˈpendənt] N personne *f* à charge, charge *f* de famille; **he had many ~s** il avait de nombreuses personnes à (sa) charge

dependence [dɪˈpendəns] N **a** (= state of depending: also **dependency**) dépendance *f* (**on, à** l'égard de, envers), sujétion *f* (**on** à); ~ **on one's parents** dépendance *f* à l'égard de or envers ses parents; ~ **on drugs** (état *m* de) dépendance *f* à l'égard de la drogue **b** **the ~ of success upon effort** le rapport entre le succès et l'effort fourni

dependency [dɪˈpendənsɪ] **1** N **a** = **dependence a b** (Ling) dépendance *f* **c** (= country) dépendance *f*, colonie *f* **2** COMP ► **dependency allowance** N (Jur) indemnité *f* pour charges de famille ► **dependency grammar** N (Ling) grammaire *f* dépendancielle

dependent [dɪˈpendənt] **1** ADJ **a** (= reliant) [person] dépendant (**on** de); **to be (heavily) ~ on sth** dépendre (beaucoup or fortement) de qch; **to be ~ on sb to do sth** dépendre de qn pour faire qch; **drug-~** ◊ **chemically ~** (on illegal drugs) toxicomane; (on medical drugs) en état de dépendance aux médicaments; **insulin-~** insulinodépendant **b** (financially) [child, relative] à charge; **families with ~ children** les familles ayant des enfants à charge; **to be financially ~ on sb** dépendre financièrement de qn **c** (= contingent) **to be ~ on or upon sth** dépendre de qch; **the results are ~ upon which programme you follow** les résultats dépendent du programme que vous

suivez [d] (*Gram*) [*clause*] subordonné
[e] (*Math*) dépendant; **~ variable** variable *f*
dépendante [2] N = **dependant**

depersonalize [diːˈpɜːsənəlaɪz]   VT dépersonnaliser

depict [dɪˈpɪkt]   VT (*in words*) dépeindre, décrire; (*in picture*) représenter; **surprise was ~ed
on his face** la surprise se lisait sur son visage,
son visage exprimait la surprise

depiction [dɪˈpɪkʃən] N (*pictorial*) représentation *f*; (*written*) description *f*; **the artist's ~ of
war as a roaring lion** la représentation de la
guerre par l'artiste sous la forme d'un lion rugissant; **the ~ of socialists as Utopian dream-
ers** l'image de rêveurs utopistes que l'on
donne des socialistes

depilate [ˈdepɪleɪt] VT épiler

depilatory [dɪˈpɪlətərɪ] ADJ, N dépilatoire *m*

deplane [ˌdiːˈpleɪn] VI descendre d'avion

deplenish [dɪˈplenɪʃ] VT (= *reduce*) dégarnir;
(= *empty*) vider

deplete [dɪˈpliːt] VT [a] (= *reduce*) [+ *supplies,
funds*] réduire; [+ *strength*] diminuer, réduire;
(= *exhaust*) [+ *supplies, strength*] épuiser;
(*Comm*) **our stock is very ~d** nos stocks sont
très bas; (*Mil*) **the regiment was greatly ~d** (*by
cuts etc*) l'effectif du régiment était très réduit; (*by war, sickness*) le régiment a été déci-
mé; **numbers were greatly ~d** les effectifs
étaient très réduits [b] (*Med*) décongestionner

depletion [dɪˈpliːʃən] N [*of resources, nutrients*]
diminution *f*; [*of funds*] réduction *f* → **ozone**

deplorable [dɪˈplɔːrəbl]   ADJ déplorable, lamentable

deplorably [dɪˈplɔːrəblɪ] ADV (*with vb*) [*behave*]
de façon déplorable; (*with adj*) déplorablement; **ours is a ~ materialistic society** notre
société est d'un matérialisme déplorable; **~,
he refused to take action** il a refusé d'agir, ce
qui est déplorable

▼ **deplore** [dɪˈplɔːr]   VT déplorer, regretter vivement; **to ~ the fact that ...** déplorer le fait que
... (+ *indic*), regretter vivement que ... (+ *subj*)

deploy [dɪˈplɔɪ] [1] VT (*Mil*) [+ *missiles, ships,
tanks, troops etc*] déployer; (*gen*) [+ *resources,
equipment*] faire usage de, utiliser; [+ *staff*]
utiliser (les services de); [+ *skills, talents*] déployer, faire preuve de [2] VI (*Mil*) être déployé

deployment [dɪˈplɔɪmənt] N (*Mil*) déploiement *m*; (*fig*) usage *m*, utilisation *f* → **rapid**

depolarization [ˈdiːˌpəʊləraɪˈzeɪʃən] N dépolarisation *f*

depolarize [diːˈpəʊləraɪz] VT dépolariser

depoliticize [ˌdiːˈpɒlɪtɪsaɪz] VT dépolitiser

deponent [dɪˈpəʊnənt] [1] N [a] (*Gram*) déponent *m* [b] (*Jur*) déposant(e) *m(f)* [2] ADJ
(*Gram*) déponent

depopulate [ˌdiːˈpɒpjʊleɪt] VT dépeupler; **to
become ~d** se dépeupler

depopulation [ˈdiːˌpɒpjʊˈleɪʃən] N dépopulation *f*, dépeuplement *m*; **rural ~** dépeuplement *m* des campagnes

deport [dɪˈpɔːt] VT [a] (= *expel*) expulser (**from**
de); (= *transport*) déporter (**from** de, **to** à);
(*Hist*) [+ *prisoner*] déporter [b] (= *behave*) **to ~
o.s.**† se comporter, se conduire

deportation [ˌdiːpɔːˈteɪʃən] [1] N expulsion *f*;
(*Hist*) déportation *f*; (*Jur*) [2] COMP
► **deportation order** N arrêt *m* d'expulsion

deportee [ˌdiːpɔːˈtiː] N déporté(e) *m(f)*

deportment [dɪˈpɔːtmənt] N maintien *m*, tenue *f*; **~ lessons** leçons *fpl* de maintien

depose [dɪˈpəʊz] [1] VT [+ *king*] déposer, détrôner; [+ *official*] destituer [2] VTI (*Jur*) déposer, attester par déposition

deposit [dɪˈpɒzɪt] [1] VT [a] (= *put down*) [+
parcel etc] déposer, poser
[b] (*in bank account*) [+ *money*] verser, déposer;

[+ *cheque*] déposer; (*for safekeeping*) [+ *money,
valuables*] déposer, laisser or mettre en dépôt
(**with sb** chez qn); **I ~ed £200 in my account**
j'ai versé 200 livres à or sur mon compte, j'ai
déposé 200 livres à sur mon compte; **I ~ed a
cheque in my account** j'ai déposé un chèque
sur mon compte; **to ~ valuables in** or **with the
bank** déposer des objets de valeur à la
banque, laisser des objets de valeur en dépôt
à la banque
[c] (*Geol*) déposer, former un dépôt de
[2] N [a] (*in bank*) dépôt *m*; **to make a ~ of £50**
déposer or verser 50 livres
[b] (= *part payment*) (*on goods, holiday*) arrhes
fpl, acompte *m*; (*on house purchase*) acompte
m; (*in hire purchase* = *down payment*) premier
versement *m*; (*in hiring goods, renting
accommodation: against damage etc*) caution *f*;
(*on bottle, container*) consigne *f*; (*Brit Pol*) cautionnement *m* électoral; **to leave a ~ of £40** or
a £40 ~ on a washing machine verser 40 livres
d'arrhes or d'acompte sur un lave-linge; **to
pay a 5% ~** or **a ~ of 5% on a property** verser
5 % d'acompte sur une propriété; (*Comm*) **a
small ~ will secure any goods** on peut faire
mettre tout article de côté moyennant (le
versement d')un petit acompte; (*Brit Pol*) **to
lose one's ~** perdre son cautionnement (*en
obtenant un très faible score*)
[c] (*in wine, Chem, Geol*) dépôt *m*; [*of mineral,
oil*] gisement *m*; (*Anat*) **fat/cholesterol ~s** dépôt *m* graisseux/de cholestérol; **calcium ~s**
calcifications *fpl*; **to form a ~** se déposer
[3] COMP ► **deposit account** N (*Brit*)
compte *m* sur livret ► **deposit bank** N
banque *f* de dépôt ► **deposit loan** N prêt *m*
en nantissement ► **deposit slip** N bulletin
m de versement

depositary [dɪˈpɒzɪtərɪ] N [a] (= *person*) dépositaire *mf* [b] = **depository**

deposition [ˌdiːpəˈzɪʃən] N [a] (*NonC*) [*of king,
official*] déposition *f* [b] (*Jur*) déposition *f* sous
serment, témoignage *m*

depositor [dɪˈpɒzɪtər] N déposant(e) *m(f)*

depository [dɪˈpɒzɪtərɪ] N dépôt *m*, entrepôt
m

depot [ˈdepəʊ] [1] N [a] (*Mil*) dépôt *m* [b] (=
warehouse) dépôt *m*, entrepôt *m*; **coal ~** dépôt
m or entrepôt *m* de charbon [c] (= *railway station*) gare *f*; (= *bus station*) gare *m* [2] COMP
► **depot ship** N (navire *m*) ravitailleur *m*

depravation [ˌdeprəˈveɪʃən] N dépravation *f*,
corruption *f*

deprave [dɪˈpreɪv] VT dépraver, corrompre

depraved [dɪˈpreɪvd] ADJ dépravé, perverti; **to
become ~** se dépraver

depravity [dɪˈprævɪtɪ] N dépravation *f*,
perversion *f*

deprecate [ˈdeprɪkeɪt] VT [+ *action, behaviour*]
désapprouver, s'élever contre

deprecating [ˈdeprɪkeɪtɪŋ] ADJ (= *disapproving*)
désapprobateur (-trice *f*); (= *condescending*)
condescendant; (= *modest*) modeste

deprecatingly [ˈdeprɪkeɪtɪŋlɪ] ADV (= *disparagingly*) avec désapprobation; (= *condescendingly*) avec condescendance; (= *modestly*) avec
modestie

deprecatory [ˈdeprɪkətərɪ] ADJ = **deprecating**

depreciate [dɪˈpriːʃɪeɪt] [1] VT (*Fin*) [+ *property,
currency*] déprécier, dévaloriser; (= *write off
asset investment*) amortir; (*fig*) [+ *help, talent*]
déprécier, dénigrer; **to ~ sth by 25% a year**
amortir qch de 25 % or à un rythme de 25 %
par an [2] VI (*Fin, fig*) se déprécier, se dévaloriser

depreciation [dɪˌpriːʃɪˈeɪʃən] N [*of property,
car*] dépréciation *f*, perte *f* de valeur; [*of
currency*] dépréciation *f*, dévalorisation *f*;
(*Comm, Econ*) [*of goods*] moins-value *f*; (=
writing off) [*asset, investment*] amortissement
m; (*fig*) [*of talent etc*] dépréciation *f*, dénigrement *m*

depredation [ˌdeprɪˈdeɪʃən] N (*gen pl*) dépré-
dation(s) *f(pl)*, ravage(s) *m(pl)*

depress [dɪˈpres] VT [a] [+ *person*] déprimer
[b] [+ *lever*] abaisser [c] [+ *status*] réduire; [+
trade] réduire, (faire) diminuer; [+ *the market,
prices*] faire baisser

depressant [dɪˈpresnt] ADJ, N (*Med*) dé-
presseur *m*

depressed [dɪˈprest] ADJ [a] [*person*] déprimé
(**about** à cause de); **to feel ~** être or se sentir
déprimé; **to get ~** se laisser abattre; **to become ~** faire une dépression; **clinically ~** qui
souffre de dépression [b] [*region, market,
economy*] déprimé; [*industry*] en déclin; [*share
price*] bas [c] (= *sunken*) déprimé

depressing [dɪˈpresɪŋ] ADJ déprimant, décourageant; **I find it very ~** je trouve cela très déprimant or décourageant

depressingly [dɪˈpresɪŋlɪ] ADV **~ obvious**
d'une évidence déprimante; **~ familiar/
predictable** tellement familier/prévisible que
c'en est déprimant; **~, the new drug is no
more effective than the previous one** malheureusement, ce nouveau médicament n'est pas
plus efficace que le précédent

depression [dɪˈpreʃən] N [a] (*NonC*) (*Med*)
dépression *f* (nerveuse), état *m* dépressif;
(*Med*) **to suffer from ~** souffrir de dépression,
faire de la dépression; (*gen*) **to be in a bit of a
~** être déprimé; **her ~ at this news** son découragement en apprenant la nouvelle [b] (*Econ*)
dépression *f*; (*Hist*) **the Depression** la Grande
dépression; **the country's economy was in a
state of ~** l'économie du pays était en pleine
dépression [c] (*Geog*) dépression *f*; (*Met*) dépression *f* (atmosphérique); (*Met*) **a deep/
shallow** or **weak ~** une forte/faible dépression
[d] (= *hollow: in ground*) creux *m*

depressive [dɪˈpresɪv] ADJ, N (*Med*) dépressif
m, -ive *f*

depressurization [dɪˌpreʃəraɪˈzeɪʃən] N dépressurisation *f*

depressurize [dɪˈpreʃəˌraɪz] VT (*Phys etc*) dépressuriser; (*fig* = *take strain off*) [+ *person*] faciliter la vie à

deprivation [ˌdeprɪˈveɪʃən] N (= *act, state*) privation *f*; (= *loss*) perte *f*; (*Psych*) carence *f*
affective; (*Jur*) **~ of office** destitution *f* de
fonction → **maternal**

deprive [dɪˈpraɪv] VT (*of sleep, food, company*)
priver (**of** de); (*of right*) priver, déposséder (**of**
de); (*of asset*) ôter (**of** à), enlever (**of** à); **to be
~d of sth/sb** être privé de qch/qn; **to ~ o.s. of
...** se priver de ...

deprived [dɪˈpraɪvd] ADJ [*area, background,
child*] défavorisé

deprogramme,   **deprogram**   (*US*)
[ˌdiːˈprəʊɡræm] VT [+ *person*] déconditionner

dept ABBR = **department**

depth [depθ] [1] N [a] (= *deepness*) [*of water,
hole, shelf, cupboard*] profondeur *f*; [*of snow*]
épaisseur *f*; [*of edge, border*] largeur *f*; **at a ~ of
3 metres** à 3 mètres de profondeur, par 3 mètres de fond; **the water is 3 metres in ~** l'eau a
3 mètres de profondeur, il y a 3 mètres de
fond; (*lit, fig*) **to get out of one's ~** perdre
pied; (*in swimming pool etc*) **don't go out of
your ~** ne va pas là où tu n'as pas pied; (*fig*)
I'm completely out of my ~ je nage complètement*, je suis complètement dépassé*
[b] (= *lowness*) [*of voice, tone*] registre *m* grave
[c] (= *intensity*) [*of colour*] intensité *f*; **in the ~
of winter** au plus fort or au cœur de l'hiver;
wine with an excellent ~ of flavour vin *m* qui a
une belle complexité; **cheese with an excellent ~ of flavour** fromage *m* bien affiné
[d] (= *strength, profundity*) [*of knowledge, feeling,
sorrow, relief*] profondeur *f*; **a great ~ of feeling** une grande profondeur de sentiment; **he
had no idea of the ~ of feeling against him** il
ne se rendait pas compte du ressentiment
qu'il suscitait; **she has a tremendous breadth**

and ~ **of knowledge** ses connaissances sont extrêmement étendues et approfondies; **this illustrated the ~ of concern among young people for the elderly** cela a montré à quel point les jeunes gens se souciaient des personnes âgées; **politicians acknowledge the ~ of public interest in the environment** les hommes politiques se rendent compte à quel point le public s'intéresse à l'environnement; **there was little emotional ~ to their relationship** leurs sentiments l'un pour l'autre n'étaient pas très profonds; **to have intellectual ~** [*book, film*] être profond; [*person*] être (un esprit) profond; **to lack intellectual ~** manquer de profondeur; **he has no ~ of character** il manque de caractère; **in ~** en profondeur; **to interview sb in ~** faire une interview en profondeur de qn → **in** [e] (*Phot*) **~ of field** profondeur *f* de champ; **~ of focus** distance *f* focale

[2] **depths** NPL [a] (= *deep place*) **the ~s of the ocean** les profondeurs *fpl* océaniques; **from the ~s of the earth** des profondeurs *fpl* or des entrailles *fpl* de la terre; **in the ~s of the forest** au plus profond or au cœur de la forêt [b] (*fig*) fond *m*; **to be in the ~s of despair** toucher le fond du désespoir; **the country is in the ~s of recession** le pays est plongé dans une profonde récession; **to sink to new ~s of depravity** tomber encore plus bas dans la perversité; **in the ~s of winter** au plus fort or au cœur de l'hiver; **in the ~s of night** au milieu or au plus profond de la nuit; **I would never sink to such ~s as to do that** je ne tomberais jamais assez bas pour faire cela

[3] COMP ► **depth charge** N grenade *f* sous-marine ► **depth psychology** N psychologie *f* des profondeurs

deputation [ˌdepjʊˈteɪʃən] N délégation *f*, députation *f*

depute [dɪˈpjuːt] VT [+ *power, authority*] déléguer; [+ *person*] députer, déléguer (**sb to do** qn pour faire)

deputize [ˈdepjʊtaɪz] [1] VI assurer l'intérim (**for sb** de qn) [2] VT députer (**sb to do** qn pour faire)

deputy [ˈdepjʊtɪ] [1] N [a] (= *second in command*) adjoint(e) *m(f)*; (= *replacement*) remplaçant(e) *m(f)*, suppléant(e) *m(f)*; (*in business*) fondé *m* de pouvoir [b] (= *member of deputation*) délégué(e) *m(f)* [c] (*French Pol*) député *m* [d] (*US*) shérif *m* adjoint, ≈ gendarme *m* [2] ADJ [3] COMP ► **deputy chairman** N (*pl* deputy chairmen) vice-président *m* ► **deputy director** N sous-directeur *m*, -trice *f* ► **deputy head** N (*Scol*) (*gen*) directeur *m*, -trice *f* adjoint(e); (*of lycée*) censeur *m* ► **deputy headmaster, deputy headmistress** N (*Scol*) = **deputy head** ► **deputy judge** N juge *m* suppléant ► **deputy mayor** N maire *m* adjoint ► **Deputy Secretary** (*US*) ministre *m* adjoint ► **deputy sheriff** N (*US*) = **deputy 1d**

derail [dɪˈreɪl] [1] VT [+ *train*] faire dérailler; [+ *plan, negotiations*] faire avorter [2] VI dérailler

derailleur [dəˈreɪljər] N dérailleur *m*; **to have ~ gears** être muni d'un dérailleur

derailment [dɪˈreɪlmənt] N déraillement *m*

derange [dɪˈreɪndʒ] VT [a] [+ *plan*] déranger, troubler; [+ *machine*] dérégler [b] (*Med*) déranger (le cerveau de), aliéner

deranged [dɪˈreɪndʒd] ADJ dérangé; **to be (mentally) ~** avoir le cerveau dérangé

derangement [dɪˈreɪndʒmənt] N [a] (*Med*) aliénation *f* mentale [b] [*of machine*] dérèglement *m*

derate [diːˈreɪt] VT (*Tax*) [+ *land, property*] dégrever

derby [ˈdɑːbɪ, (*US*) ˈdɜːbɪ] N [a] (*Sport*) **local ~** match *m* entre équipes voisines; (*Brit Racing*) **the Derby** le Derby (d'Epsom) [b] (*US*) **~ (hat)** (chapeau *m*) melon *m*

Derbys. ABBR = **Derbyshire**

deregulate [diːˈregjʊˌleɪt] VT [+ *prices*] libérer; [+ *transport system*] déréglementer

deregulation [diːˌregjʊˈleɪʃən] N [*of prices*] libération *f*; [*of transport system*] déréglementation *f*

derelict [ˈderɪlɪkt] [1] ADJ [a] (= *abandoned*) abandonné; (= *ruined*) (tombé) en ruines [b] (*frm* = *neglectful of duty*) négligent [2] N [a] (*Naut*) navire *m* abandonné (*en mer*) [b] [*person*] épave *f* (humaine)

dereliction [ˌderɪˈlɪkʃən] [1] N [*of property*] état *m* d'abandon; [*of person*] délaissement *m* [2] COMP ► **dereliction of duty** N négligence *f* (dans le service), manquement *m* au devoir

derestricted [ˌdiːrɪˈstrɪktɪd] ADJ (*Brit*) [*road, area*] sans limitation de vitesse

deride [dɪˈraɪd] VT rire de, tourner en ridicule

derision [dɪˈrɪʒən] N dérision *f*; **object of ~** objet *m* de dérision or de risée

derisive [dɪˈraɪsɪv] ADJ [a] [*smile, person*] moqueur, railleur [b] [*amount, offer*] dérisoire

derisively [dɪˈraɪsɪvlɪ] ADV [*speak*] d'un ton moqueur; **he laughed ~** il eut un petit rire moqueur; **known ~ as "Dumbo"** connu sous le sobriquet de « Dumbo »

derisory [dɪˈraɪsərɪ] ADJ [a] [*amount, offer*] dérisoire [b] [*smile, person*] moqueur, railleur

derivation [ˌderɪˈveɪʃən] N dérivation *f*

derivative [dɪˈrɪvətɪv] [1] ADJ [a] (*Chem, Ling, Math*) dérivé; (*fig*) [*literary work etc*] peu original [2] N (*Chem, Ling*) dérivé *m*; (*Math*) dérivée *f*

derive [dɪˈraɪv] [1] VT [+ *profit, satisfaction*] tirer (**from** de), trouver (**from** dans); [+ *comfort, ideas*] puiser (**from** dans); [+ *name, origins*] tenir (**from** de); [+ *word*] (faire) dériver (**from** de); **to ~ one's happiness from ...** devoir son bonheur à ..., trouver son bonheur dans ...; **to be ~d from → 2** [2] VI **to ~ from** (*also* **be ~d from**) dériver de, provenir de, venir de; [*power, fortune*] provenir de; [*idea*] avoir sa source or ses origines dans; [*word*] dériver de; **it all ~s from the fact that ...** tout cela tient au fait que or provient du fait que ...

dermatitis [ˌdɜːməˈtaɪtɪs] N dermatite *f*, dermite *f*

dermatologist [ˌdɜːməˈtɒlədʒɪst] N dermatologue *mf*, dermatologiste *mf*

dermatology [ˌdɜːməˈtɒlədʒɪ] N dermatologie *f*

dermis [ˈdɜːmɪs] N derme *m*

derogate [ˈderəgeɪt] VI **to ~ from** porter atteinte à; **without derogating from his authority/his merits** sans rien enlever à or sans vouloir diminuer son autorité/ses mérites; (*liter*) **to ~ from one's position** déroger (à son rang) (*liter*)

derogation [ˌderəˈgeɪʃən] N [a] (= *reduction*) atteinte *f* (**from, of** à); **a ~ of sovereignty** une atteinte à la souveraineté [b] (*Pol* = *temporary exception: from a law, a rule*) report *m* d'application (**from** de)

derogatory [dɪˈrɒgətərɪ] ADJ [*remark*] désobligeant (**of, to** à), dénigrant; [*attitude*] de dénigrement

derrick [ˈderɪk] N [a] (= *lifting device, crane*) mât *m* de charge; (*above oil well*) derrick *m*

derring-do†† [ˈderɪŋˈduː] N bravoure *f*; **deeds of ~** hauts faits *mpl*, prouesses *fpl*

derringer [ˈderɪndʒər] N (*US*) pistolet *m* (court et à gros calibre), Derringer *m*

derv [dɜːv] N (*Brit Aut*) gasoil *m*

dervish [ˈdɜːvɪʃ] N derviche *m*

DES [ˌdiːiːˈes] N (*Brit: formerly*) (ABBR = **Department of Education and Science**) ≈ ministère *m* de l'Éducation

desalinate [diːˈsælɪneɪt] VT dessaler

---

desalination [diːˌsælɪˈneɪʃən] [1] N dessalement *m* [2] COMP ► **desalination plant** N usine *f* de dessalement

descale [diːˈskeɪl] [1] VT détartrer [2] COMP ► **descaling agent, descaling product** N (produit *m*) détartrant *m*

descant [ˈdeskænt] N déchant *m*; **to sing ~** chanter une partie du déchant

descend [dɪˈsend] [1] VI [a] (= *go down, come down*) [*person, vehicle, road, hill etc*] descendre (**from** de); [*rain, snow*] tomber; **in ~ing order of importance** par ordre d'importance décroissante; **to ~ into** [+ *alcoholism, madness, chaos, anarchy*] sombrer dans; **gloom ~ed (up)on him** il s'est assombri; **silence ~ed (up)on us** le silence se fit [b] (*by ancestry*) descendre, être issu (**from** de); [*plan, event etc*] tirer son origine (**from** de); **his family ~s from William the Conqueror** sa famille descend de Guillaume le Conquérant [c] (= *pass by inheritance*) [*property, customs, rights*] passer (par héritage) (**from** de, **to** à) [d] (= *attack or arrive suddenly: Mil, fig*) faire une descente (**on** sur); **the moment the news was out, reporters ~ed** dès que la nouvelle a été connue, les reporters ont afflué (sur les lieux); **to ~ (up)on sb** tomber sur qn les (up)on a town [*reporters, journalists, tourists, army*] envahir une ville; **to ~ (up)on a building** [*reporters, journalists, tourists*] se précipiter or affluer vers un bâtiment; [*army, police*] faire une descente dans un bâtiment; **visitors ~ed upon us** des gens sont arrivés (chez nous) sans crier gare [e] (= *lower o.s. to*) **to ~ to lies** or **to lying** s'abaisser à mentir; **I'd never ~ to that level** je ne m'abaisserais pas ainsi [2] VT [a] [+ *stairs*] descendre [b] **to be ~ed from** [+ *species*] descendre de; [+ *person*] descendre de, être issu de

descendant [dɪˈsendənt] N descendant(e) *m(f)*

descendeur [desɑːnˈdɜːr] N (*Climbing*) descendeur *m*

descendible [dɪˈsendəbl] ADJ (*Jur*) transmissible

descent [dɪˈsent] N [a] (= *going down*) [*of person*] descente *f* (**into** dans); (*fig: into crime etc*) chute *f*; (*Aviat, Sport*) descente *f*; [*of hill*] descente *f*, pente *f*; **the street made a sharp ~** la rue était très en pente or descendait en pente très raide; **~ by parachute** descente *f* en parachute [b] (= *ancestry*) origine *f*, famille *f*; **of noble ~** de noble extraction; **to trace one's ~ back to ...** faire remonter sa famille à ...; **to trace back the ~ of ...** établir la généalogie de ... [c] [*of property, customs etc*] transmission *f* (par héritage) (**to** à) [d] (*Mil etc* = *attack*) descente *f*, irruption *f*; **to make a ~ on the enemy camp** faire une descente sur or faire irruption dans le camp ennemi; **to make a ~ on the enemy** faire une descente sur l'ennemi

descramble [diːˈskræmbl] VT (*Telec*) désembrouiller; (*TV*) décoder, décrypter; **~d programme** émission *f* en clair

descrambler [diːˈskræmblər] N (*TV*) décodeur *m*

describe [dɪsˈkraɪb] VT [a] [+ *scene, person*] décrire; **~ what it is like** racontez or dites comment c'est; **~ him for us** décrivez-le-nous; **which cannot be ~d** indescriptible, qu'on ne saurait décrire [b] (= *represent*) décrire, représenter (**as** comme); **he ~s himself as a doctor** il se dit or se prétend docteur; **she ~s herself as ordinary** elle se présente or se décrit comme quelqu'un d'ordinaire [c] (*Math*) décrire

description [dɪsˈkrɪpʃən] N [a] [*of person, scene, object, event, situation*] description *f*; (*Police*) signalement *m*; **to give an accurate/lively ~** faire or donner une description exacte/vivante; **he gave a ~ of what happened/how he had escaped** il a décrit ce qui s'était

passé/la façon dont il s'était évadé ; **police have issued a ~ of the man they are looking for** la police a diffusé le signalement de l'homme qu'elle recherche ; **do you know anyone of this ~?** (*gen*) connaissez-vous quelqu'un qui ressemble à cette description ? ; (*Police*) connaissez-vous quelqu'un qui réponde à ce signalement ? ; **beyond** or **past ~** indescriptible, qu'on ne saurait décrire → **answer, beggar, defy, fit, job**
[b] (= *sort*) sorte *f* ; **people/vehicles of every ~** or **of all ~s** des gens/des véhicules de toutes sortes ; **food of every ~** or **of all ~s** toutes sortes d'aliments ; **he's a poet of some ~** c'est une sorte de poète ; **I need a bag of some ~** il me faut un sac, n'importe lequel

descriptive [dɪsˈkrɪptɪv] ADJ (*gen, also Ling*) descriptif ; **~ geometry/linguistics** géométrie *f*/linguistique *f* descriptive

descriptively [dɪsˈkrɪptɪvlɪ] ADV **the nickname "abominable snowman" is not so much ~ accurate as evocative** « l'abominable homme des neiges » n'est pas tant une description fidèle qu'un surnom évocateur ; **linguists try to study language ~, not prescriptively** les linguistes essaient d'étudier le langage d'un point de vue descriptif et non pas normatif ; **a cliff known ~ as "the Black Ladders"** une falaise connue sous le nom pittoresque de « Échelles noires »

descriptivism [dɪˈskrɪptɪvɪzəm] N (*Ling*) descriptivisme *m*

descriptivist [dɪˈskrɪptɪvɪst] N (*Ling*) descriptiviste *mf*

descry [dɪsˈkraɪ] VT discerner, distinguer

desecrate [ˈdesɪkreɪt] VT [+ *shrine, memory*] profaner, souiller (*liter*)

desecration [ˌdesɪˈkreɪʃən] N profanation *f*

deseed [diːˈsiːd] VT [+ *fruit*] épépiner

desegregate [ˌdiːˈsegrɪgeɪt] VT abolir or supprimer la ségrégation raciale dans ; **~d schools** écoles *fpl* où la ségrégation raciale n'est plus pratiquée

desegregation [ˈdiːˌsegrɪˈgeɪʃən] N déségrégation *f*

deselect [ˌdiːsɪˈlekt] VT (*Brit Pol*) [+ *candidate*] ne pas resélectionner

desensitize [ˌdiːˈsensɪtaɪz] VT désensibiliser

desert[1] [ˈdezət] [1] N (*lit, fig*) désert *m* [2] COMP [*region, climate, animal, plant*] désertique ► **desert boot** N chaussure *f* montante (*en daim et à lacets*) ► **desert island** N île *f* déserte ► **desert rat** N (*Zool*) gerboise *f* ► **the Desert Rats*** NPL les Rats *mpl* du désert (*forces britanniques en Libye pendant la Seconde Guerre mondiale, ou au Koweït pendant la guerre du Golfe*)

desert[2] [dɪˈzɜːt] [1] VT [+ *post, people, land*] déserter, abandonner ; [+ *cause, party*] déserter ; [+ *spouse, family*] abandonner ; [+ *friend*] délaisser ; **his courage ~ed him** son courage l'a abandonné [2] VI (*Mil*) déserter ; (*from one's party*) faire défection ; **to ~ to the rebels** passer du côté des rebelles

deserted [dɪˈzɜːtɪd] ADJ [*road, place*] désert ; [*wife etc*] abandonné

deserter [dɪˈzɜːtə] N (*Mil*) déserteur *m* ; (*to the enemy*) transfuge *m*

desertification [dɪˈzɜːtɪfɪˈkeɪʃən] N désertification *f*

desertion [dɪˈzɜːʃən] N [a] (*Mil*) désertion *f* [b] (*by supporters, friends*) désertion *f* (**by** de) [c] (*by husband, mother etc*) abandon *m* du domicile conjugal

deserts [dɪˈzɜːts] NPL dû *m*, ce que l'on mérite ; (= *reward*) récompense *f* méritée ; (= *punishment*) châtiment *m* mérité ; **according to his ~** selon ses mérites ; **to get one's (just) ~** avoir or recevoir ce que l'on mérite

deserve [dɪˈzɜːv] [1] VT [*person*] mériter, être digne de ; [*object, suggestion*] mériter ; **he ~s to**

win il mérite de gagner ; **he ~s to be pitied** il mérite qu'on le plaigne, il est digne de pitié ; **he ~s more money** il mérite plus d'argent ; **he got what he ~d** il n'a eu que ce qu'il méritait ; **the idea ~s consideration** l'idée mérite réflexion → **well**[2] [2] VI [a] **deserving of → deserving** [b] (*frm*) **to ~ well of one's country** bien mériter de la patrie (*liter*)

deservedly [dɪˈzɜːvɪdlɪ] ADV **the film was a flop, and ~ so** ce film a fait un flop* mérité ; **~, she was awarded an Oscar** elle a reçu un Oscar bien mérité ; **she told him off, and ~ so** elle l'a grondé, à juste titre

deserving [dɪˈzɜːvɪŋ] ADJ [*person*] méritant ; [*action, cause*] méritoire, louable ; **she's a ~ case** c'est une personne méritante ; **the ~ poor** les pauvres *mpl* méritants ; **to be ~ of respect** être digne de respect ; **to be ~ of support/help/recognition** mériter d'être soutenu/aidé/reconnu ; **a matter ~ of our careful attention** une affaire qui mérite toute notre attention ; **he has committed crimes ~ of punishment** il a commis des crimes pour lesquels il mérite d'être puni

deshabille [ˌdezaˈbiːl] N = **dishabille**

desiccant [ˈdesɪkənt] N dessiccatif *m*

desiccate [ˈdesɪkeɪt] [1] VT dessécher, sécher [2] COMP ► **desiccated coconut** N noix *f* de coco séchée

desiccation [ˌdesɪˈkeɪʃən] N dessiccation *f*

desiderata [dɪˌzɪdəˈrɑːtə] NPL desiderata *mpl*

design [dɪˈzaɪn] [1] N [a] (= *ornamental pattern*) motif *m*, dessin *m* (**on** sur) ; **the ~ on the material/the cups** le dessin or le motif du tissu/des tasses ; **a leaf ~** un motif de feuille(s) [b] (= *plan drawn in detail*) [*of building, machine, car etc*] plan *m*, dessin *m* (**of, for** de) ; [*of dress, hat*] croquis *m*, dessin *m* (**of, for** de) ; (= *preliminary sketch*) ébauche *f*, étude *f* (**for** de) ; **have you seen the ~(s) for the new cathedral?** avez-vous vu les plans or les dessins or les ébauches de la nouvelle cathédrale ? [c] (= *way in which sth is planned and made*) [*of building, book*] plan *m*, conception *f* (**of** de) ; [*of clothes*] style *m*, ligne *f* (**of** de) ; [*of car, machine etc*] conception *f* ; (= *look*) esthétique *f*, design *m* ; **the ~ was faulty** la conception était défectueuse, c'était mal conçu ; **the ~ of the apartment facilitates ...** le plan de l'appartement facilite ... ; **the general ~ of "Paradise Lost"** le plan général or l'architecture *f* du « Paradis perdu » ; **a dress in this summer's latest ~** une robe dans le style de cet été ; **the ~ of the car allows ...** la conception de la voiture or la façon dont la voiture est conçue permet ... ; **a car in a very sporty ~** une voiture au design très sport ; **the grand** or **overall ~** le plan d'ensemble ; **this is a very practical ~** c'est conçu de façon très pratique ; **these shoes are not of (a) very practical ~** ces chaussures ne sont pas très pratiques [d] (= *completed model*) modèle *m* ; **a new ~ of car** un nouveau modèle de voiture ; **the dress is an exclusive ~ by ...** cette robe est un modèle exclusif de ... [e] (= *subject of study*) (*for furniture, housing*) design *m* ; (*for clothing*) stylisme *m* ; **industrial ~** l'esthétique *f* or la création industrielle [f] (= *intention*) intention *f*, dessein *m* ; **his ~s became obvious when ...** ses intentions or ses desseins sont devenu(e)s manifestes quand ... ; **to form a ~ to do** former le projet or le dessein de faire ; **by ~** (= *deliberately*) délibérément, à dessein ; **whether by ~ or accident he arrived just at the right moment** que ce soit à dessein or délibérément ou par hasard, il est arrivé juste au bon moment ; **truly important events often occur not by ~ but by accident** les événements vraiment importants sont souvent le fruit du hasard plutôt que d'une volonté précise ; **to have ~s on sb/sth** avoir des visées sur qn/qch ; **to have evil ~s on sb/sth** nourrir de noirs desseins à l'encontre de

qn/qch ; **imperialist ~s against** or **on Ruritania** les visées impérialistes sur la Ruritanie ; **we believe they have aggressive ~s on our country** nous pensons qu'ils ont l'intention d'attaquer notre pays
[2] VT [a] (= *think out*) [+ *object, car, model, building*] concevoir ; [+ *scheme*] élaborer ; **well-~ed** bien conçu [b] (= *draw on paper*) [+ *object, building*] concevoir, dessiner ; [+ *dress, hat*] créer, dessiner [c] (= *destine for particular purpose*) **room ~ed as a study** pièce conçue comme cabinet de travail ; **car seats ~ed for maximum safety** des sièges *mpl* de voiture conçus pour une sécurité maximale ; **software ~ed for use with a PC** un logiciel conçu pour être utilisé sur un PC ; **to be ~ed for sb** (= *aimed at particular person*) s'adresser à qn ; **a course ~ed for foreign students** un cours s'adressant aux étudiants étrangers ; **to be ~ed to do** (= *be made for sth*) être fait or conçu pour faire ; (= *be aimed at sth*) être destiné à faire, viser à faire ; **~ed to hold wine** fait or conçu pour contenir du vin ; **a peace plan ~ed to end the civil war** un plan de paix visant à mettre fin à la guerre civile ; **the legislation is ~ed as a consumer protection measure** cette loi vise à protéger les consommateurs ; **clothes that are ~ed to appeal to young people** des vêtements qui sont conçus pour plaire aux jeunes
[3] COMP ► **design award** N prix *m* de la meilleure conception or du meilleur dessin ► **design engineer** N ingénieur *m* concepteur ► **design fault** N défaut *m* de conception ► **design office** N (*Ind*) bureau *m* d'études

designate [ˈdezɪgneɪt] [1] VT [a] (= *indicate, specify, appoint*) [+ *person, thing*] désigner (**as** comme, **to sth** à qch, **to do** pour faire) ; **he was ~d to take charge of the operations** on l'a désigné comme responsable des opérations ; **these posts ~ the boundary between ...** ces poteaux montrent la frontière entre ... [b] (= *entitle*) [+ *person, thing*] désigner ; **this area was ~d a priority development region** cette région a été classée zone de développement prioritaire [2] [ˈdezɪgnɪt] ADJ désigné ; **the chairman ~** le président désigné

designation [ˌdezɪgˈneɪʃən] N (*gen*) désignation *f* ; (*Jur, Comm*) **~ of origin** appellation *f* d'origine

designedly [dɪˈzaɪnɪdlɪ] ADV à dessein, exprès

designer [dɪˈzaɪnə] [1] N (*Archit, Art*) dessinateur *m*, -trice *f*, créateur *m*, -trice *f* ; (*Comm, Ind*) concepteur-projeteur *m* ; (*esp Advertising*) créatif *m* ; (*for furniture etc*) designer *m* ; (*for clothes*) styliste *mf*, modéliste *mf* ; (*very famous*) grand couturier *m* ; (*Cine, Theat*) décorateur *m*, -trice *f* [2] COMP [*jeans, gloves, scarves etc*] haute couture ; (= *fashionable*) [*lager, mineral water*] branché* ► **designer drug** N (= *synthetic narcotic*) drogue *f* de synthèse ► **designer stubble** N barbe *f* de trois jours (*d'un négligé savamment entretenu*)

designing [dɪˈzaɪnɪŋ] ADJ (= *scheming*) intrigant ; (= *crafty*) rusé

desirability [dɪˌzaɪərəˈbɪlɪtɪ] N [*of plan, action, measures*] charme *m*, attrait *m* ; [*of person*] charmes *mpl*, sex-appeal *m*

▼ **desirable** [dɪˈzaɪərəbl] ADJ [*position*] enviable ; [*offer*] tentant, séduisant ; [*person*] désirable, séduisant ; [*action, progress*] désirable, souhaitable ; **it is ~ that** il est désirable or souhaitable que ... (+ *subj*) ; **~ residence for sale** belle propriété à vendre

desirably [dɪˈzaɪərəblɪ] ADV **this property is ~ located** cette propriété est située dans un lieu très prisé or coté ; **rugby was thought of as ~ aggressive** on considérait que le rugby faisait appel à une agressivité salutaire

▼ **desire** [dɪˈzaɪə] [1] N désir *m* (**for** de, **to do** de faire) ; (*sexual*) désir *m* ; **a ~ for peace** un désir (ardent) de paix ; **it is my ~ that ...** c'est mon

► LANGUAGE IN USE: **desirable** 1.1, 8.4   **desire** 8.4

désir que ... (+ *subj*); **I have no ~** *or* **I haven't the least ~ to do it** je n'ai nullement envie de le faire [2] VT [a] (= *want*) désirer (**to do** faire, **that** que + *subj*); (*in instructions, recipes etc*) **if ~d** si vous le désirez; **his work leaves much** *or* **a lot/something to be ~d** son travail laisse beaucoup à désirer/laisse à désirer; **cut the fabric to the ~d length** coupez la longueur voulue de tissu; **the ~d effect/outcome** *or* **result** l'effet *m*/le résultat voulu [b] (*frm* = *request*) prier (**sb to do** qn de faire)

desirous [dɪˈzaɪərəs] ADJ désireux (**of** de); **to be ~ of sth/of doing** désirer qch/faire

desist [dɪˈzɪst] VI cesser, s'arrêter (**from doing** de faire); **to ~ from sth** cesser qch; (*Jur*) se désister de qch; (= **from criticism** renoncer à *or* cesser de critiquer; **to ~ from one's efforts** abandonner ses efforts

desk [desk] [1] N [a] (*for pupil*) pupitre *m*; (*for teacher*) bureau *m*, chaire *f*; (*in office, home*) bureau *m*; (*bureau-type*) secrétaire *m*; (*Mus*) pupitre *m* → **roll**
[b] (*Brit: in shop, restaurant*) caisse *f*; (*in hotel, at airport*) réception *f*; **ask at the ~** demandez à la caisse (*or* à la réception); (*Press*) **the ~** le secrétariat de rédaction; (*Press*) **the news/city ~** le service des informations/financier; (*Foreign Office, State Department*) **he's on the West African ~** il est à la direction des affaires ouest-africaines → **cash desk**
[2] COMP ► **desk blotter** N sous-main *m inv* ► **desk-bound** ADJ sédentaire ► **desk clerk** N (*US*) réceptionniste *mf* ► **desk diary** N agenda *m* de bureau ► **desk job** N travail *m* de bureau; **he's got a ~ job** il a un travail de bureau ► **desk lamp** N lampe *f* de bureau ► **desk pad** N bloc *m* de bureau, bloc-notes *m* ► **desk study** N (*Brit fig: Econ etc*) étude *f* sur documents

deskill [dɪˈskɪl] VT déqualifier

deskilling [dɪˈskɪlɪŋ] N déqualification *f*

deskside computer [ˈdesksaɪdkəmˈpjuːtəʳ] N ordinateur *m* tour

desktop [ˈdesktɒp] [1] ADJ [*model, computer*] de table, de bureau [2] COMP ► **desktop publishing** N publication *f* assistée par ordinateur, microédition *f*

desolate [ˈdesəlɪt] [1] ADJ [a] (= *deserted*) [*place*] désolé; [*landscape*] désert; [*beauty*] sauvage [b] [*person*] (= *grief-stricken*) désespéré; (= *lost*) perdu; **he was ~ without her** il était perdu sans elle; **to feel ~** se sentir perdu [2] [ˈdesəleɪt] VT [+ *country*] désoler, ravager; [+ *person*] désoler, affliger

desolately [ˈdesəlɪtlɪ] ADV [*say etc*] d'un air désespéré

desolation [ˌdesəˈleɪʃən] N [a] (= *grief*) abattement *m*, affliction *f*; (= *friendlessness*) solitude *f*; [*of landscape*] aspect *m* désert, solitude *f* [b] [*of country*] (*by war*) désolation *f* (*liter*), dévastation *f*

despair [dɪsˈpɛəʳ] [1] N [a] (*NonC*) désespoir *m* (**about, at, over** au sujet de, **at having done** d'avoir fait); **to be in ~** être au désespoir, être désespéré; **in ~ she killed him** de désespoir elle l'a tué; **to drive sb to ~** réduire qn au désespoir, désespérer qn [b] (= *cause of despair*) désespoir *m*; **this child is the ~ of his parents** cet enfant fait *or* est le désespoir de ses parents [2] VI (se) désespérer, perdre l'espoir; **don't ~!** ne te désespère pas!; **to ~ of (doing) sth** désespérer de (faire) qch; **his life was ~ed of** on désespérait de le sauver

despairing [dɪsˈpɛərɪŋ] ADJ [*person*] désespéré; [*look, gesture*] de désespoir, désespéré

despairingly [dɪsˈpɛərɪŋlɪ] ADV [*say, agree, answer*] d'un ton désespéré; [*think*] avec désespoir; [*shake one's head*] de façon désespérée; **to sigh ~** pousser un soupir de désespoir; **Emma looked ~ at Vanessa** Emma jeta à Vanessa un regard désespéré; **~, she waited**

for him to phone elle attendait désespérément qu'il téléphone

dispatch [dɪsˈpætʃ] N = **dispatch**

desperado [ˌdespəˈrɑːdəʊ] N (*pl* **desperado(e)s**) desperado *m*

desperate [ˈdespərɪt] ADJ [a] [*situation, attempt, act, struggle*] désespéré; [*criminal*] prêt à tout, capable de tout; **he's a ~ man** il est prêt à tout *or* capable de tout; **there was no sign of my taxi and I was getting ~** mon taxi n'arrivait pas et je devenais fou; **to resort to ~ measures** recourir à des mesures désespérées; **to do something ~** commettre un acte désespéré; **I was ~ to see my children again** je voulais à tout prix revoir mes enfants; **both countries are ~ to avoid war** les deux pays veulent à tout prix éviter la guerre; **to be ~ for sb to do sth** vouloir à tout prix que qn fasse qch; (*for the lavatory*) **I'm ~*** j'ai une envie pressante* [b] (* = *very bad*) épouvantable

desperately [ˈdespərɪtlɪ] ADV [a] [*struggle, regret*] désespérément; [*say, look*] avec désespoir [b] (= *appallingly*) [*hard, poor*] extrêmement; [*unhappy, worried, cold*] terriblement; **~ shy** d'une timidité maladive; **it's ~ hard work** c'est un travail extrêmement pénible; **to be ~ ill** être très gravement malade; **to be ~ short of sth** manquer cruellement de qch [c] (* = *very*) **I'm not ~ happy about it** ça ne me plaît pas trop; **I'm not ~ keen** ça ne me dit pas grand-chose; **are you hungry? — not ~** as-tu faim? — pas trop

desperation [ˌdespəˈreɪʃən] N (*NonC*) [a] (= *state*) désespoir *m*; **to be in ~** être au désespoir; **to drive sb to ~** pousser qn à bout; **in ~ she killed him** poussée à bout elle l'a tué; **in sheer ~** en désespoir de cause [b] (= *recklessness*) désespoir *m*, rage *f* or fureur *f* du désespoir; **to fight with ~** combattre avec la rage du désespoir

despicable [dɪsˈpɪkəbl] ADJ [*action, person*] ignoble, abject, méprisable

despicably [dɪsˈpɪkəblɪ] ADV [*behave*] ignoblement, d'une façon ignoble; **that was a ~ cruel thing to say** c'était ignoble et cruel de dire une chose pareille; **that is ~ underhand behaviour!** ce comportement sournois est ignoble!

despise [dɪsˈpaɪz] VT [+ *danger, person*] mépriser; **to ~ sb for sth/for having done sth** mépriser qn pour qch/pour avoir fait qch

despisingly [dɪsˈpaɪzɪŋlɪ] ADV avec mépris, dédaigneusement

▼ **despite** [dɪsˈpaɪt] [1] PREP malgré, en dépit de; **~ our objecting to this, they decided ...** bien que nous ayons fait des objections *or* malgré nos objections, ils ont décidé ... [2] N (*liter*) dépit *m*

despoil [dɪsˈpɔɪl] VT (*liter*) [+ *person*] dépouiller, spolier (**of** de); [+ *country*] piller

despoiler [dɪsˈpɔɪləʳ] N (*liter*) spoliateur *m*, -trice *f*

despoiling [dɪsˈpɔɪlɪŋ] N spoliation *f*

despondence [dɪsˈpɒndəns], **despondency** [dɪsˈpɒndənsɪ] N découragement *m*, abattement *m*

despondent [dɪsˈpɒndənt] ADJ découragé, déprimé (**about** par)

despondently [dɪsˈpɒndəntlɪ] ADV (*with vb*) [*speak*] d'un ton découragé; **out-of-work actors trudging ~ from one audition to the next** des acteurs au chômage qui se traînent, complètement découragés, d'une audition à l'autre

despot [ˈdespɒt] N (*lit, fig*) despote *m*

despotic [desˈpɒtɪk] ADJ (*lit, fig*) despotique

despotically [desˈpɒtɪkəlɪ] ADV [*behave*] d'une manière despotique, despotiquement; [*govern*] despotiquement, en despote

despotism [ˈdespətɪzəm] N despotisme *m*

des res [dez rez] N (ABBR = **desirable residence**) → **desirable**

dessert [dɪˈzɜːt] [1] N dessert *m* [2] COMP ► **dessert apple** N pomme *f* à couteau ► **dessert chocolate** N chocolat *m* à croquer ► **dessert plate** N assiette *f* à dessert ► **dessert wine** N vin *m* de dessert

dessertspoon [dɪˈzɜːtspuːn] N (*Brit*) cuiller *f* à dessert

destabilization [diːˌsteɪbɪlaɪˈzeɪʃən] N déstabilisation *f*

destabilize [diːˈsteɪbɪlaɪz] VT (*Pol*) [+ *regime etc*] déstabiliser

de-Stalinization [diːˌstɑːlɪnaɪˈzeɪʃən] N déstalinisation *f*

de-Stalinize [diːˈstɑːlɪnaɪz] VT déstaliniser

destination [ˌdestɪˈneɪʃən] N destination *f*

destine [ˈdestɪn] VT [+ *person, object*] destiner (**for** à)

destined [ˈdestɪnd] ADJ [a] (*by fate*) destiné (**to** à); **they were ~ to meet again later** ils étaient destinés à se rencontrer plus tard; **I was ~ never to see them again** je devais ne plus jamais les revoir; **~ for greatness** promis à un grand avenir; (*liter*) **at the ~ hour** à l'heure fixée par le destin [b] (= *heading for*) **~ for London** à destination de Londres; **a letter ~ for her** une lettre qui lui est (*or* était *etc*) destinée

destiny [ˈdestɪnɪ] N destin *m*, destinée *f*; **Destiny** le destin; **the destinies of France during this period** le destin de la France pendant cette période; **it was his ~ to die in battle** il était écrit qu'il devait mourir au combat; **a man of ~** un homme promis à une grande destinée

destitute [ˈdestɪtjuːt] [1] ADJ [a] (= *poverty-stricken*) indigent, sans ressources; **to be utterly ~** être dans le dénuement le plus complet [b] (= *lacking*) dépourvu, dénué (**of** de) [2] **the destitute** NPL les pauvres *mpl*, les indigents *mpl*

destitution [ˌdestɪˈtjuːʃən] N dénuement *m*, indigence *f*, misère *f* noire

destroy [dɪsˈtrɔɪ] VT [a] (= *spoil completely*) [+ *building, town, forest, document*] détruire; [+ *toy, gadget*] démolir; **~ed by bombing** détruit par bombardement; **the village was ~ed by a fire** un incendie a ravagé le village [b] (= *kill*) [+ *enemy*] détruire, anéantir; [+ *population*] détruire, exterminer; [+ *dangerous animal, injured horse*] abattre; [+ *cat, dog*] supprimer, faire piquer; **to ~ o.s.** se suicider, se tuer [c] (= *put an end to*) [+ *reputation, mood, beauty, influence, faith*] détruire; [+ *hope, love*] anéantir, détruire

destroyer [dɪsˈtrɔɪəʳ] N [a] (*Naut*) contre-torpilleur *m*, destroyer *m* [b] (= *person*) destructeur *m*, -trice *f*; (= *murderer*) meurtrier *m*, -ière *f* [2] COMP ► **destroyer escort** N escorteur *m*

destruct [dɪsˈtrʌkt] [1] VT [+ *missile*] détruire volontairement [2] VI être détruit volontairement [3] N destruction *f* volontaire [4] COMP ► **destruct button** N télécommande *f* de destruction ► **destruct mechanism** N mécanisme *m* de destruction

destructible [dɪsˈtrʌktəbl] ADJ destructible

destruction [dɪsˈtrʌkʃən] N [a] (*NonC* = *act*) [*of town, building*] destruction *f*; [*of enemy*] destruction *f*, anéantissement *m*; [*of people, insects*] destruction *f*, extermination *f*; [*of documents*] destruction *f*; [*of reputation, hope*] destruction *f*, ruine *f*; [*of character, soul*] ruine *f*, perte *f*; **~ by fire** destruction *f* par un incendie *or* par le feu [b] (*NonC* = *damage*) (*from fire*) dégâts *mpl*; (*from war*) ravages *mpl*; **a scene of utter ~ met our gaze** nous avions devant les yeux un spectacle de dévastation totale

destructive [dɪsˈtrʌktɪv] ADJ (= *damaging*) [*person, behaviour, effect, emotion, comment*] destructeur (-trice *f*); [*power, force*] destructeur (-trice *f*), destructif; **he's very ~**

[*child*] il casse tout; **environmentally ~ projects** des projets *mpl* destructeurs pour l'environnement; **to be ~ of the environment** détruire l'environnement

destructively [dɪsˈtrʌktɪvlɪ] ADV de façon destructrice; **any power can be used creatively or ~** tout pouvoir peut être utilisé de façon créative ou destructrice

destructiveness [dɪsˈtrʌktɪvnɪs] N [*of fire, war, criticism etc*] caractère *m* or effet *m* destructeur; [*of child etc*] penchant *m* destructeur

destructor [dɪsˈtrʌktəʳ] N (*Brit*: also **refuse ~**) incinérateur *m* (à ordures)

desuetude [dɪˈsjʊɪtjuːd] N (*liter*) désuétude *f*

desultorily [ˈdesəltərɪlɪ] ADV [*say, look for*] sans conviction; [*wander around*] sans but précis; **to talk** or **chat ~** échanger des propos décousus

desultory [ˈdesəltərɪ] ADJ [*reading*] décousu, sans suite; [*attempt*] peu suivi, peu soutenu; [*firing, contact*] irrégulier, interrompu; **to have a ~ conversation** échanger des propos décousus

det. ABBR = **detective**

detach [dɪˈtætʃ] VT [+ *hook, rope, cart*] détacher, séparer (**from** de); **to ~ o.s. from a group** se détacher d'un groupe; **a section became ~ed from ...** une section s'est détachée de ...; **troops were ~ed to protect the town** on a envoyé un détachement de troupes pour protéger la ville → **detached**

detachable [dɪˈtætʃəbl] **1** ADJ [*part of machine, section of document*] détachable (**from** de); [*collar, lining*] amovible **2** COMP ► **detachable lens** N (*Phot*) objectif *m* mobile

detached [dɪˈtætʃt] **1** ADJ **a** (= *separate*) [*part, section*] détaché, séparé; **~ from the world of racing** coupé du monde des courses; **~ from reality** coupé de la réalité **b** (= *unbiased*) [*opinion*] neutre, objectif, (= *unemotional*) [*manner*] détaché, indifférent; **he seemed very ~ about it** il semblait ne pas du tout se sentir concerné **2** COMP ► **detached house** N (*Brit*) maison *f* individuelle (entourée d'un jardin), pavillon *m* ► **detached retina** N décollement *m* de la rétine

detachment [dɪˈtætʃmənt] N **a** (*NonC*) [*of part, section etc*] séparation *f* (**from** de); (*Med*) **~ of the retina** décollement *m* de la rétine **b** (*NonC: fig*) (*in manner*) détachement *m*, indifférence *f*; (*towards pleasure, friends*) indifférence *f* (**towards** à, à l'égard de) **c** (*Mil*) détachement *m*

detail [ˈdiːteɪl] **1** N **a** (*also Archit, Art*) détail *m*; (= *information on sth wanted*) renseignement *m*; **in ~** en détail; **in great ~** dans les moindres détails; **his attention to ~** l'attention qu'il porte aux détails; **to go into ~(s)** entrer dans les détails; **in every ~ it resembles ...** ça ressemble dans le moindre détail à ...; **but that's a tiny ~!** mais ce n'est qu'un (petit) détail! **b** (*Mil*) détachement *m* **2 details** NPL (*gen*) renseignements *mpl*; (= *personal facts*) coordonnées *fpl*; **let me take down the ~s** je vais noter les renseignements nécessaires; (*Comm etc*) **please send me ~s of ...** veuillez m'envoyer des renseignements sur or concernant ...; **she took down my ~s** elle a noté mes coordonnées **3** VT **a** [+ *reason, fact*] exposer en détail; [+ *story, event*] raconter en détail; [+ *items, objects*] énumérer, détailler **b** (*Mil*) [+ *troops*] affecter (**for** à, **to do** à or pour faire), détacher, désigner (**for** pour, **to do** pour faire) **4** COMP ► **detail drawing** N (*Archit, Tech*) épure *f*

detailed [ˈdiːteɪld] ADJ détaillé; [*investigation, examination*] minutieux; **the police made a ~**

search of the scene of the crime la police a minutieusement fouillé le lieu du crime or a passé le lieu du crime au peigne fin

detain [dɪˈteɪn] VT **a** (= *keep back*) retenir; **he has been ~ed at the office** il a été retenu au bureau; **I don't want to ~ you any longer** je ne veux pas vous retenir or retenir plus longtemps **b** (*in captivity*) détenir; (*Scol*) mettre en retenue, consigner

detainee [ˌdiːteɪˈniː] N détenu(e) *m(f)*; (*political*) prisonnier *m* politique

detect [dɪˈtekt] VT (= *perceive presence of*) [+ *substance, gas*] détecter, découvrir; [+ *explosive*] découvrir; [+ *disease*] dépister; [+ *sadness*] déceler; (= *see or hear*) distinguer, discerner; **they ~ed traces of poison in the body** on a découvert des traces de poison dans le cadavre; **I thought I could ~ a note of sarcasm in his voice** j'avais cru déceler une note sarcastique dans sa voix; **I could just ~ his pulse** je sentais tout juste son pouls

detectable [dɪˈtektəbl] ADJ → **detect**; qu'on peut détecter or découvrir *etc*

detection [dɪˈtekʃən] N [*of criminal, secret*] découverte *f*; [*of gas, mines*] détection *f*; (*Med*) dépistage *m*; **the ~ of crime** la chasse aux criminels; **the bloodstains led to the ~ of the criminal** les taches de sang ont mené à la découverte du criminel; **to escape ~** [*criminal*] échapper aux recherches; [*mistake*] passer inaperçu

detective [dɪˈtektɪv] **1** N policier *m* (en civil); (*also* **private ~**) détective *m* (privé) **2** COMP ► **detective chief inspector** N (*Brit*) ≈ inspecteur *m* divisionnaire (de police) ► **detective chief superintendent** N (*Brit*) ≈ commissaire *m* divisionnaire (de police) ► **detective constable** N (*Brit*) inspecteur *m* de police ► **detective device** N dispositif *m* de détection or de dépistage ► **detective inspector** N (*Brit*) ≈ inspecteur *m* principal (de police) ► **detective sergeant** N (*Brit*) ≈ inspecteur(-chef) *m* (de police) ► **detective story** N roman *m* policier, polar* *m* ► **detective superintendent** N (*Brit*) ≈ commissaire *m* (de police) ► **detective work** N (*lit, fig*) investigations *fpl*; **a bit of ~ work** quelques investigations

detector [dɪˈtektəʳ] **1** N (= *device, person*) détecteur *m* → **lie²**, **mine²** **2** COMP ► **detector van** N (*Brit TV*) camion *m* de détection radiogoniométrique

detente [deɪˈtɑːnt] N détente *f* (*Pol*)

detention [dɪˈtenʃən] **1** N (= *captivity*) [*of criminal, spy*] détention *f*; (*Mil*) arrêts *mpl*; (*Scol*) retenue *f*, consigne *f*; **to give a pupil two hours' ~** donner à un élève deux heures de retenue or de consigne → **preventive 2** COMP ► **detention centre** N (*Jur*) centre *m* de détention pour mineurs ► **detention home** N (*US*) = **detention centre**

deter [dɪˈtɜːʳ] VT (= *prevent*) détourner (**from sth** de qch), dissuader (**from doing** de faire); (= *discourage*) décourager (**from doing** de faire); (*Mil*) [+ *attack*] prévenir; [+ *enemy*] dissuader; **I was ~red by the cost** le coût m'a fait reculer; **don't let the weather ~ you** ne vous laissez pas arrêter par le temps; **a weapon which ~s no one** une arme qui ne dissuade personne

detergent [dɪˈtɜːdʒənt] ADJ, N détersif *m*, détergent *m*

deteriorate [dɪˈtɪərɪəreɪt] **1** VT [+ *material, machine*] détériorer, abîmer **2** VI [*material*] se détériorer, s'abîmer; [*species, morals*] dégénérer; [*one's health, relationships, weather*] se détériorer; [*situation*] se dégrader; **his schoolwork is deteriorating** il y a un fléchissement dans son travail scolaire

deterioration [dɪˌtɪərɪəˈreɪʃən] N [*of goods, weather, friendship*] détérioration *f*; [*of situation, relations*] dégradation *f*; [*of species*] dégé-

nération *f*; (*in morality*) dégénérescence *f*; (*in taste, art*) déchéance *f*, décadence *f*

determinable [dɪˈtɜːmɪnəbl] ADJ **a** [*quantity*] déterminable **b** (*Jur*) résoluble

determinant [dɪˈtɜːmɪnənt] ADJ, N déterminant *m*

determinate [dɪˈtɜːmɪnɪt] ADJ (= *fixed*) déterminé

determination [dɪˌtɜːmɪˈneɪʃən] N (*NonC*) **a** (= *firmness of purpose*) détermination *f*, résolution *f* (**to do** de faire); **an air of ~** un air résolu **b** (*gen, Math etc*) détermination *f*; [*of frontiers*] délimitation *f*

determinative [dɪˈtɜːmɪnətɪv] **1** ADJ déterminatif; (*Gram*) déterminant **2** N facteur *m* déterminant; (*Gram*) déterminatif *m*

determine [dɪˈtɜːmɪn] VT **a** (= *settle, fix*) [+ *conditions, policy, date*] fixer, déterminer; [+ *price*] fixer, régler; [+ *frontier*] délimiter; [+ *cause, nature, meaning*] déterminer, établir; [+ *sb's character, future*] décider de, déterminer; (*Jur*) [+ *contract*] résoudre **b** (= *resolve*) décider (**to do** de faire), se déterminer, se résoudre (**to do** à faire); (= *cause to decide*) [+ *person*] décider, amener (**to do** à faire) ► **determine (up)on** VT FUS décider de, résoudre de (**doing** faire); [+ *course of action*] se résoudre à; [+ *alternative*] choisir

▼**determined** [dɪˈtɜːmɪnd] ADJ **a** [*person, appearance*] résolu, déterminé; **to make ~ efforts** or **a ~ attempt to do sth** faire un gros effort pour faire qch; **to be ~ to do sth** être bien décidé à faire qch; **to be ~ that ...** être bien décidé à ce que ... (+ *subj*) **b** [*quantity*] déterminé, établi

determinedly [dɪˈtɜːmɪndlɪ] ADV [*say*] d'un ton déterminé or résolu; [*try*] résolument; [*walk, stride*] d'un pas (ferme et) résolu; **~ optimistic** résolument optimiste; **~ cheerful** d'une gaieté inébranlable

determiner [dɪˈtɜːmɪnəʳ] N (*Gram*) déterminant *m*

determining [dɪˈtɜːmɪnɪŋ] ADJ déterminant

determinism [dɪˈtɜːmɪnɪzəm] N déterminisme *m*

determinist [dɪˈtɜːmɪnɪst] ADJ, N déterministe *mf*

deterministic [dɪˌtɜːmɪˈnɪstɪk] ADJ déterministe

deterrence [dɪˈterəns] N (*Mil*) force *f* de dissuasion

deterrent [dɪˈterənt] **1** N (*also Mil*) force *f* de dissuasion; **to act as a ~** exercer un effet de dissuasion → **nuclear**, **ultimate 2** ADJ de dissuasion, préventif

detest [dɪˈtest] VT détester; **to ~ doing** détester faire, avoir horreur de faire; **I ~ that sort of thing!** j'ai horreur de ce genre de chose!

detestable [dɪˈtestəbl] ADJ détestable, odieux

detestably [dɪˈtestəblɪ] ADV [*rude*] odieusement, horriblement; [*ugly*] horriblement

detestation [ˌdiːtesˈteɪʃən] N **a** (*NonC*) haine *f* **b** (= *object of hatred*) abomination *f*, chose *f* détestable

dethrone [diːˈθrəʊn] VT détrôner

dethronement [diːˈθrəʊnmənt] N déposition *f* (d'un souverain)

detonate [ˈdetəneɪt] **1** VI détoner **2** VT faire détoner or exploser

detonation [ˌdetəˈneɪʃən] N détonation *f*, explosion *f*

detonator [ˈdetəneɪtəʳ] N détonateur *m*, amorce *f*, capsule *f* fulminante; (*Rail*) pétard *m*

detour [ˈdiːtʊəʳ] **1** N (*lit, fig*) détour *m*; (*for traffic*) déviation *f* **2** VI faire un détour **3** VT (*US*) [+ *traffic*] dévier

detox* [ˈdiːtɒks] ABBR = **detoxicate, detoxication, detoxification, detoxify**

detoxicate [diː'tɒksɪkeɪt] VT désintoxiquer

detoxi(fi)cation [diːˌtɒksɪ(fɪ)'keɪʃən] [1] N désintoxication f [2] COMP ► **detoxi(fi)cation centre** N centre m de désintoxication ► **detoxi(fi)cation programme** N cure f de désintoxication

detoxify [diː'tɒksɪfaɪ] VT = **detoxicate**

detract [dɪ'trækt] VI **to ~ from** [+ quality, merit] diminuer ; [+ reputation] porter atteinte à ; **it ~s from the pleasure of walking** cela diminue le plaisir de se promener

detraction [dɪ'trækʃən] N détraction f

detractor [dɪ'træktə˙] N détracteur m, -trice f, critique m

detrain [diː'treɪn] [1] VT débarquer (d'un train) [2] VI [troops] débarquer (d'un train) ; [passengers] descendre (d'un train)

detriment ['detrɪmənt] N (= handicap) handicap m ; **my qualifications proved to be a ~ rather than an asset** mes diplômes se sont avérés être un handicap plutôt qu'un atout ; **to the ~ of** au détriment de, au préjudice de ; **this policy ultimately worked to his own ~** cette politique a fini par lui porter préjudice ; **without ~ to** sans porter préjudice à ; **that is no ~ to ...** cela ne nuit en rien à ...

detrimental [ˌdetrɪ'mentl] ADJ nuisible ; **to be ~ for sb/sth** ◊ **to have a ~ effect on sb/sth** être nuisible or préjudiciable à qn/qch, nuire à qn/qch ; **to be ~ to sth** nuire à qch ; **this could be ~ in its effect** ◊ **this could have a ~ effect** cela pourrait avoir un effet néfaste

detritus [dɪ'traɪtəs] N (Geol) roches fpl détritiques, pierraille f ; (fig) détritus m

detumescent [ˌdiːtjʊ'mesnt] ADJ (frm) détumescent

deuce¹ [djuːs] N [a] (Cards, Dice etc) deux m [b] (Tennis) égalité f ; **to be at ~** être à égalité

deuce²†* [djuːs] N (euph) = **devil**

deuced†* ['djuːsɪd] [1] ADJ satané (before n), sacré* (before n) [2] ADV diablement†; **what ~ bad weather!** quel sale temps !

deuterium [djuː'tɪərɪəm] [1] N deutérium m [2] COMP ► **deuterium oxide** N eau f lourde

Deuteronomy [ˌdjuːtə'rɒnəmɪ] N le Deutéronome

Deutschmark ['dɔɪtʃmɑːk], **Deutsche Mark** [ˌdɔɪtʃə'mɑːk] N mark m

devaluate [diː'væljʊeɪt] VT = **devalue**

devaluation [ˌdiːvæljʊ'eɪʃən] N dévaluation f

devalue [diː'væljuː] VT (Fin, fig) dévaluer

devastate ['devəsteɪt] VT [+ town, land] dévaster, ravager ; [+ opponent, opposition] anéantir ; (fig) [+ person] terrasser, foudroyer ; **he was absolutely ~d when he heard the news** cette nouvelle lui a porté un coup terrible

devastating ['devəsteɪtɪŋ] ADJ [war, attack, wind, storm, effect] dévastateur (-trice f) ; [consequence, result, loss] désastreux (**to, for** pour) ; [grief] profond ; [news, reply] accablant ; [logic] implacable ; [wit, charm] irrésistible ; **to have a ~ effect (on sb/sth)** avoir un effet dévastateur (sur qn/qch) ; **with** or **to ~ effect** avec un effet dévastateur ; **(to deal) a ~ blow (to sth)** (porter) un coup fatal (à qch)

devastatingly ['devəsteɪtɪŋlɪ] ADV ► **funny** irrésistiblement drôle ; **a ~ attractive woman** une femme au charme ravageur ; ► **effective** d'une efficacité foudroyante ; **to be ~ successful** avoir un succès foudroyant ; **the German guns were ~ accurate** les canons allemands étaient terriblement précis ; **a frank appraisal** une évaluation d'une franchise implacable

devastation [ˌdevə'steɪʃən] N dévastation f

develop [dɪ'veləp] [1] VT [a] [+ mind, body] développer, former ; [+ argument, thesis, business, market] développer ; (Math, Phot) développer → **developed**
[b] [+ region] exploiter, mettre en valeur ; (= change and improve) aménager (**as** en) ; (= build

on) **this land is to be ~ed** on va construire or bâtir sur ce terrain → **developed**
[c] (= acquire, get) [+ tic, boil, cold] attraper ; [+ symptoms, signs] présenter ; [+ disease, swollen ankles etc] commencer à souffrir de, développer ; [+ habit] contracter ; **to ~ a taste for sth** prendre goût à qch ; **to ~ a talent for** faire preuve de talent pour ; **to ~ a tendency to** manifester une tendance à
[2] VI [person, embryo, tendency, town, region] se développer ; [disease] se déclarer ; [talent] s'épanouir ; [friendship] s'établir ; [jealousy] s'installer ; [Phot] [negative, print, image] se développer ; [story, plotline] se développer ; [event, situation] se produire ; **a crack was ~ing in the wall** le mur se lézardait ; **to ~ into** devenir

developed [dɪ'veləpt] ADJ [a] [economy, country] développé ; **highly ~** [ideas, theories] mûrement pensé ; [sense of humour, sense of the absurd] très développé [b] [breasts] développé ; [girl] formé

developer [dɪ'veləpə˙] N [a] (also **property ~**) promoteur m (de construction) [b] (Phot) révélateur m

developing [dɪ'veləpɪŋ] [1] ADJ [crisis, storm] qui se prépare ; [country] en voie de développement ; [industry] en expansion [2] N [a] = **development 1a** [b] (Phot) développement m ; **"~ and printing"** « développement et tirage », « travaux photographiques » [3] COMP ► **developing bath** N (Phot) (bain m) révélateur m ► **developing tank** N (Phot) cuve f à développement

development [dɪ'veləpmənt] [1] N [a] (NonC = growth, progress) [of person, body] développement m ; [of mind] développement m, formation f ; [of idea] évolution f ; [of region] exploitation f, mise f en valeur ; [of site] mise f en exploitation ; [of technique, technology] mise f au point ; [of industry] développement m, expansion f ; **at every stage in his ~** à chaque stade de son développement ; **economic ~** développement m économique ; **product ~** développement m de produits ; **business ~** (= creation of new businesses) création f d'entreprise(s) ; **to promote business ~** promouvoir la création d'entreprise(s) ; **business ~ advice** (= building of existing business) aide f au développement de l'entreprise ; **career ~** évolution f professionnelle
[b] (NonC = unfolding, exposition) [of subject, theme] développement m, exposé m ; [of idea] développement m ; [of plot, story] déroulement m, développement m
[c] (NonC: Math, Mus, Phot) développement m
[d] (NonC: Med) [of disease] (= onset) développement m, apparition f ; (= progression) développement m ; **this has been linked with the ~ of breast cancer** cela a été associé au développement or à l'apparition du cancer du sein
[e] (esp Press = event) fait m nouveau ; **a new ~** des développements mpl ; **there have been no (new) ~s** il n'y a pas de changements or nouveaux développements ; **the latest ~** les derniers développements ; **to await ~s** attendre la suite des événements ; **an unexpected or a surprise ~** un rebondissement
[f] (= advance) progrès m ; **recent ~s in the treatment of skin cancer** les progrès récents or les récents développements en matière de traitement du cancer de la peau
[g] (Constr = building complex) zone f aménagée ; **an industrial ~** une zone industrielle ; **housing** or **residential ~** [of houses] lotissement m ; [of blocks of flats] cité f ; **shopping ~** centre m commercial ; **office ~** immeuble(s) m(pl) de bureaux
[2] COMP ► **development area** N (Brit) zone f à urbaniser en priorité, ZUP f ► **development bank** N banque f de développement ► **development company** N société f d'exploitation ► **development grant** N aide f au développement ► **development**

period N [of project, company] phase f de démarrage ► **development planning** N planification f du développement

developmental [dɪˌveləp'mentl] ADJ de croissance

deviance ['diːvɪəns], **deviancy** ['diːvɪənsɪ] N (gen, also Psych) déviance f (**from** de)

deviant ['diːvɪənt] [1] ADJ [behaviour] déviant ; [development] anormal ; (sexually) perverti ; (Ling) [sentence, form] déviant [2] N déviant(e) m(f)

deviate ['diːvɪeɪt] VI [a] (from truth, former statement etc) dévier, s'écarter (**from** de) ; **to ~ from the norm** s'écarter de la norme [b] [ship, plane, projectile] dévier

deviation [ˌdiːvɪ'eɪʃən] N [a] (= straying) (from principle, disciple, custom) manquement m (**from** à) ; (from course, trajectory: also Pol) déviation f (**from** de) ; (from law, instructions) dérogation f (**from** à) ; (from social norm) déviance f (**from** de) ; **there have been many ~s from the general rule** on s'est fréquemment écarté de la règle générale [b] (sexual) déviation f [c] (Math) déviation f ; **standard ~** écart type m [d] (Aut = diversion) déviation f

deviationism [ˌdiːvɪ'eɪʃənɪzəm] N déviationnisme m

deviationist [ˌdiːvɪ'eɪʃənɪst] ADJ, N déviationniste mf

device [dɪ'vaɪs] N [a] (= gadget) appareil m ; (= mechanism) mécanisme m (**for** pour) ; (Comput) dispositif m, unité f physique → **safety** [b] (= scheme, plan) moyen m (**to do de** faire) ; **to leave sb to his own ~s** laisser qn se débrouiller ; **left to his own ~s, he'd never have finished** tout seul or livré à lui-même, il n'aurait jamais fini [c] (Literat) procédé m ; **plot** or **narrative ~** procédé m narratif [d] (Her = emblem) devise f, emblème m [e] (also **explosive ~**) engin m (explosif) ; **nuclear ~** engin m nucléaire

devil ['devl] [1] N [a] (= evil spirit) diable m, démon m ; **the Devil** le Diable, Satan m
[b] * **poor ~!** pauvre diable ! ; **he's a little ~!** c'est un petit démon ! ; **he's a nice little ~** c'est un bon petit diable ; **he's a stubborn/handsome** etc ~ il est sacrément* entêté/beau etc ; **you little ~!** petit monstre, va ! ; (hum) **go on, be a ~!*** vas-y, vis dangereusement !
[c] (†*: as intensifier) → **deuce²**, **dickens** ; **he had the ~ of a job to find it** il a eu toutes les peines du monde or un mal fou à le trouver ; **the ~ of a wind** un vent du diable or de tous les diables ; **he lives the ~ of a long way away** il habite au diable* ; **it's the ~ of a job** or **it's the very ~ to get him to understand** c'est toute une affaire pour le faire comprendre ; **why the ~ didn't you say so?** pourquoi diable ne l'as-tu pas dit ? ; **how the ~ would I know?** comment voulez-vous que je (le) sache ? ; **where the ~ is he?** où diable peut-il bien être ? ; **what the ~ are you doing?** mais enfin qu'est-ce que tu fabriques ?* ; **who the ~ are you?** qui diable êtes-vous ? ; **the ~ take it!** au diable ! ; **to work/run/shout** etc **like the ~** travailler/courir/crier etc comme un fou ; (fig) **there will be the ~ to pay (if/when ...)** cela va faire du grabuge* (si/quand ...), ça va barder* (si/quand ...)
[d] (phrases) **between the ~ and the deep blue sea** entre Charybde et Scylla ■ (PROV) **the ~ finds work for idle hands (to do)** l'oisiveté est la mère de tous les vices (PROV) ■ (PROV) **(every man for himself and) the ~ take the hindmost** sauve qui peut ; **go to the ~!:** va te faire voir !*, va te faire cuire un œuf !* ; (hum) **speak** or **talk of the ~ (and he appears)!** quand on parle du loup (on en voit la queue) ! ; **to play** or **be the ~'s advocate** se faire l'avocat du diable ; **(to) give the ~ ~ his due ...** pour être honnête, il faut reconnaître que ... ; **he has the luck of the ~*** or **the ~'s own luck*** il a une veine insolente or une veine de cocu: ■ (PROV)

better the ~ you know (than the ~ you don't) mieux vaut un danger que l'on connaît qu'un danger que l'on ne connaît pas, ≈ un homme averti en vaut deux **e** (*also* **printer's ~**) apprenti *m* imprimeur; (= *hack writer*) nègre* *m* (*d'un écrivain etc*); (*Jur*) ≈ avocat *m* stagiaire **2** VI **to ~ for sb** (*Literat etc*) servir de nègre* à qn; (*Jur*) ≈ faire office d'avocat stagiaire auprès de qn **3** VT **a** (*Culin*) [+ *kidneys*] (faire) griller au poivre et à la moutarde; **~led** (*Brit*) or **~ed** (*US*) **egg** œuf *m* à la diable **b** (*US* = *nag*) harceler (*verbalement*) **4** COMP ► **devil-may-care** ADJ insouciant, je-m'en-foutiste* ► **devil's food cake** N (*US*) gâteau *au* chocolat ► **Devil's Island** N l'île *f* du Diable ► **devils-on-horseback** NPL (*Culin*) pruneaux entourés de lard servis sur toast

devilfish ['devlfɪʃ] N (*pl* **devilfish** or **devilfishes**) (= *manta*) mante *f*

devilish ['devlɪʃ] **1** ADJ [*idea, act, invention, cunning*] diabolique **2** ADV (†* = *very*) diablement*, rudement*; **it's ~ cold** il fait un froid du diable or de canard*

devilishly ['devlɪʃlɪ] ADV **a** (= *wickedly*) **she grinned/laughed ~** elle eut un sourire/un rire diabolique; **~ cunning/handsome/clever** (*d'une astuce/beauté/intelligence diabolique **b** (* = *extremely*) = **devilish 2**

devilishness ['devlɪʃnɪs] N [*of invention*] caractère *m* diabolique; [*of behaviour*] méchanceté *f* diabolique

devilment ['devlmənt] N (*NonC*) (= *mischief*) diablerie *f*; espièglerie *f*; (= *spite*) méchanceté *f*, malice *f*; **a piece of ~** une espièglerie; **out of sheer ~** par pure malice or méchanceté

devilry ['devlrɪ], **deviltry** (*US*) ['devltrɪ] N **a** (= *daring*) (folle) témérité *f*; (= *mischief*) diablerie *f*, espièglerie *f*; (= *wickedness*) méchanceté *f* (diabolique) **b** (= *black magic*) magie *f* noire, maléfices *mpl*

devious ['diːvɪəs] ADJ **a** (= *sly*) [*means*] détourné; [*person, behaviour*] retors, sournois; [*mind*] retors, tortueux **b** (= *tortuous*) [*route*] détourné

deviously ['diːvɪəslɪ] ADV [*act, behave*] de manière sournoise, sournoisement

deviousness ['diːvɪəsnɪs] N [*of person*] fourberie *f*, sournoiserie *f*; [*of scheme, method*] complexité(s) *f(pl)*

devise [dɪ'vaɪz] **1** VT [+ *scheme, style*] imaginer, concevoir; [+ *plotline*] imaginer; (*Jur*) léguer; **of his own devising** de son invention **2** N (*Jur*) legs *m* (*de biens immobiliers*)

devisee [dɪvaɪ'ziː] N (*Jur*) légataire *mf* (*qui reçoit des biens immobiliers*)

deviser [dɪ'vaɪzəʳ] N [*of scheme, plan*] inventeur *m*, -trice *f*, auteur *m*

devisor [dɪ'vaɪzəʳ] N (*Jur*) testateur *m*, -trice *f* (*qui lègue des biens immobiliers*)

devitalization [diːˌvaɪtəlaɪ'zeɪʃən] N affaiblissement *m*

devitalize [diː'vaɪtəlaɪz] VT affaiblir

devoice [diː'vɔɪs] VT (*Phon*) assourdir

devoiced [diː'vɔɪst] ADJ (*Phon*) [*consonant*] dévoisé

devoicing [diː'vɔɪsɪŋ] N (*Phon*) dévoisement *m*

devoid [dɪ'vɔɪd] ADJ (*frm*) **~ of** [*ornament, charm, talent, qualities, imagination*] dépourvu de; [*scruples, compassion, good sense, humour, interest, meaning*] dénué de

devolution [ˌdiːvə'luːʃən] N [*of power, authority*] délégation *f*; (*Jur*) [*of property*] transmission *f*, dévolution *f*; (*Pol etc*) décentralisation *f*; (*Bio*) dégénérescence *f*

devolve [dɪ'vɒlv] **1** VI (*frm*) [*duty, responsibility*] incomber (**on, upon** à); (*by chance*) échoir (**on, upon** à); **it ~d on** or **upon me to take the final decision** c'est à moi qu'il incombait de prendre la décision définitive;

the cost of the operation ~s upon the patient le coût de l'opération est à la charge du patient **b** (*Jur*) [*property*] passer (**on, upon** à), être transmis (**on, upon** à) **c** (= *secede*) devenir autonome, faire sécession **d** (= *dissolve*) **the union ~d into a looser confederation of states** l'union s'est scindée or s'est fractionnée en une confédération d'États plus indépendants **2** VT [+ *power, responsibility, authority*] déléguer (**on, upon** à); **to ~ power away from central government** déléguer le pouvoir du gouvernement central; **a ~d government** un gouvernement décentralisé

Devonian [də'vəʊnɪən] ADJ (*Geol*) [*period*] dévonien

devote [dɪ'vəʊt] VT [+ *time, life, book, magazine*] consacrer (**to** à); [+ *resources*] affecter (**to** à), consacrer (**to** à), réserver (**to** pour); **to ~ o.s. to** [+ *a cause*] se vouer à, se consacrer à; [+ *pleasure*] se livrer à; [+ *study, hobby*] s'adonner à, se consacrer à, se livrer à; **the money ~d to education** l'argent consacré à l'éducation; **two chapters ~d to his childhood** deux chapitres consacrés à son enfance

devoted [dɪ'vəʊtɪd] ADJ **a** (= *loyal*) [*husband, mother, friend*] dévoué; [*friendship*] solide, profond; [*follower*] fidèle; **~ care** dévouement *m*; **to be a ~ admirer of sb/sth** être un fervent admirateur de qn/qch; **Joyce is a ~ Star Trek fan** Joyce est une inconditionnelle de Star Trek; **to be ~ to sb** être dévoué à qn; **to be ~ to sth** être fidèle à qch; **they are ~ to one another** ils sont très attachés l'un à l'autre **b** **~ to** (= *concerned with*) consacré à; **a museum ~ to ecology** un musée consacré à l'écologie

devotedly [dɪ'vəʊtɪdlɪ] ADV avec dévouement

devotee [ˌdevəʊ'tiː] N [*of doctrine, theory*] partisan(e) *m(f)*; [*of religion*] adepte *mf*; [*of sport, music, poetry*] passionné(e) *m(f)*

devotion [dɪ'vəʊʃən] **1** N (*NonC*) (*to duty*) dévouement *m* (**to** à); (*to friend*) dévouement *m* (**to** à, envers), (profond) attachement *m* (**to** pour); (*to work*) dévouement *m* (**to** à), ardeur *f* (**to** pour, à); (*Rel*) dévotion *f*, piété *f*; **with great ~** avec un grand dévouement **2** **devotions** NPL (*Rel*) dévotions *fpl*, prières *fpl*

devotional [dɪ'vəʊʃənl] ADJ [*book*] de dévotion, de piété; [*attitude*] de prière, pieux

devour [dɪ'vaʊəʳ] VT **a** [+ *food*] dévorer, engloutir; (*fig*) [+ *money*] engloutir, dévorer; [+ *book*] dévorer; **to ~ sb/sth with one's eyes** dévorer qn/qch des yeux **b** [*fire*] dévorer, consumer; (*fig*) **~ed by jealousy** dévoré de jalousie

devouring [dɪ'vaʊərɪŋ] ADJ [*hunger, passion*] dévorant; [*zeal*] ardent; [*enthusiasm*] débordant

devout [dɪ'vaʊt] ADJ **a** (= *pious*) [*person*] pieux, dévot; [*faith, Christianity, Catholicism etc*] dévot; [*prayer, attention, hope*] fervent **b** (*fig* = *committed*) [*supporter, opponent*] fervent

devoutly [dɪ'vaʊtlɪ] ADV **a** (= *fervently*) [*hope, believe, wish*] sincèrement **b** (= *piously*) avec dévotion; **the islanders are ~ religious** les habitants de l'île sont profondément religieux; **he was a ~ Christian prince** c'était un prince chrétien très pieux

DEW, dew¹ [djuː] **1** (*US*) ABBR = **distant early warning 2** COMP ► **DEW line** N DEW *f* (*système de radars*)

dew² [djuː] N rosée *f* → **mountain**

dewclaw ['djuːklɔː] N ergot *m*

dewdrop ['djuːdrɒp] N goutte *f* de rosée

dewlap ['djuːlæp] N [*of cow, person*] fanon *m*

dewpoint ['djuːpɔɪnt] N point *m* de rosée or de condensation

dewpond ['djuːpɒnd] N mare *f* (*alimentée par la condensation*)

dewy ['djuːɪ] **1** ADJ [*grass*] couvert de or humide de rosée; (*liter*) **~ lips** lèvres *fpl* fraîches

2 COMP ► **dewy-eyed** ADJ (= *innocent*) aux grands yeux ingénus; (= *credulous*) trop naïf (naïve *f*)

dex* [deks] N (*Drugs*) Dexédrine® *f*

Dexedrine® [deksɪ'driːn] N Dexédrine® *f*

dexie* ['deksɪ] N (*Drugs*) comprimé *m* de Dexédrine®

dexterity [deks'terɪtɪ] N (*intellectual*) habileté *f*; (*manual, physical*) dextérité *f*, adresse *f*; **~ in doing sth** habileté or dextérité à faire qch, adresse avec laquelle on fait qch; **a feat of ~** un tour d'adresse; **verbal ~** éloquence *f*

dexterous ['dekstrəs] ADJ [*person*] adroit, habile; [*movement*] adroit, agile; **by the ~ use of** par l'habile emploi de

dexterously ['dekstrəslɪ] ADV adroitement, habilement

dextrin ['dekstrɪn] N dextrine *f*

dextrose ['dekstrəʊs] N dextrose *m*

dextrous(ly) ['dekstrəs(lɪ)] = **dexterous(ly)**

DF (ABBR = **direction finder**) → **direction**

DFC [ˌdiːef'siː] N (ABBR = **Distinguished Flying Cross**) médaille décernée aux aviateurs militaires

DFE [ˌdiːef'iː] N (*Brit*) (ABBR = **Department for Education**) → **education**

DG **a** (ABBR = **director general**) → **director** **b** (ABBR = **Deo gratias**) par la grâce de Dieu

dg (ABBR = **decigram(s)**) dg *m*

DH [diː'eɪtʃ] N (*Brit*) (ABBR = **Department of Health**) → **department**

dhoti ['dəʊtɪ] N dhotî *m*

dhow [daʊ] N boutre *m*

DHSS [ˌdiːeɪtʃes'es] N (*Brit: formerly*) (ABBR = **Department of Health and Social Security**) → **health**

DI [diː'aɪ] N **a** (ABBR = **Donor Insemination**) → **donor** **b** (*Brit Police*) (ABBR = **Detective Inspector**) → **detective**

di... PREF *di...*

diabetes [ˌdaɪə'biːtiːz] N diabète *m*; **to have ~** être diabétique, avoir du diabète

diabetic [ˌdaɪə'betɪk] **1** N diabétique *mf* **2** ADJ **a** (= *person*) diabétique **b** (= *for diabetics*) [*chocolate, dessert, jam etc*] pour diabétiques

diabolic [ˌdaɪə'bɒlɪk] ADJ = **diabolical a**

diabolical [ˌdaɪə'bɒlɪkəl] ADJ **a** [*act, invention, plan, power*] diabolique, infernal, satanique; [*laugh, smile*] satanique, diabolique **b** (* = *dreadful*) [*child*] infernal*; [*weather*] atroce*, épouvantable

diabolically [ˌdaɪə'bɒlɪkəlɪ] ADV **a** (* = *horribly*) [*hot, difficult*] horriblement **b** (= *wickedly*) diaboliquement; **~ clever** d'une astuce diabolique; **she grinned/laughed ~** elle eut un sourire/rire diabolique **c** (* = *very badly*) [*drive, sing, cook etc*] horriblement mal

diachronic [ˌdaɪə'krɒnɪk] ADJ diachronique

diacid [daɪ'æsɪd] N biacide *m*, diacide *m*

diacritic [ˌdaɪə'krɪtɪk] **1** ADJ diacritique **2** N signe *m* diacritique

diacritical [ˌdaɪə'krɪtɪkəl] ADJ diacritique

diadem ['daɪədem] N (*lit, fig*) diadème *m*

diaeresis, dieresis (*US*) [daɪ'erɪsɪs] N (*pl* **diaereses, diereses** (*US*) [daɪ'erɪˌsiːz]) (*Ling*) diérèse *f*; (*Typ* = *symbol*) tréma *m*

diagnose ['daɪəgnəʊz] VT (*Med, fig*) diagnostiquer; **his illness was ~d as bronchitis** on a diagnostiqué une bronchite

diagnosis [ˌdaɪəg'nəʊsɪs] N (*pl* **diagnoses** [ˌdaɪəg'nəʊsiːz]) (*Med, fig*) diagnostic *m*; (*Bio, Bot*) diagnose *f*

diagnostic [ˌdaɪəg'nɒstɪk] ADJ diagnostique; (*Comput*) **~ program** programme *m* de diagnostic

diagnostician [ˌdaɪəgnɒs'tɪʃən] N diagnostiqueur *m*

diagnostics [ˌdaɪəg'nɒstɪks] N (*NonC: Comput etc*) diagnostic *m*

diagonal [daɪˈægənl] [1] ADJ diagonal [2] N diagonale f

diagonally [daɪˈægənəlɪ] ADV (with vb) [write, cross, cut, fold] en diagonale; [park] en épi; **the car was struck ~ by a lorry** la voiture a été prise en écharpe par un camion; **a sash worn ~ across the chest** une grande écharpe portée en travers de la poitrine; **the bank is ~ opposite the church, on the right/left** par rapport à l'église, la banque est de l'autre côté de la rue, sur la droite/gauche

diagram [ˈdaɪəɡræm] N (gen) diagramme m, schéma m; (Math) diagramme m, figure f; **as shown in the ~** comme le montre le diagramme or le schéma

diagrammatic [ˌdaɪəɡrəˈmætɪk] ADJ schématique

▼ **dial** [daɪəl] [1] N cadran m → **sundial** [2] VT (Telec) [+ number] faire, composer; **you must ~ 336 1295** il faut faire or composer le 336 12 95; (Brit) **to ~ 999** ≈ appeler police-secours; **to ~ a wrong number** faire un faux or mauvais numéro; **to ~ direct** appeler par l'automatique; **can I ~ London from here?** est-ce que d'ici je peux avoir Londres par l'automatique? [3] COMP ▶ **dial code** N (US Telec) indicatif m ▶ **dial tone** N (US Telec) tonalité f ▶ **dial-up service** N (Comput) service m de télétraitement

dial. ABBR = **dialect**

dialect [ˈdaɪəlekt] [1] N (regional) dialecte m, parler m; (local, rural) patois m; **the Norman ~** le dialecte normand, les parlers mpl normands; **in ~** en dialecte, en patois; **social-class ~** sociolecte m [2] COMP [word] dialectal ▶ **dialect atlas** N atlas m linguistique ▶ **dialect survey** N étude f de dialectologie

dialectal [ˌdaɪəˈlektl] ADJ dialectal

dialectical [ˌdaɪəˈlektɪkəl] [1] ADJ dialectique [2] COMP ▶ **dialectical materialism** N matérialisme m dialectique

dialectician [ˌdaɪəlekˈtɪʃən] N dialecticien(ne) m(f)

dialectic(s) [ˌdaɪəˈlektɪk(s)] N (NonC) dialectique f

dialectology [ˌdaɪəlekˈtɒlədʒɪ] N (NonC) dialectologie f

dialling, dialing (US) [ˈdaɪəlɪŋ] [1] N (Telec) composition f d'un numéro (de téléphone) [2] COMP ▶ **dialling code** N (Brit) indicatif m ▶ **dialling tone** N (Brit) tonalité f

dialogue, dialog (US) [ˈdaɪəlɒɡ] [1] N (lit, fig) dialogue m [2] COMP ▶ **dialogue box** N (Comput) boîte f de dialogue

dialysis [daɪˈælɪsɪs] [1] N (pl **dialyses** [daɪˈælɪˌsiːz]) dialyse f [2] COMP ▶ **dialysis machine** N rein m artificiel

diamagnetism [ˌdaɪəˈmæɡnɪtɪzəm] N diamagnétisme m

diamanté [ˌdaɪəˈmæntɪ] [1] N strass m [2] ADJ [brooch etc] en strass

diameter [daɪˈæmɪtər] N diamètre m; **the circle is one metre in ~** le cercle a un mètre de diamètre

diametrical [ˌdaɪəˈmetrɪkəl] ADJ (Math, fig) diamétral

diametrically [ˌdaɪəˈmetrɪkəlɪ] ADV [a] **~ opposed** or **opposite** diamétralement opposé (**to** à) [b] (Math) diamétralement

diamond [ˈdaɪəmənd] [1] N [a] (= stone) diamant m → **rough** [b] (= shape, figure) losange m [c] (Cards) carreau m; **the ace/six of ~s** l'as/le six de carreau → **club 1d** [d] (Baseball) diamant m, terrain m (de base-ball) [2] COMP [clip, ring] de diamant(s) ▶ **diamond-cutting** N taille f du diamant ▶ **diamond district** N **the ~ district of New York/Amsterdam** le quartier des diamantaires à New York/Amsterdam ▶ **diamond drill** N foreuse f à pointe de diamant ▶ **diamond jubilee** N

➤ LANGUAGE IN USE: **dial** 27.1, 27.5, 27.7

(célébration f du) soixantième anniversaire m (d'un événement) ▶ **diamond merchant** N diamantaire m ▶ **diamond necklace** N rivière f de diamants ▶ **diamond-shaped** ADJ en losange ▶ **diamond wedding** N noces fpl de diamant

diamorphine [ˌdaɪəˈmɔːfiːn] N (Med) diamorphine f

Diana [daɪˈænə] N Diane f

diapason [ˌdaɪəˈpeɪzən] N diapason m; (of organ) **open/stopped ~** diapason m large/étroit

diaper [ˈdaɪəpər] [1] N (US) couche f (de bébé) [2] COMP ▶ **diaper service** N service m de couches à domicile

diaphanous [daɪˈæfənəs] ADJ (liter) diaphane

diaphoretic [ˌdaɪəfəˈretɪk] ADJ, N (Med) diaphorétique m

diaphragm [ˈdaɪəfræm] N (all senses) diaphragme m

diarist [ˈdaɪərɪst] N [of personal events] auteur m d'un journal intime; [of contemporary events] mémorialiste mf, chroniqueur m

diarrhoea, diarrhea (US) [ˌdaɪəˈriːə] N diarrhée f; **to have ~** avoir la diarrhée or la colique

diarrhoeal, diarrheal (US) [ˌdaɪəˈrɪəl] ADJ diarrhéique

diary [ˈdaɪərɪ] N (record of events) journal m (intime); (for engagements) agenda m; **to keep a ~** tenir un journal; **I've got it in my ~** je l'ai noté sur mon agenda

diaspora [daɪˈæspərə] N diaspora f

diastole [daɪˈæstəlɪ] N diastole f

diatonic [ˌdaɪəˈtɒnɪk] ADJ diatonique

diatribe [ˈdaɪətraɪb] N diatribe f (**against** contre)

dibasic [daɪˈbeɪsɪk] ADJ bibasique, dibasique

dibber [ˈdɪbər] N (esp Brit) = **dibble**

dibble [ˈdɪbl] [1] N plantoir m [2] VT repiquer

dibs [dɪbz] NPL [a] (= game) osselets mpl; (Cards = counters) jetons mpl [b] (Brit‡ = money) fric‡ m [c] (US‡) **to have ~ on sth** avoir des droits sur qch; **~ on the cookies!** prem'‡ pour les petits gâteaux!

dice [daɪs] [1] N (pl inv) dé m; **to play ~** jouer aux dés; (esp US fig) **no ~!** pas question! → **load** [2] VI jouer aux dés; (fig) **he was dicing with death** il jouait avec la mort [3] VT [+ vegetables] couper en dés or en cubes

dicey* [ˈdaɪsɪ] ADJ (Brit) risqué; **it's ~ ◊ it's a ~ business** c'est bien risqué

dichotomy [daɪˈkɒtəmɪ] N dichotomie f

Dick [dɪk] N (dim of **Richard**) Richard m

dick [dɪk] N [a] (‡‡ = detective) détective m → **clever, private** [b] (‡‡ = penis) bite‡‡ f

dickens ‡† [ˈdɪkɪnz] N (euph) = **devil 1c**

Dickensian [dɪˈkenzɪən] ADJ à la Dickens

dicker [ˈdɪkər] VI (US) marchander

dickey [ˈdɪkɪ] [1] N* [of shirt] faux plastron m (de chemise) [2] COMP ▶ **dickey bird*** N (baby talk) petit zoziau m (baby talk); (Phot) **watch the ~ bird!** le petit oiseau va sortir!; **not a ~ bird*** que dalle‡; **I won't say a ~ bird about it*** je n'en piperai pas mot ▶ **dickey-bow*** N (= bow tie) nœud m pap* ▶ **dickey seat** N (Brit) strapontin m; (Aut) spider m

dickhead‡‡ [ˈdɪkhed] N tête f de nœud‡‡

dicky¹ [ˈdɪkɪ] = **dickey**

dicky²* [ˈdɪkɪ] ADJ (Brit) [person] patraque*, pas solide*; [health, heart] qui flanche*, pas solide*; [situation] pas sûr*, pas solide*

dicta [ˈdɪktə] NPL = **dictum**

Dictaphone® [ˈdɪktəfəʊn] N dictaphone® m; **~ typist** dactylo f qui travaille au dictaphone®

dictate [dɪkˈteɪt] [1] VT [a] [+ letter, passage] dicter (**to** à) [b] (= demand, impose) [+ terms,

conditions] dicter, imposer; **his action was ~d by circumstances** il a agi comme le lui dictaient les circonstances; **reason/common sense ~s that …** la raison/le bon sens veut que … [2] VI [a] dicter; **she spent the morning dictating to her secretary** elle a passé la matinée à dicter des lettres (or des rapports etc) à sa secrétaire [b] (= order about) **to ~ to sb** imposer sa volonté à qn, régenter qn; **I won't be ~d to!** je n'ai pas d'ordres à recevoir! [3] [ˈdɪkteɪt] N (gen pl) **~s** ordre(s) m(pl), précepte(s) m(pl) (de la raison etc); **the ~s of conscience** la voix de la conscience

dictation [dɪkˈteɪʃən] N (in school, office etc) dictée f; **to write to sb's ~** écrire sous la dictée de qn

dictator [dɪkˈteɪtər] N (fig, Pol) dictateur m

dictatorial [ˌdɪktəˈtɔːrɪəl] ADJ (lit, fig) [person] tyrannique; [régime, powers] dictatorial

dictatorially [ˌdɪktəˈtɔːrɪəlɪ] ADV (fig, Pol) autoritairement, dictatorialement, en dictateur

dictatorship [dɪkˈteɪtəʃɪp] N (fig, Pol) dictature f

diction [ˈdɪkʃən] N [a] (Literat = style) style m, langage m; **poetic ~** langage m poétique [b] (= pronunciation) diction f, élocution f; **his ~ is very good** il a une très bonne diction

dictionary [ˈdɪkʃənrɪ] [1] N dictionnaire m; **to look up a word in a ~** chercher un mot dans un dictionnaire; **it's not in the ~** ce n'est pas dans le dictionnaire; **French ~** dictionnaire m de français; **English-French ~** dictionnaire m anglais-français; **monolingual/bilingual ~** dictionnaire m monolingue/bilingue [2] COMP ▶ **dictionary definition** N **the ~ definition of "art"** le mot «art» tel qu'on le définit dans le dictionnaire ▶ **dictionary-maker** N (= person) lexicographe mf ▶ **dictionary-making** N lexicographie f

dictum [ˈdɪktəm] N (pl **dictums** or **dicta**) (= maxim) dicton m, maxime f; (= pronouncement) proposition f, affirmation f; (Jur) remarque f superfétatoire

did [dɪd] VB pt of **do¹**

didactic [dɪˈdæktɪk] ADJ didactique

didactically [dɪˈdæktɪkəlɪ] ADV [speak] sur un ton didactique; [write] de façon didactique

diddle* [ˈdɪdl] VT (Brit = cheat) [+ person] rouler (dans la farine)*, escroquer; **you've been ~d** tu t'es fait rouler* or avoir*; **to ~ sb out of sth ◊ to ~ sth out of sb** carotter* qch à qn

diddler‡ [ˈdɪdlər] N (Brit) carotteur* m, -euse* f, escroc m

diddly(-squat)‡ [ˈdɪdlɪ(ˈskwɒt)] N (US) **you don't know ~ (about that)** t'y connais que dalle‡; **that doesn't mean ~ (to me)** (pour moi,) c'est du vent tout ça; **their promises mean ~** leurs promesses ne sont que du vent

didn't [ˈdɪdənt] = **did not**; → **do¹**

Dido [ˈdaɪdəʊ] N Didon f

die¹ [daɪ] VI [a] [person] mourir, décéder (frm); [animal, plant] mourir, crever; [engine, motor] caler, s'arrêter; **he ~d in hospital** il est mort or décédé à l'hôpital; **to be dying** être en train de mourir; (= nearly dead) être à l'article de la mort; **doctors told him he was dying and had only a year to live** les médecins lui ont dit qu'il était condamné et qu'il n'avait plus qu'un an à vivre; **they were left to ~** on les a laissés mourir; **to ~ for one's country/beliefs** mourir pour son pays/ses idées; **Christ ~d for us/for our sins** le Seigneur est mort pour nous/pour expier nos péchés; **to ~ of or from cancer/AIDS/malaria** mourir du cancer/du sida/de la malaria; **to ~ of hunger/cold** mourir de faim/froid; **to ~ from one's injuries** mourir des suites de ses blessures; **to ~ of a broken heart** mourir de chagrin or de tristesse; **I almost ~d of shame/fright** j'étais mort de honte/peur; **we nearly ~d of boredom** on s'ennuyait à mourir; (frm) **to ~ by one's own hand** se suicider, mettre fin à ses jours; (fig) **to ~ with one's boots on*** mourir debout; **he ~d a hero** il est mort en héros; **he ~d a pauper** il est mort dans la misère; **he ~d happy** or **a happy man** (= died in peace) il est mort en paix, il est mort heureux; **to ~ like a dog**† mourir comme un chien; **never say ~!*** il ne faut jamais désespérer!; **you only ~ once** on ne meurt qu'une fois; (fig) **I'd rather** or **sooner ~!** plutôt mourir!; **I nearly** or **could have ~d!** (lit) j'ai failli mourir!; (* fig: of embarrassment) j'étais mort de honte!; **I want to ~!** (lit) (pain, depression etc) je voudrais mourir or être mort!; (embarrassment) je suis mort de honte!; **he'd ~ for her** il donnerait sa vie pour elle; **I'd ~ for a body/car** etc **like that!** je ferais n'importe quoi pour avoir un corps/ une voiture etc comme celui-là/celle-là!; **a body/car** etc **to ~ for*** un corps/une voiture de rêve; **it's to ~ for!*** ça me fait craquer!* → **natural**

[b] * [+ performer] faire un bide* or un four

[c] (* fig = long) **to be dying** or **to do sth** mourir d'envie de faire qch; **I'm dying for a cigarette/a cup of coffee** j'ai une envie folle de fumer une cigarette/de boire une tasse de café; **she's dying for him for holidays** elle meurt d'envie de partir en vacances; **she was dying for him to kiss her** elle n'attendait qu'une chose: qu'il l'embrasse (subj)

[d] (fig = die out) [fire, love, memory, daylight] s'éteindre, mourir; [custom, language] mourir, disparaître; [sound] s'éteindre; **her smile ~d on her lips** son sourire s'est évanoui or a disparu; (liter) **her words ~d on her lips** elle est restée bouche bée; **the secret ~d with him** il a emporté le secret dans la tombe; **to ~ hard** [tradition, attitude, prejudice] avoir la vie dure ■ (PROV) **old habits ~ hard** les vieilles habitudes ont la vie dure

[2] VT **to ~ a natural/violent death** mourir de mort naturelle/de mort violente; **to ~ a slow** or **lingering death** mourir d'une mort lente; **to ~ a painful death** mourir dans la souffrance; **to ~ the death** [person] faire un bide*; [idea, plan] tomber à l'eau; (fig) **he ~d the death*** il aurait voulu rentrer sous terre; (Theat) [performer] il a fait un bide* or un four; (liter) **to ~ a thousand deaths** être au supplice, souffrir mille morts

▶ **die away** VI [sound, voice, laughter] s'éteindre; [breeze, wind] tomber; **his footsteps ~d away** le bruit de ses pas s'est éteint

▶ **die back** VI [plant] perdre ses feuilles et sa tige

▶ **die down** VI [emotion, protest] se calmer, s'apaiser; [wind] tomber, se calmer; [fire] (in blazing building) diminuer, s'apaiser; (in grate etc) baisser, tomber; [noise] diminuer; [applause] se taire; [violence, conflict] s'atténuer; **the fuss quickly ~d down** l'agitation est vite retombée

▶ **die off** VI mourir or être emportés les uns après les autres

▶ **die out** VI [species, race, family] disparaître; [custom, language, skill, technique] disparaître, se perdre; **to be dying out** [species, race, tribe] être en voie d'extinction; [custom, language, skill] être en train de disparaître or de se perdre

die² [daɪ] **[1]** N **a** (pl **dice** [daɪs]) dé m; **the ~ is cast** le sort en est jeté, les dés sont jetés; (Brit) **as straight as a ~** (person) franc comme l'or; (street, tree trunk) droit comme un i → **dice** **[b]** (pl **dies**) (in minting) coin m; (Tech) matrice f; **stamping ~** étampe f **[2]** COMP ▶ **die-casting** N moulage m or coulage m sous pression ▶ **die-sinker** N graveur m de matrices ▶ **die-stamp** VT graver

dièdre [dɪˈedə] N (Climbing) dièdre m

diehard [ˈdaɪhɑːd] **[1]** N (= one who resists to the last) jusqu'au-boutiste mf; (= opponent of change) conservateur m, -trice f (à tout crin); (= obstinate politician etc) dur(e) m(f) à cuire*,

réactionnaire mf **[2]** ADJ intransigeant, inébranlable; (Pol) réactionnaire

dielectric [ˌdaɪəˈlektrɪk] ADJ, N diélectrique m

dieresis [daɪˈerɪsɪs] N (US) = **diaeresis**

diesel [ˈdiːzəl] **[1]** N **a** diesel m **b** = **diesel fuel, diesel oil** **[2]** COMP ▶ **diesel-electric** ADJ diesel-électrique ▶ **diesel engine** N (Aut) moteur m diesel; (Rail) motrice f ▶ **diesel fuel, diesel oil** N gasoil m ▶ **diesel train** N autorail m

diestock [ˈdaɪstɒk] N (= frame) cage f (de filière à peignes); (= tool) filière f à main

diet¹ [ˈdaɪət] **[1]** N **a** (= restricted food) régime m; **to be/go on a ~** être/se mettre au régime or à la diète; **he's on a special ~** il suit un régime spécial; **a high/low-protein ~** un régime à haute/basse teneur en protéines **b** (= customary food) alimentation f, nourriture f; (lit) **to live on a (constant) ~ of** vivre or se nourrir de; (fig) **she lives on a constant ~ of TV soap operas** elle passe son temps à regarder des feuilletons à la télévision; **for years they have fed us a staple ~ of propaganda** cela fait des années qu'ils nous assènent leur propagande; **children who are fed a relentless ~ of violence on TV** des enfants qui regardent sans arrêt des images violentes à la télévision

[2] VI suivre un régime

[3] VT mettre au régime

[4] COMP ▶ **diet drink** N (low calorie) boisson f basses calories or light inv; (for special or restricted diet) boisson f diététique ▶ **diet foods** (low calorie) N aliments mpl basses calories; (for special or restricted diet) aliments mpl diététiques

diet² [ˈdaɪət] N (esp Pol) diète f

dietary [ˈdaɪətərɪ] **[1]** ADJ (gen) de régime, diététique **[2]** N régime m alimentaire (d'un hôpital, d'une prison etc) **[3]** COMP ▶ **dietary fibre** N cellulose f végétale, fibres fpl alimentaires

dieter [ˈdaɪətə] N personne f qui suit un régime; **she's a keen ~** elle est souvent au régime

dietetic [ˌdaɪəˈtetɪk] ADJ diététique

dietetics [ˌdaɪəˈtetɪks] N (NonC) diététique f

dietician [ˌdaɪəˈtɪʃən] N spécialiste mf de diététique, diététicien(ne) m(f)

differ [ˈdɪfə] VI **a** (= be different) différer, se distinguer (**from** de); **the herring gull ~s from the common gull in the colour of its legs** le goéland argenté se distingue du goéland cendré par la couleur de ses pattes **b** (= disagree) ne pas être d'accord, ne pas s'entendre (**from sb** avec qn, **on** or **about sth** sur qch); **the two points of view do not ~ much** les deux points de vue ne se distinguent guère l'un de l'autre or ne sont pas très différents l'un de l'autre; **they ~ in their approach to the problem** ils diffèrent en or sur leur manière d'appréhender le problème; **I beg to ~** permettez-moi de ne pas partager cette opinion or de ne pas être de votre avis; **the texts ~** les textes ne s'accordent pas; (Jur) **to ~ from the rules** déroger aux règles → **agree**

difference [ˈdɪfrəns] N **a** (= dissimilarity) différence f (**in** de, **between** entre); **that makes a big ~ to me** c'est très important pour moi, ça ne m'est pas du tout égal, cela compte beaucoup pour moi; **to make a ~ in sb/sth** changer qn/qch; **that makes all the ~** voilà qui change tout; **what ~ does it make?** ◊ **what's the ~?** quelle différence (cela fait-il)?; **what ~ does it make if ...?** qu'est-ce que cela peut faire que ... (+ subj)?, quelle importance cela a-t-il si ... (+ indic)?; **it makes no ~** peu importe, cela ne change rien (à l'affaire); **it makes no ~ to me** cela m'est égal, ça ne (me) fait rien; **for all the ~ it makes** pour ce que cela change or peut changer; **it makes no ~ what colour/how expensive your car is** peu importe la couleur/le prix de votre voiture; **same ~!*** c'est du pareil au même!*,

c'est kif-kif!*; **with this ~, that ...** à la différence que ..., à ceci près que ...; **a car with a ~** une voiture pas comme les autres*; **test-drive a Jaguar and feel the ~!** essayez une Jaguar et vivez la différence!; **~ of opinion** différence f or divergence f d'opinions → **know** **[b]** (= quarrel) différend m **[c]** (Math) différence f (**in** de, **between** entre); **to pay the ~** payer la différence → **split**

different [ˈdɪfrənt] **[1]** ADJ **a** (= not the same) différent (**from, to,** (US) **than** de); (= other) autre; **completely ~** totalement différent, tout autre; **completely ~ from** totalement différent de; **he wore a ~ tie each day** il portait chaque jour une cravate différente; **go and put on a ~ tie** va mettre une autre cravate; **I feel a ~ person** je me sens revivre, je me sens tout autre; **let's do something ~** faisons quelque chose de différent; **quite a ~ way of doing** une tout autre manière de faire; **that's quite a ~ matter** ça c'est une autre affaire, c'est tout autre chose; **she's quite ~ from what you think** elle n'est pas du tout ce que vous croyez; **he wants to be ~** il veut se singulariser; (US) **~ strokes for ~ folks*** chacun son truc* **[b]** (= various) différent, divers; (= several) plusieurs; **~ people had noticed this** plusieurs personnes l'avaient remarqué; **in the ~ countries I've visited** dans les différents or divers pays que j'ai visités

[2] ADV (tout) autrement; **if it had happened to them, I'm sure they would think ~** si cela leur était arrivé, je suis sûr qu'ils penseraient tout autrement; **she believes this, but I know ~** c'est ce qu'elle croit mais je sais qu'il n'en est rien or qu'il en va tout autrement; **children behave like that because they don't know any ~*** les enfants se comportent ainsi parce qu'ils ignorent que ça ne se fait pas; **to me things seemed normal because I didn't know any ~*** les choses me semblaient normales car je ne savais pas que ça pouvait être différent

differential [ˌdɪfəˈrenʃəl] **[1]** ADJ différentiel **[2]** N différentielle f; (esp Brit) (in pay) écart m salarial; (Aut) différentiel m **[3]** COMP ▶ **differential calculus** N (Math) calcul m différentiel ▶ **differential equation** N équation f différentielle ▶ **differential gear** N (engrenage m) différentiel m ▶ **differential housing** N boîtier m de différentiel ▶ **differential operator** N opérateur m différentiel ▶ **differential pricing** N (Econ) tarification f différentielle

differentially [ˌdɪfəˈrenʃəlɪ] ADV (Tech) par action différentielle

differentiate [ˌdɪfəˈrenʃɪeɪt] **[1]** VI faire la différence or la distinction (**between** entre); **he cannot ~ between red and green** il ne fait pas la différence entre le rouge et le vert, il ne distingue pas le rouge du vert; **in his article he ~s between ...** dans son article, il fait la distinction entre ...; **we must ~ between the meanings of this term** il nous faut différencier les sens de ce mot **[2]** VT [+ people, things] différencier, distinguer (**from** de); (Math) différentier, calculer la différentielle de; **this is what ~s the two brothers** c'est ce qui différencie les deux frères; **this is what ~s one brother from the other** c'est ce qui distingue or différencie un frère de l'autre

differentiation [ˌdɪfərenʃɪˈeɪʃən] N différenciation f; (Math) différentiation f

differently [ˈdɪfrəntlɪ] ADV **a** différemment (**from** de); **she was never treated ~ from the men** on ne l'a jamais traitée différemment des hommes; **he thinks ~ from you** (= has different mentality) il ne pense pas comme vous; (= disagrees) il n'est pas de votre avis; **we all react ~ to stress** nous réagissons tous différemment face au stress, nous avons tous des réactions différentes face au stress; **if only things had turned out ~!** si seulement les choses s'étaient passées différemment ! **b** ~ **coloured/shaped** (= *of various colours/shapes*) de différentes couleurs/formes; (= *having other colours/shapes*) de couleurs différentes/ aux formes différentes **c** (*in politically correct language*) ~ **abled** (= *physically handicapped*) handicapé

▼**difficult** ['dɪfɪkəlt] ADJ **a** [*problem, situation, decision, task, writer*] difficile; **there's nothing ~ about it** ça n'a rien de difficile; **it's ~ being a man today** c'est difficile d'être un homme aujourd'hui; **this work is ~ to do** ce travail est difficile à faire; **it's ~ to do that** c'est difficile de faire ça; **it is ~ to deny that ...** il est difficile de nier que ... (+ *indic*); **he finds it ~ to apologize** cela lui coûte de s'excuser, il a du mal à s'excuser; **to find it ~ to do sth** avoir du mal à faire qch; **the climate makes it ~ to grow crops** le climat rend les cultures difficiles; **his injury makes it ~ (for him) to get around** il se déplace difficilement à cause de sa blessure; **he's ~ to get on with** il est difficile à vivre; **it is ~ to see what they could have done** on voit mal ce qu'ils auraient pu faire; **the ~ thing is knowing** *or* **to know where to start** le (plus) difficile *or* dur est de savoir par où commencer **b** (= *awkward, uncooperative*) [*person, child*] difficile; **come on now, don't be ~!** allez, ne crée pas de problèmes !

difficulty ['dɪfɪkəltɪ] N difficulté *f*; **with/ without ~** avec/sans difficulté *or* peine; **it's feasible, but with ~** c'est faisable, mais ce sera difficile; **she has ~ in walking** elle marche difficilement *or* avec difficulté, elle a de la difficulté *or* elle éprouve de la difficulté *or* elle a du mal à marcher; **slight ~ (in) breathing** un peu de gêne dans la respiration; **there was some ~ in finding him** on a eu du mal à le trouver; **the ~ is (in) choosing** le difficile *or* la difficulté c'est de choisir; **to make difficulties for sb** créer des difficultés à qn; **without meeting any difficulties** sans rencontrer d'obstacles *or* la moindre difficulté, sans accrocs; **to get into ~** *or* **difficulties** se trouver en difficulté; **to get into all sorts of difficulties** se trouver plongé dans toutes sortes d'ennuis; **to get out of a ~** se tirer d'affaire *or* d'embarras; **I am in ~** j'ai des difficultés, j'ai des problèmes; **to be in (financial) difficulties** être dans l'embarras, avoir des ennuis d'argent; **he was in ~** *or* **difficulties over the rent** il était en difficulté pour son loyer; **he was working under great difficulties** il travaillait dans des conditions très difficiles; **I can see no ~ in what you suggest** je ne vois aucun obstacle à ce que vous suggérez; **he's having ~** *or* **difficulties with his wife/his car/his job** il a des ennuis *or* des problèmes avec sa femme/avec sa voiture/dans son travail

diffidence ['dɪfɪdəns] N manque *m* de confiance en soi, manque *m* d'assurance, timidité *f*

diffident ['dɪfɪdənt] ADJ [*person*] qui manque de confiance *or* d'assurance, timide; [*smile*] embarrassé; **to be ~ about doing sth** hésiter à faire qch (par modestie *or* timidité)

diffidently ['dɪfɪdntlɪ] ADV [*speak, ask*] d'un ton mal assuré; [*behave*] avec timidité

diffract [dɪ'frækt] VT diffracter

diffraction [dɪ'frækʃən] N diffraction *f*; ~ **grating** réseau *m* de diffraction

diffuse [dɪ'fjuːz] **1** VT [+ *light, heat, perfume, news*] diffuser, répandre; ~**d lighting** éclairage *m* diffus *or* indirect **2** VI [*light, heat, perfume, news*] se diffuser, se répandre **3** [dɪ'fjuːs] ADJ [*light, thought*] diffus; [*style, writer*] prolixe, diffus

diffuseness [dɪ'fjuːsnɪs] N **a** [*of light, thought*] qualité *f* diffuse **b** [*of style, writer*] prolixité *f*

diffuser [dɪ'fjuːzər] N (*for light, hair dryer*) diffuseur *m*

diffusion [dɪ'fjuːʒən] N diffusion *f*

dig [dɪg] (*vb: pret, ptp* **dug**) **1** N **a** (*with hand/ elbow*) coup *m* de poing/de coude; **to give sb a ~ in the ribs** donner un coup de coude dans les côtes de qn **b** (= *sly comment*) pique *f*; **to have** *or* **take a ~ at sb** envoyer *or* lancer une pique à qn; **was that a ~ at me?** cette pique m'était destinée? **c** (*with spade*) coup *m* de bêche **d** (*Archeol*) fouilles *fpl*; **to go on a ~** aller faire des fouilles **2** VT **a** [+ *ground*] (*gen*) creuser; (*with spade*) bêcher; [+ *grave, trench, hole*] creuser; [+ *tunnel*] creuser, percer; [+ *potatoes etc*] arracher; **they dug their way out of prison** ils se sont évadés de prison en creusant un tunnel; (*lit, fig*) **to ~ one's own grave** creuser sa propre tombe **b** (= *thrust*) [+ *fork, pencil etc*] enfoncer (**sth into sth** qch dans qch); **to ~ sb in the ribs** donner un coup de coude dans les côtes de qn **c** (*US‡*) (= *understand*) piger*; (= *take notice of*) viser*; **you ~?** tu piges ?*; ~ **that guy!** vise un peu ce mec !*; (= *enjoy*) **I ~ that!** ça me botte !*; **I don't ~ football** le football ne me dit rien *or* me laisse froid **3** VI **a** [*dog, pig*] fouiller, fouir; [*person*] creuser (**into** dans); (*Tech*) fouiller; (*Archeol*) faire des fouilles; **to ~ for minerals** creuser pour extraire du minerai **b** (*fig*) **to ~ in one's pockets for sth** (*searching for sth*) fouiller dans ses poches pour trouver qch; **to ~ into one's pockets** *or* **purse** (= *spend money*) (*for oneself*) piocher dans ses économies; (*to help other people*) mettre la main au porte-monnaie; **to ~ deep** (= *search hard*) mener une enquête approfondie; (= *try hard*) [*athlete etc*] puiser dans ses réserves; (= *give generously*) mettre la main au porte-monnaie; **to ~ into the past** fouiller dans le passé

▶**dig in 1** VI **a** (*Mil*) se retrancher; (*fig*) être fin prêt; **the pickets are ~ging in for a long strike** les piquets de grève se préparent à un conflit prolongé **b** (*‡ = eat*) attaquer*; ~ **in!** allez-y, attaquez !; **let's ~ in!** allez, on attaque ! **2** VT SEP **a** (*into ground*) [+ *compost, manure*] mélanger à la terre, enterrer **b** (= *push, thrust in*) [+ *blade, knife*] enfoncer; (*fig*) **to ~ one's heels in** se braquer, se buter; (*fig*) **to ~ the knife in** remuer le couteau dans la plaie

▶**dig into** VT FUS [+ *sb's past*] fouiller dans; (*‡ = eat*) [+ *food*] attaquer deux mots à*, attaquer

▶**dig out** VT SEP [+ *tree, plant*] déterrer; [+ *animal*] déloger; (*fig*) [+ *facts, information*] déterrer, dénicher; **to ~ sb out of the snow/ rubble** sortir qn de la neige/des décombres; **where did he ~ out* that old hat?** où a-t-il été pêcher *or* dénicher ce vieux chapeau ?

▶**dig over** VT SEP [+ *earth*] retourner; [+ *garden*] bêcher, retourner

▶**dig up** VT SEP [+ *weeds, vegetables*] arracher; [+ *treasure, body*] déterrer; [+ *earth*] retourner; [+ *garden*] bêcher, retourner; (*fig*) [+ *fact, solution, idea*] déterrer, dénicher

digest [daɪ'dʒest] **1** VT [+ *food, idea*] digérer, assimiler; [+ *insult*] digérer*; **this kind of food is not easy to ~** *or* **easily ~ed** ce genre de nourriture est un peu indigeste **2** VI digérer **3** ['daɪdʒest] N (= *summary*) [*of book, facts*] sommaire *m*, résumé *m*; (= *magazine*) digest *m*; (*Jur*) digeste *m*; **in ~ form** en abrégé

digestible [daɪ'dʒestəbl] ADJ (*lit, fig*) facile à digérer, digeste

digestion [daɪ'dʒestʃən] N (*Anat, Chem, fig*) digestion *f*

digestive [daɪ'dʒestɪv] **1** ADJ digestif **2** N (*Brit: also* ~ **biscuit**) ≈ (sorte *f* de) sablé *m* → **juice 3** COMP ▶ **digestive system** N système *m* digestif ▶ **digestive tract** N appareil *m* digestif

digger ['dɪgər] N **a** (= *machine*) excavatrice *f*, pelleteuse *f* **b** (= *miner*) ouvrier mineur *m*; (= *navvy*) terrassier *m* **c** (‡ = *Australian/New Zealander*) Australien *m*/Néo-Zélandais *m* **d*** (*Mil Hist*) soldat australien ou néo-zélandais de la première guerre mondiale → **gold**

digging ['dɪgɪŋ] **1** N (*NonC*) (*with spade*) bêchage *m*; [*of hole etc*] forage *m*; (*Min*) creusement *m*, excavation *f* **2** **diggings** NPL (*Min*) placer *m*; (*Archeol*) fouilles *fpl*

digit ['dɪdʒɪt] N **a** (*Math*) chiffre *m*; **double-/ triple-~** à deux/trois chiffres **b** (= *finger*) doigt *m*; (= *toe*) orteil *m* **c** (*Astron*) doigt *m*

digital ['dɪdʒɪtl] **1** ADJ **a** (*Comput etc*) [*readout, recording etc*] numérique; [*tape, recorder*] audionumérique; [*clock, watch*] à affichage numérique; ~ **computer** calculateur *m* numérique **b** (*Anat*) digital **2** COMP ▶ **digital audio tape** N bande *f* audionumérique *or* DAT ▶ **digital compact cassette** N cassette *f* compacte numérique

digitalin [ˌdɪdʒɪ'teɪlɪn] N digitaline *f*

digitalis [ˌdɪdʒɪ'teɪlɪs] N (*Bot*) digitale *f*; (*Pharm*) digitaline *f*

digitally ['dɪdʒɪtəlɪ] ADV (*Audio, Mus*) [*record, transmit etc*] en numérique; ~ **remastered** mixé en numérique; (*on CD cover*) "~ **remastered (version)**" « remix numérique », « mixage numérique »

digitize ['dɪdʒɪtaɪz] VT (*Comput*) digitaliser

digitizer [ˌdɪdʒɪtaɪzər] N (*Comput*) digitaliseur *m*, convertisseur *m* numérique

diglossia [daɪ'glɒsɪə] N diglossie *f*

diglossic [daɪ'glɒsɪk] ADJ diglossique

dignified ['dɪgnɪfaɪd] ADJ [*person, manner*] plein de dignité, digne; [*pause, silence*] digne; **a ~ old lady** une vieille dame très digne; **he is very ~** il a beaucoup de dignité

dignify ['dɪgnɪfaɪ] VT donner de la dignité à; **to ~ sth/sb with the name of ...** honorer qch/ qn du nom de ...

dignitary ['dɪgnɪtərɪ] N dignitaire *m*

dignity ['dɪgnɪtɪ] N **a** (*NonC*) [*of person, occasion, character, manner*] dignité *f*; **he thinks that's beneath his ~** il se croit au-dessus de ça; **it would be beneath his ~ to do such a thing** il s'abaisserait en faisant une chose pareille; **to stand on one's ~** prendre de grands airs; **to (be allowed to) die with ~** (se voir accorder le droit de) mourir dignement *or* dans la dignité **b** (= *high rank*) dignité *f*, haut rang *m*; (= *title*) titre *m*, dignité *f*

digress [daɪ'gres] VI s'écarter, s'éloigner (**from** de), faire une digression; **... but I ~** ... mais je m'écarte du sujet

digression [daɪ'greʃən] N digression *f*; **this by way of ~** ceci (soit) dit en passant

digressive [daɪ'gresɪv] ADJ digressif

digs †* [dɪgz] NPL (*Brit* = *lodgings*) chambre *f* meublée (*avec ou sans pension*); **I'm looking for ~** je cherche une chambre meublée à louer; **to be in ~** loger en garni†

dihedral [daɪ'hiːdrəl] ADJ, N dièdre *m*

dike [daɪk] N = **dyke**

diktat [dɪk'taːt] N diktat *m*

dilapidated [dɪ'læpɪdeɪtɪd] ADJ [*house*] délabré; [*clothes*] dépenaillé; [*book*] déchiré; **in a ~ state** dans un état de délabrement

dilapidation [dɪˌlæpɪ'deɪʃən] N [*of buildings*] délabrement *m*, dégradation *f*; (*Jur: gen pl*) détérioration *f* (*causée par un locataire*); (*Geol*) dégradation *f*

dilate [daɪ'leɪt] **1** VT dilater; **to ~ the cervix** dilater le col (de l'utérus); (*in labour*) **to be 3cm ~d** être dilaté de 3 cm **2** VI **a** se dilater **b** (= *talk at length*) **to ~ (up)on sth** s'étendre sur qch, raconter qch en détail

dilation [daɪ'leɪʃən] N dilatation *f*; (*Med*) ~ **and curettage** (dilatation *f* et) curetage *m*

dilatoriness ['dɪlətərɪnɪs] N lenteur *f* (**in doing** à faire), caractère *m* dilatoire

dilatory ['dɪlətərɪ] [1] ADJ [*person*] traînard, lent ; [*action, policy*] dilatoire ; **they were very ~ about it** ils ont fait traîner les choses (en longueur) [2] COMP ► **dilatory motion** N (*Pol*) manœuvre *f* dilatoire

dildo ['dɪldəʊ] N godemiché *m*

dilemma [daɪ'lemə] N dilemme *m* ; **to be in a ~** ◊ **to be on the horns of a ~** être pris dans un dilemme

dilettante [,dɪlɪ'tæntɪ] [1] N (*pl* **dilettantes** *or* **dilettanti** [,dɪlɪ'tæntɪ]) dilettante *mf* [2] COMP de dilettante

dilettantism ['dɪlɪ'tæntɪzəm] N dilettantisme *m*

diligence ['dɪlɪdʒəns] N zèle *m*, diligence *f* (*frm*) ; **his ~ in his work** le zèle *or* la diligence (*frm*) dont il fait preuve dans son travail ; **to work with ~** faire preuve d'assiduité dans son travail

diligent ['dɪlɪdʒənt] ADJ [*student, worker, work*] appliqué ; [*search*] minutieux ; **to be ~ in doing sth** faire qch avec zèle *or* diligence (*frm*)

diligently ['dɪlɪdʒəntlɪ] ADV avec zèle *or* diligence (*frm*)

dill [dɪl] N aneth *m*, fenouil *m* bâtard

dilly* ['dɪlɪ] N (*US*) **it's/he's a ~** c'est/il est sensationnel* *or* vachement* bien ; **we had a ~ of a storm** nous avons eu une sacrée* tempête ; (*of problem*) **it's a ~** c'est un casse-tête

dillydally ['dɪlɪdælɪ] VI (= *dawdle*) lanterner, lambiner* ; (= *fritter time away*) musarder ; (= *vacillate*) tergiverser, atermoyer

dillydallying ['dɪlɪdælɪɪŋ] N (= *vacillation*) tergiversation(s) *f(pl)* ; (= *dawdling*) **no ~!** ne traînez pas !

dilute [daɪ'luːt] [1] VT [+ *liquid*] diluer ; [+ *wine*] couper ; [+ *sauce*] délayer, allonger ; (*Pharm*) diluer ; (*fig*) diluer, édulcorer ; **"~ to taste"** « à diluer selon votre goût » [2] ADJ [*liquid*] coupé, dilué ; (*fig*) dilué, édulcoré

diluter [daɪ'luːtə'] N diluant *m*

dilution [daɪ'luːʃən] N dilution *f* ; [*of wine, milk*] coupage *m*, mouillage *m* ; (*fig*) édulcoration *f*

dim [dɪm] [1] ADJ [a] (= *not bright*) [*light, lamp*] faible ; [*room, place*] sombre ; (*fig*) [*prospects, outlook*] sombre. [b] (= *vague*) [*shape, outline*] vague, imprécis ; [*recollection, memory*] vague → **view**. [c] (*liter*) [*eyes, sight*] faible ; **Elijah's eyes were growing ~** la vue d'Élie baissait. [d] (*Brit* = *stupid*) bouché* [2] VT [a] (= *turn down*) [+ *light*] réduire, baisser ; [+ *lamp*] mettre en veilleuse ; [+ *sb's sight*] brouiller, troubler ; (*Theat*) **to ~ the lights** baisser les lumières ; (*US Aut*) **to ~ the headlights** se mettre en code(s). [b] (= *make dull*) [+ *colours, metals, beauty*] ternir, obscurcir ; [+ *sound*] assourdir ; [+ *memory, outline*] effacer, estomper ; [+ *mind, senses*] affaiblir, troubler ; [+ *glory*] ternir [3] VI (*also* **grow ~**) [a] [*light*] baisser, décliner ; [*sight*] baisser, se troubler. [b] [*metal, beauty, glory*] se ternir ; [*colours*] devenir terne ; [*outlines, memory*] s'effacer, s'estomper [4] COMP ► **dim-out** N (*US*) black-out *m* partiel ► **dim-sighted** ADJ à la vue basse ► **dim-witted** ADJ crétin*, idiot ; **a ~-witted* mechanic** un crétin* de mécanicien

►**dim out** (*US*) [1] VT SEP [+ *city*] plonger dans un black-out partiel [2] **~-out** N → **dim**

dimbo* ['dɪmbəʊ] N (*Brit*) (*man*) ballot* *m* ; (*woman*) godiche* *f*

dime [daɪm] [1] N (pièce *f* de) dix cents ; (*US*) **it's not worth a ~*** cela ne vaut pas un clou* *or* un radis* ; (*fig*) **they're a ~ a dozen*** il y en a *or* on en trouve à la pelle [2] COMP ► **dime**

novel N (*US*) roman *m* de gare, roman *m* de quatre sous ► **dime store** N (*in US*) ≈ Prisunic® *m*

dimension [daɪ'menʃən] N (= *size, extension in space*) dimension *f* ; (*Archit, Geom*) dimension *f*, cote *f* ; (*fig* = *scope, extent*) [*of problem, epidemic*] étendue *f*

diminish [dɪ'mɪnɪʃ] [1] VT [+ *strength, power*] amoindrir ; [+ *effect*] diminuer, atténuer ; [+ *numbers, cost, speed*] réduire ; [+ *enthusiasm, optimism*] tempérer ; (*Mus*) diminuer [2] VI [*strength, power*] s'amoindrir ; [*effect*] s'atténuer ; [*numbers, cost*] se réduire ; [*resources, supply*] s'amenuiser

diminished [dɪ'mɪnɪʃt] [1] ADJ [a] [*strength, power*] amoindri ; [*value, budget, capacity, cost, numbers, staff, resources, supply*] réduit ; [*enthusiasm, optimism*] tempéré ; [*reputation*] terni ; **a ~ staff** un personnel réduit. [b] (*Mus*) [*interval, fifth, seventh*] diminué [2] COMP ► **diminished responsibility** N (*Jur*) responsabilité *f* atténuée

diminishing [dɪ'mɪnɪʃɪŋ] [1] ADJ [*amount, importance*] qui diminue, qui va en diminuant ; [*strength, power*] qui s'amoindrit ; [*resources, supply*] qui s'amenuise ; [*numbers, value, cost*] en baisse ; [*effect*] qui s'atténue ; (*Art*) **~ scale** échelle *f* fuyante *or* de perspective ; (*Econ*) **law of ~ returns** loi *f* des rendements décroissants [2] N diminution *f*

diminuendo [dɪ,mɪnjʊ'endəʊ] [1] N diminuendo *m* *inv* [2] VI faire un diminuendo

diminution [,dɪmɪ'njuːʃən] N [*of value*] baisse *f*, diminution *f* ; [*of speed*] réduction *f* ; [*of strength, enthusiasm*] diminution *f*, affaiblissement *m* (**in** de) ; [*of temperature*] baisse *f*, abaissement *m* (**in** de) ; [*of authority*] baisse *f* (**in** de) ; (*Mus*) diminution *f*

diminutive [dɪ'mɪnjʊtɪv] [1] ADJ [a] [*person, object*] tout petit, minuscule ; [*house, garden*] tout petit, exigu (-guë *f*), minuscule [b] (*Ling* = *shortened*) diminutif [2] N (*Ling*) diminutif *m*

dimity ['dɪmɪtɪ] N basin *m*

dimly ['dɪmlɪ] [1] ADV [a] (= *not brightly*) [*shine*] faiblement ; **~ lit** mal éclairé [b] (= *vaguely*) [*see, hear, recollect*] vaguement ; **the hills were ~ visible through the mist** on apercevait confusément les collines dans la brume ; **I was ~ aware that someone was talking to me** j'étais vaguement conscient que quelqu'un me parlait ; **she was ~ aware of Gavin's voice** elle entendait vaguement la voix de Gavin [2] COMP ► **dimly-remembered** ADJ dont on se souvient mal

dimmer ['dɪmə'] N [a] (*Elec: also* **~ switch**) variateur *m* (de lumière) [b] (*US Aut*) **~s** phares *mpl* code *inv*, codes *mpl* ; (= *parking lights*) feux *mpl* de position

dimming ['dɪmɪŋ] N [a] [*of light*] affaiblissement *m*, atténuation *f* ; [*of mirror, reputation*] ternissement *m* [b] (*US Aut*) [*of headlights*] mise *f* en code(s)

dimness ['dɪmnɪs] N [a] [*of light, sight*] faiblesse *f* ; [*of room, forest*] obscurité *f* ; [*of outline, memory*] flou *m* ; [*of colour, metal*] aspect *m* terne ; [*of intelligence*] faiblesse *f* [b] (* = *stupidity*) stupidité *f*

dimorphism [daɪ'mɔːfɪzəm] N dimorphisme *m*

dimple ['dɪmpl] [1] N (*in chin, cheek*) fossette *f* (**on** sur) ; (*in water*) ride *f* [2] VI [*water*] se rider ; **she ~d** ◊ **her cheeks ~d** ses joues se creusèrent de deux fossettes [3] VT **the wind ~d the water** le vent ridait la surface de l'eau

dimpled ['dɪmpld] ADJ [*cheek, chin*] à fossette

dimwit* ['dɪmwɪt] N imbécile *mf*, crétin(e)* *m(f)*

DIN [dɪn] N (ABBR = **Deutsche Industrie Normen**) DIN

din [dɪn] [1] N vacarme *m*, chahut *m* ; **the ~ of battle** le fracas de la bataille ; **to make** *or* **kick up a ~*** faire du boucan* [2] VT **to ~ sth into**

sb rebattre les oreilles à qn de qch ; **she ~ned (it) into the child that he mustn't speak to strangers** elle répétait sans cesse à l'enfant qu'il ne devait pas parler à des inconnus ; **I had it ~ned into me that it was wrong to lie** on m'a dit et répété mille fois qu'il ne fallait pas mentir ; **try to ~ it into her that ...** essayez de lui enfoncer dans la tête que ...

dinar ['diːnɑː] N dinar *m*

din-dins ['dɪndɪnz] N (*Brit: baby talk*) miam-miam *m* (*baby talk*) ; **it's time for ~** ◊ **your ~ is ready** c'est l'heure de faire miam-miam

dine [daɪn] [1] VI dîner (**off, on** de) ; **they ~d off** *or* **on a chicken** ils ont dîné d'un poulet [2] VT inviter à dîner → **wine** [3] COMP ► **dining car** N (*Brit Rail*) wagon-restaurant *m* ► **dining hall** N salle *f* à manger ► **dining room** N salle *f* à manger ; (*in hotel*) salle *f* de restaurant ► **dining room suite** N salle *f* à manger (*meubles*) ► **dining room table**, **dining table** N table *f* de salle à manger

►**dine in** VI dîner à la maison *or* chez soi

►**dine out** VI dîner en ville *or* au restaurant ; (*fig*) **he ~d out on that story for a long time afterwards** il a resservi cette histoire trente-six fois par la suite

diner ['daɪnə'] N [a] (= *person*) dîneur *m*, -euse *f* [b] (*Rail*) wagon-restaurant *m* [c] (*US*) petit restaurant *m*

dinero* [dɪ'neərəʊ] N (*US*) pognon* *m*, fric* *m*

dinette [daɪ'net] N coin-repas *m* → **kitchen**

ding-a-ling ['dɪŋəlɪŋ] N [a] [*of bell, telephone*] dring dring *m* [b] (*US* * = *fool*) cloche* *f*

dingbat ['dɪŋbæt] N (*US*) imbécile *mf*, andouille* *f*

ding-dong ['dɪŋ'dɒŋ] [1] N [a] (= *noise*) ding dong *m* [b] (* = *quarrel*) prise *f* de bec [2] ADJ* [*fight*] acharné, dans les règles (*fig*) [3] ADV ding dong

dinghy ['dɪŋgɪ] N youyou *m*, petit canot *m* ; (*collapsible*) canot *m* pneumatique ; (*also* **sailing ~**) dériveur *m*

dinginess ['dɪndʒɪnɪs] N aspect *m* minable* *or* miteux

dingo ['dɪŋgəʊ] N (*pl* **dingoes**) dingo *m*

dingus* ['dɪŋgəs] N (*US*) truc* *m*, machin* *m*

dingy ['dɪndʒɪ] ADJ miteux

dink [dɪŋk] N (*US baby talk* = *penis*) zizi* *m*

dinkie* ['dɪŋkɪ] ABBR = **double income no kids** [1] N **~s** jeune(s) couple(s) *m(pl)* salarié(s) sans enfant, ≈ couple(s) *m(pl)* yuppie(s) [2] ADJ [*attitude, lifestyle*] ≈ de yuppie

dinkum* ['dɪŋkəm] ADJ (*Austral*) **he's a (fair) ~ Aussie** il est australien jusqu'au bout des ongles ; **fair ~!** (= *seriously!*) sans blague* !

dinky* ['dɪŋkɪ] [a] ADJ (*Brit*) mignon, gentil [b] (*US pej*) de rien du tout

dinner ['dɪnə'] [1] N (= *evening meal*) dîner *m* ; (= *lunch*) déjeuner *m* ; (*for dog, cat*) pâtée *f* ; **have you given the dog his ~?** tu as donné à manger au chien ? ; **he was having his ~** (*in evening*) il était en train de dîner ; (*at lunch*) il était en train de déjeuner ; **to be at ~†** être en train de dîner ; **we're having people to ~** nous avons du monde à dîner ; **~'s ready!** le dîner est prêt !, à table ! ; **we had a good ~** nous avons bien dîné (*or* déjeuné) ; **to go out to ~** dîner au restaurant ; (*at friends*) dîner chez des amis ; **a formal ~** un dîner officiel, un grand dîner ; (*Austral: in contest etc*) **to be done like a ~*** prendre une déculottée*

[2] COMP ► **dinner bell** N **the ~ bell has gone** on a sonné (pour) le dîner ► **dinner-dance** N dîner *m* dansant ► **dinner duty** N (*Scol*) service *m* de réfectoire ; (*Scol*) **to do ~ duty** *or* **to be on ~ duty** faire de service *or* de surveillance au réfectoire ► **dinner jacket** N (*Brit*) smoking *m* ► **dinner knife** N (*pl* **dinner knives**) grand couteau *m* ► **dinner lady** N (*Brit Scol*) femme *f* de service (*à la cantine*) ► **dinner money** N (*Brit Scol*) argent *m* pour

la cantine ► **dinner party** N dîner *m* (*sur invitation*); **to give a ~ party** avoir du monde à dîner, donner un dîner ► **dinner plate** N (grande) assiette *f* ► **dinner roll** N petit pain *m* ► **dinner service** N service *m* de table ► **dinner table** N **at the ~ table** pendant le dîner (*or* déjeuner), au dîner (*or* déjeuner) ► **dinner theater** N (*US*) cabaret *m*, café-théâtre *m* ► **dinner at ~ time** à l'heure du dîner (*or* déjeuner); **it's ~ time** c'est l'heure du *or* de dîner (*or* déjeuner) ► **dinner trolley, dinner wagon** N table *f* roulante

dinnertime ['dɪnətaɪm]   N = **dinner time**; → **dinner**

dinnerware ['dɪnəwɛəʳ] N (*US*) vaisselle *f*

dinosaur ['daɪnəsɔːʳ] N dinosaure *m*

dint [dɪnt] [1] N [a] = **dent 1** [b] **by ~ of (doing) sth** à force de (faire) qch [2] VT = **dent 2**

diocesan [daɪ'ɒsɪsən] [1] ADJ diocésain [2] N (*évêque m*) diocésain *m*

diocese ['daɪəsɪs] N diocèse *m*

diode ['daɪəʊd] N diode *f*

dioptre, diopter (*US*) [daɪ'ɒptəʳ] N dioptrie *f*

diorama [daɪə'rɑːmə] N diorama *m*

dioxide [daɪ'ɒksaɪd] N bioxyde *m*, dioxyde *m*

dioxin [daɪ'ɒksɪn] N dioxine *f*

DIP [dɪp] [1] N (*Comput*) ABBR = **Dual-In-Line Package** [2] COMP ► **DIP switch** N commutateur *m* en boîtier DIP

dip [dɪp] [1] VT [a] (*into liquid*) [+ *pen, hand, fingers, toes, clothes*] tremper (**into** dans); [+ *spoon*] plonger (**into** dans); (*Tech*) tremper, décaper; [+ *candle*] fabriquer; **to ~ a brush into paint** tremper un pinceau dans de la peinture; **she ~ped her hand into the bag** elle a plongé sa main dans le sac; **walnuts ~ped in chocolate** noix *fpl* enrobées de chocolat; ~ **the meat in flour** farinez la viande; (*fig*) **to ~ a** *or* **one's toe in the water** s'aventurer prudemment
[b] [+ *sheep*] traiter contre les parasites
[c] (= *bend*) [+ *one's head*] incliner
[d] (*Brit Aut*) **to ~ one's headlights** se mettre en code(s); (*Naut*) **to ~ one's flag** saluer avec le pavillon
[2] VI [a] [*ground*] descendre, s'incliner; [*road*] descendre; [*temperature, pointer on scale etc*] baisser; [*prices*] fléchir, baisser; [*boat, raft*] tanguer, piquer du nez*; **the sun ~ped below the horizon** le soleil a disparu à l'horizon; **sales ~ped (by) 6% last month** les ventes ont fléchi *or* baissé de 6 % le mois dernier
[b] **she ~ped into her handbag for money** elle a cherché de l'argent dans son sac à main; (*fig*) **to ~ into one's savings** puiser dans ses économies; **to ~ into a book** feuilleter un livre
[3] N [a] (*: in sea etc*) baignade *f*, bain *m* (*de mer etc*); **to have a (quick) ~** faire trempette*
[b] (*Agr: for treating animals*) bain *m* parasiticide
[c] (*in ground*) déclivité *f*; (*Geol*) pendage *m*; (*in prices, figures, unemployment, support, enthusiasm*) fléchissement *m*; (*in temperature*) baisse *f*; (*Phys: also* **angle of ~**) inclinaison *f* magnétique; **share prices have recovered after a slight ~ yesterday** les cours des actions sont remontés après un léger fléchissement hier; **an after-lunch ~ in concentration** une baisse de concentration après le déjeuner
[d] (*Culin*) sauce *f* froide (*dans laquelle on trempe des crudités, des chips*) ► **avocado ~** purée *f* *or* mousse *f* d'avocat, guacamole *m*; **hot cheese ~** fondue *f* savoyarde *or* au fromage
[e] → **lucky**
[4] COMP ► **dip needle** N aiguille *f* aimantée (de boussole) ► **dipped headlights** NPL codes *mpl*, feux *mpl* de croisement; **to drive on ~ped headlights** rouler en code(s) ► **dipping needle** N = **dip needle** ► **dip switch** N (*Aut*) basculeur *m* de phares

Dip. ABBR = **diploma**

Dip Ed ['dɪped] N (*Brit Univ*) (ABBR = **Diploma in Education**) diplôme *d'enseignement*

diphtheria [dɪf'θɪərɪə] [1] N diphtérie *f* [2] COMP ► **diphtheria vaccine** N vaccin *m* antidiphtérique

diphthong ['dɪfθɒŋ] N diphtongue *f*

diphthongize ['dɪfθɒŋaɪz] [1] VT diphtonguer [2] VI se diphtonguer

diploid ['dɪplɔɪd] ADJ diploïde

diploma [dɪ'pləʊmə] N diplôme *m*; **teacher's/nurse's ~** diplôme *m* d'enseignement/d'infirmière; **to hold** *or* **have a ~ in ...** être diplômé de *or* en ...

diplomacy [dɪ'pləʊməsɪ] N (*Pol, fig*) diplomatie *f*; (*fig*) **to use ~** user de diplomatie

diplomat ['dɪpləmæt] N (*Pol*) diplomate *m*, femme *f* diplomate; (*fig*) diplomate *mf*

diplomatic [ˌdɪplə'mætɪk] [1] ADJ [a] [*mission, relations*] diplomatique [b] (= *tactful*) [*person*] diplomate; [*action, behaviour*] diplomatique, plein de tact; [*answer*] diplomatique, habile; **to be ~ in dealing with sth** s'occuper de qch avec tact *or* en usant de diplomatie [2] COMP ► **diplomatic bag** N valise *f* diplomatique ► **diplomatic corps** N corps *m* diplomatique ► **diplomatic immunity** N immunité *f* diplomatique ► **diplomatic pouch** N = **diplomatic bag** ► **diplomatic service** N diplomatie *f*, service *m* diplomatique ► **diplomatic shuttle** N navette *f* diplomatique

diplomatically [ˌdɪplə'mætɪkəlɪ] ADV [a] (= *tactfully*) avec diplomatie, diplomatiquement; **~, he refrained from mentioning the divorce** il a fait preuve de diplomatie en s'abstenant de mentionner le divorce [b] (*Pol = by diplomacy*) diplomatiquement; [*isolated, active etc*] sur le plan diplomatique; **~, the Franco-German alliance has proved unshakeable** sur le plan diplomatique, l'alliance franco-allemande s'est avérée inébranlable

diplomatist [dɪ'pləʊmətɪst] N = **diplomat**

dipole ['daɪpəʊl] ADJ, N dipôle *m*

dipper ['dɪpəʳ] N [a] (*Orn*) cincle *m* (plongeur) [b] (= *ladle*) louche *f* [c] (*Aut: for headlamps*) basculeur *m* (de phares) [d] (*US Astron*) **the Big** *or* **Great Dipper** la Grande Ourse; **the Little Dipper** la Petite Ourse → **big**

dippy: ['dɪpɪ] ADJ toqué*

dipso: ['dɪpsəʊ] N (ABBR = **dipsomaniac**) soûlard(e)* *m(f)*

dipsomania [ˌdɪpsəʊ'meɪnɪə] N (*Med*) dipsomanie *f*

dipsomaniac [ˌdɪpsəʊ'meɪnɪæk] N (*Med*) dipsomane *mf*

dipstick ['dɪpstɪk] N (*Aut*) jauge *f* (de niveau d'huile)

diptera ['dɪptərə] NPL diptères *mpl*

dipterous ['dɪptərəs] ADJ diptère

dir. ABBR = **director**

dire ['daɪəʳ] ADJ [a] (= *desperate, appalling*) [*situation, consequences, effects*] désastreux; [*warning, prediction, threat*] sinistre; [*poverty*] extrême; **(in) ~ poverty** (dans) la misère; **to do sth from** *or* **out of ~ necessity** faire qch par nécessité; **to be in ~ need of sth** avoir terriblement besoin de qch; **to be in ~ straits** être dans une situation désastreuse [b] (* = *awful*) nul*

direct [dɪ'rɛkt] [1] ADJ [a] (= *without detour*) [*road, route, train, flight*] direct; **~ hit** (*Sport*) coup *m* (en plein) dans le mille; (*Mil*) coup *m* au but, tir *m* de plein fouet; **to score** *or* **make a ~ hit** mettre dans le mille; **the building took** *or* **received** *or* **suffered a ~ hit** le bâtiment a été touché de plein fouet
[b] (= *immediate*) [*cause, result*] direct, immédiat; [*contact, control, responsibility, access, talks, negotiations*] direct; [*danger*] immédiat, imminent; **this has a ~ effect on the environment** cela a un impact direct sur l'environnement;

the army is under his ~ control l'armée est sous son contrôle direct; **the two companies are in ~ competition (with each other)** ces deux sociétés sont en concurrence directe; **to have ~ access to sth** avoir directement accès à qch; **to come into** *or* **be in ~ contact with ...** être *or* entrer en contact direct avec ...; **this was his first ~ involvement in politics** c'était la première fois qu'il se mêlait directement de politique; **keep away from ~ heat** éviter l'exposition directe à la chaleur; **"keep out of ~ sunlight"** « ne pas exposer directement à la lumière du soleil »; **to be a ~ descendant of sb** ◊ **to be descended in a ~ line from sb** descendre en droite ligne *or* en ligne directe de qn
[c] (= *straightforward, not evasive*) [*person, character, answer*] franc (franche *f*), direct; [*question*] direct; (= *outright*) [*refusal*] catégorique, absolu; (= *explicit*) [*attack, reference, link*] direct; [*evidence*] tangible; **there has been no ~ challenge to the chairman** le directeur n'a pas été ouvertement contesté; **this is the most ~ challenge yet to UN authority** jusqu'à maintenant, l'autorité des Nations unies n'avait jamais été aussi directement remise en cause
[2] VT [a] (= *give directions to*) **to ~ sb to sth** indiquer le chemin de qch à qn; **can you ~ me to the town hall?** pourriez-vous m'indiquer le chemin de la mairie?
[b] (= *address, aim*) [+ *remark, question, abuse, letter*] adresser (**to** à); [+ *threat*] proférer (**at** contre); [+ *efforts*] orienter (**towards** vers); [+ *torch*] diriger (**on** sur); **to ~ sb's attention to sth** attirer l'attention de qn sur; **to ~ one's attention to sth** concentrer *or* reporter son attention sur qch; **the violence was ~ed against the police** les actes de violence étaient dirigés contre la police; **she ~ed an angry glance at him** elle lui a jeté un regard noir; **don't ~ your anger at me** ne vous en prenez pas à moi; **he ~ed his energies to winning the election** il a tout fait pour remporter l'élection; **we need to ~ more money into research** il faut que nous affections davantage d'argent à la recherche; **a policy ~ed towards improving public transport** une politique ayant pour but d'améliorer *or* visant à améliorer les transports publics
[c] (= *control*) [+ *sb's work*] diriger; [+ *business*] diriger, gérer; [+ *movements*] guider; (*Theat*) [+ *play*] mettre en scène; (*Cine, Rad, TV*) [+ *film, programme*] réaliser; [+ *group of actors*] diriger
[d] (= *instruct*) charger (**sb to do** qn de faire), ordonner (**sb to do** à qn de faire); **he did it as ~ed** il l'a fait comme on le lui avait dit *or* comme on l'en avait chargé; **to ~ that sth (should) be done** ordonner que qch soit fait; **the judge ~ed that this remark be deleted from the record** le juge a ordonné que cette remarque soit retirée du procès-verbal; **the judge ~ed the jury to find the accused not guilty** le juge imposa au jury un verdict d'acquittement; (*US Jur*) **~ed verdict** *verdict rendu par le jury sur la recommandation du juge*; (*Med: on medicines*) **"to be taken as ~ed"** « respecter les doses prescrites »; **"to be taken as ~ed by your doctor"** « se conformer à la prescription du médecin »
[3] VI **who is ~ing?** (*Theat*) qui est le metteur en scène?; (*Cine, Rad, TV*) qui est le réalisateur?
[4] ADV [*go, write*] directement; **to fly ~ from Glasgow to Paris** prendre un vol direct de Glasgow à Paris
[5] COMP ► **direct access** N (*Comput*) accès *m* direct ► **direct action** N (*Ind, Pol*) action *f* directe ► **direct addressing** N (*Comput*) adressage *m* direct ► **direct broadcasting by satellite** N diffusion *f* en direct par satellite ► **direct broadcasting satellite** N satellite *m* de diffusion directe ► **direct current** N (*Elec*) courant *m* continu ► **direct**

debit N (*Comm, Fin*) prélèvement *m* automatique ▸ **direct dialling** N composition *f* directe (*des numéros de téléphone*) ▸ **direct discourse** N (*US*) = **direct speech** ▸ **direct grant school** N (*Brit: formerly*) établissement scolaire sous contrat avec l'État, ≈ école *f* libre ▸ **direct mail** N publipostage *m* ▸ **direct marketing** N marketing *m* direct ▸ **the direct method** N (*Educ*) la méthode directe, l'immersion *f* linguistique ▸ **direct motion** N (*Astron*) mouvement *m* direct ▸ **direct object** N (*Gram*) complément *m* d'objet direct ▸ **direct rule** N (*Pol*) administration *f* directe (*par le pouvoir central*) ▸ **direct sales** NPL = **direct selling** ▸ **direct selling** N vente *f* directe ▸ **direct speech** N (*Gram*) discours *m* or style *m* direct ▸ **direct tax** N impôt *m* direct ▸ **direct taxation** N (*NonC*) imposition *f* directe

direction [dɪˈrekʃən] **1** N **a** (= *way*) direction *f*, sens *m*; (*fig*) direction *f*, voie *f*; **in every ~** dans toutes les directions, en tous sens; **in the wrong/right ~** (*lit*) dans le mauvais/bon sens, dans la mauvaise/bonne direction; (*fig*) sur la mauvaise/bonne voie; **it's a move** or **step in the right ~** c'est un pas dans la bonne direction; **in the opposite ~** en sens inverse; **in the ~ of ...** dans la direction de ..., en direction de ...; **what ~ did he go in?** quelle direction a-t-il prise ? → **sense** **b** (= *management*) direction *f*, administration *f*; **under the ~ of ...** sous la direction de ..., sous la conduite de ... **c** (*Theat*) mise *f* en scène; (*Cine, Rad, TV*) réalisation *f*; **"under the ~ of ..."** (*Theat*) « mise en scène de ... »; (*Cine, Rad, TV*) « réalisation de ... » **d** (= *instruction*) instruction *f*, indication *f*; **~s for use** mode *m* d'emploi → **stage** **2** COMP ▸ **direction finder** N radiogoniomètre *m* ▸ **direction finding** N radiogoniométrie *f* ▸ **direction indicator** N (*Aut*) clignotant *m*

directional [dɪˈrekʃənl] ADJ directionnel

directionless [dɪˈrekʃənlɪs] ADJ [*person*] sans but; [*activity*] qui ne mène nulle part

directive [dɪˈrektɪv] N directive *f*, instruction *f*

directly [dɪˈrektlɪ] **1** ADV **a** (= *straight*) [*go, affect, communicate, pay*] directement; **~ involved/responsible** directement impliqué/responsable; **the two murders are not ~ related** ces deux meurtres n'ont pas de rapport direct; **to be ~ descended from sb** descendre en droite ligne or en ligne directe de qn; **to come ~ to the point** aller droit au but **b** (= *frankly*) [*speak, ask*] directement **c** (= *completely, exactly*) [*opposed*] diamétralement, directement; **~ contrary to** diamétralement opposé à, exactement contraire à; **~ opposite points of view** des points de vue diamétralement opposés; **the bus stops ~ opposite** le bus s'arrête juste en face; **~ opposite the railway station** juste en face de la gare; **if a planet is at opposition, it is ~ opposite the sun** si une planète est en opposition, elle est directement à l'opposé du soleil **d** (*Brit* = *immediately, very soon*) tout de suite; **~ after supper** tout de suite après le dîner; **she'll be here ~** elle sera là tout de suite **2** CONJ (*esp Brit*) aussitôt que, dès que; **he'll come ~ he's ready** il viendra dès qu'il sera prêt

directness [dɪˈrektnɪs] N [*of character, reply*] franchise *f*; [*of person*] franchise *f*, franc-parler *m*; [*of attack, question*] caractère *m* direct; **the ~ of his refusal** son refus catégorique; **to speak with great ~** parler en toute franchise

director [dɪˈrektəʳ] **1** N **a** (= *person*) (*Brit*) [*of company*] directeur *m*, -trice *f*, administrateur *m*, -trice *f*; [*of institution*] directeur *m*, -trice *f*; (*Theat*) metteur *m* en scène; (*Cine, Rad, TV*) réalisateur *m*, -trice *f*; (*Rel*) directeur *m* de

conscience; **~ general** directeur *m* général → **board, managing, stage** **b** (= *device*) guide *m* **2** COMP ▸ **director of admissions** N (*US Univ etc*) responsable *mf* du service des inscriptions ▸ **Director of Education** N (*Brit*) ≈ recteur *m* d'académie ▸ **director of music** N (*Mil*) chef *m* de musique ▸ **Director of Public Prosecutions** N (*Brit Jur*) ≈ procureur *m* général ▸ **director of studies** N (*Univ*) (*for course*) directeur *m*, -trice *f* d'études; (*for thesis*) directeur *m*, -trice *f* de thèse ▸ **director's chair** N fauteuil *m* de metteur en scène ▸ **director's cut** N (*Cine*) version *f* du réalisateur, version *f* longue

directorate [dɪˈrektərɪt] N (= *board of directors*) conseil *m* d'administration

directorial [ˌdɪrekˈtɔːrɪəl] ADJ directorial, de directeur

directorship [dɪˈrektəʃɪp] N poste *m* or fonctions *fpl* de directeur or d'administrateur, direction *f*

▾ **directory** [dɪˈrektərɪ] **1** N **a** [*of addresses*] répertoire *m* (d'adresses); (*also* **street ~**) guide *m* des rues; (*Telec*) annuaire *m* (des téléphones); (*Comm*) annuaire *m* du commerce; (*Comput*) répertoire *m* (de dossiers) **b** (*Hist*) **Directory** Directoire *m* **2** COMP ▸ **directory assistance** N (*US*) = **directory inquiries** ▸ **directory inquiries** NPL (*Brit Telec*) (service *m* des) renseignements *mpl*

directrix [dɪˈrektrɪks] N (*Math*) (ligne *f*) directrice *f*

direful [ˈdaɪəfʊl] ADJ sinistre, menaçant

dirge [dɜːdʒ] N (*lit*) hymne *m* or chant *m* funèbre; (*fig*) chant *m* lugubre

dirigible [ˈdɪrɪdʒəbl] ADJ, N dirigeable *m*

dirk [dɜːk] N (*Scot*) dague *f*, poignard *m*

dirndl [ˈdɜːndəl] ADJ, N = **(skirt)** large jupe *f* froncée

dirt [dɜːt] **1** N **a** (*on skin, clothes, objects*) saleté *f*, crasse *f*; (= *earth*) terre *f*; (= *mud*) boue *f*; (= *excrement*) crotte *f*; (*Ind*) impuretés *fpl*, corps *mpl* étrangers; (*on machine, in engine*) encrassement *m*; **covered with ~** (*gen*) très sale, couvert de crasse; [*clothes, shoes, mudguards*] couvert de boue, tout crotté; [*cog, stylus*] encrassé; **a layer of ~** une couche de saleté or de crasse; **dog ~** crotte *f* de chien; (*fig*) **to eat ~** faire ses excuses les plus plates, ramper; **to treat sb like ~** traiter qn comme un chien; (*US fig*) **to do the ~ on sb*** ◊ **to do sb ~*** faire une vacherie‡ or une saloperie‡ à qn, jouer un tour de cochon* à qn **b** (*fig* = *obscenity*) obscénité *f* **c** (* = *scandal*) cancans *mpl*, ragots* *mpl*; **to dig up ~ on sb*** ◊ **to dig the ~ on sb*** (*Brit*) essayer de salir (la réputation de) qn; (*esp Brit*) **to dish the ~* (on sb)** colporter des ragots* (sur qn); **what's the ~ on ...?*** qu'est-ce que l'on raconte sur ... ? **2** COMP ▸ **dirt-cheap** ADV pour rien, pour une bouchée de pain; **I bought it ~-cheap** je l'ai acheté pour une bouchée de pain ♦ ADJ très bon marché *inv*; **it was ~-cheap** c'était donné ▸ **dirt farmer** N (*US*) petit fermier *m* ▸ **dirt road** N chemin *m* non macadamisé ▸ **dirt track** N (*gen*) piste *f*; (*Sport*) cendrée *f* ▸ **dirt track racing** N courses *fpl* motocyclistes or de motos sur cendrée

dirtily [ˈdɜːtɪlɪ] ADV [*eat, live*] salement, malproprement; (*fig*) [*act, behave*] bassement; [*play, fight*] déloyalement

dirtiness [ˈdɜːtɪnɪs] N saleté *f*

dirty [ˈdɜːtɪ] **1** ADJ **a** (= *soiled, unhygienic*) [*object, place, person, habit*] sale; [*job, work*] salissant; [*hypodermic needle*] usagé; [*plug, contact*] encrassé; **to get ~** se salir; **to get sth ~** salir qch; **to get one's hands ~** (*lit, fig*) se salir les mains; **to do** or **wash one's ~ linen** or **laundry in public** ◊ **to do one's ~ washing in public** laver son linge sale en public; **let's not**

wash our ~ linen or **laundry in public** il vaut mieux laver son linge sale en famille **b** [*colour*] **a ~ brown/grey** un marron/gris sale; **the morning light was ~ grey** la lumière du matin était d'un gris sale **c** (= *smutty*) [*book, film, joke, story, magazine, picture*] cochon*; [*language*] grossier; (*lit, fig*) **a ~ word** un gros mot; **"communist" was a ~ word for them** « communiste » était presque une injure pour eux; **he's got a ~ mind** il a l'esprit mal tourné **d** (= *unpleasant, underhand*) sale (*before n*); **politics is a ~ business** la politique est un sale métier; **it's a ~ job, but someone's got to do it** c'est un sale boulot, mais il faut bien que quelqu'un le fasse; **a very ~ election** les coups bas n'ont pas manqué dans cette élection; **to give sb a ~ look** regarder qn de travers; (*US*) **~ pool:** tour *m* de cochon*; **you ~ rat!*** sale type !*; **that was a ~ trick** c'était un sale tour or un tour de cochon*; **~ weather** sale temps *m*; **to do sb's ~ work (for them)** faire le sale boulot* de qn; **there's been some ~ work here!** il y a quelque chose de pas catholique* là-dessous ! → **hand** **2** ADV **a** (* = *unfairly*) **to play ~** faire des coups en vache*; **to fight ~** donner des coups en vache* **b** (= *smuttily*) **to talk ~*** dire des cochonneries **c** (*intensifier*) **a ~ great tractor:** un vachement gros tracteur* **3** VT [+ *hands, clothes, reputation*] salir; [+ *machine*] encrasser; **he's never had to ~ his hands to make a living** il n'a jamais eu à retrousser ses manches pour gagner sa vie **4** N (*Brit*) **to do the ~ on sb:** faire une vacherie‡ à qn, jouer un tour de cochon* à qn **5** COMP ▸ **dirty-faced** ADJ à or qui a la figure sale ▸ **dirty-minded** ADJ à or qui a l'esprit mal tourné ▸ **dirty old man*** N (*pl* **dirty old men**) vieux cochon* *m* ▸ **dirty weekend*** N week-end *m* coquin

disability [ˌdɪsəˈbɪlɪtɪ] **1** N **a** (*NonC*) (*physical*) invalidité *f*, incapacité *f*; (*mental*) incapacité *f*; **complete/partial ~** incapacité *f* totale/partielle **b** (= *infirmity*) infirmité *f*; (= *handicap*) désavantage *m*, handicap *m*; **his ~ made him eligible for a pension** son infirmité lui donnait droit à une pension **2** COMP ▸ **disability allowance** N allocation *f* d'invalidité ▸ **disability pension** N pension *f* d'invalidité

disable [dɪsˈeɪbl] VT [*illness, accident, injury*] rendre infirme; (= *maim*) estropier, mutiler; [+ *tank, gun*] mettre hors de combat; [+ *ship*] (*gen*) avarier, mettre hors d'état; (*by enemy action*) mettre hors de combat; (*Jur* = *make/pronounce incapable*) rendre/prononcer inhabile (**from doing** à faire)

disabled [dɪsˈeɪbld] **1** ADJ **a** (*permanently*) handicapé; (*esp Admin* = *unable to work*) invalide; (= *paralyzed*) estropié; (= *maimed*) mutilé; (*Mil*) mis hors de combat; **~ ex-servicemen** mutilés *mpl* or invalides *mpl* de guerre; **severely/partially ~** souffrant d'un handicap sévère/léger **b** (*Naut*) **to be ~** [*ship*] avoir des avaries, être immobilisé pour cause d'avaries; [*propeller*] être bloqué **c** (*Jur*) incapable (**from** de), inhabile (**from** à) **2** NPL **the disabled** les handicapés *mpl*; **the severely ~** les personnes *fpl* souffrant d'un handicap sévère; **the war ~** les mutilés *mpl* or les invalides *mpl* de guerre

disablement [dɪsˈeɪblmənt] **1** N invalidité *f* **2** COMP ▸ **disablement benefit** N allocation *f* d'invalidité ▸ **disablement insurance** N assurance *f* invalidité ▸ **disablement pension** N pension *f* d'invalidité

disabuse [ˌdɪsəˈbjuːz] VT (*frm*) désenchanter; **to ~ sb of sth** détromper qn de qch

▸ LANGUAGE IN USE: **directory** 27.1, 27.6

disadvantage [ˌdɪsədˈvɑːntɪdʒ] **1** N **a** (NonC) désavantage m, inconvénient m; **to be at a ~** être défavorisé; **you've got me at a ~** vous avez l'avantage sur moi; **to catch sb at a ~** surprendre qn en position de faiblesse; **to put sb at a ~** désavantager or défavoriser qn, mettre qn en position de faiblesse **b** (= prejudice, injury) préjudice m, désavantage m; (Comm = loss) perte f; **it would be** or **work to your ~ to be seen with him** cela vous porterait préjudice or vous ferait du tort si on vous voyait avec lui; **to sell at a ~** vendre à perte **2** VT désavantager, défavoriser

disadvantaged [ˌdɪsədˈvɑːntɪdʒd] **1** ADJ défavorisé; **educationally/socially/economically ~** défavorisé sur le plan scolaire/social/économique **2 the disadvantaged** NPL les classes fpl défavorisées; (economically) les économiquement faibles mpl

disadvantageous [ˌdɪsædvɑːnˈteɪdʒəs] ADJ désavantageux, défavorable (**to** à)

disadvantageously [ˌdɪsædvɑːnˈteɪdʒəslɪ] ADV d'une manière désavantageuse, désavantageusement

disaffected [ˌdɪsəˈfektɪd] ADJ (= discontented) mécontent, mal disposé

disaffection [ˌdɪsəˈfekʃən] N désaffection f, mécontentement m

disagree [ˌdɪsəˈɡriː] VI **a** (= be of different opinion) ne pas être d'accord (**with** avec, **on**, **about** sur), ne pas être du même avis (**with** que, **on**, **about** sur), être en désaccord (**with** avec, **on**, **about** sur); **I ~** je ne suis pas de cet avis, je ne suis pas d'accord; **I ~ completely with you** je ne suis pas du tout d'accord avec vous or pas du tout de votre avis; **they always ~ (with each other)** ils ne sont jamais du même avis or d'accord; (always quarrelling) ils sont incapables de s'entendre; **to ~ with the suggestion that ...** être contre la suggestion que ...; **she ~s with everything he has done** elle se trouve en désaccord avec tout ce qu'il a fait **b** (= be different) [explanations, reports, sets of figures] ne pas concorder (**with** avec) **c** **to ~ with sb** [climate, food] ne pas convenir or réussir à qn; **mutton ~s with him** il ne digère pas le mouton, le mouton ne lui réussit pas; **the mutton ~d with him** il a mal digéré le mouton, le mouton n'est pas bien passé*

disagreeable [ˌdɪsəˈɡrɪəbl] ADJ désagréable

disagreeableness [ˌdɪsəˈɡrɪəblnɪs] N [of work, experience] nature f désagréable or fâcheuse; [of person] mauvaise humeur f, maussaderie f, attitude f or manière(s) f(pl) désagréable(s)

disagreeably [ˌdɪsəˈɡrɪəblɪ] ADV désagréablement; **~ pungent** d'une âcreté désagréable

disagreement [ˌdɪsəˈɡriːmənt] N **a** (of opinion, also between accounts etc) différence f **b** (= quarrel) désaccord m, différend m; **to have a ~ with sb (about sth)** avoir un différend avec qn (à propos de qch); **to be in ~ (over sth)** [people] être en désaccord (sur qch)

disallow [ˌdɪsəˈlaʊ] VT (gen) rejeter; (Sport) [+ goal etc] refuser; (Jur) débouter, rejeter

disambiguate [ˌdɪsæmˈbɪɡjʊˌeɪt] VT désambiguïser

disambiguation [ˌdɪsæmˌbɪɡjʊˈeɪʃən] N désambiguïsation f

disappear [ˌdɪsəˈpɪər] **1** VI [person, vehicle, lost object, snow, objection] disparaître; [memory] disparaître, s'effacer; [difficulties] disparaître, s'aplanir; [custom] disparaître, tomber en désuétude; (Ling) [sound] s'amuïr; **he ~ed from view** or **sight** on l'a perdu de vue; **the ship ~ed over the horizon** le navire a disparu à l'horizon; **to make sth ~** faire disparaître qch; [conjurer] escamoter qch; (fig) **to do a ~ing trick*** s'éclipser, s'esquiver **2** VT (Pol*) [+ dissident] faire disparaître

disappearance [ˌdɪsəˈpɪərəns] N disparition f; (Ling) [of sound] amuïssement m

disappeared [ˌdɪsəˈpɪəd] NPL (Pol) **the ~** les disparus mpl

disappoint [ˌdɪsəˈpɔɪnt] VT **a** (= let down) [+ person] décevoir; (after promising) manquer à sa parole envers; **~ed me several times** il m'avait promis de me rencontrer mais il m'a fait faux bond plusieurs fois **b** (= confound) [+ expectations, hope] décevoir; **his schemes were ~ed** ses plans ont été contrecarrés

▼ **disappointed** [ˌdɪsəˈpɔɪntɪd] ADJ [person, hope, ambition] déçu; **to be ~ that ...** être déçu que ... (+ subj); **to be ~ to find/learn** etc être déçu de trouver/d'apprendre etc; **he was ~ with her reply** sa réponse l'a déçu; **to be ~ at having to do sth** être déçu de devoir faire qch; **we were ~ at not seeing her** or **not to see her** nous avons été déçus de ne pas la voir; **to be ~ in sb/sth** être déçu par qn/qch; **I'm (very) ~ in you** tu me déçois (beaucoup); **to be ~ in one's hopes/in love** être déçu dans ses espoirs or en amour

disappointing [ˌdɪsəˈpɔɪntɪŋ] ADJ décevant; **how ~!** quelle déception!, comme c'est décevant!

disappointingly [ˌdɪsəˈpɔɪntɪŋlɪ] ADV **progress has been ~ slow** les progrès ont été d'une lenteur décevante; **the house was ~ small** la taille de la maison était décevante; **the number of new jobs created was ~ low** le nombre de nouveaux emplois créés était décevant; **the boat performed ~ badly** le bateau s'est comporté de manière décevante; **~, she couldn't come** à notre grande déception or à la grande déception de tous, il n'a pas pu venir; **~ for his parents/teachers, he failed all his exams** à la grande déception de ses parents/professeurs, il a échoué à tous ses examens

disappointment [ˌdɪsəˈpɔɪntmənt] N **a** (NonC) déception f; **to my great ~** à ma grande déception **b** (= setback, source of disappointment) déception f, déboires mpl; **~s in love** déboires mpl amoureux; **he/that was a great ~ to me** il/cela a été une grosse déception pour moi, il/cela m'a beaucoup déçu

disapprobation (liter) [ˌdɪsæprəˈbeɪʃən], **disapproval** [ˌdɪsəˈpruːvl] N désapprobation f; **murmur** etc **of ~** murmure m etc désapprobateur or de désapprobation; **to show one's ~ of sb/sth** marquer sa désapprobation à l'égard de qn/qch; **the crowd were loud in their ~** la foule désapprouva bruyamment

▼ **disapprove** [ˌdɪsəˈpruːv] **1** VI **to ~ of sb/sth** désapprouver qn/qch; **to ~ of sb('s) doing sth** désapprouver or trouver mauvais que qn fasse qch; **your mother would ~** ta mère n'approuverait pas, ta mère ne trouverait pas ça bien; **he entirely ~s of drink** il est tout à fait contre la boisson **2** VT [+ action, event] désapprouver

disapproving [ˌdɪsəˈpruːvɪŋ] ADJ [expression, look] désapprobateur (-trice f); **she seemed ~** elle avait l'air de désapprouver; **Giles announced to his ~ mother that he would be marrying Kay** Giles a annoncé à sa mère, qui était contre, qu'il se mariait avec Kay; **to be ~ of sb/sth** désapprouver qn/qch; (fig) **to make ~ noises** manifester sa désapprobation

disapprovingly [ˌdɪsəˈpruːvɪŋlɪ] ADV [look, behave] d'un air désapprobateur; [speak] d'un ton désapprobateur

disarm [dɪsˈɑːm] VTI (also fig) désarmer

disarmament [dɪsˈɑːməmənt] **1** N désarmement m **2** COMP ► **disarmament talks** NPL conférence f sur le désarmement

disarmer [dɪsˈɑːmər] N (nuclear) **~** partisan(e) m(f) du désarmement nucléaire

disarming [dɪsˈɑːmɪŋ] **1** N (Mil) désarmement m **2** ADJ [smile] désarmant

disarmingly [dɪsˈɑːmɪŋlɪ] ADV [smile, admit] de façon désarmante; **~ modest/frank/simple** d'une modestie/franchise/simplicité désarmante

disarrange [ˌdɪsəˈreɪndʒ] VT déranger, mettre en désordre

disarranged [ˌdɪsəˈreɪndʒd] ADJ [bed] défait; [hair, clothes] en désordre

disarray [ˌdɪsəˈreɪ] N (frm) désordre m, confusion f; **the troops were in (complete) ~** le désordre or la confusion régnait parmi les troupes, les troupes étaient en déroute; **a political party in ~** un parti politique en plein désarroi or en proie au désarroi; **she was** or **her clothes were in ~** ses vêtements étaient en désordre; **to fall into ~** sombrer dans le chaos

disassemble [ˌdɪsəˈsembl] VT désassembler, démonter

disassociate [ˌdɪsəˈsəʊʃɪeɪt] VT = **dissociate**

disassociation [ˌdɪsəsəʊsɪˈeɪʃən] N = **dissociation**

disaster [dɪˈzɑːstər] **1** N (gen, also fig) désastre m, catastrophe f; (from natural causes) catastrophe f, sinistre m; **air ~** catastrophe f aérienne; **the Madrid airport ~** la catastrophe de l'aéroport de Madrid; **an environmental ~** une catastrophe écologique; **a financial/political ~** un désastre financier/politique; **on the scene of the ~** sur les lieux du désastre or de la catastrophe or du sinistre; **to be heading** or **headed for ~** courir au désastre; **their marriage/her hairstyle was a ~*** leur couple/sa coiffure était une catastrophe* or un (vrai) désastre **2** COMP ► **disaster area** N (lit) région f sinistrée; (fig) **a (walking) ~ area*** une catastrophe (ambulante)* ► **disaster fund** N collecte f au profit des sinistrés; **earthquake ~ fund** collecte f au profit des victimes du tremblement de terre ► **disaster movie** N film m catastrophe ► **disaster victim** N sinistré(e) m(f), victime f de la catastrophe

disastrous [dɪˈzɑːstrəs] ADJ désastreux (**for** pour); **with ~ consequences** avec des conséquences désastreuses

disastrously [dɪˈzɑːstrəslɪ] ADV de manière désastreuse; **the match started ~ for the French** le match a commencé de manière désastreuse pour les Français; **the Socialists fared ~ in the elections** les socialistes ont obtenu des résultats désastreux aux élections; **~ low/high prices** des prix dramatiquement bas/élevés; **to go ~ wrong** tourner à la catastrophe; **to get it ~ wrong** faire une erreur monumentale

disavow [ˌdɪsəˈvaʊ] VT (frm) [+ one's words, opinions] désavouer, renier; [+ faith, duties] renier

disavowal [ˌdɪsəˈvaʊəl] N (frm) [of one's words, opinions] désaveu m; [of faith, duties] reniement m

disband [dɪsˈbænd] **1** VT [+ army, corporation, club] disperser **2** VI [army] se disperser; [organization] se dissoudre

disbar [dɪsˈbɑːr] VT [+ barrister] radier de l'ordre des avocats; **to be ~red** se faire radier de l'ordre des avocats

disbarment [dɪsˈbɑːmənt] N (Jur) radiation f de l'ordre des avocats

disbelief [ˌdɪsbəˈliːf] N incrédulité f; **in ~** avec incrédulité

disbelieve [ˌdɪsbəˈliːv] **1** VT [+ person] ne pas croire; [+ news etc] ne pas croire à **2** VI (also Rel) ne pas croire (**in** à)

disbeliever [ˌdɪsbəˈliːvər] N (also Rel) incrédule mf

disbelieving [ˌdɪsbəˈliːvɪŋ] ADJ incrédule

disbud [dɪsˈbʌd] VT ébourgeonner

disburden [dɪs'bɜːdn] VT (*lit, fig*) décharger, débarrasser (**of** de) ; (= *relieve*) soulager ; **to ~ one's conscience** se décharger la conscience

disburse [dɪs'bɜːs] VTI (*frm*) débourser, décaisser

disbursement [dɪs'bɜːsmənt] N (*frm*) (= *paying out*) déboursement *m*, décaissement *m* ; (= *money paid*) débours *mpl*

disc [dɪsk] 1 N a (*also of moon etc*) disque *m* b (*Anat*) disque *m* (intervertébral) → **slip** c (*Mil: also* **identity ~**) plaque *f* d'identité d (= *gramophone record*) disque *m* 2 COMP ▶ **disc brakes** NPL freins *mpl* à disque ▶ **disc camera** N appareil *m* photo à disque ▶ **disc film** N film *m* disque ▶ **disc harrow** N pulvériseur *m* ▶ **disc jockey** N disc-jockey *m*, animateur *m*, -trice *f* ▶ **disc shutter** N (*Cine*) [*of projector*] obturateur *m* à disque

discard [dɪs'kɑːd] 1 VT a (= *get rid of*) se débarrasser de ; (= *throw out*) jeter ; [+ *jacket etc*] se débarrasser de ; [+ *idea, plan*] renoncer à, abandonner ; [+ *rocket, part of spacecraft*] larguer b (*Bridge etc*) se défausser de, défausser ; (*Cribbage*) écarter ; **he was ~ing clubs** il se défaussait à trèfle ; **he ~ed the three of hearts** il s'est défaussé du trois de cœur 2 VI (*Bridge etc*) se défausser ; (*Cribbage*) écarter 3 ['dɪskɑːd] N a (*NonC*) [*of cargo*] déchargement *m* ; (*Elec*) décharge *f* ; [*of weapon*] décharge *f* ; [*of liquid*] écoulement *m* b (*Bridge*) défausse *f* ; (*Cribbage*) écart *m* b (*Comm, Ind*) pièce *f* de rebut, déchet *m*

discern [dɪ'sɜːn] VT [+ *person, object, difference*] discerner, distinguer, percevoir ; [+ *feelings*] discerner

discernible [dɪ'sɜːnəbl] ADJ [*object*] visible ; [*likeness, fault*] perceptible, sensible

discernibly [dɪ'sɜːnəblɪ] ADV sensiblement

discerning [dɪ'sɜːnɪŋ] ADJ [*person*] judicieux, sagace, doué de discernement ; [*taste*] délicat ; [*look*] clairvoyant, perspicace

discernment [dɪ'sɜːnmənt] N (*fig*) discernement *m*, pénétration *f*

discharge [dɪs'tʃɑːdʒ] 1 VT a [+ *ship, cargo*] décharger ; [*ship, bus etc*] [+ *passengers*] débarquer b [+ *liquid*] déverser ; (*Elec*) décharger ; [*factory, chimney, pipe*] [+ *gas*] dégager, émettre ; [+ *liquid, pollutants, sewage*] déverser ; **the factory was discharging toxic gas into the atmosphere** l'usine rejetait des gaz toxiques dans l'atmosphère ; **the pipe was discharging sewage into the sea** le tuyau déversait les eaux usées dans la mer c (*Med*) [*wound*] [+ *mucus, blood*] laisser écouler ; **to ~ pus** suppurer d (*Ind*) [+ *employee*] renvoyer, congédier ; (*Mil*) [+ *soldier*] rendre à la vie civile ; (*for health reasons*) réformer ; (*Jur*) [+ *prisoner*] libérer, élargir (*Jur*) ; [+ *jury*] congédier ; [+ *accused*] relaxer ; [+ *bankrupt*] réhabiliter ; (*Med*) [+ *patient*] (*from hospital*) renvoyer (guéri) de l'hôpital ; **to ~ o.s.** (*from hospital*) signer sa décharge e [+ *gun*] décharger, faire partir ; [+ *arrow*] décocher f (*Fin*) [+ *debt, bill*] acquitter, régler g (*frm* = *fulfil*) [+ *obligation, duty*] remplir, s'acquitter de ; [+ *function*] remplir ; [+ *responsibilities*] exercer 2 VI [*wound*] suinter 3 ['dɪstʃɑːdʒ] N a (*NonC*) [*of cargo*] déchargement *m* ; (*Elec*) décharge *f* ; [*of liquid*] écoulement *m* b (*Med*) (*gen*) suintement *m* ; (*vaginal*) pertes *fpl* (blanches) ; [*of pus*] suppuration *f* ; **nipple ~** écoulement *m* mammaire c [*of employee*] renvoi *m* ; [*of prisoner*] libération *f*, élargissement *m* (*Jur*) ; [*of patient*] renvoi *m* ; **the soldier got his ~ yesterday** le soldat a été libéré hier d (*frm* = *fulfilment*) (*gen*) **the ~ of one's duty** l'accomplissement *m* de son devoir ; (*official tasks*) **the ~ of one's duties** l'exercice *m* de ses fonctions e [*of debt*] acquittement *m*

disci ['dɪskaɪ] NPL *of* **discus**

disciple [dɪ'saɪpl] N disciple *m*

disciplinarian [ˌdɪsɪplɪ'nɛərɪən] N personne *f* stricte en matière de discipline

disciplinary ['dɪsɪplɪnərɪ] ADJ (*gen*) disciplinaire ; **a ~ offence** une faute passible de mesures disciplinaires ; **~ matters/problems** questions *fpl*/problèmes *mpl* de discipline ; **to take ~ action** prendre des mesures disciplinaires

discipline ['dɪsɪplɪn] 1 N a (*NonC*) discipline *f* ; **to keep ~** maintenir la discipline b (= *branch of knowledge*) discipline *f*, matière *f* 2 VT (= *control*) discipliner ; [+ *person*] discipliner ; (= *punish*) punir ; [+ *mind*] former, discipliner

disciplined ['dɪsɪplɪnd] ADJ [*person, group*] discipliné ; (= *methodical*) méthodique

disclaim [dɪs'kleɪm] VT a [+ *news, statement*] démentir ; [+ *responsibility*] rejeter, nier ; [+ *authorship*] nier ; [+ *paternity*] désavouer ; **to ~ all knowledge of sth** nier toute connaissance de qch b (*Jur*) se désister de, renoncer à

disclaimer [dɪs'kleɪmər] N a (= *denial*) démenti *m* ; (*Jur*) désistement *m* (**of** de), renonciation *f* (**of** à) ; **to issue a ~** publier un démenti b (= *exclusion clause*) décharge *f* (de responsabilité)

disclose [dɪs'kləʊz] 1 VT [+ *secret*] divulguer, dévoiler ; [+ *news*] divulguer ; [+ *intentions*] dévoiler ; [+ *contents of envelope, box etc*] dévoiler, montrer 2 COMP ▶ **disclosing agent** N (*Dentistry*) révélateur *m* de plaque dentaire

disclosure [dɪs'kləʊʒər] N a (*NonC*) (*by newspaper etc*) divulgation *f*, révélation *f* ; (*by individual to press etc*) communication *f* (de renseignements) (**to** à) b (= *fact etc revealed*) révélation *f*

disco* ['dɪskəʊ] 1 N (ABBR = **discotheque**) disco *m* 2 COMP ▶ **disco dancing** N disco *m*

discography [dɪs'kɒgrəfɪ] N discographie *f*

discolour, discolor (*US*) [dɪs'kʌlər] 1 VT (= *spoil colour of, fade: gen*) décolorer ; [+ *white material, teeth*] jaunir 2 VI (*gen*) se décolorer ; [*white material, teeth*] jaunir ; [*mirror*] se ternir

discolouration, discoloration (*esp US*) [dɪsˌkʌlə'reɪʃən] N décoloration *f*

discombobulate [ˌdɪskəm'bɒbjʊˌleɪt] VT (*esp US*) [+ *plans*] chambouler* ; [+ *person*] déconcerter

discomfit [dɪs'kʌmfɪt] VT (= *disappoint*) décevoir, tromper les espoirs de ; (= *confuse*) déconcerter, décontenancer, confondre

discomfiture [dɪs'kʌmfɪtʃər] N (= *disappointment*) déconvenue *f* ; (= *confusion*) embarras *m*, déconfiture* *f*

discomfort [dɪs'kʌmfət] N a (*NonC: physical, mental*) gêne *f* ; (*stronger*) malaise *m* ; **I feel some ~ from it but not real pain** ça me gêne mais ça ne me fait pas vraiment mal ; **much to my ~, he announced he would accompany me** à mon grand embarras, il a annoncé qu'il m'accompagnerait b (= *uncomfortable thing*) désagrément *m* ; **the ~s of camping in wet weather** les désagréments *mpl* du camping par temps de pluie

discomposure [ˌdɪskəm'pəʊʒər] N trouble *m*, confusion *f*

disconcert [ˌdɪskən'sɜːt] VT déconcerter, décontenancer

disconcerting [ˌdɪskən'sɜːtɪŋ] ADJ déconcertant, troublant, déroutant

disconcertingly [ˌdɪskən'sɜːtɪŋlɪ] ADV d'une manière déconcertante ; **~, I found I rather liked him** j'ai été surpris de me rendre compte que je l'aimais bien ; **the policemen's faces were ~ young** les policiers étaient d'une jeunesse déconcertante

disconnect [ˌdɪskə'nekt] VT [+ *electrical apparatus, pipe*] débrancher ; [+ *railway carriages*] décrocher ; (= *cut off*) [+ *gas, electricity, water supply, telephone*] couper ; (*Telec*) **to ~ a call** couper *or* interrompre une communication ; (*Telec*) **we've been ~ed** (*for non-payment etc*) on nous a coupé le téléphone ; (*in mid-conversation*) nous avons été coupés ; **to be/feel ~ed from reality** être/se sentir coupé de la réalité ; **their proposal is ~ed from scientific reality** leur proposition n'est fondée sur aucune réalité scientifique

disconnected [ˌdɪskə'nektɪd] ADJ [*speech*] décousu ; [*thoughts*] sans suite ; [*facts, events*] sans rapport

disconnection [ˌdɪskə'nekʃən] N (*Telec*) suspension *f* de ligne ; [*of gas, electricity*] coupure *f*

disconsolate [dɪs'kɒnsəlɪt] ADJ inconsolable

disconsolately [dɪs'kɒnsəlɪtlɪ] ADV a (= *dejectedly*) d'un air abattu ; **"I'm bored", he said ~** « je m'ennuie » dit-il d'un air abattu b (= *inconsolably*) [*trudge, wander*] l'air inconsolable ; **"there's no point going on", she said ~** « ça ne sert à rien de continuer » dit-elle inconsolable ; **she wept ~** elle pleurait, inconsolable

discontent [ˌdɪskən'tent] N mécontentement *m* ; (*Pol*) malaise *m* (social) ; **cause of ~** grief *m*

discontented [ˌdɪskən'tentɪd] ADJ mécontent (**with, about** de)

discontentedly [ˌdɪskən'tentɪdlɪ] ADV d'un air mécontent

discontentment [ˌdɪskən'tentmənt] N mécontentement *m*

discontinuance [ˌdɪskən'tɪnjʊəns], **discontinuation** [ˌdɪskən,tɪnjʊ'eɪʃən] N (*gen*) interruption *f* ; [*of production etc*] arrêt *m*

discontinue [ˌdɪskən'tɪnjuː] VT (*gen*) cesser ; [+ *product*] (= *stop manufacture of*) arrêter la production de ; (= *stop sales of*) ne plus vendre ; [+ *service*] supprimer ; (*Jur*) [+ *case, legal proceedings*] abandonner ; (*Med*) [+ *treatment*] arrêter ; **to ~ one's subscription to a newspaper** résilier son abonnement à un journal ; (*Comm*) **a ~d line** une série *or* un article qui ne se fait plus ; (*on sale article*) **"~d"** « fin de série »

discontinuity [ˌdɪskɒntɪ'njuːɪtɪ] N (*gen, Math*) discontinuité *f* ; (*Geol*) zone *f* de discontinuité

discontinuous [ˌdɪskən'tɪnjʊəs] ADJ discontinu (*also Ling*)

discord ['dɪskɔːd] N a discorde *f*, dissension *f* ; **civil ~** dissensions *fpl* civiles b (*Mus*) dissonance *f*

discordant [dɪs'kɔːdənt] ADJ a [*opinions*] incompatible ; [*sounds, colours*] discordant b (*Mus*) dissonant

discotheque ['dɪskəʊtek] N discothèque *f* (*dancing*)

discount ['dɪskaʊnt] 1 N escompte *m* ; (*on article*) remise *f*, rabais *m* ; (*rebate on transaction not shown on invoice*) ristourne *f* ; (*St Ex: also* **share ~**) décote *f* ; (*in forward markets*) déport *m* ; **to give a ~** faire une remise (**on** sur) ; **to buy at a ~** acheter au rabais ; **~ for cash** escompte *m* au comptant ; **at a ~** (*Fin*) en perte, au-dessous du pair ; (*in forward markets*) avec un déport ; (*fig*) mal coté ; (*St Ex*) **a ~ of 25% below the nominal value of the shares** une décote de 25% par rapport à la valeur nominale de l'action 2 ['dɪskaʊnt] VT [+ *sum of money*] faire une remise de, escompter ; [+ *bill, note*] prendre à l'escompte, escompter ; (*fig*) ne pas tenir compte de ; **I ~ half of what he says** je divise par deux tout ce qu'il dit 3 COMP ▶ **discount house** N magasin *m* de vente au rabais ▶ **discount rate** N taux *m* d'escompte ▶ **discount store** N = **discount house**

discounter [dɪs'kaʊntər] N (*Fin, Banking*) escompteur *m* ; (*Comm*) magasin *m* discount

discourage [dɪsˈkʌrɪdʒ] VT [a] (= dishearten) décourager, abattre; **to become ~d** se laisser décourager or rebuter, se laisser aller au découragement; **he isn't easily ~d** il ne se décourage pas facilement [b] (= advise against) décourager, (essayer de) dissuader (**sb from sth/from doing** qn de qch/de faire) [c] [+ suggestion] déconseiller; [+ offer of friendship] repousser; **she ~d his advances** elle a repoussé or décourage ses avances

discouragement [dɪsˈkʌrɪdʒmənt] N (= act) désapprobation f (**of** de); (= depression) découragement m, abattement m

discouraging [dɪsˈkʌrɪdʒɪŋ] ADJ décourageant, démoralisant

discourse [ˈdɪskɔːs] [1] N [a] discours m; (written) dissertation f, traité m [b]†† conversation f [2] [dɪsˈkɔːs] VI (= hold forth) discourir (**on** sur), traiter (**on de**) [3] COMP ► **discourse analysis** N (Ling) analyse f du discours

discourteous [dɪsˈkɜːtɪəs] ADJ impoli, peu courtois, discourtois (**towards** envers, avec)

discourteously [dɪsˈkɜːtɪəslɪ] ADV de façon discourtoise

discourtesy [dɪsˈkɜːtɪsɪ] N manque m de courtoisie

discover [dɪsˈkʌvər] VT [+ country, planet, treasure, reason, cause, secret, person hiding] découvrir; [+ mistake, loss] s'apercevoir de, se rendre compte de; (after search) [+ house, book] dénicher; **to ~ that ...** (= find out) apprendre que ...; (= notice) s'apercevoir que ...; (= understand) comprendre que ...

discoverer [dɪsˈkʌvərər] N **the ~ of America/penicillin** celui qui a découvert l'Amérique/la pénicilline, le découvreur de l'Amérique/la pénicilline

discovery [dɪsˈkʌvərɪ] N [a] (NonC) [of fact, place, person] découverte f; **it led to the ~ of penicillin** cela a conduit à la découverte de la pénicilline → **voyage** [b] (= happy find) trouvaille f [c] (Jur) ~ **of documents** communication f des pièces du dossier avant l'audience [d] (Scol: subject) activités fpl d'éveil; **to learn through ~** apprendre par des activités d'éveil

discredit [dɪsˈkredɪt] [1] VT (= cast slur on) discréditer, déconsidérer; (= disbelieve) ne pas croire, mettre en doute [2] N discrédit m, déconsidération f; **to bring ~ upon sb** jeter le discrédit sur qn; **without any ~ to you** sans que cela vous nuise en rien; **to be a ~ to ...** être une honte pour ..., faire honte à ...; **to be to sb's ~** discréditer qn

discreditable [dɪsˈkredɪtəbl] ADJ peu honorable, indigne, déshonorant

discredited [dɪsˈkredɪtɪd] ADJ discrédité

discreet [dɪsˈkriːt] ADJ [person, action, presence, silence, decor, colour] discret (-ète f) (**about** sur); **at a ~ distance** à distance respectueuse

discreetly [dɪsˈkriːtlɪ] ADV [speak, behave] discrètement; [dress] avec sobriété; **~, she said nothing until her visitor had left** par discrétion, elle n'a rien dit avant le départ de son visiteur

discrepancy [dɪsˈkrepənsɪ] N contradiction f, divergence f

discrete [dɪsˈkriːt] ADJ (gen, Math, Med) discret (-ète f)

discretion [dɪsˈkreʃən] N [a] (= tact) discrétion f; (= prudence) discrétion f, sagesse f ■ (PROV) **~ is the better part of valour** prudence est mère de sûreté (PROV) [b] (= freedom of decision) discrétion f; **to leave sth to sb's ~** laisser qch à la discrétion de qn; **use your own ~** faites comme bon vous semblera, c'est à vous de juger; **at the ~ of the judge/the chairman** etc **it is possible to ...** c'est au juge/au président etc de décider s'il est possible de ...; **the age of ~** l'âge m de raison; **to reach the age of ~** atteindre l'âge de raison

discretionary [dɪsˈkreʃənərɪ] ADJ [powers] discrétionnaire

discriminant [dɪsˈkrɪmɪnənt] N (Math) discriminant m

discriminate [dɪsˈkrɪmɪneɪt] [1] VI [a] (= make unfair distinction) introduire une discrimination (**against** contre, **in favour of** en faveur de); **to be ~d against** être victime d'une discrimination [b] (= be discerning) **the public should ~** le public ne devrait pas accepter n'importe quoi or devrait exercer son sens critique; **he is unable to ~** il est incapable d'exercer son sens critique [2] VT distinguer (**from** de), discriminer (liter) (**from** de)

discriminating [dɪsˈkrɪmɪneɪtɪŋ] ADJ [a] (= discerning) [person, audience, clientele] plein de discernement, averti; [palate] exercé; [judgement, mind] perspicace; **he's not very ~** (about books, TV) il manque d'esprit critique; (about food) il n'a pas un goût très fin [b] [tariff, tax] différentiel

discrimination [dɪsˌkrɪmɪˈneɪʃən] N [a] (= prejudice) discrimination f (**against** contre, **in favour of** en faveur de); **religious ~** discrimination f religieuse or d'ordre religieux → **racial**, **sex** [b] (= distinction) distinction f (**between** entre), séparation f [c] (NonC = judgement) discernement m

discriminatory [dɪsˈkrɪmɪnətərɪ] ADJ discriminatoire

discursive [dɪsˈkɜːsɪv] ADJ, **discursory** [dɪsˈkɜːsərɪ] ADJ discursif, décousu (pej)

discus [ˈdɪskəs] [1] N (pl **discuses** or **disci**) disque m [2] COMP ► **discus thrower** N lanceur m de disque, discobole m (Hist)

discuss [dɪsˈkʌs] VT (= examine in detail) discuter, examiner; (= talk about) [+ problem, project, price] discuter; [+ topic] discuter de or sur, débattre de; **we were ~ing him** nous parlions de lui; **I ~ed it with him** j'en ai discuté avec lui; **I won't ~ it any further** je ne veux plus en parler

discussant [dɪsˈkʌsənt] N (US) participant(e) m(f) (à une discussion etc)

discussion [dɪsˈkʌʃən] [1] N discussion f, débat m (**of, about** sur, au sujet de); **under ~** en discussion; **a subject for ~** un sujet de discussion [2] COMP ► **discussion document** N avant-projet m ► **discussion group** N groupe m de discussion ► **discussion paper** N = **discussion document**

disdain [dɪsˈdeɪn] [1] VT dédaigner (**to do** de faire) [2] N dédain m, mépris m; **in ~** avec dédain

disdainful [dɪsˈdeɪnfʊl] ADJ [person] dédaigneux; [tone, look] dédaigneux, de dédain

disdainfully [dɪsˈdeɪnfəlɪ] ADV avec dédain, dédaigneusement

disease [dɪˈziːz] N (Med: mental, physical) maladie f, affection f; (Bot, Vet) maladie f; (fig) maladie f, mal m → **heart**, **occupational**, **venereal**, **virus**

diseased [dɪˈziːzd] ADJ malade

diseconomy [ˌdɪsɪˈkɒnəmɪ] N déséconomie f

disembark [ˌdɪsɪmˈbɑːk] VTI débarquer

disembarkation [ˌdɪsemˈbɑːˈkeɪʃən] N débarquement m

disembodied [ˌdɪsɪmˈbɒdɪd] ADJ désincarné

disembowel [ˌdɪsɪmˈbaʊəl] VT éventrer, éviscérer, étriper*

disenchant [ˌdɪsɪnˈtʃɑːnt] VT désabuser, désenchanter, désillusionner

disenchantment [ˌdɪsɪnˈtʃɑːntmənt] N désenchantement m, désillusion f

disencumber [ˌdɪsɪnˈkʌmbər] VT [+ mortgage] payer; [+ property] déshypothéquer

disenfranchise [ˌdɪsɪnˈfræntʃaɪz] VT = **disfranchise**

disengage [ˌdɪsɪnˈgeɪdʒ] [1] VT [+ object, hand] dégager, libérer (**from** de); (Tech) [+ machine] déclencher, débrayer; **to ~ o.s. from** se dégager de; (Aut) **to ~ the clutch** débrayer [2] VI (Fencing) dégager (le fer); (Tech) se déclencher

disengaged [ˌdɪsɪnˈgeɪdʒd] ADJ libre, inoccupé; (Tech) débrayé

disengagement [ˌdɪsɪnˈgeɪdʒmənt] N (Pol) désengagement m

disentangle [ˌdɪsɪnˈtæŋgl] [1] VT [+ wool, problem, mystery] débrouiller, démêler; [+ plot] dénouer; (lit, fig) **to ~ o.s. from** se dépêtrer de, se sortir de [2] VI se démêler

disequilibrium [ˌdɪsekwɪˈlɪbrɪəm] N instabilité f

disestablish [ˌdɪsɪsˈtæblɪʃ] VT séparer de l'État; **to ~ the Church** séparer l'Église de l'État

disestablishment [ˌdɪsɪsˈtæblɪʃmənt] N séparation f (de l'Église et de l'État)

disfavour, disfavor (US) [dɪsˈfeɪvər] [1] N désapprobation f, défaveur f; **to fall into ~** tomber en défaveur; **to fall into ~ with sb** tomber en défaveur auprès de qn; **to be in ~ with sb** être mal vu de qn; **to look with ~ on sth** regarder qch avec désapprobation; **to look with ~ on sb** désapprouver qn [2] VT [a] (= dislike) désapprouver [b] (US = disadvantage) être défavorable à, défavoriser

disfigure [dɪsˈfɪgər] VT [+ face] défigurer; [+ scenery] défigurer, déparer

disfigured [dɪsˈfɪgəd] ADJ défiguré (**by** par)

disfigurement [dɪsˈfɪgəmənt] N défigurement m, enlaidissement m

disfranchise [dɪsˈfræntʃaɪz] VT [+ person] priver du droit électoral; [+ town] priver de ses droits de représentation

disgorge [dɪsˈgɔːdʒ] [1] VT [+ food] dégorger, rendre; [+ contents, passengers] déverser [2] VI [river] se dégorger, se décharger

disgrace [dɪsˈgreɪs] [1] N [a] (NonC) (= dishonour) honte f, déshonneur m; (= disfavour) disgrâce f, défaveur f; **there is no ~ in doing that** il n'y a aucune honte à faire cela; **to be in ~** [public figure, politician] être en disgrâce; [child, dog] être en pénitence; **to bring ~ on sb** déshonorer qn [b] (= cause of shame) honte f; **it's a ~!** c'est une honte!, c'est honteux!; **it's a ~ to our country** c'est une honte pour or cela déshonore notre pays; **she's a ~ to her family** c'est la honte de sa famille; **you're a ~!** tu devrais avoir honte de toi! [2] VT [+ family] faire honte à; [+ name, country] déshonorer, couvrir de honte or d'opprobre (liter); **don't ~ us** ne nous fais pas honte; **to ~ o.s.** se couvrir de honte; **he ~d himself by losing his temper** il s'est couvert de honte en se mettant en colère; **to be ~d** [officer, politician] être disgracié

disgraceful [dɪsˈgreɪsfʊl] ADJ scandaleux, honteux

disgracefully [dɪsˈgreɪsfəlɪ] ADV [behave] de manière scandaleuse; (= bad, badly etc) scandaleusement; **~ low wages** des salaires mpl scandaleusement bas; **~ badly paid** scandaleusement mal payé

disgruntled [dɪsˈgrʌntld] ADJ [person] (= discontented) mécontent (**about, with** de); (= in bad temper) de mauvaise humeur, mécontent (**about, with** à cause de); [expression] maussade, renfrogné

disguise [dɪsˈgaɪz] [1] VT [+ person] déguiser (**as** en); [+ mistake, voice] déguiser, camoufler; [+ building, vehicle, ship] camoufler (**as** en); [+ facts, feelings] masquer, dissimuler, déguiser (liter); **to ~ o.s. as a woman** se déguiser en femme; **to be ~d as a woman** être déguisé en femme; **there is no disguising the fact that ...** on ne peut pas se dissimuler que ..., il faut avouer que ... [2] N (lit) déguisement m; (fig) masque m; (NonC) artifice m; **his attitude was just a ~ for his true feelings** son attitude n'était qu'un masque qui cachait ses véritables sentiments; **a novel about secrecy and ~**

un roman sur le secret et l'artifice ; (*lit, fig*) **in ~ déguisé** ; **in the ~ of ...** déguisé en ...

disgust [dɪs'gʌst] **1** N dégoût *m*, répugnance *f* (**for, at** pour) ; (*lit, fig*) **he left in ~** il est parti dégoûté *or* écœuré ; **to his ~ they left** il était écœuré de les voir partir ; **to my ~ he refused to do it** il a refusé et cela m'a dégoûté **2** VT dégoûter, écœurer ; (= *infuriate*) dégoûter, révolter

disgusted [dɪs'gʌstɪd] ADJ dégoûté, écœuré (**at** de, **par**)

disgustedly [dɪs'gʌstɪdlɪ] ADV [*look at*] avec dégoût, d'un air dégoûté ; **"you really are pathetic", he said ~** « tu es vraiment minable », dit-il écœuré *or* dégoûté

disgusting [dɪs'gʌstɪŋ] ADJ **a** (= *revolting*) [*food, habit, behaviour, toilet, person*] dégoûtant ; [*taste, smell*] répugnant, infect ; **it looks ~** ça a l'air dégoûtant ; **it tastes ~** c'est dégoûtant *or* infect ; **it smells ~** ça pue **b** (= *obscene*) dégoûtant **c** (* = *disgraceful*) dégoûtant ; **~!** c'est dégoûtant ! ; **you're ~!** tu es dégoûtant ! ; **I think it's ~ that we have to pay** je trouve ça dégoûtant qu'on doive payer ; **I think it's ~ how much money they've got** je trouve (que c'est) dégoûtant qu'ils aient tant d'argent

disgustingly [dɪs'gʌstɪŋlɪ] ADV d'une manière dégoûtante ; **~ dirty** d'une saleté répugnante

dish [dɪʃ] **1** N **a** (= *serving plate*) plat *m* ; (= *dinner plate*) assiette *f* ; (*in laboratory etc*) récipient *m* ; **vegetable ~** plat *m* à légumes, légumier *m* ; **the ~es** la vaisselle ; **to do the ~es** faire la vaisselle ; **to clear away the breakfast ~es** débarrasser la table du petit déjeuner **b** (= *food*) plat *m*, mets *m* (*frm*) ; **fish/pasta/ vegetable ~** plat *m* de poisson/de pâtes/de légumes ; (*US fig*) **this is not my ~** ce n'est pas mon truc* **c** (*also* = **aerial, ~ antenna**) → 3 **d** (* *fig* = *attractive person*) (*man*) beau mec *m* ; (*woman*) belle nana* *f* ; **she's quite a ~** c'est vraiment une belle nana* **2** VT **a** [+ *food, meal*] mettre dans un plat ; **to ~ the dirt (on sb)*** colporter des ragots* (sur qn) **b** * [+ *opponent*] enfoncer*, écraser ; [+ *sb's chances, hopes*] flanquer par terre* **3** COMP ► **dish aerial, dish antenna** (*US*) N antenne *f* parabolique, parabole *f*

► **dish out** VT SEP [+ *food*] servir ; (* *fig*) [+ *money, sweets, books etc*] distribuer ; [+ *punishment*] administrer ; **to ~ out a hiding to sb*** flanquer* une correction à qn ; (*fig*) **to ~ it out to sb*** (= *smack etc*) flanquer* une correction à qn ; (*verbally*) passer un savon* à qn

► **dish up** VT SEP **a** [+ *food, meal*] servir, verser dans un plat ; **the meal was ready to ~ up** le repas était prêt à servir **b** * [+ *facts, statistics*] resservir

dishabille [ˌdɪsə'biːl] N (*frm*) déshabillé *m*, négligé† *m* ; **in ~** en déshabillé, en négligé

disharmony [dɪs'hɑːmənɪ] N désaccord *m*, manque *m* d'harmonie

dishcloth [ˈdɪʃklɒθ] N (*for washing*) lavette *f* ; (*for drying*) torchon *m* (à vaisselle)

dishearten [dɪs'hɑːtn] VT décourager, abattre, démoraliser ; **don't be ~ed** ne vous laissez pas décourager *or* abattre

disheartening [dɪs'hɑːtnɪŋ] ADJ décourageant, démoralisant

dished [dɪʃt] ADJ **a** (= *dish-shaped*) concave **b** (* *fig*) [*person, hopes*] fichu*, foutu*

dishevelled [dɪ'ʃevəld] ADJ (= *ruffled*) [*person*] échevelé, ébouriffé ; [*hair*] ébouriffé ; [*clothes*] en désordre ; (= *scruffy*) [*person*] débraillé

dishmop [ˈdɪʃmɒp] N lavette *f*

dishoard [dɪs'hɔːd] VT [+ *money*] déthésauriser, remettre en circulation

dishonest [dɪs'ɒnɪst] ADJ (= *unscrupulous*) malhonnête ; (= *insincere*) déloyal, de mauvaise foi ; **to be ~ with sb** être de mauvaise foi avec qn, être malhonnête avec qn

dishonestly [dɪs'ɒnɪstlɪ] ADV [*behave*] malhonnêtement ; [*obtain*] par des moyens malhonnêtes

dishonesty [dɪs'ɒnɪstɪ] N (= *unscrupulousness*) malhonnêteté *f* ; (= *insincerity*) mauvaise foi *f*

dishonour [dɪs'ɒnəʳ] **1** N déshonneur *m* **2** VT **a** [+ *family*] déshonorer, porter atteinte à l'honneur de ; [+ *woman*] déshonorer **b** [+ *bill, cheque*] refuser d'honorer ; **a ~ed cheque** un chèque impayé *or* non honoré

dishonourable [dɪs'ɒnərəbl] **1** ADJ [*person*] sans honneur ; [*act, behaviour*] déshonorant **2** COMP ► **dishonourable discharge** N (*Mil*) exclusion de l'armée pour conduite déshonorante

dishonourably [dɪs'ɒnərəblɪ] ADV de façon déshonorante ; (*Mil*) **to be ~ discharged** être exclu de l'armée pour conduite déshonorante

dishpan [ˈdɪʃpæn] N (*US*) bassine *f* (à vaisselle)

dishrack [ˈdɪʃræk] N égouttoir *m* (à vaisselle)

dishrag [ˈdɪʃræg] N lavette *f*

dishtowel [ˈdɪʃtaʊəl] N (*US*) torchon *m* (à vaisselle)

dishwasher [ˈdɪʃwɒʃəʳ] N **a** (= *machine*) lave-vaisselle *m inv* **b** (= *washer-up*) (*in restaurant*) plongeur *m*, -euse *f* ; **to work as a ~** travailler à la plonge

dishwater [ˈdɪʃwɔːtəʳ] N eau *f* de vaisselle ; **this coffee's like** *or* **as weak as ~*** c'est du jus de chaussettes* *or* de la lavasse* ce café → **dull**

dishy* [ˈdɪʃɪ] ADJ (*Brit*) [*person*] sexy*, appétissant

disillusion [ˌdɪsɪ'luːʒən] **1** VT désillusionner, désabuser ; **to be ~ed** être désillusionné *or* désabusé *or* désenchanté (**with** en ce qui concerne, quant à) ; **to grow ~ed** perdre ses illusions **2** N désillusion *f*, désenchantement *m*

disillusionment [ˌdɪsɪ'luːʒənmənt] N = **disillusion 2**

disincentive [ˌdɪsɪn'sentɪv] **1** N **it's a real ~** cela a un effet dissuasif *or* de dissuasion ; **this is a ~ to work** cela n'incite pas à travailler *or* au travail **2** ADJ dissuasif

disinclination [ˌdɪsɪnklɪ'neɪʃən] N manque *m* d'enthousiasme (**to do** à faire, **for sth** pour qch)

disinclined [ˌdɪsɪn'klaɪnd] ADJ peu disposé, peu porté, peu enclin (**for** à, **to do** à faire)

disinfect [ˌdɪsɪn'fekt] VT désinfecter

disinfectant [ˌdɪsɪn'fektənt] ADJ, N désinfectant *m*

disinfection [ˌdɪsɪn'fekʃən] N désinfection *f*

disinflation [ˌdɪsɪn'fleɪʃən] N déflation *f*

disinflationary [ˌdɪsɪn'fleɪʃənərɪ] ADJ de déflation, déflationniste

disinformation [ˌdɪsɪnfə'meɪʃən] N désinformation *f*

disingenuous [ˌdɪsɪn'dʒenjʊəs] ADJ fourbe

disingenuously [ˌdɪsɪn'dʒenjʊəslɪ] ADV (*frm*) avec fourberie

disingenuousness [ˌdɪsɪn'dʒenjʊəsnɪs] N fourberie *f*

disinherit [ˌdɪsɪn'herɪt] VT déshériter

disintegrate [dɪs'ɪntɪgreɪt] **1** VI se désintégrer, se désagréger ; (*Phys*) se désintégrer **2** VT désintégrer, désagréger ; (*Phys*) désintégrer

disintegration [dɪsˌɪntɪ'greɪʃən] N désintégration *f*, désagrégation *f* ; (*Phys*) désintégration *f*

disinter [ˌdɪsɪn'tɜːʳ] VT déterrer, exhumer

disinterest [dɪs'ɪntrɪst] N **a** (= *impartiality*) désintéressement *m* **b** (* = *lack of interest*) indifférence *f*

disinterested [dɪs'ɪntrɪstɪd] ADJ **a** (= *impartial*) désintéressé **b** (* = *uninterested*) indifférent

disinterestedly [dɪs'ɪntrɪstɪdlɪ] ADV **a** (= *im-*

partially) de façon désintéressée **b** (* = *uninterestedly*) avec indifférence

disinterestedness [dɪs'ɪntrɪstɪdnɪs] N **a** (= *impartiality*) désintéressement *m* **b** (* = *lack of interest*) indifférence *f*

disinterment [ˌdɪsɪn'tɜːmənt] N déterrement *m*, exhumation *f*

disintoxicate [ˌdɪsɪn'tɒksɪkeɪt] VT désintoxiquer

disintoxication [dɪsɪnˌtɒksɪ'keɪʃən] N désintoxication *f*

disinvest [ˌdɪsɪn'vest] VI désinvestir (**from** de)

disinvestment [ˌdɪsɪn'vestmənt] N désinvestissement *m* (**from** de)

disjoint [dɪs'dʒɔɪnt] ADJ (*Math*) disjoint

disjointed [dɪs'dʒɔɪntɪd] ADJ [*film, lecture, style, conversation, sentence, thoughts*] décousu, incohérent

disjunction [dɪs'dʒʌŋkʃən] N disjonction *f*

disjunctive [dɪs'dʒʌŋktɪv] ADJ disjonctif ; **~ pronoun** forme *f* tonique du pronom

disk [dɪsk] **1** N **a** (*esp US*) = **disc** **b** (*Comput*) disque *m* ; **on ~** sur disque → **double, floppy, hard 2** COMP ► **disk capacity** N (*Comput*) capacité *f* du disque ► **disk drive** N lecteur *m* de disques ► **disk pack** N unité *f* de disques ► **disk space** N (*Comput*) espace *m* disque

diskette [dɪs'ket] N (*Comput*) disquette *f*

▼**dislike** [dɪs'laɪk] **1** VT [+ *person, thing*] ne pas aimer ; **to ~ doing sth** ne pas aimer faire qch ; **I don't ~ it** cela ne me déplaît pas ; **I ~ her** elle me déplaît ; **I ~ this intensely** j'ai cela en horreur **2** N antipathie *f* ; **his ~ of sb** l'antipathie qu'il éprouve pour qn ; **his ~ of sth** son aversion pour qch ; **one's likes and ~s** ce que l'on aime et ce que l'on n'aime pas ; **to take a ~ to sb/sth** prendre qn/qch en grippe ; **to take an instant ~ to sb/sth** prendre tout de suite qn/qch en grippe

dislocate [ˈdɪsləʊkeɪt] VT **a** [+ *limb etc*] [*person*] se disloquer, se démettre, se luxer ; [*fall, accident*] disloquer, démettre, luxer **b** (*fig*) [+ *traffic, business*] désorganiser ; [+ *plans, timetable*] bouleverser

dislocation [ˌdɪsləʊ'keɪʃən] N **a** (*Med*) dislocation *f*, déboîtement *m*, luxation *f* ; **congenital ~** luxation *f* congénitale **b** (= *disruption: of life, society*) bouleversement *m*

dislodge [dɪs'lɒdʒ] VT [+ *object*] déplacer ; [+ *enemy*] déloger ; [+ *dictator*] chasser (**from** de)

disloyal [dɪs'lɔɪəl] ADJ [*person, behaviour*] déloyal (**to** envers)

disloyalty [dɪs'lɔɪəltɪ] N déloyauté *f*, infidélité *f*

dismal [ˈdɪzməl] ADJ **a** (= *dreary*) [*place, building*] lugubre ; [*thought, prospects*] sombre ; [*weather*] maussade ; **the ~ science** (= *economics*) la science funeste **b** (* = *awful*) lamentable ; **a ~ failure** un échec lamentable

dismally [ˈdɪzməlɪ] ADV* [*fail, perform*] lamentablement

dismantle [dɪs'mæntl] VT [+ *machine, furniture*] démonter ; [+ *company, department*] démanteler (*also Mil*)

dismantling [dɪs'mæntlɪŋ] N [*of company, department*] démantèlement *m*

dismast [dɪs'mɑːst] VT démâter

▼**dismay** [dɪs'meɪ] **1** N consternation *f*, désarroi *m* ; **to my ~** à ma grande consternation ; **in ~** d'un air consterné **2** VT consterner

dismayed [dɪs'meɪd] ADJ [*person*] consterné (**by** par)

dismember [dɪs'membəʳ] VT (*lit, fig*) démembrer

dismemberment [dɪs'membəmənt] N démembrement *m*

dismiss [dɪs'mɪs] VT **a** [+ *employee*] renvoyer, licencier ; [+ *official, officer*] destituer, casser ; [+ *class, visitors*] laisser partir, congédier ; [+

assembly] dissoudre; [+ *troops*] faire rompre les rangs à; (*Mil*) **to be ~ed (from) the service** être renvoyé de l'armée *or* rayé des cadres; (*Mil*) **~!** rompez (les rangs)!; (*Scol*) **class ~!** le cours est terminé! **b** [+ *thought, possibility, suggestion, objection*] écarter; [+ *request*] rejeter **c** (*gen*) [+ *sb's appeal, claim*] rejeter; (*Jur*) [+ *accused*] relaxer; [+ *jury*] congédier; (*Jur*) **to ~ sb's appeal** débouter qn de son appel; **to ~ a case** rendre une fin de non-recevoir; **to ~ a charge** rendre un arrêt de *or* une ordonnance de non-lieu

dismissal [dɪsˈmɪsəl] N **a** [*of employee*] licenciement *m*, renvoi *m*; [*of civil servant*] destitution *f*, révocation *f*; **unfair** *or* **wrongful ~** licenciement *m* abusif **b** (= *permission to leave*) congé *m*; **he made a gesture of ~** il a fait un geste pour les (*or* nous *etc*) congédier **c** (= *brushing-aside*) rebuffade *f*; **I was annoyed by his curt ~ of my objections** cette façon qu'il a eue d'écarter sèchement mes objections m'a agacé **d** (*Jur*) [*of appeal*] rejet *m*; [*of jury*] congédiement *m*; **the ~ of the charges against him** le non-lieu dont il a bénéficié

dismissive [dɪsˈmɪsɪv] ADJ (= *disdainful*) dédaigneux

dismissively [dɪsˈmɪsɪvlɪ] ADV **a** (= *disdainfully*) [*speak*] d'un ton dédaigneux, avec dédain; [*wave, nod, shrug, laugh*] avec dédain; [*describe, refer to*] dédaigneusement, avec dédain **b** (*sending sb away*) **he nodded ~ at the butler** d'un signe de tête, il congédia le maître d'hôtel; **"thank you sergeant, that will be all", she said ~** « merci, sergent, ce sera tout », dit-elle, et sur ces mots, elle le congédia

dismount [dɪsˈmaʊnt] **1** VI descendre (**from** de), mettre pied à terre **2** VT [+ *rider*] démonter, désarçonner; [+ *troops, gun, machine*] démonter (**from** de)

disobedience [ˌdɪsəˈbiːdɪəns] N (*NonC*) désobéissance *f*, insoumission *f* (**to** à); **an act of ~** une désobéissance

disobedient [ˌdɪsəˈbiːdɪənt] ADJ [*child*] désobéissant (**to** à); [*soldier*] indiscipliné, insubordonné; **he has been ~** il a été désobéissant, il a désobéi

disobey [ˌdɪsəˈbeɪ] VT [+ *parents, officer*] désobéir à, s'opposer à; [+ *law*] enfreindre, violer

disobliging [ˌdɪsəˈblaɪdʒɪŋ] ADJ (*frm*) désobligeant

disorder [dɪsˈɔːdər] **1** N **a** (*NonC*) (= *untidiness*) [*of room, plans etc*] désordre *m*; **to throw sth into ~** semer *or* jeter le désordre dans qch; **in ~** en désordre; (*Mil*) **to retreat in ~** être en déroute **b** (*NonC: Pol etc = unrest*) troubles *mpl* **c** (*Med*) troubles *mpl*; **kidney/stomach/mental ~** troubles *mpl* rénaux/gastriques/psychiques; **speech/sleep/personality ~** troubles *mpl* de l'élocution/du sommeil/de la personnalité; **eating ~** troubles *mpl* du comportement alimentaire; **skin ~** maladie *f* de la peau **2** VT [+ *room*] mettre en désordre; (*Med*) troubler, déranger

disordered [dɪsˈɔːdəd] ADJ **a** (= *untidy, disorderly*) [*room, hair*] en désordre; [*life*] désordonné **b** (= *deranged*) [*mind*] dérangé; [*imagination*] désordonné; **mentally ~** atteint de troubles mentaux

disorderly [dɪsˈɔːdəlɪ] **1** ADJ **a** (= *untidy*) [*room*] en désordre; [*mind*] confus **b** (= *unruly*) [*person, crowd, meeting*] agité; [*behaviour*] désordonné, indiscipliné → **drunk 2** COMP ▶ **disorderly conduct** N (*Jur*) trouble *m* à l'ordre public; **the marchers were charged with ~ conduct** les manifestants ont été inculpés de trouble à l'ordre public ▶ **disorderly house** N (*Jur*) (= *brothel*) maison *f* close; (= *gambling den*) maison *f* de jeu, tripot *m*

disorganization [dɪsˌɔːɡənaɪˈzeɪʃən] N désorganisation *f*

disorganize [dɪsˈɔːɡənaɪz] VT désorganiser, déranger

disorganized [dɪsˈɔːɡənaɪzd] ADJ [*person*] désorganisé; [*room*] mal rangé, en désordre

disorient [dɪsˈɔːrɪent] VT désorienter

disorientate [dɪsˈɔːrɪenteɪt] VT désorienter

disorientation [dɪsˌɔːrɪənˈteɪʃən] N désorientation *f*

disown [dɪsˈəʊn] VT [+ *child, country, opinion, document*] désavouer, renier; [+ *debt, signature*] nier, renier

disparage [dɪsˈpærɪdʒ] VT (*frm*) décrier, déprécier

disparagement [dɪsˈpærɪdʒmənt] N (*frm*) dénigrement *m*, dépréciation *f*

disparaging [dɪsˈpærɪdʒɪŋ] ADJ (*frm*) désobligeant, (plutôt) méprisant (**to** pour); **to be ~ about** faire des remarques désobligeantes *or* peu flatteuses sur

disparagingly [dɪsˈpærɪdʒɪŋlɪ] ADV (*frm*) d'une manière méprisante

disparate [ˈdɪspərɪt] ADJ disparate

disparity [dɪsˈpærɪtɪ] N disparité *f*, inégalité *f*, écart *m*

dispassionate [dɪsˈpæʃənɪt] ADJ (= *unemotional*) calme, froid; (= *unbiased*) impartial, objectif

dispassionately [dɪsˈpæʃənɪtlɪ] ADV (= *unemotionally*) sans émotion; (= *unbiasedly*) sans parti pris, impartialement

▼ **dispatch** [dɪsˈpætʃ] **1** VT **a** (= *send*) [+ *letter, goods*] expédier, envoyer; [+ *messenger*] dépêcher; (*Mil*) [+ *troops*] envoyer, faire partir; [+ *convoy*] mettre en route; (*fig*) [+ *food, drink*] expédier **b** (= *finish off*) [+ *job*] expédier, en finir avec; (= *kill*) [+ *person, animal*] tuer, abattre **2** N **a** [*of letter, messenger, telegram etc*] envoi *m*, expédition *f*; **date of ~** date *f* d'expédition; **office of ~** bureau *m* d'origine **b** (= *official report: also Mil*) dépêche *f*; (*Press*) dépêche *f* (de presse); (*Mil*) **mentioned** *or* **cited in ~es** cité à l'ordre du jour **c** (= *promptness*) promptitude *f* **3** COMP ▶ **dispatch box** N (*Brit Parl*) ≈ tribune *f* (*d'où parlent les membres du gouvernement*); (= *case*) valise *f* officielle (*à documents*) ▶ **dispatch case** N serviette *f*, porte-documents *m inv* ▶ **dispatch documents** NPL (*Comm*) documents *mpl* d'expédition ▶ **dispatch rider** N estafette *f*

dispatcher [dɪsˈpætʃər] N expéditeur *m*, -trice *f*

dispel [dɪsˈpel] VT dissiper, chasser

dispensable [dɪsˈpensəbl] ADJ dont on peut se passer; (*Rel*) dispensable

dispensary [dɪsˈpensərɪ] N (*Brit*) (*in hospital*) pharmacie *f*; (*in chemist's*) officine *f*; (= *clinic*) dispensaire *m*

dispensation [ˌdɪspenˈseɪʃən] N **a** (= *handing out*) [*of food*] distribution *f*; [*of justice, charity*] exercice *m*, pratique *f* **b** (= *exemption*) (*gen, Jur, Rel*) dispense *f* (**from** de); (*Univ, Scol: from exam etc*) dispense *f*, dérogation *f*

dispense [dɪsˈpens] VT [+ *person*] [+ *food*] distribuer; [+ *charity*] pratiquer; [+ *justice, sacrament*] administrer; [+ *hospitality*] offrir; [*machine*] [+ *product*] distribuer; **to ~ alms** faire l'aumône (**to sb** à qn) (*Pharm*) [+ *medicine, prescription*] préparer **c** (*also Rel* = *exempt*) dispenser (**sb from sth/from doing** qn de qch/de faire)

▶ **dispense with** VT FUS (= *do without*) se passer de; (= *make unnecessary*) rendre superflu

dispenser [dɪsˈpensər] N (*Brit*) (= *person*) pharmacien(ne) *m(f)*; (= *device*) distributeur *m*

dispensing chemist [dɪsˌpensɪŋˈkemɪst] N (= *person*) pharmacien(ne) *m(f)*; (= *shop*) pharmacie *f*

dispersal [dɪsˈpɜːsəl] N dispersion *f*

dispersant [dɪsˈpɜːsənt] N (*Chem*) dispersant *m*

disperse [dɪsˈpɜːs] **1** VT [+ *crowd, mist*] disperser; [+ *clouds*] dissiper; [+ *demonstrators, protesters, demonstration*] disperser; [+ *seeds*] disséminer, disperser; [+ *heat*] répandre; [+ *knowledge*] répandre, propager; (*Chem, Opt*) décomposer **2** VI [*crowd, journalists, demonstrators, protesters*] se disperser; [*fog, cloud, smoke*] se dissiper; [*chemicals, oil*] se propager; [*pain, tension*] se dissiper

dispersion [dɪsˈpɜːʃən] N (*also Phys*) dispersion *f*; (*Hist*) **the Dispersion** la dispersion des Juifs, la diaspora

dispirit [dɪsˈpɪrɪt] VT décourager, déprimer, abattre

dispirited [dɪsˈpɪrɪtɪd] ADJ découragé, déprimé, abattu

dispiritedly [dɪsˈpɪrɪtɪdlɪ] ADV avec découragement, d'un air découragé; **~, they turned round and went home** découragés, ils ont fait demi-tour et sont rentrés chez eux

dispiriting [dɪsˈpɪrɪtɪŋ] ADJ décourageant, désolant

displace [dɪsˈpleɪs] **1** VT **a** (= *move out of place*) [+ *refugees*] déplacer; [+ *furniture*] déplacer, changer de place **b** (= *deprive of office*) [+ *officer*] destituer; [+ *official*] déplacer; (= *replace*) supplanter, remplacer **c** (*Naut, Phys*) [+ *water*] déplacer **2** COMP ▶ **displaced person** N personne *f* déplacée

displacement [dɪsˈpleɪsmənt] **1** N **a** (= *replacement*) remplacement *m* **b** [*of people, population*] déplacement *m* **c** (*Math, Phys, Naut, Med*) déplacement *m*; (*Geol*) rejet *m* (*horizontal*) **2** COMP ▶ **displacement activity** N (*Zool*) activité *f* de substitution; (*Psych*) déplacement *m* ▶ **displacement tonnage** N (*Naut*) déplacement *m*

display [dɪsˈpleɪ] **1** VT **a** (= *show*) [+ *object*] montrer; (*pej: ostentatiously*) exhiber (*pej*); **she ~ed the letter she had received from the President** elle a montré *or* brandi la lettre qu'elle avait reçue du président **b** (= *set out visibly*) exposer; [+ *goods for sale*] exposer, mettre à l'étalage; [+ *items in exhibition*] exposer; [+ *notice, results, poster*] afficher; **she bought a cabinet to ~ her china collection in** elle a acheté une vitrine pour y exposer sa collection de porcelaines **c** (= *give evidence of*) [+ *courage, interest, ignorance*] faire preuve de; (*pej*) faire étalage de, exhiber **d** (*Comput*) visualiser; [*electronic device, watch etc*] afficher **2** VI (*Zool: gen*) parader; [*peacock*] faire la roue

3 N **a** (*pej: ostentatious*) étalage *m*; [*of goods for sale, items in exhibition*] exposition *f*; [*of food products, wealth*] étalage *m*; [*of notices, results, posters*] affichage *m*; [*of courage, interest, emotion etc*] manifestation *f*; [*of unity, support*] manifestation *f*, démonstration *f*; [*of strength, loyalty etc*] démonstration *f*; **on ~** exposé; **to go on (public) ~** être exposé; (*Mil*) **a ~ of force** une démonstration de force; (*pej*) **to make a great ~ of learning** faire étalage de son érudition; **she was not given to public ~s of affection** elle n'avait pas pour habitude de prodiguer son affection en public; **to be embarrassed by public ~s of affection** être gêné par des démonstrations publiques d'affection; **a fine ~ of paintings/china** *etc* une belle exposition de tableaux/de porcelaines *etc*; (*in shop window*) **the ~ of fruit** l'étalage *m* de fruits, les fruits *mpl* à l'étalage **b** (= *group, arrangement*) arrangement *m* **c** (= *event, ceremony*) **~ of gymnastics/dancing** *etc* spectacle *m* de gymnastique/de danse *etc*; **military ~** parade *f* militaire; **a dazzling ~ of fireworks lit up the sky** d'éblouissants feux d'artifice ont illuminé le ciel → **air**, **firework**

d̲ (Comput etc) affichage m
e̲ (Zool) parade f

4 COMP (Comm) [goods] d'étalage ► **display advertising** N (Press) placards mpl (publicitaires) ► **display cabinet**, **display case** N vitrine f (meuble) ► **display pack** N (dummy) emballage m de démonstration; (attractive) emballage m de luxe ► **display panel** N écran m d'affichage ► **display unit** N (Comput) écran m de visualisation ► **display window** N étalage m, vitrine f (de magasin)

displease [dɪs'pliːz] VT mécontenter, contrarier

displeased [dɪs'pliːzd] ADJ ~ **at** or **with** mécontent de

displeasing [dɪs'pliːzɪŋ] ADJ désagréable (**to** à), déplaisant (**to** pour); **to be ~ to sb** déplaire à qn

displeasure [dɪs'pleʒəʳ] N mécontentement m, déplaisir m; **to incur sb's ~** provoquer le mécontentement de qn; **to my great ~** à mon grand mécontentement or déplaisir

disport [dɪs'pɔːt] VT **to ~ o.s.** s'amuser, s'ébattre, folâtrer

disposable [dɪs'pəʊzəbl] **1** ADJ a̲ [razor, syringe etc] jetable; **today's ~ society** notre société du tout-jetable b̲ (* fig = unimportant, ephemeral) sans importance; **people should not be treated as if they were ~** on ne devrait pas traiter les gens comme s'ils étaient des objets facilement remplaçables or comme s'ils n'avaient aucune importance c̲ (= available) [time, money] disponible **2** **disposables** NPL a̲ (= containers) emballages m perdus or à jeter; (= bottles) verre m perdu; (= nappies) couches fpl à jeter, couches-culottes fpl **3** COMP ► **disposable income** N revenu(s) m(pl) disponible(s)

disposal [dɪs'pəʊzəl] N a̲ (NonC) [of rubbish] (= collection) enlèvement m; (= destruction) destruction f; [of goods for sale] vente f; (Jur) [of property] disposition f, cession f; [of problem, question] résolution f; [of matters under discussion, current business] expédition f, exécution f → **bomb**, **refuse²** b̲ (= arrangement) [of ornaments, furniture] disposition f, arrangement m; [of troops] disposition f c̲ (= control) [of resources, funds, personnel] disposition f; **the means at one's ~** les moyens dont on dispose; **to put o.s./be at sb's ~** se mettre/être à la disposition de qn

dispose [dɪs'pəʊz] VT a̲ (= arrange) [+ papers, ornaments] disposer, arranger; [+ troops] disposer; [+ forces] déployer ■ (PROV) **man proposes, God ~s** l'homme propose, Dieu dispose (PROV) b̲ (= influence, encourage) disposer (**sb to do** qn à faire); **this does not ~ me to like him** cela ne me rend pas bien disposé à son égard

► **dispose of** VT FUS a̲ (= get rid of) [+ sth no longer wanted or used] se débarrasser de, se défaire de; (by selling) vendre; [+ workers, staff] congédier, renvoyer; [+ rubbish] [householder etc] jeter, se débarrasser de; (= destroy) détruire; [+ chemical, industrial waste etc] éliminer; [shop] [+ stock] écouler, vendre; [+ body] se débarrasser de; **how did the murderer ~ of the body?** comment le meurtrier s'est-il débarrassé du corps? b̲ (*: fig = kill) liquider*; (Jur) [+ property] aliéner c̲ (= deal with) [+ bomb] désamorcer; [+ question, problem, business] expédier; [+ one's opponent, opposing team] régler son compte à; [+ meal] liquider*, expédier d̲ (= control) [+ time, money] disposer de; (= settle) [+ sb's fate] décider de

disposed [dɪs'pəʊzd] ADJ a̲ (frm) **to be ~ to do sth** être disposé à faire qch b̲ **to be well-~ towards sb/sth** être bien disposé envers qn/qch; **to be favourably** or **kindly ~ to(wards) sb/sth** être bien disposé à l'égard de qn/qch → **ill-disposed** c̲ (frm = arranged, distributed) [objects, people] disposé

disposition [ˌdɪspə'zɪʃən] N a̲ (= temperament) naturel m, caractère m, tempérament m b̲ (= readiness) inclination f (**to do** à faire) c̲ (= arrangement) [of ornaments etc] disposition f, arrangement m; [of troops] disposition f d̲ (Jur) [of money, property] distribution f

dispossess [ˌdɪspə'zes] VT déposséder, priver (**of** de); (Jur) exproprier

dispossession [ˌdɪspə'zeʃən] N dépossession f; (Jur) expropriation f

disproportion [ˌdɪsprə'pɔːʃən] N disproportion f

disproportionate [ˌdɪsprə'pɔːʃnɪt] ADJ disproportionné (**to** par rapport à)

disproportionately [ˌdɪsprə'pɔːʃnɪtlɪ] ADV [react, suffer] de manière disproportionnée; **~ small** d'une petitesse disproportionnée; **~ large numbers of blind people are unemployed** un nombre disproportionné d'aveugles sont au chômage

disprove [dɪs'pruːv] VT établir or démontrer la fausseté de, réfuter

disputable [dɪs'pjuːtəbl] ADJ discutable, contestable

disputably [dɪs'pjuːtəblɪ] ADV de manière contestable

disputant [dɪs'pjuːtənt] N (US Jur) **the ~s** les parties fpl en litige

disputation [ˌdɪspjuː'teɪʃən] N a̲ (= argument) débat m, controverse f, discussion f b̲ (†† = formal debate) dispute† f

disputatious [ˌdɪspjuː'teɪʃəs] ADJ (frm) raisonneur (liter)

dispute [dɪs'pjuːt] **1** N a̲ (NonC) (= controversy) discussion f; **beyond ~** (adj) incontestable ♦ (adv) incontestablement; **without ~** sans conteste; **there is some ~ about why he did it/what he's earning** on n'est pas d'accord sur ses motifs/le montant de son salaire; **there is some ~ about which horse won** il y a contestation sur le gagnant; **in** or **under ~** [matter] en discussion; [territory, facts, figures] contesté; (Jur) en litige; **a statement open to ~** une affirmation sujette à caution, une affirmation contestable; **it is open to ~ whether he knew** on peut se demander s'il savait
b̲ (= quarrel) dispute f; (= argument) discussion f, débat m; (Jur) litige m
c̲ (Ind, Pol) conflit m; **to have a ~ with sb about sth** se disputer avec qn à propos de qch; (Ind) **industrial ~** conflit m social; **the miners'/postal workers' ~** le conflit des mineurs/des employés des postes; **the transport/Post Office ~** le conflit dans les transports/dans les services postaux; **the United Shipping Company ~** le conflit chez United Shipping; **wages ~** conflit m salarial or sur les salaires
2 VT a̲ (= cast doubt on) [+ statement, claim] contester, mettre en doute; (Jur) [+ will] attaquer, contester; **I do not ~ the fact that …** je ne conteste pas (le fait) que … (+ subj)
b̲ (= debate) [+ question, subject] discuter, débattre
c̲ (= try to win) [+ victory, possession] disputer (**with sb** à qn)

disputed [dɪs'pjuːtɪd] ADJ [decision] contesté, en discussion; [territory, fact] contesté; (Jur) en litige

disqualification [dɪsˌkwɒlɪfɪ'keɪʃən] N a̲ (gen) disqualification f (also Sport), exclusion f (**from** de); **his lack of experience is not a ~** son manque d'expérience n'est pas rédhibitoire b̲ (Jur) incapacité f; (Aut) **his ~ (from driving)** le retrait de son permis (de conduire)

disqualify [dɪs'kwɒlɪfaɪ] VT a̲ (= debar) rendre inapte (**from sth** à qch, **from doing** à faire); rendre inhabile (**from sth** à qch, **from doing** à faire); (Sport) disqualifier b̲ (Aut, Jur) **to ~ sb from driving** retirer à qn son or le permis de conduire; **he was disqualified for speeding** on lui a retiré son permis pour excès de vitesse; **he was accused of driving while disqualified** il a été accusé d'avoir conduit alors qu'on lui avait retiré son permis c̲ (= incapacitate) rendre incapable, mettre hors d'état (**from doing** de faire); **his lack of experience does not ~ him** son manque d'expérience n'est pas rédhibitoire

disquiet [dɪs'kwaɪət] **1** VT inquiéter, troubler; **to be ~ed about** s'inquiéter de **2** N (NonC) inquiétude f, trouble m; (= unrest) agitation f

disquieting [dɪs'kwaɪətɪŋ] ADJ inquiétant, alarmant, troublant

disquietude [dɪs'kwaɪətjuːd] N (NonC) inquiétude f, trouble m

disquisition [ˌdɪskwɪ'zɪʃən] N (= treatise) traité m, dissertation f, étude f (**on** sur); (= discourse) communication f (**on** sur); (= investigation) étude f approfondie (**on** de)

disregard [ˌdɪsrɪ'gɑːd] **1** VT [+ fact, difficulty, remark] ne tenir aucun compte de, ne pas s'occuper de; [+ danger] mépriser, ne pas faire attention à; [+ feelings] négliger, faire peu de cas de; [+ authority, rules, duty] méconnaître, passer outre à **2** N [of difficulty, comments, feelings] indifférence f (**for** à); [of danger] mépris m (**for** de); [of money] mépris m, dédain m (**for** de); [of safety] négligence f (**for** en ce qui concerne); [of rule, law] désobéissance f (**for** à), non-observation f (**for** de)

disrepair [ˌdɪsrɪ'pɛəʳ] N (NonC) mauvais état m, délabrement m; **in (a state of) ~** [building] délabré; [road] en mauvais état; **to fall into ~** [building] tomber en ruines, se délabrer; [road] se dégrader

disreputable [dɪs'repjʊtəbl] ADJ a̲ (= shady, dishonorable) [establishment, area, person] peu recommandable, louche*; [behaviour] déshonorant b̲ (* = shabby) miteux

disreputably [dɪs'repjʊtəblɪ] ADV [behave] d'une manière peu honorable; [dress] minablement*

disrepute [ˌdɪsrɪ'pjuːt] N discrédit m, déshonneur m; **to bring sth into ~** jeter le discrédit sur qch; **to fall into ~** tomber en discrédit

disrespect [ˌdɪsrɪs'pekt] **1** N manque m de respect, irrespect m; **no ~ (to …)** avec tout le respect que je dois (à …); **to show ~ to sb/sth** manquer de respect envers qn/qch **2** VT manquer de respect envers

disrespectful [ˌdɪsrɪs'pektfʊl] ADJ irrespectueux, irrévérencieux (**to** envers); **to be ~ to sb/sth** manquer de respect envers qn/qch, se montrer irrespectueux envers qn/qch

disrespectfully [ˌdɪsrɪs'pektfʊlɪ] ADV de façon irrespectueuse; **to treat sb ~** manquer de respect à qn; **he was treated ~** on lui a manqué de respect

disrobe [dɪs'rəʊb] **1** VI se dévêtir, enlever ses vêtements; (= undress) se déshabiller **2** VT enlever les vêtements (de cérémonie) à, dévêtir, déshabiller

disrupt [dɪs'rʌpt] VT [+ peace, relations, train service] perturber; [+ conversation] interrompre; [+ plans] déranger; (stronger) mettre or semer la confusion dans; [+ communications] couper, interrompre

disruption [dɪs'rʌpʃən] N perturbation f

disruptive [dɪs'rʌptɪv] **1** ADJ a̲ [child, behaviour] perturbateur (-trice f); **to be a ~ influence** avoir une influence perturbatrice b̲ (Elec) disruptif **2** COMP ► **disruptive action** N action f perturbatrice

diss: [dɪs] VT (US = treat with contempt) se payer la tête de*

dissatisfaction [ˌdɪssætɪs'fækʃən] N mécontentement m, insatisfaction f; **growing/widespread ~** mécontentement m croissant/général (**at, with** devant, provoqué par)

dissatisfied [ˌdɪs'sætɪsfaɪd] ADJ mécontent, peu satisfait (**with** de)

dissect [dɪ'sekt] VT [+ animal, plant, truth] disséquer; [+ book, article] éplucher

dissected [dɪ'sektɪd] ADJ (Bot) découpé

dissection [dɪ'sekʃən] N (Anat, Bot, fig) dissection f

dissemble [dɪ'sembl] [1] VT (= conceal) dissimuler; (= feign) feindre, simuler [2] VI (in speech) dissimuler or déguiser or masquer sa pensée; (in behaviour) agir avec dissimulation

disseminate [dɪ'semɪneɪt] [1] VT disséminer, semer [2] COMP ► **disseminated cancer** N (Med) cancer m généralisé ► **disseminated sclerosis** N (Med) sclérose f en plaques

dissemination [dɪˌsemɪ'neɪʃən] N [of seeds] dissémination f; [of ideas] dissémination f, propagation f

dissension [dɪ'senʃən] N dissension f, discorde f

dissent [dɪ'sent] [1] VI différer (d'opinion or de sentiment) (**from sb** de qn); (Rel) être en dissidence, être dissident [2] N dissentiment m, différence f d'opinion; (Rel) dissidence f

dissenter [dɪ'sentər] N (esp Rel) dissident(e) m(f)

dissentient [dɪ'senʃɪənt] [1] ADJ dissident, opposé [2] N dissident(e) m(f), opposant(e) m(f)

dissenting [dɪ'sentɪŋ] ADJ [voice] dissident; **a long ~ tradition** une longue tradition de dissidence; (US Jur) **~ opinion** avis m minoritaire de l'un des juges (divergeant sur des questions de fond)

dissertation [ˌdɪsə'teɪʃən] N [a] (written) mémoire m (**on** sur); (spoken) exposé m (**on** sur) [b] (Univ) (Brit) mémoire m; (US) thèse f (de doctorat)

disservice [dɪs'sɜːvɪs] N mauvais service m; **to do sb/sth a ~** (= be unhelpful to) rendre un mauvais service à qn/qch, desservir qn/qch; (= be unfair to) faire du tort à qn/qch

dissidence ['dɪsɪdəns] N dissidence f (also Pol), désaccord m, divergence f d'opinion

dissident ['dɪsɪdənt] ADJ, N dissident(e) m(f)

dissimilar [dɪ'sɪmɪlər] ADJ dissemblable (**to** à), différent (**to** de)

dissimilarity [ˌdɪsɪmɪ'lærɪtɪ] N différence f, dissemblance f (**between** entre)

dissimulate [dɪ'sɪmjʊleɪt] VTI dissimuler

dissimulation [dɪˌsɪmjʊ'leɪʃən] N dissimulation f

dissipate ['dɪsɪpeɪt] [1] VT [+ fog, clouds, fears, suspicions] dissiper; [+ hopes] anéantir; [+ energy, efforts] disperser, gaspiller; [+ fortune] dissiper, dilapider [2] VI se dissiper

dissipated ['dɪsɪpeɪtɪd] ADJ [person] débauché, qui mène une vie dissipée; [activity] dépravé; [life, behaviour] dissipé, dissolu; [appearance] de débauché; **to lead a ~ life** mener une vie dissipée or dissolue, vivre dans la dissipation (liter)

dissipation [ˌdɪsɪ'peɪʃən] N [of clouds, fears] dissipation f; [of energy, efforts] gaspillage m; [of fortune] dilapidation f; (= debauchery) dissipation f, débauche f

▼ **dissociate** [dɪ'səʊʃɪeɪt] VT dissocier, séparer (**from** de); (Chem, Psych) dissocier; **to ~ o.s. from** se dissocier de, se désolidariser de

dissociation [dɪˌsəʊsɪ'eɪʃən] N (all senses) dissociation f

dissoluble [dɪ'sɒljʊbl] ADJ soluble

dissolute ['dɪsəluːt] ADJ [person] débauché, dissolu (liter); [way of life] dissolu, déréglé, de débauche

dissolution [ˌdɪsə'luːʃən] N (all senses) dissolution f

dissolvable [dɪ'zɒlvəbl] ADJ soluble (**in** dans)

dissolve [dɪ'zɒlv] [1] VT [a] [water etc] [+ substance] dissoudre (**in** dans); [person] [+ che-

mical etc] faire dissoudre (**in** dans); (Culin) [+ sugar etc] faire fondre (**in** dans) [b] [+ alliance, marriage, assembly] dissoudre [2] VI [a] (Chem) se dissoudre; (Culin) fondre [b] (fig) [hopes, fears] disparaître, s'évanouir; (Jur, Pol) se dissoudre; (fig) **to ~ into thin air** s'en aller or partir en fumée; (fig) **to ~ into tears** fondre en larmes [c] (Cine) se fondre [3] N (Cine, TV) fondu m (enchaîné); **~ in/out** ouverture f/ fermeture f en fondu

dissolvent [dɪ'zɒlvənt] [1] ADJ dissolvant [2] N dissolvant m, solvant m

dissonance ['dɪsənəns] N dissonance f, discordance f

dissonant ['dɪsənənt] ADJ dissonant, discordant

dissuade [dɪ'sweɪd] VT dissuader (**sb from doing** qn de faire), détourner (**sb from sth** qn de qch)

dissuasion [dɪ'sweɪʒən] N dissuasion f

dissuasive [dɪ'sweɪsɪv] ADJ (gen) dissuasif; [voice, person] qui cherche à dissuader; [powers] de dissuasion

distaff ['dɪstɑːf] N quenouille f; (fig) **on the ~ side** du côté maternel or des femmes

distance ['dɪstəns] [1] N [a] (in space) distance f (**between** entre); **what ~ is it from London?** c'est à quelle distance de Londres?; **what ~ is it from here to London?** nous sommes à combien de kilomètres de Londres?; **it's a good ~** c'est assez loin; **a short ~ away** à une faible distance; **it's no ~** c'est à deux pas, c'est tout près; **to cover the ~ in two hours** franchir or parcourir la distance en deux heures; **at an equal ~ from each other** à égale distance l'un de l'autre; **at a ~** assez loin, à quelque distance; **at a ~ of 2 metres** à une distance de 2 mètres; **the ~ between the boys/the houses/the towns** la distance qui sépare les garçons/les maisons/les villes; **the ~ between the eyes/rails/posts** l'écartement m des yeux/ des rails/des poteaux; **from a ~** de loin; **seen from a ~** vu de loin; **to go part of the ~ alone** faire une partie du trajet seul; (Sport, fig) **to go** or **last the ~** tenir la distance → **long[1]**, **middle**; **in the ~** au loin, dans le lointain; **it's within walking/cycling ~** on peut y aller à pied/en vélo → **spitting** [b] (in time) intervalle m; **from a ~ of 40 years, I can look back on it and say ...** 40 ans plus tard or 40 ans après, je peux y repenser et dire ... [c] (in rank etc) distance f; **to keep sb at a ~** tenir qn à distance; **to keep one's ~ (from sb/ sth)** garder ses distances (par rapport à qn/ qch)

[2] VT (Sport etc) distancer; (fig) **to ~ o.s. from sth** se distancier de qch

[3] COMP ► **distance learning** N (Educ) téléenseignement m ► **distance race** N (Sport: also **long-~ race**) épreuve f de fond ► **distance teaching** N (Educ) enseignement m à distance, téléenseignement m

distancing ['dɪstənsɪŋ] N distanciation f

distant ['dɪstənt] [1] ADJ [a] (in space, time) lointain; **there was a ~ view of the church** on apercevait l'église au loin; **the nearest hospital was 200km** ≈ l'hôpital le plus proche était à 200 km; **the school is 2km ~ from the church** l'école est à 2 km (de distance) de l'église; **a ~ memory** un lointain souvenir; **in the ~ future/past** dans un avenir/un passé lointain; **in the not too** or **very ~ future** dans un avenir assez proche [b] [connection] lointain; [resemblance] vague; [cousin, relative, relationship] éloigné [c] (= distracted) [person, manner] distrait; **there was a ~ look in her eyes** elle avait un regard distrait [d] (= cool, reserved) [person, manner] distant [2] COMP ► **distant early warning line** N (US Mil) ligne f DEW (système de radars)

distantly ['dɪstəntlɪ] ADV [a] (= in the distance) [hear] dans le lointain, au loin; **~, she heard the front door bell ring** elle entendit au loin qu'on sonnait à la porte d'entrée; **the sound of a flute was ~ audible** on entendait au loin le son d'une flûte; **she was ~ aware of Gavin's voice** elle entendait vaguement la voix de Gavin [b] [resemble] vaguement, un peu; **I am ~ related to her** c'est une parente éloignée, nous sommes vaguement apparentés; **the lion and the domestic cat are ~ related** le lion et le chat domestique ont des ancêtres communs [c] (= absently) [nod, smile] d'un air distrait [d] (= in a reserved way) [speak] d'un ton distant; **to smile/behave ~** avoir un sourire distant/une attitude distante

distaste [dɪs'teɪst] N dégoût m, répugnance f (**for** pour)

distasteful [dɪs'teɪstfʊl] ADJ déplaisant, désagréable; **to be ~ to sb** déplaire à qn

distastefully [dɪs'teɪstfʊlɪ] ADV [look at] d'un air dégoûté

distemper[1] [dɪs'tempər] [1] N (= paint) détrempe f [2] VT peindre à la détrempe; **~ed walls** murs mpl peints à la détrempe

distemper[2] [dɪs'tempər] N (Vet) maladie f des jeunes chiens or de Carré

distend [dɪs'tend] [1] VT (gen) ballonner; (with gas) distendre [2] VI (gen) se distendre; (with gas) se ballonner

distension [dɪs'tenʃən] N distension f, dilatation f

distich ['dɪstɪk] N distique m

distil, distill (US) [dɪs'tɪl] [1] VT [a] [+ alcohol, knowledge] distiller [b] (= drip slowly) laisser couler goutte à goutte [2] VI se distiller, couler goutte à goutte [3] COMP ► **distilled water** N (Aut etc) eau f déminéralisée

distillate ['dɪstɪlɪt] N (Chem, Ind) distillat m

distillation [ˌdɪstɪ'leɪʃən] N (Chem etc, fig) distillation f

distiller [dɪs'tɪlər] N distillateur m

distillery [dɪs'tɪlərɪ] N distillerie f

distinct [dɪs'tɪŋkt] ADJ [a] (= definite) [impression, preference, likeness, advantage, disadvantage] net (before n); [increase, progress] sensible, net (before n); [possibility] réel; **there was a ~ lack of enthusiasm for that idea** il y avait un net manque d'enthousiasme pour cette idée [b] (= different, separate) distinct (**from** de); **as ~ from** par opposition à, contrairement à [c] (= clear) [silhouette, voice, memory] distinct

distinction [dɪs'tɪŋkʃən] N [a] (= difference) distinction f, différence f; (= act of keeping apart) distinction f (**of** ... **from** de ..., **between** entre); **to draw** or **make a ~ between two things** faire la or une distinction entre deux choses [b] (NonC) (= pre-eminence) distinction f, mérite m; (= refinement) distinction f; **to win ~** se distinguer, acquérir une or de la réputation; **a pianist of ~** un pianiste réputé or de renom; **she has great ~** elle est d'une grande distinction [c] (Univ etc) **he got a ~ in French** il a été reçu en français avec mention très bien

distinctive [dɪs'tɪŋktɪv] ADJ [a] (= idiosyncratic) caractéristique [b] (= differentiating: also Ling) distinctif; **to be ~ of** or **to sth** caractériser qch

distinctively [dɪs'tɪŋktɪvlɪ] ADV ► **English/ masculine** etc typiquement anglais/masculin etc; **~ dressed** habillé de façon originale; **~ patterned** au motif caractéristique; **to be ~ different from sth** se démarquer nettement de qch

distinctiveness [dɪs'tɪŋktɪvnɪs] N caractère m distinctif

distinctly [dɪs'tɪŋktlɪ] ADV [a] (with vb = clearly) [speak, hear, see] distinctement; [remember] clairement; (with adj = decidedly) particulièrement; **it is ~ possible** c'est très possible, c'est une réelle possibilité ; ~ **different/better** nettement différent/mieux

▼ **distinguish** [dɪs'tɪŋgwɪʃ] **1** VT **a** (= *discern*) [+ *landmark*] distinguer, apercevoir ; [+ *change*] discerner, percevoir **b** [+ *object, series, person*] (= *make different*) distinguer (**from** de) ; (= *characterize*) caractériser ; **to ~ o.s.** se distinguer (**as** comme, en tant que) ; (*also iro*) **you've really ~ed yourself!** tu t'es vraiment distingué ! (*also iro*) → **distinguished**, **distinguishing 2** VI **to ~ between A and B** distinguer *or* faire la distinction entre A et B, distinguer A de B

distinguishable [dɪs'tɪŋgwɪʃəbl] ADJ **a** (= *distinct*) **to be ~ from sth (by sth)** se distinguer de qch (par qch) ; **the two political parties are now barely ~ (from each other)** maintenant, les deux partis politiques se distinguent à peine (l'un de l'autre) ; **to be ~ by sth** être reconnaissable à qch, se reconnaître à qch ; **easily** *or* **readily ~** facile à distinguer **b** (= *discernible*) [*shape, words, outline*] perceptible

distinguished [dɪs'tɪŋgwɪʃt] **1** ADJ **a** (= *elegant, sophisticated*) [*person, appearance*] distingué ; **to look ~** avoir l'air distingué **b** (= *eminent*) [*pianist, scholar*] distingué ; [*career, history*] brillant ; **in ~ company** en illustre compagnie ; **20 years of ~ service** 20 ans de bons et loyaux services ; **~ for his bravery** remarquable par *or* remarqué pour son courage ; (*US Univ*) **~ service professor** professeur *m* à titre personnel **2** COMP ▶ **Distinguished Flying Cross** N *médaille décernée aux aviateurs militaires* ▶ **distinguished-looking** ADJ à l'air distingué ▶ **Distinguished Service Cross** N *médaille militaire* ▶ **Distinguished Service Medal** N *médaille militaire* ▶ **Distinguished Service Order** N (*Brit*) *médaille militaire*

distinguishing [dɪs'tɪŋgwɪʃɪŋ] ADJ distinctif, caractéristique ; **~ mark** caractéristique *f* ; (*on passport*) signe *m* particulier

distort [dɪs'tɔːt] **1** VT (*physically*) déformer, altérer ; (*fig*) [+ *truth*] défigurer, déformer ; [+ *text*] déformer ; [+ *judgement*] fausser ; [+ *words, facts*] dénaturer, déformer **2** VI [*face*] se crisper

distorted [dɪs'tɔːtɪd] ADJ **a** [*object, image, sound*] déformé ; **his face was ~ with rage** ses traits étaient déformés par la colère **b** (= *biased*) [*report, impression*] faux (fausse *f*) ; **a ~ version of the events** une version déformée des événements **c** (= *perverted*) [*morality, sexuality*] dévoyé

distortion [dɪs'tɔːʃən] N (*gen, Elec, Med, Opt*) distorsion *f* ; [*of tree etc*] déformation *f* ; [*of features*] distorsion *f*, altération *f* ; [*of shape, facts, text*] déformation *f*, altération *f* ; **by ~ of the facts** en dénaturant les faits

distract [dɪs'trækt] VT [+ *person*] distraire, déconcentrer ; (= *interrupt*) déranger ; **the noise ~ed her from working** le bruit la distrayait de son travail ; **the noise was ~ing him** le bruit le déconcentrait *or* l'empêchait de se concentrer ; **she's busy, you mustn't ~ her** elle est occupée, il ne faut pas la déranger ; **to ~ sb's attention** détourner l'attention de qn

distracted [dɪs'træktɪd] ADJ **a** (= *worried*) éperdu, égaré ; [*look*] égaré, affolé ; **to drive sb ~** faire perdre la tête à qn, rendre qn fou ; **~ with worry** *etc* fou d'anxiété *etc* ; **she was quite ~** elle était dans tous ses états **b** († = *mad*) fou (folle *f*)

distractedly [dɪs'træktɪdlɪ] ADV **a** (= *absently*) [*speak*] d'un ton distrait, distraitement ; [*behave*] éperdument, distraitement **b** (*liter* = *wildly*) [*behave, run*] comme un fou (*or* une folle) ; [*speak*] d'un air affolé ; [*weep*] éperdument ; **~, he ran his hands through his hair** il se passa la main dans les cheveux, l'air affolé

distracting [dɪs'træktɪŋ] ADJ gênant, qui empêche de se concentrer

distraction [dɪs'trækʃən] N **a** (*NonC* = *lack of attention*) distraction *f*, inattention *f* **b** (= *interruption: to work etc*) interruption *f* **c** (= *entertainment*) divertissement *m*, distraction *f* **d** (*NonC* = *madness*) affolement *m* ; **to love sb to ~** aimer qn à la folie ; **to drive sb to ~** rendre qn fou

distrain [dɪs'treɪn] VI (*Jur*) **to ~ upon sb's goods** saisir les biens de qn, opérer la saisie des biens de qn

distrainee [ˌdɪstreɪ'niː] N (*Jur*) saisi *m*

distrainor [dɪs'treɪnər] N (*Jur*) saisissant *m*

distraint [dɪs'treɪnt] N (*Jur*) saisie *f*, saisie-exécution *f* (*sur les meubles d'un débiteur*)

distraught [dɪs'trɔːt] ADJ éperdu, égaré, affolé (**with, from** de)

distress [dɪs'tres] **1** N **a** (*physical*) douleur *f* ; (*mental*) détresse *f*, affliction *f* (*liter*) ; **to be in great ~** (*physical*) souffrir beaucoup ; (*mental*) être bouleversé, être (plongé) dans l'affliction ; **to be in great ~ over sth** être bouleversé *or* profondément affligé de qch ; **to cause ~ to** causer une grande peine *or* douleur à **b** (= *poverty*) détresse *f* ; **in ~** dans la détresse **c** (= *danger*) péril *m*, détresse *f* ; **a ship in ~** un navire en perdition ; **a plane in ~** un avion en détresse ; **a damsel in ~** une demoiselle en détresse **d** (*Jur*) saisie *f* **2** VT affliger, peiner **3** COMP ▶ **distress rocket** N fusée *f* de détresse ▶ **distress sale** N vente *f* de biens saisis ▶ **distress signal** N signal *m* de détresse

distressed [dɪs'trest] ADJ **a** (= *upset*) affligé, peiné (**by** par, **de**) ; **she was very ~** elle était bouleversée **b** († = *poverty-stricken*) **in ~ circumstances** dans la détresse *or* la misère ; **~ gentlewomen** dames *fpl* de bonne famille dans le besoin

distressful [dɪs'tresfʊl] ADJ = **distressing**

distressing [dɪs'tresɪŋ] ADJ [*situation, experience*] pénible ; [*poverty, inadequacy*] lamentable

distressingly [dɪs'tresɪŋlɪ] ADV **the trapped animal howled ~** les cris de l'animal pris au piège étaient déchirants ; **~, it took him over an hour to die** chose horrible, il a mis plus d'une heure à mourir ; **a ~ high/low percentage** un pourcentage tristement élevé/bas ; **she looked ~ thin** sa maigreur faisait peine à voir ; **the solution is ~ simple/obvious** la solution est d'une simplicité/évidence désespérante

distributary [dɪs'trɪbjʊtərɪ] **1** N (*Geog*) défluent *m* **2** ADJ de distribution

distribute [dɪs'trɪbjuːt] VT [+ *leaflets, prizes, type*] distribuer ; [+ *dividends, load, weight*] répartir ; [+ *money*] distribuer, partager ; (*Comm*) [+ *goods*] être concessionnaire de ; [+ *films*] être distributeur de ; **~ the almonds over the top of the cake** étaler les amandes sur le dessus du gâteau ; **to ~ sth into categories** répartir qch en catégories

distribution [ˌdɪstrɪ'bjuːʃən] **1** N **a** [*of food, supplies, newspaper*] distribution *f* (*also Comm, Ling, Econ*) ; [*of resources, wealth, power*] répartition *f* ; **weight/heat ~** répartition *f* du poids/de la chaleur ; **geographical ~** répartition *f* *or* distribution *f* géographique ; (*Econ*) **the ~ of wealth** la répartition *or* distribution des richesses **2** COMP ▶ **distribution network** N réseau *m* de distribution

distributional [ˌdɪstrɪ'bjuːʃənəl] ADJ (*Comm*) de distribution ; (*Ling*) distributionnel

distributive [dɪs'trɪbjʊtɪv] **1** ADJ (*Comm, Gram, Philos etc*) distributif ; (*Econ*) **the ~ trades** le secteur de la distribution **2** N (*Gram*) pronom *m* *or* adjectif *m* distributif

distributor [dɪs'trɪbjʊtər] **1** N **a** (*Comm*) [*of goods over an area*] concessionnaire *mf* ; [*of films*] distributeur *m* **b** (*Tech* = *device*) distributeur *m* ; (*Aut*) delco® *m* **2** COMP ▶ **distributor cap** N (*Aut*) tête *f* de delco®

▶ **distributor network** N réseau *m* de distributeurs

distributorship [dɪs'trɪbjʊtəʃɪp] N (*Comm*) **a** (= *company*) distributeur *m* **b** (= *right to supply*) contrat *m* de distribution

district ['dɪstrɪkt] **1** N (*of a country*) région *f* ; (*in town*) quartier *m* ; (= *administrative area*) district *m* ; (*in Paris etc*) arrondissement *m* ; (*US Pol*) circonscription *f* électorale (*or* administrative) → **electoral**, **postal 2** COMP ▶ **district attorney** N (*US Jur*) représentant *m* du ministère public, ≈ procureur *m* de la République ▶ **district commissioner** N (*Brit*) commissaire *m* ▶ **district council** N (*Brit: local government*) ≈ conseil *m* général ▶ **district court** N (*US Jur*) cour *f* fédérale (de grande instance) ▶ **district heating** N ≈ chauffage *m* urbain ▶ **district manager** N (*Comm*) directeur *m* régional ▶ **district nurse** N infirmière *f* visiteuse *or* à domicile ▶ **District of Columbia** N (*US*) district *m* (fédéral) de Columbia

> DISTRICT OF COLUMBIA

Le **District of Columbia** (ou **DC**) est un territoire autonome de 180 km², qui n'a pas le statut d'État mais où s'étend la capitale fédérale, Washington (ou Washington **DC**), et qui contient donc les grandes institutions politiques des États-Unis et en particulier la Maison-Blanche et le Capitole.

distrust [dɪs'trʌst] **1** VT se méfier de, se défier de **2** N méfiance *f* ; **to feel some ~ of sb/sth** éprouver de la méfiance à l'égard de qn/qch

distrustful [dɪs'trʌstfʊl] ADJ méfiant, qui se méfie (**of** de)

disturb [dɪs'tɜːb] VT **a** (= *inconvenience*) [+ *person*] déranger ; **sorry to ~ you** excusez-moi de vous déranger ; **"(please) do not ~"** « (prière de) ne pas déranger » **b** (= *trouble*) [+ *person*] troubler, inquiéter ; **the news ~ed him greatly** la nouvelle l'a beaucoup troublé **c** (= *interrupt*) [+ *silence, balance*] rompre ; [+ *sleep, rest*] troubler **d** (= *disarrange*) [+ *waters, sediment, atmosphere*] troubler ; [+ *papers, evidence*] déranger

disturbance [dɪs'tɜːbəns] N **a** (*political, social*) troubles *mpl*, émeute *f* ; (*in house, group*) bruit *m*, tapage *m* ; **to cause a ~** faire du bruit *or* du tapage ; **~ of the peace** atteinte *f* à l'ordre public **b** (*NonC*) [*of routine, papers*] dérangement *m* ; [*of liquid*] agitation *f* ; [*of air, atmosphere*] perturbation *f* **c** (*NonC* = *alarm, uneasiness*) trouble *m* (d'esprit), perturbation *f* (de l'esprit)

disturbed [dɪs'tɜːbd] ADJ **a** (*Psych*) perturbé ; **emotionally/mentally ~** présentant des troubles affectifs/mentaux **b** (= *concerned*) inquiet (-ète *f*) (**about** au sujet de, **at, by** par) **c** (= *unsettled*) [*childhood, period, night, sleep*] troublé ; [*background*] perturbé

disturbing [dɪs'tɜːbɪŋ] ADJ (= *alarming*) inquiétant, troublant ; (= *distracting*) gênant, ennuyeux

disturbingly [dɪs'tɜːbɪŋlɪ] ADV **a ~ high number/percentage** un nombre/pourcentage inquiétant ; **~, the data suggests that ...** chose inquiétante, les données suggèrent que ...

disunite [ˌdɪsjuː'naɪt] VT désunir

disunity [dɪs'juːnɪtɪ] N désunion *f*

disuse [dɪs'juːs] N désuétude *f* ; **to fall into ~** tomber en désuétude

disused [dɪs'juːzd] ADJ [*building*] désaffecté, abandonné

disyllabic [ˌdɪsɪ'læbɪk] ADJ dissyllabe, dissyllabique

ditch [dɪtʃ] **1** N **a** (*by roadside, between fields etc*) fossé *m* ; (*for irrigation*) rigole *f* ; (*around castle*) douve *f* **b** (*Aviat*) **the ~**: la baille* → **last¹ 2** VT **a** (* = *get rid of*) [+ *lover*] plaquer*, laisser tomber* ; [+ *car etc*] abandonner ; **to ~**

a plane faire un amerrissage forcé b (US*) [+ class] sécher*

ditcher ['dɪtʃəʳ] N terrassier m

ditching ['dɪtʃɪŋ] N a (= making ditches) creusement m de fossés; **hedging and ~** entretien m des haies et fossés b (Aviat) amerrissage m forcé (d'un avion)

ditchwater ['dɪtʃwɔːtəʳ] N → dull

dither* ['dɪðəʳ] (esp Brit) 1 N **to be in a ~** ◊ **to be all of a ~** être dans tous ses états 2 VI hésiter, se tâter; **to ~ over a decision** se tâter pour prendre une décision; **stop ~ing and get on with it!** il n'y a pas à tortiller*, il faut que tu t'y mettes!
► **dither about*, dither around*** VI tourner en rond (fig)

ditherer* ['dɪðərəʳ] N (Brit) indécis(e) m(f); **don't be such a ~!** ne sois pas si indécis!

dithery* ['dɪðərɪ] ADJ (pej) indécis, qui tourne autour du pot

ditsy* ['dɪtsɪ] ADJ (esp US) = ditzy

ditto ['dɪtəʊ] 1 ADV idem; **restaurants are expensive here, and ~ the cinemas** or **the cinemas ~** les restaurants sont chers ici et les cinémas idem* 2 COMP ► **ditto mark, ditto sign** N guillemets mpl de répétition

ditty ['dɪtɪ] N chansonnette f

ditzy* ['dɪtsɪ] ADJ (esp US) évaporé

diuresis [ˌdaɪjʊˈriːsɪs] N diurèse f

diuretic [ˌdaɪjʊəˈretɪk] ADJ, N diurétique m

diurnal [daɪˈɜːnl] 1 ADJ (Astron, Bot) diurne 2 N (Rel) diurnal m

diva ['diːvə] N (pl **divas** or **dive**) diva f

divan [dɪˈvæn] 1 N divan m 2 COMP ► **divan bed** N (Brit) divan-lit m

dive[1] [daɪv] 1 N a (= of swimmer, goalkeeper) plongeon m; (of submarine, deep-sea diver etc) plongée f; (of aircraft) piqué m; (fig) **to make a ~** foncer (tête baissée); **to go into a ~** (profits, sales etc) dégringoler, plonger; (Ftbl) **to take a ~*** faire du chiqué* b (* = disreputable club, café etc) bouge m 2 VI a (diver etc) plonger, faire un plongeon; (submarine) plonger; (aircraft) piquer; **he ~d in head first** il a piqué une tête dans l'eau; **to ~ for pearls** pêcher des perles b (= plunge) **to ~ in/out** etc entrer/sortir etc tête baissée; **he ~d for the exit** il a foncé (tête baissée) vers la sortie; **he ~d into the crowd** il a plongé dans la foule; **he ~d under the table** il s'est jeté sous la table; **to ~ for cover** se précipiter pour se mettre à l'abri; (Ftbl) **the keeper ~d for the ball** le gardien de but a plongé pour bloquer le ballon; (fig) **to ~ into one's pocket** plonger la main dans sa poche 3 COMP ► **dive-bomb** VT bombarder en piqué ► **dive bomber** N bombardier m (qui bombarde en piqué) ► **dive bombing** N bombardement m en piqué
► **dive in** VI a (diver) plonger b (= start to eat) **~ in!*** attaquez!*

dive[2] ['diːvɪ] NPL of diva

diver ['daɪvəʳ] N a (= person) plongeur m; (also **deep-sea ~**) scaphandrier m → scuba, skin b (Orn) plongeon m, plongeur m

diverge [daɪˈvɜːdʒ] VI (lines, paths, opinions, explanations) diverger

divergence [daɪˈvɜːdʒəns] N divergence f

divergent [daɪˈvɜːdʒənt] 1 ADJ divergent 2 COMP ► **divergent thinking** N raisonnement m divergent

divers ['daɪvɜːz] ADJ (liter) divers, plusieurs

diverse [daɪˈvɜːs] ADJ divers

diversification [daɪˌvɜːsɪfɪˈkeɪʃən] N diversification f

diversify [daɪˈvɜːsɪfaɪ] 1 VT diversifier, varier 2 VI [farmer, businessman] diversifier ses activités

diversion [daɪˈvɜːʃən] N a (Brit = redirecting) [of traffic] déviation f; [of stream] dérivation f,

détournement m; [of ship] (gen) déroutement m; [of profits] détournement m b (Aut) déviation f c (= relaxation) divertissement m, distraction f; **it's a ~ from work** cela change or distrait du travail d (Mil etc) diversion f; **to create a ~** (Mil) opérer une diversion; (in class, during argument etc) faire diversion

diversionary [daɪˈvɜːʃnərɪ] ADJ (also Mil) de diversion; **~ tactics** manœuvres fpl de diversion

diversity [daɪˈvɜːsɪtɪ] N diversité f

divert [daɪˈvɜːt] VT a (= redirect) [+ stream] détourner; [+ train, plane, ship] dérouter; (Brit) [+ traffic] dévier; [+ attention, eyes] détourner; [+ conversation] détourner; [+ blow] écarter; [+ phone call] transférer b (= amuse) divertir, amuser

diverting [daɪˈvɜːtɪŋ] ADJ divertissant, amusant

divest [daɪˈvest] VT (of clothes, weapons) dévêtir, dépouiller (**of** de); (of rights, property) dépouiller, priver (**of** de); [+ room] dégarnir

divide [dɪˈvaɪd] 1 VT a (= separate) séparer (**from** de); **the Pyrenees ~ France from Spain** les Pyrénées séparent la France de l'Espagne b (= split: also **~ up**: gen) diviser (**into** en, **among, between** entre); [+ people] répartir; [+ money, work] diviser, partager, répartir; [+ property, kingdom] diviser, démembrer, morceler; [+ house] diviser, partager (**into** en); [+ apple, room] diviser, couper (**into** en); [+ one's time, attention] partager (**between** entre); **they ~d it (amongst themselves)** ils se le sont partagé c (Math) diviser; **to ~ 36 by 6** ◊ **to ~ 6 into 36** diviser 36 par 6 d (= cause disagreement among) [+ friends, political parties etc] diviser; (Brit) **~ and rule** or **conquer** (politique f consistant à) diviser pour mieux régner e (Brit Parl) **to ~ the House** faire voter la Chambre 2 VI a (river) se diviser; (road) bifurquer b (also **~ up**) [people] se répartir; (Bio) [cells etc] se diviser c (Math) être divisible (**by** par) d (Brit Parl) **the House ~d** la Chambre a procédé au vote ou a voté 3 N a (= division, bar) fossé m; **to bridge the ~ between ...** combler le fossé entre ...; **the racial/social/cultural ~** le fossé racial/social/culturel; **to cross the great ~** (= die) passer de vie à trépas b (Geog) ligne f de partage des eaux; (in US) **the Great Divide** la ligne de partage des montagnes Rocheuses
► **divide off** 1 VI se séparer (**from** de) 2 VT SEP séparer (**from** de)
► **divide out** VT SEP répartir, distribuer (**among** entre)
► **divide up** 1 VI = divide 2b 2 VT SEP = divide 1b

divided [dɪˈvaɪdɪd] 1 ADJ a (= in two parts) divisé b (Bot) découpé c (= disunited, in disagreement) [people, country] divisé (**on, over** sur); [opinion] partagé (**on, over** sur); **to have** or **suffer from ~ loyalties** être déchiré; **opinion is** or **opinions are** ~ **on** or **over** or **over that** les avis sont partagés sur ce point; **opinions are ~ on what to do/on how long it will take (to do it)** les avis sont partagés quant à ce qu'il convient de faire/quant au temps que cela prendra; **I feel ~ (in my own mind)** je suis or je me sens partagé 2 COMP ► **divided highway** N (US) (route f à) quatre voies f inv → ROADS ► **divided skirt** N jupe-culotte f

dividend ['dɪvɪdend] N (Fin, Math) dividende m → pay

divider [dɪˈvaɪdəʳ] N **~s** compas m à pointes sèches b → room

dividing [dɪˈvaɪdɪŋ] 1 ADJ [wall, fence] mitoyen 2 COMP ► **dividing line** N ligne f de démarcation

divination [ˌdɪvɪˈneɪʃən] N (lit, fig) divination f

divine[1] [dɪˈvaɪn] 1 ADJ a (Rel, fig) divin; **Divine Providence** la divine Providence; (Hist) **(the) ~ right of kings** le droit divin, la monarchie de droit divin; **by ~ right** en vertu de droit divin; (Rel) **~ service/office** service m/office m divin; **darling you look simply ~!** chérie, tu es absolument divine!; **the mousse tasted absolutely ~!*** la mousse était absolument divine! 2 N ecclésiastique m, théologien m

divine[2] [dɪˈvaɪn] 1 VT a (= foretell) [+ the future] présager, prédire b (= make out) [+ sb's intentions] deviner, pressentir c (= search for) **to ~ for water** etc chercher à découvrir une source etc à l'aide de baguettes (or d'un pendule) or par rhabdomancie 2 COMP
► **divining rod** N baguette f de sourcier

divinely [dɪˈvaɪnlɪ] ADV a (Rel) **~ inspired** divinement inspiré; **~ ordained/sanctioned** décrété/sanctionné par la volonté divine b († = wonderfully) divinement; **your friend waltzes ~!** votre ami valse divinement; **~ handsome** divinement beau; **~ happy** aux anges

diviner [dɪˈvaɪnəʳ] N [of future etc] devin m, devineresse f; [of water] radiesthésiste mf

diving ['daɪvɪŋ] 1 N a (underwater) plongée f sous-marine; (= skill) art m du plongeur; (= trade) métier m de plongeur sous-marin → scuba, skin b (from diving board) plongeon m; (Sport) **platform high ~** plongeon m de haut vol 2 COMP ► **diving bell** N cloche f à plongeur ► **diving board** N plongeoir m; (= springboard) tremplin m ► **diving suit** N scaphandre m

divining [dɪˈvaɪnɪŋ] N divination f à l'aide de baguettes (or d'un pendule), rhabdomancie f

divinity [dɪˈvɪnɪtɪ] N a (quality = god) divinité f; **the Divinity** la Divinité b (= theology) théologie f

divisible [dɪˈvɪzəbl] ADJ divisible (**by** par)

division [dɪˈvɪʒən] 1 N a (= act, state) division f, séparation f (**into** en); (= sharing) partage m, répartition f, distribution f (**between, among** entre); (Bot, Math) division f; **~ of labour** division f du travail → long[1], short, simple b (= section: gen, Admin, Comm, Mil, Naut) division f; (= category) classe f, catégorie f, section f; (Ftbl etc) division f; (in box, case) division f, compartiment m; **the bank's European ~** la division européenne de la banque; **the sales ~** le département des ventes; **several armoured** or **tank ~s** plusieurs divisions fpl blindées c (= divider) séparation f; (in room) cloison f; (fig: between social classes etc) fossé m; (= dividing line: lit, fig) division f d (NonC = discord) division f, désaccord m e (Brit Parl) **to call a ~** passer au vote; **to call for a ~** demander la mise aux voix; **the ~ took place at midnight** la Chambre a procédé au vote à minuit; **without a ~** sans procéder au vote; **to carry a ~** avoir la majorité des voix 2 COMP ► **division bell** N (Brit Parl) sonnerie f qui annonce la mise aux voix ► **division sign** N (Math) signe m de division

divisional [dɪˈvɪʒənl] 1 ADJ divisionnaire 2 COMP ► **divisional coin** N monnaie f divisionnaire ► **Divisional Court** N (Brit Jur) juridiction supérieure composée d'au moins deux juges statuant en appel

divisive [dɪˈvaɪsɪv] ADJ qui entraîne la division, qui sème la discorde

divisiveness [dɪˈvaɪsɪvnɪs] N **the ~ of this decision** les dissensions causées par cette décision

divisor [dɪˈvaɪzəʳ] N (Math) diviseur m

divorce [dɪˈvɔːs] 1 N (Jur, fig) divorce m (**from** d'avec, avec); **to get a ~ from** obtenir le divorce d'avec 2 VT (Jur) divorcer de or d'avec;

(*fig*) séparer (**from** de); **she ~d her husband** elle a divorcé de *or* d'avec son mari; (*fig*) **one cannot ~ this case from ...** on ne peut pas séparer ce cas de ... ③ VI divorcer ④ COMP ► **divorce court** N ≈ tribunal *m* de grande instance ► **divorce proceedings** NPL procédure *f* de divorce; **to start ~ proceedings** entamer une procédure de divorce, demander le divorce ► **divorce settlement** N (*mutually agreed*) règlement *m* de divorce; (*imposed by court*) jugement *m* de divorce

divorcé [dɪ'vɔːseɪ] N divorcé *m*

divorced [dɪ'vɔːst] ADJ (*Jur*) divorcé (**from** d'avec)

divorcee [dɪˌvɔː'siː] N divorcé(e) *m(f)*

divot ['dɪvət] N (*esp Golf*) motte *f* de gazon

divulge [daɪ'vʌldʒ] VT divulguer, révéler

divvy* ['dɪvɪ] ① N (*Brit**) ABBR = **dividend** ② VT (*: also ~ up*) partager

Diwali [dɪ'wɑːlɪ] N Dipavali *m*

Dixie ['dɪksɪ] N (*US*) les États *mpl* du Sud; **the Heart of ~** l'Alabama *m*; **I'm not just whistling ~*** ce ne sont pas des paroles en l'air, je ne plaisante pas ② COMP (*US*) du Sud ► **Dixie cup**® N (*US*) gobelet *m* en carton ► **Dixie Democrat** N (*US Pol*) démocrate *mf* du Sud

---
DIXIE

Surnom donné aux onze États du sud des États-Unis qui constituaient la Confédération pendant la guerre de Sécession: Alabama, Arkansas, Géorgie, Floride, Louisiane, Mississippi, Caroline du Nord, Caroline du Sud, Tennessee, Texas et Virginie. L'adjectif **Dixie** *est employé pour caractériser ces États et leurs habitants: on dira ainsi que Scarlett O'Hara est l'exemple de la féminité* **Dixie**.

---

dixie* ['dɪksɪ] N (*Brit Mil: also ~ can*) gamelle *f*

Dixieland ['dɪksɪlænd] ① N = **Dixie** ② COMP ► **Dixieland jazz** N le (jazz) Dixieland

DIY [diːaɪ'waɪ] (*Brit*) (ABBR = **do-it-yourself**) bricolage *m*

dizzily ['dɪzɪlɪ] ADV ⓐ (= *giddily*) [*walk, sway, slump*] en proie au vertige; [*rise, fall, spin, swirl*] vertigineusement; **her head was spinning ~** la tête lui tournait follement ⓑ (= *in a scatterbrained way*) étourdiment; (= *in a silly way*) bêtement

dizziness ['dɪzɪnɪs] N (= *state*) vertige(s) *m(pl)*; **an attack of ~** des vertiges; **to be overcome by ~** pris de vertiges

dizzy ['dɪzɪ] ① ADJ ⓐ [*person*] (*from illness, hunger etc*) pris de vertiges *or* d'étourdissements; (*from vertigo*) pris de vertige; **to feel ~** avoir le vertige, avoir la tête qui tourne; **he was so ~ he couldn't move** (*from illness, hunger etc*) il était pris de tels vertiges *or* étourdissements qu'il ne pouvait plus avancer; (*from vertigo*) il avait tellement le vertige qu'il ne pouvait plus avancer; (*lit, fig*) **it makes me ~** cela me donne le vertige, j'en ai la tête qui tourne; **he was ~ from the heat/effort** la chaleur/l'effort lui faisait tourner la tête *or* lui donnait des vertiges *or* des étourdissements; **he was ~ with success** le succès l'avait grisé; **she was ~ with grief** elle était hébétée de douleur ⓑ [*height, speed, rise in price*] vertigineux ⓒ [*person*] (= *scatterbrained*) étourdi, écervelé; (= *silly*) bête; **a ~ blonde** une blonde évaporée ② VT (= *disorientate, confuse*) [+ *person*] étourdir, donner le vertige à; (*fig*) **to be dizzied by success** être grisé par le succès ③ COMP ► **a dizzy spell** N un vertige, un étourdissement

DJ [diː'dʒeɪ] N (ABBR = **disc jockey**) → **disc**

Djakarta [dʒə'kɑːtə] N = **Jakarta**

Djibouti [dʒɪ'buːtɪ] N Djibouti *m*; **in ~** à Djibouti

djinn [dʒɪn] N djinn *m*

dl (ABBR = **decilitre(s)**) dl

DLit(t) [diː'lɪt] N (ABBR = **Doctor of Literature** and **Doctor of Letters**) doctorat ès Lettres

DM N (ABBR = **Deutschmark**) DM *m*

dm (ABBR = **decimetre(s)**) dm

D-mark [diː'mɑːk] N (ABBR = **Deutschmark**) mark *m*

DMus N (ABBR = **Doctor of Music**) doctorat de musique

DMZ N (ABBR = **Demilitarized Zone**) → **demilitarize**

DNA [ˌdiːen'eɪ] ① N (*Med*) (ABBR = **deoxyribonucleic acid**) ADN *m* ② COMP ► **DNA fingerprinting**, **DNA profiling** N analyse *f* de l'empreinte génétique ► **DNA testing** N (*NonC*) tests *mpl* d'ADN

Dnieper ['dniːpə] N Dniepr *m*

D-notice ['diːnəʊtɪs] N (*Brit Govt*) consigne officielle à la presse de ne pas publier certaines informations relatives à la sécurité nationale

---
do¹ [duː]

vb: 3rd pers sg pres **does**, *pret* **did**, *ptp* **done**

①	AUXILIARY VERB	④	NOUN
②	TRANSITIVE VERB	⑤	PLURAL NOUN
③	INTRANSITIVE VERB	⑥	PHRASAL VERBS

① AUXILIARY VERB

ⓐ

> *There is no equivalent in French to the use of* **do** *in questions, negative statements and negative commands.*

do you understand? (est-ce que) vous comprenez?, comprenez-vous?; **I do not** *or* **don't understand** je ne comprends pas; **didn't you like it?** tu n'as pas aimé ça?; **don't worry!** ne t'en fais pas!

ⓑ **in tag questions: seeking confirmation** n'est-ce pas; **you know him, don't you?** vous le connaissez, n'est-ce pas?; **you do agree, don't you?** vous êtes d'accord, n'est-ce pas?, vous êtes bien d'accord?; **she said that, didn't she?** elle a bien dit ça, n'est-ce pas?, c'est bien ce qu'elle a dit?

> *The tag is sometimes not translated.*

he didn't go, did he? il n'y est pas allé(, n'est-ce pas)?; **he didn't agree, did he?** il n'était pas d'accord(, n'est-ce pas)?; (*conveying interest, surprise, indignation etc*) (*so*) **you know him, do you?** alors comme ça vous le connaissez?; **she said that, did she?** alors comme ça elle a dit ça? **et** elle a dit ça?

ⓒ **in tag responses** **they speak French — oh, do they?** ils parlent français — ah oui *or* ah bon *or* vraiment?; **he wanted £1,000 for it — did he really?** il en demandait 1 000 livres — vraiment *or* non?; **who broke the mirror? — I did** qui est-ce qui a cassé la glace? — (c'est) moi; **may I come in? — please do!** puis-je entrer? — je t'en prie *or* je vous en prie!; **shall I ring her again? — no, don't!** est-ce que je la rappelle? — ah non *or* surtout pas!; **I'll tell him — don't!** je vais le lui dire — surtout pas!

> *oui or non alone are often used to answer questions.*

do you see them often? —**yes, I do** vous les voyez souvent? — oui; **did you see him? — no I didn't** est-ce tu l'as vu? — non

ⓓ **substitute for another verb** faire; **he's always saying he'll stop smoking, but he never does** il dit toujours qu'il va s'arrêter de fumer mais il ne le fait pas; **she always says she'll come but she never does** elle dit toujours qu'elle viendra mais elle n'en fait rien *or* mais elle ne vient jamais; **you drive faster than I do** tu conduis plus vite que moi; **I like this colour, don't you?** j'aime bien cette couleur, pas toi?; **they said he would object and indeed he did** on a dit qu'il s'y opposerait et c'est bien ce qui s'est passé *or* et c'est bien ce qu'il a fait

ⓔ **encouraging, inviting** **DO come!** venez donc!; **DO tell him that ...** dites-lui bien que ...

ⓕ **used for emphasis** **I DO wish I could come with you** je voudrais tant pouvoir vous accompagner; **but I DO like pasta!** mais si j'aime bien les pâtes!; **I am sure he never said that — he DID say it** je suis sûr qu'il n'a jamais dit ça — je t'assure que si *or* mais si, il l'a dit!; **so you DO know them!** alors comme ça tu les connais!

② TRANSITIVE VERB

ⓐ faire; **what are you doing in the bathroom?** qu'est-ce que tu fais dans la salle de bains?; **what do you do (for a living)?** que faites-vous dans la vie?; **I don't know what to do** je ne sais pas quoi faire; **I don't know how she does it** je ne sais pas comment elle fait; **the work is being done by a local builder** c'est un entrepreneur du coin qui fait les travaux; **I've only done three pages** je n'ai fait que trois pages; **we only do one make of gloves** nous ne faisons qu'une marque de gants; **are you doing anything this evening?** vous faites quelque chose ce soir?, êtes-vous pris ce soir?; **the car was doing 100mph** la voiture faisait du 160 km/h; **we did London to Edinburgh in eight hours** nous avons fait (le trajet) Londres-Édimbourg en huit heures; **we've done 200km since 2 o'clock** nous avons fait 200 km depuis 2 heures cet après-midi; **to do the sights** faire du tourisme; **to do six years (in jail)** faire six ans de prison; *BUT* **to do again** refaire; **it's all got to be done again** tout est à refaire *or* à recommencer; **now you've done it!** c'est malin!; **that's done it!*** (*dismay*) c'est foutu!*; (*satisfaction*) (voilà) ça y est!

> *Some do + noun combinations require a more specific French verb.*

to do the flowers arranger les fleurs; **to do one's hair** se coiffer; **to do a play** (= *put on*) monter une pièce; **to do the nine subjects** étudier neuf matières; **to do one's teeth** se laver *or* se brosser les dents

◆ **to do** + *person* (= *study*) faire *or* étudier un auteur; **we're doing Orwell this term** on fait *or* étudie Orwell ce trimestre; (= *attend to*) **the barber said he'd do me next** le coiffeur a dit qu'il me prendrait après; (= *hurt*) **I'll do you* if I get hold of you!** attends un peu que je t'attrape!, tu auras affaire à moi si je t'attrape!; (= *act*) **she does the worried mother very convincingly** elle est très convaincante quand elle joue les mères inquiètes; (= *imitate*) **he does his maths master to perfection** il imite son professeur de math à la perfection; (= *serve*) **they do you very well at that restaurant** on mange rudement* bien dans ce restaurant; (= *kill*) **to do sb to death** tuer qn

ⓑ = **finish** **to get done with sth** en finir avec qch; **have you done moaning?*** tu as fini de te plaindre?; **when all's said and done** au bout du compte, en fin de compte

ⓒ **Culin** (= *cook*) faire; (= *peel*) éplucher; (= *prepare*) faire, préparer; **I'll do some pasta** je vais faire des pâtes; *BUT* **how do you like your steak done?** comment voulez-vous votre bifteck?; **I like steak well done** j'aime le bifteck bien cuit

ⓓ **Brit*** = **cheat** **he realized they'd done him** il s'aperçut qu'il s'était fait avoir*; **to be done se faire avoir***; **you've been done!** tu t'es fait avoir!*, on t'a eu *or* refait!*; **he was afraid he'd be done** il avait peur de se faire avoir

ⓔ = **suffice, suit** aller; **will a kilo do you?** un kilo, ça ira?; **that will do me nicely** ça ira très bien

ⓕ **SET STRUCTURES**

◆ **to do** + *preposition* **there's nothing I can do about it** je n'y peux rien y faire; **he's been badly done by** on s'est très mal conduit avec lui; **what are we going to do for money?** comment allons-nous faire pour trouver de l'argent?; **what can I do for you?** qu'est-ce que je peux faire pour vous?, en quoi puis-je vous aider?; **could you do something for me?** est-ce que tu peux me rendre un service?; **I could see what the stress was doing to him** je voyais qu'il était très stressé; **what are you doing to that poor cat?** qu'est-ce que tu es en train de faire à ce pauvre chat?; **this theme has been done to death** c'est un sujet rebattu; **what have you done with my gloves?** qu'as-tu fait de mes gants?; **what are you doing with yourself these days?** qu'est-ce que tu deviens?; **he didn't know what to do with himself** il ne savait pas quoi faire de sa peau*; **what am I going to do with you?** qu'est-ce que je vais bien pouvoir faire de toi?

3 INTRANSITIVE VERB

a = act faire, agir; **do as your friends do** faites comme vos amis; **do as I say** fais ce que je dis; **he did well by his mother** il a bien agi or il s'est bien comporté envers sa mère; **he did well to take advice** il a bien fait de prendre conseil; **you would do well to rest more** vous feriez bien de vous reposer davantage; **he did right** il a bien fait; **he did right to go** il a bien fait d'y aller; _BUT_ **she was up and doing at 6 o'clock** elle était sur pied dès 6 heures du matin ■ (_PROV_) **do as you would be done by** ne faites pas aux autres ce que vous ne voudriez pas qu'on vous fasse

♦ **nothing doing***: **there's nothing doing in this town** il ne se passe jamais rien dans cette ville; **could you lend me £50?** — **nothing doing!** tu pourrais me prêter 50 livres? — pas question _or_ rien à faire!*

♦ **to have to do with** (= _to be connected with_) **what has that got to do with it?** et alors, qu'est-ce que ça a à voir?; **that has nothing to do with it!** cela n'a rien à voir!, cela n'a aucun rapport!; **they say crime has nothing to do with unemployment** ils prétendent que la criminalité n'a rien à voir _or_ n'a aucun rapport avec le chômage; **this debate has to do with the cost of living** ce débat porte sur le coût de la vie; **that's got a lot to do with it!** ça y est pour beaucoup!; **money has a lot to do with it** l'argent y est pour beaucoup; **his business activities have nothing to do with how much I earn** ses affaires n'ont rien à voir avec ce que je gagne; **that has nothing to do with you!** ça ne vous regarde pas!; **I won't have anything to do with it** je ne veux pas m'en mêler; **a doctor has to do with all kinds of people** un médecin a affaire à toutes sortes de gens

b = get on aller, marcher; (_as regards health_) se porter; **how are you doing?** comment ça va?; **how's he doing?** comment va-t-il?; **the patient is doing better now** le malade va or se porte mieux; **he's doing well at school** il a de bons résultats à l'école, il marche bien* en classe; **he** or **his business is doing well** ses affaires vont or marchent bien; **hi, what's doing?*** salut, comment ça va?; _BUT_ **the patient is doing very well** le malade est en très bonne voie; (_on being introduced_) **how do you do?** enchanté or très heureux (de faire votre connaissance); **the roses are doing well this year** les roses sont belles cette année

c = finish finir, terminer; **have you done?** vous avez terminé?, ça y est?

♦ **to have done with**: **I've done with all that nonsense** je ne veux plus entendre parler de ces bêtises; **have you done with that book?** vous n'avez plus besoin de ce livre?, vous avez fini avec ce livre?

d = suit, be convenient aller, faire l'affaire; **this room will do** cette chambre fera l'affaire; **that will do for the moment** ça ira pour le moment; _BUT_ **that will never do!** il n'en est pas question!; **it would do well to tell him what you think of him** ce n'est pas une bonne idée de lui dire ce qu'on pense de lui; **this coat will do for** or **as a blanket** ce manteau peut servir de couverture

e = be sufficient suffire; **three bottles of wine should do** trois bouteilles de vin devraient suffire, trois bouteilles de vin, ça devrait aller; **can you lend me some money?** — **will £10 do?** peux-tu me prêter de l'argent? — dix livres, ça te suffira or ça ira?; **that will do!** ça suffira!, ça ira!

f † = do housework faire le ménage; **the woman who does for me** la personne qui fait mon ménage, ma femme de ménage

4 NOUN

a esp Brit fête _f_; **they had a big do for their twenty-fifth anniversary** ils ont fait une grande fête pour leur vingt-cinquième anniversaire de mariage

b Brit = swindle escroquerie _f_; **the whole business was a real do from start to finish** toute l'affaire n'a été qu'une escroquerie du début jusqu'à la fin

c **it's a poor do!** c'est plutôt minable!*

5 **dos** PLURAL NOUN

a **the dos and don'ts** ce qu'il faut faire ou ne pas faire

b **fair dos!*** il faut être juste!

6 PHRASAL VERBS

► **do away with** VT FUS **a** (= _get rid of_) [+ _law, controls_] abolir; [+ _nuclear weapons_] démanteler; [+ _subsidies_] supprimer; [+ _building_] démolir; **this will do away with the need for a UN presence** cela rendra la présence des Nations unies superflue

b (* = _kill_) [+ _person_] liquider*, supprimer; **to do away with o.s.** se suicider

► **do down** VT SEP (Brit) [+ _person_] dénigrer; **she's always doing herself down** il faut toujours qu'elle se déprécie or se rabaisse

► **do for*** VT FUS [+ _person_] (= _kill_) liquider*, supprimer; (= _ruin_) [+ _hopes, chances, project_] ficher* or foutre∗ en l'air, bousiller*; **he's/it's done for** il est/c'est fichu* or foutu∗ → do¹

► **do in**∗ VT SEP **a** (= _kill_) buter∗, liquider*

b **it does my head in** ça me prend la tête*

c (_gen pass_ = _exhaust_) épuiser; **to be** or **feel done in** être claqué* or épuisé

► **do out** VT SEP (Brit) [+ _room_] (= _clean_) nettoyer à fond; (= _decorate_) refaire

► **do out of*** VT SEP **to do sb out of £100** arnaquer* qn de 100 livres, refaire* qn de 100 livres; **to do sb out of a job** piquer son travail à qn

► **do over** VT SEP **a** (US* = _redo_) refaire

b (Brit∗) [+ _person_] (= _beat up_) tabasser*, passer à tabac*; [+ _room, house_] (= _ransack_) fouiller de fond en comble, mettre sens dessus dessous; **the door was open: they had done the place over** la porte était ouverte: ils avaient fouillé la maison de fond en comble or ils avaient mis la maison sens dessus dessous

c (= _redecorate_) [+ _house_] refaire

► **do up** **1** VI [_dress, jacket_] se fermer

2 VT SEP **a** (= _fasten_) [+ _buttons_] boutonner; [+ _zip_] fermer, remonter; [+ _dress_] fermer; [+ _shoes_] nouer (les lacets de)

b (= _parcel up_) [+ _goods_] emballer, empaqueter; **to do sth up in a parcel** emballer or empaqueter qch; **to do up a parcel** faire un paquet

c * (= _renovate_) [+ _house, room_] remettre à neuf, refaire; (= _dress_) arranger; **she was done up in a bizarre outfit** elle était bizarrement affublée; **to do o.s. up** se faire beau (belle _f_)

► **do with*** VT SEP **a** **I could do with a cup of tea** je prendrais bien une tasse de thé; **the house could do with a coat of paint** la maison a besoin d'un bon coup de peinture; **to do sth up** se faire beau (belle _f_)

b (= _tolerate_) supporter; **I can't do with** or **be doing with whining children** je ne peux pas supporter les enfants qui pleurnichent

► **do without** VT FUS se passer de; **you'll have to do without then!** alors il faudra bien que tu t'en passes (_subj_)!; **I can do without your ad-**

vice! je vous dispense de vos conseils!; **I could have done without that!** je m'en serais très bien passé!

do² [dəʊ] N (_Mus_) do _m_, ut _m_

do. (ABBR = **ditto**) id, idem

DOA [ˌdiːəʊˈeɪ] (ABBR = **dead on arrival**) → **dead**

d.o.b. (ABBR = **date of birth**) → **date¹**

Doberman ['dəʊbəmən] N (_also_ **~ pinscher**) doberman _m_

doc* [dɒk] N (_US_) (ABBR = **doctor**) docteur _m_, toubib* _m_; **yes ~** oui docteur

docile ['dəʊsaɪl] ADJ docile, maniable

docilely ['dəʊsaɪlɪ] ADV docilement

docility [dəʊˈsɪlɪtɪ] N docilité _f_, soumission _f_

dock¹ [dɒk] **1** N (_for berthing_) bassin _m_, dock _m_; (_for loading, unloading, repair_) dock _m_; (_Brit fig_) **my car is in ~*** ma voiture est en réparation → **dry**, **graving dock** **2** VT [+ _ship_] mettre à quai; [+ _spacecraft_] amarrer, arrimer **3** VI **a** (_Naut_) arriver or se mettre à quai; **the ship has ~ed** le bateau est à quai **b** (_Space_) [_two spacecraft_] s'arrimer (**with** à); **the shuttle ~ed with the space station** la navette s'est arrimée à la station spatiale **4** COMP ► **dock house** N bureaux _mpl_ des docks ► **dock labourer** N docker _m_, débardeur _m_ ► **dock strike** N grève _f_ des dockers ► **dock-worker** N = **dock labourer**

dock² [dɒk] N (_Brit Jur_) banc _m_ des accusés; **"prisoner in the ~"** « accusé »; (_lit_) **in the ~** au banc des accusés; (_fig_) **to be in the ~** être sur la sellette, être au banc des accusés

dock³ [dɒk] VT **a** [+ _dog, horse_] écourter; [+ _tail_] couper **b** (_Brit_) [+ _wages_] faire une retenue sur; **to ~£25 off sb's wages** retenir 25 livres sur le salaire de qn; **he had his wages ~ed for repeated lateness** on lui a fait une retenue sur son salaire à cause de ses retards répétés; **to ~ a soldier two days' pay/leave** supprimer deux jours de solde/de permission à un soldat; (_Sport_) **the club was ~ed six points for cheating** on a enlevé six points au club pour avoir triché

dock⁴ [dɒk] N (_Bot_) patience _f_

docker ['dɒkə'] N (_Brit_) docker _m_, débardeur _m_

docket ['dɒkɪt] **1** N **a** (= _paper: on document, parcel etc_) étiquette _f_, fiche _f_ (indiquant le contenu d'un paquet etc) **b** (_Jur_) (= _register_) registre _m_ des jugements rendus; (_esp US_) (= _list of cases_) rôle _m_ des causes; (= _abstract of letters patent_) table _f_ des matières, index _m_ **c** (_Brit Customs_ = _certificate_) récépissé _m_ de douane, certificat _m_ de paiement des droits de douane **2** VT **a** [+ _contents_] résumer; (_Jur_) [+ _judgement_] enregistrer or consigner sommairement; (_fig_) [+ _information etc_] consigner, prendre note de **b** [+ _packet, document_] faire une fiche pour, étiqueter

docking ['dɒkɪŋ] N (_Space_) arrimage _m_, amarrage _m_

dockland ['dɒklænd] N (_Brit_) **the ~** le quartier des docks, les docks _mpl_

dockwalloper* ['dɒk‚wɒləpə'] N (_US_) = **dock labourer**

dockyard ['dɒkjɑːd] N chantier _m_ naval → **naval**

doctor ['dɒktə'] **1** N **a** (_Med_) médecin _m_, docteur _m_; **he/she is a ~** il/elle est médecin or docteur; **a woman ~** une femme médecin; **who is your ~?** qui est votre docteur?, qui est votre médecin traitant?; **Doctor Allan** le docteur Allan, Monsieur (or Madame) le docteur Allan; **yes ~** oui docteur; **to send for the ~** appeler or faire venir le médecin or le docteur; **to be under the ~*** (for sth) suivre un traitement (contre qch); (_Scol etc_) **~'s line** or **note** (_Brit_) ◊ **~'s excuse** (_US_) dispense _f_; **at the ~'s** chez le médecin; (_US_) **~'s office** cabinet _m_ médical; (_fig hum_) **it's just what the ~ ordered*** c'est exactement ce qu'il me (or te etc) fallait → **Dr**

b (Univ etc) docteur m; (Univ) **~'s degree** doctorat m; **Doctor of Law/of Science** etc docteur m en droit/ès sciences etc; **Doctor of Philosophy** ≈ titulaire m d'un doctorat d'État → **medicine**

2 VT **a** [+ sick person] soigner **b** (Brit* = castrate) [+ cat etc] couper, châtrer **c** (* pej = mend) rafistoler* (pej) **d** (= tamper with) [+ wine] trafiquer*, frelater; [+ food] trafiquer*; [+ text, document, figures, accounts] tripatouiller*

doctoral ['dɒktərəl] **1** ADJ de doctorat **2** COMP ► **doctoral dissertation** N (US) = **doctoral thesis** ► **doctoral thesis** N (Univ) thèse f de doctorat

doctorate ['dɒktərɪt] N doctorat m; **~ in science/in philosophy** doctorat m ès sciences/ en philosophie

doctrinaire [,dɒktrɪ'nɛəʳ] ADJ, N doctrinaire mf

doctrinal [dɒk'traɪnl] ADJ doctrinal

doctrine ['dɒktrɪn] N doctrine f

docudrama [,dɒkju'drɑːmə] N (TV etc) docudrame m

document ['dɒkjumənt] **1** N (gen, also Comput) document m; **the ~s relating to a case** le dossier d'une affaire; **official ~** document m officiel; (Jur) acte m authentique public; (Jur) **judicial ~** acte m judiciaire **2** ['dɒkjoment] VT **a** [+ case, article, report] documenter; **well-~ed** solidement documenté; (Jur) **complaints must be ~ed** les plaintes doivent être accompagnées de pièces justificatives **b** [+ ship] munir des papiers nécessaires **3** COMP ► **document case** N porte-documents m inv ► **document imaging** N reproduction de document sous forme d'image ► **document reader** N (Comput) lecteur m de documents

documentary [,dɒkju'mentərɪ] **1** ADJ documentaire m **2** N (Cine, TV) (film m) documentaire m **3** COMP ► **documentary evidence** N (Jur) documents mpl, preuve f documentaire or par écrit ► **documentary letter of credit** N crédit m documentaire

documentation [,dɒkjumen'teɪʃən] N documentation f; (Comm) documents mpl (à fournir etc)

DOD [,diːəʊ'diː] (US) (ABBR = **Department of Defense**) → **defence**

do-dad ['duːdæd] N = **doodah**

dodder ['dɒdəʳ] VI ne pas tenir sur ses jambes; (fig) tergiverser, atermoyer

dodderer ['dɒdərəʳ] N vieux (or vieille f) gaga*, croulant(e)* m(f), gâteux m, -euse f

doddering ['dɒdərɪŋ], **doddery** ['dɒdərɪ] ADJ (= trembling) branlant; (= senile) gâteux

doddle ['dɒdl] N (Brit) **it's a ~** c'est simple comme bonjour*, c'est du gâteau*

Dodecanese [,dəʊdɪkə'niːz] N Dodécanèse m

dodge [dɒdʒ] **1** N **a** (= movement) mouvement m de côté, détour m; (Boxing, Ftbl) esquive f **b** (Brit*) (= trick) tour m, truc* m; (= ingenious scheme) combine* f, truc* m; **he's up to all the ~s** il connaît (toutes) les ficelles; **that's an old ~** c'est le coup classique*; **I've got a good ~ for making money** j'ai une bonne combine* pour gagner de l'argent

2 VT [+ blow, ball] esquiver; [+ pursuer] échapper à; (fig = avoid ingeniously) [+ question, difficulty] esquiver, éluder; [+ tax] éviter de payer; (= shirk) [+ work, duty] esquiver; **he ~d the issue** il a éludé la question; **I managed to ~ him before he saw me** j'ai réussi à m'esquiver avant qu'il ne me voie

3 VI faire un saut de côté or un brusque détour; (Boxing, Fencing) esquiver; (Ftbl, Rugby) faire une feinte du corps, feinter; **to ~ out of sight** or **out of the way** s'esquiver; **to ~ behind a tree** disparaître derrière un arbre; **to ~**

through the traffic/the trees se faufiler entre les voitures/les arbres; **he saw the police and ~d round the back (of the house)** il a vu les agents et s'est esquivé (en faisant le tour de la maison) par derrière

dodge about VI aller et venir, remuer

dodgems ['dɒdʒəmz] NPL (Brit) autos fpl tamponneuses

dodger ['dɒdʒəʳ] N **a** (* = trickster) roublard(e)* m(f), finaud(e) m(f); (= shirker) tire-au-flanc m inv → **artful b** (Naut) toile f de passerelle de commandement **c** (US = handbill) prospectus m

dodgy* ['dɒdʒɪ] ADJ **a** (Brit = uncertain, tricky) [situation, plan, finances, weather] douteux; [health] précaire; **he's got a ~ back/heart** etc il a des problèmes de dos/de cœur etc, son dos/ cœur etc lui joue des tours; **her health is ~ ◊ she's in ~ health** sa santé lui joue des tours, elle n'a pas la santé* **b** (= dubious, suspicious) [person, deal, district] louche*

dodo ['dəʊdəʊ] N (pl **dodos** or **dodoes**) dronte m, dodo m → **dead**

DOE [,diːəʊ'iː] **a** (Brit) (ABBR = **Department of the Environment**) → **environment b** (US) (ABBR = **Department of Energy**) → **energy**

doe [dəʊ] N (pl **does** or **doe**) **a** (= deer) biche f **b** (= rabbit) lapine f; (= hare) hase f; **~-eyed** [person] aux yeux de biche; [look] de biche

doer ['duː(ː)əʳ] N **a** (= author of deed) auteur m de l'action; **~s of good deeds often go unrewarded** ceux qui font le bien ne sont pas souvent récompensés **b** (= active person) personne f efficace or dynamique; **he's a ~, not a thinker** il préfère l'action à la réflexion

does [dʌz] → **do¹**

doeskin ['dəʊskɪn] N peau f de daim

doesn't ['dʌznt] = **does not**; → **do¹**

doff [dɒf] VT (†, hum) [+ garment, hat] ôter, enlever

dog [dɒg] **1** N **a** (Zool) chien(ne) m(f); **the ~'s dinner** = **dog's food** la pâtée du chien = **dogfood**; (fig) **it's a real ~'s dinner** or **breakfast** c'est le bordel‡; **he's all done up like a ~'s dinner** regarde comme il est attifé*, il est attifé* n'importe comment; **to lead a ~'s life** mener une vie de chien; **it's a ~'s life** c'est une vie de chien; (Brit Sport) **the ~s** les courses fpl de lévriers; **to go to the ~s** [person] gâcher sa vie, mal tourner; [institution, business] aller à vau-l'eau, péricliter; (fig) **to throw sb to the ~s** abandonner qn à son sort; **he is being a ~ in the manger** il joue l'empêcheur de tourner en rond ■ (PROV) **every ~ has his day** à chacun vient sa chance, à chacun son heure de gloire; **he hasn't a ~'s chance*** il n'a pas la moindre chance (de réussir); **it's (a case of) ~ eat ~** c'est un cas où les loups se mangent entre eux ■ (PROV) **give a ~ a bad name (and hang him)** qui veut noyer son chien l'accuse de la rage (PROV); (US) **to put on the ~*** faire de l'épate* → **cat, hair**

b (= male) [of fox etc] mâle m
c * **lucky ~** veinard(e)* m(f); **dirty ~** sale type* m; **sly ~** (petit) malin m, (petite) maligne f
d (‡ = unattractive woman) cageot‡ m, boudin* m
e (Tech) (= clamp) crampon m; (= pawl) cliquet m

2 VT **a** (= follow closely) [+ person] suivre (de près); **he ~s my footsteps** il marche sur mes talons, il ne me lâche pas d'une semelle **b** (= harass) harceler; **~ged by ill fortune** poursuivi par la malchance

3 COMP ► **dog and pony show** N (US fig) un spectacle fait pour impressionner ► **dog basket** N panier m pour chien ► **dog biscuit** N biscuit m pour chien ► **dog breeder** N éleveur m, -euse f de chiens ► **dog collar** N (lit) collier m de chien; (hum: clergyman's) col m de pasteur, (faux) col m d'ecclésiastique

► **dog days** NPL canicule f ► **dog-eared** ADJ écorné ► **dog fancier** N (= connoisseur) cynophile mf; (= breeder) éleveur m, -euse f de chiens ► **dog fox** N renard m (mâle) ► **dog guard** N (Aut) barrière f pour chien (à l'arrière d'une voiture) ► **dog handler** N (Police etc) maître-chien m ► **dog Latin*** N latin m de cuisine ► **dog licence** N redevance payable par les propriétaires de chiens ► **dog paddle** N nage f en chien ♦ VI nager en chien ► **dog rose** N (= flower) églantine f; (= bush) églantier m ► **Dog Star** N Sirius m ► **dog tag*** N (US Mil) plaque f d'identification (portée par les militaires) ► **dog-tired*** ADJ claqué*, crevé* ► **dog track** N piste f (de course de lévriers) ► **dog wolf** N loup m

dogcart ['dɒgkɑːt] N charrette f anglaise, dog-cart m

doge [dəʊdʒ] N doge m

dogfight ['dɒgfaɪt] N (lit) combat m de chiens; (Aviat) combat m entre avions de chasse; (between people) bagarre f

dogfish ['dɒgfɪʃ] N (pl **dogfish** or **dogfishes**) chien m de mer, roussette f

dogfood ['dɒgfuːd] N nourriture f pour chiens

dogged ['dɒgɪd] ADJ [person, character] tenace; [courage, determination, persistence, refusal] obstiné; [resistance, battle] acharné

doggedly ['dɒgɪdlɪ] ADV [say, fight] avec ténacité; [refuse] obstinément; **~ determined** résolu envers et contre tout; **he is ~ loyal** il fait preuve d'une loyauté à toute épreuve; **he was ~ optimistic** il était résolument optimiste

doggedness ['dɒgɪdnɪs] N obstination f, ténacité f

Dogger Bank ['dɒgəbæŋk] N Dogger Bank m

doggerel ['dɒgərəl] N vers mpl de mirliton

doggie ['dɒgɪ] N = **doggy 1**

doggo* ['dɒgəʊ] ADV (Brit) **to lie ~** se tenir coi; [fugitive, criminal] se terrer

doggone(d)* [,dɒg'gɒn(d)] ADJ (US euph) = **damn, damned**; → **damn 1, 2c, 3, 4, 5**

doggy* ['dɒgɪ] **1** N (baby talk) toutou* m (baby talk) **2** ADJ [smell] de chien mouillé; **she is a very ~ woman** elle a la folie des chiens; **I'm not really a ~ person** je n'aime pas trop les chiens **3** COMP ► **doggy bag*** N petit sac pour emporter les restes après un repas au restaurant ► **doggy fashion*** ADV [have sex] en levrette ► **doggy paddle*** N nage f en chien ♦ VI nager en chien ► **doggy style*** ADV = **doggy fashion**

doghouse ['dɒghaʊs] N (US) chenil m, niche f à chien; (fig) **he is in the ~*** il n'est pas en odeur de sainteté

dogie ['dəʊgɪ] N (US) veau m sans mère

dogleg ['dɒgleg] **1** N (in road etc) coude m, angle m abrupt **2** ADJ [turn, bend] en coude, en épingle à cheveux

doglike ['dɒglaɪk] ADJ [appearance] canin; [devotion, fidelity] inconditionnel

dogma ['dɒgmə] N (pl **dogmas** or **dogmata** ['dɒgmətə]) dogme m

dogmatic [dɒg'mætɪk] ADJ (Rel, fig) dogmatique; **to be very ~ about sth** être très dogmatique sur qch

dogmatically [dɒg'mætɪkəlɪ] ADV [speak, write, argue] sur un ton dogmatique; [follow rule, apply principle] dogmatiquement, d'une manière dogmatique

dogmatism ['dɒgmətɪzəm] N (Philos, Rel, fig) dogmatisme m

dogmatist ['dɒgmətɪst] N dogmatique mf

dogmatize ['dɒgmətaɪz] VI (Rel, fig) dogmatiser

do-gooder [,duː'gʊdəʳ] N (slightly pej) pilier m de bonnes œuvres, bonne âme f (iro)

dogsbody* ['dɒgzbɒdɪ] N (Brit) **she's the general ~** c'est la bonne à tout faire

dogshow ['dɒgʃəʊ] N exposition f canine

dog's-tooth check [,dɒgztu:θ'tʃek], **dog-tooth check** [,dɒgtu:θ'tʃek] N (Tex) pied-de-poule m

dogtrot ['dɒgtrɒt] N petit trot m; (US = passageway) passage m couvert

dogwatch ['dɒgwɒtʃ] N (Naut) petit quart m, quart m de deux heures

dogwood ['dɒgwʊd] N cornouiller m

doh [dəʊ] N (Mus) = **do²**

doily ['dɔɪlɪ] N (under plate) napperon m; (on plate) dessus m d'assiette

doing ['du:ɪŋ] **1** N (NonC) this is your ~ c'est vous qui avez fait cela; **it was none of my ~** je n'y suis pour rien, ce n'est pas moi qui l'ai fait; **that takes some ~** ce n'est pas facile or commode, (il) faut le faire !* **2 doings** NPL **a** faits mpl et gestes mpl **b** (Brit* = thingummy) **~s** machin* m, truc* m; **that ~s over there** ce machin* là-bas

do-it-yourself ['du:ɪtjə'self] **1** N bricolage m **2** ADJ **a** [shop] de bricolage; **~ enthusiast** bricoleur m, -euse f; **the ~ craze** la passion du bricolage, l'engouement m pour le bricolage; **~ kit** kit m (prêt-à-monter) **b** (fig) [divorce, conveyancing, will] dont on s'occupe soi-même (sans employer les services d'un professionnel)

do-it-yourselfer* [,du:ɪtjə'selfə'] N bricoleur m, -euse f

Dolby® ['dɒlbɪ] N Dolby® m

doldrums ['dɒldrəmz] NPL **a** (Naut etc) (= area) zone f des calmes; (= weather) calme m équatorial **b** (fig) **to be in the ~** [person] avoir le cafard*, broyer du noir; [business] être dans le marasme; **to come out of the ~** [person] reprendre le dessus; [business] sortir du marasme

dole [dəʊl] **1** N allocation f or indemnité f de chômage; (Brit) **to go/be on the ~** s'inscrire/être au chômage; **how much do you get a week on the ~?** combien touche-t-on d'allocation or d'indemnités de chômage par semaine? **2** COMP ► **dole queue** N (Brit) **the ~ queues are lengthening** le nombre de chômeurs augmente

►**dole out** VT SEP distribuer or accorder au compte-gouttes

doleful ['dəʊlfʊl] ADJ [person, face, expression, voice] dolent (liter), plaintif; [song] triste; **a ~ prospect** une triste perspective

dolefully ['dəʊlfʊlɪ] ADV d'un air malheureux

dolichocephalic ['dɒlɪkəʊsə'fælɪk] ADJ dolichocéphale

doll [dɒl] **1** N **a** poupée f; **to play with a ~** or **~s** jouer à la poupée **b** (esp US* = girl) nana* f, pépée† f; (= pretty girl) poupée* f; (= attractive person) **he's/she's a ~** il/elle est chou*, il/elle est adorable; (US) **you're a ~ to help me*** tu es un ange de m'aider **2** COMP ► **doll buggy**, **doll carriage** N (US) landau m de poupée ► **doll's house** N maison f de poupée ► **doll's pram** N landau m de poupée

►**doll up** VT SEP [+ person, thing] bichonner; **to ~ o.s. up ◊ to get ~ed up** se faire (tout) beau* (or (toute) belle*), se bichonner; **all ~ed up** sur son trente et un (for pour); **she was ~ed up for the party** elle s'était mise sur son trente et un pour la soirée

dollar ['dɒlə'] **1** N dollar m; (US) **it's ~s to doughnuts that ...*** c'est couru d'avance* que ... → **half, sixty** **2** COMP ► **dollar area** N zone f dollar ► **dollar bill** N billet m d'un dollar ► **dollar diplomacy** N (US Pol) diplomatie f à coups de dollars ► **dollar gap** N déficit m de la balance dollar ► **dollar rate** N (Fin) cours m du dollar ► **dollar sign** N signe m du dollar

dollop ['dɒləp] N [of butter, cheese etc] gros or bon morceau m; [of cream, jam etc] bonne cuillerée f

dolly ['dɒlɪ] **1** N **a** (*: baby talk) (= doll) poupée f **b** (for washing clothes) agitateur m; **~ tub** (for washing) baquet m à lessive; (Min) cuve f à rincer **c** (= wheeled frame) chariot m; (Cine, TV) chariot m, travelling m (dispositif); (Rail = truck) plate-forme f **2** ADJ (Sport* = easy) facile **3** VT (Cine, TV) **to ~ the camera in/out** avancer/reculer la caméra **4** COMP ► **dolly bird** N (Brit) jolie nana* f, poupée* f

dolman ['dɒlmən] **1** N dolman m **2** COMP ► **dolman sleeve** N (sorte f de) manche f kimono inv

dolmen ['dɒlmen] N dolmen m

dolomite ['dɒləmaɪt] N dolomite f, dolomie f; (Geog) **the Dolomites** les Dolomites fpl

dolphin ['dɒlfɪn] N (Zool) dauphin m

dolphinarium [,dɒlfɪ'nɛərɪəm] N aquarium m pour dauphins savants

dolt [dəʊlt] N balourd(e) m(f)

doltish ['dəʊltɪʃ] ADJ gourde*, cruche*, balourd

domain [dəʊ'meɪn] N (lit, fig) domaine m; **in the ~ of science** dans le domaine des sciences

dome [dəʊm] N (Archit: on building) dôme m, coupole f; (liter = stately building) édifice m; [of hill] sommet m arrondi, dôme m; [of skull] calotte f; [of heaven, branches] dôme m

domed [dəʊmd] ADJ [forehead] bombé; [building] à dôme, à coupole

Domesday Book ['du:mzdeɪ,bʊk] N Domesday Book m

domestic [də'mestɪk] **1** ADJ **a** (= household) (gen) domestique; [fuel] à usage domestique; [quarrel] (within family) de famille; (between married couple) conjugal; **~ bliss** les joies fpl de la vie de famille; **the ~ chores** les travaux mpl ménagers, les tâches fpl ménagères; **~ harmony** l'harmonie f du ménage **b** (= home-loving) **she was never a very ~ sort of person** elle n'a jamais vraiment été une femme d'intérieur **c** (Econ, Pol = internal) [policy, affairs, flight, politics, news, problems, market] intérieur (-eure f); [currency, economy, production] national; [sales] sur le marché intérieur; **(intended) for ~ consumption** (lit) [product, commodity] destiné à la consommation intérieure; (fig) [speech, statement] réservé au public national **d** (= domesticated) **the ~ cat/rabbit/chicken** etc le chat/lapin/poulet etc domestique **2** N **a** (= worker) domestique mf **b** (Brit Police* = fight) querelle f domestique **3** COMP ► **domestic appliance** N appareil m ménager ► **domestic heating oil** N fioul m domestique ► **domestic rates** NPL (Brit) anciens impôts locaux ► **domestic science** N arts mpl ménagers ► **domestic science college** N école f d'arts ménagers ► **domestic science teaching** N enseignement m ménager ► **domestic servants** NPL domestiques mfpl, employé(e)s m(f)pl de maison ► **domestic service** N **she was in ~ service** elle était employée de maison or domestique ► **domestic spending** N (NonC) dépenses fpl intérieures ► **domestic staff** N [of hospital, institution] personnel m auxiliaire; [of private house] domestiques mfpl ► **domestic violence** N violence f domestique or familiale

domestically [də'mestɪkəlɪ] ADV **only two of the banks are ~ owned** seules deux de ces banques sont détenues par des capitaux nationaux; **~ produced goods** biens mpl produits à l'intérieur du pays; **he's not very ~ inclined** ce n'est pas vraiment un homme d'intérieur

domesticate [də'mestɪkeɪt] VT **a** (lit) [+ animal] domestiquer **b** (* fig, hum) [+ person] apprivoiser

domesticated [də'mestɪkeɪtɪd] ADJ **a** [animal] domestiqué **b*** [person] **she's very ~** c'est une vraie femme d'intérieur; **he's not**

very ~ ce n'est pas vraiment un homme d'intérieur

domestication [dəmestɪ'keɪʃən] N [of animal] domestication f

domesticity [,dəʊmes'tɪsɪtɪ] N **a** (= home life) vie f de famille, vie f casanière (slightly pej) **b** (= love of household duties) attachement m aux tâches domestiques

domicile ['dɒmɪsaɪl] (Admin, Fin, Jur) **1** N domicile m **2** VT domicilier; **~d at** [person] domicilié à, demeurant à; **he is currently ~d in Berlin** il est actuellement domicilié à Berlin, il demeure actuellement à Berlin; **to ~ a bill with a bank** domicilier un effet à une banque

domiciliary [,dɒmɪ'sɪlɪərɪ] ADJ domiciliaire

domiciliation [,dɒmɪsɪlɪ'eɪʃən] N [of bill, cheque] domiciliation f

dominance ['dɒmɪnəns] N (gen: Ecol, Genetics, Psych) dominance f (**over** sur); [of person, country etc] prédominance f

dominant ['dɒmɪnənt] **1** ADJ **a** (= predominant, assertive) dominant; **she is the ~ partner in their marriage** dans leur couple, c'est elle qui commande **b** (Mus) de dominante; **~ seventh** septième f de dominante **c** (Genetics) dominant **d** (Zool) [individual, species] dominant; **the ~ male of the group** le mâle dominant du groupe **2** N (Mus) dominante f; (Ecol, Genetics) dominance f

dominate ['dɒmɪneɪt] VTI dominer

dominating ['dɒmɪneɪtɪŋ] ADJ [character, personality] dominateur (-trice f)

domination [,dɒmɪ'neɪʃən] N domination f

dominatrix [,dɒmɪ'neɪtrɪks] N (pl dominatrices [,dɒmɪnə'traɪsi:z]) (= sexual partner) dominatrice f; (= dominant woman) femme f dominatrice, maîtresse femme f

domineer [,dɒmɪ'nɪə'] VI agir en maître, se montrer autoritaire

domineering [,dɒmɪ'nɪərɪŋ] ADJ dominateur (-trice f), impérieux, autoritaire

Dominica [,dɒmɪ'ni:kə] N (Geog) la Dominique

Dominican¹ [də'mɪnɪkən] **1** ADJ (Geog) dominicain **2** N Dominicain(e) m(f) **3** COMP ► **the Dominican Republic** N la République dominicaine

Dominican² [də'mɪnɪkən] ADJ, N (Rel) dominicain(e) m(f)

dominion [də'mɪnɪən] **1** N **a** (NonC) domination f, empire m (**over** sur); **to hold ~ over sb** maintenir qn sous sa domination or sous sa dépendance **b** (= territory) territoire m, possessions fpl; (Brit Pol) dominion m **2** COMP ► **Dominion Day** N (Can) fête f de la Confédération

domino ['dɒmɪnəʊ] **1** N (pl dominoes) **a** domino m; **to play ~es** jouer aux dominos **b** (= costume, mask, person) domino m **2** COMP ► **domino effect** N effet m d'entraînement ► **domino theory** N (Pol) théorie f des dominos, théorie f du proche en proche

Don [dɒn] N (= river) Don m

don¹ [dɒn] N **a** (Brit Univ*) professeur m d'université (surtout à Oxford et à Cambridge) **b** (= Spanish nobleman) don m; **a Don Juan** un don Juan **c** (US) chef m de la Mafia

don² [dɒn] VT [+ garment] revêtir, mettre

donate [dəʊ'neɪt] VT faire don de, donner; **to ~ blood** donner son sang; **~d by ...** offert par ...

donation [dəʊ'neɪʃən] N **a** (NonC = act of giving) donation f **b** (= gift) don m; **to make a ~ to a fund** faire un don à une caisse

done [dʌn] **1** VB (ptp of **do¹**) **what's ~ cannot be undone** ce qui est fait est fait; **that's just not ~!** cela ne se fait pas!; **it's as good as ~** c'est comme si c'était fait ■ (PROV) **a woman's work is never ~** une femme n'est jamais au bout de sa tâche; (Comm) **~!** marché conclu!, entendu! ; **consider it ~!** c'est comme si c'était fait ! 2 ADJ ▶ **do¹** a **the ~ thing** ce qui se fait b (* = *tired out*) claqué*, crevé* ; **I'm absolutely ~!** je n'en peux plus !, je suis crevé !* c (= *cooked, ready*) cuit ; **is it ~ yet?** est-ce que c'est cuit ? ; **well ~** [*steak*] à point

donee [ˌdəʊ'niː] N (*Jur*) donataire *mf*

doner ['dɒnə'] N (*also* ~ **kebab**) doner kebab *m*

dong [dɒŋ] N a (= *sound of bell*) dong *m* b (= *unit of currency*) dông *m* c (** = *penis*) zob** *m*

dongle ['dɒŋgl] N (*Comput*) boîtier *m* de sécurité

donjon ['dʌndʒən] N donjon *m*

donkey ['dɒŋkɪ] 1 N a (= *ass*) âne(sse) *m(f)*, baudet* *m* ; (*Brit*) **she hasn't been here for ~'s years*** il y a une éternité *or* ça fait une paye* qu'elle n'est pas venue ici → **hind²** b (* = *fool*) âne *m*, imbécile *mf* 2 COMP ▶ **donkey derby** N (*Brit*) course *f* à dos d'âne ▶ **donkey engine** N (*Tech*) auxiliaire *m*, petit cheval *m*, cheval *m* alimentaire ▶ **donkey jacket** N (*Brit*) grosse veste *f* ▶ **donkey ride** N promenade *f* à dos d'âne ▶ **donkey-work** N (*Brit*) **the ~-work** le gros du travail

donnish ['dɒnɪʃ] ADJ [*person*] cérébral ; [*humour, manner*] d'intellectuel

donor ['dəʊnə'] N a (*to charity etc*) donateur *m*, -trice *f* ; (*Med*) [*of blood, organ for transplant*] donneur *m*, -euse *f* 2 COMP ▶ **donor card** N carte *f* de donneur d'organes ▶ **donor insemination** N insémination *f* artificielle ▶ **donor organ** N organe *m* de donneur

don't [dəʊnt] 1 VB = **do not** ; → **do¹** 2 N **~s** choses *fpl* à ne pas faire → **do¹** 3 COMP ▶ **don't knows*** NPL (*gen*) sans opinion *mpl* ; (= *voters*) indécis *mpl* ; **there were ten in favour, six against, and three "~ knows"** il y avait dix pour, six contre et cinq « sans opinion »

donut ['dəʊnʌt] N (*US*) = **doughnut**

doodah* ['duːdɑː], **doodad*** (*US*) ['duːdæd] N (= *gadget*) petit bidule*

doodle ['duːdl] 1 VI griffonner (distraitement) 2 N griffonnage *m*

doodlebug* ['duːdlbʌg] N (*Brit*) bombe *f* volante ; (*US*) petit véhicule *m*

doohickey* [ˌduːˈhɪkɪ] N (*US*) machin* *m*, truc* *m*, bidule* *m*

doolally* [duːˈlælɪ] ADJ dingo**, barjo**

doom [duːm] 1 N (= *ruin*) ruine *f*, perte *f* ; (= *fate*) destin *m*, sort *m* 2 VT condamner (**to** à), destiner (**to** à) ; **~ed to failure** voué à l'échec ; **the project was ~ed from the start** le projet était voué à l'échec dès le début 3 COMP ▶ **doom-laden** ADJ lugubre, sinistre

doomsayer ['duːmseɪə'] N prophète *m* de malheur

doomsday ['duːmzdeɪ] N jour *m* du Jugement dernier ; (*fig*) **till ~** jusqu'à la fin des temps

doomwatch ['duːmwɒtʃ] N attitude *f* pessimiste, catastrophisme *m*

doomwatcher ['duːmwɒtʃə'] N prophète *m* de malheur, oiseau *m* de mauvais augure

door [dɔː'] 1 N a [*of house, room, cupboard*] porte *f* ; [*of train, plane, car*] portière *f* ; **he shut** *or* **closed the ~ in my face** il m'a fermé la porte au nez ; **he came through** *or* **in the ~** il est passé par la porte ; (*Theat etc*) **"pay at the ~"** « billets à l'entrée » ; **to get tickets on the ~** prendre les billets à l'entrée ; **to go from ~ to ~** (*gen*) aller de porte en porte ; [*salesman*] faire du porte à porte ; **he lives two ~s down** *or* **up the street** il habite deux portes plus loin ; **out of ~s** (au-)dehors → **answer, front, next door** b [*phrases*] **to lay sth at sb's ~** imputer qch à qn, charger qn de qch ; **to open the ~ to further negotiations** ouvrir la voie à des négociations ultérieures ; **to leave** *or* **keep the ~ open for further negotiations** laisser la porte ouverte à des négociations ultérieures ; **to close**

or **shut the ~ on** *or* **to sth** barrer la route à qch, rendre qch irréalisable ; (*Brit*) **there was resistance to the idea at first but now we're pushing at an open ~** cette idée a rencontré beaucoup de réticences au départ, mais maintenant tout marche comme sur des roulettes ; **as one ~ closes, another one opens** il y aura d'autres occasions ; (*Theat etc*) **to be on the ~** être à l'entrée ; (*fig*) **to open ~s** ouvrir des portes ; **a Harvard degree opens ~s** un diplôme de l'université de Harvard ouvre beaucoup de portes → **death, show** 2 COMP ▶ **door chain** N chaîne *f* de sûreté ▶ **door curtain** N portière *f* (*tenture*) ▶ **door handle** N poignée *f* *or* bouton *m* de porte ; (*Aut*) poignée *f* de portière ▶ **door-knocker** N marteau *m* (de porte), heurtoir *m* ▶ **door-locking mechanism** N (*Aut, Rail*) dispositif *m* de verrouillage des portières ▶ **door scraper** N grattoir *m* ▶ **door-to-door** ADJ ~**-to-~** delivery livraison *f* à domicile ; **we deliver ~-to-~** nous livrons à domicile ; ~**-to-~ salesman** = doorstep salesman ; → **doorstep** ; (*Brit*) ~**-to-~ selling** démarchage *m*, vente *f* à domicile, porte-à-porte *m inv*

doorbell ['dɔːbel] N sonnette *f* ; **he heard the ~ ring** il entendit sonner (à la porte) ; **there's the ~!** on sonne (à la porte) !

doorframe ['dɔːfreɪm] N chambranle *m*, châssis *m* de porte

doorjamb ['dɔːdʒæm] N montant *m* de porte, jambage *m*

doorkeeper ['dɔːkiːpə'] N = **doorman**

doorknob ['dɔːnɒb] N poignée *f* *or* bouton *m* de porte

doorman ['dɔːmən] N (*pl* **-men**) [*of hotel*] portier *m* ; [*of block of flats*] concierge *m*

doormat ['dɔːmæt] N a (*lit*) paillasson *m* b (* = *downtrodden person*) paillasson *m*, carpette* *f*

doornail ['dɔːneɪl] N clou *m* de porte → **dead**

doorpost ['dɔːpəʊst] N montant *m* de porte, jambage *m* → **deaf**

doorstep ['dɔːstep] 1 N a (*lit*) pas *m* de porte, seuil *m* ; **he left it on my ~** il l'a laissé devant ma porte ; **the bus stop is just at my ~** l'arrêt du bus est (juste) devant ma porte ; (*fig*) **we don't want trouble/a motorway on our ~** nous ne voulons pas d'embêtements dans notre voisinage/d'autoroute dans notre arrière-cour b (* *hum* = *hunk of bread, sandwich*) grosse tartine *f* 2 VT (*Brit*) **to ~ sb** (*Pol*) faire du démarchage électoral chez qn ; (*Press*) aller chez qn pour l'interviewer (*contre son gré*) 3 COMP ▶ **doorstep salesman** N (*pl* **doorstep salesmen**) (*Brit*) démarcheur *m*, vendeur *m* à domicile

doorstepping* ['dɔːstepɪŋ] N a (*Pol*) démarchage *m* électoral b (*Press*) porte-à-porte pratiqué par certains journalistes

doorstop(per) ['dɔːstɒp(ə')] N butoir *m* de porte

doorway ['dɔːweɪ] N (*gen*) porte *f* ; **in the ~** dans l'embrasure de la porte

dopamine ['dəʊpəmiːn] N dopamine *f*

dope [dəʊp] 1 N a (** = *drugs, esp marijuana*) dope* *f* ; (*for athlete, horse*) dopant *m* (produit *m* dopant) ; (*US*** = *drug addict*) drogué(e) *m(f)*, toxico* *mf* ; **to take ~**◊ *or* **to be on ~**◊ *or* **to do ~**◊ (*US*) se droguer ; (*NonC*◊ = *information*) tuyaux* *mpl* ; **to give sb the ~** tuyauter* *or* affranchir* qn ; **what's the ~ on ...?** qu'est-ce qu'on a comme tuyaux* sur ...? c (* = *stupid person*) andouille* *f* d (= *varnish*) enduit *m* ; (*Aut, Chem*) dopant *m* e (*for explosives*) absorbant *m* 2 VT [+ *horse, person*] doper ; [+ *food, drink*] mettre une drogue *or* un dopant dans ; **he was ~d (up) to the eyeballs*** il était complètement défoncé* 3 COMP ▶ **dope fiend**†* N drogué(e) *m(f)* ▶ **dope peddler*, dope pusher*** N revendeur *m*, -euse *f* de drogue, dealer* *m* ▶ **dope test*** N test *m* antidopage

♦ VT faire subir un test antidopage à ▶ **dope out*** VT SEP (*US*) deviner, piger*

dopey* ['dəʊpɪ] ADJ (= *drugged*) drogué, dopé ; (= *very sleepy*) (à moitié) endormi ; (= *stupid*) abruti*

doping ['dəʊpɪŋ] N dopage *m*

Doppler effect ['dɒplə'ɪˌfekt] N effet *m* Doppler *or* Doppler-Fizeau

dopy ['dəʊpɪ] ADJ = **dopey**

Dordogne [dɔː'dɒn] N (= *region*) la Dordogne ; (= *river*) **the ~** la Dordogne

Doric ['dɒrɪk] ADJ (*Archit*) dorique

dork‡ [dɔːk] N abruti(e)* *m(f)*

dorm* [dɔːm] N (*Scol*) = **dormitory**

dormancy ['dɔːmənsɪ] N [*of volcano*] inactivité *f* ; [*of plant*] dormance *f* ; [*of virus*] latence *f*

dormant ['dɔːmənt] ADJ a [*animal, plant, passion*] dormant ; [*virus*] latent ; [*volcano*] endormi ; [*law*] inappliqué ; [*title*] tombé en désuétude ; (*Banking*) [*account*] sans mouvement ; (*Bot*) **the ~ season** la saison de dormance ; **to lie ~** [*plan, organization*] être en sommeil ; [*disease*] être latent ; [*bacterium, virus*] être à l'état latent b (*Her*) dormant ; **a lion ~** un lion dormant

dormer (window) [dɔː'mə('wɪndəʊ)] N lucarne *f*

dormice ['dɔːmaɪs] NPL of **dormouse**

dormie ['dɔːmɪ] ADJ (*Golf*) dormie

dormitory ['dɔːmɪtrɪ] 1 N dortoir *m* ; (*US Univ*) résidence *f* universitaire 2 COMP ▶ **dormitory suburb** N (*esp Brit*) banlieue *f* dortoir ▶ **dormitory town** N (*esp Brit*) ville *f* dortoir

Dormobile® ['dɔːməbiːl] N (*Brit*) camping-car *m*

dormouse ['dɔːmaʊs] N (*pl* **dormice**) loir *m*

Dors ABBR = **Dorset**

dorsal ['dɔːsl] ADJ dorsal

dory¹ ['dɔːrɪ] N (= *fish*) dorée *f*, saint-pierre *m inv*

dory² ['dɔːrɪ] N (= *boat*) doris *m*

DOS [dɒs] N (ABBR = **disk operating system**) DOS *m*

dosage ['dəʊsɪdʒ] N (= *dosing*) dosage *m* ; (= *amount*) dose *f* ; (*on medicine bottle*) posologie *f*

dose [dəʊs] 1 N a (*Pharm*) dose *f* ; **give him a ~ of medicine** donne-lui son médicament ; **in small/large ~s** à faible/haute dose ; (*hum*) **it went through her like a ~ of salts*** ça lui a donné la courante** ; **she's all right in small ~s*** elle est supportable à petites doses ; (*fig*) **to give sb a ~ of his own medicine** rendre à qn la monnaie de sa pièce b (= *bout of illness*) attaque *f* (of de) ; **to have a ~ of flu** avoir une bonne grippe* 2 VT [+ *person*] administrer un médicament à ; **she's always dosing herself (up)** elle se bourre de médicaments

dosh‡ [dɒʃ] N (*Brit* = *money*) fric* *m*, pognon* *m*

doss‡ [dɒs] (*Brit*) 1 N a (= *bed*) pieu* *m* ; (= *place*) endroit *m* où pioncer* ; (= *sleep*) roupillon* *m* b (= *easy task*) **he thought the course would be a ~** il croyait que ce stage serait du gâteau* *or* serait fastoche* 2 VI a (= *sleep*) pioncer* ; (*in dosshouse*) coucher à l'asile (de nuit) b (= *pass time aimlessly: also* **around**) glander‡ ▶ **doss down** VI pioncer* (quelque part)

dosser‡ ['dɒsə'] N (*Brit* = *vagrant*) clochard(e) *m(f)*

dosshouse‡ ['dɒshaʊs] N asile *m* (de nuit)

dossier ['dɒsɪeɪ] N dossier *m*, documents *mpl*

Dosto(y)evsky [ˌdɒstɔɪ'efskɪ] N Dostoïevski *m*

DOT [ˌdiːəʊ'tiː] N (*US*) (ABBR = **Department of Transportation**) → **transportation**

dot [dɒt] 1 N (*over i, on horizon, Math, Mus*) point *m* ; (*on material*) pois *m* ; (*in Morse code*) **~s and dashes** points *mpl* et traits *mpl* ; (*in* punctuation) ~, ~, ~ points de suspension; **they arrived on the ~ of 9pm** or **at 9pm on the ~** ils sont arrivés à 9 heures pile or tapantes; (*Brit*) **in the year ~*** il y a belle lurette*; **he's wanted to be a barrister since the year ~** ça fait belle lurette* qu'il veut devenir avocat; **she's been a socialist since the year ~*** elle est socialiste depuis toujours, c'est une socialiste de la première heure

[2] VT [a] [+ *paper, wall*] pointiller; **to ~ an i** mettre un point sur un i; (*fig*) **to ~ one's i's (and cross one's t's)** mettre les points sur les i; **a field ~ted with flowers** un champ parsemé de fleurs; **hotels ~ted around the island** des hôtels éparpillés dans l'île; **there were paintings ~ted around the room** il y avait des tableaux un peu partout sur les murs de la pièce → **dotted**
[b] **to ~ sb one*** flanquer un gnon à qn*
[3] COMP ► **dot-matrix printer** N (*Comput*) imprimante *f* matricielle

dotage ['dəʊtɪdʒ] N [a] (= *senility*) gâtisme *m*; **to be in one's ~** être gâteux [b] (= *old age*) vieux jours *mpl*; **he's spending his ~ in southern France** il passe ses vieux jours dans le sud de la France [c] (= *blind love*) adoration *f* folle (**on** pour)

dote [dəʊt] VI (= *be senile*) être gâteux, être gaga*
► **dote on** VT FUS [+ *person*] être fou de; [+ *thing*] raffoler de

doting ['dəʊtɪŋ] ADJ [a] (= *devoted*) **her ~ father** son père qui l'adore [b] (= *senile*) gâteux; **a ~ old fool** un vieux gâteux

dotted ['dɒtɪd] ADJ [a] **~ line** ligne *f* pointillée or en pointillé; (*Aut*) ligne *f* discontinue; **to tear along the ~ line** détacher suivant le pointillé; **to sign on the ~ line** (*lit*) signer sur la ligne pointillée or sur les pointillés; (*fig* = *agree officially*) donner son consentement (en bonne et due forme); **a ~ bow tie** un nœud papillon à pois [b] (*Mus*) **~ note** note *f* pointée; **~ rhythm** notes *fpl* pointées

dotterel ['dɒtrəl] N pluvier *m* (guignard)

dotty* ['dɒtɪ] (*Brit*) ADJ toqué*, piqué*; **to be ~ about sb/sth** être toqué* de qn/qch; **to go ~** perdre la boule*

double ['dʌbl] [1] ADJ [a] (= *twice as great*) double (*gen before n*); **a ~ helping of ice cream** une double part de glace; **a ~ whisky/brandy** *etc* un double whisky/cognac *etc*; **three ~ brandies** trois doubles cognacs
[b] (= *twofold; in pairs*) double (*gen before n*); (*Dice, Dominoes etc*) **the ~ six** le double-six; **a box with a ~ bottom** une boîte à double fond; **with a ~ meaning** à double sens; **to serve a ~ purpose** avoir une double fonction → **7**
[c] (= *for two people*) pour deux personnes; **a ~ ticket** un billet pour deux personnes → **7**
[d] (*in numerals, letters*) **~ oh seven** (= *007*) zéro zéro sept; **~ three four seven** (= *3347*) trois mille trois cent quarante-sept; (*in phone number*) trente-trois quarante-sept; **my name is Bell, B E ~ L** mon nom est Bell, B, E, deux L; **spelt with a "p"** écrit avec deux « p »
[e] (= *underhand, deceptive*) **to lead a ~ life** mener une double vie; **to play a ~ game** jouer un double jeu → **7**

[2] ADV [a] (= *twice*) deux fois; **to cost/pay ~** coûter/payer le double or deux fois plus; **it costs ~ what it did last year** ça coûte deux fois plus que l'année dernière; **she earns ~ what I get** elle gagne deux fois plus que moi, elle gagne le double de ce que je gagne; **he's ~ your age** il est deux fois plus âgé que toi, il a le double de ton âge; **her salary is ~ what it was five years ago** son salaire est le double de ce qu'il était il y a cinq ans
[b] (= *in two, twofold*) **to fold sth ~** plier qch en deux; **to bend ~** se plier en deux; **bent ~ with pain** tordu de douleur, plié en deux par la douleur; **to see ~** voir double

[3] N [a] (= *twice a quantity, number, size etc*) double *m*; **12 is the ~ of 6** 12 est le double de 6; **~ or quits** quitte ou double; (*fig* = *quickly*) **at** or **on the ~** au pas de course
[b] [*of whisky etc*] double *m*
[c] (= *exactly similar thing*) réplique *f*; (= *exactly similar person*) double *m*, sosie *m*; (*Cine* = *stand-in*) doublure *f* → **body**, **stunt**; (*Theat = actor taking two parts*) acteur *m*, -trice *f* qui tient deux rôles (*dans la même pièce*); (*Cards*) contre *m*; (*other games*) double *m*; (*Betting*) pari *m* doublé (*sur deux chevaux dans deux courses différentes*)
[d] (*also* **~ bedroom**) chambre *f* pour deux personnes
[4] **doubles** NPL (*Tennis*) double *m*; **mixed ~s** double *m* mixte; **ladies'/men's ~s** double *m* dames/messieurs; **a ~s player** un joueur or une joueuse de double
[5] VT [a] (= *multiply by two*) [+ *number, salary, price*] doubler
[b] (= *fold in two: also* **~ over**) plier en deux, replier, doubler
[c] (*Theat*) **he ~s the parts of courtier and hangman** il joue les rôles or il a le double rôle du courtisan et du bourreau; **he's doubling the hero's part for Tony Brennan** il est la doublure de Tony Brennan dans le rôle du héros
[d] (*Cards*) [+ *one's opponent, his call*] contrer; [+ *one's stake*] doubler; (*Bridge*) **~!** contre!
[6] VI [a] [*prices, incomes, quantity etc*] doubler
[b] (= *run*) courir, aller au pas de course
[c] (*Cine*) **to ~ for sb** doubler qn
[d] (*Bridge*) contrer
[e] (*US fig*) **to ~ in brass*** avoir une corde supplémentaire à son arc

[7] COMP ► **double act** N duo *m*
► **double-acting** ADJ à double effet
► **double agent** N agent *m* double
► **double album** N (*Mus*) double album *m*
► **double bar** N (*Mus*) double barre *f*
► **double-barrelled** ADJ [*shotgun*] à deux coups; (*fig*) [*plan, question*] à deux volets; (*Brit*) [*surname*] à rallonge* ► **double bass** N contrebasse *f* ► **double bassoon** N contrebasson *m* ► **double bed** N grand lit *m*, lit *m* à deux places ► **double bedroom** N chambre *f* pour deux personnes; (*in hotel*) chambre *f* double ► **double bend** N (*Brit Aut*) virage *m* en S ► **double bill** N (*Cine etc*) double programme *m* ► **double bind*** N situation *f* insoluble or sans issue, impasse *f* ► **double-blind** ADJ [*test, experiment, method*] en double aveugle ► **double bluff** N **it's actually a ~ bluff** il (*or* elle *etc*) dit la vérité en faisant croire que c'est du bluff ► **double boiler** N = **double saucepan** ► **double-book** N [*hotel, airline etc*] faire du surbooking or de la surréservation ♦ VT [+ *room, seat*] réserver pour deux personnes différentes ► **double booking** N surréservation *f*, surbooking *m* ► **double bounce** N (*Tennis*) double rebond *m* ♦ VI [*ball*] doubler ► **double-breasted** ADJ [*jacket*] croisé ► **double chin** N double menton *m* ► **double-chinned** ADJ qui a un double menton ► **double-click** VI (*Comput*) cliquer deux fois (**on** sur), double-cliquer (**on** sur) ► **double-clutch** VI (*US*) = **double-declutch** ► **double consonant** N consonne *f* double or redoublée or géminée ► **double cream** N (*Brit*) crème *f* fraîche épaisse or à fouetter ► **double-cross*** VT trahir, doubler* ♦ N traîtrise *f*, duplicité *f* ► **double-date** VI sortir à deux couples ► **double-dealer** N fourbe *m* ► **double-dealing** N double jeu *m*, duplicité *f* ♦ ADJ hypocrite, faux jeton* ► **double-decker** N (= *bus*) autobus *m* à impériale; (= *aircraft*) deux-ponts *m inv*; (= *sandwich*) sandwich *m* club ► **double-declutch** VI (*Aut*) faire un double débrayage ► **double density** N → **density** ► **double-digit** ADJ (*gen*) à deux chiffres ► **double-dipper** N (*US pej*) cumulard(e)* *m(f)*

► **double-dipping** N (*US pej*) cumul *m* d'emplois or de salaires ► **double door** N porte *f* à deux battants ► **double Dutch*** N (*Brit*) baragouin* *m*, charabia* *m*; **to talk ~ Dutch** baragouiner; **it was ~ Dutch to me** c'était de l'hébreu pour moi* ► **double eagle** N (*Golf*) albatros *m* ► **double entendre** N ambiguïté *f*, mot *m* (or expression *f*) à double sens ► **double-entry book-keeping** N comptabilité *f* en partie double ► **double exposure** N (*Phot*) surimpression *f*, double exposition *f* ► **double-faced** ADJ [*material*] réversible; (*pej*) [*person*] hypocrite ► **double fault** N (*Tennis*) double faute *f* ♦ VI faire une double faute ► **double feature** N (*Cine*) programme comportant deux longs métrages ► **double-figure** ADJ = **double-digit** ► **double first** N (*Univ*) mention *f* très bien dans deux disciplines ► **double flat** N (*Mus*) double bémol *m* ► **double-glaze** VT (*Brit*) **to ~-glaze a window** poser un double vitrage ► **double glazing** N (*Brit: gen*) double vitrage *m*; **to put in ~ glazing** (faire) installer un double vitrage ► **double helix** N double hélice *f* ► **double indemnity** N (*US Insurance*) indemnité *f* double ► **double jeopardy** N (*US Jur*) mise en cause de l'autorité de la chose jugée ► **double-jointed** ADJ désarticulé ► **double-knit(ting)** N (= *wool*) laine *f* épaisse ♦ ADJ en laine épaisse ► **double knot** N double nœud *m* ► **double lock** N serrure *f* de sécurité ► **double-lock** VT fermer à double tour ► **double major** N (*US Univ*) double *f* dominante ► **double marking** N (*Educ*) double correction *f* ► **double negative** N double négation *f* ► **double-park** VT (*Aut*) garer en double file ♦ VI stationner or se garer en double file ► **double-parking** N (*Aut*) stationnement *m* en double file ► **double pneumonia** N (*Med*) pneumonie *f* double ► **double room** N chambre *f* double or pour deux personnes ► **double saucepan** N casserole *f* pour bain-marie or à double fond ► **double sharp** N (*Mus*) double dièse *m* ► **double-sided** ADJ (*Comput*) [*disk*] double face ► **double-space** VT (*Typ*) taper avec un double interligne; **~-spaced** à double interligne ► **double spacing** N **in ~ spacing** à double interligne ► **double standard** N **to have ~ standards** faire deux poids, deux mesures; **there's a ~ standard operating here** il y a deux poids, deux mesures ici; **they were accused of (operating) ~ standards** on les a accusés de partialité or discrimination ► **double star** N étoile *f* double ► **double stopping** N (*Mus*) doubles cordes *fpl* ► **double take*** N **to do a ~ take** devoir y regarder à deux fois ► **double talk** N (= *gibberish*) charabia *m*; (= *deceptive talk*) paroles *fpl* ambiguës or trompeuses ► **double taxation agreement** N (*Fin, Jur*) convention *f* relative aux doubles impositions ► **double time** N (*Ind*) **to earn ~ time** être payé (au tarif) double; **to get/pay ~ time** gagner/payer le double; (*US Mil*) **in ~ time** au pas redoublé → **time** ► **double track** N (*Cine*) double bande *f*; (= *tape*) double piste *f* ► **double track line** N (*Rail*) ligne *f* à deux voies ► **double vision** N vision *f* double; **to get/have ~ vision** voir double ► **double wedding** N double mariage *m* ► **double whammy*** N double coup *m* dur* ► **double white lines** NPL lignes *fpl* blanches continues ► **double windows** NPL doubles fenêtres *fpl* ► **double yellow lines** NPL (*Aut*) double bande *f* jaune (*marquant l'interdiction de stationner*) ► **double yolk** N egg with a ~ yolk œuf *m* à deux jaunes
►**double back** [1] VI [*animal, person*] revenir sur ses pas; [*road*] faire un brusque crochet; **to ~ back on itself** [*line*] former une boucle en épingle à cheveux [2] VT SEP [+ *blanket*] rabattre, replier; [+ *page*] replier
►**double over** [1] VI = **double up a** [2] VT SEP =

double 5b

▶**double up** VI [a] (= *bend over sharply*) se plier, se courber; **to ~ up with laughter/pain** être plié en deux or se tordre de rire/de douleur [b] (= *share room*) partager une chambre (**with** avec) [c] (*Brit Betting*) parier sur deux chevaux

double-check [ˌdʌblˈtʃek] [1] VTI revérifier [2] N revérification f

double-edged [ˌdʌblˈedʒd] ADJ (*lit, fig*) [*blade, remark, praise, benefit*] à double tranchant; (*lit, fig*) **a ~ sword** une arme à double tranchant

double-quick* [ˌdʌblˈkwɪk] [1] ADV en deux temps trois mouvements* [2] ADJ **in ~ time** en deux temps trois mouvements*

doublespeak [ˈdʌblspiːk] N (*pej*) double langage m

doublet [ˈdʌblɪt] N [a] (*Dress*) pourpoint m, justaucorps m [b] (*Ling*) doublet m

doublethink* [ˈdʌblθɪŋk] N **to do a ~** tenir un raisonnement ou suivre une démarche où l'on s'accommode de contradictions flagrantes

doubleton [ˈdʌblɪtən] N (*Cards*) deux cartes fpl d'une (même) couleur, doubleton m

doubling [ˈdʌblɪŋ] N [*of number, letter*] redoublement m, doublement m

doubloon [dʌˈbluːn] N (*Hist*) doublon m

doubly [ˈdʌblɪ] ADV doublement; **divorce is always traumatic, and ~ so when there are children** le divorce est toujours traumatisant, et il est doublement quand il y a des enfants; **in order to make ~ sure** pour plus de sûreté; **to work ~ hard** travailler deux fois plus dur

▼**doubt** [daʊt] [1] N doute m, incertitude f; **his honesty is in ~** (*in this instance*) son honnêteté est en doute; (*in general*) son honnêteté est sujette à caution; **it is not in ~** [*outcome, result etc*] cela ne fait aucun doute; **I am in (some) ~ about his honesty** j'ai des doutes sur son honnêteté; **the outcome is in ~** l'issue est indécise; **I am in no ~ about** or **as to what he means** je n'ai aucun doute sur ce qu'il veut dire; **to be in great ~ about sth** avoir de sérieux doutes au sujet de qch, douter fortement de qch; **there is room for ~** il est permis de douter; **there is some ~ about whether he'll come** or **not** on ne sait pas très bien s'il viendra ou non; **to have one's ~s about sth** avoir des doutes sur or au sujet de qch; **I have my ~s (about) whether he will come** je doute qu'il vienne; **to cast** or **throw ~(s) on sth** mettre qch en doute, jeter le doute sur qch; **I have no ~(s) about it** je n'en doute pas; **no ~ about it!** cela va sans dire!; **this leaves no ~ that ...** on ne peut plus douter que ... (+ *subj*); **there is no ~ that ...** il n'y a pas de doute que ... (+ *indic*); **he'll come without any ~** ◊ **there's no ~ that he'll come** il viendra sûrement, il n'y a pas de doute qu'il viendra; **no ~ he will come tomorrow** sans doute viendra-t-il demain; **no ~** sans doute; **without (a) ~** sans aucun doute, sans le moindre doute; **it is beyond all doubt** c'est indéniable or incontestable; **beyond ~** (*adv*) indubitablement, à n'en pas douter ♦ (*adj*) indubitable; **if** or **when in ~** en cas de doute → **benefit**

[2] VT [a] [+ *person, sb's honesty, truth of statement*] douter de; **I ~ it (very much)** j'en doute (fort); **I ~ed (the evidence of) my own eyes** je n'en croyais pas mes yeux [b] (*with ne*) **I ~ whether he will come** je doute qu'il vienne; **I don't ~ that he will come** je ne doute pas qu'il vienne; **she didn't ~ that he would come** elle ne doutait pas qu'il viendrait; **I ~ he won't come now** je crains qu'il ne vienne pas maintenant; **I ~ if that is what she wanted** je doute que ce soit ce qu'elle voulait

[3] VI douter (**of** de), avoir des doutes (**of** sur), ne pas être sûr (**of** de); **~ing Thomas** Thomas l'incrédule; **don't be a ~ing Thomas** ne fais pas ton (petit) saint Thomas

doubter [ˈdaʊtər] N incrédule mf, sceptique mf

▼**doubtful** [ˈdaʊtfʊl] ADJ [a] (= *unconvinced*) [*person*] peu convaincu; **to be ~ of sth** douter de qch; **to be ~ about sb/sth** douter de qn/qch, avoir des doutes sur qn/qch; **I'm a bit ~ (about it)** je n'en suis pas si sûr, j'ai quelques doutes (à ce sujet); **to be ~ about doing sth** hésiter à faire qch; **he was ~ that** or **whether ... il doutait que ... (+ *subj*); **he was ~ that** or **whether he could ever manage it** il doutait qu'il puisse jamais réussir, il doutait pouvoir jamais réussir [b] (= *questionable, unlikely*) douteux; **it is ~ that** or **whether ...** il est douteux que ... (+ *subj*); **of ~ reliability/quality** d'une fiabilité/qualité douteuse; **in ~ taste** d'un goût douteux; (*Sport = unlikely to play*) **he's ~ (for the match)** sa participation (au match) est encore incertaine

doubtfully [ˈdaʊtfəlɪ] ADV [*frown, shake head etc*] d'un air sceptique; [*speak*] d'un ton sceptique

doubtfulness [ˈdaʊtfʊlnɪs] N [a] (= *uncertainty*) incertitude f [b] (= *suspicious quality*) caractère m équivoque or suspect or louche

doubtless [ˈdaʊtlɪs] ADV sans doute, certainement

douceur [duːˈsɜːr] N (= *gift, tip etc*) petit cadeau m

douche [duːʃ] [1] N [a] (= *shower*) douche f; (*US*) **take a ~!** va te faire foutre! [b] (*Med*) (*vaginal*) douche f vaginale; (*fig*) **it was (like) a cold ~** cela a fait l'effet d'une douche froide* [2] VT doucher

dough [dəʊ] [1] N [a] pâte f; **bread ~** pâte à pain [b] (‡ = *money*) fric‡ m, pognon‡ m [2] COMP ▶ **dough-hook** N crochet m de pétrissage

doughboy [ˈdəʊbɔɪ] N [a] (*Culin*) boulette f (de pâte) [b] (*US Mil*) sammy m (*soldat américain de la Première Guerre mondiale*)

doughnut [ˈdəʊnʌt] N beignet m; **jam** (*Brit*) or **jelly** (*US*) **~** beignet m à la confiture

doughty [ˈdaʊtɪ] ADJ (*liter*) preux (*liter*), vaillant; **~ deeds** hauts faits mpl (*liter*)

doughy [ˈdəʊɪ] ADJ [*consistency*] pâteux; [*complexion*] terreux

dour [dʊər] ADJ (= *austere*) austère, dur; (= *stubborn*) buté; **a ~ Scot** un Écossais austère

dourly [ˈdʊəlɪ] ADV [*say*] d'un ton maussade; [*smile, look at*] d'un air renfrogné; **a ~ conventional man** un homme au conformisme austère

douse [daʊs] VT [a] (= *drench*) tremper, inonder [b] (= *extinguish*) [+ *flames, light*] éteindre

dove [dʌv] [1] N colombe f; (*esp US: Pol fig*) colombe f → **turtledove** [2] COMP ▶ **dove-grey** ADJ gris perle *inv*

dovecot [ˈdʌvkɒt], **dovecote** [ˈdʌvkəʊt] N colombier m, pigeonnier m

Dover [ˈdəʊvər] [1] N Douvres → **strait** [2] COMP ▶ **Dover sole** N sole f

dovetail [ˈdʌvteɪl] [1] N (*Carpentry*) queue f d'aronde [2] VT [a] (*Carpentry*) assembler à queue d'aronde [b] (*fig*) [+ *plans etc*] faire concorder, raccorder [3] VI [a] (*Carpentry*) se raccorder (**into** à) [b] (*fig*) bien cadrer, concorder (**with** avec) [4] COMP ▶ **dovetail joint** N (*Carpentry*) assemblage m à queue d'aronde

dovish* [ˈdʌvɪʃ] ADJ (*esp US: Pol fig*) [*person*] partisan(e) m(f) de la négociation et du compromis; [*speech, attitude*] de compromis

Dow* [daʊ] N **the ~** = Dow Jones average or index; → Dow Jones

dowager [ˈdaʊədʒər] [1] N douairière f [2] COMP ▶ **dowager duchess** N duchesse f douairière

dowdiness [ˈdaʊdɪnɪs] N manque m de chic

dowdy [ˈdaʊdɪ] ADJ [*person, clothes*] démodé, sans chic

dowel [ˈdaʊəl] [1] N cheville f (en bois), goujon m [2] VT assembler avec des goujons, goujonner

dower house [ˈdaʊəhaʊs] N (*Brit*) petit manoir m

Dow Jones [ˌdaʊˈdʒəʊnz] N **the ~ average** or **index** l'indice m Dow Jones, le Dow Jones

down¹ [daʊn]

> When **down** is an element in a phrasal verb, eg **back down**, **glance down**, **play down**, look up the verb.

[1] ADV [a] (*indicating movement to lower level*) en bas, vers le bas; (= *down to the ground*) à terre, par terre; (*said to a dog*) **~!** couché!; **~ with traitors!** à bas les traîtres!; **to come** or **go ~** descendre; **to fall ~** tomber (à terre); **to go/ fall ~ and ~** descendre/tomber de plus en plus bas; **to run ~** descendre en courant → **bend down, knock down, slide down**

[b] (*indicating position at lower level*) en bas; **~ there** en bas (là-bas); **I shall stay ~ here** je vais rester ici; **the blinds were ~** les stores étaient baissés; **Douglas isn't ~ yet** Douglas n'est pas encore descendu; (*Boxing*) **to be ~ for the count** être K.-O.; **to kick somebody when they are ~** frapper un homme à terre; **don't hit** or **kick a man when he is ~** on ne frappe pas un homme à terre → **face, head, stay down**

[c] (*indicating larger town, the north, university etc*) **he came ~ from London yesterday** il est arrivé de Londres hier; **we're going ~ to the sea tomorrow** demain nous allons à la mer; **we're going ~ to Dover tomorrow** demain nous descendons à Douvres; (*Univ*) **he came ~ from Oxford in 1993** il est sorti d'Oxford en 1993; (*US*) **~ East** du ou au nord-est de la Nouvelle-Angleterre; (*Brit*) **~ under*** (= *in Australia/New Zealand*) en Australie/Nouvelle-Zélande, aux antipodes; **from ~ under*** d'Australie/de Nouvelle-Zélande → **come down, go down, send down**

[d] (*indicating diminution in volume, degree, activity*) **the heels of her shoes were quite worn ~** les talons de ses chaussures étaient tout usés; **the tyres are ~/right ~** les pneus sont dégonflés/à plat; **his temperature has gone ~** sa température a baissé; **I'm £2 ~ on what I expected** j'ai 2 livres de moins que je ne pensais; **prices are ~ on last year's** les prix sont en baisse par rapport à (ceux de) l'année dernière; (*Fin*) **the pound is ~ against the dollar** la livre est en baisse par rapport au dollar; **she's very run ~** elle n'a pas la forme; **I am ~ on my luck** je n'ai pas de chance or de veine, je suis dans une mauvaise passe; **we are ~ to our last £5** il ne nous reste plus que 5 livres → **close down, put down**

[e] (*in writing*) **I've got it (noted) ~ in my diary** je l'ai or c'est marqué sur mon agenda; **let's get it ~ on paper** mettons-le par écrit; **did you get ~ what he said?** as-tu noté ce qu'il a dit?; **to be ~ for the next race** être inscrit dans la prochaine course → **note, take down, write down**

[f] (*indicating a series or succession*) **~ to** jusqu'à; **from 1700 ~ to the present** de 1700 à nos jours; **from the biggest ~ to the smallest** du plus grand (jusqu')au plus petit; **from the king ~ to the poorest beggar** depuis le roi jusqu'au plus pauvre des mendiants

[g] **~ to*** (= *due to, up to*): **it's ~ to him to do it** c'est à lui de le faire; **it's ~ to him now** c'est à lui de jouer maintenant; **our success is all ~ to him/hard work** c'est à lui seul/à notre travail acharné que nous devons notre succès → **cash, come down, put down, suit, up**

[h] **to be ~ on sb*** avoir une dent contre qn, en vouloir à qn

[2] PREP [a] (*indicating movement to lower level*) du haut en bas de; (*lit*) **he went ~ the hill** il a descendu la colline → **come down**; **her hair hung ~ her back** ses cheveux lui tombaient dans le dos; **he ran his eye ~ the list** il a parcouru la liste du regard or des yeux

b (= at a lower part of) **he's ~ the hill** il est au pied or en bas de la colline ; **she lives ~ the street (from us)** elle habite plus bas or plus loin (que nous) dans la rue ; **it's just ~ the road** c'est tout près, c'est à deux pas ; (fig) **~ the ages** au cours des siècles

c (= along) le long de ; **he was walking ~ the street** il descendait la rue ; **he has gone ~ (to) town** il est allé or descendu en ville ; **let's go ~ the pub*** allons au pub ; **looking ~ this street, you can see ...** si vous regardez le long de cette rue, vous verrez ...

3 N (Brit) **to have a ~ on sb*** avoir une dent contre qn, en vouloir à qn → **up**

4 ADJ **a** **to be** or **feel ~** avoir le cafard*, être déprimé

b (Comput) en panne

c (Brit†) [train] en provenance de la grande ville ; **the ~ line** la ligne de la grande ville

5 VT* **to ~ an opponent** terrasser or abattre un adversaire ; **he ~ed three enemy planes** il a descendu* trois avions ennemis ; (Brit) **to ~ tools** (= stop work) cesser le travail ; (= strike) se mettre en grève, débrayer ; **he ~ed a glass of beer** il a vidé or descendu* un verre de bière

6 COMP ► **down-and-out** N SDF mf ♦ ADJ **to be ~-and-out** (Boxing) aller au tapis pour le compte, être hors de combat ; (= destitute) être sur le pavé or à la mie ► **down-at-heel** ADJ (US) [person] miteux ; [shoe] éculé ► **down-bow** N (Mus) tiré ► **down-cycle** N (Econ) cycle m de récession ► **down-in-the-mouth*** ADJ abattu, tout triste ; **to be ~-in-the-mouth** être abattu or tout triste, avoir le moral à zéro* ; **to look ~-in-the-mouth** avoir l'air abattu, faire une sale tête ► **down-market** ADJ [goods, car] bas de gamme inv ; [newspaper] populaire ; **it's rather ~-market** [programme etc] c'est plutôt du genre public de masse ♦ ADV **to go** or **move ~-market** [company] se tourner vers le bas de gamme ; [house purchaser etc] acheter quelque chose de moins bien ► **down payment** N (Fin) acompte m, premier versement m ; **to make a ~ payment of £100** payer un acompte de 100 livres, payer 100 livres d'acompte ► **down-river** ADJ, ADV = **downstream** ► **down time** N (Comput) → **downtime** ► **down-to-earth** ADJ réaliste ; **he's a very ~-to-earth person** il a les pieds sur terre

down² [daʊn] N [of bird, person, plant] duvet m ; [of fruit] peau f (veloutée) → **eiderdown**, **thistledown**

down³ [daʊn] N **a** (= hill) colline f dénudée ; (Brit) **the Downs** les Downs fpl (collines herbeuses du sud de l'Angleterre) **b** (Brit = Straits of Dover) **the Downs** les Dunes fpl

downbeat [ˈdaʊnbiːt] **1** N (Mus) temps m frappé **2** ADJ (= gloomy) [person] abattu ; [ending] pessimiste

downcast [ˈdaʊnkɑːst] **1** ADJ **a** (= discouraged) abattu, démoralisé, découragé **b** (= looking down) [eyes] baissé **2** N (Min) aérage m

downcry: [ˈdaʊnkraɪ] VT (US = denigrate) décrier, dénigrer

downdraught, **downdraft** (US) [ˈdaʊndrɑːft] N (Met) courant m descendant

downer [ˈdaʊnəʳ] N **a** (* = tranquilliser) tranquillisant m, sédatif m **b** (‡: fig = depressing experience) expérience f déprimante ; **for divorced people, Christmas can be a ~** Noël peut donner le bourdon* aux divorcés ; **to be on a ~** faire de la déprime*

downfall [ˈdaʊnfɔːl] N [of person, empire] chute f, ruine f, effondrement m ; [of hopes] ruine f ; [of rain] chute f de pluie

downgrade [ˈdaʊngreɪd] **1** VT [+ employee] rétrograder (dans la hiérarchie) ; [+ hotel] déclasser ; [+ work, job] dévaloriser, déclasser **2** N (Rail etc) rampe f, descente f ; (fig) **on the ~** sur le déclin

downhearted [ˌdaʊnˈhɑːtɪd] ADJ abattu, découragé ; **don't be ~!** ne te laisse pas abattre !

downhill [ˈdaʊnˈhɪl] **1** ADJ **a** **during the ~ journey** au cours de la descente ; **the course includes a steep ~ slope** le circuit comprend une descente or pente abrupte ; **it's just a short ~ walk to the station** il n'y a que quelques mètres à descendre pour arriver à la gare, la gare est à deux pas, en bas de la côte ; **the accident happened on a ~ stretch of the track** l'accident s'est produit alors que le train descendait une côte

b (fig) **it was ~ all the way after that** (= got easier) après cela, tout a été plus facile ; (= got worse) après cela, tout est allé en empirant or de mal en pis

c (Ski) **~ competition** épreuve f de descente ; **~ course** piste f de descente ; **~ race** (épreuve f de) descente f ; **~ racer** descendeur m, -euse f ; **~ skier** skieur m, -euse f alpin(e) ; **~ ski(ing)** ski m alpin or de piste

2 ADV **to go ~** [person, vehicle] descendre (la or une pente) ; [road] descendre, aller en descendant ; (fig = get worse) [person] être sur une or la mauvaise pente ; [company, business etc] péricliter ; [economy] se dégrader ; **things just went ~ from there** par la suite les choses n'ont fait qu'empirer

downhome: [ˌdaʊnˈhəʊm] ADJ (US) (from south) du Sud, sudiste ; (pej) péquenaud*

Downing Street [ˈdaʊnɪŋstriːt] N (Brit) Downing Street (résidence du Premier ministre britannique)

DOWNING STREET

Downing Street, dans le quartier de Westminster, est la rue où résident officiellement le Premier ministre (au nº 10) et le chancelier de l'Échiquier (au nº 11). Les médias utilisent souvent les expressions Downing Street, « Number Ten » ou « Ten Downing Street », pour désigner le Premier ministre ou le gouvernement, à la façon dont on parlerait de « Matignon » en France.
---

downlighter [ˈdaʊnlaɪtəʳ] N lampe f or applique f à faisceau descendant

download [ˈdaʊnləʊd] VT (Comput) télécharger

downloading [ˈdaʊnləʊdɪŋ] N (Comput) téléchargement m

downpipe [ˈdaʊnpaɪp] N (Brit) (tuyau m de) descente f

downplay [ˈdaʊnpleɪ] VT (fig) minimiser (l'importance de)

downpour [ˈdaʊnpɔːʳ] N pluie f torrentielle

downright [ˈdaʊnraɪt] **1** ADJ pur et simple ; **a ~ refusal** un refus catégorique ; **it's a ~ lie for him to say that ...** il ment carrément or effrontément quand il dit que ... ; **it's ~ cheek on his part*** il a un sacré culot* or toupet* **2** ADV carrément ; **it's ~ impossible** c'est carrément impossible, c'est purement et simplement impossible

downshift [ˈdaʊnʃɪft] (US Aut) **1** VI rétrograder **2** N rétrogradation f

downside [ˈdaʊnsaɪd] **1** N **a** (US) **~ up** sens dessus dessous **b** (= negative aspect) inconvénient m, désavantage m ; **on the ~** côté inconvénients, pour ce qui est des inconvénients **2** COMP ► **downside risk** N [of investment] risque m de baisse or de chute du cours

downsize [ˈdaʊnsaɪz] **1** VT [+ company] réduire les effectifs de, dégraisser* ; (Comput) réduire la taille or l'encombrement de **2** VI [company] réduire ses effectifs, dégraisser*

downspout [ˈdaʊnspaʊt] N (US) = **downpipe**

Down's syndrome [ˈdaʊnzsɪndrəʊm] N trisomie f (Med), mongolisme m ; **a person with ~** un(e) trisomique ; **a ~ baby** ◊ a baby with ~ un bébé trisomique

downstage [ˈdaʊnsteɪdʒ] ADV [stand, be] sur l'avant-scène ; [move, point] vers l'avant-scène ; **to face ~** faire face au public

downstairs [ˈdaʊnˈsteəz] **1** ADV (gen) en bas ; (= to or on floor below) à l'étage en-dessous or du dessous ; (= to or on ground floor) au rez-de-chaussée ; **to go/come ~** descendre (l'escalier) ; **to run/crawl** etc **~** descendre (l'escalier) en courant/en rampant etc ; **to rush ~** dévaler l'escalier ; **to fall ~** tomber dans les escaliers ; **the people ~** (= below) les gens mpl du dessous ; (= on ground floor) les gens mpl d'en bas or du rez-de-chaussée **2** ADJ (= on ground floor) **they've got a ~ lavatory** ils ont des toilettes en bas ; **the ~ phone** le téléphone d'en bas or du rez-de-chaussée ; **the ~ rooms** les pièces fpl du bas or du rez-de-chaussée ; **a ~ flat** un appartement au rez-de-chaussée **3** N **the ~*** (= ground floor) le rez-de-chaussée ; (= lower floors) les étages mpl inférieurs

downstate [ˈdaʊnsteɪt] (US) **1** N campagne f, sud m de l'État **2** ADJ (= southern) du sud de l'État ; **~ New York** le sud de l'État de New York **3** ADV [be] dans le sud ; [go] vers le sud ; **they live ~** ils habitent dans le sud de l'État ; **to go ~** aller dans le sud de l'État

downstream [ˈdaʊnstriːm] ADJ, ADV en aval ; **to go/move ~** descendre le courant ; (fig) **~ industries** industries fpl d'aval

downstroke [ˈdaʊnstrəʊk] N **a** (in writing) plein m **b** [of piston etc] course f descendante, descente f

downswept [ˈdaʊnswept] ADJ (Aviat) [wings] surbaissé

downswing [ˈdaʊnswɪŋ] N (fig) baisse f, phase f descendante

downtime [ˈdaʊntaɪm] N [of machine] temps m or durée f d'immobilisation ; (Comput) temps m d'arrêt

downtown [ˈdaʊnˈtaʊn] (US) **1** ADV dans le centre ; **to go ~** descendre or aller en ville **2** ADJ **~ Chicago** le centre de Chicago

downtrend [ˈdaʊntrend] N tendance f à la baisse

downtrodden [ˈdaʊntrɒdən] ADJ (fig) [person, nation] opprimé

downturn [ˈdaʊntɜːn] N = **downswing**

downward [ˈdaʊnwəd] **1** ADJ [movement, stroke, pull] vers le bas ; **there was a ~ slope from the house to the road** la maison était en hauteur par rapport à la route ; **they were on a fairly steep ~ slope** ils étaient sur une pente assez raide or qui descendait assez fort ; **the rain made our ~ path extremely treacherous** la pluie rendait notre descente extrêmement dangereuse ; **in a ~ direction** vers le bas ; (St Ex) **a ~ trend** une tendance à la baisse ; **I'm convinced the economy's on the ~ slope** je suis convaincu que l'économie est sur une mauvaise pente ; (Fin) **the dollar resumed its ~ path today** le dollar a recommencé à baisser aujourd'hui **2** ADV = **downwards**

downwards [ˈdaʊnwədz] ADV [go] vers le bas, en bas ; **to slope (gently) ~** descendre (en pente douce) ; **to look ~** regarder en bas or vers le bas ; **looking ~** les yeux baissés, la tête baissée ; **place the book face ~** posez le livre face en dessous ; (fig) **from the king ~** depuis le roi (jusqu'au plus humble), du haut en bas de l'échelle sociale

downwind [ˈdaʊnˈwɪnd] ADV [be] sous le vent (of, from par rapport à) ; [move] dans la direction du vent ; [sail] sous le vent ; **the sparks drifted ~** les étincelles étaient emportées par le vent

downy [ˈdaʊnɪ] ADJ **a** (= furry) [skin, peach] duveté ; [leaf] duveteux ; **covered with fine, ~ hair** couvert de poils fins et soyeux ; **~ softness** douceur f soyeuse **b** (= feathery) [chick] couvert de duvet **c** (= down-filled) garni de duvet

dowry [ˈdaʊrɪ] N dot f

dowse [daʊz] ① VI pratiquer la rhabdomancie ② VT = **douse**

dowser ['daʊzə'] N rhabdomancien(ne) m(f); (for water) sourcier m

dowsing ['daʊzɪŋ] ① N rhabdomancie f ② COMP ► **dowsing rod** N baguette f (de sourcier)

doxology [dɒk'sɒlədʒɪ] N doxologie f

doxy†† ['dɒksɪ] N catin† f

doyen ['dɔɪən] N doyen m; **the ~ of ...** le doyen des ...

doyenne ['dɔɪen] N doyenne f

doz. ['dʌz] ABBR = **dozen**

doze [daʊz] ① N somme m; **to have a ~** faire un petit somme ② VI sommeiller; **to be dozing** être assoupi
► **doze off** VI s'assoupir, s'endormir

dozen ['dʌzn] N douzaine f; **three ~** trois douzaines; **a ~ shirts** une douzaine de chemises; **a round ~** une douzaine tout juste; **half a ~ ◊ a half-~** une demi-douzaine; **£1 a ~** une livre la douzaine; **~s of times** des dizaines or douzaines de fois; **there are ~s like that** des choses (or des gens) comme cela, on en trouve à la douzaine → **baker, nineteen, six**

dozy ['daʊzɪ] ADJ ⓐ (= sleepy) à moitié endormi, somnolent ⓑ (Brit* = stupid) empoté*, pas très dégourdi*; **you ~ prat!** imbécile!, espèce d'empoté!

DP [di:'pi:] N (ABBR = **data processing**) → **data**

DPhil [di:'fɪl] N (ABBR = **Doctor of Philosophy**) ≈ doctorat m (d'état dans une discipline autre que le droit, la médecine ou la théologie)

DPM [di:pi:'em] N (ABBR = **Diploma in Psychiatric Medicine**) diplôme m de psychiatrie

DPP [di:pi:'pi:] N (Brit Jur) (ABBR = **Director of Public Prosecutions**) → **director**

DPT [di:pi:'ti:] N (Med) (ABBR = **diphtheria, pertussis, tetanus**) DT Coq m

Dr ['dɒktə'] (ABBR = **Doctor**) (on envelope) **Dr R. Stephenson** Dr R. Stephenson; (in letters) **Dear Dr Stephenson** (man) Cher Monsieur; (woman) Chère Madame; (if known to writer) Cher Docteur

dr (Comm) ABBR = **debtor, dram, drachma**

drab [dræb] ① ADJ (colour) morne; (clothes) terne; (surroundings, existence) terne, morne ② N (NonC: Tex) grosse toile f bise

drabness ['dræbnɪs] N (of place, surroundings, existence) aspect m morne, grisaille f; (of clothes) aspect m terne

drachm [dræm] N ⓐ (Measure, Pharm) drachme f ⓑ = **drachma**

drachma ['drækmə] N (pl **drachmas** or **drachmae** ['drækmi:]) (= coin) drachme f

draconian [drə'kəʊnɪən] ADJ draconien

Dracula ['drækjʊlə] N Dracula m

draft [drɑ:ft] ① N ⓐ (= outline; gen) avant-projet m; (of letter) brouillon m; (of novel) premier jet m, ébauche f ⓑ (Comm, Fin: for money) traite f, effet m; **to make a ~ on** tirer sur ⓒ (Mil = group of men) détachement m ⓓ (US Mil = conscript intake) contingent m; **to be ~ age** être en âge de faire son service ⓔ (US) = **draught**
② VT ⓐ (also ~ **out**) (+ letter) faire le brouillon de; (+ speech) (gen) écrire, préparer; (first draft) faire le brouillon de; (final version) rédiger; (Parl) (+ bill) (Comm, Fin) (+ contract) rédiger, dresser; (+ plan) esquisser, dresser; (+ diagram) esquisser ⓑ (US Mil + conscript) appeler (sous les drapeaux), incorporer; (esp Mil) **to ~ sb to a post/to do sth** détacher or désigner qn à un poste/pour faire qch
③ COMP ► **draft board** N (US Mil) conseil m de révision ► **draft card** N (US Mil) ordre m d'incorporation ► **draft dodger** N (US Mil) insoumis m ► **draft letter** N brouillon m de

lettre; (more frm) projet m de lettre ► **draft version** N version f préliminaire

draftee [drɑ:f'ti:] N (US Mil, fig) recrue f

draftiness ['drɑ:ftɪnɪs] N (US) = **draughtiness**

draftsman ['drɑ:ftsmən] N (pl **-men**) (US) = **draughtsman a**

draftsmanship ['drɑ:ftsmənʃɪp] N (US) = **draughtsmanship**

draftswoman ['drɑ:ftswʊmən] N (pl **-women**) (US) = **draughtswoman**

drafty ['drɑ:ftɪ] ADJ (US) = **draughty**

drag [dræg] ① N ⓐ (for dredging etc) drague f; (Naut = cluster of hooks) araignée f; (= heavy sledge) traîneau m; (Agr = harrow) herse f ⓑ = **dragnet** ⓒ (Aviat, Naut etc = resistance) résistance f, traînée f ⓓ (Aut, Rail etc = brake) sabot m or patin m de frein ⓔ (Hunting) drag m ⓕ (= hindrance) frein m (on à); **he's an awful ~ on them** ils le traînent comme un boulet ⓖ (= person) raseur* m, -euse* f, casse-pieds* mf inv; (= tedium) corvée f; **what a ~ to have to go there!** quelle corvée or quelle barbe* d'avoir à y aller!; **this thing is a ~!** quelle barbe ce truc-là! ⓗ (* = pull on cigarette, pipe) taffe* f; **here, have a ~** tiens, tire une taffe* ⓘ (* = women's clothing worn by men) habits mpl de femme; **a man in ~** un homme habillé en femme; (= transvestite) un travesti ⓙ (* = influence) piston m; **to use one's ~** travailler dans la coulisse, user de son influence ⓚ (US) **the main ~** la grand-rue
② VI ⓐ (= trail along) (object) traîner (à terre); (anchor) chasser ⓑ (= lag behind) rester en arrière, traîner ⓒ (Aut) (brakes) frotter, (se) gripper ⓓ (fig) (time, work, an entertainment) traîner; (conversation) (se) traîner, languir; **the minutes ~ged (past or by)** les minutes s'écoulaient avec lenteur
③ VT ⓐ (+ person, object) traîner, tirer; (+ person) entraîner; **he ~ged her out of/into the car** il l'a tirée de la voiture/entraînée dans la voiture; **he could barely ~ his injured leg behind him** il se traînait péniblement avec sa jambe blessée; (lit) **to ~ one's feet** or **one's heels** traîner les pieds; (fig) **to ~ one's feet** or **one's heels** traîner les pieds; **she accused the government of ~ging its feet** or **heels on reforms** elle a accusé le gouvernement de tarder à introduire des réformes; **the government is ~ging its feet** or **heels over introducing new legislation** le gouvernement tarde à mettre en place de nouvelles lois; (Naut) **to ~ anchor** chasser sur ses ancres; **to ~ the truth from** or **out of sb** finir par faire avouer la vérité à qn; (US) **to ~ ass*** glander*, traînasser ⓑ (+ river, lake etc) draguer (**for** à la recherche de) ⓒ (fig = involve) (+ person) entraîner; (+ issue, question etc) mêler; **don't ~ me into your affairs!** ne me mêle pas à tes histoires!; **to ~ politics into sth** mêler la politique à qch
④ COMP ► **drag and drop** N (Comput) glisser-poser m ► **drag artist** N travesti m ► **drag coefficient, drag factor** N (Aut) coefficient m de pénétration dans l'air, CX m ► **drag lift** N (Ski) tire-fesses m inv ► **drag queen*** N travelo* m ► **drag race** N (Aut) course f de dragsters ► **drag shoe** N (Aut, Rail etc) sabot m or patin m (de frein) ► **drag show** N (Theat) spectacle m de travestis

► **drag about** ① VI traîner ② VT SEP traîner

► **drag along** VT SEP (+ person) entraîner (à contrecœur); (+ toy etc) tirer; **to ~ o.s. along** se traîner, avancer péniblement

► **drag apart** VT SEP séparer de force

► **drag away** VT SEP arracher (**from** à), emmener de force (**from** de); **she ~ged him away from**

the television* elle l'a arraché de devant* la télévision; **she ~ged him away from his work*** elle l'a arraché à son travail; **if you manage to ~ yourself away from the bar*** si tu arrives à t'arracher du bar*

► **drag down** VT SEP tirer du haut, entraîner (en bas); (fig) **to ~ sb down to one's own level** rabaisser qn à son niveau; **he was dragged down by the scandal** le scandale l'a discrédité; **his illness is ~ging him down** sa maladie l'affaiblit

► **drag in** VT SEP (fig) (+ subject, remark) tenir à placer, amener à tout prix

► **drag on** VI (meeting, conversation) traîner en longueur, s'éterniser; (conflict) s'éterniser

► **drag out** ① VI = **drag on** ② VT SEP (+ discussion) faire traîner

► **drag up** VT SEP ⓐ (* pej) (+ child) élever à la diable; **where were you ~ged up?** d'où tu sors*? ⓑ (* scandal, story) remettre sur le tapis, déterrer; **the letter ~ged up painful memories for Rose** la lettre a fait res(s)urgir des souvenirs douloureux pour Rose

draggy* ['drægɪ] ADJ rasoir* inv, barbant*

dragnet ['drægnet] N ⓐ (for fish) seine f, drège f; (for birds) tirasse f ⓑ (fig: by police) coup m de filet

dragoman ['drægəʊmən] N (pl **-mans**) drogman m

dragon ['drægən] N ⓐ (Myth, Zool, also fig = fierce person) dragon m ⓑ (Mil = armoured tractor) tracteur m blindé

dragonfly ['drægənflaɪ] N libellule f, demoiselle f

dragoon [drə'gu:n] ① N (Mil) dragon m ② VT **to ~ sb into doing sth** contraindre or forcer qn à faire qch; **she had been ~ed into the excursion** on l'avait contrainte or forcée à prendre part à l'excursion

dragster ['drægstə'] N (Aut) dragster m

dragstrip ['drægstrɪp] N (Aut) piste f de vitesse (pour dragsters)

dragsville‡ ['drægzvɪl] N (US) **it's just ~** c'est casse-pieds* or barbant*, on s'emmerde‡

dragway ['drægweɪ] N = **dragstrip**

drain [dreɪn] ① N ⓐ (in town) égout m; (in house) canalisation f sanitaire, tuyau m d'écoulement; (on washing machine etc) tuyau m d'écoulement; (Agr, Med) drain m; (= drain cover) (in street) bouche f d'égout; (beside house) puisard m; **~s** (in town) égouts mpl; (in house) canalisations fpl sanitaires; (Agr) drains mpl; **open ~** égout m à ciel ouvert; (fig) **to throw one's money down the ~** jeter son argent par les fenêtres; (fig) **to go down the ~** tomber à l'eau*; **all his hopes have gone down the ~** tous ses espoirs ont été anéantis* ⓑ (fig) (on resources, manpower) ponction f (**on** sur, dans); (on strength) épuisement m (**on** de); **looking after her father has been a great ~ on her** s'occuper de son père l'a complètement épuisée → **brain**
② VT (+ land, marshes) drainer, assécher; (+ vegetables, dishes) égoutter; (+ mine) vider, drainer; (+ reservoir) vider; (+ boiler) vidanger; (Med) (+ wound) drainer; (+ glass, drink) vider; (Comm) **~ed weight** poids m net égoutté; (fig) **to ~ sb of strength** épuiser qn; **to ~ a country of resources** ponctionner les ressources d'un pays
③ VI (liquid) s'écouler; (stream) s'écouler (**into** dans); (vegetables) (s')égoutter; (energy) s'épuiser
④ COMP ► **draining board** N égouttoir m, paillasse f ► **draining spoon** N écumoire f

► **drain away, drain off** ① VI (liquid) s'écouler; (strength) s'épuiser ② VT SEP (+ liquid) faire couler (pour vider un récipient)

drainage ['dreɪnɪdʒ] ① N (= act of draining) drainage m, assèchement m; (= system of drains) (on land) système m de fossés or de tuyaux de drainage; (of town) système m d'égouts; (of house) système m d'écoulement des eaux ; (= *sewage*) eaux *fpl* usées ; (Geol) système *m* hydrographique fluvial 2 COMP ► **drainage area, drainage basin** N (Geol) bassin *m* hydrographique ► **drainage channel** N (Constr) barbacane *f* ► **drainage tube** N (Med) drain *m*

drainboard ['dreɪnbɔːd] N (US) = **draining board**; → **drain**

drainer ['dreɪnəʳ] N égouttoir *m*

drainpipe ['dreɪnpaɪp] N tuyau *m* d'écoulement *or* de drainage

drainpipes ['dreɪnpaɪps], **drainpipe trousers** (Brit) NPL pantalon-cigarette *m*

drake [dreɪk] N canard *m* (mâle) → **duck¹**

Dralon® ['dreɪlɒn] N Dralon® *m*

DRAM, D-RAM ['diːræm] (Comput) (ABBR = **dynamic random access memory**) (mémoire *f*) DRAM *f*

dram [dræm] N (Brit) a (Measure, Pharm) drachme *f* b (* = *small drink*) goutte *f*, petit verre *m*

drama ['drɑːmə] 1 N a (NonC: gen) théâtre *m* ; **to study ~** étudier l'art *m* dramatique ; **English ~** le théâtre anglais b (= play) drame *m*, pièce *f* de théâtre ; (fig) drame *m* c (NonC = quality of being dramatic) drame *m* 2 COMP ► **drama critic** N critique *m* dramatique ► **drama queen**: N (pej) **she's such a ~ queen!** quelle comédienne !, elle fait toujours tout un cinéma ; **stop being such a ~ queen** arrête ton cinéma* ► **drama school** N école *f* d'art dramatique ► **drama student** N étudiant(e) *m(f)* en art dramatique

drama-doc* ['drɑːmədɒk] N (TV) docudrame *m*

dramatic [drə'mætɪk] ADJ a (Literat, Theat) [*art, artist, work*] dramatique ; (Literat) **~ irony** ironie *f* dramatique → **amateur** b (fig) (= *spectacular*) [*change, decline, event, moment*] spectaculaire ; (= *theatrical*) [*effect, entry, gesture*] théâtral

dramatically [drə'mætɪkəlɪ] ADV a (= *spectacularly*) [*change, improve, worsen, increase, affect, alter*] de façon spectaculaire ; [*different, effective, successful*] extraordinairement b (Literat, Theat) [*effective, compelling, powerful*] du point de vue théâtral

dramatics [drə'mætɪks] NPL a (Theat) art *m* dramatique b (* = *fuss*) comédie *f* (fig) → **amateur**

dramatis personae ['dræmətɪspɜː'səʊnaɪ] NPL personnages *mpl* (*d'une pièce etc*)

dramatist ['dræmətɪst] N auteur *m* dramatique, dramaturge *m*

dramatization [ˌdræmətaɪ'zeɪʃən] N a (Theat, TV) (for theatre) adaptation *f* pour la scène ; (for TV) adaptation *f* pour la télévision ; (for cinema) adaptation *f* cinématographique b (= *exaggeration*) dramatisation *f*

dramatize ['dræmətaɪz] VT a [+ *novel*] adapter pour la scène *or* (Ciné) pour le grand écran *or* (TV) pour la télévision *or* le petit écran ; **they ~d several episodes from his life** plusieurs épisodes de sa vie ont été portés à la scène (*or* à l'écran) b (esp US) (= *make vivid*) [+ *event*] rendre dramatique *or* émouvant ; (= *exaggerate*) dramatiser

Drambuie® [dræm'bjuːɪ] N Drambuie® *m*

drank [dræŋk] VB *pt of* **drink**

drape [dreɪp] 1 VT [+ *window, statue, person*] draper (**with** de) ; [+ *room, altar*] tendre (**with** de) ; [+ *curtain, length of cloth*] draper ; **she ~d herself over the settee*** elle s'est allongée langoureusement sur le canapé 2 **drapes** NPL (Brit = *hangings*) tentures *fpl* ; (US = *curtains*) rideaux *mpl*

draper ['dreɪpəʳ] N (Brit) marchand(e) *m(f)* de nouveautés

drapery ['dreɪpərɪ] N a (= *material*) draperie *f*, étoffes *fpl* ; (= *hangings*) tentures *fpl*, draperies

fpl b (Brit: also **draper's shop**) magasin *m* de nouveautés

drastic ['dræstɪk] ADJ [*reform, measures, reduction*] drastique, draconien ; [*remedy*] drastique ; [*surgery, change, improvement*] radical ; [*consequences, decline*] dramatique ; [*increase*] considérable, dramatique ; **to make ~ cuts in defence spending** faire *or* opérer des coupes claires dans le budget de la défense

drastically ['dræstɪkəlɪ] ADV [*cut, increase, reduce*] considérablement, drastiquement ; [*change, improve*] radicalement ; [*increase*] considérablement, dramatiquement ; **defence spending has been ~ cut** on a fait *or* opéré des coupes claires dans le budget de la défense ; **~ different** radicalement différent ; **it** *or* **things went ~ wrong** les choses ont très mal tourné

drat* [dræt] EXCL (euph = *damn*) sapristi !*, diable ! ; **~ the child!** au diable cet enfant !, quelle peste* cet enfant !

dratted* ['drætɪd] ADJ sacré* (before n), maudit (before n)

draught, draft (US) [drɑːft] 1 N a (= *breeze*) courant *m* d'air ; (for fire) tirage *m* ; **beer on ~** bière *f* à la pression ; (fig: financially) **to feel the ~*** devoir se serrer la ceinture* ; (esp US: fig = *unfriendliness*) **I felt a ~*** j'ai senti un froid *or* qu'il *etc* me traitait avec froideur b (Naut) tirant *m* d'eau c (= *drink*) coup *m* ; [*of medicine*] potion *f*, breuvage *m* ; **a ~ of cider** un coup de cidre ; **to drink in long ~s** boire à longs traits d (Brit) (*game of*) **~s** (jeu *m* de) dames *fpl* e (= *rough sketch*) = **draft 1a** 2 COMP [*animal*] de trait ; [*cider, beer*] à la pression ► **draught excluder** N bourrelet *m* (*de porte, de fenêtre*)

draughtboard ['drɑːftbɔːd] N (Brit) damier *m*

draughtiness, draftiness (US) ['drɑːftɪnɪs] N (NonC) courants *mpl* d'air

draughtproof ['drɑːftpruːf] 1 ADJ calfeutré 2 VT calfeutrer

draughtproofing ['drɑːftpruːfɪŋ] N calfeutrage *m*

draughtsman ['drɑːftsmən] N (pl **-men**) a (Art) dessinateur *m*, -trice *f* ; (in drawing office) dessinateur *m*, -trice *f* industriel(le) b (Brit: in game) pion *m*

draughtsmanship, draftsmanship (US) ['drɑːftsmənʃɪp] N [*of artist*] talent *m* de dessinateur, coup *m* de crayon ; (in industry) art *m* du dessin industriel

draughtswoman, draftswoman (US) ['drɑːftswʊmən] N (pl **-women**) (Art) dessinatrice *f* ; (in drawing office) dessinatrice *f* industrielle

draughty, drafty (US) ['drɑːftɪ] ADJ [*room*] plein de courants d'air ; [*street corner*] exposé à tous les vents *or* aux quatre vents

draw [drɔː] (pret **drew**, ptp **drawn**) 1 VT a (= *pull: gen*) [+ *object, cord, string, bolt*] tirer ; **to ~ a bow** bander un arc ; **to ~ the curtains** (= *open*) tirer *or* ouvrir les rideaux ; (= *shut*) tirer *or* fermer les rideaux ; **to ~ one's hand over one's eyes** se passer la main sur les yeux ; **I drew her arm through mine** j'ai passé *or* glissé son bras sous le mien ; **he drew a hand through his hair** il s'est passé la main dans les cheveux ; **he drew his chair nearer the fire** il a rapproché sa chaise du feu ; **he drew her close to him** il l'a attirée contre lui ; **to ~ one's finger along a surface** passer le doigt sur une surface ; **to ~ one's belt tighter** serrer sa ceinture ; **to ~ smoke into one's lungs** avaler *or* inhaler la fumée (*d'une cigarette*) ; (Med) **to ~ an abscess** faire mûrir un abcès ; (= *aim*) **to ~ a bead on sth** viser qch b (= *pull behind*) [+ *coach, cart, train, trailer etc*] tracter c (= *extract, remove*) [+ *teeth*] extraire, arracher ; [+ *cork*] retirer, enlever ; (fig) **to ~ sb's teeth** mettre qn hors d'état de nuire ; (Sewing) **to ~ threads** tirer des fils ; **to ~ a ticket out of**

a hat tirer un billet d'un chapeau ; **to ~ one's gun** dégainer son pistolet ; **he drew a gun on me** il a sorti un pistolet et l'a braqué sur moi ; (fig) **to ~ the sword** passer à l'attaque d (= *obtain from source*) [+ *wine*] tirer (**from** de) ; [+ *water*] (from tap, pump) tirer (**from** de) ; (from well) puiser (**from** dans) ; (Med) **to ~ blood from sb's arm** faire une prise de sang à qn ; **the stone hit him and drew blood** la pierre l'a frappé et l'a fait saigner ; (fig) **that remark drew blood** cette remarque blessante a porté ; **to ~ a bath**† faire couler un bain ; **to ~ (a) breath** aspirer, respirer ; (fig) souffler ; **to ~ a card from the pack** tirer une carte du jeu ; (Cards) **to ~ trumps** choisir l'atout ; **to ~ the first prize** gagner *or* décrocher le gros lot ; **to ~ inspiration from** tirer son inspiration de, puiser son inspiration dans ; **to ~ strength from sth** puiser des forces dans qch ; **to ~ comfort from sth** trouver un réconfort dans qch ; **to ~ a smile from sb** arracher un sourire à qn ; **to ~ a laugh from sb** arriver à faire rire qn ; **her performance drew tears from the audience** son interprétation a arraché des larmes au public ; **her performance drew applause from the audience** son interprétation a été saluée par les applaudissements du public ; **I could ~ no reply from him** je n'ai pu tirer de lui aucune réponse → **blank** e (Fin) **to ~ money from the bank** retirer de l'argent à la banque ; **to ~ a cheque on a bank** tirer un chèque sur une banque ; **to ~ one's salary** *or* **pay** toucher son salaire ; **to ~ one's pension** toucher sa pension f (= *attract*) [+ *attention, customer, crowd*] attirer ; **the play has ~n a lot of criticism** la pièce a donné lieu à *or* s'est attiré de nombreuses critiques ; **to feel ~n to(wards) sb** se sentir attiré par qn g (= *cause to move, do, speak etc*) **her shouts drew me to the scene** ses cris m'ont attiré sur les lieux ; **to ~ sb into a plan** entraîner qn dans un projet ; **he refuses to be ~n** (= *will not speak*) il refuse de parler ; (= *will not react*) il refuse de se laisser provoquer *or* de réagir ; **he would not be ~n on the matter** il a refusé de parler de cette affaire ; **to ~ sth to a close** *or* **an end** mettre fin à qch h [+ *picture*] dessiner ; [+ *plan, line, circle*] tracer ; (fig) [+ *situation*] faire un tableau de ; [+ *character*] peindre, dépeindre ; **to ~ sb's portrait** faire le portrait de qn ; **to ~ a map** (Geog) dresser une carte ; (Scol) faire *or* dessiner une carte ; (fig) **I ~ the line at scrubbing floors*** je n'irai pas jusqu'à *or* je me refuse à frotter les parquets ; **I ~ the line at cheating*** (myself) je n'irai pas jusqu'à *or* je me refuse à tricher ; (in others) je n'admets pas *or* je ne tolère pas que l'on triche ; **we must ~ the line somewhere** il faut se fixer une limite, il y a des limites *or* une limite à tout ; **it's hard to know where to ~ the line** il est difficile de savoir où s'arrêter i (= *establish, formulate*) [+ *conclusion*] tirer (**from** de) ; [+ *comparison, parallel, distinction*] établir, faire (**between** entre) j (Naut) **the boat ~s 4 metres** le bateau a un tirant d'eau de 4 mètres, le bateau cale 4 mètres ; **to ~ water** (= *leak*) prendre l'eau k (Sport) **to ~ a match** faire match nul ; (Chess) faire partie nulle ; **they drew one-one** ils ont fait match nul un à un partout ; **Aston Villa have ~n a Czech team in the UEFA Cup** le tirage au sort de la coupe UEFA a désigné une équipe tchèque pour jouer contre Aston Villa l (= *infuse*) [+ *tea*] faire infuser m (Culin) [+ *fowl*] vider → **hang** n (Hunting) **to ~ a fox** débusquer *or* lancer un renard o [+ *metal*] étirer ; [+ *wire*] tréfiler

2 VI a (= *move, come*) [*person*] se diriger (**towards** vers) ; **to ~ to one side** s'écarter ; **to ~ round the table** se rassembler *or* s'assembler autour de la table ; **the train drew into the sta-**

tion le train est entré en gare; **the car drew over towards the centre of the road** la voiture a dévié vers le milieu de la chaussée; **he drew ahead of the other runners** il s'est détaché des autres coureurs; **the two horses drew level** les deux chevaux sont parvenus à la même hauteur; **to ~ near** [*person*] s'approcher (**to** de); [*time, event*] approcher; **to ~ nearer (to)** s'approcher un peu plus (de); **to ~ to an end** or **a close** tirer à or toucher à sa fin

b [*chimney, pipe*] tirer; [*pump, vacuum cleaner*] aspirer

c (= *be equal*) [*two teams*] faire match nul; (*in exams, competitions*) être ex æquo *inv*; **the competitors/the teams drew for second place** les concurrents/les équipes sont arrivé(e)s deuxièmes ex æquo or ont remporté la deuxième place ex æquo; **Scotland drew with Ireland** l'Écosse a fait match nul contre l'Irlande

d (*Cards*) **to ~ for partners** tirer pour les partenaires

e (*Art*) dessiner; **he ~s well** il dessine bien, il sait bien dessiner; **to ~ from life** dessiner d'après nature

f [*tea*] infuser

3 N **a** (= *lottery*) loterie *f*, tombola *f*; (= *act of drawing a lottery*) tirage *m*; **the ~ is at three o'clock** le tirage est à trois heures; (*Sport*) **the ~ for the quarter-finals will take place this morning** le tirage se fera sport pour les quarts de finale aura lieu ce matin → **luck**

b (*Sport*) match *m* nul; **the match ended in a ~** le match s'est terminé par un match nul; **five wins and two ~s** cinq victoires et deux (matchs) nuls; **we can get at least a ~ against Holland** nous pouvons au moins faire match nul contre la Hollande

c (= *attraction*) attraction *f*, succès *m*; (*Comm*) réclame *f*; **Mel Gibson was the big ~** Mel Gibson était la grande attraction; **the pay was the big ~ of the job** le salaire était l'élément le plus intéressant dans ce travail

d **to beat sb to the ~** (*lit*) dégainer plus vite que qn; (*fig*) devancer qn; **to be quick on the ~** (*lit*) dégainer vite; (*fig*) avoir la repartie or répartie facile

e (*Drugs*) (= *hash*) herbe* *f*

4 COMP ► **draw poker** N *sorte de jeu de poker* ► **draw-sheet** N alaise *f* ► **draw(-top) table** N table *f* à rallonge

► **draw along** VT SEP [+ *cart*] tirer, traîner; (*fig*) [+ *person*] entraîner

► **draw apart** VI s'éloigner or s'écarter l'un de l'autre, se séparer

► **draw aside** **1** VI [*people*] s'écarter **2** VT SEP [+ *person*] prendre à part; [+ *object*] écarter

► **draw away** **1** VI **a** [*person*] s'éloigner, s'écarter (**from** de); [*car etc*] démarrer; **to ~ away from the kerb** s'éloigner du trottoir **b** (= *move ahead*) [*runner, racehorse etc*] se détacher (**from** de) **2** VT SEP [+ *person*] éloigner, emmener; [+ *object*] retirer, ôter

► **draw back** **1** VI (= *move backwards*) (se) reculer, s'écarter (**from** de), faire un mouvement en arrière; (*fig*) se retirer, reculer (**at, before, from** devant) **2** VT SEP [+ *person*] faire reculer; [+ *object, one's hand*] retirer **3** **~back** N → **drawback**

► **draw down** VT SEP [+ *blind*] baisser; (*fig*) [+ *blame, ridicule*] attirer (**on** sur)

► **draw in** **1** VI **a** (*Aut*) **to ~ in by the kerb** (= *pull over*) se rapprocher du trottoir; (= *stop*) s'arrêter le long du trottoir **b** (*Brit* = *get shorter*) **the days** or **nights are ~ing in** les jours raccourcissent **2** VT SEP **a** [+ *air*] aspirer, respirer **b** (= *attract*) [+ *crowds*] attirer; **the play is ~ing in huge returns** la pièce fait des recettes énormes; (*fig*) **to ~ sb in on a project** recruter qn pour un projet **c** (= *pull in*) rentrer; [+ *reins*] tirer sur; **to ~ in one's claws** (*gen, also fig*) rentrer ses griffes; [*cat*] faire patte de velours → **horn**

► **draw off** **1** VI [*army, troops*] se retirer **2** VT

SEP **a** [+ *gloves, garment*] retirer, enlever **b** [+ *beer etc*] (*from keg*) tirer; (*Med*) [+ *blood*] prendre

► **draw on** **1** VI [*time*] avancer **2** VT SEP **a** [+ *stockings, gloves, garment*] enfiler; [+ *shoes*] mettre **b** (*fig* = *encourage*) [+ *person*] entraîner, encourager **3** VT FUS **a** = **draw upon** **b** **he drew on his cigarette** il a tiré sur sa cigarette

► **draw out** **1** VI (= *become longer*) **the days are ~ing out** les jours rallongent **2** VT SEP **a** (= *bring out, remove*) [+ *handkerchief, purse*] sortir, tirer (**from** de); [+ *money*] (*from bank etc*) retirer (**from** à, de); [+ *secret, plan*] soutirer (**from** à); (*fig*) [+ *person*] faire parler; **he's shy, try and ~ him out (of his shell)** il est timide, essayez de le faire sortir de sa coquille **b** (= *stretch, extend*) [+ *wire*] étirer, tréfiler; (*fig*) [+ *speech, meeting*] prolonger; [+ *meal*] prolonger

► **draw up** **1** VI (= *stop*) [*car etc*] s'arrêter, stopper **2** VT SEP **a** [+ *chair*] approcher; [+ *troops*] aligner, ranger; [+ *boat*] tirer à sec; **to ~ o.s. up (to one's full height)** se dresser de toute sa hauteur **b** (= *formulate, set out*) [+ *inventory*] dresser; [+ *list, contract, agreement*] dresser, rédiger; [+ *plan, scheme*] formuler, établir; (*Fin*) [+ *bill*] établir, dresser

► **draw upon** VT FUS **to ~ upon one's savings** prendre or tirer sur ses économies; **to ~ upon one's imagination** faire appel à son imagination

drawback ['drɔːbæk] N **a** (= *disadvantage*) inconvénient *m*, désavantage *m* (**to** à) **b** (*Tax* = *refund*) drawback *m*

drawbridge ['drɔːbrɪdʒ] N pont-levis *m*, pont *m* basculant or à bascule

drawee [drɔː'iː] N (*Fin*) tiré *m*

drawer[1] ['drɔːʳ] N [*of furniture*] tiroir *m* → **bottom, chest**[1]

drawer[2] ['drɔːəʳ] N **a** [*of cheque etc*] tireur *m* **b** (*Art*) [*of pictures*] dessinateur *m*, -trice *f*

drawers† ['drɔːz] NPL [*of men*] caleçon *m*; [*of women*] culotte *f*, pantalon(s)† *m(pl)*

drawing ['drɔːɪŋ] **1** N **a** (*Art*) dessin *m*; **a pencil ~** un dessin au crayon; **a chalk ~** un pastel; **rough ~** esquisse *f* **b** (*NonC* = *extending, tapering*) [*of metals*] étirage *m* **2** COMP ► **drawing board** N planche *f* à dessin; (*fig*) **the scheme is still on the ~ board** le projet est encore à l'étude; (*fig*) **back to the ~ board!** retour à la case départ! ► **drawing office** N (*Brit*) bureau *m* de dessin industriel ► **drawing paper** N (*Art*) papier *m* à dessin ► **drawing pen** N (*Art*) tire-ligne *m* ► **drawing pin** N (*Brit*) punaise *f* ► **drawing room** N salon *m*; (*larger*) salle *f* or salon *m* de réception

drawl [drɔːl] **1** VI parler d'une voix traînante **2** VT dire or prononcer d'une voix traînante **3** N voix *f* traînante; **with a Southern/an aristocratic ~** avec la voix traînante des gens du Sud des États-Unis/des aristocrates; **... he said with a ~** ... dit-il d'une voix traînante

drawn [drɔːn] **1** VB ptp of **draw**; → **long 2** ADJ **a** [*curtains, blinds*] tiré **b** (= *unsheathed*) [*sword, dagger*] dégainé; **pictures of dragoons charging with ~ sword** des images de dragons chargeant sabre au clair; **the police waited with ~ truncheons** or **with truncheons ~** les policiers attendaient, matraque en main → **dagger c** (= *haggard*) [*features*] tiré; [*person, face*] aux traits tirés; **to look ~** avoir les traits tirés; **face ~ with pain** visage *m* crispé par la douleur **d** (*Sport* = *equal*) [*match*] nul **3** COMP ► **drawn butter** N (*Culin*) beurre *m* fondu ► **drawn-thread work, drawn work** N (*Sewing*) ouvrage *m* à fils tirés or à jour(s)

drawstring ['drɔːstrɪŋ] N cordon *m*

dray [dreɪ] N [*of brewer*] haquet *m*; [*of wood, stones*] fardier *m*; [*of quarry work*] binard *m*

dread [dred] **1** VT redouter, appréhender; **to ~ doing sth** redouter de faire qch; **to ~ that ...** redouter que ... ne (+ *subj*); **the ~ed Mrs Mitch** la redoutable Mme Mitch; (*hum*) **the ~ed exam/medicine** l'examen/le médicament tant redouté (*hum*) **2** N terreur *f*, effroi *m*; **in ~ of doing sth** dans la crainte de faire qch; **to be** or **stand in ~ of sth** redouter qch, vivre dans la crainte de qch **3** ADJ (*liter*) redoutable, terrible

dreadful ['dredfʊl] ADJ **a** (= *horrible, appalling*) [*crime, sight, suffering*] affreux, atroce; [*disease*] affreux, horrible; [*weapon*] redoutable; **a ~ mistake** une erreur terrible; **a ~ waste** un gaspillage épouvantable; **he's a ~ coward!** qu'est-ce qu'il peut être lâche!; **what a ~ thing to happen!** quelle horreur! **b** (= *bad*) [*person, place, moment, situation, weather conditions*] affreux; [*food*] épouvantable; [*film, book, play etc*] lamentable; [*child*] insupportable; (= *ill, tired*) **you look ~!** tu n'as pas l'air bien du tout!; (= *unattractive*) **you look ~ (in that hat/with that haircut)!** tu es vraiment moche (avec ce chapeau/avec cette coupe de cheveux)!; (= *ill*) **I feel ~!** je ne me sens pas bien du tout!; (= *guilty*) **I feel ~ (about it)!** je m'en veux!; **I feel ~ about John/about what has happened** je m'en veux de ce qui est arrivé à John/de ce qui s'est passé → **penny**

dreadfully ['dredfʊlɪ] ADV **a** (= *badly*) [*behave, treat sb*] de façon abominable; [*suffer*] affreusement, atrocement; **I miss him ~** il me manque terriblement; **I had a feeling that something was ~ wrong** j'ai senti que quelque chose de terrible venait de se passer **b** (* = *very*) [*boring, late etc*] affreusement; **I'm ~ sorry** je suis terriblement désolé

dreadlocks ['dredlɒks] NPL dreadlocks *fpl*

dreadnought ['drednɔːt] N (*Naut*) cuirassé *m* (d'escadre)

▼ **dream** [driːm] (*vb: pret, ptp* **dreamed** or **dreamt**) **1** N **a** rêve *m*; **to have a ~ about sb/sth** rêver de qn/qch; **I've had a bad ~** j'ai fait un mauvais rêve or un cauchemar; **the whole business was (like) a bad ~** c'était un vrai cauchemar; **sweet ~s!** fais de beaux rêves!; **to see sth in a ~** voir qch en rêve; **life is but a ~** la vie n'est qu'un songe **b** (*when awake*) **to be in a ~*** (= *not paying attention*) être dans les nuages or la lune; (= *daydreaming*) rêvasser **c** (= *fantasy*) rêve *m*; **the man/woman/house of my ~s** l'homme/la femme/la maison de mes rêves; **my ~ is to have a house in the country** mon rêve serait d'avoir une maison à la campagne; **his fondest ~ was to see her again** son vœu le plus cher était de la revoir; **to have ~s of doing sth** rêver de faire qch; **it was like a ~ come true** c'était le rêve; **to make a ~ come true for sb** réaliser le rêve de qn; **in your ~s!*** tu peux toujours rêver!*; **all his ~s came true** tous ses rêves se sont réalisés; **idle ~s** rêvasseries *fpl*; **rich beyond his wildest ~s** plus riche que dans ses rêves les plus fous; **she achieved success beyond her wildest ~s** son succès a dépassé ses espoirs les plus fous; **never in my wildest ~s would I have thought that ...** jamais, même dans mes rêves les plus fous, je n'aurais imaginé que ...; **everything went like a ~*** tout est allé comme sur des roulettes* **d** * (= *lovely person*) amour* *m*; (= *lovely thing*) merveille *f*; **isn't he a ~?** n'est-ce pas qu'il est adorable or que c'est un amour?; **a ~ of a dress** une robe de rêve

2 ADJ **a ~ house** une maison de rêve; **his ~ house** la maison de ses rêves

3 VI **a** (*in sleep*) rêver; **to ~ about** or **of sb/sth** rêver de qn/qch; **to ~ about** or **of doing sth** rêver qu'on a fait qch; **~ on!*** tu peux toujours rêver!* **b** (*when awake*) rêvasser, être dans les nuages or la lune **c** (= *imagine, envisage*) songer (**of** à), avoir l'idée (**of** de); **I should never have dreamt of**

► ► **LANGUAGE IN USE:** **dream** 8.4

doing such a thing je n'aurais jamais songé à or eu l'idée de faire une chose pareille; **I wouldn't ~ of telling her!** jamais il ne me viendrait à l'idée de lui dire cela!; **will you come? — I wouldn't ~ of it!** vous allez venir? — jamais de la vie or pas question!; **I wouldn't ~ of making fun of you** il ne me viendrait jamais à l'idée de me moquer de vous **4** VT **a** (in sleep) rêver, voir en rêve; **to ~ a dream** faire un rêve; **I dreamt that she came** j'ai rêvé qu'elle venait; **you must have dreamt it!** vous avez dû (le) rêver! **b** (= imagine) imaginer; **if I had dreamt you would do that ...** si j'avais pu imaginer un instant que tu ferais cela ...; **I didn't ~ he would come!** je n'ai jamais songé or imaginé un instant qu'il viendrait! **5** COMP ► **dream ticket*** N (esp Pol) équipe f idéale ► **dream world** N (ideal) monde m utopique; (imagination) monde m imaginaire; **he lives in a ~ world** il est complètement détaché des réalités

► **dream away** VT SEP [+ time] perdre en rêveries; **to ~ one's life away** passer sa vie à rêvasser

► **dream up*** VT SEP [+ idea] imaginer, concevoir; **where did you ~ that up?** où est-ce que vous êtes allé pêcher cela?*

dreamboat* ['driːmbəʊt] N **he's a ~** il est beau comme un dieu

dreamer ['driːmər] N **a** (lit) rêveur m, -euse f **b** (fig) rêveur m, -euse f, songe-creux m inv; (politically) utopiste mf

dreamily ['driːmɪlɪ] ADV [say] d'un ton rêveur; [smile, sigh, look] d'un air rêveur

dreamland ['driːmlænd] N pays m des rêves or des songes; (= beautiful place) pays m de rêve

dreamless ['driːmlɪs] ADJ sans rêves

dreamlike ['driːmlaɪk] ADJ onirique

dreamt [dremt] VB pt, ptp of **dream**

dreamy ['driːmɪ] ADJ **a** (= relaxed, otherworldly) [smile, look, expression] rêveur; [voice, music] doux (douce f), qui fait rêver **b** (* pej = impractical, idealistic) rêveur, dans la lune or les nuages **c** (* = wonderful) [house, car, dress] de rêve; **he's ~!** il est tellement séduisant!

drearily ['drɪərɪlɪ] ADV [speak] d'un ton morne; [dress] de façon terne; **it was a ~ familiar scenario** c'était un scénario trop connu

dreariness ['drɪərɪnɪs] N [of surroundings, life] grisaille f, monotonie f; [of weather] grisaille f

dreary ['drɪərɪ] ADJ [place, landscape] morne; [job, work, life] monotone; [day, person] ennuyeux; [weather] maussade

dredge¹ [dredʒ] **1** N (= net, vessel) drague f **2** VT [+ river, mud] draguer **3** VI draguer

► **dredge up** VT SEP **a** (lit) draguer **b** (fig) [+ unpleasant facts] déterrer, ressortir

dredge² [dredʒ] VT (Culin) saupoudrer (**with** de, **on to**, **over** sur)

dredger¹ ['dredʒər] N **a** (Naut) (= ship) dragueur m; (= machine) drague f

dredger² ['dredʒər] N (Culin) saupoudreuse f, saupoudroir m

dredging¹ ['dredʒɪŋ] N (Naut) dragage m

dredging² ['dredʒɪŋ] N (Culin) saupoudrage m

dregs [dregz] NPL (lit, fig) lie f; **the ~ of society** la lie de la société

drench [drentʃ] **1** VT **a** tremper; **to get ~ed to the skin** se faire tremper jusqu'aux os, se faire saucer* **b** (Vet) administrer or faire avaler un médicament à **2** N (Vet) (dose f de) médicament m (pour un animal)

drenching ['drentʃɪŋ] **1** N **to get a ~** se faire tremper or saucer* **2** ADJ **~ rain** pluie f battante or diluvienne

Dresden ['drezdən] N (also **~ china**) porcelaine f de Saxe, saxe m; **a piece of ~** un saxe

dress [dres] **1** N **a** robe f; **a long/silk/summer ~** une robe longue/de soie/d'été → **cocktail, wedding**

b (NonC = clothing, way of dressing) tenue f; **articles of ~** vêtements mpl; **in eastern/traditional ~** en tenue orientale/traditionnelle; **to be careless in one's ~** avoir une tenue négligée; **he's always very careful in his ~** il s'habille toujours avec beaucoup de recherche, il est toujours élégamment vêtu → **evening, full, national**

2 VT **a** (= clothe) [+ child, family, recruits, customer] habiller; **to get ~ed** s'habiller; **he's old enough to ~ himself** [child] il est assez grand pour s'habiller tout seul → **dressed** **b** (Theat) [+ play] costumer **c** (= arrange, decorate) [+ gown] parer, orner; (Naut) [+ ship] pavoiser; **to ~ a shop window** faire la vitrine; **to ~ sb's hair** coiffer qn **d** (Culin) [+ salad] assaisonner; [+ chicken, crab, game] préparer **e** [+ skins] préparer, apprêter; [+ material] apprêter; [+ leather] corroyer; [+ timber] dégrossir; [+ stone] tailler, dresser **f** (Agr) [+ field] façonner **g** [+ troops] aligner **h** [+ wound] panser; **to ~ sb's wound** panser la blessure de qn

3 VI **a** s'habiller; **to ~ in black** s'habiller en noir; **to ~ in jeans** porter des jeans; **to ~ as a man** s'habiller en homme; **she ~es very well** elle s'habille avec goût; **to ~ for dinner** se mettre en tenue de soirée → **dressed** **b** [soldiers] s'aligner; **right ~!** à droite, alignement!

4 COMP ► **dress circle** N (Theat) premier balcon m, corbeille f ► **dress coat** N habit m, queue-de-pie f ► **dress code** N code m vestimentaire ► **dress designer** N couturier m ► **dress length** N (of material) hauteur f (de robe) ► **dress parade** N (US Mil) défilé m en grande tenue ► **dress rehearsal** N (Theat) (répétition f) générale f; (fig) répétition f générale ► **dress sense** N **he has no ~ sense at all** il ne sait absolument pas s'habiller; **her ~ sense is appalling** elle s'habille d'une façon épouvantable ► **dress shield** N dessous-de-bras m ► **dress shirt** N chemise f de soirée ► **dress suit** N habit m or tenue f de soirée or de cérémonie ► **dress uniform** N (Mil) tenue f de cérémonie → **dressed**

► **dress down** **1** VT SEP **a** (* = scold) passer un savon à* **b** [+ horse] panser **2** VI (Brit) s'habiller décontracté **3** **~ing-down*** N → **dressing**

► **dress up** **1** VI **a** (= put on smart clothes) se mettre sur son trente et un, s'habiller; **there's no need to ~ up*** il n'y a pas besoin de se mettre sur son trente et un → **dressed** **b** (= put on fancy dress) se déguiser; **to ~ up as ...** se déguiser or se costumer en ...; **the children love ~ing up** les enfants adorent se déguiser **2** VT SEP **a** (= disguise) déguiser (**as** en) **b** **it ~es up the skirt** cela rend la jupe plus habillée

dressage ['dresaːʒ] N dressage m

dressed [drest] **1** ADJ habillé; **casually ~** habillé de façon décontractée; **fully ~** entièrement habillé; **smartly ~** vêtu avec élégance, élégamment vêtu; **well-~** bien habillé; **~ in a suit/in white** vêtu d'un costume/de blanc; **to be ~ for the country/for town/for jogging/for gardening** être habillé pour la campagne/pour la ville/pour faire du jogging/pour jardiner; **~ as a man/a cowboy/an astronaut** etc habillé en homme/cow-boy/astronaute etc; (Brit) **to be ~ up to the nines*** ◊ **to be all ~ up*** être sur son trente et un*; (hum) **all ~ up and nowhere to go*** fringué(e)* comme un prince (or une princesse) et tout ça pour rien; **she was ~ to kill*** elle était superbement habillée, prête à faire des ravages → **dress 3a** **2** COMP ► **dressed crab** N crabe m tout préparé

dresser¹ ['dresər] N **a** (Theat) habilleur m, -euse f; (Comm: also **window ~**) étalagiste mf **b** **she's a stylish ~** elle s'habille avec chic;

→ **hairdresser** **c** (= tool) (for wood) raboteuse f; (for stone) rabotin m

dresser² ['dresər] N **a** (= furniture) buffet m, vaisselier m **b** (US) = **dressing table** → **dressing**

dressing ['dresɪŋ] **1** N **a** (= providing with clothes) habillement m; **~ always takes me a long time** je mets beaucoup de temps à m'habiller → **hairdressing** **b** (Med) pansement m **c** (Culin) (= presentation) présentation f; (= seasoning) assaisonnement m, sauce f; (= stuffing) farce f; **oil and vinegar ~** vinaigrette f → **salad** **d** (= manure) engrais m, fumages mpl **e** (for material, leather) apprêt m **f** (Constr) parement m

2 COMP ► **dressing case** N nécessaire m de toilette, trousse f de toilette or de voyage ► **dressing-down*** N **to give sb a ~-down** passer un savon à qn*; **to get a ~-down** recevoir or se faire passer un savon*, se faire enguirlander* ► **dressing gown** N (Brit) robe f de chambre; (made of towelling) peignoir m; (= negligée) déshabillé m ► **dressing room** N (in house) dressing(-room) m; (Theat) loge f; (US: in shop) cabine f d'essayage ► **dressing station** N (Mil) poste m de secours ► **dressing table** N coiffeuse f ► **dressing table set** N accessoires mpl pour coiffeuse ► **dressing-up** N déguisement m

dressmaker ['dresmeɪkər] N couturière f

dressmaking ['dresmeɪkɪŋ] N couture f

dressy* ['dresɪ] ADJ chic

drew [druː] VB pt of **draw**

dribble ['drɪbl] **1** VI **a** [liquid] tomber goutte à goutte, couler lentement; [baby] baver; **to ~ back/in** etc [people] revenir/entrer etc par petits groupes or un par un **b** (Sport) dribbler **2** VT **a** (Sport) [+ ball] dribbler **b** **he ~d his milk all down his chin** son lait lui dégoulinait le long du menton **3** N **a** (of water) petite goutte f **b** (Sport) dribble m

dribbler ['drɪblər] N (Sport) dribbleur m

driblet ['drɪblɪt] N (of liquid) gouttelette f; **in ~s** (lit) goutte à goutte; (fig) au compte-gouttes

dribs and drabs ['drɪbzən'dræbz] NPL petites quantités fpl; **in ~** (gen) petit à petit, peu à peu; [arrive] en or par petits groupes; [pay, give] au compte-gouttes

dried [draɪd] **1** VB pt, ptp of **dry** **2** ADJ [flowers, mushrooms, onions, tomatoes] séché; [beans] sec (sèche f); [eggs, milk, yeast] en poudre; **~ fruit** fruits mpl secs **3** COMP ► **dried out*** ADJ [alcoholic] désintoxiqué

dried-up [,draɪd'ʌp] ADJ **a** (= dry) [food] ratatiné; [river-bed, stream, oasis] desséché; [well, spring] tari **b** (= wizened) [person] ratatiné; **a little ~ old man** un petit vieillard ratatiné

drier ['draɪər] N = **dryer**

drift [drɪft] **1** VI **a** (on sea, river etc) aller à la dérive, dériver; (in wind/current) être poussé or emporté (par le vent/le courant); (Aviat) dériver; [snow, sand etc] s'amonceler, s'entasser; [sounds] se faire entendre; **to ~ downstream** descendre la rivière emporté par le courant; **to ~ away/out/back** etc [person] partir/sortir/revenir etc d'une allure nonchalante; **he was ~ing aimlessly about** il flânait (sans but), il déambulait **b** (fig) [person] se laisser aller, aller à la dérive; [events] tendre (**towards** vers); **to let things ~** laisser les choses aller à la dérive or à vau-l'eau; **he ~ed into marriage** il s'est retrouvé marié; **to ~ into crime** sombrer peu à peu dans la délinquance; **to ~ from job to job** aller d'un travail à un autre; **the nation was ~ing towards a crisis** le pays allait vers la crise **c** (Rad) se décaler **2** N **a** (NonC) (= driving movement or force) mouvement m, force f; [of air, water current] poussée f; **the ~ of the current** (= *speed*) la vitesse du courant; (= *direction*) le sens or la direction du courant; **carried north by the ~ of the current** emporté vers le nord par le courant; (*fig*) **the ~ towards the cities** le mouvement vers les villes; (*fig*) **the ~ of events** le cours or la tournure des événements

[b] (= *mass*) [*of clouds*] traînée f; [*of dust*] nuage m; [*of falling snow*] rafale f; [*of fallen snow*] congère f, amoncellement m; [*of sand, leaves*] amoncellement m; (*Geol* = *deposits*) apports mpl

[c] (*NonC*) (= *act of drifting*) [*of ships, aircraft*] dérive f, dérivation f; [*of projectile*] déviation f, dérivation f; (= *deviation from course*) dérive f; (*Ling*) évolution f (de la langue); **continental ~** dérive f des continents

[d] (* = *general meaning*) **to get** or **catch** or **follow sb's ~** comprendre où qn veut en venir, comprendre le sens général des paroles de qn; **(you) get my ~?** tu as pigé?*, tu vois ce que je veux dire?

[e] (*Min*) galerie f chassante

[3] COMP ► **drift anchor** N ancre f flottante ► **drift ice**, **drifting ice** N glaces fpl flottantes ► **drift net** N filet m dérivant, traîne f

► **drift apart** VI (*fig*) s'éloigner l'un de l'autre

► **drift off** VI (*fig* = *fall asleep*) se laisser gagner par le sommeil

drifter ['drɪftər] N [a] (= *boat*) chalutier m, drifter m [b] (= *person*) personne f qui se laisse aller or qui n'a pas de but dans la vie; **he's a bit of a ~** il manque un peu de stabilité

driftwood ['drɪftwʊd] N bois m flotté

drill¹ [drɪl] [1] N (*for metal, wood*) foret m, mèche f; (*for oil well*) trépan m; (*for DIY*) perceuse f; (*Min*) perforatrice f, foreuse f; (*for roads*) marteau-piqueur m; [*of dentist*] roulette f, fraise f (de dentiste); **electric (hand) ~** perceuse f électrique → **pneumatic** [2] VT [+ *wood, metal*] forer, percer; [+ *tooth*] fraiser; **to ~ an oil well** forer un puits de pétrole [3] VI forer, effectuer des forages (**for** pour trouver)

drill² [drɪl] [1] N (*NonC*) (*esp Mil* = *exercises etc*) exercice(s) m(pl), manœuvre(s) f(pl); (*in grammar etc*) exercices m; (*fig*) **what's the ~?** quelle est la marche à suivre?; **he doesn't know the ~** il ne connaît pas la marche à suivre [2] VT [+ *soldiers*] faire faire l'exercice à; **these troops are well-~ed** ces troupes sont bien entraînées; **to ~ pupils in grammar** faire faire des exercices de grammaire à des élèves; **to ~ good manners into a child** inculquer les bonnes manières à un enfant; **I ~ed it into him that he must not ...** je lui ai bien enfoncé dans la tête qu'il ne doit pas ... [3] VI (*Mil*) faire l'exercice, être à l'exercice [4] COMP ► **drill sergeant** N (*Mil*) sergent m instructeur

drill³ [drɪl] (*Agr*) [1] N (= *furrow*) sillon m; (= *machine*) drill m, semoir m [2] VT [+ *seeds*] semer en sillons; [+ *field*] tracer des sillons dans

drill⁴ [drɪl] N (*Tex*) coutil m, treillis m

drilling¹ ['drɪlɪŋ] [1] N (*NonC*) [*of metal, wood*] forage m, perçage m; (*by dentist*) fraisage m; **~ for oil** forage m (pétrolier) [2] COMP ► **drilling platform** N plateforme f de forage ► **drilling rig** N derrick m; (*at sea*) plateforme f ► **drilling ship** N navire m de forage

drilling² ['drɪlɪŋ] N (*Mil*) exercices mpl, manœuvres fpl

drillion ['drɪljən] N (*US*) **a ~ dollars** des tonnes de dollars, des milliards et des milliards de dollars

drily ['draɪlɪ] ADV [a] (= *with dry humour*) [*say, observe*] d'un air or d'un ton pince-sans-rire [b] (= *unemotionally*) flegmatiquement

drink [drɪŋk] (*vb: pret* **drank**, *ptp* **drunk**) [1] N [a] (= *liquid to drink*) boisson f; **have you got ~s for the children?** est-ce que tu as des boissons pour les enfants?; **there's food and ~ in the kitchen** il y a de quoi boire et manger à la cuisine; **may I have a ~?** est-ce que je

pourrais boire quelque chose?; **to give sb a ~** donner à boire à qn; **he's a big ~ of water*** quelle (grande) asperge!*

[b] (= *glass of alcoholic drink*) verre m; (*before meal*) apéritif m; (*after meal*) digestif m; **have a ~!** tu prendras bien un verre?; **let's have a ~** allons prendre or boire un verre; **let's have a ~ on it** allons boire un verre pour fêter ça; **I need a ~!** j'ai besoin de boire un verre!; **he likes a ~** il aime bien boire un verre; **to ask friends in for ~s** inviter des amis à venir prendre un verre; **to stand sb a ~** offrir un verre à qn, offrir à boire à qn; **to stand a round of ~s** ◊ **to stand ~s all round** payer une tournée générale; **he had a ~ in him*** il avait un coup dans le nez* → **short**, **soft**, **strong**

[c] (*NonC* = *alcoholic liquor*) la boisson, l'alcool m; **to be under the influence of ~** être en état d'ébriété; **to be the worse for ~** avoir un coup dans le nez*; **to take to ~** se mettre à boire; **to smell of ~** sentir l'alcool; **his worries drove him to ~** ses soucis l'ont poussé à boire or l'ont fait sombrer dans la boisson; **it's enough to drive you to ~!** ça vous donne envie de boire pour oublier! → **demon**

[d] (* = *sea*) baille* f; **to be in the ~** être à la baille*

[2] VT [+ *wine, coffee*] boire, prendre; [+ *soup*] manger; **would you like something to ~?** voulez-vous boire quelque chose?; **give me something to ~** donnez-moi (quelque chose) à boire; **is the water fit to ~?** est-ce que l'eau est potable?; **this coffee isn't fit to ~** ce café n'est pas buvable; **to ~ sb's health** boire à la santé de qn; **this wine should be drunk at room temperature** ce vin se boit chambré; (*fig*) **he ~s all his wages** il boit tout ce qu'il gagne; **to ~ sb under the table** faire rouler qn sous la table → **death**, **toast**

[3] VI **he doesn't ~** il ne boit pas; **his father drank** son père buvait; **to ~ from the bottle** boire à (même) la bouteille; **to ~ out of a glass** boire dans un verre; (*on notice*) **"don't ~ and drive"** «boire ou conduire, il faut choisir»; **to ~ like a fish*** boire un trou*; **to ~ to sb/to sb's success** boire à or porter un toast à qn/au succès de qn

[4] COMP ► **drink driver** N (*Brit*) conducteur m, -trice f en état d'ébriété or d'ivresse ► **drink-driving** N (*Brit*) conduite f en état d'ébriété or d'ivresse ► **drink-driving campaign** N (*Brit*) campagne f contre l'alcool au volant ► **drink problem** N **the ~ problem** le problème de l'alcoolisme; **to have a ~ problem** trop boire

► **drink away** VT SEP [+ *fortune*] boire; [+ *sorrows*] noyer (dans l'alcool)

► **drink down** VT SEP avaler, boire d'un trait

► **drink in** VT SEP [*plants, soil*] absorber, boire; (*fig*) [+ *story*] avaler*; **he drank in the fresh air** il a respiré or humé l'air frais; (*fig*) **the children were ~ing it all in** les enfants n'en perdaient pas une miette* or une goutte*

► **drink up** [1] VI boire, vider son verre; **~ up!** finis or bois ton verre! [2] VT SEP **to ~ sth up** finir son verre or sa tasse de qch

drinkable ['drɪŋkəbl] ADJ (= *not poisonous*) [*water*] potable; (= *palatable*) [*wine etc*] buvable

drinker ['drɪŋkər] N buveur m, -euse f; **whisky ~** buveur m, -euse f de whisky; **he's a hard** or **heavy ~** il boit beaucoup, il boit sec

drinking ['drɪŋkɪŋ] [1] N (fait m de) boire m; (= *drunkenness*) boisson f; **eating and ~** manger et boire m; **he wasn't used to ~** il n'avait pas l'habitude de boire; **there was a lot of heavy ~** on a beaucoup bu; **his problem was ~** son problème c'était qu'il buvait; **his ~ caused his marriage to break up** son penchant pour la boisson est responsable de l'échec de son mariage; **she left him because of his ~** elle l'a quitté parce qu'il buvait; **I don't object to ~ in moderation** je ne vois pas d'inconvénient à boire or à ce que l'on boive avec modération; **~ by the under-18s must be**

stopped il faut empêcher les jeunes de moins de 18 ans de boire

[2] COMP ► **drinking bout** N beuverie f ► **drinking chocolate** N chocolat m (en poudre) ► **drinking companion** N one of his ~ **companions** un de ses compagnons de beuverie ► **drinking fountain** N (*in street*) fontaine f publique; (*in office, toilets etc*) jet m d'eau potable ► **drinking session** N = **drinking bout** ► **drinking song** N chanson f à boire ► **drinking spree** N = **drinking bout** ► **drinking straw** N paille f ► **drinking trough** N abreuvoir m, auge f ► **drinking-up time** N (*Brit*) *dernières minutes pour finir son verre avant la fermeture d'un pub* ► **drinking water** N eau f potable

drip [drɪp] [1] VI [*water, sweat, rain*] dégoutter, dégouliner; [*tap*] couler, goutter; [*cheese, washing*] s'égoutter; [*hair, trees etc*] ruisseler (**with** de); **the rain was ~ping down the wall** la pluie dégouttait or dégoulinait le long du mur; **sweat was ~ping from his brow** son front ruisselait de sueur; **to be ~ping with sweat** ruisseler de sueur, être en nage; **his hands were ~ping with blood** ses mains ruisselaient de sang; **the walls were ~ping (with water)** les murs suintaient; (*liter*) **his voice was ~ping with sarcasm** il avait un ton profondément sarcastique → **dripping**

[2] VT [+ *liquid*] faire tomber or laisser tomber goutte à goutte; [+ *washing, cheese*] égoutter; **you're ~ping paint all over the place** tu mets de la peinture partout

[3] N [a] (= *sound*) [*of water, rain*] bruit m de l'eau qui tombe goutte à goutte; [*of tap*] bruit m d'un robinet qui goutte

[b] (= *drop*) goutte f

[c] (* *fig* = *spineless person*) lavette* f

[d] (*Med*) (= *liquid*) perfusion f; (= *device*) goutte-à-goutte m inv; **to put up a ~** mettre un goutte-à-goutte; **to be on a ~** être sous perfusion → **intravenous**

[e] (*Archit: also* **~stone**) larmier m

[4] COMP ► **drip-dry** ADJ [*shirt*] qui ne nécessite aucun repassage ♦ VT (*Comm: on label*) « ne pas repasser » ► **drip-feed** VT (*Med*) alimenter par perfusion ► **drip mat** N dessous-de-verre m inv ► **drip pan** N (*Culin*) lèchefrite f

dripping ['drɪpɪŋ] [1] N [a] (*Culin*) graisse f (de rôti); **bread and ~** tartine f à la graisse [b] (= *action*) [*of water etc*] égouttement m, égouttage m [2] ADJ [a] (= *leaking*) [*tap, gutter*] qui goutte or coule [b] (= *soaking*) [*person, hair, clothes, washing*] trempé; [*tree*] ruisselant, qui dégoutte; **he's ~ wet*** il est trempé jusqu'aux os; **my coat is ~ wet*** mon manteau est trempé → **drip** [3] COMP ► **dripping pan** N (*Culin*) lèchefrite f

drippy* ['drɪpɪ] ADJ [*person*] gnangnan* inv; [*music, book*] cucul*

drivability [ˌdraɪvə'bɪlɪtɪ] N maniabilité f, manœuvrabilité f

drive [draɪv] (*vb: pret* **drove**, *ptp* **driven**) [1] N [a] (= *car journey*) promenade f or trajet m en voiture; **to go for a ~** faire une promenade en voiture; **it's about one hour's ~ from London** c'est à environ une heure de voiture de Londres

[b] (= *private road: into house, castle*) allée f

[c] (*Golf*) drive m; (*Tennis*) coup m droit, drive m

[d] (= *energy*) dynamisme m, énergie f; (*Psych*) besoin m, instinct m; **the sex ~** les pulsions fpl sexuelles; **to have plenty of ~** avoir du dynamisme or de l'énergie; **to lack ~** manquer de dynamisme or d'énergie

[e] (*Pol, Comm*) campagne f; (*Mil*) poussée f; **a ~ to boost sales** une campagne de promotion des ventes; **an output ~** un effort de production; **a recruitment ~** une campagne de recrutement; **the ~ towards democracy** le

mouvement en faveur de la démocratie → **export**, **whist**

f (*Tech* = *power transmission*) commande *f*, transmission *f* → **front**, **left**, **rear**

g (*Comput*) (*for disk*) unité *f* de disques; (*for tape*) dérouleur *m*

2 VT **a** [+ *cart, car, train*] conduire; [+ *racing car*] piloter; [+ *passenger*] emmener (en voiture); (*for a living*) **he ~s a lorry/taxi** il est camionneur/chauffeur de taxi; **he ~s a Peugeot** il a une Peugeot; **he ~s racing cars** il est pilote de course; (*in car*) **to ~ sb back/off etc** ramener/emmener *etc* qn en voiture; **I'll ~ you home** je vais vous ramener (en voiture), je vais vous reconduire chez vous; **she drove me down to the coast** elle m'a conduit *or* emmené (en voiture) jusqu'à la côte; **he drove his car straight at me** il s'est dirigé *or* a dirigé sa voiture droit sur moi; (*esp Brit*) **measures that would ~ a coach and horses through the reforms** des mesures qui sonneraient le glas des réformes

b [+ *people, animals*] chasser *or* pousser (devant soi); (*Hunting*) [+ *game*] rabattre; [+ *clouds*] charrier, chasser; [+ *leaves*] chasser; **to ~ sb out of the country** chasser qn du pays; **the dog drove the sheep into the farm** le chien a fait rentrer les moutons à la ferme; **the gale drove the ship off course** la tempête a fait dériver le navire; **the wind drove the rain against the windows** le vent rabattait la pluie contre les vitres → **corner**

c (= *operate*) [+ *machine*] [*person*] actionner, commander; [*steam etc*] faire fonctionner; **machine driven by electricity** machine fonctionnant à l'électricité

d [+ *nail*] enfoncer; [+ *stake*] enfoncer, ficher; [+ *rivet*] poser; (*Golf, Tennis*) driver; [+ *tunnel*] percer, creuser; [+ *well*] forer, percer; **to ~ a nail home** enfoncer un clou à fond; (*fig*) **to ~ a point home** réussir à faire comprendre un argument; (*fig*) **to ~ sth into sb's head** enfoncer qch dans la tête de qn; **to ~ sth out of sb's head** faire sortir qch de la tête de qn; **to ~ a bargain** conclure un marché; **to ~ a hard bargain with sb** soutirer le maximum à qn; **he ~s a hard bargain** il ne fait pas de cadeau

e (*fig*) **to ~ sb hard** surcharger qn de travail, surmener qn; **to ~ sb mad** rendre qn fou; **to ~ sb potty*** rendre qn dingue*; **to ~ sb to despair** réduire qn au désespoir; **to ~ sb to rebellion** pousser *or* inciter qn à la révolte; **to ~ sb to do** *or* **into doing sth** pousser qn à faire qch; **I was driven to it** j'y ai été poussé malgré moi, j'y ai été contraint → **distraction**

3 VI **a** (= *be the driver*) conduire; (= *go by car*) aller en voiture; **to ~ away/back** *etc* partir/revenir *etc* (en voiture); **she drove down to the shops** elle est allée faire les courses (en voiture); **can you ~?** ◊ **do you ~?** savez-vous conduire?, vous conduisez?; **to ~ at 50km/h** rouler à 50 km/h; **to ~ on the right** rouler à droite; **did you come by train? — no, we drove** êtes-vous venus en train? — non, (nous sommes venus) en voiture; **we have been driving all day** nous avons roulé toute la journée; **she was about to ~ under the bridge** elle s'apprêtait à s'engager sous le pont

b **the rain was driving in our faces** la pluie nous fouettait le visage

4 COMP ► **drive-by shooting** N coups de feu tirés d'une voiture en marche ► **drive-in** ADJ, N drive-in *m inv*; ► **~-in cinema** ciné-parc *m*, drive-in *m inv* ► **drive-through** (*Brit*), **drive-thru** N (= *restaurant*) drive-in *m inv* ♦ ADJ [*restaurant, drugstore*] drive-in ► **drive-time** N (*Rad*) heure *f* de pointe ► **drive-up window** N (*US*) guichet *m* pour automobilistes

►**drive along 1** VI [*vehicle*] rouler, circuler; [*person*] rouler **2** VT SEP [*wind, current*] chasser, pousser

►**drive at** VT FUS (*fig* = *intend, mean*) en venir à,

vouloir dire; **what are you driving at?** où voulez-vous en venir?, que voulez-vous dire?

►**drive away 1** VI [*car*] démarrer; [*person*] s'en aller *or* partir en voiture **2** VT SEP (*lit, fig*) [+ *person, suspicions, cares*] chasser

►**drive back 1** VI [*car*] revenir; [*person*] rentrer en voiture **2** VT SEP **a** (= *cause to retreat*: *Mil etc*) repousser, refouler; **the storm drove him back** la tempête lui a fait rebrousser chemin **b** (= *convey back*) ramener *or* reconduire (en voiture)

►**drive in 1** VI [*car*] entrer; [*person*] entrer (en voiture) **2** VT SEP [+ *nail*] enfoncer; [+ *screw*] visser **3** **~-in** ADJ, N → **drive**

►**drive off 1** VI **a** = **drive away 1 b** (*Golf*) driver **2** VT SEP = **drive away 2 3** VT FUS [+ *ferry*] débarquer de

►**drive on 1** VI [*person, car*] poursuivre sa route; (*after stopping*) reprendre sa route, repartir **2** VT SEP (= *incite, encourage*) pousser (**to** à, **to do, to doing** à faire)

►**drive on to** VT FUS [+ *ferry*] embarquer sur

►**drive out 1** VI [*car*] sortir; [*person*] sortir (en voiture) **2** VT SEP [+ *person*] faire sortir, chasser; [+ *thoughts, desires*] chasser

►**drive over 1** VI venir *or* aller en voiture; **we drove over in two hours** nous avons fait le trajet en deux heures **2** VT SEP (= *convey*) conduire en voiture **3** VT FUS (= *crush*) écraser

►**drive up 1** VI [*car*] arriver; [*person*] arriver (en voiture) **2** VT FUS **the car drove up the road** la voiture a remonté la rue

driveability [ˌdraɪvəˈbɪlɪtɪ] N = **drivability**

drivel* [ˈdrɪvl] **1** N (*NonC*) bêtises *fpl*, imbécillités *fpl*; **what (utter) ~!** quelles bêtises *or* imbécillités! **2** VI radoter; **what's he ~ling (on) about?** qu'est-ce qu'il radote?*

driveline [ˈdraɪvlaɪn] N (*Aut*) transmission *f*

driven [ˈdrɪvn] VB *ptp of* **drive**

-driven [ˈdrɪvn] ADJ (*in compounds*) fonctionnant à; **chauffeur-driven** conduit par un chauffeur; **electricity-driven** fonctionnant à l'électricité; **steam-driven** à vapeur

driver [ˈdraɪvə^r] **1** N **a** [*of car*] conducteur *m*, -trice *f*; [*of taxi, truck, bus*] chauffeur *m*, conducteur *m*, -trice *f*; [*of racing car*] pilote *m*; (*Brit*) [*of train*] mécanicien *m*, conducteur *m*, -trice *f*; [*of cart*] charretier *m*; (*Sport: in horse race etc*) driver *m*; **car ~s** les automobilistes *mpl*; **to be a good ~** bien conduire; **he's a very careful ~** il conduit très prudemment → **back**, **lorry**, **racing** **b** [*of animals*] conducteur *m*, -trice *f* → **slave** **c** (= *golf club*) driver *m* **2** COMP ► **driver education** N (*US Scol*) cours *mpl* de conduite automobile (*dans les lycées*) ► **driver's license** N (*US*) = **driving licence** ► **driver's seat** N = **driving seat**

driveshaft [ˈdraɪvʃɑːft] N (*Aut etc*) arbre *m* de transmission

drivetrain [ˈdraɪvtreɪn] N = **driveline**

driveway [ˈdraɪvweɪ] N = **drive 1b**

driving [ˈdraɪvɪŋ] **1** N conduite *f*; **his ~ is awful** il conduit très mal; **bad ~** conduite *f* imprudente *or* maladroite; **~ is his hobby** conduire est sa distraction favorite

2 ADJ **a** [*necessity*] impérieux, pressant; [*ambition*] sans bornes, démesurée; **the ~ force behind the reforms** le moteur des réformes

b **~ rain** pluie *f* battante

3 COMP ► **driving belt** N courroie *f* de transmission ► **driving instructor** N moniteur *m*, -trice *f* d'auto-école ► **driving lesson** N leçon *f* de conduite ► **driving licence** N (*Brit*) permis *m* de conduire ► **driving mirror** N rétroviseur *m* ► **driving range** N (*Golf*) practice *m* ► **driving school** N auto-école *f* ► **driving seat** N place *f* du conducteur; **to be in the ~ seat** (*lit*) être au volant; (*fig*) être aux commandes, diriger les opérations ► **driving test** N examen *m* du permis de conduire; **to pass one's ~ test** avoir son permis (de conduire); **to fail one's ~ test** rater

son permis (de conduire) ► **driving wheel** N (*Tech*) roue *f* motrice

*En Grande-Bretagne, le permis de conduire (**driving licence**) s'obtient en deux étapes, les apprentis conducteurs n'ayant pendant un certain temps qu'un permis provisoire (« provisional licence »). Le permis ne comporte pas la photographie du titulaire, et il n'est pas obligatoire de l'avoir sur soi (mais il faut pouvoir le présenter au commissariat dans les sept jours qui suivent une interpellation).*

*Aux États-Unis, l'âge d'obtention du permis (**driver's license**) varie suivant les États de quinze à vingt et un ans. Les apprentis conducteurs ou les adolescents peuvent obtenir un permis spécial (« learner's license » ou « junior's license ») qui n'est valable que pour certains trajets précis, celui du lycée par exemple. Le permis de conduire américain sert souvent de carte d'identité et doit être porté par son titulaire. Il doit être renouvelé tous les quatre, cinq ou six ans selon les États.*

drizzle [ˈdrɪzl] **1** N bruine *f*, crachin *m* **2** VI bruiner, pleuviner **3** VT (*Culin*) **~ the salad with oil** ◊ **~ some oil over the salad** verser un filet d'huile sur la salade

drizzly [ˈdrɪzlɪ] ADJ **~ rain** bruine *f*, crachin *m*

droll [drəʊl] ADJ (= *comic*) drôle

dromedary [ˈdrɒmɪdərɪ] N dromadaire *m*

drone [drəʊn] **1** N **a** (= *bee*) abeille *f* mâle, faux-bourdon *m*; (*pej* = *idler*) fainéant(e) *m(f)* **b** (= *sound*) [*of bees*] bourdonnement *m*; [*of engine, aircraft*] ronronnement *m*; (*louder*) vrombissement *m*; (*fig* = *monotonous speech*) débit *m* monotone **c** (*Mus*) bourdon *m* **d** (= *robot plane*) avion *m* téléguidé, drone *m* **2** VI [*bee*] bourdonner; [*engine, aircraft*] ronronner; (*louder*) vrombir; (= *speak monotonously: also* **~ away**, **~ on**) faire de longs discours; **he ~d on about politics** il n'a pas arrêté de parler politique; **he ~d on and on for hours** il a parlé pendant des heures et des heures **3** VT **to ~ a speech** débiter un discours d'un ton monotone

drongo [ˈdrɒŋgəʊ] N **a** (*esp Austral**) crétin(e)* *m(f)* **b** (= *bird*) drongo *m*

drool [druːl] VI (*lit*) baver; (* *fig*) radoter; (*fig*) **to ~ over sth*** baver d'admiration *or* s'extasier devant qch

droop [druːp] **1** VI [*body*] s'affaisser; [*shoulders*] tomber; [*head*] pencher; [*eyelids*] s'abaisser; [*flowers*] commencer à se faner; [*feathers, one's hand*] retomber; **his spirits ~ed** ça l'a déprimé; **the heat made him ~** il était accablé par la chaleur **2** VT [+ *head*] baisser **3** N [*of body*] attitude *f* penchée *or* affaissée; [*of eyelids*] abaissement *m*; [*of spirits*] langueur *f*, abattement *m*

droopy [ˈdruːpɪ] ADJ [*moustache, tail, breasts*] pendant; (*hum* = *tired*) mou (molle *f*)

drop [drɒp] **1** N **a** [*of liquid*] goutte *f*; (*Med*) **~s** gouttes *fpl*; **~ by ~** goutte à goutte; **there's only a ~ left** il n'en reste qu'une goutte; **to fall in ~s** tomber en gouttes; **we haven't had a ~ of rain** nous n'avons pas eu une goutte de pluie; **would you like a whisky? — just a ~!** un petit whisky? — (juste) une goutte *or* une larme!; **he's had a ~ too much*** il a bu un coup de trop* → **nose**, **teardrop**

b (= *pendant*) [*of chandelier*] pendeloque *f*; [*of earring*] pendant *m*, pendeloque *f*; [*of necklace*] pendentif *m*

c (= *fall*) [*of temperature*] baisse *f* (**in** de); [*of prices*] baisse *f*, chute *f* (**in** de); (*Elec*) **~ in voltage** chute *f* de tension → **hat**

d (= *difference in level*) dénivellation *f*, descente *f* brusque; (= *abyss*) précipice *m*; (= *fall*) chute *f*; (= *distance of fall*) hauteur *f* de chute; (*Climbing*) vide *m*; [*of gallows*] trappe *f*; (= *parachute jump*) saut *m* (en parachute); **there's a ~ of 10 metres between the roof and the**

ground il y a (une hauteur de) 10 mètres entre le toit et le sol; **sheer ~** descente f à pic; (US fig) **to have/get the ~ on sb** avoir/prendre l'avantage sur qn

[e] (= delivery) livraison f; (from plane) parachutage m, droppage m; **to make a ~** [gangster] faire une livraison

[f] (= hiding place: for secret letter etc) cachette f

[g] (Theat: also ~ **curtain**) rideau m d'entracte → **backdrop**

[h] (= sweet) → **acid, chocolate**

[2] VT [a] [+ rope, ball, cup etc] (= let fall) laisser tomber; (= release, let go) lâcher; [+ bomb] lancer, larguer; [+ liquid] verser goutte à goutte; [+ one's trousers etc] baisser; [+ price] baisser; (from car) [+ person, thing] déposer; (from boat) [+ cargo, passengers] débarquer; (from car etc) **I'll ~ you here** je vous dépose or laisse ici; **to ~ one's eyes/voice** baisser les yeux/la voix; **to ~ a letter in the postbox** poster une lettre, mettre une lettre à la boîte; **to ~ soldiers/supplies by parachute** parachuter des soldats/du ravitaillement; **to be ~ped** [parachutist] sauter; (Tennis) **he ~ped the ball over the net** il a fait un amorti derrière le filet; (Rugby) **to ~ a goal** marquer un drop; (US fig) **to ~ the ball** ne pas être à la hauteur → **anchor, brick, curtain, curtsy, stitch**

[b] (* = kill) [+ bird] abattre; [+ person] descendre*

[c] (= utter casually) [+ remark, clue] laisser échapper; **to ~ a word in sb's ear** glisser un mot à l'oreille de qn; **he let ~ that he had seen her** (accidentally) il a laissé échapper qu'il l'avait vue; (deliberately) il a fait comprendre qu'il l'avait vue → **hint**

[d] [+ letter, card] envoyer, écrire (**to** à); **to ~ sb a line** écrire un (petit) mot à qn; **~ me a note** écrivez-moi or envoyez-moi un petit mot

[e] (= omit) [+ word, syllable] (spoken) avaler; (written) omettre; **to ~ one's h's or aitches** ne pas prononcer les « h »

[f] (= abandon) [+ habit, idea] renoncer à; [+ work] abandonner; (Scol etc) [+ subject] abandonner, laisser tomber; [+ plan] renoncer à, ne pas donner suite à; [+ discussion, conversation] abandonner; [+ programme, word, scene from play] supprimer; [+ friend, girlfriend, boyfriend] laisser tomber; **to ~ everything** tout laisser tomber; **to ~ sb from a team** écarter qn d'une équipe; **let's ~ the subject** parlons d'autre chose, n'en parlons plus; **~ it!*** laisse tomber !*

[g] (= lose) [+ money] perdre, laisser; (Cards, Tennis etc) [+ game] perdre; **to ~ a set/one's serve** perdre un set/son service

[h] (= give birth to) [animal] mettre bas; (* hum) [person] accoucher; **has she ~ped the sprog yet?*** est-ce qu'elle a déjà eu son gosse ?*

[i] **to ~ acid**: prendre du LSD

[3] VI [a] [object] tomber, retomber; [liquids] tomber goutte à goutte; [person] descendre, se laisser tomber; (= sink to ground) se laisser tomber, tomber; (= collapse) s'effondrer, s'affaisser; **to ~ into sb's arms** tomber dans les bras de qn; **to ~ on one's knees** tomber à genoux; **she ~ped into an armchair** elle s'est effondrée dans un fauteuil; **I'm ready to ~*** je suis claqué*; **~ dead!**: va te faire voir !*, va te faire foutre!*; **to ~ on sb (like a ton of bricks)*** secouer les puces à qn* → **curtain, fly¹, penny, pin**

[b] (= decrease) [wind] se calmer, tomber; [temperature, voice] baisser; [price] baisser, diminuer

[c] (= end) [conversation, correspondence] en rester là, cesser; **there the matter ~ped** l'affaire en est restée là; **let it ~!*** laisse tomber!*

[4] COMP ► **drop-add** N (US Univ etc) remplacement m d'un cours par un autre ► **drop cloth** N (US) bâche f de protection ► **drop-dead**: ADV vachement*; (Brit) **~-dead**

gorgeous* super* beau (belle f) ► **drop-forge** N marteau-pilon m ► **drop goal** N (Rugby) drop m; **to score a ~ goal** passer un drop ► **drop hammer** N = **drop-forge** ► **drop handlebars** NPL guidon m de course ► **drop-in centre** N (Brit) centre m d'accueil (où l'on peut se rendre sans prendre rendez-vous) ► **drop kick** N coup m de pied tombé, drop m ► **drop-leaf table** N table f à abattants ► **drop-off** N (in sales, interest etc) diminution f (**in** de) ► **drop-out** N (Rugby) renvoi m aux 22 mètres → **dropout** ► **dropping out** N (Univ etc) abandon m ► **drop shipment** N (Comm) drop shipment m ► **drop shot** N (Tennis) amorti m ► **drop tag** VT (US) démarquer ► **drop zone** N (Aviat) zone f de droppage

► **drop across*** VI **we ~ped across to see him** nous sommes passés or allés le voir; **he ~ped across to see us** il est passé or venu nous voir

► **drop away** VI [numbers, attendance] diminuer

► **drop back, drop behind** VI rester en arrière, se laisser devancer or distancer; (in work etc) prendre du retard

► **drop by** VI **to ~ by somewhere/on sb** faire un saut* or passer quelque part/chez qn; **we'll ~ by if we're in town** nous passerons si nous sommes en ville

► **drop down** VI tomber

► **drop in** VI **to ~ in on sb** passer voir qn, faire un saut* chez qn; **to ~ in at the grocer's** passer or faire un saut chez l'épicier; **do ~ in if you're in town** passez me voir (or nous voir) si vous êtes en ville

► **drop off** [1] VI [a] (= fall asleep) s'endormir [b] [leaves] tomber; [sales, interest] diminuer [c] (* = alight) descendre [2] VT SEP (= set down from car etc) [+ person, parcel] déposer, laisser [3] ~-off N → **drop**

► **drop out** [1] VI [contents etc] tomber; (fig) se retirer, renoncer; (from college etc) abandonner ses études; **to ~ out of a competition** se retirer d'une compétition, abandonner une compétition; **to ~ out of circulation** or **out of sight** disparaître de la circulation; **to ~ out (of society)** vivre en marge de la société, se marginaliser [2] ~**out** N → **dropout**

► **drop round*** VI **we ~ drop across** [2] VT SEP déposer chez moi (or toi etc)

droplet ['drɒplɪt] N gouttelette f

dropout ['drɒpaʊt] [1] N (from society) dropout mf, marginal(e) m(f); (from college etc) étudiant(e) m(f) qui abandonne ses études [2] ADJ **the ~ rate** le taux d'abandon

dropper ['drɒpə'] N (Pharm) compte-gouttes m inv

droppings ['drɒpɪŋz] NPL [of bird] fiente f; [of animal] crottes fpl; [of fly] chiures fpl, crottes fpl

dropsical ['drɒpsɪkəl] ADJ hydropique

dropsy ['drɒpsɪ] N hydropisie f

drosophila [drɒ'sɒfɪlə] N (pl **drosophilas** or **drosophilae** [drɒ'sɒfɪ,liː]) drosophile f

dross [drɒs] N (NonC) (Metal) scories fpl, crasse f, laitier m; (= coal) menu m (de houille or de coke), poussier m; (= refuse) impuretés fpl, déchets mpl; (fig = sth worthless) **the film was total ~*** ce film était complètement nul

drought [draʊt] N sécheresse f

drove [drəʊv] [1] VB pt of **drive** [2] N [a] [of animals] troupeau m en marche; **~s of people** des foules fpl de gens; **they came in ~s** ils arrivèrent en foule [b] (= channel) canal m or rigole f d'irrigation

drover ['drəʊvə'] N toucheur m or conducteur m de bestiaux

drown [draʊn] [1] VI se noyer [2] VT [a] [+ person, animal] noyer; [+ land] inonder, submerger; **because he couldn't swim he was ~ed** il s'est noyé parce qu'il ne savait pas nager; **he's like or he looks like a ~ed rat*** il est

trempé jusqu'aux os or comme une soupe; **to ~ one's sorrows** noyer son chagrin; (of whisky etc) **don't ~ it!*** n'y mets pas trop d'eau !, ne le noie pas!; **they were ~ed with offers of help*** ils ont été inondés or submergés d'offres d'assistance [b] = **drown out**

► **drown out** VT SEP [+ voice, sound, words] couvrir, étouffer

drowning ['draʊnɪŋ] [1] ADJ qui se noie ■ (PROV) **a ~ man will clutch at a straw** un homme qui se noie se raccroche à un fétu de paille [2] N [a] (= death) noyade f; **there were three ~s here last year** trois personnes se sont noyées ici or il y a eu trois noyades ici l'année dernière [b] [of noise, voice] étouffement m

drowse [draʊz] VI être à moitié endormi or assoupi, somnoler; **to ~ off** s'assoupir

drowsily ['draʊzɪlɪ] ADV [speak] d'une voix endormie; **~, she set the alarm clock and went to bed** à moitié endormie, elle mit le réveil et alla se coucher

drowsiness ['draʊzɪnɪs] N somnolence f, engourdissement m

drowsy ['draʊzɪ] ADJ [a] (= half-asleep) [person, smile, look] somnolent; [voice] ensommeillé; **he was still very ~** il était encore à moitié endormi; **these tablets will make you ~** ces comprimés vous donneront envie de dormir; **~ with sleep** tout ensommeillé; **to grow ~** s'assoupir; **to feel ~** avoir envie de dormir [b] (= soporific) [afternoon, atmosphere] soporifique; [countryside, stillness] assoupi

drub* [drʌb] VT (= thrash) rosser*, rouer de coups; (= abuse) injurier, traiter de tous les noms; (= defeat) battre à plate(s) couture(s); (fig) **to ~ an idea into sb** enfoncer une idée dans la tête de qn; (fig) **to ~ an idea out of sb** faire sortir une idée de la tête de qn

drubbing* ['drʌbɪŋ] N (= thrashing, defeat) raclée* f; **they suffered a 5-0 ~** ils ont été battus à plate(s) couture(s) 5 à 0; (lit, fig) **to give sb a ~** donner une belle raclée* à qn; (fig) **to take a ~** être battu à plate(s) couture(s)

drudge [drʌdʒ] [1] N bête f de somme (fig); **the household ~** la bonne à tout faire [2] VI trimer*, peiner

drudgery ['drʌdʒərɪ] N (NonC) corvée f, travail m pénible et ingrat; **it's sheer ~!** c'est une vraie corvée!

drug [drʌg] [1] N drogue f; (Med, Pharm) médicament m; (Police, Jur) stupéfiant m; **he's on ~s ◊ he's taking ~s** (illegal) il se drogue; (Med) il est sous médication (for contre); **to do ~s*** se droguer; **to push ~s** revendre de la drogue; (fig) **a ~ on the market** un article or une marchandise invendable; **television is a ~** la télévision est une drogue → **hard, soft**

[2] VT [+ person] droguer (also Med); [+ food, wine etc] mettre une drogue dans; **his wine had been ~ged with sleeping tablets** on avait mis des somnifères dans son vin; **to be in a ~ged sleep** dormir sous l'effet d'une drogue; (fig) **to be ~ged with sleep/from lack of sleep** être abruti de sommeil/par le manque de sommeil

[3] COMP ► **drug abuse** N usage m de stupéfiants ► **drug abuser** N drogué(e) m(f) ► **drug addict** N drogué(e) m(f), toxicomane mf ► **drug addiction** N toxicomanie f ► **drug company** N compagnie f pharmaceutique; **the ~ companies** l'industrie f pharmaceutique ► **drug czar** N responsable mf de la lutte contre la drogue, Monsieur anti-drogue ► **drug dealer** N revendeur m, -euse f de drogue ► **drug dependency** N pharmacodépendance f ► **drug habit** N **to have a ~ habit** se droguer ► **drug peddler, drug pusher** N revendeur m, -euse f de drogue, dealer* m ► **drug raid** N (US) = **drugs raid** ► **drug runner** N trafiquant(e) m(f) (de drogue) ► **drug-running** N = **drug traffic** ► **drugs czar** N = **drug czar** ► **Drug Squad** N (Police) brigade f des stupéfiants ► **drugs**

raid N (*Brit*) opération *f* antidrogue ► **drugs ring** N réseau *m* de trafiquants de drogue ► **Drugs Squad** N = **Drug Squad** ► **drugs test** N contrôle *m* antidopage ► **drugs tsar** N = **drug czar** ► **drug-taker** N = **drug user** ► **drug-taking** N usage *m* de drogue(s) or de stupéfiants ► **drug test** N = **drugs test** ► **drug traffic(king)** N trafic *m* de drogue ► **drug tsar** N = **drug czar** ► **drug user** N usager *m* de drogue

drugged [drʌgd] ADJ [*person, food, drink*] drogué; [*sleep*] provoqué par une drogue

druggist ['drʌgɪst] N [a] pharmacien(ne) *m(f)*; **~'s** pharmacie *f* [b] (*US*) gérant(e) *m(f)* de drugstore

druggy* ['drʌgɪ] [1] N camé(e)‡ *m(f)*, drogué(e) *m(f)* [2] ADJ [*person*] qui se drogue, qui se camé‡; [*music*] de camé‡

drugster ['drʌgstər] N = **druggy 1**

drugstore ['drʌgstɔːr] [1] N (*US*) drugstore *m* [2] COMP ► **drugstore cowboy*** N (*US fig*) glandeur‡ *m*, traîne-savates* *m*

druid ['druːɪd] N druide *m*

druidic [druːˈɪdɪk] ADJ druidique

druidism ['druːɪdɪzəm] N druidisme *m*

drum [drʌm] [1] N [a] (*Mus = instrument, player*) tambour *m*; **the big ~** la grosse caisse; (*Mil Mus, Jazz, Rock*) **the ~s** la batterie; **to beat the ~** battre le or du tambour; (*fig*) **to beat** or **bang the ~ for sb/sth** prendre fait et cause pour qn/qch → **kettledrum, tight** [b] (*for oil*) bidon *m*; (*for tar*) gonne *f*; (= *cylinder for wire etc*) tambour *m*; (= *machine part*) tambour *m*; (*Aut: also* **brake ~**) tambour *m* (de frein); (*Comput*) tambour *m* magnétique; (= *box: of figs, sweets*) caisse *f* [c] (= *sound*) = **drumming** [d] = **eardrum**

[2] VI (*Mus*) battre le or du tambour; [*person, fingers*] tambouriner, pianoter (**with** de, avec, **on** sur); [*insect etc*] bourdonner; **the noise was ~ming in my ears** le bruit bourdonnait à mes oreilles; **rain ~med on the roof of the car** la pluie tambourinait sur le toit de la voiture

[3] VT [+ *tune*] tambouriner; **to ~ one's fingers on the table** tambouriner or pianoter des doigts or avec les doigts sur la table; **to ~ one's feet on the floor** taper des pieds; (*fig*) **to ~ sth into sb** seriner qch à qn; **I had tidiness ~med into me** on m'a seriné qu'il fallait être ordonné

[4] COMP ► **drum brake** N (*Aut*) frein *m* à tambour ► **drum kit** N batterie *f* ► **drum machine** N boîte *f* à rythme ► **drum major** N (*Brit Mil*) tambour-major *m*; (*US*) chef *m* des tambours ► **drum majorette** N (*US*) majorette *f* ► **drum roll** N roulement *m* de tambour ► **drum set** N = **drum kit**

► **drum out** VT SEP (*Mil, fig*) expulser (à grand bruit) (**of** de)

► **drum up** VT SEP (*fig*) [+ *enthusiasm, support*] susciter; [+ *support*] rassembler, battre le rappel de; [+ *customers*] racoler, attirer; **to ~ up business** attirer la clientèle

drumbeat ['drʌmbiːt] N battement *m* de tambour

drumfire ['drʌmfaɪər] N (*Mil*) tir *m* de barrage, feu *m* roulant

drumhead ['drʌmhed] [1] N (*Mus*) peau *f* de tambour [2] COMP ► **drumhead court-martial** N (*Mil*) conseil *m* de guerre prévôtal ► **drumhead service** N (*Mil*) office *m* religieux en plein air

drumlin ['drʌmlɪn] N drumlin *m*

drummer ['drʌmər] [1] N [a] (joueur *m* de) tambour *m*; (*Jazz, Rock*) batteur *m*; (*fig*) **to march to** or **hear a different ~** marcher en dehors des sentiers battus [b] (*US Comm**) commis *m* voyageur [2] COMP ► **drummer boy** N petit tambour *m*

drumming ['drʌmɪŋ] N [*of drum*] bruit *m* du tambour; [*of insect*] bourdonnement *m*; (*in*

the ears) bourdonnement *m*; [*of fingers*] tapotement *m*, tambourinage *m*

drumstick ['drʌmstɪk] N [a] (*Mus*) baguette *f* de tambour [b] [*of chicken, turkey*] pilon *m*

drunk [drʌŋk] [1] VB *ptp of* **drink** [2] ADJ [a] (*lit*) ivre, soûl*; **he was ~ on champagne** il s'était soûlé au champagne; **to get ~ (on champagne)** se soûler* (au champagne); **to get sb ~ (on champagne)** soûler* qn (au champagne); **as ~ as a lord*** (*Brit*) ◊ **as ~ as a skunk*** (*US*) soûl comme une grive* or un Polonais*; (*Jur*) **~ and disorderly** ≈ en état d'ivresse publique; **to be ~ in charge** (*of vehicle*) conduire en état d'ébriété or d'ivresse; (*at work*) être en état d'ébriété dans l'exercice de ses fonctions → **blind, dead** [b] (*fig, liter*) **~ with** or **on success/power** enivré or grisé par le succès/pouvoir [3] N* ivrogne *mf*; (*on one occasion*) homme *m* or femme *f* soûl(e)* [4] COMP ► **drunk driver** N conducteur *m*, -trice *f* en état d'ébriété or d'ivresse ► **drunk driving** N (*esp US*) conduite *f* en état d'ébriété or d'ivresse

drunkard ['drʌŋkəd] N ivrogne *mf*

drunken ['drʌŋkən] [1] ADJ [a] [*person*] (= *habitually*) ivrogne; (= *on one occasion*) ivre; **a ~ old man** (= *old drunk*) un vieil ivrogne; **her ~ father** son ivrogne de père [b] [*party*] très arrosé; [*quarrel, brawl*] d'ivrogne(s); [*night, evening*] d'ivresse; [*voice*] aviné; [*state*] d'ivresse, d'ébriété; [*violence*] dû à l'ivresse; **a ~ orgy** une beuverie; **in a ~ rage** or **fury** dans un état de fureur dû à l'alcool; **in a ~ stupor** dans une stupeur éthylique [c] (*fig = crooked*) **at a ~ angle** de travers [2] COMP ► **drunken driving** N conduite *f* en état d'ébriété or d'ivresse

drunkenly ['drʌŋkənlɪ] ADV [a] (= *while drunk*) [*speak, say, sing*] d'une voix avinée [b] (*fig = unsteadily*) [*stumble, stagger*] comme un ivrogne; [*walk*] en titubant comme un ivrogne; [*lean*] de travers; **the boat lurched ~** le bateau tanguait dangereusement

drunkenness ['drʌŋkənnɪs] N (= *state*) ivresse *f*, ébriété *f*; (= *problem, habit*) ivrognerie *f*

drunkometer [drʌŋˈkɒmɪtər] N (*US*) alcootest® *m*

druthers‡ ['drʌðəz] N (*US*) **if I had my ~** s'il ne tenait qu'à moi

dry [draɪ] [1] ADJ [a] [*object, clothes, ground, air, wind, heat, burn*] sec (sèche *f*); **wait till the glue is ~** attendez que la colle sèche; **her throat/mouth was ~** elle avait la gorge/la bouche sèche; **his mouth was ~ with fear** la peur lui desséchait la bouche; (*lit, fig*) **her eyes were ~** elle avait les yeux secs; (*Theat, Cine etc*) **there wasn't a ~ eye in the house** toute la salle était en larmes; **for ~ skin/hair** pour les peaux sèches/cheveux secs; **on ~ land** sur la terre ferme; **to wipe sth ~** essuyer qch; **to keep sth ~** tenir qch au sec; (*on label*) **"keep in a ~ place"** «tenir au sec»; **as ~ as a bone** complètement sec → **high, powder** [b] (= *dried-up*) [*riverbed, lake, well*] à sec; [*spring, river, valley*] sec (sèche *f*); [*oasis*] tari; [*cow*] qui ne donne plus de lait; **to run ~** [*river, well*] tarir, s'assécher; [*resources*] s'épuiser; **her breasts were ~** ses seins ne donnaient plus de lait [c] (= *not rainy*) [*climate, weather, country, period*] sec (sèche *f*); [*day*] sans pluie; **a ~ spell** une période sèche or de sécheresse; **the ~ season** la saison sèche; **it was ~ and warm** le temps était sec et chaud → **2** [d] (= *without butter etc*) **a piece of ~ toast** une tranche de pain grillé sans beurre [e] [*wine, sherry, vermouth, Madeira*] sec (sèche *f*); [*champagne, cider*] brut; **a ~ sherry/white wine** un xérès/vin blanc sec [f] (* *fig*) [*country, state*] où l'alcool est prohibé; **due to a storm, the island was ~ for a week** à cause d'une tempête, l'île n'a pu être ravitaillée en alcool pendant une semaine; (= *thirsty*) **to be** or **feel ~*** avoir le gosier sec* or la

bouche sèche [g] [*humour, wit, person*] pince-sans-rire *inv*; **he has a ~ sense of humour** il est pince-sans-rire, c'est un pince-sans-rire [h] (= *not lively*) [*book, subject, speech, lecture*] aride; **as ~ as dust** ennuyeux comme la pluie [i] (= *harsh*) [*sound, voice, cough*] sec (sèche *f*); **it broke with a ~ snapping sound** ça s'est cassé avec un bruit sec [j] (= *cold, unemotional*) [*voice, manner*] flegmatique [k] (*Brit Pol: hum*) pur et dur; **a ~ Tory** un ultraconservateur, une ultraconservatrice

[2] N [a] (*esp Brit*) **at least you're in the warm and the ~** au moins vous êtes au chaud et au sec [b] (*Brit Pol: hum*) ultraconservateur *m*, -trice *f*

[3] VT [+ *paper, fruit, skin*] sécher; (*with cloth*) essuyer, sécher; [+ *clothes*] (faire) sécher; (*on label*) **"~ away from direct heat"** «ne pas sécher près d'une source de chaleur»; **to ~ one's eyes** or **one's tears** sécher ses larmes or ses pleurs; **to ~ the dishes** essuyer la vaisselle; **to ~ o.s.** s'essuyer, se sécher

[4] VI sécher; (*esp Brit**) [*actor, speaker*] sécher*

[5] COMP ► **dry-as-dust** ADJ aride, sec (sèche *f*) ► **dry-bulk cargo ship** N vraquier *m* ► **dry cell** N (*Elec*) pile *f* sèche ► **dry-clean** VT nettoyer à sec; (*on label*) **"~-clean only"** «nettoyage à sec» ► **to have a dress ~-cleaned** donner une robe à nettoyer or au pressing ► **dry-cleaner** N teinturier *m*; **to take a coat to the ~-cleaner's** porter un manteau au pressing ► **dry-cleaning** N nettoyage *m* à sec, pressing *m* ► **dry dock** N (*Naut*) cale *f* sèche, bassin *m* or cale *f* de radoub ► **dry-eyed** ADJ (*lit, fig*) qui a les yeux secs ► **dry farming** N (*Agr*) culture *f* sèche, dry farming *m* ► **dry fly** N (*Fishing*) mouche *f* sèche ► **dry ginger** N ≈ Canada dry® *m* ► **dry goods** NPL (*Comm*) tissus *mpl* et articles *mpl* de mercerie ► **dry goods store** N (*US Comm*) magasin *m* de tissus et d'articles de mercerie ► **dry ice** N neige *f* carbonique ► **dry measure** N mesure *f* de capacité pour matières sèches ► **dry-roasted** ADJ [*peanuts*] grillé à sec ► **dry rot** N pourriture *f* sèche (*du bois*) ► **dry run** (*fig*) N (= *trial, test*) galop *m* d'essai; (= *rehearsal*) répétition *f* ♦ **dry shampoo** N shampooing *m* sec ► **dry-shod** ADV à pied sec ► **dry ski slope** N piste *f* (de ski) artificielle ► **dry-stone wall** N mur *m* de pierres sèches

► **dry off** VI, VT SEP sécher

► **dry out** [1] VI [a] (= *dry off*) sécher [b]* [*alcoholic*] se faire désintoxiquer, suivre une cure de désintoxication [2] VT SEP* [+ *alcoholic*] désintoxiquer

► **dry up** VI [a] [*stream, well*] se dessécher, (se) tarir; [*moisture*] s'évaporer; [*clay*] sécher; [*cow*] ne plus donner de lait; [*source of supply, inspiration*] se tarir [b] (= *dry the dishes*) essuyer la vaisselle [c] (* = *fall silent*) se taire; [*actor, speaker, writer*] sécher*; **~ up!** tais-toi!, boucle-la!‡

dryer ['draɪər] N [a] (= *apparatus*) (*Tech*) séchoir *m*; (*for hands*) sèche-mains *m inv*; (*for clothes*) sèche-linge *m inv*; (*for hair*) sèche-cheveux *m inv* → **spin, tumble** [b] (*for paint*) siccatif *m*

drying ['draɪɪŋ] [1] N [*of fruit, crop, wood, clothes*] séchage *m*; (*with a cloth*) essuyage *m* [2] COMP ► **drying cupboard, drying room** N séchoir *m* ► **drying-up** N to do the **~-up** essuyer la vaisselle ► **drying-up cloth** N torchon *m*

dryly ['draɪlɪ] ADV = **drily**

dryness ['draɪnɪs] N [*of soil, weather*] sécheresse *f*, aridité *f*; [*of clothes, skin*] sécheresse *f*; [*of wit, humour, humorist*] style *m* pince-sans-rire *inv*

drysalter ['draɪsɔːltər] N (*Brit*) marchand *m* de couleurs

DS [di:es] N (*Brit: Police*) (ABBR = **Detective Sergeant**) → **detective**

DSC [ˌdi:es'si:] N (ABBR = **Distinguished Service Cross**) *médaille militaire*

DSc [ˌdi:es'si:] N (*Univ*) (ABBR = **Doctor of Science**) *doctorat ès sciences*

DSM [ˌdi:es'em] N (ABBR = **Distinguished Service Medal**) *médaille militaire*

DSO [ˌdi:es'əʊ] N (*Brit*) (ABBR = **Distinguished Service Order**) *médaille militaire*

DSS [ˌdi:es'es] N (*Brit*) (ABBR = **Department of Social Security**) → **department**

DSS

En Grande-Bretagne, le DSS (Department of Social Security) est l'administration des affaires sociales. Cette administration comprend plusieurs services : la « Benefit Agency », qui verse les prestations sociales aux ayants-droit, la « Contributions Agency », qui perçoit les cotisations sociales et la « Child Support Agency » qui gère les pensions alimentaires versées par les parents divorcés ou séparés. → NATIONAL INSURANCE

DST [ˌdi:es'ti:] (*US*) (ABBR = **Daylight Saving Time**) → **daylight**

DT (*Comput*) (ABBR = **data transmission**) → **data**

DTI [ˌdi:ti:'aɪ] N (*Brit Admin*) (ABBR = **Department of Trade and Industry**) → **trade**

DTP [ˌdi:ti:'pi:] N (ABBR = **desktop publishing**) PAO *f*

DT's [ˌdi:'ti:z] NPL (ABBR = **delirium tremens**) delirium tremens *m*

dual ['djʊəl] **1** ADJ [*role, function, strategy, income*] double (*before n*) **2** N (*Gram*) duel *m* **3** COMP ▶ **dual admissions** NPL (*US Univ etc*) double système *m* d'inscriptions (*avec sélection moins stricte pour étudiants défavorisés*) ▶ **dual carriageway** N (*Brit*) (route *f* à) quatre voies *f inv* → ROADS ▶ **dual-control** ADJ à double commande ▶ **dual controls** NPL (*Aut, Aviat*) double commande *f* ▶ **dual national** N personne *f* ayant la double nationalité, binational(e) *m(f)* ▶ **dual nationality** N double nationalité *f* ▶ **dual ownership** N copropriété *f* ▶ **dual personality** N dédoublement *m* de la personnalité ▶ **dual-purpose** ADJ à double usage

dualism ['djʊəlɪzəm] N (*Philos, Pol, Rel*) dualisme *m*

dualist ['djʊəlɪst] ADJ, N (*Philos*) dualiste *mf*

duality [djʊ'ælɪtɪ] N dualité *f*, dualisme *m*

dub [dʌb] VT **a** **to ~ sb a knight** donner l'accolade à qn ; (*Hist*) adouber *or* armer qn chevalier ; (= *nickname*) **to ~ sb "Ginger"** surnommer qn « Poil de Carotte » **b** (*Cine*) doubler, postsynchroniser

Dubai [du:'baɪ] N Dubaï *m*

dubbin ['dʌbɪn] N dégras *m*, graisse *f* pour les chaussures

dubbing ['dʌbɪŋ] N (*Cine*) doublage *m*, postsynchronisation *f*

dubiety [djʊ'baɪətɪ] N doute *m*, incertitude *f*

dubious ['dju:bɪəs] ADJ **a** (= *suspect*) [*deal, claim, reputation, quality, origin, morality*] douteux ; [*privilege, pleasure*] discutable ; **these measures are of ~ benefit** les avantages de ces mesures sont discutables **b** (= *unsure*) **to be ~ about sth** se montrer dubitatif quant à qch, douter de qch ; **I was ~ at first** au début, j'avais des doutes ; **I am ~ that** *or* **whether the new law will achieve anything** je doute que cette nouvelle loi serve (*subj*) à quelque chose ; **to look/sound ~** avoir l'air/parler d'un ton dubitatif

dubiously ['dju:bɪəslɪ] ADV [*look at, smile, frown*] d'un air dubitatif ; [*say*] d'un ton dubitatif ; **a piece ~ attributed to Albinoni** un morceau attribué de façon douteuse à Albinoni

Dublin ['dʌblɪn] **1** N Dublin **2** COMP ▶ **Dublin Bay prawn** N langoustine *f*

Dubliner ['dʌblɪnər] N habitant(e) *m(f)* *or* natif *m*, -ive *f* de Dublin

ducal ['dju:kəl] ADJ ducal, de duc

ducat ['dʌkət] N ducat *m*

duchess ['dʌtʃɪs] N duchesse *f*

duchy ['dʌtʃɪ] N duché *m*

duck¹ [dʌk] **1** N (*pl* **ducks** *or* **duck**) **a** canard *m* ; (*female*) cane *f* ; **wild ~** canard *m* sauvage ; (*Culin*) **roast ~** canard *m* rôti ; (*Brit*) **to play ~s and drakes** faire des ricochets (sur l'eau) ; (*Brit*) **to play ~s and drakes with sb** (= *treat badly*) traiter qn par-dessus la jambe ; (*Brit*) **to play at ~s and drakes with one's money** jeter son argent par les fenêtres, gaspiller son argent ; (*US*) **to get one's ~s in a row*** maîtriser la situation ; **he took to it like a ~ to water** c'était comme s'il avait fait ça toute sa vie ; (*Brit*) **yes ~s*** oui mon chou* ; **he's a ~*** c'est un chou* *or* un amour → **Bombay, dying, lame**
b (*Brit Cricket*) **to make a ~** ◊ *or* **to be out for a ~** faire un score nul
c (*St Ex*) spéculateur *m*, -trice *f* insolvable
d (*Mil* = *vehicle*) véhicule *m* amphibie
2 VI **a** (*also ~ down*) se baisser vivement ; (*in fight etc*) esquiver un coup ; **to ~ (down) under the water** disparaître sous l'eau
b **he ~ed into his office** (= *popped in*) il est passé au bureau ; (*to hide*) il s'est réfugié dans son bureau ; **he ~ed out of the rain** il s'est vite mis à l'abri de la pluie
3 VT **a** **to ~ sb** pousser qn sous l'eau
b [+ *one's head*] baisser vivement ; [+ *blow, question etc*] éviter, esquiver ; [+ *responsibility*] se dérober à ; [+ *decision*] éluder
4 COMP ▶ **duck-billed platypus** N ornithorynque *m* ▶ **duck-egg blue** ADJ gris-bleu *inv* ▶ **duck pond** N mare *f* aux canards ; (*Brit*) **duck shooting** N chasse *f* au canard ▶ **duck soup*** N (*US fig*) **that was ~ soup!** c'était du gâteau !*

▶ **duck out of** VT FUS esquiver ; **she ~ed out of going with them** elle s'est esquivée pour ne pas les accompagner ; **he ~ed out of the commitment he'd made** il s'est dérobé à ses engagements

duck² [dʌk] N (*Tex*) coutil *m*, toile *f* fine ; (*Brit*) **~s** pantalon *m* de coutil

duckbill ['dʌkbɪl] N = **duck-billed platypus**; → **duck**

duckboard ['dʌkbɔ:d] N caillebotis *m*

duckie* ['dʌkɪ] **1** N (*Brit*) **yes ~** oui mon chou* **2** ADJ (*US*) = **ducky**

ducking ['dʌkɪŋ] N plongeon *m*, bain *m* forcé ; **to give sb a ~** (= *push under water*) pousser qn sous l'eau ; (= *push into water*) pousser qn dans l'eau ; **~ and diving** dérobades *fpl*

duckling ['dʌklɪŋ] N (*also Culin*) caneton *m* ; (*female*) canette *f* ; (*older*) canardeau *m*

duckweed ['dʌkwi:d] N lentille *f* d'eau, lenticule *f*

ducky* ['dʌkɪ] ADJ (*US* = *cute*) mignon tout plein

duct [dʌkt] N (*for liquid, gas, electricity*) conduite *f*, canalisation *f* ; (*Bot*) trachée *f* ; (*Anat*) canal *m*, conduit *m*

ductile ['dʌktaɪl] ADJ [*metal*] ductile ; [*person*] docile

ductless gland [ˌdʌktlɪs'glænd] N glande *f* endocrine

dud* [dʌd] **1** ADJ (= *defective*) [*shell, bomb, battery, fuse etc*] qui foire* ; (= *worthless*) [*cheque*] en bois* ; [*loan*] non remboursé ; [*film, teacher, student*] nul (nulle *f*) ; (= *counterfeit*) [*note, coin*] faux (fausse *f*) **2** N (= *shell*) obus *m* non éclaté ; (= *bomb*) bombe *f* non éclatée ; (= *person*) raté(e) *m(f)* ; **this coin is a ~** cette pièce est fausse ; **this watch is a ~** c'est de la camelote* cette montre ; **Phil was a complete**

~ at school Phil était complètement nul à l'école ; **to be a ~ at geography** être nul en géographie ; **to be a ~ at tennis** être nul au tennis **3** **duds** †‡ NPL (= *clothes*) nippes† * *fpl*

dude* [d(j)u:d] (*US*) **1** N **a** (= *man*) type* *m*, mec* *m* **b** (= *dandy*) dandy *m* ; (*young*) gommeux* *m* **c** (= *Easterner*) habitant(e) *m(f)* de la côte Est **2** COMP ▶ **dude ranch** N (hôtel *m*) ranch *m*

DUDE RANCH

Sorte de ranch, authentique ou reconstitué, où les touristes peuvent goûter les joies du Far West. Les amateurs viennent y retrouver la vie du cow-boy : monter à cheval, s'occuper du bétail et dîner autour d'un feu de camp. En argot, un dude est un citadin, ou un habitant de la côte Est trop soigné et trop bien habillé.

dudgeon † ['dʌdʒən] N **in (high) ~** offensé dans sa dignité, furieux

▼ **due** [dju:] **1** ADJ **a** (= *expected, scheduled*) **the train is ~ (to arrive) at 2.19** le train doit arriver à 14 h 19 ; **the plane was ~ (to land) two hours ago** l'avion devait atterrir il y a deux heures ; **to be ~ in** [*train, ferry, plane*] devoir arriver ; **to be ~ out** [*magazine, record, film etc*] devoir sortir ; **I am ~ there tomorrow** je dois être là-bas demain ; **when is the baby ~?** quand doit naître le bébé ? ; **the results are ~ next week** les résultats doivent être rendus la semaine prochaine ; **there's an election ~ in March** des élections sont prévues en mars ; **he's ~ back tomorrow** il doit être de retour demain
b (= *payable*) [*sum, money*] dû (due *f*) ; **when is the rent ~?** quand faut-il payer le loyer ? ; **to fall ~** arriver à échéance ; **the sum ~ to me** la somme qui m'est due *or* qui me revient
c (= *owed, expecting*) **I am ~ £300/six days' holiday** on me doit 300 livres/six jours de congé ; **she is ~ (for) promotion/a rise** (= *will get one*) elle doit être promue/augmentée ; (= *ought to get one*) elle devrait être promue/augmentée ; **to be ~ for completion/demolition/release in 1999** devoir être terminé/démoli/libéré en 1999 ; **I feel I'm about ~ a holiday!** je pense que je mérite bien des vacances ! ; **our thanks are ~ to Mr Bertillon** nous tenons à remercier M. Bertillon, notre gratitude va à M. Bertillon ; **they must be treated with the respect ~ to their rank/age** ils doivent être traités avec le respect dû à leur rang/âge
d (= *proper, suitable*) **to give** *or* **pay ~ attention to sb** prêter à qn l'attention qu'il mérite ; **to receive ~ credit (for sth)** être reconnu comme il se doit (pour qch) ; **after ~ consideration** après mûre réflexion ; **to have ~ regard to** *or* **for sth** respecter pleinement qch ; **with/without ~ regard to** *or* **for sth** en tenant pleinement compte/sans tenir pleinement compte de qch ; **in ~ course** *or* **time** (= *when the time is ripe*) en temps utile *or* voulu ; (= *in the long run*) à la longue ; **in ~ course, she found out that ...** elle finit par découvrir que ... ; **with (all) ~ respect** sauf votre respect ; **with (all) ~ respect to Mrs Harrison** malgré tout le respect que je dois à Mme Harrison ; (*Jur*) **driving without ~ care and attention** conduite *f* imprudente → **credit**
e **~ to** dû (due *f*) à, attribuable à ; **it is ~ to his ineptitude that ...** c'est à cause de son incompétence que ... ; **the accident was ~ to a drunken driver** l'accident a été provoqué par un conducteur en état d'ivresse ; **the accident was ~ to the icy road** l'accident était dû au verglas ; **it is ~ to you that he is alive today** c'est grâce à vous qu'il est en vie aujourd'hui ; **what's it ~ to?** à quoi est-ce dû ?
2 ADV ▶ **north/south** *etc* plein nord/sud *etc* (**of** par rapport à) ; **to face ~ north** [*building*] être (en) plein nord ; [*person*] faire face au nord

---
▶ LANGUAGE IN USE: **due** 20.6, 26.3
---

3 N a **to give sb his ~** être juste envers qn, faire or rendre justice à qn; **(to) give him his ~, he did try hard** il faut (être juste et) reconnaître qu'il a quand même fait tout son possible → **devil**

4 **dues** NPL (= *fees*) [*of club etc*] cotisation *f*; [*of harbour*] droits *mpl* (de port)

5 COMP ► **due process** N (*Jur: also* ~ **process of law**) application de la loi selon les procédures prévues

duel ['djʊəl] 1 N (*lit, fig*) duel *m*; **~ to the death** duel *m* à mort → **challenge, fight** 2 VI se battre en duel (**with** contre, avec) 3 COMP ► **duelling pistol** N pistolet *m* de duel

duellist ['djʊəlɪst] N duelliste *m*

duet [dju:'et] 1 N = duo *m*; **to sing/play a ~** chanter/jouer en duo, **violin** ~ duo *m* de violon; **piano** ~ morceau *m* à quatre mains

duff[1] [dʌf] N (*Culin*) pudding *m*; **up the ~**: en cloque: → **plum**

duff[2] [dʌf] (*Brit*) 1 ADJ a (= *non-functional*) [*machine, watch, gene etc*] détraqué* b (= *useless*) [*suggestion, idea, film, book, record*] nul (nulle *f*) c (= *failed*) [*shot etc*] raté, loupé* 2 VT (: = *alter, fake*) [+ *stolen goods*] maquiller, truquer

► **duff up** VT SEP casser la gueule à:

duff[3] [dʌf] N (*US = buttocks*) postérieur *m*; **he just sits on his ~ all day** il ne fiche* rien de la journée; **get off your ~!** magne-toi le train !:

duffel ['dʌfəl] 1 N gros tissu de laine 2 COMP ► **duffel bag** N sac *m* de paquetage, sac *m* marin ► **duffel coat** N duffel-coat *m*

duffer* ['dʌfə'] N nullard(e)* *m(f)*; **he is a ~ at French** il est nul en français

duffle ['dʌfəl] ADJ = **duffel**

dug[1] [dʌg] N mamelle *f*, tétine *f*; [*of cow*] pis *m*

dug[2] [dʌg] VB pt, ptp of **dig**

dugong ['du:gɒn] N dugong *m*

dugout ['dʌgaʊt] N (*Mil* = *trench*) tranchée-abri *f*; (= *canoe*) pirogue *f*

duke [dju:k] 1 N (= *nobleman*) duc *m* 2 **dukes**: NPL (*esp US* = *fists*) poings *mpl*

dukedom ['dju:kdəm] N (= *territory*) duché *m*; (= *title*) titre *m* de duc

dulcet ['dʌlsɪt] ADJ (*liter*) suave

dulcimer ['dʌlsɪmə'] N tympanon *m*

dull [dʌl] 1 ADJ a (= *boring, uneventful*) [*book, lecture, party, person*] ennuyeux; [*life, job*] ennuyeux, monotone; [*place*] morne; [*food*] quelconque; [*style*] terne; (*St Ex*) [*market*] morose; **there's never a ~ minute** or **life is never ~ (with Janet here)** on ne s'ennuie jamais (lorsque Janet est là); **as ~ as ditchwater** or **dishwater** ennuyeux comme la pluie → **deadly**

b (= *not bright or shiny*) [*light, glow*] faible; [*colour, eyes, hair, skin, metal*] terne; [*weather, sky, day*] maussade, gris

c (= *vague*) [*pain, sound, feeling*] sourd; **with a ~ thud** or **thump** avec un bruit sourd

d (= *lethargic, withdrawn*) [*person*] abattu

e (= *slow-witted*) [*person, mind*] borné; **his senses/faculties are growing ~** ses sens/facultés s'émoussent or s'amoindrissent

f (= *blunt*) [*blade, knife*] émoussé

2 VT a (= *blunt*) [+ *edge, blade*] émousser; [+ *senses*] émousser, engourdir; [+ *mind*] engourdir; [+ *appetite*] calmer; [+ *pain, grief, impression*] atténuer; [+ *memories*] estomper; [+ *pleasure*] émousser; [+ *sound*] assourdir, amortir; (*in colour, brightness*) [+ *colour, mirror, metal*] ternir

3 VI [*eyes*] se voiler; [*appetite*] diminuer; [*edge, blade*] s'émousser; [*light*] baisser

4 COMP ► **dull-witted** ADJ dur à la détente*

dullard† ['dʌləd] N nullard(e)* *m(f)*

dullness ['dʌlnɪs] N a (= *slow-wittedness*) lourdeur *f* d'esprit; [*of senses*] affaiblissement *m*; **~ of hearing** dureté *f* d'oreille b (= *tedium, lack of interest*) [*of book, evening, lecture*] ca-

ractère *m* ennuyeux, manque *m* d'intérêt; [*of person*] personnalité *f* terne; [*of life*] grisaille *f*; [*of landscape, room*] tristesse *f* c [*of colour, metal, mirror etc*] manque *m* or peu *m* d'éclat, aspect *m* terne; [*of sound*] caractère *m* sourd or étouffé; [*of weather*] grisaille *f*

dullsville: ['dʌlzvɪl] N (*US*) **it's ~ here** on s'emmerde ici:, c'est pas la joie ici*

dully ['dʌlɪ] ADV a (= *with a muffled sound*) avec un bruit sourd b (= *dimly*) [*glow, gleam*] faiblement c (= *without enthusiasm*) [*say, reply*] d'un ton morne; [*look, nod*] d'un air morne; [*think*] avec lassitude d (= *boringly*) [*talk, write*] d'une manière ennuyeuse

duly ['dju:lɪ] ADV a (= *properly*) [*recorded, completed, authorized, rewarded*] dûment, en bonne et due forme; **~ elected** dûment élu, élu en bonne et due forme b (= *as expected*) comme prévu; **the visitors were ~ impressed** comme prévu, les visiteurs ont été impressionnés; **I asked him for his autograph and he ~ obliged** je lui ai demandé un autographe et il a accepté

dumb [dʌm] 1 ADJ a (*lit*) muet; **~ animals**† les bêtes *fpl*; **our ~ friends** nos amies les bêtes → **deaf, strike** b (*fig* = *silent*) muet (**with, from** de), abasourdi (**with, from** de, par); **~ insolence** mutisme *m* insolent c (*esp US*: = *stupid*) [*person*] bête; [*action, idea, joke*] stupide; [*question*] idiot; [*object, present*] ringard*; **a ~ blonde** une blonde évaporée; **to act ~** faire l'innocent **the dumb** NPL les muets *mpl* 3 COMP ► **dumb-ass**: (*US*) N con: *m*, conne: *f* ♦ ADJ à la con: ► **dumb cluck**: N imbécile *mf* ► **dumb ox**: N (*US*) ballot* *m*, andouille* *f* ► **dumb show** N in ~ **show** en mimant, par (des) signes ► **dumb terminal** N (*Comput*) terminal *m* passif

dumbbell ['dʌmbel] N (*Sport*) haltère *m*

dumbfound [dʌm'faʊnd] VT abasourdir, ahurir

dumbfounded [dʌm'faʊndɪd] ADJ ahuri, sidéré; **I'm ~** je suis sidéré, je n'en reviens pas

dumbly ['dʌmlɪ] ADV [*stare, stand, nod*] (= *silently*) en silence; (*with surprise*) avec stupeur

dumbness ['dʌmnɪs] N a mutisme *m*; (: = *stupidity*) bêtise *f*, niaiserie *f*

dumbo: ['dʌmbəʊ] N ballot* *m*, andouille* *f*

dumbstruck ['dʌmstrʌk] ADJ frappé de stupeur

dumbwaiter [ˌdʌm'weɪtə'] N (= *lift*) monteplat *m*; (*Brit*) (= *trolley*) table *f* roulante; (= *revolving stand*) plateau *m* tournant

dum-dum ['dʌmdʌm] N a (= *bullet*) balle *f* dum-dum *inv* b (: = *stupid person*) crétin(e) *m(f)*, andouille* *f*

dummy ['dʌmɪ] 1 N a (*Comm* = *sham object*) objet *m* factice; [*of book*] maquette *f*; (*Comm, Sewing* = *model*) mannequin *m*; [*of ventriloquist*] marionnette *f*; (*Theat*) personnage *m* muet, figurant *m*; (*Fin etc* = *person replacing another*) prête-nom *m*, homme *m* de paille; (*Bridge*) mort *m*; (*Sport*) feinte *f*; (*Sport*) **to sell the ~** feinter, faire une feinte de passe; **to sell sb the ~** feinter qn; (*Bridge*) **to be ~** faire or être le mort; (*Bridge*) **to play from ~** jouer du mort

b (*Brit* = *baby's teat*) sucette *f*, tétine *f*

c (* = *idiot*) andouille* *f*, imbécile *mf*; **"you're a ~, Mack," she yelled** « Mack, tu es une andouille* or un imbécile » hurla-t-elle

2 ADJ faux (fausse *f*), factice

3 VI (*Sport*) feinter, faire une feinte de passe

4 COMP ► **dummy bridge** N (*Cards*) bridge *m* à trois ► **dummy element** N (*Ling*) postiche *m* ► **dummy pass** N (*Sport*) feinte *f* de passe ► **dummy run** N (*Brit*) (*Aviat*) attaque *f* or bombardement *m* simulé(e); (*Comm, Ind*) (coup *m* d')essai *m* ► **dummy symbol** N = **dummy element**

dump [dʌmp] 1 N a (= *pile of rubbish*) tas *m* or amas *m* d'ordures; (= *place*) décharge *f*, dé-

potoir *m*; (*fig*) **to be (down) in the ~s** avoir le cafard* b (*Mil*) dépôt *m* → **ammunition** c (* *pej* = *place*) trou *m* perdu*; (= *house, hotel*) trou *m* à rats* d (*Comput*) vidage *m* e **to have a ~**: (= *defecate*) couler un bronze:, chier:: 2 VT a [+ *rubbish*] déposer, jeter; [+ *sand, bricks*] décharger, déverser; (*Comm*) [+ *goods*] vendre or écouler à bas prix (*sur les marchés extérieurs*), pratiquer le dumping pour b (* = *set down*) [+ *package*] déposer; [+ *passenger*] poser, larguer*; **~ your bag on the table** fiche* ton sac sur la table c (* = *get rid of*) [+ *thing*] bazarder*; [+ *boyfriend, girlfriend*] larguer*, plaquer: d (*Comput*) [+ *data file etc*] vider; **to ~ to the printer** transférer sur l'imprimante 3 VI (: = *defecate*) couler un bronze:, chier:: 4 COMP ► **dump bin** N (*Comm*) présentoir *m* d'articles en vrac ► **dump truck** N = **dumper**

► **dump on**: VT FUS (*US* = *mistreat*) traiter comme du poisson pourri*; (= *offload problems on*) se défouler sur

dumper ['dʌmpə'] N (*Brit*: *also* ~ **truck**) tombereau *m* automoteur, dumper *m*

dumping ['dʌmpɪŋ] 1 N [*of load, rubbish*] décharge *f*; (*Ecol: in sea etc*) déversement *m* (de produits nocifs); (*Comm*) dumping *m* 2 COMP ► **dumping ground** N (*lit, fig*) dépotoir *m*

dumpling ['dʌmplɪŋ] N (*Culin: savoury*) boulette *f* (de pâte); (* = *person*) boulot *m*, -otte *f*

Dumpster® ['dʌmpstə'] N (*US*) benne *f* (à ordures)

dumpy* ['dʌmpɪ] ADJ courtaud, boulot

dun[1] [dʌn] 1 ADJ (= *colour*) brun foncé *inv*, brun grisâtre *inv* 2 N cheval *m* louvet, jument *f* louvette

dun[2] [dʌn] 1 N (= *claim*) demande *f* de remboursement 2 VT [+ *debtor*] harceler, relancer; **to ~ sb for money owed** harceler or relancer qn pour lui faire payer ses dettes

dunce [dʌns] 1 N âne *m*, cancre* *m*; **to be a ~ at maths** être nul en math 2 COMP ► **dunce's cap** N bonnet *m* d'âne

dunderhead ['dʌndəhed] N imbécile *mf*

Dundonian [dʌn'dəʊnɪən] 1 ADJ de Dundee 2 N habitant(e) *m(f)* or natif *m*, -ive *f* de Dundee

dune [dju:n] 1 N dune *f* 2 COMP ► **dune buggy** N buggy *m*

dung [dʌŋ] 1 N (*NonC*) (= *excrement*) excrément(s) *m(pl)*, crotte *f*; [*of horse*] crottin *m*; [*of cattle*] bouse *f*; [*of bird*] fiente *f*; [*of wild animal*] fumées *fpl*; (= *manure*) fumier *m* 2 COMP ► **dung beetle** N bousier *m*

dungarees [ˌdʌŋgə'ri:z] NPL salopette *f*

dungeon ['dʌndʒən] N (*underground*) cachot *m* (souterrain); (*Hist: castle tower*) donjon *m*

dungheap ['dʌŋhi:p], **dunghill** ['dʌŋhɪl] N tas *m* de fumier

dunk [dʌŋk] VT tremper; **to ~ one's bread in one's coffee** tremper son pain dans son café

Dunkirk [dʌn'kɜ:k] N Dunkerque

dunlin ['dʌnlɪn] N bécasseau *m* variable

dunno: [də'nəʊ] = **don't know**

dunnock ['dʌnək] N (*Brit*) accenteur *m* mouchet, fauvette *f* d'hiver or des haies

dunny* ['dʌnɪ] N (*Austral*) chiottes: *fpl*, W.-C.* *mpl*

Duns Scotus ['dʌnz'skɒtəs] N Duns Scot *m*

duo ['dju:əʊ] N (*pl* **duos** or **dui** ['dju:i:]) (*Mus, Theat*) duo *m*

duodecimal [ˌdju:əʊ'desɪməl] ADJ duodécimal

duodenal [ˌdju:əʊ'di:nl] 1 ADJ duodénal 2 COMP ► **duodenal ulcer** N ulcère *m* du duodénum

duodenum [ˌdju:əʊ'di:nəm] N (*pl* **duodenums** or **duodena** [ˌdju:əʊ'di:nə]) duodénum *m*

duopoly [djʊ'ɒpəlɪ] N duopole *m*

dupe [dju:p] ① VT duper, tromper; **to ~ sb into doing sth** amener qn à faire qch en le dupant ② N dupe f

duple ['dju:pl] ① ADJ (gen) double; (Mus) binaire ② COMP ► **duple time** N (Mus) rythme m or mesure f binaire

duplex ['dju:pleks] ① ADJ duplex inv ② N (US) (also ~ **house**) maison f jumelle; (also ~ **apartment**) duplex m → HOUSE ③ COMP ► **duplex paper** N (Phot) bande f protectrice

duplicate ['dju:plɪkeɪt] ① VT [+ document, map, key] faire un double de; [+ film] faire un contretype de; (on machine) [+ document] polycopier; [+ action etc] répéter exactement; **duplicating machine** machine f à polycopier, duplicateur m; **that is merely duplicating work already done** cela revient à refaire le travail qu'on a déjà fait ② ['dju:plɪkɪt] N [of document, map, key, ornament, chair] double m; (Jur etc) duplicata m inv; **in ~** en deux exemplaires ③ ['dju:plɪkɪt] ADJ [copy] en double; **a ~ cheque/receipt** un duplicata du chèque/du reçu; **I've got a ~ key** j'ai un double de la clé ④ COMP ► **duplicate bridge** N bridge m de compétition or de tournoi

duplication [ˌdju:plɪ'keɪʃən] N (NonC) [of document] action f de copier; (on machine) polycopie f; [of efforts, work] répétition f inutile; **there is some ~ between television and magazine advertising** il y a un certain recoupement entre les publicités à la télévision et dans les magazines

duplicator ['dju:plɪkeɪtər] N duplicateur m

duplicitous [dju:'plɪsɪtəs] ADJ fourbe

duplicity [dju:'plɪsɪtɪ] N duplicité f, fourberie f

Dur. ABBR = **Durham**

durability [ˌdjʊərə'bɪlɪtɪ] N [of product, material, institution, friendship, solution] durabilité f, caractère m durable

durable ['djʊərəbl] ① ADJ durable; **CDs are more ~ than cassettes** les CD sont plus solides que les cassettes, les CD durent plus longtemps que les cassettes; (Comm) **~ goods** biens mpl de consommation durables ② **durables** NPL = **durable goods**

Duralumin® [djʊə'ræljʊmɪn] N duralumin m

duration [djʊə'reɪʃən] N durée f; **of long ~** de longue durée; **for the ~ of ...** pendant toute la durée de ...; **he stayed for the ~*** (= for ages) il est resté une éternité

Durban ['dɜ:bæn] N Durban

duress [djʊə'res] N contrainte f, coercition f; **under ~** sous la contrainte, contraint et forcé (Jur)

Durex® ['djʊəreks] N (pl inv) préservatif m

during ['djʊərɪŋ] PREP pendant, durant

durst†† [dɜ:st] VB pt of **dare**

durum ['djʊərəm] N (also ~ **wheat**) blé m dur

dusk [dʌsk] N (= twilight) crépuscule m; (= gloom) (semi-)obscurité f; **at ~** au crépuscule, à la tombée de la nuit; **shortly after ~** peu de temps après la tombée de la nuit; **in the ~** entre chien et loup

duskiness ['dʌskɪnɪs] N [of complexion] teint m mat or basané

dusky ['dʌskɪ] ADJ ⓐ (= dark-skinned) [person] à la peau basanée, au teint basané; [complexion] basané ⓑ [colour] mat; **~ pink** vieux rose inv, rose cendré inv ⓒ (= dim) [room] sombre

dust [dʌst] ① N (NonC) ⓐ (on furniture, ground) poussière f; **there was thick ~ ◊ the ~ lay thick** il y avait une épaisse couche de poussière; **I've got a speck of ~ in my eye** j'ai une poussière dans l'œil; **to raise a lot of ~** (lit) faire de la poussière; (fig) faire tout un scandale, faire beaucoup de bruit; **to lay the ~** (lit) mouiller la poussière; (fig) ramener le calme, dissiper la fumée; (fig) **to throw ~ in sb's eyes** jeter de la poudre aux yeux de qn; **to kick up** or **raise a ~:** faire un or du foin*;

(Brit) **you couldn't see him for ~*** il s'était volatilisé → **ash²**, **bite**, **shake off**
ⓑ [of coal, gold] poussière f, poudre f
② VT ⓐ [+ furniture] épousseter, essuyer; [+ room] essuyer la poussière dans; (Brit, Austral) **it's done and ~ed*** l'affaire est classée
ⓑ (with talc, sugar etc) saupoudrer (**with** de)
③ VI épousseter
④ COMP ► **dust bag** N sac m à poussière (d'aspirateur) ► **dust-bath** N **to take a ~-bath** [bird] s'ébrouer dans la poussière, prendre un bain de poussière ► **dust bowl** N (Geog) désert m de poussière, cratère(s) m(pl) de poussière ► **dust cloth** N (US) chiffon m (à poussière) ► **dust cloud** N nuage m de poussière ► **dust cover** N [of book] jaquette f; [of furniture] housse f (de protection) ► **dust devil** N tourbillon m de poussière ► **dust jacket** N jaquette f ► **dust sheet** N housse f (de protection) ► **dust storm** N tempête f de poussière ► **dust-up*** N (Brit) accrochage* m, bagarre* f; (Brit) **to have a ~up with sb** avoir un accrochage* or se bagarrer* avec qn

► **dust down**, **dust off** VT SEP épousseter

► **dust out** VT SEP [+ box, cupboard] épousseter

dustbin ['dʌstbɪn] ① N (Brit) poubelle f, boîte f à ordures ② COMP ► **dustbin man** N (pl **dustbin men**) (Brit) = **dustman**

dustcart ['dʌstkɑ:t] N (Brit) benne f à ordures, camion m des éboueurs or des boueux*

duster ['dʌstər] N ⓐ (Brit) chiffon m (à poussière); (also **blackboard ~**) chiffon m (pour effacer) → **feather** ⓑ (US) (= overgarment) blouse f; (= housecoat) robe f d'intérieur ⓒ (= device: also **crop ~**) pulvérisateur m d'insecticide (souvent un avion)

dustheap ['dʌsthi:p] N (lit) tas m d'ordures; (fig) poubelle f, rebut m

dusting ['dʌstɪŋ] ① N ⓐ [of furniture] époussetage m; **to do the ~** épousseter, essuyer (la poussière); **to give sth a ~** donner un coup de chiffon à qch ⓑ (Culin etc = sprinkling) saupoudrage m ② COMP ► **dusting down** N **to give sb a ~ down** passer un savon à qn; **to get a ~ down** recevoir un savon ► **dusting-powder** N talc m

dustman ['dʌstmən] N (pl **-men**) (Brit) éboueur m, boueux* m

dustpan ['dʌstpæn] N pelle f (à poussière)

dustproof ['dʌstpru:f] ADJ antipoussière

dusty ['dʌstɪ] ADJ ⓐ (= covered in dust) poussiéreux; **to get ~** se couvrir de poussière ⓑ [colour] cendré; **~ blue** bleu cendré inv; **~ pink** vieux rose inv, rose cendré inv ⓒ **to give sb a ~ answer*** envoyer paître qn*; **to get** or **receive a ~ answer (from sb)*** se faire envoyer paître (par qn)*; **not so ~** ◊ **not too ~*** pas mal

Dutch [dʌtʃ] ① ADJ (gen) néerlandais, hollandais; [ambassador, embassy] des Pays-Bas; [teacher] de néerlandais; (Art) **the ~ School** l'école f hollandaise; **~ cheese** fromage m de Hollande, hollande m
② N ⓐ (Ling) hollandais m, néerlandais m; (fig) **it's (all) ~ to me*** c'est du chinois or de l'hébreu pour moi → **double**
ⓑ (US fig) **to be in ~ with sb:** être en disgrâce auprès de qn; **to get one's ~ up:** se mettre en rogne*; **to get into ~:** avoir des ennuis, se mettre dans le pétrin*
③ **the Dutch** NPL (loosely) les Hollandais mpl; (more correctly) les Néerlandais mpl
④ ADV **to go ~*** (in restaurant) payer chacun sa part; (in cinema, theatre) payer chacun sa place
⑤ COMP ► **Dutch auction** N (fig) enchères fpl au rabais ► **Dutch barn** N hangar m à récoltes ► **Dutch cap** N diaphragme m ► **Dutch courage** N (fig) courage m puisé dans la bouteille; **the whisky gave him ~ courage** le whisky lui a donné du courage

► **Dutch door** N (US) porte f à double vantail, porte f d'étable ► **the Dutch East Indies** NPL les Indes fpl néerlandaises ► **Dutch elm disease** N champignon m parasite de l'orme ► **Dutch master** N maître m de l'école hollandaise ► **Dutch oven** N (= casserole) grosse cocotte f (en métal) ► **Dutch treat** N **to go on a ~ treat** partager les frais ► **Dutch uncle**†* N **to talk to sb like a ~ uncle** dire ses quatre vérités à qn

Dutchman ['dʌtʃmən] N (pl **-men**) Hollandais m; **if he's a professional footballer, then I'm a ~** je veux bien être pendu si c'est un footballeur professionnel → **flying**

Dutchwoman ['dʌtʃˌwʊmən] N (pl **-women**) Hollandaise f

dutiable ['dju:tɪəbl] ADJ taxable; (Customs) soumis à des droits de douane

dutiful ['dju:tɪfʊl] ADJ [child] obéissant; [husband, wife] dévoué; [employee] consciencieux

dutifully ['dju:tɪfəlɪ] ADV consciencieusement; **we laughed/applauded ~** nous avons ri/applaudi consciencieusement

▼ **duty** ['dju:tɪ] ① N ⓐ (NonC: moral, legal) devoir m, obligation f; **to do one's ~** s'acquitter de or faire son devoir (**by sb** envers qn); **it is my ~ to say that ...** ◊ **I feel (in) ~ bound to say that ...** il est de mon devoir de dire que ...; **~ calls** le devoir m'appelle; **the** or **one's ~ to one's parents** le or son devoir envers ses parents; **what about your ~ to yourself?** et ton devoir envers toi-même?; **to make it one's ~ to do sth** se faire un devoir de faire qch
ⓑ (gen pl = responsibility) fonction f, responsabilité f; **to take up one's duties** entrer en fonction; **to neglect one's duties** négliger ses fonctions; **my duties consist of ...** mes fonctions consistent à ...; **his duties as presidential adviser** ses fonctions de conseiller du président; **his duties have been taken over by his colleague** ses fonctions ont été reprises par son collègue
ⓒ (NonC) **on ~** (Mil, Admin etc) de service; (Med) de garde; **to be on ~** être de service or de garde; **to be off ~** ne pas être de service or de garde; (Mil) avoir quartier libre; **to go on/off ~** prendre/quitter son service; **in the course of (one's) ~** dans l'exercice de mes (or ses etc) fonctions; **to do ~ for sb** ◊ **to do sb's ~** remplacer qn; (fig) **the reading room also does ~ as** or **for a library** la salle de lecture fait également fonction or office de bibliothèque → **report**, **spell²**, **tour**
ⓓ (Fin = tax) droit m, taxe f; (at Customs) frais mpl de douane; **to pay ~ on sth** payer un droit or une taxe sur qch → **death**, **estate**
② COMP ► **duty call** N visite f de politesse ► **duty-free** ADJ hors taxes ► **duty-free allowance** N quantité autorisée de produits hors taxes (par personne) ► **duty-frees*** NPL (Brit) marchandises fpl hors taxes ► **duty-free shop** N boutique f hors taxes ► **duty-free shopping** N (NonC) achat m de marchandises hors taxes ► **duty officer** N (Mil) officier m de permanence; (Police) officier m de police de service; (Admin) officiel m or préposé m de service ► **duty paid** N dédouané ► **duty roster**, **duty rota** N liste f de service; (esp Mil) tableau m de service

duvet ['du:veɪ] ① N (Brit) couette f ② COMP ► **duvet cover** N housse f de couette

DV [di:'vi:] ADV (ABBR = **Deo volente**) Dieu voulant

DVLA [ˌdi:vi:el'eɪ] N (Brit) (ABBR = **Driver and Vehicle Licensing Agency**) service des immatriculations et permis de conduire

DVM [ˌdi:vi:'em] N (US Univ) (ABBR = **Doctor of Veterinary Medicine**) doctorat vétérinaire

dwarf [dwɔ:f] ① N (pl **dwarfs** or **dwarves** [dwɔ:vz]) (= person, animal) nain(e) m(f); (= tree) arbre m nain ② ADJ [person, tree, star] nain ③ VT ⓐ [skyscraper, person] rapetisser, écraser (fig); [achievement] écraser, éclipser **b** [+ plant] empêcher de croître

dwarfish ['dwɔːfɪʃ] ADJ (pej) nabot

dweeb: [dwiːb] N (esp US) pauvre mec* m

dwell [dwel] (pret, ptp **dwelt** or **dwelled**) VI (liter) **a** habiter, demeurer; **to ~ in Glasgow/in France** habiter or demeurer à Glasgow/en France **b** (fig) [interest, difficulty] résider (**in** dans)

► **dwell on** VT FUS (= think about) ne pouvoir s'empêcher de penser à; (= talk at length on) s'étendre sur; (Mus) [+ note] appuyer sur; **don't ~ on it** n'y pense plus; **to ~ on the past** s'appesantir sur le passé, revenir sans cesse sur le passé; **to ~ on the fact that ...** ressasser le fait que ...; **don't let's ~ on it** passons là-dessus, ne nous attardons pas sur ce sujet

► **dwell upon** VT FUS = **dwell on**

dweller ['dwelə'] N habitant(e) m(f) → **country**

dwelling ['dwelɪŋ] **1** N (Admin or liter: also ~ **place**) habitation f, résidence f; **to take up one's ~** s'installer, élire domicile (Admin) **2** COMP ► **dwelling house** N maison f d'habitation

dwelt [dwelt] VB pt, ptp of **dwell**

DWEM N (esp US) (ABBR = **Dead White European Male**) homme célèbre qui devrait sa réputation à son appartenance au sexe masculin et à la race blanche

dwindle ['dwɪndl] VI [strength] diminuer, décroître; [numbers, resources, supplies, interest] diminuer

► **dwindle away** VI diminuer; [person] dépérir

dwindling ['dwɪndlɪŋ] **1** N diminution f (graduelle) **2** ADJ [number, interest, popularity] décroissant; [resources, supplies, funds] en baisse; [population] en baisse, décroissant; **~ audiences** un public de moins en moins nombreux

dye [daɪ] **1** N (= substance) teinture f, colorant m; (= colour) teinte f; **hair ~** teinture f pour les cheveux; **fast ~** grand teint m; **the ~ will come out in the wash** cela déteindra au lava-

ge; (fig liter) **a villain of the deepest ~** une canaille or crapule de la pire espèce **2** VT teindre; **to ~ sth red** teindre qch en rouge; **to ~ one's hair** se teindre les cheveux → **dyed, tie** **3** VI [cloth etc] prendre la teinture, se teindre **4** COMP ► **dyed-in-the-wool** ADJ (fig) bon teint inv, invétéré

dyed [daɪd] ADJ [hair, fabric] teint; **~ blond/blue** teint en blond/bleu

dyeing ['daɪɪŋ] N (NonC) teinture f

dyer ['daɪə'] N teinturier m; **~'s and cleaner's** teinturier m

dyestuffs ['daɪstʌfs] NPL colorants mpl

dyeworks ['daɪwɜːks] NPL teinturerie f

dying ['daɪɪŋ] **1** ADJ **a** [person, animal, plant, fire] mourant; **the ~ daylight** les dernières lueurs fpl du jour; (Ballet) **the Dying Swan** la Mort du Cygne; **the ~ embers** les tisons mpl; (hum) **to look like a ~ duck (in a thunderstorm)*** avoir l'air pitoyable **b** (= declining) [custom, industry] en train de disparaître; **it's a ~ art** c'est un art en voie de disparition; (lit, fig) **they are a ~ breed** c'est une espèce en voie de disparition **c** (= final) [words, wish] dernier; **with his ~ breath** sur son lit de mort; **till** or **until** or **to my ~ day** jusqu'à mon dernier jour; **in the ~ minutes of the game** pendant les dernières minutes du match **2** N (= death) mort f; (just before death) agonie f **3** **the dying** NPL les mourants mpl; **prayer for the ~** prière f des agonisants

dyke [daɪk] N **a** (= channel) fossé m; (= wall, barrier) digue f; (= causeway) levée f, chaussée f; (Geol) filon m stérile, dyke m; (Scot dial = wall) mur m **b** (‡ pej = lesbian) gouine‡ f (pej)

dynamic [daɪˈnæmɪk] ADJ (gen, Phys) dynamique

dynamically [daɪˈnæmɪkəlɪ] ADV **a** [develop] de façon dynamique; [work] avec dynamisme **b** (Phys) dynamiquement, du point de vue de la dynamique

dynamics [daɪˈnæmɪks] N (NonC) dynamique f

(also Mus)

dynamism ['daɪnəmɪzəm] N dynamisme m

dynamite ['daɪnəmaɪt] **1** N **a** (NonC) dynamite f → **stick b** (* fig = dangerous) **that business is ~** c'est de la dynamite cette affaire; **it's political ~** du point de vue politique, c'est un sujet explosif or une affaire explosive; **the book is ~!** ce livre, c'est de la dynamite!*; **asking him to give evidence is potential ~** lui demander de témoigner pourrait amener une situation explosive **c** (fig) **she's ~** (= terrific) elle est super*; (= full of energy) elle pète le feu*; (= sexy) elle est supersexy*; **there are some ~ songs on this album*** il y a des chansons à tout casser* dans cet album **2** VT faire sauter à la dynamite, dynamiter

dynamo ['daɪnəməʊ] N (esp Brit) dynamo f; **he is a human ~** il déborde d'énergie

dynastic [daɪˈnæstɪk] ADJ dynastique

dynasty ['dɪnəstɪ] N dynastie f

dyne [daɪn] N dyne f

d'you [djuː] (ABBR = **do you**) → **do¹**

dysenteric [ˌdɪsənˈterɪk] ADJ dysentérique

dysentery ['dɪsɪntrɪ] N dysenterie f

dysfunction [dɪsˈfʌŋkʃən] N dysfonctionnement m

dysfunctional [dɪsˈfʌŋkʃnl] ADJ dysfonctionnel

dyslexia [dɪsˈleksɪə] N dyslexie f

dyslexic [dɪsˈleksɪk] ADJ, N dyslexique mf

dysmenorrhoea, **dysmenorrhea** (US) [ˌdɪsmenəˈrɪə] N dysménorrhée f

dyspepsia [dɪsˈpepsɪə] N dyspepsie f

dyspeptic [dɪsˈpeptɪk] ADJ, N dyspeptique mf, dyspepsique mf

dysphasia [dɪsˈfeɪzɪə] N dysphasie f

dysprosium [dɪsˈprəʊsɪəm] N dysprosium m

dystopia [dɪsˈtəʊpɪə] N contre-utopie f

dystrophy ['dɪstrəfɪ] N dystrophie f

E

E, e [i:] **1** N **a** (= letter) E, e m; **E for Easy** ≈ E comme Émile **b** (Mus) mi m → **key** **c** (ABBR = **East**) E, est m **d** (Scol) ≈ faible **e** (Brit) (ABBR = **elbow**) **to give sb/get the big E*** [+ lover] plaquer***** or laisser tomber qn*/se faire plaquer*****; [+ employee] virer qn*/se faire virer***** **f** (Drugs* = ecstasy) **E** ecstasy m **2** COMP ► **E numbers** NPL (Brit) ≈ additifs mpl (alimentaires)

EA [ˌiːˈeɪ] N (US Scol) (ABBR = **educational age**) → **educational**

each [iːtʃ] **1** ADJ chaque; **~ passport** chaque passeport, tout passeport; **~ day** chaque jour, tous les jours; **~ one of us** chacun(e) de or d'entre nous; **~ and every one of us** chacun(e) de nous sans exception

2 PRON **a** (= thing, person, group) chacun(e) m(f); **~ of the boys** chacun des garçons; **~ of us** chacun(e) m(f) de or d'entre nous; **~ of them gave their opinion** chacun a donné son avis, ils ont donné chacun leur avis; **we had our own idea about it** nous avions chacun notre idée là-dessus; **~ more beautiful than the next** or **the other** tous plus beaux les uns que les autres; **~ of them was given a present** on leur a offert à chacun un cadeau, chacun d'entre eux a reçu un cadeau; **a little of ~ please** un peu de chaque s'il vous plaît **b** (= apiece) chacun(e); **we gave them one apple ~** nous leur avons donné une pomme chacun; **two classes of 20 pupils ~** deux classes de 20 élèves (chacune); **the books are £12 ~** les livres coûtent 12 livres chacun or chaque; **carnations at one franc ~** des œillets à un franc (la) pièce **c** **~ other** l'un(e) l'autre m(f), les uns les autres mpl, les unes les autres fpl; **they love ~ other** ils s'aiment (l'un l'autre); **they write to ~ other often** ils s'écrivent souvent; **they were sorry for ~ other** ils avaient pitié l'un de l'autre; **they respected ~ other** ils avaient du respect l'un pour l'autre, ils se respectaient mutuellement; **you must help ~ other** il faut vous entraider; **separated from ~ other** séparés l'un de l'autre; **they used to carry ~ other's books** ils s'aidaient à porter leurs livres

3 COMP ► **each way** (Brit Racing etc) ADJ [bet] sur un cheval placé ♦ ADV **to bet on** or **back a horse ~ way** jouer un cheval placé

eager [ˈiːgəʳ] **1** ADJ [person, buyer] empressé; [worker, volunteer] enthousiaste; [lover] ardent, passionné; [search] avide; [pursuit, discussion] âpre; [face] impatient; **~ anticipation** pleine d'impatience; **she is an ~ student of English** elle étudie l'anglais avec enthousiasme or ardeur; **~ supporters** (of cause) défenseurs mpl ardents; (Sport) supporters mpl passionnés or enthousiastes; **to be ~ for** [+ happiness] rechercher avidement; [+ affection, information] être avide de; [+ vengeance, knowledge] avoir soif de; [+ power, honour] briguer, convoiter; [+ pleasure] être assoiffé de; [+ praise, fame, nomination] désirer vivement; **to be ~ for change** avoir soif de changement; **to be ~ for sb to do sth** avoir hâte que qn fasse qch; **to be ~ for sth to happen** avoir hâ-

te que qch arrive (subj); **to be ~ to do sth** (= keen) désirer vivement faire qch; (= impatient) brûler or être impatient or être pressé de faire qch; **she is ~ to help** elle ne demande qu'à aider; **she is ~ to please** (= make people happy) elle ne demande qu'à faire plaisir; (= be helpful) elle ne demande qu'à rendre service

2 COMP ► **eager beaver*** N (gen) personne f enthousiaste et consciencieuse; (at work) **he's an ~ beaver** il en veut*, il se donne du mal pour réussir

eagerly [ˈiːgəlɪ] ADV [await, anticipate] avec impatience; [accept] avec enthousiasme; [say] avec empressement

eagerness [ˈiːgənɪs] N (NonC) (= excitement) excitation f; (= impatience) impatience f; (= impetuousness) ardeur f; **~ for sth** soif f de qch; **~ to succeed** vif désir m de réussir; **~ to learn** soif f or vif désir m d'apprendre; **~ to leave/help/please** empressement m à partir/aider/faire plaisir

eagle [ˈiːgl] **1** N (Orn) aigle mf (gen m); (Rel = lectern) aigle m; (Her, Hist, Mil) aigle f; (Golf) eagle m; (US† = coin) pièce de 10 dollars → **golden** **2** COMP ► **eagle eye** N **to keep an ~ eye on sb/sth** surveiller qn/qch d'un œil attentif; **nothing escapes her ~ eye** rien n'échappe à son œil vigilant ► **eagle-eyed** ADJ aux yeux d'aigle or de lynx ► **eagle owl** N grand-duc m ► **eagle ray** N aigle m de mer ► **Eagle Scout** N (US) scout du plus haut grade

eaglet [ˈiːglɪt] N aiglon(ne) m(f)

E & OE [ˌiːəndˈəʊiː] (ABBR = **errors and omissions excepted**) se & o

ear¹ [ɪəʳ] **1** N (also fig) oreille f; (fig) **I'm all ~s!*** je suis tout oreilles or tout ouïe!; **projectiles buzzed around his ~s** des projectiles lui sifflaient aux oreilles; **it all came crashing down around** or **about his ~s** tout s'est effondré autour de lui; **your ~s must have been burning!*** vous avez dû entendre vos oreilles siffler!; **if that should come to his ~s** si cela venait à ses oreilles; **to close** or **shut one's ~s to sth** ne pas vouloir entendre qch; **to close** or **shut one's ~s to sb** refuser d'écouter qn; (fig) **to have** or **keep one's ~ to the ground** se tenir au courant; **to have an ~ for music** avoir l'oreille musicale; (for music) **to have a good ~** avoir une bonne oreille; **to have an ~** or **a good ~ for languages** avoir de l'oreille or une bonne oreille pour les langues; **he has the ~ of the President** il a l'oreille du Président; (fig) **it goes in one ~ and out (of) the other*** cela lui (or vous etc) entre par une oreille et lui (or vous etc) sort par l'autre; **to keep one's ~s open** ouvrir l'oreille; **you'll be out on your ~* if you're not careful** tu vas te faire vider* si tu ne fais pas attention; (Mus) **to play by ~** jouer d'oreille; (fig) **I'll play it by ~** je déciderai quoi faire or j'improviserai le moment venu; (US) **to set** or **put sb on his ~** (= irritate) exaspérer qn; (= shock) atterrer qn; **that set them by the ~s!** ça a semé la zizanie (entre eux)!; (hum) **they practically had steam com-**

ing out of their ~s* ils étaient à cran or profondément exaspérés; **to find/lend a sympathetic ~** trouver/prêter une oreille attentive; **his proposal found few sympathetic ~s** sa proposition a rencontré peu d'échos; **to be up to the** or **one's ~s in work*** avoir du travail par-dessus la tête; **to be up to the** or **one's ~s in debt** être endetté jusqu'au cou; (hum) **he's got money/houses** etc **coming out of his ~s*** il a de l'argent/des maisons etc à ne plus savoir qu'en faire; **he's got nothing between his ~s*** il n'a rien dans la tête (fig) → **bend, box², clip, deaf, half**

2 COMP [operation] à l'oreille ► **ear, nose and throat department** N (Med) service m d'oto-rhino-laryngologie ► **ear, nose and throat specialist** N oto-rhino-laryngologiste mf, oto-rhino* mf ► **ear piercing** N perçage m d'oreilles ► **ear-piercing** ADJ = **ear-splitting** ► **ear shell** N (Zool) ormeau m ► **ear-splitting** ADJ [sound, scream] strident, perçant; [din] fracassant ► **ear stoppers** NPL = **earplugs** ► **ear trumpet** N cornet m acoustique

ear² [ɪəʳ] N [of grain, plant] épi m

earache [ˈɪəreɪk] N mal m d'oreille(s); **to have (an) ~** avoir mal à l'oreille or aux oreilles

eardrops [ˈɪədrɒps] NPL (Med) gouttes fpl pour les oreilles

eardrum [ˈɪədrʌm] N (Anat) tympan m

earful* [ˈɪəfʊl] N **to give sb an ~** (= talk a lot) casser les oreilles* à qn; (= scold) passer un savon* à qn

earhole* [ˈɪəhəʊl] N (Brit) esgourde* f; **to give sb a clip** or **clout round the ~** filer une claque à qn*

earl [ɜːl] **1** N comte m **2** COMP ► **Earl Grey (tea)** N Earl Grey m

earldom [ˈɜːldəm] N (= title) titre m de comte; (= land) comté m

earlier [ˈɜːlɪəʳ] compar of **early** **1** ADJ **a** (in past) [chapter, edition, meeting, efforts, attempts] précédent; **at an ~ date** (= formerly) autrefois, plus tôt; (than that specified) précédemment; **in ~ times** autrefois; **his ~ symphonies** ses premières symphonies fpl; **an ~ train** un train plus tôt; **the ~ train** le train précédent **b** (in future) **at an ~ date** à une date plus rapprochée **2** ADV **a** (= nearer beginning of day) [get up] plus tôt **b** (= previously) [leave] auparavant, plus tôt; **she had left ten minutes ~** elle était partie dix minutes auparavant or plus tôt; **~ in the evening** plus tôt dans la soirée; **~ on** (= formerly) autrefois; (before specified moment) plus tôt, précédemment; **~ today** plus tôt dans la journée; **I said ~ that ...** tout à l'heure j'ai dit que ...; **not** or **no ~ than Thursday** pas avant jeudi

earliest [ˈɜːlɪɪst] superl of **early** **1** ADJ **a** (= first) [novel, film] tout premier; **the ~ in a series of murders** le premier en date or le tout premier d'une série de meurtres **b** (= first possible) **the ~ date he could do it was 31 July** le plus tôt qu'il pouvait le faire était le 31 juillet; **the ~ possible date for the**

election la première date possible pour la tenue des élections; **at the ~ possible moment** le plus tôt possible, au plus tôt; **the ~ time you may leave is 4pm** vous ne pouvez pas partir avant 16 heures (au plus tôt); (*Comm*) **at your ~ convenience** dans les meilleurs délais; (*Comm*) **the ~ delivery time** le délai de livraison le plus court, le meilleur délai de livraison

2 ADV **to arrive/get up ~** arriver/se lever le tout premier *or* la toute première, être le tout premier *or* la toute première à arriver/se lever; **to flower ~** être le tout premier *or* la toute première à fleurir

3 N **at the ~** au plus tôt; **the ~ he can come is Monday** le plus tôt qu'il puisse venir c'est lundi

earlobe ['ɪələʊb] N lobe *m* d'oreille

early ['ɜːlɪ] **1** ADJ **a** (= *near beginning of period*) [*years, months, days, settlers, film, book*] premier; [*childhood*] petit; **it's too ~ to say** *or* **tell** il est trop tôt pour le dire; **it is too ~ to say** *or* **know what will happen** il est trop tôt pour dire *or* savoir ce qui va se passer; **the ~ (19)60s** au début des années soixante; **in the ~ afternoon** en début d'après-midi; **at an ~ age** (très) jeune; **from an ~ age** dès mon/son/leur *etc* plus jeune âge; **in ~ childhood** pendant la petite enfance; **his ~ career** les débuts *mpl* de sa carrière; **in the ~ 18th century** au début du 18ᵉ siècle; **in the ~ days** au début, au commencement (**of** de); **the ~ days** *or* **stages of the project** les débuts *mpl* du projet; (*esp Brit*) **it's ~ days (yet)*** il est (encore) trop tôt pour en juger; **it was ~ evening when we finished** nous avons fini tôt dans la soirée; **to be an ~ example of sth** être un des premiers exemples de qch; **an ~ form of ...** une forme ancienne de ...; **two ~ goals** deux buts *mpl* en début de match; **~ January** début janvier; **by ~ January** d'ici début janvier; **in the ~ morning** tôt le matin; **an ~-morning drive** une promenade matinale en voiture; **in the ~ part of the century** au début *or* au commencement du siècle; **in its ~ stages** à ses débuts; **this is in a very ~ stage of development** c'en est au tout début; **in ~ summer** au début de l'été; **in his ~ teens** au début de son adolescence, dès treize ou quatorze ans; **to be in one's ~ thirties** avoir un peu plus de trente ans; **the ~ Tudors** les premiers Tudor *mpl*; **the ~ Victorians** les Victoriens *mpl* du début du règne; **an ~ Victorian table** une table du début de l'époque victorienne; **in his ~ youth** dans sa première *or* prime jeunesse → **earlier, earliest, life**

b (= *near beginning of day*) tôt; **don't go, it's still ~** ne t'en va pas, il est encore tôt *or* il n'est pas tard; **at an ~ hour** de bonne heure, très tôt; **at an ~ hour of the morning** à une heure matinale; **(in) the ~ hours (of the morning)** (dans) les premières heures *fpl* (de la matinée); **we've got an ~ start tomorrow** nous partons tôt *or* de bonne heure demain; **I caught an ~ train** j'ai pris un train tôt le matin; **I caught the ~ train** j'ai pris le premier train (du matin)

c (= *before expected time*) [*departure, death, marriage, menopause*] prématuré; [*spring, flowers, cabbages, crop*] précoce; **to be ~** [*person*] (*gen*) être en avance; (*arriving*) arriver en avance; **I'm ~** (*gen*) je suis en avance; (*menstrual period*) mes règles ont de l'avance; **I'm a week ~** (*gen*) je suis une semaine en avance, j'ai une semaine d'avance; (*menstrual period*) mes règles sont une semaine en avance; **I was two hours ~** j'étais deux heures en avance, j'avais deux heures d'avance; **you're ~ today** vous arrivez de bonne heure *or* tôt aujourd'hui; **too ~** trop tôt, trop en avance; **to be ~ for an appointment** (*gen*) être en avance à un rendez-vous; (*arriving*) arriver en avance à un rendez-vous; **to be ~ in arriving** arriver avec de l'avance *or* en avance; **to be ~ with sth** avoir de l'avance dans qch; **I was ~ with**

the rent j'ai payé mon loyer en avance; **both my babies were ~** mes deux bébés sont arrivés avant terme; **Easter is ~ this year** Pâques est tôt cette année; **spring was ~** le printemps était en avance *or* était précoce; **the train is ~** le train est en avance *or* a de l'avance; **the train is 30 minutes ~** le train est 30 minutes en avance *or* a 30 minutes d'avance; **we're having an ~ holiday this year** nous partons en vacances cette année; **to have an ~ lunch** déjeuner tôt; **to have an ~ night** (aller) se coucher tôt; (*Brit fig*) **to take an ~ bath*** (withdraw) prendre une retraite anticipée; (*Brit Ftbl, Rugby*) **to send sb for an ~ bath** mettre qn sur la touche; (*Comm*) **~ fruit** primeurs *mpl*; (*Comm*) **~ vegetables** primeurs *mpl*

d (= *occurring in near future*) **at an ~ date** bientôt, prochainement; (*Comm*) **to promise ~ delivery** promettre une livraison rapide; (*Comm*) **"hoping for an ~ reply"** « dans l'espoir d'une prompte réponse » → **earlier, earliest**

2 ADV **a** (= *near beginning of period*) [*start*] tôt; **as ~ as next week** dès la semaine prochaine; **~ in 1915** au début de 1915; **~ in the year** au début de l'année; **~ in May** début mai; **~ in life** tôt dans la vie; **~ in his life** dans ses jeunes années; **~ in the book** au début du livre; **~ in the meeting** au début de la réunion; **~ next month/year** au mois prochain/l'année prochaine; **~ on (in life)** très tôt; **~ on in his career** au début de sa carrière; **~ this month/year** tôt dans le mois/l'année; **~ today** tôt dans la journée; **~ yesterday** tôt dans la journée d'hier → **earlier**

b (= *near beginning of day*) [*get up, go to bed, set off*] tôt, de bonne heure; **~ in the morning/day** tôt le matin/dans la journée; **next day** tôt le lendemain; **too ~** trop tôt, de trop bonne heure ■ (*PROV*) **~ to bed, ~ to rise (makes a man healthy, wealthy and wise)** l'avenir appartient à ceux qui se lèvent tôt (*PROV*) → **bright, earlier, earliest**

c (= *before usual time*) [*arrive, end*] en avance; [*flower, harvest*] tôt; **an ~ flowering gladiolus** un glaïeul à floraison précoce; **to arrive ~ for sth** arriver en avance pour qch; **to arrive five minutes ~** arriver cinq minutes en avance *or* avec cinq minutes d'avance; **post ~** expédiez votre courrier à l'avance; **book ~ to avoid disappointment** réservez rapidement *or* le plus tôt possible; **he took his summer holiday ~ this year** il a pris ses vacances d'été tôt cette année; **the peaches are ripening ~ this year** les pêches seront mûres tôt cette année; **too ~** trop tôt *or* earliest

d (= *soon*) **as ~ as possible** le plus tôt possible, dès que possible

3 COMP ► **early admission** N (*US Univ*) inscription *f* anticipée ► **early bird*** *mf inv* ■ (*PROV*) **it's the ~ bird that catches the worm** l'avenir appartient à ceux qui se lèvent tôt (*PROV*) ► **Early Christian** ADJ, N paléochrétien(ne) *m(f)*; **the ~ Christians** les premiers chrétiens *mpl* ► **the Early Church** N l'Église *f* primitive ► **early closing (day)** N (*Brit*) jour de fermeture l'après-midi; **it's ~ closing (day) today** aujourd'hui les magasins ferment l'après-midi ► **Early English** N (*Archit*) premier gothique *m* anglais ► **early man** N les premiers hommes *mpl*, l'homme *m* primitif ► **early music** N la musique ancienne ► **early retirement** N (*gen*) retraite *f* anticipée; (*Admin*) préretraite *f*; **to take ~ retirement** (*gen*) prendre une retraite anticipée; (*Admin*) partir en préretraite ► **early riser** N lève-tôt* *mf inv* ► **early warning system** N (*Mil, fig*) système *m* d'alerte anticipée à grande distance

earmark ['ɪəmɑːk] **1** N (*fig*) marque *f*, signe *m* distinctif, caractéristique *f* **2** VT [+ *cattle*] marquer (au fer rouge); (*fig*) [+ *object, seat*] réserver (**for** à); [+ *funds, person*] assigner, affecter, destiner (**for** à)

earmuff ['ɪəmʌf] N cache-oreilles *m inv*

earn [ɜːn] **1** VT [+ *money*] gagner; [+ *salary*] toucher; (*Fin*) [+ *interest*] rapporter; [+ *praise, rest*] mériter, gagner; **to ~ one's living (doing sth)** gagner sa vie (en faisant qch); **she ~s** *or* **her living as a freelance TV producer** elle gagne sa vie comme réalisatrice indépendante pour la télévision; (*Brit hum*) **to ~ a** *or* **one's crust** gagner sa croûte*; (*Brit hum*) **to ~ an honest crust** gagner honnêtement sa vie *or* son pain; (*Brit*) **he has already ~ed his corn** il nous a déjà rapporté plus qu'il ne nous a coûté; **his success ~ed him praise** sa réussite lui a valu des éloges **2** VI **to be ~ing** gagner sa vie **3** COMP ► **earned income** N revenus *mpl* salariaux, traitement(s) *m(pl)*, salaire(s) *m(pl)* ► **earning power** N (*Econ*) productivité *f* financière; **his ~ing power** son salaire *etc* potentiel

earner ['ɜːnə'] N **high/low ~s** gens *mpl* qui gagnent bien leur vie/qui ont des revenus modestes; (*Brit*) **it's a nice little ~*** ça rapporte (bien)

earnest ['ɜːnɪst] **1** ADJ [*person, hope, desire, conversation, discussion*] sérieux; [*prayer*] fervent **2** N **a in ~** (= *with determination*) sérieusement; (= *without joking*) sans rire; **this time I am in ~** cette fois je ne plaisante pas; **it is snowing in ~** il neige pour de bon **b** (*fig* = *guarantee*) garantie *f*, gage *m*; **as an ~ of his good intentions** en gage de ses bonnes intentions **c** (*also ~ money*) arrhes *fpl*

earnestly ['ɜːnɪstlɪ] ADV [*say, explain, look at*] avec sérieux; [*talk, discuss, ask*] sérieusement; [*hope*] sincèrement; [*beseech*] instamment; [*pray*] avec ferveur

earnestness ['ɜːnɪstnɪs] N [*of person, tone*] gravité *f*, sérieux *m*; [*of effort*] ardeur *f*; [*of demand*] véhémence *f*

earnings ['ɜːnɪŋz] **1** NPL [*of person*] salaire *m*, gain(s) *m(pl)*; [*of business*] profits *mpl*, bénéfices *mpl* **2** COMP ► **earnings-related** ADJ [*pension, contributions*] proportionnel au salaire

earphone ['ɪəfəʊn] N (*Rad, Telec etc*) écouteur *m*; **to listen on ~s** écouter au casque

earpiece ['ɪəpiːs] N (*Rad, Telec etc*) écouteur *m*

earplugs ['ɪəplʌgz] N (*for sleeping*) boules *fpl* Quiès®; (*for underwater*) protège-tympans *mpl*

earring ['ɪərɪŋ] N boucle *f* d'oreille

earshot ['ɪəʃɒt] N **out of ~** hors de portée de voix; **within ~** à portée de voix

earth [ɜːθ] **1** N **a** (*NonC* = *ground, soil*) terre *f* (*also Elec*); **to fall to ~** tomber à terre *or* par terre *or* au sol; (*fig*) **to come down** *or* **be brought down to ~ (with a bump)** revenir *or* redescendre (brutalement) sur terre (*fig*); (*hum*) **the ~ moved** ça a été le grand frisson → **down**¹

b (= *planet*) **(the) Earth** la Terre; **on ~** sur terre; **here on ~** ici-bas, en ce bas monde; (*fig*) **it's heaven on ~** c'est le paradis sur terre; **to the ends of the ~** au bout du monde; **where/why/how on ~ ...?** où/pourquoi/comment diable ...?; **nowhere on ~ will you find ...** nulle part au monde vous ne trouverez ...; **nothing on ~** rien au monde; **she looks like nothing on ~!** à quoi elle ressemble!; **it tasted like nothing on ~** ça avait un goût vraiment bizarre; (*fig*) **to promise sb the ~** promettre la lune à qn; **it must have cost the ~!*** ça a dû coûter les yeux de la tête!*

c [*of fox, badger etc*] terrier *m*, tanière *f*; (*lit, fig*) **to run** *or* **go to ~** [*fox, criminal*] se terrer (*fig*); **to run sb to ~** dépister qn; (*hum*) **she finally ran him to ~ in the pub** elle a fini par le dénicher au pub; **he ran the quotation to ~ in "Hamlet"** il a déniché la citation dans « Hamlet »

2 VT (*Brit Elec*) [+ *apparatus*] mettre à la masse *or* à la terre

3 COMP ► **earth closet** N fosse f d'aisances ► **earth mother** N (Myth) déesse f de la fertilité; (fig) mère f nourricière ► **earth-moving equipment** N engins mpl de terrassement ► **earth sciences** NPL sciences fpl de la terre ► **earth-shaking***, **earth-shattering*** ADJ (fig) stupéfiant ► **earth tremor** N secousse f sismique ► **earth up** VT SEP [+ plant] butter

earthborn ['ɜːθbɔːn] ADJ (liter) humain

earthbound ['ɜːθbaʊnd] ADJ (= moving towards earth) qui se dirige vers la terre; (= stuck on earth) attaché à la terre; (fig = unimaginative) terre à terre inv, terre-à-terre inv

earthed [ɜːθt] ADJ (Brit Elec) relié à la terre

earthen ['ɜːθən] ADJ de terre, en terre

earthenware ['ɜːθənwɛəʳ] **1** N poterie f, terre f cuite; (glazed) faïence f **2** COMP [jug etc] en terre cuite (or en faïence)

earthiness ['ɜːθɪnɪs] N (fig) [of person] caractère m terre à terre or terre-à-terre; (fig) [of humour] truculence f

earthling* ['ɜːθlɪŋ] N terrien(ne) m(f) (par opposition à extraterrestre)

earthly ['ɜːθlɪ] **1** ADJ **a** [being, paradise, possessions] terrestre **b** (* fig = possible) there is no ~ reason to think that ... il n'y a pas la moindre raison de croire que ...; for no ~ reason sans aucune raison; he doesn't stand or hasn't an ~ chance of succeeding il n'a pas la moindre chance de réussir; of no ~ use d'aucune utilité, sans aucun intérêt; it's no ~ use telling him that ça ne sert absolument à rien de lui dire ça **2** N (Brit) not an ~* pas la moindre chance, pas l'ombre d'une chance

earthman* ['ɜːθmæn] N (pl -men) terrien m (par opposition à extraterrestre)

earthmover ['ɜːθmuːvəʳ] N bulldozer m

earthquake ['ɜːθkweɪk] N tremblement m de terre, séisme m → damage

earthward(s) ['ɜːθwəd(z)] ADV dans la direction de la terre, vers la terre

earthwork ['ɜːθwɜːk] N (Mil, Archeol) ouvrage m de terre; (Constr) terrassement m

earthworm ['ɜːθwɜːm] N ver m de terre

earthy ['ɜːθɪ] ADJ **a** (= like earth) [colour] ocré; [flavour] légèrement terreux; [smell] terreux, de terre **b** (= frank) [humour, language] truculent

earwax ['ɪəwæks] N cérumen m, cire f

earwig ['ɪəwɪg] N perce-oreille m

ease [iːz] **1** N (NonC) **a** (= well-being, relaxation) (mental) tranquillité f; (physical) bien-être m; at ~ (one's) ~ à l'aise; she put me at (my) ~ elle m'a mis à l'aise; not at ~ mal à l'aise; my mind is at ~ at last j'ai enfin l'esprit tranquille; to put or set sb's mind at ~ tranquilliser qn; to be at ~ with sb être à l'aise avec qn; I like Spain, but I don't feel at ~ with the language j'aime bien l'Espagne, mais je ne suis pas à l'aise en espagnol; I'm not really at ~ with the idea of flying l'idée de prendre l'avion m'angoisse un peu; to be or feel at ~ with oneself être bien dans sa peau; (Mil) (stand) at ~! repos!; he lives a life of ~ il a une vie facile; to take one's ~ prendre ses aises → ill
b (= lack of difficulty) aisance f, facilité f; ~ of use/reference/access facilité f d'emploi/de consultation/d'accès; for ~ of reference/access/storage pour faciliter la consultation/l'accès/le rangement, pour une consultation/un accès/un rangement facile; we tested them for ~ of use nous les avons testés pour voir s'ils étaient faciles à utiliser; with ~ aisément, facilement; with the greatest of ~ avec la plus grande facilité, sans la moindre difficulté
2 VT **a** (= relieve) [+ pain] atténuer, soulager; [+ mind] calmer, tranquilliser; [+ pressure, tension] diminuer, réduire; [+ sanctions] assou-

plir; [+ restrictions] relâcher; [+ shortage, overcrowding] pallier; [+ problem] atténuer; [+ suffering] soulager; [+ situation] détendre; [+ fears] apaiser; ways to ~ the food shortage des moyens de pallier la pénurie alimentaire; to ~ traffic congestion in Bangkok/on the motorway décongestionner Bangkok/on the autoroute; to ~ the overcrowding in the universities décongestionner les universités; to ~ sb's burden soulager qn d'un poids
b (= make easier) [+ transition] faciliter
c (= move gently) to ~ a key into a lock introduire doucement or délicatement une clé dans une serrure; to ~ in the clutch embrayer en douceur; she ~d the car into gear elle a passé la première en douceur; she ~d out the screw elle a enlevé doucement or délicatement la vis; he ~d himself into the chair il s'est laissé glisser dans le fauteuil; he ~d himself through the gap in the fence il s'est glissé par le trou de la barrière; he ~d himself into his jacket il a passé or enfilé doucement sa veste
3 VI [pressure, tension, fighting] diminuer; the situation has ~d la situation s'est détendue; prices have ~d les prix ont baissé, il y a eu une baisse des prix

►**ease back** VI (US) to ~ back on sb/sth montrer moins strict envers qn/en ce qui concerne qch
►**ease off** **1** VI [person] (= slow down) ralentir; (= work less hard) se relâcher; (= subside) [rain, wind] se calmer; [pressure] diminuer; [work, business] devenir plus calme; [traffic] diminuer; [pain] se calmer; [demand] baisser **2** VT SEP [+ bandage, stamp etc] enlever délicatement; [+ lid] enlever doucement
►**ease up** VI [person] (= relax) se détendre, se reposer; (= make less effort) relâcher ses efforts; (= calm down) [situation] se détendre; ~ up a bit! vas-y plus doucement!; to ~ up on sb/sth se montrer moins strict envers qn/en ce qui concerne qch

easel ['iːzl] N chevalet m

easement ['iːzmənt] N (US Jur) droit m de passage

easily ['iːzɪlɪ] ADV **a** (= without difficulty, quickly) [accessible, available, recognizable] facilement; to tire/break ~ se fatiguer/se casser facilement; I can ~ fetch him je peux facilement aller le chercher; he makes friends ~ il se fait facilement des amis; just as ~ aussi bien; as ~ as (if ...) aussi facilement que (si ...); (fig) he is ~ led il est très influençable
b (= very possibly) bien; he may ~ change his mind il pourrait bien changer d'avis; he could ~ be right il pourrait bien avoir raison
c (with superl = unquestionably) sans aucun doute, de loin; he was ~ the best candidate il était de loin le meilleur candidat
d (with amounts, measurements etc) facilement; that's ~ 50km ça fait facilement 50 km
e (= in relaxed manner) [talk, smile, breathe] avec décontraction; "yes", he said ~ «oui», dit-il avec décontraction

easiness ['iːzɪnɪs] N facilité f

east [iːst] **1** N est m, orient m (frm); the East (gen) l'Orient m; (Pol = Iron Curtain) les pays mpl de l'Est; (US Geog) (les États mpl de) l'Est m; the mysterious East l'Orient m mystérieux; to the ~ of ... à l'est de ...; in the ~ of Scotland dans l'est de l'Écosse; house facing the ~ maison f exposée à l'est; to veer to the ~ ◊ to go into the ~ [wind] tourner à l'est; the wind is in the ~ le vent est à l'est; the wind is (coming or blowing) from the ~ le vent vient or souffle de l'est; to live in the ~ habiter dans l'Est → far, middle
2 ADJ [coast, wing] est inv; ~ wind vent m d'est; on the ~ side du côté est; East Asia l'Asie f de l'Est; in ~ Devon dans l'est du Devon; East London l'est m de Londres; a room with an ~ aspect une pièce exposée à l'est;

(Archit) ~ transept/door transept m/portail m est or oriental → 4
3 ADV [go, travel, fly] vers l'est; go ~ till you get to Manchester allez vers l'est jusqu'à Manchester; we drove ~ for 100km nous avons roulé vers l'est pendant 100 km; to be (due) ~ of Paris être (en plein) à l'est de Paris; to head due ~ (gen) se diriger plein est; (Aviat, Naut) avoir le cap à l'est; to sail due ~ avoir le cap à l'est; further ~ plus à l'est; ~ by north/south est quart nord/sud; ~ by north-~ est quart nord-est
4 COMP ► **East Africa** N l'Afrique f orientale, l'Est m de l'Afrique ► **East African** ADJ d'Afrique orientale ◆ N Africain(e) m(f) de l'Est ► **East Berlin** N Berlin-Est ► **East Berliner** N habitant(e) m(f) de Berlin-Est ► **the East End** N (also **the East End of London**) les quartiers mpl est de Londres (quartiers surtout pauvres) ► **East Ender** (Brit) N habitant(e) m(f) de l'East End (de Londres) ► **East Europe** N (esp US) l'Europe f de l'Est ► **East European** ADJ d'Europe de l'Est ◆ N Européen(ne) m(f) de l'Est ► **east-facing** ADJ exposé à l'est ► **East German** ADJ est-allemand ◆ N Allemand(e) m(f) de l'Est ► **East Germany** N l'Allemagne f de l'Est ► **East Indian** des Indes orientales ► **the East Indies** NPL les Indes fpl orientales ► **east-north-east** N, ADJ est-nord-est m ► **(the) East Side** N [of New York] les quartiers mpl est de New York ► **east-south-east** N, ADJ est-sud-est m

eastbound ['iːstbaʊnd] ADJ [traffic, vehicles] (se déplaçant) en direction de l'est; [carriageway] est inv; to be ~ on the M8 être sur la M8 en direction de l'est

Easter ['iːstəʳ] **1** N **a** (Rel: also ~ Day) Pâques m; ~ is celebrated between ... Pâques est célébré entre ... **b** Pâques fpl; at ~ à Pâques; Happy ~! joyeuses Pâques! **2** COMP [egg] de Pâques; [holidays] pascal, de Pâques ► **Easter bonnet** N chapeau m de printemps ► **Easter communion** N to make one's ~ communion faire ses pâques ► **Easter Day** N le jour de Pâques ► **Easter Island** N l'île f de Pâques; the ~ Island statues les statues fpl de l'île de Pâques ► **Easter Monday** N le lundi de Pâques ► **Easter parade** N défilé m pascal ► **Easter Sunday** N le dimanche de Pâques ► **Easter week** N la semaine pascale

easterly ['iːstəlɪ] **1** ADJ [wind] d'est; [situation] à l'est, à l'orient (frm); in an ~ direction en direction de l'est, vers l'est; ~ aspect exposition f à l'est **2** ADV vers l'est

eastern ['iːstən] ADJ est inv, de l'est; the ~ coast la côte est or orientale; a house with an ~ outlook une maison exposée à l'est; ~ wall mur m exposé à l'est; ~ Africa l'Afrique f orientale; ~ France la France de l'est, l'Est m de la France; (Pol) the Eastern bloc les pays de l'Est; the Eastern Church l'Église f d'Orient; (US) Eastern Daylight Time heure f d'été de l'Est; Eastern European Time heure f de l'Europe orientale; (US) Eastern Standard Time heure f de l'Est

easterner ['iːstənəʳ] N (esp US) homme m or femme f de l'Est; he is an ~ il vient de l'Est; the ~s les gens mpl de l'Est

easternmost ['iːstənməʊst] ADJ le plus à l'est

Eastertide ['iːstətaɪd] N le temps pascal, la saison de Pâques

eastward ['iːstwəd] **1** ADJ [route] en direction de l'est; [slope] exposé à l'est; in an ~ direction en direction de l'est, vers l'est **2** ADV (also ~s) vers l'est

easy ['iːzɪ] **1** ADJ **a** (= not difficult) [work, decision, access, victory, option, target] facile; [solution] facile, aisé; there are no ~ answers il n'y a pas de réponses faciles; as ~ as anything* or pie* or ABC or falling off a log* facile comme tout; in ~ circumstances dans l'aisance; to be far from ~ or none too ~ or no ~ matter or no ~ task être loin d'être facile; he came in an ~ **first** il est arrivé bon premier ; ~ **to get on with** facile à vivre ; **reducing inflation is a relatively ~ job** réduire l'inflation est chose relativement facile ; ~ **living** ◊ **the ~ life** la vie facile ; **to be ~ meat* (for sb)** être une cible facile (pour qn) ; **it was an ~ mistake to make** c'était une erreur facile à faire ; **it's none too ~** ◊ **it's no ~ task** ce n'est pas simple or évident ; ~ **on the eye*** (Brit) or **on the eyes*** (US) [person] bien balancé* ; [thing] agréable à regarder ; ~ **on the ear*** agréable à entendre ; **to be ~ on the stomach** ne pas être lourd pour l'estomac ; **to take the ~ option** or **the ~ way out** choisir la solution de facilité ; (euph) **to take the ~ way out** (= commit suicide) mettre fin à ses jours ; **at an ~ pace** à une allure modérée ; **that's the ~ part** c'est ce qu'il y a de plus facile ; **burglars hoping for ~ pickings*** cambrioleurs espérant pouvoir faucher* facilement ; **there were ~ pickings* to be made in the property market** on pouvait faire de bonnes affaires sur le marché de l'immobilier ; **within ~ reach of sth** à distance commode de qch ; **to make ~ reading** être facile à lire ; **to have an ~ ride** avoir la vie facile ; **in** or **by ~ stages** par petites étapes ; (esp US) **to be on ~ street*** se la couler douce* ; **to have an ~ time (of it)** avoir la vie belle ; **it is ~ for him to do that** il lui est facile de faire cela ; **that's ~ for you to say** pour toi, c'est facile à dire ; **it is ~ to see that ...** on voit bien que ..., cela se voit que ... ; **it's ~ to see why** il est facile de comprendre pourquoi ; **it was ~ to get them to be quiet** on a eu vite fait de les faire taire ; **he is ~ to work with** il est agréable or accommodant dans le travail → **mark²**

b (= relaxed) [temperament, disposition] placide ; [conversation] tranquille ; [voice, tone] paisible ; [laugh, laughter] décontracté ; [style] facile, aisé ; [relationship] facile ; [manners] aisé ; **on ~ terms with sb** en bons termes avec qn ; **I'm ~*** ça m'est égal

c (= happy) **I don't feel ~ about it** ça me gêne un peu ; **I don't feel ~ about leaving the kids with that woman** ça me gêne un peu de laisser les gosses avec cette femme ; **to feel ~ in one's mind (about sth)** être tout à fait tranquille or ne pas se faire de souci (à propos de qch)

d (Comm, Fin, St Ex) **on ~ terms** ◊ **by ~ payments** avec facilités de paiement ; ~ **credit** fonds mpl aisément disponibles ; ~ **market** marché m tranquille or mou ; **prices are ~ today** les prix sont un peu moins hauts aujourd'hui

e (* pej = promiscuous) [person] facile (pej) ; **she had a reputation for being ~** elle avait la réputation d'être (une femme) facile ; **to be an ~ lay** or (US) **make** être une Marie-couche-toi-là ; (euph) **a woman of ~ virtue†** une femme de petite vertu†

2 ADV **a** (* = gently) **to go ~ on sb/sth** y aller doucement avec qn/qch ; **to take it ~** ◊ **to take things ~** (= rest) se la couler douce* ; **take it ~!** (= relax) t'énerve pas !* ; (esp US: when saying goodbye) à plus !* ; ~ **does it!** ◊ ~ **there!** doucement !

b (= without difficulty) **to have it ~** se la couler douce* ; **that's easier said than done!** c'est plus facile à dire qu'à faire ! ; **just get rid of it — easier said than done!** tu n'as qu'à t'en débarrasser — facile à dire ! ; (fig) **to breathe ~** (= relax) souffler ; ~ **come, ~ go!*** ce n'est que de l'argent !, c'est fait pour être dépensé ! → **3**

c (Mil) **stand ~!** repos !

3 COMP ► **easy-care** ADJ d'entretien facile ► **easy chair** N fauteuil m (rembourré) ► **easy-going** ADJ accommodant ; [person] facile à vivre, qui ne s'en fait pas ; [attitude] complaisant ► **easy listening** N (Mus) musique f légère ► **easy-listening** ADJ (Mus) [album, CD] de musique légère ► **~-listening music** musique f légère ► **easy money** N (in prospect) argent m facile à gagner ; (already

made) argent m gagné facilement ► **easy-peasy*** ADJ (Brit) fastoche*

eat [iːt] (pret **ate**, ptp **eaten**) **1** VT **a** [+ food] manger ; **to ~ (one's) breakfast** déjeuner, prendre son petit déjeuner ; **to ~ (one's) lunch** déjeuner ; **to ~ (one's) dinner** dîner ; **to ~ a meal** prendre un repas ; **to have nothing to ~** n'avoir rien à manger or à se mettre sous la dent ; **to ~ one's fill** manger à sa faim ; **fit to ~** mangeable, bon à manger ; (fig) **she looks good enough to ~** elle est belle à croquer ; (fig) **to ~ one's words** se rétracter, ravaler ses paroles ; (fig) **to make sb ~ his words** faire rentrer ses mots dans la gorge à qn ; **I'll ~ my hat if ...*** je veux bien être pendu si ... ; **I could ~ a horse*** j'ai une faim de loup* ; **he won't ~ you*** il ne va pas te manger ; **what's ~ing you?*** qu'est-ce qui ne va pas ?, qu'est-ce qui te tracasse ? ; **he left the other runners ~ing his dust*** il a laissé les autres coureurs loin derrière lui

b (‡ = perform oral sex on) sucer‡

2 VI manger ; **we ~ at eight** nous dînons à 20 heures ; **to ~ like a horse** manger comme quatre or comme un ogre ; **to ~ like a bird** picorer ; **to ~ like a pig** manger comme un porc ; **he's ~ing us out of house and home*** son appétit va nous mettre à la rue ; (fig) **to ~ out of sb's hand** faire les quatre volontés de qn ; **I've got him ~ing out of my hand** il fait tout ce que je lui dis or tout ce que je veux

3 **eats‡** NPL (Brit) bouffe‡ f ; (on notice) snacks mpl ; **let's get some ~s** mangeons quelque chose or un morceau

► **eat away** VT SEP [sea] saper, éroder ; [acid, mice] ronger

► **eat away at** VT FUS [waves, sea] éroder ; [acid, rust, pest] ronger ; [rot, damp] attaquer ; **a cancer ~ing away at society** un cancer qui ronge la société ; **jealousy was ~ing away at her** elle était rongée de jalousie ; **inflation was ~ing away at their capital** l'inflation rongeait leur capital

► **eat in** **1** VI manger chez soi **2** VT consommer sur place

► **eat into** VT FUS [acid, insects] ronger ; [moths] manger ; [expenditure] [+ savings] entamer, écorner

► **eat out** **1** VI aller au restaurant, déjeuner or dîner en ville **2** VT SEP (fig) **to ~ one's heart out** (= pine away) se ronger d'inquiétude ; **I've written a novel: Marcel Proust, ~ your heart out!** j'ai écrit un roman : Marcel Proust peut aller se rhabiller !*

► **eat up** **1** VI ~ **up!** mangez ! **2** VT SEP (= finish off) finir ; ~ **up your meat** finis ta viande ; ~ **up your meal** finis ton repas, finis de manger ; (fig) **to be ~en up with envy** être dévoré d'envie or rongé par l'envie **3** VT FUS (fig = consume heavily) [+ fuel] consommer beaucoup de, être gourmand en* ; [+ resources, profits] absorber ; [+ savings] engloutir ; **this car ~s up the miles** cette voiture dévore la route ; **this car ~s up petrol** cette voiture est gourmande* (en essence) or consomme beaucoup (d'essence) ; **it ~s up the electricity/coal** cela consomme beaucoup d'électricité/de charbon

eatable ['iːtəbl] **1** ADJ **a** (= not poisonous) [mushroom, berries etc] comestible, bon à manger **b** (= not disgusting) [meal etc] mangeable **2** **eatables*** NPL comestibles mpl, victuailles fpl (hum)

eaten ['iːtn] VB ptp of **eat**

eater ['iːtəʳ] N **a** (= person) mangeur m, -euse f ; **to be a big ~** être un grand or gros mangeur ; **to be a big meat ~** être un gros mangeur de viande **b** (* = eating apple) pomme f à couteau

eatery* ['iːtərɪ] N (café-)restaurant m

eating ['iːtɪŋ] **1** N **these apples make good ~** ces pommes sont bonnes à manger **2** COMP [apple] à couteau, de dessert ► **eating**

chocolate N chocolat m à croquer ► **eating disorder** N troubles mpl du comportement alimentaire ► **eating hall** N (US) réfectoire m ► **eating house**, **eating place** N (café-) restaurant m

eau de Cologne ['əʊdəkə'ləʊn] N eau f de Cologne

eaves ['iːvz] NPL avant-toit(s) m(pl)

eavesdrop ['iːvzdrɒp] VI écouter aux portes ; **to ~ on a conversation** écouter une conversation privée

eavesdropper ['iːvzdrɒpəʳ] N oreille f indiscrète

ebb [eb] **1** N (of tide) reflux m ; (Naut) jusant m ; ~ **and flow** le flux et le reflux ; **the tide is on the ~** la marée descend ; (fig) **to be at a low ~** [person] être bien bas ; [business] aller mal ; **his spirits were at a low ~** il avait le moral très bas or à zéro* ; **his funds were at a low ~** ses fonds étaient bien bas or bien dégarnis **2** VI **a** [tide] refluer, descendre ; **to ~ and flow** monter et baisser **b** (fig: also ~ **away**) [enthusiasm, strength etc] décliner, baisser **3** COMP ► **ebb tide** N marée f descendante, reflux m ; (Naut) jusant m

Ebola [ɪˈbəʊlə] N (Med: also ~ **virus**) virus m Ebola

ebonite ['ebənaɪt] N ébonite f

ebony ['ebənɪ] **1** N ébène f **2** COMP (= ebony-coloured) noir d'ébène ; (= made of ebony) en ébène, d'ébène

EBRD [ˌiːbiːɑːˈdiː] N (ABBR = European Bank for Reconstruction and Development) BERD f

ebullience [ɪˈbʌlɪəns] N exubérance f

ebullient [ɪˈbʌlɪənt] ADJ [person] plein de vie, exubérant ; [spirits, mood] exubérant

EC [ˌiːˈsiː] **1** N (ABBR = European Community) CE f **2** COMP [directive, membership, states etc] de la CE ► **EC-wide** ADJ, ADV à l'échelle de (toute) la CE

eccentric [ɪkˈsentrɪk] **1** ADJ (also Math, Astron) excentrique **2** N **a** (= person) original(e) m(f), excentrique mf **b** (Tech) excentrique m

eccentrically [ɪkˈsentrɪkəlɪ] ADV [behave, dress] de façon excentrique, excentriquement ; [decorate] de façon originale

eccentricity [ˌeksənˈtrɪsɪtɪ] N (also Math, Astron) excentricité f

Eccles cake ['ekəlz,keɪk] N (in Brit) pâtisserie fourrée de fruits secs

Ecclesiastes [ɪˌkliːzɪˈæstiːz] N (Bible) (the Book of) ~ (le livre de l')Ecclésiaste m

ecclesiastic [ɪˌkliːzɪˈæstɪk] ADJ, N ecclésiastique m

ecclesiastical [ɪˌkliːzɪˈæstɪkəl] ADJ ecclésiastique

ecdysis ['ekdɪsɪs] N (pl **ecdyses** ['ekdɪˌsiːz]) ecdysis f

ECG, **EKG** (US) [ˌiːkeɪˈdʒiː] N (ABBR = electrocardiogram, electrocardiograph) ECG m

echelon ['eʃəlɒn] N échelon m

echinoderm [ɪˈkaɪnədɜːm] N échinoderme m

echo ['ekəʊ] **1** N (pl **echoes**) écho m ; (fig) écho m, rappel m ; **to cheer to the ~** applaudir à tout rompre **2** VT (lit) répercuter, renvoyer ; (fig) **he ~ed my words incredulously** il a répété ce que j'avais dit d'un ton incrédule ; **"go home?", he ~ed** « rentrer ? », répéta-t-il ; **to ~ sb's ideas/remarks** se faire l'écho de l'écho de la pensée/des remarques de qn **3** VI [sound] (= resonate) retentir, résonner ; (= bounce back) se répercuter, faire écho ; [place] renvoyer l'écho ; (liter) **to ~ with music** retentir de musique ; (liter) **the valley ~ed with their laughter** la vallée résonnait or retentissait de leurs rires **4** COMP ► **echo chamber** N (Rad, TV) chambre f sonore ► **echo-sounder** N (Naut) sondeur m (à ultrasons) ► **echo-sounding** N sondage m par ultrasons

éclair [eɪ'klɛəʳ, ɪ'klɛəʳ] N (Culin) éclair m (à la crème)

eclampsia [ɪ'klæmpsɪə] N éclampsie f

eclectic [ɪ'klektɪk] ADJ, N éclectique mf

eclecticism [ɪ'klektɪsɪzəm] N éclectisme m

eclipse [ɪ'klɪps] **1** N (Astron, fig) éclipse f; **to be in ~** être éclipsé; **to fall** or **go into ~** être éclipsé; **partial/total ~** éclipse f partielle/totale **2** VT éclipser **3** COMP ► **eclipsing binary** N étoile f double

ecliptic [ɪ'klɪptɪk] ADJ écliptique

eclogue ['eklɒg] N églogue f

eclosion [ɪ'kləʊʒən] N éclosion f

eco... ['iːkəʊ] PREF éco...

ecocide ['iːkəʊsaɪd] N écocide m

eco-friendly ['iːkəʊˌfrendlɪ] ADJ [detergent, hairspray etc] respectueux de l'environnement

E-coli [iː'kəʊlaɪ] N (Med) E. coli m, bactérie f Escherischia coli

ecological [ˌiːkə'lɒdʒɪkəl] ADJ **a** [damage, problem, disaster] écologique **b** (= ecologically sound) écologique

ecologically [ˌiːkə'lɒdʒɪkəlɪ] ADV [unacceptable] écologiquement, d'un point de vue écologique; **~ aware** sensibilisé aux problèmes écologiques; **~ harmful** qui nuit à l'environnement; **~ minded** soucieux de l'environnement; **~ sound** écologique, respectueux de l'environnement; **~ speaking** d'un point de vue écologique

ecologist [ɪ'kɒlədʒɪst] N écologiste mf

ecology [ɪ'kɒlədʒɪ] N écologie f

ecomovement ['iːkəʊˌmuːvmənt] N (Pol) mouvement m écologique

econometer [ˌɪkə'nɒmətəʳ] N (Aut) économètre m

econometric [ˌɪˌkɒnə'metrɪk] ADJ économétrique

econometrician [ˌɪˌkɒnəmə'trɪʃən] N économétricien(ne) m(f)

econometrics [ˌɪˌkɒnə'metrɪks] N (NonC) économétrie f

econometrist [ˌɪˌkɒnə'metrɪst] N = **econometrician**

economic [ˌiːkə'nɒmɪk] **1** ADJ **a** (Econ) [growth, policy, system, crisis, recovery, sanctions, aid] économique; **the ~ situation** or **outlook** la conjoncture (économique) **b** (= viable, cost-effective) [system, factory, mine etc] rentable (**for sb** pour qn); **this business is no longer ~** or **an ~ proposition** cette affaire n'est plus rentable; **it is not ~ to do that** ce n'est pas rentable de faire cela; **► rate of return** taux m de rentabilité économique **c** (= market-driven) [price, rent] déterminé par le marché **2** COMP ► **economic analyst** N spécialiste mf de l'analyse économique ► **economic indicator** N indicateur m économique ► **economic management** N gestion f de l'économie ► **economic migrant, economic refugee** N migrant(e) m(f) économique

economical [ˌiːkə'nɒmɪkəl] ADJ [person] économe; [method, vehicle, machine, speed] économique; (fig) [style, writing] sobre, concis; **to be ~ with** sth économiser qch, ménager qch; **to be ~ with the truth** (= not tell whole truth) ne pas dire toute la vérité; (hum = lie) prendre ses aises avec la vérité

economically [ˌiːkə'nɒmɪkəlɪ] ADV (Econ) [viable, depressed] économiquement; [feasible, powerful, important] d'un point de vue économique; [develop, suffer] économiquement, d'un point de vue économique; **~ speaking** d'un point de vue économique **b** (= without waste) [use, operate, live] de façon économe **c** (= concisely) [write] avec sobriété

economics [ˌiːkə'nɒmɪks] N (NonC) (= science) économie f politique, science f économique; (= financial aspect) côté m économique; **the ~**

of the situation/the project le côté économique de la situation/du projet → **home**

economist [ɪ'kɒnəmɪst] N économiste mf, spécialiste mf d'économie politique

economize [ɪ'kɒnəmaɪz] **1** VI économiser (**on** sur), faire des économies **2** VT [+ time, money] économiser (sur), épargner; **to ~ 20% on the costs** faire or réaliser une économie de 20 % sur les coûts

economy [ɪ'kɒnəmɪ] **1** N **a** (= saving: in time, money etc) économie f (**in** de); **to make economies in ...** faire des économies de ...; **economies of scale** économies fpl d'échelle **b** (NonC = system) économie f, système m économique; **the country's ~ depends on ...** l'économie du pays dépend de ... → **black, political 2** COMP ► **economy class** N (esp Aviat) classe f touriste ► **economy drive** N [of government, firm] (campagne f de) restrictions fpl budgétaires; **I'm going on** or **having an ~ drive this month** ce mois-ci je m'efforce de faire des économies ► **economy pack** N (Comm) paquet m économique ► **economy size** N (Comm) taille f économique

ecosphere ['iːkəʊˌsfɪə] N écosphère f

ecosystem ['iːkəʊˌsɪstəm] N écosystème m

ecotone ['iːkəʊˌtəʊn] N écotone m

eco-tourism [ˌiːkəʊ'tʊərɪzəm] N écotourisme m

ecotype ['iːkəʊˌtaɪp] N écotype m

ecru ['ekruː] ADJ, N écru m

ECSC [ˌiːsiːes'siː] N (formerly) (ABBR = **European Coal and Steel Community**) CECA f

ecstasy ['ekstəsɪ] N **a** (= joy) extase f (also Rel), ravissement m; **with ~** avec ravissement, avec extase; **to be in ecstasies over** [+ object] s'extasier sur; [+ person] être en extase devant **b** (Drugs) ecstasy m

ecstatic [eks'tætɪk] ADJ [crowd] en délire; [welcome, reception] enthousiaste; **to be ~ over** or **about sth** être follement heureux de qch

ecstatically [eks'tætɪkəlɪ] ADV [applaud, react] avec extase; [listen, say] d'un air extasié; **~ happy** follement heureux

ECT [ˌiːsiː'tiː] N ABBR = **electroconvulsive therapy**

ectomorph ['ektəʊˌmɔːf] N ectomorphe mf

ectopic [ek'tɒpɪk] ADJ ► **pregnancy** grossesse f extra-utérine

ectoplasm ['ektəʊplæzəm] N ectoplasme m

ECU ['eɪkjuː, ˌiːsiː'juː] N (ABBR = **European Currency Unit**) ECU m, écu m; **hard ~** écu m fort; **weights of currencies in the ~** pieds m des devises au sein de l'écu

Ecuador ['ekwədɔːʳ] N l'Équateur m

Ecuador(i)an [ˌekwə'dɔːr(ɪ)ən] **1** ADJ équatorien **2** N Équatorien(ne) m(f)

ecumenical [ˌiːkjuː'menɪkəl] ADJ œcuménique

ecumenicism [ˌiːkjuː'menɪsɪzəm], **ecumenism** [iː'kjuːmənɪzəm] N œcuménisme m

eczema ['eksɪmə] N eczéma m; **~ sufferer** personne f sujette à l'eczéma

ed. a (ABBR = **edition**) éd.; **3rd ~** 3ᵉ éd. **b** (ABBR = **editor**) **"Chèvrefeuille", ~ J. Lefèvre** « Chèvrefeuille », annoté et commenté par J. Lefèvre; **"Essays in Welsh History", eds. Dodd and Jenkins** « Essays in Welsh History », sous la direction de Dodd et Jenkins

EDC [ˌiːdiː'siː] N (ABBR = **European Defence Community**) CED f

eddy ['edɪ] **1** N [of water, air] remous m, tourbillon m; [of snow, dust, smoke] tourbillon m; [of leaves] tournoiement m, tourbillon m **2** VI [air, smoke, leaves, snow, dust] tourbillonner; [people] tournoyer; [water] faire des remous or des tourbillons

edelweiss ['eɪdlvaɪs] N edelweiss m inv

edema [ɪ'diːmə] N (pl **edemata** [ɪ'diːmətə]) (esp US) œdème m

Eden ['iːdn] N Éden m, paradis m terrestre → **garden**

edentate [iː'denteɪt] ADJ, N édenté m

edge [edʒ] **1** N **a** [of table, plate, cloth, river, lake] bord m; [of road] bord m, côté m; [of town] abords mpl; [of cloth, coin] tranche f; [of page] bord m; (= margin) marge f; [of cube, brick] arête f; [of cliff] bord m; [of forest] lisière f, orée f; **at the water's ~** au bord de l'eau; **to stand sth on its ~** poser qch de chant; **the trees at the ~ of the road** les arbres au bord or en bordure de la route; **the film had us on the ~ of our seats** or (US) **chairs** le film nous a tenus en haleine **b** (= blade) [of knife, razor] tranchant m, fil m; **a blade with a sharp ~** une lame bien affilée; **to put an ~ on** [+ knife, blade etc] aiguiser, affiler; affûter **c** [of ski] arête f; (= metal strip) carre f **d** (fig = brink, verge) **to be on the ~ of disaster** être au bord du désastre, courir au désastre; **that pushed him over the ~** ça a été plus qu'il ne pouvait supporter, ça a été le comble; **to live life on the ~*** être or marcher sur le fil du rasoir **e** on **~: he's on ~** il est énervé or à cran*; **my nerves are all on ~** j'ai les nerfs à vif or en pelote* or en boule*; (lit, fig) **it sets my teeth on ~** cela me fait grincer les dents **f** (fig = advantage) **the company has lost its competitive ~** la société est devenue moins compétitive; **the party has lost its radical ~** le parti n'est plus aussi radical qu'avant; **to have the ~ on** or **over** avoir un (léger) avantage sur, l'emporter de justesse sur; **to give sb the ~ on** or **over the competition** donner à qn un avantage sur la concurrence **g** (fig = sharpness) **to take the ~ off** [+ sensation] émousser; [+ appetite] calmer, émousser; **there was an ~ to his voice** on sentait à sa voix qu'il était tendu; **panic gave a sharp ~ to his voice** sous l'effet de la panique, sa voix est devenue tendue; **there was a slightly caustic ~ to his voice** il y avait des intonations caustiques dans sa voix → **cutting, rough 2** VT **a** (= put a border on) border (**with** de); **~d with lace** bordé de dentelle **b** **to ~ one's chair nearer the door** rapprocher sa chaise tout doucement de la porte; **to ~ one's way through** or **into** → 3; **to ~ sb out of his** (or **her**) **job** déloger progressivement qn de son poste; **wage rises have ~d up inflation** la hausse des salaires a entraîné une légère augmentation du taux d'inflation **3** VI se glisser, se faufiler; **to ~ through/into** etc se glisser or se faufiler à travers/dans etc; **to ~ forward** avancer petit à petit; **to ~ away** s'éloigner tout doucement or furtivement; **to ~ up to sb** (furtively) s'approcher tout doucement or furtivement de qn; (shyly) s'approcher timidement de qn; **share prices ~d up** il y a eu une tendance à la hausse des valeurs boursières; **to ~ out of a room** se glisser hors d'une pièce, sortir furtivement d'une pièce

-edged [edʒd] ADJ (in compounds) **a** [paper, fabric] bordé de, avec une bordure de **b** [knife etc] **blunt-/sharp-edged** émoussé/bien aiguisé

edgeways ['edʒweɪz], **edgewise** ['edʒwaɪz] ADV de côté; **I couldn't get a word in ~*** je n'ai pas réussi à placer un mot or à en placer une*

edginess ['edʒɪnɪs] N (NonC) nervosité f, énervement m, irritation f

edging ['edʒɪŋ] **1** N **a** (gen) bordure f; [of ribbon, silk] liseré or liséré m **b** (Ski) prise f de carres **2** COMP ► **edging shears** NPL (Hort) cisailles fpl à gazon

edgy ['edʒɪ] ADJ [person, mood] énervé, à cran*, crispé

edibility [ˌedɪ'bɪlɪtɪ] N comestibilité f

edible ['edɪbl] **1** ADJ **a** (= not poisonous) [mushroom, berries etc] comestible, bon à manger **b** (= not disgusting) [meal etc] mangeable [2] COMP ► **edible crab** N dormeur m, tourteau m ► **edible snail** N escargot m comestible

edict [ˈiːdɪkt] N (gen, Jur, Pol) décret m; (Hist) édit m

edification [ˌedɪfɪˈkeɪʃən] N édification f, instruction f

edifice [ˈedɪfɪs] N édifice m

edify [ˈedɪfaɪ] VT édifier

edifying [ˈedɪfaɪɪŋ] ADJ édifiant

Edinburgh [ˈedɪnbərə] [1] N Édimbourg [2] COMP ► **the Edinburgh Festival** N le Festival d'Édimbourg

---
EDINBURGH FESTIVAL

Le Festival d'Édimbourg, qui se tient chaque année durant trois semaines au mois d'août, est l'un des grands festivals européens. Il est réputé pour son programme officiel mais aussi pour son festival « off » (the Fringe) qui propose des spectacles aussi bien traditionnels que résolument d'avant-garde. Pendant la durée du Festival se tient par ailleurs, sur l'esplanade du château, un grand spectacle de musique militaire, le « Military Tattoo ».

---

edit [ˈedɪt] [1] VT [+ newspaper, magazine] être le rédacteur (or la rédactrice) en chef de; [+ article] mettre au point, préparer; [+ series of texts] diriger la publication de; [+ text, author] éditer, donner une édition de; [+ dictionary, encyclopedia] assurer la rédaction de; (Rad, TV) [+ programme] réaliser; [+ film] monter; [+ tape] mettre au point, couper et recoller; (Comput) [+ file] éditer [2] N révision f
► **edit out** VT SEP supprimer (**of** de); [+ text, film] couper (**of** de)

editing [ˈedɪtɪŋ] N [of magazine] direction f; [of newspaper, dictionary] rédaction f; [of article, series of texts, tape] mise f au point; [of text, author] édition f; [of film] montage m; (Comput) édition f

edition [ɪˈdɪʃən] N [of newspaper, book] édition f; [of print, etching] tirage m; **revised ~** édition f revue et corrigée; **to bring out an ~ of a text** publier or faire paraître l'édition d'un texte → **first**

editor [ˈedɪtər] [1] N [a] (Press) [of newspaper, magazine] rédacteur m, -trice f en chef [b] (Publishing) [of writer, text, anthology] directeur m, -trice f de la publication; [of dictionary, encyclopedia] rédacteur m, -trice f [c] (Rad, TV) [of programme] réalisateur m, -trice f [d] (Cine) monteur m, -euse f; (Press) **political ~** rédacteur m, -trice f politique; **sports ~** rédacteur m sportif, rédactrice f sportive; **"letters to the ~"** « courrier des lecteurs », « lettres à la rédaction » → **news** [2] COMP ► **editor-in-chief** N rédacteur m, -trice f en chef

editorial [ˌedɪˈtɔːrɪəl] [1] ADJ [budget, board, meeting, comment, control, decision] de la rédaction; [office] de (la) rédaction; [page] de l'éditorial; [policy] éditorial; **~ assistant** rédacteur m, -trice f adjoint(e); **~ staff** (as team) rédaction f; (as individuals) personnel m de la rédaction; **the ~ "we"** le « nous » de modestie or d'auteur [2] N (in newspaper etc) éditorial m, article m de tête

editorialist [ˌedɪˈtɔːrɪəlɪst] N (US) éditorialiste mf

editorialize [ˌedɪˈtɔːrɪəlaɪz] VI exprimer une opinion

editorially [ˌedɪˈtɔːrɪəlɪ] ADV [a] (= in approach, content) [independent, selective] du point de vue éditorial [b] (in opinion piece) **the Times commented ~ that ...** le Times a affirmé dans un éditorial que ...

editorship [ˈedɪtəʃɪp] N [a] (= position of editor) [of newspaper, magazine] poste m de rédacteur en chef; (Rad, TV) poste m de réalisateur [b] (NonC = act or style of editing) [of newspaper, magazine] direction f; [of dictionary, ency-

clopedia] rédaction f; [of text] édition f; **under sb's ~ or the ~ of sb** sous la direction de qn

Edmund [ˈedmənd] N Edmond m

EDP [ˌiːdiːˈpiː] N (ABBR = **Electronic Data Processing**) → **electronic**

EDT [ˌiːdiːˈtiː] N (US) (ABBR = **Eastern Daylight Time**) → **eastern**

educable [ˈedjʊkəbl] ADJ éducable

educate [ˈedjʊkeɪt] VT (= teach) [teacher, school] [+ pupil] assurer l'instruction de, instruire; (= bring up) [+ family, children] élever, éduquer; [+ the mind, one's tastes] former; **the parents' role in educating their children** le rôle des parents dans l'éducation de leurs enfants; **he is being ~d in Paris/at Cambridge** il fait ses études à Paris/Cambridge; **to ~ the public** éduquer le public; **we need to ~ our children about drugs/the environment** il faut que nous sensibilisions nos enfants au problème de la drogue/aux questions d'écologie; **a campaign to ~ people about the dangers of smoking** une campagne de sensibilisation du public aux dangers du tabac or du tabagisme; (fig) **to ~ sb to believe that ...** enseigner à qn que ...

educated [ˈedjʊkeɪtɪd] [1] VB ptp of **educate** [2] ADJ [person] (= cultured) cultivé; (= learned, trained) instruit; [work force] ayant un bon niveau d'éducation or d'instruction; [voice] cultivé; [palate, ear] averti; **he's hardly ~ at all** il n'a guère d'instruction; **an ~ mind** un esprit cultivé → **guess, well**

education [ˌedjʊˈkeɪʃən] [1] N (gen) éducation f; (= teaching) enseignement m; (= learning) instruction f; (= studies) études fpl; (= training) formation f; (= knowledge) culture f; (Univ etc = subject) pédagogie f; **he had a good ~** il a reçu une bonne éducation; **his ~ was neglected** on a négligé son éducation; **physical/political ~** éducation f physique/politique; **he has had very little ~** il n'a pas fait beaucoup d'études; **his ~ was interrupted** ses études ont été interrompues; **she has or has had a university ~** elle est diplômée d'université, elle a fait des études supérieures; **the ~ he received at school** l'instruction qu'il a reçue à l'école or au lycée etc); **literary/professional ~** formation f littéraire/professionnelle; **primary/secondary ~** enseignement m primaire/secondaire; **~ is free in Britain** l'instruction est gratuite en Grande-Bretagne, l'enseignement est gratuit en Grande-Bretagne; **the crisis in ~** ◊ **the ~ crisis** la crise de l'enseignement; (gen) **the ~ system** le système éducatif or d'éducation; **the French ~ system** ◊ **the ~ system in France** le système éducatif or l'enseignement en France; **people working in ~** les personnes qui travaillent dans l'enseignement; **Department or Ministry of Education** ministère m de l'Éducation; **Secretary of State for or Minister of Education** (Brit) ◊ **Secretary for Education** (US) ministre m de l'Éducation → **adult, further**

[2] COMP [theory, method] d'enseignement, pédagogique; [standards] d'instruction, scolaire; [costs] de l'enseignement; (Pol) [budget, minister] de l'Éducation nationale ► **the Education Act** N (Brit) la loi sur l'enseignement ► **education authority** N (Brit) ≈ délégation f départementale de l'enseignement ► **Education Committee** N (Brit Scol Admin) commission f du conseil régional chargée des affaires scolaires ► **education correspondent** N (Press) correspondant(e) m(f) chargé(e) des questions de l'enseignement ► **education department** N (Brit: of local authority) ≈ délégation f départementale de l'enseignement; (= ministry) ministère m de l'Éducation ► **education page** N (Press) rubrique f de l'enseignement ► **Education Welfare Officer** N (Brit Scol Admin) assistant(e) m(f) social(e) scolaire

educational [ˌedjʊˈkeɪʃənl] [1] ADJ [system, needs, film, book, toy, game] éducatif; [institution, establishment] d'enseignement; [standards] de l'enseignement; [achievement] (at school) scolaire; (at university) universitaire; [supplies] scolaire; [theory] de l'éducation; [role, function] éducateur (-trice f); [method, methodology, issue, material] pédagogique; [experience] instructif; [visit, day] (for adults) instructif; (for children) éducatif; **~ opportunities** possibilité f de faire des études; **~ qualifications** diplômes mpl; **falling ~ standards** la baisse du niveau de l'enseignement

[2] COMP ► **educational adviser** N (Scol Admin) conseiller m, -ère f pédagogique ► **educational age** N (US Scol) niveau m scolaire (d'un élève) ► **educational park** N (US) complexe scolaire et universitaire ► **educational psychologist** N psychopédagogue mf ► **educational psychology** N psychopédagogie f ► **educational television** N (gen) télévision f éducative; (US) chaîne de télévision f éducatif

educationalist [ˌedjʊˈkeɪʃnəlɪst] N (esp Brit) éducateur m, -trice f, pédagogue mf

educationally [ˌedjʊˈkeɪʃnəlɪ] ADV [subnormal, deprived etc] sur le plan éducatif; **~ sound principles** des principes sains du point de vue pédagogique

educationist [ˌedjʊˈkeɪʃnɪst] N = **educationalist**

educative [ˈedjʊkətɪv] ADJ éducatif, éducateur (-trice f)

educator [ˈedjʊkeɪtər] N (esp US) éducateur m, -trice f

educe [ɪˈdjuːs] VT (frm) dégager, faire sortir

edutainment* [ˌedjʊˈteɪnmənt] N (esp US) (= games) jeux mpl éducatifs; (= TV etc programmes) émissions fpl éducatives pour enfants

Edward [ˈedwəd] N Édouard m; (Brit Hist) **~ the Confessor** Édouard le Confesseur

Edwardian [edˈwɔːdɪən] (Brit) [1] ADJ [England, house, furniture, picture, literature] édouardien, du début du (20ᵉ) siècle; [lady, gentleman] de l'époque d'Édouard VII; **~ clothes** vêtements mpl style 1900; **in ~ days** à l'époque d'Édouard VII, au début du (20ᵉ) siècle; **the ~ era** → la Belle Époque [2] N personne qui vivait sous le règne d'Édouard VII ou qui a les caractéristiques de cette époque

EEC [ˌiːiːˈsiː] N (ABBR = **European Economic Community**) CEE f

EEG [ˌiːiːˈdʒiː] N (ABBR = **electroencephalogram**) EEG m

eek* [iːk] EXCL ah !

eel [iːl] N anguille f → **electric**

eelworm [ˈiːlwɜːm] N anguillule f

e'en [iːn] ADV (liter) = **even² 2**

EEOC [ˌiːiːəʊˈsiː] N (US) (ABBR = **Equal Employment Opportunity Commission**) → **equal**; → EOC, EEOC

e'er [ɛər] ADV (liter) = **ever 1**

eerie [ˈɪərɪ] ADJ sinistre, qui donne le frisson

eerily [ˈɪərɪlɪ] ADV [deserted, empty] sinistrement; [similar, familiar] étrangement; **~ quiet/silent** d'un calme/d'un silence inquiétant; **to echo/gleam ~** résonner/luire sinistrement

eery [ˈɪərɪ] ADJ = **eerie**

EET [ˌiːiːˈtiː] N (ABBR = **Eastern European Time**) → **eastern**

eff* [ef] VI **he was ~ing and blinding** il jurait comme un charretier* → **effing**
► **eff off*** VI aller se faire voir*

efface [ɪˈfeɪs] VT (lit, fig) effacer, oblitérer (liter)

effect [ɪˈfekt] [1] N [a] (= result) effet m, conséquence f (**on** sur); (Phys) effet m; [of wind, chemical, drug] action f (**on** sur); **this rule will have the ~ of preventing ...** ◊ **the ~ of this rule will be to prevent ...** cette règle aura pour effet d'empêcher ...; (frm) **the ~ of all this is**

that ... il résulte de tout ceci que ...; **to feel the ~s of an accident** ressentir les effets d'un accident, se ressentir d'un accident; **the ~s of the new law are already being felt** les effets de la nouvelle loi se font déjà sentir; **in ~** de fait, en réalité; **to put into ~** mettre à exécution or en application; **to come** or **go into ~** [law] prendre effet, entrer en vigueur; [policy] être appliqué; **to have no ~** ne produire aucun effet; **to be of no ~** (= have no effect) être inefficace; [law etc] être inopérant, rester sans effet; **to have an ~ on sth** avoir or produire un effet sur qch; **it won't have any ~ on him** ça ne lui fera aucun effet, ça n'aura aucun effet sur lui; **to take ~** [drug] agir, produire or faire son effet; [law] prendre effet, entrer en vigueur; **to little ~** sans grand résultat; **to no ~** en vain; **to use to good** or **great ~** savoir tirer avantage de; **to such good ~ that ...** si bien que ...; (esp Brit) **with ~ from April** à compter du mois d'avril; (esp Brit: frm) **with immediate ~** avec effet immédiat

⌊b⌋ (= impression) effet m; **he said it just for ~** il ne l'a dit que pour faire de l'effet or pour impressionner; **to give a good ~** faire (un) bon effet; **to make an ~** faire effet or de l'effet → **sound, special, stage**

⌊c⌋ (Cine, Rad, Theat, TV) (also **sound ~**) effet m sonore; (also **special ~**) effet m spécial

⌊d⌋ (= meaning) sens m; **his letter is to the ~ that ...** sa lettre nous apprend que ...; **an announcement to the ~ that ...** un communiqué annonçant que ... or selon lequel ...; **orders to the ~ that ...** ordres suivant lesquels ...; **he used words to that ~** il s'est exprimé dans ce sens; **... or words to that ~** ... ou quelque chose d'analogue or de ce genre; **we got a letter to the same ~** nous avons reçu une lettre dans le même sens

⌊e⌋ (frm = property) (**personal**) **~s** effets mpl personnels; (Banking) **"no ~s"** « sans provision » → **personal**

⌊2⌋ VT (gen) [+ reform, reduction, payment] effectuer; [+ cure] obtenir; [+ improvement] apporter; [+ transformation] opérer, effectuer; [+ reconciliation, reunion] amener; [+ sale, purchase] réaliser, effectuer; **to ~ change** procéder à des changements; **to ~ a saving** faire une économie; **to ~ a settlement** arriver à un accord; **negotiation ~ed the release of the hostages** les négociations ont abouti à or ont permis la libération des otages; (frm) **to ~ an entry** entrer de force

effective [ɪˈfektɪv] ⌊1⌋ ADJ ⌊a⌋ (= successful) [action, method, treatment, policy, deterrent, government, politician] efficace (**against sth** contre qch, **in doing sth** pour faire qch); [word, remark, argument] qui porte, qui a de l'effet; (Pharm) **~ life** durée f effective ⌊b⌋ (= striking) [decoration, pattern, combination] frappant; **to look ~** faire de l'effet ⌊c⌋ (= actual) [control] effectif; [leader] véritable ⌊d⌋ (Econ, Fin) [demand, income] effectif; [interest rate] net, réel ⌊e⌋ (= operative) [law, ceasefire, insurance cover] en vigueur (**from** à compter de, à partir de); **to become ~** entrer en vigueur; **to be** or **become ~ immediately** prendre effet immédiatement; **~ date** date f d'entrée en vigueur ⌊f⌋ (Mil) **~ troops** hommes mpl valides ⌊2⌋ **effectives** NPL (Mil) effectifs mpl

effectively [ɪˈfektɪvlɪ] ADV ⌊a⌋ (= successfully) [treat, teach, work] efficacement; **to function ~** bien fonctionner ⌊b⌋ (= strikingly) [contrast] de manière frappante ⌊c⌋ (= in effect) [prevent, stop] en réalité

effectiveness [ɪˈfektɪvnɪs] N (= efficiency) efficacité f; (= striking quality) effet m frappant or saisissant

effector [ɪˈfektə*] ⌊1⌋ ADJ effecteur (-trice f) ⌊2⌋ N effecteur m

effectual [ɪˈfektjʊəl] ADJ (frm) [remedy, punishment] efficace; [document, agreement] valide

effectually [ɪˈfektjʊəlɪ] ADV (frm) efficacement

effectuate [ɪˈfektjʊeɪt] VT (frm) effectuer, opérer, réaliser

effeminacy [ɪˈfemɪnəsɪ] N caractère m efféminé

effeminate [ɪˈfemɪnɪt] ADJ efféminé

efferent [ˈefərənt] ADJ efférent

effervesce [ˌefəˈves] VI ⌊a⌋ (= fizz) [liquid] être or entrer en effervescence; [drinks] pétiller, mousser; [gas] se dégager (en effervescence) ⌊b⌋ (fig) [person] déborder (**with** de), être tout excité

effervescence [ˌefəˈvesns] N ⌊a⌋ (= fizziness) effervescence f, pétillement m ⌊b⌋ (fig = liveliness) excitation f

effervescent [ˌefəˈvesnt] ADJ ⌊a⌋ (= fizzy) [liquid, tablet] effervescent; [drink] gazeux ⌊b⌋ (fig = lively) plein d'entrain

effete [ɪˈfiːt] ADJ (frm) [person] mou (molle f), veule; [empire, civilization] décadent; [government] affaibli; [method] (devenu) inefficace, stérile

effeteness [ɪˈfiːtnɪs] N (frm) [of person] mollesse f, veulerie f (liter); [of group, civilization] décadence f

efficacious [ˌefɪˈkeɪʃəs] ADJ (frm) efficace (**for sth** pour qch, **against sth** contre qch)

efficacy [ˈefɪkəsɪ], **efficaciousness** [ˌefɪˈkeɪʃəsnɪs] N efficacité f

efficiency [ɪˈfɪʃənsɪ] ⌊1⌋ N [of person] capacité f, compétence f; [of method] efficacité f; [of organization, system] efficacité f, bon fonctionnement m; [of machine] bon rendement m, bon fonctionnement m ⌊2⌋ COMP ► **efficiency apartment** N (US) studio m

efficient [ɪˈfɪʃənt] ADJ [person, machine, organization, service, method, use] efficace; [car] d'un bon rendement; **to be ~ in** or **at doing sth** faire qch avec efficacité; **to be ~ in one's use of sth** utiliser qch avec efficacité

efficiently [ɪˈfɪʃəntlɪ] ADV [use, manage] efficacement; [deal with] avec efficacité; **to work ~** [person] travailler efficacement; [machine] avoir un bon rendement

effigy [ˈefɪdʒɪ] N effigie f; **in ~** en effigie

effing [ˈefɪŋ] (Brit euph) ⌊1⌋ ADJ **this ~ phone!** ce fichu* téléphone!; **what an ~ waste of time!** merde!‡ quelle perte de temps! → **eff** ⌊2⌋ N **~ and blinding** grossièretés fpl

effloresce [ˌeflɒˈres] VI (Chem) effleurir

efflorescence [ˌeflɒˈresns] N (Chem, Med: also liter) efflorescence f; (Bot) floraison f

efflorescent [ˌeflɒˈresnt] ADJ (Chem) efflorescent; (Bot) en fleur(s)

effluence [ˈefluəns] N émanation f, effluence f (liter)

effluent [ˈefluənt] ADJ, N effluent m

effluvium [eˈfluːvɪəm] N (pl **effluviums** or **effluvia** [eˈfluːvɪə]) effluve(s) m(pl), émanation f, exhalaison f; (pej) exhalaison f or émanation f fétide

efflux [ˈeflʌks] N **~ of capital** fuite f or exode m de capitaux

effort [ˈefət] N ⌊a⌋ effort m; **getting up was an ~** j'ai eu (or il a eu etc) du mal à me (or se etc) lever; **it's not bad for a first ~** ça n'est pas (si) mal pour un début; **that's a good ~** ça n'est pas mal (réussi); **in an ~ to solve the problem/be polite** etc pour essayer de résoudre le problème/d'être poli etc; **what do you think of his latest ~?** qu'est-ce que tu penses de ce qu'il vient de faire?; **it's a pretty poor ~** ça n'est pas une réussite or un chef-d'œuvre; **the famine relief ~** la lutte contre la famine; **the government's ~ to avoid ...** les efforts mpl or les tentatives fpl du gouvernement pour éviter ...; **the war ~** l'effort m de guerre; **to do sth by ~ of will** faire qch dans un effort de volonté; **with ~** avec difficulté, non sans mal; **without ~** sans peine, sans effort; **it's not worth the ~** cela n'en vaut pas la peine; **it is well worth the ~** cela en vaut

vraiment la peine

⌊b⌋ **to make an ~ to do sth** faire un effort pour faire qch, s'efforcer de faire qch; **to make an ~ to concentrate/to adapt** faire un effort de concentration/d'adaptation; **to make every ~ to do sth** (= try hard) faire tous ses efforts or (tout) son possible pour faire qch, s'évertuer à faire qch; (= take great pains) se donner beaucoup de mal or de peine pour faire qch; **to make little ~ to do sth** ne pas faire beaucoup d'effort pour faire qch; **little ~ has been made to investigate this case** on ne s'est pas vraiment donné la peine d'enquêter sur cette affaire; **he made no ~ to be polite** il ne s'est pas donné la peine d'être poli; (Scol) **he makes no ~** il ne fait aucun effort, il ne s'applique pas; **do make some ~ to help!** fais un petit effort pour aider!, essaie d'aider un peu!; **to make the ~ to do sth** faire l'effort de faire qch, se donner le mal de faire qch

effortless [ˈefətlɪs] ADJ [movement, style] fluide; [success, victory] facile; [charm, elegance, skill, superiority] naturel; **with ~ ease** avec une parfaite aisance

effortlessly [ˈefətlɪslɪ] ADV [lift, succeed, beat] sans effort

effrontery [ɪˈfrʌntərɪ] N effronterie f

effusion [ɪˈfjuːʒən] N [of liquid] écoulement m; [of blood, gas] effusion f; (fig) effusion f, épanchement m

effusive [ɪˈfjuːsɪv] ADJ [thanks, greeting, welcome] chaleureux; [praise] enthousiaste; [person] expansif; **to be ~ in one's thanks/apologies** se confondre en remerciements/excuses

effusively [ɪˈfjuːsɪvlɪ] ADV [greet, welcome, praise] avec effusion; **to thank sb ~** se confondre en remerciements auprès de qn

EFL [ˌiːefˈel] N (ABBR = **English as a Foreign Language**) → **English**; → |TEFL, TESL, TESOL, ELT|

EFT [ˌiːefˈtiː] N (ABBR = **electronic funds transfer**) TEF m, transfert m électronique de fonds

eft [eft] N (Zool) triton m (crêté), salamandre f d'eau

EFTA [ˈeftə] N (ABBR = **European Free Trade Association**) AELE f, Association f européenne de libre-échange

EFTPOS [ˈeftpɒs] N (ABBR = **electronic funds transfer at point of sale**) TEF/TPV m

EFTS [ˌiːefˈtiːes] N (ABBR = **electronic funds transfer system**) → **electronic**

eg, e.g. [ˌiːˈdʒiː] ADV (ABBR = **exempli gratia**) (= for example) par ex.

EGA [ˌiːdʒiːˈeɪ] N (ABBR = **enhanced graphics adaptor**) → **enhance**

egad†† [ɪˈgæd] EXCL Dieu du ciel!†

egalitarian [ɪˌgælɪˈtɛərɪən] ⌊1⌋ N égalitariste mf ⌊2⌋ ADJ [person] égalitariste; [society, principle, spirit, relationship, policy] égalitaire

egalitarianism [ɪˌgælɪˈtɛərɪənɪzəm] N égalitarisme m

egest [iːˈdʒest] VT évacuer

egg [eg] ⌊1⌋ N ⌊a⌋ (Culin, Zool) œuf m; **in the ~** dans l'œuf; **~s and bacon** œufs mpl au bacon; **a three-minute ~** un œuf à la coque; **to lay an ~** (lit) [bird etc] pondre (un œuf); (‡ fig = fail) faire un fiasco or un bide‡; (fig) **to put all one's ~s in one basket** mettre tous ses œufs dans le même panier; **as sure as ~s is ~s**‡ c'est sûr et certain*; (fig) **to have ~ on one's face** avoir l'air plutôt ridicule; **he's a good/bad ~**†* c'est un brave/sale type* → **boil**¹, **Scotch** ⌊2⌋ VT* pousser, inciter (**to do** à faire)

⌊3⌋ COMP ► **egg-and-spoon race** N course f (à l'œuf et) à la cuillère ► **egg custard** N ≈ crème f renversée ► **egg flip** N lait m de poule ► **egg roll** N (= sandwich) petit pain m aux œufs (durs); (Chinese) pâté m impérial ► **egg sandwich** N sandwich m aux œufs (durs) ► **eggs Benedict** N (NonC: Culin) œufs pochés sur toast et jambon recouverts de sauce hollandaise ► **egg-shaped** ADJ en forme d'œuf, ovoïde ► **egg-timer** N (sand) sablier m; (automatic) minuteur m ► **egg whisk** N fouet m ► **egg white** N blanc m d'œuf ► **egg yolk** N jaune m d'œuf

►**egg on** VT SEP pousser, inciter (**to do** à faire)

eggbeater ['egbiːtər] N (rotary) batteur m (à œufs); (whisk) fouet m; (US: = helicopter) hélico* m, hélicoptère m

eggcup ['egkʌp] N coquetier m

egghead* ['eghed] N intello* mf, intellectuel(le) m(f)

eggnog ['egnɒg] N lait m de poule

eggplant ['egplɑːnt] N (esp US) aubergine f

eggshell ['egʃel] 1 N coquille f (d'œuf); **when I'm with him I feel I'm walking on ~s** quand je suis avec lui, je marche sur des œufs or j'ai toujours peur de dire un mot de travers 2 COMP ► **eggshell china** N coquille f d'œuf (porcelaine) ► **eggshell paint** N peinture f coquille d'œuf

egis ['iːdʒɪs] N (US) = aegis

eglantine ['eglæntaɪn] N (= flower) églantine f; (= bush) églantier m

EGM [,iːdʒiː'em] N (ABBR = extraordinary general meeting) AGE f

ego ['iːgəʊ] N (= pride) amour-propre m; (Psych) **the ~** l'ego m, le moi 2 COMP ► **ego trip*** N having his name all over the papers is a **great ~ trip for him** avoir son nom dans tous les journaux flatte son amour-propre; **this lecture is just an ~ trip for him** cette conférence ne sert qu'à flatter son amour-propre

egocentric(al) [,egəʊ'sentrɪk(əl)] ADJ égocentrique

egocentricity [,egəʊsen'trɪsɪtɪ] N égocentrisme m

egoism ['egəʊɪzəm] N égoïsme m

egoist ['egəʊɪst] N égoïste mf

egoistic(al) [,egəʊ'ɪstɪk(əl)] ADJ égoïste

egomania [,egəʊ'meɪnɪə] N manie f égocentrique

egomaniac [,egəʊ'meɪnɪæk] N égotiste mf

egotism ['egəʊtɪzəm] N égotisme m

egotist ['egəʊtɪst] N égotiste mf

egotistic(al) [,egəʊ'tɪstɪk(əl)] ADJ égotiste

egregious [ɪ'griːdʒəs] ADJ (pej) énorme (iro), fameux* (before n) (iro); [folly] extrême; [blunder] monumental

egress ['iːgres] N (gen: frm) sortie f, issue f; (Astron) émersion f

egret ['iːgrɪt] N aigrette f

Egypt ['iːdʒɪpt] N l'Égypte f

Egyptian [ɪ'dʒɪpʃən] 1 ADJ égyptien, d'Égypte 2 N Égyptien(ne) m(f)

Egyptologist [,iːdʒɪp'tɒlədʒɪst] N égyptologue mf

Egyptology [,iːdʒɪp'tɒlədʒɪ] N égyptologie f

eh [eɪ] EXCL a (= what did you say?) quoi?, hein?* b **it's hot, eh?** il fait chaud, n'est-ce pas or hein*?

eider ['aɪdər] N (also **~ duck**) eider m

eiderdown ['aɪdədaʊn] N a (= quilt) édredon m b (NonC: down) duvet m (d'eider)

eidetic [aɪ'detɪk] ADJ eidétique

Eiffel Tower [,aɪfəl'taʊər] N tour f Eiffel

Eiger ['aɪgər] N Eiger m

eight [eɪt] 1 ADJ huit inv; (Ind etc) **an ~-hour day** la journée de huit heures; (Ind etc) **to do** or **work ~-hour shifts** faire des postes mpl or des roulements mpl de huit heures 2 N huit m inv (also Rowing); (fig) **he's had one over the ~*** il a du vent dans les voiles*, il a un coup dans le nez* → **figure**; for other phrases see **six** 3 PRON huit m; **there are ~** il y en a huit

eighteen ['eɪ'tiːn] 1 ADJ dix-huit inv 2 N dix-huit m inv; for phrases see **six** 3 PRON dix-huit m; **there are ~** il y en a dix-huit

eighteenth ['eɪ'tiːnθ] 1 ADJ dix-huitième 2 N dix-huitième mf; (= fraction) dix-huitième m; for phrases see **sixth**

eighth [eɪtθ] 1 ADJ huitième; (US Mus) **~ note** croche f 2 N huitième mf; (= fraction) huitième m; for phrases see **sixth**

eightieth ['eɪtɪəθ] 1 ADJ quatre-vingtième 2 N quatre-vingtième mf; (= fraction) quatre-vingtième m; for phrases see **sixth**

eightsome reel ['eɪtsəm'riːl] N danse folklorique écossaise avec huit danseurs

eighty ['eɪtɪ] 1 ADJ quatre-vingts inv; **about ~ books** environ or à peu près quatre-vingts livres 2 N quatre-vingts m; **about ~** environ or à peu près quatre-vingts; **~-one** quatre-vingt-un; **~-two** quatre-vingt-deux; **~-first** quatre-vingt-unième; **page ~** la page quatre-vingt; for other phrases see **sixty** 3 PRON quatre-vingts; **there are ~** il y en a quatre-vingts 4 COMP ► **eighty-six*** VT (US) (= refuse to serve) refuser de servir; (= eject) vider*

Einsteinian [aɪn'staɪnɪən] ADJ einsteinien

einsteinium [aɪn'staɪnɪəm] N einsteinium m

Eire ['ɛərə] N la République d'Irlande, l'Eire f

eisteddfod [aɪ'stedfəd] N concours de musique et de poésie en gallois

either ['aɪðər, 'iːðər] 1 ADJ a (= one or other) l'un(e) ou l'autre, n'importe lequel (laquelle f) (des deux); **~ day would suit me** l'un ou l'autre jour me conviendrait, l'un de ces deux jours me conviendrais; **I don't like ~ book** je n'aime ni l'un ni l'autre de ces livres; **do it ~ way** faites-le de l'une ou l'autre façon; **~ way***, **I can't do anything about it** de toute façon or quoi qu'il arrive, je n'y peux rien b (= each) chaque; **in ~ hand** dans chaque main; **on ~ side of the street** des deux côtés or de chaque côté de la rue; **on ~ side lay fields** de part et d'autre s'étendaient des champs

2 PRON l'un(e) m(f) ou l'autre, n'importe lequel (laquelle f) (des deux); **which bus will you take?** — **~** quel bus prendrez-vous? — n'importe lequel; **there are two boxes on the table, take ~** il y a deux boîtes sur la table, prenez celle que vous voulez or n'importe laquelle; **I don't believe ~ of them** je ne les crois ni l'un ni l'autre; **give it to ~ of them** donnez-le soit à l'un soit à l'autre; **if ~ is attacked the other helps him** si l'un des deux est attaqué l'autre l'aide

3 ADV (after neg statement) non plus; **he sings badly and he can't act ~** il chante mal et il ne sait pas jouer non plus or et il ne joue pas mieux; **I have never heard of him — no, I haven't ~** je n'ai jamais entendu parler de lui — moi non plus

4 CONJ a **~ ... or** ou (bien) ... ou (bien), soit ... soit; (after neg) ni ... ni; **he must be ~ lazy or stupid** il doit être ou paresseux ou stupide; **he must ~ change his policy or resign** il faut soit qu'il change (subj) de politique soit qu'il démissionne (subj); **~ be quiet or go out!** tais-toi ou sors d'ici!, ou (bien) tu te tais ou (bien) tu sors d'ici!; **I have never been ~ to Paris or to Rome** je ne suis jamais allé ni à Paris ni à Rome; **it was ~ him or his sister** c'était soit lui soit sa sœur, c'était ou (bien) lui ou (bien) sa sœur b (= moreover) **she got a sum of money, and not such a small one ~** elle a reçu une somme d'argent, plutôt rondelette d'ailleurs

ejaculate [ɪ'dʒækjʊleɪt] VTI a (= cry out) s'exclamer, s'écrier b (Physiol) éjaculer

ejaculation [ɪ,dʒækjʊ'leɪʃən] N a (= cry) exclamation f, cri m b (Physiol) éjaculation f

ejaculatory [ɪ'dʒækjʊlətərɪ] ADJ (Physiol) éjaculatoire

eject [ɪ'dʒekt] 1 VT (Aviat, Tech etc) éjecter; [+ tenant, troublemaker] expulser; [+ trespasser] chasser, éconduire; [+ customer] expulser, vider* 2 VI [pilot] s'éjecter

ejection [ɪ'dʒekʃən] 1 N (NonC) [of person] expulsion f; (Aviat, Tech) éjection f 2 COMP ► **ejection seat** (US) N = **ejector seat**

ejector [ɪ'dʒektər] 1 N (Tech) éjecteur m 2 COMP ► **ejector seat** N (Aviat) siège m éjectable

eke [iːk] VT **to ~ out** (by adding) accroître, augmenter; (by saving) économiser, faire durer; (= supplement) **he ~s out his pension by doing odd jobs** il fait des petits travaux pour arrondir sa pension or ses fins de mois; **to ~ out a living** vivoter

EKG [,iːkeɪ'dʒiː] N (US) = **ECG**

el [el] N (US) (ABBR = **elevated railroad**) → **elevated**

elaborate [ɪ'læbərɪt] 1 ADJ [system, ritual, preparations, drawing, meal, hoax, joke] élaboré; [costume, clothes, style] recherché; [excuse, plan] compliqué; [precautions] minutieux; **with ~ care** avec un soin minutieux 2 [ɪ'læbəreɪt] VT élaborer 3 [ɪ'læbəreɪt] VI donner des détails (on sur), entrer dans or expliquer les détails (on de) 4 COMP ► **elaborated code** N (Ling) code m élaboré

elaborately [ɪ'læbərɪtlɪ] ADV [decorated, dressed] avec recherche; [carved, planned] avec minutie

elaboration [ɪ,læbə'reɪʃən] N élaboration f

élan [eɪ'lɑːn, eɪ'læn] N allant m

elapse [ɪ'læps] VI s'écouler, (se) passer

elastic [ɪ'læstɪk] 1 ADJ élastique (also fig) 2 N a (NonC) élastique m b (also **baggage** or **luggage ~**) tendeur m, sandow® m 3 COMP ► **elastic band** N (esp Brit) élastique m, caoutchouc m ► **elastic stockings** NPL bas mpl à varices

elasticated [ɪ'læstɪkeɪtɪd] ADJ (Brit) élastiqué, à élastique

elasticity [,iːlæs'tɪsɪtɪ] N (also Econ) élasticité f

Elastoplast® [ɪ'læstə,plɑːst] N (Brit) sparadrap m

elate [ɪ'leɪt] VT transporter, ravir, enthousiasmer

elated [ɪ'leɪtɪd] ADJ transporté or rempli de joie; **to be ~** exulter

elation [ɪ'leɪʃən] N allégresse f, exultation f

Elba ['elbə] N (also **the Island of ~**) (l'île f d')Elbe f

Elbe [elb] N (also **the River ~**) l'Elbe f

elbow ['elbəʊ] 1 N [of person, road, river, pipe, garment] coude m; **to lean one's ~s on** s'accouder à or sur, être accoudé à; **to lean on one's ~** s'appuyer sur le coude; **at his ~** à ses côtés; **worn at the ~s** usé aux coudes; (Brit) **to give sb/get the ~*** [lover] plaquer or laisser tomber qn*/se faire plaquer*; [employee] virer qn*/se faire virer*; (euph hum) **he lifts his ~ a bit*** il lève le coude*, il picole‡ 2 VI **to ~ through** jouer des coudes 3 VT **to ~ sb (in the face)** donner à qn un coup de coude (au visage); **to ~ sb aside** (lit) écarter qn du coude or d'un coup de coude; (fig) pousser qn pour écarter qn; **to ~ one's way through** etc = **to elbow through**; → **2**; (fig) **to ~ one's way to the top** jouer des coudes pour arriver au sommet 4 COMP ► **elbow grease** N **to use a bit of ~ grease** mettre de l'huile de coude* ► **elbow joint** N articulation f du coude ► **elbow-rest** N accoudoir m ► **elbow room** N **to have enough ~ room** (lit) avoir de la place pour se retourner; (fig) avoir les coudées franches; **to have no ~ room** (lit) être à l'étroit; (fig) ne pas avoir les coudées franches, ne pas avoir de liberté d'action

elder[1] ['eldər] 1 ADJ aîné (de deux); **my ~ sister** ma sœur aînée; **Pliny the ~** Pline l'Ancien; **Alexander Dumas the ~** Alexandre Dumas père; **~ statesman** vétéran m de la politique, homme m politique chevronné 2 N a (= older person) aîné(e) m(f); **one's ~s and betters**

ses aînés [b] (*Rel etc*) [*of Presbyterian Church*] membre *m* du conseil d'une église presbytérienne ; [*of tribe, Church*] **~s** anciens *mpl*

elder² ['eldə'] N (*Bot*) sureau *m*

elderberry ['eldəberı] N baie *f* de sureau ; **~ wine** vin *m* de sureau

elderflower ['eldəflauə'] N fleur *f* de sureau

elderly ['eldəlı] [1] ADJ [*person*] âgé ; [*vehicle, machine etc*] plutôt vieux ; **he's getting ~** il prend de l'âge, il se fait vieux [2] **the elderly** NPL les personnes *fpl* âgées

eldest ['eldıst] ADJ, N aîné(e) ; **their ~ (child)** leur aîné(e), l'aîné(e) de leurs enfants ; **my ~ brother** l'aîné de mes frères

Eleanor ['elınə'] N Éléonore *f*

elec ABBR = **electric, electricity**

elect [ı'lekt] [1] VT [a] (*by vote*) élire ; **he was ~ed chairman/MP** il a été élu président/député [b] (*frm* = *choose*) **to ~ to smoke/stand/stay** *etc* choisir de *or* décider de fumer/rester debout/rester *etc* [2] ADJ futur (*before n*) ; **the president ~** le président désigné, le futur président [3] **the elect** NPL (*esp Rel*) les élus *mpl* [4] COMP ► **elected member** N (*Brit Local Govt*) conseiller *m*, -ère *f* municipal(e) *or* régional(e) ► **elected official** N élu(e) *m(f)*

election [ı'lekʃən] [1] N élection *f* ; **to hold an ~** tenir une élection ; **to stand for ~ (to Parliament)** se présenter aux élections législatives ; **her ~ as Tory leader** son élection à la tête du parti conservateur ; **his ~ to the presidency** son élection à la présidence → **general** [2] COMP [*speech, agent*] électoral ; [*day, results*] du scrutin ; [*publication*] de propagande électorale ► **election campaign** N campagne *f* électorale ► **elections judge** N (*US Pol*) scrutateur *m*, -trice *f*

electioneer [ı,lekʃə'nıə'] VI mener une campagne électorale, faire de la propagande électorale

electioneering [ı,lekʃə'nıərıŋ] [1] N (= *campaign*) campagne *f* électorale ; (= *propaganda*) propagande *f* électorale [2] COMP [*propaganda, publicity*] électoral ; [*speech*] de propagande électorale

elective [ı'lektıv] [1] ADJ [a] (*frm* = *elected*) [*post, official, body, democracy, dictatorship*] électif ; (*US*) **to hold ~ office** avoir une fonction élective [b] (*frm* = *with power to elect*) [*body, assembly, power*] électoral [c] (*Med*) [*surgery*] non urgent [d] (*esp US Scol, Univ*) [*course*] facultatif ; [*subject*] facultatif, en option [2] N (*US Scol, Univ*) (= *course*) cours *m* facultatif

elector [ı'lektə'] N (*gen, Parl*) électeur *m*, -trice *f* ; (*US Parl*) membre *m* du collège électoral ; (*Hist*) **Elector** Électeur *m*, prince *m* électeur

electoral [ı'lektərəl] [1] ADJ électoral [2] COMP ► **electoral boundaries** NPL limites *fpl* des circonscriptions (électorales) ► **electoral college** N collège *m* électoral ► **electoral district, electoral division** N (*US*) circonscription *f* (électorale) ► **the electoral map** N (*US*) la carte électorale ► **electoral register, electoral roll** N liste *f* électorale ► **electoral vote** N (*US*) vote *m* des grands électeurs

---

ELECTORAL COLLEGE

Selon la constitution des États-Unis, les Américains n'élisent pas directement leur président et leur vice-président, mais élisent des grands électeurs qui forment ensemble le collège électoral et qui s'engagent à voter pour tel ou tel candidat. Chaque grand électeur dispose d'un certain nombre de voix, compris entre 3 et 54 selon l'importance démographique de l'État qu'il représente.

---

electorally [ı'lektərəlı] ADV sur le plan électoral

electorate [ı'lektərıt] N électorat *m*, électeurs *mpl*

Electra [ı'lektrə] [1] N Électre *f* [2] COMP ► **Electra complex** N (*Psych*) complexe *m* d'Électre

electric [ı'lektrık] [1] ADJ électrique ; (*fig*) **the atmosphere was ~** l'ambiance était électrique [2] **the electrics*** NPL (*Brit*) l'installation *f* électrique [3] COMP ► **electric arc welding** N soudure *f* électrique à l'arc ► **electric blanket** N couverture *f* chauffante ► **electric blue** N bleu *m* électrique ► **electric-blue** ADJ bleu électrique *inv* ► **electric chair** N chaise *f* électrique ► **electric charge** N charge *f* électrique ► **electric current** N courant *m* électrique ► **electric eel** N (*Zool*) anguille *f* électrique, gymnote *m* ► **electric eye** N cellule *f* photoélectrique ► **electric fence** N clôture *f* électrifiée ► **electric field** N champ *m* électrique ► **electric fire** N (*Brit*) radiateur *m* électrique ► **electric furnace** N four *m* électrique ► **electric guitar** N guitare *f* électrique ► **electric heater** N = **electric fire** ► **electric light** N lumière *f* électrique ; (*NonC* = *lighting*) éclairage *m* électrique ► **electric mixer** N mixeur *m* ► **electric organ** N (*Mus*) orgue *m* électrique ; (*in fish*) organe *m* électrique ► **electric piano** N piano *m* électrique ► **electric potential** N potentiel *m* électrique ► **electric ray** N (*Zool*) raie *f* électrique ► **electric shock** N décharge *f* électrique ; **to get an ~ shock** recevoir une décharge électrique ; **to give sb an ~ shock** donner une décharge électrique à qn ; (*Med*) **~ shock treatment*** (traitement *m* par) électrochocs *mpl* ► **electric socket** N prise *f* électrique *or* de courant ► **electric storm** N orage *m* (électrique) ► **electric welding** N soudure *f* électrique ► **electric wiring** N installation *f* électrique

electrical [ı'lektrıkəl] [1] ADJ électrique [2] COMP ► **electrical engineer** N ingénieur *m* électricien ► **electrical engineering** N électrotechnique *f* ► **electrical failure** N panne *f* dans le circuit électrique ► **electrical fault** N défaut *m* du circuit électrique ► **electrical fitter** N monteur *m* électricien ► **electrical power** N électricité *f* ► **electrical storm** N orage *m* (électrique)

electrically [ı'lektrıkəlı] ADV [*heated*] à l'électricité ; [*charged, neutral, self-sufficient*] électriquement ; **~ controlled** à commande électrique ; **~ operated** *or* **powered** électrique

electrician [ılek'trıʃən] N électricien *m*

electricity [ılek'trısətı] [1] N (*gen*) électricité *f* ; (*also fig*) **to switch off/on the ~** couper/rétablir le courant *or* l'électricité → **supply¹** [2] COMP ► **electricity board** N (*Brit*) office *m* régional de l'électricité ► **electricity strike** N grève *f* des employés de l'électricité

electrification [ı,lektrıfı'keıʃən] N électrification *f*

electrify [ı'lektrıfaı] [1] VT [a] (*Rail*) électrifier ; (= *charge with electricity*) électriser ; **to be electrified** [*village etc*] avoir l'électricité [b] (*fig*) [+ *audience*] électriser, galvaniser [2] COMP ► **electrified fence** N barrière *f* électrifiée

electrifying [ı'lektrıfaıŋ] ADJ (*fig*) électrisant, galvanisant

electro... [ı,lektrəʊ] PREF électro...

electrocardiogram [ı,lektrəʊ'kɑːdıəgræm] N électrocardiogramme *m*

electrocardiograph [ı,lektrəʊ'kɑːdıəgrɑːf] N électrocardiographe *m*

electrochemical [ı,lektrəʊ'kemıkəl] ADJ électrochimique

electrochemistry [ı,lektrəʊ'kemıstrı] N électrochimie *f*

electroconvulsive therapy [ı'lektrəʊkən,vʌlsıv'θerəpı] N (traitement *m* par) élec-

trochocs *mpl* ; **to give sb/have ~** traiter qn/être traité par électrochocs

electrocute [ı'lektrəkjuːt] VT électrocuter

electrocution [ı,lektrə'kjuːʃən] N électrocution *f*

electrode [ı'lektrəʊd] N électrode *f*

electrodialysis [ı,lektrəʊdaı'ælısıs] N électrodialyse *f*

electrodynamic [ı,lektrəʊdaı'næmık] ADJ électrodynamique

electrodynamics [ı,lektrəʊdaı'næmıks] N (*NonC*) électrodynamique *f*

electrodynamometer [ı,lektrəʊ,daınə'mɒmıtə'] N électrodynamomètre *m*

electroencephalogram [ı,lektrəʊen'sefələ,græm] N électro-encéphalogramme *m*

electroencephalograph [ı,lektrəʊen'sefələ,grɑːf] N appareil permettant de faire des électro-encéphalogrammes

electroencephalography [ı,lektrəʊ,ınsefə'lɒgrəfı] N électro-encéphalographie *f*

electroforming [ı'lektrəʊfɔːmıŋ] N électroformage *m*

electrolyse [ı'lektrəʊ,laız] VT électrolyser

electrolyser [ı'lektrəʊ,laızə'] N électrolyseur *m*

electrolysis [ılek'trɒlısıs] N électrolyse *f*

electrolyte [ı'lektrəʊ,laıt] N électrolyte *m*

electrolytic [ı,lektrəʊ'lıtık] ADJ électrolytique

electrolyze [ı'lektrəʊ,laız] VT (*US*) = **electrolyse**

electromagnet [ı,lektrəʊ'mægnıt] N électroaimant *m*

electromagnetic [ı,lektrəʊmæg'netık] ADJ électromagnétique ; **~ wave** faisceau *m* hertzien

electromagnetism [ı,lektrəʊ'mægnı,tızəm] N électromagnétisme *m*

electromechanical [ı,lektrəʊmı'kænıkəl] ADJ électromécanique

electromechanics [ı,lektrəʊmı'kænıks] N (*NonC*) électromécanique *f*

electrometallurgical [ı,lektrəʊ,metə'lɜːdʒıkəl] ADJ électrométallurgique

electrometallurgist [ı,lektrəʊmı'tælədʒıst] N électrométallurgiste *m*

electrometallurgy [ı,lektrəʊmı'tælədʒı] N électrométallurgie *f*

electrometer [ılek'trɒmıtə'] N électromètre *m*

electromotive [ı,lektrəʊ'məʊtıv] ADJ électromoteur (-trice *f*)

electron [ı'lektrɒn] [1] N électron *m* [2] COMP [*telescope*] électronique ► **electron beam** N faisceau *m* électronique ► **electron camera** N caméra *f* électronique ► **electron engineering** N génie *m* électronique ► **electron gun** N canon *m* à électrons ► **electron microscope** N microscope *m* électronique

electronegative [ı,lektrəʊ'negətıv] ADJ électronégatif

electronic [ılek'trɒnık] [1] ADJ électronique [2] COMP ► **the electronic age** N l'ère *f* de l'électronique ► **electronic banking** N opérations *fpl* bancaires électroniques ► **electronic data processing** N traitement *m* électronique de l'information *or* des données ► **electronic engineer** N ingénieur *m* électronicien, électronicien(ne) *m(f)* ► **electronic engineering** N électronique *f* ► **electronic flash** N (*Phot*) flash *m* électronique ► **electronic funds transfer** N transfert *m* électronique de fonds ► **electronic funds transfer system** N système *m* de transfert électronique de fonds ► **electronic game** N jeu *m* électronique ► **electronic keyboard** N clavier *m* électronique ► **electronic mail** N courrier *m* électronique ► **electronic mailbox** N boîte *f* aux lettres électronique ► **electronic music** N musique *f* électronique ► **electronic**

news gathering N journalisme *m* électronique ▶ **electronic organ** N orgue *m* électronique ▶ **electronic point of sale** N point *m* de vente électronique ▶ **electronic publishing** N édition *f* électronique ▶ **electronic surveillance** N surveillance *f* électronique ▶ **electronic tag** N (*on prisoner*) étiquette *f* électronique ▶ **electronic tagging** N (*of prisoner*) étiquetage *m* électronique ▶ **electronic transfer of funds** N transfert *m* électronique de fonds ▶ **electronic typewriter** N machine *f* à écrire électronique

electronically [ɪlek'trɒnɪkəlɪ] ADV électroniquement

electronics [ɪlek'trɒnɪks] N (*NonC*) électronique *f* ; ~ **engineer** ingénieur *m* électronicien, électronicien(ne) *m(f)*

electrophysiological [ɪ,lektrəʊ,fɪzɪəʊ'lɒdʒɪkəl] ADJ électrophysiologique

electrophysiologist [ɪ,lektrəʊ,fɪzɪ'ɒlədʒɪst] N électrophysiologiste *mf*

electrophysiology [ɪ,lektrəʊ,fɪzɪ'ɒlədʒɪ] N électrophysiologie *f*

electroplate [ɪ'lektrəʊpleɪt] **1** VT plaquer par galvanoplastie ; (*with gold*) dorer par galvanoplastie ; (*with silver*) argenter par galvanoplastie ; **~d nickel silver** ruolz *m* **2** N (*NonC*) articles *mpl* plaqués *etc* par galvanoplastie ; (= *silver*) articles *mpl* de ruolz

electroplating [ɪ'lektrəʊ,pleɪtɪŋ] N (= *process*) galvanoplastie *f*

electropositive [ɪ,lektrəʊ'pɒzɪtɪv] ADJ électropositif

electropuncture [ɪ,lektrəʊ'pʌŋktʃəʳ] N électroponcture *or* électropuncture *f*

electroshock [ɪ'lektrəʊʃɒk] **1** N électrochoc *m* **2** COMP ▶ **electroshock baton** N matraque *f* électrique ▶ **electroshock therapy**, **electroshock treatment** N (traitement *m* par) électrochocs *mpl* ; **to give sb ~ therapy** *or* **treatment** traiter qn par électrochocs

electrostatic [ɪ,lektrəʊ'stætɪk] ADJ électrostatique

electrostatics [ɪ,lektrəʊ'stætɪks] N (*NonC*) électrostatique *f*

electrosurgery [ɪ,lektrəʊ'sɜːdʒərɪ] N électrochirurgie *f*

electrotechnological [ɪ,lektrəʊ,teknə'lɒdʒɪkəl] ADJ électrotechnique

electrotechnology [ɪ,lektrəʊtek'nɒlədʒɪ] N électrotechnique *f*

electrotherapeutics [ɪ,lektrəʊ,θerə'pjuːtɪks] N (*NonC*) électrothérapie *f*

electrotherapist [ɪ,lektrəʊ'θerəpist] N électrothérapeute *mf*

electrotherapy [ɪ,lektrəʊ'θerəpɪ] N électrothérapie *f*

electrotype [ɪ'lektrəʊ,taɪp] **1** N galvanotype *m* **2** VT clicher par galvanotypie

electrovalency [ɪ,lektrəʊ'veɪlənsɪ] N électrovalence *f*

electrovalent bond [ɪ,lektrəʊ'veɪləntbɒnd] N liaison *f* électrostatique

electrum [ɪ'lektrəm] N électrum *m*

eleemosynary [,elɪiː'mɒsɪnərɪ] ADJ (*frm*) de bienfaisance, charitable

elegance ['elɪgəns] N (*NonC*) élégance *f*

elegant ['elɪgənt] ADJ (*lit, fig*) élégant

elegantly ['elɪgəntlɪ] ADV [*dressed*] élégamment, avec élégance ; [*furnished, decorated*] élégamment ; [*written, described*] dans un style élégant ; **an ~ simple room** une pièce élégante par sa simplicité ; **an ~ simple idea** une idée d'une élégante simplicité

elegiac [,elɪ'dʒaɪək] **1** ADJ élégiaque **2** **elegiacs** NPL poèmes *mpl* élégiaques **3** COMP ▶ **elegiac couplet** N distique *m* élégiaque ▶ **elegiac stanza** N strophe *f* élégiaque

elegy ['elɪdʒɪ] N élégie *f*

element ['elɪmənt] N **a** (*Chem, Gram, Med, Phys*) élément *m* ; (*Elec*) [*of heater, kettle*] résistance *f* ; (*Met*) **the ~s** les éléments *mpl* ; **the four ~s** (= *earth, air, fire, water*) les quatre éléments *mpl* ; **to be in/out of one's ~** être/ne pas être dans son élément ; **the ~s of mathematics** les éléments *mpl* *or* les rudiments *mpl* des mathématiques **b** (= *aspect*) dimension *f* ; (= *factor*) élément *m*, facteur *m* ; (= *small part*) part *f* ; (= *group*) élément *m*, composante *f* ; **the comic/tragic/sexual ~ in his poetry** la dimension comique/tragique/sexuelle dans sa poésie ; **the human ~** l'élément *m* humain ; **one of the key ~s of the peace plan** un des éléments clés du plan de paix ; **the ~ of chance** le facteur chance ; **it's the personal ~ that matters** c'est le rapport personnel qui compte ; **an ~ of danger/truth** une part de danger/de vérité ; **the communist ~ in the trade unions** la composante communiste dans les syndicats ; **the hooligan ~** les éléments *mpl* incontrôlés, les hooligans *mpl* ; **the criminal ~** les (éléments *mpl*) criminels *mpl* **c** (*Rel*) **the Elements** les espèces *fpl*

elemental [,elɪ'mentl] ADJ **a** (*liter* = *primal*) [*drive, need*] fondamental ; [*truth*] fondamental, premier (*after n*) ; [*emotion*] brute ; **the ~ violence/fury of the storm** la violence/fureur brute de l'orage **b** (*Chem, Phys, Astron*) élémentaire

elementary [,elɪ'mentərɪ] **1** ADJ élémentaire ; **~ geometry course** cours *m* de géométrie élémentaire ; **~, my dear Watson!** élémentaire, mon cher Watson! **2** COMP ▶ **elementary education**†† N ≈ enseignement *m* primaire ▶ **elementary particle** N (*Phys*) particule *f* élémentaire *or* fondamentale ▶ **elementary school**† N école *f* primaire ▶ **elementary schooling**† N enseignement *m* primaire ▶ **elementary student** N (*US*) ≈ élève *mf* du primaire ▶ **elementary teacher** N (*US: Educ*) professeur *m* des écoles

elephant ['elɪfənt] N (*pl* **elephants** *or* **elephant**) éléphant *m* ; **bull/cow ~** éléphant *m* mâle/femelle ; **African/Indian ~** éléphant *m* d'Afrique/d'Asie → **white 2** COMP ▶ **elephant seal** N éléphant *m* de mer

elephantiasis [,elɪfən'taɪəsɪs] N éléphantiasis *f*

elephantine [,elɪ'fæntaɪn] ADJ (= *large*) éléphantesque ; (= *heavy, clumsy*) gauche, lourd ; [*wit*] lourd

elevate ['elɪveɪt] VT hausser, élever (*also Rel, fig*) ; [*voice*] hausser ; [*mind*] élever ; [*soul*] élever, exalter ; **to ~ to the peerage** élever à la pairie, anoblir

elevated ['elɪveɪtɪd] **1** ADJ **a** (= *exalted*) [*position, status, rank, tone, style, thoughts*] élevé **b** (= *raised*) [*position, platform, walkway, track*] surélevé **2** COMP ▶ **elevated railroad** N (*US*) métro *m* aérien ▶ **elevated train** N (*US*) rame *f* de métro aérien

elevating ['elɪveɪtɪŋ] ADJ [*reading*] qui élève l'esprit

elevation [,elɪ'veɪʃən] N **a** (*NonC* = *raising*) [*of person, standards, temperature*] (*also Astron, Rel, Shooting, Surv*) élévation *f* ; [*of blood pressure*] augmentation *f* ; **her ~ to the Cabinet/to the rank of Prime Minister** son accession au gouvernement/au rang de Premier ministre ; **his ~ to the papacy/to the peerage** son accession à la dignité de pape/au rang de pair ; **the ~ of trash to the status of fine art** la camelote élevée au rang des beaux-arts ; (*Shooting*) **angle of ~** angle *m* de hausse **b** (*frm* = *hill, rise*) hauteur *f*, élévation *f* **c** (= *altitude*) altitude *f* ; **at an ~ of ...** à une altitude de ... **d** (*Archit*) (= *drawing*) élévation *f* ; [*of building*] façade *f* ; **front/north ~** élévation *f* frontale/nord ; **sectional ~** coupe *f* (verticale) **e** (*NonC: frm* = *loftiness*) [*of mind, spirit*] élévation *f*

elevator ['elɪveɪtəʳ] **1** N **a** (*esp US* = *lift*) ascenseur *m* ; (= *hoist*) monte-charge *m inv* **b** (*US* = *grain storehouse*) silo *m* (à élévateur pneumatique) **c** (*Aviat*) gouvernail *m* de profondeur **d** (*US: also* ~ **shoe**) soulier *m* à talonnette **2** COMP ▶ **elevator car** N (*US*) cabine *f* d'ascenseur ▶ **elevator operator** N (*US*) liftier *m*, -ière *f* ▶ **elevator shaft** N (*US*) cage *f* d'ascenseur

eleven [ɪ'levn] **1** ADJ onze *inv* **2** N **a** (= *number*) onze *m inv* ; **number ~** le numéro onze, le onze ; (*Brit Scol*) **the ~ plus** ≈ l'examen m d'entrée en sixième **b** (*Sport*) **the French ~** le onze de France ; **the first ~** le onze, la première équipe ; **the second ~** la deuxième équipe ; *for other phrases see* **six 3** PRON onze ; **there are ~** il y en a onze

elevenses* [ɪ'levnzɪz] NPL (*Brit*) ≈ pause-café *f* (*dans la matinée*)

eleventh [ɪ'levnθ] **1** ADJ onzième ; (*fig*) **at the ~ hour** à la onzième heure, à la dernière minute **2** N onzième *mf* ; (= *fraction*) onzième *m* ; *for phrases see* **sixth**

elf [elf] N (*pl* **elves**) (*lit*) elfe *m*, lutin *m*, farfadet *m* ; (*fig*) lutin *m*

elfin ['elfɪn] ADJ **a** (= *delicately attractive*) [*person*] aux traits délicats ; [*face*] délicat **b** (*Myth*) [*light, music, dance, creature*] féerique

El Greco [el'grekəʊ] N le Greco

elicit [ɪ'lɪsɪt] VT [+ *reply, explanation, information*] obtenir (**from** de) ; [+ *reaction, support*] susciter (**from** de la part de) ; [+ *admission, promise*] arracher (**from** à) ; **to ~ sympathy from sb** s'attirer la sympathie de qn ; **to ~ public sympathy** s'attirer la sympathie du public ; **to ~ the facts of a case** tirer une affaire au clair ; **to ~ the truth about a case** jeter la lumière sur une affaire

elide [ɪ'laɪd] VT **a** (*Ling*) élider ; **to be ~d** s'élider **b** [+ *distinctions*] gommer

eligibility [,elɪdʒə'bɪlɪtɪ] N (*for election*) éligibilité *f* ; (*for employment*) admissibilité *f*

eligible ['elɪdʒəbl] ADJ (*for membership, office*) éligible (**for** à) ; (*for job*) admissible (**for** à) ; **to be ~ for a pension** avoir droit à la retraite, pouvoir faire valoir ses droits à la retraite (*frm*) ; **to be ~ for promotion** remplir les *or* satisfaire aux conditions requises pour obtenir de l'avancement ; **an ~ bachelor** un beau *or* bon parti ; **he's very ~*** c'est un très bon parti

Elijah [ɪ'laɪdʒə] N Élie *m*

eliminate [ɪ'lɪmɪneɪt] VT **a** [+ *alternative, suspicion, competitor, candidate*] éliminer, écarter ; [+ *possibility*] écarter, exclure ; [+ *competition, opposition, suspect*] éliminer ; [+ *mark, stain*] enlever, faire disparaître ; [+ *bad language, expenditure, detail*] éliminer, supprimer ; (*Math, Physiol*) éliminer **b** (* = *kill*) supprimer, éliminer

elimination [ɪ,lɪmɪ'neɪʃən] N élimination *f* ; **by (the process of) ~** par élimination

eliminator [ɪ'lɪmɪneɪtəʳ] N (*Sport*) (épreuve *f*) éliminatoire *f*

Elisha [ɪ'laɪʃə] N Élisée *m*

elision [ɪ'lɪʒən] N élision *f*

elite [ɪ'liːt] **1** N (= *select group*) élite *f* **2** ADJ **a** (= *select*) [*group, unit, force, troops*] d'élite ; [*school, university*] prestigieux **b** (*Typ*) élite *inv*

elitism [ɪ'liːtɪzəm] N élitisme *m*

elitist [ɪ'liːtɪst] ADJ, N élitiste *mf*

elixir [ɪ'lɪksəʳ] N élixir *m* ; **the ~ of life** l'élixir *m* de (longue) vie

Elizabeth [ɪ'lɪzəbəθ] N Élisabeth *f*

Elizabethan [ɪ,lɪzə'biːθən] **1** ADJ élisabéthain **2** N Élisabéthain(e) *m(f)*

elk [elk] N (*pl* **elk** *or* **elks**) (*Zool*) élan *m* ; **Canadian ~** orignac *m* (*Can*), orignal *m*

ellipse [ɪ'lɪps] N (*Math*) ellipse *f*

ellipsis [ɪ'lɪpsɪs] N (*pl* **ellipses** [ɪ'lɪpsiːz]) (*Gram*) ellipse *f*

ellipsoid [ɪ'lɪpsɔɪd] ADJ, N ellipsoïde *m*

elliptic(al) [ɪ'lɪptɪk(əl)] ADJ (*Gram, Math, fig*) elliptique

elliptically [ɪ'lɪptɪk(ə)lɪ] ADV a (= *in elliptical path*) [*move*] en ellipse b (= *not explicitly*) [*speak, write*] de manière elliptique

elm [elm] N (= *tree, wood*) orme *m*; **young ~** ormeau *m* → **Dutch**

elocution [ˌelə'kjuːʃən] N élocution *f*, diction *f*

elocutionist [ˌelə'kjuːʃənɪst] N (= *teacher*) professeur *m* d'élocution or de diction; (= *entertainer*) diseur *m*, -euse *f*

elongate ['iːlɒŋgeɪt] 1 VT (*gen*) allonger, étirer; [+ *line*] prolonger 2 VI s'allonger, s'étirer

elongation [ˌiːlɒŋ'geɪʃən] N (*gen*) allongement *m*; [*of line etc*] prolongement *m*; (*Astron, Med*) élongation *f*

elope [ɪ'ləʊp] VI [*man, woman*] s'enfuir; **they ~d** ils se sont enfuis ensemble

elopement [ɪ'ləʊpmənt] N fugue *f* (amoureuse)

eloquence ['eləkwəns] N éloquence *f*

eloquent ['eləkwənt] ADJ [*person, speech, look, gesture, silence, proof*] éloquent; [*hands*] expressif; **to be ~ about** or **on sth** parler avec éloquence de qch → **wax²**

eloquently ['eləkwəntlɪ] ADV [*speak, express*] éloquemment, avec éloquence; [*write*] avec éloquence; [*demonstrate*] éloquemment

El Salvador [el'sælvəˌdɔːr] N le Salvador; **to ~** au Salvador; **in ~** au Salvador

else [els] ADV a (= *other, besides, instead*) d'autre; **if all ~ fails** si rien d'autre ne marche; **anybody ~ would have done it** tout autre or n'importe qui d'autre l'aurait fait; **is there anybody ~ there?** y a-t-il quelqu'un d'autre?, y a-t-il encore quelqu'un?; **I'd prefer anything ~** tout mais pas ça!; **have you anything ~ to say?** avez-vous encore quelque chose à dire?, avez-vous quelque chose à ajouter?; **will there be anything ~ sir?** désirez-vous autre chose monsieur?, monsieur ne désire rien d'autre?; **I couldn't do anything ~ but leave** il ne me restait plus qu'à partir; **anywhere ~ nobody would have noticed, but ...** n'importe où ailleurs personne ne s'en serait aperçu mais ...; **can you do it anywhere ~?** pouvez-vous le faire ailleurs?; **you won't find this flower anywhere ~** vous ne trouverez cette fleur nulle part ailleurs; **how ~ can I do it?** de quelle autre façon est-ce que je peux le faire?, comment est-ce que je peux le faire autrement?; **there is little ~ to be done** il n'y a or il ne reste plus grand-chose d'autre à faire; **they sell books and toys and much ~ (besides)** ils vendent des livres, des jouets et bien d'autres choses (encore) or et que sais-je encore; **not much ~** pas grand-chose d'autre; **nobody ~ ◊ no one ~** personne d'autre; **nothing ~** rien d'autre; **nothing ~, thank you** rien d'autre, merci; **it was fun if nothing ~** au moins on s'est amusé; **nowhere ~** nulle part ailleurs; **someone** or **somebody ~** quelqu'un d'autre; **may I speak to someone ~?** puis-je parler à quelqu'un d'autre?; **this is someone ~'s umbrella** c'est le parapluie de quelqu'un d'autre; **something ~** autre chose, quelque chose d'autre; (*fig*) **she is/it is something ~*** elle est/c'est vraiment fantastique or terrible*; **somewhere ~ ◊ someplace ~** (*US*) ailleurs, autre part; **what ~ could I do?** que pouvais-je faire d'autre or de plus?; **where ~?** à quel autre endroit?; **who ~?** qui encore?, qui d'autre?

b **or ~** ou bien, sinon, autrement; **do it or ~ let me** faites-le, ou bien laissez-moi faire; **do it now or ~ you'll be punished** fais-le tout de suite, sinon tu seras puni; **do it or ~!*** vous avez intérêt à le faire!

elsewhere [ˌels'wɛər] ADV ailleurs, autre part; **from ~** (venu) d'ailleurs; **to go ~** aller ailleurs

---

ELT [ˌiːel'tiː] N (ABBR = **English Language Teaching**) → **English**; → *TEFL, TESL, TESOL, ELT*

elucidate [ɪ'luːsɪdeɪt] VT [+ *text*] élucider; [+ *mystery*] élucider, tirer au clair

elucidation [ɪˌluːsɪ'deɪʃən] N élucidation *f*

elude [ɪ'luːd] VT [+ *enemy, pursuit, arrest*] échapper à; [+ *question*] éluder; [+ *police, justice*] se dérober à; **to ~ sb's grasp** échapper aux mains de qn; **the name ~s me** le nom m'échappe; **success ~d him** le succès restait hors de sa portée; **sleep ~d her** elle n'arrivait pas à trouver le sommeil

elusive [ɪ'luːsɪv] ADJ [*person*] difficile à joindre; [*animal, truth, happiness*] insaisissable; [*quality*] indéfinissable; [*goal, target, success, happiness*] difficile à atteindre

elusively [ɪ'luːsɪvlɪ] ADV **to behave ~** se dérober; **... he said ~** ... dit-il pour s'esquiver or pour éluder la question

elusiveness [ɪ'luːsɪvnɪs] N nature *f* insaisissable, caractère *m* évasif

elusory [ɪ'luːsərɪ] ADJ = **elusive**

elver ['elvər] N civelle *f*

elves [elvz] NPL of **elf**

Elysian [ɪ'lɪzɪən] ADJ élyséen

elytron ['elɪtrɒn] N (*pl* **elytra** ['elɪtrə]) élytre *m*

EM [ˌiː'em] N (*US*) a (ABBR = **Engineer of Mines**) → **engineer** b (ABBR = **enlisted man**) → **enlist**

em [em] N (*Typ*) cicéro *m*

'em* [əm] PERS PRON = **them**

emaciated [ɪ'meɪsɪeɪtɪd] ADJ [*person, face*] émacié; [*limb*] décharné; **to become ~** s'émacier

emaciation [ɪˌmeɪsɪ'eɪʃən] N émaciation *f*, amaigrissement *m*

e-mail ['iːmeɪl] 1 N (*Comput*) (ABBR = **electronic mail**) e-mail *m*, courrier *m* électronique 2 VT **to ~ sb** envoyer un courrier électronique or un e-mail à qn; **to ~ sth** envoyer qch par courrier électronique

emanate ['eməneɪt] VI [*light, odour*] émaner (**from** de); [*rumour, document, instruction*] émaner, provenir (**from** de)

emanation [ˌemə'neɪʃən] N émanation *f*

emancipate [ɪ'mænsɪpeɪt] VT [+ *women*] émanciper; [+ *slaves*] affranchir; (*fig*) émanciper, affranchir, libérer; **to be ~d from sth** s'affranchir or s'émanciper de qch

emancipated [ɪ'mænsɪpeɪtɪd] ADJ (*fig*) émancipé, libéré

emancipation [ɪˌmænsɪ'peɪʃən] N (*NonC*) [*of mankind, women*] émancipation *f*; [*of slaves*] affranchissement *m*, émancipation *f*; **black/female ~** émancipation *f* des Noirs/de la femme

emasculate [ɪ'mæskjʊleɪt] 1 VT (*lit, fig*) émasculer 2 [ɪ'mæskjʊlɪt] ADJ (*lit, fig*) émasculé

emasculation [ɪˌmæskjʊ'leɪʃən] N (*lit, fig*) émasculation *f*

embalm [ɪm'bɑːm] VT (*all senses*) embaumer

embalmer [ɪm'bɑːmər] N embaumeur *m*

embalming [ɪm'bɑːmɪŋ] 1 N embaumement *m* 2 COMP ► **embalming fluid** N bain *m* de natron

embankment [ɪm'bæŋkmənt] N [*of path, railway line*] talus *m*, remblai *m*; [*of road*] banquette *f* (de sûreté); [*of canal, dam*] digue *f*, chaussée *f* (de retenue); [*of river*] (= *mound of earth*) berge *f*; [*of wall of earth*] quai *m*; (*in London*) **the Embankment** l'un des quais le long de la Tamise

embargo [ɪm'bɑːgəʊ] 1 N (*pl* **embargoes**) a (*Pol, Comm, Naut etc*) embargo *m*; **to impose an ~ on** [+ *country etc*] imposer un embargo contre; [+ *goods*] imposer un embargo sur; **arms ~** embargo *m* sur les armes; **an oil ~** un embargo pétrolier; **to lift an ~** lever l'embargo; **to enforce an ~** appliquer l'embargo b (*fig = prohibition*) interdiction *f*, restriction *f*; **to put an ~ on sth** mettre l'embargo sur qch, interdire qch 2 VT mettre l'embargo sur; (*fig = prohibit*) interdire

embark [ɪm'bɑːk] 1 VT [+ *passengers*] embarquer, prendre à bord; [+ *goods*] embarquer, charger 2 VI (*Aviat, Naut*) embarquer (**on** à bord de, sur); (*fig*) **to ~ on** [+ *journey*] commencer; [+ *business undertaking, deal*] s'engager dans, se lancer dans; [+ *doubtful or risky affair, explanation, story*] se lancer dans, s'embarquer dans*; [+ *discussion*] se lancer dans

embarkation [ˌembɑː'keɪʃən] N [*of passengers*] embarquement *m*; [*of cargo*] embarquement *m*, chargement *m*; (*Aviat, Naut*) **~ card** carte *f* d'embarquement

embarrass [ɪm'bærəs] VT [+ *person, government*] embarrasser, gêner

embarrassed [ɪm'bærəst] ADJ a (= *person, silence, laugh*) gêné, embarrassé; **there was an ~ silence** il y eut un silence gêné, un ange est passé; **he looked ~** il avait l'air gêné or embarrassé; **I feel ~ about it** cela me gêne or m'embarrasse; **he was ~ about discussing his financial difficulties** cela le gênait or l'embarrassait de parler de ses problèmes financiers; **she was ~ about her spots** ses boutons étaient une source d'embarras pour elle or la rendaient mal à l'aise; **he was ~ at** or **about being the focus of attention** cela le gênait or le mettait dans l'embarras d'être au centre de l'attention; **I was ~ for him** j'étais gêné pour lui; **she was ~ to be seen with him** cela la gênait d'être vue en sa compagnie b **to be financially ~** être dans l'embarras financièrement, avoir des ennuis d'argent

embarrassing [ɪm'bærəsɪŋ] ADJ embarrassant, gênant; **to get out of an ~ situation** se tirer d'embarras

embarrassingly [ɪm'bærəsɪŋlɪ] ADV **~ short/few/bad** si court/peu/mauvais que c'en est (or était) embarrassant; **for him, he ...** à son grand embarras, il ...; **~, he ...** au grand embarras de tous, il ...

embarrassment [ɪm'bærəsmənt] N a (= *emotion*) embarras *m*, gêne *f* (**at** devant); **to cause sb ~** mettre qn dans l'embarras, embarrasser qn; **financial ~** des ennuis *mpl* d'argent, des embarras *mpl* financiers; **it is an ~ of riches: Zola, Flaubert, Balzac, Stendhal** on peut dire qu'on a l'embarras du choix: Zola, Flaubert, Balzac, Stendhal b (= *source of embarrassment*) **her son is an ~ to her** son fils est une source d'embarras pour elle; **her scar is an ~ to her** sa cicatrice est une source d'embarras pour elle or la rend mal à l'aise

embassy ['embəsɪ] N ambassade *f*; **the French Embassy** l'ambassade *f* de France

embattled [ɪm'bætld] ADJ a (= *beleaguered*) [*city, country, people, army*] assiégé b (= *troubled*) [*person, government*] aux prises avec des difficultés, en difficulté

embed [ɪm'bed] VT (*in wood*) enfoncer; (*in cement*) noyer; (*in stone*) sceller; [+ *jewel*] enchâsser; (*Ling*) enchâsser; (*fig*) **~ded in the memory/mind** gravé dans la mémoire/l'esprit

embedding [ɪm'bedɪŋ] N action *f* de sceller, fixation *f*; (*Ling*) enchâssement *m*

embellish [ɪm'belɪʃ] VT (= *adorn*) embellir, orner (**with** de); [+ *manuscript*] relever, enjoliver (**with** de); (*fig*) [*tale, account*] enjoliver, embellir; [+ *truth*] broder sur, orner

embellishment [ɪm'belɪʃmənt] N a (= *adornment*) embellissement *m*, ornement *m*; **stripped of ~** dépouillé de tout ornement b (= *added detail*) [*of story, truth*] embellissement *m*, enjolivement *m* c (*Mus*) fioriture *f*

ember ['embər] N charbon *m* ardent; **the ~s** la braise; **the dying ~s** les tisons *mpl* → **fan¹**

Ember days ['embəˌdeɪz] NPL (*Rel*) quatre-temps *mpl*

embezzle [ɪm'bezl] 1 VT détourner 2 VI détourner des fonds

embezzlement [ɪm'bezlmənt] N détournement m de fonds

embezzler [ɪm'bezlər] N escroc m

embitter [ɪm'bɪtər] VT [+ person] aigrir, remplir d'amertume ; [+ relations, disputes] envenimer

embittered [ɪm'bɪtəd] ADJ [person, relationship] aigri, plein d'amertume

embittering [ɪm'bɪtərɪŋ] ADJ qui laisse amer

embitterment [ɪm'bɪtəmənt] N amertume f, aigreur f

emblazon [ɪm'bleɪzən] VT (= extol) chanter les louanges de ; (Her) blasonner

emblem ['embləm] N (all senses) emblème m

emblematic [,emblə'mætɪk] ADJ (= characteristic) typique ; (= symbolic) **dogs are ~ of faithfulness** les chiens sont un symbole de fidélité

embodiment [ɪm'bɒdɪmənt] N a incarnation f, personnification f ; **to be the ~ of progress** incarner le progrès ; **he is the ~ of kindness** c'est la bonté incarnée or personnifiée b (= inclusion) incorporation f

embody [ɪm'bɒdɪ] VT a [+ spirit, quality] incarner ; [+ one's thoughts, theories] [person] exprimer, concrétiser, formuler (in dans, en) ; [work] exprimer, donner forme à, mettre en application (in dans) b (= include) [+ ideas] [person] résumer (in dans) ; [work] renfermer ; [+ features] [machine] réunir

embolden [ɪm'bəʊldən] VT a enhardir ; **to ~ sb to do** donner à qn le courage de faire, enhardir qn à faire b (Typ) imprimer en gras (or mi-gras)

embolism ['embəlɪzəm] N embolie f

emboss [ɪm'bɒs] VT [+ metal] travailler en relief, repousser, estamper ; [+ leather, cloth] frapper, gaufrer ; [+ velvet, paper] frapper

embossed [ɪm'bɒst] ADJ [lettering, letters, design] en relief ; [paper, wallpaper, card] gaufré ; [leather] (with stamp) gaufré ; (with tool) repoussé ; [metal] (with stamp) estampé ; (with tool) repoussé ; **~ writing paper** papier m à lettres à en-tête m ; **to be ~ with sth** avoir qch en relief ; **leather books ~ in gold** des livres à reliure de cuir estampée d'or

embouchure [,ɒmbʊ'ʃʊər] N (Mus) embouchure f

embrace [ɪm'breɪs] 1 VT a (= hug) étreindre ; (amorously) enlacer, étreindre b (fig) [+ religion] embrasser ; [+ opportunity] saisir ; [+ cause] épouser, embrasser ; [+ offer] profiter de c (= include) [person] [+ theme, experience] embrasser ; [+ topics, hypotheses] inclure ; [work] [+ theme, period] embrasser, englober ; [+ ideas, topics] renfermer, comprendre ; **his charity ~s all mankind** sa charité s'étend à l'humanité tout entière ; **an all-embracing review** une revue d'ensemble 2 VI s'étreindre, s'embrasser 3 N (= hug) étreinte f ; **they were standing in a tender ~** ils étaient tendrement enlacés ; **he held her in a tender ~** il l'enlaçait tendrement ; **to greet sb with a warm ~** accueillir qn en l'étreignant chaleureusement ; **locked in an ~** enlacé

embrasure [ɪm'breɪʒər] N embrasure f

embrocation [,embrəʊ'keɪʃən] N embrocation f

embroider [ɪm'brɔɪdər] 1 VT broder ; (fig: also ~ on) [+ facts, truth] broder sur ; [+ story] enjoliver 2 VI faire de la broderie

embroidery [ɪm'brɔɪdərɪ] 1 N broderie f 2 COMP ► **embroidery frame** N métier m or tambour m à broder ► **embroidery silk** N soie f à broder ► **embroidery thread** N fil m à broder

embroil [ɪm'brɔɪl] VT entraîner (in dans), mêler (in à) ; **to get (o.s.) ~ed in** se laisser entraîner dans, se trouver mêlé à

embroilment [ɪm'brɔɪlmənt] N implication f (in dans), participation f (in à)

embryo ['embrɪəʊ] N (lit, fig) embryon m ; **in ~** (lit) à l'état or au stade embryonnaire ; (fig) en germe

embryological [,embrɪə'lɒdʒɪkəl] ADJ embryologique

embryologist [,embrɪ'ɒlədʒɪst] N embryologiste mf

embryology [,embrɪ'ɒlədʒɪ] N embryologie f

embryonic [,embrɪ'ɒnɪk] ADJ a (Zool) embryonnaire b (fig) en germe

embus [ɪm'bʌs] 1 VT (faire) embarquer dans un car 2 VI s'embarquer dans un car

emcee ['em'siː] (US) ABBR = **master of ceremonies** 1 N (gen) maître m de cérémonies ; (in show etc) animateur m, meneur m de jeu 2 VT [+ show etc] animer

emend [ɪ'mend] VT [+ text] corriger

emendation [,iːmen'deɪʃən] N correction f

emerald ['emərəld] 1 N (= stone) émeraude f ; (= colour) (vert m) émeraude m 2 COMP (= set with emeralds) (serti) d'émeraudes ; (also ~ green) émeraude inv ► **the Emerald Isle** N (liter) l'île f d'Émeraude (Irlande) ► **emerald necklace** N collier m d'émeraudes

emerge [ɪ'mɜːdʒ] VI [person, animal] émerger (from de), sortir (from de) ; (fig) [truth, facts] émerger (from de), se dégager ; [difficulties] surgir, apparaître ; [new nation] naître ; [theory, school of thought] apparaître, naître ; **it ~s (from this) that ...** il (en) ressort que ..., il (en) résulte que ... ; **to ~ as ...** (= turn out to be) se révéler être ...

emergence [ɪ'mɜːdʒəns] N [of truth, facts] émergence f ; [of new nation, theory, school of thought] naissance f

emergency [ɪ'mɜːdʒənsɪ] 1 N cas m urgent, imprévu m (NonC) ; **in case of ~** ◊ **in an ~** en cas d'urgence or d'imprévu or de nécessité ; **to be prepared for any ~** être prêt à or parer à toute éventualité ; **in this ~** dans cette situation critique, dans ces circonstances critiques ; **state of ~** état m d'urgence ; **to declare a state of ~** déclarer l'état d'urgence 2 COMP [measures, treatment, operation, repair] d'urgence ; [brake, airstrip] de secours ; (= improvised) [mast] de fortune ; (Med) **an ~ case** une urgence ► **emergency centre** N poste m de secours ► **emergency exit** N issue f or sortie f de secours ► **emergency force** N (Mil) force f d'urgence or d'intervention ► **emergency landing** N (Aviat) atterrissage m forcé ► **emergency powers** (Pol) pouvoirs mpl extraordinaires ► **emergency rations** NPL vivres mpl de réserve ► **emergency room** N (US Med) = **emergency ward** ► **emergency service** N (Med) service m des urgences ; (Aut) service m de dépannage ► **emergency services** NPL (= police etc) services mpl d'urgence, ≈ police-secours f ► **emergency stop** N (Aut) arrêt m d'urgence ► **emergency tax** N impôt m extraordinaire ► **emergency telephone** N dispositif m or borne f d'urgence ► **emergency ward** N (Med) salle f des urgences

emergent [ɪ'mɜːdʒənt] ADJ [democracy, movement, group, sexuality] naissant ; [nation, country] (gen) naissant ; (= recently independent) nouvellement indépendant ; (Opt, Philos) émergent

emeritus [ɪ'merɪtəs] ADJ (Univ) **~ professor** ◊ **professor ~** professeur m émérite† or honoraire

emery ['emərɪ] 1 N émeri m 2 COMP ► **emery board** N lime f à ongles ► **emery cloth** N toile f (d')émeri ► **emery paper** N papier m (d')émeri, papier m de verre

emetic [ɪ'metɪk] ADJ, N émétique m

emigrant ['emɪgrənt] 1 N (just leaving) émigrant(e) m(f) ; (established) émigré(e) m(f) 2 COMP [ship, family] d'émigrants

emigrate ['emɪgreɪt] VI émigrer

emigration [,emɪ'greɪʃən] N émigration f

émigré ['emɪgreɪ] N émigré(e) m(f)

Emilia-Romagna [ɪ'miːlɪərəʊ'mɑːnjə] N l'Émilie-Romagne f

eminence ['emɪnəns] N a (NonC = distinction) distinction f ; **to achieve ~ in one's profession** parvenir à un rang éminent dans sa profession ; **to win ~ as a surgeon** acquérir un grand renom comme chirurgien ; **the ~ of his position** sa position éminente ; (Rel) **His/Your Eminence** Son/Votre Éminence b (= high ground) éminence f, élévation f, butte f

eminent ['emɪnənt] ADJ a (= distinguished) [person] éminent ; **she is ~ in the field of avionics** c'est une sommité dans le domaine de l'avionique b (frm = great) remarquable ; **his ~ good sense** son remarquable bon sens c (Rel) **Most Eminent** éminentissime

eminently ['emɪnəntlɪ] ADV [sensible, reasonable, capable] parfaitement ; [respectable, qualified] éminemment ; [practical, readable, desirable] tout à fait ; [forgettable] absolument ; **to be ~ suitable** convenir parfaitement

emir [e'mɪər] N émir m

emirate [e'mɪərɪt] N émirat m

emissary ['emɪsərɪ] N émissaire m

emission [ɪ'mɪʃən] 1 N (NonC) dégagement m 2 **emissions** NPL (= substances) émissions fpl 3 COMP ► **emission spectrum** N spectre m d'émission

emit [ɪ'mɪt] VT [+ gas, heat, smoke] émettre, dégager ; [+ light, waves] émettre ; [+ smell] dégager, exhaler ; [+ lava] répandre ; [+ sound, chuckle] émettre

emitter [ɪ'mɪtər] N (Elec) émetteur m

Emmanuel [ɪ'mænjʊəl] N Emmanuel m

Emmy ['emɪ] N (pl Emmys or Emmies) oscar de la télévision américaine

emollient [ɪ'mɒlɪənt] 1 N émollient m 2 ADJ [cream] émollient ; (fig) [person] conciliant

emolument [ɪ'mɒljʊmənt] N émoluments mpl

emote [ɪ'məʊt] VI donner dans le sentiment*

emoticon [ɪ'məʊtɪkən] N (Comput) emoticon m, smiley m

emotion [ɪ'məʊʃən] N émotion f, sentiment m ; **a voice full of ~** une voix émue

emotional [ɪ'məʊʃənl] 1 ADJ a (= psychological) [problem, support, development, detachment, bond, intensity] affectif ; [shock, disturbance, impact] émotif, affectif ; **his ~ state** son état émotionnel ; **to make an ~ commitment to sb** s'engager vis-à-vis de qn sur le plan affectif ; **on an ~ level** sur le plan affectif ; **to be on an ~ high/low*** être dans un état d'exaltation or sur un petit nuage*/ déprimé b (= emotive) **it is an ~ issue** cette question soulève les passions c (= full of emotion) [person] (by nature) émotif ; (on specific occasion) ému ; [moment, situation] de grande émotion ; [experience, story, appeal, speech, farewell, welcome, outburst, scene, response] plein d'émotion ; [decision] guidé par les sentiments ; **he became very ~** il a été très ému ; **to be ~ about sth** (by nature) s'émouvoir facilement de qch ; **his behaviour was very ~** il a eu un comportement très émotionnel 2 COMP ► **emotional baggage*** N (pej) expériences fpl personnelles ; **his ~ baggage** le poids de son vécu personnel ► **emotional blackmail*** N chantage m affectif ► **emotional cripple*** N (pej) **to be an ~ cripple** être bloqué sur le plan émotionnel ► **emotional roller coaster** N **to be on an ~ roller coaster** être pris dans un tourbillon d'émotions ► **emotional wreck** N loque f sur le plan affectif

emotionalism [ɪ'məʊʃnəlɪzəm] N émotivité f,

sensiblerie f (pej) ; **the article was sheer ~** l'article n'était qu'un étalage de sensiblerie

emotionally [ɪ'məʊʃnəlɪ] ADV **a** (= psychologically) [mature, stable, distant, drained] sur le plan affectif or émotionnel ; **~ deprived** privé d'affection ; **to be ~ disturbed** souffrir de troubles émotifs or affectifs ; **an ~ disturbed child** un(e) enfant caractériel(le) ; **as a doctor, one should never become ~ involved** un médecin ne doit jamais s'impliquer au niveau affectif or émotionnel ; **to be ~ involved with sb** (= be in relationship) avoir une liaison avec qn ; **~ I was a wreck** sur le plan émotionnel j'étais une loque **b** (= with emotion) [speak, describe, react] avec émotion ; **an ~ charged atmosphere** une atmosphère chargée d'émotion ; **an ~ worded article** un article qui fait appel aux sentiments

emotionless [ɪ'məʊʃənlɪs] ADJ [expression, tone etc] impassible ; [person] imperturbable

emotive [ɪ'məʊtɪv] ADJ [issue, question, subject] qui soulève les passions ; [language, word] à connotations émotionnelles

empanel [ɪm'pænl] VT (Jur) [+ jury] constituer ; **to ~ a juror** inscrire quelqu'un sur la liste du jury

empanelment [ɪm'pænlmənt] N [of jury] constitution f

empathetic [ˌempə'θetɪk] ADJ compréhensif (**to** envers)

empathetically [ˌempə'θetɪkəlɪ] ADV avec compréhension or sympathie

empathic [em'pæθɪk] ADJ = **empathetic**

empathize [ˈempəθaɪz] VI **to ~ with sb** comprendre ce que ressent qn

empathy [ˈempəθɪ] N empathie f, communion f d'idées (or de sentiments etc) ; **our ~ with the pain she was suffering** notre compassion f pour la douleur qui était la sienne

emperor [ˈempərə^r] **1** N empereur m **2** COMP ► **emperor moth** N paon m de nuit ► **emperor penguin** N manchot m empereur

emphasis [ˈemfəsɪs] N (pl **emphases** [ˈemfəsiːz]) (in word, phrase) accentuation f, accent m d'intensité ; (fig) accent m ; **to speak with ~** parler sur un ton d'insistance ; **the ~ is on the first syllable** l'accent d'intensité or l'accentuation tombe sur la première syllabe ; **to lay on a word** souligner un mot, insister sur or appuyer sur un mot ; (fig) **to lay ~ on one aspect of ...** mettre l'accent sur or insister sur or attacher de l'importance à un aspect de ... ; **the ~ is on sport** on accorde une importance particulière au sport ; (Fashion) **this year the ~ is on femininity** cette année l'accent est sur la féminité → **shift**

emphasize [ˈemfəsaɪz] VT (= stress) [+ word, fact, point] insister sur, souligner ; [+ syllable] accentuer ; (= draw attention to: gen) accentuer ; [+ sth pleasant or flattering] mettre en valeur, faire valoir ; **this point cannot be too strongly ~d** on ne saurait trop insister sur ce point ; **I must ~ that ...** je dois souligner le fait que ... ; **the long coat ~d his height** le long manteau faisait ressortir sa haute taille ; **to ~ the eyes with mascara** mettre les yeux en valeur avec du mascara

emphatic [ɪm'fætɪk] ADJ **a** (= forceful) [person] catégorique ; [condemnation, denial, rejection, response, statement, declaration] énergique ; **the answer is an ~ yes/no** la réponse est un oui/ non catégorique ; **to be ~ about sth** insister sur qch ; **she's ~ that business is improving** elle affirme catégoriquement que les affaires reprennent ; **they were quite ~ that they were not going to** ils ont refusé catégoriquement d'y aller ; **he was ~ in his defence of the system** il a vigoureusement défendu le système ; **they were ~ in denying their involvement** ils ont vigoureusement démenti être impliqués **b** (=

emphasizing) [tone, gesture, nod] emphatique **c** (= decisive) [victory, defeat] écrasant ; [result, winner] incontestable

emphatically [ɪm'fætɪkəlɪ] ADV **a** (= forcefully) [say, reply, shake one's head] énergiquement ; [deny, reject, refuse] catégoriquement, énergiquement ; **to nod ~** acquiescer énergiquement de la tête **b** (= definitely) [democratic] clairement ; **politics is most ~ back on the agenda** la politique fait bel et bien un retour en force ; **~ not** absolument pas ; **yes, ~!** oui, tout à fait! ; **~ no!** non, en aucun cas!, non, absolument pas!

emphysema [emfɪ'siːmə] N emphysème m

Empire [ˈempaɪə^r] ADJ [costume, furniture] Empire inv

empire [ˈempaɪə^r] **1** N (all senses) empire m **2** COMP ► **empire-builder** N (fig) bâtisseur m d'empires ► **empire-building** N (fig) he is **~-building** ◊ it is **~-building on his part** il joue les bâtisseurs d'empire ► **the Empire State** N (US) l'État m de New York ► **the Empire State Building** N l'Empire State Building m

empiric [em'pɪrɪk] **1** ADJ empirique **2** N empiriste mf ; (Med) empirique m

empirical [em'pɪrɪkəl] ADJ empirique

empirically [em'pɪrɪkəlɪ] ADV [test] empiriquement ; [invalid, testable] d'un point de vue empirique ; **an ~ grounded approach** une approche fondée sur un raisonnement empirique ; **~ based knowledge** connaissances fpl fondées sur un raisonnement empirique ; **~, therefore, four is the answer** empiriquement, donc, la réponse est quatre

empiricism [em'pɪrɪsɪzəm] N empirisme m

empiricist [em'pɪrɪsɪst] ADJ, N empiriste mf

emplacement [ɪm'pleɪsmənt] N (Mil) emplacement m (d'un canon)

employ [ɪm'plɔɪ] **1** VT [+ person] employer (**as** comme) ; [+ means, method, process] employer, utiliser ; [+ time] employer (**in** or **by doing** à faire) ; [+ force, cunning] recourir à, employer ; [+ skill] faire usage de, employer ; **to be ~ed in doing sth** être occupé à faire qch **2** N **to be in sb's ~** être employé par qn, travailler chez or pour qn ; (of domestic staff) être au service de qn

employable [ɪm'plɔɪəbəl] ADJ [person] capable d'entrer sur le marché de l'emploi ; **~ skills** compétences fpl utilisables

employee [ˌɪmplɔɪ'iː] **1** N salarié(e) m(f) ; **to be an ~ of ...** travailler chez ... **2** COMP ► **employee stock ownership plans** NPL (US) actionnariat m ouvrier or des salariés

employer [ɪm'plɔɪə^r] N (Comm, Ind, also domestic) patron(ne) m(f) ; (Jur) employeur m, -euse f ; (Ind: collectively) **~s** le patronat ; **~s'** federation syndicat m patronal, fédération f patronale ; (Insurance) **~'s contribution** cotisation f patronale

employment [ɪm'plɔɪmənt] **1** N (NonC = jobs collectively) emploi m (NonC) ; (= a job) emploi m, travail m ; (modest) place f ; (important) situation f ; **full ~** le plein emploi ; **in ~** qui travaille, qui a un emploi ; **the numbers in ~** les actifs mpl ; **in sb's ~** employé par qn ; (domestic staff) au service de qn ; **without ~** sans emploi, au chômage ; **conditions/place of ~** conditions fpl/lieu m de travail ; **to seek/find/ take up ~ (with)** chercher/trouver/prendre un emploi (chez) ; **Department** or **Ministry of Employment** ministère m de l'Emploi ; **Secretary (of State) for** or **Minister of Employment** (Brit) ◊ **Secretary for Employment** (US) ministre m de l'Emploi **2** COMP ► **employment agency** N agence f de placement ► **employment exchange**† N (Brit) bourse f du travail ► **employment office** N (Brit) ≈ bureau m de l'Agence nationale pour l'emploi ► **Employment Service** N (US) ≈ Agence f nationale pour l'emploi

emporium [em'pɔːrɪəm] N (pl **emporiums** or **emporia** [em'pɔːrɪə]) (= shop) grand magasin m, bazar m ; (= market) centre m commercial, marché m

empower [ɪm'paʊə^r] VT **a** (= authorize) **to ~ sb to do sth** autoriser qn à faire qch ; (Jur) habiliter qn à faire qch ; **to be ~ed to do sth** avoir pleins pouvoirs pour faire qch **b** **to ~ sb** (= make stronger) rendre qn plus fort ; (= make more independent) permettre à qn de s'assumer

empowering [ɪm'paʊərɪŋ] ADJ **such experiences can be ~** ce type d'expérience peut aider les gens à s'assumer

empowerment [ɪm'paʊəmənt] N **a** (Pol, Sociol) émancipation f ; **female ~** ◊ **the ~ of women** l'émancipation f des femmes **b** (Ind) délégation f des responsabilités

empress [ˈemprɪs] N impératrice f

emptiness [ˈemptɪnɪs] N vide m ; [of pleasures etc] vanité f ; **the ~ of life** le vide de l'existence

empty [ˈemptɪ] **1** ADJ **a** (= containing nothing) [place, building, container, seat, vehicle, hand, days] vide (**of sth** de qch) ; [ship] lège (Naut) ; [landscape] désert ; (Ling) vide ; **she was staring into ~ space** elle regardait fixement dans le vide ; **there was an ~ space at the table** il y avait une place vide à la table ; **on an ~ stomach** l'estomac vide, à jeun ; **his face and eyes were ~ of all expression** son visage et ses yeux étaient dénués de toute expression ; **~ of emotion** or **feeling** incapable de ressentir la moindre émotion ; **to be running on ~** (Aut) avoir le réservoir pratiquement vide ; (fig) [person] avoir l'estomac vide ; [organization] être à bout de souffle ■ (PROV) **~ vessels make most noise** ce sont les tonneaux vides qui font le plus de bruit → **5** **b** (= meaningless) [phrase, words, rhetoric] creux ; [dream, hope, exercise] vain ; **~ talk** verbiage m ; **~ promises/threats** promesses fpl/menaces fpl en l'air ; **it's an ~ gesture** c'est un geste vide de sens or un geste qui ne veut rien dire ; **my life is ~ without you** ma vie est vide sans toi **c** (= numb) [person] vidé ; [feeling] de vide ; **when I heard the news I felt ~** quand j'ai appris la nouvelle, je me suis senti vidé **2** **empties** NPL (= bottles) bouteilles fpl vides ; (= boxes etc) boîtes fpl or emballages mpl vides ; (= glasses: in pub etc) verres mpl vides **3** VT **a** (= discharge) [+ box, glass, bin, pond, pocket] vider ; [+ tank] vider, vidanger ; [+ vehicle] décharger ; **the burglars emptied the shop** les voleurs ont dévalisé le magasin ; **television has emptied the cinemas** la télévision a vidé les cinémas ; **his singing emptied the room** la salle s'est vidée quand il a chanté **b** (also **~ out**) [+ bricks, books] sortir ; [+ rubbish] vider (**of, from** de, **into** dans) ; [+ liquid] vider (**from** de), verser (**from** de, **into** dans), transvaser (**into** dans) **4** VI [water] se déverser, s'écouler ; [river] se jeter (**into** dans) ; [building, room, container] se vider **5** COMP ► **empty calories** NPL calories fpl inutiles ► **empty-handed** ADJ les mains vides ; **to return ~-handed** revenir bredouille or les mains vides ► **empty-headed** ADJ sot (sotte f), sans cervelle ; **an ~-headed girl** une écervelée, une évaporée ► **empty-nester*** N personne dont les enfants ont quitté la maison

empyema [ˌempaɪ'iːmə] N (pl **empyemas** or **empyemata** [ˌempaɪ'iːmətə]) empyème m

empyrean [ˌempaɪ'riːən] N (liter) **the ~** l'empyrée m (liter)

EMS [ˌiːem'es] N (ABBR = **European Monetary System**) SME m

EMU [ˌiːemˈjuː] N (ABBR = **economic and monetary union**) UME f

emu [ˈiːmjuː] N émeu m

emulate [ˈemjʊleɪt] VT imiter ; (Comput) émuler

emulation [ˌemjʊˈleɪʃən] N imitation f ; (Comput) émulation f

emulator [ˈemjʊleɪtə^r] N (Comput) émulateur m

emulsifier [eˈmʌlsɪˌfaɪə^r] N émulsifiant m

emulsify [eˈmʌlsɪfaɪ] VTI émulsionner

emulsion [ɪˈmʌlʃən] **1** N (also Phot) émulsion f ; ~ (paint) peinture-émulsion f **2** VT peindre (avec une peinture-émulsion)

en [en] N (Typ) n m, lettre f moyenne

enable [ɪˈneɪbl] **1** VT to ~ sb to do sth (= give opportunity) permettre à qn de faire qch, donner à qn la possibilité de faire qch ; (= give means) permettre à qn de faire qch, donner à qn le moyen de faire qch ; (Jur etc = authorize) habiliter qn à faire qch, donner pouvoir à qn de faire qch **2** COMP ► **enabling legislation** N loi f d'habilitation

enact [ɪˈnækt] **1** VT **a** (Jur) [+ law, decree] promulguer, passer ; **as by law ~ed** aux termes de la loi, selon la loi **b** (= perform) [+ play] représenter, jouer ; [+ part] jouer ; (fig) **the drama which was ~ed yesterday** le drame qui s'est déroulé hier **2** COMP ► **enacting terms** NPL dispositif m d'un jugement

enactment [ɪˈnæktmənt] N promulgation f

enamel [ɪˈnæməl] **1** N (NonC: most senses) émail m ; **nail ~** vernis m à ongles (laqué) ; **tooth ~** émail m dentaire **b** (Art) **an ~** un émail **2** VT émailler **3** COMP [ornament, brooch] en émail ► **enamel paint** N peinture f laquée ► **enamel painting** N (Art) peinture f sur émail ► **enamel saucepan** N casserole f en fonte émaillée

enamelled [ɪˈnæməld] ADJ [jewellery, bath, saucepan] en émail ; [metal] émaillé

enamelling [ɪˈnæməlɪŋ] N émaillage m

enamelware [ɪˈnæməlweə^r] N (NonC) articles mpl en métal émaillé

enamoured, enamored (US) [ɪˈnæməd] ADJ (liter or hum) **to be ~ of** [+ person] être amoureux or épris de ; [+ thing] être enchanté de, être séduit par ; (hum) **she was not ~ of the idea** l'idée ne l'enchantait pas

encamp [ɪnˈkæmp] **1** VI camper **2** VT faire camper

encampment [ɪnˈkæmpmənt] N campement m

encapsulate [ɪnˈkæpsjʊleɪt] VT incarner (l'essence de) ; (Pharm, Space) mettre en capsule

encase [ɪnˈkeɪs] VT (= contain) enfermer, enchâsser (**in** dans) ; (= cover) enrober (**in** de)

encash [ɪnˈkæʃ] VT (Brit) [+ cheque] encaisser, toucher

encashment [ɪnˈkæʃmənt] N (Brit) encaissement m

encaustic [enˈkɔːstɪk] **1** ADJ [painting] à l'encaustique ; [tile, brick] vernissé **2** N (= painting) encaustique f

encephala [enˈsefələ] NPL of **encephalon**

encephalic [ensɪˈfælɪk] ADJ encéphalique

encephalitis [ˌensefəˈlaɪtɪs] N encéphalite f

encephalogram [enˈsefələgræm] N encéphalogramme m

encephalon [enˈsefəlɒn] N (pl **encephala**) encéphale m

enchant [ɪnˈtʃɑːnt] VT **a** (= put under spell) enchanter, ensorceler ; **the ~ed wood** le bois enchanté **b** (fig = delight) enchanter, ravir

enchanter [ɪnˈtʃɑːntə^r] N enchanteur m

enchanting [ɪnˈtʃɑːntɪŋ] ADJ ravissant

enchantingly [ɪnˈtʃɑːntɪŋlɪ] ADV [dress, dance] d'une façon ravissante ; [smile] d'une façon charmante ; **the ~ named "via della Gatta"** la rue au nom charmant de « via della Gatta » ;

she is ~ pretty elle est jolie et pleine de charme ; **she is ~ beautiful** elle est belle à ravir

enchantment [ɪnˈtʃɑːntmənt] N **a** (= spell) enchantement m, ensorcellement m **b** (fig = appeal) charme m ; **the forest had its own peculiar ~** la forêt avait son charme bien particulier ; **the many ~s of Venice** les nombreux charmes mpl or enchantements mpl de Venise

enchantress [ɪnˈtʃɑːntrɪs] N enchanteresse f

enchilada* [ˌentʃɪˈlɑːdə] N (US) **big ~** huile* f, grosse légume* f, gros bonnet* m

encircle [ɪnˈsɜːkl] VT (gen) entourer ; [troops, men, police] encercler, cerner, entourer ; [walls, belt, bracelet] entourer, ceindre

encirclement [ɪnˈsɜːklmənt] N encerclement m

encircling [ɪnˈsɜːklɪŋ] **1** N encerclement m **2** ADJ qui encercle ; ~ **movement** manœuvre f d'encerclement

enc(l). (ABBR = **enclosure(s)**) PJ, pièce(s) f(pl) jointe(s)

enclave [ˈenkleɪv] N enclave f

enclitic [ɪnˈklɪtɪk] N enclitique m

▼ **enclose** [ɪnˈkləʊz] VT **a** (= fence in) enclore, clôturer ; (= surround) entourer, ceindre (**with** de) ; (Rel) cloîtrer ; **to ~ within** enfermer dans **b** (with letter etc) joindre (**in, with** à) ; **to ~ sth in a letter** joindre qch à une lettre, inclure qch dans une lettre ; **letter enclosing a receipt** lettre f contenant un reçu ; **please find ~d** veuillez trouver ci-joint ; **the ~d cheque** le chèque ci-joint or ci-inclus

enclosed [ɪnˈkləʊzd] **1** ADJ [area] fermé ; [garden] clos, clôturé ; [path] clôturé ; **an ~ space** un espace clos ; **an ~ community** une communauté retirée **2** COMP ► **enclosed order** N (Rel) ordre m cloîtré

enclosure [ɪnˈkləʊʒə^r] **1** N **a** (NonC) [of land] fait m de clôturer ; (Brit Hist) enclosure f **b** (= document etc enclosed) pièce f jointe, document m ci-joint or ci-inclus ; (= ground enclosed) enclos m, enceinte f ; [of monastery] clôture f ; (= fence etc) enceinte f, clôture f ; [of racecourse] **the ~** le pesage ; **the public ~** la pelouse ; **the royal ~** l'enceinte f réservée à la famille royale **2** COMP ► **enclosure wall** N mur m d'enceinte

encode [ɪnˈkəʊd] VTI coder ; (Comput) coder, encoder ; (Ling) encoder

encoder [ɪnˈkəʊdə^r] N (Comput) encodeur m

encoding [ɪnˈkəʊdɪŋ] N [of message] codage m ; (Comput, Ling) encodage m

encomium [ɪnˈkəʊmɪəm] N (pl **encomiums** or **encomia** [ɪnˈkəʊmɪə]) panégyrique m, éloge m

encompass [ɪnˈkʌmpəs] VT (gen) couvrir ; (= include) englober, comprendre

encore [ɒŋˈkɔː^r] **1** EXCL bis ! **2** [ˈɒŋkɔː^r] N bis m, rappel m ; **to call for an ~** bisser, crier « bis » ; **to play an ~** jouer or faire un bis ; **the pianist gave several ~s** le pianiste a interprété plusieurs morceaux en rappel or a donné plusieurs rappels **3** VT [+ song, act] bisser

encounter [ɪnˈkaʊntə^r] **1** VT [+ person] rencontrer (à l'improviste), tomber sur ; [+ enemy] affronter, rencontrer ; [+ opposition] se heurter à ; [+ difficulties] rencontrer, éprouver ; [+ danger] affronter ; **to ~ enemy fire** essuyer le feu de l'ennemi **2** N rencontre f (inattendue) ; (Mil) rencontre f, engagement m, combat m **3** COMP ► **encounter group** N (Psych) atelier m de psychothérapie de groupe

encourage [ɪnˈkʌrɪdʒ] VT [+ person] encourager ; [+ arts, industry, projects, development, growth] encourager, favoriser ; [+ bad habits] encourager, flatter ; **to ~ sb to do** encourager or inciter or pousser qn à faire ; **to ~ sb in his belief that ...** confirmer or conforter qn dans sa croyance que ... ; **to ~ sb in his desire to do** encourager le désir de qn de faire

encouragement [ɪnˈkʌrɪdʒmənt] N encouragement m ; (to a deed) incitation f (**to** à) ; (= support) encouragement m, appui m, soutien m

encouraging [ɪnˈkʌrɪdʒɪŋ] ADJ encourageant

encouragingly [ɪnˈkʌrɪdʒɪŋlɪ] ADV [say, smile, nod] de manière encourageante ; **the theatre was ~ full** le public était nombreux, ce qui était encourageant ; **~, inflation is slowing down** l'inflation est en baisse, ce qui est encourageant

encroach [ɪnˈkrəʊtʃ] VI (on sb's land, time, rights) empiéter (**on** sur) ; **the sea is ~ing (on the land)** la mer gagne du terrain (sur la terre ferme) ; (US fig) **to ~ on sb's turf** marcher sur les plates-bandes de qn

encroachment [ɪnˈkrəʊtʃmənt] N empiètement m (**on** sur)

encrustation [ɪnkrʌˈsteɪʃən] N [of earth, cement etc] croûte f

encrusted [ɪnˈkrʌstɪd] ADJ ~ **with** [+ jewels, gold] incrusté de ; [+ moss, snow] recouvert (d'une couche) de

encrypt [ɪnˈkrɪpt] VT (Comput, Telec, TV) crypter

encryption [ɪnˈkrɪpʃən] N (Comput, Telec, TV) cryptage m

encumber [ɪnˈkʌmbə^r] VT [+ person, room] encombrer (**with** de) ; ~**ed with debts** [person] criblé de dettes

encumbrance [ɪnˈkʌmbrəns] N (= burden) fardeau m ; (inhibiting career etc) handicap m, gêne f ; [furniture, skirts etc] gêne f ; (mortgage) charge f hypothécaire ; (fig) **to be an ~ to sb** être un fardeau pour qn, être une gêne pour qn

encyclical [ɪnˈsɪklɪkəl] ADJ, N encyclique f

encyclop(a)edia [ɪnˌsaɪkləʊˈpiːdɪə] N encyclopédie f → **walking**

encyclop(a)edic [ɪnˌsaɪkləʊˈpiːdɪk] ADJ encyclopédique ; **to have an ~ knowledge of sth** avoir une connaissance encyclopédique de qch

encyclop(a)edist [enˌsaɪkləʊˈpiːdɪst] N encyclopédiste mf

end [end]

1 NOUN		**4** COMPOUNDS	
2 TRANSITIVE VERB		**5** PHRASAL VERBS	
3 INTRANSITIVE VERB			

1 NOUN

a = **farthest part** [of road, string, table, branch, finger] bout m, extrémité f ; [of procession, line of people] bout m, queue f ; [of garden] fond m ; [of telephone line] bout m ; [of spectrum] extrémité f ; **the fourth from the ~** le quatrième en partant de la fin ; **from ~ to ~** d'un bout à l'autre, de bout en bout ; **~ to ~** bout à bout ; **the southern ~ of the town** l'extrémité sud de la ville ; **the ships collided ~ on** les bateaux se sont heurtés de front ; **to the ~s of the earth** jusqu'au bout du monde ; (Sport) **to change ~s** changer de côté or de camp ; **you've opened the packet at the wrong ~** vous avez ouvert le paquet par le mauvais bout or du mauvais côté ; (fig) **to be on the wrong ~ of sth** faire les frais de qch ; (fig) **the ~ of the road** or **line** la fin du voyage ; (fig) **to reach the ~ of the line** être au bout du rouleau ; (Telec) **there was silence at the other ~ of the line** il y eut un silence à l'autre bout du fil ; **at the other ~ of the social scale** à l'autre bout de l'échelle sociale ; (fig) **he can't see beyond the ~ of his nose** il ne voit pas plus loin que le bout de son nez ; **to keep one's ~ up*** se défendre (assez bien) ; (fig) **to make (both) ~s meet** (faire) joindre les deux bouts ; **to play both ~s against the middle*** jouer les uns contre les autres ; **how are things at your ~?** comment vont les choses de ton côté ? ; **to get one's ~ away*** s'envoyer en l'air*

b = **conclusion** [of story, chapter, month] fin f ; [of work] achèvement m, fin f ; [of efforts] fin f, aboutissement m; [of meeting] fin f, issue f; **the ~ of a session** la clôture d'une séance; **the ~ of the world** la fin du monde; (fig) **it's not the ~ of the world!*** ce n'est pas la fin du monde!; **to** or **until the ~ of time** jusqu'à la fin des temps; **to read a book to the very ~** lire un livre de A à Z or jusqu'à la dernière page; **to get to the ~ of** [+ supplies, food] finir; [+ work, essay] venir à bout de; [+ troubles] (se) sortir de; [+ holiday] arriver à la fin de; **we shall never hear the ~ of it** on n'a pas fini d'en entendre parler; **that's the ~ of the matter** ◊ **that's an ~ to the matter** on n point c'est tout, on n'en parle plus; **that was the ~ of that!** on n'en a plus reparlé; **to put an ~ to sth** ◊ **to make an ~ of sth** mettre fin à qch, mettre fin à qch; **that was the ~ of him** on n'a plus reparlé de lui, on ne l'a plus revu; (euph, liter) **to be nearing one's ~** être à (l'article de) la mort, se mourir (liter); **that was the ~ of my watch** ma montre était fichue*

[c] **= remnant** [of rope, candle] bout m; [of loaf, meat] reste m, restant m

[d] **= purpose** but m, fin f; **with this ~ in view** ◊ **to this ~** dans ce but, à cette fin, à cet effet; **to no ~** en vain ∎ (PROV) **the ~ justifies the means** la fin justifie les moyens (PROV)

[e] Sport (of pitch) côté m

[f] Ftbl ailier m

[g] SET STRUCTURES

♦ **at the end of**: **at the ~ of the day** à la fin de la journée; (fig) **en fin de compte**; **at the ~ of three weeks** au bout de trois semaines; **at the ~ of December** à la fin (du mois) de décembre; (Comm) **fin décembre**; **at the ~ of the winter** à la fin ou au sortir de l'hiver; **at the ~ of the century** à or vers la fin du siècle; **to be at the ~ of one's patience/strength** être à bout de patience/forces

♦ **in the end**: **it succeeded in the ~** cela a réussi finalement or en fin de compte; **he got used to it in the ~** il a fini par s'y habituer; **in the ~ they decided to ...** ils ont décidé en définitive de ..., ils ont fini par décider de ...

♦ **no end**: **there is no ~ to it all** cela n'en finit plus; **there was no ~* of ...** il y avait une masse* de or un tas de or énormément de ...; **it pleased her no ~*** cela lui a fait un plaisir fou or énorme → **d**

♦ **on end** (= upright) debout; (= continuously) de suite; **to stand a box etc on ~** mettre une caisse etc debout; **his hair stood on ~** ses cheveux se dressèrent sur sa tête; **for two hours on ~** deux heures de suite or d'affilée; **for days on ~** jour après jour, pendant des jours et des jours; **for several days on ~** pendant plusieurs jours de suite

♦ **to be at an end** [action] être terminé or fini; [time, period] être écoulé; [material, supplies] être épuisé; **my patience is at an ~** ma patience est à bout

♦ **to bring sth to an end** = end 2

♦ **to come to an end** = end 3

[2] TRANSITIVE VERB

= **bring to an end** [+ work] finir, terminer; [+ period of service] accomplir; [+ speech, writing] conclure, achever (**with** avec, par); [+ broadcast, series] terminer (**with** par); [+ speculation, rumour] mettre fin à, mettre un terme à; [+ quarrel, war] mettre fin à, faire cesser; **to ~ one's days** (**in Paris/in poverty**) finir ses jours (à Paris/dans la misère); **to ~ it all** (= kill oneself) en finir (avec la vie); **that was the lie to ~ all lies!** comme mensonge on ne fait pas mieux!* (iro); **the film to ~ all films** le meilleur film qu'on ait jamais fait; **the deal to ~ all deals** l'affaire f du siècle*

[3] INTRANSITIVE VERB

= **come to an end** [speech, programme, holiday, marriage, series] finir, se terminer; [road] se terminer; [insurance cover etc] expirer, arriver à échéance; **the winter is ~ing** l'hiver tire à sa fin; (fig) **where's it all going to ~?** ◊ **where will it**

all ~? comment tout cela finira-t-il?; **word ~ing in an "s"/in "re"** mot se terminant par un «s»/en «re»; **it ~ed in a fight** cela s'est terminé par une bagarre*; **the plan ~ed in failure** le projet s'est soldé par un échec; **the film ~s with the heroine dying** le film se termine par la mort de l'héroïne

[4] COMPOUNDS

► **end-all** N → be ► **end game** N (Cards, Chess) fin f de partie, phase f finale du jeu ► **end house** N **the ~ house in the street** la dernière maison de la rue ► **end line** N (Basketball) ligne f de fond ► **end product** N (Comm, Ind) produit m fini; (fig) résultat m ► **end result** N résultat m final or définitif ► **end run** N (US fig) moyen m détourné ► **end table** N (US) table f basse ► **end user** N (Comput etc) utilisateur m final

[5] PHRASAL VERBS

► **end off** VT SEP finir, achever, terminer
► **end up** VI [a] finir, se terminer (**in** en, par); [road] aboutir (**in** à); **it ~ed up in a fight** cela s'est terminé par une bagarre*
[b] (= finally arrive at) se retrouver, échouer (**in** à, en); (= finally become) finir par devenir; **he ~ed up in Paris** il s'est retrouvé à Paris; **you'll ~ up in jail** tu vas finir en prison; **he ~ed up a policeman** il a fini par devenir agent de police; **they ~ed up arresting us** ils ont fini par nous arrêter; **the book she had planned ~ed up (being)** just an article son projet de livre a fini en simple article; **this oil spill could ~ up as the largest in history** cette marée noire pourrait se révéler (être) la plus importante de l'histoire; **he broke his leg and ~ed up being rushed to hospital** il s'est cassé la jambe et a été emmené d'urgence à l'hôpital

endanger [ɪnˈdeɪndʒəʳ] [1] VT [+ life, interests, reputation] mettre en danger, exposer; [+ future, chances, health] compromettre [2] COMP ► **endangered species** N espèce f en voie de disparition or d'extinction

endear [ɪnˈdɪəʳ] VT faire aimer (**to** de); **this ~ed him to the whole country** cela l'a fait aimer de tout le pays; **what ~s him to me is ...** ce qui me plaît en lui c'est ...; **to ~ o.s. to everybody** se faire aimer de tout le monde; **that speech didn't ~ him to the public** ce discours ne l'a pas fait apprécier du public

endearing [ɪnˈdɪərɪŋ] ADJ [person, quality, characteristic] attachant; [habit, manner] touchant; [smile] engageant

endearingly [ɪnˈdɪərɪŋlɪ] ADV [say, smile] de façon engageante; [admit] de façon touchante; **~ shy** d'une timidité touchante; **she is ~ unpretentious/childlike** elle est sans prétentions/comme une enfant, ce qui la rend sympathique

endearment [ɪnˈdɪəmənt] N **term of ~** terme m d'affection; **words of ~** paroles fpl tendres; **~s** (= words) paroles fpl affectueuses or tendres; (= acts) paroles fpl d'affection

endeavour, endeavor (US) [ɪnˈdevəʳ] [1] N (frm) [a] (NonC = effort) effort m; **in all fields** or **areas of human ~** dans toutes les branches or tous les secteurs de l'activité humaine [b] (= attempt) tentative f (**to do** pour faire); **he made every ~ to go** il a fait tout son possible pour y aller, il a tout fait pour y aller; **in an ~ to please** dans l'intention de plaire, dans un effort pour plaire [2] VI s'efforcer, tenter (**to do** de faire); (stronger) s'évertuer, s'appliquer (**to do** à faire)

endemic [enˈdemɪk] [1] ADJ endémique (**to** à) [2] N endémie f

ending [ˈendɪŋ] N [a] [of story, book] fin f, dénouement m; [of events] fin f, conclusion f; [of day] fin f; (= outcome) issue f; [of speech etc] conclusion f; **a story with a happy ~** une histoire qui finit bien → **nerve** [b] (Ling) terminaison f, désinence f; **feminine ~** termi-

naison f féminine; **the accusative ~** la flexion de l'accusatif

endive [ˈendaɪv] N (curly) chicorée f; (smooth, flat) endive f

endless [ˈendlɪs] [1] ADJ [a] (= interminable) [day, summer, queue, speech, series, road] interminable; [expanse, stretch, forest, variety, patience] infini; [desert, plain] infini, sans fin; [cycle, list] sans fin; [supply, resources] inépuisable; [discussion, argument] continuel, incessant; [chatter] intarissable; **an ~ stream of traffic** un flot interminable de voitures; **an ~ round of meetings** une interminable série de réunions; **to go to ~ trouble over sth** se donner un mal fou pour qch; **this job is ~** c'est à n'en plus finir, on n'en voit pas la fin [b] (= countless) [meetings, questions, problems, hours] innombrable; [possibilities] innombrable, illimité; [times, attempts, arguments] innombrable, sans nombre [2] COMP ► **endless belt** N (Tech) courroie f sans fin

endlessly [ˈendlɪslɪ] ADV [a] (= continually) [repeat] sans cesse; [talk, discuss, debate] sans arrêt; [chatter, argue] continuellement [b] (= without limit) [stretch] sans fin, à perte de vue; [recycle] continuellement; **~ long streets** des rues fpl qui n'en finissent pas; **~ curious/kind/willing** d'une curiosité/d'une bonté/d'une bonne volonté sans limites; **I find this subject ~ fascinating** ce sujet ne cesse (pas) de me fasciner or exerce sur moi une fascination sans fin

endocardia [ˌendəʊˈkɑːdɪə] NPL of **endocardium**

endocarditis [ˌendəʊkɑːˈdaɪtɪs] N endocardite f

endocardium [ˌendəʊˈkɑːdɪəm] N (pl **endocardia**) endocarde m

endocarp [ˈendəkɑːp] N endocarpe m

endocrine [ˈendəʊkraɪn] ADJ endocrine; **~ gland** glande f endocrine

endocrinologist [ˌendəʊkraɪˈnɒlədʒɪst] N endocrinologue mf, endocrinologiste mf

endocrinology [ˌendəʊkrɪˈnɒlədʒɪ] N endocrinologie f

endogamy [enˈdɒɡəmɪ] N (Sociol) endogamie f

endogenous [enˈdɒdʒɪnəs] ADJ [factor] endogène

endolymph [ˈendəʊˌlɪmf] N (Anat) endolymphe f

endometrium [ˌendəʊˈmiːtrɪəm] N (pl **endometria** [ˌendəʊˈmiːtrɪə]) (Anat) endomètre m

endomorph [ˈendəʊˌmɔːf] N (Anat) endomorphe mf

endorphin [enˈdɔːfɪn] N endorphine f

endorse [ɪnˈdɔːs] VT [a] (= sign) [+ document, cheque] endosser; (= guarantee) [+ bill] avaliser; **to ~ an insurance policy** faire un avenant à une police d'assurance; (Brit Jur) **he has had his licence ~d** on (lui) a retiré des points sur son permis [b] (= approve) [+ claim, candidature] appuyer; [+ opinion] souscrire à, adhérer à; [+ action, decision] approuver, sanctionner; (= advertise) [+ product, company] recommander

endorsee [ˌɪndɔːˈsiː] N endossataire mf, bénéficiaire mf d'un endossement

endorsement [ɪnˈdɔːsmənt] [1] N [a] (= approval) [of proposal, policy] adhésion f (**of sth** à qch); [of movement, claim, candidate] appui m (**of sb/sth** de qn/qch); [of action, decision, efforts] approbation f (**of sth** de qch); **a letter of ~** une lettre d'approbation
[b] (NonC = ratification) [of treaty] ratification f
[c] (Comm) [of product] recommandation f publicitaire; [of book] recommandation f; **to receive ~ from sb** être recommandé par qn; **celebrity ~** recommandation f publicitaire faite par une personnalité connue

d (Brit Jur: on driving licence) infraction mentionnée sur le permis de conduire ; **he's already got three ~s** il a déjà perdu des points pour trois infractions au code de la route **e** (on cheque, document) endossement m **f** [of insurance policy] avenant m (**to sth à** qch) **2** COMP ► **endorsement advertising** N technique publicitaire faisant intervenir des personnalités connues

endoscope ['endəʊˌskəʊp] N endoscope m

endoscopy [en'dɒskəpɪ] N endoscopie f

endoskeleton [ˌendəʊ'skelɪtən] N squelette m interne, endosquelette m

endothermic [ˌendəʊ'θɜːmɪk] ADJ endothermique

endow [ɪn'daʊ] VT [+ institution, church] doter (**with** de) ; [+ hospital bed, prize, chair] fonder ; (fig) **to be ~ed with brains/beauty** etc être doté d'intelligence/de beauté etc → **well**

endowment [ɪn'daʊmənt] **1** N **a** (Fin) (money, school, college) dotation f ; (hospital bed, prize, university chair) fondation f **b** (= portion) **to have a generous ~ of sth** être généreusement pourvu ou doté de qch ; **a sense of fair play, the natural ~ of every Briton** un sens du fair-play, la qualité naturelle de tout Britannique **2** COMP ► **endowment assurance, endowment insurance** N assurance f à capital différé ► **endowment mortgage** N (Brit) hypothèque f liée à une assurance-vie ► **endowment policy** N = **endowment assurance**

endpapers ['endˌpeɪpəz] NPL (Typ) gardes fpl, pages fpl de garde

endurable [ɪn'djʊərəbl] ADJ supportable, endurable

endurance [ɪn'djʊərəns] **1** N endurance f ; **to have great powers of ~** avoir beaucoup d'endurance, être très endurant ; **a test of human ~** une mise à l'épreuve de l'endurance humaine ; **he has come to the end of his ~** il n'en peut plus, il est à bout ; **beyond ~** ◊ **past ~** intolérable, au-delà de ce que l'on peut supporter ; **tried beyond ~** excédé **2** COMP ► **endurance race** N (Sport) épreuve f de fond ► **endurance test** N (Sport, Tech, fig) épreuve f de résistance ; (Aut) épreuve f d'endurance

endure [ɪn'djʊər] **1** VT **a** (= put up with) [+ pain] endurer, supporter ; [+ insults] supporter, tolérer ; [+ hardships] supporter ; **she can't ~ being teased** elle ne peut pas supporter ou souffrir qu'on la taquine (subj) ; **I cannot ~ him** je ne peux pas le supporter ou le voir ; **it was more than I could ~** c'était plus que je ne pouvais supporter **b** (= suffer) subir ; **the company ~d heavy financial losses** la société a subi de grosses pertes financières **2** VI (frm = last) [building, peace, friendship] durer ; [book, memory] rester

enduring [ɪn'djʊərɪŋ] ADJ [appeal, legacy, quality, peace, friendship, fame, love] durable ; [image, grudge] tenace ; [illness, hardship] persistant, qui persiste

endways ['endweɪz], **endwise** ['endwaɪz] ADV (endways on) en long, par le petit bout ; (= end to end) bout à bout

ENEA [ˌiːniːˈeɪ] N (ABBR = **European Nuclear Energy Authority**) AENE f

enema ['enɪmə] N (pl **enemas** or **enemata** ['enɪmətə]) (= act) lavement m ; (= apparatus) poire f ou bock m à lavement ; **to give sb an ~** faire un lavement à qn

enemy ['enəmɪ] **1** N (Mil) ennemi m ; (gen) ennemi(e) m(f), adversaire mf ; **to make enemies** se faire or s'attirer des ennemis ; **to make an ~ of sb** (se) faire un ennemi de qn ; **he is his own worst ~** il est son pire ennemi, il n'a de pire ennemi que lui-même ; **they are deadly enemies** ils sont à couteaux tirés, ils sont ennemis jurés ; (fig) **corruption is the ~**

of the state la corruption est l'ennemie de l'État → **public** **2** COMP [tanks, forces, tribes] ennemi ; [morale, strategy] de l'ennemi ► **enemy action** N attaque f ennemie ; **killed by ~ action** tombé à l'ennemi ► **enemy alien** N ressortissant(e) m(f) d'un pays ennemi ► **enemy-occupied** ADJ occupé par l'ennemi

energetic [ˌenə'dʒetɪk] ADJ [person, government, action, measure, denial, refusal] énergique ; [performance, campaign] plein d'énergie ; [activity, sport, game] énergétique ; **he is an ~ campaigner for road safety** il milite énergiquement en faveur de la sécurité sur les routes ; **I don't feel very ~** je ne me sens pas d'attaque

energetically [ˌenə'dʒetɪkəlɪ] ADV [deny, campaign] énergiquement, avec vigueur ; [nod, wave] énergiquement

energetics [ˌenə'dʒetɪks] N (NonC) énergétique f

energize ['enədʒaɪz] VT [+ person] regonfler ; (Elec) alimenter (en courant)

energizing ['enədʒaɪzɪŋ] ADJ énergisant

energy ['enədʒɪ] **1** N **a** (gen) énergie f, vigueur f ; **he has a lot of ~** il a beaucoup d'énergie, il est très dynamique ; **he seems to have no ~ these days** il semble sans énergie ou à plat* en ce moment ; (Brit) **I haven't the ~ to start again** je n'ai pas le courage de (tout) recommencer ; **to concentrate one's energies on doing sth** appliquer toute son énergie à faire qch ; **with all one's ~** de toutes ses forces ; **to put all one's ~ or energies into sth/into doing sth** se consacrer tout entier à qch/à faire qch, appliquer toute son énergie à qch/à faire qch ; **to save one's ~ for sth** économiser ses forces pour qch ; **he used up all his ~ doing it** il a épuisé ses forces à le faire ; **don't waste your ~*** ne te fatigue pas*, ne te donne pas du mal pour rien **b** (Phys) énergie f ; **potential/kinetic ~** énergie f potentielle/cinétique ; **in order to save ~** pour faire des économies d'énergie ; **Department** or **Ministry of Energy** ministère m de l'Énergie ; **Secretary (of State) for** or **Minister of Energy** ministre m de l'Énergie → **atomic** **2** COMP ► **energy conservation** N conservation f de l'énergie ► **energy conversion** N conversion f de l'énergie ► **energy crisis** N crise f énergétique or de l'énergie ► **energy-giving** ADJ [food etc] énergétique ► **energy-intensive industry** N industrie f grande consommatrice d'énergie ► **energy level** N (Phys) niveau m d'énergie ► **energy-saving** N économies fpl d'énergie ◊ ADJ d'économie d'énergie ► **energy-saving campaign** N campagne f pour les économies d'énergie

enervated ['enɜːveɪtɪd] ADJ affaibli, mou (molle f)

enervating ['enɜːveɪtɪŋ] ADJ débilitant, amollissant

enfeeble [ɪn'fiːbl] VT affaiblir

enfeeblement [ɪn'fiːblmənt] N affaiblissement m

enfilade [ˌenfɪ'leɪd] (Mil) **1** VT soumettre à un tir d'enfilade **2** N tir m d'enfilade

enfold [ɪn'fəʊld] VT envelopper (**in** de) ; **to ~ sb in one's arms** entourer qn de ses bras, étreindre qn

enforce [ɪn'fɔːs] VT [+ ruling, the law] faire obéir or respecter ; [+ decision, policy] mettre en application or en vigueur, appliquer ; [+ discipline] imposer ; [+ argument, rights] faire valoir ; **to ~ obedience** se faire obéir ; **these laws aren't usually ~d** ces lois ne sont généralement pas appliquées

enforceable [ɪn'fɔːsəbl] ADJ [law] exécutoire ; [rules] applicable

enforced [ɪn'fɔːst] ADJ (= forcible) forcé, obligé

enforcement [ɪn'fɔːsmənt] **1** N [of decision, policy, law] mise f en application or en vigueur ; [of discipline] imposition f ; (Jur, Fin) **of securities** réalisation f des sûretés → **law** **2** COMP ► **enforcement action** N (Jur) mesure f coercitive

enfranchise [ɪn'fræntʃaɪz] VT (= give vote to) accorder le droit de vote à ; (= set free) affranchir

enfranchisement [ɪn'fræntʃaɪzmənt] N **a** (Pol) octroi m du droit de vote (**of sb** à qn) **b** (= emancipation) [of slave] affranchissement m

ENG [ˌiːen'dʒiː] N (ABBR = **electronic news gathering**) → **electronic**

engage [ɪn'geɪdʒ] **1** VT **a** (= employ, hire) [+ servant] engager ; [+ workers] embaucher ; [+ lawyer] prendre ; **to ~ sb's services** s'adjoindre les services de qn ; (frm) **to ~ o.s. to do sth** s'engager à faire qch **b** (= attract) [+ sb's attention, interest] éveiller ; **to ~ sb in conversation** engager la or lier conversation avec qn **c** (Mil) [+ enemy] engager le combat avec, attaquer **d** (Aut, Mechanics) engager ; [+ gearwheels] mettre en prise ; (Aut: frm) **to ~ a gear** engager une vitesse ; **to ~ gear** mettre en prise ; **to ~ the clutch** embrayer ; **to ~ the four-wheel drive** passer en quatre roues motrices intégrales or en rapport court **2** VI [person] s'engager (**to do** à faire) ; (Aut, Mechanics) [wheels] s'engrener ; [bolt] s'enclencher ; **to ~ in (a) discussion/conversation** se lancer dans une discussion/conversation (**with** avec) ; **the clutch didn't ~** l'embrayage n'a pas fonctionné ; **to ~ in** [+ politics, transaction] se lancer dans, s'embarquer dans ; [+ controversy] s'engager dans, s'embarquer dans ; **to ~ in competition** entrer en concurrence (**with** avec) ; **to ~ with sb/sth** s'engager auprès de qn/dans qch ; **she found it hard to ~ with office life** elle a eu du mal à se faire à la vie de bureau

▼ **engaged** [ɪn'geɪdʒd] **1** ADJ **a** (= betrothed) **to be ~ (to be married)** être fiancé (**to** à) ; **to get ~ (to sb)** se fiancer (à qn) ; **the ~ couple** les fiancés mpl **b** (Brit Telec) [line, number, telephone] occupé ; **it's ~** ça sonne « occupé » **c** (= not vacant) [toilet] occupé **d** (frm = unavailable) [person] occupé, pris ; **to be otherwise ~** être déjà pris **e** (= involved) **~ in sth** [+ task] occupé à qch ; [+ criminal activity] engagé dans qch ; **~ in doing sth** occupé à faire qch ; **~ on sth** pris par qch **2** COMP ► **engaged tone** N (Brit Telec) tonalité f « occupé » ; **I got the** or **an ~ tone** ça sonnait « occupé »

▼ **engagement** [ɪn'geɪdʒmənt] **1** N **a** (= appointment) rendez-vous m inv ; [of actor etc] engagement m ; **public ~** obligation f officielle ; **previous ~** engagement m antérieur ; **I have an ~** or **a previous ~** j'ai un rendez-vous, je ne suis pas libre, je suis pris **b** (= betrothal) fiançailles fpl ; **a long/short ~** de longues/courtes fiançailles ; **to break off one's ~** rompre ses fiançailles **c** (frm = undertaking) engagement m, obligation f ; **to give an ~ to do sth** s'engager à faire qch **d** (Mil) combat m, engagement m **2** COMP ► **engagement book** N agenda m ► **engagement ring** N bague f de fiançailles

engaging [ɪn'geɪdʒɪŋ] ADJ [person] charmant ; [smile, frankness] engageant ; [personality] attachant ; [manner] aimable

engender [ɪn'dʒendər] VT occasionner, créer

engine ['endʒɪn] **1** N (Tech) machine f, moteur m ; [of ship] machine f ; (Rail) locomotive f ; (Aut, Aviat) moteur m ; (Rail) **to sit facing the ~/with one's back to the ~** être assis dans le sens de la marche/le sens contraire à la marche → **jet¹** **2** COMP ► **engine block** N (Aut) bloc-moteur m ► **engine driver** N (Brit Rail) mécanicien m ► **engine house** N (US Rail) =

engine shed ► **engine room** N (*Naut*) salle *f* or chambre *f* des machines; (*over speaking tube*) **hello, ~ room?** allô, les machines? ► **engine shed** N (*Brit Rail*) rotonde *f* ► **engine unit** N bloc-moteur *m*

-engined ['endʒɪnd] ADJ (*in compounds*) **twin-engined** à deux moteurs, bimoteur → **single**

engineer [,endʒɪ'nɪəʳ] **1** N **a** (*professional*) ingénieur *m*; (= *tradesman*) technicien *m*; (= *repairer: for domestic appliances etc*) dépanneur *m*, réparateur *m*; **woman ~** (femme *f*) ingénieur *m*; (*Mil*) **the Engineers** le génie; (*US*) **~ of mines** ingénieur *m* des mines; **the TV ~ came** le dépanneur est venu pour la télévision → **civil, heating, highway b** (*Merchant Navy, US Rail*) mécanicien *m*; (*Navy*) mécanicien *m* de la marine → **chief 2** VT [+ *sb's dismissal etc, scheme, plan*] machiner, manigancer

engineering [,endʒɪ'nɪərɪŋ] **1** N **a** (*NonC*) ingénierie *f*, engineering *m*; **to study ~** faire des études d'ingénieur → **civil, electrical, mechanical b** (*fig, gen pej*) machination(s) *f(pl)*, manœuvre(s) *f(pl)* **2** COMP ► **engineering consultant** N ingénieur-conseil *m* ► **engineering factory** N atelier *m* de construction mécanique ► **engineering industries** NPL industries *fpl* d'équipement ► **engineering works** N (*pl inv* = **engineering factory**

England ['ɪŋglənd] N l'Angleterre *f*

Englander ['ɪŋgləndə] N → **little, new**

English ['ɪŋglɪʃ] **1** ADJ (*gen*) anglais; [*monarch*] d'Angleterre; [*teacher, dictionary*] d'anglais

2 N anglais *m*; **the King's** *or* **Queen's ~** l'anglais *m* correct; **in plain** *or* **simple ~** en termes très simples, ≈ en bon français; **~ as a Foreign Language** l'anglais *m* langue étrangère; **~ as a Second Language** l'anglais *m* seconde langue; **~ for Special Purposes** l'anglais *m* langue de spécialité; **~ Language Teaching** l'enseignement *m* de l'anglais → TEFL *etc*

3 **the English** NPL les Anglais *mpl*

4 COMP ► **English breakfast** N (*in hotel etc*) petit déjeuner *m* anglais ► **the English Channel** N la Manche ► **English Heritage** N *organisme britannique de protection du patrimoine historique* ► **English horn** N (*US*) cor *m* anglais ► **English muffin** N (*US Culin*) muffin *m* ► **English-speaker** N anglophone *mf* ► **English-speaking** ADJ anglophone

Englishman ['ɪŋglɪʃmən] N (*pl* **-men**) Anglais *m* ■(*PROV*) **an ~'s home is his castle** charbonnier est maître chez soi (*PROV*)

Englishwoman ['ɪŋglɪʃwʊmən] N (*pl* **-women**) Anglaise *f*

Eng Lit ['ɪŋ'lɪt] N (*ABBR* = **English Literature**) littérature *f* anglaise

---

engorged [ɪn'gɔːdʒd] ADJ (*frm*) gonflé; **~ with blood** gonflé de sang

engraft [ɪn'grɑːft] VT (*Agr, Surg, fig*) greffer (**into, on** sur)

engram ['engræm] N engramme *m*

engrave [ɪn'greɪv] VT [+ *wood, metal, stone*] graver; (*Typ*) graver au burin; (*fig*) graver, empreindre; **~d on the heart/the memory** gravé dans le cœur/la mémoire

engraver [ɪn'greɪvəʳ] N graveur *m*

engraving [ɪn'greɪvɪŋ] **1** N gravure *f* → **wood** **2** COMP ► **engraving plate** N (*Typ*) cliché *m* typo

engross [ɪn'grəʊs] VT **a** [+ *attention, person*] absorber, captiver; **to be ~ed in** [+ *work*] être absorbé par, s'absorber dans; [+ *reading, thoughts*] être plongé dans, s'abîmer dans (*liter*) **b** (*Jur*) grossoyer

engrossing [ɪn'grəʊsɪŋ] ADJ absorbant

engrossment [ɪn'grəʊsmənt] N (*US Pol*) rédaction *f* définitive d'un projet de loi

engulf [ɪn'gʌlf] VT engouffrer, engloutir; **to be ~ed in** s'engouffrer dans, sombrer dans

enhance [ɪn'hɑːns] VT **a** (= *improve, augment*) [+ *attraction, beauty, status*] mettre en valeur; [+ *powers*] accroître, étendre; [+ *value, pleasure*] augmenter; [+ *position, chances*] améliorer; [+ *prestige, reputation*] accroître, rehausser; **~d graphics adaptor** adaptateur *m* de graphique amélioré **b** (*Admin, Fin* = *increase*) majorer (**by** de)

enhancement [ɪn'hɑːnsmənt] N [*of pension entitlement*] majoration *f*; [*of conditions*] amélioration *f*

enhancer [ɪn'hɑːnsəʳ] N (*also* **flavour ~**) agent *m* de sapidité

enharmonic [,enhɑː'mɒnɪk] ADJ enharmonique

enigma [ɪ'nɪgmə] N énigme *f*

enigmatic [,enɪg'mætɪk] ADJ énigmatique

enigmatically [,enɪg'mætɪkəlɪ] ADV [*say*] de façon énigmatique; [*smile*] d'un air énigmatique

enjambement [ɪn'dʒæmmənt] N enjambement *m*

enjoin [ɪn'dʒɔɪn] VT **a** (= *urge*) [+ *silence, obedience*] imposer (**on** à); [+ *discretion, caution*] recommander (**on** à); **to ~ sb to do sth** ordonner *or* prescrire à qn de faire qch **b** (*US* = *forbid*) **to ~ sb from doing** interdire à qn de faire, enjoindre à qn de ne pas faire

enjoy [ɪn'dʒɔɪ] VT **a** (= *take pleasure in*) [+ *theatre, cinema, football, music, book*] aimer, apprécier; [+ *game, pastime*] aimer, trouver agréable; [+ *evening, walk, holiday, company, conversation*] aimer, prendre plaisir à; [+ *meal*] apprécier, trouver bon; **to ~ doing sth** trouver du plaisir *or* prendre plaisir à faire qch, aimer faire qch, trouver agréable de faire qch; **I ~ed doing it** cela m'a fait plaisir (de le faire); **to ~ greatly** se délecter (**sth** de qch, **doing** à faire); **to ~ life** jouir de *or* profiter de la vie; **to ~ a weekend/an evening/holidays** passer un bon week-end/une soirée très agréable/de bonnes vacances; **did you ~ the concert?** le concert vous a-t-il plu?; **to ~ one's dinner** bien manger *or* dîner; **the children ~ed their meal** les enfants ont bien mangé *or* ont mangé de bon appétit

b **to ~ o.s.** s'amuser, prendre *or* se donner du bon temps; **did you ~ yourself in Paris?** est-ce que tu t'es bien amusé à Paris?; **~ yourself!** amusez-vous bien!; **~ yourself tonight/ this weekend!** ◊ **~ your evening/weekend!** passez une bonne soirée/un bon week-end!; **she always ~s herself in the country** elle se plaît toujours à la campagne, elle est toujours contente d'être à la campagne

c (*frm* = *benefit from*) [+ *income, rights, health, advantage*] jouir de

---

enjoyable [ɪn'dʒɔɪəbl] ADJ agréable; [*meal*] excellent; **~ sex** rapports *mpl* satisfaisants

enjoyably [ɪn'dʒɔɪəblɪ] ADV agréablement

enjoyment [ɪn'dʒɔɪmənt] N (*NonC*) **a** (= *pleasure*) plaisir *m*; **to get ~ from** (**doing**) **sth** trouver du plaisir à (faire) qch **b** (= *possession*) [*of income, rights etc*] jouissance *f*, possession *f* (**of** de)

enlarge [ɪn'lɑːdʒ] **1** VT [+ *house, territory*] agrandir; [+ *empire, influence, field of knowledge, circle of friends*] étendre; [+ *business*] développer; [+ *hole*] élargir, agrandir; [+ *numbers, majority*] augmenter; (*Med*) [+ *organ*] hypertrophier; (*Phot*) agrandir **2** VI **a** (= *grow bigger*) [*territory*] s'agrandir; [*empire, influence, field of knowledge, circle of friends*] s'étendre; [*business*] se développer; [*hole*] s'élargir; [*Med*] [*organ*] s'hypertrophier; [*pore, pupil*] se dilater **b** (= *explain*) **to ~ (up)on** [+ *subject, difficulties etc*] s'étendre sur; [+ *idea*] développer

enlarged [ɪn'lɑːdʒd] ADJ [*photograph, group, building*] agrandi; [*force*] plus important; [*majority*] accru; [*edition*] augmenté; [*prostate, gland, organ*] hypertrophié; [*pore*] dilaté

enlargement [ɪn'lɑːdʒmənt] N **a** (*NonC* = *expansion*) [*of building, city*] agrandissement *m*; [*of organization*] élargissement *m*; [*of majority*] élargissement *m*, accroissement *m* **b** (*NonC: Med*) [*of organ, gland, prostate*] hypertrophie *f*; [*of pore*] dilatation *f*; [*of vein*] gonflement *m* → **breast c** (*Phot* = *photograph, process*) agrandissement *m*

enlarger [ɪn'lɑːdʒəʳ] N (*Phot*) agrandisseur *m*

enlighten [ɪn'laɪtn] VT éclairer (**sb on sth** qn sur qch)

enlightened [ɪn'laɪtnd] ADJ [*person, society, approach, views*] éclairé; **in this ~ age** ◊ **in these ~ times** (*esp iro*) en ce siècle de lumières; **~ self-interest** individualisme *m* constructif, égoïsme *m* à visage humain

enlightening [ɪn'laɪtnɪŋ] ADJ instructif

enlightenment [ɪn'laɪtnmənt] N (*NonC*) (= *explanations*) éclaircissements *mpl*; (= *knowledge*) instruction *f*, édification *f*; (*Rel*) illumination *f*; **we need some ~ on this point** nous avons besoin de quelques éclaircissements *or* lumières sur ce point; **the Age of Enlightenment** le Siècle des lumières

enlist [ɪn'lɪst] **1** VI (*Mil etc*) s'engager, s'enrôler (**in** dans) **2** VT [+ *recruits*] enrôler, engager; [+ *soldiers, supporters*] recruter; **to ~ sb's support/sympathy** s'assurer le concours/la sympathie de qn **3** COMP ► **enlisted man** N (*US Mil*) simple soldat *m*, militaire *m* du rang; (*woman*) ≈ caporal *m*

enlistment [ɪn'lɪstmənt] N **a** (*Mil* = *enrolment*) enrôlement *m*, engagement *m* (**in sth** dans qch) **b** (*Mil* = *period*) engagement *m*; **a normal five-year ~** un engagement normal pour cinq ans **c** (*NonC* = *finding*) [*of helpers*] recrutement *m*

enliven [ɪn'laɪvn] VT [+ *conversation, visit, evening*] animer; [+ *décor, design*] mettre une note vive dans, égayer

en masse [ãmæs] ADV en masse

enmesh [ɪn'meʃ] VT (*lit, fig*) prendre dans un filet; **to get ~ed in ...** s'empêtrer dans ...

enmity ['enmɪtɪ] N inimitié *f*, hostilité *f* (**towards** envers, **for** pour)

enneathlon [,enɪ'æθlɒn] N (*Sport*) ennéathlon *m*

ennoble [ɪ'nəʊbl] VT (*lit*) anoblir; (*fig*) [+ *person, mind*] ennoblir, élever

ennui ['ɒnwiː] N (*NonC*) ennui *m* (*also Literat*)

enologist [iː'nɒlədʒɪst] N (*US*) = **oenologist**

enology [iː'nɒlədʒɪ] N (*US*) = **oenology**

enormity [ɪ'nɔːmɪtɪ] N **a** (*NonC*) [*of action, offence*] énormité *f* **b** (= *crime*) crime *m* très grave, outrage *m*; (= *blunder*) énormité *f*

enormous [ɪˈnɔːməs] ADJ [*person, animal, object, amount, number, power, difference*] énorme; [*patience*] immense; [*strength*] prodigieux; [*stature*] colossal; [*talent, interest*] formidable

enormously [ɪˈnɔːməslɪ] ADV [*enjoy, vary etc*] énormément; [*enjoyable, variable etc*] extrêmement; **to be ~ helpful** être d'un immense secours

enosis [ˈenəʊsɪs] N Enôsis *m*

enough [ɪˈnʌf] **1** ADJ, N assez (de); **~ books** assez de livres; **~ money** assez or suffisamment d'argent; **I haven't ~ room** je n'ai pas assez de place; **~'s ~!** ça suffit comme ça!; **it is ~ for us to know that ...** il nous suffit de savoir que ...; **I've had ~** (*eating*) j'ai assez mangé; (*protesting*) j'en ai assez; **I've read ~ Proust to last me a lifetime** (= fed up with it) j'en ai assez de ce roman/de lui obéir; **you can never have ~ of this music** on ne se lasse jamais de cette musique; **you can never have ~ friends** on n'a jamais trop d'amis; **I've had more than ~ wine** j'ai bu plus de vin que je n'aurais dû, j'ai bu un peu trop de vin; **there's more than ~ for all** il y en a largement (assez) or plus qu'assez pour tous; **I had not seen ~ of his work** je n'avais pas vu assez de son travail; **~ of this!** ça suffit comme ça!; **said!*** assez parlé!*; **I think you have said ~** je pense que vous en avez assez dit; **that's ~,** **thanks** ça suffit, merci; **that's ~!** ◊ **~ already!*** (*esp US*) ça suffit!; **~ to eat** assez à manger; **he earns ~ to live on** il gagne de quoi vivre; **one song was ~ to show he couldn't sing** une chanson a suffi à prouver qu'il ne savait pas chanter; **this noise is ~ to drive you mad** ce bruit est à (vous) rendre fou; **I've got ~ to worry about (already)** j'ai assez de soucis comme ça ∎ (*PROV*) **~ is as good as a feast** il ne faut pas abuser des bonnes choses

2 ADV **a** (= *sufficiently*) assez; **he was close ~ now to see them clearly** il était maintenant assez près pour les voir clairement; **the proposed changes don't go far ~** les changements proposés ne vont pas assez loin; **I was fool ~** or **~ of a fool to believe him** j'ai été assez bête pour le croire; **your work is good ~** votre travail est assez bon; **that's a good ~ excuse** c'est une assez bonne excuse; **he is good ~ to win** il est assez bon pour gagner; **he is old ~ to go alone** il est assez grand pour y aller tout seul; **are you warm ~?** avez-vous assez chaud?; **he was well ~ to leave hospital** il allait assez bien pour quitter l'hôpital; **I couldn't get out of there quick ~** je n'avais qu'une envie or je n'attendais qu'une chose, c'était de partir; **we have waited long ~** nous avons assez attendu; **it's proof ~ that ...** c'est une preuve suffisante que ...; **he knows well ~ what I've said** il sait très bien ce que j'ai dit → **fair, sure**

b (*offhand* = *tolerably*) assez; **she is pretty ~** elle est assez jolie, elle n'est pas mal; **he writes well ~** il écrit assez bien, il n'écrit pas mal; **it's good ~ in its way** ce n'est pas (si) mal dans son genre*

c (*intensifying*) **oddly** or **funnily ~, I saw him too** chose curieuse or c'est curieux, je l'ai vu aussi → **sure**

enprint [ˈenprɪnt] N (*Phot*) tirage *m* normal

enquire [ɪnˈkwaɪəʳ] = **inquire**

enrage [ɪnˈreɪdʒ] VT mettre en rage or en fureur, rendre furieux; **he was ~d by this suggestion** cette proposition l'a rendu furieux; **it ~s me to think that ...** j'enrage de penser que ...

enrapture [ɪnˈræptʃəʳ] VT ravir, enchanter; **~d by ...** ravi de ..., enchanté par ...

enrich [ɪnˈrɪtʃ] **1** VT [+ *person, language, collection, mind*] enrichir (**with** en); [+ *soil*] fertiliser, amender; (*Phys*) enrichir; **vitamin-/**

iron-~ed enrichi en vitamines/en fer **2** COMP ► **enriched uranium** N uranium *m* enrichi

enrichment [ɪnˈrɪtʃmənt] N enrichissement *m*

enrol, enroll (*US*) [ɪnˈrəʊl] **1** VT [+ *worker*] embaucher; [+ *student*] immatriculer, inscrire; [+ *member*] inscrire; [+ *soldier*] enrôler **2** VI [*worker etc*] se faire embaucher (**as** comme); [*student*] se faire immatriculer or inscrire, s'inscrire (**in** à, **for** pour); [*soldier*] s'enrôler, s'engager (**in** dans); **to ~ as a member of a club/party** s'inscrire à un club/un parti **3** COMP ► **enrolled bill** N (*US Pol*) projet *m* de loi ratifié par les deux Chambres

enrolment, enrollment (*US*) [ɪnˈrəʊlmənt] **1** N (*at school, college, in club, scheme*) inscription *f* (**at** or **in** à qch); (*Mil*) enrôlement *m* (**in sth** dans qch), engagement *m* (**in sth** dans qch); (*Educ*) **enrol(l)ment for** or **on** (*Brit*) or **in** (*US*) **a course** inscription *f* à un cours; **the school has an ~ of 600 pupils** l'école a un effectif de 600 élèves; **the ideal would be 1,100 members** l'effectif idéal serait de 1 100 membres; **~ has** or **~s have doubled** (*at college, in club, scheme*) les inscriptions ont doublé; (*Mil*) les enrôlements or les engagements ont doublé **2** COMP ► **enrolment fee** N (*at school, university*) frais *mpl* de scolarité; (*in club*) frais *mpl* d'adhésion ► **enrolment figures** NPL effectif *m*

ensconce [ɪnˈskɒns] VT **to ~ o.s.** bien se caler, bien s'installer; **to be ~d** être bien installé

ensemble [ɑ̃ːˈnsɑ̃ːmbl] **1** N (*Dress, Mus* = *collection*) ensemble *m* **2** ADJ (*Theat*) [*acting, playing*] d'ensemble

enshrine [ɪnˈʃraɪn] VT [+ *custom, principle, rights*] sauvegarder; (*Rel*) enchâsser; **to be ~d in law** être garanti par la loi

enshroud [ɪnˈʃraʊd] VT (*liter*) **grey clouds ~ the city** la ville est ensevelie sous des nuages gris; **mist ~ed the land** la terre était noyée sous la brume; (*fig*) **~ed in mystery** enveloppé de mystère

ensign [ˈensaɪn] **1** N **a** [ˈensən] (= *flag*) drapeau *m*; (*Naut*) pavillon *m*; (*Brit*) **Red/White Ensign** pavillon *m* de la marine marchande/de la marine de guerre **b** (= *emblem*) insigne *m*, emblème *m* **c** (*Mil Hist*) (officier *m*) porte-étendard *m* **d** (*US Naut*) enseigne *m* de vaisseau de deuxième classe **2** COMP ► **ensign-bearer** N porte-étendard *m inv*

enslave [ɪnˈsleɪv] VT (*lit*) réduire en esclavage, asservir; (*fig*) asservir; **to be ~d by tradition** être l'esclave de la tradition

enslavement [ɪnˈsleɪvmənt] N asservissement *m*

ensnare [ɪnˈsnɛəʳ] VT (*lit, fig*) prendre au piège; [*woman, charms*] séduire

ensue [ɪnˈsjuː] VI s'ensuivre, résulter (**from** de)

ensuing [ɪnˈsjuːɪŋ] ADJ [*battle, violence, discussion, argument, chaos*] qui s'ensuit (or s'ensuivait); [*months, weeks*] suivant, qui suivent (or suivaient etc)

en suite [ɑ̃ːˈswiːt] ADJ **with bathroom ~** ◊ **with an ~ bathroom** avec salle de bains (attenante)

ensure [ɪnˈʃʊəʳ] VT **a** assurer, garantir; [+ *safety*] veiller sur, assurer; **he did everything to ~ that she came** il a tout fait pour qu'elle vienne or pour s'assurer qu'elle viendrait **b** = **insure b**

ENT [iːenˈtiː] (*Med*) (ABBR = **Ear, Nose and Throat**) ORL *f*

entail [ɪnˈteɪl] VT **a** (*gen, Philos*) entraîner; [+ *expense, work, delay*] occasionner; [+ *inconvenience, risk, difficulty*] comporter; [+ *suffering, hardship*] imposer, entraîner; **it ~ed buying a car** cela nécessitait l'achat d'une voiture **b** (*Jur*) **to ~ an estate** substituer un héritage; **~ed estate** biens *mpl* inaliénables

entangle [ɪnˈtæŋgl] VT **a** (= *catch up*) empêtrer, enchevêtrer; (= *twist together*) [+ *hair*] emmêler; [+ *wool, thread*] emmêler, em-

brouiller; **to become ~d in ropes** s'empêtrer dans des cordages **b** (*fig*) [+ *person*] entraîner, impliquer (**in** dans), mêler (**in** à); **to become ~d in an affair** s'empêtrer or se laisser entraîner dans une affaire; **to become ~d in lies/explanations** s'empêtrer dans des mensonges/des explications

entanglement [ɪnˈtæŋglmənt] N **a** (*NonC* = *entwining*) enchevêtrement *m*, emmêlement *m* **b** (*Mil*) **barbed-wire ~s** (réseau *m* de) barbelés *mpl* **c** (*sexual*) liaison *f* compliquée; **romantic ~** histoire *f* d'amour compliquée **d** (= *difficulty*) imbroglio *m*; **his ~ with the police** son imbroglio avec la police

entente [ɒnˈtɒnt] N **entente** *f*; **~ cordiale** entente *f* cordiale

enter [ˈentəʳ] **1** VT **a** (= *come or go into*) [+ *house etc*] entrer dans, pénétrer dans; [+ *vehicle*] monter dans, entrer dans; [+ *path, road*] s'engager dans; **he ~ed the grocer's** il est entré chez l'épicier or dans l'épicerie; (*Naut*) **to ~ harbour** entrer au port or dans le port; **the thought never ~ed my head** or **mind** cette pensée ne m'est jamais venue à l'esprit; **he is ~ing his sixtieth year** il entre dans sa soixantième année **b** (= *become member of*) [+ *profession, the army*] entrer dans; [+ *university, college*] s'inscrire à, se faire inscrire à or dans; **to ~ the Church** se faire prêtre, recevoir la prêtrise; **to ~ society** faire ses débuts dans le monde **c** (= *submit, write down*) [+ *amount, name, fact, order*] (*on list*) inscrire; (*in notebook*) noter; (*Comput*) [+ *data*] introduire, entrer; **to ~ an item in the ledger** porter un article sur le livre de comptes; (*Comm*) **~ these purchases to me** mettez or portez ces achats à or sur mon compte; **to ~ a horse for a race** engager or inscrire un cheval dans une course; **to ~ a dog for a show** présenter un chien dans un concours; **to ~ a pupil for an exam/a competition** présenter un élève à un examen/à un concours; **he has ~ed his son for Eton** il a inscrit son fils (à l'avance) à Eton; **to ~ a protest** élever une protestation; (*Jur*) **to ~ an appeal** interjeter appel; (*Jur*) **to ~ an appearance** comparaître (en justice)

2 VI **a** entrer; (*Theat*) **~ Macbeth** entre Macbeth **b** **to ~ for a race** s'inscrire pour une course; **to ~ for an exam** s'inscrire à un examen

► **enter into** VT FUS **a** [+ *explanation, apology*] se lancer dans; [+ *correspondence, conversation*] entrer en; [+ *plot*] prendre part à; [+ *negotiations*] entamer; [+ *contract*] passer; [+ *alliance*] conclure **b** [+ *sb's plans, calculations*] entrer dans; (*lit, fig*) **to ~ into the spirit of the game** entrer dans le jeu; **her money doesn't ~ into it at all** son argent n'y est pour rien or n'a rien à voir là-dedans

► **enter on** VT FUS = **enter upon**

► **enter up** VT SEP [+ *sum of money, amount*] inscrire; [+ *diary, ledger*] tenir à jour

► **enter upon** VT FUS [+ *course of action*] s'engager dans; [+ *career*] débuter dans, entrer dans; [+ *negotiations*] entamer; [+ *alliance*] conclure; (*Jur*) [+ *inheritance*] prendre possession de

enteric [enˈterɪk] **1** ADJ entérique **2** COMP ► **enteric fever** N (fièvre *f*) typhoïde *f*

enteritis [ˌentəˈraɪtɪs] N entérite *f*

enterostomy [ˌentəˈrɒstəmɪ] N entérostomie *f*

enterotomy [ˌentəˈrɒtəmɪ] N entérotomie *f*

enterovirus [ˌentərəʊˈvaɪrəs] N entérovirus *m*

enterprise [ˈentəpraɪz] **1** N **a** (= *undertaking, company*) entreprise *f* **b** (*NonC* = *initiative*) (esprit *m* d')initiative *f*, esprit *m* entreprenant → **free 2** COMP ► **Enterprise Allowance Scheme** N (*Brit*) aide à la création d'entreprise accordée aux chômeurs

enterprising [ˈentəpraɪzɪŋ] ADJ [*person, compa-*

ny] plein d'initiative; [*idea*] hardi; **that was ~ of you!** vous avez fait preuve d'initiative!

enterprisingly ['entǝpraɪzɪŋlɪ] ADV (= *showing initiative*) de sa (*or* leur *etc*) propre initiative; (*daringly*) hardiment, audacieusement

entertain [,entǝ'teɪn] **1** VT **a** (= *amuse*) [+ *audience*] amuser, divertir; (= *keep occupied*) [+ *guests, children*] distraire; **Liverpool ~ed the crowd with some brilliant football** Liverpool a diverti le public avec un football brillant **b** (= *offer hospitality to*) [+ *guests*] recevoir; (*frm*) **to ~ sb to dinner** (*at restaurant*) offrir à dîner à qn; (*at home*) recevoir qn à dîner **c** (= *have in mind*) [+ *possibility*] envisager; [+ *intention, suspicion, doubt, hope*] nourrir; [+ *proposal*] accueillir; **to ~ the thought of doing sth** envisager de faire qch; **she doesn't really want to ~ the thought** elle ne veut pas vraiment considérer cette éventualité; **I wouldn't ~ it for a moment** je repousserais tout de suite une telle idée; (*Insurance, Jur etc*) **to ~ a claim** admettre une réclamation, faire droit à une réclamation

2 VI **a** (= *amuse*) [+ *comic, entertainer, book, film*] divertir **b** (= *offer hospitality*) recevoir; **do you ~ often?** vous recevez beaucoup?

entertainer [,entǝ'teɪnǝʳ] N artiste *mf* (de music-hall *etc*), fantaisiste *mf*; **a well-known radio ~** un(e) artiste bien connu(e) à la radio; **he's a born ~** c'est un amuseur né

entertaining [,entǝ'teɪnɪŋ] **1** ADJ divertissant **2** N she loves ~ recevoir; (*more formal occasions*) elle adore donner des réceptions; **this is a lovely room for ~** c'est la pièce idéale pour recevoir *or* pour des réceptions; **this dish is ideal for ~** c'est un plat idéal quand on reçoit

entertainingly [,entǝ'teɪnɪŋlɪ] ADV [*say, talk*] d'une façon divertissante; **~ cynical** d'un cynisme divertissant

entertainment [,entǝ'teɪnmǝnt] **1** N **a** (*NonC = amusement*) divertissements *mpl*; **the cinema is their favourite form of ~** le cinéma est leur loisir *or* divertissement préféré; **this was not his idea of an evening's ~** ce n'était pas comme ça qu'il voyait un divertissement pour une soirée; **family/popular ~** divertissement familial/populaire; **much to the ~ of ...** au grand divertissement de ...; **for your ~ we have invited ...** (*gen*) pour vous divertir nous avons invité ...; (*on TV, radio show*) pour vous faire plaisir nous avons invité ...; **to make one's own ~** se divertir soi-même → **light b** (= *show*) spectacle *m*; **the world of ~** le monde du spectacle **c** (*Comm*) [*of clients, guests*] réception *f*

2 COMP ► **entertainment allowance** N = **entertainment expenses** ► **entertainment expenses** NPL frais *mpl* de représentation ► **entertainment tax** N taxe *f* sur les spectacles

enthral(l) [ɪn'θrɔːl] VT **a** [*book, film, talk, performance, spectacle, story*] captiver; [*scenery, entertainer, actor*] charmer; [*idea, thought*] enchanter; [*beauty, charm*] séduire, ensorceler **b** (†† = *enslave*) asservir

enthral(l)ed [ɪn'θrɔːld] ADJ (*by book, film, talk, performance, spectacle, story*) captivé; (*by scenery, entertainer, actor*) charmé; (*by idea*) enchanté; **the children listened, ~** les enfants écoutaient, captivés; **to hold sb ~** captiver qn

enthralling [ɪn'θrɔːlɪŋ] ADJ [*story, film, day*] passionnant; [*beauty*] ensorcelant

enthrone [ɪn'θrǝʊn] VT [+ *king*] placer sur le trône, introniser; [+ *bishop*] introniser; (*liter*) **to sit ~d** trôner; (*fig*) **~d in the hearts of his countrymen** vénéré par ses compatriotes

enthronement [ɪn'θrǝʊnmǝnt] N (*lit*) couronnement *m*, intronisation *f*; (*fig*) consécration *f*

enthuse [ɪn'θuːz] **1** VI **to ~ over sb/sth** porter qn/qch aux nues, parler avec (beaucoup d')enthousiasme de qn/qch **2** VT enthousiasmer

enthusiasm [ɪn'θuːzɪæzǝm] N **a** (*NonC*) enthousiasme *m* (**for** pour); **without ~** sans enthousiasme; **her visit generated little ~ among local people** sa visite a provoqué peu d'enthousiasme parmi les habitants; **they showed little ~ for the scheme** ils ont manifesté peu d'enthousiasme pour le projet, ils n'ont pas vraiment été enthousiasmés par le projet; **the idea filled her with ~** l'idée l'a enthousiasmée; **she has great ~ for life** elle a une véritable passion pour la vie **b** (= *pet interest*) passion *f*; **photography is one of her many ~s** la photographie est une de ses nombreuses passions

enthusiast [ɪn'θuːzɪæst] N enthousiaste *mf*; **he is a jazz/bridge/sport** *etc* **~** il se passionne pour le *or* il est passionné de jazz/bridge/sport *etc*; **all these football ~s** tous ces passionnés de football; **a Vivaldi ~** un(e) fervent(e) de Vivaldi

enthusiastic [ɪn,θuːzɪ'æstɪk] ADJ enthousiaste; **~ about** [+ *painting, chess, botany*] passionné de; [+ *plan, suggestion*] enthousiasmé par; **he was very ~ about the plan** le projet l'a beaucoup enthousiasmé; **~ about doing sth** enthousiaste à l'idée de faire qch; **he was ~ in his praise** il a fait des éloges enthousiastes; **he was less than ~ (about/about doing)** il n'était pas du tout enthousiaste (à propos de/pour faire); **to make sb ~ (about sth)** enthousiasmer qn (pour qch); **to wax ~ (about sth)** s'enthousiasmer (pour qch)

enthusiastically [ɪn,θuːzɪ'æstɪkǝlɪ] ADV avec enthousiasme

entice [ɪn'taɪs] VT attirer, entraîner; (*with food, false promises*) allécher; (*with prospects*) séduire; **to ~ sb to do** entraîner qn (par la ruse) à faire; **to ~ sb away from sb/sth** éloigner qn de qn/qch

enticement [ɪn'taɪsmǝnt] N (= *act*) séduction *f*; (= *attraction*) attrait *m*

enticing [ɪn'taɪsɪŋ] ADJ [*prospect, invitation, offer, idea*] séduisant; **to look ~** [*person*] être séduisant; [*food*] être appétissant; [*water*] être tentant

enticingly [ɪn'taɪsɪŋlɪ] ADV [*display*] de façon attrayante; **an ~ simple way of life** un style de vie d'une simplicité séduisante

entire [ɪn'taɪǝʳ] ADJ **a** (= *whole, complete*) [*time, world, family*] entier; [*body, company, community, house, object, country, area*] tout entier; [*cost*] total; **the ~ city/street** toute la ville/rue; **his ~ life/career** toute sa vie/carrière; **the greatest thief in the ~ history of the world** le plus grand voleur de toute l'histoire du monde; **he has my ~ confidence** j'ai entièrement confiance en lui, il a mon entière confiance **b** (= *uncastrated*) [*animal*] entier

entirely [ɪn'taɪǝlɪ] ADV [*change*] du tout au tout; [*depend on, devote to*] entièrement; [*satisfied, different, clear, possible, happy, convinced*] tout à fait; [*new*] totalement; [*free*] absolument; **I ~ agree** je suis entièrement *or* tout à fait d'accord; **made ~ of wood** entièrement fait en bois; **it's ~ up to you** c'est à toi de décider, c'est toi qui décides; **she's ~ the wrong person for the job** ce n'est vraiment pas la personne qui convient pour ce travail; **the accident was ~ the fault of the other driver** l'accident était entièrement de la faute de l'autre conducteur; **to be ~ a matter for sb/ sth** relever entièrement de la compétence de qn/qch; **to be another matter ~** ◊ **to be an ~ different matter** être une tout autre affaire; **was she right? — not ~** avait-elle raison? — pas entièrement *or* complètement

entirety [ɪn'taɪǝrǝtɪ] N intégralité *f*, totalité *f*; **in its ~** en (son) entier, intégralement

entitle [ɪn'taɪtl] VT **a** (= *bestow right on*) autoriser, habiliter (*Jur*) (**to do** à faire); **to ~ sb to sth** donner droit à qch à qn; **this voucher ~s you to three half-price recordings** ce bon vous donne droit à trois disques à moitié prix; **to be ~d to sth** avoir droit à qch; **you should claim all that you're ~d to** vous devriez réclamer tout ce à quoi vous avez droit; **you're ~d to a bit of fun!** tu as bien le droit de t'amuser un peu!; **I'm ~d to my own opinion** j'ai bien le droit d'avoir ma propre opinion; **to ~ sb to do sth** donner à qn le droit de faire qch; **to be ~d to do sth** (*by position, qualifications*) avoir qualité pour faire qch, être habilité à faire qch (*Jur*); (*by conditions, rules*) avoir droit *or* être en droit de faire qch; **he is quite ~d to believe that ...** il est tout à fait en droit de croire que ...; **to be ~d to vote** (*Pol* = *have right of suffrage*) avoir le droit de vote; (*in union election, for committee etc*) avoir voix délibérative **b** [+ *book*] intituler; **to be ~d** s'intituler

entitlement [ɪn'taɪtlmǝnt] **1** N droit *m* (**to** à) **2** COMP ► **entitlement program** N (*US Pol*) programme *m* social

entity ['entɪtɪ] N entité *f* → **legal**

entomb [ɪn'tuːm] VT mettre au tombeau, ensevelir; (*fig*) ensevelir

entombment [ɪn'tuːmmǝnt] N mise *f* au tombeau, ensevelissement *m*

entomological [,entǝmǝ'lɒdʒɪkǝl] ADJ entomologique

entomologist [,entǝ'mɒlǝdʒɪst] N entomologiste *mf*

entomology [,entǝ'mɒlǝdʒɪ] N entomologie *f*

entourage [,ɒntʊ'rɑːʒ] N entourage *m*

entr'acte ['ɒntrækt] N entracte *m*

entrails ['entreɪlz] NPL (*lit, fig*) entrailles *fpl*

entrain [ɪn'treɪn] **1** VT (*Rail*) faire monter dans un train; (= *carry along*) entraîner **2** VI monter dans un train

entrance[1] ['entrǝns] **1** N **a** (= *way in*) (*gen*) entrée *f* (**to** de); [*of cathedral*] portail *m*; (= *hall*) entrée *f*, vestibule *m* → **tradesman b** (= *act of entering*) entrée *f*; **on his ~** à son entrée; (*esp Theat*) **to make an ~** faire son entrée; **his ~ into politics** son entrée dans la politique **c** (= *right to enter*) admission *f*; **~ to a school** admission *f* à *or* dans une école; **to gain ~ to a university** être admis à *or* dans une université; **children get free ~ (to the zoo)** l'entrée (du zoo) est gratuite pour les enfants

2 COMP ► **entrance card** N carte *f or* billet *m* d'entrée *or* d'admission ► **entrance examination** N examen *m* d'entrée; (*Admin*) concours *m* de recrutement ► **entrance fee** N (*at museum, cinema etc*) prix *m or* droit *m* d'entrée; (*Brit: for club, association etc*) droit *m* d'inscription ► **entrance hall** N hall *m* (d'entrée) ► **entrance qualifications** NPL (*Educ*) diplômes *mpl* exigés à l'entrée ► **entrance ramp** N (*US Aut*) bretelle *f* d'accès ► **entrance requirements** NPL (*Educ*) qualifications *f* exigées à l'entrée ► **entrance ticket** N billet *m* d'entrée

entrance[2] [ɪn'trɑːns] VT ravir, enchanter; **she stood there ~d** elle restait là extasiée *or* en extase

entrancing [ɪn'trɑːnsɪŋ] ADJ enchanteur (-teresse *f*), ravissant

entrancingly [ɪn'trɑːnsɪŋlɪ] ADV [*dance, sing*] à ravir; [*smile*] d'une façon ravissante *or* séduisante; **she is ~ beautiful** elle est belle à ravir; **it's ~ simple** c'est d'une merveilleuse simplicité

entrant ['entrǝnt] N (*to profession*) nouveau venu *m*, nouvelle venue *f* (**to** dans, en); (*in race*) concurrent(e) *m(f)*, participant(e) *m(f)*; (*in competition*) candidat(e) *m(f)*, concurrent(e) *m(f)*; (*in exam*) candidat(e) *m(f)*

entrap [ɪn'træp] VT prendre au piège ; **to ~ sb into doing sth** amener qn à faire qch par la ruse or la feinte

entrapment [ɪn'træpmənt] N (Jur) incitation policière à commettre un délit qui justifiera ensuite l'arrestation de son auteur

entreat [ɪn'triːt] VT supplier, implorer (**sb to do** qn de faire) ; **listen to him, I ~ you** écoutez-le, je vous en supplie or je vous en conjure ; **to ~ sth of sb** demander instamment qch à qn ; **to ~ sb for help** implorer le secours de qn

entreating [ɪn'triːtɪŋ] ① ADJ suppliant, implorant ② N supplications fpl

entreatingly [ɪn'triːtɪŋlɪ] ADV [look] d'un air suppliant ; [ask] d'un ton suppliant, d'une voix suppliante

entreaty [ɪn'triːtɪ] N prière f, supplication f ; **at his ~** sur ses instances fpl ; **a look/gesture of ~** un regard/un geste suppliant

entrée ['ɒntreɪ] N (Culin) entrée f

entrench [ɪn'trentʃ] VT (Mil) retrancher

entrenched [ɪn'trentʃd] ADJ ⓐ (pej = established) [position, idea, attitude] arrêté ; [belief, behaviour, practice, racism, suspicion] enraciné ; [interests, power, bureaucracy] bien établi ; [person] inflexible ; **to become ~** [position, idea, attitude] devenir trop arrêté ; [belief, behaviour, practice, racism, suspicion] s'enraciner ; [interests, power, bureaucracy] s'établir fermement ; [person] se retrancher sur ses positions ; **the recession is still well ~** la récession s'est installée, la récession dure ; **you're too ~ in the past** vous êtes trop replié sur le passé ; **he remained ~ in his position** il ne démordait pas de son point de vue ; **to be ~ in the belief/view that ...** ne pas démordre de l'idée que .../du point de vue selon lequel ... ⓑ (Mil) [troops, position] retranché

entrenchment [ɪn'trentʃmənt] N ⓐ (Mil) retranchement m ⓑ (= establishment) [of rights, standards] (gen) établissement m ; (by constitution, law) validation f

entrepôt ['ɒntrəpəʊ] N entrepôt m

entrepreneur [ˌɒntrəprə'nɜːʳ] N entrepreneur m (chef d'entreprise)

entrepreneurial [ˌɒntrəprə'nɜːrɪəl] ADJ [person, company] entreprenant ; [initiative] audacieux ; **to have ~ flair** avoir l'esprit d'entreprise, avoir le sens de l'initiative

entrepreneurship [ˌɒntrəprə'nɜːʃɪp] N esprit m d'entreprise

entropy ['entrəpɪ] N entropie f

entrust [ɪn'trʌst] VT [+ secrets, valuables, letters] confier (**to** à) ; [+ child] confier (**to sb** à qn, à la garde de qn) ; [+ prisoner] confier (**to** à la garde de) ; **to ~ sb/sth to sb's care** confier or remettre qn/qch aux soins de qn ; **to ~ sb with a task** charger qn d'une tâche, confier à qn une tâche ; **to ~ sb with the job of doing** charger qn de faire qch, confier à qn le soin de faire qch

entry ['entrɪ] ① N ⓐ (= action) entrée f ; (in competition) participation f ; **to make an ~** faire son entrée ; (Theat) **to make one's ~** entrer en scène ; **"no ~"** (on gate etc) « défense d'entrer », « entrée interdite » ; (in one-way street) « sens interdit » ⓑ (= way in: gen) entrée f ; [of cathedral] portail m ⓒ (= item) [of list] inscription f ; [of account book, ledger] écriture f ; [of dictionary, encyclopedia] (= term) article m ; (= headword) adresse f, entrée f ; (Accounts) **single/double ~** comptabilité f en partie simple/double ; (Naut) **~ in the log** entrée f du journal de bord ⓓ (Sport etc = participant(s)) **there is a large ~ for the 200 metres** il y a une longue liste de concurrents pour le 200 mètres ; **there are only three entries** (for race, competition) il n'y a que trois concurrents ; (for exam) il n'y a que trois candidats

② COMP ► **entry condition** N (Ling) condition f d'admission (à un système) ► **entry examination** N examen m d'entrée ► **entry fee** N (at museum, cinema etc) prix m or droit m d'entrée ; (Brit: for club, association etc) droit m d'inscription ► **entry form** N feuille f d'inscription ► **entry-level** ADJ (Comput) de base ► **entry permit** N visa m d'entrée ► **entry phone** N interphone m ► **entry qualifications** NPL (Educ) diplômes mpl exigés à l'entrée ► **entry requirements** NPL (Educ) qualifications fpl exigées à l'entrée ► **entry visa** N = entry permit ► **entry word** N (US Lexicography) entrée f, adresse f

entryism ['entrɪɪzəm] N entrisme m

entryist ['entrɪɪst] N, ADJ entriste mf

entwine [ɪn'twaɪn] ① VT [+ stems, ribbons] entrelacer ; [+ garland] tresser ; (= twist around) enlacer (**with** de) ; **to ~ itself around** s'enrouler autour de ② VI s'entrelacer, s'enlacer (**around** autour de)

enumerate [ɪ'njuːməreɪt] VT énumérer, dénombrer

enumeration [ɪˌnjuːmə'reɪʃən] N énumération f, dénombrement m

enunciate [ɪ'nʌnsɪeɪt] VT [+ sound, word] prononcer, articuler ; [+ principle, theory] énoncer, exposer ; **to ~ clearly** bien articuler

enunciation [ɪˌnʌnsɪ'eɪʃən] N [of sound, word] articulation f ; [of theory] énonciation f, formulation f ; [of problem] énoncé m ; **he has good ~** il articule bien

enuresis [ˌenjʊ'riːsɪs] N énurésie f

enuretic [ˌenjʊ'retɪk] ADJ énurétique

envelop [ɪn'veləp] VT envelopper (also fig) ; **~ed in a blanket** enveloppé dans une couverture ; **~ed in clouds/snow** enveloppé de nuages/neige ; **~ed in mystery** enveloppé or entouré de mystère

envelope ['envələʊp] N [of letter, balloon, airship] enveloppe f ; [Bio, Bot] enveloppe f, tunique f ; (Math) enveloppe f ; **to put a letter in an ~** mettre une lettre sous enveloppe ; **in a sealed ~** sous pli cacheté ; **in the same ~** sous le même pli ; **it sounds as if it was written on the back of an ~** on dirait que ça a été rédigé à la hâte

envelopment [ɪn'veləpmənt] N enveloppement m

envenom [ɪn'venəm] VT (lit, fig) envenimer

enviable ['envɪəbl] ADJ enviable

enviably ['envɪəblɪ] ADV **~ slim** d'une minceur enviable ; **a city with ~ little crime** une ville dont on peut envier le faible taux de criminalité ; **an ~ high academic standard** un niveau scolaire élevé qui fait envie

envious ['envɪəs] ADJ [person, glance] envieux ; **you're going to Barbados? — I'm very ~** tu vas à la Barbade ? — je t'envie beaucoup ; **to be ~ of sb/sth** envier qn/qch ; **people were ~ of his success** son succès a fait des envieux ; **to be ~ that ...** être envieux du fait que ... (+ subj) ; **to cast ~ eyes** or **an ~ eye at sb/sth** jeter un regard envieux sur qn/qch

enviously ['envɪəslɪ] ADV avec envie

environment [ɪn'vaɪərənmənt] N (Bio, Bot, Geog) milieu m ; (Admin, Pol, Ling) environnement m ; (physical) cadre m, environnement m ; (social, moral) milieu m ; **cultural ~** milieu m culturel ; **he has a good working ~** il travaille dans un cadre agréable ; (fig) **hostile ~** climat m d'hostilité, ambiance f hostile ; **natural ~** milieu m naturel ; **his normal ~** son cadre or son milieu normal ; **working-class ~** milieu m ouvrier ; **heredity or ~** l'hérédité f ou l'environnement m ; **pollution/protection of the ~** la pollution/la protection de l'environnement ; **~-friendly** qui respecte l'environnement ; (Brit) **Secretary (of State) for** or **Minister of the Environment** ministre m de l'Environnement ; **Department** or **Ministry of the Environment** ministère m de l'Environnement

environmental [ɪnˌvaɪərən'mentl] ① ADJ ⓐ (= ecological) [issues, matters, problems] écologique, environnemental ; [impact, effects, research] sur l'environnement ; [change] d'écosystème ; [policy] de l'environnement ; [group, movement] écologiste ; [disaster] écologique ; **~ awareness** conscience f écologique ; **to take account of ~ concerns** tenir compte des considérations écologiques or environnementales ; **~ damage** dommages mpl causés à l'environnement ; **~ regulations** lois fpl sur (la protection de) l'environnement ⓑ (= situational) [factors] lié à l'environnement ; [influence] de l'environnement ; **the illness is caused by genetic rather than ~ factors** cette maladie est due à des facteurs génétiques plutôt qu'au milieu ambiant

② COMP ► **environmental health** N (Brit) hygiène f publique ► **Environmental Health Department** N (Brit) département m d'hygiène publique ► **Environmental Health Officer** N (Brit) inspecteur m de l'hygiène publique ► **Environmental Health Service** N (Brit) service m d'hygiène publique ► **Environmental Protection Agency** N (US Admin) ≈ ministère m de l'Environnement ► **environmental studies** NPL étude f de l'environnement, études fpl écologiques

environmentalism [ɪnˌvaɪərən'mentəˌlɪzəm] N écologie f, science f de l'environnement

environmentalist [ɪnˌvaɪərən'mentəlɪst] N écologiste mf, environnementaliste mf

environmentally [ɪnˌvaɪərən'mentəlɪ] ADV ⓐ (= ecologically) [sensitive] écologiquement ; **to be ~ conscious** or **aware** être sensibilisé aux problèmes de l'environnement ; **to be ~ friendly** or **correct** respecter l'environnement ; **to be ~ harmful** nuire à l'environnement ; **~ sound policies** des politiques respectueuses de l'environnement ⓑ (= from living conditions) **to suffer from an ~ acquired** or **induced disease** souffrir d'une maladie due aux conditions de vie

environs [ɪn'vaɪərənz] NPL abords mpl, alentours mpl

envisage [ɪn'vɪzɪdʒ] VT (= foresee) prévoir ; (= imagine) envisager ; **I ~d that ...** on prévoit que ... ; **an increase is ~d next year** on prévoit une augmentation pour l'année prochaine ; **it is hard to ~ such a situation** il est difficile d'envisager une telle situation

envision [ɪn'vɪʒən] VT (esp US) (= conceive of) imaginer ; (= foresee) prévoir

envoy¹ ['envɔɪ] N (gen) envoyé(e) m(f), émissaire m ; (= diplomat: also = **extraordinary**) ministre m plénipotentiaire, ambassadeur m extraordinaire

envoy² ['envɔɪ] N (Poetry) envoi m

envy ['envɪ] ① N envie f, jalousie f ; **out of ~** par envie, par jalousie ; **filled with ~** dévoré de jalousie ; **it was the ~ of everyone** cela faisait or excitait l'envie de tout le monde → **green** ② VT [+ person, thing] envier ; **to ~ sb sth** envier qch à qn

enzyme ['enzaɪm] N enzyme f

EOC [ˌiːəʊ'siː] N (Brit) ABBR = **Equal Opportunities Commission**

EOC, EEOC

La Commission pour l'égalité des chances (Equal Opportunities Commission ou EOC) est un organisme britannique chargé de veiller à ce que les femmes perçoivent à travail égal un salaire égal à celui des hommes et qu'elles ne fassent pas l'objet d'une discrimination sexiste. La Commission pour l'égalité des races (« Commission for Racial Equality ») veille pour sa part à ce qu'il n'y ait pas de discrimination sur la base de la race ou de la religion.

Aux États-Unis, la Commission pour l'égalité

des chances (**Equal Employment Opportunity Commission** ou **EEOC**) lutte contre toutes les formes de discrimination raciale, religieuse ou sexuelle sur le lieu de travail. Les entreprises pratiquant une quelconque discrimination peuvent être poursuivies devant la justice fédérale.

Eocene ['i:əʊ,si:n] ADJ, N (Geol) éocène m

eolithic [,i:əʊ'lɪθɪk] ADJ éolithique

eon ['i:ɒn] N = **aeon**

eosin(e) ['i:əʊsɪn] N éosine f

EP [,i:'pi:] N (ABBR = **extended play**) 45 tours m double durée

EPA [,i:pi:'eɪ] (US Admin) (ABBR = **Environmental Protection Agency**) → **environmental**

epaulet(te) ['epɔ:let] N épaulette f

épée ['epeɪ] N fleuret m

ephedrine ['efɪdrɪn] N éphédrine f

ephemera [ɪ'femərə] ① N (pl **ephemeras** or **ephemerae** [ɪ'femə,ri:]) (Zool) éphémère m ② NPL (= transitory items) choses fpl éphémères; (= collectables) babioles fpl (d'une époque donnée)

ephemeral [ɪ'femərəl] ADJ (Bot, Zool, fig) éphémère

ephemerid [ɪ'femərɪd] N éphémère m

ephemeris [ɪ'femərɪs] N (pl **ephemerides** [,efɪ'merɪ,di:z]) éphéméride f

Ephesians [ɪ'fi:ʒənz] N Éphésiens mpl

Ephesus ['efɪsəs] N Éphèse

epic ['epɪk] ① ADJ (Literat) épique; (fig) héroïque, épique; (hum) épique, homérique ② N épopée f, poème m or récit m épique; (Cine) **an ~ of the screen** un film à grand spectacle

epicarp ['epɪkɑ:p] N épicarpe m

epicene ['episi:n] ADJ (frm) [manners, literature] efféminé; (Gram) épicène

epicentre, epicenter (US) ['episentər] N épicentre m

epicure ['epɪkjʊər] N (fin) gourmet m, gastronome mf

epicurean [,epɪkjʊə'ri:ən] ADJ, N épicurien(ne) m(f)

epicureanism [,epɪkjʊə'ri:ənɪzəm] N épicurisme m

Epicurus [,epɪ'kjʊərəs] N Épicure m

epicyclic [epɪ'saɪklɪk] ADJ **~ gear** or **train** train m épicycloïdal

epidemic [,epɪ'demɪk] ① N épidémie f ② ADJ épidémique; **to reach ~ proportions** atteindre des proportions épidémiques

epidemiologist [,epɪdemɪ'ɒlədʒɪst] N épidémiologiste mf

epidemiology [,epɪdemɪ'ɒlədʒɪ] N épidémiologie f

epidermis [,epɪ'dɜ:mɪs] N (Anat, Bot, Zool) épiderme m

epidiascope [,epɪ'daɪə,skəʊp] N épidiascope m

epididymis [,epɪ'dɪdɪmɪs] N (pl **epididymides** [,epɪdɪ'dɪmɪ,di:z]) (Anat) épididyme m

epidural [,epɪ'djʊərəl] ADJ, N **~ (anaesthetic)** péridurale f

epigenesis [,epɪ'dʒenɪsɪs] N (Bio) épigénèse f; (Geol) épigénie f

epiglottis [,epɪ'glɒtɪs] N (pl **epiglottises** or **epiglottides** [,epɪ'glɒtɪ,di:z]) épiglotte f

epigram ['epɪgræm] N épigramme f

epigrammatic(al) [,epɪgrə'mætɪk(əl)] ADJ épigrammatique

epigraph ['epɪgrɑ:f] N épigraphe f

epilator ['epɪleɪtər] N épilateur m

epilepsy ['epɪlepsɪ] N épilepsie f

epileptic [,epɪ'leptɪk] ① ADJ épileptique; **~ fit** crise f d'épilepsie ② N épileptique mf

epilogue ['epɪlɒg] N (Literat) épilogue m

epinephrine [,epə'nefrɪn] N (US) adrénaline f

Epiphany [ɪ'pɪfənɪ] N Épiphanie f, jour m des Rois

epiphytic [,epɪ'fɪtɪk] ADJ épiphyte

episcopacy [ɪ'pɪskəpəsɪ] N épiscopat m

Episcopal [ɪ'pɪskəpəl] ADJ (Rel: of Church) épiscopalien

episcopal [ɪ'pɪskəpəl] ADJ (of bishop) épiscopal

Episcopalian [ɪ'pɪskə'peɪlɪən] ① ADJ épiscopalien ② N membre m de l'Église épiscopalienne; **the ~s** les épiscopaliens mpl

episcopate [ɪ'pɪskəpɪt] N épiscopat m

episcope ['epɪ,skəʊp] N (Brit) épiscope f

episiotomy [ə,pɪzɪ'ɒtəmɪ] N épisiotomie f

episode ['epɪsəʊd] N (= event) (TV) épisode m; (Med) crise f

episodic [,epɪ'sɒdɪk] ADJ épisodique

epistemic [,epɪ'sti:mɪk] ADJ épistémique

epistemological [ɪ,pɪstɪmə'lɒdʒɪkəl] ADJ épistémologique

epistemology [ɪ,pɪstə'mɒlədʒɪ] N épistémologie f

epistle [ɪ'pɪsl] N épître f; (Admin = letter) courrier m; (Bible) **Epistle to the Romans/Hebrews** etc Épître f aux Romains/Hébreux etc

epistolary [ɪ'pɪstələrɪ] ADJ épistolaire

epitaph ['epɪtɑ:f] N épitaphe f

epithelium [,epɪ'θi:lɪəm] N (pl **epitheliums** or **epithelia** [,epɪ'θi:lɪə]) épithélium m

epithet ['epɪθet] N épithète f

epitome [ɪ'pɪtəmɪ] N [of idea, subject] quintessence f; **she's the ~ of virtue** elle est la vertu incarnée or personnifiée, elle est l'exemple même de la vertu

epitomize [ɪ'pɪtəmaɪz] VT [+ quality, virtue] incarner, personnifier; **it ~d everything he hated** c'était l'illustration parfaite de tout ce qu'il détestait

EPNS [,i:pi:en'es] (ABBR = **electroplated nickel silver**) → **electroplate**

epoch ['i:pɒk] ① N époque f, période f; (fig) **to mark an ~** faire époque, faire date ② COMP **► epoch-making** ADJ qui fait époque, qui fait date

eponym ['epənɪm] N éponyme m

eponymous [ɪ'pɒnɪməs] ADJ éponyme

EPOS ['i:pɒs] N (ABBR = **electronic point of sale**) TPV m, terminal m point de vente; **has the shop got ~?** est-ce que le magasin est équipé d'un TPV?

epoxide [ɪ'pɒksaɪd] N époxyde m; **~ resin** = **epoxy resin**; → **epoxy**

epoxy [ɪ'pɒksɪ] N (also = **resin**) résine f époxyde

EPROM ['i:prɒm] N (Comput) (ABBR = **erasable programmable read only memory**) EPROM f

Epsom salts ['epsəm'sɔ:ltz] NPL epsomite f, sulfate m de magnésium

equable ['ekwəbl] ADJ [temperament, climate] égal, constant; **he is very ~** il a un tempérament très égal

equably ['ekwəblɪ] ADV [say] tranquillement, calmement; [respond to] calmement

▼ equal ['i:kwəl] ① ADJ ⒜ (gen, Math) égal; **to be ~ to sth** être égal à qch, égaler qch → **1b**; **~ in number** égal en nombre; **to be ~ in size** être de la même taille; **~ pay for ~ work** à travail égal salaire égal; **~ pay for women** salaire égal pour les femmes; **~ rights** égalité f des droits; **an ~ sum of money** une même somme d'argent; **with ~ indifference** avec la même indifférence; **with ~ enthusiasm** avec le même enthousiasme; **each party has ~ access to the media** chaque parti a le même accès aux médias; **they are about ~** (in value etc) ils se valent à peu près; **to talk to sb on ~ terms** parler d'égal à égal; **other or all things being ~** toutes choses (étant) égales par ailleurs; **to be on ~ terms** or **an ~ footing (with sb)** être sur un pied d'égalité (avec qn); **to**

come ~ first/second etc être classé premier/deuxième etc ex æquo

⒝ (= capable) **to be ~ to sth** être à la hauteur de qch; **the guards were ~ to anything** les gardes pouvaient faire face à n'importe quoi; **to be ~ to doing sth** être de force à or de taille à faire qch; **she did not feel ~ to going out** elle ne se sentait pas le courage or la force de sortir

⒞ (†† = equable) [temperament] égal

② N égal(e) m(f); **our ~s** nos égaux mpl; **to treat sb as an ~** traiter qn d'égal à égal; **she has no ~** elle n'a pas sa pareille, elle est hors pair; **she is his ~** (in rank, standing) elle est son égale

③ VT (gen, Math) égaler (**in** en); **not to be ~led** sans égal, qui n'a pas son égal; **there is nothing to ~ it** il n'y a rien de tel or de comparable; (Math) **let x ~ y** si x égale y

④ COMP **► Equal Employment Opportunity Commission** N (US) Commission f pour l'égalité des chances → EOC, EEOC; **► equal opportunities** NPL chances fpl égales **► Equal Opportunities Commission** N (Brit) Commission f pour l'égalité des chances → EOC, EEOC; QUANGO; **► equal opportunities employer, equal opportunity employer** N employeur m qui ne fait pas de discrimination **► Equal Rights Amendment** N (US) amendement constitutionnel en faveur de l'égalité des droits **► equal(s) sign** N (Math) signe m d'égalité or égal **► equal time** N (US Rad, TV) droit m de réponse (à l'antenne)

equality [ɪ'kwɒlɪtɪ] N égalité f; **~ in the eyes of the law** égalité f devant la loi; **~ of opportunity** l'égalité f des chances; **the Equality State** le Wyoming

equalization [i:kwəlaɪ'zeɪʃən] N (NonC) [of wealth] répartition f; [of income, prices] égalisation f; [of retirement ages] nivellement m; [of account] régularisation f; **to work towards the ~ of opportunities** œuvrer pour l'égalité des chances

equalize ['i:kwəlaɪz] ① VT [+ rights, opportunities] garantir l'égalité de; [+ chances] équilibrer; [+ wealth, possessions] niveler; [+ income, prices] égaliser; [+ accounts] régulariser ② VI (Brit Sport) égaliser

equalizer ['i:kwəlaɪzər] N ⒜ (Sport) but m (or point m) égalisateur ⒝ (US‡) (= revolver) pétard* m, revolver m; (= rifle) flingue* m

▼ equally ['i:kwəlɪ] ADV ⒜ (= evenly) [divide, share] en parts égales; **~ spaced** à espaces réguliers

⒝ (= in the same way) [treat] de la même manière; **this applies ~ to everyone** ceci s'applique à tout le monde de la même manière; **this applies ~ to men and to women** ceci s'applique aussi bien aux hommes qu'aux femmes

⒞ (= just as) [important, impressive, true, difficult] tout aussi; [clear] également; **her mother was ~ disappointed** sa mère a été tout aussi déçue; **~ qualified candidates** des candidats mpl ayant les mêmes qualifications; **to be ~ successful** [person] réussir aussi bien; [artist, exhibition] avoir autant de succès; **~ gifted brothers** frères mpl également or pareillement doués; **they were ~ guilty** (gen) ils étaient aussi coupables l'un que l'autre; (Jur) ils étaient coupables au même degré; **she did ~ well in history** elle a eu de tout aussi bons résultats en histoire; **~ as good/bad** tout aussi bon/mauvais, aussi bon/mauvais l'un que l'autre

⒟ (= by the same token) **the country must find a solution to unemployment. Equally, it must fight inflation** le pays doit trouver une solution au chômage; de même, il doit lutter contre l'inflation; **she cannot marry him, but ~ she cannot live alone** elle ne peut pas l'épouser mais elle ne peut pas non plus vivre seule

➤ LANGUAGE IN USE: **equal** 5.2 **equally** 26.1, 26.2

equanimity [ˌekwəˈnɪmɪtɪ] N égalité f d'humeur, équanimité f (frm); **with ~** avec sérénité, d'une âme égale

equate [ɪˈkweɪt] VT (= identify) assimiler (**with** à); (= compare) mettre sur le même pied (**with** que); (Math) mettre en équation (**to** avec); (= make equal) égaler, égaliser; **to ~ Eliot with Shakespeare** mettre Eliot sur le même pied que Shakespeare; **to ~ black with mourning** assimiler le noir au deuil; **to ~ supply and demand** égaler or égaliser l'offre et la demande

equation [ɪˈkweɪʒən] 1 N a (Math, Chem) équation f; **that doesn't even enter the ~** ça n'entre même pas en ligne de compte → **quadratic, simple, simultaneous** b (= comparison) **the ~ of sth with sth** ◊ **the ~ between sth and sth** l'assimilation f de qch à qch 2 COMP ► **equation of time** N (Astron) équation f du temps

equator [ɪˈkweɪtər] N équateur m (terrestre), ligne f équinoxiale; **at the ~** sous l'équateur

equatorial [ˌekwəˈtɔːrɪəl] ADJ équatorial; **Equatorial Guinea** la Guinée équatoriale

equerry [ɪˈkwerɪ] N écuyer m (au service d'un membre de la famille royale)

equestrian [ɪˈkwestrɪən] 1 ADJ équestre 2 N (gen) cavalier m, -ière f; (in circus) écuyer m, -ère f

equestrianism [ɪˈkwestrɪəˌnɪzəm] N (Sport) hippisme m, sports mpl équestres

equi... [ˈiːkwɪ] PREF équi...

equidistant [ˈiːkwɪˈdɪstənt] ADJ équidistant, à égale distance; **Orléans is ~ from Tours and Paris** Orléans est à égale distance de Tours et de Paris

equilateral [ˌiːkwɪˈlætərəl] ADJ équilatéral

equilibrium [ˌiːkwɪˈlɪbrɪəm] N (pl **equilibriums** or **equilibria** [ˌiːkwɪˈlɪbrɪə]) (physical, mental) équilibre m; **to lose one's ~** (physically) perdre l'équilibre; (mentally) devenir déséquilibré; **in ~** en équilibre

equine [ˈekwaɪn] ADJ [species, profile] chevalin

equinoctial [ˌiːkwɪˈnɒkʃəl] ADJ équinoxial; [gales, tides] d'équinoxe

equinox [ˈiːkwɪnɒks] N équinoxe m; **vernal** or **spring ~** équinoxe m de printemps, point m vernal; **autumnal ~** équinoxe m d'automne

equip [ɪˈkwɪp] VT a (= fit out) [+ factory] équiper, outiller; [+ kitchen, laboratory, ship, soldier, worker, astronaut] équiper; **to ~ a room as a laboratory** aménager une pièce en laboratoire; **to ~ a household** monter un ménage; **to be ~ped to do** [factory etc] être équipé pour faire; (fig) **to be ~ped for a job** avoir les compétences nécessaires pour un emploi → **ill, well** b (= provide) **to ~ with** [+ person] équiper de, pourvoir de; [+ ship, car, factory, army etc] équiper de, doter de; **to ~ o.s. with** s'équiper de, se munir de; **he is well ~ped with cookery books** il est bien monté or pourvu en livres de cuisine; **to ~ a ship with radar** installer le radar sur un bateau

equipage [ˈekwɪpɪdʒ] N équipage m (chevaux et personnel)

equipment [ɪˈkwɪpmənt] N (gen) équipement m; (for office, laboratory, camping etc) matériel m; **factory ~** outillage m; **lifesaving ~** matériel m de sauvetage; **electrical ~** appareillage m électrique; **domestic ~** appareils mpl ménagers; **~ grant** prime f or subvention f d'équipement

equipoise [ˈekwɪpɔɪz] N (frm) équilibre m

equisetum [ˌekwɪˈsiːtəm] N (pl **equisetums** or **equiseta** [ˌekwɪˈsiːtə]) equisetum m, prèle f

equitable [ˈekwɪtəbl] ADJ équitable

equitably [ˈekwɪtəblɪ] ADV équitablement

equitation [ˌekwɪˈteɪʃən] N (frm) équitation f

equity [ˈekwɪtɪ] 1 N a (NonC = fairness) équité f b (Econ) (also **owner's ~, shareholder's ~, ~ capital**) fonds mpl or capitaux mpl propres, capital m actions; (Brit St Ex) **equities** actions fpl cotées en bourse c (Jur = system of law) équité f d (Brit) **Equity** syndicat des acteurs 2 COMP ► **Equity card** N (Brit Theat) carte de membre du syndicat des acteurs ► **equity issue** N (Econ) émission f de capital ► **equity-linked policy** N (Econ) police f d'assurance-vie indexée sur le cours des valeurs boursières

equivalence [ɪˈkwɪvələns] N équivalence f

▼ **equivalent** [ɪˈkwɪvələnt] 1 ADJ équivalent; **to be ~ to** être équivalent à, équivaloir à 2 N équivalent m (in en); **the French ~ of the English word** l'équivalent en français du mot anglais; (Ind) **man ~** unité-travailleur f

equivocal [ɪˈkwɪvəkəl] ADJ [reply, statement, attitude, behaviour, results, evidence] équivoque, ambigu (-guë f); [person] (= ambiguous) équivoque; (= undecided) indécis (**about sth** quant à qch)

equivocally [ɪˈkwɪvəkəlɪ] ADV d'une manière équivoque or ambiguë

equivocate [ɪˈkwɪvəkeɪt] VI user de faux-fuyants or d'équivoques, parler (or répondre etc) de façon équivoque

equivocation [ɪˌkwɪvəˈkeɪʃən] N (often pl) paroles fpl équivoques; **without ~** sans équivoque or ambiguïté

ER a (ABBR = **Elizabeth Regina**) la reine Élisabeth b (US Med) (ABBR = **emergency room**) (salle f des) urgences fpl

er [ɜːr] INTERJ euh

ERA [ˌiːɑːrˈeɪ] a (US) (ABBR = **Equal Rights Amendment**) → **equal** b (Brit) (ABBR = **Education Reform Act**) loi f sur la réforme de l'enseignement

era [ˈɪərə] N (Geol, Hist) ère f; (gen) époque f, temps m; **the Christian ~** l'ère f chrétienne; **the end of an ~** la fin d'une époque; **the ~ of crinolines** le temps des crinolines; **to mark an ~** marquer une époque, faire époque

eradicate [ɪˈrædɪkeɪt] VT [+ injustice, discrimination, poverty] éradiquer, supprimer; [+ disease] éradiquer, éliminer; [+ weeds] éliminer

eradication [ɪˌrædɪˈkeɪʃən] N (NonC) [of injustice, discrimination] suppression f; [of poverty, disease, corruption] éradication f; [of weeds] élimination f

erasable [ɪˈreɪzəbl] 1 ADJ effaçable 2 COMP ► **erasable programmable read only memory** N (Comput) mémoire f morte programmable effaçable

erase [ɪˈreɪz] 1 VT a [+ writing, marks] effacer, gratter; (with rubber) gommer; (Comput, Recording) effacer; [+ memory] bannir b (US‡ = kill) liquider‡, tuer 2 COMP ► **erase head** N tête f d'effacement

eraser [ɪˈreɪzər] N (esp US = rubber) gomme f

Erasmus [ɪˈræzməs] N Érasme m

erasure [ɪˈreɪʒər] N grattage m, effacement m

erbium [ˈɜːbɪəm] N erbium m

ere [ɛər] (††, liter) 1 PREP avant; **~ now** déjà; **~ then** d'ici là; **~ long** sous peu 2 CONJ avant que (+ subj)

erect [ɪˈrekt] 1 ADJ a (= upright) [person, head, plant, stem] droit; [tail, ears] dressé; **her posture is very ~** elle se tient très droite; **to hold o.s.** or **stand ~** se tenir droit b (Physiol) [penis, clitoris] en érection; [nipples] durci 2 ADV [walk] (= on hind legs) debout; (= not slouching) droit 3 VT [+ temple, statue] ériger, élever; [+ wall, flats, factory] bâtir, construire; [+ machinery, traffic signs] installer; [+ scaffolding, furniture] monter; [+ altar, tent, mast, barricade] dresser; (fig) [+ theory] bâtir; [+ obstacles, barrier] élever

erectile [ɪˈrektaɪl] ADJ érectile

erection [ɪˈrekʃən] N a [of penis] érection f; **to have** or **get an ~** avoir une érection; **to maintain an ~** maintenir une érection b (NonC = construction) [of statue, monument] érection f; [of building, wall, fence] construction f; [of scaffolding] montage m; [of altar, tent, mast, barricade] dressage m; (fig) [of theory, obstacle, barrier] édification f c (= structure) structure f

erectly [ɪˈrektlɪ] ADV droit

erector [ɪˈrektər] 1 N (= muscle) érecteur m 2 COMP ► **erector set** N (US = toy) jeu m de construction

erg [ɜːg] N (Phys, Geol) erg m

ergative [ˈɜːgətɪv] ADJ (Ling) ergatif

ergo [ˈɜːgəʊ] CONJ (frm, hum) par conséquent

ergonomic [ˌɜːgəʊˈnɒmɪk] ADJ ergonomique

ergonomically [ˌɜːgəʊˈnɒmɪkəlɪ] ADV [designed] conformément à l'ergonomie; [sound, sensible] du point de vue ergonomique

ergonomics [ˌɜːgəʊˈnɒmɪks] N (NonC) ergonomie f

ergonomist [ɜːˈgɒnəmɪst] N ergonome mf

ergot [ˈɜːgət] N (Agr) ergot m; (Pharm) ergot m de seigle

ergotism [ˈɜːgətɪzəm] N ergotisme m

Erie [ˈɪərɪ] N **Lake ~** le lac Érié

Erin [ˈɪərɪn] N (††, liter) l'Irlande f

Eritrea [erɪˈtreɪə] N l'Érythrée f

Eritrean [erɪˈtreɪən] 1 ADJ érythréen 2 N Érythréen(ne) m(f)

erk‡ [ɜːk] N (Brit) (Aviat) bidasse m; (Naut) mataf m

ERM [ˌiːɑːrˈem] N (ABBR = **Exchange Rate Mechanism**) → **exchange**

ermine [ˈɜːmɪn] N (pl **ermines** or **ermine**) (= animal, fur, robes) hermine f

ERNIE [ˈɜːnɪ] N (Brit) (ABBR = **Electronic Random Number Indicator Equipment**) ordinateur qui sert au tirage des numéros gagnants des bons à lots

erode [ɪˈrəʊd] 1 VT a [water, wind, sea] éroder; [acid, rust] ronger, corroder b (fig) [+ power, authority, support] éroder; [+ confidence] saper; [+ advantages] grignoter; [inflation] [+ value] amoindrir 2 VI [rock, soil] s'éroder; [value] s'amoindrir

► **erode away** 1 VT désagréger 2 VI se désagréger

erogenous [ɪˈrɒdʒənəs] ADJ érogène

Eroica [ɪˈrəʊɪkə] N (Mus) **the ~ Symphony** la symphonie Héroïque

Eros [ˈɪərɒs] N Éros m

erosion [ɪˈrəʊʒən] N a [of soil, rock, cliff] érosion f; [of metal] corrosion f, érosion f; (Med) érosion f; **coastal ~** érosion f littorale; **soil ~** érosion f du sol; **wind ~** érosion f éolienne; **cervical ~** érosion f cervicale; **gum ~** érosion f gingivale or des gencives b (= reduction) [of power, authority, support, confidence, belief, freedom, rights] érosion f; [of moral standards] dégradation f; **the ~ of the French franc through inflation** l'érosion f or l'effritement m du franc français du fait de l'inflation

erosive [ɪˈrəʊzɪv] ADJ [power] d'érosion; [effect] de l'érosion

erotic [ɪˈrɒtɪk] ADJ érotique

erotica [ɪˈrɒtɪkə] NPL (Art) art m érotique; (Literat) littérature f érotique; (Cine) films mpl érotiques

erotically [ɪˈrɒtɪkəlɪ] ADV érotiquement; **an ~ charged novel** un roman plein d'érotisme

eroticism [ɪˈrɒtɪsɪzəm] N érotisme m

erotomania [ɪˌrɒtəʊˈmeɪnɪə] N érotomanie f

err [ɜːr] VI (= be mistaken) se tromper; (= sin) pécher, commettre une faute; **to ~ in one's judgement** faire une erreur de jugement; **to ~ on the side of caution** pécher par excès de prudence; **to ~ is human** l'erreur est humaine

errand [ˈerənd] 1 N commission f, course f; **to go on** or **run ~s** faire des commissions or des courses; **to be on an ~** être en course; **~ of mercy** une mission de charité → **fool[1]** 2 COMP ► **errand boy** N garçon m de courses

errant ['erənt] ADJ (= *sinful*) dévoyé ; (= *wandering*) errant → **knight**

errata [e'rɑːtə] NPL of **erratum**

erratic [ɪ'rætɪk] ADJ [*person, behaviour, moods*] fantasque ; [*driving, performance, progress, movements, sales, pulse*] irrégulier ; [*nature*] irrégulier, changeant ; **we work ~ hours** nos heures de travail sont très irrégulières

erratically [ɪ'rætɪkəlɪ] ADV [*behave, act*] de manière fantasque ; [*work, play*] de façon irrégulière ; [*drive*] de manière imprévisible, dangereusement

erratum [e'rɑːtəm] N (pl **errata**) erratum m (errata pl)

erroneous [ɪ'rəʊnɪəs] ADJ erroné

erroneously [ɪ'rəʊnɪəslɪ] ADV à tort, erronément

error ['erər] N **a** (= *mistake*) erreur f (*also Math*), faute f ; **to make** or **commit an ~** faire (une) erreur, commettre une erreur, se tromper ; **it would be an ~ to underestimate him** on aurait tort de le sous-estimer ; **~ of judgement** erreur f de jugement ; **~ in calculation** erreur f de calcul ; (*Naut*) **compass ~** variation f du compas ; (*Comm*) **~s and omissions excepted** sauf erreur ou omission ; (*Comput*) **~ message** message m d'erreur ; **margin, spelling b** (*NonC*) erreur f ; **in ~** par erreur, par méprise ; (*Rel*) **to be in/fall into ~** être/tomber dans l'erreur ; **to see the ~ of one's ways** revenir de ses erreurs

ersatz ['eazæts] **1** N ersatz m, succédané m **2** ADJ **this is ~ coffee** c'est de l'ersatz or du succédané de café ; **this coffee is ~** ce café est un ersatz or de l'ersatz or un succédané

erstwhile ['ɜːstwaɪl] († or *liter*) **1** ADJ d'autrefois, d'antan (*liter*) **2** ADV autrefois, jadis

eructate [ɪ'rʌkteɪt] VI (*frm*) éructer

erudite ['eroda ͜ıt] ADJ [*person, work*] érudit, savant ; [*word*] savant

eruditely ['erodaɪtlɪ] ADV d'une manière savante, avec érudition

erudition [,ero'dɪʃən] N érudition f

erupt [ɪ'rʌpt] VI **a** [*volcano*] (*begin*) entrer en éruption ; (*go on erupting*) faire éruption ; **~ing volcano** volcan m en éruption **b** [*war, fighting, violence, riots, argument, protests, scandal*] éclater ; [*crisis*] se déclencher ; **to ~ in(to) violence** tourner à la violence ; **the town ~ed in riots** la ville est devenue (subitement) le théâtre de violentes émeutes ; **the car ~ed in flames** la voiture s'est embrasée ; **she ~ed (in anger) when she heard the news** sa colère a explosé quand elle a entendu la nouvelle ; **the crowd ~ed into applause/laughter** la foule a éclaté en applaudissements/de rire ; **the children ~ed into the room** les enfants ont fait irruption dans la pièce **c** (*Med*) [*spots*] sortir, apparaître ; [*tooth*] percer ; **his face had ~ed (in spots)** son visage s'était soudain couvert de boutons ; **a rash had ~ed across his chest** sa poitrine s'était soudain couverte de boutons

eruption [ɪ'rʌpʃən] N **a** [*of volcano*] éruption f ; **a volcano in a state of ~** un volcan en éruption **b** [*of violence, laughter*] explosion f ; [*of crisis*] déclenchement m ; [*of anger*] explosion f, accès m ; [*of radicalism, fundamentalism*] vague f ; **since the ~ of the scandal/the war** depuis que le scandale/la guerre a éclaté ; **this could lead to the ~ of civil war** cela pourrait faire éclater une guerre civile **c** (*Med*) [*of spots, rash*] éruption f, poussée f ; [*of tooth*] percée f

erysipelas [,err'sɪpɪləs] N érysipèle or érésipèle m

erythrocyte [ɪ'rɪθrəʊ,saɪt] N (*Anat*) érythrocyte m

ES [iː'es] N (ABBR = **expert system**) SE m

ESA [,iː'eɪ] N (ABBR = **European Space Agency**) ASE f

Esau ['iːsɔː] N Ésaü m

escalate ['eskəleɪt] **1** VI [*fighting, bombing, violence*] s'intensifier ; [*tension, hostilities*] monter ; [*costs*] monter en flèche ; **the war is escalating** c'est l'escalade de la guerre ; **prices are escalating** c'est l'escalade des prix **2** VT [+ *fighting, violence*] intensifier ; [+ *prices, wage claims*] faire monter en flèche

escalation [,eskə'leɪʃən] **1** N (= *intensification*) [*of violence*] escalade f, intensification f ; [*of fighting, conflict, war*] intensification f ; [*of tension, hostilities*] montée f ; [*of costs, prices*] montée f en flèche ; **nuclear ~** surenchère f dans la course aux armements nucléaires **2** COMP ► **escalation clause** N (*Comm*) clause f d'indexation or de révision

escalator ['eskəleɪtər] **1** N escalier m roulant or mécanique, escalator m **2** COMP ► **escalator clause** N (*Comm*) clause f d'indexation or de révision

escalope [eskə'lɒp] N (*Brit*) escalope f ; **veal ~** escalope f de veau

escapade ['eskə,peɪd] N (= *misdeed*) fredaine f ; (= *prank*) frasque f ; (= *adventure*) équipée f

escape [ɪs'keɪp] **1** VI **a** (= *get away*) [*person, animal*] (*from person, incident, accident*) échapper (**from sb** à qn) ; (*from place*) s'échapper (**from** de) ; [*prisoner*] s'évader (**from** de) ; **to ~ from sb/from sb's hands** échapper à qn/des mains de qn ; **to ~ from captivity** [*person*] s'évader ; [*animal*] s'échapper (*du zoo etc*) ; **an ~d prisoner** un évadé ; **to ~ from a country** fuir un pays ; **to ~ to a neutral country** s'enfuir dans or gagner un pays neutre ; **to ~ with a warning** s'en tirer avec un (simple) avertissement ; **he ~d with a few scratches** il s'en est tiré avec quelques égratignures ; **he only just ~d with his life** il a failli y laisser la vie, il a failli y rester* ; **to ~ from poverty** échapper à la pauvreté ; **to ~ from the world/ the crowd** fuir le monde/la foule ; **to ~ from reality** s'évader (du réel) ; **to ~ from o.s.** se fuir ; **she wanted to ~ from her marriage** elle voulait échapper à la vie de couple **b** [*water, steam, gas*] s'échapper, fuir **2** VT **a** (= *avoid*) ► *pursuit, death, arrest, capture, prosecution, poverty, criticism*] échapper à ; [+ *consequences*] éviter ; [+ *punishment*] se soustraire à ; **he narrowly ~d injury/being run over** il a failli être blessé/écrasé ; **he ~d death or serious injury by no more than a few centimetres** quelques centimètres de plus et il était tué ou gravement blessé ; **to ~ detection** or **notice** ne pas se faire repérer ; **to ~ one's pursuers** échapper à ses poursuivants ; **this species has so far managed to ~ extinction** cette espèce a jusqu'à présent réussi à échapper à l'extinction **b** (= *elude, be forgotten by*) échapper à ; **his name ~s me** son nom m'échappe ; **nothing ~s him** rien ne lui échappe ; **it had not ~d her or her notice that ...** elle n'avait pas été sans s'apercevoir que ..., il ne lui avait pas échappé que ... **3** N [*of person*] fuite f, évasion f ; [*of animal*] fuite f ; [*of water, gas*] fuite f ; [*of steam, gas in machine*] échappement m ; **to plan an ~** combiner un plan d'évasion ; **to make an** or **one's ~** (*from person, incident, accident*) s'échapper ; (*from place*) s'évader ; [*prisoner*] s'évader ; **to have a lucky** or **narrow ~** l'échapper belle, s'en tirer de justesse ; **~ from reality** évasion f (hors de la réalité) ; (*Comput*) **~ (key)** touche f d'échappement **4** COMP ► **escape artist** N = **escapologist** ► **escape chute** N (*Aviat*) toboggan m de secours ► **escape clause** N (*Jur*) clause f dérogatoire or de sauvegarde ► **escape device** N dispositif m de sortie or de secours ► **escape hatch** N (*Naut*) sas m de secours ► **escape key** N (*Comput*) → **3** ► **escape mechanism** N (*lit*) mécanisme m de défense or de protection ; (*Psych*) fuite f (*devant la réalité*)

► **escape pipe** N tuyau m d'échappement or de refoulement, tuyère f ► **escape plan** N plan m d'évasion ► **escape route** N (*Aut*) voie f de détresse ; (*fig*) échappatoire f ► **escape valve** N soupape f d'échappement ► **escape velocity** N (*Space*) vitesse f de libération

escapee [ɪskeɪ'piː] N (*from prison*) évadé(e) m(f)

escapement [ɪs'keɪpmənt] N [*of clock, piano*] échappement m

escapism [ɪs'keɪpɪzəm] N envie f de fuir la réalité ; **it's sheer ~!** c'est simplement s'évader du réel !

escapist [ɪs'keɪpɪst] **1** N personne f qui fuit la réalité or qui se réfugie dans l'imaginaire **2** ADJ [*film, reading etc*] d'évasion

escapologist [,eskə'pɒlədʒɪst] N (*lit*) virtuose mf de l'évasion ; (*fig*) champion(ne) m(f) de l'esquive

escarpment [ɪs'kɑːpmənt] N escarpement m

eschatology [,eskə'tɒlədʒɪ] N eschatologie f

eschew [ɪs'tʃuː] VT (*frm*) éviter ; [+ *wine etc*] s'abstenir de ; [+ *temptation*] fuir

escort ['eskɔːt] **1** N **a** (*Mil, Naut*) escorte f ; (= *guard of honour*) escorte f, cortège m ; **under the ~ of ...** sous l'escorte de ... ; **under ~** sous escorte **b** (*female*) hôtesse f ; (*male*) (*at dance*) cavalier m ; (= *prostitute*) call-boy m **2** [ɪs'kɔːt] VT (*Mil, Naut, gen*) escorter ; (= *accompany*) accompagner, escorter ; **to ~ sb in** (*Mil, Police*) faire entrer qn sous escorte ; (*gen*) (= *accompany*) faire entrer qn ; **to ~ sb out** (*Mil, Police*) faire sortir qn sous escorte ; (*gen*) raccompagner qn jusqu'à la sortie **3** COMP ► **escort agency** N agence f de rencontres ► **escort duty** N **to be on ~ duty** [*soldiers*] être assigné au service d'escorte ; [*ship*] être en service d'escorte ► **escort vessel** N (*Naut*) vaisseau m or bâtiment m d'escorte, (*vaisseau m*) escorteur m

escrow ['eskrəʊ] **1** N (*Jur*) dépôt m fiduciaire or conditionnel ; **in ~** en dépôt fiduciaire, en main tierce **2** COMP ► **escrow account** N (*Fin*) compte m bloqué

escudo [es'kuːdəʊ] N (*pl* **escudos**) escudo m

escutcheon [ɪs'kʌtʃən] N (*Her*) écu m, écusson m → **blot**

esker ['eskər] N (*Geol*) os m

Eskimo ['eskɪməʊ] **1** N **a** Esquimau(de) m(f) **b** (*Ling*) esquimau m **2** ADJ esquimau (-au(de) f), eskimo inv ; **~ dog** chien m esquimau

ESL [,iːes'el] N (*Educ*) (ABBR = **English as a Second Language**) → **English**

esophagus [ɪ'sɒfəgəs] N (*pl* **esophaguses** or **esophagi** [ɪ'sɒfə,dʒaɪ]) œsophage m

esoteric [,esəʊ'terɪk] ADJ ésotérique

esoterica [,esəʊ'terɪkə] NPL objets mpl ésotériques

ESP [,iːes'piː] N **a** (ABBR = **extrasensory perception**) → **extrasensory** **b** (ABBR = **English for Special Purposes**) → **English**

esp. ABBR = **especially**

espadrille [,espə'drɪl] N espadrille f

espalier [ɪ'spælɪər] **1** N (= *trellis*) treillage m d'un espalier ; (= *tree*) arbre m en espalier ; (= *method*) culture f en espalier **2** VT cultiver en espalier

esparto [e'spɑːtəʊ] N (*also* **~ grass**) alfa m

especial [ɪs'peʃəl] ADJ particulier, spécial

▼ **especially** [ɪs'peʃəlɪ] ADV **a** (= *particularly*) surtout, en particulier ; **the garden is beautiful, ~ in summer** le jardin est beau, surtout en été ; **~ as** or **since it's so late** d'autant plus qu'il est tard ; **skincare becomes vitally important, ~ as we get older** les soins de la peau deviennent d'une importance vitale, surtout or en particulier quand on vieillit ; **he has mellowed considerably, ~ since he got married** il est beaucoup plus détendu, surtout depuis son mariage ; **more ~ as ...** d'autant plus que

...; **you ~ ought to know** tu devrais le savoir mieux que personne; **why me ~?** pourquoi moi en particulier?
b (= *expressly*) spécialement; **I came ~ to see you** je suis venu spécialement pour te voir; **to do sth ~ for sb/sth** faire qch spécialement pour qn/qch
c (= *more than usual*) particulièrement; **is she pretty? — not ~** elle est jolie? — pas particulièrement *or* spécialement; **read this passage ~ carefully** lisez ce passage avec un soin tout particulier

Esperantist [ˌespəˈræntɪst] N espérantiste *mf*

Esperanto [ˌespəˈræntəʊ] **1** N espéranto *m* **2** ADJ en espéranto

espionage [ˌespɪəˈnɑːʒ] N espionnage *m*

esplanade [ˌespləˈneɪd] N esplanade *f*

espousal [ɪˈspaʊzəl] N [*of cause, values, theory*] adhésion *f* (**of** à)

espouse [ɪsˈpaʊz] VT **a** [+ *cause, values, theory*] épouser, embrasser **b** (†† = *marry*) [+ *person*] épouser

espresso [esˈpresəʊ] **1** N (café *m*) express *m* **2** COMP ► **espresso bar** N café *m* (où l'on sert du café express)

espy [ɪsˈpaɪ] VT († *or frm*) apercevoir, aviser (*frm*)

Esq. N (*Brit frm*) (ABBR = **esquire**) **Brian Smith ~** M. Brian Smith (*sur une enveloppe etc*)

...esque [esk] SUF **Kafkaesque** kafkaïen

esquire [ɪsˈkwaɪəʳ] N **a** (*Brit: on envelope etc*) → **Esq. b** (*Brit Hist*) écuyer *m*

essay [ˈeseɪ] **1** N **a** (*Literat*) essai *m* (**on** sur); (*Scol*) rédaction *f* (**on** sur); (*longer*) dissertation *f* (**on** sur); (*US Univ*) mémoire *m* **b** (*liter* = *attempt*) essai *m* **2** [eˈseɪ] VT (*liter*) (= *try*) essayer, tenter (**to do** de faire); (= *test*) mettre à l'épreuve **3** COMP ► **essay test** N (*US Educ*) épreuve *f* écrite

essayist [ˈeseɪɪst] N essayiste *mf*

essence [ˈesəns] **1** N (*gen, Chem, Philos*) essence *f*; (*Culin*) extrait *m*; **the ~ of what was said** l'essentiel *m* de ce qui a été dit; **the novel captures the ~ of life in the city** le roman rend l'essence de la vie dans la ville; **the ~ of stupidity*** le comble de la stupidité; **he embodies the very ~ of socialism** il incarne l'essence même du socialisme; **the divine ~** l'essence *f* divine; **speed/accuracy is of the ~** la vitesse/la précision est essentielle *or* s'impose; **in ~** essentiellement **2** COMP ► **essence of violets** N essence *f* de violette

▼ **essential** [ɪˈsenʃəl] **1** ADJ [*equipment, action*] essentiel, indispensable (**to** à); [*fact*] essentiel; [*role, point*] capital, essentiel; [*question*] essentiel, fondamental; [*commodities*] essentiel, de première nécessité; (*Chem*) essentiel; **speed/accuracy is ~** la vitesse/la précision est essentielle; **it is ~ to act quickly** il est indispensable *or* essentiel d'agir vite; **it is ~ that ...** il est indispensable que ... (+ *subj*); **it's not ~** ce n'est pas indispensable; **the ~ thing is to act** l'essentiel est d'agir; **man's goodness** la bonté essentielle de l'homme **2** N qualité *f* (*or* objet *m etc*) indispensable; **the ~s** l'essentiel *m*; **in (all) ~s** pour l'essentiel, de manière générale; **to see to the ~s** s'occuper de l'essentiel; **accuracy is an ~** *or* **one of the ~s** la précision est une des qualités indispensables *or* est indispensable; **the ~s of German grammar** (= *basics*) des notions *fpl* fondamentales de grammaire allemande **3** COMP ► **essential oil** N huile *f* essentielle

essentially [ɪˈsenʃəlɪ] ADV [*correct, good, different*] essentiellement; **it's ~ a landscape of rolling hills and moors** c'est essentiellement un paysage de collines ondulantes et de landes; **she was ~ a generous person** au fond c'était quelqu'un de généreux; **~, it is a story of ordinary people** c'est avant tout l'histoire de gens ordinaires; **things will remain ~ the same** pour l'essentiel, les choses ne changeront pas

► **LANGUAGE IN USE:** **essential** 10.1, 10.3

EST [ˌiːesˈtiː] (*US*) (ABBR = **Eastern Standard Time**) → **eastern**

est [est] N (ABBR = **Erhard Seminars Training**) thérapie de groupe mise au point par Werner Erhard

est. **a** (*Comm etc*) (ABBR = **established**) ~ **1900** ≈ maison *f* fondée en 1900 **b** ABBR = **estimate(d)**

establish [ɪsˈtæblɪʃ] **1** VT **a** (= *set up*) [+ *government*] constituer, établir; [+ *state, business*] fonder, créer; [+ *factory*] établir, monter; [+ *society, tribunal*] constituer; [+ *laws, custom*] instaurer; [+ *relations*] établir, nouer; [+ *post*] créer; [+ *power, authority*] asseoir; [+ *peace, order*] faire régner; [+ *list*] dresser; [+ *sb's reputation*] établir; **to ~ one's reputation as a scholar/writer** se faire une réputation de savant/comme écrivain; **to ~ o.s. as a grocer** s'établir épicier **b** (= *prove*) [+ *fact, identity, one's rights*] établir; [+ *necessity, innocence, guilt*] établir, démontrer **2** COMP ► **establishing shot** N (*Cine*) plan *m* de situation

established [ɪsˈtæblɪʃt] **1** ADJ [*order, authority, religion, tradition, company, reputation, truth*] établi; [*clientele*] régulier; **it's an ~ fact that ...** c'est un fait établi que ...; (*Comm*) **1850** ≈ maison fondée en 1850 → **long 2** COMP ► **the Established Church** N (*Brit*) l'Église *f* anglicane

establishment [ɪsˈtæblɪʃmənt] **1** N **a** (*NonC* = *creation*) [*of organization, business, system, scheme, post*] création *f*; [*of regime, custom*] instauration *f*; [*of relations, reputation, identity, peace, order*] établissement *m*; [*of tribunal*] constitution *f* **b** (*NonC* = *proving*) [*of innocence, guilt*] établissement *m*, preuve *f* **c** (= *institution, business*) établissement *m*; **commercial/educational ~** établissement *m* commercial/scolaire; **research ~** institut *m* de recherche; **military ~** centre *m* militaire **d** (= *ruling class*) **the Establishment** l'establishment *m*; **to be against the Establishment** être contre l'establishment; **to join the Establishment** rejoindre l'establishment; **a pillar of the French Establishment** un pilier de l'establishment français; **the medical/political/religious ~** l'establishment *m* médical/politique/religieux **e** (*Mil, Naut* = *personnel*) effectif *m*; **a peacetime ~ of 132,000 men** un effectif en temps de paix de 132 000 hommes; **war ~** effectif *m* en temps de guerre **f** [*in household*] maisonnée *f*; **to keep up a large ~** avoir un grand train de maison **2** ADJ **the ~ view of history** la vue de l'histoire selon l'establishment; **~ figure** personnalité *f* de l'establishment

estate [ɪsˈteɪt] **1** N **a** (= *land*) propriété *f*, domaine *m*; (*esp Brit: also* **housing ~**) lotissement *m*, cité *f*; **country ~** terre(s) *f(pl)* → **real b** (*Jur* = *possessions*) bien(s) *m(pl)*; [*of deceased*] succession *f*; **he left a large ~** il a laissé une grosse fortune (en héritage); **to liquidate the ~** liquider la succession **c** (= *order, rank, condition*) état *m*; **the three ~s** les trois états; **the third ~** le Tiers État, la bourgeoisie; **the fourth ~** la presse, le quatrième pouvoir; (*liter*) **a man of high/low ~** un homme de haut rang/de basse extraction; (*liter*) **to grow to** *or* **reach man's ~** parvenir à l'âge d'homme, atteindre sa maturité **d** (*Brit*) = **estate car 2** COMP ► **estate agency** N (*esp Brit*) agence *f* immobilière ► **estate agent** N (*esp Brit*) agent *m* immobilier ► **estate car** N (*Brit*) break *m* ► **estate duty**, **estate tax** (*US*) N (*Jur*) droits *mpl* de succession

esteem [ɪsˈtiːm] **1** VT **a** (= *think highly of*) [+ *person*] avoir de l'estime pour, estimer; [+ *quality*] apprécier; **our (highly) ~ed colleague** notre (très) estimé collègue *or* confrère **b** (= *consider*) estimer, considérer; **I ~ it an**

honour (that ...) je m'estime très honoré (que ... (+ *subj*)); **I ~ it an honour to do** je considère comme un honneur de faire **2** N estime *f*, considération *f*; **to hold sb in high ~** tenir qn en haute estime, avoir une haute opinion de qn; **to hold sth in high ~** avoir une haute opinion de qch; **he went up/down in my ~** il est monté/a baissé dans mon estime

ester [ˈestəʳ] (*Chem*) N ester *m*

Esther [ˈestəʳ] N Esther *f*

esthete [ˈiːsθiːt] N = **aesthete**

Esthonia [esˈtəʊnɪə] N = **Estonia**

estimable [ˈestɪməbl] ADJ (*frm*) estimable, digne d'estime

estimate [ˈestɪmət] **1** N **a** estimation *f*; (*Comm*) devis *m*; **this figure is five times the original ~** ce chiffre est cinq fois supérieur à l'estimation initiale; **at a conservative ~** au bas mot; **the painting is worth £28 million at the lowest ~** le tableau vaut 28 millions de livres au bas mot *or* vaut au minimum 28 millions de livres; (*Comm*) **give me an ~ for (building) a greenhouse** donnez-moi *or* établissez-moi un devis pour la construction d'une serre; **give me an ~ of what your trip will cost** donnez-moi une idée du coût de votre voyage; **to form an ~ of sb's capabilities** évaluer les capacités de qn; **his ~ of 400 people was very far out** il s'était trompé de beaucoup en évaluant le nombre de gens à 400; **this price is only a rough ~** ce prix n'est que très approximatif; **at a rough ~** approximativement → **preliminary b** (*Admin, Pol*) **the ~s** le budget; **the Army ~s** le budget de l'armée **2** [ˈestɪmeɪt] VT estimer, juger (**that** que); [+ *cost, number, price, quantity*] estimer, évaluer; [+ *distance, speed*] estimer, apprécier; **his fortune is ~d at ...** on évalue sa fortune à ...; **I ~ that there must be 40 of them** j'estime qu'il doit y en avoir 40, à mon avis il doit y en avoir 40

estimated [ˈestɪmeɪtɪd] ADJ [*number, cost, figure*] estimé; **an ~ 60,000 refugees have crossed the border** environ 60 000 réfugiés auraient traversé la frontière; **~ time of arrival/departure** horaire *m* prévu d'arrivée/de départ; **~ cost** coût *m* estimé

estimation [ˌestɪˈmeɪʃən] N **a** jugement *m*, opinion *f*; **in my ~** à mon avis, selon moi **b** (= *esteem*) estime *f*, considération *f*; **he went up/down in my ~** il est monté/a baissé dans mon estime

estimator [ˈestɪmeɪtəʳ] N expert *m* (*de compagnie d'assurances*)

Estonia [eˈstəʊnɪə] N l'Estonie *f*

Estonian [eˈstəʊnɪən] **1** ADJ estonien **2** **a** Estonien(ne) *m(f)* **b** (*Ling*) estonien *m*

estrange [ɪsˈtreɪndʒ] VT brouiller (**from** avec), éloigner (**from** de); **to become ~d (from)** se brouiller (avec); **the ~d couple** le couple désuni; **her ~d husband** son mari, dont elle est séparée

estrangement [ɪsˈtreɪndʒmənt] N [*of people*] séparation *f* (**from sb** d'avec qn); [*of couple*] désunion *f*; [*of countries*] brouille *f*; **a feeling of ~** un sentiment d'éloignement; **the ~ between the two countries** la brouille entre les deux pays; **the ~ between the couple** la désunion du couple

estrogen [ˈestrədʒən, ˈiːstrədʒən] N (*US*) = **oestrogen**

estrus [ˈiːstrəs] N (*US*) = **oestrus**

estuary [ˈestjʊərɪ] **1** N estuaire *m* **2** COMP ► **Estuary English** N (*Brit*) façon de parler chez certaines personnes de la région de Londres, où les *t*, *l* et *h* ne se prononcent pas

ET [iːˈtiː] (*US*) (ABBR = **Eastern Time**) heure sur la côte est

ETA [ˌiːtiːˈeɪ] N (ABBR = **estimated time of arrival**) → **estimated**

et al [et'æl] (ABBR = **and others**) et autres

etc [ɪt'setərə] (ABBR = **et cetera**) etc

et cetera, **etcetera** [ɪt'setərə] ① ADV et caetera ② **the etceteras** NPL les extras *mpl*

etch [etʃ] VTI (*Art, Typ*) graver à l'eau forte ; (*fig*) ~**ed on his memory** gravé dans sa mémoire

etching ['etʃɪŋ] ① N ⓐ (*NonC*) gravure *f* à l'eau-forte ⓑ (= *picture*) (gravure *f* à l')eauforte *f* ② COMP ► **etching needle** N pointe *f* (sèche)

ETD [,i:ti:'di:] N (ABBR = **estimated time of departure**) → **estimated**

eternal [ɪ'tɜ:nl] ① ADJ [*beauty, love, life, youth*] éternel ; **can't you stop this ~ quarrelling?** allez-vous cesser vos querelles perpétuelles ? ; **he was the ~ practical joker** c'était l'éternel farceur ② **the Eternal** l'Éternel *m* ③ COMP ► **the eternal triangle** N l'éternel triangle *m* amoureux

eternally [ɪ'tɜ:nəlɪ] ADV ⓐ (= *everlastingly*) [*exist, be damned*] éternellement ⓑ (= *constantly*) [*grateful, optimistic, cheerful, young*] éternellement ; **he's ~ complaining** il est perpétuellement en train de se plaindre

eternity [ɪ'tɜ:nɪtɪ] ① N éternité *f* ; **it seemed like an ~ that we had to wait** nous avons eu l'impression d'attendre une éternité ; **we waited an ~*** nous avons attendu une éternité ② COMP ► **eternity ring** N bague offerte en gage de fidélité

ETF [,i:ti:'ef] N (ABBR = **electronic transfer of funds**) TEF *m*

ethane ['i:θeɪn] N éthane *m*

ethanol ['eθənɒl] N alcool *m* éthylique, éthanol *m*

ether ['i:θəʳ] N (*Chem, Phys*) éther *m* ; (*liter*) **the ~** l'éther *m*, les espaces *mpl* célestes ; (*Rad*) **over the ~** sur les ondes

ethereal [ɪ'θɪərɪəl] ADJ ⓐ (= *delicate*) éthéré, aérien ; (= *spiritual*) éthéré, sublime

ethic ['eθɪk] ① N morale *f*, éthique *f* → **work** ② ADJ = **ethical**

ethical ['eθɪkəl] ① ADJ (= *moral*) éthique, moral ; **not ~** contraire à la morale ② COMP ► **ethical code** N (*Med*) code *m* déontologique, déontologie *f* ► **ethical drug** N médicament *m* sur ordonnance

ethically ['eθɪklɪ] ADV [*behave, act*] conformément à l'éthique ; [*sound, unacceptable, wrong*] sur le plan éthique, d'un point de vue éthique ; [*opposed*] d'un point de vue éthique

ethics ['eθɪks] ① N (*NonC* = *study*) éthique *f*, morale *f* ② NPL (= *system, principles*) morale *f* ; (= *morality*) moralité *f* ; **medical ~** éthique *f* médicale, code *m* déontologique → **code**

Ethiopia [,i:θɪ'əʊpɪə] N l'Éthiopie *f*

Ethiopian [,i:θɪ'əʊpɪən] ① ADJ éthiopien ② N Éthiopien(ne) *m(f)*

ethnic ['eθnɪk] ① ADJ ⓐ (= *racial*) [*origin, community, group, conflict, tension*] ethnique ⓑ (= *expatriate*) [*population*] d'ethnie différente ; **~ Germans** personnes *fpl* d'ethnie allemande ⓒ (= *non-Western*) [*music, food, jewellery*] exotique ② N (*esp US*) membre *m* d'une minorité ethnique ③ COMP ► **ethnic cleansing** N (*euph*) purification *f* ethnique ► **ethnic minority** N minorité *f* ethnique

ethnically ['eθnɪklɪ] ADV [*diverse, distinct, pure, clean, homogeneous, divided*] sur le plan ethnique ; **~ based republics** républiques *fpl* fondées sur l'origine ethnique *or* sur des critères ethniques ; **an ~ mixed country** un pays comprenant divers groupes ethniques ; **~ related violence** violences *fpl* ethniques ; **the town had been ~ cleansed** la ville avait subi une purification ethnique

ethnicity [eθ'nɪsɪtɪ] N ⓐ (*NonC*) ethnicité *f* ⓑ (= *ethnic group*) ethnie *f*

ethnocentric ['eθnəʊ'sentrɪk] ADJ ethnocentrique

ethnographer [eθ'nɒɡrəfəʳ] N ethnographe *mf*

ethnographic(al) [,eθnə'ɡræfɪk(əl)] ADV ethnographique

ethnography [eθ'nɒɡrəfɪ] N ethnographie *f*

ethnolinguistics [,eθnəʊlɪŋ'ɡwɪstɪks] N (*NonC*) ethnolinguistique *f*

ethnologic(al) [,eθnə'lɒdʒɪk(əl)] ADJ ethnologique

ethnologist [eθ'nɒlədʒɪst] N ethnologue *mf*

ethnology [eθ'nɒlədʒɪ] N ethnologie *f*

ethologist [ɪ'θɒlədʒɪst] N éthologue *mf*

ethology [ɪ'θɒlədʒɪ] N éthologie *f*

ethos ['i:θɒs] N philosophie *f* ; **the company/party ~** la philosophie de l'entreprise/du parti

ethyl ['i:θaɪl] ① N éthyle *m* ② COMP ► **ethyl acetate** N acétate *m* d'éthyle

ethylene ['eθɪli:n] N éthylène *m*

etiolated ['i:tɪəleɪtɪd] ADJ (*Bot, fig frm*) étiolé

etiology [,i:tɪ'ɒlədʒɪ] N = **aetiology**

etiquette ['etɪket] N étiquette *f*, convenances *fpl* ; **~ demands that ...** les convenances exigent *or* l'étiquette exige que ... (+ *subj*) ; **diplomatic ~** protocole *m* ; **court ~** cérémonial *m* de cour ; **that isn't ~** c'est contraire aux convenances, c'est un manquement à l'étiquette ; **it's against medical ~** c'est contraire à la déontologie médicale ; **it's not professional ~** c'est contraire aux usages de la profession

Etna ['etnə] N (*also* **Mount ~**) l'Etna *m*

Etonian [i:'təʊnɪən] (*Brit*) ① N élève du collège d'Eton ② ADJ du collège d'Eton

étrier [eɪtrɪ'eɪ] N (*Climbing*) étrier *m*, escarpolette *f*

Etruria [ɪ'trʊərɪə] N l'Étrurie *f*

Etruscan [ɪ'trʌskən] ① ADJ étrusque ② N ⓐ (= *person*) Étrusque *mf* ⓑ (*Ling*) étrusque *m*

ETU [,i:ti:'ju:] N (*Brit*) (ABBR = **Electrical Trades Union**) syndicat

ETV [,i:ti:'vi:] N (*US TV*) (ABBR = **Educational Television**) → **educational**

etymological [,etɪmə'lɒdʒɪkəl] ADJ étymologique

etymologically [,etɪmə'lɒdʒɪkəlɪ] ADV étymologiquement

etymology [,etɪ'mɒlədʒɪ] N étymologie *f*

EU [i:'ju:] N (ABBR = **European Union**) UE *f*

eucalyptus [,ju:kə'lɪptəs] ① N (*pl* **eucalyptuses** *or* **eucalypti** [,ju:kə'lɪptaɪ]) (*Bot, Pharm*) eucalyptus *m* ② COMP ► **eucalyptus oil** N huile *f* essentielle d'eucalyptus

Eucharist ['ju:kərɪst] N Eucharistie *f*

Eucharistic [,ju:kə'rɪstɪk] ADJ eucharistique

euchre ['ju:kəʳ] (*US*) ① N euchre *m* (*jeu de cartes*) ② VT (= *cheat*) **to ~ sb out of sth*** carotter* qch à qn

Euclid ['ju:klɪd] N Euclide *m*

Euclidean [ju:'klɪdɪən] ADJ euclidien

eugenic [ju:'dʒenɪk] ADJ eugénique

eugenics [ju:'dʒenɪks] N (*NonC*) eugénique *f*, eugénisme *m*

eulogistic [,ju:lə'dʒɪstɪk] ADJ (*frm*) élogieux

eulogize ['ju:lədʒaɪz] ① VT faire l'éloge *or* le panégyrique de ② VI faire l'éloge *or* le panégyrique (**about, over** de)

eulogy ['ju:lədʒɪ] N (*gen*) panégyrique *m* ; (*at funeral service*) oraison *f* or éloge *m* funèbre

eunuch ['ju:nək] N eunuque *m*

euphemism ['ju:fəmɪzəm] N euphémisme *m* (**for** pour)

euphemistic [,ju:fə'mɪstɪk] ADJ euphémique

euphemistically [,ju:fə'mɪstɪkəlɪ] ADV euphémiquement, par euphémisme ; **described/known as ...** décrit/connu par euphémisme comme ...

euphonic [ju:'fɒnɪk] ADJ euphonique

euphonium [ju:'fəʊnɪəm] N euphonium *m*

euphonius [ju:'fəʊnɪəs] ADJ = **euphonic**

euphony ['ju:fənɪ] N euphonie *f*

euphorbia [ju:'fɔ:bɪə] N euphorbe *f*

euphoria [ju:'fɔ:rɪə] N euphorie *f*

euphoric [ju:'fɒrɪk] ADJ euphorique

Euphrates [ju:'freɪti:z] N Euphrate *m*

euphuism ['ju:fju:ɪzəm] N préciosité *f*, euphuisme *m*

Eurasia [jʊə'reɪʒə] N l'Eurasie *f*

Eurasian [jʊə'reɪʃn] ① ADJ [*population*] eurasien ; [*continent*] eurasiatique ② N Eurasien(ne) *m(f)*

Euratom [jʊə'rætəm] N (ABBR = **European Atomic Energy Community**) Euratom *m*, CEEA *f*

eureka [jʊə'ri:kə] EXCL eurêka !

eurhythmics [ju:'rɪðmɪks] N (*NonC*) gymnastique *f* rythmique

Euripides [jʊə'rɪpɪdi:z] N Euripide *m*

euro ['jʊərəʊ] N (= *currency*) euro *m*

euro... ['jʊərəʊ] PREF euro...

Eurobond ['jʊərəʊ,bɒnd] N euro-obligation *f*

Eurocentric [,jʊərəʊ'sentrɪk] ADJ eurocentrique

Eurocheque ['jʊərəʊ,tʃek] ① N eurochèque *m* ② COMP ► **Eurocheque card** N carte *f* Eurochèque

Eurocommunism ['jʊərəʊ,kɒmjʊnɪzəm] N eurocommunisme *m*

Eurocrat ['jʊərəʊ,kræt] N eurocrate *mf*

eurocredit ['jʊərəʊ,kredɪt] N eurocrédit *m*

Eurocurrency ['jʊərəʊ,kʌrənsɪ] N eurodevise *f*

Eurodollar ['jʊərəʊ,dɒləʳ] N eurodollar *m*

Euromarket ['jʊərəʊ,mɑ:kɪt] N Communauté *f* économique européenne

Euro MP ['jʊərəʊem'pi:] N député(e) *m(f)* européen(ne)

Europe ['jʊərəp] N l'Europe *f* ; (*Brit Pol*) **to go into ◊ to join ~** entrer dans l'Union européenne

European [,jʊərə'pi:ən] ① ADJ européen ② N Européen(ne) *m(f)* ③ COMP ► **European Atomic Energy Community** N Communauté *f* européenne de l'énergie atomique ► **European Bank for Reconstruction and Development** N Banque *f* européenne pour la reconstruction et le développement ► **European Coal and Steel Community** N Communauté *f* européenne du charbon et de l'acier ► **European Commission** N Commission *f* des communautés européennes ► **European Community** N Communauté *f* européenne ► **European Court of Human Rights** N Cour *f* européenne des droits de l'homme ► **European Court of Justice** N Cour *f* de justice européenne *or* des communautés européennes ► **European Currency Unit** N unité *f* de compte européenne, unité *f* monétaire européenne ► **European Defence Community** N Communauté *f* européenne de défense ► **European Economic Community** N Communauté *f* économique européenne ► **European Free Trade Association** N Association *f* européenne de libre-échange ► **European Monetary System** N Système *m* monétaire européen ► **European monetary union** N Union *f* monétaire européenne ► **European Parliament** N Parlement *m* européen ► **European plan** N (*US: in hotel*) chambre *f* sans les repas ► **European Regional Development Fund** N Fonds *m* européen de développement régional ► **European Space Agency** N Agence *f* spatiale européenne ► **European standard** N (*Ind*) norme *f* européenne ► **European Union** N Union *f* européenne

Europeanize [,jʊərə'pɪə,naɪz] VT européaniser

europium [jʊə'rəʊpɪəm] N europium *m*

Eurosceptic [ˈjʊərəʊˌskeptɪk] N eurosceptique *mf*

Euro-size [ˈjʊərəʊˌsaɪz] N (*Comm*) ~ **1** modèle *m* E 1

Eurostar® [ˈjʊərəʊˌstɑːʳ] N Eurostar® *m*

Eurosterling [ˈjʊərəʊˌstɜːlɪŋ] N eurosterling *m*

Eurotunnel® [ˈjʊərəʊˌtʌnl] N Eurotunnel® *m*

Eurovision [ˈjʊərəʊˌvɪʒən] **1** N Eurovision *f* **2** COMP ► **Eurovision Song Contest** N Concours *m* Eurovision de la chanson

Eurydice [jʊˈrɪdɪsɪ] N Eurydice *f*

Eustachian tube [juːˈsteɪʃəntjuːb] N trompe *f* d'Eustache

eustatic [juːˈstætɪk] ADJ eustatique

euthanasia [ˌjuːθəˈneɪzɪə] N euthanasie *f* → **voluntary**

evacuate [ɪˈvækjʊeɪt] VT (*all senses*) évacuer

evacuation [ɪˌvækjʊˈeɪʃən] N évacuation *f*

evacuee [ɪˌvækjʊˈiː] N évacué(e) *m(f)*

evade [ɪˈveɪd] VT [+ *blow, difficulty*] esquiver, éviter ; [+ *pursuers*] échapper à, tromper ; [+ *obligation*] se soustraire à ; [+ *punishment*] échapper à, se soustraire à ; [+ *sb's gaze*] éviter ; [+ *question*] éluder ; [+ *law*] tourner, contourner ; **to ~ military service** se soustraire à ses obligations militaires ; **to ~ taxation/ customs duty** frauder le fisc/la douane

evaluate [ɪˈvæljʊeɪt] VT [+ *damages*] évaluer (**at** à), calculer le montant de ; [+ *property, worth*] évaluer (**at** à), déterminer la valeur de ; [+ *effectiveness, usefulness*] mesurer ; [+ *evidence, reasons, argument*] peser, évaluer ; [+ *sb's work, performance*] évaluer ; (*in essay etc*) **try to ~ the achievements of Victorian architects** essayez d'évaluer l'apport des architectes de l'époque victorienne ; **the market situation is difficult to ~** les tendances du marché sont difficiles à apprécier

evaluation [ɪˌvæljʊˈeɪʃən] N évaluation *f*

evaluative [ɪˈvæljʊətɪv] ADJ [*criteria, research, report*] d'évaluation ; **~ judgement** *or* **assessment** évaluation *f*

evanescent [ˌevəˈnesnt] ADJ (*liter*) évanescent

evangelical [ˌiːvænˈdʒelɪkəl] **1** ADJ (*Rel*) évangélique ; (*fig*) **with ~ fervour** avec une verve de tribun **2** N évangélique *mf*

evangelicalism [ˌiːvænˈdʒelɪkəlɪzəm] N évangélisme *m*

evangelism [ɪˈvændʒəlɪzəm] N évangélisation *f*

evangelist [ɪˈvændʒəlɪst] N (*Bible*) évangéliste *m* ; (= *preacher*) évangélisateur *m*, -trice *f* ; (= *itinerant*) évangéliste *m*

evangelize [ɪˈvændʒəlaɪz] **1** VT évangéliser, prêcher l'Évangile à **2** VI prêcher l'Évangile

evaporate [ɪˈvæpəreɪt] **1** VT [+ *liquid*] faire évaporer **2** VI [*liquid*] s'évaporer ; [*hopes*] s'envoler ; [*dreams, fear, anger*] se dissiper **3** COMP ► **evaporated milk** N lait *m* condensé non sucré

evaporation [ɪˌvæpəˈreɪʃən] N évaporation *f*

evasion [ɪˈveɪʒən] N dérobade *f* (**of** devant) → **tax**

evasive [ɪˈveɪzɪv] ADJ [*person, answer*] évasif (**about sth** à propos de qch) ; [*eyes*] fuyant ; **to take ~ action** (*Mil*) user de manœuvres dilatoires ; (*gen*) esquiver *or* contourner la difficulté

evasively [ɪˈveɪzɪvlɪ] ADV [*reply*] évasivement ; [*smile*] d'un air évasif

evasiveness [ɪˈveɪzɪvˌnɪs] N manières *fpl* évasives

Eve [iːv] N Ève *f*

eve[1] [iːv] N veille *f* ; (*Rel*) vigile *f* ; (*lit, fig*) **on the ~ of sth/of doing** à la veille de qch/de faire → **Christmas**

eve[2] [iːv] N (*liter* = *evening*) soir *m*

even[1] [ˈiːvən] N = **eve**[2]

even[2] [ˈiːvən] **1** ADJ **[a]** (= *smooth, flat*) [*surface*] plat, plan ; [*ground*] plat ; **to make ~** égaliser → **keel**
[b] (= *regular*) [*progress*] régulier ; [*temperature, breathing, step, temper, distribution*] égal ; **his work is not ~** son travail est inégal
[c] (= *equal*) [*quantities, distances, values*] égal ; **our score is ~** nous sommes à égalité ; **they are an ~ match** (*Sport*) la partie est égale ; (*fig*) ils sont (bien) assortis ; **to get ~ with sb** rendre à qn la monnaie de sa pièce, rendre la pareille à qn ; **don't get mad, get ~*** inutile de se mettre en colère, il faut plutôt rendre la pareille ; **I'll get ~ with you for that** je te revaudrai ça ; (*fig*) **the odds** *or* **chances are about ~** les chances sont à peu près égales ; **I'll give you ~ money** *or* **~ odds** (*US*) **that ...** il y a une chance sur deux pour que ... (+ *subj*)
[d] (= *calm*) [*voice, tones, temper*] égal
[e] ► **number/date** nombre *m*/jour *m* pair
2 ADV **[a]** même ; **~ in the holidays** même pendant les vacances ; **~ the most optimistic** même les plus optimistes ; **~ the guards were asleep** même les gardes dormaient ; **I have ~ forgotten his name** j'ai oublié jusqu'à son nom, j'ai même oublié son nom ; **they ~ denied his existence** ils ont été jusqu'à nier *or* ils ont même nié son existence
[b] (+ *compar adj or adv*) encore ; **~ better** encore mieux ; **~ more easily** encore plus facilement ; **~ less money** encore moins d'argent
[c] (+ *neg*) même ; **without ~ saying goodbye** sans même dire au revoir ; **he can't ~ swim** il ne sait même pas nager
[d] (*phrases*) **~ if** même si (+ *indic*) ; **~ though** quand bien même (+ *cond*), même si (+ *indic*) ; **~ though** *or* **~ if he came himself I would not do it** quand bien même il viendrait en personne *or* même s'il venait en personne, je ne le ferais pas ; **if he ~ made an effort** si encore *or* si au moins il faisait un effort ; **... and ~ then she wasn't happy** ... mais elle n'était toujours pas contente ; **~ so he was disappointed** il a quand même *or* pourtant été déçu ; **yes but ~ so ...** oui mais quand même ... ; **~ as he spoke, the door opened** au moment même où il disait cela *or* alors même qu'il disait cela, la porte s'ouvrit ; (*liter*) **~ as he had wished it** précisément comme il l'avait souhaité ; (*liter*) **~ as ... so ...** de même que ... même ...
3 VT [+ *surface*] égaliser
4 evens NPL (*esp Brit*) **the bookmakers are offering ~s** les bookmakers le donnent un contre un
5 COMP ► **even-handed** ADJ impartial, équitable ► **even-handedly** ADV impartialement, équitablement ► **even-handedness** N impartialité *f*, équité *f* ► **evens favourite** N (*esp Brit*) favori *m* à un contre un ► **even-steven*** ADV [*divide*] en deux (parts égales) ♦ ADJ (= *quits*) quitte (**with** avec) ; **it's ~-steven*** **whether we go or stay** peut-être qu'on partira, peut-être qu'on restera ► **even-tempered** ADJ d'humeur égale, placide

► **even out** VT SEP [+ *burden, taxation*] répartir *or* distribuer plus également (**among** entre) ; [+ *prices*] égaliser

► **even up** VT SEP égaliser ; **that will ~ things up** cela rétablira l'équilibre ; (*financially*) cela compensera

evening [ˈiːvnɪŋ] **1** N soir *m* ; (*length of time*) soirée *f* ; **all ~** toute la soirée ; **every ~** tous les soirs, chaque soir ; **every Monday ~** tous les lundis soir(s) ; **the previous ~** la veille au soir ; **that ~** ce soir-là ; **this ~** ce soir ; **tomorrow ~** demain soir ; **one fine summer ~** (par) une belle soirée d'été ; **the warm summer ~s** les chaudes soirées d'été ; **a long winter ~** une longue soirée d'hiver ; **in the ~(s)** le soir ; **to go out in the ~** sortir le soir ; **6 o'clock in the ~** 6 heures du soir ; (*liter*) **in the ~ of life** au soir de la vie ; **on the ~ of his birthday** le soir de son anniversaire ; **on the ~ of the next day** le lendemain soir ; **on the ~ of the twenty-ninth** le vingt-neuf au soir ; **to spend one's ~ reading** passer sa soirée à lire ; **let's have an ~ out** (*tonight*) si on sortait ce soir ? ; (*some time*) nous devrions sortir un de ces soirs ; **it's her ~ out** c'est le soir où elle sort → **good**
2 COMP ► **evening class** N cours *m* du soir ► **evening dress** N [*of man*] tenue *f* de soirée, habit *m* ; [*of woman*] robe *f* du soir ; **in ~ dress** (*man*) en tenue de soirée ; (*woman*) en robe du soir ► **evening fixture, evening match** N (*Sport*) (match *m* en) nocturne *f* ► **evening paper** N journal *m* du soir ► **evening performance** N (représentation *f* en) soirée *f* ► **evening prayer(s)** N(PL) office *m* du soir ► **evening primrose oil** N huile *f* d'onagre ► **evening service** N (*Rel*) service *m* (religieux) du soir ► **evening star** N étoile *f* du berger

evenly [ˈiːvənlɪ] ADV **[a]** (= *equally*) [*distribute*] également ; [*mix*] de façon homogène ; (= *steadily*) [*breathe, beat, flow*] régulièrement ; **to divide/split sth ~** diviser/répartir qch en parts égales ; **~ matched** de force égale ; **~ spaced** à intervalles réguliers ; **an ~ grey sky** un ciel uniformément gris ; **keep your weight ~ balanced** répartissez bien votre poids ; **spread the butter ~** étalez le beurre uniformément ; **the cuts were ~ spread throughout the various departments** les réductions budgétaires ont été réparties uniformément entre les divers services **[b]** (= *calmly*) [*say, ask, reply*] d'une voix égale ; [*watch*] d'un air égal

evenness [ˈiːvənnɪs] N [*of movements, performance*] régularité *f* ; [*of ground*] caractère *m* plan, planéité *f* ; **~ of temper** égalité *f* d'humeur

evensong [ˈiːvənsɒŋ] N (*Rel*) vêpres *fpl*, office *m* du soir (*de l'Église anglicane*)

event [ɪˈvent] **1** N **[a]** (= *happening*) événement *m* ; **course of ~s** (déroulement *m* des) événements *mpl* ; **in the course of ~s** par la suite ; **in the normal** *or* **ordinary course of ~s** normalement ; **after the ~** après coup ; **it's quite an ~** c'est un (véritable) événement → **happy**
[b] (= *case*) cas *m* ; **in the ~ of death** en cas de décès ; (*frm*) **in the ~ of his failing** au cas où il échouerait ; **in the unlikely ~ that ...** dans l'hypothèse improbable où ... ; (*Brit*) **in the ~** (= *confirming sth*) ainsi ; (= *contradicting sth*) en fait, en réalité ; **in this case** dans ce cas ; **in any ~** en tout cas, de toute façon ; **in either ~** dans l'un ou l'autre cas ; (*Jur*) **~ of default** cas *m* de défaillance, manquement *m*
[c] (*Sport*) épreuve *f* ; (*Racing*) course *f* ; **field ~s** lancers *mpl* et sauts *mpl* ; **track ~s** épreuves *fpl* sur piste → **three**
2 COMP ► **event horizon** N (*Astron*) horizon *m* des événements

eventer [ɪˈventəʳ] N (*Horse-riding*) participant(e) *m(f)* à un concours complet

eventful [ɪˈventfʊl] ADJ [*life, day, period, journey*] mouvementé, fertile en événements

eventide [ˈiːventaɪd] **1** N (*liter*) tombée *f* du jour, soir *m* **2** COMP ► **eventide home** N maison *f* de retraite

eventing [ɪˈventɪŋ] N (*Horse-riding*) concours *m* complet

eventual [ɪˈventʃʊəl] ADJ **[a]** (= *resulting*) [*death, failure*] qui s'ensuit ; [*success*] final ; **the ~ winner of the election** le candidat qui a finalement remporté les élections ; **he lost in the semi-final to the ~ winner, McCormack** il a perdu en demi-finale contre McCormack qui a fini par gagner le tournoi ; **it resulted in the ~ disappearance of ...** cela a abouti finalement à la disparition de ... **[b]** (= *possibly resulting*) éventuel ; **any ~ profits** les profits *mpl* éventuels **[c]** (= *ultimate*) [*aim*] ultime

eventuality [ɪˌventʃʊˈælɪtɪ] N éventualité *f*

eventually [ɪˈventʃʊəlɪ] ADV finalement ; **to do sth ~** finir par faire qch ; **he ~ became Prime Minister** il est finalement devenu *or* il a fini par devenir Premier ministre ; **he ~ agreed that she was right** il a fini par admettre qu'elle avait raison

eventuate [ɪˈventʃʊˌeɪt] VI (*US*) (finir par) se produire ; **to ~ in ...** se terminer par ...

ever [ˈevər] ADV [a] (*with negation, doubt*) jamais ; (*with interrogation*) jamais, déjà ; **nothing ~ happens** il ne se passe jamais rien ; **if you ~ see her** si jamais vous la voyez ; **do you ~ see her?** est-ce qu'il vous arrive de la voir ? ; **have you ~ seen her?** l'avez-vous jamais *or* déjà vue ? ; **I haven't ~ seen her** je ne l'ai jamais vue ; **we seldom if ~ go** nous n'y allons pour ainsi dire jamais ; **now if ~ is the moment to do** c'est le moment ou jamais de faire ; **he's a liar if ~ there was one** c'est le dernier des menteurs

[b] (*after compar or superl*) jamais ; **more beautiful than ~** plus beau que jamais ; **faster than ~** plus vite que jamais ; **the best meal I have ~ eaten** le meilleur repas que j'aie jamais fait ; **the best grandmother ~** la meilleure grandmère du monde ; **the coldest night ~** la nuit la plus froide qu'on ait jamais connue

[c] (*at all times*) toujours, sans cesse ; **~ ready** toujours prêt ; **~ after** à partir de ce jour ; **they lived happily ~ after** ils vécurent (toujours) heureux ; **~ since I was a boy** depuis mon enfance ; **~ since I have lived here** depuis que j'habite ici ; **~ since (then) they have been very careful** depuis (lors) *or* depuis ce moment-là ils sont très prudents ; **all he ~ does is sleep** il ne fait que dormir, tout ce qu'il sait faire c'est dormir ; **as ~** comme toujours ; (*Brit: in letters*) **yours ~** amical souvenir, cordialement (à vous) ; **~ increasing anxiety** inquiétude *f* qui ne cesse d'augmenter ; **she is ~ present** elle est toujours là ; **her ~ present anxiety** son angoisse constante *or* de tous les instants ; († , *frm*) **he was ~ courteous** il était toujours poli ; († , *liter*) **~ and anon** de temps à autre, parfois → **forever**

[d] (*intensive*) (*esp Brit*) **although he is** *or* (*frm*) **be he ~ so charming ...** quelque *or* si *or* pour charmant qu'il soit ... ; **as quickly as ~ you can** aussi vite que vous le pourrez ; **as soon as ~ he arrives** aussitôt *or* dès qu'il arrivera ; **the first ~** le tout premier ; **before ~ she came in** avant même qu'elle (ne) soit entrée ; (*esp Brit*) **~ so slightly drunk** (un) tant soit peu ivre ; (*esp Brit*) **so pretty** joli comme tout ; (*esp Brit*) **he is ~ so nice** il est tout ce qu'il y a de plus gentil ; (*esp Brit*) **I'm ~ so sorry** je regrette infiniment, je suis (vraiment) désolé ; (*esp Brit*) **it's ~ such a pity** c'est vraiment dommage ; (*esp Brit*) **thank you ~ so much** ◊ **thanks ~ so*** merci mille fois, merci bien ; (*esp Brit*) **she is ~ so much prettier than her sister** elle est autrement plus jolie que sa sœur ; **as if I ~ would!** comme si je ferais ça !, moi, faire ça ! ; **what ~ shall we do?**† qu'allons nous bien faire ? ; **where ~ can he have got to?**† où a-t-il bien pu passer ? ; **when ~ will they come?**† quand donc viendront-ils ? ; **why ~ not?** mais enfin, pourquoi pas ?, pourquoi pas, Grand Dieu ? ; **did you ~!*** a-t-on jamais vu cela ?, (ça) par exemple !

Everest [ˈevərɪst] N (**Mount**) **~** le mont Everest, l'Everest *m*

everglade [ˈevəɡleɪd] N (*US*) terres *fpl* marécageuses

Everglades [ˈevəɡleɪdz] N Everglades *mpl*

evergreen [ˈevəɡriːn] [1] ADJ [a] [*tree, shrub*] vert, à feuilles persistantes [b] (*fig*) [*song*] qui ne vieillit pas ; [*subject of conversation*] qui revient toujours [2] N [a] (= *tree*) arbre *m* vert *or* à feuilles persistantes ; (= *plant*) plante *f* à feuilles persistantes [b] (*fig* = *song etc*) chanson *f etc* qui ne vieillit pas [c] (*US*) crédit *m* permanent non confirmé [3] COMP
► **evergreen oak** N yeuse *f*, chêne *m* vert

► **the Evergreen State** N (*US*) l'État *m* de Washington

everlasting [ˌevəˈlɑːstɪŋ] [1] ADJ (*God*) éternel ; [*gratitude, mercy*] infini, éternel ; [*fame, glory*] éternel, immortel ; [*materials*] inusable, qui ne s'use pas [2] COMP
► **everlasting flower** N immortelle *f*

everlastingly [ˌevəˈlɑːstɪŋlɪ] ADV éternellement

evermore [ˌevəˈmɔːr] ADV toujours ; **for ~** à tout jamais

every [ˈevrɪ] ADJ [a] (= *each*) tout, chaque, tous (*or* toutes) les ; **~ shop in the town** tous les magasins *or* chaque magasin de la ville ; **not ~ child has the same advantages** les enfants n'ont pas tous les mêmes avantages ; **not ~ child has the advantages you have** tous les enfants n'ont pas les avantages que tu as ; **he spends ~ penny he earns** il dépense tout ce qu'il gagne (jusqu'au dernier sou) ; **~ (single) one of them** chacun d'eux, tous, sans exception ; **~ one of them had brought something** chacun d'entre eux avait apporté quelque chose, ils avaient tous apporté quelque chose ; **~ child had brought something** chaque enfant avait apporté quelque chose ; **~ movement causes him pain** chaque *or* tout mouvement lui fait mal ; **from ~ country** de tous (les) pays ; **at ~ moment** à tout moment, à chaque instant ; **at ~ opportunity** à chaque occasion ; **of ~ sort** de toute sorte ; **from ~ side** de toute part ; **of ~ age** de tout âge ; **he became weaker ~ day** il devenait chaque jour plus faible *or* plus faible de jour en jour

[b] (*for emphasis*) **I have ~ confidence in him** j'ai pleine confiance en lui ; **there is ~ chance that he will come** il y a toutes les chances qu'il vienne ; **you have ~ reason to complain** vous avez tout lieu de vous plaindre ; **I have ~ reason to think that ...** j'ai toutes les raisons de penser que ..., j'ai tout lieu de penser que ... ; **there was ~ prospect of success** tout laissait augurer d'un succès

[c] (*showing recurrence*) tout ; **~ fifth day** ◊ **~ five days** tous les cinq jours, un jour sur cinq ; **~ second** *or* **~ other child** un enfant sur deux ; **one man in ~ ten** un homme sur dix ; **~ quarter of an hour** tous les quarts d'heure ; **~ other** *or* **second day** tous les deux jours, un jour sur deux ; **~ other Wednesday** un mercredi sur deux ; **to write on ~ other line** écrire en sautant une ligne sur deux ; **~ few days** tous les deux ou trois jours ; **once ~ week** une fois par semaine ; **~ 15 metres** tous les 15 mètres

[d] (*after poss*) tout, chacun, moindre ; **his ~ action** chacune de ses actions, tout ce qu'il faisait ; **his ~ wish** son moindre désir, tous ses désirs

[e] (*in phrases*) **he is ~ bit as clever as his brother** il est tout aussi intelligent que son frère ; **he is ~ bit as much of a liar as his brother** il est tout aussi menteur que son frère ; **~ now and then** *or* **~ now and again** ◊ **so often** de temps en temps, de temps à autre ; **~ time (that) I see him** chaque fois que je le vois ; **~ single time** chaque fois sans exception ; **you must examine ~ one** il faut les examiner tous, sans exception ; **~ single one of these peaches is bad** toutes ces pêches sans exception sont pourries ; **~ last biscuit/chocolate** *etc* tous les biscuits/chocolats *etc* jusqu'au dernier ; **~ one of us is afraid of something** tous autant que nous sommes nous craignons quelque chose ; **~ one of them was there** ils étaient tous là ■ (*PROV*) **~ little helps** les petits ruisseaux font les grandes rivières (*PROV*) ; **~ man for himself (and the devil take the hindmost)** chacun pour soi ; (= *save yourself*) sauve qui peut ! ; **~ man to his trade** à chacun son métier ; **in ~ way** (= *from every point of view*) à tous (les) égards, en tous points ; (= *by every means*) par tous les moyens → **bit[1]**

everybody [ˈevrɪbɒdɪ] PRON tout le monde, chacun ; **~ has finished** tout le monde a fini ; **~ has his** *or* **their own ideas about it** chacun a ses idées là-dessus ; **~ else** tous les autres ; **~ knows ~ else here** tout le monde se connaît ici ; **~ knows that** tout le monde *or* n'importe qui sait cela ; **~ who is anybody** tous les gens qui comptent

everyday [ˈevrɪdeɪ] ADJ [*thing, clothes, object, world*] de tous les jours ; [*situation, language*] courant ; [*activity, task, life*] de tous les jours, quotidien ; [*occurrence, problem*] quotidien ; **fabrics for ~ use** des tissus *mpl* pour tous les jours ; **it's too expensive for ~ use** c'est trop cher pour un usage courant ; **words in ~ use** mots *mpl* d'usage courant ; **~ people** gens *mpl* ordinaires

everyman [ˈevrɪmæn] N Monsieur *m* tout-le-monde

everyone [ˈevrɪwʌn] PRON = **everybody**

everyplace [ˈevrɪpleɪs] ADV (*US*) = **everywhere**

everything [ˈevrɪθɪŋ] PRON tout ; **~ is ready** tout est prêt ; **~ you have** tout ce que vous avez ; **stamina is ~** l'endurance compte plus que tout, l'essentiel c'est l'endurance ; **success isn't ~** le succès n'est pas tout ; **and ~ (like that)*** et tout et tout*

everywhere [ˈevrɪwɛər] ADV partout ; **~ in the world** partout dans le monde, dans le monde entier ; **~ you go you meet the British** où qu'on aille *or* partout où l'on va, on rencontre des Britanniques

evict [ɪˈvɪkt] VT (*from house, lodgings, meeting*) expulser

eviction [ɪˈvɪkʃən] [1] N expulsion *f* [2] COMP
► **eviction order** N mandat *m* d'expulsion

evidence [ˈevɪdəns] [1] N (*NonC*) [a] (= *ground for belief*) évidence *f* ; (= *testimony*) témoignage *m* ; **the clearest possible ~** la preuve manifeste ; **the ~ of the senses** le témoignage des sens ; **on the ~ of this document** à en croire ce document

[b] (*Jur*) (= *data*) preuve *f* ; (= *testimony*) témoignage *m*, déposition *f* ; **to give ~** témoigner, déposer ; **to give ~ for/against sb** témoigner *or* déposer en faveur de/contre qn ; **to call sb to give ~** convoquer qn pour qu'il témoigne ; **to take sb's ~** recueillir la déposition de qn ; **to turn King's** *or* **Queen's ~** (*Brit*) ◊ **to turn State's ~** (*US*) témoigner contre ses complices ; **whatever you say may be held in ~ against you** tout ce que vous direz pourra être retenu contre vous

[c] signe *m*, marque *f* ; **to show ~ of** [+ *impatience, worry*] montrer des signes de ; **his kidneys showed ~ of infection** on a trouvé dans ses reins des signes d'infection ; **his features bore ~ of the agony he had endured** ses traits étaient marqués par les épreuves qu'il avait subies

[d] **to be in ~** [*object*] être en évidence ; **his father was nowhere in ~** il n'y avait aucune trace de son père ; **a man very much in ~ at the moment** un homme très en vue à l'heure actuelle

[2] VT manifester, témoigner de

evident [ˈevɪdənt] ADJ évident ; **that is very ~** c'est l'évidence même ; **we must help her, that's ~** il faut l'aider, c'est évident *or* cela va de soi ; **he's guilty, that's ~** il est coupable, c'est évident *or* cela saute aux yeux ; **it was ~ from the way he walked** cela se voyait à sa démarche ; **it is ~ from his speech that ...** il ressort de son discours que ...

▼ **evidently** [ˈevɪdəntlɪ] ADV [a] (= *apparently*) apparemment ; **~ he feared I was going to refuse** il craignait apparemment que je refuse ; **was it suicide? — ~ not** était-ce un suicide ? — apparemment non ; **are they going too? — ~** ils y vont aussi ? — apparemment oui [b] (= *obviously*) manifestement, de toute évidence ; **they ~ knew each other** manifestement *or* de toute évidence, ils se connaissaient ; **that is ~**

► LANGUAGE IN USE: **evidently** 15.1

not the case ce n'est manifestement pas le cas, de toute évidence or à l'évidence ce n'est pas le cas ; **~, such men are usually extremely wealthy** manifestement or de toute évidence or à l'évidence, de tels hommes sont généralement extrêmement riches

evil ['iːvl] [1] ADJ [person] méchant, malfaisant ; [deed, practice, system, consequence, influence] néfaste ; [power] malfaisant ; [place] maléfique ; [spell, reputation] mauvais ; [smell] infect ; **to have an ~ tongue** [person] être mauvaise langue ; (hum) **he had his ~ way with her** il est arrivé à ses fins avec elle ; **to have an ~ temper** avoir un sale caractère ; **(to put off) the ~ day** or **hour** (remettre à plus tard) le moment fatidique

[2] N mal m ; **the powers** or **forces of ~** les forces fpl du mal ; **to wish sb ~** vouloir du mal à qn ; **to speak ~ of sb** dire du mal de qn ; **of two ~s one must choose the lesser** de deux maux, il faut choisir le moindre ; **it's the lesser ~** c'est le moindre mal ; **social ~s** maux mpl sociaux ; **the ~s of drink** les conséquences fpl funestes de la boisson ; **one of the great ~s of our time** un des grands fléaux de notre temps

[3] COMP ► **the evil eye** N le mauvais œil ; **to give sb the ~ eye** jeter le mauvais œil à qn ► **evil-minded** ADJ malveillant, mal intentionné ► **the Evil One** N le Malin ► **evil-smelling** ADJ nauséabond ► **evil spirit** N esprit m malfaisant

evildoer [ˌiːvlˈduːəʳ] N personnage m infâme

evilly ['iːvlɪ] ADV avec malveillance

evince [ɪˈvɪns] VT (frm) [+ surprise, desire] manifester ; [+ qualities, talents] faire preuve de

eviscerate [ɪˈvɪsəreɪt] VT (frm) éventrer, éviscérer

evocation [ˌevəˈkeɪʃən] N évocation f

evocative [ɪˈvɒkətɪv] ADJ [a] (= reminiscent) [name, description, memory, atmosphere, scent] évocateur (-trice f) ; **to be ~ of sth** évoquer qch [b] (Occultism) [incantation, magic] évocatoire

evocatively [ɪˈvɒkətɪvlɪ] ADV [describe] dans un style évocateur

evoke [ɪˈvəʊk] VT [+ spirit, memories] évoquer ; [+ admiration] susciter

evolution [ˌiːvəˈluːʃən] N [a] (Bio, Zool etc) évolution f (from à partir de) ; [of language, events] évolution f ; [of culture, technology, machine] évolution f, développement m [b] [of troops, skaters etc] évolutions fpl

evolutionary [ˌiːvəˈluːʃnərɪ] ADJ (Bio, Zool etc) évolutionniste ; (gen) [stage, process] d'évolution

evolve [ɪˈvɒlv] [1] VT [+ system, theory, plan] élaborer, développer [2] VI (gen, Bio) évoluer ; **to ~ from** se développer à partir de

ewe [juː] [1] N brebis f [2] COMP ► **ewe lamb** N agnelle f

ewer ['juːəʳ] N aiguière f

ex [eks] [1] PREP (Comm) ≈ départ, ≈ sortie ; **price ex factory** ◊ **price ex works** (Brit) prix m départ or sortie usine ; **price ex warehouse** prix m départ or sortie entrepôt → **ex dividend, ex officio** [2] N* ex* mf

ex- [eks] PREF ex-, ancien ; **ex-chairman** ancien président m, ex-président m ; **he's my ex-boss** c'est mon ancien patron → **ex-husband, ex-service**

exacerbate [ɪgˈzæsəˌbeɪt, ɪkˈsæsəˌbeɪt] VT [+ problem, situation] aggraver ; [+ pain, disease, hatred] exacerber

exact [ɪgˈzækt] [1] ADJ [a] (= precise) [number, amount, cause, time, translation, details] exact ; [copy] conforme à l'original, exact ; **to be ~ about sth** préciser qch ; **can you be more ~?** pouvez-vous préciser un peu ? ; **can you be more ~ about how many came?** pouvez-vous préciser le nombre des gens qui sont venus ? ; **he's 44, to be ~** il a 44 ans,

pour être précis ; **he gave ~ instructions as to what had to be done** il a donné des instructions précises sur ce qu'il fallait faire ; **what were his ~ instructions?** quelles étaient ses instructions exactes ? ; **to be an ~ likeness of sb/sth** ressembler parfaitement à qn/qch ; **until this ~ moment** jusqu'à ce moment précis ; **to be the ~ opposite of sb/sth** être aux antipodes or tout le contraire de qn/qch ; **the ~ same thing*** exactement la même chose ; **these were his ~ words** c'est ce qu'il a dit, mot pour mot

[b] (= meticulous) [person, study, work] méticuleux ; [analysis, instrument] précis

[2] VT [+ money, obedience etc] exiger (**from** de) ; **to ~ revenge** se venger ; **to ~ a high price for sth** faire payer qch cher

[3] COMP ► **exact science** N science f exacte

exacting [ɪgˈzæktɪŋ] ADJ [person] exigeant ; [task, activity, profession, work] astreignant, qui exige beaucoup d'attention

exaction [ɪgˈzækʃən] N (= act) exaction f (pej) ; (= money exacted) impôt m, contribution f ; (= excessive demand) extorsion f

exactitude [ɪgˈzæktɪtjuːd] N exactitude f

▼**exactly** [ɪgˈzæktlɪ] ADV (= precisely) [match, imitate] exactement ; **to look ~ like sb** ressembler trait pour trait à qn, être tout le portrait de qn ; **I wanted to get things ~ right** je voulais que tout soit parfait ; **at ~ 5 o'clock** à 5 heures pile or précises ; **it is 3 o'clock ~** il est 3 heures pile or précises, il est exactement 3 heures ; **~ one hour** une heure exactement ; **I had ~ £3** j'avais exactement 3 livres ; **~ the same thing** exactement la même chose ; **that's ~ what I was thinking** c'est exactement ce que je pensais ; **I found it somewhere over there — where ~?** je l'ai trouvé quelque part par là — où exactement ? ; **~ what are you implying?** qu'est-ce que tu veux dire par là or au juste ? ; **so I was wrong — ~** alors j'avais tort — exactement ; **he didn't ~ say no, but ...** il n'a pas vraiment dit non, mais ... ; **we don't ~ know** nous ne savons pas au juste ; **is she sick? — not ~** est-elle malade ? — pas exactement or pas vraiment ; **it's easy work, but not ~ interesting** c'est facile, mais pas vraiment ce qu'on appelle intéressant

exactness [ɪgˈzæktnɪs] N (NonC) [of measurement, words, definition] précision f ; [of translation] fidélité f ; [of copy, description] exactitude f

exaggerate [ɪgˈzædʒəreɪt] [1] VT [a] (= overstate) [+ dangers, fears, size, beauty, story, importance, effect] exagérer ; [+ problem] exagérer l'importance de ; **the press ~d the number of victims** les médias ont gonflé le nombre des victimes [b] (= emphasize) accentuer ; **the dress ~d her paleness** la robe accentuait sa pâleur [2] VI exagérer, forcer la note ; **he always ~s a little** il exagère or il en rajoute* toujours un peu

exaggerated [ɪgˈzædʒəreɪtɪd] ADJ [claim, view, politeness, gesture, report] exagéré ; [praise] outré ; **an ~ sense of one's own importance** une trop haute opinion de soi-même

exaggeratedly [ɪgˈzædʒəreɪtɪdlɪ] ADV [polite] exagérément ; [laugh] d'une manière exagérée

exaggeration [ɪgˌzædʒəˈreɪʃən] N exagération f

exalt [ɪgˈzɔːlt] VT (in rank, power) élever (à un rang plus important) ; (= extol) porter aux nues, exalter

exaltation [ˌegzɔːlˈteɪʃən] N (NonC) exaltation f

exalted [ɪgˈzɔːltɪd] ADJ (= high) [rank, position, style] élevé ; [person] haut placé, de haut rang ; (= elated) [mood, person] exalté

exam [ɪgˈzæm] N (ABBR = **examination 1a**) examen m, exam* m

examination [ɪgˌzæmɪˈneɪʃən] [1] N [a] (Scol, Univ) (= test) examen m ; (each paper) épreuve f ; (Scol) **class ~** composition f ; (Univ etc) **the**

June/September ~s la session de juin/de septembre

[b] (= study, inspection) examen m ; [of machine, premises] inspection f, examen m ; [of question] étude f, considération f ; [of accounts] vérification f ; [of passports] contrôle m ; **Custom's ~** fouille f douanière ; **expert's ~** expertise f ; **close ~** examen m approfondi or détaillé ; **on ~ après examen** ; **on close ~, his papers proved to be false** un examen approfondi or détaillé révéla que ses papiers étaient des faux → **medical**

[c] (Jur) [of suspect, accused] interrogatoire m ; [of witness] audition f ; [of case, documents] examen m ; **legal ~** examen m légal → **cross**

[2] COMP ► **examination board** N (Brit Scol) comité chargé de l'organisation des examens scolaires nationaux ► **examination candidate** N (Scol etc) candidat(e) m(f) ► **examination paper** N (= exam) examen m, épreuve f ; (= question paper) questions fpl or sujet m d'examen ; (= answer paper) copie f ► **examination script** N (Brit) (= answer paper) copie f ; (= question paper) questions fpl or sujet m d'examen

▼**examine** [ɪgˈzæmɪn] [1] VT [a] (gen, Med) examiner ; [+ machine] inspecter ; [+ document, dossier, question, problem, proposition] examiner ; [+ accounts] vérifier ; [+ passport] contrôler ; (Customs) [+ luggage] inspecter, fouiller ; **to ~ a question thoroughly** examiner une question à fond [b] [+ pupil, candidate] faire passer un examen à ; (orally) interroger (**on** sur) [c] (Jur) [+ witness] interroger ; [+ accused] interroger, faire subir un interrogatoire à ; [+ case, document, evidence] examiner

[2] COMP ► **examining board** N (Brit Scol) = **examination board** ; (Univ: for doctorates) jury m de thèse ► **examining magistrate** N (Jur. in France) juge m d'instruction

examinee [ɪgˌzæmɪˈniː] N candidat(e) m(f)

examiner [ɪgˈzæmɪnəʳ] N examinateur m, -trice f (**in** de) → **board, oral, outside**

▼**example** [ɪgˈzaːmpl] N exemple m ; **for ~** par exemple ; **to set a good ~** donner l'exemple ; **to be an ~** [person, sb's conduct, deeds] être un exemple (**to** pour) ; **she's an ~ to us all** c'est un exemple pour nous tous ; **to take sb as an ~** prendre exemple sur qn ; **to follow sb's ~** suivre l'exemple de qn ; **following the ~ of ...** à l'instar de ... ; **to hold sb/sth up as an ~** ériger qn/qch en exemple ; **to make an ~ of sb** punir qn pour l'exemple ; **to punish sb as an ~ to others** punir qn pour l'exemple ; **to quote the ~ of ...** citer l'exemple de ... ; **to quote sth as an ~** citer qch en exemple ; **here is an ~ of the work** voici un échantillon du travail

exasperate [ɪgˈzaːspəreɪt] VT [+ person] exaspérer ; [+ feeling] exaspérer, exacerber

exasperated [ɪgˈzaːspəreɪtɪd] ADJ exaspéré ; **~ at** or **by** or **with sb/sth** exaspéré par qn/qch

exasperating [ɪgˈzaːspəreɪtɪŋ] ADJ exaspérant

exasperatingly [ɪgˈzaːspəreɪtɪŋlɪ] ADV de manière exaspérante ; **~ slow/stupid** d'une lenteur/d'une stupidité exaspérante

exasperation [ɪgˌzaːspəˈreɪʃən] N exaspération f ; **"hurry!" he cried in ~** « dépêchez-vous ! » cria-t-il, exaspéré

ex cathedra [ˌekskəˈθiːdrə] ADJ, ADV ex cathedra

excavate ['ekskəveɪt] [1] VT [+ ground] creuser, excaver ; (Archeol) fouiller ; [+ trench] creuser ; [+ remains] déterrer [2] VI (Archeol) faire des fouilles

excavation [ˌekskəˈveɪʃən] N [a] (NonC) [of tunnel etc] creusement m, percement m ; **~ work** excavations fpl [b] (Archeol = activity, site) fouilles fpl

excavator ['ekskəveɪtəʳ] N [a] (= machine) excavateur m or excavatrice f [b] (Archeol = person) fouilleur m, -euse f

exceed [ɪkˈsiːd] VT (*in value, amount, length of time etc*) dépasser, excéder (**in** en, **by** de); [+ *powers*] [*person*] outrepasser; [*decision etc*] excéder; [+ *expectations, limits, capabilities*] dépasser; [+ *desires*] aller au-delà de, dépasser; **to ~ one's authority** commettre un abus de pouvoir; **to ~ the speed limit** dépasser la vitesse permise, commettre un excès de vitesse; **a fine not ~ing £50** une amende ne dépassant pas or n'excédant pas 50 livres

exceedingly [ɪkˈsiːdɪŋlɪ] ADV extrêmement; **his behaviour troubles me ~** je suis extrêmement troublé par son comportement

excel [ɪkˈsel] [1] VI briller, exceller; **to ~ in** or **at French/tennis** briller en français/au tennis [2] VT **to ~ o.s.** se surpasser, se distinguer

excellence [ˈeksələns] N excellence f

Excellency [ˈeksələnsɪ] N Excellence f; **Your/His** or **Her ~** Votre/Son Excellence

▼ **excellent** [ˈeksələnt] ADJ excellent; **what an ~ idea!** (quelle) excellente idée!; **~!** parfait!; **that's ~!** c'est parfait!

excellently [ˈeksələntlɪ] ADV admirablement

excelsior [ekˈselsjɔʳ] N (*US* = *wood shavings*) copeaux *mpl* d'emballage

except [ɪkˈsept] [1] PREP [a] sauf, excepté, à l'exception de; **all ~ the eldest daughter** tous, excepté la fille aînée, tous, la fille aînée exceptée; **~ (for)** à part, à l'exception de; **~ (that)** sauf que, excepté que; **~ if** sauf si; **~ when** sauf quand, excepté quand [b] (*after neg and certain interrogs*) sinon; **what can they do ~ wait?** que peuvent-ils faire sinon attendre? [2] CONJ (†, *liter*) à moins que + ne (+ *subj*); **~ he be a traitor** à moins qu'il ne soit un traître [3] VT excepter, exclure (**from** de), faire exception de; **not** or **without ~ing** sans excepter, sans oublier; **always ~ing** à l'exception (bien entendu) de, exception faite (bien entendu) de; **present company ~ed** exception faite des personnes présentes

excepting [ɪkˈseptɪŋ] PREP, CONJ = **except 1, 2**

exception [ɪkˈsepʃən] N [a] (*NonC*) exception f; **without ~** sans exception; **with the ~ of ...** à l'exception de ..., exception faite de ...; **to take ~ to** (= *demur*) trouver à redire à, désapprouver; (= *be offended*) s'offenser de, s'offusquer de; **I take ~ to that remark** je suis indigné par cette remarque [b] (= *singularity*) exception f; **to make an ~** faire une exception (**to sth** à qch, **for sb/sth** pour qn/qch); **these strokes of luck are the ~** ces coups de chance sont l'exception; **this case is an ~ to the rule** ce cas est or constitue une exception à la règle; **the ~ proves the rule** l'exception confirme la règle; **with this ~** à cette exception près, à ceci près; **apart from a few ~s** à part quelques exceptions, à de rares exceptions près

exceptionable [ɪkˈsepʃnəbl] ADJ (= *open to objection*) [*conduct*] répréhensible, blâmable; [*proposal*] inadmissible, inacceptable

exceptional [ɪkˈsepʃənl] [1] ADJ (*gen*) exceptionnel; (*Jur*) [*provisions*] dérogatoire; (*Jur*) **to apply ~ arrangements (to)** appliquer un régime dérogatoire (à) [2] COMP ► **exceptional child** N (*pl* **exceptional children**) (*US Scol*) (*gifted*) enfant *mf* surdoué(e); (*handicapped*) (*mentally*) enfant *mf* handicapé(e) mental(e); (*physically*) enfant *mf* handicapé(e)

exceptionally [ɪkˈsepʃənəlɪ] ADV exceptionnellement

excerpt [ˈeksɜːpt] [1] N (*Literat, Mus etc*) extrait *m*, passage *m* [2] VT (*Literat, Mus*) extraire

excess [ɪkˈses] [1] N [a] (*NonC*) [*of precautions, enthusiasm*] excès *m*; [*of details, adjectives*] luxe *m*, surabondance *f*; **to ~** (= *jusqu'*)à l'excès; **to take** or **carry to ~** pousser à l'excès, pousser trop loin; **carried to ~** outré; **in ~ of** [*number*] supérieur à; **in ~ of 50 people have died** plus de 50 personnes sont mortes; **to drink to ~**

boire à l'excès or avec excès; **the ~ of imports over exports** l'excédent *m* des importations sur les exportations [b] (*Brit Insurance*) franchise f [c] **~es** (= *debauchery*) excès *mpl*; (= *cruelty, violence*) excès *mpl*, abus *m*; (= *overindulgence*) excès *mpl*, écart *m*; **the ~es of the regime** les abus or excès du régime [2] COMP [*weight, production*] excédentaire ► **excess baggage** N (*NonC*) excédent *m* de bagages ► **excess demand** N (*Econ*) demande f excédentaire ► **excess employment** N suremploi *m* ► **excess fare** N (*Transport*) supplément *m* ► **excess luggage** N = **excess baggage** ► **excess postage** N (*Brit*) surtaxe f (*pour affranchissement insuffisant*) ► **excess profits tax** N impôt *m* sur les bénéfices exceptionnels ► **excess supply** N (*Econ*) excès *m* de l'offre

excessive [ɪkˈsesɪv] ADJ [*amount, quantity, use, force, speed, demands*] excessif; [*ambition*] démesuré; [*praise*] outré; **~ drinking** abus *m* d'alcool or de boissons alcoolisées

excessively [ɪkˈsesɪvlɪ] ADV [*drink, eat*] à l'excès, avec excès; [*optimistic, proud, ambitious, cautious, centralized*] par trop; [*boring, pretty*] excessivement; **do you worry ~ about work?** avez-vous tendance à vous faire trop de souci pour votre travail?; **his behaviour was impeccable, sometimes ~ so** il se conduisait de manière irréprochable, parfois jusqu'à l'excès

exchange [ɪksˈtʃeɪndʒ] [1] VT [+ *gifts, letters, glances, blows*] échanger; [+ *houses, cars, jobs*] faire un échange de; **to ~ one thing for another** échanger une chose contre une autre; **they ~d a few words** ils échangèrent quelques mots; (*euph*) **to ~ words with sb** (= *quarrel*) avoir des mots avec qn; (*Conveyancing*) **to ~ contracts** ≈ signer les contrats [2] N [a] [*of objects, prisoners, ideas, secrets, notes, greetings*] échange *m*; **in ~** en échange (**for** de); **to give one thing in ~ for another** échanger une chose contre une autre; **to gain/lose on the ~** gagner/perdre au change; (*Conveyancing*) **~ of contracts** ≈ signature f des contrats → **fair¹, part** [b] (*Fin*) change *m*; **foreign ~ office** bureau *m* de change; **at the current rate of ~** au cours actuel du change; **the dollar ~** le change du dollar; **on the (stock) ~** à la Bourse → **bill¹, foreign** [c] (*also* **telephone ~**) central *m*; (*also* **labour ~**) bourse f du travail [d] = **exchange visit** [3] COMP [*student, teacher*] participant(e) *m(f)* à un échange ► **exchange control** N (*Fin*) contrôle *m* des changes; (*Econ*) **~ control regulations** réglementation f des changes ► **exchange law** N droit *m* cambial ► **exchange rate** N taux *m* de change ► **exchange rate mechanism** N mécanisme *m* du taux de change ► **exchange restrictions** NPL restrictions *fpl* de change ► **exchange value** N contre-valeur f ► **exchange visit** N (*Educ etc*) échange *m*; **to be on an ~ visit** faire partie d'un échange

exchangeable [ɪksˈtʃeɪndʒəbl] ADJ échangeable (**for** contre)

exchequer [ɪksˈtʃekəʳ] [1] N [a] (= *state treasury*) ministère *m* des Finances → **chancellor** [b] (* = *one's own funds*) fonds *mpl*, finances *fpl* [2] COMP ► **exchequer bond** N obligation f du Trésor

excisable [ekˈsaɪzəbl] ADJ imposable, soumis aux droits de régie

excise¹ [ˈeksaɪz] [1] N taxe f (**on** sur), accise f (*Belg, Can*); (*Brit*) **the Excise** ≈ l'administration f des impôts indirects [2] COMP ► **excise duties** NPL (*Brit*) impôts *mpl* indirects ► **excise laws** NPL (*US*) lois sur le commerce des boissons

excise² [ekˈsaɪz] VT [a] (*gen*) retrancher, supprimer [b] (*Med*) exciser

exciseman [ˈeksaɪzmæn] N (*pl* **-men**) (*Brit*) agent *m* du fisc (*chargé du recouvrement des impôts indirects*)

excision [ekˈsɪʒən] N (*frm*) [a] (*Med*) excision f [b] (*NonC* = *act of deletion*) [*of words, clause*] suppression f [c] (= *deleted passage: in film, play, book*) coupure f

excitability [ɪkˌsaɪtəˈbɪlɪtɪ] N excitabilité f, nervosité f

excitable [ɪkˈsaɪtəbl] ADJ [*person, animal, temperament*] (*also Med*) excitable; **to be in an ~ state** être tendu

excitableness [ɪkˈsaɪtəblnɪs] N excitabilité f, nervosité f

excite [ɪkˈsaɪt] VT [a] [+ *person, animal*] (*gen, also sexually*) exciter; (= *rouse enthusiasm in*) passionner; **to ~ o.s.** s'exciter, s'énerver [b] [+ *sentiments, envy, attention, pity*] exciter; [+ *imagination, passion*] exciter, enflammer; [+ *desire, anger*] exciter, aviver; [+ *admiration*] exciter, susciter; [+ *curiosity*] exciter, piquer; **to ~ enthusiasm/interest in sb** enthousiasmer/intéresser qn; **the issue has ~d a great deal of debate** le sujet a suscité de nombreux débats [c] (*Med*) [+ *nerve*] exciter, stimuler

excited [ɪkˈsaɪtɪd] ADJ [a] (= *exhilarated*) [*person, voice, shout, laugh, imagination*] excité; [*chatter*] animé; (*sexually*) excité; **he was ~ to hear of this development** il était tout excité d'apprendre ce fait nouveau; **he is ~ at the prospect** il est tout excité à cette idée; **I'm really ~ about it** je suis tout excité à cette idée; **he was ~ about going on holiday** il était tout excité à l'idée de partir en vacances; **to become** or **get ~** s'exciter; **it's nothing to get ~ about** il n'y a pas de quoi s'énerver [b] (= *agitated*) [*person, gesture*] nerveux; [*state*] de nervosité; **to get ~ (about sth)** s'énerver (à propos de qch); **don't get ~!** du calme!, ne t'énerve pas! [c] (*Phys*) [*atom, molecule*] excité

excitedly [ɪkˈsaɪtɪdlɪ] ADV [*say, talk, chatter*] sur un ton animé, avec animation; [*grin*] d'un air excité; [*laugh*] avec excitation; [*behave*] avec agitation; [*run*] tout excité; **to wave ~** gesticuler

excitement [ɪkˈsaɪtmənt] N [*of people*] excitation f; [*of event*] fièvre f; **the ~ of the departure** l'excitation or la fièvre du départ; **the ~ of a trip to the fair** la perspective excitante d'une visite à la fête foraine; **the ~ of the elections** la fièvre des élections; **to be in a state of great ~** être dans un état de très grande excitation; **the ~ of victory** l'ivresse f de la victoire; **the book caused great ~ in literary circles** le livre a fait sensation dans les milieux littéraires; **there was great ~ when she announced that ...** elle a suscité un grand émoi lorsqu'elle a annoncé que ...; **he likes ~** il aime les émotions fortes; **she's looking for a bit of ~ in her life** elle cherche à donner un peu de piquant à sa vie; **this sport has plenty of ~s** ce sport est excitant à bien des égards; **the ~ of getting a book published** l'excitation que l'on ressent à la publication d'un livre; **the ~ of being in love** l'ivresse f que l'on ressent lorsqu'on est amoureux; **sexual ~** excitation f sexuelle; **with growing ~ he turned the key in the lock** de plus en plus excité, il a tourné la clé dans la serrure

exciting [ɪkˈsaɪtɪŋ] ADJ (= *exhilarating*) [*activity, experience, opportunity, idea, news, book*] passionnant; (*sexually*) [*person*] excitant; **he's ~ to be with** c'est passionnant d'être avec lui; **how ~!** comme c'est excitant or passionnant!; **we had an ~ time** nous avons passé des moments passionnants; **to be ~ to sb** être excitant or palpitant pour qn

excitingly [ɪkˈsaɪtɪŋlɪ] ADV [*describe*] de façon passionnante; **an ~ original writer** un écrivain d'une originalité passionnante

excl. ABBR = **excluding, exclusive (of)**

exclaim [ɪksˈkleɪm] [1] VI (*gen*) s'exclamer; **he ~ed in surprise when he saw it** il a laissé échapper une exclamation de surprise en le voyant; **to ~ at sth** (*indignantly*) s'exclamer d'indignation devant qch; (*admiringly*) s'exclamer d'admiration devant qch 2 VT s'écrier (**that** que); **"at last!" she ~ed** « enfin ! » s'écria-t-elle

exclamation [,eksklə'meɪʃən] 1 N exclamation f 2 COMP ► **exclamation mark**, **exclamation point** (US) N point m d'exclamation

exclamatory [ɪks'klæmətərɪ] ADJ exclamatif

exclude [ɪks'klu:d] VT (*from team, society*) exclure (**from** de); (*Brit: from school*) exclure temporairement; (*from list*) écarter (**from** de), ne pas retenir; (*from meeting, discussions, process*) écarter, exclure; [+ *possibility*] exclure, écarter; [+ *sun's rays, germs*] faire écran à; **red meat is ~d from this diet** ce régime interdit la viande rouge; **women were ~d from participation/from competing** les femmes n'avaient pas le droit de participer/de prendre part à la compétition; **to ~ sth from consideration** refuser de prendre qch en considération; **to ~ from the jurisdiction of** soustraire à la compétence de; **the price ~s VAT** le prix est hors taxe; **£200, excluding VAT** 200 livres, hors taxe; **a meal here costs about £15 per head excluding wine** un repas ici coûte environ 15 livres par personne, vin non compris

excluding [ɪks'klu:dɪŋ] PREP à l'exclusion de, à part

exclusion [ɪks'klu:ʒən] 1 N exclusion f (**from** de); **to the ~ of ...** à l'exclusion de ... 2 COMP ► **exclusion clause** N clause f d'exclusion ► **exclusion order** N (Brit Jur) (*from country*) interdiction f de territoire *or* de séjour; (*against spouse*) interdiction f de domicile conjugal ► **exclusion zone** N zone f d'exclusion

exclusionary [ɪks'klu:ʒənərɪ] ADJ [*practice*] d'exclusive

exclusive [ɪks'klu:sɪv] 1 ADJ a (= *select*) [*person, friendship, interest, occupation*] exclusif; [*club*] fermé; [*district, resort, hotel, restaurant*] chic inv; [*gathering*] sélect b (= *sole*) [*use, offer, contract, property, story, picture*] exclusif; **~ to readers of ...** exclusivement pour les lecteurs de ...; **this special offer is ~ to (readers of) this magazine** cette offre spéciale est réservée à nos lecteurs; **an interview ~ to ...** une interview exclusive accordée à ...; **to have ~ rights to sth** avoir l'exclusivité de qch c (= *not including*) **to be ~ of sth** exclure qch; **~ of postage and packing** frais d'expédition non compris; **from 15 to 20 June** = du 15 au 19 juin inclus; (*Comm*) **~ of taxes** hors taxes, taxes non comprises → **mutually** 2 N (*Press*) exclusivité f

exclusively [ɪks'klu:sɪvlɪ] ADV exclusivement; **available ~ from ...** en vente exclusivement chez ...; **~ available to readers of ...** réservé exclusivement aux lecteurs de ...

exclusivity [ɪksklu:'sɪvətɪ] N exclusivité f

excommunicate [,ekskə'mju:nɪkeɪt] VT excommunier

excommunication ['ekskə,mju:nɪ'keɪʃən] N excommunication f

ex-con: [,eks'kɒn] N ancien taulard: m

excoriate [ɪk'skɔ:rɪeɪt] VT (*frm*) [+ *person*] chapitrer; [+ *organization*] condamner; [+ *idea*] fustiger

excrement ['ekskrɪmənt] N excrément m

excrescence [ɪks'kresns] N (*lit, fig*) excroissance f

excreta [ɪks'kri:tə] NPL excrétions fpl; (= *excrement*) excréments mpl, déjections fpl

excrete [ɪks'kri:t] VT excréter; [*plant*] sécréter

excretion [ɪks'kri:ʃən] N excrétion f, sécrétion f

excretory [ɪk'skri:tərɪ] ADJ (*Physiol*) excréteur (-trice f), excrétoire

excruciating [ɪks'kru:ʃɪeɪtɪŋ] ADJ [*pain, suffering, sight, sound, boredom*] insoutenable; [*death*] atroce; [*joke*] lamentable; **I was in ~ pain** je souffrais comme un damné; **in ~ detail** dans les moindres détails

excruciatingly [ɪks'kru:ʃɪeɪtɪŋlɪ] ADV [*painful*] atrocement; [*difficult, humiliating*] affreusement; **~ funny** désopilant

exculpate ['ekskʌlpeɪt] VT [+ *person*] disculper, innocenter (**from** de); **to ~ sb of** *or* **from responsibility** juger qn non responsable

excursion [ɪks'kɜ:ʃən] 1 N excursion f, balade* f; (*on foot, cycle*) randonnée f; (*fig* = *digression*) digression f 2 COMP ► **excursion ticket** N billet m excursion ► **excursion train** N train m spécial (*pour excursions*)

excusable [ɪks'kju:zəbl] ADJ excusable, pardonnable

▼**excuse** [ɪks'kju:z] 1 VT a (= *justify*) [+ *action, person*] excuser; **such rudeness cannot be ~d** une telle impolitesse est inexcusable; **to ~ o.s.** s'excuser (**for** de), présenter ses excuses b (= *pardon*) excuser (**sb for having done** qn d'avoir fait); **to ~ sb's insolence** excuser l'insolence de qn, pardonner à qn son insolence; **one can be ~d for not understanding what she says** il est excusable de ne pas comprendre ce qu'elle dit; **if you will ~ the expression** ◊ **~ my French** (*hum*) passez-moi l'expression; **and now if you will ~ me, I have work to do** et maintenant, si vous voulez bien m'excuser, j'ai du travail à faire; **~ me for wondering if ...** permettez-moi de me demander si ...; **~ me!** excusez-moi!, (*je vous demande*) pardon!; **~ me, but I don't think this is true** excusez-moi, mais je ne crois pas que ce soit vrai; **~ me for not seeing you out** excusez-moi si je ne vous raccompagne pas *or* de ne pas vous raccompagner c (= *exempt*) exempter (**sb from sth** qn de qch), dispenser (**sb from sth** qn de qch, **sb from doing** qn de faire), excuser; (*to children*) **you are ~d** vous pouvez vous en aller; **he ~d himself after ten minutes** au bout de dix minutes, il s'est excusé et est parti; **to ask to be ~d** demander à être excusé; **he was ~d from the afternoon session** on l'a dispensé d'assister à la séance de l'après-midi; **to ~ sb from an obligation** dispenser qn d'une obligation

2 [ɪks'kju:s] N a (= *reason, justification*) excuse f; **there is no ~ for it** ◊ **it admits of no ~** (*frm*) c'est inexcusable; **his only ~ was that ...** sa seule excuse était que ...; **that is no ~ for his leaving so abruptly** cela ne l'excuse pas d'être parti si brusquement; **in ~ for** pour s'excuser de; **without ~** sans excuse → **ignorance** b (= *pretext*) excuse f, prétexte m; **a lame ~** une piètre excuse, une excuse boiteuse; **to find an ~ for sth** trouver une excuse à qch; **I have a good ~ for not going** j'ai une bonne excuse pour ne pas y aller; (*gen*) **to make an ~ for sth/for doing** trouver une *or* des excuse(s) à qch/pour faire; **he's just making ~s** il se cherche des excuses; **he is always making ~s to get away** il trouve *or* invente toujours des excuses pour s'absenter; **what's your ~ this time?** qu'avez-vous comme excuse cette fois-ci ?; **he gave the bad weather as his ~ for not coming** il a prétexté *or* allégué le mauvais temps pour ne pas venir; **it's only an ~** ce n'est qu'un prétexte; **his success was a good ~ for a family party** ce succès a fourni le prétexte à une fête de famille

3 COMP ► **excuse-me (dance)** N (*Brit*) danse où l'on change de partenaire, ≈ danse f du balai

▼**ex-directory** [,eksdɪ'rektərɪ] ADJ (*Brit Telec*) qui ne figure pas dans l'annuaire, ≈ qui est sur la liste rouge; **he's gone ~** il s'est fait mettre sur la liste rouge

ex dividend ['eks'dɪvɪ,dend] ADJ (*St Ex*) ex-dividende

execrable ['eksɪkrəbl] ADJ exécrable

execrably ['eksɪkrəblɪ] ADV exécrablement

execrate ['eksɪkreɪt] VT (*liter*) a (= *hate*) exécrer b (= *curse*) maudire

execration [,eksɪ'kreɪʃən] N (*liter*) a (*NonC*) exécration f (*liter*), horreur f; **to hold in ~** exécrer (*liter*) b (= *curse*) malédiction f, imprécation f

executable ['eksɪkju:təbl] ADJ exécutable; (*Comput*) **~ program** application f

executant [ɪg'zekjutənt] N (*Mus*) interprète mf, exécutant(e) m(f)

execute ['eksɪkju:t] VT a (= *carry out*) [+ *order, piece of work, dance, movement*] exécuter; [+ *work of art*] réaliser; [+ *project, plan*] exécuter, mettre à exécution; [+ *purpose, sb's wishes*] accomplir; [+ *duties*] exercer, remplir; [+ *task*] accomplir, s'acquitter de; (*Mus*) exécuter, interpréter; (*Jur*) [+ *will*] exécuter; [+ *document*] valider; [+ *deed*] signer; [+ *contract*] valider b (= *put to death*) exécuter

execution [,eksɪ'kju:ʃən] N a (= *carrying out*) [*of task, order, will, warrant, dance, sculpture*] exécution f; [*of plan*] exécution f, réalisation f; [*of wishes*] accomplissement m; [*of song*] interprétation f; [*of treaty*] application f; **in the ~ of his duties** dans l'exercice m de ses fonctions; **to carry** *or* **put sth into ~** mettre qch à exécution b → **stay**

executioner [,eksɪ'kju:ʃnə] N (*also* **public ~**) bourreau m, exécuteur m des hautes œuvres

executive [ɪg'zekjutɪv] 1 ADJ a (*Govt, Ind, Comm*) [*power, decision, function, role*] directorial; [*position, pay*] de cadre; [*car*] de fonction; **the ~ arm of the organization** l'organe exécutif de l'organisation; **~ capability** capacité f d'exécution b (*esp Brit* = *up-market*) [*briefcase, chair*] de luxe

2 N a (*Admin, Ind etc* = *person*) cadre m; **senior/junior ~** cadre m supérieur/moyen; **a Shell/IBM ~** un cadre (de chez) Shell/IBM; **a sales/production ~** un cadre du service des ventes/du service production; **a woman** *or* **female ~** une femme cadre → **chief** b (= *managing group: of organization*) bureau m; **to be on the ~** faire partie du bureau; **the trade union/party ~** le bureau du syndicat/du parti c (= *part of government*) (pouvoir m) exécutif m

3 COMP ► **executive agreement** N (*US Pol*) accord conclu entre chefs d'État ► **executive board** N (*Admin, Ind*) conseil m de direction ► **executive branch** N (*Admin, Ind, Govt*) organe m exécutif ► **executive burnout** N épuisement m du cadre ► **executive chairman** N (*pl* **executive chairmen**) directeur m exécutif ► **executive committee** N (*Admin, Ind*) comité m exécutif ► **executive council** N (*Admin, Ind*) conseil m exécutif *or* de direction; (*US Pol*) conseil m exécutif ► **executive director** N directeur m exécutif ► **executive lounge** N salon m classe affaires ► **the Executive Mansion** (*US*) (= *White House*) la Maison-Blanche; (= *Governor's house*) la résidence officielle du gouverneur (*d'un État américain*) ► **executive member** N membre m du bureau exécutif ► **the Executive Office of the President** N (*US*) le cabinet du président (*des États-Unis*), la Présidence (*des États-Unis*) ► **executive officer** N [*of organization*] cadre m administratif; (*US Mil, Naut*) commandant m en second ► **executive order** N (*US*) décret-loi m ► **executive president** N président m exécutif ► **executive privilege** N (*US Pol*) privilège du président de ne pas communiquer certaines informations ► **executive producer** N (*Cine, Theat, TV*) producteur m exécutif ► **executive relief** N (*NonC: euph*) ≈ le cinq

à sept du cadre ► **executive secretary** N secrétaire *mf* de direction ► **executive session** N (*US Govt*) séance *f* à huis clos ► **the executive suite (of offices)** N les bureaux *mpl* de la direction ► **executive toy** N (*for play*) gadget *m* de bureau ; (*as status symbol*) gadget *m* de luxe

┌─ **EXECUTIVE PRIVILEGE** ─┐

Le «privilège de l'exécutif» est le droit dont bénéficie le président des États-Unis de ne pas divulguer au Congrès ou au pouvoir judiciaire certaines informations jugées confidentielles ou devant rester secrètes pour des raisons de sécurité nationale. Plusieurs présidents ont tenté d'obtenir un droit au secret total, y compris pour des motifs personnels, mais la Cour suprême s'y est opposée. Ainsi, pendant l'affaire du Watergate, elle a rejeté la requête du président Nixon, qui invoquait ce privilège pour refuser de livrer des enregistrements à la commission d'enquête du Sénat.

executor [ɪgˈzekjʊtər] N (*Jur*) exécuteur *m* testamentaire

executrix [ɪgˈzekjʊtrɪks] N (*pl* **executrixes** or **executrices** [ɪg,zekjʊˈtraɪsiːz]) (*Jur*) exécutrice *f* testamentaire

exegesis [,eksɪˈdʒiːsɪs] N (*pl* **exegeses** [,eksɪˈdʒiːsiːz]) exégèse *f*

exemplar [ɪgˈzemplɑː] N (= *model*) exemple *m*, modèle *m*

exemplary [ɪgˈzemplərɪ] ① ADJ exemplaire ; **~ in one's conduct** d'une conduite exemplaire ② COMP ► **exemplary damages** NPL (*Jur*) dommages-intérêts *mpl* pour préjudice moral

exemplification [ɪg,zemplɪfɪˈkeɪʃən] N exemplification *f*

exemplify [ɪgˈzemplɪfaɪ] VT (= *illustrate*) exemplifier, illustrer ; (= *be example of*) servir d'exemple de, être un exemple de ; (*Jur*) **exemplified copy** expédition *f*, copie *f* certifiée

exempt [ɪgˈzempt] ① ADJ exempt (**from** de) ② VT exempter (**from sth** de qch), dispenser (**from doing** de faire)

exemption [ɪgˈzempʃən] N exonération *f* (**from** de) ; (*Educ*) dispense *f* (**from** de) ; (*Jur*) dérogation *f* ; **tax ~** exonération *f* fiscale

exercise [ˈeksəsaɪz] ① N ⓐ (*NonC* = *putting into practice*) [*of right, caution, power*] exercice *m* ; [*of religion*] pratique *f*, exercice *m* ; **in the ~ of his duties** dans l'exercice de ses fonctions ⓑ (= *physical exertion*) exercice *m* ; **to take ~** faire de l'exercice ; **to do (physical) ~s every morning** faire de la gymnastique tous les matins ⓒ (= *task*) exercice *m* ; **a grammar ~** un exercice de grammaire ⓓ (*Mil etc: gen pl*) exercice *m*, manœuvre *f* ; **to go on (an) ~** (*Mil*) aller à l'exercice ; (*Naut*) partir en manœuvre ; **NATO ~s** manœuvres *fpl* de l'OTAN ⓔ (= *sth carried out*) opération *f* ; **an ~ in public relations/in management** *etc* une opération de relations publiques/de gestion des affaires *etc* ; **a cost-cutting ~** une opération de réduction des coûts ; **an ~ in futility** le type même de l'entreprise inutile ② **exercises** NPL (*US* = *ceremony*) cérémonies *fpl* ③ VT ⓐ (= *exert*) [+ *body, mind*] exercer ; [+ *troops*] faire faire l'exercice à ; [+ *horse*] exercer ; **to ~ one's dog** faire courir son chien ⓑ (= *use, put into practice*) [+ *one's authority, control, power*] exercer ; [+ *a right*] exercer, user de ; [+ *one's talents*] employer, exercer ; [+ *patience, tact, restraint*] faire preuve de ; **to ~ care in doing** apporter du soin à faire, s'appliquer à bien faire ⓒ (*frm = preoccupy*) préoccuper ; **the problem which is exercising my mind** le problème qui me préoccupe ④ VI faire de l'exercice

⑤ COMP ► **exercise bike** N vélo *m* d'appartement ► **exercise book** N (*for writing in*) cahier *m* (d'exercices or de devoirs) ; (= *book of exercises*) livre *m* d'exercices ► **exercise yard** N [*of prison*] cour *f* (de prison)

exerciser [ˈeksəsaɪzə] N (= *person*) personne *f* qui fait de l'exercice ; (= *machine*) exerciseur *m*

exercycle [ˈeksəsaɪkl] N vélo *m* d'appartement

exert [ɪgˈzɜːt] VT ⓐ [+ *pressure*] exercer ; [+ *force*] employer ; [+ *talent, influence*] exercer, déployer ; [+ *authority*] exercer, faire sentir ⓑ **to ~ o.s.** (*physically*) se dépenser ; (= *take trouble*) se donner du mal, s'appliquer ; **to ~ o.s. to do** s'appliquer à or s'efforcer de faire ; **he didn't ~ himself unduly** il ne s'est pas donné trop de mal, il ne s'est pas trop fatigué ; (*iro*) **don't ~ yourself!** ne vous fatiguez pas !

exertion [ɪgˈzɜːʃən] N ⓐ effort *m* ; **by his own ~s** par ses propres moyens ; **after the day's ~s** après les fatigues *fpl* de la journée ; **it doesn't require much ~** cela n'exige pas un grand effort ⓑ (*NonC*) [*of force, strength*] emploi *m* ; [*of authority, influence*] exercice *m* ; **by the ~ of a little pressure** (*lit*) en exerçant une légère pression ; (*fig*) en utilisant la manière douce

exeunt [ˈeksɪʌnt] VI (*Theat*) ils sortent ; **~ Macbeth and Lady Macbeth** Macbeth et Lady Macbeth sortent

exfoliate [eksˈfəʊlɪeɪt] ① VT (*Bio, Geol*) exfolier ; (*Cosmetics*) gommer ② VI (*Bio, Geol*) s'exfolier ; (*Cosmetics*) se faire un gommage (de la peau) ③ COMP ► **exfoliating cream** N crème *f* exfoliante

exfoliation [eks,fəʊlɪˈeɪʃən] N (*Bio, Geol*) exfoliation *f* ; (*Cosmetics*) gommage *m* ; **frequent ~ is good for the skin** un gommage fréquent est bon pour la peau

ex gratia [,eksˈgreɪʃə] ADJ [*payment*] à titre gracieux

exhalation [,ekshəˈleɪʃən] N ⓐ (= *act*) exhalation *f* ⓑ (= *odour, fumes etc*) exhalaison *f*

exhale [eksˈheɪl] ① VT ⓐ (= *breathe out*) expirer (*Physiol*) ⓑ (= *give off*) [+ *smoke, gas, perfume*] exhaler ② VI expirer ; **~ please** expirez s'il vous plaît ; **he ~d slowly in relief** il a laissé échapper un long soupir de soulagement

exhaust [ɪgˈzɔːst] ① VT ⓐ (= *use up*) [+ *supplies, energy, mine, subject*] épuiser ; **to ~ sb's patience** pousser qn à bout ⓑ (= *tire*) épuiser, exténuer ; **to ~ o.s. (doing)** s'épuiser (à faire) ② (*Aut*) (= *system*) échappement *m* ; (= *pipe*) tuyau *m* or pot *m* d'échappement ; (= *fumes*) gaz *m* d'échappement

exhausted [ɪgˈzɔːstɪd] ADJ ⓐ (= *tired out*) [*person*] épuisé (**from doing** d'avoir fait) ; **their horses were ~ from** or **with the chase** la poursuite avait épuisé leurs chevaux ; **I'm ~** je suis épuisé, je n'en peux plus ⓑ (= *used up*) [*supplies, savings, mine*] épuisé ; **my patience is ~** ma patience est à bout ; **until funds are ~** jusqu'à épuisement des fonds

exhaustible [ɪgˈzɔːstɪbl] ADJ [*resources*] non renouvelable ; [*patience*] limité, qui a des limites

exhausting [ɪgˈzɔːstɪŋ] ADJ épuisant

exhaustion [ɪgˈzɔːstʃən] N épuisement *m*

exhaustive [ɪgˈzɔːstɪv] ADJ [*list, study, report, analysis, research, investigation*] exhaustif ; [*coverage*] exhaustif, complet (-ète *f*) ; [*search*] minutieux ; [*tests*] approfondi, poussé ; **to make an ~ study of sth** étudier qch à fond or de manière exhaustive

exhaustively [ɪgˈzɔːstɪvlɪ] ADV [*research, cover, list, describe*] de manière exhaustive ; [*study*] à fond, de manière exhaustive ; **they searched the area ~** ils ont minutieusement fouillé la région

exhaustiveness [ɪgˈzɔːstɪvnɪs] N exhaustivité *f*

exhibit [ɪgˈzɪbɪt] ① VT ⓐ (= *put on display*) [+ *painting, handicrafts*] exposer ; [+ *merchandise*] exposer, étaler ; [+ *animal*] montrer ⓑ [+ *courage, skill, ingenuity*] faire preuve de, déployer ; [+ *tendencies*] montrer, afficher ; [+ *behaviour*] afficher ; [+ *symptoms*] présenter ; **some people may ~ allergic reactions to this substance** certaines personnes développent or présentent des réactions allergiques à cette substance ② VI [*artist, sculptor*] exposer ; **dog breeders who ~ all over the country** des éleveurs de chiens qui participent à des concours dans tout le pays ③ N ⓐ (= *object on display: in exhibition*) pièce *f* exposée (*dans un musée etc*) ⓑ (*Jur*) pièce *f* à conviction ; **~ A** première pièce *f* à conviction ⓒ (*US* = *exhibition*) exposition *f* ; **a photography ~** une exposition de photographies ; **a retrospective ~** une rétrospective

exhibition [,eksɪˈbɪʃən] ① N ⓐ (= *show*) [*of paintings, furniture etc*] exposition *f* ; [*of articles for sale*] étalage *m* ; **the Van Gogh ~** l'exposition *f* Van Gogh ; (*fig*) **to make an ~ of o.s.** se donner en spectacle ⓑ (= *act of exhibiting*) [*of technique etc*] démonstration *f* ; [*of film*] présentation *f* ; **what an ~ of bad manners!** quel étalage de mauvaises manières ! ⓒ (*Brit Univ*) bourse *f* (d'études) ② COMP ► **exhibition centre** N centre *m* d'expositions ► **exhibition match** N (*Sport*) match-exhibition *m*

exhibitioner [,eksɪˈbɪʃənə] N (*Brit Univ*) boursier *m*, -ière *f*

exhibitionism [,eksɪˈbɪʃənɪzəm] N exhibitionnisme *m*

exhibitionist [,eksɪˈbɪʃənɪst] ADJ, N exhibitionniste *mf*

exhibitor [ɪgˈzɪbɪtər] N exposant(e) *m(f)* (*dans une exposition*)

exhilarate [ɪgˈzɪləreɪt] VT [*sea air etc*] vivifier ; [*music, wine, good company*] rendre euphorique ; **to be** or **feel ~d** être en pleine euphorie

exhilarating [ɪgˈzɪləreɪtɪŋ] ADJ [*experience, time, feeling, ride*] grisant ; [*air, breeze*] vivifiant ; [*activity*] exaltant ; **it is ~ to do that** c'est grisant de faire cela

exhilaration [ɪg,zɪləˈreɪʃən] N ivresse *f*, euphorie *f*

exhort [ɪgˈzɔːt] VT exhorter (**sb to sth** qn à qch, **sb to do** qn à faire)

exhortation [,egzɔːˈteɪʃən] N exhortation *f* (**to sth** à qch, **to do sth** à faire qch) ; **despite ~s to investors to buy** bien que l'on ait exhorté les investisseurs à acheter

exhumation [,ekshjuːˈmeɪʃən] ① N exhumation *f* ② COMP ► **exhumation order** N (*Jur*) autorisation *f* d'exhumer

exhume [eksˈhjuːm] VT exhumer

ex-husband [,eksˈhʌzbənd] N ex-mari *m*

exigence [ˈeksɪdʒəns], **exigency** [ˈeksɪdʒənsɪ] N (*frm*) (= *urgency*) urgence *f* ; (= *emergency*) circonstance *f* or situation *f* critique ; (*gen pl* = *demand*) exigence *f* ; **according to the exigencies of the situation** selon les exigences de la situation

exigent [ˈeksɪdʒənt] ADJ (*frm*) (= *urgent*) urgent, pressant ; (= *exacting*) exigeant

exiguity [,egzɪˈgjuːɪtɪ] N (*frm*) exiguïté *f*

exiguous [ɪgˈzɪgjʊəs] ADJ (*frm*) [*space*] exigu (-güe *f*) ; [*savings, income, revenue*] maigre

exile [ˈeksaɪl] ① N ⓐ (= *person*) exilé(e) *m(f)* ⓑ (*NonC* = *condition: lit, fig*) exil *m* ; **in ~** en exil ; **to send into ~** envoyer en exil, exiler ; **to go into ~** s'exiler ② VT exiler, bannir (**from** de)

exiled [ˈeksaɪld] ADJ exilé, en exil

exist [ɪgˈzɪst] VI ⓐ (= *be in existence: gen, Philos*) exister ; **everything that ~s** tout ce qui existe ; **does God ~?** est-ce que Dieu existe ? ; **might life ~ on Mars?** est-ce qu'il peut y avoir de la vie sur Mars?; **it only ~s in her imagination** cela n'existe que dans son imagination; **the understanding which ~s between the two countries** l'entente qui règne or existe entre les deux pays; **the ceasefire now ~s only on paper** or **in name only** à présent, le cessez-le-feu n'existe plus que sur le papier; **to continue to ~** [*situation, conditions, doubt*] subsister; [*institution*] rester en place; [*person*] (*after death*) continuer à exister; **to cease to ~** cesser d'exister, disparaître; **there ~s a large number of people who ...** il existe un grand nombre de gens qui ...; **there ~s a possibility** or **the possibility ~s that she is still alive** il se peut qu'elle soit toujours vivante **b** (= *live*) vivre, subsister; **we cannot ~ without water** nous ne pouvons pas vivre or subsister sans eau; **we ~ on an income of just £90 per week** nous vivons or subsistons avec seulement 90 livres par semaine; **she ~s on junk food** elle se nourrit de cochonneries

existence [ɪgˈzɪstəns] N **a** (*NonC*) [*of God, person, object, institution*] existence *f*; **to be in ~** exister; **to come into ~** voir le jour; **to call into ~** faire naître, créer; **it passed** or **went out of ~ ten years ago** cela n'existe plus depuis dix ans; **the only one in ~** le seul or la seule qui existe (*subj*) or qui soit **b** (= *life*) existence *f*, vie *f*

existent [ɪgˈzɪstənt] ADJ (*frm*) existant

existential [ˌegzɪˈstenʃəl] ADJ existentiel

existentialism [ˌegzɪˈstenʃəlɪzəm] N existentialisme *m*

existentialist [ˌegzɪˈstenʃəlɪst] ADJ, N existentialiste *mf*

existing [ɪgˈzɪstɪŋ] ADJ [*system, arrangements, customers, facilities, product, border*] actuel; [*law, order*] existant; **under ~ circumstances** dans les circonstances actuelles

exit [ˈeksɪt] **1** N **a** (*from stage, competition, motorway*) sortie *f*; **to make one's ~** (*Theat*) quitter la scène, faire sa sortie; (*gen*) sortir, quitter les lieux **b** (= *way out, door*) sortie *f* → **emergency c** (*voluntary euthanasia society*) **Exit** ≈ Mourir dans la Dignité **2** VI **a** (*Theat*) **~ the King** le roi sort **b** (= *leave*) sortir, faire sa sortie **c** (*Comput*) sortir **3** VT (*Comput*) [+ *file, program, application*] sortir de, quitter **4** COMP ▸ **exit permit** N permis *m* de sortie ▸ **exit poll** N (*at election*) sondage *m* effectué à la sortie des bureaux de vote ▸ **exit ramp** N (*US Aut*) bretelle *f* d'accès ▸ **exit visa** N visa *m* de sortie

ex nihilo [ˌeksˈnɪhɪləʊ] ADV ex nihilo

exocrine [ˈeksəʊˌkraɪn] ADJ exocrine

exodus [ˈeksədəs] N exode *m*; **there was a general ~** il y a eu un exode massif; (*Bible*) **Exodus** l'Exode *m*

ex officio [ˌeksəˈfɪʃɪəʊ] (*frm*) **1** ADV [*act*] ès qualités **2** ADJ [*member*] de droit

exonerate [ɪgˈzɒnəreɪt] VT (= *prove innocent*) disculper (**from** de), innocenter; (= *release from obligation*) dispenser (**from** de)

exoneration [ɪgˌzɒnəˈreɪʃən] N disculpation *f* (**from sth** de qch)

exorbitance [ɪgˈzɔːbɪtəns] N [*of demands*] outrance *f*; [*of price*] énormité *f*

exorbitant [ɪgˈzɔːbɪtənt] ADJ [*price, cost, charge, demands*] exorbitant; [*profit*] faramineux

exorbitantly [ɪgˈzɔːbɪtəntlɪ] ADV [*expensive*] démesurément; **an ~ high salary** un salaire exorbitant; **~ priced** d'un prix exorbitant; **to pay sb/charge sb ~** payer qn/faire payer à qn des sommes exorbitantes

exorcise [ˈeksɔːsaɪz] VT exorciser (**of** de)

exorcism [ˈeksɔːsɪzəm] N exorcisme *m*

exorcist [ˈeksɔːsɪst] N exorciste *mf*

exoskeleton [ˌeksəʊˈskelɪtən] N exosquelette *m*

exosphere [ˈeksəʊˌsfɪər] N exosphère *f*

exoteric [ˌeksəʊˈterɪk] ADJ [*doctrine*] exotérique; [*opinions*] populaire

exothermic [ˌeksəʊˈθɜːmɪk] ADJ exothermique

exotic [ɪgˈzɒtɪk] **1** ADJ exotique; **an ~ sounding name** un nom aux consonances exotiques **2** N (*Bot*) plante *f* exotique

exotica [ɪgˈzɒtɪkə] NPL objets *mpl* exotiques

exotically [ɪgˈzɒtɪklɪ] ADV [*dressed*] d'une manière exotique; **~ named** au nom exotique

exoticism [ɪgˈzɒtɪsɪzəm] N exotisme *m*

expand [ɪkˈspænd] **1** VT [+ *gas, liquid, metal*] dilater; [+ *one's business, trade, ideas*] développer; [+ *production*] accroître, augmenter; [+ *number*] augmenter; [+ *study*] élargir; [+ *influence, empire*] étendre; [+ *range*] élargir, étendre; (*Math*) [+ *formula*] développer; **to ~ one's knowledge** élargir ses connaissances; **to ~ one's experience** élargir son expérience; **exercises to ~ one's chest** exercices *mpl* physiques pour développer le torse; **she ~ed the story into a novel** elle a développé l'histoire pour en faire un roman; **they have ~ed their workforce to 300** ils ont porté le nombre de leurs employés à 300; **this ~ed board membership to 21** cela a porté à 21 le nombre de membres du conseil d'administration

2 VI **a** [*gas, liquid, metal*] se dilater; [*business, trade, ideas*] se développer; [*production*] s'accroître, augmenter; [*study*] s'élargir; [*influence, empire*] s'étendre; [*knowledge*] s'élargir; **the market is ~ing** le marché est en expansion; **the market is ~ing rapidly** le marché connaît une rapide expansion; **the economy ~ed by 3.9% in 1996** l'économie a connu une croissance de 3,9 % en 1996; **they've ~ed into the European market** ils ont étendu leur activités au marché européen; **they've ~ed into new products** ils ont diversifié leurs produits; **a former radio presenter who has ~ed into television** un ancien présentateur de radio qui s'est reconverti dans la télévision → **expanding**
b **to ~ (up)on** développer

expanded [ɪkˈspændɪd] ADJ (*Metal, Tech*) expansé; **~ polystyrene** polystyrène *m* expansé

expander [ɪkˈspændər] N → **chest**

expanding [ɪkˈspændɪŋ] ADJ [*metal etc*] qui se dilate; [*bracelet*] extensible; [*market, industry, profession*] en expansion; **the ~ universe** l'univers *m* en expansion; **the ~ universe theory** la théorie de l'expansion de l'univers; **~ file** classeur *m* extensible; **a job with ~ opportunities** un emploi qui offre un nombre croissant de débouchés; **a rapidly ~ industry** une industrie en pleine expansion

expanse [ɪkˈspæns] N étendue *f*

expansion [ɪkˈspænʃən] **1** N [*of gas*] expansion *f*, dilatation *f*; [*of business*] expansion *f*, agrandissement *m*; [*of trade*] développement *m*, expansion *f*; [*of production*] accroissement *m*, augmentation *f*; (*territorial, economic, colonial*) expansion *f*; [*of subject, idea*] développement *m*; [*of business*] développement *m*; (*Gram*) expansion *f* **2** COMP ▸ **expansion bottle** N (*Aut*) vase *m* d'expansion ▸ **expansion card** N (*Comput*) carte *f* d'extension ▸ **expansion slot** N (*Comput*) emplacement *m* or logement *m* pour carte supplémentaire ▸ **expansion tank** N = **expansion bottle**

expansionary [ɪkˈspænʃənərɪ] ADJ expansionniste

expansionism [ɪkˈspænʃənɪzəm] N expansionnisme *m*

expansionist [ɪkˈspænʃənɪst] ADJ, N expansionniste *mf*

expansive [ɪkˈspænsɪv] ADJ **a** (= *affable*) [*person, mood, gesture*] expansif; [*smile*] chaleureux **b** (*frm* = *grand*) [*area, lawn*] étendu; [*room*] spacieux; [*view*] étendu, bien dégagé **c** (= *expanding*) [*economy, business*] en expansion; [*phase*] d'expansion; **to have ~ ambitions** avoir des ambitions conquérantes **d** (*Phys*) (= *causing expansion*) expansif; (= *capable of expanding*) expansible, dilatable

expansively [ɪkˈspænsɪvlɪ] ADV **a** (= *affably*) [*say, smile*] chaleureusement, avec chaleur; **to gesture ~** faire de grands gestes **b** (= *in detail*) **he wrote ~ to his son** il a écrit de longues lettres à son fils; **he talked ~ of his travels** il a longuement raconté ses voyages

expansiveness [ɪkˈspænsɪvnɪs] N [*of person*] expansivité *f*; [*of welcome, smile*] chaleur *f*

expat[*] [eksˈpæt] N (ABBR = **expatriate**) expatrié(e) *m(f)*; **the ~ community** la communauté des expatriés

expatiate [ɪkˈspeɪʃɪeɪt] VI discourir, disserter (**upon** sur)

expatriate [eksˈpætrɪət] **1** N expatrié(e) *m(f)*; **British ~s** ressortissants *mpl* britanniques établis à l'étranger **2** ADJ [*person*] expatrié; [*family, community*] d'expatriés **3** VT [eksˈpætrɪeɪt] expatrier

expect [ɪkˈspekt] VT → **expected a** (= *anticipate*) s'attendre à; (= *predict*) prévoir; (*with confidence*) escompter; (= *count on*) compter sur; (= *hope for*) espérer; **I ~ that ◊ I ~ed as much** je m'y attendais; **he failed, as we had ~ed** il a échoué, comme nous l'avions prévu; **this suitcase is not as heavy as I ~ed** cette valise n'est pas aussi lourde que je le croyais, je m'attendais à ce que cette valise soit plus lourde; **I did not ~ that from him** je ne m'attendais pas à cela de lui; **we were ~ing rain** nous nous attendions à de la pluie; **he did not have the success he ~ed** il n'a pas eu le succès qu'il escomptait; **to ~ that ...** s'attendre à ce que ... (+ *subj*); **I ~ that he'll come** je pense qu'il viendra; **to ~ to do sth** penser or compter faire qch; **I ~ him to come** je m'attends à ce qu'il vienne; **we were ~ing war** on attendait la guerre; **I know what to ~** je sais à quoi m'attendre or m'en tenir; **well what do** or **did you ~?** il fallait t'y attendre!, ce n'est pas surprenant!; **to ~ the worst** s'attendre au pire; **as ~ed** comme on s'y attendait, comme prévu; **as might have been ~ed ◊ as was to be ~ed** comme on pouvait or comme il fallait s'y attendre; **that was to be ~ed** c'était à prévoir, il fallait s'y attendre; **it is ~ed that ...** on s'attend à ce que ... (+ *subj*); **it is hardly to be ~ed that ...** il ne faut pas or guère s'attendre à ce que ... (+ *subj*); **the talks are ~ed to last two or three days** les négociations devraient durer or on s'attend à ce que les négociations durent (*subj*) deux ou trois jours; **she is ~ed to make an announcement this afternoon** elle doit faire une déclaration cet après-midi; **inflation is ~ed to rise this year** on s'attend à ce que l'inflation augmente (*subj*) cette année

b (= *suppose*) **I ~ so** je crois que oui, je crois*; **we're not going to win — I ~ not** nous n'allons pas gagner — je crois bien que non; **this work is very tiring — yes, I ~ it is** ce travail est très fatigant — oui, je m'en doute or je veux bien le croire; **I ~ he'll soon have finished** je pense or suppose qu'il aura bientôt fini; **I ~ you're tired** vous devez être fatigué, je suppose que vous êtes fatigué

c (= *demand*) attendre (**sth from sb** qch de qn), demander (**sth from sb** qch à qn); (*stronger*) exiger (**sth from sb** qch de qn); **you can't ~ too much from him** il ne faut pas trop lui en demander; **the company ~s employees to be punctual** l'entreprise attend de ses employés qu'ils soient ponctuels; **what do you ~ of me?** qu'attendez-vous or qu'exigez-vous de moi?; **to ~ sb to do sth** vouloir que qn fasse qch; (*stronger*) exiger or demander que qn fasse qch; **I ~ you to tidy your own room** tu devras ranger ta chambre toi-même; **what do you ~ me to do about it?** que voulez-vous que j'y fasse?; **you can't ~ them to take it/him seriously** comment voulez-vous qu'ils prennent cela/qu'il le prennent au sérieux?; **are we**

~ed to leave now? est-ce que nous sommes censés or est-ce qu'on doit partir tout de suite ? **d** (= *await*) [+ *person, thing, action, letter, phone call*] attendre ; **I am ~ing her tomorrow/ this evening/at 7pm** elle doit venir demain/ce soir/à 19 heures ; (*Comm etc*) **we are ~ing it this week** nous devons le recevoir cette semaine ; **I am ~ing them for dinner** ils doivent venir dîner ; **~ me when you see me!*** vous (me) verrez bien quand je serai là !*, ne m'attendez pas ! ; **we'll ~ you when we see you*** on ne t'attend pas à une heure précise **e** **to be ~ing a baby** attendre un enfant **2** VI **she is ~ing*** elle attend un enfant

expectancy [ɪkˈspektənst] N attente *f* ; (= *hopefulness*) espoir *m* ; **an air of ~** une atmosphère d'impatience contenue ; **a look of ~** un regard plein d'espoir ; **awaited with eager ~** attendu avec une vive impatience → **life**

expectant [ɪkˈspektənt] ADJ **a** (= *future*) [*mother, father*] futur (*before n*) **b** (= *excited*) [*person, crowd*] impatient ; [*silence, hush, face, eyes, smile*] plein d'attente ; **with an ~ look on one's face** le visage plein d'attente ; **an ~ atmosphere** une atmosphère d'impatience contenue

expectantly [ɪkˈspektəntlɪ] ADV [*look at, smile*] avec l'air d'attendre quelque chose ; **to wait ~** attendre avec impatience

expectation [ˌekspekˈteɪʃən] N **a** (*NonC*) attente *f*, espérance *f* ; **in ~ of ...** en prévision de ... ; **to live in ~** vivre dans l'expectative ; **happiness in ~** du bonheur en perspective ; **there is every ~ of/no ~ of a cold winter** il y a toutes les chances/peu de chances que l'hiver soit rude **b** (= *sth expected*) attente *f*, espérance *f* ; **contrary to all ~(s)** contre toute attente ; **to come up to sb's ~s** répondre à l'attente or aux espérances de qn ; **beyond ~** au-delà de mes or (de nos *etc*) espérances ; **his (financial) ~s are good** ses perspectives financières sont bonnes

expected [ɪkˈspektɪd] ADJ [*phone call, letter, news*] qu'on attendait ; [*change, growth*] attendu ; [*arrival*] prévu ; [*profit, loss*] escompté ; **the ~ letter never came** la lettre qu'on attendait n'est jamais arrivée ; **their ~ time of arrival is 6 o'clock** on les attend à 6 heures, ils doivent arriver à 6 heures ; **what is their ~ time/date of arrival?** à quelle heure/ quand doivent-ils arriver ? ; **six weeks was the ~ time it would take to resolve such an inquiry** six semaines était le temps qu'il fallait escompter pour répondre à une demande de ce genre ; **she had been born before the ~ time** elle était née avant terme ; **less than half the ~ number turned out to the demonstration** les manifestants étaient moitié moins nombreux que prévu ; **next year's ~ £1.8 billion deficit** le déficit escompté de 1,8 milliard de livres pour l'année prochaine

expectorant [ɪkˈspektərənt] N, ADJ expectorant *m*

expectorate [ɪkˈspektəreɪt] VTI expectorer

expedience [ɪkˈspiːdɪəns], **expediency** [ɪkˈspiːdɪənsɪ] N (= *convenience*) opportunité *f* ; (= *self-interest*) opportunisme *m* ; (= *advisability*) [*of project, course of action*] opportunité *f*

expedient [ɪkˈspiːdɪənt] **1** ADJ **a** (= *suitable, convenient*) indiqué, opportun **b** (= *politic*) politique, opportun ; **this solution is more ~ than just** cette solution est plus politique que juste ; **it would be ~ to change the rule** il serait opportun de changer le règlement **2** N expédient *m*

expedite [ˈekspɪdaɪt] VT [+ *preparations, process*] accélérer ; [+ *work, operations, legal or official matters*] activer, hâter ; [+ *business, task*] expédier ; [+ *deal*] s'efforcer de conclure ; († *or frm = dispatch*) expédier

expedition [ˌekspɪˈdɪʃən] N **a** (= *journey*) expédition *f* ; (= *shorter trip*) tour *m* ; (= *group of* people) (membres *mpl* d'une) expédition *f* ; **a fishing ~** une partie de pêche **b** (*NonC*:† *or frm = speed*) promptitude *f*

expeditionary [ˌekspɪˈdɪʃənrɪ] ADJ expéditionnaire ; (*Mil*) **~ force** corps *m* expéditionnaire

expeditious [ˌekspɪˈdɪʃəs] ADJ (*frm*) expéditif

expeditiously [ˌekspɪˈdɪʃəslɪ] ADV (*frm*) promptement (*liter*) ; **as ~ as possible** aussi rapidement que possible

expel [ɪkˈspel] VT (*from country, meeting*) expulser ; (*from society, party*) exclure ; (*from school*) renvoyer ; [+ *the enemy*] chasser ; [+ *gas, liquid*] évacuer, expulser ; (*from the body*) évacuer ; [+ *foetus*] expulser

expend [ɪkˈspend] VT **a** (= *spend*) [+ *time, energy*] consacrer (**on sth** à qch, **on doing** à faire) ; [+ *money*] dépenser (**on sth** pour qch, **on doing** pour faire) **b** (= *use up*) [+ *ammunition, resources*] épuiser

expendability [ɪkˌspendəˈbɪlɪtɪ] N **its ~** le peu de valeur qu'on y attache

expendable [ɪkˈspendəbl] **1** ADJ (= *not indispensable*) [*person, luxury, troops, aircraft*] dont on peut se passer ; (= *disposable*) [*rocket, launcher*] non récupérable ; (*Mil*) **~ stores** matériel *m* de consommation **2** N consommable *m*

expenditure [ɪkˈspendɪtʃəʳ] N (*NonC*) **a** (= *money spent*) dépense(s) *f(pl)* ; (*Accounts = outgoings*) sortie *f* ; **public ~** dépenses *fpl* publiques ; **to limit one's ~** limiter ses dépenses ; **a project which involves heavy ~** un projet qui entraîne de grosses dépenses ; **income and ~** recettes *fpl* et dépenses *fpl* **b** (= *spending*) [*of money, time, energy*] dépense *f* ; [*of resources*] utilisation *f* ; **the ~ of public funds on this project** l'utilisation *f* des fonds publics pour ce projet **c** (= *using up*) [*of ammunition, resources*] épuisement *m*

expense [ɪkˈspens] **1** N **a** (*NonC*) dépense *f*, frais *mpl* ; (*Accounts: on account statement*) charge *f*, frais *mpl* ; **regardless of ~** même si ça revient cher ; **that will involve him in some ~** cela lui occasionnera des frais ; **at my ~** à mes frais ; **at public ~** aux frais de l'État ; **at little ~** à peu de frais ; **at great ~** à grands frais ; **to go to the ~ of buying a car** aller jusqu'à acheter une voiture ; **to put sb to ~** faire faire or causer des dépenses à qn ; **to put sb to great ~** occasionner de grosses dépenses à qn ; **to go to great ~ on sb's account** engager de grosses dépenses pour qn ; **to go to great ~ (to repair the house)** faire beaucoup de frais (pour réparer la maison) ; **don't go to any ~ over our visit** ne faites pas de frais pour notre visite ; **to live at other people's ~** vivre aux frais or à la charge des autres → **spare** **b** (*fig*) **at the ~ of** [+ *person, one's health, happiness, peace of mind*] au détriment de ; **to have a good laugh at sb's ~** bien rire aux dépens de qn ; **to get rich at other people's ~** s'enrichir aux dépens d'autrui or au détriment des autres **2 expenses** NPL frais *mpl*, dépenses *fpl* ; **he gets all his ~s paid** il se fait rembourser tous ses frais or toutes ses dépenses ; **your ~s will be entirely covered** vous serez défrayé entièrement or en totalité ; **after all ~s have been paid** tous frais payés **3** COMP ► **expense account** N (*Comm*) frais *mpl* de représentation ; **this will go on his ~ account** cela passera aux frais de représentation or sur sa note de frais ; **~ account lunch** déjeuner *m* qui passe aux frais de représentation or sur la note de frais ► **expenses sheet** N note *f* de frais

expensive [ɪkˈspensɪv] ADJ [*goods, shop, restaurant, country, city*] cher ; [*journey*] qui coûte cher, onéreux ; [*hobby, holiday, undertaking*] coûteux ; [*mistake*] qui coûte cher ; **to be ~** coûter cher, valoir cher ; **to come ~*** revenir cher ; **to have ~ tastes** avoir des goûts de luxe ; **it is very ~ to live in London** c'est très cher or ça revient très cher de vivre à Londres ; **bringing up children is an ~ business** c'est cher or ça revient cher d'élever des enfants

expensively [ɪkˈspensɪvlɪ] ADV [*buy, sell*] très cher ; [*equipped, furnished, educated*] à grands frais ; [*dressed*] de façon coûteuse ; **to live ~** mener grand train

expensiveness [ɪkˈspensɪvnɪs] N cherté *f*

▼ **experience** [ɪkˈspɪərɪəns] **1** N **a** (*NonC = knowledge, wisdom*) expérience *f* ; **~ of life/of men** expérience *f* du monde/des hommes ; **~ shows that ...** l'expérience montre que ... ; **in my ~** d'après mon expérience ; **I know by ~** je sais par expérience ; **from my own or personal ~** d'après mon expérience personnelle ; **I know from bitter ~ that ...** j'ai appris à mes dépens que ... ; **he has no ~ of real grief** il n'a jamais éprouvé or ressenti un vrai chagrin ; **he has no ~ of living in the country** il ne sait pas ce que c'est que de vivre à la campagne **b** (*NonC = practice, skill*) pratique *f*, expérience *f* ; **practical ~** pratique *f* ; **business ~** expérience *f* des affaires ; **he has a lot of teaching ~** il a une longue pratique or expérience de l'enseignement ; **he has considerable ~ in selecting ...** il possède une expérience considérable dans la sélection de ... ; **he has considerable driving ~** c'est un conducteur très expérimenté ; **he lacks ~** il manque d'expérience or de pratique ; **have you any previous ~ (in this kind of work)?** avez-vous déjà fait ce genre de travail ? ; **I've (had) no ~ of driving this type of car** je n'ai jamais conduit une voiture de ce type ; (*in job advert*) **~ preferred (but not essential)** expérience souhaitable (mais non indispensable or essentielle) **c** (= *event experienced*) expérience *f*, aventure *f* ; **I had a pleasant/frightening ~** il m'est arrivé une aventure agréable/effrayante ; **she's had or gone through some terrible ~s** elle a subi de rudes épreuves ; **it was a new ~ for me** c'était une nouveauté or une expérience nouvelle pour moi ; **we had many unforgettable ~s there** nous y avons vécu or passé bien des moments inoubliables ; **she swam in the nude and it was an agreeable ~** elle a nagé toute nue et a trouvé l'expérience agréable ; **it wasn't an ~ I would care to repeat** ça n'est pas une aventure que je tiens à recommencer ; **unfortunate ~** mésaventure *f* **2** VT **a** (= *undergo*) [+ *misfortune, hardship*] connaître ; [+ *setbacks, losses*] essuyer ; [+ *privations*] souffrir de ; [+ *conditions*] être confronté à ; [+ *ill treatment*] subir ; [+ *difficulties*] rencontrer ; **he doesn't know what it is like to be poor for he has never ~d it** il ne sait pas ce que c'est que d'être pauvre car il n'en a jamais fait l'expérience or cela ne lui est jamais arrivé ; **he ~s some difficulty in speaking** il a du mal or il éprouve de la difficulté à parler **b** (= *feel*) [+ *sensation, terror, remorse*] éprouver ; [+ *emotion, joy, elation*] ressentir

experienced [ɪkˈspɪərɪənst] ADJ [*person*] expérimenté ; **we need someone more ~** il nous faut quelqu'un qui ait plus d'expérience or quelqu'un de plus expérimenté ; **she is not ~ enough** elle n'a pas assez d'expérience ; **"~ driver required"** « on recherche chauffeur : expérience exigée » ; **with an ~ eye** d'un œil exercé ; **to the ~ eye/ear** pour un œil exercé/ une oreille exercée ; **to be sexually ~** être expérimenté (sexuellement) ; **to be ~ in sth** être expérimenté en or dans qch, être rompu à qch ; **to be ~ in the trade** avoir du métier ; **to be ~ in doing sth** avoir l'habitude de faire qch

experiential [ɪkˌspɪərɪˈenʃəl] ADJ (*frm, Philos*) qui résulte de l'expérience, dont on a fait l'expérience

experiment [ɪkˈsperɪmənt] **1** N (*Chem, Phys*) expérience *f* ; (*fig*) expérience *f*, essai *m* ; **to carry out an ~** faire une expérience ; **by way of**

► LANGUAGE IN USE: **experience** 19.2

~ ◊ **as an ~** à titre d'essai or d'expérience [2] [ɪk'sperɪˌment] VI (*Chem, Phys*) faire une expérience, expérimenter ; (*fig*) faire une or des expérience(s) ; **to ~ with a new vaccine** expérimenter un nouveau vaccin ; **to ~ on guinea pigs** faire des expériences sur des cobayes ; **they are ~ing with communal living** ils font l'expérience de la vie communautaire

experimental [ɪk,sperɪ'mentl] ADJ [*technique, method, evidence, research, novel*] expérimental ; **~ scientist/psychologist/physicist** expert *m* en sciences expérimentales/ psychologie expérimentale/physique expérimentale ; **to be at** or **in the ~ stage** en être au stade expérimental ; **he gave a ~ tug at the door handle** il a tiré un peu sur la porte pour voir

experimentally [ɪk,sperɪ'mentəlɪ] ADV [a] (= *scientifically*) [*study, test*] expérimentalement [b] (= *to see what happens*) [*try out, introduce*] pour voir, à titre expérimental ; **he lifted the cases ~ to see how heavy they were** il a soupesé les valises pour voir si elles étaient lourdes

experimentation [ɪk,sperɪmen'teɪʃən] N expérimentation *f*

experimenter [ɪk'sperɪmentə'] N expérimentateur *m*, -trice *f*

expert ['eksp3:t] [1] N spécialiste *mf* (**in, on, at** en), connaisseur *m* (**in, on** en) ; (= *officially qualified*) expert *m* ; **he is an ~ on wines** or **a wine ~** c'est un grand or fin connaisseur en vins ; **he is an ~ on the subject** c'est un expert en la matière ; **~ at pigeon shooting** spécialiste *mf* du tir aux pigeons ; **19th century ~** spécialiste *mf* du 19ᵉ siècle ; **he's an ~ at repairing watches** il est expert à réparer les montres ; **he's an ~ at that sort of negotiation** il est spécialiste de ce genre de négociations ; **with the eye of an ~** [*examine*] d'un œil or regard connaisseur ; [*judge*] en connaisseur, en expert ; **~'s report** or **valuation** expertise *f* [2] ADJ [*carpenter, acrobat, hands, approach*] expert (**at** or **in sth** en qch, **at** or **in doing sth** à faire qch) ; [*advice, opinion, help, attention, knowledge, evidence*] d'un expert ; [*treatment*] spécialisé ; **to be ~ at** or **in sth/in** or **at doing sth** être expert en qch/à faire qch ; **he ran an ~ eye over the photographs** il a regardé les photographies d'un œil expert ; **not noticeable except to the ~ eye** que seul un œil expert peut remarquer ; **with an ~ touch** avec une habileté d'expert or l'habileté d'un expert ; **he is ~ in this field** il est expert en la matière [3] COMP ▸ **expert appraisal** N expertise *f* ▸ **expert system** N (*Comput*) système *m* expert ▸ **expert valuation** N = **expert appraisal** ▸ **expert witness** N témoin *m* expert

expertise [,eksp3:'ti:z] N (= *knowledge*) expertise *f* ; (= *competence*) compétence *f* (**in** en)

expertly ['eksp3:tlɪ] ADV de façon experte

expertness ['eksp3:tnɪs] N = **expertise**

expiate ['ekspɪeɪt] VT expier

expiation [,ekspɪ'eɪʃən] N expiation *f* ; **in ~ of ...** en expiation de ...

expiatory ['ekspɪətərɪ] ADJ expiatoire

expiration [,ekspaɪə'reɪʃən] N [a] = **expiry** [b] (= *breathing out*) expiration *f* [c] († = *death*) trépas *m* (*liter*), décès *m*

expire [ɪk'spaɪə'] VI [a] [*lease, passport, licence, insurance, contract*] expirer ; [*period, time limit*] arriver à terme [b] (*liter* = *die*) expirer, rendre l'âme or le dernier soupir [c] (= *breathe out*) expirer

expiry [ɪk'spaɪərɪ] N [*of time limit, period, term of office*] expiration *f*, fin *f* ; [*of passport, lease*] expiration *f* ; **date of ~** ◊ **~ date** (*gen*) date *f* d'expiration ; (*on label*) à utiliser avant ... ; **date of ~ of the lease** expiration *f* or terme *m* du bail

▼ **explain** [ɪk'spleɪn] VT [a] (= *make clear*) [+ *how sth works, rule, meaning of a word, situation, motives, thoughts*] expliquer ; [+ *mystery*] élucider, éclaircir ; [+ *reasons, points of view*] exposer ; **~**

what you want to do expliquez ce que vous voulez faire ; **"it's raining" she ~ed** « il pleut » expliqua-t-elle ; **that is easy to ~ ◊ that is easily ~ed** cela s'explique facilement ; **this may seem confused, I will ~ myself** ceci peut paraître confus, je m'explique donc ; **I can ~** je peux (m')expliquer ; **let me ~** je m'explique ; **to ~ why/how** etc expliquer pourquoi/ comment etc ; **he ~ed to us why he had been absent** il nous a expliqué pourquoi il avait été absent ; **to ~ to sb how to do sth** expliquer à qn comment (il faut) faire qch [b] (= *account for*) [+ *phenomenon*] expliquer ; [+ *behaviour*] expliquer, justifier ; **the bad weather ~s why he is absent** le mauvais temps explique son absence or qu'il soit absent ; **come now, ~ yourself!** allez, expliquez-vous !

▸ **explain away** VT SEP justifier, trouver une explication convaincante à

explainable [ɪk'spleɪnəbl] ADJ explicable ; **that is easily ~** cela s'explique facilement

explanation [,eksplə'neɪʃən] N [a] (= *act, statement*) explication *f*, éclaircissement *m* ; **a long ~ of what he meant by democracy** une longue explication de ce qu'il entendait par la démocratie ; **these instructions need some ~** ces instructions demandent quelques éclaircissements [b] (= *cause, motive*) explication *f* ; **to find an ~ for sth** trouver l'explication de qch [c] (*NonC* = *justification*) explication *f*, justification *f* ; **has he something to say in ~ of his conduct?** est-ce qu'il peut fournir une explication à sa conduite ? ; **what do you have to say in ~?** comment expliquez-vous la chose ?

explanatory [ɪk'splænətərɪ] ADJ explicatif

expletive [ɪk'spli:tɪv] [1] N (= *exclamation*) exclamation *f*, interjection *f* ; (= *oath*) juron *m* ; (*Gram*) explétif *m* [2] ADJ (*Gram*) explétif

explicable [ɪk'splɪkəbl] ADJ explicable

explicably [ɪk'splɪkəblɪ] ADV d'une manière explicable

explicate ['eksplɪˌkeɪt] VT (*frm*) expliciter

explicit [ɪk'splɪsɪt] ADJ explicite (**about sth** à propos de qch, **in sth** dans qch) ; **to be ~ in doing sth** faire qch de façon explicite ; **he was ~ on this point** il a été explicite sur ce point ; **in ~ detail** avec des détails explicites ; **sexually ~** sexuellement explicite

explicitly [ɪk'splɪsɪtlɪ] ADV explicitement

explode [ɪk'spləʊd] [1] VI [*bomb, boiler, plane*] exploser, éclater ; [*gas*] exploser, détoner ; [*building, ship, ammunition*] exploser, sauter ; [*joy, anger*] éclater ; [*person*] (*: from rage, impatience*) exploser ; **to ~ with laughter** éclater de rire [2] VT [+ *bomb*] faire exploser ; (*fig*) [+ *theory, argument*] faire voler en éclats ; [+ *rumour*] couper court à ; **to ~ the myth that ...** démolir le mythe selon lequel ... [3] COMP ▸ **exploded drawing**, **exploded view** N (*Art etc*) éclaté *m*

exploit ['eksplɔɪt] [1] N (*heroic*) exploit *m*, haut fait *m* ; (= *feat*) prouesse *f* ; **~s** (= *adventures*) aventures *fpl* [2] [ɪk'splɔɪt] VT [a] (= *use unfairly*) [+ *workers, sb's credulity*] exploiter [b] (= *make use of*) [+ *minerals, land, talent*] exploiter ; [+ *situation*] profiter de, tirer parti de

exploitable [ɪk'splɔɪtəbl] ADJ exploitable

exploitation [,eksplɔɪ'teɪʃən] N exploitation *f*

exploitative [ɪk'splɔɪtətɪv] ADJ exploiteur (-trice *f*)

exploration [,eksplə'reɪʃən] N (*Med, lit, fig*) exploration *f* ; **voyage of ~** voyage *m* d'exploration or de découverte ; **preliminary ~** [*of ground, site*] reconnaissance *f*

exploratory [ɪk'splɒrətərɪ] ADJ (= *investigative*) [*expedition, digging, drilling*] d'exploration ; (= *preliminary*) [*talks*] exploratoire ; [*meeting, trip, approach, stage*] préliminaire ; **the ~ nature of the discussions** la nature préliminaire des discussions ; (*Jur*) **~ study** étude *f* prospective ; (*Med*) **to have ~ surgery** or **an ~ operation** subir une exploration

explore [ɪk'splɔ:'] VT [+ *territory, house, question, matter*] explorer ; (*Med*) sonder ; (*fig*) [+ *issue, proposal*] étudier sous tous ses aspects ; **to go exploring** partir en exploration or à la découverte ; **to ~ every corner of a house/garden** explorer chaque recoin d'une maison/d'un jardin ; (*lit, fig*) **to ~ the ground** tâter or sonder le terrain ; (*fig*) **to ~ every avenue** examiner toutes les possibilités ; **to ~ the possibilities** étudier les possibilités ; **to ~ an agreement** examiner les modalités d'un éventuel accord

explorer [ɪk'splɔ:rə'] N [a] (= *person*) explorateur *m*, -trice *f* [b] (*US* = *dental probe*) sonde *f*

explosion [ɪk'spləʊʒən] N [a] [*of bomb, boiler, plane*] explosion *f* ; **nuclear ~** explosion *f* nucléaire ; **to carry out a nuclear ~** effectuer un essai nucléaire [b] [*of anger, laughter, joy*] explosion *f* ; [*of violence*] flambée *f* ; **an ~ of colour/light** une soudaine débauche de couleurs/de lumière ; **an ~ in demand for sth** une explosion de la demande en qch ; **an ~ of interest in sth** une explosion d'intérêt pour qch ; **price ~** flambée *f* des prix → **population**

explosive [ɪk'spləʊsɪv] [1] ADJ [a] (*lit, fig*) [*device, charge, power, applause, growth, situation, issue, person, temper*] explosif ; [*gas, matter*] explosible ; [*mixture*] (*lit*) détonant, explosif ; (*fig*) détonant [b] (*Phon*) = **plosive** [2] N (*gen, Chem*) explosif *m* → **high**

explosively [ɪk'spləʊsɪvlɪ] ADV (= *with bang*) [*react, erupt*] en explosant [b] (= *angrily*) **"are you mad?" he asked ~** « tu es fou, ou quoi ? » demanda-t-il furieux or aboya-t-il

explosiveness [ɪk'spləʊsɪvlɪs] N explosibilité *f*

expo ['ekspəʊ] N (ABBR = **exposition b**) expo *f*

exponent [ɪk'spəʊnənt] N [*of theory etc*] champion(ne) *m(f)* ; (*Math, Gram*) exposant *m* ; **the principal ~ of this movement/this school of thought** le chef de file or le principal représentant de ce mouvement/de cette école de pensée

exponential [,ekspəʊ'nenʃəl] ADJ exponentiel ; (*Stat*) **~ distribution** distribution *f* exponentielle

exponentially [,ekspəʊ'nenʃəlɪ] ADV de manière exponentielle

export [ɪk'spɔ:t] [1] VT [a] [+ *product*] exporter (**to** vers) ; **countries which ~ coal** pays *mpl* exportateurs de charbon [b] (*Comput*) [+ *document*] exporter [2] VI exporter (**to** vers) [3] ['ekspɔ:t] N [a] (*NonC*) exportation *f* ; **for ~ only** réservé à l'exportation [b] (= *object, commodity*) (article *m* d')exportation *f* ; **invisible ~s** exportations *fpl* invisibles ; **ban on ~s ◊ ~ ban** interdiction *f* des exportations [c] (= *beer*) bière forte [4] ['ekspɔ:t] COMP [*goods, permit, agent*] d'exportation ; [*manager, director*] du service export, des exportations ▸ **export credit** N crédit *m* à l'exportation ▸ **export drive** N campagne *f* pour (encourager) l'exportation ▸ **export duty** N droit *m* de sortie ▸ **export earnings** NPL recettes *fpl* d'exportation ▸ **export-orientated**, **export-oriented** ADJ à vocation exportatrice ▸ **export reject** N article *m* impropre à l'exportation ▸ **export trade** N commerce *m* d'exportation, export *m*

exportable [ɪk'spɔ:təbl] ADJ exportable

exportation [,ekspɔ:'teɪʃən] N (*NonC*) exportation *f*, sortie *f*

exporter [ɪk'spɔ:tə'] N (= *person*) exportateur *m*, -trice *f* ; (= *country*) pays *m* exportateur

expose [ɪk'spəʊz] VT [a] (= *uncover, leave unprotected*) découvrir, exposer ; [+ *wire, nerve, body part*] mettre à nu, dénuder ; **to ~ to radiation/rain/sunlight** exposer à des radiations/à la pluie/au soleil ; **to ~ to danger** mettre en danger ; **to ~ o.s. to criticism/ridicule**

s'exposer à la critique/au ridicule ; **a dress which leaves the back ~d** une robe qui découvre or dénude le dos ; **to be ~d to view** s'offrir à la vue ; **apples turn brown when ~d to air** les pommes brunissent au contact de l'air ; **digging has ~d the remains of a temple** les fouilles ont mis au jour les restes d'un temple ; (*Tech*) **~d parts** parties *fpl* apparentes ; (*Hist*) **to ~ a child (to die)** exposer un enfant ; **he ~d himself to the risk of losing his job** il s'est exposé à perdre sa place, il a risqué de perdre sa place ; (*Jur: indecently*) **to ~ o.s.** commettre un outrage à la pudeur
b (= *display*) [+ *goods*] étaler, exposer ; [+ *pictures*] exposer ; [+ *one's ignorance*] afficher, étaler
c (= *unmask, reveal*) [+ *vice*] mettre à nu ; [+ *scandal, plot, lie*] révéler, dévoiler ; [+ *secret*] éventer ; (= *denounce*) [+ *person*] démasquer, dénoncer (**as** comme étant) ; **the affair ~d him as a fraud** cette affaire a montré que c'était un imposteur
d (*Phot*) exposer

exposé [eks'pəʊzeɪ] N révélation *f*

exposed [ɪk'spəʊzd] ADJ a (= *unprotected*) [*troops, flank*] à découvert, exposé ; [*location, hillside, garden*] exposé ; [*ground*] découvert ; (*Climbing*) [*passage, section*] aérien ; (= *uncovered*) [*brickwork, plaster, wire, skin, nerve*] à nu ; [*body part*] dénudé ; [*machine part*] apparent ; **the house is in a very ~ position** la maison est très exposée ; (*Mil*) **an ~ position** un (lieu) découvert ; **~ to the wind** exposé au vent b (= *vulnerable*) [*person*] exposé aux regards ; **to feel ~** [*person*] se sentir exposé ; **his position is very ~** sa position l'expose aux regards c (*Phot*) [*film*] exposé

exposition [ˌekspə'zɪʃən] N a (*NonC*) [*of facts, theory, plan*] exposition *f* ; [*of text*] exposé *m*, commentaire *m*, interprétation *f* ; (*Mus*) exposition *f* b (= *exhibition*) exposition *f*

expostulate [ɪk'spɒstjʊleɪt] (*frm*) 1 VT protester 2 VI **to ~ with sb about sth** faire des remontrances à qn au sujet de qch

expostulation [ɪkˌspɒstjʊ'leɪʃən] N (*frm*) protestation *f*

exposure [ɪk'spəʊʒəʳ] 1 N a (*NonC*) contact: *to substance, radiation, sunlight, noise*) exposition *f* (**to sth** à qch) ; **to risk ~ to a virus** risquer d'être en contact avec un virus ; **to undergo ~ to new ideas** être exposé à de nouvelles idées ; **avoid the ~ of children to violent images on television** évitez d'exposer les enfants aux images violentes de la télévision → **indecent**
b (*NonC: Med*) hypothermie *f* ; **to die of ~** mourir de froid ; **to suffer from ~** souffrir d'hypothermie
c (*NonC* = *revelation, unmasking*) [*of secret, corruption, scandal*] révélation *f* ; [*of person*] dénonciation *f* ; **public ~** [*of affair, corruption, scandal*] révélation *f* publique ; [*of person*] dénonciation *f* publique
d (*NonC* = *publicity*) **media ~** couverture *f* médiatique ; **to get an enormous amount of ~ on television** être l'objet d'une abondante couverture télévisée
e (*Phot* = *photograph*) pose *f* ; **a 36-~ film** ◊ **a film with 36 ~s** une pellicule 36 poses ; **to make an ~** (= *take photograph*) prendre une photo ; (= *develop photograph*) développer un cliché
f (*NonC: Phot* = *amount of light*) exposition *f* → **double, multiple**
g (*NonC: Phot: also ~ time*) temps *m* de pose
h (*NonC* = *position*) [*of house*] exposition *f* ; **southern/eastern ~** exposition *f* au sud/à l'est ; **a house with a northern ~** une maison exposée au nord
2 COMP ► **exposure index** N (*Phot*) indice *m* de pose ► **exposure meter** N posemètre *m*, photomètre *m* ► **exposure value** N indice *m* de lumination

expound [ɪk'spaʊnd] VT [+ *theory*] expliquer ; [+ *one's views*] exposer ; [+ *the Bible*] expliquer, interpréter

ex-president [ˌeks'prezɪdənt] N ex-président *m*, ancien président *m*

▼**express** [ɪk'spres] 1 VT a (= *make known*) [+ *appreciation, feelings, sympathy*] exprimer ; [+ *opinions*] émettre, exprimer ; [+ *surprise, displeasure*] exprimer, manifester ; [+ *thanks*] présenter, exprimer ; [+ *a truth, proposition*] énoncer ; [+ *wish*] formuler ; **to ~ o.s.** s'exprimer ; **I haven't the words to ~ my thoughts** les mots me manquent pour traduire ma pensée ; **they have ~ed (an) interest in ...** ils se sont montrés intéressés par ..., ils ont manifesté de l'intérêt pour ...
b (*in another language or medium*) rendre, exprimer ; [*face, actions*] exprimer ; (*Math*) exprimer ; **this ~es exactly the meaning of the word** ceci rend exactement le sens du mot ; **you cannot ~ that so succinctly in French** on ne peut pas l'exprimer aussi succinctement en français
c [+ *juice*] exprimer, extraire ; [+ *breast milk*] tirer
d (= *send*) [+ *letter, parcel*] expédier par exprès
2 ADJ a (= *explicit*) [*order, instruction*] exprès (-esse *f*) ; [*purpose, intention*] délibéré ; **with the ~ purpose of doing sth** dans le seul but or dans le but délibéré de faire qch
b (= *fast*) [*letter, delivery, mail*] exprès *inv* ; [*service*] express *inv*
3 ADV [*send*] en exprès or par Chronopost®
4 N a [= *train*] rapide *m*
b **to send sth by ~** envoyer qch en exprès
5 COMP ► **express coach** N (*auto*)car *m* express ► **express company** N compagnie *f* de messageries exprès ► **express delivery**, **express mail** N (*Brit Post* = *system*) distribution *f* exprès ; **to send sth by ~ delivery** or **mail** envoyer qch en exprès or par Chronopost® ► **express rifle** N fusil *m* de chasse express ► **express train** N train *m* express

expressage [ɪk'spresɪdʒ] N (*US*) (= *service*) service *m* de messagerie exprès ; (= *charge for service*) frais *mpl* de messagerie exprès

expression [ɪk'spreʃən] 1 N a (*NonC*) [*of opinions*] expression *f* ; [*of friendship, affection*] témoignage *m* ; [*of joy*] manifestation *f* ; **to give ~ to one's fears** formuler ses craintes ; **to find ~ (in)** se manifester (dans or par) ; **from Cairo came ~s of regret at the attack** Le Caire a exprimé ses regrets après cette attaque
b (= *facial expression*) expression *f* ; **a face devoid of ~** un visage sans expression
c (*NonC* = *feeling*) expression *f* ; **to play with ~** jouer avec expression
d (= *phrase*) expression *f* ; (= *turn of phrase*) tournure *f* ; (*Math*) expression *f* ; **an original/common ~** une tournure originale/expression courante ; **it's an ~ he's fond of** c'est une expression or une tournure qu'il affectionne ; **a figurative ~** une expression figurée ; **set** or **fixed ~** locution *f*
2 COMP ► **expression mark** N (*Mus*) signe *m* d'expression

expressionism [ɪk'spreʃəˌnɪzəm] N expressionnisme *m*

expressionist [ɪk'spreʃəˌnɪst] ADJ, N expressionniste *mf*

expressionless [ɪk'spreʃənlɪs] ADJ [*person*] sans expression ; [*face, eyes, look*] sans expression, inexpressif ; [*voice*] monotone, monocorde ; [*playing, style*] plat

expressive [ɪk'spresɪv] ADJ [*face, look, voice, gesture, music, language*] expressif ; [*power, ability, capability, skill*] d'expression ; **she's very ~** elle est très éloquente ; (*frm*) **to be ~ of sth** exprimer qch

expressively [ɪk'spresɪvlɪ] ADV d'une manière expressive

expressiveness [ɪk'spresɪvnɪs] N [*of face*] caractère *m* expressif, expressivité *f* ; [*of words*] force *f* expressive ; [*of music, language*] expressivité *f* ; [*of gesture*] éloquence *f* ; **a picture remarkable for its ~** un tableau remarquable par (la force de) l'expression

expressly [ɪk'spreslɪ] ADV [*forbid, exclude, allow, design, make, write*] expressément ; [*state*] explicitement ; **~ illegal** expressément interdit par la loi

expressman [ɪk'spresmæn] N (*pl* **-men**) (*US*) employé *m* de messageries exprès

expresso [ɪk'spresəʊ] N = **espresso**

expressway [ɪk'spreswei] N (*esp US*) voie *f* express, autoroute *f* urbaine → ROADS

expropriate [eks'prəʊprɪeɪt] VT [+ *person, land*] exproprier

expropriation [eksˌprəʊprɪ'eɪʃən] N expropriation *f*

expulsion [ɪk'spʌlʃən] 1 N expulsion *f*, bannissement *m* ; (*Scol etc*) renvoi *m*, exclusion *f* définitive 2 COMP ► **expulsion order** N arrêté *m* d'expulsion

expunge [ɪk'spʌndʒ] VT (*frm: from book*) supprimer ; **to ~ sth from the record** supprimer or effacer qch

expurgate ['ekspɜːgeɪt] VT (*frm*) expurger ; **~d edition** édition *f* expurgée

exquisite [ɪk'skwɪzɪt] ADJ a (= *fine*) exquis ; **a woman of ~ beauty** une femme d'une exquise beauté ; **in ~ detail** dans les moindres détails b (*liter* = *intense*) [*pleasure, satisfaction*] exquis ; [*pain*] lancinant ; [*care*] minutieux

exquisitely [ɪk'skwɪzɪtlɪ] ADV [*dress, make, decorate, paint, embroider, describe*] de façon exquise ; **~ beautiful/delicate/polite** d'une beauté/délicatesse/politesse exquise ; **~ detailed** [*picture, tapestry etc*] plein de détails exquis ; **he gave us an ~ detailed account of the accident** il nous a raconté l'accident dans ses moindres détails

ex-service [ˌeks'sɜːvɪs] ADJ (*Brit Mil*) ayant servi dans l'armée

ex-serviceman [ˌeks'sɜːvɪsmæn] N (*pl* **ex-servicemen**) ancien militaire *m* ; (= *war veteran*) ancien combattant *m*

ex-servicewoman [ˌeks'sɜːvɪswʊmən] N (*pl* **ex-servicewomen**) femme *f* militaire à la retraite ; (= *war veteran*) ancienne combattante *f*

ext (*Telec*) (ABBR = **extension**) poste *m*

extant [ek'stænt] ADJ (*frm*) qui existe encore, existant ; **the only ~ manuscript** le seul manuscrit conservé ; **a few examples are still ~** quelques exemples subsistent (encore)

extemporaneous [ɪkˌstempə'reɪnɪəs], **extemporary** [ɪk'stempərərɪ] ADJ improvisé, impromptu

extempore [ɪk'stempərɪ] 1 ADV impromptu, sans préparation 2 ADJ improvisé, impromptu ; **to give an ~ speech** improviser un discours, faire un discours au pied levé

extemporize [ɪk'stempəraɪz] VTI improviser

extend [ɪk'stend] 1 VT a (= *enlarge*) [+ *house, property*] agrandir ; [+ *research*] porter or pousser plus loin ; [+ *powers*] étendre, augmenter ; [+ *business*] étendre, accroître ; [+ *knowledge*] élargir, accroître ; [+ *limits*] étendre ; [+ *period, time allowed*] prolonger ; [+ *insurance cover*] augmenter le montant de ; **to ~ the field of human knowledge/one's sphere of influence** élargir le champ des connaissances/sa sphère d'influence ; **to ~ the frontiers of a country** reculer les frontières d'un pays ; **a course that ~s students' understanding of British history** un cours qui permet aux étudiants d'approfondir leur connaissance de l'histoire britannique ; **to ~ one's vocabulary** enrichir or élargir son vocabulaire ; **to ~ a time limit (for sth)** accorder un délai (pour qch)
b (= *prolong*) [+ *street, line*] prolonger (**by** de) ;

[+ *visit, leave*] prolonger; **to ~ one's stay by two weeks** prolonger son séjour de deux semaines; **to be fully ~ed** [*ladder, telescope*] être entièrement déployé

c (= *offer, give*) [+ *help*] apporter; [+ *hospitality, friendship*] offrir; [+ *thanks, condolences, congratulations*] présenter; [+ *credit, loan*] consentir; **to ~ a welcome to sb** souhaiter la bienvenue à qn; **to ~ an invitation** faire or lancer une invitation

d (= *stretch out*) [+ *arm*] étendre; **to ~ one's hand (to sb)** tendre la main (à qn)

e (= *make demands on*) [+ *person, pupil*] pousser à la limite de ses capacités, faire donner son maximum à

2 VI [*wall, estate*] s'étendre (**to, as far as** jusqu'à); [*table*] s'allonger; [*meeting, visit*] se prolonger, continuer (**over** pendant, **for** durant); **the caves ~ for some 10 kilometres** les grottes s'étendent sur quelque 10 kilomètres; **a footballing career that ~ed from 1974 to 1990** une carrière de footballeur qui a duré de 1974 à 1990; **holidays which ~ into September** des vacances qui durent or se prolongent jusqu'en septembre; **the table ~s to 220cm** la table peut s'allonger jusqu'à 220 cm, avec ses rallonges, cette table fait 220 cm; **enthusiasm which ~s even to the children** enthousiasme qui gagne même les enfants

extendable [ɪkˈstendəbl] ADJ [*ladder*] à rallonge; [*contract, lease*] renouvelable

extended [ɪkˈstendɪd] **1** ADJ prolongé; [*holiday, leave*] longue durée; **for an ~ period** pendant une période supplémentaire; **an ~ play record** un disque double (durée); (*US Med*) **~ care facilities** soins *mpl* pour convalescents; (*Sociol*) **the ~ family** la famille étendue **2** COMP ▶ **extended memory** N (*Comput*) mémoire *f* étendue

extendible [ɪkˈstendəbl] ADJ = **extendable**

extensible [ɪkˈstensɪbl] ADJ extensible

▼ **extension** [ɪkˈstenʃən] **1** N **a** (*to building*) **to build an ~ (to a building)** agrandir (un bâtiment); **to have an ~ built onto a house** faire agrandir une maison; **there is an ~ at the back of the house** la maison a été agrandie à l'arrière; **come and see our ~** venez voir, nous avons fait agrandir; **the kitchen/bathroom ~** la nouvelle partie de la maison occupée par la cuisine/la salle de bains; **a new ~ to the library** une nouvelle annexe de la bibliothèque **b** (= *continuation*) prolongement *m* (**to** or **of** *sth* de qch); (= *extra part*) (*for table, electric flex, pipe*) rallonge *f*; (*also* **hair ~**) (*clip-on*) postiche *m*; (*permanent*) extension *f*; **motorway ~** prolongement *m* d'une autoroute; **the building of an ~ to a golf course** l'agrandissement *m* d'un terrain de golf; **~ to an insurance policy** (= *extra cover*) extension *f* d'une assurance; (*in duration*) prolongation *f* d'une assurance; **an ~ of o.s./one's personality** un prolongement de soi-même/sa personnalité **c** (= *extra time*) prolongation *f* (**to** or **of** *sth* de qch); **there will be no ~ of the deadline** le délai ne sera pas prolongé; **to grant an ~ of a deadline** accorder un délai supplémentaire; **to get an ~ (of time for payment)** obtenir un délai; (*Jur, Fin*) **~ of due date** report *m* d'échéance, délai *m* **d** (= *development*) [*of rights, powers*] extension *f*; [*of idea, concept*] développement *m*; **the role of women within the family and, by ~, within the community** le rôle des femmes dans la famille et, par extension, au sein de la communauté; **the logical ~ of sth** la suite logique de qch **e** (*Telec*) (*in house*) appareil *m* supplémentaire; (*in office*) poste *m*; **you can get me on ~ 308** vous pouvez me joindre au poste 308 **f** (= *provision*) [*of credit*] allocation *f*

2 COMP ▶ **extension cable, extension cord** (*US*) N (*Elec*) rallonge *f* ▶ **extension courses** NPL cours dispensés par l'institut

▶ LANGUAGE IN USE: **extension** 27.2, 27.4

d'éducation permanente d'une université
▶ **extension ladder** N échelle *f* coulissante
▶ **extension lead** N = **extension cable**
▶ **extension light** N (lampe *f*) baladeuse *f*
▶ **extension tube** N (*Phot*) tube-allonge *m*

extensive [ɪkˈstensɪv] ADJ [*area, grounds, knowledge, powers, range, collection*] étendu; [*damage, alterations, experience*] considérable; [*plans, reforms*] de grande envergure; [*research, discussions*] approfondi; [*tests*] nombreux; [*list*] long (longue *f*); [*menu*] varié; [*tour*] complet (-ète *f*); **to make ~ use of sth** beaucoup utiliser qch; **her visit got ~ coverage in the press** sa visite a fait l'objet de très nombreux articles dans la presse or d'une large couverture médiatique; **to undergo ~ surgery** (= *one operation*) subir une opération longue et complexe; (= *series of operations*) subir une série d'interventions chirurgicales

extensively [ɪkˈstensɪvlɪ] ADV [*travel, work, write*] beaucoup; [*alter, damage*] considérablement; [*revise, discuss*] en profondeur; [*grow, quote, report*] abondamment; **to use sth ~** beaucoup utiliser qch; **an ~ used method** une méthode très répandue; **the story was covered ~ in the press** cette histoire a fait l'objet de nombreux articles dans la presse or d'une large couverture médiatique; **the subject has been ~ researched** cette question a fait l'objet de recherches approfondies; **the band has toured ~** le groupe a fait des tournées un peu partout; **to advertise ~ in the papers** [*company*] faire énormément de publicité dans les journaux; [*individual*] faire passer de nombreuses annonces dans les journaux

extensor [ɪkˈstensə ʳ] N (muscle *m*) extenseur *m*

extent [ɪkˈstent] N **a** (= *size*) étendue *f*, superficie *f*; (= *length*) longueur *f*; **an avenue lined with trees along its entire ~** une allée bordée d'arbres sur toute sa longueur; **to open to its fullest ~** ouvrir entièrement or tout grand; **over the whole ~ of the ground** sur toute la superficie du terrain; **she could see the full ~ of the park** elle voyait le parc dans toute son étendue **b** (= *range, scope*) [*of damage*] importance *f*, ampleur *f*; [*of commitments, losses*] importance *f*; [*of knowledge, activities, power, influence*] étendue *f* **c** (= *degree*) mesure *f*, degré *m*; **to what ~?** dans quelle mesure?; **to a certain ~** jusqu'à un certain point or degré, dans une certaine mesure; **to a large ~** en grande partie; **to a small** or **slight ~** dans une faible mesure, quelque peu; **to the** or **such an ~ that ...** à tel point que ..., au point que ...; **to the ~ of doing** au point de faire

extenuate [ɪkˈstenjʊeɪt] VT atténuer; **extenuating circumstances** circonstances *fpl* atténuantes

extenuation [ɪkˌstenjʊˈeɪʃən] N atténuation *f*

exterior [ɪkˈstɪərɪə ʳ] **1** ADJ [*wall, door, lighting, paint, decorating, world*] extérieur (-eure *f*); [*surface*] extérieur (-eure *f*), externe; **~ to sth** extérieur à qch; **paint for ~ use** peinture *f* pour l'extérieur **2** N [*of house, box*] extérieur *m*; (*Art, Cine*) extérieur *m*; **on the ~** à l'extérieur; **underneath his rough ~, he ...** sous ses dehors rudes, il ... **3** COMP ▶ **exterior angle** N (*Math*) angle *m* externe ▶ **exterior decoration** N peintures *fpl* extérieures

exteriorize [ɪkˈstɪərɪəˌraɪz] VT (*Med, Psych*) extérioriser

exterminate [ɪkˈstɜːmɪˌneɪt] VT [+ *pests, group of people*] exterminer; [+ *race*] anéantir; [+ *disease, beliefs, ideas*] éradiquer

extermination [ɪkˌstɜːmɪˈneɪʃən] **1** N [*of race, animals*] extermination *f*; [*of disease*] éradication *f*; **mass ~** extermination *f* massive **2** COMP ▶ **extermination camp** N camp *m* d'extermination

exterminator [ɪkˈstɜːmɪˌneɪtə ʳ] N (*US = rat-catcher etc*) employé(e) *m(f)* de la désinfection

extern [ˈekstɜːn] N (*US Med*) externe *mf*

external [ɪkˈstɜːnl] **1** ADJ **a** (= *outer, exterior*) [*wall*] extérieur (-eure *f*); [*surface*] extérieur (-eure *f*), externe; [*injury*] superficiel; (*Zool, Anat*) [*ear, gills*] externe; **~ skeleton** exosquelette *m*; (*Pharm*) **"for ~ use only"** « à usage externe » **b** (= *outside, from outside*) [*pressure, factor, reality, world*] extérieur (-eure *f*); (*Comm*) [*mail*] externe; [*phone call*] (*outgoing*) vers l'extérieur; (*incoming*) de l'extérieur **c** (= *foreign*) [*debt*] extérieur (-eure *f*); **the European commissioner for ~ affairs** le commissaire européen aux affaires or chargé des affaires extérieures **2** N (*fig*) **the ~s** l'extérieur *m*, les apparences *fpl*; **the ~s of our faith** les manifestations *fpl* extérieures de notre foi; **to look at the ~s of an issue** ne voir que l'aspect superficiel d'une question **3** COMP ▶ **external auditor** N (*Brit Fin*) vérificateur *m*, -trice *f* de comptes (externe) ▶ **external degree** N (*Brit Univ*) diplôme délivré par une université à des personnes non régulièrement inscrites ▶ **external examiner** N (*Brit Univ*) examinateur *m*, -trice *f* extérieur(e) ▶ **external student** N (*Brit Univ*) étudiant(e) *mf* externe ▶ **external trade** N (*US*) commerce *m* extérieur

externalize [ɪkˈstɜːnəˌlaɪz] VT extérioriser

externally [ɪkˈstɜːnəlɪ] ADV [*impose*] de l'extérieur; [*express*] extérieurement; **~ mounted cameras** des caméras *fpl* installées à l'extérieur; **he remained ~ calm** il est resté calme extérieurement; **a cream to be applied ~** une crème à usage externe; **"to be used ~"** « à usage externe »

extinct [ɪkˈstɪŋkt] ADJ **a** (= *no longer existing*) [*animal, species, tribe, way of life, language*] disparu; [*custom*] tombé en désuétude; **to be ~** avoir disparu; **to become ~** disparaître; **to be nearly ~** être en voie d'extinction; **are good manners ~?** les bonnes manières n'existent-elles plus? **b** (= *not active*) [*volcano*] éteint

extinction [ɪkˈstɪŋkʃən] N (*NonC*) [*of animal, species, race, family*] extinction *f*, disparition *f*; [*of hopes*] anéantissement *m*; [*of debt*] amortissement *m*; [*of fire*] extinction *f*

extinguish [ɪkˈstɪŋgwɪʃ] VT [+ *fire, light*] éteindre; [+ *candle*] éteindre, souffler; [+ *hopes*] anéantir, mettre fin à; [+ *debt*] amortir

extinguisher [ɪkˈstɪŋgwɪʃə ʳ] N extincteur *m* → **fire**

extirpate [ˈekstəˌpeɪt] VT extirper

extirpation [ˌekstəˈpeɪʃən] N (*NonC*) extirpation *f*

extirpator [ˈekstəˌpeɪtə ʳ] N (*Agr, Tech*) extirpateur *m*

extn (*Telec*) (ABBR = **extension**) poste *m*

extol [ɪkˈstəʊl] VT [+ *person*] porter aux nues, chanter les louanges de; [+ *act, quality*] prôner, exalter; **to ~ the virtues of ...** chanter les louanges de ...

extort [ɪkˈstɔːt] VT [+ *promise, money*] extorquer, soutirer (**from** à); [+ *consent, promise, confession, secret*] arracher (**from** à); [+ *signature*] extorquer

extortion [ɪkˈstɔːʃən] N (*also Jur*) extorsion *f*; (*fig*) **this is sheer ~!** c'est du vol (manifeste)!

extortionate [ɪkˈstɔːʃənɪt] ADJ exorbitant

extortioner [ɪkˈstɔːʃənə ʳ], **extortionist** [ɪkˈstɔːʃənɪst] N extorqueur *m*, -euse *f*

extra [ˈekstrə] **1** ADJ **a** (= *additional*) [*homework, bus, chair, costs, troops, effort*] supplémentaire; **to work ~ hours** faire des heures supplémentaires; **take an ~ pair of shoes** prends une autre paire de chaussures; **I've set an ~ place at table** j'ai ajouté un couvert; **for**

~ safety pour plus de sécurité; **take ~ care!** fais bien attention!; **to earn an ~ £20 a week** gagner 20 livres de plus par semaine; **there is an ~ charge for wine** ◊ **the wine is ~** le vin est en supplément; **there's no ~ charge for the wine** il n'y a pas de supplément pour le vin, le vin est compris; **take some ~ money just to be on the safe side** prends un peu plus d'argent, on ne sait jamais *or* au cas où*; **the ~ money will come in handy** l'argent en plus *or* l'argent supplémentaire pourra toujours servir; **the ~ money required to complete the project** le montant supplémentaire *or* l'argent requis pour terminer le projet; **to go to ~ expense** faire des frais; **~ pay** supplément *m* de salaire, sursalaire *m*; (*Mil*) supplément *m* de solde; **postage and packing ~** frais d'expédition en sus; **95p ~ for postage and packing** 95 pence de plus pour les frais d'expédition
[b] (= *spare*) **these copies are ~** ces exemplaires sont en surplus
[2] ADV **[a]** (= *more money*) **to pay/charge ~ (for sth)** payer/faire payer un supplément (pour qch); **a room with a bath costs ~** les chambres avec salle de bains coûtent plus cher, il y a un supplément pour les chambres avec salle de bains
[b] (= *especially*) [*cautious*] encore plus; **he was ~ polite/nice to her** il a été tout poli/gentil avec elle; **take ~ special care when washing those glasses** faites très attention en lavant ces verres; **he expected to do ~ well in the exam** il s'attendait à réussir brillamment à l'examen; **to work ~ hard** travailler d'arrache-pied; **~ large** [*garment*] très grand; [*eggs, tomatoes etc*] très gros
[3] N **[a]** (= *perk*) à-côté *m*; (= *expenses*) **~s** frais *mpl* supplémentaires; (= *options*) **singing and piano are ~s** les leçons de chant et de piano sont en option; (= *luxuries*) **those little ~s** ces petites gâteries *fpl*; **there are no hidden ~s** il n'y a pas de frais supplémentaires
[b] (*in restaurant* = *extra dish*) supplément *m*
[c] (*Cine, Theat* = *actor*) figurant(e) *m(f)*
[d] (*US* = *gasoline*) super(carburant) *m*
[4] COMP ► **extra time** N (*esp Brit Sport*) prolongations *fpl*; **the match went to ~ time** on a joué les prolongations; **after ~ time** après prolongation(s)

extra... ['ekstrə] PREF **[a]** (= *outside*) extra... → **extramarital [b]** (= *specially, ultra*) extra...; **~dry** [*wine etc*] très sec; [*champagne, vermouth*] extra-dry *inv*; **~fine** extrafin; **~smart** ultrachic *inv*; **~strong** [*person*] extrêmement fort; [*material*] extrasolide → **extra-special**

extract [ik'strækt] **[1]** VT [+ *juice, minerals, oil, bullet, splinter*] extraire (**from** de); [+ *tooth*] arracher (**from** à); [+ *cork*] tirer (**from** de); [+ *confession, permission, promise*] arracher (**from** à); [+ *information*] tirer (**from** de); [+ *money*] tirer (**from** de), soutirer (**from** à); [+ *meaning*] tirer, dégager (**from** de); **to ~ pleasure from sth** tirer du plaisir de qch; **to ~ DNA from sth** extraire l'ADN de qch; (*Math*) **to ~ the square root** extraire la racine carrée **[2]** ['ekstrækt] N **[a]** [*of book, film, play etc*] extrait *m*; **~s from Voltaire** morceaux *mpl* choisis de Voltaire **[b]** (*Pharm*) extrait *m*; (*Culin*) extrait *m*, concentré *m*; **meat ~** extrait *m* de viande

extraction [ik'strækʃən] N **[a]** (*NonC*) [*of minerals, coal, oil*] extraction *f*; [*of fluid, bone marrow*] prélèvement *m*; **the ~ of confessions through torture** le fait d'arracher des aveux par la torture **[b]** (*NonC* = *descent*) origine *f*; **to be of Scottish ~** ◊ **to be Scottish by ~** être d'origine écossaise **[c]** (*Dentistry*) extraction *f*

extractor [ik'stræktə^r] **[1]** N extracteur *m* **[2]** COMP ► **extractor fan** N (*Brit*) ventilateur *m* ► **extractor hood** N (*Brit*) hotte *f* aspirante

extracurricular [ˌekstrəkə'rɪkjʊlə^r] ADJ (*Scol*)

parascolaire, hors programme; [*sports*] en dehors des heures de classe

extraditable ['ekstrəˌdaɪtəbl] ADJ [*offence*] qui peut donner lieu à l'extradition; [*person*] passible *or* susceptible d'extradition

extradite ['ekstrəˌdaɪt] VT extrader

extradition [ˌekstrə'dɪʃən] **[1]** N extradition *f* **[2]** COMP ► **extradition warrant** N mandat *m* d'extradition

extragalactic [ˌekstrəgə'læktɪk] **[1]** ADJ extragalactique **[2]** COMP ► **extragalactic nebula** N nébuleuse *f* extragalactique

extralinguistic [ˌekstrəlɪŋ'gwɪstɪk] ADJ extralinguistique

extramarital ['ekstrə'mærɪtl] ADJ en dehors du mariage

extramural ['ekstrə'mjʊərəl] ADJ **[a]** (*esp Brit*) [*course*] hors faculté (*donné par des professeurs accrédités par la faculté et ouvert au public*); **~ lecture** conférence *f* publique; (*Brit Univ*) **Department of Extramural Studies** ≈ Institut *m* d'éducation permanente; (*US Scol*) **~ sports** sports pratiqués entre équipes de différents établissements **[b]** [*district*] extra-muros *inv*

extraneous [ik'streɪnɪəs] ADJ **[a]** (= *irrelevant*) [*matter, issue, detail, thought*] sans rapport avec le sujet; **~ to** étranger à **[b]** (*frm* = *external*) [*noise*] extérieur (-eure *f*)

extraordinaire [eks,trɔːdɪ'neə^r] ADJ (*after n: esp hum*) **George Kuchar, film-maker ~** George Kuchar, cinéaste hors du commun

extraordinarily [ik'strɔːdnrɪlɪ] ADV extraordinairement; **~, nobody was killed in the explosion** fait extraordinaire, personne n'a été tué par l'explosion

extraordinary [ik'strɔːdnrɪ] ADJ [*person, behaviour, appearance, success, courage, tale, speech*] extraordinaire; [*insults*] incroyable; [*violence*] inouï; **there's nothing ~ about that** cela n'a rien d'extraordinaire, il n'y a rien d'extraordinaire à cela; **I find it ~ that he hasn't replied** je trouve inouï qu'il n'ait pas répondu; **it's ~ to think that ...** il est extraordinaire de penser que ...; **it's ~ how much he resembles his brother** c'est inouï ce qu'il peut ressembler à son frère; **what an ~ thing to say!** quelle idée saugrenue!; **the ~ thing is that he's right** ce qu'il y a d'extraordinaire c'est qu'il a *or* ait raison; **an ~ meeting of the shareholders** une assemblée extraordinaire des actionnaires; (*Brit*) **an Extraordinary General Meeting of the Union** une assemblée générale extraordinaire du syndicat → **envoy**

extrapolate [ik'stræpəleit] VT extrapoler (**from** à partir de)

extrapolation [ik,stræpə'leiʃən] N extrapolation *f*

extrasensory ['ekstrə'sensərɪ] **[1]** ADJ extrasensoriel **[2]** COMP ► **extrasensory perception** N perception *f* extrasensorielle

extra-special [ˌekstrə'speʃəl] ADJ exceptionnel; **to take ~ care over sth** apporter un soin tout particulier à qch; **~ occasion** grande occasion *f*

extraterrestrial [ˌekstrətɪ'restrɪəl] ADJ, N extraterrestre *mf*

extraterritorial ['ekstrə,terɪ'tɔːrɪəl] ADJ d'extraterritorialité, d'extraterritorialité

extravagance [ik'strævəgəns] N **[a]** (= *excessive spending*) prodigalité *f*; (= *thing bought*) dépense *f* excessive, folie *f*; **gross mismanagement and financial ~** une mauvaise gestion flagrante et des dépenses excessives; **buying a yacht is sheer ~** acheter un yacht est une pure folie **[b]** (= *wastefulness*) gaspillage *m* **[c]** (= *action, notion*) extravagance *f*, fantaisie *f*

extravagant [ik'strævəgənt] ADJ **[a]** (*financially*) [*person*] dépensier; [*tastes*] de luxe; [*gift*] somptueux; [*price*] exorbitant, prohibitif; **~ spending** dépenses *fpl* excessives; **it seems ~ to hire a car** ça paraît exagéré de louer une

voiture; **it was very ~ of him to buy this ring** il a fait une folie en achetant cette bague; **to lead an ~ lifestyle** mener un train de vie fastueux; **to be ~ with one's money** être dépensier; **to be ~ with electricity** gaspiller l'électricité **[b]** (= *exaggerated*) [*person, behaviour, dress, talk, claims*] extravagant; [*praise*] outré; **to be ~ in one's praise of sb/sth** faire un éloge outré de qn/qch

extravagantly [ik'strævəgəntlɪ] ADV [*spend*] sans compter; [*use*] avec prodigalité; [*entertain*] sans regarder à la dépense; [*furnish*] avec luxe; [*behave, dress*] d'une façon extravagante; [*praise, thank*] à outrance; [*expensive*] excessivement; [*eccentric, gifted*] extrêmement; **to live ~** mener un train de vie fastueux; **an ~ large bouquet of flowers** un énorme bouquet de fleurs; **~ elegant** d'une élégance extravagante

extravaganza [ik,strævə'gænzə] N (*Literat, Mus*) fantaisie *f*; (= *story*) histoire *f* extravagante *or* invraisemblable; (= *show*) spectacle *m* somptueux; (= *whim*) folie *f*, caprice *m*

extravehicular [ˌekstrəvɪ'hɪkjʊlə^r] ADJ (*Space*) extravéhiculaire

extravert ['ekstrə,vɜːt] N, ADJ = extrovert

extreme [ik'striːm] **[1]** ADJ (*gen*) extrême; [*praise, flattery*] outré (*after n*); **of ~ importance** d'une extrême importance; **of ~ urgency** d'une extrême urgence, extrêmement urgent; **in ~ danger** en très grand danger; **the ~ end** l'extrémité *f*; **~ old age** l'extrême vieillesse *f*; **he died in ~ poverty** il est mort dans une misère extrême; **in the ~ distance** au loin; **the ~ north** l'extrême nord *m*; **to the ~ right** à l'extrême droite; (*Pol*) **the ~ left/right** l'extrême gauche *f*/droite *f*; **to be ~ in one's opinions** avoir des opinions extrêmes, être extrémiste
[2] N extrême *m*; **in the ~** [*difficult, irritating, obstinate, wealthy, helpful, interesting*] à l'extrême; **to go from one ~ to the other** passer d'un extrême à l'autre; **~s of temperature** écarts *mpl* extrêmes de température; **~s meet** les extrêmes se touchent; **to go to ~s** pousser les choses à l'extrême; **I won't go to that ~** je ne veux pas aller jusqu'à ces extrémités
[3] COMP ► **extreme sport** N sport *m* extrême ► **extreme unction** N (*Rel*) extrême-onction *f*

extremely [ik'striːmlɪ] ADV [*happy, difficult, important, high, helpful*] extrêmement; **to be ~ talented/successful** avoir énormément de talent/succès

extremism [ik'striːmɪzəm] N extrémisme *m*

extremist [ik'striːmɪst] ADJ, N extrémiste *mf*

extremity [ik'stremɪtɪ] N **[a]** (= *furthest point*) extrémité *f*, bout *m or* partie *m* le plus éloigné; **extremities** (= *hands and feet*) extrémités *fpl* **[b]** [*of despair, happiness*] extrême *or* dernier degré *m*; (= *extreme act*) extrémité *f*; **to drive sb to extremities** pousser qn à une extrémité **[c]** (= *danger, distress*) extrémité *f*; **to help sb in his ~** venir en aide à qn qui est aux abois

extricate ['ekstrɪkeɪt] VT [+ *object*] dégager (**from** de); **to ~ o.s.** s'extirper (**from** de); (*fig*) se tirer (**from** de); **to ~ sb from a nasty situation** tirer qn d'un mauvais pas

extrication [ˌekstrɪ'keɪʃən] N [*of object*] dégagement *m*; (*fig*) **to be in debt without hope of ~** être endetté sans espoir de s'en sortir

extrinsic [ek'strɪnsɪk] ADJ extrinsèque

extroversion [ˌekstrə'vɜːʃən] N extraversion *or* extroversion *f*

extrovert ['ekstrəʊ,vɜːt] (*esp Brit*) **[1]** ADJ extraverti *or* extroverti **[2]** N extraverti(e) *or* extroverti(e) *m(f)*; **he's an ~** il s'extériorise (beaucoup)

extroverted ['ekstrəʊ,vɜːtɪd] ADJ (*esp US*) = extrovert 1

extrude [ik'struːd] VT rejeter (**from** hors de), expulser (**from** de); [+ *metal, plastics*] extruder

extrusion [ɪk'stru:ʒən] N (Tech) extrusion f

extrusive [ɪk'stru:sɪv] ADJ extrusif

exuberance [ɪg'zju:bərəns] N [of person] exubérance f; [of vegetation] exubérance f, luxuriance f; [of words, images] richesse f, exubérance f

exuberant [ɪg'zju:bərənt] ADJ [person, personality, mood, style, film, music] exubérant; [growth, vegetation] exubérant, luxuriant; [colour] vif; [painting] d'un style exubérant

exuberantly [ɪg'zju:bərəntlɪ] ADV **a** (= highspiritedly) [laugh, embrace] avec exubérance; **to be ~ happy** manifester une joie exubérante **b** (Bot = vigorously) **to grow ~** être luxuriant

exude [ɪg'zju:d] **1** VI suinter, exsuder (from de) **2** VT [+ resin, blood] exsuder; **to ~ water** or **moisture** suinter; **he ~d charm** le charme lui sortait par tous les pores; **he ~s confidence** il respire la confiance en soi

exult [ɪg'zʌlt] VI (= rejoice) se réjouir (**in** de, **over** à propos de), exulter; (= triumph) jubiler, chanter victoire; **to ~ at finding** or **to find** se réjouir grandement or exulter de trouver

exultant [ɪg'zʌltənt] ADJ [person, mood, tone, expression] jubilant, triomphant; [joy] triomphant; **to be** or **feel ~** ◊ **to be in an ~ mood** être d'humeur joyeuse

exultantly [ɪg'zʌltəntlɪ] ADV en exultant, en jubilant

exultation [ˌegzʌl'teɪʃən] N exultation f, jubilation f

exurbia [eks'ɜ:bɪə] N (US) la banlieue aisée

ex-wife [ˌeks'waɪf] N (pl **ex-wives**) ex-femme f

ex-works [ˌeks'wɜ:ks] ADJ (Brit Comm) [price] départ usine → **ex 1**

---

eye [aɪ]

1 NOUN	**3** COMPOUNDS
2 TRANSITIVE VERB	**4** PHRASAL VERBS

1 NOUN

a of person, animal œil m (yeux pl); **to have brown ~s** avoir les yeux marron; **a girl with blue ~s** une fille aux yeux bleus; **before my very ~s** sous mes yeux; **it's there in front of your very ~s** il l'a sous les yeux, c'est sous ton nez*; **with tears in her ~s** les larmes aux yeux; **to have the sun in one's ~s** avoir le soleil dans les yeux; **I haven't got ~s in the back of my head** je n'ai pas des yeux dans le dos; **he must have ~s in the back of his head!** il n'a pas les yeux dans sa poche!; **to let one's ~s rest on sb/sth** poser son regard sur qn/qch; **I've never set** or **clapped*** or **laid ~s on him** je ne l'ai jamais vu de ma vie; **why don't you use your ~s?** tu es aveugle?; (Mil) **~s front!** fixe!; (Mil) **~s right!** tête (à) droite!; **an ~ for an ~ and a tooth for a tooth** œil pour œil, dent pour dent

b of object [of needle] chas m, œil m (œils pl); [of potato, peacock's tail] œil m (yeux pl); [of hurricane] œil m; [of camera] objectif m; (= photoelectric cell) œil m électrique; (fig) **the ~ of the storm** l'œil m du cyclone

c SET STRUCTURES

♦ **to close** or **shut one's eyes to**: **to close** or **shut one's ~s to sb's shortcomings** fermer les yeux sur les faiblesses de qn; **to close** or **shut one's ~s to the evidence** refuser or nier l'évidence; **to close** or **shut one's ~s to the dangers of sth/to the truth** refuser de voir les écueils de qch/la vérité en face; **one can't close** or **shut one's ~s to the fact that ...** il faut bien reconnaître que ...; **he preferred to close his ~s to the possibility of war** il refusait d'envisager la guerre

♦ **to get one's eye in** ajuster son coup d'œil

♦ **to give sb the eye*** faire de l'œil* à qn

♦ **to have an eye for**: **she has an ~ for a bargain** elle flaire or elle reconnaît tout de suite une bonne affaire; **she has** or **she's got an ~ for antiques** elle a le coup d'œil pour les antiquités

♦ **to have eyes for**: **he only had ~s for her** il n'avait d'yeux que pour elle; **they only have ~s for the championship** ils ne pensent qu'au championnat

♦ **to have (got) one's/an eye on**: **he's got his ~ on the championship** il lorgne le championnat; **I've already got my ~ on a house** j'ai déjà une maison en vue; **to have an ~ on sb for a job** avoir qn en vue pour un poste; **he had his ~ on a job in the Foreign Office** il visait un poste au ministère des Affaires étrangères

♦ **to keep an eye/one's eye(s) ...**: **he couldn't keep his ~s open*** il dormait debout; **to keep one's ~s wide open** garder les yeux grand(s) ouverts; **to keep one's ~ on the ball** (lit) fixer la balle; (fig) rester vigilant; **keeping his ~ on the bear, he seized his gun** sans quitter l'ours des yeux, il a empoigné son fusil; **keep your ~ on the main objective** ne perdez pas de vue le but principal; **to keep an ~ on things** or **on everything*** garder la boutique*; **will you keep an ~ on the baby/shop?** vous pouvez surveiller le bébé/le magasin?; **to keep an ~ on expenditure** surveiller ses dépenses; **to keep one's ~s open** or **peeled*** or **skinned*** ouvrir l'œil; **keep your ~s open for** or **keep an ~ out for a hotel*** essayez de repérer* un hôtel; **to keep a strict ~ on sb** surveiller qn de près, tenir qn à l'œil*

♦ **to make eyes at sb*** faire de l'œil à qn*

♦ **to open sb's eyes to**: **this will open his ~s to the truth** ça va lui ouvrir or dessiller les yeux

♦ **to take one's eye off**: **he didn't take his ~s off her** il ne l'a pas quittée des yeux; **he couldn't take his ~s off the cakes** il ne pouvait pas s'empêcher de lorgner les gâteaux, il dévorait les gâteaux des yeux; **to take one's ~ off the ball** (lit) arrêter de fixer le ballon; (fig) avoir un moment d'inattention

♦ **all eyes**: **all ~s are on him** tous les regards sont tournés vers lui; **all ~s are on the conference** tous les regards convergent sur la conférence; **to be all ~s*** être tout yeux

♦ **eye to eye**: **to see ~ to ~ with sb** (on specific issue) partager le point de vue de qn, être d'accord avec qn; **we rarely see ~ to ~** nous sommes rarement d'accord

♦ **my eye**: **my ~!** mon œil!*; **it's all my ~** tout ça, c'est des foutaises*

♦ **for your eyes only** (fig) ultraconfidentiel; (US: on documents) "~s only" « top secret »

♦ **in the eye(s)** (fig) **it hits you in the ~** cela saute aux yeux; **that's one in the ~ for him*** c'est bien fait pour lui or pour sa poire*; **in the ~s of ...** aux yeux de ...; **in his ~s** à ses yeux; **in the ~s of the law** au regard de or aux yeux de la loi

♦ **through sb's eyes**: **to look at sth through someone else's ~s** examiner qch du point de vue de quelqu'un d'autre; **to look at a question through the ~s of an economist** envisager une question du point de vue de l'économiste

♦ **under the eye of**: **under the ~ of** sous la surveillance de, sous l'œil de

♦ **up to the/one's eyes**: **to be up to one's ~s in work** être débordé (de travail); **to be up to one's ~s in paperwork** être dans la paperasse jusqu'au cou*; **to be up to one's ~s in debt** être endetté jusqu'au cou; (in crime, plot, conspiracy) **he's in it up to the** or **his ~s*** il est mouillé jusqu'au cou

♦ **with an eye/one's eyes**: **with one's ~s closed** or **shut** les yeux fermés; **with ~s half-closed** or **half-shut** les yeux mi-clos; **with my own ~s** de mes propres yeux; **I saw him with my own ~s** je l'ai vu de mes propres yeux; **he went into it with his ~s wide open** or **with open ~s** il s'y est lancé en toute connaissance de cause; (fig) **I could do it with my ~s shut** je pourrais le faire les yeux fermés; **with an ~ to the future** en prévision de l'avenir; **to look at a house with an ~ to buying** visiter une maison que l'on envisa-

ge d'acheter; **he's a man with an ~ for quality** c'est un homme qui sait reconnaître la bonne qualité; **a writer with an ~ for detail** un auteur qui a le sens du détail; **with a critical/a jealous/an uneasy** etc **~** d'un œil critique/jaloux/inquiet etc → **catch, fall, far, half, look, main, mind, open, private, run**

2 TRANSITIVE VERB
[+ person] regarder, mesurer du regard; [+ thing] regarder, observer; **to ~ sb from head to toe** toiser qn de la tête aux pieds

3 COMPOUNDS
► **eye-catcher** N personne f (or chose f) qui attire l'œil ► **eye-catching** ADJ [dress, colour] qui attire l'œil; [publicity, poster] accrocheur ► **eye contact** N **to establish/avoid ~ contact with sb** regarder/éviter de regarder qn dans les yeux ► **eye doctor** N (US) oculiste mf; (prescribing) ophtalmologue mf ► **eye job*** N opération de chirurgie esthétique aux yeux ► **eye level** N **at ~ level** au niveau des yeux ► **eye-level grill** N gril m surélevé ► **eye-opener*** N (= surprise) révélation f, surprise f; (US = drink) petit verre m pris au réveil; **that was an ~-opener for him** cela lui a ouvert les yeux; **his speech was an ~-opener** son discours a été très révélateur ► **eye-patch** N cache m, bandeau m ► **eye socket** N orbite f ► **eye test** N examen m de la vue

4 PHRASAL VERBS
► **eye up** VT SEP (Brit) reluquer*; **he was ~ing up the girls** il reluquait les filles

---

eyeball ['aɪbɔ:l] **1** N globe m oculaire; (fig) **to stand ~ to ~ with sb*** se trouver nez à nez avec qn; **to be up to one's ~s in work*** être débordé (de travail); **to be up to one's ~s in debt/paperwork*** être endetté/être dans la paperasse jusqu'au cou* **2** VT* zieuter*

eyebank ['aɪbæŋk] N (Med) banque f des yeux

eyebath ['aɪbɑ:θ] N (esp Brit) œillère f

eyebrow ['aɪbraʊ] **1** N sourcil m **2** COMP ► **eyebrow pencil** N crayon m à sourcils ► **eyebrow tweezers** NPL pince f à épiler

eyecup ['aɪkʌp] N (US) = **eyebath**

-eyed [aɪd] ADJ (in compounds) **big-eyed** aux grands yeux; **brown-eyed** aux yeux marron; **one-eyed** (lit) borgne; (* fig) miteux, minable → **dry, hollow**

eyedrops ['aɪdrɒps] NPL gouttes fpl pour les yeux, collyre m

eyeful ['aɪfʊl] N **he got an ~ of mud** il a reçu de la boue plein les yeux; **she's quite an ~*** cette fille, c'est un régal pour l'œil, elle est vraiment canon*; **get an ~ of this!*** vise un peu ça!*

eyeglass ['aɪglɑ:s] N monocle m

eyeglasses ['aɪglɑ:sɪz] NPL (esp US) lunettes fpl

eyelash ['aɪlæʃ] N cil m

eyelet ['aɪlɪt] N œillet m (dans du tissu etc)

eyelid ['aɪlɪd] N paupière f

eyeliner ['aɪlaɪnər] N eye-liner m

eyepiece ['aɪpi:s] N oculaire m

eyeshade ['aɪʃeɪd] N visière f

eyeshadow ['aɪʃædəʊ] N fard m à paupières

eyesight ['aɪsaɪt] N vue f; **to have good ~** avoir une bonne vue or de bons yeux; **to lose one's ~** perdre la vue; **his ~ is failing** sa vue baisse

eyesore ['aɪsɔ:r] N horreur f; **these ruins are an ~** ces ruines sont une horreur or sont hideuses

eyestrain ['aɪstreɪn] N **to have ~** avoir les yeux fatigués

eyetooth ['aɪtu:θ] N (pl **eyeteeth** ['aɪti:θ]) canine f supérieure; (fig) **I'd give my eyeteeth* for a car like that/to go to China** qu'est-ce que je ne donnerais pas pour avoir une voiture comme ça/pour aller en Chine

eyewash [ˈaɪwɒʃ] N a (*Med*) collyre *m* b (*fig*) **that's a lot of ~** (= *nonsense*) ce sont des fadaises, c'est du vent; (*to impress*)

c'est de la frime*, c'est de la poudre aux yeux

eyewitness [ˈaɪˌwɪtnɪs] 1 N témoin *m* oculaire *or* direct 2 COMP ► **eyewitness account** N (*in media*) récit *m* de témoin

oculaire; (*to police*) déposition *f* de témoin oculaire

eyrie [ˈɪərɪ] N aire *f* (*d'aigle*)

Ezekiel [ɪˈziːkɪəl] N Ézéchiel *m*

F

F, f [ef] N **a** (= *letter*) F, f *m or f*; **F for Freddy** ◊ **F for fox** (*US*) F comme François → **f-word, f-number** **b** (*Mus*) fa *m* **c** (*Scol* = *mark*) faible **d** ABBR = **Fahrenheit**

FA [ef'eɪ] (*Brit*) **a** (ABBR = **Football Association**) fédération *f* anglaise et galloise de football **b**⁎ (ABBR = **Fanny Adams**) → **Fanny**

fa [fɑː] N (*Mus*) fa *m*

FAA [,efer'eɪ] (*US*) (ABBR = **Federal Aviation Administration**) → **federal**

fab⁎ [fæb] ADJ (*Brit*) (ABBR = **fabulous**) sensass⁎, terrible⁎

Fabian ['feɪbɪən] **1** N (*Pol*) Fabien(ne) *m(f)* **2** ADJ fabien **3** COMP ► **Fabian Society** N Association *f* fabienne

fable ['feɪbl] N (*Literat, fig*) fable *f* → **fact**

fabled ['feɪbld] ADJ légendaire

fabric ['fæbrɪk] **1** N **a** (= *cloth*) tissu *m*, étoffe *f*; **cotton ~s** cotonnades *fpl*; **woollen ~s** lainages *mpl* **b** [*of building, system, society*] structure *f*; **the social ~ of our country** le tissu social de notre pays **2** COMP ► **fabric conditioner, fabric softener** N produit *m* assouplissant

fabricate ['fæbrɪkeɪt] VT **a** (= *manufacture*) [+ *goods*] fabriquer **b** (= *invent*) [+ *story, account*] inventer, fabriquer; [+ *evidence*] fabriquer; [+ *document*] fabriquer, forger; **to ~ an allegation** avancer une allégation

fabrication [,fæbrɪ'keɪʃən] N **a** (= *lie*) **it is (a) pure ~** c'est une invention pure et simple **b** (*NonC* = *invention*) [*of story, account*] invention *f*; [*of document*] fabrication *f*; (*Jur*) **~ of evidence** fabrication *f* de (fausses) preuves **c** (= *manufacturing*) [*of goods*] fabrication *f*

fabulist ['fæbjʊlɪst] N (*Literat*) fabuliste *m*

fabulous ['fæbjʊləs] ADJ **a** (= *incredible*) fabuleux **b** (⁎ = *wonderful*) [*prize, holiday, opportunity, weather*] fabuleux; **a ~ price** un prix fabuleux *or* astronomique; **~!** chouette!⁎, sensass!⁎ **c** (*liter* = *mythical*) [*beast, monster*] fabuleux (*liter*)

fabulously ['fæbjʊləslɪ] ADV [*wealthy, rich*] fabuleusement; [*expensive*] incroyablement; **to be ~ successful** avoir un succès fabuleux

façade [fə'sɑːd] N (*Archit, fig*) façade *f*

---

face [feɪs]

1	NOUN	4	COMPOUNDS
2	TRANSITIVE VERB	5	PHRASAL VERBS
3	INTRANSITIVE VERB		

1 NOUN

a Anat visage *m*; **a pleasant ~** un visage agréable; **he stuck his ~ out of the window** il a passé la tête par la fenêtre; **I know that ~** ◊ **that ~ is familiar** ce visage me dit quelque chose; **injuries to the ~** blessures *fpl* à la face *or* au visage; **to have one's ~ lifted** se faire faire un lifting; **to put one's ~ on**⁎ se faire une beauté⁎; **he won't show his ~ here again** il ne remettra plus les pieds ici; **to go red in the ~** rougir; (*fig*) **I could never look him in the ~ again** je ne pourrais plus le regarder en face; **to be written**

across *or* all over *or* on sb's **~** se lire sur le visage de qn; **you're lying, it's written all over your ~!** tu mens, ça se lit sur ton visage!

◆ **in one's face**: **the rain was blowing in our ~s** la pluie nous fouettait le visage *or* la figure; (*lit*) **it blew up in my ~** ça m'a explosé à la figure; (*fig*) **his plan blew up in his ~** son plan s'est retourné contre lui → **in-your-face**

◆ **in the face of**: **courage in the ~ of the enemy** courage *m* face à l'ennemi; **they remained defiant in the ~ of international condemnation** ils persistaient à défier la condamnation internationale; **in the ~ of this threat** devant cette menace, face à cette menace; **he succeeded in the ~ of great difficulties** il a réussi en dépit de grandes difficultés

◆ **to sb's face**: **he told him so to his ~** il le lui a dit en face *or* sans détour; **he told him the truth to his ~** il lui a dit la vérité sans détour

◆ **face to face**: **to come ~ to ~ with** (= *meet*) se trouver face à face *or* nez à nez avec; (*fig* = *confront*) [+ *problem, difficulty*] devoir affronter; **to bring two people ~ to ~** confronter deux personnes → **4**

◆ **to be off one's face**⁎ (*Brit*) être bourré⁎

◆ **out of sb's face**⁎: **get out of my ~!** fous-moi la paix!⁎

b = front **he was lying ~ down(wards)** (*on ground*) il était face contre terre *or* à plat ventre; (*on bed, sofa*) il était à plat ventre; **he was lying ~ up(wards)** il était allongé sur le dos; **to fall (flat) on one's ~** (*lit*) tomber à plat ventre, tomber face contre terre; (*fig*) se planter⁎

c = expression mine *f*; **to make** *or* **pull ~s (at)** faire des grimaces (à); **to make** *or* **pull a (disapproving) ~** faire la moue; **to put a bold** *or* **brave ~ on things** faire bonne contenance; **you'll just have to put a good ~ on it** tu n'auras qu'à faire contre mauvaise fortune bon cœur; **to set one's ~ against sth** s'élever contre qch; **to set one's ~ against doing** se refuser à faire

d = appearance visage *m*; **to change the ~ of a town** changer le visage d'une ville; **the changing ~ of Malaysian politics** le visage changeant de la politique malaise; **the unacceptable ~ of capitalism** la face inacceptable du capitalisme; **on the ~ of it** his evidence is false à première vue, son témoignage est faux

e ⁎ = person visage *m*; (= *celebrity*) nom *m* (connu); **a familiar ~** un visage familier; **among familiar ~s** parmi des visages familiers *or* connus; **the new committee includes many of the same old ~s** on retrouve les mêmes visages dans le nouveau comité; **we need some new** *or* **fresh ~s on the team** notre équipe a besoin de sang neuf

f of building façade *f*

g of clock cadran *m*

h Climbing [*of mountain*] face *f*; [*of cliff*] paroi *f*; **the north ~ of the Eiger** la face nord de l'Eiger

i = surface [*of coin*] côté *m*; [*of the earth*] surface *f*; [*of document*] recto *m*; [*of playing card*] face *f*, dessous *m*; **it fell ~ up/down** [*playing card, photo*] elle est tombée face en

dessus/en dessous; [*coin*] elle est tombée côté face/pile; **to turn sth ~ up** retourner *or* mettre qch à l'endroit; **he vanished off the ~ of the earth** il a complètement disparu

j Typ œil *m*

k = prestige **to lose ~**⁎ perdre la face → **loss**

l = impertinence **to have the ~**⁎ **to do sth** avoir le toupet⁎ de faire qch

2 TRANSITIVE VERB

a = turn one's face towards faire face à; **he turned and ~d the man** il se retourna et fit face à l'homme; **~ this way!** tournez-vous de ce côté!

b = have one's face towards faire face à, être en face de; **he was facing me** il me faisait face; **facing one another** en face l'un de l'autre, l'un en face de l'autre; **the two boys ~d each other** les deux garçons se faisaient face *or* étaient face à face; **he was facing the wall** il était face au mur; (*fig*) **to ~ both ways** ménager la chèvre et le chou

c = have its front towards (*gen*) faire face à; (= *look out onto*) [*building, window*] faire face à, donner sur; **the seats were all facing the platform** les sièges faisaient tous face à l'estrade; **the picture facing page 16** l'illustration en regard de *or* en face de la page 16; **which way does the house ~?** comment la maison est-elle orientée?; **the house ~s north** la maison est orientée au nord

d = confront [*problem, task, situation*] se présenter à; **two problems/tasks ~d them** deux problèmes/tâches se présentaient à eux, ils se trouvaient devant deux problèmes/tâches; **the problem facing us** le problème devant lequel nous nous trouvons *or* qui se pose à nous; **the economic difficulties facing the country** les difficultés économiques que rencontre le pays *or* auxquelles le pays doit faire face

◆ **faced with**: **the government, ~d with renewed wage demands ...** le gouvernement, confronté à de nouvelles revendications salariales ...; **he was ~d with a class who refused to cooperate** il se trouvait face à *or* confronté à une classe qui refusait de coopérer; **~d with the task of deciding, he ...** se trouvant dans l'obligation de prendre une décision, il ...; **he was ~d with having to pay £100** *or* **with a bill for £100** il se voyait contraint *or* obligé de payer (une note de) 100 livres; **he was ~d with the possibility that they might refuse** il risquait de les voir refuser; **he was ~d with the prospect of doing it himself** il risquait d'avoir à le faire lui-même; **~d with the prospect of having to refuse, he ...** face à *or* devant la perspective d'avoir à refuser, il ...

◆ **to face sb with sth**: **you must ~ him with this choice/the decision** vous devez le contraindre à faire face à ce choix/cette décision; **you must ~ him with the truth** vous devez le contraindre à regarder la vérité en face

e = look at honestly [+ *problem*] faire face à; [+ *truth*] regarder en face; **she ~d the problem at last** elle a enfin fait face au problème; **to ~ the music** braver l'orage *or* la tempête; **sooner**

or later he'll have to ~ **the music** tôt ou tard, il va devoir braver l'orage or la tempête; **to ~ (the) facts** regarder les choses en face, se rendre à l'évidence; **she won't ~ the fact that he's not going to come back** elle ne veut pas se rendre à l'évidence et admettre qu'il ne reviendra pas; **let's ~ it** regardons les choses en face

♦ **can't/couldn't face**: **I can't ~ doing it** je n'ai pas le courage de le faire; **I can't ~ breakfast this morning** je ne peux rien avaler ce matin; **I can't ~ him/the washing up** je n'ai pas le courage de le voir/de faire la vaisselle; **I couldn't ~ this alone** je ne pourrais pas y faire face tout seul

|f| **= risk incurring** [+ *fine, charges, prison, defeat, death*] risquer; [+ *unemployment, redundancy*] être menacé de; **he ~s life in prison if convicted** il risque la prison à vie s'il est reconnu coupable; **many people were facing redundancy** beaucoup de gens étaient menacés de licenciement or risquaient d'être licenciés

|g| **= line** [+ *wall*] revêtir (**with** de); (*Sewing*) doubler; **the hood is ~d with silk** la capuche est doublée de soie

③ INTRANSITIVE VERB

|a| |person| (= *turn one's face*) se tourner (**towards** vers); (= *be turned*) faire face (**towards** à); **he was facing towards the audience** il faisait face au public; (*US Mil*) **right ~!** à droite, droite!; (*US Mil*) **about ~!** demi-tour!

|b| |house| être exposé or orienté; **a window facing south** une fenêtre orientée au sud; **a room facing towards the sea** une chambre donnant sur la mer

④ COMPOUNDS

► **face card** N (*US*) figure *f* (*de jeu de cartes*) ► **face cloth** N = **face flannel** ► **face cream** N crème *f* pour le visage ► **face flannel** N (*Brit*) ≈ gant *m* de toilette ► **face guard** N (*Baseball*) visière *f* de protection ► **face-lift** N lifting *m*; **to have a ~-lift** se faire faire un lifting; (*fig*) **to give a ~-lift*** **to** [+ *house*] (*exterior*) ravaler la façade de; (*interior*) retaper; [+ *political party, company*] rajeunir l'image de; **the town/the park/the garden has been given a ~-lift*** la ville/le parc/le jardin a fait peau neuve ► **face mask** N masque *m*; (*Cosmetics*) masque *m* (de beauté) ► **face-off** N (*Hockey*) remise *f* en jeu; (*fig*) confrontation *f* ► **face pack** N masque *m* (de beauté) ► **face powder** N poudre *f* de riz ► **face-saver** N → face-saving ► **face-saving** ADJ qui sauve la face ♦ **it was clearly a piece of ~-saving** or **a ~-saver on their part** ils ont visiblement fait cela pour sauver la face ► **face-to-face** ADJ face à face, nez à nez; (*TV etc*) ~-to-~ discussion face à face *m inv*, face-à-face *m inv* ► **face value** N valeur *f* nominale; (*fig*) **to take a statement at (its) ~ value** prendre une déclaration au pied de la lettre; **to take sb at ~ value** juger qn sur les apparences; **you can't take it at (its) ~ value** il ne faut pas vous laisser tromper par les apparences

⑤ PHRASAL VERBS

► **face about** VI (*Mil*) faire demi-tour

► **face down** VT SEP (*esp US*) défier du regard

► **face out*** VT SEP (*Brit*) **to ~ it out** faire front; **to ~ out a crisis** faire face à or affronter une crise

► **face up to** VT FUS [+ *danger, difficulty*] faire face à, affronter; [+ *responsibilities*] faire face à; **to ~ up to the fact that ...** admettre or accepter (le fait) que ...

faceless ['feɪslɪs] ADJ anonyme

facer* ['feɪsəʳ] N (*Brit*) **it was a real ~** c'était un sacré* problème

facet ['fæsɪt] N (*lit, fig*) facette *f*

faceted ['fæsɪtɪd] ADJ à facettes

facetious [fə'siːʃəs] ADJ [*person*] facétieux, plaisant; [*remark*] plaisant, bouffon

facetiously [fə'siːʃəslɪ] ADV facétieusement

facetiousness [fə'siːʃəsnɪs] N [*of person*] esprit *m* facétieux; [*of remark*] caractère *m* or côté *m* facétieux; (= *jokes*) facéties *fpl*

facia ['feɪʃə] N = fascia

facial ['feɪʃəl] ① ADJ [*nerve, muscles, massage*] facial; [*expression*] du visage; [*injury*] au visage; **~ features** traits *mpl* (du visage) ② N* soin *m* (complet) du visage; **to have a ~** se faire faire un soin du visage; **to give o.s. a ~** se faire un nettoyage de peau ③ COMP ► **facial hair** N poils *mpl* du visage ► **facial scrub** N exfoliant *m*, produit *m* gommant (pour le visage) ► **facial wash** N lotion *f* (pour le visage)

facially ['feɪʃəlɪ] ADV **~ disfigured** défiguré; **to be ~ scarred** avoir une (or des) cicatrice(s) au visage; **they are ~ similar** leurs visages se ressemblent

facies ['feɪʃiːz] N (*pl inv*) faciès *m*

facile ['fæsaɪl] ADJ (*pej*) [*person, talk, idea, style*] superficiel; [*optimism, solution, comparison*] facile (*pej*); [*question*] simpliste; **it is ~ to suggest that ...** c'est un peu facile de suggérer que ...

facilely ['fæsaɪllɪ] ADV complaisamment

facilitate [fə'sɪlɪteɪt] VT faciliter

facilitator [fə'sɪlɪteɪtəʳ] N (*Pol, Ind*) médiateur *m*, -trice *f*, conciliateur *m*, -trice *f*; (*Psych, Educ*) animateur *m*, -trice *f*

facility [fə'sɪlɪtɪ] N |a| **facilities** (= *equipment, material*) équipements *mpl* (**for** de); (= *place, installation*) installations *fpl*; **military facilities** installations *fpl* militaires; **sports/educational facilities** équipements *mpl* sportifs/scolaires; **storage facilities** (*Ind*) installations *fpl* d'entreposage, entrepôts *mpl*; (*in house* = *wardrobes, cupboards etc*) espaces *mpl* de rangement; **a large hotel with all facilities** un grand hôtel doté de tout le confort moderne; **toilet facilities** toilettes *fpl*, sanitaires *mpl*; **health care facilities** services *mpl* de santé, infrastructure *f* médicale; **child care facilities** (= *crèches*) crèches *fpl*; (*for older children*) garderies *fpl*; **we offer facilities for childminding from 8am to 8pm** nous proposons une crèche or garderie pour les enfants de 8 heures à 20 heures; **play facilities for young children** un espace de jeu pour les petits enfants; **there are no facilities for children/the disabled** ce n'est pas aménagé pour les enfants/les handicapés; **the flat has no cooking facilities** l'appartement n'est pas équipé pour faire la cuisine

|b| (= *means* (*of doing sth*)) moyens *mpl* (**for** de), possibilité *f* (**for doing** de faire); **transport/production facilities** moyens *mpl* de transport/de production; **a ~ for converting part of one's pension into ...** la possibilité de convertir une partie de sa retraite en ...; **the bank offers the ~ to pay over 50 weeks** la banque offre la possibilité d'étaler les paiements sur 50 semaines; **we have no ~ or facilities for disposing of toxic waste** nous ne sommes pas en mesure d'éliminer les déchets toxiques; **you will have all facilities or every ~ for study** vous aurez toutes facilités or tout ce qu'il faut pour étudier; **a computer with the ~ to reproduce speech** un ordinateur capable de reproduire le son de la voix; **the machine does not have the ~ to run this program** l'appareil ne permet pas d'exécuter ce programme → overdraft

|c| (*Tech etc* = *device*) mécanisme *m*; (*Comput*) fonction *f*; **the clock has a stopwatch ~** le réveil peut aussi servir de chronomètre; **the oven has an automatic timing ~** le four est doté d'un minuteur automatique; (*Comput*) **there's a ~ for storing data** il y a une fonction de mise en mémoire des données

|d| (= *place, building*) **the museum has a ~ where students can work** le musée met à la disposition des étudiants un endroit où travailler; **student facilities include a library and**

language laboratory les étudiants disposent notamment d'une bibliothèque et d'un laboratoire de langues; **a newly-built manufacturing ~** une nouvelle usine; **nuclear ~** (= *arms factory*) usine *f* nucléaire; (= *power station*) centrale *f* nucléaire

|e| (*NonC* = *ease*) facilité *f*; **to write/speak/express o.s. with ~** écrire/parler/s'exprimer avec facilité or aisance

|f| (= *person's talent, ability*) **her ~ in** or **for learning** ◊ **her learning ~** sa facilité à apprendre; **he has a great ~ for languages/maths** il est très doué pour les langues/les maths, il a beaucoup de facilité en langues/maths

facing ['feɪsɪŋ] N (*Constr*) revêtement *m*; (*Sewing*) revers *m*

-facing ['feɪsɪŋ] ADJ (*in compounds*) **south-facing** exposé au sud

facsimile [fæk'sɪmɪlɪ] ① N fac-similé *m*; **in ~** en fac-similé ② COMP ► **facsimile machine** N télécopieur *m* ► **facsimile transmission** N télécopie *f*

▼ **fact** [fækt] ① N |a| (= *sth known, accepted as true*) fait *m*; **the ~ that he is here** le fait qu'il est là or qu'il soit là; **it is a ~ that ...** il est de fait que ...; **in view of the ~ that ...** étant donné que ...; **despite the ~ that ...** bien que ... (+ *subj*); **is it a ~ that ...?** est-il vrai que ... (+ *subj* or *indic*)?; (*iro*) **is that a ~?** vraiment?; **(and) that's a ~** c'est certain or sûr; **I know it for a ~** j'en suis sûr; **to know (it) for a ~ that ...** être certain que ...; **let's stick to the ~s** tenons-nous-en aux faits; **we haven't got all the ~s and figures yet** nous ne disposons pas encore de tous les éléments; **interesting ~s and figures about the different peoples of Africa** des informations intéressantes sur les différents peuples d'Afrique; **it's a ~ of life (that ...)** la vie est ainsi faite (que ...); **it's time he knew the ~s of life** (*gen*) il est temps de lui apprendre les choses de la vie or qu'on le mette devant les réalités de la vie; (*about sex*) il est temps qu'il sache comment les enfants viennent au monde → face

|b| (*NonC* = *reality*) faits *mpl*, réalité *f*; **story founded on ~** histoire *f* basée sur des faits or sur la réalité; **~ and fiction** le réel et l'imaginaire; **he can't tell ~ from fiction** or **from fable** il ne sait pas séparer le vrai du faux; **the ~ of the matter is that ...** le fait est que ...; **I accept what he says as ~** je ne mets en doute la véracité de ses propos

|c| **in ~** en fait; (*reinforcing sth*) effectivement; **he had promised to send the books and in ~ they arrived the next day** il avait promis d'envoyer les livres et ils sont effectivement arrivés le lendemain; **it was a terrible party, in ~ I only stayed for half an hour** la soirée était nulle, en fait, je ne suis resté qu'une demi-heure; **only I knew that Phyllis was, in ~, David's sister** j'étais le seul à savoir que Phyllis était en fait la sœur de David; **it sounds rather simple, but in (actual) ~** or **in point of ~ it's very difficult** cela paraît plutôt simple, mais en fait or en réalité, c'est très difficile

|d| (*Jur*) fait *m*, action *f* → accessary

② COMP ► **fact-finding** ADJ **~-finding committee** commission *f* d'enquête; **they were on a ~-finding mission** or **trip** or **visit to the war front** ils étaient partis en mission d'inspection au front; **~-finding session** séance *f* d'information ► **fact sheet** N fiche *f* d'informations

faction[1] ['fækʃən] N |a| (= *group*) faction *f* |b| (*NonC* = *strife*) discorde *f*, dissension *f*

faction[2] ['fækʃən] N (*Theat, Cine* = *mixture of fact and fiction*) docudrame *m*

factional ['fækʃənl] ADJ [*fighting, violence, rivalry*] entre factions; [*leader*] de faction

factionalism ['fækʃənlɪzəm] N querelles *fpl* intestines

► LANGUAGE IN USE: **fact** 26.1, 26.3

factionalize ['fækʃənlaɪz] VT diviser (en factions)

factious ['fækʃəs] ADJ factieux

factitious [fæk'tɪʃəs] ADJ artificiel

factitive ['fæktɪtɪv] ADJ (*Gram*) factitif

factor ['fæktə'] **1** N **a** (*gen, Bio, Math*) facteur *m*, élément *m*; **risk ~** facteur *m* de risque; (*Tech*) **~ of safety** ◊ **safety ~** facteur *m* de sécurité; **the human ~** le facteur humain; **determining** or **deciding ~** facteur *m* déterminant or décisif; **a (crucial) ~ in determining/deciding sth** un facteur (essentiel) lorsqu'il s'agit de déterminer/décider qch; **price is very much a determining ~ in deciding which car to buy** le prix est un critère important or déterminant lors de l'achat d'une voiture; **the scandal was a contributing ~ in his defeat** le scandale a contribué à sa défaite; **output has risen by a ~ of ten** la production a été multipliée par dix → **common, prime**
b (*of sun cream*) (**sun protection**) **~ 9/17** *etc* indice *m* (de protection) 9/17 etc
c (= *agent*) agent *m*; (*Scot* = *estate manager*) régisseur *m*, intendant *m*
2 COMP ► **factor analysis** N (*Stat*) analyse *f* factorielle ► **factor VIII, factor 8** N (*Med*) facteur *m* 8
► **factor in** VT SEP (*esp US*) prendre en compte

factorage ['fæktərɪdʒ] N **a** (*Comm*) commission *f* **b** (*Fin*) commission *f* d'affacturage or de factoring

factorial [fæk'tɔːrɪəl] **1** ADJ factoriel **2** N factorielle *f*

factoring ['fæktərɪŋ] N affacturage *m*, factoring *m*

factorize ['fæktə,raɪz] VT (*Math*) mettre en facteurs

factory ['fæktərɪ] **1** N usine *f*; **shoe/soap** *etc* **~** usine *f* or fabrique *f* de chaussures/de savon *etc*; **car/textile** *etc* **~** usine *f* d'automobiles/de textile *etc*; **arms/china/tobacco ~** manufacture *f* d'armes/de porcelaine/de tabac **2** COMP ► **Factory Acts** NPL (*Brit*) législation *f* industrielle ► **factory chimney** N cheminée *f* d'usine ► **factory farm** N ferme *f* industrielle ► **factory farming** N élevage *m* industriel ► **factory floor** N ateliers *mpl*; **workers on the ~ floor** ouvriers *mpl* ► **factory-fresh** ADJ tout droit sorti de l'usine ► **factory hand** N = **factory worker** ► **factory inspector** N inspecteur *m* du travail ► **factory outlet** N magasin *m* d'usine ► **factory ship** N navire-usine *m* ► **factory work** N (*NonC*) travail *m* en or d'usine ► **factory worker** N ouvrier *m*, -ière *f* (d'usine)

factotum [fæk'təʊtəm] N factotum *m*, intendant *m*; (*hum*) **general ~** bonne *f* à tout faire (*fig, hum*)

factual ['fæktjʊəl] ADJ [*information, basis, evidence, account*] factuel; [*error*] sur les faits, de fait; [*knowledge*] des faits

factually ['fæktjʊəlɪ] ADV [*accurate, correct, wrong*] dans les faits; **~ based** fondé or basé sur des faits réels; **she told her story ~ and without emotion** elle a raconté son histoire factuellement et sans trace d'émotion

faculty ['fækəltɪ] **1** N **a** faculté *f*; **the mental faculties** les facultés *fpl* mentales; **to have all one's faculties** avoir toutes ses facultés; **critical ~** le sens critique **b** (*NonC* = *aptitude*) aptitude *f*, facilité *f* (**for doing** à faire) **c** (*Univ*) faculté *f*; **the Faculty of Arts** la faculté des Lettres; **the medical ~** la faculté de médecine; (*US*) **the Faculty** le corps enseignant → **law, science 2** COMP ► **faculty advisor** N (*US Univ*) (*for student*) directeur *m*, -trice *f* d'études; (*for club*) animateur *m*, -trice *f* ► **Faculty board** N (*Univ*) Conseil *m* de faculté ► **Faculty board meeting** N réunion *f* du Conseil de faculté ► **faculty lounge** N (*US Scol*) salle *f* des professeurs ► **Faculty meeting** N = **Faculty board meeting**

► LANGUAGE IN USE: **fail** 11.2

fad [fæd] N (*personal*) marotte *f*, manie *f*; (*in society in general*) engouement *m*, mode *f*; **she has her ~s** elle a ses (petites) marottes or manies; **her latest food ~** sa dernière lubie en matière de nourriture; **a passing ~** un engouement, une lubie

faddish ['fædɪʃ], **faddy** ['fædɪ] ADJ (*Brit*) [*person*] capricieux, à marottes; [*distaste, desire*] capricieux

fade [feɪd] **1** VI **a** [*colour*] passer, perdre son éclat; [*material*] passer, se décolorer; [*light*] baisser, diminuer; [*flower*] se faner, se flétrir; (*Tex*) **guaranteed not to ~** garanti bon teint; **the daylight was fast fading** le jour baissait rapidement
b (*also ~ away*) [*thing remembered, vision*] s'effacer; [*interest, enthusiasm*] diminuer, décliner; [*sound*] s'affaiblir; [*smile*] s'évanouir; [*one's sight, memory, hearing etc*] baisser; **the castle ~d from sight** le château disparut aux regards; **her voice ~d into silence** sa voix s'est éteinte; (*Rad*) **the sound is fading** il y a du fading; **our hopes had ~d** nos espoirs s'étaient évanouis; **hopes are fading of finding any more survivors** l'espoir de découvrir d'autres survivants s'amenuise; **to ~ into the background** [*person*] se fondre dans le décor; **my fears for Philip ~d into the background** mes craintes pour Philip furent reléguées au second plan; **a singer who ~d into obscurity after just one hit record** un chanteur qui est retombé dans l'anonymat après seulement un tube*
c (*liter = die*) [*person*] dépérir
2 VT **a** [+ *curtains etc*] décolorer; [+ *colours, flowers*] faner
b (*Rad*) [+ *conversation*] couper par un fondu sonore; (*Cine, TV*) **to ~ one scene into another** faire un fondu enchaîné
3 N = **fade-out**
4 COMP ► **fade-in** N (*Cine*) fondu *m* en ouverture; (*Rad*) apparition *f* graduelle; (*Rad*) fondu *m* sonore ► **fade in-fade out** N (*Cine*) fondu *m* enchaîné ► **fade-out** N (*Cine*) fondu *m* en fermeture; (*TV*) disparition *f* graduelle; (*Rad*) fondu *m* sonore
► **fade away** VI = **fade 1b**
► **fade in 1** VI (*Cine, TV*) apparaître en fondu **2** VT SEP (*Cine, TV*) faire apparaître en fondu; (*Rad*) monter **3** **~-in** N → **fade**
► **fade out 1** VI (*Cine, TV*) [*picture*] disparaître en fondu; (*Rad*) [*music, dialogue*] être coupé par un fondu sonore **2** VT SEP (*Cine, TV*) faire disparaître en fondu; (*Rad*) couper par un fondu sonore **3** **~-out** N → **fade**

faded ['feɪdɪd] ADJ [*material*] décoloré, passé; [*jeans*] délavé; [*flowers*] fané, flétri; [*beauty*] défraîchi, fané

faecal, fecal (*US*) ['fiːkəl] ADJ fécal

faeces, feces (*US*) ['fiːsiːz] NPL fèces *fpl*

faerie, faery ['fɛərɪ] († *or liter*) **1** N féerie *f* **2** ADJ imaginaire, féerique

Faeroes ['fɛərəʊz] NPL = **Faroes**

faff [fæf] VI (*Brit*) **to ~ about** or **around** glandouiller*

fag [fæg] **1** N **a** (*Brit* ‡ = *cigarette*) clope* *f*
b (*esp US* ‡ *pej* = *homosexual*) pédé‡ *m*
c (*NonC: Brit* ‡) corvée *f*; **what a ~!** quelle corvée! **d** (*Brit Scol*) petit élève au service d'un grand **2** VT (*Brit*) **a** (*also ~ out*) [+ *person, animal*] éreinter, épuiser; **to be ~ged (out)** être claqué* or crevé* **b** **I can't be ~ged:** j'ai la flemme* (**to do** de faire) **3** VI (*Brit Scol*) **to ~ for sb** faire les menues corvées de qn **4** COMP ► **fag end** N **a** ‡ [*of cigarette*] mégot* *m* **b** (= *remainder*) restant *m*, reste *m*; [*of conversation*] dernières bribes *fpl* ► **fag hag:** N **she's a ~ hag** elle a des amis homos*

faggot¹, fagot (*US*) ['fægət] N **a** (= *wood*) fagot *m* **b** (*Brit Culin*) ≈ crépinette *f*

faggot²: ['fægət] N (*esp US pej*) (= *homosexual*) pédé‡ *m*, tante‡ *f*

fah [fɑː] N (*Mus*) fa *m*

Fahrenheit ['færənhaɪt] ADJ Fahrenheit *inv*; **~ thermometer/scale** thermomètre *m*/échelle *f* Fahrenheit; **degrees ~** degrés *mpl* Fahrenheit

▼ **fail** [feɪl] **1** VI **a** (= *be unsuccessful*) [*person*] (*gen*) échouer; (*in exam*) échouer, être recalé* or collé*; [*plans, attempts, treatment*] échouer, ne pas réussir; [*negotiations*] ne pas aboutir, échouer; [*play, show*] faire or être un four; [*bank, business*] faire faillite; **to ~ in an exam/in Latin** échouer or être recalé* à un examen/en latin; **to ~ by five votes/by ten minutes** échouer à cinq voix près/à dix minutes près; **to ~ miserably or dismally** échouer lamentablement; **he ~ed in his attempt to take control of the company** sa tentative de prendre le contrôle de la société a échoué; **to ~ in one's duty** faillir à or manquer à son devoir
b (= *grow weak*) [*hearing, eyesight, health*] faiblir; [*person, invalid, voice*] s'affaiblir; **his eyes are ~ing** sa vue faiblit or baisse; **his heart/lungs/liver ~ed** il a eu une défaillance cardiaque/pulmonaire/hépatique; **the daylight was beginning to ~** le jour commençait à baisser
c (= *run short*) [*power, gas, electricity, water supply*] manquer; **crops ~ed because of the drought** la sécheresse a causé la perte des récoltes
d (= *break down*) [*engine*] tomber en panne; [*brakes*] lâcher
2 VT **a** [+ *examination*] échouer à, être recalé* or collé* à; **to ~ Latin** échouer or être recalé* en latin; **to ~ one's driving test** échouer à or être recalé* à son permis (de conduire); **he's a ~ed writer** c'est un écrivain raté
b [+ *candidate*] recaler*, coller*
c (= *let down*) [+ *business partner*] manquer à ses engagements envers; [+ *friend, colleague, loved one*] (= *disappoint*) décevoir; (= *neglect*) délaisser; **don't ~ me!** je compte sur vous!; **he felt that he'd ~ed his family** il avait le sentiment d'avoir manqué à ses devoirs envers sa famille; **his heart ~ed him** le cœur lui a manqué; **words ~ me!** les mots me manquent!; **his memory often ~s him** sa mémoire lui fait souvent défaut, sa mémoire le trahit souvent
d (= *omit*) **to ~ to do** manquer de faire; **he never ~s to write** il ne manque jamais d'écrire; **he ~ed to visit her** il a omis de lui rendre visite; **he ~ed to meet the deadline** il n'est pas parvenu à respecter les délais; **he ~ed to keep his word** il a manqué à sa parole; **he ~ed to turn up for dinner** il ne s'est pas montré au dîner; **they ~ed to make any progress/to get an agreement** ils n'ont absolument pas progressé/ne sont pas parvenus à un accord; **she never ~s to amaze me** elle me surprendra toujours; **I ~ to see why** je ne vois pas pourquoi; **I ~ to understand** je n'arrive pas à comprendre; (*Jur*) **to ~ to appear** faire défaut; (*Jur*) **he was fined for ~ing to stop at a red light** il a eu une amende or contravention pour avoir brûlé un feu rouge
3 N **a** **without ~** [*happen, befall*] immanquablement; [*come, do*] chaque fois, sans exception; (*implying obligation*) sans faute; **every morning without ~, she takes the dog for a walk** chaque matin sans exception, elle sort son chien; **I'll bring you the money first thing in the morning without ~** je vous apporterai l'argent sans faute, demain à la première heure; **you must take these tablets every day without ~** il faut que vous preniez ces cachets tous les jours sans faute or sans exception
b (*Scol, Univ*) échec *m*; **she got a ~ in history** elle a échoué or a été recalée* or a été collée* en histoire
4 COMP ► **fail-safe** ADJ (*Tech*) à sûreté intégrée

failing [ˈfeɪlɪŋ] **1** N défaut m **2** PREP à défaut de ; **~ this** sinon ; **~ which we ...** sinon or faute de quoi nous ... ; **drugs can often help. Failing this, surgery may be required** les médicaments sont souvent efficaces, sinon, or dans le cas contraire, on peut avoir recours à la chirurgie **3** ADJ [eyesight, health, memory] défaillant ; [marriage] qui va à vau-l'eau ; [light] qui baisse ; [economy] déprimé, en récession ; (US Scol) "**~**" « faible »

failure [ˈfeɪljəʳ] **1** N **a** (= lack of success) [of person, plan] échec m ; [of bank, business] faillite f ; [of discussions, negotiations] échec m, fiasco m ; **academic ~** l'échec m scolaire (or universitaire) ; **I was surprised by her ~ in the exam** j'ai été surpris qu'elle échoue à cet examen ; **after two ~s he gave up** il a abandonné après deux échecs ; **the play was a ~** la pièce a fait un four or a été un fiasco ; **this new machine/this plan is a total ~** cette nouvelle machine/ce projet est un fiasco complet ; **his ~ to convince them** son incapacité or son impuissance à les convaincre → **rate¹**
b (= unsuccessful person) raté(e) m(f) ; **to be a ~ at maths** être nul en math ; **to be a ~ at gardening** ne pas être doué pour le jardinage ; **he's a ~ as a writer** (= poor writer) il ne vaut rien comme écrivain ; (= unsuccessful writer) il n'a pas eu de succès en tant qu'écrivain
c (= insufficiency) [of electricity] panne f ; **~ of oil/water supply** manque de pétrole/d'eau ; **~ of the crops** perte f des récoltes
d (Med) **heart/kidney/liver ~** défaillance f cardiaque/rénale/hépatique
e (= breakdown) [of engine] panne f
f (= omission) **his ~ to answer** le fait qu'il n'a pas répondu ; **because of his ~ to help us** du fait qu'il ne nous a pas aidés ; **the government's ~ to comply with EU legal obligations** le non-respect des lois de l'UE de la part du gouvernement ; (Jur) **~ to appear** défaut m de comparution or de comparaître ; **~ to observe a bylaw** inobservation f d'un règlement (de police)

fain †† [feɪn] ADV volontiers ; **I would ~ be dead** puissé-je périr

faint [feɪnt] **1** ADJ **a** (= slight, not pronounced) [sound, smell, trace, breathing] léger ; [marking, writing] à peine visible ; [colour] pâle ; (= vague) [recollection, memory, idea] vague ; [suspicion] léger ; [hope] faible, léger ; (= weak) [voice, light, breathing, smile] faible ; [protest] sans conviction ; **to grow ~er** s'affaiblir, diminuer ; **a ~ feeling of unease** un vague sentiment de gêne ; **she made a ~ attempt to make him laugh** elle a essayé vaguement de le faire rire ; **I haven't the ~est idea (about it)** je n'en ai pas la moindre idée ; **I never felt the ~est desire to cry** je n'ai jamais eu la moindre envie de pleurer ■ (PROV) **~ heart never won fair lady** qui n'ose rien n'a rien (PROV) → **damn**
b (= unwell) [person] prêt à s'évanouir or à défaillir ; **to feel ~** se sentir mal ; **to be/grow ~ with hunger** défaillir/commencer à défaillir de faim
2 N évanouissement m, défaillance f ; **to fall in a ~** s'évanouir, avoir une défaillance
3 VI (= lose consciousness) s'évanouir ; **he ~ed from the shock/the pain** le choc/la douleur lui a fait perdre connaissance ; **to be ~ing** (= feel weak : from hunger etc) défaillir (**from** de)
4 COMP ► **fainting fit, fainting spell** (US) N évanouissement m ► **faint-ruled paper** N papier m réglé (en impression légère)

fainthearted [ˌfeɪntˈhɑːtɪd] ADJ pusillanime, timoré ; **it's not for the ~** [venture, investment] ça demande un certain courage ; (= not for the oversensitive) ce n'est pas pour les personnes sensibles

faintheartedly [ˌfeɪntˈhɑːtɪlɪ] ADV sans courage, avec pusillanimité

faintheartedness [ˌfeɪntˈhɑːtɪdnɪs] N pusillanimité f

faintly [ˈfeɪntlɪ] ADV **a** (= slightly) [glow, smell of] légèrement ; [odd, strange, silly] un peu ; [ridiculous, absurd, familiar] vaguement ; [surprised, embarrassed, annoyed, uncomfortable] légèrement ; **~ amusing** vaguement amusant ; **in a ~ disappointed tone** d'un ton un peu déçu, avec une nuance de déception dans la voix ; **to be ~ reminiscent of sth** rappeler vaguement qch **b** (= lightly) [breathe, write] légèrement ; (= weakly) [breathe, say, call] faiblement ; **to smile ~** esquisser un faible or un vague sourire ; **to sigh ~** pousser un léger soupir

faintness [ˈfeɪntnɪs] N **a** [of sound, voice etc] faiblesse f ; [of breeze etc] légèreté f **b** (= dizziness) vertiges mpl

fair¹ [fɛəʳ] **1** ADJ **a** (= just) [person, decision] juste, équitable ; [price] juste ; [deal] équitable, honnête ; [competition, match, fight, player] loyal, correct ; [profit] justifié, mérité ; **he is strict but ~** il est sévère mais juste or équitable ; **be ~: it's not their fault** sois juste : ce n'est pas de leur faute ; **it's not ~** ce n'est pas juste ; **as is (only) ~** et ce n'est que justice, comme de juste ; **to be ~ (to him)** or **let's be ~ (to him)**, **he thought he had paid for it** rendons-lui cette justice, il croyait l'avoir payé ; **it wouldn't be ~ to his brother** ce ne serait pas juste vis-à-vis de son frère ; **this isn't ~ on anyone/either of us** ce n'est juste pour personne/ni pour toi ni pour moi ; **it's ~ to say that ...** il est juste de dire que ... ; **it's (a) ~ comment** la remarque est juste ; **to get** or **have a ~ crack of the whip** avoir la chance de montrer de quoi on est capable ; **to give sb a ~ deal** agir équitablement envers qn, être fair-play inv avec qn ; **~ enough!** d'accord !, très bien ! ; **all this is ~ enough, but ...** tout cela est très bien mais ..., d'accord mais ... ; **it's a ~ exchange** c'est équitable, c'est un échange honnête ■ (PROV) **~ exchange is no robbery** échange n'est pas vol ; **he was ~ game for the critics** c'était une proie rêvée or idéale pour les critiques ; **~'s ~!** ce n'est que justice ! ; **all's ~ in love and war** en amour comme à la guerre, tous les coups sont permis ; **by ~ means or foul** par tous les moyens, par n'importe quel moyen ; **that's a ~ point** c'est juste ; (US) **to give sb a ~ shake** agir équitablement envers qn, être fair-play inv avec qn ; **he got his ~ share of the money** il a eu tout l'argent qui lui revenait (de droit) ; **he's had his ~ share of trouble*** il a eu sa part de soucis ; **~ shares for all** (à) chacun son dû ; **it was all ~ and square** tout était très correct or régulier ; **he's ~ and square** il est honnête or franc ; **to get a ~ trial** bénéficier d'un procès équitable ; **to give sb ~ warning of sth** prévenir qn honnêtement de qch
b (= considerable) [sum] considérable ; [number] respectable ; **their garden's a ~ size** leur jardin est de taille respectable ; **there's a ~ amount of money left** il reste pas mal d'argent ; **he's travelled a ~ amount** il a pas mal voyagé ; **we've travelled a ~ distance** or **way** avoir fait un bon bout de chemin ; **to go at a ~ pace** aller bon train, aller à (une) bonne allure
c (= average) [work, achievements] passable ; (Scol : as mark) "**~**" « passable » ; **it's ~ to middling** c'est passable, ce n'est pas mal ; **in ~ condition** en assez bon état
d (= reasonable) [guess, assessment] juste ; [idea] précis ; **he has a ~ chance of success** il a des chances de réussir ; **he is in a ~ way to doing** il a de bonnes chances pour qu'il fasse ; **~ sample** échantillon m représentatif
e (= light-coloured) [hair] blond ; [complexion, skin] clair, de blond(e) ; **she's ~** elle est blonde, c'est une blonde
f (= fine) [weather] beau (belle f) ; [wind] propice, favorable ; **it will be ~ and warm tomorrow** il fera beau et chaud demain ; **it's set ~** le temps est au beau fixe

g († or liter = beautiful) [person, place] beau (belle f) ; **~ words** belles phrases fpl or paroles fpl ; **the ~ lady of some brave knight of old** la belle dame de quelque brave chevalier du temps jadis ; **this ~ city of ours** cette belle ville qui est la nôtre ; **~ promises** belles promesses fpl ; (hum) **with one's own ~ hands** de ses blanches mains
h (= clean, neat) propre, net ; **~ copy** (rewritten) copie f au propre or au net ; (= model answer) corrigé m ; **to make a ~ copy of sth** recopier qch au propre or au net
2 ADV **a** **to play ~** jouer franc jeu ; **to act ~ and square** se montrer juste ; **the branch struck him ~ and square in the face** la branche l'a frappé au beau milieu du visage or en plein (milieu du) visage ; **the car ran ~ and square into the tree** la voiture est entrée de plein fouet or en plein dans l'arbre
b (‡ or dial) = **fairly** c
c †† [speak] courtoisement ; **~ spoken** qui parle avec courtoisie
3 COMP ► **fair-haired** ADJ blond, aux cheveux blonds ; **~-haired girl** blonde f ; (US fig) **the ~-haired boy*** le chouchou*, le chéri ► **fair-minded** ADJ impartial, équitable ► **fair play** N fair-play m ► **fair-sized** ADJ assez grand, d'une bonne taille ► **fair-skinned** ADJ à la peau claire ► **fair-trade price** N (US) prix m imposé ► **fair-weather friends** NPL (fig) des amis mpl des beaux jours

fair² [fɛəʳ] N (gen) foire f ; (Comm) foire f ; (for charity) fête f, kermesse f ; (Brit : also **funfair**) fête f foraine ; (Comm) **the Book Fair** le Salon or la Foire du livre → **world**

fairground [ˈfɛəgraʊnd] N champ m de foire

fairing [ˈfɛərɪŋ] N (Aut, Aviat) carénage m

fairly [ˈfɛəlɪ] ADV **a** (= moderately) assez ; **he plays ~ well** il joue assez bien ; **he's ~ good** il est assez bon, il n'est pas mauvais ; **they lead a ~ quiet life** ils mènent une vie plutôt tranquille ; **I'm ~ sure that ...** je suis presque sûr que ... ; **~ soon** d'ici peu de temps **b** (= justly) [treat, compare, judge, share, distribute] équitablement ; [obtain] honnêtement, loyalement ; [call, describe] honnêtement ; [claim, argue] à juste titre **c** († = positively) carrément ; **he was ~ beside himself with rage** il était carrément hors de lui ; **he ~ flew across the room** il a traversé la pièce en trombe **d** **~ and squarely** = **fair and square** ; → **fair¹**

fairness [ˈfɛənɪs] **1** N **a** (= lightness) [of hair] couleur f blonde, blondeur f ; [of skin] blancheur f **b** (= honesty, justice) équité f ; [of decision, judgment] équité f, impartialité f ; **in** or **out of all ~** en toute justice ; **in ~ to him** pour être juste envers lui **2** COMP ► **Fairness Doctrine** N (US) principe m de l'impartialité

┌─────────────────────┐
│ **FAIRNESS DOCTRINE** │
└─────────────────────┘

Aux États-Unis, le principe de l'impartialité ou Fairness Doctrine impose aux stations de radio et aux chaînes de télévision de faire entendre différents points de vue sur les grandes questions de société et de respecter un certain équilibre dans le temps d'antenne accordé aux principaux candidats lors des élections locales et nationales. Il ne s'agit pas d'une loi, mais d'un principe déontologique qui bénéficie du soutien du Congrès.

fairway [ˈfɛəweɪ] N (Naut) chenal m, passe f ; (Golf) fairway m

fairy [ˈfɛərɪ] **1** N **a** fée f ; **the wicked ~** la fée Carabosse ; **she's his good ~** elle est sa bonne fée ; (hum) **he's away with the fairies*** il a une araignée au plafond* **b** (‡ pej = homosexual) pédé* m, tapette‡ f **2** ADJ [helper, gift] magique **3** COMP ► **fairy cycle** N bicyclette f d'enfant ► **fairy footsteps** NPL (iro) pas mpl (légers) de danseuse (iro) ► **fairy godmother** N (lit) bonne fée f ; (fig) marraine f gâteau* inv ► **fairy lights** NPL guirlande f électrique

► **fairy-like** ADJ féerique, de fée ► **fairy queen** N reine *f* des fées ► **fairy story, fairy tale** N conte *m* de fées; (= *untruth*) histoire à dormir debout* ► **fairy-tale** ADJ [*character, place*] (*lit*) de conte de fées; (*fig*) enchanteur (-teresse *f*); **the hotel is set in ~-tale surroundings** l'hôtel est situé dans un cadre enchanteur; **a ~-tale ending** un dénouement romanesque

fairyland ['fɛərɪlænd] N royaume *m* des fées; (*fig*) féerie *f*

faith [feɪθ] **1** N **[a]** (*NonC* = *trust, belief*) foi *f*, confiance *f*; **Faith, Hope and Charity** la foi, l'espérance et la charité; **~ in God** foi *f* en Dieu; **to have ~ in sb** avoir confiance en qn; **to have ~ in sb's ability/judgement** se fier aux compétences/au jugement de qn; **I've lost ~ in him** je ne lui fais plus confiance; **to put one's ~ in ◊ to pin one's ~ on*** mettre tous ses espoirs en **[b]** (= *religion*) religion *f*; **the Christian ~** la religion *or* la foi chrétienne; **people of different ~s** des gens de confessions différentes **[c]** (*NonC*) **to keep ~ with sb** tenir ses promesses envers qn; **to break ~ with sb** manquer à sa parole envers qn **[d]** (*NonC*) **good ~** bonne foi *f*; **to do sth in all good ~** faire qch en toute bonne foi; **bad ~** mauvaise foi *f*; **to act in bad ~** agir de mauvaise foi **2** COMP ► **faith healer** N guérisseur *m*, -euse *f* ► **faith healing** N guérison *f* par la foi

faithful ['feɪθfʊl] **1** ADJ [*person, translation, copy, account*] fidèle (**to** à); **to be ~ to sb's wishes** respecter les désirs de qn; **26 years' service** 26 années de bons et loyaux services; **my ~ old car** ma bonne vieille voiture **2** **the faithful** NPL (*Rel*) (= *Christians*) les fidèles *mpl*; (= *Muslims*) les croyants *mpl*; (*Pol*) **the (party) ~** les fidèles *mpl* du parti

faithfully ['feɪθfəlɪ] ADV [*report, translate, reproduce*] fidèlement; [*serve*] loyalement; **to promise ~** donner sa parole; (*esp Brit: in letter writing*) **Yours ~** Veuillez agréer, Messieurs, mes salutations distinguées, Je vous prie d'agréer, Messieurs, l'expression de mes sentiments distingués

faithfulness ['feɪθfʊlnɪs] N [*of person*] fidélité *f* (**to** à), loyauté *f* (**to** envers); [*of account, translation*] fidélité *f*, exactitude *f*; [*of copy*] conformité *f*

faithless ['feɪθlɪs] ADJ déloyal, perfide

faithlessness ['feɪθlɪsnɪs] N (*NonC*) déloyauté *f*, perfidie *f*

fake [feɪk] **1** N **[a]** faux *m*; **the passport/document/certificate was a ~** le passeport/le document/le certificat était (un) faux; **the diamond was a ~** c'était un faux diamant; **the pistol was a ~** le pistolet était faux, c'était un faux pistolet; **the bomb was a ~** c'était une fausse bombe; **he's a ~** c'est un imposteur **[b]** (*US Sport*) feinte *f* **2** ADJ [*document, passport, painting, beam*] faux (fausse *f*); [*blood*] factice; [*elections, trial, photograph*] truqué; (*Rad, TV*) [*interview*] truqué, monté d'avance; **a ~ suntan** un bronzage artificiel; **a ~ Mackintosh chair** une fausse chaise Mackintosh; **a ~ £10 note** un faux billet de 10 livres; **~ fur** fausse fourrure *f*; **~ pearls** fausses perles *fpl* **3** VT **[a]** [*+ document*] (= *counterfeit*) faire un faux de; (= *alter*) maquiller, falsifier; (*Art*) [*+ picture*] faire un faux de, contrefaire; [*+ beam, furniture, signature*] imiter; [*+ photograph, sound tape, trial*] truquer; [*+ accounts*] falsifier; (*Rad, TV*) [*+ interview*] truquer, monter d'avance; **to ~ illness/death** faire semblant d'être malade/mort; **to ~ orgasm** simuler l'orgasme; (*US Sport*) **to ~ a pass** feinter **[b]** (*US* = *ad-lib*) [*+ tune*] improviser **4** VI faire semblant; (*US Sport*) feinter

fakir ['fɑːkɪəʳ] N fakir *m*

falcon ['fɔːlkən] N faucon *m*

falconer ['fɔːlkənəʳ] N fauconnier *m*

falconry ['fɔːlkənrɪ] N fauconnerie *f*

Falkland ['fɔːlklənd] **1** **the Falklands** NPL = **the Falkland Islands 2** COMP ► **Falkland Islander** N habitant(e) *m(f)* des (îles) Malouines *or* Falkland ► **the Falkland Islands** NPL les îles *fpl* Malouines *or* Falkland

fall [fɔːl] (*vb: pret* **fell**, *ptp* **fallen**) **1** N **[a]** (*lit, fig* = *tumble*) chute *f*; **to have a ~** tomber, faire une chute; (*fig*) **to be heading** *or* **riding for a ~** courir à l'échec, aller au-devant de la défaite → **free** **[b]** (= *lowering: in price, demand, temperature*) baisse *f* (**in** de); (*more drastic*) chute *f* (**in** de); (*Fin*) dépréciation *f*, baisse *f* **[c]** (= *shower of objects etc*) [*of rocks, snow*] chute *f*; **~ of earth** éboulement *m*, éboulis *m* **[d]** (*Mil* = *defeat*) chute *f*, prise *f*; **the ~ of Saigon** la chute *or* la prise de Saigon; **the ~ of the Bastille** la prise de la Bastille **[e]** (*Rel*) **the Fall (of Man)** la chute (de l'homme) **[f]** (= *slope*) [*of ground, roof*] pente *f*, inclinaison *f* **[g]** (*US* = *autumn*) automne *m*; **in the ~** en automne **2** **falls** NPL (= *waterfall*) chute *f* d'eau, cascade *f*; **the Niagara Falls** les chutes du Niagara **3** VI **[a]** (= *tumble*) [*person, object*] tomber; **he fell into the river** [*person*] il est tombé dans la rivière; **to ~ out of a tree/off a bike** tomber d'un arbre/de vélo; **to ~ over a chair** tomber en butant contre une chaise; **he let the cup ~** il a laissé tomber la tasse; (*lit, fig*) **to ~ on one's feet** retomber sur ses pieds; (*US: lit, fig*) **to ~ on one's ass✲✲** se casser la gueule✲; **to ~ on stony ground** ne rien donner → **wayside** **[b]** (= *collapse*) [*building*] s'écrouler, s'effondrer; **he fell into bed exhausted** il s'est effondré sur son lit, épuisé **[c]** (= *find o.s.*) **he fell among thieves** il est tombé aux mains de voleurs **[d]** (= *rain down*) [*rain, leaves, bombs*] tomber **[e]** (= *drop*) [*temperature, price, level*] baisser, tomber; [*wind*] tomber; [*voice*] baisser; **his face fell** son visage s'est assombri *or* s'est allongé; **to let ~ a hint that ...** laisser entendre que ..., donner à entendre que ... **[f]** (= *hang*) **her hair fell to her shoulders** les cheveux lui tombaient sur les épaules; **the curtains ~ to the floor** les rideaux vont jusqu'au sol **[g]** (= *descend*) [*night, darkness*] tomber **[h]** (*also* **~ away**) [*ground*] descendre en pente; **the ground fell steeply to the valley floor** le terrain descendait en pente raide vers le fond de la vallée **[i]** (= *be defeated*) [*country, city, fortress*] tomber; [*government*] tomber, être renversé **[j]** (*Rel* = *sin*) tomber, pécher → **grace** **[k]** (*Mil* = *die*) [*soldier etc*] tomber (au champ d'honneur) **[l]** (= *throw o.s.*) **they fell into each other's arms** ils sont tombés dans les bras l'un de l'autre; **to ~ to** *or* **on one's knees** tomber à genoux; **he was ~ing over himself to be polite*** il faisait de gros efforts pour être poli; **they were ~ing over each other to get it*** ils se battaient pour l'avoir → **neck** **[m]** (= *occur*) tomber; **Christmas Day ~s on a Sunday** Noël tombe un dimanche; **the accent ~s on the second syllable** l'accent tombe sur la deuxième syllabe; **the students ~ into three categories** les étudiants se divisent en trois catégories → **stool** **[n]** (*with adjective*) **to ~ ill** *or* **sick** tomber malade; **to ~ pregnant** tomber enceinte; **to ~ lame** se mettre à boiter; [*job*] devenir vacant, se libérer; [*room, flat*] devenir libre; **to ~ asleep** s'endormir; **to ~ silent** se taire; **his work fell short of what we had expected**

son travail n'a pas répondu à notre attente; **the copy fell far short of the original** la copie était loin de valoir l'original; **to ~ short of perfection** ne pas atteindre la perfection → **flat, foul** **4** COMP ► **fall-back position** N solution *f* de secours *or* de réserve ► **fall guy✲** N (= *scapegoat*) bouc *m* émissaire; (= *easy victim*) pigeon* *m*, dindon *m* (de la farce), dupe *f* ► **fall line** N (*Geog*) ligne *f* de séparation entre un plateau et une plaine côtière; (*Ski*) ligne *f* de plus grande pente ► **fall-off** N = **falling-off** → **falling**

► **fall about*** VI (*Brit fig: also* **~ about laughing**) se tordre de rire

► **fall apart** VI [*house, furniture*] s'effondrer; [*scheme, plan, deal*] tomber à l'eau; [*person, one's life*] s'effondrer; (*in exam etc*) perdre tous ses moyens; **their marriage is ~ing apart** leur couple est en train de se briser

► **fall away** VI [*ground*] descendre en pente; [*plaster*] s'écailler; [*numbers, attendances*] diminuer; [*anxiety, fears*] se dissiper, s'évanouir; **his supporters are ~ing away** ses partisans sont en train de le déserter *or* de l'abandonner

► **fall back 1** VI (= *retreat, also Mil*) reculer, se retirer; (*fig*) **to ~ back on sth** avoir recours à qch; **some money to ~ back on** un peu d'argent en réserve; **gold shares fell back a point** les mines d'or ont reculé *or* se sont repliées d'un point **2** **~back** N → **fallback**

► **fall behind 1** VI rester en arrière, être à la traîne; [*racehorse, runner*] se laisser distancer; (*in cycle race*) décrocher; **to ~ behind with one's work** prendre du retard dans son travail; **she fell behind with the rent** elle était en retard pour son loyer **2** VT FUS **to ~ behind sb** (*in work etc*) prendre du retard sur qn

► **fall down** VI **[a]** [*person, book*] tomber (par terre); [*building*] s'effondrer, s'écrouler; [*tree*] tomber; (*fig = fail*) [*person*] échouer; [*plans*] tomber à l'eau; [*hopes*] s'évanouir; **to ~ down on the job** se montrer incapable de faire ce travail, ne pas être à la hauteur; **he fell down badly that time** il s'est vraiment pris les pieds dans le tapis cette fois; **that was where we fell down** c'est là que nous avons achoppé; **she fell down on the last essay** elle a raté la dernière dissertation

► **fall for** VT FUS **[a]** (= *become very keen on*) **to ~ for sb*** tomber amoureux de qn; **to ~ for an idea*** etc s'enthousiasmer pour une idée *etc* **[b]** (*pej = be taken in by*) **to ~ for a suggestion** se laisser prendre à une suggestion; **he really fell for it!*** il s'est vraiment laissé prendre!, il s'est vraiment fait avoir!*

► **fall in 1** VI **[a]** [*building*] s'effondrer, s'écrouler; **she leaned over the pool and fell in** elle s'est penchée au-dessus de la piscine et elle est tombée dedans **[b]** (*Mil*) [*troops*] former les rangs; [*one soldier*] rentrer dans les rangs; **~ in!** à vos rangs! **2** VT SEP [*+ troops*] (faire) mettre en rangs

► **fall into** VT FUS [*+ trap, ambush*] tomber dans; [*+ disfavour, disgrace, disuse*] tomber en; [*+ despair, anarchy*] sombrer dans; [*+ recession*] s'enfoncer dans; **to ~ into a deep sleep** tomber dans un profond sommeil; **to ~ into conversation with sb** entamer une conversation avec qn, se mettre à parler avec qn; **to ~ into debt** s'endetter; **to ~ into bad habits** prendre *or* contracter de mauvaises habitudes; **to ~ into temptation** (= *be tempted*) être tenté; (= *give in to temptation*) succomber à la tentation; **she fell into a deep depression** elle a sombré dans la dépression, elle a fait une grave dépression; **to ~ into decline** connaître le déclin; **the city fell into decline at the end of the 16th century** le déclin de la ville remonte à la fin du 16ᵉ siècle; **to ~ into ruin** tomber en ruine; **the mansion fell into decay** *or* **ruin 20 years ago** le manoir a commencé à se délabrer *or* à tomber en ruine il y a 20 ans,

le manoir est délabré depuis 20 ans; **ancient civilizations that fell into decay** les civilisations anciennes qui ont connu le déclin → **line**
► **fall in with** VT FUS [a] (= *meet*) [+ *person*] rencontrer; [+ *group*] se mettre à fréquenter; **he fell in with a bad crowd** il s'est mis à avoir de mauvaises fréquentations [b] (= *agree to*) [+ *proposal, suggestion*] accepter; **to ~ in with sb's views** se ranger au point de vue de qn [c] (= *fit in*) **this decision fell in very well with our plans** cette décision a cadré avec nos projets
► **fall off** [1] VI [a] (*lit*) tomber; (*Climbing*) dévisser [b] [*supporters*] déserter; [*sales, numbers, attendances*] diminuer; [*curve on graph*] décroître; [*interest*] se relâcher, tomber; [*enthusiasm*] baisser, tomber [2] **~-off** N = **falling-off,** → **falling**
► **fall on** VT FUS [a] (= *alight on, encounter*) **her eyes fell on a strange object** son regard est tombé sur un objet étrange; **strange sounds fell on our ears** des bruits étranges parvinrent à nos oreilles; **to ~ on bad** *or* **hard times** tomber dans la misère, avoir des revers de fortune [b] = **fall upon**
► **fall out** [1] VI [a] (= *quarrel*) se brouiller, se fâcher (**with** avec) [b] (*Mil*) rompre les rangs; **~ out!** rompez! [c] (= *come to pass*) advenir, arriver; **everything fell out as we had hoped** tout s'est passé comme nous l'avions espéré [2] VT SEP [+ *troops*] faire rompre les rangs à
► **fall over** VI tomber (par terre)
► **fall through** VI **all their plans have ~en through** tous leurs projets ont échoué *or* sont tombés à l'eau
► **fall to** [1] VI [a] (= *begin*) **he fell to wondering if ...** il s'est mis à se demander si ... [b] (= *start eating*) se mettre à l'œuvre, attaquer (un repas) [2] VT FUS (= *be one's duty*) **it ~s to me to say** il m'appartient de dire, c'est à moi de dire
► **fall under** VT FUS (= *be subject to*) **to ~ under suspicion** devenir suspect
► **fall upon** VT FUS [a] (= *attack*) se jeter sur, se lancer sur; (*Mil*) **to ~ upon the enemy** fondre *or* s'abattre sur l'ennemi; (*liter*) **the wrath of God fell upon them** la colère de Dieu s'abattit sur eux [b] (= *be incumbent on*) **the responsibility ~s upon you** la responsabilité retombe sur vous [c] (= *find*) trouver, découvrir; **to ~ upon a way of doing sth** trouver *or* découvrir un moyen de faire qch

fallacious [fə'leɪʃəs] ADJ fallacieux

fallaciousness [fə'leɪʃəsnɪs] N caractère *m* fallacieux

fallacy [ˈfæləsɪ] N (= *false belief*) erreur *f*, illusion *f*; (= *false reasoning*) faux raisonnement *m*, sophisme *m*

fallback [ˈfɔːlbæk] N recul *m*, repli *m*; **as a ~ they will start building their own dealer network** ils vont mettre sur pied un réseau de distribution pour avoir une position de repli

fallen [ˈfɔːlən] [1] VB ptp of **fall** [2] ADJ [a] [*object*] tombé; **~ leaf** feuille *f* morte [b] (*morally*) perdu; [*angel*] déchu; **~ idol** idole *f* déchue [3] **the fallen** NPL (*Mil*) ceux *mpl* qui sont morts à la guerre, ceux *mpl* qui sont tombés au champ d'honneur [4] COMP ► **fallen arches** NPL (*Med*) affaissement *m* de la voûte plantaire

fallibility [ˌfælɪˈbɪlɪtɪ] N faillibilité *f*

fallible [ˈfæləbl] ADJ faillible; **everyone is ~** tout le monde peut se tromper

falling [ˈfɔːlɪŋ] [1] VB prp of **fall** [2] ADJ [*prices, profits, standards, inflation*] en baisse; [*water, snow, leaf*] qui tombe; **"beware (of) ~ rocks"** « attention : chutes de pierres » [3] COMP ► **falling evil**†† N = **falling sickness** ► **falling-off** N réduction *f*, diminution *f*, décroissance *f* (**in** de) ► **falling-out**†† N **to have a ~out (with sb)** se brouiller (avec qn) ► **falling sickness**†† N (= *epilepsy*) haut

mal†† *m*, mal caduc†† *m* ► **falling star** N étoile *f* filante

Fallopian [fəˈləʊpɪən] ADJ **~ tube** trompe *f* utérine *or* de Fallope

fallout [ˈfɔːlaʊt] [1] N (*NonC*) retombées *fpl* (*radioactives*); (*fig*) retombées *fpl*, répercussions *fpl* [2] COMP ► **fallout shelter** N abri *m* antiatomique

fallow [ˈfæləʊ] [1] N (*Agr*) jachère *f* [2] ADJ [a] (*Agr*) [*land*] en jachère; **the land lay ~** la terre était en jachère [b] (= *inactive*) **a ~ period** *or* **time** un passage à vide [3] ► **fallow deer** N daim *m*

false [fɔːls] [1] ADJ [a] (= *artificial, fake*) [*beard, eyelashes, passport, banknote*] faux (fausse *f*); **a box with a ~ bottom** une boîte à double fond; **~ ceiling** faux plafond *m*; **~ hem** faux ourlet *m* [b] (= *wrong*) [*information, accusation, impression, hope, rumour*] faux (fausse *f*); (= *untrue*) [*promise*] faux (fausse *f*), mensonger; **to give ~ evidence** fournir un faux témoignage; **to make a ~ confession** faire de faux aveux; **he was forced into a ~ confession** on lui a extorqué des aveux; **he gave the police a ~ name** il a donné un faux nom à la police; **he had assumed a ~ identity** il vivait sous une fausse identité; **to bear ~ witness**†† porter un faux témoignage; **under ~ pretences** (*gen*) sous des prétextes fallacieux; (*Jur*) par des moyens frauduleux; **to put a ~ interpretation on sth** mal interpréter qch; **~ expectations** faux espoirs *mpl*; **a ~ sense of security** une illusion de sécurité; **~ move** *or* **step** faux pas *m*; **to make a ~ move** ◊ **to take a ~ step** faire un faux pas [c] (*Jur* = *wrongful*) **~ arrest/imprisonment** arrêt *m*/détention *f* arbitraire [d] (= *insincere*) [*person*] faux (fausse *f*); **~ laughter** rire *m* forcé; **~ modesty** fausse modestie *f*; **to ring ~** sonner faux; **in a ~ position** en porte-à-faux [e] (= *unfaithful*) **to be ~ to one's wife**† tromper sa femme

[2] ADV (*liter*) **to play sb ~** trahir qn

[3] COMP ► **false alarm** N (*lit, fig*) fausse alerte *f* ► **false dawn** N lueurs *fpl* annonciatrices de l'aube; (*fig*) lueur *f* d'espoir trompeuse ► **false economy** N fausse économie *f* ► **false friend** N (*also Ling*) faux ami *m* ► **false-hearted** ADJ fourbe ► **False Memory Syndrome** N (*Psych*) syndrome *m* du faux souvenir ► **false negative** (*Med*) N résultat *m* faussement négatif, faux négatif *m* ◊ ADJ [*result*] faussement négatif ► **false positive** (*Med*) N résultat *m* faussement positif, faux positif *m* ◊ ADJ [*result*] faussement positif ► **false ribs** NPL fausses côtes *fpl* ► **false start** N (*Sport, also fig*) faux départ *m* ► **false teeth** NPL fausses dents *fpl*, dentier *m*

falsehood [ˈfɔːlshʊd] N [a] (= *lie*) mensonge *m*; **to tell a ~** mentir, dire un mensonge [b] (*NonC*) faux *m*; **truth and ~** le vrai et le faux [c] (*NonC*) = **falseness**

falsely [ˈfɔːlslɪ] ADV [*claim, declare, report*] faussement; [*accuse*] à tort, faussement; [*convict, imprison, believe*] à tort; **~ cheerful** d'une gaieté feinte

falseness [ˈfɔːlsnɪs] N fausseté *f*; († *or liter*) [of *lover*] infidélité *f*

falsetto [fɔːlˈsetəʊ] [1] N (*Mus*) fausset *m* [2] ADJ [*voice, tone*] de fausset, de tête

falsies* [ˈfɔːlsɪz] NPL faux seins *mpl*

falsification [ˌfɔːlsɪfɪˈkeɪʃən] N falsification *f*

falsify [ˈfɔːlsɪfaɪ] VT [a] (= *forge*) [+ *document*] falsifier; [+ *evidence*] maquiller; (= *misrepresent*) [+ *story, facts*] dénaturer; [+ *accounts, figures, statistics*] truquer [b] (= *disprove*) [+ *theory*] réfuter

falsity [ˈfɔːlsɪtɪ] N = **falseness**

falter [ˈfɔːltər] [1] VI [*voice, speaker*] hésiter, s'entrecouper; (= *waver*) vaciller, chanceler;

[*courage, memory*] faiblir; **her steps ~ed** elle chancela [2] VT (*also ~ out*) [+ *words, phrases*] bredouiller

faltering [ˈfɔːltərɪŋ] ADJ [*voice*] hésitant, entrecoupé; [*steps*] chancelant

falteringly [ˈfɔːltərɪŋlɪ] ADV [*speak*] d'une voix hésitante *or* entrecoupée; [*walk*] d'un pas chancelant *or* mal assuré

fame [feɪm] N (*gen*) gloire *f*, renommée *f*; (= *celebrity*) célébrité *f*; **he wanted ~** il était avide de gloire, il voulait se faire un nom; **to win ~ for o.s.** se rendre célèbre; **this book brought him ~** ce livre l'a rendu célèbre, c'est à ce livre qu'il doit sa célébrité; **~ and fortune** la gloire et la fortune; **Margaret Mitchell of "Gone with the Wind" ~** Margaret Mitchell, connue pour son livre « Autant en emporte le vent » *or* l'auteur célèbre de « Autant en emporte le vent »; **Bader of 1940 ~** Bader, célèbre pour ses prouesses *or* exploits en 1940 → **ill**

famed [feɪmd] ADJ célèbre, renommé (**for** pour)

familial [fəˈmɪlɪəl] ADJ (*frm*) familial

familiar [fəˈmɪljər] [1] ADJ [a] (= *usual, well-known*) [*sight, scene, street*] familier; [*complaint, event, protest*] habituel; **the problems are all too ~** ces problèmes sont, hélas, bien connus; **his face is ~** je l'ai déjà vu quelque part, son visage me dit quelque chose*; **his voice seems ~ (to me)** il me semble connaître sa voix; **he's a ~ figure in the town** c'est un personnage bien connu *or* tout le monde le connaît de vue dans la ville; **it's a ~ feeling** c'est une sensation bien connue → **face** [b] (= *conversant*) **to be ~ with sth** bien connaître qch, être au fait de qch; **to make o.s. ~ with** se familiariser avec; **he is ~ with our customs** il connaît bien nos coutumes [c] (= *intimate*) familier, intime; **~ language** langue *f* familière; **to be on ~ terms with sb** bien connaître qn; **~ spirit** démon *m* familier; (*pej*) **he got much too ~** il s'est permis des familiarités (**with** avec)

[2] N [a] (= *familiar spirit*) démon *m* familier [b] (= *friend*) familier *m*

familiarity [fəˌmɪlɪˈærɪtɪ] N [a] (*NonC*) [of *sight, event etc*] caractère *m* familier *or* habituel [b] (*NonC: with book, poem, customs etc*) familiarité *f* (**with** avec), (parfaite) connaissance *f* (**with** de); ► (*PROV*) **~ breeds contempt** la familiarité engendre le mépris [c] (= *intimacy*) familiarité *f*; **the ~ with which she greeted the head waiter** la familiarité avec laquelle elle a salué le maître d'hôtel; (*pej: gen pl*) **familiarities** familiarités *fpl*, privautés *fpl*

familiarize [fəˈmɪlɪəraɪz] VT **to ~ sb with sth** familiariser qn avec qch, habituer qn à qch; **to ~ o.s. with** se familiariser avec

familiarly [fəˈmɪljəlɪ] ADV [*say, greet*] avec familiarité; **the "Jade Palace", ~ known as "Jo's Place"** le « Jade Palace », « Jo's Place » pour les intimes

family [ˈfæmɪlɪ] [1] N (*all senses*) famille *f*; **has he any ~?** (= *relatives*) a-t-il de la famille?; (= *children*) a-t-il des enfants?; **it runs in the ~** cela tient de famille; **my ~ are all tall** dans ma famille tout le monde est grand; **they'd like to start a ~** ils aimeraient avoir des enfants; **of good ~** de bonne famille; **he's one of the ~** il fait partie *or* il est de la famille

[2] COMP [*dinner, jewels, likeness, name*] de famille; [*Bible, life*] familial, de famille ► **family allowance** N (*Brit Admin: formerly*) allocations *fpl* familiales ► **family business** N entreprise *f* familiale, affaire *f* de famille ► **family butcher** N boucher *m* de quartier ► **family circle** N [a] (= *family members*) cercle *m* familial [b] (*US Theat*) deuxième balcon *m* ► **family court** N (*US Jur*) ≈ tribunal *m* de grande instance (*s'occupant des affaires familiales*) ► **family credit** N (*Brit Admin*) ≈ complément *m* familial ► **Family Crisis Intervention Unit** N (*US Police*) ≈ police-secours *f*

(intervenant en cas de drames familiaux) ► **the Family Division** N (Brit Jur) tribunal m des affaires familiales ► **family doctor** N médecin m de famille, généraliste m ► **family friend** N ami(e) m(f) de la famille ► **family grouping** N (Scol) regroupement de classes de primaire de sections différentes ► **Family Health Services Authority** N (Brit) autorité supervisant les professions de santé ► **family hotel** N pension f de famille ► **family income supplement** N (Brit Admin: formerly) ≈ complément m familial ► **family man** N (pl family men) he's a ~ **man** il aime la vie de famille ► **family-minded** ADJ to be ~-minded avoir le sens de la famille ► **family name** N nom m de famille ► **family planning** N planning m familial ► **family planning clinic** N centre m de planning familial ► **family practice** N (US Med) médecine f générale ► **family practitioner** N (US Med) médecin m de famille, (médecin) généraliste m ► **family room** N a (esp US: in house) salle f de séjour (réservée à la famille plutôt qu'aux invités) b (Brit) (in pub) salle autorisée aux enfants; (in hotel) chambre f familiale ► **family-size(d) packet** N (Comm) paquet m familial ► **family therapy** N thérapie f familiale ► **family tree** N arbre m généalogique ► **family unit** N (Sociol) cellule f familiale ► **family viewing** N (TV) it's (suitable for) ~ viewing c'est un spectacle familial or pour toute la famille ► **family way**†* N she's in the ~ way elle est enceinte, elle attend un enfant

famine ['fæmɪn] N famine f

famished ['fæmɪʃt] ADJ affamé; I'm absolutely ~* je meurs de faim, j'ai une faim de loup; ~ **looking** d'aspect famélique

famous ['feɪməs] ADJ a (= well-known) célèbre (for pour); (iro) ~ **last words!*** on verra bien!, c'est ce que tu crois!; (iro) **so when's this ~ party going to be?** alors, cette fameuse soirée, quand est-ce qu'elle va avoir lieu? b (†* = excellent) fameux, formidable*

famously ['feɪməslɪ] ADV **a ~ rich/arrogant film star** une vedette de cinéma connue pour sa richesse/son arrogance; **Quentin Tarantino, who once ~ said ...** Quentin Tarantino, dont tout le monde connaît la fameuse boutade ...; **Marlon Brando ~ refused an Oscar in 1972** Marlon Brando, comme chacun le sait, a refusé un oscar en 1972; **there have been hurricanes in England, most ~ in 1987** il y a eu des ouragans en Angleterre, dont le plus connu en 1987 b (†* = well) **to get on** or **along** ~ s'entendre comme larrons en foire*; **to get on** or **along ~ with sb** s'entendre à merveille avec qn; **to go** ~ marcher rudement* bien

fan¹ [fæn] 1 N éventail m; (mechanical) ventilateur m; (Agr) tarare m; **electric ~** ventilateur m électrique 2 VT a [+ person, object] éventer; **to ~ the fire** attiser le feu; **to ~ the embers** souffler sur la braise; **to ~ o.s.** s'éventer b (fig) [+ violence, hatred] attiser; [+ fears] entretenir c (US* = smack) corriger, flanquer* une fessée à 3 COMP ► **fan-assisted oven** N four m à chaleur tournante ► **fan belt** N (Aut) courroie f de ventilateur ► **fan heater** N (Brit) radiateur m soufflant ► **fan light** N imposte f (semi-circulaire) ► **fan oven** N four m à chaleur pulsée ► **fan-shaped** ADJ en éventail ► **fan vaulting** N (Archit) voûte(s) f(pl) en éventail
► **fan out** 1 VI [troops, searchers] se déployer (en éventail) 2 VT SEP [+ cards etc] étaler (en éventail)

fan² [fæn] 1 N [of person] (gen) admirateur m, -trice f; [of personality, pop star, music style] fan mf; [of sports team] supporter m; [of work of art] amateur m; **I'm definitely not one of his ~s** je suis loin d'être un de ses admirateurs; **he is a jazz/bridge/sports/rugby ~** c'est un mordu* or un fana* de jazz/bridge/sport/rugby etc; **football ~** amateur m or fan m de

football; **movie ~** cinéphile mf, passionné(e) m(f) de cinéma; **a Vivaldi ~** un grand amateur de Vivaldi 2 COMP ► **fan club** N (Cine etc) cercle m or club m de fans; (fig) cercle m d'adorateurs or de fervents (admirateurs); **the Colin Smith ~ club** le club des fans de Colin Smith ► **fan letters** NPL = fan mail ► **fan mail** N courrier m des fans; **she receives lots of ~ mail** elle reçoit beaucoup de lettres d'admirateurs

fanatic [fə'nætɪk] N fanatique mf; **a religious ~** un fanatique religieux; **(s)he's a football ~** c'est un(e) fana* de football

fanatical [fə'nætɪkl] ADJ fanatique; **to be ~ about sth** être un(e) fanatique de qch

fanatically [fə'nætɪklɪ] ADV fanatiquement

fanaticism [fə'nætɪsɪzəm] N fanatisme m

fanciable* ['fænsɪəbl] ADJ (Brit) pas mal du tout*

fancied ['fænsɪd] ADJ imaginaire → **fancy**

fancier ['fænsɪə'] N **dog ~** (= connoisseur) connaisseur m, -euse f en chiens; (= breeder) éleveur m, -euse f de chiens

fanciful ['fænsɪfʊl] ADJ (= whimsical) [person] capricieux, fantasque; [ideas] fantasque; (= imaginative) [design, drawing] plein d'imagination, imaginatif; [story, account] fantaisiste

fancy ['fænsɪ] 1 N a (= whim) caprice m, fantaisie f; **a passing ~** une lubie; **as the ~ takes her** comme l'idée la prend; **he only works when the ~ takes him** il ne travaille que quand cela lui plaît or lui chante* b (= taste, liking) goût m, envie f; **to take a ~ to sb** (gen) se prendre d'affection pour qn; (= have a crush on) avoir le béguin* or une tocade* pour qn; **to take a ~ to sth** se mettre à aimer qch, prendre goût à qch; **it took** or **caught my ~** cela m'a fait envie or m'a tapé dans l'œil*; **the hat took** or **caught my ~** ce chapeau m'a fait envie or m'a tapé dans l'œil; **the story caught the public's ~** cette histoire a frappé les esprits c (NonC = fantasy) imagination f, fantaisie f; **that is in the realm of ~** cela appartient au domaine de l'imaginaire, c'est chimérique d (= delusion) chimère f, fantasme m; (= whimsical notion) idée f fantasque; **I have a ~ that ...** j'ai idée que ... e (Culin) gâteau m à la crème (fait de génoise fourrée)
2 VT a (esp Brit) (= want) avoir envie de; (= like) aimer; **do you ~ going for a walk?** as-tu envie or ça te dit* d'aller faire une promenade?; **do you ~ a drink?** ça vous dirait de prendre un verre?; **I don't ~ the idea** cette idée ne me dit rien; (Brit) **he fancies himself*** il ne se prend pas pour rien (iro); **he fancies himself as an actor*** il se prend pour un acteur; (Brit) **he fancies her*** il s'est entiché* d'elle; (Racing) **Omar is strongly fancied for the next race** Omar est très coté or a la cote pour la prochaine course b (= imagine) se figurer, s'imaginer; (= rather think) croire, penser; **he fancies he can succeed** il se figure pouvoir réussir, il s'imagine qu'il peut réussir; **I rather ~ he's gone out** je crois (bien) qu'il est sorti; **he fancied he heard the car arrive** il a cru entendre arriver la voiture; **I ~ we've met before** j'ai l'impression que nous nous sommes déjà rencontrés; **~ that!*** voyez-vous ça!; **~ anyone doing that!** les gens font de ces choses!; **~ seeing you here!*** tiens! vous ici!; **~ him winning!** qui aurait cru qu'il allait gagner!
3 ADJ a [clothes, shoes, hat, pattern] (= sophisticated) sophistiqué; (= showy) tape-à-l'œil inv; **~ food** des plats compliqués; **good plain food, nothing ~** de la nourriture simple, sans chichis; **~ cakes** pâtisseries fpl b (gen pej = expensive) [restaurant, shop, school] chic inv; **with his ~ house and his ~ car how can he know what being poor is like?** avec sa belle maison et sa belle voiture,

comment peut-il savoir ce que c'est que d'être pauvre? c (pej = pretentious) [idea, cure] fantaisiste; [word, language] recherché d (= high) [price] exorbitant e (= high-quality) [products, foodstuffs] de luxe 4 COMP ► **fancy dress** N (NonC) déguisement m; **in ~ dress** déguisé, travesti; **to go in ~ dress** se déguiser ► **fancy-dress ball** N bal m masqué or costumé ► **fancy-free** ADJ **he is ~-free** c'est un cœur à prendre → **footloose** ► **fancy goods** NPL (Comm) articles mpl de luxe ► **fancy man*** N (pl fancy men) (pej) amant m, jules* m ► **fancy woman*** N (pl fancy women) (pej) maîtresse f, poule* f (pej) ► **fancy work** N (NonC) ouvrages mpl d'agrément

fandango [fæn'dæŋgəʊ] N (pl fandangos) fandango m

fanfare ['fænfeə'] N fanfare f (morceau de musique); (fig) **a ~ of publicity** un déploiement de publicité

fanfold paper ['fænfəʊld'peɪpə'] N (Comput) papier m accordéon

fang [fæŋ] N [of dog, vampire] croc m, canine f; [of snake] crochet m

Fanny ['fænɪ] N a ABBR = **Frances** b (Brit) **sweet ~ Adams‡** que dalle‡

fanny ['fænɪ] N (US:* = buttocks) cul** m, fesses* fpl b (Brit:* = vagina) chatte** f

fantabulous‡ [fæn'tæbjʊləs] ADJ superchouette*

fantail ['fænteɪl] N (also ~ pigeon) pigeon-paon m

fantasia [fæn'teɪzjə] N (Literat, Mus) fantaisie f

fantasist ['fæntəzɪst] N doux rêveur m

fantasize ['fæntəsaɪz] VI (gen, Psych) se livrer à des fantasmes, fantasmer (about sur)

fantastic [fæn'tæstɪk] ADJ a (* = fabulous, terrific) [person, achievement, opportunity, news] fantastique, formidable; **it's ~ to see you again!** c'est formidable de te revoir!; **you look ~!** (= healthy) tu as une mine superbe; (= attractive) tu es superbe! b (* = huge) [amount, profit, speed] phénoménal c (= exotic) [creature, world] fantastique → **trip** d (= improbable) [story, adventure, idea] invraisemblable

fantastical [fæn'tæstɪkl] ADJ [story, place, world] fantastique; [account, architecture] fantasque

fantastically [fæn'tæstɪkəlɪ] ADV a (= extraordinarily) [complicated] fantastiquement, extraordinairement; [expensive, rich] fabuleusement b (= imaginatively) [wrought, coloured] fantastiquement

fantasy ['fæntəzɪ] N a (NonC) imagination f, fantaisie f b idée f fantasque; (Psych) fantasme m c (Literat, Mus) fantaisie f

fanzine ['fænziːn] N (ABBR = fan magazine) fanzine m

FAO [ˌefeɪ'əʊ] (ABBR = **Food and Agriculture Organization**) FAO f

FAQ 1 (Comm) (ABBR = **free alongside quay**) FLQ 2 N (Comput) (ABBR = **frequently asked questions**) FAQ f

far [fɑː'] (compar **farther** or **further**, superl **farthest** or **furthest**) 1 ADV a (lit) loin; **how ~ is it to Glasgow?** combien y a-t-il de kilomètres jusqu'à Glasgow?; **how ~ is it from Glasgow to Edinburgh?** combien y a-t-il (de kilomètres) de Glasgow à Édimbourg?; **is it ~?** c'est loin?; **is it ~ to London?** c'est loin pour aller à Londres?; **we live not ~ from here** nous habitons tout près d'ici; **we live quite ~** nous habitons assez loin; **have you come from ~?** vous venez de loin?; **how ~ are you going?** jusqu'où allez-vous?
b (fig) **how ~ have you got with your plans?** où en êtes-vous de vos projets?; **he'll go ~** (= do well) il ira loin; **to make one's money go ~** faire durer son argent; **£10 doesn't go ~**

these days avec 10 livres, on ne va pas bien loin de nos jours ; **that will go ~ towards placating him** cela contribuera beaucoup à le calmer ; **this scheme does not go ~ enough** ce projet ne va pas assez loin ; **I would even go so ~ as to say that ...** j'irais même jusqu'à dire que ..., je dirais même que ... ; **that's going too ~** cela dépasse les bornes *or* la mesure ; **I wouldn't go that ~** je n'irais pas jusque-là ; **now you're going a bit too ~** alors là vous allez un peu trop loin ; **he's gone too ~ this time!** il est vraiment allé trop loin cette fois ! ; **he has gone too ~ to back out now** il est trop engagé pour reculer maintenant ; **he carried** *or* **took the joke too ~** il a poussé trop loin la plaisanterie ; **he was ~ gone** (= *ill*) il était bien bas ; (* = *drunk*) il était bien parti* ; **just so ~ ◊ so ~ and no further** jusque-là mais pas plus loin ; **so ~ so good** jusqu'ici ça va ; **so ~ this year** jusqu'ici cette année ; **we have ten volunteers so ~** nous avons dix volontaires pour l'instant *or* jusqu'à présent ; **~ be it from me to try to dissuade you** loin de moi l'idée de vous dissuader

c **as ~ as : we went as ~ as the town** nous sommes allés jusqu'à la ville ; **we didn't go as** *or* **so ~ as the others** nous ne sommes pas allés aussi loin que les autres ; **as** *or* **so ~ as I know** (pour) autant que je le sache ; **as ~ as I can** dans la mesure du possible ; **as** *or* **so ~ as I can tell** d'après moi ; **as ~ as the eye can see** à perte de vue ; **as** *or* **so ~ as that goes** pour ce qui est de cela ; **as** *or* **so ~ as I'm concerned** en ce qui me concerne, pour ma part ; **as ~ back as I can remember** d'aussi loin que je m'en souvienne ; **as ~ back as 1945** dès 1945, déjà en 1945 ; **~ and away ◊ ~ and wide ◊ ~ and near** de tous côtés, partout → **1d** ; **they came from ~ and wide** *or* **~ and near** ils sont venus de partout ; **~ above** loin au-dessus ; **~ above the hill** loin au-dessus de la colline ; **he is ~ above the rest of the class** il est de loin supérieur *au* *or* il domine nettement le reste de la classe ; **~ away in the distance** au loin, dans le lointain ; **he wasn't ~ away when I saw him** il n'était pas loin quand je l'ai vu ; **~ beyond** bien au-delà ; **~ beyond the forest** très loin au-delà de la forêt ; **it's ~ beyond what I can afford** c'est bien au-dessus de mes moyens ; (*fig*) **I can't look ~ beyond May** je ne sais pas très bien ce qui se passera après le mois de mai ; **~ from** loin de ; **your work is ~ from satisfactory** votre travail est loin d'être satisfaisant ; **~ from it!** loin de là !, tant s'en faut ! ; **~ from liking him I find him rather objectionable** bien loin de l'aimer, je le trouve (au contraire) tout à fait désagréable ; **I am ~ from believing him** je suis très loin de le croire ; **~ into the night** tard dans la nuit ; **they went ~ into the forest** ils se sont enfoncés (loin) dans la forêt, ils ont pénétré très avant dans la forêt ; **~ off** au loin, dans le lointain ; **he wasn't ~ off when I caught sight of him** il n'était pas loin quand je l'ai aperçu ; **his birthday is not ~ off** c'est bientôt son anniversaire, son anniversaire approche ; **she's not ~ off fifty** elle n'est pas loin de la cinquantaine ; **~ out at sea** au (grand) large ; **~ out on the branch** tout au bout de la branche

d (= *very much*) beaucoup, bien ; **~ too expensive/too slow/too dangerous** beaucoup *or* bien trop cher/trop lent/trop dangereux ; **this is ~ better** c'est beaucoup *or* bien mieux ; **by ~** de loin, de beaucoup ; **this is ~ (and away) the best ◊ this is by ~ the best** *or* **the best by ~** ceci est de très loin ce qu'il y a de mieux ; **he's the oldest by ~** c'est de loin le plus âgé, il est beaucoup plus âgé que les autres ; **it is ~ more serious** c'est (bien) autrement sérieux ; **she is ~ prettier than her sister** elle est bien plus jolie que sa sœur ; **to be ~ out** *or* **~ off** (= *wrong*) [*person*] se tromper lourdement, être loin du compte ; [*estimates, guesses*] être loin du compte ; [*opinion polls*] se tromper lourdement ; [*calculations*] être complètement

erroné ; **to be not ~ wrong** *or* **out** *or* **off** [*person*] ne pas s'être trompé de beaucoup, ne pas être très loin de la vérité ; **it's not ~ wrong** *or* **out** [*figures, change*] il n'y a pas beaucoup de différence

2 ADJ **a** (= *distant*) (*liter*) [*country, land*] lointain, éloigné ; (*fig*) **it's a ~ cry from what he promised** on est loin de ce qu'il a promis **b** (= *further away*) autre, plus éloigné ; **on the ~ side of** de l'autre côté de ; **at the ~ end of** à l'autre bout de, à l'extrémité de ; **in the ~ north of Scotland** tout au nord de l'Écosse **c** (*Pol*) **the ~ right/left** l'extrême droite *f*/ gauche *f*

3 COMP ► **the Far East** N l'Extrême-Orient *m* ► **the Far North** N le Grand Nord ► **the Far West** N (*US*) le Far West, l'Ouest *m* américain

far- [fɑːʳ] PREF **~distant** lointain ; **Far-Eastern** d'Extrême-Orient ; **~fetched** [*explanation, argument*] forcé, tiré par les cheveux ; [*idea, scheme, suggestion*] bizarre ; **~flung** vaste, très étendu ; **~off** lointain, éloigné ; **~out*** (= *modern*) d'avant-garde ; (= *superb*) super*, génial ; (*fig*) **~reaching** d'une portée considérable, d'une grande portée ; **~seeing ◊ ~sighted** [*person*] prévoyant, qui voit loin ; [*decision, measure*] pris avec clairvoyance ; (*lit*) **~sighted** hypermétrope ; (*in old age*) presbyte → **farsightedness**

farad ['færæd] N farad *m*

faraway ['fɑːrəweɪ] ADJ **a** (*lit*) [*country*] lointain ; [*village, house*] éloigné **b** (*fig*) [*look*] distrait, absent ; [*voice*] lointain

farce [fɑːs] N **a** (*fig*) **the whole thing's a ~!** tout ça c'est grotesque ; **the elections were a ~** les élections furent une mascarade ; **the election campaign degenerated into a ~** la campagne électorale a tourné à la farce **b** (*Theat*) farce *f*

farcical ['fɑːsɪkəl] ADJ **a** (= *comical*) [*episode, attempt, scene*] burlesque ; (= *ridiculous, grotesque*) risible ; [*situation*] grotesque, risible **b** (*Theat*) **~ comedy** farce *f*

fare [fɛəʳ] **1** N **a** (= *charge*) (*on tube, subway, bus etc*) prix *m* du ticket *or* du billet ; (*on train, boat, plane*) prix *m* du billet ; (*in taxi*) prix *m* de la course ; (*in bus*) **~s, please!** ≈ les billets, s'il vous plaît ! ; **~s are going to go up** les tarifs *mpl* (des transports) vont augmenter ; **let me pay your ~** laissez-moi payer pour vous ; **I haven't got the ~** je n'ai pas assez d'argent pour le billet → **half, return** **b** (= *passenger*) voyageur *m*, -euse *f* ; (*of taxi*) client·e *m(f)* **c** (*NonC = food*) chère† *f*, nourriture *f* ; **hospital ~** régime *m* d'hôpital ; **traditional Christmas ~** les plats *mpl* traditionnels de Noël ; **vegetarian dishes are now standard ~ in many restaurants** les plats végétariens figurent désormais au menu de nombreux restaurants ; **old black-and-white films are standard ~ on late-night TV** les vieux films en noir et blanc figurent régulièrement au programme de fin de soirée à la télévision → **bill¹**

2 VI **he ~d better at his second attempt** il a mieux réussi à sa deuxième tentative ; **she has ~d better in France than in Britain** elle a mieux réussi en France qu'en Grande-Bretagne ; **the dollar ~d well on the stock exchange today** le dollar s'est bien comporté à la Bourse aujourd'hui ; († *or hum*) **how did you ~?** comment ça s'est passé ?, comment ça a marché ?*

3 COMP ► **fare-dodger** N (*Brit*) voyageur *m*, -euse *f* sans billet, resquilleur* *m*, -euse* *f* ► **fare-dodging** N resquillage* *m* ► **fare stage** N [*of bus*] section *f* ► **fare war** N guerre *f* des tarifs ► **fare zone** N (*US*) = **fare stage**

fare-thee-well [ˌfɛəðiːˈwel], **fare-you-well** [ˌfɛəjuːˈwel] N (*US*) **to a ~** (= *to perfection*) [*imi-*

tate etc] à la perfection ; (= *very much, very hard*) au plus haut point

farewell [fɛəˈwel] **1** N, EXCL adieu *m* ; **to say** *or* **make one's ~s** faire ses adieux ; **to take one's ~ of** faire ses adieux à ; (*lit*) **to say** *or* **bid† ~ to** dire adieu à ; (*fig*) **you can say ~ to your chances of promotion** tu peux dire adieu à tes chances de promotion !, ta promotion, tu peux faire une croix dessus !* **2** COMP [*dinner etc*] d'adieu

farinaceous [ˌfærɪˈneɪʃəs] ADJ farinacé, farineux

farm [fɑːm] **1** N (*Agr*) ferme *f*, exploitation *f* agricole ; **pig/chicken/trout ~** élevage *m* de porcs/poulets/truites ; **to work on a ~** travailler dans une ferme ; **~ fish, sheep** **2** VT [+ *land*] cultiver ; [+ *fish, salmon, deer*] faire l'élevage de → **farmed** **3** VI être agriculteur *m*, -trice *f* **4** COMP ► **farm animal** N animal *m* de (la) ferme ► **farm gate price** N (*Econ*) prix *m* à la production *or* au producteur ► **farm labourer** N = **farm worker** ► **farm produce** N (*NonC*) produits *mpl* agricoles *or* de la ferme ► **farm worker** N ouvrier *m*, -ière *f* agricole

► **farm out*** VT SEP [+ *shop*] mettre en gérance ; **to ~ out work** recourir à un sous-traitant ; **the firm ~ed out the plumbing to a local tradesman** l'entreprise a confié la plomberie à un sous-traitant local ; **she ~ed her children out on her sister-in-law** elle a donné ses enfants à garder à sa belle-sœur

farmed [fɑːmd] ADJ [*fish etc*] d'élevage

farmer ['fɑːməʳ] N agriculteur *m*, -trice *f*, fermier *m*, -ière *f*

farmhand ['fɑːmhænd] N = **farm worker**

farmhouse ['fɑːmhaʊs] **1** N ferme *f* **2** COMP ► **farmhouse loaf** N (*Brit*) pain *m* de campagne

farming ['fɑːmɪŋ] **1** N (*gen*) agriculture *f* ; **he's always been interested in ~** il s'est toujours intéressé à l'agriculture ; **vegetable/fruit ~** culture *f* maraîchère/fruitière ; **pig/mink ~** élevage *m* de porcs/de visons ; **the ~ of this land** la culture *or* l'exploitation de cette terre → **dairy, factory, mixed** **2** COMP [*methods, techniques*] de culture, cultural ► **farming communities** NPL collectivités *fpl* rurales

farmland ['fɑːmlænd] N terres *fpl* cultivées *or* arables

farmstead ['fɑːmsted] N ferme *f*

farmyard ['fɑːmjɑːd] N cour *f* de ferme

Faroes ['fɛərəʊz] NPL **the ~** (*also* **the Faroe Islands**) les îles *fpl* Féroé *or* Faeroe

Faroese [ˌfɛərəʊˈiːz] **1** N **a** (*pl inv = person*) Féroïen(ne) *m(f)*, Féringien(ne) *m(f)* **b** (*Ling*) féroïen *m* **2** ADJ féroïen, féringien, des îles Féroé

farrago [fəˈrɑːgəʊ] N (*pl* **farragos** *or* **farragoes**) méli-mélo* *m*, mélange *m*

farrier ['færɪəʳ] N (*esp Brit*) maréchal-ferrant *m*

farrow ['færəʊ] **1** VTI mettre bas **2** N portée *f* (de cochons)

Farsi ['fɑːsiː] N farsi *m*

farsightedness [ˌfɑːˈsaɪtɪdnɪs] N **a** (*fig*) prévoyance *f* **b** (*lit*) hypermétropie *f* ; (*in old age*) presbytie *f*

fart: [fɑːt] **1** N pet* *m* ; (*pej = person*) **he's a boring old ~** c'est un mec rasoir* *or* un vieux schnoque* **2** VI péter*

► **fart about:, fart around:** VI glander* ; **stop ~ing about and do some work!** arrête de glander*, et bosse un peu ! ; (= *play with*) **to ~ about** *or* **around with sth** déconner* avec qch

farther ['fɑːðəʳ] *compar of* **far** **1** ADV plus loin ; **how much ~ is it?** c'est encore loin ? ; **it's ~ than I thought** c'est plus loin que je ne pensais ; **have you got much ~ to go?** est-ce que vous avez encore loin à aller ? ; **we will go no ~** (*lit*) nous n'irons pas plus loin ; (*fig*) nous en resterons là ; **I can't go any ~** (*lit*) je ne peux pas aller plus loin; (fig) je n'en peux plus; **I got no ~ with him** je ne suis arrivé à rien de plus avec lui; **nothing could be ~ from the truth** rien n'est plus éloigné de la vérité; **nothing is ~ from my thoughts** rien n'est plus éloigné de ma pensée; **I can't see any ~ than the next six months** je n'arrive pas à voir au-delà des six prochains mois; **to get ~ and ~ away** s'éloigner de plus en plus; **~ back** plus (loin) en arrière; **push it ~ back** repousse-le plus loin; **move ~ back** reculez-vous; **~ back than 1940** avant 1940; **a little ~ up** (on wall etc) un peu plus haut; (along path) un peu plus loin; **~ away ◊ ~ off** plus éloigné, plus loin; **he went ~ off than I thought** il est allé plus loin que je ne pensais; **~ on ◊ ~ forward** plus en avant, plus loin; (fig) **we're no ~ forward after all that** on n'est pas plus avancé après tout ça

[2] ADJ plus éloigné, plus lointain; **at the ~ end of the room** à l'autre bout de la salle, au fond de la salle; **at the ~ end of the branch** à l'autre bout or à l'extrémité de la branche

farthest ['fɑːðɪst] superl of **far** [1] ADJ le plus éloigné; **in the ~ depths of the forest** au fin fond de la forêt; **they went by boat to the ~ point of the island** ils se sont rendus en bateau à l'extrémité de l'île; **the ~ way** la route la plus longue; **it's 5km at the ~** il y a 5 km au plus or au maximum [2] ADV le plus loin

farthing ['fɑːðɪŋ] N quart d'un ancien penny; **I haven't a ~** je n'ai pas le sou → **brass**

FAS [,efeɪ'es] (Comm) (ABBR = **free alongside ship**) FLB

fascia ['feɪʃə] N (pl **fasciae** ['feɪʃɪ,iː]) (Brit) [a] (on building) panneau m [b] (Aut) tableau m de bord

fascicle ['fæsɪkl], **fascicule** ['fæsɪkjuːl] N (Bot) rameau m fasciculé; [of book] fascicule m

fascinate ['fæsɪneɪt] VT [a] (= interest) [speaker, tale] fasciner, captiver; [sight] fasciner [b] [snake] fasciner

fascinated ['fæsɪneɪtɪd] ADJ [person] fasciné, captivé; [look, smile] fasciné

fascinating ['fæsɪneɪtɪŋ] ADJ [person, place, sight, story] fascinant; [book, film] captivant; [subject] passionnant; **it'll be ~ to see how she reacts** ce sera très intéressant de voir sa réaction

fascinatingly ['fæsɪneɪtɪŋlɪ] ADV **~ interesting** d'un intérêt exceptionnel; **~, his thesis is that ...** chose très intéressante, sa thèse est que ...

fascination [,fæsɪ'neɪʃən] N fascination f; **his ~ with the cinema** la fascination qu'exerce sur lui le cinéma; **I don't understand the ~ of this book** je ne comprends pas la fascination que ce livre exerce sur les gens; **he listened in ~** il écoutait, fasciné; **she has developed a ~ for Impressionist painting** elle se passionne maintenant pour la peinture impressionniste

fascism ['fæʃɪzəm] N fascisme m

fascist ['fæʃɪst] ADJ, N fasciste mf

fascistic [fə'ʃɪstɪk] ADJ fasciste

fashion ['fæʃən] [1] N [a] (NonC = manner) façon f, manière f; **in a strange ~** d'une façon or manière bizarre; **in (a) similar ~** d'une façon or manière similaire or semblable, pareillement; **after a ~** [manage] tant bien que mal; **I can cook after a ~** je sais à peu près faire la cuisine, je me débrouille en cuisine, sans plus; **it worked, after a ~** ça a marché plus ou moins bien; **after the ~ of** à la manière de; **in the French ~** à la française; **in his own ~** à sa manière or façon; (frm) **it's not my ~ to lie** ce n'est pas mon genre de mentir

[b] (lit, fig = latest clothes, style, ideas etc) mode f; **in ~** à la mode; **it's the latest ~** c'est la dernière mode or le dernier cri; **she always wears the latest ~s** elle est toujours habillée à la dernière mode; **the Paris ~s** les collections fpl (de mode) parisiennes; **a man of ~** un homme élégant; **~s have changed** la mode a

changé; **out of ~** démodé, passé de mode; **to set the ~ for** lancer la mode de; **to bring sth into ~** mettre qch à la mode; **to come into ~** devenir à la mode; **to go out of ~** se démoder; **it is the ~ to say** il est de bon ton de dire; **it's no longer the ~ to send children away to school** ça ne se fait plus de mettre les enfants en pension

[c] (= habit) coutume f, habitude f; **as was his ~** selon sa coutume or son habitude

[2] VT [+ carving] façonner; [+ model] fabriquer; [+ dress] confectionner

[3] COMP ► **fashion-conscious** ADJ **to be ~-conscious** suivre la mode ► **fashion designer** N (gen) styliste mf, modéliste mf; **the great ~ designers** (= Givenchy etc) les grands couturiers mpl ► **fashion editor** N rédacteur m, -trice f de mode ► **fashion house** N maison f de couture ► **fashion magazine** N magazine m or journal m de mode ► **fashion model** N mannequin m (personne) ► **fashion parade** N défilé m de mannequins, présentation f de collections ► **fashion plate** N gravure f de mode; **she's a real ~ plate*** on dirait une gravure de mode, elle a l'air de sortir d'un magazine de mode ► **fashion show** N présentation f de modèles or de collections; **to go to the Paris ~ shows** faire les collections parisiennes ► **fashion victim*** N victime f de la mode

fashionable ['fæʃnəbl] ADJ [clothes, shop, restaurant, subject, idea] à la mode; [hotel] chic inv; [district] prisé; [person] (= stylish) à la mode; (= in the public eye) en vue; [artist, writer] à la mode; **it is ~ to criticize these theories** il est à la mode de critiquer ces théories

fashionably ['fæʃnəblɪ] ADV [dress] à la mode; **~ long hair** des cheveux longs comme c'est la mode; **she was ~ late** elle était en retard, juste ce qu'il faut

fast¹ [fɑːst] [1] ADJ [a] (= speedy) rapide; **she's a ~ walker/runner/reader** elle marche/court/lit vite; **~ train** rapide m; **he's a ~ thinker** il a l'esprit très rapide; (Tennis) **a grass court is ~er** le jeu est plus rapide sur gazon; (Phot) **~ film** pellicule f rapide; **to pull a ~ one on sb*** rouler qn*, avoir qn* → 3

[b] **to be ~** [clock, watch] avancer; **my watch is five minutes ~** ma montre avance de cinq minutes

[c] († = dissipated) [person] léger, de mœurs légères; **~ life** vie f dissolue (liter); **~ woman** femme f légère or aux mœurs légères; **a ~ set** une bande de noceurs*; **one of the ~ set** un noceur or une noceuse

[d] (= firm) [rope, knot, grip] solide; **to make a boat ~** amarrer un bateau; **they're ~ friends** ils sont très amis

[e] [colour] bon teint inv, grand teint inv; **is the dye ~?** est-ce que ça déteindra?, est-ce que la teinture s'en ira?

[2] ADV [a] (= quickly) vite, rapidement; **don't speak so ~** ne parlez pas si vite; **how ~ can you type?** à quelle vitesse pouvez-vous taper (à la machine)?; **the environment is ~ becoming a major political issue** l'environnement est en train de prendre une place importante dans les débats politiques; **he ran off as ~ as his legs could carry him** il s'est sauvé à toutes jambes; (interrupting) **not so ~!** doucement!, minute!*; **he'd do it ~ enough if ...** il ne se ferait pas prier si ...; **the holidays can't come ~ enough for me** vivement les vacances!; **as ~ as I advanced he drew back** à mesure que j'avançais, il reculait → **furious**

[b] (= firmly, securely) ferme, solidement; **to be ~ asleep** dormir à poings fermés; **to be stuck ~** [person, door, window, lid] être coincé; **a door shut ~** une porte bien close; **to stand ~** tenir bon or ferme, ne pas lâcher pied; **to play ~ and loose with sb** se jouer de qn, traiter qn à la légère → **hard**, **hold**

[c] **~ by the church** †† qui jouxte† l'église

[3] COMP ► **fast breeder (reactor)** N (Phys) (réacteur m) surgénérateur m, (réacteur m) surrégénérateur m ► **fast-flowing** ADJ [river, stream] au cours rapide ► **fast food** N (= food) prêt-à-manger m; (= place: also **~-food restaurant**) fast-food m ► **fast-food chain** N chaîne f de fast-foods ► **fast-food industry**, **fast-food trade** N secteur m des fast-foods, restauration f rapide ► **fast forward** N avance f rapide ► **fast-forward** VT faire avancer rapidement ♦ VI [tape] avancer rapidement ► **the fast lane** N (Aut) ≈ la voie de gauche; (fig) **to be in the ~ lane** avoir une vie trépidante, vivre à 100 à l'heure*; **life in the ~ lane** la vie trépidante ► **fast-moving** ADJ (gen) rapide; (fig = active, rapidly-changing) [industry, sector] en mouvement constant; **~-moving consumer goods** biens mpl de consommation à rotation rapide ► **fast-selling** ADJ à écoulement rapide ► **fast-track** N (in organization) filière f ultrarapide; **her career was on the ~-track** elle progressait rapidement dans sa carrière; **this put the company on a ~-track to privatization** cela a accéléré la privatisation de l'entreprise ♦ ADJ [approach] expéditif; (Univ) **~-track degree** diplôme m de formation accélérée ► **fast-tracking** N [of personnel] avancement m rapide

fast² [fɑːst] [1] VI jeûner, rester à jeun; (Rel) jeûner, faire maigre [2] N jeûne m; **to break one's ~** rompre le jeûne; (Rel) **~ day** jour m maigre or de jeûne

fastback ['fɑːstbæk] N (Brit Aut) voiture f à hayon

fasten ['fɑːsn] [1] VT [a] (lit) attacher (**to** à); (with rope, string etc) lier (**to** à); [+ dress] fermer, attacher; [+ shoelaces] attacher, nouer; [+ box] fermer (solidement); **to ~ two things together** attacher deux choses ensemble or l'une à l'autre; **to ~ one's seat belt** attacher or mettre sa ceinture de sécurité; (fig) [+ responsibility] attribuer (**on sb** à qn); [+ crime] imputer (**on sb** à qn); **to ~ the blame on sb** rejeter la faute sur (le dos de) qn; **you can't ~ it on me!** tu ne peux pas me mettre ça sur le dos!; **to ~ one's hopes on sb/sth** placer or mettre tous ses espoirs dans qn/qch; **to ~ one's eyes on sth** fixer son regard or les yeux sur qch [2] VI [dress] s'attacher; [box, door, lock, window] se fermer

► **fasten down** VT SEP fixer en place

► **fasten on** [1] VT SEP fixer (en place) [2] VT FUS = **fasten upon**

► **fasten on to** VT FUS [a] = **fasten upon** [b] se cramponner à, s'accrocher à; **he ~ed on to my arm** il s'est cramponné or accroché à mon bras

► **fasten up** VT SEP [+ dress, coat] fermer, attacher

► **fasten upon** VT FUS saisir; **to ~ upon an excuse** saisir un prétexte; **to ~ upon the idea of doing** se mettre en tête (l'idée de) faire

fastener ['fɑːsnə⁷], **fastening** ['fɑːsnɪŋ] N [of box, bag, necklace, book] fermoir m; [of garment] fermeture f; (= button) bouton m; (= hook) agrafe f; (= press stud) bouton-pression m, pression f; (= zip) fermeture f éclair® inv; **a zip ~** une fermeture éclair®; **a Velcro ~** une fermeture velcro®; **a snap ~** un bouton-pression, une pression

fastidious [fæs'tɪdɪəs] ADJ [work, research] minutieux; [person] (= meticulous) méticuleux, minutieux; (= demanding about detail) tatillon, pointilleux; (= particular about cleanliness) tatillon; (= easily disgusted) délicat; **their inspectors are very ~** leurs inspecteurs sont très pointilleux or tatillons; **he's ~ about security/hygiene** il est pointilleux en ce qui concerne la sécurité/l'hygiène; **she's too ~ to eat there** elle est trop délicate pour manger là; **this film is not for the ~** ce film n'est pas pour les esprits délicats or pour les personnes trop délicates

fastidiously [fæs'tɪdɪəslɪ] ADV [a] (= meticulously) [check, copy] méticuleusement ; **~ clean** d'une propreté méticuleuse ; **his ~ tidy flat** son appartement impeccablement rangé [b] (pej = with distaste) [examine] en faisant le délicat

fastidiousness [fæs'tɪdɪəsnɪs] N (= meticulousness) méticulosité f (liter), minutie f ; (= concern about detail) caractère m tatillon

fastigiate [fæ'stɪdʒɪɪt] ADJ fastigié

fastness ['fɑːstnɪs] N [a] [of colours] solidité f ; **to test a fabric for colour ~** tester la résistance au lavage d'un tissu [b] (NonC = speed) rapidité f, vitesse f [c] (= stronghold) place f forte ; **mountain ~** repaire m de montagne

fat [fæt] [1] N (gen, also Anat) graisse f ; (on raw meat) graisse f, gras m ; (on cooked meat) gras m ; (for cooking) matière grasse f ; **try to cut down the amount of ~ in your diet** essayez de manger moins gras or moins de matières grasses ; **to fry sth in deep ~** (faire) frire or cuire qch dans un bain de friture ; **animal/vegetable ~** graisse f animale/végétale ; **beef/mutton ~** graisse f de bœuf/de mouton ; **pork ~** saindoux m ; **body ~** tissu m adipeux ; **he's got rolls of ~ round his waist** il a des bourrelets de graisse autour de la taille ; (fig) **the ~'s in the fire** ça va barder* or chauffer* ; (fig) **to live off the ~ of the land** vivre grassement

[2] ADJ [a] (= overweight) [person, animal, stomach, thighs, cheeks] gros (grosse f) ; [face] joufflu ; **to get** or **grow** or **become ~** devenir gros, grossir ; **she has got a lot ~ter** elle a beaucoup grossi ; (fig) **to grow ~ (on sth)** s'engraisser (de qch) ; (hum) **it's not** or **the show's not over until the ~ lady sings*** il ne faut jamais désespérer

[b] (= fatty) [meat, bacon] gras (grasse f)
[c] (= thick) [book, volume] gros (grosse f), épais (épaisse f) ; [wallet] bien garni
[d] (* = large) [profit, fee, cheque, salary] gros (grosse f)
[e] (= prosperous) [year] bon
[f] (* pej = stupid) **can't you get that into your ~ head?** tu ne peux pas te mettre ça dans la caboche* ? ; **get it into your ~ head that you can't come with us** mets-toi bien dans la tête que tu ne peux pas venir avec nous
[g] (* iro) (a) **~ lot: a ~ lot he cares!** comme si ça lui faisait quelque chose ! ; **a ~ lot of good that did!** nous voilà bien avancés ! ; **a ~ lot of good lying did you!** ça t'a avancé à quoi, de mentir ? ; **a ~ lot of good such a promise will be!** ça nous fait une belle jambe ! ; **it'll be a ~ lot of good to phone now** tu parles si ça sert à quelque chose de téléphoner maintenant ! (iro) ; (a) **~ lot of help she was (to me)!** c'est fou ce qu'elle m'a aidé ! (iro) ; **a ~ lot you did to help!** tu as vraiment été d'un précieux secours ! (iro) ; **a ~ lot he knows about it!** comme s'il y connaissait quelque chose ! ; **that's a ~ lot of use!** pour ce à quoi ça sert ! (iro) ; **that's a ~ lot of use to me!** c'est fou ce que ça m'aide ! (iro) ; **a ~ lot that's worth!** c'est fou ce que ça a comme valeur ! (iro), ça ne vaut pas tripette !*
[h] (* iro) **~ chance (of that)!** ça m'étonnerait ! ; **he wants to be a racing driver — chance!** il veut être pilote de course — il n'a aucune chance ! ; **a ~ chance he's got of winning the lottery!** tu parles qu'il risque de gagner à la loterie !* ; **you've got a ~ chance of seeing her!** comme si tu avais la moindre chance de la voir !

[3] VT ‡‡ [a] = **fatten 1**
[b] **to kill the ~ted calf** tuer le veau gras
[4] COMP ► **fat-ass**‡ (US pej) N (man) gros lard* m (pej) ; (woman) grosse vache* f (pej) ♦ ADJ obèse (pej) ► **fat cat** N gros richard* m ► **fat city**‡ N (US) **to be in ~ city** être plein aux as* ► **fat farm**‡ N (esp US) clinique f d'amaigrissement ► **fat-free** ADJ [diet] sans

matières grasses, sans corps gras ► **fat-headed*** ADJ idiot, imbécile → **fathead**

fatal ['feɪtl] ADJ [a] (= causing death) [injury, illness, accident, shot, dose] mortel, fatal ; [blow] mortel, fatal ; [consequences, result, delay] fatal ; **to be ~ to** or **for sb** être fatal pour or à qn [b] (= disastrous) [mistake, weakness] fatal ; [flaw] malheureux ; [influence] néfaste, pernicieux ; **~ attraction** attraction f irrésistible ; **to be ~ to** or **for sb/sth** porter un coup fatal or le coup de grâce à qn/qch ; **it would be ~ to do that** ce serait une erreur fatale de faire cela [c] (= fateful) [day] fatidique

fatalism ['feɪtəlɪzəm] N fatalisme m

fatalist ['feɪtəlɪst] N, ADJ fataliste mf

fatalistic [ˌfeɪtə'lɪstɪk] ADJ fataliste

fatality [fə'tælɪtɪ] N [a] (= fatal accident) accident m mortel ; (= person killed) mort m ; **there were no fatalities** il n'y a pas eu de morts ; **bathing fatalities** noyades fpl ; **road fatalities** accidents mpl mortels de la route [b] (NonC) fatalisme m ; **a growing sense of pessimism and ~** un sentiment croissant de pessimisme et de fatalisme

fatally ['feɪtlɪ] ADV [a] (= mortally) [wounded, injured] mortellement ; **~ ill** condamné [b] (= irrevocably) [undermine, damage, weaken] irrémédiablement ; **~ flawed** voué à l'échec [c] (= disastrously) [disastrously] désastreusement ; **to be ~ attracted to sb/sth** être irrésistiblement attiré par qn/qch

fatback ['fætbæk] N ≈ lard m maigre

fate [feɪt] N [a] (= force) destin m, sort m ; (Myth) **the Fates** les Parques fpl ; **what ~ has in store for us** ce que le destin or le sort nous réserve → **tempt** [b] (= one's lot) sort m ; **to leave sb to his ~** abandonner qn à son sort ; **to meet one's ~** trouver la mort ; **it met with a strange ~** cela a eu une destinée curieuse ; **to meet with** or **suffer the same ~** connaître or subir le même sort ; **to face a similar ~** risquer de subir le même sort ; **to settle** or **seal sb's ~** décider du sort de qn/qch ; **it was a ~ worse than death** c'était un sort pire que la mort, la mort eût été mille fois préférable

fated ['feɪtɪd] ADJ [friendship, person] voué au malheur ; **they were ~ to meet again** il était dit qu'ils se reverraient

fateful ['feɪtfʊl] ADJ [day, night, moment, words] fatidique ; [decision, consequence, journey] fatal ; [meeting] décisif ; **to be ~ for sb** être fatal pour qn

fathead* ['fæthed] N imbécile mf, cruche* f

father ['fɑːðəʳ] [1] N [a] père m ; **from ~ to son** de père en fils (PROV) **like ~ like son** tel père tel fils (PROV) ; **to act like a ~** agir en père or comme un père ; **he was like a ~ to me** il était comme un père pour moi ; **there was the ~ and mother of a row!*** il y a eu une dispute épouvantable ! → 4
[b] (= founder, leader) père m, créateur m ; **the ~ of modern jazz/French Impressionism** le père du jazz moderne/de l'impressionnisme français ; **the Fathers of the Church** les Pères mpl de l'Église → **city**
[c] (Rel = priest, monk etc) père m ; **Father Paul** le (révérend) père Paul, l'abbé m Paul ; **yes, Father** oui, mon père ; **the Capuchin Fathers** les pères mpl capucins → **holy**
[d] (Rel) (= God) **Our Father** Notre Père ; (= prayer) **the Our Father** le Notre Père
[2] **fathers** NPL ancêtres mpl, pères mpl
[3] VT [+ child] engendrer ; **he ~ed three children** il a eu trois enfants ; **he was unable to ~ a child** il ne pouvait pas avoir d'enfants
[4] COMP ► **Father Christmas** N (Brit) le père Noël ► **father confessor** N (Rel) directeur m de conscience, père m spirituel ► **father figure** N figure f de père ; **he is the ~ figure** il joue le rôle du père ► **father-in-law** N (pl fathers-in-law) beau-père m ► **Father's Day** N

la fête des Pères ► **Father Time** N (also **Old Father Time**) le Temps

fatherhood ['fɑːðəhʊd] N paternité f

fatherland ['fɑːðəlænd] N patrie f

fatherless ['fɑːðəlɪs] ADJ orphelin de père, sans père

fatherly ['fɑːðəlɪ] ADJ paternel

fathom ['fæðəm] [1] N (Naut) brasse f (= 1,83 m) ; **a channel with five ~s of water** un chenal de 9 m de fond ; **to lie 25 ~s deep** or **down** reposer par 45 m de fond [2] VT (Naut) sonder ; (fig: also **~ out**) [+ mystery] pénétrer ; [+ person] (finir par) comprendre ; **I just can't ~ it (out)** je n'y comprends absolument rien

fathomless ['fæðəmlɪs] ADJ (lit) insondable ; (fig) insondable, impénétrable

fatigue [fə'tiːg] [1] N [a] fatigue f, épuisement m [b] (= jadedness) **donor ~** ◊ **charity ~** la lassitude des donateurs ; **compassion ~ has set in** la compassion s'est émoussée ; **they blamed the low election turn-out on voter ~** ils ont attribué la faible participation électorale à la lassitude des électeurs → **battle, combat** [c] (Mil) corvée f ; **to be on ~** être de corvée [2] **fatigues** NPL (Mil) = **fatigue dress** [3] VT fatiguer, lasser ; (Tech) [+ metals etc] fatiguer [4] COMP ► **fatigue dress** N (Mil) tenue f de corvée, treillis m ► **fatigue duty** N (Mil) corvée f ► **fatigue limit** N (Tech) limite f de fatigue ► **fatigue party** N (Mil) corvée f

fatigued [fə'tiːgd] ADJ las (lasse f), fatigué

fatiguing [fə'tiːgɪŋ] ADJ fatigant, épuisant

fatness ['fætnɪs] N [of person] embonpoint m, corpulence f

fatso‡ ['fætsəʊ] N (pl fatsos or fatsoes) (pej) gros lard‡ m

fatstock ['fætstɒk] N (Agr) animaux mpl de boucherie

fatten ['fætn] [1] VT (also **~ up**) [+ cattle, chickens] engraisser ; [+ geese] gaver [2] VI (also **~ out**) engraisser, grossir

fattening ['fætnɪŋ] [1] ADJ [food] qui fait grossir [2] N (also **~-up**) [of cattle, chickens] engraissement m ; [of geese] gavage m

fatty ['fætɪ] [1] ADJ (= greasy) [food] gras (grasse f) ; **they have a fattier diet than us** ils mangent plus gras que nous [b] (Anat, Bio) [tissue] adipeux [2] N* gros m (bonhomme), grosse f (bonne femme) ; **hey ~!** eh toi le gros (or la grosse) ! [3] COMP ► **fatty acid** N acide m gras ► **fatty degeneration** N (Med) dégénérescence f graisseuse

fatuity [fə'tjuːɪtɪ] N stupidité f, sottise f

fatuous ['fætjʊəs] ADJ [person, remark] idiot, stupide ; [smile] stupide, niais

fatuously ['fætjʊəslɪ] ADV sottement, stupidement

fatuousness ['fætjʊəsnɪs] N = **fatuity**

fatwa ['fætwə] N (Rel) fatwa f

faucet ['fɔːsɪt] N (US) robinet m

faugh [fɔː] EXCL pouah !

fault [fɔːlt] [1] N [a] (in person, scheme) défaut m ; (in machine) anomalie f, défaut m ; (= mistake) erreur f ; **in spite of all her ~s** malgré tous ses défauts ; **her big ~ is ...** son gros défaut est ... ; **a mechanical ~** un défaut technique ; **a ~ has been found in the engine** une anomalie a été constatée dans le moteur ; **the ~ lay in the production process** l'anomalie se situait au niveau de la production ; **there is a ~ in the gas supply** il y a un défaut dans l'arrivée du gaz ; **an electrical ~** un défaut du circuit électrique ; **to be at ~** être fautif, coupable ; **you were at ~ in not telling me** vous avez eu tort de ne pas me le dire ; **he's at ~ in this matter** il est fautif or c'est lui le fautif dans cette affaire ; **my memory was at ~** ma mémoire m'a trompé or m'a fait défaut ; **to find ~ with sth** trouver à redire à qch, critiquer qch ; **to find ~ with sb** critiquer qn ; **I have no ~ to find with him** je n'ai rien à lui reprocher; **he is always finding ~** il trouve toujours à redire; **she is generous to a ~** elle est généreuse à l'excès

[b] (NonC = blame, responsibility) faute f; **whose ~ is it?** c'est la faute à qui?, qui est fautif?; (iro) **whose ~ is it if we're late?** et à qui la faute si nous sommes en retard?; **the ~ lies with him** c'est de sa faute, c'est lui le responsable; **it's not my ~** ce n'est pas (de) ma faute; **it's all your ~** c'est entièrement (de) ta faute; **it's your own ~** vous n'avez à vous en prendre qu'à vous-même; **it happened through no ~ of mine** ce n'est absolument pas de ma faute si c'est arrivé; **through no ~ of her own, she ...** sans qu'elle y soit pour quelque chose, elle ...

[c] (Tennis) faute f
[d] (Geol) faille f

[2] VT **to ~ sth/sb** trouver des défauts à qch/chez qn; **you can't ~ him** on ne peut pas le prendre en défaut; **you can't ~ her on her handling of the situation** la manière dont elle a géré la situation est irréprochable; **I can't ~ his reasoning** je ne trouve aucune faille dans son raisonnement

[3] COMP ► **fault-find** VI **she's always ~-finding** elle trouve toujours à redire, elle est toujours en train de critiquer ► **fault-finder** N mécontent(e) m(f), grincheux m, -euse f ► **fault-finding** ADJ chicanier, grincheux ♦ N critiques fpl ► **fault line** N (Geol) ligne f de faille ► **fault plane** N (Geol) plan m de faille ► **fault-tolerant** ADJ (Comput) à tolérance de pannes, insensible aux défaillances

faultless ['fɔːltlɪs] ADJ [person, behaviour] irréprochable; [work, manners, dress] impeccable, irréprochable; [performance] parfait; **he spoke ~ English** il parlait un anglais impeccable

faultlessly ['fɔːltlɪslɪ] ADV impeccablement

faulty ['fɔːltɪ] ADJ [work] défectueux, mal fait; [machine] défectueux; [style] incorrect, mauvais; [reasoning] défectueux, erroné

faun [fɔːn] N faune m

fauna ['fɔːnə] N (pl **faunas** or **faunae** ['fɔːniː]) faune f

Faust [faʊst] N Faust m

Faustian ['faʊstɪən] ADJ faustien

faux pas [fəʊ'pɑː] N (pl inv) impair m, bévue f, gaffe* f

fava bean ['fɑːvəbiːn] N (US) fève f

▼ **favour, favor** (US) ['feɪvər] [1] N [a] (= act of kindness) (small) service m; (more major) faveur f; **to do sb a ~** ◊ **to do a ~ for sb** rendre (un) service à qn, faire or accorder une faveur à qn; **to ask sb a ~** ◊ **to ask a ~ of sb** demander un service à qn, solliciter une faveur de qn (frm); **he did it as a ~ to his brother** il l'a fait pour rendre service à son frère; **I'll return this ~** je vous revaudrai ça; **I would consider it a ~ if you ...** je vous serais très reconnaissant si vous ...; **do me a ~ and ...** sois gentil et ...; **you're not doing yourself any ~s (by refusing to cooperate)** tu ne te facilites pas les choses (en refusant de coopérer); (iro) **do me a ~!** tu te fous de moi!*; **a woman's ~s** les faveurs fpl d'une femme; **(your) ~ of the 7th inst.** votre honorée† du 7 courant

[b] (NonC = approval, regard) faveur f, approbation f; **to be in ~** être en faveur, avoir la cote*; [style, fashion] être à la mode or en vogue; **to be out of ~** [person] ne pas être en faveur, ne pas avoir la cote*; [style, fashion] être démodé or passé de mode; **to be in ~ with sb** être bien vu de qn, jouir des bonnes grâces de qn; **to win sb's ~** ◊ **to find ~ with sb** [person] s'attirer les bonnes grâces de qn; [suggestion] gagner l'approbation de qn; **to get back into sb's ~** rentrer dans les bonnes grâces de qn; **to look with ~ on sth** approuver qch; **to look with ~ on sb** bien considérer qn

[c] (NonC = support, advantage) faveur f, avantage m; **the court decided in her ~** le tribunal lui a donné gain de cause; **the decision/judgement went in his ~** la décision a

été prise/le jugement a été rendu en sa faveur; **it's in our ~ to act now** c'est (à) notre avantage d'agir maintenant; **the exchange rate is in our ~** le taux de change joue en notre faveur or pour nous; **the traffic lights are in our ~** les feux sont pour nous; **circumstances were all working in her ~** les circonstances lui étaient (entièrement) favorables; **that's a point in his ~** c'est quelque chose à mettre à son actif, c'est un bon point pour lui; **he's got everything in his ~** il a tout pour lui; **will in ~ of sb** testament m en faveur de qn; **cheque in ~ of sb** chèque m payable à qn; (Banking) **"balance in your ~"** « solde en votre faveur »

[d] **to be in ~ of sth** être pour qch, être partisan(e) de qch; **to be in ~ of doing sth** être d'avis de faire qch; **they voted in ~ of accepting the pay offer** ils ont voté en faveur de la proposition de salaire

[e] (NonC = partiality) faveur f, indulgence f; **to show ~ to sb** accorder un traitement de faveur à qn, favoriser qn → curry², fear

[f] (= ribbon, token) faveur f

[2] VT [+ political party, scheme, suggestion] être partisan de; [+ undertaking] favoriser, appuyer; [+ person] préférer; [+ candidate, pupil] montrer une préférence pour; [+ team, horse] être pour; († or dial = resemble) ressembler à; **I don't ~ the idea** je ne suis pas partisan de cette idée; **he ~ed us with a visit** il a eu l'amabilité or la bonté de nous rendre visite; (iro) **he did not ~ us with a reply** il n'a même pas eu l'amabilité or la bonté de nous répondre; **the weather ~ed the journey** le temps a favorisé le voyage; **circumstances that ~ this scheme** circonstances fpl favorables à ce projet; **tax cuts which ~ the rich** des réductions d'impôts qui avantagent or favorisent les riches

▼ **favourable, favorable** (US) ['feɪvrəbl] ADJ [a] (= positive) [reaction, impression, opinion, report] favorable; [comparison] flatteur; **to be ~ to sb/sth** être favorable à qn/qch; **to show sth in a ~ light** montrer qch sous un jour favorable [b] (= beneficial) [terms, deal] avantageux (for sb/sth pour qn/qch); [position] bon; [treatment] (gen) bon; (= preferential) de faveur [c] [climate] favorable (for, to à); [weather, wind] propice (for, to à)

▼ **favourably, favorably** (US) ['feɪvrəblɪ] ADV [a] (= approvingly) [respond, react, receive] favorablement; [look upon, consider] d'un œil favorable; **to impress sb ~** faire une impression favorable à qn; **~ disposed** bien disposé [b] (= advantageously) [placed] bien; **to compare ~ with sb/sth** soutenir la comparaison avec qn/qch; **he was always being compared ~ with his sister** on l'a toujours trouvé mieux que sa sœur; **few would compare themselves ~ with him** peu de personnes se jugeraient meilleures que lui

favoured, favored (US) ['feɪvəd] ADJ favorisé; **the ~ few** les élus mpl; **most ~ nation clause** clause f de la nation la plus favorisée

▼ **favourite, favorite** (US) ['feɪvərɪt] [1] N (gen) favori(te) m(f), préféré(e) m(f); (at court, Racing) favori(te) m(f); **he's his mother's ~** c'est le préféré de sa mère; **he's a universal ~** tout le monde l'adore; **that song is a great ~ of mine** cette chanson est une de mes préférées; **he sang a lot of old ~s** il a chanté beaucoup de vieux succès → hot [2] ADJ favori(te) m(f), préféré; (US) **~ son** (Pol) candidat à la présidence soutenu officiellement par son parti dans son État; (gen) enfant m chéri (de sa ville natale etc)

favouritism, favoritism (US) ['feɪvərɪtɪzəm] N favoritisme m

fawn¹ [fɔːn] [1] N faon m [2] ADJ (= colour) fauve

fawn² [fɔːn] VI **to ~ (up)on sb** [dog] faire fête à qn; [person] flatter qn (servilement), lécher les bottes de qn*

fawning ['fɔːnɪŋ] ADJ [person, manner] servile, flagorneur; [dog] trop démonstratif, trop affectueux

fax [fæks] [1] N (= machine) télécopieur m; (= transmission) fax m, télécopie f; **~ number** numéro m de fax or de télécopie or de télécopieur; **by ~** par fax or télécopie [2] VT [+ document] faxer, envoyer par fax or par télécopie or par télécopieur; [+ person] envoyer un fax à; **~ me your reply** répondez-moi par fax

fay [feɪ] N († or liter) fée f

faze: [feɪz] VT déboussoler*

FBI [ˌefbiː'aɪ] N (US) (ABBR = **Federal Bureau of Investigation**) FBI m

FCC [ˌefsiː'siː] N (US) (ABBR = **Federal Communications Commission**) → federal

FCO [ˌefsiː'əʊ] (Brit) (ABBR = **Foreign and Commonwealth Office**) → foreign

FD [ef'diː] [a] N (US) (ABBR = **Fire Department**) → fire [b] (Brit) (ABBR = **Fidei Defensor**) Défenseur m de la foi [c] (Comm) (ABBR = **free delivered at dock**) livraison f franco à quai

FDA [ˌefdiː'eɪ] N (US) (ABBR = **Food and Drug Administration**) FDA f

FDA
La Food and Drug Administration ou FDA est l'organisme qui a pour mission de tester l'innocuité des aliments, additifs alimentaires, médicaments et cosmétiques aux États-Unis, et de délivrer les autorisations de mise sur le marché.

FDD N (Comput) (ABBR = **floppy disk drive**) → floppy

FE [ef'iː] N (ABBR = **Further Education**) → further

fealty ['fiːəltɪ] N (Hist) fidélité f, allégeance f

▼ **fear** [fɪər] [1] N [a] (= fright) peur f; (= worry, apprehension) crainte f; **he obeyed out of ~** il a obéi sous l'effet de la peur; **I couldn't move from or for ~** j'étais paralysé de peur; **a sudden ~ came over him** la peur s'est soudain emparée de lui; **~ of death/failure/rejection** la peur de la mort/de l'échec/du rejet or d'être rejeté; **~ of flying** la peur des voyages en avion or de l'avion; **~ of heights** vertige m; **grave ~s have arisen for the safety of the hostages** on est dans la plus vive inquiétude en ce qui concerne le sort des otages; **there are ~s that ...** on craint que ... ne (+ subj); **there are ~s that many more refugees will die** on craint que beaucoup d'autres réfugiés ne meurent; **he has ~s for his sister's life** il craint pour la vie de sa sœur; **to have a ~ of** avoir peur de; **have no ~(s)** ne craignez rien, soyez sans crainte; **without ~ or favour** impartialement, sans distinction de personnes; **to stand in ~ of sb/sth** craindre or redouter qn/qch; **he lived in ~ of being discovered** il craignait toujours d'être découvert, il a vécu dans la peur d'être découvert; **to go in ~ of one's life** craindre pour sa vie; **in ~ and trembling** en tremblant de peur; **for ~ of waking him** de peur de le réveiller; **for ~ (that ...)** de peur que ... ne (+ subj)

[b] (NonC = awe) crainte f, respect m; **the ~ of God** la crainte or le respect de Dieu; **to put the ~ of God into sb*** (= frighten) faire une peur bleue à qn; (= scold) passer à qn une semonce or un savon* qu'il n'oubliera pas de si tôt

[c] (= risk, likelihood) risque m, danger m; **there's not much ~ of his coming** il est peu probable qu'il vienne, il ne risque guère de venir; **there's not much ~ of us making that kind of money!** nous ne risquons pas de gagner des sommes pareilles!; **there's no ~ of that!** ça ne risque pas d'arriver!; **no ~!*** jamais de la vie!, pas de danger!*

[2] VT [a] craindre, avoir peur de; **to ~ the worst** redouter or craindre le pire; **to ~ that** avoir peur que or craindre que ... ne (+ subj); **I ~ that a war now looks inevitable** je crains or

j'ai bien peur que la guerre ne soit maintenant inévitable ; **I ~ he won't come** j'ai (bien) peur *or* je crains (bien) qu'il ne vienne pas ; **many women ~ to go out at night** beaucoup de femmes ont peur de sortir le soir ; **I ~ so** je crains que oui, hélas oui ; **I ~ not** je crains que non, hélas non ; *(apologizing)* **I ~ I'm late** je crois bien que je suis en retard, je suis désolé d'être en retard ; **it's raining, I ~** il pleut, hélas ; **he's a man to be ~ed** c'est un homme redoutable

[b] (= *awe for God*) [+ *gods*] craindre, avoir le respect de

[3] VI **to ~ for one's life** craindre pour sa vie ; **I ~ for him** j'ai peur *or* je tremble pour lui ; **he ~s for the future of the country** l'avenir du pays lui inspire des craintes *or* des inquiétudes ; **we ~ for their safety** nous craignons pour leur sécurité ; **never ~!** ne craignez rien !, n'ayez crainte ! ; *(hum)* **not !**† n'ayez crainte !

fearful ['fɪəfʊl] ADJ [a] (= *frightening*) [*spectacle, noise*] effrayant, affreux ; [*accident*] épouvantable [b] († = *extreme*) affreux ; **it really is a ~ nuisance** c'est vraiment empoisonnant* *or* embêtant* ; **she's a ~ bore** Dieu ! qu'elle est *or* peut être ennuyeuse ! [c] (= *timid*) [*person*] peureux, craintif ; **I was ~ of waking her** je craignais de la réveiller

fearfully ['fɪəfəlɪ] ADV [a] (= *timidly*) [*say, ask*] craintivement [b] († = *extremely*) [*expensive, hot*] affreusement, terriblement ; **she's ~ ugly** elle est laide à faire peur

fearfulness ['fɪəfʊlnɪs] N (= *fear*) crainte *f*, appréhension *f* ; (= *shyness*) extrême timidité *f*

fearless ['fɪəlɪs] ADJ intrépide, courageux ; *(liter)* **~ of** sans peur *or* appréhension de

fearlessly ['fɪəlɪslɪ] ADV [*fight*] courageusement ; **to be ~ outspoken** avoir le courage de ses opinions

fearlessness ['fɪəlɪsnɪs] N intrépidité *f*

fearsome ['fɪəsəm] ADJ [*opponent*] redoutable ; [*apparition*] terrible, effroyable

fearsomely ['fɪəsəmlɪ] ADV effroyablement, affreusement

feasibility [ˌfiːzəˈbɪlɪtɪ] [1] N [a] (= *practicability*) [*of plan, suggestion*] faisabilité *f*, possibilité *f* (de réalisation) ; **~ of doing** possibilité *f* de faire ; **to doubt the ~ of a scheme** douter qu'un plan soit réalisable [b] (= *plausibility*) [*of story, report*] vraisemblance *f*, plausibilité *f* [2] COMP ► **feasibility study** N étude *f* de faisabilité

feasible ['fiːzəbl] ADJ [a] (= *practicable*) [*plan, suggestion*] faisable, possible ; **can we do it? — yes, it's quite ~** pouvons-nous le faire ? — oui, c'est tout à fait possible *or* faisable ; **it would be ~ to put all the data on one disk** il serait possible de rassembler toutes les données sur une seule disquette ; **it was not economically ~ to keep the school open** il n'était pas économiquement viable de maintenir ouverte cette école [b] (= *likely, probable*) [*story, theory*] plausible, vraisemblable

feasibly ['fiːzəblɪ] ADV **he could ~ still be alive** il se pourrait bien qu'il soit encore vivant

feast [fiːst] [1] N [a] (*lit, fig*) festin *m*, banquet *m* ; *(Brit)* **to be the spectre** *or* **ghost** *or* **skeleton at the ~** jeter une ombre sur les réjouissances ; **it's ~ or famine** c'est l'abondance ou la famine [b] *(Rel)* fête *f* ; **~ day** (jour *m* de) fête *f* ; **the ~ of St John** la Saint-Jean ; **the ~ of the Assumption** la fête de l'Assomption → **movable** [2] VI banqueter, festoyer ; **to ~ on sth** (*lit*) se régaler de qch ; (*fig*) se délecter de qch [3] VT († *or liter*) [+ *guest*] fêter, régaler ; **to ~ o.s.** se régaler ; **to ~ one's eyes on** repaître ses yeux de, se délecter à regarder

feat [fiːt] N exploit *m*, prouesse *f* ; **~ of architecture** *etc* chef-d'œuvre *m* *or* triomphe *m* de l'architecture *etc* ; **~ of arms** fait *m* d'armes ; **~ of skill** tour *m* d'adresse ; **getting him to speak**

was quite a ~ cela a été un tour de force *or* un exploit de (réussir à) le faire parler

feather ['feðə'] [1] N [*of wing, tail*] plume *f* ; penne *f* ; **the scholarship was a ~ in his cap** il pouvait être fier d'avoir obtenu la bourse ; **you could have knocked me down** *or* **over with a ~!*** les bras m'en sont tombés, j'en suis resté baba* *inv* → **bird, light²,white**

[2] VT [a] [+ *arrow etc*] empenner ; *(fig)* **to ~ one's nest** faire sa pelote ; **to ~ one's nest at sb's expense** s'engraisser sur le dos de qn [b] *(Aviat)* [+ *propeller*] mettre en drapeau ; *(Rowing)* **to ~ an oar** plumer

[3] COMP [*mattress etc*] de plumes ; [*headdress*] à plumes ► **feather bed** N lit *m* de plume(s) ; (* = *sinecure*) sinécure *f*, bonne planque* *f* ► **feather-bed** VT *(fig)* [+ *person, project*] surprotéger ; [+ *child*] élever dans du coton ; *(Ind)* protéger *(afin de lutter contre les licenciements économiques)* ► **feather boa** N boa *m* (de plumes) ► **feather cut** N *(Hairdressing)* dégradé *m* court ► **feather duster** N plumeau *m* ► **feather-edged** ADJ en biseau

featherbedding ['feðəbedɪŋ] N *(Ind)* protection *f* excessive de la main-d'œuvre

featherbrain ['feðəbreɪn] N écervelé(e) *m(f)*

featherbrained ['feðəbreɪnd] ADJ écervelé

feathered ['feðəd] ADJ [*bird*] à plumes ; **our ~ friends** nos amis à plumes

featheredge ['feðəredʒ] N *(Carpentry)* biseau *m*

feathering ['feðərɪŋ] N plumage *m*, plumes *fpl*

featherweight ['feðəweɪt] *(Boxing)* [1] N poids *m* plume *inv* [2] ADJ [*championship etc*] poids plume *inv*

feathery ['feðərɪ] ADJ [*texture, feel*] duveteux, doux (douce *f*) comme la plume ; [*mark, design*] plumeté

feature ['fiːtʃə'] [1] N [a] (*facial*) trait *m* (du visage) ; **the ~s** la physionomie ; **to have delicate ~s** avoir les traits fins [b] [*of person*] (*physical*) trait *m* ; [*of personality*] caractéristique *f* ; [*of machine, countryside, building*] caractéristique *f*, particularité *f* ; **her most striking ~ is her hair** son trait le plus frappant ce sont ses cheveux ; **one of his most outstanding ~s is his patience** une de ses caractéristiques les plus remarquables est sa patience ; **one of the main ~s in the kidnapping story was ...** un des éléments les plus frappants dans l'affaire du kidnapping a été ... ; **scepticism is a ~ of our age** le scepticisme est caractéristique *or* un trait de notre temps ; **personal attacks have been a ~ of these elections** ces élections ont été marquées par une série d'attaques personnelles

[c] *(Cine)* grand film *m*, long métrage *m* ; *(Press)* [*of column*] chronique *f* ; **this cartoon is a regular ~ in "The Observer"** cette bande dessinée paraît régulièrement dans « The Observer »

[d] *(Ling: also* **distinctive ~***)* trait *m* distinctif

[2] VT [a] (= *give prominence to*) [+ *person, event, story*] mettre en vedette ; [+ *name, news*] faire figurer ; **this film ~s an English actress** ce film a pour vedette une actrice anglaise ; **a film featuring John Wayne** un film avec John Wayne ; **the murder was ~d on the front page** le meurtre était à la une ; **a new album featuring their latest hit single** un nouvel album où figure leur dernier tube*

[b] (= *depict*) représenter

[c] (= *have as one of its features*) [*machine etc*] être doté *or* équipé de

[3] VI [a] *(Cine)* jouer (**in** dans) [b] (*gen*) figurer ; **fish often ~s on the menu** le poisson figure souvent au menu ; **the story ~d on all of today's front pages** cette histoire faisait aujourd'hui la une de tous les journaux

[4] COMP ► **feature article** N *(Press)* article *m* de fond ► **feature(-length) film** N *(Cine)* long métrage *m* ► **feature story** N = **feature article** ► **feature writer** N *(Press)* journaliste *mf*

-featured ['fiːtʃəd] ADJ *(in compounds)* **delicate/heavy-featured** aux traits délicats/lourds

featureless ['fiːtʃəlɪs] ADJ [*landscape, building*] monotone

Feb. ABBR = **February**

febrifuge ['febrɪfjuːdʒ] ADJ, N fébrifuge *m*

febrile ['fiːbraɪl] ADJ fébrile, fiévreux

February ['febrʊərɪ] N février *m* ; *for phrases see* **September**

fecal ['fiːkəl] ADJ *(US)* = **faecal**

feces ['fiːsiːz] NPL *(US)* = **faeces**

feckless ['feklɪs] ADJ [*person*] inepte, incapable ; [*attempt*] maladroit ; **a ~ girl** une tête sans cervelle, une évaporée

fecund ['fiːkənd] ADJ fécond

fecundity [frˈkʌndɪtɪ] N fécondité *f*

Fed [fed] [1] (*esp US*) ABBR = **Federal, Federated** *and* **Federation** [2] N [a] *(US*)* (ABBR = **federal officer**) agent *m* or fonctionnaire *m* fédéral [b] *(US)* (ABBR = **Federal Reserve Bank**) → **federal**

fed [fed] [1] VB (*pret, ptp of* **feed**) **well ~** bien nourri [2] COMP ► **fed up*** ADJ **to be ~ up** en avoir assez, en avoir marre* ; **I'm ~ up waiting for him** j'en ai marre* de l'attendre ; **he got ~ up with it** il en a eu assez, il en a eu marre* ; **to be ~ up to the back teeth**‡ en avoir ras le bol‡ (**with doing** de faire)

fedayee [feˈdɑːjiː] N (*pl* **fedayeen**) fedayin *m* *inv*

federal ['fedərəl] [1] ADJ fédéral [2] N *(US Hist)* fédéral *m*, nordiste *m* [3] COMP ► **Federal Aviation Administration** N *(US)* Direction *f* générale de l'aviation civile ► **Federal Bureau of Investigation** N *(US)* FBI *m* ► **Federal Communications Commission** N *(US Admin)* ≈ Conseil *m* supérieur de l'audiovisuel ► **Federal court** N *(US Jur)* cour *f* fédérale ► **federal crop insurance** N *(US)* système fédéral d'indemnisation des agriculteurs en cas de catastrophe naturelle ► **Federal Housing Administration** N *(US)* commission *f* de contrôle des prêts au logement ► **Federal Insurance Contributions Act** N *(US)* (= *law*) loi sur les cotisations de Sécurité sociale ; (= *contribution*) ≈ cotisations *fpl* de Sécurité sociale ► **federal land bank** N *(US Fin)* banque *f* fédérale agricole ► **Federal Maritime Board** N *(US)* Conseil *m* supérieur de la Marine marchande ► **Federal Republic of Germany** N Allemagne *f* fédérale, République *f* fédérale d'Allemagne ► **Federal Reserve Bank** N Federal Reserve Bank *f*

federalism ['fedərəlɪzəm] N fédéralisme *m*

federalist ['fedərəlɪst] ADJ, N fédéraliste *mf*

federate ['fedəreɪt] [1] VT fédérer [2] VI se fédérer [3] ['fedərɪt] ADJ fédéré

federation [ˌfedəˈreɪʃən] N fédération *f*

federative ['fedərətɪv] ADJ fédératif ; **the Federative Republic of ...** la République fédérative de ...

fedora [fəˈdɔːrə] N chapeau *m* mou, feutre *m* mou

fee [fiː] [1] N [*of doctor, lawyer*] honoraires *mpl* ; [*of artist, speaker, footballer*] cachet *m* ; [*of director, administrator*] honoraires *mpl*, jeton *m* (de présence) ; [*of private tutor*] appointements *mpl* ; *(Scol, Univ etc)* (for tuition) frais *mpl* de scolarité ; (for *examination*) droits *mpl* ; (for *board*) prix *m* de la pension ; **what's his ~?** combien prend-il ? ; **is there a ~?** est-ce qu'il faut payer ? ; **you can borrow more books for a small ~** *or* **on payment of a small ~** contre une somme modique vous pouvez emprunter d'autres livres ; *(Jur)* **~ or other charges** redevances *fpl* ou autres droits; (*Jur*) ~ **for appeal** taxe *f* de recours → **entrance, licence, membership**

[2] COMP ► **fee-paying school** N établissement *m* (d'enseignement) privé ► **fee-splitting** N (*US: gen*) partage *m* des honoraires; [*of doctors*] dichotomie *f*

feeble ['fiːbl] [1] ADJ [a] (= *weak*) [*person, light, voice*] faible [b] (*pej* = *pathetic*) [*excuse, response*] piètre; [*attempt*] vague; [*joke*] médiocre; **don't be so ~!** quelle mauviette tu fais! [2] COMP ► **feeble-minded** ADJ imbécile ► **feeble-mindedness** N imbécillité *f*

feebleness ['fiːblnɪs] N [*of person, pulse, light, voice*] faiblesse *f*

feebly ['fiːblɪ] ADV [*smile, shine*] faiblement; [*say, explain*] sans grande conviction

feed [fiːd] (*vb: pret, ptp* **fed**) [1] N [a] (*NonC*) (*gen*) nourriture *f*; (= *pasture*) pâture *f*; (= *hay etc*) fourrage *m*; **animal/cattle/chicken** etc ~ nourriture *f* or aliments *mpl* pour animaux/ bétail/volailles *etc*; **he's off his ~*** [*baby*] il n'a pas d'appétit [b] (= *portion of food*) ration *f*; [*of baby*] (*breast-fed*) tétée *f*; (*bottle-fed*) biberon *m*; (*solid*) repas *m*; **~ of oats** picotin *m* d'avoine; **we had a good ~*** on a bien bouffé* [c] (*Theat** = *comedian's cue line*) réplique *f*; (= *straight man*) faire-valoir *m inv* [d] (= *part of machine*) mécanisme *m* d'alimentation; (*Comput*) **sheet paper ~** chargeur *m* feuille à feuille

[2] VT [a] (= *provide food for*) (*gen*) nourrir; [+ *army*] nourrir, ravitailler; (= *give food to*) [+ *child, invalid, animal*] donner à manger à; (*Brit*) [+ *baby*] nourrir; [+ *baby bird*] donner la becquée à; **there are six people/mouths to ~ in this house** il y a six personnes/bouches à nourrir dans cette maison; **I have three hungry mouths to ~** j'ai trois bouches à nourrir; **what do you ~ your cat on?** que donnez-vous à manger à votre chat?; **he can ~ himself now** [*child*] il sait manger tout seul maintenant; **to ~ sth to sb** donner qch à manger à qn; **you shouldn't ~ him that** vous ne devriez pas lui donner cela à manger [b] [+ *plant*] [*ground, sap etc*] nourrir; (*with fertilizer, plant food*) donner de l'engrais à [c] (*fig*) **to ~ sb information** fournir des informations à qn; **to ~ sb lies** raconter des mensonges à qn; **we've fed him all the facts*** nous lui avons fourni toutes les données; **to ~ sb a line*** essayer de faire avaler une histoire à qn; **to ~ one's habit*/one's heroin habit*** se procurer sa drogue/son héroïne [d] [+ *fire*] entretenir, alimenter; [+ *furnace, machine*] alimenter; **two rivers ~ this reservoir** deux rivières alimentent ce réservoir; **to ~ the parking meter*** rajouter une pièce dans le parcmètre; **to ~ sth into a machine** mettre or introduire qch dans une machine; **to ~ data into a computer** entrer des données dans un ordinateur; **blood vessels that ~ blood to the brain** des vaisseaux sanguins qui irriguent le cerveau → **flame** [e] (*Theat** = *comedian*) donner la réplique à; (= *prompt*) souffler à

[3] VI [*animal*] manger, se nourrir; (*on pasture*) paître, brouter; [*baby*] manger; (*at breast*) téter; (*lit, fig*) **to ~ on** se nourrir de; **nationalism ~s on old hatreds** le nationalisme se nourrit de vieilles haines

[4] COMP ► **feed grains** NPL céréales *fpl* fourragères

► **feed back** [1] VT SEP [+ *information, results*] donner (en retour) [2] **~back** N → **feedback**

► **feed in** VT SEP [+ *tape, wire*] introduire (**to** dans); [+ *facts, information*] fournir (**to** à)

► **feed up** [1] VT SEP [+ *animal*] engraisser; [+ *geese*] gaver; [+ *person*] faire manger plus or davantage [2] **fed up*** ADJ → **fed**

feedback ['fiːdbæk] N [a] (*gen*) réactions *fpl*; (*Comm: from questionnaire etc*) information *f*

en retour, retour *m* d'information; **I haven't had any ~ from him yet** je n'ai encore eu aucune réaction de sa part; **to give sb ~ on sth** faire part à qn de ses réactions or impressions sur qch [b] (*Elec*) réaction *f*; (*unwanted*) réaction *f* parasite; (*Cybernetics*) rétroaction *f*, feed-back *m*

feedbag ['fiːdbæg] N [*of livestock*] sac *m* de nourriture; (*US = nosebag*) musette *f*

feeder ['fiːdəʳ] [1] N [a] (= *eater: person, animal*) mangeur *m*, -euse *f*; **peonies are quite heavy ~s** (= *need water*) les pivoines ont besoin de beaucoup d'eau; (= *need fertilizer*) les pivoines ont besoin de beaucoup d'engrais [b] (= *device*) (*for chickens*) mangeoire *f* automatique; (*for cattle*) nourrisseur *m* automatique; (*for machine*) chargeur *m* [c] (*Elec*) ligne *f* d'alimentation [d] (*Brit*) (= *bib*) bavoir *m*; (= *bottle*) biberon *m* [2] COMP ► **feeder canal** N d'amenée; [*railway*] secondaire; [*road*] d'accès; [*team, league*] servant de réservoir, jouant le rôle de réservoir ► **feeder primary (school)** N (*Brit Scol*) école primaire *f* d'où sont issus les élèves d'un collège donné ► **feeder stream** N affluent *m*

feeding ['fiːdɪŋ] [1] N (= *food*) alimentation *f*; (= *action of feeding animal*) nourrissage *m* [2] COMP ► **feeding bottle** N (*esp Brit*) biberon *m* ► **feeding frenzy** N (*fig*) **the press was in a ~ frenzy** les organes de presse se sont déchaînés ► **feeding grounds** NPL (*gen*) aire *f* de nourrissage; [*of grazing animals*] pâtures *fpl*, pâturages *mpl* ► **feeding stuffs** NPL nourriture *f* or aliments *mpl* (pour animaux) ► **feeding time** N [*of baby*] (*breast-feeding*) heure *f* de la tétée; (*bottle-feeding*) heure *f* du biberon; [*of toddler*] heure *f* du repas; [*of animal*] (*in zoo*) heure *f* de nourrir les animaux

feedpipe ['fiːdpaɪp] N tuyau *m* d'amenée

feedstuffs ['fiːdstʌfs] NPL nourriture *f* or aliments *mpl* (pour animaux)

▼**feel** [fiːl]

vb: pret, ptp **felt**

[1] NOUN	[3] INTRANSITIVE VERB
[2] TRANSITIVE VERB	[4] PHRASAL VERBS

[1] NOUN

[a] = *texture* toucher *m*; **to know sth by the ~ (of it)** reconnaître qch au toucher; **the fabric has a papery ~** le grain de ce tissu ressemble à celui du papier

[b] = *sensation* sensation *f*; **she liked the ~ of the sun on her face** elle aimait sentir le soleil sur son visage; **I don't like the ~ of wool against my skin** je n'aime pas le contact de la laine contre ma peau, je n'aime pas porter de la laine à même la peau

[c] = *impression* **he wants to get the ~ of the factory** il veut se faire une impression générale de l'usine; **you have to get the ~ of a new car** il faut se faire à une nouvelle voiture; **the palms bring a Mediterranean ~ to the garden** les palmiers donnent un aspect méditerranéen au jardin; **the room has a cosy ~** on se sent bien dans cette pièce; **there's a nostalgic ~ to his music** il y a quelque chose de nostalgique dans sa musique; **I don't like the ~ of it** ça ne me dit rien de bon or rien qui vaille

[d] = *intuition* **to have a ~ for languages** être doué pour les langues; **to have a ~ for English** être doué en anglais; **to have a ~ for music** avoir l'oreille musicale; **to have a ~ for doing sth** savoir s'y prendre pour faire qch

[2] TRANSITIVE VERB

[a] = *touch* toucher; (= *explore with one's fingers*) palper; **she felt the jacket to see if it was made of wool** elle a palpé or touché la veste pour voir si c'était de la laine; **~ the envelope and see if there's anything in it** palpez l'enveloppe pour voir s'il y a quelque chose dedans; **to ~ sb's pulse** tâter le pouls de qn

♦ **to feel one's way** (*lit*) avancer or marcher à

tâtons; **he got out of bed and felt his way to the telephone** il s'est levé et a avancé or marché à tâtons jusqu'au téléphone; (*fig*) **you'll have to ~ your way** il faut y aller à tâtons; **we are ~ing our way towards an agreement** nous tâtons le terrain pour parvenir à un accord; (*fig*) **I'm still ~ing my way around** j'essaie de m'y retrouver; **she's still ~ing her way in her new job** elle n'est pas encore complètement habituée à son nouveau travail, elle est encore en train de se familiariser avec son nouveau travail

[b] = *experience physically* [+ *blow, caress*] sentir; [+ *pain*] sentir, ressentir; **I felt a few drops of rain** j'ai senti quelques gouttes de pluie; **I'm so cold I can't ~ anything** j'ai si froid que je ne sens plus rien; **she could ~ the heat from the radiator** elle sentait la chaleur du radiateur → c; **I can ~ something pricking me** je sens quelque chose qui me pique; **he felt it move** il l'a senti bouger

[c] = *be affected by, suffer from* **to ~ the heat/ cold** être sensible à la chaleur/au froid; **I don't ~ the heat much** la chaleur ne me gêne pas beaucoup; **she really ~s the cold** elle est très frileuse; **she felt the loss of her father greatly** elle a été très affectée par la mort de son père

[d] = *experience emotionally* [+ *sympathy, grief*] éprouver, ressentir; **you must ~ the beauty of this music before you can play it** il faut que vous sentiez (*subj*) la beauté de cette musique avant de pouvoir la jouer vous-même; **the effects will be felt later** les effets se feront sentir plus tard; **he felt a great sense of relief** il a éprouvé or ressenti un grand soulagement; **I ~ no interest in it** cela ne m'intéresse pas du tout; **I do ~ the importance of this** je pleinement conscience de l'importance de ceci; **he started to ~ the importance of the match** il a commencé à prendre conscience de l'importance du match; **to ~ o.s. doing sth** (*involuntarily*) se sentir faire qch, se rendre compte qu'on fait qch

[e] = *think, believe* **I ~ he has spoilt everything** à mon avis, il a tout gâché; **I ~ that he ought to go** j'estime qu'il devrait partir; **he felt it necessary to point out ...** il a jugé or estimé nécessaire de faire remarquer ...; **I ~ strongly that ...** je suis convaincu que ...; **if you ~ strongly about it** si cela vous tient à cœur, si cela vous semble important; **what do you ~ about this idea?** que pensez-vous de cette idée?; **I can't help ~ing that something is wrong** je ne peux m'empêcher de penser que quelque chose ne va pas; **I ~ it in my bones*** or **waters*** that Scotland will score l'Écosse va marquer, je le sens!, quelque chose me dit que l'Écosse va marquer

[3] INTRANSITIVE VERB

[a] *physically* se sentir; **how do you ~ today?** comment vous sentez-vous aujourd'hui?; **I ~ much better** je me sens beaucoup mieux; **you'll ~ all the better for a rest** vous vous sentirez mieux après vous être reposé; **he doesn't ~ quite himself today** il ne se sent pas tout à fait dans son assiette aujourd'hui; **to ~ old/ill** se sentir vieux/malade; **to ~ cold/hot/hungry/ thirsty/sleepy** avoir froid/chaud/faim/soif/ sommeil; **he felt like a young man again** il se sentait redevenu jeune homme; **I ~ like a new man/woman** je me sens un autre homme/une autre femme

[b] *emotionally, intellectually* **I couldn't help ~ing envious** je ne pouvais pas m'empêcher d'éprouver de la jalousie; **I ~ sure that ...** je suis sûr que ...; **they don't ~ able to recommend him** ils estiment qu'ils ne peuvent pas le recommander; **he ~s confident of success** il s'estime capable de réussir; **we felt very touched by his remarks** nous avons été très touchés par ses remarques; **I don't ~ ready to see her again yet** je ne me sens pas encore prêt à la revoir; **I ~ very bad about leaving you here** cela m'ennuie beaucoup de vous laisser ici; **how do you ~ about him?** que pensez-vous de

lui ? ; **what does it ~ like** or **how does it ~ to know that you are a success?** quel effet cela vous fait-il de savoir que vous avez réussi ?

♦ **to feel for sb** compatir aux malheurs de qn ; **we ~ for you in your sorrow** nous partageons votre douleur ; **I ~ for you!** comme je vous comprends !

♦ **to feel like sth/doing sth** (= want) avoir envie de qch/de faire qch ; **I ~ like an ice cream** j'ai envie d'une glace ; **do you ~ like a walk?** ça vous dit d'aller vous promener ? ; **if you ~ like it** si ça te dit ; **I don't ~ like it** je n'en ai pas envie, ça ne me dit rien

[c] = have impression I **felt as if I was going to faint** j'avais l'impression que j'allais m'évanouir ; **I ~ as if there's nothing we can do** j'ai le sentiment or j'ai bien l'impression que nous ne pouvons rien faire

[d] = give impression **to ~ hard/soft** [object] être dur/doux au toucher ; **the house ~s damp** la maison donne l'impression d'être humide ; **his shirt ~s as though it's made of silk** on dirait que sa chemise est en soie (quand on la touche) ; **the car travelled so fast it felt like flying** la voiture filait si rapidement qu'on avait l'impression de voler ; **it ~s like rain** on dirait qu'il va pleuvoir ; **it ~s like thunder** on dirait qu'il va y avoir de l'orage

[e] = grope (also **~ about, ~ around**) tâtonner, fouiller ; **she felt (about** or **around) in her pocket for some change** elle a fouillé dans sa poche pour trouver de la monnaie ; **he was ~ing (about** or **around) in the dark for the door** il tâtonnait dans le noir pour trouver la porte

[4] PHRASAL VERBS

►**feel out** VT SEP [+ person] sonder, tâter le terrain auprès de

►**feel up** VT SEP **to ~ sb up** peloter* qn

feeler ['fiːlə^r] [1] N [of insect] antenne f ; [of octopus] tentacule m ; (fig) **to put out** or **throw out ~s (to discover)** tâter le terrain (pour essayer de découvrir) [2] COMP ► **feeler gauge** N (Tech) calibre m (d'épaisseur)

feelgood ['fiːlgʊd] N (after exercise) sensation f de bien-être ; (pej) autosatisfaction f ; (Pol) euphorie f passagère

▼**feeling** ['fiːlɪŋ] N [a] (NonC: physical) sensation f ; **I've lost all ~ in my right arm** j'ai perdu toute sensation dans le bras droit, mon bras droit ne sent plus rien ; **a ~ of cold** ◊ **a cold ~** une sensation de froid

[b] (= awareness, impression) sentiment m ; **a ~ of isolation** un sentiment d'isolement ; **he had a ~ (that) something terrible was going to happen to him** il avait le sentiment qu'il allait lui arriver quelque chose de terrible ; **I've got a funny ~ she will succeed** j'ai comme l'impression qu'elle va réussir ; **I know the ~!** je sais ce que c'est or ce que ça fait ! ; **the ~ of the meeting was against the idea** dans l'ensemble, les participants (à la réunion) étaient contre l'idée ; **there was a general ~ that ...** on avait l'impression que ..., le sentiment général a été que ... → **strong**

[c] (= emotion) sentiment m ; **~s** sentiments mpl, sensibilité f ; **he appealed to their rather than their reason** il faisait appel à leurs sentiments plutôt qu'à leur raison ; **a ~ of joy/horror came over her** un sentiment de joie/d'horreur l'a envahie ; **you can imagine my ~s** tu t'imagines ce que je ressens (or j'ai ressenti etc) ; **~s ran high about the new motorway** la nouvelle autoroute a déchaîné les passions ; **his ~s were hurt** il était blessé ; **I didn't mean to hurt your ~s** je ne voulais pas te blesser or te vexer → **hard**

[d] (NonC) (= sensitivity) émotion f, sensibilité f ; (= compassion) sympathie f ; **a woman of great ~** une femme très sensible ; **she sang with ~** elle a chanté avec sentiment ; **he spoke with great ~** il a parlé avec chaleur or avec émotion ; **he doesn't show much ~ for his sis-**

ter il ne fait pas preuve de beaucoup de sympathie pour sa sœur ; **he has no ~ for the suffering of others** les souffrances d'autrui le laissent insensible ; **he has no ~ for music** il n'apprécie pas du tout la musique ; **he has a certain ~ for music** il est assez sensible à la musique ; **ill** or **bad ~** animosité f, hostilité f

feelingly ['fiːlɪŋlɪ] ADV [speak, write] avec émotion, avec chaleur

feet [fiːt] NPL of **foot**

FEFC [ˌefiːefˈsiː] N (Brit) (ABBR = **Further Education Funding Council**) → **further**

feign [feɪn] VT [+ surprise] feindre ; [+ madness] simuler ; **to ~ illness/sleep** faire semblant d'être malade/de dormir ; **~ed modesty** fausse modestie f, modestie f feinte

feint [feɪnt] [1] N (Boxing, Fencing, Mil) feinte f ; **to make a ~** faire une feinte (**at** à) [2] VI feinter [3] COMP ► **feint-ruled paper** N papier m à réglure fine

feist* [faɪst] N (US) roquet m (chien)

feisty* ['faɪstɪ] ADJ [a] (= lively) fougueux [b] (US = quarrelsome) bagarreur*

feldspar ['feldspɑː^r] N = **felspar**

felicitate [fɪˈlɪsɪteɪt] VT (frm) féliciter, congratuler

felicitous [fɪˈlɪsɪtəs] ADJ (frm) heureux

felicity [fɪˈlɪsɪtɪ] N (frm) (= happiness) félicité f, bonheur m ; (= aptness) bonheur m

feline ['fiːlaɪn] ADJ, N félin(e) m(f)

fell[1] [fel] VB pt of **fall**

fell[2] [fel] VT [+ tree, enemy] abattre ; [+ ox] assommer, abattre

fell[3] [fel] N (Brit) (= mountain) montagne f, mont m ; (= moorland) **the ~s** la lande

fell[4] [fel] ADJ (liter) [blow] féroce, cruel ; [disease] cruel → **swoop**

fell[5] [fel] N (= hide, pelt) fourrure f, peau f (d'animal)

fella* ['felə] N (= chap) type* m ; (= boyfriend) petit ami m

fellate [fɪˈleɪt] VT faire une fellation à

fellatio [fɪˈleɪʃɪəʊ], **fellation** [fɪˈleɪʃən] N fellation f

fellow ['feləʊ] [1] N [a]* type* m, homme m ; **a nice ~** un brave type* ; **an old ~** un vieux (bonhomme) ; **a poor old ~** un pauvre vieux ; **some poor ~ will have to rewrite this** il y aura un pauvre malheureux qui devra récrire cela ; **poor little ~** pauvre petit m (bonhomme m or gars m) ; **a young ~** un jeune homme ; **a ~ must have a bit of a rest!** il faut bien qu'on se repose (subj) un peu ! ; **my dear** or **good ~!** mon cher ; **look here, old ~!**† écoute, mon vieux ; **this journalist ~** un journaliste

[b] (= comrade) camarade m, compagnon m ; (= equal, peer) pair m, semblable m ; **~s in misfortune** frères mpl dans le malheur, compagnons mpl d'infortune → **schoolfellow**

[c] (= of association, society etc) membre m, associé m (d'une société savante, d'une académie)

[d] (US Univ) boursier m, -ière f ; (Brit Univ) ≈ chargé m de cours (souvent membre du conseil d'administration) → **research**

[2] COMP ► **fellow being** N semblable mf, pareil(le) m(f) ► **fellow citizen** N concitoyen(ne) m(f) ► **fellow countryman** (pl fellow countrymen) , **fellow countrywoman** (pl fellow countrywomen) N compatriote mf ► **fellow creature** N semblable mf, pareil(le) m(f) ► **fellow feeling** N sympathie f ► **fellow inmate** N codétenu(e) m(f) ► **fellow member** N confrère m, consœur f ► **fellow men** NPL semblables mpl ► **fellow passenger** N compagnon m de voyage, compagne f de voyage ► **fellow student** N condisciple mf ► **fellow traveller** N (lit) compagnon m de voyage, compagne f de voyage ; (Pol) (with communists) communisant(e) m(f), cryptocommuniste m(f) ; (gen) sympathisant(e) m(f) ► **fellow worker** N (in office) collègue mf ; (in factory) camarade mf (de travail)

fellowship ['feləʊʃɪp] N [a] (NonC) (= comradeship) camaraderie f ; (Rel etc) communion f [b] (= society etc) association f, corporation f ; (Rel) confrérie f [c] (= membership of learned society) titre m de membre or d'associé (d'une société savante) [d] (US Univ = scholarship) bourse f universitaire ; (Brit Univ = post) poste m d'enseignement et de recherche → **fellow 1d**

felon ['felən] N (Jur) criminel(le) m(f)

felonious [fɪˈləʊnɪəs] ADJ (Jur) criminel

felony ['felənɪ] N (Jur) crime m, forfait m

felspar ['felspɑː^r] N feldspath m

felt[1] [felt] VB pt, ptp of **feel**

felt[2] [felt] [1] N feutre m → **roofing** [2] COMP de feutre ► **felt hat** N feutre m (chapeau) ► **felt-tip (pen)** N feutre m (crayon)

fem: [fem] N = **femme b**

fem. [fem] [a] ABBR = **female** [b] ABBR = **feminine**

female ['fiːmeɪl] [1] ADJ [a] (Biol, Zool = of feminine gender) [animal, plant] femelle ; [subject, slave] du sexe féminin ; **a ~ child** une fille, un enfant du sexe féminin ; **~ labour** main-d'œuvre f féminine ; **~ students** étudiantes fpl ; **~ cat/camel** chatte f/chamelle f [b] (= relating to women) [company, vote] des femmes ; [sex, character, quality, organs, health problems] féminin [c] (Elec) femelle [2] N (= person) femme f, fille f ; (= animal, plant) femelle f ; (pej) **there was a ~ there who ...** * il y avait là une espèce de bonne femme qui ...* (pej) [3] COMP ► **female circumcision** N excision f ► **female condom** N préservatif m féminin ► **female impersonator** N (Theat) travesti m

feminine ['femɪnɪn] [1] ADJ (also Gram) féminin [2] N (Gram) féminin m ; **in the ~** au féminin [3] COMP ► **feminine hygiene** N (euph) hygiène f féminine

femininity [ˌfemɪˈnɪnɪtɪ] N féminité f

feminism ['femɪnɪzəm] N féminisme m

feminist ['femɪnɪst] N féministe mf

feminize ['femɪnaɪz] VT féminiser

femme [fæm, fem] N [a] **~ fatale** femme f fatale [b]* partenaire f passive (dans un couple de lesbiennes)

femoral ['femərəl] ADJ fémoral

femur ['fiːmə^r] N (pl **femurs** or **femora** ['femərə]) fémur m

fen [fen] N (Brit: also **~land**) marais m, marécage m ; **the Fens** les plaines fpl marécageuses du Norfolk

fence [fens] [1] N [a] barrière f, clôture f ; (Racing) obstacle m ; (fig) **to sit on the ~** ménager la chèvre et le chou, s'abstenir de prendre position ; (fig) **to mend one's ~s* with sb** se réconcilier avec qn ; **they're mending their ~s* (with each other)** ils sont en train de se réconcilier → **barbed** [b] (= machine guard) barrière f protectrice [c]* [of stolen goods] receleur m, fourgue* m [2] VT [a] (also **~ in**) [+ land] clôturer, entourer d'une clôture [b] (fig) [+ question] éluder [3] VI (Sport) faire de l'escrime ; (fig) éluder la question, se dérober ; (Sport) **to ~ with sword/sabre** etc tirer à l'épée/au sabre etc [4] COMP ► **fence-mending** N (fig: esp Pol) rétablissement m de bonnes relations, réconciliation f

►**fence in** VT SEP [a] (lit) = **fence 2a** [b] (fig) **to feel ~d in by restrictions** se sentir gêné or entravé par des restrictions

►**fence off** VT SEP [+ piece of land] séparer par une clôture

fencer ['fensə^r] N escrimeur m, -euse f

fencing ['fensɪŋ] [1] N [a] (Sport) escrime f [b] (for making fences) matériaux mpl pour clôture [2] COMP ► **fencing master** N maître m d'armes ► **fencing match** N assaut m d'escrime ; (fig) prise f de bec ► **fencing school** N salle f d'armes

fend [fend] VI **to ~ for o.s.** se débrouiller (tout seul)

►**fend off** VT SEP [+ *blow*] parer ; [+ *attack*] détourner ; [+ *attacker*] repousser ; [+ *question*] écarter, éluder

fender [ˈfendəʳ] [1] N (*in front of fire*) garde-feu *m inv* ; (*US Aut*) aile *f* ; (*US Rail*) chasse-pierres *m inv* ; (*Naut*) défense *f*, pare-battage *m inv* [2] COMP ► **fender-bender*** N accrochage *m* ; **it was just a ~-bender** ce n'était qu'un accrochage *or* que de la tôle froissée*

fenestration [ˌfenɪsˈtreɪʃən] N (*Archit*) fenêtrage *m* ; (*Med*) fenestration *f* ; (*Bot, Zool*) aspect *m* fenêtré

feng shui [ˌfeŋˈʃuːɪ] N feng-shui *m*

fennel [ˈfenl] N fenouil *m*

fenugreek [ˈfenjʊˌgriːk] N fenugrec *m*

feral [ˈfɪərəl] ADJ sauvage

ferment [fəˈment] [1] VI (*lit, fig*) fermenter [2] VT (*lit, fig*) faire fermenter [3] [ˈfɜːment] N (*lit*) ferment *m* ; (*fig*) agitation *f*, effervescence *f* ; **to be in (a state of) ~** être en ébullition

fermentation [ˌfɜːmenˈteɪʃən] N (*lit, fig*) fermentation *f*

fermium [ˈfɜːmɪəm] N fermium *m*

fern [fɜːn] N fougère *f*

ferocious [fəˈrəʊʃəs] ADJ [a] (= *fierce*) [*animal, person, battle, fighting*] féroce ; [*attack, assault*] violent ; [*knife, teeth*] redoutable [b] (= *intense*) [*competition*] acharné ; [*debate*] houleux ; [*argument*] violent ; [*energy*] farouche [c] (= *severe*) [*heat*] accablant ; [*weather, violent storm*] épouvantable ; [*thirst*] terrible

ferociously [fəˈrəʊʃəslɪ] ADV [a] (= *violently*) [*beat, kick, struggle*] violemment ; **to fight ~** [*person*] se battre âprement ; [*animal*] se battre férocement *or* avec férocité [b] (= *extremely*) [*independent*] farouchement ; [*difficult, complicated*] furieusement ; [*clever, intelligent, funny*] terriblement ; **to be ~ competitive** avoir un esprit de compétition acharné ; **~ determined** d'une détermination farouche ; **~ loyal** d'une fidélité à toute épreuve

ferociousness [fəˈrəʊʃəsnɪs], **ferocity** [fəˈrɒsɪtɪ] N férocité *f*

Ferrara [fəˈrɑːrə] N Ferrare

ferret [ˈferɪt] [1] N (*Zool*) furet *m* [2] VI [a] (*also* **~ about, ~ around**) fouiller, fureter ; **she was ~ing (about** *or* **around) among my books** elle furetait dans mes livres [b] **to go ~ing** chasser au furet

►**ferret out** VT SEP [+ *secret, person*] dénicher, découvrir

ferric [ˈferɪk] ADJ ferrique

Ferris wheel [ˈferɪswiːl] N grande roue *f* (*dans une foire*)

ferrite [ˈferaɪt] N ferrite *f*

ferro- [ˈferəʊ] PREF ferro-

ferroconcrete [ˈferəʊˈkɒŋkriːt] N béton *m* armé

ferrous [ˈferəs] ADJ ferreux

ferrule [ˈferuːl] N virole *f*

ferry [ˈferɪ] [1] N (*also* **~boat**) (*large*) ferry-boat *m* ; (*small*) bac *m* ; (*Can*) traversier *m* ; (*between ship and quayside*) va-et-vient *m inv* → **air, car** [2] VT [a] (*also* **~ across, ~ over**) [+ *person, car, train*] faire passer *or* traverser (en bac *or* par bateau *or* par avion *etc*) [b] (*fig = transport*) [+ *people*] transporter, emmener ; [+ *things*] porter, apporter ; **he ferried voters to and from the polls** il a fait la navette avec sa voiture pour emmener les électeurs au bureau de vote

ferryman [ˈferɪmən] N (*pl* **-men**) passeur *m*

fertile [ˈfɜːtaɪl] [1] ADJ [*soil, land*] fertile ; [*person*] fertile, fécond ; [*animal, egg, mind*] fécond ; **the ~ period** *or* **time** la période de fécondité ; (*gen, pej*) **to have a ~ imagination** avoir une imagination fertile ; (*fig*) **to be (a) ~ ground for sb/sth** être un terrain propice pour qn/qch [2] COMP ► **the Fertile Crescent** N le Croissant fertile

fertility [fəˈtɪlɪtɪ] [1] N [*of soil, land, man*] fertilité *f* ; [*of woman, animal*] fécondité *f*, fertilité *f* ; (*frm*) **~ of invention** fertilité *f* d'imagination [2] COMP [*cult, symbol*] de fertilité ► **fertility drug** N (*Med*) médicament *m* contre la stérilité

fertilization [ˌfɜːtɪlaɪˈzeɪʃən] N [*of land, soil*] fertilisation *f* ; [*of animal, plant, egg*] fécondation *f*

fertilize [ˈfɜːtɪlaɪz] VT [+ *land, soil*] fertiliser, amender ; [+ *animal, plant, egg*] féconder

fertilizer [ˈfɜːtɪlaɪzəʳ] N engrais *m*, fertilisant *m* ; **artificial ~** engrais *m* chimique

fervent [ˈfɜːvənt] ADJ [*admirer, advocate, prayer*] fervent ; [*supporter, belief, desire*] ardent ; **to be a ~ believer in sth** être un adepte de qch ; **my ~ hope is that ...** je souhaite vraiment *or* ardemment que ... ; **it is my ~ wish that ...** je souhaite ardemment que ...

fervently [ˈfɜːvəntlɪ] ADV [*hope, believe*] ardemment ; [*say, pray, support*] avec ferveur ; [*religious, anti-Communist*] profondément ; **~ opposed to sth** profondément opposé à qch ; **~ patriotic** d'un ardent patriotisme

fervid [ˈfɜːvɪd] ADJ = **fervent**

fervour, fervor (*US*) [ˈfɜːvəʳ] N ferveur *f*

fest* [fest] N [a] (= *festival*) **jazz/film ~** festival *m* de jazz/de cinéma [b] (= *extravaganza*) festival *m*, débauche *f* ; **gore ~** film *m* d'horreur (*où le sang coule à flots*)

fester [ˈfestəʳ] VI [*cut, wound*] suppurer ; [*anger*] gronder ; [*resentment*] couver ; **resentments are starting to ~** le ressentiment couve

festival [ˈfestɪvəl] N (*Rel etc*) fête *f* ; (*Mus etc*) festival *m* ; **the Edinburgh Festival** le festival d'Édimbourg

festive [ˈfestɪv] ADJ de fête ; **the ~ season** la période des fêtes ; **to be in a ~ mood** avoir envie de faire la fête

festivity [fesˈtɪvɪtɪ] N [a] (*also* **festivities**) fête *f*, réjouissances *fpl* ; **an air of ~** un air de fête [b] (= *festival*) fête *f*

festoon [fesˈtuːn] [1] N feston *m*, guirlande *f* [2] VT festonner, orner de festons ; [+ *building, town*] pavoiser ; **a room ~ed with posters** une pièce tapissée d'affiches

feta [ˈfetə] N (*also* **~ cheese**) feta *f*

fetal [ˈfiːtl] ADJ (*US*) = **foetal**

fetch [fetʃ] [1] VT [a] (= *go and get*) [+ *person, thing*] aller chercher ; (= *bring*) [+ *person*] amener ; [+ *thing*] apporter ; (*to dog*) **~ (it)!** rapporte !, va chercher ! [b] (= *sell for*) [+ *money*] rapporter ; **they won't ~ much** ils ne rapporteront pas grand-chose ; **it ~ed a good price** ça a atteint un bon prix [c] [+ *blow*] flanquer* [2] VI [a] (*fig*) **to ~ and carry for sb** faire la bonne pour qn [b] (*Naut*) manœuvrer [3] N (*Naut*) fetch *m*

►**fetch in*** VT SEP [+ *person*] faire (r)entrer ; [+ *thing*] rentrer

►**fetch out*** VT SEP [+ *person*] faire sortir ; [+ *thing*] sortir (**of** de)

►**fetch up** [1] VI* finir par arriver, se retrouver (**at** à, **in** dans) [2] VT SEP [a] [+ *object*] apporter, monter ; [+ *person*] faire monter [b] (*Brit** *fig = vomit*) rendre, vomir

fetching* [ˈfetʃɪŋ] ADJ [*person*] ravissant, charmant ; [*dress, hat*] seyant, ravissant

fetchingly [ˈfetʃɪŋlɪ] ADV d'une façon charmante

fête [feɪt] [1] N (*Brit*) fête *f* ; (*for charity*) fête *f*, kermesse *f* ; **village ~** fête *f* de village [2] VT [+ *person*] faire fête à ; [+ *success, arrival*] fêter

fetid [ˈfetɪd] ADJ fétide, puant

fetish [ˈfetɪʃ] N fétiche *m* ; (*Psych*) objet *m* de fétichisation ; **she makes a real ~ of** *or* **has a real ~ about cleanliness** elle est obsédée par la propreté, c'est une maniaque de la propreté

fetishism [ˈfetɪʃɪzəm] N fétichisme *m*

fetishist [ˈfetɪʃɪst] N fétichiste *mf* ; **to be a silk/foot ~** être fétichiste de la soie/du pied

fetishistic [ˌfetɪˈʃɪstɪk] ADJ fétichiste

fetlock [ˈfetlɒk] N (= *joint*) boulet *m* ; (= *hair*) fanon *m*

fetoscope [ˈfiːtəʊˌskəʊp] N fœtoscope *m*

fetoscopy [fiːˈtɒskəpɪ] N fœtoscopie *f*

fetter [ˈfetəʳ] [1] VT [+ *person*] enchaîner, lier ; [+ *horse, slave*] entraver ; (*fig*) entraver [2] **fetters** NPL [*of prisoner*] fers *mpl*, chaînes *fpl* ; [*of horse, slave*] (*fig*) entraves *fpl* ; **in ~s** dans les fers *or* les chaînes ; **to put a prisoner in ~s** mettre un prisonnier aux fers

fettle [ˈfetl] N **in fine** *or* **good ~** en pleine forme

fettucine [ˌfetəˈtʃiːnɪ] N (*NonC*) fettucine *fpl*

fetus [ˈfiːtəs] N (*US*) = **foetus**

feu [fjuː] [1] N (*Scot Jur*) bail *m* perpétuel (*à redevance fixe*) [2] COMP ► **feu duty** N loyer *m* (de la terre)

feud[1] [fjuːd] [1] N querelle *f* (*entre deux clans*), vendetta *f* ; **family ~s** querelles *fpl* de famille [2] VI se quereller, se disputer ; **to ~ with sb** être l'ennemi juré de qn, être à couteaux tirés avec qn

feud[2] [fjuːd] N (*Hist*) fief *m*

feudal [ˈfjuːdl] ADJ féodal ; **the ~ system** le système féodal

feudalism [ˈfjuːdəlɪzəm] N (*Hist*) féodalité *f* ; (*fig*) [*of society, institution*] féodalisme *m*

fever [ˈfiːvəʳ] N (*Med, fig*) fièvre *f* ; **to run a ~** avoir de la fièvre ; **he has no ~** il n'a pas de fièvre ; (*fig*) **gambling ~** le démon du jeu ; **a ~ of impatience** une impatience fébrile ; **enthusiasm reached ~ pitch** l'enthousiasme était à son comble → **glandular, scarlet**

fevered [ˈfiːvəd] ADJ [a] (*liter*) [*brow*] brûlant de fièvre [b] (*fig*) [*imagination*] exalté, enfiévré

feverish [ˈfiːvərɪʃ] ADJ [a] (*Med*) [*person*] fiévreux, fébrile ; [*illness*] accompagné de fièvre [b] (*fig*) [*person, excitement, atmosphere, activity*] fiévreux ; [*speculation, pace*] effréné ; **~ with excitement** dans un état d'excitation fiévreuse *or* fébrile

feverishly [ˈfiːvərɪʃlɪ] ADV [*work*] fiévreusement, fébrilement ; [*try*] fébrilement

feverishness [ˈfiːvərɪʃnɪs] N [a] (*Med*) état *m* fébrile [b] (*fig*) fébrilité *f*

few [fjuː] ADJ, PRON [a] (= *not many*) peu (de) ; **~ books** peu de livres ; **very ~ books** très peu de livres ; **~ of them came** peu d'entre eux sont venus, quelques-uns d'entre eux seulement sont venus ; **~ (people) come to see him** peu de gens viennent le voir ; **he is one of the ~ people who is able to do this** c'est l'une des rares personnes qui puisse le faire *or* à pouvoir le faire ; **we have worked hard in the past ~ days** nous avons travaillé dur ces jours-ci *or* ces derniers jours ; **these past ~ weeks** ces dernières semaines ; **the next ~ days** les (quelques) jours qui viennent ; **with ~ exceptions** à de rares exceptions près ; **the exceptions are ~** les exceptions sont rares *or* peu nombreuses ; **she goes to town every ~ days** elle va à la ville tous les deux ou trois jours ; **~ and far between** rares ; **such occasions are ~ and far between** de telles occasions sont rares ; **we are very ~ (in number)** nous sommes peu nombreux ; (*liter*) **our days are ~** nos jours sont comptés ; **I'll spend the remaining ~ minutes alone** je passerai seul le peu de *or* les quelques minutes qui me restent ; **there are always the ~ who think that ...** il y a toujours la minorité qui croit que ... ; **the ~ who know him** les rares personnes qui le connaissent ; (*Brit Aviat Hist*) **the Few** *les héros de la Bataille d'Angleterre* → **happy, word**

[b] (*after adv*) **I have as ~ books as you** j'ai aussi peu de livres que vous ; **I have as ~ as you** j'en ai aussi peu que vous ; **there were as ~ as six objections** il n'y a eu en tout et pour tout que six objections ; **how ~ there are!** il n'y en a (vraiment) pas beaucoup ! ; **how ~ they are!** il n'y en a (vraiment) pas beau-

coup!; **however ~ books you (may) buy** même si l'on achète peu de livres; **however ~ there may be** si peu qu'il y en ait; **I've got so ~ already (that ...)** j'en ai déjà si peu (que ...); **so ~ have been sold** on en a (or ils en ont) vendu si peu; **so ~ books** tellement peu or si peu de livres; **there were too ~** il y en avait trop peu; **too ~ cakes** trop peu de gâteaux; **there were three too ~** il en manquait trois; **ten would not be too ~** dix suffiraient, il (en) suffirait de dix; **I've got too ~ already** j'en ai déjà (bien) trop peu; **he has too ~ books** il a trop peu de livres; **there are too ~ of you** vous êtes trop peu nombreux, vous n'êtes pas assez nombreux; **too ~ of them realize that ...** trop peu d'entre eux sont conscients que ... [c] (= *some, several*) **a ~** quelques(-uns), quelques(-unes); **a ~ books** quelques livres *mpl*; **I know a ~ of these people** je connais quelques-unes de ces personnes; **a ~** or (*liter*) **some ~ thought otherwise** certains or (*liter*) d'aucuns pensaient autrement; **I'll take just a ~** j'en prendrai quelques-uns (or quelques-unes) seulement; **I'd like a ~ more** j'en voudrais quelques-un(e)s de plus; **quite a ~ books** pas mal* de livres; **quite a ~ did not believe me** pas mal* de gens ne l'ont pas cru; **I saw a good ~** or **quite a ~ people there** j'y ai vu pas mal* de gens; **he has had a good ~ (drinks)** il a pas mal* bu; **we'll go in a ~ minutes** nous partirons dans quelques minutes; **a ~ of us** quelques-un(e)s d'entre nous; **there were only a ~** il nous n'étions qu'une poignée; **a good ~ of the books are ...** (un) bon nombre de ces livres sont ...; **we must wait a ~ more days** il nous faut attendre encore quelques jours or attendre quelques jours de plus

fewer ['fjuːəʳ] ADJ, PRON (*compar of* **few**) moins (de); **we have sold ~ this year** nous en avons moins vendu cette année; **he has ~ books than you** il a moins de livres que vous; **we are ~ (in number) than last time** nous sommes moins nombreux que la dernière fois; **~ people than we expected** moins de gens que nous n'en attendions; **there are ~ opportunities for doing it** les occasions de le faire sont plus rares, il y a moins d'occasions de le faire; **no ~ than 37 pupils were ill** il y a eu pas moins de 37 élèves malades; **the ~ the better** moins il y en a mieux c'est or mieux ça vaut; **few came and ~ stayed** peu sont venus et encore moins sont restés

fewest ['fjuːɪst] ADJ, PRON (*superl of* **few**) le moins (de); **he met her on the ~ occasions possible** il l'a rencontrée le moins souvent possible; **we were ~ in number then** c'est à ce moment-là que nous étions le moins nombreux; **we sold ~ last year** c'est l'année dernière que nous en avons le moins vendu; **I've got (the) ~** c'est moi qui en ai le moins; **he has (the) ~ books** c'est lui qui a le moins de livres

fey [feɪ] ADJ (*pej = affected*) mignard, minaudier

fez [fez] N (*pl* **fezzes**) fez *m*

ff (ABBR = **and the following**) sqq

FFA [‚efef'eɪ] (ABBR = **Future Farmers of America**) *club agricole*

FFV [‚efef'viː] (ABBR = **First Families of Virginia**) *descendants des premiers colons de Virginie*

FH N (ABBR = **fire hydrant**) → **fire**

FHA [‚efeɪtʃ'eɪ] (*US*) (ABBR = **Federal Housing Administration**) → **federal**; **~ loan** *prêt à la construction*

FHSA [‚efeɪtʃes'eɪ] N (*Brit*) (ABBR = **Family Health Services Authority**) → **family**

fiancé [fɪ'ɑ̃ːŋseɪ] N fiancé *m*

fiancée [fɪ'ɑ̃ːŋseɪ] N fiancée *f*

fiasco [fɪ'æskəʊ] N (*pl* **fiascos** or **fiascoes**) fiasco *m*; **the whole undertaking was a ~** or **ended in a ~** l'entreprise a tourné au désastre or a été

un fiasco total; **the play was a ~** la pièce a fait un four

fiat ['faɪæt] N décret *m*, ordonnance *f*

fib* [fɪb] [1] N bobard* *m* [2] VI raconter des bobards*; **you're ~bing!** tu plaisantes!

fibber ['fɪbəʳ] N blagueur* *m*, -euse *f*, menteur *m*, -euse *f*; **you ~!** espèce de menteur!

fibre, fiber (*US*) ['faɪbəʳ] [1] N [a] [*of wood, cotton, muscle*] fibre *f*; [*cotton*] ~ fibre *f* de coton; **synthetic ~s** fibres *fpl* synthétiques, synthétiques *mpl*; (*fig*) **a man of ~** un homme qui a de la trempe; **a man of great moral ~** un homme d'une grande force morale [b] (*dietary*) fibres *fpl* alimentaires; **a diet high in ~** (= *eating régime*) un régime riche en fibres; (= *food eaten*) une alimentation riche en fibres [2] COMP ► **fibre optics** NPL la fibre optique ► **fibre-tip (pen)** N (*Brit*) stylo *m* pointe fibre

fibreboard, fiberboard (*US*) ['faɪbəbɔːd] N panneau *m* de fibres

fibrefill, fiberfill (*US*) ['faɪbəfɪl] N rembourrage *m* synthétique

fibreglass, fiberglass (*US*), **Fiberglas®** (*US*) ['faɪbəglɑːs] N fibre *f* de verre

fibreoptic cable, fiberoptic cable (*US*) [‚faɪbərɒptɪk'keɪbl] N câble *m* en fibres optiques

fibreoptic link, fiberoptic link (*US*) [‚faɪbərɒptɪk'lɪŋk] N liaison *f* par fibre optique

fibrescope, fiberscope (*US*) ['faɪbəskəʊp] N fibroscope *m*

fibril ['faɪbrɪl], **fibrilla** [faɪ'brɪlə] N fibrille *f*

fibrillation [‚faɪbrɪ'leɪʃən] N fibrillation *f*

fibrin ['faɪbrɪn] N fibrine *f*

fibrinogen [fɪ'brɪnədʒən] N fibrinogène *m*

fibroid ['faɪbrɔɪd] N = **fibroma**

fibroma [faɪ'brəʊmə] N (*pl* **fibromas** or **fibromata** [faɪ'brəʊmətə]) (*Med*) fibrome *m*

fibrositis [‚faɪbrə'saɪtɪs] N aponévrite *f*

fibrous ['faɪbrəs] ADJ fibreux

fibula ['fɪbjʊlə] N (*pl* **fibulas** or **fibulae** ['fɪbjʊ‚liː]) péroné *m*

FICA [‚efaɪsiː'eɪ] N (*US*) (ABBR = **Federal Insurance Contributions Act**) → **federal**

fickle ['fɪkl] ADJ [*friend, follower, supporter*] inconstant; [*lover, husband*] volage, inconstant; [*fate, weather*] changeant, capricieux

fickleness ['fɪklnɪs] N inconstance *f*

fiction ['fɪkʃən] N [a] (NonC: *Literat*) (**works of**) **~** œuvres *fpl* de fiction; **a writer of ~** un romancier; **light ~** romans *mpl* faciles à lire = **science, truth** [b] (= *fabrication*) fiction *f*; **his account was a complete ~** son récit était une invention du début à la fin; (= *unjustified belief*) **there is still this ~ that you can find a job if you try hard enough** il y a encore des gens qui s'imaginent qu'il suffit d'un peu de persévérance pour trouver du travail; **total recycling is a ~** l'idée de pouvoir tout recycler relève du mythe [c] (NonC: = *the unreal*) le faux → **fact**

fictional ['fɪkʃənl] ADJ (*Literat*) [*character*] imaginaire, fictif; [*hero, setting*] imaginaire; [*film, drama*] de fiction; [*account, device*] romanesque; (= *unreal*) [*plans, figures*] fictif

fictionalize ['fɪkʃənəlaɪz] VT romancer

fictitious [fɪk'tɪʃəs] ADJ (= *false*) [*name, address*] faux (fausse *f*); [*character, story*] imaginaire, fictif; [*setting*] imaginaire

Fid. Def. (ABBR = **Fidei Defensor**) (= *Defender of the Faith*) Défenseur *m* de la foi

fiddle ['fɪdl] [1] N [a] (= *violin*) violon *m* → **fit'**, **second'** [b] (*esp Brit* = *cheating*) truc* *m*, combine* *f*; **it was all a ~** tout ça c'était une combine*; **tax ~** fraude *f* fiscale; **he's on the ~** il traficote* [2] (*Mus*) jouer du violon; **to ~ while Rome burns** se perdre en futilités au lieu d'agir [b] **do stop fiddling (about** or **around)!** tiens-toi donc tranquille!; **to ~**

(**about** or **around**) **with a pencil** tripoter un crayon; **he's fiddling (about** or **around) with the car** il bricole la voiture [c] (*esp Brit* = *cheat*) faire de la fraude, traficoter* [3] VT [a] (*esp Brit*) [+ *accounts, expenses claim*] truquer; **to ~ one's tax return** truquer sa déclaration d'impôts [b] (*Mus*) jouer du violon [4] COMP ► **fiddle-faddle*** EXCL quelle blague!*

► **fiddle about, fiddle around** VI **he's fiddling about in the garage** il est en train de bricoler dans le garage; **we just ~d about yesterday** on n'a rien fait de spécial hier, on a seulement traînassé hier → **fiddle 2b**

fiddler ['fɪdləʳ] N [a] joueur *m*, -euse *f* de violon, violoneux* *m* (*gen pej*) [b] (*esp Brit* = *cheat*) combinard* *m*

fiddlesticks* ['fɪdlstɪks] EXCL quelle blague!*

fiddling ['fɪdlɪŋ] [1] ADJ futile, insignifiant; **little jobs** menus travaux *mpl* sans importance [2] N (NonC: = *dishonesty*) combine(s)* *f(pl)*

fiddly* ['fɪdlɪ] ADJ [*job, task*] minutieux, délicat; [*machinery*] difficile à manier; **~ to open** difficile à ouvrir; **prawns are ~ to eat** les crevettes ne sont pas pratiques à manger

fidelity [fɪ'delɪtɪ] N fidélité *f* → **high**

fidget ['fɪdʒɪt] [1] VI (= *wriggle: also* **~ about, ~ around**) remuer, gigoter*; (= *grow impatient*) donner des signes d'impatience; **stop ~ing!** reste donc tranquille!, arrête de bouger!; **to ~ (about** or **around) with sth** tripoter qch [2] N **to be a ~** [*child*] être très remuant, ne pas tenir en place; [*adult*] ne pas tenir en place; **to have the ~s*** avoir la bougeotte*

fidgety ['fɪdʒɪtɪ] ADJ (= *jittery*) agité; (*physically*) remuant, agité; **to feel ~** ne pas tenir en place, être agité

fiduciary [fɪ'djuːʃɪərɪ] ADJ, N fiduciaire *mf*

fie [faɪ] EXCL (†† or *hum*) **~ (up)on you!** honni sois-tu!†† (*also hum*)

fief [fiːf] N fief *m*

fiefdom ['fiːfdəm] N (*Hist, fig*) fief *m*

field [fiːld] [1] N [a] (*Agr etc*) champ *m*; (*Miner*) gisement *m*; **in the ~s** dans les champs, aux champs → **coalfield, goldfield, oilfield** [b] (= *real environment*) terrain *m*; **this machine had a year's trial in the ~** cette machine a eu un an d'essais sur le terrain; (*Comm*) **to be first in the ~ with sth** être le premier à lancer qch; **work in the ~** enquête *f* sur place or sur le terrain [c] (*Mil*) champ *m*; **~ of battle** champ *m* de bataille; **~ of honour** champ *m* d'honneur; **to take the ~** entrer en campagne; **to hold the ~** se maintenir sur ses positions; **to die in the ~** tomber or mourir au champ d'honneur [d] (*Sport*) terrain *m*; **the ~** (*Racing*) les concurrents *mpl* (sauf le favori); (*Hunting*) les chasseurs *mpl*; **football ~** terrain *m* de football; **to take the ~** entrer en jeu; **to hold off the ~** (*Sport*) tenir bon face à ses adversaires; (*fig*) tenir bon face à la concurrence [e] (= *sphere of activity, knowledge*) domaine *m*; **in the ~ of painting** dans le domaine de la peinture; **it's outside my ~** ce n'est pas de mon domaine; **his particular ~ is Renaissance painting** la peinture de la Renaissance est sa spécialité, son domaine de spécialité est la peinture de la Renaissance [f] (*Phys: also* **~ of force**) champ *m*; **~ of vision** champ *m* visuel or de vision; **gravitational ~** champ *m* de gravitation → **magnetic** [g] (*Comput*) champ *m*; (*Ling*) (**semantic**) **~** champ *m* (sémantique) [h] (= *expanse*) étendue *f*; (*Her*) champ *m*; (*Her*) **on a ~ of blue** en champ d'azur [2] VT (*Sport*) [+ *ball*] attraper; [+ *team*] faire jouer; (*fig*) **to ~ questions** répondre au pied levé (à des questions) [3] VI (*Sport*) être joueur de champ

④ COMP ► **field day** N (*Mil*) jour *m* de grandes manœuvres; (*gen*) jour *m* faste, grand jour *m*; (*fig*) **to have a ~ day** s'en donner à cœur joie; **the ice-cream sellers had a ~ day*** les marchands de glaces ont fait des affaires en or *or* d'or ce jour-là; **the press had a ~ day with the story** la presse a fait ses choux gras de cette histoire ► **field event** N (*Athletics*) concours *m* ► **field glasses** NPL jumelles *fpl* ► **field grown** ADJ de plein champ ► **field gun** N canon *m* (de campagne) ► **field hand** N (*US*) ouvrier *m*, -ière *f* agricole ► **field hockey** N (*US*) hockey *m* sur gazon ► **field hospital** N (*Mil*) antenne *f* chirurgicale; (*Hist*) hôpital *m* de campagne ► **field house** N (*US*) (*for changing*) vestiaire *m*; (= *sports hall*) complexe *m* sportif (couvert) ► **field kitchen** N (*Mil*) cuisine *f* roulante ► **field label** N (*Ling*) (indication *f* de) domaine *m* ► **field marshal** N (*Brit Mil*) ≈ maréchal *m* ► **field mushroom** agaric *m* champêtre ► **field officer** N (*Mil*) officier *m* supérieur ► **field service** N (*US Admin*) antenne *f* (*d'un service administratif*) ► **field sports** NPL activités *fpl* de plein air (*surtout la chasse et la pêche*) ► **field study** N étude *f* or enquête *f* sur le terrain ► **field term** N (*US Univ*) stage *m* pratique ► **field-test** VT soumettre aux essais sur le terrain, tester sur le terrain ► **field tests** NPL essais *mpl* sur le terrain ► **field trials** NPL [*of machine etc*] essais *mpl* sur le terrain; (*Med*) essais *mpl* cliniques ► **field trip** N (*Educ*) sortie *f* éducative; (*longer*) voyage *m* d'étude ► **field work** N (*Archeol, Geol*) recherches *fpl* or enquête *f* sur le terrain; (*Social Work*) travail *m* social (*sur le terrain*) ► **field worker** N (*Archeol, Geol*) archéologue *mf* (*or* géologue *mf etc*) de terrain; (*Social Work*) ≈ travailleur *m*, -euse *f* social(e) (*allant sur le terrain*)

fielder ['fiːldər] N (*Cricket*) joueur *m* de champ

fieldfare ['fiːldfɛər] N (*Orn*) litorne *f*

fieldmouse ['fiːldmaʊs] N (*pl* **-mice**) (*Zool*) mulot *m*, rat *m* des champs

fieldsman ['fiːldzmən] N (*pl* **-men**) (*Cricket*) joueur *m* de champ

fieldstrip ['fiːldstrɪp] VT (*US Mil*) [+ *firearm*] démonter (*pour inspection*)

fiend [fiːnd] N ⓐ démon *m*; (= *cruel person*) monstre *m*, démon *m*; (*Rel* = the *Devil*) **the Fiend** le Malin; **that child's a real ~*** cet enfant est un petit monstre *or* est infernal* ⓑ (* = *fanatic*) enragé(e) *m(f)*, mordu(e)* *m(f)*; **tennis ~** enragé(e) *m(f)* or mordu(e)* *m(f)* de tennis; **drug ~†** toxicomane *mf* → **sex**

fiendish ['fiːndɪʃ] ADJ ⓐ (= *cruel*) [*despot*] monstrueux; [*act, look*] diabolique; [*cruelty*] extrême; **to take a ~ delight in doing sth** prendre un malin plaisir à faire qch ⓑ (= *ingenious*) [*plot, device*] diabolique ⓒ (* = *difficult*) [*problem, difficulty*] infernal

fiendishly ['fiːndɪʃlɪ] ADV ⓐ (= *evilly*) **to laugh ~** éclater d'un rire diabolique ⓑ (* = *extremely*) [*difficult, complicated, expensive*] abominablement; [*simple*] diaboliquement; [*funny*] terriblement; **~ clever** [*person*] d'une intelligence redoutable; [*plot, device*] extrêmement ingénieux

fierce [fɪəs] ADJ [*animal, person, look, tone, battle*] féroce; [*attack, argument*] violent; [*debate*] houleux, acharné; [*opposition, opponent, resistance, determination*] farouche; [*loyalty*] à toute épreuve; [*criticism, critic*] virulent; [*heat, storm*] terrible; [*wind*] violent; **to take a ~ pride in sth** être extrêmement fier de qch; **he has a ~ temper** il est d'un tempérament explosif; **competition for the post was ~** la concurrence pour le poste a été rude

fiercely ['fɪəslɪ] ADV [*resist, fight, defend*] avec acharnement; [*oppose*] farouchement; [*criticize*] violemment; [*say*] d'un ton féroce; **to burn ~** flamber; **~ independent** farouchement

indépendant; **to be ~ competitive** avoir un esprit de compétition acharné

fierceness ['fɪəsnɪs] N ⓐ (= *savageness*) [*of animal, gaze, expression*] férocité *f*; [*of person*] férocité *f*; **his ~ of manner** son abord *m* féroce ⓑ (= *intensity*) [*of passion, sun*] ardeur *f*; [*of love, fighting, competition, opposition, heat, fire*] intensité *f*; [*of blow, shot*] violence *f*

fiery ['faɪərɪ] ① ADJ [*colour*] rougeoyant; [*sunset*] embrasé; [*hair, eyes*] flamboyant; [*person, character, personality, nature*] fougueux; [*temper*] explosif; [*speech, rhetoric*] enflammé; [*food*] (très) épicé, qui emporte la bouche; [*drink*] qui emporte la bouche; (*Bible*) **the ~ furnace** la fournaise ardente; **a ~ inferno** un terrible brasier; **the ~ heat of the desert** la chaleur torride du désert; **~ orange/red** orange/rouge flamboyant *inv* ② ► **fiery-tempered** ADJ irascible, coléreux

fiesta [fɪˈestə] N fiesta *f*

FIFA ['fiːfə] N (ABBR = **Fédération internationale de football-association**) FIFA *f*

fife [faɪf] N fifre *m* (*instrument*)

FIFO ['faɪfəʊ] N (ABBR = **first in, first out**) PEPS *m*

fifteen [fɪf'tiːn] ① ADJ quinze *inv*; **about ~ books** une quinzaine de livres ② N ⓐ quinze *m inv*; **about ~** une quinzaine ⓑ (*Rugby*) quinze *m*; **the French ~** le quinze de France; *for other phrases see* **six** ③ PRON quinze; **there are ~** il y en a quinze

fifteenth [fɪf'tiːnθ] ① ADJ quinzième ② N quinzième *mf*; (= *fraction*) quinzième *m*; *for phrases see* **sixth**

fifth [fɪfθ] ① ADJ cinquième; (*fig*) **~-rate** de dernier ordre, de dernière catégorie; *for other phrases see* **sixth** ② N ⓐ (*gen*) cinquième *mf*; (= *fraction*) cinquième *m*; (*US Jur*) **to take the Fifth** invoquer le cinquième amendement pour refuser de répondre → FIFTH AMENDMENT; (* *fig*) refuser de parler; *for other phrases see* **sixth** ⓑ (*Mus*) quinte *f* ⓒ (*US*) (= *measurement*) cinquième d'un gallon (= 75 cl); (= *bottle*) bouteille *f* (d'alcool) ③ COMP ► **Fifth Amendment** N (*US Jur*) cinquième amendement *m* (de la constitution); **to plead the Fifth Amendment** invoquer le cinquième amendement pour refuser de répondre ► **fifth column** N cinquième colonne *f* ► **fifth columnist** N membre *m* de la cinquième colonne

┌─────────────────┐
│ **FIFTH AMENDMENT** │
└─────────────────┘

Le cinquième amendement de la constitution des États-Unis protège le citoyen contre certains abus de pouvoir. Ainsi, on ne peut incarcérer une personne ou lui confisquer ses biens sans procès; on ne peut non plus la juger deux fois pour un même délit. Enfin, tout citoyen peut invoquer cet amendement (« to plead the Fifth Amendment » ou « to take the Fifth ») pour refuser de fournir des éléments de preuve susceptibles de se retourner contre lui. À l'époque du maccarthysme, le cinquième amendement a été invoqué par diverses personnalités présumées coupables d'activités antiaméricaines. → BILL OF RIGHTS

fiftieth ['fɪftɪɪθ] ① ADJ cinquantième ② N cinquantième *mf*; (= *fraction*) cinquantième *m*; *for phrases see* **sixth**

fifty ['fɪftɪ] ① ADJ cinquante *inv*; **about ~ books** une cinquantaine de livres ② N cinquante *m inv*; **about ~** une cinquantaine; *for other phrases see* **sixty** ③ PRON cinquante; **there are ~** il y en a cinquante ④ COMP ► **fifty-fifty** ADJ, ADV moitié-moitié, fifty-fifty*; **to go ~~ with sb** partager moitié-moitié *or* fifty-fifty* avec qn; **we have a ~~ chance of success** nous avons cinquante pour cent de chances *or* une chance sur deux de réussir; **it was a ~~ deal** ils ont (*or* nous avons *etc*) fait moitié-moitié *or* fifty-fifty*

fig [fɪg] ① N ⓐ (= *fruit*) figue *f*; (*also* **~ tree**) figuier *m* ⓑ (*†* *fig*) **I don't care a ~** je m'en fiche*; **I don't give a ~ what people think** je me fiche* de ce que les gens pensent; **I don't give a ~ for that** je m'en moque comme de ma première chemise*; **a ~ for all your principles!** vos principes, je m'asseois dessus!* ② COMP ► **fig leaf** N (*pl* **fig leaves**) (*Bot*) feuille *f* de figuier; (*on statue etc*) feuille *f* de vigne; (*fig*) couverture *f*, camouflage *m*; **the agreement was merely a ~ leaf for the government to hide behind** l'accord n'a fait que servir de couverture au gouvernement

fig. ABBR = **figure 1b**

fight [faɪt] (*vb*: pret, ptp **fought**) ① N ⓐ (*between persons*) bagarre* *f*; (*Mil*) combat *m*, bataille *f*; (*Boxing*) combat *m*; (*against disease, poverty etc*) lutte *f* (**against** contre); (= *quarrel*) dispute *f*; **to have a ~ with sb** se battre avec qn, se bagarrer* avec qn; (= *argue*) se disputer avec qn; (*lit, fig*) **he put up a good ~** il s'est bien défendu; **~ for life** (*of sick person*) lutte *f* contre la mort; **the ~ for survival** la lutte pour la survie; **the country's ~ for independence** la lutte du pays pour son indépendance; **we're going to make a ~ of it** nous n'allons pas nous laisser faire, nous allons contre-attaquer; **we won't go down without a ~** nous n'abandonnerons pas sans nous être battus → **pick** ⓑ (*NonC* = *spirit*) **there was no ~ left in him** il n'avait plus envie de lutter, il n'avait plus de ressort; **he certainly shows ~** il faut reconnaître qu'il sait montrer les dents *or* qu'il ne se laisse pas faire

② VI [*person, animal*] se battre (**with** avec, **against** contre); [*troops, countries*] se battre (**against** contre); (*fig*) lutter (**for** pour, **against** contre); (= *quarrel*) se disputer (**with** avec); **the boys were ~ing in the street** les garçons se battaient *or* se bagarraient* dans la rue; **the dogs were ~ing over a bone** les chiens se disputaient un os; **he went down ~ing** il s'est battu jusqu'au bout; (*fig*) **to ~ against sleep** lutter contre le sommeil; **to ~ against disease** lutter contre *or* combattre la maladie; (*lit, fig*) **to ~ for sb** se battre pour qn; (*lit, fig*) **to ~ for one's life** lutter contre la mort; **to be ~ing for breath** respirer à grand-peine; (*fig*) **to ~ shy of sth/sb** fuir devant qch/qn, tout faire pour éviter qch/qn; **to ~ shy of doing sth** éviter à tout prix de *or* répugner à faire

③ VT [+ *person, army*] se battre avec *or* contre; [+ *fire, disease*] lutter contre, combattre; **to ~ a battle** livrer bataille; (*fig*) **to ~ a losing battle against sth** mener un combat perdu d'avance contre qch; **we're ~ing a losing battle** c'est un combat perdu d'avance; **to ~ a duel** se battre en duel; (*Pol etc*) **to ~ a campaign** mener une campagne, faire campagne; (*Jur*) **to ~ a case** [*plaintiff*] aller en justice; [*defendant*] se défendre; [*defence lawyer*] plaider une cause; **we shall ~ this decision all the way** nous combattrons cette décision jusqu'au bout; **to ~ one's way out through the crowd** sortir en se frayant un passage à travers la foule

► **fight back** ① VI (*in fight*) rendre les coups, répondre; (*Mil*) se défendre, résister; (*in argument*) répondre, se défendre; (*after illness*) se remettre, réagir; (*Sport*) se reprendre, effectuer une reprise ② VT SEP [+ *tears*] refouler; [+ *despair*] lutter contre; [+ *doubts*] vaincre ③ **~back** N → **fightback**

► **fight down** VT SEP [+ *anxiety, doubts*] vaincre; [+ *desire*] refouler, réprimer

► **fight off** VT SEP ⓐ (*lit, Mil*) [+ *attack*] repousser; **she fought off her attackers** elle a repoussé *or* mis en fuite ses agresseurs ⓑ (*fig*) [+ *disease, sleep*] lutter contre, résister à; [+ *criticisms*] répondre à

► **fight on** VI continuer le combat *or* la lutte

► **fight out** VT SEP **they fought it out** (*lit*) ils se sont bagarrés* pour régler la question; (*fig*) ils ont réglé la question en se disputant

fightback ['faɪtbæk] N (Brit Sport) reprise f

fighter ['faɪtə^r] **1** **a** (Boxing) boxeur m, pugiliste m; (fig) **he's a ~** c'est un lutteur; **prize¹** **b** (also **~ aircraft, ~ plane**) avion m de chasse, chasseur m **2** COMP ► **fighter-bomber** N (Aviat) chasseur m bombardier, avion m de combat polyvalent ► **fighter pilot** N pilote m de chasse

fighting ['faɪtɪŋ] **1** N (Mil) combat m; (in classroom, pub etc) bagarres* fpl; **there was some ~ in the town** il y a eu des échauffourées dans la ville; **~ broke out between police and demonstrators** des incidents ont éclaté entre la police et les manifestants → **street** **2** ADJ [person] combatif; (Mil) [troops] de combat; (Mil) **~ soldier** or **man** combattant m; **he's got a lot of ~ spirit** c'est un lutteur, il a du cran*; **there's a ~ chance for her recovery** elle a une assez bonne chance de s'en tirer; **~ cock/dog** coq m/chien m de combat; **to live like a ~ cock** vivre comme un coq en pâte; (esp Brit) **~ fit** en pleine forme; (Mil) **~ forces** forces fpl armées; **~ fund** fonds m de soutien; **~ line** front m; **~ strength** effectif m mobilisable; **~ talk** or **words** paroles fpl de défi

figment ['fɪgmənt] N **a ~ of the imagination** une invention or création de l'imagination; **it's all a ~ of his imagination** il l'a purement et simplement inventé, il a inventé ça de toutes pièces

figurative ['fɪgjʊrətɪv] ADJ **a** (= metaphorical) [language] figuré, métaphorique; **in the literal and in the ~ sense** or **meaning** au (sens) propre et au (sens) figuré **b** (Art) figuratif

figuratively ['fɪgjʊrətɪvlɪ] ADV au sens figuré; **both literally and ~** au propre comme au figuré; **~ speaking** métaphoriquement parlant

figure ['fɪgə^r] **1** N **a** chiffre m; **in round ~s** en chiffres ronds; **I can't give you the exact ~s** je ne peux pas vous donner les chiffres exacts; **the crime/unemployment** etc **~s** les chiffres de la criminalité/du chômage etc; **to put a ~ to sth** chiffrer qch; **can you put a ~ to** or **on that?** est-ce que vous pouvez me donner un chiffre?; **he's good at ~s** il est doué pour le calcul; **there's a mistake in the ~s** il y a une erreur de calcul; **a three-~ number** un nombre or un numéro de trois chiffres; **to get into double ~s** atteindre la dizaine; **to reach three ~s** atteindre la centaine; **he earns well into five ~s** il gagne bien plus de dix mille livres; **to bring** or **get inflation/unemployment** etc **down to single ~s** faire passer l'inflation/le chômage etc en dessous (de la barre) des 10%; **to sell sth for a high ~** vendre qch cher or à un prix élevé; **I got it for a low ~** je l'ai eu pour pas cher or pour peu de chose

b (= diagram, drawing) [of animal, person etc] figure f, image f; (Math) figure f; **he drew the ~ of a bird** il a dessiné (la silhouette d')un oiseau; **draw a ~ of eight** dessinez un huit → **1h**

c (= human form) forme f, silhouette f; **I saw a ~ approach** j'ai vu une forme or une silhouette s'approcher; **she's a fine ~ of a woman** c'est une belle femme; **he cut a poor** or **sorry ~** il faisait piètre figure; **she cuts a fine ~ in that dress** elle a grand air (frm) or elle a beaucoup d'allure dans cette robe

d (= shape: of person) ligne f, formes fpl; **to improve one's ~** soigner sa ligne; **to keep one's ~** garder la ligne; **she has a good ~** elle est bien faite or bien tournée; **remember your ~!** pense à ta ligne!; **she doesn't have the ~ for that dress** elle n'est pas faite pour porter cette robe

e (= important person) figure f, personnage m; **the great ~s of history** les grandes figures fpl or les grands personnages mpl de l'histoire; **a ~ of fun** un guignol → **public**

f (Literat) figure f; **~ of speech** figure f de rhétorique; (fig) **it's just a ~ of speech** ce n'est qu'une façon de parler

g (Mus) figure f mélodique

h (Dancing, Skating) figure f; **~ of eight** ◊ **~ eight** (US) huit m

2 VT **a** (esp US = guess) penser, supposer; **I ~ it like this** je vois la chose comme ceci; **I ~ he'll come** je pense or suppose qu'il va venir **b** (= imagine) penser, s'imaginer **c** (= represent) représenter; (= illustrate by diagrams) illustrer par un or des schéma(s), mettre sous forme de schéma **d** (= decorate) orner; [+ silk etc] brocher, gaufrer; **~d velvet** velours m façonné **e** (Mus) **~d bass** basse f chiffrée

3 VI **a** (= appear) figurer; **he ~d in a play of mine** il a joué or tenu un rôle dans une de mes pièces; **his name doesn't ~ on this list** son nom ne figure pas sur cette liste **b** (esp US* = make sense) **it doesn't ~** ça n'a pas de sens; **that ~s** ça paraît logique

4 COMP ► **figure-conscious*** ADJ **to be ~-conscious** penser à sa ligne ► **figure-hugging** ADJ [dress] moulant ► **figure-skate** VI (in competition) faire les figures imposées (en patinage); (in display etc) faire du patinage artistique ► **figure skater** N patineur m, -euse f artistique ► **figure skating** N (in competition) figures fpl imposées; (in display etc) patinage m artistique

► **figure in*** VT SEP (US) inclure, compter; **it's ~d in** c'est inclus, c'est compris

► **figure on** VT FUS (esp US) (= take account of) tenir compte de; (= count on) compter sur; (= expect) s'attendre (**doing** à faire); **you can ~ on 30** tu peux compter sur 30; **I was figuring on doing that tomorrow** je pensais faire ça demain; **I hadn't ~d on that** je n'avais pas tenu compte de ça; **I wasn't figuring on having to do that** je ne m'attendais pas à devoir faire ça

► **figure out** VT SEP **a** (= understand) arriver à comprendre; (= resolve) résoudre; **I can't ~ that guy out at all** je n'arrive pas du tout à comprendre ce type*; **I can't ~ out how much it comes to** je n'arrive pas à (bien) calculer à combien ça s'élève; **I can't ~ it out** ça me dépasse* **b** (= work out, plan) calculer; **they had it all ~d out** ils avaient calculé leur coup

figurehead ['fɪgəhed] N **a** (gen) chef m de file **b** [of ship] figure f de proue

figurine [,fɪgə'riːn] N figurine f

Fiji ['fiːdʒiː] N Fidji; (also **the ~ Islands**) les îles fpl Fidji; **in ~** à or aux Fidji

Fijian ['fiːdʒiːən] **1** ADJ fidjien **2** N **a** Fidjien(ne) m(f) **b** (Ling) fidjien m

filament ['fɪləmənt] N filament m

filariasis [,fɪlə'raɪəsɪs] N filariose f

filbert ['fɪlbɜːt] N aveline f

filch* [fɪltʃ] VT voler, chiper*

file¹ [faɪl] **1** N (for wood, fingernails etc) lime f; **triangular ~** tiers-point m → **nailfile** **2** VT limer; **to ~ one's nails** se limer les ongles; **to ~ through the bars** limer les barreaux

► **file away** VT SEP limer (pour enlever)

► **file down** VT SEP limer (pour raccourcir)

file² [faɪl] **1** N (= folder) dossier m, chemise f; (with hinges) classeur m; (for drawings) carton m; (for card index) fichier m; (= cabinet) classeur m; (= papers) dossier m; (Comput) fichier m; **to put a document on the ~** joindre une pièce au dossier; **do we have a ~ on her?** est-ce que nous avons un dossier sur elle?; **there's something in** or **on the ~ about him** le dossier contient des renseignements sur lui; **to be on ~** [person, fingerprints] être fiché; **to be on police ~s** être fiché par la police; **to keep sb's details on ~** garder les coordonnées de qn; **to keep information about sth on ~** avoir un dossier or des renseignements sur qch; **to keep a ~ on sb/sth** avoir un dossier sur qn/qch; **they closed the ~ concerning his death** ils ont classé le dossier concernant sa mort; **they closed the ~ on that case** ils ont

classé cette affaire; (Comput) **data on ~** données fpl fichées → **student, single**

2 VT **a** (also **~ away**) [+ notes] classer; [+ letters] ranger, classer; (into file) joindre au dossier **b** (Comput) classer, stocker **c** (Jur) **to ~ a claim** déposer or introduire une requête or demande; **to ~ a claim for damages** intenter un procès en dommages-intérêts; (Insurance) **to ~ an accident claim** faire une déclaration d'accident; **to ~ a petition** déposer or introduire une requête or demande; **to ~ a petition (in bankruptcy)** déposer son bilan; **to ~ a suit against sb** intenter un procès à qn → **submission**

3 COMP ► **file cabinet** N (US) classeur m (meuble) ► **file card** N fiche f ► **file clerk** N (US) documentaliste mf ► **file management** N (Comput) gestion f de fichiers ► **file manager** N (Comput) gestionnaire m de fichiers ► **file transfer protocol** N (Comput) protocole m de transfert de fichiers

► **file for** VT FUS (Jur) **to ~ for divorce** demander le divorce; **to ~ for bankruptcy** déposer son bilan; **to ~ for custody (of the children)** demander la garde des enfants

file³ [faɪl] **1** N file f; **in Indian ~** à la or en file indienne; **in single ~** à la or en file → **rank¹** **2** VI **to ~ in/out** etc entrer/sortir etc en file; **to ~ past** défiler; **they ~d past the general** les soldats ont défilé devant le général; **they ~d slowly past the ticket collector** ils sont passés lentement les uns après les autres devant le contrôleur

filename ['faɪlneɪm] N (Comput) nom m de fichier

filet [fɪ'leɪ] (US) = **fillet**

filial ['fɪlɪəl] ADJ filial

filiation [,fɪlɪ'eɪʃən] N filiation f

filibuster ['fɪlɪbʌstə^r] **1** N **a** (Pol) obstruction f parlementaire **b** (= pirate) flibustier m **2** VI (Pol) faire de l'obstruction parlementaire

filibusterer ['fɪlɪbʌstərə^r] N (Pol) obstructionniste mf

filigree ['fɪlɪgriː] **1** N filigrane m (en métal) **2** COMP en filigrane

filing ['faɪlɪŋ] **1** N **a** [of documents] classement m; **to do the ~** s'occuper du classement **b** (Jur) [of claim etc] enregistrement m **2** COMP ► **filing box** N fichier m (boîte) ► **filing cabinet** N classeur m (meuble) ► **filing clerk** N (esp Brit) documentaliste mf

filings ['faɪlɪŋz] NPL limaille f; **iron ~** limaille f de fer

Filipino [,fɪlɪ'piːnəʊ] **1** ADJ philippin **2** N **a** (= person) Philippin(e) m(f) **b** (Ling) tagalog m

fill [fɪl] **1** VT **a** [+ bottle, bucket, hole] remplir (**with** de); [+ cake, pastry] fourrer (**with** de); [+ teeth] plomber; **smoke ~ed the room** la pièce s'est remplie de fumée; **the wind ~ed the sails** le vent a gonflé les voiles; **to ~ o.s. with** [+ chocolate etc] se gaver de; **the thought ~s me with pleasure/horror/hope** cette pensée me réjouit/m'horrifie/me remplit d'espoir; **~ed with admiration** rempli or plein d'admiration; **~ed with emotion/anger** très ému/en colère; **~ed with despair** désespéré, plongé dans le désespoir

b [+ post, job] [employer] pourvoir; **to ~ a vacancy** [employer] pourvoir un emploi; [employee] prendre un poste vacant; **the position is already ~ed** le poste est déjà pourvu or pris; **he ~s all our requirements** il répond à toutes nos conditions; **to ~ a need** répondre à un besoin; **to ~ a void** or **a gap** remplir or combler un vide; (esp US: Comm) **to ~ an order** livrer une commande

2 VI (also **~ up**) [bath] se remplir, s'emplir; [bus, hall] se remplir; **to ~ with water/mud**

[*hole*] se remplir d'eau/de boue ; **her eyes ~ed with tears** ses yeux se sont remplis de larmes

3 ▷ **to eat one's ~** manger à sa faim, se rassasier ; **he had eaten his ~** il était rassasié ; **to have/drink one's ~** avoir/boire tout son content ; **she's had her ~ of married life** elle en a assez de la vie conjugale ; **we've had our ~ of disappointments** nous avons trop souvent été déçus

4 COMP ▶ **fill-in** N (*gen = temporary employee*) remplaçant(e) *m(f)* ; (*fig*) **I'm only a ~-in** je fais office de bouche-trou*
▶ **fill in** **1** VI **to ~ in for sb** remplacer qn (temporairement) **2** VT SEP **a** [*+ form, questionnaire*] remplir ; [*+ account, report*] compléter ; (*fig*) **would you ~ in the details for us?** (*on questionnaire*) pourriez-vous compléter le questionnaire ? ; (*verbally*) pourriez-vous nous donner quelques précisions ? ; **to ~ sb in on sth*** mettre qn au courant de qch **b** [*+ hole*] boucher ; **we had that door ~ed in** nous avons fait murer *or* condamner cette porte ; **to ~ in gaps in one's knowledge** combler des lacunes dans ses connaissances ; **he was trying to ~ in the day** il essayait de trouver à s'occuper jusqu'au soir ; **draw the outline in black and ~ it in in red** dessinez le contour en noir et remplissez-le en rouge **c** (⸎ *fig = beat up*) casser la gueule à⸎ ; **3** ▶ **~-in** N → **fill**
▶ **fill out** **1** VI **a** [*sails etc*] gonfler, s'enfler **b** (*= become fatter*) [*person*] forcir, se fortifier ; **her cheeks** *or* **her face had ~ed out** elle avait pris de bonnes joues **2** VT SEP **a** [*+ form, questionnaire*] remplir **b** [*+ story, account, essay*] étoffer
▶ **fill up** **1** VI **a** = **fill 2 b** (*with petrol*) faire le plein (d'essence) **2** VT SEP **a** [*+ tank, cup*] remplir ; **to ~ o.s. up with** [*+ chocolates etc*] se gaver de ; (*with petrol*) **~ it** *or* **her up!*** (faites) le plein ! **b** [*+ hole*] boucher **c** (*Brit*) [*+ form, questionnaire*] remplir

-filled [fɪld] ADJ (*in compounds*) **cream/chocolate-filled** fourré à la crème/au chocolat ; **foam-filled** rempli de mousse ; **tear-filled** plein de larmes ; **hate-filled eyes** des yeux pleins de haine ; **he was found dead in his fume-filled car** il a été trouvé mort dans sa voiture remplie de gaz d'échappement

filler [ˈfɪlə*] **1** N **a** (*= utensil*) récipient *m* (de remplissage) ; [*of bottle*] remplisseuse *f* ; (*= funnel*) entonnoir *m* **b** (*NonC: for cracks in wood, plaster etc*) enduit *m or* produit de rebouchage **c** (*TV, Rad*) intermède *m* (*entre deux programmes*) ; (*Press*) article *m* bouche-trou *inv* **2** COMP ▶ **filler cap** N (*Aut*) bouchon *m* de réservoir

-filler [ˈfɪlə*] N (*in compounds*) **the team is a real stadium-filler** cette équipe fait le plein chaque fois qu'elle joue ; **Beethoven's Second Piano Concerto, the standard programme-filler** le Deuxième concerto pour piano de Beethoven, qui figure souvent au programme des concerts ; **space-filler*** bouche-trou* *m*

fillet [ˈfɪlɪt], **filet** (*US*) [fɪˈleɪ] **1** N **a** (*Culin*) [*of beef, pork, fish*] filet *m* ; **veal ~** (*NonC*) longe *f* de veau ; (*one piece*) escalope *f* de veau ; **~ of beef/sole** filet *m* de bœuf/de sole **b** (*for the hair*) serre-tête *m inv* **2** VT [*+ meat*] désosser ; [*+ fish*] découper en filets ; **~ed sole** filets *mpl* de sole **3** COMP ▶ **fillet steak** N (*NonC*) filet *m* de bœuf ; (*one slice*) bifteck *m* dans le filet ; (*thick*) chateaubriand *m*

filling [ˈfɪlɪŋ] **1** N **a** (*in tooth*) plombage *m* ; **my ~'s come out** mon plombage est parti *or* a sauté **b** (*in pie, tart, sandwich*) garniture *f* ; (*= stuffing*) farce *f* ; **chocolates with a coffee ~** chocolats *mpl* fourrés au café **2** ADJ [*food*] substantiel **3** COMP ▶ **filling station** N station-service *f*, poste *m* d'essence

fillip [ˈfɪlɪp] N (*with finger*) chiquenaude *f*, pichenette *f* ; (*fig*) coup *m* de fouet (*fig*) ; **our advertisements gave a ~ to our business** notre

publicité a donné un coup de fouet à nos affaires

filly [ˈfɪlɪ] N pouliche *f* ; (†* = *girl*) jeune fille *f*
film [fɪlm] **1** N **a** (*esp Brit: Cine* = *movie*) film *m* ; **to go to a ~** aller voir un film ; **the ~ is on at the Odeon just now** le film passe actuellement à l'Odéon ; **he's in ~s** il travaille dans le cinéma ; **he's been in many ~s** il a joué dans beaucoup de films → **feature**
b (*Phot, Cine*) film *m*, pellicule *f* ; (*Typ*) film *m* **c** (*for wrapping food*) film *m* transparent (*pour envelopper les aliments*) ; (*in goods packaging etc*) film *m* plastique **d** (*= thin layer*) [*of dust, mud*] couche *f*, pellicule *f* ; [*of mist*] voile *m* ; [*of oil, water*] film *m*
2 VT (*gen*) [*+ news, event, play*] filmer ; [*+ scene*] [*director*] filmer, tourner ; [*camera*] tourner
3 VI **a** [*windscreen, glass*] (*also* ~ **over**) se voiler, s'embuer **b** (*Cine* = *make a film*) faire *or* tourner un film ; **they were ~ing all day** ils ont tourné toute la journée ; **they were ~ing in Spain** le tournage avait lieu en Espagne ; **the story ~ed very well** l'histoire a bien rendu au cinéma *or* en film ; **she ~s well** elle est photogénique
4 COMP [*archives, history etc*] du cinéma ▶ **film camera** N (*Cine*) caméra *f* ▶ **film fan** N cinéphile *mf*, amateur *mf* de cinéma ▶ **film festival** N festival *m* du cinéma *or* du film ▶ **film library** N cinémathèque *f* ▶ **film-maker** N cinéaste *mf* ▶ **film-making** N (= *filming*) tournage *m* ; (*more gen*) le cinéma ▶ **film première** N première *f* ▶ **film rating** N (*Brit*) système *m* de classification des films → MOVIE RATING ▶ **film rights** NPL droits *mpl* d'adaptation (cinématographique) ▶ **film script** N scénario *m* ▶ **film sequence** N séquence *f* (de film) ▶ **film set** N (*Cine*) plateau *m* de tournage ▶ **filmset** N → **film speed** N sensibilité *f* de la pellicule ▶ **film star** N vedette *f* (de cinéma), star *f* ▶ **film studio** N studio *m* (de cinéma) ▶ **film test** N bout *m* d'essai ; **to give sb a ~ test** faire tourner un bout d'essai à qn

filming [ˈfɪlmɪŋ] N (*Cine*) tournage *m*
filmography [fɪlˈmɒɡrəfɪ] N filmographie *f*
filmset [ˈfɪlmset] VT (*Typ*) photocomposer
filmsetter [ˈfɪlmsetə*] N (*Typ*) photocomposeuse *f*
filmsetting [ˈfɪlmsetɪŋ] N (*Typ*) (= *machine*) photocomposition *f* ; (= *person*) photocompos(it)eur *m*
filmstrip [ˈfɪlmstrɪp] N film *m* (pour projection) fixe
filmy [ˈfɪlmɪ] ADJ [*fabric, material*] léger, vaporeux ; [*clothing*] léger et transparent ; **~ curtains** voilages *mpl*
Filofax® [ˈfaɪləʊfæks] N Filofax® *m*
filter [ˈfɪltə*] **1** N **a** (*gen, also Phot*) filtre *m* → **colour, oil**
b (*Brit: in traffic lights*) flèche *f* (*permettant à une file de voitures de tourner*)
2 VT [*+ liquids*] filtrer ; [*+ air*] purifier, épurer
3 VI [*light, liquid, sound*] filtrer ; **the light ~ed through the shutters** la lumière filtrait à travers les volets ; **to ~ back/in/out** [*people*] revenir/entrer/sortir par petits groupes ; **horror stories were beginning to ~ out of the prison** des récits effroyables commençaient à filtrer de la prison → **filter out**; **news of the attack quickly ~ed through the college** la nouvelle de l'agression s'est vite répandue dans tout le collège → **filter through**; **to ~ to the left** [*car, driver*] prendre la voie *or* la file de gauche pour tourner
4 COMP ▶ **filter bed** N bassin *m* de filtration ▶ **filter cigarette** N cigarette *f* (à bout) filtre ▶ **filter coffee** N café *m* filtre ▶ **filter lane** N (= *matérialisée sur la chaussée*) ▶ **filter light** N (*Aut*) flèche *f* (*de feux de signalisation*) ▶ **filter paper** N papier *m* filtre

▶ **filter tip** N (= *cigarette, tip*) bout *m* filtre
▶ **filter-tipped** ADJ à bout filtre
▶ **filter in** VI **the news of the massacre began to ~ in** on a commencé petit à petit à avoir des renseignements sur le massacre
▶ **filter out** VT SEP [*+ impurities*] éliminer par filtrage ; (*fig*) éliminer
▶ **filter through** VI [*light*] filtrer ; **the news ~ed through at last** les nouvelles ont fini par se savoir

filth [fɪlθ] N **a** (*lit*) saleté *f*, crasse *f* ; (= *excrement*) ordure *f* **b** (*fig*) saleté *f*, ordure *f* (*liter*) ; (*fig*) **this book is sheer ~** ce livre est une vraie saleté ; **the ~ shown on television** les saletés *or* les grossièretés *fpl* que l'on montre à la télévision ; **all the ~ he talks** toutes les grossièretés qu'il débite

filthy [ˈfɪlθɪ] ADJ **a** (= *dirty*) crasseux ; **to live in ~ conditions** vivre dans la crasse ; **~ with mud** couvert *or* maculé de boue ; **~ dirty** d'une saleté répugnante *or* dégoûtante **b** (= *disgusting*) [*creature, insect, habit*] dégoûtant ; [*substance*] infect ; **you ~ liar!** espèce de sale menteur ! ; **~ rich*** bourré* de fric → **lucre c** (= *obscene*) [*joke, book*] obscène ; [*language*] ordurier ; **to have a ~ mind** avoir l'esprit mal tourné ; **~ talk** grossièretés *fpl*, propos *mpl* orduriers **d** (= *angry*) **to give sb a ~ look** lancer un regard noir à qn ; **to have a ~ temper** avoir un tempérament explosif ; **to be in a ~ temper** être d'une humeur massacrante **e*** [*weather, night*] dégueulasse*

filtrate [ˈfɪltreɪt] N filtrat *m*
filtration [fɪlˈtreɪʃən] N filtration *f*
fin [fɪn] N **a** [*of fish*] nageoire *f* ; [*of shark*] aileron *m* ; [*of aircraft, spacecraft*] empennage *m* ; [*of ship*] dérive *f* ; [*of radiator*] ailette *f* ; [*of diver*] palme *f* **b** (*US⸎* = *five-dollar bill*) billet *m* de cinq dollars

finagle [fɪˈneɪɡl] (*US*) **1** VI resquiller **2** VT **to ~ sb out of sth** carotter* qch à qn
finagler [fɪˈneɪɡlə*] N (*US*) resquilleur *m*, -euse *f*

▼ **final** [ˈfaɪnl] **1** ADJ **a** (= *last*) [*minute, stage, match, chapter*] dernier ; **to make a ~ attempt to do sth** faire une dernière tentative pour faire qch ; (*in speech, lecture*) **one ~ point** enfin, un dernier point ; **to put the ~ touches to sth** mettre la dernière main à qch ; **a ~-year student** un étudiant de dernière année **b** (= *conclusive*) [*decree, result, approval, answer, draft*] définitif ; **the judges' decision is ~** la décision des arbitres est sans appel ; **to have the ~ say** avoir le dernier mot ; **and that's ~!** un point c'est tout !, point final ! → **analysis, arbiter, say c** (= *ultimate*) [*humiliation*] suprême ; **the ~ irony is that he …** comble de l'ironie, il … ; **he paid for the ~ penalty for his crime** il a payé son crime de sa vie **d** (*Philos*) [*cause*] final
2 N **a** (*Sport: US: also* ~**s**) finale *f* **b** (*Press*) **late night ~** dernière édition *f* (du soir)
3 **finals** NPL (*Univ*) examens *mpl* de dernière année
4 COMP ▶ **the final curtain** N (*Theat*) la chute du rideau ▶ **final demand** N (*Comm*) dernier rappel *m* ▶ **final dividend** N (*Fin*) solde *m* de dividende ▶ **final edition** N (*Press*) dernière édition *f* ▶ **final examinations** NPL (*Univ*) examens *mpl* de dernière année ▶ **the Final Four** NPL (*US Basketball*) les demi-finalistes *mpl* ▶ **final instalment** N (*Fin*) versement *m* libératoire ▶ **final notice** N (*Comm*) dernier rappel *m* ▶ **the Final Solution** N (*Hist*) la solution finale ▶ **the final whistle** N (*Ftbl*) le coup de sifflet final

finale [fɪˈnɑːlɪ] N (*Mus, fig*) finale *m* ; (*fig*) **the grand ~** l'apothéose *f*

finalist [ˈfaɪnəlɪst] N (*Sport*) finaliste *mf* ; (*Univ*)

▶ LANGUAGE IN USE: **final** 26.1

étudiant qui passe ses examens de la dernière année

finality [faɪˈnælɪtɪ] N [of decision etc] caractère m définitif, irrévocabilité f; **to say sth with an air of ~** dire qch sur un ton sans réplique

finalization [ˌfaɪnəlaɪˈzeɪʃən] N [of deal] finalisation f; [of text, report] rédaction f définitive; [of details] mise f au point; [of arrangements, plans] mise f au point des détails

finalize [ˈfaɪnəlaɪz] VT [+ text, report] rédiger la version définitive de, finaliser; [+ arrangements, plans, preparations] mettre au point les derniers détails de, mettre la dernière main à; [+ details] mettre au point; [+ decision] confirmer; [+ date] fixer de façon définitive; **their divorce is now ~d** le divorce est maintenant prononcé

▼ **finally** [ˈfaɪnəlɪ] ADV a (= eventually) enfin, finalement; **women ~ got the vote in 1918** les femmes ont enfin or finalement obtenu le droit de vote en 1918 b (= lastly) pour finir, pour terminer; **~ I would like to say ...** pour terminer or pour finir je voudrais dire ... c (= definitively) [decide, settle] définitivement

finance [faɪˈnæns] 1 N (NonC) finance f; **high ~** la haute finance; **Minister/Ministry of Finance** ministre m/ministère m des Finances 2 **finances** NPL finances fpl; **his ~s aren't sound** ses finances ne sont pas solides; **the country's ~s** la situation financière du pays; **he hasn't the ~ to do that** il n'a pas les finances or les fonds mpl pour cela 3 VT [+ scheme etc] (= supply money for) financer, commanditer; (= obtain money for) trouver des fonds pour 4 COMP (Press) [news, page] financier ► **finance bill** N (Parl) projet m de loi de finances ► **finance company**, **finance house** N compagnie f financière, société f de financement

financial [faɪˈnænʃəl] 1 ADJ (gen) financier; **to depend on sb for ~ support** dépendre financièrement de qn 2 COMP ► **financial accounting** N (Comm) comptabilité f générale ► **financial aid office** N (US Univ Admin) service m des bourses ► **financial management** N (Comm) gestion f financière ► **financial plan** N plan m de financement ► **financial services** NPL services mpl financiers ► **Financial Times index**, **Financial Times Stock Exchange 100 Index** N (Brit St Ex) indice m FT ► **financial year** N (Brit) exercice m budgétaire

financially [faɪˈnænʃəlɪ] ADV [secure, independent, viable] financièrement; **to benefit ~** profiter financièrement; **to be struggling ~** avoir des problèmes financiers; **~, things are a bit tight** financièrement, la situation n'est pas facile

financier [faɪˈnænsɪəʳ] N financier m

finch [fɪntʃ] N fringillidé m (pinson, bouvreuil, gros-bec etc)

find [faɪnd] (pret, ptp **found**) 1 VT a (gen) trouver; [+ lost person or object] retrouver; **he was trying to ~ his gloves** il cherchait ses gants, il essayait de retrouver ses gants; **I never found my keys** je n'ai jamais retrouvé mes clés; **your book is not** or **nowhere to be found** on ne parvient pas à retrouver votre livre, votre livre reste introuvable; **to ~ one's place in a book** retrouver sa page dans un livre; **they soon found him again** ils l'ont vite retrouvé; **they couldn't ~ the way back** ils n'ont pas pu trouver le chemin du retour; **I'll ~ my way about all right by myself** je trouverai très bien mon chemin tout seul; **can you ~ your own way out?** pouvez-vous trouver la sortie tout seul?; **to ~ one's way into a building** trouver l'entrée d'un bâtiment; **it found its way into my bag** ça s'est retrouvé or ça a atterri* dans mon sac; **it found its way into his essay** ça s'est glissé dans sa dissertation; **we left everything as we found it** nous avons tout laissé tel quel; **he was found dead in bed** on l'a trouvé

mort dans son lit; **the castle is to be found near Tours** le château se trouve près de Tours; **this flower is found all over England** on trouve cette fleur or cette fleur se trouve partout en Angleterre; **to ~ one's** or **its mark** atteindre son but; **to ~ work** trouver du travail

b (reflexive vb) **he found himself in Paris** il s'est retrouvé à Paris; **I found myself smiling/looking/wondering** je me suis surpris à sourire/regarder/me demander; **I found myself thinking that ...** je me suis surpris à penser que ...; **to my surprise, I found myself having fun** à mon grand étonnement, je me suis amusé; **I found myself quite at sea among all those scientists** je me suis senti complètement perdu au milieu de tous ces scientifiques; (fig) **he found himself at last** il a enfin trouvé sa voie

c (fig: gen) trouver (that que); **I can never ~ anything to say to him** je ne trouve jamais rien à lui dire; **to ~ the courage to do** trouver le courage de faire; **I can't ~ time to read** je n'arrive pas à trouver le temps de lire; (fig) **to ~ one's voice** trouver son style; (fig) **to ~ one's feet** s'adapter, s'acclimater; **to ~ some difficulty in doing** éprouver une certaine difficulté à faire; **I couldn't ~ it in my heart to refuse** je n'ai pas eu le cœur de refuser; **how did you ~ him?** (in health) comment l'avez-vous trouvé?; **how did you ~ the steak?** comment avez-vous trouvé le bifteck?; **I ~ her very pleasant** je la trouve très agréable; **he found it impossible to leave** il n'arrivait pas à partir; **he ~s it difficult/impossible to walk** il lui est difficile/impossible de marcher; **he ~s it tiring/encouraging** etc il trouve que c'est fatigant/encourageant etc; **you won't ~ it easy** vous ne trouverez pas cela facile; **we're sure you'll ~ the film exciting** nous sommes sûrs que vous trouverez ce film captivant!; **I ~ that I have plenty of time** il se trouve que j'ai tout le temps qu'il faut → **expression**, **fault**, **favour**

d (= perceive, realize) constater (that que); (= discover) constater, constater (that que); [+ cure] découvrir; [+ solution] trouver, découvrir; [+ answer] trouver; **you will ~ that I am right** vous verrez or vous constaterez que j'ai raison; **it has been found that one person in ten does this** on a constaté qu'une personne sur dix fait cela; **I went there yesterday, only to ~ her out** j'y suis allé hier, pour constater qu'elle était sortie

e (Jur) **to ~ sb guilty** déclarer qn coupable; **how do you ~ the accused?** quel est votre verdict?; **to ~ a verdict of guilty** rendre or prononcer un verdict de culpabilité; **the court found that ...** le tribunal a conclu que ...

f (= supply) fournir; (= obtain) obtenir, trouver; **wages £150 all found** salaire de 150 livres logé (et) nourri; (US) **wages 500 dollars and found** salaire de 500 dollars logé (et) nourri; **who will ~ the money for the trip?** qui va trouver l'argent pour le voyage?; **I can't ~ the money to do it** je ne peux pas trouver l'argent nécessaire pour le faire; **go and ~ me a needle** va me chercher une aiguille; **can you ~ me a pen?** peux-tu me trouver un stylo?; **there are no more to be found** il n'en reste plus

2 VI (Jur) **to ~ for/against the accused** se prononcer en faveur de/contre l'accusé

3 N trouvaille f; **that was a lucky ~** nous avons (or vous avez etc) eu de la chance de trouver or de découvrir cela

▶ **find out** 1 VI a (= make enquiries) se renseigner (about sur) b (= discover) **we didn't ~ out about it in time** nous ne l'avons pas su or appris à temps; **your mother will ~ out if you ... ** ta mère le saura si tu ... 2 VT SEP a (= discover) découvrir (that que); [+ answer] trouver; [+ sb's secret, character] découvrir; **I found out what he was really like** j'ai découvert son vrai caractère b (= discover the misdeeds etc of) [+ person] démasquer; **he thought we**

wouldn't know, but we found him out il pensait que nous ne saurions rien, mais nous l'avons démasqué or nous avons découvert le pot aux roses*; **this affair has really found him out** il s'est bel et bien révélé tel qu'il est or sous son vrai jour dans cette affaire

finder [ˈfaɪndəʳ] 1 N a (of lost object) personne f qui trouve; (Jur) inventeur m, -trice f; **~s keepers (losers weepers)!** (celui) qui le trouve le garde (et tant pis pour celui qui l'a perdu)! b [of telescope] chercheur m → **viewfinder** 2 COMP ► **finder's fee** N (US) prime f d'intermédiaire

findings [ˈfaɪndɪŋz] NPL a (= conclusions, deductions) [of person, committee] conclusions fpl, constatations fpl; [of scientist, researcher] conclusions fpl, résultats mpl (des recherches); (Jur) conclusions fpl, verdict m b (= objects etc unearthed) découvertes fpl

fine¹ [faɪn] 1 N amende f, contravention f (esp Aut); **I got a ~ for going through a red light** j'ai eu une amende or j'ai attrapé une contravention pour avoir brûlé un feu rouge 2 VT condamner à une amende, donner une contravention à (esp Aut); **he was ~d £30** il a eu une amende de 30 livres, il a eu 30 livres d'amende; **they ~d him heavily** ils l'ont condamné à une lourde amende; **he was ~d for exceeding the speed limit** il a eu une amende or une contravention pour excès de vitesse; **she was ~d for possession of drugs** elle a été condamnée à une amende pour détention de stupéfiants

fine² [faɪn] 1 ADJ a (= excellent) [performer, player, piece of work] excellent; [place, object, example] beau (belle f); [view] superbe; **the ~st footballer of his generation** le meilleur footballeur de sa génération; **to be in ~ form** être en pleine forme; **you're doing a ~ job** vous faites un excellent travail; **to be in ~ health** être en bonne santé; **it's a ~ thing to help others** c'est beau d'aider autrui; **it was his ~st hour** or **moment** ce fut son heure de gloire → **finest**; → **fettle**, **figure** b (= acceptable) bien inv; **how was I? — you were ~** comment je me suis débrouillé? — bien; **the wallpaper looks ~** le papier peint est bien; **you look ~** tu es très bien; **your idea sounds ~** votre idée semble bonne; **the coffee's just ~** le café est parfait; **everything's ~** tout va bien; **everything's going to be just ~** tout va bien se passer; **isn't the basket a bit too small?** — **it'll be ~** est-ce que le panier n'est pas un peu trop petit? — ça ira; **any questions? no? ~!** des questions? non? parfait!; **it's ~ to interrupt me** vous pouvez m'interrompre; **it's ~ for men to cry** il n'y a rien de mal à ce que les hommes pleurent; **it's ~ for two** c'est très bien pour deux personnes; **the hotel is ~ for a weekend break** l'hôtel convient pour un séjour d'un week-end; **this bike is ~ for me** ce vélo me convient; **these apples are ~ for cooking** ces pommes sont parfaites comme pommes à cuire; **that's all very ~, but ...** c'est bien beau or bien joli mais ... c (= not unwell) **to be ~** aller bien; **a glass of water and I'll be ~** un verre d'eau et ça ira; **don't worry, I'm sure he'll be ~** ne t'inquiète pas, je suis sûr qu'il se remettra; **to feel ~** se sentir bien; **he looks ~** il a l'air en forme; **how are you? — ~ thanks** comment allez-vous? — bien, merci d (= without problems) **she'll be ~, the others will look after her** il ne lui arrivera rien, les autres s'occuperont d'elle; **I'll be ~ on my own** je me débrouillerai très bien tout seul e (expressing agreement) très bien; **I'll be back by lunchtime — ~!** je serai de retour à l'heure du déjeuner — très bien!; **that's ~ by** or **with me** d'accord; **if you want to give me a hand, that's ~ by me** tu veux me donner un coup de main, je veux bien; **it'll take me a couple of days — that's ~ by** or **with me** ça va

► LANGUAGE IN USE: **finally** 26.1, 26.2

me prendre quelques jours — d'accord ; **anything she wanted was usually ~ with me** il était en général d'accord avec tout ce qu'elle demandait ; **shall we have another beer? — ~ by me** or **sounds ~ to me!** on prend encore une bière ? — bonne idée !

[f] (iro) **that's ~ for you to say** c'est facile à dire ; **a ~ friend you are!** c'est beau l'amitié ! ; **that's another ~ mess you've got(ten) me into!** tu m'as encore mis dans un beau pétrin ! ; **you're a ~ one!** t'es bon, toi !* ; **you're a ~ one to talk!** ça te va bien de dire ça ! ; **~ words** belles paroles fpl

[g] (= honourable, refined) [person] bien inv ; [feelings] raffiné ; **he has no ~r feelings** il n'a aucune noblesse de sentiment

[h] (= superior) [food, ingredients] raffiné ; [wine] fin ; [furniture, china, fabric, clothes] beau (belle f), raffiné ; [jewellery] précieux ; [metal] pur ; [workmanship] délicat ; **~ gold** or **~ fin** ; **meat of the ~st quality** viande f de première qualité ; **~ ladies and gentlemen** les beaux messieurs mpl et les belles dames fpl ; **she likes to play at being the ~ lady** elle aime jouer les grandes dames

[i] (= delicate) [fabric, powder, rain, hair, features, bones] fin ; [net, mesh] à mailles fines ; [mist] léger → **print**

[j] (= subtle) [adjustment] minutieux ; [detail, distinction] subtil ; **there's a ~ line between genius and madness/fact and fiction** entre le génie et la folie/la réalité et la fiction, la marge est étroite or la distinction est subtile ; **not to put too ~ a point on it** pour parler franchement ; **the ~r points of English grammar** les subtilités de la grammaire anglaise

[k] [weather, day] beau (belle f) ; **it's been ~ all week** il a fait beau toute la semaine ; **all areas will be ~ tomorrow** il fera beau partout demain ; **coastal areas will be ~** il fera beau sur la côte ; **I hope it keeps ~ for you!** j'espère que vous continuerez à avoir beau temps ! ; **one ~ day** un beau jour ; (fig) **one of these ~ days** un de ces quatre matins, un de ces jours

[2] ADV [a] (* = well) bien ; **you're doing ~!** tu te débrouilles bien !* ; **we get on ~** nous nous entendons bien ; **that suits me ~** ça me convient très bien

[b] (= not coarsely) **to chop sth ~** hacher qch menu ; (lit) **to cut sth ~** couper qch en tranches fines ; (fig) **to cut it ~** ne pas se laisser de marge ; **you're cutting it too ~** vous comptez trop juste

[3] COMP ► **fine art** N (= subject) beaux-arts mpl ; (= works) objets mpl d'art ; **the ~ arts** les beaux-arts mpl ; **a ~ art** un véritable art ; **to get sth down** or **off to a ~ art** faire qch à la perfection ► **fine-drawn** ADJ [wire, thread] finement étiré ► **fine-grained** ADJ [wood] au grain fin ; (Phot) à grain fin ► **fine-spun** ADJ [yarn] très fin, ténu ► **fine-toothcomb** N peigne m fin ; **he went through the documents with a ~toothcomb** il a passé les documents au peigne fin or au crible ► **fine-tune** VT (fig) [+ production, the economy] régler avec précision ► **fine-tuning** N réglage m minutieux

►**fine down** [1] VI (= get thinner) s'affiner [2] VT SEP (= reduce) réduire ; (= simplify) simplifier ; (= refine) raffiner

finely ['faɪnlɪ] ADV [a] (= exquisitely) [crafted, carved] finement ; [written, painted] avec finesse ; **~ detailed** aux détails précis [b] (= not coarsely) [chop] menu ; [cut, slice] en tranches fines ; [grate, grind] fin ; **to dice sth ~** couper qch en petits dés [c] (= delicately) **the case was ~ balanced** l'issue du procès était tangente ; **the distinction was ~ drawn** la distinction était très subtile ; **a ~ judged speech** un discours avec des propos bien choisis ; **a ~ tuned car** une voiture réglée avec précision ; **a ~ tuned mind** un esprit aiguisé

fineness ['faɪnnɪs] N [a] [of hair, powder, features, wine, material, china, clothes] finesse f ; [of workmanship] délicatesse f ; [of feelings] no-

blesse f ; [of detail, point, distinction] subtilité f [b] [of metal] titre m

finery ['faɪnərɪ] N parure† f ; **she wore all her ~** elle était parée de ses plus beaux atours† ; **wedding guests in all their ~** les invités d'un mariage vêtus de leurs plus beaux habits

finesse [fɪ'nes] [1] N finesse f ; (Cards) impasse f [2] VI (Cards) **to ~ against the King** faire l'impasse au roi [3] VT [a] (= manage skilfully) [+ details] peaufiner ; [+ problem, questions] aborder avec finesse ; (= avoid) esquiver ; **the skier ~d the difficulties of the mountain** le skieur s'est joué des difficultés de la montagne ; (pej) **no doubt he will try to ~ the problem** il cherchera sans doute à esquiver le problème [b] (Cards) **to ~ the Queen** faire l'impasse en jouant la dame

finest ['faɪnɪst] NPL (US: iro = police) **Chicago's/the city's ~** la police de Chicago/de la ville ; **one of New York's ~** un agent de police newyorkais

finger ['fɪŋgəʳ] [1] N [a] (Anat) doigt m ; **first** or **index ~** index m → **little, middle, ring** ; **between ~ and thumb** entre le pouce et l'index ; **to count on one's ~s** compter sur ses doigts ; **I can count on the ~s of one hand the number of times he has …** je peux compter sur les doigts d'une main le nombre de fois où il a … ; **to point one's ~ at sb** montrer qn du doigt → **1b**

[b] (fig phrases) **he wouldn't lift a ~ to help me** il ne lèverait pas le petit doigt pour m'aider ; **to point the ~ at sb** (= accuse) montrer qn du doigt ; (= identify) identifier qn ; **to point the ~ of suspicion at sb** faire peser des soupçons sur qn ; **to point the ~ of blame at sb** faire porter le blâme à qn ; **to keep one's ~s crossed** croiser les doigts ; **(keep your) ~s crossed!** croisons les doigts ! ; **keep your ~s crossed for me!** souhaite-moi bonne chance ! ; **to put** or **stick two ~s up at sb** (Brit) ◊ **to give sb the ~** (US) ≈ faire un bras d'honneur* à qn ; **to put one's ~ on the difficulty** mettre le doigt sur la difficulté ; **there's something wrong, but I can't put my ~ on it** il y a quelque chose qui cloche* mais je ne peux pas mettre le doigt dessus ; **to put the ~ on sb** (= betray) dénoncer qn ; (= indicate as victim) désigner qn comme victime ; **to pull** or **get one's ~ out** se décarcasser* ; **pull your ~ out!** remue-toi !* → **green, pie, pulse, thumb**

[c] [of cake etc] petite part f ; [of whisky] doigt m ; [of land] langue f

[2] VT [a] (= touch) toucher or manier (des doigts) ; (pej) tripoter ; [+ money] palper ; [+ keyboard, keys] toucher

[b] (Mus = mark fingering on) doigter, indiquer le doigté sur

[c] (esp US‡ = betray) moucharder*, balancer‡

[3] COMP ► **finger alphabet** N alphabet m des sourds-muets ► **finger board** N (Mus) touche f (de guitare ou de violon etc) ► **finger bowl** N rince-doigts m inv ► **finger buffet** N buffet m d'amuse-gueule(s) ► **finger-dry** VT **to ~-dry one's hair** passer les doigts dans ses cheveux pour les faire sécher ► **finger exercises** NPL (for piano etc) exercices mpl de doigté ► **finger food** N amuse-gueule(s) m(pl) ► **finger painting** N peinture f avec les doigts ► **finger plate** N (on door) plaque f de propreté ► **finger print** N empreinte f digitale

fingering ['fɪŋgərɪŋ] N [a] (Mus) doigté m [b] (= fine wool) laine f (fine) à tricoter [c] [of goods in shop etc] maniement m

fingermark ['fɪŋgəmaːk] N trace f or marque f de doigts

fingernail ['fɪŋgəneɪl] N ongle m

fingerprint ['fɪŋgəprɪnt] [1] N empreinte f digitale [2] VT [+ car, weapon] relever les empreintes digitales sur ; [+ room, building] relever les empreintes digitales dans ; [+ person] relever les empreintes digitales de [3] COMP

► **fingerprint expert** N spécialiste mf en empreintes digitales, expert m en dactyloscopie

fingerstall ['fɪŋgəstɔːl] N doigtier m

fingertip ['fɪŋgətɪp] [1] N bout m du doigt ; **all the basic controls are at your ~s** toutes les commandes principales sont à portée de votre main ; **I had the information at my ~s** (= near to hand) j'avais ces informations à portée de main ; **he's a politician to his ~s** c'est un homme politique jusqu'au bout des ongles [2] COMP ► **fingertip control** N **a machine with ~ control** une machine d'un maniement (très) léger ► **fingertip hold** N (Climbing) gratton m

finial ['faɪnɪəl] N fleuron m, épi m (de faîtage)

finicky ['fɪnɪkɪ] ADJ [person] pointilleux, tatillon ; [work, job] minutieux, qui demande de la patience ; **don't be so ~!** ne fais pas le (or la) difficile ! ; **she is ~ about her food** elle est difficile pour or sur la nourriture

finish ['fɪnɪʃ] [1] N [a] (= end) fin f ; [of race] arrivée f ; (Climbing) sortie f ; (Hunting) mise à mort f ; (fig) **to be in at the ~** assister au dénouement (d'une affaire) ; **to fight to the ~** se battre jusqu'au bout ; **from start to ~** du début à la fin → **photo**

[b] (= surface, look) [of woodwork, manufactured articles] finition f ; **it's a solid car but the ~ is not good** la voiture est solide mais les finitions sont mal faites ; **a car with a two-tone ~** une voiture (peinte) en deux tons ; **paint with a matt ~** peinture f mate ; **paint with a gloss ~** laque f ; **table with an oak ~** (stained) table f teintée chêne ; (veneered) table f plaquée or à placage chêne ; **a table with rather a rough ~** une table à la surface plutôt rugueuse

[2] VT [+ activity, work, letter, game, meal, supplies, cake] finir, terminer ; **~ your soup** finis or mange ta soupe ; **to ~ doing sth** finir de faire qch ; **I'm in a hurry to get this job ~ed** je suis pressé de finir or de terminer ce travail ; **to ~ a book** finir or terminer un livre ; **to put the ~ing touch** or **touches to sth** mettre la dernière main or la touche finale à qch ; **that last mile nearly ~ed me** ces derniers quinze cents mètres ont failli m'achever or m'ont mis à plat* → **finished**

[3] VI [a] [book, film, game, meeting] finir, se terminer ; [holiday, contract] prendre fin ; [runner, horse] arriver, terminer ; (St Ex) clôturer, terminer ; (Climbing) sortir ; **the meeting was ~ing** la réunion tirait à sa fin ; (St Ex) **our shares ~ed at $70** nos actions cotaient 70 dollars en clôture or en fin de séance ; **he ~ed by saying that …** il a terminé en disant que … ; (in race) **to ~ well** arriver en bonne position ; **to ~ first** arriver or terminer premier

[b] **I've ~ed with the paper** je n'ai plus besoin du journal ; **I've ~ed with politics once and for all** j'en ai fini avec la politique, j'ai dit une fois pour toutes adieu à la politique ; (in relationship) **she's ~ed with him*** elle l'a plaqué* ; **you wait till I've ~ed with you!** attends un peu que je te règle ton compte !*

►**finish off** [1] VI terminer, finir ; **let's ~ off now** maintenant finissons-en ; **to ~ off with a glass of brandy** terminer par or sur un verre de cognac ; **the meeting ~ed off with a prayer** la réunion a pris fin sur une prière, à la fin de la réunion on a récité une prière [2] VT SEP [a] [+ work] terminer, mettre la dernière main à [b] [+ food, meal] terminer, finir ; **~ off your potatoes!** finis or mange tes pommes de terre ! [c] (* fig = kill) [+ person, wounded animal] achever ; **his illness last year almost ~ed him off** sa maladie de l'année dernière a failli l'achever

►**finish up** [1] VI [a] = **finish off 1** [b] se retrouver ; **he ~ed up in Rome** il s'est retrouvé à Rome, il a fini à Rome [2] VT SEP = **finish off 2b**

finished ['fɪnɪʃt] ADJ [a] (= at end of activity) **to be ~** [person] avoir fini ; (US) **to be ~ doing sth** avoir fini de or terminé de faire qch ; (= have completed) **to be ~ with sth** avoir fini qch ; **he was ~ with marriage** le mariage, pour lui, c'était fini ; **to be ~ with sb** (after questioning) en avoir fini avec qn ; (= have had enough of) ne plus vouloir entendre parler de qn [b] (= at its end) [fighting, life] être fini ; [performance, trial] être fini or terminé [c] (= tired) **to be ~*** être crevé* [d] (= without a future) **to be ~** [politician, sportsperson, career] être fini [e] (= decorated) **the room is ~ in red** la pièce a des finitions rouges ; **the bedroom is ~ with cream curtains** les rideaux crème complètent harmonieusement le décor de la chambre ; **the jacket is beautifully ~ with hand-sewn lapels** la veste est joliment finie avec des revers cousus main ; **beautifully ~ wood** du bois magnifiquement fini [f] (= final) [product, goods, painting, film] fini ; [result] final ; **the ~ article** (= product) le produit fini ; (= piece of writing) la version finale ; **he's the ~ article*** il est génial*

finisher ['fɪnɪʃə'] N (Sport) **a fast ~** un finisseur or une finisseuse rapide ; **a strong ~** un bon finisseur, une bonne finisseuse ; **a good ~** (Ftbl) un bon buteur ; (Rugby, Hockey etc) un bon marqueur, une bonne marqueuse

finishing ['fɪnɪʃɪŋ] [1] N (Ftbl) dons mpl de buteur ; (Rugby, Hockey etc) dons mpl de marqueur ; **his ~ is excellent** c'est un très bon buteur or marqueur [2] COMP ► **finishing line** N ligne f d'arrivée ; **to cross the ~ line** (Sport) franchir la ligne d'arrivée ; (fig) toucher au but ► **finishing school** N institution f pour jeunes filles (de bonne famille)

finite ['faɪnaɪt] [1] ADJ [a] (= limited) [number, set, being, world, universe] fini ; [amount, period, life, resources] limité [b] (Gram) [verb] dont la forme est fixée par le temps et la personne ; [clause] à forme verbale fixée par le temps et la personne [2] COMP ► **finite state grammar** N grammaire f à états finis

fink: [fɪŋk] (US pej) [1] N (= strikebreaker) jaune* m ; (= informer) mouchard* m, indic* m ; (= unpleasant person) sale type m [2] VT moucharder*, dénoncer

► **fink out:** VI (US) échouer, laisser tomber

Finland ['fɪnlənd] N la Finlande

Finn [fɪn] N (gen) Finlandais(e) m(f) ; (also ~ish speaker) Finnois(e) m(f)

Finnish ['fɪnɪʃ] [1] ADJ (gen) finlandais ; [ambassador, embassy] de Finlande ; [teacher] de finnois ; [literature, culture, civilization] finnois [2] N (Ling) finnois m

Finno-Ugric ['fɪnəʊ'uːɡrɪk], **Finno-Ugrian** ['fɪnəʊ'uːɡrɪən] N, ADJ (Ling) finno-ougrien m

fiord [fjɔːd] N fjord or fiord m

fir [fɜː'] N (also ~ tree) sapin m ; ~ **cone** pomme f de pin

fire [faɪə'] [1] N [a] (gen) feu m ; (= blaze) incendie m ; **~!** au feu ! ; **the house was on ~** la maison était en feu or en flammes ; **the chimney was on ~** il y avait un feu de cheminée ; **forest ~** incendie m de forêt ; **to insure o.s. against ~** s'assurer contre l'incendie ; **to lay/light/make up the ~** préparer/allumer/faire le feu ; **come and sit by the ~** venez vous installer près du feu or au coin du feu ; **I was sitting in front of a roaring ~** j'étais assis devant une belle flambée ; **to set ~ to sth ◊ to set sth on ~** mettre le feu à qch ; (fig) **to set the world on ~** révolutionner le monde ; **he'll never set the world** or **the Thames** (Brit) or **the heather** (Scot) **on ~** il n'impressionnera jamais par ses prouesses ; **to catch ~** (lit) prendre feu ; (fig) [play, film, idea] décoller ; **her dress caught ~** sa robe s'est enflammée or a pris feu ; (fig) **the issue caught ~** la question est devenue brûlante or délicate ; (fig) **~ and brimstone** les tourments mpl (liter) de l'enfer → **4** ; **by ~ and**

sword par le fer et par le feu ; **he would go through ~ and water for her** il se jetterait dans le feu pour elle ; **to have ~ in one's belly** avoir le feu sacré → **play**
[b] (Brit = heater) radiateur m → **electric**
[c] (Mil) feu m ; **to open ~** ouvrir le feu, faire feu ; **~!** feu ! ; (fig) **between two ~s** entre deux feux ; **under ~** sous le feu de l'ennemi ; **to come under ◊ ~** (Mil) essuyer le feu (de l'ennemi) ; (fig = be criticized) essuyer des critiques ; **to return ~** riposter par le feu ; **to hang** or **hold ~** [guns] faire long feu ; (on plans etc) traîner (en longueur) ; **to hold one's ~** (= stop firing) suspendre le tir ; (= hold back) ne pas tirer ; **to fight ~ with ~** combattre le feu par le feu → **ceasefire, line¹**
[d] (NonC = passion) ardeur f, feu m (liter) ; **to speak with ~** parler avec feu (liter) or avec ardeur
[2] VT [a] (= set fire to) incendier, mettre le feu à ; (fig) [+ imagination, passions, enthusiasm] enflammer, exciter ; **~d with the desire to do** brûlant de faire → **gas, oil**
[b] [+ gun] décharger, tirer ; [+ rocket] tirer ; (* = throw) balancer* ; **to ~ a gun at sb** tirer (un coup de fusil) sur qn ; **to ~ a shot** tirer un coup de feu (at sur) ; **without firing a shot** sans tirer un coup (de feu) ; **to ~ a salute** or a salvo lancer or tirer une salve ; **to ~ a salute of 21 guns** saluer de 21 coups de canon ; **she ~d an elastic band at me*** elle m'a tiré dessus* avec un élastique ; **to ~ (off) questions at sb** bombarder qn de questions ; **"your name?" suddenly ~d at me** « votre nom ? » me demanda-t-il à brûle-pourpoint
[c] (* = dismiss) virer*, renvoyer ; **you're ~d!** vous êtes viré* or renvoyé !
[d] [+ pottery] cuire ; [+ furnace] chauffer
[3] VI [a] [person] (gen) tirer ; (Mil, Police) faire feu (at sur) ; [gun] partir ; **the revolver failed to ~** le coup n'est pas parti ; (fig) **~ away** vas-y !, tu peux y aller
[b] [engine] tourner ; **it's only firing on two cylinders** il n'y a que deux cylindres qui marchent → **cylinder** ; **the engine is firing badly** le moteur tourne mal
[4] COMP ► **fire alarm** N alarme f d'incendie ► **fire-and-brimstone** ADJ [sermon, preacher] apocalyptique ► **fire appliance** N voiture f de pompiers ► **fire brigade** N (esp Brit) (brigade f des) (sapeurs-)pompiers mpl ► **fire chief** N (US) capitaine m des pompiers ► **fire clay** N (Brit) argile f réfractaire ► **fire curtain** N (Theat) rideau m de fer ► **fire department** N (US) = fire brigade ► **fire door** N porte f coupe-feu ► **fire drill** N exercice m d'évacuation (en cas d'incendie) ► **fire-eater** N (lit) cracheur m de feu ; (fig) belliqueux m, -euse f ► **fire engine** N (= vehicle) voiture f de pompiers ; (= apparatus) pompe f à incendie ► **fire escape** N (= staircase) escalier m de secours ; (= ladder) échelle f d'incendie ► **fire exit** N sortie f de secours ► **fire extinguisher** N extincteur m ► **fire fighter** N (= fireman) pompier m ; (volunteer) pompier m volontaire ► **fire-fighting** N lutte f contre les incendies or anti-incendie ♦ ADJ [equipment, team] de lutte contre les incendies or anti-incendie ► **fire hazard** N **it's a ~ hazard** cela pourrait provoquer un incendie ► **fire hydrant** N bouche f d'incendie ► **fire insurance** N assurance-incendie f ► **fire irons** NPL garniture f de foyer, accessoires mpl de cheminée ► **fire marshal** N (US) = fire chief ► **fire power** N (Mil) puissance f de feu ► **fire practice** N = fire drill ► **fire prevention** N mesures fpl de sécurité or de prévention contre l'incendie ► **fire-raiser** N (Brit) incendiaire mf, pyromane mf ► **fire-raising** N (Brit) pyromanie f ► **fire regulations** NPL consignes fpl en cas d'incendie ► **fire retardant** ADJ, N ignifuge m ► **fire sale** N (lit) vente de marchandises légèrement endommagées dans un incendie ;

(fig) braderie f ; **~-sale prices** prix mpl massacrés ► **fire screen** N écran m de cheminée ► **fire service** N = fire brigade ► **fire station** N caserne f de pompiers ► **fire trap** N **it's a ~ trap** c'est une véritable souricière en cas d'incendie ► **fire truck** N (US) = fire engine ► **fire warden** N (US) responsable mf de la lutte contre les incendies or anti-incendie ► **fire watcher** N guetteur m (dans la prévention contre les incendies) ► **fire watching** N surveillance f contre les incendies
► **fire away** VI → fire 3a
► **fire off** VT SEP → fire 2b

firearm ['faɪər,ɑːm] N arme f à feu

fireback ['faɪəbæk] N (of chimney) contrecœur m, contre-feu m

fireball ['faɪəbɔːl] N (= meteor) bolide m ; (= lightning, nuclear) boule f de feu ; (Mil) bombe f explosive ; (fig) **he's a real ~** il pète le feu*

Firebird ['faɪəbɜːd] N **The ~** (Mus) l'Oiseau m de feu

firebomb ['faɪəbɒm] [1] N bombe f incendiaire [2] VT lancer une (or des) bombe(s) incendiaire(s) sur

firebrand ['faɪəbrænd] N (lit) brandon m ; **he's a real ~** (= energetic person) il pète le feu* ; (causing unrest) c'est un fauteur de troubles

firebreak ['faɪəbreɪk] N pare-feu m, coupe-feu m

firebrick ['faɪəbrɪk] N brique f réfractaire

firebug* ['faɪəbʌg] N incendiaire mf, pyromane mf

firecracker ['faɪə,krækə'] N pétard m

firedamp ['faɪədæmp] N (Min) grisou m

firedogs ['faɪədɒgz] NPL chenets mpl

firefight ['faɪəfaɪt] N (Mil) échange m de coups de feu

firefly ['faɪəflaɪ] N luciole f

fireguard ['faɪəgɑːd] N (in hearth) pare-feu m, pare-étincelles m ; (in forest) pare-feu m, coupe-feu m

firehouse ['faɪəhaʊs] N (US) = fire station ; → fire

firelight ['faɪəlaɪt] N lueur f du feu ; **by ~** à la lueur du feu

firelighter ['faɪə,laɪtə'] N allume-feu m ; (= sticks) ligot m

fireman ['faɪəmən] [1] N (pl -men) (in fire brigade) (sapeur-)pompier m ; (Rail) chauffeur m [2] COMP ► **fireman's lift** N **to give sb a ~'s lift** (Brit) porter qn sur l'épaule

fireplace ['faɪəpleɪs] N cheminée f, foyer m

fireplug ['faɪəplʌg] N (US) = fire hydrant ; → fire

fireproof ['faɪəpruːf] [1] VT ignifuger [2] ADJ [material] ignifugé, ininflammable [3] COMP ► **fireproof dish** N (Culin) plat m allant au feu ► **fireproof door** N porte f ignifugée or à revêtement ignifuge

fireside ['faɪəsaɪd] N foyer m, coin m du feu ; **~ chair** fauteuil m club ; (without arms) chauffeuse f

firestorm ['faɪəstɔːm] N (lit) incendie m dévastateur ; (US fig) **a ~ of protest** un tollé (général), une levée de boucliers ; **a ~ of criticism** une avalanche de critiques ; **a ~ of controversy** une vive controverse

firewater* ['faɪə,wɔːtə'] N alcool m, gnôle* f

firewood ['faɪəwʊd] N bois m de chauffage, bois m à brûler

firework ['faɪəwɜːk] [1] N (fusée f de) feu m d'artifice [2] **fireworks** NPL (also ~(s) display) feux mpl d'artifice

firing ['faɪərɪŋ] [1] N [of pottery] cuite f, cuisson f [b] (Mil) tir m ; (= gun battle) fusillade f [2] COMP ► **firing hammer** N [of firearm] percuteur m ► **firing line** N ligne f de tir ; **to be in the ~ line** (lit) être dans la ligne de tir ; (fig) être sous le feu des attaques ; (fig) **to be in sb's ~ line** être la cible de qn ; (fig) **to be out**

of the ~ line ne plus être sous le feu des attaques ► **firing pin** N = **firing hammer** ► **firing
squad** N peloton m d'exécution

firm¹ [fɜːm] N (Comm) entreprise f; (Brit Med)
there are four doctors in the ~* quatre médecins partagent le cabinet; (= Mafia) **the Firm***
la Mafia

firm² [fɜːm] **1** ADJ **a** (= hard) [fruit, ground,
muscles, breasts, handshake] ferme; **the cake
should be ~ to the touch** le gâteau doit être
ferme au toucher

b (= steady, secure) [table, ladder] stable;
[voice] ferme; **a sofa that provides ~ support
for the back** un canapé qui maintient bien le
dos; (lit) **to get** or **take a ~ grip** or **hold on**
[object, person] saisir fermement; (lit) **to have**
or **keep a ~ grip** or **hold on** [object, person] tenir fermement → **1c**

c (= strong, solid) [grasp, understanding] bon;
[foundation, base, support] solide; **to be on a ~
footing** [finances, relationship] être sain; **to put
sth on a ~ footing** établir qch sur une base solide; **to be in ~ control of sth** or **to keep sth
under ~ control** tenir qch bien en main; **it is
my ~ belief that ...** je crois fermement que ...;
to be a ~ believer in sth croire fermement à
qch; **it is my ~ conviction that ...** je suis
fermement convaincu que ...; **to have a ~
grasp of sth** [subject, theory] avoir une
connaissance solide de qch; **they became ~
friends** ils sont devenus de grands amis; **he's
a ~ favourite (with the young)** c'est une(e)
grand(e) favori(te) m(f) (parmi or chez les jeunes); **to have** or **keep a ~ grip on power** tenir
(fermement) les rênes du pouvoir; **to have** or
keep a ~ grip on spending surveiller de près
les dépenses

d (= resolute, determined) [person, leadership]
ferme; [action, measure] sévère; **to be ~ about
sth** être ferme à propos de qch; **with a ~ hand**
d'une main ferme; **to be ~ with sb** ◊ **to take a
~ hand with sb** être ferme avec qn ◊ **to take a
line** or **stand (against sth)** adopter une attitude ferme (contre qch); **to hold** or **stand ~
(against sth)** tenir bon (face à qch)

e (= definite, reliable) [agreement, conclusion,
decision] définitif; [commitment, intention]
ferme; [promise] formel; [information, news]
sûr; [evidence] solide; [date] fixé, arrêté;
(Comm) **~ offer** offre f ferme

f (Fin) [price] ferme, stable; [currency] stable;
the pound was ~ against the dollar la livre
était ferme par rapport au dollar; **to hold ~**
rester stable or ferme

2 VT = **firm up 2**
3 VI = **firm up 1**
► **firm up 1** VI [plans, programme] se préciser;
[muscles, stomach] se raffermir; (Fin) [currency]
se consolider **2** VT SEP [+ plans etc] préciser;
[+ muscles, stomach] raffermir; (Fin) [+ currency]
consolider

firmament [ˈfɜːməmənt] N firmament m; (fig)
she's a rising star in the political/movie ~ c'est
une étoile montante du monde politique/du
monde du cinéma

firmly [ˈfɜːmlɪ] ADV [fix, base] solidement; [an-
chor] profondément, solidement; [root] profondément; [shut, establish, stick] bien; [hold,
believe, maintain, reject, tell] fermement;
[speak, say] avec fermeté; [deny] formellement; **~ in place** bien en place; **legs ~ planted on the ground** les jambes bien plantées sur
le sol; **the jelly is ~ set** la gelée est bien
ferme; **to be ~ committed to doing sth** s'être
engagé à faire qch; **to be ~ in control of the
situation** avoir la situation bien en main; **~
entrenched attitudes** des attitudes très arrêtées; **~ held opinions** des convictions fpl; **~
opposed to sth** fermement opposé à sth; **she
had her sights ~ set on a career** elle avait bien
l'intention de faire carrière

firmly [ˈfɜːmlɪ]

firmness [ˈfɜːmnɪs] N [of person, object,
handshake, currency] fermeté f; [of step, voice,

manner] fermeté f, assurance f; **~ of purpose**
détermination f

firmware [ˈfɜːmweəʳ] N (Comput) microprogramme m

first [fɜːst] **1** ADJ premier; **the ~ of May** le premier mai; **the twenty-~ time** la vingt et unième fois; **Charles the First** Charles Premier,
Charles Iᵉʳ; **in the ~ place** en premier lieu,
d'abord; **~ principles** principes mpl premiers;
(Climbing) **~ ascent** première f; **he did it the
very ~ time** il l'a fait du premier coup; **it's not
the ~ time and it won't be the last** ce n'est pas
la première fois et ce ne sera pas la dernière;
they won for the ~ and last time in 1932 ils
ont gagné une seule et unique fois en 1932 or
pour la première et la dernière fois en 1932;
there's always a ~ time il y a un début à tout;
I haven't got the ~ idea* je n'en ai pas la
moindre idée; **she doesn't know the ~ thing
about it** elle est complètement ignorante là-
dessus; **he goes out ~ thing in the morning** (=
at early hour) il sort très tôt le matin; (= soon
after waking) il sort dès qu'il est levé; **I'll do it
~ thing in the morning** or **~ thing tomorrow**
je le ferai dès demain matin, je le ferai demain
à la première heure; **take the pills ~ thing in
the morning** prenez les pilules dès le réveil; **~
things ~!** les choses importantes d'abord!
(hum) **she's past her ~ youth** elle n'est plus
de la première or prime jeunesse; (fig) **of the
~ water** de tout premier ordre → **4**; → **first-
class, floor, love, offender, sight**

2 ADV **a** (= at first) d'abord; (= firstly)
d'abord, premièrement; (= in the beginning)
au début; (= as a preliminary) d'abord, au
préalable; **~ you take off the string, then you
...** d'abord on enlève la ficelle, ensuite ..., premièrement on enlève la ficelle, deuxièmement on ...; **when we ~ lived here** quand nous
sommes venus habiter ici; **he accepted but ~
he wanted ...** il a accepté mais au préalable or
d'abord il voulait ...; **~ of all** ◊ **~ off*** tout
d'abord; **~ and foremost** tout d'abord, en
tout premier lieu; **he's a patriot ~ and a socialist second** il est patriote avant d'être socialiste, chez lui, le patriote l'emporte sur le
socialiste; **she arrived ~** elle est arrivée la première; **to come ~** (= arrive) arriver le premier;
(in exam, competition) être reçu premier; **my
family comes ~** ma famille passe avant tout or
compte plus que tout le reste; **one's health
comes ~** il faut penser à sa santé d'abord, la
santé est primordiale; **she comes ~ with him**
pour lui, elle compte plus que tout or elle
passe avant tout le reste; **it comes ~ with him**
pour lui, c'est ça qui compte avant tout or
c'est ça qui passe en premier; **~ come ~
served** les premiers arrivés seront les premiers
servis; **you go ~!** (gen) allez-y d'abord!; (in
doorway) passez devant!, après vous!; **ladies
~!** les dames d'abord!, place aux dames!;
women and children ~ les femmes et les
enfants d'abord; **he says ~ one thing and then
another** il se contredit sans cesse, il dit tantôt
ceci, tantôt cela; **she looked at ~ one thing
then another** elle regardait tantôt ceci, tantôt
cela; **~ you agree, then you change your mind!**
d'abord or pour commencer tu acceptes, et
ensuite tu changes d'avis!; **~ and last** avant
tout; **I must finish this ~** il faut que je termine
(subj) ceci d'abord

b (= for the first time) pour la première fois;
when did you ~ meet him? quand est-ce que
vous l'avez rencontré pour la première fois?

c (= in preference) plutôt; **I'd die ~!** plutôt
mourir!; **I'd resign ~!** je préfère démissionner!, plutôt démissionner!; **I'd give
up my job ~, rather than do that** j'aimerais
mieux renoncer à mon travail que de faire
cela

3 N **a** premier m, -ière f; **he was among the
very ~ to arrive** il est arrivé parmi les tout premiers; **they were the ~ to come** ils sont arrivés les premiers; **he was among the ~ to meet

her** il a été l'un des premiers à la rencontrer;
(= achievement) **another ~ for Britain** une nouvelle première pour la Grande-Bretagne;
(Ind) **~ in, ~ out** premier entré, premier sorti

b (NonC) commencement m, début m; **at ~**
d'abord, au commencement, au début; **from
~ to last** du début or depuis le début (jusqu')à
la fin; **they liked him from the ~** ils l'ont aimé
dès le début or dès le premier jour; **the ~ I
heard of it was when ...** je n'étais pas au courant, je l'ai appris quand ...; **that's the ~ I've
heard of it!** c'est la première fois que
j'entends parler de ça!

c (Aut: also **~ gear**) première f (vitesse); **in ~**
en première

d (Brit Univ) **he got a ~** ≈ il a eu sa licence
avec mention très bien; **to get a double ~**
obtenir sa licence avec mention très bien
dans deux disciplines

4 COMP ► **first aid** N → **first aid** ► **first
aider** N → **first aider** ► **the First Amendment (of the Constitution)** N (in US) le premier amendement de la constitution des
États-Unis ► **first base** N (Baseball) première
base f; (fig) **he didn't even get to ~ base*** il
n'a même pas franchi le premier obstacle
(fig); **these ideas didn't even get to ~ base** ces
idées n'ont jamais rien donné ► **first-born**
ADJ, N premier-né m, première-née f ► **first-
class** ADJ → **first-class** ► **the first couple** N
(US Pol) le couple présidentiel ► **first cousin**
N cousin(e) m(f) germain(e) ou au premier degré ► **first-day cover** N (Post) émission f du
premier jour ► **first edition** N première édition f; (valuable) édition f originale or
princeps ► **first-ever** ADJ tout premier
► **the first family** N (US Pol) la famille du
président ► **first floor** N **on the ~ floor** (Brit)
au premier (étage); (US) au rez-de-chaussée
► **first-foot** N (Scot) première personne à franchir le seuil d'une maison le premier janvier ♦ VI
rendre visite à ses parents ou amis après minuit
à la Saint-Sylvestre ► **first-footing** N (Scot)
coutume écossaise de rendre visite à ses parents
ou amis après minuit à la Saint-Sylvestre →
HOGMANAY ► **first form** N (Brit Scol) ≈
(classe f de) sixième f ► **first fruits** NPL (fig)
premiers résultats mpl ► **first-generation**
ADJ de première génération; **he's a ~-
generation American** c'est un Américain de
première génération ► **first grade** N (US
Scol) cours m préparatoire ► **first hand** N **I
got it at ~ hand** je l'ai appris de première
main ► **first-hand** ADJ [article, news, informa-
tion] de première main ► **first lady** N première dame f; (US Pol) présidente f des États-
Unis (ou personne servant d'hôtesse à sa place);
the ~ lady of jazz la plus grande dame du jazz
► **first language** N première langue f
► **first lieutenant** N (Brit Naut) lieutenant m
de vaisseau; (US Aviat) lieutenant m ► **first
mate** N (Naut) second m ► **first name** N prénom m, nom m de baptême; **my ~ name is
Ellis** mon prénom est Ellis ► **first-name** ADJ
to be on ~-name terms with sb appeler qn par
son prénom ► **the first-named** N (frm) le
premier, la première ► **first night** N (Theat
etc) première f ► **first-nighter** N (Theat etc)
habitué(e) m(f) des premières ► **first officer**
N (Naut) = **first mate** ► **first-past-the-post
system** N (Pol) système m majoritaire à un
tour ► **first performance** N (Cine, Theat)
première f; (Mus) première audition f ► **first
person** N (Gram) première personne f
► **first-rate** ADJ → **first-rate** ► **first school**
N (Brit) école f primaire (pour enfants de 5 à 8
ou 9 ans) ► **first strike capability** N (Mil)
capacité f de première frappe ► **first-time
buyer** N (primo-)accédant m à la propriété
► **first-timer*** N **a** (= novice) débutant(e)
m(f) **b** = **first-time buyer** ► **first violin** N
premier violon m ► **the First World** N les
pays mpl industrialisés ► **the First World
War** N la première guerre mondiale ► **first

year infants NPL (*Brit Scol*) cours *m* préparatoire ► **-first** [fɜːst] ADV (*in compounds*) **feet-first** les pieds devant → **head**

first aid [ˈfɜːstˈeɪd] **1** N premiers secours *mpl* or soins *mpl*, secours *mpl* d'urgence *m*; (= *subject of study*) secourisme *m*; **to give ~** donner des soins *or* secours d'urgence **2** COMP ► **first-aid box** N = **first-aid kit** ► **first-aid classes** NPL cours *mpl* de secourisme ► **first-aid kit** N trousse *f* de premiers secours *or* à pharmacie ► **first-aid post**, **first-aid station** N poste *m* de secours ► **first-aid worker** N secouriste *mf*

first aider [ˈfɜːstˈeɪdər] N secouriste *mf*

first-class [ˌfɜːstˈklɑːs] **1** ADJ **a** (= *first-rate*) [*food, facilities, service, hotel*] excellent; [*candidate, administrator*] remarquable, exceptionnel; **to have a ~ brain** être d'une intelligence exceptionnelle **b** [*Rail, Aviat, Naut*] [*travel, flight*] en première (classe); [*ticket, passenger, carriage, compartment*] de première (classe) **c** (*Post*) [*mail, letter, stamp*] en tarif prioritaire **d** (*Univ*) **a ~ (honours) degree** ≈ une licence avec mention très bien; **a ~ honours graduate** ≈ un(e) diplômé(e) qui a obtenu la mention très bien; **to graduate with ~ honours** ≈ obtenir son diplôme avec la mention très bien **2** ADV [*travel, fly*] en première classe; (*Post*) [*send, go*] en tarif prioritaire

▼ **firstly** [ˈfɜːstlɪ] ADV d'abord, premièrement, en premier lieu

first-rate [ˈfɜːstˈreɪt] ADJ excellent; **to do a ~ job** faire un excellent travail; **he's a ~ translator** c'est un traducteur de premier ordre *or* un excellent traducteur

firth [fɜːθ] N (*gen Scot*) estuaire *m*, bras *m* de mer; **the Firth of Clyde** l'estuaire *m* de la Clyde

FIS [ˌefaɪˈes] (*Brit*) ABBR = **Family Income Supplement**) → **family**

fiscal [ˈfɪskəl] **1** ADJ fiscal; **~ drag** ralentissement de l'économie dû à une fiscalisation excessive, fiscal drag *m* (*SPEC*); **~ year** année *f* fiscale, exercice *m* fiscal → **procurator** **2** N (*Scot Jur*) ≈ procureur *m* de la République

fiscalist [ˈfɪskəlɪst] N fiscaliste *mf*

fish [fɪʃ] **1** N (*pl* **fish** or **fishes**) **a** poisson *m*; **I caught two ~** j'ai pris deux poissons; **to play a ~** fatiguer un poisson; (*fig*) **I've got other ~ to fry** j'ai d'autres chats à fouetter; **there are plenty more ~ in the sea** (*gen*) les occasions ne manquent pas; (*relationship*) un(e) de perdu(e) dix de retrouvé(e)s; (*fig*) **it's neither ~ nor fowl** (*or nor flesh*) nor good red herring ce n'est ni chair ni poisson; **he's like a ~ out of water** il est comme un poisson hors de l'eau; **he's a queer ~!*** c'est un drôle de numéro* *or* de lascar* (celui-là)!; **poor ~!*** pauvre type!*; (*Astron*) **the Fishes** les Poissons *mpl* → **big, cold, drink, goldfish, kettle** **b** (*NonC: Culin*) poisson *m*
2 VI pêcher; **to go ~ing** aller à la pêche; **to go salmon ~ing** aller à la pêche au saumon; **to ~ for trout** pêcher la truite; (*fig*) **to ~ in troubled waters** pêcher en eau trouble (*fig*); **to ~ for compliments** chercher les compliments; **to ~ for information** aller à la pêche (aux informations); (*US*) **~ or cut bait*** allez, décide-toi!
3 VT [+ *trout, salmon*] pêcher; [+ *river, pool*] pêcher dans; (*fig*) **they ~ed the cat from the well** ils ont repêché le chat du puits; **he ~ed a handkerchief from his pocket** il a extirpé un mouchoir de sa poche; **where on earth did you ~ that (up) from?*** où diable as-tu été pêcher ça?*
4 COMP ► **fish and chips** N (*pl inv*) poisson *m* frit et frites ► **fish-and-chip shop** N friterie *f* ► **fish cake** N (*Culin*) croquette *f* de poisson ► **fish-eye** N (*in door*) œil *m* panoramique ► **fish-eye lens** N (*Phot*) fish-eye *m* ► **fish factory** N conserverie *f* de poisson ► **fish farm** N centre *m* de pisciculture, établissement *m* piscicole ► **fish farmer** N pisciculteur *m*, -trice *f* ► **fish farming** N pisciculture *f*, élevage *m* de poissons ► **fish fingers** NPL (*Brit*) bâtonnets *mpl* de poisson ► **fish fork** N fourchette *f* à poisson → **fish knife** ► **fish fry** N (*US*) pique-nique *m* (*où l'on fait frire du poisson*) ► **fish glue** N colle *f* de poisson ► **fish hook** N hameçon *m* ► **fish kettle** N (*Culin*) poissonnière *f* ► **fish knife** N (*pl* **fish knives**) couteau *m* à poisson; **~ knife and fork** couvert *m* à poisson → **fish fork** ► **fish ladder** N échelle *f* à poissons ► **fish manure** N engrais *m* de poisson ► **fish market** N (*retail*) marché *m* au poisson; (*wholesale*) criée *f* ► **fish meal** N (= *fertilizer*) guano *m* de poisson; (= *feed*) farine *f* de poisson ► **fish paste** N (*Culin*) beurre *m* de poisson ► **fish-pole** N (*US*) canne *f* à pêche ► **fish shop** N poissonnerie *f* ► **fish slice** N (*Brit Culin*) pelle *f* à poisson ► **fish sticks** NPL (*US*) = **fish fingers** ► **fish store** N (*US*) = **fish shop** ► **fish story*** N (*US*) histoire *f* de pêcheur, histoire *f* marseillaise ► **fish-tail** VI (*US*) [*car*] chasser ► **fish tank** N aquarium *m*

► **fish out** VT SEP (*from water*) sortir, repêcher; (*from box, drawer etc*) sortir, extirper (**from** de); **he ~ed out a piece of string from his pocket** il a extirpé un bout de ficelle de sa poche; **to ~ sb out of a river** repêcher qn d'une rivière

► **fish up** VT SEP (*from water*) pêcher, repêcher; (*from bag etc*) sortir → **fish 3**

fishbone [ˈfɪʃbəʊn] N arête *f*

fishbowl [ˈfɪʃbəʊl] N bocal *m* (à poissons)

fisher [ˈfɪʃər] N pêcheur *m*

fisherman [ˈfɪʃəmən] N (*pl* **-men**) pêcheur *m*; **he's a keen ~** il aime beaucoup la pêche; (*Brit fig*) **~'s tale** histoire *f* de pêcheur, histoire *f* marseillaise

fishery [ˈfɪʃərɪ] N pêcherie *f*, pêche *f*

fishing [ˈfɪʃɪŋ] **1** N pêche *f*; **"~ prohibited"** « pêche interdite », « défense de pêcher »; **"private ~"** « pêche réservée » **2** COMP ► **fishing boat** N barque *f* de pêche; (*bigger*) bateau *m* de pêche ► **fishing expedition** N **to go on a ~ expedition** (*lit*) aller à la pêche; (*fig*) chercher à en savoir plus long ► **fishing fleet** N flottille *f* de pêche ► **fishing grounds** NPL pêches *fpl*, lieux *mpl* de pêche ► **fishing harbour** N port *m* de pêche ► **fishing line** N ligne *f* de pêche ► **fishing net** N (*on fishing boat*) filet *m* (de pêche); [*of angler, child*] épuisette *f* ► **fishing permit** N permis *m* or licence *f* de pêche ► **fishing port** N port *m* de pêche ► **fishing rod** N canne *f* à pêche ► **fishing tackle** N attirail *m* de pêche

fishmonger [ˈfɪʃˌmʌŋgər] N (*esp Brit*) marchand(e) *m(f)* de poisson, poissonnier *m*, -ière *f*

fishnet [ˈfɪʃnet] **1** N (*on fishing boat*) filet *m* (de pêche); [*of angler*] épuisette *f* **2** COMP [*tights, stockings*] résille *inv*

fishplate [ˈfɪʃpleɪt] N (*Rail*) éclisse *f*

fishpond [ˈfɪʃpɒnd] N bassin *m* à poissons; (*in fish farming*) vivier *m*

fishwife [ˈfɪʃwaɪf] N (*pl* **-wives**) marchande *f* de poisson, poissonnière *f*; (*pej*) harengère *f*, poissarde *f*; (*pej*) **she talks like a ~** elle a un langage de poissarde, elle parle comme une marchande de poisson

fishy [ˈfɪʃɪ] ADJ **a** [*smell*] de poisson; **it smells ~ in here** ça sent le poisson ici **b** (* = *suspicious*) louche, douteux; **the whole business seems** *or* **smells very ~ to me** toute cette histoire m'a l'air bien louche; **it seems** *or* **smells rather ~** ça ne me paraît pas très catholique*

fissile [ˈfɪsaɪl] ADJ fissile

fission [ˈfɪʃən] N fission *f* → **nuclear**

fissionable [ˈfɪʃnəbl] ADJ fissible

fissure [ˈfɪʃər] N (*gen*) fissure *f*, crevasse *f*; (*Anat: in brain*) scissure *f*

fissured [ˈfɪʃəd] ADJ fissuré

fist [fɪst] **1** N poing *m*; **he hit me with his ~** il m'a donné un coup de poing; **he shook his ~ at me** il m'a menacé du poing **2** COMP ► **fist fight** N pugilat *m*, bagarre *f* à coups de poing; **to have a ~ fight (with sb)** se battre à coups de poing (avec qn)

fistful [ˈfɪstfʊl] N poignée *f*

fisticuffs [ˈfɪstɪkʌfs] NPL coups *mpl* de poing

fistula [ˈfɪstjʊlə] N (*pl* **fistulas** or **fistulae** [ˈfɪstjʊliː]) fistule *f*

fit¹ [fɪt] **1** ADJ **a** [*person*] (= *suitable, suited*) capable (**for** de); (= *worthy*) digne (**for** de); **he isn't ~ to rule the country** (= *not capable*) il n'est pas capable de gouverner le pays; (= *not worthy*) il n'est pas digne de gouverner le pays; **he's not ~ to drive** il n'est pas en mesure de conduire; **I'm not ~ to be seen** je ne suis pas présentable; **that shirt isn't ~ to wear** cette chemise n'est pas mettable; **~ to eat** (= *palatable*) mangeable; (= *not poisonous*) comestible, bon à manger; **~ to drink** (= *palatable*) buvable; (= *not poisonous*) potable; **~ for habitation** ◊ **~ to live in** habitable; **~ for (human) consumption** propre à la consommation; (= *qualified*) **to be ~ for a job** avoir la compétence nécessaire pour faire un travail; **a meal ~ for a king** un repas digne d'un roi; **to be ~ for nothing** être incapable de faire quoi que ce soit, être bon à rien; **to be ~ for the bin** être bon à jeter à la poubelle **b** (= *right and proper*) convenable, correct; [*time, occasion*] propice; (*frm*) **it is not ~ that you should be here** votre présence est inconvenante (*frm*); **it is not a ~ moment to ask that question** ce n'est pas le moment de poser cette question; **he's not ~ company for my son** ce n'est pas une bonne fréquentation pour mon fils; **to see** *or* **think ~ to do** trouver *or* juger bon de faire; **I'll do as I think** *or* **see ~** je ferai comme bon me semblera; **will she come? — if she sees ~** est-ce qu'elle viendra? — oui, si elle le juge bon **c** (= *healthy*) en bonne santé; (= *in trim*) en forme; **to be as ~ as a fiddle** être en pleine forme, se porter comme un charme; **she is not yet ~ to travel** elle n'est pas encore en état de voyager; **~ for duty** (*after illness*) en état de reprendre le travail; (*Mil*) en état de reprendre le service; **will he be ~ for Saturday's match?** (*footballer etc*) sera-t-il en état de jouer samedi?, sera-t-il suffisamment en forme pour le match de samedi? → **keep** **d** (= *ready*) **to laugh ~ to burst** se tenir les côtes, rire comme un(e) bossu(e)* *or* une baleine*; **she was crying ~ to break your heart** elle sanglotait à (vous) fendre le cœur; **to be ~ to drop** tomber de fatigue; (*US*) **~ to be tied*** (= *angry*) furibard*

2 N **your dress is a very good ~** votre robe est tout à fait à votre taille; **these trousers aren't a very good ~** ce pantalon n'est pas vraiment à ma (*or* sa *etc*) taille; **the crash helmet was a tight ~ on his head** (= *too tight*) le casque était un peu trop juste pour lui; (= *good fit*) le casque était exactement à sa taille

3 VT **a** (= *be the right size for*) [*clothes, shoes*] aller à; **this coat ~s you well** ce manteau vous va bien *or* est bien à votre taille; **the dress ~s her like a glove** cette robe lui va comme un gant; **the washing machine is too big to ~ this space** la machine à laver est trop grande pour entrer dans cet espace; **the key doesn't ~ the lock** cette clé ne correspond pas à la serrure; **you can put these units together to ~ the shape of your kitchen** vous pouvez assembler les éléments en fonction de la forme de votre cuisine; **the cover is tailored to ~ the seat** la housse est faite pour s'adapter au siège; **roll out the pastry to ~ the top of the pie** abaisser

► LANGUAGE IN USE: **firstly** 26.1, 26.2

la pâte au rouleau pour recouvrir la tourte; **sheets to ~** des draps pour un grand lit; **"one size ~s all"** « taille unique »; **"to ~ ages 5 to 6"** « 5-6 ans »; **"to ~ waist sizes 70 to 75cm"** « tour de taille 70-75 cm » → **cap**

b (= find space or time for) **you can ~ five people into this car** il y a de la place pour cinq dans cette voiture; **to ~ a dental appointment into one's diary** trouver un créneau dans son emploi du temps pour un rendez-vous chez le dentiste, caser* un rendez-vous chez le dentiste dans son emploi du temps; **I can't ~ any more meetings into my schedule** je n'ai pas le temps pour d'autres réunions dans mon emploi du temps, il m'est impossible de caser* d'autres réunions dans mon emploi du temps

c (= correspond to, match) [+ mood, definition, stereotype] correspondre à; [+ needs] répondre à; **the building has been adapted to ~ the needs of disabled people** ce bâtiment a été adapté pour répondre aux besoins des handicapés; **his speech was tailored to ~ the mood of the conference** son discours était adapté à l'ambiance du congrès; **a man ~ting this description** un homme répondant à ce signalement; **to ~ the circumstances** être adapté aux circonstances; **this hypothesis appears to ~ the facts** cette hypothèse semble concorder avec les faits; **the facts ~ the theory** les faits concordent avec la théorie; **she doesn't ~ the profile** or **picture of a typical drug smuggler** elle ne correspond pas à l'idée que l'on se fait or à l'image que l'on a d'un trafiquant de drogue; **he doesn't ~ my image of a good teacher** il ne correspond pas à l'idée que je me fais d'un bon professeur; **the punishment should ~ the crime** le châtiment doit être proportionné au crime; **the curtains won't ~ the colour scheme** les rideaux n'iront pas avec les couleurs de la pièce, la couleur des rideaux va jurer avec le reste

d [+ garment] ajuster; **her brother ~ted the dress on her** son frère a ajusté la robe sur elle **e** (= put in place) mettre; (= fix) fixer (**on** sur); (= install) poser, mettre; **he ~ted it to the side of the instrument** il l'a mis or fixé sur le côté de l'instrument; **to ~ a key in the lock** engager une clé dans la serrure; **to ~ two things together** assembler or ajuster deux objets; **~ part A to part B** assemblez la pièce A avec la pièce B; **to ~ sth into place** mettre qch en place; **I had a new window ~ted on** m'a posé or installé une nouvelle fenêtre; **to have a new kitchen ~ted** se faire installer une nouvelle cuisine; **car ~ted with a radio** voiture f équipée d'une radio; **to ~ lights to a bicycle** ◊ **to ~ a bicycle with lights** installer des feux sur un vélo; **he has been ~ted with a new hearing aid** on lui a mis or posé un nouvel appareil auditif

f (frm) **to ~ sb for sth/to do sth** préparer qn or rendre qn apte à qch/à faire qch; **to ~ o.s. for a job** se préparer à un travail

4 VI **a** **the dress doesn't ~ very well** cette robe n'est pas à sa taille or ne lui va pas; **it ~s like a glove** [garment] cela me (or vous etc) va comme un gant; [suggestion] cela me (or leur etc) convient parfaitement

b (= be the right size, shape etc) **this key/part doesn't ~** ce n'est pas la bonne clé/pièce; **the saucepan lid doesn't ~** le couvercle ne va pas sur la casserole; **it should ~ on this end somewhere** cela doit aller or se mettre là au bout (quelque part)

c (= have enough room) entrer, tenir; **it's too big to ~ into the box** c'est trop grand pour entrer or tenir dans la boîte; **the clothes won't ~ into the suitcase** les vêtements ne vont pas entrer or tenir dans la valise; **a computer small enough to ~ into your pocket** un ordinateur qui tient dans la poche; **my CV ~s onto one page** mon CV tient en une page; **seven people in one car? We'll never ~!** sept

personnes dans une voiture? Il n'y aura jamais assez de place!

d (fig = add up, match) [facts] cadrer; **it doesn't ~ with what he said to me** ça ne correspond pas à or ne cadre pas avec ce qu'il m'a dit; **how does this idea ~ into your overall plan?** comment cette idée s'inscrit-elle dans votre plan d'ensemble?; **people don't always ~ neatly into categories** les gens ne rentrent pas toujours facilement dans des catégories bien définies; **his face doesn't ~ here** il détonne ici; **suddenly everything ~ted into place** soudain, tout est devenu clair; **it all ~s (into place) now!** tout s'explique!

▶ **fit in** **1** VI **a** (= add up, match) [fact] cadrer; **this doesn't ~ in with what I was taught at school** ceci ne correspond pas à or ne cadre pas avec ce que l'on m'a appris à l'école

b (= integrate) **at school she has problems ~ting in** (with other children) à l'école elle a du mal à s'intégrer; (= getting used to lessons etc) elle a du mal à s'adapter à l'école; **he has ~ted in well with the other members of our team** il s'est bien entendu avec les autres membres de notre équipe, il s'est bien intégré dans notre équipe

c (= have room: into room, car etc) **will we all ~ in?** y aura-t-il assez de place pour nous tous?, allons-nous tous entrer or tenir?; **will the toys all ~ in?** y aura-t-il assez de place pour tous les jouets?; **the box is too small for all his toys to ~ in** la boîte est trop petite pour contenir tous ses jouets

2 VT SEP **a** (= find room for) [+ object, person] faire entrer, trouver de la place pour; **can you ~ another book in?** y a-t-il encore de la place pour un livre?

b (= adapt) adapter, faire concorder; **I'll try to ~ my plans in with yours** je tâcherai de m'adapter en fonction de tes plans

c (= find time for) [+ person] prendre, caser*; **the doctor can ~ you in tomorrow at three** le docteur peut vous prendre demain à 15 heures; **have you got time to ~ in a quick meeting?** avez-vous le temps d'assister à une réunion rapide?

▶ **fit on** **1** VI **the bottle top won't ~ on** le bouchon de la bouteille n'est pas adapté **2** VT SEP [+ object] mettre

▶ **fit out** VT SEP **a** [+ expedition, person] équiper **b** (= furnish) [+ room, office, building] aménager; **to ~ a room/building out with sth** installer qch dans une pièce/un bâtiment; **they've ~ted one room out as an office** ils ont transformé or aménagé une pièce en bureau **c** [+ ship] armer

▶ **fit up** VT SEP **they've ~ted their house up with a burglar alarm** ils ont installé une alarme dans leur maison; **they've ~ted one room up as an office** ils ont transformé or aménagé une pièce en bureau

fit² [fɪt] N **a** (Med) attaque f; [of epilepsy] crise f; **~ of coughing** quinte f de toux; **to have** or **throw* a ~** avoir or piquer* une crise; **to fall down in a ~** tomber en convulsions; (fig) **she'll have a ~ when we tell her*** elle va avoir une attaque or va piquer une crise quand on lui dira ça* → **blue, epileptic, faint b** (= outburst) mouvement m, accès m; **in a ~ of anger** dans un mouvement or accès de colère; **~ of crying** crise f de larmes; **to be in ~s (of laughter)** se tordre de rire; **to get a ~ of the giggles** se tordre le fou rire; **he has ~s of enthusiasm** il a des accès d'enthousiasme; **in ~s and starts** par à-coups

fitful [ˈfɪtfʊl] ADJ [sleep] troublé, agité; [showers] intermittent; [breeze] capricieux, changeant; **~ enthusiasm/anger** des accès mpl d'enthousiasme/de colère; **to have a ~ night** passer une nuit agitée

fitfully [ˈfɪtfʊlɪ] ADV [sleep, doze] de façon intermittente; [work] par à-coups; **the sun shone ~** le soleil faisait de brèves apparitions

fitment [ˈfɪtmənt] N **a** (Brit) (= built-in furniture) meuble m encastré; (= cupboard) placard m encastré; (in kitchen) élément m (de cuisine); **you can't move the table, it's a ~ on** on ne peut pas déplacer la table, elle est encastrée **b** (= part: for vacuum cleaner, mixer etc) accessoire m; **it's part of the light ~** cela fait partie du luminaire

fitness [ˈfɪtnɪs] **1** N **a** (= health) santé f; (= physical trimness) forme f **b** (= suitability) [of remark] à-propos m, justesse f; [of person] aptitude f (**for** à) **2** COMP ▶ **fitness fanatic***, **fitness freak*** N (pej) fana* mf d'exercices physiques ▶ **fitness test** N (Sport) test m de condition physique

fitted [ˈfɪtɪd] **1** ADJ **a** (Brit) [wardrobe, kitchen units] encastré; [kitchen] intégré; [bedroom] meublé; [bathroom] aménagé; **a fully-~ kitchen** une cuisine entièrement équipée **b** (= tailored) [jacket, shirt] ajusté **c** (frm = suited) ~ **to do sth** apte à faire qch; **well/ill ~ to do sth** vraiment/pas vraiment fait pour faire qch; **~ for** or **to a task** apte pour une tâche **2** COMP ▶ **fitted carpet** N moquette f; **the room has a ~ carpet** la pièce est moquettée ▶ **fitted sheet** N drap-housse m

fitter [ˈfɪtər] N **a** [of machine, device] monteur m; [of carpet] poseur m **b** (Dress) essayeur m, -euse f

fitting [ˈfɪtɪŋ] **1** ADJ [remark] pertinent, juste **2** N **a** (Dress) essayage m **b** (Brit: gen pl: in house etc) ~**s** installations fpl; **bathroom ~s** installations fpl sanitaires; **electrical ~s** installations fpl électriques, appareillage m électrique; **furniture and ~s** mobilier m et installations fpl; **office ~s** équipement m de bureau → **light¹ 3** COMP ▶ **fitting room** N salon m d'essayage

-fitting [ˈfɪtɪŋ] ADJ (in compounds) **ill-fitting** qui ne va pas; **wide-fitting** large → **close¹, loose, tight**

fittingly [ˈfɪtɪŋlɪ] ADV [dress] convenablement (pour l'occasion); [titled, named] de façon appropriée; **a ~ exciting finish to a magnificent match** une fin passionnante à la hauteur de la qualité du match; **the speech was ~ solemn** le discours avait la solennité qui convenait; **~, he won his first world title before his home crowd** comme il convient, il a remporté son premier titre mondial devant son public

five [faɪv] **1** ADJ cinq inv **2** N cinq m; (esp US) **to take ~*** faire une pause; for other phrases see **six 3 fives** NPL (Sport) sorte de jeu de pelote (à la main) **4** PRON cinq; **there are ~** il y en a cinq **5** COMP ▶ **five-and-dime, five-and-ten** N (US) bazar m ▶ **five-a-side (football)** N (Brit) football à cinq ▶ **five-by-five*** ADJ (US fig) aussi gros que grand ▶ **Five Nations Tournament** N (Rugby) tournoi m des cinq nations ▶ **five-o'clock shadow** N barbe f d'un jour ▶ **five spot*** N (US) billet m de cinq dollars ▶ **five-star hotel** N hôtel m cinq étoiles ▶ **five-star restaurant** N ≈ restaurant m trois étoiles ▶ **five-year** ADJ quinquennal ▶ **five-year man*** N (US Univ: hum) éternel redoublant m ▶ **five-year plan** N plan m quinquennal

fiver* [ˈfaɪvər] N (Brit) billet m de cinq livres; (US) billet m de cinq dollars

fix [fɪks] **1** VT **a** (= make firm) (with nails etc) fixer; (with ropes etc) attacher; **to ~ a stake in the ground** enfoncer un pieu en terre; (Mil) **to ~ bayonets** mettre (la) baïonnette au canon → **fixed**

b (= direct, aim) [+ gun, camera, radar] diriger (**on** sur); [+ attention] fixer (**on** sur); **to ~ one's eyes on sb/sth** fixer qn/qch du regard; **all eyes were ~ed on her** tous les regards or tous les yeux étaient fixés sur elle; **he ~ed him with an angry glare** il l'a fixé d'un regard furieux; **to ~ sth in one's mind** graver or imprimer qch dans son esprit; **to ~ one's hopes on sth** mettre tous ses espoirs en qch; **to ~ the blame on**

sb attribuer *or* faire endosser la responsabilité à qn ► [c] (= *arrange, decide*) décider, arrêter; [+ *time, price*] fixer, arrêter; [+ *limit*] fixer, établir; **on the date ~ed** à la date convenue; **nothing has been ~ed yet** rien n'a encore été décidé, il n'y a encore rien d'arrêté *or* de décidé ► [d] (*Phot*) fixer ► [e] * arranger, préparer; **to ~ one's hair** se passer un coup de peigne; **can I ~ you a drink?** vous prendrez bien un verre?; **I'll go and ~ us something to eat** je vais vite (nous) préparer un petit quelque chose à manger ► [f] (= *deal with*) arranger; (= *mend*) réparer; **don't worry, I'll ~ it all** ne vous en faites pas, je vais tout arranger; **he ~ed it with the police before he organized the demonstration** il a attendu d'avoir le feu vert* de la police *or* il s'est arrangé avec la police avant d'organiser la manifestation; **I'll soon ~ him*** ◊ **I'll ~ his wagon*** (*US*) je vais lui régler son compte; **to ~ a flat tyre** réparer un pneu ► [g] (* = *rig, corrupt*) [+ *person, witness, jury*] (*gen*) corrompre; (= *bribe*) acheter, soudoyer; [+ *match, fight, election, trial*] truquer; [+ *prices*] fixer (de manière déloyale)

[2] VI (*US* = *intend*) **to be ~ing to do sth*** avoir l'intention de faire qch, compter faire qch

[3] N [a]* ennui *m*, embêtement* *m*; **to be in/get into a ~** être/se mettre dans le pétrin* *or* dans de beaux draps; **what a ~!** nous voilà dans de beaux draps *or* dans le pétrin!* ► [b] (* = *dose*) [*of drugs*] (= *injection*) piqûre *f*, piquouse* *f*; [*of coffee, chocolate, caffeine*] dose* *f*; (*Drugs*) **to get** *or* **give o.s. a ~** se shooter*, se piquer; (*hum*) **I need my daily ~ of coffee/chocolate** *etc* il me faut ma dose quotidienne de café/chocolat *etc* ► [c] (*Aviat, Naut*) position *f*; **I've got a ~ on him now** j'ai sa position maintenant; (*Naut*) **to take a ~ on** déterminer la position de; (*fig*) **I can't get a ~ on it*** je n'arrive pas à m'en faire une idée claire ► [d] (= *trick*) **it's a ~*** c'est truqué, c'est une combine

[4] COMP ► **fixing bath** N (*Phot*) (= *liquid*) bain *m* de fixage, fixateur *m*; (= *container*) bac *m* de fixateur

► **fix on** [1] VT FUS choisir; **they finally ~ed on that house** leur choix s'est finalement arrêté sur cette maison [2] VT SEP [+ *lid*] fixer, attacher

► **fix up** [1] VI s'arranger (**to do** pour faire) [2] VT SEP arranger, combiner; **I'll try to ~ something up** je tâcherai d'arranger quelque chose; **let's ~ it all up now** décidons tout de suite; (= *sb up with sth* trouver qch pour qn; **we ~ed them up for one night** (= *put them up*) nous les avons logés pour une nuit; (= *found them a place to stay*) nous leur avons trouvé à coucher pour une nuit

fixated [fɪk'seɪtɪd] ADJ (*Psych*) qui fait une fixation; (*fig*) obsédé (**on** par)

fixation [fɪk'seɪʃən] N (*Chem, Phot, Psych*) fixation *f*; (*fig*) obsession *f*; **to have a ~ about** (*Psych*) faire une fixation sur; (*fig*) être obsédé par

fixative [ˈfɪksətɪv] N fixatif *m*

fixed [fɪkst] [1] ADJ [a] (= *set*) [*amount, position, time, intervals, stare, price*] fixe; [*smile, grin*] figé; [*idea*] arrêté; (*Ling*) [*stress, word order*] fixe; (*Jur*) **(of) no ~ abode** *or* **address** sans domicile fixe; **there's no ~ agenda** il n'y a pas d'ordre du jour bien arrêté; **with ~ bayonets** baïonnette au canon ► [b] (= *rigged*) [*election, trial, match, race*] truqué; [*jury*] soudoyé, acheté ► [c] * **how are we ~ for time?** on a combien de temps?, on en est où question temps*?; **how are you ~ for cigarettes?** il te reste combien de cigarettes?, tu en es où question cigarettes*?; **how are you ~ for tonight?** tu es libre ce soir?, tu as prévu quelque chose ce soir?;

how are you ~ for transport? comment fais-tu question transport*?

[2] COMP ► **fixed assets** NPL (*Comm*) immobilisations *fpl* ► **fixed cost contract** N marché *m* à prix forfaitaire ► **fixed costs** NPL (*Comm*) frais *mpl* fixes ► **fixed decimal point** N virgule *f* fixe ► **fixed disk** N (*Comput*) disque *m* fixe ► **fixed exchange rate** N (*Econ*) taux *m* de change fixe ► **fixed menu** N (menu *m* à) prix *m* fixe ► **fixed point** N = **fixed decimal point** ► **fixed-point notation** *or* **representation** N (*Comput*) notation *f* en virgule fixe ► **fixed-rate financing** N financement *m* à taux fixe ► **fixed star** N étoile *f* fixe ► **fixed-term contract** N contrat *m* à durée déterminée ► **fixed-term tenancy** N location *f* à durée déterminée ► **fixed-wing aircraft** N aéronef *m* à voilure fixe

fixedly [ˈfɪksɪdlɪ] ADV [*stare*] fixement; **to smile ~** avoir un sourire figé

fixer [ˈfɪksər] N [a] (*Phot*) fixateur *m* [b] (* : = *person*) combinard(e)* *m(f)*

fixings [ˈfɪksɪŋz] NPL [a] (= *nuts and bolts*) vis, boulons *et écrous* [b] (*US Culin*) garniture *f*, accompagnement *m*

fixity [ˈfɪksɪtɪ] N [*of stare*] fixité *f*; **his ~ of purpose** sa détermination inébranlable

fixture [ˈfɪkstʃər] N [a] (*gen pl: in building*) installation *f* fixe; (*Jur*) immeuble *m*, bien *m* immeuble; (*Brit*) **the house was sold with ~s and fittings** on a vendu la maison avec toutes les installations; (*Brit*) **£2000 for ~s and fittings** 2 000 livres de reprise; **lighting ~s** appareillage *m* électrique; (*fig*) **she's a ~*** elle fait partie du mobilier* [b] (*Brit Sport*) match *m* (prévu), rencontre *f*; **~ list** calendrier *m*

fizz [fɪz] [1] VI [*drink*] pétiller, mousser; [*steam etc*] siffler [2] N [a] pétillement *m*, sifflement *m* [b] (*fig*) punch* *m*, piment *m* (*fig*); **they need to put some ~ into their election campaign** leur campagne électorale a besoin d'un peu plus de nerf [c] * champ* *m*, champagne *m*; (*US*) eau *f or* boisson *f* gazeuse

► **fizz up** VI monter (en pétillant), mousser

► **fizzle** [ˈfɪzl] VI pétiller

► **fizzle out** VI [*firework*] rater (*une fois en l'air*); [*party, event*] se terminer; [*book, film, plot*] se terminer en queue de poisson; [*plans*] tomber à l'eau; [*enthusiasm, interest*] tomber

fizzy [ˈfɪzɪ] ADJ (*esp Brit*) [*soft drink*] pétillant, gazeux; [*wine*] mousseux, pétillant

fjord [fjɔːd] N = **fiord**

FL ABBR = **Florida**

Fla. ABBR = **Florida**

flab* [flæb] N (= *fat*) graisse *f* superflue, lard* *m*

flabbergast* [ˈflæbəgɑːst] VT sidérer*; **I was ~ed at this** ça m'a sidéré*

flabbiness [ˈflæbɪnɪs] N [*of muscle, flesh*] aspect *m* flasque; (*fig*) mollesse *f*

flabby [ˈflæbɪ] ADJ [a] (*physically*) [*thighs, face, stomach, muscles*] mou (molle *f*), flasque; [*person, skin*] flasque [b] (= *ineffectual*) [*country, economy*] mou (molle *f*)

flaccid [ˈflæksɪd] ADJ [*muscle, flesh*] flasque, mou (molle *f*)

flaccidity [flæk'sɪdɪtɪ] N flaccidité *f*

flack [flæk] [1] N (*US Cine, Press*) attaché(e) *m(f)* de presse [2] VI être attaché(e) de presse

flag[1] [flæg] [1] N [a] drapeau *m*; (*Naut*) pavillon *m*; **~ of truce** ◊ **white ~** drapeau *m* blanc; **black ~** [*of pirates*] pavillon *m* noir; **~ of convenience** ◊ **~ of necessity** (*US*) pavillon *m* de complaisance; (*Brit fig*) **they put the ~s out*** ils ont fêté ça; (*fig*) **with (all) ~s flying** en pavoisant; **to go down with ~s flying** (*Naut*) couler pavillon haut; (*fig*) mener la lutte jusqu'au bout; (*fig*) **to keep the ~ flying** maintenir les traditions; **to fly the ~ for one's country** défendre les couleurs de son pays; (*esp US*) **to wrap** *or* **drape o.s. in the ~** servir

ses intérêts personnels sous couvert de patriotisme → **red, show** ► [b] [*of taxi*] **the ~ was down** ≈ le taxi était pris ► [c] (*for charity*) insigne *m* (*d'une œuvre charitable*) ► [d] (*Comput*) drapeau *m*

[2] VT [a] orner *or* garnir de drapeaux; [+ *street, building, ship*] pavoiser ► [b] (= *mark page*) signaler (*avec une marque*); (*Comput*) signaler (*avec un drapeau*)

[3] COMP ► **flag carrier** N (= *airline*) compagnie *f* nationale ► **Flag Day** N (*US*) le 14 juin (*anniversaire du drapeau américain*) ► **flag day** N (*Brit*) journée *f* de vente d'insignes (*pour une œuvre charitable*); **~ day in aid of the war-blinded** journée *f* des *or* pour les aveugles de guerre ► **flag officer** N (*Naut*) officier *m* supérieur ► **flag-waving** (*fig*) N déclarations *fpl* cocardières ♦ ADJ [*politicians, patriots etc*] cocardier

► **flag down** VT SEP [+ *taxi, bus, car*] héler, faire signe à; [*police*] faire signe de s'arrêter à

flag[2] [flæg] VI [*athlete, walker*] faiblir; [*worker*] fléchir, se relâcher; [*conversation*] traîner, languir; [*interest, spirits*] faiblir; [*enthusiasm*] tomber; [*sales*] fléchir; [*market*] faiblir; [*economy, economic recovery*] s'essouffler; [*film, novel, album*] faiblir; **he's ~ging** il ne va pas fort; **the film begins well but starts ~ging towards the middle** le film commence bien mais se met à faiblir vers le milieu

flag[3] [flæg] N (*Bot*) iris *m* (des marais)

flag[4] [flæg] N (*also* **~stone**) dalle *f*

flagellant [ˈflædʒələnt] N [a] (*Rel*) flagellant *m* [b] (*sexual*) adepte *mf* de la flagellation

flagellate [ˈflædʒəleɪt] [1] ADJ, N (*Bio*) flagellé *m* [2] VT flageller

flagellation [ˌflædʒə'leɪʃən] N flagellation *f*

flagellum [fləˈdʒeləm] N (*pl* **flagellums** *or* **flagella** [fləˈdʒelə]) flagelle *m*

flageolet [ˌflædʒəʊ'let] N [a] (*Mus*) flageolet *m* [b] (*also* **~ bean**) flageolet *m*

flagged [flægd] ADJ [*floor*] dallé

flagon [ˈflægən] N [*of glass*] (grande) bouteille *f*; (*larger*) bonbonne *f*; (= *jug*) (grosse) cruche *f*

flagpole [ˈflægpəʊl] N mât *m* (*portant le drapeau*); (*fig*) **to run an idea/proposal up the ~*** lancer une idée/proposition pour tâter le terrain; **let's run this up the ~ (and see who salutes it)** proposons cela (et voyons les réactions)

flagrant [ˈfleɪgrənt] ADJ flagrant

flagrante delicto [fləˈgræntɪdɪ'lɪktəʊ] **in ~** (*adv*) en flagrant délit

flagrantly [ˈfleɪgrəntlɪ] ADV [*abuse, disregard*] de manière flagrante; [*silly, untrue, unequal*] manifestement; [*provocative*] ouvertement; **~ unjust/indiscreet** d'une injustice/d'une indiscrétion flagrante

flagship [ˈflægʃɪp] [1] N (*Naut*) vaisseau *m* amiral; (*Comm*) produit *m* phare [2] COMP (*Comm*) [*product, store, company, TV programme*] phare

flagstaff [ˈflægstɑːf] N mât *m* (*portant le drapeau*); (*Naut*) mât *m* de pavillon

flail [fleɪl] [1] N (*Agr*) fléau *m* [2] VT (*Agr*) [+ *corn*] battre au fléau [3] VI [*arms*] (*also* **~ about**) battre l'air

flair [fleər] N [a] (= *talent*) flair *m*; (= *perceptiveness*) perspicacité *f*; **to have a ~ for** avoir un don pour [b] (= *style, elegance*) style *m*

flak [flæk] [1] N [a] (*Mil*) (= *firing*) tir *m* antiaérien *or* de DCA; (= *guns*) canons *mpl* antiaériens *or* de DCA; (= *flashes*) éclairs *mpl* (* = *criticism*) critiques *fpl*; **he got a lot of ~ (for that)** il s'est fait descendre en flammes (pour ça); **he got a lot of ~ from ...** il s'est fait éreinter par ... [2] COMP ► **flak-jacket** N gilet *m* pare-balles *inv* ► **flak ship** N bâtiment *m* de DCA

flake [fleɪk] **1** N **a** [of snow, cereal] flocon m; [of paint] écaillure f; [of metal] paillette f, écaille f → **cornflakes** **b** (* = eccentric) barjo* mf **2** VI (also ~ **off**) [stone, plaster] s'effriter, s'écailler; [paint] s'écailler; [skin] peler, se desquamer (Med) **3** VT (also ~ **off**) effriter, écailler; (Culin) **~d almonds** amandes fpl effilées **4** COMP ► **flake-white** N blanc m de plomb
► **flake off** VI **a** → flake 3 **b** (US) ~ **off!**‡ fous le camp !‡, de l'air !*
► **flake out**‡ VI (Brit) (= faint) tomber dans les pommes*, tourner de l'œil*; (= fall asleep) s'endormir or tomber (tout d'une masse); **to be ~d out** être crevé* or à plat*

flakey‡ ['fleɪkɪ] ADJ = **flaky b**

flaky ['fleɪkɪ] **1** ADJ **a** [paint] floconneux **b**‡ bizarre, excentrique **2** COMP ► **flaky pastry** N pâte f feuilletée

flambé ['flɒːmbeɪ] **1** ADJ flambé **2** VT flamber; **~ed steaks** steaks mpl flambés

flamboyance [flæm'bɔɪəns] N extravagance f

flamboyant [flæm'bɔɪənt] ADJ **a** [colour] flamboyant, éclatant; [person, character] haut en couleur; [rudeness] ostentatoire; [speech] retentissant; [style, dress, manners] extravagant **b** (Archit) flamboyant

flame [fleɪm] **1** N **a** flamme f; (fig) [of passion, enthusiasm] flamme f, ardeur f; **to feed** or **fan the ~s** (lit) attiser le feu; (fig) jeter de l'huile sur le feu; **in ~s** en flammes, en feu; **to go up in ~s** (lit) = catch fire) s'embraser; (= be destroyed by fire) être détruit par le feu; (fig) partir en fumée → **burst, fuel** **b** **she's one of his old ~s*** c'est une de ses anciens béguins* **2** VI [fire] flamber; [passion] brûler; **her cheeks ~d** ses joues se sont empourprées **3** COMP ► **flame-coloured** ADJ (rouge) feu inv ► **flame gun** N = flamethrower ► **flame-proof dish** N plat m allant au feu ► **flame red** N rouge feu m vif ► **flame-red** ADJ rouge vif ► **flame retardant** ADJ, N ignifuge m
► **flame up** VI [fire] flamber

flamenco [flə'meŋkəʊ] ADJ, N flamenco m

flamethrower ['fleɪm,θrəʊə'] N lance-flammes m inv

flaming ['fleɪmɪŋ] **1** ADJ **a** (= burning) [sun, fire] ardent; [torch] allumé **b** (in colour) [sunset] embrasé; **~ red hair** des cheveux d'un roux flamboyant **c** (* = furious) [row] violent **d** (esp Brit* = damn) fichu*, satané*; **the ~ car's locked** cette fichue or satanée voiture est fermée à clé; **it's a ~ nuisance!** c'est vraiment enquiquinant !* c'est vraiment emmerdant !** **2** ADV (esp Brit*) **he's ~ useless!** il est complètement nul !*; **you get so ~ worked up about everything!** c'est pas possible de s'énerver comme ça pour un rien !*

flamingo [flə'mɪŋɡəʊ] N (pl **flamingos** or **flamingoes**) flamant m (rose)

flammable ['flæməbl] ADJ inflammable

flan [flæn] N (= tart) tarte f; (savoury) ≈ quiche f; (US = custard) flan m au caramel

Flanders ['flɑːndəz] **1** N les Flandres fpl, la Flandre **2** COMP ► **Flanders poppy** N coquelicot m

flange [flændʒ] N (on wheel) boudin m; (on pipe) collerette f, bride f; (on I-beam) aile f; (on railway rail) patin m; (on tool) rebord m, collet m

flanged [flændʒd] ADJ [wheel] à boudin, à rebord; [tube] à brides; [radiator] à ailettes

flank [flæŋk] **1** N **a** (Anat, Geog, Mil) flanc m; (Culin) flanchet m **2** VT **a** flanquer; **~ed by two policemen** flanqué de or encadré par deux gendarmes **b** (Mil) flanquer; (= turn the flank of) contourner le flanc de

flanker ['flæŋkə'] N (Rugby) ailier m

flannel ['flænl] **1** N **a** (NonC: Tex) flanelle f **b** (Brit: also **face ~**) ≈ gant m de toilette **c** (Brit* fig = waffle) baratin* m **2** **flannels**

NPL (Brit = trousers) pantalon m de flanelle **3** VI (Brit* = waffle) baratiner* **4** COMP de flanelle

flannelette [,flænə'let] **1** N finette f, pilou m **2** COMP [sheet] de finette, de pilou

flap [flæp] **1** N **a** [of wings] battement m, coup m; [of sails] claquement m **b** [of pocket, envelope, hat, tent, book cover] rabat m; [of counter, table] abattant m; (= door in floor) trappe f; (for cats) chatière f; (Aviat) volet m **c** (* = panic) **to be in a ~** être dans tous ses états; **to get into a ~** se mettre dans tous ses états, paniquer **d** (Phon) battement m **2** VI **a** [wings] battre; [shutters] battre, claquer; [sails] claquer; **his cloak ~ped about his legs** sa cape lui battait les jambes; (fig) **his ears must be ~ing*** ses oreilles doivent siffler* **b** (* = be panicky) paniquer; **stop ~ping!** pas de panique!, t'affole pas !* **3** VT [bird] **to ~ its wings** battre des ailes

flapdoodle* ['flæp,duːdəl] N blague* f, balivernes fpl

flapjack ['flæpdʒæk] N (Culin) (= biscuit) galette f (à l'avoine); (US = pancake) crêpe f épaisse

flapper†* ['flæpə'] N garçonne des années 1920

flare [fleə'] **1** N **a** (= light) [of torch, fire, sun] éclat m, flamboiement m **b** (= signal) feu m, signal m (lumineux); (Mil) fusée f éclairante, fusée-parachute f; (Aviat) (for target) bombe f éclairante or de jalonnement; (for runway) balise f **c** (Dress) évasement m **2** **flares*** NPL = **flared trousers** **3** VI **a** [match] s'enflammer; [candle] briller; [sunspot] brûler **b** (fig) [violence, fighting] éclater; **tempers ~d** les esprits se sont (vite) échauffés **c** [sleeves, skirt] s'évaser, s'élargir; [nostrils] se dilater, se gonfler **4** VT [+ skirt, trouser legs] évaser; [+ nostrils] dilater, gonfler; **~d skirt** jupe f évasée; **~d trousers** pantalon m à pattes d'éléphant **5** COMP ► **flare path** N (Aviat) piste f balisée ► **flare-up** N [of fire] recrudescence f; [of fighting] intensification f (soudaine); (= outburst of rage) accès m de colère; (= sudden dispute) altercation f, prise f de bec*
► **flare out** VI → flare 3c
► **flare up** **1** VI [fire] s'embraser, prendre (brusquement); [person] s'emporter; [political situation] exploser; [anger, fighting, revolt] éclater; [disease] se réveiller, reprendre; [epidemic] éclater, se déclarer (soudain); (fig) **he ~s up at the slightest thing** il est très soupe au lait **2** → **flare-up** N

flash [flæʃ] **1** N **a** (= sudden light) (from torch, car headlights, explosion, firework) lueur f soudaine; (of flame, jewels) éclat m; **a ~ of light** un jet de lumière; **a ~ of lightning** ◊ **a lightning ~** un éclair **b** (fig = brief moment) **it happened in a ~** c'est arrivé en un clin d'œil; **it came to him in a ~ that ...** l'idée lui est venue tout d'un coup que ...; **~ of genius** or **inspiration** (gen) éclair m de génie; (= brainwave) idée f de génie; (with) **a ~ of anger** or **temper** (dans) un mouvement de colère; **staring at the photo of him, I had a sudden ~ of recognition** en le regardant sur la photo, je l'ai subitement reconnu; **in a ~ of memory, she saw ...** la mémoire lui revenant soudain, elle a vu ...; **a ~ of humour** un trait d'humour; **a ~ of wit** une boutade; (fig) **a ~ in the pan** (Pol etc: for new movement, idea, party) un feu de paille (fig); (= person's fad) lubie f → **hot** **c** (= brief glimpse) coup m d'œil; **a ~ of colour/of blue** (= briefly seen colour) une note soudaine de couleur/de bleu; (= small amount of colour) une note de couleur/de bleu; **give us a ~!**‡ fais voir !‡; **despite his illness, there were ~es of the old Henry** malgré sa maladie, il y avait des moments où Henry redevenait lui-même; **she has ~es of the future** elle a des vi-

sions fugitives de l'avenir **d** (also **newsflash**) flash m (d'information) **e** (Mil) écusson m **f** (Phot) flash m **g** (US) = **flashlight** **h** (US = bright student) petit(e) doué(e) m(f) **2** VI **a** [light] (on and off) clignoter; [jewels] étinceler; [eyes] lancer des éclairs; **lightning was ~ing** il y avait des éclairs; **a beam of light ~ed across his face** un trait de lumière éclaira soudain son visage; **the sunlight ~ed on the water** l'eau scintillait (au soleil); **the blade of the knife ~ed in the sunlight** la lame du couteau brillait au soleil; **to ~ on and off** clignoter; **~ing light** [of police car, ambulance etc] gyrophare m; [of answerphone, warning signal] lumière f clignotante; **her eyes ~ed with anger** ses yeux lançaient des éclairs **b** (= move quickly) **to ~ in/out/past** etc [person, vehicle] entrer/sortir/passer etc comme un éclair; **the day ~ed by** or **past** on n'a pas vu la journée passer; **the thought ~ed through** or **across his mind that ...** un instant, il a pensé que ...; **his whole life ~ed before him** il a revu le film de sa vie; **a look of terror/anger ~ed across her face** une expression de terreur/de colère passa fugitivement sur son visage; **a message ~ed (up) onto the screen** un message est apparu sur l'écran **3** VT **a** [+ light] projeter; **to ~ a torch on** diriger une lampe torche sur; **to ~ a torch in sb's face** diriger une lampe torche dans les yeux de qn; **to ~ one's headlights** ◊ **to ~ the high beams** (US) faire un appel de phares (**at sb** à qn) **b** (= show quickly) **to ~ one's passport/ID card** montrer rapidement son passeport/sa carte d'identité; **the screen was ~ing a message at me** l'écran m'envoyait un message; **these images were ~ed across television screens all around the world** ces images sont apparues sur les écrans de télévision du monde entier; **she ~ed him a look of contempt** elle lui a jeté un regard de mépris; **to ~ a smile at sb** lancer un sourire éclatant à qn **c** (= flaunt) [+ diamond ring] étaler (aux yeux de tous), mettre (bien) en vue; **don't ~ all that money around** n'étale pas tout cet argent comme ça **4** ADJ* = **flashy** **5** COMP ► **flash bulb** N (Phot) ampoule f de flash ► **flash burn** N (Med) brûlure f (causée par un flux thermique) ► **flash card** N (Scol) fiche f (support pédagogique) ► **flash flood** N crue f subite ► **flash-forward** N projection f dans le futur ► **flash gun** N (Phot) flash m ► **flash Harry**†* N (Brit pej) frimeur* m ► **flash meter** N (Phot) flashmètre m ► **flash pack** N emballage m promotionnel ► **flash photography** N (Phot) photographie f au flash ► **flash point** N (Chem) point m d'ignition; (fig) **the situation had nearly reached ~ point** la situation était explosive ► **flash powder** N (Phot) photopoudre m

flashback ['flæʃbæk] N **a** (Cine) flash-back m inv, retour m en arrière **b** (Psych) flash-back m inv

flashcube ['flæʃkjuːb] N (Phot) flash m (cube)

flasher ['flæʃə'] N **a** (= light, device) clignotant m **b** (* = person committing indecent exposure) exhibitionniste m

flashily ['flæʃɪlɪ] ADV de façon tape-à-l'œil

flashing ['flæʃɪŋ] N **a** (on roof) revêtement m de zinc, noue f **b** (* = indecent exposure) exhibitionnisme m

flashlight ['flæʃlaɪt] N (Phot) flash m; (esp US = torch) torche f or lampe f électrique; (on lighthouse etc) fanal m

flashy ['flæʃɪ] ADJ (pej) [person] tapageur; [jewellery, car] tape-à-l'œil inv, clinquant; [dress] tape-à-l'œil inv, voyant; [colour, taste] criard, tapageur

flask [flɑːsk] N (*Pharm*) fiole *f*; (*Chem*) ballon *m*; (= *bottle*) bouteille *f*; (*for pocket*) flasque *f*; (*also* **vacuum ~**) bouteille *f* isotherme, (bouteille *f*) thermos® *f*

flat¹ [flæt] **1** ADJ **a** [*countryside, surface, the earth*] plat; [*tyre*] dégonflé, à plat; **a ~ dish** un plat creux; **~ roof** toit *m* plat or en terrasse; **~ nose** nez *m* épaté or camus; **a ~ stomach** un ventre plat; **he was lying ~ on the floor** il était (étendu) à plat par terre; **to fall ~** [*event, joke*] tomber à plat; [*scheme*] ne rien donner; **lay the book ~ on the table** pose le livre à plat sur la table; **the earthquake laid the whole city ~** le tremblement de terre a rasé la ville entière; **as ~ as a pancake*** [*tyre*] plat comme une galette; [*surface, countryside*] tout plat; (*after bombing*) complètement rasé; (*Brit fig*) **to be in a ~ spin*** être dans tous ses états → **4** **b** (= *dull*) [*taste, style*] monotone, plat; (= *unexciting*) [*event, experience*] morne, sans intérêt; [*battery*] à plat; (= *not fizzy*) [*beer etc*] éventé; **I was feeling rather ~** je n'avais pas la pêche*; **the beer tastes ~** (= *not fizzy*) la bière est éventée; (= *insipid*) la bière a un goût fade **c** (*Mus*) (= *off-key*) faux (fausse *f*), trop bas (basse *f*); (= *semitone lower*) **B ~** si *m* bémol **d** [*refusal, denial*] net (nette *f*), catégorique; **and that's ~!** un point c'est tout!* **e** (*Comm*) **~ rate of pay** salaire *m* fixe; [*of price, charge*] **~ rate** forfait *m* **f** (= *not shiny*) [*colour*] mat **g** (*US = penniless*) **to be ~:** être fauché (comme les blés)*, n'avoir plus un rond*

2 ADV **a** **he told me ~ that ...** il m'a dit carrément or sans ambages que ...; **he turned it down ~** il l'a carrément refusé, il a refusé tout net; **to be ~ broke:** être fauché (comme les blés)*, n'avoir plus un rond*; **in ten seconds ~** en dix secondes pile **b** **to go ~ out** (*esp Brit*) [*person*] courir à fond de train; [*car*] rouler à fond de train; (*esp Brit*) **to go ~ out for sth** faire tout son possible pour avoir qch; **to be ~ out** (= *exhausted*) être à plat* or vidé*; (= *asleep*) dormir, ronfler* (*fig*); (= *drunk*) être complètement rétamé, être K.-O.*; (*esp Brit*) **to be working ~ out** travailler d'arrache-pied; (= *lying down*) être étendu or couché de tout son long → **4** **c** (*Mus*) [*sing, play*] faux (fausse *f*), trop bas (basse *f*)

3 N **a** [*of hand, blade*] plat *m* **b** (*Geog*) (= *dry land*) plaine *f*; (= *marsh*) marécage *m* → **salt** **c** (*Mus*) bémol *m*; **A ~** la *m* bémol **d** (*Aut*) crevaison *f*, pneu *m* crevé **e** (*Racing*) **the ~ = flat racing, flat season**; **on the ~** sur le plat

4 COMP ► **flat bed** N [*of lorry*] plateau *m* ► **flat-bed lorry** N camion *m* à plateau ► **flat-bottomed boat** N bateau *m* à fond plat ► **flat cap** N (*Brit*) casquette *f* ► **flat car** N (*US Rail*) wagon *m* plat ► **flat-chested** ADJ **she is ~-chested** elle est plate, elle n'a pas de poitrine ► **flat feet** NPL **to have ~ feet** avoir les pieds plats ► **flat-iron** N fer *m* à repasser ► **flat-out:** (*US*) ADJ complet, absolu ◆ ADV complètement ► **flat pack** N meuble *m* en kit; **it arrives as a ~ pack** c'est livré en kit ► **flat-pack** ADJ en kit ► **flat race** N course *f* de plat ► **flat racing** N course *f* de plat ► **flat rate amount** N (*Fin, Jur*) montant *m* forfaitaire ► **flat screen** N (*TV*) écran *m* plat ► **flat season** N (*Racing*) saison *f* des courses de plat ► **flat silver** N (*US*) couverts *mpl* en argent ► **flat top** N (= *haircut*) coupe *f* en brosse

flat² [flæt] **1** N (*Brit*) appartement *m* **2** COMP ► **flat-hunting** N **to go ~-hunting** chercher un appartement

flatfish ['flætfɪʃ] N (*pl* **flatfish** or **flatfishes**) poisson *m* plat

flatfoot: ['flætfʊt] N (*pl* **-foots** or **-feet**) (*US* = *policeman*) flic* *m*

flatfooted [ˌflæt'fʊtɪd] **1** ADJ (*lit*) aux pieds plats; (* *fig* = *tactless*) [*person, approach*] maladroit **2** ADV (= *wholeheartedly*) tout de go*; (*fig*) **to catch sb ~*** prendre qn par surprise

flatlet ['flætlɪt] N (*Brit*) studio *m*

flatly ['flætlɪ] ADV **a** (= *firmly*) [*refuse, deny, reject*] catégoriquement; **to be ~ against sth** être catégoriquement contre qch; **to be ~ opposed to sth** être catégoriquement opposé à qch **b** (= *unemotionally*) [*say, state*] avec impassibilité **c** (= *absolutely*) **to be ~ inconsistent with sth** être absolument incompatible avec qch

flatmate ['flætmeɪt] N **my ~** la personne avec qui je partage mon appartement; (*both renting*) mon colocataire, ma colocataire

flatness ['flætnɪs] N **a** [*of countryside, surface*] manque *m* de relief, aspect *m* plat; [*of curve*] aplatissement *m* **b** [*of refusal*] netteté *f* **c** (= *dullness*) monotonie *f*

flatten ['flætn] VT **a** (= *make less bumpy*) [+ *path, road*] aplanir; [+ *metal*] aplatir **b** (= *destroy*) [*wind, storm*] [+ *crops*] coucher, écraser; [+ *tree*] abattre; [*bombing, earthquake*] [+ *town, building*] raser; [+ *knock over*] [+ *person*] étendre*; **to ~ o.s. against** s'aplatir or se plaquer contre **c** (* = *defeat*) écraser* **d** (*Mus*) [+ *tone, pitch, note*] bémoliser **e** [+ *battery*] mettre à plat

► **flatten out** **1** VI [*countryside, road*] s'aplanir; [*aircraft*] se redresser; [*curve*] s'aplatir **2** VT SEP [+ *path*] aplanir; [+ *metal*] aplatir; [+ *map, newspaper*] ouvrir à plat

flatter ['flætə'] VT (*all senses*) flatter; **he ~s himself he's a good musician** il se flatte d'être bon musicien; **you ~ yourself!** tu te flattes!

flatterer ['flætərə'] N flatteur *m*, -euse *f*, flagorneur *m*, -euse *f* (*pej*)

flattering ['flætərɪŋ] ADJ **a** [*person, remark, behaviour*] flatteur (*to sb* pour qn); **they listened to him with a ~ interest** ils l'ont écouté avec un intérêt flatteur; **to be ~ about sb** parler de qn en termes flatteurs **b** [*clothes, colour*] flatteur; **it wasn't a very ~ photo (of him)** ce n'était pas une photo qui l'avantageait beaucoup; **lighter shades are more ~ to your complexion** les tons clairs sont plus flatteurs pour votre teint or conviennent mieux à votre teint

flatteringly ['flætərɪŋlɪ] ADV flatteusement

flattery ['flætərɪ] N flatterie *f*; (*hum*) **~ will get you nowhere/everywhere** la flatterie ne mène à rien/mène à tout

flatties* ['flætɪz] NPL chaussures *fpl* basses or à talon plat

flattop* ['flættɒp] N (*US*) porte-avions *m*

flatulence ['flætjʊləns] N flatulence *f*

flatulent ['flætjʊlənt] ADJ flatulent

flatware ['flætwɛə'] N (*US*) (= *plates*) plats *mpl* et assiettes *fpl*; (= *cutlery*) couverts *mpl*

flatworm ['flætwɜːm] N plathelminthe *m*, ver *m* plat

flaunt [flɔːnt] VT [+ *wealth*] étaler, afficher; [+ *jewels*] faire étalage de; [+ *knowledge*] faire étalage or parade de; [+ *boyfriend etc*] afficher; **she ~ed her femininity at him** elle lui jetait sa féminité à la tête; **to ~ o.s.** poser (pour la galerie)

flautist ['flɔːtɪst] N (*esp Brit*) flûtiste *mf*

flavour, flavor (*US*) ['fleɪvə'] **1** N goût *m*, saveur *f*; [*of ice cream, sweet, yoghurt, jelly*] parfum *m*; **with a rum ~** (parfumé au rhum); (*fig*) **a slight ~ of irony** une légère pointe d'ironie; **the film gives the ~ of Paris in the twenties** le film rend bien l'atmosphère du Paris des années vingt; (*fig*) **to be (the) ~ of the month** être la coqueluche du moment **2** VT (*with fruit, spirits*) parfumer (**with** à); (*with herbs, spices*) aromatiser, assaisonner; **to ~ a sauce with garlic** relever une sauce avec de l'ail; **pineapple-~ed** (parfumé) à l'ananas **3** COMP ► **flavour enhancer** N agent *m* de sapidité, exhausteur *m* de goût or de saveur

flavourful, flavorful (*US*) ['fleɪvə,fʊl] ADJ goûteux

flavouring, flavoring (*US*) ['fleɪvərɪŋ] N (*in cake, yoghurt, ice cream*) parfum *m*; **vanilla ~** parfum *m* vanille

flavourless, flavorless (*US*) ['fleɪvəlɪs] ADJ insipide, sans saveur

flaw [flɔː] **1** N (*in character*) défaut *m*, imperfection *f*; (*in argument, reasoning*) faille *f*; (*in wood*) défaut *m*, imperfection *f*; (*in gemstone, marble*) défaut *m*, crapaud *m*; (*Jur: in contract, procedure*) vice *m* de forme; (= *obstacle*) problème *m*; **everything seems to be working out, but there's just one ~** tout semble s'arranger, il n'y a qu'un problème **2** VT **the plan was ~ed by its dependence on the actions of others** le plan avait un point faible: il dépendait des actions des autres; **his career was ~ed by this incident** cet incident a nui à sa carrière; **the elections were ~ed by widespread irregularities** les élections ont été entachées de très nombreuses irrégularités; **the team's performance was seriously ~ed by their inexperience** le manque d'expérience de l'équipe a sérieusement nui à ses résultats

flawed [flɔːd] ADJ [*person, character*] imparfait; [*object, argument, reasoning, plot*] défectueux

flawless ['flɔːlɪs] ADJ parfait, sans défaut; **he spoke ~ English** il parlait un anglais impeccable, il parlait parfaitement l'anglais

flax [flæks] N lin *m*

flaxen ['flæksən] ADJ [*hair*] (blond) filasse *inv*, de lin (*liter*); (*Tex*) de lin; **~-haired** aux cheveux (blond) filasse, aux cheveux de lin (*liter*)

flay [fleɪ] VT **a** (= *beat*) [+ *person, animal*] fouetter, rosser; (= *criticize*) éreinter **b** [+ *animal*] (= *skin*) écorcher

flea [fliː] **1** N puce *f*; **to send sb away** or **off with a ~ in his ear*** envoyer promener* qn, envoyer qn sur les roses* → **sand** **2** COMP ► **flea collar** N [*of dog, cat*] collier *m* antipuces ► **flea market** N marché *m* aux puces ► **flea-pit:** N (*Brit* = *cinema*) ciné* *m* miteux ► **flea powder** N poudre *f* antipuces ► **flea-ridden** ADJ (*lit*) [*person, animal*] couvert de puces; [*place*] infesté de puces; (*fig*) miteux

fleabag: ['fliːbæg] N (*Brit* = *person*) souillon *mf*; (*US* = *hotel*) hôtel *m* minable

fleabite ['fliːbaɪt] N (*lit*) piqûre *f* de puce; (*fig*) vétille *f*, broutille *f*

fleabitten ['fliː,bɪtn] N (*lit*) infesté de puces; (*fig*) miteux

fleck [flek] **1** N [*of colour*] moucheture *f*; [*of foam*] flocon *m*; [*of blood, light*] petite tache *f*; [*of dust*] particule *f* **2** VT tacheter, moucheter; **dress ~ed with mud** robe *f* éclaboussée de boue; **blue ~ed with white** bleu moucheté de blanc; **sky ~ed with little clouds** ciel *m* pommelé; **hair ~ed with grey** cheveux *mpl* qui commencent à grisonner

fled [fled] VB *pt, ptp* of **flee**

fledged [fledʒd] ADJ → **fully**

fledg(e)ling ['fledʒlɪŋ] **1** N **a** (*Orn*) oiselet *m*, oisillon *m* **b** (*fig* = *novice*) novice *mf*, débutant(e) *m(f)* **2** COMP [*industry, democracy*] jeune; [*dancer, writer, poet*] débutant

flee [fliː] (*pret, ptp* **fled**) **1** VI fuir (*before* devant), s'enfuir (*from* de); **they fled** ils ont fui, ils se sont enfuis; **they fled to Britain/to their parents'** ils se sont enfuis en Grande-Bretagne/chez leurs parents; **I fled when I heard she was expected** je me suis sauvé or j'ai pris la fuite lorsque j'ai appris qu'elle devait venir; **to ~ from temptation** fuir la tentation **2** VT [+ *town, country*] s'enfuir de; [+ *famine, war, temptation, danger*] fuir

fleece [fliːs] **1** N **a** [*of sheep*] toison *f* → **golden** **b** (= *garment*) (laine *f*) polaire *f* **2** VT

a (= rob) voler; (= swindle) escroquer, filouter; (= overcharge) estamper* **b** [+ sheep] tondre **3** COMP ► **fleece-lined** ADJ doublé de mouton

fleecy ['fliːsɪ] ADJ [blanket, lining] laineux; [jacket] doublé de laine; [cloud] floconneux

fleet¹ [fliːt] **1** N (Naut) flotte f; [of cars, buses, lorries] parc m → **admiral, fishing 2** COMP ► **fleet admiral** N (US) amiral m ► **Fleet Air Arm** N (Brit) aéronavale f ► **fleet chief petty officer** N (Brit) major m

fleet² [fliːt] ADJ (also ~-footed, ~ of foot) rapide, au pied léger

fleeting ['fliːtɪŋ] ADJ [smile, glance, thought] fugitif; [memory] fugace; **a ~ visit** une visite en coup de vent; **to catch** or **get a ~ glimpse of sb/sth** entrapercevoir qn/qch; **to make a ~ appearance** faire une brève apparition; **for a ~ moment** l'espace d'un instant; (liter) **the ~ years** les années fpl qui fuient

fleetingly ['fliːtɪŋlɪ] ADV [think, wonder] un bref or court instant; [see, appear] fugitivement; **to smile ~ at sb** adresser un sourire fugitif à qn

Fleet Street [fliːt,striːt] N (Brit) les milieux de la presse londonienne

Fleming ['flemɪŋ] N Flamand(e) m(f)

Flemish ['flemɪʃ] **1** ADJ flamand **2** N (Ling) flamand m **3** the Flemish NPL les Flamands mpl

flesh [fleʃ] **1** N **a** [of person, animal] chair f; [of fruit, vegetable] chair f, pulpe f; **to put on ~** [animal] engraisser; (fig) **to make sb's ~ creep** or **crawl** donner la chair de poule à qn; **creatures of ~ and blood** êtres mpl de chair et de sang; **I'm only ~ and blood** je ne suis qu'un homme (or qu'une femme) comme les autres; **my own ~ and blood** la chair de ma chair; **it is more than ~ and blood can stand** c'est plus que la nature humaine ne peut endurer; **in the ~** en chair et en os, en personne; **to put ~ on the bare bones of a proposal** étoffer une proposition → **pound** **b** (Rel liter) **he's gone the way of all ~** (= died) il a payé son tribut à la nature†; **the sins of the ~** les péchés mpl de la chair; **the ~ is weak** la chair est faible **2** COMP ► **flesh colour** N couleur f chair; (Art) carnation f ► **flesh-coloured** ADJ (couleur f) chair inv ► **flesh tints** NPL (Art) carnations fpl ► **flesh wound** N blessure f superficielle

► **flesh out** VT SEP (fig) [+ essay, speech] étoffer; [+ idea, proposal, agreement] développer; **to ~ out the details of an agreement** développer les éléments d'un accord; **the author needs to ~ out his characters more** il faut que l'auteur étoffe davantage ses personnages

fleshly ['fleʃlɪ] ADJ (liter) [creature, love] charnel; [pleasures] charnel, de la chair

fleshpots ['fleʃpɒts] NPL lieux mpl de plaisir

fleshy ['fleʃɪ] ADJ [face] rebondi, joufflu; [cheeks] rebondi; [nose, fruit, leaf] charnu; [person] grassouillet

flew [fluː] VB pt of fly³

flex [fleks] **1** VT [+ body, knees] fléchir, ployer (pour assouplir); **to ~ one's muscles** (lit) faire jouer ses muscles, bander (liter) ses muscles; (fig) faire étalage de sa force **2** N (Brit) [of lamp, iron] fil m (souple); [of telephone] cordon m; [heavy duty] câble m

flexi* ['fleksɪ] = **flexitime**

flexibility [,fleksɪ'bɪlɪtɪ] N [of material, person, attitude, approach] souplesse f, flexibilité f; [of body] souplesse f; [of working hours, system] flexibilité f; [of machine, device] flexibilité f, souplesse f d'emploi

flexible ['fleksəbl] **1** ADJ **a** [object, material] flexible, souple; [person, limbs, joints, body] souple **b** (fig) [person, approach, system, plans] flexible, souple; [working hours, budget] flexible; (fig) **I'm ~** je peux toujours m'arranger;

to be ~ in one's approach faire preuve de souplesse **2** COMP ► **flexible response** N (Mil) riposte f graduée

flexibly ['fleksəblɪ] ADV [respond, adapt, apply] avec souplesse; [work] avec flexibilité; **to interpret a rule ~** interpréter une règle avec une certaine souplesse

flexion ['flekʃən] N flexion f, courbure f

flexitime ['fleksɪ,taɪm] N (esp Brit) horaire m flexible or à la carte; **to work ~** avoir un horaire flexible or à la carte; **we work 35 hours' ~ a week** on travaille 35 heures hebdomadaires en horaire flexible

flexor ['fleksə] ADJ, N fléchisseur m

flibbertigibbet ['flɪbətɪ'dʒɪbɪt] N tête f de linotte, étourdi(e) m(f)

flick [flɪk] **1** N **a** [of tail, duster] petit coup m; (with finger) chiquenaude f, pichenette f; (with wrist) petit mouvement m (rapide); **at the ~ of a switch** rien qu'en appuyant sur un bouton **b** (Brit* = film) film m; **the ~s** le ciné*, le cinoche* **2** VT donner un petit coup à; **he ~ed the horse lightly with the reins** il a donné au cheval un (tout) petit coup avec les rênes; **I'll just ~ a duster round the sitting room** je vais passer un petit coup de chiffon dans le salon; **to ~ a ball of paper at sb** envoyer d'une chiquenaude une boulette de papier à qn; **he ~ed his cigarette ash into the ashtray** il a fait tomber la cendre de sa cigarette dans le cendrier **3** COMP ► **flick knife** N (pl **flick knives**) (Brit) (couteau m à) cran m d'arrêt

► **flick off** VT SEP [+ dust, ash] enlever d'une chiquenaude

► **flick out** VI, VT SEP **the snake's tongue ~ed out** ◊ **the snake ~ed its tongue out** le serpent a dardé sa langue

► **flick over** VT SEP [+ pages of book] feuilleter, tourner rapidement

► **flick through** VT FUS [+ pages of book, document] feuilleter, lire en diagonale; **to ~ through the TV channels** zapper

flicker ['flɪkə] **1** VI [flames, light] danser; (before going out) trembloter, vaciller; [needle on dial] osciller; [eyelids] ciller; **the snake's tongue ~ed in and out** le serpent a dardé sa langue **2** N [of flames, light] danse f; (before going out) vacillement m; (fig) **without a ~** sans sourciller or broncher; **a ~ of hope** une lueur d'espoir; **a ~ of doubt** l'ombre f d'un doute; **a ~ of annoyance** un geste d'humeur; **without a ~ of a smile** sans l'ombre d'un sourire **3** VT **to ~ one's eyelids** battre des cils

flickering ['flɪkərɪŋ] ADJ (gen) tremblant; [flames] dansant; (before going out) vacillant; [needle] oscillant

flickertail ['flɪkə,teɪl] **1** N (US) spermophile m d'Amérique du Nord **2** COMP ► **the Flickertail State** N le Dakota du Nord

flier ['flaɪə] N **a** (Aviat = person) aviateur m, -trice f; **to be a good ~** [passenger] supporter (bien) l'avion; **to be a bad ~** ne pas supporter or mal supporter l'avion → **high b** (US) (= fast train) rapide m; (= fast coach) car m express **c** **to take a ~** (= leap) sauter avec élan; (US* fig = take a risk) foncer tête baissée **d** (US Ex) (folle) aventure f **e** (= handbill) prospectus m

flight¹ [flaɪt] **1** N **a** (NonC = action, course) [of bird, insect, plane] vol m; [of ball, bullet] trajectoire f; **the principles of ~** les rudiments mpl du vol or de la navigation aérienne; **in ~** en plein vol; (Mus) **the Flight of the Bumblebee** le Vol du bourdon **b** (= plane trip) vol m; **~ number 776 from/to Madrid** le vol numéro 776 en provenance/à destination de Madrid; **did you have a good ~?** le vol s'est bien passé?, vous avez fait (un) bon voyage? **c** (fig) **a ~ of fancy** (= harebrained idea) une idée folle; (= figment of imagination) une pure invention; **to indulge** or **engage in a ~ of fancy** avoir des idées folles; **in my wildest ~s of**

fancy dans mes rêves les plus fous → **reconnaissance, test** **d** (= group) [of birds] vol m, volée f; [of planes] escadrille f; (in the first or **top ~ of scientists/novelists** parmi les scientifiques/les romanciers les plus marquants; **a firm in the top ~** une entreprise prestigieuse **e** **~ of stairs** escalier m, volée f d'escalier; **we had to climb three ~s to get to his room** nous avons dû monter trois étages pour arriver à sa chambre; **he lives three ~s up** il habite au troisième; **~ of hurdles** série f de haies; **~ of terraces** escalier m de terrasses **2** COMP ► **flight attendant** N steward m/hôtesse f de l'air, agent m de bord ► **flight bag** N (petit) sac m de voyage, bagage m à main ► **flight control** N (on ground) contrôle m aérien; (in aircraft) commande f de vol ► **flight crew** N équipage m ► **flight deck** N [of plane] poste m or cabine f de pilotage; [of aircraft carrier] pont m d'envol ► **flight engineer** N mécanicien m de bord ► **flight lieutenant** N (Brit) capitaine m (de l'armée de l'air) ► **flight log** N suivi m de vol ► **flight path** N trajectoire f (de vol) ► **flight plan** N plan m de vol ► **flight recorder** N enregistreur m de vol ► **flight sergeant** N (Brit) ≈ sergent-chef m (de l'armée de l'air) ► **flight simulator** N simulateur m de vol ► **flight-test** VT essayer en vol

flight² [flaɪt] N (NonC = act of fleeing) fuite f; **to put to ~** mettre en fuite; **to take (to) ~** prendre la fuite, s'enfuir; (Fin) **the ~ of capital abroad** la fuite or l'exode m des capitaux à l'étranger

flightless ['flaɪtlɪs] ADJ incapable de voler; **~ bird** ratite m, oiseau m coureur

flighty ['flaɪtɪ] ADJ (gen) frivole; (in love) volage, inconstant

flimflam* ['flɪm,flæm] (US) **1** N (= nonsense) balivernes fpl, blague* f **2** ADJ **a ~ man** or **artist** un filou, un escroc **3** VT (= swindle) rouler*, blouser*

flimsily ['flɪmzɪlɪ] ADV **~ built** or **constructed** (d'une construction) peu solide; **his thesis was ~ argued** sa thèse était assez faiblement étayée

flimsiness ['flɪmzɪnɪs] N [of dress] finesse f; [of house] caractère m peu solide; [of paper] minceur f; [of excuse, reasoning] faiblesse f, futilité f

flimsy ['flɪmzɪ] **1** ADJ **a** (= fragile) [object, structure, construction] peu solide; [fabric] peu résistant **b** (= thin) [fabric] léger, mince; [garment] léger, fin; [paper] mince **c** (= feeble) [evidence] peu convaincant; [excuse] piètre; [grounds] peu solide **2** N (Brit = type of paper) papier m pelure inv

flinch [flɪntʃ] VI broncher, tressaillir; **to ~ from a task** reculer devant une tâche; **he didn't ~ from warning her** il ne s'est pas dérobé au devoir de la prévenir; **without ~ing** sans sourciller or broncher

fling [flɪŋ] (vb: pret, ptp **flung**) **1** N* **a** (= spree) **to go on a ~** aller faire la noce or la foire*; (in shops) faire des folies; **youth must have its ~** il faut que jeunesse se passe (PROV); **to have a last** or **final ~** (= do sth foolish) faire une dernière folie; [sportsman etc] faire un dernier exploit; **to have a final ~ at beating one's opponent/winning the championship** tenter une dernière fois de battre son adversaire/de remporter le championnat → **highland** **b** (= affair) aventure f; **he had a brief ~ with my sister** il a eu une brève aventure avec ma sœur **2** VT [+ object, stone] jeter, lancer (at sb à qn, at sth sur qch); (fig) [+ remark, insult] lancer (at sb à qn); **he flung his opponent to the ground** il a jeté son adversaire à terre; **to ~ sb into jail** jeter or flanquer* qn en prison; **to ~ the window open** ouvrir toute grande la fenêtre; **the door was flung open** la porte s'est ouverte brusquement; **to ~ one's arms round sb** or **sb's neck** sauter or se jeter au cou de qn; **to ~ a coat over one's shoulders** jeter un manteau sur ses épaules; **to ~ one's coat on/off** enfiler/enlever son manteau d'un geste brusque; **to ~ an accusation at sb** lancer une accusation contre qn; **to ~ o.s. off a bridge/under a train** se jeter d'un pont/sous un train; **to ~ o.s. to the ground/to one's knees** se jeter à terre/à genoux; **to ~ o.s. into a job/a hobby** se jeter or se lancer à corps perdu dans un travail/une activité; (fig) **she flung herself* at him** elle s'est jetée à sa tête

▶ **fling away** VT SEP [+ unwanted object] jeter, ficher en l'air*; (fig) [+ money] gaspiller, jeter par les fenêtres

▶ **fling back** VT SEP [+ ball etc] renvoyer; [+ one's head] rejeter en arrière; [+ curtains] ouvrir brusquement

▶ **fling off** VT SEP (fig liter) se débarrasser de

▶ **fling out** VT SEP [+ person] flanquer* or mettre à la porte; [+ unwanted object] jeter, ficher en l'air*

▶ **fling up** VT SEP jeter en l'air; **to ~ one's arms up in exasperation** lever les bras en l'air ou au ciel d'exaspération

flint [flɪnt] **1** N (gen) silex m; (for cigarette lighter) pierre f (à briquet) → **clay 2** COMP [axe] de silex ▶ **flint glass** N flint(-glass) m

flintlock ['flɪntlɒk] N fusil m à silex

flinty ['flɪntɪ] ADJ **a** (Geol) [soil, ground, rocks] siliceux **b** (= cruel) [person] dur, insensible; [heart] de pierre; [eyes, look] dur

flip [flɪp] **1** N **a** chiquenaude f, petit coup m; **to decide/win sth on the ~ of a coin** décider/gagner qch en tirant à pile ou face **b** (Aviat*) petit tour m en zinc* **2** VT donner un petit coup à, donner une chiquenaude à; (US) [+ pancake] faire sauter; **to ~ a coin** tirer à pile ou face; **to ~ a book open** ouvrir un livre d'une chiquenaude or d'une pichenette; **to ~ one's lid*** ◊ **to ~ one's wig*** or (US) **one's top*** éclater, exploser (fig) **3** VI (*: also **~ out**) (angrily) piquer une crise* (**over** à cause de); (ecstatically) devenir dingue* (**over** de) **4** ADJ [remark, repartee] désinvolte **5** EXCL* zut!* **6** COMP ▶ **flip-flop** → **flip-flop** ▶ **flip side** N [of record] autre face f, face f B; (fig) envers m ▶ **flip-top bin** N poubelle f à couvercle pivotant

▶ **flip out** VI → **flip 3**

▶ **flip over** VT SEP [+ stone] retourner d'un coup léger; [+ pages] feuilleter

▶ **flip through** VT FUS [+ book] feuilleter

flipboard ['flɪpbɔːd], **flipchart** ['flɪptʃaːt] N tableau m de conférence

flip-flop ['flɪpflɒp] **1** N **a** (Comput) bascule f (bistable); **b** (esp US fig = change of opinion) volte-face f **2** **flip-flops** NPL (= sandals) tongs fpl **3** VI (US fig) faire volte-face

flippancy ['flɪpənsɪ] N [of attitude] désinvolture f; [of speech, remark] irrévérence f, légèreté f

flippant ['flɪpənt] ADJ [person, remark] désinvolte; **to sound ~** sembler désinvolte

flippantly ['flɪpəntlɪ] ADV avec désinvolture, irrévérencieusement, cavalièrement

flipper ['flɪpə'] N [of seal, whale, penguin] nageoire f; **~s** [of swimmer] palmes fpl

flipping* ['flɪpɪŋ] (Brit) **1** ADJ [+ fichu* (before n), maudit (before n) **2** ADV (Brit) [rude, stupid, cold] drôlement*; **it's ~ impossible!** c'est vraiment impossible! **; ~ heck!** ◊ **~ hell!** zut!*

flirt [flɜːt] **1** VI flirter (**with** avec); **to ~ with danger** flirter avec le danger; **to ~ with an idea** caresser une idée **2** N **he's a ~** c'est un dragueur*, il aime flirter

flirtation [flɜː'teɪʃən] N flirt m, amourette f

flirtatious [flɜː'teɪʃəs] ADJ flirteur

flirty* ['flɜːtɪ] ADJ [person, behaviour] dragueur*; [clothes] sexy inv

flit [flɪt] **1** VI **a** [bats, butterflies] voleter, voltiger; **the idea ~ted through his head** l'idée lui

a traversé l'esprit **b** [person] **to ~ in/out** etc (Brit: lightly) entrer/sortir etc avec légèreté; (US: affectedly) entrer/sortir etc en minaudant; **to ~ about** (Brit) se déplacer avec légèreté; (US) marcher à petits pas maniérés **c** (Brit = move house stealthily) déménager à la cloche de bois; (N Engl, Scot = move house) déménager **2** N **a** (N Engl, Scot = house move) déménagement m; (Brit) **to do a (moonlight) ~** déménager à la cloche de bois **b** (US*: = homosexual) pédale* f, tapette* f

flitch [flɪtʃ] N flèche f (de lard)

flitting ['flɪtɪŋ] N (N Engl, Scot) déménagement m

flivver* ['flɪvə'] N (US) tacot* m, guimbarde* f

float [fləʊt] **1** N **a** (Fishing, Plumbing) flotteur m, flotte f; (of cork) bouchon m; (of seaplane) flotteur m

b (= vehicle in a parade) char m → **milk**

c (also **cash ~**) fonds m de caisse

d (esp US = drink) milk-shake ou soda contenant une boule de glace

2 VI (on water, in air) flotter; [ship] être à flot; [swimmer] faire la planche; (Fin) [currency] flotter; **the raft ~ed down the river** le radeau a descendu la rivière; **to ~ back up to the surface** remonter à la surface (de l'eau); **the balloon ~ed up into the sky** le ballon s'est envolé dans le ciel; **music ~ed through the air** une musique flottait dans l'air; **the idea ~ed into his mind** l'idée lui a traversé l'esprit

3 VT **a** [+ boat] faire flotter, mettre à flot or sur l'eau; (= refloat) remettre à flot or sur l'eau; [+ wood etc] faire flotter; (fig) [+ idea] lancer; **to ~ logs downstream** faire flotter des rondins au fil de l'eau

b (Fin) [+ currency] laisser flotter; [+ company] fonder, créer; **to ~ a share issue** émettre des actions; **to ~ a loan** lancer or émettre un emprunt

▶ **float around*** VI [rumour, news] circuler, courir; **have you seen my glasses ~ing around anywhere?** as-tu vu mes lunettes quelque part?

▶ **float away** VI dériver, partir à la dérive

▶ **float off 1** VI [wreck] se renflouer, se déséchouer **2** VT SEP [+ wreck] renflouer, remettre à flot

▶ **float round*** VI = **float around**

floatation [fləʊ'teɪʃən] = **flotation**

floating ['fləʊtɪŋ] **1** ADJ [leaves, debris etc] flottant; [population] fluctuant

2 N **a** [of boat] mise f en flottement **b** (Fin) [of loan] lancement m; [of currency] flottement m, flottaison f

3 COMP ▶ **floating assets** NPL (Fin) capitaux mpl circulants ▶ **floating currency** N (Fin) devise f flottante ▶ **floating currency rate** N (Fin) taux m de change flottant ▶ **floating debt** N (Fin) dette f à court terme or flottante ▶ **floating decimal (point)** N (Math) virgule f flottante ▶ **floating dock** N (Naut) dock m flottant ▶ **floating exchange** (Fin) change m flottant ▶ **floating point representation** N (Comput) notation f en virgule flottante ▶ **floating restaurant** N restaurant m flottant ▶ **floating rib** N (Anat) côte f flottante ▶ **floating vote** N (Brit Pol) vote m flottant ▶ **floating voter** N (Brit Pol) électeur m, -trice f indécis(e)

flocculent ['flɒkjʊlənt] ADJ floconneux

flock¹ [flɒk] **1** N [of sheep, geese] troupeau m; [of birds] vol m, volée f; [of people] foule f, troupeau m (pej); (Rel) ouailles fpl; **they came in ~s** ils sont venus en masse **2** VI aller or venir en masse or en foule, affluer; **to ~ in/out** etc entrer/sortir etc en foule; **to ~ together** s'assembler; **to ~ round sb** s'attrouper or s'assembler autour de qn

flock² [flɒk] **1** N (NonC) [of wool] bourre f de laine; [of cotton] bourre f de coton **2** COMP

▶ **flock (wall)paper** N papier m velouté or tontisse

floe [fləʊ] N banquise f, glaces fpl flottantes

flog [flɒg] VT **a** flageller, fustiger; **to ~ an idea to death*** or **into the ground*** rabâcher une idée → **dead b** (Brit*: = sell) fourguer*; **how much did you ~ it for?** tu en as tiré combien ?*

flogging ['flɒgɪŋ] N flagellation f, fustigation f; (Jur) fouet m (sanction)

flood [flʌd] **1** N **a** (gen) inondation f; (also **~ tide**) marée f haute; (notice on road) **"~"** ≈ «attention route inondée »; (Bible) **the Flood** le déluge; **river in ~** rivière f en crue; **~s of tears** un torrent or déluge de larmes; **a ~ of light** un flot de lumière; **a ~ of letters/protests** un déluge de lettres/de protestations; **a ~ of immigrants** une marée d'immigrants

b = **floodlight**

2 VT **a** [+ fields, town] inonder, submerger; (fig) inonder; **he was ~ed with letters/applications** il a été inondé de lettres/de demandes; **room ~ed with light** pièce f inondée de lumière

b [storm, rain] [+ river, stream] faire déborder; (Comm) **to ~ the market** [suppliers, goods] inonder le marché (**with** de)

c (Aut) [+ carburettor] noyer

3 VI [river] déborder, être en crue; **the crowd ~ed into the streets** la foule a envahi les rues or s'est répandue dans les rues; **refugees ~ed across the border** les réfugiés ont franchi la frontière en masse, des flots de réfugiés ont franchi la frontière

4 COMP ▶ **flood control** N prévention f des inondations ▶ **flood damage** N dégâts mpl des eaux ▶ **flood plain** N zone f inondable ▶ **flood tide** N marée f haute

▶ **flood back** VI [memories, worries] (also **come ~ing back**) resurgir; **it brought all the memories ~ing back** cela a fait resurgir tous les souvenirs

▶ **flood in** VI [sunshine] entrer à flots; [people] entrer en foule, affluer

▶ **flood out** VT SEP [+ house] inonder; **the villagers were ~ed out** les inondations ont forcé les villageois à évacuer leurs maisons

floodgate ['flʌdgeɪt] N vanne f, porte f d'écluse; (fig) **these changes would open the ~s to ...** ces changements seraient la porte ouverte à ...

flooding ['flʌdɪŋ] N inondation f

floodlight ['flʌdlaɪt] (pret, ptp **floodlit**) **1** VT [+ buildings] illuminer; (Sport) [+ match] éclairer (aux projecteurs) **2** N (= device) projecteur m; (= light) lumière f (des projecteurs); **to play a match under ~s** jouer un match en nocturne

floodlighting ['flʌdlaɪtɪŋ] N [of building] illumination f; [of match] éclairage m (aux projecteurs)

floodlit ['flʌdlɪt] VB pt, ptp of **floodlight**

floodwater(s) ['flʌd,wɔːtə(z)] N(PL) eaux fpl de crue

flooey* ['fluːɪ] ADJ **to go ~** se détraquer*

floor [flɔː'] **1** N **a** (gen) sol m; (wooden) plancher m, parquet m; (for dance) piste f (de danse); [of valley, ocean] fond m; (fig) [of prices] plancher m; **stone/tiled ~** sol m dallé/carrelé; **put it on the ~** pose-le par terre or sur le sol; **she was sitting on the ~** elle était assise par terre or sur le sol; **to take to the ~** (= dance) aller sur la piste (de danse); **last year, sales went through the ~** l'année dernière les ventes ont chuté; **property prices have dropped through the ~** les prix sur le marché immobilier se sont effondrés → **wipe**

b (in public speaking) **a question from the ~ of the house** une question de l'auditoire m or de l'assemblée f; **to hold the ~** garder la parole; **to take the ~** (= speak) prendre la parole; (Parl) **to cross the ~ (of the House)** ≈ s'inscrire à un parti opposé

[c] (= storey) étage m; **first ~** (Brit) premier étage m; (US) rez-de-chaussée m; **on the first ~** (Brit) au premier (étage); (in two-storey building) à l'étage; (US) au rez-de-chaussée; **he lives on the second ~** (Brit) il habite au deuxième étage or au second; (US) il habite au premier (étage); **we live on the same ~** nous habitons au même étage or sur le même palier → **ground**[1]

[d] (St Ex) enceinte f de la Bourse; **on/off the ~** en/hors Bourse

[2] VT [a] faire le sol de; (with wooden boards) planchéier, parqueter

[b] (= knock down) [+ opponent] terrasser; (Boxing) envoyer au tapis

[c] (* = silence) réduire au silence; (* = baffle, perplex) désorienter, dérouter; (Sport = defeat) battre à plates coutures; **this argument ~ed him** il n'a rien trouvé à répondre

[3] COMP ► **floor area** N [of flat, offices etc] surface f au sol ► **floor covering** N revêtement m de sol ► **floor exercises** NPL exercices mpl au sol ► **floor lamp** N (US) lampadaire m ► **floor leader** N (US Pol) chef m de file ► **floor manager** N (TV) régisseur m de plateau; (in shop) chef m de rayon ► **floor plan** N (Archit) plan m de niveau ► **floor polish** N encaustique f, cire f ► **floor polisher** N (= tool) cireuse f ► **floor show** N attractions fpl, spectacle m de variétés (dans un restaurant, cabaret etc) ► **floor space** N (gen) place f (par terre); (Comm) surface f au sol

floorboard ['flɔːbɔːd] N planche f (de plancher), latte f

floorcloth ['flɔːklɒθ] N serpillière f

flooring ['flɔːrɪŋ] N (= floor) sol m; (made of wood) plancher m, parquet m; (tiled) carrelage m; (= material) revêtement m (de sol)

floorwalker ['flɔːˌwɔːkəʳ] N (US Comm) chef m de rayon

floozy* ['fluːzɪ] N poule* f, pouffiasse: f

flop [flɒp] [1] VI [a] (= drop) s'effondrer, s'affaler; **he ~ped down on the bed/in a chair** il s'est effondré or s'est affalé sur le lit/dans un fauteuil; **his hair ~ped over his left eye** ses cheveux lui tombaient sur l'œil gauche [b] (US: = sleep) roupiller* [c] (= fail) [play, film, record] faire un four or un flop; [scheme etc] être un fiasco or un bide*; **he ~ped as Hamlet** son interprétation d'Hamlet a fait un four [2] N [a] (= failure) [of business venture, scheme] fiasco m; **the play was a ~** la pièce a été un four or un bide*; **he was a terrible ~** il a lamentablement raté son coup

► **flop over*** (US) [1] VI **to ~ over to a new idea** adopter une nouvelle idée [2] **~over** N → **flopover**

flophouse* ['flɒphaʊs] N (US) asile m de nuit

flopover* ['flɒpəʊvəʳ] N (US TV) cascade f d'images

floppy ['flɒpɪ] [1] ADJ [hat] à bords flottants; [clothes] lâche, flottant; [rabbit, dog ears] tombant [2] N = **floppy disk** [3] COMP ► **floppy disk** N (Comput) disquette f ► **floppy (disk) drive** N (Comput) lecteur m de disquettes

flora ['flɔːrə] N (pl **floras** or **florae** ['flɔːriː]) flore f

floral ['flɔːrəl] [1] ADJ [fabric, dress, wallpaper, curtains] à fleurs, à fleurs; [print] à fleurs; [design] à fleurs, floral; [fragrance, perfume] de fleurs; [arrangement, display] floral; **material with a ~ pattern** étoffe f à motifs floraux [2] COMP ► **floral tributes** NPL fleurs fpl et couronnes fpl

Florence ['flɒrəns] N Florence

Florentine ['flɒrəntaɪn] ADJ florentin

floret ['flɒrɪt] N (Bot) fleuron m; **cauliflower/broccoli ~s** morceaux mpl de chou-fleur/brocoli

floribunda [ˌflɒrəˈbʌndə] N polyanta floribunda m

florid ['flɒrɪd] ADJ [a] (= ornate) [language, literary style, wallpaper, architecture] très chargé [b] (= ruddy) [person, face, complexion] rubicond, rougeaud

Florida ['flɒrɪdə] N la Floride; **in ~** en Floride

florin ['flɒrɪn] N florin m (ancienne pièce de deux shillings)

florist ['flɒrɪst] N fleuriste mf; **~'s shop** magasin m de fleurs, fleuriste m

floss [flɒs] [1] N bourre f de soie; (also dental ~) fil m dentaire → **candy** [2] VTI **to ~ (one's teeth)** utiliser du fil dentaire

flossy* ['flɒsɪ] ADJ (US) ultrachic inv, d'un brillant superficiel

flotation [fləʊˈteɪʃən] [1] N [a] (lit) [of boat] action f de flotter; [of log] flottage m [b] (Fin) [of shares, loan] lancement m; [of company] constitution f, création f [2] COMP ► **flotation collar** N (Space) flotteur m (de module lunaire) ► **flotation compartment** N caisse f de flottaison ► **flotation tank** N caisse f de flottaison

flotilla [fləˈtɪlə] N flottille f

flotsam ['flɒtsəm] N (NonC) épave f (flottante); (lit) **~ and jetsam** épaves fpl flottantes et rejetées; (fig) **the ~ and jetsam of our society** les laissés-pour-compte de notre société

flounce [flaʊns] [1] VI **to ~ in/out** etc entrer/sortir etc dans un mouvement d'humeur (or d'indignation etc) [2] N [a] (= gesture) geste m impatient, mouvement m vif [b] (= frill: on clothes, curtain) volant m

flounced [flaʊnst] ADJ [skirt, dress] à volants

flounder[1] ['flaʊndəʳ] N (pl **flounder** or **flounders**) (= fish) flet m

flounder[2] ['flaʊndəʳ] VI (= move with difficulty) patauger (péniblement); (violently) se débattre; **we ~ed along in the mud** nous avons poursuivi notre chemin en pataugeant dans la boue; **I watched him ~ing about in the water** je le regardais se débattre dans l'eau; **he ~ed through the rest of the speech** il a fini le discours en bredouillant; **he ~ed on in bad French** il continuait de baragouiner en mauvais français; **his career was ~ing** sa carrière traversait une mauvaise passe; **the company/economy was ~ing** la société/l'économie battait de l'aile

flour [flaʊəʳ] [1] N farine f [2] VT fariner [3] COMP ► **flour bin** N boîte f à farine ► **flour mill** N minoterie f ► **flour shaker** N saupoudreuse f (à farine) ► **flour sifter** N tamis m à farine

flourish ['flʌrɪʃ] [1] VI [plant, animal] bien venir, se plaire; [business, town, market] prospérer; [person] s'épanouir; [literature, the arts, painting] fleurir, être en plein essor; **the children were all ~ing** les enfants étaient épanouis or en pleine forme; **the local fox population was ~ing** les renards prospéraient or se multipliaient dans la région; **racism and crime ~ed in poor areas** le racisme et la criminalité se développaient dans les quartiers pauvres; **drug traffickers continued to ~** les trafiquants de drogue ont continué à prospérer or à faire des affaires

[2] VT [+ stick, book, object] brandir

[3] N (= curve, decoration) fioriture f, ornement m; (in handwriting) fioriture f; (under signature) parafe m or paraphe m; (Mus) fioriture f; **he took the lid off with a ~** il a enlevé le couvercle avec un grand geste du bras

flourishing ['flʌrɪʃɪŋ] ADJ [business, economy, career] prospère, florissant; [garden] florissant; [plant, town] qui prospère; [market] en expansion → **flourish**

floury ['flaʊərɪ] ADJ [hands] enfariné; [potatoes]

farineux; [loaf, dish] saupoudré de farine, fariné

flout [flaʊt] VT [+ orders, advice] faire fi de, passer outre à; [+ conventions, society] mépriser, se moquer de

flow [fləʊ] [1] VI [a] (= run) [river, blood from wound] couler; [tide] monter, remonter; **to ~ back** refluer; **to ~ out of** [liquid] s'écouler de, sortir de; **to ~ past sth** passer devant qch; **the river ~s into the sea** le fleuve se jette dans la mer; **the water ~ed over the fields** l'eau s'est répandue dans les champs; **tears were ~ing down her cheeks** les larmes coulaient or ruisselaient sur ses joues

[b] (= circulate) [electric current, blood in veins] circuler; **traffic ~ed freely** la circulation était fluide

[c] (= move, stream) **to ~ in** [people] affluer, entrer à flots; **refugees continue to ~ in from the war zone** les réfugiés continuent à affluer de la zone des conflits; **the money keeps ~ing in** l'argent continue à rentrer; **let the music ~ over you** laissez la musique vous envahir, laissez-vous envahir par la musique; **a surge of hatred ~ed through my blood** j'ai soudain ressenti une bouffée de haine → **land**

[d] (= abound) **the wine ~ed all evening** le vin a coulé à flots toute la soirée; **his words ~ed readily** les mots lui venaient facilement

[e] [dress, hair etc] flotter, ondoyer

[f] (fig) **to ~ from** (= result) découler de, résulter de

[2] N [a] [of tide] flux m; [of river] courant m; **he stopped the ~ of blood** il a arrêté l'écoulement m or l'épanchement m du sang; **(menstrual) ~** flux m menstruel

[b] (= circulation) [of electric current, blood in veins] circulation f; **it hindered the ~ of traffic** ça a ralenti la circulation

[c] (fig = movement, flood) [of donations, orders, replies, words] flot m; **the interruption in the ~ of oil from Iran** l'arrêt de l'approvisionnement en pétrole iranien; **the phone rang, interrupting the ~ of conversation** le téléphone a sonné, interrompant le déroulement de la conversation; **the ~ of information** le flux d'informations; **to be in full ~** [speaker] être sur sa lancée; (fig) **to go with the ~** suivre le mouvement → **ebb**

[3] COMP ► **flow chart, flow diagram, flow sheet** N (gen) organigramme m; (Comput) ordinogramme m; (Admin, Ind) organigramme m, graphique m d'évolution

flower ['flaʊəʳ] [1] N [a] (lit) fleur f; **in ~** en fleurs; **to say sth with ~s** dire qch avec des fleurs; **"no ~s by request"** « ni fleurs ni couronnes »

[b] (fig) [of group, generation] (fine) fleur f, élite f; **the ~ of the army** la (fine) fleur or l'élite f de l'armée → **bunch**

[2] VI (lit, fig) fleurir

[3] COMP ► **flower arrangement** N (= art) art m floral; (= exhibit) composition f florale, arrangement m floral ► **flower arranging** N art m floral ► **flower bed** N platebande f, parterre m ► **flower children** NPL = **flower people** ► **flower garden** N jardin m d'agrément ► **flower head** N capitule m ► **flower people** NPL (fig) hippies mpl, babas cool* mpl ► **flower power** N power m ► **flower seller** N marchand(e) m(f) de fleurs ambulant(e), bouquetière† f ► **flower shop** N fleuriste m, magasin m de fleurs; **at the ~ shop** chez le fleuriste ► **flower show** N floralies fpl; (smaller) exposition f de fleurs

flowered ['flaʊəd] ADJ [fabric, garment] à fleurs

flowering ['flaʊərɪŋ] [1] N (lit) floraison f; (fig) floraison f, épanouissement m; **the ~ of creative genius** l'épanouissement m du génie créateur [2] ADJ (= in flower) en fleurs; (= which flowers) à fleurs [3] COMP ► **flowering shrub** N arbuste m à fleurs

flowerpot ['flaʊəpɒt] N pot m de fleurs

flowery ['flaʊərɪ] ADJ [a] [*fragrance, perfume*] fleuri, de fleurs; [*fabric, dress, wallpaper*] fleuri, à fleurs; [*meadow, field*] fleuri, couvert de fleurs [b] (*fig = elaborate*) [*speech, language*] fleuri

flowing ['flaʊɪŋ] ADJ [*water*] qui coule; [*tide*] montant; [*hair, beard, skirt*] flottant; [*movement*] fluide, plein d'aisance; [*style*] coulant, fluide; **the car's ~ lines** les lignes douces or fluides de la voiture → **fast**

flown [fləʊn] VB ptp of **fly³**; → **high**

fl. oz (ABBR = **fluid ounce**) → **fluid**

flu [fluː] N (ABBR = **influenza**) grippe f → **Asian**

flub* [flʌb] (*US*) [1] VT louper*, rater* [2] VI rater* [3] N ratage* m, erreur f

fluctuate ['flʌktjʊeɪt] VI [*prices, rate, temperature*] varier, fluctuer; [*person, attitude*] varier (**between** entre)

fluctuation [ˌflʌktjʊ'eɪʃən] N fluctuation f, variation f

flue [fluː] [1] N [*of chimney*] conduit m (de cheminée); [*of stove*] tuyau m (de poêle) [2] COMP ► **flue brush** N hérisson m (de ramoneur)

fluency ['fluːənsɪ] N (*in speech*) facilité f or aisance f (d'élocution); (*in writing*) facilité f, aisance f; **his ~ in English** son aisance (à s'exprimer) en anglais

fluent ['fluːənt] ADJ [a] (*in foreign language*) **he is ~ in Italian ◊ he speaks ~ Italian ◊ his Italian is ~** il parle couramment l'italien; **to become ~ in German** acquérir une bonne maîtrise de l'allemand [b] (= *eloquent*) [*style*] coulant; [*talker, debater*] éloquent; **to be a ~ speaker** parler avec aisance; **to be a ~ reader** lire avec facilité or aisance; **to be a ~ writer** avoir la plume facile; **she speaks in ~ sentences** [*baby*] elle fait des phrases [c] (= *graceful*) [*movement*] fluide, plein d'aisance

fluently ['fluːəntlɪ] ADV [*speak foreign language*] couramment; [*speak, read, write, move, play*] avec facilité, avec aisance

fluey* ['fluːɪ] ADJ (*Brit*) **to feel ~** se sentir grippé

fluff [flʌf] [1] N (NonC: *on birds, young animals*) duvet m; (*from material*) peluche f; (= *dust on floors*) mouton(s) m(pl) (de poussière); (*fig = girl*) **a bit of ~*** une nénette f [2] VT [a] (*also ~ out*) [+ *feathers*] ébouriffer; [+ *pillows, hair*] faire bouffer [b] (* = *do badly*) [+ *audition, lines in play, exam*] rater*, louper*

fluffy ['flʌfɪ] ADJ [a] (= *soft*) [*wool*] doux (douce f); [*slipper*] molletonné; [*sweater, towel*] pelucheux; [*hair*] duveteux; [*kitten, rabbit*] au pelage duveteux; [*cloud*] floconneux; **~ toy** (= *soft toy*) peluche f [b] (= *light*) [*cake, rice, mashed potatoes*] léger; [*egg, mixture*] mousseux; [*omelette*] soufflé

fluid ['fluːɪd] [1] ADJ [*substance*] liquide; [*shape*] doux (douce f); [*style*] fluide, coulant; [*drawing, outline*] fluide; [*movement*] fluide, plein d'aisance; [*situation*] fluide, fluctuant; [*plan*] flou [2] N fluide m (*also Chem*), liquide m; **he's on ~s only** (*as diet*) il ne prend que des (aliments) liquides [3] COMP ► **fluid assets** NPL (*US Fin*) liquidités fpl, disponibilités fpl ► **fluid ounce** N mesure de capacité (*Brit: 0,028 litres, US : 0,030 litres*)

fluidity [fluː'ɪdɪtɪ] N [*of gas, liquid, situation*] fluidité f; [*of style, speech*] aisance f, fluidité f

fluke¹ [fluːk] [1] N (= *chance event*) coup m de chance or de veine* extraordinaire, hasard m extraordinaire; **by a (sheer) ~** par un hasard extraordinaire [2] ADJ [*coincidence, circumstances*] extraordinaire; **he scored a ~ goal** il a marqué un but tout à fait par hasard

fluke² [fluːk] N [*of anchor*] patte f (d'ancre); [*of arrow, harpoon*] barbillon m

fluke³ [fluːk] N (*Zool*) douve f (du foie *etc*)

fluky ['fluːkɪ] ADJ [a] [*wind*] capricieux [b] → **fluke¹**

flume [fluːm] N [a] (= *ravine*) ravin m [b] (= channel) chenal m [c] (*in swimming pool*) toboggan m

flummery ['flʌmərɪ] N (*Culin*) bouillie f; (*fig*) flagornerie f

flummox* ['flʌməks] VT [+ *person*] démonter, couper le sifflet à*; **he was ~ed** ça lui avait coupé le sifflet*, il était complètement démonté

flung [flʌŋ] VB pret, ptp of **fling**; → **far-**

flunk* [flʌŋk] (*esp US*) [1] VI (= *fail*) être recalé* or collé*; (= *shirk*) se dégonfler* [2] VT [a] (= *fail*) to ~ **French/an exam** être recalé* or être collé* en français/à un examen; **they ~ed ten candidates** ils ont recalé* or collé* dix candidats [b] (= *give up*) laisser tomber

► **flunk out*** (*US*) [1] VI se faire virer* (**of** de) [2] VT SEP virer*, renvoyer

flunk(e)y ['flʌŋkɪ] N (*lit*) laquais m; (*fig*) larbin m

fluorescein [ˌfluə'resɪn] N fluorescéine f

fluorescence [fluə'resns] N fluorescence f

fluorescent [fluə'resnt] [1] ADJ [*lighting, bulb, colour, dye, paint*] fluorescent; [*clothes*] fluorescent, fluo* *inv* [2] COMP ► **fluorescent strip** N tube m fluorescent or au néon

fluoridation [ˌfluərɪ'deɪʃən] N fluoration f

fluoride ['fluəraɪd] [1] N fluorure m [2] COMP ► **fluoride toothpaste** N dentifrice m fluoré or au fluor

fluorine ['fluəriːn] N fluor m

fluorite ['fluəraɪt] N (*US*) fluorite f, spath m fluor

fluorspar ['fluəspɑːʳ] N spath m fluor, fluorite f

flurry ['flʌrɪ] [1] N [*of snow*] rafale f; [*of wind*] rafale f, risée f; (*fig*) agitation f, émoi m; **a ~ of activity** un débordement d'activité; **a ~ of protest** une vague de protestations; **in a ~ of excitement** dans un frisson d'agitation [2] VT agiter, effarer; **to get flurried** perdre la tête, s'affoler (**at** pour)

flush¹ [flʌʃ] [1] N [a] (*in sky*) lueur f rouge, rougeoiement m; [*of blood*] afflux m; (= *blush*) rougeur f; (*Med*) (**hot**) **~es** bouffées fpl de chaleur; [*of beauty, health, youth*] éclat m; [*of joy*] élan m; [*of excitement*] accès m; **in the (first) ~ of victory** dans l'ivresse de la victoire; **she's not in the first ~ of youth** elle n'est pas dans sa première jeunesse [c] [*of lavatory*] chasse f (d'eau) [2] VI [a] [*face, person*] rougir; **to ~ crimson** s'empourprer, rougir jusqu'aux oreilles; **to ~ with shame/anger** rougir de honte/de colère [b] **the toilet won't ~** la chasse d'eau ne marche pas [3] VT nettoyer à grande eau; [+ *drain, pipe*] curer à grande eau; **to ~ the toilet** or **lavatory** tirer la chasse (d'eau); **to ~ sth down the toilet** or **lavatory** faire passer qch dans les toilettes

► **flush away** VT SEP (*down sink/drain*) faire partir par l'évier/par l'égout; (*down lavatory*) faire partir (en tirant la chasse d'eau)

► **flush out** VT SEP (*with water*) nettoyer à grande eau

flush² [flʌʃ] [1] ADJ [a] au même niveau (**with** que), au or à ras (**with** de); **~ with the ground** à ras de terre, au ras de terre; **a door ~ with the wall** une porte dans l'alignement du mur; **a cupboard ~ with the wall** un placard encastré dans le mur; **~ against** tout contre [b] **to be ~ (with money)*** être en fonds, avoir des sous* [2] VT **to ~ a door** affleurer une porte

flush³ [flʌʃ] VT (*also ~ out*) [+ *game, birds*] lever; [+ *person*] forcer à se montrer

► **flush out** VT FUS **they ~ed them out of their hiding places** ils les ont forcés à sortir de leur cachette, ils les ont fait sortir de leur cachette; **they tried to ~ out illegal workers operating in the country** ils ont essayé de chasser les travailleurs clandestins du pays

flush⁴ [flʌʃ] N (*Cards*) flush m → **royal**

flushed ['flʌʃt] ADJ [*person*] tout rouge; [*face, cheeks*] tout rouge, enflammé; **~ with anger** rouge or empourpré de colère; **~ with fever/embarrassment/excitement** rouge de fièvre/d'embarras/d'excitation; **~ with success** grisé par le succès; **white flowers ~ with pink** des fleurs blanches colorées de rose

fluster ['flʌstəʳ] [1] VT énerver, troubler; **to get ~ed** s'énerver, se troubler [2] N agitation f, trouble m; **in a ~** énervé, troublé

flute [fluːt] N (= *musical instrument, wine glass*) flûte f

fluted ['fluːtɪd] ADJ [a] [*pillar*] cannelé; [*flan dish*] à cannelures [b] [*tone, note*] flûté

fluting ['fluːtɪŋ] N cannelures fpl

flutist ['fluːtɪst] N (*US*) flûtiste mf

flutter ['flʌtəʳ] [1] VI [a] [*flag, ribbon*] flotter; [*bird, moth, butterfly*] voleter, voltiger; [*wings*] battre; **the bird ~ed about the room** l'oiseau voletait çà et là dans la pièce; **the butterfly ~ed away** le papillon a disparu en voletant or voltigeant; **a leaf came ~ing down** une feuille est tombée en tourbillonnant [b] [*person*] papillonner, virevolter [c] [*heart, pulse*] palpiter [2] VT [+ *fan, paper*] jouer de; **the bird ~ed its wings** l'oiseau a battu des ailes; **to ~ one's eyelashes** battre des cils (**at sb** dans la direction de qn) [3] N [a] [*of eyelashes, wings*] battement m; [*of heart, pulse*] palpitation f; **there was a ~ of fear in her voice** sa voix trahissait la peur; **to feel a ~ of excitement at the prospect of ...** être tout excité à l'idée de ...; **(all) in a ~** tout troublé, dans un grand émoi [b] (*Brit** = *gamble*) **to have a ~** parier (de petites sommes) (**on** sur); (*St Ex*) boursicoter

fluvial ['fluːvɪəl] ADJ fluvial

flux [flʌks] N (NonC) [a] changement m continuel, fluctuation f; **to be in a state of ~** changer sans arrêt, fluctuer continuellement [b] (*Med*) flux m, évacuation f (de sang *etc*); (*Phys*) flux m; (*Metal*) fondant m

fly¹ [flaɪ] [1] N (= *insect, Fishing*) mouche f; **they were dropping*** or **dying like flies** ils tombaient* or mouraient comme des mouches; **small businesses were dropping like flies in the recession*** les petites entreprises faisaient faillite les unes après les autres à cause de la récession; **he wouldn't harm** or **hurt a ~** il ne ferait pas de mal à une mouche; **I wish I were a ~ on the wall** j'aimerais être une petite souris (pour pouvoir écouter or voir) ►2; (*fig*) **there's a ~ in the ointment** il y a un ennui or un hic* or un os*; **he's the ~ in the ointment** c'est lui l'empêcheur de tourner en rond; **there are no flies on him*** il n'est pas né d'hier, il n'est pas tombé de la dernière averse or pluie → **housefly** [2] COMP ► **fly-blown** ADJ (*lit*) couvert or plein de chiures de mouches; (*fig*) très défraîchi ► **fly fishing** N pêche f à la mouche ► **fly-on-the-wall documentary** N document m pris sur le vif ► **fly paper** N papier m tue-mouches ► **fly rod** N (*Fishing*) canne f à mouche ► **fly spray** N bombe f insecticide ► **fly swat(ter)** N tapette f ► **fly trap** N (= *device*) attrape-mouches m inv → **Venus**

fly² [flaɪ] ADJ (*esp Brit* = *astute*) malin (-igne f), rusé

fly³ [flaɪ] (pret **flew**, ptp **flown**) [1] VI [a] [*bird, insect, plane*] voler; [*air passenger*] aller or voyager en avion; [*pilot*] piloter un (or des) avion(s); **I don't like ~ing** je n'aime pas (prendre) l'avion; **I always ~** je voyage toujours en avion, je prends toujours l'avion; **how did you get here? — I flew** comment es-tu venu? — par or en avion; **to ~ over London** survoler Londres, voler au-dessus de Londres; **the planes flew past** or **over at 3pm** les avions sont passés à 15 heures; **to ~ over the Channel**

survoler la Manche; **to ~ across the Channel** [*bird, plane*] traverser la Manche; [*passenger*] traverser la Manche (en avion); **to ~ away** [*bird*] s'envoler; (*fig*) **all her worries flew away** tous ses soucis se sont envolés; **we flew in from Rome this morning** nous sommes venus de Rome en *or* par avion ce matin; **to ~ off** [*bird, plane*] s'envoler; [*passenger*] partir en avion, s'envoler (**to** pour); **a bee flew in through the window** une abeille est entrée par la fenêtre; (*fig*) **fur was ~ing** ◊ **feathers were ~ing** ça bardait*, il y avait du grabuge*; **that will make the fur** *or* **feathers ~!** il va y avoir du grabuge!*; (*fig*) **he is ~ing high** il a beaucoup de succès, il réussit très bien; **the company is ~ing high** l'entreprise marche très bien; (*fig*) **to find that the bird has flown** trouver l'oiseau envolé; (*US fig*) **~ right, sonny*** surtout pas de bêtises, fiston* → **fury**

b (*fig*) [*time*] passer vite, filer*; [*sparks*] jaillir, voler; [*car, people*] filer*; **to ~ in/out/back** *etc* [*person*] entrer/sortir/retourner *etc* à toute vitesse *or* à toute allure; **it's late, I must ~!** il est tard, il faut que je me sauve (*subj*)!; **to ~ to sb's assistance** voler au secours de qn; **to ~ in the face of danger/accepted ideas** défier le danger/les idées reçues; **to ~ in the face of authority** battre en brèche l'ordre établi; **to ~ into a rage** *or* **a passion** s'emporter, se mettre dans une violente colère; **to ~ off the handle*** s'emporter, sortir de ses gonds; **to let ~ at sb** (*in angry words*) s'en prendre violemment à qn, prendre qn violemment à partie; (*by shooting*) tirer sur qn; **to ~ at sb** sauter *or* se ruer sur qn; **to ~ at sb's throat** sauter à la gorge de qn; **the door flew open** la porte s'est ouverte brusquement; **the handle flew off** la poignée s'est détachée brusquement *or* soudain → **send, spark**

c (= *flee*) fuir (**before** devant), s'enfuir (**from** de); **to ~ from temptation** fuir la tentation; **~ for your life!** fuyez!

d [*flag*] se déployer; **her hair was ~ing in the wind** ses cheveux flottaient au vent → **flag¹**

2 VT **a** [+ *aircraft*] piloter; [+ *person*] emmener en avion; [+ *goods*] transporter par avion; [+ *standard, admiral's flag*] arborer; (*Naut*) **to ~ the French flag** battre pavillon français; **the building was ~ing the French flag** le drapeau français flottait sur l'immeuble; **to ~ a kite** (*lit*) faire voler un cerf-volant; (*fig*) lancer un ballon d'essai (*fig*); **to ~ great distances** faire de longs voyages en avion; **to ~ the Atlantic/the Channel** *etc* traverser l'Atlantique/la Manche *etc* en avion; **to ~ Air France** voler sur Air France; **we will ~ you to Italy and back for £350** nous vous proposons un vol aller et retour pour l'Italie pour 350 livres

b **to ~ the country** s'enfuir du pays → **coop, nest**

3 N **a** (*on trousers: also* **flies**) braguette *f*; (*on tent*) auvent *m*

b (= *vehicle*) fiacre *m*

c [*of flag*] battant *m*

d (*US*) **on the ~** (= *quickly*) sur-le-champ; (= *while busy*) tout en faisant autre chose; **people who can make decisions on the ~** les gens capables de prendre des décisions sur-le-champ

4 **flies** NPL (*Theat*) cintres *mpl*, dessus *mpl*

5 COMP ► **fly-button** N bouton *m* de braguette ► **fly-by-night** N (= *irresponsible person*) tout-fou* *m*; (= *decamping debtor*) débiteur *m*, -trice *f* qui déménage à la cloche de bois *or* qui décampe en douce* ♦ ADJ [*person*] tout-fou* *m* only; (*Comm, Fin*) [*firm, operation*] véreux ► **fly-drive** N (*Travel*) formule *f* avion plus voiture ► **fly-drive holiday** N (vacances *fpl* en) formule *f or* forfait *m* avion plus voiture ► **fly hack** N (*Rugby*) = **fly kick** ► **fly half** N (*Rugby*) demi *m* d'ouverture ► **fly kick** N (*Rugby*) coup *m* de pied à suivre ► **fly-post** VT (*Brit*) coller des affiches illégalement

► **fly-posting** N (*Brit*) affichage *m* illégal ► **fly sheet** N (*Brit*) feuille *f* volante ► **fly-tipping** N décharge *f* sauvage

flyaway ['flaɪə,weɪ] ADJ [*hair*] rebelle, difficile; (= *frivolous*) frivole, futile

flyboy ['flaɪbɔɪ] N (*US*) pilote *m* (*de l'armée de l'air*)

flyby ['flaɪbaɪ] N (*US*) (*pl* **flybys**) = **flypast**

flycatcher ['flaɪ,kætʃəʳ] N **a** (= *bird*) gobe-mouches *m inv* **b** (= *plant*) plante *f* carnivore **c** (= *trap*) attrape-mouches *m inv*

flyer ['flaɪəʳ] N = **flier**

flying ['flaɪɪŋ] **1** N (= *action*) vol *m*; (= *activity*) aviation *f*; **he likes ~** [*passenger*] il aime (prendre) l'avion; [*pilot*] il aime piloter; **he's afraid of ~** il a peur de prendre l'avion; **to go ~** (*lit*) faire de l'avion; (*fig* = *fall over*) aller valdinguer* → **formation, stunt**

2 ADJ [*animal, insect*] volant; [*debris*] projeté; **~ glass** éclats *mpl* de verre; **~ jump** *or* **leap** saut *m* avec élan; **to take a ~ jump** *or* **leap** sauter avec élan; **~ visit** visite *f* éclair *inv*; **with ~ colours** haut la main

3 COMP ► **flying ambulance** N (= *plane*) avion *m* sanitaire; (= *helicopter*) hélicoptère *m* sanitaire ► **flying boat** N hydravion *m* ► **flying bomb** N bombe *f* volante ► **flying buttress** N arc-boutant *m* ► **flying doctor** N médecin *m* volant ► **the Flying Dutchman** N (*Mus*) le Vaisseau fantôme; (= *legend*) le Hollandais volant ► **flying fish** N poisson *m* volant, exocet *m* ► **flying fortress** N forteresse *f* volante ► **flying fox** N roussette *f* ► **flying machine** N machine *f* volante, appareil *m* volant ► **flying officer** N (*Brit Mil*) lieutenant *m* de l'armée de l'air ► **flying picket** N (*Ind*) piquet *m* de grève volant ► **flying saucer** N soucoupe *f* volante ► **Flying Squad** N (*Brit Police*) brigade *f* volante (*de la police judiciaire*) ► **flying start** N (*Sport*) départ *m* lancé; (*fig*) **to get off to a ~ start** [*racing car, runner*] prendre un départ très rapide *or* en flèche; [*scheme, plan*] prendre un bon *or* un excellent départ ► **flying suit** N combinaison *f* (de vol) ► **flying time** N heures *fpl or* temps *m* de vol ► **flying trapeze** N trapèze *m* volant

flyleaf ['flaɪliːf] N (*pl* **-leaves**) page *f* de garde

flyover ['flaɪ,əʊvəʳ] N (*Brit Aut*) autopont *m*; (*temporary*) toboggan *m*; (*US Aviat*) défilé *m* aérien

flypast ['flaɪpaːst] N (*Brit*) défilé *m* aérien

flyweight ['flaɪweɪt] N (*Boxing*) poids *m* mouche

flywheel ['flaɪwiːl] N volant *m* (*Tech*)

FM [ef'em] **a** (ABBR = **Field Marshal**) → **field** **b** (ABBR = **frequency modulation**) FM **c** (ABBR = **Foreign Minister**) → **foreign**

FMB [,efem'biː] N (*US*) (ABBR = **Federal Maritime Board**) → **federal**

FMCG, fmcg [,efemsiː'dʒiː] (ABBR = **fast-moving consumer goods**) → **fast¹**

f-number ['ef,nʌmbəʳ] N (*Phot*) ouverture *f* (*du diaphragme*)

FO (*Brit*) (ABBR = **Foreign Office**) → **foreign**

foal [fəʊl] **1** N (= *horse*) poulain *m*; (= *donkey*) ânon *m*; **the mare is in ~** la jument est pleine **2** VI mettre bas

foam [fəʊm] **1** N [*of beer etc*] mousse *f*; [*of sea*] écume *f*; (*in fire fighting*) mousse *f* (carbonique); (*at mouth*) écume *f*; (*liter*) **the ~** les flots *mpl* (*liter*) **2** VI [*sea*] écumer, moutonner; [*soapy water*] mousser, faire de la mousse; **to ~ at the mouth** [*animal*] baver, écumer; [*person*] (*lit*) avoir de l'écume aux lèvres; (*fig*) écumer de rage **3** COMP ► **foam-backed** ADJ [*carpet*] à sous-couche de mousse ► **foam bath** N bain *m* moussant ► **foam plastic** N mousse *f* de plastique ► **foam rubber** N caoutchouc *m* mousse® ► **foam**

sprayer N extincteur *m* à mousse ► **foam up** VI [*liquid in container*] mousser

foamy ['fəʊmɪ] ADJ [*waves, sea*] écumeux; [*beer*] mousseux

FOB [efəʊ'biː] (*Comm*) (ABBR = **free on board**) FOB

fob [fɒb] **1** VT **to ~ sth off on sb** ◊ **to ~ sb off with sth** refiler* *or* fourguer‡ qch à qn; **to ~ sb off with promises** se débarrasser de qn par de belles promesses **2** N († = *pocket*) gousset *m* (*de pantalon*); (= *ornament*) breloque *f* **3** COMP ► **fob watch** N montre *f* de gousset

FOC [efəʊ'siː] (*Comm*) (ABBR = **free of charge**) → **free**

focal ['fəʊkəl] **1** ADJ focal **2** COMP ► **focal distance** N = **focal length** ► **focal infection** N (*Med*) infection *f* focale ► **focal length** N distance *f* focale, focale *f* ► **focal plane** N plan *m* focal ► **focal plane shutter** N (*Phot*) obturateur *m* focal *or* à rideau ► **focal point** N (*Opt*) foyer *m*; (*in building, gardens*) point *m* de convergence; (*fig* = *main point*) [*of meeting, discussions etc*] point *m* central ► **focal ratio** N diaphragme *m*

foci ['fəʊkaɪ] NPL of **focus**

fo'c'sle ['fəʊksl] N = **forecastle**

focus ['fəʊkəs] **1** N (*pl* **focuses** *or* **foci**) **a** (*Math, Phys*) foyer *m* **b** (*Phot*) **the picture is in/out of ~** l'image est nette/floue, l'image n'est/n'est pas au point; **to bring a picture into ~** mettre une image au point **c** (*fig* = *main point*) [*of illness, unrest*] foyer *m*, siège *m*; **to keep sth in ~** ne pas perdre de vue qch; **to bring sth into ~** centrer l'attention sur qch; **he was the ~ of attention** il était le point de mire **d** (*fig* = *purpose, direction*) [*of person, policy*] objectif *m*; [*of film, play, plot*] cohérence *f* **2** VT **a** [+ *instrument, camera*] mettre au point; **to ~ the camera** faire le point **b** (= *direct*) [+ *light, heat rays*] faire converger; [+ *beam, ray*] diriger (**on** sur); (*fig*) [+ *attention*] concentrer (**on** sur); **to ~ one's eyes on sth** fixer ses yeux sur qch; **all eyes were ~ed on him** il était le point de mire de tous **3** VI **a** (*Phot*) mettre au point (**on** sur) **b** (*on eyes*) se fixer sur, accommoder sur; [*person*] fixer son regard sur; **my eyes won't ~** ◊ **I can't ~ properly** je vois trouble, je ne peux pas accommoder **c** [*heat, light, rays*] converger (**on** sur) **d** (*fig*) **we must ~ on raising funds** il faut nous concentrer sur la collecte des fonds; **the meeting ~ed on the problems of the unemployed** la réunion a surtout porté sur les problèmes des chômeurs

fodder ['fɒdəʳ] N fourrage *m* → **cannon**

FOE, FoE (ABBR = **Friends of the Earth**) → **friend**

foe [fəʊ] N (*liter, lit, fig*) ennemi(e) *m(f)*, adversaire *mf*

foetal, fetal (*esp US*) ['fiːtl] ADJ fœtal; **in a ~ position** dans la position du fœtus, dans une position fœtale

foetid ['fiːtɪd] ADJ = **fetid**

foetus ['fiːtəs] N fœtus *m*

fog [fɒg] **1** N **a** (*Met*) brouillard *m*; (*Naut*) brume *f*, brouillard *m* (de mer) **b** (*fig*) brouillard *m*, confusion *f*; **to be in a ~** être dans le brouillard, ne plus savoir où l'on en est **c** (*Phot*) voile *m* **2** VT **a** [+ *mirror, glasses*] embuer **b** (*fig*) [+ *person*] embrouiller, brouiller les idées à; **to ~ the issue** (*accidentally*) embrouiller *or* obscurcir la question; (*purposely*) brouiller les cartes **c** [+ *photo*] voiler **3** VI **a** [*mirror, glasses*] (*also* **~ over** *or* **up**) s'embuer; [*landscape*] s'embrumer **b** (*Phot*) [*negative*] se voiler **4** COMP ► **fog bank** N banc *m* de brume ► **fog signal** N (*Naut*) signal *m* de brume; (*Rail*) pétard *m*

fogbound ['fɒgbaʊnd] ADJ pris dans la brume, bloqué par le brouillard

fogey* ['fəʊgɪ] N **old ~** vieille baderne* f; **young ~** personne très vieux jeu dans ses goûts et ses opinions

foggy ['fɒgɪ] ADJ a (= misty) [night] de brouillard; [landscape, weather] brumeux; [street] enveloppé de brouillard; **it is ~** il y a du brouillard; **on a ~ day** par un jour de brouillard b (fig = confused) [brain] embrumé; [state] de confusion; **I haven't the foggiest (idea** or **notion)!*** je n'en ai pas la moindre idée

Foggy Bottom* [ˌfɒgɪ'bɒtəm] N (US hum) surnom du ministère américain des Affaires étrangères

foghorn ['fɒghɔːn] N corne f or sirène f de brume; **she has a voice like a ~** elle a une voix tonitruante or de stentor

foglamp (Brit) ['fɒglæmp], **foglight** ['fɒglaɪt] N (Aut) feu m de brouillard

foible ['fɔɪbl] N marotte f, petite manie f

foil¹ [fɔɪl] N a (NonC = metal sheet) feuille f or lame f de métal; (also **cooking** or **kitchen ~**) papier m d'aluminium, (papier m) alu* m; **fish cooked in ~** poisson m cuit (au four) dans du papier d'aluminium → **tinfoil** b (fig) repoussoir m; **to act as a ~ to sb/sth** servir de repoussoir à qn/qch, mettre qn/qch en valeur

foil² [fɔɪl] N (Fencing) fleuret m

foil³ [fɔɪl] VT [+ attempts] déjouer; [+ plans] contrecarrer

foist [fɔɪst] VT **to ~ sth (off) on sb** refiler* or repasser* qch à qn; **this job was ~ed (off) on to me** c'est moi qui ai hérité de ce boulot*; **to ~ o.s. on (to) sb** s'imposer à qn; (as uninvited guest) s'imposer or s'installer chez qn

fold¹ [fəʊld] 1 N (in paper, cloth, skin, earth's surface) pli m; (Geol) **~s** plissement m
2 VT a [+ paper, blanket, bed, chair] plier; [+ wings] replier; **to ~ a page in two** plier une feuille en deux; **to ~ one's arms** (se) croiser les bras; (in prayer) **to ~ one's hands** joindre les mains
b (= wrap up) envelopper (**in** dans), entourer (**in** de); **to ~ sb/sth in one's arms** serrer qn/qch dans ses bras, étreindre qn/qch; (liter) **hills ~ed in mist** des collines enveloppées de brume
c (Culin) [+ eggs, flour] incorporer (**into** à)
3 VI a [chair, table] se (re)plier
b (* = fail) [newspaper] disparaître, cesser de paraître; [business] fermer (ses portes); [play] quitter l'affiche, être retiré de l'affiche; **they ~ed last year** [business etc] ils ont mis la clé sous la porte l'année dernière
4 COMP ► **fold-up** ADJ [chair, table etc] pliant, escamotable
► **fold away** 1 VI [table, bed] (être capable de) se (re)plier 2 VT SEP [+ clothes, newspaper] plier et ranger 3 **~-away** ADJ → **foldaway**
► **fold back** VT SEP [+ shutters] ouvrir, rabattre; [+ bedclothes, collar] replier, rabattre
► **fold down** VT SEP [+ chair] plier; **to ~ down the corner of a page** corner une page
► **fold in** VT SEP (Culin) [+ eggs, flour] incorporer
► **fold over** VT SEP [+ paper] plier, replier; [+ blanket] replier, rabattre
► **fold up** 1 VI = **fold¹ 3** 2 VT SEP [+ paper etc] plier, replier

fold² [fəʊld] N (= enclosure) parc m à moutons; (Rel) sein m de l'Église; (fig) **to come back to the ~** rentrer au bercail

...fold [fəʊld] SUF **twentyfold** (adj) par vingt ♦ (adv) vingt fois → **twofold**

foldaway ['fəʊldəˌweɪ] ADJ [bed] pliant, escamotable

folder ['fəʊldər] N a (= file) chemise f; (with hinges) classeur m; (for drawings) carton m; (papers) dossier m b (= leaflet) dépliant m, brochure f

folding ['fəʊldɪŋ] 1 ADJ [bed, table, bicycle, screen] pliant 2 COMP ► **folding door** N

---

porte f (en) accordéon ► **folding money*** N (US) billets mpl de banque ► **folding seat** (gen: also **~ stool**) N pliant m; (Aut, Theat) strapontin m

foldout ['fəʊldaʊt] N encart m

foliage ['fəʊlɪɪdʒ] N feuillage m

foliation [ˌfəʊlɪ'eɪʃən] N (Bot) foliation f, feuillaison f; [of book] foliotage m; (Geol) foliation f; (Archit) rinceaux mpl

folic acid [ˌfəʊlɪk'æsɪd] N acide m folique

folio ['fəʊlɪəʊ] N (= sheet) folio m, feuillet m; (= volume) (volume m) in-folio m

folk [fəʊk] 1 N a (pl = people: also **~s**) gens mpl (f adj before n); **they are good ~(s)** ce sont de braves gens; **a lot of ~(s) believe ...** beaucoup de gens croient ...; **there were a lot of ~ at the concert** il y avait beaucoup de gens or de monde au concert; **old ~(s)** les personnes fpl âgées, les vieux mpl (pej); **young ~(s)** les jeunes mpl, les jeunes gens mpl; **my old ~s** (= parents) mes vieux* mpl; **hello ~s!*** bonjour tout le monde!* → **country, old**
b (pl = people in general: also **~s**) les gens mpl, on; **what will ~(s) think?** qu'est-ce que les gens vont penser?, qu'est-ce qu'on va penser?; **~ get worried when they see that** les gens s'inquiètent quand ils voient ça
c (*: pl = relatives) **~s** famille f, parents mpl; **my ~s** ma famille, mes parents mpl, les miens mpl
d (NonC) **folk music**
2 COMP ► **folk art** N art m populaire ► **folk dance, folk dancing** N danse f folklorique ► **folk etymology** N étymologie f populaire ► **folk medicine** N médecine f populaire ► **folk memory** N mémoire f collective ► **folk music** N (gen) musique f folklorique; (contemporary) musique f folk inv, folk m ► **folk rock** N folk-rock m ► **folk singer** N (gen) chanteur m, -euse f de chansons folkloriques; (contemporary) chanteur m, -euse f folk inv ► **folk tale** N conte m populaire ► **folk wisdom** N bon sens m or sagesse f populaire

folklore ['fəʊklɔːr] N folklore m

folksong ['fəʊksɒŋ] N (gen) chanson f or chant m folklorique; (contemporary) chanson f folk inv

folksy* ['fəʊksɪ] ADJ a (= rustic) [furniture, charm] rustique; [clothes] de style rustique b (US = affable) [person] sans façon(s); [manner] sans prétentions; [comment, story, speech, humour] plein de sagesse populaire

follicle ['fɒlɪkl] N follicule m

▼ **follow** ['fɒləʊ] 1 VT a [+ person, road, vehicle, roadsigns] suivre; (in procession) aller or venir à la suite de, suivre; [+ suspect] filer; **to ~ sb in/out** etc suivre qn (qui entre/sort etc); **he ~ed me into the room** il m'a suivi dans la pièce; **we're being ~ed** on nous suit; **~ that car!** suivez cette voiture!; **~ me** suivez-moi; **they ~ed the guide** ils ont suivi le guide; (fig) **he'll be a difficult man to ~** il sera difficile de lui succéder; **to have sb ~ed** faire filer qn; **the detectives ~ed the suspect for a week** les détectives ont filé le suspect pendant une semaine; **a bodyguard ~ed the president everywhere** un garde du corps accompagnait le président partout; **he arrived first, ~ed by the ambassador** il est arrivé le premier, suivi de l'ambassadeur; **this was ~ed by a request for ...** ceci a été suivi d'une demande de ...; **the boat ~ed the coast** le bateau suivait or longeait la côte; **~ your nose*** continuez tout droit; **he ~ed his father into the business** il est entré dans l'affaire sur les traces de son père; **the earthquake was ~ed by an epidemic** une épidémie a suivi le tremblement de terre; **the dinner will be ~ed by a concert** le dîner sera suivi d'un concert; **the years ~ed one another** les années se suivaient or se succédaient; **night ~s day** la nuit succède au jour
b [+ fashion] suivre, se conformer à; [+ in-

---

structions, course of study] suivre; [+ sb's orders] exécuter; [+ serial, strip cartoon] lire (régulièrement); [+ speech, lecture] suivre, écouter (attentivement); **to ~ sb's advice/example** suivre les conseils/l'exemple de qn; (fig) **to ~ suit** en faire autant, faire de même; (Cards) **to ~ suit (in clubs** etc) fournir (à trèfle etc); **do you ~ football?** vous suivez le football?; **which team do you ~?** tu es supporter de quelle équipe?
c [+ profession] exercer, suivre; [+ career] poursuivre; (liter) **to ~ the sea** être or devenir marin
d (= understand) suivre, comprendre; **do you ~ me?** vous me suivez?; **I don't quite ~ (you)** je ne vous suis pas bien or pas tout à fait
2 VI a (= come after) suivre; **to ~ right behind sb** ◊ **to ~ hard on sb's heels** être sur les talons de qn; (fig) **to ~ in sb's footsteps** or **tracks** suivre les traces or marcher sur les traces de qn; (at meals) **what is there to ~?** qu'est-ce qu'il y a après?, qu'est-ce qui suit?; **we had ice cream to ~** après or ensuite nous avons eu de la glace; (gen) **as ~s** comme suit; **his argument was as ~s** son raisonnement était le suivant
b (= result) s'ensuivre, résulter (**from** de); **it ~s that ...** il s'ensuit que ... (+ indic); **it doesn't ~ that ...** il ne s'ensuit pas nécessairement que ... (+ subj or indic), cela ne veut pas forcément dire que ... (+ subj or indic); **that doesn't ~** pas forcément, les deux choses n'ont rien à voir; **that ~s from what he said** cela découle de ce qu'il a dit
c (= understand) suivre, comprendre
3 COMP ► **follow-my-leader** N (Brit) jeu où les enfants doivent imiter tous les mouvements d'un joueur désigné ► **follow-on** N (Cricket) nouveau tour à la défense du guichet ► **follow-the-leader** N (US) = **follow-my-leader** ► **follow-through** N (to a project, survey) suite f, continuation f; (Billiards) coulé m; (Golf, Tennis) accompagnement m (du coup) ► **follow-up** N (on file, case) suivi m (**on, of** de); [of event, programme] (coming after another) suite f (**to** de); [of letter, circular] rappel m; (by sales representative) relance f; (= visit) → **follow-up visit; this course is a ~-up to the beginners' course** ce cours fait suite au cours pour débutants ► **follow-up call** N **to make a ~-up call** appeler pour donner suite à une lettre (or un fax etc) ► **follow-up care** N (Med) soins mpl posthospitaliers or de postcure ► **follow-up interview** N entretien m complémentaire, second entretien m ► **follow-up letter** N lettre f de rappel or relance ► **follow-up study, follow-up survey** N étude f complémentaire ► **follow-up telephone call** N → **follow-up call** ► **follow-up visit** N (Med, Social Work etc) visite f de contrôle
► **follow about, follow around** VT SEP suivre (partout), être toujours sur les talons de
► **follow on** VI a (= come after) suivre; **you go ahead and I'll ~ on when I can** allez-y, je vous suivrai quand je pourrai b (= result) résulter (**from** de); **it ~s on from what I said** cela découle de ce que j'ai dit, c'est la conséquence logique de ce que j'ai dit
► **follow out** VT SEP [+ idea, plan] poursuivre jusqu'au bout or jusqu'à sa conclusion; [+ order] exécuter; [+ instructions] suivre
► **follow through** a (Billiards) faire or jouer un coulé; (Golf, Tennis) accompagner son coup or sa balle 2 VT SEP [+ idea, plan] poursuivre jusqu'au bout or jusqu'à sa conclusion 3 **~-through** → **follow**
► **follow up** 1 VI a (= pursue an advantage) exploiter un or tirer parti d'un avantage b [Ftbl etc] suivre l'action
2 VT SEP a (= benefit from) [+ advantage, success, victory] exploiter, tirer parti de; [+ offer] donner suite à b (= not lose track of)

suivre; **we must ~ this business up** il faudra suivre cette affaire; **this is a case to ~ up** (gen, Police, Jur) c'est un cas à suivre; (Med) c'est une affaire à suivre; **"to be ~ed up"** (gen, Police, Jur) « affaire à suivre »; (Med) « cas à suivre » [c] (= reinforce) [+ victory] asseoir; [+ remark] faire suivre (**with** de), compléter (**with** par); **they ~ed up the programme with another equally good** ils ont donné à cette émission une suite qui a été tout aussi excellente; **they ~ed up their insults with threats** ils ont fait suivre leurs insultes de menaces [3] **~up** N, ADJ → **follow**

follower ['fɒləʊəʳ] N [a] [of political, military leader] partisan(e) m(f); [of religious leader, artist, philosopher] disciple m; [of religion, theory, tradition] adepte mf; **~s of fashion** les adeptes mfpl de la mode; **as all football ~s know** comme le savent tous les amateurs de football [b] († = admirer) amoureux m, -euse f, admirateur m, -trice f

following ['fɒləʊɪŋ] [1] ADJ suivant; **the ~ day** le jour suivant, le lendemain; **he made the ~ remarks** il a fait les remarques suivantes or les remarques que voici [2] N [a] [of political, military leader] partisans mpl; [of religion, theory, tradition] adeptes mpl; [of religious leader, artist, philosopher] disciples mpl; (Sport) supporters mpl; **he has a large ~** il a de nombreux partisans or disciples [b] **he said the ~** il a dit ceci; (in documents) **see the ~ for an explanation** voir ce qui suit pour toute explication; **his argument was the ~** son raisonnement était le suivant; **the ~ have been chosen** (= people) les personnes suivantes ont été retenues; (= books) les livres suivants ont été retenus [3] PREP [a] (= after) après; **~ the concert there will be ...** après le concert il y aura ... [b] (= as a result of) (comme) suite à; (Comm) **~ your letter ...** (comme) suite à or en réponse à votre lettre ...; **~ our meeting** (comme) suite à notre entretien [4] COMP ► **following wind** N vent m arrière

folly ['fɒlɪ] N [a] (NonC = foolishness) folie f, sottise f; **it's sheer ~ to do that** c'est de la pure folie or de la démence de faire cela [b] (= foolish thing, action) sottise f, folie f [c] (Archit) folie f

foment [fəʊ'ment] VT (lit, fig) fomenter

fomentation [ˌfəʊmen'teɪʃən] N (lit, fig) fomentation f

fond [fɒnd] ADJ [a] **to be ~ of sb** bien aimer qn; **to become** or **grow ~ of sb** se prendre d'affection pour qn; **to be ~ of sth** aimer beaucoup qch; **to become** or **grow ~ of sth** se mettre à aimer qch; **to be very ~ of music** aimer beaucoup la musique, être très mélomane; **to be ~ of sweet things** être friand de sucreries, aimer les sucreries; (gen) **to be ~ of doing sth** aimer beaucoup faire qch [b] (= loving, believe, smile) [look] tendre; **to bid a ~ farewell to sb/sth** faire de tendres adieux à qn/qch → **absence** [c] (= pleasant) [memory] très bon, très agréable [d] (= foolish) [belief] naïf (naïve f); [hope] fou (folle f) [e] (= dear) [hope] fervent; [dream, wish] cher

fondant ['fɒndənt] [1] N (bonbon m) fondant m [2] COMP ► **fondant icing** N glaçage m fondant

fondle ['fɒndl] VT caresser

fondly ['fɒndlɪ] ADV [a] (= affectionately) [remember, think of] avec tendresse; [say] affectueusement, tendrement; **to smile ~ at sb** faire un tendre sourire à qn [b] (= foolishly) [imagine, believe, hope] naïvement

fondness ['fɒndnɪs] N (for things) prédilection f, penchant m (**for** pour); (for people) affection f, tendresse f (**for** pour)

fondue ['fɒndu:] N fondue f

font [fɒnt] N [a] (Rel) fonts mpl baptismaux [b] (Typ) = **fount b**

fontanel(le) [ˌfɒntə'nel] N fontanelle f

food [fu:d] [1] N [a] (NonC = sth to eat) nourriture f; **there was no ~ in the house** il n'y avait rien à manger or il n'y avait pas de nourriture dans la maison; **there's not enough ~** il n'y a pas assez à manger, il n'y a pas assez de nourriture; **most of the ~ had gone bad** la plus grande partie de la nourriture or des vivres s'était avariée; **to give sb ~** donner à manger à qn; **to give the horses their ~** faire manger les chevaux, donner à manger aux chevaux; **what's that? — it's ~ for the horse** qu'est-ce que c'est? — c'est de la nourriture pour or c'est de quoi manger pour le cheval; **to buy ~** acheter à manger, faire des provisions; **the cost of ~** le prix des denrées alimentaires; **~ and clothing** la nourriture et les vêtements; **to be off one's ~*** avoir perdu l'appétit, n'avoir plus d'appétit; **the ~ is very good here** la nourriture est très bonne ici, on mange très bien ici; **he likes plain ~** il aime les nourritures simples, il aime se nourrir simplement; (fig) **it gave me ~ for thought** cela m'a donné à penser or à réfléchir [b] (= specific substance) (gen) aliment m; (soft, moist, for poultry, dogs, cats, pigs etc) pâtée f; **a new ~ for babies/for pigs** un nouvel aliment pour les bébés/pour les cochons; **pet ~** aliments mpl pour animaux; **tins of dog/cat ~** des boîtes de pâtée pour chiens/chats; **all these ~s must be kept in a cool place** tous ces aliments doivent être conservés au frais → **frozen, health** [c] (for plants) engrais m [2] COMP ► **food additive** N additif m alimentaire ► **food aid** N aide f alimentaire ► **Food and Agriculture Organization** N Organisation f des Nations Unies pour l'alimentation et l'agriculture ► **Food and Drug Administration** N (US) FDA f → **FDA** ► **food chain** N (Ecol) chaîne f alimentaire ► **food colouring** N colorant m alimentaire ► **food counter** N (in shop) rayon m (d')alimentation ► **food crop** N culture f vivrière ► **food grains** NPL céréales fpl vivrières ► **food mixer** N mixer m, mixeur m ► **food parcel** N colis m de vivres ► **food poisoning** N intoxication f alimentaire ► **food prices** NPL prix mpl des denrées alimentaires or de la nourriture ► **food processing** N (industrial) transformation f des aliments; **the ~ processing industry** l'industrie f agro-alimentaire ► **food processor** N robot m ménager or de cuisine ► **food rationing** N rationnement m alimentaire ► **food shares** NPL (St Ex) valeurs fpl de l'agroalimentaire ► **food stamps** NPL (US) bons mpl de nourriture (pour indigents) ► **food subsidy** N subvention f sur les denrées alimentaires ► **food supplies** NPL vivres mpl ► **food value** N valeur f nutritive

foodie* ['fu:dɪ] N fana* mf de la (grande) cuisine

foodstuffs ['fu:dstʌfs] NPL denrées fpl alimentaires, aliments mpl

foofaraw ['fu:fə‚rɔː] N histoires* fpl, cirque* m, pétard* m

fool[1] [fu:l] [1] N [a] imbécile mf, idiot(e) m(f); **stupid ~!** espèce d'imbécile or d'idiot!; **don't be a ~!** ne sois pas stupide!; **I felt such a ~** je me suis vraiment senti bête; **some ~ of a doctor*** ◊ **some ~ doctor*** un imbécile or un abruti* de médecin; **he was a ~ not to accept** il a été bête or stupide de ne pas accepter; **what a ~ I was to think ...** ce que j'ai pu être bête de penser ...; **he's more of a ~ than I thought** il est (encore) plus bête que je ne pensais; **he was ~ enough to accept** il a été assez stupide pour accepter, il a eu la bêtise d'accepter; **to play** or **act the ~** faire l'imbécile; **he's no ~** il est loin d'être bête; **he's nobody's ~** il n'est pas né d'hier or tombé de la dernière pluie; **more ~ you!*** ce que tu es

bête!; **he made himself look a ~** or **he made a ~ of himself in front of everybody** il s'est rendu ridicule devant tout le monde; **to make a ~ of sb** (= ridicule) ridiculiser qn, se payer la tête de qn*; (= trick) avoir* or duper qn; **to play sb for a ~** mener qn en bateau*, rouler* qn; **I went on a ~'s errand** (= go somewhere) j'y suis allé pour rien; (= do something) je me suis dépensé en pure perte; **any ~ can do that** n'importe quel imbécile peut faire ça; **to live in a ~'s paradise** se bercer d'illusions or d'un bonheur illusoire ■ (PROV) **a ~ and his money are soon parted** aux idiots l'argent file entre les doigts ■ (PROV) **there's no ~ like an old ~** il n'y a pire imbécile qu'un vieil imbécile ■ (PROV) **~s rush in (where angels fear to tread)** c'est de l'inconscience [b] (= jester) bouffon m, fou m [2] VI [a] (= act silly) faire l'imbécile or l'idiot; **stop ~ing!** arrête de faire l'idiot or l'imbécile!; **no ~ing*, he really said it** sans blague*, il a vraiment dit ça; **I was only ~ing** je ne faisais que plaisanter, c'était pour rire [b] **~ with** (= mess with) [+ drugs, drink, electricity] toucher à*; **she's not someone you should ~ with** avec elle on ne plaisante pas [3] VT berner, duper; **you won't ~ me so easily!** vous n'arriverez pas à me berner or duper si facilement!; **it ~ed nobody** personne n'a été dupe [4] ADJ (US*) = **foolish** [5] COMP ► **fooling about, fooling around** N bêtises fpl ► **fool's gold** N (Geol) pyrite f; (fig) **to go after ~'s gold** se lancer dans un projet insensé en espérant faire de l'argent

► **fool about, fool around** [1] VI [a] (= waste time) perdre son temps; **stop ~ing about and get on with your work** cesse de perdre ton temps et fais ton travail [b] (= play the fool) faire l'imbécile; **stop ~ing about!** arrête de faire l'imbécile!, cesse tes pitreries!; **to ~ about with sth** (= play with) faire l'imbécile avec qch; (= mess with) [+ drugs, drink, electricity] toucher à qch* [c] (= have an affair) avoir une liaison or une aventure; (= have affairs) avoir des liaisons or des aventures [2] **~ing about** or **around** N → **fool**[1]

fool[2] [fu:l] N (Brit Culin: also **fruit ~**) (sorte de) mousse f de fruits; **gooseberry ~** ≈ mousse f de groseilles à maquereaux

foolery ['fu:lərɪ] N (NonC) (= foolish acts) sottises fpl, bêtises fpl; (= behaviour) bouffonnerie f, pitrerie(s) f(pl)

foolhardiness ['fu:l‚hɑːdɪnɪs] N témérité f, imprudence f

foolhardy ['fu:l‚hɑːdɪ] ADJ téméraire, imprudent

foolish ['fu:lɪʃ] ADJ [a] (= foolhardy) [person] idiot, bête; [action, decision, statement, mistake] stupide; **don't be so ~** ne fais pas l'idiot(e), ne sois pas bête; **don't do anything ~** ne faites pas de bêtises; **she had done something very ~** elle avait fait une grosse bêtise; **what a ~ thing to do!** quelle bêtise!; **it would be ~ to believe her** ce serait stupide de la croire; **I was ~ enough to do it** j'ai été assez bête pour le faire; **it was ~ of him to say such a thing** c'était stupide de sa part de dire une chose pareille [b] (= ridiculous) [person, question] ridicule; **to make sb look ~** rendre qn ridicule

foolishly ['fu:lɪʃlɪ] ADV [a] (= unwisely) [behave, act, ignore, forget, admit] bêtement; **~ romantic** d'un romantisme stupide; **~, I allowed myself to be persuaded** bêtement, je me suis laissé persuader [b] (= ridiculously) [say, grin] bêtement, sottement

foolishness ['fu:lɪʃnɪs] N (NonC) bêtise f, sottise f

foolproof ['fu:lpru:f] ADJ [method] infaillible; [piece of machinery] indéréglable

foolscap ['fu:lskæp] [1] N (also **~ paper**) ≈ papier m ministre [2] COMP ► **foolscap en-**

velope N enveloppe f longue ► **foolscap sheet** N feuille f de papier ministre ► **foolscap size** N format m ministre

foot [fʊt] 1 N (pl **feet**) a [of person, horse, cow etc] pied m; [of dog, cat, bird] patte f; **to be on one's feet** (lit) être or se tenir debout; (fig: after illness) être sur pied, être rétabli; **I'm on my feet all day long** je suis debout toute la journée; (lit, fig) **to fall** or **land on one's feet** retomber sur ses pieds; (lit, fig) **to think on one's feet** agir sur le moment; (fig) **to stand on one's own (two) feet** voler de ses propres ailes, se débrouiller tout seul; **to have a ~ in both camps** or **each camp** avoir un pied dans chaque camp; **to go on ~** aller à pied; **to get** or **rise to one's feet** se lever, se mettre debout; **to bring sb to his feet** faire lever qn; (fig) **to put** or **set sb on his feet again** (healthwise) remettre qn d'aplomb or sur pied; (financially) remettre qn en selle; **to keep one's feet** garder l'équilibre; (fig) **to keep one's feet on the ground** garder les pieds sur terre; (US fig) **to get one's feet on the ground** (= establish o.s.) trouver ses marques; (= re-establish o.s.) retrouver ses marques; **feet first** les pieds devant; **it's very wet under ~** c'est très mouillé par terre; **he was trampled under ~ by the horses** les chevaux l'ont piétiné; (fig) **to get under sb's feet** venir dans les jambes de qn; **the children have been under my feet the whole day** les enfants ont été dans mes jambes toute la journée; (in car) **to put one's ~ down*** (= accelerate) appuyer sur le champignon*; (fig) **you've got to put your ~ down** (= be firm) il faut réagir; **he let it go on for several weeks before finally putting his ~ down** il l'a supporté pendant plusieurs semaines avant d'y mettre le holà; (fig) **to put one's ~ in it*** mettre les pieds dans le plat; (fig) **to put one's best ~ forward** (= hurry) se dépêcher, allonger or presser le pas; (= do one's best) faire de son mieux; (fig) **he didn't put a ~ wrong** il n'a pas commis la moindre erreur or maladresse; **to start off** or **get off on the right/wrong ~** [people, relationship] être bien/mal parti; **I got off on the wrong ~ with him** j'ai mal commencé avec lui; (fig) **to get one's** or **a ~ in the door** faire le premier pas, établir un premier contact; (Brit fig) **to get one's feet under the table*** s'installer; **to put one's feet up*** (s'étendre or s'asseoir pour) se reposer un peu; **to take the weight off one's feet** (s'asseoir pour) se reposer un peu; (fig) **to have one ~ in the grave*** avoir un pied dans la tombe; **to be dying** or **dead on one's feet*** (= exhausted) être (complètement) à plat; **the business is dying on its feet*** c'est une affaire qui périclite; **to run sb off his feet*** fatiguer or éreinter qn; **she is absolutely run off her feet*** elle est débordée, elle n'en peut plus, elle ne sait plus où donner de la tête; **to set ~ on land** poser le pied sur la terre ferme; **I've never set ~ there** je n'y ai jamais mis le(s) pied(s); **never set ~ here again!** ne remettez jamais les pieds ici!; **my ~!*** mon œil!*, à d'autres!; **the boot** (Brit) or **the shoe** (US) **is on the other ~ now** les rôles sont inversés maintenant → **cold, drag, find, ground**

b [of hill, bed, stocking, sock] pied m; [of table] bout m; [of page, stairs] bas m; **at the ~ of the page** au or en bas de la page

c (= measure) pied m (anglais) (= 30,48 cm)

d (NonC: Mil) infanterie f; **ten thousand ~** dix mille fantassins mpl or soldats mpl d'infanterie; **the 91st of ~** le 91e (régiment) d'infanterie

e (Poetry) pied m

2 VT **to ~ the bill*** payer (la note or la douloureuse*); **to ~ it*** (= walk) (y) aller à pied or à pinces* ; (= dance) danser

3 COMP ► **foot-and-mouth (disease)** N fièvre f aphteuse ► **foot brake** N frein m à pied ► **foot-dragging** N lenteurs fpl,

atermoiements mpl ► **foot fault** N (Tennis) faute f de pied ► **foot fault judge** N juge m de ligne de fond ► **foot passengers** NPL [of ferry] passagers mpl sans véhicule ► **foot patrol** N (Police, Mil) patrouille f à pied ► **foot patrolman** N (pl **foot patrolmen**) (US Police) agent m de police ► **foot rot** N piétin m ► **foot soldier** N fantassin m

footage ['fʊtɪdʒ] N (gen, also Cine = length) ≈ métrage m; (Cine = material on film) séquences fpl (about, on sur); (TV) **they showed some ~ of the riots/the concert** ils ont diffusé quelques séquences sur les émeutes/le concert

football ['fʊtbɔːl] 1 N a (= sport) (Brit) football m, foot* m; (US) football m américain → **table**

b (= ball) ballon m (de football) → **political**

2 COMP [ground, match, team, coach] de football ► **football hooligan** N (Brit) hooligan m, houligan m ► **football hooliganism** N (NonC: Brit) hooliganisme m, houliganisme m ► **football league** N championnat m de football; (Brit) **the Football League** la fédération britannique de football ► **football player** N (Brit) joueur m de football, footballeur m; (US) joueur m de football américain ► **football pools** NPL (Brit) ≈ loto m sportif, ≈ pronostics mpl (sur les matchs de football); **to do the ~ pools** ≈ jouer au loto sportif; **he won £200 on the ~ pools** ≈ il a gagné 200 livres au loto sportif ► **football season** N saison f de football ► **football special** N (Brit Rail) train m de supporters (d'une équipe de football)

footballer ['fʊtbɔːləʳ] N (Brit) joueur m de football, footballeur m

footballing ['fʊtbɔːlɪŋ] ADJ [skills, career] de footballeur; [hero] du football; **the great ~ nations** les grandes nations du football; **he's got a ~ injury** il s'est blessé lors d'un match de football

footbath ['fʊtbɑːθ] N bain m de pieds

footboard ['fʊtbɔːd] N marchepied m

footbridge ['fʊtbrɪdʒ] N passerelle f

-footed ['fʊtɪd] ADJ (in compounds) light-footed au pied léger → **four**

footer ['fʊtəʳ] N (Typ, Comput) titre m en bas de page

-footer ['fʊtəʳ] N (in compounds) **a 15-footer** (= boat) ≈ un bateau de 5 mètres de long → **six**

footfall ['fʊtfɔːl] N (bruit m de) pas mpl

footgear ['fʊtgɪəʳ] N chaussures fpl

foothills ['fʊthɪlz] NPL contreforts mpl

foothold ['fʊthəʊld] N prise f (de pied); **to get** or **gain a ~** (lit) prendre pied; (fig) [newcomer] se faire (progressivement) accepter; [idea, opinion, fascism etc] se répandre, se propager; (Comm) **to gain a ~ in a market** prendre pied sur un marché

footing ['fʊtɪŋ] N a (lit) prise f (de pied); **to lose** or **miss one's ~** perdre pied or son équilibre or l'équilibre; b (= position, basis) **to get a ~ in society** se faire une position dans le monde; **to be on a friendly ~ with sb** être en termes amicaux avec qn; **on an equal ~** sur un pied d'égalité; **on a war ~** sur le pied de guerre; **to put sth on an official ~** officialiser qch, rendre qch officiel; (Jur) **on the ~ that ...** en supposant que ...

footle* ['fuːtl] VI **to ~ about** (= clown around) faire l'âne; (= waste time) perdre son temps à des futilités

footlights ['fʊtlaɪts] NPL (Theat) rampe f; (fig) **the lure of the ~** l'attrait du théâtre or des planches*

footling ['fuːtlɪŋ] ADJ insignifiant, futile

footlocker ['fʊt͵lɒkəʳ] N (US Mil) cantine f

footloose ['fʊtluːs] ADJ libre de toute attache; (fig) **~ and fancy-free** libre comme l'air

footman ['fʊtmən] N (pl **-men**) valet m de pied

footmark ['fʊtmɑːk] N empreinte f (de pied)

footnote ['fʊtnəʊt] N (lit) note f en bas de (la) page; (fig) post-scriptum m

footpath ['fʊtpɑːθ] N (= path) sentier m → **public**; (Brit) (= pavement) trottoir m; (by highway) chemin m

footplate ['fʊtpleɪt] 1 N (esp Brit Rail) plate-forme f (d'une locomotive) 2 COMP ► **footplate workers** NPL = **footplatemen**

footplatemen ['fʊtpleɪtmən] NPL (esp Brit Rail) agents mpl de conduite

footprint ['fʊtprɪnt] N (lit) empreinte f (de pied); (fig) (of computer) surface f d'encombrement; (of satellite) empreinte f

footpump ['fʊtpʌmp] N pompe f à pied

footrest ['fʊtrest] N (= part of chair) repose-pieds m inv; (= footstool) tabouret m (pour les pieds)

Footsie* ['fʊtsɪ] N (Fin) (ABBR = **Financial Times Stock Exchange 100 Index**) → **financial**; **(the) ~ Index** l'indice m Footsie

footsie* ['fʊtsɪ] N **to play ~ with sb** faire du pied à qn

footslog*: ['fʊtslɒg] VI **I've been ~ging around town** j'ai fait toute la ville à pied

footslogger*: ['fʊtslɒgəʳ] N (= walker) marcheur m, -euse f; (= soldier) pousse-cailloux† ‡ m inv

footsore ['fʊtsɔːʳ] ADJ aux pieds endoloris or douloureux; **to be ~** avoir mal aux pieds

footstep ['fʊtstep] N pas m → **follow**

footstool ['fʊtstuːl] N tabouret m (pour les pieds)

footway ['fʊtweɪ] N = **footpath**

footwear ['fʊtwɛəʳ] N chaussures fpl

footwork ['fʊtwɜːk] N (NonC) (Sport, Dancing) jeu m de jambes; (fig) **legal/financial/political ~** manœuvre f juridique/financière/politique

fop [fɒp] N dandy m

foppish ['fɒpɪʃ] ADJ [manners, behaviour, clothes] de dandy; **a ~ man** un dandy

FOR [͵efəʊˈɑːʳ] (Comm) (ABBR = **free on rail**) → **free**

---

for [fɔːʳ]

| 1 PREPOSITION | 2 CONJUNCTION |

When **for** *is part of a phrasal verb, eg* look for, make for, stand for, *look up the verb. When it is part of a set combination, eg* a gift/taste for, for sale/pleasure, eager/fit/noted for, *look up the other word.*

1 PREPOSITION

a pour; **a letter ~ you** une lettre pour toi; **is this ~ me?** c'est pour moi?; **a collection ~ the homeless** une quête pour les or en faveur des sans-abri; **he went there ~ a rest** il y est allé pour se reposer; **it is warm ~ January** il fait bon pour (un mois de) janvier; **he's tall ~ his age** il est grand pour son âge; **it's okay ~ a first attempt** ce n'est pas mal pour une première tentative; **there is one French passenger ~ every ten English** il y a un passager français pour dix Anglais; **~ or against** pour ou contre; **I'm ~ helping him** je suis pour l'aider, je suis partisan de l'aider; **I've got some news ~ you** j'ai du nouveau à t'apprendre, j'ai des nouvelles pour toi; **a cloth ~ polishing silver** un chiffon pour astiquer l'argenterie; **it's not ~ cutting wood** ça n'est pas fait pour couper du bois; (BUT) **what's this knife ~?** à quoi sert ce couteau?; **he had a bag ~ a pillow** il avait un sac en guise d'oreiller; **it's time ~ dinner** c'est l'heure du dîner, il est l'heure de dîner; **I decided that it was the job ~ me** j'ai décidé que ce travail était fait pour moi or que c'était le travail qu'il me fallait

b (= going to) pour; **is this the train ~ Paris?** c'est bien le train pour Paris?; **this isn't the bus ~ Lyons** ce n'est pas le bus pour Lyon; **trains ~ Paris go from platform one** les trains pour Paris *or* à destination de Paris partent du quai numéro un; [BUT] **he swam ~ the shore** il a nagé vers le rivage; **where are you ~?** où allez-vous?

[c] **= on behalf of** ~ **me/you** *etc* à ma/ta *etc* place; **I'll see her ~ you if you like** je peux aller la voir à ta place si tu veux; **will you go ~ me?** est-ce que vous pouvez y aller à ma place?

[d] **= as in** comme; **D ~ Daniel** D comme Daniel

[e] **= in exchange for** **I'll give you this book ~ that one** je vous échange ce livre-ci contre celui-là; **he'll do it ~ £25** il le fera pour 25 livres

When used with **pay** *and* **sell**, **for** *is not translated.*
to pay 50 francs ~ a ticket payer un billet 50 F; **I sold it ~ £20** je l'ai vendu 20 livres

[f] **= because of** pour; ~ **this reason** pour cette raison; **to go to prison ~ theft** aller en prison pour vol; **to choose sb ~ his ability** choisir qn pour *or* en raison de sa compétence

[g] **= from** de; ~ **fear of being left behind** de peur d'être oublié; **to jump ~ joy** sauter de joie

[h] **= up to** à; **that's ~ him to decide** c'est à lui de décider; **it's not ~ you to blame him** ce n'est pas à vous de le critiquer; **it's not ~ me to say** ce n'est pas à moi de le dire

[i] **= in spite of** malgré; ~ **all his wealth** malgré toute sa richesse; ~ **all that, you should have warned me** malgré tout, vous auriez dû me prévenir, vous auriez quand même dû me prévenir; ~ **all he promised to come, he didn't** malgré ses promesses, il n'est pas venu, bien qu'il ait promis de venir, il ne l'a pas fait

[j] **= for a distance of** sur, pendant; **a road lined with trees ~ 3km** une route bordée d'arbres sur 3 km; **there was nothing to be seen ~ miles** il n'y avait rien à voir pendant des kilomètres; **we walked ~ 2km** nous avons marché (pendant) 2 km; **there were small drab houses ~ mile upon mile** des petites maisons monotones se succédaient pendant *or* sur des kilomètres et des kilomètres

[k] [time in the past or future] pendant; **he suffered terribly ~ six months** il a horriblement souffert pendant six mois

With certain verbs **pendant** *may be omitted.*
I worked/stayed there ~ three months j'y ai travaillé/j'y suis resté (pendant) trois mois; **he went away ~ two weeks** il est parti (pendant) quinze jours; **I'll be away ~ a month** je serai absent (pendant) un mois

When **for** *indicates an intention, the translation is* **pour**.
Christian went ~ a week, but stayed ~ a year Christian était parti pour une semaine, mais il est resté un an

When **for** *refers to future time, it is translated by* **pour** *after* **aller** *and* **partir**.
he's going there ~ six months il va là-bas pour six mois; **I am going away ~ a few days** je pars (pour) quelques jours; [BUT] **he won't be back ~ a week** il ne sera pas de retour avant huit jours

[l] [uncompleted states and actions] depuis, ça fait ... que (*less frm*)

French generally uses the present and imperfect where English uses the perfect and past perfect.
he's been here ~ ten days il est ici depuis dix jours, ça fait dix jours qu'il est ici; **I have known her ~ five years** je la connais depuis cinq ans, ça fait cinq ans que je la connais; **I have been working here ~ three months** je travaille ici depuis trois mois, ça fait trois mois que je travaille ici; **I had known her ~ years** je la connaissais depuis des années; **I had been working there ~ three months when ...** je travaillais là depuis trois mois quand ...; **he hasn't worked ~ two years** il n'a pas travaillé

depuis deux ans, ça fait deux ans qu'il ne travaille pas; **she hadn't seen him ~ three months** elle ne l'avait pas vu depuis trois mois, cela faisait trois mois qu'elle ne l'avait pas vu

[m] [phrases with infinitive] **their one hope is ~ him to return** leur seul espoir est qu'il revienne; **the best would be** *or* **it would be best ~ you to go away** le mieux serait que vous vous en alliez (*subj*); ~ **this to be possible** pour que cela soit possible; **I brought it ~ you to see** je l'ai apporté pour que vous le voyiez (*subj*); **there is still time ~ him to come** il a encore le temps d'arriver

[n] [exclamations]
◆ **for it!***: **now ~ it!** (bon, alors) on y va!; **you're ~ it!** qu'est-ce que tu vas prendre!*, ça va être ta fête!*; **I'll be ~ it if he catches me here!** qu'est-ce que je vais prendre* s'il me trouve ici!

◆ **oh for ...!**: **oh ~ a cup of tea!** je donnerais n'importe quoi pour une tasse de thé!; **oh ~ a chance of revenge!** si seulement je pouvais me venger!

[2] CONJUNCTION
[liter] **= because** car; **I avoided him, ~ he was rude and uncouth** je l'évitais car il était impoli et grossier

forage ['fɒrɪdʒ] [1] N fourrage *m* [2] VI fourrager, fouiller (**for** pour trouver) [3] COMP
► **forage cap** N (*Mil*) calot *m*

foray ['fɒreɪ] [1] N (*Mil*) incursion *f*, raid *m* (**into** en); (*fig: into business, politics, acting etc*) incursion *f* (**into** dans); (*Mil*) **to go on** *or* **make a ~** faire une incursion *or* un raid; **we made a short ~ into town** on a fait une petite expédition en ville [2] VI faire une incursion *or* un raid

forbad(e) [fə'bæd] VB *pret of* **forbid**

forbear [fɔː'beər] (*pret* **forbore**, *ptp* **forborne**) VI (*frm*) s'abstenir; **to ~ from doing** ◊ **to ~ to do** s'abstenir *or* se garder de faire; **he forbore to make any comment** il s'abstint de tout commentaire

forbearance [fɔː'beərəns] N patience *f*, tolérance *f*

forbearing [fɔː'beərɪŋ] ADJ patient, tolérant

forbears ['fɔːbeəz] NPL = **forebears**

▼ **forbid** [fə'bɪd] (*pret* **forbad(e)**, *ptp* **forbidden**) VT
[a] (**= not allow**) défendre, interdire; **to ~ sb to do sth** ◊ **to ~ sb from doing sth** interdire à qn de faire qch; **to ~ sb alcohol** défendre *or* interdire l'alcool à qn; **I ~ you to!** je vous l'interdis!; **it is ~den to do sth** il est défendu *or* interdit de faire cela; **they are ~den to do that** ils n'ont pas le droit de faire cela, il leur est défendu *or* interdit de faire cela; **~den** c'est défendu *or* interdit; **~den by law** interdit par la loi; **smoking is (strictly) ~den** il est (formellement) interdit de fumer; (*on sign*) **"smoking ~den"** «défense de fumer»; **preaching was ~den to women** il était défendu *or* interdit aux femmes de prêcher

[b] (**= prevent**) empêcher; **his pride ~s him to ask for** *or* **from asking for help** ◊ **his pride ~s his asking for help** (*more frm*) sa fierté l'empêche de demander de l'aide; **custom ~s any modernization** la coutume empêche toute modernisation; **God** *or* **Heaven ~!*** grands dieux non!; (*liter*) **God** *or* **Heaven ~ that this might be true!** pourvu que ça ne soit pas vrai! (*liter*); **God** *or* **Heaven ~ that he should come here!** pourvu qu'il ne vienne pas ici!; **God** *or* **Heaven ~ (that) I should do anything illegal** Dieu me garde de faire quoi que ce soit d'illégal

▼ **forbidden** [fə'bɪdn] [1] VB *pt of* **forbid** [2] ADJ [*food, book, place, love*] interdit; [*subject, word*] tabou; [*feelings*] défendu; (*fig*) **that's ~ territory** *or* **ground** c'est un sujet tabou [3] COMP
► **the Forbidden City** N la Cité interdite
► **forbidden fruit** N (*Bible or fig*) fruit *m* défendu

forbidding [fə'bɪdɪŋ] ADJ [*person*] à l'allure sévère; [*expression*] sévère; [*place*] inhospitalier; [*building*] menaçant

forbiddingly [fə'bɪdɪŋli] ADV [*look at, frown*] de façon rébarbative; **a ~ prison-like building** un bâtiment aux allures rébarbatives de prison

forbore [fɔː'bɔː] VB *pt of* **forbear**

forborne [fɔː'bɔːn] VB *ptp of* **forbear**

▼ **force** [fɔːs] [1] N [a] (*NonC*) (**= strength**) force *f*, violence *f*; (*Phys*) force *f*; [*of phrase, word*] force *f*, poids *m*; (*Phys*) (**= gravity**) pesanteur *f*; **centrifugal/centripetal ~** force *f* centrifuge/centripète; **to use ~** employer la force (**to do** pour faire); **by sheer ~** de vive force; **by ~ of** à force de; ~ **of circumstances** force *f* des choses; **from ~ of habit** par la force de l'habitude; **through** *or* **by sheer ~ of will** purement à force de volonté; **by (sheer) ~ of personality** uniquement grâce à sa personnalité; ~ **of a blow** violence *f* d'un coup; **by ~** de vive force, par la force; **to resort to ~** avoir recours à la force; **to settle a dispute by ~** régler une querelle par la force; **his argument lacked ~** son argument manquait de conviction; **I don't quite see the ~ of his argument** je ne vois pas bien la force de son argument; **to come into ~** [*law, prices*] entrer en vigueur *or* en application; **the rule is now in ~** le règlement est désormais en vigueur; **the police were there in ~** la police était là en force; **they came in ~ to support him** ils sont venus en force pour lui apporter leur soutien → **brute**

[b] (**= power**) force *f*; **the ~s of Nature** les forces *fpl* de la nature; **he is a powerful ~ in the Trade Union movement** il exerce un grand pouvoir au sein du mouvement syndical; **there are several ~s at work** plusieurs influences entrent en jeu → **life**

[c] (*body of men*) force *f*; (*Brit Mil*) **the ~s** les forces *fpl* armées; (*Brit Mil*) **allied ~s** armées *fpl* alliées; (*Police*) **the ~*** la police → **police**; → **join, land, sale**

[2] VT [a] (**= constrain**) forcer, obliger (**sb to do** qn à faire); **to be ~d to do sth** être contraint *or* forcé *or* obligé de faire qch; **to ~ o.s. to do sth** se forcer *or* se contraindre à faire qch; **I find myself ~d to say that ...** je me vois contraint de dire que ...; **he was ~d to conclude that ...** il a été forcé de conclure que ..., force lui a été de conclure que ...

[b] (**= impose**) [+ *conditions, obedience*] imposer (**on sb** à qn); **the decision was ~d on me by events** cette décision m'a été imposée par les événements, ce sont les événements qui m'ont dicté cette décision; **they ~d action on the enemy** ils ont contraint l'ennemi à se battre; **I don't want to ~ myself on you, but ...** je ne veux pas m'imposer, mais ...; **to ~ the issue** enfoncer le clou

[c] (**= push, thrust**) pousser; **to ~ books into a box** fourrer des livres dans une caisse; **he ~d himself through the gap in the hedge** il s'est frayé un passage par un trou dans la haie; **to ~ one's way into** entrer *or* pénétrer de force dans; **to ~ one's way through sth** se frayer un passage à travers qch; **to ~ a bill through Parliament** forcer la Chambre à voter une loi; **the lorry ~d the car off the road** le camion a forcé la voiture à quitter la route

[d] (**= break open**) [+ *lock*] forcer; **to ~ (open) a drawer/a door** forcer un tiroir/une porte; (*fig*) **to ~ sb's hand** forcer la main à qn

[e] (**= extort**) arracher; (*stronger*) extorquer (**from** à); **he ~d a confession from me** il m'a arraché *or* extorqué une confession; **we ~d the secret out of him** nous lui avons arraché le secret

[f] [+ *plants*] forcer, hâter; **to ~ the pace** forcer l'allure *or* le pas

[g] **he ~d a reply/a smile** ◊ **he ~d himself to reply/smile** il s'est forcé à répondre/à sourire

[3] VI (*Bridge*) faire un forcing

4 COMP ► **force-feed** VT (gen) nourrir de force ; [+ animal] gaver ; **he was ~-fed** on l'a nourri de force ; (fig) **as a child she was ~-fed (on) Shakespeare** quand elle était petite elle a été gavée de Shakespeare ► **forcing bid** N (Bridge) annonce f forcée or de forcing ► **forcing house** N (Agr) forcerie f ; (fig) pépinière f

► **force back** VT SEP a (Mil) [+ enemy] obliger à reculer, faire reculer ; [+ crowd] repousser, faire reculer b **to ~ back one's desire to laugh** réprimer son envie de rire ; **to ~ back one's tears** refouler ses larmes

► **force down** VT SEP a [+ aircraft] forcer à atterrir b [+ prices, inflation, unemployment] faire baisser c **to ~ food down** se forcer à manger ; **if you ~ the clothes down you will get more into the suitcase** si tu tasses les vêtements tu en feras entrer plus dans la valise

► **force out** VT SEP a faire sortir (de force) ; **he ~d the cork out** il a sorti le bouchon en forçant ; **they ~d the rebels out into the open** ils ont forcé or obligé les insurgés à se montrer ; **small farmers will be ~d out of the market** les petits exploitants seront éliminés du marché b **he ~d out a reply/an apology** il s'est forcé à répondre/à s'excuser

► **force up** [fɔ:s] VT SEP [+ prices, inflation, unemployment] faire monter

▼ **forced** [fɔ:st] 1 ADJ a (= imposed) [marriage, repatriation] forcé b (= artificial) [smile, laughter] forcé ; [conversation] peu naturel ; **to sound ~** [words] faire peu naturel ; [laughter] sembler forcé c [plant] forcé 2 COMP ► **forced entry** N (Law) entrée f avec effraction ► **forced labour** N travaux mpl forcés ► **forced landing** N (Aviat) atterrissage m forcé ► **forced march** N (Mil) marche f forcée ► **forced savings** NPL épargne f forcée

forceful ['fɔ:sfʊl] ADJ a (= hard) [blow, kick, punch] violent b (= vigorous) [person, personality, intervention] énergique ; [action, reminder] vigoureux ; [argument] convaincant ; [statement, speech] énergique ; **to be ~ in doing sth** faire qch énergiquement ; **he was ~ in condemning the regime** or **in his condemnation of the regime** il a condamné énergiquement le régime

forcefully ['fɔ:sfʊlɪ] ADV a (= using force) [push, knock] avec force, violemment ; [remove, administer] avec fermeté ; (= forcibly) de force b [say, express, remind] avec force ; [argue] avec force, avec vigueur ; [act, intervene] avec détermination ; **it struck him ~ that ...** il lui est apparu avec force or avec une évidence frappante que ...

forcefulness ['fɔ:sfʊlnɪs] N a (= force) [of blow, kick, punch] force f, violence f b (= vigour) [of person] détermination f ; [of argument, attack] force f

forcemeat ['fɔ:smi:t] N (Culin) farce f, hachis m (de viande et de fines herbes)

forceps ['fɔ:seps] NPL (also **pair of ~**) forceps m ; **~ delivery** accouchement m au forceps

forcible ['fɔ:səbl] 1 ADJ a (= forced) [repatriation, feeding] forcé b (= powerful) [affirmation, speech] vigoureux 2 COMP ► **forcible entry** N (by thief) entrée f par effraction ; (by police) **to make a ~ entry** entrer de force

forcibly ['fɔ:səblɪ] ADV a (= by force) [remove, eject, annex] de force, par la force ; [repatriate, separate, feed] de force ; [restrain] par la force b (= powerfully) [strike] avec force ; [argue, express] énergiquement ; **to bring sth ~ home to sb** forcer qn à prendre conscience de qch

ford [fɔ:d] 1 N gué m 2 VT passer à gué

fordable ['fɔ:dəbl] ADJ guéable

fore [fɔ:ʳ] 1 ADJ a (Zool) [foot, limb] antérieur ; **near ~** antérieur gauche ; **off ~** antérieur droit → **foreleg** b (Naut, Aviat) avant inv ; (Naut) **the ~ watch** le quart de proue 2 N

a **to come to the ~** [person] se mettre en évidence, se faire remarquer ; [sb's courage] se manifester ; **he was well to the ~ during the discussion** il a été très en évidence pendant la discussion ; **to the ~** (= at hand) à portée de main b (Naut) avant m 3 ADV (Naut) à l'avant ; **~ and aft** de l'avant à l'arrière 4 EXCL (Golf) gare !, attention ! 5 COMP ► **fore and aft rig** N (Naut) gréement m aurique ► **fore and aft sail** N (Naut) voile f aurique

forearm ['fɔ:rɑ:m] N avant-bras m inv

forebears ['fɔ:bɛəz] NPL (liter) aïeux mpl (liter)

forebode [fɔ:'bəʊd] VT présager, annoncer

foreboding [fɔ:'bəʊdɪŋ] 1 N pressentiment m, prémonition f ; **to have a ~ that** avoir le pressentiment que, pressentir que ; **to have ~s** avoir des pressentiments or des prémonitions ; **with many ~s he agreed to do it** il a consenti à le faire en dépit de or malgré toutes ses appréhensions 2 ADJ qui ne présage rien de bon, menaçant

forecast ['fɔ:kɑ:st] (pret, ptp forecast) 1 VT (Met) prévoir 2 N a (gen, Comm) prévisions fpl ; (Betting) pronostic m ; **according to all the ~s** selon toutes les prévisions ; (Comm) **sales ~** prévisions fpl de vente ; **the racing ~** les pronostics mpl hippiques or des courses b (also **weather ~**) bulletin m météorologique, météo* f ; **the ~ is good** les prévisions sont bonnes, la météo* est bonne

forecaster ['fɔ:kɑ:stəʳ] N (Met) météorologue mf ; (Econ, Pol) prévisionniste mf ; (Sport) pronostiqueur m, -euse f

forecastle ['fəʊksl] N (Naut) gaillard m d'avant ; (Merchant Navy) poste m d'équipage

foreclose [fɔ:'kləʊz] 1 VT (Jur) saisir ; **to ~ (on) a mortgage** saisir un bien hypothéqué 2 VI saisir le bien hypothéqué ; **to ~ on → 1**

foreclosure [fɔ:'kləʊʒəʳ] N saisie f

forecourt ['fɔ:kɔ:t] N (esp Brit) avant-cour f, cour f de devant ; [of petrol station] devant m

foredoomed [fɔ:'du:md] ADJ (liter) condamné d'avance, voué à l'échec

forefathers ['fɔ:ˌfɑ:ðəz] NPL aïeux mpl (liter), ancêtres mpl

forefinger ['fɔ:ˌfɪŋgəʳ] N index m

forefoot ['fɔ:fʊt] N (pl **-feet**) [of horse, cow] pied m antérieur or de devant ; [of cat, dog] patte f antérieure or de devant

forefront ['fɔ:frʌnt] N **in** or **at the ~ of** [+ research, technology, progress] à la pointe de ; **in** or **at the ~ of their minds** au premier plan or au centre de leurs préoccupations ; **to bring sth to the ~** mettre qch en évidence, faire ressortir qch

foregather [fɔ:'gæðəʳ] VI se réunir, s'assembler

forego [fɔ:'gəʊ] (pret forewent, ptp foregone) VT renoncer à, se priver de

foregoing ['fɔ:gəʊɪŋ] ADJ précédent ; (in legal document) susdit ; **according to the ~** d'après ce qui précède

foregone [fɔ:'gɒn] ADJ **it was a ~ conclusion** c'était à prévoir, c'était couru d'avance

foreground ['fɔ:graʊnd] 1 N (Art, Phot) premier plan m ; **in the ~** au premier plan 2 VT (lit) [+ object in photo, picture] mettre en premier plan ; (fig) [+ issue, problem] mettre en avant

forehand ['fɔ:hænd] (Tennis) 1 N coup m droit 2 COMP ► **forehand drive** N coup m droit ► **forehand volley** N volée f de coup droit

forehead ['fɒrɪd] N front m ; **on his ~** au front

foreign ['fɒrən] 1 ADJ a [person, country, language, food, car] étranger ; [holiday, travel] à l'étranger ; [goods, produce] de l'étranger ; [politics, trade, debt] extérieur ; (incoming) étranger ; (abroad) à l'étranger ; [news] du monde ; **he comes from a ~ country** il vient de l'étranger ;

our relations with ~ countries nos rapports avec l'étranger b (= alien) ~ to étranger à ; **lying is quite ~ to him** or **to his nature** le mensonge lui est (complètement) étranger c (= extraneous) [matter, object, substance] étranger 2 COMP ► **foreign affairs** NPL affaires fpl étrangères ; **Minister of Foreign Affairs** ministre m des Affaires étrangères ; **Ministry of Foreign Affairs** ministère m des Affaires étrangères ; (Brit) **Secretary (of State) for Foreign Affairs** ≈ ministre m des Affaires étrangères ► **foreign agent** N (= spy) agent m étranger ; (Comm) représentant m à l'étranger ► **Foreign and Commonwealth Office** (Brit) ministère m des Affaires étrangères et du Commonwealth ► **foreign body** N (Med) corps m étranger ► **foreign correspondent** N correspondant(e) m(f) à l'étranger ► **foreign currency** N devises fpl étrangères ► **foreign exchange** N (= system) change m ; (= currency) devises fpl ; **the ~ exchange market** le marché des changes ► **Foreign Legion** N Légion f (étrangère) ► **Foreign Minister** N ministre m des Affaires étrangères ► **Foreign Ministry** N ministère m des Affaires étrangères ► **foreign national** N ressortissant(e) m(f) étranger (-ère f) ► **Foreign Office** N (Brit) ≈ ministère m des Affaires étrangères ► **foreign-owned** ADJ (Econ, Comm) sous contrôle étranger ► **foreign policy** N politique f étrangère or extérieure ► **foreign relations** NPL relations fpl extérieures ► **Foreign Secretary** N (Brit) ≈ ministre m des Affaires étrangères ► **foreign service** N (esp US) service m diplomatique

foreigner ['fɒrənəʳ] N étranger m, -ère f

foreknowledge ['fɔ:'nɒlɪdʒ] N fait m de savoir à l'avance, connaissance f anticipée ; **I had no ~ of his intentions** je ne savais pas à l'avance ce qu'il avait l'intention de faire ; **it presupposes a certain ~ of ...** ceci présuppose une certaine connaissance anticipée de ...

foreland ['fɔ:lənd] N (= headland) cap m, promontoire m

foreleg ['fɔ:leg] N [of horse, cow] jambe f antérieure ; [of dog, cat] patte f de devant

forelock ['fɔ:lɒk] N mèche f, toupet m ; (Brit) **to touch** or **tug one's ~ to sb** (lit) saluer qn en portant la main à son front ; (fig) faire des courbettes à or devant qn ; (liter) **to take Time by the ~** saisir l'occasion aux cheveux

foreman ['fɔ:mən] N (pl **-men**) a (Ind) contremaître m, chef m d'équipe ; [of jury] président m

foremast ['fɔ:mɑ:st] N (Naut) mât m de misaine

foremost ['fɔ:məʊst] 1 ADJ a (= chief) [authority, expert, writer, scholar] plus grand, plus éminent ; **~ among contemporary writers is ...** le premier d'entre tous les écrivains contemporains est ... ; **to be ~ in sb's mind** être au premier plan des pensées or des préoccupations de qn ; **they were ~ in calling for an end to the war** ils ont été les plus actifs pour appeler à la fin de la guerre b (Naut) le or la plus en avant 2 ADV a (= above all) tout d'abord ; **first and ~** d'abord et avant tout b (= forwards) en avant

forename ['fɔ:neɪm] N prénom m

forenoon ['fɔ:nu:n] N matinée f

forensic [fə'rensɪk] 1 ADJ a (also **~s**: Med, Jur) [test, laboratory] médicolégal b (frm = lawyerly) [skill, eloquence] du barreau 2 **forensics** N (NonC) (= science) médecine f légale ; (= police department) département m médicolégal 3 COMP ► **forensic evidence** N preuves fpl relevées lors d'une expertise médicolégale ► **forensic expert** N expert m médicolégal ► **forensic medicine** N médecine f légale ► **forensic science** N expertise f médicolégale ; **~ science laboratory** ≈ laboratoire *m* de police scientifique ► **forensic scientist** N expert *m* légiste ► **forensics expert** N = forensic expert

forepaw ['fɔːpɔː] N (*Zool*) patte *f* antérieure *or* de devant

foreplay ['fɔːpleɪ] N préliminaires *mpl* (amoureux)

forequarters ['fɔːˌkwɔːtəz] NPL quartiers *mpl* de devant

forerunner ['fɔːˌrʌnər] N **a** (= *sign, indication*) signe *m* avant-coureur, présage *m* ; (= *person*) précurseur *m* ; [*of machine, invention*] ancêtre *m* **b** (*Ski*) ouvreur *m*

foresail ['fɔːseɪl] N (*Naut*) (voile *f* de) misaine *f*

foresee [fɔːˈsiː] (*pret* **foresaw**, *ptp* **foreseen**) VT prévoir

foreseeable [fɔːˈsiːəbl] ADJ prévisible ; **in the ~ future** dans un avenir prévisible

foreshadow [fɔːˈʃædəʊ] VT [*event etc*] présager, annoncer, laisser prévoir

foreshore ['fɔːʃɔːr] N [*of beach*] plage *f* ; (*Geog*) estran *m*

foreshorten [fɔːˈʃɔːtn] VT **a** (*Art*) [+ *perspective, view, image, figure*] faire un raccourci de ; (*Phot*) déformer par un effet de téléobjectif ; **~ed view** raccourci *m* **b** (*frm: in duration, size*) raccourcir

foreshortening [fɔːˈʃɔːtnɪŋ] N (*Art, Phot*) raccourci *m*

foresight ['fɔːsaɪt] N prévoyance *f* ; **lack of ~** imprévoyance *f* ; **to have the ~ to do sth** faire preuve de prévoyance en faisant qch, avoir la bonne idée de faire qch au bon moment

foreskin ['fɔːskɪn] N prépuce *m*

forest ['fɒrɪst] **1** N forêt *f* ; (*US fig*) **he can't see the ~ for the trees** les arbres lui cachent la forêt **2** COMP ► **Forest Enterprise** N (*Brit*) ≈ l'Office *m* des forêts ► **forest ranger** N garde *m* forestier

forestall [fɔːˈstɔːl] VT [+ *competitor*] devancer ; [+ *desire, eventuality, objection*] anticiper, prévenir

forested ['fɒrɪstɪd] ADJ boisé

forester ['fɒrɪstər] N forestier *m*

forestry ['fɒrɪstrɪ] **1** N sylviculture *f*, foresterie *f* **2** COMP ► **the Forestry Commission** N (*Brit*) ≈ l'Office *m* des Forêts

foretaste ['fɔːteɪst] N avant-goût *m*

foretell [fɔːˈtel] (*pret, ptp* **foretold**) VT prédire

forethought ['fɔːθɔːt] N prévoyance *f* ; **lack of ~** imprévoyance *f*

forever, for ever [fərˈevər] ADV **a** (= *eternally*) [*live, last, remember*] toujours ; **I'll love you ~** je t'aimerai toujours ; **Manchester United ~!** vive Manchester United ! ; **~ and ever** à jamais, éternellement **b** (= *definitively*) [*go, change, disappear, lose, close*] définitivement, pour toujours ; **he left ~** il est parti pour toujours **c** (* = *a long time*) [*take*] une éternité ; [*wait*] jusqu'à la saint-glinglin* ; **the meeting lasted ~** la réunion n'en finissait pas **d** (= *constantly*) **to be ~ doing sth** être sans arrêt en train de faire qch **e** (= *unfailingly*) [*cheerful, suspicious*] toujours

forewarn [fɔːˈwɔːn] VT prévenir, avertir ■ (*PROV*) **~ed is forearmed** un homme averti en vaut deux (*PROV*)

foreword ['fɔːwɜːd] N avant-propos *m inv*, avertissement *m* (au lecteur)

forfeit ['fɔːfɪt] **1** VT (*Jur*) [+ *property*] perdre (par confiscation) ; [+ *one's rights*] perdre, être déchu de ; (*fig*) [+ *one's life, health*] payer de ; [+ *sb's respect*] perdre **2** N **a** (*gen*) prix *m*, peine *f* **b** (*for non-performance of contract*) dédit *m* ; (= *game*) **~s** gages *mpl* (jeu de société) ; (*in game*) **to pay a ~** avoir un gage **3** ADJ (*liter*) (= *liable to be taken*) susceptible d'être confisqué ; (= *actually taken*) confisqué ; **his life was ~** (= *he died*) il le paya de sa vie ; (= *he might die*) il pourrait le payer de sa vie

forfeiture ['fɔːfɪtʃər] N [*of property*] perte *f* (par confiscation) ; [*of right etc*] perte *f*, déchéance *f*

forgather [fɔːˈgæðər] VI = foregather

forgave [fəˈgeɪv] VB *pt of* **forgive**

forge [fɔːdʒ] **1** VT **a** (= *fake*) [+ *signature, banknote*] contrefaire ; [+ *document*] faire un faux de ; [+ *painting*] faire un faux de, contrefaire ; [+ *evidence*] fabriquer ; (= *alter*) maquiller, falsifier ; **a ~d passport/ticket** un faux passeport/billet ; **to ~ a certificate** (= *create new one*) faire un faux certificat ; (= *alter existing one*) maquiller *or* falsifier un certificat ; **the date on the certificate had been ~d** la date figurant sur le certificat avait été falsifiée ; **to ~ a Renoir** faire un faux Renoir ; **a ~d painting** un faux (*tableau*) ; **a ~d Renoir** un faux Renoir ; **it's ~d** c'est un faux **b** [+ *metal*] forger **c** (= *establish*) [+ *alliance, ties, links*] forger ; [+ *coalition*] former ; [+ *agreement, compromise*] établir ; [+ *solution*] parvenir à ; **to ~ one's identity** construire son identité **2** VI **to ~ ahead** prendre de l'avance ; (*Racing*) foncer **3** N forge *f*

forger ['fɔːdʒər] N faussaire *mf* ; (*Jur*) contrefacteur *m*

forgery ['fɔːdʒərɪ] N **a** (*NonC*) [*of banknote, signature, document, will*] (= *counterfeiting*) contrefaçon *f* ; (= *altering*) falsification *f* ; [*of story*] invention *f* ; (*Jur*) contrefaçon *f* (frauduleuse) ; **to prosecute sb for ~** poursuivre qn pour faux (et usage de faux) ; **art/cheque/banknote ~** contrefaçon d'œuvres d'art/de chèques/de billets de banque **b** (= *thing forged: work of art, document, passport, will*) faux *m* ; **the signature was a ~** la signature était fausse

▼ **forget** [fəˈget] (*pret* **forgot**, *ptp* **forgotten**) **1** VT **a** [+ *name, fact, experience*] oublier ; **I've forgotten all my Spanish** j'ai oublié tout l'espagnol que je savais *or* tout mon espagnol ; **she never ~s a face** elle a la mémoire des visages ; **I shall never ~ what he said** je n'oublierai jamais ce qu'il a dit ; **I ~ who said ...** je ne sais plus qui a dit ... ; **not ~ting ...** sans oublier ... ; **we completely forgot the time** nous avons complètement oublié l'heure ; **and don't you ~ it!*** et tâche de ne pas oublier !, tu as intérêt à ne pas oublier ! ; **she'll never let him ~ it** elle ne manque pas une occasion de le lui rappeler ; **let's ~ it!** passons *or* on passe l'éponge ! ; (= *let's drop the subject*) ça n'a aucune importance ; **~ it!** (*to sb thanking*) ce n'est rien ! ; (*to sb pestering*) laissez tomber ! ; (*to sb hopeful*) n'y comptez pas ! ; **to ~ to do** oublier *or* omettre de faire ; **I've forgotten how to do it** je ne sais plus comment on fait ; **it's easy to ~ how to do it** c'est facile d'oublier comment on fait ; **I forgot (that) I'd seen her** j'ai oublié que je l'avais vue

b **to ~ o.s.** (= *be altruistic*) s'oublier, oublier son propre intérêt ; **to ~ o.s.** *or* **one's manners** oublier toutes ses bonnes manières, s'oublier (*liter*) ; **he drinks to try to ~ himself** il boit pour oublier ; (*gen*) **he forgot himself and ...** (= *be distracted*) dans un moment de distraction, il ...

c (= *leave behind*) [+ *umbrella, passport, gloves etc*] oublier, laisser

2 VI oublier ; **I completely forgot ◊ I forgot all about it** j'ai complètement oublié, ça m'est complètement sorti de l'esprit ; **I've forgotten all about it (already)** je n'y pense (déjà) plus ; **~ about it!*** n'y pensez plus ! ; **he seemed willing to ~ about the whole business** il semblait prêt à passer l'éponge sur l'affaire ; **if that's the kind of work you're going to produce, you can ~ about your promotion** si c'est comme ça que tu vas travailler, tu peux dire adieu à ta promotion

3 COMP ► **forget-me-not** N (*Bot*) myosotis

m ► **forget-me-not blue** N (bleu *m*) myosotis *m inv*

forgetful [fəˈgetful] ADJ **a** (= *absent-minded*) distrait ; (= *careless*) négligent, étourdi ; **he is very ~** il a très mauvaise mémoire, il oublie tout ; **how ~ of me!** que je suis étourdi ! ; **~ of the danger** oublieux du danger

forgetfulness [fəˈgetfulnɪs] N (= *absent-mindedness*) manque *m* de mémoire ; (= *carelessness*) négligence *f*, étourderie *f* ; **in a moment of ~** dans un moment d'oubli *or* d'étourderie

forgettable [fəˈgetəbəl] ADJ peu mémorable

forgivable [fəˈgɪvəbl] ADJ pardonnable

forgivably [fəˈgɪvəblɪ] ADV **to act** *or* **behave ~** avoir un comportement pardonnable *or* excusable ; **he was ~ tense/rude** il était tendu/malpoli, ce qu'on pouvait lui pardonner

forgive [fəˈgɪv] (*pret* **forgave**, *ptp* **forgiven** [fəˈgɪvn]) VT **a** [+ *person, sin, mistake*] pardonner ; **to ~ sb (for) sth** pardonner qch à qn ; **to ~ sb for doing** pardonner à qn de faire ; **~ me for asking, but ...** excuse-moi de demander, mais ... ; **you must ~ him his rudeness** pardonnez-lui son impolitesse ; **one could be ~n for thinking ...** on serait excusable *or* pardonnable de penser ... ; **~ me, but ...** pardonnez-moi *or* excusez-moi, mais ... ; **we must ~ and forget** nous devons pardonner et oublier **b** (*frm*) **to ~ (sb) a debt** faire grâce (à qn) d'une dette

forgiveness [fəˈgɪvnɪs] N (*NonC*) (= *pardon*) pardon *m* ; (= *compassion*) indulgence *f*, clémence *f*

forgiving [fəˈgɪvɪŋ] ADJ indulgent, clément

forgo [fɔːˈgəʊ] VT = forego

forgot [fəˈgɒt] VB *pt of* **forget**

forgotten [fəˈgɒtn] VB *ptp of* **forget**

fork [fɔːk] **1** N **a** (*at table*) fourchette *f* ; (*for digging*) fourche *f* **b** [*of branches*] fourche *f* ; [*of roads, railways*] embranchement *m* ; (*giving directions*) **take the left ~** prenez à gauche à l'embranchement **2** VT **a** (*also ~ over*) [+ *hay, ground*] fourcher **b** **he ~ed the beans into his mouth** il enfournait* ses haricots (à coups de fourchette) **3** VI [*roads*] bifurquer ; **we ~ed right on leaving the village** nous avons pris *or* bifurqué à droite à la sortie du village ; **~ left for Oxford** prenez *or* bifurquez à gauche pour Oxford **4** COMP ► **fork-lift truck** N chariot *m* élévateur (à fourche)

► **fork out*** **1** VI casquer* ; **2** VT SEP [+ *money*] allonger*, abouler*

► **fork over** VT SEP = fork 2a

► **fork up** VT SEP **a** [+ *soil*] fourcher **b*** = fork out 2

forked [fɔːkt] **1** ADJ fourchu ; (*fig*) **to speak with (a) ~ tongue** avoir la langue fourchue **2** COMP ► **forked lightning** N éclair *m* en zigzags

forkful ['fɔːkfʊl] N **a ~ of mashed potato** une pleine fourchette de purée

forlorn [fəˈlɔːn] ADJ **a** (= *miserable*) [*person*] solitaire et malheureux, triste et délaissé ; [*voice*] triste ; [*expression*] de tristesse et de délaissement ; **to look ~** avoir l'air triste et délaissé **b** (= *desolate*) [*area*] désolé ; [*building*] abandonné ; [*road*] désert **c** (= *despairing*) [*attempt, effort*] désespéré, vain ; **it is a ~ hope** c'est un mince espoir ; **in the ~ hope of sth/doing sth** dans le fol espoir de qch/de faire qch

forlornly [fəˈlɔːnlɪ] ADV **a** (= *miserably*) [*stand, sit, wait, stare*] d'un air triste et délaissé, tristement **b** (= *despairingly*) [*hope*] en vain ; [*try*] désespérément

form [fɔːm] **1** N **a** (= *type, particular kind*) forme *f*, sorte *f* ; **the various ~s of energy** les différentes formes d'énergie ; **you could say it was a ~ of apology** on pourrait appeler cela une sorte d'excuse ; **a new ~ of government**

une nouvelle forme de gouvernement ; **a different ~ of life** (= *life-form*) une autre forme de vie ; (= *way of life*) un autre mode de vie

[b] (= *style, condition*) forme *f* ; **in the ~ of** sous forme de ; **medicine in the ~ of tablets** *or* **in tablet ~** médicament *m* sous forme de comprimés ; **the first prize will take the ~ of a trip to Rome** le premier prix sera un voyage à Rome ; **what ~ should my application take?** comment dois-je présenter *or* formuler ma demande ? ; **their discontent took various ~s** leur mécontentement s'est manifesté de différentes façons ; **the same thing in a new ~** la même chose sous une forme nouvelle *or* un aspect nouveau ; **her letters are to be published in book ~** ses lettres doivent être publiées sous forme de livre ; (*Gram*) **the plural ~** la forme du pluriel

[c] (*NonC: Art, Literat, Mus etc*) forme *f* ; **~ and content** la forme et le fond

[d] (*NonC = shape*) forme *f* ; **to take ~** prendre forme ; **his thoughts lack ~** ses pensées manquent d'ordre

[e] (= *figure*) forme *f* ; **the human ~** la forme humaine ; **I saw a ~ in the fog** j'ai vu une forme *or* une silhouette dans le brouillard

[f] (*Philos*) (= *structure, organization*) forme *f* ; (= *essence*) essence *f* ; (*Ling*) forme *f*

[g] (*NonC: esp Brit = étiquette*) forme *f*, formalité *f* ; **for ~'s sake ◊ as a matter of ~** pour la forme ; **it's good/bad ~ to do that** cela se fait/ ne se fait pas

[h] (= *formula, established practice*) forme *f*, formule *f* ; **he pays attention to the ~s** il respecte les formes ; **choose another ~ of words** choisissez une autre expression *or* tournure ; **the correct ~ of address for a bishop** la manière correcte de s'adresser à un évêque ; **~ of worship** liturgie *f*, rites *mpl* ; **what's the ~?**†* quelle est la marche à suivre ?

[i] (= *document*) (*gen: for applications etc*) formulaire *m* ; (*for telegram, giro transfer*) formule *f* ; (*for tax returns*) feuille *f* ; (= *card*) fiche *f* ; **printed ~** imprimé *m* ; **to fill up** *or* **in** *or* **out a ~** remplir un formulaire → **application, tax**

[j] (*NonC: esp Brit = fitness*) forme *f* ; **on ~** en forme ; **he's not on ~** *or* **he's off ~** *or* **out of ~** il n'est pas en forme ; **in fine** *or* **great ~** ◊ **on top ~** en pleine forme

[k] **to study (the)** ~ (*Brit Racing*) ≈ préparer son tiercé ; (*fig*) établir un pronostic

[l] (*Brit* = *bench*) banc *m*

[m] (*Brit Scol* = *class*) classe *f* ; **he's in the sixth ~** ≈ il est en première

[n] (*NonC: Brit = criminal record*) **he's got ~:** il a fait de la taule:

[2] VT [a] (= *shape*) former, construire ; **he ~s his sentences well** il construit bien ses phrases ; **he ~ed the clay into a ball** il a roulé *or* pétri l'argile en boule ; (*liter*) **he ~ed it out of a piece of wood** il l'a façonné *or* fabriqué dans un morceau de bois

[b] (= *train, mould*) [+ *child*] former, éduquer ; [+ *sb's character*] façonner, former

[c] (= *develop*) [+ *habit*] contracter ; [+ *plan*] mettre sur pied ; **to ~ an opinion** se faire *or* se former une opinion ; **to ~ an impression** se faire une impression ; **you mustn't ~ the idea that ...** il ne faut pas que vous vous mettiez dans la tête que ...

[d] (= *organize, create*) [+ *government*] former ; [+ *coalition, alliance*] constituer ; (*Comm*) [+ *company*] former, créer ; **to ~ a committee** former un comité ; **to ~ a new political party** former *or* créer un nouveau parti politique

[e] (= *constitute*) composer, former ; **to ~ part of** faire partie de ; **the ministers who ~ the government** les ministres qui composent *or* constituent le gouvernement ; **those who ~ the group** les gens qui font partie du groupe ; **to ~ a** *or* **the basis for** former *or* constituer la base de, servir de base à

[f] (= *take the shape or order of*) [+ *pattern, picture*] former, faire ; **to ~ a line** se mettre en ligne, s'aligner ; **~ a circle please** mettez-vous en cercle s'il vous plaît ; **to ~ a queue** se mettre en file, former la queue ; (*Mil*) **to ~ fours** se mettre par quatre ; **the road ~s a series of curves** la route fait *or* dessine une série de courbes

[g] (*Gram*) **to ~ the plural** former le pluriel

[3] VI [*queue, group, company, crystal, deposits, blood clots*] se former ; [*idea*] prendre forme ; **an idea ~ed in his mind** une idée a pris forme dans son esprit

[4] COMP ► **form feeder** N (*Comput*) dispositif *m* de changement de page ► **form leader** N (*Brit Scol*) ≈ chef *m* de classe ► **form letter** N lettre *f* type ► **form master, form mistress** N ≈ professeur *m* principal ► **form room** N salle *f* de classe (*affectée à une classe particulière*) ► **form tutor** N = **form master** *or* **mistress**

►**form up** VI se mettre *or* se ranger en ligne, s'aligner ; **~ up behind your teacher** mettez-vous *or* rangez-vous en ligne derrière votre professeur

formal ['fɔ:məl] [1] ADJ [a] (= *polite, ceremonial*) [*person*] cérémonieux, protocolaire ; [*behaviour, handshake, welcome, relationship*] cérémonieux ; [*dinner, occasion, function*] protocolaire, officiel ; [*clothes*] habillé ; [*letter*] respectant les convenances ; [*politeness*] formel ; [*language, style*] soutenu ; [*word*] de style soutenu ; **don't be so ~** ne faites pas tant de cérémonies ; **lunch was a ~ affair** le déjeuner était protocolaire ; **a ~ dance** un bal habillé

[b] (= *official*) [*talks, statement, request, complaint, acceptance, surrender*] officiel ; **~ contract** contrat *m* en bonne et due forme ; **~ denial** démenti *m* formel *or* officiel ; **~ instructions** instructions *fpl* formelles

[c] (= *in design*) [*garden*] à la française ; [*room*] solennel

[d] (= *professional*) **he had no ~ training/ qualifications** il n'avait pas vraiment de formation/de qualifications ; **he had little ~ education** *or* **schooling** il a suivi une scolarité très incomplète

[e] (= *structural*) [*perfection*] formel

[f] (= *superficial, in form only*) de forme ; **a certain ~ resemblance** une certaine ressemblance dans la forme

[2] COMP ► **formal dress** N tenue *f* de cérémonie ; (= *evening dress*) tenue *f* de soirée ► **formal grammar** N (*Ling*) grammaire *f* formelle ► **formal logic** N (*Philos*) logique *f* formelle

formaldehyde [fɔ:'mældɪhaɪd] N formaldéhyde *m*

formalin(e) ['fɔ:məlɪn] N formol *m*

formalism ['fɔ:məlɪzəm] N formalisme *m*

formalist ['fɔ:məlɪst] ADJ, N formaliste *mf*

formalistic [ˌfɔ:məˈlɪstɪk] ADJ formaliste

formality [fɔ:'mælɪtɪ] N [a] (*NonC*) (= *convention*) formalité *f* ; (= *stiffness*) raideur *f*, froideur *f* ; (= *ceremoniousness*) cérémonie *f* (*NonC*) [b] formalité *f* ; **it's a mere** *or* **just a ~** ce n'est qu'une simple formalité ; **the formalities** les formalités *fpl* ; **let's do without the formalities!** dispensons-nous des formalités !, faisons au plus simple !

formalize ['fɔ:məlaɪz] VT formaliser

formally ['fɔ:məlɪ] ADV [a] (= *politely*) [*say, shake hands*] cérémonieusement ; **~ courteous** d'une courtoisie cérémonieuse ; **his behaviour was ~ correct** son comportement était cérémonieux [b] (= *officially*) [*announce, agree, approve, open, launch*] officiellement ; **~ charged** mis en examen ; **we have been ~ invited** nous avons reçu une invitation officielle [c] **to be ~ dressed** (= *smartly*) être en tenue de cérémonie ; (= *in evening dress*) être en tenue de soirée [d] (= *academically*) [*teach*] en tant que matière spécifique ; **to have been ~ trained** avoir reçu

une formation professionnelle [e] (*in design*) **a ~ laid-out garden** un jardin à la française

format ['fɔ:mæt] [1] N [a] (= *type, kind*) [*of computer data, document, camera film, publication*] format *m* ; [*of video*] système *m* ; **newspapers in tabloid or broadsheet ~** des journaux de format tabloïd ou de grand format ; **the film will be shown in wide-screen ~** (*Cine*) le film sera projeté sur grand écran ; (*TV*) le film sera diffusé en format grand écran ; **dictionaries published in both paper and electronic ~** des dictionnaires publiés à la fois en version papier et en version électronique ; **available in cassette or CD ~** disponible en cassette ou CD

[b] (= *structure, presentation*) [*of book, newspaper, page*] présentation *f* ; [*of TV, radio programme*] forme *f*, présentation *f* ; [*of event, competition*] forme *f* ; **dictionaries published in three-column ~** des dictionnaires publiés dans une présentation sur trois colonnes ; **large-~ books** livres *mpl* grand format

[2] VT [a] (*Comput*) formater

[b] (*gen*) concevoir le format *or* la présentation de

formation [fɔ:'meɪʃən] [1] N [a] (*NonC*) [*of child, character*] formation *f* ; [*of plan*] élaboration *f* ; [*of government*] formation *f* ; [*of classes, courses*] organisation *f*, mise *f* en place ; [*of club*] création *f* ; [*of committee*] création *f*, mise *f* en place [b] (*NonC: Mil etc*) formation *f*, disposition *f* ; **battle ~** formation *f* de combat ; **in close ~** en ordre serré [c] (*Geol*) formation *f* [2] COMP ► **formation dance, formation dancing** N danse *f* de groupe ► **formation flying** N (*Aviat*) vol *m* en formation

formative ['fɔ:mətɪv] [1] ADJ formateur (-trice *f*) [2] N (*Gram*) formant *m*, élément *m* formateur

formatting ['fɔ:mætɪŋ] N (*Comput*) formatage *m*

-formed ['fɔ:md] ADJ (*in compounds*) **fully-formed** [*baby, animal*] complètement formé *or* développé ; **half-formed** à moitié formé *or* développé → **well²**

former¹ ['fɔ:mə] N (*Tech*) gabarit *m*

▼**former²** ['fɔ:mə] [1] ADJ [a] (= *previous*) [*president, employee, home*] ancien (*before n*) ; [*strength, authority*] d'autrefois ; **the ~ Soviet Union** l'ex-Union *f* soviétique ; **the ~ Yugoslavia** l'ex-Yougoslavie *f* ; **my ~ wife/husband** mon ex-femme/ex-mari ; **the college is a ~ mansion** le collège est un ancien manoir ; **to restore sth to its ~ glory** redonner à qch sa splendeur d'autrefois ; **the buildings have now been restored to their ~ glory** les bâtiments rénovés ont retrouvé leur ancienne splendeur *or* leur splendeur d'antan (*liter*) ; **he was a (pale) shadow of his ~ self** il n'était plus que l'ombre de lui-même ; **he was very unlike his ~ self** il ne se ressemblait plus du tout ; **in a ~ life** au cours d'une vie antérieure ; **in ~ years** *or* **times** *or* **days** autrefois ; **the radicals of ~ days** les radicaux d'autrefois

[b] (*as opposed to latter*) **the ~ option/ alternative** la première option/alternative ; **your ~ suggestion** votre première suggestion

[2] PRON celui-là, celle-là ; **the ~ ... the latter** celui-là ... celui-ci ; **of the two ideas I prefer the ~** des deux idées je préfère celle-là *or* la première ; **the ~ is the more expensive of the two systems** ce premier système est le plus coûteux des deux, des deux systèmes, c'est le premier le plus coûteux ; **of the two possible solutions, I prefer the ~** entre les deux solutions, je préfère la première, entre les deux, je préfère la première solution

[3] COMP ► **former pupil** N (*Scol*) ancien(ne) élève *m(f)*

-former ['fɔ:mə] N (*in compounds: Scol*) élève *mf* de ... ; **fourth-former** ≈ élève *mf* de troisième

formerly ['fɔːməlɪ] ADV autrefois ; **Lake Malawi, ~ Lake Nyasa** le lac Malawi, anciennement or autrefois lac Nyassa

formic ['fɔːmɪk] ADJ formique

Formica® [fɔː'maɪkə] N formica® m, plastique m laminé

formidable ['fɔːmɪdəbl] ADJ [a] (= daunting) [person, opposition] redoutable, terrible ; [task, challenge] redoutable ; [obstacle] terrible [b] (= prodigious) [person, talent, reputation] phénoménal ; [combination] impressionnant

formidably ['fɔːmɪdəblɪ] ADV (= extremely) terriblement, redoutablement ; **~ armed** redoutablement bien armé, aux armes redoutables

formless ['fɔːmlɪs] ADJ [a] (= amorphous) [shape, image] informe ; [terror, apprehension] indéfini [b] (pej = unstructured) [book, play, film, record] dépourvu de structure

Formosa [fɔː'məʊsə] N (formerly) Formose m or f

Formosan [fɔː'məʊsən] ADJ formosan

formula [fɔː'mjʊlə] N (pl **formulas** or **formulae** ['fɔːmjʊliː]) (gen, also Chem, Math etc) formule f ; **a ~ for averting** or **aimed at averting the strike** une formule visant à éviter la grève ; **winning ~** formule f idéale ; **peace ~** forme f de paix ; **pay/pricing ~** système m de fixation des salaires/prix [b] (= baby milk) lait m maternisé [c] (Aut) **Formula One/Two/Three** la formule un/deux/trois ; **a ~-one car** une voiture de formule un

formulaic [,fɔːmjʊ'leɪɪk] ADJ [language, plot, response, TV programme] convenu, stéréotypé ; **~ phrase** or **expression** expression f convenue

formulate ['fɔːmjʊleɪt] VT formuler

formulation [,fɔːmjʊ'leɪʃən] N [a] (NonC = forming, creation) [of idea, theory, proposal] formulation f [b] (= formula) [of policy, plan, product] élaboration f ; [of treaty, settlement] formule f ; **this ~ was acceptable to both sides** cette formule convenait aux deux parties [c] (= medicine) formule f [d] (= saying) formule f

fornicate ['fɔːnɪkeɪt] VI forniquer

fornication [,fɔːnɪ'keɪʃən] N fornication f

forsake [fə'seɪk] (pret **forsook**, ptp **forsaken**) VT (liter) [+ person] abandonner, délaisser ; [+ place] quitter ; [+ habit] renoncer à

forsaken [fə'seɪkən] [1] VB pt of **forsake** ; **→ godforsaken** [2] ADJ **an old ~ farmhouse** une vieille ferme abandonnée

forsook [fə'sʊk] VB pt of **forsake**

forsooth [fə'suːθ] ADV (†† or hum) en vérité, à vrai dire ; **~!** par exemple !

forswear [fɔː'swɛə'] (pret **forswore** [fɔː'swɔː'], ptp **forsworn** [fɔː'swɔːn]) VT (frm) (= renounce) renoncer à, abjurer ; (= deny) désavouer ; (= perjure) **to ~ o.s.** se parjurer

forsythia [fɔː'saɪθɪə] N forsythia m

fort [fɔːt] N (Mil) fort m ; (small) fortin m ; (fig) **to hold the ~** monter la garde (hum), assurer la permanence

forte[1] ['fɔːtɪ, (US) fɔːt] N fort m ; **generosity is not his ~** la générosité n'est pas son fort

forte[2] ['fɔːtɪ] ADJ, ADV (Mus) forte

forth [fɔːθ] ADV

> When **forth** is an element in a phrasal verb, eg **pour forth, sally forth, venture forth**, look up the verb.

[a] († or frm = out) de l'avant ; **to go back and ~ between ...** aller et venir entre ..., faire la navette entre ... ; **the thunderstorm burst ~** l'orage a éclaté ; **to come ~** (= forward) s'avancer ; (= outside) sortir ; **to pour ~ a torrent of invective** vomir un torrent d'injures ; **to stretch ~ one's hand** tendre la main → **bring forth, hold forth** [b] (= onward) **and so ~** et ainsi de suite ; (frm) **from this day ~** dorénavant, désormais

forthcoming [fɔː'kʌmɪŋ] ADJ [a] (= imminent) [event, visit, election, album etc] prochain ; **in a ~ book/film, he examines ...** dans un prochain livre/film ou dans un livre/film qui va bientôt sortir, il examine ... [b] (= available) **to be ~** [money, funds, aid, support] être disponible ; **no evidence of this was ~** on n'avait aucune preuve de cela ; **no answer was ~** il n'y a pas eu de réponse [c] (= communicative) [person] communicatif ; **to be ~ on** or **about sth** être disposé à parler de qch

forthright ['fɔːθraɪt] ADJ [person, manner, answer, remark] franc (franche f), direct ; [language] direct ; [statement] sans détour ; **in ~ terms** sans détour ; **to be ~ in one's response** donner une réponse franche ; **to be ~ in saying sth** dire qch ouvertement ; **to be ~ about sth** ne pas mâcher ses mots à propos de qch

forthwith [fɔːθ'wɪθ] ADV (frm) sur-le-champ

fortieth ['fɔːtɪɪθ] [1] ADJ quarantième [2] N quarantième mf ; (= fraction) quarantième m ; for phrases see **sixth**

fortification [,fɔːtɪfɪ'keɪʃən] N fortification f

fortify ['fɔːtɪfaɪ] VT [a] (+ place) fortifier, armer (against contre) ; [+ person] réconforter ; **fortified place** place f forte ; (hum) **have a drink to ~ you** prenez un verre pour vous remonter [b] [+ wine] accroître la teneur en alcool de ; [+ food] renforcer en vitamines ; **fortified wine** ≈ vin m doux, vin m de liqueur

fortitude ['fɔːtɪtjuːd] N courage m, force f d'âme

Fort Knox [,fɔːt'nɒks] N Fort Knox m (réserve d'or des États-Unis) ; (fig) **they have turned their home into (a) ~** ils ont transformé leur maison en une véritable forteresse

fortnight ['fɔːtnaɪt] N (esp Brit) quinzaine f, quinze jours mpl ; **a ~'s holiday** quinze jours de vacances ; **a ~ tomorrow** demain en quinze ; **adjourned for a ~** remis à quinzaine ; **for a ~** pour une quinzaine, pour quinze jours ; **in a ~ ◊ in a ~'s time** dans quinze jours ; **a ~ ago** il y a quinze jours

fortnightly ['fɔːtnaɪtlɪ] (esp Brit) [1] ADJ [newspaper] bimensuel ; [visit] tous les quinze jours ; [cycle] de quinze jours [2] ADV tous les quinze jours

FORTRAN, Fortran ['fɔːtræn] N fortran m

fortress ['fɔːtrɪs] N (= prison) forteresse f ; (= medieval castle) château m fort ; **~ Europe** forteresse f Europe → **flying**

fortuitous [fɔː'tjuːɪtəs] ADJ fortuit, accidentel

fortuitously [fɔː'tjuːɪtəslɪ] ADV fortuitement, par hasard

fortunate ['fɔːtʃənɪt] ADJ [coincidence, choice] heureux ; [circumstances] favorable ; **to be ~** [person] avoir de la chance ; **we are ~ that ...** nous avons de la chance que ... ; **it is ~ that ...** c'est une chance que ... ; **it was ~ for him that ...** heureusement pour lui que ... ; **they were ~ to escape** ils ont eu de la chance de s'échapper ; **I was ~ enough to go to a good school** j'ai eu la chance de fréquenter une bonne école ; **to be ~ in one's career** avoir de la chance dans sa carrière ; **to be ~ in having a wonderful mother** avoir la chance d'avoir une mère merveilleuse ; **she is in the ~ position of having plenty of choice** elle a la chance d'avoir plein d'options ; **how ~!** quelle chance !

▼ **fortunately** ['fɔːtʃənɪtlɪ] ADV heureusement (for pour)

fortune ['fɔːtʃən] [1] N [a] (= chance) fortune f, chance f ; **the ~s of war** la fortune des armes ; **by good ~** par chance, par bonheur ; **I had the good ~ to meet him** j'ai eu la chance or le bonheur de le rencontrer ; **to try one's ~** tenter sa chance ; **~ favoured him** la fortune or la chance lui a souri ; **to tell sb's ~** dire la bonne aventure à qn ; **to tell ~s** dire la bonne aventure ; **whatever my ~ may be** quel que soit le sort qui m'est réservé → **seek**

[b] (= riches) fortune f ; **to make a ~** faire fortune ; **he made a ~ on it** il a gagné une fortune avec ça ; **to come into a ~** hériter d'une fortune ; **a man of ~** un homme d'une fortune or d'une richesse considérable ; **to marry a ~** épouser une grosse fortune ; **to spend/cost/lose etc a (small ~ tidy) ~** dépenser/coûter/perdre etc une (petite) fortune

[2] COMP ► **fortune cookie** N (US) beignet m chinois (renfermant un horoscope ou une devise) ► **fortune hunter** N (man) coureur m de dot ; (woman) femme f intéressée ► **fortune-teller** N diseur m, -euse f de bonne aventure ; (with cards) tireuse f de cartes ► **fortune-telling** N (art m de la) divination ; (with cards) cartomancie f

forty ['fɔːtɪ] [1] ADJ quarante inv ; **about ~ books** une quarantaine de livres ; **to have ~ winks** faire un petit somme, piquer un roupillon* [2] N quarante m inv ; **about ~** une quarantaine ; (US = states) **the lower ~-eight** les quarante-huit États américains (à l'exclusion de l'Alaska et de Hawaï) ; for other phrases see **sixty** [3] PRON quarante ; **there are ~** il y en a quarante [4] COMP ► **forty-niner** N (US) prospecteur m d'or (de la ruée vers l'or de 1849)

forum ['fɔːrəm] N (pl **forums** or **fora** ['fɔːrə]) (Hist) forum m ; (fig) tribune f

forward ['fɔːwəd]

> When **forward** is an element in a phrasal verb, eg **bring forward, come forward, step forward**, look up the verb.

[1] ADV (also **~s**) en avant ; **to rush ~** se précipiter or s'élancer (en avant) ; **to go ~** avancer ; **to go straight ~** aller tout droit devant soi ; **~! ◊ ~ march!** (Mil) en avant, marche! ; **from that moment ~** à partir de ce moment-là ; (lit, fig) **to push o.s. ~** se mettre en avant ; (fig) **to come ~** se présenter ; **he went backward(s) and ~(s) between the station and the house** il allait et venait entre or il faisait la navette entre la gare et la maison ; **to put the clocks ~** avancer les pendules → **bring forward**

[2] PREP **~ of** à l'avant de

[3] ADJ [a] (= in front, ahead) [movement] en avant, vers l'avant ; **the ~ ranks of the army** les premiers rangs de l'armée ; **this seat is too far ~** ce siège est trop en avant [b] (= well-advanced) [season, plant] précoce ; [child] précoce, en avance ; **I'm no further ~ (with this problem)** me voilà bien avancé ! (iro) [c] (= bold) effronté ; **that was rather ~ of him** c'était assez effronté de sa part [d] (Comm) [prices, delivery] à terme

[4] N (Sport) avant m

[5] VT [a] (= advance) [+ career, cause, interests] favoriser, faire avancer [b] (= dispatch) [+ goods] expédier, envoyer ; (= send on) [+ letter, parcel] faire suivre ; **please ~** faire suivre SVP, prière de faire suivre

[6] COMP ► **forward buying** N achat m à terme ► **forward gears** NPL vitesses fpl avant ► **forwarding address** N (gen) adresse f de réexpédition ; (Comm) adresse f pour l'expédition ; **he left no ~ing address** il est parti sans laisser d'adresse ► **forwarding agent** N (Comm) transitaire m ► **forward line** N (Mil) première ligne f ; (Sport) ligne f des avants ► **forward-looking** ADJ [person] ouvert sur or tourné vers l'avenir ; [plan] tourné vers l'avenir ► **forward pass** N (Rugby) (passe f) en-avant m inv ► **forward planning** N planification f ► **forward post** N (Mil) avant-poste m, poste m avancé ► **forward sale** N vente f à terme

forwardness ['fɔːwədnɪs] N [of seasons, plants, children] précocité f ; (= boldness) effronterie f

forwards ['fɔːwədz] ADV = **forward 1**

Fosbury flop ['fɒzbərɪ,flɒp] N (Sport) rouleau m dorsal

fossil ['fɒsl] **1** N fossile m; (fig) **he's an old ~**! c'est un vieux fossile* or une vieille croûte*! **2** COMP ► **fossil energy** N énergie f fossile ► **fossil fuel** N combustible m fossile ► **fossil hunter** N collectionneur m de fossiles

fossilization [,fɒsɪlaɪ'zeɪʃən] N fossilisation f

fossilized ['fɒsɪlaɪzd] ADJ fossilisé; (fig, pej) [person, customs] fossilisé, figé; (Ling) [form, expression] figé

foster ['fɒstə'] **1** VT **a** (Jur = care for) [+ child] élever (sans obligation d'adoption); **the authorities ~ed the child with Mr and Mrs Moore** les autorités ont placé l'enfant chez M. et Mme Moore **b** (= encourage) [+ friendship, development] favoriser, encourager **c** (= entertain) [+ idea, thought] entretenir, nourrir **2** COMP [child] adoptif, placé dans une famille; [father, parents, family] adoptif, nourricier; [brother, sister] adoptif ► **foster home** N famille f nourricière or de placement familial ► **foster mother** N mère f nourricière or adoptive (d'un enfant placé)

fostering ['fɒstərɪŋ] N placement m familial or en famille d'accueil; **the couple has been approved for ~** le couple a obtenu l'autorisation d'accueillir un enfant (en placement familial)

fought [fɔːt] VB pt, ptp of **fight**

foul [faʊl] **1** ADJ **a** (= disgusting) [place] immonde, dégoûtant; [water] croupi; [air] vicié; [breath] fétide; [person] infect, ignoble; [smell] infect, nauséabond; [taste, food] infect; **to smell ~** puer **b** (esp Brit* = bad) [day] épouvantable; **~ luck** terrible malchance f; **~ weather** (gen) sale temps m, temps m de chien; (Naut) gros temps m; **the weather was ~** le temps était infect **c** (esp liter = vile) [crime] ignoble, odieux; [behaviour] odieux, vil (vile f); **~ deed** acte m crapuleux **d** (= offensive) [language, abuse] grossier; **to have a ~ mouth** être mal embouché; **to have a ~ temper** avoir un sale caractère; **in a ~ mood** or **temper** d'une humeur massacrante **e** (= unfair: Sport) [shot] mauvais; [tackle] irrégulier; **by ~ means** par des moyens déloyaux → **fair**; **a ~ blow** un coup déloyal or en traître → **cry** **f** **to fall** or **run ~ of sb** se mettre qn à dos; **to fall** or **run ~ of the law/authorities** avoir maille à partir avec la justice/les autorités; (Naut) **to fall** or **run ~ of a ship** entrer en collision avec un bateau

2 N (Sport) coup m défendu or irrégulier; (Boxing) coup m bas; (Ftbl) faute f; (Basketball) **technical/personal ~** faute f technique/personnelle

3 VT **a** (= pollute) [+ air, water] polluer; [+ beaches] polluer, souiller **b** [dog] [+ pavement, garden, grass] souiller; (fig) **to ~ one's own nest** causer sa propre perte **c** (= entangle) [+ fishing line, rope] emmêler; [+ mechanism, propeller, anchor] s'emmêler dans **d** (= clog) [+ pipe, chimney, gun barrel] encrasser, obstruer **e** (Sport) commettre une faute contre **f** (Naut = collide with) [+ ship] entrer en collision avec

4 VI (= become entangled or jammed) **to ~ on sth** [rope, line] s'emmêler dans qch, s'entortiller dans qch; [mechanism] se prendre dans qch

5 COMP ► **foul-mouthed** ADJ mal embouché ► **foul play** N (Sport) jeu m irrégulier; (Cards) tricherie f; (Jur) acte m criminel; **he suspected ~ play** il soupçonnait qu'il y avait quelque chose de louche; **the police found a body but do not suspect ~ play** la police a découvert un cadavre mais écarte l'hypothèse d'un meurtre ► **foul-smelling** ADJ puant, nauséabond, fétide ► **foul-tasting** ADJ infect ► **foul-tempered** ADJ **to be ~-tempered** (habitually) avoir un caractère de cochon; (on one occasion) être d'une humeur massacrante ► **foul-up*** N confusion f
► **foul out** VI (Basketball) être exclu (pour cinq fautes personnelles)
► **foul up 1** VT SEP **a** = **foul 3a b*** [+ relationship] ficher en l'air*; **that has ~ed things up** ça a tout fichu en l'air* or gâché **2** **~-up*** N → **foul**

found¹ [faʊnd] VB pt, ptp of **find**

found² [faʊnd] VT [+ town, school] fonder, créer; [+ hospital] fonder; [+ business enterprise] fonder, constituer; [+ colony] établir, fonder; (fig) [+ belief, opinion] fonder, baser (on sur); [+ suspicion] baser; **our society is ~ed on this** notre société est fondée là-dessus; **the novel is/my suspicions were ~ed on fact** le roman est basé/mes soupçons reposaient sur or étaient basés sur des faits réels

found³ [faʊnd] VT (Metal) fondre

foundation [faʊn'deɪʃən] **1** N **a** (NonC = founding) [of town, school, hospital, business] fondation f, création f **b** (= establishment) fondation f; **Carnegie Foundation** fondation f Carnegie; **research ~** fondation f consacrée à la recherche; **charitable ~** organisation f or fondation f caritative **c** (Constr) **~s** fondations fpl; (lit) **to lay the ~s of** faire or jeter les fondations de → **1d** **d** (fig = basis) [of career, social structure] base f; [of idea, religious belief, theory] base f, fondement m; **agriculture is the ~ of their economy** l'agriculture est la base de leur économie; **to lay the ~s of sth** poser les bases or les fondements de qch; **his work laid the ~(s) of our legal system** son travail a posé les bases de notre système judiciaire; **without ~** [rumour, allegation, report, fears etc] sans fondement; **to rock** or **shake sth to its ~s** profondément secouer or ébranler qch **e** (also ~ **cream**) fond m de teint **2** COMP ► **foundation course** N (Brit Univ) cours m d'initiation or d'introduction ► **foundation cream** N fond m de teint ► **foundation garment** N gaine f, combiné m ► **foundation stone** N (Brit) pierre f commémorative; (lit, fig) **to lay the ~ stone** poser la première pierre

founder¹ ['faʊndə'] **1** N fondateur m, -trice f **2** COMP ► **founder member** N (Brit) membre m fondateur

founder² ['faʊndə'] VI [ship] sombrer; [horse] (in mud etc) s'embourber, s'empêtrer; (from fatigue) (se mettre à) boiter; [plans] s'effondrer, s'écrouler; [hopes] s'en aller en fumée

founding ['faʊndɪŋ] **1** N = **foundation 1a** **2** COMP ► **founding fathers** NPL (US) pères mpl fondateurs (qui élaborèrent la Constitution fédérale des États-Unis)

foundling ['faʊndlɪŋ] N enfant m(f) trouvé(e); **~ hospital** hospice m pour enfants trouvés

foundry ['faʊndrɪ] N fonderie f

fount [faʊnt] N **a** (liter = spring) source f; **the ~ of knowledge/wisdom** la source du savoir/de la sagesse **b** (Brit Typ) fonte f

fountain ['faʊntɪn] **1** N **a** (lit) fontaine f **b** (also **drinking ~**) fontaine f d'eau potable **c** (fig) [of light, sparks, flowers] gerbe f, source f → **soda 2** COMP ► **fountain pen** N stylo m (à) plume

fountainhead ['faʊntɪnhed] N source f, origine f; **to go to the ~** aller (directement) à la source, retourner aux sources

four [fɔː'] **1** ADJ quatre inv; **it's in ~ figures** c'est dans les milliers; **open to the ~ winds** ouvert à tous les vents or aux quatre vents; **to the ~ corners of the earth** aux quatre coins du monde; (US) **the Four Hundred** l'élite sociale → **stroke**

2 N quatre m inv; **on all ~s** à quatre pattes; (Rowing) **a ~** un quatre; **will you make up a ~ for bridge?** voulez-vous faire le quatrième au bridge?; (Cricket) **to hit a ~** marquer quatre courses or points; **he hit three ~s** il a marqué trois fois quatre courses or points → **form**; for other phrases see **six**

3 PRON quatre; **there are ~** il y en a quatre

4 COMP ► **four-ball** ADJ, N (Golf) fourball m ► **four-by-four** N (= vehicle) 4 x 4 m ► **four-colour (printing) process** N (Typ) quadrichromie f ► **four-door** ADJ [car] (à) quatre portes ► **four-engined** ADJ [plane] quadrimoteur; **~-engined plane** quadrimoteur m ► **four-eyes*** N binoclard(e)* m(f) ► **four-flush*** VI bluffer* ► **four-flusher*** N (US) bluffeur* m, -euse* f ► **four-footed** ADJ quadrupède, à quatre pattes ► **four-four time** N (Mus) **in ~~ time** à quatre/quatre ► **four-handed** ADJ [piano music] à quatre mains ► **Four-H club** N (US) club éducatif de jeunes ruraux ► **four-in-hand** N (= coach) attelage m à quatre ► **four-leaf clover, four-leaved clover** N trèfle m à quatre feuilles ► **four-legged** ADJ à quatre pattes, quadrupède (frm) ► **four-legged friend** N (hum) compagnon m à quatre pattes ► **four-letter word** N (fig) obscénité f, gros mot m; **he let out a ~-letter word** il a sorti le mot de cinq lettres (euph) ► **four-minute mile** N (Sport) course d'un mille courue en quatre minutes ► **four-part** ADJ [song] à quatre voix; [serial] en quatre épisodes ► **four-part harmony** N (Mus) harmonie f à quatre voix ► **four-poster** N lit m à baldaquin or à colonnes ► **four-seater** N (= car) (voiture f à) quatre places f inv ► **four-star** ADJ (= high-quality) de première qualité ♦ N = **four-star petrol** ► **four-star general** N (US) général m à quatre étoiles ► **four-star petrol** N (Brit) super(carburant) m ► **four-stroke** ADJ, N (Aut) (moteur m) à quatre temps ► **four-way stop** N (US = crossroads) carrefour sans priorité autre que l'ordre d'arrivée ► **four-wheel drive** N (NonC) propulsion f à quatre roues motrices; (= car) voiture f à quatre roues motrices; **with ~-wheel drive** à quatre roues motrices

fourchette [fʊə'ʃet] N fourchette f vulvaire

fourfold ['fɔːfəʊld] **1** ADJ quadruple **2** ADV au quadruple

fourscore ['fɔː'skɔː'] ADJ, N (liter) quatre-vingts m; **~ and ten** quatre-vingt-dix m

foursome ['fɔːsəm] N (= game) partie f à quatre; (= two women, two men) deux couples mpl; **we went in a ~** nous y sommes allés à quatre

foursquare ['fɔː'skwɛə'] ADJ (= square) carré; (= firm) [attitude, decision] ferme, inébranlable; (= forthright) [account, assessment] franc (franche f)

fourteen ['fɔː'tiːn] **1** ADJ, N quatorze m inv; for phrases see **six 2** PRON quatorze; **there are ~** il y en a quatorze

fourteenth ['fɔː'tiːnθ] **1** ADJ quatorzième; **Louis the Fourteenth** Louis Quatorze or XIV **2** N quatorzième mf; (= fraction) quatorzième m; **the ~ of July** le quatorze juillet, la fête du quatorze juillet; for other phrases see **sixth**

fourth [fɔːθ] **1** ADJ quatrième; **the ~ dimension** la quatrième dimension; **he lives on the ~ floor** (Brit) il habite au quatrième (étage); (US) il habite au cinquième (étage); **to change into ~ gear** passer en quatrième; **the ~ estate** le quatrième pouvoir **2** N quatrième mf; (US) (= fraction) quart m; (Mus) quarte f; **we need a ~ for our game of bridge** il nous faut un quatrième pour notre bridge; (US) **the Fourth of July** le 4 juillet (fête nationale américaine); for other phrases see **sixth 3** COMP ► **fourth-class matter** N (US Post) paquet-poste m ordinaire ► **fourth finger** N annulaire m ► **fourth-rate** ADJ (fig) de dernier ordre, de dernière catégorie ► **the Fourth World** N (*Pol*) le quart-monde

<table><tr><td>FOURTH OF JULY</td></tr></table>

Le 4 juillet, ou jour de l'indépendance (« Independence Day ») est la grande fête nationale des États-Unis. Marquant la signature de la déclaration d'indépendance en 1776 (et, par conséquent, la naissance du pays), cette commémoration est l'occasion de manifestations patriotiques diverses: feux d'artifice, défilés etc.

fourthly ['fɔːθlɪ] ADV quatrièmement, en quatrième lieu

fowl [faʊl] [1] N [a] (= *hens etc: collective n*) volaille *f*, oiseaux *mpl* de basse-cour; (= *one bird*) volatile *m*, volaille *f*; **roast ~** volaille *f* rôtie [b] †† oiseau *m*; (*liter*) **the ~s of the air** les oiseaux *mpl* → **fish, waterfowl, wildfowl** [2] VI **to go ~ing** chasser le gibier à plumes [3] COMP ► **fowling piece** N fusil *m* de chasse léger, carabine *f* ► **fowl pest** N peste *f* aviaire

fox [fɒks] [1] N [a] (= *animal*) renard *m*; (*fig*) **a (sly) ~** un fin renard [b] (*US* *f* = *girl*) fille *f* sexy*, jolie fille *f* [2] VT (= *puzzle: esp Brit*) rendre perplexe, mystifier; (= *deceive*) tromper, berner [3] COMP ► **fox cub** N renardeau *m* ► **fox fur** N (fourrure *f* de) renard *m* ► **fox terrier** N fox-terrier *m*, fox-terrier *m*

foxed [fɒkst] ADJ [*book, paper*] marqué de rousseurs

foxglove ['fɒksglʌv] N (*Bot*) digitale *f* (pourprée)

foxhole ['fɒkshəʊl] N terrier *m* de renard, renardière *f*; (*Mil*) gourbi *m*

foxhound ['fɒkshaʊnd] N chien *m* courant, fox-hound *m*

foxhunt ['fɒkshʌnt] N chasse *f* au renard

foxhunting ['fɒks,hʌntɪŋ] N chasse *f* au renard; **to go ~** aller à la chasse au renard

foxtrot ['fɒkstrɒt] N fox-trot *m*

foxy ['fɒksɪ] ADJ [a] (= *crafty*) finaud, rusé [b] (*esp US**) **~ lady** fille *f* sexy*, jolie fille *f*

foyer ['fɔɪeɪ] N [*of theatre*] foyer *m*; [*of hotel*] foyer *m*, hall *m*; (*US*) [*of house*] vestibule *m*, entrée *f*

FP [ef'piː] (*US*) ABBR = **fireplug**

FPA [,efpiː'eɪ] (ABBR = **Family Planning Association**) Mouvement *m* pour le planning familial

fr (ABBR = **franc**) F; **10fr** 10 F

Fr. (*Rel*) (ABBR = **Father**) (*on envelope*) ~ **R. Frost** le Révérend Père R. Frost

fracas ['fræka:] N (= *scuffle*) rixe *f*, échauffourée *f*; (= *noise*) fracas *m*

fractal ['fræktəl] N (*Math*) objet *m* fractal, fractale *f*

fraction ['frækʃən] N (*Math*) fraction *f*; (*fig*) fraction *f*, partie *f*; **for a ~ of a second** pendant une fraction de seconde; **she only spends a ~ of what she earns** elle ne dépense qu'une infime partie de ce qu'elle gagne; **can you move it a ~ higher/to the left?** peux-tu le déplacer un tout petit peu vers le haut/vers la gauche? → **decimal, vulgar**

fractional ['frækʃənl] [1] ADJ (*Math*) fractionnaire; (*fig*) infime, tout petit [2] COMP ► **fractional distillation** N (*Chem*) distillation *f* fractionnée ► **fractional note** N (*US*) petite coupure *f* ► **fractional part** N fraction *f*

fractionally ['frækʃnəlɪ] ADV un tout petit peu; **to be ~ ahead** avoir un tout petit peu d'avance; **to be ~ behind** être un tout petit peu en arrière, être très légèrement derrière; **to move sth ~ higher/to the left** déplacer qch un tout petit peu vers le haut/vers la gauche

fractious ['frækʃəs] ADJ [*child*] grincheux, pleurnicheur; [*old person*] grincheux, hargneux

fracture ['fræktʃə'] [1] N fracture *f* [2] VT

fracturer; **she ~d her hip** elle s'est fracturé la hanche [3] VI se fracturer

frag* [fræg] (*US Mil*) [1] N grenade *f* offensive [2] VT tuer *or* blesser d'une grenade (*un officier etc*)

fragile ['frædʒaɪl] ADJ [a] (= *delicate*) [*object, beauty, health, economy*] fragile; [*person*] fragile; (*from age, ill health*) frêle; [*truce, peace, happiness*] précaire, fragile; [*situation*] délicat; (*notice on boxes*) **"~: handle with care"** « fragile » [b] (* *gen hum* = *weak*) patraque*, mal fichu*

fragility [frə'dʒɪlɪtɪ] N fragilité *f*

fragment ['frægmənt] [1] N [*of china, bone*] fragment *m*; [*of paper, metal, glass*] fragment *m*, (petit) morceau *m*; [*from bomb*] éclat *m*; [*of information*] élément *m*; **he smashed it to ~s** il l'a réduit en miettes; **the window smashed into ~s** le fenêtre s'est brisée en mille morceaux; **~s of food/DNA** ◊ **food/DNA ~s** fragments *mpl* de nourriture/d'ADN; **~s of conversation** bribes *fpl* de conversation [2] [fræg'ment] VT [a] (*lit*) fragmenter [b] (*fig*) [*or-ganization, system*] faire éclater [3] [fræg-'ment] VI [a] (*lit*) se fragmenter [b] (*fig*) [*organization, system*] éclater

fragmental [fræg'mentl] ADJ fragmentaire; (*Geol*) clastique

fragmentary ['frægməntərɪ] ADJ fragmentaire

fragmentation [,frægmen'teɪʃən] [1] N fragmentation *f* [2] COMP ► **fragmentation grenade** N (*Mil*) grenade *f* à fragmentation

fragmented [fræg'mentɪd] ADJ [*story, version*] morcelé, fragmentaire; [*organization, system*] éclaté

fragrance ['freɪgrəns] N (= *smell*) parfum *m*, senteur *f*; (= *perfume*) parfum *m*; **a new ~ by Chanel** un nouveau parfum de Chanel

fragrant ['freɪgrənt] ADJ [*flowers, herbs, spices, food*] parfumé, odorant; **the air was ~ with the scent of roses** le parfum des roses embaumait l'air

fraidy-cat* ['freɪdɪkæt] ADJ (*US: baby talk*) trouillard(e)* *m(f)*, poule *f* mouillée

frail [freɪl] ADJ [*person*] frêle; [*object*] frêle, fragile; [*health, happiness, ego*] fragile; [*hope*] faible

frailty ['freɪltɪ] N [*of person, health, happiness*] fragilité *f*; (*morally*) faiblesse *f*

frame [freɪm] [1] N [a] (= *supporting structure*) [*of building*] charpente *f*; [*of bicycle*] cadre *m*; [*of boat*] carcasse *f*; [*of car*] châssis *m*; [*of racket*] armature *f*, cadre *m* [b] (= *border, surround*) [*of picture*] cadre *m*, encadrement *m*; [*of embroidery, tapestry*] cadre *m*; [*of window, door*] châssis *m*, chambranle *m* [c] **~s** [*of spectacles*] monture *f* [d] (*Cine*) photogramme *m*; (*Phot*) image *f* [e] [*of human, animal*] (= *body*) corps *m*; (= *skeleton*) ossature *f*; **his large ~** son grand corps [f] (*fig* = *structure*) cadre *m*; **this proposal is beyond the ~ of the peace agreement** cette proposition dépasse le cadre du traité de paix; **the new ~ of government** la nouvelle structure du gouvernement; **~ of mind** humeur *f*, disposition *f* d'esprit; **I'm not in the right ~ of mind for this job** *or* **to do this job** je ne suis pas d'humeur à faire ce travail; **to be in a positive/relaxed ~ of mind** être positif/décontracté; (*Math, fig*) **~ of reference** système *m* de référence [g] (*in garden*) châssis *m*, cloche *f* [h] (* = *set-up: also* **~-up**) coup *m* monté [i] (*for weaving*) métier *m* [2] VT [a] [+ *picture*] encadrer; **he appeared ~d in the doorway** il apparut dans l'encadrement de la porte; **her face was ~d by a mass of curls** son visage était encadré par une profusion de boucles; **a lake ~d by trees** un lac entouré d'arbres *or* encadré par des arbres [b] (= *construct*) [+ *house*] bâtir *or* construire la charpente de

[c] (= *conceive*) [+ *idea, plan*] concevoir, formuler; [+ *plot*] combiner; [+ *sentence*] construire; [+ *question, issue*] formuler; **she ~d the issue rather differently** elle a formulé la question assez différemment; **the debate is being ~d in terms of civil rights** on aborde la question du point de vue des droits civils [d] (*Phot*) **to ~ a subject** cadrer un sujet [e] (* : *also* **~ up**) **to ~ sb (up)** ◊ **to have sb ~d** monter un coup contre qn (*pour faire porter l'accusation contre lui*); **he claimed he had been ~d** il a prétendu être victime d'un coup monté [3] COMP ► **frame house** N maison *f* à charpente de bois ► **frame rucksack** N sac *m* à dos à armature ► **frame tent** N tente *f* à armature intégrée ► **frame-up*** N coup *m* monté, machination *f*

frameless ['freɪmlɪs] ADJ [*spectacles*] à monture à griffes

framer ['freɪmə'] N (*also* **picture ~**) encadreur *m*

framework ['freɪmwɜːk] [1] N [a] (*lit* = *frame*) (*gen*) structure *f*; (*for building, system*) charpente *f* [b] (*fig* = *basis*) cadre *m*; **within the ~ of ...** dans le cadre de ...; **to establish the legal ~ for sth** établir le cadre légal de qch; **the ~ of society** la structure de la société [2] COMP ► **framework agreement** N (*Ind, Pol*) accord-cadre *m*

framing ['freɪmɪŋ] N [a] (= *frame of picture, photo*) encadrement *m* [b] (*Art, Phot* = *composition of picture*) cadrage *m*

franc [fræŋk] [1] N franc *m* [2] COMP ► **franc area** N zone *f* franc

France [fra:ns] N la France; **in ~** en France

Frances ['fra:nsɪs] N Françoise *f*

franchise ['fræntʃaɪz] [1] N [a] (*Pol*) droit *m* de vote [b] (*Comm*) franchise *f* [2] VT franchiser

franchisee [,fræntʃaɪ'zi:] N franchisé(e) *m(f)*

franchiser ['fræntʃaɪzə'] N franchiseur *m*

Francis ['fra:nsɪs] N François *m*, Francis *m*; **Saint ~ of Assisi** saint François d'Assise

Franciscan [fræn'sɪskən] ADJ, N franciscain *m*

francium ['frænsɪəm] N francium *m*

Franco* ['fræŋkəʊ] ADJ (*Can*) canadien français

franco ['fræŋkəʊ] ADV (*Comm*) franco; **~ frontier/domicile** franco frontière/domicile

Franco- ['fræŋkəʊ] PREF franco-; **~British** franco-britannique

francophile ['fræŋkəʊfaɪl] ADJ, N francophile *mf*

francophobe ['fræŋkəʊfəʊb] ADJ, N francophobe *mf*

francophone ['fræŋkəʊfəʊn] ADJ, N francophone *mf*

frangipane ['frændʒɪpeɪn], **frangipani** [,frændʒɪ'pɑ:nɪ] N (*pl* **frangipanes** *or* **frangipane**) (= *perfume, pastry*) frangipane *f*; (= *shrub*) frangipanier *m*

Franglais* ['frɑ̃:gleɪ] N franglais *m*

Frank [fræŋk] N (*Hist*) Franc *m*, Franque *f*

frank¹ [fræŋk] ADJ [*person, comment, admission*] franc (franche *f*); **to be ~ (with you) ...** franchement ...; **I'll be quite ~ with you** je vais être très franc avec vous

frank² [fræŋk] [1] VT [+ *letter*] affranchir [2] COMP ► **franking machine** N machine *f* à affranchir

frank³* [fræŋk] N (*US*) (saucisse *f* de) Francfort *f*

Frankenstein ['fræŋkənstaɪn] N Frankenstein *m*

frankfurter ['fræŋk,fɜ:tə'] N (= *sausage*) saucisse *f* de Francfort

Frankfurt(-on-Main) ['fræŋkfɜːt,ɒn'meɪn] N Francfort(-sur-le-Main)

frankincense ['fræŋkɪnsens] N encens *m*

Frankish ['fræŋkɪʃ] [1] ADJ (*Hist*) franc (franque *f*) [2] N (*Ling*) francique *m*, langue *f* franque

frankly ['fræŋklɪ] ADV franchement ; **~, I don't give a damn** franchement, je m'en fiche complètement

frankness ['fræŋknɪs] N franchise f

frantic ['fræntɪk] ADJ [person] dans tous ses états ; [shout, phone call] désespéré ; [search] affolé ; [desire, pace] effréné ; [effort, activity, rush] frénétique ; [week, day] fou (folle f) ; **to become** or **get ~** s'affoler ; **~ with worry** fou (folle f) d'inquiétude ; **he/it drives me ~** il/ça me rend dingue*

frantically ['fræntɪkəlɪ] ADV [try, search] désespérément ; [work, write] comme un(e) forcené(e) ; [scramble] comme un fou or une folle ; **to be ~ busy** avoir un boulot* fou, être débordé ; **to wave ~ to sb** faire des gestes frénétiques de la main à qn

frappé ['fræpeɪ] N (US) boisson f glacée

frat* [fræt] N (US Univ) = **fraternity 1a**

fraternal [frə'tɜːnl] ADJ fraternel ; **~ twins** faux jumeaux mpl

fraternity [frə'tɜːnɪtɪ] **1** N **a** (NonC) fraternité f ; (US Univ) association f d'étudiants → SORORITY, FRATERNITY **b** (= group) confrérie f ; **the hunting ~** la confrérie des chasseurs ; **the yachting ~** le monde de la navigation de plaisance ; **the criminal ~** la pègre **2** COMP ► **fraternity pin** N (US Univ) insigne m de confrérie

fraternization [,frætənaɪ'zeɪʃən] N fraternisation f

fraternize ['frætənaɪz] VI fraterniser (**with** avec)

fratricidal [,frætrɪ'saɪdl] ADJ fratricide

fratricide ['frætrɪsaɪd] N (= act) fratricide m ; (frm, liter = person) fratricide mf

fraud [frɔːd] **1** N **a** (= criminal deception) fraude f, supercherie f ; (financial) escroquerie f ; (Jur) fraude f ; **tax ~** fraude f fiscale ; **credit card ~** escroquerie f à la carte de crédit **b** (= person) imposteur m, fraudeur m, -euse f ; (= object) attrape-nigaud m ; **he isn't a ~ doctor, he's a ~** ce n'est pas un médecin, c'est un imposteur ; **he's not ill, he's a ~** il n'est pas malade, il joue la comédie* or c'est un simulateur ; **this whole thing is a ~!** c'est de la frime* or de la fumisterie*! **2** COMP ► **Fraud Squad** N (Police) service m de la répression des fraudes

fraudster ['frɔːdstər] N fraudeur m, -euse f

fraudulence ['frɔːdjʊləns], **fraudulency** ['frɔːdjʊlənsɪ] N caractère m frauduleux

fraudulent ['frɔːdjʊlənt] **1** ADJ frauduleux **2** ► **fraudulent conversion** N (Jur) malversation f, détournement m de fonds

fraudulently ['frɔːdjʊləntlɪ] ADV frauduleusement

fraught [frɔːt] ADJ **a** (= filled) **~ with difficulty/danger** plein de difficultés/dangers ; **~ with tension** lourd de tension **b** (= anxious) [person] tendu, angoissé ; [situation, meeting, relationship, morning] tendu

fray¹ [freɪ] N rixe f, échauffourée f ; (Mil) combat m ; (lit, fig) **ready for the ~** prêt à se battre ; (fig) **to enter the ~** descendre dans l'arène, entrer en lice

fray² [freɪ] **1** VT [+ cloth, garment] effilocher, effiler ; [+ cuff] user le bord de, râper ; [+ trousers] user le bas de, râper ; [+ rope] user, raguer (Naut) ; **tempers were getting ~ed** on commençait à perdre patience or s'énerver ; **my nerves are ~ed** je suis à bout (de nerfs) **2** VI [cloth, garment] s'effilocher, s'effiler ; [rope] s'user, se raguer (Naut) ; **his sleeve was ~ing at the cuff** sa manche était usée or râpée au poignet ; (fig) **to ~ at** or **around the edges** [marriage, alliance] battre de l'aile ; **he looked rather ~ed around the edges*** il ne semblait pas en grande forme

frazzle ['fræzl] **1** N **a** **worn to a ~** claqué*, crevé* ; **she's worn to a ~ getting ready for the**

---

competition la préparation de la compétition la crève* ; **she had worn herself to a ~** elle s'était crevée à la tâche* **b** **burnt to a ~** carbonisé, calciné **2** VT **a** (= exhaust) crever* ; **my brain's ~d** j'ai la tête farcie!* ; **his nerves were ~d** il était à bout (de nerfs) **b** (= burn) (faire) carboniser, (faire) cramer*

FRCP [,efɑːsiː'piː] N (Brit) (ABBR = **Fellow of the Royal College of Physicians**) membre de l'Académie royale de médecine

FRCS [,efɑːsiː'es] N (Brit) (ABBR = **Fellow of the Royal College of Surgeons**) membre de l'Académie royale de chirurgie

freak [friːk] **1** N **a** (= abnormal person or animal) monstre m, phénomène m ; (= eccentric) phénomène m ; (= absurd idea) lubie f, idée f saugrenue or farfelue* ; **~ of nature** accident m de la nature ; **his winning was really just a ~** il n'a gagné que grâce à un hasard extraordinaire **b** (‡ = fanatic) **he's an acid ~** il est accro* à l'acide ; **a jazz ~** un(e) dingue* or un(e) fana* du jazz ; **a health food ~** un(e) fana* de l'alimentation naturelle or de la bouffe bio* ; **a speed ~** un(e) fana* de la vitesse **2** ADJ [storm, weather] anormal, insolite ; [error] bizarre ; [victory] inattendu **3** COMP ► **freak-out‡** N défonce f ► **freak show** N exhibition f de monstres (dans une foire)

► **freak out‡ 1** VI **a** (= get angry) piquer une de ces crises* **b** (= get high on drugs) se défoncer‡ ; **to ~ out on LSD** se défoncer‡ au LSD **2** VT SEP **to ~ sb out** (= surprise) en boucher un coin à qn* ; (= make angry) foutre qn en boule‡ or en pétard‡ **3** **~-out‡** N → **freak**

freakish ['friːkɪʃ] ADJ (gen) bizarre ; [weather] anormal ; [idea] saugrenu, insolite

freakishly ['friːkɪʃlɪ] ADV [hot, cold] anormalement

freaky* ['friːkɪ] ADJ bizarre

freckle ['frekl] **1** N tache f de rousseur **2** VI se couvrir de taches de rousseur

freckled ['frekld] ADJ plein de taches de rousseur, taché de son

Frederick ['fredrɪk] N Frédéric m

free [friː]

1 ADJECTIVE	4 NOUN
2 ADVERB	5 COMPOUNDS
3 TRANSITIVE VERB	6 PHRASAL VERBS

1 ADJECTIVE

a = **at liberty, not captive or tied** [person, animal] libre ; **they tied him up but he managed to get ~** ils l'ont attaché mais il a réussi à se libérer ; **to go ~** [prisoner] être relâché, être mis en liberté ; **all these dangerous people still go ~** tous ces gens dangereux sont encore en liberté ; **to set a prisoner ~** libérer or mettre en liberté un prisonnier ; **they had to cut the driver ~ from the wreckage** ils ont dû dégager le conducteur du véhicule accidenté ; **he left the end of the rope ~** il a laissé libre le bout de la corde ; **she opened the door with her ~ hand** elle a ouvert la porte avec sa main libre ; (lit, fig) **to have one's hands ~** avoir les mains libres ; (fig) **to have a ~ hand to do sth** avoir carte blanche pour faire qch ; **to give sb a ~ hand** donner carte blanche à qn

b = **unrestricted, unhindered** [person] libre ; [choice, access] libre (before n) ; **~ elections** élections fpl libres ; **~ press** presse f libre ; **~ translation** traduction f libre ; **the fishing is ~** la pêche est autorisée ; **to be/get ~ of sb** se débarrasser/être débarrassé de qn ; **~ and easy** décontracté, désinvolte ; (Brit) **as ~ as a bird** or **(the) air** libre comme l'air → **5**

♦ **(to be) free to do** : **I'm not ~ to do it** je ne suis pas libre de le faire ; **he was ~ to refuse** il était libre de refuser ; **you're ~ to choose** vous êtes libre de choisir, libre à vous de choisir ; **I am leaving you ~ to do as you please** je vous laisse libre de faire comme bon vous semble, je vous laisse carte blanche ; **her aunt's death**

---

set her ~ to follow her own career la mort de sa tante lui a donné toute liberté pour poursuivre sa carrière

♦ **to feel free (to do)** : **can I borrow your pen? — feel ~*** est-ce que je peux vous emprunter votre stylo ? — je vous en prie or faites ; **please feel ~ to ask questions** n'hésitez pas à poser des questions ; **a school where children feel ~ to express themselves** une école où les enfants se sentent libres de s'exprimer

♦ **free from** or **of** (= without) **to be ~ from** or **of care/responsibility** être dégagé de tout souci/de toute responsabilité ; **to be ~ from** or **of pain** ne pas souffrir ; **~ from the usual ruling** non soumis au règlement habituel ; **a surface ~ from** or **of dust** une surface dépoussiérée ; **area ~ of malaria** zone f non touchée par la malaria ; **a world ~ of nuclear weapons** un monde sans armes nucléaires or dénucléarisé ; **the elections have been ~ of violence** les élections se sont déroulées sans violence ; **the company is now ~ of government control** la société n'est plus contrôlée par le gouvernement ; **~ of tax** or **duty** exonéré, hors taxe

c = **Pol = autonomous, independent** [country, state] libre ; [government] autonome, libre ; (Hist) **the Free French** les Français mpl libres ; **the ~ world** le monde libre ; (fig) **it's a ~ country!** on est en république !*, on peut faire ce qu'on veut ici !

d = **costing nothing** [object, ticket, sample] gratuit ; **he got a ~ ticket** il a eu un billet gratuit ; **"~ mug with each towel"** « une chope gratuite pour tout achat d'une serviette » ; **admission ~** ◊ **admission** entrée f gratuite or libre ; **it's ~ of charge** c'est gratuit → **5** ; (Comm) **~ delivery** ◊ **delivery** ~ livraison f gratuite, franco de port ; (Comm) **~ delivered at dock** livraison f franco à quai ; (Comm) **as a ~ gift** en prime, en cadeau ; **~ offer** offre f gratuite ; (Comm) **~ sample** échantillon m gratuit ; **there's no such thing as a ~ lunch** tout se paie ; (fig) **to get a ~ ride*** profiter de la situation

e = **not occupied** [room, seat, hour, person] libre ; **there are only two ~ seats left** il ne reste que deux places de libre ; **is this table ~?** cette table est-elle libre ? ; **I will be ~ at 2 o'clock** je serai libre à 14 heures

f = **lavish, profuse** généreux, prodigue ; **to be ~ with one's money** dépenser son argent sans compter ; (iro) **you're very ~ with your advice** vous êtes particulièrement prodigue de conseils (iro) ; **he makes ~ with all my things** il ne se gêne pas pour se servir de mes affaires ; **to make ~† with a woman** prendre des libertés or se permettre des familiarités avec une femme

g Ling [morpheme] libre

h Chem [gas] libre, non combiné

2 ADVERB

a = **without payment** [give, get, travel] gratuitement, gratis ; **we got in ~** or **for ~*** nous sommes entrés gratuitement or gratis or à l'œil* ; **they'll send it ~ on request** ils l'enverront gratuitement or franco sur demande

b = **without restraint** [run about] en liberté

c = **expressing release** **the screw had worked itself ~** la vis s'était desserrée ; **to pull ~** se dégager, se libérer ; **to wriggle ~** [person] se libérer en se tortillant ; [fish] se libérer en frétillant or à force de frétillements

3 TRANSITIVE VERB

a = **liberate** [+ nation, slave] affranchir, libérer

b = **untie** [+ person, animal] détacher ; [+ knot] défaire, dénouer ; [+ tangle] débrouiller

c = **release** [+ caged animal, prisoner] libérer ; [+ person] (from wreckage) dégager, désincarcérer ; (from burden) soulager, débarrasser ; (from tax) exempter, exonérer ; (lit, fig) **to ~ o.s. from** se débarrasser de, se libérer de ; **to ~ sb from anxiety** libérer or délivrer qn de l'angoisse

d = unblock [+ pipe] débloquer, déboucher
4 NOUN
the land of the ~ le pays de la liberté
5 COMPOUNDS
► **free agent** N to be a ~ agent avoir toute liberté d'action ► **free alongside quay** ADJ (Comm) franco à quai ► **free alongside ship** ADJ (Comm) franco le long du navire ► **free association** N (Psych) libre association f ► **Free Church** (Brit) N église f non-conformiste ♦ ADJ non-conformiste ► **free climbing** N escalade f libre ► **free clinic** (US Med) dispensaire m ► **free collective bargaining** N (Ind) négociation f salariale libre (sans limite imposée par l'État) ► **free enterprise** N libre entreprise f ► **free-enterprise economy** N économie f de marché ► **free fall** N (Space, Parachuting, Econ) chute f libre; in ~ fall en chute libre; to go into ~ fall entamer une chute libre ► **free fight** N mêlée f générale ► **free-fire zone** N (Mil) secteur m or zone f de tir libre ► **free flight** N (Aviat) vol m libre ► **free-floating** ADJ (in water) qui flotte librement; (in outer space) qui flotte librement dans l'espace; (fig) [person] sans attaches ► **free-for-all** N mêlée f générale ► **free-form jazz** N (Mus) free jazz m ► **free hit** N (Sport) coup m franc ► **free house** N (Brit) pub m (qui n'appartient pas à une chaîne) → PUB ► **free kick** N (Sport) coup m franc ► **free labour** N (Ind) main-d'œuvre f non syndiquée ► **free love** N amour m libre ► **free market, free-market economy** N économie f de marché ► **free marketeer** N partisan m de l'économie de marché ► **free of charge** ADV (Comm) gratuitement ► **free on board** ADJ (Comm) franco à bord ► **free on rail** ADJ (Comm) franco wagon ► **free period** N (Educ) heure f de libre or sans cours ► **free port** N port m franc ► **free-range egg** N œuf m de poule élevée en plein air ► **free-range poultry** N poulets mpl élevés en plein air ► **free shot** N lancer m franc, coup m franc ► **free speech** N liberté f de parole ► **free spirit** N esprit m libre ► **free-spirited** ADJ [person] libre d'esprit; [ways] libre ► **free-standing** ADJ [furniture] sur pied ► **the Free State** N (US) le Maryland ► **free-styling** N (Ski) ski m acrobatique ► **free throw** N (US Sport) lancer m franc ► **free trade** N (Econ) libre-échange m ► **free-trader** N (Econ) libre-échangiste m ► **free-trade zone** N (Econ) zone f franche ► **free verse** N (Literat) vers m libre ► **free vote** N vote m en conscience (sans consigne de vote) ► **free will** N (Philos) libre arbitre m; he did it of his own ~ will il l'a fait de son propre gré ► **free-will gift** N don m volontaire ► **free-will offering** N offrande f volontaire
6 PHRASAL VERBS
► **free up** VT SEP [+ money, resources] dégager; [+ staff] libérer; to ~ up some time to do sth trouver du temps pour faire qch

-free [fri:] ADJ (in compounds) salt-free sans sel; stress-free sans stress; trouble-free sans problèmes
freebase* ['fri:beɪs] (Drugs) **1** N freebase* m (forme de cocaïne purifiée) **2** VT to ~ cocaine fumer du freebase* **3** VI fumer du freebase*
freebie* ['fri:bɪ] **1** N (= free gift) (petit) cadeau m; (= free trip) voyage m gratis* or à l'œil*; (= free newspaper) journal m gratis* **2** ADJ gratis*
freeboard ['fri:bɔ:d] N (hauteur f de) franc-bord m
freebooter ['fri:,bu:tər] N (= buccaneer) pirate m; (Hist) flibustier m
freedom ['fri:dəm] **1** N liberté f; ~ of action liberté f d'action or d'agir; ~ of association liberté f d'association; ~ of information liberté f d'information; ~ of the press liberté f de la

presse; ~ of speech liberté f de parole; ~ of worship liberté f religieuse or du culte; ~ of the seas franchise f des mers; to give sb ~ to do as he wishes laisser les mains libres à qn, donner carte blanche à qn; to speak with ~ parler en toute liberté; to give sb the ~ of a city nommer qn citoyen d'honneur d'une ville; he gave me the ~ of his house il m'a laissé la libre disposition de sa maison
2 COMP ► **freedom fighter** N guérillero m, partisan m ► **Freedom of Information Act** N (US: Jur) loi f sur la liberté d'information

---
FREEDOM OF INFORMATION ACT

Aux États-Unis, la loi sur la liberté d'information ou **Freedom of Information Act** oblige les organismes fédéraux à divulguer les informations qu'ils détiennent à quiconque en fait la demande, sauf pour des raisons spécifiques liées au secret-défense, aux secrets de fabrication ou à la protection de la vie privée. Cette loi, particulièrement utile pour les journalistes, a permis la publication de renseignements jusqu'alors gardés secrets sur certaines affaires délicates comme la guerre du Vietnam et les activités d'espionnage illégales du FBI.

Freefone® ['fri:fəʊn] **1** N (Brit Telec) ≈ numéro m vert **2** VT **to find out more, freefone 77 88 99** pour plus de renseignements, appelez le 77 88 99 (numéro vert) or appelez notre numéro vert 77 88 99
freehand ['fri:hænd] ADJ, ADV à main levée
freehold ['fri:həʊld] (Brit) **1** N propriété f foncière libre (à perpétuité) **2** ADV en propriété libre
freeholder ['fri:həʊldər] N (Brit) propriétaire mf foncier (-ière f) (à perpétuité)
freelance ['fri:lɑ:ns] **1** N free-lance mf, collaborateur m, -trice f indépendant(e); (= journalist) pigiste mf **2** ADJ [journalist, designer, player] indépendant, free-lance inv; [work, writing] en indépendant, en free-lance **3** VI travailler en free-lance or en indépendant **4** ADV [work] en free-lance, en indépendant; to go ~ se mettre à travailler en free-lance or en indépendant
freelancer ['fri:lɑ:nsər] N free-lance mf, collaborateur m, -trice f indépendant(e); (= journalist) pigiste mf
freeload* ['fri:ləʊd] VI vivre en parasite
freeloader* ['fri:ləʊdər] N parasite m, pique-assiette mf
freely ['fri:lɪ] ADV a (= unrestrictedly) [travel, elect] en toute liberté; [operate] librement, en toute liberté; [express, translate, adapt] librement; [talk, speak] franchement, librement; to move ~ [person] se déplacer en toute liberté; [machine part] jouer librement; traffic is moving or flowing ~ la circulation est fluide; to be ~ available [drugs, commodity, help, information] être facile à trouver b (= willingly) [give, share] généreusement; [lend, admit] volontiers c (= liberally) [spend] sans compter; [use, perspire] abondamment; the wine was flowing ~ le vin coulait à flots
freeman ['fri:mən] N (pl -men) (Hist) homme m libre; ~ of a city citoyen m d'honneur d'une ville
freemason ['fri:,meɪsn] N franc-maçon m
freemasonry ['fri:,meɪsnrɪ] N franc-maçonnerie f
Freephone® ['fri:fəʊn] = **Freefone**
Freepost® ['fri:pəʊst] N (Brit) port m payé
freesia ['fri:zɪə] N freesia m
freestone ['fri:stəʊn] N (NonC) pierre f de taille
freestyle ['fri:staɪl] N (also ~ swimming) nage f libre

freethinker [,fri:'θɪŋkər] N libre-penseur m, -euse f
freethinking [,fri:'θɪŋkɪŋ] **1** ADJ libre penseur **2** N libre pensée f
freeway ['fri:weɪ] N (US) autoroute f (sans péage) → ROADS
freewheel [,fri:'wi:l] (Brit) **1** VI [cyclist] se mettre en roue libre, être en roue libre; [motorist] rouler au point mort **2** N [of bicycle] roue f libre
freewheeler [,fri:'wi:lər] N (fig) insouciant(e) m(f)
freewheeling [,fri:'wi:lɪŋ] ADJ [person] insouciant; [scheme] hardi; [discussion] libre
freeze [fri:z] (pret **froze**, ptp **frozen**) **1** VI a [liquid] (lit) geler; [food] se congeler; it will ~ hard tonight il gèlera dur cette nuit; to ~ to death mourir de froid; the lake has frozen le lac est gelé; the windscreen was frozen le pare-brise était givré; this dish ~s well ce plat se congèle bien; the fallen apples had frozen to the ground les pommes tombées étaient collées au sol par le gel b (fig = stop) se figer; he froze (in his tracks or to the spot) il est resté figé sur place; the smile froze on his lips son sourire s'est figé sur ses lèvres; ~! pas un geste! → freezing, frozen **2** VT a [+ liquid] geler; [+ food] congeler; (industrially) surgeler; (fig) she froze him with a look elle lui a lancé un regard qui l'a glacé sur place b (= stop, block) [+ assets, credit, wages] geler, bloquer; [+ prices, bank account] bloquer; (Cine = hold image) can you ~ it? tu peux t'arrêter sur l'image? → frozen **3** N a (Met) temps m de gelée, gel m; the big ~ of 1948 le grand gel de 1948 b (Econ) [of prices, wages, credit] blocage m, gel m; a wage(s)/price(s) ~ ◊ a ~ on wages/prices un blocage or gel des salaires/des prix; a ~ on new staff appointments un gel de l'embauche; a ~ on nuclear weapons testing/programmes un gel des essais nucléaires/des programmes d'armes nucléaires **4** COMP ► **freeze-dry** VT lyophiliser ► **freeze-frame** N [of film, video] arrêt m sur image ► **freeze-up** N
► **freeze out** VT SEP to ~ sb out (from sth) tenir qn à l'écart (de qch)
► **freeze over** VI [lake, river] geler; [windscreen] givrer; the river has frozen over la rivière est gelée
► **freeze up 1** VI [pipes, lake, river] geler **2** VT SEP the pipes were frozen up last winter les conduits ont gelé l'hiver dernier **3** ~-up N → freeze
freezer ['fri:zər] **1** N a (domestic) congélateur m; (industrial) surgélateur m b (in fridge: also ~ compartment) (one-star) freezer m; (two-star) conservateur m; (three-star) congélateur m c (US = ice cream maker) sorbetière f **2** COMP ► **freezer bag** N sac m congélation ► **freezer container** N barquette f congélation ► **freezer film** N plastique m spécial congélation ► **freezer foil** N aluminium m spécial congélation ► **freezer tray** N bac m à glace
freezing ['fri:zɪŋ] **1** ADJ a (= icy) [temperatures, weather, wind, rain, night] glacial b (also ~ cold) [person] gelé; [water, room] glacial; my hands are ~ j'ai les mains gelées; it's ~ il fait un froid glacial; it's ~ in here on gèle ici; in the ~ cold dans le froid glacial **2** N [of food] congélation f, gel m **3** COMP ► **freezing fog** N (Met) brouillard m givrant ► **freezing point** N point m de congélation; below ~ point au-dessous de zéro (centigrade)
freight [freɪt] **1** N (= transporting) transport m; (= price, cost) fret m; (= goods moved) fret m, cargaison f; (esp Brit = ship's cargo) fret m; (Comm) ~ **paid** port m payé; (US Comm) ~ **and delivery paid** franco de port; to send sth by ~ faire transporter qch; **air** ~ transport m par

avion, fret *m* aérien [2] VT [+ *goods*] transporter [3] COMP ► **freight agent** N transitaire *mf* ► **freight car** (*US Rail*) wagon *m* de marchandises, fourgon *m* ► **freight charges** NPL frais *mpl* de transport, fret *m* ► **freight forwarder** N transporteur *m* ► **freight note** N bordereau *m* d'expédition ► **freight plane** N avion-cargo *m*, avion *m* de fret ► **freight terminal** N terminal *m* de fret ► **freight train** N train *m* de marchandises ► **freight yard** N dépôt *m* des marchandises

freightage ['freɪtɪdʒ] N (= *charge*) fret *m*; (= *goods*) fret *m*, cargaison *f*

freighter ['freɪtər] N (*Naut*) cargo *m*, navire *m* de charge; (*Aviat*) avion-cargo *m*, avion *m* de fret

freightliner ['freɪt,laɪnər] N train *m* de marchandises en conteneurs

French [frentʃ] [1] ADJ (*gen*) français; [*ambassador, embassy, monarch*] de France; [*teacher*] de français; **the ~ way of life** la vie française; **~ cooking** la cuisine française; **the ~ people** les Français *mpl* → **4**
[2] N (*Ling*) français *m*; (*apologizing for swearing*) **excuse** or **pardon my ~*** passez-moi l'expression
[3] **the French** NPL les Français *mpl* → **free**
[4] COMP ► **the French Academy** N l'Académie *f* française ► **French bean** N (*Brit*) haricot *m* vert ► **French bread** N pain *m* à la française ► **French Canadian** ADJ canadien français ♦ N (= *person*) Canadien(ne) français(e) *m(f)*; (*Ling*) français *m* canadien ► **French chalk** N craie *f* de tailleur ► **French cricket** N *forme simplifiée du cricket jouée par les enfants* ► **French door** N (*US*) porte-fenêtre *f* ► **French dressing** N (*Culin*) (= *vinaigrette*) vinaigrette *f*; (*US = salad cream*) sauce *f* (à) salade ► **French Equatorial Africa** N l'Afrique *f* équatoriale française ► **French fried potatoes, French fries** NPL (pommes *fpl* de terre) frites *fpl* ► **French-fry** VT (*US*) frire à la friteuse ► **French Guiana** N la Guyane française ► **French horn** N (*Mus*) cor *m* d'harmonie ► **French kiss*** N baiser *m* profond or avec la langue, patin* *m* ♦ VT embrasser avec la langue, rouler un patin* à ♦ VI s'embrasser avec la langue, se rouler un patin* ► **French knickers** NPL (petite) culotte-short *f* ► **French leave** N **to take ~** **leave filer** à l'anglaise* ► **French letter*** N (= *contraceptive*) capote *f* anglaise* ► **French loaf** N baguette *f* (*de pain*) ► **French marigold** N œillet *m* d'Inde ► **French pastry** N pâtisserie *f* ► **French pleat** N (*Hairdressing*) chignon *m* banane ► **French polish** N (*Brit*) vernis *m* (à l'alcool) ► **French-polish** VT (*Brit*) vernir (à l'alcool) ► **the French Riviera** N la Côte d'Azur ► **French seam** N (*Sewing*) couture *f* anglaise ► **French-speaking** ADJ francophone → **Switzerland** ► **French stick** N = **French loaf** ► **French toast** N (*Brit*) (= *toast*) pain *m* grillé d'un seul côté; (= *fried bread in egg*) pain *m* perdu ► **French West Africa** N l'Afrique *f* occidentale française ► **French window** N porte-fenêtre *f*

Frenchify ['frentʃɪfaɪ] VT franciser; (*pej*) **his Frenchified ways** ses maniérismes copiés sur les Français

Frenchman ['frentʃmən] N (*pl* -**men**) Français *m*

Frenchwoman ['frentʃwʊmən] N (*pl* -**women**) Française *f*

frenetic [frə'netɪk] ADJ [*person*] très agité; [*activity, pace, applause, shouts*] frénétique; [*effort*] désespéré; [*period, time*] trépidant

frenetically [frə'netɪklɪ] ADV [*work, rush, think, try*] frénétiquement; [*busy*] extrêmement

frenzied ['frenzɪd] ADJ [*attack*] sauvage; [*activity, atmosphere, haste, applause, crowd, fans*] frénétique; [*efforts, shouts*] désespéré

frenziedly ['frenzɪdlɪ] ADV [*run, shake, dance*] frénétiquement; [*work*] comme un fou or une folle; **a ~ busy** or **hectic time** une période d'activité frénétique

frenzy ['frenzɪ] N frénésie *f*; **~ of delight** transport *m* de joie; **to be in a ~** être au comble de l'excitation; **a ~ of activity** une activité folle; **a religious/media ~** un délire religieux/médiatique

frequency ['friːkwənsɪ] [1] N fréquence *f* → **high, ultrahigh, very** [2] COMP ► **frequency band** N (*Elec*) bande *f* de fréquence ► **frequency distribution** N (*Stat*) distribution *f* des fréquences ► **frequency modulation** N (*Elec*) modulation *f* de fréquence

frequent ['friːkwənt] [1] ADJ [*rests, breaks, changes, trains*] fréquent, nombreux; [*absences, headaches, colds, occurrence, use*] fréquent; [*reports*] nombreux; [*complaint, criticism*] courant, que l'on entend souvent; **it's quite ~** c'est très courant, cela arrive souvent; **to make ~ visits** or **trips to ...** ◊ **to be a ~ visitor to ...** aller fréquemment à ...; **he is a ~ visitor (to our house)** c'est un habitué de la maison [2] [frɪ'kwent] VT fréquenter, hanter [3] COMP ► **frequent flyer** N **he's a ~ flyer** il prend beaucoup l'avion ► **frequent-flyer** ADJ [*scheme, programme*] de fidélisation ► **frequent wash shampoo** N shampoing *m* (pour) usage fréquent

frequentative [frɪ'kwentətɪv] ADJ, N (*Gram*) fréquentatif *m*, itératif *m*

frequenter [frɪ'kwentər] N [*of restaurant, pub*] habitué(e) *m(f)*; **~s of theatres/public libraries** habitués *mpl* des théâtres/des bibliothèques municipales; **he was a great ~ of night clubs** il courait les boîtes de nuit, c'était un habitué des boîtes de nuit

frequently ['friːkwəntlɪ] [1] ADV fréquemment [2] COMP ► **frequently asked questions** NPL (*Comput*) questions *fpl* fréquentes

fresco ['freskəʊ] N (*pl* **frescoes** or **frescos**) (= *pigment, picture*) fresque *f*; **to paint in ~** peindre à fresque

fresh [freʃ] [1] ADJ [a] (= *not stale*) [*food, flavour, smell*] frais (fraîche *f*); [*clothes, towel*] propre; **is this milk ~?** ce lait est-il frais?; **is my breath ~?** ai-je l'haleine fraîche?
[b] (= *recent*) [*blood, tracks, scent, news*] frais (fraîche *f*); [*scar, wound*] récent; [*memories*] proche; **it's still in my mind** or **memory** c'est encore tout frais dans ma mémoire; **a ~ coat of paint** une nouvelle couche de peinture; **"~ paint"** « peinture fraîche »
[c] (= *new, renewed*) [*evidence, approach, fighting, outbreak, supplies*] nouveau (nouvelle *f*); **a ~ sheet of paper** une nouvelle feuille de papier; **she applied ~ lipstick** elle a remis du rouge à lèvres; **to make a ~ pot of tea** refaire du thé; **he poured himself a ~ drink** il s'est reversé à boire; **to take a ~ look at sth** regarder qch sous un jour nouveau; **(to make) a ~ start** (prendre) un nouveau départ; **a ~ face** (= *new person*) un nouveau visage; **~ fields (and pastures new)** nouveaux horizons *mpl* → **break, heart**
[d] (= *not dried or processed*) [*pasta, fruit, vegetables, herbs, juice, cream, flowers*] frais (fraîche *f*); **~ coffee** café *m* (*moulu*)
[e] (= *rested*) [*person, horse*] frais (fraîche *f*); **to feel ~** être frais et dispos; **he/she is as ~ as a daisy** il est frais comme un gardon/elle est fraîche comme une rose; **to have a ~ complexion** avoir le teint frais
[f] (= *refreshing, original*) [*approach, style, humour, writing*] original
[g] (= *cool, invigorating*) [*day, wind, breeze*] frais (fraîche *f*)
[h] (†* = *cheeky*) culotté*; **that's enough of that ~ talk!** ça suffit avec ces familiarités!; **to be** or **get ~ (with sb)** (= *cheeky*) être impertinent (avec qn); (*sexually*) prendre des libertés

(avec qn), se permettre des familiarités (avec qn)
[2] ADV [a] (= *straight*) **milk ~ from the cow** du lait fraîchement trait; **fish ~ from the lake** du poisson qui sort tout juste du lac; **the bread is ~ from the oven** le pain sort à l'instant or est frais sorti du four; **~ from** or **out of school** frais émoulu du lycée; **~ from the war** tout juste de retour de la guerre; **tourists ~ off the plane** des touristes tout juste débarqués de l'avion; **to come ~ to sth** aborder qch sans idées préconçues
[b] **to be ~ out of sth*** être en panne* de qch
[3] COMP ► **fresh air** N air *m* frais; **I'm going out for some ~ air** or **for a breath of ~ air** je sors prendre l'air or le frais; **in the ~ air** au grand air, en plein air ► **breath ► fresh-air fiend*** N amoureux *m*, -euse *f* du grand air ► **fresh breeze** N (*Naut*) bonne brise *f* ► **fresh-faced** ADJ au visage juvénile ► **fresh gale** N (*Naut*) coup *m* de vent ► **fresh water** N (= *not salt*) eau *f* douce

freshen ['freʃn] [1] VI (*Met*) [*wind, air*] fraîchir [2] VT [+ *air*] désodoriser; [+ *breath, complexion*] rafraîchir; **can I ~ your drink for you?** je vous en ressers?, encore une goutte?
► **freshen up** [1] VI (= *wash o.s.*) faire un brin de toilette; (= *touch up make-up*) se refaire une beauté* [2] VT SEP [+ *invalid etc*] faire un brin de toilette à; [+ *child*] débarbouiller; [+ *room, paintwork*] rafraîchir; **accessories to ~ up your summer wardrobe** des accessoires pour égayer votre garde-robe estivale; **the new players will ~ up the team** les nouveaux joueurs vont apporter du sang neuf dans or à l'équipe; **chewing gum to ~ the breath up** du chewing-gum pour rafraîchir l'haleine; **to ~ o.s. up** or **to freshen up**; → **1**

freshener ['freʃnər] N (*also* **skin ~**) lotion *f* tonique; (*also* **air ~**) désodorisant *m*

fresher ['freʃər] [1] N (*Brit Univ*) bizut(h) *m*, étudiant(e) *m(f)* de première année [2] ► **freshers' week** N (*Brit Univ*) semaine *f* d'accueil des étudiants

freshet ['freʃɪt] N (= *flood*) crue *f* rapide, inondation *f* brutale; (*into sea*) (petit) cours *m* d'eau qui se jette dans la mer

freshly ['freʃlɪ] ADV [*ground, grated, dug*] fraîchement; **~ baked bread** du pain qui sort or frais sorti du four; **~ caught fish** du poisson fraîchement pêché; **~-cut flowers** des fleurs fraîchement cueillies or qui viennent d'être coupées; **~ made coffee** du café qui vient d'être fait; **~ painted** qui vient d'être peint; **~ squeezed orange juice** du jus d'oranges pressées

freshman ['freʃmən] N (*pl* -**men**) (*US Univ*) ≈ bizut(h) *m*

freshness ['freʃnɪs] N [*of air, food, fruit, milk, wind*] fraîcheur *f*; [*of manner*] franchise *f*, spontanéité *f*; [*of outlook, approach*] fraîcheur *f*, jeunesse *f*; [*of colour*] fraîcheur *f*, gaieté *f*

freshwater ['freʃ,wɔːtər] ADJ [*fish, plant, lake*] d'eau douce

fret[1] [fret] [1] VI [a] (= *become anxious*) se tracasser (**about** à propos de); [*baby*] pleurer, geindre; **don't ~!** ne t'en fais pas!, ne te tracasse pas!; **she ~s over the slightest thing** elle se fait du mauvais sang or elle se tracasse pour un rien; **the child is ~ting for its mother** le petit réclame sa mère en pleurant [b] **to ~ (at the bit)** [*horse*] ronger le mors [2] VT **to ~ o.s.*** se tracasser, se faire de la bile [3] N **to be in a ~*** se biler*

fret[2] [fret] VT [+ *wood*] découper, chantourner; **the stream has ~ted its way through the rock** le ruisseau s'est frayé un passage dans le rocher

fret[3] [fret] N [*of guitar*] touchette *f*

fretful ['fretfʊl] ADJ [*person*] irritable; [*baby, child*] grognon, pleurnicheur; [*sleep*] agité; [*tone*] plaintif

fretfully ['frɛtfəlɪ] ADV [say] (= anxiously) d'un ton irrité ; (= complainingly) d'un ton plaintif or pleurnichard ; **to cry ~** [baby] pleurnicher, être grognon

fretfulness ['frɛtfʊlnɪs] N irritabilité f

fretsaw ['frɛtsɔː] N scie f à chantourner or à découper

fretwork ['frɛtwɜːk] N (= piece) pièce f chantournée ; (= work) découpage m

Freudian ['frɔɪdɪən] [1] ADJ (Psych, fig) freudien ; **that's very ~!** c'est révélateur ! [2] N disciple mf de Freud [3] COMP ► **Freudian slip** N lapsus m

FRG [ˌefɑːˈdʒiː] N (ABBR = **Federal Republic of Germany**) RFA f

Fri. N ABBR = **Friday**

friable ['fraɪəbl] ADJ friable

friar ['fraɪəʳ] N moine m, frère m ; **Friar John** frère Jean

friary ['fraɪərɪ] N confrérie f

fricassee ['frɪkəsiː] N fricassée f

fricative ['frɪkətɪv] (Ling) [1] ADJ spirant, fricatif [2] N spirante f, fricative f

friction ['frɪkʃən] [1] N a (Phys) friction f, frottement m ; (Ling) friction f ; (fig) friction f ; (fig) **there is a certain amount of ~ between them** il y a des frictions entre eux b (also ~ **climbing**) adhérence f [2] COMP ► **friction feed** N (on printer) entraînement m par friction ► **friction tape** N (US) chatterton m

Friday ['fraɪdɪ] N vendredi m ; **the thirteenth** vendredi treize → **good** ; for other phrases see **Saturday**

fridge [frɪdʒ] [1] N (esp Brit) (ABBR = **refrigerator**) frigo* m, frigidaire® m [2] COMP ► **fridge-freezer** N réfrigérateur m avec partie congélateur

fried [fraɪd] VB pt, ptp of **fry²**

friend [frɛnd] N ami(e) m(f) ; (= schoolmate, workmate) camarade mf, copain* m, copine* f ; (= helper, supporter) ami(e) m(f) ; **a ~ of mine** un de mes amis ; **~s of ours** des amis (à nous) ; **he's one of my son's ~s** c'est un ami or un copain* de mon fils ; **her best ~** sa meilleure amie ; (fig) **it's a girl's best ~** c'est le rêve de chaque femme ; **he's no ~ of mine** je ne le compte pas au nombre de mes amis ; **to make ~s with sb** devenir ami avec qn, se lier d'amitié avec qn ; **he made a ~ of him** il en a fait son ami ; **he makes ~s easily** il se fait facilement des amis, il se lie facilement ; **to be ~s with sb** être ami or lié avec qn ; **let's be ~s again** on fait la paix ? ; **close ~s** amis mpl intimes ; **we're just good ~s** on est simplement amis ; **we're all ~s here** nous sommes entre amis ; **a ~ of the family** un ami de la famille ■ (PROV) **a ~ in need (is a ~ indeed)** c'est dans le besoin que l'on connaît ses vrais amis ; **the best of ~s must part** il n'est si bonne compagnie qui ne se sépare (PROV) ; **he's been a true ~ to us** il a fait preuve d'une véritable amitié envers nous ; (fig) **a ~ at court** un ami influent ; (fig) **to have ~s at court** avoir des amis influents or des protections ; **my honourable ~** (Parl) ◊ **my learned ~** (Jur) mon cher or distingué confrère, ma distinguée collègue ; **~ of the poor** bienfaiteur m or ami m des pauvres ; **Friends of the Earth** les Amis mpl de la Terre ; **Friends of the National Theatre** (Société f des) Amis du Théâtre National ; (Rel) **Society of Friends** Société f des Amis

friendless ['frɛndlɪs] ADJ seul, isolé, sans amis

friendliness ['frɛndlɪnɪs] N gentillesse f

friendly ['frɛndlɪ] [1] ADJ a (= amiable) [person] gentil (**to sb** avec qn) ; [child] gentil, affectueux ; [cat, dog] affectueux ; [manner, smile, gesture, atmosphere, argument, fight] amical ; [face] avenant ; [welcome] chaleureux ; [service] sympathique ; [advice] d'ami ; [place] accueillant ; **that wasn't a very ~ thing to do** ce n'était pas très gentil de faire cela ; **unions ~**

to management syndicats favorables à la direction ; **to feel ~ towards sb** être bien disposé envers qn ; **it's nice to see a ~ face!** ça fait plaisir de voir un visage sympathique ! → **neighbourhood** b (= friends) **we're quite ~** nous sommes assez amis ; **to be ~ with sb** être ami avec qn ; **to become** or **get ~ with sb** se lier d'amitié avec qn ; **to be on ~ terms with sb** avoir des rapports d'amitié avec qn ; (sexually) **to get ~** se permettre des familiarités (pej) c (Pol) [country, nation, government] ami ; [port] de pays ami [2] N (also ~ **match**: Brit) → 3 [3] COMP ► **friendly fire** N (Mil, fig) tirs mpl de son propre camp ► **the Friendly Islands** NPL les îles fpl des Amis ► **friendly match** N (Sport) match m amical ► **friendly society** N (Brit) société f de prévoyance, mutuelle f

-friendly ['frɛndlɪ] ADJ (in compounds) **customer-friendly** [shop] soucieux de sa clientèle, accueillant ; [policy, prices] favorable aux consommateurs ; **child-friendly** [shop] aménagé pour les enfants ; [beach, kitchen] sûr or non dangereux pour les enfants ; **dolphin-friendly tuna** thon m pêché en respectant les dauphins ; **reader-friendly** soucieux de ses lecteurs → **environment, ozone, user**

friendship ['frɛndʃɪp] N amitié f ; **out of ~** par amitié

fries* [fraɪz] NPL (esp US) frites fpl

Friesian ['friːʒən] = **Frisian**

frieze¹ [friːz] N (Archit) frise f

frieze² [friːz] N (Tex) ratine f

frig: [frɪg] VI **to ~ about** or **around** déconner*

frigate ['frɪgɪt] N frégate f (Naut)

frigging** ['frɪgɪŋ] [1] ADV foutrement* [2] ADJ foutu*

fright [fraɪt] N a frayeur f, peur f ; **to take ~** prendre peur, s'effrayer (**at** de) ; **to get** or **have a ~** avoir peur ; **to get the ~ of one's life** avoir la frayeur de sa vie ; **to give sb a ~** faire peur à qn ; **it gave me such a ~** ça m'a fait une de ces peurs* or une belle peur → **stage** b (* = person) horreur* f, épouvantail m ; **she's** or **she looks a ~** elle est à faire peur

frighten ['fraɪtn] VT effrayer, faire peur à ; **did he ~ you?** est-ce qu'il vous a fait peur ? ; **it nearly ~ed him out of his wits*** or **his skin*** ◊ **it ~ed the life out of him*** cela lui a fait une peur bleue ; **to ~ sb into doing sth** faire peur à qn pour qu'il fasse qch ; **he was ~ed into doing it** il l'a fait sous le coup de la peur ; **she is easily ~ed** elle prend peur facilement, elle est peureuse

► **frighten away, frighten off** VT SEP [+ birds] effaroucher ; [+ children etc] chasser (en leur faisant peur) ; (fig) [+ buyers, investors etc] décourager (en leur faisant peur)

frightened ['fraɪtnd] ADJ effrayé ; **to be ~ (of sb/sth)** avoir peur (de qn/qch) ; **to be ~ of doing** or **to do sth** avoir peur de faire qch ; **to be ~ about (doing) sth** avoir peur à l'idée de (faire) qch ; **to be ~ that ...** avoir peur que ... ; **to be ~ to death* (that ...)** être mort de peur (que ...) ; **to be ~ to death* of sb/sth** avoir une peur bleue de qn/qch ; **to be ~ out of one's wits*** avoir une peur bleue ; **like a ~ rabbit** comme un animal effarouché

frighteners: ['fraɪtnəz] NPL (Brit) **to put the ~ on sb** foutre les jetons* à qn

frightening ['fraɪtnɪŋ] ADJ effrayant ; **it is ~ to think that ...** ça fait peur de penser que ...

frighteningly ['fraɪtnɪŋlɪ] ADV [ugly, thin] à faire peur ; [expensive] effroyablement ; **we came ~ close to losing all our money** nous avons vraiment failli perdre tout notre argent

frightful ['fraɪtfʊl] ADJ a (liter = horrifying) [sight, experience] épouvantable, effroyable b [† * = awful] [mistake, prospect, possibility, clothes, hat, wallpaper] affreux ; [person] détestable ; **he's a ~ bore** il est terriblement

ennuyeux ; **I know I'm being a ~ nuisance, but ...** je ne voudrais pas vous importuner davantage, mais ...

frightfully ['fraɪtfəlɪ] ADV a (liter = horrifyingly) [suffer] effroyablement b (Brit:† * = very) terriblement ; **I'm ~ sorry** je suis vraiment désolé ; **it's ~ nice of you** c'est vraiment trop gentil à vous

frightfulness ['fraɪtfʊlnɪs] N [of crime, situation, behaviour] atrocité f, horreur f

frigid ['frɪdʒɪd] ADJ a (sexually) frigide b (= unfriendly) [smile, stare, atmosphere, silence] glacial c (Geog, Met) glacial

frigidity [frɪˈdʒɪdɪtɪ] N (sexual) frigidité f ; (gen) froideur f

frill [frɪl] N [of dress] ruche f, volant m ; [of shirt front] jabot m ; [of cuff] ruche f ; (Culin) papillote f ; (fig) ~**s** chichis* mpl ; (fig) **without any ~s** [ceremony etc] simple, sans façon → **furbelow, no**

frilly ['frɪlɪ] ADJ [shirt, dress, cushion] à fanfreluches ; [underwear] à dentelle ; (fig) [style, speech] plein de fioritures

fringe [frɪndʒ] [1] N a (Brit = hair) frange f b [of rug, shawl] frange f c (= edge) [of forest] bordure f, lisière f ; [of crowd] derniers rangs mpl ; **on the ~ of the forest** en bordure de forêt, à la lisière de la forêt ; **to live on the ~(s) of society** vivre en marge de la société ; **a party on the ~(s) of British politics** un parti en marge de la politique britannique ; **the outer ~s** [of town] la périphérie → **lunatic** [2] VT a [+ rug, shawl] franger (**with** de) b (fig) **a lake ~d with trees** un lac bordé d'arbres [3] COMP ► **fringe area** N (TV) zone f limite (de réception) ► **fringe benefits** NPL avantages mpl divers ; (company car etc) avantages mpl en nature ► **fringe festival** N festival m off → EDINBURGH FESTIVAL ► **fringe group** N groupe m marginal ► **fringe meeting** N (Pol) réunion f d'un groupe marginal ► **fringe theatre** N (Brit) théâtre m d'avant-garde or expérimental ► **fringing reef** N (Geog) récif m frangeant

frippery ['frɪpərɪ] N (esp Brit: pej) (= cheap ornament) colifichets mpl ; (on dress) fanfreluches fpl ; (= ostentation) préciosité f, maniérisme m

Frisbee® ['frɪzbɪ] N frisbee® m

Frisian ['frɪʒən] [1] ADJ frison ; **the ~ Islands** les îles fpl Frisonnes [2] N a Frison(ne) m(f) b (Ling) frison m

frisk [frɪsk] [1] VI gambader [2] VT [+ criminal, suspect] fouiller

friskiness ['frɪskɪnɪs] N vivacité f

frisky ['frɪskɪ] ADJ (= lively) vif, sémillant ; (hum) **to be feeling ~** (sexually) être d'humeur folâtre

frisson ['friːsɒn] N frisson m

fritillary [frɪˈtɪlərɪ] N fritillaire f

fritter¹ ['frɪtəʳ] VT (also ~ **away**) [+ money, time, energy] gaspiller

fritter² ['frɪtəʳ] N (Culin) beignet m ; **apple ~** beignet m aux pommes

fritz: [frɪts] (US) N **on the ~** en panne ► **fritz out:** VI tomber en panne

frivolity [frɪˈvɒlɪtɪ] N frivolité f

frivolous ['frɪvələs] ADJ [person, object, activity] (= lighthearted) frivole ; (= futile) futile ; [attitude, behaviour, remark] frivole, léger

frivolously ['frɪvələslɪ] ADV de façon frivole, frivolement

frizz [frɪz] VT [+ hair] faire friser or frisotter

frizzle ['frɪzl] [1] VI grésiller [2] VT [+ food] faire trop griller, laisser brûler or calciner ; **a man with ~d white hair** un homme aux cheveux blancs frisés

frizzy ['frɪzɪ] ADJ [hair] crépu, crêpelé

fro [frəʊ] ADV **to and ~** de long en large ; **to go to and ~** aller et venir ; **to and ~ between** aller et venir entre, faire la navette entre; **journeys to and ~ between London and Edinburgh** allers *mpl* et retours *mpl* entre Londres et Edimbourg

frock [frɒk] **1** N **a** † [*of woman, baby*] robe *f* **b** [*of monk*] froc† *m* **2** COMP ► **frock coat** N redingote *f*

frog¹ [frɒg] **1** N **a** (*Zool*) grenouille *f*; (*fig*) **to have a ~ in one's throat** avoir un chat dans la gorge **b** (*pej*) **Frog:** franchouillard(e)* *m(f)* (*pej*), Français(e) *m(f)* **2** COMP ► **frog-march** VT **to ~-march sb in/out** *etc* (= *hustle*) faire entrer/sortir qn de force ► **frogs' legs** NPL (*Culin*) cuisses *fpl* de grenouilles

frog² [frɒg] N (*Dress*) brandebourg *m*, soutache *f*

frogging ['frɒgɪŋ] N (*Dress*) soutaches *fpl*

Froggy: ['frɒgɪ] N (*Brit pej*) franchouillard(e)* *m(f)* (*pej*), Français(e) *m(f)*

frogman ['frɒgmən] N (*pl* **-men**) homme-grenouille *m*

frogspawn ['frɒgspɔːn] N frai *m* de grenouille

frolic ['frɒlɪk] **1** VI (*also* **~ about**, **~ around**) [*people*] (*gen, hum*) batifoler*; [*lambs*] gambader **2** N [*of lambs*] gambades *fpl*; (= *prank*) espièglerie *f*, gaminerie *f*; (= *merrymaking*) ébats *mpl*; (*hum: sexual*) batifolage *m*

frolicsome ['frɒlɪksəm] ADJ folâtre, badin

from [frɒm] PREP **a** (*place: starting point*) de; **~ house to house** de maison en maison; **~ town to town** de ville en ville; **to jump ~ a wall** sauter d'un mur; **to travel ~ London to Paris** voyager de Londres à Paris; **train ~ Manchester** train *m* (en provenance) de Manchester; **programme transmitted ~ Lyons** émission *f* retransmise depuis Lyon; **he comes ~ London** il vient de Londres, il est (originaire) de Londres; **he comes ~ there** il en vient; **where are you ~?** ◊ **where do you come ~?** d'où êtes-vous (originaire)?; **I see where you're coming ~*** (= *understand*) je comprends maintenant **b** (*time: starting point*) à partir de, de; **(as) ~ 14 July** à partir du 14 juillet; **~ that day onwards** à partir de ce jour-là; **~ beginning to end** du début (jusqu')à la fin; **~ her childhood onwards ...** dès son enfance ...; **~ time to time** de temps en temps; **~ day to day** de jour en jour; **~ year to year** d'année en année; **counting ~ last Monday** à dater de lundi dernier; **five years ~ now** dans cinq ans **c** (*distance: lit, fig*) de; **the house is 10km ~ the coast** la maison est à 10 km de la côte; **it is 10km ~ here** c'est à 10 km de là; **to go away ~ home** quitter la maison; **not far ~ here** pas loin d'ici; **far ~ blaming you** loin de vous le reprocher **d** (*origin = coming from*) de, de la part de; (= *inspired by*) d'après; **a letter ~ my mother** une lettre de ma mère; **tell him ~ me** dites-lui de ma part; **an invitation ~ the Smiths** une invitation (de la part) des Smith; **memories ~ his childhood** des souvenirs *mpl* de son enfance; **painted ~ life** peint d'après nature; **a picture by Picasso** d'après un tableau de Picasso **e** (*used with prices, numbers*) à partir de, depuis; **wine ~ 10 francs a bottle** vins à partir de 10 F la bouteille; **there were ~ 10 to 15 people there** il y avait là entre 10 et 15 personnes *or* de 10 à 15 personnes; (*Math*) **take 12 ~ 18** soustrayez 12 de 18; (*Math*) **3 ~ 8 leaves 5** 8 moins 3 égalent 5 **f** (*source*) **to drink ~ a stream/a glass** boire à un ruisseau/dans un verre; **to drink straight ~ the bottle** boire à (même) la bouteille; **he took it ~ the cupboard** il l'a pris dans le placard; **he put the box down and took a book ~ it** il a posé la caisse et en a sorti *or* tiré un livre; **to take sth ~ a shelf** prendre qch sur une étagère; **to pick sb ~ the crowd** choisir qn dans la foule; **a quotation ~ Racine** une citation (tirée) de Racine; **here's an extract ~ it** en voici un extrait; **to speak ~ notes** parler avec des notes; **~ your point of view** à *or* de votre point de vue; **to draw a conclusion ~**

the information tirer une conclusion des renseignements **g** (*prevention, escape, deprivation etc*) à, de; **take the knife ~ that child!** enlevez *or* prenez le couteau à cet enfant!; **he took/stole it ~ them** il le leur a pris/volé; **he prevented me ~ coming** il m'a empêché de venir; **the news was kept ~ her** on lui a caché la nouvelle; **to shelter ~ the rain** s'abriter de la pluie **h** (*change*) de; **~ bad to worse** de mal en pis; **price increase ~ one franc to one franc fifty** augmentation de prix d'un franc à un franc cinquante; **he went ~ office boy to director in five years** de garçon de bureau, il est passé directeur en cinq ans **i** (*cause, reason*) **to die ~ fatigue** mourir de fatigue; **he died ~ his injuries** il est mort des suites de ses blessures; **~ what I heard ...** d'après ce que j'ai entendu ...; **~ what I can see ...** à ce que je vois ...; **~ the look of things ...** à en juger par les apparences ...; **~ the way he talks you would think that ...** à l'entendre, on penserait que ... **j** (*difference*) de; **he is quite different ~ the others** il est complètement différent des autres; **to distinguish the good ~ the bad** distinguer le bon du mauvais **k** (*with other preps and advs*) **seen ~ above** vu d'en haut; **~ above the clouds** au-dessus des nuages; **I saw him ~ afar** je l'ai vu de loin; **she was looking at him ~ over the wall** elle le regardait depuis l'autre côté du mur; **~ under the table** de dessous la table

frond [frɒnd] N [*of fern*] fronde *f*; [*of palm*] feuille *f*

front [frʌnt] **1** N **a** (= *leading section*) [*of boat, car, train etc*] avant *m*; [*of class, crowd, audience*] premier rang *m*; (= *part facing forward*) [*of cupboard, shirt, dress*] devant *m*; [*of building*] façade *f*, devant *m*; [*of book*] (= *beginning*) début *m*; (= *cover*) couverture *f*; [*of postcard, photo*] recto *m*; **in ~** [*be, stand, walk, put*] devant; [*send, move, look*] en avant; **in ~ of the table** devant la table; **to send sb on in ~** envoyer qn en avant; **he was walking in ~** il marchait devant; (*Sport*) **to be in ~** mener; (*fig*) **to come to the ~** se faire connaître *or* remarquer, percer; **to sit in the ~ (of the car)** ◊ **to sit in ~** être assis à l'avant (de la voiture); **to sit in the ~ of the train/bus** s'asseoir en tête de *or* à l'avant du bus; **in the ~ of the class** au premier rang de la classe; **let's go and sit up ~** allons nous asseoir devant; **in the ~ of the book** au début du livre; **she was lying on her ~** elle était couchée sur le ventre; **it fastens at the ~** cela se ferme devant; **she spilt it down the ~ of her dress** elle l'a renversé sur le devant de sa robe; **he pushed his way to the ~ of the crowd** il s'est frayé un chemin jusqu'au premier rang de la foule **b** (*Mil, Pol*) front *m*; **to fall at the ~** mourir au front; **there was fighting on several ~s** on se battait sur plusieurs fronts; (*gen, Mil, Pol etc*) **on all ~s** sur tous les fronts, de tous côtés; (*Pol, fig*) **we must present a common ~** nous devons offrir un front uni, il faut faire front commun → **home c** (*Met*) front *m*; **cold/warm ~** front *m* froid/chaud **d** (*Brit: also* **sea ~**) (= *beach*) bord *m* de mer, plage *f*; (= *prom*) front *m* de mer; **along the ~** (= *on the beach*) en bord de mer; (= *on the prom*) sur le front de mer; **a house on the ~** une maison sur le front de mer **e** (*liter* = *forehead*) front *m* **f** [*of spy, criminal*] couverture *f* (*fig*); (*fig*) **it's all just a ~ with him** ◊ **he's just putting on a ~** ce n'est qu'une façade; **he's putting on a brave ~** il fait bonne contenance **2** ADJ **a** de devant, (en) avant; **~ garden** jardin *m* de devant; **on the ~ cover** en couverture; **~ door** [*of house*] porte *f* d'entrée *or* principale; [*of car*] porte *f* avant; **in the ~ end**

of the train en tête de *or* du train, à l'avant du train; (*Mil*) **~ line(s)** front *m*; (*fig*) **to be in the ~ line** être en première ligne, être aux avant-postes; (*Press*) **the ~ page** la première page, la une*; (*Press*) **on the ~ page** en première page, à la une* → **6**; **the ~ panel** [*of machine*] le panneau de devant, la face avant; (*fig*) **in the ~ rank** parmi les premiers; **~ room** pièce *f* donnant sur la rue, pièce *f* de devant; (= *lounge*) salon *m*; **in the ~ row** au premier rang; **to have a ~ seat** (*lit*) avoir une place (assise) au premier rang; (*fig*) être aux premières loges (*fig*); **~ tooth** dent *f* de devant; **~ wheel** roue *f* avant → **6**; → **row¹ b** de face; **~ view** vue *f* de face; (*Archit*) **~ elevation** élévation *f* frontale **3** ADV par devant; **to attack ~ and rear** attaquer par devant et par derrière; (*Mil*) **eyes ~!** fixe! **4** VI **a** **to ~ on to** donner sur; **the house ~s north** la maison fait face *or* est exposée au nord; **the windows ~ on to the street** les fenêtres donnent sur la rue **b** **to ~ for sb** servir de façade à qn **5** VT **a** [+ *building*] donner une façade à; **house ~ed with stone** maison *f* avec façade en pierre **b** (*Brit* = *lead, head*) [+ *company, organization, team*] diriger, être à la tête de; [+ *rock group*] être le chanteur *or* la chanteuse de **c** (*TV*) [+ *show*] présenter **6** COMP ► **the front bench** N (*Brit Parl* = *people*) (*government*) les ministres *mpl*; (*opposition*) les membres *mpl* du cabinet fantôme ► **the front benches** NPL (*Brit Parl*) (= *place*) le banc des ministres et celui des membres du cabinet fantôme; (= *people*) ≈ les chefs de file des partis politiques ► **front burner** N **to be on the ~ burner** être une question prioritaire, être au centre des préoccupations; **it's on my ~ burner** j'y pense, je m'en occupe ► **front crawl** N (*Swimming*) crawl *m* ► **front-end financing** N financement *m* initial ► **front-end payment** N versement *m* initial ► **front-end processor** N (*Comput*) (processeur *m*) frontal *m* ► **front-line** ADJ [*troops, news*] du front; [*countries, areas*] limitrophe *or* voisin (*d'un pays en guerre*) ► **front-line player** N (*US Sport*) avant *m* ► **front-loader, front-loading washing machine** N lave-linge *m* à chargement frontal ► **front matter** N pages *fpl* liminaires ► **front money** N acompte *m*, avance *f* ► **front office** N (*US Comm*) (= *place*) administration *f*; (= *managers*) direction *f* ► **front organization** N **it's merely a ~ organization** cette organisation n'est qu'une façade *or* une couverture ► **front-page news** N gros titres *mpl*, manchettes *fpl*; **it was ~-page news for a month** cela a fait la une* (des journaux) pendant un mois ► **front-rank** ADJ de premier plan ► **front runner** N (*Athletics*) coureur *m* de tête; **he is a ~ runner for the party leadership** c'est l'un des favoris pour la présidence du parti ► **front-to-back engine** N (*Aut*) moteur *m* longitudinal ► **front vowel** N (*Ling*) voyelle *f* antérieure ► **front-wheel drive** N (*Aut* = *car, system*) traction *f* avant

frontage ['frʌntɪdʒ] N [*of shop*] devanture *f*, façade *f*; [*of house*] façade *f*; (*US*) **~ road** contre-allée *f*

frontal ['frʌntl] **1** ADJ **a** (*Mil*) [*assault, attack*] de front; **to make a ~ assault** *or* **attack on sth** attaquer qch de front; (*Aut*) **~ impact** choc *m* frontal **b** (*Anat, Met*) frontal **c** [*nudity*] de face → **full 2** N (*Rel*) parement *m*

frontbencher [ˌfrʌnt'bentʃər] N (*Brit Parl*) (*government*) ministre *m*; (*opposition*) membre *m* du cabinet fantôme → BACKBENCHER

frontier ['frʌntɪər] **1** N (*lit, fig*) frontière *f*; **they're pushing back the ~s of science** ils font reculer les frontières de la science; (*US Hist*) **the ~** *la limite des terres colonisées*, la Frontière

2 COMP [town, zone] frontière inv; [tribe] frontalier ► **frontier dispute** N incident m de frontière ► **frontier post, frontier station** N poste m frontière ► **frontier technology** N (fig) technologie f de pointe

frontiersman ['frʌntɪəzmən] N (pl **-men**) (US Hist) habitant m de la Frontière → **frontier 1**

frontispiece ['frʌntɪspiːs] N frontispice m

frontman ['frʌntmən] N (pl **-men**) (TV etc) présentateur m

frontwards ['frʌntwədz] ADV en avant, vers l'avant

frosh* [frɒʃ] N (US Univ) ≈ bizut(h) m

frost [frɒst] 1 N gel m, gelée f; (also **hoarfrost**) givre m, gelée f blanche; **late ~s** gelées fpl tardives or de printemps; (Brit) **ten degrees of ~** dix degrés au-dessous de zéro → **ground**[1], **jack** 2 VT (= ice) [+ cake] glacer → **frosted** 3 COMP ► **frost-free** ADJ [fridge] à dégivrage automatique ► **frost over, frost up** VI [window] se givrer, se couvrir de givre

frostbite ['frɒstbaɪt] N engelures fpl; **to get ~ in one's hands** avoir les mains gelées

frostbitten ['frɒstbɪtn] ADJ [hands, feet] gelé; [rosebushes, vegetables] gelé, grillé par la gelée or le gel

frostbound ['frɒstbaʊnd] ADJ [ground] gelé

frosted ['frɒstɪd] 1 ADJ a (= frost-covered) [grass, plants, windows, windscreen] couvert de givre b (Cosmetics) [eyeshadow, nail varnish, lipstick] nacré c (Culin) (= iced) recouvert d'un glaçage; (= sugared) recouvert de sucre 2 COMP ► **frosted glass** N (for window) verre m dépoli; (for drink) verre m givré

frostily ['frɒstɪlɪ] ADV [greet, reply] sur un ton glacial; **she smiled ~ at him** elle lui a adressé un sourire glacial

frosting ['frɒstɪŋ] N (Culin) (= icing) glace f, glaçage m; (= icing sugar) sucre m glace

frosty ['frɒstɪ] ADJ a (= cold) [night, morning, weather] de gelée, glacial; [air, weather] glacial; **it is ~** il gèle b (= frost-covered) [ground, grass, window, windscreen] couvert de givre c (= unfriendly) [person] glacial, froid; [atmosphere, reception, response, relations, smile] glacial; [look] froid

froth [frɒθ] 1 N a [of liquids in general] écume f, mousse f; [of beer] mousse f; (around the mouth) écume f; **a ~ of lace** un bouillon de dentelle b (fig = frivolous talk) propos mpl frivoles, paroles fpl creuses; **his speech was all ~ and no substance** son discours n'était que du vent et n'avait aucune substance; **the novel is nothing but silly romantic** ~ ce roman est d'un romantisme mièvre et stupide; **falling in love the first time is all ~ and fantasy** les premières histoires d'amour sont pleines de rêves naïfs 2 VI écumer, mousser; **the beer ~ed over the edge of the glass** la mousse débordait du verre (de bière); **waves ~ed over the deck** des vagues passaient par-dessus le pont dans un nuage d'écume; **a cup of ~ing coffee** une tasse de café mousseux; **to ~ at the mouth** [dog] avoir de l'écume à la gueule; [angry person] écumer de rage

frothy ['frɒθɪ] ADJ a (= bubbly) [beer, milk shake, coffee, mixture] mousseux; [water] mousseux, écumeux; [sea] moutonneux b (= frilly) [dress, underwear, lace] léger, vaporeux c (= not serious) [operetta, comedy] léger

frown [fraʊn] 1 N froncement m (de sourcils); **to give a ~** froncer les sourcils; **he looked at her with a disapproving ~** il l'a regardée en fronçant les sourcils d'un air désapprobateur; **a puzzled/worried ~ crossed his face** il fronça les sourcils d'un air perplexe/inquiet 2 VI froncer les sourcils; **to ~ at sb** regarder qn en fronçant les sourcils; (at child) faire les gros yeux à qn; **he ~ed at the news/the interruption** la nouvelle/l'interruption l'a

fait tiquer

► **frown (up)on** VT FUS (fig) [+ person, suggestion, idea] désapprouver

frowning ['fraʊnɪŋ] ADJ [person, face, expression] renfrogné; [look, glance] sombre

frowsty* ['fraʊstɪ] ADJ (Brit) = **frowsy a**

frowsy, frowzy ['fraʊzɪ] ADJ a [room] qui sent le renfermé b [person, clothes] négligé, peu soigné

froze [frəʊz] VB pt of **freeze**

frozen ['frəʊzn] 1 VB ptp of **freeze** 2 ADJ a (lit) [lake, ground, pipe, corpse] gelé; **to be ~ solid** or **hard** être complètement gelé b (= preserved) [vegetables, meat, meal] (industrially) surgelé; (at home) congelé; [embryo, sperm] congelé c (* = very cold) [person, fingers] gelé; **I'm ~ (stiff)** je suis gelé (jusqu'aux os); **my hands are ~ (stiff)** j'ai les mains (complètement) gelées; **~ to death*** frigorifié* → **bone, marrow** d (= immobile) figé; **in horror/with fear** glacé d'horreur/de peur; **~ to the spot** cloué sur place; **~ in time** figé dans le temps e (Econ, Fin) [prices, wages, account, credit] gelé, bloqué 3 COMP ► **frozen assets** NPL (Fin) actifs mpl gelés or bloqués ► **frozen food** N (industrially) aliments mpl surgelés; (at home) aliments mpl congelés ► **frozen food compartment** N partie f congélateur ► **frozen shoulder** N (Med) épaule f ankylosée ► **frozen wastes** NPL déserts mpl de glace ► **frozen yoghurt** N glace f au yaourt

FRS [,efɑːr'es] (ABBR = **Fellow of the Royal Society**) ≈ membre m de l'Académie des sciences

fructification [,frʌktɪfɪ'keɪʃən] N fructification f

fructify ['frʌktɪfaɪ] VI fructifier

frugal ['fruːgəl] ADJ [person] (gen) économe (**with sth** de qch); (pej) pingre; [life, meal] frugal; **to be ~ with one's money** faire attention à la dépense; (pej) être pingre

frugality [fruː'gælɪtɪ] N [of meal] frugalité f; [of person] frugalité f; (fig) parcimonie f

frugally ['fruːgəlɪ] ADV [live] simplement; [eat] frugalement; [use] parcimonieusement

fruit [fruːt] 1 N a (collective n) fruit m; **may I have some ~?** puis-je avoir un fruit?; **a piece of ~** (= whole fruit) un fruit; (= segment) un morceau or quartier de fruit; **~ is good for you** les fruits sont bons pour la santé; **several ~s have large stones** plusieurs espèces de fruits ont de gros noyaux; **the ~s of the earth** les fruits de la terre; **to be in ~** [tree, bush] porter des fruits → **bear**[1], **dried, forbidden** b (= benefits) fruit m; **the ~(s) of his labour(s)** les fruits de son travail; **it is the ~ of much hard work** c'est le fruit d'un long travail; **the ~s of victory** les fruits de la victoire; **one of the main ~s of the meeting was ...** un des principaux acquis de la réunion a été ...; **to enjoy the ~s of one's success** savourer sa réussite; (liter) **the ~ of thy womb** or **loins** le fruit de tes entrailles → **bear**[1], **first, reap** c **hullo, old ~!**[†]* salut, mon pote!* d (US*: pej) pédé* m, tapette* f 2 VI [tree] donner 3 COMP ► **fruit basket** N corbeille f à fruits ► **fruit bat** N roussette f ► **fruit bowl** N coupe f à fruits ► **fruit cocktail** N macédoine f de fruits (en boîte) ► **fruit cup** N (drink) boisson f aux fruits (parfois faiblement alcoolisée); (US) (coupe f de) fruits mpl rafraîchis ► **fruit dish** N (for dessert) (small) petite coupe f or coupelle f à fruits; (large) coupe f à fruits, compotier m; (basket) corbeille f à fruits ► **fruit drop** N bonbon m au fruit ► **fruit farm** N exploitation f or entreprise f fruitière ► **fruit farmer** N arboriculteur m (fruitier) ► **fruit farming** N arboriculture f (fruitière), culture f fruitière ► **fruit fly** N mouche f du vinaigre, drosophile f ► **fruit**

gum N (Brit) boule f de gomme (bonbon) ► **fruit juice** N jus m de fruit(s) ► **fruit knife** N (pl **fruit knives**) couteau m à fruits ► **fruit machine** N (Brit) machine f à sous ► **fruit salad** N salade f de fruits ► **fruit salts** NPL (Med) sels mpl purgatifs ► **fruit tree** N arbre m fruitier

fruitcake ['fruːtkeɪk] N a (Culin) cake m b (Brit*: = eccentric person) cinglé(e)* m(f); **he's as nutty as a ~** il est complètement timbré*

fruiterer ['fruːtərər] N (Brit) marchand(e) m(f) de fruits, fruitier m, -ière f; **at the ~'s (shop)** chez le fruitier, à la fruiterie

fruitful ['fruːtfʊl] ADJ a (= profitable) [relationship, discussion, career] fructueux; [meeting] utile, fécond; [life] productif; **a ~ source of information** une mine de renseignements; **it would be more ~ to do that** il serait plus utile or avantageux de faire cela b [land, soil, plant] fécond (liter)

fruitfully ['fruːtfʊlɪ] ADV fructueusement

fruitfulness ['fruːtfʊlnɪs] N a [of discussion, partnership] caractère m fructueux or profitable b [of soil] fertilité f, fécondité f; [of plant] fécondité f

fruition [fruː'ɪʃən] N [of aims, plans, ideas] réalisation f; **to bring to ~** réaliser, concrétiser; **to come to ~** se réaliser

fruitless ['fruːtlɪs] ADJ a (= vain) [search, quest, effort, attempt, exercise] vain; [discussion, talks] stérile; **she spent a ~ morning trying to ...** elle a perdu toute une matinée à essayer de ...; **it is ~ to try** il est vain d'essayer b (= infertile) [plant] stérile

fruity ['fruːtɪ] ADJ a (= like fruit) [flavour, taste, smell] fruité, de fruit; [wine, oil] fruité b (= mellow) [voice] bien timbré; [laugh] chaleureux c (Brit* = lewd) [remark] salé; [joke] corsé, salé d (* = crazy) dingue* e (US*: pej = homosexual) homo*

frump [frʌmp] N bonne femme f mal fagotée or mal ficelée*; **old ~** vieux tableau m, vieille sorcière f or rombière* f

frumpish ['frʌmpɪʃ], **frumpy** ['frʌmpɪ] ADJ mal fagoté, mal ficelé*

frustrate [frʌs'treɪt] VT a (= thwart) [+ attempts, plans] contrecarrer, faire échouer; [+ plot] déjouer, faire échouer; **he was ~d in his efforts to win** malgré tous ses efforts, il n'a pas réussi à gagner; **to ~ sb's hopes** frustrer or tromper les espoirs de qn; **a stumbling block which has ~d the peace process** un obstacle qui a entravé le processus de paix; **rescuers were ~d in their search by bad weather** (= hindered) le mauvais temps a gêné les sauveteurs dans leurs recherches; (= stopped) le mauvais temps a empêché les sauveteurs de mener leurs recherches à bien b (= irritate, annoy) [+ person] contrarier, énerver; **it really ~s me when people interrupt me** ça me contrarie or ça m'énerve que l'on m'interrompe

frustrated [frʌs'treɪtɪd] ADJ a (= thwarted, unfulfilled) [person, love, desire] frustré; [ambition] déçu, contrarié; **in a ~ effort to speak to him** dans une vaine effort pour lui parler; **he's a ~ poet/intellectual** c'est un poète/un intellectuel frustré or manqué; **to be ~ in one's ambitions** être frustré dans ses ambitions; **he feels very ~ in his present job** il se sent très frustré dans son poste actuel b (= irritated) énervé; **I get ~ when people criticize my work** cela m'énerve quand les gens critiquent mon travail c (sexually) frustré

frustrating [frʌs'treɪtɪŋ] ADJ [situation, experience, morning] contrariant; **how ~! I've lost my keys** que c'est contrariant, j'ai perdu mes clés!; **it's very ~ having** or **to have no money** c'est vraiment frustrant de ne pas avoir d'argent

frustration [frʌs'treɪʃən] N frustration f (also Psych)

fry¹ [fraɪ] COLLECTIVE N [*of fish*] fretin *m*; [*of frogs*] têtards *mpl* → **small**

fry² [fraɪ] (*pret, ptp* **fried**) [1] VT [+ *meat, fish, vegetables, bread*] (= *deep-fry*) (faire) frire; (= *shallow-fry*) faire revenir; **to ~ eggs** faire des œufs sur le plat; **fried eggs** œufs *mpl* sur le plat; **fried fish** poisson *m* frit; **fried food is fattening** les fritures *fpl* font grossir; **fried potatoes** (= *chips*) pommes *fpl* (de terre) frites; (= *sauté*) pommes *fpl* (de terre) sautées; **fried rice** ≈ riz *m* frit, riz *m* cantonais → **fish, French** [2] VI frire [3] N friture *f* [4] COMP ► **fry-pan** N (*US*) poêle *f* (à frire) ► **fry-up*** N (*Brit* = *dish*) plat composé de saucisses, œufs, bacon etc cuits à la poêle

frying ['fraɪɪŋ] [1] N **there was a smell of ~** il y avait une odeur de friture [2] COMP ► **frying pan** N poêle *f* (à frire); (*fig*) **to jump out of the ~ pan into the fire** tomber de mal en pis, tomber de Charybde en Scylla (*liter*) ► **frying steak** N steak *m* (à frire)

f-stop ['ɛfstɒp] N (*Phot*) ouverture *f* (du diaphragme)

FT [ɛf'tiː] (ABBR = **Financial Times**) → **financial**

ft. ABBR = **foot** *or* **feet**

FTSE 100 index [ˌfʊtsɪwʌn,hʌndrəd'ɪndɛks] N (*Brit St Ex*) indice *m* FTSE *or* FT

fuchsia ['fjuːʃə] N fuchsia *m*

fuck** [fʌk] [1] N (= *act*) baise** *f*; **she's a good ~** c'est un bon coup*; [b] **charge me? like ~ (you will)!** moi payer? mon cul!**; **~ knows!** je n'en sais foutrement rien!* [c] (*US* = *person*) **you dumb ~!** espèce de pauvre débile*! [2] VT baiser**; **~!** ◊ **~ it!** putain de merde!**; **~ me!** putain!*, merde alors!*; **~ you!** va te faire foutre!** [3] VI baiser** [4] COMP ► **fuck-all**** N (*Brit*) rien *m* de rien; **I know ~-all about it** j'en sais foutrement rien ► **fuck about****, **fuck around** [1] VI déconner*; **to ~ about** *or* **around with sth** tripoter* qch [2] VT SEP emmerder* ► **fuck off**** VI foutre le camp*; **~ off!** va te faire foutre!**, va te faire enculer!** ► **fuck up**** [1] VT SEP [+ *plans*] foutre la merde dans*; [+ *people*] foutre dans la merde* [2] VI merder*

fucker** ['fʌkə] N connard* *m*, connasse* *f*

fucking** ['fʌkɪŋ] [1] ADJ **~ hell!** putain de bordel!**, putain de merde!**; **~ bastard/bitch** espèce *f* de salaud**/salope**; **this ~ machine** cette putain* de machine; **this ~ phone** ce putain* de téléphone; **where's the ~ phonebook?** où est le foutu* annuaire?; **I haven't a ~ clue** je n'en sais foutrement* rien [2] ADV foutrement*; **it's ~ cold** il fait un putain* de froid; **this is a ~ great idea** c'est une putain* de bonne idée; **it's ~ brilliant!** putain*, c'est génial *or* chié!; **don't be ~ stupid!** fais pas le con*!; **you ~ well know what I mean!** mais putain*, tu sais très bien ce que je veux dire!; **I don't ~ know!** j'en sais foutrement* rien!; **I don't ~ believe this!** putain, c'est pas possible!*

fuckwit** ['fʌkwɪt] N peigne-cul* *m*

fuddled ['fʌdld] ADJ [*ideas*] embrouillé, confus; [*person*] (= *muddled*) désorienté, déconcerté; (= *tipsy*) éméché, gris

fuddy-duddy* ['fʌdɪ,dʌdɪ] [1] ADJ (= *old-fashioned*) [*person, ideas*] vieux jeu *inv*; (= *fussy*) [*person*] tatillon, maniaque [2] N vieux machin* *m*, vieux (vieille *f*) schnock* *mf or* schnoque* *mf*

fudge [fʌdʒ] [1] N [a] (*Culin*) caramel(s) *m(pl)*; **a piece of ~** un caramel [b] (*Press*) (= *space for stop press*) emplacement *m* de la dernière heure; (= *stop press news*) (insertion *f* de) dernière heure, dernières nouvelles *fpl* [c] (* = *dodging*) faux-fuyants *mpl*, échappatoires *fpl*; **the wording is a total ~** le libellé est très vague *or* flou [2] EXCL* baliverses! (*liter*) [3] VT* [a] (= *fake up*) [+ *story, excuse*] monter; (= *tamper with*) [+

accounts, figures, results] truquer [b] (= *dodge*) [+ *question, issue*] esquiver, tourner [4] VI (* = *dodge issue*) esquiver le problème

fuel [fjʊəl] [1] N (*NonC*) (*Aviat, Space, also for heating*) combustible *m*; (*for car engine*) carburant *m*; **what kind of ~ do you use in your central heating?** quel combustible utilisez-vous dans votre chauffage central?; **it's no longer a cheap ~** ce n'est plus une forme *or* une source d'énergie économique; (*fig*) **to add ~ to the flames** *or* **fire** jeter de l'huile sur le feu; **the statistics gave him ~ for further attacks on the government** les statistiques lui ont fourni des munitions pour renforcer ses attaques contre le gouvernement [2] VT [a] [+ *stove, furnace*] alimenter (en combustible); [+ *ships, aircraft*] ravitailler (en combustible *or* carburant) [b] (*fig*) [+ *anger, tension, speculation, controversy, fears*] attiser [3] VI [*ship, engine, aircraft*] s'approvisionner *or* se ravitailler en combustible *or* en carburant; (*Aviat etc*) **a ~ling stop** une escale technique [4] COMP [*bill, costs*] de chauffage ► **fuel-efficient** ADJ économique ► **fuel gauge** N (*Aut, Aviat*) jauge *f* de carburant ► **fuel injection** N injection *f* (de carburant) ► **fuel injection engine** N moteur *m* à injection ► **fuel injector** N injecteur *m* (de carburant) ► **fuel oil** N mazout *m*, fioul *m* ► **fuel pump** N pompe *f* d'alimentation ► **fuel rod** N crayon *m* combustible ► **fuel saving** N économies *fpl* de carburant (*or* de combustible *etc*) ► **fuel-saving** ADJ qui réduit la consommation de carburant (*or* de combustible *etc*) ► **fuel-saving device** N (*Aut*) économiseur *m* de carburant ► **fuel tank** N réservoir *m* à carburant; [*of ship*] soute *f* à mazout

fug* [fʌg] N (*esp Brit* = *smell*) (*stale*) forte odeur *f* de renfermé; (*smoky*) forte odeur *f* de fumée; **what a ~!** (*ce que*) ça pue le renfermé *or* la fumée!

fuggy* ['fʌgɪ] ADJ (*esp Brit*) [*room*] (= *stale*) qui sent le renfermé, mal aéré; (= *smoky*) enfumé; [*atmosphere*] confiné

fugitive ['fjuːdʒɪtɪv] [1] N fugitif *m*, -ive *f*, fuyard(e) *m(f)*; **he was a ~ from justice** il fuyait la justice [2] ADJ [a] (= *running away*) [*person*] fugitif, en fuite [b] (*liter* = *fleeting*) [*thought, impression*] fugitif; [*happiness*] fugace, éphémère

fugue [fjuːg] N (*Mus, Psych*) fugue *f*

fulcrum ['fʌlkrəm] N (*pl* **fulcrums** *or* **fulcra** ['fʌlkrə]) [a] (*lit*) pivot *m*, point *m* d'appui [b] (*fig*) pivot *m*; **she is the ~ of our team** elle est le pivot de notre équipe

fulfil, fulfill (*US*) [fʊl'fɪl] VT [+ *task, prophecy*] accomplir, réaliser; [+ *order*] exécuter; [+ *condition, function*] remplir; [+ *plan, ambition*] réaliser; [+ *desire*] satisfaire, répondre à; [+ *promise*] tenir; [+ *one's duties*] s'acquitter de, remplir; [+ *contract*] remplir, respecter; **all my prayers have been ~led** toutes mes prières ont été exaucées; **he ~s all my hopes** il répond à *or* satisfait toutes mes espérances, il comble tous mes espoirs; **to feel** *or* **be ~led** se sentir profondément satisfait, se réaliser (dans la vie)

fulfilling [fʊl'fɪlɪŋ] ADJ [*job, career, experience, life*] épanouissant

fulfilment, fulfillment (*US*) [fʊl'fɪlmənt] N [*of duty, desire*] accomplissement *m*; [*of prayer, wish*] exaucement *m*; [*of conditions, plans*] réalisation *f*, exécution *f*; (= *satisfied feeling*) épanouissement *m*, (sentiment *m* de) contentement *m*; **to have a sense of ~** se sentir *or* être épanoui

full [fʊl]

[1]	ADJECTIVE	[3]	NOUN
[2]	ADVERB	[4]	COMPOUNDS

[1] ADJECTIVE

[a] = **filled** [*container, stomach*] plein, rempli;

[*room, hall, theatre*] comble, plein; [*hotel, bus, train*] complet (-ète *f*); **we're ~ (up) for July** nous sommes complets pour juillet; (= *not hungry*) **I'm ~ (up)!*** je n'en peux plus!, j'ai trop mangé!; **you'll work better on a ~ stomach** tu travailleras mieux le ventre plein *or* après avoir mangé; (*Theat*) **to play to a ~ house** jouer à guichets fermés; (*Theat*) **"house ~"** « complet »; **I have a ~ day/morning ahead of me** j'ai une journée/matinée chargée devant moi; **he's had a ~ life** il a eu une vie (bien) remplie; (*liter*) **his heart was ~** il avait le cœur gros

♦ **full of** plein de; **pockets ~ of money** des poches pleines d'argent; **the house was ~ of people** la maison était pleine de monde; **she was/the papers were ~ of the murder** elle ne parlait/les journaux ne parlaient que du meurtre; **a look ~ of hate** un regard plein *or* chargé de haine; **he's ~ of hope** il est plein *or* rempli d'espoir; **he's ~ of good ideas** il est plein de *or* il déborde de bonnes idées; **~ of one's own importance** pénétré de son importance, plein de suffisance; **~ of oneself** imbu de soi-même; (*liter*) **to die ~ of years** mourir chargé d'ans (*liter*) → **life**

[b] = **complete** **I waited two ~ hours** j'ai attendu deux bonnes heures; **a ~ 10 kilometres** 10 bons kilomètres, pas moins de 10 kilomètres; **~ employment** plein emploi *m*; **to pay ~ fare** payer plein tarif; **in ~ flight** en plein vol; **~ and frank discussions** un franc échange de vues; **ask for ~ information** demandez des renseignements complets; **we must have ~er information** il nous faut des informations plus complètes *or* un complément d'information; **until ~er information is available** en attendant d'en savoir plus; **the ~ particulars** tous les détails; **to pay ~ price for sth** (*for goods*) acheter qch au prix fort; (*for tickets, fares*) payer qch plein tarif; **at ~ speed** à toute vitesse; **~ speed ahead** ◊ **~ steam ahead!** (*Naut*) en avant toute!; (*fig*) **to go ~ steam ahead** avancer à plein régime; **battalion at ~ strength** bataillon *m* au (grand) complet; **in ~ uniform** en grande tenue → **4**

[c] in titles **a ~ colonel** un colonel; **a ~ general** un général d'armée; ≈ un général à cinq étoiles; **~ member** membre *m* à part entière; (*Univ: esp US*) **~ professor** professeur *m* (titulaire d'une chaire)

[d] = **ample** [*lips*] charnu; [*face*] plein, joufflu; [*figure*] replet (-ète *f*), rondelet; [*skirt, trousers, blouse*] large, ample; (*Naut*) [*sails*] plein, gonflé; **clothes for the ~er figure** des vêtements pour personnes fortes

[2] ADVERB

to hit sb ~ in the face frapper qn en plein visage; **to look sb ~ in the face** regarder qn droit dans les yeux; **to go ~ out** mettre la gomme*; **to turn the volume/sound up ~** mettre le volume/le son à fond; **~ well** [*know, understand*] fort bien, parfaitement; **to realize ~ well that ...** se rendre parfaitement compte que ...

[3] NOUN

to write one's name in ~ écrire son nom en entier; **to publish a letter in ~** publier une lettre intégralement; **text in ~** texte *m* intégral; **he paid in ~** il a tout payé; **to the ~** pleinement → **life**

[4] COMPOUNDS

► **full beam** N (*Brit Aut*) **to drive (with one's headlights) on ~ beam** rouler en pleins phares ► **full-blooded** ADJ (= *vigorous*) [*person*] vigoureux, robuste; (= *of unmixed race*) de race pure ► **full-blown** ADJ [*flower*] épanoui; (*fig*) [*crisis, disaster, war, epidemic*] généralisé; **he has ~-blown Aids** il a un sida avéré *or* déclaré; **he's a ~-blown doctor/architect** il est médecin/architecte diplômé ► **full-bodied** ADJ [*wine*] qui a du corps ► **full-court press** N (*US fig*) **to give sb the ~-court press*** exercer une forte pression sur qn ► **full-cream milk** N lait *m* entier *or* non écrémé ► **full dress** N (*Mil*) grande tenue *f*; (= *evening dress*) tenue *f* de soirée ► **full-dress** ADJ [*clothes*] de cérémonie; (*Parl*) ~-dress debate débat *m* dans les règles; they had a ~-dress discussion on what should be done ils ont eu un débat de fond pour décider de la conduite à tenir ► **full-face** ADJ [*photograph*] de face; [*helmet*] intégral ► **full-fashioned** ADJ (*US*) = fully-fashioned; → **fully** ► **full-fledged** ADJ (*US*) = fully-fledged; → **fully** ► **full frontal** N nu *m* intégral de face ► **full-frontal** ADJ [*photograph*] d'un nu intégral de face; [*view*] de face; ~-frontal assault *or* attack attaque *f* de front ► **full-grown** ADJ [*child*] parvenu au terme de sa croissance; [*animal, man, woman*] adulte ► **full house** N (*Cards*) full *m* ► **full-length** ADJ [*portrait, mirror*] en pied; [*dress, coat*] long; [*curtains*] tombant jusqu'au sol; [*film*] (de) long métrage ► **full moon** N pleine lune *f* ► **full name** N nom *m* et prénom(s) *m(pl)* ► **full-page** ADJ [*advert, article*] (en) pleine page ► **full pay** N to be suspended on ~ pay être suspendu de ses fonctions sans perte de salaire ► **full-scale** ADJ → full-scale ► **full score** N (*Mus*) grande partition *f*; (*Brit Sport*) = full-time score ► **full-size(d)** ADJ (= *life-sized*) [*model, drawing*] grandeur nature *inv*; (= *adult-sized*) [*bicycle, violin, bed*] en grandeur réelle ► **full stop** N (*Brit Gram*) point *m*; (*fig*) I'm not going, ~ stop!* je n'y vais pas, un point c'est tout!; his career seems to have come to a ~ stop il semble que sa carrière soit au point mort ► **full-strength** ADJ [*cigarettes*] très fort; [*solution*] non dilué ► **full term** N to come *or* go to ~ term [*baby*] arriver à terme; [*pregnancy*] arriver à terme, être mené à terme ♦ ADV to be carried ~ term [*baby*] arriver à terme; to go ~ term [*woman*] accoucher à terme ► **full-term** ADJ [*baby*] né à terme; [*pregnancy, delivery, birth*] à terme ► **full-throated** ADJ [*laugh, shout*] retentissant ► **full time** ADV [*work*] à temps plein, à plein temps ♦ N (*Brit Sport*) fin *f* de match ► **full-time** ADJ [*employment*] à plein temps; she's a ~-time secretary elle est secrétaire à plein temps; it's a ~-time job looking after those children* s'occuper de ces enfants est un travail à temps plein; (*Sport*) ~-time score score *m* final ► **full word** N (*Ling*) mot *m* principal

fullback ['fʊlbæk] N (*Sport*) arrière *m*
fuller's earth [,fʊləz'ɜːθ] N terre *f* savonneuse
fullness ['fʊlnɪs] N a [*of details*] abondance *f*; [*of description*] (*in novel, story*) richesse *f*; [*of voice, sound, garment*] ampleur *f*; the police were impressed by the ~ of her description of the suspect la police a été impressionnée par l'exhaustivité de sa description du suspect; ~ of flavour richesse *f* de goût; this cut gives some ~ to the hairstyle cette coupe donne du volume *or* du gonflant à la coiffure b (*liter*) out of the ~ of his sorrow le cœur débordant de chagrin; in the ~ of time (= *eventually*) avec le temps; (= *at predestined time*) en temps et lieu
full-scale ['fʊl'skeɪl] ADJ a (= *thorough-going*) [*war, conflict*] total, généralisé; [*riot*] véritable; [*attack, search, negotiations, debate, investigation*] de grande envergure; [*review, retreat*] complet (-ète *f*); [*industrial production*] à plein rendement b (= *life-size*) [*drawing, model, replica*] grandeur nature *inv*
fully ['fʊlɪ] 1 ADV a (= *completely*) [*use, load*] au maximum, à plein; [*justify*] complètement; [*understand*] très bien; [*convinced, satisfied*] entièrement, complètement → **laden** b (= *at least*) au moins, bien; ~ 600 600 au moins; ~ half une bonne moitié, la moitié au moins; it is ~ two hours since he went out il y a au moins *or* bien deux heures qu'il est sorti 2 COMP ► **fully-fashioned** ADJ (*Dress*) moulant ► **fully-fitted kitchen** N cuisine *f*

entièrement équipée ► **fully-fledged** ADJ a ~-fledged bird oiseau *m* qui a toutes ses plumes b (*fig*) [*system*] véritable, à part entière; (*Brit*) he's now a ~-fledged doctor/architect il est maintenant médecin/architecte diplômé; (*Brit*) a ~-fledged British citizen un citoyen britannique à part entière
fulmar ['fʊlmər] N fulmar *m*
fulminate ['fʌlmɪneɪt] 1 VI fulminer, pester (against contre) 2 COMP ► **fulminate of mercury** N fulminate *m* de mercure
fulmination [,fʊlmɪ'neɪʃən] N (*also* ~s) invective(s) *f(pl)* (against sb/sth contre qn/qch)
fulness ['fʊlnɪs] N = fullness
fulsome ['fʊlsəm] ADJ (*gen pej* = *extravagant*) [*praise, tribute, welcome, compliments, thanks*] outré, excessif; [*tone*] excessivement élogieux; [*manner*] obséquieux; to be ~ in one's praise faire des éloges outrés
fulsomely ['fʊlsəmlɪ] ADV abondamment, excessivement
fumarole ['fjuːmərəʊl] N fumerolle *f*
fumble ['fʌmbl] 1 VI (*also* ~ about, around) (*in the dark*) tâtonner; (*in one's pockets*) fouiller; to ~ (about) for sth in the dark chercher qch à tâtons dans l'obscurité; to ~ (about) for sth in a pocket/a drawer fouiller dans une poche/un tiroir pour trouver qch; to ~ with sth manier *or* tripoter qch (maladroitement); to ~ for words chercher ses mots 2 VT [+ *object*] manier gauchement *or* maladroitement; he ~d the key in the lock il tentait maladroitement d'engager la clé dans la serrure; (*Sport*) to ~ the ball mal attraper la balle; their fumbling attempts to arrange a settlement leurs tentatives maladroites pour arriver à un accord; I ~d the question I was trying to ask je me suis emmêlé les pinceaux* en essayant de poser ma question
fume [fjuːm] 1 VI a [*liquids, gases*] exhaler des vapeurs, fumer b (* = *be furious*) rager; he's fuming il est furibard* *or* furax* *inv* 2 N ~s (*gen*) exhalaisons *fpl*, émanations *fpl*; factory ~s fumées *fpl* d'usine; petrol ~s vapeurs *fpl* d'essence; car exhaust ~s gaz *m* d'échappement
fumigate ['fjuːmɪgeɪt] VT désinfecter par fumigation, fumiger (*frm*)
fumigation [,fjuːmɪ'geɪʃən] N fumigation *f*
fun [fʌn] 1 N (*NonC* = *amusement*) amusement *m*; he had great *or* good ~ il s'est bien *or* beaucoup amusé; have ~!* amusez-vous bien!; he's great *or* good ~ il est très drôle, on s'amuse bien avec lui; the book is great *or* good ~ le livre est très amusant; sailing is good ~ c'est amusant de faire de la voile; what ~! ce que c'est drôle *or* amusant!; for ~ ◊ in ~ pour rire *or* plaisanter; I don't see the ~ of it je ne trouve pas cela drôle; I only did it for the ~ of it je ne l'ai fait que pour m'amuser; I'm not doing this for the ~ of it je ne fais pas cela pour m'amuser *or* pour mon plaisir; it's not much ~ for us ce n'est pas très amusant, cela ne nous amuse pas beaucoup; it's only his ~ il fait cela pour rire, c'est tout; to spoil the ~ ◊ to spoil his (*or* our *etc*) ~ [*person*] jouer les trouble-fête *or* les rabat-joie; [*event, weather*] gâter *or* gâcher son (*or* notre *etc*) amusement; the children had ~ and games at the picnic les enfants se sont follement amusés pendant le pique-nique; (*iro*) there'll be ~ and games over this decision* cette décision va faire du potin* *or* du boucan*; (*euph*) he's having ~ and games with the au pair girl* il ne s'ennuie pas avec la jeune fille au pair (*euph*); (= *difficulty*) she's been having ~ and games with the washing machine* la machine à laver lui en a fait voir de toutes les couleurs*; (= *difficulty*) we had a bit of ~ getting the car started* pour faire partir la voiture ça n'a pas été de la rigolade* *or* ça n'a pas été une partie de plaisir; to make ~ of *or* poke ~ at sb/sth se

moquer de qn/qch; did he go? — like ~ he did!* y est-il allé? — tu rigoles *or* tu parles!* 2 ADJ* marrant*, rigolo*; it's a ~ thing to do c'est marrant à faire*; she's a really ~ person elle est vraiment marrante* *or* rigolote* 3 COMP ► **fun fur** N similifourrure *f* ♦ ADJ en similifourrure ► **fun house** N (*US*) attraction foraine comprenant des planchers mouvants, des miroirs déformants, etc ► **fun-loving** ADJ she's a ~-loving girl elle aime s'amuser ► **fun run** N course *f* de fond pour amateurs
function ['fʌŋkʃən] 1 N a (= *role*) [*of heart, tool etc*] fonction *f*; [*of person*] fonction *f*, charge *f*; in his ~ as judge en sa qualité de juge; it is not part of my ~ to do that cela n'entre pas dans mes fonctions, il ne m'appartient pas de faire cela → **bodily** b (= *meeting*) réunion *f*; (= *reception*) réception *f*; (= *official ceremony*) cérémonie *f* publique c (*Math, Ling, Comput*) fonction *f* d (*fig* = *depend on*) to be a ~ of sth être en fonction de qch 2 VI fonctionner, marcher; to ~ as [*person, thing*] faire fonction de, servir de, jouer le rôle de 3 COMP ► **function key** N (*Comput*) touche *f* de fonction ► **function room** N salle *f* de réception ► **function word** N (*Ling*) mot-outil *m*
functional ['fʌŋkʃnəl] ADJ fonctionnel
functionalism ['fʌŋkʃnəlɪzəm] N fonctionnalisme *m*
functionalist ['fʌŋkʃnəlɪst] ADJ, N fonctionnaliste *mf*
functionally ['fʌŋkʃnəlɪ] ADV fonctionnellement
functionary ['fʌŋkʃənərɪ] N employé(e) *m(f)* (*d'une administration*); (*in civil service, local government*) fonctionnaire *mf*
fund [fʌnd] 1 N a (*Fin*) caisse *f*, fonds *m*; to start a ~ lancer une souscription; ~s fonds *mpl*; to be in ~s être en fonds; the public ~s les fonds publics; (*Banking*) no ~s défaut *m* de provision; he hasn't the ~s to buy a house il n'a pas les fonds nécessaires pour acheter une maison → **raise, secret** b (= *supply*) [*of humour, good sense etc*] fond *m*; a ~ of knowledge un trésor de connaissances; he has a ~ of funny stories il connaît des quantités d'histoires 2 VT [+ *debt*] consolider; [+ *project*] financer, assurer le financement de; [+ *firm*] doter en capital; [+ *account*] alimenter 3 COMP ► **fund manager** N gestionnaire *mf* de fonds *or* de portefeuille ► **fund-raiser** N (= *person*) collecteur *m*, -trice *f* de fonds; (= *dinner etc*) dîner *m etc* organisé pour collecter des fonds ► **fund-raising** N collecte *f* de fonds ♦ ADJ [*dinner, event*] organisé pour collecter des fonds
fundamental [,fʌndə'mentl] 1 ADJ a [*belief, principle, right, question, issue, concern, importance*] fondamental; a ~ mistake *or* error une erreur capitale; this is ~ to the smooth running of the company c'est essentiel pour la bonne marche de l'entreprise; it is ~ to our understanding of the problem c'est fondamental *or* essentiel si nous voulons comprendre le problème b (*Mus*) fondamental 2 N a principe *m* essentiel *or* de base; when you get down to (the) ~s quand on en vient à l'essentiel b (*Mus*) fondamental *m* 3 COMP ► **fundamental particle** N (*Phys*) particule *f* fondamentale ► **fundamental research** N recherche *f* fondamentale
fundamentalism [,fʌndə'mentəlɪzəm] N intégrisme *m*
fundamentalist [,fʌndə'mentəlɪst] ADJ, N intégriste *mf*
fundamentally [,fʌndə'mentəlɪ] ADV [*different, wrong*] fondamentalement, radicalement; [*agree, affect, alter*] fondamentalement; ~ important d'une importance capitale; he is ~

good il a un bon fond ; **the plan is ~ flawed** le plan est vicié à la base ; **to disagree ~ with sb/ sth** être en profond désaccord avec qn/qch ; **~, it's a love story** au fond, c'est une histoire d'amour

fundholder ['fʌnd,həʊldəʳ] N (gen) rentier m, -ière f ; [of public funds] détenteur m, -trice f de fonds publics

fundholding doctor [,fʌndhəʊldɪŋ'dɒktəʳ], **fundholding GP** [,fʌndhəʊldɪŋdʒiː'piː] N (Brit Admin) généraliste ayant obtenu le droit de gérer son propre budget

funding ['fʌndɪŋ] N financement m ; **they're hoping to get government ~ for the scheme** ils espèrent obtenir un financement or des fonds du gouvernement pour ce programme

fundus ['fʌndəs] N (pl fundi ['fʌndaɪ]) fond m (de l'utérus)

funeral ['fjuːnərəl] **1** N (gen) obsèques fpl (frm) ; (grander) funérailles fpl ; (= burial) enterrement m ; (= cremation) incinération f ; (in announcements) obsèques fpl ; **that's your ~!*** c'est ton problème ! → **state 2** COMP ► **funeral director** N entrepreneur m de pompes funèbres ► **funeral home** N (US) = **funeral parlour** ► **funeral march** N marche f funèbre ► **funeral oration** N oraison f funèbre ► **funeral parlour** N funérarium m, salon m funéraire m (Can) ► **funeral procession** N (on foot) cortège m funèbre ; (in car) convoi m mortuaire ► **funeral pyre** N bûcher m (funéraire) ► **funeral service** N service m or cérémonie f funèbre

funerary ['fjuːnərərɪ] ADJ funéraire

funereal [fjuː'nɪərɪəl] ADJ [expression, atmosphere] funèbre, lugubre ; [voice] sépulcral, lugubre

funfair ['fʌnfɛəʳ] N (Brit) fête f (foraine)

fungal ['fʌŋɡəl] ADJ [infection] fongique

fungi ['fʌŋɡaɪ] NPL of **fungus**

fungible ['fʌndʒɪbəl] ADJ fongible

fungicide ['fʌndʒɪsaɪd] N fongicide m

fungoid ['fʌŋɡɔɪd], **fungous** ['fʌŋɡəs] ADJ (Med) fongueux ; (Bot) cryptogamique

fungus ['fʌŋɡəs] N (pl fungi or funguses) (Bot: generic term) (= mushrooms etc) champignon m ; (= mould) moisissure f ; (Med) mycose f ; (‡ hum = beard) barbe f

funicular [fjuː'nɪkjʊləʳ] **1** ADJ funiculaire **2** N (also = **railway**) funiculaire m

funk¹ [fʌŋk] N (Mus) **~ (music)** funk m

funk²* [fʌŋk] **1** N (Brit) **to be in a (blue) ~†** (= frightened) avoir la trouille* **2** VT **he ~ed it** il s'est dégonflé*, il a cané‡

funker* ['fʌŋkəʳ] N (= skiver) planqué(e)* m(f)

funky¹ ['fʌŋkɪ] ADJ [music, rhythm] funky inv

funky²* ['fʌŋkɪ] (US) ADJ **a** (= excellent) super* inv, génial* ; (= fashionable) à la page, qui a le look* **b** (= smelly) qui cocotte‡, qui pue

funnel ['fʌnl] **1** N **a** (for pouring through) entonnoir m **b** (Brit) [of ship, engine] cheminée f **2** VT (faire) passer dans un entonnoir ; (fig) canaliser

funnily* ['fʌnɪlɪ] ADV **a** (= strangely) [behave, walk] bizarrement ; **~ enough ...** curieusement ... **b** (= amusingly) drôlement, comiquement

funny ['fʌnɪ] **1** ADJ **a** (= amusing) [person, joke, story, book, film, play] drôle, amusant ; [accent, voice, walk] comique ; **it's not ~** ça n'a rien de drôle, qu'est-ce qu'il y a de drôle ? ; **don't (try to) be ~** n'essaie pas d'être drôle ; **to make a ~ face** faire une grimace amusante → **1b** ; **to see the ~ side of sth** voir le côté amusant or comique de qch **b** (* = strange) bizarre ; **~-peculiar (or ~-haha)?** drôle bizarre (ou drôle amusant) ? ; **he's ~ that way** il est bizarre pour ça ; **the meat tastes ~** la viande a un drôle de goût ; **a ~ idea** une drôle d'idée ; **to feel ~** (= ill) ne pas être dans son assiette ; **to go ~** [machine] se détraquer ; **to make a ~ face** faire une drôle de tête → **1a** ;

I have a ~ feeling I'm going to regret this j'ai comme l'impression que je vais le regretter ; **(it's) ~ you should say that** c'est bizarre que vous disiez (subj) cela ; **the ~ thing (about it) is that ...** ce qu'il y a de drôle c'est que ... ; **~! I thought he'd left** bizarre ! je croyais qu'il était parti ; **it's a ~ old world** c'est tout de même bizarre or curieux **c** (* = fishy) louche* ; **~ business** magouilles* fpl ; **don't try anything ~!*** ne fais pas le malin or la maligne ! **2** N (US Press‡: gen pl) **the funnies** les bandes fpl dessinées **3** COMP ► **funny bone*** N petit juif* m ► **funny cigarette*** N joint* m ► **funny farm*** N maison f de fous ► **funny girl*** N (= comedian) comique f ► **funny handshake*** N poignée f de main rituelle ► **funny man*** N (pl funny men) (= comedian) comique m ► **funny money*** N (= large amount) sommes fpl astronomiques ; (= counterfeit) fausse monnaie f

fur [fɜːʳ] **1** N **a** [of animal] pelage m, fourrure f ; **the cat has beautiful ~** le chat a un beau pelage or une belle fourrure → **fly³ b** (often pl = animal skins) fourrure(s) f(pl) ; **she was dressed in ~s** elle portait des fourrures or de la fourrure **c** (= limescale) incrustation f, (dépôt m de) tartre m ; **to have ~ on one's tongue** avoir la langue pâteuse or chargée **2** VI (also = **up**) [kettle, pipe, boiler] s'entartrer **3** VT **his tongue is ~red** sa langue est chargée or pâteuse **4** COMP [jacket etc] de fourrure ► **fur coat** N manteau m de fourrure ► **fur trade** N industrie f de la fourrure

furbelow† ['fɜːbɪləʊ] N falbala m ; **(frills and) ~s** fanfreluches fpl, falbalas mpl

furbish ['fɜːbɪʃ] VT (= polish) fourbir, astiquer, briquer ; (= smarten) remettre à neuf, rénover

furious ['fjʊərɪəs] ADJ **a** (= angry) [person] furieux (about or at or over sth de qch) ; **she was ~ at being disturbed** elle était furieuse d'avoir été dérangée ; **to be ~ at or with sb (for doing sth)** être furieux contre qn (parce qu'il a fait qch) ; **to be ~ with o.s. for doing sth** s'en vouloir d'avoir fait qch ; **I was ~ that I'd lost** j'étais furieux d'avoir perdu ; **I was ~ that he'd come** j'étais furieux qu'il soit venu ; **she was ~ to find that ...** elle a été furieuse de découvrir que ... ; **to get ~** se mettre en rage (**with sb** contre qn) **b** (= energetic) [pace] effréné ; [speed] fou (folle f) ; [activity] débordant, frénétique ; [effort] vigoureux, acharné ; **the action of the film was fast and ~** le rythme du film était endiablé ; **the fun was fast and ~** la fête battait son plein **c** (= violent) [row, reaction, attack, protest] violent ; [debate] houleux ; [battle, struggle] acharné ; [storm, sea] déchaîné

furiously ['fjʊərɪəslɪ] ADV **a** (= angrily) [say] d'un ton furieux, furieusement ; [react] furieusement ; [argue] avec emportement ; **to be ~ angry** être dans une colère noire, être hors de soi **b** (= frantically) [work, scribble] comme un(e) forcené(e) ; [fight, lobby] avec acharnement ; [drive] à une allure folle ; [ride] à bride abattue ; **~ busy/jealous** extrêmement occupé/jaloux ; **her heart was beating ~** son cœur battait la chamade

furl [fɜːl] VT (Naut) [+ sail] ferler, serrer ; [+ umbrella, flag] rouler ; **the flags are ~ed** les drapeaux sont en berne

furlong ['fɜːlɒŋ] N furlong m (201,17 m)

furlough ['fɜːləʊ] (US) **1** N **a** (Mil) permission f, congé m ; **on ~** en permission **b** (Ind) chômage m technique **2** VT (Ind) mettre au chômage technique

furnace ['fɜːnɪs] **1** N (industrial) fourneau m, four m ; (for central heating) chaudière f ; **this room is like a ~** cette pièce est une vraie fournaise **2** COMP ► **furnace room** N chaufferie f

furnish ['fɜːnɪʃ] **1** VT **a** [+ house] meubler (with de) ; **~ed flat** (Brit) ◊ **~ed apartment** (US) appartement m meublé ; **in ~ed rooms** en meublé **b** (= supply) [+ object, information, excuse, reason] fournir ; **to ~ sb with sth** pourvoir or munir qn de qch ; **to ~ an army with provisions** ravitailler une armée **2** COMP ► **furnishing fabrics** NPL tissus mpl d'ameublement

furnishings ['fɜːnɪʃɪŋz] NPL mobilier m, ameublement m ; **house sold with ~ and fittings** maison f vendue avec objets mobiliers divers

furniture ['fɜːnɪtʃəʳ] **1** N (NonC) meubles mpl, mobilier m ; **a piece of ~** un meuble ; **I must buy some ~** il faut que j'achète des meubles ; **the ~ was very old** les meubles étaient très vieux, le mobilier était très vieux ; **the ~ was scanty** l'ameublement était insuffisant, c'était à peine meublé ; **one settee and three chairs were all the ~** un sofa et trois chaises constituaient tout l'ameublement or le mobilier ; **he treats her as part of the ~** il la traite comme si elle faisait partie du décor ; **he's like part of the ~** (regular: in pub etc) il fait partie des meubles ; **dining-room ~** des meubles mpl or du mobilier m de salle à manger **2** COMP ► **furniture depot** N garde-meubles m inv ► **furniture mover** N (US) déménageur m ► **furniture polish** N encaustique f ► **furniture remover** N déménageur m ► **furniture shop** N magasin m d'ameublement or de meubles ► **furniture store** N = **furniture depot** and **furniture shop** ► **furniture van** N camion m de déménagement

furore [fjʊəˈrɔːrɪ], **furor** (US) [fjʊˈrɔːʳ] N (= protests) scandale m ; (= enthusiasm) débordement m d'enthousiasme ; **the incident caused a ~** cet incident a fait scandale

furrier ['fʌrɪəʳ] N fourreur m

furrow ['fʌrəʊ] **1** N (Agr) sillon m ; (in garden etc) rayon m ; (on brow) ride f ; (liter: on sea) sillage m → **ridge 2** VT [+ earth] sillonner ; [+ face, brow] rider

furry ['fɜːrɪ] **1** ADJ **a** [animal] à poil ; [body, tail] poilu ; [leaf] duveteux **b** (= fleecy) [hat, slippers] en fausse fourrure ; [material] qui ressemble à de la fourrure ; **~ toy** (= soft toy) peluche f **c** (fig) [kettle, pipe] entartré ; (Brit) [tongue] chargé, pâteux ; [teeth] recouvert de tartre, entartré **2** COMP ► **furry dice** NPL (Brit) dés mpl en feutrine (qu'on accroche au rétroviseur) ► **furry friend** N (hum) ami m à fourrure

▼ **further** ['fɜːðəʳ] compar of **far** **1** ADV **a** = **farther 1 b** (= more) davantage, plus ; **he questioned us no ~** il ne nous a pas interrogés davantage, il ne nous a pas posé d'autres questions ; **without troubling any ~** sans se tracasser davantage, sans plus se tracasser ; **I got no ~ with him** je ne suis arrivé à rien de plus avec lui ; **unless I hear any ~** à moins qu'on ne me prévienne du contraire, sauf avis contraire ; **until you hear ~** jusqu'à nouvel avis ; **we heard nothing ~ from him** nous n'avons plus rien reçu de lui, nous n'avons pas eu d'autres nouvelles de lui or de sa part ; (fig) **this mustn't go any ~** il ne faut pas que cela aille plus loin ; **I think we should take this matter ~** je pense que nous devrions poursuivre cette affaire or que nous ne devrions pas nous en tenir là ; **and ~ I believe ...** et de plus je crois ... ; **he said that he would do it and ~ that he wanted to** il a dit qu'il le ferait en outre or et en plus qu'il avait envie de le faire ; **to study/examine an issue ~** approfondir l'étude/l'examen d'une question ; (Comm) **~ to your letter** comme suite à votre lettre

2 ADJ **a** = **farther 2 b** (= additional) nouveau (nouvelle f), supplémentaire ; **until ~ notice** jusqu'à nouvel ordre ; (Jur) **to refer or remand a case for ~ inquiry** renvoyer une cause pour complément

► LANGUAGE IN USE: **further** 19.1, 20.2, 21.1

d'information *or* d'instruction ; **without ~ delay** sans autre délai, sans plus attendre ; **without ~ ado** sans plus de cérémonie ; **upon ~ consideration** après plus ample réflexion, à la réflexion ; **awaiting ~ details** en attendant de plus amples détails ; **one or two ~ details** un ou deux autres points ; (*in letter*) **please send me ~ details of ...** veuillez m'envoyer de plus amples renseignements sur *or* concernant ... ; **there are one or two ~ things I must say** il y a encore une ou deux remarques que j'aimerais faire, j'ai encore une ou deux remarques à faire

③ VT [+ *one's interests, a cause*] servir, favoriser

④ COMP ► **Further Education, further education** N enseignement *m* postscolaire → **college** ► **Further Education Funding Council** N (*Brit*) *organisme de financement de l'enseignement postscolaire*

furtherance ['fɜ:ðərəns] N avancement *m* ; **in ~ of sth** pour avancer *or* servir qch

▼ **furthermore** [,fɜ:ðə'mɔ:ʳ] ADV en outre, de plus

furthermost ['fɜ:ðəməʊst] ADJ le plus éloigné, le plus lointain

furthest ['fɜ:ðɪst] = **farthest**

furtive ['fɜ:tɪv] ADJ [*action, behaviour, look*] furtif ; [*person*] sournois ; **she sneaked out for a ~ cigarette** elle s'éclipsa pour fumer furtivement une cigarette *or* pour fumer en douce*

furtively ['fɜ:tɪvlɪ] ADV furtivement, à la dérobée

fury ['fjʊərɪ] N [*of person*] fureur *f*, furie *f* ; [*of storm, wind*] fureur *f*, violence *f* ; [*of struggle*] acharnement *m* ; **to be in a ~** être en furie, être dans une rage *or* colère folle ; **to put sb into a ~** mettre qn dans une colère folle ; **to fly into a ~** entrer en fureur *or* en furie, se mettre dans une rage folle ; **she's a little ~** c'est une petite furie *or* harpie ; (*Myth*) **the Furies** les Furies *fpl*, les Euménides *fpl* ; **to work like ~*** travailler d'arrache-pied *or* comme un fou ; **to run like ~*** courir comme un dératé

furze [fɜ:z] N (*NonC*) ajoncs *mpl*

fuse, fuze (*US*) [fju:z] ① VT ⓐ (= *unite*) [+ *metal*] fondre, mettre en fusion
ⓑ (*fig*) faire fusionner, réunir
ⓒ (*Brit Elec*) faire sauter ; **to ~ the television** (*or* **the iron** *or* **the lights** *etc*) faire sauter les plombs
ⓓ (= *fit with fuse*) [+ *bomb*] amorcer ; **to ~ a plug** équiper une prise d'un fusible
② VI ⓐ [*metals*] fondre ; (*fig: also* **~ together**) fusionner
ⓑ (*Brit Elec*) **the television** (*or* **the lights** *etc*) **~d** les plombs ont sauté
③ N ⓐ (*Elec* = *wire*) fusible *m*, plomb *m* ; (*fig*) **to light the ~** mettre la machine en marche, mettre les choses en branle ; **this incident lit the ~ which led to the war** cet incident a été le détonateur de la guerre ; (*fig*) **to have a short ~* ◊ to be on a short ~*** se mettre facilement en rogne*, être soupe au lait
ⓑ (*Elec* = *blow-out*) **there's been a ~ somewhere** il y a un fusible de sauté quelque part
ⓒ [*of bomb etc*] amorce *f*, détonateur *m* ; (*Min*) cordeau *m*
④ COMP ► **fuse box** N (*gen*) boîte *f* à fusibles, coupe-circuit *m inv* ; (*Aut*) boîte *f* à fusibles ► **fuse wire** N fusible *m*

fused [fju:zd] ADJ (*Elec*) [*electrical equipment, plug*] avec fusible incorporé

fusel ['fju:zl] N (*also* **~ oil**) fusel *m*, huile *f* de fusel

fuselage ['fju:zəlɑ:ʒ] N fuselage *m*

fusible ['fju:zɪbl] ADJ **~ metal** *or* **alloy** alliage *m* fusible

fusilier [,fju:zɪ'lɪəʳ] N (*Brit*) fusilier *m*

fusillade [,fju:zɪ'leɪd] N fusillade *f*

fusion ['fju:ʒən] N (*Metal*) fonte *f*, fusion *f* ; (*Phys*) fusion *f* ; (*Mus*) fusion *f* ; [*of parties, races*] fusion *f*, fusionnement *m*

fuss [fʌs] ① N (*NonC*) (= *commotion stirred up*) tapage *m* ; (= *excitement, agitation in reaction to sth*) agitation *f* ; (= *complaints, objections, difficulties*) histoires *fpl* ; **I think all this ~ is only a publicity stunt** je pense que tout ce tapage n'est qu'un truc publicitaire ; **the company introduced new working conditions with the minimum of ~** la société a mis en place de nouvelles conditions de travail sans que cela provoque trop d'agitation *or* de remous ; **the government's proposals have caused a great deal of ~** les propositions du gouvernement ont provoqué beaucoup d'agitation *or* de remous ; **I'm sick of all this ~!** j'en ai assez de toute cette agitation *or* de toutes ces histoires ! ; **I don't know what all the ~ is about** je ne sais pas pourquoi on fait tant d'histoires ; **a lot of ~ about nothing** beaucoup de bruit pour rien ; **what a ~ just to get a passport!** que d'histoires rien que pour obtenir un passeport ! ; **we got married very quietly. We didn't want a big ~** nous nous sommes mariés sans cérémonie. Nous voulions quelque chose de simple ; **without (any) ~** [*marry, be buried etc*] simplement, en toute simplicité ; **he just gets down to work without any ~** il se met au travail sans faire toute une histoire ; **to make a ~ ◊ to kick up a ~*** faire un tas d'histoires* ; **to make a ~ about** *or* **over sth** (*justifiably*) protester à propos de qch, ne pas laisser passer qch ; (*unjustifiably*) faire des histoires pour qch, faire tout un plat de qch* ; **you were quite right to make a ~** vous avez eu tout à fait raison de protester *or* de ne pas laisser passer ça ; **don't make such a ~ about accepting** ne faites pas tant de manières pour accepter ; **to make a ~ of** (*Brit*) *or* **over** (*US*) **sb** être aux petits soins pour qn
② VI (= *become excited*) s'agiter ; (= *rush around busily*) s'affairer, faire la mouche du coche ; (= *worry*) se tracasser, s'en faire* ; **to ~ over sb** être aux petits soins pour qn ; (*pej*) **don't ~ over him** laisse-le tranquille
③ VT [+ *person*] ennuyer, embêter*

► **fuss about, fuss around** VI s'affairer, faire la mouche du coche

fussbudget* [fʌs,bʌdʒɪt] N (*US*) = **fusspot**

fussed* [fʌst] ADJ (*Brit*) **I'm not ~ (about going)** ça m'est égal (d'y aller)

fussily ['fʌsɪlɪ] ADV (*pej*) ⓐ (= *painstakingly*) [*check, adjust*] de façon tatillonne ⓑ (*pej* = *overelaborately*) **~ ornate** tarabiscoté ; **~ dressed** habillé de façon apprêtée

fussiness ['fʌsɪnɪs] N [*of person*] caractère *m* tatillon *or* pointilleux ; [*of style*] caractère *m* tarabiscoté *or* surchargé

fusspot* ['fʌspɒt] N (= *nuisance*) enquiquineur* *m*, -euse* *f* ; (= *finicky person*) coupeur *m*, -euse *f* de cheveux en quatre ; **don't be such a ~!** ne fais pas tant d'histoires !, arrête d'enquiquiner le monde !*

fussy ['fʌsɪ] ADJ ⓐ (= *exacting*) [*person, cat*] tatillon (**about sth** sur qch), pointilleux ; **to be a ~ eater** être difficile sur la nourriture ; **tea or coffee? — I'm not ~*** thé ou café ? — ça m'est égal ⓑ (*pej* = *overelaborate*) [*design, style, furnishings, details*] trop recherché ; [*food*] (*trop*) élaboré ; **that dress is too ~** cette robe n'est pas assez simple

fustian ['fʌstɪən] N futaine *f*

fusty ['fʌstɪ] ADJ ⓐ (*pej* = *old-fashioned*) [*person*] vieux jeu *inv* ; [*organization*] poussiéreux, vieillot ; [*image, ideas*] suranné, vieillot ⓑ (= *musty*) [*smell*] de renfermé, de moisi ; [*place,*

clothes, furnishings] qui sent le renfermé

futile ['fju:taɪl] ADJ [*remark*] futile, vain ; [*attempt*] vain

futility [fju:'tɪlɪtɪ] N futilité *f* ; **the ~ of this attempt/measure** l'inutilité *f* de cette tentative/mesure

futon ['fu:tɒn] N futon *m*

future ['fju:tʃəʳ] ① N ⓐ avenir *m* ; **what the ~ holds for us** ce que l'avenir nous réserve ; **does Britain's ~ lie within the EU?** l'avenir de la Grande-Bretagne est-il dans l'UE ? ; **there is a real ~ for bright young people in this firm** cette entreprise offre de réelles possibilités d'avenir pour des jeunes gens doués ; (*in relationship, business*) **he believed his ~ lay with her** il pensait que son avenir était lié à elle ; **in (the) ~** à l'avenir ; **in the near ~ ◊ in the not too distant ~** bientôt, dans un proche avenir (*more frm*) ; **there's no ~ in this type of research** ce type de recherche n'a aucun avenir ; **there's no ~ in it*** [+ *product, method, relationship*] cela n'a aucun avenir ; [+ *measures, way of behaving*] ça n'aboutira à rien, ça ne servira à rien
ⓑ (*Gram*) futur *m* ; **in the ~** au futur
② **futures** NPL (*St Ex*) marchandises *fpl* (achetées) à terme ; **~s market** marché *m* à terme ; **coffee ~s** café *m* (acheté) à terme
③ ADJ [*prospects, plans, role*] futur ; [*king, queen*] futur (*before n*) ; **her ~ husband** son futur mari ; **~ generations** les générations *fpl* futures *or* à venir ; **at a** *or* **some ~ date** à une date ultérieure ; **in ~ years** dans les années à venir ; **for ~ reference** pour référence ultérieure
④ COMP ► **future perfect (tense)** N futur *m* antérieur ► **future tense** N futur *m* ; **in the ~ tense** au futur

futurism ['fju:tʃərɪzəm] N futurisme *m*

futurist ['fju:tʃərɪst] N ⓐ (*esp US = futurologist*) futurologue *mf* ⓑ (*Art*) futuriste *mf*

futuristic [,fju:tʃə'rɪstɪk] ADJ futuriste

futurity [fju:'tjʊərɪtɪ] N (*frm = future time*) futur *m*

futurologist [fju:tʃər'ɒlədʒɪst] N futurologue *mf*

futurology [,fju:tʃər'ɒlədʒɪ] N futurologie *f*, prospective *f*

fuze [fju:z] (*US*) = **fuse**

fuzz [fʌz] ① N (*NonC = light growth*) (*on body*) duvet *m*, poils *mpl* fins ; (*on head*) duvet *m*, cheveux *mpl* fins ; (= *frizzy hair*) cheveux *mpl* crépus *or* crêpelés (et bouffants) ② **the fuzz*** NPL (= *police*) la flicaille*, les flics* *mpl*

fuzzily ['fʌzɪlɪ] ADV [*worded*] de manière confuse ; **you're thinking ~** vous n'avez pas les idées claires

fuzzy ['fʌzɪ] ① ADJ ⓐ (= *indistinct*) [*photograph, picture*] flou ; [*sound, voice*] confus, indistinct ; [*writing*] indistinct ⓑ (= *confused*) [*idea, brain, details, distinction*] confus ; [*memory*] imprécis, vague ; **to be ~ about** *or* **on sth** n'avoir qu'une idée confuse de qch ⓒ (= *downy*) duveteux ; (= *frizzy*) [*hair*] crépu ⓓ (= *furry*) [*material, sweater*] pelucheux ⓔ **to be** *or* **feel ~(-headed)*** (*from drink*) être dans les vapes* ② COMP ► **fuzzy dice** NPL (*US*) = **furry dice** ► **fuzzy logic** N (*Comput*) logique *f* floue

fwd (*esp Comm*) ABBR = **forward**

f-word ['ef,wɜ:d] N (*euph = fuck*) **the ~** le mot « fuck »**, un gros mot

FX* [ef'eks] NPL (*Cine = special effects*) effets *mpl* spéciaux

FY N (*Fin*) (ABBR = **fiscal year**) → **fiscal**

FYI (ABBR = **for your information**) → **information**

G

G, g [dʒiː] **1** N **a** (= letter) G, g m; **G for George** ≈ G comme Gaston **b** (Mus) sol m → **key** **c** (Phys = gravity, acceleration) g m **d**‡ (ABBR = **grand**) (Brit) mille livres fpl; (US) mille dollars mpl **e** (Scol = mark) (ABBR = **good**) bon **2** COMP ► **G7** N G7 m; **G7 summit** sommet m du G7 ► **G8** N G8 m ► **G-force** N force f gravitationnelle ► **G-man**‡ N (pl **G-men**) (US) agent m du FBI ► **G spot** N point m G ► **G-string** N (Mus) (corde f de) sol m; (= garment) cache-sexe m inv, string m ► **G-suit** N (Space) combinaison f spatiale or anti-g

g. **a** (ABBR = **gram(s)**) g inv **b** (ABBR = **gravity**) g

GA ABBR = **Georgia**

gab‡ [gæb] **1** N bagou(t)‡ m; **to have a ~ (about sth)** papoter (à propos de qch) → **gift** **2** VI (= chatter) papoter (**about** à propos de); (= reveal secret) vendre la mèche

gabardine [,gæbə'diːn] N gabardine f

gabble ['gæbl] **1** VT **a** (= talk indistinctly) bafouiller; (= talk unintelligibly) baragouiner*; (= talk quickly) **he ~d on about the accident** il nous a fait une description volubile de l'accident; **he ~d (out) an excuse** il a bafouillé une excuse; **"where are they, where are they?", he ~d** « où sont-ils, où sont-ils ? », a-t-il bafouillé; **they were gabbling away in French** ils jacassaient en français **2** N baragouin* m, charabia* m

gabbro ['gæbrəʊ] N gabbro m

gabby‡ ['gæbɪ] ADJ jacasseur, bavard comme une pie

gable ['geɪbl] **1** N pignon m **2** COMP ► **gable end** N pignon m ► **gable roof** N comble m sur pignon(s)

gabled ['geɪbld] ADJ à pignon(s)

Gabon [gə'bɒn] N le Gabon

Gabonese [,gæbə'niːz] **1** ADJ gabonais **2** N Gabonais(e) m(f)

gad[1] [gæd] N (Agr) aiguillon m

gad[2] [gæd] VI **to ~ about** vadrouiller*; **she spent the summer ~ding about (in) Italy** elle a passé l'été à vadrouiller* en Italie

gad[3]‡ [gæd] EXCL (also **by ~**) sapristi !†, bon sang !

gadabout ['gædə,baʊt] N vadrouilleur* m, -euse* f

gadfly ['gædflaɪ] N taon m; (fig = harassing person) mouche f du coche

gadget ['gædʒɪt] N **a** (= device) (petit) appareil m **b** (* = thingummy) (petit) truc* m or bidule* m, gadget m

gadgetry ['gædʒɪtrɪ] N (of car etc) gadgets mpl

gadolinium [,gædə'lɪnɪəm] N gadolinium m

Gael [geɪl] N Gaël mf

Gaelic ['geɪlɪk, 'gælɪk] **1** ADJ gaélique **2** N (Ling) gaélique m **3** COMP ► **Gaelic coffee** N irish coffee m

gaff[1] [gæf] **1** N (Fishing) gaffe f; (Naut) corne f; (US fig) **to stand the ~**‡ encaisser*, tenir **2** VT gaffer, harponner

gaff[2]‡ [gæf] N (Brit) (= home) piaule* f; (= music hall etc) beuglant‡ m

gaff[3]‡ [gæf] N (= nonsense) foutaises‡ fpl → **blow**[1]

gaffe [gæf] N gaffe f, impair m

gaffer‡ ['gæfə] N **a** **an old ~** un vieux (bonhomme) **b** (Brit) (= foreman) contremaître m; (= boss) patron m, chef m **c** (Cine) chef m électricien

gag [gæg] **1** N **a** (in mouth) bâillon m; (Med) ouvre-bouche m inv; (fig) **the new law will effectively put a ~ on the free press** la nouvelle loi aura pour effet de bâillonner la presse libre **b*** (= joke) blague f, plaisanterie f; (= hoax) canular m; (by comedian) (unscripted) improvisation f comique; (visual) gag m **2** (lit) bâillonner; (fig = silence) bâillonner, museler; **he was bound and ~ged** on l'a attaché et bâillonné **3** VI **a** (* = retch) avoir des haut-le-cœur; **to be ~ging for it**‡ être en chaleur‡ **b** (* = joke) plaisanter, blaguer; (comedian) faire une or des improvisation(s) comique(s) **4** COMP ► **gag law**‡, **gag rule**‡ N (US) loi f limitant la durée des délibérations

gaga‡ ['gɑːgɑː] ADJ (= senile) gaga* f inv, gâteux; (= crazy) cinglé*

gage [geɪdʒ] **1** N **a** (= challenge) défi m; (= glove) gant m **b** (= pledge) gage m, garantie f; (= article pledged) gage m **c** (US Tech) = **gauge 1 2** VT (US Tech) = **gauge 2**

gaggle ['gægl] **1** N (lit, hum) troupeau m **2** VI [geese] cacarder

gaiety ['geɪtɪ] N (NonC) gaieté f

gaily ['geɪlɪ] ADV **a** (= brightly) [painted, dressed] de couleurs vives; [decorated] de façon gaie; **~ coloured** aux couleurs vives **b** (= cheerily) [chatter] gaiement **c** (= thoughtlessly) tranquillement

gain [geɪn] **1** N (Comm, Fin) (= profit) gain m, profit m; (= increase in value of asset) plus-value f; (fig) avantage m; (= increase) augmentation f; (in wealth) accroissement m (in de); (in knowledge etc) acquisition f (in de); **to do sth for (financial) ~** faire qch pour le profit; **his loss is our ~** là où il perd nous gagnons; **a ~ in weight** une augmentation de poids; (St Ex) **there have been ~s of up to three points** des hausses allant jusqu'à trois points ont été enregistrées; (in election) **Labour made ~s in the South** les travaillistes ont progressé or sont en progression dans le sud **2** **gains** NPL (= profits) bénéfices mpl, gains mpl; (= winnings) gains mpl **3** VT **a** [+ money, approval, respect] gagner, obtenir; [+ liberty] obtenir; [+ support, supporters] s'attirer; [+ friends] se faire; **what have you ~ed by doing that?** qu'est-ce que tu as gagné à faire ça ?; **he'll ~ nothing by being rude** il ne gagnera rien à être impoli; (St Ex) **these shares have ~ed three points** ces valeurs ont enregistré une hausse de trois points; **my watch has ~ed five minutes** ma montre a pris cinq minutes d'avance; **we were unable to ~ access to his files** nous n'avons pas pu avoir accès à ses fichiers; **did they ~ access to the property?** ont-ils réussi à entrer dans la propriété ?; **to ~ sb's confidence** gagner la confiance de qn; **to ~ control (of)** prendre le contrôle (de); **his troops ~ed control after heavy fighting** ses troupes ont pris le contrôle après des combats acharnés; **to ~ back control over sth** reprendre le contrôle de qch; **to ~ entry** (to building) réussir à entrer; **she ~ed entry to the system by using a stolen password** elle s'est introduite dans le système à l'aide d'un mot de passe volé; **to ~ sb's goodwill** gagner les bonnes grâces de qn; **to ~ a hearing** (= make people listen) se faire écouter; (with king etc) obtenir une audience; **Cyprus ~ed independence from Britain in 1960** Chypre, ancienne colonie britannique, est devenue indépendante en 1960; **to ~ one's objective** atteindre son objectif; (in election) **Labour has ~ed three seats** les travaillistes ont gagné trois nouveaux sièges; **Labour has ~ed three seats from the Conservatives** les travaillistes ont pris trois sièges aux conservateurs **b** (= acquire more) **to ~ ground** (Mil) gagner du terrain; (fig) gagner du terrain, progresser; **to ~ momentum** (lit) prendre de la vitesse; (fig) prendre de l'ampleur, gagner du terrain; **to ~ speed** prendre de la vitesse; **to ~ time** gagner du temps (by doing en faisant); **to ~ experience** acquérir de l'expérience; **to ~ popularity** gagner en popularité; **to ~ prestige** gagner en prestige; **to ~ strength** [person, movement] devenir plus fort; [storm, hurricane] devenir plus violent; (Fin) [market] se raffermir; **to ~ weight** prendre du poids; **she's ~ed 3kg (in weight)** elle a pris 3 kg **d** (= reach) [+ place] atteindre, parvenir à **4** VI **a** (= benefit) gagner **b** **to ~ in** (= acquire more) → **1c** **c** [watch] avancer; [runners] prendre de l'avance; **he hasn't ~ed by the exchange** il n'a pas gagné au change

► **gain (up)on** VT FUS **a** (Sport, fig) (= catch up with) rattraper; (= outstrip) prendre de l'avance sur **b** [sea] gagner sur

gainer ['geɪnə] N (= person) gagnant(e) m(f); (St Ex) valeur f en hausse; **there were more losers than ~s** il y avait davantage de perdants que de gagnants; **he is the ~ by it** c'est lui qui y gagne

gainful ['geɪnfʊl] ADJ [occupation] (= worthwhile) utile, profitable; (= lucrative) lucratif, rémunérateur (-trice f); **to be in ~ employment** avoir un emploi rémunéré

gainfully ['geɪnfʊlɪ] ADV **to be ~ employed** (= in paid work) avoir un emploi rémunéré; (= doing sth useful) ne pas perdre son temps; **there was nothing that could ~ be said** il n'y avait pas grand-chose à dire

gainsay ['geɪn'seɪ] VT (pret, ptp **gainsaid** [,geɪn'sed]) [+ person] contredire; [+ account, statement] contredire, démentir; [+ fact] nier; **the facts cannot be gainsaid** on ne peut pas nier les faits, ces faits sont indéniables; **the evidence cannot be gainsaid** ces preuves sont irrécusables; **her argument cannot be gainsaid** son argument est irréfutable; **there's no ~ing it** c'est indéniable, on ne peut pas le nier

gait [geɪt] N démarche f; **with an awkward ~** d'une démarche or d'un pas gauche; **to have a rolling ~** rouler or balancer les hanches; **to have a shuffling ~** marcher en traînant les pieds

gaiter ['geɪtə'] N guêtre f

gal †* [gæl] N = **girl 1**

gal. (pl **gal.** or **gals.**) ABBR = **gallon**

gala ['gɑːlə] **1** N fête f, gala m; **opening/ closing ~** gala m d'ouverture/de clôture; **swimming/sports ~** grand concours m de natation/d'athlétisme **2** COMP [evening, dinner, concert] de gala ▸ **gala day** N jour m de gala or de fête ▸ **gala dress** N tenue f de gala ▸ **gala night** N (Theat) soirée f de gala ▸ **gala occasion** f grande occasion f

galactic [gəˈlæktɪk] ADJ galactique

galantine ['gælantiːn] N galantine f

Galapagos [gəˈlæpəgəs] NPL **the ~ (Islands)** les (îles fpl) Galapagos fpl

Galatians [gəˈleɪʃənz] NPL (Bible) Galates mpl

galaxy ['gæləksɪ] N (Astron) galaxie f; (fig) [of talent] constellation f, brillante assemblée f

gale [geɪl] **1** N coup m de vent, grand vent m; (Met) **a force 8 ~** un vent de force 8; **it was blowing a ~** le vent soufflait très fort; **there's a ~ blowing in through that window** c'est une véritable bourrasque qui entre par cette fenêtre; (fig) **~s of laughter** grands éclats mpl de rire **2** COMP ▸ **gale force winds** NPL vent m soufflant en tempête, coups mpl de vent ▸ **gale warning** N (Met) avis m de coup de vent

galena [gəˈliːnə] N galène f

Galicia [gəˈlɪʃɪə] N (in Central Europe) la Galicie; (in Spain) la Galice

Galician [gəˈlɪʃɪən] **1** ADJ galicien **2** N Galicien(ne) m(f)

Galilean [gælɪˈliːən] **1** ADJ (Bible, Geog) galiléen **2** N (Astron) de Galilée **2** N Galiléen(ne) m(f); (Bible) **the ~** le Christ

Galilee ['gælɪliː] N la Galilée; **the Sea of ~** le lac de Tibériade, la mer de Galilée

Galileo [gælɪˈleɪəʊ] N Galilée m

gall[1] [gɔːl] **1** N (Med) bile f; (Zool) bile f, fiel m; (fig = bitterness) fiel m, amertume f; **she had the ~ to say that ...** elle a eu l'effronterie de dire que ... **2** COMP ▸ **gall-bladder** N vésicule f biliaire

gall[2] [gɔːl] **1** N (on animal) écorchure f, excoriation f; (Bot) galle f **2** VT (fig) irriter, exaspérer; **it ~s me that ...** cela m'irrite or m'exaspère que ...; **it ~s me to have to admit it** cela m'irrite or m'exaspère d'avoir à le reconnaître

gall. (pl **gall.** or **galls.**) ABBR = **gallon**

gallant ['gælənt] **1** ADJ **a** († = brave) [soldier] brave, vaillant; (liter) **~ conduct** bravoure f, vaillance f (liter); **a ~ deed** une action d'éclat **b** (= plucky) [effort, attempt] courageux, héroïque; [fight] héroïque **c** (liter = elegant) [appearance, dress] élégant **d** [gəˈlænt] (= chivalrous) [gentleman, gesture] galant **2** N [gəˈlænt] galion m

gallantly ['gæləntlɪ] ADV **a** (= bravely) [fight, battle] bravement, vaillamment (liter) **b** [gəˈlæntlɪ] (= chivalrously) galamment

gallantry † ['gæləntrɪ] N **a** (= bravery) bravoure f, vaillance f (liter) **b** (= chivalrousness) galanterie f

galleon ['gælɪən] N galion m

gallery ['gælərɪ] N **a** (Archit) (= passageway, long room, outside balcony) galerie f; (= inside balcony) tribune f; (in cave, mine) galerie f → **minstrel, press, shooting b** (also **art ~**) (state-owned) musée m (d'art); (private, selling paintings) galerie f (de tableaux or d'art); (US = auction room) salle f des ventes **c** (Theat) dernier balcon m, poulailler* m; **in the ~** au dernier balcon, au poulailler*; (fig) **to play to the ~** poser or parler pour la galerie

---

galley ['gælɪ] **1** N **a** (= ship) galère f; (= ship's kitchen) coquerie f **b** (Typ) galée f; (also **~ proof**) (épreuve f en) placard m **2** COMP ▸ **galley slave** N galérien m

galley west ['gælɪˌwest] ADV (US) **to knock sth ~** chambarder* qch, mettre la pagaille dans qch

Gallic ['gælɪk] ADJ (= of Gaul) gaulois; (= French) français; **~ charm** charme m latin; **the ~ Wars** la guerre des Gaules

gallic ['gælɪk] ADJ (Chem) gallique

Gallicism ['gælɪsɪzəm] N gallicisme m

gallimaufry [gælɪˈmɔːfrɪ] N fatras m

galling ['gɔːlɪŋ] ADJ (= irritating) irritant, exaspérant

gallinule ['gælɪnjuːl] N **common ~** poule f d'eau

gallium ['gælɪəm] N gallium m

gallivant [gælɪˈvænt] VI (also **~ about, ~ around**: for pleasure) se balader; **I have to earn my living while you go ~ing around Europe!** il faut que je gagne ma vie pendant que tu te balades en Europe!

gallon ['gælən] N gallon m (Brit = 4,546 l, US = 3,785 l)

gallop ['gæləp] **1** N galop m; **to go for a ~** aller galoper; **to break into a ~** prendre le galop, se mettre au galop; **at a or the ~** au galop; **at full ~** (horse) au grand galop, ventre à terre; (rider) au grand galop, à bride abattue; (fig) **after a quick ~ through the history of the Roman Empire, the author turns to ...** après avoir évoqué rapidement l'histoire de l'empire romain, l'auteur en vient à ... **2** VI [horse, rider] galoper; **to ~ away/back** etc partir/revenir etc au galop; (fig) **to go ~ing down the street** descendre la rue au galop; **to ~ through a book*** lire un livre à toute vitesse **3** VT [+ horse] faire galoper

galloping ['gæləpɪŋ] ADJ **a** [horse] au galop; [hooves, pace] de cheval au galop **b** (Med) [pneumonia, pleurisy, consumption] galopant; (Econ) [economy, interest rates, prices] qui s'emballe; **~ inflation** inflation f galopante

gallows ['gæləʊz] **1** N (pl **gallowses** or **gallows**) (NonC: also **~ tree**) gibet m, potence f; **he'll end up on the ~** il finira à la potence or par la corde **2** COMP ▸ **gallows bird*** N gibier m de potence ▸ **gallows humour** N (fig) humour m macabre

gallstone ['gɔːlstəʊn] N calcul m biliaire

Gallup ['gæləp] N Gallup m **2** COMP ▸ **Gallup poll**® N sondage m Gallup

galop ['gæləp] N galop m (danse)

galore [gəˈlɔː'] ADV en abondance, à gogo*; **bargains ~** de bonnes affaires à profusion

galosh [gəˈlɒʃ] N (gen pl) **~es** caoutchoucs mpl (enfilés par-dessus les chaussures)

galumph* [gəˈlʌmf] VI **to go ~ing in/out** etc (clumsily) entrer/sortir etc en courant maladroitement; (happily) entrer/sortir etc en sautillant gaiement; **a ~ing great girl** une grande fille à la démarche gauche

galvanic [gælˈvænɪk] ADJ (Elec) galvanique; [jerk] crispé; (fig) [effect] galvanisant, électrisant

galvanism ['gælvənɪzəm] N galvanisme m

galvanization [gælvənaɪˈzeɪʃən] N galvanisation f

galvanize ['gælvənaɪz] VT **a** (Elec, Med) galvaniser; **~d iron** fer m galvanisé **b** (fig) [+ person, group] galvaniser; [+ discussions, debate] animer; [+ market, economy] stimuler, donner une impulsion à; **to ~ sb into action** pousser qn à agir; **to ~ sb to do sth** ◊ **to ~ sb into doing sth** pousser qn à faire qch

galvanometer [gælvəˈnɒmɪtə'] N galvanomètre m

---

galvanoscope [ˈgælvənəˌskəʊp] N galvanoscope m

Gambia ['gæmbɪə] N **(the) ~** la Gambie

Gambian ['gæmbɪən] **1** N Gambien(ne) m(f) **2** ADJ gambien

gambit ['gæmbɪt] N (Chess) gambit m; (fig) manœuvre f, ruse f → **opening**

gamble ['gæmbl] **1** N entreprise f risquée, pari m; **a political ~** un pari politique; **life's a ~** la vie est un jeu de hasard; **it's a pure ~** c'est affaire de chance; **it was a bit of a ~ but ...** c'était un peu risqué mais ...; **the ~ came off** or **paid off** ça a payé de prendre ce risque; **to take a ~** prendre un risque; **to take a ~ on it** prendre le risque; **we're really taking a ~ with him** nous prenons vraiment un risque avec lui; **the party is taking a ~ that they will be elected** le parti mise sur le fait qu'il remportera les élections; **to have a ~ on a horse** miser sur un cheval; **to have a ~ on the stock exchange** jouer à la Bourse **2** VI **a** (lit) jouer (on sur, with avec); **to ~ on the stock exchange** jouer à la Bourse **b** (fig) **to ~ on** miser sur; **we had been gambling on fine weather** nous avions misé sur le beau temps; **to ~ on doing sth** (confident of success) compter faire qch; (less sure) penser faire qch; **Labour was gambling on winning support from the trade unions** les travaillistes comptaient or pensaient obtenir le soutien des syndicats; **he was gambling on her being late** or **that she would be late** il comptait sur le fait qu'elle serait en retard; **to ~ with sb's life** jouer avec la vie de qn; **to ~ with one's future** mettre en jeu son avenir

▸ **gamble away** VT SEP [+ money etc] perdre or dilapider au jeu

gambler ['gæmblə'] **1** N (lit) joueur m, -euse f; (fig = risk-taker) **he's a bit of a ~** il a le goût du risque, il aime prendre des risques → **big 3** **2** COMP ▸ **Gamblers Anonymous** N association venant en aide aux joueurs invétérés

gambling ['gæmblɪŋ] **1** N (= action) jeu m; (= games played) jeux mpl d'argent; **his ~ ruined his family** sa passion du jeu a entraîné la ruine de sa famille; **he believes ~ is wrong** il pense que les jeux d'argent sont un vice **2** COMP ▸ **gambling debts** NPL dettes fpl de jeu ▸ **gambling den, gambling hell***, **gambling house, gambling joint:** (US) N (pej) maison f de jeu, tripot m (pej) ▸ **gambling losses** NPL pertes fpl au jeu

gamboge [gæmˈbuːʒ] N gomme-gutte f

gambol ['gæmbəl] **1** N gambade f, cabriole f **2** VI gambader, cabrioler; **to ~ away/back** etc partir/revenir etc en gambadant or cabriolant

gambrel ['gæmbrəl] N (also **~ roof**) toit m brisé

game[1] [geɪm] **1** N **a** (gen) jeu m; (= match) [of football, rugby, cricket etc] match m; [of tennis, billiards, chess] partie f; [of bridge] manche f; **a ~ of cards** une partie de cartes; **card ~s** mpl de cartes; **video ~s** jeux mpl vidéo inv; **the wonderful ~ of football** le jeu merveilleux qu'est le football; **a ~ of skill/of chance** un jeu d'adresse/de hasard; **to have** or **play a ~ of** (chess etc) faire une partie de; (football etc) jouer un match de; **he plays a good ~ of football** il est bon au football; **they were ~ all** (Tennis) ils étaient à un jeu partout; (Bridge) ils étaient à une manche partout; **it was three ~s all** (Tennis) on était à trois jeux partout; (Bridge) on était à trois manches partout; (Tennis) **~, set and match** jeu, set et match; (Tennis) **~ (to) Johnston** jeu Johnston; **it isn't a ~, you know!** ce n'est pas un jeu tu sais!; **it's all part of the ~** cela fait partie des règles du jeu; (fig) **he's just playing silly ~s** il n'est pas sérieux; (lit, fig) **to have the ~ in one's hands** être sur le point de gagner → **highland, indoor** **b** (* = style of playing) **he's off his ~** il n'est pas en forme; **to put sb off his** (or **her** etc) **~** troubler qn

[c] (fig) (= scheme, plan) plan m, projet m; (= dodge, trick) (petit) jeu m, manège m; (* = occupation) travail m, boulot* m; **it's a profitable ~** c'est une entreprise rentable; **the ~ is up** tout est fichu* or à l'eau; **they saw the ~ was up** ils ont vu que la partie était perdue; **OK, the ~'s up!** ça suffit maintenant, tu es démasqué!; **don't play his ~** n'entre pas dans son jeu; **we soon saw through his ~** nous avons vite vu clair dans son (petit) jeu; **two can play at that ~** à bon chat bon rat (PROV); **what's the ~?*** (= what's happening?) qu'est-ce qui se passe?; (= what are you doing?) à quoi tu joues?*; **what's your (little) ~?*** à quoi tu joues?*; **I wonder what his ~ is*** je me demande ce qu'il mijote* or manigance; (Brit) **don't come that ~ with me*** ne jouez pas ce petit jeu-là avec moi; **to beat sb at his** (or her etc) **own ~** battre qn sur son propre terrain; **to spoil sb's ~** déjouer les manigances or machinations de qn; **how long have you been in this ~?*** cela fait combien de temps que vous faites ça?; (esp US) **to be the only ~ in town** [person, company, plan] être le seul valable or digne de considération; **to be on the ~:** [prostitute] faire le trottoir* → **fun, give away, play, waiting**

[d] (Culin, Hunting) gibier m; **big/small ~** gros/petit or menu gibier m → **big, fair[1]**

[2] **games** NPL (Brit Scol) sport m, activités fpl physiques et sportives; **to be good at ~s** être sportif; **we get ~s on Thursdays** nous avons APS le jeudi

[3] VI (= gamble) jouer

[4] ADJ [a] (= brave) courageux; **to be ~** avoir du cran*, avoir du cœur au ventre

[b] (= ready, prepared) prêt (**to do** à faire); **are you ~?** tu en as envie?; **I'm ~ if you are** je marche si tu marches; **he's ~ for anything** il est prêt à tout, il ne recule devant rien

[5] COMP ► **game birds** NPL gibier m (NonC) à plume ► **game fish** N poissons mpl d'eau douce ► **game laws** NPL réglementation f de la chasse ► **game park** N = **game reserve** ► **game pie** N (Culin) pâté m de gibier en croûte ► **game plan** N (lit, fig) stratégie f; (fig) **what's the ~ plan?** comment va-t-on s'organiser? ► **game reserve** N réserve f naturelle ► **games console** N (Comput) console f de jeux (TV) ► **game show** N jeu m télévisé; (Rad) jeu m radiophonique ► **games master, games mistress** N (Scol) professeur m d'éducation physique ► **game theory** N théorie f des jeux ► **game warden** N garde-chasse m; (on reserve) gardien m chargé de la protection des animaux

game² [geɪm] ADJ (= lame) [arm, leg] estropié

gamebag [ˈgeɪmbæg] N gibecière f, carnassière f

gamecock [ˈgeɪmkɒk] N coq m de combat

gamekeeper [ˈgeɪmˌkiːpəʳ] N garde-chasse m

gamely [ˈgeɪmlɪ] ADV hardiment

gamesmanship [ˈgeɪmzmənʃɪp] N **a successful piece of ~** un stratagème couronné de succès; **an element of political ~** une part de stratégie politique; **to be good at ~** savoir utiliser les règles (du jeu) à son avantage

gamester [ˈgeɪmstəʳ] N joueur m, -euse f

gamete [ˈgæmiːt] N gamète m

gamin [ˈgæmɛ̃] N gamin m

gamine [gæˈmiːn] [1] N (= cheeky girl) gamine f (espiègle); (= tomboy) garçon m manqué [2] COMP [appearance, hat] gamin ► **gamine haircut** N **she had a ~ haircut** elle avait les cheveux coupés à la garçonne

gaming [ˈgeɪmɪŋ] [1] N = **gambling** [2] COMP ► **gaming laws** NPL réglementation f des jeux d'argent

gamma [ˈgæmə] [1] N gamma m [2] COMP ► **gamma radiation** N rayons mpl gamma ► **gamma rays** NPL = **gamma radiation**

gammon [ˈgæmən] [1] N (Brit) (= bacon) quartier m de lard fumé; (= ham) jambon m fumé [2] COMP ► **gammon steak** N (épaisse) tranche f de jambon fumé or salé

gammy* [ˈgæmɪ] ADJ (Brit) = **game²**

gamp: [gæmp] N (Brit hum) pépin* m, pébroc m

gamut [ˈgæmət] N (Mus, fig) gamme f; (fig) **to run the ~** passer par toute la gamme de; **his facial expressions ran the ~ from pain to terror** son visage est passé par toute la gamme des expressions de la douleur à la terreur

gamy [ˈgeɪmɪ] ADJ [meat etc] au goût de gibier

gander [ˈgændəʳ] N [a] (= bird) jars m → **sauce** [b] (= look) **to take a ~:** filer* un coup d'œil (at vers)

ganef: [ˈgɑːnəf] N (US) escroc m, filou m

gang [gæŋ] [1] N [of workmen] équipe f; [of criminals] bande f, gang m; [of youths, children, friends etc] bande f; [of prisoners] convoi m; (Tech) série f (d'outils multiples); **do you want to be in our ~?** veux-tu faire partie de notre bande?; **they roam the streets in ~s** ils traînent dans les rues en bandes → **chain** [2] COMP ► **the Gang of Four** N (Pol) la bande des Quatre ► **gang rape** N viol m collectif ► **gang warfare** N guerre f des gangs

► **gang together*** VI se mettre ensemble or à plusieurs (**to do** pour faire)

► **gang up*** VI se mettre à plusieurs (**to do** pour faire); **to ~ up on** or **against sb:** se liguer contre qn, se mettre à plusieurs contre qn

gangbang: [ˈgæŋˌbæŋ] N (= rape) viol m collectif

ganger [ˈgæŋəʳ] N (Brit) chef m d'équipe (de travailleurs)

Ganges [ˈgændʒiːz] N Gange m

gangland* [ˈgæŋˌlænd] N **~ boss** chef m de gang; **~ killing** règlement m de comptes (entre gangs)

ganglia [ˈgæŋglɪə] NPL of **ganglion**

gangling [ˈgæŋglɪŋ] ADJ [person] dégingandé; **a ~ boy** un échalas, une perche (hum)

ganglion [ˈgæŋglɪən] N (pl **ganglia** or **ganglions**) ganglion m; (fig) [of activity] centre m

gangly [ˈgæŋglɪ] ADJ = **gangling**

gangplank [ˈgæŋˌplæŋk] N passerelle f (de débarquement); (Naut) échelle f de coupée

gangrene [ˈgæŋgriːn] N gangrène f

gangrenous [ˈgæŋgrɪnəs] ADJ gangreneux; **to go ~** se gangrener

gangsta rap [ˈgæŋstəˌræp] N (Mus) gangsta rap m

gangster [ˈgæŋstəʳ] [1] N gangster m, bandit m [2] COMP [story, film] de gangsters

gangsterism [ˈgæŋstərɪzəm] N gangstérisme m

gangway [ˈgæŋˌweɪ] N passerelle f; (Brit) (in bus etc) couloir m; (in theatre) allée f; **~!** dégagez!

ganja [ˈgændʒə] N ganja f

gannet [ˈgænɪt] N (Orn) fou m (de Bassan)

gantry [ˈgæntrɪ] N (for crane) portique m; (Space) tour f de lancement; (Rail) portique m (à signaux); (for barrels) chantier m

gaol [dʒeɪl] (Brit) = **jail**

gaoler [ˈdʒeɪləʳ] N (Brit) = **jailer**

gap [gæp] [1] N [a] (= hole) trou m, vide m; (in wall) trou m, brèche f; (in hedge) trou m, ouverture f; (in print, text) espace m, blanc m; (between floorboards) interstice m; (in pavement) brèche f; (between curtains) intervalle m; (in clouds, fog) trouée f; (between teeth) écart m, interstice m; (= mountain pass) trouée f; (in writing) blanc m; **to stop up** or **fill in a ~** boucher un trou, combler un vide

[b] (fig) (in time) intervalle m; (in timetable) trou m; (in conversation, narrative) interruption f, vide m; (in education) lacune f, manque m; **a ~ in his memory** un trou de mémoire; **he left a ~ which will be hard to fill** il a laissé un vide

qui sera difficile à combler; **the four-month ~ between the ceasefire and the elections** l'intervalle de quatre mois entre le cessez-le-feu et les élections; **production was resumed after a three-year ~** or **a ~ of three years** la production a repris après une interruption de trois ans; **after a ~ of three years** or **a three-year ~, Henry was born** trois ans plus tard, Henry est né; **she returned after a ~ of four years** elle est rentrée après une absence de quatre ans; **on the last lap she closed the ~ (between them) to 4.2 seconds** au dernier tour de piste elle est revenue à 4,2 secondes de sa concurrente; **policies designed to close the ~ between the salaries of public and private sector employees** des mesures visant à réduire l'écart entre les salaires du secteur public et ceux du secteur privé; **tax increases to close the ~ between spending and revenue** des augmentations d'impôt afin de réduire l'écart entre les dépenses et les recettes; **to close the ~ in the balance of payments** supprimer le déficit dans la balance des paiements; **the ~ between rich and poor is closing/widening** l'écart entre les riches et les pauvres se réduit/se creuse; (Comm) **a ~ in the market** un créneau; **the software ~ is the biggest problem** l'insuffisance en matière de logiciel constitue le problème majeur; **the trade ~** le déficit commercial → **bridge¹, credibility, generation**

[2] COMP ► **gap financing** N (Fin) crédit m (de) relais ► **gap-toothed** ADJ [person] (teeth wide apart) aux dents écartées; (= teeth missing) brèche-dent†, à qui il manque une (or des) dent(s); [smile, grin] édenté

gape [geɪp] [1] VI [a] (= open mouth) [person] bâiller, ouvrir la bouche toute grande; [bird] ouvrir le bec tout grand; [seam etc] bâiller; [chasm, abyss] être béant [b] (= stare) rester bouche bée, bayer aux corneilles; **to ~ at sb/sth** regarder qn/qch bouche bée [2] N (= stare) regard m ébahi

gaping [ˈgeɪpɪŋ] ADJ [hole, chasm, wound] béant; [mouth, eyes] grand ouvert; [onlooker, tourist] bouche bée inv

gappy [ˈgæpɪ] ADJ [teeth] écartés; [structure, hedge] avec des vides

garage [ˈgærɑːʒ] [1] N [a] garage m [b] (also **~ music**) garage m [2] VT garer, mettre au garage [3] COMP [door, wall] de garage ► **garage band** N (Mus) groupe m de musique garage ► **garage mechanic** N mécanicien m ► **garage proprietor** N garagiste m ► **garage sale** N vente f d'objets usagés (chez un particulier), vide-grenier m → CAR-BOOT SALE, GARAGE SALE ► **garage space** N (NonC) place f pour se garer; **there is ~ space for three cars** il y a de la place pour trois voitures

garageman [ˈgærɑːʒmən] N (pl **-men**) mécanicien m

garaging [ˈgærɑːʒɪŋ] N (NonC) place f pour se garer; **there is ~ for three cars** il y a de la place pour trois voitures

garb [gɑːb] [1] N (NonC: gen hum) costume m, atours mpl (liter); **in medieval ~** en costume médiéval [2] VT (gen passive) vêtir (**in** de)

garbage [ˈgɑːbɪdʒ] [1] N (NonC: esp US) ordures fpl, détritus mpl; (= food waste) déchets mpl; (fig) (= worthless objects) rebut m; (= nonsense) foutaises* fpl; (Comput) (information) parasites mpl; (Comput) **~ in, ~ out** qualité d'entrée égale qualité de sortie, garbage in garbage out [2] COMP ► **garbage can** N (US) boîte f à ordures, poubelle f ► **garbage chute** N (US) vide-ordures m inv ► **garbage collector** N (US) éboueur m, boueux* m ► **garbage disposal unit** N (US) broyeur m d'ordures ► **garbage man** N (pl **garbage men**) (US) = **garbage collector** ► **garbage shute** N (US) = **garbage chute**

► **garbage truck** N (US) camion m des éboueurs

garble ['gɑːbl] VT embrouiller

garbled ['gɑːbld] ADJ [account, version, message] embrouillé; [words, speech] confus

Garda[1] ['gɑːdə] N Lake ~ le lac de Garde

Garda[2] ['gɑːdə] N (pl **Gardaí** ['gɑːdiː]) (Ir) agent m de police; **the** ~ or ~ la police irlandaise

garden ['gɑːdn] [1] N jardin m; **the Garden of Eden** le Paradis terrestre, le jardin d'Éden; ~**s** (public) parc m, jardin m public; [of manor house etc] jardin m; **herb** ~ jardin m d'herbes aromatiques; **vegetable** ~ (jardin m) potager m; **in the** ~ dans le jardin, au jardin; (fig) **everything in the ~'s lovely** or **rosy** tout va pour le mieux → **back, flower, kitchen** [2] VI jardiner, faire du jardinage; **I like ~ing** j'aime le jardinage, j'aime jardiner [3] COMP ► **garden apartment** N (US) = **garden flat** ► **garden centre** N jardinerie f ► **garden city** N (Brit) cité-jardin f ► **garden flat** N appartement m en rez-de-jardin ► **garden gnome** N nain m de jardin ► **garden hose** N tuyau m d'arrosage ► **garden of remembrance** N jardin m du souvenir (dans un cimetière) ► **garden party** N garden-party f, réception f en plein air ► **garden path** N (fig) **to lead sb up the ~path*** mener qn en bateau* ► **garden produce** N (NonC) produits mpl maraîchers ► **garden seat** N banc m de jardin ► **garden shears** NPL cisaille f de jardinier ► **garden snail** N escargot m ► **the Garden State** N (US) le New Jersey ► **garden suburb** N banlieue f résidentielle (aménagée par un paysagiste) ► **garden tools** NPL outils mpl de jardinage ► **garden-variety** ADJ (US) (= ordinary) simple, ordinaire; (= standard) d'un modèle standard or ordinaire ► **garden wall** N mur m de jardin; **he lives just over the ~ wall from us** il habite juste à côté de chez nous

gardener ['gɑːdnə] N jardinier m, -ière f; **I'm no ~** je ne connais rien au jardinage; **he's a good ~** il est très bon jardinier → **landscape**

gardenia [gɑːˈdiːnɪə] N gardénia m

gardening ['gɑːdnɪŋ] [1] N jardinage m → **garden, landscape** [2] COMP ► **gardening tools** NPL = **garden tools**; → **garden**

garfish ['gɑːfɪʃ] N (pl **garfish** or **garfishes**) orphie f

gargantuan [gɑːˈgæntjʊən] ADJ gargantuesque

gargle ['gɑːgl] [1] VI se gargariser (**with** à); faire un gargarisme (**with** avec) [2] N gargarisme m

gargoyle ['gɑːgɔɪl] N gargouille f

garish ['gɛərɪʃ] ADJ (pej) [colour] criard; [clothes] aux couleurs criardes, tapageur; [décor] criard, tapageur; [light] cru

garishly ['gɛərɪʃlɪ] ADV [decorated, painted, dressed] de couleurs criardes; ~ **coloured** aux couleurs criardes; ~ **lit** crûment éclairé

garishness ['gɛərɪʃnɪs] N [of clothes, décor, building] aspect m criard or tapageur; [of colours] crudité f, violence f

garland ['gɑːlənd] [1] N guirlande f; **a ~ of flowers/holly** une guirlande de fleurs/de houx [2] VT orner de guirlandes, enguirlander

garlic ['gɑːlɪk] [1] N (NonC) ail m → **clove** [2] COMP ► **garlic bread** N pain m à l'ail ► **garlic mushrooms** NPL champignons mpl à l'ail ► **garlic press** N presse-ail m inv ► **garlic salt** N sel m d'ail ► **garlic sausage** N saucisson m à l'ail

garlicky ['gɑːlɪkɪ] ADJ [flavour, smell] d'ail; [sauce] à l'ail; [food] aillé; [breath] qui sent l'ail

garment ['gɑːmənt] N vêtement m

garner ['gɑːnə] [1] VT (also ~ **in**, ~ **up**) [+ grain etc] rentrer, engranger; (fig) [+ information, reviews] recueillir [2] N (liter) (= granary) grenier m; (= anthology) recueil m

garnet ['gɑːnɪt] [1] N (= gem, colour) grenat m [2] ADJ (also ~-**coloured**) grenat inv [3] COMP [ring] de grenat(s) ► **garnet-coloured** ADJ → 2

garnish ['gɑːnɪʃ] [1] VT orner, parer (**with** de); (Culin) décorer (**with** avec) [2] N décoration f

garnishee [gɑːnɪˈiː] N (Jur) saisi m

garnishing ['gɑːnɪʃɪŋ] N (Culin) décoration f

garnishment ['gɑːnɪʃmənt] N (Jur) saisie-arrêt f

garnishor ['gɑːnɪʃə] N (Jur) saisissant m

garotte [gəˈrɒt] = **garrotte**

garret ['gærət] N (= room) mansarde f; (= attic) grenier m

garrison ['gærɪsən] [1] N garnison f [2] VT [+ fort etc] placer une garnison dans; [+ troops] mettre en garnison; [regiment] être en garnison dans [3] COMP ► **garrison life** N vie f de garnison ► **garrison town** N ville f de garnison ► **garrison troops** NPL troupes fpl de garnison

garrotte [gəˈrɒt] [1] VT (= strangle) étrangler; (Spanish Hist) faire périr par le garrot [2] N (gen) cordelette f (pour étrangler); (Spanish Hist) garrot m

garrulous ['gærʊləs] ADJ [person] loquace, volubile; [liter] [stream] babillard (liter)

garrulously ['gærʊləslɪ] ADV [talk] avec volubilité

garrulousness ['gærʊləsnɪs] N loquacité f, volubilité f

garter ['gɑːtə] [1] N (gen) jarretière f; (for men's socks) fixe-chaussette m; (US: from belt) jarretelle f; (Brit) **Order of the Garter** Ordre m de la Jarretière; (Brit) **Knight of the Garter** chevalier m de l'Ordre de la Jarretière [2] COMP ► **garter belt** N (US) porte-jarretelles m inv ► **garter stitch** N (Knitting) point m mousse

gas [gæs] [1] N (pl **gas(s)es**) [a] (Chem, Culin, Phys, Med etc) gaz m inv; (Min) méthane m, grisou m; (Mil) gaz m (asphyxiant or vésicant etc); (= anaesthetic) (gaz m) anesthésique m; **to cook by** or **with** ~ faire la cuisine au gaz; **to turn on/off the** ~ allumer/fermer or éteindre le gaz; **the dentist gave me** ~ le dentiste m'a fait une anesthésie au gaz; (**combined**) ~ **and electric cooker** cuisinière f mixte → **laughing, natural, supply** [b] (US: also ~**oline**) essence f; **to step on the ~*** (Aut) appuyer sur le champignon*; (fig) se magner*, se presser; **to take one's foot off the ~*** ralentir [c] (= chat) **to have a ~** tailler une bavette* (**about** à propos de) [d] (* = fun) rigolade* f; **it was a real ~!** quelle rigolade!*, ce qu'on s'est marrés! [2] VT (gen) asphyxier; (Mil) gazer; **to ~ o.s.** (gen) s'asphyxier; (= commit suicide) se suicider au gaz [3] VI [a] (Chem) dégager des gaz [b] (= talk, chat) papoter [4] COMP [industry] du gaz, gazier; [engine] à gaz ► **gas bracket** N applique f à gaz ► **gas burner** N = **gas jet** ► **gas carrier** N (= ship) méthanier m ► **gas central heating** N = **gas-fired central heating** ► **gas chamber** N chambre f à gaz ► **gas cooker** N cuisinière f à gaz, gazinière f; (portable) réchaud m à gaz ► **gas-cooled reactor** N réacteur m graphite-gaz ► **gas cylinder** N bonbonne f de gaz ► **gas explosion** N (gen) explosion f (causée par une fuite) de gaz; (in coal mine) explosion f or coup m de grisou ► **gas fire** N appareil m de chauffage à gaz; **to light the ~ fire** allumer le gaz ► **gas-fired** ADJ chauffé au gaz ► **gas-fired central heating** N chauffage m central au gaz ► **gas fitter** N installateur m, -trice f d'appareils à gaz ► **gas fittings** NPL installation f de gaz ► **gas fixture** N = **gas bracket** ► **gas guzzler*** N (= car) voiture f qui consomme énormément d'essence or qui suce* beaucoup ► **gas heat-**

er N appareil m de chauffage à gaz; (for heating water) chauffe-eau m inv (à gaz) ► **gas hog*** N (US) = **gas guzzler** ► **gas jet** N brûleur m à gaz ► **gas lamp** N lampe f à gaz ► **gas lighter** N (for cooker etc) allume-gaz m inv; (for cigarettes) briquet m à gaz ► **gas lighting** N éclairage m au gaz ► **gas main** N canalisation f de gaz ► **gas mantle** N manchon m à incandescence ► **gas meter** N compteur m à gaz ► **gas mileage** N (US Aut) consommation f (d'essence) ► **gas oil** N gasoil m ► **gas oven** N four m à gaz; **he put his head in the** ~ **oven** il s'est suicidé en se mettant la tête dans le four à gaz; **she felt like putting her head in the** ~ **oven** elle avait envie de se jeter par la fenêtre ► **gas pedal** N (US Aut) (pédale f d')accélérateur m ► **gas-permeable** ADJ [lens] perméable à l'oxygène ► **gas pipeline** N tuyau m à gaz ► **gas pipeline** N gazoduc m ► **gas pump** N (US Aut) pompe f à essence ► **gas range** N fourneau m à gaz ► **gas ring** N (= part of cooker) brûleur m; (= small stove) réchaud m à gaz ► **gas station** N (US) station-service f ► **gas stove** N (portable) réchaud m à gaz; (larger) cuisinière f or fourneau m à gaz ► **gas tank** N (US) réservoir m à essence ► **gas tap** N (on pipe) robinet m à gaz; (on cooker) bouton m (de cuisinière à gaz) ► **gas turbine** N turbine f à gaz ► **gas worker** N gazier m

► **gas up*** VI (US Aut) faire le plein (de carburant)

gasbag ['gæsbæg] N (enveloppe f de) ballon m à gaz; (* pej) (= talkative person) moulin m à paroles* (pej); (= boastful person) baratineur* m, -euse* f

Gascon ['gæskən] [1] ADJ gascon [2] N Gascon(ne) m(f)

Gascony ['gæskənɪ] N la Gascogne

gaseous ['gæsɪəs] ADJ gazeux

gash [gæʃ] [1] N (in flesh) entaille f, estafilade f; (on face) balafre f; (in cloth, leather) grande déchirure f [2] VT [+ flesh] entailler, entamer; [+ face] balafrer; [+ cloth, leather] déchirer; **she ~ed her arm** elle s'est entaillé or s'est entamé le bras [3] ADJ (Brit* = surplus) de trop, en surplus

gasholder ['gæs,həʊldə] N gazomètre m

gasket ['gæskɪt] N [a] [of piston] garniture f de piston; [of joint] joint m d'étanchéité; [of cylinder head] joint m de culasse → **blow**[1] [b] (Naut) raban m de ferlage

gaslight ['gæslaɪt] N lumière f du gaz; **by** ~ au gaz, à la lumière du gaz

gaslit ['gæslɪt] N éclairé au gaz

gasman* ['gæsmæn] N (pl -**men**) employé m du gaz, gazier m

gasmask ['gæsmɑːsk] N masque m à gaz

gasohol ['gæsəhɒl] N (US) carburol m

gasoline ['gæsəliːn] (US) [1] N essence f [2] COMP ► **gasoline gauge** N jauge f d'essence ► **gasoline-powered** ADJ à essence

gasometer [gæˈsɒmɪtə] N (Brit) gazomètre m

gasp [gɑːsp] [1] N halètement m; **to give a ~ of surprise/fear** etc avoir le souffle coupé par la surprise/la peur etc; **to be at one's last ~** être au bout du rouleau; **to the last ~** jusqu'au dernier souffle; **11,000 years ago, at the last ~ of the ice age** il y a 11 000 ans, juste à la fin de l'ère glaciaire [2] VI (= choke) haleter, suffoquer; (from astonishment) avoir le souffle coupé; (lit, fig) **to make sb** ~ couper le souffle à qn; **to ~ for breath** or **air** haleter, suffoquer; (= want desperately) **I'm ~ing for a cup of tea/a cigarette** je meurs d'envie de boire une tasse de thé/de fumer une cigarette; **I was ~ing!** (= thirsty) je mourais de soif [3] VT (in quiet voice) souffler; **"no!" she ~ed** « non! » souffla-t-elle; (in strangled voice) **the young man ~ed his thanks** le jeune homme remercia d'une voix entrecoupée ; **"you're beau-tiful," he ~ed out** «vous êtes belle» dit-il d'une voix entrecoupée

gasper: ['gɑːspəʳ] N (*Brit*) sèche: *f*, clope: *f* or *m*

gassed: ['gæst] ADJ (= *drunk*) bourré:

gassy ['gæsɪ] ADJ gazeux ; (: *pej*) [*person*] bavard, jacasseur

gastric ['gæstrɪk] 1 ADJ gastrique 2 COMP
► **gastric flu** N grippe *f* gastro-intestinale
► **gastric juices** NPL sucs *mpl* gastriques
► **gastric ulcer** N ulcère *m* de l'estomac

gastritis [gæs'traɪtɪs] N gastrite *f*

gastro... ['gæstrəʊ] PREF gastro...

gastroenteritis [,gæstrəʊ,entə'raɪtɪs] N gastro-entérite *f*

gastroenterologist ['gæstrəʊ'entə,rɒlədʒɪst] N gastroentérologue *mf*

gastroenterology ['gæstrəʊ'entə,rɒlədʒɪ] N gastroentérologie *f*

gastronome ['gæstrənəʊm] N gastronome *mf*

gastronomic [,gæstrə'nɒmɪk] ADJ gastronomique

gastronomist [gæs'trɒnəmɪst] N gastronome *mf*

gastronomy [gæs'trɒnəmɪ] N gastronomie *f*

gastropod ['gæstrəpɒd] N gastéropode *m*

gasworks ['gæswɜːks] N (*pl inv*) usine *f* à gaz

gat¹ †† [gæt] VB *pt of* **get**

gat² †‡ [gæt] N (*US = gun*) flingue: *m*, pétard: *m*

gate [geɪt] 1 N a [*of castle, town, airport*] porte *f* ; [*of field, level crossing*] barrière *f* ; [*of garden*] porte *f*, portail *m* ; (*large, metallic*) grille *f* (d'entrée) ; (*low*) portillon *m* ; [*tall, into courtyard etc*) porte *f* cochère ; (*in Metro*) portillon *m* ; [*of lock, sluice*] vanne *f*, porte *f* (d'écluse) ; [*of sports ground*] entrée *f* ; (= *entrance*) **the factory/castle** *etc* ~ l'entrée *f* de l'usine/du château *etc* ; **five-bar** ~ ≈ barrière *f* ; (*US*) **to give sb the ~**‡ [+ *employee*] virer* qn ; [+ *boyfriend etc*] plaquer* qn ; (*US*) **to get the ~**‡ (= *be dismissed*) être viré*
b (*Sport*) (= *attendance*) spectateurs *mpl* ; (= *money*) recette *f*, entrées *fpl* ; **there was a ~ of 5,000** il y avait 5 000 spectateurs ; **the match got a good ~** le match a fait beaucoup d'entrées
c (*Ski*) porte *f*
d (*Comput*) porte *f*
2 VT (*Brit*:) *Scol, Univ*) consigner, coller*
3 COMP ► **gate-leg(ged) table** N table *f* anglaise, table *f* à abattants ► **gate money** N (*Sport*) recette *f*, (montant *m* des) entrées *fpl*

...gate [-geɪt] N (*in compounds*) **Dianagate** scandale *m* Diana ; **Irangate** Irangate *m* → **Watergate**

gâteau ['gætəʊ] N (*pl* **gâteaux** ['gætəʊz]) (*Brit*) grand gâteau *m* fourré

gatecrash ['geɪtkræʃ] 1 VI (*without invitation*) s'introduire sans invitation ; (*without paying*) resquiller* 2 VT s'introduire (sans invitation) dans ; **to ~ a match** assister à un match sans payer

gatecrasher ['geɪt,kræʃəʳ] N (*without invitation*) intrus(e) *m(f)* ; (*without paying*) resquilleur* *m*, -euse* *f*

gatefold ['geɪtfəʊld] N (*US Publishing*) dépliant *m* encarté

gatehouse ['geɪthaʊs] N [*of castle*] corps *m* de garde ; [*of park etc*] loge *f*

gatekeeper ['geɪt,kiːpəʳ] N [*of block of flats etc*] portier *m*, -ière *f* ; [*of factory etc*] gardien(ne) *m(f)* ; (*Rail*) garde-barrière *mf*

gatepost ['geɪtpəʊst] N montant *m* (de porte) ; (*fig*) **between you, me and the ~*** soit dit entre nous

gateway ['geɪtweɪ] N entrée *f* ; (*fig*) **New York, the ~ to America** New York, porte de l'Amérique ; **it proved the ~ to success/fame/fortune** cela ouvrit toutes grandes les portes du succès/de la gloire/de la fortune

gather ['gæðəʳ] 1 VT a (*also* **~ together**) [+ *people*] rassembler, réunir ; [+ *objects*] rassembler, ramasser ; [+ *troops*] amasser
b (= *draw, attract*) attirer ; (*Typ*) [+ *pages*] assembler ; **the programme ~ed an audience of 20 million viewers** cette émission a été regardée par 20 millions de téléspectateurs ; **the accident ~ed quite a crowd** l'accident a attiré pas mal de monde
c (= *collect*) [+ *flowers*] cueillir ; [+ *wood, sticks, mushrooms*] ramasser ; [+ *taxes*] percevoir ; [+ *information, data, evidence*] réunir ; **to ~ dirt** s'encrasser ; (*lit, fig*) **to ~ dust** prendre la poussière ; **to ~ momentum** (*lit*) prendre de la vitesse ; (*fig*) [*political movement, pressure group*] prendre de l'ampleur ; **to ~ one's thoughts** se concentrer ; **to ~ speed**◊ **to ~ way** (*Naut*) prendre de la vitesse ; **to ~ strength** [*person*] reprendre des forces ; [*feeling, movement*] se renforcer ; **she is trying to ~ support for her ideas/her candidacy** elle essaie d'obtenir des appuis pour ses idées/sa candidature ; **to ~ volume** croître en volume
d **she ~ed him in her arms** elle l'a serré dans ses bras ; **he ~ed her to him** il l'a serrée contre lui ; **he ~ed his cloak around him** il a ramené son manteau contre lui ; **she ~ed up her skirts** elle a ramassé ses jupes ; **her hair was ~ed into a bun** ses cheveux étaient ramassés en chignon ; (*liter, euph*) **he was ~ed to his fathers** il alla rejoindre ses ancêtres *or* aïeux
e (*Sewing*) froncer ; **a ~ed skirt** une jupe froncée
f (= *infer*) déduire, conclure ; **I ~ from this report (that) ...** je conclus *or* je déduis de ce rapport (que) ... ; **I ~ from the papers that ...** d'après ce que disent les journaux, je déduis *or* je crois comprendre que ... ; **I ~ from him that ...** je comprends d'après ce qu'il me dit que ... ; **what are we to ~ from that?** que devons-nous en déduire ? ; **as far as I can ~**◊ **from what I could ~** à ce que je comprends ; **I ~ she won't be coming** d'après ce que j'ai compris, elle ne viendra pas ; **as you will have ~ed** comme vous avez dû le deviner ; **as will be ~ed from my report** comme il ressort de mon rapport ; **so I ~** c'est ce que j'ai cru comprendre ; **I ~ed that** j'avais compris
2 VI a (= *collect*) [*people*] se rassembler, se réunir ; [*troops*] s'amasser ; [*objects*] s'accumuler ; [*clouds*] se former, s'amonceler ; [*dust*] s'accumuler, s'amasser ; **they ~ed round him** ils se sont groupés *or* se sont rassemblés autour de lui ; **a crowd had ~ed in front of the embassy** une foule s'était formée devant l'ambassade ; **a crowd of demonstrators had ~ed** des manifestants s'étaient rassemblés
b (= *increase*) (*in volume, intensity etc*) croître, grandir ; (*in size, content etc*) grossir → **gathering**
c [*abscess*] mûrir ; [*pus*] se former ; **tears ~ed in her eyes** ses yeux se remplirent de larmes
3 N (*Sewing*) fronce *f*
► **gather in** VT SEP [+ *crops*] rentrer, récolter ; [+ *money, taxes*] faire rentrer, percevoir ; [+ *contributions*] recueillir ; [+ *papers, essays*] ramasser ; **the dress ~ed in at the waist** la robe est froncée à la taille
► **gather round** VI faire cercle, s'approcher ; **~ round!** approchez-vous ! ; **~ round, children!** approchez-vous les enfants !
► **gather together** 1 VI s'amasser, se rassembler 2 VT SEP = **gather 1a** ; **to ~ o.s. together** (= *collect one's thoughts*) se recueillir, se concentrer ; (*for jump etc*) se ramasser
► **gather up** VT SEP [+ *papers, clothes, toys*] ramasser ; **to ~ up the threads of a discussion** rassembler les principaux arguments d'une discussion ; **to ~ up one's courage** rassembler son courage ; **to ~ up one's dignity** essayer de paraître digne ; **to ~ up one's strength** rassembler ses forces ; **to ~ o.s. up** (*for jump etc*) se ramasser ; **he ~ed himself up to his full height** il s'est redressé de toute sa hauteur → **gather 1c**

gatherer ['gæðərəʳ] N cueilleur *m*, -euse *f* → **hunter-gatherer**

gathering ['gæðərɪŋ] 1 N a (*NonC* = *act*) [*of people*] rassemblement *m* ; [*of objects*] accumulation *f*, amoncellement *m* ; [*of fruits etc*] cueillette *f* ; [*of crops*] récolte *f* ; **the ~ of information/evidence may take several weeks** réunir les informations/les preuves pourrait prendre plusieurs semaines
b (= *group of people*) assemblée *f*, réunion *f* ; (= *act of meeting*) rassemblement *m* ; **a family ~** une réunion de famille ; **a ~ of 12 heads of state** une rencontre de 12 chefs d'État ; **~s of more than 20 people were forbidden** les rassemblements de plus de 20 personnes étaient interdits
c (*NonC: Sewing*) fronces *fpl*, froncis *m*
2 ADJ [*dusk, darkness, gloom*] grandissant ; [*crowd*] en train de se former ; **the ~ clouds** les nuages qui s'amoncellent (*or* s'amoncelaient) ; **the ~ storm** l'orage qui se prépare (*or* se préparait) ; **with ~ speed** de plus en plus vite

-gathering [-'gæðərɪŋ] N (*in compounds*) **information-** *or* **intelligence-gathering** collecte *f* de renseignements

gator* ['geɪtəʳ] N (*US*) = **alligator**

GATT [gæt] N (ABBR = **General Agreement on Tariffs and Trade**) GATT *m*

gauche [gəʊʃ] ADJ gauche, maladroit

gaucheness ['gəʊʃnɪs] N gaucherie *f*, maladresse *f*

gaucho ['gaʊtʃəʊ] N gaucho *m*

gaudily ['gɔːdɪlɪ] ADV [*decorated, painted, dressed*] de couleurs voyantes ; **~ coloured** aux couleurs voyantes *or* crues ; **~ patterned** aux motifs voyants

gaudy ['gɔːdɪ] 1 ADJ [*clothes*] aux couleurs voyantes ; [*bird, fish*] aux couleurs éclatantes ; [*colour*] voyant, cru ; [*display etc*] tapageur 2 N (*Brit Univ*) fête *f* annuelle (de collège)

gauge [geɪdʒ] 1 N a (= *standard measure*) calibre *m* ; (*Rail*) écartement *m* ; (*Tex*) jauge *f* ; (= *instrument*) jauge *f*, indicateur *m* ; **oil ~** indicateur *m* or jauge *f* du niveau d'huile ; (*fig*) **the survey was seen as a good ~ of employment trends** l'enquête a été considérée comme un bon indicateur des tendances de l'emploi ; **opinion polls are not an accurate ~ of popular feeling** les sondages ne permettent pas de d'évaluer avec justesse le sentiment populaire
2 VT a (= *measure*) [+ *nut, temperature*] mesurer ; [+ *oil*] jauger ; [+ *wind*] mesurer la vitesse de ; [+ *screw, gun*] calibrer ; [+ *sb's abilities*] évaluer ; [+ *course of events*] prévoir ; **to ~ a distance** (*by looking*) évaluer une distance à vue d'œil ; **"she's out," he said, gauging my reaction** « elle est sortie, » dit-il, essayant de deviner ma réaction ; **I tried to ~ whether she was pleased or not** j'ai essayé de deviner si elle était contente ou pas ; **we must try to ~ how strong public opinion is** nous devons essayer d'évaluer le poids de l'opinion publique ; **to ~ the right moment** calculer le bon moment
b [+ *tools*] standardiser

-gauge [geɪdʒ] SUF (*in compounds*) **narrow-/standard-/broad-gauge railway** voie *f* étroite/à écartement normal/à grand écartement

Gaul [gɔːl] N (= *country*) la Gaule ; (= *person*) Gaulois(e) *m(f)*

Gaullism ['gəʊlɪzəm] N gaullisme *m*

Gaullist ['gəʊlɪst] ADJ, N gaulliste *mf*

gaunt [gɔːnt] ADJ a (= *thin and pale*) [*person, face, features*] hâve ; [*body, figure*] émacié ; **he looks ~** il a les traits tirés b (= *grim*) [*building*] austère ; [*tree*] squelettique

gauntlet ['gɔːntlɪt] N [*of glove*] gant *m* (à crispin) ; (= *part of glove*) crispin *m* ; [*of armour*] gantelet *m* ; (*Hist, also fig*) **to throw down/take up the ~** jeter/relever le gant ; **to run the ~** (*Mil Hist*) passer par les baguettes ; (*Naut Hist*) courir la bouline ; (*fig*) **they ran the ~ of enemy submarines** ils risquaient d'être la cible de sous-marins ennemis ; (*fig*) **he had to run the ~ through the crowd** il a dû foncer à travers une foule hostile ; (*fig*) **he ran the ~ of public criticism** il essuya le feu des critiques du public

gauss [gaʊs] N (*pl inv*) gauss *m*

Gaussian ['gaʊsɪən] ADJ gaussien

gauze [gɔːz] N (*all senses*) gaze *f*

gauzy ['gɔːzɪ] ADJ vaporeux

gave [geɪv] VB *pt of* **give**

gavel [gævl] N marteau *m* (*de président de réunion, de commissaire-priseur*)

gavotte [gə'vɒt] N gavotte *f*

Gawd: [gɔːd] EXCL (*Brit = God*) mon Dieu !, bon Dieu !*

gawk [gɔːk] **1** N godiche* *f*, grand dadais* *m* **2** VI rester bouche bée (**at** devant)

gawker* [gɔːkər] N badaud *m*

gawky ['gɔːkɪ] ADJ godiche*, empoté

gawp* [gɔːp] VI (*Brit*) = **gape 1**

gay [geɪ] **1** ADJ **a** (= *homosexual*) [*person, community, movement*] homosexuel, gay *inv* ; [*group*] gay *inv* ; [*club, bar*] gay *inv*, pour homosexuels ; **~ men and women** homosexuels *mpl* et lesbiennes *fpl* ; **~ rights** droits *mpl* des homosexuels ; **~ sex** rapports *mpl* homosexuels **b** († = *cheerful*) [*person, company, occasion*] joyeux ; [*music, party, appearance, colour*] gai ; [*laughter*] enjoué, gai ; [*costume*] aux couleurs gaies ; **to become ~(er)** s'égayer ; **with ~ abandon** avec une belle désinvolture ; **to lead a** *or* **the ~ life** mener une vie de plaisirs, mener joyeuse vie ; **to have a ~ time** prendre du bon temps **2** N homosexuel(le) *m(f)* ; **Gay Liberation (Movement)** ◊ **Gay Lib*** (mouvement *m* pour) la libération des homosexuels *or* la libération gay

gayness ['geɪnɪs] N [*of homosexual*] homosexualité *f*

Gaza strip ['gɑːzə'strɪp] N bande *f* de Gaza

gaze [geɪz] **1** N regard *m* (fixe) ; **his ~ met mine** son regard a croisé le mien **2** VI regarder ; **to ~ into space** regarder dans *or* fixer le vide ; **to ~ at** *or* (*liter*) **upon sth** regarder *or* contempler qch ; **they ~d into each other's eyes** ils se regardaient les yeux dans les yeux ; **to ~ out of the window** regarder fixement par la fenêtre ; **to ~ at o.s. in the mirror** se regarder fixement dans le miroir

► **gaze about, gaze around** VI regarder autour de soi

gazebo [gə'ziːbəʊ] N (*pl* **gazebos** *or* **gazeboes**) belvédère *m* (*pavillon*)

gazelle [gə'zel] N (*pl* **gazelles** *or* **gazelle**) gazelle *f*

gazette [gə'zet] **1** N (= *official publication*) (journal *m*) officiel *m* ; (= *newspaper*) gazette *f* **2** VT publier à l'Officiel ; (*Mil etc*) **to be ~d** avoir sa nomination publiée à l'Officiel

gazetteer [ˌgæzɪ'tɪər] N index *m* (géographique)

gazpacho [gəz'pætʃəʊ] N gaspacho *m*

gazump [gə'zʌmp] VT (*Brit*) **he was ~ed** le vendeur est revenu sur sa promesse de vente en acceptant une meilleure offre

gazumping [gə'zʌmpɪŋ] N (*Brit*) le fait de revenir sur une promesse de vente d'une maison pour accepter une offre plus élevée

GB [dʒiː'biː] (ABBR = **Great Britain**) GB

GBH [dʒiːbiː'eɪtʃ] (*Brit = crime*) (ABBR = **grievous bodily harm**) → **grievous**

GBS [dʒiːbiː'es] (*Brit*) ABBR = **George Bernard Shaw**

GC ['dʒiːsiː] N (*Brit*) (ABBR = **George Cross**) → **George**

GCE [dʒiːsiː'iː] N (*Brit Educ*) (ABBR = **General Certificate of Education**) (*formerly*) ~ **"O" level** ≈ brevet *m* ; **~ "A" level** ≈ baccalauréat *m*

GCH N (ABBR = **gas(-fired) central heating**) → **gas**

GCHQ [ˌdʒiːsiːeɪtʃ'kjuː] N (*Brit*) (ABBR = **Government Communications Headquarters**) service gouvernemental d'interception des communications

GCSE [ˌdʒiːsiːes'iː] N (*Brit Educ*) (ABBR = **General Certificate of Secondary Education**) ≈ brevet *m* des collèges

┌─────────┐
│ GCSE   │
└─────────┘

En Angleterre, au Pays de Galles et en Irlande du Nord, le **General Certificate of Secondary Education** ou **GCSE** est l'équivalent du brevet des collèges français. À l'issue de cet examen, qui se passe généralement à l'âge de seize ans, l'élève peut soit quitter l'école, soit préparer les « A levels », qui correspondent au baccalauréat français. L'équivalent écossais du **GCSE** porte le nom de « Standard Grades ». → A LEVELS

Gdansk [gdænsk] N Gdansk

GDI [dʒiːdiː'aɪ] (ABBR = **gross domestic income**) → **gross**

Gdns ABBR = **Gardens**

GDP [dʒiːdiː'piː] (ABBR = **gross domestic product**) → **gross**

GDR [dʒiːdiː'ɑːr] (ABBR = **German Democratic Republic**) → **German**

gear [gɪər] **1** N **a** (*NonC*) (= *equipment*) équipement *m*, matériel *m* ; (= *harness*) harnachement *m* ; (*for camping, skiing, climbing, photography*) matériel *m*, équipement *m* ; (*for sewing, painting*) matériel *m* ; (*for gardening*) matériel *m*, outils *mpl* ; **fishing** *etc* **~** matériel *m or* équipement *m* de pêche *etc* **b** (*NonC:* * = *belongings*) effets *mpl* (personnels), affaires *fpl* ; **he leaves his ~ all over the house** il laisse traîner ses affaires dans toute la maison **c** (*NonC: Brit = clothing*) vêtements *mpl* ; **he had his tennis ~ on** il était en tenue de tennis ; **put on your tennis ~** mets tes affaires de tennis **d** (*NonC: Brit* * = *modern clothes*) fringues* *fpl* ; **he was wearing all the ~** il portait toute la panoplie **e** (*NonC* = *apparatus*) mécanisme *m*, dispositif *m* ; **safety ~** mécanisme *m or* dispositif *m* de sécurité → **landing, steering** **f** (*Tech*) engrenage *m* ; **in ~** engréné, en prise ; **it's out of ~** c'est désengréné, ce n'est pas *or* plus en prise **g** (*Aut*) (= *mechanism*) embrayage *m* ; (= *speed*) vitesse *f* ; **in ~** en prise ; **not in ~** au point mort ; **she put the car into ~** elle a mis (la voiture) en prise ; **the car slipped** *or* **jumped out of ~** la vitesse a sauté ; **to accelerate** *or* **move (up) through the ~s** accélérer en passant toutes les vitesses les unes après les autres ; **to move down through the ~s** ralentir en rétrogradant ; **to change** *or* (*US*) **to shift ~** changer de vitesse ; **first** *or* **bottom** *or* **low ~** première *f* (vitesse) ; **second/third/fourth ~** deuxième *f*/troisième *f*/quatrième *f* (vitesse) ; **top ~** (*Brit*) ◊ **high ~** (*US*) (= *fourth*) quatrième *f* (vitesse) ; (= *fifth*) cinquième *f* (vitesse) ; **in second ~** en seconde ; **to change** *or* (*US*) **to shift into third ~** passer en troisième (vitesse) ; (*fig*) **to change** *or* (*US*) **to shift ~s** se réadapter ; (*fig*) **to get in(to) ~*** [*person, process*] se mettre en branle ; **he helped her get her life back in(to) ~*** after the divorce il l'a aidée à commencer une vie nouvelle après le divorce ; **to get one's brain in(to) ~*** faire travailler ses méninges* ; **to get one's arse** (*Brit*) *or* **ass** (*US*) **in(to) ~** se remuer le cul ; **I'm pretty much in ~ now*** c'est relativement bien parti pour moi, maintenant ; **she war life suddenly moved into top ~** après la guerre, la vie a soudain pris un rythme effréné ; **military production moved into high ~** la production militaire a atteint sa vitesse maximale → **engage, reverse**

h : (= *drugs*) came* *f* ; (= *heroin*) héro* *f* **2** ADJ (*US* * = *great*) super* **3** VT **a** adapter ; **they ~ed their output to seasonal demands** ils ont adapté leur production à la demande saisonnière ; **classrooms ~ed to the needs of disabled students** des salles de classe adaptées aux besoins des étudiants handicapés ; **the factory was not ~ed to cope with an increase of production** l'usine n'était pas à même de faire face à une augmentation de la production ; (*Econ, Ind*) **~ed to the cost of living** indexé ; **we both ~ our lives to the children** nous aménageons tous les deux notre vie en fonction des enfants ; **movies ~ed primarily to a US audience** des films s'adressant essentiellement à un public américain ; **training is ~ed to make staff more efficient** la formation est conçue pour rendre le personnel plus compétent **b** [+ *wheel*] engrener **4** VI s'engrener **5** COMP ► **gear change** N (*Brit Aut*) changement *m* de vitesse ► **gear lever** N (*Brit Aut*) levier *m* de (changement de) vitesse ► **gear ratio** N [*of cycle*] braquet *m* ► **gear stick** N = **gear lever**

► **gear down** VI (*Tech*) démultiplier

► **gear up** **1** VI **a** (*Tech*) produire une multiplication **b** (= *get ready*) **they are ~ing up for a general election** ils se préparent pour des législatives ; **Japan is ~ing up to produce 2 million cars a year** le Japon se prépare à produire 2 millions de voitures par an **c** (*Brit Fin*) [*company*] s'endetter, augmenter le taux d'endettement **2** VT SEP (* = *make ready*) **he is ~ing himself up for the presidential elections** il se prépare pour les élections présidentielles ; **satellites that are ~ed up to look for missiles** des satellites équipés pour la détection des missiles ; **the club is ~ed up for success** le club est fin prêt et compte bien gagner ; **they were all ~ed up for the new sales campaign** ils étaient parés *or* fin prêts pour la nouvelle campagne de ventes

gearbox ['gɪəbɒks] N (*Aut*) boîte *f* de vitesses

gearing ['gɪərɪŋ] N (*Tech*) embrayage *m* ; (*Brit Fin*) taux *m* d'endettement

gearshift ['gɪəʃɪft] N (*US*) = **gear lever, gear change**

gearwheel ['gɪəwiːl] N [*of bicycle*] pignon *m*

gecko ['gekəʊ] N (*pl* **geckos** *or* **geckoes**) gecko *m*

GED N (*US Educ*) (ABBR = **general equivalency diploma**) diplôme d'études secondaires obtenu en candidat libre

geddit: ['gedɪt] EXCL **~?** tu piges ?*

gee[1]* [dʒiː] **1** EXCL (*esp US*) eh bien ! ; **~ whiz!** mince alors !* **2** COMP ► **gee-whiz** ADJ (*US*) [*product, gadget*] tape-à-l'œil *inv*

gee[2] [dʒiː] **1** EXCL (*to horse*) **~ up!** hue ! **2** COMP ► **gee-gee** N (*baby talk*) dada *m*

geek* [giːk] N (*esp US*) débile* *mf*

geeky* ['giːkɪ] ADJ (*esp US*) débile*

geese [giːs] NPL *of* **goose**

geezer †‡ ['giːzər] N (*esp Brit*) bonhomme* *m*, gus* *m* ; (*silly*) **old ~** vieux schnock* *m*

gefilte [gə'fɪltə] ADJ (*US*) **~ fish** ≈ boulettes *fpl* de poisson

Geiger counter ['gaɪgəˌkaʊntər] N compteur *m* Geiger

geisha ['geɪʃə] N (*pl* **geisha** *or* **geishas**) geisha *f*

gel[1] [dʒel] **1** N (*Chem*) colloïde *m* ; (*Cosmetics*) gel *m* ; (*gen*) gelée *f* **2** VI **a** [*jelly*] prendre **b** [*plan*] prendre tournure ; [*people*] (*into team, group*) s'intégrer (**with** à) ; [*partnership, team*] se souder

gel[2] [gel] N († *or hum*) = **girl 1**

gelatin(e) ['dʒelətiːn] N gélatine *f*

gelatinous [dʒɪ'lætɪnəs] ADJ gélatineux

geld [geld] VT [+ *horse*] hongrer ; [+ *pig etc*] châtrer

gelding ['geldɪŋ] N [a] (= *horse*) (cheval *m*) hongre *m* [b] (*NonC*) castration *f*

gelignite ['dʒelɪgnaɪt] N plastic *m*

gelt⁎ [gelt] N (*US*) fric⁎ *m*

gem [dʒem] [1] N [a] (*lit*) gemme *f*, pierre *f* précieuse [b] (*fig* = *work of art*) (vrai) bijou *m*, merveille *f* ; **this painting is a real ~** ce tableau est une merveille ; **the cathedral is a ~ of Gothic architecture** la cathédrale est un joyau de l'architecture gothique ; **a perfect ~ of a hotel** un hôtel absolument charmant ; **Duval is a ~ of a writer** Duval est un écrivain remarquable ; **I must read you this little ~ from the newspaper** il faut que je te lise cette perle dans le journal ; **thanks, Pat, you're a ~** merci, Pat, tu es un amour *or* un ange ; **Naomi's a ~ of a girl!** Naomi est un amour ! [2] COMP ► **the Gem State** N (*US*) l'Idaho *m*

Gemini ['dʒemɪnaɪ] NPL (*Astron*) les Gémeaux *mpl* ; (*Astrol*) **I'm (a) ~** je suis (des) Gémeaux

Geminian [,dʒemɪ'naɪən] [1] N **to be a ~** être (des) Gémeaux [2] ADJ [*person*] du signe des Gémeaux ; [*tendency, characteristic*] propre aux Gémeaux

gem(m)ology [dʒe'mɒlədʒɪ] N gemmologie *f*

gemstone ['dʒemstəʊn] N gemme *f*

gen⁎ [dʒen] (*Brit*) N **to give sb the ~ on sth** donner à qn tous les tuyaux⁎ sur qch ; **what's the ~ on this?** qu'est-ce qu'on sait là-dessus ? ; **I want all the ~ on him** je veux tout savoir sur lui ; **have you got the ~ on the new house?** avez-vous une documentation sur la nouvelle maison ?

► **gen up⁎** [1] VI **to ~ up on sth** se rancarder sur qch⁎ [2] VT SEP **to be ~ned up on sth** être tout à fait au courant de, être bien renseigné sur

Gen. (*Mil*) (ABBR = **general**) (*on envelope*) **~ J. Smith** le général Smith

gen. ABBR = **general** and **generally**

gendarme [dʒɒndɑːm] N (*Climbing*) gendarme *m*

gender ['dʒendər] [1] N [a] (*Gram*) genre *m* ; **common ~⁎** genre *m* commun ; (*Gram*) **to agree in ~** s'accorder en genre [b] (= *sex*) sexe *m* ; **discrimination on grounds of ~** discrimination *f* sexuelle [2] COMP ► **gender bender⁎** N *personne qui s'habille de façon androgyne* ► **gender bias** N parti pris *m* contre les femmes (*or* les hommes) ► **the gender gap** N le décalage entre hommes et femmes ► **gender reassignment** N changement *m* de sexe

gene [dʒiːn] [1] N gène *m* [2] COMP ► **gene mapping** N (*Bio*) cartographie *f* génétique *or* génique ► **gene pool** N bagage *m or* patrimoine *m* héréditaire (de l'espèce) ► **gene therapy** N thérapie *f* génétique

genealogical [,dʒiːnɪə'lɒdʒɪkəl] ADJ généalogique

genealogist [,dʒiːnɪ'ælədʒɪst] N généalogiste *mf*

genealogy [,dʒiːnɪ'ælədʒɪ] N généalogie *f*

genera ['dʒenərə] NPL *of* **genus**

general ['dʒenərəl] [1] ADJ [a] (= *widespread*) [*approval, attitude, interest, decline*] général ; **this type of behaviour is fairly ~** ce genre de comportement est assez répandu ; **the rain has been fairly ~** il a plu un peu partout ; **there was ~ agreement** il y avait un consensus ; **our aim is to raise ~ awareness of the problems** notre but est de sensibiliser les gens *or* le grand public aux problèmes ; **the book was a ~ favourite** tout le monde aimait ce livre ; **in ~ use** d'usage courant ; **for ~ use** pour l'usage du public ; **a ~ ache** une douleur généralisée [b] (= *overall*) **the ~ idea** l'idée *f* générale ; **to give sb a ~ idea of a subject** donner à qn un aperçu d'un sujet ; **I've got the ~ idea** j'ai une

idée d'ensemble sur la question ; **I get the ~ idea⁎** je vois ; **to give sb a ~ outline of a subject** exposer à qn les grandes lignes de qch [c] (= *unspecific*) [*answer, discussion, enquiry*] d'ordre général ; **in ~ terms** d'une manière générale ; **as a ~ rule** en règle générale [d] (= *non-specialist*) [*labourer*] non spécialisé ; **the ~ reader** le lecteur moyen ; **~ maintenance** maintenance *f* générale → **secretary** [e] (= *rough, approximate*) **in the ~ direction of the village** dans la direction approximative du village [f] (*after official title*) général, en chef [2] N [a] général *m* ; **in ~** en général [b] (*Brit, US etc: Mil*) général *m* ; (*US*) **~ (of the Air Force)** général *m* de l'armée de l'air → **brigadier** [c] (⁎ = *servant*) bonne *f* à tout faire [3] COMP ► **general anaesthetic** N (*Med*) anesthésique *m* général ► **the General Assembly** N l'assemblée *f* générale ► **General Certificate of Education** N (*Brit Educ*) *examen passé à 18 ans,* ≈ baccalauréat *m* → **GCE** ► **General Certificate of Secondary Education** N (*Brit Educ*) *examen passé à 16 ans,* ≈ *brevet m des collèges* → GCSE ► **general confession** N (*Rel*) (*Church of England*) confession *f* collective (*lors de la prière en commun*) ; (*Roman Catholic Church*) confession *f* générale ► **general costs** NPL frais *mpl* généraux ► **general dealer** N (*US*) = **general shop** ► **general degree** N (*Univ*) licence non spécialisée ► **general delivery** N (*US, Can Post*) poste *f* restante ► **general election** N élections *fpl* législatives ► **general expenses** NPL dépenses *fpl* générales ► **general factotum** N (*Brit*) (*lit*) factotum *m* ; (*fig*) bonne *f* à tout faire ► **general headquarters** NPL (*Mil*) quartier *m* général ► **general holiday** N jour *m* férié ► **general hospital** N centre *m* hospitalier ► **general insurance** N assurances *fpl* IARD (*incendies, accidents, risques divers*) ► **general knowledge** N connaissances *fpl* générales, culture *f* générale ► **general linguistics** N (*NonC*) linguistique *f* générale ► **General Manager** N directeur *m* général ► **general medicine** N médecine *f* générale ► **general meeting** N assemblée *f* générale → **annual** ► **General Officer Commanding** N (*Mil*) général *m* commandant en chef ► **general partnership** N (*Jur, Fin*) société *f* en nom collectif ► **General Post Office** N (*Brit Govt: formerly*) Postes *fpl* et Télécommunications *fpl* ; (= *building*) poste *f* centrale ► **general practice** N (*Brit Med*) (= *work*) médecine *f* générale ; (= *place*) cabinet *m* de médecine générale ; **to be in ~ practice** faire de la médecine générale ► **general practitioner** N (*Med*) (*médecin m*) généraliste *m* → **the general public** N le grand public ► **general-purpose** ADJ [*tool, substance*] universel, multi-usages ; [*dictionary*] général ► **general science** N (*Scol*) *physique, chimie et biologie* ; **~ science teacher** professeur *m* de physique, chimie et biologie ► **General Secretary** N secrétaire *m* général ► **general servant** N domestique *mf* (*non spécialisé*) ► **general shop** N épicerie *f* générale ► **general staff** N (*Mil*) état-major *m* ► **general store** N (*US*) épicerie *f* générale ► **general strike** N grève *f* générale ► **General Studies** NPL (*Brit Scol*) *cours de culture générale pour élèves spécialisés*

generalissimo [,dʒenərə'lɪsɪməʊ] N généralissime *m*

generality [,dʒenə'rælɪtɪ] N [a] (*gen pl*) généralité *f*, considération *f* générale ; **we talked only of generalities** nous n'avons parlé que de généralités *or* qu'en termes généraux ; **to talk in generalities** dire des généralités [b] **the ~ of** (= *most of*) la plupart de [c] (*NonC*) caractère *m* général ; **a rule of great ~** une règle très générale

generalization [,dʒenərəlaɪ'zeɪʃən] N généralisation *f*

generalize ['dʒenərəlaɪz] VTI (*gen, Med*) généraliser

generally ['dʒenərəlɪ] ADV [a] (= *on the whole*) [*accurate*] en général, généralement ; [*true*] en règle générale ; **~, the course is okay** dans l'ensemble, le cours est bien [b] (= *usually*) d'une manière générale, d'habitude ; **I ~ get the bus to work** d'habitude je vais au travail en bus [c] (= *widely*) [*available*] partout ; [*accepted*] généralement, communément [d] (= *in general terms*) **to talk ~ about sth** dire des généralités sur qch ; **~ speaking** en règle générale

generalship ['dʒenərəlʃɪp] N (*Mil*) tactique *f*

generate ['dʒenəreɪt] [1] VT [+ *electricity, heat*] produire ; [+ *income, wealth*] générer ; [+ *interest*] susciter ; [+ *publicity*] faire ; [+ *work, jobs*] créer ; **to ~ excitement** susciter l'enthousiasme [2] COMP ► **generating set** N groupe *m* électrogène ► **generating station** N centrale *f* électrique ► **generating unit** N groupe *m* électrogène

generation [,dʒenə'reɪʃən] [1] N [a] génération *f* ; **the younger ~** la jeune génération ; **the postwar ~** la génération d'après-guerre ; **the leading artist of his ~** l'artiste le plus en vue de sa génération ; **within a ~** en l'espace d'une génération ; **a new ~ of computers** une nouvelle génération d'ordinateurs ; (*Comput etc*) **first-/second-~** de la première/de la seconde génération ; **he is a first-/second-~ American** c'est un Américain de première/seconde génération → **rising** [b] (*NonC*) (= *generating*) [*of electricity, heat*] production *f* ; [*of hatred etc*] engendrement *m* ; (*Ling*) génération *f* [2] COMP ► **the generation gap** N le conflit des générations

generational [,dʒenə'reɪʃənl] ADJ (= *within one generation*) de sa (*or* leur *etc*) génération ; (= *between generations*) des générations

generative ['dʒenərətɪv] [1] ADJ (*Ling*) génératif [2] COMP ► **generative grammar** N grammaire *f* générative

generator ['dʒenəreɪtər] N (*Elec*) groupe *m* électrogène ; (*in power station*) génératrice *f* ; (*for steam*) générateur *m* ; (*for gas*) gazogène *m*

generatrix ['dʒenə,reɪtrɪks] N (*pl* **generatrices** ['dʒenə,reɪtrɪˌsiːz]) (*Math*) génératrice *f*

generic [dʒɪ'nerɪk] [1] ADJ (*gen, Ling, Med*) générique [2] N (*Med* = *drug*) (médicament *m*) générique *m*

generically [dʒɪ'nerɪkəlɪ] ADV génériquement

generosity [,dʒenə'rɒsɪtɪ] N (*NonC*) générosité *f*, libéralité *f*

generous ['dʒenərəs] ADJ [*person, amount, gift, offer*] généreux ; [*supply*] ample ; **to be in a ~ mood** être d'humeur généreuse ; **to be ~ in one's praise of sth** ne pas tarir d'éloges pour qch ; **that's very ~ of you** c'est très généreux de ta part ; **to be ~ with one's time** ne pas être avare de son temps

generously ['dʒenərəslɪ] ADV [*give, reward, offer, pardon, season*] généreusement ; [*say*] avec générosité ; **~ cut** [*garment*] ample

genesis ['dʒenɪsɪs] N (*pl* **geneses** ['dʒenɪsiːz]) genèse *f*, origine *f* ; (*Bible*) **Genesis** la Genèse

genetic [dʒɪ'netɪk] [1] ADJ (*Bio*) (= *of the genes*) génétique, génique ; (= *hereditary*) (*Philos*) génétique [2] COMP ► **genetic code** N (*Bio*) code *m* génétique ► **genetic counselling** N conseil *m* génétique ► **genetic engineering** N génie *m* génétique, manipulations *fpl* génétiques ► **genetic fingerprint** N empreinte *f* génétique ► **genetic fingerprinting** N système *m* d'empreinte génétique ► **genetic map** N carte *f* génétique ► **genetic screening** N test *m* de dépistage génétique

genetically [dʒɪ'netɪkəlɪ] ADV (*gen*) [*deter-*

mined, programmed] génétiquement; ~ **engineered** génétiquement manipulé

geneticist [dʒɪˈnetɪsɪst] N généticien(ne) m(f)

genetics [dʒɪˈnetɪks] N (NonC) génétique f

Geneva [dʒɪˈniːvə] **1** N Genève; **Lake ~** le lac Léman or de Genève **2** COMP ► **Geneva Convention** N convention f de Genève

genial [ˈdʒiːnɪəl] ADJ [person, atmosphere] cordial; [face] avenant; [smile, look, tone] engageant; [climate] doux (douce f), clément; [warmth] réconfortant; **a ~ host** un hôte sympathique

geniality [ˌdʒiːnɪˈælɪtɪ] N [of person, smile] cordialité f; [of climate] douceur f, clémence f

genially [ˈdʒiːnɪəlɪ] ADV cordialement

genie [ˈdʒiːnɪ] N (pl **genii**) génie m, djinn m; (fig) **the ~ is out of the bottle** le mal est fait; **to let the ~ out of the bottle** commettre l'irréparable; **to put the ~ back in the bottle** chercher à réparer l'irréparable

genii [ˈdʒiːnɪaɪ] NPL of **genie** and **genius** d

genital [ˈdʒenɪtl] **1** ADJ génital **2** **genitals** NPL organes mpl génitaux **3** COMP ► **genital herpes** N herpès m génital ► **genital warts** NPL vésicules fpl génitales

genitalia [ˌdʒenɪˈteɪlɪə] NPL organes mpl génitaux

genitive [ˈdʒenɪtɪv] (Gram) **1** ADJ [case] génitif; **~ ending** flexion f du génitif **2** N génitif m; **in the ~** au génitif

genius [ˈdʒiːnɪəs] N **a** (NonC) (= cleverness) génie m; (= ability, aptitude) génie m (for de), don m extraordinaire (for pour); **man of ~** (homme m de) génie m; **his ~ lay in his ability to assess …** il était supérieurement doué pour juger …; **her real ~ as a designer** son véritable génie en design; **he has a ~ for publicity** il a le génie de la publicité; **to have ~** avoir du génie; **to have a ~ for doing** avoir le don de faire; **she has a ~ for controversy** elle a le don de la polémique; **he's got a ~ for saying the wrong thing** il a le don de or un don pour dire ce qu'il ne faut pas; **a flash** or **stroke of ~** un trait de génie **b** (pl **geniuses**) génie m; **he's a ~** c'est un génie, il est génial **c** (NonC = distinctive character) [of period, country etc] génie m (particulier) **d** (pl **genii**) (= spirit) génie m; **evil ~** mauvais génie m

Genoa [ˈdʒenəʊə] N Gênes

genocidal [ˌdʒenəʊˈsaɪdl] ADJ génocide

genocide [ˈdʒenəʊsaɪd] N génocide m

Genoese [ˌdʒenəʊˈiːz] **1** ADJ génois **2** N (pl inv) Génois(e) m(f)

genome [ˈdʒiːnəʊm] N (Bio) génome m

genotype [ˈdʒenəʊtaɪp] N génotype m

genre [ˈʒɑ̃ːrə] N genre m; (also **~ painting**) tableau m de genre

gent [dʒent] N ABBR = **gentleman** **a** (Comm) **~s' outfitters** magasin m d'habillement or de confection pour hommes; (Comm) **~s' shoes** etc chaussures fpl etc (pour hommes); (Brit) **the ~s** les toilettes fpl (pour hommes); (Brit: sign) **"~s"** « messieurs » **b** monsieur m, type m; **he's a (real) ~** c'est un monsieur (tout ce qu'il y a de) bien

genteel [dʒenˈtiːl] ADJ **a** (= refined) [person, behaviour, manners] distingué; [upbringing, resort, district] comme il faut; [atmosphere] raffiné; [institution] respectable; **to live in ~ poverty** vivre dignement dans la pauvreté **b** (= affected) affecté; **she has a very ~ way of holding her glass** elle a une façon très affectée de tenir son verre; **~ shabby**

genteelly [dʒenˈtiːlɪ] ADV **a** (= with refinement) [sit, eat, drink] de façon distinguée **b** (= affectedly) [behave] d'une manière affectée; **she coughed ~ behind her hand** elle toussa d'une manière affectée derrière sa main

gentian [ˈdʒenʃən] N gentiane f; **~ blue** bleu m gentiane; **~ violet** bleu m de méthylène

Gentile [ˈdʒentaɪl] **1** N Gentil(e) m(f) **2** ADJ des Gentils

gentility [dʒenˈtɪlɪtɪ] N (iro) prétention f à la distinction or au bon ton; († = good birth) bonne famille f, bonne naissance f

gentle [ˈdʒentl] **1** ADJ **a** (= kind, mild) [person, animal, voice, smile] doux (douce f); **to be ~ with sb** être doux avec qn; **be ~ with me** vas-y doucement; **to have a ~ disposition** être doux de nature; **her ~ manner** sa douceur; **(as) ~ as a lamb** doux comme un agneau; († or hum) **~ reader** aimable lecteur m **b** (= not violent or strong) [movement, touch, sound, breeze] léger; [transition] sans heurts; [exercise] modéré; [slope, curve, colour] doux (douce f); [landscape] d'une grande douceur; **to cook over a ~ heat** faire cuire à feu doux; **to apply ~ pressure** presser légèrement; **the car came to a ~ stop** la voiture s'est arrêtée doucement; **a ~ stroll** une petite promenade tranquille **c** (= not harsh) [detergent, cleaning product, beauty product] doux (douce f); **it is ~ on the skin** ça n'irrite pas la peau **d** (= discreet) [hint, rebuke, reminder] discret (-ète f); **to poke ~ fun at sb** se moquer gentiment de qn; **to use a little ~ persuasion** utiliser la manière douce; **a little ~ persuasion will get him to help** si nous le persuadons en douceur il nous aidera **e** († = wellborn: also of **~ birth**) bien né (liter); **~ knight** †† noble chevalier m **2** COMP ► **the gentle** or **gentler sex** † N (liter) le beau sexe†

gentlefolk [ˈdʒentlfəʊk] NPL gens mpl de bonne famille

gentleman [ˈdʒentlmən] (pl **-men**) **1** N **a** (= man) monsieur m; **there's a ~ to see you** il y a un monsieur qui voudrait vous voir; (US Pol) **the ~ from …** Monsieur le député de …; (sign) **"gentlemen"** « messieurs » **b** (= man of breeding) homme m bien élevé, gentleman m; **he is a perfect ~** c'est un vrai gentleman; **a ~ never uses such language** un monsieur bien élevé ne se sert jamais de mots pareils; **one of nature's gentlemen** un gentleman né; **to behave like a ~** se comporter en gentleman; **be a ~ and take Emily home** sois galant or comporte-toi en gentleman et ramène Emily chez elle; **he's no ~!** ce n'est pas un gentleman!; (hum) **~'s ~** valet m de chambre **c** (= man of substance) rentier m; **to lead the life of a ~** vivre de ses rentes **d** (at court etc) gentilhomme m **2** COMP ► **gentleman-at-arms** N (pl **gentlemen-at-arms**) gentilhomme m de la garde ► **gentleman-farmer** N (pl **gentlemen-farmers**) gentleman-farmer m ► **gentleman-in-waiting** N (pl **gentlemen-in-waiting**) gentilhomme m (attaché à la personne du roi etc) ► **gentleman's agreement** N gentleman's agreement m, accord m reposant sur l'honneur ► **gentlemen's club** N (esp Brit) club privé réservé aux hommes

gentlemanly [ˈdʒentlmənlɪ] ADJ [man] bien élevé; [manner, behaviour, conduct] courtois; [voice, appearance, sport] distingué

gentlemen [ˈdʒentlmən] NPL of **gentleman**

gentleness [ˈdʒentlnɪs] N douceur f

gentlewoman [ˈdʒentlwʊmən] N (pl **-women**) (by birth) dame f or demoiselle f de bonne famille; (in manner) dame f or demoiselle f très bien or comme il faut*; (at court) dame f d'honneur or de compagnie

gently [ˈdʒentlɪ] ADV **a** (= kindly) [say, rebuke] avec douceur, gentiment; [smile, remind, suggest] gentiment **b** (= not violently or strongly) [move, shake, caress] doucement; [push, touch] doucement, avec douceur; [exercise] doucement, sans forcer; **~ does it!** douce-

ment!; **~ sloping hills** des collines en pente douce; **the road slopes ~ down to the river** la route descend en pente douce vers la rivière; **to simmer ~** faire cuire à feu doux; **to deal ~ with sb** ménager qn, ne pas bousculer qn **c** (= nobly) **~ born†** de bonne naissance†

gentrification [ˌdʒentrɪfɪˈkeɪʃən] N [of area of a town or city] embourgeoisement m

gentrified [ˈdʒentrɪfaɪd] ADJ [area, houses etc] embourgeoisé

gentrify [ˈdʒentrɪfaɪ] VT [+ area] embourgeoiser

gentry [ˈdʒentrɪ] N (Hist: of good birth) gentry f; (fig pej) gens mpl bien

genuflect [ˈdʒenjʊflekt] VI (lit) faire une génuflexion; (fig) **to ~ to** or **in front of** se prosterner devant

genuflexion, genuflection (US) [ˌdʒenjʊˈflekʃən] N génuflexion f

genuine [ˈdʒenjʊɪn] **1** ADJ **a** (= authentic) [refugee, picture, manuscript, antique, coin] authentique; (Comm) [democracy, leather, wool, silver] véritable; (Comm) [goods] garanti d'origine; **a ~ Persian rug** un authentique tapis persan; **it's the ~ article*** c'est du vrai **b** (= real) [emotion, belief, enthusiasm, interest, offer] sincère; [laughter, disbelief] franc (franche f); [tears] vrai, sincère; [difficulty] véritable; **this was a ~ mistake** c'était vraiment une erreur; (Comm) **a ~ buyer** un acheteur sérieux **c** (= sincere) [person, relationship] sincère **2** COMP ► **genuine assets** NPL (Accounts) actif m réel

genuinely [ˈdʒenjʊɪnlɪ] ADV [interested] sincèrement, vraiment; [concerned, surprised] réellement; [worried, upset, sorry, democratic] vraiment, [funny, pleased] vraiment; **she ~ believed that …** elle croyait vraiment or sincèrement que …; **I ~ want to help** je veux vraiment or sincèrement aider; **he is ~ committed to reform** il est profondément partisan de la réforme

genuineness [ˈdʒenjʊɪnnɪs] N **a** (= authenticity) authenticité f **b** (= sincerity) sincérité f

genus [ˈdʒenəs] N (pl **genera** or **genuses**) (Bio) genre m

ge(o)… [ˈdʒiː(əʊ)] PREF géo…

geocentric [ˌdʒiːəʊˈsentrɪk] ADJ géocentrique

geochemical [ˌdʒiːəʊˈkemɪkəl] ADJ géochimique

geochemist [ˌdʒiːəʊˈkemɪst] N géochimiste mf

geochemistry [ˌdʒiːəʊˈkemɪstrɪ] N géochimie f

geode [ˈdʒiːəʊd] N géode f

geodesic [ˌdʒiːəʊˈdesɪk] ADJ géodésique; **~ dome** dôme m géodésique; **~ line** géodésique f

geodesy [dʒiːˈɒdɪsɪ] N géodésie f

geodetic [ˌdʒiːəʊˈdetɪk] ADJ = **geodesic**

geographer [dʒɪˈɒɡrəfəʳ] N géographe mf

geographic(al) [dʒɪəˈɡræfɪk(əl)] ADJ géographique; **~ mile** mille m marin or nautique

geographically [dʒɪəˈɡræfɪkəlɪ] ADV [isolated] géographiquement

geography [dʒɪˈɒɡrəfɪ] N (= science) géographie f; **policemen who knew the local ~** des policiers qui connaissaient la topographie du quartier

geological [dʒɪəˈlɒdʒɪkəl] ADJ géologique; (US) **~ survey** Bureau m de recherches géologiques et minières

geologically [dʒɪəˈlɒdʒɪkəlɪ] ADV géologiquement

geologist [dʒɪˈɒlədʒɪst] N géologue mf

geology [dʒɪˈɒlədʒɪ] N géologie f

geomagnetic [ˌdʒiːəʊmæɡˈnetɪk] ADJ géomagnétique; **~ storm** orage m géomagnétique

geomagnetism [ˌdʒiːəʊˈmæɡnɪtɪzəm] N géomagnétisme m

geometric(al) [ˌdʒɪəˈmetrɪk(əl)] ADJ géométrique ; (Math) ~ **mean** moyenne f géométrique ; **by ~ progression** selon une progression géométrique ; ~ **series** série f géométrique

geometrically [ˌdʒɪəˈmetrɪkəlɪ] ADV [arranged] géométriquement ; ~ **patterned** à motifs géométriques

geometrician [ˌdʒɪˌɒmɪˈtrɪʃən] N géomètre mf

geometry [dʒɪˈɒmɪtrɪ] N géométrie f

geomorphic [ˌdʒɪːəˈmɔːfɪk] ADJ géomorphique

geomorphologic(al) [ˌdʒɪːəˈmɔːfəˈlɒdʒɪkəl] ADJ géomorphologique

geomorphology [ˌdʒɪːəʊmɔːˈfɒlədʒɪ] N géomorphologie f

geonomics [ˌdʒiːəʊˈnɒmɪks] N (NonC) géographie f économique

geophysical [ˌdʒiːəʊˈfɪzɪkəl] ADJ géophysique

geophysicist [ˌdʒiːəʊˈfɪzɪsɪst] N géophysicien(ne) m(f)

geophysics [ˌdʒiːəʊˈfɪzɪks] N (NonC) géophysique f

geopolitical [ˌdʒiːəʊpəˈlɪtɪkəl] ADJ géopolitique

geopolitics [ˌdʒiːəʊˈpɒlɪtɪks] N (NonC) géopolitique f

Geordie⁎ [ˈdʒɔːdɪ] N (Brit) natif de Tyneside

George [dʒɔːdʒ] N Georges m ; **by ~!**⁎† mon Dieu! ; (Brit) ~ **Cross** or **Medal** ≈ médaille f du courage

georgette [dʒɔːˈdʒet] N (also ~ **crêpe**) crêpe f georgette

Georgia [ˈdʒɔːdʒə] N (= country and US state) la Géorgie ; **in ~** en Géorgie

Georgian [ˈdʒɔːdʒɪən] ADJ a (Brit Hist) [period] des rois George Iᵉʳ à George IV (1714-1830) ; (Archit) [architecture, house, style] géorgien (entre 1714 et 1830) b (Geog) [person, language] géorgien ; [town] de Géorgie ; [capital] de la Géorgie

geoscience [ˌdʒiːəˈsaɪəns] N science(s) f(pl) de la terre

geoscientist [ˌdʒiːəˈsaɪəntɪst] N spécialiste mf des sciences de la terre

geostationary [ˌdʒiːəʊˈsteɪʃənərɪ] ADJ géostationnaire

geosynchronous [ˌdʒiːəʊˈsɪŋkrənəs] ADJ géosynchrone

geosyncline [ˌdʒiːəʊˈsɪnklaɪn] N géosynclinal m

geothermal [ˌdʒiːəʊˈθɜːməl] ADJ géothermal ; ~ **power** énergie f géothermique

geothermally [ˌdʒiːəʊˈθɜːməlɪ] ADV géothermiquement

geotropic [ˌdʒiːəʊˈtrɒpɪk] ADJ géotropique

geotropically [ˌdʒiːəʊˈtrɒpɪkəlɪ] ADV géotropiquement

geotropism [dʒɪˈɒtrəpɪzəm] N géotropisme m

geranium [dʒɪˈreɪnɪəm] 1 N géranium m 2 ADJ (colour: also ~ **red**) rouge géranium inv

gerbil [ˈdʒɜːbɪl] N gerbille f

geriatric [ˌdʒerɪˈætrɪk] 1 ADJ a [hospital] gériatrique ; [ward] de gériatrie ; [patient] de service de gériatrie ; [nurse] spécialisé en gériatrie ; ~ **care** or **nursing** soins mpl aux vieillards ; ~ **medicine** gériatrie f ; ~ **social work** aide f sociale aux vieillards b (* pej) [judge, rock star] gaga⁎ (pej) ; [government] de vieux gâteux⁎ (pej) ; **a ~ car** un vieux tacot⁎ (pej) ; **a ~ horse** un vieux canasson⁎ (pej) 2 N a (Med) malade mf gériatrique b (* pej) vieillard(e) m(f)

geriatrics [ˌdʒerɪˈætrɪks] N (NonC: Med) gériatrie f

germ [dʒɜːm] 1 N a (Bio, also fig) germe m ; **the ~ of an idea** un embryon d'idée, le germe d'une idée b (Med) microbe m, germe m 2 COMP ► **germ carrier** N (Med) porteur m de microbes ► **germ cell** N (Bio) cellule f ger-

minale or reproductrice, gamète m ► **germ-free** ADJ (Med) stérile, stérilisé ► **germ-killer** N germicide m ► **germ warfare** N (NonC) guerre f bactériologique

German [ˈdʒɜːmən] 1 ADJ (gen) allemand ; [ambassador, embassy] d'Allemagne ; [teacher] d'allemand ; **East/West ~** d'Allemagne de l'Est/de l'Ouest, est-/ouest-allemand 2 N a Allemand(e) m(f) b (Ling) allemand m 3 COMP ► **the German Democratic Republic** N (formerly) la République démocratique allemande ► **German measles** N (Med) rubéole f ► **German sheep dog, German shepherd** N chien m loup, berger m allemand ► **German speaker** N germanophone mf ► **German-speaking** ADJ qui parle allemand ; [nation] germanophone → **Switzerland**

germane [dʒɜːˈmeɪn] ADJ pertinent (**to** pour, par rapport à)

Germanic [dʒɜːˈmænɪk] ADJ germanique

germanium [dʒɜːˈmeɪnɪəm] N germanium m

germanophile [dʒɜːˈmænəʊfaɪl] N germanophile mf

germanophobe [dʒɜːˈmænəʊfəʊb] N germanophobe mf

Germany [ˈdʒɜːmənɪ] N l'Allemagne f ; **East/West ~** l'Allemagne f de l'Est/de l'Ouest

germicidal [ˌdʒɜːmɪˈsaɪdl] ADJ germicide

germicide [ˈdʒɜːmɪsaɪd] N germicide m

germinal [ˈdʒɜːmɪnl] ADJ embryonnaire

germinate [ˈdʒɜːmɪneɪt] 1 VI germer 2 VT faire germer

germination [ˌdʒɜːmɪˈneɪʃən] N germination f

germproof [ˈdʒɜːmpruːf] ADJ résistant aux microbes

gerontocracy [ˌdʒerɒnˈtɒkrəsɪ] N gérontocratie f

gerontologist [ˌdʒerɒnˈtɒlədʒɪst] N gérontologue mf

gerontology [ˌdʒerɒnˈtɒlədʒɪ] N gérontologie f

gerrymander [ˈdʒerɪmændəʳ] 1 VI faire du charcutage électoral 2 N = **gerrymandering**

gerrymandering [ˈdʒerɪmændərɪŋ] N charcutage m électoral

gerund [ˈdʒerənd] N (in English) gérondif m, substantif m verbal ; (in Latin) gérondif m

gerundive [dʒɪˈrʌndɪv] 1 ADJ du gérondif 2 N adjectif m verbal

gesso [ˈdʒesəʊ] N [of moulding etc] plâtre m (de Paris) ; (Art) gesso m

Gestalt [gəˈʃtaːlt] N (pl **Gestalts** or **Gestalten** [gəˈʃtaːltən]) gestalt f ; ~ **psychology** gestaltisme m

Gestapo [gesˈtaːpəʊ] N Gestapo f

gestate [dʒesˈteɪt] 1 VI être en gestation 2 VT (Bio) garder en gestation ; [+ work of art] mûrir ; [+ anger] couver

gestation [dʒesˈteɪʃən] N gestation f

gesticulate [dʒesˈtɪkjʊleɪt] 1 VI faire de grands gestes (**at sb** pour attirer l'attention de qn) 2 VT exprimer par gestes

gesticulation [dʒesˌtɪkjʊˈleɪʃən] N gesticulation f

gestural [ˈdʒestʃərəl] ADJ gestuel

gesture [ˈdʒestʃəʳ] 1 N (lit, fig) geste m ; **a ~ of good will** un geste de bonne volonté ; **friendly ~** geste m or témoignage m d'amitié ; **a ~ of defiance** un signe de méfiance ; **they did it as a ~ of support** ils l'ont fait pour manifester leur soutien ; **what a nice ~!** quelle délicate attention ! 2 VI **to ~ to sb to do sth** faire signe à qn de faire qch ; **he ~d towards the door** il désigna la porte d'un geste ; **he ~d with his head towards the safe** il a indiqué le coffre d'un signe de tête ; **he ~d at Derek to**

remain seated il a fait signe à Derek de rester assis 3 VT mimer, exprimer par gestes

get [get]

┌─────────────────────────────────────┐
│ vb: pret, ptp **got**, ptp (US) **gotten** │
│ 1 TRANSITIVE VERB   3 COMPOUNDS │
│ 2 INTRANSITIVE VERB 4 PHRASAL VERBS │
└─────────────────────────────────────┘

1 TRANSITIVE VERB

When **get** is part of a set combination, eg **get the sack, get hold of, get sth right**, look up the other word.

a = have, receive, obtain avoir

avoir covers a wide range of meanings, and like **get** is unspecific.

I **go** whenever I ~ the chance j'y vais dès que j'en ai l'occasion ; he's got a cut on his finger il a une coupure au doigt ; he got a fine il a eu une amende ; she ~s a good salary il a un bon salaire ; not everyone ~s a pension tout le monde n'a pas la retraite ; you need to ~ permission from the owner il faut avoir la permission du propriétaire ; I got a lot of presents j'ai eu beaucoup de cadeaux ; he got first prize il a eu le premier prix ; you may ~ a surprise tu pourrais avoir une surprise

Some **get** + noun combinations may take a more specific French verb.

we can ~ sixteen **channels** nous pouvons recevoir seize chaînes ; it was impossible to ~ **help** il était impossible d'obtenir de l'aide ; he got **help** from the others il s'est fait aider par les autres ; first I need to ~ a better **idea** of the situation je dois d'abord me faire une meilleure idée de la situation ; I think he got the wrong **impression** je pense qu'il s'est fait des idées ; they ~ **lunch** at school ils déjeunent or ils mangent à l'école ; he got his **money** by exploiting others il s'est enrichi en exploitant les autres ; if I'm not working I ~ no **pay** si je ne travaille pas je ne suis pas payé ; this area doesn't ~ much **rain** il ne pleut pas beaucoup dans cette région ; she got a **reputation** for infallibility elle a acquis une réputation d'infaillibilité ; they got interesting **results** ils ont obtenu des résultats intéressants ; we'll ~ a **sandwich** in town on prendra or mangera un sandwich en ville ; this room ~s a lot of **sun** cette pièce est très ensoleillée ; I didn't ~ a very good **view** of it je ne l'ai pas bien vu ; he got two **years** il s'est pris⁎ deux ans de prison

♦ **have/has got** : I've got toothache j'ai mal aux dents ; I have got three sisters j'ai trois sœurs ; how many have you got? combien en avez-vous ? ; she's got too much to do elle a trop (de choses) à faire ; I've got it! (= have safely) (ça y est) je l'ai !, je le tiens ! ; you're okay, I've got you! ne t'en fais pas, je te tiens ! → **have**

b = find trouver ; they can't ~ jobs ils n'arrivent pas à trouver de travail ; he got me a job il m'a trouvé un emploi ; it's difficult to ~ a hotel room in August c'est difficile de trouver une chambre d'hôtel en août ; you ~ different kinds of ... on trouve plusieurs sortes de ... ; you'll ~ him at home if you phone this evening tu le trouveras chez lui si tu appelles ce soir ; **BUT** I've been trying to ~ you all week ça fait une semaine que j'essaie de t'avoir ; you can ~ me on this number/the mobile tu peux m'appeler à ce numéro/sur mon portable

c = buy acheter ; where do they ~ their raw materials? où est-ce qu'ils achètent leurs matières premières ? ; to ~ sth cheap acheter qch bon marché ; I'll ~ some milk je prendrai or j'achèterai du lait

d = fetch aller chercher ; I must go and ~ some bread il faut que j'aille chercher or acheter du pain ; quick, ~ help! allez vite chercher de l'aide ! ; can you ~ my coat from the cleaners? est-ce que tu peux aller chercher mon manteau au pressing ? ; **BUT** can I ~ you a drink? est-ce que je peux vous offrir quelque chose ?

e = take prendre; I'll ~ the bus je vais prendre le bus; I don't ~ the local paper je ne prends pas le journal local

f = pick up aller chercher; phone me when you arrive and I'll come and ~ you appelle-moi quand tu arrives et j'irai te chercher

g = call in appeler; we had to ~ the doctor/a plumber nous avons dû appeler le médecin/un plombier

h = prepare préparer; she was ~ting breakfast elle préparait le petit déjeuner

i = catch [+ disease, fugitive] attraper; [+ name] entendre, comprendre; [+ details] comprendre; you'll ~ a cold tu vas attraper un rhume; they've got the thief ils ont attrapé le voleur; I didn't ~ your name je n'ai pas entendu or compris votre nom; BUT to ~ sb alone or to o.s. être seul à seul avec qn; it ~s me here [pain] ça me fait mal ici; we'll ~ them yet! on leur revaudra ça!; I'll ~ you! je te revaudrai ça!; he'll ~ you for that! qu'est-ce que tu vas prendre!*; he's got it bad for her* il est fou d'elle

j = understand ~ it?* t'as pigé?*, tu saisis?*; I don't ~ it* je ne comprends pas, je ne saisis pas*; you've got it in one!* tu as tout compris!; I don't ~ you* je ne vois pas*; I don't ~ the joke je ne vois pas ce qu'il y a de drôle; I don't ~ your meaning* je ne vous suis pas; he got the point immediately il a tout de suite tout compris; let me ~ this right, you're saying that ... alors, si je comprends bien, tu dis que ...; don't ~ me wrong comprenez-moi bien

k = answer can you ~ the phone? est-ce que tu peux répondre?; I'll ~ it! j'y vais!

l * = annoy agacer; that's what really ~s me c'est ce qui m'agace le plus

m SET STRUCTURES

◆ **to get** + *adjective*

This construction is often translated by a verb alone. Look up the relevant adjective.

don't ~ the carpet **dirty!** ne salis pas la moquette!; to ~ one's hands **dirty** se salir les mains; to ~ sb **drunk** enivrer or soûler qn; you're ~ting me **worried** tu m'inquiètes

◆ **to get sth done** (*by someone else*) faire faire qch; to ~ one's hair cut se faire couper les cheveux; I need to ~ my car serviced je dois faire réviser ma voiture; he knows how to ~ things done! il sait faire activer les choses!; (*do oneself*) when do you think you'll ~ it finished? quand penses-tu avoir fini?; you can't ~ anything done round here il est impossible de travailler ici

◆ **to get sb/sth to do sth**: ~ him to clean the car fais-lui laver la voiture; I'll ~ her to ring you back je lui demanderai de te rappeler

réussir or pouvoir may be used when speaking of achieving a result.

we eventually got her to change her mind nous avons finalement réussi à or pu la faire changer d'avis; I couldn't ~ the washing machine to work je n'ai pas réussi à or pu faire marcher la machine à laver; I couldn't ~ the sauce to thicken je n'ai pas réussi à or pu épaissir la sauce; to ~ sth going [+ *machine*] (réussir à or pouvoir) faire marcher qch

◆ **to get sb/sth somewhere**: to ~ sth **downstairs** descendre qch; they got him home somehow ils l'ont ramené chez lui tant bien que mal; how can we ~ it **home?** comment faire pour l'apporter à la maison?; threatening me will ~ you **nowhere** tu n'obtiendras rien en me menaçant; to ~ sth **upstairs** monter qch; **where** does that ~ us? où est-ce que ça nous mène?

◆ **to get sb/sth** + *preposition*: to ~ sb **by** the arm saisir qn par le bras; to ~ sb **by** the throat prendre qn à la gorge; I didn't ~ much **for** it on ne m'en a pas donné grand-chose; he ~s a lot of money **for** his paintings il gagne beaucoup d'argent avec ses tableaux; he ~s his red hair **from** his mother il a les cheveux roux de sa mère; I don't ~ much **from** his lectures je ne tire pas grand-chose de ses cours; the bullet got him **in** the arm la balle l'a atteint au bras; try to ~ him **into** a good mood essaie de le mettre de bonne humeur; he managed to ~ the card **into** the envelope il a réussi à faire entrer la carte dans l'enveloppe; to ~ o.s. **into** a difficult position se mettre dans une situation délicate; we got him **on to** the subject of the war nous l'avons amené à parler de la guerre; she ~s a lot of pleasure **out of** gardening elle prend beaucoup de plaisir à jardiner; we'll never ~ anything **out of** him nous n'en tirerons jamais rien, nous ne tirerons jamais rien de lui; I couldn't ~ the stain **out of** the tablecloth je n'ai pas réussi à enlever la tache sur la nappe; to ~ sth **past** the customs réussir à passer qch à la douane; I don't know how it got **past** the inspectors je ne sais pas comment ça a échappé à la surveillance des inspecteurs; to ~ sb **round** the throat prendre qn à la gorge; I'll never ~ the car **through** here je n'arriverai jamais à faire passer la voiture par ici; to ~ sth **to** sb faire parvenir qch à qn; to ~ a child **to** bed mettre un enfant au lit, coucher un enfant

2 INTRANSITIVE VERB

a = go aller (to à, from de); (= *arrive*) arriver; (= *be*) être; how do you ~ **there?** comment fait-on pour y aller?; **can** you ~ there from London by bus? est-ce qu'on peut y aller de Londres en bus?; what **time** do you ~ to Sheffield? à quelle heure arrivez-vous à Sheffield?; he should ~ here soon il devrait bientôt être là; (*lit, fig*) to ~ to the top arriver or parvenir au sommet → top

◆ **to get** + *adverb/preposition*: to ~ **after** sb essayer d'attraper qn; we won't ~ **anywhere** with him nous n'arriverons à rien avec lui; you won't ~ **anywhere** if you behave like that tu n'arriveras à rien en te conduisant comme ça; I got **as far as** speaking to him je lui ai même parlé; how did that box ~ **here?** comment cette boîte est elle arrivée ici?; what's got **into** him? qu'est-ce qui lui prend?; we're ~ting **nowhere** on n'avance pas; we're ~ting **nowhere** fast* on fait du sur place*; now we're ~ting **somewhere!*** enfin du progrès!; how's your thesis going? — I'm ~ting **there** où en es-tu avec ta thèse? — ça avance; your garden is lovely! — yes, we're ~ting **there!** votre jardin est très joli! — oui, ça prend tournure!; where did you ~ **to?** où étais-tu donc passé?; where can he have got **to?** où est-il passé? (*in book, work*) where have you got **to?** où en êtes-vous?; don't let it ~ **to you*** ne te fais pas de bile* pour ça; to ~ **with** it* se mettre à la mode or dans le vent*; this is serious business and the government had better ~ **with** it (= *become aware*) c'est là un problème grave et le gouvernement ferait bien d'en prendre conscience

b = go away ~!* fous le camp!*

c SET STRUCTURES

◆ **to get** + *adjective*

This construction is often translated by a verb alone.

I hope you'll ~ **better** soon j'espère que tu vas vite te remettre; things are ~ting **complicated** les choses se compliquent; this is ~ting **expensive** ça commence à faire cher; she's afraid of ~ting **fat** elle a peur de grossir; it's ~ting **late** il se fait tard; how do people ~ **like** that? comment peut-on en arriver là?; I'm ~ting **nervous** je commence à avoir le trac; he's ~ting **old** il vieillit, il se fait vieux; this is ~ting **ridiculous** ça devient ridicule; how **stupid** can you ~? il faut vraiment être stupide!; he soon ~s **tired** il se fatigue vite; to ~ **used** to sth/to doing sth s'habituer à qch/à faire

◆ **to get** + *past participle* (*passive*) she often ~s asked for her autograph on lui demande souvent son autographe; he got beaten up il s'est fait tabasser*; several windows got broken plusieurs fenêtres ont été brisées; to ~ **killed** se faire tuer; to ~ **paid** se faire payer

Reflexive verbs are used when the sense is not passive.

to ~ **dressed** s'habiller; to ~ **married** se marier; to ~ **washed** se laver

◆ **to get to** + *infinitive*: it got to be quite pleasant after a while c'est devenu assez agréable au bout d'un moment; he's ~ting to be an old man il se fait vieux; it's ~ting to be impossible ça devient impossible; she never ~s to drive the car* on ne la laisse jamais conduire; to ~ to know sb apprendre à connaître qn; we soon got to like them nous les avons vite appréciés; we got to like him in the end nous avons fini par l'apprécier; students only ~ to use the library between 2pm and 8pm les étudiants ne peuvent utiliser la bibliothèque qu'entre 14 heures et 20 heures

◆ **have got to** + *infinitive* (= *must*) you've got to come il faut que vous veniez (*subj*); have you got to go and see her? est-ce que vous êtes obligé d'aller la voir?; I haven't got to leave yet je ne suis pas obligé de partir tout de suite; you've got to be joking! tu plaisantes!

◆ **to get** + *-ing* (= *begin*) to ~ going se mettre en route, partir; I got talking to him in the train j'ai parlé avec lui dans le train, nous avons engagé la conversation dans le train; I got to thinking that ...* je me suis dit que ...

3 COMPOUNDS

► **get-at-able*** ADJ [*place*] accessible, d'accès facile; [*person*] accessible ► **get-rich-quick scheme*** N projet pour faire fortune rapidement ► **get-together** N (petite) réunion f ► **get-up-and-go*** N he's got lots of ~-up-and-go il a beaucoup d'allant or de dynamisme, il est très dynamique ► **get-well card** N carte f de vœux (pour un prompt rétablissement)

4 PHRASAL VERBS

► **get about** VI a (= *move about*) [*person*] se déplacer; he ~s about with a stick/on crutches il marche or se déplace avec une canne/des béquilles; she ~s about quite well despite her handicap elle arrive assez bien à se déplacer malgré son handicap; she's old, but she still ~s about quite a bit elle est âgée mais elle est encore très active; (*after illness*) he's ~ting about again now il est de nouveau sur pied b (= *travel*) voyager; she ~s about a lot elle voyage beaucoup c [*news*] circuler; the story had got about that ... des rumeurs circulaient selon lesquelles ...; it has got about that ... le bruit court que ...; I don't want it to ~ about je ne veux pas que ça s'ébruite

► **get above** VT FUS to ~ above o.s. avoir la grosse tête*; you're ~ting above yourself! pour qui te prends-tu?

► **get across** 1 VI (*lit*) traverser; [*meaning, message*] I think the message is ~ting across je pense que le message commence à passer; the message is ~ting across that people must ... les gens commencent à comprendre qu'on doit ...; that was what got across to me c'est ce que j'ai compris; he didn't ~ across to the audience le courant n'est pas passé entre le public et lui; he managed to ~ across to her at last il a enfin réussi à se faire entendre d'elle 2 VT SEP (*lit*) faire traverser, faire passer; [+ *ideas, intentions, desires*] communiquer (**to sb** à qn); to ~ sth across to sb faire comprendre qch à qn 3 VT FUS (= *annoy*) to ~ across sb se faire mal voir de qn

► **get ahead** VI (*lit*) prendre de l'avance; (*in career*) monter en grade

► **get along** VI a (= *go*) aller (**to** à); (= *leave*) s'en aller; I must be ~ting along il faut que je m'en aille; ~ along with you!* (= *go away*) va-t-en!, file!*; (*Brit = stop joking*) à d'autres! b (= *manage*) se débrouiller; to ~ along without sth/sb se débrouiller sans qch/qn

|c| (= *progress*) [*work*] avancer; [*student, invalid*] faire des progrès; **he's ~ting along well in French** il fait de gros progrès en français
|d| (= *be on good terms*) (bien) s'entendre; **they ~ along very well** ils s'entendent très bien; **I don't ~ along with him at all** je ne m'entends pas du tout avec lui

▶ **get around** |1| VI = get about
|2| VT SEP = get round 2
|3| VT FUS = get round 3

▶ **get at** VT FUS |a| (= *reach*) [+ *object, component, person, place*] atteindre; **sometimes children are used to ~ at their parents** on se sert parfois des enfants pour atteindre leurs parents; **the dog got at the meat** le chien a touché à la viande; **the goat was trying to ~ at the cabbages** la chèvre essayait de manger les choux; **the rich and powerful are difficult to ~ at** les riches et les puissants sont difficiles à approcher; **let me ~ at him!*** attends un peu que je l'attrape (*subj*)!
|b| (= *find, ascertain*) [+ *facts, truth*] découvrir
|c| (= *suggest*) **what are you ~ting at?** où voulez-vous en venir?
|d| (*Brit* = *attack, jibe at*) s'en prendre à; **she's always ~ting at her brother** elle s'en prend toujours à son frère; **I feel got at** je me sens visé
|e| (* = *influence*) suborner; **there's a danger witnesses will be got at** les témoins risquent d'être subornés

▶ **get away** |1| VI |a| (= *leave*) s'en aller, partir; [*vehicle*] partir; **to ~ away from a place** quitter un endroit; **I usually ~ away from work/the office at six** je quitte généralement (le travail/le bureau) à 6 heures; **I'll try to ~ away from work early** j'essaierai de quitter plus tôt; **I couldn't ~ away any sooner** je n'ai pas pu me libérer plus tôt; **we are not going to be able to ~ away this year** nous n'allons pas pouvoir partir en vacances cette année; **~ away!** allez-vous-en!; **~ away (with you)!*** à d'autres!
|b| (= *escape*) s'échapper; **to ~ away from** [+ *prison*] s'échapper de; [+ *people, situation*] échapper à; [+ *idea*] renoncer à; **he was trying to ~ away when he was shot** il essayait de s'échapper quand on lui a tiré dessus; **she moved here to ~ away from the stress of city life** elle est venue s'installer ici pour échapper au stress de la vie citadine; **it's time we got away from this idea** il est temps que nous renoncions à cette idée; **he went to the Bahamas to ~ away from it all** il est allé aux Bahamas pour laisser tous ses ennuis *or* problèmes derrière lui; **the doctor told her she must ~ away from it all** le médecin lui a ordonné de partir se reposer loin de tout; **the thief got away with the money** le voleur est parti avec l'argent; **you can't ~ away from it!** ◊ **there's no ~ting away from it!** on ne peut pas y couper!*
|2| VT SEP |a| (= *take*) emmener; (= *move away*) éloigner; (= *send off*) expédier; **you must ~ her away to the country for a while** il faut que vous l'emmeniez (*subj*) passer quelque temps à la campagne
|b| (= *remove*) **to ~ sth away from sb** enlever qch à qn

▶ **get away with** VT (= *suffer no consequences*) **she got away with saying outrageous things** elle a tenu impunément des propos choquants; **he broke the law and got away with it** il violait la loi sans être inquiété *or* en toute impunité; **you'll never ~ away with that!** on ne te laissera pas passer ça!*; **he ~s away with murder*** il peut se permettre de faire n'importe quoi; (= *escape lightly*) **he got away with a mere apology** il en a été quitte pour une simple excuse; **we can ~ away with just repainting it** on pourrait se contenter de le repeindre

▶ **get back** |1| VI |a| (= *return*) revenir; **to ~ back (home)** rentrer chez soi; **to ~ back to bed** se recoucher, retourner au lit; **to ~ back upstairs** remonter, retourner en haut; **life is starting to ~ back to normal** la vie reprend son cours; **to ~ back to work** se remettre au tra-

vail, reprendre le travail; **to ~ back to the point** revenir au sujet; **let's ~ back to why you didn't come yesterday** revenons à la question de savoir pourquoi vous n'êtes pas venu hier; **to ~ back to sb*** recontacter qn; (*on phone also*) rappeler qn; **can I ~ back to you on that?*** puis-je vous recontacter à ce sujet?; (*on phone*) puis-je vous rappeler à ce sujet? → get on 3
|b| (= *move backwards*) reculer; **~ back!** reculez!
|2| VT SEP |a| (= *recover*) [+ *sth lent*] récupérer; [+ *sth lost, stolen*] retrouver, récupérer; [+ *strength*] reprendre; [+ *one's husband, partner etc*] faire revenir; **he's trying desperately to ~ her back** il essaie désespérément de la faire revenir; **now that we've got you back** maintenant que tu nous es revenu; **I won't ~ my car back until Thursday** je n'aurai pas ma voiture avant jeudi; **I was afraid I wouldn't ~ my passport back** j'avais peur qu'on ne me rende pas mon passeport; **to ~ one's money back** se faire rembourser, récupérer son argent
|b| (= *replace*) remettre en place
|c| (= *return*) rendre; **I'll ~ it back to you as soon as I can** je vous le rendrai dès que possible
|d| (= *take home*) [+ *person*] raccompagner, reconduire; **he was drunk and I was trying to ~ him back home** il était ivre et j'essayais de le raccompagner chez lui

▶ **get back at*** VT FUS (= *retaliate against*) prendre sa revanche sur

▶ **get by** VI |a| (= *pass*) passer; **let me ~ by** laissez-moi passer
|b| (= *manage*) arriver à s'en sortir*; **by doing two part-time jobs she just ~s by** elle arrive tout juste à s'en sortir* avec deux emplois à mi-temps; **she ~s by on very little money** elle arrive à s'en sortir* *or* elle se débrouille* avec très peu d'argent; **he'll ~ by!** il s'en sortira!*

▶ **get down** |1| VI |a| descendre (**from, off** de); (*at table*) **may I ~ down?** est-ce que je peux sortir de table?; **to ~ down on one's knees** se mettre à genoux; **~ down!** (= *climb down*) descends!; (= *lie down*) couche-toi!
|b| (*esp US* = *enjoy oneself*) s'éclater‡
|2| VT SEP |a| (*from upstairs, attic*) descendre; (*from shelf*) prendre
|b| (* = *swallow*) [+ *food, pill*] avaler
|c| (= *make note of*) noter, prendre (en note)
|d| (= *depress*) déprimer; **he ~s me down** il me fiche le cafard*, il me déprime; **all the worry has got him down** tous les soucis l'ont déprimé *or* lui ont mis le moral à zéro*; **don't let it ~ you down!** ne te laisse pas abattre!

▶ **get down to** VT FUS **to ~ down to doing sth** se mettre à faire qch; **to ~ down to work** se mettre au travail; **you'll have to ~ down to it** il faut vous y mettre; **when you ~ down to it there's not much difference between them** en y regardant de plus près il n'y a pas grande différence entre eux; **to ~ down to business** passer aux choses sérieuses; **let's ~ down to the details** regardons ça de plus près

▶ **get in** |1| VI |a| [*person*] (= *enter*) entrer; (= *be admitted to university, school*) être admis; (= *reach home*) rentrer; [*rain, water*] pénétrer, s'introduire; **do you think we'll ~ in?** tu crois qu'on réussira à entrer?
|b| (= *arrive*) [*train, bus, plane*] arriver
|c| (*Parl* = *be elected*) [*member*] être élu; [*party*] accéder au pouvoir
|2| VT SEP |a| (*lit*) faire entrer; [+ *screw, nail*] enfoncer; [+ *crops, harvest*] rentrer; (*into case*) **I managed to ~ it in** j'ai réussi à le faire entrer dedans *or* à le caser; **did you ~ your essay in on time?** as-tu rendu *or* remis ta dissertation à temps?
|b| (= *plant*) [+ *seeds*] planter, semer; [+ *bulbs*] planter
|c| (= *buy*) [+ *groceries, beer*] acheter; **to ~ in supplies** s'approvisionner, faire des provisions
|d| (= *summon*) [+ *doctor, police, tradesman*]

faire venir
|e| (= *fit in*) glisser; **he got in a reference to his new book** il a glissé une allusion à son dernier livre; **it was hard to ~ a word in** c'était difficile de placer un mot; **he managed to ~ in a game of golf** il a réussi à trouver le temps de jouer une partie de golf → eye, hand

▶ **get in on*** VT FUS **he managed to ~ in on the deal/the trip** il s'est débrouillé pour se joindre à l'affaire/au voyage → act 1c

▶ **get into** VT FUS |a| (= *enter*) [+ *house, park*] entrer dans, pénétrer dans; [+ *car, train*] monter dans; **to ~ into a club** devenir membre d'un club; **he got into a good university** il a été admis dans une bonne université; **to ~ into politics** entrer en politique; **how did I ~ into all this?** comment me suis-je fourré là-dedans?; **to ~ into the way of doing sth** (= *make a habit of*) prendre l'habitude de faire qch; **I don't know what has got into him** je ne sais pas ce qui lui a pris → company, habit, mischief
|b| [+ *clothes*] mettre; **I can't ~ into these jeans any more** je ne peux plus rentrer dans ce jean

▶ **get in with** VT FUS |a| (= *gain favour of*) (réussir à) se faire bien voir de; **he tried to ~ in with the headmaster** il a essayé de se faire bien voir du directeur
|b| (= *become friendly with*) se mettre à fréquenter; **he got in with local drug dealers** il s'est mis à fréquenter les trafiquants de drogue du quartier

▶ **get off** |1| VI |a| (*from vehicle*) descendre; **to tell sb where to ~ off*** envoyer promener qn*, envoyer qn sur les roses*
|b| (= *depart*) [*person*] partir; [*car*] démarrer; [*plane*] décoller; **to ~ off to a good start** (*lit*) prendre un bon départ; (*fig*) partir du bon pied; **to ~ off (to sleep)** s'endormir
|c| (= *escape*) s'en tirer; **to ~ off with a reprimand/a fine** en être quitte pour une réprimande/une amende
|d| (= *leave work*) finir, quitter; (= *take time off*) se libérer; **we ~ off at 5 o'clock** nous finissons *or* nous quittons à 5 heures; **I can't ~ off early today** je ne peux pas m'en aller de bonne heure aujourd'hui; **can you ~ off tomorrow?** est-ce que tu peux te libérer demain?
|2| VT SEP |a| [+ *bus, train*] descendre de
|b| (= *remove*) [+ *clothes, shoes*] enlever; [+ *stains*] faire partir, enlever
|c| (= *dispatch*) [+ *mail*] expédier, envoyer; **I'll phone you once I've got the children off to school** je t'appellerai une fois que les enfants seront partis à l'école; **to ~ a child off to sleep** faire dormir un enfant
|d| (= *save from punishment*) faire acquitter; **a good lawyer will ~ him off** un bon avocat le tirera d'affaire *or* le fera acquitter
|e| (= *learn*) **to ~ sth off (by heart)** apprendre qch (par cœur)
|f| (*from shore*) [+ *boat*] renflouer; (*from boat*) [+ *crew, passengers*] débarquer
|3| VT FUS |a| **to ~ off a bus/a bike** descendre d'un bus/d'un vélo; **to ~ off a ship** descendre à terre; **he got off his horse** il est descendu de cheval; **to ~ off a chair** se lever d'une chaise; **~ (up) off the floor!** levez-vous!; (*fig*) **I wish he would ~ off my back!*** si seulement il pouvait me ficher la paix*!; **let's ~ off this subject of conversation** parlons d'autre chose; **we've rather got off the subject** nous nous sommes plutôt éloignés du sujet
|b| (* = *be excused*) **to ~ off gym** se faire dispenser des cours de gym; **to ~ off work** se libérer

▶ **get off on‡** VT FUS [+ *pornography, power, violence*] prendre son pied avec‡; **these guys ~ off on other guys** ces mecs, ce sont les hommes qui les excitent

▶ **get off with*** VT FUS (*Brit*) draguer*

▶ **get on** |1| VI |a| (*on to bus, bike*) monter; (*on to ship*) monter à bord
|b| (= *advance, make progress*) avancer, pro-

gresser; **how are you ~ting on?** comment ça marche?*; **how did you ~ on?** ça a bien marché?*, comment ça s'est passé?; **she's ~ting on very well with Russian** elle fait de gros progrès en russe; **to be ~ting on*** se faire vieux, prendre de la bouteille*; **he's ~ting on for 40** il approche de la quarantaine; **time is ~ting on** il se fait tard; **it's ~ting on for 3 o'clock** il n'est pas loin de 3 heures; **I must be ~ting on now** il faut que j'y aille; **this will do to be ~ting on with** ça ira pour le moment; **there were ~ting on for 100 people** il y avait pas loin de 100 personnes; **we have ~ting on for 500 copies** nous avons près de or pas loin de 500 exemplaires

[c] (*esp Brit* = *succeed*) réussir, arriver; **if you want to ~ on, you must** ... si tu veux réussir, tu dois ...; **to ~ on in life** or **in the world** réussir dans la vie or faire son chemin

[d] (= *agree*) s'entendre (**with** avec); **we don't ~ on** nous ne nous entendons pas; **I ~ on well with her** je m'entends bien avec elle

[2] VT SEP [a] (= *put on*) [+ *clothes, shoes*] mettre, enfiler

[b] (*Culin*) **I've got the potatoes on** j'ai mis les pommes de terre sur le feu; **I've got the dinner on** j'ai mis le repas en route

[3] VT FUS **to ~ on a horse** monter sur un cheval; **to ~ on a bicycle** monter sur or enfourcher une bicyclette; **to ~ on a ship** monter à bord (d'un navire); **to ~ on a bus/train** monter dans un bus/un train; **to ~ back on one's feet** se remettre debout

► **get on to** VT FUS [a] = get on 3

[b] (*esp Brit* = *get in touch with*) se mettre en rapport avec; (= *speak to*) parler à; (= *ring up*) téléphoner à

[c] (= *start talking about*) aborder; **we got on to (the subject of) money** nous avons abordé le sujet de l'argent

► **get on with** VT FUS [a] (= *continue*) continuer; **while he talked she got on with her work** pendant qu'ils parlaient, elle continua à travailler; **while he was ~ting on with the job** pendant qu'il continuait à travailler; **~ on with it!** ◊ **~ on with the job!** allez, au travail !

[b] (= *start on*) se mettre à; **I'd better ~ on with the job!** il faut que je m'y mette !

► **get out** [1] VI [a] sortir (**of** de); (*from vehicle*) descendre (**of** de); **~ out!** sortez !; **~ out of here!** (*lit*) sors d'ici !; (*US** = *I don't believe it*) à d'autres !

[b] (= *escape*) s'échapper (**of** de); (*fig*) **to ~ out of** [+ *task, obligation*] échapper à; [+ *difficulty*] surmonter; **you'll have to do it, you can't ~ out of it** il faut que tu le fasses, tu ne peux pas y échapper or y couper*; **some people will do anything to ~ out of paying taxes** certaines personnes feraient n'importe quoi pour éviter de payer des impôts; **he's trying to ~ out of going to the funeral** il essaie de trouver une excuse pour ne pas aller à l'enterrement

[c] [*news*] se répandre, s'ébruiter; [*secret*] être éventé; **wait till the news ~s out!** attends que la nouvelle soit ébruitée !

[2] VT SEP [a] (= *bring out*) [+ *object*] sortir (**of** de); [+ *words, speech*] prononcer, sortir*; [+ *book*] [*publisher*] publier, sortir; [*library-user*] emprunter, sortir; **~ the cards out and we'll have a game** sors les cartes et on va faire une partie; **he got his diary out of his pocket** il sortit son agenda de sa poche

[b] (= *remove*) [+ *nail*] arracher; [+ *tooth*] extraire, arracher; [+ *stain*] enlever, faire partir; **to ~ the cork out of a bottle** déboucher une bouteille; **I can't ~ it out of my mind** je ne peux pas chasser cela de mon esprit, ça me trotte dans la tête* sans arrêt

[c] (= *free*) [+ *person*] faire sortir (**of** de); **they hope he'll ~ them out of their difficulties** ils espèrent qu'il les sortira de ce mauvais pas; **it ~s me out of the house** ça me fait sortir (de chez moi)

---

[d] (= *prepare*) [+ *list*] établir, dresser

► **get over** [1] VI [a] (= *go*) aller; (= *come*) venir; (= *cross*) traverser; [*message, meaning*] passer*; [*speaker*] faire entendre

[2] VT FUS [a] (= *cross*) [+ *river, road*] traverser; [+ *fence*] [*horse*] franchir, sauter par-dessus; [*person*] escalader, passer par-dessus

[b] (= *recover from*) **to ~ over an illness** guérir or se remettre d'une maladie; **to ~ over sb's death** se consoler or se remettre de la mort de qn; **I can't ~ over it** je n'en reviens pas; **I can't ~ over the fact that** ... je n'en reviens pas que ... (+ *subj*); **I can't ~ over how much he's changed** je n'en reviens pas de voir combien il a changé; **you'll ~ over it!** tu n'en mourras pas !; **she never really got over him*** elle ne l'a jamais vraiment oublié

[c] (= *overcome*) [+ *obstacle, difficulty*] surmonter; [+ *problem*] résoudre

[3] VT SEP [a] (*lit*) [+ *person, animal, vehicle*] faire passer; **we couldn't ~ the car over** nous n'avons pas pu faire passer la voiture

[b] (= *communicate*) faire comprendre; [+ *ideas*] communiquer; **I couldn't ~ it over to him that he had to come** je n'ai pas pu lui faire comprendre qu'il devait venir; **he couldn't ~ his ideas over to his readers** il était incapable de communiquer ses idées à ses lecteurs

► **get over with** VT SEP (= *have done with*) en finir; **let's ~ it over with** finissons-en; **I was glad to ~ the injections over with** j'étais content d'en avoir fini avec ces piqûres

► **get round** [1] VI = get about

[2] VT SEP **to ~ sb round to one's way of thinking** rallier qn à son point de vue

[3] VT FUS [a] (= *circumvent*) [+ *obstacle, difficulty, law, regulation*] contourner

[b] (= *coax, persuade*) [+ *person*] amadouer*

► **get round to*** VT FUS **to ~ round to doing sth** trouver le temps de faire qch; **I don't think I'll ~ round to it before next week** je ne pense pas trouver le temps de m'en occuper avant la semaine prochaine

► **get through** [1] VI [a] [*news*] parvenir (**to** à); [*signal*] être reçu; **I think the message is ~ting through to him** je pense qu'il commence à comprendre

[b] (= *be accepted, pass*) [*candidate*] être reçu, réussir; [*motion, bill*] passer, être voté; **to ~ through to the third round** [*team*] se qualifier pour le troisième tour

[c] (*Telec*) obtenir la communication; **I phoned you several times but couldn't ~ through** je t'ai appelé plusieurs fois mais je n'ai pas pu t'avoir; **I got through to him straight away** j'ai réussi à lui parler tout de suite

[d] (= *communicate with*) **to ~ through to sb** se faire comprendre de qn; **he can't ~ through to his son at all** il n'arrive pas du tout à se faire comprendre de son fils

[e] (= *finish*) terminer, finir; **I won't ~ through before 6 o'clock** je n'aurai pas terminé or fini avant 6 heures; **to ~ through with sb/sth*** en finir avec qn/qch

[2] VT FUS [a] [+ *hole, window*] passer par; [+ *hedge*] traverser, passer à travers; [+ *crowd*] se frayer un chemin dans or à travers; (*Mil*) [+ *enemy lines*] enfoncer, franchir

[b] (= *do*) [+ *work*] faire; [+ *book*] lire (en entier); **we've got a lot of work to ~ through** nous avons beaucoup de travail à faire; **he got through a lot of work** il a abattu beaucoup de besogne

[c] (= *consume, use, spend*) [+ *supplies*] utiliser, consommer; [+ *money*] dépenser; [+ *food*] manger; [+ *drink*] boire; **we ~ through a lot of nappies** nous utilisons beaucoup de couches; **we ~ through £150 per week** nous dépensons 150 livres par semaine

[d] (= *survive*) **how are they going to ~ through the winter?** comment vont-ils passer l'hiver?; **we couldn't ~ through a day without arguing** pas un jour ne se passait sans que nous ne disputions

---

[3] VT SEP [a] [+ *person, object*] faire passer; **we couldn't ~ the sofa through the door** on ne pouvait pas faire passer le sofa par la porte; **to ~ the message through to sb that** ... faire comprendre à qn que ...; **I can't ~ it through to him that** ... je n'arrive pas à lui faire comprendre que ...

[b] (= *have approved*) **to ~ a bill through** faire adopter un projet de loi

[c] (*Scol*) **he got his pupils through** il y est pour beaucoup dans le succès de ses élèves à l'examen; **it was his English that got him through** c'est grâce à son anglais qu'il a été reçu

► **get together** [1] VI se retrouver; **let's ~ together on Thursday and decide what to do** si on se retrouvait jeudi pour décider de ce qu'on va faire?; **this is the only place where villagers can ~ together** c'est le seul endroit où les gens du village peuvent se retrouver or se réunir; **you'd better ~ together with him before you decide** vous feriez bien de le voir avant de prendre une décision

[2] VT SEP [+ *people*] rassembler, réunir; [+ *thoughts, ideas*] rassembler; [+ *team, group*] former; [+ *money*] rassembler, collecter; **let me just ~ my things together** je rassemble mes affaires et j'arrive

► **get under** [1] VI (= *pass underneath*) passer par-dessous

[2] VT FUS **to ~ under a fence/a rope** etc passer sous une barrière/une corde etc

► **get up** [1] VI [a] (= *rise*) [*person*] se lever (**from** de); [*wind*] se lever; **the sea is ~ting up** la houle se lève; **what time did you ~ up?** à quelle heure t'es-tu levé?

[b] (*on a chair, on stage*) monter

[2] VT FUS [+ *tree, ladder*] monter à; [+ *hill*] monter, grimper

[3] VT SEP [a] (*lit*) [+ *person*] (*up stairs, hill*) faire monter; [+ *thing*] monter; [+ *sail*] hisser; **to ~ up speed** prendre de la vitesse

[b] (*from bed*) [+ *person*] faire lever; (= *wake*) réveiller

[c] (= *organize*) [+ *play, show*] monter; [+ *concert*] organiser; [+ *story*] fabriquer, forger; **to ~ up a petition** organiser une pétition

[d] (= *prepare, arrange*) [+ *article for sale*] apprêter, préparer; [+ *book*] présenter

[e] (= *dress*) **she was very nicely got up** elle était très bien mise; **a tramp got up in a velvet jacket** un clochard affublé d'une veste de velours; **to ~ o.s. up as** se déguiser en

[f] (= *study*) [+ *history, literature* etc] travailler, bûcher*; [+ *speech, lecture*] préparer

► **get up to** VT FUS [a] (= *catch up with*) rattraper

[b] (= *reach*) arriver à; **I've got up to page 17** j'en suis à la page 17; **where did we ~ up to last week?** où en étions-nous or où en sommes-nous arrivés la semaine dernière?

[c] (* = *be involved in, do*) **to ~ up to mischief** faire des bêtises or des sottises; **you never know what he'll ~ up to next** on ne sait jamais ce qu'il va inventer or fabriquer*; **do you realize what they've been ~ting up to?** est-ce que tu sais ce qu'ils ont trouvé le moyen de faire?; (*hum*) **what have you been ~ting up to lately?** qu'est-ce que tu deviens?

---

getaway ['getəweɪ] N [a] (= *start*) (*Aut*) démarrage m; (*Racing*) départ m [b] (= *escape*) [of *criminals*] fuite f; **to make a** or **one's ~** filer, décamper; **they had a ~ car waiting** ils avaient une voiture pour filer; **the gangsters' ~ car was later found abandoned** on a retrouvé abandonnée la voiture qui avait permis aux gangsters de s'enfuir [c] (= *short holiday*) escapade f

Gethsemane [geθ'semənɪ] N Gethsémani

getup* ['getʌp] N (= *clothing*) mise f, tenue f, accoutrement m (*pej*); (= *fancy dress*) déguisement m; (= *presentation*) présentation f

geum ['dʒiːəm] N benoîte f

gewgaw ['gju:gɔː] N bibelot *m*, babiole *f*

geyser ['gi:zəʳ, (US) 'gaɪzəʳ] N (Geol) geyser *m*; (Brit: in house) chauffe-eau *m inv*

Ghana ['gɑːnə] N le Ghana

Ghanaian [gɑːˈneɪən] [1] ADJ ghanéen [2] N Ghanéen(ne) *m(f)*

ghastly ['gɑːstlɪ] ADJ [a] (= awful, horrendous) [person] horrible; [war, murder, news, clothes, wallpaper, building] horrible, affreux; [situation, experience] épouvantable [b] (= frightening) effrayant [c] (= serious) [mistake, headache, pain] terrible, épouvantable [d] (= pale) [appearance] mortellement pâle; [pallor] mortel; [light] spectral; **to look ~** avoir une mine de déterré

ghee [gi:] N beurre *m* clarifié

Ghent [gent] N Gand

gherkin ['gɜːkɪn] N (Culin) cornichon *m*

ghetto ['getəʊ] [1] N (pl **ghettos** or **ghettoes**) (lit, fig) ghetto *m* [2] COMP ▶ **ghetto-blaster*** N (gros) radiocassette *m*

ghettoization [ˌgetəʊaɪˈzeɪʃən] N ghettoïsation *f*; (fig) marginalisation *f*

ghettoize ['getəʊˌaɪz] ♦VT ghettoïser; (fig) marginaliser

Ghibelline ['gɪbɪˌlaɪn] N Gibelin *m*

ghost [gəʊst] [1] N (= apparition) fantôme *m*; (fig) ombre *f*; (TV) filage *m*; (†† = soul) âme *f*; **I don't believe in ~s** je ne crois pas aux fantômes; **he gave the ~ of a smile** il a eu un vague sourire; **I haven't a ~ of a chance** je n'ai pas la moindre chance or pas l'ombre d'une chance; (liter, hum) **to give up the ~*** (= die) rendre l'âme; (= stop trying) baisser les bras; **my alarm clock's finally given up the ~** mon réveil a fini par rendre l'âme; **you look like or as if you've seen a ~!** on dirait que tu as vu un revenant! → **holy**
[2] VT **his book was ~ed by a journalist** c'est un journaliste qui lui a servi de nègre pour (écrire) son livre
[3] COMP [film, story] de revenants, de fantômes; [ship] fantôme ▶ **ghost image** N (TV) filage *m* ▶ **ghost town** N ville *f* morte ▶ **ghost train** N (Brit: at funfair) train *m* fantôme ▶ **ghost-write** VT → **ghost 2** ▶ **ghost writer** N nègre *m*

ghostly ['gəʊstlɪ] ADJ [a] spectral, fantomatique [b] (†† : Rel etc) spirituel

ghoul [gu:l] N goule *f*; (= grave robber) déterreur *m* de cadavres; (fig) **he's a ~** il est morbide, il a des goûts dépravés

ghoulish ['gu:lɪʃ] ADJ (= morbid, ghoul-like) de goule; (fig, pej) [person, curiosity, desire, humour, tastes] morbide

ghoulishly ['gu:lɪʃlɪ] ADV (= morbidly) de façon morbide

GHQ [ˌdʒiːeɪtʃˈkjuː] N (Mil etc) (ABBR = **General Headquarters**) GQG *m*

GI* [dʒiːˈaɪ] (US) [1] N (also **GI Joe**) soldat *m* (américain), GI *m* [2] ADJ militaire; (Univ) **GI bill** loi sur les bourses pour anciens combattants; **GI bride** épouse étrangère d'un GI

giant ['dʒaɪənt] [1] N géant *m*; **he is a ~ of a man** c'est un géant; **the ~ of opera, Luciano Pavarotti** le monstre sacré de l'opéra, Luciano Pavarotti; (Geog) **the Giant's Causeway** la chaussée des Géants; (fig) **electronics/chemicals ~** géant *m* de l'électronique/de l'industrie chimique [2] ADJ [tree, star etc] géant; [strides] de géant; [helping, amount] gigantesque; [packet, size] géant [3] COMP ▶ **giant-killer** N (Sport) vainqueur *m* surprise (équipe de second plan qui parvient à battre une grande équipe) ▶ **giant-killing** ADJ **the team's ~-killing act against Manchester United** la victoire surprise de l'équipe contre le géant Manchester United; **Spain's ~-killing French Open champion** l'outsider espagnol qui a tombé les meilleurs joueurs aux Internationaux de France ▶ **giant panda** N grand

panda *m* ▶ **giant slalom** N (Ski) slalom *m* géant

giantess ['dʒaɪəntɪs] N géante *f*

gibber ['dʒɪbəʳ] VI [person, ape etc] baragouiner*; **to ~ with rage/fear** bégayer or bafouiller de colère/de peur; **~ing idiot*** crétin *m* patenté*; **I was a ~ing wreck by this stage** j'étais alors à bout de nerfs

gibberish ['dʒɪbərɪʃ] N (NonC) charabia* *m*, baragouin* *m*

gibbet ['dʒɪbɪt] N potence *f*, gibet *m*

gibbon ['gɪbən] N gibbon *m*

gibbous ['gɪbəs] ADJ (= hump-backed) gibbeux (liter), bossu; **~ moon** lune *f* dans le deuxième or troisième quartier

gibe [dʒaɪb] [1] VI [a] **to ~ at sb** railler qn, se moquer de qn [b] (Naut) [boat] virer lof pour lof; [sail] passer d'un bord à l'autre du mât [2] N raillerie *f*, moquerie *f*

giblets ['dʒɪblɪts] NPL abattis *mpl*, abats *mpl* (de volaille)

Gibraltar [dʒɪˈbrɔːltəʳ] N Gibraltar; **in ~** à Gibraltar → **rock²**, **strait**

giddily ['gɪdɪlɪ] ADV (= unsteadily) en titubant; (= dizzyingly) à donner/à en avoir le vertige; **to be ~ high** [figures etc] atteindre des sommets vertigineux

giddiness ['gɪdɪnɪs] N (NonC) (Med) vertiges *mpl*, étourdissements *mpl*; (= lightheadedness) légèreté *f*; (= heedlessness) étourderie *f*; **a bout of ~** un vertige, un étourdissement

giddy¹ ['gɪdɪ] ADJ [person] (= dizzy) pris de vertige or d'un étourdissement; (= heedless) étourdi, écervelé; (= not serious) léger; [height] vertigineux, qui donne le vertige; **I feel ~** la tête me tourne; **to turn** or **go ~** être pris de vertige; **to make sb ~** donner le vertige à qn; **~ spells** vertiges *mpl*, étourdissements *mpl*; **being there gave me a ~ pleasure** être là me procurait un plaisir grisant; **she was ~ with excitement** l'idée (or l'émerveillement etc) la grisait; (fig, iro) **the ~ heights of senior management** les hautes sphères de la direction générale; **that's the ~ limit!‡** ça c'est le bouquet!* → **spell²**

giddy² ['gɪdɪ] EXCL (to horse) **~ up!** hue!

Gideon Bible [ˌgɪdɪən ˈbaɪbəl] N bible placée dans les hôtels par la Gideon Society

GIFT [gɪft] N (ABBR = **Gamete Intrafallopian Transfer**) fivète *f*

gift [gɪft] [1] N [a] (= present) cadeau *m*, présent *m*; (Comm) prime *f*, cadeau *m*; **New Year ~** étrennes *fpl*; **it was a ~** (lit) c'était un cadeau; (* fig = it was easy) c'était du gâteau*; **I wouldn't have it as a ~** on m'en ferait cadeau que je n'en voudrais pas; (Comm) **"free ~ inside the packet"** « ce paquet contient un cadeau »
[b] (Jur etc) don *m*, donation *f*; **to make sb a ~ of sth** faire don or cadeau de qch à qn; **in the ~ of** à la discrétion de → **deed**
[c] (= talent) don *m* (for de, pour), talent *m* (for pour); **he has a ~ for maths** il a un don pour les maths or le don des maths; **she has a ~ for teaching** elle a un don pour l'enseignement, elle est très douée pour l'enseignement; **he has great artistic ~s** il a de grands dons artistiques; **to have the ~ of the gab*** avoir la langue bien pendue, avoir du bagout*
[2] VT (esp Jur) donner; (fig) **to be ~ed with patience** etc être doué de patience etc
[3] COMP ▶ **gift horse** N ▪ (PROV) **don't look a ~ horse in the mouth** à cheval donné on ne regarde point la bouche (PROV), on ne critique pas le cadeau qu'on reçoit (PROV) ▶ **gift shop** N boutique *f* de cadeaux ▶ **gift token**, **gift voucher** N chèque-cadeau *m*

gifted ['gɪftɪd] ADJ (fig) doué (**for** pour); **the ~ child** l'enfant *m* surdoué

giftwrap ['gɪftræp] [1] VT **to ~ a package** faire un paquet-cadeau; **could you ~ it for me?** pouvez-vous me faire un paquet-cadeau? [2] N = **giftwrapping**

giftwrapped ['gɪftræpt] ADJ sous emballage-cadeau

giftwrapping ['gɪftræpɪŋ] N emballage-cadeau *m*

gig [gɪg] [1] N [a] (= vehicle) cabriolet *m*; (= boat) petit canot *m*, youyou *m* [b] (Mus* = jazz, pop concert) concert *m*; **they had a regular ~ at the Cavern** ils jouaient régulièrement au Cavern; (Theat) **comedy ~s** numéros *mpl* de comique [c] (US fig:*) job* *m* temporaire [2] VI (Mus*) jouer live or sur scène; **he spent ten years ~ging in bars** [stand-up comedian] il a passé dix ans à jouer dans les bars

gigabyte ['dʒɪgəˌbaɪt] N gigaoctet *m*

gigaflop ['gɪgəˌflɒp] N milliard *m* d'opérations en virgule flottante par seconde

gigahertz ['dʒɪgəˌhɜːts] N gigahertz *m*

gigantic [dʒaɪˈgæntɪk] ADJ gigantesque

gigantically [dʒaɪˈgæntɪkəlɪ] ADV **~ fat** démesurément gros; **to be ~ successful** avoir un succès énorme

gigantism [dʒaɪˈgæntɪzəm] N gigantisme *m*

gigawatt ['dʒɪgəˌwɒt] N gigawatt *m*

giggle ['gɪgl] [1] VI rire sottement, glousser; **stop giggling!** ne riez pas sottement comme ça!; **she was giggling helplessly** elle ne pouvait pas se retenir de rire sottement or de glousser; **"stop that!" she ~d** « arrête! » dit-elle en gloussant [2] N petit rire *m* sot or nerveux, gloussement *m* sot or nerveux; **to have/get the ~s** avoir/attraper le fou rire; **she had a fit of the ~s** elle avait le fou rire; (Brit) **it was a bit of a ~*** ça nous a bien fait rigoler*; (Brit) **he did it for a ~*** il a fait ça pour rigoler*

giggly ['gɪglɪ] ADJ qui rit bêtement or glousse (sans arrêt)

GIGO ['gi:gəʊ, ˌdʒiːaɪdʒiːˈəʊ] (ABBR = **garbage in, garbage out**) → **garbage**

gigolo ['ʒɪgələʊ] N (sexually) gigolo *m*; (= dancing partner) danseur *m* mondain

gigot ['ʒiːgəʊ, dʒɪgət] N (Culin) gigot *m*

Gila ['hiːlə] N **~ monster** monstre *m* de Gila, héloderme *m*

Gilbertian [gɪlˈbɜːtɪən] ADJ (Brit) ≈ vaudevillesque

gild [gɪld] VT (pret **gilded**, ptp **gilded** or **gilt**) dorer; (fig) **to ~ the lily** renchérir sur la perfection; **to ~ the pill** dorer la pilule; **~ed youth** la jeunesse dorée

gilding ['gɪldɪŋ] N dorure *f*

Giles [dʒaɪlz] N Gilles *m*

gill¹ [gɪl] N [of mushrooms] lamelle *f*; **~s** [of fish] ouïes *fpl*, branchies *fpl*; **he was looking somewhat green** or **pale around the ~s*** il était (devenu) vert

gill² [dʒɪl] N (Brit = measure) quart *m* de pinte (= 0,142 l)

gillie ['gɪlɪ] N (Scot) gillie *m*, accompagnateur *m* (d'un chasseur, d'un pêcheur etc)

gillyflower ['dʒɪlɪˌflaʊəʳ] N giroflée *f*

gilt [gɪlt] [1] VB ptp of **gild** [2] N (= gold) dorure *f*; (fig) **to take the ~ off the gingerbread** enlever tout le charme, gâter le plaisir [3] **gilts** NPL (Brit Fin) = **gilt-edged securities** [4] ADJ doré [5] COMP ▶ **gilt-edged** ADJ [book] doré sur tranche; (fig) de tout premier ordre ▶ **gilt-edged securities** NPL (Brit Fin) (government-issued) fonds *mpl* or obligations *fpl* d'État; (= safe investment) valeurs *fpl* de tout repos or de père de famille ▶ **gilt-edged stock** N = **gilt-edged securities** ▶ **gilt-head** N (= fish) daurade *f*, dorade *f*

gimbal(s) ['dʒɪmbəl(z)] N (Aut, Naut) cardan *m*

gimcrack ['dʒɪmkræk] ADJ ringard

gimlet ['gɪmlɪt] N vrille *f*; **to have eyes like**

~s ◊ **to be ~-eyed** avoir des yeux perçants, avoir un regard perçant

gimme ['gɪmɪ] = **give me**

gimmick ['gɪmɪk]   N *(gen)* truc* *m* ; *(Theat = catch phrase)* réplique *f* à effet ; *(= gadget)* gadget *m* ; *(US = trick)* truc* *m*, combine *f* ; **advertising ~** truc* *m* or procédé *m* publicitaire ; **election ~** procédé *m* pour s'attirer des suffrages ; **it's just a sales ~** c'est simplement un gadget promotionnel or une astuce promotionnelle

gimmickry ['gɪmɪkrɪ]   N gadgets *mpl*

gimmicky ['gɪmɪkɪ]   ADJ *(pej)* qui relève du gadget

gimp* [gɪmp] *(US)*   [1]   N *(= person)* boiteux *m*, -euse *f* ; **to walk with a ~** boiter   [2]   VI boiter

gimpy ['gɪmpɪ]   ADJ *(US)* boiteux

gin[1] [dʒɪn]   [1]   N   [a]   gin *m* ; **~ and tonic** gin-tonic *m* ; *(Brit)* **~ and it** gin-vermouth *m* → **pink**   [b]   *(Cards: also* **~ rummy***)* variante du rami   [2]   COMP ► **gin mill** N *(US)* bar *m*, saloon *m* ► **gin sling** N gin-fizz *m*

gin[2] [dʒɪn]   N   [a]   *(Brit: also* **~ trap***)* piège *m*   [b]   *(Tech: also* **cotton ~***)* égreneuse *f* (de coton)

ginger ['dʒɪndʒə^r]   [1]   N   [a]   gingembre *m* ; *(fig)* énergie *f*, pêche* *f* ; *(= nickname)* **Ginger** Poil de Carotte   [2]   ADJ   [a]   *[hair]* roux (rousse *f*), rouquin* ; **a ~ tom** un chat roux   [b]   *(Culin) [biscuit etc]* au gingembre   [3]   COMP ► **ginger ale, ginger beer** *(Brit)* N boisson *f* gazeuse au gingembre ► **ginger group** N *(Brit: esp Pol)* groupe *m* de pression ► **ginger nut** N *(Brit)* gâteau *m* sec au gingembre ► **ginger pop*** N = **ginger ale** ► **ginger snap** N = **ginger nut**

► **ginger up** VT SEP *(Brit)* *[+ person]* secouer, secouer les puces à* ; *[+ action, event]* mettre de la vie or de l'entrain dans ; **the banks are desperately trying to ~ up the housing market** les banques essaient désespérément de stimuler or dynamiser le marché de l'immobilier ; **he ~ed up his talk with a few jokes** il a relevé or égayé sa causerie de quelques plaisanteries

gingerbread ['dʒɪndʒəbred]   [1]   N pain *m* d'épice   [2]   ADJ *(Culin)* en pain d'épice ; *(Archit* *)* *[style]* tarabiscoté ; **~ man** bonhomme *m* en pain d'épice

gingerly ['dʒɪndʒəlɪ]   [1]   ADJ *[prod]* léger, doux (douce *f*) ; *[touch]* délicat   [2]   ADV avec précaution

gingery ['dʒɪndʒərɪ]   ADJ   [a]   *(= colour) [hair]* avec des reflets roux ; *[cloth etc]* dans les tons roux   [b]   *[taste]* de gingembre ; **it tastes (very) ~** ça a (fort) goût de gingembre

gingham ['gɪŋəm]   N *(Tex)* vichy *m*

gingivitis [,dʒɪndʒɪ'vaɪtɪs]   N gingivite *f*

gink* [gɪŋk]   N *(US pej)* (drôle de) type* *m*

ginormous* [dʒaɪ'nɔːməs]   ADJ gigantesque, maous(se)* *m(f)*

ginseng [dʒɪn'seŋ]   [1]   N ginseng *m*   [2]   COMP *[tea, tablets]* au ginseng

Gioconda [dʒɔ'kɒndə]   N **La ~** la Joconde ; **~ smile** sourire *m* énigmatique or sibyllin

gippy* ['dʒɪpɪ]   ADJ *(Brit)* **to have a ~ tummy** avoir la courante*

gipsy ['dʒɪpsɪ]   [1]   N *(gen)* bohémien(ne) *m(f)* ; *(Spanish)* gitan(e) *m(f)* ; *(Central European)* Tsigane or Tzigane *mf* ; *(pej)* romanichel(le) *m(f)*   [2]   COMP *[caravan, custom]* de bohémien, de gitan, tsigane, de romanichel *(pej)* ; *[music]* des gitans, tsigane ► **gipsy cab** N *(US)* taxi *m* clandestin ► **gipsy driver** N *(US)* chauffeur *m* de taxi clandestin ► **gipsy moth** N *(Zool)* zigzag *m*

giraffe [dʒɪ'rɑːf]   N *(pl* **giraffes** *or* **giraffe***)* girafe *f* ; **baby ~** girafeau *m*

gird [gɜːd]   *(pret, ptp* **girded** *or* **girt***)* VT *(liter = encircle)* ceindre *(liter)* ; *(†† = clothe)* revêtir **(with** de) ; *(fig = get ready)* **to ~ o.s. for a fight** se préparer au combat ; *(liter)* **to ~ (up) one's loins** se préparer ; **(to do sth** à faire qch, **for sth** pour qch)

► **gird on** VT SEP *[+ sword etc]* ceindre *(liter)*
► **gird up** VT SEP *[+ robe]* ceindre → **gird**

girder ['gɜːdə^r]   N poutre *f* ; *(smaller)* poutrelle *f*

girdle[1] ['gɜːdl]   [1]   N *(= belt: lit, fig)* ceinture *f* ; *(= corset)* gaine *f*   [2]   VT *(fig liter)* ceindre **(with** de)

girdle[2] ['gɜːdl]   N *(Culin)* = **griddle 1**

girl [gɜːl]   [1]   N   [a]   (jeune) or (petite) fille *f* ; **the ~ who looks after the children** la jeune fille qui s'occupe des enfants ; **a little ~** une petite fille, une fillette ; **that ~ gets on my nerves** cette fille m'énerve ; **a ~ of 17** une (jeune) fille de 17 ans ; **an English ~** une jeune Anglaise ; **a little English ~** une petite Anglaise ; **poor little ~** pauvre petite *f* ; **the Smith ~s** les filles des Smith ; **I'll really give you something to cry about, my ~** je vais te donner une bonne raison de pleurer, ma fille* ; **~s' school** école *f* (or lycée *m* etc) de filles   [b]   *(= daughter)* fille *f* ; *(= pupil)* élève *f* ; *(= servant)* bonne *f* ; *(= factory-worker)* ouvrière *f* ; *(= shop assistant)* vendeuse *f*, jeune fille *f* ; *(* = sweetheart)* petite amie *f* ; *(Brit Scol)* **old ~** ancienne élève *f* ; **yes, old ~*** oui, ma vieille* ; **the old ~*** *(= wife)* la patronne*, la bourgeoise* ; *(= mother)* ma mère or vieille* ; **the old ~ next door** la vieille dame or la vieille* d'à côté   [2]   COMP ► **girl Friday** N *(in office)* aide *f* de bureau ► **girl guide** N *(Brit)* éclaireuse *f* ; *(Roman Catholic)* guide *f* ► **girl's blouse*** N **he's a big ~'s blouse** c'est une vraie mauviette ; **you big ~'s blouse!** quelle mauviette tu fais ! ► **girl scout** N *(US)* → **girl guide** ► **girl-watching** N *(US)* **to go ~-watching** aller reluquer* les filles

girlfriend ['gɜːlfrend]   N *[of boy]* petite amie *f* ; *[of girl]* amie *f*, copine *f*

girlhood ['gɜːlhʊd]   N enfance *f*, jeunesse *f*

girlie* ['gɜːlɪ]   N fillette *f* ; **~ magazine** magazine *m* de fesse*

girlish ['gɜːlɪʃ]   ADJ *[boy]* efféminé ; *[behaviour, appearance]* *(woman's)* de petite fille, de jeune fille ; *(man's, boy's)* efféminé

giro ['dʒaɪrəʊ]   N *(Brit*: also* **~ cheque***)* ≈ mandat *m* postal *(servant au paiement des prestations de chômage ou de maladie)* ; **bank ~ system** système *m* de virement bancaire ; **National Giro** ≈ Comptes *mpl* Chèques Postaux ; *(Fin)* **by ~ transfer** par virement postal *(or bancaire)*

girt [gɜːt]   [1]   VB *pt, ptp of* **gird**   [2]   N = **girth b**

girth [gɜːθ]   N   [a]   *(= circumference) [of tree]* circonférence *f* ; *[of waist/hips etc]* tour *m* (de taille/de hanches etc) ; **in ~** de circonférence, de tour ; **his (great) ~** sa corpulence   [b]   *[of saddle]* sangle *f* ; **to loosen the ~s** dessangler

gist [dʒɪst]   N *(NonC) [of report, conversation etc]* fond *m*, essentiel *m* ; *[of question]* point *m* principal ; **to get the ~ of sth** comprendre l'essentiel de qch ; **give me the ~ of what he said** résumez-moi ce qu'il a dit, en deux mots

git* [gɪt]   N *(Brit pej)*   [a]   *(= idiot) (man)* con* *m* ; *(woman)* conne* *f* ; **stupid ~!** espèce de con(ne)!* ;   [b]   *(= unpleasant person) (man)* salaud* *m* ; *(woman)* salope* *f* ; **he's a miserable old ~** c'est un vieux con*

give [gɪv]

---

vb: pret **gave**, ptp **given**

[1] TRANSITIVE VERB	[4] COMPOUNDS
[2] INTRANSITIVE VERB	[5] PHRASAL VERBS
[3] NOUN	

---

[1] TRANSITIVE VERB

When **give** *is part of a set combination, eg* **give evidence, give a party, give a yawn,** *look up the other word.*

[a]   donner (**to** à) ; *[+ gift]* offrir (**to** à) ; *[+ one's time]* consacrer, donner (**to** à) ; **to ~ sb something to eat/drink** donner à manger/à boire à qn ; **can you ~ him something to do?** pouvez-vous lui donner quelque chose à faire ? ; **what**

are you going to ~ her? qu'est-ce que tu vas lui offrir ? ; **to ~ one's daughter in marriage†** donner sa fille en mariage† ; **she gave herself to him†** elle s'est donnée à lui† ; **it was not ~n to him to achieve happiness** il ne lui a pas été donné de trouver le bonheur ; **to ~ sb one's trust** donner or accorder sa confiance à qn ; **he gave his life/himself to helping the poor** il a consacré sa vie aux pauvres ; *BUT* **she gave us a wonderful meal** elle nous a préparé un délicieux repas ; **to ~ sb a look** jeter or lancer un regard à qn ; **~ me a gas cooker every time!*** pour moi rien ne vaut une gazinière ! ; **children? ~ me dogs any time!** des enfants ? je préfère de loin les chiens !

> **give + noun may be translated by a verb alone.** **can you ~ me a bed for the night?** pouvez-vous me loger pour la nuit ? ; **they gave us a lot of help** ils nous ont beaucoup aidés ; **I'll ~ you a call** je vous appellerai, je vous passerai un coup de fil

♦ **to be given** *(= receive)*

> *In French the recipient is not made the subject of a passive construction.* **she was ~n a huge bouquet** on lui a donné or offert un énorme bouquet ; **we were ~n a warm reception** on nous a accueillis chaleureusement ; **the suggestion will be ~n serious consideration** cette suggestion sera soigneusement examinée ; **six footballers were ~n honours** six footballeurs ont reçu une distinction honorifique ; *BUT* **he was ~n a knighthood** il a été fait chevalier

♦ **to give and take**: **one must ~ and take** il faut faire des concessions → **4**

♦ **give or take**: **~ or take a few minutes** à quelques minutes près ; **a hundred people, ~ or take a few** à peu près cent personnes

[b]   *= cause, cause to feel* faire ; **it gave me a shock** ça m'a fait un choc ; **keying ~s me a pain in my wrist** si je tape au clavier, ça me fait mal au poignet ; **it gave me a funny feeling** ça m'a fait un drôle d'effet ; *BUT* **to ~ sb to believe sth** donner à croire qch à qn, laisser entendre qch à qn ; **I was ~n to understand that ...** on m'avait laissé entendre que ..., on m'avait donné à croire que ... ; **her grandchildren ~ her a lot of pleasure** ses petits-enfants lui procurent beaucoup de plaisir ; **it ~s me great pleasure to introduce ...** c'est avec grand plaisir que je vous présente ... ; **it gave us a good laugh*** on a bien rigolé

[c]   *= pass on* OK, **I'll ~ him the message** d'accord, je lui ferai la commission, d'accord, je le lui dirai ; **you've ~n me your cold** tu m'as passé or refilé* ton rhume ; **~ him my love** faites-lui mes amitiés

[d]   *= put through to* passer ; **could you ~ me Mr Smith/extension 231?** pouvez-vous me passer M. Smith/le poste 231 ?

[e]   *with time expressions* **~ him time to get home** laissez-lui le temps de rentrer ; **~ me time and I'll manage it** laissez-moi du temps et j'y arriverai ; **~ yourself time to think about it before you decide** prends le temps de réfléchir avant de te décider ; *(just)* **~ me time!** attends un peu !, ne me bouscule pas ! ; **I can't ~ you any longer, you must pay me now** je ne peux plus vous accorder de délai, il faut que vous payiez maintenant ; **I can ~ you half an hour tomorrow** je peux vous consacrer une demi-heure demain ; **the doctors gave him two years (to live)** les médecins lui ont donné deux ans (à vivre) ; **how long do you ~ that marriage?** combien de temps crois-tu que ce mariage tiendra ? ; *(in age)* **I can ~ him ten years*** il est de dix ans mon cadet

[f]   *+ name, address, description* donner (**to** à) ; **what name did he ~?** quel nom a-t-il donné ? ; **she was unable to ~ the police a description of her attacker** elle a été incapable de donner une description de son agresseur à la police ; **to ~ one's decision** rendre or faire connaître sa

décision ; **he gave the cause of death as asphyxia** il a conclu à une mort par asphyxie ; *(Jur)* **~n under my hand and seal** signé

g = **utter** [+ *answer*] donner ; [+ *sigh, cry*] pousser ; **they haven't yet ~n their answer** ils n'ont pas encore donné de réponse, ils n'ont pas encore rendu leur réponse

h = **pay** payer ; (= *offer*) offrir, donner ; **what did you ~ for it?** combien l'avez-vous payé ? ; **I'd ~ a lot/anything to know** je donnerais gros/ n'importe quoi pour savoir ; **what will you ~ me for it?** combien m'en offrez-vous *or* m'en donnez-vous ? ; **I don't ~ much for his chances** je ne donne pas cher de ses chances

i = **punish with** [+ *lines, detention*] donner (**to** à) ; **the teacher gave him 100 lines** le professeur lui a donné 100 lignes ; *BUT* **the judge gave him five years** le juge l'a condamné à cinq ans de prison

j = **perform, do, deliver** [+ *lecture*] faire, donner ; [+ *play*] donner, présenter

k = **produce** donner, produire ; **cows ~ more milk when ...** les vaches donnent *or* produisent plus de lait lorsque ... ; **two surveys gave good results** deux études ont donné *or* produit de bons résultats ; *BUT* **it ~s a total of 100** cela fait 100 en tout ; **this lamp doesn't ~ much light** cette lampe éclaire mal

l *frm* = **toast** **I ~ you the Queen!** je lève mon verre à la santé de la Reine !

m **idiomatic expressions** **he gave as good as he got** il a rendu coup pour coup ; **~ it all you've got!** mets-y le paquet ! * ; **I wouldn't have it if you gave it to me** * tu m'en ferais cadeau que je n'en voudrais pas ; **I'll ~ him something to cry about!** * je lui apprendrai à pleurer ! ; **to ~ sb what for** * ◊ **to ~ it to sb** * passer un savon à qn* , faire sa fête à qn* ; *(iro)* **he wants £100?** I'll ~ **him £100!** * il veut 100 livres ? il peut toujours courir ! * ; *(agreeing)* **I'll ~ you that** je suis d'accord là-dessus ; **don't ~ me that!** * ne me raconte pas d'histoires ! * ; *(US)* **OK, now ~!** * allez accouche ! *

n **SET STRUCTURES**

◆ **to give way** [1] (= *collapse*) [*bridge, beam, ceiling, floor*] s'effondrer (**beneath, under** sous) ; [*ground*] céder, se dérober (**beneath, under** sous) ; [*cable, rope*] céder, (se) casser ; [*legs*] fléchir, mollir ; *BUT* **his strength gave way** les forces lui ont manqué ; **after months of stress his health gave way** après des mois de stress, il a eu de graves problèmes de santé *or* sa santé a flanché

◆ **to give way** [2] (= *yield*) [*person*] céder (**to sth** à qch) ; (= *stand back*) s'écarter, se pousser ; (= *agree*) finir par donner son accord, finir par consentir ; [*troops*] (= *withdraw*) reculer, se retirer ; [*car, traffic*] céder le passage (**to** à) ; *(Aut)* **"~ way"** « cédez le passage », « vous n'avez pas la priorité » ; *(Aut)* **"~ way to traffic from the right"** « priorité à droite » ; **I gave way to temptation** j'ai cédé à la tentation ; **he gave way to their demands** il a cédé à leurs revendications ; **don't ~ way to despair** ne cédez pas au désespoir, ne désespérez pas ; **to ~ way to an impulse** céder à une impulsion ; *BUT* **she gave way to tears** elle n'a pas pu retenir ses larmes ; **his shock gave way to anger** sa surprise a fait place *or* laissé place à la colère

[2] **INTRANSITIVE VERB**

a = **collapse** céder (**beneath, under** sous) ; **the axle gave and fell on me** l'essieu a cédé et m'est tombé dessus ; **the chair gave under his weight** la chaise a cédé sous son poids

b = **yield** [*floor*] fléchir ; [*cloth, elastic*] se détendre, se relâcher ; **the floor gave slightly under his feet** le parquet fléchissait légèrement sous son poids

c *esp US* **what ~s?** * alors, qu'est-ce qui se passe ?

[3] **NOUN**

* = **flexibility** **there is a lot of ~ in this rope** cette corde est très élastique ; **there isn't a lot of ~ in**

these proposals il n'y a pas beaucoup de souplesse dans ces propositions ; **how much ~ has there been on their side?** est-ce qu'ils se sont montrés prêts à faire des concessions ?

[4] **COMPOUNDS**

► **give-and-take** N (*NonC*) concessions *fpl* mutuelles ; **there must be a certain amount of ~-and-take** il faut que chacun fasse des concessions *or* y mette un peu du sien

[5] **PHRASAL VERBS**

► **give away** VT SEP **a** (= *bestow, distribute*) [+ *prizes*] distribuer ; [+ *bride*] conduire à l'autel ; [+ *money, goods*] donner ; **we've got 200 CDs to ~ away** nous avons 200 CD à donner ; **at this price I'm giving it away** à ce prix-là c'est un cadeau *or* c'est donné

b (= *concede*) faire cadeau de ; **we gave away a silly goal** nous leur avons bêtement fait cadeau d'un but

c (= *tell, betray*) [+ *names, details*] donner ; [+ *secrets*] révéler ; **to ~ sb away** [+ *person, accomplice*] dénoncer *or* donner* qn ; [*reaction, expression*] trahir qn ; **to ~ o.s. away** se trahir ; **don't ~ anything away** ne dis rien ; **his face gave nothing away** son visage ne trahissait aucune émotion ; **to ~ the game away** * vendre la mèche*

► **give back** VT SEP [+ *object, freedom*] rendre (**to** à) ; [+ *echo*] renvoyer ; [+ *image*] refléter ; **they have been ~n back their property** leurs biens leur ont été restitués *or* rendus

► **give forth** VT SEP [+ *sound*] émettre, faire entendre

► **give in** [1] VI (= *surrender*) capituler ; (= *yield*) céder (**to** à) ; **the troops gave in after three weeks** les troupes ont capitulé au bout de trois semaines ; **I pestered my parents until they gave in** j'ai harcelé mes parents jusqu'à ce qu'ils cèdent *or* capitulent ; **I ~ in!** *(in games)* j'abandonne ! ; *(in guessing)* je donne ma langue au chat ! *

[2] VT SEP [+ *essay, exam paper, key*] rendre ; [+ *manuscript, report*] remettre

► **give off** VT SEP [+ *heat*] dégager, émettre ; [+ *gas, smell, aura*] dégager ; **the carpets and curtains gave off a smell of mould** la moquette et les rideaux dégageaient une odeur de moisi ; **they gave off a sense of assurance** on sentait chez eux une assurance naturelle

► **give on to** VT FUS [*door, window*] donner sur

► **give out** [1] VI [*supplies*] s'épuiser ; [*patience*] être à bout ; [*heart*] lâcher ; **after two weeks their food had ~n out** au bout de deux semaines leurs provisions étaient épuisées ; **one of his lungs gave out entirely** un de ses poumons a lâché ; **all machines ~ out eventually** les machines ne sont pas éternelles ; **my strength is giving out** je suis à bout de forces, je n'en peux plus

[2] VT SEP **a** (= *distribute*) [+ *books, food*] distribuer

b (= *make known*) [+ *information, details*] donner ; **it was ~n out that ...** on a annoncé que ...

c *(Rad)* [+ *signal*] émettre

d (= *utter*) **he gave out a scream of pain** il poussa un cri de douleur → **give 1g**

e = **give off**

► **give over** * VT FUS (= *stop*) [+ *studies, activities*] arrêter ; **to ~ over doing sth** cesser de faire qch, arrêter de faire qch ; **~ over!** arrête !, ça suffit !

► **give over to** VT SEP (= *dedicate, devote*) consacrer ; **most of the garden is ~n over to vegetables** la majeure partie du jardin est consacrée au potager ; **many cinemas are ~n over to bingo** de nombreux cinémas ont été transformés en salles de bingo ; **to ~ o.s. over to** [+ *activity, drink*] s'adonner à ; [+ *children, family*] se consacrer à

► **give up** [1] VI abandonner, laisser tomber* ; **they were on the point of giving up when ...** ils étaient sur le point d'abandonner *or* de laisser tomber* lorsque ... ; **I ~ up** j'abandonne, je capitule ; *(in guessing)* je

donne ma langue au chat* ; **don't ~ up!** tenez bon !

[2] VT SEP **a** (= *renounce*) [+ *interests*] abandonner ; [+ *seat, territory*] céder ; [+ *habit, idea, hope, claim*] renoncer à ; [+ *job*] quitter ; [+ *business*] se retirer de ; [+ *subscription*] résilier ; **when she went to university she gave up her old friends** quand elle est entrée à l'université elle a cessé de voir ses vieux amis ; **to ~ up the struggle** abandonner la partie ; **I gave it up as a bad job** (comme ça ne menait à rien) j'ai laissé tomber* ; **she gave him up as a bad job** * comme elle n'arrivait à rien avec lui elle l'a laissé tomber*

b (= *stop*) arrêter, cesser ; **to ~ up smoking** arrêter de fumer, renoncer au tabac ; **I've ~n up trying to persuade her** j'ai renoncé à essayer de la convaincre ; **eventually he gave up trying** au bout d'un moment il a renoncé

c (= *deliver, hand over*) **to ~ o.s. up** se rendre, se constituer prisonnier ; **she gave the baby up for adoption** elle a fait adopter le bébé

d (= *abandon hope for*) [+ *expected visitor*] ne plus attendre ; **the doctors had ~n him up** les médecins le croyaient condamné ; **to ~ sb up for lost** considérer qn comme perdu ; **to ~ sb up for dead** croire qn mort

► **give up on** VT FUS **a** (= *renounce*) [+ *idea*] renoncer à ; **I finally gave up on it** j'ai fini par y renoncer ; **the car/washing machine has ~n up on me** la voiture/la machine à laver m'a lâché*

b (= *stop expecting*) [+ *visitor*] ne plus attendre ; (= *lose faith in*) perdre espoir en

giveaway ['gɪvəweɪ] [1] N *(fig)* révélation *f* involontaire ; *(Comm* = *free gift*) cadeau *m* (publicitaire) ; *(US Rad, TV)* jeu *m* radiophonique *or* télévisé (doté de prix) [2] ADJ [*price*] dérisoire ; **it was a real ~ when he said that ...** il s'est vraiment trahi en disant que ... ; **the fact that she knew his name was a ~** le simple fait qu'elle sache son nom était révélateur ; **what a ~!** là tu t'es trahi (*or* il s'est trahi ! *etc*)

▼ **given** ['gɪvn] [1] VB *ptp of* **give** [2] ADJ **a** donné, déterminé ; **at a ~ time** à un moment donné ; **of a ~ size** d'une taille donnée *or* bien déterminée ; **under the ~ conditions** compte tenu des conditions ; **~ name** prénom *m*, nom *m* de baptême **b** **the triangle ABC** soit *or* étant donné le triangle ABC ; **~ that he is capable of learning** à supposer qu'il soit capable d'apprendre **c** (= *having inclination*) **I am not ~ to lying** je n'ai pas l'habitude de mentir ; **he's ~ to laziness** il est enclin à la paresse [3] PREP (= *the opportunity*) si l'occasion se présentait ; **~ patience** avec de la patience

giver ['gɪvə'] N donateur *m*, -trice *f* ; *(St Ex)* preneur *m*, -euse *f* d'option, optionnaire *mf*

giving ['gɪvɪŋ] ADJ généreux

gizmo * ['gɪzməʊ] N machin* *m*, truc* *m*

gizzard ['gɪzəd] N gésier *m* → **stick**

glacé ['glæseɪ] ADJ *(Culin)* [*fruit*] glacé, confit ; **~ icing** glaçage *m*

glacial ['gleɪsɪəl] ADJ **a** *(Geol)* glaciaire ; [*wind, winter*] glacial ; *(Chem)* cristallisé, en cristaux ; **at a ~ pace** ◊ **with ~ slowness** incroyablement lentement **b** [*person, stare, atmosphere*] glacial

glaciated ['gleɪsɪeɪtɪd] ADJ *(Geol)* **~ landscape** relief *m* glaciaire

glaciation [,gleɪsɪ'eɪʃən] N glaciation *f*

glacier ['glæsɪə'] N glacier *m*

glaciological [,glæsɪə'lɒdʒɪkəl] ADJ glaciologique

glaciologist [,glæsɪ'ɒlədʒɪst] N glaciologue *mf*

glaciology [,glæsɪ'ɒlədʒɪ] N glaciologie *f*

glad [glæd] [1] ADJ **a** (= *pleased*) **to be ~ (about sth)** être bien content (de qch) ; **I had a great time — I'm ~** j'en suis beaucoup amusé — j'en suis ravi *or* bien content ; **he was ~ of a chance to change the subject** il était

> **LANGUAGE IN USE**: **given** 17.1

content de pouvoir changer de sujet ; **I'd be ~ of some help with this** j'aimerais bien qu'on m'aide (à faire ça) ; **I'm ~ that you came** je suis bien content que vous soyez venu ; **I'm ~ that I've come** je suis bien content d'être venu ; **to be ~ to do sth** (= happy) être bien content de faire qch ; (= willing) se faire un plaisir de faire qch ; **I shall be ~ to come** ça me fera plaisir de venir ; **~ to know you!** très heureux de faire votre connaissance ; **to be only too ~ to do sth** ne pas demander mieux que de faire qch [b] (†, liter = happy) [news] heureux ; [occasion] joyeux ; **to give sb the ~ tidings** annoncer à qn la bonne nouvelle [2] COMP ▶ **glad eye**† N (Brit) **to give sb the ~ eye*** faire de l'œil* à qn ▶ **glad hand*** N (esp US) **to give sb the ~ hand** accueillir à bras ouverts ▶ **glad-hand*** VT (US) accueillir avec effusion ▶ **glad rags*** NPL belles fringues* fpl ; **to put on one's ~ rags** mettre ses plus belles fringues

gladden ['glædn] VT [+ person] réjouir ; **to ~ sb's heart** réjouir qn ; **it ~s the heart** ça fait chaud au cœur ; **to be ~ed to see** etc être heureux de voir etc

glade [gleid] N clairière f

gladiator ['glædieitə'] N gladiateur m

gladiatorial [,glædiə'tɔːriəl] ADJ (fig) conflictuel ; **~ politics** politique f de la confrontation

gladiolus [,glædi'əʊləs] N (pl **gladiolus** or **gladioluses** or **gladioli** [,glædi'əʊlai]) glaïeul m

▼ **gladly** ['glædli] ADV (= happily) avec plaisir ; (= willingly) volontiers ; **will you help me? —** voulez-vous m'aider ? — volontiers or avec plaisir

gladness ['glædnis] N joie f, contentement m

glam* [glæm] [1] ADJ ABBR = **glamorous** [2] COMP ▶ **glam rock*** N (Mus) glam-rock m (mouvement musical des années 70)

glamor ['glæmə'] (US) = **glamour**

glamorize ['glæməraiz] VT [+ place, event, act etc] montrer or présenter sous des couleurs séduisantes

glamorous ['glæmərəs] ADJ [person, clothes, photo, atmosphere] glamour inv ; [life(style)] de star ; [restaurant, café] chic ; [occasion] éclatant ; [production] somptueux ; [job] prestigieux

glamour ['glæmə'] [1] N [of person] glamour m ; [of occasion] éclat m ; [of situation etc] prestige m ; [of distant countries, journeys] séduction f ; **the ~ of show biz** le côté glamour du monde du showbiz ; **the ~ of life in Hollywood** le côté glamour de la vie d'Hollywood ; **the ~ of being on television** le prestige que confère un passage à la télévision [2] COMP ▶ **glamour boy*** N beau mec* m ▶ **glamour girl*** N pin-up* f inv, beauté f ▶ **glamour model** N pin-up f inv

glamourpuss* ['glæməpʊs] N (female) pin-up f inv ; (male) beau mec* m

glance [glɑːns] [1] N [a] regard m, coup m d'œil ; **Susan and I exchanged a ~** Susan et moi avons échangé un regard ; **at a ~** d'un coup d'œil ; **at first ~** au premier coup d'œil, à première vue ; **without a backward ~** (lit) sans se retourner ; (fig) sans plus de cérémonie ; **to have** or **take a ~ at** jeter un coup d'œil sur or à ; **to steal a ~ at sb/sth** jeter un coup d'œil furtif sur or à qn/qch [b] (= gleam) [of light] lueur f ; [of metal] reflet m ; **a ~ of sunlight** un rayon de soleil [2] VI [a] (= look) jeter un coup d'œil (**at** sur, à), lancer un regard (**at** à) ; **she ~d in my direction** elle a jeté un coup d'œil vers moi ; **he picked up the book and ~d through it** il a pris le livre et l'a feuilleté [b] (= glint) étinceler [c] **to ~ off** [bullet] ricocher sur ; [arrow, sword] dévier sur

▶ **glance away** VI détourner le regard

▶ **glance down** VI jeter un coup d'œil en bas, regarder en bas

▶ **glance off** VI [bullet etc] ricocher, dévier

[arrow, sword] dévier

▶ **glance round** VI (= behind) regarder en arrière ; (= round about) jeter un coup d'œil autour de soi

▶ **glance up** VI (= raise eyes) lever les yeux ; (= look upwards) regarder en l'air

glancing ['glɑːnsiŋ] ADJ [blow] oblique

gland [glænd] N glande f ; (Tech) presse-étoupe m inv

glanders ['glændəz] N (Vet) morve f

glandes ['glændiːz] NPL of **glans**

glandular ['glændjʊlə'] [1] ADJ glandulaire [2] COMP ▶ **glandular fever** N mononucléose f infectieuse

glans [glænz] N (pl **glandes**) **~ (penis)** gland m

glare [glɛə'] [1] VI [a] [person] lancer un regard furieux (**at** à) [b] [sun, lights] être éblouissant, briller avec éclat [2] VT **to ~ daggers at sb** foudroyer qn du regard [3] N [a] [of person] regard m furieux ; **"no" he said with a ~** «non », dit-il en lançant un regard furieux ; **he gave me an angry ~** il m'a lancé un regard furieux [b] [of light] éclat m aveuglant, lumière f éblouissante ; (Aut) éblouissement m ; **the ~ of publicity** le feu des projecteurs (fig)

glaring ['glɛəriŋ] ADJ (= angry) [eyes, look] brillant de colère ; (= blinding) [light, sun] éblouissant ; (pej = blatant) [example, error, contradiction] flagrant ; [omission] manifeste ; **the ~ weakness of that argument** la faiblesse manifeste de cet argument

glaringly ['glɛəriŋli] ADV (pej) **it is ~ obvious (that ...)** c'est une évidence aveuglante (que ...) ; **a ~ obvious error** une erreur d'une évidence aveuglante

glasnost ['glæznɒst] N glasnost f

glass [glɑːs] [1] N [a] (NonC) verre m ; **pane of ~** carreau m, vitre f ; **window ~** vitre f ; **I cut myself on the broken ~** je me suis coupé avec l'éclat de verre ; **there was some broken ~ in the dustbin** il y avait du verre cassé dans la poubelle → **glassed** ; → **cut, plate** [b] (= tumbler) verre m ; (= glassful) (plein) verre m ; **a ~ of wine** un verre de vin ; **a wine ~** un verre à vin ; **she cut her hand on a broken ~** elle s'est coupé la main avec un verre cassé → **balloon, beer, champagne** [c] (NonC: also **~ware**) (gen) verrerie f, objets mpl de or en verre ; (= glasses) gobeleterie f [d] (= mirror) miroir m, glace f ; (Opt) lentille f ; (also **magnifying ~**) verre m grossissant, loupe f ; (= telescope) longue-vue f ; (= barometer) baromètre m ; (Comm etc) vitrine f ; (Met) **the ~ is falling** le baromètre baisse ; (Hort) **under ~** sous châssis ; **object displayed under ~** objet m exposé en vitrine [2] VT (Brit*) frapper avec une bouteille (or un verre) [3] COMP [bottle, ornament] de verre, en verre ▶ **glass case** N (Comm) vitrine f ; [of clock etc] globe m ; **to keep sth in a ~ case** garder qch sous verre or sous globe ▶ **glass ceiling*** N niveau professionnel où les femmes ont tendance à plafonner ▶ **glass door** N porte f vitrée ▶ **glass eye** N œil m de verre ▶ **glass factory** N = **glassworks** ▶ **glass fibre** N fibre f de verre ♦ COMP en fibre de verre ▶ **glass industry** N industrie f du verre, verrerie f ▶ **glass slipper** N pantoufle f de verre ▶ **glass wool** N laine f de verre

glassblower ['glɑːsbləʊə'] N souffleur m (de verre)

glassblowing ['glɑːsbləʊiŋ] N soufflage m (du verre)

glasscloth ['glɑːsklɒθ] N essuie-verres m inv, torchon m à verres

glasscutter ['glɑːskʌtə'] N (= tool) diamant m, coupe-verre m inv ; (= person) vitrier m

glassed [glɑːst], **glassed-in** ['glɑːstin] ADJ [cubicle] vitré ; **~-in shower** cabine f de douche (à parois de verre) ; **~-in porch** véranda f

glasses ['glɑːsiz] NPL (= spectacles) lunettes fpl ; (= binoculars) jumelles fpl → **sunglasses**

glassful ['glɑːsfʊl] N (plein) verre m

glasshouse ['glɑːshaʊs] N (Brit: for plants) serre f ; (US = glassworks) verrerie f (fabrique) ; (Brit Mil) **in the ~:** au trou* ■ (PROV) **people who live in glass houses shouldn't throw stones** avant de critiquer, tu ferais bien de balayer devant ta porte

glasspaper ['glɑːspeipə'] N (Brit) papier m de verre

glassware ['glɑːswɛə'] N verrerie f, objets mpl de or en verre

glassworks ['glɑːswɜːks] N (pl inv) verrerie f (fabrique)

glassy ['glɑːsi] [1] ADJ [substance] vitreux ; [surface] uni, lisse ; [water, sea] transparent, lisse comme un miroir ; **~ eyes** or **look** regard m perdu or vague ; (from drink, drugs) regard m vitreux or terne ; (from displeasure) regard m froid [2] COMP ▶ **glassy-eyed** ADJ au regard vide ; (from drugs, drink) au regard terne or vitreux ; (from displeasure) au regard froid

Glaswegian [glæs'wiːdʒən] [1] N **he's a ~** il est de Glasgow [2] ADJ de Glasgow

glaucoma [glɔː'kəʊmə] N glaucome m

glaucous ['glɔːkəs] ADJ glauque

glaze [gleiz] [1] VT [a] [+ door, window] vitrer ; [+ picture] mettre sous verre → **double** [b] [+ pottery, tiles] vernisser ; [+ leather] vernir ; [+ cotton etc] satiner, lustrer ; [+ paper, photograph, cake, meat] glacer [2] N [a] (NonC) (on pottery, leather, tiles etc) vernis m ; (on cotton etc) lustre m ; (on paper, photograph) glacé m ; (Culin) glaçage m [b] (= substance) (for tiles etc) glaçure f ; (for pottery) vernis m [c] (US = ice) verglas m

▶ **glaze over** VI [person] prendre un air absent ; **his eyes ~d over** (boredom) il prit un air absent ; (dying) ses yeux sont devenus vitreux

glazed [gleizd] ADJ [door, window etc] vitré ; [picture] sous verre [pottery, tiles] vernissé ; [leather] glacé, verni ; [material] lustré, satiné ; [paper, photograph] brillant ; [cake, meat] glacé ; (US‡ = drunk) bourré‡, ivre ; **his eyes** or **he had a ~ look** il avait les yeux ternes or vitreux

glazier ['gleiziə'] N vitrier m

glazing ['gleiziŋ] N [a] (= act) [of windows] vitrage m, pose f de vitres ; [of pottery] vernissage m [b] (= glass) vitrage m, vitres fpl → **double, triple**

GLC [,dʒiːel'siː] N (Brit: formerly) (ABBR = **Greater London Council**) ancienne administration centrale à Londres

gleam [gliːm] [1] N lueur f, rayon m (de lumière) ; [of metal] reflet m ; [of water] miroitement m ; **a ~ of hope/interest** une lueur d'espoir / d'intérêt ; **with a fanatical ~ in his eye** avec une lueur fanatique dans le regard ; **there was a ~ in her eye when she looked at me** il y avait une lueur dans ses yeux quand elle m'a regardé ; **the product is still only a ~ in an engineer's eye** ce produit n'est encore qu'une idée en germe dans la tête d'un ingénieur ; (hum) **almost 20 years before you were even a ~ in your father's eye** près de 20 ans avant que ton père n'ait même imaginé de te concevoir

[2] VI [lamp, star, eyes etc] luire ; [polished metal, shoes etc] reluire ; [knife, blade etc] luire, briller ; [water] miroiter ; **his eyes ~ed with mischief** ses yeux luisaient or brillaient de malice ; **his eyes ~ed almost wickedly** il y avait une sorte de lueur mauvaise dans les yeux ; **his hair ~ed in the sun** ses cheveux brillaient au soleil ; **his forehead ~ed with sweat** son front était luisant de sueur ; **his skin ~ed with health** sa peau resplendissait de santé

gleaming ['gliːmiŋ] ADJ [lamp, star, metal, shoes] brillant ; [kitchen] étincelant

glean [gliːn] VTI (lit, fig) glaner

gleaner ['gli:nə'] N glaneur *m*, -euse *f*

gleanings ['gli:nɪŋz] NPL glanure(s) *f(pl)*

glebe [gli:b] N (*Rel*) terre *f* attachée à un bénéfice ecclésiastique; (*liter*) terre *f*, glèbe *f* (*liter*)

glee [gli:] N ⓐ (*NonC*) joie *f*, jubilation *f*; **his victory was greeted with ~** sa victoire a été accueillie dans l'allégresse; **in great ~** jubilant; **they were rubbing their hands in ~** ils se frottaient les mains en jubilant ⓑ (*Mus*) chant *m* choral à plusieurs voix; **~ club** chorale *f*

gleeful ['gli:fʊl] ADJ jubilant; [*smile, look*] de jubilation

gleefully ['gli:fəlɪ] ADV [*say, point out*] en jubilant; **to laugh ~** rire avec jubilation

glen [glen] N vallée *f*, vallon *m*

glib [glɪb] ADJ (*pej*) [*answer, style, excuse*] désinvolte; [*speech, phrase, lie*] facile, désinvolte; [*person*] qui a la langue bien pendue or la parole facile; **~ talk** propos *mpl* or paroles *fpl* en l'air; **to make ~ promises** faire des promesses en l'air

glibly ['glɪblɪ] ADV (*pej*) avec désinvolture

glibness ['glɪbnɪs] N [*of answer, speech, style*] désinvolture *f*; [*of person*] facilité *f* de parole

glide [glaɪd] ① VI ⓐ **to ~ in/out** *etc* [*person*] (*silently*) entrer/sortir *etc* sans bruit; (*in stately way, gracefully*) entrer/sortir *etc* avec grâce; [*ghost*] entrer/sortir *etc* en flottant; [*car, ship*] entrer/sortir *etc* en glissant; (*fig*) **time ~d past** le temps s'écoula ⓑ (*Ski*) glisser ⓒ [*birds*] planer; (*Aviat*) planer, faire du vol plané; (*Aviat*) **he ~d down to land** il a atterri en vol plané ② VT faire glisser, faire avancer en douceur ③ N ⓐ glissement *m*; (*Dancing*) glissé *m*, glissade *f*; (*Ski*) glisse *f* ⓑ (*Mus*) port *m* de voix; (*Phon*) glissement *m* ⓒ (*Aviat*) vol *m* plané

glider ['glaɪdə'] N ⓐ (*Aviat*) planeur *m*; **~ pilot** pilote *m* de planeur ⓑ (*US = swing*) balancelle *f*

gliding ['glaɪdɪŋ] ① N (*Sport*) vol *m* à voile; (*Aviat*) vol *m* plané; (*gen = movement*) glissement *m* ② ADJ (*Anat*) **~ joint** arthrodie *f*

glimmer ['glɪmə'] ① VI [*lamp, light, fire*] luire; [*water*] miroiter ② N [*of light, candle etc*] lueur *f*; [*of water*] miroitement *m*; **a ~ of hope** une lueur d'espoir; **not a ~ of intelligence** pas la moindre lueur d'intelligence

glimmering ['glɪmərɪŋ] ① N = **glimmer 2** ② ADJ étincelant, scintillant

glimpse [glɪmps] ① N [*of the truth, the future, sb's meaning*] aperçu *m*; **a ~ into the future** un aperçu de l'avenir; **to catch a ~ of** (*person, thing*) entrevoir or apercevoir (un bref instant); (*the truth, the future etc*) entrevoir, pressentir ② VT entrevoir or apercevoir (un bref instant)

glint [glɪnt] ① N [*of light*] trait *m* de lumière, éclair *m*; [*of metal*] reflet *m*; **he had a ~ in his eye** il avait une étincelle or une lueur dans le regard; **with the ~ of triumph in his eye** avec une étincelle or une lueur de triomphe dans les yeux ② VI [*metal object, glass, wet road*] luire, briller; [*eyes*] briller; **the sea ~ed in the sun** la mer miroitait au soleil; **sunlight ~ed on his spectacles** ses lunettes renvoyaient la lumière éblouissante du soleil

glissade [glɪ'seɪd] (*Climbing*) ① N (*also* **standing ~**) ramasse *f* ② VI descendre en ramasse

glissando [glɪ'sændəʊ] ADV glissando

glisten ['glɪsn] ① VI [*water*] miroiter, scintiller; [*wet surface*] luire; [*light*] scintiller; [*metal object*] briller, miroiter; **her eyes ~ed (with tears)** ses yeux brillaient (de larmes); **his face was ~ing with sweat** son visage était luisant de sueur ② N miroitement *m*, scintillement *m*

glister†† ['glɪstə'] = **glitter**

glitch* [glɪtʃ] N pépin *m*

glitter ['glɪtə'] ① VI [*snow, ice, lights*] scintiller, briller; [*jewel*] chatoyer, rutiler, scintiller; [*water*] miroiter, scintiller; **her eyes ~ed (with hatred)** ses yeux brillaient de haine; (*with greed*) ses yeux brillaient de convoitise ■ (*PROV*) **all that ~s is not gold** tout ce qui brille n'est pas or (*PROV*) ② N scintillement *m*; (*fig*) éclat *m*

glitterati* [,glɪtə'rɑ:tɪ] NPL **the ~** le beau monde, les célébrités *fpl*

glittering ['glɪtərɪŋ] ADJ [*stars, lights, ice*] étincelant, scintillant; [*jewel*] étincelant; [*eyes*] brillant, étincelant; (*fig*) [*career, future*] brillant; [*occasion, social event*] somptueux; **~ prizes** prix *mpl* fabuleux; **a ~ array of celebrities** une brillante assemblée de célébrités

glittery ['glɪtərɪ] ADJ (*lit, fig*) étincelant

glitz* [glɪts] N faste *m*

glitzy* ['glɪtsɪ] ADJ fastueux

gloaming ['gləʊmɪŋ] N (*liter*) crépuscule *m*; **in the ~** au crépuscule, entre chien et loup

gloat [gləʊt] VI (*pej*) exulter, jubiler*; **to ~ over** (*money, possessions*) jubiler* à la vue (or à l'idée) de; **he was ~ing over or about his success** son succès le faisait jubiler*; **that's nothing to ~ over or about!** il n'y a pas de quoi jubiler!*; **he was ~ing that he was going to win** il affirmait en jubilant* qu'il allait gagner

gloating ['gləʊtɪŋ] (*pej*) ① N exultation *f* or jubilation *f* malveillante ② ADJ jubilatoire

glob [glɒb] N [*of liquid*] globule *m*; [*of clay etc*] petite boule *f*

global ['gləʊbl] ① ADJ ⓐ (*= worldwide*) [*economy, trade, market, recession, climate, system, problem, issue*] mondial; [*peace*] universel, mondial; **a ~ ban on nuclear testing** une interdiction totale des essais nucléaires; **on a ~ scale** à l'échelle mondiale ⓑ (*= comprehensive*) [*sum, view*] global, entier; (*Comput*) **~ search and replace** recherche *f* et remplacement *m* automatiques ② COMP ► **the global village** N le village planétaire ► **global warming** N réchauffement *m* de la planète

globalization [,gləʊbəlaɪ'zeɪʃən] N mondialisation *f*

globalize ['gləʊbəlaɪz] ① VI [*company*] passer à l'échelle mondiale ② VT [+ *market, business*] mondialiser

globally ['gləʊbəlɪ] ADV ⓐ (*= worldwide, in world terms*) [*sell, compete, think*] à l'échelle mondiale; **a ~ familiar trade name** une marque mondialement connue or connue dans le monde entier; **~, the risks are huge** à l'échelle planétaire, les risques sont énormes ⓑ (*= universally*) universellement

globe [gləʊb] ① N ⓐ (*= sphere*) globe *m*, sphère *f*; (*with map on it*) globe *m*; (*= lampshade etc*) globe *m*; (*= fishbowl*) bocal *m*; (*Anat*) globe *m*; (*Geog*) **the ~** le globe, la terre; **all over the ~** sur toute la surface du globe; **countries on the far side of the ~** les pays à l'autre bout du monde ② COMP ► **globe artichoke** N artichaut *m* ► **globe lightning** N éclair *m* en boule ► **globe-trotter** N globe-trotter *mf* ► **globe-trotting** N voyages *mpl* à travers le monde

globefish ['gləʊbfɪʃ] N (*pl* **globefish** or **globefishes**) poisson-globe *m*

globular ['glɒbjʊlə'] ADJ globulaire; (*= like globe*) en forme de globe

globule ['glɒbjuːl] N gouttelette *f*

glockenspiel ['glɒkən,spiːl] N glockenspiel *m*

gloom [gluːm] N (*= darkness*) obscurité *f*, ténèbres *fpl*; (*= melancholy*) mélancolie *f*, tristesse *f*; **to cast a ~ over sth** assombrir qch; **to cast a ~ over sb** rendre qn sombre, attrister qn; **a ~ descended on us** la tristesse s'est abattue sur nous; **it was all ~ and doom*** tout allait mal; **economic ~** morosité *f* économique

gloomily ['gluːmɪlɪ] ADV [*say*] d'un air sombre

gloomy ['gluːmɪ] ADJ [*person, thoughts, sky, look, mood*] sombre; (*stronger*) lugubre; [*weather, day, outlook*] morose, déprimant; [*voice, place*] morne; (*stronger*) lugubre; **to feel ~** se sentir morose; **to look ~** [*person*] avoir l'air sombre or morose; [*future*] être sombre; **he took a ~ view of everything** il voyait tout en noir

glorification [,glɔːrɪfɪ'keɪʃən] N glorification *f*

glorified ['glɔːrɪfaɪd] ADJ **the drug is nothing but a ~ painkiller** ce médicament n'est rien de plus qu'un vulgaire calmant; **the referendum was no more than a ~ opinion poll** le référendum n'était qu'un vulgaire sondage; **the "luxury hotel" was nothing but a ~ boarding house** le soi-disant «hôtel de luxe» n'était qu'une pension de famille; **he's a sort of ~ secretary** il ne fait que du secrétariat amélioré

glorify ['glɔːrɪfaɪ] VT [+ *God*] glorifier, rendre gloire à; [+ *person*] glorifier, célébrer; (*fig*) [+ *event, place etc*] glorifier, embellir; [+ *war, violence, rape, death*] glorifier; **songs ~ing war** des chansons glorifiant la guerre

gloriole ['glɔːrɪəʊl] N nimbe *m*

glorious ['glɔːrɪəs] ① ADJ ⓐ (* = *beautiful*) [*view, scenery*] splendide, magnifique; [*sunshine, weather, day*] radieux, magnifique; (*iro*) **a ~ mess** un joli or beau gâchis ⓑ (* = *enjoyable*) [*feeling, holiday*] merveilleux ⓒ (* = *illustrious*) [*career, future*] brillant; [*years, days, era*] glorieux; [*victory*] éclatant; **~ deed** action *f* d'éclat ② COMP ► **the Glorious Revolution** N (*Brit Hist*) la Glorieuse Révolution, la Seconde Révolution d'Angleterre (*1688-89*)

gloriously ['glɔːrɪəslɪ] ADV ⓐ (* = *wonderfully*) [*happy*] merveilleusement; **a ~ sunny day** une journée radieuse; **~ hot weather** un temps chaud et radieux ⓑ (* = *triumphantly*) [*succeed, win*] glorieusement; **~ successful** glorieusement réussi

glory ['glɔːrɪ] ① N ⓐ (*NonC*) gloire *f* (*also Rel*); (* = *magnificence*) splendeur *f*, magnificence *f*; **to give ~ to God** rendre gloire à Dieu; **to the greater ~ of God** pour la plus grande gloire de Dieu; **Christ in ~** le Christ en majesté or en gloire; **the saints in ~** les glorieux *mpl*; **Solomon in all his ~** Salomon dans toute sa gloire; **covered with ~** couvert de gloire; **Rome at the height of its ~** Rome à l'apogée or au sommet de sa gloire; **there she was in all her ~*, dressed in gold from head to foot** elle était là dans toute sa splendeur, vêtue d'or de la tête aux pieds; **she was in her ~* as president of the club** elle était tout à fait à son affaire en tant que présidente du club; **she led her team to Olympic ~** elle a mené son équipe à la gloire lors des Jeux olympiques; **a moment of ~** un moment de gloire; **to have one's moment of ~** avoir son heure de gloire; **to go to ~†*** (* = *die*) aller ad patres*; **~ be!*** Seigneur!, grand Dieu!; (*US*) **Old Glory*** le drapeau américain → **former** ⓑ (*gen pl*) **the glories of the past** ◊ **past glories** la gloire passée; **the church was the village's greatest ~** l'église était le principal titre de gloire du village; **the artistic glories of the Italian Renaissance** les chefs-d'œuvre or les joyaux artistiques de la renaissance italienne; **this sonnet is one of the glories of English poetry** ce sonnet est un des chefs-d'œuvre or fleurons de la poésie anglaise → **crowning** ② VI **to ~ in sth** (* = *be proud of*) être très fier de qch; (* = *revel in*) se glorifier de qch; (* = *enjoy*) savourer qch; **he gloried in his reputation as a troublemaker** il se glorifiait de sa réputation de fauteur de troubles; (*iro*) **the café glories in the name of "The Savoy"** le café porte le nom ronflant de «Savoy» ③ COMP ► **glory hole*** N capharnaüm* *m*; (*Naut*) cambuse *f*

Glos ABBR = **Gloucestershire**

gloss¹ [glɒs] ① N ⓐ (* = *shine*) [*of metal, ceramic, paintwork, polished surface*] lustre *m*; [*of silk,*

satin] lustre m, éclat m; [of person's hair, animal's coat] brillant m; **to take the ~ off** (metal etc) dépolir; (fig) (event, success) retirer or enlever tout son charme or attrait à; (victory, compliment) gâcher; **to lose its ~** [metal etc] se dépolir; (fig) [event, success] perdre tout son charme or son attrait; (fig) **to put a ~** or **an optimistic ~ on sth** présenter qch sous un jour favorable, enjoliver qch [b] (= paint) peinture f brillante or laquée [2] VT [+ metal etc] faire briller, polir [3] COMP [paint] brillant, laqué; [paper] glacé, brillant ► **gloss finish** N brillant m
► **gloss over** VT FUS (= play down) glisser sur, passer sur; (= cover up) dissimuler

gloss² [glɒs] [1] N (= insertion) glose f; (= note) commentaire m; (= interpretation) paraphrase f, interprétation f [2] VT commenter, gloser

glossary ['glɒsərɪ] N glossaire m, lexique m

glossematics [ˌglɒsə'mætɪks] N (NonC) glossématique f

glossily ['glɒsɪlɪ] ADV ~ **packaged** luxueusement conditionné; **a ~ presented** or **produced brochure** une brochure luxueusement présentée

glossolalia [ˌglɒsə'leɪlɪə] N glossolalie f

glossy ['glɒsɪ] [1] ADJ [fur, material] luisant, lustré; [photograph] sur papier brillant; [paint] brillant, laqué; [hair] brillant; [leaves] vernissé; [metal] brillant, poli; [red, black etc] brillant; **~ magazine/brochure** magazine m/ brochure f de luxe (sur papier couché); **~ paper** (Typ) papier m couché, (esp Phot) papier m brillant or glacé; (film) **~ production** superproduction f (luxueuse) [2] N (Brit) **the glossies*** les magazines mpl de luxe

glottal ['glɒtl] [1] ADJ (Anat) glottique; (Ling) glottal [2] COMP ► **glottal stop** N (Ling) coup m de glotte

glottis ['glɒtɪs] N (pl **glottises** or **glottides** ['glɒtɪˌdiːz]) glotte f

Gloucs ABBR = **Gloucestershire**

glove [glʌv] [1] N (gen, also Baseball, Boxing) gant m; (fig) **the ~s are off!** j'y vais (or il y va etc) sans prendre de gants! → **fit, hand, kid, rubber** [2] VT ganter; **his ~d hand** sa main gantée; **white~d** ganté de blanc [3] COMP ► **glove box, glove compartment** N (Aut) boîte f à gants, vide-poches m ► **glove factory** N ganterie f (fabrique) ► **glove maker** N gantier m, -ière f ► **glove puppet** N marionnette f (à gaine) ► **glove shop** N ganterie f (magasin)

glover ['glʌvə'] N gantier m, -ière f

glow [gləʊ] [1] VI [coal, fire] rougeoyer; [sky] rougeoyer, s'embraser; [metal] luire; [cigarette end, lamp] luire; [colour, jewel] rutiler; [complexion, face] rayonner; [eyes] rayonner, flamboyer; **her cheeks ~ed** elle avait les joues toutes rouges; **to ~ red** rougeoyer; **the autumn leaves ~ed red and yellow in the sunlight** le feuillage rouge et jaune de l'automne resplendissait sous la lumière du soleil; **streetlamps ~ing orange in the dusk** les réverbères répandant leur lumière orange au crépuscule; **he was ~ing with health** il était florissant (de santé); **to ~ with enthusiasm** brûler d'enthousiasme; **she ~ed with pride** elle rayonnait de fierté; **his face ~ed with pleasure** son visage rayonnait de plaisir; **~ing with confidence** respirant la confiance [2] N [of coal, fire, metal] rougeoiement m; [of sun] feux mpl, embrasement m; [of complexion, skin] éclat m; [of colour, jewel] éclat m; [of lamp] lueur f; [of passion] feu m; [of youth] ardeur f; **a ~ of enthusiasm** un élan d'enthousiasme [3] COMP ► **glow-worm** N ver m luisant

glower ['glaʊə'] [1] VI lancer des regards mauvais or noirs; **to ~ at sb/sth** lancer à qn/qch des regards mauvais or noirs, regarder qn/qch de travers [2] N regard m noir

glowering ['glaʊərɪŋ] ADJ [look] mauvais, noir

glowing ['gləʊɪŋ] ADJ [coals, fire] rougeoyant; [sky] rougeoyant, embrasé; [colour, jewel] rutilant; [lamp, cigarette end] luisant; [eyes] brillant, flamboyant, de braise; [complexion, skin] rayonnant, éclatant; [person] florissant (de santé); [words, report, tribute, review, praise] élogieux; **to give a ~ account/description of sth** raconter/décrire qch en termes élogieux; **to speak of sb/sth in ~ terms** parler de qn/qch en termes élogieux; (fig) **to paint sth in ~ colours** présenter qch en rose; (from job) **to get ~ references** être chaudement recommandé

gloxinia [glɒk'sɪnɪə] N gloxinia m

glucose ['gluːkəʊs] N glucose m

glue [gluː] [1] N colle f
[2] VT coller (**to, on** à); **she ~d the pieces together** (from broken object) elle a recollé les morceaux; (from kit etc) elle a collé les morceaux ensemble; **I ~d the plate back together** j'ai recollé l'assiette; **to ~ sth back on** recoller qch; **to ~ sth down** coller qch; **the fabric is ~d in place** le tissu est fixé avec de la colle; (fig) **he stood there ~d to the spot*** il était la comme s'il avait pris racine; **his face was ~d to the window** son visage était collé à la vitre; **to keep one's eyes ~d to sb/sth*** avoir les yeux fixés sur qn/qch, ne pas détacher les yeux de qn/qch; (fig) **~d to the television*** cloué devant or rivé à la télévision; **we were ~d to our seats*** nous étions cloués à nos sièges
[3] COMP ► **glue ear** N (Med) otite f séreuse ► **glue-sniffer** N sniffeur* m, -euse* f de colle ► **glue-sniffing** N intoxication f à la colle or aux solvants

gluey ['gluːɪ] ADJ gluant, poisseux

glum [glʌm] ADJ [person, face] sombre; (stronger) lugubre; [appearance] sombre, morne; [thoughts] noir; **to feel ~** avoir des idées noires, avoir le cafard; **a ~ silence** un silence lugubre

glumly ['glʌmlɪ] ADV [say, look at] d'un air sombre or abattu

glut [glʌt] [1] VT (gen) gaver; (Comm) [+ market, economy] saturer (**with** de); **~ted with food** repu, gavé (de nourriture) [2] N [of foodstuffs, goods] surplus m, excès m; **there is a ~ of ...** il y a excès de ...

glutamate ['gluːtəmeɪt] N → **monosodium glutamate**

glutamic [gluː'tæmɪk] ADJ ► **acid** acide m glutamique

gluteal [gluː'tiːəl] ADJ fessier

gluten ['gluːtən] [1] N gluten m [2] COMP ► **gluten-free** ADJ sans gluten

glutenous ['gluːtənəs] ADJ glutineux

gluteus ['gluːtɪəs] [1] N (pl **glutei** ['gluːtɪaɪ]) fessier m [2] COMP ► **gluteus maximus/medius/minimus** N grand/moyen/petit fessier m

glutinous ['gluːtɪnəs] ADJ visqueux, gluant

glutton ['glʌtn] N glouton(ne) m(f), gourmand(e) m(f); (fig) **to be a ~ for work** être un bourreau de travail; **he's a ~ for punishment** il est masochiste

gluttonous ['glʌtənəs] ADJ glouton, goulu

gluttony ['glʌtənɪ] N gloutonnerie f

glycerin(e) [ˌglɪsə'riːn] N glycérine f

glycerol ['glɪsərɒl] N glycérol m

glycin(e) ['glaɪsɪːn] N glycine f

glycogen ['glaɪkəʊdʒen] N glycogène m

glycol ['glaɪkɒl] N glycol m

GM [ˌdʒiː'em] N [a] (ABBR = **General Manager**) DG m [b] (ABBR = **George Medal**) → **George**

gm ABBR = **gram(me)** g inv

GMAT [ˌdʒiːem'eɪtiː] N (US Univ) (ABBR = **Graduate Management Admission Test**) test d'admission pour des études de commerce de troisième cycle

GMT [ˌdʒiːem'tiː] (ABBR = **Greenwich Mean Time**) GMT

GMWU [ˌdʒiːemdʌbliuː'juː] N (Brit) (ABBR = **General and Municipal Workers Union**) syndicat

gnarled [nɑːld] ADJ [tree, roots, hands, fingers] noueux; [old man, old woman] ratatiné

gnash [næʃ] [1] VT **to ~ one's teeth** [person] grincer des dents; [animal] montrer ses dents en grognant [2] VI [person's teeth] grincer; **its teeth were ~ing** [animal's teeth] il (or elle) montrait ses dents en grognant

gnashing ['næʃɪŋ] [1] N **~ of teeth** grincement m de dents [2] ADJ grinçant

gnat [næt] [1] N moucheron m [2] COMP ► **gnat's piss** N pisse f d'âne*

gnaw [nɔː] [1] VI (lit, fig) ronger; **to ~ at** or **on a bone** ronger un os; **the rat had ~ed through the electric cable** le rat avait complètement rongé la câble électrique; **remorse/desire ~ed at him** le remords/le désir le rongeait; **the secret still ~ed at her** le secret la tourmentait toujours [2] VT [+ bone etc] ronger; (fig) **~ed by remorse** rongé par le remords
► **gnaw off** VT SEP ronger complètement

gnawing ['nɔːɪŋ] ADJ [fear, doubt, guilt, hunger, pain] tenaillant; **I had a ~ feeling that something had been forgotten** j'étais tenaillé par le sentiment qu'on avait oublié quelque chose

gneiss [naɪs] N gneiss m

gnocchi ['nɒkɪ] NPL gnocchis mpl

gnome [nəʊm] [1] N gnome m, lutin m [2] COMP ► **the Gnomes of Zurich** NPL (Brit fig = bankers) les gnomes de Zurich

gnomic ['nəʊmɪk] ADJ gnomique

gnostic ['nɒstɪk] ADJ, N gnostique mf

gnosticism ['nɒstɪˌsɪzəm] N gnosticisme m

GNP [ˌdʒiːen'piː] N (Econ) (ABBR = **gross national product**) PNB m

gnu [nuː] N (pl **gnus** or **gnu**) gnou m

GNVQ [ˌdʒiːenviː'kjuː] N (Brit Scol) (ABBR = **General National Vocational Qualification**) diplôme professionnel national

go [gəʊ]

vb: 3rd person sg pres **goes**, pret **went**, ptp **gone**

[1] INTRANSITIVE VERB	[5] ADJECTIVE
[2] MODAL VERB	[6] COMPOUNDS
[3] TRANSITIVE VERB	[7] PHRASAL VERBS
[4] NOUN	

When **go** is part of a set combination, eg **go cheap, go to the bad, go too far, go down the tubes, go smoothly**, look up the other word.

[1] INTRANSITIVE VERB

[a] (= proceed, travel, move) aller; [vehicle] (referring to speed/manner of moving) rouler; **where are you going?** où allez-vous?; **to go to do sth** aller faire qch; **he's gone to see his mother** il est allé or parti voir sa mère; **who goes there?** qui va là?; **I wouldn't go as far as to say that** je n'irais pas jusque là; **she was going too fast** elle roulait or allait trop vite; [BUT] **there he goes!** le voilà!; **we can talk as we go** nous pouvons parler en chemin; **you can go next** vous pouvez passer devant; (in game) **whose turn is it to go?** c'est à qui de jouer?; **add the sugar, stirring as you go** ajoutez le sucre, en remuant au fur et à mesure
♦ **to go + preposition**: **the train goes at 90km/h** le train roule à or fait du 90 km/h; **to go down the hill** descendre la colline; **to go for a walk** (aller) se promener, (aller) faire une promenade; **the train goes from London to Glasgow** le train va de Londres à Glasgow; **where do we go from here?** qu'est-ce qu'on fait maintenant?; **to go on a journey** faire un voyage; (US) **it's going on three** il est bientôt trois heures, il va bientôt être trois heures; **to go to France/to Canada/to Rome** aller en France/au Canada/à Rome; **to go to the swimming pool/cinema/Champs Élysées** aller à la piscine/ au cinéma/aux Champs Élysées; **he went to**

Paris/to his aunt's il est allé *or* il s'est rendu à Paris/chez sa tante; **she went to the headmaster** elle est allée voir *or* trouver le principal; **to go to the doctor** aller chez le *or* voir le médecin; **to go to sb for sth** aller demander qch à qn, aller trouver qn pour qch; **the child went to his mother** l'enfant est allé vers sa mère; **to go up the hill** monter la colline; (*at auction*) **I went up to £1,000** je suis monté jusqu'à 1 000 livres → **7**

♦ **to go** + *-ing*: **to go fishing/shooting** aller à la pêche/à la chasse; **to go riding** (aller) faire du cheval; **to go swimming** (aller) nager; **don't go looking for trouble!** ne va pas t'attirer des ennuis!; **don't go getting upset*** ne te mets pas dans ces états

♦ **go and ...**: **I'll go and check the train times** je vais vérifier les horaires de trains; **go and get me it!** va me le chercher!; **don't go and tell her I gave it you*** ne va pas lui dire *or* raconter que je te l'ai donné

> go and *is often not translated.*
> **go and shut the door!** ferme *or* va fermer la porte!; **don't go and do that!*** ne fais pas ça!

> *Note how indignation, regret etc are expressed in the following:*
> **now you've gone and broken the zip!** ça y est*, tu as cassé la fermeture éclair!; **I wish I hadn't gone and spent all that money!*** si seulement je n'avais pas dépensé tout cet argent!; **what have you gone and done to him?*** qu'est-ce qu'ils ont bien pu lui faire?

b **= depart** partir, s'en aller; (= *disappear*) disparaître; [*time*] passer, s'écouler; (= *be sacked*) être licencié; (= *be abolished*) être aboli *or* supprimé; (= *be finished*) [*money*] filer; **when does the train go?** quand part le train?; **everybody had gone** tout le monde était parti; **my bag has gone** mon sac a disparu; **we must go** nous devons partir, il faut qu'on y aille; (*Sport*) **go!** partez!; **50 workers are to go at ...** 50 ouvriers doivent être licenciés à ...; *BUT* **after I go** *or* **have gone** après mon départ; **after a week all our money had gone** en l'espace d'une semaine, nous avions dépensé tout notre argent; **he'll have to go** [*employee*] on ne peut pas le garder; [*official, minister*] il doit démissionner; **the car will have to go** on va devoir se séparer de la voiture; **there goes my chance of promotion!** je peux faire une croix sur ma promotion!; (*at auction*) **going, going, gone!** une fois, deux fois, trois fois, adjugé, vendu!

♦ **to let sb go** (= *allow to leave*) laisser partir qn; (*euph* = *make redundant*) se séparer de qn; (= *stop gripping*) lâcher qn

♦ **to let go** *or* **leave go** lâcher prise; **let go!** ◊ **leave go!** lâchez!

♦ **to let go** *or* **leave go of sth/sb** lâcher qch/qn; (*psychologically*) **eventually parents have to let go of their children** tôt ou tard, les parents doivent laisser leurs enfants voler de leurs propres ailes

♦ **to let sth go**: **they have let their garden go** ils ont laissé leur jardin à l'abandon; **we'll let it go at that** n'en parlons plus; **you're wrong, but let it go** vous avez tort, mais passons

♦ **to let o.s. go** se laisser aller

c **= operate** (= *start*) [*car, machine*] démarrer; (= *function*) [*machine, watch, car*] marcher; **how do you make this go?** comment est-ce que ça marche?; **to be going** [*machine, engine*] être en marche; **the washing machine was going so I didn't hear the phone** la machine à laver était en marche, si bien que je n'ai pas entendu le téléphone; *BUT* **to make a party go** mettre de l'ambiance dans une soirée

♦ **to get going** [*person*] (= *leave*) **let's get going!** allons-y!; (= *start*) **to get going on** *or* **with sth** s'occuper de qch; **I've got to get going on my tax** il faut que je m'occupe (*subj*) de mes impôts; **once he gets going ...** une fois lancé ...

♦ **to get sth going** [+ *machine*] mettre en marche; [+ *car*] faire démarrer; [+ *work, dinner*] mettre en train; **to get things going** activer les choses

♦ **to keep going** (= *continue*) [*person*] continuer; [*business*] réussir à se maintenir à flot; **it's okay, keep going!** ne te dérange pas, continue!; **the police signalled her to stop but she kept going** la police lui a fait signe de s'arrêter mais elle a continué son chemin; *BUT* **she was under great strain but kept going somehow** elle avait beaucoup de soucis mais réussissait malgré cela à tenir le coup; **will the Prime Minister be able to keep going until the spring?** est-ce que le Premier ministre pourra se maintenir au pouvoir jusqu'au printemps?; **it wouldn't keep going** [*machine*] elle s'arrêtait tout le temps, [*car*] elle n'arrêtait pas de caler

♦ **to keep sb/sth going**: **this medicine/hope kept her going** ce médicament/cet espoir lui a permis de tenir (le coup); **a cup of coffee is enough to keep her going all morning** elle réussit à tenir toute la matinée avec un café; **I gave them enough money to keep them going for a week or two** je leur ai donné assez d'argent pour tenir une semaine ou deux; **to keep a factory going** maintenir une usine en activité

d **= begin** **there he goes again!** le voilà qui recommence!; **here goes!*** allez, on y va!

e **= progress** aller, marcher; **the project was going well** le projet marchait bien; **how's it going?** ◊ **how goes it?** (comment) ça va?; **the way things are going** au train où vont les choses, si ça continue comme ça; **I hope all will go well** j'espère que tout ira bien; **all went well for him until ...** tout a bien marché *or* s'est bien passé pour lui jusqu'au moment où...

f **= turn out** [*events*] se passer; **how did your holiday go?** comment se sont passées tes vacances?; **the evening went very well** la soirée s'est très bien passée; **let's wait and see how things go** attendons de voir ce qui va se passer; **I don't know how things will go** je ne sais pas comment ça va se passer, je ne sais pas comment les choses vont tourner*; *BUT* **that's the way things go, I'm afraid** c'est malheureux mais c'est comme ça; (*esp US*) **what goes?*** quoi de neuf?

g **= extend** aller, s'étendre; **the garden goes as far as the river** le jardin va *or* s'étend jusqu'à la rivière; **£50 does not go very far** on ne va pas très loin avec 50 livres

h **= belong** aller; **the books go in that cupboard** les livres vont dans ce placard-là; **this screw goes here** cette vis va là

i **= become** devenir; **the biscuits have gone soft** les biscuits sont devenus mous *or* ont ramolli; **have you gone mad?** tu es (devenu) fou?; **she went pale** elle est devenue pâle, elle a pâli; *BUT* **don't go all sentimental/shy/religious on me!*** tu ne vas pas me faire le coup* des grands sentiments/de la timidité/de la ferveur religieuse!; **the lights went red** les feux sont passés au rouge; **the constituency went Labour at the last election** aux dernières élections la circonscription est passée aux travaillistes

j **= break, yield** [*rope, cable*] céder; [*fuse*] sauter; [*bulb*] griller; [*material*] être usé; **the lining's going** la doublure est usée; **jeans tend to go at the knees** les jeans ont tendance à s'user aux genoux; **this jumper has gone at the elbows** ce pull est troué aux coudes; **there goes another button!** encore un bouton de décousu!

k **= fail** [*sight*] baisser; [*strength*] manquer; **his mind is going** il n'a plus toute sa tête; **his nerve is beginning to go** il commence à paniquer *or* à perdre la tête; **my voice has gone** je n'ai plus de voix; **my voice is going** je n'ai presque plus de voix; **his health is going** il

commence à avoir des problèmes de santé; **his hearing is going** il devient sourd

l **euph = die** partir; **after I go** *or* **have gone** quand je serai parti, quand je ne serai plus là; **he's gone!** il est parti, c'est fini!

m **= be sold** **how much do you think the house will go for?** combien crois-tu que la maison va être vendue?

n **= be given** [*prize, reward, inheritance*] aller, revenir (to à)

o **= be current, be accepted** [*story, rumour*] circuler; **the story goes that ...** le bruit court *or* circule que ...; **anything goes these days*** tout est permis de nos jours; **that goes without saying** cela va sans dire; **what he says goes** c'est lui qui fait la loi; **what I say goes around here** c'est moi qui commande ici

p *** = say** sortir*, faire*; **he goes to me: "what do you want?"** il me sort* *or* il me fait: «qu'est-ce que tu veux?»

q **= apply** **she mustn't say a word, and that goes for you too** elle ne doit pas dire un mot et c'est valable pour toi aussi; **that goes for me too** (= *I agree with that*) je suis (aussi) de cet avis; **as far as your suggestion goes ...** pour ce qui est de ta suggestion ...

♦ **as far as it goes**: **this explanation is fine, as far as it goes, but ...** cette explication n'est pas mauvaise, mais ...

r **= available**

♦ **to be going**: **are there any jobs going?** y a-t-il des postes vacants?; **there just aren't any jobs going** il n'y a pas de travail; **is there any coffee going?** est-ce qu'il y a du café?; **I'll have whatever's going** donnez-moi *or* je prendrai de ce qu'il y a

s **= be sung, played** **the tune goes like this** voici l'air; **I don't know how the song goes** je ne connais pas cette chanson; **how does it go?** c'est comment *or* quoi la chanson?

t **= make specific sound or movement** faire; [*bell, clock*] sonner; **go like that with your left foot** faites comme ça avec votre pied gauche

u **= serve** **the money will go to compensate the accident victims** cet argent servira à dédommager les victimes de l'accident; **the qualities that go to make a great man** les qualités qui font un grand homme

v **Math** **4 into 12 goes 3 times** 12 divisé par 4 égale 3; **2 won't go exactly into 11** 11 divisé par 2, ça ne tombe pas juste

w *** euph** aller aux toilettes; **do you need to go?** tu as envie d'aller aux toilettes?; **I need to go** j'ai une envie pressante

x **implying comparison**

♦ **as ... go**: **he's not bad, as estate agents go** il n'est pas mauvais pour un agent immobilier; **it's a fairly good garage as garages go** comme garage cela peut aller *or* ce n'est pas trop mal

y **= be disposed of, elapse** **seven down and three to go** en voilà sept de faits, il n'en reste plus que trois; **there is a week to go before the election** il reste une semaine avant les élections

z **US = take away** **to go** à emporter; **two hotdogs to go** deux hot-dogs à emporter

2 MODAL VERB

indicating future

♦ **to be going to** + *infinitive* aller; **I'm going to phone him this afternoon** je vais l'appeler cet après-midi; **it's going to rain** il va pleuvoir; **I was just going to do it** j'allais le faire, j'étais sur le point de le faire; **I was going to do it yesterday but I forgot** j'allais le faire *or* j'avais l'intention de le faire hier mais j'ai oublié

3 TRANSITIVE VERB

a **= travel** [+ *distance*] faire; **we had gone only 3km** nous n'avions fait que 3 km; *BUT* **the car was fairly going it*** la voiture roulait *or* filait à bonne allure

♦ **to go it alone** (*gen*) se débrouiller tout seul; (*Pol etc*) faire cavalier seul

◆ **to go one better** aller encore plus loin, renchérir

[b] Cards, Gambling he went three spades il a annoncé trois piques; he went £50 on the red il a misé 50 livres sur le rouge; I can only go £15 je ne peux mettre que 15 livres

[c] = make sound faire; he went "psst", « psst », fit-il

[4] NOUN
(pl **goes**)

[a] NonC = energy to be full of go être plein d'énergie, être très dynamique; there's no go about him il n'a aucun ressort, il est mou

[b] NonC:* = activity, motion it's all go! ça n'arrête pas!; to be always on the go être toujours sur la brèche; to keep sb on the go ne pas laisser souffler qn; he's got two projects on the go at the moment il a deux projets en chantier actuellement

[c] * = attempt tentative f, coup m; at one or a go d'un seul coup; BUT it's your go (in games) c'est à toi (de jouer)

◆ **to have a go** (= try) essayer, tenter le coup; to have a go at sth essayer de faire qch; to have another go réessayer, faire une nouvelle tentative, ressayer; have another go! essaie encore une fois!, réessaie!; to have a go at sb (verbally) s'en prendre à qn*; (physically) se jeter sur qn; (at criminal) the public is warned not to have a go il est demandé au public de ne rien tenter or de ne pas s'approcher du criminel

[d] * = event, situation it's a rum go c'est une drôle de situation; they've had a rough go of it ils ont traversé une mauvaise période

[e] = success to make a go of sth réussir qch; they decided to try to make a go of their marriage ils ont décidé de donner une chance à leur couple; no go!* rien à faire!; it's all the go* ça fait fureur, c'est le dernier cri

[5] ADJECTIVE

esp Space* paré pour la mise à feu; (gen) all systems (are) go tout est OK; you are go for moon-landing vous avez le feu vert pour l'alunissage

[6] COMPOUNDS

► **go-ahead** ADJ (esp Brit) [person, government] dynamique, qui va de l'avant; [business, attitude] dynamique ♦ N to give sb the go-ahead (for sth/to do)* donner le feu vert à qn (pour qch/pour faire) ► **go-between** N intermédiaire mf ♦ N to give sb/sth the go-by laisser tomber* qch/qn ► **go-cart** N (= vehicle) kart m; (= toy) chariot m (que se construisent les enfants); (= handcart) charrette f; (= pushchair) poussette f; (= baby-walker) trotteur m ► **go-carting** N (Sport) karting m ► **go-faster stripe*** N (Aut) liseré m sport (sur la carrosserie d'une voiture) ► **go-getter*** N fonceur* m, -euse* f ► **go-getting*** ADJ [person] fonceur* ► **go-slow (strike)** N (Brit) grève f perlée

[7] PHRASAL VERBS

► **go about** [1] VI [a] circuler, aller; he goes about in a Rolls il roule en Rolls; to go about barefoot/in torn jeans se promener pieds nus/en jean déchiré; they go about in gangs ils vont or circulent en bandes; he's going about with disreputable people il fréquente des gens peu recommandables; he always goes about telling people what to do il est toujours en train de dire aux gens ce qu'ils doivent faire [b] [rumour] courir, circuler [c] (Naut = change direction) virer de bord [2] VT FUS [a] (= deal with) [+ task, duties] he went about the task methodically il a procédé or il s'y est pris de façon méthodique; he knows how to go about it il sait s'y prendre; we must go about it carefully nous devons y aller doucement; how does one go about getting seats? comment s'y prend-on or comment fait-on pour avoir des places? [b] (= be occupied with) to go about one's work

vaquer à ses occupations or travaux; to go about one's business vaquer à ses affaires

► **go across** [1] VI (= cross) traverser; she went across to Mrs. Smith's elle est allée en face chez Mme Smith

[2] VT FUS [+ river, road] traverser

► **go after** VT FUS (= follow) suivre; (= attack) attaquer; go after him! suivez-le!; we're not going after civilian targets nous n'attaquons pas les cibles civiles; the press went after him mercilessly la presse s'est acharnée contre lui; to go after a job poser sa candidature à un poste, postuler à un emploi; he saw the job advertised and decided to go after it il a vu une annonce pour ce poste et a décidé de poser sa candidature

► **go against** VT FUS [a] (= prove hostile to) [vote, judgement, decision] être défavorable à; the decision went against him la décision lui a été défavorable; everything began to go against us tout se liguait contre nous

[b] (= oppose) aller à l'encontre de; conditions which went against national interests des conditions qui allaient à l'encontre des intérêts nationaux; to go against the tide aller contre le courant or à contre-courant; to go against public opinion aller à contre-courant de l'opinion (publique); to go against sb's wishes s'opposer à la volonté or aux volontés de qn; it goes against my conscience ma conscience s'y oppose; it goes against my principles cela va à l'encontre de mes principes, c'est contre mes principes

► **go ahead** VI (also **go on ahead**) passer devant or en tête; go ahead! allez-y!; the exhibition will go ahead as planned l'exposition aura lieu comme prévu; to go ahead with a plan/project mettre un plan/projet à exécution

► **go along** VI aller; why don't you go along too? pourquoi n'iriez-vous pas aussi?; I'll tell you as we go along je vous le dirai en cours de route or en chemin; I check as I go along je vérifie au fur et à mesure; to go along with sb (lit) aller avec qn, accompagner qn; (= agree with) être d'accord avec qn; I'd go along with you on that je suis d'accord avec toi sur ce point; I don't go along with you there là, je ne suis pas d'accord avec vous; I can't go along with that at all je ne suis pas du tout d'accord là-dessus, je suis tout à fait contre; the other parties are unlikely to go along with the plan il est peu probable que les autres partis acceptent ce projet

► **go around** VI [a] = go about 1a and 1b, go round

[b] what goes around comes around tout finit par se payer

► **go at** VT FUS (= attack) [+ person] attaquer, se jeter sur; (= undertake) [+ task] s'atteler à; he went at it with a will il s'y est mis avec acharnement

► **go away** VI partir, s'en aller; (on holiday) partir (en vacances), aller en vacances; [pain] disparaître; he's gone away with my keys il est parti avec mes clés; we're not going away this year nous n'allons nulle part or nous ne partons pas cette année; don't go away with the idea that ...* n'allez pas penser que ...; I think we need to go away and think about this je pense que nous devons prendre le temps d'y réfléchir

► **go back** VI [a] (= return) retourner; we went back to the beach after lunch nous sommes retournés à la plage après le déjeuner; shall we go back now? it's getting dark il est peut-être temps qu'on rentre or qu'on y aille, il commence à faire nuit; to go back to a point revenir sur un point; to go back to the beginning revenir au début; to go back to work reprendre le travail

[b] (= retreat) reculer

[c] (in time) remonter; my memories don't go back so far mes souvenirs ne remontent pas aussi loin; the family goes back to the Norman

Conquest la famille remonte à la conquête normande; we go back a long way on se connaît depuis longtemps

[d] (= revert) revenir (to à); I don't want to go back to the old system je ne veux pas revenir à l'ancien système; to go back to one's former habits retomber dans ses anciennes habitudes

[e] (= extend) s'étendre; the garden goes back to the river le jardin s'étend jusqu'à la rivière; the cave goes back 300 metres la grotte a 300 mètres de long

► **go back on** VT FUS [+ decision, promise] revenir sur

► **go before** VI (lit) aller au devant; (fig = happen earlier) all that has gone before tout ce qui s'est passé avant; (euph = die) those who are or have gone before ceux qui sont partis avant nous; to go before a court/judge comparaître devant un tribunal/juge

► **go below** VI (Naut) descendre dans l'entrepont

► **go by** [1] VI [person] passer; [period of time] (se) passer, s'écouler; we've let the opportunity go by nous avons raté or laissé passer l'occasion; as time goes by à mesure que le temps passe, avec le temps; in days (or years) gone by autrefois, jadis

[2] VT FUS [a] (= judge by) if first impressions are anything to go by s'il faut se fier à sa première impression; that's nothing to go by ce n'est pas une référence; you can't go by what he says on ne peut pas se fier à ce qu'il dit; to go by appearances juger d'après les apparences; the only thing the police have got to go by ... le seul indice dont dispose la police ...

[b] (= be guided by) suivre; to go by the instructions suivre les instructions; if they prove I was wrong I'll go by what they say s'ils prouvent que j'avais tort, je me rallierai à leur point de vue

► **go down** VI [a] (= descend) descendre; to go down to the coast aller or descendre sur la côte

[b] (= fall) [person] tomber; [boxer] aller au tapis; [building] s'écrouler

[c] (= sink) [ship] couler, sombrer; [person] couler

[d] (= crash) [plane] s'écraser

[e] (Brit Univ) [student] (= go on holiday) partir en vacances; (= finish studies) terminer (ses études), quitter l'université; the university goes down on 20 June les vacances universitaires commencent le 20 juin

[f] (= set) [sun, moon] se coucher

[g] (= be swallowed) it went down the wrong way j'ai (or il a etc) avalé de travers

[h] (= be accepted, approved) I wonder how that will go down with her parents je me demande comment ses parents vont prendre ça; to go down well/badly être bien/mal accueilli; it went down well ça a été bien accueilli; the suggestion didn't go down well with the locals cette proposition a été mal accueillie par la population locale

[i] (= subside) [tide] descendre; [temperature] baisser; the floods are going down les eaux commencent à se retirer

[j] (= lessen) [amount, numbers, rate] diminuer; [value, price, standards] baisser; the house has gone down in value la maison s'est dépréciée; this neighbourhood has gone down ce quartier s'est dégradé

[k] (= be defeated, fail) être battu (to par); (Bridge) chuter; (= fail examination) échouer, être recalé (in en); (Ftbl) Spain went down to Scotland 2-1 l'Espagne a été battue 2 à 1 par l'Écosse

[l] (= be relegated) [team] être relégué; (Scol) to go down a class redescendre d'une classe

[m] (Comput = break down) tomber en panne

[n] (Theat) [curtain] tomber; when the curtain goes down lorsque le rideau tombe; [lights] s'éteindre

[o] (= *go as far as*) aller ; **go down to the bottom of the page** allez *or* reportez-vous au bas de la page

[p] [*balloon, tyre*] se dégonfler ; **my ankle's OK, the swelling has gone down** ma cheville va bien, elle a désenflé

[q] (= *be noted, remembered*) **to go down to posterity** passer à la postérité

[r] (*Mus* = *lower pitch*) **can you go down a bit?** vous pouvez chanter (*or* jouer) un peu plus bas ?

▶ **go down as** VT FUS (= *be regarded as*) être considéré comme ; (= *be remembered as*) passer à la postérité comme ; **the victory will go down as one of the highlights of the year** cette victoire restera dans les mémoires comme l'un des grands moments de l'année

▶ **go down on***** VT FUS sucer*⁎*

▶ **go down with*** VT FUS attraper ; **to go down with flu** attraper la grippe → **go down h**

▶ **go for** VT FUS [a] (= *attack*) attaquer ; **he went for me with a knife** il m'a attaqué avec un couteau ; (*to dog*) **go for him!** mors-le !

[b] (⁎ = *like*) **she went for him in a big way** elle en pinçait* pour lui, elle a craqué* pour lui ; **I don't go for that sort of talk** je n'aime pas qu'on parle comme ça ; **I don't go much for poetry** je ne raffole pas de la poésie ; **to tend to go for** avoir tendance à préférer

[c] (= *strive for*) essayer d'avoir ; (= *choose*) choisir ; **go for it!*** vas-y ! ; **I decided to go for it*** j'ai décidé de tenter le coup

[d] **he's got a lot going for him*** il a beaucoup d'atouts ; **the theory has a lot going for it** cette théorie a de nombreux mérites

▶ **go forth** VI (*liter, frm*) [a] [*person*] s'en aller ; **they went forth to battle** ils s'en sont allés à la bataille

[b] **the order went forth that ...** il fut décrété que ... ; **the word went forth that ...** il a été annoncé que ...

▶ **go forward** VI [a] (= *move ahead*) [*person, vehicle*] avancer ; [*economy*] progresser ; [*country*] aller de l'avant

[b] (= *take place*) avoir lieu

[c] (= *continue*) maintenir ; **if they go forward with these radical proposals** s'ils maintiennent ces propositions radicales

▶ **go in** VI [a] (= *enter*) entrer ; **they went in by the back door** ils sont entrés par la porte de derrière ; **I must go in now** il faut que je rentre (*subj*) maintenant ; **go in and win!** allez, bonne chance !

[b] (= *attack*) attaquer ; **the troops are going in tomorrow** les troupes attaquent demain ; **British troops will not go in alone** les troupes britanniques ne seront pas les seules à se battre

[c] [*sun, moon*] se cacher (**behind** derrière)

▶ **go in for** VT FUS [a] [+ *examination*] se présenter à ; [+ *position, job*] poser sa candidature à, postuler à *or* pour ; [+ *competition, race*] prendre part à

[b] [+ *sport*] pratiquer ; [+ *hobby*] se livrer à ; [+ *style*] être sur, affectionner ; [+ *medicine, accounting, politics*] faire ; **she goes in for very high heels** elle affectionne les très hauts talons ; **I don't go in for bright colours** je ne suis pas (très) porté sur les couleurs vives, je ne raffole pas des couleurs vives ; **he doesn't go in much for reading** il n'aime pas beaucoup lire ; **we don't go in for eating in expensive restaurants** nous n'avons pas pour habitude de manger dans des restaurants chers ; **he's going in for science** il va faire des sciences

▶ **go into** VT FUS [a] (= *take up*) [+ *profession, field*] **he doesn't want to go into industry** il ne veut pas travailler dans l'industrie

[b] (= *embark on*) [+ *explanation*] se lancer dans ; **he went into a long explanation** il s'est lancé *or* embarqué dans une longue explication ; **to go into details** rentrer dans les détails ; **let's not go into that now** laissons cela pour le moment ; **to go into fits of laughter** être pris de fou rire

[c] (= *investigate*) étudier ; **this matter is being gone into** on étudie la question ; **we haven't got time to go into that now** nous n'avons pas le temps de nous pencher sur ce problème ; **to go into a question in detail** approfondir une question

[d] (= *be devoted to*) [*time, money, effort*] être investi dans ; **a lot of money went into the research** on a investi beaucoup d'argent dans la recherche

▶ **go in with** VT FUS (= *share costs*) se cotiser avec ; **she went in with her sister to buy the present** elle s'est cotisée avec sa sœur pour acheter le cadeau

▶ **go off** [1] VI [a] (= *leave*) partir, s'en aller ; (*Theat*) quitter la scène ; **they went off together** ils sont partis ensemble ; (= *go off duty*) **she went off at 3 o'clock** elle est partie à 3 heures, elle a quitté (son travail) à 3 heures

[b] [*alarm clock*] sonner ; [*alarm*] se déclencher ; **the gun didn't go off** le coup n'est pas parti ; **the pistol went off in his hand** le coup est parti alors qu'il tenait le pistolet dans sa main

[c] (= *stop*) [*light, radio, TV*] s'éteindre ; [*heating*] s'arrêter, s'éteindre

[d] (*Brit* = *deteriorate*) [*meat*] s'avarier, se gâter ; [*milk*] tourner ; [*butter*] rancir ; [*athlete*] être en méforme

[e] (= *lose intensity*) [*pain*] s'apaiser, passer

[f] (= *go to sleep*) s'endormir

[g] [*event*] se passer ; **the evening went off very well** la soirée s'est très bien passée

[2] VT FUS (*Brit*⁎) **I'm starting to go off the idea** ça ne me dit plus grand-chose ; **I've gone off skiing** le ski ne me tente plus beaucoup ; **I used to like him, but I've gone off him lately** je l'aimais bien mais depuis un certain temps il m'agace

▶ **go off with** VT FUS [+ *thing, person*] partir avec ; **she went off with my umbrella** elle est partie avec mon parapluie ; **his wife went off with another man** sa femme est partie avec un autre homme

▶ **go on** [1] VI [a] (= *fit*) **the lid won't go on** le couvercle ne ferme pas bien ; **the cover won't go on** ça ne rentre pas dans la housse

[b] (= *proceed on one's way*) (*without stopping*) poursuivre son chemin ; (*after stopping*) continuer sa route ; (*by car*) reprendre la route ; **after a brief chat she went on to church** après avoir bavardé quelques instants, elle a continué sa route vers l'église ; **go on, it's fun!*** vas-y, tu vas voir, c'est super !* → **go ahead**

[c] (= *continue*) continuer (**doing** de *or* à faire) ; **to go on speaking** continuer de *or* à parler ; (*after pause*) reprendre (la parole) ; **go on with your work** continuez votre travail ; **go on trying!** essaie encore ! ; **go on!** continue ! ; **go on (with you)!*** allons donc !, à d'autres !* ; **the war went on until 1945** la guerre a continué *or* s'est prolongée jusqu'en 1945 ; **if you go on doing that, you'll get into trouble** si tu continues à faire ça, tu vas avoir des ennuis ; **that's enough to be going on with** ça suffit pour l'instant

[d] (⁎ = *talk*) **to go on about sth** ne pas arrêter de parler de qch ; **don't go on about it!** ça va, j'ai compris ! ; **she just goes on and on** elle radote ; **he goes on and on about it** il n'arrête pas d'en parler

[e] (⁎ = *nag*) **to go on at sb** s'en prendre à qn ; **she went on (and on) at him** elle n'a pas cessé de s'en prendre à lui ; **she's always going on at him about doing up the kitchen** elle n'arrête pas de le harceler pour qu'il refasse la cuisine

[f] (= *proceed*) passer ; **to go on to another matter** passer à une autre question ; **he went on to say that ...** puis il a dit que ... ; **he retired from football and went on to become a journalist** il a abandonné le football et est devenu journaliste ; **he goes on to Holland tomorrow** il repart demain pour la Hollande

[g] (= *happen*) se dérouler ; (*for a stated time*) durer ; **several matches were going on at the same time** plusieurs matchs se déroulaient en même temps ; **how long has this been going on?** depuis combien de temps est-ce que ça dure ? ; **the rioting went on all night** les émeutes ont duré toute la nuit ; **while this was going on** pendant ce temps, au même moment ; **what's going on here?** qu'est-ce qui se passe ici ?

[h] (= *pass*) **things got easier as time went on** avec le temps les choses sont devenues plus faciles ; **as the day went on he became more and more anxious** au fil des heures, il devenait de plus en plus inquiet

[i] (⁎: *gen pej* = *behave*) **that's no way to go on** c'est une conduite inacceptable ! ; **what a way to go on!** en voilà des manières !

[j] (*Theat* = *enter*) entrer en scène

[k] (= *progress*) [*person, patient*] se porter, aller ; **how is he going on?** comment va-t-il *or* se porte-t-il ? ; **life went on uneventfully** la vie poursuivit son cours paisiblement

[l] (⁎ = *approach*) **she's going on 50** elle va sur la cinquantaine, elle frise* la cinquantaine ; **Ann's 25 going on 50** Ann a 25 ans mais elle a les réactions d'une femme de 50 ans

[2] VT FUS [a] (= *be guided by*) **you've got to go on the facts** il faut s'appuyer sur les faits ; **what have you got to go on?** de quels indices *or* de quelles pistes disposez-vous ? ; **we don't have much to go on yet** nous n'avons pas beaucoup d'indices pour l'instant ; **the police had no clues to go on** la police n'avait aucun indice sur lequel s'appuyer

[b] (= *appreciate, be impressed by*) **I don't go much on that*** ça ne me dit pas grand-chose*

▶ **go on for** VT FUS **it's going on for 100km** c'est à une centaine de kilomètres ; **it's going on for 5 o'clock** il est près de 5 heures ; **he's going on for 50** il va sur la cinquantaine

▶ **go out** VI [a] (= *leave*) sortir ; **to go out of a room** sortir d'une pièce ; **to go out shopping** aller faire des courses ; **to go out for a meal** aller au restaurant ; **he goes out a lot** il sort beaucoup ; **she doesn't go out with him any more** elle ne sort plus avec lui ; **to go out to work** (aller) travailler ; **most mothers have to go out to work** la plupart des mères de famille doivent travailler

[b] [*style*] passer de mode, se démoder ; [*custom*] disparaître ; [*fire, light*] s'éteindre ; **he was so tired he went out like a light*** il était si fatigué qu'il s'est endormi comme une masse* ; **all the fun has gone out of it now** ce n'est plus aussi drôle maintenant

[c] (= *travel*) aller (**to** à) ; **she went out to Bangkok to join her husband** elle est allée rejoindre son mari à Bangkok

[d] [*sea*] se retirer ; [*tide*] descendre ; **the tide** *or* **the sea goes out 2km** la mer se retire sur 2 km

[e] **my heart went out to him** j'ai été vraiment désolé pour lui ; **all our sympathy goes out to you** nous pensons à vous en ces moments douloureux

[f] (*Cards etc*) terminer

[g] (= *be issued*) [*pamphlet, circular*] être distribué ; [*invitation*] envoyer ; (= *be broadcast*) [*radio programme, TV programme*] être diffusé ; **an appeal has gone out for people to give blood** un appel a été lancé pour encourager les dons de sang ; **the programme goes out on Friday evenings** l'émission passe *or* est diffusée le vendredi soir

[h] (*Sport* = *be eliminated*) être éliminé, se faire sortir* ; **our team went out to a second division side** notre équipe a été éliminée *or* s'est fait sortir* par une équipe de deuxième division

[i] (= *end*) [*year*] finir, se terminer

▶ **go over** [1] VI [a] (= *cross*) aller ; **to go over to France** aller en France ; **she went over to Mrs Smith's** elle est allée chez Mme Smith ; **his speech went over well** son discours a été bien reçu *or* est bien passé ; **the ball went over into** the field le ballon est passé par-dessus la haie (or le mur etc) et il est tombé dans le champ [b] (= be overturned) [vehicle] se retourner; [boat] chavirer, se retourner [2] VT FUS [a] (= examine) [+ accounts, report] examiner, vérifier; [doctor] [+ patient] examiner; to go over a house visiter une maison; I went over his essay with him j'ai regardé sa dissertation avec lui

[b] (= rehearse, review) [+ speech] revoir; [+ facts, points] récapituler; to go over sth in one's mind repasser qch dans son esprit; to go over the events of the day repasser les événements de la journée; let's go over the facts again récapitulons les faits

[c] (= touch up) retoucher, faire des retouches à; to go over a drawing in ink repasser un dessin à l'encre

▶ **go over to** VT FUS passer à; we're going over to a new system nous passons à un nouveau système; I've gone over to a new brand of coffee j'ai changé de marque de café; to go over to the enemy passer à l'ennemi

▶ **go round** VI [a] (= turn) tourner; my head is going round j'ai la tête qui tourne

[b] (= go the long way) faire le tour; (= make a detour) faire un détour; there's no bridge, we'll have to go round il n'y a pas de pont, il faut faire le tour; we went round by Manchester nous avons fait un détour par Manchester

[c] to go round to sb's house/to see sb aller chez qn/voir qn

[d] (= be sufficient) suffire (pour tout le monde); there's enough food to go round il y a assez à manger pour tout le monde; to make the money go round joindre les deux bouts*

[e] (= circulate) [bottle, document, story] circuler; [rumour] courir, circuler

[f] = go about 1a

▶ **go through** [1] VI (= be agreed, voted) [proposal] être accepté; [law, bill] passer, être voté; [business deal] être conclu, se faire; the deal did not go through l'affaire n'a pas été conclue or ne s'est pas faite

[2] VT FUS [a] (= suffer, endure) subir, endurer; after all he's gone through après tout ce qu'il a subi or enduré; we've all gone through it nous sommes tous passés par là, nous avons tous connu cela; he's going through a very difficult time il traverse une période difficile

[b] (= examine) [+ list] éplucher; [+ book] parcourir; [+ mail] regarder, dépouiller; [+ subject, plan] étudier; [+ one's pockets] fouiller dans; [+ suitcases, trunks] fouiller; I went through my drawers looking for a pair of socks j'ai cherché une paire de chaussettes dans mes tiroirs; I went through his essay with him j'ai regardé sa dissertation avec lui

[c] (= use up) [+ money] dépenser; (= wear out) user; to go through a fortune engloutir une fortune; he goes through a pair of shoes a month il use une paire de chaussures par mois; he has gone through the seat of his trousers il a troué le fond de son pantalon; this book has already gone through 13 editions ce livre en est déjà à sa 13ᵉ édition

[d] (= carry out) [+ routine, course of study] suivre; [+ formalities] remplir, accomplir; [+ apprenticeship] faire

▶ **go through with** VT FUS (= persist with) [+ plan, threat] mettre à exécution; in the end she couldn't go through with it en fin de compte elle n'a pas pu le faire; he pleaded with her not to go through with the divorce il la suppliée de ne pas continuer la procédure de divorce

▶ **go to** [1] VI go to!†† allons donc! [2] VT FUS go to it! allez-y!

▶ **go together** VI [colours] aller (bien) ensemble; [events, conditions, ideas] aller de pair; poor living conditions and TB go together la tuberculose va de pair avec les mauvaises conditions de vie; they go well together ils

vont bien ensemble; Ann and Peter are going together Ann et Peter sortent ensemble

▶ **go under** VI [a] (= sink) [ship] sombrer, couler; [person] couler

[b] (= fail) [business person] faire faillite; [business] couler, faire faillite

▶ **go up** VI [a] (= rise) [price, value, temperature] monter, être en hausse; (Theat) [curtain] se lever; [lights] s'allumer; [cheer] s'élever; three teams are hoping to go up to the second division trois équipes espèrent monter or passer en deuxième division; houses are going up near the park on construit des maisons près du parc; when the curtain goes up lorsque le rideau se lève; to go up in price augmenter; (Scol) to go up a class monter d'une classe

[b] (= climb) monter, aller en haut; (= go upstairs to bed) monter se coucher

[c] (= travel north) aller, monter; I'm going up to Manchester tomorrow demain je vais or je monte à Manchester

[d] (= approach) I wanted to go up and talk to him je voulais m'approcher de lui et lui parler; a man went up to him and asked him the time un homme s'est approché et lui a demandé l'heure

[e] (= explode, be destroyed) [building] sauter, exploser

[f] (Brit Univ) entrer à l'université; he went up to Oxford il est entré à Oxford

[2] VT FUS [+ hill] monter, gravir; to go up the stairs monter l'escalier, monter les marches d'un escalier; to go up the street monter la rue

▶ **go with** VT FUS [a] (= accompany) [circumstances, event, conditions] aller (de pair) avec; ill health goes with poverty la pauvreté et la mauvaise santé vont de pair; the house goes with the job le logement va avec le poste; to go with the times vivre avec son temps; to go with the crowd suivre la foule; (fig) faire comme tout le monde

[b] (= harmonize with, suit) [colours] aller bien avec, se marier avec; [furnishings] être assorti à; [behaviour, opinions] cadrer avec, s'accorder avec; I want a hat to go with my new coat je cherche un chapeau assorti à mon or qui aille avec mon nouveau manteau; his accent doesn't go with his appearance son accent ne correspond pas à son apparence

[c] (= agree with) [+ person] être de l'avis de; [+ idea] souscrire à; I'll go with you there là, je suis de votre avis; yes, I'd go with that je suis d'accord sur ce point

[d] (* = choose) opter pour, choisir; we decided to go with the first option nous avons décidé d'opter pour la première solution or de choisir la première option

[e] (*: also go steady with) sortir avec

▶ **go without** [1] VI se priver de tout; mothers feed their children and go without themselves les mères nourrissent leurs enfants et se privent elles-mêmes de tout

[2] VT FUS se priver de, se passer de

---

goad [gəʊd] [1] N [a] (lit) aiguillon m [b] (fig) (= spur, impetus) aiguillon m, stimulation f; (= irritant) source f d'agacement, cause f d'irritation [2] VT [a] [+ cattle] aiguillonner, piquer [b] (fig) aiguillonner, stimuler; to ~ sb into doing sth talonner or harceler qn jusqu'à ce qu'il fasse qch; he was ~ed into replying il a été piqué au point de répondre; his insults ~ed her into action ses insultes l'ont fait passer à l'action

▶ **goad on** VT SEP aiguillonner, stimuler; to ~ sb on to doing inciter qn à faire

goal [gəʊl] [1] N [a] (gen = aim) but m, objectif m; his ~ was to become president son objectif or son but était de devenir président, il avait pour ambition or pour but de devenir président; her ~ was in sight elle approchait du but; the ~ is to raise as much money as possible le but or l'objectif est d'obtenir autant

d'argent que possible; to set a ~ fixer un objectif; to set o.s. a ~ se fixer un but or un objectif

[b] (Sport) but m; to keep ~ ◊ to play in ~ être gardien de but; to win by three ~s to two gagner par trois buts à deux; the ball went into the ~ le ballon est entré dans le but

[2] COMP ▶ **goal-area** N (Sport) surface f de but ▶ **goal average**, **goal difference** N (Brit Ftbl) goal-average m ▶ **goal-kick** N (Ftbl) coup m de pied de renvoi (aux six mètres) ▶ **goal-line** N ligne f de but ▶ **goal post** N montant m or poteau m de but; (fig) to move the ~ posts changer les règles du jeu ▶ **goal scorer** N buteur m; the main ~ scorer was Jones c'est Jones qui a marqué le plus de buts

goalie* ['gəʊlɪ] N (ABBR = **goalkeeper**) goal m

goalkeeper ['gəʊlkiːpər] N gardien m de but, goal m

goalkeeping ['gəʊlkiːpɪŋ] N jeu m du gardien de but

goalless ['gəʊllɪs] ADJ [a] (Sport) [match] au score vierge, sans but marqué; a ~ draw un match nul zéro à zéro [b] (= aimless) sans but

goalmouth ['gəʊlmaʊθ] N in the ~ juste devant les poteaux

goat [gəʊt] [1] N [a] chèvre f; (= he-goat) bouc m; (= young goat) chevreau m, chevrette f → sheep [b] (Brit) to act the ~* faire l'imbécile or l'andouille* [c] (fig = irritate) to get sb's ~* taper sur le système* or les nerfs* de qn [2] COMP ▶ **the goat God** N (Myth) le divin chèvre-pied, le dieu Pan ▶ **goat('s) cheese** N fromage m de chèvre

goatee [gəʊ'tiː] N barbiche f, bouc m

goatherd ['gəʊthɜːd] N chevrier m, -ière f

goatskin ['gəʊtskɪn] N (= clothing) peau f de chèvre or de bouc; (= container) outre f en peau de bouc

goatsucker ['gəʊtsʌkər] N (US Orn) engoulevent m

gob [gɒb] [1] N [a] (‡ = spit) crachat m, mollard‡ m [b] (esp Brit:‡ = mouth) gueule‡ f; shut your ~! ferme-la !*, ta gueule !‡ [c] (US Navy‡) marin m, mataf‡ [2] VI (‡ = spit) cracher (at sur) [3] COMP ▶ **gob-stopper*** N (Brit) (gros) bonbon m

gobbet* ['gɒbɪt] N petit bout m

gobble ['gɒbl] [1] N [of turkey] glouglou m [2] VI [turkey] glousser, glouglouter [3] VT (also ~ down, ~ up) [+ food] engloutir, engouffrer; don't ~! ne mange pas si vite !

gobbledegook, **gobbledygook*** ['gɒbldɪguːk] N charabia* m

gobbler* ['gɒblər] N (= turkey) dindon m

Gobi ['gəʊbɪ] N ~ **Desert** désert m de Gobi

goblet ['gɒblɪt] N (= stem glass) verre m à pied; (= cup) coupe f

goblin ['gɒblɪn] N lutin m, farfadet m

gobshite‡ ['gɒbʃaɪt] N (= idiot) peigne-cul‡ m

gobsmacked‡ [gɒb,smækd] ADJ (Brit) sidéré*, estomaqué*

goby ['gəʊbɪ] N (pl ~ **goby** or **gobies**) gobie m

GOC [,dʒiːəʊ'siː] N (Mil) (ABBR = **General Officer Commanding**) → **general**

god [gɒd] [1] N [a] dieu m, divinité f; (fig) dieu m, idole f; (fig) **money is his ~** l'argent est son dieu

[b] **God** Dieu m; **God the Father, the Son, the Holy Spirit** Dieu le Père, le Fils et le Saint-Esprit; **he thinks he's God** il se prend pour Dieu; **he thinks he's God's gift*** to women il se prend pour Don Juan; (pej) **to play God with people's lives** jouer avec la vie des gens; **God's acre**† (= cemetery) cimetière m; (US) **God's own country*** les États-Unis mpl

[c] (phrases) **(my) God!*** mon Dieu !; **God help him!** (que) Dieu lui vienne en aide !; **God help you*** (if your mother ever finds out about this!) (si ta mère apprend ça) je te souhaite bien de la chance !; **God (only) knows*** Dieu

seul le sait, allez donc savoir* ; **and God (only) knows what else** et Dieu sait quoi ; **God knows I've tried*** Dieu sait si j'ai essayé ; **God knows where he's got to*** allez savoir or Dieu sait où il est passé! ; **he went God knows where*** il est parti Dieu sait où ; **for God's sake!*** ◊ **for the love of God!*** (crossly) nom d'un chien!* ; (imploringly) par l'amour du ciel! ; **by God, I'll get you for this!*** nom d'un chien or nom de Dieu je te le ferai payer!* ; **God willing** s'il plaît à Dieu ; **I wish to God I hadn't told him!*** si seulement je ne lui avais rien dit! ; **would to God that ...**† plût à Dieu que ... (+ subj) ; **ye ~s!**†† grands dieux! → **help, hope, love, man, name, thank, tin**

d (Brit Theat) **the ~s** le poulailler*

2 COMP ► **god-awful**‡ ADJ (gen) vraiment affreux ; [weather, place] pourri ; [book, film etc] complètement nul(le) m(f) ► **god-botherer*** N (pej) bigot(e)* m(f) (pej) ► **god-fearing** ADJ (très) religieux, (très) croyant ; **any ~-fearing man** tout croyant digne de ce nom ► **god-slot*** N (Brit TV) créneau m horaire des émissions religieuses

godchild ['gɒdtʃaɪld] N (pl **-children**) filleul(e) m(f)

goddammit [gɒ'dæmɪt] EXCL (US) nom de Dieu!‡, bon sang!*

goddam(n) ['gɒdæm], **goddamned**‡ ['gɒdæmd] ADJ sacré (before n), fichu* (before n), foutu‡ (before n) ; **it's no goddam(ned) use!** ça sert à rien!*

goddaughter ['gɒdɔːtər] N filleule f

goddess ['gɒdɪs] N déesse f ; (fig) idole f

godfather ['gɒdfɑːðər] N (lit, fig) parrain m ; **to stand ~ to a child** être parrain d'un enfant ; (at ceremony) tenir un enfant sur les fonts baptismaux

godforsaken ['gɒdfəseɪkən] ADJ [town, place] perdu, paumé* ; [person] malheureux, misérable ; **~ existence** chienne f de vie* ; **~ spot** trou m perdu or paumé*

godhead ['gɒdhed] N divinité f

godless ['gɒdlɪs] ADJ [person, action, life] impie

godlike ['gɒdlaɪk] ADJ divin

godliness ['gɒdlɪnɪs] N dévotion f → **cleanliness**

godly ['gɒdlɪ] ADJ [person] dévot(e) m(f), pieux ; [actions, life] pieux

godmother ['gɒdmʌðər] N marraine f ; **to stand ~ to a child** être marraine d'un enfant ; (at ceremony) tenir un enfant sur les fonts baptismaux → **fairy**

godparent ['gɒdpɛərənt] 1 N (= godfather) parrain m ; (= godmother) marraine f 2 **godparents** NPL **his ~s** son parrain et sa marraine

godsend ['gɒdsend] N aubaine f, bénédiction f ; **to be a** or **come as a ~** être une bénédiction or aubaine (**to** pour)

godson ['gɒdsʌn] N filleul m

godspeed† ['gɒdspiːd] EXCL bonne chance!, bon voyage!

godsquad* ['gɒdskwɒd] N (pej) bande f d'illuminés (pej), ≈ les bigots* mpl (pej)

goer ['gəʊər] N a (= horse, runner) fonceur m, -euse f b (* = feasible idea) bon plan* m, bonne idée f c (* = woman) **she's a real ~**‡ elle démarre au quart de tour*

...goer ['gəʊər] N (in compounds) **cinemagoer** cinéphile mf → **opera-goer**

goes [gəʊz] VB → **go**

Goethe ['gøːtə] N Goethe m

gofer ['gəʊfər] N coursier m, -ière f

goggle ['gɒgl] 1 VI* [person] rouler de gros yeux ronds ; [eyes] être exorbités, sortir de la tête ; **to ~ at sb/sth** regarder qn/qch en roulant de gros yeux ronds 2 **goggles** NPL [of motorcyclist] lunettes fpl protectrices or de motocycliste ; [of skindiver] lunettes fpl de plongée ; (industrial) lunettes fpl protectrices or de protection ; (* = glasses) besicles fpl

(hum) 3 COMP ► **goggle-box**‡ N (Brit) télé* f ► **goggle-eyed** ADJ (gen) aux yeux exorbités ; **he sat ~-eyed in front of the TV*** il était assis devant la télé*, les yeux exorbités

go-go ['gəʊgəʊ] 1 N a (US St Ex) [market, stocks] spéculatif ; (* = dynamic) [team] plein d'allant ; [years, days] prospère, de vaches grasses ; **the ~ 1980s** la décennie prospère des années 1980 b (Brit Fin) [investment, fund] à haut rendement et à haut risque, hautement spéculatif 2 COMP ► **go-go dance** N danse exécutée par des personnes légèrement vêtues (pour les clients d'une boîte de nuit etc) ► **go-go dancer, go-go girl** N jeune fille qui danse légèrement vêtue (pour les clients d'une boîte de nuit etc)

going ['gəʊɪŋ] 1 N a (= departure) départ m → **coming**

b (= progress) (lit, fig) **that was good ~** ça a été rapide ; **it was slow ~** on n'avançait pas ; (in work, task) les progrès étaient lents ; **it was hard ~** on a eu du mal, ça a été dur* ; **the meeting was hard** or **tough ~** la réunion était laborieuse

c (= conditions) (gen) état m du sol or du terrain (pour la marche etc) ; (Racing) état m du sol or du terrain ; **it's rough ~** (walking) on marche mal ; (in car) la route est mauvaise ; **he got out while the ~ was good*** il est parti au bon moment ■ (PROV) **when the ~ gets tough, the tough get ~** quand ça se met à être dur, les durs s'y mettent (PROV) → **heavy**

2 ADJ a **the ~ rate/price** le tarif/le prix normal

b (after superlative adj.*) **it's the best thing ~** il n'y a rien de mieux (à l'heure actuelle) ; **the best computer game ~** le meilleur jeu électronique du moment or sur le marché ; **you must be the biggest fool ~** tu es vraiment le roi des imbéciles

3 COMP ► **a going concern** N (Comm) une affaire florissante or qui marche ; (fig) **the Empire was still a ~ concern** l'Empire était toujours une réalité ► **going-over** N (pl **goings-over**) [of accounts] vérification f, révision f ; (medical) examen m ; (= cleaning) [of rooms, house etc] nettoyage m ; (fig = beating) brutalités fpl, passage m à tabac* ; **to give sth a good** or **thorough ~-over** (= check) inspecter qch soigneusement ; (= clean) nettoyer qch à fond ► **goings-on*** NPL (pej) [of behaviour] activités fpl (louche), manigances fpl ; (= happenings) événements mpl ; **fine ~s-on!*** c'est du joli! ; **your letters keep me in touch with ~s-on at home** tes lettres me tiennent au courant de ce qui se passe à la maison

-going ['gəʊɪŋ] 1 ADJ (in compounds) **churchgoing Christian** chrétien m pratiquant ; **the theatre-going public** le public amateur de théâtre, les amateurs de théâtre → **easy, ocean** 2 N (in compounds) **church-going/theatre-going has declined over the last ten years** depuis dix ans les gens vont de moins en moins à l'église/au théâtre

goitre, goiter (US) ['gɔɪtə] N goitre m

Golan ['gəʊlæn] N **the ~ Heights** le plateau du Golan

gold [gəʊld] 1 N a (NonC) or m ; **£500 in ~** 500 livres en or ; **a pot** or **crock of ~** (= money) une mine d'or ; (= desired object etc) un oiseau rare → **good, heart, rolled**

b = **gold medal**

2 ADJ a (= made of gold) [watch, tooth] en or ; [coin, ingot, bullion] d'or ; [letters, lettering] d'or, doré

b (= yellow) [paint] doré ; **a green and ~ flag** un drapeau vert et or inv → **3**

3 COMP ► **gold braid** N (Mil) galon m or ► **Gold Card** N (Fin) ≈ Gold Card, Gold MasterCard® ► **gold-clause loan** N (Jur, Fin) emprunt m avec garantie-or ► **Gold Coast** N (Hist: in Africa) Côte-de-l'Or f ; (US:

fig) quartiers mpl chic (souvent en bordure d'un lac) ► **gold digger** N a (lit) chercheur m d'or b (fig pej) **she's a ~ digger** c'est une aventurière ► **gold disc** N (Mus) disque m d'or ► **gold dust** N (lit) poudre f d'or ; (esp Brit fig) **to be like ~ dust** être une denrée rare ► **gold-exchange standard** N (Econ) étalon m de change-or ► **gold fever** N la fièvre de l'or ► **gold-filled** ADJ [tooth] aurifié ► **gold filling** N (Dentistry) obturation f en or, aurification f ► **gold foil** N feuille f d'or ► **gold-headed cane** N canne f à pommeau d'or ► **gold lace** N (on uniform) = **gold braid** ► **gold leaf** N feuille f d'or, or m en feuille d'or ► **gold medal** N médaille f d'or ► **gold mine** N (lit, fig) mine f d'or ; (fig) **he's sitting on a ~ mine** il est assis sur une véritable mine d'or ► **gold miner** N mineur m (dans une mine d'or) ► **gold mining** N extraction f de l'or ► **gold plate** N (= coating) mince couche f d'or ; (= dishes) vaisselle f d'or ; (fig) **to eat off ~ plates** rouler sur l'or, nager dans l'opulence ► **gold-plated** ADJ (lit) plaqué or inv ; (* fig) [deal, contract] qui doit rapporter gros ► **the gold pool** N (Fin) le pool de l'or ► **gold record** N = **gold disc** ► **gold reserves** NPL (Econ) réserves fpl d'or ► **gold-rimmed spectacles** NPL lunettes fpl à montures en or ► **gold rush** N ruée f vers l'or ► **gold standard** N étalon-or m ; **to come off** or **leave the ~ standard** abandonner l'étalon-or ► **Gold Star Mother** N (US Hist) mère f d'un soldat mort au combat ► **gold stone** N aventurine f

goldbrick ['gəʊldbrɪk] 1 N a (lit) barre f d'or b (US fig) (= good deal) affaire f en or ; (* = shirker) tire-au-flanc* m 2 VI (US* = shirk) tirer au flanc*

goldcrest ['gəʊldkrest] N roitelet m huppé

golden ['gəʊldən] 1 ADJ a (= yellow) [hair] doré, d'or ; [suntan, sand, light, colour] doré ; (Culin: also **~-brown**) bien doré

b (liter = made of gold) [cross, chain, locket] en or ; (fig) [voice] d'or, en or

c (= happy, prosperous) [years] doré ; [future] en or ; **a ~ era** un âge d'or ; **~ hours** heures fpl précieuses or merveilleuses → **golden age, goose, silence**

2 COMP ► **golden age** N âge m d'or ► **golden boy*** N (popular) enfant m chéri ; (gifted) jeune prodige m ; (financially successful) golden boy m ► **golden-brown** ADJ [tan, skin] brun doré inv ; (Culin) bien doré ► **the golden calf** N le veau d'or ► **golden deed** N action f d'éclat ► **Golden Delicious (apple)** N (pomme f) golden f ► **golden eagle** N aigle m royal or doré ► **the Golden Fleece** N la Toison d'or ► **Golden Gate** N (US Geog) **the Golden Gate (Bridge)** le pont de la Golden Gate ► **golden girl*** N (popular) enfant f chérie ; (gifted, successful) jeune prodige m ► **golden handcuffs*** NPL (Ind) prime d'encouragement (à rester à un poste) ► **golden handshake** N (Ind) grosse prime f de départ ► **golden hello** N (Ind) prime f d'embauche ► **golden jubilee** N (Brit) cinquantième m anniversaire, jubilé m ► **the golden mean** N le juste milieu ► **golden number** N nombre m d'or ► **golden oldie*** N (= pop song, performer, sportsperson) vieille star f ► **golden opportunity** N occasion f en or ► **golden oriole** N loriot m d'Europe ► **golden parachute*** N (Ind) prime de licenciement (prévue dans le contrat d'un cadre en cas de rachat de l'entreprise) ► **golden pheasant** N faisan m doré ► **golden remedy** N remède m souverain or infaillible ► **golden retriever** N golden retriever m (chien) ► **golden rod** N (Bot) verge f d'or ► **golden rule** N règle f d'or ► **golden share** N (St Ex) action f privilégiée ► **the Golden State** N (US) la Californie ► **golden syrup** N (Brit) sirop m de sucre roux ► **the Golden Triangle** N le Triangle

d'or ► **golden wedding (anniversary)** N noces fpl d'or ► **golden yellow** ADJ jaune d'or

goldfield ['gəuldfiːld] N région f or terrain m aurifère

goldfinch ['gəuldfɪntʃ] N (Orn) chardonneret m

goldfish ['gəuldfɪʃ] (pl **goldfish** or **goldfishes**) 1 N poisson m rouge, cyprin m (doré) 2 COMP ► **goldfish bowl** N bocal m (à poissons); (fig) **to live in a ~ bowl** vivre comme dans un bocal en verre

Goldilocks ['gəuldɪlɒks] N Boucles d'Or f

goldsmith ['gəuldsmɪθ] N orfèvre m; **~'s shop** magasin m or atelier m d'orfèvre; **~'s trade** orfèvrerie f

golf [gɒlf] 1 N golf m → **clock** 2 VI faire du golf, jouer au golf 3 COMP ► **golf ball** N balle f de golf; (on typewriter) boule f, sphère f; **~ ball typewriter** machine f à écrire à boule or à sphère ► **golf club** N (= stick) club m or crosse f (de golf); (= place) club m de golf ► **golf course** N (terrain m de) golf m ► **golf links** NPL = **golf course** ► **golf widow** N she's a ~ **widow** son mari la délaisse pour aller jouer au golf, son mari lui préfère le golf

golfer ['gɒlfər] N joueur m, -euse f de golf, golfeur m, -euse f

golfing ['gɒlfɪŋ] 1 ADJ [equipment, trousers] de golf; **to go on a ~ holiday** partir en vacances faire du golf 2 N golf m

Golgotha ['gɒlgəθə] N Golgotha

Goliath [gəu'laɪəθ] N (lit, fig) Goliath m

golliwog ['gɒlɪwɒg] N (Brit) poupée f nègre de chiffon (aux cheveux hérissés)

golly* ['gɒlɪ] 1 EXCL **(by) ~!** mince (alors)!*, bon sang!*; **and by ~ he did it!** et il l'a fait nom de Dieu! 2 N (Brit) = **golliwog**

golosh [gə'lɒʃ] N = **galosh**

Gomorrah [gə'mɒrə] N Gomorrhe

gonad ['gəunæd] N (Med) gonade f

gonadotrop(h)in [,gɒnədəu'trəufɪn] N gonadotrophine f

gonadotropic [,gɒnədəu'trəupɪk] ADJ gonadotrope

gondola ['gɒndələ] N a (= boat) gondole f b [of balloon, airship] nacelle f c (in supermarket) gondole f; (US Rail: also ~ **car**) wagon-tombereau m

gondolier [,gɒndə'lɪər] N gondolier m

Gondwana [gɒnd'wɑːnə] N (also ~**land**) le Gondwana

gone [gɒn] 1 VB ptp of **go** 2 ADJ a **to be ~** [object, enthusiasm etc] avoir disparu; **the coffee is all ~** il n'y a plus de café; **the trees have been ~ for years** cela fait des années qu'il n'y a plus d'arbres; **~ are the days when ...** le temps n'est plus où ...; **he is ~** il est parti; (euph = dead) il n'est plus; **to be long ~** ne plus exister depuis longtemps; **to be far ~** (= ill) être très bas or mal; (* = drunk, on drugs) être cassé*; (= pregnant) **she was six months ~*** elle était enceinte de six mois; **to be ~ on sb*** en pincer pour qn*; (†† or hum) **be ~!** allez-vous-en! b **"Gone with the Wind"** « Autant en emporte le vent » b (Brit = after) **it's just ~ three** il est 3 heures et quelques; **it was ~ four before he came** il était plus de 4 heures or 4 heures passées quand il est arrivé

goner* ['gɒnər] N **to be a ~** être fichu* or foutu*

gong [gɒŋ] N a (Boxing) gong m b (Brit hum = medal) médaille f

gonna* ['gɒnə] (esp US) = **going to**

gonorrhoea [,gɒnə'rɪə] N blennorragie f

gonzo* ['gɒnzəu] ADJ (US) bizarre

goo* [guː] 1 N matière f visqueuse or gluante; (= sentimentality) sentimentalité f à l'eau de rose 2 COMP ► **goo-goo eyes*** (US hum) **to make ~-~ eyes at sb** faire les yeux doux à qn

---

good [gud]

compar **better**, superl **best**	
1 ADJECTIVE	4 PLURAL NOUN
2 ADVERB	5 COMPOUNDS
3 NOUN	

1 ADJECTIVE

When **good** is part of a set combination, eg a good thrashing, in a good temper, a good deal of, good heavens, look up the noun.

a = **pleasant** [trip, holiday, news, mood] bon; [weather, life] beau (belle f); **his ~ nature** son bon caractère; **I've got some ~ news for you** j'ai de bonnes nouvelles pour toi; **have you had a ~ day?** est-ce que tu as passé une bonne journée?; **I've had a ~ life** j'ai eu une belle vie; **we had a ~ time** nous nous sommes bien amusés; **there are ~ times ahead** l'avenir est prometteur; **he's a ~ chap*** c'est un brave or chic type*; **it's too much** or **you can have too much of a ~ thing** c'est presque trop

♦ **it's good to**: **it's ~ to be here** cela fait plaisir d'être ici; **it's ~ to see you looking so well** ça fait plaisir de te voir en si bonne forme; **it's ~ to see you** je suis content de te voir; **it's ~ to talk** ça fait du bien de parler; **it's ~ to be alive** il fait bon vivre; **it's too ~ to be true** c'est trop beau pour être vrai

b = **kind** gentil; **be ~ to him** soyez gentil avec lui; **that's very ~ of you** c'est très gentil de votre part, vous êtes bien gentil; BUT **I tried to find something ~ to say about him** j'ai essayé de trouver quelque chose de bien à dire sur lui; **would you be ~ enough to tell me** auriez-vous l'obligeance de me dire; **perhaps you'd be ~ enough to check your facts before accusing me** vous feriez peut-être mieux de vérifier les faits avant de m'accuser

c = **efficient, competent** bon; **she was a ~ wife and mother** elle a été une bonne épouse et une bonne mère; **I've got a ~ teacher/doctor/lawyer** j'ai un bon professeur/médecin/avocat; **I think I'm as ~ as him** je pense que je suis aussi bon que lui; **40% of candidates are not ~ enough to pass** 40% des candidats ne sont pas assez bons pour être reçus; BUT **he's as ~ a player as his brother** il joue aussi bien que son frère

♦ **good at** (academic subject) bon en; **~ at French** bon en français; **he's ~ at everything** il est bon en tout; **he's ~ at singing** elle chante bien; **she's ~ at putting people at their ease** elle sait mettre les gens à l'aise

♦ **good with**: **good ~ with children/dogs** elle sait s'y prendre avec les enfants/les chiens; **she's ~ with her hands** elle est habile de ses mains

d = **upright, virtuous** **he's a ~ man** c'est un homme bon; **a ~ and holy man** un saint homme; **to live** or **lead a ~ life** mener une vie vertueuse; **he sounds too ~ to be true!** mais c'est une vraie perle!; **to do ~ works** faire de bonnes œuvres; **the 12 ~ men and true** les 12 jurés

e = **respected** **send us a photo of your ~ self** envoyez-nous une photo de vous; (hum) **your ~ lady (wife)** Madame votre épouse; **yes, my ~ man** oui, mon brave

f = **well-behaved** [child, animal] sage; **be ~!** sois sage!; **be a ~ girl!** sois sage!; **Andrew was as ~ as gold** Andrew a été sage comme une image

g = **at ease** **I feel ~** je me sens bien; **I don't feel too ~ about that*** (= ashamed) j'ai un peu honte de moi; **I started to feel ~ about myself** j'ai commencé à me sentir bien dans ma peau*

h = **close** [friend] bon; **he's a ~ friend of mine** c'est un bon ami à moi; **my ~ friend Laura** ma bonne amie Laura

i = **high quality** de qualité; **always use ~ ingredients** utilisez toujours des ingrédients de qualité; **it's made of ~ leather** c'est en cuir de bonne qualité; **it's important to have ~ equipment** il est important d'avoir du matériel de qualité or du bon matériel; BUT **nothing was too ~ for his wife** rien n'était trop beau pour sa femme; **this is my only ~ dress** c'est la seule robe habillée que j'aie

j = **creditable** [result, mark] bon; **200 was a ~ score in those conditions** 200 était un bon résultat dans ces conditions; BUT **he came in a third** il s'est honorablement classé troisième

k = **satisfactory** [reason, excuse] bon, valable; **unless you have a ~ excuse** à moins que vous n'ayez une bonne excuse or une excuse valable; BUT **it's as ~ a way as any other** c'est une façon comme une autre

♦ **good enough**: **that's ~ enough for me** cela me suffit; **that's not ~ enough** ça ne suffit pas; **a refreshment voucher! that's not ~ enough!** un bon pour une boisson! mais vous vous moquez de moi!; **it's just not ~ enough!** (indignantly) c'est lamentable!, c'est inadmissible!; **it is not ~ enough to say parents control what children watch** cela ne suffit pas de dire que les parents doivent surveiller ce que regardent leurs enfants

l = **beneficial** bon (for pour); **milk is ~ for children** le lait est bon pour les enfants; **it's ~ for you** c'est bon pour la santé; **this climate is not ~ for one's health** ce climat est mauvais pour la santé or est insalubre; BUT **the shock was ~ for him** le choc lui a été salutaire; (hum) **all this excitement isn't ~ for me!** toutes ces émotions, ça ne me vaut rien!; (hum) **it's ~ for the soul!** ça forme le caractère!

♦ **what's good for**: **if you know what's ~ for you you'll say yes** si tu as le moindre bon sens tu accepteras; **what's ~ for the consumer isn't necessarily ~ for the economy** ce qui bon pour le consommateur ne l'est pas forcément pour l'économie

♦ **more than is good for**: **they tend to eat and drink more than is ~ for them** ils ont tendance à boire et à manger plus que de raison; **some children know more than is ~ for them** certains enfants en savent plus qu'ils ne le devraient

m = **wholesome, in sound condition** bon; **the water of the well is still ~** l'eau du puits est encore bonne or saine; **their stock of food is still ~** leurs stocks de nourriture sont encore bons; **how ~ is her eyesight?** est-ce qu'elle a une bonne vue?; BUT **his hearing is ~** il entend bien; **to stay ~** [food] (bien) se conserver

n = **attractive** joli, beau (belle f); **she's got a ~ figure** elle a un joli corps, elle est bien faite; **you've got ~ hair** tu as de beaux cheveux; **she's got ~ legs** elle a de jolies jambes; BUT **you have to be of ~ appearance** vous devez bien présenter; **you look ~ in that** ◊ **that looks ~ on you** ça vous va bien; **you look ~!** (= healthy) tu as bonne mine!; (= well-dressed) tu es très bien comme ça!

o **the ~ ship Domino** le Domino

p = **advantageous, favourable** [terms, deal, offer] intéressant; [omen, opportunity] bon; **it would be a ~ thing to ask him** il serait bon de lui demander; BUT **it's a ~ chance to sort things out** c'est l'occasion ou jamais de régler le problème; (Gambling) **I've had a ~ day** la chance était avec moi aujourd'hui; **he's on to a ~ thing*** il a trouvé le filon* or un bon filon*; **this is as ~ a time as any to do it** autant le faire maintenant; **you've never had it so ~!*** la vie n'a jamais été aussi facile

q = **lucky** **it's a ~ thing** or **job I was there** heureusement que j'étais là, c'est une chance que j'aie été là; **that's a ~ thing!** tant mieux!, très bien!

r = **upper-class** **to live at a ~ address** habiter dans un beau quartier; **he's got no money but** he's of ~ **family** il n'a pas d'argent mais il est de bonne famille

|s| **= reliable, valid** [car, tools, machinery] bon ; it's a ~ **little car** c'est une bonne petite voiture ; |BUT| **he is a ~ risk** (financially) c'est un client sûr ; **is his credit ~?** peut-on lui faire crédit

◆ **good for**: **this ticket is ~ for three months** ce billet est valable trois mois ; **he's ~ for another 20 years yet** il en a encore bien pour 20 ans ; **my car is ~ for another few years** ma voiture fera or tiendra bien encore quelques années ; **I'm ~ for another mile or two** je me sens de force à faire quelques kilomètres de plus ; **he is or his credit is ~ for £9,000** on peut lui faire crédit jusqu'à 9 000 livres ; **what or how much is he ~ for?** de combien (d'argent) dispose-t-il ? ; **he's ~ for £500** (= will lend) il nous (or vous etc) prêtera bien 500 livres ; **are you ~ for another beer?** tu reprendras bien une autre bière ? → **5**

|t| **= thorough** **to have a ~ cry** pleurer un bon coup or tout son soûl

Verb + adverb may be used in French, instead of adjective + noun. For combinations other than the following, look up the noun.

give it a ~ **rinse** rincez-le bien or à grande eau ; give it a ~ **stir** mélangez-le bien

|u| **= considerable, not less than** bon, grand ; **a ~ distance** une bonne distance ; **it will take you a ~ hour** il vous faudra une bonne heure ; **we waited a ~ fifteen minutes** nous avons attendu un bon quart d'heure ; **a ~ 8 kilometres** 8 bons kilomètres, 8 kilomètres au moins

|v| **in greetings** **~ afternoon** (early) bonjour ; (later) bonsoir ; (on leaving) bonsoir ; **~ day**† (= goodbye) au revoir ; (= good morning) bonjour ; **~ evening** bonsoir ; **~ morning** bonjour ; **Robert sends (his) ~ wishes** Robert envoie ses amitiés ; (in letter) **with every ~ wish** ◊ **with all ~ wishes** cordialement

|w| **in exclamations** **oh ~,** Tom's just arrived tiens justement, Tom vient d'arriver ; **very ~, sir!** (très) bien monsieur ! ; **~ for YOU!** ◊ **~ on you!** bravo ! ; **(that's) ~!** bien !, excellent ! ; [joke, story] **that's a ~ one!** elle est (bien) bonne celle-là ! ; (iro) à d'autres ! ; **~ one!** (= well done, well said) bravo ! (also iro)

|x| **emphatic use** **we had a ~ long talk** nous avons bien or longuement discuté ; **a ~ long walk** une bonne or une grande promenade ; **they're expecting it to take a ~ long time** ils pensent que ça va prendre un bon bout de temps ; **~ old Charles!** (= bon) vieux Charles ! ; **~ strong shoes** de bonnes chaussures

◆ **good and ...**: **the soup was served ~ and hot** la soupe a été servie bien chaude ; **I'll go when I'm ~ and ready** je partirai quand ça me chante ; **I told him off ~ and proper** je lui ai passé un bon savon, je l'ai bien engueulé

|y| SET STRUCTURES

◆ **as good as** (= practically) pratiquement, pour ainsi dire ; **his career is as ~ as over** sa carrière est pratiquement terminée ; **the matter is as ~ as settled** c'est comme si l'affaire était réglée, l'affaire est pour ainsi dire or pratiquement réglée ; **she as ~ as told me that ...** elle m'a dit à peu de chose près que ..., elle m'a pour ainsi dire déclaré que ... ; |BUT| **it was as ~ as a holiday** c'étaient presque des vacances ; **he as ~ as called me a liar** il n'a pas dit que je mentais mais c'était tout comme, il m'a pratiquement traité comme menteur ; **it's as ~ as saying that ...** autant dire que ... ; **he was as ~ as his word** il a tenu promesse

◆ **as good as new** [thing] comme neuf (neuve f) ; [person] **in a day or so he'll be as ~ as new** dans un jour ou deux il sera complètement rétabli

◆ **to make good** (= succeed) faire son chemin, réussir ; [ex-criminal] s'acheter une conduite ; (= compensate for) [+ deficit] combler ; [+ deficiency, losses] compenser ; [+

expenses] rembourser ; (= put right) [+ injustice, damage] réparer ; **to make ~ an assertion** justifier une affirmation ; **to make ~ one's escape** réussir son évasion ; **to make ~ a loss** to sb dédommager qn d'une perte ; **to make ~ a promise** tenir une promesse ; **they were sure he would make ~ his threat** ils étaient sûrs qu'il mettrait sa menace à exécution

|2| ADVERB

~ = well bien ; **you did ~** tu as bien fait ; (esp US) **how are you? — ~!** comment vas-tu ? bien ! ; **to be in ~ with sb** être dans les petits papiers de qn

|3| NOUN

|a| **= virtue, righteousness** bien m ; **~ and evil may co-exist within one family** le bien et le mal peuvent se côtoyer au sein d'une même famille ; **for ~ or ill** pour le meilleur et or ou pour le pire ; |BUT| **he is a power for ~** il exerce une bonne influence ; **there's some ~ in him** il a de bons côtés

|b| **= good deeds** **to do ~** faire le bien ; **she's up to no ~** elle prépare un mauvais coup

|c| **= advantage, profit** bien m ; **it's for his own ~** c'est pour son bien ; **I did it for your ~** je l'ai fait pour son bien ; **for the ~ of the country** pour le bien du pays ; |BUT| **the common ~** l'intérêt m commun ; **a lot of ~ that's done!** nous voilà bien avancés ! ; **a lot of ~ that's done you!** te voilà bien avancé ! ; **he'll come to no ~** il finira mal

◆ **to do sb good** faire du bien à qn ; **that will do you ~** cela vous fera du bien ; |BUT| **what will that do you?** ça t'avancera à quoi ? ; **a (fat) lot of ~ that will do (you)!** tu seras bien avancé !, ça te fera une belle jambe ! ; **much may it do you!** grand bien t'en fasse ! ; **a lot of ~ that's done him!** le voilà bien avancé ! ; **it does my heart ~ to see him** ça me réjouit de le voir

|d| **= use** **what's the ~?** à quoi bon ? ; **what's the ~ of hurrying?** à quoi bon se presser ? ; **it's not much ~** to me [advice, suggestion] ça ne m'avance pas à grand-chose ; [object, money] ça ne me sert pas à grand-chose ; **if that is any ~ to you** si ça peut t'être utile or te rendre service ; **is he any ~?** [worker/singer etc] est-ce qu'il est bon ?

◆ **no good** (= useless) à rien ; **~ to no ~** ça ne sert à rien ; **it's no ~ saying that** ça ne sert à rien de dire cela, inutile de dire cela ; **it's no ~ worrying** ça ne sert à rien de se faire du souci ; **it's no ~, I'll never get it finished in time** il n'y a rien à faire, je n'arriverai jamais à le finir à temps ; **that's no ~** ça ne va pas ; **that's no ~, it's too thick** ça ne va pas, c'est trop épais ; **that won't be much ~** cela ne servira pas à grand-chose ; **I'm no ~ at maths** je suis mauvais en maths

|e| → **goods**

|f| SET STRUCTURES

◆ **for good** pour de bon ; **he's gone for ~** il est parti pour de bon ; **for ~ and all** une (bonne) fois pour toutes ; |BUT| **to settle down for ~** se fixer définitivement

◆ **to the good**: **we were £50 to the ~** nous avions fait 50 livres de bénéfice ; **that's all to the ~!** tant mieux !, c'est autant de gagné !

|4| **the good** NPL **= people** les bons mpl ; **the ~ and the bad** les bons mpl et les méchants mpl ; |BUT| **the ~ die young** ce sont toujours les meilleurs qui partent les premiers

|5| COMPOUNDS

▶ **the Good Book** N la Bible ▶ **good-for-nothing** ADJ bon or propre à rien ◆ N bon m, bonne f à rien, propre mf à rien ▶ **Good Friday** N Vendredi m saint ▶ **good-hearted** ADJ qui a bon cœur, bon ▶ **good-heartedness** N bonté f ▶ **good-humoured** ADJ [person] de bonne humeur, jovial ; [appearance, smile etc] jovial ; [joke] sans malice ▶ **good-humouredly** ADV avec bonne humeur, avec bonhomie ▶ **good-looker** N (= man) beau gosse m ; (= woman) belle or jolie fille f ; (= horse) beau cheval m ▶ **good-**

looking ADJ beau (belle f), bien inv ▶ **good looks** NPL beauté f ▶ **good-natured** ADJ [person] accommodant, facile à vivre ; [smile, laughter] bon enfant inv ▶ **good-tempered** ADJ [person] qui a bon caractère ; [smile, look] aimable, gentil ▶ **good-time girl** N (pej) fille f qui ne pense qu'à s'amuser or qu'à prendre du bon temps

goodbye [gʊdˈbaɪ] EXCL au revoir ; **to say or bid ~ to sb** dire au revoir à qn, faire ses adieux à qn (frm) ; **~ to all that!** fini tout cela ! ; **you can say ~ to all your hopes** tu peux dire adieu à toutes tes espérances ; **you can ~ to peace and quiet!** tu peux dire adieu à ta tranquillité ! ; **you can kiss it ~!** tu peux faire une croix dessus !

goodie ['gʊdɪ] = **goody**

goodish ['gʊdɪʃ] ADJ assez bon or bien

goodly ['gʊdlɪ] ADJ |a| (= reasonable) [number, supply] considérable ; [portion, amount] gros (grosse f) ; [size] grand ; **to have a ~ share of sth** avoir plus que sa part de qch |b| († or liter = attractive) [appearance] beau (belle f), gracieux

goodness ['gʊdnɪs] N [of person] bonté f ; [of foodstuff] valeur f nutritive ; **out of the ~ of his heart** par pure gentillesse ; **(my) ~!** ◊ **~ gracious!** juste ciel !, bonté divine ! ; **~ (only) knows** Dieu (seul) sait ; **for ~' sake** pour l'amour de Dieu ; **I wish to ~ I had gone there!** si seulement j'y étais allé ! ; **I wish to ~ I had never met him!** si seulement j'avais pu ne jamais le rencontrer !, si seulement je ne l'avais jamais rencontré ! → **surely**, **thank**

goodnight [gʊdˈnaɪt] EXCL bonsoir, bonne nuit ; **to bid sb ~** souhaiter le or dire bonsoir à qn ; **to give sb a ~ kiss** embrasser qn (en lui disant bonne nuit)

goods [gʊdz] |1| NPL |a| (Comm) marchandises fpl, articles mpl ; **leather ~** articles mpl de cuir, maroquinerie f ; **knitted ~** articles mpl en tricot ; **that's just the ~!** c'est exactement ce qu'il (nous or vous etc) faut ! ; **he's just the ~!** c'est exactement l'homme qu'il nous (or vous etc) faut ! ; (US) **to have the ~ on sb** en savoir long sur qn → **consumer**, **deliver** |b| (Jur) biens mpl, meubles mpl ; **all his ~ and chattels** tous ses biens et effets

|2| COMP ▶ **goods service** N (Brit Rail) **to send by fast/slow ~ service** envoyer en grande/petite vitesse ▶ **goods siding** N (Brit Rail) voie f de garage pour wagons de marchandises ▶ **goods station** N (Brit Rail) gare f de marchandises ▶ **goods train** N (Brit Rail) train m de marchandises ▶ **goods wagon** N (Brit Rail) wagon m de marchandises ▶ **goods yard** N (Brit Rail) dépôt m or cour f des marchandises

goodwill [ˌgʊdˈwɪl] N |a| bonne volonté f, bon vouloir m, bienveillance f ; **to gain sb's ~** se faire bien voir de qn ; (Pol) **~ mission or tour** visite f d'amitié |b| (= willingness) zèle m ; **to work with ~** travailler de bon cœur or avec zèle |c| (Comm = customer connections) (biens mpl) incorporels mpl, clientèle f ; (Accounts = intangible assets) survaloir m, goodwill m ; **the ~ goes with the business** les incorporels sont vendus or la clientèle est vendue avec le fonds de commerce

goody ['gʊdɪ] |1| EXCL (also **~ ~**) chic ! , chouette ! |2| N |a| (= person) **the goodies and the baddies** les bons mpl et les méchants mpl |b| **goodies** (= treats) friandises fpl ; (Culin = gifts) petits cadeaux mpl |3| COMP ▶ **goody bag** N sachet m de cadeaux, pochette f de cadeaux promotionnels ▶ **goody two-shoes** N (pej) modèle m de vertu (iro), petit(e) saint(e) m(f)

goody-goody ['gʊdɪˌgʊdɪ] |1| ADJ (pej) **to be ~** [child] être l'image du petit garçon (or de la petite fille) modèle ; [adult] être un vrai petit saint [2] N (pl **goody-goodies**) modèle m de vertu (iro), petit(e) saint(e)* m(f)

gooey* ['guːɪ] ADJ (= sticky) [substance, mess] gluant; [cake, dessert] fondant; (pej = sentimental) [film, story] à l'eau de rose (pej); **to go (all) ~** devenir bêtement sentimental; **women went ~ over him** il faisait fondre toutes les femmes

goof* [guːf] [1] N (= idiot) toqué(e)‡ m(f) [2] VI faire une gaffe, gaffer*
► **goof around*** VI (US) faire l'imbécile
► **goof off*** VI (US) tirer au flanc
► **goof up*** [1] VI (US) faire une gaffe, gaffer* [2] VT SEP gâcher‡

goofball* [1] N [a] (= drug) barbiturique m [b] (US = eccentric person) fantaisiste mf, numéro* m

goofy* ['guːfɪ] ADJ (= mad) maboul‡, toqué‡; (esp US = silly) niais

googly ['guːglɪ] N (Cricket) balle lancée de manière à tromper le batteur sur la direction qu'elle va prendre

gook‡ [guːk] N (US) [a] (= slime etc) substance f visqueuse; (= dirt) crasse f; **what's this ~?** qu'est-ce que c'est que cette saloperie‡? [b] (pej = Asian etc) Asiate mf (pej)

goolies‡ ['guːlɪz] NPL couilles‡ fpl

goon‡ [guːn] N (= fool) idiot(e) m(f), imbécile mf; (US) (= hired thug) homme m de main; (= prison camp guard) garde-chiourme m

gooney bird‡ ['guːnɪˌbɜːd] N (US) albatros m

goop‡ [guːp] N (esp US) substance f visqueuse

goosander [guːˈsændəʳ] N harle m bièvre

goose [guːs] (pl **geese**) [1] N oie f; (fig) **all his geese are swans** il exagère tout le temps, il en rajoute toujours; (fig) **to kill the ~ that lays the golden eggs** tuer la poule aux œufs d'or; **don't be such a ~!**‡† ne sois pas si bébête!‡; **silly little ~!*** petite dinde!‡ → **boo, cook, mother** [2] VT (esp US‡ = prod) donner un petit coup sur les fesses de qn [3] COMP ► **goose bumps** NPL → **goose pimples** ► **goose chase** N → **wild** ► **goose flesh** N = **goose pimples** ► **goose pimples** NPL **to come out in ~ pimples** avoir la chair de poule; **that gives me ~ pimples** cela me donne la chair de poule ► **goose-step** N pas m de l'oie ► **to ~-step along/in** etc avancer/entrer etc au pas de l'oie

gooseberry ['guzbərɪ] N (= fruit) groseille f à maquereau; (also ~ **bush**) groseillier m; (Brit) **to play ~** tenir la chandelle

goosegog‡ ['guzgɒg] N (Brit) = **gooseberry**

GOP [ˌdʒiːəʊˈpiː] N (US) (ABBR = **Grand Old Party**) → **grand**

gopher ['gəʊfəʳ] [1] N [a] (= squirrel) spermophile m; (= rodent) gauphre m, gaufre m [b] **gofer** [c] (Comput) gopher m [2] COMP ► **the Gopher State** N (US) le Minnesota

gorblimey‡ [ɡɔːˈblaɪmɪ] [1] ADJ (accent) populaire [2] EXCL (Brit) nom d'un chien!*

Gordian ['ɡɔːdɪən] N **to cut** or **untie the ~ knot** trancher le nœud gordien

gore[1] [ɡɔːʳ] N (= blood) sang m

gore[2] [ɡɔːʳ] VT (= injure) encorner, blesser d'un coup de corne; **~d to death** tué d'un coup de corne

gore[3] [ɡɔːʳ] [1] N (Sewing) godet m; [of sail] pointe f [2] VT (+ sail) mettre une pointe à; **~d skirt** jupe f à godets

gorge [ɡɔːdʒ] [1] N [a] (Geog) gorge f, défilé m [b] (Anat) gorge f, gosier m; (fig) **it makes my ~ rise** cela me soulève le cœur [2] VT **to ~ o.s.** se gaver (**with** de) [3] VI se gaver (**on** de)

gorgeous ['ɡɔːdʒəs] ADJ [a] (= beautiful) [scenery, sunset, colour, house] superbe, splendide; [weather, day] formidable, superbe; [food, wine] sensationnel; **to look ~** avoir l'air superbe; **to smell ~** sentir délicieusement bon [b] (* = attractive) [person] superbe; [eyes, hair] splendide; **a ~ blonde** une superbe blonde; **a**

~ hunk un mec* superbe; **hi, ~!** (to female) salut, beauté!*; (to male) salut, playboy!* → **drop-dead** [c] (liter = sumptuous) [clothes, fabric, jewellery, building] somptueux

gorgeously ['ɡɔːdʒəslɪ] ADV [embroidered, dressed] superbement, splendidement; **~ coloured** aux couleurs superbes or splendides

Gorgons ['ɡɔːgənz] NPL (Myth) Gorgones fpl

gorilla [ɡəˈrɪlə] N [a] (Zool) gorille m [b] (‡ pej) (= man) brute f; (= thug) gangster m; (= bodyguard) gorille* m

Gorki, Gorky ['ɡɔːkɪ] N Gorki m

gormandize ['ɡɔːməndaɪz] VI (pej) se goinfrer‡, s'empiffrer‡

gormless* ['ɡɔːmlɪs] ADJ (Brit) empoté

gorse [ɡɔːs] N (NonC) ajoncs mpl; **~ bush** ajonc m

gory ['ɡɔːrɪ] ADJ sanglant; (hum) **tell me all the ~ details!*** raconte-moi tous les détails sordides! (hum)

gosh* [ɡɒʃ] EXCL dites donc!, mince alors!*

goshawk ['ɡɒshɔːk] N autour m

gosling ['ɡɒzlɪŋ] N oison m

gospel ['ɡɒspəl] [1] N [a] évangile m; **the Gospel according to St John** l'Évangile selon saint Jean; (fig) **that's ~*** c'est parole d'évangile; (fig) **to take** or **accept sth as ~*** accepter qch comme or prendre qch pour parole d'évangile [b] (= music) gospel m [2] COMP ► **gospel music** N gospel m ► **Gospel oath** N serment m prêté sur l'Évangile ► **gospel song** N gospel m, negro-spiritual m ► **gospel truth** N (fig) **it's the ~ truth*** c'est parole d'évangile, c'est la vérité pure

gossamer ['ɡɒsəməʳ] [1] N (NonC) (= cobweb) fils mpl de la Vierge; (= gauze) gaze f; (= light fabric) tulle m, gaze f [b] (US = waterproof) imperméable m léger [2] ADJ [thread, garment, wings] (= light) arachnéen (liter), léger; **~ thin** très fin, fin comme de la gaze

gossip ['ɡɒsɪp] [1] N [a] (NonC: pej = rumours) commérages mpl (pej), cancans mpl (pej); (in newspaper) échos mpl, potins mpl (pej); **I never listen to ~** je n'écoute jamais les commérages or les cancans; **what's the latest ~?** quels sont les derniers potins?; **a piece of ~** un cancan, un ragot [b] (= chat) **we had a good old ~** on a bien bavardé* [c] (= person) bavard(e) m(f), pipelette f, commère f (pej); **he's a real ~** c'est une vraie commère or une vraie pipelette* [2] VI [a] (= chat) bavarder, papoter [b] (pej: maliciously) cancaner, faire des commérages (**about** sur) [3] COMP ► **gossip column** N (Press) échos mpl ► **gossip columnist, gossip writer** N échotier m, -ière f

gossiping ['ɡɒsɪpɪŋ] [1] ADJ (= chatting) bavard; (pej) cancanier [2] N (idle) bavardage m, papotage m; (pej: malicious) commérage m

gossipy* ['ɡɒsɪpɪ] ADJ [style, book, letter] plein de bavardages; (pej) [person] cancanier (pej)

got [ɡɒt] VB pt, ptp of **get**; → **have**

gotcha‡ ['ɡɒtʃə] EXCL [a] (= I've got you) [a] (= I see) pigé!*; [b] (when catching sb, catching sb out) je te tiens!*; (when hitting, killing sb) je t'ai eu!*

Goth[1] [ɡɒθ] N Goth m

Goth[2], **goth** [ɡɒθ] (esp Brit) [1] N [a] (= person) fan mf de goth [b] (Mus) goth m (mouvement musical des années 80) [c] (= fashion) mode f goth [2] ADJ goth

Gothic ['ɡɒθɪk] [1] ADJ [a] (Archit, Literat, Cine) (genuine) gothique; (in Gothic style) de style gothique [b] (Hist) des Goths [2] N (Archit, Ling etc) gothique m [3] COMP ► **Gothic Revival** N (Archit) néogothique m ► **Gothic script** N (Printing) écriture f gothique

gotta* ['ɡɒtə] MODAL AUX VB (esp US = have got to) **I/he's/they ~ go** je dois/il doit/ils doivent partir

gotten ['ɡɒtn] VB (US) ptp of **get**

gouache [ɡuˈɑːʃ] N gouache f

gouge [ɡaʊdʒ] [1] N gouge f [2] VT [a] (+ wood etc) gouger; **to ~ a hole in sth** creuser un trou dans qch [b] (US* fig = overcharge etc) estamper*, arnaquer
► **gouge out** VT SEP (with gouge) gouger; (with thumb, pencil etc) évider; **to ~ sb's eyes out** arracher les yeux à qn

goulash ['ɡuːlæʃ] N goulache m, goulasch m

gourd [ɡʊəd] N (= fruit) gourde f; (= container) gourde f, calebasse f

gourmand ['ɡʊəmənd] N gourmand(e) m(f), glouton(ne) m(f)

gourmet ['ɡʊəmeɪ] [1] N gourmet m, gastronome mf [2] ADJ [food, restaurant] gastronomique

gout [ɡaʊt] N (Med) goutte f

gouty ['ɡaʊtɪ] ADJ [person, joint, condition] goutteux

gov: [ɡʌv] N ABBR = **governor** b

Gov. N ABBR = **governor** a

govern ['ɡʌvn] [1] VT [a] (= rule) [person, government] gouverner, diriger; [+ country] gouverner, diriger; [+ province, city] administrer; (= direct) [+ household, business, company] diriger, gérer; [+ affairs] administrer, gérer; **she ~ed Britain from 1979 to 1990** elle a gouverné la Grande-Bretagne de 1979 à 1990 [b] (= control) [law, rule, principle] [+ conduct, behaviour, treatment] régir; (Jur) **~ed by the laws of England** régi par le droit anglais; **international guidelines ~ing the export of arms** les directives internationales régissant l'exportation des armes; **there are strict rules ~ing how much lawyers can charge** il existe des règles strictes fixant le montant des honoraires des avocats [c] (= influence) [+ events] déterminer, régir; [+ opinions] guider; [+ speed] déterminer [d] (fig frm) [+ passions, emotions] maîtriser, dominer; **to ~ one's temper** se maîtriser [e] (Gram) régir [2] VI (Pol) gouverner

governance ['ɡʌvənəns] N (frm) (= governing) gouvernement m; (= authority) autorité f

governess ['ɡʌvənɪs] N gouvernante f, institutrice f (à domicile)

governing ['ɡʌvənɪŋ] [1] ADJ [party, coalition] au pouvoir; [council, board] d'administration; [committee] directeur (-trice f) → **self-governing** [2] COMP ► **governing body** N [of sport] comité m directeur; [of professional association] conseil m d'administration; [of school] conseil m d'établissement; [of university] conseil m d'université ► **governing class** N classe f gouvernante ► **governing principle** N principe m directeur

government ['ɡʌvənmənt] [1] N [of country] gouvernement m; [of province, city] administration f; (= Cabinet of ministers) gouvernement m; (= the State: also **central ~**) État m, pouvoirs mpl publics; (= local, municipal, regional) administration f territoriale; (= political régime) régime m politique; **a project financed by the ~** un projet financé par l'État; **a presidential/democratic system of ~** un régime présidentiel/démocratique; **we've had five years of socialist ~** on a eu cinq années de gouvernement or gestion socialiste → **local** [2] COMP [policy, decision, intervention, spending] gouvernemental, du gouvernement; [backing] du gouvernement; [grant] gouvernemental, d'État; [responsibility, loan] de l'État, public (-ique f) ► **Government Accounting Office** N (US) ≈ Cour f des comptes ► **government action** N (gen) action f gouvernementale; (Insurance) fait m du prince ► **government bond** N (Fin) obligation f d'État ► **government corporation** N (US) régie f d'État ► **government department** N département m or service m gouvernemental ► **government expenditure** N dépenses fpl publiques ► **Government House** N (*Brit*) palais *m* or résidence *f* du gouverneur ► **government issue** ADJ [*equipment*] fourni par le gouvernement; [*bonds etc*] émis par le gouvernement ► **government monopoly** N monopole *m* d'État ► **government-owned corporation** N établissement *m* public autonome ► **Government Printing Office** N (*US*) ≈ Imprimerie *f* nationale ► **government securities** NPL (*Fin*) fonds *mpl* or titres *mpl* publics or d'État ► **government stock** N (*Fin*) fonds *mpl* publics or d'État

governmental [ˌgʌvənˈmentl] ADJ gouvernemental, du gouvernement

governor [ˈgʌvənə] N a [*of state, bank*] gouverneur *m*; (*esp Brit*) [*of prison*] directeur *m*, -trice *f*; [*of institution*] administrateur *m*, -trice *f*; (*Brit Scol*) ≈ membre *m* d'un conseil d'établissement (*de lycée ou d'IUT*); ~ **general** gouverneur *m* général b (*Brit**) (= *employer*) patron *m*; (= *father*) paternel* *m*; **thanks ~!** merci chef or patron! c (*Tech*) régulateur *m*; (*Aut, Rail* = *speed control device*) limiteur *m* de vitesse

governorship [ˈgʌvənəʃɪp] N fonctions *fpl* de gouverneur; **during my ~** pendant la durée de mes fonctions (de gouverneur)

govt. ABBR = **government**

gown [gaʊn] 1 N robe *f*; (*Jur, Univ*) toge *f* → **town** 2 VT (*liter*) revêtir (**in** de), habiller (**in** de)

goy [gɔɪ] N (*pl* **goys** or **goyim** [ˈgɔɪm]) goy *mf*

GP [dʒiːˈpiː] N (ABBR = **General Practitioner**) (médecin *m*) généraliste *m*; **he's/she's a GP** il/elle est (médecin) généraliste; **to go to one's GP** aller voir son médecin généraliste or traitant

GPMU [ˌdʒiːpiːemˈjuː] N (*Brit*) (ABBR = **Graphical, Paper and Media Union**) syndicat

GPO [dʒiːpiːˈəʊ] N a (*Brit Govt: formerly*) (ABBR = **General Post Office**) → **general** b (*US*) (ABBR = **Government Printing Office**) → **government**

gr. ABBR = **gross 1e**

grab [græb] 1 N **to make a ~ for** or **at sth** faire un geste or un mouvement vif pour saisir qch; **to be up for ~s*** (= *available*) être disponible; **there are big money prizes up for ~s** il y a de grosses sommes d'argent à gagner b (*esp Brit Tech*) benne *f* preneuse

2 VT a (*lit* = *take hold of*) [+ *object, one's belongings*] saisir; **to ~ sth away from sb** arracher qch à qn, enlever qch à qn d'un geste brusque; **he ~bed the pen from me** il m'a arraché le stylo; **~ hold of this for a minute** tiens ça une minute; **he ~bed (hold of) me** il m'a empoigné; **she ~bed (hold of) him by the arm** elle l'a saisi or empoigné par le bras; (*fig*) **I managed to ~ him before he left** j'ai réussi à lui mettre la main dessus avant qu'il s'en aille b (= *seize unlawfully*) [+ *land, power*] s'emparer de c (* = *snatch*) [+ *quick snack, sandwich*] avaler; [+ *cigarette*] fumer rapidement; [+ *seat*] prendre; **I'll ~ a quick shower** je vais prendre une douche vite fait*; **to ~ a quick nap** piquer un roupillon* d (*fig* = *attract, win*) [+ *sb's attention*] attirer, accaparer; (= *take*) [+ *opportunity*] saisir; **to ~ the headlines** [*person, story*] faire la une; **they're trying to ~ a share of the market** ils essaient de prendre une part de marché; **he ~bed the audience at once** il a tout de suite captivé l'auditoire; **that really ~bed* me** ça m'a vraiment emballé*; **how does that ~ you?*** qu'est-ce que tu en dis?*

3 VI **to ~ at a rope** essayer d'agripper une corde; (*to child*) **don't ~!** doucement!, ne te jette pas dessus!

4 COMP ► **grab bag*** N (*US*) (*lit*) sac *m* (pour

jouer à la pêche miraculeuse); (*fig*) mélange *m* hétéroclite

grabby* [ˈgræbɪ] ADJ (= *greedy*) [*person*] gourmand (*fig*), accapareur

grace [greɪs] 1 N a (*NonC*) [*of person, animal, movement*] grâce *f* b (*Rel*) grâce *f*; **by the ~ of God** par la grâce de Dieu; **there but for the ~ of God go I** cela aurait tout aussi bien pu être moi; **in a state of ~** en état de grâce; **to fall from ~** (*Rel*) perdre la grâce; (*fig hum*) tomber en disgrâce, ne plus avoir la cote*; **to say ~** (*before meals*) dire le bénédicité; (*after meals*) dire les grâces → **year** c (*phrases*) **to be in sb's good/bad ~s** être bien/mal vu de qn, être en faveur/défaveur auprès de qn; **to get into sb's good/bad ~s** se faire bien/mal voir de qn; **to do sth with good/bad ~** faire qch de bonne/mauvaise grâce; **he had the (good) ~ to apologize** il a eu la bonne grâce de s'excuser; **his saving ~** ce qui le rachète (or rachetait *etc*) → **air** d (*NonC* = *respite*) grâce *f*, répit *m*; **a day's ~** un jour de grâce or de répit; (*Comm*) **days of ~** jours *mpl* de grâce; (*Jur*) **as an act of ~, he ...** en exerçant son droit de grâce, il ... e (= *title*) **His Grace (the Archbishop)** Monseigneur l'Archevêque, Son Excellence l'Archevêque; **His Grace (the Duke)** Monsieur le duc; **Her Grace (the Duchess)** Madame la duchesse; **yes, your Grace** oui, Monseigneur (*or* Monsieur le duc *or* Madame la duchesse) f (*Myth*) **the (three) Graces** les trois Grâces *fpl*

2 VT a (= *adorn*) orner, embellir (**with** de) b honorer (**with** de); **the queen ~d the performance with her presence** la reine honora la représentation de sa présence

3 COMP ► **grace-and-favour** N (*Brit*) **~-and-favour residence** résidence attribuée à une personne pour la durée de sa vie par un roi ou un noble; (*fig*) **he has the use of the room on a ~-and-favour basis** il a l'usage de cette pièce (à titre gratuit) ► **grace note** N (*Mus*) (note *f* d')ornement *m* ► **grace period** N (*Jur, Fin*) délai *m* de grâce or de carence

graceful [ˈgreɪsfʊl] ADJ [*movement, animal, person*] gracieux; [*building, apology, retraction, refusal*] élégant

gracefully [ˈgreɪsfəlɪ] ADV [*move*] avec grâce, gracieusement; [*dance, accept, withdraw*] avec grâce; [*retire*] avec dignité; [*apologize*] élégamment, avec grâce; **to admit defeat ~** s'avouer vaincu de bonne grâce; **to grow old ~** vieillir avec grâce

gracefulness [ˈgreɪsfʊlnɪs] N = **grace 1a**

graceless [ˈgreɪslɪs] ADJ [*dance, movement, building*] sans grâce; [*person, refusal*] inélégant, peu courtois

gracious [ˈgreɪʃəs] 1 ADJ a (*frm* = *kindly*) [*person*] bienveillant; [*smile, gesture*] gracieux, bienveillant; (= *courteous*) [*person, smile, gesture*] courtois, affable; [*action*] courtois, plein de bonne grâce; **our ~ Queen** notre gracieuse souveraine; **by the ~ consent of** par la grâce de; **to be ~ to sb** se montrer bienveillant à l'égard de qn b (= *elegant*) [*house, room, gardens*] d'une élégance raffinée; [*era*] fastueux; **~ living** vie de luxe c († = *merciful*) [*God*] miséricordieux; **Lord be ~ unto him** Seigneur, accordez-lui votre miséricorde 2 EXCL (**good** or **goodness**) **~!** juste ciel!, bonté divine!; (**good** or **goodness**) **~ yes!** bien sûr que oui!; (**good** or **goodness**) **~ no!** jamais de la vie!; (**good** or **goodness**) **~ me!** oh, mon Dieu!

graciously [ˈgreɪʃəslɪ] ADV a (*frm* = *courteously*) [*wave, smile*] gracieusement, avec grâce; [*accept, agree*] de bonne grâce; [*consent, allow*] gracieusement; (*frm*) **the king was ~ pleased to accept** le roi eut la bonté d'accepter, le roi accepta gracieusement

b (= *elegantly*) [*live*] avec raffinement c (= *mercifully*) miséricordieusement

graciousness [ˈgreɪʃəsnɪs] N (*NonC*) [*of person*] bienveillance *f* (**towards** envers); [*of house*] élégance *f* raffinée; [*of God*] miséricorde *f*

grad* [græd] N (*US*) ABBR = **graduate 3a**

gradate [grəˈdeɪt] 1 VT graduer 2 VI être gradué

gradation [grəˈdeɪʃən] N gradation *f*

grade [greɪd] 1 N a (*Comm*) [*of goods*] (= *quality*) qualité *f*; (= *size*) calibre *m*; **high-~ meat/fruit** viande *f*/fruits *mpl* de premier choix or de première qualité; **high-~ steel/coal** acier *m*/charbon *m* de haute qualité; **small-/large-~ eggs** œufs *mpl* de petit/gros calibre b (*in hierarchy: in company etc*) échelon *m*; (*Mil* = *rank*) rang *m*; **to go up a ~** monter d'un échelon; **the lowest ~ of skilled worker** la catégorie la plus basse des ouvriers qualifiés; **the highest ~ of clerical post** la catégorie supérieure or la plus élevée des employés de bureau; (*fig*) **to make the ~** se montrer à la hauteur, y arriver; **he'll never make the ~** il n'y arrivera jamais, il ne sera jamais à la hauteur; **salary ~** échelon *m* (salarial); **she's on salary ~ three** elle est à l'indice trois c (= *mark*) note *f*; **~s for effort** *etc* note *f* d'application *etc*; **to get good/poor ~s** avoir de bonnes/mauvaises notes d (*US Scol* = *class*) année *f* → ⌐GRADE⌐ e (= *gradation on scale*) degré *m* f (*Climbing*) degré *m* (de difficulté) g (*US* = *slope*) rampe *f*, pente *f* h (*US* = *ground level*) **at ~** au niveau du sol

2 VT a (= *sort out*) [+ *produce, accommodation, colours, questions*] classer; (*by size*) [+ *apples, eggs etc*] calibrer; **the exercises are ~d according to difficulty** les exercices sont classés selon leur degré de difficulté; (*Comm*) **to ~ sb according to performance/seniority** classer qn en fonction de son rendement/ancienneté b (= *make progressively easier, more difficult, darker, lighter etc*) [+ *work, exercises, colours etc*] graduer → **graded** c (*Scol* = *mark*) [+ *pupil, work*] noter d (*US Agr: also* = **up**) améliorer par sélection e (*US* = *level*) [+ *ground*] niveler

3 COMP ► **grade book** N (*US Scol*) registre *m* or cahier *m* de notes ► **grade crossing** N (*US Rail*) passage *m* à niveau ► **grade inflation** N (*US Educ*) surnotation *f* ► **grade point (average)** N (*US Educ*) (note *f*) moyenne *f* ► **grade school** N (*US*) école *f* primaire ► **grade separation** N (*US Aut*) séparation *f* des niveaux de circulation ► **grade sheet** N (*US Educ*) relevé *m* de notes ► **grade down** VT SEP mettre or placer dans une catégorie inférieure ► **grade up** VT SEP mettre or placer dans une catégorie supérieure → **grade 2d**

⌐GRADE⌐

Aux États-Unis et au Canada, on désigne sous le nom de **grade** *chacune des douze années de la scolarité obligatoire, depuis le cours préparatoire (first* **grade***) jusqu'à la terminale (twelfth* **grade***). On notera les surnoms donnés aux élèves des quatre dernières années: «freshman» (petit nouveau) en 9ᵉ année (la première année du deuxième cycle du secondaire), «sophomore» en 10ᵉ année, «junior» en 11ᵉ et «senior» en terminale.*

---

graded [ˈgreɪdɪd] ADJ [*charges, rates, tax*] (= *increasing*) progressif; (= *decreasing*) dégressif; [*tests, exercises*] classé par degré de difficulté; **a ~ series of transformations** une série progressive de transformations; **~ reader** méthode *f* de lecture progressive

grader ['greɪdə'] N (US Scol) correcteur m; (Constr) niveleuse f

gradient ['greɪdɪənt] N (esp Brit) pente f, inclinaison f; (Math, Phys) gradient m; **a ~ of one in ten** or **10%** une inclinaison or une déclivité de 10%

grading ['greɪdɪŋ] N (gen) classification f; (by size) calibrage m; (Scol etc) notation f

gradual ['grædjʊəl] [1] ADJ [process, progress] graduel; [change, improvement, withdrawal, reduction] graduel, progressif; [decline, recovery, reform] progressif; [slope] doux (douce f) [2] N (Rel) graduel m

gradualism ['grædjʊəlɪzm] N (Pol, Geol etc) gradualisme m

gradually ['grædjʊəlɪ] ADV peu à peu, petit à petit, progressivement

graduate ['grædjʊeɪt] [1] VT [a] (= mark out) [+ thermometer, container] graduer (**in** en) [b] (= make progressively easier, more difficult, darker etc) [+ work, exercises, colours etc] graduer; **to ~ payments** [buyer] payer par fractionnements progressifs (or dégressifs) [c] (US Scol, Univ) conférer un diplôme à [2] VI [a] (Univ) ≈ obtenir sa licence (or son diplôme etc); (US Scol) ≈ obtenir son baccalauréat; **he ~d as an architect/a teacher** etc il a eu son diplôme d'architecte/de professeur etc [b] [colours etc] se changer graduellement; **to ~ to ...** virer progressivement à ... [3] ['grædjʊɪt] N [a] (Univ) ≈ licencié(e) m(f), diplômé(e) m(f) [b] (Pharm) verre m (or bocal m etc) gradué [4] ['grædjʊɪt] ADJ (Univ) [teacher, staff] ≈ diplômé, ≈ licencié; **~ assistant** étudiant(e) m(f) chargé(e) de travaux dirigés, moniteur m, -trice f; **~ course** études fpl de troisième cycle; (US Univ) **Graduate Record Examination** examen d'entrée dans le second cycle; (US) **~ school** troisième cycle m d'université; (US) **~ student** étudiant(e) m(f) de troisième cycle; **~ studies** études fpl de troisième cycle

graduated ['grædjʊeɪtɪd] [1] ADJ [tube, flask] gradué; [tax] progressif; **in ~ stages** par paliers, progressivement [2] COMP ► **graduated pension scheme** N (Brit) ≈ régime m de retraite complémentaire

graduation [,grædjʊ'eɪʃən] [1] N [a] (Univ, also US Scol) (= ceremony) cérémonie f de remise des diplômes; (by student) obtention f du diplôme; **I'm hoping to get a good job after ~** j'espère trouver un bon emploi une fois que j'aurai (obtenu) mon diplôme [b] (on container, instrument) graduation f [2] COMP ► **graduation ceremony** N cérémonie f de remise des diplômes ► **graduation day** N jour m de la remise des diplômes

---

┌─ **GRADUATION** ─┐

La graduation est la cérémonie de remise des diplômes universitaires. C'est un événement important, où les étudiants, revêtus de leur toge et de leur toque noires, reçoivent officiellement leurs diplômes des mains du recteur. Les familles assistent à la cérémonie et les photos prises à cette occasion occupent généralement une place d'honneur dans les intérieurs anglo-saxons.

Aux États-Unis, le terme désigne aussi la cérémonie qui marque la fin des études secondaires.

Graeco- (Brit), **Greco-** (esp US) ['gri:kəʊ-] [1] PREF gréco- [2] COMP ► **Graeco-Roman** ADJ [art, sculpture] gréco-romain ► **Graeco-Roman wrestling** N lutte f gréco-romaine

graffiti [grə'fi:tɪ] N (NonC) graffiti mpl; **~ artist** graffiteur m, -euse f (artiste)

graft [grɑːft] [1] N [a] (Agr) greffe f, greffon m, ente f; (Med) greffe f; **they did a skin ~** ils ont fait une greffe de la peau; **they did a kidney ~ on him** on lui a greffé un rein [b] (NonC: esp US = bribery etc) corruption f [c] (Brit* = work)

dure besogne f; **hard ~*** boulot* m acharné [2] VT [a] (Agr, Med) greffer (**on** sur) [b] (= get by bribery) obtenir par la corruption; (= get by swindling) obtenir par (l')escroquerie [3] VI (= engage in bribery) donner (or recevoir) des pots-de-vin or enveloppes*; (= swindle) faire de l'escroquerie

grafter ['grɑːftə'] N [a] (= swindler etc) escroc m, chevalier m d'industrie (liter) [b] (Brit* = hard worker) bourreau m de travail

graham cracker ['greɪəmkrækə'] N (US) biscuit m à la farine complète

graham flour ['greɪəmflaʊə'] N farine f complète

grail [greɪl] N **the Holy Grail** le Saint Graal

grain [greɪn] [1] N [a] (NonC) céréale(s) f(pl); (US) blé m [b] (= single grain) [of cereal, salt, sand etc] grain m; (fig) [of sense, malice] grain m, brin m; [of truth] ombre f, miette f; **a few ~s of rice** quelques grains de riz; **that's a ~ of comfort** c'est une petite consolation → **salt** [c] (in leather, also Phot) grain m; (in wood, meat) fibre f; (in cloth) fil m; (in stone, marble) veine f; **with the ~** dans le sens de la fibre (or de la veine etc); **against the ~** en travers de la fibre (or de la veine etc); (fig) **it goes against the ~ for him to apologize** cela va à l'encontre de sa nature de s'excuser; **I'll do it, but it goes against the ~** je le ferai, mais ça de bon cœur or mais cela va à l'encontre de mes idées [d] (= weight) mesure de poids (= 0,065 gramme) [2] VT [a] (+ salt etc) grener, grainer; [+ powder] granuler; **finely ~ed** à grain fin; **coarse ~ed** à gros grain [b] (+ leather, paper) greneler; (= paint in imitation of wood) veiner [3] COMP ► **grain alcohol** N alcool m de grain ► **grain elevator** N (US) silo m à céréales

graininess ['greɪnɪnɪs] N (Phot) grain m

grainy ['greɪnɪ] ADJ (Phot) qui a du grain; [substance] granuleux

gram [græm] N gramme m

grammar ['græmə'] [1] N [a] (NonC) grammaire f; **that is bad ~** cela n'est pas grammatical → **generative** [b] (also ~ **book**) (livre m de) grammaire f [2] COMP ► **grammar checker** N correcteur m grammatical ► **grammar school** N (Brit) ≈ lycée m (avec examen d'entrée); (US) ≈ école f primaire → COMPREHENSIVE SCHOOL

grammarian [grə'mεərɪən] N grammairien(ne) m(f)

grammatical [grə'mætɪkəl] ADJ [a] [structure, sentence] grammatical; [rule, error] de grammaire, grammatical [b] (= correct) grammaticalement correct; **he speaks perfectly ~ English** il parle un anglais parfaitement correct du point de vue grammatical

grammaticality [grəmætɪ'kælɪtɪ] N grammaticalité f

grammatically [grə'mætɪkəlɪ] ADV [correct] du point de vue grammatical; **to write ~** écrire des phrases grammaticalement correctes; **to speak ~** s'exprimer correctement d'un point de vue grammatical

grammaticalness [grə'mætɪkəlnɪs] N grammaticalité f

grammatologist [,græmə'tɒlədʒɪst] N grammatologue mf

grammatology [,græmə'tɒlədʒɪ] N grammatologie f

gramme [græm] N (Brit) = **gram**

Grammy ['græmɪ] N (pl **Grammys** or **Grammies**) (US) prix récompensant les meilleurs disques

gramophone ['græməfəʊn] [1] N (esp Brit) phonographe m [2] COMP ► **gramophone needle** N aiguille f de phonographe ► **gramophone record** N disque m

Grampian ['græmpɪən] N **the ~ Mountains** ◊ **the ~s** les (monts mpl) Grampians mpl

gramps* [græmps] N (US) pépé* m, papy* m

grampus ['græmpəs] N (pl **grampuses**) dauphin m de Risso

gran* [græn] N (Brit) mémé* f, mamie* f

Granada [grə'nɑːdə] N Grenade

granary ['grænərɪ] [1] N grenier m (à blé etc) [2] COMP **Granary** ® [bread, loaf, roll] complet (-ète f) (avec grains concassés)

grand [grænd] [1] ADJ [a] (= impressive) [architecture] grandiose; [building, staircase] majestueux; [person] éminent; [job] prestigieux; [occasion, chorus, concert] grand; **to make a ~ entrance** faire une entrée majestueuse; **in the ~ manner** en souverain(e) m(f); **on a ~ scale** à très grande échelle; **to do things on a ~ scale** faire les choses en grand; **to live in ~ style** mener la grande vie; (fig) **to make a ~ gesture** faire un geste grandiose [b] (= ambitious) [scheme, strategy, design] ambitieux [c] (†* = excellent) [person] super* inv; **we had a ~ time** c'était formidable; **it was a ~ game** le match a été magnifique [d] (in names) **the Grand Hotel** le Grand Hôtel [2] N [a] (pl inv:*) (Brit) mille livres fpl; (US) mille dollars mpl [b] (also ~ **piano**) piano m à queue or de concert → **baby** [3] COMP ► **the Grand Canyon** N le Grand Canyon; **the Grand Canyon State** l'Arizona m ► **grand duchy** N grand-duché m ► **grand duke** N grand-duc m ► **grand finale** N grande finale f ► **grand jury** N (in US) jury m d'accusation ► **grand larceny** N (US Jur) vol m qualifié ► **grand master** N (Chess) grand maître m ► **the Grand National** N (Brit Racing) le Grand National ► **grand old man** N (pl **grand old men**) **the ~ old man of English politics** le grand monsieur de la politique anglaise ► **the Grand Old Party** N (US) le parti républicain ► **grand opening** N grande inauguration f ► **grand opera** N grand opéra m ► **grand piano** N piano m à queue or de concert ► **grand slam** N (Bridge, Sport) grand chelem m ► **grand staircase** N escalier m d'honneur ► **grand total** N (gen) somme f globale; (Math) résultat m final; (fig) **we get to the ~ total of ...** nous arrivons au chiffre impressionnant de ... ► **the Grand Tour** N (Hist) le tour d'Europe; **we did a** or **the ~ tour of the Louvre** nous avons fait le tour complet or une visite complète du Louvre ► **Grand Unified Theory** N (Phys) théorie f de la grande unification ► **grand vizier** N grand vizier m

---

┌─ **GRAND JURY** ─┐

Dans le système judiciaire américain, le grand jury est le jury d'accusation, qui décide si une personne devra comparaître devant le jury de jugement («trial jury» ou «petit jury»), qui statuera sur son éventuelle culpabilité.

Composé de 12 à 23 personnes, le grand jury se réunit à huis clos; il a le droit de citer des témoins à comparaître.

---

grandchild ['græntʃaɪld] [1] N petit(e)-enfant m(f), petit-fils m, petite-fille f [2] **grandchildren** NPL petits-enfants mpl

grand(d)ad* ['grændæd], **grand(d)addy*** (US) ['grændædɪ] N grand-papa* m, pépé* m, papi* m, bon-papa* m

granddaughter ['grændɔːtə'] N petite-fille f

grandee [græn'diː] N (in Spain) grand m d'Espagne; (fig) grand personnage m

grandeur ['grændjə'] N [of person] grandeur f; [of scenery, house] splendeur f, magnificence f; [of character, style] noblesse f; [of position] éminence f; **an air of ~** une allure grandiose

grandfather ['grænfɑːðər] **1** N grand-père m **2** COMP ► **grandfather clause** N (US fig: in law) clause f d'antériorité ► **grandfather clock** N (horloge f) comtoise f, horloge f de parquet

grandiloquence [græn'dɪləkwəns] N grandiloquence f

grandiloquent [græn'dɪləkwənt] ADJ (frm) grandiloquent

grandiloquently [græn'dɪləkwəntlɪ] ADV (frm) avec grandiloquence

grandiose ['grændɪəʊz] ADJ grandiose; [style] grandiloquent, pompeux

grandly ['grændlɪ] ADV **a** (= impressively) [stand] majestueusement; **to live** ~ mener grand train; ~ **decorated** au décor majestueux **b** (= pompously) [announce] solennellement; [speak, say, call] pompeusement; [behave] avec majesté

grand mal ['grɑːnmæl] N (= illness) épilepsie f (essentielle); (= seizure) crise f (d'épilepsie) convulsive

grand(ma)ma* ['grænd(mə)mɑː] N grandmaman* f, mémé* f, mamie* f, bonnemaman* f

grandmother ['grænmʌðər] N grand-mère f

grand(pa)pa ['græn(pə)pɑː] N = **grand(d)ad**

grandparent ['grændpɛərənt] **1** N (= grandfather) grand-père m; (= grandmother) grandmère f **2** **grandparents** NPL grands-parents mpl

Grand Prix [grɒn'priː] N (Motor Racing) Grand Prix m; **the French/Monaco** etc ~ le Grand Prix de France/de Monaco etc

grandson ['grænsʌn] N petit-fils m

grandstand ['grændstænd] **1** N (Sport) tribune f; (fig) **to have a ~ view** être aux premières loges (fig) (**of sth** pour voir qch) **2** VI (US* fig) jouer pour la galerie; (US fig) ~ **play*** amusement m pour la galerie

grange [greɪndʒ] N **a** (esp Brit = country house) château m, manoir m **b** (US = farm) ferme f; (US Hist) **the Grange** la Fédération agricole **c** = **granary 1**

granger ['greɪndʒər] N (US) fermier m

granite ['grænɪt] **1** N granit m **2** COMP de granit ► **the Granite City** N (Brit) Aberdeen ► **the Granite State** N (US) le New Hampshire

grannie, granny ['grænɪ] **1** N* mamie f, grand-maman f **2** COMP ► **granny bond*** N ≈ bon m du Trésor indexé ► **granny flat*** N petit appartement m indépendant (en annexe) ► **granny glasses*** NPL petites lunettes fpl cerclées de métal ► **granny knot** N nœud m de vache ► **Granny Smith (apple)** N granny smith f inv ► **granny specs*** NPL = **granny glasses**

granola [grə'nəʊlə] N (US) muesli m (aux céréales légèrement caramélisées)

grant [grɑːnt] **1** VT **a** (= accord) [+ favour, permission, wish] accorder; [+ prayer] exaucer; [+ request] accéder à, faire droit à; [+ pension] accorder, allouer; **to ~ sb permission to do sth** accorder à qn l'autorisation de faire qch; **to ~ sb his request** accéder à la requête de qn; **they were ~ed an extension of three weeks** on leur a accordé un délai de trois semaines; **to ~ sb political asylum** accorder l'asile politique à qn; **I beg your pardon!** — ~**ed!** je vous demande pardon! — je vous en prie!; **God ~ that ...** plaise à Dieu que ... (+ subj) **b** (= admit) admettre, concéder; **to ~ a proposition** admettre la vérité d'une proposition; **it must be ~ed that ...** il faut admettre or reconnaître que ...; **I ~ you that** je vous l'accorde; **I ~ that he is honest** je vous accorde qu'il est honnête → **granted c** **to take sb/sth for ~ed**: he takes her for ~ed il la considère comme faisant partie du

décor; **stop taking me for ~ed!** j'existe moi aussi!, tu pourrais avoir quelques égards pour moi!; **to take details/sb's agreement** etc for ~ed considérer les détails/l'accord de qn etc comme allant de soi; **we may take it for ~ed that he will come** nous ne pouvons tenir pour certain et nous pouvons compter qu'il viendra; **he takes it for ~ed that ...** il trouve tout naturel que ... (+ subj); **you take too much for ~ed** (= take too many liberties) vous vous croyez tout permis, vous prenez trop de libertés; (= assume things are further forward than they are) si vous croyez que c'est facile ...

2 N **a** (NonC) [of favour, permission] octroi m; [of land] concession f; (Jur) [of property] cession f; [of money, pension] allocation f; (Jur) ~ **of a patent** délivrance f d'un brevet **b** (= sum given) subvention f, allocation f; (Brit = scholarship) bourse f; **they have a government ~ to aid research** ils ont une subvention gouvernementale d'aide à la recherche; **to be on a ~** [student] avoir une bourse; **he's on a ~ of £900** il a une bourse de 900 livres → **improvement**

3 COMP ► **grant-aided** ADJ subventionné par l'État ► **grant-in-aid** N (pl grants-in-aid) subvention f de l'État ► **grant-maintained school** N (Brit) établissement scolaire financé par l'État plutôt que par une collectivité locale

granted ['grɑːntɪd] **1** CONJ ~ **that this is true** en admettant que ce soit vrai **2** ADV ~, **he doesn't look too bad for his age** c'est vrai, il n'est pas mal pour son âge **3** EXCL soit!, d'accord!

grantee [grɑːn'tiː] N (Jur: gen) bénéficiaire mf; [of patent] impétrant m

granular ['grænjʊlər] ADJ granuleux

granulate ['grænjʊleɪt] **1** VT [+ metal, powder] granuler; [+ salt, sugar, soil] grener, grainer; [+ surface] rendre grenu **2** COMP ► **granulated paper** N papier m grenelé ► **granulated sugar** N sucre m semoule ► **granulated surface** N surface f grenue

granule ['grænjuːl] N granule m

grape [greɪp] **1** N (grain m de) raisin m; ~**s** raisin m (NonC), raisins mpl; **to harvest the** ~**s** vendanger, faire la (or les) vendange(s) → **bunch, sour 2** COMP ► **grape harvest** N vendange f ► **grape hyacinth** N muscari m ► **grape juice** N jus m de raisin

grapefruit ['greɪpfruːt] N (pl **grapefruit** or **grapefruits**) pamplemousse m

grapeshot ['greɪpʃɒt] N mitraille f

grapevine ['greɪpvaɪn] N **a** (lit) vigne f **b** (fig) **I hear on** or **through the ~ that ...** j'ai appris par le téléphone arabe or par mes services de renseignement que ...

graph [grɑːf] **1** N (gen) graphique m; (Ling) graphe m **2** VT tracer le graphique or la courbe de **3** COMP ► **graph paper** N papier m quadrillé; (in millimetres) papier m millimétré ► **graph plotter** N table f traçante

grapheme ['græfiːm] N graphème m

graphic ['græfɪk] **1** ADJ **a** (= vivid) [account, description] imagé; **to describe sth in ~ detail** faire une description très crue de (Art, Math) graphique **2** COMP ► **graphic artist** N graphiste mf ► **the graphic arts** NPL les arts mpl graphiques ► **graphic design** N graphisme m ► **graphic designer** N maquettiste mf, graphiste mf ► **graphic display** N (Comput) visualisation f graphique ► **graphic equalizer** N égaliseur m graphique ► **graphic novel** N roman m illustré

graphical ['græfɪkəl] **1** ADJ (gen, also Math) graphique **2** COMP ► **graphical display unit** N (Comput) visuel m graphique ► **graphical user interface** N (Comput) interface f graphique, interface f GUI

graphically ['græfɪkəlɪ] ADV [describe, explain] de manière très réaliste; [illustrate, demon-

strate, display] très clairement; **to be ~ clear** être tout à fait évident

graphics ['græfɪks] **1** N **a** (NonC) (= art of drawing) art m graphique; (Math etc = use of graphs) (utilisation f des) graphiques mpl; (Comput) traitement m graphique, graphiques mpl **b** (pl = sketches) représentations fpl graphiques, graphisme m; (TV etc) ► **by** ... art m graphique (de) ... → **computer 2** COMP ► **graphics card** N (Comput) carte f graphique

graphite ['græfaɪt] N graphite m, mine f de plomb

graphologist [græ'fɒlədʒɪst] N graphologue mf

graphology [græ'fɒlədʒɪ] N graphologie f

grapnel ['græpnəl] N grappin m

grapple ['græpl] **1** N (Tech: also **grappling hook** or **iron**) grappin m **2** VT (Tech) saisir avec un grappin or au grappin **3** VI **to ~ with** [+ person] lutter avec; [+ problem, task, book, subject] se colleter avec, se débattre avec

grasp [grɑːsp] **1** VT **a** (= seize) [+ object] saisir, empoigner; **to ~ sb's hand** saisir or empoigner la main de qn → **nettle b** (fig) [+ power] s'emparer de; [+ opportunity] saisir **c** (= understand) saisir, comprendre **2** N **a** (= hold) prise f; (stronger) poigne f; **a strong ~** une forte poigne; (lit) **to lose one's ~** lâcher prise; (lit) **to lose one's ~ on** or **of sth** lâcher qch; (fig) ne plus être au fait de qch; (fig) **to let sth/sb slip out of** or **from one's ~** laisser échapper qch/qn; **to have sb/sth in one's ~** (= have power over) avoir or tenir qn/ qch sous son emprise; (lit, fig) **to have sth within one's ~** avoir qch à portée de la main; **peace is now within our ~** la paix est à présent à notre portée **b** (= understanding) compréhension f; **he has a good ~ of basic mathematics** il a de bonnes bases en mathématiques; **he has no ~ of our difficulties** il ne se rend pas compte de nos difficultés, il ne saisit pas la nature de nos difficultés; **it is beyond my ~** je n'y comprends rien, cela me dépasse; **this subject is within everyone's ~** ce sujet est à la portée de tout le monde

► **grasp at** VT FUS **a** (lit) essayer d'agripper **b** (fig) [+ hope] chercher à se raccrocher à; [+ opportunity] chercher à saisir → **straw**

grasping ['grɑːspɪŋ] ADJ [arm, hand] crochu; (fig) cupide, avide

grass [grɑːs] **1** N **a** (NonC) herbe f; (= lawn) gazon m, pelouse f; (= grazing) herbage m, pâturage m; **"keep off the ~"** «défense de marcher sur la pelouse »; **at** ~ au vert; (Agr) **to put under ~** enherber, mettre en pré; **to put out to ~** [+ horse] mettre au vert; (fig) [+ person] mettre sur la touche; (Tennis) **to play on ~** jouer sur herbe or sur gazon; **to let the ~ grow under one's feet** laisser traîner les choses, laisser passer son temps; **he can hear the ~ growing*** rien ne lui échappe; **the ~ is (always) greener on the other side of the fence** ailleurs, l'herbe est toujours plus verte → **blade, green b** (Bot) ~**es** graminées fpl **c** (‡ = marijuana) herbe* f **d** ‡ (= telltale) balance‡ f, mouchard* m; (= informer) indic* m **2** VT (also ~ **over**) [+ garden, square] gazonner; [+ field, land] couvrir d'herbe, enherber **3** VI‡ moucharder*; **to ~ on sb** donner* or vendre* qn **4** COMP ► **grass court** N (Tennis) court m (en gazon); **to play on a ~ court** jouer sur herbe or sur gazon ► **grass cutter** N (grosse) tondeuse f à gazon ► **grass green** N vert m pré ► **the grass roots** NPL (esp Pol fig) [of movement, party] la base; (Pol) ~**-roots**

candidate/movement *etc* candidat *m*/ mouvement *m etc* populaire ▶ **grass skirt** N pagne *m* végétal (*des Hawaïennes*) ▶ **grass snake** N couleuvre *f* ▶ **grass widow** N (*esp US*) (*divorced*) divorcée *f*; (*separated*) femme *f* séparée (de son mari); (*Brit fig*) **I'm a ~ widow this week*** cette semaine je suis célibataire *f* (*hum*) or sans mari ▶ **grass widower** N (*esp US*) (*divorced*) divorcé *m*; (*separated*) homme *m* séparé (de sa femme)

grasshopper ['grɑːʃɒpəʳ] N sauterelle *f*

grassland ['grɑːslænd] N (*NonC*) prairie *f*, herbages *mpl*

grassy ['grɑːsɪ] ADJ a [*land*] herbeux, herbu b [*wine, flavour*] herbacé

grate¹ [greɪt] N (= *metal framework*) grille *f* de foyer; (= *fireplace*) âtre *m*, foyer *m*; **a fire in the ~** un feu dans l'âtre

grate² [greɪt] 1 VT a (*Culin*) [+ *cheese, carrot etc*] râper b (= *make noise with*) [+ *metallic object*] faire grincer; [+ *chalk*] faire grincer or crisser 2 VI [*metal*] grincer; [*chalk*] grincer, crisser (**on** sur); **to ~ on the ears** écorcher les oreilles; **it ~d on his nerves** cela lui tapait sur les nerfs* or le système*; **his constant chatter ~d on me** son bavardage incessant me tapait sur les nerfs* or m'agaçait

▼ **grateful** ['greɪtfʊl] ADJ [*person*] reconnaissant (**to** à, **for** de); [*smile*] de reconnaissance; **I am ~ for your support** je vous suis reconnaissant de votre soutien; **I should be ~ if you would come** je serais très heureux si vous pouviez venir; **he sent me a very ~ letter** il m'a envoyé une lettre exprimant sa vive reconnaissance; **with ~ thanks** avec mes (*or nos etc*) plus sincères remerciements; (*in letter*) **I would be ~ if you could send me ...** je vous saurais gré de bien vouloir m'envoyer ...; **he was ~ that she had told him the truth** il était heureux qu'elle lui ait dit la vérité

gratefully ['greɪtfəlɪ] ADV avec gratitude; **all donations ~ received** tous les dons seront les bienvenus

grater ['greɪtəʳ] N râpe *f*; **cheese ~** râpe *f* à fromage

gratification [ˌɡrætɪfɪˈkeɪʃən] N (= *pleasure*) satisfaction *f*, plaisir *m*; (= *fulfilment*) [*of desires etc*] assouvissement *m*; **to his ~ he learnt that ...** à sa grande satisfaction il apprit que ...; **sensual ~** le plaisir sensuel; **sexual ~** la satisfaction sexuelle, le plaisir sexuel

gratify ['grætɪfaɪ] VT (= *please*) [+ *person*] faire plaisir à, être agréable à; (= *fulfil*) [+ *desire etc*] satisfaire, assouvir; [+ *whim*] satisfaire; **I was gratified to hear that ...** cela m'a fait plaisir d'apprendre que ...

gratifying ['grætɪfaɪɪŋ] ADJ (= *pleasing*) agréable, plaisant; (= *flattering*) [*attentions*] flatteur; **it is ~ to learn that ...** il est très agréable d'apprendre que ..., j'ai (*or nous avons*) appris avec plaisir que ...

grating¹ ['greɪtɪŋ] N grille *f*

grating² ['greɪtɪŋ] 1 ADJ [*voice, sound*] grinçant 2 N (*NonC* = *sound*) grincement *m*

gratis ['grætɪs] 1 ADV gratuitement 2 ADJ gratuit

▼ **gratitude** ['grætɪtjuːd] N reconnaissance *f*, gratitude *f* (**towards** envers, **for** de)

gratuitous [grəˈtjuːɪtəs] ADJ gratuit

gratuitously [grəˈtjuːɪtəslɪ] ADV **~ violent/ nasty/cruel** d'une violence/méchanceté/ cruauté gratuite; **~ offensive** qui cherche à choquer sans justification

gratuity [grəˈtjuːɪtɪ] N a (*Brit Mil*) prime *f* de démobilisation b (= *tip*) pourboire *m*, gratification *f* c (*to a retiring employee*) prime *f* de départ

gravamen [grəˈveɪmen] N (*pl* **gravamina** [grəˈvæmɪnə]) (*Jur*) ≈ principal chef *m* d'accusation

grave¹ [greɪv] N tombe *f*; (*more elaborate*) tombeau *m*; **from beyond the ~** d'outre-tombe; **he'll come to an early ~** il aura une fin prématurée; **he sent her to an early ~** il est responsable de sa mort prématurée; (*hum*) **you'll send me to an early ~!** tu veux ma mort?; **someone is walking over my ~*** j'ai eu un frisson; **Mozart must be turning in his ~*** Mozart doit se retourner dans sa tombe* → **dig, foot, silent**

grave² [greɪv] ADJ (= *serious, solemn*) grave; **to have ~ doubts about sth** douter sérieusement de qch

grave³ [grɑːv] ADJ (*Typ*) [*accent*] grave

gravedigger ['greɪvdɪɡəʳ] N fossoyeur *m*

gravel ['grævəl] 1 N a (*NonC*) gravier *m*; (*finer*) gravillon *m* b (*Med*) lithiase *f* 2 VT couvrir de gravier 3 COMP ▶ **gravel path** allée *f* de gravier ▶ **gravel pit** N carrière *f* de cailloux

gravelly ['grævəlɪ] ADJ a (= *stony*) [*road, soil, riverbed*] graveleux b (*fig* = *rough*) [*voice*] râpeux

gravely ['greɪvlɪ] ADV a (= *solemnly*) [*say, ask, nod*] gravement b (= *badly, extremely*) **~ ill** gravement malade; **~ wounded** grièvement blessé; **~ displeased** extrêmement mécontent; **~ concerned** extrêmement or profondément inquiet

graven †† ['greɪvən] ADJ taillé, sculpté; (*Rel etc*) **~ image** image *f* (gravée); (*fig*) **~ on his memory** gravé dans sa mémoire

graveness ['greɪvnɪs] N (*NonC: all senses*) gravité *f*

graverobber ['greɪvrɒbəʳ] N déterreur *m* de cadavres

graveside ['greɪvsaɪd] N **at the ~** (= *beside the grave*) près de la tombe; (= *at the burial ceremony*) à l'enterrement

gravestone ['greɪvstəʊn] N pierre *f* tombale

graveyard ['greɪvjɑːd] N cimetière *m*; (*fig*) **the ~ of so many political careers** la ruine de tant de carrières politiques; (*fig*) **a ~ cough** une toux caverneuse or qui sent le sapin*; (*US fig hum*) **~ shift*** le poste or l'équipe *f* de nuit

gravid ['grævɪd] ADJ (*frm*) gravide

graving dock ['greɪvɪŋdɒk] N (*Naut*) bassin *m* de radoub

gravitas ['grævɪtæs] N [*of person*] gravité *f*

gravitate ['grævɪteɪt] VI a (*Phys*) graviter (**round** autour de); **to ~ to the bottom** se déposer or descendre au fond (*par gravitation*) b (*fig*) graviter (**round** autour de), être attiré (**towards** par)

gravitation [ˌɡrævɪˈteɪʃən] N (*Phys, fig*) gravitation *f* (**round** autour de, **towards** vers)

gravitational [ˌɡrævɪˈteɪʃənl] 1 ADJ gravitationnel; **~ constant/field/force** constante *f*/ champ *m*/force *f* de gravitation 2 COMP ▶ **gravitational pull** N gravitation *f*

gravity ['grævɪtɪ] N a (*NonC*) (*Phys*) pesanteur *f*; **~ feed** alimentation *f* par gravité → **centre, law, specific** b (= *seriousness*) gravité *f*, sérieux *m*; **to lose one's ~** perdre son sérieux

gravy ['greɪvɪ] 1 N a (*Culin*) sauce *f* au jus de viande b (*US**) (= *easy money*) profit *m* facile, bénéf* *m*; (= *dishonest money*) argent *m* mal acquis 2 COMP ▶ **gravy boat** N saucière *f* ▶ **gravy train*** N (*fig*) **to be on** or **ride the ~ train** avoir trouvé le bon filon*; **to get on the ~ train** trouver une bonne planque*

gray [greɪ] (*esp US*) = **grey**

grayish ['greɪɪʃ] ADJ (*esp US*) = **greyish**

grayling ['greɪlɪŋ] N (*pl* **grayling** or **graylings**) (= *fish*) ombre *m* (de rivière)

graze¹ [greɪz] 1 VI brouter, paître 2 VT a [*cattle*] [+ *grass*] brouter, paître; [+ *field*] pâturer (dans) b [*farmer*] [+ *cattle*] paître, faire paître

graze² [greɪz] 1 VT a (= *touch lightly*) frôler, raser, effleurer; **it only ~d him** cela n'a fait

que l'effleurer; (*Naut*) **to ~ bottom** labourer le fond b (= *scrape*) [+ *skin, hand etc*] érafler, écorcher; **to ~ one's knees** s'écorcher les genoux; **the bullet ~d his arm** la balle lui a éraflé le bras 2 N écorchure *f*, éraflure *f*

grazing ['greɪzɪŋ] N (*NonC: also* **~ land**) pâturage *m*; (= *act*) pâture *f*

GRE [ˌdʒiːɑːˈriː] N (*US Univ*) (ABBR = **Graduate Record Examination**) → **graduate**

grease [griːs] 1 N (*gen, also Culin*) graisse *f*; (*Aut, Tech*) lubrifiant *m*, graisse *f*; (= *dirt*) crasse *f*, saleté *f*; **to remove the ~ from sth** dégraisser qch; **his hair is thick with ~** il a les cheveux très gras 2 VT graisser; (*Aut, Tech*) lubrifier, graisser; **like ~d lightning*** en quatrième vitesse*, à toute pompe*; (*US*) **to move like a ~d pig*** filer comme un zèbre* → **palm¹, wheel** 3 COMP ▶ **grease gun** N (pistolet *m*) graisseur *m* ▶ **grease monkey*** N mécano* *m* ▶ **grease nipple** N (*Aut*) graisseur *m* ▶ **grease remover** N dégraisseur *m* ▶ **grease-stained** ADJ graisseux

greasepaint ['griːspeɪnt] N fard *m* gras; **stick of ~** crayon *m* gras

greaseproof paper ['griːsˌpruːfˈpeɪpəʳ] N papier *m* sulfurisé

greaser* ['griːsəʳ] N a (= *mechanic*) mécano* *m* b (= *motorcyclist*) motard* *m* c (*pej* = *ingratiating person*) lèche-bottes* *m* d (*US pej* = *Latin American*) Latino-Américain *m*, ≈ métèque* *m*

greasiness ['griːsɪnɪs] N aspect *m* or état *m* graisseux; (= *slipperiness*) [*of road*] surface *f* grasse or glissante

greasy ['griːsɪ] 1 ADJ a (= *oily*) [*hair, skin, ointment, food, surface*] gras (grasse *f*); [*overalls, tools*] graisseux; **~ hands** mains *fpl* pleines de graisse, mains *fpl* graisseuses; **the road (surface) was ~** la chaussée était grasse b (*pej* = *smarmy*) obséquieux 2 COMP ▶ **greasy pole** N (*lit*) mât *m* de cocagne; (*Brit fig*) **to climb (up) the ~ pole** progresser au prix de grands efforts ▶ **greasy spoon*** N (*pej*) gargote* *f* (*pej*)

great [greɪt] 1 ADJ a (= *large*) [*building, tree, cloud*] grand; **A or B, whichever is the ~er** choisir entre A et B le chiffre ayant la valeur la plus élevée

b (= *considerable*) [*effort, success*] grand; **a player of ~ ability** un joueur très doué; **to live to a ~ age** parvenir à un âge avancé; **he did not live to a ~ age** il n'a pas vécu très vieux; **despite his ~ age, he ...** malgré son grand âge, il ...; **with ~ care** avec grand soin, avec beaucoup de soin; **a ~ deal** beaucoup; **a ~ deal of sth** beaucoup or énormément de qch; **to study sth in ~ depth** étudier qch à fond; **with ~ difficulty** avec de grandes difficultés; **to a ~ extent** dans une large mesure; **she has a ~ eye for detail** elle a vraiment le coup d'œil pour les détails; **I have a ~ hatred of ...** j'éprouve une violente haine pour ...; **to be a ~ help** être d'une grande aide; **to take a ~ interest in sb/sth** s'intéresser énormément à qn/qch; **a ~ many** un grand nombre; **a ~ many people** un grand nombre de gens; **a ~ many of us** beaucoup d'entre nous; **there is a ~ need for improvement** des améliorations s'imposent; **I have no ~ opinion of ...** je n'ai pas une haute opinion de ...; **at a ~ pace** à vive allure; **are you in ~ pain?** avez-vous très mal?; **a ~ sense of team spirit** un esprit d'équipe remarquable; **it was all a ~ shock** tout cela fut un choc terrible; **a ~ variety of opinions** des avis très variés; **she has ~ willpower** elle a une forte volonté

c (= *important*) [*achievement, event, issue, city, country*] grand; **America can be ~ again** l'Amérique peut retrouver sa grandeur

d (= *eminent*) [*scientist, footballer etc*] éminent; **a ~ man** un grand homme; **he has a ~ future** il a un bel or grand avenir (devant lui);

the ~ **masters** les grands maîtres; **the ~est names in football/poetry** etc les plus grands noms du football/de la poésie etc

e (* = excellent) [person, place] super* inv; [holiday, idea] sensationnel*, génial*; **you were ~!** tu as été sensationnel!*; **he's the ~est!** il est formidable!; (lit, iro) **that's ~!** c'est super!*; **I feel ~** je me sens en pleine forme; **my wife isn't feeling so ~** ma femme ne se sent pas trop bien; **this cook book is ~ for desserts** ce livre de cuisine est excellent pour les desserts; **you look ~** (= healthy) tu as vraiment bonne mine; (= attractive) tu es superbe; **we had a ~ time** c'était merveilleux; **it was ~ fun** c'était très amusant; **wouldn't it be ~ to live here?** ça ne serait pas merveilleux de vivre ici? → **gun, shake**

f (= enthusiastic) **he's a ~ angler** il est passionné de pêche; **he's a ~ arguer** il est toujours prêt à discuter; **he was a ~ friend of Huxley** c'était un grand ami de Huxley; **they are ~ friends** ce sont de grands amis; **he's a ~ one for cathedrals*** il adore visiter les cathédrales; **he's a ~ one for criticizing others*** il ne rate pas une occasion de critiquer les autres; **he was a ~ womaniser** c'était un grand coureur de jupons; (US) **he's ~ on jazz*** il est mordu* de jazz

g (* = expert) **he's a ~ teacher** c'est un excellent professeur; **he's ~ at football/maths** il est doué pour le football/les maths; **he's ~ on baroque music** il est incollable* en musique baroque

h (in exclamations) **Great Scott** or **Heavens!**† grands dieux!

i (in titles) **Alexander the Great** Alexandre le Grand; **Catherine the Great** Catherine II la Grande

j (= pregnant) **to be ~ with child**†† être enceinte

2 ADV* a (= excellently) super bien*; **she's doing ~** elle s'en tire super bien*; **we get on ~** nous nous entendons super bien*; **everything's going ~** [life] tout va super bien*; [activity, business] tout marche comme sur des roulettes*

b **~ big** [object, animal, kiss] énorme; **a ~ big Italian wedding** un mariage italien en grand

3 EXCL* (= brilliant) super*, génial*; **oh ~, just what I need!** super*, j'avais vraiment besoin de ça!

4 N (Oxford Univ) **Greats** ≈ licence f de lettres classiques

5 **the great** NPL les grands mpl

6 COMP ► **great ape** N grand singe m, anthropoïde m ► **great auk** N (Zool) grand pingouin m ► **great-aunt** N grand-tante f ► **the Great Australian Bight** N la Grande Baie Australienne ► **the Great Barrier Reef** N la Grande Barrière de corail ► **the Great Bear** N (Astron) la Grande Ourse ► **Great Britain** N la Grande-Bretagne → GREAT BRITAIN ► **Great Dane** N (= dog) danois m ► **the Great Dividing Range** N la cordillère australienne ► **Greater London** N (in Brit) le grand Londres ► **Greater Manchester** N (in Brit) l'agglomération f de Manchester ► **greatest common divisor, greatest common factor** N (Math) plus grand commun diviseur m ► **great-grandchild** N (pl **great-grandchildren**) arrière-petit-fils m, arrière-petite-fille f; **my ~grandchildren** mes arrière-petits-enfants mpl ► **great-granddaughter** N arrière-petite-fille f ► **great-grandfather** N arrière-grand-père m, bisaïeul m (liter) ► **great-grandmother** N arrière-grand-mère f, bisaïeule f (liter) ► **great-grandparent** N (= grandfather) arrière-grand-père m; (= grandmother) arrière-grand-mère f; **~ grandparents** arrière-grands-parents mpl ► **great-grandson** N arrière-petit-fils m ► **great-great-grandfather** N arrière-arrière-grand-père m, trisaïeul m (liter) ► **great-great-grandson** N arrière-arrière-

petit-fils m ► **great-hearted** ADJ au grand cœur, magnanime ► **the Great Lakes** NPL les Grands Lacs mpl ► **Great Leap Forward** N (in China) le Grand Bond en avant ► **great-nephew** N petit-neveu m ► **great-niece** N petite-nièce f ► **the Great Plains** NPL les Grandes Plaines fpl ► **the Great Powers** NPL (Pol) les grandes puissances fpl ► **great tit** N (Orn) mésange f charbonnière ► **great-uncle** N grand-oncle m ► **the Great Wall of China** N la Grande Muraille de Chine ► **the Great War** N la Grande Guerre, la guerre de 14-18 ► **the Great White Way*** N (esp US) Broadway m

greatcoat ['greɪtkəʊt] N pardessus m; (Mil) manteau m, capote f

greater ['greɪtəʳ], **greatest** ['greɪtɪst] ADJ compar, superl of **great**

greatly ['greɪtlɪ] ADV [regret] vivement; [surprise] beaucoup; [prefer] de beaucoup; [admire, influence, increase] énormément; [improve] considérablement; [exaggerate] largement; [diminish] fortement, considérablement; **to be ~ superior to sb/sth** être nettement supérieur à qn/qch; (frm) **this is ~ to be feared/regretted** il y a tout lieu de le craindre/de le regretter

greatness ['greɪtnɪs] N [of person, achievement, country, city] grandeur f; [of work of art] grandeur f, splendeur f

grebe [gri:b] N grèbe m

Grecian ['gri:ʃən] (liter) 1 ADJ grec (grecque f); **hair in a ~ knot** coiffure f à la grecque 2 N (= Greek) Grec(que) m(f)

Greco- ['gri:kəʊ-] (esp US) = **Graeco-**

Greece [gri:s] N la Grèce

greed [gri:d] N (NonC) (for food) gourmandise f; (for money, power etc) avidité f, cupidité f

greedily ['gri:dɪlɪ] ADV [eat, drink] goulûment; **he eyed the food ~** il a regardé la nourriture d'un air vorace or goulu; **he licked his lips ~** il s'est léché les babines

greediness ['gri:dɪnɪs] N = **greed**

greedy ['gri:dɪ] ADJ (for food) gourmand; (for money, power etc) avide (**for** de), rapace, cupide; **~ for gain** âpre au gain; **don't be ~!** (at table) ne sois pas si gourmand!; (gen) n'en demande pas tant!; (pej) **~ guts**‡ goinfre m, bâfreur* m → **hog**

Greek [gri:k] 1 ADJ (gen) grec (grecque f); [ambassador, embassy, monarch] de Grèce; [teacher] de grec; **~ scholar** or **expert** helléniste mf 2 N a Grec(que) m(f) b (Ling) grec m; **ancient/modern ~** grec m classique/moderne; (fig) **that's (all) ~ to me*** tout ça c'est de l'hébreu or du chinois pour moi* 3 COMP ► **Greek god** N (Myth) dieu m grec; (= handsome man) **to be a ~ god** être beau comme un dieu ► **Greek-letter soci-**

ety N (US Univ) association d'étudiants désignée par une combinaison de lettres grecques → PHI, BETA, KAPPA ► **Greek Orthodox Church** N Église f orthodoxe grecque ► **Greek tragedy** N (Theat) tragédie f grecque

green [gri:n] 1 ADJ a (in colour) vert; **dark ~** vert inv foncé inv; **light ~** vert inv clair inv; **pale ~** vert inv pâle inv; **the ~ shoots of recovery** les premiers signes mpl de reprise; (fig) **he looked quite ~** il était vert; **to turn** or **go ~** [person] verdir; **she went ~** elle or son visage a verdi; (fig) **to be/turn ~ with envy** être/devenir vert de jalousie; **to make sb ~ with envy** rendre qn vert de jalousie → 5

b (= unripe) [fruit] vert, pas mûr; [banana, tomato, wood] vert; [bacon] non fumé; **~ corn** blé m en herbe; **~ meat** viande f crue

c * (= inexperienced) jeune, inexpérimenté; (= naïve) naïf (naïve f); **I'm not as ~ as I look!** je ne suis pas si naïf que j'en ai l'air!; **he's as ~ as grass** c'est un blanc-bec*

d (* = ecological) [issues, movement, company, policy, product] écologique; [vote, voters] vert; [party] écologique, vert; [person] écolo* inv; **~ awareness** prise f de conscience des problèmes écologiques

e (liter = flourishing) vert, vigoureux; **to keep sb's memory ~** chérir la mémoire de qn; **memories still ~** souvenirs mpl encore vivaces or vivants

2 N a (= colour) vert m; **dressed in ~** habillé de or en vert

b (= lawn) pelouse f, gazon m; (also **village ~**) ≈ place f (du village) (gazonnée); (Golf) vert m; (also **bowling ~**) terrain gazonné pour le jeu de boules

3 **greens** NPL a (Brit = vegetables) légumes mpl verts

b (Pol) **the Greens** les Verts mpl

4 ADV (Pol*) **to vote ~** voter vert; **to think ~** penser écologie

5 COMP ► **green bean** N haricot m vert ► **green belt** N (Brit Town Planning) ceinture f verte ► **the Green Berets** NPL (Mil) les bérets mpl verts ► **green card** N (in Brit = driving insurance) carte f verte; (in US = work permit) permis m de travail ► **Green Cross Code** N (Brit) code de prévention routière destiné aux enfants ► **green currency** N monnaie f verte ► **green-eyed** ADJ aux yeux verts; (fig) jaloux, envieux; (fig) **the ~-eyed monster** la jalousie ► **green fingers** NPL (Brit) **he's got ~ fingers** il a la main verte or le pouce vert ► **green goddess*** N (Brit) voiture f de pompiers (de l'armée) ► **green light** N (traffic light) feu m vert; (fig) **to give sb/sth the ~ light** donner le feu vert à qn/qch; **to get the ~ light from sb** obtenir or recevoir le feu vert de qn ► **Green Mountain State** N (US) le Vermont ► **green onion** N (US) ciboule f ► **Green Paper** N (Brit Pol) ≈ livre m blanc ► **the Green Party** N (Brit Pol) les Verts mpl ► **green peas** NPL petits pois mpl ► **green pepper** N poivron m vert ► **the green pound** N (Econ) la livre verte ► **green power** N (US fig) [of money] puissance f de l'argent ► **green revolution** N (Econ, Agr) révolution f verte ► **green room** N (Theat) foyer m des acteurs or des artistes ► **green salad** N salade f (verte) ► **green tea** N thé m vert ► **green thumb** N (US) = **green fingers** ► **green vegetables** NPL légumes mpl verts ► **the green-wellie brigade** N la haute société ► **green woodpecker** N pivert m, picvert m

parfois utilisée pour évoquer certains aspects déplaisants du comportement de la haute société.

greenback* ['gri:nbæk] N (US = dollar) dollar m

greenery ['gri:nərɪ] N verdure f

greenfield site ['gri:nfi:ldsaɪt] N (Ind) terrain m en dehors de la ville

greenfinch ['gri:nfɪntʃ] N verdier m

greenfly ['gri:nflaɪ] N (pl **greenfly** or **greenflies**) puceron m (des plantes)

greengage ['gri:ngeɪdʒ] N (Brit) reine-claude f

greengrocer [gri:ngrəʊsər] N (Brit) marchand(e) m(f) de fruits et légumes; **~'s (shop)** magasin m de fruits et légumes

greenhorn ['gri:nhɔ:n] N blanc-bec m

greenhouse ['gri:nhaʊs] N serre f; (Ecol) **the ~ effect** l'effet m de serre; (Ecol) **~ gas** gaz m contribuant à l'effet de serre

greening ['gri:nɪŋ] N (NonC) sensibilisation f à l'environnement

greenish ['gri:nɪʃ] ADJ tirant sur le vert, verdâtre (pej); **~-blue/-yellow/-brown** bleu/jaune/brun tirant sur le vert

Greenland ['gri:nlənd] [1] N le Groenland [2] ADJ groenlandais

Greenlander ['gri:nləndər] N Groenlandais(e) m(f)

Greenlandic [gri:n'lændɪk] [1] ADJ groenlandais [2] N (Ling) groenlandais m

greenmail ['gri:nmeɪl] N (US St Ex) chantage m financier (pour revendre au prix fort à une société les actions qui ont été achetées lors d'un raid)

greenness ['gri:nnɪs] N couleur f verte, vert m; [of countryside etc] verdure f; [of wood, fruit etc] verdeur f

Greenpeace ['gri:n,pi:s] N Greenpeace m

greenshank ['gri:nʃænk] N (Orn) chevalier m aboyeur

greenstick fracture ['gri:nstɪkfræktʃər] N (Med) fracture f incomplète or en bois vert

greenstuff ['gri:nstʌf] N verdure f; (Culin) légumes mpl verts, verdure f

greensward†† ['gri:nswɔ:d] N pelouse f, gazon m, tapis m de verdure

Greenwich ['grenɪtʃ, 'grenɪdʒ] N **~ (mean) time** heure f de Greenwich

greenwood ['gri:nwʊd] N (liter) **the ~** la forêt verdoyante

greeny* ['gri:nɪ] ADJ = **greenish**

greet¹ [gri:t] VT [+ person] (= say or wave hello to) saluer; (= invite, welcome) accueillir; **they ~ed him with cries of delight** ils l'ont accueilli avec des cris de joie; **he ~ed me with the news that ...** il m'a accueilli en m'apprenant que ...; **the statement was ~ed with laughter** la déclaration fut accueillie or saluée par des rires; **this was ~ed with relief by everyone** ceci a été accueilli avec soulagement par tous; **to ~ the ear** parvenir à l'oreille; **an awful sight ~ed me** or **my eyes** un spectacle affreux s'offrit à mes regards

greet² [gri:t] VI (Scot = weep) pleurer

greeting ['gri:tɪŋ] N salut m, salutation f; (= welcome) accueil m; **~s** compliments mpl, salutations fpl; **Xmas ~s** vœux mpl de Noël; **~(s) card** carte f de vœux; **he sent ~s to my brother** il s'est rappelé au bon souvenir de mon frère; **my mother sends you her ~s** ma mère vous envoie son bon souvenir

gregarious [grɪ'gɛərɪəs] ADJ [animal, instinct, tendency] grégaire; [person] sociable; **man is ~** l'homme est un animal grégaire

Gregorian [grɪ'gɔ:rɪən] [1] ADJ grégorien [2] COMP ▶ **Gregorian calendar** N calendrier m grégorien ▶ **Gregorian chant** N chant m grégorien

Gregory ['gregərɪ] N Grégoire m

gremlin* ['gremlɪn] N (hum) diablotin m (malfaisant)

Grenada [gre'neɪdə] N la Grenade; **in ~** à la Grenade

grenade [grɪ'neɪd] N (Mil) grenade f → **hand**, **stun**

Grenadian [gre'neɪdɪən] [1] ADJ grenadin [2] N Grenadin(e) m(f)

grenadier [,grenə'dɪər] N grenadier m (soldat)

grenadine ['grenədɪn] N grenadine f

grew [gru:] VB pt of **grow**

grey, gray (US) [greɪ] [1] ADJ [a] (in colour) gris; **dark ~** gris inv foncé inv; **light ~** gris inv clair inv; **pale ~** gris inv pâle inv; (hair) **he is totally ~** il a les cheveux complètement gris; **he** or **his hair is going** or **turning ~** il grisonne, ses cheveux grisonnent; **he nearly went ~ over it** il s'en est fait des cheveux blancs; **~ skies** ciel m gris; **it was a ~ day** (lit) c'était un jour gris; (fig) c'était un jour triste; (Pol hum) **the men in ~ suits** les membres influents du parti conservateur [b] (= ashen) [person, face, complexion] blême; **to turn ~** blêmir [c] (= bleak) [time, world] morne; [outlook, prospect] sombre, morne; (= boring) [person, image] terne; [city, town] morne, triste [2] N [a] (= colour) gris m; **dressed in ~** habillé de or en gris; **hair touched with ~** cheveux mpl grisonnants [b] (= horse) cheval m gris [3] VI [hair] grisonner; **~ing hair** cheveux mpl grisonnants; **a ~ing man** un homme aux cheveux grisonnants; **he was ~ing at the temples** il avait les tempes grisonnantes [4] COMP ▶ **grey area** N zone f d'ombre or d'incertitude ▶ **Grey Friar** N franciscain m ▶ **grey-haired** ADJ aux cheveux gris, grisonnant ▶ **grey market** N (St Ex) marché m gris ▶ **grey matter** N (Anat) substance f grise; (* = intelligence) matière f grise ▶ **grey mullet** N mulet m, muge m ▶ **grey seal** N phoque m gris ▶ **grey squirrel** N écureuil m gris, petit-gris m ▶ **grey wagtail** N bergeronnette f des ruisseaux ▶ **grey wolf** N loup m (gris)

greybeard ['greɪbɪəd] N (liter) vieil homme m

Greyhound ['greɪhaʊnd] N Greyhound mpl

�b—— GREYHOUND ——

Les cars de tourisme de la compagnie **Greyhound** sillonnent tout le territoire des États-Unis. Ce moyen de transport très répandu et bon marché perpétue symboliquement la tradition des grandes migrations américaines. La compagnie propose un abonnement forfaitaire appelé « Ameripass » qui permet de voyager sans restriction dans l'ensemble du pays.

greyhound ['greɪhaʊnd] [1] N (= dog) lévrier m; (= bitch) levrette f [2] COMP ▶ **greyhound racing** N courses fpl de lévriers

greying ['greɪɪŋ] ADJ → **grey 3**

greyish ['greɪɪʃ] ADJ tirant sur le gris, grisâtre (pej); [hair, beard] grisonnant

greylag goose ['greɪlæggu:s] N oie f cendrée

greyness ['greɪnɪs] N (= colour) couleur f grise; (= semi-dark) pénombre f; [of atmosphere, weather, day] morosité f; [of person] fadeur f

grid [grɪd] [1] N [a] (= grating) grille f, grillage m; (= network of lines on chart, map etc, also Rad) grille f; (Surv) treillis m; (Brit Elec = system) réseau m; (Surv) treillis m; (Brit Elec) **the (national) ~** le réseau électrique (national) [b] = **gridiron** [2] COMP ▶ **grid map** N carte f or plan m quadrillé(e) or à grille ▶ **grid reference** N référence f de grille

griddle ['grɪdl] [1] N (Culin) plaque f en fonte (pour cuire); (= part of stove) plaque f chauffante [2] VT (Culin) cuire sur une plaque [3] COMP ▶ **griddle cake** N (sorte f de) crêpe f épaisse

gridiron ['grɪdaɪən] N [a] (= utensil) gril m [b] (American Ftbl) terrain m de football américain

gridlock ['grɪdlɒk] N (US) bouchon m; (fig: in talks etc) impasse f

gridlocked ['grɪdlɒkt] ADJ (esp US) [a] (lit) [road] embouteillé; [traffic] bloqué [b] (fig) [government, negotiations] dans une impasse

grief [gri:f] [1] N [a] (NonC) chagrin m, peine f; **to come to ~** [vehicle, rider, driver] avoir un accident; [plan, marriage etc] tourner mal, échouer; **we came to ~** il nous est arrivé malheur; **good ~!*** ciel!, grands dieux! [b] (= cause of grief) (cause f de) chagrin m [c] (* = trouble) embêtements* mpl, ennuis mpl; **to give sb ~** embêter* qn, en faire voir de toutes les couleurs à qn; **the bank's been giving me ~ about my overdraft** la banque m'a fait des histoires à cause de mon découvert [2] COMP ▶ **grief-stricken** ADJ accablé de douleur, affligé

grievance ['gri:vəns] N (= ground for complaint) grief m, sujet m de plainte; (= complaint) doléance f; (Ind) différend m, conflit m; **to have a ~ against sb** avoir un grief or un sujet de plainte contre qn, en vouloir à qn; **he was filled with a sense of ~** il avait le sentiment profond d'être victime d'une injustice → **redress**

grieve [gri:v] [1] VT peiner, chagriner; **it ~s us to see** nous sommes peinés de voir; **it ~s us to learn that ...** nous avons la douleur d'apprendre que ..., c'est avec beaucoup de peine que nous apprenons que ...; **in a ~d tone** d'un ton peiné or chagriné [2] VI avoir de la peine or du chagrin (at, about, over à cause de); **to ~ for sb/sth** pleurer qn/qch; **I didn't have any time to ~** je n'avais pas le temps de pleurer

grieving ['gri:vɪŋ] ADJ [family, relatives] éploré; **the ~ process** le deuil

grievous ['gri:vəs] (frm) [1] ADJ [injury, damage, error, injustice] grave; [wound] grave, sérieux; [setback] sérieux; [loss] cruel; [blow] sévère; [news] pénible, affreux; [crime, offence] odieux [2] COMP ▶ **grievous bodily harm** N (Jur) ≈ coups mpl et blessures fpl

grievously ['gri:vəslɪ] ADV (frm) [hurt, offend] terriblement; **~ injured** or **wounded** grièvement blessé; **to wrong sb ~** gravement léser qn; **to be ~ mistaken** se tromper lourdement

griffin ['grɪfɪn] N (Myth) griffon m

griffon ['grɪfən] N (Myth, Zool) griffon m

grift* [grɪft] (US) [1] N filouterie* f, escroquerie f [2] VI filouter*, vivre d'escroquerie

grifter* ['grɪftər] N (US) escroc m, filou m

grill [grɪl] [1] N [a] (= cooking utensil) gril m; (= food) grillade f; (= restaurant: also **~room**) rôtisserie f, grill m; **brown it under the ~** faites-le dorer au gril → **mixed** [b] = **grille** [2] VT [a] (Culin) (faire) griller; **~ed fish** poisson m grillé [b] (fig = interrogate) cuisiner*, mettre sur la sellette [3] VI (Culin) griller [4] COMP ▶ **grill pan** N (Brit) plateau m à grillades (avec poignée)

grille [grɪl] N (= grating) grille f; [of convent etc] grille f; [of door] judas m; (Aut: also **radiator ~**) calandre f

grilling ['grɪlɪŋ] N (fig = interrogation) interrogatoire m serré; **to give sb a ~** cuisiner* qn, mettre qn sur la sellette

grim [grɪm] ADJ [1] [a] (= dire, gloomy) [place, situation, warning, outlook, news] sinistre; **to hold** or **hang** or **cling on to sth like** or **for ~ death** se cramponner à qch de toutes ses forces; **things are looking pretty ~** les perspectives ne sont guère réjouissantes; **~ necessity** la dure or cruelle nécessité; **the ~ reality of hospital work** la dure réalité du travail à l'hôpital; **the ~ truth** la vérité brutale [b] [person, face, expression] (= stern, angry) sévère; (= worried) sombre; [smile] sans joie;

[*humour*] macabre; [*voice*] sombre; **to look ~** (= *angry*) avoir une mine sévère; (= *worried*) avoir une mine sombre; **with ~ determination** avec une volonté inflexible [c] (* = *bad*) nul*; **his singing's pretty ~** il chante comme une casserole; **to feel ~** (= *unwell*) ne pas être dans son assiette [2] COMP ► **the Grim Reaper** N la Faucheuse (*liter*)

grimace [grɪ'meɪs] [1] N grimace *f* [2] VI (*from disgust, pain etc*) grimacer, faire la grimace; (*for fun*) faire des grimaces; **he ~d at the taste/the sight of ...** il a fait une grimace en goûtant/voyant ...

grime [graɪm] N (*NonC*) crasse *f*, saleté *f*

grimly ['grɪmlɪ] ADV [*frown, look at*] d'un air sévère; [*continue, hold on*] avec détermination; [*fight, struggle*] farouchement; **~ determined** farouchement déterminé; **to smile ~** avoir un sourire amer; **he nodded ~** l'air sombre, il acquiesça d'un signe de tête; **"no surrender", they said ~** «nous ne nous rendrons pas», dirent-ils, farouchement déterminés; **"this is not good enough" he said ~** «ça ne va pas» dit-il d'un air sévère

grimness ['grɪmnɪs] N [*of situation*] caractère *m* sinistre; [*of sight, face, person*] aspect *m* lugubre or sinistre

grimy ['graɪmɪ] ADJ crasseux

grin [grɪn] [1] VI [a] (= *smile*) sourire; (*broadly*) avoir un large or grand sourire; **~ning** [*face, person*] souriant; (*broader*) arborant un large or grand sourire; **to ~ broadly at sb** adresser un large sourire à qn; **to ~ from ear to ear** ◊ **to ~ like a Cheshire cat** avoir un sourire fendu jusqu'aux oreilles; **we must just ~ and bear it** il faut le prendre avec le sourire, il faut faire contre mauvaise fortune bon cœur [b] (*in pain*) avoir un rictus, grimacer; [*snarling dog*] montrer les dents [2] VT **he ~ned his approval** il a manifesté son approbation d'un large sourire [3] N (= *smile*) (large) sourire *m*; (*in pain*) rictus *m*, grimace *f* de douleur

grind [graɪnd] (*pret, ptp* **ground**) [1] N [a] (= *sound*) grincement *m*, crissement *m* [b] (* = *dull hard work*) boulot* *m* pénible; (*particular task*) corvée *f*; **the daily ~** le boulot* quotidien; **she found housework a ~** le ménage était une corvée pour elle; **the tiresome ~ of preparing for exams** la vraie corvée que sont les révisions pour les examens [c] (*US* = *swot*) bûcheur *m*, -euse *f*

[2] VT [a] (= *corn, coffee, pepper etc*) moudre; (= *crush*) écraser, broyer; (*US*) [+ *meat*] hacher; (*in mortar*) piler, concasser; **to ~ sth to a powder** pulvériser qch, réduire qch en poudre; **the metal will have to be ground into tiny pieces** il faudra réduire le métal en petits morceaux; **to ~ one's teeth** grincer des dents; **dirt ground into the carpet** saleté *f* incrustée dans le tapis; **he ground his heel into the soil** il a enfoncé son talon dans la terre; **to ~ the faces of the poor** opprimer les pauvres → **ground²** [b] (= *polish*) [+ *gems*] égriser, polir; [+ *knife, blade*] aiguiser or affûter (à la meule), meuler; [+ *lens*] polir → **axe** [c] (= *turn*) [+ *handle*] tourner; [+ *barrel organ*] faire jouer, jouer de; **to ~ a pepper mill** tourner un moulin à poivre

[3] VI [a] grincer; **the ship was ~ing against the rocks** le navire heurtait les rochers en grinçant; **tanks were ~ing south** des chars progressaient péniblement en direction du sud; **to ~ to a halt** or **a standstill** [*vehicle*] s'arrêter or s'immobiliser dans un grincement de freins; [*process, production, negotiations etc*] s'enliser; **the traffic had ground to a halt** or **a standstill** il y avait un bouchon [b] (* = *work hard*) bûcher* (dur or ferme)

► **grind away*** VI bûcher* or boulonner* (dur or ferme); **to ~ away at grammar** bûcher* or potasser* la grammaire

► **grind down** VT SEP [a] (*lit*) pulvériser [b] (*fig*)

(= *oppress*) opprimer, écraser; (= *wear down*) [+ *one's opponents etc*] avoir à l'usure; **ground down by poverty** accablé par la misère; **he gradually ground down all opposition to his plans** il a écrasé petit à petit toute tentative d'opposition à ses plans → **grind 3a**

► **grind on** VI [*person*] continuer péniblement or laborieusement; [*year, week, day etc*] s'écouler péniblement; [*war*] s'éterniser implacablement

► **grind out** VT SEP **to ~ out a tune on a barrel organ** jouer un air sur un orgue de Barbarie; (*fig*) **he ground out an oath** il a proféré un juron entre ses dents; **he managed to ~ out two pages of his essay** il est laborieusement arrivé à pondre* or à écrire deux pages de sa dissertation

► **grind up** VT SEP pulvériser

grinder ['graɪndə*] N [a] (= *apparatus*) broyeur *m*, moulin *m*; (= *tool*) meuleuse *f*; (*for sharpening*) affûteuse *f*, meule *f* à aiguiser [b] (= *person*) broyeur *m*, -euse *f*; (*for knives*) rémouleur *m*, -euse *f* → **organ** [c] (= *tooth*) molaire *f* [d] (*US Culin*) grand sandwich *m* mixte

grinding ['graɪndɪŋ] [1] N (*NonC* = *sound*) grincement *m* [2] ADJ [a] (= *oppressive*) **~ poverty** misère *f* noire; **~ hard work** travail *m* très pénible; **~ tedium** ennui *m* mortel [b] (= *grating*) [*noise*] grinçant; **to make a ~ noise** grincer; **to come to a ~ halt** [*process, production, negotiations*] s'enrayer brusquement; [*vehicle*] s'arrêter brusquement; **to bring sth to a ~ halt** [+ *process, production, negotiations*] mettre brusquement un terme à qch; [+ *vehicle*] arrêter qch dans un grincement; **the traffic came to** or **was brought to a ~ halt** la circulation a fini par se bloquer

grindingly ['graɪndɪŋlɪ] ADV **to be ~ hard work** être terriblement dur; **to be a ~ slow process** être terriblement long; **the routine became ~ familiar** la routine est devenue terriblement pesante

grindstone ['graɪndstəʊn] N meule *f* (à aiguiser); **to keep sb's nose to the ~** faire travailler qn sans répit or relâche; **to keep one's nose to the ~** travailler sans répit or relâche

gringo ['grɪŋgəʊ] N (*US pej*) gringo *m*, Ricain(e) *m(f)*

grip [grɪp] [1] N [a] (*lit*) (= *handclasp*) poigne *f*; (= *hold*) prise *f*; (*Wrestling*) prise *f*; **he held my arm in a vice-like ~** il me tenait le bras d'une poigne d'acier, il me serrait le bras comme un étau; **he has a strong ~** il a la poigne forte or une bonne poigne; (*Wrestling*) **arm etc ~** prise *f* de bras *etc*; **to get a ~ on** or **of sth** empoigner qch; **to lose one's ~** lâcher prise → **b**; **he lost his ~ on the rope** il a lâché la corde [b] (*fig*) **in the ~ of winter** paralysé par l'hiver; **country in the ~ of a general strike** pays paralysé par une grève générale; **cold weather had a firm ~ on the capital** un froid intense régnait dans la capitale; **environmentalism has taken a firm ~ on Europe** l'écologisme est solidement implanté en Europe; **to fall into the ~ of sb** tomber entre les or aux mains de qn; **to get a ~ on** [+ *inflation*] contrôler; [+ *party, power*] prendre le contrôle de; [+ *situation*] prendre en main; **the President was losing his ~ on power** le président perdait le contrôle du pouvoir; **to lose one's ~ on reality** perdre le sens de la réalité; **to get a ~ on** or **of o.s.** se ressaisir; **get a ~ on yourself!** ressaisis-toi!; **to keep a ~ on o.s.** se maîtriser, se contrôler; **he's losing his ~** il baisse*; (*hum*) **I must be losing my ~!** je ne fais que des bêtises! [c] (= *device*) serrage *m* [d] (= *handle*) poignée *f*; (*on racket*) prise *f* de raquette; (*on golf club, bat*) prise *f* [e] (= *suitcase*) valise *f*; (*US* = *bag: also* **~sack**) sac *m* de voyage [f] (*TV, Cine: also* **key ~**: *US*) machiniste *mf* caméra

[2] **grips** NPL **to come** or **get to ~s with a problem** s'attaquer à un problème, s'efforcer de résoudre un problème; **we have never had to come to ~s with such a situation** nous n'avons jamais été confrontés à pareille situation

[3] VT [a] (= *grasp*) [+ *rope, handrail, sb's arm*] saisir; [+ *pistol, sword etc*] saisir, empoigner; (= *hold*) serrer, tenir serré; **to ~ sb's hand** (= *grasp*) saisir la main de qn; (= *hold*) tenir la main de qn serrée; **to ~ the road** [*tyres*] adhérer à la chaussée; **the car ~s the road well** la voiture tient bien la route [b] [*fear etc*] saisir, étreindre; **~ped by terror** saisi de terreur [c] (= *interest strongly*) [*film, story etc*] captiver; **a film that really ~s you** un film vraiment palpitant, un film qui vous prend vraiment [4] VI [*wheels*] adhérer, mordre; [*screw, vice, brakes*] mordre; [*anchor*] crocher (sur le fond) [5] COMP ► **grip strip** N (*for carpet*) bande *f* adhésive (*pour tapis*)

gripe [graɪp] [1] VT (= *anger*) **this ~d him*** cela lui a mis l'estomac en boule* [2] VI (* = *grumble*) ronchonner, rouspéter* (**at** contre) [3] N [a] (*Med: also* **~s**) coliques *fpl* [b] (*NonC*) **his main ~ was that ...*** son principal sujet de plainte or de rogne* était que ... [4] COMP ► **gripe water** N (*Brit*) calmant *m* (*pour coliques infantiles*)

griping ['graɪpɪŋ] [1] ADJ **~ pain(s)** coliques *fpl* [2] N (*NonC:* * = *grumbling*) rouspétance* *f*, ronchonnements* *mpl*

grippe [grɪp] N (*US*) grippe *f*

gripping ['grɪpɪŋ] ADJ (= *exciting*) palpitant

grisly ['grɪzlɪ] ADJ (= *gruesome*) macabre, sinistre; (= *terrifying*) horrible, effroyable

grist [grɪst] N blé *m* (à moudre); (*fig*) **it's all ~ for** or **to his mill** cela apporte de l'eau à son moulin; **any media coverage is useful - it's all ~ to the mill** toute couverture médiatique est utile: c'est toujours bon à prendre

gristle ['grɪsl] N (*NonC*) tendons *mpl*, nerfs *mpl* (*surtout dans la viande cuite*)

gristly ['grɪslɪ] ADJ [*meat*] tendineux

grit [grɪt] [1] N (*NonC*) [a] (= *sand*) sable *m*; (= *gravel*) gravillon *m*; (= *rock: also* **~stone**) grès *m*; (*for fowl*) gravier *m*; **I've got (a piece of) ~ in my eye** j'ai une poussière dans l'œil [b] (* *fig* = *courage*) cran* *m*; **he's got ~** il a du cran* [2] **grits** NPL (*US*) gruau *m* de maïs [3] VI craquer, crisser [4] VT [a] **to ~ one's teeth** serrer les dents [b] **to ~ a road** sabler une route, répandre du sable sur une route

gritter ['grɪtə*] N camion *m* de sablage

gritty ['grɪtɪ] ADJ [a] (= *stony, grainy*) [*soil, ash*] graveleux; [*road*] sablé; [*floor*] plein de grains de sable; [*texture*] grumeleux; [*fruit*] graveleux, grumeleux [b] (* = *courageous*) [*person, determination*] solide; **the team's ~ display** la performance courageuse de l'équipe [c] (= *unsentimental*) [*realism*] cru; [*film, drama, account*] réaliste

grizzle ['grɪzl] VI (*Brit*) (= *whine*) pleurnicher, geindre; (= *complain*) ronchonner*

grizzled ['grɪzld] ADJ [*hair, beard, man*] grisonnant

grizzly ['grɪzlɪ] [1] ADJ [a] (= *grey*) grisâtre; [*hair, person*] grisonnant [b] (= *whining*) pleurnicheur, geignard [2] N (*also* **~ bear**) ours *m* gris

groan [grəʊn] [1] N [*of pain*] gémissement *m*, plainte *f*; [*of disapproval, dismay*] grognement *m*; **this news was greeted with ~s** cette nouvelle a été accueillie par des murmures (désapprobateurs) [2] VI [a] (*in pain*) gémir, pousser un or des gémissement(s) (**with** de); (*in disapproval, dismay*) grogner; **he ~ed inwardly at the thought** il étouffa un grognement à cette idée [b] (= *creak*) [*planks*] gémir; [*door*] crier; **the table ~ed under the weight of the food** la table ployait sous le poids de la nourriture; (hum) **the ~ing board** la table ployant sous l'amoncellement de victuailles [3] VT (in pain) dire en gémissant; (in disapproval, dismay) dire en grommelant

groat [grəʊt] N (Brit) ancienne petite pièce de monnaie

groats [grəʊts] NPL gruau m d'avoine or de froment

grocer ['grəʊsər] N épicier m, -ière f; **at the ~'s (shop)** à l'épicerie, chez l'épicier

grocery ['grəʊsərɪ] N [a] (= shop) épicerie f; **he's in the ~ business** il est dans l'épicerie [b] **I spent £25 on groceries** (= provisions) j'ai dépensé 25 livres en épicerie (NonC) or en provisions; **all the groceries are in this basket** toute l'épicerie est dans ce panier

grog [grɒg] N grog m

groggy ['grɒgɪ] ADJ [person] (= weak) faible; (= unsteady) groggy*; (from blow etc) groggy*, sonné*; [voice] faible; **I still feel a bit ~** je me sens toujours un peu sonné* or groggy*

grogram ['grɒgrəm] N gros-grain m

groin [grɔɪn] N [a] (Anat) aine f [b] (Archit) arête f [c] = **groyne**

grommet ['grɒmɪt] N [a] (= metal eyelet) œillet m [b] (Med) drain m transtympanique

groom [gru:m] [1] N [a] (for horses) valet m d'écurie, palefrenier m [b] (also **bridegroom**) (just married) (jeune) marié m; (about to be married) (futur) marié m [c] (in royal household) chambellan m [2] VT [+ horse] panser; **the cat was ~ing itself** le chat faisait sa toilette; **to ~ o.s.** [person] se pomponner, s'arranger; **well-~ed** [person] très soigné; [hair] bien coiffé; (fig) **to ~ sb for a post** etc préparer or former qn pour un poste etc; **she is being ~ed for stardom** on la prépare à devenir une star; **he is ~ing him as his successor** il en fait son poulain

grooming ['gru:mɪŋ] N [a] (gen) soins mpl de toilette or de beauté; (= well-groomedness) apparence f (impeccable); **~ products** produits mpl de toilette or de beauté [b] [of horse] pansage m; [of dog] toilettage m

groove [gru:v] [1] N [a] (in wood, plank, head of screw, for sliding door) rainure f; (for pulley) gorge f; (in column) cannelure f; (in record) sillon m; (in penknife blade) onglet m [b] (Mus* = rhythm) groove m; **to get into the ~** trouver son rythme [c]* **to be in the ~** (= up-to-date) [person, place] être dans le vent* or coup*; **he's in the or a ~** il a le vent en poupe*; **he's (stuck) in a ~** il s'est encroûté [d] (US = great) **it's a ~!** c'est sensationnel*, c'est le pied* [2] VT [a] (= put groove in) rainurer, rainer [b] (SPEC) [3] VI [a] (US = like) **I ~ it!** ça me botte* [3] VI [a] (US*) prendre son pied* [b] (* = dance) danser; **to ~ to the music** danser au rythme de la musique

groovy ['gru:vɪ] ADJ (= marvellous) sensass* inv, vachement bien*; (= up-to-date) dans le vent*

grope [grəʊp] [1] VI tâtonner, aller à l'aveuglette; **to ~ (around) for sth** (in a room etc) chercher qch à tâtons or à l'aveuglette; **I ~d (around) in my bag for the keys** j'ai fouillé dans mon sac pour trouver les clés; **to ~ for words** chercher ses mots; **scientists are groping towards a cure** les chercheurs s'efforcent de trouver un remède; (fig) **to be groping in the dark** être dans le brouillard [2] VT [a] **to ~ one's way towards** avancer à tâtons or à l'aveuglette vers; **to ~ one's way in/out** etc entrer/sortir etc à tâtons or à l'aveuglette [b] (*, pej = touch sexually) peloter*, tripoter* [3] N (pej: sexual) **to have a ~*** [couple] se peloter*

groping ['grəʊpɪŋ] [1] ADJ [a] (= tentative) [attempt] tâtonnant, timide; **we have a ~ awareness of how it works** nous commençons plus ou moins à comprendre comment cela fonctionne [b] (pej) **~ hands*** mains fpl bala-

---

deuses [2] N [a] (also **~s** = tentative attempts) tâtonnements mpl [b] (*, pej) pelotage* m

gropingly ['grəʊpɪŋlɪ] ADV en tâtonnant, à tâtons

grosgrain ['grəʊgreɪn] N gros-grain m

gross [grəʊs] [1] ADJ [a] (= flagrant) [injustice] flagrant; [inequalities, abuse, violation] choquant; [exaggeration, mismanagement] manifeste; [simplification] grossier; [error] gros (grosse f), lourd; **~ ignorance** ignorance f crasse; **that is a ~ understatement** c'est le moins que l'on puisse dire [b] (* = disgusting) [person, behaviour, food] dégoûtant, répugnant; [clothes] moche* [c] (= crude) [remarks, jokes] grossier [d] (pej = fat) énorme [e] [income, profit, weight etc] brut [2] ADV [pay, weigh] brut; **she earns £30,000 ~ per annum** elle gagne 30 000 livres brut par an [3] N **in (the) ~** (= wholesale) en gros, en bloc; (fig) en général, à tout prendre [b] (pl inv = twelve dozen) grosse f, douze douzaines fpl [4] VT (Comm) réaliser or dégager un bénéfice brut de [5] COMP ▸ **gross domestic income** N (Econ) revenu m intérieur brut ▸ **gross domestic product** N (Econ) produit m intérieur brut ▸ **gross national product** N (Econ) produit m national brut ▸ **gross negligence** N (gen) extrême négligence f; (Jur) ≈ faute f grave ▸ **gross output** N (Ind, Econ) production f brute

▸ **gross out*** VT (US) débecter*
▸ **gross up** VT FUS [+ interest, dividend, amount] calculer le montant brut or la valeur brute de

grossly ['grəʊslɪ] ADV [a] (= very much) [exaggerate, overestimate, underestimate] grossièrement; [overpaid, underpaid] nettement; [inadequate] nettement, largement; [inaccurate] totalement; [misleading, inefficient, irresponsible] terriblement; **~ unfair** d'une injustice flagrante; **to be ~ negligent** (gen) commettre une négligence grave; (Jur) ≈ commettre une faute grave; **the health service is ~ underfunded** les services de santé manquent cruellement de fonds [b] (= disgustingly) [behave, talk] de façon grossière, grossièrement [c] (gen, Med) ▸ **overweight** obèse

grossness ['grəʊsnɪs] N [a] (= coarseness) grossièreté f [b] (= fatness) obésité f

grot* ['grɒt] N (NonC) (= dirt) crasse f; (fig) inepties fpl

grotesque [grəʊ'tesk] [1] ADJ [a] (= hideous) [appearance] monstrueux; [idea, proposal] grotesque; [sight, spectacle] choquant [b] (Art) grotesque [2] N grotesque m

grotesquely [grəʊ'tesklɪ] ADV (= hideously) [distorted, deformed, swollen] monstrueusement; [simplistic] ridiculement

grotto ['grɒtəʊ] N (pl **grottos** or **grottoes**) grotte f

grotty* ['grɒtɪ] ADJ (Brit) (= dirty) [clothes] cradingue*; (= horrible) [place, food] minable*; **to feel ~** (= unwell) être mal fichu*

grouch* [graʊtʃ] [1] VI râler* [2] N (= person) râleur* m, -euse f; (= complaint) **his main ~ is that ...** il râle* surtout parce que ...

grouchiness* ['graʊtʃɪnɪs] N caractère m ronchon* or grincheux

grouchy* ['graʊtʃɪ] ADJ ronchon*, grincheux

ground[1] [graʊnd] [1] N [a] (NonC) **the ~** (= surface for walking on) la terre, le sol; **above ~** en surface; **below (the) ~** sous terre; **to fall to the ~** tomber par terre; **to knock sb to the ~** faire tomber qn (par terre); **burnt to the ~** réduit en cendres; **to lie/sit (down) on the ~** se coucher/s'asseoir par terre or sur le sol; (fig) **to have one's feet (firmly) on the ~** avoir les pieds sur terre; **to get off the ~** [plane etc] décoller; [scheme etc] démarrer; (fig) **to get sth**

---

off the ~ (faire) démarrer qch; (lit, fig) **to go to ~** se terrer; **to run a fox to ~** poursuivre un renard jusqu'à son terrier; (fig) **to run sb to ~** mettre la main sur qn; **that suits me down to the ~*** ça me va tout à fait; **to run** or **drive a car into the ~** user une voiture jusqu'à ce qu'elle soit bonne pour la casse; **to run a business into the ~** laisser péricliter une entreprise; **to run sb into the ~** user or épuiser qn; **to run o.s. into the ~ (with work)** s'épuiser (au travail); **to cut the ~ from under sb's feet** couper l'herbe sous le pied de qn → **ear**, **high**, **thick**, **thin**

[b] (NonC) (= piece of land) terrain m; (larger) domaine m, terres fpl; (= soil) sol m, terre f, terrain m; (fig) terrain m; **to till the ~** labourer la terre; **stony ~** sol m or terrain m caillouteux → **stony**; **all this ~ is owned by Lord Carrick** toutes ces terres appartiennent à Lord Carrick; (lit, fig) **neutral ~** terrain m neutre; (fig) **to meet sb on his own ~** affronter qn sur son propre terrain; **to be sure of one's ~** être sûr de son fait; **to be on dangerous ~** être sur un terrain glissant; **on familiar ~** en terrain familier or connu; **we're on fairly firm** or **solid ~** nous sommes sur un terrain assez solide; (fig) **to change one's ~** changer son fusil d'épaule; (Mil, also fig) **to give ~** céder du terrain; (fig: in discussion etc) **to go over the same ~ again** ressasser les mêmes questions; **to hold one's ~** tenir bon, ne pas lâcher prise; **to lose ~** (Mil, also fig) perdre du terrain; [party, politician] être en perte de vitesse; **sterling lost ~ against the other European currencies** la livre a perdu du terrain face aux autres monnaies européennes; (fig) **to clear the ~** déblayer le terrain; **to shift one's ~** changer son fusil d'épaule; **to stand one's ~** tenir bon → **break**, **common**, **cover**, **gain**

[c] (= area for special purpose) terrain m; **football ~** terrain m de football → **landing**, **parade**, **recreation**

[d] **~s** (= gardens etc) → **grounds**

[e] (US Elec) terre f; (in car etc) masse f

[f] (gen pl = reason) motif m, raison f; **~s for divorce/dismissal** motifs mpl de divorce/licenciement; **~s for prosecution** chefs mpl d'accusation; **~(s) for complaint** grief m; **there are ~s for believing that ...** il y a lieu de penser que ...; **the situation gives ~s for anxiety** la situation est préoccupante; **the latest figures give (us) ~s for optimism** les derniers chiffres (nous) permettent d'être optimistes; **on personal/medical ~s** pour (des) raisons personnelles/médicales; **on what ~s?** à quel titre?; **on the ~(s) of** pour raison de; **on the ~(s) that ...** en raison du fait que ...; (Jur) **on the ~ that ...** au motif que ...

[g] (= background) fond m; **on a blue ~** sur fond bleu

[2] VT [a] [+ plane, pilot] empêcher de voler, interdire de voler à; (= keep on ground) retenir au sol

[b] (*: as punishment) [+ teenager] priver de sortie

[c] [+ ship] faire s'échouer; **the tanker was ~ed (on the rocks)** le pétrolier s'était échoué (sur les rochers)

[d] (US Elec) mettre à la terre; (in car etc) mettre à la masse

[e] (= base) fonder (**on**, **in** sur); **her argument was ~ed in** or **on fact** son argument était fondé sur des faits; **the story isn't ~ed in reality** cette histoire n'est pas fondée sur la réalité → **well**

[3] VI [ship] s'échouer

[4] COMP ▸ **ground angle shot** N (Phot, Cine) contre-plongée f ▸ **ground attack** N (Mil) offensive f terrestre ▸ **ground bait** N (Fishing) amorce f de fond ▸ **ground bass** N (Mus) basse f contrainte or obstinée ▸ **ground cloth** N (US) tapis m de sol ▸ **ground colour** N (= background colour) fond m ▸ **ground control** N (Aviat) contrôle

m au sol ► **ground crew** N (*Aviat*) équipe *f* au sol ► **ground floor** N (*esp Brit*) rez-de-chaussée *m* ; (*fig*) **he got in on the ~ floor** il est là depuis le début ► **ground-floor** ADJ (*esp Brit*) [*flat, room*] au rez-de-chaussée ; [*window*] du rez-de-chaussée ► **ground forces** NPL (*Mil*) forces *fpl* terrestres ► **ground frost** N gelée *f* blanche ► **ground ice** N glaces *fpl* de fond ► **ground ivy** N lierre *m* terrestre ► **ground level** N **at ~ level** au niveau du sol ► **ground plan** N (= *scale drawing*) plan *m* (au sol) ; (= *basic sketch*) esquisse *f* ► **ground rent** N (*esp Brit*) redevance *f* foncière ► **ground rules** NPL (*gen*) procédure *f* ; (*fig*) **we can't change the ~ rules at this stage** on ne peut pas changer les règles du jeu maintenant ► **ground staff** N (*Aviat*) personnel *m* au sol ► **ground-to-air missile** N (*Mil*) missile *m* sol-air ► **ground-to-ground missile** N (*Mil*) missile *m* sol-sol ► **ground troops** NPL (*Mil*) armée *f* de terre ► **ground water** N (*Geol*) nappe *f* phréatique ► **ground wire** N (*US Elec*) fil *m* de terre ; (*in car etc*) fil *m* de masse ► **ground zero** N (*Mil: of nuclear explosion*) point *m* de radiation maximum au sol

ground² [graʊnd] **1** VB *pt, ptp* of **grind 2** ADJ [*coffee, spices etc*] moulu ; (*US Culin*) **~ beef** bœuf *m* haché ; **~ glass** (*rough surface*) verre *m* dépoli ; (*powdered*) verre *m* pilé ; **~ rice** farine *f* de riz

groundbreaking [ˈgraʊndbreɪkɪŋ] ADJ révolutionnaire

groundhog [ˈgraʊndhɒg] **1** N (*US*) marmotte *f* d'Amérique **2** COMP ► **Groundhog Day** N (*US*) jour *m* de la marmotte d'Amérique

---
GROUNDHOG DAY

Groundhog Day est une tradition américaine selon laquelle on peut prédire l'arrivée du printemps en observant le comportement de la marmotte d'Amérique, censée sortir de son hibernation le 2 février. Si le soleil brille ce jour-là, la marmotte est tellement effrayée par son ombre qu'elle prolonge son hibernation de six semaines, ce qui signifie que l'hiver se prolongera d'autant. La sortie de la marmotte est filmée chaque année à Punxsutawney, en Pennsylvanie, et l'événement est diffusé à l'échelle nationale.

---

grounding [ˈgraʊndɪŋ] N **a** (*in education*) bases *fpl* (**in** en) ; **she had a good ~ in French** elle avait de bonnes bases en français **b** [*of ship*] échouage *m* **c** [*of plane*] interdiction *f* de vol

groundless [ˈgraʊndlɪs] ADJ sans fondement, non fondé, infondé

groundnut [ˈgraʊndnʌt] **1** N (*esp Brit*) arachide *f* **2** COMP ► **groundnut oil** N huile *f* d'arachide

grounds [graʊndz] NPL **a** (*also* **coffee ~**) marc *m* (de café) **b** (= *gardens etc*) parc *m*

groundsel [ˈgraʊnsl] N séneçon *m*

groundsheet [ˈgraʊndʃiːt] N tapis *m* de sol

ground(s)keeper [ˈgraʊndzkiːpər] N (*US*) = **groundsman**

groundsman [ˈgraʊndzmən] (*pl* **-men**) N [*of playing field*] gardien *m* (de stade) ; [*of park*] garde *m* (de parc) ; [*of cemetery*] gardien *m* (de cimetière)

groundspeed [ˈgraʊndspiːd] N (*Aviat*) vitesse *f* au sol

groundswell [ˈgraʊndswel] N (*lit, fig*) lame *f* de fond

groundwork [ˈgraʊndwɜːk] N (*gen*) travail *m* préparatoire, préparation *f* ; [*of novel, play etc*] plan *m*, canevas *m*

group [gruːp] **1** N (*gen, also Gram, Comm, Mus*) groupe *m* ; **in ~s of four** par groupes de quatre ; **to stand in ~s** former des petits groupes ; **to form a ~ round sth/sb** se grouper *or* se

rassembler autour de qch/qn ; **literary ~** cercle *m* littéraire → **blood, in, pressure**

2 VI (*also* **~ together**) [*people*] se grouper, se regrouper ; **to ~ round sth/sb** se grouper *or* se rassembler autour de qch/qn

3 VT (*also* **~ together**) [+ *objects, people*] rassembler, réunir ; **the children ~ed themselves around the teacher** les enfants se sont groupés *or* rassemblés autour du professeur ; **pupils are ~ed according to age and ability** les élèves sont répartis en groupes en fonction de leur âge et de leurs aptitudes

4 COMP ► **group booking** N réservation *f* de groupe ► **group captain** N (*Brit Aviat*) colonel *m* de l'armée de l'air ► **group dynamics** N dynamique *f* de(s) groupe(s) ► **group insurance** N (*NonC*) assurance *f* groupe ► **the Group of Eight** N (*Pol*) le groupe des Huit ► **the Group of Seven** N (*Pol*) le groupe des Sept ► **group practice** N (*Med*) cabinet *m* (de groupe *or* d'association) ► **group sex** N **to take part in ~ sex** faire l'amour à plusieurs ► **group theory** N (*Math*) théorie *f* des ensembles ► **group therapist** N (*Psych*) (psycho)thérapeute *mf* (de groupe) ► **group therapy** N (*Psych*) (psycho)thérapie *f* de groupe ► **group work** N (*Social Work*) travail *m* en groupe *or* en équipe

grouper [ˈgruːpər] N mérou *m*

groupie* [ˈgruːpɪ] N groupie* *f*

grouping [ˈgruːpɪŋ] N groupement *m* ; (*Fin, Jur*) **~s of companies** regroupements *mpl* d'entreprises

groupware [ˈgruːpwɛər] **1** N (*NonC: Comput*) groupware *m* **2** COMP ► **groupware package** N logiciel *m* de productivité de groupe

grouse¹ [graʊs] (*Orn*) **1** N (*pl* **grouse** *or* **grouses**) grouse *f* → **black, red 2** COMP ► **grouse-beating** N **to go ~-beating** faire le rabatteur (*à la chasse à la grouse*) ► **grouse moor** N chasse *f* réservée (*où l'on chasse la grouse*) ► **grouse-shooting** N **to go ~-shooting** chasser la grouse, aller à la chasse à la grouse

grouse²* [graʊs] **1** VI (= *grumble*) rouspéter*, râler* (**at, about** contre) ; **stop grousing!** arrête de rouspéter !* **2** N **to have a ~ (about sth)** (= *complain*) rouspéter* *or* râler* (contre qch) ; **I have a big ~ about the firm's attitude** j'ai de bonnes raisons de rouspéter* *or* râler* contre l'attitude de l'entreprise

grout [graʊt] **1** N enduit *m* de jointoiement ; (*on floor*) coulis *m*, enduit *m* de ragréage **2** VT jointoyer

grouting [ˈgraʊtɪŋ] N jointoiement *m*

grove [grəʊv] N bosquet *m* ; **olive ~** oliveraie *f* ; **chestnut ~** châtaigneraie *f* ; **pine ~** pinède *f*

grovel [ˈgrɒvl] VI (*lit*) être à plat ventre ; (*searching for something*) ramper ; (*fig* = *humble oneself*) se mettre à plat ventre, ramper (**to, before** devant)

grovelling [ˈgrɒvlɪŋ] ADJ (*lit*) rampant ; (*fig*) servile

grow [grəʊ] (*pret* **grew**, *ptp* **grown**) **1** VI **a** (= *get taller, bigger, longer etc physically*) [*plant, hair*] pousser ; [*person*] grandir ; [*animal*] grandir, grossir ; [*tumour*] grossir ; [*crystal*] se former ; **she's letting her hair ~** elle se laisse pousser les cheveux ; **that plant does not ~ in England** cette plante ne pousse pas en Angleterre ; **the plant ~s from a bulb/from seed** c'est une plante à bulbe/que l'on sème ; **to ~ to a height of 60cm** atteindre 60 cm (de haut) ; **he has ~n (by) 5cm** il a grandi de 5 cm ; **haven't you ~n!** comme tu as grandi *or* poussé !* → **grow into**

b (= *increase, develop*) [*numbers, amount*] augmenter, grandir ; [*club, group*] s'agrandir ; [*population, rage, fear, love, influence, knowledge*] augmenter, s'accroître ; [*economy, market*] être en expansion ; **their friendship grew as time**

went on leur amitié a grandi avec le temps ; **our friendship grew from a common interest in gardening** notre amitié s'est développée à partir d'un goût commun pour le jardinage ; **fears are ~ing for the safety of the hostages** on craint de plus en plus pour la sécurité des otages ; **pressure is ~ing on him to resign** on fait de plus en plus pression sur lui pour qu'il démissionne ; **their policies kept the economy ~ing** grâce à leur politique, la croissance de l'économie s'est maintenue ; **the economy/market is ~ing at** *or* **by 3% a year** l'économie/le marché connaît une croissance de 3 % par an ; **the population is ~ing at** *or* **by 2% a year** la population augmente de 2 % par an ; **we have ~n away from each other** avec le temps, nous nous sommes éloignés l'un de l'autre

c **to ~ in: to ~ in popularity** devenir plus populaire ; **to ~ in confidence** prendre de l'assurance ; **to ~ in strength** se renforcer ; (*liter*) **to ~ in wisdom/beauty** croître en sagesse/beauté

d **to ~ to do** commencer à faire ; **to ~ to like/dislike/fear sth** commencer à aimer/détester/redouter qch ; **I'm ~ing to like him a bit more** je commence à l'apprécier un peu plus ; **I had ~n to like him** j'avais fini par l'apprécier

e (+ *adj*) devenir ; **to ~ big(ger)** grandir ; **to ~ old(er)** vieillir ; **to ~ red(der)** rougir ; **to ~ angry** se fâcher, se mettre en colère ; **to ~ rare(r)** se faire (plus) rare ; **to ~ used to sth** s'habituer *or* s'accoutumer à qch

2 VT [+ *plants, crops*] cultiver, faire pousser ; [+ *one's hair, beard, nails*] laisser pousser ; [+ *crystal*] fabriquer ; **organically-~n vegetables** légumes *mpl* biologiques ; **she has ~n her hair (long)** elle s'est laissé pousser les cheveux ; **it's ~n a new leaf** une nouvelle feuille vient de pousser *or* d'apparaître ; **to ~ horns** commencer à avoir des cornes

3 COMP ► **grow bag** N (*Hort*) sac contenant du terreau enrichi où l'on peut faire pousser directement des plantes

► **grow apart** VI s'éloigner peu à peu (l'un de l'autre *or* les uns des autres)

► **grow in** VI [*nail*] s'incarner ; [*hair*] repousser

► **grow into** VT FUS **a** (= *become*) devenir ; **to ~ into a man** devenir un homme ; **he's ~n into quite a handsome boy** il est devenu très beau garçon (en grandissant) **b** [+ *clothes*] devenir assez grand pour mettre ; **he grew into the job** peu à peu, il a appris les ficelles du métier ; **to ~ into the habit of doing** prendre (avec le temps) l'habitude de faire

► **grow on** VT FUS [*habit etc*] s'imposer peu à peu à ; [*book, music etc*] plaire de plus en plus à ; **his paintings ~ on you** plus on regarde ses tableaux, plus on les apprécie

► **grow out** **1** VI **to let one's dyed hair ~ out** laisser repousser ses cheveux (pour éliminer la teinture), attendre que ses cheveux retrouvent leur couleur naturelle **2** VT SEP **if you don't like the perm, you'll just have to ~ it out** si la permanente ne vous plaît pas, vous n'avez qu'à vous laisser repousser les cheveux

► **grow out of** VT FUS [+ *clothes*] devenir trop grand pour ; **he's ~n out of this jacket** cette veste est (devenue) trop petite pour lui ; **he grew out of his asthma/acne** son asthme/acné lui a passé avec le temps ; **to ~ out of the habit of doing** perdre l'habitude de faire

► **grow up** VI **a** [*person, animal*] devenir adulte ; **when I ~ up I'm going to be a doctor** quand je serai grand je serai médecin ; **~ up!*** arrête les enfantillages ! **b** [*friendship, hatred etc*] se développer ; [*custom*] se répandre

grower [ˈgrəʊər] N **a** (= *person*) producteur *m*, -trice *f*, cultivateur *m*, -trice *f* ; **vegetable ~** maraîcher *m*, -ère *f* → **rose b** **this plant is a slow ~** c'est une plante à croissance lente

growing [ˈgrəʊɪŋ] **1** ADJ **a** [*plant*] qui pousse ; **~ crops** récoltes *fpl* sur pied ; **fast-/slow-~** à croissance rapide/lente **b** [*child*] en cours de croissance, qui grandit ; **he's a ~ boy**

il est en pleine croissance [c] (= increasing) [number, amount] grandissant, qui augmente; [friendship, hatred] grandissant, croissant; **a ~ opinion** une opinion de plus en plus répandue; **a ~ feeling of frustration** un sentiment croissant or grandissant de frustration; **to have a ~ desire to do sth** avoir de plus en plus envie de faire qch [2] N (= getting bigger) croissance f; (Agr) culture f [3] COMP ► **growing pains** NPL (Med) douleurs fpl de croissance; [of business, project] difficultés fpl de croissance ► **growing season** N (Agr) période f de croissance

growl [graʊl] [1] VI [animal] grogner, gronder (**at** contre); [person] grogner, ronchonner*; [thunder] gronder [2] VT [+ reply etc] grogner, grommeler [3] N grognement m, grondement m; **to give a ~** grogner

grown [grəʊn] [1] VB ptp of **grow**; → **home 4** [2] ADJ [person] adulte; **he's a ~ man** il est adulte

grown-up [ˈgrəʊnʌp] [1] ADJ [a] (= adult) [children] adulte; **when he is ~** quand il sera grand [b] (= mature) [child, adolescent] mûr; [behaviour] de grande personne; **your brother's very ~ for his age** ton frère est très mûr pour son âge; **you think you're so ~!** tu te prends pour une grande personne!; **she looks very ~** elle fait très grande personne or très adulte; **try to be more ~ about it** ne sois pas aussi puéril [c] [talk, subject] d'adultes [2] N grande personne f, adulte mf; **the ~s** les grandes personnes fpl

growth [grəʊθ] [1] N [a] (NonC = development) [of plant] croissance f, développement m; [of person] croissance f; **to reach full ~** [plant] atteindre sa taille maximale; [person] avoir fini de grandir [b] (NonC = increase) [of numbers, amount] augmentation f; [of business, trade] expansion f, croissance f (in de); [of club, group] croissance f; [of influence, economy] croissance f, développement m; [of knowledge, love, friendship] développement m; (Econ) **these measures encourage ~** ces mesures favorisent la croissance; **the ~ of public interest in ...** l'intérêt croissant du public pour ... [c] (= what has grown) pousse f, poussée f; **a thick ~ of weeds** des mauvaises herbes qui ont poussé dru; **a five days' ~ of beard** une barbe de cinq jours; **she had a new ~ of hair** ses cheveux se sont mis à repousser [d] (Med = tumour) tumeur f; **benign/malignant ~** tumeur f bénigne/maligne [2] COMP [potential, prospects, forecast] de croissance, d'expansion ► **growth area** N (= sector of economy) secteur m en (pleine) expansion; (= region) région f en (pleine) expansion ► **growth factor** N (Med) facteur m de croissance ► **growth hormone** N hormone f de croissance ► **growth industry** N secteur m en (pleine) expansion or en plein essor ► **growth market** N marché m en (pleine) expansion or en plein essor ► **growth rate** N taux m de croissance ► **growth shares** NPL (Brit) valeurs fpl de croissance ► **growth stock** N (US) = **growth shares**

groyne [grɔɪn] N (esp Brit) brise-lames m inv

Grozny [ˈgrɒznɪ] N Grozny

grub [grʌb] [1] N [a] (= larva) larve f; (in apple etc) ver m, asticot m [b] (NonC: = food) bouistifaille* f, bouffe* f; **~'s up!** à la soupe!* [2] VT [animal] [+ ground, soil] fouir [3] VI (also ~ **about, ~ around**) fouiller, fouiner (**in, among** dans); **he was ~bing (about or around) in the earth for a pebble** il fouillait le sol pour trouver un caillou [4] COMP ► **Grub Street** N (Brit) le monde des écrivaillons ► **grub up** VT SEP [+ soil] fouir; [+ object] déterrer

grubbiness [ˈgrʌbɪnɪs] N saleté f

grubby [ˈgrʌbɪ] ADJ (= dirty) [person, object] malpropre, sale; (pej = sordid) sale, sordide; **I don't want him to get his ~ hands on it** je ne veux pas qu'il y touche (avec ses pattes sales); **the ~ business of selling arms** le sordide commerce des armes

grubstake [ˈgrʌbsteɪk] [1] N (US) (Hist) avance f faite à un prospecteur; (Fin) **to put up a ~ for sb** fournir les fonds nécessaires à qn (pour le lancement d'une entreprise ou d'un projet) [2] VT accorder une avance à; (Fin) financer (pendant la phase de lancement)

grudge [grʌdʒ] [1] VT **to ~ doing sth** faire qch à contrecœur, rechigner à faire qch; **she ~s paying £20 a ticket** cela lui fait mal au cœur de payer 20 livres le billet; **he ~s her even the food she eats** il lui mesure jusqu'à sa nourriture, il lésine même sur sa nourriture; **do you ~ me these pleasures?** me reprochez-vous ces (petits) plaisirs?; **they ~d him his success** ils lui en voulaient de sa réussite; **I won't ~ you $5** je ne vais pas te refuser 5 dollars [2] N rancune f; **to bear** or **have a ~ against sb** en vouloir à qn, garder rancune à qn [3] COMP ► **grudge match** N (pl **grudge matches**) (Sport, fig) règlement m de comptes

grudging [ˈgrʌdʒɪŋ] ADJ [consent, approval, support] réticent; [apology, praise] fait à contrecœur; **he won their ~ admiration/respect** ils ont fini par l'admirer/le respecter; **to be ~ in one's support for sth** apporter un soutien réticent à qch

grudgingly [ˈgrʌdʒɪŋlɪ] ADV à contrecœur

gruel [ˈgrʊəl] N gruau m

gruelling, **grueling** (US) [ˈgrʊəlɪŋ] ADJ éreintant

gruesome [ˈgruːsəm] ADJ horrible, épouvantable; **in ~ detail** jusque dans les plus horribles détails

gruesomely [ˈgruːsəmlɪ] ADV (with vb) d'une manière horrible; (with adj) horriblement

gruff [grʌf] ADJ bourru

gruffly [ˈgrʌflɪ] ADV [say] d'un ton bourru

gruffness [ˈgrʌfnɪs] N [of person, manner] brusquerie f; [of voice] ton m bourru

grumble [ˈgrʌmbl] [1] VI [person] maugréer (**at, about** contre); [thunder] gronder [2] N [a] grognement m, ronchonnement* m; **to do sth without a ~** faire qch sans ronchonner*; **after a long ~ about ...** après avoir longtemps maugréé contre ... [b] **~s** récriminations fpl

grumbling [ˈgrʌmblɪŋ] [1] N (NonC) récriminations fpl [2] ADJ [person] grognon, grincheux; **a ~ sound** un grondement [3] COMP ► **grumbling appendix** N appendicite f chronique

grummet [ˈgrʌmɪt] N = **grommet**

grump [grʌmp] [1] N (= person) grognon m, ronchon m [2] **grumps** NPL **to have the ~s** être de mauvais poil*

grumpily [ˈgrʌmpɪlɪ] ADV [say] d'un ton maussade

grumpiness [ˈgrʌmpɪnɪs] N (permanent) mauvais caractère m; **sorry for my ~ yesterday** désolé d'avoir été de mauvais poil* hier

grumpy [ˈgrʌmpɪ] ADJ grognon, bougon

grunge [grʌndʒ] N grunge m

grungy [ˈgrʌndʒɪ] ADJ crado* inv, cradingue*

grunt [grʌnt] [1] VTI grogner; **to ~ a reply** grommeler or grogner une réponse; **"no", he ~ed** «non», grommela-t-il [2] N grognement m; **to give a ~** pousser or faire entendre un grognement; (in reply) répondre par un grognement [b] (US: = soldier) fantassin m, biffin* m

gruppetto [gruˈpetəʊ] N (pl **gruppetti** [gruˈpetiː]) (Mus) gruppetto m

gryphon [ˈgrɪfən] N = **griffin**

GSOH N (ABBR = good sense of humour) sens m de l'humour

GT [ˌdʒiːˈtiː] N (ABBR = gran turismo) GT f

Gt (ABBR = **Great**) gd (gde f), grand; **Gt Britain** la Grande-Bretagne; **Gt Yarmouth** Great Yarmouth

GTi [ˌdʒiːtiːˈaɪ] N (ABBR = gran turismo injection) GTi f

GU (US Post) ABBR = **Guam**

guacamole [ˌgwɑːkəˈməʊlɪ] N (Culin) guacamole m

Guadeloupe [ˌgwɑːdəˈluːp] N la Guadeloupe

Guam [gwɑːm] N Guam

guano [ˈgwɑːnəʊ] N (NonC) guano m

guarantee [ˌgærənˈtiː] [1] N [a] (gen, Comm = promise, assurance) garantie f; **to be under ~** être sous garantie; **there is a year's ~ on this watch** cette montre est garantie un an, cette montre a une garantie d'un an; **a ~ against defective workmanship** une garantie contre les malfaçons; **"money-back ~ with all items"** «remboursement garanti sur tous les articles»; **you have** or **I give you my ~ that ...** je vous garantis que ...; **there's no ~ that it will happen** il n'est pas garanti or dit que cela arrivera; **there's no ~ that it actually happened** il n'est pas certain que cela soit arrivé; **health is not a ~ of happiness** la santé n'est pas une garantie de bonheur [b] (Jur etc = pledge, security) garantie f, caution f; (Fin) **~ for a bill** aval m d'une traite; **to give sth as (a) ~** donner qch en garantie; **he left his watch as a ~ of payment** il a laissé sa montre en gage; **what ~ can you offer?** quelle caution pouvez-vous donner? [c] = **guarantor** [2] VT [a] (Comm) [+ goods etc] garantir (**against** contre); **to ~ sth for two years** garantir qch (pour) deux ans; **~d not to rust** garanti inoxydable; **~d price** prix m garanti [b] (= assure) [+ sb's safety, freedom, rights] garantir; **I will ~ his good behaviour** je me porte garant de sa bonne conduite; **I ~ that it won't happen again** je vous garantis que cela ne se reproduira pas; **I can't ~ that he will come** je ne peux pas garantir qu'il viendra; **we can't ~ good weather** nous ne pouvons pas garantir le beau temps or qu'il fera beau [c] (Fin) **to ~ a loan** se porter garant or caution d'un emprunt; **I will ~ him for a £500 loan** je lui servirai de garant or de caution pour un emprunt de 500 livres; (US Univ) **~d student loan** prêt m d'honneur (à un étudiant) [3] COMP ► **guarantee form** N garantie f (fiche)

guarantor [ˌgærənˈtɔːr] N garant(e) m(f), caution f; **to stand ~ for sb** se porter garant or caution de qn; **will you be my ~ for the loan?** me servirez-vous de garant or de caution pour cet emprunt?

guaranty [ˈgærəntɪ] N (Fin) garantie f, caution f; (= agreement) garantie f; (= person) garant(e) m(f)

guard [gɑːd] [1] N [a] (NonC) garde f, surveillance f; (Mil) garde f; **to put a ~ on sb/sth** faire surveiller qn/qch; **to come off ~** finir son tour de garde; **to be on ~** être de garde or de faction; **to go on ~** prendre son tour de garde; **to keep** or **stand ~** être de garde, monter la garde; **to keep** or **stand ~ on** (against attack) garder; (against theft, escape) surveiller; **to stand ~ over sb/sth** monter la garde auprès de qn/qch; **to be under ~** être sous surveillance or sous bonne garde; **to keep sb under ~** garder qn sous surveillance; **he was taken under ~ to ...** il a été emmené sous escorte à ... → **mount** [b] (NonC) (Boxing, Fencing) garde f; (Sport) **on ~!** en garde! [c] (= as protection) **he wears goggles as a ~ against accidents** il porte des lunettes protectrices [d] (= wariness) **to be on one's ~** se méfier (**against** de), être or se tenir sur ses gardes (**against** contre) ; **to put sb on his ~** mettre qn en garde (**against** contre) ; **to be off (one's) ~** ne pas être or ne pas se tenir sur ses gardes ; **to catch sb off (his) ~** prendre qn au dépourvu ; **to put sb off (his) ~** tromper la vigilance de qn

e (Mil etc) (= squad of men) garde f ; (= one man) garde m ; (Mil) **to change (the) ~** faire la relève de la garde ; **one of the old ~** un vieux de la vieille* ; (Brit Mil) **the Guards** les régiments mpl de la garde royale → **lifeguard, security**

f (Brit Rail) chef m de train

g (on machine) dispositif m de sûreté ; (on sword) garde f → **fireguard**

h (Basketball) **left/right ~** arrière m gauche/droit

2 VT (against attack) garder (**from, against** contre) ; (against theft, escape) surveiller ; (Cards, Chess) garder ; (fig) [+ one's tongue, passions etc] surveiller ; **the frontier is heavily ~ed** la frontière est solidement gardée ; **the dog ~ed the house** le chien gardait la maison ; **~ it with your life!** veillez bien dessus ! ; (fig) **to ~ o.s. against sth** se prémunir contre qch

3 COMP ► **guard dog** N chien m de garde ► **guard duty** N (Mil) **to be on ~ duty** être de garde or de faction ► **guard of honour** N (lit, fig) garde f d'honneur ; (on either side) haie f d'honneur ► **guard's van** N (Brit Rail) fourgon m

►**guard against** VT FUS se protéger contre, se prémunir contre ; **to ~ against doing** (bien) se garder de faire ; **in order to ~ against this** pour éviter cela ; **we must try to ~ against this happening again** nous devons essayer d'empêcher que cela ne se reproduise

guarded ['gɑːdɪd] ADJ [person] sur ses gardes ; [response, remark] circonspect, prudent ; [support, smile] réservé ; [optimism] prudent ; **he is ~ about his intentions** il se garde de trop révéler ses intentions ; **a closely or carefully ~ secret** un secret bien gardé ; **to give a ~ welcome to sth** accueillir qch avec réserve

guardedly ['gɑːdɪdlɪ] ADV [say] avec circonspection, prudemment ; **~ optimistic** d'un optimisme prudent

guardedness ['gɑːdɪdnɪs] N circonspection f

guardhouse ['gɑːdhaʊs] N (Mil) (for guards) corps m de garde ; (for prisoners) salle f de police

guardian ['gɑːdɪən] **1** N **a** gardien(ne) m(f), protecteur m, -trice f **b** [of minor] tuteur m, -trice f **2** ADJ gardien **3** COMP ► **guardian angel** N ange m gardien ► **Guardian reader** N (Brit) lecteur m, -trice f du Guardian

┌─────────────────────┐
│ **GUARDIAN READER** │
└─────────────────────┘

« Dis-moi quel quotidien tu lis, et je te dirai qui tu es » : cet adage est particulièrement valable en Grande-Bretagne, où les gens ont une image stéréotypée des lecteurs des différents quotidiens. Les lecteurs du **Guardian**, quotidien de centre gauche, se comptent surtout parmi la gauche bourgeoise et intellectuelle, les enseignants, les travailleurs sociaux etc. Le « Sun » se situerait à l'autre extrême.

guardianship ['gɑːdɪənʃɪp] N (Jur) tutelle f

guardrail ['gɑːdreɪl] N [of staircase] rampe f ; [of balcony] balustrade f, rambarde f ; [of road] glissière f de sécurité

guardroom ['gɑːdrʊm] N (Mil) corps m de garde

guardsman ['gɑːdzmən] N (pl **-men**) (Brit Mil) soldat m de la garde royale, garde m ; (US) soldat m de la garde nationale

Guatemala [,gwɑːtɪ'mɑːlə] N le Guatemala

Guatemalan [,gwɑːtɪ'mɑːlən] **1** ADJ guatémaltèque **2** N Guatémaltèque mf

---

guava ['gwɑːvə] N (= fruit) goyave f ; (= tree) goyavier m

gubbins* ['gʌbɪnz] N (Brit) **a** (= thing) machin* m, truc* m **b** (= silly person) crétin* m, imbécile m

gubernatorial [,guːbənə'tɔːrɪəl] ADJ (esp US) de or du gouverneur

gudgeon¹ ['gʌdʒən] N (= fish) goujon m

gudgeon² ['gʌdʒən] **1** N (Tech) tourillon m ; (Naut) goujon m **2** COMP ► **gudgeon pin** N (Brit Aut) axe m de piston

guelder rose [,geldə'rəʊz] N (Bot) boule-de-neige f

Guelf, Guelph [gwelf] N guelfe m

Guernsey ['gɜːnzɪ] N **a** (Geog) Guernesey f ; **in ~** à Guernesey **b** (also **~ cow**) vache f de Guernesey

guernsey ['gɜːnzɪ] N (= garment) ≈ pull m marin

guerrilla [gə'rɪlə] **1** N guérillero m **2** COMP [tactics etc] de guérilla ► **guerrilla band** N troupe f de partisans or de guérilleros ► **guerrilla financing** N (US) financement m indépendant ► **guerrilla group** N = **guerrilla band** ► **guerrilla strike** N (Ind) grève f sauvage ► **guerrilla war(fare)** N guérilla f

guess [ges] **1** N supposition f, conjecture f ; **to have** or **make a ~ (at sth)** essayer de deviner (qch) ; **he made a wild ~** il a lancé une réponse au hasard ; **(I'll give you) three ~es!** essaie de deviner ! ; **that was a good ~!** tu as deviné juste ! ; **that was a good ~ but ...** c'est une bonne idée, mais ... ; **how did you know? — it was just a lucky ~** comment as-tu deviné ? — j'ai dit ça au hasard ; **my ~ is that he refused** d'après moi, il aura or a refusé ; **it's anyone's ~ who will win*** impossible de prévoir qui va gagner ; **will he come tomorrow? — it's anyone's ~*** viendra-t-il demain ? — qui sait ? or Dieu seul le sait ; **at a ~ I would say there were 200** à vue de nez, il y en avait 200 ; **at a rough ~** à vue de nez ; **an educated ~** une supposition éclairée ; **your ~ is as good as mine!*** je n'en sais pas plus que toi !

2 VT **a** (also **~ at**) [+ answer, name etc] deviner ; (= estimate) [+ height, numbers etc] estimer, évaluer ; (= surmise) supposer, conjecturer (**that** que) ; **you've ~ed (it)!** tu as deviné !, c'est ça ! ; **I ~ed as much** je m'en doutais ; **I don't weigh the ingredients, I just ~ the quantities** je ne pèse pas les ingrédients, je le fais au pif* ; **I ~ed him to be about 20** ◊ **I ~ed (that) he was about 20** je lui donnais à peu près 20 ans ; **~ how heavy he is** devine combien il pèse ; **can you ~ what it means?** devine ce que ça veut dire ; **~ what!*** tu sais quoi ? ; **~ who!*** devine qui c'est ! ; **you'll never ~ who's coming to see us!** tu ne devineras jamais qui va venir nous voir !

b (= believe, think) supposer, penser ; **he'll be about 40 I ~** je lui donnerais la quarantaine ; **I ~ she's decided not to come** je suppose qu'elle a décidé de ne pas venir ; **I ~ so** sans doute, oui ; **I ~ not** non

3 VI deviner ; **(try to) ~!** essaie de deviner ! , devine un peu ! ; **you'll never ~!** tu ne devineras jamais ! ; **to ~ right** deviner juste ; **to ~ wrong** tomber à côté ; **to keep sb ~ing** laisser qn dans le doute ; **to ~ at the height of a building/the number of people present** évaluer or estimer (au jugé) la hauteur d'un bâtiment/le nombre de personnes présentes

4 COMP ► **guessing game** N **to play a ~ing game** jouer aux devinettes

guesstimate* ['gestɪmɪt] **1** N (NonC) estimation f approximative **2** VT calculer au pifomètre*

guesswork ['geswɜːk] N conjecture f, hypothèse f ; **it was sheer ~** ce n'étaient que des conjectures ; **by ~** en devinant, au jugé

---

guest [gest] **1** N (at home) invité(e) m(f), hôte mf ; (at table) convive mf ; (in hotel) client(e) m(f) ; (in boarding house) pensionnaire mf ; (TV, Rad) invité(e) m(f) ; **~ of honour** invité(e) m(f) d'honneur ; **we were their ~s last summer** nous avons été invités chez eux l'été dernier ; **be my ~!*** je vous en prie ! → **houseguest, paying**

2 VI (TV, Rad) **to ~ on sb's show** être invité sur le plateau de qn ; **and ~ing on tonight's show we have Linda Roberts** et pour l'émission de ce soir, notre invitée est Linda Roberts

3 COMP ► **guest appearance** N **to make a ~ appearance on sb's show** être invité sur le plateau de qn ► **guest artist** N invité(e) m(f) spécial(e) ► **guest book** N livre m d'or ► **guest list** N liste f des invités ► **guest night** N soirée où les membres d'un club peuvent inviter des non-membres ► **guest room** N chambre f d'amis ► **guest speaker** N conférencier m, -ière f (invité(e) par un club, une organisation)

guesthouse ['gesthaʊs] N (Brit: gen) pension f de famille ; (in monastery etc) hôtellerie f

guestworker ['gestwɜːkəʳ] N travailleur m, -euse f immigré(e)

guff* [gʌf] N (NonC) idioties fpl, conneries: fpl

guffaw [gʌ'fɔː] **1** VI s'esclaffer **2** N gros (éclat m de) rire m

GUI ['guːɪ] N (Comput) (ABBR = **graphical user interface**) interface f graphique, interface f GUI

Guiana [gaɪ'ænə] N les Guyanes fpl

guidance ['gaɪdəns] **1** N **a** conseils mpl ; (= counselling) guidance f ; **he needs some ~ about how** or **as to how to go about it** il a besoin de conseils quant à la façon de procéder ; **your ~ was very helpful** vos conseils ont été très utiles ; **for your ~** pour votre gouverne, à titre d'indication or d'information → **child, vocational b** [of rocket etc] guidage m **2** COMP ► **guidance counselor** N (US Scol) conseiller m, -ère f d'orientation ► **guidance system** N (Tech) système m de guidage

guide [gaɪd] **1** N **a** (= person) guide m ; **you must let reason be your ~** il faut vous laisser guider par la raison **b** (= indication) guide m, indication f ; **this figure is only a ~** ce chiffre n'est donné qu'à titre indicatif ; **last year's figures will be a good ~** les statistiques de l'année dernière serviront d'indication générale ; **these statistics are not a very good ~ as to his ability** ces résultats ne reflètent pas vraiment ses compétences ; **as a rough ~, count four apples to the pound** comptez en gros quatre pommes par livre

c (= guidebook) guide m (touristique) ; **~ to Italy** guide m d'Italie

d (= book of instructions) guide m, manuel m ; **beginner's ~ to sailing** manuel m d'initiation à la voile

e (for curtains etc) glissière f ; (on sewing machine) pied-de-biche m

f (Brit: also **girl ~**) éclaireuse f ; (Roman Catholic) guide f

2 VT **a** [+ stranger, visitor] guider, piloter ; [+ blind person] conduire, guider ; **he ~d us through the town** il nous a pilotés or guidés à travers la ville ; **he ~d us to the main door** il nous a montré le chemin jusqu'à la porte d'entrée ; (lit, fig) **to be ~d by sb/sth** se laisser guider par qn/qch

b [+ rocket, missile] guider

3 COMP ► **guide dog** N chien m d'aveugle ► **guide line** N (for writing) ligne f (permettant une écriture horizontale régulière) ; (= rope) main f courante → **guideline** ► **guide price** N prix m indicatif

guidebook ['gaɪdbʊk] N guide m (touristique)

guided ['gaɪdɪd] **1** ADJ [rocket etc] téléguidé **2** COMP ► **guided missile** N missile m téléguidé ► **guided tour** N visite f guidée

guideline ['gaɪdlaɪn] N **a** (= rough guide) indication f; (= advice) conseil m; **an IQ test is merely a ~** un test de QI ne donne qu'une indication (générale); **I gave her a few ~s on how to look after a kitten** je lui ai donné quelques conseils sur la manière de s'occuper d'un chaton; **follow these simple ~s for a healthy diet** pour vous alimenter sainement, il suffit de suivre ces conseils **b** (= official directive) directive f (**on** sur); **safety/health ~s** directives fpl concernant la santé/sécurité, directives fpl de santé/sécurité

guidepost ['gaɪdpəʊst] N poteau m indicateur

guiding ['gaɪdɪŋ] ADJ [idea, principle] directeur (-trice f); [ideology] dominant; [policy, rule] de base; **he assumed a ~ role in his nephew's life** il a servi de mentor à son neveu; (fig) ► **light, ~ star** guide m; ► **force** moteur m; **he is the ~ force behind these reforms** il est le moteur de ces réformes; **he needs a ~ hand from time to time** de temps en temps, il faut le remettre sur la bonne voie

guild [gɪld] N **a** (Hist) guilde f, corporation f; **goldsmiths' ~** guilde f des orfèvres **b** association f, confrérie f; **the church ~** le conseil paroissial; **women's ~** association f féminine

guilder ['gɪldə'] N (pl **guilders** or **guilder**) florin m

guildhall ['gɪldhɔːl] N (Hist) maison f des corporations; (= town hall) hôtel m de ville

guile [gaɪl] N (NonC) (= deceit) fourberie f, duplicité f; (= cunning) ruse f

guileful ['gaɪlfʊl] ADJ (= deceitful) fourbe, trompeur; (= cunning) rusé

guileless ['gaɪllɪs] ADJ candide, sans malice

guillemot ['gɪlɪmɒt] N guillemot m

guillotine ['gɪlə'tiːn] **1** N (for beheading) guillotine f; (for paper-cutting) massicot m; (Parl) **a ~ was imposed on the bill** la durée des débats sur le projet de loi a été limitée **2** VT [+ person] guillotiner; [+ paper] massicoter; (Parl) **to ~ a bill** limiter la durée des débats sur un projet de loi

guilt [gɪlt] **1** N (NonC) culpabilité f; **he was tormented by ~** il était torturé par un sentiment de culpabilité; **to have ~ feelings about sth/sb** avoir un sentiment de culpabilité à cause de qch/envers qn **2** COMP ► **guilt complex** N (Psych) complexe m de culpabilité

guiltily ['gɪltɪlɪ] ADV [say] d'un ton coupable; [look away] d'un air coupable; [think] avec un sentiment de culpabilité

guiltless ['gɪltlɪs] ADJ innocent (**of** de)

guilty ['gɪltɪ] **1** ADJ **a** (also Jur) [person] coupable (**of** de); **I've been ~ of that myself** j'ai moi-même commis la même erreur; **he was ~ of taking the book without permission** il s'est rendu coupable d'avoir pris le livre sans permission; **to be found ~/not ~ (of sth)** être déclaré coupable/non coupable (de qch); **to plead ~/not ~ (to sth)** plaider coupable/non coupable (de qch); **how do you plead? ~ or not ~?** plaidez-vous coupable ou non coupable?; **a ~ verdict ◊ a verdict of ~** un verdict de culpabilité; **a not ~ verdict ◊ a verdict of not ~** un verdict d'acquittement; **the judge took into account his ~ plea** or **his plea of ~** le juge a tenu compte du fait qu'il avait plaidé coupable; **the court accepted a not ~ plea** or **a plea of not ~** la cour l'a acquitté **b** (= ashamed) [smile, thought] coupable; [silence] chargé de culpabilité; **to look ~** avoir l'air coupable; **he had a ~ look on his face** il avait une expression coupable; **to feel ~** culpabiliser, avoir mauvaise conscience; **to make sb feel ~** culpabiliser qn, donner mauvaise conscience à qn; **to feel ~ about sth** se sentir coupable de qch; **I felt ~ that I had not thanked her** je culpabilisais or j'avais mauvai-

se conscience de ne pas l'avoir remerciée **c** (= shameful) [secret] honteux; [pleasure] inavouable, coupable **2** COMP ► **guilty conscience** N mauvaise conscience f; **I have a ~ conscience about not writing** j'ai mauvaise conscience de ne pas avoir écrit ► **the guilty party** N le coupable

Guinea ['gɪnɪ] **1** N (Geog) (the Republic of) ~ la (République f de) Guinée f → **equatorial 2** COMP ► **Guinea-Bissau** N la Guinée-Bissau ► **guinea-fowl** N (pl inv) pintade f ► **guinea-pig** N (Zool) cochon m d'Inde, cobaye m; (fig) cobaye m; (fig) **to be a guinea-pig** servir de cobaye

guinea ['gɪnɪ] N (Brit: formerly = money) guinée f (= 21 shillings)

Guinean ['gɪnɪən] **1** ADJ guinéen **2** N Guinéen(ne) m(f)

guise [gaɪz] N **in a new ~** sous une autre forme; **in** or **under the ~ of scientific research** sous l'apparence de or sous couvert de recherche scientifique; **under the ~ of doing sth** sous prétexte de faire qch; **a portrait of the king in the ~ of a Roman emperor** un portrait du roi en empereur romain

guitar [gɪ'tɑː'] N guitare f

guitarist [gɪ'tɑːrɪst] N guitariste mf

Gujarat, Gujerat [,gʊdʒə'rɑːt] N le Gujarat, le Gujarat

Gujarati, Gujerati [,gʊdʒə'rɑːtɪ] **1** ADJ du Gujarat **2** N **a** (= person) Gujarati mf **b** (Ling) gujarati m

gulch [gʌlʃ] N (US) ravin m

gulf [gʌlf] **1** N **a** (in ocean) golfe m; **the (Persian) Gulf** le golfe Persique, le Golfe **b** (= abyss: lit, fig) gouffre m, abîme m **2** COMP ► **the Gulf of Aden** N le golfe d'Aden ► **the Gulf of Alaska** N le golfe d'Alaska ► **the Gulf of Mexico** N le golfe du Mexique ► **the Gulf States** NPL (Middle East) les États mpl du Golfe; (in US) les États mpl du golfe du Mexique ► **the Gulf Stream** N le Gulf Stream ► **the Gulf War** N la guerre du Golfe ► **Gulf War syndrome** N (NonC: Med) syndrome m de la guerre du Golfe

gull¹ [gʌl] **1** N (= bird) goéland m, mouette f; **common ~** goéland m or mouette f **2** COMP ► **gull-wing door** N (Aut) porte f papillon

gull² [gʌl] **1** VT duper, rouler* **2** N (= dupe) gogo* m

gullet ['gʌlɪt] N (Anat) œsophage m; (= throat) gosier m; (fig) **it really stuck in my ~** ça m'est resté en travers de la gorge*

gulley ['gʌlɪ] N = **gully**

gullibility [,gʌlɪ'bɪlɪtɪ] N crédulité f

gullible ['gʌlɪbl] ADJ crédule

gully ['gʌlɪ] N **a** (= ravine) ravine f, couloir m; (Climbing) couloir m **b** (= drain) caniveau m, rigole f

gulp [gʌlp] **1** N **a** (= action) coup m de gosier; (from emotion) serrement m de gorge; **to swallow sth in one ~** avaler qch d'un seul coup; **he emptied the glass in one ~** il a vidé le verre d'un (seul) trait; **"yes" he replied with a ~** « oui » répondit-il la gorge serrée or avec une boule dans la gorge **b** (= mouthful) [of food] bouchée f; [of drink] gorgée f, lampée f; **he took a ~ of milk** il a avalé une gorgée de lait **2** VT **a** (also **~ down**) [+ food] engloutir, avaler tout rond; [+ drink] avaler d'un trait, lamper*; **don't ~ your food** mâche ce que tu manges **b** **"I'm sorry," he ~ed** « désolé », répondit-il la gorge serrée or avec une boule dans la gorge **3** VI essayer d'avaler; (from emotion) avoir un serrement à la gorge; **he ~ed** sa gorge s'est serrée or s'est contractée
► **gulp back** VT SEP **to ~ back one's tears/sobs** ravaler or refouler ses larmes/sanglots

gum¹ [gʌm] **1** N (Anat) gencive f **2** COMP ► **gum disease** N gingivite f ► **gum shield** N protège-dents m

gum² [gʌm] **1** N **a** (NonC) (Bot) gomme f; (esp Brit = glue) gomme f, colle f; (= rubber) caoutchouc m **b** (NonC) chewing-gum m **c** (= sweet: also **~drop**) boule f de gomme **2** VT (= put gum on) gommer; (= stick) coller (**to** à); **~med envelope/label** enveloppe f/ étiquette f collante or gommée; **to ~ sth back on** recoller qch; **to ~ down an envelope** coller or cacheter une enveloppe **3** COMP ► **gum arabic** N gomme f arabique ► **gum tree** N gommier m; (Brit fig) **to be up a ~ tree*** être dans le pétrin*
► **gum up*** VT SEP (+ machinery, plans) bousiller*; (fig) **it's ~med up the works** ça a tout bousillé*

gum³* [gʌm] N (euph) **by ~!** nom d'un chien!*, mince alors!*

gumball* ['gʌmbɔːl] N (US) (= chewing gum) boule f de chewing-gum; (pej = person) andouille* f; (hum: on police car) gyrophare m, bulle* f

gumbo ['gʌmbəʊ] N (US, Can) (Bot) gombo m; (Culin) soupe f au gombo

gumboil ['gʌmbɔɪl] N fluxion f dentaire, abcès m à la gencive

gumboots ['gʌmbuːts] NPL (esp Brit) bottes fpl de caoutchouc

gumdrop ['gʌmdrɒp] N boule f de gomme

gummy ['gʌmɪ] ADJ [substance, surface] collant

gumption* ['gʌmpʃən] N (NonC) jugeote* f, bon sens m; **use your ~!** un peu de jugeote!*; **he's got a lot of ~** il sait se débrouiller

gumshoe: ['gʌmʃuː] N (US = detective) privé* m

gumshoes ['gʌmʃuːz] NPL (US) (= overshoes) caoutchoucs mpl; (= sneakers) (chaussures fpl de) tennis mpl

gun [gʌn] **1** N **a** (= handgun) revolver m, pistolet m; (= rifle) fusil m; (= cannon) canon m; **he's got a ~!** il est armé!; **the thief was carrying a ~** le voleur avait une arme (à feu), le voleur était armé; **to draw a ~ on sb** braquer une arme sur qn; (fig) **to hold** or **put a ~ to sb's head** mettre le couteau or le pistolet sous la gorge de qn; **a 21-~ salute** une salve de 21 coups de canon; (Mil) **the ~s** les canons mpl, l'artillerie f; (Mil) **the big ~s** les gros canons mpl, l'artillerie f lourde; (* fig = people) les grosses légumes* fpl, les huiles* fpl; (fig) **to bring out the big ~s** brandir un argument massue; **to be going great ~s*** [business] marcher très fort*; [person] être en pleine forme → **blow**; **he's the fastest ~ in the West** c'est la meilleure gâchette de l'Ouest; **with (all) ~s blazing** tout feu tout flamme inv; (esp US) **to be under the ~** être dans une situation critique → **jump, son, stick b** (Brit = member of shooting party) fusil m **c** (US:: also **~man**) bandit m armé **d** (Tech) pistolet m; **paint ~** pistolet m à peinture → **grease**

2 VT (esp US Aut) **to ~ the engine** faire ronfler le moteur; **to ~ it*** appuyer sur le champignon*

3 VI (* fig) **to be ~ning for sb** chercher qn*, essayer d'avoir qn; **watch out, he's ~ning for you!** fais gaffe, il te cherche!*

4 COMP ► **gun barrel** N canon m de fusil or de revolver ► **gun carriage** N affût m de canon; (at funeral) prolonge f d'artillerie ► **gun control** N (US) réglementation f du port d'armes ► **gun cotton** N fulmicoton m, coton-poudre m ► **gun crew** N (Mil) peloton m or servants mpl de pièce ► **gun dog** N chien m de chasse ► **the gun laws** NPL (US) les lois fpl sur le port d'armes ► **gun licence, gun license** (US) N permis m de port d'armes ► **gun room** N (in house) armurerie f; (Brit Naut) poste m des aspirants ► **gun-shy** ADJ qui a peur des coups de feu or des détonations; (fig) qui n'a pas le courage de ses

opinions ► **gun turret** N (*Mil etc*) tourelle *f*
► **gun down** VT SEP abattre

| GUN CONTROL |

Aux États-Unis, la réglementation du port d'armes est un sujet très controversé. Le droit pour tous les citoyens de détenir des armes à feu est inscrit dans la constitution et certains lobbies encouragent fortement la pratique de l'autodéfense. Cependant, la montée de la violence préoccupe de nombreux Américains et a conduit à mettre en place une législation plus restrictive; en particulier, beaucoup d'armes semi-automatiques ont été interdites.

gunboat ['gʌnbəʊt] ▢1 N (*Naut*) canonnière *f*
▢2 COMP ► **gunboat diplomacy** N politique *f* de la canonnière, politique *f* de force

gunfight ['gʌnfaɪt] N échange *m* de coups de feu, fusillade *f*

gunfighter ['gʌnfaɪtər] N (*esp US*) professionnel *m* de la gâchette, tireur *m*

gunfire [gʌnfaɪər] N [*of rifles etc*] coups *mpl* de feu, fusillade *f*; [*of cannons*] feu *m* or tir *m* d'artillerie

gunge* [gʌndʒ] N (*NonC: Brit*) magma *m* infâme*

gung ho* ['gʌŋ 'h ʃ] ADJ fonceur

gunk* [gʌŋk] N (*NonC*) = **gunge**

gunmaker ['gʌnmeɪkər] N armurier *m*

gunman ['gʌnmən] N (*pl* **-men**) bandit *m* armé; (*Pol*) terroriste *m*

gunmetal ['gʌnmetl] ▢1 N bronze *m* à canon ▢2 ADJ (= *colour*) vert-de-gris *inv*

gunnel ['gʌnl] N = **gunwale**

gunner ['gʌnər] N (*Mil, Naut*) artilleur *m*; (*Brit Mil*) canonnier *m*

gunnery ['gʌnərɪ] ▢1 N ▢a (= *science, art, skill*) tir *m* au canon, canonnage *m* ▢b (*Mil* = *guns*) artillerie *f* ▢2 COMP ► **gunnery officer** N (*Mil*) officier *m* de tir

gunny ['gʌnɪ] N (*NonC*) toile *f* de jute grossière; (*also* ~ **bag**, ~ **sack**) sac *m* de jute

gunplay ['gʌnpleɪ] N (*US*) échange *m* de coups de feu

gunpoint ['gʌnpɔɪnt] N **to have** or **hold sb at** ~ tenir qn sous la menace d'un revolver or d'un fusil; **he did it at** ~ il l'a fait sous la menace d'un revolver or d'un fusil

gunpowder ['gʌnpaʊdər] N poudre *f* à canon; (*Brit Hist*) **the Gunpowder Plot** la conspiration des Poudres

gunrunner ['gʌnrʌnər] N trafiquant *m* d'armes

gunrunning ['gʌnrʌnɪŋ] N contrebande *f* or trafic *m* d'armes

gunsel* ['gʌnsl] N (*US* = *gunman*) flingueur* *m*

gunship ['gʌnʃɪp] N (*also* **helicopter** ~) hélicoptère *m* de combat

gunshot ['gʌnʃɒt] ▢1 N (= *sound*) coup *m* de feu; **within** ~ à portée de fusil; **out of** ~ hors de portée de fusil ▢2 COMP ► **gunshot wound** N blessure *f* de or par balle; **to get a** ~ **wound** être blessé par balle, recevoir un coup de feu

gunslinger* ['gʌnslɪŋər] N (*US* = *gunman*) flingueur* *m*

gunsmith ['gʌnsmɪθ] N armurier *m*

gunwale ['gʌnl] N (*Naut*) plat-bord *m*

guppy ['gʌpɪ] N guppy *m*

gurgle ['gɜ:gl] ▢1 N [*of water, rain*] gargouillis *m*, glouglou *m*; [*of stream*] murmure *m*; [*of laughter*] gloussement *m*; [*of baby*] gazouillis *m*; **to give a** ~ **of delight** gazouiller de joie ▢2 VI [*water*] glouglouter, gargouiller; [*stream*] murmurer; [*person*] (*with delight*) gazouiller; (*with laughter*) glousser

Gurkha ['gɜ:kə] N Gurkha *m*

gurnard ['gɜ:nəd] N (*pl* **gurnard** or **gurnards**) grondin *m*

gurney ['gɜ:nɪ] N (*US*) lit *m* à roulettes

guru ['gʊru:] N (*lit, fig*) gourou *m*

gush [gʌʃ] ▢1 N [*of oil, water, blood*] jaillissement *m*, bouillonnement *m*; [*of tears, words*] flot *m*; (* *pej*) effusion(s) *f(pl)*, épanchement(s) *m(pl)* ▢2 VI ▢a (*lit, fig*) jaillir; **to** ~ **in/out/through** etc [*water etc*] entrer/sortir/traverser etc ▢b (* *pej*) [*person*] se répandre en compliments (**over/about** sur/au sujet de), en rajouter*

gusher* ['gʌʃər] N ▢a (= *oil well*) puits *m* jaillissant (de pétrole) ▢b (= *effusive person*) **to be a** ~ être trop exubérant

gushing ['gʌʃɪŋ] ADJ [*water etc*] jaillissant; (*pej*) [*person, enthusiasm, welcome*] trop exubérant

gushy* ['gʌʃɪ] ADJ [*person*] trop exubérant; [*language*] dithyrambique

gusset ['gʌsɪt] N (*Sewing*) soufflet *m*

gussy* ['gʌsɪ] VT (*US*) **to** ~ **sth up** retaper* qch

gust [gʌst] ▢1 N ▢a [*of wind*] rafale *f*, bourrasque *f*; [*of smoke*] bouffée *f*; [*of flame*] jet *m*; **a** ~ **of rain** une averse; **the wind was blowing in** ~**s** le vent soufflait en rafales; ~**s of 100km/h** des rafales de 100 km/h ▢b [*of rage etc*] accès *m*, bouffée *f*; **a** ~ **of laughter** un grand éclat de rire ▢2 VI [*wind*] souffler en rafales; (*Met*) **wind** ~**ing to force 7** vent *m* (en rafales) atteignant force 7

gustatory ['gʌstətərɪ] ADJ gustatif

gusto ['gʌstəʊ] N (*NonC*) enthousiasme *m*, plaisir *m*; **with** ~ avec brio or verve; **he ate his meal with great** ~ il a dévoré son repas

gusty ['gʌstɪ] ADJ [*weather*] venteux; **a** ~ **day** un jour de grand vent; ~ **wind** du vent en rafales

gut [gʌt] ▢1 N (*Anat*) boyau *m*, intestin *m*; (*Med: for stitching*) catgut *m*; (*Mus etc*) (corde *f* de) boyau *m*; (*Anat*) ~**s** boyaux *mpl*; **my** ~**s ache!** j'ai mal au bide*; (*fig*) **to work** or **sweat one's** ~**s out** se crever* au travail; **I hate his** ~**s!** je ne peux pas le blairer*; **the** ~**s of the problem** l'essentiel de son discours/du problème → **bust**

▢2 **guts*** NPL (= *courage*) cran* *m*; **he's got** ~**s** il a du cran*; **he's got no** ~**s** il n'a rien dans le ventre*, il manque de cran*; **it takes a lot of** ~**s to do that** il faut beaucoup de cran* pour faire ça

▢3 ADJ (*fig*) [*reaction*] instinctif; (*negative*) viscéral; **I've got a** ~ **feeling about it** je le sens au fond de moi-même; **my** ~ **feeling** or **instinct is that** ... instinctivement, je sens que ...

▢4 VT (*Culin*) [+ *animal*] vider, étriper; [+ *fish*] vider; * [+ *book etc*] piller*; **fire** ~**ted the house** le feu n'a laissé que les quatre murs de la maison; **the vandals** ~**ted the hall** les vandales n'ont laissé de la salle que les murs → **gutted**

▢5 COMP ► **gut-churning** ADJ abominable, effroyable ► **gut course*** N (*US Univ*) enseignement *m* de base ► **gut-wrenching** ADJ abominable, effroyable

gutless* ['gʌtlɪs] ADJ (= *cowardly*) dégonflé*

gutsy* ['gʌtsɪ] ADJ ▢a (= *plucky*) courageux ▢b (= *substantial*) [*food, wine*] corsé; [*music, song*] musclé*

gutta-percha [,gʌtə'pɜ:tʃə] N (*NonC*) gutta-percha *f*

gutted* ['gʌtɪd] ADJ (*Brit* = *disappointed*) écœuré

gutter ['gʌtər] ▢1 N [*of roof*] gouttière *f*; [*of road*] caniveau *m*; **the language of the** ~ le langage de la rue; **to rise from the** ~ sortir du ruisseau ▢2 VI [*candle*] couler; [*flame*] vaciller, crachoter ▢3 COMP ► **gutter-press** N presse *f* de bas étage or à scandales

guttering ['gʌtərɪŋ] N (*NonC*) gouttières *fpl*

guttersnipe ['gʌtəsnaɪp] N gamin(e) *m(f)* des rues

guttural ['gʌtərəl] ▢1 ADJ guttural ▢2 N (*Phon*†) gutturale *f*

guv* [gʌv] N = **gov**; → **governor** b

guvnor* ['gʌvnər] N = **governor** b

Guy [gaɪ] ▢1 N Guy *m* ▢2 COMP ► **Guy Fawkes Night** N (*Brit*) fête célébrée le 5 novembre

---
| GUY FAWKES NIGHT |
---

*En Grande-Bretagne, **Guy Fawkes Night** se fête le 5 novembre en mémoire de l'exécution du principal conjuré de la Conspiration des poudres (1605). Cette fête est prétexte à feux d'artifices et à feux de joie sur lesquels on brûle traditionnellement une effigie de **Guy Fawkes** (the guy) sous la forme d'une poupée de chiffon. Dans les jours qui précèdent, les enfants promènent cette effigie dans les rues et abordent les passants pour leur demander « a penny for the guy ».*

guy[1] [gaɪ] ▢1 N ▢a (*esp US**) type* *m*, mec* *m*; **the good/bad** ~**s** les bons *mpl*/les méchants *mpl*; **nice** ~ chic type* *m*, type *m* bien*; **hi,** ~**s!** salut les mecs!*; **what are you** ~**s doing tonight?** qu'est-ce que vous faites ce soir, les mecs?*; (*US* = *friends*) **the** ~**s** les copains *mpl* → **fall** ▢b (*Brit*) effigie de Guy Fawkes → GUY FAWKES NIGHT ▢2 VT (= *make fun of*) tourner en ridicule

guy[2] [gaɪ] N (*also* ~ **rope**) corde *f* de tente

Guyana [gaɪˈænə] N la Guyana

Guyanese [,gaɪəˈni:z] ▢1 ADJ guyanais ▢2 N Guyanais(e) *m(f)*

guzzle ['gʌzl] VT ▢a [*person*] [+ *food*] bâfrer*, bouffer*; [+ *drink*] siffler* ▢b (* *fig*) [*car*] [+ *fuel, petrol*] bouffer*

guzzler ['gʌzlər] N goinfre *mf* → **gas**

gybe [dʒaɪb] VI = **gibe** 1b

gym [dʒɪm] ▢1 N ▢a (ABBR = **gymnastics**) gymnastique *f*, gym* *f* ▢b (ABBR = **gymnasium**) gymnase *m*; (*Scol*) salle *f* de gym* ▢2 COMP ► **gym shoes** NPL chaussures *fpl* de gym* ► **gym slip** (*Brit*), **gym suit** (*US*) N tunique *f* (d'écolière)

gymkhana [dʒɪmˈkɑ:nə] N (*esp Brit*) gymkhana *m*

gymnasium [dʒɪmˈneɪzɪəm] N (*pl* **gymnasiums** or **gymnasia** [dʒɪmˈneɪzɪə]) gymnase *m*; (*Scol*) gymnase *m*, salle *f* de gymnastique

gymnast ['dʒɪmnæst] N gymnaste *mf*

gymnastic [dʒɪmˈnæstɪk] ADJ [*ability*] en gymnastique; [*exercise, routine, championship*] de gymnastique; [*leap*] acrobatique

gymnastics [dʒɪmˈnæstɪks] N ▢a (*pl* = *exercises*) gymnastique *f*; **to do** ~ faire de la gymnastique; **mental** ~ gymnastique *f* intellectuelle ▢b (*NonC* = *art, skill*) gymnastique *f*

gynae* ['gaɪnɪ] ABBR = **gynaecological, gynaecology**

gynaecological, gynecological (*US*) [,gaɪnɪkəˈlɒdʒɪkəl] ADJ gynécologique

gynaecologist, gynecologist (*US*) [,gaɪnɪˈkɒlədʒɪst] N gynécologue *mf*

gynaecology, gynecology (*US*) [,gaɪnɪˈkɒlədʒɪ] N gynécologie *f*

gyp* [dʒɪp] ▢1 N ▢a (*US*) (= *swindler*) arnaqueur* *m*; (= *swindle*) escroquerie *f* ▢b (*Brit*) **my leg is giving me** ~ j'ai atrocement or sacrément* mal à la jambe ▢c (*Brit Univ*) domestique *m* ▢2 VT (*US*) **to** ~ **sb out of sth** escroquer qch à qn

gyppo* ['dʒɪpəʊ] N (*Brit*) manouche* *mf*

gypsophila [dʒɪpˈsɒfɪlə] N gypsophile *f*

gypsum ['dʒɪpsəm] N (*NonC*) gypse *m*

gypsy ['dʒɪpsɪ] N = **gipsy**

gyrate [,dʒaɪəˈreɪt] VI (= *dance*) tournoyer

gyration [,dʒaɪəˈreɪʃən] N giration *f*

gyratory [,dʒaɪəˈreɪtərɪ] ADJ giratoire

gyro ['dʒaɪərəʊ] N ABBR = gyrocompass, gyroscope

gyro... ['dʒaɪə'rəʊ] PREF gyro...

gyrocompass ['dʒaɪərəʊ'kʌmpəs] N gyrocompas *m*

gyrofrequency [,dʒaɪərəʊ'friːkwənsɪ] N gyrofréquence *f*

gyromagnetic [,dʒaɪrəʊmæg'netɪk] ADJ gyromagnétique

gyroscope ['dʒaɪərəskəʊp] N gyroscope *m*

gyroscopic ['dʒaɪərəʊ] ADJ gyroscopique

gyrostabilizer [,dʒaɪərəʊ'steɪbɪlaɪzə] N gyrostabilisateur *m*

gyrostat ['dʒaɪərəʊ,stæt] N gyrostat

H

H, h [eɪtʃ] **1** N **a** (= *letter*) H, h *m*; **H for Harry** ◊ **H for How** (*US*) ≈ H comme Hector → **drop b** (*Drugs*) **H*** poudre* *f* (*Drugs*), héroïne *f* **2** COMP ► **H-bomb** N bombe *f* H ► **H grade** N (*Scot Scol*) = **Higher Grade**; → **higher**

ha [hɑ:] EXCL ha!, ah!; **ha, ha!** (*surprise, irony*) ha! ha!; (*laughter*) hi! hi! hi! hi!

habeas corpus ['heɪbɪəs'kɔ:pəs] N (*Jur*) habeas corpus *m* → **writ¹**

haberdasher ['hæbədæʃə'] N (= *person*) (*Brit*) mercier *m*, -ière *f*; (*US*) chemisier *m*, -ière *f*; **~'s** (*Brit*) mercerie *f*; (*US*) confection *f* pour hommes

haberdashery [,hæbə'dæʃərɪ] N (*Brit*) mercerie *f*; (*US*) confection *f* pour hommes

habit ['hæbɪt] **1** N **a** habitude *f*; **good ~s** bonnes habitudes *fpl*; **eating ~s** habitudes *fpl* alimentaires; **a survey of British reading ~s** une étude sur ce que lisent les Britanniques; **I'm worried about his drinking ~s** je m'inquiète de son penchant pour la boisson; **to be in the ~ of doing sth** avoir pour habitude *or* avoir l'habitude de faire qch; **he was talking very loudly, as he was in the ~ of doing when nervous** il parlait très fort comme il avait l'habitude de le faire quand il était tendu; **I don't make a ~ of it** je ne le fais pas souvent; **you can do it this time, but don't make a ~ of it** d'accord pour cette fois, mais il ne faut pas que cela devienne une habitude; **let's hope he doesn't make a ~ of it** espérons qu'il n'en prendra pas l'habitude; **to get** *or* **fall into bad ~s** prendre de mauvaises habitudes; **to get into/out of the ~ of doing sth** prendre/perdre l'habitude de faire qch; **to get sb into the ~ of doing sth** faire prendre à qn l'habitude de faire qch, habituer qn à faire qch; **to get out of a ~** (= *lose the habit*) perdre une habitude; (= *get rid of a habit*) se débarrasser *or* se défaire d'une habitude; **I've got out of the ~ of going to the cinema** j'ai perdu l'habitude d'aller au cinéma, je ne vais pratiquement plus au cinéma; **to have a ~ of doing sth** avoir l'habitude de faire qch; **his ~ of staring at people unnerved her** cette habitude qu'il avait de fixer les gens la troublait; **he had a bad ~ of listening in to other people's conversations** il avait la mauvaise habitude d'écouter les conversations des autres; **history has a ~ of repeating itself** l'histoire a tendance à se répéter; **to do sth out of** *or* **from ~** faire qch par habitude; **~ of mind** tournure *f* d'esprit ■ (*PROV*) **old ~s die hard** les mauvaises habitudes ont la vie dure (*PROV*) → **creature, force**

b **to have a ~** (= *drug-taking*) être toxicomane; (= *smoking*) avoir une dépendance à la nicotine; **they couldn't cure him of the ~** ils n'ont pas réussi à le désaccoutumer *or* le faire décrocher* → **kick**

c (= *costume*) [*of monk, nun*] habit *m*; (*also* **riding ~**) tenue *f* d'équitation

2 COMP ► **habit-forming** ADJ qui crée une accoutumance

habitability [,hæbɪtə'bɪlɪtɪ] N habitabilité *f*

habitable ['hæbɪtəbl] ADJ habitable

habitat ['hæbɪtæt] N habitat *m*

habitation [,hæbɪ'teɪʃən] N **a** (*NonC*) habitation *f*; **the house showed signs of ~** la maison avait l'air habitée; **unfit for human ~** inhabitable **b** (= *dwelling-place*) habitation *f*, domicile *m*; (= *settlement*) établissement *m*, colonie *f*

habitual [hə'bɪtjʊəl] ADJ **a** (= *customary*) [*action, smile, expression, practice, courtesy*] habituel; **to become ~** devenir une habitude **b** (= *regular*) [*drug user, drinker, liar*] invétéré; **~ criminal** *or* **offender** multirécidiviste *mf*

habitually [hə'bɪtjʊəlɪ] ADV habituellement

habituate [hə'bɪtjʊeɪt] VT habituer, accoutumer (**sb to sth** qn à qch)

hacienda [,hæsɪ'endə] N (*US*) hacienda *f*

hack¹ [hæk] **1** N **a** (= *cut*) entaille *f*; (= *blow*) (grand) coup *m*; (= *kick*) coup *m* de pied **b** (= *cough*) toux *f* sèche **c** (*Comput*) = **hacker**

2 VT **a** (= *cut*) hacher, tailler; **to ~ sth to pieces** tailler qch en pièces; **the victims had been ~ed to death** les victimes avaient été massacrées à coups de hache; **we ~ed our way through the jungle** nous nous sommes frayé un chemin dans la jungle à coups de machette

b (*Brit Sport* = *kick*) **to ~ the ball away** renvoyer le ballon

c ‡ **he just can't ~ it** (= *can't manage it*) il est complètement largué‡; (= *can't stand it*) il déteste ça, ça lui donne des boutons*; **can he ~ it as a police chief?** est-ce qu'il tiendra le choc* en tant que chef de la police?

d (*Brit*‡) **I'm ~ed off** (= *fed up*) j'en ai ras le bol‡ (**with sb/sth** de qn/qch); (= *annoyed*) je l'ai mauvaise*; (= *annoyed*) **I'm really ~ed off with her!** je suis en rogne* contre elle!

e (*Comput*) [+ *system, file*] s'introduire dans

3 VI **a** (= *cut*) **to ~ at sth** (essayer de) couper qch (au couteau *or* à la hache *etc*)

b (= *cough*) tousser (d'une toux sèche)

c (= *be computer enthusiast*) être un(e) mordu(e)* d'informatique; **she had managed to ~ into the system** (= *break into system*) elle avait réussi à s'introduire dans le système

4 COMP ► **hacking cough** N toux *f* sèche

► **hack around** VI (*US*) traîner

► **hack down** VT SEP [+ *person*] massacrer à coups de couteau (*or* de hache *or* d'épée *etc*); [+ *tree*] abattre

► **hack out** VT SEP enlever grossièrement à coups de couteau (*or* de hache *or* d'épée *etc*)

► **hack up** VT SEP hacher, tailler en pièces

hack² [hæk] **1** N **a** (*Brit*) (= *horse*) cheval *m* de selle; (*hired*) cheval *m* de louage; (*worn-out*) haridelle *f*, rosse *f*; (= *ride*) promenade *f* à cheval; **to go for a ~** (aller) se promener à cheval **b** (*pej*) (= *journalist*) journaleux *m*, -euse *f* (*pej*); (= *politician*) politicard(e) *m(f)* (*pej*); (*Pol*) **the party ~s** les politicards *mpl* (*pej*) du parti; **a ~ writer** ◊ **a literary ~** un écrivaillon, un plumitif **c** (*US*‡) (= *vehicle*) taxi *m*; (= *driver*) chauffeur *m* de taxi **2** VI (*Brit* = *ride*) monter (à cheval); **to go ~ing** (aller) se promener à cheval **b** (*US* = *operate cab*) faire

le taxi* **3** COMP ► **hacking jacket** N (*Brit*) veste *f* de cheval *or* d'équitation ► **hack reporter** N **to be a ~ reporter** tenir la rubrique des chiens écrasés, faire les chiens écrasés ► **hack work** N = **hack writing** ► **hack writer** N (*pej*) → **1b** ► **hack writing** N (*NonC*) écrits *mpl* alimentaires; (*pej*) travail *m* d'écrivaillon (*pej*)

► **hack up** VI [*horse*] (= *win easily*) l'emporter facilement; **the favourite ~ed up by 12 lengths** le favori l'a emporté facilement avec 12 longueurs d'avance

hacker ['hækə'] N (*Comput*) (= *enthusiast*) mordu(e)* *m(f)* d'informatique; (= *pirate*) pirate *m* informatique

hacking ['hækɪŋ] N (*Comput*) (= *enthusiasm*) engouement *m* pour l'informatique; (= *piracy*) piratage *m* informatique

hackle ['hækl] **1** N plume *f* du cou **2** **hackles** NPL poils *mpl* du cou; (*fig*) **his ~s rose at the very idea** ça le hérissait d'y penser; **to get sb's ~s up** ◊ **to raise sb's ~s** hérisser qn

hackman ['hækmən] N (*pl* **-men**) (*US* = *cabdriver*) chauffeur *m* de taxi

hackney cab ['hæknɪkæb], **hackney carriage** ['hæknɪkærɪdʒ] N voiture *f* de place *or* de louage

hackneyed ['hæknɪd] ADJ [*word, image*] banal; [*theme, subject*] rebattu; [*metaphor*] usé; **~ expression** *or* **phrase** cliché *m*, lieu *m* commun

hacksaw ['hæksɔ:] N scie *f* à métaux

had [hæd] VB *pt, ptp of* **have**

haddock ['hædək] N (*pl* **haddock** *or* **haddocks**) églefin *m* *or* aiglefin *m*; **smoked ~** haddock *m*

Hades ['heɪdi:z] N (*Myth*) (= *the underworld*) les enfers *mpl*; (= *god*) Hadès *m*

hadj [hædʒ] N = **hajj**

hadn't ['hædnt] = **had not**; → **have**

Hadrian **1** ['heɪdrɪən] N Hadrien *m* **2** COMP ► **Hadrian's Wall** N le mur d'Hadrien

haematemesis, hematemesis (*US*) [,hi:mə'temɪsɪs] N hématémèse *f*

haematic, hematic (*US*) [hi:'mætɪk] ADJ hématique

haematite, hematite (*US*) ['hi:mə,taɪt] N hématite *f*

haematological, hematological (*US*) [,hi:mətə'lɒdʒɪkəl] ADJ hématologique

haematologist, hematologist (*US*) [,hi:mə'tɒlədʒɪst] N hématologue *mf*, hématologiste *m*

haematology, hematology (*US*) [,hi:mə'tɒlədʒɪ] N hématologie *f*

haematolysis, hematolysis (*US*) [,hi:mə'tɒlɪsɪs] N = **haemolysis**

haematoma, hematoma (*US*) [,hi:mə'təʊmə] N (*pl* **haematomas** *or* **haematomata** [,hi:mə'təʊmətə]) hématome *m*

haemodialyser, hemodialyzer (*US*) [,hi:məʊ'daɪə,laɪzə'] N rein *m* artificiel

haemodialysis, hemodialysis (*US*) [,hi:məʊdaɪ'ælɪsɪs] N hémodialyse *f*

haemoglobin, hemoglobin (US) [ˌhiːməʊˈgləʊbɪn] N hémoglobine f

haemolysis, hemolysis (US) [hɪˈmɒlɪsɪs] N (pl **haemolyses** [hɪˈmɒlɪˌsiːz]) hémolyse f

haemophilia, hemophilia (US) [ˌhiːməʊˈfɪlɪə] N hémophilie f

haemophiliac, hemophiliac (US) [ˌhiːməʊˈfɪlɪæk] ADJ, N hémophile mf

haemoptysis, hemoptysis (US) [hɪˈmɒptɪsɪs] N (pl **haemoptyses** [hɪˈmɒptɪˌsiːz]) hémoptysie f

haemorrhage, hemorrhage (US) [ˈhemərɪdʒ] ① N hémorragie f ② VI faire une hémorragie

haemorrhoids, hemorrhoids (US) [ˈhemərɔɪdz] NPL hémorroïdes fpl

haemostasis, hemostasis (US) [ˌhiːməʊˈsteɪsɪs] N hémostase f

hafnium [ˈhæfnɪəm] N hafnium m

haft [hɑːft] ① N [of knife] manche m; [of sword] poignée f ② VT emmancher, mettre un manche à

hag [hæg] ① N (= ugly old woman) vieille sorcière f; (= witch) sorcière f; (* = unpleasant woman) mégère f ② COMP ► **hag-ridden** ADJ (gen) tourmenté; (henpecked husband) **he's ~-ridden** sa femme n'arrête pas de le houspiller

haggard [ˈhægəd] ADJ (= careworn) défait; (= wild in appearance) hagard; **to look ~** avoir la mine défaite

haggis [ˈhægɪs] N (Culin) haggis m (saucisse écossaise à base de panse de brebis)

haggle [ˈhægl] VI (= bargain) marchander; (= quibble) chicaner; **to ~ about** or **over the price** (= bargain) débattre le prix; (= quibble) chicaner sur le prix; **they ~d over the terms of the agreement** ils ont chicané sur les termes de l'accord

haggling [ˈhæglɪŋ] N (= bargaining) marchandage m; (= quibbling) ergotage m

hagiographer [ˌhægɪˈɒɡrəfəʳ] N hagiographe mf

hagiography [ˌhægɪˈɒɡrəfɪ] N hagiographie f

Hague [heɪg] N **The ~** La Haye

hah [hɑː] EXCL ha!, ah!

ha-ha [ˈhɑːˈhɑː] N (Brit) (= fence) clôture f en contrebas; (= ditch) saut-de-loup m

haiku [ˈhaɪkuː] N (pl inv) haïku m

hail¹ [heɪl] ① N ⓐ (NonC: Met) grêle f ⓑ (fig) [of stones, bullets, blows] grêle f, pluie f; **a ~ of gunfire** une pluie or grêle de balles ② VI grêler; **it is ~ing** il grêle

hail² [heɪl] ① VT ⓐ (= acclaim) saluer (as comme); **she has been ~ed as the greatest novelist of her generation** elle a été saluée comme la plus grande romancière de sa génération; **the agreement was ~ed as a breakthrough** l'accord a été salué comme un événement capital ⓑ † (= acknowledge) acclamer (as comme); **he was ~ed as emperor** on l'acclama or il fut acclamé comme empereur ⓒ (all) ~!† salut à vous!, je vous salue! ⓓ (= call loudly) [+ ship, taxi, person] héler; **within ~ing distance** à portée de (la) voix ② VI (frm) **to ~ from** [ship] être en provenance de; [person] être originaire de; **a ship ~ing from London** un navire en provenance de Londres; **they ~ from Leeds** ils sont originaires de Leeds; **where do you ~ from?** d'où êtes-vous? ③ N appel m ④ COMP ► **hail-fellow-well-met** ADJ **to be ~-fellow-well-met** se montrer d'une familiarité excessive ► **Hail Mary** N (Rel) Je vous salue Marie m inv, Ave m inv

► **hail down** VT SEP [+ taxi] héler

hailstone [ˈheɪlstəʊn] N grêlon m

hailstorm [ˈheɪlstɔːm] N averse f de grêle

hair [heəʳ] ① N ⓐ (NonC) [of human] (on head) cheveux mpl; (on body) poils mpl; **he has black ~** il a les cheveux noirs; **a man with long ~** un homme aux cheveux longs; **a fine head of ~** une belle chevelure; **to wash one's ~** se laver les cheveux; **to do one's ~** se coiffer; **her ~ always looks nice** elle est toujours bien coiffée; **to have one's ~ done** se faire coiffer; **she always does my ~ very well** elle me coiffe toujours très bien; **to get one's ~ cut** se faire couper les cheveux; **to put one's ~ up** relever ses cheveux; (fig) **to let one's ~ down*** se laisser aller; (Brit) **keep your ~ on!*** du calme!; **he gets in my ~*** (= is annoying) il me tape sur les nerfs* or sur le système*; **I wish you'd get out of my ~*** while I'm working j'aimerais bien que tu ne sois pas tout le temps dans mes jambes quand je travaille; **to get sb out of one's ~** (= get rid of them) se débarrasser de qn; **it made my ~ stand on end** cela m'a fait dresser les cheveux sur la tête

ⓑ [of human] (= single hair) (on head) cheveu m; (on body) poil m; **I'm starting to get some grey ~s** je commence à avoir des cheveux gris or à grisonner; **(with) not a ~ out of place** tiré à quatre épingles; **not a ~ of his head was harmed** on n'a pas touché à un seul de ses cheveux; (hum) **this will put ~s on your chest*** (spicy food, strong drink etc) ça te rendra plus viril; (fig) **it was hanging by a ~** cela ne tenait qu'à un cheveu; **he won the race by a ~** il a gagné la course de justesse or d'un cheveu → **hair's breadth, split, turn**

ⓒ [of animal] (= single hair) poil m; (NonC) pelage m; [of horse] pelage m, robe f; (= bristles) soies fpl; **I'm allergic to cat ~** je suis allergique aux poils de chat; (fig) **try a ~ of the dog (that bit you)*** reprends un petit verre pour faire passer ta gueule de bois*

② COMP [sofa, mattress] de crin ► **hair appointment** N rendez-vous m chez le coiffeur ► **hair bulb** N bulbe m pileux ► **hair care** N soins mpl capillaires or du cheveu ► **hair clippers** NPL tondeuse f (de coiffeur) ► **hair conditioner** N après-shampooing m, baume m démêlant ► **hair cream** N crème f capillaire ► **hair-curler** N bigoudi m ► **hair-dryer** N (hand-held) sèche-cheveux m inv, séchoir m (à cheveux); (freestanding) casque m ► **hair extension** N (clip-on) postiche m; (permanent) extension f ► **hair follicle** N follicule m pileux ► **hair gel** N gel m (coiffant or pour les cheveux) ► **hair grip** N (Brit) pince f à cheveux ► **hair implant** N implants mpl capillaires ► **hair lacquer** N laque f (pour cheveux) ► **hair oil** N huile f capillaire ► **hairraising*** ADJ [experience, story] terrifiant, à (vous) faire dresser les cheveux sur la tête; **driving in Paris is a ~-raising business** c'est terrifiant de conduire dans Paris ► **hair remover** N crème f dépilatoire ► **hair restorer** N antichute m ► **hair roller** N rouleau m (bigoudi) ► **hair shirt** N (Rel) haire f, cilice m ► **hair slide** N (Brit) barrette f ► **hair specialist** N capilliculteur m, -trice f ► **hairsplitter** N coupeur m, -euse f de cheveux en quatre ► **hair-splitting** N ergotage m, pinaillage* m ► **hair spray** N laque f (pour cheveux) ► **hair style** N coiffure f ► **hair stylist** N coiffeur m, -euse f ► **hair transplant** N implants mpl capillaires ► **hair-trigger** ADJ [temper] explosif

hairball [ˈheəbɔːl] N [of cat] boule f de poils

hairband [ˈheəbænd] N bandeau m

hairbrained [ˈheəbreɪnd] ADJ = **harebrained**

hairbrush [ˈheəbrʌʃ] N brosse f à cheveux

haircloth [ˈheəklɒθ] N étoffe f de crin

haircut [ˈheəkʌt] N **to have** or **get a ~** se faire couper les cheveux; **I'd like a ~** je voudrais une coupe; **I like your ~** j'aime bien ta coupe de cheveux

hairdo* [ˈheəduː] N coiffure f; **do you like my**

~? tu aimes ma coiffure?, tu aimes mes cheveux comme ça?*

hairdresser [ˈheədresəʳ] ① N coiffeur m, -euse f; **I'm going to the ~'s** je vais chez le coiffeur ② COMP ► **hairdresser's (salon** or **shop)** N salon m de coiffure

hairdressing [ˈheədresɪŋ] ① N (NonC = skill, job) coiffure f (métier) ② COMP ► **hairdressing appointment** N rendez-vous m chez le coiffeur ► **hairdressing salon** N salon m de coiffure

-haired [heəd] ADJ (in compounds) **long-haired** [person] aux cheveux longs; [animal] à longs poils; **short-haired** [person] aux cheveux courts; [animal] à poils ras → **curly, fair**

hairless [ˈheəlɪs] ADJ [head] chauve; [face, chin] imberbe; [body, legs] glabre; [animal] sans poils

hairline [ˈheəlaɪn] ① N (on head) naissance f des cheveux; (in handwriting) délié m → **recede** ② COMP ► **hairline crack** N (gen) fine fissure f; (Med) mince or légère fêlure f ► **hairline fracture** N (Med) fêlure f

hairnet [ˈheənet] N résille f, filet m à cheveux

hairpiece [ˈheəpiːs] N postiche m

hairpin [ˈheəpɪn] ① N épingle f à cheveux ② COMP ► **hairpin bend, hairpin curve** (US) N virage m en épingle à cheveux

hair's breadth [ˈheəzbredθ] ① N **the bullet missed him by a ~** la balle l'a manqué de justesse or d'un cheveu; **the car missed the taxi by a ~** la voiture a évité le taxi de justesse; **the country is within a ~ of civil war** le pays est à deux doigts de la guerre civile; **she was within a ~ of selling the business** elle était à deux doigts de vendre l'affaire ② ADJ **they won the election with a ~ majority** ils ont remporté les élections d'un cheveu or de justesse; **this performance earned him a ~ victory** grâce à cette performance, il l'a emporté or il a gagné de justesse; **they had a ~ escape from their pursuers** ils ont échappé à leurs poursuivants de justesse

hairspring [ˈheəsprɪŋ] N (ressort m) spiral m (de montre)

hairy [ˈheərɪ] ADJ ⓐ (= covered with hair) [person, body] poilu; [animal] très poilu; [chest, legs, spider, leaf] velu; **a mammal's coat** le pelage épais d'un mammifère ⓑ* (= scary) **his driving is a bit ~** sa façon de conduire file la pétoche*; **there were some ~ moments on the mountain bends** on a eu de sueurs froides dans les virages de montagne

Haiti [ˈheɪtɪ] N Haïti f or m; **in ~** en Haïti

Haitian [ˈheɪʃən] ① ADJ haïtien ② N Haïtien(ne) m(f)

hajj [hædʒ] N (pl **hajjes**) hadj m

hake [heɪk] N (pl **hake** or **hakes**) (Brit) colin m, merlu m

halal [hæˈlæl] ADJ [meat, butcher] halal inv or hallal inv

halberd [ˈhælbəd] N hallebarde f

halcyon [ˈhælsɪən] ① N (Myth, Orn) alcyon m ② ADJ [years, period] de bonheur; **~ days** jours mpl de bonheur, jours mpl heureux

hale [heɪl] ADJ [person] vigoureux, robuste; **to be ~ and hearty** (gen) être en pleine santé; [old person] avoir bon pied bon œil

half [hɑːf] (pl **halves**) ① N ⓐ (of one whole) moitié f; **would you like one ~ of my apple?** veux-tu la moitié de ma pomme?; **to take ~ of sth** prendre la moitié de qch; **two halves make a whole** deux demis font un entier; **the two halves of the brain** les deux hémisphères du cerveau; **inflation rose in the first ~ of this year** l'inflation a augmenté au cours du premier semestre de l'année; **two and a ~** deux et demi; **two and a ~ hours/weeks** ◊ **two hours/weeks and a ~** deux heures/semaines et demie; **two and a ~ kilos** ◊ **two kilos and a ~** deux kilos et demi; **to cut sth in ~** [+ object] couper qch en deux ; **to cut in** *or* **by ~** [+ *costs, prices, budget, workforce*] réduire de moitié ; **the plate broke in ~** l'assiette s'est cassée en deux ; **I spent ~ the night thinking about it** j'ai passé la moitié de la nuit à y penser ; **she was working with ~ her usual energy** elle travaillait avec beaucoup moins d'énergie que de coutume ; (*fig*) **in ~ a second*** en moins de rien ; **to listen with ~ an ear** n'écouter que d'une oreille ; **you can see that with ~ an eye** ça saute aux yeux, ça crève les yeux

[b] (*of a number of things or people*) moitié *f* ; **~ of the books are in French** la moitié des livres sont en français ; **nearly ~ of all marriages end in divorce** près de la moitié des couples divorcent ; **100 employees, ~ of whom are part-time** 100 employés, dont la moitié sont à temps partiel ; **they don't know how to drive, ~ of them** la plupart d'entre eux ne savent pas conduire

[c] [*of rail ticket*] **outward ~** billet *m* aller ; **return ~** billet *m* de retour

[d] (*phrases*) **he doesn't do things by halves** il ne fait pas les choses à moitié *or* à demi ; **will you go halves with me in buying the book?** veux-tu qu'on achète ce livre ensemble, en payant chacun la moitié ?, est-ce que tu partagerais avec moi le prix de ce livre ? ; **we always go halves on the phone bill** nous partageons toujours la note de téléphone en deux ; **we went halves on a taxi** nous avons partagé un taxi ; **and that's not the ~ of it!*** ◊ **I haven't told you the ~ of it yet!*** et c'est pas tout !* ; **that was a day/an exam and a ~!*** ça a été une sacrée journée/un sacré examen !*, je te raconte pas ma journée/mon examen !* ; **he's too clever/cheeky by ~*** c'est un petit malin/impertinent ; **the film was too sentimental by ~*** ce film était bien trop sentimental ; (*hum*) **my better** *or* **other ~*** ma douce moitié ; (*fig*) **to see how the other ~ lives*** voir comment vivent les autres

[e] (*Sport* = *part of match*) mi-temps *f* ; **the first/second ~** la première/seconde mi-temps

[f] (*Sport* = *player*) demi *m* ; (*Ftbl*) **left/right ~** demi *m* gauche/droite

[g] (*Scol* = *term*) semestre *m*

[h] (*Brit: also* **~-pint**) demi *m* ; **a ~ of Guinness please** un demi de Guinness, s'il vous plaît

2 ADJ demi ; **a ~ cup** ◊ **~ a cup** une demi-tasse ; **two and a ~ cups** deux tasses et demie ; **three ~ cups** trois demi-tasses ; **a bottle of wine** une demi-bouteille de vin ; **a ~-point cut in interest rates** une réduction d'un demi pour cent des taux d'intérêt ; **~ one thing ~ another** ni chair ni poisson ; **~ man ~ beast** mi-homme mi-bête ; **there are no ~ measures** il n'y a pas de demi-mesures ; **this plan smacks of ~ measures** ce plan ne propose que des demi-mesures ; **he never does anything by ~ measures** ◊ **there are no ~ measures with him** il ne fait jamais les choses à moitié → **4, tick¹**

3 ADV [a] (= *50%*) **a mixture of ~ milk, ~ cream** un mélange moitié lait moitié crème, un mélange de lait et de crème, moitié-moitié ; **a ~-million dollars/people** un demi-million de dollars/personnes ; **the book was ~ in French, ~ in English** le livre était à moitié en français, à moitié en anglais ; **he's ~ French ~ English** il est de père français et de mère anglaise (*or* de père anglais et de mère française) ; **he is ~ as big as his sister** il est deux fois plus petit que sa sœur ; **he earns ~ as much as you** il gagne deux fois moins que vous ; **she earns ~ as much again as him** elle gagne une fois et demi(e) son salaire ; **a PC costs ~ as much again in Europe as in America** les PC coûtent une fois et demi(e) plus cher en Europe qu'en Amérique ; **his company's sales fell ~ as much again as last year** les ventes de son entreprise ont connu une baisse de 50 % de plus que l'année dernière → **4**

[b] (= *partially, partly*) à moitié ; **~ asleep** à

moitié endormi ; **~-buried** à moitié *or* à demi enterré ; **the work is only ~ done** le travail n'est qu'à moitié fait ; **she has only ~ recovered from her illness** elle n'est qu'à moitié remise de sa maladie ; **he only ~ understands** il ne comprend qu'à moitié ; **I've only ~ read it** (= *didn't read carefully*) je ne l'ai lu qu'à moitié ; (= *haven't finished reading*) je n'en ai lu que la moitié ; **she was ~ laughing ~ crying** elle était partagée entre le rire et les larmes, elle était entre rire et larmes ; **~ angry, ~ amused** mi-fâché, mi-amusé

[c] (= *rather, almost*) un peu ; **I'm ~ afraid that ...** j'ai un peu peur que ... + ne (+ *subj*) ; **he was ~ ashamed to admit it** il avait un peu honte de l'admettre ; **I ~ think (that) ...** je serais tenté de penser que ... ; **I'm ~ inclined to do it** je suis tenté de le faire ; **I ~ suspect that ...** je soupçonne que ... → **4**

[d] (*Brit*: emphatic*) **he wasn't ~ bad to look at!** il était rudement* *or* drôlement* beau ! ; **she didn't ~ swear!** elle a juré comme un charretier ! ; **she didn't ~ cry!** elle a pleuré comme une Madeleine ! ; **not ~!*** tu parles !*, et comment !

[e] (*in telling the time*) **it is ~ past three** il est trois heures et demie ; **what time is it? — ~ past** quelle heure est-il ? — la demie → **4**

4 COMP ► **half-a-crown** N (*Brit: formerly = value*) demi-couronne *f* → **half-crown** ► **half-a-dollar** N (*US = value*) un demi-dollar ; (*Brit: formerly*) une demi-couronne → **half-dollar** ► **half-a-dozen** N une demi-douzaine → **half-dozen** ► **half-and-half** ADV moitié-moitié ◆ N (*US = milk and cream*) mélange mi-crème mi-lait ► **half-an-hour** N une demi-heure → **half-hour** ► **half-assed** ADJ (*US*) foireux*, nul ► **half-baked** ADJ (*Culin*) à moitié cuit ; (*fig, pej*) [*plan, idea*] qui ne tient pas debout, à la noix* ; [*attempt*] maladroit ; **a ~-baked philosopher/politician** un philosophe/politicien à la manque* ► **half-binding** N [*of book*] demi-reliure *f* ► **half-blind** ADJ à moitié aveugle ► **half-blood** N (*US*) = **half-breed** ► **half-board** N (*Brit: in hotel*) demi-pension *f* ► **half-breed** N (= *person*) métis(se) *m(f)* ◆ ADJ (*also* **~-bred**) [*person*] métis(se) ; [*animal*] hybride ► **half-brother** N demi-frère *m* ► **half-caste** N métis(se) *m(f)* ► **half-century** N demi-siècle *m* ► **half-circle** N demi-cercle *m* ► **half-clad** ADJ à demi vêtu ► **half-closed** ADJ à demi fermé, à moitié fermé ► **half-cock** N **to go off at ~-cock** (*fig*) [*plan etc*] rater ► **half-cocked** ADJ [*gun*] à moitié armé, au cran de sûreté ; (*fig*) [*plan, scheme*] mal préparé, bâclé ; (*fig*) **to go off ~-cocked** rater ► **half-convinced** ADJ à demi convaincu, à moitié convaincu ► **half-cooked** ADJ à moitié cuit ► **half-crazy** ADJ à moitié fou (folle *f*) ► **half-crown** N (*Brit: formerly = coin*) demi-couronne *f* → **half-a-crown** ► **half-cup bra** N soutien-gorge *m* à balconnet ► **half-cut** ‡* ADJ (*Brit*) bourré* ► **half-day** N demi-journée *f* ; **to have a ~-day (holiday)** avoir une demi-journée (de congé) ► **half-dazed** ADJ à demi hébété ► **half-dead** ADJ (*lit, fig*) à moitié mort, à demi mort (**with** de) ► **half-deaf** ADJ à moitié sourd ► **half-deck** N (*Naut*) demi-pont *m* ► **half-digested** ADJ (*lit, fig*) mal digéré ► **half-dollar** N (*US = coin*) demi-dollar *m* → **half-a-dollar** ► **half-dozen** N demi-douzaine *f* → **half-a-dozen** ► **half-dressed** ADJ à demi vêtu ► **half-drowned** ADJ à moitié noyé ► **half-educated** ADJ **he is ~-educated** il n'est pas très instruit ► **half-empty** ADJ à moitié vide ◆ VT vider à moitié ► **half-fare** N demi-tarif *m* ◆ ADV [*pay*] demi-tarif ► **half-fill** VT remplir à moitié ► **half-forgotten** ADJ à moitié oublié ► **half-frozen** ADJ à moitié gelé ► **half-full** ADJ à moitié plein ► **half-grown** ADJ à mi-croissance ► **half-hearted** ADJ [*person, welcome*] peu enthousiaste ; [*manner*] tiède ;

[*attempt*] timide ► **half-heartedly** ADV [*welcome*] sans enthousiasme ; [*try*] sans conviction ► **half-heartedness** N tiédeur *f* ; [*of person, welcome*] manque *m* d'enthousiasme ; [*of attempt*] manque *m* de conviction ► **half-hitch** N demi-clef *f* ► **half holiday** N (*Brit*) demi-journée *f* de congé ► **half-hour** N demi-heure *f* ; **the clock struck the ~-hour** l'horloge a sonné la demie (de l'heure) ; **on the ~-hour** à la demie ◆ ADJ [*wait, delay*] d'une demi-heure → **half-an-hour** ► **half-hourly** ADV toutes les demi-heures ◆ ADJ d'une demi-heure ► **half-jokingly** ADV en plaisantant à moitié ► **half-landing** N palier *m* de repos ► **half-length** N (*Swimming*) demi-longueur *f* ◆ ADJ [*portrait*] en buste ► **half-lie** N demi-mensonge *m* ► **half-life** N (*Phys*) demi-vie *f* ► **half-light** N demi-jour *m* ► **half-mad** ADJ à moitié fou (folle *f*) ► **half-marathon** N semi-marathon *m* ► **half-mast** N **at ~-mast** [*flag*] en berne ; [*trousers*] qui tombe ► **half-moon** N demi-lune *f* ; (*on fingernail*) lunule *f* ► **half-naked** ADJ à demi nu, à moitié nu ► **half-nelson** N (*Wrestling*) étranglement *m* ► **half-note** N (*US Mus*) blanche *f* ► **half open** VT entrouvrir, entrebâiller ► **half-open** ADJ [*eye, mouth*] entrouvert ; [*window, door*] entrouvert, entrebâillé ► **half pay** N **to be on ~ pay** (*gen*) toucher un demi-salaire ; (*Mil*) toucher une demi-solde ► **half-pint** N ≈ quart *m* de litre ; (* = *small person*) demi-portion* *f* ; **a ~-pint (of beer)** ≈ un demi ► **half price** N **at ~ price** à moitié prix ; **the goods were reduced to ~ price** le prix des articles était réduit de moitié ; **children are admitted (at) ~ price** les enfants paient demi-tarif ; **a ~-price hat** un chapeau à moitié prix ► **half-raw** ADJ à moitié cru ► **half rest** N (*US: Mus*) demi-pause *f* ► **half seas over**†‡ ADJ parti*, dans les vignes du Seigneur ► **half-serious** ADJ à moitié sérieux ► **half-shut** ADJ à moitié fermé ► **half-sister** N demi-sœur *f* ► **half-size** N [*of shoes*] demi-pointure *f* ◆ ADJ **~-size(d) model** modèle *m* réduit de moitié ► **half-sleeve** N manche *f* mi-longue ► **half-staff** N (*US*) **at ~-staff** en berne ► **half-starved** ADJ à demi mort de faim, affamé ► **half term** N (*Brit Educ*) congé *m* en milieu de trimestre, petites vacances *fpl* ► **half-timbered** ADJ à colombage ► **half time** N (*Sport*) mi-temps *f* ; **at ~ time** à la mi-temps [b] (= *work*) mi-temps *m* ; **on ~ time** à mi-temps ; **they are working ~ time** ils travaillent à mi-temps ► **half-time** N **time score** score *m* à la mi-temps ► **half-tone** N (*US Mus*) demi-ton *m* ; (*Art*) demi-teinte *f* ; (*Phot*) similigravure *f* ► **half-track** N (= *tread*) chenille *f* ; (= *vehicle*) half-track *m* ► **half-truth** N demi-vérité *f* ► **half-understood** ADJ compris à moitié, mal compris ► **half volley** N (*Tennis*) demi-volée *f* ◆ ADV tous les six mois, chaque semestre

halfback ['hɑːfbæk] N (*Sport*) demi *m*

halfpenny ['heɪpnɪ] 1 N (*pl* **halfpennies** *or* **halfpence** ['heɪpəns]) demi-penny *m* ; **he hasn't got a ~** il n'a pas le *or* un sou 2 ADJ d'un demi-penny

halfway ['hɑːf'weɪ] 1 ADV (*in distance*) à mi-chemin ; **to be ~ along the road** être à mi-chemin ; **~ along (the line of cars etc)** vers le milieu (de la file de voitures etc) ; (*lit, fig*) **~ between ... and ...** à mi-chemin entre ... ; **~ down (the hill)** à mi-pente, à mi-côte ; **~ up (the pipe/tree etc)** à mi-hauteur (du tuyau/de l'arbre etc) ; **he was ~ down/up the stairs** il avait descendu/monté la moitié de l'escalier ; **her hair reaches ~ down her back** ses cheveux lui arrivent au milieu du dos ; **to stretch ~ around the world** faire la moitié de la terre ; **they've travelled ~ around the world** (*lit*) ils ont fait la moitié du tour de la terre ; (*fig*) ils ont beaucoup voyagé ; **(to be) ~ there** (être) à mi-chemin ; **~ through the book/film** au milieu du livre/du film ; **turn the fish over ~ through** retourner le poisson en milieu de cuisson ; **~ to Paris** à mi-chemin de Paris ; **anything ~ decent will be incredibly expensive** pour avoir quelque chose d'à peu près correct, il faut compter une fortune ; (lit) **to go ~** faire la moitié du chemin ; (fig) **the decision goes ~ to giving the strikers what they want** cette décision va dans le sens des revendications des grévistes ; **I'll meet you ~** (lit) j'irai à votre rencontre, je ferai la moitié du chemin ; (fig) coupons la poire en deux, faisons un compromis ; **to meet trouble ~** se créer des ennuis

[2] COMP ► **halfway hostel** N = **halfway house** a ► **halfway house** N [a] (for rehabilitation) centre m de réadaptation [b] (= compromise) compromis m ; **it's a ~ house between dance and drama** c'est à mi-chemin entre la danse et le théâtre [c] (Hist = inn) hôtellerie f relais ► **halfway line** N (Ftbl) ligne f médiane

halfwit ['hɑːfwɪt] N idiot(e) m(f), imbécile mf
halfwitted [hɑːf'wɪtɪd] ADJ idiot, imbécile
halibut ['hælɪbət] N (pl halibut or halibuts) flétan m
halitosis [ˌhælɪ'təʊsɪs] N mauvaise haleine f

hall [hɔːl] [1] N [a] (= large public room) salle f ; (of castle, public building) (grande) salle f ; (also **village ~, church ~**) salle f paroissiale ; (Brit Univ = refectory) réfectoire m → **concert, music, town** [b] (= mansion) château m, manoir m [c] (Theat) **to play the ~s** faire du music-hall [d] (= entrance way) (of house) entrée f ; (of hotel) hall m [e] (Univ: also **~ of residence** (Brit), **residence ~** (US)) résidence f universitaire ; **to live** or **be in ~** habiter en résidence universitaire or en cité universitaire [2] COMP ► **Hall of Fame** N (esp US: lit, fig) panthéon m ► **hall porter** N (Brit) (in blocks of flats) concierge mf ; (in hotel) portier m ► **hall tree** N (US) = **hallstand**

hallelujah [ˌhælɪ'luːjə] EXCL, N alléluia m
hallmark ['hɔːlmɑːk] [1] N [a] (of gold, silver) poinçon m [b] (fig) marque f ; **the ~ of genius** la marque du génie [2] VT poinçonner
hallo [hə'ləʊ] EXCL (Brit) = **hello**
halloo [hə'luː] [1] EXCL (Hunting) taïaut ! ; (gen) ohé ! [2] N appel m [3] VI (Hunting) crier taïaut ; (gen) appeler (à grands cris)
hallow ['hæləʊ] VT sanctifier, consacrer ; **~ed be Thy name** que Ton nom soit sanctifié
hallowed ['hæləʊd] ADJ [a] (= holy) saint, béni ; **on ~ ground** en terre sacrée [b] (= venerable) [right, tradition, institution] sacré ; (hum) **the ~portals of the headmaster's office** l'entrée de ce lieu sacré qu'est le bureau du directeur
Halloween, Hallowe'en [ˌhæləʊ'iːn] N Halloween m

HALLOWEEN

La fête d'**Halloween**, célébrée le 31 octobre (jour où, pensait-on, les morts venaient rendre visite aux vivants), est une très ancienne tradition dans les pays anglo-saxons. À cette occasion, les enfants déguisés en sorcières et en fantômes frappent aux portes de leurs voisins pour leur demander des bonbons et de l'argent ; aux États-Unis, cette coutume est connue sous le nom de « trick or treat », car les enfants menacent de vous jouer un mauvais tour (« trick ») si vous ne leur donnez pas un petit cadeau (« treat »), en général des bonbons.

hallstand ['hɔːlstænd] N portemanteau m
hallucinant [hə'luːsɪnənt] N hallucinogène m
hallucinate [hə'luːsɪneɪt] VI avoir des hallucinations
hallucination [hə,luːsɪ'neɪʃən] N hallucination f
hallucinatory [hə'luːsɪnətərɪ] ADJ (drug) hallucinogène ; (state, effect, vision) hallucinatoire

hallucinogen [ˌhælʊː'sɪnədʒən] N hallucinogène m
hallucinogenic [hə,luːsɪnəʊ'dʒenɪk] ADJ hallucinogène
hallway ['hɔːlweɪ] N = **hall 1d**
halo ['heɪləʊ] N (pl **halo(e)s**) (of saint) auréole f, nimbe m ; (Astron) halo m
halogen ['hælə,dʒen] [1] N halogène m [2] COMP ► **halogen lamp** N lampe f (à) halogène
halt[1] [hɔːlt] [1] N [a] halte f, arrêt m ; **five minutes' ~** cinq minutes d'arrêt ; **to come to a ~** [person] faire halte, s'arrêter ; [vehicle] s'arrêter ; [process] être interrompu ; **the commander called a ~** le commandant a ordonné que l'on s'arrête ; (Ftbl etc) **the referee called a ~** l'arbitre a sifflé un arrêt de jeu ; **to call a ~ to sth** mettre fin à qch ; **to call for a ~ to sth** demander l'arrêt de qch ; **her government called for an immediate ~ to the fighting** son gouvernement a demandé l'arrêt immédiat des combats [b] (Brit = Rail) halte f [2] VI faire halte, s'arrêter ; **~!** halte ! [3] VT (vehicle) faire arrêter ; (+ process) interrompre [4] COMP ► **halt sign** N (Aut) (panneau m) stop m
halt[2] †† [hɔːlt] [1] ADJ (= lame) boiteux [2] **the halt** NPL les estropiés mpl
halter ['hɔːltə'] [1] N [a] (of horse) licou m, collier m ; (= hangman's noose) corde f (de pendaison) [b] (Dress: also **~neck**) **a dress with a ~ top** une robe dos nu [2] ADJ (Dress: also **~neck**) (top, dress) dos nu inv
halterneck ['hɔːltə'nek] [1] N dos-nu m inv [2] ADJ dos nu inv
halting ['hɔːltɪŋ] ADJ (speech, efforts, progress) hésitant ; (voice) haché, hésitant ; (verse) boiteux ; (style) heurté ; **in ~ French/German** dans un français/allemand hésitant
haltingly ['hɔːltɪŋlɪ] ADV (speak) de façon hésitante
halve [hɑːv] [1] VT [a] (= divide in two) (+ object) couper en deux [b] (= reduce by half) (+ expense, time) réduire or diminuer de moitié [2] VI (sales, figures) être réduit de moitié
halves [hɑːvz] NPL of **half**
halyard ['hæljəd] N (Naut) drisse f
ham [hæm] [1] N [a] (Culin) jambon m ; **~ and eggs** œufs mpl au jambon [b] (Anat) (of animal) cuisse f [c] (Theat*: pej) cabotin(e)* m(f) (pej) [d] (Rad*) radioamateur m [2] COMP (sandwich) au jambon ► **ham acting** N cabotinage* m ► **ham-fisted, ham-handed** ADJ maladroit, gauche
► **ham up*** VT SEP (Theat) (+ part, speech) forcer ; **to ~ it up** forcer son rôle
Hamburg ['hæmbɜːg] N Hambourg
hamburger ['hæm,bɜːgə'] N (gen) hamburger m ; (US: also **~ meat**) viande f hachée
Hamitic [hæ'mɪtɪk] ADJ chamitique
Hamlet ['hæmlət] N Hamlet m
hamlet ['hæmlɪt] N (village) hameau m
hammer ['hæmə'] [1] N [a] (= tool: also Sport, of piano) marteau m ; (of gun) chien m ; **the ~ and sickle** la faucille et le marteau ; **they were going at it ~ and tongs** (= fighting) ils se battaient comme des chiffonniers ; (= working) ils y mettaient tout leur cœur ; (= arguing, debating) ils discutaient âprement ; **to come under the ~** (at auction) être mis aux enchères [2] VT [a] (+ metal) battre au marteau, marteler ; **to ~ a nail into a plank** enfoncer un clou dans une planche (à coups de marteau) ; **to ~ the table with one's fists** frapper du poing sur la table ; (fig) **to ~ sb/sth into the ground** venir à bout de qn/qch ; (fig) **to ~ a point home** insister sur un point ; **to ~ into shape** (+ metal) façonner (au marteau) ; (fig) (+ plan, agreement) mettre au point ; **I tried to ~ some sense into him** j'ai essayé de lui faire entendre raison ; **I'd had it ~ed into me that ...** on m'avait enfoncé dans la tête que ...

[b] (Brit* fig) (= defeat) battre à plate(s) couture(s) ; (= criticize severely) descendre en flammes, éreinter ; (= damage severely) frapper de plein fouet ; **the firm had been ~ed by the recession** l'entreprise avait été frappée de plein fouet par la récession ; **the report ~s motorists who drink and drive** le rapport incrimine les automobilistes qui conduisent en état d'ivresse
[c] (St Ex) (+ stockbroker) déclarer failli or en faillite
[3] VI (lit) donner des coups de marteau ; (fig) **he was ~ing at the door** il frappait à la porte à coups redoublés ; **he was ~ing away on the piano** il tapait sur le piano (comme un sourd) ; **to ~ away at a problem** s'acharner à résoudre un problème ; **my heart was ~ing** mon cœur battait très fort
[4] COMP ► **hammer blow** N (lit) coup m de marteau ; (fig) coup m terrible (for pour) ► **hammer drill** N perceuse f à percussion
► **hammer down** VT SEP (+ nail) enfoncer ; (+ metal) aplatir au marteau ; (+ loose plank) fixer
► **hammer in** VT SEP enfoncer (au marteau) ; **he ~ed the nail in with his shoe** il a enfoncé le clou avec sa chaussure
► **hammer out** VT SEP (+ metal) étirer (au marteau) ; (fig) (+ plan, agreement) élaborer (avec difficulté) ; (+ difficulties) démêler ; (+ verse, music) marteler ; **to ~ out a solution** finir par trouver une solution
► **hammer together** VT SEP (+ pieces of wood etc) assembler au marteau
hammerhead ['hæməhed] N (= shark) requin m marteau
hammering ['hæmərɪŋ] N [a] (lit) (= action) martelage m ; (= sound) martèlement m [b] (*: fig) (= defeat) raclée* f, dérouillée‡ f ; (= criticism) éreintement m, descente f en flammes ; **to take a ~*** (team, boxer, player) prendre une raclée‡ or une dérouillée‡ ; (book, play, film) se faire esquinter* or éreinter
hammertoe ['hæmə'təʊ] N orteil m en marteau
hammock ['hæmək] N hamac m
hammy* ['hæmɪ] ADJ (actor) qui force son rôle ; (performance) trop théâtral
hamper[1] ['hæmpə'] N panier m d'osier, manne f ; (for oysters, fish, game) bourriche f ; **a ~ of food** un panier garni (de nourriture) → **picnic**
hamper[2] ['hæmpə'] VT (+ person) gêner, handicaper ; (+ movement, efforts) gêner, entraver
hamster ['hæmstə'] N hamster m
hamstring ['hæmstrɪŋ] [1] N tendon m du jarret [2] VT couper les jarrets à ; (fig) (+ person) couper ses moyens à, paralyser ; (+ activity) paralyser [3] COMP ► **hamstring injury** N claquage m (au jarret)

▼**hand** [hænd]

| [1] NOUN | [3] COMPOUNDS |
| [2] TRANSITIVE VERB | [4] PHRASAL VERBS |

[1] NOUN

[a] = part of body main f ; **he took her by the ~** il l'a prise par la main ; **to take sth with both ~s** prendre qch à deux mains ; **he's very good with his ~s** il est très adroit de ses mains ; **give me your ~** donne-moi la main ; **my ~s are tied** j'ai les mains liées ; **I could do it with one ~ tied behind my back** je pourrais le faire les yeux fermés ; **we're forced to do it with one ~ or both ~s** or **our ~s tied behind our back** nous sommes pieds et poings liés
[b] in marriage main f ; **he asked for her ~†** il a demandé sa main ; **to give sb one's ~†** accorder sa main à qn†
[c] = help coup m de main ; **could you give** or **lend me a ~?** tu peux me donner un coup de main ? ; **would you give me a ~ with moving that?** tu veux un coup de main pour déplacer ça ? ; **to lend a ~** donner un coup de main

► LANGUAGE IN USE: **hand** 26.2

d = influence influence f; **you could see his ~ in everything the committee did** on reconnaissait son influence dans tout ce que faisait le comité

e person (= worker) ouvrier m, -ière f; (= member of crew) membre m d'équipage; **I sailed round Java, with a couple of ~s** j'ai fait le tour de Java en voilier avec un équipage de deux personnes; **the ship was 26 ~s short of her complement** il manquait 26 hommes à l'équipage du bateau; **the ship was lost with all ~s** le navire a disparu corps et biens; **all ~s on deck** tout le monde sur le pont; (fig) **the wedding's next week, so it's all ~s on deck** la mariage a lieu la semaine prochaine, alors on a besoin de tout le monde

f of clock, watch aiguille f; **the ~s of the clock were pointing to midday** les aiguilles de l'horloge indiquaient midi; **the big/little ~** la grande/petite aiguille

g Cards (= cards one has) main f, jeu m; (= game) partie f; **I've got a good ~** j'ai une belle main or un beau jeu; **we played a ~ of bridge** nous avons fait une partie de bridge

h = handwriting écriture f; **she recognized his neat ~** elle a reconnu son écriture bien nette; BUT **the letter was written in his own ~** la lettre était écrite de sa propre main

i Measure paume f; **a horse 13 ~s high** un cheval de 13 paumes

j Culin **~ of bananas** régime m de bananes; **~ of pork** jambonneau m

k SET STRUCTURES

♦ preposition/article/possessive + **hand**: **many suffered at the ~s of the secret police** beaucoup de gens ont souffert aux mains de la police secrète; (Sport) **their defeat at the ~s of Manchester** leur défaite face à Manchester; **to lead sb by the ~** conduire qn par la main; (Mus) **for four ~s** à quatre mains; **she had a book in her ~** elle avait un livre à la main; **she was holding the earrings in her ~** elle tenait les boucles d'oreilles dans sa main; **he wanted £100 in his ~** il a demandé 100 livres de la main à la main; **my life is in your ~s** ma vie est entre vos mains; **in one's own ~s** entre ses mains; **our destiny is in our own ~s** notre destinée est entre nos mains; **to put o.s. in sb's ~s** s'en remettre à qn; **to put sth into sb's ~s** confier qch à qn; **she put the firm into her daughter's ~s** elle a confié l'entreprise à sa fille; **to fall into the ~s of** tomber aux mains or entre les mains de; **the children are now off our ~s** maintenant nous n'avons plus besoin de nous occuper des enfants; **to get sth off one's ~s** se débarrasser or se décharger de qch; **I'll take it off your ~s** je vous en débarrasse; **we've got a difficult job on our ~s** une tâche difficile nous attend; **he'll have a real battle on his ~s** un véritable combat l'attend; **he had time on his ~s** il avait du temps de reste; **to sit on one's ~s** rester sans rien faire; **goods left on our** (or their etc) **~s** marchandises fpl invendues; **the hedgehog ate out of his ~** le hérisson lui mangeait dans la main; **she's got the boss eating out of her ~** elle fait marcher le patron au doigt et à l'œil; **it is out of his ~s** ce n'est plus lui qui s'en occupe

♦ **hand** + preposition/adverb: **she won ~s down** elle a gagné haut la main; (fig) **in ~** se faire la main; **to have a ~ in** [+ task, achievement] jouer un rôle dans; [+ crime] être mêlé à, être impliqué dans; **Lee scored a goal and had a ~ in two others** Lee a marqué un but et a contribué à en marquer deux autres; **the president himself had a ~ in the massacre** le président lui-même était impliqué dans le massacre; **I had no ~ in it** je n'y suis pour rien; **to take a ~ in sth/in doing sth** contribuer à qch/à faire qch; **everybody took a ~ in the preparations for the party** tout le monde a participé aux préparatifs de la fête; **the government took a ~ in drawing up the plan** le gou-

vernement a contribué à l'élaboration du projet; **to keep one's ~ in** garder la main; **he can't keep his ~s off the money** il ne peut pas s'empêcher de toucher à l'argent; **keep your ~s off my sweets!*** touche pas à mes bonbons!*; **~s off!** bas les pattes!*; **~s off our village!*** laissez notre village tranquille!; **to get one's ~s on sth** mettre la main sur qch; **just wait till I get my ~s on him!*** attends un peu que je lui mette la main dessus!; **I wish I could lay my ~s on a good dictionary** si seulement je pouvais mettre la main sur or dénicher un bon dictionnaire; **she read everything she could get** or **lay her ~s on** elle a lu tout ce qui lui tombait sous la main; **to put** or **set one's ~ to sth** entreprendre qch; **he can set his ~ to most things** il y a peu de choses qu'il ne sache (pas) faire; **~s up!** (at gun point) haut les mains!; (in school) levez la main!; **~s up who'd like some chocolate!** levez la main si vous voulez du chocolat!

♦ adjective + **hand**: **she's no bad ~ at acting** ce n'est pas une mauvaise actrice; **they gave him a big ~** ils l'ont applaudi bien fort; **a big ~, please, for Mr John Turner** applaudissez bien fort M. John Turner; **he grabbed the opportunity with both ~s** il a sauté sur l'occasion; **I am leaving you in Penny's very capable ~s** je vous laisse entre les mains de Penny; **on every ~** partout; **to rule with a firm ~** gouverner d'une main ferme; **at first ~** de première main; **I've got my ~s full at the moment** je suis débordé en ce moment; **to have one's ~s full** avoir fort à faire avec; **to be in good ~s** être en (de) bonnes mains; **King Henry ruled with a heavy ~** le roi Henri a dirigé le pays d'une main de fer; **on the left ~** du côté gauche, à gauche; **he's an old ~ (at this game)!** il connaît la musique!; **he's an old ~ at blackmail** le chantage, ça le connaît; **the director was an old ~ at Racine** il (or elle) n'en était pas à sa première mise en scène de Racine; **to give with one ~ and take away with the other** donner d'un côté or d'une main et reprendre de l'autre; **on the one ~ ..., on the other ~** d'une part ..., d'autre part; **yes, but on the other ~ he is very rich** oui, mais (par ailleurs) il est très riche; **on the right ~** du côté droit, à droite; **to gain** or **get the upper ~** prendre l'avantage or le dessus; **to get into the wrong ~s** tomber dans or entre de mauvaises mains → **left, right**

♦ **hand** + noun: **he's making money ~ over fist** il fait des affaires en or; **we're losing money ~ over fist** nous perdons de l'argent à une vitesse phénoménale; **he was bound ~ and foot** il était pieds et poings liés; **I refuse to wait on my husband ~ and foot** je refuse d'être l'esclave de mon mari; **she expected to be waited on ~ and foot** elle voulait être servie comme une princesse; **they are ~ in glove** ils sont de mèche; **he's ~ in glove with them** il est de mèche avec eux; **the authorities often work ~ in glove with criminals** les autorités ont souvent travaillé en étroite collaboration avec des criminels; **they were walking along hand in hand** ils marchaient (la) main dans la main; **research and teaching go hand in hand** la recherche et l'enseignement vont de pair or sont indissociables; **she hauled herself up the rope hand over hand** elle a grimpé à la corde en s'aidant des deux mains; **from hand to hand** de main en main; **on (one's) ~s and knees** à quatre pattes; **to live from ~ to mouth** vivre au jour le jour; **he doesn't like putting his ~ in his pocket** il n'aime pas mettre la main à la poche; (Brit) **he never does a ~'s turn*** il ne fiche* jamais rien

♦ verb + **hand**: **to force sb's ~** forcer la main à qn; **to show one's ~** dévoiler son jeu; (liter) **to stay one's ~** se retenir; **he turned his ~ to writing** il s'est mis à écrire; **he can turn his ~ to anything** il sait tout faire

♦ **at hand** (= close by) à portée de (la) main; **having the equipment at ~ will be very helpful** ce sera très pratique d'avoir l'équipement à

portée de (la) main; BUT **summer is (close) at ~** † l'été m est (tout) proche

♦ **by hand** à la main; **made by ~** fait (à la) main; **the letter was written by ~** la lettre était manuscrite or écrite à la main; BUT **the letter was delivered by ~** quelqu'un a apporté la lettre

♦ **in hand**: **Guy was at the door, briefcase in ~** Guy était à la porte, son attaché-case à la main; **he opened the door, gun in ~** il a ouvert la porte, pistolet au poing; **he had the situation well in ~** il avait la situation bien en main; **to take sb/sth in ~** prendre qn/qch en main; **to take o.s. in ~** se prendre en main; **Scotland are behind, but have a game in ~** l'Écosse est derrière, mais il lui reste un match à jouer; **he had £6,000 in ~** il avait 6000 livres de disponibles; **let's concentrate on the job in ~** revenons à nos moutons

♦ **off hand**: **I don't know off ~** je ne pourrais pas le dire de tête

♦ **on hand** sur place; **there are experts on ~ to give you advice** il y a des experts sur place pour vous conseiller

♦ **out of hand** (= instantly) d'emblée; **to dismiss sth out of ~** rejeter qch d'emblée; BUT **to get out of ~** [situation, spending, crowd] échapper à tout contrôle

♦ **to hand** sous la main; **I haven't got the letter to ~** je n'ai pas la lettre sous la main; BUT **the information to ~** les renseignements mpl disponibles; **she seized the first weapon to ~** elle s'est emparée de la première arme venue

2 TRANSITIVE VERB

= give donner (**to** à); (= hold out) tendre (**to** à); **to ~ sb sth ◊ to ~ sth to sb** donner qch à qn; (fig) **you've got to ~ it to him*** - he did it very well il faut reconnaître qu'il l'a très bien fait, il n'y a pas à dire, il l'a très bien fait; (fig) **it was ~ed to him on a plate*** on le lui a apporté sur un plateau (d'argent)

3 COMPOUNDS

► **hand-baggage** N = hand-luggage ► **hand controls** NPL commandes fpl manuelles ► **hand cream** N crème f pour les mains ► **hand-drier, hand-dryer** N sèche-mains m inv ► **hand grenade** N (Mil) grenade f ► **hand-held** ADJ portable ► **hand-knitted** ADJ tricoté à la main ► **hand lotion** N lotion f pour les mains ► **hand-luggage** N (NonC) bagages mpl à main ► **hand-me-down*** N vêtement m déjà porté; **it's a ~-me-down from my sister** c'est un vêtement qui me vient de ma sœur ► **hand-out** N (= leaflet) prospectus m; (at lecture, meeting) polycopié m; (= press release) communiqué m; (= money: from government, official body) aide f, subvention f; (= alms) aumône f ► **hand-painted** ADJ peint à la main ► **hand-pick** VT [+ fruit, vegetables etc] cueillir à la main; (fig) trier sur le volet ► **hand-picked** ADJ [fruit, vegetables etc] cueilli à la main; (fig) trié sur le volet ► **hand print** N empreinte f de main ► **hand-printed** ADJ imprimé à la main ► **hand puppet** N marionnette f à gaine ► **hand-reared** ADJ [animal] élevé or nourri au biberon ► **hand signal** N **a** (gen) geste m, signe m **b** (Aut) signe m de la main ► **hands-off** ADJ (fig) [policy etc] de non-intervention ► **hands-on** ADJ [experience] pratique; [exhibition] interactif (où l'on peut toucher les objets) ► **hand-spray** N (= shower attachment) douchette f (amovible); (= plant spray) spray m ► **hand-stitched** ADJ cousu (à la) main ► **hand-to-hand** ADJ, ADV **to fight ~-to-~** combattre corps à corps; **a ~-to-~ fight** un corps à corps; **~-to-~ fighting** du corps à corps ► **hand-to-mouth** ADJ **to lead a ~-to-mouth existence** vivre au jour le jour ► **hand towel** N essuie-mains m inv ► **hand wash** VT laver à la main; **"~ wash only"** « lavage à la main » ► **hand-woven** ADJ tissé à la main

4 PHRASAL VERBS

► **hand around** VT SEP = hand round

►**hand back** VT SEP rendre (**to** à)

►**hand down** VT SEP ⓐ (*lit*) ~ me down the vase descends-moi le vase; **he ~ed me down the dictionary from the top shelf** il a pris le dictionnaire qui était en haut de l'étagère et me l'a passé

ⓑ (*fig*) transmettre; **the farm's been ~ed down from generation to generation** cette ferme s'est transmise de génération en génération; **these tales are ~ed down from mother to daughter** ces histoires se transmettent de mère en fille ⓒ (*Jur*) [+ *decision*] rendre

►**hand in** VT SEP remettre (**to** à); ~ **this in at the office** remettez cela à quelqu'un au bureau; [+ *lost item*] **your wallet's been ~ed in at reception** on a rapporté votre portefeuille à la réception

►**hand on** VT SEP ⓐ (= *pass to sb else*) donner (**to** à), passer (**to** à)
ⓑ = **hand down** b

►**hand out** VT SEP distribuer; **to ~ out advice** donner des conseils

►**hand over** ① VI (*fig*) **to ~ over to sb** (*gen*) passer le relais à qn; (*at meeting*) passer le micro à qn; (*Rad, TV*) passer l'antenne à qn
② VT SEP [+ *book, object*] remettre (**to** à); [+ *criminal, prisoner*] livrer (**to** à); [+ *authority, powers*] (= *transfer*) transmettre (**to** à); [+ *surrender*] céder (**to** à); [+ *property, business*] céder (**to** à)

►**hand round** VT SEP [+ *bottle, papers*] faire circuler; [+ *cakes*] (faire) passer (à la ronde); [*hostess*] offrir

►**hand up** VT SEP passer (*de bas en haut*)

handbag [ˈhændbæg] N sac *m* à main
handball [ˈhændbɔːl] N ⓐ (= *sport*) handball *m* ⓑ (*Ftbl*) faute *f* de main
handbasin [ˈhændˌbeɪsn] N lavabo *m*
handbasket [ˈhændbɑːskɪt] N → **hell**
handbell [ˈhændbel] N sonnette *f*
handbill [ˈhændbɪl] N prospectus *m*
handbook [ˈhændbʊk] N ⓐ (= *manual*) manuel *m* → **teacher** ⓑ (= *guidebook*) (*for tourist*) guide *m*; (*to museum*) catalogue *m*
handbrake [ˈhændbreɪk] ① N (*Brit Aut*) frein *m* à main ② COMP ► **handbrake turn** N (*Aut*) virage *m* au frein à main
h. & c. (ABBR = **hot and cold (water)**) → **hot**
handcar [ˈhændkɑːʳ] N (*Rail*) draisine *f*
handcart [ˈhændkɑːt] N charrette *f* à bras → **hell**
handclap [ˈhændklæp] N (*Brit*) **a thunderous ~** un tonnerre d'applaudissements; **to get the slow ~** se faire siffler
handclasp [ˈhændklɑːsp] N poignée *f* de main
handcraft [ˈhændkrɑːft] N = **handicraft**
handcuff [ˈhændkʌf] ① N menotte *f* ② VT mettre or passer les menottes à; **to be ~ed** avoir les menottes aux poignets
-handed [ˈhændɪd] ADJ (*in compounds*) one-handed d'une main, avec une main → **empty**, **left²**, **short**
Handel [ˈhændəl] N Händel or Haendel *m*
handful [ˈhændfʊl] N ⓐ (= *fistful*) [*of coins, objects etc*] poignée *f*; **his hair started falling out by the ~** or **in ~s** il a commencé à perdre ses cheveux par poignées; **she was swallowing sleeping pills by the ~** elle se bourrait de somnifères ⓑ (= *small number*) poignée *f*; **there was only a ~ of people at the concert** il n'y avait qu'une poignée de gens au concert; **only a tiny ~ of companies did well in the recession** très peu d'entreprises ont prospéré pendant la récession ⓒ (= *nuisance*) **the children can be a ~** les enfants me donnent parfois du fil à retordre
handgrip [ˈhændgrɪp] N (*on cycle, machine etc*) poignée *f*; (= *handshake*) poignée *f* de main
handgun [ˈhændgʌn] N pistolet *m*
handhold [ˈhændhəʊld] N prise *f*

handicap [ˈhændɪkæp] ① N ⓐ (= *disability*) handicap *m*; (= *disadvantage*) désavantage *m*; **his appearance is a great ~** son aspect physique le handicape beaucoup; **to be under a great ~** avoir un désavantage or un handicap énorme → **physical** ⓑ (*Sport*) handicap *m*; **weight ~** [*of racehorse*] surcharge *f*; **time ~** handicap *m* (de temps) ② VT (*also Sport, fig*) handicaper; **the industry was ~ped by antiquated machinery** la vétusté des machines constituait un handicap pour ce secteur
handicapped [ˈhændɪkæpt] ① ADJ handicapé; **a physically ~ child** un enfant handicapé physique ② **the handicapped** NPL les handicapés *mpl*; **the mentally/physically ~** les handicapés *mpl* mentaux/physiques
handicraft [ˈhændɪkrɑːft] ① N (= *work*) artisanat *m*, travail *m* artisanal; (= *skill*) habileté *f* manuelle ② **handicrafts** NPL (= *products*) objets *mpl* artisanaux
handily [ˈhændɪlɪ] ADV ⓐ (= *conveniently*) [*placed*] commodément ⓑ (*US* = *easily*) [*win*] haut la main
handiness [ˈhændɪnɪs] N ⓐ (= *usefulness*) [*of object, method, approach*] côté *m* pratique, commodité *f*; (= *ease of control*) [*of car, boat*] maniabilité *f* ⓑ (= *nearness*) **because of the ~ of the library** parce que la bibliothèque est tout près ⓒ (= *skill*) [*of person*] adresse *f*, dextérité *f*
handiwork [ˈhændɪwɜːk] N œuvre *f*; **the architect stepped back to admire his ~** l'architecte a fait un pas en arrière pour admirer son œuvre; (*fig*) **the fire was the ~ of an arsonist** l'incendie était l'œuvre d'un pyromane
handjob⁑ [ˈhænddʒɒb] N **to give sb a ~** branler qn⁑; **to give o.s. a ~** se branler⁑
handkerchief [ˈhæŋkətʃɪf] N mouchoir *m*; (*fancy*) pochette *f*
handle [ˈhændl] ① N ⓐ [*of basket, bucket*] anse *f*; [*of broom, spade, knife*] manche *m*; [*of door, drawer, suitcase*] poignée *f*; [*of handcart*] brancard *m*; [*of saucepan*] queue *f*; [*of pump, stretcher, wheelbarrow*] bras *m*; (**starting**) **~** [*of car*] manivelle *f*
ⓑ (*fig* = *understanding*) **to have a ~ on** [+ *problem, state of affairs*] comprendre; (= *control*) [+ *situation, spending*] maîtriser; **my subject is something not many people have a ~ on** peu de gens ont une idée de mon sujet
ⓒ **to have a ~ to one's name**† avoir un nom à rallonge* → **fly³**
② VT ⓐ (= *touch*) [+ *fruit, food etc*] toucher à; (= *move etc by hand: esp Ind*) manipuler, manier; **please do not ~ the goods** prière de ne pas toucher aux marchandises; **her hands are black from handling newsprint** elle a les mains noires à force de manier or manipuler des feuilles de journaux; (*label*) **"~ with care"** « fragile »; **the crowd ~d him roughly** (*lit*) la foule l'a malmené; (*fig*) la foule l'a hué; (*Ftbl*) **to ~ the ball** toucher le ballon de la main, faire une faute de main
ⓑ (= *control, deal with*) [+ *ship*] manœuvrer, gouverner; [+ *car*] conduire, manœuvrer; [+ *weapon, money*] manier, se servir de; [+ *person, animal*] manier, s'y prendre avec; **the boat was very easy to ~** le bateau était très facile à manœuvrer or gouverner; **he knows how to ~ a gun** il sait se servir d'un revolver or manier un revolver; **she ~s large sums of money in her job** elle manie de grosses sommes d'argent dans son travail; **the hospital doesn't ~ emergencies** l'hôpital n'a pas de service d'urgences; **he ~d the situation very well** il a très bien géré la situation; **I could have ~d it better than I did** j'aurais pu mieux m'y prendre; **you didn't ~ that very well!** vous ne vous y êtes pas bien pris!; **I'll ~ this** je m'en charge, je vais m'en occuper; **we don't ~ that type of business** nous ne traitons pas ce type d'affaires; **do you ~ tax matters?** est-ce que vous vous occupez de fiscalité?; **which**

judge is handling the case? quel juge est chargé de l'affaire?; **three lawyers had already refused to ~ the case** trois avocats avaient déjà refusé de s'occuper de l'affaire; **they doubt the government's ability to ~ the economy** ils doutent de la capacité du gouvernement à gérer l'économie; **he knows how to ~ his son** il sait s'y prendre avec son fils; **this child is very hard to ~** cet enfant est très difficile
ⓒ (*Comm etc*) [+ *commodity, product*] avoir, faire; **we don't ~ that type of product** nous ne faisons pas ce genre de produit; **to ~ stolen goods** receler des objets volés; **to ~ drugs** être revendeur de drogue; **she was convicted of handling explosives** elle a été reconnue coupable de détention d'explosifs; **Orly ~s 5 million passengers a year** 5 millions de voyageurs passent par Orly chaque année; **we ~ 200 passengers a day** 200 voyageurs par jour passent par nos services; **can the port ~ big ships?** le port peut-il accueillir les gros bateaux?
③ VI **to ~ well/badly** [*ship*] être facile/difficile à manœuvrer; [*car, gun*] être facile/difficile à manier; [*horse*] répondre bien/mal aux aides
handlebar [ˈhændlbɑːʳ] ① N (*also* **~s**) guidon *m* ② COMP ► **handlebar moustache** N (*hum*) moustache *f* en guidon de vélo*
-handled [ˈhændld] ADJ (*in compounds*) **a wooden-handled spade** une pelle au manche de bois or avec un manche de bois
handler [ˈhændləʳ] N ⓐ (*also* **dog ~**) maître-chien *m* ⓑ [*of stock*] manutentionnaire *mf*
handling [ˈhændlɪŋ] ① N [*of ship*] manœuvre *f*; [*of car*] maniement *m*; (*Ind*) [*of goods, objects*] manutention *f*; (= *fingering*) maniement *m*, manipulation *f*; [*of stolen goods*] recel *m*; **~ of drugs** trafic *m* de drogue; **his ~ of the matter** la façon dont il a géré l'affaire; **the judge's ~ of witnesses was criticized** on a critiqué la manière dont le juge a traité les témoins; **a new system to speed up the ~ of complaints** un nouveau système pour accélérer le traitement des réclamations; **the government's ~ of the economy** la manière dont le gouvernement gère l'économie; **toxic waste requires very careful ~** les déchets toxiques doivent être manipulés avec beaucoup de précaution; **to get some rough ~** [*person, object*] se faire malmener
② COMP (*Comm*) ► **handling charges** NPL frais *mpl* de manutention
handmade [ˌhændˈmeɪd] ADJ fait (à la) main
handmaid(en) [ˈhændmeɪd(ə)n] N († *or liter: lit, fig*) servante *f*
handover [ˈhændəʊvə] N [*of company, colony*] cession *f*; **the ~ of power** la passation des pouvoirs; **during the prisoner's ~ to the police ...** lorsque le prisonnier a été remis à la police ...
handrail [ˈhændreɪl] N [*of stairs*] rampe *f*, main *f* courante; [*of bridge, quay*] garde-fou *m*
handsaw [ˈhændsɔː] N scie *f* à main, scie *f* égoïne
handset [ˈhændset] N (*Telec*) combiné *m*
handshake [ˈhændʃeɪk] N ⓐ poignée *f* de main → **golden** ⓑ (*Comput*) prise *f* de contact
handsome [ˈhænsəm] ADJ ⓐ (= *attractive*) [*man, face, features, building, object*] beau (belle *f*); **a ~ woman** une belle femme ■ (*PROV*) **~ is as ~ does** l'air ne fait pas la chanson, l'habit ne fait pas le moine ⓑ (= *large*) [*sum*] coquet; **a ~ price/salary** un bon prix/salaire; **to win a ~ victory** remporter une belle victoire; **to win by a ~ margin** gagner haut la main ⓒ (= *generous*) [*conduct, compliment, gift*] généreux; **to make a ~ apology for sth** se confondre en excuses pour qch
handsomely [ˈhænsəmlɪ] ADV ⓐ (= *attractively*) [*illustrated*] joliment; [*dressed*] avec élégance ⓑ (= *generously*) [*pay, reward, behave*]

généreusement ; [*contribute*] généreusement, avec générosité ; **to apologize** ~ se confondre en excuses [c] (= *convincingly*) [*win*] haut la main ; **this strategy paid off** ~ cette stratégie s'est révélée payante

handspring ['hændsprɪŋ] N saut *m* de mains

handstand ['hændstænd] N appui *m* renversé, équilibre *m* sur les mains ; **to do a** ~ faire un appui renversé *or* un équilibre sur les mains

handwork ['hændwɜːk] N = **handiwork**

handwrite ['hændraɪt] VT écrire à la main

handwriting ['hændraɪtɪŋ] N écriture *f* ; (*US fig*) **he has seen the** ~ **on the wall** il a mesuré la gravité de la situation ; (*US fig*) **the** ~ **is on the wall** la catastrophe est imminente

handwritten ['hændrɪtən] ADJ manuscrit, écrit à la main

handy ['hændɪ] [1] ADJ [a] (= *useful*) [*tool, hint, method*] pratique ; **a** ~ **little car** une petite voiture bien pratique ; **I brought a torch just in case — that's** ~! j'ai apporté une lampe de poche à tout hasard — bonne idée! ; **he's coming to see us tomorrow — that's** ~! il vient nous voir demain — ça tombe bien ! ; **to come in** ~ être bien utile [b]* (= *conveniently close*) proche ; **in a** ~ **place** à portée de (la) main ; **the shops are very** ~ les magasins sont tout près ; **to be** ~ **for the shops** être à proximité des magasins ; **to keep** *or* **have sth** ~ avoir qch à portée de (la) main [c] (= *skilful*) adroit (de ses mains) ; **he's** ~ **around the home** il est bricoleur ; **he's** ~ **in the kitchen** il se débrouille bien en cuisine ; **to be** ~ **with sth** savoir bien se servir de qch [d] [*ship*] maniable [2] COMP ► **handy-pack** N emballage *m* à poignée

handyman ['hændɪmæn] N (*pl* **-men**) (*do-it-yourself*) bricoleur *m* ; (= *servant*) factotum *m*, homme *m* à tout faire

hang [hæŋ] (*pret, ptp* **hung**) [1] VT [a] (= *suspend*) [*lamp*] suspendre, accrocher (**on** à) ; [+ *curtains, hat, decorations*] accrocher ; [+ *painting*] (*gen*) accrocher ; (*in gallery = exhibit*) exposer ; [+ *door*] monter ; [+ *wallpaper*] poser, tendre ; [+ *dangling object*] laisser pendre ; **to** ~ **clothes on the line** pendre des vêtements sur la corde à linge, mettre des vêtements à sécher ; **he hung the rope over the side of the boat** il a laissé pendre le cordage par-dessus bord ; **to** ~ **one's head** baisser la tête [b] (*Culin*) [+ *game*] faire faisander [c] (= *decorate*) décorer (**with** de) ; **trees hung with lights** des arbres décorés de lumières ; **walls hung with modern paintings** des murs décorés de tableaux modernes ; **a study hung with hessian** un bureau tapissé *or* tendu de jute ; **balconies hung with flags** des balcons pavoisés [d] (*pret, ptp* **hanged**) [+ *criminal*] pendre ; **he was ~ed for murder** il a été pendu pour meurtre ; **he was ~ed, drawn and quartered** il a été pendu, éviscéré et écartelé ; **he ~ed himself** il s'est pendu ; **(may) as well be ~ed for a sheep as a lamb** autant être punis, autant l'être pour un crime qui en vaille la peine [e] (†*: in phrases*) ~ **him!** qu'il aille se faire voir !* ; **(I'll be) ~ed if I know!** je veux bien être pendu si je le sais !* ; **I'm ~ed if I'm waiting until he decides to come back** je serais fou d'attendre *or* je ne vois pas pourquoi j'attendrais qu'il décide à revenir ; ~ **it (all)!** zut !* [2] VI [a] [*rope, dangling object*] pendre, être accroché *or* suspendu (**on, from** à) ; [*drapery*] tomber ; **a suit that ~s well** un costume qui tombe bien ; **her hair hung down her back** (*not put up*) elle avait les cheveux dénoués ; (*long*) ses cheveux lui tombaient dans le dos ; **her hair hung loose about her shoulders** ses cheveux flottaient sur ses épaules ; **a picture ~ing on the wall** un tableau accroché au mur ; **to** ~ **out of the window** [*person*] se pencher à la fenêtre ; [*thing*] pendre à la fenêtre ; **I was left ~ing by my fingertips** (*lit*) je me suis retrouvé

agrippé *or* cramponné au rocher (*or* au bord de la fenêtre *etc*) ; (*fig*) je n'avais plus qu'un mince espoir de m'en tirer ; (*esp US*) **just ~ loose!**‡ essaie d'être relax !‡ → **balance** [b] (= *hover*) planer, peser ; **a damp fog hung over the valley** un brouillard chargé d'humidité planait *or* pesait sur la vallée ; **a haze of expensive perfume ~s around her** les effluves d'un parfum de luxe flottent autour d'elle ; **the hawk hung motionless in the sky** le faucon était comme suspendu dans le ciel ; **a constant threat of unemployment ~s over us** *or* **our heads** une menace constante de chômage pèse sur nous ; **the question was left ~ing in the air** la question est restée en suspens ; **time hung heavy (on his hands)** le temps lui durait *or* pesait, il trouvait le temps long [c] [*criminal*] être pendu, peser ; **he ought to** ~ il devrait être pendu ; **he'll** ~ **for it** cela lui vaudra la corde *or* d'être pendu ; **to be sentenced to** ~ être condamné à la corde (**for sth** pour qch) ; **he was sentenced to** ~ **for killing a young woman** il a été condamné à la corde pour avoir tué une jeune femme [d] (*US*‡) = **hang out** [3] N* [a] **to get the** ~ **of** (= *learn to use*) [+ *machine, tool, device*] piger* comment utiliser ; (= *grasp meaning of*) [+ *letter, book*] (arriver à) comprendre ; **to get the** ~ **of doing sth** attraper le coup pour faire qch ; **you'll soon get the** ~ **of it** (*of device, process etc*) tu auras vite fait de t'y mettre ; **she's getting the** ~ **of her new job** elle commence à s'habituer à son nouveau travail ; **I am getting the** ~ **of it!** ça y est, je saisis ! [b] **I don't give a** ~† je m'en fiche* [4] COMP ► **hang-glider** N (= *aircraft*) deltaplane® *m*, aile *f* delta ; (= *person*) libériste *mf* ► **hang-gliding** N deltaplane® *m*, vol *m* libre ; **to go ~-gliding** faire du deltaplane®, pratiquer le vol libre ► **hang-out*** N (= *place*) lieu *m* de prédilection ► **hang-up*** N (= *complex*) complexe *m* (**about** en ce qui concerne) ; **to have a ~-up about one's body** être mal dans son corps, être complexé ; **to have a ~-up about spiders** avoir la phobie des araignées, avoir une peur maladive des araignées ; **to have sexual ~-ups** avoir des blocages (sexuels)

► **hang about, hang around** [1] VI (= *loiter, pass time*) traîner ; (= *wait*) attendre ; **he's always ~ing about here** il est toujours à traîner par ici ; **he got sick of ~ing around waiting for me** il en a eu marre* de m'attendre ; **they always ~ around together** ils sont toujours ensemble ; **Ann used to** ~ **around with the boys** Ann traînait avec les garçons ; **to keep sb ~ing about** faire attendre *or* poireauter* qn ; **this is where they usually** ~ **about** c'est là qu'ils se trouvent habituellement ; ~ **about!*** attends ! ; ~ **about*, this fellow's a crook** attends, ce type* est un escroc [2] VT FUS **the crowd who hung around the cafe** les habitués du café

► **hang back** VI (*in walking etc*) rester en arrière, hésiter à aller de l'avant ; (*fig*) **she hung back from suggesting this** elle hésitait à le proposer ; **they hung back on closing the deal** ils tardaient à conclure l'affaire ; **he should not ~ back (on this decision) any longer** il est temps qu'il prenne une décision *or* qu'il se décide

► **hang down** VI pendre

► **hang in*** VI (*also* ~ **in there**) s'accrocher ; ~ **in there, Bill, you're going to make it** accroche-toi, Bill, tu vas t'en sortir

► **hang on** [1] VI [a] (* = *wait*) attendre ; ~ **on!** attendez ! ; (*on phone*) ne quittez pas ! ; ~ **on a sec, I'll come with you** attends une seconde, je viens avec toi ; (*on phone*) **I had to** ~ **on for ages** j'ai dû attendre des siècles [b] (= *hold out*) tenir bon ; **he managed to** ~ **on till help came** il réussit à tenir bon jusqu'à l'arrivée des secours ; **Manchester United hung on to take the Cup** Manchester United a tenu

bon et a remporté le championnat ; **to** ~ **on by one's fingernails** *or* **fingertips** (*lit*) être agrippé *or* cramponné au rocher (*or* au bord de la fenêtre *etc*) ; (*fig*) n'avoir plus qu'un mince espoir de s'en tirer ; ~ **on in there** ; → **hang in there** ; → **hang in** [c] **to** ~ **on to sth*** (= *cling on to*) s'accrocher à qch, rester cramponné à qch ; (= *keep, keep after*) garder qch ; ~ **on to the branch** cramponne-toi à la branche, ne lâche pas la branche ; (*fig*) **to** ~ **on to one's lead** conserver son avance ; **to** ~ **on to power** s'accrocher au pouvoir [2] VT FUS [a] (*lit, fig*) se cramponner à, s'accrocher à ; **to** ~ **on sb's arm** se cramponner *or* s'accrocher au bras de qn ; **to** ~ **on sb's words** *or* **every word** boire les paroles de qn, être suspendu aux lèvres de qn [b] (= *depend on*) dépendre de ; **everything ~s on his decision** tout dépend de sa décision ; **everything ~s on whether he saw her or not** le tout est de savoir s'il l'a vue ou non [3] VT SEP (*esp US fig*) **to** ~ **one on*** se cuiter*, se biturer*

► **hang out** [1] VI [a] [*tongue*] pendre ; [*shirt tails etc*] pendre (dehors), pendouiller* ; (*fig*) **let it all** ~ **out!**‡ défoulez-vous ! [b]* (= *live*) percher*, crécher* ; (= *loiter aimlessly*) traîner [c] (= *resist*) **they are ~ing out for a 5% rise*** ils insistent pour obtenir une augmentation de 5 % [2] VT SEP [+ *streamer*] suspendre (dehors) ; [+ *washing*] étendre (dehors) ; [+ *flag*] arborer ; (*fig*) **to** ~ **sb out to dry*** (= *abandon them*) abandonner qn à son sort [3] ~**-out*** N → **hang**

► **hang together** VI [a] (= *unite*) [*people*] se serrer les coudes [b] (= *be consistent*) [*argument*] se tenir ; [*story*] tenir debout ; [*statements*] s'accorder, concorder ; **her ideas don't always ~ together very well as a plot** ses intrigues sont souvent décousues

► **hang up** [1] VI (*Telec*) raccrocher ; **to** ~ **up on sb** raccrocher au nez de qn → **hung** [2] VT SEP [+ *hat, picture*] accrocher, pendre (**on** à, **sur**) ; (*Telec*) **to** ~ **up the receiver** raccrocher ; (*fig*) ~ **up one's hat** (= *retire*) raccrocher* ; (*fig*) **the goalkeeper announced he was ~ing up his boots for good** le gardien de but a annoncé qu'il raccrochait pour de bon → **hung** [3] ~**-up*** N → **hang**

hangar ['hæŋəʳ] N (*Aviat*) hangar *m*

hangdog ['hæŋdɒg] N **to have a** ~ **look** *or* **expression** avoir un air de chien battu

hanger ['hæŋəʳ] [1] N (*also* **coat** ~) cintre *m* ; (= *hook*) patère *f* [2] COMP ► **hanger-on** N (*pl* **hangers-on**) parasite *m* ; (= *person*) **he's just one of the ~s-on** c'est juste l'un de ces parasites ; **there was a crowd of ~s-on** il y avait toute une foule de parasites

hanging ['hæŋɪŋ] [1] N [a] (= *execution*) pendaison *f* [b] (*NonC*) accrochage *m*, suspension *f* ; [*of bells, wallpaper*] pose *f* ; [*of door*] montage *m* ; [*of picture*] accrochage *m* [c] (= *curtains etc*) ~s tentures *fpl*, draperies *fpl* ; **bed ~s** rideaux *mpl* de lit [2] ADJ [*bridge, staircase*] suspendu ; [*door*] battant ; [*lamp, light*] pendant ; [*sleeve*] tombant [3] COMP ► **hanging basket** N panier *m* suspendu ► **hanging committee** N (*Art*) jury *m* d'exposition ► **the Hanging Gardens of Babylon** NPL les jardins *mpl* suspendus de Babylone ► **hanging judge** N (*Hist*) juge *qui* envoyait régulièrement à la potence ► **hanging offence** N (*lit*) crime *m* pendable ; (*fig*) **it's not a ~ offence** ce n'est pas grave, ce n'est pas un cas pendable ► **hanging wardrobe** N penderie *f*

hangman ['hæŋmən] N (*pl* **-men**) [a] (= *executioner*) bourreau *m* [b] (= *game*) pendu *m* ; **to play** ~ jouer au pendu

hangnail ['hæŋneɪl] N petite peau *f*, envie *f*

hangover ['hæŋəʊvəʳ] N [a] (*after drinking*) **to have a** ~ avoir la gueule de bois* [b] (*fig* = *relic*) this problem is a ~ from the previous adminis-tration c'est un problème que nous avons hé-rité de l'administration précédente

Hang Seng Index [ˌhænseŋˈɪndeks] N indice m Hang Seng

hank [hæŋk] N (of wool) écheveau m

hanker ['hæŋkə'] VI to ~ for or after rêver de

hankering ['hæŋkərɪŋ] N to have a ~ for sth/to do sth rêver de qch/de faire qch

hankie*, **hanky*** ['hæŋkɪ] N ABBR = handker-chief

hanky-panky* ['hæŋkɪ'pæŋkɪ] N (suspicious) entourloupes* fpl; (= fooling around) bêtises fpl; (sexual) batifolage m; (suspicious) there's some ~ going on il se passe quelque chose de louche, il y a là quelque chose de pas très ca-tholique*; there were reports of political ~ le bruit courait qu'il se passait des choses lou-ches en politique

Hannibal ['hænɪbəl] N Hannibal m

Hanoi [hæˈnɔɪ] N Hanoi

Hanover ['hænəʊvə'] N Hanovre; (Brit Hist) the house of ~ la maison or la dynastie de Hano-vre

Hanoverian [ˌhænəʊˈvɪərɪən] ADJ hanovrien

Hansard ['hænsɑːd] N Hansard m (procès verbal des débats du parlement britannique)

Hanseatic [ˌhænzɪˈætɪk] ADJ the ~ League la Hanse, la Ligue hanséatique

hansom ['hænsəm] N (also ~ cab) cab m

Hants [hænts] ABBR = Hampshire

Hanukkah ['hɑːnəkə] N (Rel) Hanoukka f

ha'pence† ['heɪpəns] NPL of ha'penny

ha'penny† ['heɪpnɪ] N = halfpenny

haphazard [ˌhæp'hæzəd] ADJ in a somewhat ~ fashion un peu n'importe comment; the whole thing was very ~ tout était fait au petit bonheur; a ~ approach to film-making une approche de la réalisation de films peu mé-thodique

haphazardly [ˌhæp'hæzədlɪ] ADV [arrange, se-lect] au hasard

hapless ['hæplɪs] ADJ infortuné (before n), malheureux (before n)

happen ['hæpən] VI **a** arriver, se passer; something ~ed il est arrivé or il s'est passé quelque chose; what's ~ed? qu'est-ce qui s'est passé?, qu'est-il arrivé?; just as if nothing had ~ed comme si de rien n'était; whatever ~s quoi qu'il arrive (subj) ou advienne; don't let it ~ again! et que cela ne se reproduise pas!; these things ~ ce sont des choses qui arri-vent; what has ~ed to him? (= befallen) qu'est-ce qui lui est arrivé?; (= become of) qu'est-ce qu'il est devenu?; if anything ~ed to me my wife would have enough money s'il m'arrivait quelque chose ma femme aurait assez d'argent; something has ~ed to him il lui est arrivé quelque chose; a funny thing ~ed to me this morning il m'est arrivé quelque chose de bizarre ce matin; let's pre-tend it never ~ed faisons comme si rien ne s'était passé; she switched on the ignition. Nothing ~ed elle a mis le contact. Il ne s'est rien passé; it's all ~ing!* il s'en passe des cho-ses!

b (= come about, chance) how does it ~ that ...? comment se fait-il que ... (+ subj)?; it might ~ that ... il se pourrait que ... (+ subj); it so ~ed that ... il s'est trouvé que ... (+ indic); it so ~s that I'm going there today ◊ as it ~s I'm going there today il se trouve que j'y vais au-jourd'hui; he ~ed to tell me that ... il me di-sait justement que ...; do you ~ to have a pen? aurais-tu par hasard un stylo?; how did you ~ to go? comment se fait-il que tu y sois allé?; we ~ed to discover we had a friend in common nous avons découvert par hasard que nous avions un ami commun; I looked in the nearest paper, which ~ed to be the Dai-ly Mail j'ai regardé dans le premier journal

qui m'est tombé sous la main. Il s'est trouvé que c'était le Daily Mail; I ~ to know he is not rich je sais qu'en fait, il n'est pas riche; if he does ~ to see her s'il lui arrive de la voir

happen (up)on† VT FUS [+ object] trouver par hasard; [+ person] rencontrer par hasard

happening ['hæpnɪŋ] **1** N événement m; (Theat) happening m **2** ADJ* branché*

happenstance* ['hæpənstæns] N by ~ par ha-sard

happily ['hæpɪlɪ] ADV **a** [say, talk, play] (= contentedly) d'un air heureux; (= merrily) gaie-ment; to smile ~ avoir un sourire épanoui or de bonheur; it all ended ~ tout s'est bien terminé; I'm a ~ married man je suis heureux en ménage; they lived ~ ever after ils vé-curent heureux **b** (= without difficulty) [live to-gether, work together etc] sans problème **c** (= willingly) [offer, lend] volontiers **d** (= fortunate-ly) heureusement; ~, no one was hurt heureu-sement, personne n'a été blessé; ~ for him, he can afford it heureusement pour lui, il peut se le permettre **e** (= felicitously) [express, word] avec bonheur; a ~ chosen word un mot choi-si avec bonheur

▼ **happiness** ['hæpɪnɪs] N bonheur m

▼ **happy** ['hæpɪ] **1** ADJ **a** (= joyful, glad) [person, smile, time] heureux; a ~ feeling un sentiment de bonheur; to have a ~ ending bien se terminer; to have ~ memories of sb/ sth garder un bon souvenir or de bons souve-nirs de qn/qch; to be ~ about sth être heu-reux de qch; as ~ as Larry or a sandboy or (US) a clam or a lark ◊ ~ as the day is long heureux comme un poisson dans l'eau, heureux comme un roi; (firm, school etc) we're just one big ~ family nous formons une grande fa-mille, nous sommes comme une grande fa-mille; to be ~ for sb se réjouir pour qn; can't you just be ~ for me? tu ne peux pas te ré-jouir pour moi?; I'm ~ that I came je suis content d'être venu; I'm ~ that you came je suis content que vous soyez venu; I'm ~ to say that ... j'ai le plaisir de vous dire que ...; I'm just ~ to have a job je m'estime heureux d'avoir un emploi

b (= contented, at ease) [person] content, heu-reux; [childhood, old age, marriage, retirement, fami-ly] heureux; I'm ~ here reading je suis très bien ici à lire; we like to keep the customers/ sponsors ~ nous voulons que nos clients/ sponsors soient satisfaits; you're not just say-ing that to keep me ~? tu ne dis pas ça juste pour me faire plaisir?; to be ~ with or about sth être satisfait de qch; I'm not ~ with this new car je ne suis pas satisfait de cette nou-velle voiture; I'm not ~ about leaving him alone ça ne me plaît pas trop de le or je n'ai-me pas trop le laisser seul

c (= willing, glad) to be ~ to do sth bien vou-loir faire qch; she was quite ~ to stay there alone cela ne l'ennuyait or la dérangeait pas (du tout) de rester là toute seule; I'm always ~ to oblige je suis à votre service; I would be ~ to have your comments n'hésitez pas à me faire part de vos commentaires; I'd be more than or only too ~ to do that je le ferais volontiers → slap, trigger

d (in greetings) ~ birthday! bon anniversai-re!; (in song) "~ birthday to you!" « joyeux anniversaire! »; (on card) "~ 40th birthday" « 40 ans: joyeux anniversaire! »; ~ Christmas! joyeux Noël!; ~ Easter! joyeuses Pâques!; ~ New Year! bonne année!; (US) ~ holidays! joyeuses fêtes!; (as toast) ~ days!* tchin-tchin!* → return

e * (euph = tipsy) éméché*, gris*

f (= fortunate) [chance, coincidence] heureux; the ~ few les rares privilégiés mpl

g (= felicitous) [phrase, words, outcome] heu-reux; it's not a ~ thought ce n'est pas une perspective réjouissante

2 COMP ► happy-clappy ADJ (pej) [service] qui se déroule dans une allégresse collective

► the happy couple N les jeunes mariés mpl ► the happy event N (= birth) l'heureux événement m ► happy families N (= card game) jeu m des sept familles ► happy-go-lucky ADJ [person, attitude] insouciant; the ar-rangements were very ~-go-lucky c'était orga-nisé au petit bonheur (la chance); to do sth in a ~-go-lucky way faire qch au petit bonheur (la chance) or à la va comme je te pousse* ► happy hour N (US) heure f du cocktail or de l'apéritif; (Brit) heure, généralement en début de soirée, pendant laquelle les consommations sont à prix réduit ► happy hunting ground N (of Native Americans) paradis m des Indiens d'Amérique; (fig) a ~ hunting ground for col-lectors le paradis des collectionneurs ► happy medium N juste milieu m; to strike a ~ medium trouver le juste milieu

Hapsburg ['hæpsbɜːg] N Habsbourg; the ~s les Habsbourg mpl

hara-kiri ['hærəˈkɪrɪ] N hara-kiri m; to commit ~ faire hara-kiri

harangue [həˈræŋ] **1** VT [+ crowd] haranguer (about à propos de); [+ individual] sermonner (about à propos de); he tried to ~ the crowd into action il a essayé de haranguer la foule pour qu'elle agisse **2** N (to crowd) harangue f; (to individual) sermon m

harass ['hærəs] VT **a** (= harry) [+ troops, the enemy, crowd etc] harceler; they complained of being routinely ~ed by the police ils se sont plaints de harcèlements répétés de la part de la police; he sexually ~ed her il la harcelait sexuellement **b** (= worry) tracasser; (stronger) harceler, tourmenter; ~ed by doubts harcelé de doutes

harassed ['hærəst] ADJ (= hassled) harcelé; (= overburdened) surmené; to feel ~ être harcelé

harassment ['hærəsmənt] N harcèlement m; police ~ harcèlement m de la part de la police → sexual

harbinger ['hɑːbɪndʒə'] N (liter) signe m avant-coureur (liter), présage m; a ~ of doom un funeste présage

harbour, harbor (US) ['hɑːbə'] **1** N (for boats) port m; (fig) havre m (liter), refuge m; (in names) Dover Harbour port m de Douvres; the ship was lying in the ~ le navire était au port or avait mouillé dans le port → outer **2** VT **a** (= give shelter to) héberger, abriter; to ~ a criminal receler un criminel (Jur); (fig) they accused the government of ~ing terror-ists ils ont accusé le gouvernement d'avoir fermé les yeux sur la présence de terroristes **b** [+ suspicions] entretenir, nourrir; [+ fear, hope] entretenir; to ~ a grudge against sb garder rancune à qn; she ~s no regrets elle ne nourrit aucun regret **c** [+ dirt, dust] retenir, garder; the river still ~s crocodiles des crocodiles habitent encore le fleuve; the cat's fur ~s various parasites di-vers parasites trouvent refuge dans la fourru-re du chat **3** COMP ► harbour dues, harbour fees NPL (Jur, Comm) droits mpl de port ► harbour master N capitaine m de port ► harbour station N gare f maritime

hard [hɑːd] **1** ADJ **a** (= firm) [object, substance, ground, bed, fruit] dur; [mud, snow] durci; [muscle] ferme; [cheese] à pâte pressée or f; to become or get or go or grow ~ durcir; the ground was baked/frozen ~ le sol était durci par la chaleur/par le gel; the lake was frozen ~ le lac était complètement gelé; to set ~ [plaster, concrete, clay etc] bien prendre **b** (= difficult) [problem, question, exam, choice, decision, work] difficile; [task] pénible, dur; [battle, fight] rude; [match] âprement disputé; it is ~ to do that il est difficile de faire cela; to find it ~ to do sth avoir du mal à faire qch, trouver difficile de faire qch; I find it ~ to be-lieve that ... j'ai du mal à croire que ...; their prices are ~ to beat leurs prix sont imbattables; **to be ~ to open/close/translate** etc être difficile or dur à ouvrir/fermer/traduire etc; **good managers are ~ to find these days** il est difficile de trouver de bons cadres de nos jours; **that's a ~ question to answer** c'est une question à laquelle il est difficile de répondre; **it was a ~ decision to make** c'était une décision difficile à prendre; **I've had a ~ day** ma journée a été dure; **a ~ day's work** une rude journée de travail; **it's ~ work!** c'est dur!; (hum) **a ~ day's sunbathing on the beach** une rude journée or une journée fatigante passée à bronzer sur la plage (hum); **she's had a very ~ life** elle a eu une vie très dure; (also iro) **it's a ~ life** la vie est dure; (also iro) **it's a ~ life being a man** c'est dur d'être un homme; **she's having a ~ time at the moment** elle traverse une période difficile; **she had a ~ time of it after her husband's death** elle a traversé une période difficile après la mort de son mari; **you'll have a ~ time doing sth** avoir du mal or des difficultés à faire qch; **you'll have a ~ time trying to get him to help you** vous allez avoir du mal à le persuader de vous aider; **to give sb a ~ time*** en faire voir de toutes les couleurs à qn; **the kids are giving me a ~ time at the moment*** les enfants sont vraiment pénibles en ce moment; **times are ~** les temps sont durs; **those were ~ times** c'était une époque difficile; **he always has to do it** or **things the ~ way** il faut toujours qu'il cherche (subj) la difficulté; **to learn the ~ way** l'apprendre à ses dépens; **to play ~ to get*** se faire désirer → **drive**

[c] (= committed) **he's a ~ worker** il est travailleur; **he's a ~ drinker** il boit beaucoup, il boit sec

[d] (= forceful) [blow, kick, punch] violent; **give it a ~ push** pousse fort; **she gave the rope a ~ tug** elle a tiré la corde d'un coup sec; **he had a ~ fall** il a fait une mauvaise chute; (fig) **a ~ blow** un coup dur (for, to sb/sth pour qn/qch) → **knock**

[e] (= unsympathetic) [person, face, look, smile, voice] dur; **to have a ~ heart** avoir le cœur dur; **no ~ feelings!** sans rancune!; **to show there are no ~ feelings** pour montrer qu'il n'y a pas de rancune entre nous (or eux etc); **to grow ~** s'endurcir

[f] (= harsh, severe) [winter, climate] rude, rigoureux; [frost] fort; [light, colour] cru; [treatment] dur; [rule, decision] sévère; **to take a ~ line with sb/on sth** se montrer dur or intransigeant avec qn/lorsqu'il s'agit de qch → **3**; **to be ~ on sb** [person] être dur avec qn; **aren't you being a bit ~ on yourself?** n'es-tu pas un peu trop dur avec toi-même?; (= damaging) **to be ~ on sb/sth** [situation, circumstances] être difficile or éprouvant pour qn/qch; **the light was ~ on the eyes** la lumière fatiguait les yeux; **children are ~ on their shoes** les enfants usent leurs chaussures en un rien de temps; (Brit) **~ cheese*** or **lines*!** tant pis pour toi!; **~ luck!** pas de chance or de veine*!; **it was ~ luck that he didn't win** il n'a vraiment pas eu de chance de ne pas gagner; **it's ~ luck on him** il n'a vraiment pas de chance; **he told me another ~ luck story** il m'a encore raconté ses malheurs; **his ~ luck story failed to move me** il n'a pas réussi à m'émouvoir avec ses malheurs

[g] (= tough) [person] **she thinks she's really ~*** elle se considère comme une dure

[h] (= indisputable) [information] sûr; [evidence] tangible; **there are ~ facts to support our arguments** il y a des faits concrets pour soutenir nos arguments; **the ~ facts of the matter are that ...** ce qu'il y a de sûr et certain, c'est que ...; **what we want is ~ news** ce qu'il nous faut, c'est une information sérieuse

[i] (= strong) [drink] fortement alcoolisé, fort; [drug] dur; **~ porn*** porno m hard*; **the ~ stuff*** (= whisky) le whisky; (= drugs) les drogues dures

[j] (Chem) [water] dur

[k] (Med) [tissue] sclérosé, scléreux

[l] (esp Brit Pol) **the ~ left/right** la gauche/droite dure

[m] (Phon, Ling) [sound] dur; [consonant] (= not palatalized) dur; (= velar) fort, dur†

[n] (St Ex) [market, stock, rate] soutenu, ferme → **3**

2 ADV [a] (= energetically, assiduously) [push, pull, rain, snow] fort; [work] dur; [study] assidûment; [laugh] aux éclats; [cry] à chaudes larmes; [listen] de toutes ses oreilles; [think] bien; **tug the rope** ~ tire sur la corde d'un coup sec; **she slammed the door** ~ elle a claqué violemment la porte; **to fall down** ~ tomber lourdement; **to run** ~ courir de toutes ses forces; **to hold on** ~ tenir bon; **to hit** ~ frapper fort, cogner dur → **hit**; **to beg** ~ supplier; **to look** ~ **at** [+ person] dévisager; [+ thing] bien regarder; **to try** ~ faire or fournir un gros effort; **no matter how** ~ **I try, I ...** j'ai beau essayer, je ...; **as** ~ **as one can** de toutes ses forces; **to be** ~ **at work** or **at it*** travailler or bosser* dur; **she works** ~ **at keeping herself fit** elle fait de gros efforts pour rester en forme; **he likes to work** ~ **and play** ~ il met autant d'énergie à travailler qu'à s'amuser; **to clamp down** ~ **on sb** prendre des sanctions très sévères contre qn; **to be** ~ **pushed** or **put (to it)** or **pressed to do sth** avoir beaucoup de mal à faire qch; **to be** ~ **pressed for time/money** être vraiment à court de temps/d'argent

[b] (= as far as possible) [turn] ~ **left** à fond à gauche; ~ **right** à fond à droite; (Naut) ~ **a-port** bâbord toute; (Naut) ~ **a-starboard** tribord toute; (Naut) ~ **astern** arrière toute; (Naut) ~ **about** demi-tour toute

[c] (= badly) **to take sth** ~ être très affecté par qch; **it'll go** ~ **for him if ...** ça ira mal pour lui si ...; **she feels** ~ **done by** (by person) elle se sent brimée; (by life) elle trouve qu'elle n'a pas eu de chance dans la vie

[d] (= closely) **to follow** or **come** ~ **behind** or **upon sth** suivre qch de très près; ~ **by sth†** tout près de qch; **it was** ~ **on 10 o'clock†** il était bientôt 10 heures → **heel**

3 COMP ► **hard-and-fast** ADJ [timetable] strict; [position] inflexible; [conclusion] définitif; [evidence] concluant; [rule] absolu ► **hard-ass*'** N (US) dur(e) m(f) à cuire* ► **hard-bitten** ADJ (fig) dur à cuire* ► **hard-boiled** ADJ [egg] dur; (fig) [person] dur à cuire* ► **hard cash** N (Fin) espèces fpl, argent m liquide ► **hard copy** N (Comput) tirage m, sortie f papier ► **hard core** N (= committed group) [of supporters, advocates, objectors] noyau m dur; (within organization, political party) éléments mpl durs, inconditionnels mpl → **hardcore** ► **hard-core** ADJ [reactionary] (Marxism etc) pur et dur; [support, opposition] inconditionnel; **~-core pornography** pornographie f hard ► **hard court** N (Tennis) court m en dur ► **hard currency** N (Fin) devise f forte ► **hard disk** N (Comput) disque m dur ► **hard disk drive** N (Comput) unité f de disque dur ► **hard-drinking** ADJ qui boit beaucoup or sec ► **hard-earned** ADJ [money, salary] durement gagné; [holiday] bien mérité ► **hard-faced**, **hard-featured** ADJ au visage sévère, aux traits durs ► **hard-fought** ADJ [battle] acharné; [election, competition] âprement disputé ► **hard hat** N [of motorcyclist, construction worker] casque m; (= riding hat) bombe f; (esp US fig = construction worker) ouvrier m du bâtiment ► **hard-hat** ADJ (esp US fig) réactionnaire ► **hard-headed** ADJ réaliste, qui a la tête sur les épaules; **~-headed businessman** homme m d'affaires réaliste → **hardhead** ► **hard-hearted** ADJ insensible, au cœur dur; **he was very ~-hearted towards them** il était très dur avec eux ► **hard-hitting** ADJ (fig) [report, news programme] sans complaisance ► **hard labour**, **hard labor**

(US) N (Jur) travaux mpl forcés ► **hard-line** ADJ (pur et) dur ► **hard-liner** N pur(e) m(f) et dur(e) m(f) ► **hard loan** N (Fin) prêt m aux conditions commerciales or du marché ► **hard mint candy** N (US) bonbon à la menthe ► **hard-nosed** ADJ dur ► **hard of hearing** ADJ dur d'oreille ► **the hard-of-hearing** NPL les malentendants mpl ► **hard-on**⁕ N **to have a ~-on** bander⁕ ► **hard-packed snow** N neige f tassée; (by wind) congère f ► **hard palate** N voûte f du palais, palais m dur ► **hard rock** N (Mus) hard rock m ► **hard sauce** N (US) crème au beurre ► **hard-sell** N (Comm) vente f agressive; **~-sell tactics** stratégie f de vente agressive; (gen) **~-sell approach** approche f agressive ► **hard shoulder** N (esp Brit Aut) bande f d'arrêt d'urgence ► **hard-up*** ADJ (= penniless) fauché*, sans le sou; **I'm ~-up** je suis fauché* or à sec*; (fig) **they must be ~-up if ...** les choses doivent aller mal (pour eux) si ...; (gen) **to be ~-up for sth** être à court de qch, manquer de qch ► **hard-wearing** ADJ [shoes, clothes, material] solide, résistant ► **hard-wired** ADJ (Comput) câblé ► **hard-won** ADJ [victory, battle, freedom, independence] durement gagné, remporté de haute lutte; [promotion] bien mérité ► **hard-working** ADJ (gen) travailleur; [student, pupil] travailleur, bûcheur*

hardback ['hɑːdbæk] **1** ADJ [book] relié, cartonné **2** N livre m relié or cartonné

hardball ['hɑːdbɔːl] N (US) base-ball m; (fig) **to play ~*** employer la manière forte, ne pas prendre de gants

hardboard ['hɑːdbɔːd] N (NonC) isorel® m, panneau m dur (de fibres de bois)

hardcore [ˌhɑːdˈkɔːʳ] N [a] (for roads) matériaux mpl pour assise, couche f de fondation [b] (Mus) hardcore m → **hard**

hardcover ['hɑːdˌkʌvəʳ] ADJ, N (US) = **hardback**

harden ['hɑːdn] **1** VT [a] [+ substance] durcir; [+ steel] tremper; [+ muscle] affermir, durcir; **his years in the Arctic ~ed him considerably** les années qu'il a passées dans l'Arctique l'ont considérablement endurci; **to ~ o.s. to sth** s'endurcir or s'aguerrir à qch; **to ~ one's heart** s'endurcir; **this ~ed his heart** cela lui a endurci le cœur; **my heart ~ed against her** je lui ai fermé mon cœur [b] (Fin) **to ~ credit** restreindre le crédit → **hardened** [c] (Med) [+ arteries] scléroser **2** VI [a] [substances] durcir; [steel] se tremper; **his voice ~ed** sa voix se fit dure; **the look on his face ~ed** son regard s'est durci [b] (Fin) [shares, prices] se raffermir; **the market ~ed** le marché s'affermit [c] (Med) [arteries] se scléroser

hardened ['hɑːdnd] ADJ [substance] durci; [steel] trempé; [criminal, sinner] endurci; [drinker] invétéré; **~ drug addicts** des toxicomanes endurcis; **I'm ~ to it** j'ai l'habitude, ça ne me fait plus rien; **a world ~ to political injustice** un monde qui est devenu insensible à l'injustice politique

hardening ['hɑːdnɪŋ] **1** N [a] [of substance] durcissement m; [of steel] trempe f; (fig) durcissement m, endurcissement m; **I noticed a ~ of his attitude** j'ai remarqué que son attitude se durcissait [b] (Fin) [of currency, prices] raffermissement m [c] (Med) induration f, sclérose f **2** COMP ► **hardening of the arteries** N (Med) artériosclérose f

hardhead ['hɑːdhed] N (= person) réaliste mf → **hard**

hardihood ['hɑːdɪhʊd] N hardiesse f

hardiness ['hɑːdɪnɪs] N robustesse f

hardly ['hɑːdlɪ] ADV [a] (gen) à peine, ne ... guère; (= only just) à peine, tout juste; **he can ~ write** il sait à peine écrire, c'est à peine s'il sait écrire; **I can ~ hear you** je vous entends à peine; **I ~ know you** je vous connais à peine, je ne vous connais presque pas; **he had ~ spoken when ...** à peine avait-il parlé que ..., il n'eut pas plus tôt parlé que ...; **you'll ~ be-**

lieve it vous aurez de la peine *or* du mal à le croire; **it's ~ his business if ...** ce n'est guère son affaire si ...; **I need ~ point out that ...** je n'ai pas besoin de faire remarquer que ...; **he was given ~ 24 hours to pack his bags** c'est à peine si on lui a donné 24 heures pour faire ses bagages; **their two faces were ~ more than 18 inches apart** leurs visages étaient à moins de 50 centimètres l'un de l'autre; **~ anyone** presque personne; **~ anywhere** presque nulle part; **~ a day goes by without a visit from someone** il est rare qu'une journée se passe sans qu'il y ait une visite; **~ had he got home than the phone started ringing** à peine était-il rentré chez lui que le téléphone se mit à sonner; **you have ~ eaten anything** tu n'as presque rien mangé; **Nicki had ~ slept** Nicki avait à peine dormi; **~ ever** presque jamais; **~!** (= *not at all*) certainement pas!; (= *not exactly*) pas précisément!; **he would ~ have said that** il n'aurait tout de même pas dit cela; **it's ~ surprising his ideas didn't catch on** il n'est guère surprenant que ses idées ne soient pas devenues populaires
b (*frm* = *harshly*) durement, sévèrement; **to treat sb ~** se montrer sévère avec qn

hardness ['hɑːdnɪs] N dureté *f*; **~ of hearing** surdité *f* (partielle); (*fig*) **his ~ of heart** sa dureté de cœur; (*Fin*) **the ~ of the market** le raffermissement du marché

hardscrabble ['hɑːd,skræbəl] ADJ (*US*) [*farmer, farm*] misérable

hardship ['hɑːdʃɪp] **1** N **a** (*NonC*) (= *circumstances*) épreuves *fpl*; (= *suffering*) souffrance *f*; (= *poverty*) pauvreté *f*; (= *deprivation*) privation *f*; **he has suffered great ~** il a connu de dures épreuves; **periods of economic ~** des périodes de difficultés économiques; **many students are experiencing severe financial ~** beaucoup d'étudiants ont de gros problèmes d'argent; **there's a certain amount of ~ involved but it's worth it** ça sera dur mais ça en vaut la peine; **a life of ~** une vie pleine d'épreuves; **being posted to Cairo was no ~ at all** être posté au Caire n'avait rien de désagréable; **it's no great ~ to go and see her once a month** ce n'est pas la mer à boire d'aller la voir une fois par mois
b **~s** épreuves *fpl*, privations *fpl*; **the ~s of war** les privations *fpl or* les rigueurs *fpl* de la guerre; **many families are suffering economic ~s** de nombreuses familles ont des problèmes financiers
2 COMP ▶ **hardship clause** N (*Jur*) clause *f* de sauvegarde

hardtack ['hɑːdtæk] N (*Mil*) biscuit *m*; (*Naut*) galette *f*

hardtop ['hɑːdtɒp] N (*Aut*) voiture *f* à hardtop

hardware ['hɑːdwɛəʳ] **1** N (*NonC*) (*Comm*) quincaillerie *f* (*marchandises*); (*Mil etc*) matériel *m*; (*Comput, Space*) matériel *m*, hardware *m* **2** COMP ▶ **hardware dealer** N quincaillier *m*, -ière *f* ▶ **hardware shop** (*Brit*), **hardware store** (*US*) N quincaillerie *f*

hardwood ['hɑːdwʊd] **1** N (= *tree*) feuillu *m*; (= *wood*) bois *m* dur, bois *m* de feuillu **2** COMP de feuillu, de bois dur

hardy ['hɑːdɪ] **1** ADJ **a** (= *tough*) [*person, animal*] robuste; [*plant*] rustique **b** (= *brave*) [*person*] hardi, intrépide **2** COMP ▶ **hardy annual** N (*Bot*) annuelle *f* rustique; (*fig* = *topic*) sujet *m* rebattu, sujet *m* bateau ▶ **hardy perennial** N (*Bot*) vivace *f* rustique; (*fig*) sujet *m* rebattu, sujet *m* bateau

hare [hɛəʳ] **1** N (*pl* **hares** *or* **hare**) lièvre *m*; **~ and hounds** (= *game*) (sorte de) jeu *m* de piste; **to run with the ~ and hunt with the hounds** ménager la chèvre et le chou → **jug, mad 2** VI (*Brit*) **to ~ away** *or* **off*** partir en trombe *or* à fond de train **3** COMP ▶ **hare coursing** N chasse *f* au lièvre

harebell ['hɛəbel] N campanule *f*

---

harebrained ['hɛəbreɪnd] ADJ [*person*] écervelé; [*plan, scheme*] insensé; **to be ~** [*person*] être une tête de linotte, être écervelé

harelip [,hɛə'lɪp] N (*Med*) bec-de-lièvre *m*

harem ['hɑːriːm] N harem *m*

haricot ['hærɪkəʊ] N (*Brit*: *also* **~ bean**) haricot *m* blanc; **~ mutton** haricot *m* de mouton

hark [hɑːk] VI (*liter*) **to ~ to** écouter, prêter une oreille attentive à; († *or liter*) **~!** écoutez!; (*Brit*) **~ at him!*** mais écoutez-le (donc)!*
▶ **hark back** VI revenir (**to** à); **to ~ back to sth** revenir sur qch, ressasser qch

harken ['hɑːkən] VI = **hearken**

Harlequin ['hɑːlɪkwɪn] N (*Theat*) Arlequin *m*; **~ costume** costume *m* bigarré *or* d'Arlequin

Harley Street ['hɑːlɪ,striːt] N (*Brit*) Harley Street (*haut lieu de la médecine privée à Londres*)

harlot†† ['hɑːlət] N courtisane *f*

harm [hɑːm] **1** N mal *m*; **to do sb ~** faire du mal à qn; **he never did any ~ to anyone** il n'a jamais fait de mal à personne; **a bit of exercise never did anyone any ~** un peu d'exercice physique n'a jamais fait de mal à personne; **the ~'s done now** le mal est fait maintenant; **no ~ done!** il n'y a pas de mal!; **it can't do you any ~** ça ne peut pas te faire de mal; **it will do more ~ than good** cela fera plus de mal que de bien; **to cut taxes would do the economy more ~ than good** une réduction des impôts ferait plus de mal que de bien à l'économie; **he means no ~** il n'a pas de mauvaises intentions; **he doesn't mean us any ~** il ne nous veut pas de mal; **you will come to no ~** il ne t'arrivera rien; **make sure that no ~ comes to him** fais en sorte qu'il ne lui arrive rien de mal; **I don't see any ~ in it** ◊ **I see no ~ in it** je n'y vois aucun mal; **there's no ~ in an occasional drink** un petit verre de temps en temps ne peut pas faire de mal; **there's no ~ in asking** un renseignement ne coûte rien; **in ~'s way** en danger; **they'd been put in ~'s way** on les avait mis en danger; **keep** *or* **stay out of ~'s way** (= *out of danger*) mettez-vous en sûreté; (= *out of the way*) ne restez pas dans les parages; **to keep a child out of ~'s way** mettre un enfant à l'abri du danger; **put the vase out of ~'s way** mets ce vase en lieu sûr
2 VT [+ *person*] (= *damage*) faire du tort à, nuire à; (= *hurt*) faire du mal à; [+ *crops, harvest, building*] endommager; [+ *object*] abîmer; [+ *reputation, interests, cause*] nuire à; **this will ~ his case considerably** cela desservira ses intérêts; **products which ~ the environment** des produits nocifs pour l'environnement → **fly**

harmful ['hɑːmfʊl] ADJ [*substance, rays, effects*] nocif; **to be ~ to** (*physically*) être nuisible à *or* mauvais pour; (*morally*) porter préjudice à

harmless ['hɑːmlɪs] ADJ [*animal, substance, device, joke*] inoffensif (**to** pour); [*hobby, pleasure, entertainment, diversion*] innocent; [*rash, cyst, growth*] bénin -igne *f*); **it's just a bit of ~ fun** ce n'est pas bien méchant; **he's ~*** il n'est pas bien méchant; (*Jur*) **to hold ~** tenir à couvert

harmlessly ['hɑːmlɪslɪ] ADV **a** (= *without causing damage*) [*explode*] sans dommages **b** (= *inoffensively*) [*gossip*] de façon inoffensive; **it all started ~ enough** au début ce n'était qu'un jeu

harmonic [hɑː'mɒnɪk] **1** ADJ (*Math, Mus, Phys*) harmonique **2 harmonics** NPL **a** (= *science*) harmonie *f*; (= *overtones*) harmoniques *mpl* **b** (*Phys*) harmoniques *mpl or fpl*

harmonica [hɑː'mɒnɪkə] N harmonica *m*

harmonious [hɑː'məʊnɪəs] ADJ (*gen, Mus*) harmonieux

harmoniously [hɑː'məʊnɪəslɪ] ADV **a** (*live together, work together*) en harmonie; [*blend, combine*] harmonieusement, avec harmonie **b** [*sing*] harmonieusement

harmonium [hɑː'məʊnɪəm] N harmonium *m*

---

harmonize ['hɑːmənaɪz] **1** VI (*Mus*) chanter en harmonie; [*colours etc*] s'harmoniser (**with** avec) **2** VT (*gen, Mus*) harmoniser

harmony ['hɑːmənɪ] N (*Mus*) harmonie *f*; (*fig*) harmonie *f*, accord *m*; **in perfect ~** en parfaite harmonie, en parfait accord; **they work together in ~** ils travaillent ensemble en harmonie; **in ~ with** en harmonie *or* en accord avec; **to live in ~ with nature** vivre en harmonie avec la nature → **close**¹

harness ['hɑːnɪs] **1** N [*of horse*] harnais *m*, harnachement *m*; [*of parachute*] harnais *m*; (*Climbing*) baudrier *m*; (*fig*) **to get back in(to) ~*** (= *back to work*) reprendre le collier; (*fig*) **to die in ~*** mourir debout *or* à la tâche; (*fig*) **to work in ~ (with sb)** travailler en tandem (avec qn) **2** VT **a** [+ *horse*] harnacher; **to ~ a horse to a carriage** atteler un cheval à une voiture **b** (*fig*) [+ *river, resources, energy, power, anger*] exploiter; [+ *talents*] employer à bien

Harold ['hærəld] N Harold *m*

harp [hɑːp] **1** N harpe *f* **2** VI* **to ~ on (about)** sth rabâcher qch; **stop ~ing on about it!** cesse de nous rebattre les oreilles avec ça!; **she's always ~ing on about her problems** elle ne cesse de rebattre les oreilles de ses problèmes; **I don't want to ~ on about it** je ne veux pas revenir toujours là-dessus; **to ~ back to sth** revenir sur qch, ressasser qch

harpist ['hɑːpɪst] N harpiste *mf*

harpoon [hɑː'puːn] **1** N harpon *m* **2** VT harponner

harpsichord ['hɑːpsɪkɔːd] N clavecin *m*

harpsichordist ['hɑːpsɪkɔːdɪst] N claveciniste *mf*

harpy ['hɑːpɪ] N (*Myth*) harpie *f*; (*pej*) **old ~** vieille harpie *f or* sorcière *f*

harridan ['hærɪdən] N (*frm*) harpie *f*, sorcière *f*

harried ['hærɪd] ADJ [*look, expression*] soucieux

harrier ['hærɪəʳ] N **a** (= *dog*) harrier *m*; **~s** meute *f* **b** **~s** (= *cross-country runners*) coureurs *mpl* de cross **c** (= *bird*) busard *m*

Harris Tweed® [,hærɪs'twiːd] N (*gros*) tweed *m* (*des Hébrides*)

harrow ['hærəʊ] **1** N herse *f* **2** VT **a** (*Agr*) herser **b** (*fig*) [+ *person*] tourmenter, torturer

harrowing ['hærəʊɪŋ] **1** ADJ [*story, account, film*] poignant; [*experience*] extrêmement pénible; [*photo, picture*] difficile à supporter **2** N (*Agr*) hersage *m*

Harry ['hærɪ] N (ABBR = **Henry**) → **flash**

harry ['hærɪ] VT [+ *country*] dévaster, ravager; [+ *person*] harceler; (*Mil*) harceler

harsh [hɑːʃ] ADJ **a** (= *severe*) [*words, criticism, reality, truth, measures*] dur; [*person, verdict, sentence, punishment*] sévère; **the ~ facts of ...** la dure réalité de ...; **he said many ~ things about his opponents** il n'a pas été tendre avec ses adversaires; **to be ~ on sb** être dur avec qn **b** (= *inhospitable*) [*conditions, environment*] dur; [*climate, winter, weather*] rude, rigoureux **c** (= *rough, hard*) [*colour, voice, cry*] criard; [*sound*] discordant; [*light*] cru; [*whisper, breathing*] rauque; [*contrast*] heurté; [*wool, fabric*] rêche; [*wine, whisky, tobacco*] âpre, âpreux; [*cleaner, detergent*] corrosif; **the ~ glare of the sun** l'éclat éblouissant du soleil

harshly ['hɑːʃlɪ] ADV [*treat, criticize, judge*] sévèrement; [*say*] rudement, durement; [*laugh*] d'un rire jaune *or* amer

harshness ['hɑːʃnɪs] N **a** (= *severity*) [*of manner*] rudesse *f*; [*of words, conditions*] dureté *f*; [*of fate, climate*] rigueur *f*; [*of punishment, laws*] sévérité *f* **b** (= *roughness*) (*to the touch*) rudesse *f*, dureté *f*; (*to the taste*) âpreté *f*; (*to the ear*) discordance *f*

hart [hɑːt] N (*pl* **harts** *or* **hart**) cerf *m*

harum-scarum* ['hɛərəm'skɛərəm] **1** ADJ tête de linotte *inv* **2** N tête *f* de linotte

harvest ['hɑːvɪst] [1] N [of corn] moisson f; [of fruit] récolte f, cueillette f; [of grapes] vendange f; (fig) moisson f; **to get in the ~** faire la moisson, moissonner; **a bumper potato ~** une récolte de pommes de terre exceptionnelle; **poor ~s** mauvaises récoltes fpl → **reap** [2] VT [+ corn] moissonner; [+ fruit] récolter, cueillir; [+ grapes] vendanger, récolter; (fig) [+ reward] moissonner; [+ information] récolter; **to ~ the fields** faire les moissons, moissonner (les champs) [3] VI faire la moisson, moissonner [4] COMP ► **harvest festival** N fête f de la moisson ► **harvest home** N (= festival) fête f de la moisson; (= season) fin f de la moisson ► **harvest moon** N pleine lune f (de l'équinoxe d'automne) ► **harvest time** N **at ~ time** pendant or à la moisson

harvester ['hɑːvɪstəʳ] N (= machine) moissonneuse f; (= person) moissonneur m, -euse f → **combine**

harvestman ['hɑːvɪstmən] N (pl **-men**) (= insect) faucheur m

has [hæz] [1] → **have** [2] COMP ► **has-been** N (= person) has been* m inv; (= hat, carpet etc) vieillerie f, vieux truc* m; **he's/she's a ~-been*** il/elle a fait son temps

hash [hæʃ] [1] N [a] (* = mess) gâchis m; **he made a ~ of it** il a raté son affaire; **I'll settle his ~**¡ je vais lui régler son compte* [b] (Culin) plat en sauce à base de viande hachée et de légumes [c] (Drugs*: also **~ish**) hasch* m [2] VT (Culin) hacher [3] COMP ► **hash browns** NPL (Culin) pommes fpl de terre sautées (servies au petit déjeuner) ► **hash house*** N (US) gargote f ► **hash house slinger*** N (US) serveur m, -euse f dans une gargote

► **hash out*** VT SEP [a] = **hash over** [b] (= solve) finir par résoudre

► **hash over*** VT SEP [+ problem, plan, difficulty] discuter ferme de; **this subject has been ~ed over a great deal** on a discuté en long et en large de ce sujet

► **hash up** [1] VT SEP [a] (Culin) hacher menu [b] (= spoil) **he really ~ed it up** il a raté son affaire [2] **~-up** N = **hash 1a**

hashish ['hæʃɪʃ] N haschisch or haschich m

hasn't ['hæznt] = **has not**; → **have**

hasp [hɑːsp] N [of door, lid, window] moraillon m; [of book cover, necklace] fermoir m

Hassidic [hæ'sɪdɪk] ADJ hassidique

hassle* ['hæsl] [1] N [a] (= fuss) histoire f; (= worries) tracas mpl; **what a ~!** quelle histoire!; **legal ~s** tracas mpl juridiques; **it's a ~!** c'est toute une histoire or affaire!; **it's no ~!** ce n'est pas un problème!; **it isn't worth the ~** ça ne vaut pas la peine*; **preparing for a wedding is such a ~** la préparation d'un mariage, c'est toute une affaire!; **commuting's a bit of a ~** les trajets quotidiens sont un peu embêtants; **charcoal's a real ~ to light** ce n'est pas une mince affaire d'allumer du charbon de bois [b] (US) (= squabble) chamaillerie* f, bagarre* f; (= bustle, confusion) pagaille f [2] VT (= harass) embêter, enquiquiner*; **stop hassling me, will you?** arrête donc de m'embêter or de m'enquiquiner*; **he was continually being ~d for money** on l'embêtait sans arrêt pour lui demander de l'argent [3] VI (US = quarrel) se battre (**with sb** avec qn, **over sth** à propos de qch)

hassock ['hæsək] N coussin m (d'agenouilloir)

hast†† [hæst] (liter) **thou ~** = **you have**; → **have**

haste [heɪst] N hâte f; (excessive) précipitation f; **why all this ~?** pourquoi tant de précipitation?; **to do sth in ~** faire qch à la hâte or en hâte; **in their ~ to explain what had happened, they ...** dans leur précipitation à expliquer ce qui s'était passé, ils ...; **in great ~** en toute hâte; **to make ~†** se hâter (**to do sth** de faire qch). ■(PROV) **more ~ less speed** hâtez-vous lentement ■(PROV) **marry in ~, repent at leisure** qui se marie sans réfléchir aura tout le loisir de s'en repentir

hasten ['heɪsn] [1] VI se hâter, s'empresser (**to do sth** de faire qch); **... I ~ to add** ... je m'empresse d'ajouter, ... j'ajoute tout de suite; **to ~ down/away** etc se hâter de descendre/partir etc, descendre/partir etc à la hâte [2] VT (gen) hâter, accélérer; [+ reaction] activer; **to ~ one's step** presser le pas, accélérer l'allure or le pas; **to ~ sb's departure** hâter le départ de qn; **to ~ sb's/sth's demise** précipiter la fin de qn/qch; **the strikes that ~ed the collapse of the Soviet Union** les grèves qui ont précipité l'effondrement de l'Union soviétique

hastily ['heɪstɪlɪ] ADV hâtivement; (= excessively quickly) précipitamment; **a ~ arranged press conference** une conférence de presse organisée à la hâte; **he ~ suggested that ...** il s'est empressé de suggérer que ..., il a suggéré précipitamment que ...; **to act ~ in doing sth** agir avec précipitation or à la hâte en faisant qch

Hastings ['heɪstɪŋz] N **the Battle of ~** la bataille de Hastings

hasty ['heɪstɪ] ADJ [a] (= hurried) [departure, escape, retreat] précipité; [glance, examination, visit, sketch, kiss] rapide; **to eat a ~ breakfast** prendre son petit déjeuner en hâte; **to bid a ~ goodbye to sb** dire précipitamment au revoir à qn [b] (= rash) [action, decision, words] hâtif; [marriage] précipité; **don't be ~** pas de précipitation; **perhaps I was a bit ~** (in actions) j'ai sans doute agi avec précipitation; (in speaking) j'ai sans doute parlé trop vite; **to have a ~ temper** s'emporter facilement

hat [hæt] [1] N chapeau m; **to put on one's ~** mettre son chapeau; **~ in hand** (lit) chapeau bas; (fig) obséquieusement; **~s off!** chapeau bas!; (fig) **to take one's ~ off to sb** tirer son chapeau à qn; **~s off to them for helping the homeless!** leur action en faveur des SDF mérite un (grand) coup de chapeau; (fig) **to keep sth under one's ~** garder qch pour soi; (fig) **keep it under your ~!** motus!; **to pass round the ~** or (US) **to pass the ~ for sb** faire la quête pour qn; (fig) **she wears two ~s** elle a deux casquettes; (fig) **speaking with my accountant's ~ on** (si je te parlais) en tant que comptable; **putting on my nationalistic ~ ...** en tant que nationaliste ...; (fig) **at the drop of a ~** [act, make speech etc] au pied levé; [leave, shoot, get angry] pour un oui pour un non → **bowler²**, **eat**, **old**, **pull out**, **talk**, **top** [2] COMP ► **hat shop** N (for women) boutique f de modiste; (for men) chapellerie f ► **hat tree** N (US) = **hatstand** ► **hat trick** N [a] **to score a ~ trick** (gen Sport) réussir trois coups (or gagner trois matchs etc) consécutifs; (Ftbl) marquer trois buts dans un match; (Cricket) éliminer trois batteurs en trois balles [b] (Conjuring) tour m du chapeau

hatband ['hætbænd] N ruban m de chapeau

hatbox ['hætbɒks] N carton m à chapeaux

hatch¹ [hætʃ] [1] VT [a] [+ chick, egg] faire éclore [b] [+ plan] ourdir (liter), tramer; [+ plan] couver [2] VI (also **~ out**) [chick, egg] éclore [3] N (= brood) couvée f

hatch² [hætʃ] N [a] (Naut: also **~way**) écoutille f; [= floodgates] vanne f d'écluse; (fig) **down the ~!**¡ cul sec!* [b] (Brit: also **service** or **serving ~**) passe-plats m inv, guichet m [c] (= car) = **hatchback**

hatch³ [hætʃ] VT (Art) hachurer

hatchback ['hætʃbæk] N (= car) voiture f à hayon

hatcheck ['hætʃek] N (also **~ girl**, **~ man**) préposé(e) m(f) au vestiaire

hatchery ['hætʃərɪ] N couvoir m

hatchet ['hætʃɪt] [1] N hachette f → **bury** [2] COMP ► **hatchet-faced** ADJ au visage en lame de couteau ► **hatchet job** N (fig) démolissage m; **to do a ~ job on sb** démolir qn ► **hatchet man*** N (pl **hatchet men**) (US = hired killer) tueur m (à gages); (fig: in industry etc) homme m de main; **he was the company's ~ man when they sacked 200 workers** c'est lui que l'entreprise a chargé de faire tomber les têtes quand elle a licencié 200 ouvriers

hatching¹ ['hætʃɪŋ] N [of chicks, eggs] (= act) éclosion f; (= brood) couvée f

hatching² ['hætʃɪŋ] N (Art) hachures fpl

hatchway ['hætʃweɪ] N passe-plats m inv

▼**hate** [heɪt] [1] VT haïr; (weaker) détester, avoir horreur de; **she ~s him like poison** elle le hait à mort; (weaker) elle ne peut pas le voir en peinture*; **what he ~s most of all is ...** ce qu'il déteste le plus au monde c'est ...; **I ~ it when people accuse me of lying** je déteste or j'ai horreur que les gens m'accusent de mentir; **to ~ o.s.** s'en vouloir (**for doing sth** de faire qch); **I ~d myself for writing that letter** je m'en voulais d'avoir écrit cette lettre; **to ~ doing sth** ◊ **to ~ to do sth** détester faire qch, avoir horreur de faire qch; **he ~s being or to be ordered about** il a horreur or il ne peut pas souffrir qu'on lui donne (subj) des ordres; **I ~ being late** je déteste être en retard, j'ai horreur d'être en retard; **she ~s me having any fun** elle ne supporte pas que je m'amuse; **I ~ to tell you this, but ...** je suis désolé (de vous le dire), mais ...; **I ~ to admit it, but you were right** je suis obligé d'admettre que vous aviez raison; **I ~ seeing her in pain** je ne peux pas supporter de la voir souffrir; **I would ~ to keep him waiting** je ne voudrais surtout pas le faire attendre; **I ~ to rush you but I have another appointment later on** je ne voudrais pas vous bousculer mais j'ai un autre rendez-vous plus tard; **I would ~ him to think that ...** je voudrais surtout pas qu'il pense que ... [2] N (NonC) haine f → **pet** [3] COMP ► **hate campaign** N campagne f de dénigrement or de haine ► **hate mail** N lettres fpl d'injures

hated ['heɪtɪd] ADJ haï, détesté

hateful ['heɪtfʊl] ADJ [a] (= horrible) odieux [b] (= full of hate) haineux

hath†† [hæθ] = **has**; → **have**

hatless ['hætlɪs] ADJ sans chapeau

hatpin ['hætpɪn] N épingle f à chapeau

hatrack ['hætræk] N porte-chapeaux m inv

hatred ['heɪtrɪd] N (NonC) haine f; **racial ~** la haine raciale; **he developed a bitter ~ of the police** il s'est mis à vouer une haine féroce à la police; **the brothers killed their father out of ~** la haine a poussé les frères à tuer leur père; **to feel ~ for sb/sth** haïr qn/qch

hatstand ['hætstænd] N portemanteau m

hatter ['hætəʳ] N chapelier m → **mad**

haughtily ['hɔːtɪlɪ] ADV [say, reply, dismiss, ignore] avec arrogance, avec morgue (liter)

haughtiness ['hɔːtɪnɪs] N arrogance f, morgue f (liter)

haughty ['hɔːtɪ] ADJ (pej) [person, manner, tone, look] hautain

haul [hɔːl] [1] N [a] (= journey) **the long ~ between Paris and Grenoble** le long voyage entre Paris et Grenoble; (lit, fig) **it's a long ~** la route est longue; **revitalizing the economy will be a long ~** relancer l'économie prendra beaucoup de temps; (esp US fig) **over the long ~** sur le long terme [b] (= catch) [of fish] prise f; **a good ~** une belle prise, un beau coup de filet [c] (= booty) butin m; **the thieves made a good ~** les voleurs ont eu un beau butin; **a drugs ~** une saisie de drogue; **police have recovered a ~ of machine guns** la police a récupéré tout un stock de mitraillettes; (fig) **what a ~!** quelle récolte!

2 VT **a** (= *pull*) traîner, tirer; **he ~ed himself to his feet** il s'est levé à grand-peine; (fig) **to ~ sb over the coals** passer un savon* à qn, réprimander sévèrement qn; **she was ~ed before magistrates for refusing to pay the fine*** elle a été traînée devant les tribunaux parce qu'elle avait refusé de payer l'amende; (US) **to ~ ass*** se barrer‡, mettre les bouts‡

b (= *transport by truck*) camionner

c (*Naut*) haler; **to ~ a boat into the wind** faire lofer un bateau

3 VI (*Naut*) [*boat*] lofer; [*wind*] refuser

▶**haul down** VT SEP (*gen*) [+ *object*] descendre (*en tirant*); [+ *flag, sail*] affaler, amener

▶**haul in** VT SEP [+ *line, catch*] amener; [+ *drowning man*] tirer (de l'eau)

▶**haul up** VT SEP (*gen*) [+ *object*] monter (*en tirant*); [+ *flag, sail*] hisser; **to ~ o.s. up** se hisser; (*Naut*) **to ~ up a boat** (*aboard ship*) rentrer une embarcation (à bord); (*on to beach*) tirer un bateau au sec; **to be ~ed up in court*** être traîné devant les tribunaux; **he was ~ed up for speeding*** il a été interpellé parce qu'il roulait trop vite

haulage ['hɔ:lɪdʒ] **1** N (= *business*) transport *m* routier; (= *charge*) frais *mpl* de transport **2** COMP ▶ **haulage company** N (*Brit*) entreprise *f* de transports (routiers) ▶ **haulage contractor** N = **haulier**

hauler ['hɔ:lə'] N (US) **a** = **haulier b** (= *vehicle*) camion *m*, poids *m* lourd

haulier ['hɔ:lɪə'] N (*Brit*) (= *company*) entreprise *f* de transports (routiers); (= *person in charge*) entrepreneur *m* de transports (routiers), transporteur *m*; (= *driver*) camionneur *m*, routier *m*

haunch [hɔ:ntʃ] N hanche *f*; **~es** [*of animal*] derrière *m*, arrière-train *m*; **(squatting) on his ~es** (*person*) accroupi; (*dog etc*) assis (sur son derrière); (*Culin*) **~ of venison** cuissot *m* de chevreuil

haunt [hɔ:nt] **1** VT (*lit, fig*) hanter; (fig) **he used to ~ the café in the hope of seeing her** il hantait le café dans l'espoir de la voir; **to be ~ed by memories** être hanté par des souvenirs; **he is ~ed by the fear of losing all his money** il est hanté par la peur de *or* il a la hantise de perdre tout son argent; **the decision to leave her children now ~s her** elle est hantée par le remords parce qu'elle a décidé d'abandonner ses enfants; **lack of money ~ed successive projects** le manque d'argent a été la plaie de *or* a nui à tous les projets → **haunted**

2 N [*of criminals*] repaire *m*; **one of the favourite ~s of this animal is ...** un des lieux où l'on trouve souvent cet animal est ...; **it is a favourite ~ of artists** c'est un lieu fréquenté par les artistes; **that café is one of his favourite ~s** ce café est un de ses lieux favoris *or* de prédilection; **familiar childhood ~s** des lieux de prédilection de son (*or* mon *etc*) enfance

haunted ['hɔ:ntɪd] ADJ [*house*] hanté; [*look, expression*] égaré; [*face, eyes*] hagard; **he looks ~** il a un air égaré *or* hagard

haunting ['hɔ:ntɪŋ] **1** ADJ [*tune*] obsédant, qui vous hante; [*image, beauty, memory, doubt, cry*] lancinant **2** N **there have been several ~s here** il y a eu plusieurs apparitions ici

hauntingly ['hɔ:ntɪŋlɪ] ADV **~ beautiful** d'une beauté envoûtante

haute couture [,əʊt ku:'tʊə'] N haute couture *f*

haute cuisine [,əʊt kwɪ'zi:n] N haute cuisine *f*

hauteur [əʊ'tɜ:] N hauteur *f* (*pej*), morgue *f* (*liter*)

Havana [hə'vænə] N **a** La Havane **b a ~ (cigar)** un havane

▼**have** [hæv]

---
vb: 3rd pers sg pres **has**, *pret, ptp* **had**
1 AUXILIARY VERB　　**4** NOUN
2 MODAL VERB　　　　**5** PHRASAL VERBS
3 TRANSITIVE VERB

When **have** *is part of a set combination, eg* **have a look/walk, have a good time, have breakfast/ lunch,** *look up the noun.*

---

1 AUXILIARY VERB

a avoir

avoir is the auxiliary used with most verbs to form past tenses. For important exceptions see **b**.

I ~ eaten j'ai mangé; **I ~ been** j'ai été; **I had been** j'avais été; **I had eaten** j'avais mangé; **haven't you grown!** comme tu as grandi!; **once he'd explained the situation I felt better** une fois qu'il m'eut expliqué la situation, je me suis senti mieux

Note the agreement of the past participle with the preceding direct object.

I haven't seen him je ne l'ai pas vu; **I haven't seen her** je ne l'ai pas vue; **I hadn't seen him** je ne l'avais pas vu; **had I seen her** *or* **if I had seen her** I would have spoken to him si je l'avais vue, je lui aurais parlé; **having seen them** les ayant vus

When describing uncompleted states or actions, French generally uses the present and imperfect where English uses the perfect and past perfect.

I ~ lived *or* **~ been living here for ten years/since January** j'habite ici depuis dix ans/depuis janvier; **I had lived** *or* **had been living there for ten years** j'habitais là depuis dix ans

◆ **to have just ...** venir de ...; **I ~ just seen him** je viens de le voir; **I had just spoken to him** je venais de lui parler; *BUT* **I've just come from London** j'arrive à l'instant de Londres

b être

être is the auxiliary used with all reflexives, and the following verbs when used intransitively: **aller, arriver, descendre, devenir, entrer, monter, mourir, naître, partir, passer, rentrer, rester, retourner, revenir, sortir, tomber, venir.**

I ~ gone je suis allé; **I've made a mistake** je me suis trompé; **I had gone** j'étais allé; **I had made a mistake** je m'étais trompé; **I left immediately after I had seen him** je suis parti tout de suite après l'avoir vu

c in tag questions: seeking confirmation n'est-ce pas; **you've seen her, haven't you?** vous l'avez vue, n'est-ce pas?; **he hasn't told anyone, has he?** il n'en a parlé à personne, n'est-ce pas?; **you haven't lost it, ~ you?** tu ne l'as pas perdu, n'est-ce pas?

d in tag responses **he's got a new job — oh has he?** il a un nouveau travail — ah bon?; **you've dropped your book — so I ~!** vous avez laissé tomber votre livre — en effet *or* ah oui, c'est vrai!

(mais) si *or* **(mais) non** *are used to contradict.*

you haven't seen her — yes I ~! vous ne l'avez pas vue — (mais) si!; **you've made a mistake — no I haven't!** vous vous êtes trompé — (mais) non!

oui *or* **non** *are often sufficient when answering questions.*

have you met him? — yes I ~ est-ce que tu l'as rencontré? — oui; **has he arrived? — no he hasn't** est-ce qu'il est arrivé? — non

e avoiding repetition of verb **~ you ever been there? if you ~ ...** y êtes-vous déjà allé? si oui, ...; **~ you tried it? if you haven't ...** est-ce que vous avez goûté ça? si vous ne l'avez pas fait, ... → **so, neither, nor**

2 MODAL VERB

◆ **to have to** + *infinitive* devoir, falloir

---

falloir is always used in the third person singular, in an impersonal construction.

they ~ to work hard ils doivent travailler dur, il faut qu'ils travaillent (*subj*) dur; **they had to work hard** ils ont dû travailler dur, il a fallu qu'ils travaillent (*subj*) dur; **you're going to ~ to work hard!** tu vas devoir travailler dur!, il va falloir que tu travailles (*subj*) dur!; **I ~ (got) to speak to you at once** je dois vous parler *or* il faut que je vous parle (*subj*) immédiatement; **I'll ~ to leave now or I'll miss the train** il faut que je parte, sinon je vais rater mon train; **he had to pay all the money back** il a dû tout rembourser; **don't you ~ to get permission?** est-ce qu'on ne doit pas demander la permission?; **do you ~ to go now?** ◊ **~ you got to go now?** est-ce que vous devez partir tout de suite?; **she was having to get up at six each morning** elle devait se lever à 6 heures tous les matins; **we've had to work late twice this week** nous avons dû rester travailler tard deux fois cette semaine; **we shall ~ to find an alternative** nous allons devoir *or* il nous faudra trouver une autre solution; **the locks will ~ to be changed** il va falloir changer les serrures; **what kind of equipment would you ~ to have?** quel type de matériel vous faudrait-il?; *BUT* **it's got to be** *or* **it has to be the biggest scandal this year** c'est sans aucun doute le plus gros scandale de l'année; **it still has to be proved** ça reste à prouver; **do you ~ to make such a noise?** vous êtes vraiment forcé de faire tout ce bruit?, tu ne pourrais pas faire un peu moins de bruit?

◆ **don't/doesn't have to** + *infinitive*

Note that falloir and devoir are not used.

he doesn't ~ to work il n'a pas besoin de travailler; **you didn't ~ to tell her!** tu n'avais pas besoin de le lui dire!; **if you're a member you don't ~ to pay** si vous êtes membre vous n'avez pas besoin de payer; **it's nice not to ~ to work on Saturdays** c'est agréable de ne pas avoir à travailler le samedi; **I don't ~ to do it** je ne suis pas obligé *or* forcé de le faire

3 TRANSITIVE VERB

a = possess avoir; **I ~** *or* **I've got three books** j'ai trois livres; **~ you got** *or* **do you ~ a suitcase?** avez-vous une valise?; **she has blue eyes** elle a les yeux bleus; **he's got big feet** il a de grands pieds; **I've got an idea** j'ai une idée; **~ you got this jumper in black?** est-ce que vous avez ce pull en noir?; **sorry, that's all I ~** désolé, c'est tout ce que j'ai; **I haven't (got) any more** je n'en ai plus; **she has** *or* **she's got a shop** elle tient *or* a une boutique; **~ you got the time (on you)?** est-ce que vous avez *or* avez-vous l'heure?; **I ~ (got) nothing to do** je n'ai rien à faire; **I ~ (got) letters to write** j'ai des lettres à écrire; (*Cards*) **I didn't ~ any spades** je n'avais pas de piques; **he has flu** il a la grippe; **I've (got) a headache** j'ai mal à la tête; **I had my camera ready** j'avais mon appareil tout prêt; *BUT* **I'll ~ everything ready** je veillerai à ce que tout soit prêt; **I ~ (got) no German** je ne parle pas un mot d'allemand

b = eat, drink, take **he had an egg for breakfast** il a mangé un œuf au petit déjeuner; **I'll just ~ a sandwich** je vais juste prendre *or* manger un sandwich; **I've had some more** j'en ai repris; **shall we ~ a coffee?** est-ce qu'on prend un café?; **to ~ tea with sb** prendre le thé avec qn; **I've had a couple of aspirins** j'ai pris deux aspirines

◆ **will you have ...?** (*in offers*) will you ~ tea or coffee? voulez-vous *or* prendrez-vous du thé ou du café?; **will you ~ some more?** voulez-vous en reprendre?

c = spend passer; **what sort of day have you had?** est-ce que tu as passé une bonne journée?; **to ~ a pleasant evening** passer une bonne soirée

d = smoke fumer; **he had a cigarette** il a fumé une cigarette

---

➤ LANGUAGE IN USE: **have** 10.1, 10.2, 10.3

[e] **= receive, obtain, get** avoir, recevoir; **to ~ news from sb** avoir or recevoir des nouvelles de qn; **we had a lot of visitors** nous avons eu or reçu beaucoup de visites; [BUT] **I had a birthday card from him** il m'a envoyé une carte d'anniversaire; **there are no newspapers to be had** on ne trouve pas de journaux

Note the use of **falloir** *to translate* **must have/ have to have.**

I must ~ £50 at once il me faut 50 livres immédiatement; **I must** or **~ to have them by this afternoon** il me les faut pour cet après-midi; **I must ~ more time** il me faut davantage de temps

[f] **= hold, catch** tenir; **he had me by the throat/the hair** il me tenait à la gorge/par les cheveux; **the dog had (got) him by the ankle** le chien le tenait par la cheville; **I ~** or **I've got him where I want him!*** je le tiens!; [BUT] **there you ~ me!** là tu me poses une colle!

[g] **= to give birth to** **to ~ a child** avoir un enfant; **she is having a baby in April** elle va avoir un bébé en avril; **our cat has had kittens** notre chatte a eu des petits

[h] *** = to have sex with** coucher* avec

[i] SET STRUCTURES

- **to let sb have** (= give) donner à qn; **let me ~ your address** donnez-moi votre adresse; **I'll let you ~ the books tomorrow** je vous donnerai les livres demain; [BUT] **I'll let you ~ it for 100 francs** je vous le cède pour 100 F

- **to have it that**: **he will ~ it that Paul is guilty** il soutient que Paul est coupable; **he won't ~ it that Paul is guilty** il n'admet pas que Paul soit coupable; **rumour has it that ...** le bruit court que ...

- **won't have** or **am not having** (= refuse to accept) **I won't ~** or **am not having this nonsense!** je ne tolérerai pas ces enfantillages!; **I won't ~** or **am not having this sort of behaviour!** je ne tolérerai pas une conduite pareille!; **I won't ~ it!** je ne tolérerai pas ça!; **I won't ~ him risking his neck on that motorbike** je ne tolérerai pas qu'il risque sa vie sur cette moto; **I'm not having any!** ça ne prend pas!

- **would have** (= wish) **as fate would ~ it, he did not get the letter** la fatalité a voulu qu'il ne reçoive pas la lettre; **what would you ~ me do?** que voulez-vous que je fasse?; **I would ~ you know that ...** sachez que ...

- **to have sth done** faire faire qch; **to ~ sth mended** faire réparer qch; **~ it mended!** fais-le réparer!; **to ~ one's hair cut** se faire couper les cheveux; **they killed him, or had him killed** ils l'ont tué ou ils l'ont fait tuer; **I've had the brakes checked** j'ai fait vérifier les freins

- **to have sb do sth** faire faire qch à qn; **I had him clean the car** je l'ai fait nettoyer la voiture

- **to have sb doing sth**: **he had us all helping with the dinner** il nous avait tous mis à contribution pour préparer le dîner; **she soon had them all reading and writing** elle réussit très rapidement à leur apprendre à lire et à écrire

- **to have sth stolen/broken** etc: **he had his car stolen** il s'est fait voler sa voiture, on lui a volé sa voiture; **he had his worst fears confirmed** ses pires craintes se sont réalisées; **I've had three windows broken this week** j'ai eu trois fenêtres cassées cette semaine

- **had better** (= should) **I had better go now** il vaut mieux que j'y aille; **you'd better not tell him that!** tu ferais mieux de ne pas lui dire ça!

- **to be had*** se faire avoir; **you've been had** tu t'es fait avoir*, on t'a eu*

- **to have had it***: **I've had it** (= am done for) je suis fichu* or foutu‡; (= fed up: also **I've had it up to here** or **I've had that**) j'en ai par-dessus la tête!*, j'en ai marre!*, j'en ai ras-le-bol!*

- **to have to do with**: **I ~ (got) nothing to do with it** je n'y suis pour rien; **that has nothing to do with it** ça n'a rien à voir

---

[4] NOUN

the ~s and the ~-nots les riches mpl et les pauvres mpl; **the ~-nots** les démunis mpl, les déshérités mpl

[5] PHRASAL VERBS

▶ **have at** VT FUS (in swordfight etc) **~ at thee!** ††défends-toi!

▶ **have away‡** VT SEP (Brit) = **have off**

▶ **have down** VT SEP **we are having the Smiths down for a few days** nous avons invité les Smith à venir passer quelques jours chez nous

▶ **have in** VT SEP [a] [+ doctor] faire venir; **we'll ~ them in and discuss it** nous allons les faire venir pour en discuter

     [b] **to ~ it in for sb*** garder or avoir une dent contre qn

     [c] **to ~ it in one** en être capable; **she has got it in her** elle en est capable

▶ **have off** VT SEP (Brit) **to ~ it off with sb‡** s'envoyer‡ qn, se taper‡ qn

▶ **have on** VT SEP [a] [+ clothes] porter; **he had nothing on** il était tout nu

     [b] (Brit = have planned) **I've got so much on this week that ...** j'ai tant à faire cette semaine que ...; **I've (got) nothing on this evening** je suis libre ce soir

     [c] (Brit = tease) [+ person] faire marcher*

     [d] * **Richard has nothing on him!** Richard ne lui arrive pas à la cheville!; **the police ~ nothing on me** la police n'a pas de preuve contre moi

▶ **have out** VT SEP [a] **to ~ a tooth out** se faire arracher une dent

     [b] **to ~ it out with sb** s'expliquer avec qn

▶ **have round** VT SEP [+ friends, neighbours] inviter

▶ **have up** VT SEP **to be had up** passer en jugement (**for sth** pour qch, **for doing sth** pour avoir fait qch)

---

have-a-go* ['hævə,gəʊ] ADJ ▶ **~ hero** intrépide qui n'hésite pas à intervenir lorsqu'il est témoin d'un délit

haven ['heɪvn] N [a] **a ~ of** [+ peace, tranquillity etc] un havre de; **a ~ for** [+ animals, refugees] un refuge pour; [+ artists, writers] un refuge de [b] (liter = harbour) port m → **safe, tax**

haven't ['hævnt] = **have not**; → **have**

haver ['heɪvər] VI (N Engl, Scot) dire des âneries

haversack ['hævəsæk] N (over shoulder) musette f; (on back) sac m à dos; (Mil) havresac m, musette f

havoc ['hævək] N (NonC) ravages mpl; (less serious) dégâts mpl; **to cause** or **create ~** faire des dégâts; **to wreak ~** causer des ravages; **violent storms wreaked ~ on the French Riviera** de violents orages ont ravagé la Côte d'Azur or ont causé des ravages sur la Côte d'Azur; **stress can wreak ~ on the immune system** le stress peut perturber sérieusement or dérégler le système immunitaire; **this wreaked ~ with their plans** cela a bouleversé tous leurs projets; **to wreak ~ on sb's life** complètement bouleverser la vie de qn; **to play ~ with** (schedule, routine, plans) bouleverser; (health, skin) être très mauvais pour; **spicy food can play ~ with your stomach** les aliments épicés peuvent vous déranger l'estomac; **his drug habit played ~ with his career** sa toxicomanie a gravement perturbé sa carrière

haw¹ [hɔː] N (Bot) cenelle f

haw² [hɔː] VI **to hem and ~** ◊ **to hum and ~** balancer

Hawaii [həˈwaɪ] N Hawaï or Hawaii; **in ~** à Hawaï or Hawaii

Hawaiian [həˈwaɪjən] [1] ADJ hawaïen; **the ~ Islands** les îles fpl Hawaï or Hawaii [2] N [a] Hawaïen(ne) m(f) [b] (Ling) hawaïen m [3] COMP ▶ **Hawaiian guitar** N guitare f hawaïenne ▶ **Hawaiian shirt** N chemise f hawaïenne ▶ **Hawaiian Standard Time** N (US) heure f de Hawaï

hawfinch ['hɔːfɪntʃ] N gros-bec m

---

hawk¹ [hɔːk] [1] N [a] (Orn) faucon m; **to have eyes like a ~** avoir un regard d'aigle or des yeux de lynx; **to watch sb like a ~** surveiller qn de près, avoir qn à l'œil* [b] (Pol fig) faucon m; **~s and doves** faucons mpl et colombes fpl [2] VI chasser au faucon [3] COMP ▶ **hawk-eyed** ADJ au regard d'aigle, aux yeux de lynx

hawk² [hɔːk] VI (also **~ up** = clear one's throat) se racler la gorge

hawk³ [hɔːk] VT (= peddle) colporter; (in street) crier (des marchandises)

hawker ['hɔːkər] N (street) colporteur m; (door-to-door) démarcheur m, -euse f

Hawkeye ['hɔːkaɪ] [1] N (US) habitant(e) m(f) de l'Iowa [2] COMP ▶ **the Hawkeye State** N l'Iowa m

hawkish ['hɔːkɪʃ] ADJ belliciste

hawser ['hɔːzər] N haussière or aussière f

hawthorn ['hɔːθɔːn] N aubépine f

hay [heɪ] [1] N foin m; (Agr) **to make ~** faner, faire les foins ■ (PROV) **to make ~ while the sun shines** ≈ battre le fer pendant qu'il est chaud; **to make ~ of*** (argument) démolir*; (enemy, team) battre à plate(s) couture(s); (US fig) **that ain't ~‡** c'est pas rien* → **hit, roll** [2] COMP ▶ **hay fever** N (Med) rhume m des foins ▶ **hay fork** N fourche f à foin

haycock ['heɪkɒk] N meulon m (de foin)

hayloft ['heɪlɒft] N grenier m à foin, fenil m

haymaker ['heɪmeɪkər] N (= worker) faneur m, -euse f; (Boxing = blow) uppercut m magistral

haymaking ['heɪmeɪkɪŋ] N fenaison f, foins mpl

hayrick ['heɪrɪk] N = **haystack**

hayride ['heɪraɪd] N (esp US) promenade dans une charrette de foin

hayseed‡ ['heɪsiːd] N (US pej) péquenaud‡ m

haystack ['heɪstæk] N meule f de foin

haywire* ['heɪwaɪər] ADJ **to go ~** [person] perdre la tête or la boule*; [plans] être perturbé; [equipment etc] se détraquer

hazard ['hæzəd] [1] N [a] (= risk) risque m; (stronger) danger m, péril m; **natural ~s** risques mpl naturels; **to be a safety ~ (to children)** constituer un danger (pour les enfants), être dangereux (pour les enfants); **to pose a ~ (to sb/sth)** présenter un risque (pour qn/qch); **these waste materials pose an environmental ~** ces déchets présentent un risque pour l'environnement → **fire, health, occupational** [b] (= chance) hasard m, chance f; **it was pure ~ that he ...** ce fut pur hasard qu'il (+ subj) ... [c] (Golf etc) obstacle m naturel, hazard m [2] VT [a] (= venture to make) [+ remark, forecast] hasarder; **to ~ a suggestion** hasarder une proposition; **to ~ an attempt** risquer une tentative; **to ~ a guess** hasarder une hypothèse; **she ~ed a guess that ...** elle a hasardé l'hypothèse que ...; **"I could do it," she ~ed** « je pourrais le faire, » se risqua-t-elle à dire [b] (= risk) [+ life, reputation] hasarder, risquer; [+ one's fortune] risquer [3] COMP ▶ **hazard (warning) lights** NPL (Aut) feux mpl de détresse

hazardous ['hæzədəs] [1] ADJ dangereux (**to** or **for sb/sth** pour qn/qch) [2] COMP ▶ **hazardous waste** N déchets mpl dangereux

haze¹ [heɪz] N brume f (légère); **a ~ of cigarette smoke filled the room** de la fumée de cigarette emplissait la pièce; **a ~ of dust** un nuage de poussière; (fig) **to be in a ~** être dans le brouillard; **in a ~ of alcohol** dans les brumes de l'alcool → **heat**

haze² [heɪz] VT (US Univ) bizuter

hazel ['heɪzl] [1] N (Bot) noisetier m, coudrier m [2] ADJ (colour) (couleur) noisette inv; **~ eyes** yeux mpl (couleur) noisette [3] COMP ▶ **hazel grouse** N gélinotte f (des bois) ▶ **hazel grove** N coudraie f

hazelnut ['heɪzlnʌt] N noisette f

hazelwood ['heɪzlwʊd] N (bois m de) noise-tier m

haziness ['heɪzɪnɪs] N **a** (= mist) brume f **b** (= lack of clarity) [of ideas, memory] flou m, manque m de précision

hazing ['heɪzɪŋ] N (US Univ) bizutage m

hazy ['heɪzɪ] ADJ **a** (= misty) [sunshine, sun] voilé; [day, sky] brumeux; [view] (with mist) brumeux; (with heat, vapour, dust) flou; **it's very ~ today** (with mist) il y a beaucoup de brume aujourd'hui; (with vapour, heat, dust) l'air est vaporeux aujourd'hui; **~ blue** bleu pastel inv **b** (= indistinct) [outline, vision, details] flou; [notion, idea, memory] vague; **to be ~ about sth** [person] n'avoir qu'une vague idée de qch

HC (ABBR = **hot and cold (water)**) → **hot**

HDD N (Comput) (ABBR = **hard disk drive**) → **hard**

HDTV N (ABBR = **high definition television**) TVHD f

HE [eɪtʃ'iː] **a** (ABBR = **His or Her Excellency**) SE **b** (ABBR = **high explosive**) → **high**

he, He (Rel) [hiː] **1** PERS PRON **a** (unstressed) il; **he has come** il est venu; **here he is** le voici; **he is a doctor** il est médecin, c'est un médecin; **he is a small man** c'est un homme petit **b** (stressed) lui; (frm) **it is he** c'est lui; (frm) **if I were he** si j'étais lui, si j'étais à sa place; (frm) **younger than he** plus jeune que lui; **HE didn't do it** ce n'est pas lui qui l'a fait **c** (+ rel pron) celui; **he who** or **that can** celui qui peut **2** N **a*** mâle m; (animal) c'est un mâle; (baby) c'est un garçon **b** (Scol) **you're he!*** (c'est toi le) chat! **3** COMP mâle ► **he-bear** N ours m mâle; **it's a he*** **► he-goat** N bouc m ► **he-man*** N (pl **he-men**) (vrai) mâle m, macho* m

head [hed]

┌─────────────────────────────┐
│ **1** NOUN   **4** COMPOUNDS │
│ **2** TRANSITIVE VERB   **5** PHRASAL VERBS │
│ **3** INTRANSITIVE VERB │
└─────────────────────────────┘

1 NOUN
a Anat tête f; **to hit sb on the ~** frapper qn à la tête; **~ down** (= upside down) la tête en bas; (= looking down) la tête baissée; **to keep one's ~ down*** (= avoid trouble) garder un profil bas; (= work hard) travailler dur; **~ hanging** la tête baissée; **~ downwards** la tête en bas; **~ first** ◊ **~ foremost** la tête la première; **my ~ aches** ◊ **I've got a bad ~*** j'ai mal à la tête or au crâne*; **I've got a bit of a ~*** j'ai un peu mal au crâne*; **~ of hair** chevelure f; **to stand on one's ~** faire le poirier; **I could do it standing on my ~** c'est simple comme bonjour; **to stand** or **turn sth on its ~** prendre le contre-pied de qch; **she is a ~ taller than her sister** ◊ **she is taller than her sister by a ~** elle dépasse sa sœur d'une tête; **to win by a (short) ~** [horse] gagner d'une (courte) tête; **to give a horse its ~** lâcher la bride à un cheval; **to give sb his ~** lâcher la bride à qn; (esp US) **to give (sb) ~**** tailler une pipe** (à qn); **to keep one's ~ above water** (lit) garder la tête au-dessus de l'eau; (fig) se maintenir à flot; (fig) **to have a big** or **swollen ~** avoir la grosse tête*; (fig) **to put** or **lay one's ~ on the block** risquer gros; (fig) **it's completely above my ~** cela me dépasse complètement; **to get in** or **be in over one's ~*** être complètement dépassé; **he gave orders over my ~** il a donné des ordres sans me consulter; **he went over my ~ to the director** il m'a court-circuité pour parler au directeur; **his ideas went right over my ~** ses idées me dépassaient complètement; (fig) **he's got his ~ in the sand** il pratique la politique de l'autruche; (Brit) **to have one's ~ up one's arse**** (= be confused) dérailler*; (US) **to have one's ~ up one's ass**** (= be heedless) marcher à côté de ses pompes*; **he was talking his ~ off*** il n'arrêtait pas de parler; **to sing/shout one's ~ off*** chanter/crier à tue-tête; **to laugh**

one's ~ off rire aux éclats or à gorge déployée; **on your own ~ be it!** à vos risques et périls!; (Naut) **~ to wind** vent debout; **~ on** = **head-on**
♦ **a head** ◊ **per head** par tête; **they paid 10 francs a ~** or **per ~** ils ont payé 10 F par tête
♦ **from head to foot** or **toe** de la tête aux pieds; **covered from ~ to foot** or **toe in mud** couvert de boue de la tête aux pieds; **he was dressed in black from ~ to foot** or **toe** il était habillé en noir de la tête aux pieds; **he was trembling from ~ to foot** il tremblait de tout son corps
♦ **head and shoulders**: **he stands ~ and shoulders above everybody else** (lit) il dépasse tout le monde d'une tête; (fig) il surpasse tout le monde; **she is ~ and shoulders above her sister in maths** elle est cent fois meilleure que sa sœur en maths
♦ **head over heels**: **to turn** or **go ~ over heels** (accidentally) faire la culbute; (on purpose) faire une galipette; **to be/fall ~ over heels in love with sb** être follement or éperdument amoureux de qn
b = **mind, intellect** tête f; **weak** or **soft*** **in the ~** un peu demeuré* or de tête; **to count in one's ~** calculer mentalement or de tête; **I can't do it in my ~** je ne peux pas faire or calculer ça de tête; **to get sth into one's ~*** s'enfoncer or se mettre qch dans la tête; **I wish he would get it into his ~*** **that** … j'aimerais qu'il se mette dans la tête que …; **I can't get that into his ~*** je ne peux pas lui mettre ça dans la tête; **he has taken it into his ~ that** … il s'est mis dans la tête que …; **to take it into one's ~ to do sth** se mettre en tête de or s'aviser de faire qch; **it didn't enter his ~ that** …/**to do it** il ne lui vint pas à l'idée or à l'esprit que …/de faire; **you never know what's going on in his ~** on ne sait jamais ce qui lui passe par la tête; **what put that (idea) into his ~?** qu'est-ce qui lui a mis cette idée-là dans la tête?; **that tune has been running through my ~ all day** j'ai eu cet air dans la tête or cet air m'a trotté dans la tête toute la journée; **she's got her ~ screwed on (right)*** elle a la tête sur les épaules; **two ~s are better than one** deux avis valent mieux qu'un; **we put our ~s together*** nous y avons réfléchi ensemble; **don't bother** or **worry your ~ about it*** ne vous en faites pas pour cela; **to keep one's ~** garder son sang-froid; **to lose one's ~** perdre la tête; **the wine/his success went to his ~** le vin/son succès lui est monté à la tête; **he has gone** or **he is off his ~*** il a perdu la boule*; **to get one's ~ together** or **straight*** reprendre le dessus; **to get one's ~ round sth*** (= understand) piger* qch; (= come to accept) accepter qch; **it does my ~ in*** ça me prend la tête*
♦ **a (good) head (for)**: **she has a good ~ for figures** elle a des dispositions pour or elle est douée pour le calcul; **she has a good ~ for heights** elle n'a jamais le vertige; **he has no ~ for heights** il a le vertige; **she has a good business ~** elle a le sens des affaires; **she has a good ~ on her shoulders** elle a de la tête
♦ **out of one's head**: **I can't get it out of my ~** je ne peux pas me sortir ça de la tête, ça me trotte dans la tête; **he couldn't get her out of his ~** il ne pouvait pas s'empêcher de penser à elle; **his name has gone out of my ~** son nom m'est sorti de la tête or de la mémoire; **it's gone right out of my ~** ça m'est tout à fait sorti de la tête; **to be out of one's ~*** (= mad) être cinglé* or dingue*; (= drunk) être bituré* or pété*; (= high on drugs) être défoncé* or pété*
c of cattle (pl inv) **20 ~ of cattle** 20 têtes fpl or pièces fpl de bétail; **20 ~ of oxen** 20 bœufs mpl
d specific part [of flower, nail, pin, hammer, mast] tête f; [of arrow] pointe f; [of spear] fer m; [of cane] pommeau m; [of bed] chevet m, tête f; [of violin] crosse f; (on beer) mousse f, faux col* m; (on tape recorder) tête f (de lecture, d'enregistrement)
e = top end [of page, staircase] haut m; [of pillar] chapiteau m; [of jetty, pier] extrémité f;

at the ~ of (lake, valley) à l'extrémité de; (table) au (haut†) bout de; (procession) en tête de; (fig = in charge of: army, organization, company) à la tête de; **at the ~ of the list/the queue** en tête de liste/de file; (Sport) **to be at the ~ of the field** or **pack** mener la course
f of vegetable [of lettuce, cabbage] pomme f; [of celery] pied m
g of abscess, pimple tête f; **it's coming to a ~** [abscess, pimple] ça mûrit; (fig, gen) ça devient critique; **it all came to a ~ when he met her yesterday** les choses sont arrivées au point critique quand il l'a rencontrée hier; **to bring things to a ~** précipiter les choses
h = leader (Comm, Pol) [of family] chef m; **~ of department** [of company] chef m de service; [of shop] chef m de rayon → **i**; **~ of state** chef m d'État; **the ~ of the government** le chef du gouvernement
i esp Brit Scol = headmaster or headmistress; (Scol) **~ of French/Maths** etc ≈ professeur m coordinateur de français/de maths etc; **~ of department** [of school, college] chef m de section
j = title titre m; (= subject heading) rubrique f; **under this ~** sous ce titre or cette rubrique
k of coin face f; **to toss ~s or tails** jouer à pile ou face; **~s or tails?** pile ou face?; **~s I win!** face je gagne!; **he called ~s** il a annoncé « face »; **I can't make ~ (n)or tail of what he's saying** je ne comprends rien à ce qu'il dit; **I can't make ~ (n)or tail of it** je n'y comprends rien, pour moi ça n'a ni queue ni tête
l Drugs → **acid**
m Comput tête f; **reading/writing ~** tête f de lecture/d'écriture

2 TRANSITIVE VERB
a + group of people être à la tête de; [+ procession, list, poll] venir or être en tête de; **Dr Grey ~s our research team** le docteur Grey est à la tête de notre équipe de chercheurs; **a coalition government ~ed by the former opposition leader** un gouvernement de coalition dirigé par l'ancien leader de l'opposition
b = direct **he got in the car and ~ed it towards town** il est monté dans la voiture et a pris la direction de or il s'est dirigé vers la ville; (Naut) **to ~ a ship for port** mettre le cap sur le port
c = put at head of [+ chapter] intituler; **to ~ a chapter/a letter** etc **with sth** mettre qch en tête d'un chapitre/d'une lettre etc
d Ftbl **to ~ the ball** faire une tête

3 INTRANSITIVE VERB
= go, move **to ~ for** or **towards** ◊ **to be ~ed for** or **towards** [person, vehicle] se diriger vers; [ship] mettre le cap sur; **he ~ed up the hill** il s'est mis à monter la colline; **he was ~ing home(wards)** il était sur le chemin du retour; **they were ~ing back to town** ils rentraient or retournaient à la ville; (fig) **he's ~ing for a disappointment** il va vers une déception; **he's ~ing for trouble** il va avoir des ennuis; **they're ~ing for victory** ils sont partis pour gagner; **they're ~ing straight for disaster** ils vont droit au désastre

4 COMPOUNDS
[buyer, assistant etc] principal ► **head-banger*** N (= heavy metal fan) enragé(e)* m(f) de heavy metal; (= mad person) cinglé(e)* m(f) ► **head boy** N (Brit Scol) élève de terminale chargé d'un certain nombre de responsabilités ► **head clerk** N (Comm) premier commis m, chef m de bureau; (Jur) principal m ► **head cold** N rhume m de cerveau ► **head gardener** N jardinier m en chef ► **head girl** N (Brit Scol) élève de terminale chargée d'un certain nombre de responsabilités ► **head-guard** N (Sport) casque m de protection ► **head height** N **at ~ height** à hauteur d'homme ► **head lad** N (Racing) premier garçon m ► **head nurse** N (US) infirmier m, -ière f en

chef ► **head office** N siège m social, agence f centrale ► **head of steam** N pression f; (fig) **to build up** or **work up a ~ of steam** (= get worked up) se mettre dans tous ses états; (= build momentum) [movement] prendre de l'ampleur; (fig) **to get** or **build up a ~ of steam for sth** obtenir un ferme soutien pour qch ► **head of water** N colonne f d'eau, hauteur f de chute ► **head-on** → head-on ► **head post office** N bureau m central des postes, poste f principale ► **head restraint** N (Aut) = headrest ► **head shop** N (US) boutique f hippie ► **head start** N (fig) **to have a ~ start** être avantagé dès le départ (over or on sb par rapport à qn) ► **head teacher** N (Brit Scol) = headmaster or headmistress ► **head to head** ADV **to compete ~ to ~ with sb** affronter directement qn; (Comm) être en concurrence directe avec qn ► **head-to-head** ADJ [contest, competition] direct ◆ N affrontement m direct (with avec) ► **head waiter** N maître m d'hôtel

5 PHRASAL VERBS

► **head off** **1** VI partir (**for** pour, **towards** vers); (fig) **he ~ed off onto the subject of ...** il est passé à la question de ...

2 VT SEP [+ enemy] forcer à se rabattre; [+ person] (lit) détourner de son chemin; (fig) détourner (**from** de); [+ questions] parer, faire dévier

► **head up** VT FUS [+ organization, team] diriger

headache ['hedeɪk] N **a** (lit) mal m de tête; **to have a ~** avoir mal à la tête; **he suffers from terrible ~s** il souffre de terribles maux de tête **b** (fig) problème m; **at least that's not my ~** au moins ce n'est pas mon problème; **it was a real ~** ça n'a pas été une mince affaire; **the decision created a major ~ for the Government** cette décision a sérieusement compliqué la tâche du gouvernement; **his teenage daughter is a real ~** sa fille est une adolescente impossible

headband ['hedbænd] N bandeau m

headboard ['hedbɔːd] N [of bed] dosseret m

headbutt ['hedbʌt] **1** N coup m de tête **2** VT donner un coup de tête à

headcase* ['hedkeɪs] N cinglé(e) m(f)

headcheese ['hedtʃiːz] N (US Culin) fromage m de tête

headcount ['hedkaʊnt] N comptage m, vérification f du nombre de personnes présentes; **let's do a ~** comptons-les, comptons combien ils sont

headdress ['heddres] N [of lace] coiffe f; [of feathers] coiffure f

headed ['hedɪd] ADJ (Brit) **~ writing paper** or **notepaper** papier m à lettres à en-tête

-headed ['hedɪd] ADJ (in compounds) **bareheaded** nu-tête inv; **curly-headed** frisé, aux cheveux frisés → **hard**

header ['hedə'] N **a*** (= dive) plongeon m; (= fall) chute f or plongeon m (la tête la première); **to take a ~** (= fall) tomber par terre la tête la première; **to take** or **do a ~ into the water** piquer une tête dans l'eau; **the dollar took a ~ in share trading today** le dollar a chuté en Bourse aujourd'hui **b** (Ftbl) tête f **c** (Constr) boutisse f **d** (Comput) en-tête m

headfirst [ˌhedˈfɜːst] ADV (lit) la tête la première; (fig) **she rushed ~ into marriage** elle s'est précipitée dans le mariage

headgear ['hedgɪə'] N (NonC) couvre-chef m

headhunt ['hedhʌnt] **1** VI (fig) recruter des cadres pour une entreprise **2** VT recruter; **she has been ~ed by several firms** plusieurs entreprises ont essayé de la recruter

headhunter ['hedhʌntə'] N (lit) chasseur m de têtes; (fig: in recruiting personnel) chasseur m de têtes, recruteur m de cadres

headhunting ['hedhʌntɪŋ] N chasse f aux or de têtes

headiness ['hedɪnɪs] N **a** (= strength) [of wine] goût m capiteux; **the ~ of her perfume was almost intoxicating** son parfum capiteux était presque enivrant **b** (= exhilaration) exaltation f; **the ~ of the unknown** l'exaltation de l'inconnu

heading ['hedɪŋ] N (= title: at top of page, chapter, article, column of figures) titre m; (= subject title) rubrique f; (printed: on letter, document) en-tête m; **chapter ~** (gen) tête f de chapitre; (= title) titre m; **under this ~** sous ce titre or cette rubrique; **this comes under the ~ of ...** cela se classe sous la rubrique de ..., cela vient au chapitre de ...; **under the ~ of "Science" may be found ...** sous la rubrique « Sciences » on peut trouver ...; **the essay was divided into several ~s** la dissertation était divisée en plusieurs chapitres → **tariff**

headlamp ['hedlæmp] N = headlight

headland ['hedlənd] N promontoire m, cap m

headless ['hedlɪs] ADJ [body, nail] sans tête; (Zool) acéphale → **chicken**

headlight ['hedlaɪt] N (Brit Aut) phare m; [of train] fanal m, feu m avant

headline ['hedlaɪn] **1** N [of newspaper] gros titre m; (Rad, TV) grand titre m; **it's in the ~s in the papers** c'est en gros titre or en manchette dans les journaux; **the ~s were full of the story** cette histoire faisait les gros titres or la une de tous les journaux; **to hit the ~s*** [story, person] faire les gros titres or la une; [scandal, crime etc] défrayer la chronique; **the story never made the ~s** cette histoire n'a jamais fait les gros titres or la une; **have you seen the ~s?** as-tu vu les (gros) titres?; (Rad, TV) **here are the news ~s** voici les titres de l'actualité or de notre journal; **here are the ~s again** et maintenant le rappel des titres; **I only heard the ~s** je n'ai entendu que les (grands) titres

2 VT [+ story] mettre en manchette; **a story ~d "Fraud in high places"** un article intitulé « Fraude en haut lieu »

3 COMP ► **headline news** N **to be** or **make ~ news** faire les gros titres ► **headline rate of inflation** N (Econ) l'indice des prix prenant notamment en compte les taux d'intérêt des emprunts logement

headliner* ['hedlaɪnə'] N (US Mus, Theat) vedette f

headlock ['hedlɒk] N **to get/have sb in a ~** cravater qn/avoir cravaté qn

headlong ['hedlɒŋ] **1** ADV (lit, fig) [run, rush, plunge] tête baissée; **she fell ~ down the stairs** elle est tombée la tête la première dans les escaliers; **avoid rushing ~ into another relationship** évitez de vous précipiter tête baissée dans une nouvelle liaison **2** ADJ (lit, fig) [fall] vertigineux; **~ dash** or **rush** ruée f; **they made a ~ dash for the door** ils se sont rués vers la porte; **the army was in ~ flight** l'armée était en pleine débandade

headman ['hedmən] N (pl -men) chef m (d'une tribu or)

headmaster ['hedmɑːstə'] N (Brit gen) directeur m; [of French lycée] proviseur m; [of college] principal m; (US Scol) directeur m d'école privée

headmistress ['hedmɪstrɪs] N (Brit gen) directrice f; [of French lycée] proviseur m; [of college] principale f; (US Scol) directrice f d'école privée

head-on ['hedˈɒn] **1** ADV **a** (physically) **to collide** or **crash ~** se heurter de plein fouet; **to collide ~ with sth** ◊ **to crash ~ into sth** heurter qch de plein fouet **b** (fig = directly) [confront, tackle, meet] de front **2** ADJ **a** (physical) [smash, collision] frontal **b** (fig = direct) [conflict, clash, confrontation] direct

headphones ['hedfəʊnz] NPL (Rad, Telec) casque m (à écouteurs)

headquarter ['hedkwɔːtə'] VT **the company is ~ed in Chicago** la société a son siège à Chicago

headquarters ['hedkwɔːtəz] **1** NPL [of bank, company, political party] siège m; (Mil) quartier m général **2** COMP ► **headquarters staff** N (Mil) état-major m

headrest ['hedrest] N appui-tête m, repose-tête m

headroom ['hedrʊm] N (Aut) hauteur f de l'habitacle; (gen) **there is not enough ~** le plafond est trop bas or n'est pas assez haut; **have you got enough ~?** vous avez assez d'espace (en hauteur)?; (on roadsign) **"5 metres ~"** « hauteur limite: 5 mètres »

headscarf ['hedskɑːf] N foulard m

headset ['hedset] N = headphones

headship ['hedʃɪp] N (= post) poste m de directeur or de directrice (gén) or de proviseur (lycée); **under the ~ of Mr Winfield** sous la direction de M. Winfield

headshrinker* ['hedʃrɪŋkə'] N psy* mf

headsman† ['hedzmən] N (pl -men) bourreau m

headsquare ['hedskwɛə'] N foulard m

headstand ['hedstænd] N **to do a ~** faire le poirier

headstone ['hedstəʊn] N **a** [of grave] pierre f tombale **b** (Archit) clef f de voûte, pierre f angulaire

headstrong ['hedstrɒŋ] ADJ (= obstinate) têtu; (= rash) impétueux

headwaters ['hedwɔːtəz] NPL sources fpl

headway ['hedweɪ] N progrès m; **to make ~** (in journey, studies etc) avancer, faire des progrès; [ship] faire route; **I didn't make much ~ with him** je n'ai pas fait beaucoup de progrès avec lui

headwind ['hedwɪnd] N vent m contraire; (Naut) vent m debout

headword ['hedwɜːd] N entrée f, adresse f

heady ['hedɪ] ADJ [scent, wine] capiteux; [days, experience, atmosphere, brew, mixture] grisant; **the ~ delights of ...** les plaisirs grisants de ...; **the ~ heights of ...** les sommets vertigineux de ...; **it's ~ stuff* (for sb)** c'est grisant (pour qn); **to be ~ with success** être grisé par le succès; **the air was ~ with spices** les épices rendaient l'air enivrant

heal [hiːl] **1** VI (also ~ **over**, ~ **up**) [wound] se cicatriser **2** VT [+ person] guérir (**of** de); [+ wound] cicatriser; (fig) [+ differences] régler; [+ troubles] apaiser; **time will ~ the pain** votre chagrin s'estompera avec le temps; (fig) **to ~ the breach** combler le fossé, effectuer une réconciliation

healer ['hiːlə'] N guérisseur m, -euse f → **faith**

healing ['hiːlɪŋ] **1** N [of person] guérison f; [of wound] cicatrisation f **2** ADJ [ointment] cicatrisant; [properties] médicinal, curatif; [powers] de guérison; [words] apaisant; **the ~ process** le processus de guérison; **to have ~ hands** avoir des talents de guérisseur

health [helθ] **1** N (Med, fig) santé f; **in good/ poor ~** en bonne/mauvaise santé; **poverty can cause poor ~** la pauvreté peut être la cause de problèmes de santé; **he suffers from poor ~** il est en mauvaise santé; **to have ~ problems** avoir des problèmes de santé; **the ~ benefits of a vegetarian diet** les effets bénéfiques pour la santé d'un régime végétarien → **2**; **to regain one's ~** recouvrer la santé, guérir; (fig) **the ~ of the economy** la santé de l'économie; **to drink (to) sb's ~** boire à la santé de qn; **your ~!** ◊ **good ~!** à votre santé!; **Department of/Secretary of State for Health and Social Security** (Brit: formerly) ◊ **Department/Secretary of Health and Human Services** (US) ministère m/ministre m de la Santé et des Affaires sociales; (Brit) **De-**

partment of Health ≈ ministère *m* de la Santé → **national**, **restore**

2 COMP ► **the Health and Safety Executive** N (*Brit*) ≈ l'inspection *f* du travail ► **Health Authority** N (*Brit*) administration *f* régionale de la santé publique ► **health benefits** NPL (*Admin*) prestations *fpl* maladie ► **health care** N services *mpl* médicaux ► **health care worker** N membre *m* du personnel soignant ► **health centre** N ≈ centre *m* médicosocial ► **health check** N visite *f* médicale; (*more thorough*) bilan *m* de santé ► **health club** N club *m* de (re)mise en forme ► **health education** N (*Scol*) hygiène *f* ► **health farm** N établissement *m* de remise en forme ► **health foods** NPL aliments *mpl* naturels *or* diététiques *or* bio* ► **health food shop, health food store** (*US*) N magasin *m or* boutique *f* de produits diététiques ► **health-giving** ADJ → **healthful** ► **health hazard** N risque *m* pour la santé ► **health insurance** N assurance *f* maladie ► **health maintenance organization** N (*US*) *organisme médical privé* ► **health officer** N inspecteur *m*, -trice *f* de la santé (publique) ► **health resort** N (= *spa town*) station *f* thermale, ville *f* d'eau; (*in mountains*) station *f* climatique ► **health risk** N = **health hazard** ► **Health Service** N (*Brit*) → [NHS] **I got my glasses on the Health Service** ≈ la Sécurité sociale m'a remboursé mes lunettes ► **health service** N (*US Univ*) infirmerie *f* ► **Health Service doctor** N (*Brit*) ≈ médecin *m* conventionné ► **health spa** N centre *m* de cure, station *f* thermale ► **health visitor** N (*Brit*) ≈ infirmière *f* visiteuse ► **health warning** N (*on cigarette packet*) mise en garde du ministère de la Santé

HEALTH MAINTENANCE ORGANIZATION

Aux États-Unis, les health maintenance organizations sont des organismes privés qui dispensent des soins médicaux (y compris hospitaliers) à leurs adhérents. Dans une volonté de maîtrise des coûts, ces organismes insistent sur la médecine préventive et obligent à consulter des médecins agréés. En ce sens, ils diffèrent des assurances médicales privées avec lesquelles on les assimile parfois.

healthful ['helθfʊl] ADJ sain

healthily ['helθɪlɪ] ADV [*live, eat, grow*] sainement; **a recipe which is ~ low in fat** une recette saine du fait de sa faible teneur en graisses; **~ cynical/irreverent** d'un cynisme/ d'une irrévérence salutaire; **to be ~ contemptuous of sth** montrer un mépris sain de qch; **to be ~ sceptical of sth** faire preuve d'un scepticisme salutaire à l'égard de qch

healthy ['helθɪ] ADJ **a** (= *in good health*) [*person, animal, plant*] en bonne santé; [*body, skin, hair, cell, sexuality*] sain; [*appetite*] solide; **he is very ~** il est en très bonne santé; **to stay ~** rester en bonne santé; **her skin/she had a ~ glow** sa peau/elle éclatait de santé; **a ~ mind in a ~ body** un esprit sain dans un corps sain **b** (*fig = thriving*) [*economy, bank, relationship*] sain; [*bank account*] bien approvisionné; **to make** *or* **earn a ~ living** gagner confortablement sa vie **c** (= *health-giving*) [*food, lifestyle, attitude*] sain; [*climate, air*] salubre; [*exercise*] bon pour la santé, salutaire; **to have a ~ diet** manger sainement; **advice on ~ living** conseils *mpl* pour vivre sainement **d** (= *wholesome, desirable*) [*profit*] substantiel; [*scepticism*] salutaire, bon; [*doubts*] légitime; **to have a ~ respect for sb/sth** apprécier qn/qch à sa juste valeur; **the economy is showing ~ growth** l'économie connaît une croissance équilibrée; **a ~ dose of caution/ scepticism** *etc* une bonne dose de prudence/

► LANGUAGE IN USE: **hear** 21.1

scepticisme *etc*; **his interest in this is not very ~** l'intérêt qu'il y porte n'est pas très sain

heap [hiːp] **1** N **a** tas *m*; **in a ~** en tas; **to collapse/fall in a ~** [*person*] s'effondrer/tomber comme une masse **b** (* *fig*) tas* *m*, masse *f*; **~s of** (*money, people, ideas*) des tas* de; **she has ~s of enthusiasm** elle déborde d'enthousiasme; **they got ~s of criticism for this decision** ils ont été très critiqués pour cette décision; **we've got ~s of time** nous avons largement le temps, nous avons tout notre temps; **~s of times** des tas* de fois, mille fois; **to have ~s of** *or* **a whole ~ of things to do** avoir un tas* *or* des masses* de choses à faire; **~s better** drôlement* mieux; **(to be in) a whole ~ of trouble** (avoir) tout un tas* d'ennuis; **to be at the top/the bottom of the ~** être en haut/en bas de l'échelle; (*fig*) **the news struck him all of a ~:** la nouvelle lui a coupé bras et jambes *or* l'a éberlué*; (*fig*) **he was struck all of a ~:** il en est resté baba* **c** (: = *car*) tas *m* de ferraille*

2 VT **a** = **heap up** **b** (*fig*) **to ~ gifts on sb** couvrir qn de cadeaux; **to ~ praise/favours on sb** combler qn d'éloges/de faveurs; **to ~ abuse/scorn on sb** accabler *or* couvrir qn d'injures/de mépris; **to ~ work on sb** accabler qn de travail; (*fig*) **to ~ coals of fire on sb's head** rendre le bien pour le mal à qn

► **heap up** VT SEP empiler; **to ~ sth up on top of sth** empiler *or* entasser qch sur qch; **she ~ed her plate up with cakes** elle a empilé des gâteaux sur son assiette, elle a chargé son assiette de gâteaux

heaped [hiːpt] ADJ **a** [*basket*] très chargé; **shelves ~ with piles of old books** des étagères *fpl* croulant sous des piles de vieux livres; **a sofa ~ with cushions** un canapé où s'entassent des coussins *or* disparaissant sous les coussins **b** (*Culin*) **a ~ spoonful** une grosse cuillerée; **a ~ teaspoonful** une cuiller à café bien pleine

heaping [hiːpɪŋ] ADJ (*US*) = **heaped b**

▼ **hear** [hɪər] (*pret, ptp* **heard**) **1** VT **a** entendre; **did you ~ what he said?** avez-vous entendu ce qu'il a dit?; **can you ~ him?** vous l'entendez (bien)?; **I can't ~ you!** je ne vous entends pas!; **I ~ you speaking** je vous entends parler; **I heard him say that ...** je l'ai entendu dire que ...; **I heard someone come in** j'ai entendu entrer quelqu'un *or* quelqu'un entrer; **a noise was heard** un bruit se fit entendre; **he was heard to say that ...** on l'a entendu dire que ...; **to make o.s. heard** se faire entendre; **I couldn't ~ myself think*** je ne m'entendais plus penser; **to ~ him (talk) you'd think he was an expert** à l'entendre, on dirait que c'est un expert; **I have heard it said that ...** ◊ **I've heard tell that ...** j'ai entendu dire que ...; **I've heard tell of ...** j'ai entendu parler de ...; (*lit, fig*) **to ~ voices** entendre des voix; (*call for applause*) **let's ~ it for ...*** un grand bravo pour ..., on applaudit bien fort ... **b** (= *learn*) [+ *piece of news, facts*] apprendre; **have you heard the news?** connaissez-vous la nouvelle?; **have you heard the rumour that they're going to leave?** avez-vous entendu la rumeur selon laquelle ils partiraient?; **we've been ~ing reports of roads blocked by snow** nous avons entendu à la radio que les routes étaient bloquées par la neige; **have you heard the story about her trip to Paris?** tu as entendu ce qui s'est passé quand elle est allée à Paris?; **have you heard the one about the Scotsman who ...** tu connais l'histoire de l'Écossais qui ...; **we've heard it all before** ce n'est pas la première fois qu'on entend cette histoire; **I've been ~ing bad things about him** on m'a dit du mal de lui; **I've never heard such rubbish!** jamais je n'ai entendu pareilles âneries!; **he had heard that they had left** on lui avait dit qu'ils étaient partis; **I ~ you've been ill** il paraît que vous avez été malade, on m'a dit que vous avez été malade; **did you ~**

whether or not she's accepted the job? savez-vous si elle a accepté (ou non) le poste?
c (= *listen to*) [+ *lecture etc*] assister à, écouter; (*Jur*) **to ~ a case** entendre une cause; **the court has been ~ing evidence that he was ...** le tribunal a entendu des témoignages selon lesquels il aurait été ...; (*Rel*) **to ~ mass** assister à *or* entendre la messe; **Lord, ~ our prayers** Seigneur, écoutez nos prières; **to ~ a child's lessons** faire répéter *or* réciter ses leçons à un enfant

2 VI **a** entendre; **he does not** *or* **cannot ~ very well** il n'entend pas très bien **b** (= *get news*) recevoir *or* avoir des nouvelles (**from** de); **I ~ from my daughter every week** je reçois *or* j'ai des nouvelles de ma fille chaque semaine; **you will ~ from me soon** vous aurez bientôt de mes nouvelles; **hoping to ~ from you** (*in informal letter*) en espérant avoir bientôt de tes nouvelles; (*in formal letter*) dans l'attente de vous lire; (*threatening*) **you'll be ~ing from me!** tu vas avoir de mes nouvelles!, tu vas entendre parler de moi!; **to ~ about** *or* **of sb/sth** (*gen*) entendre parler de qn/qch; (= *have news of*) avoir des nouvelles de qn/qch; **I ~ about** *or* **of him from his mother** j'ai de ses nouvelles par sa mère, sa mère me donne de ses nouvelles; **he wasn't heard of for a long time** on n'entendit plus parler de lui pendant longtemps; **he was never heard of again** on n'a plus jamais entendu parler de lui; **the ship was never heard of again** on n'a jamais retrouvé trace du navire; **I've never heard of him!** je ne le connais pas!, connais pas!*; **everyone has heard of him** tout le monde a entendu parler de lui; **I've never heard of such a thing!** je n'ai jamais entendu parler d'une chose pareille!; **I ~ about nothing else!** j'en ai les oreilles rebattues!; **I won't ~ of you going there** je ne veux absolument pas que tu y ailles; **no! I won't ~ of it!** non, je ne veux pas en entendre parler!; **can I help you with the washing-up? — I wouldn't ~ of it!** je peux vous aider à faire la vaisselle? — (il n'en est) pas question!

3 EXCL **~, ~!** bravo!

► **hear out** VT SEP [+ *person, story*] écouter jusqu'au bout

heard [hɜːd] VB *pt, ptp* of **hear**

hearer ['hɪərər] N auditeur *m*, -trice *f*; **~s** auditoire *m*, auditeurs *mpl*

hearing ['hɪərɪŋ] **1** N **a** (*NonC* = *sense*) ouïe *f*; **to have good ~** avoir l'ouïe fine; **his ~'s not very good** il n'entend pas très bien; **within ~ (distance)** à portée de voix; **in my ~** en ma présence, devant moi → **hard b** (= *chance to be heard*) **to give sb a fair ~** (*gen*) écouter ce que qn a à dire; **he was refused a ~** on refusa de l'entendre, on refusa d'écouter ce qu'il avait à dire; **to condemn sb without a ~** condamner qn sans l'entendre; **he got a sympathetic ~** on l'a écouté avec bienveillance **c** (= *meeting*) [*of commission, committee etc*] séance *f*; (*Jur*) **court ~** audience *f*; **to give sb a fair ~** accorder à qn un procès équitable; **they demanded a proper ~ of their complaint** ils ont exigé que leur plainte soit correctement entendue; **disciplinary ~** conseil *m* de discipline; (*Jur*) **full ~** audience *f* contradictoire **2** ADJ [*person*] qui entend (bien) **3** COMP ► **hearing aid** N appareil *m* acoustique, audiophone *m*, sonotone® *m* ► **hearing-impaired** ADJ (= *deaf*) sourd; (= *hard of hearing*) malentendant ♦ N **the ~-impaired** (= *deaf*) les sourds *mpl*; (= *hard of hearing*) les malentendants *mpl*

hearken ['hɑːkən] VI († *or liter*) prêter l'oreille (**to** à)

hearsay ['hɪəseɪ] **1** N **from** *or* **by ~** par ouï-dire; **it's only ~** ce ne sont que des rumeurs *or* des on-dit **2** COMP [*report, account*] fondé sur des ouï-dire ► **hearsay evidence** N (*Jur*) preuve *f* par commune renommée *or* par ouï-dire

hearse [hɜːs] N corbillard *m*, fourgon *m* mortuaire

▼ heart [hɑːt]

| 1 NOUN | 3 COMPOUNDS |
| 2 PLURAL NOUN | |

1 NOUN

a Anat cœur *m*; **to have a weak ~** avoir le cœur malade, être cardiaque; (*liter*) **to clasp sb to one's ~** serrer qn sur son cœur

b *fig: seat of feelings, emotions* cœur *m*; **it did my ~ good to see them** cela m'a réchauffé le cœur de les voir; **I didn't have the ~ to tell him** ◊ **I couldn't find it in my ~ to tell him** je n'ai pas eu le cœur de le lui dire; **he knew in his ~ that it was a waste of time** au fond de lui-même, il savait bien que c'était une perte de temps; **in his ~ of ~s he thought ...** dans son for intérieur *or* au fond de lui-même, il pensait ...; **his ~ isn't in it** le cœur n'y est pas; **his ~ isn't in his work** il n'a pas le cœur à l'ouvrage; **his ~ is in the right place** il a bon cœur; **this is an issue which is close to** *or* **dear to his ~** c'est un sujet qui lui tient à cœur; **that part of the country was very dear to her ~** cette région du pays était très chère à son cœur; **to be in good ~** avoir le moral; **a man after my own ~** un homme selon mon cœur; **with all my ~** de tout mon cœur; **have a ~!*** pitié!*; **to lose one's ~ to sb** tomber amoureux de qn; **to take sth to ~** prendre qch à cœur; **don't take it to ~** ne prenez pas cela trop à cœur; **it cut me to the ~** cela m'a profondément blessé; **he has set his ~ on a new car** ◊ **his ~ is set on a new car** il veut à tout prix une nouvelle voiture; **he has set his ~ on going to Paris** son vœu le plus cher est d'aller à Paris, il rêve d'aller à Paris; **my ~ was in my mouth** ◊ **I had my ~ in my mouth** mon cœur battait la chamade; **to eat/drink to one's ~'s content** manger/boire tout son soûl; **it was his ~'s desire** c'était son plus cher désir *or* ce qu'il désirait le plus au monde; **to have a ~ of gold/stone** avoir un cœur en or/de pierre; **~ and soul** corps et âme; **he put his ~ and soul into his work** il s'est donné à son travail corps et âme

♦ **from the heart** du cœur; **a cry from the ~** un cri du cœur; **a plea from the ~** un appel du fond du cœur; **to speak from the ~** parler du fond du cœur; **from the bottom of one's ~** du fond du cœur

♦ **at heart** au fond; **I'm an optimist at ~** au fond je suis optimiste; **she's still a child at ~** elle est restée très enfant; **we have your (best) interests at ~** vos intérêts nous tiennent à cœur

♦ **by heart** par cœur; **to know by ~** *or* **off by ~*** [+ *text, song, poem*] savoir par cœur; [+ *subject, plan, route*] connaître par cœur; **to learn sth by ~** *or* **off by ~*** apprendre qch par cœur

c = *courage* courage *m*; **to put new** *or* **fresh ~ into sb** redonner (du) courage à qn; **to lose/ take ~** perdre/prendre courage; **we may take ~ from the fact that ...** le fait que ... devrait nous encourager

d = *centre* [*of town*] cœur *m*, centre *m*; **in the ~ of the forest** au cœur *or* au (beau) milieu de la forêt, en pleine forêt; **in the ~ of the desert** au cœur *or* au (fin) fond du désert; **in the ~ of the country** en pleine campagne; **the ~ of the matter** le fond du problème, le vif du sujet

e = *middle part* [*of cabbage, lettuce, celery*] cœur *m*; [*of artichoke*] fond *m*, cœur *m*

2 hearts NPL Cards cœur *m*; **queen/six of ~s** dame *f*/six de cœur; *for other phrases see* **club**

3 COMPOUNDS

► **heart attack** N crise *f* cardiaque ► **heart case** N cardiaque *mf* ► **heart complaint**, **heart condition** N maladie *f* de cœur; **to have a ~ complaint** *or* **condition** être cardiaque ► **heart disease** N maladie *f* de cœur

► **heart failure** N (*gen*) insuffisance *f* cardiaque; (= *cardiac arrest*) arrêt *m* du cœur ► **heart-lung machine** N cœur-poumon *m* (artificiel) ► **heart-rate** N rythme *m* cardiaque ► **heart-rate monitor** N moniteur *m* cardiaque ► **heart-searching** N **after much ~-searching he ...** après s'être longuement interrogé, il ... ► **heart-shaped** ADJ en (forme de) cœur ► **heart surgeon** N chirurgien *m* cardiologue ► **heart surgery** N chirurgie *f* du cœur ► **heart-throb*** N (= *person*) idole *f*, coqueluche *f*; (*US*) = heartbeat ► **heart-to-heart** ADJ intime, à cœur ouvert ♦ ADV à cœur ouvert ♦ N **to have a ~-to-~ (with sb)*** parler à cœur ouvert (avec qn) ► **heart transplant** N greffe *f* du cœur ► **heart trouble** N **to have ~ trouble** souffrir du cœur, être cardiaque; **~ trouble in the over-50s** les troubles cardiaques dont on souffre après la cinquantaine

heartache ['hɑːteɪk] N chagrin *m*, peine *f*

heartbeat ['hɑːtbiːt] N **a** (= *single beat*) battement *m* de *or* du cœur, pulsation *f* **b** (= *rhythm of heart, pulse*) battements *mpl* de *or* du cœur, pouls *m*; **her ~ is very weak** son pouls est très faible

heartbreak ['hɑːtbreɪk] N immense chagrin *m* *or* douleur *f*

heartbreaker ['hɑːtbreɪkəʳ] N (*man*) bourreau *m* des cœurs; (*woman*) femme *f* fatale

heartbreaking ['hɑːtbreɪkɪŋ] ADJ [*story, sight*] qui fend le cœur; [*appeal, cry, sound*] déchirant, qui fend le cœur; **it was ~ to see him like that** c'était à fendre le cœur de le voir comme ça

heartbroken ['hɑːtbrəʊkn] ADJ **to be ~** avoir un immense chagrin; (*stronger*) avoir le cœur brisé; [*child*] avoir un gros chagrin; **she was ~ about it** elle en a eu un immense chagrin; (*stronger*) elle en a eu le cœur brisé

heartburn ['hɑːtbɜːn] N brûlures *fpl* d'estomac

-hearted ['hɑːtɪd] ADJ (*in compounds*) open-hearted sincère; warm-hearted chaleureux → **broken, hard**

hearten ['hɑːtn] VT encourager, donner du courage à

heartening ['hɑːtnɪŋ] ADJ encourageant, réconfortant; **it's very ~ to see so many young writers emerging** c'est très encourageant *or* réconfortant de voir apparaître tant de jeunes écrivains; **it's ~ that the crime figures have dropped so significantly** il est encourageant *or* réconfortant de voir que la criminalité a connu une telle baisse

▼ heartfelt ['hɑːtfelt] ADJ qui vient du fond du cœur; **to make a ~ appeal** lancer un appel du fond du cœur; **~ sympathy** condoléances *fpl* sincères

hearth [hɑːθ] **1** N foyer *m*, âtre† *m* **2** COMP ► **hearth rug** N devant *m* de foyer

heartily ['hɑːtɪlɪ] ADV **a** (= *enthusiastically*) [*laugh*] de bon cœur; [*say, welcome*] chaleureusement; [*applaud*] avec enthousiasme; [*eat*] de bon appétit; [*drink, sing*] avec entrain; [*recommend*] vivement; [*agree*] pleinement; [*congratulate, endorse*] de tout cœur **b** (= *thoroughly*) [*glad, relieved, sorry*] profondément; **to be ~ sick of*** *or* **fed up with* sb/sth** en avoir vraiment par-dessus la tête* de qn/qch; **to dislike sb ~** détester cordialement qn; **to dislike sth ~** avoir une profonde aversion pour qch

heartland ['hɑːtlænd] N (*also* ~s) [*of country, continent*] cœur *m*, centre *m*; (*fig*) **the Tory ~** le bastion traditionnel des conservateurs

heartless ['hɑːtlɪs] ADJ [*person*] sans cœur; [*treatment*] cruel

heartlessly ['hɑːtlɪslɪ] ADV [*say, deceive*] sans pitié; **~ cruel** d'une cruauté impitoyable

heartlessness ['hɑːtlɪsnɪs] N [*of person*] manque *m* de cœur

heartrending ['hɑːtrendɪŋ] ADJ [*cry, appeal*] déchirant, qui fend le cœur; [*sight*] qui fend le cœur; **it was ~ to see him** c'était à fendre le cœur de le voir

heartsick ['hɑːtsɪk] ADJ **to be ~** avoir la mort dans l'âme

heartstrings ['hɑːtstrɪŋz] NPL **to pull at** *or* **tug (at)** *or* **touch sb's ~** toucher *or* faire vibrer la corde sensible de qn, prendre qn par les sentiments

heartwarming ['hɑːtwɔːmɪŋ] ADJ réconfortant, qui réchauffe le cœur

hearty ['hɑːtɪ] **1** ADJ **a** (= *enthusiastic*) [*welcome, thanks*] chaleureux; [*applause*] enthousiaste; [*slap, pat, thump*] bon (*before n*); [*appetite*] solide; **he gave a ~ laugh** il eut un bon rire franc; **to bid sb a ~ welcome** accueillir chaleureusement qn; **he's a ~ eater** c'est un gros mangeur → **hale b** (= *substantial*) [*food, soup*] consistant; [*meal*] copieux; [*helping*] généreux **c** (*pej* = *bluff*) [*person, greeting*] trop exubérant; [*voice*] retentissant **d** (= *wholehearted*) [*endorsement, condemnation*] sans réserves; **to be in ~ agreement with sb/sth** être absolument d'accord avec qn/qch; (*in letter*) **please accept my ~** *or* **heartiest congratulations** je vous adresse mes plus vives félicitations; **to have a ~ dislike of sb** détester cordialement qn; **to have a ~ dislike of sth** avoir une profonde aversion pour qch **2** N* **a** (= *person*) gai luron† *m* **b** (*Naut*) **heave ho, my hearties!** oh! hisse! les gars!*

heat [hiːt] **1** N **a** (*NonC: gen, Phys*) chaleur *f*; **extremes of ~ and cold** extrêmes *mpl* de chaleur et de froid; **I can't stand ~** je ne supporte pas la chaleur; **how can you work in this ~?** (*indoor temperature*) comment pouvez-vous travailler dans cette fournaise?; (*in hot weather*) comment pouvez-vous travailler par cette chaleur?; (*fig*) **if you can't stand the ~ get out of the kitchen** que ceux qui trouvent la situation intenable s'en aillent; **in the ~ of the day** au (moment le) plus chaud de la journée; **in the summer ~** dans la chaleur de l'été; **we were trying to stay cool in the 35-degree ~** nous essayions de nous rafraîchir alors qu'il faisait 35 degrés; (*Culin*) **at a low ~** à feu doux; **cook over a low/medium ~** cuire à feu doux/moyen; (*Culin*) **lower the ~ and allow to simmer** réduire le feu et laisser mijoter; **in the ~ of the moment/the battle/the argument** dans le feu de l'action/du combat/de la discussion; **in the ~ of his departure they forgot ...** dans l'agitation qui a entouré son départ, ils ont oublié ...; **"certainly not!" she responded with some ~** «certainement pas!» répondit-elle avec feu; **the issue was debated with some ~** cette question a fait l'objet d'un débat houleux; **we had no ~ all day at the office** nous n'avons été sans chauffage toute la journée au bureau; **to turn on the ~** (*in house, office etc*) mettre le chauffage; (*fig*) **to put** *or* **turn the ~ on sb*** faire pression sur qn; (*fig*) **to turn up the ~ on sb*** accentuer la pression sur qn; **the ~ is on*** on est sous pression; (*fig*) **it'll take the ~ off us*** ça nous permettra de souffler *or* de respirer un peu → **red, specific, white**

b (*Sport*) (épreuve *f*) éliminatoire *f* → **dead c** (*NonC: Zool*) chaleur *f*, rut *m*; **in** *or* (*Brit*) **on ~** en chaleur, en rut **d** (*US*) **the ~*** les flics‡ *mpl*

2 VT (*Culin, Phys, Tech*) chauffer; (*Med*) [+ *blood*] échauffer; (*fig*) enflammer

3 VI [*liquid etc*] chauffer; [*room*] se réchauffer

4 COMP ► **heat constant** N (*Phys*) constante *f* calorifique ► **heat efficiency** N rendement *m* thermique *or* calorifique ► **heat exchanger** N échangeur *m* de chaleur ► **heat exhaustion** N (Med) épuisement m dû à la chaleur ► **heat haze** N brume f de chaleur ► **heat lightning** N éclair(s) m(pl) de chaleur ► **heat loss** N perte f calorifique ► **heat rash** N (Med) irritation f or inflammation f (due à la chaleur) ► **heat-resistant, heat-resisting** ADJ = heatproof ► **heat-seeking** ADJ [missile] thermoguidé, guidé par infrarouge ► **heat-sensitive** ADJ sensible à la chaleur ► **heat shield** N (Space) bouclier m thermique ► **heat treatment** N (Med) traitement m par la chaleur, thermothérapie f

►**heat up** [1] VI [liquid etc] chauffer ; [room] se réchauffer [2] VT SEP réchauffer

heated ['hi:tɪd] [1] ADJ [a] [swimming pool, greenhouse, towel rail] chauffé ; [b] (= impassioned) [debate, discussion] passionné ; [argument, exchange, words] vif ; **to become** or **get** or **grow** ~ [person, debate, argument etc] s'échauffer [2] COMP ► **heated rollers** NPL bigoudis mpl or rouleaux mpl chauffants

heatedly ['hi:tɪdlɪ] ADV [say] avec emportement ; [argue] avec feu, fougueusement ; [debate] avec feu, avec passion ; [deny] farouchement

heater ['hi:tər] N (gen: for room) appareil m de chauffage, radiateur m ; (for water) chauffe-eau m inv ; [of car] chauffage m → **electric, immersion**

heath [hi:θ] N [a] (esp Brit = moorland) lande f [b] (= plant) bruyère f

heathen ['hi:ðən] (pej) [1] ADJ (= unbelieving) païen, (= barbarous) barbare, sauvage [2] N (pl **heathens** or **heathen**) païen(ne) m(f), les païens mpl, (= savages) les barbares mpl, les sauvages mpl

heathenish ['hi:ðənɪʃ] ADJ (pej) (= unbelieving) de païen, (= barbarous) barbare

heathenism ['hi:ðənɪzəm] N (pej) paganisme m

heather ['heðər] N bruyère f

Heath Robinson* [hi:θ'rɒbɪnsən] ADJ (Brit) bricolé

heating ['hi:tɪŋ] [1] N chauffage m → **central** [2] COMP ► **heating apparatus** N (= heater) appareil m de chauffage ; (= equipment) appareils mpl de chauffage ► **heating engineer** N chauffagiste m ► **heating plant** N système m or installation f de chauffage ► **heating power** N pouvoir m calorifique ► **heating system** N système m de chauffage

heatproof ['hi:tpru:f] ADJ [material] résistant inv à la chaleur ; [dish] allant inv au four

heatpump ['hi:tpʌmp] N pompe f à chaleur, thermopompe f

heatstroke ['hi:tstrəʊk] N (NonC: Med) coup m de chaleur

heatwave ['hi:tweɪv] N vague f de chaleur

heave [hi:v] (vb: pret, ptp **heaved**) [1] N [of sea] houle f ; [of bosom] soulèvement m ; (= lift, throw, tug etc) **to give a** ~ faire un effort pour soulever (or lancer or tirer etc) ; **to give sb the ~(-ho)*** [employer] sacquer* or virer* qn ; [boyfriend, girlfriend] plaquer* qn

[2] VT (= lift) lever or soulever (avec effort) ; (= pull) tirer (avec effort) ; (= drag) traîner (avec effort) ; (= throw) lancer ; **he ~d Barney to his feet** il a soulevé Barney pour le mettre debout ; **he ~d himself up off his stool** il s'est levé de son tabouret avec effort ; **to ~ a sigh of relief** pousser un gros soupir de soulagement

[3] VI [a] [sea, chest] se soulever ; [person] (= pant) haleter ; (= retch) avoir des haut-le-cœur or des nausées ; **his stomach was heaving** son estomac se soulevait [b] (Naut) (pret, ptp **hove**) **to** ~ **into sight** or **view** apparaître

[4] COMP ► **heave-ho** EXCL (Naut) oh ! hisse !
►**heave to** (pret, ptp **hove**) (Naut) [1] VI se met-

tre en panne [2] VT SEP mettre en panne
►**heave up** VT SEP (= vomit) vomir

heaven ['hevn] [1] N [a] (= paradise) ciel m, paradis m ; **to go to** ~ aller au ciel, aller au paradis ; **in** ~ au ciel, au or en paradis ; **our Father which art in** ~ notre Père qui êtes aux cieux ; **he was in** ~ il était au septième ciel or aux anges ; **I thought I'd died and gone to ~!*** j'étais au septième ciel or aux anges ; **it was** ~* c'était divin or merveilleux ; **he found a ~ on earth** il a trouvé son paradis sur terre ; **the shop was a chocolate-lover's ~!** ce magasin un paradis pour les amateurs de chocolat ! ; **an injustice that cries out to** ~ une injustice criante or flagrante ; ~ **help you*** (if your mother ever finds out about this) (si ta mère apprend ça) je te souhaite bien de la chance ; **what in** ~**'s name does that mean?*** mais qu'est-ce que ça veut bien dire ? ; ~ **(only) knows what/when** etc Dieu sait or quand etc ; **when will you come back?** — ~ **(only) knows!** quand reviendras-tu ? — Dieu seul le sait ! ; ~ **knows I've tried** Dieu sait or m'est témoin que j'ai essayé ; **(good)** ~**s!*** mon Dieu !, Seigneur !, ciel ! (hum) **for ~'s sake*** pour l'amour de Dieu* or du ciel* ; **I wish to ~* he were still here!** si seulement il était encore là ! ; **I wish to ~* I'd never met you!** si seulement je ne t'avais jamais rencontré ! → **forbid, move, stink, thank**

[b] (gen liter) **the ~s** (= sky) le ciel, le firmament (liter) ; **the ~s opened** le ciel se mit à déverser des trombes d'eau

[2] COMP ► **heaven-sent** ADJ providentiel

heavenly ['hevnlɪ] [1] ADJ (lit) céleste, du ciel ; (fig = delightful) divin, merveilleux [2] COMP ► **heavenly body** N corps m céleste ► **Heavenly Father** N (Rel) Père m céleste

heavenward(s) ['hevnwəd(z)] ADV [go] vers le ciel ; **to look** ~ lever les yeux au ciel

heavily ['hevɪlɪ] ADV [a] (= much) [rely on, influence, censor, subsidize] fortement ; [rain] à verse, très fort ; [snow] à gros flocons, très fort ; [bleed, sweat] abondamment ; [smoke, drink] beaucoup ; [gamble] gros ; [criticize] vivement ; [tax] lourdement ; [fortified] solidement ; [populated] densément ; [wooded] très ; **he spoke in** ~ **accented English** il parlait anglais avec un fort accent ; ~ **armed** fortement armé ; ~ **bandaged** entouré d'un épais pansement ; **to be** ~ **booked in advance** être en grande partie réservé à l'avance ; **his face was** ~ **bruised** il avait la figure toute meurtrie ; **in debt** fortement endetté ; **to be** ~ **defeated** subir une défaite écrasante ; **to be** ~ **disguised** avoir un déguisement très élaboré ; ~ **edited** plein de corrections ; ~ **fined** condamné à une lourde amende ; ~ **guarded** fortement gardé ; ~ **involved in** or **with** (politics, interest group) fortement engagé dans ; (drugs, illegal business) fortement impliqué dans ; ~ **laden** lourdement chargé ; **his** ~ **lined face** son visage tout parcheminé or ridé ; ~ **made-up eyes** yeux mpl très maquillés or fardés ; ~ **outnumbered** très inférieur en nombre ; ~ **pregnant** près d'accoucher, dans un état de grossesse avancée ; **a** ~ **pregnant mare** une jument près de mettre bas ; ~ **scented flowers** des fleurs au parfum lourd or capiteux ; ~ **sedated** sous l'influence de fortes doses de calmants ; ~ **spiced** fortement épicé ; ~ **underlined** souligné d'un gros trait ; ~ **weighted in sb's favour/ against sb** fortement favorable/défavorable à qn ; **the rain/snow was falling** ~ il pleuvait/ neigeait très fort ; **to borrow** ~ emprunter de fortes sommes ; **to invest** ~ beaucoup investir ; **to lose** ~ (Gambling) perdre gros ; (Sport, Pol) subir une défaite écrasante

[b] **to be** ~ **into*** [+ sports, music, computers etc] être un(e) mordu(e) de* ; **he's** ~ **into drugs/ heroin/health foods** son truc*, c'est la drogue/l'héroïne/l'alimentation bio

[c] (= deeply) [breathe, pant] bruyamment ; [sleep, sigh] profondément

[d] (= clumsily) [sit down, fall, land, lean, move] lourdement ; [walk] d'un pas lourd

[e] (= solidly) ~ **built** costaud, solidement bâti ; **her attacker is described as aged 30-40 and** ~ **built** son agresseur aurait entre 30 et 40 ans et serait de forte carrure

[f] (= slowly) [say] d'une voix accablée

[g] (= richly) [encrusted, embroidered, gilded] richement

heaviness ['hevɪnɪs] N [of person, animal, load] poids m ; **the** ~ **of his movements** la lourdeur dans ses mouvements ; **a sensation of** ~ **in the limbs** une sensation de lourdeur dans les membres ; **the** ~ **of the blood loss** l'importance f de l'hémorragie ; **hormones to reduce the** ~ **of your period** des hormones qui rendraient vos règles moins abondantes ; (fig) ~ **of heart** tristesse f

heavy ['hevɪ] [1] ADJ [a] (gen) lourd ; ~ **luggage** gros bagages mpl ; **to make heavier** alourdir ; **how** ~ **are you?** combien pesez-vous ? ; **heavier than air** plus lourd que l'air ; ~ **with young** [animal] gravide ; (liter) **to be** ~ **with child**† être grosse†

[b] (fig) [expenses, movement] lourd ; [payments, charges] important ; [step] pesant, lourd ; [crop] abondant ; [loss, fine] gros (grosse f) (before n), lourd (before n) ; [rain, shower] fort (before n), gros (grosse f) (before n) ; [fog] épais (-aisse f) ; [meal, food] lourd, indigeste ; [defeat] grave ; [book, film, lecture] (= not superficial) profond, (= difficult, tedious) indigeste ; [humour, irony] lourd ; (Theat) [part] (= demanding) lourd, difficile, (= tragic) tragique ; [population] dense ; [sigh] gros (grosse f) (before n), profond ; [silence, sleep] lourd, profond ; [sky] couvert, lourd ; [soil] lourd, gras (grasse f) ; [task] lourd, pénible ; [work] gros (grosse f) (before n) ; **to be a** ~ **drinker/smoker** boire/ fumer beaucoup, être un grand buveur/ fumeur ; **to be a** ~ **sleeper** avoir le sommeil profond or lourd ; **the** ~ **smell of incense** la forte odeur de l'encens ; **his voice was** ~ **with sarcasm** son ton était très sarcastique ; **the air was** ~ **with smoke from the factory** l'air était chargé de fumée provenant de l'usine ; **eyes** ~ **with sleep** yeux mpl lourds de sommeil ; ~ **eyes** yeux mpl battus or cernés ; **my car is** ~ **on petrol** ma voiture consomme beaucoup (d'essence) ; **salads** ~ **on carrots** des salades avec beaucoup de carottes ; **barley bread is** ~ **on the stomach** le pain d'orge pèse sur l'estomac ; **I've had a** ~ **day** j'ai eu une journée chargée ; (Mil) ~ **artillery** artillerie f lourde, grosse artillerie f ; ~ **(gun)fire** feu m nourri ; ~ **shelling** bombardements mpl intensifs ; ~ **blow** (lit) coup m violent, (fig) rude coup m ; **a man of** ~ **build** un homme solidement bâti or de forte constitution ; **there were** ~ **casualties** il y a eu de nombreuses victimes ; **a** ~ **concentration of ...** une forte concentration de ... ; (Med) ~ **cold** gros rhume m ; ~ **periods** règles fpl abondantes ; (Naut) ~ **cruiser** croiseur m lourd ; ~ **dew** forte rosée f ; ~ **features** gros traits mpl, traits mpl épais or lourds ; ~ **fighting** combats mpl acharnés ; **the going was** ~ **because of the rain** le terrain était lourd à cause de la pluie ; **the conversation was** ~ **going** la conversation languissait ; **this book is very** ~ **going** ce livre est très indigeste ; **with a** ~ **heart** le cœur gros ; (fig) **to play the** ~ **husband** jouer les maris autoritaires ; **the plane made a** ~ **landing** l'avion a fait un atterrissage brutal ; ~ **line** gros trait m, trait m épais ; ~ **sea** grosse mer f ; **a** ~ **sea was running** la mer était grosse ; (fig) **it's** ~ **stuff*** (= not superficial) c'est du solide* ; (= difficult, tedious) c'est indigeste ; **the traffic was** ~ la circulation était dense ; **I was caught up in** ~ **traffic** j'ai été pris dans un ralentissement ; (Typ) ~ **type** caractères mpl gras ; (TV) ~ **viewer** téléspectateur m, -trice f assidu(e) ; (Naut) ~ **weather** gros temps m ; (fig) **he made** ~ **weather of it** il s'est compliqué la tâche or l'existence* ; **he made** ~

weather of cleaning the car il s'est compliqué la vie pour laver la voiture; **~ wine** vin *m* corsé *or* lourd; **he did all the ~ work** c'est lui qui a fait le gros travail; *(Ind)* **~ workers** travailleurs *mpl* de force

2 ADV lourd, lourdement; **to weigh** *or* **lie ~ on** peser lourd sur; *(US fig)* **he's ~ into* health foods** il est à fond dans l'alimentation bio*, son truc, c'est l'alimentation bio* → **lie¹**

3 N **a** *(Boxing)* poids *m* lourd **b** (* = *bouncer etc*) costaud* *m* **c** *(Brit* = newspaper)* grand journal *m*

4 COMP ► **heavy bodies** NPL *(Phys)* corps *mpl* graves ► **heavy breather** N *(on phone)* personne qui fait des appels téléphoniques anonymes obscènes ► **heavy cream** N *(US)* crème *f* fraîche épaisse *or* à fouetter ► **heavy crude (oil)** N brut *m* lourd ► **heavy-duty** ADJ [*carpet*] résistant; [*equipment*] à usage industriel ► **heavy goods vehicle** N poids *m* lourd ► **heavy-handed** ADJ *(lit, fig)* **to be ~-handed** être maladroit ► **heavy-hearted** ADJ **to be ~-hearted** avoir le cœur gros ► **heavy industry** N industrie *f* lourde ► **heavy-laden** ADJ lourdement chargé ► **heavy metal** N *(Chem)* métal *m* lourd; *(Mus)* heavy metal *m* ► **heavy-set** ADJ costaud ► **heavy water** N eau *f* lourde

heavyweight ['hevɪweɪt] **1** N *(Boxing)* poids *m* lourd; (* *fig* = *influential person*) (grosse) pointure *f* **2** ADJ **a** *(Boxing)* [*bout, champion, class*] poids lourds *inv*; **a ~ boxer** un poids lourd **b** (= *serious*) [*issue, subject, newspaper, interviewer, political commentator*] sérieux **c** (= *thick*) [*cloth, plastic*] épais (-aisse *f*); [*wallpaper*] fort

Hebe⸸ ['hiːbɪ] N *(US pej)* youpin(e)⸸ *m(f)*

Hebraic [hɪ'breɪk] ADJ hébraïque

Hebrew ['hiːbruː] **1** ADJ hébreu *m* only, hébraïque **2** N **a** *(Hist)* Hébreu *m*, Israélite *mf*; *(Bible)* **~s** Hébreux *mpl* **b** *(Ling)* hébreu *m*

Hebrides ['hebrɪdiːz] N **the ~** les Hébrides *fpl*

heck* [hek] **1** EXCL zut!*, flûte!* **2** N **a ~ of a lot** une sacrée quantité*; **I'm in one ~ of a mess** je suis dans un sacré pétrin*; **what the ~ is he doing?** que diable* peut-il bien faire?; **what the ~ did he say?** qu'est-ce qu'il a bien pu dire?; **what the ~!** et puis flûte* *or* zut*!

heckle ['hekl] VTI chahuter

heckler ['heklər] N *(Pol etc)* (élément *m*) perturbateur *m*

heckling ['heklɪŋ] N chahut *m*

hectare ['hektaːr] N hectare *m*

hectic ['hektɪk] **1** ADJ **a** [*life, lifestyle*] (= *busy*) trépidant; (= *eventful*) mouvementé; [*journey, day*] mouvementé; [*schedule*] très chargé; [*activity*] fiévreux; [*pace*] trépidant; [*traffic*] intense; **we've had three ~ days** on n'a pas arrêté pendant trois jours **b** *(Med)* [*person, colour*] fiévreux **2** COMP ► **hectic fever** N fièvre *f* hectique

hectogramme, hectogram *(US)* ['hektəʊgræm] N hectogramme *m*

hectolitre, hectoliter *(US)* ['hektəʊˌliːtər] N hectolitre *m*

Hector ['hektər] N Hector *m*

hector ['hektər] **1** VT harceler **2** VI **stop ~ing!** arrête de harceler les gens!

hectoring ['hektərɪŋ] ADJ **in a ~ voice** d'un ton autoritaire *or* impérieux

Hecuba ['hekjʊbə] N Hécube *f*

he'd [hiːd] = **he had, he would**; → **have, would**

hedge [hedʒ] **1** N **a** haie *f*; **beech ~** haie *f* de hêtres

b *(fig)* **a ~ against inflation** une protection contre l'inflation

2 VI **a** (= *not be direct*) *(in answering)* se dérober; *(in explaining, recounting etc)* expliquer *or* raconter *etc* avec des détours; **don't ~** dis-le franchement *or* directement; **to ~ on a question/promise** éviter de répondre à une

question/de s'engager

b (= *protect o.s.*) **to ~ against sth** se prémunir contre qch

3 VT **a** (*also* **~ about, ~ in**) entourer d'une haie, enclore; *(fig)* **~d (about** *or* **in) with difficulties** plein de difficultés; **the offer was ~d around with conditions** l'offre était assortie d'une série de conditions

b [+ *bet, risk*] couvrir; *(fig)* **to ~ one's bets** se couvrir *(fig)*; **"I can't give you an answer now", he ~d** « je ne peux pas vous répondre maintenant », dit-il en se dérobant

c **to ~ the issue** esquiver la question

4 COMP ► **hedge clippers** NPL cisailles *fpl* à haie ► **hedge trimmer** N taille-haie *m*

►**hedge off** VT SEP [+ *garden*] entourer d'une haie; [+ *part of garden*] séparer par une haie (**from** de)

hedgehog ['hedʒˌhɒg] N hérisson *m*

hedgehop ['hedʒhɒp] VI *(Aviat)* faire du rase-mottes

hedger ['hedʒər] N *(St Ex, Fin)* arbitragiste *m* (en couverture de risques)

hedgerow ['hedʒrəʊ] N haie *f*

hedgesparrow ['hedʒspærəʊ] N fauvette *f* des haies *or* d'hiver

hedonism ['hiːdənɪzəm] N hédonisme *m*

hedonist ['hiːdənɪst] ADJ, N hédoniste *mf*

hedonistic [ˌhiːdəʊ'nɪstɪk] ADJ hédoniste

heebie-jeebies⸸ ['hiːbɪ'dʒiːbɪz] NPL **to give sb the ~** *(revulsion)* donner la chair de poule à qn; *(fright, apprehension)* flanquer la frousse* *or* la trouille* à qn

heed [hiːd] **1** VT tenir compte de **2** N **to take ~ of sth** ◊ **to pay** *or* **give ~ to sth** tenir compte de qch; **take no ~ of what they say** ne faites pas attention à ce qu'ils disent; **to pay no ~ to sb** ne pas écouter qn; **pay no ~ to these rumours** ne faites pas attention à ces rumeurs, ne tenez pas compte de ces rumeurs; **he paid no ~ to the warning** il n'a tenu aucun compte de cet avertissement; **to take ~ to do** prendre soin de faire

heedless ['hiːdlɪs] ADJ (= *not thinking*) étourdi; (= *not caring*) insouciant; **~ of what was going on** inattentif à ce qui se passait; **~ of danger, she ...** sans se soucier du danger, elle ...; **~ of complaints** sans tenir compte des réclamations

heedlessly ['hiːdlɪslɪ] ADV sans faire attention

heehaw ['hiːhɔː] **1** N hi-han *m* **2** VI faire hi-han, braire

heel¹ [hiːl] **1** N **a** [*of foot, sock, shoe, tool, golf club, bow etc*] talon *m*; [*of hand*] hypothénar *m* *(Anat)*; **high ~s** talons *mpl* hauts; **shoes with high ~s** chaussures *fpl* à talons hauts; **at sb's ~s** sur les talons de qn; **to be (hot) on sb's ~s** marcher sur les talons de qn; **they followed close** *or* **hard on his ~s** ils étaient sur ses talons; **this meeting follows hot on the ~s of last month's talks** cette réunion arrive juste après les négociations du mois dernier; *(fig)* **to be snapping at sb's ~s*** essayer de prendre la place de qn; **to take to one's ~s** prendre ses jambes à son cou; **to show a clean pair of ~s** prendre ses jambes à son cou; **he turned on his ~ and left** il a tourné les talons et est parti; *(fig)* **under the ~ of** sous le joug *or* la botte de; *(to dog)* **~!** au pied!; **he brought the dog to ~** il a fait venir le chien à ses pieds; *(fig)* **to bring sb to ~** rappeler qn à l'ordre, faire rentrer qn dans le rang → **click, cool down, kick**

b (†* = *unpleasant man*) salaud⸸ *m*

2 VT **a** [+ *shoes*] remettre *or* refaire un talon à

b *(Rugby)* [+ *ball*] talonner → **back**

3 COMP ► **heel-bar** N talon-minute *m* ► **heel-piece** N [*of sock etc*] talon *m* (renforcé)

heel² [hiːl] VI (*also* **~ over**) [*ship*] gîter, donner

de la bande; [*truck, structure*] s'incliner *or* pencher (dangereusement)

heeled [hiːld] ADJ **a** → **well** **b** *(US* = armed)* armé

heeling ['hiːlɪŋ] N *(Rugby)* talonnage *m*

heft* [heft] VT (= *lift*) soulever; (= *feel weight of*) soupeser

hefty* ['heftɪ] ADJ **a** (= *big*) [*person*] costaud*, maous* (-ousse* *f*); [*object, fine, increase, meal*] de taille*; [*profit*] gros (grosse *f*); [*bill*] salé*; [*fees*] très élevé; **a ~ sum** une jolie somme, une coquette somme **b** (= *powerful*) [*kick, slap, punch*] formidable

Hegelian [hɪ'geɪlɪən] ADJ hégélien

hegemony [hɪ'gemənɪ] N hégémonie *f*

Hegira ['hedʒɪrə] N hégire *f*

heifer ['hefər] N génisse *f*

heigh [heɪ] EXCL hé!, eh!; **~-ho!** eh bien!

height [haɪt] **1** N **a** [*of object, building*] hauteur *f*; [*of person*] taille *f*; [*of mountain*] altitude *f*; [*of star, sun*] élévation *f*; **what ~ are you?** combien mesurez-vous?; **he is 5 foot 9 inches in ~** ◊ **his ~ is 5 foot 9 inches** il fait 1 mètre 75; **of average ~** de taille moyenne; **her weight is about normal for her ~** son poids est à peu près normal par rapport à sa taille; **he drew himself up to his full ~** il s'est dressé de toute sa hauteur; **a building 40 metres in ~** un bâtiment qui a *or* un bâtiment de 40 mètres de haut; **at shoulder ~** à hauteur des épaules; **~ above sea level** altitude *f* au-dessus du niveau de la mer

b (= *high place*) éminence *f*, hauteur *f*; **the ~s** les sommets *mpl*; *(gen)* **fear of ~s** vertige *m*; **to be afraid of ~s** avoir le vertige; *(fig)* **his performance never reached the ~s** il n'a jamais brillé → **giddy, head**

c (= *altitude*) [*of plane*] altitude *f*; **to gain/lose ~** gagner *or* prendre/perdre de l'altitude

d *(fig = best point)* [*of fortune*] apogée *m*; [*of success*] point *m* culminant; [*of glory*] sommet *m*; [*of grandeur*] sommet *m*, faîte *m*; [*of absurdity, folly*] comble *m*; **at the ~ of his power** au summum de sa puissance; **at the ~ of his career** à l'apogée *or* au sommet de sa carrière; **at the ~ of his fame** au sommet de sa gloire; **he is at the ~ of his powers** il est en pleine possession de ses moyens; **at the ~ of summer/the storm/the battle** au cœur de l'été/l'orage/la bataille; **at the ~ of the season** au plus fort de la saison; **the season is at its ~** la saison bat son plein; **the ~ of fashion** la toute dernière mode, le dernier cri; **the ~ of luxury** le comble du luxe; **the ~ of bad manners/arrogance/bad taste** le comble de l'impolitesse/de l'arrogance/du mauvais goût; **during the war emigration was at its ~** pendant la guerre l'émigration a atteint son niveau le plus haut; **at its ~ the company employed 12,000 people** à son apogée la société employait 12 000 personnes; **the crisis was at its ~** la crise avait atteint son paroxysme

2 COMP ► **height gauge** N *(Aviat etc)* altimètre *m*

heighten ['haɪtn] **1** VT (= *raise*) relever, rehausser; *(Med)* [+ *fever*] faire monter, aggraver; [+ *effect, absurdity, interest, tension, fear*] augmenter, intensifier; [+ *flavour*] relever; **~ed emotions** des sentiments *mpl* plus vifs; **~ed sensations** des sensations *fpl* plus vives; **she looked at him with ~ed interest** elle l'a regardé avec un intérêt accru; **this gave her a ~ed awareness of ...** cela lui a permis de mieux se rendre compte de ...; **with ~ed colour** [*person*] le teint animé **2** VI [*tension*] augmenter, monter; [*fear*] s'intensifier, devenir plus vif

heinous ['heɪnəs] ADJ odieux, atroce

heir [ɛər] **1** N héritier *m*, légataire *mf* (**to** de); **he is ~ to a fortune** il héritera d'une fortune; **~ to the throne** héritier *m* du trône *or* de la couronne; **rightful ~** héritier *m* légitime *or* na-

turel; **to fall ~ to sth** hériter de qch **2** COMP
► **heir apparent** N (pl **heirs apparent**) héritier m présomptif ► **heir-at-law** N (pl **heirs-at-law**) (Jur) héritier m légitime or naturel ► **heir presumptive** N (pl **heirs presumptive**) héritier m présomptif (sauf naissance d'un héritier en ligne directe)

heiress ['ɛəres] N héritière f

heirloom ['ɛəlu:m] N héritage m; **this silver is a family ~** c'est de l'argenterie de famille

heist* [haɪst] (esp US) **1** N (= robbery) hold-up m inv; (= burglary) casse* m **2** VT voler

held [held] VB pt, ptp of **hold**

Helen ['helɪn] N Hélène f; **~ of Troy** Hélène f de Troie

helical ['helɪkəl] ADJ hélicoïdal; **~ spring** ressort m hélicoïdal

helices ['helɪ,si:z] NPL of **helix**

helicopter ['helɪkɒptə'] **1** N hélicoptère m; **transfer** or **transport by ~** héliportage m; **transferred** or **transported by ~** héliporté **2** VT (esp US) [+ person, goods] transporter en hélicoptère; **to ~ in/out** etc amener/évacuer etc par hélicoptère **3** COMP [patrol, rescue] en hélicoptère; [pilot] d'hélicoptère ► **helicopter gunship** N hélicoptère m de combat ► **helicopter station** N héligare f

heliograph ['hi:lɪəɡrɑ:f] N héliographe m

heliostat ['hi:lɪəʊstæt] N héliostat m

heliotrope ['hi:lɪətrəʊp] **1** N **a** (Bot) héliotrope m **b** (= colour) ≈ violet m **2** ADJ ≈ violet

helipad ['helɪ,pæd] N hélistation f

heliport ['helɪpɔ:t] N héliport m

helium ['hi:lɪəm] N hélium m

helix ['hi:lɪks] N (pl **helixes** or **helices** ['helɪ,si:z]) (Anat) hélix m

he'll [hi:l] = **he will**; → **will**

hell [hel] **1** N **a** (Rel) enfer m; (Myth) les enfers mpl; **in ~** (gen, Rel) en enfer; (Myth) aux enfers; **the ~ of the labour camps** l'enfer des camps de travail; **to make sb's life ~** rendre la vie de qn infernale; **when ~ freezes over** quand les poules auront des dents, à la Saint-Glinglin; **all ~ broke** or **was let loose** ça a été une pagaille* monstre; **when he heard about it all ~ broke** or **was let loose** quand il l'a appris il a fait une scène épouvantable; **life became ~** la vie est devenue infernale; **it's ~ on earth** c'est l'enfer; **a living ~** un véritable enfer; **we've been to ~ and back*** ça a été l'enfer or l'horreur (mais on s'en est sortis); **we're going to ~ in a handbasket** or **handcart*** la situation est catastrophique* pour nous ■ (PROV) **~ hath no fury like a woman scorned** rien n'est plus à craindre qu'une femme blessée; **come ~ or high water** en dépit de tout, contre vents et marées; **the boyfriend from ~*** le pire des petits amis; **the holiday from ~*** des vacances de cauchemar; **to ride ~ for leather** aller à un train d'enfer; **he went off home ~ for leather** il est rentré chez lui au triple galop → **raise, road**

b (‡: emphatic phrases) **to make a ~ of a noise** faire un boucan or un raffut du diable*; **a ~ of a lot of cars** tout un tas de bagnoles*; **a ~ of a lot of people** des masses* de gens; **he's a ~ of a nice guy** c'est un type vachement bien*; **we had a ~ of a time** (= bad) ça n'a pas été marrant‡, on en a bavé‡; (= good) on s'est vachement marrés‡, ça a été terrible‡ or du tonnerre‡; **they had one ~ of a fight** ils se sont étripés; **there'll be ~ to pay** ◊ **there'll be a ~ of a row** ça va barder*; **he did it for the ~ of it** (gen) il l'a fait parce que ça lui chantait; (= to annoy people) il l'a fait pour embêter le monde; **to play (merry) ~ with** [+ plans, routine, schedule] bouleverser; [+ health, skin] être très mauvais pour; **they beat the ~ out of me** ils m'ont roué de coups; **to work like ~** travailler comme un forçat; **to run like ~** courir comme

un dératé* or un fou; **it hurts like ~** ça fait vachement* mal; **I missed her like ~** elle me manquait vachement*; **I was angry as ~** j'étais vraiment en boule*; **it's (as) hot/cold as ~** on crève* de chaud/froid; **they sure as ~ haven't been trained properly** une chose est sûre, ils n'ont pas été correctement formés; **I hope to ~ you're right** j'espère sacrément* que tu as raison; **to give sb ~** (= make their life a misery) faire mener une vie infernale à qn; (= scold) faire sa fête à qn (iro), passer une engueulade* à qn; **my back's giving me ~** mon dos me fait horriblement mal*; **the children give her ~** les enfants lui en font voir de toutes les couleurs; **to go through ~** vivre un enfer or l'enfer; **I put Brian through ~** j'en ai fait voir de toutes les couleurs à Brian; **oh ~!** flûte!*, merde!‡; (Brit) **~'s bells** or **teeth!**† sacrebleu!*; **to ~ with him!** qu'il aille se faire voir!*; **to ~ with it!** la barbe!*; **get the ~ out of here!** fous le camp!‡; **let's get the ~ out of here** barrons-nous*; **he got the ~ out** il a foutu le camp‡; **to scare the ~ out of sb** faire une peur bleue à qn*, ficher la frousse à qn*; **what the ~!** (in surprise) merde alors!‡; (dismissive) qu'est-ce que ça peut bien faire!; **what the ~ does he want now?** qu'est-ce qu'il peut bien vouloir maintenant?; **what the ~ is he doing?** qu'est-ce qu'il peut bien fabriquer* or foutre‡?; **what the ~ did he say?** qu'est-ce qu'il a bien pu raconter?; **what the ~'s going on?** mais enfin qu'est-ce qui se passe?, mais bon sang* qu'est-ce qui se passe?; **where the ~ have I put it?** où est-ce que j'ai bien pu le foutre?‡; **where the ~ have you been?** d'où tu sors, toi?*; **how the ~ did you get in?** comment diable tu as fait pour entrer?; **why the ~ did you do it?** qu'est-ce qui t'a pris de faire ça?; **go to ~!** va te faire voir* or foutre‡!; **will you do it? — like ~ (I will)** or **the ~ I will!** tu le feras? — tu parles* or tu rigoles‡ or pas si con**‡**!

2 COMP ► **hell-raiser‡** N **to be a ~-raiser** mener une vie de patachon* or de bâton de chaise* ► **hell-raising‡** N vie f de patachon* or de bâton de chaise* ► **hell's angel** N (= person) Hell's Angel m

hellacious‡ [he'leɪʃəs] ADJ (US) **a** (= terrible) [fighting] infernal; [car crash] effroyable **b** (= wild) [party] dingue* **c** (= excellent) [vacation] d'enfer*

hellbent [,hel'bent] ADJ **to be ~ on doing sth** or (US) **to do sth** vouloir à tout prix faire qch

hellcat ['helkæt] N harpie f, mégère f

hellebore ['helɪbɔ:'] N (h)ellébore m

Hellene ['heli:n] N Hellène mf

Hellenic [he'li:nɪk] ADJ hellénique

Hellenistic [,helɪ'nɪstɪk] ADJ hellénistique

heller‡ ['helə'] N (US) vrai démon* m

hellfire ['helfaɪə'] N flammes fpl de l'enfer

hellhole* ['helhəʊl] N bouge m

hellion* ['heljən] N (US) chahuteur m, trublion m

hellish ['helɪʃ] **1** ADJ (lit) [vision] cauchemardesque; [intentions, actions] diabolique; (* fig = very unpleasant) [time, place, job] infernal; [problems] épouvantable **2** ADV†* [expensive, difficult] sacrément

hellishly* ['helɪʃlɪ] ADV horriblement

▼**hello** [hə'ləʊ] EXCL (in greeting) bonjour!; (Telec) allo!; (to attract attention) hé!, ohé!; (in surprise) tiens!

helluva‡ ['heləvə] = **hell of a**; → **hell**

helm [helm] **1** N (Naut) barre f; **to be at the ~** (Naut) être à or tenir la barre; (fig) être à or tenir la barre or les rênes; (fig) **to take (over) the ~** prendre la barre **2** VT tenir la barre de **3** VI être à or tenir la barre, barrer

helmet ['helmɪt] N casque m → **crash¹**

helmeted ['helmɪtɪd] ADJ casqué m

helminth ['helmɪnθ] N helminthe m

helmsman ['helmzmən] N (pl **-men**) (Naut) timonier m, homme m de barre

▼**help** [help] **1** N **a** (gen) aide f; (in emergency) secours m; **~!** (in danger etc) au secours!, à l'aide!; (in dismay) mince!; **thank you for your ~** merci de votre aide; **with his brother's ~** avec l'aide de son frère; **~ was at hand in the form of my sister** ma sœur est venue à mon secours; **with the ~ of a knife/a computer** à l'aide d'un couteau/d'un ordinateur; **he did it without ~** il l'a fait tout seul; **to shout for ~** appeler or crier au secours, appeler à l'aide; **to ask sb for ~** demander de l'aide à qn; **ask the pharmacist for ~** demandez conseil au pharmacien; **to go to sb's ~** aller au secours de qn, prêter secours or assistance à qn; **to come to sb's ~** venir à l'aide de qn or en aide à qn; **to be of ~ to sb** [person, machine, training] rendre service à qn; **can I be of ~?** je peux vous aider?; **I was glad to be of ~** j'ai été content d'avoir pu rendre service; **it was of no ~ (at all)** cela n'a servi à rien (du tout); **you've been a great ~** vous m'avez vraiment rendu service; (iro) **you're a great ~!** tu es d'un précieux secours! (iro); **you can't get decent (domestic) ~ nowadays** on ne trouve plus de bons employés de maison de nos jours; **she has no ~ in the house** elle n'a personne pour l'aider à la maison; **we need more ~ in the shop** il nous faut davantage de personnel au magasin; (fig) **he's beyond ~** on ne peut plus rien pour lui; **there's no ~ for it** il n'y a rien à faire, on n'y peut rien → **voluntary**

b (= cleaner) femme f de ménage → **daily, home, mother**

2 VT **a** (gen) aider (**sb to do** qn à faire); (in emergency) secourir; **let me ~ you with that suitcase** je vais vous aider avec votre valise; **she ~s her son with his homework** elle aide son fils à faire ses devoirs; **he got his brother to ~ him** il s'est fait aider par son frère; **that doesn't ~ much** cela ne sert pas à or n'arrange pas grand-chose; **that won't ~ you** cela ne vous servira à rien ■ (PROV) **God ~s those who ~ themselves** aide-toi et le ciel t'aidera (PROV); **so ~ me God!** je le jure devant Dieu!; **so ~ me* I'll kill him!** je te le jurerai, je le jure!; **this money will ~ to save the church** cet argent contribuera à sauver l'église; **every little ~s** les petits ruisseaux font les grandes rivières (PROV); (in shop) **can I ~ you?** (to customer at counter) vous désirez?; (to customer browsing) je peux vous aider?; **to ~ each other** or **one another** s'entraider; (euph) **he is ~ing the police with their inquiries** il est en train de répondre aux questions de la police; **to ~s industry/exports** cela favorise l'industrie/les exportations; **to ~ sb across/down/in** etc aider qn à traverser/à descendre/à entrer etc; **to ~ sb up/down/out with a suitcase** aider qn à monter/à descendre/à sortir une valise; **to ~ sb (up) to his feet** aider qn à se lever; **to ~ sb on/off with his coat** aider qn à mettre/à enlever son manteau

b (= serve) **to ~ o.s.** se servir; **he ~ed himself to vegetables** il s'est servi de légumes; **~ yourself to wine/bread** prenez du vin/du pain, servez-vous de vin/de pain; **just ~ yourself to leaflets** voilà des prospectus, servez-vous; **~ yourself!** servez-vous!; (euph) **he ~ed himself to my pencil*** il m'a piqué mon crayon*

c (with "can" or "cannot") **I couldn't ~ laughing** je ne pouvais pas m'empêcher de rire; **one cannot ~ wondering whether ...** on ne peut s'empêcher de se demander si ...; **one can't ~ but wonder/be impressed** on ne peut s'empêcher de se demander/d'être impressionné; **it can't be ~ed** tant pis!, on n'y peut rien!; **I can't ~ it if he always comes late** je n'y peux rien or ce n'est pas de ma faute s'il arrive toujours en retard; **he can't ~ it** ce n'est pas de sa faute, il n'y peut rien; **why are you laughing? — I can't ~ it** pourquoi riez-vous? — c'est plus fort que moi; **we just can't ~ ourselves**

c'est plus fort que nous ; **not if I can ~ it!** sûrement pas !, il faudra d'abord me passer sur le corps ! (*hum*) **he won't come if I can ~ it** je vais faire tout mon possible pour l'empêcher de venir ; **can I ~ it if it rains?** est-ce que c'est de ma faute s'il pleut ? ; **it's rather late now — I can't ~ that, you should have come earlier** il est un peu tard maintenant — je n'y peux rien, tu aurais dû venir plus tôt ; **he can't ~ his temperamental nature** il n'arrive pas à se corriger de son humeur instable ; **he can't ~ his deafness** ce n'est pas de sa faute s'il est sourd ; **he can't ~ being stupid** ce n'est pas de sa faute s'il est idiot ; **don't say more than you can ~** n'en dites pas plus qu'il ne faut

[3] COMP ► **help desk** N service *m* d'assistance ► **help menu** N (*Comput*) menu *m* d'assistance

► **help along** VT SEP [+ *person*] aider à marcher ; [+ *scheme*] (faire) avancer, faire progresser

► **help out** [1] VI aider, donner un coup de main ; (*financially*) dépanner* ; **I ~ out with the secretariat work** j'aide à la secrétariat [2] VT SEP (*gen*) aider, donner un coup de main à ; (*financially*) dépanner*, tirer d'embarras ; **to ~ each other out** s'entraider

► **help up** VT SEP **to ~ sb up** aider qn à se lever

helper ['hɛlpə'] N aide *mf*

helpful ['hɛlpʊl] ADJ [a] (= *cooperative*) [*person, staff*] obligeant (**to sb** avec qn) ; **you have been most ~** c'était très aimable à vous [b] (= *useful*) [*suggestion, book, tool*] utile ; [*medicine*] efficace ; **to be ~ in doing sth** contribuer à faire qch

helpfully ['hɛlpʊlɪ] ADV [*say*] avec obligeance ; [*provide, suggest, explain*] obligeamment

helpfulness ['hɛlpʊlnɪs] N obligeance *f*

helping ['hɛlpɪŋ] [1] N (*at table*) portion *f* ; **to take a second ~ of sth** reprendre de qch ; **I've had three ~s** j'en ai repris deux fois ; **the public appetite for huge ~s of nostalgia** le goût du public pour de grosses bouffées de nostalgie [2] ADJ secourable ; **to give** or **lend a ~ hand (to)** aider, donner un coup de main (à)

helpless ['hɛlplɪs] ADJ [*victim, baby, old person*] sans défense (**against sth** contre qch) ; [*invalid*] impotent, sans défense ; [*situation*] désespéré ; [*feeling, gesture*] d'impuissance ; **he is quite ~ (in this matter)** il n'y peut rien, il ne peut rien y faire ; **she looked at him with a ~ expression** elle lui jeta un regard d'impuissance ; **to feel ~ (against sth)** se sentir désarmé (devant qch) ; **he was ~ to resist** il a été incapable de résister ; **to be ~ with laughter** être mort de rire

helplessly ['hɛlplɪslɪ] ADV [a] (= *impotently*) [*struggle, try, say*] désespérément ; [*stand, look on*] sans pouvoir rien faire ; [*agree*] en désespoir de cause ; **he was lying ~ on the ground** il était allongé par terre, sans pouvoir bouger [b] (= *uncontrollably*) [*sob, cry, sneeze*] sans pouvoir se retenir ; [*drift*] inexorablement ; **to laugh ~** être mort de rire ; **to get ~ drunk** se soûler jusqu'à ne plus pouvoir tenir debout ; **to feel ~ angry** être en proie à une colère impuissante

helplessness ['hɛlplɪsnɪs] N [*of victim, baby, old person*] impuissance *f* (**against sth** face à qch, **before sth** devant qch) ; [*of invalid*] impotence *f* ; **feelings of ~** un sentiment d'impuissance ; **the ~ of the situation** le fait que la situation soit désespérée

helpline ['hɛlplaɪn] N (*esp Brit*) service *m* d'assistance téléphonique ; (*Comm*) = numéro *m* vert (*pour renseignements sur un produit*)

helpmate ['hɛlpmeɪt], **helpmeet**† ['hɛlp-miːt] N (= *spouse*) époux *m*, épouse *f* ; (= *female companion*) dame *f* de compagnie

Helsinki [hɛl'sɪŋkɪ] N Helsinki

helter-skelter ['hɛltə'skɛltə'] [1] ADV [*run*] pêle-mêle [2] ADJ [*rush*] désordonné [3] N

---

[a] (= *rush*) débandade *f*, bousculade *f* [b] (*Brit: in fairground*) toboggan *m*

hem[1] [hɛm] [1] N ourlet *m* ; (= *edge*) bord *m* ; **I've let the ~ down on my skirt** j'ai défait l'ourlet de ma jupe pour la rallonger, j'ai rallongé ma jupe [2] VT (= *sew*) ourler

► **hem in** VT SEP [+ *houses, objects, people*] cerner ; [*rules etc*] entraver ; **I feel ~med in** je me sens oppressé ; **they are ~med in by rigid contracts** ils sont pris dans le carcan de contrats rigides

hem[2] [hɛm] VI → **haw**[2]

hema(t)... ['hiːmə(t)] PREF (*US*) = **haema(t)...**

hemato... ['hiːmətəʊ] PREF (*US*) = **haemato...**

hemicycle ['hɛmɪsaɪkl] N hémicycle *m*

hemiplegia [ˌhɛmɪ'pliːdʒɪə] N hémiplégie *f*

hemiplegic [ˌhɛmɪ'pliːdʒɪk] ADJ, N hémiplégique *mf*

hemisphere ['hɛmɪsfɪə'] N hémisphère *m* ; **the northern ~** l'hémisphère *m* nord or boréal ; **the southern ~** l'hémisphère *m* sud or austral

hemispheric ['hɛmɪsfɛrɪk] ADJ [a] (*Geog*) **Northern ~ summers** les étés *mpl* de l'hémisphère nord or boréal [b] (*US Pol*) [*relations, solidarity*] entre pays du nord et du sud de l'Amérique ; [*policy*] concernant les relations entre pays du nord et du sud de l'Amérique ; **a sense of ~ identity** un sentiment d'identité américaine [c] (*Med, Psych*) [*asymmetry*] hémisphérique ; [*specialization, activity*] de l'un des hémisphères (du cerveau)

hemistich ['hɛmɪstɪk] N hémistiche *m*

hemline ['hɛmlaɪn] N (bas *m* de l')ourlet *m* ; **~s are lower this year** les robes rallongent cette année

hemlock ['hɛmlɒk] N [a] (= *plant, poison*) ciguë *f* [b] (= *tree*: also **~ spruce**) sapin *m* du Canada, sapin-ciguë *m*

hem(o)... ['hiːm(əʊ)] PREF (*US*) = **haem(o)...**

hemp [hɛmp] N (= *plant, fibre*) chanvre *m* ; (= *drug*) chanvre *m* indien

hemstitch ['hɛmstɪtʃ] [1] VT ourler à jour [2] N point *m* d'ourlet

hen [hɛn] [1] N [a] poule *f* ; (= *female bird*) femelle *f* ; **~ bird** oiseau *m* femelle [b] (*Scot*) **here you are, ~!** voilà, ma petite dame* [2] COMP ► **hen harrier** N busard *m* Saint-Martin ► **hen night***, **hen party*** N (*esp Brit*) soirée *f* entre femmes (*or* filles)

henbane ['hɛnbeɪn] N (*Bot*) jusquiame *f* (noire), herbe *f* aux poules

▼ **hence** [hɛns] ADV [a] (*frm* = *therefore*) d'où ; **~ the name** d'où son nom ; **inflation is rising: ~, new economic policies are needed** l'inflation est en hausse ; d'où la nécessité de prendre de nouvelles mesures économiques ; **it will drive up the price of oil, and ~ the price of petrol** ça fera monter le prix du pétrole, et par là or et par conséquent, celui de l'essence ; **the lack of blood, and ~ oxygen, in the brain** le manque de sang, et par conséquent or et donc d'oxygène, dans le cerveau [b] (*frm* = *from now*) d'ici ; **two years ~** d'ici deux ans [c] (†† = *from here*) d'ici ; **(get thee) ~!** hors d'ici !

henceforth ['hɛns'fɔːθ], **henceforward** ['hɛns'fɔːwəd] ADV (*frm*) dorénavant, désormais

henchman ['hɛntʃmən] N (*pl* **-men**) (*pej*) homme *m* de main ; (*Hist*) écuyer *m*

hencoop ['hɛnkuːp] N cage *f* à poules

henhouse ['hɛnhaʊs] N poulailler *m*

henna ['hɛnə] [1] N henné *m* [2] VT [+ *hair*] teindre au henné ; **to ~ one's hair** se faire un henné

henpecked ['hɛnpɛkt] ADJ **he's a ~ husband** sa femme le mène par le bout du nez

Henry ['hɛnrɪ] N Henri *m* → **hooray**

hep†* [hɛp] ADJ dans le vent* ; (*US*) **to be ~ to sth** être au courant de qch

heparin ['hɛpərɪn] N héparine *f*

---

hepatitis [ˌhɛpə'taɪtɪs] N hépatite *f* ; **~ A/B/C** hépatite *f* A/B/C

heptagon ['hɛptəgən] N (*Geom*) heptagone *m*

heptagonal [hɛp'tægənəl] ADJ (*Geom*) heptagonal

heptathlon [hɛp'tæθlən] N heptathlon *m*

her [hɜː'] [1] PERS PRON [a] (*direct*) (*unstressed*) la ; (*before vowel*) l' ; (*stressed*) elle ; **I see ~** je la vois ; **I have seen ~** je l'ai vue ; **I know HIM but I have never seen HER** lui je le connais, mais elle je ne l'ai jamais vue [b] (*indirect*) lui ; **I gave ~ the book** je lui ai donné le livre ; **I'm speaking to ~** je lui parle [c] (*after prep etc*) elle ; **I am thinking of ~** je pense à elle ; **without ~** sans elle ; **she took her books with ~** elle a emporté ses livres ; **if I were ~** si j'étais elle ; **it's ~** c'est elle ; **younger than ~** plus jeune qu'elle [d] celle ; **to ~ who might complain, I should point out that ...** à celle qui se plaindrait, je ferais remarquer que ... ; **the articles are of no value except to ~ who had once owned them** ces articles n'ont aucune valeur sauf pour celle à qui ils appartenaient autrefois [2] POSS ADJ son, sa, ses ; **~ book** son livre ; **~ table** sa table ; **~ friend** son ami(e) *m(f)* ; **~ clothes** ses vêtements

Hera ['hɪərə] N Héra *f*

Heracles ['hɛrəˌkliːz] N Héraclès *m*

Heraclitus [ˌhɛrə'klaɪtəs] N Héraclite *m*

herald ['hɛrəld] [1] N héraut *m* ; (*fig, liter*) **the ~ of spring** le messager du printemps (*liter*) [2] VT annoncer ; **to ~ (in)** annoncer l'arrivée de ; (*Ftbl*) **tonight's game is being ~ed as the match of the season** on présente le match de ce soir comme le plus important de la saison

heraldic [he'rældɪk] ADJ héraldique ; **~ bearing** armoiries *fpl*, blason *m*

heraldry ['hɛrəldrɪ] N (*NonC*) (= *science*) héraldique *f* ; (= *coat of arms*) blason *m* ; (*ceremonial*) pompe *f* héraldique ; **book of ~** armorial *m*

herb [hɜːb, (*US*) ɜːb] [1] N herbe *f* ; (*Culin*) **~s** fines herbes *fpl* ; **pot ~s** herbes *fpl* potagères ; **medicinal ~s** herbes *fpl* médicinales, simples *mpl* [2] COMP ► **herb garden** N jardin *m* d'herbes aromatiques ► **herb tea** N infusion *f*, tisane *f*

herbaceous [hɜː'beɪʃəs] ADJ herbacé ; **~ border** bordure *f* de plantes herbacées

herbage ['hɜːbɪdʒ] N (*Agr*) herbages *mpl* ; (*Jur*) droit *m* de pacage

herbal ['hɜːbəl] [1] ADJ d'herbes [2] N herbier *m* (*livre*) [3] COMP ► **herbal medicine** N phytothérapie *f* ► **herbal remedy** N remède *m* à base de plantes ► **herbal tea** N infusion *f*, tisane *f*

herbalism ['hɜːbəlɪzəm] N phytothérapie *f*

herbalist ['hɜːbəlɪst] N herboriste *mf*

herbarium [hɜː'bɛərɪəm] N (*pl* **herbariums** or **herbaria** [hɜː'bɛərɪə]) herbier *m* (*collection*)

herbicide ['hɜːbɪsaɪd] N herbicide *m*

herbivore ['hɜːbɪvɔː'] N herbivore *m*

herbivorous [hɜː'bɪvərəs] ADJ herbivore

Herculean [ˌhɜːkjʊ'liːən] ADJ herculéen

Hercules ['hɜːkjuliːz] N (*Myth*) Hercule *m* ; (*fig = strong man*) hercule *m*

herd [hɜːd] [1] N [a] [*of cattle, goats, elephants etc*] troupeau *m* ; [*of stags*] harde *f* ; [*of horses*] troupe *f*, bande *f* ; (*US*) **to ride ~ on sb** avoir l'œil sur qn [b]* [*of people*] troupeau *m*, foule *f* ; (*fig*) **to follow the ~** être comme un mouton de Panurge → **common** [c] (†† = *person*) pâtre *m* (*liter*) → **cowherd**[1], **goatherd** [2] VT [+ *animals*] mener en troupeau ; **to ~ into/onto etc** [+ *people*] faire entrer/monter etc en troupeau dans [3] COMP ► **herd instinct** N instinct *m* grégaire

► **herd together** [1] VI [*animals, people*] s'attrouper, s'assembler en troupeau [2] VT SEP [+ *animals, people*] rassembler en troupeau

herdsman [ˈhɜːdzmən] N (pl **-men**) gardien m de troupeau; (= *shepherd*) berger m; (= *cowman*) vacher m, bouvier m

here [hɪəʳ] **1** ADV **a** (*place*) ici; **I live** ~ j'habite ici; **come** ~ venez ici; (*at roll call*) ~! présent!; ~ **I am** me voici; ~ **is my brother** voici mon frère; ~ **are the others** voici les autres; ~ **we are at last** nous voici enfin arrivés; (*bringing sth*) ~ **we are!** voici!; (*giving sth*) ~ **you are!** tenez!; ~ **come my friends** voici mes amis qui arrivent; **he's** ~ **at last** le voici enfin, il est enfin là or arrivé; **spring is** ~ c'est le printemps, le printemps est là; **my sister says …** ma sœur que voici dit …; **this man** ~ saw it cet homme-ci l'a vu; ~**'s to you!** voici!; ~**'s to your success!** à votre succès!; **about** or **around** ~ par ici; **far from** ~ loin d'ici; **put it in** ~ mettez-le ici; **come in** ~ venez (par) ici; **in** ~ **please** par ici s'il vous plaît; **near** ~ près d'ici; **over** ~ ici; **it's cold up** ~ il fait froid ici (en haut); **up to** or **down to** ~ jusqu'ici; **from** ~ **to London** d'ici (jusqu')à Londres; **it's 10km from** ~ **to Paris** il y a 10 km d'ici à Paris; **Mr Moore is not** ~ **just now** M. Moore n'est pas là or ici en ce moment; **are you there? — yes I'm** ~ vous êtes là? — oui je suis là; **I shan't be** ~ **this afternoon** je ne serai pas là cet après-midi; **I'm** ~ **to help** je suis là pour vous aider; **I'm** ~ **to tell you (that) …** je suis venu vous dire (que) …; ~, **and there and everywhere** un peu partout; (*fig*) **it's neither** ~ **nor there** tout cela n'a aucun rapport; ~ **goes!*** allons-y!, c'est parti!*; ~ **we go again!** c'est reparti!*, (et) voilà que ça recommence!; ~ **and now** sur-le-champ; **I must warn you** ~ **and now that …** il faut que je vous prévienne sans plus tarder que …; ~ **below** ici-bas; ~ **lies** ci-gît → **look**

b (*time*) alors, à ce moment-là; **it's** ~ **that the real test will come** ce sera l'épreuve de vérité; ~ **I think it is appropriate to draw your attention to …** je pense qu'il convient maintenant d'attirer votre attention sur …

2 EXCL ~, **I didn't promise that at all!** écoutez or dites donc, je n'ai jamais promis cela!; ~, **you try to open it*** tiens, essaie de l'ouvrir, alors; ~, **hold this a minute*** tiens-moi ça une minute

3 COMP ► **the here and now** N le présent, l'instant m présent

hereabouts [ˌhɪərəˈbaʊts] ADV par ici

hereafter [ˌhɪərˈɑːftəʳ] **1** ADV (= *in the future*) après, plus tard; (*in document* = *following this*) ci-après; (= *after death*) dans l'autre monde or vie **2** N **the** ~ l'au-delà m

hereby [hɪəˈbaɪ] ADV (*Comm, Jur*) (*in letter*) par la présente; (*in document*) par le présent document; (*in act*) par le présent acte; (*in will*) par le présent testament; (*in declaration*) par la présente (déclaration)

hereditaments [ˌherɪˈdɪtəmənts] NPL (*Jur*) biens meubles ou immeubles transmissibles par héritage

hereditary [hɪˈredɪtərɪ] ADJ héréditaire; **a** ~ **peer** un lord héréditaire

heredity [hɪˈredɪtɪ] N hérédité f

herein [hɪəˈrɪn] ADV (*frm*) (= *in this matter*) en ceci, en cela; (= *in this writing*) ci-inclus

hereinafter [ˌhɪərɪnˈɑːftəʳ] ADV (*Jur*) ci-après, dans la suite des présentes

hereof [hɪərˈɒv] ADV (*frm*) de ceci, de cela; **the provisions** ~ les dispositions fpl des présentes

heresy [ˈherəsɪ] N hérésie f; **an act of** ~ une hérésie

heretic [ˈheretɪk] N hérétique mf

heretical [hɪˈretɪkəl] ADJ hérétique

hereto [hɪəˈtuː] ADV (*Jur*) à ceci, à cela; (*Jur*) **the parties** ~ les parties fpl aux présentes

heretofore [ˌhɪətʊˈfɔːʳ] ADV (*frm*) (= *up to specified point*) jusque-là; (= *up to now*) jusqu'ici; (= *previously*) ci-devant

hereupon [ˌhɪərəˈpɒn] ADV (*frm*) là-dessus, sur ce

herewith [ˌhɪəˈwɪð] ADV (*frm*) avec ceci; **I am sending you** ~ je vous envoie ci-joint or sous ce pli; **I enclose** ~ **a copy of …** veuillez trouver ci-joint une copie de …

heritable [ˈherɪtəbl] ADJ [*objects, property*] transmissible; [*intelligence*] héréditaire

heritage [ˈherɪtɪdʒ] **1** N (*lit, fig*) héritage m, patrimoine m; **our national** ~ notre patrimoine national **2** COMP ► **heritage centre** N (*Brit*) petit musée m local

hermaphrodite [hɜːˈmæfrədaɪt] ADJ, N hermaphrodite m

hermaphroditic [hɜːmæfrəˈdɪtɪk] ADJ hermaphrodite

Hermes [ˈhɜːmiːz] N Hermès m

hermetic [hɜːˈmetɪk] ADJ (*gen, also Literat*) hermétique

hermetically [hɜːˈmetɪkəlɪ] ADV hermétiquement; ~ **sealed** hermétiquement fermé

hermit [ˈhɜːmɪt] **1** N (*lit, fig*) ermite m **2** COMP ► **hermit crab** N bernard-l'(h)ermite m inv

hermitage [ˈhɜːmɪtɪdʒ] N ermitage m

hernia [ˈhɜːnɪə] N (pl **hernias** or **herniae** [ˈhɜːnɪˌiː]) hernie f

hero [ˈhɪərəʊ] (pl **heroes**) **1** N **a** (*all senses*) héros m; **his boyhood** ~ le héros de son enfance; **the** ~ **of the hour** le héros du jour **b** = **hero sandwich 2** COMP ► **hero sandwich** N (*US*) grand sandwich m mixte ► **hero's welcome** N **to give sb a** ~**'s welcome** accueillir qn comme un héros ► **hero-worship** N culte m (du héros) ♦ VT aduler, idolâtrer

Herod [ˈherəd] N Hérode m → **out-Herod**

heroic [hɪˈrəʊɪk] **1** ADJ héroïque; **to put up** ~ **resistance** résister héroïquement **2** COMP ► **heroic couplet** N (*Poetry*) distique m héroïque ► **heroic verse** N (*NonC: Poetry*) vers mpl héroïques; **in** ~ **verse** en décasyllabes

heroically [hɪˈrəʊɪkəlɪ] ADV héroïquement; (*hum*) **she managed,** ~, **to keep a straight face** elle réussit, à grand-peine, à garder son sérieux

heroics [hɪˈrəʊɪks] NPL actes mpl de bravoure; **no** ~! ne joue pas les héros!

heroin [ˈherəʊɪn] **1** N héroïne f (*drogue*) **2** COMP ► **heroin addict** N héroïnomane mf ► **heroin addiction** N héroïnomanie f ► **heroin user** N consommateur m, -trice f d'héroïne, héroïnomane mf

heroine [ˈherəʊɪn] N héroïne f (*femme*)

heroism [ˈherəʊɪzəm] N héroïsme m

heron [ˈherən] N héron m

herpes [ˈhɜːpiːz] N herpès m → **genital**

herring [ˈherɪŋ] **1** N (pl **herrings** or **herring**) hareng m → **fish, red 2** COMP ► **herring boat** N harenguier m ► **herring gull** N goéland m argenté ► **the herring-pond*** N (= *Atlantic*) la mare aux harengs (*hum*), l'Atlantique nord

herringbone [ˈherɪŋbəʊn] **1** N (*lit*) arête f de hareng; (*Archit*) appareil m en épi; (*Ski: also* ~ **climb**) montée f en canard **2** COMP ► **herringbone pattern** N (dessin m à) chevrons mpl ► **herringbone stitch** N point m d'épine (en chevron)

hers [hɜːz] POSS PRON le sien, la sienne, les siens, les siennes; **my hands are clean,** ~ **are dirty** mes mains sont propres, les siennes sont sales; ~ **is a specialized department** sa section est une section spécialisée; **this book is** ~ ce livre est à elle, ce livre est le sien; **the house became** ~ la maison est devenue la sienne; **it is not** ~ **to decide** ce n'est pas à elle de décider, il ne lui appartient pas de décider; **a friend of** ~ un de ses amis (à elle); **it's**

no fault of ~ ce n'est pas de sa faute (à elle); **no advice of** ~ **could prevent him** aucun conseil de sa part ne pouvait l'empêcher; **is this poem** ~? ce poème est-il d'elle?; (*pej*) **that car of** ~ sa fichue* voiture; (*pej*) **that stupid son of** ~ son idiot de fils; (*pej*) **that temper of** ~ son sale caractère

herself [hɜːˈself] PERS PRON (*reflexive*) (*direct and indirect*) se; (*emphatic*) elle-même; (*after prep*) elle; **she has hurt** ~ elle s'est blessée; **she poured** ~ **a whisky** elle s'est servie un whisky; **"why not?" she said to** ~ «pourquoi pas?» se dit-elle; **she told me** ~ elle me l'a dit elle-même; **I saw the girl** ~ j'ai vu la jeune fille elle-même or en personne; **she kept three for** ~ elle s'en est réservé trois; **he asked her for a photo of** ~ il lui a demandé une photo d'elle; **(all) by** ~ toute seule; **she hasn't been** ~ **lately** (= *not behaving normally*) elle n'est pas dans son état normal ces temps-ci; (= *not feeling well*) elle n'est pas dans son assiette ces temps-ci

Herts [hɑːts] ABBR = **Hertfordshire**

hertz [hɜːts] N (pl inv) hertz m

he's [hiːz] = **he is, he has**; → **be, have**

hesitancy [ˈhezɪtənsɪ] N hésitation f

hesitant [ˈhezɪtənt] ADJ hésitant; **to be** ~ **to do sth** or **about doing sth** hésiter à faire qch

hesitantly [ˈhezɪtəntlɪ] ADV [*say*] avec hésitation; [*enter*] en hésitant; **she stood** ~ **in the doorway** elle se tenait indécise sur le pas de la porte

▼**hesitate** [ˈhezɪteɪt] VI hésiter (**over, about, at** sur, devant, **to do** à faire); **he didn't** ~ **at the idea of leaving her** il l'a quittée sans hésiter; **he never once** ~**d over publishing the article** il n'a pas hésité une seconde avant de publier cet article; **the President has been hesitating over whether to attend the conference** le président hésite à assister à la conférence; **I will not** ~ **to take unpopular decisions** je n'hésiterai pas à prendre des décisions impopulaires; **she** ~**d about going in for politics** elle hésitait à entrer dans la politique; **don't** ~ **to ask me** n'hésitez pas à me demander; **please do not** ~ **to contact our Customer Service Department** n'hésitez pas à contacter notre service clientèle; **he** ~**s at nothing** il ne recule devant rien, rien ne l'arrête ■ (*PROV*) **he who** ~**s is lost** une minute d'hésitation peut coûter cher

hesitation [ˌhezɪˈteɪʃən] N hésitation f; **without the slightest** ~ sans la moindre hésitation; **I have no** ~ **in saying that …** je n'hésite pas à dire que …; ~, **he said after some** ~ … dit-il après un moment d'hésitation; **I had no** ~ **about taking the job** j'ai accepté le travail sans la moindre hésitation

Hesperides [heˈsperɪˌdiːz] NPL **the** ~ les Hespérides fpl

hessian [ˈhesɪən] (*esp Brit*) **1** N (toile f de) jute m **2** COMP (= *made of hessian*) en (toile de) jute

hetero* [ˈhetərəʊ] N, ADJ hétéro* mf

hetero… [ˈhetərəʊ] PREF hétér(o)…

heterodox [ˈhetərədɒks] ADJ hétérodoxe

heterodoxy [ˈhetərədɒksɪ] N hétérodoxie f

heterogeneity [ˌhetərəʊdʒəˈniːɪtɪ] N hétérogénéité f

heterogeneous [ˌhetərəʊˈdʒiːnɪəs] ADJ hétérogène

heterosexism [ˈhetərəʊˈseksɪzm] N discrimination f à l'égard des homosexuels

heterosexual [ˌhetərəʊˈseksjʊəl] ADJ, N hétérosexuel(le) m(f)

heterosexuality [ˌhetərəʊˌseksjʊˈælɪtɪ] N hétérosexualité f

het up* [ˈhetˈʌp] ADJ excité, énervé; **he gets** ~ **about the slightest thing** il se met dans tous ses états à propos d'un rien

heuristic [hjʊəˈrɪstɪk] ADJ heuristique

heuristics [hjʊəˈrɪstɪks] NPL heuristique f

► LANGUAGE IN USE: hesitate 3.1, 20.2, 21.2

hew [hjuː] **1** VT (pret **hewed**, ptp **hewn** or **hewed** [hjuːn]) [+ stone] tailler, équarrir; [+ wood] couper; [+ coal] abattre; **to ~ sth out of wood/stone** tailler qch dans du bois/la pierre **2** VI (pret, ptp **hewed**) (US) **to ~ to sth** se conformer à qch, suivre qch

hewer ['hjuːə] N [of stone, wood] équarrisseur m; [of coal] haveur m, piqueur m

hex¹ [heks] (esp US) **1** N (= spell) sort m; (= witch) sorcière f **2** VT jeter un sort à

hex² [heks] N (Comput) ~ **code** code m hexadécimal

hexadecimal [,heksə'desɪməl] ADJ, N hexadécimal m

hexagon ['heksəgən] N hexagone m

hexagonal [hek'sægənəl] ADJ hexagonal

hexagram ['heksə,græm] N hexagramme m

hexameter [hek'sæmɪtə] N hexamètre m

hexathlon [hek'sæθlən] N hexathlon m

hey [heɪ] EXCL hé!, ohé!; ~ **presto!** (said by magician) passez muscade!; (fig) ô miracle!

heyday ['heɪdeɪ] N [of the music hall, the railways etc] âge m d'or, beaux jours mpl; **in his ~** (= in his prime) quand il était dans la force de l'âge; (= at his most famous) à l'apogée de sa gloire; **in the ~ of punk/of the theatre** à l'âge d'or du punk/du théâtre; **in the ~ of flares** à la grande époque des pantalons à pattes d'éléphant

Hezbollah ['hezbə'lɑː] **1** N Hezbollah m **2** ADJ [guerrillas, leader, stronghold] du Hezbollah

HGV [,eɪtʃdʒiː'viː] N (Aut) (ABBR = **heavy goods vehicle**) → **heavy**

HHS [eɪtʃeɪtʃ'es] N (US) (ABBR = **Health and Human Services**) ministère de la Santé et des Affaires sociales

HI ABBR = **Hawaii**

hi* [haɪ] EXCL **a** (= greeting) salut!* **b** (= hey) hé!, ohé!

hiatus [haɪ'eɪtəs] **1** N (pl **hiatuses** or **hiatus**) (in series, manuscript etc) lacune f; (Ling, Phon, Poetry) hiatus m; (fig) (= interruption) interruption f, pause f; (= difference) hiatus m, décalage m; **after a two-week ~** après une interruption de deux semaines; **there was an ~ in his acting life** il y a eu une coupure dans sa carrière d'acteur **2** COMP ► **hiatus hernia** N (Med) hernie f hiatale

hibernate ['haɪbəneɪt] VI hiberner

hibernation [,haɪbə'neɪʃən] N hibernation f; **in ~** en hibernation

Hibernian [haɪ'bɜːnɪən] **1** ADJ irlandais **2** N Irlandais(e) m(f)

hibiscus [hɪ'bɪskəs] N (pl **hibiscuses**) hibiscus m

hic [hɪk] EXCL hic!

hiccup, hiccough† ['hɪkʌp] **1** N **a** hoquet m; **to have ~s** avoir le hoquet **b** (= minor setback) contretemps m, ratés mpl; **the recent sales ~** la baisse momentanée des ventes que nous avons connue récemment **2** VI hoqueter **3** VT dire en hoquetant

hick* [hɪk] (US) **1** N péquenaud(e)* m(f) (pej) **2** ADJ [ideas] de péquenaud* (pej) **3** COMP ► **hick town** N bled* m (pej)

hickey* ['hɪkɪ] N (US) (= pimple) petit bouton m; (= lovebite) suçon m

hickory ['hɪkərɪ] N hickory m, noyer m blanc d'Amérique

hide¹ [haɪd] (pret **hid** [hɪd], ptp **hidden** ['hɪdn] or **hid††**) **1** VT cacher (**from sb** à qn); [+ feelings] dissimuler (**from sb** à qn); **to ~ o.s.** se cacher; **I've got nothing to ~** je n'ai rien à cacher or à dissimuler; **he's hiding something** il a une idée quelque chose; **to ~ one's face** se cacher le visage; **to ~ sth from sight** dérober qch aux regards; **hidden from sight** dérobé aux regards; **to ~ one's light under a bushel** cacher ses talents; **he doesn't ~ his light under a**

bushel ce n'est pas la modestie qui l'étouffe; **clouds hid the sun** des nuages cachaient or voilaient le soleil; **the building was hidden by trees and shrubs** le bâtiment était caché par des arbres et des arbustes; **he tried to ~ his disappointment** il a essayé de dissimuler sa déception; **a hidden meaning** un sens caché; **"no hidden extras"** «garanti sans suppléments»; **hidden tax** impôt m déguisé **2** VI se cacher (**from sb** de qn); (fig) **he's hiding behind his boss** il se réfugie derrière son patron (fig) **3** N (Brit) cachette f **4** COMP ► **hidden agenda** N intentions fpl non déclarées ► **hide-and-(go-)seek** N cache-cache m

► **hide away 1** VI se cacher (**from** de) **2** VT SEP cacher **3** ~ **away** N → **hideaway**

► **hide out, hide up 1** VI se cacher (**from** de) **2** ~ **out** N → **hideout**

hide² [haɪd] **1** N (= skin) peau f; (= leather) cuir m; **they found neither ~ nor hair of him** ils n'ont pas trouvé la moindre trace de son passage; **I haven't seen ~ nor hair of him*** je ne l'ai vu nulle part, il a complètement disparu de la circulation; **when I went to Australia I didn't see ~ nor hair of a kangaroo** quand je suis allé en Australie, je n'ai pas vu l'ombre d'un kangourou → **tan 2** COMP [chair etc] de or en cuir

hideaway ['haɪdəweɪ] N cachette f, planque* f

hidebound ['haɪdbaʊnd] ADJ [person] borné, obtus; [view] étroit, borné

hideous ['hɪdɪəs] ADJ [appearance, sight, person] hideux, affreux; [crime, attack] abominable, horrible; (fig) terrible*; **it's been a truly ~ day** ça a été une journée absolument épouvantable

hideously ['hɪdɪəslɪ] ADV [deformed, ugly] hideusement; [embarrassed] affreusement; [expensive] horriblement

hideout ['haɪdaʊt] N = **hideaway**

hidey-hole* ['haɪdɪhəʊl] N planque* f

hiding¹ ['haɪdɪŋ] **1** N [of object] fait m de cacher; [of feelings] dissimulation f; [of criminals] recel m; **to be in ~** se tenir caché; **to go into ~** se cacher; **to come out of ~** sortir de sa cachette **2** COMP ► **hiding place** N cachette f

hiding² ['haɪdɪŋ] N (gen) raclée* f; (= punishment) correction f; **to give sb a good ~** donner une bonne raclée* or correction à qn; (fig) **to take or get a ~** prendre une raclée*; (Brit) **to be on a ~ to nothing*** être sûr de se ramasser or prendre une gamelle*

hie†† [haɪ] VI se hâter; ~ **thee hence!** hors d'ici!

hierarchic(al) [,haɪə'rɑːkɪk(əl)] ADJ hiérarchique

hierarchically [,haɪə'rɑːkɪkəlɪ] ADV hiérarchiquement

hierarchy ['haɪərɑːkɪ] N hiérarchie f

hieratic [haɪə'rætɪk] ADJ (frm) hiératique

hieroglyph ['haɪərəglɪf] N hiéroglyphe m

hieroglyphic [,haɪərə'glɪfɪk] **1** ADJ hiéroglyphique **2** N hiéroglyphe m

hieroglyphics [,haɪərə'glɪfɪks] NPL (lit) écriture f hiéroglyphique; (fig) hiéroglyphes mpl, écriture f hiéroglyphique

hifalutin* [,haɪfə'luːtɪn] ADJ = **highfalutin(g)**

hi-fi ['haɪ'faɪ] ABBR = **high fidelity 1** N **a** (also ~ **system**) chaîne f (hi-fi inv) **b** (NonC) hi-fi f inv, haute fidélité f **2** COMP [reproduction, record] hi-fi inv, haute fidélité inv ► **hi-fi equipment** N matériel m hi-fi inv ► **hi-fi set, hi-fi system** N chaîne f (hi-fi inv)

higgledy-piggledy* ['hɪgldɪ'pɪgldɪ] ADJ, ADV pêle-mêle inv

high [haɪ] **1** ADJ **a** (in height) [building, mountain, wall, shelf, ceiling] haut; **a ~ fence/hill/block of flats** une haute clôture/colline/tour; **a building 40 metres ~** ◊ **a 40-metre ~**

building un bâtiment de 40 mètres de haut, un bâtiment haut de 40 mètres; **the wall is 2 metres ~** le mur fait 2 mètres de haut; **the door is 3 metres ~** la porte fait 3 mètres de haut; **how ~ is that tower?** quelle est la hauteur de cette tour?; **how ~ is the mountain?** quelle est l'altitude de la montagne?; **the shelf was too ~ for him to reach** l'étagère était trop haute, il n'arrivait pas à l'atteindre; **the sun was ~ in the sky** le soleil était haut dans le ciel; **at ~ altitude** à haute altitude; **when he was only so ~*** alors qu'il était haut comme trois pommes; **(a piece of) ~ ground** une hauteur; (fig) **to have or hold or occupy the (moral) ~ ground** (= moral superiority) être au-dessus de la mêlée; **to take or claim the (moral) ~ ground** se mettre dans une position moralement plus élevée, prétendre être au-dessus de la mêlée → **4**

b (in degree, number, strength etc) [frequency, latitude, tension] haut (before n); [speed, value] grand (before n); [fever] gros (grosse f) (before n), fort (before n); [pressure] élevé, haut (before n); [salary] haut (before n), gros (grosse f) (before n); [rent, price] élevé; [number] grand (before n), élevé; [sound, voice] aigu (-guë f); [note] haut; [complexion] rougeaud; [colour] vif; [polish] brillant; [respect] grand (before n); profond; [calling, character] noble; [ideal] noble, grand (before n); (Phon) [vowel] fermé; **to have ~ blood pressure** avoir de la tension; **his team were of the ~est calibre** son équipe était de très haut niveau; **of ~ caste** de caste supérieure; **official reports say casualties have been ~** selon les rapports officiels, il y a beaucoup de morts et de blessés; **the new model has been refined to the ~est degree** le nouveau modèle est hautement perfectionné; **to have ~ expectations of sth** placer de grands espoirs en qch; **to have ~ expectations of sb** beaucoup attendre de qn; ~ **official** haut fonctionnaire m; **to have a ~ opinion of sb/ sth** avoir une haute opinion de qn/qch; **she has friends in ~ places** elle a des amis en haut lieu; **allegations of corruption in ~ places** des allégations de corruption en haut lieu; **to buy sth at a ~ price** acheter qch cher; (lit, fig) **to pay a ~ price for sth** payer qch cher; **he has a ~ temperature** il a une forte température; **it boils at a ~ temperature** cela bout à une température élevée; **the temperature was in the ~ 30s** la température approchait les quarante degrés; **it's ~ time you went home** il est grand temps que tu rentres (subj); **to set a ~ value on sth** attacher une grande valeur à qch; **a ~ wind was blowing** il soufflait un vent violent, il faisait grand vent; (Aut) **in ~ gear** en quatrième (or cinquième) vitesse; (Math) **the ~est common factor** le plus grand commun diviseur → **4**; → **lord, priority, profile, very**

c (Culin) [game, meat] avancé, faisandé; [butter] fort, rance

d * (= drunk) parti*; (= on drugs) **he was ~** il planait; **to get ~ on alcohol** s'enivrer; **he was ~ on speed** il planait après avoir pris du speed; **to be (as) ~ as a kite** planer complètement*; **she was ~ on her latest success** elle était enivrée par son dernier succès

e († + fig) **to have a ~ old time** s'amuser follement; **there was a ~ old row about it** cela a provoqué une sacrée bagarre* or un sacré chambard*

2 ADV **a** (in height) [climb, jump, throw] haut; [fly] à haute altitude, à une altitude élevée; **she threw the ball ~ in the air** elle a lancé le ballon haut dans les airs; **the balloon rose ~ in the air** le ballon s'est élevé or est monté haut dans le ciel or dans les airs; ~ **above our heads** bien au-dessus de nos têtes; **how ~ can you jump?** à quelle hauteur pouvez-vous sauter?; **a plate piled ~ with sandwiches** une assiette avec une grosse pile de sandwiches;

the house was built ~ on the hillside la maison son était construite en haut de la colline ; **a house ~ up in the hills** une maison perchée dans les collines ; **grapes grown ~ up on the slope** du raisin que l'on fait pousser en haut de la pente ; **we saw a bird circling very ~ up** nous avons vu un oiseau décrire des cercles très haut dans le ciel ; **~er up** plus haut ; **~er up the hill was a small farm** plus haut sur la colline il y avait une petite ferme ; **~er and ~er** de plus en plus haut ; **unemployment is climbing ~er and ~er** le chômage augmente de plus en plus ; **she was quite ~ up in the organization** elle était assez haut placée dans l'organisation ; **economic reform is ~ (up) on the agenda** or **on the list of priorities** la réforme économique est l'une des (premières) priorités ; (fig) **to aim ~ ◊ to set one's sights ~** viser haut ; (esp US fig) **to live ~ on the hog*** vivre comme un nabab

b (in degree, number, strength etc) **the numbers go as ~ as 200** les nombres montent jusqu'à 200 ; **I had to go as ~ as 200 francs for it** j'ai dû aller or monter jusqu'à 200 F pour l'avoir ; **to hunt** or **look ~ and low for sb** chercher qn partout ; **to hunt** or **look ~ and low for sth** chercher qch partout or dans tous les coins ; **to hold one's head (up) ~** avoir la tête haute ; **to play ~** (gambler) jouer gros (jeu) ; **to live ~** mener grand train, mener la grande vie ; **the sea is running ~** la mer est grosse or houleuse ; **the river is running ~** la rivière est en crue ; **feelings ran ~** les esprits étaient échauffés → **fly**[1]

3 N **a** (= high point) **the cost of living reached a new ~** le coût de la vie a atteint une nouvelle pointe or un nouveau plafond ; **the pound closed at a new ~ against the dollar today** la livre a atteint un nouveau plafond par rapport au dollar en clôture aujourd'hui ; **his football career reached a new ~ with eight goals in ten matches** sa carrière de footballeur a atteint un nouveau sommet avec huit buts en dix matchs ; **car sales reached an all-time ~ of 2.3 million** les ventes de voitures ont atteint un niveau record : 2,3 millions ; (fig) **~s and lows** les hauts mpl et les bas mpl

b **on ~** en haut ; **from on ~** d'en haut ; **the directive had come down from on ~** la directive était venue d'en haut ; **orders from on ~** des ordres venus d'en haut ; **God on ~** Dieu qui est au ciel

c (Met = high pressure) **a ~ over the North Sea** une zone de haute pression sur la mer du Nord

d (Rel) **the Most High** le Très-Haut

4 COMP ► **high-ability** ADJ très doué ► **high altar** N maître-autel m ► **high and dry** ADJ [boat] échoué ; (fig) **to leave sb ~ and dry** laisser qn en plan* ► **high and mighty*** ADJ **to be ~ and mighty** se donner de grands airs, faire le grand seigneur (or la grande dame) ► **high-angle shot** N (Cine) plongée f ► **high beam** N (US) pleins phares mpl ► **high camp** N → **camp**[2] ► **High Church** N (Brit) Haute Église f (anglicane) ► **high-class** ADJ [hotel, food, service] de premier ordre ; [house] très bourgeois ; [neighbourhood, flat] (de) grand standing ; [person] du grand monde ; [prostitute] de luxe ► **high comedy** N (Theat) comédie f sophistiquée ; (fig) **it was ~ comedy** c'était du plus haut comique ► **high command** N (Mil) haut commandement m ► **High Commission** N (Admin) haut commissariat m ► **High Commissioner** N (Admin) haut commissaire m ► **High Court** N (Jur) ≈ Haute Cour f ► **High Court judge** N (Brit) juge m de la Haute Cour ► **high definition** N, ADJ haute définition f ► **high definition television** N télévision f haute définition ► **high-density** ADJ [printing, disk] haute densité inv ► **high-density housing** N grands ensembles mpl ► **high diving** N (NonC : Sport) plongeon(s) m(pl) de haut vol →

diving ► **high-energy** ADJ [particle] de haute énergie ► **high explosive** N explosif m (puissant) ► **high-explosive shell** N obus m explosif ► **high fibre diet** N (= eating régime) régime m riche en fibres ; (= food eaten) alimentation f riche en fibres ► **high-fidelity** N, ADJ haute fidélité f inv ► **high-five*** N geste m de salut or de félicitation où les deux personnes se tapent dans la main ► **high flier** N (fig) (in profession) jeune loup m ; (at school) crack* m ► **high-flown** ADJ [style, discourse] ampoulé ► **high flyer** N = **high flier** ► **high-flying** ADJ [aircraft] volant à haute altitude ; (fig) [aim, ambition] extravagant ; [person] qui ira loin ► **high-frequency** ADJ de or à haute fréquence ► **ultrahigh, very** ► **High German** N haut allemand m ► **high-grade** ADJ [goods] de qualité supérieure, de premier choix ► **high-grade mineral** N minerai m à haute teneur ► **high hand** N **to rule sb with a ~ hand** imposer sa loi à qn ► **high-handed** ADJ désinvolte ► **high-handedly** ADV avec désinvolture ► **high-handedness** N désinvolture f ► **high hat** N (= hat) (chapeau m) haut-de-forme m ► **high-hat*** ADJ snob, poseur ♦ VT snober, traiter de haut ♦ VI faire le snob or la snobinette ► **high-heeled shoes** N chaussures fpl à hauts talons ► **high heels** NPL (= shoes) hauts talons mpl ► **high horse** N (fig) **to get up/be on one's ~ horse** monter/ être sur ses grands chevaux ► **high-income** ADJ [group, country] à hauts revenus, à revenus élevés ► **high-interest** ADJ (Fin) à intérêt élevé ► **high jinks** †[1] NPL **to get up to** or **have ~ jinks** se payer du bon temps ; **there were ~ jinks last night** on s'est amusé comme des fous hier soir ► **high jump** N (Sport) saut m en hauteur ; (Brit fig) **he's for the ~ jump!*** (= going to be scolded, punished) il est bon pour une engueulade*, qu'est-ce qu'il va prendre !* ; (= going to be sacked) il va se faire virer !* ► **high jumper** N (Sport) sauteur m, -euse f en hauteur ► **high-level** ADJ [meeting, discussions] à un très haut niveau ; (Comput) [language, programming] de haut niveau ; **~-level committee** (with great authority) haute instance f ; (composed of high officials) comité m formé de hauts responsables ; **~-level nuclear waste** déchets mpl nucléaires à haute activité ► **high life** N **to live the ~ life** mener la grande vie ► **high living** N la grande vie ► **High Mass** N grand-messe f ► **high-minded** ADJ [person] à l'âme noble, de caractère élevé ; [ambition, wish] noble, élevé ► **high-necked** ADJ à col haut ► **high noon** N plein midi m ; (fig = crisis point) **it's ~ noon for ...** c'est l'heure de vérité pour ... ► **high-octane** ADJ [petrol] à indice d'octane élevé ► **high-performance** ADJ très performant, à haute performance ► **high-pitched** ADJ (Mus) [voice, sound, note] aigu (-guë f) ; [song] (chanté) dans les aigus ; (Archit) [roof] à forte pente ; [ambitions] noble, haut (before n) ► **high point** N (of visit, holiday) grand moment m ; **the ~ point of the show/evening** le clou du spectacle/de la soirée ► **high-powered** ADJ [car] très puissant ; (fig) [person] de haut vol ; **~-powered businessman** homme m d'affaires de haut vol ► **high-pressure** (Tech) à haute pression ; (Met) **~-pressure area** zone f de haute pression ; (fig) **a ~-pressure salesman** un vendeur de choc* ; **~-pressure salesmanship** technique f de vente agressive ► **high-priced** ADJ coûteux, cher ► **high priest** N grand prêtre m ► **high priestess** N grande prêtresse f ► **high-principled** ADJ qui a des principes élevés ► **high-profile** ADJ [position, politician] très en vue ; [role] très influent ; [issue] très discuté ► **high-protein** ADJ riche en protéines ► **high-ranking** ADJ haut placé, de haut rang ; **~-ranking official** haut fonctionnaire m ► **high resolution** N haute résolution f ► **high-resolution** ADJ haute résolution inv ► **high-rise** N (also **~-rise block, ~-rise flats**) tour f (d'habitation)

► **high-risk** ADJ à haut risque ► **high roller** N (US) (gen) casse-cou* m inv ; (Gambling) flambeur* m ► **high school** N (US) ≈ lycée m ; (Brit) collège m or établissement m d'enseignement secondaire ; (US) **~ school diploma** diplôme m de fin d'études secondaires, ≈ baccalauréat m → HIGH SCHOOL ► **high-scoring** ADJ à score élevé ► **high seas** NPL **on the ~ seas** en haute mer ► **high season** N (Brit) haute saison f ► **high-sided vehicle** N véhicule m haut (donnant prise au vent) ► **high sign*** N (US) signe m convenu or d'intelligence ; **to give sb a ~ sign** faire un signe d'intelligence à qn ► **high society** N haute société f ► **high-sounding** ADJ sonore, grandiloquent (pej), ronflant (pej) ► **high-speed** ADJ (gen) ultrarapide ; **a ~-speed chase** une course poursuite ; **~-speed lens** objectif m à obturation (ultra)rapide ; **~-speed train** train m à grande vitesse, TGV ► **high-spirited** ADJ [person] plein d'entrain or de vivacité ; [horse] fougueux, fringant ► **high spirits** NPL entrain m, vivacité f ; **in ~ spirits** (= lively, energetic) plein d'entrain or de vivacité ; (= happy) tout joyeux ► **high spot** N (fig = climax) [of visit, holiday] grand moment m ; **the ~ spot of the show/evening** le clou du spectacle/de la soirée ; **to hit the ~ spots*** faire la foire* or la noce* (dans un night-club, restaurant etc) ► **high stakes** NPL (lit, fig) **to play for ~ stakes** jouer gros (jeu) ► **high street** N (Brit) [of village] grand-rue f ; [of town] rue f principale ► **high-street** ADJ (Brit) [shop, store] qui appartient à une grande chaîne ; **the ~-street banks** les grandes banques fpl ► **high-strung** ADJ (US) = **highly strung** ; **highly** ► **high summer** N le cœur de l'été ; **in ~ summer** en plein été, au cœur de l'été, au plus chaud de l'été ► **high table** N (gen) table f d'honneur ; (Scol, Univ) table f des professeurs (au réfectoire) ► **high tea** N (Brit) repas fin d'après-midi or en début de soirée ► **high tech** N high-tech m inv ► **high-tech** ADJ [equipment, product] de pointe, de haute technologie ; [computer] sophistiqué ; [company] high-tech inv, de pointe, de haute technologie ; [industry, medicine] de pointe, high-tech inv ; [weapon] de haute technologie ; [job] dans un secteur de haute technologie ; [technique] de pointe ; **the ~-tech age** l'ère f des techniques de pointe ► **high technology** N technologie f avancée or de pointe ► **high-technology** ADJ [device] d'une haute technicité ; [sector] de pointe ► **high-tensile steel** N acier m à résistance élevée ► **high-tensile wire** N fil m à résistance élevée ► **high tension** N (Elec) haute tension f ► **high-tension** ADJ (Elec) à haute tension ► **high tide** N marée f haute ; **at ~ tide** à marée haute ► **high treason** N haute trahison f ► **high-up** ADJ [person, post] de haut rang, très haut placé ♦ N* grosse légume* f, huile* f ► **high-velocity** ADJ [rifle, bullet, jet of air] à grande vitesse ► **high voltage** N haut voltage m ► **high-voltage** ADJ haut voltage inv ► **high water** N = high tide ; → **hell** ► **high-water mark** N niveau m des hautes eaux ► **high wire** N (lit = tightrope) corde f raide ; (fig) **to be walking the ~ wire** être sur la corde raide ► **high wire act** N (lit, fig) numéro m de corde raide ► **high yellow**** N (US pej) mulâtre m au teint clair, mulâtresse f au teint clair

---

HIGH SCHOOL

Aux États-Unis, les high schools réunissent les quatre années du deuxième cycle du secondaire (15 à 18 ans). Les élèves reçus à leur examen final se voient remettre leur diplôme au cours d'une importante cérémonie appelée «graduation».

La vie des high schools a inspiré de nombreux films et téléfilms américains ; on y voit le rôle qu'y jouent les sports (en particulier le football et le basket-ball) et certaines manifestations

mondaines comme le bal de fin d'année des élèves de terminale, le « senior prom ». → GRADE; GRADUATION; PROM

-high [haɪ] ADJ (in compounds) **to be knee/ shoulder-high** arriver aux genoux/épaules

highball ['haɪbɔːl] **1** N **a** (esp US = drink) whisky m à l'eau (avec de la glace) **b** (also ~ **glass** or **tumbler**) grand verre m **2** VI (US Aut‡) foncer*

highborn ['haɪbɔːn] ADJ de haute naissance, bien né

highboy ['haɪbɔɪ] N (US) commode f (haute)

highbrow ['haɪbraʊ] (slightly pej) **1** N intellectuel(le) m(f) **2** ADJ [tastes, interests] d'intellectuel; [music] pour intellectuels

highchair ['haɪtʃɛəʳ] N chaise f haute (pour enfants)

higher ['haɪəʳ] compar of high **1** ADJ [animal, primate, species, plant] supérieur; [degree, diploma] d'études supérieures; **any number ~ than six** tout nombre supérieur à six; (Scol) **the ~ forms** or **classes** les grandes classes fpl; **the ~ income brackets** les tranches fpl de revenu(s) supérieur(s) **2** ADV plus haut → **high 3** N (Scot Scol: also **Higher**) = **Higher Grade 4** COMP ► **higher education** N enseignement m supérieur ► **Higher Grade** N (Scot Scol) diplôme m de fin d'études secondaires, ≈ baccalauréat m → A LEVELS ► **Higher National Certificate** N (Brit Educ) ≈ BTS m ► **Higher National Diploma** N (Brit Educ) ≈ DUT m ► **higher-up*** N (= senior person) supérieur(e) m(f) (hiérarchique)

highfalutin(g)* [ˌhaɪfəˈluːtɪn] ADJ [behaviour, language] affecté, prétentieux; [style] ampoulé

highjack ['haɪdʒæk] VT = **hijack**
highjacker ['haɪdʒækəʳ] N = **hijacker**
highjacking ['haɪdʒækɪŋ] N = **hijacking**

highland ['haɪlənd] **1** ADJ (Brit) **Highland** [scenery, air] des Highlands; [holiday] dans les Highlands **2 highlands** NPL région f montagneuse, montagnes fpl; (Brit Geog) **the Highlands** les Highlands mpl **3** COMP ► **Highland fling** N danse f écossaise ► **Highland games** NPL jeux mpl écossais

highlander ['haɪləndəʳ] N montagnard m; (Brit) **Highlander** natif m, -ive f des Highlands

highlight ['haɪlaɪt] **1** N **a** (= high point) **the ~s of the match/the festival** les instants mpl les plus marquants du match/du festival; **the ~ of the show/evening** le clou du spectacle/de la soirée **b** (Art, lit) rehaut m; **to have ~s put in one's hair** se faire faire un balayage or des mèches fpl **2** VT **a** (= emphasize) souligner, mettre l'accent sur; **his report ~ed the plight of the homeless** son rapport a attiré l'attention sur la situation des SDF; **the incident ~s growing concern about racism** cet incident montre que le racisme inquiète de plus en plus les gens **b** (with highlighter pen) surligner; (= underline) souligner; (on computer) sélectionner

highlighter ['haɪˌlaɪtəʳ] N **a** (= pen) surligneur m **b** (for hair) produit m éclaircissant

highly ['haɪlɪ] **1** ADV **a** (= very) (gen) extrêmement; [skilled, qualified, unlikely, professional] hautement; [prized] très; [interesting, unusual] tout à fait; **~ respected** éminemment respecté; **~ acclaimed by the critics** salué par la critique; **~ recommended** [book, film, play] hautement recommandé; **she comes ~ recommended** elle est chaudement recommandée; **~ polished** (= shiny) [furniture, wood] (bien) astiqué, briqué; [gemstone] (bien) poli; **~ charged** [atmosphere] (bien) tendu; [occasion, debate] à l'atmosphère très tendue; **~ seasoned** fortement assaisonné; **to be ~ sexed** avoir de forts appétits sexuels **b** (= at or to a high level) **~-paid** [person, job] très bien payé or rémunéré; **~-trained**

[scientist, academic] qui a une formation très poussée; [sportsman] bien entraîné; **~-placed** haut inv placé; **~-regarded** ◊ **~-rated** très estimé; **~ coloured** (lit) [picture etc] haut en couleur; (fig) [description] pittoresque **c** (with vb) **to speak/think ~ of sb/sth** dire/ penser beaucoup de bien de qn/qch; **to praise sb ~** chanter les louanges de qn; **I don't rate him very ~ at all** je n'ai pas une très haute opinion de lui; **travelling by car rates very ~ in terms of convenience** la voiture est perçue comme un moyen de transport très pratique **2** COMP ► **highly strung** ADJ (esp Brit) très nerveux

highness ['haɪnɪs] N **His** or **Her/Your Highness** Son/Votre Altesse f → **royal**

highroad ['haɪrəʊd] N (esp Brit) (lit) grand-route f; (fig) **the ~ to success** la voie de la réussite

hightail* ['haɪteɪl] VT (esp US) **they ~ed it back to town** ils sont revenus en ville à toute vitesse or à tout(e) berzingue‡

highway ['haɪweɪ] **1** N **a** (US = main road) grande route f, route f nationale **b** (also **public ~**) voie f publique; **the king's** or **queen's ~** la voie publique; **through the ~s and byways of Sussex** par tous les chemins du Sussex **2** COMP ► **highway code** N (Brit) code m de la route ► **highway patrol** N (US: also **state ~ patrol**) police f de la route ► **highway robbery** N (lit) banditisme m de grand chemin; (fig) **it's ~ robbery** c'est du vol manifeste or caractérisé ► **Highways Department** N (Admin) administration f des Ponts et Chaussées ► **highways engineer** N ingénieur m des Ponts et Chaussées

highwayman ['haɪweɪmən] N (pl **-men**) (Hist) bandit m de grand chemin

hijack ['haɪdʒæk] **1** VT (lit) détourner; (fig) récupérer **2** N (lit) détournement m; (fig) récupération f

hijacker ['haɪdʒækəʳ] N pirate m (de l'air/de la route/du rail etc), auteur m d'un détournement

hijacking ['haɪdʒækɪŋ] N (lit, fig) détournement m

hike [haɪk] **1** N **a** randonnée f (à pied); (Mil, Sport) marche f à pied; **to go on** or **for a ~** faire une randonnée (pédestre) **b** (= increase) [of prices etc] hausse f, augmentation f **2** VI **a** faire des randonnées (pédestres); **we spent our holidays hiking in France** nous avons passé nos vacances à faire des randonnées pédestres à travers la France **b** (US = increase) [price etc] augmenter **3** VT = **hike up**

► **hike up** VT SEP **a** (= hitch up) [+ skirt] remonter **b** (= increase) [+ prices, amounts] augmenter

hiker ['haɪkəʳ] N randonneur m, -euse f

hiking ['haɪkɪŋ] **1** N randonnées fpl (à pied) **2** COMP ► **hiking boots** NPL chaussures fpl de randonnée or de marche

hilarious [hɪˈlɛərɪəs] ADJ très drôle, tordant*

hilariously [hɪˈlɛərɪəslɪ] ADV comiquement; **~ funny** absolument tordant*; **~ old-fashioned** démodé et ridicule

hilarity [hɪˈlærɪtɪ] N hilarité f; **it caused a lot of ~** cela a déchaîné l'hilarité

hill [hɪl] **1** N colline f; (gen lower) coteau m; (rounded) mamelon m; (= slope) côte f, pente f; (up) montée f; (down) descente f; **he was going up the ~** il montait la colline; (liter) **up ~ and down dale** ◊ **over ~ and dale** par monts et par vaux; **as old as the ~s** vieux comme Hérode; (fig) **he's over the ~*** (= old) il se fait vieux → **ant, molehill, uphill 2** COMP ► **hill climb** N (Sport) course f de côtes ► **hill climber** N = **hill walker** ► **hill climbing** N = **hill walking** ► **hill farmer** N (esp Brit) agriculteur m pratiquant l'élevage sur hauts pâturages

► **hill start** N (Aut) démarrage m en côte ► **hill walker** N randonneur m, -euse f ► **hill walking** N randonnées fpl (en montagne)

hillbilly* ['hɪlbɪlɪ] **1** N (US: gen pej) péquenaud* m (pej), rustaud m (pej) (montagnard du sud des USA) **2** COMP ► **hillbilly music** N musique f folk inv (originaire des montagnes du sud des USA)

hilliness ['hɪlɪnɪs] N caractère m accidenté

hillock ['hɪlək] N monticule m

hillside ['hɪlsaɪd] N (flanc m de) coteau m; **on the ~** à flanc de coteau

hilltop ['hɪltɒp] N **on the ~** en haut de or au sommet de la colline

hilly ['hɪlɪ] ADJ [country] vallonné, accidenté; [road] qui monte et qui descend

hilt [hɪlt] N [of sword] poignée f; [of dagger] manche m; [of pistol] crosse f; **she's in debt up to the ~** elle est endettée jusqu'au cou; **we're mortgaged to the ~** nous nous sommes endettés jusqu'au cou avec l'achat de notre maison (or appartement); **to back** or **support sb to the ~** être derrière qn quoi qu'il arrive, soutenir qn à fond; **he played his role to the ~** il a joué son rôle avec conviction

him, Him (Rel) [hɪm] PERS PRON **a** (direct) (unstressed) le; (before vowel) l'; (stressed) lui; **I see ~** je le vois; **I have seen ~** je l'ai vu; **I know HER but I've never seen HIM** je la connais, elle, mais lui je ne l'ai jamais vu **b** (indirect) lui; **I give ~ the book** je lui donne le livre; **I'm speaking to ~** je lui parle, c'est à lui que je parle **c** (after prep etc) lui; **I am thinking of ~** je pense à lui; **I'm proud of ~** je suis fier de lui; **without ~** sans lui; **if I were ~** si j'étais lui, si j'étais à sa place; **it's ~** c'est lui; **younger than ~** plus jeune que lui **d** celui; **to ~ who might complain, I should point out that ...** à ceux qui se plaindraient, je ferais remarquer que ...

Himalayan [ˌhɪmərˈleɪən] ADJ (gen) himalayen; [expedition] dans l'Himalaya

Himalayas [ˌhɪmərˈleɪəz] NPL (chaîne f de l')Himalaya m

himself [hɪmˈself] PERS PRON (reflexive) (direct and indirect) se; (emphatic) lui-même; (after prep) lui; **he has hurt ~** il s'est blessé; **he poured ~ a whisky** il s'est servi un whisky; **"why not?" he said to ~** « pourquoi pas ? » se dit-il; **he told me ~** il me l'a dit lui-même; **I saw the teacher ~** j'ai vu le professeur lui-même or en personne; **he kept three for ~** il s'en est réservé trois; **she asked him for a photo of ~** elle lui a demandé une photo de lui; **there's no work and no future for students like ~** il n'y a pas de travail et pas d'avenir pour les étudiants comme lui; **(all) by ~** tout seul; **he hasn't been ~ lately** (= not behaving normally) il n'est pas dans son état normal ces temps-ci; (= not feeling well) il n'est pas dans son assiette ces temps-ci

hind¹ [haɪnd] N (pl **hinds** or **hind**) (Zool) biche f

hind² [haɪnd] ADJ [legs, feet, paws] de derrière; (hum) **to get up on one's ~ legs*** se lever pour parler; **she could** or **would talk the ~ leg(s) off a donkey*** c'est un vrai moulin à paroles

hinder¹ ['haɪndəʳ] ADJ compar of **hind²**

hinder² ['hɪndəʳ] VT (= obstruct, impede) entraver, gêner; (= delay) retarder; (= prevent) empêcher, arrêter; **the rescue team's efforts were ~ed by the bad weather** les efforts de l'équipe de sauveteurs ont été entravés par le mauvais temps; **we want to help, not ~**, the progress of the scheme nous voulons faire avancer le projet, pas l'entraver; **being disabled has done nothing to ~ her career** son handicap n'a pas du tout entravé sa carrière; **the heavy jacket ~ed him as he tried to swim** sa lourde veste le gênait pour nager; **poor productivity ~s economic growth** lorsque la productivité est faible, cela entrave la croissance économique; **he does not let rac-**

ism ~ him il ne se laisse pas arrêter par le racisme ; **the rocky terrain ~ed their progress** le terrain rocheux les a freinés ; **poor diet is ~ing her recovery** sa mauvaise alimentation l'empêche de guérir plus vite ; **high interest rates are ~ing recovery** les taux d'intérêt élevés font obstacle à la reprise or freinent la reprise ; (= prevent) **to ~ sb from doing sth** empêcher qn de faire qch ; (= impede) **restrictions that ~ them from doing their job** les restrictions qui les gênent dans leur travail

Hindi ['hɪndɪ] N (Ling) hindi m

hindmost ['haɪndməʊst] ADV dernier → **devil, every**

hindquarters ['haɪnd‚kwɔ:təz] NPL arrière-train m, train m de derrière

hindrance ['hɪndrəns] N obstacle m ; **to be a ~ to sb/sth** gêner qn/qch ; **he is more of a ~ than a help** il gêne plus qu'il n'aide ; **these attacks are a ~ to reconciliation** ces attaques font obstacle à la réconciliation ; **the issue has been a constant ~ to normal relations between the two countries** ce problème n'a cessé de faire obstacle à la normalisation des relations entre les deux pays ; **they crossed the border without ~** ils ont traversé la frontière sans problème or difficulté

hindsight ['haɪndsaɪt] N **with** or **in ~** ◊ **with the benefit of ~** avec du recul, rétrospectivement ; **it was, in ~, a mistaken judgement** rétrospectivement or avec du recul, je pense que c'était une erreur de jugement

Hindu ['hɪndu:] 1 ADJ hindou 2 N hindou(e) m(f)

Hinduism ['hɪndu‚ɪzəm] N hindouisme m

Hindustan [‚hɪndʊ'stɑ:n] N l'Hindoustan m

Hindustani [‚hɪndʊ'stɑ:nɪ] 1 ADJ hindou 2 N a Hindoustani(e) m(f) b (Ling) hindoustani m

hinge [hɪndʒ] 1 N [of door] gond m, charnière f ; [of box] charnière f ; (fig) pivot m, charnière f ; [of stamp hinge] charnière f ; **the door came off its ~s** la porte est sortie de ses gonds 2 VT [+ door] mettre dans ses gonds ; [+ box] mettre des charnières à ; **a ~d lid** un couvercle à charnière(s) ; **a ~d flap** [of counter] (in shop, bar) abattant m ; **the mirror was ~d to a wooden frame** le miroir était fixé à un cadre en bois par des charnières 3 VI a (Tech) pivoter (on sur) b (fig) **to ~ on** or **upon sth** dépendre de qch ; **everything ~s on his decision** tout dépend de sa décision 4 COMP ► **hinged girder** N (Tech) poutre f articulée ► **hinge joint** N (Anat) diarthrose f

hint [hɪnt] 1 N a allusion f ; **to drop a ~** ◊ **to throw out a ~** faire une allusion ; **to drop a ~ that ...** faire une allusion au fait que ... ; **he dropped me a ~ that he would like an invitation** il m'a fait comprendre or il m'a laissé entendre qu'il aimerait être invité ; **he dropped a gentle ~ about it** il y a fait une allusion discrète ; **a broad** or **strong** or **heavy ~** une allusion transparente or à peine voilée ; **there are strong ~s from the government that ...** le gouvernement a clairement laissé entendre que ... ; **I dropped heavy ~s that I'd love a new coat for my birthday** j'ai insisté lourdement sur le fait que je voulais un nouveau manteau pour mon anniversaire ; **she gave me a subtle ~ not to expect promotion** elle m'a fait comprendre discrètement qu'il ne fallait pas compter sur une promotion ; **he knows how to take a ~** il comprend à demi-mot, il comprend les allusions ; **he took the ~ and left at once** il a compris sans qu'on ait besoin de lui expliquer et est parti sur-le-champ ; **I can take a ~** (ça va,) j'ai compris ; **he can't take a ~** il ne comprend pas vite ; **I'll give you a ~ - the answer has two words** je vais vous donner un indice or vous mettre sur la piste ; **the réponse est en deux mots ; he gave no ~ of his feelings** il n'a rien laissé transparaître de ses sentiments ; **~s and tips for trav-**

ellers conseils mpl aux voyageurs ; **~s on maintenance** conseils mpl d'entretien
b (= trace) [of colour] touche f ; [of taste, flavour] soupçon m ; **she was wearing a ~ of eyeshadow** elle avait mis un peu or une touche de fard à paupières ; **there was a ~ of sadness in his smile** il y avait un je ne sais quoi de triste dans son sourire ; **there was a ~ of desperation in his voice** il y avait une pointe de désespoir dans sa voix ; **there was no ~ of apology in his voice** il n'y avait pas la moindre trace de remords dans sa voix ; **"why are you here?" she said, with no ~ of irony** « que faites-vous ici ? » dit-elle, sans la moindre ironie ; **at the first ~ of trouble** à la moindre alerte, au moindre problème ; **there's a ~ of spring in the air** il y a un petit air printanier
2 VT (= insinuate) insinuer (that que) ; **he ~ed strongly that ...** il a lourdement insinué que ... ; **he ~ed to me that he was unhappy** il m'a laissé entendre or fait comprendre qu'il était malheureux
3 VI **to ~ at sth** faire allusion à qch ; **what are you ~ing at?** qu'est-ce que vous voulez dire par là ? ; **are you ~ing at something?** c'est une allusion ? ; **the newspapers ~ed darkly at conspiracies** les journaux ont fait des allusions inquiétantes à des complots ; **the president ~ed at the possibility of tax cuts** le président a laissé entendre qu'il pourrait y avoir une baisse des impôts

hinterland ['hɪntəlænd] N arrière-pays m inv

hip¹ [hɪp] 1 N a (Anat) hanche f ; **with (one's) hands on (one's) ~s** les mains sur les hanches ; **to break one's ~** se casser le col du fémur → **shoot** b (Archit) arête f (d'un toit) 2 COMP ► **hip bath** N bain m de siège ► **hip flask** N flasque f ► **hip joint** N articulation f coxofémorale or de la hanche ► **hip measurement** N = hip size ► **hipped roof** N (Archit) toit m en croupe ► **hip pocket** N poche f revolver inv ► **hip replacement (operation)** N pose f d'une prothèse de la hanche ; **she's waiting for/she's had a ~ replacement** elle attend/on lui a posé une prothèse de la hanche ► **hip size** N tour m de hanches ; **what is her ~ size?** quel est son tour de hanches ?, combien fait-elle de tour de hanches ?

hip² [hɪp] N (Bot) cynorrhodon m

hip³ [hɪp] EXCL **~ ~ hurrah!** hip hip hip hourra !

hip⁴* [hɪp] 1 ADJ (= up-to-date) dans le vent*, à la page 2 VT (US) mettre au parfum*

hipbone ['hɪpbəʊn] N os m iliaque or de la hanche

hip-hop ['hɪphɒp] N hip-hop m

hiphuggers ['hɪphʌgəz] NPL pantalon m taille basse

hipped [hɪpt] ADJ (US) **to be ~ on sth*** être dingue* de qch

-hipped [hɪpt] ADJ (in compounds) **broad-hipped** large de hanches, aux hanches larges ; **narrow-hipped** aux hanches étroites

hippie* ['hɪpɪ] N (in the sixties) hippie mf ; (modern-day) baba mf cool ; **an ageing ~** un hippie sur le retour

hippo* ['hɪpəʊ] N ABBR = hippopotamus

Hippocrates [hɪ'pɒkrə‚ti:z] N Hippocrate m

Hippocratic oath [‚hɪpəʊ'krætɪk] N **the ~** le serment d'Hippocrate

hippodrome ['hɪpədrəʊm] N hippodrome m

Hippolytus [hɪ'pɒlɪtəs] N Hippolyte m

hippopotamus [‚hɪpə'pɒtəməs] N (pl hippopotamuses or hippopotami [‚hɪpə'pɒtəmaɪ]) hippopotame m

hippy¹* ['hɪpɪ] = hippie

hippy²* ['hɪpɪ] ADJ aux hanches larges, large de hanches

hipster ['hɪpstə'] 1 N a (Brit) **~ skirt** jupe f taille basse → **2** b (US*) jeune homme m

dans le vent (1940-50) 2 **hipsters** NPL (Brit) pantalon m taille basse

hire ['haɪə'] 1 N (NonC: Brit = act of hiring) [of car, boat, clothes, hall] location f ; **for ~** [car, boat, building] à louer ; [taxi] libre ; **on ~** en location ; **to let out sth on ~** louer qch ; **car/cycle/ski ~** location f de voitures/de vélos/de skis 2 VT a (Brit = rent) [+ car, boat, clothes, hall] louer ; **a ~d car** une voiture louée or de location b (= employ) [+ person] engager, embaucher ; **~d man** (for season) ouvrier m saisonnier ; (on daily basis) ouvrier m à la journée ; **a ~d killer** un tueur à gages 3 VI embaucher, recruter ; **she's in charge of all hiring and firing at the company** c'est elle qui est responsable du recrutement et des licenciements au sein de l'entreprise 4 COMP ► **hire car** N (Brit) voiture f de location ► **hire charges** NPL (Brit) frais mpl de location, prix m de (la) location ► **hire purchase** N (Brit) achat m or vente f à crédit, achat m or vente f à tempérament ; **on ~ purchase** à crédit ► **hire purchase agreement** N (Brit) contrat m de crédit
► **hire out** VT SEP a (Brit = rent out) [+ car, tools] louer, donner en location b (US) **he ~s himself out as a gardener** il fait des journées (or des heures) de jardinier

hireling ['haɪəlɪŋ] N (pej) mercenaire m

Hiroshima [‚hɪrɒ'ʃi:mə] N Hiroshima

hirsute ['hɜ:sju:t] ADJ velu, poilu

his [hɪz] 1 POSS ADJ son, sa, ses ; **~ book** son livre ; **~ table** sa table ; **~ friend** son ami(e) ; **~ clothes** ses vêtements ; **HIS book** son livre à lui ; **he has broken ~ leg** il s'est cassé la jambe 2 POSS PRON le sien, la sienne, les siens, les siennes ; **my hands are clean, ~ are dirty** mes mains sont propres, les siennes sont sales ; **~ is a specialized department** sa section est une section spécialisée ; **this book is ~** ce livre est à lui, ce livre est le sien ; **this poem is ~** ce poème est de lui ; **the house became ~** la maison est devenue la sienne ; **it is not ~ to decide** ce n'est pas à lui de décider, il ne lui appartient pas de décider ; **a friend of ~** un de ses amis (à lui) ; **it's no fault of ~** ce n'est pas de sa faute (à lui) ; **no advice of ~ could prevent her doing it** aucun conseil de sa part ne pouvait l'empêcher de le faire ; (pej) **that car of ~** sa fichue* voiture ; **that stupid son of ~** son idiot de fils ; **that temper of ~** son sale caractère ; **that awful laugh of ~** ce rire abominable qu'il a

Hispanic [hɪ'spænɪk] 1 ADJ (gen) hispanique ; (in America) hispano-américain 2 N Hispano-Américain(e) m(f)

Hispano... [hɪ'spænəʊ] PREF hispano-

hiss [hɪs] 1 VI [person, snake] siffler ; [cat] cracher ; [gas, steam] chuinter, siffler 2 VT [+ actor, speaker] siffler ; **"come here", he ~ed** « viens ici », siffla-t-il 3 N sifflement m ; (Theat) **~es** sifflet(s) m(pl)

histogram ['hɪstəgræm] N histogramme m

histologist [hɪ'stɒlədʒɪst] N histologiste mf

histology [hɪ'stɒlədʒɪ] N histologie f

historian [hɪ'stɔ:rɪən] N historien(ne) m(f)

historic [hɪ'stɒrɪk] 1 ADJ (gen) historique ; **site of ~ interest** site m historique ; **a ~ occasion** un événement historique 2 COMP ► **historic present** N (Gram) présent m historique or de narration

historical [hɪ'stɒrɪkəl] 1 ADJ (gen) historique ; **the ~ background to the case** le rappel historique or l'historique m de l'affaire ; **place of ~ interest** monument m or site m historique ; **of ~ importance** d'une importance historique ; **a ~ landmark** un événement historique marquant, un jalon dans l'histoire ; **a famous ~ figure** un personnage historique célèbre ; **from a ~ perspective** d'un point de vue historique; **~ research** recherche *f* historique; **a ~ record** une source historique; **there is no ~ precedent for this** sur le plan historique, il n'y a aucun précédent 2 COMP ► **historical linguistics** N (*NonC*) linguistique *f* diachronique ► **historical novel** N roman *m* historique ► **historical present** N (*Gram*) = historic present; → historic

historically [hɪˈstɒrɪkəlɪ] ADV (= *traditionally*) traditionnellement; (= *in historical terms*) [*important, accurate*] historiquement; [*consider*] sur le plan historique; **~, there is no precedent for this** sur le plan historique, ceci n'a aucun précédent; **~ speaking** historiquement parlant

historiography [ˌhɪstɒrɪˈɒɡrəfɪ] N historiographie *f*

history [ˈhɪstərɪ] N a (*NonC*) histoire *f*; **to make ~** être historique; **she will go down in ~ for what she did** elle entrera dans l'histoire pour ce qu'elle a fait; **it will go down in ~ (as ...)** [*event, day, decision*] cela entrera dans l'histoire (comme étant ...); **one of the most dramatic moments in Polish ~** un des moments les plus marquants de l'histoire polonaise; **the highest salary in television ~** le salaire le plus élevé de l'histoire de la télévision; **religious ~** l'histoire *f* des religions; **military ~** l'histoire *f* militaire; (*fig*) **that's all ancient ~** c'est de l'histoire ancienne tout cela; (*fig*) **the recent ceasefire agreement is already ~** le récent cessez-le-feu n'est déjà plus qu'un souvenir; **... and the rest is ~** ... le reste appartient à l'histoire → natural
b **I don't know the ~ of this necklace** je ne connais pas l'histoire de ce collier; **what is his medical ~?** quel est son passé médical?; **he has a ~ of psychiatric disorders** il a des antécédents de troubles psychiatriques; **the accused had a ~ of violent behaviour** l'accusé était déjà connu pour avoir commis des actes de violence → case¹

histrionic [ˌhɪstrɪˈɒnɪk] ADJ théâtral; (*pej*) histrionique, de cabotin (*pej*); **~ ability** talent *m* dramatique

histrionically [ˌhɪstrɪˈɒnɪkəlɪ] ADV d'un air théâtral *or* mélodramatique

histrionics [ˌhɪstrɪˈɒnɪks] NPL art *m* dramatique; (*pej*) **I'm tired of his ~** j'en ai assez de ses airs dramatiques *or* de son cinéma* (*fig*)

hit [hɪt] (*vb: pret, ptp* **hit**) 1 N a (= *stroke, blow*) coup *m*; (*in baseball, cricket*) coup *m* de batte; (*in tennis*) coup *m* de raquette; (*fig*) attaque *f*; **the film was a ~ at current government policy** le film était une attaque contre la politique actuelle du gouvernement → free
b (= *successful stroke*) coup *m* réussi, beau coup *m*; (*Fencing*) touche *f*; (*Mil*: *with bomb, bullet, shell*) tir *m* réussi; (*gen*) **three ~s and three misses** trois succès et trois échecs → direct, score
c (*gen*) (gros) succès *m*; (= *song*) tube* *m*; **the play/song was a big ~** la pièce/chanson a eu un énorme succès; **to make a ~ of sth*** réussir (pleinement) qch; **she was** *or* **made a big ~ with my sister** elle a beaucoup plu à ma sœur
d (* = *dose*) [*of crack, speed, caffeine etc*] dose* *f* → score
e (* = *assassination*) meurtre *m*, coup *m*

2 VT a (= *strike*) (*once*) frapper; (*repeatedly*) taper sur; (= *knock against*) heurter, cogner; (= *reach*) atteindre; (*Billiards, Fencing*) toucher; (*Typ, Comput*) [+ *key*] appuyer sur; (*fig* = *hurt, annoy*) blesser; **he ~ his brother** il a frappé son frère; **he ~ me!** (*once*) il m'a frappé!; (*repeatedly*) il m'a tapé dessus!; **his father used to ~ him** son père le battait; **to ~ sb where it hurts** (*lit: in fight*) frapper qn là où ça fait mal; (*fig*) toucher qn à son point faible; **she ~ him a blow across the face** (*with hand*) elle l'a frappé au visage; (*with truncheon etc*) elle lui a donné un coup de matraque *etc* sur le visage; **to ~**

one's **knee/elbow on** *or* **against sth** se cogner *or* se heurter le genou/coude contre qch; **his head ~ the corner of the table** ◊ **he ~ his head on the corner of the table** sa tête a cogné contre *or* heurté le coin de la table, il s'est cogné la tête sur le coin de la table; **the stone ~ the window** la pierre a cogné contre la fenêtre; **he ~ the nail with a hammer** il a tapé sur le clou avec un marteau; (*fig*) **that ~ home!** le coup a porté!; (*Brit fig*) **to ~ the buffers** [*plan, project*] s'en aller en eau de boudin; (*fig*) **to ~ the wall** [*athlete etc*] connaître un passage à vide; **to ~ the ground running*** se mettre immédiatement au travail; **he was ~ by flying glass** il a reçu des éclats de verre; **the president was ~ by three bullets** le président a reçu trois balles; **the bullet ~ him in the chest** il a reçu la balle dans la poitrine; **the house was ~ by a bomb** la maison a été atteinte par *or* a reçu une bombe; **the tree was ~ by lightning** l'arbre a été frappé par la foudre; **the hurricane ~ San Francisco yesterday evening** l'ouragan a frappé San Francisco hier soir; **my plane had been ~** mon avion avait été touché; **you won't know what's ~ you when the baby arrives!*** ta vie va être bouleversée par l'arrivée du bébé → down², mark
b (*fig* = *affect adversely*) toucher; **California was the area hardest ~ by the storms** la Californie a été la région la plus touchée par les tempêtes; **production was ~ by the strike** la production a été touchée par la grève; **the rise in prices will ~ the poorest families first** la hausse des prix affectera *or* touchera d'abord les familles les plus pauvres; **he was hard ~ by his losses** ses pertes l'ont durement touché *or* atteint; **industry has been hard ~ by the recession** l'industrie a été gravement touchée par la récession; **the public was hardest ~ by the strike** c'est le public qui a été touché le plus durement par la grève
c (*fig*) **to ~ the papers** [*news, story*] être à la une* des journaux, faire les gros titres des journaux; **what will happen when the story ~s the front page?** que se passera-t-il quand on lira cette histoire en première page des journaux?; **the car ~* 100mph just before it crashed** la voiture a atteint les 160 km/h juste avant l'accident; **oil prices ~ record levels yesterday** le prix du pétrole a atteint un niveau record hier; **then it ~ me*** (= *realization*) alors ça a fait tilt; **it suddenly ~ me*** that ... = je me suis soudain rendu compte que ..., j'ai soudain réalisé que ...; **you've ~ it!*** ça y est*, tu as trouvé!; (*US Cards*) **he ~ me with a six of spades*** il m'a flanqué un six de pique; (*US*) **to ~ sb for 10 dollars*** taper* qn de 10 dollars; **to ~ the bottle*** se mettre à picoler*; **to ~ the ceiling*** *or* **the roof*** sortir de ses gonds; **to ~ the deck*** (= *get down*) s'aplatir au sol; (= *get knocked down*) (*gen*) tomber par terre; [*boxer*] aller au tapis; **to ~ the dirt*** s'aplatir au sol; **to ~ the hay*** *or* **the sack*** se pieuter*; **to ~ the road*** *or* **the trail*** se mettre en route; **in May the candidates will ~ the campaign trail** en mai les candidats se lanceront dans la campagne électorale; **to ~ the dance floor*** aller sur la piste (de danse); **when will Jim ~ town?*** quand est-ce que Jim va débarquer* en ville?; **we should ~ Las Vegas in a couple of hours** nous devrions arriver à Las Vegas dans une ou deux heures; **to ~ the shops*** [*article*] arriver dans les magasins; [*person*] faire les magasins; **to ~ the bookshops** *or* (*US*) **bookstores** [*new publication*] sortir en librairie; **it ~s the spot*** [*food, drink*] ça fait du bien!; (= *succeeds*) ça tombe à pic!*; **to ~ sb for six*** [*cold, flu*] lessiver* qn; [*news*] faire un choc à qn → headline, high, jackpot, skid
d (= *collide with*) heurter, rentrer dans*; **the car ~ a pedestrian** la voiture a renversé un piéton
e (= *find*) trouver, tomber sur; [+ *problems,*

difficulties] rencontrer; **at last we ~ the right road** nous sommes enfin tombés sur la bonne route; **we've ~ a snag** on est tombés sur un os*
3 VI (= *collide*) se heurter, se cogner (**against** à, contre)
4 COMP ► **hit-and-miss** ADV au petit bonheur (la chance), un peu n'importe comment ◊ ADJ [*work*] fait au petit bonheur (la chance); [*attitude*] désinvolte; [*technique*] empirique; **it's a ~-and-miss affair** c'est une question de chance; **the way she painted the room was rather ~-and-miss** elle a peint la pièce un peu n'importe comment; **it was all rather ~-and-miss** tout se passait plutôt au petit bonheur (la chance), tout était à la va-comme-je-te-pousse ► **hit-and-run accident** N accident *m* avec délit de fuite ► **hit-and-run driver** N chauffard *m* coupable du délit de fuite ► **hit-and-run raid** N (*Mil*) raid *m* éclair *inv* ► **hit-and-run strike** N grève *f* éclair ► **hit list** N liste *f* noire; (*fig*) **he's on her ~ list** elle l'a dans le collimateur ► **hit-or-miss** ADV, ADJ = hit-and-miss ► **hit parade** N hit-parade *m* ► **hit show** N (*Theat*) revue *f* à succès; (*TV*) émission *f* à succès ► **hit single** N (*Mus*) tube* *m* ► **hit squad*** N commando *m* de tueurs

► **hit back** 1 VI (*lit*) frapper en retour; (*fig*) riposter; (*fig*) **to ~ back at sb** se venger de qn; **to ~ back at sb's criticism/suggestions/accusations** riposter à la critique/aux suggestions/aux accusations de qn 2 VT SEP **to ~ sb back** frapper qn en retour
► **hit off** VT SEP **to ~ it off with sb** bien s'entendre avec qn; **they ~ it off straight away** ils se sont immédiatement bien entendus; **he has never ~ it off with Douglas** il ne s'est jamais entendu avec Douglas
► **hit on** VT FUS a = hit upon b (*US*) draguer*
► **hit out** VI a (*lit*) **the police ~ out with batons and iron bars** la police a distribué des coups de matraque et de barres de fer; **to ~ out at sb** donner un coup à qn b (*fig*) riposter; **he ~ out angrily when I suggested it had been his fault** il a riposté avec colère quand j'ai suggéré que c'était de sa faute; **to ~ out at sb** s'en prendre à qn; **to ~ out at sb's criticism/suggestions/accusations** riposter à la critique/aux suggestions/aux accusations de qn
► **hit upon** VT FUS tomber sur, trouver

hitch [hɪtʃ] 1 N a (= *obstacle*) (petit) problème *m*; **there's been a ~** il y a eu un (petit) problème; **there's been a ~ in their plans** leur projet s'est heurté à un obstacle; **after some technical ~es the show finally got under way** après quelques problèmes techniques le spectacle a finalement commencé; **the only ~ is that ...** le seul ennui c'est que ...; **without a ~** sans accroc
b (*US*: *in army or in jail*) période passée dans l'armée ou en prison
c (= *knot*) (*gen*) nœud *m*; (*also* ~ **knot**) deux demi-clés *fpl*
d **to give sth a ~ (up)** remonter qch
2 VT a (*also* ~ **up**) [+ *trousers, skirt*] remonter b (= *fasten*) accrocher, attacher, fixer; (*Naut*) amarrer; **to get ~ed*** se marier; (*US*) **to ~ one's wagon to a star** aspirer à de hautes destinées; (*US*) **to ~ one's wagon to sb** chercher à profiter de la destinée de qn
c * **to ~ a lift** (= *be hitch-hiking*) faire du stop*; (= *get a lift*) être pris en stop*; **to ~ a lift** *or* **a ride to Paris** faire du stop* jusqu'à Paris, être pris en stop* jusqu'à Paris; **she ~ed a lift into town** elle a fait du stop* pour aller en ville, quelqu'un l'a déposée en ville; **I ~ed a ride with a truck driver** j'ai été pris en stop* par un camion *or* un routier
3 VI* = hitch-hike
4 COMP ► **hitch-hike** VI faire du stop* *or* de l'auto-stop; **they ~-hiked to Paris** ils sont allés à Paris en stop, ils ont fait du stop* *or* de

l'auto-stop jusqu'à Paris ► **hitch-hiker** N auto-stoppeur m, -euse f ► **hitch-hiking** N auto-stop m, stop* m

►**hitch up** VT SEP a [+ horses, oxen] atteler (**to** à) b = **hitch 2a**

hi-tec(h) ['haɪ'tek] ADJ = **high-tech**; → **high**

hither ['hɪðə'] 1 ADV a (†† = to here) [bring] ici; **come ~!** viens çà†† ► **come**; **his journey ~** son voyage en ce lieu b **~ and thither** (Brit) ◊ **~ and yon** (US) (= to and fro) çà et là 2 ADJ †† de ce côté-ci

hitherto [,hɪðə'tuː] ADV jusqu'ici

Hitler ['hɪtlə'] 1 N Hitler m 2 COMP ► **the Hitler Youth (Movement)** N les jeunesses fpl hitlériennes

Hitlerian [hɪt'lɪərɪən] ADJ hitlérien

Hitlerism ['hɪtlərɪzm] N hitlérisme m

hitman* ['hɪtmæn] N (pl **-men**) tueur m à gages

Hittite ['hɪtaɪt] 1 N a Hittite mf b (Ling) hittite m 2 ADJ hittite

HIV [,eɪtʃaɪ'viː] 1 N (Med) (ABBR = **human immunodeficiency virus**) HIV m, VIH m 2 COMP ► **HIV-negative** ADJ séronégatif ► **HIV-positive** ADJ séropositif ► **HIV-related** ADJ associé au sida ► **HIV virus** N virus m HIV

hive [haɪv] 1 N (= place, also fig) ruche f; (with bees in it) essaim m; (fig) **a ~ of activity** or **industry** une vraie ruche 2 VT mettre dans une ruche 3 VI essaimer

►**hive off** (Brit) 1 VI a (= separate) se séparer (**from** de), essaimer b (= rush off) filer*, se tirer; 2 VT SEP séparer (**from** de); **they ~d off the infant school to a different building** ils ont déplacé la maternelle pour l'installer dans un autre bâtiment; **the branch may be ~d off into a separate company** il se peut que cette succursale devienne une société indépendante

hives [haɪvz] NPL (Med) urticaire f

hiya: ['haɪjə] EXCL salut !*

Hizbollah, Hizbullah ['hɪzbə'lɑː] N = **Hezbollah**

hl (ABBR = **hectolitre(s)**) hl

HM [eɪtʃ'em] N (ABBR = **His** or **Her Majesty**) S.M., Sa Majesté

HMG [,eɪtʃem'dʒiː] N (Brit) (ABBR = **His** or **Her Majesty's Government**) → **majesty**

HMI [,eɪtʃem'aɪ] N (Brit Educ) (ABBR = **His** or **Her Majesty's Inspector**) ≈ inspecteur m, -trice f général(e) de l'enseignement secondaire

HMS [,eɪtʃem'es] N (Brit) (ABBR = **His** or **Her Majesty's Ship**) → **ship**

HMSO [,eɪtʃemes'əʊ] N (Brit) (ABBR = **His** or **Her Majesty's Stationery Office**) → **stationery**

HNC [,eɪtʃen'siː] N (Brit Educ) (ABBR = **Higher National Certificate**) ≈ BTS m

HND [,eɪtʃen'diː] N (Brit Educ) (ABBR = **Higher National Diploma**) ≈ DUT m

ho [həʊ] EXCL **ho ho!** ah ah (ah)!

hoagie, hoagy ['həʊɡɪ] N (US) grand sandwich m mixte

hoard [hɔːd] 1 N réserves fpl, provisions fpl; (pej) magot m (pej); (= treasure) trésor m; **a ~ of food** des provisions fpl, des réserves fpl; **a ~ of silver and jewels** un trésor composé d'argenterie et de bijoux; (pej) tout un stock d'argenterie et de bijoux; **a squirrel's ~ of nuts** les réserves or provisions de noisettes d'un écureuil 2 VT (also **~ up**) [+ food etc] amasser, mettre en réserve; (pej) stocker (pej); [+ money] accumuler, amasser

hoarder ['hɔːdə'] N **to be a ~** ne rien jeter

hoarding¹ ['hɔːdɪŋ] N (= act of saving) entassement m, accumulation f; [of capital] thésaurisation f

hoarding² ['hɔːdɪŋ] N a (Brit: for advertisements) panneau m d'affichage or publicitaire b (= fence) palissade f

hoarfrost ['hɔː,frɒst] N gelée f blanche, givre m

hoarse [hɔːs] ADJ [person] enroué; [voice] rauque, enroué; **to be ~** avoir la voix rauque, être enroué; **he shouted himself ~** il s'est enroué à force de crier

hoarsely ['hɔːslɪ] ADV d'une voix rauque

hoarseness ['hɔːsnɪs] N enrouement m

hoary ['hɔːrɪ] ADJ a [hair] blanchi, blanc neigeux inv; [person] (lit, liter: also **~-headed**) chenu (liter); (fig) vénérable; **a ~ old joke** une blague éculée; **a ~ old tradition** une vieille tradition surannée b (Bot) couvert de duvet blanc

hoax [həʊks] 1 N canular m; **to play a ~ on sb** monter or faire un canular à qn; **the phone call was a ~** le coup de téléphone était le fait d'un mauvais plaisant 2 VT faire or monter un canular à; **we were completely ~ed** on nous a eus*; **to ~ sb into believing sth** faire croire qch à qn

hob [hɒb] N a (on cooker) plan m de cuisson; (Brit: on old-fashioned cooker) rond m; (by fireplace) plaque f (de foyer) (où la bouilloire etc est tenue au chaud)

hobble ['hɒbl] 1 VI clopiner, boitiller; **to ~ along** aller clopin-clopant; **to ~ in/out** etc entrer/sortir etc en clopinant 2 VT (lit, fig) entraver 3 N (for horses) entrave f 4 COMP ► **hobble skirt** N jupe f entravée

hobbledehoy [,hɒbldɪ'hɔɪ] N grand dadais m

hobby ['hɒbɪ] 1 N passe-temps m inv, hobby m; **he began to paint as a ~** il a commencé la peinture comme passe-temps 2 COMP ► **hobby-horse** N (= toy) tête f de cheval (sur un manche); (= rocking horse) cheval m à bascule; (fig) sujet m favori, dada* m; (fig) **he's off on his ~-horse** le voilà reparti (sur son dada)

hobbyist ['hɒbɪɪst] N amateur m; **a photo ~** un photographe amateur

hobgoblin ['hɒb,ɡɒblɪn] N (= elf) lutin m; (fig = bugbear) croquemitaine m

hobnail ['hɒbneɪl] 1 N caboche f, clou m 2 COMP ► **hobnail(ed) boots** NPL souliers mpl cloutés or ferrés

hobnob ['hɒbnɒb] VI **to ~ with** frayer avec

hobo ['həʊbəʊ] N (pl **hobo(e)s**) (US) a (= tramp) clochard m b (= migratory worker) saisonnier m

Hobson's choice ['hɒbsənz'tʃɔɪs] N **it's ~** c'est un choix qui n'en est pas un, ce n'est un choix qu'en apparence

Ho Chi Minh City ['həʊ'tʃiː'mɪn'sɪtɪ] N Hô Chi Minh-Ville

hock¹ [hɒk] N [of animal] jarret m; [of human] creux m du genou; (Culin) jarret m (de bœuf)

hock² [hɒk] N (Brit = wine) vin m du Rhin

hock³: [hɒk] 1 VT (= pawn) mettre au clou* 2 N **in ~** [object] au clou*, au mont-de-piété; [person] endetté

hockey ['hɒkɪ] 1 N a (also **field ~**) hockey m b (also **ice ~**) hockey m sur glace 2 COMP [match, pitch] de hockey ► **hockey player** N hockeyeur m, -euse f, joueur m, -euse f de hockey ► **hockey stick** N crosse f de hockey

hocus-pocus ['həʊkəs'pəʊkəs] N (NonC) a (= trickery) **a bit of ~** des tours de passe-passe b (= mumbo-jumbo) galimatias m

hod [hɒd] N (for coal) seau m à charbon; (for bricks, mortar) oiseau m, hotte f

hodgepodge ['hɒdʒpɒdʒ] N (esp US) = **hotchpotch**

hoe [həʊ] 1 N houe f, binette f 2 VT [+ ground] biner; [+ vegetables, weeds] sarcler

hoedown ['həʊdaʊn] N (US) (= dance) danse f (villageoise); (= party) bal m populaire

hog [hɒɡ] 1 N a cochon m, porc m; (Brit: castrated) cochon m; **he's a greedy ~** c'est un vrai goinfre; (US) **to go ~ wild*** dépasser les bornes ► **high, road, whole** b (US* = motorbike) moto* f 2 VT* a (= monopolize) [+ best chair etc] accaparer, monopoliser; [+ conversa-

tion] monopoliser; **don't ~ all the sweets** ne garde pas tous les bonbons pour toi; **to ~ the credit** s'attribuer tout le mérite; **to ~ the limelight** monopoliser l'attention b [+ food] se goinfrer* de

Hogarthian [həʊ'ɡɑːθɪən] ADJ grotesque à la manière de Hogarth

Hogmanay [,hɒɡmə'neɪ] N (Scot) la Saint-Sylvestre, le réveillon du jour de l'an

┌─ HOGMANAY ─┐

Hogmanay est le nom donné aux festivités du premier de l'An en Écosse, où elles occupent une place toute particulière. La coutume veut que l'on se rende chez ses voisins après minuit en apportant symboliquement un petit cadeau, de la boisson et, parfois, un morceau de charbon en gage de prospérité pour l'année à venir; cette coutume porte le nom de « first-footing ».

hogshead ['hɒɡzhed] N barrique f

hogtie ['hɒɡtaɪ] VT (US) (lit) lier les pieds et les poings de; (fig) entraver; (lit, fig) **to be ~d** être pieds et poings liés

hogwash ['hɒɡwɒʃ] N a (= pigswill) eaux fpl grasses (pour nourrir les porcs); b (* = nonsense) inepties fpl

ho hum* ['həʊ'hʌm] 1 EXCL **~! that's life** eh oui! c'est la vie 2 ADJ (also **ho-hum**) moyen

hoick* [hɔɪk] VT (Brit = lift) **to ~ one's trousers up** remonter son pantalon; **to ~ sb out of bed** tirer qn de son lit

hoi polloi [,hɔɪpə'lɔɪ] NPL (pej) **the ~** la populace

hoist [hɔɪst] 1 VT hisser, remonter; [+ sails, flag] hisser; (fig) **to be ~ with one's own petard** être pris à son propre piège 2 N a (= equipment) appareil m de levage, palan m; (= winch) treuil m; (= crane) grue f; (for goods) monte-charge m inv; (made of rope) corde f, palan m b **to give sth a ~ (up)** hisser or remonter qch

hoity-toity ['hɔɪtɪ'tɔɪtɪ] ADJ (pej = arrogant) prétentieux, bêcheur*

hoke: [həʊk] VT (US) **to ~ up a movie** forcer les effets d'un film

hokey* ['həʊkɪ] ADJ (US) a (= phoney) bidon* inv; **it's ~** c'est du bidon* b (= corny) [story, song] cucul la praline* inv; [excuse] tiré par les cheveux

hokey-cokey ['həʊkɪ'kəʊkɪ] N sorte de ronde

hokum* ['həʊkəm] N (US) (= nonsense) foutaises: fpl; (= sentimentality) blablabla* m sentimental, niaiseries fpl; (US Cine, Theat) gros effets mpl

▼**hold** [həʊld]

vb: pret, ptp **held**
| 1 NOUN | 3 INTRANSITIVE VERB |
| 2 TRANSITIVE VERB | 4 PHRASAL VERBS |

1 NOUN

a = **grip, clutch** prise f; **he loosened his ~** il a desserré sa prise or son étreinte f; **he loosened his ~ around my arms/my throat** il a desserré son étreinte autour de mes bras/ma gorge; **I tried to break free from his ~** j'ai essayé de me dégager; **to seize ~ of sth** saisir; **to have ~ of** tenir; **I've got a good** or **firm ~ on the rope** je tiens bien or bon la corde

b = **control, influence** emprise f; **the Prime Minister's uneasy ~ over her government** la fragile emprise du Premier ministre sur son gouvernement; **the president has consolidated his ~ on the media** le président a renforcé son emprise sur les médias; **she still has a ~ on him** elle a toujours de l'emprise sur lui

c **gen, also Climbing** prise f; **the rock offered him few ~s** le rocher lui offrait peu de prises

d **Wrestling** prise f; (fig) **no ~s barred*** tous les coups sont (or étaient etc) permis; **a talk** show with no ~s barred* un débat télévisé où tous les coups sont permis

[e] of hairspray, hair gel fixation f; finish with hairspray for extra ~ pour finir, vaporisez de la laque pour obtenir une fixation parfaite

[f] Naut cale f

[g] Aviat soute f

[h] SET STRUCTURES
♦ to catch hold (of sth) attraper (qch); catch ~! attrape!; he caught ~ of her arm il l'a attrapée par le bras
♦ to get/take a hold of (= catch) prendre; to get a ~ of o.s. se maîtriser, se contrôler; get a ~ of yourself! ressaisis-toi!
♦ to get hold of (= find, trace) [+ object] dénicher*, (réussir à) se procurer, (= details, information) réussir à obtenir; (= contact) [+ person] contacter, joindre; can you get ~ of £500 by tomorrow? est-ce que tu peux te procurer 500 livres d'ici demain?*; where did you get ~ of that hat? où as-tu déniché* or été trouver ce chapeau?; children can all too easily get ~ of drugs les enfants peuvent trop facilement se procurer de la drogue; where did you get ~ of that idea? où as-tu été pêcher* or trouver cette idée?; the press got ~ of the story la presse s'empara de cette histoire; we've been trying to get ~ of him all day nous avons essayé de le contacter or le joindre toute la journée
♦ to take hold [fire] prendre; [custom, practice] se répandre; [idea] faire son chemin; [recession, economic recovery, disease] s'installer; [truce, ceasefire] tenir; the reforms taking ~ in former Communist states les réformes engagées dans les anciens États communistes; take ~! tiens!
♦ to keep hold of tenir fermement, ne pas lâcher; keep ~ of the idea that ... dites-vous bien que ...
♦ on hold [phone call, order etc] en attente; (during phone call) to put sb on ~ mettre qn en attente; nuclear testing was put on ~ les essais nucléaires ont été suspendus; he put his career on ~ to spend more time with his family il a laissé sa carrière en plan pour consacrer davantage de temps à sa famille

2 TRANSITIVE VERB
[a] = grasp tenir; ~ this for a moment tiens or prends ça un moment; he held my arm il me tenait le bras; the dog held the stick in his mouth le chien tenait le bâton dans sa gueule; (lit, fig) she was ~ing her sister's hand elle tenait la main de sa sœur; they were ~ing hands (gen) ils se tenaient par la main; [lovers] ils étaient la main dans la main; she held him tight elle l'a serré très fort; ~ him tight or he'll fall tenez-le bien pour qu'il ne tombe (subj) pas
[b] = keep in place to ~ sth in place maintenir qch en place; the nails ~ the carpet in place les clous maintiennent la moquette en place; hair held in place with a clip des cheveux attachés avec une barrette; she held the door open elle a tenu la porte (ouverte); a hat held by a ribbon tied under the chin un chapeau maintenu au moyen d'un ruban noué sous le menton
[c] = support supporter; the ladder won't ~ you or your weight l'échelle ne supportera pas ton poids
[d] = maintain, keep to ~ o.s. upright se tenir droit; (Mus) to ~ a note tenir une note; to ~ sth in mind garder qch à l'esprit; to ~ an opinion avoir une opinion; to ~ sb's attention/interest retenir l'attention/l'intérêt de qn; can he ~ an audience? est-ce qu'il sait tenir son public (en haleine)?; this car ~s the road well cette voiture tient bien la route; to ~ one's breath retenir son souffle; (fig) don't ~ your breath! n'y compte pas trop!; it's scheduled to finish in August, but don't ~ your breath il est prévu que ce soit fini en août mais je n'y compterais pas trop; (Telec) ~ the line! ne

quittez pas!; (Telec) I've been ~ing the line for several minutes cela fait plusieurs minutes que je suis en ligne or que j'attends
[e] = have, possess [+ ticket, permit, driving licence] avoir; [+ shares, record] détenir; Spain held vast territories in South America l'Espagne possédait de vastes territoires en Amérique du Sud
[f] = defend successfully (gen, Mil) tenir; the army held the bridge against the enemy l'armée a tenu le pont malgré les attaques de l'ennemi; (Tennis) to ~ one's serve défendre son service
♦ to hold one's own (gen) (bien) se débrouiller; [ill person] se maintenir; he can ~ his own in German il se débrouille très bien en allemand; he can ~ his own with anybody il ne s'en laisse pas remontrer
[g] = occupy [+ post, position] avoir, occuper; (Rel) [+ living] jouir de; he ~s the post of headmaster il occupe le poste de directeur
[h] = cause to take place [+ meeting, election, debate etc] tenir; [+ conversation] avoir, tenir; (Scol) [+ examination] organiser; the exhibition is always held here l'exposition se tient toujours or a toujours lieu ici; (Rel) to ~ a service [priest etc] célébrer un office; they are ~ing a service to mark the day when ... ils ont prévu une cérémonie pour commémorer le jour où ...; to ~ interviews [employer etc] recevoir des candidats; the interviews are being held in London les entretiens ont lieu à Londres
[i] = contain contenir; this box will ~ all my books cette caisse est assez grande pour (contenir) tous mes livres; this bottle ~s one litre cette bouteille a une contenance d'un litre or peut contenir un litre; this room ~s 20 people il y a de la place pour 20 personnes dans cette salle; what does the future ~ for us? qu'est-ce que l'avenir nous réserve?; I wonder what the future ~s je me demande ce que l'avenir nous réserve; she can ~ her drink or liquor!* c'est fou ce qu'elle supporte bien l'alcool!
[j] = keep, have charge of garder; I will ~ the money until ... je garderai l'argent jusqu'à ce que ...; my lawyer ~s these documents ces documents sont chez mon avocat; the bank ~s these bills la banque conserve ces effets; we don't ~ that information on our files nous n'avons pas ces informations dans nos fichiers; the data is held on computer ces données sont informatisées
[k] = keep back, restrain [+ person] tenir, retenir; to ~ a train empêcher un train de partir; ~ the letter until ... n'envoyez pas la lettre avant que ... (+ subj); (US: on letters) "~ for arrival" « ne pas faire suivre »; the police held him for two days la police l'a gardé (à vue) pendant deux jours; there's no ~ing him il n'y a pas moyen de l'arrêter; ~ it!* stop!
[l] = believe, assert to ~ that ... maintenir que ...; he ~s that matter doesn't exist il maintient que la matière n'existe pas; to ~ sth to be true considérer qch comme vrai; this is held to be true cela passe pour vrai; (Jur) the court held that ... la cour a statué que ...; it was held by the judge that ... le juge a statué que ...; the law ~s that ... la loi prévoit or stipule que ...; he was held guilty of the offence on pensait que c'était lui qui avait commis le délit; to ~ sb responsible for sth tenir qn pour responsable de qch; to ~ in high esteem tenir en haute estime
♦ to hold sth against sb en vouloir à qn de qch; I don't ~ it against him je ne lui en veux pas

3 INTRANSITIVE VERB
[a] = remain in place [rope, nail etc] tenir, être solide; to ~ firm or fast rester ferme; (= stay in place) tenir → tight; ~ hard! arrête!, minute!*
[b] weather se maintenir

[c] Telec can you ~, please? ne quittez pas!; I've been ~ing for several minutes cela fait plusieurs minutes que je suis en ligne or que j'attends
[d] also ~ good [statement, argument] être valable; your argument doesn't ~ (good) votre argument n'est pas valable; the theory could still ~ la théorie pourrait tout de même être valable

4 PHRASAL VERBS
► hold back [1] VI (lit) rester en arrière; (fig) se retenir (from sth de qch, from doing de faire); I held back from telling him what I really thought je me suis retenu de lui dire ce que je pensais vraiment
[2] VT SEP [a] [+ fears, emotions] maîtriser; [+ tears] retenir; the police held back the crowd la police a contenu la foule; to ~ sb back from doing sth empêcher qn de faire qch; they held back the names of the victims ils n'ont pas divulgué le nom des victimes; he was ~ing something back from me il me cachait quelque chose; his policies have held our country back economically sa politique a bloqué l'essor économique or a freiné le développement (économique) de notre pays
[b] (US Scol) [+ pupil] faire redoubler; to be held back redoubler
► hold down VT SEP [a] (= keep in place) maintenir en place; [+ person] maintenir; to ~ one's head down garder la tête baissée; we couldn't ~ him down nous ne sommes pas arrivés à le maintenir au sol
[b] (= keep low) [+ costs, prices, inflation, taxes] empêcher d'augmenter; strict government regulation will ~ down costs le gouvernement empêchera les coûts d'augmenter grâce à une réglementation stricte
[c] [+ job] (= have) avoir, occuper; (= keep) garder; she's managed to ~ down a job as well as looking after the children elle a réussi à continuer de travailler tout en s'occupant des enfants; he's ~ing down a good job il a une belle situation; he can't ~ down a job il ne garde jamais longtemps le même travail
► hold forth [1] VI faire des discours, disserter; he was ~ing forth on the subject of religion il faisait des discours or dissertait sur la religion
[2] VT SEP (frm = hold out) tendre
► hold in VT SEP retenir; ~ your stomach in! rentre ton ventre!; to ~ in one's temper se contenir, se retenir; he managed to ~ in his horse il réussit à maîtriser son cheval; depression can sometimes be traced to ~ing in anger le fait de réprimer sa colère peut entraîner la dépression; go ahead and cry, don't ~ it in laisse-toi aller et pleure, n'essaie pas de te retenir
► hold off [1] VI (fig) the rain has held off so far jusqu'ici il n'a pas plu
[2] VT SEP [a] (= prevent from approaching) tenir éloigné or à distance; they held off the enemy ils tenaient l'ennemi à distance; (fig) try to ~ him off a little longer essayez de le faire patienter encore un peu; (fig) I can't ~ him off any longer: you'll have to see him je ne peux pas le faire attendre plus longtemps: il faut que vous le voyiez
[b] (= resist) she held off all challengers to win the race elle a gagné la course malgré les autres challengers
[c] (= delay) to ~ off doing sth attendre pour faire qch; they held off eating until she had arrived ils ont attendu qu'elle soit arrivée pour manger
► hold on [1] VI [a] (= endure) tenir bon, tenir le coup; despite her aching shoulders, Nancy held on malgré ses épaules qui lui faisaient mal, Nancy a tenu bon or a tenu le coup
[b] (= wait) attendre; ~ on! attendez!; (on telephone) ne quittez pas!
[2] VT SEP maintenir (en place), tenir en place; this hinge ~s the lid on cette charnière maintient le couvercle (en place); to ~ one's hat on tenir son chapeau sur sa tête

► **hold on to** VT FUS [a] (= *cling to*) [+ *rope, raft, branch*] se cramponner à, s'accrocher à ; (*fig*) [+ *hope, idea*] se raccrocher à
[b] (= *keep*) garder ; ~ on to this for me (= *hold it*) tiens-moi ça ; (= *keep it*) garde-moi ça

► **hold out** [1] VI [a] (= *last*) [*supplies*] durer ; **how long will the food ~ out?** combien de temps est-ce que les provisions vont durer ? ; **if his luck ~s out** s'il continue à avoir de la chance
[b] (= *endure, resist*) tenir bon, tenir le coup ; **to ~ out against** [+ *enemy, attacks*] tenir bon devant ; [+ *change, improvements, progress, threats, fatigue*] résister à ; **one prisoner was still ~ing out on the roof of the jail** un prisonnier continuait à résister sur le toit de la prison ; **they are ~ing out for more pay** ils continuent de demander une augmentation
[2] VT SEP [+ *object*] tendre (**sth to sb** qch à qn) ; **"I'm Nancy" she said, ~ing out her hand** « je m'appelle Nancy » dit-elle en tendant la main ; **to ~ out one's arms** ouvrir les bras
[3] VT FUS **the doctors ~ out little hope for him** les médecins ne lui donnent pas beaucoup de chances de s'en tirer ; **she's still ~ing out hope that ...** elle conserve toujours l'espoir que ... ; **the negotiations held out little hope of a settlement** il y avait peu d'espoir que les négociations aboutissent à un accord ; **the scheme ~s out the promise of great financial reward** ce projet promet de rapporter beaucoup d'un point de vue financier

► **hold out on*** VT FUS [+ *price etc*] s'en tenir à ; **you've been ~ing out on me!** tu m'as caché quelque chose !

► **hold over** VT SEP remettre ; **the meeting was held over until Friday** la réunion a été remise à vendredi

► **hold to** [1] VT FUS s'en tenir à ; **I ~ to what I said** je m'en tiens à ce que j'ai dit ; **he held to his religious beliefs** il restait attaché à ses convictions religieuses
[2] VT SEP **to ~ sb to a promise** faire tenir parole à qn ; **I'll ~ you to that!** je te prends au mot !

► **hold together** [1] VI [*objects*] tenir (ensemble) ; [*groups, people*] rester unis ; **the coalition will never ~ together for six months** la coalition ne tiendra jamais six mois ; **we must ~ together** il faut se serrer les coudes or rester unis
[2] VT SEP [+ *objects*] maintenir (ensemble) ; (*fig*) [+ *political party*] maintenir l'union de ; **he held the family together** c'est grâce à lui que la famille est restée unie ; **she sought to ~ together the various factions in her party** elle a cherché à réconcilier les différentes factions de son parti

► **hold up** [1] VI [a] (*lit*) **that building won't ~ up much longer** ce bâtiment ne tiendra plus longtemps debout
[b] [*argument*] tenir la route ; [*economy*] tenir le coup ; **the evidence doesn't ~ up** ces preuves ne tiennent pas la route
[2] VT SEP [a] (= *raise*) lever, élever ; **~ it up higher** tiens-le plus haut ; **~ up your hand** levez la main ; **~ it up so that we can see it** soulevez-le pour que nous puissions le voir ; **to ~ sth up to the light** élever qch vers la lumière ; **I'll never be able to ~ my head up again** je ne pourrai plus jamais regarder personne en face ; **to ~ sb up to ridicule** tourner qn en ridicule ; **he had always been held up as an example to the younger ones** il avait toujours été cité en exemple aux plus jeunes
[b] (= *support*) soutenir ; **the roof is held up by pillars** le toit est soutenu par des piliers
[c] (= *stop*) arrêter ; (= *suspend*) suspendre ; (= *cause delay to*) retarder ; **the traffic was held up by the accident** l'accident a ralenti la circulation ; **I'm sorry, I was held up** excusez-moi, j'ai été retenu ; **violence on the streets could ~ up progress towards reform** la violence dans les rues pourrait retarder les réformes
[d] [*robber*] [+ *bank, shop*] faire un hold-up

dans, braquer* ; [+ *coach, person*] attaquer (à main armée), braquer*

► **hold with*** VT FUS **I don't ~ with that** je désapprouve or réprouve cela ; **she doesn't ~ with people smoking** elle n'aime pas que l'on fume (*subj*)

holdall ['həʊldɔːl] N (*Brit*) (sac *m*) fourre-tout *m inv*

holder ['həʊldə^r] N [a] [*of ticket, card*] détenteur *m*, -trice *f* ; [*of passport, office, post, title of nobility, diploma*] titulaire *mf* ; [*of stocks*] porteur *m*, -euse *f*, détenteur *m*, -trice *f* ; [*of farm*] exploitant *m* ; [*Sport etc*] [*of record*] détenteur *m*, -trice *f* ; [*of title*] détenteur *m*, -trice *f*, tenant(e) *m(f)* ; **the ~s of the European Football Championship** les détenteurs or les tenants du titre de champion d'Europe de football ; (*Banking*) **account ~** titulaire *mf* d'un compte [b] (= *object*) support *m* ; **penholder** porte-plume *m inv* → **cigarette**

holding ['həʊldɪŋ] [1] N [a] (= *act*) tenue *f* ; (*Tech*) fixation *f* [b] (= *possession*) [*of lands*] possession *f*, jouissance *f* ; [*of stocks*] possession *f* [c] (= *farm*) propriété *f*, ferme *f* [2] **holdings** NPL (*Fin*) (= *lands*) avoirs *mpl* fonciers ; (= *stocks*) intérêts *mpl*, participations *fpl* [3] COMP ► **holding company** N (*Fin*) holding *m*, société *f* de portefeuille

holdout ['həʊldaʊt] N (*US*) *personne qui fait obstacle*, obstacle *m* ; **Britain was the only ~ on this agreement** la Grande-Bretagne était le seul pays à faire obstacle à cet accord

holdover* ['həʊldəʊvə^r] N (*US: esp Pol*) rescapé(e) *m(f)* (*fig*)

holdup ['həʊldʌp] N [a] (= *robbery*) hold-up *m inv*, braquage* *m* [b] (= *delay*) retard *m* ; (*in traffic*) embouteillage *m*, bouchon *m* ; **there's been a ~ in the delivery** il y a eu un retard dans la livraison ; **a big ~ owing to roadworks** un gros embouteillage or bouchon dû aux travaux

hole [həʊl] [1] N [a] trou *m* ; (*in defences, dam*) brèche *f* ; (*in clouds*) trouée *f* ; **he spied on them through a ~ in the wall** il les a espionnés en regardant par un trou dans le mur ; **these socks are in ~s** or **full of ~s** ces chaussettes sont toutes trouées or pleines de trous ; **to wear a ~ in sth** trouer qch ; **to wear into ~s** se trouer ; **I need it like I need a ~ in the head!*** je n'ai vraiment pas besoin de ça !
[b] [*of mouse*] trou *m* ; [*of rabbit, fox*] terrier *m*
[c] (*Golf*) trou *m* ; **we played nine ~s** nous avons fait neuf trous or → **4**
[d] (*fig* = *gap*) **it made** or **blew a ~ in his savings** cela a fait un trou dans ses économies ; **to blow a ~ in sb's plans** saborder les plans de qn ; **there were some ~s in his theory/his argument** il y avait des failles *fpl* or des faiblesses *fpl* dans sa théorie/son argumentation ; **the plot is full of ~s** l'intrigue est mal ficelée ; **his story's full of ~s** sa version des faits ne tient pas debout → **burn, knock, pick**
[e] (* = *trouble*) **they were in a nasty ~** ils étaient dans un sale pétrin ; **he got me out of a ~** il m'a tiré d'embarras or d'un mauvais pas
[f] (* *pej*) (= *town*) trou *m* (paumé*) ; (= *room, house*) bouge *m*
[2] VT [a] faire un trou dans, trouer ; **the ship was ~d by a missile** un missile a fait un trou dans le bateau
[b] (*Golf*) [+ *putt*] enquiller ; **to ~ a ball in three** faire un or le trou en trois ; **he ~d the 5th in three ◊** il a fait le (trou numéro) cinq en trois coups il a fait trois sur le cinq
[3] VI [a] [*socks, pullover*] se trouer
[b] (*Golf: also ~ out*) terminer le trou ; **to ~ in one** faire le or un trou en un ~ **4** ; **he ~d from nine feet at the 18th** il a fait le 18e trou à trois mètres
[c] (*Billiards*) bloquer
[4] COMP ► **hole-and-corner** ADJ (*pej*) (= *secret*) clandestin, secret (-ète *f*) ; (= *furtive*)

furtif ; (= *underhand*) fait en douce* ► **hole in one** N (*Golf*) trou *m* en un ► **hole in the heart** N maladie *f* bleue ; **she was born with a ~ in the heart** elle est née avec une malformation cardiaque or du cœur ► **hole-in-the-heart** ADJ **~-in-the-heart baby** enfant *m(f)* bleu(e) ; **~-in-the-heart operation** opération *f* pour communication interventriculaire ► **hole-in-the-wall*** N (*Brit* = *cash dispenser*) distributeur *m* de billets

► **hole up** VI [*animal, criminal*] se terrer ; **she's been ~d up in her study all day** elle a passé toute la journée cloîtrée dans son bureau

holey ['həʊlɪ] ADJ plein de trous, (tout) troué

holiday ['hɒlɪdeɪ] [1] N (*esp Brit*) (= *vacation*) vacances *fpl* ; (= *day off*) (jour *m* de) congé *m* ; (= *public holiday*) jour *m* férié ; **to take a ~** prendre des vacances or un congé ; **on ~** en vacances, en congé ; **to take a month's ~** prendre un mois de vacances ; **~s with pay ◊ paid ~s** congés *mpl* payés ; **tomorrow is a ~** demain est un jour férié ; **the school ~(s)** les vacances *fpl* scolaires ; **the Christmas ~(s)** les vacances *fpl* de Noël → **bank²**
[2] VI (*esp Brit*) passer les vacances ; **they were ~ing at home** ils prenaient leurs vacances à la maison
[3] COMP [*mood*] gai, joyeux ► **holiday camp** N (*Brit*) (*gen*) camp *m* de vacances ; (*for children only*) colonie *f* or camp *m* de vacances ► **holiday clothes** NPL tenue *f* de vacances ► **holiday feeling** N atmosphère *f* or ambiance *f* de vacances ► **holiday home** N (*esp Brit*) maison *f* or résidence *f* secondaire ► **holiday job** N (*Brit*) emploi *m* temporaire (*pendant les vacances*) ► **holiday-maker** N (*Brit*) vacancier *m*, -ière *f* ; (*in summer*) estivant(e) *m(f)* ► **holiday pay** N (*esp Brit*) congés *mpl* payés ; **they don't get ~ pay** ils n'ont pas droit aux congés payés ► **holiday resort** N (*esp Brit*) villégiature *f*, lieu *m* de vacances ► **holiday season** N période *f* des vacances ► **holiday spirit** N air *m* or ambiance *f* de vacances ; **he's already lost his ~ spirit** il ne se sent déjà plus en vacances ► **holiday traffic** N départs *mpl* en (or retours *mpl* de) vacances

holier-than-thou* ['həʊlɪəðən'ðaʊ] ADJ [*person*] imbu de soi-même, supérieur ; (*in religious matters*) pharisien ; [*attitude*] suffisant

holiness ['həʊlɪnɪs] N sainteté *f* ; **His Holiness** Sa Sainteté

holism ['həʊlɪzəm] N holisme *m*

holistic [həʊ'lɪstɪk] ADJ holistique

Holland ['hɒlənd] N [a] la Hollande, les Pays-Bas *mpl* [b] (*Tex*) **holland** toile *f* de Hollande

holler* ['hɒlə^r] (*esp US*) [1] N braillement *m* [2] VTI (*also ~ out*) brailler, beugler* ; **to ~ at sb** (= *tell off*) crier après qn

hollow ['hɒləʊ] [1] ADJ [a] (= *empty inside*) [*tree, tooth, log, stem*] creux ; **to sound** [*object*] sonner creux ; **to have a ~ feeling in one's stomach** (*from hunger*) avoir le ventre creux ; (*from emotion*) avoir l'estomac noué
[b] (= *sunken*) [*cheeks*] creux ; [*eyes*] creux, cave
[c] (= *hollow-sounding*) [*laugh*] creux ; [*voice*] caverneux ; [*sound*] (*from box*) creux ; (*from hall, cave*) caverneux → **beat**
[d] (= *false, empty*) [*person, victory*] faux (fausse *f*) ; [*promise, threat, gesture*] vain ; **~ words** des paroles *fpl* creuses ; **to have a ~ ring ◊ to ring ~** sonner faux ; **a ~ sham** une dérisoire comédie
[2] N (*in ground*) (*gen*) creux *m* ; (= *valley*) cuvette *f* ; [*of back, hand, tree*] creux *m* ; [*of tooth*] cavité *f* ; (*fig*) **to have** or **hold sb in the ~ of one's hand** mener qn par le bout du nez
[3] VT (*also ~ out*) creuser ; (= *scoop out*) [+ *apple etc*] évider
[4] COMP ► **hollow-cheeked** ADJ aux joues creuses or creusées ► **hollow-eyed** ADJ aux yeux caves or creux

hollowly ['hɒləʊlɪ] ADV [echo] avec un bruit creux; [say] platement; **to ring ~** sonner creux; **to laugh ~** rire jaune

hollowness ['hɒləʊnɪs] N [of promise, guarantee] manque m de sincérité, vacuité f

holly ['hɒlɪ] 1 N houx m 2 COMP ► **holly berry** N baie f de houx

hollyhock ['hɒlɪˌhɒk] N rose f trémière

Hollywood ['hɒlɪˌwʊd] N Hollywood

holmium ['hɒlmɪəm] N holmium m

holm oak ['həʊm'əʊk] N chêne m vert, yeuse f

holocaust ['hɒləkɔːst] N holocauste m

hologram ['hɒləˌgræm] N hologramme m

holograph ['hɒləgrɑːf] 1 N document m (h)olographe 2 ADJ (h)olographe

holographic [ˌhɒlə'græfɪk] ADJ holographique

holography [hɒ'lɒgrəfɪ] N holographie f

holophrastic [ˌhɒlə'fræstɪk] ADJ holophrastique

hols* [hɒlz] N (Brit) (ABBR = **holidays**) vacances fpl

holster ['həʊlstər] N étui m de revolver; (on saddle) fonte f

holy ['həʊlɪ] 1 ADJ [object, place, day, book] saint; **~ war** guerre f sainte; **on ~ ground** dans un lieu saint; **the ~ month of Ramadan** le mois sacré du ramadan; **that child is a ~ terror*** cet enfant est un vrai démon; **~ cow** or **smoke** or **Moses** or **Moley** or **mackerel!*** sacrebleu!*; **~ shit!*** nom de Dieu!*; **Holy (Mary) Mother of God!*** nom de Dieu!* → **innocent**
2 N **the ~ of holies** le saint des saints
3 COMP ► **the Holy Alliance** N la Sainte-Alliance ► **the Holy Bible** N la sainte bible ► **the Holy City** N la Ville sainte ► **Holy Communion** N sainte communion f ► **Holy Eucharist** N saint sacrement m ► **the Holy Family** N la Sainte famille ► **the Holy Father** N le Saint-Père ► **the Holy Ghost** N Holy Spirit ► **the Holy Grail** N le Saint-Graal ► **Holy Joe*** N (= clergyman) curé m; (= sanctimonious person) grenouille f de bénitier (pej) ► **the Holy Land** N la Terre sainte; **in the Holy Land** en Terre sainte ► **holy man** N (pl holy men) saint homme m ► **holy matrimony** N les liens mpl sacrés du mariage; **they were joined in ~ matrimony** ils ont été unis par les liens sacrés du mariage ► **the Holy Office** N le Saint-Office ► **holy oil** N huile f bénite ► **holy orders** NPL ordres mpl; **in ~ orders** dans les ordres; **to take ~ orders** entrer dans les ordres ► **the Holy Roman Empire** N le Saint Empire romain germanique ► **the Holy Rood** N la sainte Croix ► **Holy Saturday** N samedi m saint ► **Holy Scripture** N Écriture f sainte ► **the Holy See** N le Saint-Siège ► **the Holy Sepulchre** N le Saint-Sépulcre ► **the Holy Spirit** N le Saint-Esprit, l'Esprit m saint ► **the Holy Trinity** N la sainte Trinité ► **holy water** N eau f bénite ► **Holy Week** N semaine sainte f ► **Holy Writ**† N (= scripture) Écriture f sainte; (fig) **he treats everything she says as if it were Holy Writ** pour lui, tout ce qu'elle dit est parole d'évangile

holystone ['həʊlɪstəʊn] (Naut) 1 N brique f à pont 2 VT briquer

homage ['hɒmɪdʒ] N (NonC) hommage m; **to pay ~ to sb/sth** rendre hommage à qn/qch; **in ~ to sb/sth** en hommage à qn/qch

homburg ['hɒmbɜːg] N chapeau m mou, feutre m (souple)

home [həʊm] 1 N a maison f, chez-soi m; **to have a ~ of one's own** avoir sa propre maison (or son propre appartement); **he was glad to see his ~ again** il était content de rentrer chez lui; **it is quite near my ~** c'est tout près de chez moi; **his ~ is in Paris** il habite Paris; **I live in Paris but my ~ is in London** je suis de Londres, mais j'habite à Paris en ce moment;

~ for me is Edinburgh c'est à Édimbourg que je me sens chez moi; **for some years he made his ~ in France** pendant quelques années il a habité en France; **refugees who made their ~ in Britain** les réfugiés qui se sont installés en Grande-Bretagne; **~ for them is England now ◊ they now call England ~** maintenant l'Angleterre c'est leur pays; **Warwick is ~ to some 550 international students** il y a quelque 550 étudiants étrangers à Warwick; **the building is ~ to over 1,000 students** plus de 1 000 étudiants logent dans ce bâtiment; **he is far from ~** il est loin de chez lui; **he has been away from ~ for some months** il est loin de chez lui depuis quelques mois ■ (PROV) **there's no place like ~** ■ (PROV) **~ is where the heart is** on n'est vraiment bien que chez soi; **he has no ~** il n'a pas de foyer; **to give sb/an animal a ~** recueillir qn/un animal chez soi or sous son toit; **he made a ~ for his sisters** il a accueilli ses sœurs sous son toit; **it's a ~ from ~** (Brit) or **away from ~** (US) c'est mon second chez-moi (or son second chez-soi etc); **she has a lovely ~** c'est joli chez elle; **he comes from a broken ~** il vient d'un foyer désuni; **"good ~ wanted for kitten"** «cherche foyer accueillant pour chaton»; **accidents in the ~** accidents mpl domestiques

♦ **at home** chez soi, à la maison; **I'll be at ~ this afternoon** je serai chez moi cet après-midi; **is Paul at ~?** est-ce que Paul est à la maison?; (Ftbl) **Celtic are at ~ to Rangers ◊ Celtic are playing Rangers at ~** le Celtic joue à domicile contre les Rangers, le Celtic reçoit les Rangers; (frm = not receiving visitors) **Mrs Gough is not at ~** Mme Gough ne reçoit pas; (frm) **Mrs Gough is not at ~ to anyone** Mme Gough ne reçoit personne; **to be** or **feel at ~ with sb** se sentir à l'aise avec qn; **he doesn't feel at ~ in English** il n'est pas à l'aise en anglais; **to make o.s. at ~** se mettre à l'aise, faire comme chez soi; (fig, also iro) **make yourself at ~!** faites comme chez vous!; **who's he when he's at ~?*** qui c'est celui-là?*; **what's that when it's at ~?*** qu'est-ce que c'est que ça? → **leave, set up, spiritual**

b (= country of origin) pays m natal, patrie f; **at ~ and abroad** ici et or chez nous et à l'étranger; **the Russians, at ~ and abroad** les Russes, chez eux et à l'étranger; (fig) **to bring sth closer** or **nearer (to) ~ for sb** permettre à qn de mieux se rendre compte de qch; (fig) **let's concentrate on problems closer** or **nearer to ~** occupons-nous de problèmes qui nous concernent plus directement; (fig) **her jokes about bald people were a bit too close to ~ for him** ses plaisanteries sur les chauves le touchaient au vif; (fig) **Scotland is the ~ of the haggis** l'Écosse est le pays du haggis; **Bordeaux is the ~ of some of the world's finest wines** Bordeaux produit certains des meilleurs vins du monde

c (= institution) maison f, institution f; (shorter-term) foyer m; **children's ~** maison f pour enfants → **maternity, mental, nursing**

d (Bot, Zool) habitat m

e (Racing) arrivée f

f (Baseball) base f de départ

2 ADV a chez soi, à la maison; **to go ~** rentrer (chez soi or à la maison); **to get ~** rentrer; **I got ~ at 5 o'clock** je suis rentré (chez moi or à la maison) à 5 heures; **I'll be ~ at 5 o'clock** je serai à la maison à 5 heures, je rentrerai à 5 heures; **I met him on the journey ~** je l'ai rencontré sur le chemin du retour; **I must write ~** il faut que j'écrive à ma famille; **it's nothing to write ~ about*** ça ne casse pas des briques*, ça ne casse rien*; (fig) **to be ~ and dry** or (US) **~ free** être arrivé au bout de ses peines

b (from abroad) dans son pays, chez soi; **he came ~ from abroad** il est rentré de l'étranger; **to go** or **return ~** rentrer dans son pays

c (= right in etc) à fond; **to drive a nail ~** enfoncer un clou à fond; **to bring sth ~ to sb** faire comprendre or faire voir qch à qn; **the horror of the situation was brought ~ to him when ...** l'horreur de la situation lui est apparue pleinement quand ...; (fig) **to drive** or **hammer sth ~** bien faire comprendre qch; (Ftbl) **he nodded the ball ~** il a marqué un but de la tête; (Ftbl) **he drove the ball ~ from 15 yards** il a marqué un but grâce à un tir de 15 mètres; **to push ~ an attack** pousser à fond une attaque → **hit**

3 VI revenir or rentrer chez soi; [pigeons] revenir au colombier

4 COMP [atmosphere] de famille, familial; [troubles] de famille, domestique; (Econ, Pol) du pays, national; [policy, market] intérieur (-eure f) ► **home address** N (on forms etc) domicile m (permanent); (as opposed to business address) adresse f personnelle ► **home-baked** ADJ (fait) maison inv; **~-baked bread** pain m fait maison ► **home baking** N (= cakes etc) pâtisseries fpl maison ► **home banking** N services mpl (bancaires) télématiques ► **home base** N (Baseball) base f de départ ► **home birth** N accouchement m à domicile ► **home brew** N (= beer) bière f faite à la maison; (= wine) vin m fait à la maison ► **home-buying** N achats mpl de logements; (first-time) accession f à la propriété ► **home comforts** NPL confort m du foyer ► **home computer** N ordinateur m personnel, PC m ► **home cooking** N cuisine f familiale ► **the Home Counties** NPL (Brit) les comtés qui entourent Londres ► **home country** N pays m natal or d'origine ► **home economics** N (NonC) économie f domestique ► **home front** N **on the ~ front** (Pol, Mil) à l'intérieur; (* hum = at home) à la maison ► **home ground** N (Sport) **to play at one's ~ ground** jouer sur son terrain or à domicile; (fig) **to be on ~ ground** être sur son terrain ► **home-grown** ADJ (= not foreign) du pays; (= from own garden) du jardin ► **Home Guard** N (Brit) volontaires pour la défense du territoire (1940-45) ► **home heating oil** N fuel m domestique ► **home help** N (Brit Social Work) (= person) aide f ménagère; (gen = assistance) **do you have any ~ help?** est-ce que vous avez quelqu'un pour vous aider à la maison? ► **home improvement grant** N prime f à l'amélioration de l'habitat ► **home improvement loan** N prêt m pour l'amélioration de l'habitat ► **home improvements** NPL réfection f de logements; (= DIY) bricolage m ► **home leave** N (gen) congé m au foyer; (Mil) permission f ► **home life** N vie f de famille ► **home loan** N prêt m immobilier ► **home-lover** N casanier m, -ière f; (woman) femme f d'intérieur ► **home-loving** ADJ casanier ► **home-made** ADJ (fait) maison inv ► **home-maker** N femme f d'intérieur ► **home match** N (Sport) match m à domicile ► **home movie** N vidéo f amateur ► **home news** N (gen) nouvelles fpl de chez soi; (Pol) nouvelles fpl nationales ► **the Home Office** N (Brit) ≈ le ministère de l'Intérieur ► **home owner** N propriétaire mf ► **home ownership** N **~ ownership is on the increase** de plus en plus de gens sont propriétaires de leur logement ► **home page** N (Comput) page f d'accueil ► **home port** N (Naut) port m d'attache ► **home posting** N (Brit: of diplomat, soldier) affectation f au pays ► **home rule** N autonomie f ► **home run** N [of ship, truck] voyage m de retour; (Baseball) coup m de circuit; **to hit a ~ run** (Baseball) faire or réussir un coup de circuit; (US fig) réussir un beau coup ► **home sales** NPL ventes fpl intérieures or domestiques ► **Home Secretary** N (Brit) ≈ ministre m de l'Intérieur ► **home shopping** N (by post, telephone) achat par correspondance ou par téléphone; (by computer, television) téléachats mpl

► **home side** N (Sport) = **home team** ► **home State** N (US) État m d'origine ► **home straight, home stretch** N to be in the ~ straight (Sport) être dans la (dernière) ligne droite; (fig) toucher au but ► **home team** N (Ftbl etc) équipe f qui reçoit ► **home territory** N (fig) to be on one's ~ territory être sur son terrain ► **home time** N it's ~ time c'est l'heure de rentrer à la maison ► **home town** N my ~ town (= place of birth) ma ville natale; (= where I grew up) la ville où j'ai grandi ► **home truth** N I'll tell him a few ~ truths je vais lui dire ses quatre vérités ► **home video** N vidéo f amateur ► **home visit** N (by doctor etc) visite f à domicile ► **home waters** NPL (Naut) (= territorial waters) eaux fpl territoriales; (near home port) eaux fpl voisines du port d'attache

► **home in on, home on to** VT FUS [missile] (= move towards) se diriger vers or sur; (= reach) atteindre

homebody* ['həʊmbɒdɪ] N (esp US) casanier m, -ière f, pantouflard(e)* m(f) (pej)

homebound ['həʊmbaʊnd] ADJ (= on the way home) [traveller] qui rentre chez soi

homeboy* ['həʊmbɔɪ] N (US) pote* m

homecoming ['həʊmkʌmɪŋ] N a (gen) retour m à la maison; (to one's country) retour m au pays; (of soldier etc) retour m au foyer b (US Scol, Univ) fête f annuelle (marquant le début de l'année universitaire)

homegirl* ['həʊmgɜːl] N (US) copine* f

homeland ['həʊmlænd] N (gen) patrie f; (in South Africa) homeland m

homeless ['həʊmlɪs] [1] ADJ sans foyer, sans abri [2] the homeless NPL les SDF mpl → single

homelessness ['həʊmlɪsnɪs] N ~ is on the increase il y a de plus en plus de SDF; what's the government doing about ~? que fait le gouvernement pour les SDF ?

homelike ['həʊmlaɪk] ADJ accueillant, confortable

homely ['həʊmlɪ] ADJ a (esp Brit) [person] aux goûts simples; [atmosphere, room, place] accueillant; [dish, food] simple, familial b (US = plain) [person] sans charme; [appearance] peu attrayant

homeopath ['həʊmɪəʊpæθ] N homéopathe mf

homeopathic [ˌhəʊmɪəʊ'pæθɪk] ADJ [medicine, methods] homéopathique; [doctor] homéopathe

homeopathy [ˌhəʊmɪ'ɒpəθɪ] N homéopathie f

Homer ['həʊmə'] N Homère m

homer ['həʊmə'] N a (US Baseball*) coup m de circuit b (Brit = homing pigeon) pigeon m voyageur

Homeric [həʊ'merɪk] ADJ homérique

homeroom ['həʊmrʊm] [1] N (US Scol) salle f de classe (affectée à une classe particulière) [2] COMP ► **homeroom teacher** N ≈ professeur m principal

homesick ['həʊmsɪk] ADJ nostalgique; to be ~ (for place) avoir le mal du pays; (for one's family) s'ennuyer de sa famille; to be ~ for sth avoir la nostalgie de qch

homesickness ['həʊmsɪknɪs] N mal m du pays

homespun ['həʊmspʌn] [1] ADJ [cloth] filé à domicile; (fig) simple, sans recherche [2] N homespun m

homestead ['həʊmsted] (esp US) [1] N (= house etc) propriété f; (= farm) ferme f [2] COMP ► **the Homestead Act** N (US) la loi agraire de 1862

homesteader ['həʊmstedə'] N (US) colon m (pionnier)

homeward ['həʊmwəd] [1] ADJ de retour; ~ journey (voyage m de) retour m [2] ADV (Brit:

also ~s) to head ~ partir en direction de chez soi; to hurry ~ se dépêcher de rentrer chez soi [3] COMP ► **homeward bound** ADV to be ~-bound être sur le chemin de retour; ~-bound commuters banlieusards mpl rentrant chez eux

homework ['həʊmwɜːk] [1] N (Scol) devoirs mpl [2] COMP ► **homework diary** N cahier m de textes ► **homework exercise** N devoir m ► **homework notebook** N = homework diary

homeworker ['həʊmwɜːkə'] N travailleur m, -euse f à domicile

homeworking ['həʊmwɜːkɪŋ] N travail m à domicile

homey ['həʊmɪ] ADJ (US) = homely b

homicidal [ˌhɒmɪ'saɪdl] ADJ [tendencies] homicide; [rage] meurtrier; ~ maniac fou m dangereux, folle f dangereuse

homicide ['hɒmɪsaɪd] N (= act) homicide m; (= person) homicide mf

homily ['hɒmɪlɪ] N (Rel) homélie f; (fig) sermon m, homélie f

homing ['həʊmɪŋ] [1] ADJ [missile] à tête chercheuse [2] COMP ► **homing device** N tête f chercheuse ► **homing instinct** N [of animal] instinct m de retour (à l'habitat d'origine) ► **homing pigeon** N pigeon m voyageur

hominy grits ['hɒmɪnɪ'grɪts] NPL (US) maïs m concassé et bouilli

homo†‡ ['həʊməʊ] ADJ, N (ABBR = homosexual) (pej) pédé‡ m (pej), homo* mf

homoeopath etc ['həʊmɪəʊpæθ] = homeopath etc

homoerotic [ˌhəʊməʊɪ'rɒtɪk] ADJ [image, fantasy, subtext] érotique homosexuel

homogeneity [ˌhəʊməʊdʒɪ'niːɪtɪ] N homogénéité f

homogeneous [ˌhəʊmə'dʒiːnɪəs] ADJ homogène

homogenize [hə'mɒdʒənaɪz] VT homogénéiser

homogenous [hə'mɒdʒɪnəs] ADJ = homogeneous

homograph ['hɒməʊgrɑːf] N homographe m

homographic [ˌhɒmə'græfɪk] ADJ homographique

homography [hɒ'mɒgrəfɪ] N homographie f

homonym ['hɒmənɪm] N homonyme m

homonymic [ˌhɒmə'nɪmɪk] ADJ homonymique

homonymy [hɒ'mɒnɪmɪ] N homonymie f

homophobe [ˌhəʊməʊ'fəʊb] N homophobe mf

homophobia [ˌhəʊməʊ'fəʊbɪə] N homophobie f

homophobic [ˌhəʊməʊ'fəʊbɪk] ADJ homophobe

homophone ['hɒməfəʊn] N homophone m

homophonic [ˌhɒmə'fɒnɪk] ADJ homophone

homophony [hɒ'mɒfənɪ] N homophonie f

homo sapiens ['hɒməʊ'sæpɪˌenz] N homo sapiens m

homosexual [ˌhɒməʊ'seksjʊəl] ADJ, N homosexuel(le) m(f)

homosexuality [ˌhɒməʊseksjʊ'ælɪtɪ] N homosexualité f

homunculus [hɒ'mʌŋkjʊləs] N (pl homunculi [hɒ'mʌŋkjʊlaɪ]) homoncule m or homuncule m

hon* [hʌn] N (US) (ABBR = honey) hi, ~! bonjour, chéri(e) !

Hon. (in titles) ABBR = Honorary or Honourable

honcho* ['hɒntʃəʊ] N (US) patron m, grand chef m

Honduran [hɒn'djʊərən] [1] ADJ hondurien [2] N Hondurien(ne) m(f)

Honduras [hɒn'djʊərəs] N le Honduras; in ~ au Honduras

hone [həʊn] [1] N pierre f à aiguiser [2] VT a [+ craft, abilities, wit, skill] affiner; ~d to perfection ◊ finely ~d parfaitement affiné; a finely ~d body un corps d'athlète b [+ blade] affûter, affiler; finely ~d parfaitement affûté or affilé

honest ['ɒnɪst] [1] ADJ [person, action] honnête (with sb avec qn, about sth en ce qui concerne qch); [face] franc (franche f); [answer] franc (franche f), sincère; [money, profit] honnêtement acquis or gagné; (Jur) [goods] de qualité loyale et marchande; he's (as) ~ as the day is long il est on ne peut plus honnête, il est foncièrement honnête; now, be ~! (= say what you think) allons, dis ce que tu penses !; (= tell the truth, be objective) allons, sois honnête !; ~ to goodness (with you) ... à vrai dire ...; ~ (injun)!* parole d'honneur !; ~ to goodness or God!* (expressing sincerity) parole d'honneur !; (expressing impatience) vingt dieux !*; by ~ means par des moyens honnêtes; an ~ mistake une erreur commise en toute bonne foi; I'd like your ~ opinion of it j'aimerais que vous me donniez honnêtement votre avis (là-dessus); an ~ day's work une honnête journée de travail; (hum) to earn an ~ penny or crust gagner honnêtement sa vie or son pain; I'm trying to turn an ~ penny j'essaie de me faire de l'argent honnêtement; the ~ truth la pure vérité; (the) God's ~ truth* la vérité pure; († or hum) he made an ~ woman of her il a fini par l'épouser; good, ~ home cooking de la bonne cuisine bourgeoise

[2] COMP ► **honest broker** N (Brit: esp Pol) arbitre m (impartial) ► **honest-to-God***, **honest-to-goodness*** ADJ très simple, sans chichi*

honestly ['ɒnɪstlɪ] ADV [act, behave, say, answer] honnêtement; [think, expect] vraiment; ~? c'est vrai ?; I can ~ say that ... franchement or en toute honnêteté, je peux dire que ...; I ~ believe that ... je suis convaincu que ...; no, ~, I'm fine non, vraiment, je me sens bien; ~, I don't care honnêtement or franchement, ça m'est égal; I didn't do it, ~ ce n'est pas moi, je le jure or parole d'honneur; quite ~ ... en toute honnêteté ...; ~, that woman!* celle-là, alors !*; ~, this is getting ridiculous!* enfin, ça devient ridicule !

honesty ['ɒnɪstɪ] [1] N a (= integrity, truthfulness) [of person] honnêteté f; [of words, writing] franchise f, sincérité f; (= sincerity) sincérité f; in all ~ en toute honnêteté ■ (PROV) ~ is the best policy l'honnêteté paie b (Bot) lunaire f, monnaie-du-pape f [2] COMP ► **honesty box** N boîte où l'on est invité à déposer le montant d'un journal en distribution hors kiosque, d'un trajet impayé, etc

honey ['hʌnɪ] N a miel m; clear/thick ~ miel m liquide/solide b (= person) yes, ~* oui, chéri(e); she's a ~* elle est adorable, c'est un chou*

honeybee ['hʌnɪbiː] N abeille f

honeybunch* ['hʌnɪbʌntʃ], **honeybun*** ['hʌnɪbʌn] N (esp US) hi, ~! salut, chéri(e) !

honeycomb ['hʌnɪkəʊm] [1] N a (of bees) rayon m de miel b (Tex) nid m d'abeille [2] VT (Metal) soufflure f [2] VT (fig) cribler (with de); the palace was ~ed with corridors le palais était un dédale de couloirs [3] COMP [textile, pattern] en nid d'abeille

honeydew ['hʌnɪdjuː] [1] N [of insects] miellat m; [of plants] miellée f [2] COMP ► **honeydew melon** N melon m d'hiver or d'Espagne

honeyed ['hʌnɪd] ADJ a [scent, taste] de miel b [words, voice] mielleux, doucereux

honeymoon ['hʌnɪˌmuːn] N (= trip) voyage m de noces; (= period) lune f de miel; their ~ was spent in Paris ils sont allés à Paris en voyage de noces; they spent their ~ at home ils ont passé leur lune de miel à la maison; we were on our ~ nous étions en voyage de noces; **while on ~ in Majorca they ...** pendant leur voyage de noces à Majorque, ils ... **2** VI passer son voyage de noces; **while ~ing in Majorca we ...** pendant notre voyage de noces à Majorque, nous ... **3** COMP ► **honeymoon couple** N jeunes mariés *mpl* (en voyage de noces) ► **honeymoon period** N (*fig*) lune *f* de miel ► **honeymoon suite** N suite *f* nuptiale

honeymooner ['hʌnɪ,muːnəʳ] N jeune marié(e) *m(f)* (en voyage de noces)

honeypot ['hʌnɪpɒt] N (*lit*) pot *m* à miel; (*fig*) **a tourist ~ ◊ a ~ for tourists** un lieu qui attire les touristes → **bee**

honeysuckle ['hʌnɪsʌkəl] N chèvrefeuille *m*

Hong Kong ['hɒŋ'kɒŋ] N Hong-Kong; **in ~** à Hong-Kong

honk [hɒŋk] **1** VI **a** (*car*) klaxonner; (*goose*) cacarder **b** (‡ = *stink*) chlinguer‡, cocotter*; **it's ~ing in here!** ça chlingue‡ *or* cocotte* ici! **2** VT **to ~ the** *or* **one's horn** klaxonner, corner **3** N (*of car*) coup *m* de klaxon®; (*of goose*) cri *m*; **~, ~!** (*of car*) tut-tut!; (*of goose*) coin-coin!

honkie‡, **honky**‡ ['hɒŋkɪ] N (*US pej*) sale Blanc *m*, sale Blanche *f*

honky-tonk* ['hɒŋkɪ,tɒŋk] N **a** (*US = club*) bastringue* *m*, beuglant‡ *m* **b** (*Mus*) musique *f* de bastringue

Honolulu [,hɒnə'luːluː] N Honolulu

honor ['ɒnəʳ] (*US*) = **honour**

honorable ['ɒnərəbl] ADJ (*US*) = **honourable**

honorably ['ɒnərəblɪ] ADV (*US*) = **honourably**

honorarium [,ɒnə'rɛərɪəm] N (*pl* **honorariums** *or* **honoraria** [,ɒnə'rɛərɪə]) honoraires *mpl* (*no sg*)

honorary ['ɒnərərɪ] **1** ADJ (*official, member*) honoraire; (*duties, titles*) honorifique; (*degree*) accordé à titre honorifique; (*Univ*) **to be awarded an ~ doctorate** être nommé docteur honoris causa **2** COMP ► **Honorary Secretary** N secrétaire *mf* honoraire

honorific [,ɒnə'rɪfɪk] **1** ADJ honorifique **2** N titre *m* honorifique

honour, honor (*US*) ['ɒnəʳ] **1** N **a** honneur *m*; **in ~ of ...** en l'honneur de ...; ■(*PROV*) **(there is) ~ among thieves** les loups ne se mangent pas entre eux; (*woman*) **to lose one's ~†** s'être déshonoré†; **he is the soul of ~** c'est la probité même; **on** *or* **upon my ~!†** parole d'honneur!; **to be on one's ~ to do sth** s'être engagé à faire; **she put me on my ~ to own up** je lui ai donné ma parole d'honneur que j'avouerais; **it is a great ~ for me** c'est un grand honneur pour moi; **it is an ~ for me to be here** c'est un honneur pour moi que d'être ici; **it does him ~** c'est tout à son honneur; **to what do we owe this ~?** qu'est-ce qui nous vaut cet honneur?; (*frm*) **I have the ~ to inform you** *or* **of informing you that ...** j'ai l'honneur de vous informer que ...; (*frm*) **may I have the ~ of accompanying you?** puis-je avoir l'honneur de vous accompagner?; (*frm*) **perhaps you will do me the ~ of dancing with me?** me ferez-vous l'honneur de m'accorder une danse?; **he is an ~ to his father/his regiment** il fait honneur à son père/son régiment → **debt, word** **b** **to do the ~s** (= *introductions*) faire les présentations (*entre invités*); (*of one's house*) faire les honneurs de sa maison **c** (*Mil etc*) **the last ~s** les derniers honneurs *mpl*, le dernier hommage; **with full military ~s** avec les honneurs militaires → **guard** **d** (*frm: title*) **Your/His Honour** Votre/Son Honneur **e** (*Brit Univ*) **to take ~s in English** ≈ faire une licence d'anglais; **he got first-/second-class ~s in English** ≈ il a eu sa licence d'anglais avec mention très bien/mention bien **f** (*Bridge*) honneur *m* **g** (*Brit = award*) distinction *f* honorifique

2 VT **a** (+ *person*) honorer, faire honneur à; **to feel ~ed (to do sth)** être honoré (de faire qch); **I'm ~ed** je suis très honoré, quel honneur!; **I'd be ~ed** je serais très honoré; (*gen, iro*) **she ~ed them with her presence** elle les honora de sa présence; **since you have ~ed me with your confidence** puisque vous m'avez fait l'honneur de m'accorder votre confiance; (*in dancing*) **to ~ one's partner** saluer son cavalier (*or* sa cavalière); **~ed guest** invité(e) *m(f)* d'honneur **b** (+ *cheque, contract*) honorer

3 COMP ► **honor roll** N (*US*) (*gen*) liste *f* honorifique; (*Mil*) liste *f* d'anciens combattants; (*Scol*) liste *f* des meilleurs élèves ► **honors course** N (*US*) cours réservé aux meilleurs étudiants ► **honors degree** N (*US*) licence *f* avec mention ► **honor society** N (*US Scol*) club *m* des meilleurs élèves ► **honor system** N (*US*) système *m* de l'auto-surveillance (*dans les écoles et les prisons*) ► **honour-bound** ADJ **to be ~-bound to do sth** être tenu par l'honneur de faire qch ► **honours course** N (*Brit Univ*) ≈ licence *f* ► **honours degree** N (*Brit Univ*) ≈ licence *f* ► **Honours List** N (*Brit*) liste de distinctions honorifiques conférées par le monarque

---

HONOURS LIST

La **Honours List** est la liste des personnes proposées pour recevoir une distinction honorifique telle qu'un MBE (titre de « Member of the Order of the British Empire ») ou un OBE (titre de « Officer of the Order of the British Empire »). Cette liste, établie par le Premier ministre et approuvée par le monarque, est publiée deux fois par an au moment de la nouvelle année (**New Year's Honours List**) et de l'anniversaire de la reine en juin (**Queen's Birthday Honours List**).

---

honourable, honorable (*US*) ['ɒnərəbl] ADJ [*person, action, intentions*] honorable; [*contract, debt*] d'honneur; **an ~ mention** une mention honorable; (*title*) **the Honourable ...** l'honorable ...; (*Brit Parl*) **my (right) Honourable friend** mon (très) honorable collègue; (*Brit Parl*) **the (right) Honourable member for Weston** ≈ Monsieur (*or* Madame) le député de Weston → **right**

honourably, honorably (*US*) ['ɒnərəblɪ] ADV honorablement

Hons. (*Univ*) (ABBR = **honours degree**) avec mention

Hon. Sec. N (ABBR = **Honorary Secretary**) → **honorary**

hooch‡ [huːtʃ] N (= *alcoholic drink*) gnôle* *f*

hood [hʊd] **1** N **a** (*gen*) capuchon *m*; [*of executioner etc*] cagoule *f*; (*Univ*) épitoge *f*; [*of falcon*] chaperon *m*; **rain ~** capuche *f* (*en plastique*) **b** (*Brit Aut*) capote *f*; (*US Aut*) capot *m* **c** [*of pram*] capote *f*; (*over fire, cooker etc*) hotte *f* **d** [*of cobra*] capuchon *m* **e** (‡ = *hoodlum*) truand *m* **2** VT (+ *falcon*) chaperonner, encaperonner

hooded ['hʊdɪd] **1** ADJ (*gen*) [*monk, figure, gunman*] encapuchonné; [*prisoner*] au visage couvert; [*coat etc*] à capuchon; **he has ~ eyes** il a les paupières tombantes **2** COMP ► **hooded crow** N corneille *f* mantelée ► **hooded falcon** N faucon *m* chaperonné *or* encaperonné

hoodlum ['huːdləm] N truand *m*

hoodoo* ['huːduː] **1** N (= *bad luck*) guigne* *f*, poisse* *f*; (= *object, person*) porte-guigne* *m* **2** VT porter la guigne* *or* la poisse* à

hoodwink ['hʊd,wɪŋk] VT tromper, duper; **they ~ed me into accepting** j'ai accepté sur la foi d'informations erronées

hooey* ['huːɪ] N (*US*) sornettes *fpl*, conneries‡ *fpl*; **to talk a lot of ~** dire des bêtises, déconner‡

hoof [huːf] **1** N (*pl* **hoofs** *or* **hooves**) sabot *m* (*d'animal*); **on the ~** sur pied → **cloven** **2** VT **to ~ it**‡ (= *walk*) aller à pinces*; (*US = dance*) danser, se trémousser **3** COMP ► **hoof and mouth disease** N (*US*) fièvre *f* aphteuse

hoofed [huːft] ADJ à sabots

hoofer* ['huːfəʳ] N (*esp US = dancer*) danseur *m*, -euse *f* professionnel(le)

hoo-ha* ['huː,hɑː] N (= *noise*) brouhaha *m*, boucan* *m*; (= *confusion*) pagaille* *f* or pagaïe* *f*; (= *bustle*) tohu-bohu *m*; (= *excitement*) animation *f*; (*pej* = *fuss*) **there was a great ~ about it** on en a fait tout un foin* *or* tout un plat*

hook [hʊk] **1** N **a** crochet *m*; (*for hanging coats*) patère *f*; (*on dress*) agrafe *f*; (*Fishing*) hameçon *m*; (*Sewing*) **~s and eyes** agrafes *fpl*; (*fig*) **he swallowed the story ~, line and sinker*** il a gobé* tout ce qu'on lui a raconté, il a tout avalé (*fig*); **by ~ or by crook** coûte que coûte, par tous les moyens; **to get sb off the ~*** tirer qn d'affaire *or* d'un mauvais pas; **to let sb off the ~*** [+ *wrongdoer*] ficher la paix à qn*; [+ *sb with problem*] tirer une épine du pied à qn; **he's off the ~*** il est tiré d'affaire; (*pej*) **to get one's ~s into sb/sth*** mettre le grappin sur qn/qch **b** (*Telec*) **to take the phone off the ~** décrocher le téléphone; **the phone's off the ~** on a décroché le téléphone; (*US*) **the phone was ringing off the ~*** le téléphone n'arrêtait pas de sonner **c** (*Boxing*) crochet *m*; **right ~** crochet *m* (du) droit **d** (*Golf*) coup *m* hooké **e** (*Agr*) faucille *f* **2** VT accrocher (**to** à); [+ *dress*] agrafer; (*Naut*) gaffer; (*Boxing*) donner un crochet à; (*Fishing*) prendre; (*Golf*) hooker; (*Rugby*) **to ~ the ball** talonner le ballon; **to ~ a husband*** se trouver un mari → **hooked** **3** VI **a** (*Golf*) hooker **b** (*US*‡) [*prostitute*] faire le tapin‡ *or* le trottoir* **4** COMP ► **hook-nosed** ADJ au nez recourbé *or* crochu ► **the Hook of Holland** N Hoek van Holland

► **hook on 1** VI s'accrocher (**to** à) **2** VT SEP accrocher (**to** à)

► **hook up 1** VI [*dress etc*] s'agrafer **2** VT SEP **a** [+ *dress etc*] agrafer **b** (*Rad, TV*‡) faire un duplex entre **3** **~up*** N → **hookup**

hookah ['hʊkɑː] N narguilé *m*

hooked [hʊkt] ADJ **a** (= *hook-shaped*) [*nose*] recourbé, crochu; **the end of the wire was ~** le bout du fil (de fer) était recourbé **b** (= *having hooks*) muni de crochets *or* d'agrafes *or* d'hameçons → **hook c** (* *fig*) (= *fascinated*) fasciné (**on** par), accroché*; (= *dependent*) pendant (**on** de); **he's ~ on it** il ne peut plus s'en passer; **to get ~ on** [+ *drugs*] devenir accro*; à; [+ *jazz, television*] devenir enragé* de; **he's really ~ on that girl** il est complètement dingue* de cette fille; **he's become ~ on power** il aime trop le pouvoir: il ne peut plus s'en passer; **once I'd seen the first episode I was ~** après avoir vu le premier épisode j'étais accro* **d** (‡ = *married*) casé*, marié

hooker ['hʊkəʳ] N **a** (*Rugby*) talonneur *m* **b** (‡ = *prostitute*) putain‡ *f*

hookey* ['hʊkɪ] N **to play ~** sécher les cours, faire l'école buissonnière

hookup* ['hʊkʌp] N (*Rad, TV*) relais *m* temporaire

hookworm ['hʊkwɜːm] N ankylostome *m*

hooky* ['hʊkɪ] N = **hookey**

hooligan ['huːlɪgən] N vandale *m*, hooligan *m*

hooliganism ['huːlɪgənɪzəm] N vandalisme *m*, hooliganisme *m*

hoop [huːp] N [*of barrel*] cercle *m*; (= *toy: in circus; for skirt*) cerceau *m*; (*Basketball*) cercle *m* du) panier *m*; (*Croquet*) arceau *m*; (*fig*) **they put him through the ~(s)** (= *interrogated*) ils l'ont mis sur la sellette; **they put him through** or **made him jump through ~s** (= put to test) ils l'ont mis à l'épreuve

hoopla ['hu:plɑ:] N [a] (Brit) jeu m d'anneaux (dans les foires) [b] (US*) = **hoo-ha**

hoopoe ['hu:pu:] N huppe f

hooray [hu:'reɪ] [1] EXCL hourra [2] COMP ► **Hooray Henry** N (pl **Hooray Henries**) (Brit pej) jeune homme des classes supérieures jovial et bruyant

hoosegow: ['hu:sgaʊ] N (US) taule* f or tôle* f, trou* m

Hoosier ['hu:ʒər] N (US) habitant(e) m(f) de l'Indiana; **the ~ State** l'Indiana m

hoot [hu:t] [1] N [a] (of owl) hululement m; (esp Brit) (Aut) coup m de klaxon®; [of siren] mugissement m; [of train] sifflement m; (= jeer) huée f; **she gave a ~ of laughter** elle s'est esclaffée; **I don't give or care a ~ or two ~s*** je m'en fiche* [b] (* = amusing thing, person) **it was a ~** c'était tordant* or marrant*; **she's a ~** elle est impayable* [2] VI [owl] hululer; (esp Brit) [car horn] klaxonner, corner; [siren] mugir; [train] siffler; (= jeer) huer, pousser des huées; **to ~ with laughter** s'esclaffer, rire aux éclats; **to ~ with derision/delight** pousser des cris moqueurs/de joie [3] VT [a] (also ~ **down**) [+ actor, speaker] huer, conspuer [b] **to ~ the** or **one's horn** klaxonner

hooter ['hu:tər] N [a] (of factory) sirène f; (Brit) [of car] klaxon® m; [of train] sifflet m [b] (Brit* = nose) pif* m, blair* m [c] (US) **~s:** (= breasts) roberts: mpl

Hoover® ['hu:vər] (Brit) [1] N aspirateur m [2] VT **to hoover a carpet/a room** passer l'aspirateur sur un tapis/dans une pièce

hooves [hu:vz] NPL of **hoof**

hop¹ [hɒp] [1] N [a] [of person, animal] saut m; [of bird] sautillement m; (Sport) ~ **skip and jump** ◊ ~ **step and jump** triple saut m; (fig) **it's a ~, skip** or **step and jump from here** c'est à deux pas d'ici; **with a ~, skip** or **step and jump he was gone** une pirouette et il avait disparu; (Brit fig) **to catch sb on the ~** prendre qn au dépourvu; (Brit) **to keep sb/be on the ~*** ne pas laisser à qn/ne pas avoir le temps de respirer* [b] (†* = dance) sauterie† f [c] (Aviat) étape f; **from London to Athens in two ~s** de Londres à Athènes en deux étapes; **it's a short ~ from Paris to Brussels** ce n'est qu'un saut de Paris à Bruxelles [2] VI [person] (on one foot) sauter à cloche-pied; (= jump) sauter; [animal] sauter; [bird] sautiller; **he ~ped over to the window** il est allé à cloche-pied jusqu'à la fenêtre; (in car etc) ~ **in!** montez!; **he ~ped out of bed** il a sauté du lit; (fig) **he ~ped onto a plane for London** il a attrapé un avion pour Londres → **mad** [3] VT sauter; (Brit) **to ~ it*** décamper*, mettre les bouts* or les voiles*; (Brit) ~ **it!*** fiche le camp!*; (US) **he ~ped a flight to New York** il a attrapé un avion pour New York [4] COMP ► **hop-o'-my-thumb** N le Petit Poucet

► **hop off*** VI (= leave) décamper*, ficher le camp*

hop² [hɒp] [1] N (Bot: also ~s) houblon m [2] COMP ► **hop-picker** N cueilleur m, -euse f de houblon ► **hop-picking** N cueillette f du houblon ► **hop pole** N perche f à houblon

▼ **hope** [həʊp] [1] N espoir m (**of doing** de faire), espérance f (liter, also Rel); **we must live in ~** nous devons vivre d'espoir; **she lives in (the) ~ of seeing her son again** elle continue d'espérer revoir un jour son fils; **in the ~ that ...** dans l'espoir que ...; **in the ~ of sth/of doing** dans l'espoir de qch/de faire; **to have ~s of doing** avoir l'espoir de faire; **I haven't much ~ of succeeding** je n'ai pas beaucoup d'espoir de réussir; **to give up ~** cesser d'espérer, per-

dre espoir; **you should never give up ~** il ne faut jamais perdre espoir; **to give up ~ of doing** abandonner l'espoir de faire; **past** or **beyond (all) ~** sans espoir, désespéré; **the car was smashed beyond any ~ of repair** la voiture était bonne pour la casse; **she hasn't (got) a ~ in hell:** of being promoted elle n'a pas la moindre chance d'être promue; **there is no ~ of that** c'est hors de question; **he set out with high ~s** il s'est lancé avec l'espoir de faire de grandes choses; **she had high ~s of winning** elle avait bon espoir de gagner; **her family has great** or **high ~s of her** sa famille a de grands espoirs pour elle; **to raise sb's ~s** faire naître l'espoir chez qn; **don't raise her ~s too much** ne lui laisse or donne pas trop d'espoir; **don't get your ~s up** or **raise your ~s too much** n'y compte pas trop; **to lose (all) ~ of sth/of doing** perdre l'espoir or tout espoir de qch/de faire; **my ~ is that ...** ce que j'espère or mon espoir c'est que ...; **you're my last ~** tu es mon dernier espoir; **she's now our best ~** elle représente maintenant notre plus grand espoir; **some ~(s)!*** tu parles!*, tu crois au père Noël!* → **dash, faith, hold out** [2] VI (for money/for success) espérer gagner de l'argent/avoir du succès; **they were still hoping for a peaceful solution to the crisis** ils espéraient toujours trouver une solution pacifique à la crise; **we're hoping for fine weather** nous espérons avoir du beau temps or qu'il fera beau; **if I were you I shouldn't ~ for too much from the meeting** à votre place je n'attendrais pas trop de la réunion; **don't ~ for too much** n'en attendez pas trop; **it was too much to ~ for (that ...)** ça aurait été trop beau (que ... (+ subj)); **a pay rise would be too much to ~ for** une augmentation? il ne faut pas rêver!; **to ~ for better days** espérer (connaître) des jours meilleurs; **we must ~ for better things** il faut espérer que de meilleurs jours viendront or que ça ira mieux; **to ~ for the best** espérer que tout se passe au mieux; **to ~ against ~** espérer en dépit de tout or contre tout espoir [3] VT espérer; **I ~ (that) he comes** j'espère qu'il viendra; **I ~ to see you** ◊ **I ~ I'll see you** j'espère te voir; **I ~ to God** or **hell:** she **remembers/he doesn't turn up** j'espère vraiment qu'elle s'en souvient/qu'il ne viendra pas; **what do you ~ to gain by that?** qu'espères-tu obtenir par là?; **the party cannot ~ to win more than a few seats** le parti ne peut espérer obtenir plus que quelques sièges; (in letter) **hoping to hear from you** dans l'espoir d'avoir de vos nouvelles; **I ~ so** (answer to question) j'espère que oui; (agreeing with sb's statement) je l'espère, j'espère bien; **I ~ not** (answer to question) j'espère que non; (agreeing: also **I should ~ not**) j'espère bien que non! [4] COMP ► **hope chest** N (US) (armoire f or malle f à) trousseau m

hoped-for ['həʊptfɔːr] ADJ espéré

hopeful ['həʊpfʊl] [1] ADJ [a] (= optimistic) [person, face] plein d'espoir; **to be** or **feel ~ (that ...)** avoir bon espoir (que ...); **I'll ask her but I'm not too ~** je lui demanderai mais je n'y crois pas trop; **to be ~ of doing sth** avoir bon espoir de faire qch [b] (= promising) [sign, future] prometteur; [situation, news] encourageant [2] N **the young ~s** (showing promise) les jeunes espoirs mpl; (ambitious) les jeunes ambitieux mpl; (hoping for sth) les jeunes optimistes mpl; **the British Olympic ~s** (hoping to make team) les candidats mpl à la sélection pour l'équipe olympique britannique; (hoping to win medal) les prétendants mpl britanniques à une médaille olympique; **presidential ~ Gavin Killip** le candidat à la présidence Gavin Killip

hopefully ['həʊpfəlɪ] ADV [a] (= optimistically) [say, look at] avec espoir; **... she asked ~ ...** demanda-t-elle pleine d'espoir [b] (* = one

hopes) avec un peu de chance; **~ we'll be able to find a solution** avec un peu de chance, nous trouverons une solution; **~ it won't rain** j'espère qu'il ne va pas pleuvoir; **(yes) ~!** je l'espère!, j'espère bien!; **~ not!** j'espère que non!

hopeless ['həʊplɪs] ADJ [a] (= doomed) [person, cause, situation, position, attempt] désespéré; [love, task] impossible; **it's ~!** c'est désespérant!; **a ~ muddle** or **mess** une effroyable pagaille; **in the face of** or **against ~ odds** face à une situation désespérée; (= in despair) **to feel ~** désespéré [b] (= incurable) [romantic] incorrigible; [drunk] invétéré; **he's ~** ◊ **he's a ~ case** c'est un cas désespéré [c] (* = useless) [person, work] nul; **he's a ~ teacher** il est nul comme professeur; **to be ~ at maths/sport** etc être nul en maths/sport etc; **to be ~ at doing sth** être nul quand il s'agit de faire qch

hopelessly ['həʊplɪslɪ] ADV [a] (= despairingly) avec désespoir [b] (= impossibly) [confused] totalement; [lost] complètement; **~ naïve** d'une naïveté désespérante; **supplies were ~ inadequate** les provisions manquaient cruellement; **to be ~ in love** or **besotted (with sb)** être éperdument amoureux (de qn)

hopelessness ['həʊplɪsnɪs] N [of situation] caractère m désespéré; (= powerlessness) sentiment m d'impuissance; (= despair) désespoir m

hopfield ['hɒpfiːld] N houblonnière f

hophead: ['hɒphed] N (US pej) junkie: mf

hopper ['hɒpər] [1] N [a] (= bin) trémie f [b] (Austral*) kangourou m [2] COMP ► **hopper car** N (Rail) wagon-trémie m

hopscotch ['hɒpskɒtʃ] N marelle f

Horace ['hɒrɪs] N Horace m

Horae ['hɔːriː] NPL (Myth) Heures fpl

horde [hɔːd] N horde f (also pej), foule f; **~s of people** des foules de gens

horizon [həˈraɪzn] N (lit) horizon m; (fig) vue f, horizon m; (lit, fig) **on the ~** à l'horizon; **the mountains on the distant ~** les montagnes loin à l'horizon; (fig) **a man of limited ~s** un homme aux vues étroites; (fig) **to broaden** or **expand one's ~s** élargir son horizon or ses horizons; **to open new ~s for sb** ouvrir des horizons à qn

horizontal [ˌhɒrɪˈzɒntl] [1] ADJ horizontal [2] N horizontale f [3] COMP ► **horizontal bar** N barre f fixe

horizontally [ˌhɒrɪˈzɒntəlɪ] ADV horizontalement

hormonal [hɔːˈməʊnəl] ADJ hormonal

hormone ['hɔːməʊn] [1] N hormone f [2] COMP ► **hormone replacement therapy** N traitement m hormonal substitutif ► **hormone treatment** N traitement m hormonal

horn [hɔːn] [1] N [a] corne f; (fig) **to draw in** or **pull in one's ~s** (= back down) diminuer d'ardeur; (= spend less) restreindre son train de vie → **dilemma** [b] (Mus) cor m → **French** [c] [of car] klaxon® m, avertisseur m; [of boat] sirène f; **to blow** or **sound the** or **one's ~** klaxonner, corner → **foghorn** [d] (US: = telephone) bigophone* m; **to get on the ~ to sb** passer un coup de bigophone* à qn [2] COMP [handle, saddle] corne f, pommeau m [2] COMP [handle, ornament] en corne ► **horn of plenty** N corne f d'abondance ► **horn-rimmed spectacles** NPL lunettes fpl à monture d'écaille

► **horn in:** VI (esp US) mettre son grain de sel

hornbeam ['hɔːnbiːm] N (Bot) charme m

hornbill ['hɔːnbɪl] N calao m

horned [hɔːnd] [1] ADJ (gen) cornu [2] COMP ► **horned owl** N duc m (Orn) ► **horned toad** N crapaud m cornu

hornet ['hɔːnɪt] N frelon m; (fig) **his inquiries stirred up a ~'s nest** ses investigations ont mis le feu aux poudres; **the case has opened up a**

► LANGUAGE IN USE: **hope** 8.4, 23, 25.2

~'s nest of moral and legal concerns cette affaire soulève une série de questions épineuses, tant morales que juridiques

hornless ['hɔːnlɪs] ADJ sans cornes

hornpipe ['hɔːnpaɪp] N (*Naut*) matelote *f* (*danse*)

horny ['hɔːnɪ] ADJ [a] (= *like horn*) corné; [*hands etc*] calleux [b] (‡ = *sexually aroused*) excité*; (*sexuellement*) [c] (‡ = *sexually attractive*) sexy*

horology [hɒ'rɒlədʒɪ] N horlogerie *f*

horoscope ['hɒrəskəup] N horoscope *m*

horrendous [hɒ'rendəs] ADJ épouvantable

horrible ['hɒrɪbl] ADJ [a] (= *horrific*) horrible; [*moment*] terrible; **the ~ truth** la terrible vérité [b] (= *unpleasant, awful*) épouvantable; [*clothes*] affreux; [*mistake*] terrible [c] (* = *unkind*) [*person*] méchant (**to sb** avec qn); **that's a ~ thing to say!** c'est vraiment méchant *or* terrible de dire des choses pareilles!; **all the ~ things I said to you** toutes les horreurs que je t'ai dites

horribly ['hɒrɪblɪ] ADV [a] (= *horrifically*) [*die, scream*] d'une manière horrible; [*mutilated, disfigured, injured*] horriblement; [*cruel*] très, particulièrement; [*violent*] terriblement [b] (= *unpleasantly, awfully*) [*expensive, guilty, embarrassed, uncomfortable*] terriblement; **it's all gone ~ wrong** les choses ont très mal tourné; **I'm going to be ~ late** je vais être affreusement en retard

horrid ['hɒrɪd] ADJ (= *nasty*) [*person*] ignoble; [*weather, place*] épouvantable; (= *ugly*) hideux; **a ~ child** une (petite) horreur*

horrific [hɒ'rɪfɪk] ADJ atroce, horrible

horrifically [hɒ'rɪfɪkəlɪ] ADV [*injured, burned, beaten*] horriblement; [*expensive, dangerous*] terriblement

horrified ['hɒrɪfaɪd] ADJ horrifié

horrify ['hɒrɪfaɪ] VT horrifier

horrifying ['hɒrɪfaɪɪŋ] ADJ effrayant

horrifyingly ['hɒrɪfaɪɪŋlɪ] ADV effroyablement

horror ['hɒrə'] [1] N (= *feeling, object*) horreur *f*; **to have a ~ of sth/of doing** avoir horreur de qch/de faire; **the ~s of war** les horreurs *fpl* de la guerre; **to my ~ I realized that ...** je me suis rendu compte avec horreur que ...; **to my ~ he returned with a knife** à ma grande horreur il est revenu un couteau à la main; **they watched in ~ as the train left the tracks** le train a déraillé sous leurs yeux horrifiés; **and then, ~ of ~s*, he said ...** et alors, pour comble de l'horreur, il a dit ...; **you little ~!** petit monstre!*; (*as headline*) **nine die in motorway ~** scènes d'horreur sur l'autoroute: neuf morts → **chamber** [2] COMP [*book, film, comic*] d'épouvante ► **horror story** N (*lit*) histoire *f* d'épouvante; (*fig*) horreur *f* ► **horror-stricken, horror-struck** ADJ glacé d'horreur

horse [hɔːs] [1] N [a] cheval *m*; **to work like a ~** travailler comme un forcené; (*fig*) (*straight*) **from the ~'s mouth** de source sûre; (*lit, fig*) **to back the wrong ~** miser sur le mauvais cheval; (*fig*) **that's a ~ of a different colour** cela n'a rien à voir; (*fig*) **hold your ~s!** arrêtez!, minute!*; (*Brit*) **it's (a case of) ~s for courses** chacun selon ses compétences; (*fig*) **to change** *or* **switch ~s in midstream** changer de cheval au milieu du gué ■ (*PROV*) **you can take** *or* **lead a ~ to water but you cannot make it drink** on ne peut pas forcer les gens → **dark, eat, gift, white, willing** [b] (*Gym*) cheval *m* d'arçons → **clothes** [c] (*NonC: Mil*) cavalerie *f*; **light ~** cavalerie *f* légère [d] (*Drugs* = *heroin*) blanche* *f*, héroïne *f* [2] COMP ► **horse-and-buggy** ADJ (*US*) [*approach, system*] dépassé ► **horse artillery** N troupes *fpl* montées ► **horse brass** N médaillon *m* de cuivre (*fixé à une martingale*) ► **horse-breaker** N dresseur *m*, -euse *f* de chevaux ► **horse breeder** N éleveur *m*, -euse *f* de chevaux ► **horse chestnut** N (=

nut) marron *m* (d'Inde); (*also ~ chestnut tree*) marronnier *m* (d'Inde) ► **horse-collar** N collier *m* (de harnais) ► **horse-dealer** N maquignon *m* ► **horse-doctor*** N vétérinaire *mf* ► **horse-drawn** ADJ tiré par des chevaux, à chevaux ► **the Horse Guards** NPL (*Brit Mil*) (le régiment de) la Garde à cheval ► **horse latitudes** NPL latitudes *fpl* subtropicales ► **horse-laugh** N gros rire *m* ► **horse manure** N crottin *m* de cheval ► **horse opera*** N (*US Cine, TV*) western *m* ► **horse-race** N course *f* de chevaux ► **horse-racing** N courses *fpl* de chevaux, hippisme *m* ► **horse-riding** N (*Brit*) équitation *f* ► **horse-sense*** N (= *gros*) bon sens *m* ► **horse show** N concours *m* hippique ► **horse-trade** VI (*lit*) maquignonner; (*fig*) négocier âprement ► **horse-trader** N (*lit*) maquignon *m*; (*fig*) négociateur *m*, -trice *f* redoutable ► **horse-trading** N (*lit*) maquignonnage *m*; (*fig*) âpres négociations *fpl* ► **horse trailer** N (*US*) = **horsebox** ► **horse trials** NPL concours *m* hippique ► **horse vaulting** N (*Sport*) saut *m* de cheval

► **horse about***, **horse around*** VI chahuter, jouer bruyamment; **stop horsing about!** arrêtez de chahuter!

horseback ['hɔːsbæk] [1] N **on ~** à cheval [2] COMP ► **horseback riding** N (*esp US*) équitation *f*

horsebox ['hɔːsbɒks] N (*Brit*) fourgon *m* à chevaux, van *m*; (*in stable*) box *m*

horsecar ['hɔːskɑː'] N (*US*) fourgon *m* à chevaux, van *m*

horseflesh ['hɔːsflɛʃ] N [a] (= *horses generally*) chevaux *mpl* [b] (= *horsemeat*) viande *f* de cheval

horsefly ['hɔːsflaɪ] N taon *m*

horsehair ['hɔːshɛə'] [1] N crin *m* (de cheval) [2] ADJ de *or* en crin

horsehide ['hɔːshaɪd] N cuir *m* de cheval

horseless ['hɔːslɪs] [1] ADJ sans cheval [2] COMP ► **horseless carriage**† N voiture *f* sans chevaux

horseman ['hɔːsmən] N (*pl* **-men**) cavalier *m*; **he's a good ~** c'est un bon cavalier, il monte bien (à cheval)

horsemanship ['hɔːsmənʃɪp] N (= *skill*) talent *m* de cavalier, monte *f*

horsemeat ['hɔːsmiːt] N viande *f* de cheval

horseplay ['hɔːspleɪ] N chahut *m*

horsepower ['hɔːspauə'] N puissance *f* (en chevaux); (= *unit*) cheval-vapeur *m*; **a ten-~ car** une dix-chevaux

horseradish ['hɔːsrædɪʃ] [1] N (*Bot*) raifort *m* [2] COMP ► **horseradish sauce** N sauce *f* au raifort

horseshit‡ ['hɔːsʃɪt] N (*lit*) crottin *m* (de cheval); (*fig* = *nonsense*) conneries‡ *fpl*

horseshoe ['hɔːsʃuː] [1] N fer *m* à cheval [2] ADJ en fer à cheval

horsetail ['hɔːsteɪl] N (*Bot*) prêle *f*

horsewhip ['hɔːswɪp] [1] N cravache *f* [2] VT cravacher

horsewoman ['hɔːswumən] N (*pl* **-women**) cavalière *f*, écuyère *f*; **she's a good ~** c'est une bonne cavalière, elle monte bien (à cheval)

hors(e)y* ['hɔːsɪ] ADJ [a] (= *fond of horses*) passionné de chevaux; (= *fond of riding*) passionné d'équitation [b] (*in appearance*) [*person, face*] chevalin

horticultural [ˌhɔːtɪ'kʌltʃərəl] ADJ horticole; **~ show** exposition *f* horticole *or* d'horticulture

horticulturalist [ˌhɔːtɪ'kʌltʃərəlɪst] N = **horticulturist**

horticulture ['hɔːtɪkʌltʃə'] N horticulture *f*

horticulturist [ˌhɔːtɪ'kʌltʃərɪst] N horticulteur *m*, -trice *f*

hosanna, hosannah [həʊ'zænə] [1] EXCL hosanna! [2] N hosanna *m*

hose¹ [həʊz] [1] N (*gen*) tuyau *m*; (*also* **garden ~**) tuyau *m* d'arrosage; (*also* **fire ~**) tuyau *m* d'incendie; (*Tech*) (*for water*) manche *f* à eau; (*for air*) manche *f* à air; (*Aut*) durite *f* [2] VT (*in garden*) arroser au jet; [*firemen*] arroser à la lance

► **hose down, hose out** VT SEP laver au jet

hose² [həʊz] N (*pl inv*) (*Comm* = *stockings etc*) bas *mpl*; (*Hist*) (= *tights*) chausses *fpl*; (= *knee breeches*) culotte *f* courte (*jusqu'aux genoux*)

Hosea [həʊ'zɪə] N Osée *m*

hosepipe ['həʊzpaɪp] [1] N (*in garden*) tuyau *m* d'arrosage; (*of fireman*) tuyau *m* d'incendie [2] COMP ► **hosepipe ban** N (*Brit*) interdiction d'arroser pour cause de pénurie d'eau

hosier ['həʊzɪə'] N bonnetier *m*, -ière *f*

hosiery ['həʊzɪərɪ] N (*business*) bonneterie *f*; (*Comm*) (= *stocking department*) (rayon *m* des) bas *mpl*; (= *stockings*) bas *mpl*

hosp N ABBR = **hospital**

hospice ['hɒspɪs] N (*gen*) hospice *m*; (*for terminally ill*) établissement *m* de soins palliatifs

hospitable [hɒs'pɪtəbl] ADJ [*person, place, welcome*] hospitalier; **to sb** envers qn), accueillant; [*climate, environment*] favorable (**to sth** à qch), hospitalier

hospitably [hɒs'pɪtəblɪ] ADV [*welcome*] de façon accueillante

hospital ['hɒspɪtl] [1] N hôpital *m*; **in ~** à l'hôpital; **people** *or* **patients in ~** (malades *mpl*) hospitalisés *mpl*; **to go into ~** aller à l'hôpital, être hospitalisé → **maternity, mental** [2] COMP [*treatment, staff*] hospitalier; [*bed etc*] d'hôpital; [*dispute, strike*] des hôpitaux ► **hospital administrator** N (*Brit*) administrateur *m*, -trice *f* d'hôpital; (*US*) directeur *m*, -trice *f* d'hôpital ► **hospital board** N conseil *m* d'administration de l'hôpital ► **hospital case** N **90% of ~ cases are released within three weeks** 90% des patients hospitalisés sortent dans les trois semaines; **this is a ~ case** le patient doit être hospitalisé ► **hospital doctor** N médecin *m* hospitalier; **junior ~ doctor** interne *m* des hôpitaux ► **hospital facilities** NPL structures *fpl* hospitalières ► **hospital nurse** N infirmier *m*, -ière *f* hospitalier (-ière) ► **hospital service** N service *m* hospitalier ► **hospital ship** N navire-hôpital *m* ► **hospital train** N train *m* sanitaire

hospitality [ˌhɒspɪ'tælɪtɪ] [1] N hospitalité *f* [2] COMP ► **hospitality suite** N salon *m* (*où sont offerts les rafraîchissements*)

hospitalization [ˌhɒspɪtəlaɪ'zeɪʃən] N hospitalisation *f*

hospitalize ['hɒspɪtəlaɪz] VT hospitaliser

host¹ [həʊst] [1] N [a] (= *person receiving guests*) hôte *m*; († = *innkeeper*) patron *m*; [*of TV, radio show*] animateur *m*, -trice *f*, présentateur *m*, -trice *f*; (*hum*) **mine ~** notre hôte (*hum*) [b] (*Bot, Zool*) hôte *m* [2] VT (*Rad, TV*) [+ *show*] animer [3] COMP [*plant, animal*] hôte; [*town etc*] qui reçoit ► **host country** N [*of conference, games etc*] pays *m* d'accueil

host² [həʊst] N [a] (= *crowd*) foule *f*; **a ~ of friends** une foule d'amis; **a whole ~ of reasons** toute une série *or* tout un tas* de raisons [b] †† armée *f*

host³ [həʊst] N (*Rel*) hostie *f*

hostage ['hɒstɪdʒ] N otage *m*; **to take/hold sb ~** prendre/retenir qn en otage; (*fig*) **to be a ~ to fortune** être le jouet du destin

hostel ['hɒstəl] [1] N [a] (*for students, workers*) foyer *m*; **(youth) ~** auberge *f* de jeunesse [b] († = *inn*) auberge *f* [2] VI **to go (youth) ~ling** aller passer ses vacances en auberges de jeunesse

hosteller ['hɒstələr] N ≈ ajiste *mf*

hostelry ['hɒstəlrɪ] N (*esp Brit* ††) hostellerie *f*; (*hum* = *pub*) auberge *f*

hostess ['həʊstɪs] **1** N (gen) hôtesse f; (in night club) entraîneuse f; [of TV, radio show] animatrice f, présentatrice f → **air 2** COMP ► **hostess trolley** N (Brit) table f roulante chauffante

hostile ['hɒstaɪl, (US) 'hɒstəl] **1** ADJ (gen) hostile (to à); (Mil) [fire, force, aircraft] ennemi **2** COMP ► **hostile takeover bid** N (Econ, Fin) OPA f hostile

hostility [hɒ'stɪlɪtɪ] N hostilité f

hostler†† ['ɒslə'] N (US) = **ostler**

hot [hɒt] **1** ADJ **a** (lit) chaud; **to be ~** [person] avoir (très or trop) chaud; [thing] être (très) chaud; (Met) faire (très) chaud; **it's too ~ in here** il fait trop chaud ici; **to get ~** [person] commencer à avoir (trop) chaud; [thing] devenir chaud, chauffer; (Met) commencer à faire chaud; **it was a very ~ day** c'était un jour de grande or de forte chaleur; **the ~ sun** le soleil brûlant; **in the ~ weather** pendant les grandes chaleurs; **bread ~ from the oven** pain tout chaud sorti du four; (on menu) **~ dishes** plats mpl chauds; **I can't drink ~ things** je ne peux pas boire chaud; **the food must be served ~** la nourriture doit être servie bien chaude; (fig) **he's had more trips to Paris than I've had ~ dinners*** c'est un grand habitué des voyages à Paris; **~ and cold (running water)** (eau f courante) chaude et froide; (fig) **to be in ~ water** être dans le pétrin; (fig) **to be or get into ~ water** s'attirer des ennuis; **this subject's too ~ to handle*** ce sujet est trop épineux; **she's too ~ to handle** il vaut mieux ne pas s'y frotter; (US) **that's a ~ button** c'est un sujet épineux, brûlant; **to be (all) ~ and bothered** (= perspiring) être en nage; (= flustered) être dans tous ses états (**about sth** au sujet de qch); **to be/get ~ under the collar*** être/se mettre dans tous ses états (**about sth** au sujet de qch) → **4**; → **cake, coal, iron**

b (fig) [food, curry] fort, épicé; [spices] fort; [news] tout(e) frais (fraîche f); [contest, dispute, competition] acharné; [topic] brûlant; [temperament] passionné, violent; **~ jazz** hot m; **he's got a ~ temper** il a un caractère violent, il est très coléreux; (Pol) **a ~ war*** une guerre ouverte; (Sport) **~ favourite** grand favori m; **~ tip*** tuyau m sûr*; **to be ~ on the trail** être sur la bonne piste; **to be ~ on sb's trail** être sur les talons de qn; (in guessing games etc) **you're getting ~!** tu brûles!; **news ~ from the press** informations fpl de dernière minute; **the latest designs ~ from Milan** les derniers modèles qui arrivent tout droit de Milan; **to make it** or **things ~ for sb*** mettre qn dans une situation délicate → **pursuit**

c (* = very good) (gen) terrible*, sensationnel*; (esp US) **that's ~** c'est fantastique; **not so ~** pas formidable*, pas fameux*; **how are things? — not so ~** comment ça va? — pas terrible*; **he's pretty ~ at maths** c'est un crack* en maths; **he's pretty ~ at football** il joue super bien au foot*; (sexually) **she is so ~*** elle est tellement sexy

d (= successful) [article for sale] très recherché, qui a beaucoup de succès; **the hottest show in town*** un spectacle à voir absolument; **Bardot soon became the hottest property* in show business** bientôt, on s'est arraché Bardot dans le milieu du show-business

e (= stolen) **it's ~*** c'est de la fauche*

2 ADV → **blow¹**

3 hots* NPL **to have the ~s for sb** craquer* complètement pour qn

4 COMP ► **hot air*** N (fig) (= nonsense) blablabla* m, foutaises* fpl; **to blow ~ air** brasser du vent; **he's all ~ air** c'est une grande gueule* ► **hot-air balloon** N ballon m, montgolfière f ► **hot-blooded** ADJ (fig) ardent, passionné ► **hot cross bun** N brioche f du Vendredi saint ► **hot dog** N (Culin) hot-dog m ► **hot-dogging** N (Ski) ski m acrobatique ► **hot**

► **hot flush** N (Med) bouffée f de chaleur ► **hot gospeller*** N prêcheur m évangéliste, exalté(e) m(f) ► **hot issue** N (Fin) émission f des valeurs vedettes ► **hot key** N (Comput) touche f directe ► **hot line** N (Telec) (gen) ligne f ouverte vingt-quatre heures sur vingt-quatre (**to** avec); (Pol) téléphone m rouge (**to** avec) ► **hot money** N (Fin) capitaux mpl spéculatifs or fébriles; (stolen) argent m volé ► **hot pants** NPL mini-short m ► **hot pepper** N piment m rouge ► **hot potato*** N (fig) sujet m brûlant; **he dropped the idea like a ~ potato** il a (soudain) laissé tomber cette idée ► **hot press** N (Ir = airing cupboard) placard-séchoir m ► **hot seat*** N (US = electric chair) chaise f électrique; (fig: in decision-making etc) **to be in the ~ seat** être en première ligne ► **hot-selling** ADJ qui se vend comme des petits pains ► **hot shit***** N (esp US fig) **he really thinks he's ~ shit** il ne se prend pas pour de la merde* ► **hot-shoe** N (Phot) sabot (-contact) m, porte-flash m ► **hot spot*** N (Brit) (= trouble area) point m névralgique or chaud; (= night club) boîte f (de nuit) ► **hot spring** N source f chaude ► **hot stuff*** N **to be ~ stuff** (= terrific) être terrible*; (= daring) [film etc] être osé*; **he's ~ stuff** (= clever) il est génial*; (= sexy) il est sexy* ► **hot-tempered** ADJ emporté, colérique ► **hot tub** N (esp US) jacuzzi® m ► **hot-water bottle** N bouillotte f ► **hot-wire*** VT [+ car] démarrer en faisant se toucher les fils de contact

► **hot up*** (fig) **1** VI (esp Brit) chauffer*; **things are ~ting up in the Middle East** cela commence à chauffer* au Moyen-Orient; (at a party) **things are ~ting up** l'atmosphère commence à chauffer*; **the bars rarely ~ up before 1am** il y a rarement de l'ambiance dans les bars avant une heure du matin **2** VT SEP (= to step up) **police are ~ting up their surveillance** la police renforce sa surveillance

hotbed ['hɒtbed] N **a ~ of vice** une sentine de vices; **a ~ of social unrest** un foyer d'agitation sociale

hotcake ['hɒtkeɪk] N (US) = **pancake**

hotchpotch ['hɒtʃpɒtʃ] N salmigondis m, fatras m

hotel [həʊ'tel] **1** N hôtel m; **to stay at a ~** être à l'hôtel **2** COMP [furniture, prices, porter] d'hôtel ► **hotel industry** N industrie f hôtelière, hôtellerie f ► **hotel manager** N gérant(e) m(f) or directeur m, -trice f d'hôtel ► **hotel receptionist** N réceptionniste mf d'hôtel ► **hotel room** N chambre f d'hôtel ► **hotel ship** N navire-hôtel m ► **hotel staff** N personnel m hôtelier or de l'hôtel ► **hotel work** N **he's looking for ~ work** il cherche un travail dans l'hôtellerie ► **hotel workers** NPL personnel m hôtelier

hotelier [həʊ'telɪə'], **hotelkeeper** [həʊ'tel,kiːpə'] N hôtelier m, -ière f

hotfoot ['hɒt'fʊt] **1** ADV à toute vitesse, à toute allure **2** VT **to ~ it*** galoper

hothead ['hɒthed] **1** N (fig) tête f brûlée **2** ADJ (also **~ed**) [person] impétueux; [attitude] exalté

hothouse ['hɒthaʊs] **1** N (lit) serre f (chaude); (fig) foyer m **2** ADJ (lit) de serre (chaude); (fig) **a ~ atmosphere** une ambiance très compétitive

hothousing ['hɒthaʊzɪŋ] N enseignement intensif à l'intention des enfants surdoués

hotly ['hɒtlɪ] ADV **a** (= keenly) [debated, disputed] avec passion; **~ pursued (by sb)** poursuivi de très près (par qn); **the man ~ tipped to become the next president** l'homme donné comme grand favori de la course à la présidence; **he was ~ tipped to take a gold** il était grand favori pour la médaille d'or; **to be ~ contested** être l'objet d'une lutte acharnée

b (= angrily) [deny] avec virulence; [say] avec feu

hotplate ['hɒtpleɪt] N plaque f chauffante

hotpot ['hɒtpɒt] N (Brit Culin) ragoût de viande aux pommes de terre

hotrod ['hɒtrɒd] N (US: also **~ car**) hotrod m, voiture f gonflée*

hotshot* ['hɒtʃɒt] **1** ADJ [person] génial; [performance] de virtuose; **a ~ lawyer** un ténor du barreau **2** N (= expert) as m, crack* m; (= important person) gros bonnet m

Hottentot ['hɒtntɒt] **1** ADJ hottentot **2 a** Hottentot mf **b** (Ling) hottentot m

houm(o)us ['huːməs] N = **hummus**

hound [haʊnd] **1** N **a** chien m courant, chien m de meute; (hum = any dog) chien m; (Brit) **the ~s** la meute; **to ride to ~s** chasser à courre → **foxhound, master b** († pej = person) canaille f, crapule f **2** VT [+ person] s'acharner sur or contre, harceler; **he is constantly ~ing them for advice** il les harcèle constamment pour leur demander conseil; **to be ~ed by the press** être harcelé par la presse; **he was ~ed out of his job** il a été chassé de son travail; **he was ~ed out of town** il a été forcé à quitter la ville; **they ~ed him for the money** ils n'ont pas arrêté de le harceler pour qu'il leur donne l'argent

► **hound down** VT SEP (traquer et) capturer

► **hound out** VT SEP chasser

hour ['aʊə'] **1** N **a** (= period) heure f; **a quarter of an ~** un quart d'heure; **half an ~ ◊ a half-~** une demi-heure; **an ~ and a half** une heure et demie; **~ by ~** heure par heure; **80km an ~** 80 km à l'heure; **four ~s' walk from here** à quatre heures de marche d'ici; **London is an ~ away from here** Londres est à une heure d'ici; **to do sth (for) ~ after ~** faire qch heure après or des heures d'affilée; **to pay sb by the ~** payer qn à l'heure; **she is paid £8 an ~** elle est payée 8 livres (de) l'heure; **getting there would take ~s** il faudrait des heures pour s'y rendre; **she's been waiting for ~s** elle attend depuis des heures; **to be ~s late** (lit) être en retard de plusieurs heures; (fig) être terriblement en retard

b (= time of day, point in time) heure f; (fig) heure f, moment m; **on the ~** à l'heure juste (toutes les heures); **the ~ has come** l'heure est venue, c'est l'heure; **his ~ has come** son heure est venue; **his last ~ neared** sa dernière heure approchait; **the ~ of his execution** l'heure de son exécution; **the darkest ~ of my professional life** le passage le plus noir de ma vie professionnelle; **in the early** or (wee) **small ~s (of the morning)** au petit matin or jour, aux premières heures (du jour); **at all ~s (of the day and night)** à toute heure (du jour et de la nuit); **till all ~s*** jusqu'à une heure avancée de la nuit, jusqu'à très tard; **not at this ~ surely!** tout de même pas à cette heure-ci or à l'heure qu'il est!; (fig) **at this late ~** à ce stade avancé; **in his ~ of danger** lorsqu'il était en danger; **the problems of the ~** les problèmes mpl du jour or de l'heure; **Book of Hours** livre m d'Heures → **eleventh, half**

c **to keep regular ~s** avoir une vie réglée; **to work long ~s** avoir une journée très longue; (Brit) **after ~s** (of shops, pubs) après l'heure de fermeture; (of offices) après les heures de bureau; **out of ~s** en dehors des heures d'ouverture; **out of school ~s** en dehors des heures de cours or de classe → **early, late, office, school¹**

2 COMP ► **hour hand** N [of watch, clock] petite aiguille f

hourglass ['aʊəglɑːs] **1** N sablier m **2** COMP ► **hourglass figure** N (fig) silhouette f de rêve

hourly ['aʊəlɪ] **1** ADJ **a** (= every hour) **the ~ news broadcast** les nouvelles diffusées toutes les heures; **the village has an ~ bus service** le village est desservi par un car qui passe toutes les heures; **at ~ intervals** toutes les heures; **at two-~ intervals** toutes les deux heures [b] (= *per hour*) [*earnings, wage, rate*] horaire; [*worker, job*] payé à l'heure; **paid on an ~ basis** payé à l'heure [c] (= *constant*) constant [2] ADV [a] (= *every hour*) [*fly, patrol, update*] toutes les heures [b] (= *per hour*) [*pay*] à l'heure [c] (= *constantly*) constamment [d] (= *at any moment*) [*expect*] à tout moment, d'un moment à l'autre

house [haʊs] [1] N (*pl* **houses** ['haʊzɪz]) [a] maison *f*; **at my ~** chez moi; **to my ~** chez moi; **she needs more help in the ~** il faudrait qu'elle soit plus aidée à la maison; **she looks after the ~ herself** elle tient son ménage, c'est elle qui s'occupe du ménage; **to keep ~ (for sb)** tenir la maison or le ménage (de qn); **to set up ~** s'installer, monter son ménage; **they've set up ~ together** (*gen*) ils habitent ensemble; [*couple*] ils se sont mis en ménage; (*fig*) **to put** or **set one's ~ in order** mettre de l'ordre dans ses affaires; **to play at ~** ◊ **to play ~** (*esp US*) jouer au papa et à la maman; **they got on like a ~ on fire** ils s'entendaient à merveille or comme larrons en foire; **to be (as) safe as ~s** ne pas faire tout à fait sûr, ne présenter aucun risque; **he'll be safe as ~s** il ne courra absolument aucun risque; **their jobs are safe as ~s** ils ne risquent pas du tout de perdre leur emploi, ils ont un emploi tout à fait sûr; (*Brit: fig*) **to go round the ~s** parler pour ne rien dire → **doll, eat, move, open, public** [b] (*Parl*) **the House** la Chambre → **floor** [c] (*Theat etc*) (= *place*) salle *f*; (= *audience*) spectateurs *mpl*; **is there a doctor in the ~?** y a-t-il un médecin dans la salle?; **a full** or **good ~** une salle pleine; **to play to full** or **packed ~s** faire salle pleine, jouer à guichets fermés; **"~ full"** « complet »; **the second ~** la deuxième séance; (*fig*) **to bring the ~ down** faire un tabac*, casser la baraque* → **pack** [d] (*Comm*) maison *f* (de commerce), compagnie *f*; (*of noble family*) maison *f*; (*Rel*) maison *f* religieuse; (*Brit Scol*) groupe *m* d'internes; (*fig*) **on the ~** aux frais de la maison; **the House of Windsor** la maison des Windsor; **banking ~** établissement *m* bancaire; **business ~** compagnie *f*, maison *f* (de commerce); **publishing ~** maison *f* d'édition; **steak ~** grill *m*; **the world's top fashion ~s** les plus grandes maisons *fpl* de couture du monde → **in** [e] (*Mus*) **House (music)** house *f*

[2] [haʊz] VT [+ *person*] loger, héberger; **she was housing refugees** elle logeait or hébergeait des réfugiés; **the town offered to ~ six refugee families** la ville a proposé de loger six familles de réfugiés; **this building ~s five families/a motorcycle museum** ce bâtiment abrite cinq familles/un musée de la moto; **the jail ~s more than a thousand inmates** il y a plus de mille détenus dans cette prison; **the freezer is ~d in the basement** le congélateur est au sous-sol; **the generator is ~d in a large wooden box** le générateur se trouve dans un grand châssis de bois; **the sauna is ~d in their garage** le sauna est (situé) dans leur garage

[3] COMP ► **house agent** N (*Brit*) agent *m* immobilier ► **house arrest** N assignation *f* à domicile or à résidence; **to put sb under ~ arrest** assigner qn à domicile or à résidence; **to be under ~ arrest** être assigné à domicile, être en résidence surveillée ► **house-clean** VI (*US*) faire le ménage ► **house-cleaning** N (*US*) ménage *m*, nettoyage *m* ► **house-hunt** VI (*Brit*) chercher une maison (or un appartement), être à la recherche d'une maison (or d'un appartement) ► **house-hunting** N (*Brit*) recherche *f* d'une maison (or d'un appartement) ► **house-husband** N homme *m* au foyer ► **house journal, house magazine** N [*of company, organization*] bulletin *m*, journal *m* interne ► **house manager** N (*Theat*) directeur *m*, -trice *f* de théâtre ► **house of cards** N château *m* de cartes ► **House of Commons** N (*Brit*) Chambre *f* des communes

► **house of correction** N (*US*) maison *f* d'arrêt ► **House of God** N maison *f* de Dieu ► **House of Lords** N (*Brit*) Chambre *f* des lords ► **House of Representatives** N (*US*) Chambre *f* des députés ► **house organ** N = **house journal** ► **house-owner** N propriétaire *mf* d'une maison ► **house painter** N peintre *m* en bâtiments ► **house party** N (*in country house*) partie *f* de campagne; (*gen*) **I'm having a ~ party next week** j'organise une soirée or une fête chez moi la semaine prochaine ► **house physician** N (*Brit*) (*in hospital*) ≈ interne *mf* en médecine; (*in hotel etc*) médecin *m* (attaché à un hôtel etc) ► **house plant** N plante *f* d'intérieur ► **house prices** NPL prix *mpl* de l'immobilier ► **house-proud** ADJ (*esp Brit*) **she's very ~-proud** tout est toujours impeccable chez elle ► **house red** N vin *m* rouge cuvée du patron ► **house rosé** N vin *m* rosé cuvée du patron ► **house rule** N (*gen, Comm*) règle *f* de la maison; (*Comm*) ~ **rules** règlement *m* interne ► **house sale** N vente *f* immobilière ► **house-sit** VI **to ~-sit for sb** garder la maison de qn ► **house-sitter** N *personne qui loge chez qn en son absence* ► **the Houses of Parliament** N (*in Brit*) (= *building*) le Palais de Westminster; (= *members*) le Parlement, les Chambres *fpl* ► **house sparrow** N moineau *m* domestique ► **house style** N (*Publishing*) style *m* maison ► **house surgeon** N (*Brit*) ≈ interne *mf* en chirurgie ► **house-to-house** ADJ porte à porte *inv*; **~-to-~ search** perquisition *f* systématique dans le quartier; **to make a ~-to-~ search for sb** aller de porte en porte à la recherche de qn ► **house-train** VT (*Brit*) [+ *animal*] apprendre à être propre à ► **house-trained** ADJ (*Brit*) [*animal*] propre; (*fig*) [*person*] docile, obéissant ► **House Un-American Activities Committee** N (*US Hist*) Commission *f* des activités antiaméricaines ► **house-warming (party)** N pendaison *f* de crémaillère; **to give a ~-warming (party)** pendre la crémaillère ► **house white** N vin *m* blanc cuvée du patron ► **house wine** N cuvée *f* du patron

---

HOUSE

Les types de logements portent souvent des noms différents en anglais britannique et en anglais américain; ainsi, un appartement se dit respectivement « flat » (Brit) et « apartment » (US). Un « condominium » (US) est un immeuble d'habitation dont les appartements appartiennent à des propriétaires individuels alors que les parties communes sont en copropriété.

Les rangées de maisons identiques et contiguës sont appelées « terraced houses » (Brit) ou « row houses » (US). Les « semidetached houses » (Brit) ou « duplex houses » (US) sont des maisons jumelles, tandis que la « detached house » (Brit) est un pavillon.

Deux autres types de maisons répandues aux États-Unis sont les « ranch houses » - de longues bâtisses généralement de plain-pied, et les « colonials », maisons de style 18ᵉ siècle en bardeaux ou en briques, comportant souvent un portique.

---

houseboat ['haʊsbəʊt] N house-boat *m*, péniche *f* (aménagée)

housebound ['haʊsbaʊnd] [1] ADJ confiné chez soi [2] **the housebound** NPL les personnes *fpl* confinées chez elles

houseboy† ['haʊsbɔɪ] N (= *servant*) domestique *m*; (*in former colonies*) boy *m*

housebreaker ['haʊsbreɪkər] N (= *burglar*) cambrioleur *m*

housebreaking ['haʊsbreɪkɪŋ] N (= *burglary*) cambriolage *m*

housebroken ['haʊsbrəʊkən] ADJ (*US*) = house-trained; → house

housecoat ['haʊskəʊt] N [a] (= *dress*) robe *f* d'intérieur [b] (= *dressing gown*) peignoir *m*

housedress ['haʊsdres] N = housecoat a

housefather ['haʊsfɑ:ðər] N responsable *m* (de groupe) (*dans une institution*)

housefly ['haʊsflaɪ] N mouche *f* (commune or domestique)

houseful ['haʊsfʊl] N **a ~ of people** une pleine maisonnée de gens; **a ~ of dogs** une maison pleine de chiens

houseguest ['haʊsgest] N invité(e) *m(f)*; **I've got ~s** j'ai des amis à la maison

household ['haʊsˌhəʊld] [1] N (= *persons*) (gens *mpl* de la) maison *f*, ménage *m* (*also Admin, Econ*); **there were seven people in his ~** sa maison était composée de sept personnes; **the whole ~ was there to greet him** tous les gens de la maison étaient là pour l'accueillir; **give below details of your ~** indiquez ci-dessous les personnes qui résident chez vous; **~s with more than three wage-earners** des ménages or des familles de plus de trois salariés; **poor ~s** les ménages *mpl* pauvres; **a male-only ~** un appartement (or une maison) où il n'y a que des hommes; (*Brit*) **Household** maison *f* royale

[2] COMP [*accounts, expenses, equipment*] de or du ménage ► **household ammonia** N ammoniaque *f* ► **household arts** NPL arts *mpl* ménagers ► **Household Cavalry** N (*Brit*) Cavalerie *f* de la Garde Royale ► **household chores** NPL travaux *mpl* ménagers ► **household gods** NPL dieux *mpl* du foyer, pénates *mpl* ► **household goods** NPL (*gen*) (*Comm*) appareils *mpl* ménagers; (*Econ*) biens *mpl* d'équipement ménager; (*more generally*) **all her ~ goods** ses meubles *mpl* et ses ustensiles *mpl* de ménage ► **household insurance** N assurance *f* sur le contenu de l'habitation ► **household linen** N linge *m* de maison ► **household name** N **it's a ~ name** elle est connue partout; **Kleeno is a ~ name** Kleeno est une marque très connue ► **household soap** N savon *m* de Marseille ► **Household troops** NPL (*Brit*) Garde *f* royale ► **household word** N (*fig*) **it's a ~ word** c'est un mot que tout le monde connaît

householder ['haʊsˌhəʊldər] N occupant(e) *m(f)*; (= *owner*) propriétaire *mf*; (= *lessee*) locataire *mf*; (= *head of house*) chef *m* de famille

housekeeper ['haʊski:pər] N (*in sb else's house*) gouvernante *f*; (*in institution*) économe *f*, intendante *f*; **his wife is a good ~** sa femme est bonne ménagère or maîtresse de maison

housekeeping ['haʊski:pɪŋ] N [a] (= *skill*) économie *f* domestique or ménagère; (= *work*) ménage *m* [b] (*esp Brit: also ~ money*) argent *m* du ménage [c] (*Comput*) gestion *f* des disques

houselights ['haʊslaɪts] NPL (*Theat*) lumières *fpl* or éclairage *m* de la salle

housemaid ['haʊsmeɪd] [1] N bonne *f* [2] COMP ► **housemaid's knee** N inflammation *f* du genou

houseman ['haʊsmən] N (*pl* **-men**) (*Brit: in hospital*) ≈ interne *mf*

housemartin ['haʊsmɑ:tɪn] N hirondelle *f* de fenêtre

housemaster ['haʊsmɑ:stər] N (*Brit Scol*) professeur responsable d'un groupe d'internes

housemate ['haʊsmeɪt] N **my ~** la personne avec qui je partage la maison; (*both renting*) mon or ma colocataire

housemistress ['haʊsmɪstrɪs] N (*Brit Scol*) professeur responsable d'un groupe d'internes

housemother ['haʊsmʌðər] N responsable *f* (de groupe) (*dans une institution*)

houseroom ['haʊsrʊm] N **I wouldn't give it ~** je n'en voudrais pas chez moi; (*Brit fig*) **I wouldn't give him ~** je ne veux pas de lui

housetop ['haʊstɒp] N toit *m*; (*fig*) **to shout or proclaim sth from the ~s** crier qch sur les toits

housewares ['haʊswɛəz] NPL (*esp US*) articles *mpl* ménagers

housewife ['haʊs,waɪf] N (*pl* **-wives** [waɪvz]) [a] ménagère *f*; (*as opposed to career woman*) femme *f* au foyer; **a born ~** une ménagère née, une femme au foyer type; **a bored ~** une femme au foyer qui s'ennuie, une ménagère esseulée; **housewives refuse to pay these prices** les ménagères refusent de payer ces prix; **I'd rather be a ~** j'aimerais mieux être femme au foyer [b] ['hʌzɪf] (= *sewing box*) trousse *f* de couture

housewifely ['haʊs,waɪflɪ] ADJ de ménagère

housewifery ['haʊs,wɪfərɪ] N tenue *f* du ménage

housewives ['haʊs,waɪvz] NPL *of* **housewife**

housework ['haʊswɜːk] N (*NonC*) ménage *m*, tâches *fpl* ménagères; **to do the ~** faire le ménage

housing ['haʊzɪŋ] [1] N [a] (*NonC*) logement *m*; **affordable ~ is difficult to find** les logements à des prix abordables sont difficiles à trouver; **there's a lot of new ~** il y a beaucoup de résidences *or* de constructions nouvelles; **the ~ of workers proved difficult** le logement des ouvriers a posé un problème; **Minister/ Ministry of Housing** (*Brit*) ◊ **Secretary/ Department of Housing and Urban Development** (*US*) ministre *m*/ministère *m* de l'Urbanisme et du Logement → **low¹** [b] (*Tech: for mechanism etc*) boîtier *m*; (*Archit, Constr*) encastrement *m* [2] COMP [*matters, problem, crisis*] de *or* du logement ► **housing association** N (*Brit*) (*for providing housing*) association à but non lucratif qui construit et rénove des logements pour les louer à des prix très raisonnables; (*for co-ownership*) association *f* de copropriétaires (*pour faciliter l'accession à la propriété privée*) ► **housing benefit** N (*Admin*) allocation *f* logement ► **housing conditions** NPL conditions *fpl* de logement ► **housing development** N (*US*) ensemble *m* immobilier privé ► **housing estate** N (*Brit*) (= *council-owned flats*) cité *f*; (= *privately-owned houses*) lotissement *m* ► **housing list** N (*Brit*) liste d'attente pour obtenir un logement social ► **housing project** N (*US* = *place*) ≈ cité *f* ► **housing scheme** N (*Scot*) = **housing estate** ► **housing shortage** N pénurie *f* *or* manque *m* de logements; **the current acute ~ shortage** la crise du logement actuelle ► **housing stock** N parc *m* de logements

hove [həʊv] VB pt, ptp of **heave**

hovel ['hɒvəl] N taudis *m*, masure *f*

hover ['hɒvəʳ] VI [a] [*bird, butterfly*] voltiger (**about** autour de, **over** au-dessus de); [*bird of prey, helicopter, danger, threat*] planer (**above, over** au-dessus de); [*person*] (*also* **~ about, ~ around**) rôder; [*smile*] errer; [*mist, fog*] flotter; **a waiter ~ed over** *or* **round us** un garçon (de café) rôdait *or* tournait autour de nous; **she was ~ing in the doorway** elle hésitait sur le pas de la porte; **he was ~ing between life and death** il restait suspendu entre la vie et la mort; **the exchange rate is ~ing around 140 yen to the dollar** le taux de change tourne autour de *or* avoisine les 140 yens pour un dollar [b] (= *waver*) hésiter (**between** entre)

hovercraft ['hɒvəkrɑːft] N aéroglisseur *m*

hoverport ['hɒvəpɔːt] N hoverport *m*

how [haʊ] [1] ADV [a] (= *in what way*) comment; **~ did you come?** comment êtes-vous venu?; **tell me ~ you came** dites-moi comment vous êtes venu?; **to learn ~ to do sth** apprendre à faire qch; **I know ~ to do it** je sais le faire; **~ do you like your steak?** comment aimez-vous votre bifteck?; **~ did you like the steak?** comment avez-vous trouvé le bifteck?; **~ was the play?** comment avez-vous trouvé la pièce?; **~ is it that ...?** comment se fait-il que ... (+ *subj*)?; **~ could**

you (do such a thing)? comment as-tu pu faire une chose pareille?; **~ could you do/say that?** comment as-tu pu faire/dire une chose pareille?; **~ so?** ◊ **~ can that be?** comment cela (se fait-il)?; **~ come?*** comment ça se fait?*, pourquoi?*; **~ come you aren't going out?*** pourquoi tu ne sors pas?*; **~*** *or* **~'s: about going for a walk?** et si on allait se promener?; **~ about you?** et toi?; **and ~!*** et comment!*

[b] **~'s that?*** (= *how possible, in what way*) comment ça?; (= *what is your opinion*) qu'est-ce que tu en penses?; (= *agreed*) d'accord?, ça va?; **~'s that (again)?** (= *please repeat*) vous pouvez répéter?; **~'s that for size/height?** ça va du point de vue de la taille/de la hauteur?; (*admiringly*) **~'s that for clean!** c'est ce que j'appelle propre!; **~'s that for luck?** quelle veine!

[c] (*health etc*) **~ are you?** comment allez-vous?; **tell me ~ she is** dites-moi comment elle va; (*on being introduced*) **~ do you do?** enchanté; **~ are things?*** comment ça va?; **~'s business?** comment vont les affaires?; **~'s life?*** comment ça va?

[d] (*with adj, adv: degree, quantity etc*) que, comme; **~ glad I am to see you!** que *or* comme je suis content de vous voir!; **I can't tell you ~ glad I was to leave that place** vous ne pouvez pas savoir à quel point j'étais heureux de quitter cet endroit; **~ splendid!** c'est merveilleux!; **~ nice!** comme c'est gentil!; **~ kind of you!** c'est très aimable à vous!; **~ very astute of you** (*or* **him** *etc*)! quelle finesse! (*also iro*); **~ very clever of you!** ce que vous pouvez être intelligent!; **~ he has grown!** comme il a grandi!, ce qu'il a grandi!*; **~ long is the tunnel?** quelle est la longueur du tunnel?; **~ long is this film?** combien de temps dure ce film?; **~ long will you be staying?** combien de temps resterez-vous?; **~ tall is he?** quelle est sa taille?, combien mesure-t-il?; **~ old is he?** quel âge a-t-il?; **~ soon can you come?** quand pouvez-vous venir?; **~ much does this book cost?** combien coûte ce livre?

[e] (= *that*) que; **she told me ~ she had seen the child lying on the ground** elle m'a raconté qu'elle avait vu l'enfant couché par terre [2] N **the ~ and the why of it** le comment et le pourquoi de cela [3] COMP ► **how-d'ye-do**†* N **here's a (fine) ~-d'ye-do!** en voilà une affaire!, en voilà une histoire!*; **it was a real ~-d'ye-do** c'était un joli gâchis!*

howdah ['haʊdə] N *siège sanglé sur le dos d'un éléphant*

howdy* ['haʊdɪ] EXCL (*US*) salut!

▼**however** [haʊ'evəʳ] [1] ADV [a] (= *nevertheless*) cependant, toutefois; **that is one reason. It is not, ~, the only one** c'est une raison. Ce n'est cependant pas la seule; **losing doesn't seem to matter to women. Most men, ~, can't stand it** cela ne semble pas gêner les femmes de perdre. Par contre *or* en revanche, les hommes détestent cela, cela ne semble pas gêner les femmes de perdre alors que la plupart des hommes détestent cela; **~, he remained unimpressed by my enthusiasm** pourtant, mon enthousiasme ne lui a fait ni chaud ni froid [b] (= *no matter how*) **~ tall he may be** *or* **is, ...** il a beau être grand, ..., malgré sa taille, ...; **~ much money he has ...** il a beau être riche ..., même s'il a beaucoup d'argent ...; **~ hard she tried, she couldn't remember my name** malgré tous ses efforts, elle n'arrivait pas à se souvenir de mon nom; **~ great the temptation, don't do it** même si tu es très tenté, ne le fais pas; **~ few people come, we'll do the play** même s'il n'y a pas beaucoup de monde, nous jouerons la pièce; **~ many people there are** quel que soit le nombre de personnes (présentes); **six or seven people, or ~ many are present** six ou sept personnes, ou selon le

nombre de présents

[c] (= *how on earth: in questions*) comment donc; **~ did you manage to do that?** comment donc as-tu réussi à le faire? [2] CONJ de quelque manière que (+ *subj*); **~ we tell her about this, she won't be pleased** de quelque manière que nous le lui disions, elle ne sera pas contente; **~ you may do it, it will never be right** quoi que vous fassiez *or* de toute façon, ce ne sera jamais bien; **~ that may be** quoi qu'il en soit

howitzer ['haʊɪtsəʳ] N obusier *m*

howl [haʊl] [1] N [*of person, animal*] hurlement *m*; [*of baby*] braillement *m*, hurlement *m*; [*of wind*] mugissement *m*; **there were ~s of laughter at her remark** sa remarque a provoqué d'énormes éclats de rire [2] VI [a] [*person, animal*] hurler; [*wind*] mugir; **to ~ with laughter** rire aux éclats *or* à gorge déployée; **to ~ with delight** pousser des cris de joie; **to ~ with pain/rage** hurler de douleur/de rage; **to ~ with derision** lancer des huées [b] (* = *cry*) pleurer; [*baby*] brailler* [3] VT (*also* **~ out**) hurler, crier; **they ~ed their disapproval** ils hurlaient leur désapprobation

►**howl down** VT SEP huer; **the president was ~ed down by the crowd** le président a été hué par la foule

howler* ['haʊləʳ] N gaffe* *f*, bourde *f*; **to make a ~** faire une gaffe* *or* une bourde; **schoolboy ~** perle *f* (d'écolier)

howling ['haʊlɪŋ] [1] N [*of person, animal*] hurlements *mpl*; [*of wind*] mugissement *m* [2] ADJ [a] (= *wailing*) [*person, animal*] hurlant; [*wind, blizzard*] mugissant [b] (* = *terrific*) [*success*] monstre

howsoever [haʊsəʊ'evəʳ] [1] ADV (*frm = no matter how*) **~ bad the situation may seem** quelque (*liter*) que soit la situation [b] († *or* *dial = nevertheless*) néanmoins [2] CONJ (*frm*) **~ that may be** quoi qu'il en soit

hoy [hɔɪ] EXCL ohé!

hoyden† ['hɔɪdn] N garçon *m* manqué

hoydenish† ['hɔɪdənɪʃ] ADJ garçonnier, de garçon manqué

hp [eɪtʃ'piː] N (*ABBR* = **horsepower**) CV

HP* [eɪtʃ'piː] N (*Brit*) (*ABBR* = **hire purchase**) → **hire**

HQ [eɪtʃ'kjuː] N (*ABBR* = **headquarters**) QG *m*

hr (*ABBR* = **hour**) h; **28 hrs** 28 h

HRH [eɪtʃɑːr'eɪtʃ] N (*ABBR* = **His** *or* **Her Royal Highness**) SAR

HRT [eɪtʃɑːr'tiː] N (*ABBR* = **hormone replacement therapy**) → **hormone**

HS (*US Scol*) (*ABBR* = **high school**) → **high**

HST [eɪtʃes'tiː] N [a] (*Brit*) (*ABBR* = **high speed train**) ≈ TGV *m* [b] (*US*) (*ABBR* = **Hawaiian Standard Time**) → **Hawaiian**

HT (*ABBR* = **high tension**) → **high**

ht N (*ABBR* = **height**)

HUAC N (*US Hist*) (*ABBR* = **House Un-American Activities Committee**) → **house**

hub [hʌb] [1] N [*of wheel*] moyeu *m*; (*fig*) (= *centre*) centre *m*; (= *cornerstone*) pierre *f* angulaire; **a ~ of finance/activity/operations** un centre financier/d'activité/d'opérations *or* opérationnel; **the island's social ~** le carrefour de la vie sociale de l'île; **the ~ of their environmental policy** la pierre angulaire de leur politique écologique [2] COMP ► **hub airport** N (*US*) plaque *f* tournante du transport aérien

hubba-hubba* ['hʌbə'hʌbə] EXCL (*US*) vise un peu!*

hubbub ['hʌbʌb] N tohu-bohu *m*

hubby* ['hʌbɪ] N (*ABBR* = **husband**) mari *m*

hubcap ['hʌbkæp] N (*Aut*) enjoliveur *m*

hubris ['hjuːbrɪs] N orgueil *m* (démesuré)

huckleberry ['hʌklbərɪ] N (*US*) myrtille *f*

huckster ['hʌkstə'] N (US) (= hawker) colporteur m; (fig pej) mercanti m; (* = salesman) vendeur m de choc*; (in fairground) bonimenteur m

HUD [hʌd] N (US) (ABBR = Department of Housing and Urban Development) → **housing**

huddle ['hʌdl] 1 N [of people] petit groupe m (compact); **a ~ of houses in the valley** quelques maisons blotties dans la vallée; **to go into a ~*** se réunir en petit comité (fig) 2 VI a (lit) se blottir (les uns contre les autres); **we ~d round the fire** nous nous sommes blottis autour du feu; **the baby birds ~d in the nest** les oisillons se blottissaient les uns contre les autres dans le nid; **spectators huddling under umbrellas** des spectateurs s'abritant tant bien que mal sous leurs parapluies → **huddled** b (US fig = meet and discuss) se réunir en petit comité (fig)
►**huddle down** VI (= crouch) se recroqueviller, se faire tout petit; (= snuggle) se blottir, se pelotonner
►**huddle together** VI se serrer or se blottir les uns contre les autres; **they were huddling together for warmth** ils se serraient or se blottissaient les uns contre les autres pour se tenir chaud; **they ~d together to discuss the proposal** ils ont formé un petit groupe pour discuter de la proposition → **huddled**
►**huddle up** VI se blottir, se pelotonner

huddled ['hʌdld] ADJ **the chairs were ~ in a corner** les chaises étaient rassemblées or groupées dans un coin; **small wooden sheds, ~ under tall pine trees** des petites cabanes groupées sous de hauts sapins; **he lay ~ under the blankets** il était blotti or pelotonné sous les couvertures; **the children lay ~ (together) under the blankets** les enfants étaient blottis or pelotonnés (les uns contre les autres) sous les couvertures; **she sat ~ in the corner** elle était (assise,) blottie dans le coin; **he was ~ over his books** il était penché sur ses livres

Hudson Bay ['hʌdsən'beɪ] N la baie d'Hudson

hue[1] [hju:] N **~ and cry** clameur f; **to raise a ~ and cry** crier haro (**against** sur)

hue[2] [hju:] N (= colour) teinte f, nuance f

-hued [hju:d] ADJ (in compounds) **many-hued** multicolore

huff[1]* [hʌf] N **to be in a ~** être vexé; **to go into a ~** prendre la mouche, se vexer; **he went off or left in a ~** il s'est vexé et il est parti

huff[2] [hʌf] VI (lit) **to ~ and puff** souffler comme un bœuf*; (* = show annoyance) râler*

huffily* ['hʌfɪlɪ] ADV avec (mauvaise) humeur

huffiness* ['hʌfɪnɪs] N mauvaise humeur f

huffy* ['hʌfɪ] ADJ (= annoyed) vexé; (= sulky) boudeur, qui boude; (= touchy) susceptible

hug [hʌg] 1 VT a (= hold close) serrer dans ses bras, étreindre; [bear, gorilla] écraser entre ses bras; **to ~ one another** s'étreindre; **she stood ~ging herself as if she were cold** elle avait les bras serrés contre sa poitrine comme si elle avait froid; **she ~ged her legs tight to her chest** elle a serré ses jambes contre sa poitrine; (fig) **to ~ o.s. over sth** jubiler à l'idée de qch b (= keep close to) serrer; (Naut) **to ~ the shore/wind** serrer la côte/le vent; **to ~ the kerb** [car] serrer le trottoir 2 VI s'étreindre; **we ~ged and kissed** nous nous sommes embrassés 3 N étreinte f; **to give sb a ~** serrer qn dans ses bras, étreindre qn; **he gave the child a big ~** il a serré l'enfant bien fort dans ses bras → **bear**[2]

huge [hju:dʒ] ADJ [person, object, profit, difference, amount, effort] énorme; [success] énorme, fou (folle f); [eyes] immense; [number, increase] très fort; **on a ~ scale** sur une très grande échelle

hugely ['hju:dʒlɪ] ADV [popular, expensive, important, entertaining, enjoyable] extrêmement; [enjoy o.s., vary, increase] énormément;

a ~ successful film un film qui a eu un énorme succès or un succès fou; **~ influential** très influent; **~ talented** extrêmement doué

hugeness ['hju:dʒnɪs] N immensité f

hugger-mugger†* ['hʌgə,mʌgə'] ADV (confusedly) pêle-mêle

Hugh [hju:] N Hugues m

Huguenot ['hju:gənəʊ] 1 ADJ huguenot 2 N huguenot(e) m(f)

huh [hʌ] EXCL (dismay) oh!; (surprise, disbelief) hein?; (disgust) berk!*, beuh!

Hula Hoop® ['hu:lə,hu:p] N hula-hoop m

hulk [hʌlk] N a (big) **~ of a man** mastodonte m; **I followed his big ~*** into the kitchen j'ai suivi ce géant dans la cuisine b (= prison ship) ponton m; (= wrecked ship) épave f; (= ramshackle ship) vieux rafiot* m; (= wrecked vehicle, building) carcasse f

hulking ['hʌlkɪŋ] ADJ massif, imposant; **he was a ~ great brute*** c'était un gros malabar*

hull [hʌl] 1 N a [of ship] coque f; [of plane] carlingue f; [of tank] caisse f b [of nuts] coque f; [of peas, beans] cosse f, gousse f 2 VT a [+ peas] écosser; [+ barley] monder; [+ oats, rice] décortiquer; [+ nuts] écaler; [+ berries] équeuter b [+ ship, plane] percer la coque de

hullabaloo* [,hʌləbə'lu:] N (= noise) raffut* m, chambard* m; (= fuss) **there was quite a ~ about the missing money** on a fait toute une histoire* or tout un foin* à propos de l'argent disparu; **I don't know what all the ~ is about** (= noise) je ne sais pas d'où vient ce raffut*; (= fuss) je ne comprends pas pourquoi on en fait toute une histoire

hullo [hʌ'ləʊ] EXCL (esp Brit) = **hello**

hum [hʌm] 1 VT a [insect] bourdonner; [person] fredonner, chantonner; [aeroplane, engine, machine] vrombir; [spinning top, radio] ronfler; [wire] bourdonner; (fig) **then things began to ~*** alors les choses ont commencé à chauffer* or à s'animer → **haw**[2] b (Brit* = stink) chlinguer* 2 VT [+ tune] fredonner, chantonner 3 N a [of insect, conversation] bourdonnement m; [of aeroplane, engine, machine] vrombissement m; [of spinning top, radio] ronflement m b (Brit* = stink) puanteur f 4 EXCL hem!, hum!

human ['hju:mən] 1 ADJ humain; **he's only ~ after all** après tout, ce n'est pas un surhomme; **to lack the ~ touch** manquer de chaleur humaine; **not fit for ~ consumption** impropre à la consommation → **decency** 2 N humain m 3 COMP ► **human being** N être m humain ► **human ecology** N écologie f humaine ► **human engineering** N ergonomie f ► **human interest** N dimension f humaine ► **human interest story** N (Press) histoire f à dimension f humaine ► **human nature** N nature f humaine; **it's only ~ nature to want revenge** c'est dans la nature humaine de chercher à se venger ► **human race** N race f humaine, genre m humain ► **human resource management** N gestion f des ressources humaines ► **human resources** NPL ressources fpl humaines ► **human rights** NPL droits mpl de l'homme ► **human rights campaigner** N défenseur m des droits de l'homme ► **human shield** N bouclier m humain

humane [hju:'meɪn] 1 ADJ a (= compassionate) [person] plein d'humanité; [attitude] humain, plein d'humanité; [treatment, decision, system] humain; [society] bienveillant b (= painless) **the ~ killing of cattle** l'abattage m sans cruauté du bétail 2 COMP ► **the Humane Society** N (in US) société protectrice des animaux, ≈ SPA f ► **humane studies** NPL études de lettres

humanely [hju:'meɪnlɪ] ADV (= compassionately) [treat] avec humanité, humainement; (painlessly) [kill, slaughter, rear] sans cruauté

humaneness [hju:'meɪnnɪs] N humanité f

humanism ['hju:mənɪzəm] N humanisme m

humanist ['hju:mənɪst] N, ADJ humaniste mf

humanistic [,hju:mə'nɪstɪk] ADJ humaniste

humanitarian [hju:,mænɪ'tɛərɪən] ADJ, N humanitaire mf

humanitarianism [hju:,mænɪ'tɛərənɪzəm] N humanitarisme m

humanity [hju:'mænɪtɪ] 1 N humanité f 2 **the humanities** NPL les humanités fpl, les lettres fpl

humanization [,hju:mənaɪ'zeɪʃən] N humanisation f

humanize ['hju:mənaɪz] VT humaniser

humankind [,hju:mən'kaɪnd] N humanité f, genre m humain

humanly ['hju:mənlɪ] ADV **if it is ~ possible** si c'est humainement possible; **we will do all that is ~ possible** nous ferons tout ce qui est humainement possible; **in as quick a time as is ~ possible** aussi vite qu'il est humainement possible de le faire

humanoid ['hju:mənɔɪd] ADJ, N humanoïde mf

humble ['hʌmbl] 1 ADJ a (= lowly) [person, beginnings, home, job] humble; (liter) **of ~ origins** or **birth** d'humble naissance; **the ~ potato/earthworm** l'humble pomme de terre/ver de terre; (esp iro) **in my ~ opinion** à mon humble avis; (hum) **my ~ abode** mon humble demeure (hum); (in letters) **I am** or **remain, Sir, your ~ servant**† je suis, Monsieur, votre humble serviteur† (also hum); **your ~ servant** (= oneself) votre serviteur (hum); (fig) **to eat ~ pie** faire amende honorable b (= unassuming) [person] modeste (**about sth** à propos de qch); [restaurant] sans prétention c **it makes me (feel) very ~** ça me donne un sentiment de grande humilité 2 VT (= humiliate) rabaisser; (Sport) humilier; **Ted's words ~d me** les paroles de Ted ont été une leçon d'humilité pour moi; **to ~ o.s.** se rabaisser; **millions of viewers were ~d by their story** ça a été une leçon d'humilité pour des millions de téléspectateurs; **United were ~d 3-0 at Liverpool** United a été honteusement battu 3 à 0 par Liverpool

humblebee ['hʌmblbi:] N bourdon m

humbleness ['hʌmblnɪs] N humilité f

humbly ['hʌmblɪ] ADV [say, beseech, thank, beg sb's pardon] humblement; [suggest] en toute humilité

humbug ['hʌmbʌg] 1 N a (= person) charlatan m; (= talk) sornettes fpl b (Brit = sweet) bonbon m à la menthe 2 EXCL n'importe quoi!

humdinger†* ['hʌmdɪŋə'] N **he's/she's a real ~!** il est génial/elle est géniale!*; **it's a ~!** c'est terrible* or sensass*!; **it's going to be a ~ of a match** ça va être un match sensass*; **a ~ of a hangover** une épouvantable gueule de bois*; **his latest novel is a real ~** son dernier roman est vraiment sensass*

humdrum ['hʌm,drʌm] 1 ADJ monotone, banal 2 N monotonie f, banalité f

humerus ['hju:mərəs] N (pl **humeri** ['hju:mə,raɪ]) humérus m

humid ['hju:mɪd] ADJ [climate] humide et chaud; **it's ~ today** il fait lourd aujourd'hui

humidifier ['hju:'mɪdɪfaɪə'] N humidificateur m

humidify [hju:'mɪdɪfaɪ] VT [+ room, air] humidifier

humidity [hju:'mɪdɪtɪ] N humidité f

humidor ['hju:mɪdɔ:'] N boîte f à cigares

humiliate [hju:'mɪlɪeɪt] VT humilier

humiliating [hju:'mɪlɪeɪtɪŋ] ADJ humiliant

humiliatingly [hju:'mɪlɪeɪtɪŋlɪ] ADV d'une manière humiliante, honteusement; **~, he broke down in tears** à sa grande honte, il éclata en sanglots

humiliation [hjuː‚mɪlɪ'eɪʃən] N humiliation f

humility [hjuː'mɪlɪtɪ] N humilité f

humming ['hʌmɪŋ] **1** N [of insect, voices] bourdonnement m; [of aeroplane, engine, machine] vrombissement m; [of person] fredonnement m **2** COMP ► **humming-top** N toupie f ronflante

hummingbird ['hʌmɪŋbɜːd] N oiseau-mouche m, colibri m

hummock ['hʌmək] N (= hillock) tertre m, monticule m; (in ice field) hummock m

hummus ['homəs] N houm(m)ous m

humongous [hjuː'mɒŋɡəs] ADJ maous* (-ousse* f); **a ~ row** une mégadispute*, une dispute maousse*; **a ~ box office hit** un mégasuccès* au box-office; **Streisand is such a ~ star** Streisand est vraiment une superstar

humor ['hjuːmə'] (US) = **humour**

-humored ['hjuːməd] ADJ (US: in compounds) = **-humoured**

humorist ['hjuːmərɪst] N humoriste mf

humorless(ly) ['hjuːmələs(lɪ)] ADJ, ADV (US) = **humourless(ly)**

humorous ['hjuːmərəs] ADJ **a** (= amusing) [book, comment, writer] humoristique **b** (= amused) [expression] amusé

humorously ['hjuːmərəslɪ] ADV avec humour

humour, humor (US) ['hjuːmə'] **1** N **a** (= sense of fun) humour m; **I see no ~ in it** je ne vois pas où est l'humour; **this is no time for ~** ce n'est pas le moment de faire de l'humour; **the ~ of the situation** le comique de la situation; **their own inimitable brand of ~** leur humour inimitable **b** (= temper) humeur f; **to be in (a) good/bad ~** être de bonne/mauvaise humeur; **to be out of ~** être de mauvaise humeur **c** (Med Hist) humeur f **2** VT [+ person] faire plaisir à; [+ sb's wishes, whims] se prêter à, se plier à; **just ~ him!** fais-lui plaisir!

-humoured, -humored (US) ['hjuːməd] ADJ (in compounds) **bad-humoured** de mauvaise humeur → **good**

humourless, humorless (US) ['hjuːmələs] ADJ [person] qui manque d'humour, qui n'a pas le sens de l'humour; [laugh, style] sans humour

humourlessly, humorlessly (US) ['hjuːmə-lɪslɪ] ADV sans humour

hump [hʌmp] **1** N **a** [of person, camel] bosse f **b** (= hillock) bosse f, mamelon m; (fig) **we're over the ~ now** le plus difficile est passé or fait maintenant **c** (Brit) **to have** or **get the ~*** faire la gueule* **2** VT **a** (Brit* = carry) porter, trimballer* **b** (*‡* = have sex with) baiser‡, sauter‡ **3** VI (*‡* = have sex) baiser‡

humpback ['hʌmpbæk] N **a** (= person) bossu(e) m(f); **to have a ~** être bossu **b** (also **~ whale**) baleine f à bosse

humpbacked ['hʌmpbækt] ADJ **a** [person] bossu **b** (Brit) [bridge] en dos d'âne

humph [hʌmf] EXCL hum!

humpy ['hʌmpɪ] ADJ [ground] inégal, accidenté

humungous‡ ['hjuːmʌŋgəs] ADJ = **humongous**

humus ['hjuːməs] N humus m

Hun [hʌn] N **a** (Hist) Hun m **b** (‡ pej) Boche m (pej)

hunch [hʌntʃ] **1** VT **to ~ one's back** arrondir le dos; **to ~ one's shoulders** se voûter; **~ed shoulders** épaules fpl voûtées; **with ~ed shoulders** la tête rentrée dans les épaules → **hunched 2** N **a** (* = premonition) pressentiment m, intuition f; **to have a ~ that ...** avoir (comme une petite) idée que* ...; **it's only a ~** ce n'est qu'une impression; **your ~ paid off** vous avez bien fait de vous fier à votre intuition; **his ~ proved right** son intuition était juste; **to act on a ~ ◊ to play a ~** (esp US) suivre son intuition **b** (= hump) bosse f **c** = **hunk**

hunchback ['hʌntʃbæk] N bossu(e) m(f)

hunchbacked ['hʌntʃbækt] ADJ bossu

hunched ['hʌntʃt] ADJ **she sat ~ over her typewriter** elle était penchée sur sa machine à écrire; **he sat ~ (up) over his books** il était assis courbé or penché sur ses livres; **he was ~ forward in his chair** il était penché en avant sur sa chaise → **hunch**

hundred ['hʌndrəd] **1** ADJ cent; **a ~ books/chairs** cent livres/chaises; **two ~ chairs** deux cents chaises; **about a ~ books** une centaine de livres **2** N **a** cent m; **about a ~ ◊ a ~-odd*** une centaine; **I've got a ~** j'en ai cent; **a or one ~ and one** cent un; **two ~** deux cents; **two ~ and one** deux cent un; **the ~ and first** le or la cent unième; **a ~ per cent** cent pour cent; (fig) **it was a ~ per cent successful** cela a réussi à cent pour cent; **in seventeen ~** en dix-sept cents; **in seventeen ~ and ninety-six** en dix-sept cent quatre-vingt-seize; (Comm) **sold by the ~** vendus par (lots de) cent; **to live to be a ~** devenir centenaire; **they came in (their) ~s** ils sont venus par centaines; for other phrases see **sixty b** (* fig) **~s of** des centaines de, des tas* de; **I've told you ~s of times!** je te l'ai dit mille fois! **3** COMP ► **the Hundred Days** NPL (Hist) les Cent Jours mpl ► **hundreds and thousands** NPL (Brit) vermicelles mpl en sucre ► **hundred-year-old** ADJ centenaire, séculaire (liter) ► **the Hundred Years' War** N (Hist) la guerre de Cent Ans

hundredfold ['hʌndrədfəʊld] **1** ADJ centuple **2** ADV au centuple

hundredth ['hʌndrɪdθ] **1** ADJ centième **2** N (= person, thing) centième mf; (= fraction) centième m

hundredweight ['hʌndrədweɪt] N (Brit, Can) (poids m de) cent douze livres fpl (50,7 kg); (US) (poids m de) cent livres fpl (45,3 kg)

hung [hʌŋ] **1** VB pret, ptp of **hang 2** ADJ **to be ~ like a horse** or **a donkey**‡ être bien monté‡ **3** COMP ► **hung jury** N jury m sans majorité, jury m qui ne parvient pas à une décision ► **hung over*** ADJ **to be ~ over** avoir la gueule de bois* ► **hung parliament** N parlement m sans majorité, parlement m où aucun parti n'a la majorité ► **hung up*** ADJ (= tense) complexé, inhibé; **he's ~ up about it** il en fait tout un complexe*; (= obsessed) **to be ~ up on sb/sth** être fou (folle f) de qn/qch

Hungarian [hʌŋ'ɡeərɪən] **1** ADJ (gen) hongrois; [ambassador, embassy] de Hongrie; [teacher] de hongrois **2** N **a** Hongrois(e) m(f) **b** (Ling) hongrois m

Hungary ['hʌŋɡərɪ] N la Hongrie

hunger ['hʌŋɡə'] **1** N faim f; (fig) faim f, soif f (**for** de); **~ to do sth** désir m ardent de faire qch **2** VI (liter) avoir faim; (fig) **to ~ for** or **after sth** avoir faim (fig) or soif (fig) de qch; **to ~ to do sth** désirer ardemment faire qch **3** COMP ► **the hunger marches** NPL (Brit Hist) les marches fpl de la faim ► **hunger strike** N grève f de la faim; **to go on (a) ~ strike** faire la grève de la faim ► **hunger striker** N gréviste mf de la faim

hungrily ['hʌŋɡrɪlɪ] ADV [eat, kiss, smoke] goulûment; [look, listen, wait] avidement

hungry ['hʌŋɡrɪ] ADJ **a** (for food) [person, animal] affamé; **to be** or **feel ~** avoir faim; **I'm so ~** j'ai tellement faim; **to be very ~** avoir très faim, être affamé; **you look ~** tu as l'air d'avoir faim; **to make sb ~** donner faim à qn; **to go ~** (= starve) être affamé, manquer de nourriture; (= miss a meal) sauter un repas; **when he was a child he often went ~** quand il était enfant, il ne mangeait pas toujours à sa faim; **digging the garden is ~ work** ça donne faim de bêcher **b** (= eager) **they were ~ for news** ils attendaient avidement des nouvelles; **the child is ~ for love** cet enfant a be-

soin d'amour; **~ for success** [executive] avide de réussir; [artist, writer] avide de succès

hunk [hʌŋk] N **a** [of bread, cheese] (gros) morceau m **b** (* = attractive man) beau mec* m

hunker ['hʌŋkə'] VI **to ~ down** s'accroupir

hunkers ['hʌŋkəz] NPL fesses fpl; **on one's ~** accroupi

hunky* ['hʌŋkɪ] ADJ [man] bien foutu*

hunky-dory* ['hʌŋkɪ'dɔːrɪ] ADJ au poil*; **everything's ~** tout marche comme sur des roulettes*

hunt [hʌnt] **1** N **a** (gen) recherche f **b** (Sport) (= event) chasse f; **elephant/tiger ~** chasse f à l'éléphant/au tigre; **the ~ was held on the Duke's land** la partie de chasse a eu lieu sur les terres du duc; (= hunters) **the ~ rode by** les chasseurs sont passés à cheval; **the Beaufort ~** l'équipage m Beaufort; **the ~ for the missing child** la battue pour retrouver l'enfant disparu; **the ~ for the murderer** la chasse au meurtrier; **the ~ for a husband** la chasse au mari; **I've had a ~ for my gloves** j'ai cherché mes gants partout; **to be on the ~ for a cheap house** chercher une or être à la recherche d'une maison bon marché; (fig) **the ~ is on for ...** on cherche ... **2** VT **a** (= seek) chercher; (= pursue) poursuivre, pourchasser **b** (Sport) [+ fox etc] chasser, faire la chasse à; **to ~ a horse** monter un cheval à la chasse; **astronomers ~ the sky for black holes** les astronomes cherchent des trous noirs dans le ciel; **I've ~ed my desk for it** j'ai retourné tout mon bureau pour le trouver **3** VI (Sport) chasser; **to go ~ing** aller à la chasse; **to ~ for** (Sport) faire la chasse à, chasser; (gen) [+ object, details, facts, missing person] chercher (partout), être à la recherche de; **he is ~ing for a job** il est à la recherche d'un travail; **he ~ed in his pocket for his pen** il a fouillé dans sa poche pour trouver son stylo; **we ~ed around for cardboard and glue** nous avons cherché partout du carton et de la colle; **~ around until you find what you need** fouillez jusqu'à ce que vous trouviez ce dont vous avez besoin **4** COMP ► **hunt saboteur, hunt sab*** N (Brit) activiste cherchant à saboter les chasses à courre ► **hunt sabbing*** N (Brit) sabotage m des chasses à courre

► **hunt down** VT SEP [+ animal] pourchasser; [+ person] traquer, pourchasser; [+ object, facts, details, quotation] dénicher

► **hunt out** VT SEP dénicher, découvrir

hunter ['hʌntə'] **1** N **a** (= person) (Sport) chasseur m; (gen) poursuivant m → **lion b** (= horse) cheval m de chasse **c** (= watch) (montre f à) savonnette f **2** COMP ► **hunter-gatherer** N chasseur-cueilleur m; **they were ~-gatherers** ils vivaient de chasse et de cueillette ► **hunter-killer submarine** N sous-marin m nucléaire d'attaque

hunting ['hʌntɪŋ] **1** N **a** (Sport) chasse f; (with dogs) chasse f à courre; (also **fox ~**) chasse f au renard **b** (gen = search) chasse f (**for** à), recherche f (**for** de) → **bargain, house 2** COMP ► **hunting ground** N (lit, fig) (terrain m de) chasse f → **happy** ► **hunting horn** N cor m or trompe f de chasse ► **hunting lodge** N pavillon m de chasse ► **hunting pink** N rouge m chasseur inv ► **hunting season** N saison f de chasse

Huntington's chorea [‚hʌntɪŋtənzkɔː'rɪə] N chorée f de Huntington

huntress ['hʌntrɪs] N (liter) chasseresse f

huntsman ['hʌntsmən] N (pl **-men**) chasseur m

hurdle ['hɜːdl] **1** N (for fences) claie f; (Sport) haie f; (fig) obstacle m; (Sport) **the 100-metre ~s** le 100 mètres haies; **to take a ~** (Sport) franchir une haie; (fig) franchir un obstacle; (fig) **to fall at the first ~** échouer au premier obstacle **2** VI (Sport) faire de la course de haies [3] COMP ▶ **hurdle champion** N champion(ne) *m(f)* de course de haies ▶ **hurdle race** N course *f* de haies ▶ **hurdles champion** N = **hurdle champion** ▶ **hurdles race** N = **hurdle race**

hurdler ['hɜːdlə'] N (*Sport*) coureur *m*, -euse *f* de haies

hurdling ['hɜːdəlɪŋ] N (*NonC*) course *f* de haies

hurdy-gurdy ['hɜːdɪ'gɜːdɪ] N orgue *m* de Barbarie

hurl [hɜːl] VT [+ *object, stone*] jeter *or* lancer (avec violence) (**at** contre); **they were ~ed to the ground by the blast** ils ont été précipités à terre par le souffle de l'explosion; **to ~ o.s. at sb/sth** se ruer sur qn/qch; **they ~ed themselves into the fray** ils se sont jetés dans la mêlée; **he ~ed himself from a 10th floor window** il s'est jeté *or* précipité d'une fenêtre au 10ᵉ étage; (*fig*) **they ~ed themselves into the debate** ils se sont jetés à corps perdu dans le débat; (*fig*) **her question ~ed us headlong into a moral quandary** sa question nous a plongés dans un dilemme moral; **to ~ abuse at sb** lancer des injures à qn, accabler *or* agonir qn d'injures

hurley ['hɜːlɪ], **hurling** ['hɜːlɪŋ] N *sport irlandais ressemblant au hockey sur gazon*

hurly-burly ['hɜːlɪ'bɜːlɪ] N (= *commotion*) tohu-bohu *m*; (= *uproar*) tumulte *m*; **the ~ of politics** le tourbillon de la politique; **the ~ of election campaigning** le tourbillon de la campagne électorale

Huron ['hjʊərən] N ▶ **Lake ~** le lac Huron

hurrah [hʊ'rɑː], **hurray** [hʊ'reɪ] N hourra *m*; **~ for Robert!** vive Robert!; (*US*) **last ~** (= *last appearance*) dernier tour *m* de piste; (= *last attempt*) dernière tentative *f*; (*Pol*) dernière campagne *f* → **hip³**

hurricane ['hʌrɪkən] [1] N ouragan *m* [2] COMP ▶ **hurricane-force** ADJ [*wind*] de force 12 ▶ **hurricane lamp** N lampe-tempête *f*

hurried ['hʌrɪd] ADJ [*steps*] précipité, pressé; [*remark*] dit à la hâte; [*departure*] précipité; [*decision*] pris à la hâte; [*reading, visit, meeting*] très rapide; [*work*] fait à la hâte, fait à la va-vite* (*pej*); **a ~ breakfast** un petit déjeuner pris à la hâte; **a ~ goodbye** des adieux précipités; **to pay sb a ~ visit** passer voir qn en coup de vent

hurriedly ['hʌrɪdlɪ] ADV (= *quickly*) en hâte; (*faster than one would wish*) à la hâte

hurry ['hʌrɪ] [1] N (= *haste*) hâte *f*, précipitation *f*; (= *eagerness*) empressement *m*; **to be in a ~** être pressé; **to be in a ~ to do sth** avoir hâte de faire qch; **it was done in a ~** cela a été fait à la hâte; **he left in a ~** il est parti précipitamment; **I'm in no particular ~** je ne suis pas particulièrement pressé; **I won't do that again in a ~!*** ◊ **I'm in no ~ to do that again!*** je ne recommencerai pas de sitôt!, je ne suis pas près de recommencer!; **he won't come back here in a ~!*** il ne reviendra pas de sitôt!, il n'est pas près de revenir!; **are you in a ~ for this?** vous en avez un besoin urgent?, vous en avez besoin tout de suite?; **what's the ~ your ~?*** qu'est-ce qui (vous) presse?; **there's no (great) ~** rien ne presse, il n'y a pas le feu*; **there's no ~ for it** ça ne presse pas

[2] VI se dépêcher, se presser (**to do** de faire); **do ~!** dépêchez-vous!; **don't ~** ne vous pressez *or* dépêchez pas; **I must ~** il faut que je me dépêche (*subj*) *or* presse (*subj*)
[b] **to ~ in/out/through** entrer/sortir/traverser en hâte; **she hurried (over) to her sister's** elle s'est précipitée chez sa sœur; **he hurried after her** il a couru pour la rattraper; **they hurried up the stairs** ils ont monté l'escalier quatre à quatre; **she hurried home** elle s'est dépêchée de rentrer, elle est rentrée en hâte

[3] VT [a] [+ *person*] bousculer, faire se dépêcher; [+ *piece of work*] presser; **don't ~ your meal** (= *don't feel you have to rush*) ne vous pressez pas (de manger); (= *don't eat too quickly*) ne mangez pas trop vite; **I don't want to ~ you** je ne veux pas vous bousculer; **you can't ~ him** ◊ **he won't be hurried** vous ne le ferez pas se dépêcher; **this job can't be hurried** ce travail prend du temps; **I won't be hurried into a decision** je refuse de prendre une décision précipitée → **hurried**
[b] **to ~ sb in/out/through** *etc* faire entrer/sortir/traverser *etc* qn à la hâte *or* en (toute) hâte; **they hurried him to a doctor** ils l'ont emmené d'urgence chez un médecin

▶**hurry along** [1] VI marcher d'un pas pressé; **~ along please!** pressons un peu, s'il vous plaît! [2] VT SEP = **hurry on 2**

▶**hurry back** VI se presser de revenir (*or* de retourner); (*to guest*) **~ back!** revenez-nous bientôt!; **don't ~ back: I'll be here till 6 o'clock** ne te presse pas de revenir, je serai ici jusqu'à 6 heures

▶**hurry on** [1] VI **she hurried on to the next stop** elle s'est pressée de gagner l'arrêt suivant; **they hurried on to the next question** ils sont vite passés à la question suivante; **she hurried on ahead** elle est partie devant, elle est partie en éclaireur [2] VT SEP [+ *person*] faire se dépêcher, activer, accélérer; **we're trying to ~ things on a little** nous essayons d'accélérer *or* d'activer un peu les choses

▶**hurry up** [1] VI se dépêcher, se presser; **~ up!** dépêchez-vous!; **~ up and take your bath** dépêche-toi de prendre ton bain; **~ up with that coffee** (*bringing it*) dépêche-toi d'apporter ce café; (*drinking it*) dépêche-toi de boire ton café [2] VT SEP [+ *person*] faire se dépêcher; [+ *work*] activer, pousser

hurry-scurry ['hʌrɪ'skʌrɪ] [1] VI courir dans tous les sens [2] N bousculade *f*, débandade *f* [3] ADV à la débandade

hurt [hɜːt] (*pret, ptp* **hurt**) [1] VT [a] (= *do physical damage to*) [+ *person*] faire du mal à; **to ~ o.s.** se blesser, se faire mal; **to ~ one's arm** se faire mal au bras; **I hope I haven't ~ you?** j'espère que je ne vous ai pas fait de mal *or* pas blessé?; **to get ~** se blesser, se faire mal; **someone is bound to get ~** il va y avoir quelqu'un de blessé, quelqu'un va se faire du mal → **1b, 1c**; **a little rest won't ~ him** un peu de repos ne lui fera pas de mal; **a glass of wine never ~ anyone** un verre de vin n'a jamais fait de mal à personne; **it wouldn't ~ you to be a bit more serious** ça ne te ferait pas de mal d'être un peu plus sérieux → **fly¹**
[b] (= *cause physical pain to*) [+ *person*] faire mal à; **to ~ o.s.** ◊ **to get ~** se faire mal
[c] (*emotionally*) faire de la peine à; **someone is bound to get ~** il y a toujours quelqu'un qui pâtit *or* qui écope*; **what ~ most was ... what ~ most was ...** ce qui faisait le plus mal c'était ...; **to ~ sb's feelings** blesser qn
[d] (= *damage*) [+ *thing*] abîmer, endommager; [+ *sb's reputation, career*] nuire à; **an embargo would ~ the economy** un embargo serait mauvais pour *or* aurait un effet néfaste sur l'économie

[2] VI [a] faire mal; **that ~s** ça fait mal; **my arm ~s** mon bras me fait mal; **it doesn't ~ much** ça ne fait pas très mal; **where does it ~?** où avez-vous mal?; **nothing ~s like the truth** il n'y a que la vérité qui blesse; **it won't ~ for being left for a while** il n'y aura pas de mal à laisser cela de côté un instant
[b] (= *suffer emotionally*) souffrir

[3] N (*physical*) douleur *f*; (*fig*) **the real ~ lay in his attitude to her** ce qui la blessait vraiment *or* lui faisait vraiment mal c'était l'attitude qu'il avait envers elle; **feelings of ~ and anger** la peine et la colère

[4] ADJ (*lit, fig*) blessé; **she's feeling ~ about it** ça l'a blessée, elle est blessée

hurtful ['hɜːtfʊl] ADJ nocif, nuisible (**to** à); [*remark*] blessant; **what a ~ thing (for you) to say!** c'est vraiment blessant ce que tu as dit!

hurtfully ['hɜːtfʊlɪ] ADV d'une manière blessante

hurtle ['hɜːtl] [1] VI **to ~ along** [*car, person*] avancer à toute vitesse *or* allure; **to ~ past sb** passer en trombe devant qn; **the stone ~d through the air** la pierre a fendu l'air; **she went hurtling down the hill** elle a dévalé la pente [2] VT lancer (de toutes ses forces *or* violemment)

husband ['hʌzbənd] [1] N mari *m*; (*Admin, Jur*) époux *m*; **now they're ~ and wife** ils sont maintenant mari et femme; **the ~ and wife** les conjoints *mpl*, les époux *mpl*; **they were living together as ~ and wife** (*gen*) ils vivaient maritalement; (*Jur, Admin*) ils vivaient en concubinage [2] VT (*frm*) [+ *strength*] ménager, économiser; [+ *supplies, resources*] bien gérer

husbandry ['hʌzbəndrɪ] N (*Agr*) agriculture *f*; (*fig*) économie *f*, gestion *f*; **good ~** bonne gestion *f* → **animal**

hush [hʌʃ] [1] N silence *m*; **there was a sudden ~** ◊ **a ~ fell** il y a eu un silence, tout à coup tout le monde s'est tu; **an expectant ~ fell over the crowd** les spectateurs ont retenu leur souffle; (*liter*) **in the ~ of the night** dans le silence de la nuit; **a deathly ~** un silence de mort → **hushed** [2] EXCL chut! [3] VT (= *silence*) faire taire; (= *soothe*) apaiser, calmer [4] VI se taire [5] COMP ▶ **hush-hush*** secret (-ète *f*) ▶ **hush money** N pot-de-vin *m* (*pour acheter le silence*), prix *m* du silence; **to pay sb ~ money** acheter le silence de qn ▶ **hush puppy** N (*US Culin*) *espèce de beignet*

▶**hush up** VT SEP [+ *scandal, news*] étouffer; [+ *fact*] cacher; [+ *person*] faire taire, empêcher de parler

hushed [hʌʃt] ADJ [*voice, conversation*] étouffé; **there was a ~ silence** (*of embarrassment*) un ange est passé; (*of expectation*) tout le monde a retenu son souffle; **in ~ amazement they ...** frappés de stupeur, ils ...; **we discussed the situation in ~ whispers** nous avons discuté de la situation à voix basse

husk [hʌsk] [1] N [*of wheat*] balle *f*; [*of maize, rice*] enveloppe *f*; [*of chestnut*] bogue *f*; [*of nut*] écale *f*; [*of peas*] cosse *f*, gousse *f*; **rice in the ~** riz *m* non décortiqué [2] VT [+ *maize, rice*] décortiquer; [+ *nut*] écaler; [+ *grain*] vanner; [+ *peas*] écosser; [+ *barley, oats*] monder

huskily ['hʌskɪlɪ] ADV d'une voix rauque *or* voilée

huskiness ['hʌskɪnɪs] N enrouement *m*

husky¹ ['hʌskɪ] ADJ [a] (= *hoarse*) [*person*] enroué; [*voice*] rauque, voilé [b] (= *burly*) costaud*

husky² ['hʌskɪ] N (= *dog*) chien *m* esquimau *or* de traîneau

hussar [hʊ'zɑː'] N hussard *m*

hussy ['hʌsɪ] N (*pej*) dévergondée *f*

hustings ['hʌstɪŋz] NPL (*esp Brit*) plateforme *f* électorale; **he said it on the ~** il l'a dit pendant *or* au cours de sa campagne électorale; (*fig*) **candidates are battling it out at the ~** les élections mettent aux prises les candidats

hustle ['hʌsl] [1] VT [a] [+ *person*] pousser, bousculer; **to ~ sb in/out/away** faire entrer/sortir/partir qn; **they ~d him into a car** ils l'ont poussé dans une voiture; **I won't be ~d into anything** je ne me ferai rien si on me bouscule; **I won't be ~d into making a decision** je refuse de prendre une décision précipitée [b] (= *cause to proceed*) **to ~ legislation through** faire voter des lois à la hâte; **to ~ things (on** *or* **along)** faire activer les choses [c] (*US* = *sell, pass off*) fourguer*, refiler* [2] VI [a] (* = *hurry*) se manier*, se grouiller* [b] (*esp US*) (= *make efforts*) se démener; (= *work hard*) trimer*, turbiner* [c] (*esp US*) [*prostitute*] faire le trottoir*; [*trader*] fricoter* [3] N

a (= *jostling*) bousculade *f*; (= *activity*) grande activité *f*; **~ and bustle** tourbillon *m* d'activité; **the ~ and bustle of city life** le tourbillon de la vie en ville **b** (*US*‡) racket *m*, activité *f* illégale

hustler* ['hʌslə'] N (= *swindler*) arnaqueur *m*, -euse *f*; (= *prostitute*) prostitué(e) *m(f)*; (= *go-getter*) battant(e) *m(f)*

hut [hʌt] N (= *primitive dwelling*) hutte *f*, case *f*; (= *shed*) cabane *f*; (*Mil*) baraquement *m*; (*for climbers*) refuge *m*; [*of shepherd*] cabane *f*, abri *m* → **mud**

hutch [hʌtʃ] N [*of rabbit*] clapier *m*; (*US* = *dresser*) vaisselier *m*

HV, h.v. (ABBR = **high voltage**) → **high**

hyacinth ['haɪəsɪnθ] N **a** (*Bot*) jacinthe *f*; **wild ~** jacinthe *f* des bois or sauvage, endymion *m* **b** (= *gemstone*) hyacinthe *f*

hyaena [haɪ'iːnə] N = **hyena**

hybrid ['haɪbrɪd] **1** N **a** (*gen*) hybride *m* **b** (= *bicycle*) vélo *m* hybride **2** ADJ hybride **3** COMP ► **hybrid system** N système *m* hybride

hybridism ['haɪbrɪdɪzəm] N hybridisme *m*

hybridization [ˌhaɪbrɪdaɪ'zeɪʃən] N hybridation *f*

hybridize ['haɪbrɪdaɪz] VT hybrider, croiser

hydra ['haɪdrə] N (*pl* **hydras** or **hydrae** ['haɪdriː]) hydre *f*

hydrangea [haɪ'dreɪndʒə] N hortensia *m*

hydrant ['haɪdrənt] N prise *f* d'eau; (*also* **fire ~**) bouche *f* d'incendie

hydrate ['haɪdreɪt] **1** N hydrate *m* **2** VT hydrater

hydraulic [haɪ'drɒlɪk] **1** ADJ (*gen*) hydraulique **2** COMP ► **hydraulic brake** N (*Aut*) frein *m* hydraulique ► **hydraulic circuit** N (*Aut*) circuit *m* hydraulique ► **hydraulic ramp** N (*Aut*) pont *m* élévateur ► **hydraulic suspension** N (*Aut*) suspension *f* hydraulique

hydraulics [haɪ'drɒlɪks] N (*NonC*) hydraulique *f*

hydro ['haɪdrəʊ] **1** N **a** (*Brit*†) = *hotel*) établissement *m* thermal (*hôtel*) **b** (*Can*) = *electricity*) énergie *f* hydroélectrique; (= *power station*) centrale *f* hydroélectrique **2** ADJ (*Can*) hydroélectrique

hydr(o)... ['haɪdr(əʊ)] PREF hydr(o)...

hydrocarbon [ˌhaɪdrəʊ'kɑːbən] N hydrocarbure *m*

hydrochloric [ˌhaɪdrəʊ'klɒrɪk] ADJ chlorhydrique

hydrocyanic [ˌhaɪdrəʊsaɪ'ænɪk] ADJ cyanhydrique

hydrodynamics [ˌhaɪdrəʊdaɪ'næmɪks] N (*NonC*) hydrodynamique *f*

hydroelectric [ˌhaɪdrəʊ'lektrɪk] **1** ADJ hydroélectrique **2** COMP ► **hydroelectric power** N énergie *f* hydroélectrique

hydroelectricity [ˌhaɪdrəʊlek'trɪsɪtɪ] N hydroélectricité *f*

hydrofoil ['haɪdrəʊfɔɪl] N hydroptère *m*, hydrofoil *m*

hydrogen ['haɪdrɪdʒən] **1** N hydrogène *m* **2** COMP ► **hydrogen bomb** N bombe *f* à hydrogène ► **hydrogen peroxide** N eau *f* oxygénée

hydrography [haɪ'drɒgrəfɪ] N hydrographie *f*

hydrolysis [haɪ'drɒlɪsɪs] N hydrolyse *f*

hydrometer [haɪ'drɒmɪtə'] N hydromètre *m*

hydropathic [ˌhaɪdrəʊ'pæθɪk] ADJ hydrothérapique

hydrophilic [ˌhaɪdrəʊ'fɪlɪk] ADJ hydrophile

hydrophobia [ˌhaɪdrəʊ'fəʊbɪə] N hydrophobie *f*

hydrophobic [ˌhaɪdrəʊ'fəʊbɪk] ADJ hydrophobe

hydroplane [ˌhaɪdrəʊ'pleɪn] N hydroglisseur *m*

hydroponic [ˌhaɪdrəʊ'pɒnɪk] ADJ hydroponique

hydroponics [ˌhaɪdrəʊ'pɒnɪks] N (*NonC*) culture *f* hydroponique

hydropower [ˌhaɪdrəʊ'paʊə'] N énergie *f* hydroélectrique, hydroélectricité *f*

hydrotherapy [ˌhaɪdrəʊ'θerəpɪ] N hydrothérapie *f*

hydroxide [haɪ'drɒksaɪd] N hydroxyde *m*

hyena [haɪ'iːnə] N hyène *f*

hygiene ['haɪdʒiːn] N hygiène *f*

hygienic [haɪ'dʒiːnɪk] ADJ hygiénique

hygienist ['haɪdʒiːnɪst] N hygiéniste *mf*

hymen ['haɪmen] N (*Anat*) hymen *m*

hymn [hɪm] **1** N hymne *m*, cantique *m*; (*fig* = *celebration*) **a ~ to sth** un hymne à qch **2** VT (*liter*) chanter un hymne à la gloire de **3** COMP ► **hymn book** N livre *m* de cantiques

hymnal ['hɪmnəl] N livre *m* de cantiques

hype [haɪp] **1** N **a** (*NonC*:* = *publicity*) battage *m* publicitaire; (*in media*) battage *m* médiatique; **it has been the subject of intense media ~** ça a fait l'objet d'un énorme battage médiatique; **he's always been contemptuous of marketing ~** il a toujours méprisé le battage publicitaire des campagnes de marketing **b** (* = *book, product*) livre *m* or produit *m* lancé à grand renfort de publicité **c** (*Drugs*‡) (= *syringe*) shooteuse‡ *f*; (= *injection*) shoot‡ *m*; (= *addict*) toxico* *mf*, camé(e)* *m(f)* **2** VT **a*** (*also* **~ up** = *publicize*) [+ *book, product, film*] faire un énorme battage autour de; **he felt the film was ~d up too much** il a trouvé que l'on avait fait trop de battage autour de ce film **b** (‡ = *increase*) [+ *numbers, attendance*] augmenter; **to ~ the economy** stimuler l'économie **c** (‡ = *excite*) exciter → **hyped-up** **d** (*US*‡ = *cheat*) [+ *person*] tromper, rouler* **3** VI (*Drugs*‡: *also* **~ up**) se shooter‡ ► **hype up** VI, VT SEP → **hype 3, hyped-up**

hyped-up‡ [haɪpt'ʌp] ADJ (= *excited*) surexcité; (= *anxious*) stressé

hyper* ['haɪpə'] ADJ surexcité

hyper... ['haɪpə'] PREF hyper...

hyperacidity ['haɪpərə'sɪdɪtɪ] N hyperacidité *f*

hyperactive [ˌhaɪpər'æktɪv] ADJ suractif; [*child*] hyperactif

hyperactivity [ˌhaɪpəræk'tɪvɪtɪ] N suractivité *f*; [*of child*] hyperactivité *f*, syndrome *m* hyperkinétique (*SPEC*)

hyperbola [haɪ'pɜːbələ] N (*pl* **hyperbolas** or **hyperbolae** [haɪ'pɜːbəliː]) (*Math*) hyperbole *f*

hyperbole [haɪ'pɜːbəlɪ] N (*Literat*) hyperbole *f*

hyperbolic(al) [ˌhaɪpə'bɒlɪk(əl)] ADJ hyperbolique

hypercorrection [ˌhaɪpəkə'rekʃən] N hypercorrection *f*

hypercritical [ˌhaɪpə'krɪtɪkəl] ADJ hypercritique

hyperglycaemia, hyperglycemia (*US*) [ˌhaɪpəglaɪ'siːmɪə] N hyperglycémie *f*

hyperglycaemic, hyperglycemic (*US*) [ˌhaɪpəglaɪ'siːmɪk] ADJ hyperglycémique

hyperinflation [ˌhaɪpərɪn'fleɪʃən] N hyperinflation *f*

hyperkinetic [ˌhaɪpəkɪ'netɪk] ADJ suractif; [*child*] hyperactif

hypermarket ['haɪpəmɑːkɪt] N (*Brit*) hypermarché *m*

hypermeter [haɪ'pɜːmɪtə'] N vers *m* hypermètre

hypermetropia [ˌhaɪpəmɪ'trəʊpɪə], **hypermetropy** [ˌhaɪpə'metrəpɪ] N hypermétropie *f*

hypernym ['haɪpənɪm] N hyperonyme *m*

hyperrealism [ˌhaɪpə'rɪəlɪzəm] N hyperréalisme *m*

hypersensitive [ˌhaɪpə'sensɪtɪv] ADJ hypersensible

hypersonic [ˌhaɪpə'sɒnɪk] ADJ hypersonique

hypertension [ˌhaɪpə'tenʃən] N hypertension *f*

hypertext ['haɪpətekst] N (*Comput*) hypertexte *m*

hypertrophy [haɪ'pɜːtrəfɪ] **1** N hypertrophie *f* **2** VT hypertrophier **3** VI s'hypertrophier

hyperventilate [ˌhaɪpɜː'ventɪleɪt] VI hyperventiler

hyperventilation [ˌhaɪpɜːventɪ'leɪʃən] N hyperventilation *f*

hyphen ['haɪfən] N trait *m* d'union

hyphenate ['haɪfəneɪt] VT mettre un trait d'union à; **~d word** mot *m* à trait d'union

hypnagogic, hypnogogic [ˌhɪpnə'gɒdʒɪk] ADJ hypnagogique

hypnosis [hɪp'nəʊsɪs] N (*pl* **hypnoses** [hɪp'nəʊsiːz]) hypnose *f*; **under ~** en état d'hypnose, en état hypnotique

hypnotherapist [ˌhɪpnəʊ'θerəpɪst] N hypnothérapeute *mf*

hypnotherapy [ˌhɪpnəʊ'θerəpɪ] N hypnothérapie *f*

hypnotic [hɪp'nɒtɪk] **1** ADJ [*state*] hypnotique, d'hypnose; [*trance, regression, power*] hypnotique; [*rhythm, effect, eyes, voice*] envoûtant **2** N (= *drug*) hypnotique *m*; (= *person*) sujet *m* hypnotique

hypnotism ['hɪpnətɪzəm] N hypnotisme *m*

hypnotist ['hɪpnətɪst] N hypnotiseur *m*, -euse *f*

hypnotize ['hɪpnətaɪz] VT (*lit, fig*) hypnotiser; **to ~ sb into doing sth** faire faire qch à qn sous hypnose; **to ~ o.s.** s'hypnotiser

hypo... ['haɪpəʊ] PREF hypo...

hypoallergenic [ˌhaɪpəʊælə'genɪk] ADJ hypoallergénique

hypocentre ['haɪpəʊˌsentə'] N [*of earthquake*] hypocentre *m*; [*of nuclear blast*] point *m* zéro

hypochondria [ˌhaɪpəʊ'kɒndrɪə] N (*Med*) hypocondrie *f*

hypochondriac [ˌhaɪpəʊ'kɒndrɪæk] **1** ADJ (*Med*) hypocondriaque; (*gen*) **my ~ brother** mon frère, ce malade imaginaire **2** N (*Med*) hypocondriaque *mf*; (*gen*) malade *mf* imaginaire

hypocrisy [hɪ'pɒkrɪsɪ] N hypocrisie *f*

hypocrite ['hɪpəkrɪt] N hypocrite *mf*

hypocritical [ˌhɪpə'krɪtɪkəl] ADJ hypocrite

hypocritically [ˌhɪpə'krɪtɪkəlɪ] ADV hypocritement

hypodermic [ˌhaɪpə'dɜːmɪk] **1** ADJ hypodermique **2** N (= *syringe*) seringue *f* hypodermique; (= *needle*) aiguille *f* hypodermique; (= *injection*) injection *f* hypodermique

hypoglossal [ˌhaɪpə'glɒsəl] ADJ hypoglosse

hypoglycaemia, hypoglycemia (*US*) [ˌhaɪpəʊglaɪ'siːmɪə] N (*Med*) hypoglycémie *f*

hypoglycaemic, hypoglycemic (*US*) [ˌhaɪpəʊglaɪ'siːmɪk] ADJ hypoglycémique

hyponym ['haɪpənɪm] N hyponyme *m*

hyponymy [haɪ'pɒnɪmɪ] N hyponymie *f*

hypostasis [haɪˈpɒstəsɪs] N (pl **hypostases** [haɪˈpɒstəsiːz]) (Rel) hypostase f

hypostatic [ˌhaɪpəʊˈstætɪk] ADJ (Rel) hypostatique

hypotenuse [haɪˈpɒtɪnjuːz] N hypoténuse f

hypothalamus [ˌhaɪpəˈθæləməs] N (pl **hypothalami** [ˌhaɪpəˈθæləmaɪ]) hypothalamus m

hypothermia [ˌhaɪpəʊˈθɜːmɪə] N hypothermie f

hypothesis [haɪˈpɒθɪsɪs] N (pl **hypotheses** [haɪˈpɒθɪsiːz]) hypothèse f → **working**

hypothesize [haɪˈpɒθɪˌsaɪz] [1] VT conjecturer; **it was ~d that ...** on est parti de l'hypothèse que ... [2] VI se livrer à des conjectures

hypothetic(al) [ˌhaɪpəʊˈθetɪk(əl)] ADJ hypothétique

hypothetically [ˌhaɪpəʊˈθetɪkəlɪ] ADV en théorie

hyssop [ˈhɪsəp] N (Bot) hysope f

hysterectomy [ˌhɪstəˈrektəmɪ] N hystérectomie f

hysteria [hɪsˈtɪərɪə] N (Psych) hystérie f; (= panic) **she felt a wave of mounting ~** elle se sentait or elle était au bord de la crise de nerfs; **there were signs of ~ among the crowd** la foule semblait être au bord de l'hystérie; **he was completely overcome with ~** il était complètement hystérique → **mass¹**

hysterical [hɪsˈterɪkəl] ADJ (Psych) hystérique; (gen) [person] très nerveux, surexcité; (with laughter) en proie au fou rire; [laugh, sobs, weeping] convulsif; (* = hilarious) [joke, scene, comedian] tordant*; **~ laughter** fou rire m; **~ crying** une violente crise de larmes

hysterically [hɪsˈterɪkəlɪ] ADV (Med, Psych) hystériquement; **to weep ~** avoir une violente crise de larmes; **to laugh ~** rire convulsivement, être saisi d'un rire convulsif; **"come here", she shouted ~** «viens ici» hurla-t-elle comme une hystérique; **it was ~ funny*** c'était à se tordre de rire

hysterics [hɪsˈterɪks] NPL [a] (= tears, shouts) (violente) crise f de nerfs; **to have ~ ◊ to go into ~** avoir une (violente) crise de nerfs; **she was nearly in ~** elle était au bord de la crise de nerfs [b] (* = laughter) crise f de fou rire; **to have ~ ◊ to go into ~** attraper le fou rire; **we were in ~ about it** on a ri aux larmes; **he had us all in ~** il nous a fait rire aux larmes

Hz (Rad etc) (ABBR = **hertz**) hz

I

I¹, i [aɪ] N a (= *letter*) I, i *m*; **I for Isaac** (*Brit*) ◊ **I for item** (*US*) ≈ I comme Irène → **dot** b (*Geog*) (ABBR = **Island** *and* **Isle**) I

I² [aɪ] PERS PRON (*unstressed*) je; (*before vowel*) j'; (*stressed*) moi; **he and I are going to sing** lui et moi (nous) allons chanter; **no, I'll do it** non, c'est moi qui vais le faire; (*frm*) **it is I** c'est moi

IA ABBR = **Iowa**

Ia. ABBR = **Iowa**

IAAF [ˌaɪeɪeɪˈef] N (ABBR = **International Amateur Athletic Federation**) FIAA *f*

IAEA [ˌaɪeɪiːˈeɪ] N (ABBR = **International Atomic Energy Agency**) AIEA *f*

iambic [aɪˈæmbɪk] 1 ADJ iambique 2 N iambe *m*, vers *m* iambique 3 COMP ► **iambic pentameter** N pentamètre *m* iambique

IBA [ˌaɪbiːˈeɪ] N (*Brit*) (ABBR = **Independent Broadcasting Authority**) *haute autorité contrôlant les sociétés indépendantes de radiotélévision*

Iberia [aɪˈbɪərɪə] N l'Ibérie *f*

Iberian [aɪˈbɪərɪən] 1 ADJ ibérique 2 N a Ibère *mf* b (*Ling*) ibère *m* 3 COMP ► **Iberian Peninsula** N péninsule *f* Ibérique

ibex [ˈaɪbeks] N (*pl* **ibexes** *or* **ibex** *or* **ibices** [ˈɪbɪˌsiːz]) bouquetin *m*, ibex *m*

ibid [ˈɪbɪd] (ABBR = **ibidem**) ibid

ibis [ˈaɪbɪs] N (*pl* **ibises** *or* **ibis**) ibis *m*

Ibiza [ɪˈbiːθə] N Ibiza *f*; **in ~** à Ibiza

IBRD [ˌaɪbiːɑːˈdiː] N (ABBR = **International Bank for Reconstruction and Development**) BIRD *f*

IBS [ˌaɪbiːˈes] N (ABBR = **irritable bowel syndrome**) → **irritable**

i/c (ABBR = **in charge**) → **charge**

ICA [ˌaɪsiːˈeɪ] N a (*Brit*) ABBR = **Institute of Contemporary Arts** b (*Brit*) ABBR = **Institute of Chartered Accountants** c ABBR = **International Cooperation Administration**

ICAO [ˌaɪsiːeɪˈəʊ] N (ABBR = **International Civil Aviation Organization**) OACI *f*

Icarus [ˈɪkərəs] N Icare *m*

ICBM [ˌaɪsiːbiːˈem] N (ABBR = **intercontinental ballistic missile**) → **intercontinental**

ice [aɪs] 1 N a (*NonC*) glace *f*; (*on road*) verglas *m*; (*for drink*) glaçons *mpl*; **my hands are like ~** j'ai les mains glacées; **to put sth on ~** (*lit*) [+ *melon, wine*] mettre qch à rafraîchir avec de la glace; [+ *champagne*] mettre qch à frapper; (*fig*) mettre qch en attente *or* au frigidaire*; **to keep sth on ~** (*lit*) garder qch sur *or* dans de la glace; (*fig*) garder qch en attente; (*Theat*) **"Cinderella on ~"** « Cendrillon, spectacle sur glace »; **to break the ~** (*lit*) (*also in conversation etc*) briser *or* rompre la glace; (= *broach tricky matter*) entamer le sujet délicat; **that cuts no ~** *or* **that doesn't cut much ~ with me** ça ne me fait aucun effet, ça ne m'impressionne guère → **black, cold** b (*Brit: also* **~ cream**) glace *f*; **raspberry ~** glace *f* à la framboise → **water** c (‡ = *diamonds*) diam(s)‡ *m(pl)*, diamant(s) *m(pl)*

d (‡ = *drug*) drogue à base de méthamphétamine

2 VT a [+ *cake*] glacer b (*fig*) **his words ~d her heart** ses paroles l'ont glacée → **iced**

3 COMP ► **ice age** N période *f* glaciaire ► **ice-age** ADJ (qui date) de la période glaciaire ► **ice axe** N piolet *m* ► **ice blue** N, ADJ bleu *m* métallique *inv* ► **ice bucket** N seau *m* à glace *or* à champagne ► **ice climber** N glaciériste *mf* ► **ice-cold** ADJ [*drink, hands*] glacé; [*room, manners, person*] glacial ► **ice cream** N glace *f*; **strawberry ~ cream** glace *f* à la fraise ► **ice-cream cone, ice-cream cornet** (*Brit*) N cornet *m* de glace ► **ice-cream soda** N (*US*) soda *m* avec de la crème glacée ► **ice-cream van** N camionnette *f* de vendeur de glaces ► **ice cube** N glaçon *m* ► **ice dance** N = **ice dancing** ► **ice dancer** N danseur *m*, -euse *f* sur glace ► **ice dancing** N danse *f* sur glace ► **ice field** N champ *m* de glace ► **ice floe** N banquise *f* (flottante) ► **ice hammer** N marteau-piolet *m* ► **ice hockey** N hockey *m* sur glace ► **ice lolly** N (*Brit*) sucette *f* glacée ► **ice maiden*** N glaçon* *m* (*fig*) ► **ice pack** N (*Med*) poche *f* de glace; (*Geog*) banquise *f* ► **ice pick** N pic *m* à glace ► **ice piton** N broche *f* (à glace) ► **ice rink** N patinoire *f* ► **ice show** N (*Theat*) spectacle *m* sur glace ► **ice skate** N patin *m* (à glace) ► **ice-skate** VI faire du patin (à glace) *or* du patinage (sur glace) ► **ice skater** N patineur *m*, -euse *f* (sur glace) ► **ice-skating** N patinage *m* (sur glace) ► **ice storm** N tempête *f* de pluie verglaçante ► **ice tray** N bac *m* à glaçons ► **ice water** N (*US*) eau *f* glacée ► **ice yacht** N char *m* à voile (sur patins)

►**ice over** 1 VI [*windscreen, aircraft wings*] givrer; [*river*] geler; **the lake has ~d over** le lac a gelé *or* est pris (de glace) 2 VT SEP **to be ~d over** [*windscreen, aircraft wings*] être givré; [*river, lake*] être gelé, être pris (de glace)

►**ice up** 1 VI [*windscreen, aircraft, mechanism, lock*] se givrer 2 VT SEP **to be ~d up** [*windscreen, aircraft wings*] être givré; [*river, lake*] être gelé, être pris (de glace)

iceberg [ˈaɪsbɜːg] 1 N iceberg *m*; (* *fig* = *person*) glaçon* *m* → **tip¹** 2 COMP ► **iceberg lettuce** N laitue *f* iceberg (*sorte de laitue croquante*)

iceboat [ˈaɪsbəʊt] N (*Sport*) = **ice yacht**; → **ice**; (*Naut*) = **icebreaker**

icebound [ˈaɪsbaʊnd] ADJ [*harbour*] fermé par les glaces; [*ship*] pris dans les glaces

icebox [ˈaɪsbɒks] N (*US†* = *refrigerator*) frigidaire® *m*, réfrigérateur *m*; (*Brit = freezer compartment*) compartiment *m* à glace, freezer *m*; (= *insulated box*) glacière *f*; **this room is like an ~** cette pièce est une vraie glacière, on gèle dans cette pièce

icebreaker [ˈaɪsˌbreɪkər] N (*Naut*) brise-glace(s) *m*; (*fig*) **as an ~** pour briser la glace *or* faire connaissance

icecap [ˈaɪskæp] N calotte *f* glaciaire

iced [aɪst] ADJ [*coffee, tea*] glacé; [*melon*] rafraîchi; **~ water/martini** de l'eau/un martini avec des glaçons; **~ champagne** champagne *m* frappé

icehouse [ˈaɪshaʊs] N glacière *f*

Iceland [ˈaɪslənd] N l'Islande *f*

Icelander [ˈaɪsləndər] N Islandais(e) *m(f)*

Icelandic [aɪsˈlændɪk] 1 ADJ islandais 2 N (*Ling*) islandais *m*

iceman [ˈaɪsmæn] N (*pl* **-men**) a (*US*) marchand *m* *or* livreur *m* de glace b (*Archeol*) homme *m* trouvé dans la glace

I Ching [ˈiː ˈtʃɪŋ] N Yijing *or* Yi-king *m*

ichthyologist [ˌɪkθɪˈɒlədʒɪst] N ichtyologiste *mf*

ichthyology [ˌɪkθɪˈɒlədʒɪ] N ichtyologie *f*

ichthyosaurus [ˌɪkθɪəˈsɔːrəs] N (*pl* **ichthyosauruses** *or* **ichthyosauri** [ˌɪkθɪəˈsɔːraɪ]) ichtyosaure *m*

icicle [ˈaɪsɪkl] N glaçon *m* (*naturel*)

icily [ˈaɪsɪlɪ] ADV [*say*] sur un ton glacial; [*smile, stare*] d'un air glacial; **~ polite** d'une politesse glaciale; **~ calm** d'un calme glacial

iciness [ˈaɪsɪnɪs] N a (*lit*) [*of road surface*] état *m* verglacé b (*fig*) [*of manner, tone, stare etc*] froideur *f* extrême

icing [ˈaɪsɪŋ] 1 N a (*NonC: Culin*) glace *f*, glaçage *m*; **chocolate/coffee** *etc* **~** glaçage *m* au chocolat/au café *etc* **~ polite** b (*fig*) **the ~ on the cake** la cerise sur le gâteau 2 COMP ► **icing sugar** N (*Brit*) sucre *m* glace

icky‡ [ˈɪkɪ] ADJ (= *messy*) poisseux; (*fig* = *horrible*) dégueulasse‡

icon [ˈaɪkɒn] N a (*Rel, Comput*) icône *f* b (*fig* = *symbol*) emblème *m*; (= *idol*) idole *f*; **a feminist/youth/gay ~** une idole pour les féministes/les jeunes/les homosexuels; **fashion ~** figure *f* emblématique de la mode

iconic [aɪˈkɒnɪk] ADJ a (*Ling, Comput, Psych*) iconique b (*Art*) [*portrait*] ressemblant à une icône c (*culturally*) [*figure*] emblématique; **to achieve ~ status** devenir une idole

iconoclast [aɪˈkɒnəklæst] N iconoclaste *mf*

iconoclastic [aɪˌkɒnəˈklæstɪk] ADJ iconoclaste

iconographer [ˌaɪkɒˈnɒgrəfər] N iconographe *mf*

iconography [ˌaɪkɒˈnɒgrəfɪ] N iconographie *f*

ICRC [ˌaɪsiːɑːˈsiː] N (ABBR = **International Committee of the Red Cross**) CICR *m*

ICU [ˌaɪsiːˈjuː] N (ABBR = **intensive care unit**) USI *f*

icy [ˈaɪsɪ] 1 ADJ a (= *frozen*) [*road, pavement*] verglacé; [*lake, river, sea*] gelé; **~ rain** pluie *f* mêlée de grêle; **~ conditions** (*on roads*) verglas *m*; **it's ~ this morning** il gèle ce matin b (*also* **~ cold**) [*wind, water*] glacial, glacé; [*hands, feet*] glacé; **it was ~ (cold) yesterday** il faisait un froid glacial hier; **her hands were ~ (cold)** elle avait les mains glacées; (*liter or hum*) **the ~ blast** le vent glacial c (*unfriendly*) [*stare, silence, tone, reception*] glacial 2 COMP ► **icy blue** ADJ, N bleu *m* métallique *inv*

ID [aɪ'diː] **1** ABBR = **Idaho 2** N (ABBR = **identification**) pièce *f* d'identité; **she asked me for some ID** elle m'a demandé une pièce d'identité; **I had no ID on me** je n'avais pas de pièce d'identité sur moi **3** COMP (ABBR = **identification, identity**) [*bracelet, tag, number*] d'identification ► **ID card** N (*gen*) carte *f* d'identité; (*magnetic*) carte *f* d'identification ► **ID parade** N (*Brit*) séance *f* d'identification (d'un suspect)

id [ɪd] N (*Psych*) ça *m*

I'd [aɪd] = **I had, I should, I would**; → **have, should, would**

Ida. ABBR = **Idaho**

Idaho ['aɪdəhəʊ] N l'Idaho *m*; **in ~** dans l'Idaho

IDD [ˌaɪdiː'diː] N (*Brit Telec*) (ABBR = **international direct dialling**) *automatique international*

▼ **idea** [aɪ'dɪə] N **a** (= *thought, purpose*) idée *f*; **brilliant** *or* **bright ~** idée *f* géniale *or* de génie; **good ~!** bonne idée!; **what an ~!** ◊ **the very ~ (of it)!** quelle idée!, en voilà une idée!; **I can't bear the ~ of selling it** je ne supporte pas l'idée de le vendre; **I've got an ~ for a play** j'ai une idée pour une pièce de théâtre; **I hit (up)on** *or* **I suddenly had the ~ of going to see her** d'un seul coup l'idée m'est venue d'aller la voir; **I like the ~ of helping people** l'idée d'aider les gens me plaît; **it's an ~ or a good ~ to book well in advance** c'est une (bonne) idée de réserver assez longtemps à l'avance; **it might not be a bad ~ to wait a few days** ce ne serait peut-être pas une mauvaise idée d'attendre quelques jours; **the ~ is to reduce expenditure** c'est de réduire les dépenses; **whose ~ was it to take this route?** qui a eu l'idée de prendre cet itinéraire?; **it wasn't my ~!** ce n'est pas moi qui en ai eu l'idée!; **man/woman of ~s** homme *m*/femme *f* à idées; **he's the ~s man*** *or* **the one with the ~s** c'est lui qui trouve les idées; **the ~ never entered my head** l'idée ne m'en est jamais venue *or* ne m'a jamais effleuré; **he got the ~ into his head that she wouldn't help him** il s'est mis dans la tête qu'elle ne l'aiderait pas; **where did you get the ~ that I wasn't well?** où as-tu été chercher que je n'allais pas bien?; **where did you get that ~?** où est-ce que tu as pris cette idée?; **what gave you the ~ that I couldn't come?** qu'est-ce qui t'a fait penser que je ne pourrais pas venir?; **don't get any ~s!*** ce n'est pas la peine d'y penser!; **once he gets an ~ into his head** une fois qu'il s'est mis une idée en tête; **to put ~s into sb's head** ◊ **to give sb ~s** mettre *or* fourrer* des idées dans la tête de qn; **that gave me the ~ of inviting her** cela m'a donné l'idée de l'inviter **b** (= *opinion*) idée *f*, opinion *f*; (= *way of thinking*) façon *f* de penser; **she has some odd ~s about how to bring up children** elle a de drôles d'idées sur l'éducation des enfants; **according to his ~** selon sa façon de penser; **if that's your ~ of fun** si c'est ça que tu appelles t'amuser; **that's not my ~ of a holiday** ce n'est pas ce que j'appelle des vacances **c** (= *vague knowledge*) idée *f*; **I've got some ~ of what this is all about** j'ai une vague idée de quoi il s'agit; **have you any ~ of what he meant to do?** avez-vous idée de ce qu'il voulait faire?; **I haven't the least** *or* **slightest** *or* **foggiest* ~** je n'en ai pas la moindre idée; **I had an ~ that he'd joined the army** j'avais dans l'idée qu'il s'était engagé dans l'armée; **I had no ~ they knew each other** je n'avais aucune idée *or* j'ignorais absolument qu'ils se connaissaient; **he has no ~ what he's doing!** il fait n'importe quoi!*; **it was awful, you've no ~!** c'était terrible, tu ne peux pas t'imaginer!; **can you give me a rough ~ of how many you want?** pouvez-vous m'indiquer en gros *or* approximativement combien vous en voulez?; **he gave me a general ~ of what they would do** il m'a donné une idée générale de ce qu'ils allaient faire; **this will give you an ~ of how**

much it will cost cela permettra de vous faire une idée de ce que ça va coûter; **you're getting the ~!** tu commences à comprendre *or* à piger*!; **I've got the general ~*** je vois à peu près *or* en gros (ce dont il s'agit); **that's the ~!** c'est ça!; **what's the big ~?*** ça ne va pas, non?◊

ideal [aɪ'dɪəl] **1** ADJ idéal (**for sb/sth** pour qn/qch, **for doing sth** pour faire qch) **2** N idéal *m*

idealism [aɪ'dɪəlɪzəm] N idéalisme *m*

idealist [aɪ'dɪəlɪst] ADJ, N idéaliste *mf*

idealistic [aɪ'dɪə'lɪstɪk] ADJ idéaliste

idealization [aɪ,dɪəlaɪ'zeɪʃən] N idéalisation *f*

idealize [aɪ'dɪəlaɪz] VT idéaliser

ideally [aɪ'dɪəlɪ] ADV **a** (= *preferably*) **~, you should brush your teeth after every meal** l'idéal serait de se brosser les dents après chaque repas, pour bien faire il faudrait se brosser les dents après chaque repas; **~, every child should get individual attention** l'idéal serait que chaque enfant soit suivi individuellement; **~ I'd like to leave about five** dans l'idéal *or* pour bien faire, j'aimerais partir vers cinq heures **b** (= *perfectly*) **he is ~ suited to the job** il est parfait pour ce poste; **I'm not ~ placed to give you advice** je ne suis pas le mieux placé pour vous conseiller; **the village is ~ situated** la situation du village est idéale

ident* ['aɪdent] N (*TV: also* **station ~**) clip vidéo *servant à identifier une chaîne de télévision*

identical [aɪ'dentɪkəl] ADJ identique (**to** à); **~ twins** vrais jumeaux *mpl*, vraies jumelles *fpl*

identically [aɪ'dentɪkəlɪ] ADV de façon identique; **~ dressed** vêtus de manière identique, habillés pareil*

identifiable [aɪ'dentɪ,faɪəbl] ADJ identifiable; [*goal, group*] distinct; [*person*] repérable, reconnaissable; **~ as a Frenchman** reconnaissable en tant que Français; **it is ~ as a Rembrandt** on voit tout de suite que c'est un Rembrandt; **he's easily ~** il est facilement repérable *or* reconnaissable (**as** comme, **by** à); **Chinese rugs are ~ by their design** les tapis chinois se reconnaissent à leur motifs

identification [aɪ,dentɪfɪ'keɪʃən] **1** N **a** identification *f* (**with** avec); **early ~ of a disease** l'identification précoce d'une maladie; **he's made a formal ~ of the body** il a formellement identifié le corps **b** (= *association*) association *f*; **the ~ of Spain with Catholicism** l'association de l'Espagne au catholicisme **c** (= *empathy*) **his ~ with the problem** sa compréhension profonde du problème; **an actor's ~ with his character** l'identification d'un acteur avec son personnage **d** (= *proof of identity*) pièce *f* d'identité **2** COMP ► **identification mark** N signe *m* particulier (*permettant d'identifier qn ou qch*) ► **identification papers** NPL pièces *fpl* *or* papiers *mpl* d'identité ► **identification parade** N (*Brit Police*) séance *f* d'identification (d'un suspect) ► **identification tag** N plaque *f* d'identité

identifier [aɪ'dentɪfaɪə'] N (*Comput*) identificateur *m*

identify [aɪ'dentɪfaɪ] **1** VT **a** (= *establish identity of*) identifier; **she identified him as the man who had attacked her** elle l'a identifié comme étant son agresseur; **the police have identified the man they want to question** la police a identifié *or* établi l'identité de l'homme qu'elle veut interroger; **to ~ a body** identifier un cadavre **b** (= *consider as the same*) identifier (**A with B** A avec *or* à *or* et B); **to ~ o.s. with** s'identifier à *or* avec, s'assimiler à; **he refused to ~ himself with the rebels** il a refusé de s'identifier avec les rebelles; **he refused to be identified with the rebels** il a refusé d'être identifié *or* assimilé aux rebelles **2** VI s'identifier (**with** avec, à), s'assimiler

(**with** à); **a character the audience can ~ with** un personnage auquel le public peut s'identifier

Identikit® [aɪ'dentɪkɪt] N (*also* **~ picture**) portrait-robot *m*, photo-robot *f*

identity [aɪ'dentɪtɪ] **1** N identité *f*; **proof of ~** pièce *f* d'identité; **a case of mistaken ~** une erreur d'identité; **the distinct cultural ~ of Tibetans** l'identité culturelle distincte des Tibétains **2** COMP ► **identity card** N (*gen*) carte *f* d'identité; (*magnetic*) carte *f* d'identification ► **identity crisis** N (*Psych*) crise *f* d'identité ► **identity disc** N plaque *f* d'identité ► **identity papers** NPL pièces *fpl* *or* papiers *mpl* d'identité ► **identity parade** N (*Brit*) séance *f* d'identification (d'un suspect)

ideogram ['ɪdɪəgræm], **ideograph** ['ɪdɪəgrɑːf] N idéogramme *m*

ideographic [ˌɪdɪə'græfɪk] ADJ idéographique

ideological [ˌaɪdɪə'lɒdʒɪkəl] ADJ idéologique

ideologically [ˌaɪdɪə'lɒdʒɪkəlɪ] ADV [*motivated*] idéologiquement, du point de vue idéologique; **~ sound/unsound** idéologiquement correct/incorrect, correct/incorrect sur le plan idéologique; **to be ~ opposed to sth** être hostile à qch pour des raisons idéologiques; **~, they are poles apart** du point de vue idéologique, ils sont très éloignés l'un de l'autre

ideologist [ˌaɪdɪ'ɒlədʒɪst] N idéologue *mf*

ideologue ['aɪdɪəlɒg, (*US*) 'aɪdɪəlɑːg] N idéologue *mf*

ideology [ˌaɪdɪ'ɒlədʒɪ] N idéologie *f*

ides [aɪdz] NPL ides *fpl*

idiocy ['ɪdɪəsɪ] N **a** (*NonC*) stupidité *f*, idiotie *f* (**of doing** de faire); **a piece of ~** une stupidité, une idiotie **b** (*Med*††) idiotie *f*

idiolect ['ɪdɪəʊlekt] N idiolecte *m*

idiom ['ɪdɪəm] N **a** (= *phrase, expression*) expression *f* *or* tournure *f* idiomatique, idiotisme *m* **b** (= *language*) [*of country*] idiome *m*, langue *f*; [*of region*] idiome *m*; [*of person*] idiome *m*, parler *m* **c** (= *style*) style *m*; **in a minimalist ~** dans un style minimaliste

idiomatic [ˌɪdɪə'mætɪk] ADJ idiomatique; **~ expression** expression *f* *or* tournure *f* idiomatique

idiomatically [ˌɪdɪə'mætɪkəlɪ] ADV de façon idiomatique

idiosyncrasy [ˌɪdɪə'sɪŋkrəsɪ] N particularité *f*, singularité *f*; **it's just one of his little idiosyncrasies** ça fait partie de son côté original

idiosyncratic [ˌɪdɪəsɪŋ'krætɪk] ADJ particulier, singulier

idiot ['ɪdɪət] **1** N **a** idiot(e) *m(f)*, imbécile *mf*; **to act** *or* **behave like an ~** se conduire en idiot *or* en imbécile; **to grin like an ~** sourire bêtement; **to feel like an ~** se sentir bête; **what an ~ I am!** que je suis idiot!, quel imbécile je fais! **b** (*Med*††) idiot(e) *m(f)* (de naissance) → **village 2** COMP ► **idiot board** N (*TV*) téléprompteur *m*, télésouffleur *m* ► **idiot box:** N (*US TV*) téloche* *f* ► **idiot-proof*** ADJ [*method*] infaillible; [*machine*] indétraquable, indéréglable

idiotic [ˌɪdɪ'ɒtɪk] ADJ idiot, stupide; **that was ~ of you!** ce que tu as été idiot!; **what an ~ thing to say!** c'est idiot *or* stupide de dire une chose pareille!

idiotically [ˌɪdɪ'ɒtɪkəlɪ] ADV stupidement, de façon idiote

idle ['aɪdl] **1** ADJ **a** (= *inactive*) [*person*] inactif; [*employee*] désœuvré; [*machinery*] à l'arrêt; [*factory*] arrêté; [*land*] inexploité; **this machine is never ~** cette machine n'est jamais à l'arrêt *or* ne s'arrête jamais; **he has not been ~ during his absence** il n'a pas chômé pendant son absence; **to stand ~** [*machinery, vehicle, factory*] être à l'arrêt; **to lie** *or* **sit ~** [*money*] dormir; [*land*] rester inexploité; **~ money** argent *m* qui dort → **lie¹**

► ▲ LANGUAGE IN USE: **idea** 1, 2.2, 11.2

b (= *unoccupied, at leisure*) [*person, hours, days*] oisif ; **~ time** [*of workers*] temps *m* chômé ; [*of machine*] temps *m* mort, arrêt *m* machine ; **to spend one's ~ hours doing sth** passer son temps libre à faire qch ; **in an ~ moment** pendant un moment d'oisiveté

c (*pej = lazy*) [*person*] fainéant ; (*pej*) **the ~ rich** les riches oisifs *mpl* → **bone**, **devil**

d († = *unemployed*) sans emploi ; (*Ind*) **to make sb ~** réduire qn au chômage

e (= *futile, vain*) [*threat, promise, hope*] vain (*before n*) ; [*speculation, talk, chatter*] oiseux, vain (*before n*) ; [*conversation, remark, question*] oiseux, futile ; [*rumour, fear*] sans fondement ; **out of ~ curiosity** par pure *or* simple curiosité ; **~ gossip** ragots *mpl* ; **that is no ~ boast** ce n'est pas une vaine fanfaronnade ; **an ~ dream** un vain rêve ; **it would be ~ to do** il serait vain *or* futile de faire

2 VI **a** (*also* **~ about** *or* **around**) [*person*] paresser, fainéanter ; **to ~ about the streets** traîner dans les rues

b [*engine, machine*] tourner au ralenti

3 VT (*US*) **a** mettre au chômage ; [+ *factory*] mettre à l'arrêt

► **idle away** VT SEP **to ~ away one's time** passer le temps (en occupations futiles) s'occuper pour passer le temps ; **he ~d the time away in dreamy thought** il passait le temps à rêvasser

idleness ['aɪdlnɪs] N **a** (= *leisure*) oisiveté *f* ; (*pej* = *laziness*) paresse *f*, fainéantise *f* ; **to live in ~** vivre dans l'oisiveté **b** (= *state of not working*) inaction *f*, inactivité *f* ; (= *unemployment*) chômage *m* **c** [*of threat, wish, question, speculation*] futilité *f*, inutilité *f* ; [*of promises, pleasures*] futilité *f* ; [*of fears*] manque *m* de justification ; [*of words*] manque *m* de sérieux ; [*of effort*] inutilité *f*

idler ['aɪdlə'] N **a** (= *lazy person*) paresseux *m*, -euse *f*, fainéant(e) *m(f)* **b** (*Tech*) (= *wheel*) roue *f* folle ; (= *pinion*) pignon *m* libre ; (= *pulley*) poulie *f* folle

idling ['aɪdlɪŋ] ADJ **at ~ speed** au ralenti

idly ['aɪdlɪ] ADV **a** (= *lazily*) [*sit, spend time*] sans rien faire ; **to stand** *or* **sit ~ by (while ...)** rester sans rien faire (pendant que ...) **b** (= *abstractedly*) [*wonder, speculate, think, look at*] vaguement ; [*say, play with*] négligemment ; [*talk*] pour passer le temps ; **~ curious** vaguement curieux

idol ['aɪdl] N (*lit, fig*) idole *f* ; **a teen ~** une idole des jeunes ; **a fallen ~** une idole déchue

idolater [aɪ'dɒlətə'] N idolâtre *mf*

idolatrous [aɪ'dɒlətrəs] ADJ idolâtre

idolatry [aɪ'dɒlətrɪ] N (*lit, fig*) idolâtrie *f*

idolize ['aɪdəlaɪz] VT idolâtrer

idyll ['ɪdɪl] N (*Literat, also fig*) idylle *f*

idyllic [ɪ'dɪlɪk] ADJ idyllique

i.e. [,aɪ'iː] (ABBR = **id est**) (= *that is*) c.-à-d., c'est-à-dire

if [ɪf] **1** CONJ **a** (*condition* = *supposing that*) si ; **I'll go if you come with me** j'irai si tu m'accompagnes ; **if the weather's nice I shall be pleased** s'il fait beau je serai content ; **if the weather were nice I should be pleased** s'il faisait beau je serais content ; **if the weather's nice and (if it is) not too cold I shall go with you** s'il fait beau et (s'il ne fait *or* qu'il ne fasse) pas trop froid je vous accompagnerai ; **if I had known, I would have visited them** si j'avais su, je leur aurais rendu visite ; **if you wait a minute, I'll come with you** si vous attendez *or* voulez attendre une minute, je vais vous accompagner ; **if I were a millionaire, I could ...** si j'étais (un) millionnaire, je pourrais ... ; **if I were you** si j'étais vous, (si j'étais) à votre place ; **(even) if I knew I wouldn't tell you** même si je le savais, je ne te le dirais pas ; **if they are to be believed** à les en croire ; **if it is true that ...** s'il est vrai que ... (+ *indic*), si tant est que ... (+ *subj*)

b (= *whenever*) si ; **if I asked him he helped**

me si je le lui demandais il m'aidait ; **if she wants any help she asks me** si elle a besoin d'aide elle s'adresse à moi

c (= *although*) si ; **(even) if it takes me all day I'll do it** (même) si cela doit me prendre toute la journée je le ferai ; **(even) if they are poor at least they are happy** s'ils sont pauvres du moins ils sont heureux ; **even if it is a good film it's rather long** c'est un bon film bien qu'(il soit) un peu long ; **nice weather, (even) if rather cold** temps agréable, bien qu'un peu froid ; **even if he tells me himself I won't believe it** même s'il me le dit lui-même je ne le croirai pas

d (= *granted that, admitting that*) si ; **if I am wrong, you are wrong too** si je me trompe *or* en admettant que je me trompe (*subj*), vous vous trompez aussi ; **(even) if he did say that, he didn't mean to hurt you** quand (bien) même il l'aurait dit, il n'avait aucune intention de vous faire de la peine

e (= *whether*) si ; **do you know if they have gone?** savez-vous s'ils sont partis? ; **I wonder if it's true** je me demande si c'est vrai

f (= *unless*) **if ... not** si ... ne ; **that's the house, if I'm not mistaken** voilà la maison, si je ne me trompe ; **they're coming at Christmas if they don't change their minds** ils viennent à Noël à moins qu'ils ne changent (*subj*) d'avis

g **if only** si seulement ; **if only to do** ne serait-ce que pour faire ; **if only I had known!** si seulement j'avais su! ; **if only it were that simple!** si seulement c'était aussi simple! ; **I'd better write to her, if only to let her know that ...** il faudrait que je lui écrive, ne serait-ce que pour lui faire savoir que ...

h **as if** comme, comme si ; **he acts as if he were rich** il se conduit comme s'il était riche ; **as if by chance** comme par hasard ; **he stood there as if he were dumb** il restait là comme (s'il était) muet ; **it isn't as if we were rich** ce n'est pas comme si nous étions riches, nous ne sommes pourtant pas riches

i (*phrases*) **if anything, it's even smaller** c'est peut-être encore plus petit ; **if anything, this one is bigger** c'est plutôt celui-ci qui est le plus grand ; **underpaid, if they are paid at all** mal payés, si tant est qu'on les paie ; **if necessary** s'il le faut, au besoin, si nécessaire ; **if so** ◊ **if it be so** (*liter*) s'il en est ainsi, si c'est le cas ; **if not** sinon ; **if it weren't for him, I wouldn't go** sans lui, je n'irais pas ; **if it weren't for him, I wouldn't be in this mess** sans lui, je ne serais pas dans ce pétrin ; **if it hadn't been for you, I would have despaired** sans toi, j'aurais désespéré ; **if only for a moment** ne serait-ce que pour un instant ; **well if he didn't try to steal my bag!*** (ne) voilà-t-il pas qu'il essaie de me voler mon sac!* ; **if it isn't our old friend Smith!** tiens ! mais c'est notre bon vieux Smith! ; **if I know her, she'll refuse** telle que je la connais, elle refusera

2 N **ifs and buts** les si *mpl* et les mais *mpl* ; **it's a big if** c'est un grand point d'interrogation

iffy* ['ɪfɪ] ADJ (= *uncertain*) [*outcome, future*] aléatoire, incertain ; (= *dodgy*) [*method*] qui craint* ; **an ~ neighbourhood** un quartier douteux ; **it all seems a bit ~ to me** ça me paraît un peu suspect, ça ne me paraît pas très catholique ; **I was feeling a bit ~** je n'étais pas vraiment dans mon assiette

igloo ['ɪgluː] N igloo *m or* iglou *m*

Ignatius [ɪg'neɪʃəs] N Ignace *m* ; **(St) ~ Loyola** saint Ignace de Loyola

igneous ['ɪgnɪəs] ADJ igné

ignite [ɪg'naɪt] **1** VT **a** (*lit*) mettre le feu à, enflammer **b** (*fig*) [*passions, interest*] susciter, déclencher ; [*conflict, controversy*] déclencher, être le détonateur de **2** VI **a** (*lit*) prendre feu, s'enflammer **b** (*fig*) [*conflict, controversy*] se déclencher

ignition [ɪg'nɪʃən] **1** N **a** ignition *f* **b** (*Aut*) (= *system*) allumage *m* ; (= *starting mechanism*)

contact *m* ; **to switch on/turn off the ~** mettre/couper le contact **2** COMP
► **ignition coil** N (*Aut*) bobine *f* d'allumage
► **ignition key** N clé *f* de contact
► **ignition switch** N contact *m*

ignoble [ɪg'nəʊbl] ADJ ignoble, indigne

ignominious [,ɪgnə'mɪnɪəs] ADJ (*frm*) ignominieux (*liter*)

ignominiously [,ɪgnə'mɪnɪəslɪ] ADV (*frm*) ignominieusement (*liter*)

ignominy ['ɪgnəmɪnɪ] N ignominie *f*

ignoramus [,ɪgnə'reɪməs] N ignare *mf*, ignorant(e) *m(f)*

ignorance ['ɪgnərəns] N **a** ignorance *f* (*of* de) ; **to be in ~ of sth** ignorer qch ; **they lived in blissful ~ of his true identity** ils vivaient dans l'heureuse ignorance de sa véritable identité ; **to keep sb in ~ of sth** tenir qn dans l'ignorance de qch, laisser ignorer qch à qn ; **in my ~** dans mon ignorance ; **~ of the law is no excuse** nul n'est censé ignorer la loi ; **his ~ of chemistry** son ignorance en (matière de) chimie ; **there is so much public ~ about this problem** c'est un problème totalement méconnu du grand public ; **~ is bliss** il vaut mieux ne pas savoir **b** (= *lack of education*) ignorance *f* ; **don't show your ~!** ce n'est pas la peine d'étaler ton ignorance !

ignorant ['ɪgnərənt] ADJ **a** (= *unaware*) **~ of** ignorant de ; **to be ~ of the facts** ignorer les faits, être ignorant des faits **b** (= *lacking education*) [*person*] ignorant ; [*words, behaviour*] d'(un) ignorant ; **for fear of appearing ~** par peur de paraître ignorant → **pig**

ignorantly ['ɪgnərəntlɪ] ADV par ignorance

ignore [ɪg'nɔː'] VT **a** (= *take no notice of*) [+ *interruption, remark, objection, advice, warning*] ne tenir aucun compte de, ignorer ; [+ *sb's behaviour*] ne pas prêter attention à ; [+ *person*] faire semblant de ne pas voir *or* entendre ; [+ *invitation, letter*] ne pas répondre à ; [+ *facts*] méconnaître ; [+ *question*] ne pas répondre à ; [+ *rule, prohibition*] ne pas respecter ; [+ *awkward fact*] faire semblant de ne pas connaître, ne tenir aucun compte de ; **I shall ~ your impertinence** je ne relèverai pas votre impertinence ; **we cannot ~ this behaviour any longer** nous ne pouvons plus fermer les yeux sur ce genre de comportement **b** (*Jur*) **to ~ a bill** prononcer un verdict d'acquittement

iguana [ɪ'gwɑːnə] N iguane *m*

ikon ['aɪkɒn] N = **icon**

IL ABBR = **Illinois**

ILEA [,aɪ.eliː'eɪ] N (*Brit Educ: formerly*) (ABBR = **Inner London Education Authority**) *services londoniens de l'enseignement*

ileum ['ɪlɪəm] N (*Anat*) iléon *m*

ilex ['aɪleks] N **a** (= *holm oak*) yeuse *f*, chêne *m* vert **b** (*genus* = *holly*) houx *m*

Iliad ['ɪlɪəd] N **the ~** l'Iliade *f*

Ilion ['ɪlɪən], **Ilium** ['ɪlɪəm] N Ilion

ilium ['ɪlɪəm] N (*pl* **ilia** ['ɪlɪə]) (*Anat*) ilion *m*

ilk [ɪlk] N **of that ~** de cette espèce *or* cet acabit ; **people of his ~** des gens de son espèce

I'll [aɪl] = **I shall**, **I will**; → **shall**, **will**

ill [ɪl] **1** ADJ (*compar* **worse**, *superl* **worst**) **a** (= *unwell*) malade ; (*less serious*) souffrant ; **to be ~** être malade *or* souffrant ; **to fall** *or* **take** *or* **be taken ~** tomber malade ; **to feel ~** ne pas se sentir bien ; **to look ~** avoir l'air malade *or* souffrant ; **to make sb ~** rendre qn malade ; **to be ~ with a fever/pneumonia** avoir de la fièvre/une pneumonie ; **~ with anxiety/ jealousy** *etc* malade d'inquiétude/de jalousie *etc* ; **he's seriously ~ in hospital** il est à l'hôpital dans un état grave → **mentally**, **terminally** **b** (= *bad*) mauvais, méchant ; (*liter*) **~ deed** mauvaise action *f*, méfait *m* ; **~ effects** conséquences *fpl* négatives ; (*liter*) **~ of fame** *or* **repute** [*place*] mal famé ; [*person*] de mauvaise réputation ; **house of ~ repute** maison *f* mal famée ; **~ health** mauvaise santé *f* ; **~ luck** malchance *f* ; **by ~ luck** par malheur, par malchance ; **as ~ luck would have it, he ...** le malheur a voulu qu'il ... (+ *subj*) ; **~ humour** *or* **temper** mauvaise humeur *f* ; **~ nature** méchanceté *f* ; **~ omen** mauvais augure *m* ; **~ feeling** ressentiment *m*, rancune *f* ; **no ~ feeling!** sans rancune! ; **~ will** (*gen*) malveillance *f* ; (= *grudge, resentment*) rancune *f* ; **I bear him no ~ will** je ne lui en veux pas ; **just to show there's no ~ will, I'll do it** je vais le faire, pour bien montrer que je ne suis pas rancunier ■ (*PROV*) **it's an ~ wind that blows nobody any good** à quelque chose malheur est bon (*PROV*)

2 N (*NonC* = *evil, injury*) mal *m* ; **to think/ speak ~ of sb** penser/dire du mal de qn ; **they mean you no ~** ils ne vous veulent aucun mal → **good**

3 **ills** NPL (= *misfortunes*) maux *mpl*, malheurs *mpl*

4 ADV mal ; **he can ~ afford the expense** il peut difficilement se permettre la dépense ; **we can ~ afford another scandal** nous ne pouvons guère nous permettre un autre scandale ; (*liter*) **to take sth** = prendre mal qch, prendre qch en mauvaise part ; (*liter*) **to go ~ with sb/sth** tourner mal pour qn/qch, aller mal pour qn/qch ; (*liter*) **to sit ~ with sth** aller mal avec qch ; **to bode** *or* **augur ~ for sb** être de mauvais augure pour qn ; (*frm, liter*) **it ~ becomes you to do that** il vous sied mal (*frm*) de faire cela

5 COMP ► **ill-advised** ADJ [*decision, remark, action*] peu judicieux ; **you would be ~-advised to do that** vous auriez tort de faire cela, vous seriez malavisé de faire cela ► **ill-assorted** ADJ mal assorti ► **ill-at-ease** ADJ mal à l'aise ► **ill-bred** ADJ mal élevé ► **ill-concealed** ADJ [*amusement, disdain, disgust*] mal dissimulé ► **ill-conceived** ADJ [*plan, policy*] mal conçu *or* pensé ► **ill-considered** ADJ [*action, words*] irréfléchi ; [*measures*] hâtif ► **ill-defined** ADJ [*goals, powers, task*] mal défini ► **ill-disposed** ADJ mal disposé (**towards** envers) ► **ill-equipped** ADJ mal équipé (**with** en) ; **to be ~-equipped to do sth** (*lit*) être mal équipé pour faire qch, ne pas avoir le matériel nécessaire pour faire qch ; (*fig*) [*person*] être mal armé pour faire qch ; **he's ~-equipped for the role of Macbeth** il n'a pas les qualités requises pour jouer Macbeth ► **ill-fated** ADJ [*person*] infortuné, malheureux ; [*day*] fatal, néfaste ; [*action, effort*] malheureux ► **ill-favoured**, **ill-favored** (*US*) ADJ (= *ugly*) laid, pas aidé par la nature ; (= *objectionable*) déplaisant, désagréable ; (*stronger*) répugnant ► **ill-fitting** ADJ [*shoe, garment*] qui ne va pas (bien) ; [*lid, stopper*] qui ferme mal ► **ill-formed** ADJ (*Ling*) mal formé ► **ill-founded** ADJ [*belief, argument*] mal fondé ; [*rumour*] sans fondement ► **ill-gotten gains** NPL biens *mpl* mal acquis ► **ill-humoured** ADJ de mauvaise humeur, maussade ► **ill-informed** ADJ [*person*] mal renseigné, mal informé ; [*comment, criticism*] mal fondé ; [*essay, speech*] plein d'inexactitudes ► **ill-judged** ADJ peu judicieux, peu sage ► **ill-mannered** ADJ [*person, behaviour*] grossier, impoli ► **ill-natured** ADJ [*person, reply*] désagréable ; [*child*] méchant, désagréable ► **ill-nourished** ADJ mal nourri ► **ill-omened** ADJ de mauvais augure ► **ill-prepared** ADJ mal préparé ► **ill-starred** ADJ (*liter*) [*person*] né sous une mauvaise étoile, infortuné ; [*day, undertaking*] malheureux, néfaste ► **ill-suited** ADJ **they are ~-suited to each other**) ils sont mal assortis ; **~-suited to** [*tool, computer*] mal adapté à ; **he is ~-suited to this type of work** il ne convient guère à ce genre de travail, il n'est pas vraiment fait pour ce genre de travail ► **ill-tempered** ADJ (*habitually*) désagréable, qui a mauvais caractère ; (*on one occasion*) de mauvaise humeur, maussade ► **ill-timed** ADJ inopportun ► **ill-treat** VT maltraiter ► **ill-treatment** N

mauvais traitements *mpl* ► **ill-use** VT = **ill-treat**

Ill. ABBR = **Illinois**

illegal [ɪˈliːgəl] ADJ a (= *against the law*) illégal ; **it is ~ to do that** il est illégal de faire cela ; **it is ~ to sell alcohol to children** la loi interdit la vente d'alcool aux enfants ; **to make it ~ to do sth** rendre illégal de faire qch ; **~ parking** stationnement *m* illicite *or* interdit ; **~ alien** étranger *m*, -ère *f* en situation irrégulière ; **~ immigrant** immigré(e) *m(f)* clandestin(e) b (*Sport*) **~ tackle** tacle *m* irrégulier c (*Comput*) **~ character** caractère *m* invalide ; **~ operation** opération *f* interdite

illegality [ˌɪliːˈgælɪtɪ] N illégalité *f*

illegally [ɪˈliːgəlɪ] ADV illégalement ; **to be ~ parked** être en stationnement interdit

illegible [ɪˈledʒəbl] ADJ illisible

illegibly [ɪˈledʒəblɪ] ADV illisiblement

illegitimacy [ˌɪlɪˈdʒɪtɪməsɪ] N illégitimité *f*

illegitimate [ˌɪlɪˈdʒɪtɪmɪt] ADJ a [*child*] illégitime, naturel b [*action*] illégitime ; (*fig*) [*argument*] illogique ; [*conclusion*] injustifié

illegitimately [ˌɪlɪˈdʒɪtɪmɪtlɪ] ADV illégitimement

illiberal [ɪˈlɪbərəl] ADJ [*law*] restrictif ; [*system, regime*] intolérant ; [*person*] intolérant, étroit d'esprit ; [*view*] étroit

illicit [ɪˈlɪsɪt] ADJ illicite

illicitly [ɪˈlɪsɪtlɪ] ADV illicitement

illimitable [ɪˈlɪmɪtəbl] ADJ illimité, sans limites

Illinois [ˌɪlɪˈnɔɪ] N l'Illinois *m* ; **in ~** dans l'Illinois

illiteracy [ɪˈlɪtərəsɪ] N analphabétisme *m*

illiterate [ɪˈlɪtərɪt] **1** ADJ [*person*] illettré, analphabète ; (*fig*) **he is computer ~** il ne connaît rien à l'informatique, il ne s'y connaît pas en informatique **2** N illettré(e) *m(f)*, analphabète *mf*

illness [ˈɪlnɪs] N maladie *f* ; **she died after a long ~** elle est morte à la suite d'une longue maladie

illocutionary [ˌɪləˈkjuːʃənərɪ] ADJ illocutionnaire

illogical [ɪˈlɒdʒɪkəl] ADJ illogique

illogicality [ɪˌlɒdʒɪˈkælɪtɪ] N illogisme *m*

illogically [ɪˈlɒdʒɪkəlɪ] ADV de façon illogique

illuminate [ɪˈluːmɪneɪt] VT a (*gen*) éclairer ; (*for special occasion or effect*) illuminer ; **~d sign** enseigne *f* lumineuse b (*fig*) [+ *question, subject*] éclairer, faire la lumière sur c (*Art*) [+ *manuscript*] enluminer

illuminating [ɪˈluːmɪneɪtɪŋ] ADJ (*lit, fig*) éclairant ; **his comments proved very ~** ses commentaires se sont révélés très éclairants *or* ont beaucoup éclairci la question ; **it would be ~ to compare their stories** on apprendrait beaucoup en comparant leurs histoires

illumination [ɪˌluːmɪˈneɪʃən] N a (*NonC*) (*gen*) éclairage *m* ; (*for special effect*) [*of building*] illumination *f* b (*fig*) lumière *f*, inspiration *f* c (*Brit*) **~s** (= *decorative lights*) illuminations *fpl* d [*of manuscript*] enluminure *f*

illuminator [ɪˈluːmɪneɪtər] N a (= *lighting device*) dispositif *m* d'éclairage b [*of manuscript*] enlumineur *m*

illumine [ɪˈluːmɪn] VT (*liter*) éclairer

illusion [ɪˈluːʒən] N illusion *f* ; **to be under an ~** avoir *or* se faire une illusion ; **to be under the ~ that ...** avoir *or* se faire l'illusion que ... (+ *indic*) ; **to have** *or* **to be under no ~(s)** ne se faire aucune illusion ; **I have no ~s about what will happen to him** je ne me fais aucune illusion sur le sort qui l'attend ; **no one has any ~s about winning the war** personne ne se fait d'illusions sur l'issue de la guerre ; **he cherishes the ~ that ...** il caresse l'illusion que ... ; **large wall mirrors give an ~ of space** des

grands miroirs au mur créent une impression d'espace, **a tan can give us the ~ of being slimmer** le bronzage peut donner l'impression d'être plus mince → **optical**

illusionist [ɪˈluːʒənɪst] N illusionniste *mf*

illusive [ɪˈluːsɪv], **illusory** [ɪˈluːsərɪ] ADJ (= *unreal*) illusoire, irréel ; (= *deceptive*) illusoire, trompeur

▼ **illustrate** [ˈɪləstreɪt] VT a [+ *book, story*] illustrer ; **~d paper** (journal *m* *or* magazine *m* etc) illustré *m* b (*fig* = *exemplify*) [+ *idea, problem*] illustrer ; [+ *rule*] donner un exemple de ; **this can best be ~d as follows** la meilleure illustration qu'on puisse en donner est la suivante ; **to ~ that ...** illustrer le fait que ...

▼ **illustration** [ˌɪləsˈtreɪʃən] N (*lit, fig*) illustration *f* ; (*fig*) **by way of ~** à titre d'exemple

illustrative [ˈɪləstrətɪv] ADJ [*example*] explicatif, servant d'explication ; **for ~ purposes** à titre d'illustration ; **~ of this problem** qui sert à illustrer ce problème

illustrator [ˈɪləstreɪtər] N illustrateur *m*, -trice *f*

illustrious [ɪˈlʌstrɪəs] ADJ illustre, célèbre

illustriously [ɪˈlʌstrɪəslɪ] ADV glorieusement

ILO [ˌaɪelˈəʊ] N (ABBR = **International Labour Organisation**) OIT *f*

IM, i.m. [ˈaɪˈem] (ABBR = **intramuscular(ly)**) IM, i.m.

I'm [aɪm] = **I am** ; → **be**

image [ˈɪmɪdʒ] **1** N a (= *likeness*) image *f* ; **God created man in his own ~** Dieu créa l'homme à son image ; **real/virtual ~** image *f* réelle/virtuelle ; **~ in the glass/mirror** réflexion *f* dans la vitre/le miroir ; (*fig*) **he is the (living or very or spitting*) ~ of his father** c'est le portrait (vivant) de son père, c'est son père tout craché* ; **he's the very ~ of the English aristocrat** c'est l'aristocrate anglais type, c'est l'image même de l'aristocrate anglais ; **I had a sudden (mental) ~ of her, alone and afraid** soudain je l'ai vue en imagination, seule et effrayée ; **they had quite the wrong ~ of him** ils se faisaient une idée tout à fait fausse de lui → **graven, mirror** b (*also* **public ~**) image *f* (de marque) (*fig*) ; **he has to think of his ~** il faut qu'il pense à son image (de marque) ; **the tobacco industry is trying to improve its ~** l'industrie du tabac essaie d'améliorer son image (de marque) ; (*Cine, Theat etc*) **he's got the wrong ~ for that part** le public ne le voit pas dans ce genre de rôle → **brand**

2 COMP ► **image-building** N **it's just ~-building** ça ne vise qu'à promouvoir son (*or* leur *etc*) image de marque ► **image-conscious** ADJ **he is very ~-conscious** il se soucie beaucoup de son image ► **image enhancement** N (*Tech*) enrichissement *m* d'images

imager [ˈɪmɪdʒər] N → **magnetic, thermal**

imagery [ˈɪmɪdʒərɪ] N imagerie *f* ; **language full of ~** langage *m* imagé

imaginable [ɪˈmædʒɪnəbl] ADJ imaginable ; **every activity ~** toutes les activités imaginables ; **the most horrible circumstances ~** les circonstances les plus horribles que l'on puisse imaginer ; **a place of no ~ strategic value** un endroit qui ne présente pas le moindre intérêt stratégique

imaginary [ɪˈmædʒɪnərɪ] ADJ [*danger*] imaginaire ; [*character, place*] imaginaire, fictif

imagination [ɪˌmædʒɪˈneɪʃən] N (*NonC*) imagination *f* ; **to have a lively** *or* **vivid ~** avoir une imagination fertile ; **he's got ~** il a de l'imagination ; **he has little ~** il a peu d'imagination ; **a lack of ~** un manque d'imagination ; **she lets her ~ run away with her** elle se laisse emporter *or* entraîner par son imagination ; **it existed only in his ~** cela n'existait que dans son imagination ; **to capture** *or* **catch sb's ~** frapper l'imagination de qn ; **it is only** *or* **all (your) ~!** vous vous faites des idées!, vous rêvez!; **haven't you got any ~?** tu n'as donc aucune imagination?; **use your ~!** tu n'as pas beaucoup d'imagination! → **appeal**; → **stretch**

imaginative [ɪˈmædʒɪnətɪv] ADJ [*person*] imaginatif, plein d'imagination; [*book, film, approach*] plein d'imagination; [*solution, system, device*] inventif

imaginatively [ɪˈmædʒɪnətɪvlɪ] ADV avec imagination

imaginativeness [ɪˈmædʒɪnətɪvnɪs] N [*of person*] esprit *m* imaginatif *or* inventif; [*of thing*] caractère *m* imaginatif *or* inventif

▼ **imagine** [ɪˈmædʒɪn] VT a (= *picture to o.s.*) (s')imaginer; **~ life 100 years ago** imaginez (-vous) *or* représentez-vous la vie il y a 100 ans; **try to ~ a huge house far from anywhere** essayez d'imaginer *or* de vous imaginer une immense maison loin de tout; **~ (that) you're lying on a beach** imaginez que vous êtes étendu sur une plage; **I can't ~ myself at 60** je ne m'imagine *or* ne me vois pas du tout à 60 ans; **~ a situation in which ...** imaginez(-vous) une situation où ...; **(just) ~!** tu (t')imagines!; **(you can) ~ how I felt!** imaginez *or* vous imaginez ce que j'ai pu ressentir!; **I can ~ how he must feel** j'imagine ce qu'il doit ressentir; **I can ~!** je m'en doute!; **~ my surprise when I won!** imaginez ma surprise quand j'ai gagné!; **(you can) ~ how pleased I was!** vous pensez si j'étais content!; **it's hard to ~ how bad things were** on a du mal à s'imaginer à quel point les choses allaient mal; **did you ever ~ you'd meet her one day?** est-ce que tu t'étais jamais imaginé *or* douté que tu la rencontrerais un jour?; **I can just ~ his reaction when he sees her** je vois d'ici sa réaction quand il la verra; **I can't ~ you being nasty to anyone** je ne peux pas imaginer que vous puissiez être désagréable avec qui que ce soit; **I can't ~ living there** je ne me vois pas vivre là; **he's (always) imagining things** il se fait des idées b (= *suppose, believe*) supposer, imaginer **(that** que); **you won't want to stay long, I ~** vous ne resterez pas longtemps, je suppose *or* j'imagine; **I didn't ~ he would come** je ne pensais pas qu'il viendrait; **was he meeting someone? — I ~ so** il avait un rendez-vous? — j'imagine *or* je suppose c (= *believe wrongly*) croire, s'imaginer; **don't ~ that I can help you** n'allez pas croire que *or* ne vous imaginez pas que je puisse vous aider; **he fondly ~d she was still willing to obey him** il s'imaginait naïvement qu'elle était encore prête à lui obéir; **I ~d I heard someone speak** j'ai cru entendre parler; **I ~d you to be dark-haired** je vous imaginais avec les cheveux bruns

imaging [ˈɪmɪdʒɪŋ] N (*Comput*) imagerie *f* → **document, thermal**

imaginings [ɪˈmædʒɪnɪŋz] NPL **it was beyond our wildest ~** nous n'en espérions pas tant, même dans nos rêves les plus fous

imam [ɪˈmɑːm] N imam *m*

imbalance [ɪmˈbæləns] N (*lit, fig*) déséquilibre *m*; **the ~ in trade between the two countries** le déséquilibre des échanges commerciaux entre les deux pays

imbalanced [ɪmˈbælənst] ADJ déséquilibré

imbecile [ˈɪmbəsiːl] 1 N a imbécile *mf*, idiot(e) *m(f)*; **to act/speak like an ~** faire/dire des imbécillités *or* des bêtises; **you ~!** espèce d'imbécile *or* d'idiot! b (*Med*††) imbécile *mf* 2 ADJ a [*action, words*] imbécile; [*person*] imbécile, idiot b (*Med*††) imbécile

imbecility [ˌɪmbɪˈsɪlɪtɪ] N a (*NonC*) imbécillité *f*, stupidité *f* b (= *act etc*) imbécillité *f*, stupidité *f* c (*Med*††) imbécillité *f*

imbed [ɪmˈbed] VT = **embed**

imbibe [ɪmˈbaɪb] 1 VT a (= *drink*) boire, absorber; (*fig*) [+ *ideas, information*] absorber

b (= *absorb*) [+ *water, light, heat*] absorber 2 VI (* *hum* = *drink to excess*) s'imbiber d'alcool

imbroglio [ɪmˈbrəʊlɪəʊ] N imbroglio *m*

imbue [ɪmˈbjuː] VT (*fig*) imprégner (**with** de); **~d with** imprégné de

IMF [ˌaɪemˈef] (*Econ*) (ABBR = **International Monetary Fund**) FMI *m*

imitable [ˈɪmɪtəbl] ADJ imitable

imitate [ˈɪmɪteɪt] VT imiter

imitation [ˌɪmɪˈteɪʃən] 1 N imitation *f*; **in ~ of** en imitant; **they learnt grammar by ~ of their elders** ils ont appris la grammaire en imitant leurs aînés; (*Comm*) **"beware of ~s"** « se méfier des contrefaçons »; **it's only ~** c'est de l'imitation; **I do a pretty good ~ of him** j'arrive assez bien à l'imiter ■ (*PROV*) **~ is the sincerest form of flattery** il n'est pas de louange plus sincère que l'imitation

2 COMP [*silk, ivory, gun, fruit*] faux (fausse *f*) (*before n*) ► **imitation fur coat** N manteau *m* en fourrure synthétique *or* en fausse fourrure ► **imitation gold** N similor *m* ► **imitation jewellery** N faux bijoux *mpl* ► **imitation leather** N imitation *f* cuir, similicuir *m* ► **imitation marble** N faux marbre *m*, similimarbre *m* ► **imitation mink coat** N manteau *m* (en) imitation vison ► **imitation pearl** N perle *f* synthétique, fausse perle *f* ► **imitation stone** N pierre *f* artificielle, fausse pierre *f*

imitative [ˈɪmɪtətɪv] ADJ [*word, art*] imitatif; [*person*] imitateur (-trice *f*)

imitator [ˈɪmɪteɪtə*r*] N imitateur *m*, -trice *f*

immaculate [ɪˈmækjʊlɪt] 1 ADJ a (= *clean*) [*fabric, garment, colour*] immaculé; (= *spick and span*) [*garment, house, hair, figure*] impeccable; **an ~ white shirt** une chemise blanche immaculée 2 COMP ► **the Immaculate Conception** N (*Rel*) l'Immaculée Conception *f*

immaculately [ɪˈmækjʊlɪtlɪ] ADV [*dressed, groomed, behaved*] de façon impeccable; ~ **clean** d'une propreté impeccable; **an ~ kept house/car** une maison/voiture impeccablement tenue

immanent [ˈɪmənənt] ADJ immanent

Immanuel [ɪˈmænjʊəl] N Emmanuel *m*

immaterial [ˌɪməˈtɪərɪəl] ADJ a (= *unimportant*) négligeable, sans importance; **it is ~ whether he did or not** il importe peu qu'il l'ait fait ou non; **that's (quite) ~** (= *not important*) ça n'a pas d'importance; (= *not relevant*) ça n'est pas pertinent; **that's ~ to us** peu nous importe; **my presence was ~ to him** il n'avait que faire de ma présence b (*Philos etc*) immatériel

immature [ˌɪməˈtjʊə*r*] ADJ a (= *not full-grown*) [*fruit*] (qui n'est) pas mûr, vert; [*animal, tree*] jeune b (= *childish*) immature; **he's very ~** il est très immature, il manque vraiment de maturité; **he is emotionally ~** il est affectivement immature; **she's just being childish and ~** elle se comporte d'une manière puérile et immature

immaturity [ˌɪməˈtjʊərɪtɪ] N manque *m* de maturité, immaturité *f*

immeasurable [ɪˈmeʒərəbl] ADJ [*amount, height, space*] incommensurable; [*joy, suffering*] incommensurable, infini; [*precautions, care*] infini; [*wealth, riches, value*] inestimable

immeasurably [ɪˈmeʒərəblɪ] ADV (*frm*) [*better, worse*] infiniment; [*improve*] infiniment; [*increase, rise, advance*] dans des proportions illimitées; **to help sb ~** apporter une aide inestimable à qn; **to add ~ to sth** ajouter infiniment à qch

immediacy [ɪˈmiːdɪəsɪ] N immédiateté *f*; **the ~ of live television** l'immédiateté du direct; **a sense of ~** un sentiment d'immédiateté *or* d'urgence

immediate [ɪˈmiːdɪət] 1 ADJ a (= *instant*) [*effect, impact, response, results, ceasefire, closure,*

danger] immédiat; **with ~ effect** avec effet immédiat; **to come into ~ effect** entrer immédiatement en vigueur; **to take ~ action** agir immédiatement; **for ~ delivery** à livrer immédiatement; **the matter deserves your ~ attention** cette affaire exige une attention immédiate *or* de votre part; **a savings account that allows ~ access to your money** un compte d'épargne qui vous permet d'effectuer des retraits à tout moment; **he has no ~ plans to retire** il n'envisage pas de prendre sa retraite dans l'immédiat b (= *most urgent*) [*future, needs, priority, threat, problem, issue*] immédiat; **my ~ concern was for the children** mon premier souci a été les enfants; **of more ~ concern is the state of the economy** l'état de l'économie est une préoccupation plus urgente *or* plus immédiate; **his (most) ~ task** sa tâche la plus urgente c (= *direct, nearest*) immédiat; **in sb's ~ vicinity** dans le voisinage immédiat de qn; **to the ~ south** immédiatement au sud; **her ~ predecessor** son prédécesseur immédiat; **in the ~ aftermath of the war** sitôt après la guerre, dans l'immédiat après-guerre; **my ~ family** ma famille immédiate

2 COMP ► **immediate constituent** N (*Gram*) constituant *m* immédiat

immediately [ɪˈmiːdɪətlɪ] 1 ADV a (= *at once*) immédiatement, tout de suite; **~ available/obvious/apparent** immédiatement *or* tout de suite disponible/évident/apparent; **~ before/after/afterwards** immédiatement *or* sitôt avant/après/après; **the years ~ following the Second World War** les années qui ont immédiatement suivi la Seconde Guerre mondiale; **~ upon arrival** *or* **arriving** dès l'arrivée b (= *directly*) directement; **~ behind/above** directement derrière/au-dessus 2 CONJ (*esp Brit*) dès que; **~ I returned, I ...** dès mon retour, je ...

immemorial [ˌɪmɪˈmɔːrɪəl] ADJ immémorial; **from** *or* **since time ~** de toute éternité, de temps immémorial

immense [ɪˈmens] ADJ [*space*] immense, vaste; [*size*] immense; [*possibilities, achievements, fortune, difficulty*] immense, énorme

immensely [ɪˈmenslɪ] ADV [*rich, successful, popular*] immensément, extrêmement; [*enjoy, help, vary*] énormément; **~ helpful** [*book, object etc*] extrêmement utile; [*person*] extrêmement serviable; **to improve ~** s'améliorer énormément

immensity [ɪˈmensɪtɪ] N immensité *f*

immerse [ɪˈmɜːs] VT immerger, plonger; (*Rel*) baptiser par immersion; **to ~ one's head in water** plonger la tête dans l'eau; (*fig*) **to ~ o.s. in sth** se plonger dans; **to be ~d in one's work** être absorbé *or* plongé dans son travail

immersion [ɪˈmɜːʃən] 1 N immersion *f*; (*fig*) absorption *f*; (*Rel*) baptême *m* par immersion 2 COMP ► **immersion course** N (*Educ*) stage *m* *or* cours *m* intensif (**in** de) ► **immersion heater** N (*Brit*) (= *boiler*) chauffe-eau *m inv* électrique; (= *device*) thermoplongeur *m*

immigrancy [ˈɪmɪgrənsɪ] N (*US*) condition *f* d'immigrant

immigrant [ˈɪmɪgrənt] 1 ADJ, N (*newly arrived*) immigrant(e) *m(f)*; (*well-established*) immigré(e) *m(f)* 2 COMP ► **immigrant labour** N = **immigrant workers** ► **immigrant workers** NPL (*Ind*) main-d'œuvre *f* immigrée

immigrate [ˈɪmɪgreɪt] VI immigrer

immigration [ˌɪmɪˈgreɪʃən] 1 N immigration *f*; **to go through customs and ~** passer la douane et l'immigration 2 COMP [*policy*] d'immigration; [*law*] sur l'immigration ► **immigration authorities** NPL services *mpl* de l'immigration ► **immigration border patrol** N (*US Police*) services *mpl* de l'immigration ► **immigration control** N (= *department*) (services *mpl* de) l'immigration *f*; (= *system*) contrôle *m* de l'immigration

► **Immigration Department** N services *mpl* de l'immigration *f*

imminence ['ımınəns] N imminence *f*

imminent ['ımınənt] ADJ imminent

immobile [ı'məʊbaıl] ADJ immobile

immobiliser [ı'məʊbılaızəʳ] N (*Aut*) dispositif *m* antidémarrage

immobility [ıməʊ'bılıtı] N immobilité *f*

immobilize [ı'məʊbılaız] VT (*also Fin*) immobiliser

immoderate [ı'mɒdərıt] ADJ (*frm*) [*desire, appetite*] immodéré, démesuré; [*conduct*] déréglé

immoderately [ı'mɒdərıtlı] ADV (*frm*) immodérément

immodest [ı'mɒdıst] ADJ [a] (= *indecent*) impudique, indécent [b] (= *presumptuous*) impudent, présomptueux

immodestly [ı'mɒdıstlı] ADV [a] (= *indecently*) [*dress*] de façon inconvenante; **to behave ~** avoir une conduite inconvenante [b] (= *presumptuously*) [*claim*] de façon présomptueuse

immodesty [ı'mɒdıstı] N [a] (= *indecency*) impudeur *f*, indécence *f* [b] (= *presumption*) impudence *f*, présomption *f*

immolate ['ıməʊleıt] VT (*frm*) immoler

immoral [ı'mɒrəl] [1] ADJ immoral, contraire aux bonnes mœurs; **it is ~ to do that** il est immoral de faire ça; **it would be ~ for him to take the money** il serait immoral qu'il accepte (*subj*) l'argent; **it is ~ that …** il est immoral que … (+ *subj*); **~ behaviour** un comportement contraire aux bonnes mœurs [2] COMP ► **immoral earnings** NPL (*Jur*) gains *mpl* résultant d'activités contraires à la morale

immorality [ımə'rælıtı] N immoralité *f*

immortal [ı'mɔːtl] [1] ADJ [*person, god*] immortel; [*fame*] immortel, impérissable; **in the ~ words of La Pasionaria, they shall not pass** selon le mot impérissable de la Pasionaria, ils ne passeront pas [2] N immortel(le) *m(f)*

immortality [ımɔː'tælıtı] N immortalité *f*

immortalize [ı'mɔːtəlaız] VT immortaliser

immovable [ı'muːvəbl] [1] ADJ [a] [*object*] fixe; (*Jur*) [*belongings*] immeuble, immobilier [b] (*fig*) [*courage, decision*] inflexible, inébranlable; **John was ~ in his decision** John était inflexible *or* inébranlable dans sa décision [2] **immovables** NPL (*Jur*) immeubles *mpl*, biens *mpl* immobiliers

immovably [ı'muːvəblı] ADV [a] [*fix, nail down*] de façon inamovible [b] [*determined*] de façon inébranlable; [*opposed*] irrévocablement

immune [ı'mjuːn] [1] ADJ [a] (*Med*) [*person*] immunisé (**from, to** contre) → **acquired** [b] (*fig = secure from*) **~ from** *or* **to** (*temptation, wish etc*) immunisé *or* blindé* contre; **~ to criticism** immunisé *or* blindé* contre la critique; **he never became ~ to the sight of death** il n'a jamais pu s'habituer à la vue de la mort [c] (*fig = exempt from*) **~ from taxation** exonéré d'impôt; **to be ~ from prosecution** bénéficier de l'immunité [2] COMP ► **immune body** N anticorps *m* ► **immune deficiency** N déficience *f* immunitaire ► **immune response** N réaction *f* immunitaire ► **immune serum** N immun-sérum *m* ► **immune system** N système *m* immunitaire

immunity [ı'mjuːnıtı] N (*Med, gen*) immunité *f* (**from, to** contre); **diplomatic/parliamentary ~** immunité *f* diplomatique/parlementaire

immunization [ımjʊnaı'zeıʃən] N immunisation *f* (**against** contre)

immunize ['ımjʊnaız] VT immuniser (**against** contre)

immunodeficiency [ımjʊnəʊdı'fıʃənsı] N déficience *f* immunologique

immunodepressant [ımjʊnəʊdı'presnt] N, ADJ immunodépresseur *m*

immunogenic [ımjʊnəʊ'dʒenık] ADJ immunogène

immunoglobulin [ımjʊnəʊ'glɒbjulın] N immunoglobuline *f*

immunological [ımjʊnəʊ'lɒdʒıkəl] ADJ immunologique

immunologist [ımjʊ'nɒlədʒıst] N immunologiste *mf*

immunology [ımjʊ'nɒlədʒı] N immunologie *f*

immunosuppressant [ımjʊnəʊsʌ'presnt] [1] N immunosuppresseur *m* [2] ADJ immunosuppressif

immunosuppression [ımjʊnəʊsʌ'preʃən] N immunosuppression *f*

immunosuppressive [ımjʊnəʊdı'presnt] ADJ immunosuppressif

immunotherapy [ımjʊnəʊ'θerəpı] N immunothérapie *f*

immure [ı'mjʊəʳ] VT (*frm*) (*lit*) emmurer; (*fig*) enfermer

immutability [ımjuːtə'bılıtı] N immutabilité *f*, immuabilité *f* (*frm*)

immutable [ı'mjuːtəbl] ADJ immuable, inaltérable

immutably [ı'muːtəblı] ADV immuablement

imp [ımp] N diablotin *m*, lutin *m*; (* = *child*) petit(e) espiègle *m(f)*, petit diable *m*

impact ['ımpækt] [1] N [a] (*lit*) impact *m* (**on** sur), choc *m* (**on, against** contre); **the asteroid exploded on ~** l'astéroïde a explosé au moment du choc *or* de l'impact; **the plane exploded on ~ with the sea** l'avion a explosé au moment où il a touché la mer
[b] (*fig*) (= *effect*) impact *m*, effet *m*; (= *consequences*) incidences *fpl*, conséquences *fpl*; **to make an ~ on sb** (= *affect*) produire un impact sur qn; (= *impress*) faire une forte impression sur qn; **to have an ~ on sth** avoir des incidences *or* conséquences sur qch
[2] [ım'pækt] VT [a] (= *cause to become impacted*) enfoncer, presser (**into** dans)
[b] (= *collide with*) percuter, entrer en collision avec
[c] (*fig = affect*) toucher
[3] [ım'pækt] VI [a] (= *hit*) percuter; **the missile ~ed with the ground** le missile a percuté le sol
[b] (= *become stuck*) se coincer
[c] (*fig*) influer
[4] COMP ► **impact printer** N (*Comput*) imprimante *f* à impact

► **impact on** VT FUS **to ~ on sb** produire un impact sur qn

impacted [ım'pæktıd] [1] ADJ (*gen* = *stuck*) coincé; [*tooth*] inclus, enclavé; [*fracture*] engrené [2] COMP ► **impacted area** N (*US*) quartier *m* surpeuplé

impair [ım'pɛəʳ] VT [+ *abilities, faculties*] détériorer, diminuer; [+ *negotiations, relations*] porter atteinte à; [+ *health*] abîmer, détériorer; [+ *sight, hearing*] abîmer, affaiblir; [+ *mind, strength*] diminuer

impaired [ım'pɛəd] ADJ [*sight, hearing*] abîmé, affaibli; [*faculties, health*] détérioré; [*strength*] diminué

impairment [ım'pɛəmənt] N [a] (*NonC* = *weakening*) [*of judgment, mental functions*] affaiblissement *m*, diminution *f* [b] (= *defect*) déficience *f*; **hearing/visual ~** déficience *f* auditive/visuelle; **speech** *or* **language ~s** troubles *mpl* du langage

impala [ım'pɑːlə] N (*pl* **impalas** *or* **impala**) impala *m*

impale [ım'peıl] VT empaler (**on** sur)

impalpable [ım'pælpəbl] ADJ impalpable

impanel [ım'pænl] VT = **empanel**

imparity [ım'pærıtı] N inégalité *f*

impart [ım'pɑːt] VT [a] (= *make known*) [+ *news*] communiquer, faire part de; [+ *knowledge*]

communiquer, transmettre [b] (= *bestow*) donner, transmettre

impartial [ım'pɑːʃəl] ADJ [*person, attitude, verdict, decision, speech*] impartial, objectif

impartiality [ım,pɑːʃı'ælıtı] N impartialité *f*, objectivité *f*

impartially [ım'pɑːʃəlı] ADV impartialement, objectivement

impassable [ım'pɑːsəbl] ADJ [*barrier, river*] infranchissable; [*road*] impraticable

impasse [æm'pɑːs] N (*lit, fig*) impasse *f*; **to reach an ~** se retrouver dans une impasse

impassioned [ım'pæʃnd] ADJ [*feeling*] exalté; [*plea, speech*] passionné

impassive [ım'pæsıv] ADJ [*person, attitude, face*] impassible, imperturbable

impassively [ım'pæsıvlı] ADV impassiblement, imperturbablement

impatience [ım'peıʃəns] N [a] (= *eagerness*) impatience *f* (**to do** de faire) [b] (= *intolerance*) intolérance *f* (**of sth** à l'égard de qch, **with sb** vis-à-vis de qn, à l'égard de qn)

impatiens [ım'peıʃı,enz] N (*pl inv*: *Bot*) impatiente *f*

impatient [ım'peıʃənt] ADJ [a] (= *eager*) [*person, answer*] impatient; **~ to leave** impatient de partir; **to become** *or* **get** *or* **grow ~** s'impatienter; **they are ~ for jobs** ils ont hâte d'obtenir un emploi [b] (= *intolerant*) intolérant (**of sth** à l'égard de qch, **with sb** vis-à-vis de qn, à l'égard de qn, **at** par rapport à)

impatiently [ım'peıʃəntlı] ADV [*wait, say*] impatiemment; [*nod*] avec impatience; **to look forward ~ to sth** attendre qch avec beaucoup d'impatience

impeach [ım'piːtʃ] VT [a] (*Jur* = *accuse*) [+ *public official*] mettre en accusation (*en vue de destituer*); (*US*) entamer la procédure d'impeachment contre; [+ *person*] accuser (**for** *or* **of sth** de qch, **for doing** de faire); (= *question, challenge*) [+ *sb's character*] attaquer; [+ *sb's motives, honesty*] mettre en doute; (*Jur*) **to ~ a witness** récuser un témoin

impeachable [ım'piːtʃəbl] ADJ passible des tribunaux

impeachment [ım'piːtʃmənt] N [a] (*Jur*) [*of public official*] mise *f* en accusation (*en vue d'une destitution*); (*US*) procédure *f* d'impeachment; [*of person*] accusation *f* (**for sth** de qch, **for doing** de faire) [b] [*of sb's character*] dénigrement *m*; [*of sb's honesty*] mise *f* en doute

impeccable [ım'pekəbl] ADJ [*manners, behaviour, taste*] irréprochable; [*credentials, timing, English, service, clothes*] impeccable

impeccably [ım'pekəblı] ADV [*dress*] impeccablement; [*behave*] de façon irréprochable

impecunious [ımpı'kjuːnıəs] ADJ (*frm*) impécunieux, nécessiteux

impedance [ım'piːdəns] N (*Elec*) impédance *f*

impede [ım'piːd] VT [+ *person, progress*] entraver; [+ *action, success, movement, traffic*] gêner, entraver; **to ~ sb from doing sth** empêcher qn de faire qch

impediment [ım'pedımənt] N [a] obstacle *m*, empêchement *m*; **there was no legal ~ to the marriage** il n'y avait aucun empêchement légal à ce mariage [b] (*also* **speech ~**) défaut *m* d'élocution [c] **~s** = **impedimenta**

impedimenta [ım,pedı'mentə] NPL (*also Mil*) impedimenta *mpl*

impel [ım'pel] VT [a] (= *drive forward*) pousser, faire avancer [b] (= *compel*) obliger, forcer (**to do** à faire); (= *urge*) inciter, pousser (**to do** à faire); **to ~ sb to crime** pousser qn au crime; **to ~ sb to action** pousser qn à agir

impend [ım'pend] VI [a] (= *be about to happen*) être imminent; (= *menace, hang over*) [*danger, storm*] menacer; [*threat*] planer

impending [ım'pendıŋ] ADJ imminent

impenetrability [ɪm,penɪtrə'bɪlɪtɪ] N [of forest] impénétrabilité f ; [of book, theory] caractère m hermétique

impenetrable [ɪm'penɪtrəbl] ADJ [barrier] infranchissable ; [forest] impénétrable ; [darkness, mystery] insondable ; [book, theory] inaccessible ; [accent] incompréhensible

impenetrably [ɪm'penɪtrəblɪ] ADV ~ thick d'une épaisseur impénétrable ; ~ obscure d'une obscurité insondable

impenitence [ɪm'penɪtəns] N impénitence f

impenitent [ɪm'penɪtənt] ADJ impénitent ; he was quite ~ about it il ne s'en repentait nullement

impenitently [ɪm'penɪtəntlɪ] ADV sans repentir

imperative [ɪm'perətɪv] 1 ADJ a [action, need] impératif ; [desire] pressant, impérieux ; immediate action is ~ il est impératif d'agir immédiatement ; silence is ~ le silence s'impose ; it is ~ to do this il est impératif de le faire ; it is ~ for him to do this ◊ it is ~ that he (should) do this il est impératif qu'il le fasse b (Gram) ~ form/mood forme f impérative/mode m impératif ; ~ verb verbe m à l'impératif 2 N (Gram) impératif m ; in the ~ (mood) à l'impératif, au mode impératif

imperatively [ɪm'perətɪvlɪ] ADV a [need] impérieusement ; [order] impérativement b (Gram) [use verb] à l'impératif

imperceptible [,ɪmpə'septəbl] ADJ [sight, movement, sound] imperceptible (to à) ; [difference] imperceptible, insensible

imperceptibly [,ɪmpə'septəblɪ] ADV imperceptiblement

imperceptive [,ɪmpə'septɪv] ADJ peu perspicace

imperfect [ɪm'pɜːfɪkt] 1 ADJ a (= flawed) [world, human being, system, knowledge] imparfait ; [goods, copy] défectueux b (Gram) [tense, ending] de l'imparfait ; [verb] à l'imparfait 2 N (Gram) imparfait m ; in the ~ (tense) à l'imparfait 3 COMP ► imperfect competition N (Econ) concurrence f imparfaite ► imperfect market N (Econ) marché m imparfait

imperfection [,ɪmpə'fekʃən] N (in person) (moral) défaut m ; (physical) imperfection f ; (in skin, paper, policy, system, design) imperfection f (in sth de qch) ; (in china, glass, jewel, cloth) défaut m (in sth de qch)

imperfectly [ɪm'pɜːfɪktlɪ] ADV imparfaitement

imperial [ɪm'pɪərɪəl] 1 ADJ a (Pol) impérial ; His Imperial Highness/Majesty Son Altesse/Sa Majesté Impériale b (in Brit = non-metric) ~ weights and measures système anglo-saxon de poids et mesures ; ~ gallon ≈ 4,55 litres 2 N (= beard) (barbe f à l')impériale f 3 COMP ► imperial preference N (Brit Hist) tarif m préférentiel (à l'intérieur de l'Empire britannique) ► imperial system N système anglo-saxon de poids et mesures

┌─────────────────┐
│ IMPERIAL SYSTEM │
└─────────────────┘

Le système dit « impérial » des poids et mesures reste utilisé en Grande-Bretagne, parallèlement au système métrique, officiellement adopté en 1971 et enseigné dans les écoles. Beaucoup de gens connaissent leur poids en « stones and pounds » et leur taille en « feet and inches ». Les distances sont, elles, données en « miles ».

Aux États-Unis, le système « impérial » est encore officiellement en usage pour toutes les unités de poids et mesures. Cependant, en ce qui concerne les liquides, beaucoup de noms sont les mêmes que dans le système britannique, mais la contenance est différente. D'autre part, les gens se pèsent en « pounds » plutôt qu'en « stones and pounds ».

imperialism [ɪm'pɪərɪəlɪzəm] N impérialisme m

imperialist [ɪm'pɪərɪəlɪst] ADJ, N impérialiste mf

imperialistic [ɪm,pɪərɪə'lɪstɪk] ADJ impérialiste

imperially [ɪm'pɪərɪəlɪ] ADV majestueusement ; [say, gesture] impérieusement

imperil [ɪm'perɪl] VT (liter) [+ sb's life] mettre en péril or danger ; [+ fortune, one's life] exposer, risquer ; [+ health, reputation] compromettre

imperious [ɪm'pɪərɪəs] ADJ [gesture, look, command] impérieux ; [need, desire] pressant, impérieux

imperiously [ɪm'pɪərɪəslɪ] ADV impérieusement

imperishable [ɪm'perɪʃəbl] ADJ impérissable

impermanence [ɪm'pɜːmənəns] N caractère m éphémère

impermanent [ɪm'pɜːmənənt] ADJ éphémère, transitoire

impermeable [ɪm'pɜːmɪəbl] ADJ [rock] imperméable ; [wall, roof] étanche

impersonal [ɪm'pɜːsnl] ADJ (also Gram) impersonnel

impersonality [ɪm,pɜːsə'nælɪtɪ] N côté m impersonnel

impersonalize [,ɪm'pɜːsənə,laɪz] VT déshumaniser

impersonally [ɪm'pɜːsnlɪ] ADV de façon impersonnelle

impersonate [ɪm'pɜːsəneɪt] VT (gen) se faire passer pour ; (Jur) usurper l'identité de ; (Theat) imiter

impersonation [ɪm,pɜːsə'neɪʃən] N (Theat) imitation f ; (Jur) usurpation f d'identité ; his Elvis ~ son imitation d'Elvis ; he gave a fair ~ of somebody trying to be friendly il jouait assez bien le rôle de quelqu'un qui se veut aimable

impersonator [ɪm'pɜːsəneɪtə] N (Theat) imitateur m, -trice f ; (Jur) usurpateur m, -trice f d'identité → female

impertinence [ɪm'pɜːtɪnəns] N impertinence f ; a piece of ~ une impertinence ; to ask would be an ~ il serait impertinent de demander

impertinent [ɪm'pɜːtɪnənt] ADJ (= impudent) impertinent (to sb envers qn) ; don't be ~! ne soyez pas impertinent! ; would it be ~ to ask where exactly you were? serait-il inconvenant de vous demander où vous étiez exactement?

impertinently [ɪm'pɜːtɪnəntlɪ] ADV a (= impudently) avec impertinence b (= irrelevantly) sans pertinence, hors de propos ; [reply] à côté de la question

imperturbable [,ɪmpə'tɜːbəbl] ADJ imperturbable

imperturbably [,ɪmpə'tɜːbəblɪ] ADV imperturbablement

impervious [ɪm'pɜːvɪəs] ADJ a (= impermeable) [substance, rock] imperméable (to à) ; [wall, roof] étanche (to à) b (fig) ~ to the sufferings of others insensible aux souffrances d'autrui ; ~ to reason inaccessible or sourd à la raison ; ~ to threats indifférent aux menaces ; he is ~ to criticism la critique le laisse indifférent or ne le touche pas ; (pej) il est fermé or sourd à la critique

impetigo [,ɪmpɪ'taɪgəʊ] N (Med) impétigo m ; (in children) gourme f

impetuosity [ɪm,petjʊ'ɒsɪtɪ] N impétuosité f, fougue f

impetuous [ɪm'petjʊəs] ADJ impétueux, fougueux

impetuously [ɪm'petjʊəslɪ] ADV impétueusement, fougueusement

impetuousness [ɪm'petjʊəsnɪs] N = **impetuosity**

impetus ['ɪmpɪtəs] N a (Phys) [of object] force f d'impulsion ; [of runner] élan m b (fig) impulsion f, élan m ; to give (an) ~ to donner

une impulsion or un élan à qch ; she needs a new ~ for her talent elle a besoin d'une nouvelle impulsion or d'un nouvel élan pour exprimer son talent

impiety [ɪm'paɪətɪ] N impiété f

impinge [ɪm'pɪndʒ] VI a (= make impression) to ~ on sb/sth affecter or toucher qn/qch ; it didn't ~ on his daily life cela n'affectait pas sa vie quotidienne, cela n'avait pas de répercussion sur sa vie quotidienne b to ~ on sb's rights empiéter sur les droits de qn, porter atteinte aux droits de qn ; this legislation could ~ on privacy cette législation pourrait porter atteinte à la vie privée c cosmic rays that ~ on the upper atmosphere les rayons cosmiques qui affectent la couche supérieure de l'atmosphère

impingement [ɪm'pɪndʒmənt] N empiètement m (of, on sur)

impious ['ɪmpɪəs] ADJ impie

impiously ['ɪmpɪəslɪ] ADV avec impiété

impish ['ɪmpɪʃ] ADJ espiègle, malicieux

implacable [ɪm'plækəbl] ADJ implacable (towards sb/sth envers qn/qch) ; he was ~ in his opposition to the proposal il a été implacable dans son opposition à la proposition

implacably [ɪm'plækəblɪ] ADV implacablement

implant [ɪm'plɑːnt] 1 VT a [+ idea] implanter (in sb dans la tête de qn) ; [+ principle] inculquer (in sb à qn) ; [+ desire, wish] inspirer (in sb à qn) b (Med) implanter (in dans) 2 VI s'implanter (in dans) 3 ['ɪmplɑːnt] N (under skin) implant m ; (= graft) greffe f

implantation [,ɪmplɑːn'teɪʃən] N [of ideology, culture] introduction f ; (Med) [of embryo] implantation f

implausible [ɪm'plɔːzəbl] ADJ peu plausible, peu vraisemblable

implausibly [ɪm'plɔːzəblɪ] ADV [big, fat, high] incroyablement ; his characters are ~ nice ses personnages sont d'une bonté peu vraisemblable ; they are, rather ~, good friends chose incroyable, ils sont bons amis

implement ['ɪmplɪmənt] 1 N outil m, instrument m ; ~s équipement m (NonC), matériel m (NonC) ; (for gardening, painting, carpentry) matériel m, outils mpl ; (for cooking) ustensiles mpl ; ~s of war matériel m de guerre ; farm ~s matériel m or outillage m agricole 2 ['ɪmplɪment] [+ decision, plan, recommendation] mettre en œuvre, exécuter ; [+ promise] accomplir ; [+ contract] exécuter ; [+ law] mettre en œuvre, appliquer ; [+ system] mettre en place ; [+ idea] mettre en pratique, réaliser

implementation [,ɪmplɪmen'teɪʃən] N [of plan] exécution f, réalisation f ; [of law, reform, peace agreement, policy] mise f en œuvre ; (Comput) implémentation f

implicate ['ɪmplɪkeɪt] VT impliquer, compromettre (in dans)

implication [,ɪmplɪ'keɪʃən] N a (= inference) insinuation f ; what's your ~? qu'est-ce que tu insinues (par là)? ; by ~ par voie de conséquence ; he didn't realize the full ~ of his words il n'a pas mesuré toute la portée de ses paroles b (= possible result) implication f ; what are the ~s of the new tax for the poor? quelles sont les implications or incidences du nouvel impôt pour les pauvres? ; what are the political ~s? quelles sont les incidences politiques? ; we shall have to study all the ~s il nous faudra étudier toutes les conséquences (possibles) c (NonC = involvement) implication f (in dans)

implicit [ɪm'plɪsɪt] ADJ a (= implied) [warning, message, criticism, threat, admission] implicite (in dans) ; [recognition] tacite b (= unquestioning) [belief, faith, confidence, obedience] absolu

implicitly [ɪm'plɪsɪtlɪ] ADV a (= indirectly) [accept, recognize, criticize] implicitement

b (= *unquestioningly*) [*trust*] totalement ; [*believe*] tout à fait

implied [ɪmˈplaɪd] **1** ADJ [*criticism, question*] implicite, sous-entendu ; [*threat*] implicite, voilé ; [*message*] implicite **2** COMP ► **implied reader** N (*Literat*) lecteur *m* (*à qui s'adresse implicitement le texte*) ► **implied term** N (*Jur*) clause *f* implicite *or* tacite ► **implied warranty** N (*US Jur*) garantie *f* légale

implode [ɪmˈpləʊd] **1** VI imploser **2** VT causer l'implosion de **3** COMP ► **imploded consonant** N (*Phon*) consonne *f* implosive

implore [ɪmˈplɔːʳ] VT implorer (**sb to do** qn de faire) ; **to ~ sb's help** implorer le secours de qn ; **I ~ you!** je vous en supplie *or* conjure !

imploring [ɪmˈplɔːrɪŋ] ADJ [*look, voice*] implorant, suppliant ; [*person*] suppliant

imploringly [ɪmˈplɔːrɪŋlɪ] ADV [*say*] d'un ton implorant ; **to look ~ at sb** supplier qn du regard, regarder qn d'un air implorant

implosion [ɪmˈpləʊʒən] N implosion *f*

implosive [ɪmˈpləʊzɪv] **1** ADJ implosif **2** N (*Phon*) implosive *f*

imply [ɪmˈplaɪ] VT **a** [*person*] suggérer, laisser entendre ; (= *insinuate*) insinuer (*pej*) ; **he implied that he would come** il a laissé entendre qu'il viendrait ; **he implied that I was lying** il a laissé entendre *or* insinué que je mentais ; **are you ~ing that ...?** voulez-vous suggérer *or* insinuer que ...? ; **it is implied that ...** il faut sous-entendre que ..., cela sous-entend que ... → **implied** **b** (= *indicate*) impliquer ; **that implies some intelligence** cela implique *or* suppose une certaine intelligence ; **figures ~ that the economy is getting stronger** les chiffres laissent penser *or* suggèrent que l'économie connaît une embellie → **implied**

impolite [ˌɪmpəˈlaɪt] ADJ impoli (**to** *or* **towards sb** avec *or* envers qn) ; **it is ~ to do that** il est impoli de faire cela ; **it was very ~ of you to do/say that** c'était très impoli de votre part de faire/dire cela

impolitely [ˌɪmpəˈlaɪtlɪ] ADV impoliment

impoliteness [ˌɪmpəˈlaɪtnɪs] N impolitesse *f* (**to, towards** envers)

impolitic [ɪmˈpɒlɪtɪk] ADJ (*frm*) peu politique, impolitique

imponderable [ɪmˈpɒndərəbl] ADJ, N impondérable *m*

import ['ɪmpɔːt] **1** N **a** (*Comm* = *process, goods*) importation *f* (**into** en) ; **~ of goods** importation *f* de marchandises ; **~s from England** importations *fpl* en provenance d'Angleterre **b** (= *significance*) importance *f* ; **of great/little ~** [*question, issue*] de grande/peu d'importance ; [*argument*] de poids/de peu de poids **c** (*frm* = *meaning*) [*of action, decision, speech, words*] sens *m*, signification *f* ; [*of document*] teneur *f* **2** [ɪmˈpɔːt] VT **a** (*Comm*) importer ; **~ed goods** marchandises *fpl* d'importation *or* importées **b** (*frm* = *mean, imply*) signifier, vouloir dire **3** COMP ► **import duty** N (*Comm*) droits *mpl* d'importation, taxe *f* à l'importation ► **import-export (trade)** N import-export *m* ► **import licence** N licence *f* d'importation ► **import quota** N quota *m* à l'importation, contingent *m* d'importation ► **import surcharge** N surtaxe *f* à l'importation ► **import trade** N (commerce *m* d')importation *f*

importance [ɪmˈpɔːtəns] N importance *f* ; **to be of ~** avoir de l'importance ; **of some ~** assez important, d'une certaine importance ; **of great ~** très important, de grande importance ; **it is a matter of great ~ for the future** c'est quelque chose de très important pour l'avenir ; **it is of the highest ~ that ... il**

est de la plus haute importance que ... (+ *subj*), il importe au premier chef que ... (+ *subj*) ; **it is of ~ to do** il est important de faire, il importe de faire (*frm*) ; **it is of no (great) ~** c'est sans (grande) importance ; **to give ~ to sth** [*person*] attacher de l'importance *or* du prix à qch ; [*event, development*] accorder *or* donner de l'importance à qch ; **we give** *or* **attach the greatest ~ to establishing the facts** nous accordons *or* attachons la plus haute importance à l'établissement des faits ; **man of ~** homme *m* important, personnage *m* (important) ; **person of no ~** personne *f* sans importance ; **his position gives him considerable ~** sa position lui donne une importance *or* un poids considérable ; **he is full of his own ~** il est imbu de lui-même, il est pénétré de son importance ; **the ~ of being/doing** l'importance d'être/de faire

▼ **important** [ɪmˈpɔːtənt] ADJ important (**to** *or* **for sb/sth** pour qn/qch) ; **that's not ~** ça n'a pas d'importance, cela n'est pas important ; **the ~ thing is not to win but to take part** l'important n'est pas de gagner mais de participer ; **the most ~ thing is that you should be happy** le plus important, c'est que tu sois heureux ; (*factual important*) **the most ~ thing to remember is ...** ce qu'il faut surtout retenir, c'est ... ; (*advice on interview technique etc*) **the most ~ thing to remember is to do ...** surtout n'oublie pas de faire ... ; **to make sb feel ~** donner à qn un sentiment d'importance ; **he's trying to look ~** il fait l'important, il se donne des airs importants ; **it is ~ to do sth** il est important de faire qch ; **it is ~ for sb to do sth** *or* **that sb (should) do sth** il est important que qn fasse qch

importantly [ɪmˈpɔːtəntlɪ] ADV **a** (= *significantly*) **to figure ~ in sth** occuper une place importante dans qch ; **to differ ~ from sth** présenter d'importantes différences avec qch ; **I was hungry, and, more ~, my children were hungry** j'avais faim et, surtout *or* plus important encore, mes enfants avaient faim **b** (*also* **self-~**) [*say, strut*] d'un air important

importation [ˌɪmpɔːˈteɪʃən] N (*Comm*) importation *f*

importer [ɪmˈpɔːtəʳ] N (= *person*) importateur *m*, -trice *f* ; (= *country*) (pays *m*) importateur *m*

importunate [ɪmˈpɔːtjʊnɪt] ADJ (*frm*) [*visitor, demand*] importun, gênant ; [*creditor*] harcelant

importune [ɪmˈpɔːtjuːn] **1** VT (*frm*) [*questioner, beggar*] importuner, ennuyer ; [*creditor*] harceler, presser ; (*Jur*) [*prostitute*] racoler **2** VI (*Jur*) racoler ; **she was arrested for importuning** elle a été arrêtée pour racolage

importunity [ˌɪmpɔːˈtjuːnɪtɪ] N (*frm*) importunité *f*

impose [ɪmˈpəʊz] **1** VT **a** [+ *task, conditions, constraint, rule, obedience, one's opinion*] imposer (**on** à) ; [+ *sanctions*] infliger (**on** à) ; **to ~ a fine on sb** condamner qn à une amende ; **to ~ a tax on sth** imposer qch, taxer qch ; **beware of imposing your tastes on your children** gardez-vous d'imposer vos goûts à vos enfants ; **the pressures ~d upon teachers** les pressions que subissent les professeurs ; **to ~ itself** s'imposer ; **to ~ o.s. (on sb)** s'imposer (à qn) ; **to ~ one's presence on sb** imposer sa présence à qn **b** (*Typ*) imposer **2** VI imposer ; **I don't want to ~** je ne veux pas m'imposer ; **to ~ on sb** abuser de la gentillesse de qn ; **to ~ on sb's hospitality** abuser de l'hospitalité de qn

imposing [ɪmˈpəʊzɪŋ] ADJ imposant, impressionnant

imposition [ˌɪmpəˈzɪʃən] N **a** (*NonC*) [*of sanction, rule, law, tax, conditions*] imposition *f* ; **the ~ of a ban on cycling** l'imposition d'une interdiction de rouler à bicyclette **b** (= *tax imposed*) impôt *m*, taxe *f* **c** (*fig*) **it's rather an**

~ on her c'est abuser de sa gentillesse **d** (*Typ*) imposition *f* **e** (*Scol*) punition *f*

impossibility [ɪmˌpɒsəˈbɪlɪtɪ] N impossibilité *f* (**of sth** de qch, **of doing** de faire) ; **it's an ~** c'est une chose impossible, c'est quelque chose d'impossible → **physical**

▼ **impossible** [ɪmˈpɒsəbl] **1** ADJ impossible ; **this cooker is ~ to clean!** cette cuisinière est impossible à nettoyer ! ; **it is ~ for him to leave** il lui est impossible *or* il est dans l'impossibilité de partir ; **I find it ~ to understand why ...** il m'est impossible de comprendre pourquoi ... ; **to make it ~ for sb to do sth** mettre qn dans l'impossibilité de faire qch ; **to put sb/to be in an ~ position** *or* **situation** mettre qn/être dans une position *or* situation impossible ; **it is/is not ~ that ...** il est/n'est pas impossible que ... (+ *subj*) ; **that boy is ~!*** ce garçon est impossible !* **2** N impossible *m* ; **to do/ask for the ~** faire/demander l'impossible

impossibly [ɪmˈpɒsəblɪ] ADV [*small, large, late*] incroyablement ; [*expensive*] ridiculement ; **~ rude/arrogant** d'une impolitesse/arrogance insupportable ; **~ difficult** d'une difficulté insurmontable ; **her standards were ~ high** ses exigences étaient impossibles à satisfaire ; **he's behaving ~** il se conduit d'une façon impossible ; **if, ~, he were to succeed** si, par impossible, il réussissait

impost ['ɪmpəʊst] N (*Admin, Fin, Jur*) impôt *m* ; (*Customs*) taxe *f* douanière, droit *m* de douane

imposter, impostor [ɪmˈpɒstəʳ] N imposteur *m*

imposture [ɪmˈpɒstʃəʳ] N imposture *f*

impotence ['ɪmpətəns] N (*gen, sexual, fig*) impuissance *f* ; † [*of invalid, patient*] impotence *f*

impotent ['ɪmpətənt] ADJ **a** (*sexually*) impuissant **b** (= *powerless*) [*person, organization*] impuissant ; † [*invalid, patient*] impotent ; **in ~ rage** *or* **fury**† dans une rage impuissante ; **to be ~ in the face of sth** être impuissant face à qch

impound [ɪmˈpaʊnd] VT **a** (*Jur*) [+ *property*] confisquer, saisir ; [+ *car*] mettre en fourrière **b** [+ *water*] retenir, endiguer

impoundment [ɪmˈpaʊndmənt] N **a** (*Jur*) [*of property*] saisie *f* ; [*of car*] mise *f* en fourrière **b** [*of water*] retenue *f* d'eau **c** (*US Fin*) mise en réserve de fonds votés (*par le Congrès*)

impoverish [ɪmˈpɒvərɪʃ] VT appauvrir

impoverished [ɪmˈpɒvərɪʃt] ADJ pauvre

impoverishment [ɪmˈpɒvərɪʃmənt] N appauvrissement *m*

impracticability [ɪmˌpræktɪkəˈbɪlɪtɪ] N impraticabilité *f*

impracticable [ɪmˈpræktɪkəbl] ADJ [*idea, plan, scheme, suggestion*] impraticable, irréalisable

impractical [ɪmˈpræktɪkəl] ADJ [*person*] qui manque d'esprit pratique ; [*plan, idea*] difficilement applicable ; [*clothes*] pas pratique

impracticality [ɪmˌpræktɪˈkælɪtɪ] N [*of person*] manque *m* d'esprit pratique ; [*of plan, idea*] côté *m* peu pratique

imprecation [ˌɪmprɪˈkeɪʃən] N (*frm*) imprécation *f*, malédiction *f*

imprecise [ˌɪmprɪˈsaɪs] ADJ imprécis

imprecision [ˌɪmprɪˈsɪʒən] N imprécision *f*, manque *m* de précision

impregnable [ɪmˈpregnəbl] ADJ (*Mil*) [*fortress, defences*] imprenable, inexpugnable ; (*fig*) [*person, position*] inattaquable ; [*argument*] irréfutable

impregnate ['ɪmpregneɪt] VT **a** (= *fertilize*) féconder **b** (= *saturate*) imprégner, imbiber (**with** de) ; (*fig*) imprégner, pénétrer (**with** de)

impregnation [ˌɪmpregˈneɪʃən] N **a** (= *fertilization*) fécondation *f* **b** (= *permeation*) imprégnation *f* ; **the ~ of paper with chemicals** l'imprégnation du papier par des produits chimiques

impresario [ˌɪmprɪˈsɑːrɪəʊ] N impresario *m*

impress [ɪmˈpres] **1** VT **a** (+ *person*) impressionner; **to be ~ed by sth** être impressionné par qch; **they were most ~ed by his having everything ready on time** ils ont été très impressionnés par le fait qu'il ait tout préparé à temps; **he is not easily ~ed** il ne se laisse pas facilement impressionner; (*negative opinion*) **I am not ~ed** (*by object, work of art, performance*) ça me laisse froid; (*by sb's behaviour*) ça ne m'impressionne pas; (*annoyance*) **I am NOT ~ed!** je ne suis pas du tout content!; **he ~ed me favourably/unfavourably** il m'a fait une bonne/mauvaise impression; **his novel greatly ~ed me** son roman m'a beaucoup impressionné, son roman m'a fait une forte *or* grosse impression; **he does it just to ~ people** il ne le fait que pour épater la galerie **b** imprimer, marquer (**on** sur); **to ~ a seal on wax** imprimer un sceau sur de la cire; (*fig*) **to ~ sth on sb** faire (bien) comprendre qch à qn; **that day has remained ~ed in my memory** ce jour est resté gravé dans ma mémoire **2** VI (*object, work of art, performance*) être impressionnant; (*person*) faire bonne impression **3** [ˈɪmpres] N marque *f*, empreinte *f*

impression [ɪmˈpreʃən] N **a** (= *effect*) impression *f*; **to make an ~ on sb** faire impression *or* de l'effet à qn; **to make an ~ on sth** avoir un effet sur qch; **to make a good/bad ~ on sb** faire bonne/mauvaise impression à qn; **his novel made a lasting ~ on me** son roman m'a laissé une impression durable; **what was your ~ of him?** quelle impression vous a-t-il fait?; **you have a false ~ of him** vous vous trompez sur son compte; **first ~s count** c'est la première impression qui compte; **he gave the ~ of being bored** il donnait l'impression de s'ennuyer; **to create an ~ of space** créer une impression d'espace **b** (= *vague idea*) impression *f*; **I was under the ~ that ...** ◊ **my ~ was that ...** j'avais l'impression que ..., je croyais que ...; **that wasn't my ~!** ce n'est pas l'impression que j'ai eue!; **his ~s of Paris** les impressions qu'il a gardées de Paris **c** (*of seal, stamp, footprint*) empreinte *f*, trace *f*; (*on wax*) impression *f*; (*Dentistry*) empreinte *f* **d** (*of engraving*) impression *f*; (*esp Brit*) (*of book*) tirage *m*, édition *f* **e** **to do ~s (of sb)** faire des imitations (de qn)

impressionable [ɪmˈpreʃnəbl] ADJ impressionnable; **at an ~ age** à un âge où l'on est impressionnable

impressionism [ɪmˈpreʃənɪzəm] N (*Art*) impressionnisme *m*

impressionist [ɪmˈpreʃnɪst] ADJ, N (*Art*) impressionniste *mf*

impressionistic [ɪmˌpreʃəˈnɪstɪk] ADJ [*story, account, painting*] impressionniste

impressive [ɪmˈpresɪv] ADJ [*appearance, building, ceremony, person, sight, sum*] impressionnant, imposant; [*amount, account, achievement, result, speech*] impressionnant

impressively [ɪmˈpresɪvlɪ] ADV [*big, high, brave etc*] remarquablement; [*win, perform*] d'une manière impressionnante; **~ large** remarquablement grand, d'une grandeur impressionnante

impressment [ɪmˈpresmənt] N [*of person*] enrôlement *m* forcé; [*of property, goods*] réquisition *f*

imprimatur [ˌɪmprɪˈmɑːtəʳ] N (*frm*) imprimatur *m*

imprint [ɪmˈprɪnt] **1** VT imprimer, marquer (**on** sur); (*fig*) imprimer, graver (**on** dans) **2** [ˈɪmprɪnt] N **a** (= *impression*) (*lit, fig*) empreinte *f*; (*Psych*) empreinte *f* perceptive **b** (*Publishing*) **published under the Collins ~** édité chez Collins

imprinting [ɪmˈprɪntɪŋ] N (*NonC: Psych*) empreinte *f*

imprison [ɪmˈprɪzn] VT emprisonner, écrouer; (*fig*) emprisonner; **they ~ed him for his part in the burglary** ils l'ont emprisonné *or* écroué pour avoir participé au cambriolage; **the judge ~ed him for ten years** le juge l'a condamné à dix ans de prison

imprisonment [ɪmˈprɪznmənt] N emprisonnement *m*, incarcération *f*; **to sentence sb to seven years' ~/to life ~** condamner qn à sept ans de prison/à la prison à vie *or* à perpétuité; **sentence of life ~** condamnation *f* à la prison à vie *or* à perpétuité; **the prospect of ~** la perspective de la prison

improbability [ɪmˌprɒbəˈbɪlɪtɪ] N **a** (= *unlikelihood*) [*of outcome*] improbabilité *f* **b** (= *implausibility*) [*of film, story, plot, excuse*] invraisemblance *f*

improbable [ɪmˈprɒbəbl] ADJ **a** (= *unlikely*) [*situation, victory*] improbable; **it is ~ that ...** il est improbable *or* il est peu probable que ... (+ *subj*) **b** (= *implausible*) [*explanation, story, name*] invraisemblable; **~ as it sounds ...** aussi invraisemblable que cela paraisse ...

improbably [ɪmˈprɒbəblɪ] ADV invraisemblablement; **she works, ~, in a bank** bizarrement, elle travaille dans une banque

impromptu [ɪmˈprɒmptjuː] **1** ADV impromptu **2** ADJ impromptu; **to make an ~ speech** faire un discours impromptu *or* au pied levé; **to make an ~ appearance** faire une apparition **3** N (*Mus*) impromptu *m*

improper [ɪmˈprɒpəʳ] ADJ **a** (= *unsuitable*) déplacé, malséant; **b** (= *indecent*) indécent, inconvenant; [*conduct, suggestion*] indécent; [*story*] indécent, scabreux **c** (= *dishonest*) malhonnête **d** (= *wrong*) [*diagnosis*] incorrect, erroné; [*term*] inexact, impropre; [*use, interpretation*] abusif, incorrect; (*Sport*) [*play etc*] incorrect

improperly [ɪmˈprɒpəlɪ] ADV **a** (= *indecently*) **he was ~ dressed** il était habillé de façon inconvenante **b** (= *dishonestly*) [*act*] de façon irrégulière **c** (= *incorrectly*) [*test, diagnose, treat*] mal; **a word used ~** un mot employé improprement

impropriety [ˌɪmprəˈpraɪətɪ] N **a** [*of behaviour etc*] inconvenance *f*; **to commit an ~** commettre une inconvenance; **to behave with ~** se conduire avec inconvenance; **financial ~** irrégularités *fpl* financières **b** (*Ling*) [*of expression, phrase*] impropriété *f*

improv* [ˈɪmprɒv] N sketch *m* improvisé

improve [ɪmˈpruːv] **1** VT **a** (= *make better*) [+ *situation, position, work, health, wording*] améliorer; [+ *physique*] développer; [+ *knowledge, machine, invention*] améliorer, perfectionner; [+ *building, property*] réaménager, rénover; [+ *site*] aménager, embellir; [+ *soil, land*] amender, bonifier; **to ~ sb's looks** *or* **appearance** embellir *or* avantager qn; **to ~ one's looks** s'embellir; **to ~ one's chances of doing sth** améliorer *or* augmenter ses chances de faire qch; **how can I ~ my chances at interview?** comment est-ce que je peux améliorer *or* augmenter mes chances de réussite à un entretien?; **that should ~ his chances of success** cela devrait améliorer ses chances de succès; **$60,000 worth of repairs failed to ~ matters** 60 000 dollars de réparations n'ont pas réussi à améliorer les choses; **she's trying to ~ her mind** elle essaie de se cultiver (l'esprit); **a book which ~s the mind** un livre qui élève l'esprit; **he wants to ~ his French** il veut se perfectionner en français **b** (= *make good use of*) tirer parti de, profiter de; **to ~ the occasion** ◊ **to ~ the shining hour** (*hum*) tirer parti de l'occasion, mettre l'occasion à profit

2 VI **a** (= *get better*) [*situation, position, health, prospects, chances, weather*] s'améliorer; [*physique*] se développer; [*soil*] s'amender, se bonifier; [*student, patient*] faire des progrès; **the service has ~d** la qualité du service s'est améliorée; **his work is improving** (la qualité de) son travail s'améliore; **his French is improving** il fait des progrès en français; **as medical knowledge ~s** avec l'amélioration des connaissances médicales; **mobile phones have ~d greatly** les téléphones portables se sont beaucoup améliorés; **safety/efficiency/productivity has definitely ~d** il y a eu une nette amélioration au niveau de la sécurité/de l'efficacité/du rendement; **business is improving** les affaires reprennent; **things are improving** les choses vont mieux; **matters haven't ~d much** la situation ne s'est pas beaucoup améliorée; **his chances of success are improving** ses chances de réussir s'améliorent; **to ~ with use** s'améliorer à l'usage; **this wine ~s with age** ce vin se bonifie *or* s'améliore en vieillissant; (*hum*) **he's ~d with age** il s'est amélioré *or* bonifié avec l'âge; **this book ~s on re-reading** ce livre gagne à être relu **b** **to ~ on sth** faire mieux que qch, apporter des améliorations à qch; **it can't be ~d on** on peut difficilement faire mieux; **she had ~d on her previous performance** elle s'est améliorée depuis sa dernière prestation; (*Comm, Fin*) **to ~ on sb's offer** enchérir sur qn

improved [ɪmˈpruːvd] ADJ meilleur; **much/slightly ~** nettement/légèrement meilleur; **this room looks much ~ after painting** la pièce est beaucoup mieux après avoir été repeinte; (*Comm*) **"new ~ formula"** « nouvelle formule »

improvement [ɪmˈpruːvmənt] **1** N **a** (*NonC*) [*of situation, position, health, soil, land*] amélioration *f*; [*of mind, physique*] développement *m*; [*of site*] aménagement *m*, embellissement *m*; [*of building, property*] réaménagement *m*, rénovation *f*; [*of machine*] perfectionnement *m*; (*gen*) **there's been quite an ~ on** on constate une nette amélioration; **there has been some ~ in the patient's condition** l'état du malade s'est un peu amélioré; **it is open to ~** ça peut être amélioré; **he has shown some ~ in French** il a fait quelques progrès en français; **this model is an ~ on the previous one** ce modèle est mieux que le précédent; **the new teacher is an ~ on his predecessor** le nouveau professeur est meilleur que son prédécesseur; **there is room for ~** (*in situation*) cela pourrait être mieux; (*in work*) on pourrait faire mieux **b** (*gen pl*) **~s** améliorations *fpl*, aménagements *mpl*; **to carry out ~s to a house** apporter des améliorations à *or* faire des travaux d'aménagement dans une maison **2** COMP ► **improvement grant** N subvention *f* pour l'amélioration d'un logement, ≈ prime *f* à l'amélioration de l'habitat

improvidence [ɪmˈprɒvɪdəns] N imprévoyance *f*, manque *m* de prévoyance

improvident [ɪmˈprɒvɪdənt] ADJ **a** (= *not providing for future*) imprévoyant; (= *extravagant*) prodigue, dépensier

improvidently [ɪmˈprɒvɪdəntlɪ] ADV avec imprévoyance

improving [ɪmˈpruːvɪŋ] ADJ (= *edifying*) édifiant

improvisation [ˌɪmprəvaɪˈzeɪʃən] N (*gen, Mus*) improvisation *f*

improvise [ˈɪmprəvaɪz] VTI (*gen, Mus*) improviser

imprudence [ɪmˈpruːdəns] N imprudence *f*

imprudent [ɪmˈpruːdənt] ADJ imprudent

imprudently [ɪmˈpruːdəntlɪ] ADV imprudemment

impudence [ˈɪmpjʊdəns] N impudence *f*, effronterie *f*

impudent [ˈɪmpjʊdənt] ADJ impudent, effronté

impudently [ˈɪmpjʊdəntlɪ] ADV impudemment, avec effronterie

impugn [ɪmˈpjuːn] VT (frm) [+ motives, sincerity, judgment] contester; [+ honour, reputation] porter gravement atteinte à, attaquer

impulse [ˈɪmpʌls] **1** N **a** (= sudden desire) impulsion f; **rash ~** coup m de tête; **on a sudden ~ he ...** pris d'une impulsion soudaine il ...; **a man of ~** un impulsif; **to act on (an) ~** agir par impulsion; **my first ~ was to refuse** ma première impulsion or réaction a été de refuser; **he couldn't resist the ~** il n'arrivait pas à résister à l'envie; **she resisted an ~ to smile** elle a réprimé son envie de sourire **b** (= stimulus) impulsion f, élan m; **this gave new ~ to the reform process** ça a donné une nouvelle impulsion or un nouvel élan au processus de réforme **c** (Phys, Elec, Physiol) impulsion f **2** COMP ► **impulse buy** N achat m d'impulsion ► **impulse buying** N achats mpl d'impulsion ► **impulse purchase** N = impulse buy

impulsion [ɪmˈpʌlʃən] N impulsion f

impulsive [ɪmˈpʌlsɪv] ADJ **a** (= spontaneous, acting on impulse) [movement] impulsif, spontané; [temperament] primesautier; [temper, passion] fougueux; [act] impulsif, spontané; [remark] irréfléchi; **she's very ~** elle est très impulsive **b** (= impelling) [force] irrésistible

impulsively [ɪmˈpʌlsɪvlɪ] ADV impulsivement

impulsiveness [ɪmˈpʌlsɪvnɪs] N (NonC) caractère m impulsif, impulsivité f

impunity [ɪmˈpjuːnɪtɪ] N impunité f; **with ~** impunément, avec impunité

impure [ɪmˈpjʊəʳ] ADJ [air, water, milk, motive] impur; [thought, action] impur, impudique; [drug] frelaté; (Archit etc) [style] bâtard

impurity [ɪmˈpjʊərɪtɪ] N impureté f

imputation [ˌɪmpjʊˈteɪʃən] N **a** (= accusation) imputation f **b** (NonC) attribution f, imputation f (**of sth to sb/sth** de qch à qn/qch)

impute [ɪmˈpjuːt] VT imputer, attribuer (**sth to sb/sth** qch à qn/qch); (Comm) **~d rent/value** loyer m/valeur f imputé(e) or implicite; (Comm) **~d cost** coût m supplétif, charge f supplétive

IN ABBR = **Indiana**

in [ɪn]

1 PREPOSITION	**4** PLURAL NOUN	
2 ADVERB	**5** COMPOUNDS	
3 ADJECTIVE		

1 PREPOSITION

*When **in** is the second element in a phrasal verb, eg ask in, fill in, look in, look up the verb. When it is part of a set combination, eg in the country, in ink, in danger, weak in, wrapped in, look up the other word.*

a place dans; **in the box** dans la boîte; **in the street** dans la rue; BUT **in the shop window** en vitrine; **in sb's house** chez qn

◆ **in it/them** (= inside it, inside them) dedans; **put that in it** mets-le dedans; **there's something in it** il y a quelque chose dedans; **our bags were stolen, and our passports were in them** on nous a volé nos sacs et nos passeports étaient dedans

b people chez; **a condition rare in a child of that age** une maladie rare chez un enfant de cet âge; **it's something I admire in her** c'est quelque chose que j'admire chez elle; **we find this theme in Dickens** on trouve ce thème chez Dickens; BUT **the party will have a great leader in him** le parti trouvera en lui un excellent leader

c plant, animal chez; **you find this instinct in animals** on trouve cet instinct chez les animaux; **a condition common in plants, shellfish**

and some lizards une maladie courante chez les plantes, les crustacés et certains lézards

d with geographical names

◆ **in** + fem countries, regions, islands en

*Feminine countries usually end in **-e***

in England/France en Angleterre/France; **in Brittany/Provence** en Bretagne/Provence; **in Sicily/Crete** en Sicile/Crète; **in Louisiana/Virginia** en Louisiane/Virginie; **in Cornwall/Bavaria** en Cornouailles/Bavière

en is also used with masc countries beginning with a vowel.
in Iran/Israel en Iran/Israël

◆ **in** + masc country au; **in Japan/Kuwait** au Japon/Koweït

Note also:
in the Sahara/Kashmir au Sahara/Cachemire

◆ **in** + pl country/group of islands aux; **in the United States/West Indies** aux États-Unis/Antilles

◆ **in** + town/island without article à; **in London/Paris** à Londres/Paris; **in Cuba/Malta** à Cuba/Malte

◆ **in** + masc state/French region/county dans; **in Poitou/Berry** dans le Poitou/le Berry; **in Sussex/Yorkshire** dans le Sussex/le Yorkshire

dans is also used with islands with île in their name, and many departments.
in the Drôme/the Var dans la Drôme/le Var; **in the Isle of Man/the Ile de Ré** dans l'île de Man/l'île de Ré; BUT **in Seine-et-Marne/the Vendée** en Seine-et-Marne/Vendée

e with time expressions (= in the space of) en; (= after) dans; **I can't do it in two hours** je ne peux pas le faire en deux heures; **he has written twice in three years** il a écrit deux fois en trois ans; **it'll be ready in three hours** ce sera prêt dans trois heures; **I'll be back in a week** je reviendrai dans une semaine; BUT **once in a hundred years** une fois tous les cent ans

f month, year, season en; **in May** en mai; **in 1998/September 1998** en 1998/septembre 1998; **in summer/autumn/winter** en été/automne/hiver; BUT **in spring** au printemps

*Look up the noun when translating such phrases as **in the morning, in the sixties, in a minute, in a week's time, in the end**.*

g = wearing en; **they were all in shorts** ils étaient tous en short; **in his slippers** en pantoufles, dans ses pantoufles; BUT **you look nice in that dress** cette robe te va bien, tu es jolie dans cette robe

h language, medium, material en; **in French** en français; **in marble/velvet** en marbre/velours

i ratio sur; **one man in ten** un homme sur dix; **what happened was a chance in a million** il y avait une chance sur un million que ce genre de choses arrive; **a one in fifty chance of survival** une chance sur cinquante de survie; BUT **they pay 20 pence in the pound income tax** ils payent 20 pour cent d'impôts sur le revenu

j = in respect of rough in appearance d'aspect rugueux; **in that, he resembles his father** en cela, il ressemble à son père

k following superlative de; **the best pupil in the class** le meilleur élève de la classe; **the highest mountain in Europe** la plus haute montagne d'Europe, la montagne la plus haute d'Europe

l = while en; **in saying this** ◊ **in so saying** en disant cela; **in trying to save her he fell into the water himself** en essayant de la sauver, il est tombé à l'eau

2 ADVERB

a = inside à l'intérieur; **she opened the door and they all rushed in** elle a ouvert la porte et ils se sont tous précipités à l'intérieur

*When **in** means **in it** or **in them**, it is translated by y.*

she opened her bag and put the ticket in elle a ouvert son sac et y a mis le billet

b at home, work

◆ **to be in** [person] être là; **the boss isn't in yet** le patron n'est pas encore là

*When **in** means at home, chez + pronoun can also be used.*

he's usually in on Saturday morning il est généralement là le samedi matin, il est généralement chez lui le samedi matin; **you're never in!** tu n'es jamais là!, tu n'es jamais chez toi!; **is Paul in?** est-ce que Paul est là?; BUT **there's nobody in** il n'y a personne

*to be **in** may require a more specific translation.*
the train is in le train est en gare; **he's in for tests** il est venu faire des analyses; **the essays have to be in by Friday** les dissertations doivent être rendues d'ici vendredi; **the harvest is in** la moisson est rentrée; **the socialists are in!** les socialistes sont au pouvoir!; **the fire is still in** il y a encore du feu; **the screw was not in properly** la vis n'était pas bien enfoncée

c SET STRUCTURES

◆ **in between**: **the pages in between are completely blank** les pages du milieu sont vierges; **in between he will give three concerts** entre-temps or dans l'intervalle, il donnera trois concerts

◆ **in between** + noun/pronoun entre; **he positioned himself in between the two weakest players** il s'est placé entre les deux joueurs les plus faibles; **in between adventures, he finds time for ...** entre deux aventures, il trouve le temps de ... → 5

◆ **to be in for sth** (= be threatened with) **we are in for trouble*** nous allons avoir des ennuis; **you don't know what you're in for!*** tu ne sais pas ce qui t'attend!; **he's in for it!*** il va en prendre pour son grade!*; (= to be entered for) **to be in for a competition/exam** être inscrit à un concours/examen

◆ **to be in on sth*** (= know about) **to be in on a plan/secret** être au courant d'un plan/d'un secret; **are you in on it?** tu es au courant?

◆ **in that** (= seeing that) **the new treatment is preferable in that ...** le nouveau traitement est préférable car ...

◆ **to be well in with sb*** être dans les petits papiers de qn*; **she's well in with the management** elle est bien avec la direction

3 ADJECTIVE

* = fashionable in inv, à la mode; **straw hats are in** les chapeaux de paille sont in* or en vogue or à la mode; **it's the in place to eat** c'est le restaurant branché* or à la mode en ce moment; **it's the in thing to ...** c'est très in* or à la mode de ... (+ infin)

4 the ins PLURAL NOUN

a = details

◆ **the ins and outs**: **to know the ins and outs of a matter** connaître les tenants et aboutissants d'une affaire, connaître une affaire dans ses moindres détails; **she knows the ins and outs of the system** le système n'a plus de secret pour elle, elle connaît le système dans ses moindres détails

b US Pol* le parti au pouvoir

5 COMPOUNDS

► **in-between** N **the in-betweens** ceux qui sont entre les deux ♦ ADJ **it's in-between** c'est entre les deux; **in-between times** dans les intervalles; **it was in-between* weather** c'était un temps mitigé; **a coat for in-between* weather** un manteau de demi-saison ► **in-built** ADJ (esp Brit) [feeling, tendency] inné; [feature, device] intégré; **in-built limitation** limite f inhérente au système ► **in-car entertainment system** N autoradio m ► **in-crowd*** N les branchés* mpl, les gens mpl in; **to be in with the in-crowd** faire partie des branchés* or des gens in ► **in-depth** ADJ en profondeur; **in-depth interview** interview f en profondeur ► **in-fighting** N = infighting ► **in-flight** ADJ → in-flight ► **in-goal area** N (*Rugby*) en-but *m inv* ► **in-group** N cercle *m* fermé ► **in-house** ADJ (= *designed for staff*) [*publication*] interne; [*training*] en entreprise or en interne; (= *made within company*) [*video etc*] réalisé en interne ♦ ADV [*train, produce etc*] en interne ► **in-joke** N plaisanterie *f* pour initiés ► **in-laws*** NPL (= *parents-in-law*) beaux-parents *mpl*; (*others*) belle-famille *f* ► **in-off** N (*Ftbl*) **the goal was an in-off** le but a été marqué après un cafouillage dans la surface de réparation ► **in-patient** N inpatient ► **in-service education** N (*US*) formation *f* continue ► **in-service training** N (*Ind etc*) formation *f* continue; (*Ind, Scol etc*) **to have in-service training** [*new employee*] faire un stage d'initiation; [*present employee*] faire un stage de perfectionnement; (*new subject*) faire un stage de recyclage; **to have in-service training in the use of computers** suivre un stage d'informatique dans son entreprise ► **in-store** ADJ [*detective*] employé par le magasin; [*theft*] commis par un membre du personnel ► **in-tray** N corbeille *f* « arrivée »

-in [ɪn] N (*in compounds*) particule qui désigne une réunion ou un rassemblement; **a talk-in** une réunion où l'on discute → **sit-in, teach**

in. ABBR = **inch**

inability [ˌɪnəˈbɪlɪtɪ] N incapacité *f* (**to do** de faire), inaptitude *f* (**to do** à faire)

in absentia [ˌɪnæbˈsentɪə] ADV (*frm*) en votre (*or leur etc*) absence

inaccessibility [ˈɪnækˌsesəˈbɪlɪtɪ] N inaccessibilité *f*

inaccessible [ˌɪnækˈsesəbl] ADJ (*lit, fig*) inaccessible (**to sb/sth** à qn/qch); (= **to be ~ by road/by land/by boat/by sea** être inaccessible par la route/par voie terrestre/par bateau/par voie maritime

inaccuracy [ɪnˈækjʊrəsɪ] N **a** (*NonC*) [*of calculation, information, translation, quotation, statement*] inexactitude *f*; [*of person*] imprécision *f*, manque *m* de précision; [*of expression, term, word*] inexactitude *f*, impropriété *f* **b** (= *error*) inexactitude *f*; **there are several inaccuracies in his account** son rapport contient plusieurs inexactitudes

inaccurate [ɪnˈækjʊrɪt] ADJ [*information, statement, picture, forecast*] inexact; [*method, instrument, missile, shot*] imprécis; **he is ~** il fait des erreurs; **the clock is ~** l'horloge n'est pas à l'heure; **it is ~ to say that ...** il est inexact de dire que ...

inaccurately [ɪnˈækjʊrɪtlɪ] ADV [*answer, quote, report*] avec inexactitude, inexactement; [*multiply*] incorrectement

inaction [ɪnˈækʃən] N inaction *f*, inertie *f*; **policy of ~** politique *f* de l'inaction or de non-intervention

inactive [ɪnˈæktɪv] ADJ **a** [*person, animal, lifestyle, bank account*] inactif; [*member*] non participant **b** (*Chem*) [*substance*] non actif, inerte **c** [*volcano*] (= *extinct*) inactif, éteint; (= *dormant*) assoupi

inactivity [ˌɪnækˈtɪvɪtɪ] N inactivité *f*

inadequacy [ɪnˈædɪkwəsɪ] N [*of system, punishment, resources, piece of work*] insuffisance *f*; (*Psych*) inadaptation *f* or insuffisance *f* socio-affective; **the inadequacies of the current system** les insuffisances du système actuel

inadequate [ɪnˈædɪkwɪt] **1** ADJ (= *insufficient*) [*resources, funding, protection, information, preparation, amount*] insuffisant; (= *unsatisfactory*) [*facilities, housing, training, response, diet*] inadéquat, inadapté; (= *incompetent*) incompétent; (*Psych*) mal adapté or inadapté (sur le plan socio-affectif); **he's ~** il ne fait pas le poids, il n'est pas à la hauteur; **he felt totally ~** il ne se sentait absolument pas à la hauteur; **~ staffing levels** manque *m* de personnel; **the**

proposed legislation is quite ~ for this purpose la législation en projet est tout à fait insuffisante or inadéquate pour atteindre ce but; **the amount offered is ~ to cover the expenses** la somme proposée ne suffit pas à couvrir les frais **2** N (*also* **social ~**) inadapté(e) *m(f)*

inadequately [ɪnˈædɪkwɪtlɪ] ADV insuffisamment

inadmissible [ˌɪnədˈmɪsəbl] ADJ [*attitude, opinion, behaviour*] inadmissible; [*suggestion, offer*] inacceptable; (*Jur*) **~ evidence** témoignage *m* irrecevable

inadvertence [ˌɪnədˈvɜːtəns] N manque *m* d'attention, étourderie *f*; **by** or **through ~** par inadvertance, par mégarde

inadvertent [ˌɪnədˈvɜːtənt] ADJ **a** (= *heedless*) [*person*] insouciant (**to** de); [*action*] commis par inadvertance or par mégarde; **an ~ insult** une insulte lâchée par étourderie **b** (= *inattentive*) [*person*] inattentif, étourdi

inadvertently [ˌɪnədˈvɜːtəntlɪ] ADV par inadvertance or mégarde

inadvisability [ˈɪnədˌvaɪzəˈbɪlɪtɪ] N inopportunité *f* (**of doing** de faire)

▼**inadvisable** [ˌɪnədˈvaɪzəbl] ADJ [*action, scheme*] inopportun, à déconseiller; **it is ~ to do ...** il est déconseillé de faire ...

inalienable [ɪnˈeɪlɪənəbl] ADJ (*Jur, fig*) [*rights, affection*] inaliénable

inamorata [ɪnˌæməˈrɑːtə] N (*liter*) amoureuse *f*

inane [ɪˈneɪn] ADJ [*person, action*] inepte, bête; [*question, smile, grin*] bête; **~ remark** observation *f* inepte, ineptie *f*; **what an ~ thing to do!** faut-il être bête pour faire une chose pareille!

inanely [ɪˈneɪnlɪ] ADV [*grin, laugh*] bêtement; [*talk*] sottement

inanimate [ɪnˈænɪmɪt] ADJ inanimé

inanition [ˌɪnəˈnɪʃən] N inanition *f*

inanity [ɪˈnænɪtɪ] N ineptie *f*

inapplicable [ɪnˈæplɪkəbl] ADJ inapplicable (**to** à)

inappropriate [ˌɪnəˈprəʊprɪɪt] ADJ [*action, behaviour, remark*] inopportun, déplacé; [*word, expression*] impropre; [*name*] mal choisi, impropre; [*moment*] inopportun, mauvais; **it would be ~ for me to comment** il ne m'appartient pas de commenter

inappropriately [ˌɪnəˈprəʊprɪɪtlɪ] ADV [*remark, reply*] mal à propos, inopportunément; **to behave ~** ne pas se comporter comme il faut (*or fallait etc*); **he was asking questions quite ~** il posait des questions de façon tout à fait inopportune; **he was dressed ~ for ...** il n'était pas habillé comme il fallait pour ...

inappropriateness [ˌɪnəˈprəʊprɪɪtnəs] N [*of action, behaviour, remark*] caractère *m* inopportun or déplacé; [*of word*] impropriété *f*

inapt [ɪnˈæpt] ADJ **a** [*remark, behaviour*] peu approprié **b** [*person*] inapte, incapable

inaptitude [ɪnˈæptɪtjuːd] N **a** [*of remark, behaviour*] caractère *m* peu approprié **b** [*of person*] inaptitude *f*, incapacité *f*

inarticulacy [ˌɪnɑːˈtɪkjʊləsɪ] N difficulté *f* à s'exprimer; **he was suddenly reduced to ~** il était soudain incapable de s'exprimer

inarticulate [ˌɪnɑːˈtɪkjʊlɪt] ADJ **a** (= *incoherent*) [*speech*] mal articulé; [*sound, noise*] inarticulé; [*emotion*] inexprimable; **he is ~** (= *unable to express himself*) il s'exprime mal, il n'arrive pas à s'exprimer; (*in pronunciation*) il articule mal, il avale ses mots; **~ with anger** bafouillant or bégayant de colère **b** (*Anat, Bot*) [*body, structure*] inarticulé

inarticulately [ˌɪnɑːˈtɪkjʊlɪtlɪ] ADV [*mumble*] de manière confuse

inartistic [ˌɪnɑːˈtɪstɪk] ADJ [*work*] peu artistique, sans valeur artistique; [*person*] dépourvu de sens artistique, peu artiste

inartistically [ˌɪnɑːˈtɪstɪkəlɪ] ADV sans talent (artistique), de façon peu artistique

inasmuch [ˌɪnəzˈmʌtʃ] ADV **~ as** (= *seeing that*) attendu que, vu que; (= *insofar as*) en ce sens que, dans la mesure où

inattention [ˌɪnəˈtenʃən] N manque *m* d'attention, inattention *f*; **~ to details** manque *m* d'attention pour les détails; **a moment's ~** un moment d'inattention

inattentive [ˌɪnəˈtentɪv] ADJ (= *not paying attention*) inattentif, distrait; (= *neglectful*) peu attentionné, négligent (**towards sb** envers qn); **he was ~ to details** il accordait peu d'attention aux détails; **he was ~ to her requests** il était peu attentif à ses demandes

inattentively [ˌɪnəˈtentɪvlɪ] ADV distraitement, sans prêter attention

inaudible [ɪnˈɔːdəbl] ADJ [*sound, whisper, voice*] inaudible; **he was almost ~** il était presque inaudible, on l'entendait à peine; **sounds that are ~ to humans** des sons qui ne sont pas perceptibles à l'oreille humaine

inaudibly [ɪnˈɔːdəblɪ] ADV [*speak, mumble*] de manière inaudible

inaugural [ɪˈnɔːɡjʊrəl] ADJ inaugural; (*Univ*) **~ lecture** cours *m* inaugural; **~ ceremony** cérémonie *f* d'inauguration or d'ouverture

inaugurate [ɪˈnɔːɡjʊreɪt] VT **a** [+ *policy*] inaugurer, mettre en application; [+ *new rail service etc*] inaugurer; [+ *era*] inaugurer, commencer **b** [+ *president, official*] investir dans ses fonctions; [+ *bishop, king, pope*] introniser

inauguration [ɪˌnɔːɡjʊˈreɪʃən] **1** N [*of president, governor, government*] investiture *f*; [*of bishop, king, pope*] intronisation *f*; [*of building, institution, service*] inauguration *f* **2** COMP ► **Inauguration Day** N (*US Pol*) jour *m* de l'investiture du président

inauspicious [ˌɪnɔːsˈpɪʃəs] ADJ [*beginning, event*] peu propice, de mauvais augure; [*circumstances*] malencontreux, fâcheux

inauspiciously [ˌɪnɔːsˈpɪʃəslɪ] ADV sous de mauvais auspices

inboard [ˈɪnbɔːd] (*Naut*) **1** ADV à l'intérieur, à bord **2** PREP à bord de **3** ADJ intérieur (-eure *f*) **4** COMP ► **inboard motor** N (moteur *m*) in-bord *m*

inborn [ˈɪnbɔːn] ADJ [*talent, ability, instinct, desire, fear*] inné; [*weakness, fault*] congénital

inbound [ˈɪnbaʊnd] ADJ **an ~ flight from Honduras** un vol en provenance du Honduras; **a plane/flight ~ for Heathrow Airport** un avion/vol arrivant à l'aéroport de Heathrow

inbred [ˈɪnbred] ADJ **a** (= *innate*) inné (**in sb** chez qn) **b** (*Sociol, Bio*) [*family, tribe*] qui possède un fort degré de consanguinité; [*person*] de parents ayant un fort degré de consanguinité; [*animal*] issu de la même souche

inbreeding [ˈɪnbriːdɪŋ] N [*of animals*] croisement *m* d'animaux de même souche; **there is a lot of ~ in the tribe** il y a beaucoup d'unions consanguines au sein de la tribu

inc ABBR = **including, inclusive**

Inc. (ABBR = **Incorporated**) SA; **Gough and Gautier ~** Gough et Gautier SA

Inca [ˈɪŋkə] **1** N (*pl* **Inca** *or* **Incas**) **a** Inca *mf* **b** (*Ling*) quichua *m* **2** ADJ inca *inv*

incalculable [ɪnˈkælkjʊləbl] ADJ **a** (= *immeasurable*) [*effect, consequences, damage, risk, cost, loss*] incalculable; [*value, importance, benefit*] inestimable [b] (= *unpredictable*) [*mood*] imprévisible

incandescence [ˌɪnkæn'desns] N incandescence *f*

incandescent [ˌɪnkæn'desnt] [1] ADJ [a] (*lit* = *glowing*) incandescent [b] (*fig, liter* = *radiant*) rayonnant [c] (= *furious*) **he was ~ (with rage** *or* **fury)** il était blême de rage [2] COMP [*bulb, lamp, light*] à incandescence

incantation [ˌɪnkæn'teɪʃən] N incantation *f*

incapability [ɪnˌkeɪpə'bɪlɪtɪ] N (*Jur, fig*) incapacité *f* (**of doing** de faire)

▼ **incapable** [ɪn'keɪpəbl] ADJ [*person*] incapable (**of doing sth** de faire qch); (*Jur*) incapable, inapte; **I'm not ~, I can manage** je ne suis pas invalide, je peux me débrouiller; **~ of violence/tenderness/love/murder** incapable de violence/de tendresse/d'aimer/de commettre un meurtre; **he was ~ of movement** il était incapable de bouger; (*frm*) **~ of proof/analysis** impossible à prouver/analyser; (*frm*) **to be ~ of solution** être insoluble *or* sans solution, ne pouvoir être résolu

incapacitate [ˌɪnkə'pæsɪteɪt] VT [a] handicaper; **she was ~d by diabetes** elle était handicapée par ses problèmes de diabète; **to be ~d for work** *or* **from working** être dans l'incapacité de travailler, être en invalidité; **heart problems ~d him** ses problèmes cardiaques l'empêchaient de mener une vie normale [b] (*Jur*) frapper d'incapacité

incapacitated [ˌɪnkə'pæsɪteɪtɪd] ADJ handicapé; **he was ~ with severe back pain** il était immobilisé souffrant d'un sérieux mal de dos

incapacitating [ˌɪnkə'pæsɪteɪtɪŋ] ADJ **~ headaches** des maux *mpl* de tête qui empêchent toute activité; **he had an ~ heart condition** ses problèmes cardiaques l'empêchaient de poursuivre des activités normales; **she suffered an ~ stroke** elle a eu une attaque qui l'a laissée handicapée

incapacity [ˌɪnkə'pæsɪt] N [a] incapacité *f* (**to do** de faire), incompétence *f* (**to do** pour faire), impuissance *f* (**to do** à faire, **for sth** en matière de qch) [b] (*Jur*) incapacité *f* (légale)

incarcerate [ɪn'kɑːsəreɪt] VT incarcérer

incarceration [ɪnˌkɑːsə'reɪʃən] N incarcération *f*

incarnate [ɪn'kɑːnɪt] (*Rel, fig*) [1] ADJ incarné; (*Rel*) **the Incarnate Word** le Verbe incarné; **he's evil/the devil ~** c'est le mal/le diable incarné [2] ['ɪnkɑːneɪt] VT incarner

incarnation [ˌɪnkɑː'neɪʃən] N (*Rel, fig*) incarnation *f*; **she is the ~ of virtue** c'est la vertu incarnée; **in a previous ~** dans une vie antérieure

incautious [ɪn'kɔːʃəs] ADJ [*person*] imprudent; [*remark, promise, action*] irréfléchi; [*behaviour*] inconsidéré

incautiously [ɪn'kɔːʃəslɪ] ADV imprudemment, sans réfléchir

incendiary [ɪn'sendɪərɪ] [1] ADJ (*lit, fig*) incendiaire [2] N (= *bomb*) engin *m* *or* bombe *f* incendiaire; (= *arsonist*) incendiaire *mf*; (*fig* = *agitator*) brandon *m* de discorde [3] COMP ▶ **incendiary device** N dispositif *m* incendiaire

incense¹ [ɪn'sens] VT (= *anger*) mettre en fureur; (*stronger*) mettre dans une rage folle

incense² ['ɪnsens] [1] N encens *m* [2] COMP ▶ **incense bearer** N thuriféraire *m* ▶ **incense burner** N encensoir *m*

incensed [ɪn'senst] ADJ outré (**at, by** de, par), révolté (**at, by** par)

incentive [ɪn'sentɪv] [1] N [a] (= *motivation*) motivation *f*; **he has got no ~** il n'a aucune motivation, il n'est absolument pas motivé; **this gave me an ~** cela m'a motivé *or* m'a donné une motivation; **there is no ~ to work hard** rien ne vous incite *or* ne vous pousse à

travailler dur; **what ~ is there to work faster?** pour quelle (bonne) raison se mettrait-on à travailler plus vite?; **they have little ~ to keep going** peu de choses les motivent *or* incitent à continuer; **to provide ~(s) for sth** encourager qch à l'aide de mesures incitatives

[b] (= *promised reward*) incitation *f*; **financial/ economic ~s** incitations *fpl* financières/ économiques; **they offered him an ~** ils lui ont promis qu'il serait récompensé → **tax**

[2] COMP ▶ **incentive bonus** N (*Ind*) prime *f* d'encouragement ▶ **incentive discount** N (*Comm*) remise *f* promotionnelle ▶ **incentive payment** N = **incentive bonus**

inception [ɪn'sepʃən] N commencement *m*, début *m*; **since its ~** depuis ses débuts

incertitude [ɪn'sɜːtɪtjuːd] N incertitude *f*

incessant [ɪn'sesnt] ADJ [*complaints*] incessant, perpétuel; [*rain, efforts*] incessant

incessantly [ɪn'sesntlɪ] ADV sans arrêt

incest ['ɪnsest] N inceste *m*

incestuous [ɪn'sestjʊəs] ADJ (*lit*) incestueux; (*fig*) **they're an ~ lot** ils sont très repliés sur eux-mêmes, ils vivent entre eux

inch [ɪntʃ] [1] N pouce *m* (= 2,54 cm); **he has grown a few ~es since last year** ≈ il a grandi de quelques centimètres depuis l'année dernière; **not an ~ from my face** *or* **nose** en plein *or* juste devant mon nez; **he couldn't see an ~ in front of him** il n'y voyait pas à deux pas; **not an ~ of the cloth is wasted** on ne perd pas un centimètre de tissu; **not an ~ of French territory will be conceded** on ne cédera pas un pouce de territoire français; **he knows every ~ of the district** il connaît la région comme sa poche *or* (jusque) dans ses moindres recoins; **we searched every ~ of the room** nous avons cherché partout dans la pièce, nous avons passé la pièce au peigne fin; **the police were searching the area ~ by ~** la police passait le quartier au peigne fin; **an ~ by-~ search** une fouille minutieuse; **he wouldn't budge an ~** (*lit*) il n'a pas voulu bouger d'un pouce; (*fig*) il n'a pas voulu faire la plus petite concession *or* céder d'un pouce; **he's every ~ a soldier** il a tout d'un soldat, il est soldat jusqu'à la moelle; **she's every ~ a lady** c'est une femme du monde jusqu'au bout des ongles, elle a tout d'une femme du monde; **within an ~ of succeeding/of death** *etc* à deux doigts *or* à un doigt de réussir/de la mort *etc*; **they beat him to within an ~ of his life** ils l'ont roué de coups et laissé à deux doigts de la mort; **he missed being run over by ~es** il a été à deux doigts de se faire écraser; **give him an ~ and he'll take a yard** *or* **a mile** vous lui donnez le doigt, il vous prend le bras

[2] VI **to ~ (one's way) forward/out/in** *etc* avancer/sortir/entrer *etc* peu à peu *or* petit à petit; **to ~ (one's way) through** se frayer peu à peu un passage; **prices are ~ing up** les prix augmentent petit à petit

[3] VT **to ~ sth forward/in/out** *etc* faire avancer/entrer/sortir *etc* qch peu à peu *or* petit à petit

inchoate ['ɪnkəʊeɪt] ADJ (*frm*) (= *just begun*) naissant, débutant; (= *half-formed*) vague, mal défini; (= *unfinished*) incomplet (-ète *f*), inachevé

inchoative [ɪn'kəʊətɪv] ADJ (*Ling*) [*aspect, verb*] inchoatif

inchtape ['ɪntʃteɪp] N centimètre *m* (de couturière)

incidence ['ɪnsɪdəns] N [a] [*of disease*] fréquence *f*, incidence *f*; [*of crime*] taux *m*; **the ~ of breast cancer increases with age** la fréquence *or* l'incidence des cancers du sein augmente avec l'âge; **the high ~ of heart disease in men over 40** le taux élevé des maladies cardiaques chez les hommes de plus de

40 ans; **record ~s of pneumonia and bronchitis** un nombre record de cas de pneumonie et de bronchite [b] (*Opt, Phys etc*) incidence *f* → **angle**

incident ['ɪnsɪdənt] [1] N [a] incident *m*; (*in book, play etc*) épisode *m*, péripétie *f*; **there were several ~s on the border last month** il y a eu plusieurs incidents frontaliers le mois dernier; **two students were killed in separate incidents** deux étudiants ont été tués dans deux incidents différents; **a diplomatic ~** un incident diplomatique; **the Birmingham ~** l'incident de Birmingham *or* qui a eu lieu à Birmingham; **~s of violence** actes *mpl* de violence

[b] (*NonC*) **the elections went ahead without ~** les élections se sont poursuivies sans incident; **a novel full of ~** un roman plein de péripéties; **a life full of ~** une vie mouvementée

[2] ADJ [a] (*frm*) **~ to** lié à; **costs ~ to the development of the new model** les coûts liés au développement du nouveau modèle

[b] (*Opt*) incident

[3] COMP ▶ **incident room** N (*Police*) bureau *m* de police (*provisoirement installé sur les lieux d'une enquête*)

incidental [ˌɪnsɪ'dentl] [1] ADJ (= *accompanying*) annexe; (= *secondary*) d'importance secondaire, annexe; (= *unplanned*) accidentel, fortuit; (= *relating to a particular incident*) [*detail*] accessoire, secondaire; **I don't know much about the ~ background** je connais mal les circonstances annexes; **teaching is ~ to my main occupation of translating** l'enseignement n'est pour moi qu'une activité annexe par rapport à la traduction; **these minor characters are ~ to the story** ces personnages secondaires ne sont pas essentiels à l'histoire; **the dangers ~ to such exploration** les dangers que comporte une telle exploration

[2] N [*event etc*] chose *f* fortuite; **that's just an ~** ça n'a pas de rapport avec la question; **~s** (= *expenses*) faux frais *mpl*; (= *objects*) accessoires *mpl*

[3] COMP ▶ **incidental damages** NPL (*Jur*) dommages-intérêts *mpl* accessoires ▶ **incidental expenses** NPL faux frais *mpl* ▶ **incidental music** N (*TV*) musique *f* de fond; (*Theat*) musique *f* de scène; (*Cine*) musique *f* de film; **the ~ music to the play** la musique qui accompagne la pièce

incidentally [ˌɪnsɪ'dentəlɪ] ADV [a] (= *by the way*) (*at start of sentence*) au fait, à propos; (*in middle, at end of sentence*) soit dit en passant, entre parenthèses; **~, why have you come?** au fait *or* à propos, pourquoi es-tu venu?; **the tower, ~, dates from the 12th century** la tour, entre parenthèses, date du 12ᵉ siècle [b] (= *casually*) [*mention, happen*] incidemment; **it was only ~ interesting** cela n'avait qu'un intérêt accessoire

incinerate [ɪn'sɪnəreɪt] VT incinérer

incineration [ɪnsɪnə'reɪʃən] N incinération *f*

incinerator [ɪn'sɪnəreɪtə*] N (*domestic, industrial*) incinérateur *m*; [*of crematorium*] four *m* crématoire

incipient [ɪn'sɪpɪənt] ADJ [*quarrel, disease, revolt*] naissant, qui commence; **the ~ uprising was suppressed** la révolte naissante a été étouffée, la révolte a été écrasée dans l'œuf

incise [ɪn'saɪz] VT [a] inciser, faire une incision dans [b] (*Art*) graver

incision [ɪn'sɪʒən] N incision *f*, entaille *f*; (*Surg*) incision *f*

incisive [ɪn'saɪsɪv] ADJ [*tone, analysis, comment, criticism*] incisif; [*mind*] pénétrant; **she's very ~** elle a l'esprit très vif

incisively [ɪn'saɪsɪvlɪ] ADV [*say*] sur un ton incisif; [*analyse, criticize*] de façon pénétrante

incisiveness [ɪn'saɪsɪvnɪs] N [*of person, comment, criticism, analysis*] perspicacité *f*; **the ~ of his mind** son acuité d'esprit; **the ~ of his**

tone was almost aggressive son ton était incisif au point d'en être presque agressif

incisor [ɪnˈsaɪzəʳ] N (= tooth) incisive f

incite [ɪnˈsaɪt] VT inciter, pousser (to à); to ~ sb to violence/revolt etc inciter or pousser qn à la violence/la révolte etc; to ~ sb to do inciter or pousser qn à faire; they were ~d to break the law on les a incités or poussés à enfreindre la loi

incitement [ɪnˈsaɪtmənt] N (NonC) incitation f (to à)

incivility [ˌɪnsɪˈvɪlɪtɪ] N (NonC) impolitesse f, incivilité f (also liter); there was an exchange of incivilities ils ont échangé des amabilités (iro)

incl. ABBR = including, inclusive

inclemency [ɪnˈklemənsɪ] N inclémence f

inclement [ɪnˈklemənt] ADJ inclément

inclination [ˌɪnklɪˈneɪʃən] N **a** (= liking, wish) inclination f, penchant m; (= tendency) tendance f; (= desire) envie f; children with little ~ for schooling des enfants qui montrent peu d'inclination or de penchant pour les études; she was by ~ generous elle était généreuse par inclination; I had no ~ to sleep je n'avais aucune envie de dormir; I have neither the time nor the ~ (to do) je n'ai ni le temps ni l'envie (de faire); she's a playwright by ~ elle est auteur dramatique par goût; to follow one's own ~s suivre son inclination or ses penchants (naturels); he has an ~ towards meanness il a tendance à être mesquin; her natural ~ was to help him son inclination naturelle la portait à lui venir en aide **b** (= slope, leaning) [of hill] inclinaison f, pente f; [of head, body] inclination f

incline [ɪnˈklaɪn] **1** VT **a** (= bend, bow) incliner, pencher; Jack ~d his head very slightly Jack a très légèrement incliné or penché la tête; ~d at an angle of ... incliné à un angle de ...
b (fig: gen pass) to ~ sb to do incliner or porter qn à faire; to be ~d to do (= have tendency to) avoir tendance à faire; (= feel desire to) incliner à or être enclin à faire; he's ~d to be lazy il a tendance à être paresseux; the drawer is ~d to stick le tiroir a tendance à se coincer; I'm ~d to think that ... j'ai tendance à penser que ...; I'm ~d to believe you je suis tenté de te croire; I'm more ~d to believe her than her sister j'aurais tendance à la croire elle, plutôt que sa sœur; he's that way ~d il est comme ça; to be criminally ~d avoir des tendances criminelles; to be artistically ~d avoir des dispositions pour l'art; if you feel (so) ~d si le cœur vous en dit; to be well or favourably ~d towards sb être bien disposé envers qn
2 VI **a** (= slope) s'incliner; (= bend, bow) s'incliner, se pencher
b (= tend towards) she ~s to the opinion that ... elle est plutôt d'avis que ..., elle aurait tendance à croire que ...; he ~s to laziness il incline à la paresse, il a tendance à être paresseux; his politics ~ towards socialism ses idées politiques tendent vers le socialisme
3 [ˈɪnklaɪn] N pente f, inclinaison f; (Rail) plan m incliné; a steep ~ une pente raide
4 COMP ► inclined plane N plan m incliné

inclose [ɪnˈkləʊz] VT = enclose

inclosure [ɪnˈkləʊʒəʳ] N = enclosure

include [ɪnˈkluːd] VT inclure, comprendre; your name is not ~d on the list votre nom ne figure pas sur la liste; the wine was ~d in the overall price le vin était compris or inclus dans le prix; "service ~d/not ~d" « service compris/non compris »; all or everything ~d tout compris; the hostages ~ three Britons il y a trois Britanniques parmi les otages; does that remark ~ me? est-ce que cette remarque s'adresse aussi à moi?; he ~d my mother in the invitation ma mère était comprise dans

son invitation; the invitation ~s everybody l'invitation s'adresse à tout le monde; they were all ~d in the accusation ils étaient tous visés par l'accusation; I had worked hard to be ~d in a project like this j'avais travaillé dur pour participer à un projet comme celui-ci; everyone, children ~d tout le monde, les enfants y compris; all of us, myself ~d nous tous, moi y compris; the district ~s ... la région comprend ...

► **include out*** VT SEP ~ me out! ne comptez pas sur moi!

including [ɪnˈkluːdɪŋ] PREP y compris; that comes to 200 francs ~ packing cela fait 200 F y compris l'emballage; there were six rooms ~ the kitchen il y avait six pièces y compris la cuisine; (not) ~ service charge service (non) compris; not ~ tax taxe non comprise; up to and ~ chapter five jusqu'au chapitre cinq inclus; up to and ~ 4 May jusqu'au 4 mai inclus; several projects, ~ ... plusieurs projets, dont ... or parmi lesquels ...; many conditions, ~ allergies, can be treated with homeopathic remedies beaucoup de maladies, dont or et notamment les allergies, peuvent être traitées par l'homéopathie; several people, ~ my father, had been invited plusieurs personnes, dont mon père, avaient été invitées

inclusion [ɪnˈkluːʒən] N inclusion f

inclusive [ɪnˈkluːsɪv] ADJ **a** (= comprehensive) [price, package] tout compris inv; [amount, sum] forfaitaire, global; (Comm) ~ terms (prix m) tout compris m; ~ of postage and packing port et emballage compris; all prices are ~ of VAT tous les prix incluent la TVA; cost ~ of travel prix voyage compris; the course costs £700, ~ of all food, drink and accommodation le cours coûte 700 livres, nourriture, boissons et logement compris or y compris la nourriture, les boissons et le logement; the course is fully ~ of all costs le cours inclut or comprend tous les frais → all 6
b (= included) Tuesday to Saturday ~ de mardi à samedi inclus or compris; rows A to M ~ de la rangée A à M incluse or comprise; from 1 to 6 May ~ du 1er au 6 mai inclus; up to page five ~ jusqu'à la page cinq incluse or comprise
c (= undiscriminating) a very ~ agenda un programme très riche; the conservatoire is far more ~ than before le conservatoire accueille une clientèle beaucoup plus diversifiée qu'autrefois

inclusively [ɪnˈkluːsɪvlɪ] ADV inclusivement

incognito [ˌɪnkɒɡˈniːtəʊ] **1** ADV [travel] incognito **2** ADJ to remain ~ garder l'incognito; to be an ~ traveller voyager incognito **3** N incognito m

incoherence [ˌɪnkəʊˈhɪərəns] N incohérence f

incoherent [ˌɪnkəʊˈhɪərənt] ADJ [person, speech, letter] incohérent; [style] décousu; an ~ set of objectives un ensemble incohérent d'objectifs; he was ~ with rage la fureur le rendait incohérent; ~ ramblings des divagations fpl, des propos mpl incohérents

incoherently [ˌɪnkəʊˈhɪərəntlɪ] ADV de façon incohérente

incohesive [ˌɪnkəʊˈhiːsɪv] ADJ sans cohésion

incombustible [ˌɪnkəmˈbʌstəbl] ADJ incombustible ·

income [ˈɪnkʌm] **1** N revenu(s) m(pl); families on low ~s ◊ low-~ families les familles fpl à faible revenu; an ~ of £15,000 a year un revenu de 15 000 livres par an; most of their ~ comes from ... l'essentiel de leur revenu provient de ...; private ~ rente(s) f(pl) → price, upper
2 COMP ► income group N (Econ) tranche f de revenus; the lowest ~ group les économiquement faibles mpl; the middle ~ group les revenus mpl moyens; the upper or highest ~ group les gros revenus mpl, les revenus mpl élevés ► incomes policy N politique f des

revenus ► Income Support N (Brit Admin) ≈ revenu m minimum d'insertion, ≈ RMI m ► income tax N (gen) impôt m sur le revenu; [of corporations] impôt m sur les bénéfices ► income tax inspector N inspecteur m des impôts ► income tax return N déclaration f de revenus, feuille f d'impôts

incomer [ˈɪnˌkʌməʳ] N (Brit = new arrival) (into town, area) nouveau venu m, nouvelle venue f, nouvel(le) arrivant(e) m(f); (into country) immigrant(e) m(f)

incoming [ˈɪnˌkʌmɪŋ] **1** ADJ **a** (Mil) [missile] en approche; (Phys) [light, radiation] reçu; they would not let him receive ~ calls ils ne le laissaient pas recevoir d'appels; this telephone only takes ~ calls ce téléphone ne prend que les appels de l'extérieur; ~ mail le courrier à l'arrivée **b** (= arriving: Travel) [plane, flight] à l'arrivée **c** [tide] montant; [waves] qui arrive **d** (= new) [president, government] nouveau (nouvelle f) **2** incomings NPL (Accounts) rentrées fpl, recettes fpl

incommensurable [ˌɪnkəˈmenʃərəbl] ADJ incommensurable (with avec)

incommensurate [ˌɪnkəˈmenʃərɪt] ADJ **a** (= out of proportion) sans rapport (to avec), disproportionné (to à); (= inadequate) insuffisant (to pour) **b** = incommensurable

incommode† [ˌɪnkəˈməʊd] VT (frm) incommoder, gêner

incommodious [ˌɪnkəˈməʊdɪəs] ADJ (frm) (= inconvenient) incommode; (= not spacious) [house, room] où l'on est à l'étroit

incommunicable [ˌɪnkəˈmjuːnɪkəbl] ADJ incommunicable

incommunicado [ˌɪnkəmjʊnɪˈkɑːdəʊ] **1** ADJ to be ~ être injoignable **2** ADV to be kept or held ~ être tenu au secret

incomparable [ɪnˈkɒmpərəbl] ADJ incomparable (to, with à); [talent, beauty] incomparable, sans pareil

incomparably [ɪnˈkɒmpərəblɪ] ADV [better, superior] incomparablement; ~ beautiful d'une beauté incomparable

incompatibility [ˈɪnkəmˌpætəˈbɪlɪtɪ] N (gen, Med, Comput) incompatibilité f; divorce on the grounds of ~ divorce m pour incompatibilité d'humeur

incompatible [ˌɪnkəmˈpætəbl] ADJ (gen, Med, Comput) incompatible (with sb/sth avec qn/qch); we were totally ~ il y avait incompatibilité totale entre nous, nous n'étions pas faits pour nous entendre

incompetence [ɪnˈkɒmpɪtəns], **incompetency** [ɪnˈkɒmpɪtənsɪ] N (gen, Jur) incompétence f

incompetent [ɪnˈkɒmpɪtənt] **1** ADJ **a** (gen, Jur) incompétent; ~ teachers professeurs mpl incompétents; to be ~ in business être incompétent or inapte en affaires; to be ~ at driving/drawing être mauvais conducteur/mauvais en dessin; the court declared him ~ to manage his financial affairs le tribunal l'a déclaré inapte à s'occuper de ses propres finances **2** N incompétent(e) m(f), incapable mf

incomplete [ˌɪnkəmˈpliːt] ADJ (= unfinished) incomplet (-ète f), inachevé; (= with some parts missing) [collection, series, kit, machine] incomplet (-ète f)

incompletely [ˌɪnkəmˈpliːtlɪ] ADV incomplètement

incompleteness [ˌɪnkəmˈpliːtnɪs] N inachèvement m

incomprehensible [ɪnˌkɒmprɪˈhensəbl] ADJ incompréhensible (to sb à qn)

incomprehensibly [ɪnˌkɒmprɪˈhensəblɪ] ADV [act, react] de manière incompréhensible; ~ worded formulé de façon inintelligible or incompréhensible; ~, he refused inexplicablement, il a refusé

incomprehension [ɪnˌkɒmprɪ'henʃən] N
incompréhension f

inconceivable [ˌɪnkən'siːvəbl] ADJ inconcevable

inconceivably [ˌɪnkən'siːvəblɪ] ADV ~ **stupid**
d'une stupidité inconcevable ; **almost ~, she
survived the accident** il est incroyable qu'elle
ait survécu à l'accident

inconclusive [ˌɪnkən'kluːsɪv] ADJ [outcome, results, evidence, debate] peu concluant, peu probant ; [war, fighting] sans vainqueur ni vaincu

inconclusively [ˌɪnkən'kluːsɪvlɪ] ADV [discuss]
d'une manière peu concluante ; **to end ~** ne
pas produire de résultats tangibles, ne déboucher sur rien

incongruity [ˌɪnkɒn'gruːɪtɪ] N [of behaviour,
dress, remark] incongruité f, inconvenance f ;
[of situation] absurdité f ; [of age, condition] disproportion f, incompatibilité f

incongruous [ɪn'kɒngruəs] ADJ (= out of place)
[remark, act, name] incongru, déplacé ; (=
absurd) [situation] absurde, grotesque ; **he was
an ~ figure among the tourists** il ne semblait
pas à sa place au milieu des touristes ; **it was
an ~ setting for a wedding** c'était un cadre qui
ne semblait pas convenir à un mariage ; **it
seemed ~ that they should take such a silly
idea so seriously** il semblait absurde qu'ils
prennent tellement au sérieux une idée aussi
stupide ; **~ with** peu approprié à

incongruously [ɪn'kɒngruəslɪ] ADV [say, remark, remind, dress] de façon incongrue ; **he
wore old jeans, with ~ smart shoes** il portait
un vieux jean avec des chaussures d'une élégance incongrue

inconsequent [ɪn'kɒnsɪkwənt] ADJ (frm)
[person, remark, behaviour, reasoning] inconséquent

inconsequential [ɪnˌkɒnsɪ'kwenʃəl] ADJ a =
inconsequent b (= unimportant) sans
importance, sans conséquence

inconsequentially [ɪnˌkɒnsɪ'kwenʃəlɪ] ADV
[talk, remark] de façon inconséquente

inconsiderable [ˌɪnkən'sɪdərəbl] ADJ insignifiant ; **a not ~ sum of money** une somme
d'argent non négligeable

inconsiderate [ˌɪnkən'sɪdərɪt] ADJ [person] qui
manque d'égards or de considération ; [action,
reply] inconsidéré, irréfléchi ; **to be ~ towards
sb** manquer d'égards or de considération
envers qn ; **you were very ~ ◊ that was very ~
of you** tu as agi sans aucun égard or sans
aucune considération ; **it would be ~ to wake
him up** ce serait manquer d'égards or de
considération de le réveiller

inconsistency [ˌɪnkən'sɪstənsɪ] N [of person]
inconstance f ; [of facts, accusation, behaviour,
reasoning] incohérence f ; **the ~ of the two
statements** les contradictions entre les deux
déclarations ; **the ~ of his work** le manque de
constance de son travail

inconsistent [ˌɪnkən'sɪstənt] ADJ a (pej = capricious) [person] inconstant ; [behaviour] incohérent b (= variable) [work, quality] inégal,
non constant c (= contradictory) [statements,
evidence, accounts] contradictoire ; **it is ~ to do
that** c'est incohérent or inconséquent de faire
cela ; **to be ~ with sth** (= contradict) ne pas
concorder avec qch, contredire qch ; (= be out
of keeping with) ne pas être conforme à qch,
ne pas correspondre à qch

inconsolable [ˌɪnkən'səʊləbl] ADJ inconsolable

inconsolably [ˌɪnkən'səʊləblɪ] ADV de façon
inconsolable

inconspicuous [ˌɪnkən'spɪkjʊəs] ADJ [person,
action] qui passe inaperçu ; [dress] discret (-ète
f) ; **he tried to make himself ~** il a essayé de
passer inaperçu, il s'est efforcé de ne pas se
faire remarquer

inconspicuously [ˌɪnkən'spɪkjʊəslɪ] ADV [be-

have, move, sit, wait] discrètement ; [dress] de
façon discrète

inconstancy [ɪn'kɒnstənsɪ] N (frm) (= fickleness) [of person] inconstance f ; (= instability)
instabilité f

inconstant [ɪn'kɒnstənt] ADJ a [person] (in
friendship) changeant, instable ; (in love)
inconstant, volage b (= variable) [weather]
instable, changeant ; [quality] variable

incontestable [ˌɪnkən'testəbl] ADJ
incontestable, indiscutable

incontinence [ɪn'kɒntɪnəns] 1 N (Med, also
fig frm) incontinence f 2 COMP
► **incontinence pad** N couche f pour
incontinent

incontinent [ɪn'kɒntɪnənt] ADJ a (Med)
incontinent b (fig frm) intempérant

incontrovertible [ˌɪnkɒntrə'vɜːtəbl] ADJ
[proof, evidence] irréfutable, irrécusable ; [argu-
ment] irréfutable ; [fact] indéniable ; **it is ~ that
...** il est indéniable que ...

incontrovertibly [ˌɪnkɒntrə'vɜːtəblɪ] ADV
[true, right] indéniablement, irréfutablement ;
[prove, demonstrate] de façon irréfutable, irréfutablement

inconvenience [ˌɪnkən'viːnɪəns] 1 N a (=
disadvantage) inconvénient m, désagrément
m ; **there are ~s in** or **to living in the country** il
y a des inconvénients à habiter la campagne,
habiter la campagne présente des inconvénients or des désagréments ; **it's one of the ~s
of getting old** c'est l'un des inconvénients
quand on vieillit b (NonC) dérangement m ;
**the ~ of a de-
layed flight** le dérangement occasionné par le
retard d'un vol ; **to put sb to great ~** causer
beaucoup de dérangement à qn ; **I don't want
to put you to any ~** je ne veux surtout pas
vous déranger ; **he went to a great deal of ~ to
help me** il s'est donné beaucoup de mal pour
m'aider ; **the management apologizes for any
~ caused by this work** la direction vous prie
de bien vouloir excuser la gêne occasionnée
par les travaux
2 VT (= presume on, impose on) déranger ; (=
disturb) [noise, smoke etc] incommoder ;
(stronger) gêner

inconvenient [ˌɪnkən'viːnɪənt] ADJ [time, mo-
ment] inopportun ; [visitor] gênant, importun ;
[fact, information, truth] gênant ; [arrangement,
location] peu pratique ; [house, room] peu pratique, malcommode ; **I'm sorry if I've come at an
~ time** excusez-moi si j'arrive à un moment
inopportun or au mauvais moment ; **I can
come back later if it is ~** je peux revenir plus
tard si je vous dérange ; **it is ~ for us to do
that** ce n'est pas pratique pour nous de faire
cela, cela ne nous arrange pas de faire ça

inconveniently [ˌɪnkən'viːnɪəntlɪ] ADV
[happen] malencontreusement ; **an ~ designed
room/car** une pièce/voiture conçue de façon
peu pratique ; **the hotel is ~ situated** la situation de l'hôtel est peu pratique

inconvertibility ['ɪnkənˌvɜːtɪ'bɪlɪtɪ] N non-
convertibilité f

inconvertible [ˌɪnkən'vɜːtəbl] ADJ (Fin etc)
inconvertible

incorporate¹ [ɪn'kɔːpəreɪt] 1 VT a (= introduce as part) [+ territory, suggestions, revisions]
incorporer, intégrer ; **they ~d him into their
group** ils l'ont incorporé or intégré dans leur
groupe ; **her proposals were ~d into the project plan** ses propositions ont été incorporées
dans l'ébauche du projet ; **they refused to ~
environmental considerations into their policies** ils ont refusé d'intégrer or de prendre en
compte des considérations écologiques dans
leur politique b (= include, contain) [+ articles, essays] contenir, comprendre ; [+ ideas, thoughts] rassem-
bler, réunir ; **the new cars will ~ a number of
major improvements** les nouvelles voitures se-

ront dotées de plusieurs perfectionnements
importants
c (Comm, Jur) [+ company] absorber ; (esp US)
~d company société f à responsabilité limitée ;
(in name of firm) **Smith Robinson Incorporated**
Smith Robinson SA
d (= mix, add) incorporer (**into** à) ; **to ~ eggs
into a sauce** incorporer des œufs à une sauce
2 VI (Comm) fusionner (**with** avec)

incorporate² [ɪn'kɔːpərɪt] ADJ (Philos)
incorporel

incorporation [ɪnˌkɔːpə'reɪʃən] N (gen)
incorporation f (**in(to)** sth dans qch) ; (Comm,
Jur) [of single company] incorporation f ; (=
takeover) absorption f (**of, by** de, par)

incorporator [ɪn'kɔːpəˌreɪtə'] N (Jur, Fin)
fondateur m (d'une société)

incorporeal [ˌɪnkɔː'pɔːrɪəl] ADJ (frm) incorporel

incorrect [ˌɪnkə'rekt] ADJ [information, answer,
spelling, assessment, behaviour, posture]
incorrect ; [assumption, belief] erroné ; [diet,
dress] inadapté ; [breathing] mauvais ; **he is ~
(in his assertion/belief that ...)** il se trompe (en
affirmant/croyant que ...) ; **it is ~ to say that
...** il est incorrect de dire que ... → **politically**

incorrectly [ˌɪnkə'rektlɪ] ADV [behave, act]
incorrectement ; **he sits ~** il se tient mal, il ne
se tient pas correctement ; **we assumed ~ that
...** nous avons supposé à tort que ...

incorrigible [ɪn'kɒrɪdʒəbl] ADJ incorrigible

incorrigibly [ɪn'kɒrɪdʒəblɪ] ADV incorrigiblement

incorruptible [ˌɪnkə'rʌptəbl] ADJ incorruptible

increase [ɪn'kriːs] 1 VI [price, sales, taxes,
crime, sorrow, surprise, rage, pain] augmenter ;
[amount, numbers] augmenter, croître ; [de-
mand, strength, population, supply, speed,
possessions, riches] augmenter, s'accroître ;
[trade] se développer ; [darkness] grandir ;
[noise, effort] s'intensifier ; [pride] grandir ;
[business, firm, institution, town] s'agrandir, se
développer ; [rain, wind] devenir plus violent,
redoubler ; [friendship] se renforcer, se consolider ; **industrial output ~d by 2% last year** la
production industrielle a augmenté de 2%
l'année dernière ; **to ~ in volume** augmenter
de volume, prendre du volume ; **to ~ in
weight** prendre du poids, s'alourdir ; **to ~ in
width** s'élargir ; **to ~ in height** [person] grandir ;
[tree] pousser ; [building] gagner de la hauteur
2 VT [+ numbers, strength, taxes, pain]
augmenter (**by** de) ; [+ price, sales] augmenter,
faire monter (**by** de) ; [+ demand, supply, population, possessions, riches] augmenter, accroître
(**by** de) ; [+ delight, pride, rage, sorrow, surprise]
augmenter, ajouter à ; [+ trade] développer ; [+
noise] intensifier ; [+ business] agrandir, développer ; [+ friendship] renforcer, consolider ;
how can I ~ my chances of winning? comment
puis-je augmenter mes chances de gagner ? ; **a
poor diet ~s the risk of cancer** une mauvaise
alimentation augmente le risque de cancer ; **a
greatly ~d risk of (getting) heart disease** un
risque considérablement accru de contracter
une maladie du cœur ; **they've ~d her salary
by £2,000 a year** ils l'ont augmentée or ils ont
augmenté son salaire de 2 000 livres par an ;
they've ~d her salary to £20,000 a year son salaire a été porté à 20 000 livres par an ; **his
hours were ~d to 25 per week** ses heures ont
été portées à 25 par semaine ; **to ~ speed**
accélérer ; **he ~d his speed to 90km/h** il a accéléré jusqu'à 90 km/h, il a atteint le 90* ; **she
~d her efforts** elle redoubla ses efforts or redoubla d'efforts
3 ['ɪnkriːs] N [of price, sales, numbers, pain,
workload] augmentation f ; [of demand, supply,
population, speed] augmentation f, accroissement m ; [of trade] développement m ; [of
noise] intensification f ; [of business] agrandis-

sement *m*, développement *m*; [*of crime*] augmentation *f*; [*of rain, wind*] redoublement *m*; [*of friendship*] renforcement *m*, consolidation *f*; [*of effort*] redoublement *m*, intensification *f*; **our sales figures showed no significant ~** nos chiffres de vente n'ont pas connu d'augmentation notable; **an ~ in public spending** une augmentation des dépenses publiques; **there has been an ~ in police activity** la police a intensifié ses activités; **a pay ~ ◊ an ~ in pay** une hausse de salaire, une augmentation (de salaire); **violent crime is/ racial attacks are on the ~** les crimes violents/les agressions raciales sont en augmentation; **the problem of crime is on the ~** le problème de la criminalité s'accentue; **inflation is on the ~** l'inflation est de plus en plus forte; **asthma is on the ~** les cas d'asthme sont de plus en plus nombreux; (*Fin*) **~ in value** plus-value *f*

increasing [ɪnˈkriːsɪŋ] ADJ [*number, amount*] croissant; **there is ~ concern about the effect of these drugs** on se préoccupe de plus en plus de l'effet de ces drogues; **there is ~ evidence to suggest that ...** nous disposons de plus en plus d'éléments qui tendent à prouver que ...; **there are ~ signs that ...** il semble de plus en plus que ...; **there is ~ pressure on her to resign** elle subit des pressions de plus en plus fortes qui la poussent à démissionner

increasingly [ɪnˈkriːsɪŋlɪ] ADV (= *more and more*) de plus en plus; (= *more and more often*) de plus en plus souvent; **~ well** de mieux en mieux; **~ unreliable** de moins en moins fiable

incredible [ɪnˈkredəbl] ADJ incroyable; **it is ~ that ...** il est incroyable que ... (+ *subj*); **~ though it may seem ...** aussi incroyable que cela puisse paraître ...

incredibly [ɪnˈkredəblɪ] ADV **a** (= *unbelievably*) incroyablement; **~, he refused** chose incroyable, il a refusé **b** (= *extremely*) [*big, small, fast, silly etc*] drôlement*; **it was ~ difficult** c'était drôlement* *or* extrêmement difficile

incredulity [ˌɪnkrɪˈdjuːlɪtɪ] N incrédulité *f*

incredulous [ɪnˈkredjʊləs] ADJ [*person*] incrédule; [*look*] incrédule, d'incrédulité

incredulously [ɪnˈkredjʊləslɪ] ADV [*say*] d'un ton incrédule; [*watch*] d'un air incrédule

increment [ˈɪnkrɪmənt] **1** N (*in salary*) échelon *m*; (*Math*) différentielle *f*; (*Comput*) incrément *m* → **unearned 2** VT (*gen*) augmenter; (*Comput*) incrémenter

incremental [ˌɪnkrɪˈmentl] **1** ADJ [*benefits*] supplémentaire; [*cost*] marginal, différentiel; [*rise, increase*] progressif; (*Comput*) incrémentiel **2** COMP ► **incremental plotter** N (*Comput*) traceur *m* incrémentiel ► **incremental value** N (*Comm: on index, scale*) valeur *f* indiciaire *or* de l'augmentation

incriminate [ɪnˈkrɪmɪneɪt] VT incriminer, compromettre; **the drugs had been planted to ~ him** les drogues avaient été placées là dans le but de le compromettre *or* de pouvoir l'incriminer; **he was afraid of incriminating himself** il avait peur de se compromettre

incriminating [ɪnˈkrɪmɪneɪtɪŋ] ADJ compromettant; **~ document** pièce *f* à conviction; **~ evidence** (*Jur*) pièces *fpl* à conviction, preuves *fpl* à charge; (*fig*) pièces *fpl* à conviction

incrimination [ɪnˌkrɪmɪˈneɪʃən] N incrimination *f*

incriminatory [ɪnˈkrɪmɪnətərɪ] ADJ = **incriminating**

incrustation [ˌɪnkrʌsˈteɪʃən] N incrustation *f*

incubate [ˈɪnkjubeɪt] **1** VT **a** [+ *eggs*] couver, incuber **b** (= *grow*) [+ *bacteria cultures, disease*] incuber **c** (*fig*) [+ *plan, scheme*] mûrir **2** VI [*eggs, bacteria, virus*] être en incubation; (*fig*) couver

incubation [ˌɪnkjuˈbeɪʃən] **1** N **a** [*of eggs, disease*] incubation *f* **b** (*fig*) [*of plan, scheme*] gestation *f* **2** COMP ► **incubation period** N période *f* d'incubation

incubator [ˈɪnkjubeɪtər] N (*for chicks, eggs, babies*) couveuse *f*, incubateur *m*; (*for bacteria cultures*) incubateur *m*; **to put a baby in an ~** mettre un nouveau-né en couveuse

incubus [ˈɪŋkjʊbəs] N (*pl* **incubuses** *or* **incubi** [ˈɪŋkjʊˌbaɪ]) (= *demon*) incube *m*; (*fig*) cauchemar *m*

incudes [ɪnˈkjuːdiːz] NPL *of* **incus**

inculcate [ˈɪnkʌlkeɪt] VT inculquer (**sth in sb, sb with sth** qch à qn)

inculcation [ˌɪnkʌlˈkeɪʃən] N inculcation *f*

incumbency [ɪnˈkʌmbənsɪ] N [*of president, official*] mandat *m*; (*Rel*) charge *f*; **during his ~** (*gen*) pendant son mandat; (*Rel*) pendant la durée de sa charge

incumbent [ɪnˈkʌmbənt] **1** ADJ **a** (*frm*) **to be ~ (up)on sb to do sth** incomber *or* appartenir à qn de faire qch **b** (*in office*) en exercice; (*US Pol*) **the ~ President** le président en exercice; (*before elections*) le président sortant **2** N (*Rel, Admin*) titulaire *m*; (*US Pol*) **the present ~ of the White House** l'occupant actuel de la Maison-Blanche

incunabula [ˌɪnkjuˈnæbjʊlə] NPL incunables *mpl*

incunabular [ˌɪnkjuˈnæbjʊlə] ADJ incunable

incur [ɪnˈkɜːr] VT [+ *anger, blame*] s'attirer, encourir; [+ *risk*] courir; [+ *obligation, debts*] contracter; [+ *loss*] subir; [+ *expenses, costs*] encourir

incurable [ɪnˈkjʊərəbl] **1** ADJ **a** (*Med*) incurable **b** (*fig*) incurable, incorrigible; **he's an ~ romantic** c'est un romantique incorrigible **2** N incurable *mf*

incurably [ɪnˈkjʊərəblɪ] ADV (*Med, fig*) incurablement; **the ~ ill** les incurables *mpl*

incurious [ɪnˈkjʊərɪəs] ADJ sans curiosité (**about** en ce qui concerne), incurieux (*liter*) (**about** de)

incuriously [ɪnˈkjʊərɪəslɪ] ADV sans curiosité

incursion [ɪnˈkɜːʃən] N (*Mil*) incursion *f*; (*fig*) ingérence *f*

incus [ˈɪŋkəs] N (*pl* **incudes**) (*Anat*) enclume *f*

Ind. ABBR = **Indiana**

indebted [ɪnˈdetɪd] ADJ **a** (*Fin*) endetté; (*lit, fig*) **to be ~ to sb for sth** être redevable à qn de qch; **I was ~ to the tune of £13,000** mes dettes s'élevaient à 13 000 livres; **heavily companies** des sociétés *fpl* fortement endettées; **he was ~ to his brother for a large sum** il était redevable d'une grosse somme à son frère **b** (= *grateful*) **I am ~ to him for pointing out that ...** je lui suis redevable d'avoir fait remarquer que ...; **I am greatly ~ to him for his generosity** je lui dois beaucoup pour sa générosité

indebtedness [ɪnˈdetɪdnɪs] N (*Fin, Comm*) dette(s) *f(pl)*, endettement *m*; **the company has reduced its ~ to £15 million** la société a réduit son endettement à 15 millions de livres; **the amount of our ~ to the bank is $15,000** notre dette envers la banque s'élève à 15 000 dollars **b** (*fig*) dette(s) *f(pl)*; **my ~ to my friend** ma dette envers mon ami, ce dont je suis redevable à mon ami; **De Palma's ~ to Hitchcock** ce que De Palma doit à Hitchcock

indecency [ɪnˈdiːsnsɪ] **1** N (*gen*) indécence *f*; (*Jur: also* **act of ~**) attentat *m* à la pudeur **2** COMP ► **indecency charge** N accusation *f* d'attentat à la pudeur ► **indecency law** N loi *f* sur l'attentat à la pudeur

indecent [ɪnˈdiːsnt] **1** ADJ indécent; **~ material** documents *mpl* contraires aux bonnes mœurs **2** COMP ► **indecent assault** N attentat *m* à la pudeur (**on sb** contre qn) ► **indecent behaviour** N outrage *m* aux bonnes mœurs ► **indecent exposure** N outrage *m* public à la pudeur

indecently [ɪnˈdiːsntlɪ] ADV **a** [*behave*] indécemment, de façon indécente; **they got married ~ soon after his first wife's funeral** ils se sont mariés si tôt après les obsèques de sa première femme que c'en était indécent **b** (*Jur*) [*touch*] de façon indécente; **to ~ assault sb** attenter à la pudeur de qn; **to ~ expose oneself** *or* **one's person** commettre un outrage public à la pudeur

indecipherable [ˌɪndɪˈsaɪfərəbl] ADJ indéchiffrable

indecision [ˌɪndɪˈsɪʒən] N indécision *f*, irrésolution *f*

indecisive [ˌɪndɪˈsaɪsɪv] ADJ **a** (= *uncertain*) [*person, government, manner*] indécis (**about** *or* **over sth** à propos de qch) **b** (= *inconclusive*) [*discussion, argument, result, vote*] peu concluant, peu probant

indecisively [ˌɪndɪˈsaɪsɪvlɪ] ADV de façon indécise

indecisiveness [ˌɪndɪˈsaɪsɪvnɪs] N = **indecision**

indeclinable [ˌɪndɪˈklaɪnəbl] ADJ indéclinable

indecorous [ɪnˈdekərəs] ADJ (*frm*) peu convenable, inconvenant

indecorously [ɪnˈdekərəslɪ] ADV d'une manière inconvenante *or* peu convenable

indecorum [ˌɪndɪˈkɔːrəm] N (*frm*) manquement *m* aux usages

▼**indeed** [ɪnˈdiːd] ADV **a** (*indicating confirmation, agreement*) en effet, effectivement; **he promised to help and ~ he helped us a lot** il a promis de nous aider et effectivement il nous a beaucoup aidés; **I am ~ quite tired** je suis en effet assez fatigué; **did you know him? — I did ~** vous le connaissiez? — oui, tout à fait; **are you coming? — ~ I am** *or* **yes ~!** vous venez? — mais certainement *or* (mais) bien sûr! **b** (*introducing further information*) d'ailleurs, en fait; **I don't know what she said, ~ I don't want to know** je ne sais pas ce qu'elle a dit, d'ailleurs *or* en fait je ne veux pas le savoir; **he was happy, ~ delighted, to hear the news** il était content, même ravi d'entendre la nouvelle; **I feel, ~ I know he is right** je sens, en fait je sais qu'il a raison **c** (*as intensifier*) vraiment; **that's praise ~ coming from him** venant de lui, c'est vraiment un compliment; **I am very grateful/pleased ~** je suis vraiment reconnaissant/très content; **thank you very much ~** je vous remercie infiniment; **if ~ he were wrong** s'il est vrai qu'il a tort, si tant est qu'il ait tort **d** (*showing interest, irony, surprise etc*) **(oh) ~?** vraiment?, c'est vrai?; **is it ~!** ◊ **did you** (*or he etc*) **~!** vraiment?; **who is that man? — who is he ~?** qui est cet homme? — ah, là est la question!; **what was to be done? — what ~?** que faire? — on peut effectivement se poser la question!; **I heard it on the wireless — wireless, ~! they're called radios now** je l'ai entendu à la TSF — TSF, vraiment! ça s'appelle une radio, maintenant

indefatigable [ˌɪndɪˈfætɪgəbl] ADJ infatigable, inlassable

indefatigably [ˌɪndɪˈfætɪgəblɪ] ADV inlassablement

indefensible [ˌɪndɪˈfensəbl] ADJ indéfendable

indefensibly [ˌɪndɪˈfensəblɪ] ADV d'une manière inexcusable; **he was ~ rude** il a été d'une grossièreté impardonnable *or* inexcusable

indefinable [ˌɪndɪˈfaɪnəbl] ADJ indéfinissable, vague

indefinably [ˌɪndɪˈfaɪnəblɪ] ADV vaguement

indefinite [ɪnˈdefɪnɪt] **1** ADJ **a** (= *unspecified*) [*period, postponement, size, number, duration*] indéterminé; [*strike, curfew, ban*] illimité; **for the ~ future** pour un avenir indéterminé; **to be granted ~ leave (of absence)** obtenir un congé à durée indéterminée; **at some ~ time** à un moment quelconque *or* indéterminé **b** (= *vague*) [*feelings*] indéfini; [*word*] imprécis; [*plans*] imprécis, mal défini **2** COMP

► **indefinite article** N (*Gram*) article *m* indéfini ► **indefinite pronoun** N (*Gram*) pronom *m* indéfini

indefinitely [ɪnˈdefɪnɪtlɪ] ADV [*last, continue, stay, detain*] indéfiniment; [*adjourn, cancel*] pour une durée indéterminée; **the meeting has been postponed ~** la réunion a été reportée à une date indéterminée

indelible [ɪnˈdeləbl] ADJ (*lit, fig*) indélébile

indelibly [ɪnˈdelɪblɪ] ADV (*lit, fig*) de façon indélébile

indelicacy [ɪnˈdelɪkəsɪ] N (*frm*) [a] (*NonC*) [*of person, behaviour*] (= *tactlessness*) indélicatesse *f*, manque *m* de délicatesse; (= *indiscreetness*) manque *m* de discrétion [b] [*of action, remark*] (= *impropriety*) inconvenance *f*; (= *coarseness*) grossièreté *f*; (= *tactlessness*) indiscrétion *f*

indelicate [ɪnˈdelɪkɪt] ADJ [*person*] (= *indiscreet*) indélicat, peu délicat; (= *tactless*) manquant de tact, indiscret (-ète *f*); [*act, remark*] (= *out of place*) indélicat, déplacé; (= *tactless*) indiscret (-ète *f*), manquant de tact; (= *coarse*) grossier

indemnification [ɪnˌdemnɪfɪˈkeɪʃən] N [a] (*NonC*) indemnisation *f* (**for, against** de) [b] (= *sum paid*) indemnité *f*, dédommagement *m*

indemnify [ɪnˈdemnɪfaɪ] VT [a] (= *compensate*) indemniser, dédommager (**sb for sth** qn de qch) [b] (= *safeguard*) garantir, assurer (**sb against** *or* **for sth** qn contre qch)

indemnity [ɪnˈdemnɪtɪ] N [a] (= *compensation*) indemnité *f*, dédommagement *m* [b] (= *insurance*) assurance *f*, garantie *f*

indent [ɪnˈdent] [1] VT [a] (*Typ*) [+ *word, line*] mettre en alinéa *or* en retrait; [+ *whole paragraph*] mettre en retrait; [+ *first line of paragraph*] faire un retrait de première ligne de; **~ed line** ligne *f* en alinéa *or* en retrait; **~ two spaces** renfoncez de deux espaces, mettez en alinéa *or* en retrait de deux espaces [b] [+ *border*] denteler, découper (*en dentelant*); **~ed edge** bord *m* dentelé; **~ed coastline** littoral *m* découpé [2] VI (*Brit Comm*) **to ~ on sb for sth** passer une commande de qch à qn, commander qch à qn [3] [ˈɪndent] N [a] (*Brit Comm*) commande *f* [b] = **indentation**

indentation [ˌɪndenˈteɪʃən] N [a] (*Typ*) alinéa *m* [b] (= *act*) découpage *m*; (= *notched edge*) dentelure *f*, découpure *f*; [*of coastline*] échancrures *fpl*, indentations *fpl* [c] (= *hollow mark*) empreinte *f*; (= *footprint*) trace *f* de pas; (*in metal, car*) bosse *f*; **the ~ of tyres on the soft ground** l'empreinte des pneus sur le sol mou

indenture [ɪnˈdentʃəʳ] [1] N (*Jur*) contrat *m* synallagmatique; (= *apprentice*) contrat *m* d'apprentissage [2] VT (*Jur*) lier par contrat (synallagmatique); [+ *apprentice*] mettre en apprentissage (**to** chez)

independence [ˌɪndɪˈpendəns] [1] N [a] (*gen*) indépendance *f* (**from** par rapport à); **to show ~** faire preuve d'indépendance, manifester son indépendance [b] (*Pol*) **the country's first elections since ~** les premières élections du pays depuis l'indépendance; **the country got its ~ in 1970** le pays est devenu indépendant *or* a obtenu son indépendance en 1970; **Rhodesia gained ~ from Britain in 1978** la Rhodésie s'est affranchie de la tutelle britannique en 1978 [2] COMP ► **Independence Day** N (*US*) fête *f or* anniversaire *m* de l'Indépendance américaine (*le 4 juillet*)

independent [ˌɪndɪˈpendənt] [1] ADJ [a] (*gen*) [*person, attitude, artist*] indépendant; [*radio*] libre; **she was fiercely ~** elle était farouchement indépendante; **he is an ~ thinker** c'est un penseur original; (*Pol*) **an Independent member** un député non inscrit *or* non affilié; **~ means** rentes *fpl*, revenus *mpl* indépendants; **he has ~ means** il a une fortune personnelle
[b] [*country, nation*] indépendant (**of** de), auto-

nome; **to become ~** devenir indépendant *or* autonome, s'affranchir
[c] (= *unrelated*) [*proof, research*] indépendant; [*reports*] émanant de sources indépendantes; **to ask for an ~ opinion** demander un avis indépendant; **there has been no ~ confirmation of this report** aucune source indépendante n'a confirmé cette information
[d] (*Gram*) indépendant
[2] N (*Pol*) **Independent** non-inscrit(e) *m(f)*, non-affilié(e) *m(f)*
[3] COMP ► **independent school** N (*Brit*) établissement *m* d'enseignement privé ► **independent suspension** N (*Aut*) suspension *f* indépendante ► **Independent Television Commission** N (*Brit*) ≈ Conseil *m* supérieur de l'audiovisuel

independently [ˌɪndɪˈpendəntlɪ] ADV [*act, live, think*] de façon indépendante, de façon autonome; [*research, negotiate, investigate*] séparément; **~ of sb/sth** indépendamment de qn/qch; **to be ~ wealthy** avoir une fortune personnelle; **the two scientists had discovered the virus quite ~** les deux savants avaient découvert le virus chacun de leur côté; **quite ~, he had offered to help** il avait proposé son aide sans même qu'on le lui demande, il avait spontanément proposé son aide

indescribable [ˌɪndɪsˈkraɪbəbl] ADJ indescriptible

indescribably [ˌɪndɪsˈkraɪbəblɪ] ADV **~ filthy** d'une saleté indescriptible; **it was ~ awful** c'était affreux au-delà de toute expression; **~ beautiful** d'une beauté indescriptible

indestructibility [ˌɪndɪstrʌktəˈbɪlɪtɪ] N indestructibilité *f*

indestructible [ˌɪndɪsˈtrʌktəbl] ADJ indestructible

indeterminable [ˌɪndɪˈtɜːmɪnəbl] ADJ indéterminable

indeterminacy [ˌɪndɪˈtɜːmɪnəsɪ] N indétermination *f*

indeterminate [ˌɪndɪˈtɜːmɪnɪt] [1] ADJ [*age, sex, number, period*] indéterminé; [*meaning, shape*] imprécis, vague; [*colour*] imprécis, indéterminé; (*Math*) indéterminé [2] COMP ► **indeterminate sentence** N (*US Jur*) peine *f* de prison de durée indéterminée

indeterminately [ˌɪndɪˈtɜːmɪnɪtlɪ] ADV de façon indéterminée, vaguement

index [ˈɪndeks] [1] N [a] (*pl* **indexes**) (= *list*) (*in book, map etc*) index *m*, table *f* alphabétique; (*on cards, in files: in library etc*) catalogue *m* *or* répertoire *m* (alphabétique); (*Rel*) **to put a book on the Index** mettre un livre à l'Index
[b] (*pl* **indexes**) (= *pointer*) [*of instrument*] aiguille *f*, index *m*
[c] (*pl* **indices**) (= *number expressing ratio*) indice *m*; **cost-of-living ~** indice *m* du coût de la vie; **~ of growth/of industrial activity** indice *m* de croissance/de l'activité industrielle; (*Opt*) **~ of refraction** indice *m* de réfraction
[d] (*St Ex: also* **share ~**) indice *m* boursier
[e] (*pl* **indices**) (*fig*) signe *m* (révélateur), indication *f*; **it is an ~ of how much poorer people were then** c'est un signe révélateur de la plus grande pauvreté qui régnait à l'époque; **weeds are an ~ to the character of the soil** les mauvaises herbes sont un indicateur de la nature du sol
[f] (*pl* **indexes**) **~ (finger)** index *m*
[g] (*pl* **indexes**) (*Typ*) index *m*
[h] (*pl* **indices**) (*Math*) exposant *m*
[2] VT [a] (= *put an index in*) [+ *book*] ajouter un index *or* une table alphabétique à; **the book is badly ~ed** l'index *or* la table alphabétique du livre est mal fait(e)
[b] (= *put into an index*) [+ *word*] faire figurer dans l'index *or* la table alphabétique; (*on cards, in files etc*) répertorier *or* cataloguer (alphabétiquement); [+ *books,*

diskettes, articles] classer (**under** sous, à); **it is ~ed under "Europe"** c'est classé *or* indexé sous « Europe »
[c] (*Fin, Econ*) [+ *wages, prices*] indexer
[3] COMP ► **index card** N fiche *f* ► **index figure** N (*Stat*) indice *m* ► **index finger** N index *m* ► **index-linked** ADJ (*Brit Econ*) indexé ► **index number** N = **index figure** ► **index-tied** ADJ = **index-linked**

indexation [ˌɪndekˈseɪʃən] N indexation *f*

India [ˈɪndɪə] [1] N l'Inde *f*; (*Hist*) les Indes *fpl* [2] COMP ► **India ink** N encre *f* de Chine ► **India paper** N papier *m* bible ► **India rubber** N (*NonC*) (= *substance*) caoutchouc *m*; (= *eraser*) gomme *f*

Indiaman [ˈɪndɪəmən] N (*pl* **-men**) (*Naut Hist*) navire faisant le voyage des Indes

Indian [ˈɪndɪən] [1] ADJ [a] (*in India*) indien, de l'Inde; [*ambassador, embassy*] de l'Inde; (*Hist*) des Indes
[b] (*also* **American ~**) indien, des Indiens (d'Amérique)
[2] N [a] (*in India*) Indien(ne) *m(f)*
[b] (*also* **American ~**) Indien(ne) *m(f)* (d'Amérique)
[c] (*Ling*) amérindien *m*
[3] COMP ► **Indian clubs** NPL massues *fpl* (*de gymnastique*) ► **Indian corn** N maïs *m* ► **Indian elephant** N éléphant *m* d'Asie ► **Indian Empire** N Empire *m* des Indes ► **Indian file** N in ~ file en file indienne ► **Indian giver*** N (*US pej*) personne *f* qui reprend ses cadeaux ► **Indian ink** N encre *f* de Chine ► **Indian Mutiny** N (*Hist*) révolte *f* des Cipayes ► **Indian National Congress** N Congrès *m* national indien ► **Indian Ocean** N océan *m* Indien ► **Indian rope trick** N tour d'illusionniste consistant à grimper à une corde que l'on a dressée en jouant d'un instrument de musique ► **Indian sign†** N (*US*) sort *m*; **to put an ~ sign on sb** jeter un sort à qn ► **Indian summer** N (= *warm weather*) été *m* indien *or* de la Saint-Martin; (*esp Brit: fig* = *success late in life*) réussite *f* tardive, succès *m* tardif ► **Indian tea** N thé *m* indien *or* de l'Inde ► **Indian tonic (water)** N Schweppes® *m* ► **Indian wrestling** N (*US Sport*) bras *m* de fer → **rope**

Indiana [ˌɪndɪˈænə] N l'Indiana *m*; **in ~** dans l'Indiana

indicate [ˈɪndɪkeɪt] [1] VT [a] (= *point to*) indiquer, montrer; **he ~d a chair and asked me to sit down** il a indiqué *or* montré une chaise et m'a invité à m'asseoir
[b] (= *be a sign of*) indiquer; **a change in colour ~s the presence of acid** un changement de couleur indique la présence d'acide; **opinion polls ~ (that) they are losing popularity** les sondages indiquent que leur cote de popularité est en baisse
[c] (= *make known*) [+ *intentions, opinion*] faire connaître, faire part de; [+ *feelings*] laisser voir, manifester; **he ~d that I was to leave** il m'a fait comprendre que je devais partir; **he ~d that he might resign** il a laissé entendre qu'il pourrait démissionner
[d] (= *call for*) indiquer; **the use of penicillin is clearly ~d** le recours à la pénicilline est nettement indiqué; **a new approach to the wages problem is ~d** il convient d'aborder le problème des salaires sous un nouvel angle
[2] VI (*esp Brit Aut*) mettre son clignotant; **he was indicating (left)** il avait mis son clignotant (à gauche)

indication [ˌɪndɪˈkeɪʃən] N signe *m*, indication *f*; **it was an ~ of his guilt** c'était un signe *or* une indication de sa culpabilité; **we had no ~ that it was going to take place** rien ne laissait prévoir *or* présager que cela allait arriver; **there is every ~ that she's right** tout porte à croire *or* laisse à penser qu'elle a raison; **there are few ~s that they are ready to come to an agreement** rien ne laisse présager qu'ils approchent d'un accord; **all the ~s lead one to believe that ...** tout porte à croire que ..., il y a toute raison de croire que ...; **it is some ~ of how popular she is** cela montre à quel point elle est populaire; **if this result is any ~, he ...** à en juger par ce résultat, il ...; **to give sb an ~ of one's feelings/intentions** manifester ses sentiments/faire part de ses intentions à qn; **he gave us some ~ of what he meant** il nous a donné une idée de ce qu'il voulait dire; **he gave no ~ that he was ready to compromise** il n'a aucunement laissé entendre qu'il était prêt à transiger

indicative [ɪn'dɪkətɪv] [1] ADJ [a] **to be ~ of sth** être révélateur de qch; **to be ~ of the fact that ...** montrer que ...; [b] (*Gram*) indicatif [2] N (*Gram: also ~ mood*) (mode *m*) indicatif *m*; **in the ~** à l'indicatif

indicator ['ɪndɪkeɪtə*] N (= *device*) indicateur *m*; (= *needle on scale etc*) aiguille *f*, index *m*; (= *indication*) indicateur *m*; (*Brit Aut: also ~ light*) (*flashing*) clignotant *m*; (*projecting*) flèche *f*; (*Ling*) indicateur *m*; **higher output is an ~ that the economy is recovering** *or* **of economic recovery** une augmentation de la production est un indicateur de reprise économique; **economic ~s** indicateurs *mpl* économiques; **altitude/pressure ~** indicateur *m* d'altitude/de pression

indices ['ɪndɪsiːz] NPL *of* index 1c, 1e, 1h

indict [ɪn'daɪt] VT [a] (*esp US Jur*) mettre en examen; **to ~ sb for sth** *or* **on a charge of sth** inculper qn de qch, mettre qn en examen pour qch [b] (*fig*) accuser, porter une accusation contre

indictable [ɪn'daɪtəbl] ADJ (*Jur*) [*person, action*] attaquable en justice, passible de poursuites; **an ~ offence** un délit grave, une infraction majeure

indictment [ɪn'daɪtmənt] N [a] (*Jur*) (= *bill*) acte *m* d'accusation (**for** de); (= *process*) mise *f* en examen (**for** pour); (*US*) accusation *f* (*par le jury d'accusation*) → GRAND JURY; (*Brit Hist*) **bill of ~** résumé *m* d'instruction (*présenté au jury d'accusation*); **to bring an ~ against sb (for sth)** inculper qn (de qch) [b] (*fig*) **such poverty is an ~ of the political system** une telle pauvreté est une véritable mise en cause du système politique; **his speech constituted a damning ~ of government policy** son discours a été un réquisitoire accablant contre la politique du gouvernement; **it is a sad ~ of our times that many old people are afraid to go out alone** c'est un triste signe des temps que beaucoup de personnes âgées n'osent plus sortir seules

indie• ['ɪndɪ] N (*Mus*) musique *f* *or* rock *m* indé

Indies ['ɪndɪz] NPL Indes *fpl* → east, west

indifference [ɪn'dɪfrəns] N [a] (= *lack of interest, of feeling*) indifférence *f* (**to** à, **towards** envers), manque *m* d'intérêt (**to, towards** pour, à l'égard de); **he greeted the suggestion with ~** il a accueilli la suggestion avec indifférence *or* sans manifester d'intérêt; **it is a matter of supreme ~ to me** cela m'est parfaitement indifférent *or* égal [b] (= *poor quality*) médiocrité *f*

indifferent [ɪn'dɪfrənt] ADJ [a] (= *lacking feeling, interest*) indifférent (**to** à); **the government's ~ attitude to the massacres** l'indifférence manifestée par le gouvernement vis-à-vis des massacres [b] (*pej = mediocre*) [*talent, performance, player*] médiocre, quelconque; **good, bad or ~** bon, mauvais ou quelconque [c] († = *impartial*) impartial, neutre

indifferently [ɪn'dɪfrəntlɪ] ADV [a] (= *uninterestedly*) [*say, shrug, look at*] avec indifférence [b] (*pej* = *badly*) [*perform, write*] médiocrement [c] († = *impartially*) **she went ~ to one shop or the other** elle allait indifféremment dans une boutique ou dans l'autre

indigence ['ɪndɪdʒəns] N indigence *f*

indigenous [ɪn'dɪdʒɪnəs] ADJ [*people, species, plant, culture, language*] indigène; [*population*] indigène, autochtone; **the elephant is ~ to India** l'éléphant est un animal indigène en Inde

indigent ['ɪndɪdʒənt] ADJ (*frm*) indigent, nécessiteux

indigestible [ˌɪndɪ'dʒestəbl] ADJ [a] [*food, fibre*] inassimilable (par l'organisme) [b] (*fig*) [*book, information*] indigeste

indigestion [ˌɪndɪ'dʒestʃən] N (*NonC: Med*) indigestion *f*; **to have an attack of ~** avoir une indigestion; **he gets a lot of ~** il fait souvent des indigestions

indignant [ɪn'dɪgnənt] ADJ indigné (**at** *or* **about sth** de qch, **with sb** contre qn); **they were ~ that they were not consulted/that he had not consulted them** ils étaient indignés de ne pas avoir été consultés/qu'il ne les eût pas consultés; **to become** *or* **get ~** s'indigner; **to make sb ~** indigner qn

indignantly [ɪn'dɪgnəntlɪ] ADV avec indignation; [*say*] d'un air *or* d'un ton indigné

indignation [ˌɪndɪg'neɪʃən] N indignation *f* (**at** devant, **with** contre); **she was filled with ~ at their working conditions** leurs conditions de travail la remplissaient d'indignation

indignity [ɪn'dɪgnɪtɪ] N [a] (= *act*) outrage *m*, indignité *f*; **it was the final ~** c'était le comble de l'outrage; **he suffered the ~ of having to ...** il subit l'outrage d'avoir à ... [b] (*NonC*) indignité *f*

indigo ['ɪndɪgəʊ] [1] N (*pl* indigos *or* indigoes) indigo *m* [2] ADJ (*also ~ blue*) (bleu) indigo *inv*

indirect [ˌɪndɪ'rekt] [1] ADJ indirect [2] COMP ► **indirect discrimination** N discrimination *f* indirecte ► **indirect lighting** N éclairage *m* indirect ► **indirect object** N (*Gram*) complément *m* d'objet indirect ► **indirect question** N (*gen, Gram*) question *f* indirecte ► **indirect speech** N (*Gram*) discours *m* indirect ► **indirect tax** N impôt *m* indirect ► **indirect taxation** N contributions *fpl* indirectes, impôts *mpl* indirects

indirectly [ˌɪndɪ'rektlɪ] ADV indirectement

indirectness [ˌɪndɪ'rektnɪs] N caractère *m* indirect

indiscernible [ˌɪndɪ'sɜːnəbl] ADJ indiscernable

indiscipline [ɪn'dɪsɪplɪn] N indiscipline *f*

indiscreet [ˌɪndɪs'kriːt] ADJ (= *tactless*) indiscret (-ète *f*); (= *rash*) imprudent (**about sth** à propos de qch)

indiscreetly [ˌɪndɪs'kriːtlɪ] ADV (= *tactlessly*) indiscrètement; (= *rashly*) imprudemment, avec imprudence

indiscretion [ˌɪndɪs'kreʃən] N [a] (*NonC*) (= *tactlessness*) manque *m* de discrétion, indiscrétion *f*; (= *rashness*) imprudence *f*; (= *carelessness*) indiscrétion *f* [b] (= *tactless remark, action*) indiscrétion *f*; **an act of ~** une indiscrétion; **a youthful ~** une bêtise *or* une erreur de jeunesse

indiscriminate [ˌɪndɪs'krɪmɪnɪt] ADJ [*killing, violence*] aveugle; [*punishment*] distribué à tort et à travers; **~ use of pesticides** emploi *m* sans discernement des pesticides; **to be ~ in one's attacks** lancer ses attaques au hasard; **to be ~ in one's viewing habits** ne pas être sélectif dans ses choix de programmes de télévision

indiscriminately [ˌɪndɪs'krɪmɪnɪtlɪ] ADV [*use*] sans discernement; [*kill*] sans discrimination; [*fire*] au hasard; [*read, watch TV*] de façon non sélective

indispensable [ˌɪndɪs'pensəbl] ADJ indispensable (**to** à); **nobody's ~!** personne n'est indispensable!; **you're not ~!** on peut se passer de toi!, tu n'es pas indispensable!

indisposed [ˌɪndɪs'pəʊzd] ADJ [a] (= *unwell*)

indisposé, souffrant [b] (= *disinclined*) peu disposé, peu enclin (**to do** à faire)

indisposition [ˌɪndɪspə'zɪʃən] N [a] (= *illness*) indisposition *f*, malaise *m* [b] (= *disinclination*) manque *m* d'inclination (**to do** à faire)

indisputable [ˌɪndɪs'pjuːtəbl] ADJ incontestable, indiscutable

▼ **indisputably** [ˌɪndɪs'pjuːtəblɪ] ADV incontestablement, indiscutablement

indissoluble [ˌɪndɪ'sɒljʊbl] ADJ [a] [*friendship*] indissoluble [b] (*Chem*) insoluble

indissolubly [ˌɪndɪ'sɒljʊblɪ] ADV (*gen, Jur*) indissolublement

indistinct [ˌɪndɪs'tɪŋkt] ADJ [*voice, sound, words, figure, shape*] indistinct; [*memory*] vague, flou; [*photograph*] flou

indistinctly [ˌɪndɪs'tɪŋktlɪ] ADV [*see, hear, speak*] indistinctement; [*remember*] vaguement

indistinguishable [ˌɪndɪs'tɪŋgwɪʃəbl] ADJ [a] indifférenciable (**from** de) [b] (= *very slight*) [*noise, difference, change*] imperceptible, indiscernable

indistinguishably [ˌɪndɪs'tɪŋgwɪʃəblɪ] ADV au point de ne pouvoir être différencié

indium ['ɪndɪəm] N indium *m*

individual [ˌɪndɪ'vɪdjʊəl] [1] ADJ [a] (= *separate*) [*opinion, attention, portion*] individuel; **served in ~ dishes** servi dans des plats individuels [b] (= *distinctive, characteristic*) personnel, particulier; **he has an ~ style** il a un style personnel *or* bien à lui; **the language she uses is highly ~** elle utilise un langage très personnel *or* particulier [c] (*Sport*) **~ pursuit** poursuite *f* individuelle; **~ sports** sports *mpl* individuels [2] N individu *m*; **each ~ is entitled to ...** tout individu *or* toute personne *or* chacun a droit à ...

individualism [ˌɪndɪ'vɪdjʊəlɪzəm] N individualisme *m*

individualist [ˌɪndɪ'vɪdjʊəlɪst] N individualiste *mf*

individualistic [ˌɪndɪˌvɪdjʊə'lɪstɪk] ADJ individualiste

individuality [ˌɪndɪˌvɪdjʊ'ælɪtɪ] N individualité *f*

individualize [ˌɪndɪ'vɪdjʊəlaɪz] VT individualiser, personnaliser; (*US Scol*) **~d instruction** enseignement *m* individualisé

individually [ˌɪndɪ'vɪdjʊəlɪ] ADV [a] (= *separately*) [*wrapped, numbered*] individuellement, séparément; **~ responsible for sth** individuellement *or* personnellement responsable de qch; **he spoke to them ~** il leur a parlé à chacun individuellement *or* personnellement; **they're all right ~** pris séparément ils sont très bien [b] (= *uniquely*) [*decorated*] de façon individualisée *or* personnalisée; **~ designed flats** appartements *mpl* individualisés *or* personnalisés

indivisibility [ˌɪndɪˌvɪzə'bɪlɪtɪ] N indivisibilité *f*

▼ **indivisible** [ˌɪndɪ'vɪzəbl] ADJ indivisible; (*Math, Philos*) insécable

indivisibly [ˌɪndɪ'vɪzəblɪ] ADV indivisiblement, indissolublement

Indo- ['ɪndəʊ] PREF indo- → **Indo-China**

Indo-China ['ɪndəʊ'tʃaɪnə] N l'Indochine *f*

Indo-Chinese ['ɪndəʊtʃaɪ'niːz] [1] ADJ indochinois [2] N Indochinois(e) *m(f)*

indoctrinate [ɪn'dɒktrɪneɪt] VT endoctriner; **they've all been ~d** ils sont tous endoctrinés; **to ~ sb with ideas** inculquer des idées à qn; **to ~ sb to do sth** conditionner qn à faire qch; **we have all been strongly ~d to value material things** nous avons tous été fortement conditionnés à valoriser les choses matérielles, on nous a fortement inculqué à tous le sens des choses matérielles; **to ~ sb with political ideas/with hatred of the enemy**

inculquer des doctrines politiques/la haine de l'ennemi à qn

indoctrination [ɪn,dɒktrɪˈneɪʃən] N endoctrinement *m*

Indo-European [ˈɪndəʊˌjʊərəˈpɪən] **1** ADJ indo-européen **2** N (*Ling*) indo-européen *m*

indolence [ˈɪndələns] N indolence *f*

indolent [ˈɪndələnt] ADJ indolent

indolently [ˈɪndələntlɪ] ADV indolemment

indomitable [ɪnˈdɒmɪtəbl] ADJ indomptable ; **her ~ spirit** sa ténacité à toute épreuve

indomitably [ɪnˈdɒmɪtəblɪ] ADV [*struggle, continue*] sans jamais se laisser abattre

Indonesia [,ɪndəʊˈniːzɪə] N l'Indonésie *f*

Indonesian [,ɪndəʊˈniːzɪən] **1** ADJ indonésien **2** N **a** Indonésien(ne) *m(f)* **b** (*Ling*) indonésien *m*

indoor [ˈɪndɔːʳ] ADJ [*activity, plant, shoes*] d'intérieur ; [*market, swimming pool, tennis court, cycle track*] couvert ; [*sports, athletics, championship*] en salle ; [*job*] (*in office*) dans un bureau ; (*at home*) à la maison ; (*Cine, Theat*) [*scene*] d'intérieur ; (*TV*) **~ aerial** antenne *f* intérieure ; **~ games** (*squash etc*) sports *mpl* pratiqués en salle ; (*table games*) jeux *mpl* de société ; **~ photography** photographie *f* d'intérieur

indoors [ɪnˈdɔːz] ADV [*stay*] (*in building*) à l'intérieur ; (*at home*) chez soi ; [*go, keep, spend time*] à l'intérieur ; **to go ~** rentrer ; **to take sb ~** faire entrer qn ; **I can't stay ~ forever** je ne peux pas rester enfermé tout le temps ; **bring plants ~ in October** en octobre, rentrer les plantes

indorse [ɪnˈdɔːs] VT = **endorse**

indrawn [ˈɪndrɔːn] ADJ (*lit*) **a long ~ breath** une longue inspiration ; (*fig*) **he received the news with ~ breath** l'annonce de la nouvelle lui a coupé le souffle ; **the crowd gave a gasp of ~ breath** la foule a retenu son souffle

indubitable [ɪnˈdjuːbɪtəbl] ADJ indubitable

indubitably [ɪnˈdjuːbɪtəblɪ] ADV indubitablement

induce [ɪnˈdjuːs] VT **a** (= *persuade*) persuader (**sb to do** qn de faire), inciter (**sb to do** qn à faire) ; **nothing would ever ~ me to go back there** rien ne pourrait me décider à retourner là-bas **b** (= *bring about*) [+ *reaction*] produire, provoquer ; [+ *sleep, illness, hypnosis*] provoquer ; (*Med*) **to ~ labour** déclencher l'accouchement (*artificiellement*) ; **~d labour** accouchement *m* déclenché ; **she was ~d** son accouchement a été déclenché **c** (*Philos* = *infer*) induire, conclure **d** (*Elec*) produire par induction

-induced [ɪnˈdjuːst] ADJ (*in compounds*) causé *or* provoqué par ; **drug-induced** [*sleep, fit*] causé *or* provoqué par les médicaments (*or* par la drogue *etc*) ; **self-induced** intentionnel, volontaire ; [*hypnosis*] autosuggéré

inducement [ɪnˈdjuːsmənt] N **a** (= *reward*) récompense *f* ; (*euph* = *bribe*) pot-de-vin *m* (*pej*) ; **and as an added ~ we are offering …** et comme avantage supplémentaire nous offrons … ; **he received £100 as an ~** il a reçu 100 livres à titre de gratification, il a reçu un pot-de-vin (*pej*) de 100 livres ; **financial/cash ~s** avantages *mpl* financiers/en espèces **b** (*NonC* = *reason for doing sth*) motivation *f* (**to do, for doing** pour faire), encouragement *m* (**to do, for doing** à faire)

induct [ɪnˈdʌkt] VT [+ *president*] établir dans ses fonctions, installer ; [+ *clergyman*] instituer, installer ; [+ *student*] accueillir (*au début de leur première année d'études*) ; (*US Mil*) incorporer ; **to ~ sb into the mysteries of …** initier qn aux mystères de …

induction [ɪnˈdʌkʃən] **1** N **a** (*NonC*) (*Elec, Philos*) induction *f* ; [*of sleep, hypnosis etc*] provocation *f* ; (*Med*) [*of labour*] déclenchement *m* (provoqué) **b** [*of clergyman, president*]

installation *f* ; [*of new staff members*] insertion *f*, intégration *f* ; (*US Mil*) incorporation *f* **2** COMP **► induction coil** N (*Elec*) bobine *f* d'induction **► induction course, induction training** N (*Ind*) stage *m* préparatoire (d'intégration), stage *m* d'accueil et d'orientation **► induction year** N (*Scol*) [*of teacher*] ≈ année *f* de stage

inductive [ɪnˈdʌktɪv] ADJ **a** (*Logic, Math*) [*reasoning, logic, process*] inductif **b** (*Elec*) [*load*] inductif ; [*current*] inducteur (-trice *f*)

indulge [ɪnˈdʌldʒ] **1** VT **a** (= *spoil*) [+ *person*] gâter ; (= *give way to, gratify*) [+ *person, desires, wishes, laziness*] céder à ; **he ~s her every whim** il lui passe tous ses caprices, il cède à tous ses caprices ; **on Saturdays he ~s his passion for football** le samedi il s'adonne à sa passion pour le football ; **~ yourself with a glass of chilled white wine** faites-vous plaisir avec un verre de vin blanc bien frais ; **go on, ~ yourself!** allez, laissez-vous tenter ! **b** (*Comm* = *extend for payment*) [+ *person, firm*] accorder des délais de paiement à **2** VI **to ~ in sth** se permettre qch ; **she ~d in a little harmless flirtation** elle s'est permis un petit flirt inoffensif ; **we can't afford to ~ in cheap speculation** nous ne pouvons pas nous complaire dans des suppositions gratuites ; **we don't ~ in such underhand tactics** nous ne nous abaissons pas à pratiquer ces tactiques sournoises

indulgence [ɪnˈdʌldʒəns] N **a** (*NonC* = *tolerance*) indulgence *f*, complaisance *f* **b** (= *luxury*) luxe *m* ; (= *treat, food*) gâterie *f* ; **he allowed himself the ~ of a day off work** il s'est offert le luxe de prendre un jour de congé ; **smoking was his one ~** la cigarette était son seul petit plaisir *or* son seul péché mignon **c** (*Rel*) indulgence *f*

indulgent [ɪnˈdʌldʒənt] ADJ (= *not severe*) indulgent (**to** envers, pour) ; (= *permissive*) indulgent (**to** envers, pour), complaisant (**to** à l'égard de, pour)

indulgently [ɪnˈdʌldʒəntlɪ] ADV avec indulgence

Indus [ˈɪndəs] N Indus *m*

industrial [ɪnˈdʌstrɪəl] **1** ADJ [*application, experience, psychology, research, training*] industriel ; [*expansion*] industriel, de l'industrie ; [*worker*] de l'industrie ; [*accident, injury, medicine*] du travail ; [*fabric, equipment*] pour l'industrie, industriel **2** COMP **► industrial action** N (*Brit*) action *f* revendicative ; (= *strike*) (mouvement *m* de) grève *f* ; **to take ~ action** lancer une action revendicative ; (= *go on strike*) se mettre en grève **► industrial arts** NPL (*US*) enseignement *m* technique **► industrial correspondent** N (*Brit Press, Rad, TV*) correspondant *m* industriel **► industrial design** N design *m* (industriel), esthétique *f* industrielle **► industrial designer** N concepteur-dessinateur *m* industriel, designer *m* **► industrial diamond** N diamant *m* naturel *or* industriel **► industrial disease** N maladie *f* professionnelle **► industrial dispute** N (*Brit*) conflit *m* social **► industrial engineering** N génie *m* industriel **► industrial espionage** N espionnage *m* industriel **► industrial estate** N (*Brit*) zone *f* industrielle **► industrial hygiene** N hygiène *f* du travail **► industrial injury benefit** N indemnité *f* d'accident du travail **► industrial insurance** N assurance *f* contre les accidents du travail, assurance *f* des salariés de l'industrie **► industrial park** N zone *f* industrielle **► industrial psychologist** N psychologue *mf* d'entreprise **► industrial rehabilitation** N réadaptation *f* fonctionnelle **► industrial relations** NPL relations *fpl* patronat-syndicats ; (= *field of study*) relations *fpl* sociales **► Industrial Revolution** N (*Hist*) révolution *f* industrielle **► industrial school** N (*US*) école *f* techni-

que **► industrial-strength** ADJ **a** (*Ind*) à usage industriel **b** (* *hum* = *strong*) [*elastic*] bien costaud ; [*face cream*] énergique ; **~-strength red wine** du gros rouge costaud *or* qui tache **► industrial tribunal** N ≈ conseil *m* de prud'hommes **► industrial unrest** N troubles *mpl* sociaux, agitation *f* ouvrière **► industrial vehicle** N véhicule *m* industriel **► industrial waste** N (*Brit*) déchets *mpl* industriels **► industrial wastes** NPL (*US*) = **industrial waste**

industrialism [ɪnˈdʌstrɪəlɪzəm] N industrialisme *m*

industrialist [ɪnˈdʌstrɪəlɪst] N industriel *m*

industrialization [ɪn,dʌstrɪəlaɪˈzeɪʃən] N industrialisation *f*

industrialize [ɪnˈdʌstrɪəlaɪz] VT industrialiser

industrious [ɪnˈdʌstrɪəs] ADJ assidu

industriously [ɪnˈdʌstrɪəslɪ] ADV assidûment, avec assiduité

industriousness [ɪnˈdʌstrɪəsnɪs] N = **industry 1b**

industry [ˈɪndəstrɪ] **1** N **a** industrie *f* ; **basic** *or* **heavy ~** industrie *f* lourde ; **the hotel ~** l'hôtellerie *f*, l'industrie *f* hôtelière ; **the tourist ~** le tourisme, l'industrie *f* touristique ; (*fig*) **psychoanalysis has become a real ~** la psychanalyse est devenue une véritable industrie → **coal, textile, trade b** (*NonC* = *industriousness*) assiduité *f*, application *f* ; **with great ~** avec beaucoup d'assiduité **2** COMP **► industry standard** N norme *f* industrielle **► industry-standard** ADJ aux normes industrielles

inebriate [ɪˈniːbrɪɪt] **1** N (*frm*) alcoolique *mf* **2** ADJ (*frm*) en état d'ébriété **3** [ɪˈniːbrɪeɪt] VT (*lit, fig*) enivrer, griser

inebriated [ɪˈniːbrɪ,eɪtɪd] ADJ (= *drunk*) (*lit*) ivre ; (*fig*) enivré, grisé (**by** de)

inebriation [ɪ,niːbrɪˈeɪʃən], **inebriety** [,ɪnɪˈbraɪətɪ] N état *m* d'ébriété

inedible [ɪnˈedɪbl] ADJ (= *not meant to be eaten*) non comestible ; (= *not fit to be eaten*) immangeable

ineducable [ɪnˈedjʊkəbl] ADJ inéducable

ineffable [ɪnˈefəbl] ADJ (*liter*) indicible (*liter*), ineffable

ineffably [ɪnˈefəblɪ] ADV (*liter*) ineffablement (*liter*)

ineffaceable [,ɪnɪˈfeɪsəbl] ADJ ineffaçable, indélébile

ineffective [,ɪnɪˈfektɪv] ADJ inefficace (**against sth** contre qch, **in doing sth** pour faire qch)

ineffectively [,ɪnɪˈfektɪvlɪ] ADV [*use*] inefficacement ; [*try*] vainement, en vain

ineffectiveness [,ɪnɪˈfektɪvnɪs] N inefficacité *f*

ineffectual [,ɪnɪˈfektjʊəl] ADJ = **ineffective**

ineffectually [,ɪnɪˈfektjʊəlɪ] ADV inefficacement

inefficacious [,ɪnefɪˈkeɪʃəs] ADJ inefficace

inefficacy [ɪnˈefɪkəsɪ] N inefficacité *f*

inefficiency [,ɪnɪˈfɪʃənsɪ] N [*of action, machine, measures*] inefficacité *f*, insuffisance *f* ; [*of person*] incompétence *f*, manque *m* d'efficacité

inefficient [,ɪnɪˈfɪʃənt] ADJ [*person, measures, drug*] inefficace ; [*machine, factory*] peu performant

inefficiently [,ɪnɪˈfɪʃəntlɪ] ADV inefficacement ; **work done ~** travail exécuté de façon inefficace

inelastic [,ɪnɪˈlæstɪk] ADJ **a** [*material*] non élastique **b** (*fig*) [*system, regulations*] rigide ; (*Econ*) [*demand, supply*] non élastique **c** (*Phys*) inélastique

inelegant [ɪnˈelɪgənt] ADJ inélégant, peu élégant

inelegantly [ɪnˈelɪgəntlɪ] ADV inélégamment

ineligibility [ɪn,elɪdʒə'bɪlɪtɪ] N (gen) inéligibilité f; (Fin) irrecevabilité f

ineligible [ɪn'elɪdʒəbl] ADJ [candidate] inéligible; **he's ~ for social security benefits** il n'a pas droit aux prestations de la Sécurité sociale; **he's ~ to vote** il n'a pas le droit de vote; **~ for military service** inapte au service militaire

ineluctable [,ɪnɪ'lʌktəbl] ADJ (frm) inéluctable, inévitable

inept [ɪ'nept] ADJ (= incompetent) incompétent; (= inappropriate) [remark] déplacé; **the team's ~ performance** la médiocre performance de l'équipe

ineptitude [ɪ'neptɪtjuːd] N (= incompetence) incompétence f; (= inappropriateness) [of remark] caractère m déplacé

ineptly [ɪ'neptlɪ] ADV ineptement

ineptness [ɪ'neptnɪs] N = **ineptitude**

inequality [,ɪnɪ'kwɒlɪtɪ] N inégalité f

inequitable [ɪn'ekwɪtəbl] ADJ inéquitable, injuste

inequity [ɪn'ekwɪtɪ] N injustice f, iniquité f

ineradicable [,ɪnɪ'rædɪkəbl] ADJ indéracinable, tenace

inert [ɪ'nɜːt] ① ADJ (gen, also Chem, Phys) inerte; (= dull) morne ② COMP ► **inert gas** N gaz m inerte

inertia [ɪ'nɜːʃə] ① N ⓐ [of person] inertie f, apathie f ⓑ (Chem, Phys) inertie f ② COMP ► **inertia-reel seat belts** NPL (Aut) ceintures fpl (de sécurité) à enrouleurs ► **inertia selling** N (Brit Comm) vente f forcée par correspondance

inescapable [,ɪnɪs'keɪpəbl] ADJ inéluctable, inévitable

inessential [,ɪnɪ'senʃəl] ADJ superflu, non-essentiel

inestimable [ɪn'estɪməbl] ADJ [gift, friendship] inestimable, inappréciable; [fortune, work] incalculable

inevitability [ɪn,evɪtə'bɪlɪtɪ] N caractère m inévitable

inevitable [ɪn'evɪtəbl] ① ADJ [result] inévitable, inéluctable; [day, event] fatal; **it seems that civil war has become ~** il semble que la guerre civile soit devenue inévitable or inéluctable; **it's ~ that new recruits will make errors at first** les nouvelles recrues feront inévitablement or fatalement des erreurs au début; **I'm afraid it's ~** j'ai bien peur que ce soit inévitable or inéluctable; **the tourist had the ~ camera** le touriste avait l'inévitable or l'incontournable appareil-photo ② N **the ~** l'inévitable m

inevitably [ɪn'evɪtəblɪ] ADV inévitablement

inexact [,ɪnɪg'zækt] ADJ inexact

inexactitude [,ɪnɪg'zæktɪtjuːd] N inexactitude f

inexactly [,ɪnɪg'zæktlɪ] ADV inexactement

inexcusable [,ɪnɪks'kjuːzəbl] ADJ inexcusable, impardonnable; **it is ~ that ...** il est inexcusable que ... (+ subj); **it would be ~ to make such a mistake** il serait inexcusable de faire une telle erreur; **that was ~ of you** c'était inexcusable or impardonnable de votre part

inexcusably [,ɪnɪks'kjuːzəblɪ] ADV [say, overlook, neglect] de façon inexcusable or impardonnable; **~ lazy/careless** d'une paresse/d'une négligence inexcusable

inexhaustible [,ɪnɪg'zɔːstəbl] ADJ inépuisable

inexorable [ɪn'eksərəbl] ADJ inexorable

inexorably [ɪn'eksərəblɪ] ADV inexorablement

inexpedient [,ɪnɪks'piːdɪənt] ADJ [action, decision, policy] inopportun, malavisé

inexpensive [,ɪnɪks'pensɪv] ADJ bon marché inv, pas cher

inexpensively [,ɪnɪks'pensɪvlɪ] ADV [buy] à bon marché, à bon compte; [live] à peu de frais

► LANGUAGE IN USE: **inferior** 26.3

inexperience [,ɪnɪks'pɪərɪəns] N inexpérience f, manque m d'expérience

inexperienced [,ɪnɪks'pɪərɪənst] ADJ [driver, pilot, teacher, doctor] inexpérimenté; **I am very ~ in matters of this kind** j'ai très peu d'expérience dans ce genre de choses; **doctors are ~ in dealing with this disease** les médecins ont peu d'expérience dans le traitement de cette maladie; **he's too ~ to be president** il manque trop d'expérience pour être président; **to be sexually ~** manquer d'expérience sexuelle

inexpert [ɪn'eksp3ːt] ADJ inexpert, maladroit (**in** en)

inexpertly [ɪn'eksp3ːtlɪ] ADV maladroitement

inexplicable [,ɪnɪks'plɪkəbl] ADJ inexplicable

inexplicably [,ɪnɪks'plɪkəblɪ] ADV inexplicablement

inexpressible [,ɪnɪks'presəbl] ADJ inexprimable

inexpressive [,ɪnɪks'presɪv] ADJ inexpressif

inextinguishable [,ɪnɪks'tɪŋgwɪʃəbl] ADJ [fire] impossible à éteindre or à maîtriser; [passion, enthusiasm] indéfectible; [thirst, laughter] inextinguible

in extremis [ɪnɪk'striːmɪs] ADV (frm) in extremis

inextricable [,ɪnɪks'trɪkəbl] ADJ inextricable

inextricably [,ɪnɪks'trɪkəblɪ] ADV inextricablement

infallibility [ɪn,fælə'bɪlɪtɪ] N (also Rel) infaillibilité f

infallible [ɪn'fæləbl] ADJ infaillible

infallibly [ɪn'fæləblɪ] ADV ⓐ (= without error) [pronounce, correct] infailliblement ⓑ (= always) infailliblement, immanquablement

infamous ['ɪnfəməs] ADJ [person, place] tristement célèbre (**for sth** pour qch); [incident] notoire; [case, trial, conduct] infâme; **his ~ temper** son mauvais caractère notoire

infamy ['ɪnfəmɪ] N infamie f

infancy ['ɪnfənsɪ] N ⓐ (lit) petite enfance f, bas âge m; (Jur) minorité f; **early ~** toute petite enfance f; **child still in ~** enfant mf encore en bas âge; **a quarter of these children die in ~** un quart de ces enfants meurent en bas âge ⓑ (fig) enfance f, débuts mpl; **when radio was still in its ~** quand la radio en était encore à ses débuts or à ses premiers balbutiements

infant ['ɪnfənt] ① N (= newborn) nouveau-né m; (= baby) bébé m, nourrisson m; (= young child) petit(e) enfant m(f), enfant mf en bas âge; (Jur) mineur(e) m(f); (Brit Scol) enfant mf, petit(e) m(f) (de quatre à sept ans) ② COMP [disease] infantile; (fig) [industry, movement, organization] naissant ► **infant class** N (Brit) ≈ cours m préparatoire; **the ~ classes** les classes fpl enfantines, les petites classes fpl ► **infant education** N enseignement m des petits (entre quatre et sept ans) ► **infant mortality** N mortalité f infantile ► **infant school** N (Brit) ≈ cours m préparatoire et première année de cours élémentaire (entre quatre et sept ans) ► **infant welfare clinic** N centre m médico-social pédiatrique

infanta [ɪn'fæntə] N infante f

infante [ɪn'fæntɪ] N infant m

infanticide [ɪn'fæntɪsaɪd] N (= crime) infanticide m; (frm = killer) infanticide mf

infantile ['ɪnfəntaɪl] ① ADJ (gen, Med, fig pej) infantile ② COMP ► **infantile paralysis**† (= polio) paralysie f infantile†

infantilism [ɪn'fæntɪ,lɪzəm] N (Psych) infantilisme m

infantilize [ɪn'fæntɪ,laɪz] VT infantiliser

infantry ['ɪnfəntrɪ] N (NonC: Mil) infanterie f (NonC), fantassins mpl

infantryman ['ɪnfəntrɪmən] N fantassin m → **light²**

infarct ['ɪnfɑːkt] N (Med) infarctus m

infarction [ɪn'fɑːkʃən] N (Med) ⓐ (= dead tissue) = **infarct** ⓑ (= forming of dead tissue) infarcissement m

infatuate [ɪn'fætjuet] VT (gen pass) tourner la tête à; **to be ~d with** [+ person] être fou d'amour pour; [+ idea] avoir la tête pleine de, être engoué de; **to become ~d with** [+ person] s'enticher de; [+ idea] s'engouer pour; **as soon as he met her he was ~d** il s'est entiché d'elle dès leur première rencontre

infatuation [ɪn,fætjʊ'eɪʃən] N (with person) amour m obsessionnel; (with idea, activity) engouement m (**with sth** pour qch)

infect [ɪn'fekt] VT ⓐ (lit) [+ person, wound] infecter; [+ air, well, blood] contaminer; **his wound became ~ed** sa blessure s'infecta; **a virus spread by ~ed blood** un virus qui se transmet par du sang contaminé; **to ~ sb with a disease** transmettre or communiquer une maladie à qn; **to be ~ed with malaria/hepatitis** être atteint du paludisme/de l'hépatite; **~ed with HIV** séropositif ⓑ (fig) **for a moment I was ~ed by her fear** pendant un moment elle m'a communiqué sa peur; **you can't help being ~ed with his passion for the music** sa passion pour la musique est véritablement contagieuse

infection [ɪn'fekʃən] N ⓐ (lit) [of person, wound] infection f; [of air, well, blood] contamination f; **there's some ~ in the wound** la blessure est légèrement infectée; **she has a slight ~** elle a une légère infection; **a throat ~** une angine; **an ear ~** une otite ⓑ (fig) contagion f

infectious [ɪn'fekʃəs] ① ADJ ⓐ (Med) [disease] (= transmissible) contagieux; (= caused by germs) infectieux ⓑ (fig) [person, laugh, enthusiasm, rhythm] contagieux ② COMP ► **infectious hepatitis** N hépatite f infectieuse

infectiousness [ɪn'fekʃəsnɪs] N ⓐ (Med) nature f infectieuse ⓑ (fig) contagion f

infective [ɪn'fektɪv] ADJ [disease] (= transmissible) contagieux; (= caused by germs) infectieux; [agent] infectieux

infelicitous [,ɪnfɪ'lɪsɪtəs] ADJ (frm) malheureux, fâcheux

infelicity [,ɪnfɪ'lɪsɪtɪ] N (frm) ⓐ (NonC = misfortune) malheur m ⓑ (= tactless act, remark) maladresse f

infer [ɪn'fɜː'] VT ⓐ (= conclude) déduire, conclure (**that** que); **can we ~ from this that you disagree?** pouvons-nous en déduire or en conclure que vous n'êtes pas d'accord? ⓑ (* = imply) laisser entendre, insinuer; **what are you ~ing?** qu'est-ce que vous insinuez?

inference ['ɪnfərəns] N ⓐ (= conclusion) déduction f, conclusion f; **by ~** par déduction; **the ~ is that he is unwilling to help us** on doit en conclure qu'il n'est pas disposé à nous aider; **to draw an ~ from sth** tirer une conclusion de qch ⓑ (* = implication) insinuation f

inferential [,ɪnfə'renʃəl] ADJ [method] déductif; [proof] obtenu par déduction

inferentially [,ɪnfə'renʃəlɪ] ADV par déduction

▼ **inferior** [ɪn'fɪərɪə'] ① ADJ ⓐ [person, status, quality] inférieur (-eure f) (**to sb** à qn, **in sth** en qch); [product] de qualité inférieure; [service, work] de second ordre; **he makes me feel ~** il me donne un sentiment d'infériorité ⓑ (Jur) [court] ≈ de première instance ⓒ (Bot) infère ⓓ (Typ) **~ letter** indice m ② N (in quality, social standing) inférieur m, -eure f; (in authority, rank: also Mil) subalterne mf, subordonné(e) m(f)

inferiority [ɪn,fɪərɪ'ɒrɪtɪ] ① N infériorité f (**to** par rapport à) ② COMP ► **inferiority complex** N complexe m d'infériorité

infernal [ɪn'fɜːnl] ADJ ⓐ (* = terrible) [noise] infernal; [heat, weather] abominable; [car, computer] satané; **it's an ~ nuisance** c'est vraiment empoisonnant ⓑ (*Myth, Rel, liter*) [*regions*] infernal ; [*flames*] de l'enfer

infernally* [ɪnˈfɜːnəlɪ] ADV [*difficult*] abominablement, épouvantablement ; **it is ~ hot** il fait une chaleur infernale *or* abominable

inferno [ɪnˈfɜːnəʊ] N ⓐ **an ~** ◊ **a blazing ~** un brasier ⓑ (*liter* = *hell*) enfer *m*

infertile [ɪnˈfɜːtaɪl] ADJ [*person, animal, land, soil*] stérile

infertility [ˌɪnfɜːˈtɪlɪtɪ] ① N [*of person, animal, land, soil*] stérilité *f* ② COMP ► **infertility clinic** N *service de consultation pour problèmes de stérilité* ► **infertility treatment** N (*Med*) traitement *m* de la stérilité

infest [ɪnˈfest] VT ⓐ (*lit*) [*pest, vermin*] infester ; **~ed with** infesté de ⓑ (*fig*) [*drugs, bandits*] envahir

infestation [ˌɪnfesˈteɪʃən] N infestation *f*

infidel [ˈɪnfɪdəl] ① N (*liter*) (*Hist, Rel*) infidèle† *mf* ; (*Rel*) incroyant(e) *m(f)* ② ADJ infidèle†, incroyant

infidelity [ˌɪnfɪˈdelɪtɪ] N infidélité *f* ; (*Jur*) **divorce on the grounds of ~** divorce *m* pour cause d'adultère

infighting [ˈɪnˌfaɪtɪŋ] N ⓐ (*within group*) conflits *mpl or* querelles *fpl* internes, luttes *fpl* intestines (**within** au sein de) ⓑ (*Mil*) (*hand-to-hand*) corps à corps *m* ; (*close-range*) combat *m* rapproché ; (*Boxing*) corps à corps *m*

infill [ˈɪnfɪl] N (*Constr, Geol*) remplissage *m*

infiltrate [ˈɪnfɪlˌtreɪt] ① VI [*troops, person, light, liquid, ideas*] infiltrer (**into** dans) ② VT [+ *liquid*] infiltrer (**into** dans, **through** à travers) ; (*Pol*) [+ *group, organization*] infiltrer, noyauter ; (*Mil*) [*troops*] [+ *territory, city, enemy lines*] s'infiltrer dans ; **to ~ troops into a territory** envoyer des troupes s'infiltrer dans un territoire

infiltration [ˌɪnfɪlˈtreɪʃən] N (*Pol, Mil, Med*) infiltration *f* (**into sth** dans qch)

infiltrator [ˈɪnfɪlˌtreɪtə] N (*inside organization, country*) agent *m* infiltré ; **Western ~s** agents *mpl* de l'Occident

infinite [ˈɪnfɪnɪt] ① ADJ (*gen*) [*number, patience, care*] infini, illimité ; [*possibilities*] illimité ; (*Math, Philos, Rel*) infini ; **the choice is ~** le choix est illimité ; **an ~ variety of landscapes** une variété infinie de paysages ; **God in his ~ mercy** Dieu dans son infinie miséricorde ; **it gave her ~ pleasure** cela lui a fait infiniment plaisir ; (*iro*) **the organizers, in their ~ wisdom, planned the two events for the same day** les organisateurs, dans leur infinie sagesse, ont programmé les deux manifestations le même jour ; **he seemed to have an ~ capacity for cruelty** sa cruauté semblait illimitée ② N infini *m*

infinitely [ˈɪnfɪnɪtlɪ] ADV infiniment

infiniteness [ˈɪnfɪnɪtnɪs] N = **infinity c**

infinitesimal [ˌɪnfɪnɪˈtesɪməl] ADJ (*gen*) [*amount, majority etc*] infinitésimal, infime ; (*Math*) infinitésimal

infinitesimally [ˌɪnfɪnɪˈtesɪmlɪ] ADV infiniment

infinitive [ɪnˈfɪnɪtɪv] (*Gram*) ① N infinitif *m* ; **in the ~** à l'infinitif ② ADJ infinitif

infinitude [ɪnˈfɪnɪtjuːd] N **an ~ of** une infinité de

infinity [ɪnˈfɪnɪtɪ] N ⓐ (= *that which is infinite*) infinité *f*, infini *m* ; **in time and space or in ~** dans le temps et dans l'espace ou dans l'infini *or* l'infinité *f* ; (*fig*) **an ~ of reasons/details/possibilities** une infinité de raisons/détails/possibilités ⓒ (= *infiniteness*) infinitude *f* ; **the ~ of God** l'infinitude *f* de Dieu ⓓ (*Math*) infini *m* ; **to ~** à l'infini

infirm [ɪnˈfɜːm] ① ADJ ⓐ (= *sick*) infirme ⓑ (*liter*) **~ of purpose** irrésolu, indécis ② **the infirm** NPL les infirmes *mpl* ; **the old**

and the ~ les personnes *fpl* âgées et les infirmes *mpl*

infirmary [ɪnˈfɜːmərɪ] N (= *hospital*) hôpital *m* ; (*in school etc*) infirmerie *f*

infirmity [ɪnˈfɜːmɪtɪ] N infirmité *f* ; **her grandmother's increasing ~** l'infirmité croissante de sa grand-mère ; **she bears these infirmities with fortitude** elle supporte ces infirmités avec courage

infix [ˈɪnfɪks] ① VT [+ *habit, idea*] inculquer (**in** à), implanter (**in** dans) ; (*Ling*) insérer (**in** dans) ② [ˈɪnfɪks] N (*Ling*) infixe *m*

inflame [ɪnˈfleɪm] VT ⓐ (*fig*) [+ *courage*] enflammer ; [+ *anger, desire, hatred, discord*] attiser ⓑ (*Med*) enflammer ⓒ (= *set alight*) enflammer, mettre le feu à

inflammable [ɪnˈflæməbl] ADJ ⓐ [*liquid, substance*] inflammable ⓑ (*fig*) [*situation*] explosif

inflammation [ˌɪnfləˈmeɪʃən] N (*Med, fig*) inflammation *f*

inflammatory [ɪnˈflæmətərɪ] ADJ ⓐ [*speech, remark, language*] incendiaire ⓑ (*Med*) inflammatoire

inflatable [ɪnˈfleɪtəbl] ① ADJ [*dinghy, mattress*] pneumatique, gonflable ; [*toy, rubber ring*] gonflable ② N (*gen*) objet *m* (*or* jouet *m etc*) gonflable ; (= *dinghy*) canot *m* pneumatique

inflate [ɪnˈfleɪt] ① VT ⓐ (*lit*) [+ *tyre, balloon*] gonfler (**with** de) ; (*Med*) [+ *lung*] dilater ⓑ (*fig*) [+ *prices*] gonfler, faire monter ; [+ *bill, account*] gonfler, charger ② VI [*tyre, balloon, air bag*] se gonfler

inflated [ɪnˈfleɪtɪd] ADJ ⓐ (*lit*) [*tyre, balloon*] gonflé ; [*lung*] dilaté ⓑ (*fig*) [*price, cost, salary, insurance claim*] excessif ; **~ with pride** bouffi d'orgueil ; **he has an ~ ego** il a une très haute opinion de lui-même ; **he has an ~ sense of his own importance** il se fait une idée exagérée de sa propre importance

inflation [ɪnˈfleɪʃən] ① N ⓐ (*Econ*) inflation *f* ; [*of prices*] hausse *f* ⓑ [*of tyre etc*] gonflement *m* ② COMP ► **inflation-proof** ADJ protégé contre l'inflation ► **inflation rate** N taux *m* d'inflation

inflationary [ɪnˈfleɪʃnərɪ] ADJ inflationniste

inflationist [ɪnˈfleɪʃənɪst] N partisan(e) *m(f)* d'une politique inflationniste

inflect [ɪnˈflekt] ① VT ⓐ (*Ling*) [+ *word*] mettre une désinence à ; (= *conjugate*) conjuguer ; (= *decline*) décliner ; **~ed form** forme *f* fléchie ; **~ed vowel** voyelle *f* infléchie ⓑ (= *modulate*) [+ *voice*] moduler ; (*Mus*) [+ *note*] altérer ⓒ (*Geom, Opt* = *bend*) infléchir, dévier ② (*Ling*) **a verb which ~s** un verbe flexionnel *or* qui prend des désinences ; **does this noun ~ in the plural?** ce nom prend-il la marque du pluriel ? ; **an ~ing language** une langue désinentielle *or* flexionnelle

inflection [ɪnˈflekʃən] N ⓐ (= *modulation*) [*of voice, tone*] inflexion *f* ; [*of note*] altération *f* ⓑ (*NonC: Ling*) [*of word*] flexion *f* ; **the ~ of nouns/verbs** la flexion nominale/verbale ; **vowel ~** inflexion *f* vocalique ⓒ (*Ling* = *affix*) désinence *f* ⓓ (= *curving*) [*of body*] inflexion *f*, inclination *f* ; (*Geom, Opt*) inflexion *f*, déviation *f*

inflectional [ɪnˈflekʃənəl] ADJ (*Ling*) flexionnel ; **an ~ ending** une désinence

inflexibility [ɪnˌfleksɪˈbɪlɪtɪ] N ⓐ (*lit*) rigidité *f* ⓑ (*fig*) inflexibilité *f*, rigidité *f*

inflexible [ɪnˈfleksəbl] ADJ ⓐ (*lit*) [*person*] inflexible ; [*object*] rigide ⓑ (*fig*) [*system, policy*] rigide ; [*person, rule, position*] inflexible ; [*attitude*] rigide, inflexible

inflexion [ɪnˈflekʃən] N = **inflection**

inflict [ɪnˈflɪkt] VT [+ *punishment, torture, fine, defeat*] infliger (**on** à) ; [+ *pain, suffering*] faire subir, infliger (**on** à) ; **to ~ damage** causer des dégâts ; **to ~ a wound on sb** infliger une blessure à qn ; **the enemy ~ed heavy casualties**

on us l'ennemi nous a infligé de lourdes pertes ; **to ~ one's company/one's beliefs on sb** imposer sa compagnie/ses croyances à qn

infliction [ɪnˈflɪkʃən] N (*NonC*) ⓐ **another operation would mean further ~ of pain on him** une autre opération reviendrait à lui infliger de nouvelles douleurs ⓑ (= *misfortune*) affliction *f*

in-flight [ˈɪnˌflaɪt] ADJ [*refuelling*] en vol ; [*film, entertainment*] proposé pendant le vol ; **~ meal** repas *m* servi pendant le vol ; **~ magazine** magazine *m* de voyage (*destiné aux passagers aériens*)

inflow [ˈɪnfləʊ] ① N ⓐ [*of water*] afflux *m*, arrivée *f* ⓑ = **influx a** ⓒ [*of capital*] entrée *f* ② COMP ► **inflow pipe** N tuyau *m* d'arrivée ; **water-~ pipe** arrivée *f or* adduction *f* d'eau

influence [ˈɪnfluəns] ① N (*gen*) influence *f* (**on** sur) ; **under his ~** sous son influence ; **under the ~ of his advisers, he ...** influencé par ses conseillers, il ... ; **under the ~ of drink/drugs** sous l'effet *or* l'empire de la boisson/des drogues ; (*Jur*) **convicted of driving under the ~ of drink** condamné pour conduite en état d'ébriété *or* d'ivresse ; **he was a bit under the ~*** il était pompette* ; **her book had *or* was a great ~ on him** son livre a eu beaucoup d'influence sur lui *or* l'a beaucoup influencé ; **he has got ~** il a de l'influence ; **I've got a lot of ~ with her** j'ai beaucoup d'influence *or* d'ascendant sur elle ; **to use one's ~ with sb to get sth** user de son influence auprès de qn pour obtenir qch ; **she used her ~ to persuade them to accept the deal** elle a usé de son influence pour les persuader d'accepter le marché ; **to exert ~ over sb** exercer une influence sur qn ; **he denies having exerted any political ~ over them** il a nié avoir exercé la moindre influence politique sur eux ; **I shall bring all my ~ *or* every ~ to bear on him** j'essaierai d'user de toute mon influence pour le persuader ; **a man of ~** un homme influent ; **she is a good ~ in the school/on the pupils** elle a *or* exerce une bonne influence dans l'établissement/sur les élèves ② VT [+ *attitude, behaviour, decision, person*] influencer ; **don't be ~d by him** ne vous laissez pas influencer par lui ; **he's easily ~d** il est très influençable, il se laisse facilement influencer ; **her music is strongly ~d by jazz** sa musique est fortement influencée par le jazz ; **the artist has been ~d by Leonardo da Vinci** cet artiste a été influencé par Léonard de Vinci ; **your diet may ~ your risk of getting cancer** votre alimentation peut influer sur les risques que vous avez de développer un cancer ③ COMP ► **influence peddling** N trafic *m* d'influence

influential [ˌɪnfluˈenʃəl] ADJ influent ; **to be ~** avoir de l'influence ; **she has ~ friends** elle a des amis influents *or* haut placés

influenza [ˌɪnfluˈenzə] N (*NonC*) grippe *f* ; **he's got ~** il a la grippe

influx [ˈɪnflʌks] N ⓐ [*of people*] afflux *m*, flot *m* ; [*of new ideas, attitudes*] flot *m*, flux *m* ; **a great ~ of people into the neighbourhood** un gros afflux d'arrivants dans le voisinage ; **the ~ of tourists/foreign workers** l'afflux *m or* le flot de touristes/de travailleurs étrangers ⓑ = **inflow 1a** ⓒ (= *meeting place of rivers*) confluent *m*

info* [ˈɪnfəʊ] N (*NonC*) (ABBR = **information 1a**) (*gen*) renseignements *mpl* ; (= *tips*) tuyaux* *mpl* (**about** sur)

infobahn [ˈɪnfəʊbɑːn] N autoroute *f* de l'information

infomercial [ˈɪnfəʊmɜːʃəl] N (*US*) (*for product*) publireportage *m* ; (*Pol*) *émission où un candidat présente son programme électoral*

▼ **inform** [ɪnˈfɔːm] ① VT ⓐ (*gen*) informer (**of** de) ; (= *warn*) avertir (**of** de) ; **to ~ sb of sth**

informer qn de qch, faire savoir qch à qn; **"he'd like a word with you", she ~ed me** «il aimerait vous dire un mot» m'a-t-elle dit; **we were ~ed that the factory was to close** nous avons été informés que l'usine allait fermer; **I should like to be ~ed as soon as he arrives** j'aimerais être informé or averti dès qu'il sera là, prévenez-moi dès qu'il arrivera; **keep me ~ed** tenez-moi au courant; **I'd like to be kept ~ed of progress** j'aimerais que l'on me tienne au courant de l'avancement des choses; **they tried to keep us fully ~ed** ils ont essayé de nous tenir pleinement informés; **why was I not ~ed?** pourquoi ne m'a-t-on rien dit?, pourquoi n'ai-je pas été informé?; **we must ~ the police** il faut avertir la police; **the public should be ~ed about the dangers of these drugs** il faudrait informer le public or le public devrait être informé des dangers de ces drogues; **she's better ~ed than most of her colleagues** elle est mieux informée que la plupart de ses collègues; **he was not well ~ed about what had been happening** il était mal informé or il n'était pas bien au courant de ce qui s'était passé → **informed**
[b] (= contribute to) contribuer à; (= influence) influencer; **his writing is ~ed by a sound knowledge of philosophy** ses écrits portent la marque d'une solide connaissance de la philosophie
[2] VI **to ~ against** or **on sb** dénoncer qn

informal [ɪnˈfɔːməl] ADJ [a] (= relaxed, natural) [person] décontracté, sans façons; [manner, tone, style, atmosphere] décontracté
[b] (Ling) [language, expression] familier
[c] (= unceremonious) [party, meal, visit] tout simple, sans cérémonie; [clothes] décontracté; **it was a very ~ occasion** c'était une occasion dénuée de toute formalité or de tout protocole; **it's just an ~ get-together between friends** ce sera à la bonne franquette; **it will be quite ~** ce sera sans cérémonie or en toute simplicité; **"dress ~"** «tenue de ville»
[d] (= unofficial) [talks, meeting] non officiel, informel; [agreement, acceptance, announcement, communication, visit] non officiel, officieux; [invitation] non officiel, dénué de caractère officiel; [group] à caractère non officiel; **there was an ~ arrangement that ...** il y avait une entente officieuse selon laquelle ...

informality [ˌɪnfɔːˈmælɪtɪ] N [of visit, welcome etc] simplicité f, absence f de formalité; [of style, language] simplicité f; [of arrangement, agreement, occasion] caractère m informel or officieux; **the ~ of his manners** (gen) son naturel; (pej) les familiarités qu'il se permet

informally [ɪnˈfɔːməlɪ] ADV [a] (= in relaxed manner) [talk, dress] de façon décontractée
[b] (= unceremoniously, unofficially) [invite] sans cérémonie; [meet, discuss, agree, arrange] officieusement [c] (Ling) [call] familièrement

informant [ɪnˈfɔːmənt] N [a] (gen, Press) informateur m, -trice f; **my ~ tells me ...** mon informateur me dit que ...; **who is your ~?** de qui tenez-vous cette information?, quelles sont vos sources? [b] (= informer: also **police ~**) indicateur m, -trice f (de la police); **a mafia boss turned police ~** un parrain de la mafia devenu indicateur or informateur [c] (Ling: also **native ~**) informateur m, -trice f

informatics [ˌɪnfəˈmætɪks] N (NonC) informatique f

▼ **information** [ˌɪnfəˈmeɪʃən] [1] N [a] (NonC) (= facts) renseignements mpl, information(s) f(pl); **a piece of ~** un renseignement, une information; **to give sb ~ about** or **on sth/sb** renseigner qn sur qch/qn; **to get ~ about** or **on sth/sb** se renseigner sur qch/qn, obtenir des informations sur qch/qn; **to ask for ~ about** or **on sth/sb** demander des renseignements or des informations sur qch/qn; **I need more ~ about it** il me faut des renseigne-

ments plus complets or des informations plus complètes; **we are collecting as much ~ as we can on that organization** nous sommes en train de réunir le plus d'informations or de renseignements possible(s) sur cette organisation; **we have no ~ on that point** nous n'avons aucune information or aucun renseignement là-dessus; **until more ~ is available** jusqu'à ce qu'il y ait de plus amples renseignements; **have you any ~ about the accident?** avez-vous des renseignements or des détails sur l'accident?; **the police are seeking ~ about ...** la police recherche des renseignements sur ..., la police enquête sur ...; **I have ~ that they are being held captive near the border** j'ai des informations selon lesquelles ils seraient retenus en captivité près de la frontière; **our ~ is that he has refused to talk to the press** selon nos renseignements il aurait refusé de parler à la presse; **my ~ is that the President will be making a statement this afternoon** selon mes renseignements le président fera une déclaration cet après-midi; **the police had acted on inadequate ~** la police avait agi à partir d'informations insuffisantes; **I enclose for your ~ a copy of ...** à titre d'information je joins une copie de ...; (on document) **"for your ~"** «à titre d'information», «à titre indicatif»; **for your ~, he ...** (gen) nous vous signalons or informons qu'il ...; (iro) au cas où vous ne le sauriez pas (encore), il ... → **tourist**
[b] (US Telec) (service m des) renseignements mpl
[c] (pl **informations**) (Jur) (= denunciation) dénonciation f; (= charge) plainte f; **to lay an ~ against sb** (= bring charge against) déposer plainte contre qn; (= denounce) dénoncer qn à la police
[2] COMP ▶ **information bureau** N bureau m d'informations or de renseignements ▶ **information content** N contenu m informationnel ▶ **information desk** N accueil m ▶ **information exchange** N centre m d'échange d'informations ▶ **information highway** N = **information superhighway** ▶ **information office** N = **information bureau** ▶ **information officer** N responsable mf de l'information ▶ **information overload** N surinformation f ▶ **information pack** N (Brit) documentation f, ensemble m documentaire ▶ **information processing** N informatique f, traitement m de l'information ▶ **information retrieval** N recherche f documentaire ▶ **information retrieval system** N système m de recherche documentaire ▶ **information science** N informatique f ▶ **information scientist** N informaticien(ne) m(f) ▶ **information service** N bureau m d'informations or de renseignements ▶ **information superhighway** N autoroute f de l'information ▶ **information technology** N informatique f, technologie f de l'information ▶ **information theory** N théorie f de l'information

informational [ˌɪnfəˈmeɪʃənl] ADJ [needs, meeting, documentary, programme] d'information

informative [ɪnˈfɔːmətɪv] ADJ [book, meeting, article, talk] instructif; **the talk was very ~ about ...** l'exposé était très instructif quant à or au sujet de ...

informatory [ɪnˈfɔːmətərɪ] ADJ (Bridge) d'information; **~ double** contre m d'appel

informed [ɪnˈfɔːmd] ADJ [person] informé; [debate, discussion] approfondi; [opinion, criticism, point of view] fondé; **an ~ decision** une décision prise en connaissance de cause; **to make an ~ choice** choisir en connaissance de cause; **~ sources** sources fpl bien informées; **~ observers** observateurs mpl bien informés; **there is a body of ~ opinion which claims that there is ...** certains milieux bien informés prétendent qu'il y a ..., selon certains milieux bien informés, il y aurait ...; **an ~ guess** une

hypothèse fondée sur la connaissance des faits → **inform**

informer [ɪnˈfɔːmər] N dénonciateur m, -trice f, délateur m, -trice f; **police ~** indicateur m, informateur m (de la police); **to turn ~** (on specific occasion) dénoncer or vendre ses complices; (long-term) devenir indicateur or informateur

infotainment [ˌɪnfəʊˈteɪnmənt] N info-spectacle m, info-divertissement m

infraction [ɪnˈfrækʃən] N [of law, rule] infraction f (of à)

infra dig* [ˈɪnfrəˈdɪg] ADJ au-dessous de sa (or ma etc) dignité, indigne or au-dessous de soi (or moi etc), déshonorant

infrared [ˈɪnfrəˈred] ADJ infrarouge

infrasonic [ˌɪnfrəˈsɒnɪk] ADJ infrasonore

infrastructure [ˈɪnfrəˌstrʌktʃər] N infrastructure f

infrequency [ɪnˈfriːkwənsɪ] N rareté f

infrequent [ɪnˈfriːkwənt] ADJ peu fréquent

infrequently [ɪnˈfriːkwəntlɪ] ADV peu souvent, peu fréquemment; **not ~** assez fréquemment

infringe [ɪnˈfrɪndʒ] [1] VT [+ law, rule] enfreindre, transgresser; **to ~ copyright** ne pas respecter les droits d'auteur; **to ~ a patent** commettre une contrefaçon en matière de brevet; **to ~ sb's rights** empiéter sur or léser les droits de qn [2] VI **to ~ (up)on sb's rights** empiéter sur or léser les droits de qn; **to ~ on sb's privacy** porter atteinte à la vie privée de qn

infringement [ɪnˈfrɪndʒmənt] N [of law] transgression f (of sth de qch), violation f (of sth de qch); [of rule] infraction f (of sth à qch); [of rights, liberties] atteinte f (of or on sth à qch); **to be in ~ of a law** enfreindre une loi; **~ of copyright** non-respect m des droits d'auteur; **~ of patent** contrefaçon f de brevet

infuriate [ɪnˈfjʊərɪeɪt] VT rendre furieux, mettre en fureur; **it ~s me (that ...)** cela me rend fou (que .. (+ subj)), cela m'exaspère (que ... (+ subj)); **to be ~d** être furieux; **she was ~d to hear that ...** elle était furieuse d'apprendre que ...; **to be ~d by sth/sb** être exaspéré par qch/qn

infuriating [ɪnˈfjʊərɪeɪtɪŋ] ADJ exaspérant, rageant

infuriatingly [ɪnˈfjʊərɪeɪtɪŋlɪ] ADV [say, reply, laugh] de façon exaspérante; **~ slow/cheerful** d'une lenteur/gaieté exaspérante; **~ reasonable** raisonnable à un point exaspérant

infuse [ɪnˈfjuːz] [1] VT infuser (**into** dans); (Culin) [+ tea, herbs] infuser; (fig) [+ ideas etc] infuser, insuffler (**into** à); **to ~ a project with enthusiasm** insuffler de l'enthousiasme dans un projet [2] VI (Culin) [tea, herbs] infuser

infusion [ɪnˈfjuːʒən] N infusion f

ingenious [ɪnˈdʒiːnɪəs] ADJ ingénieux, astucieux

ingeniously [ɪnˈdʒiːnɪəslɪ] ADV ingénieusement, astucieusement; **~ inventive excuses** des excuses ingénieuses

ingénue [ˌænʒeɪˈnjuː] N ingénue f

ingenuity [ˌɪndʒɪˈnjuːɪtɪ] N ingéniosité f

ingenuous [ɪnˈdʒenjʊəs] ADJ (= naïve) ingénu, naïf (naïve f); (= candid) sincère, franc (franche f)

ingenuously [ɪnˈdʒenjʊəslɪ] ADV ingénument

ingenuousness [ɪnˈdʒenjʊəsnɪs] N ingénuité f

ingest [ɪnˈdʒest] VT (Med) ingérer

ingestion [ɪnˈdʒestʃən] N (Med) ingestion f

inglenook [ˈɪŋglnʊk] [1] N coin m du feu [2] COMP ▶ **inglenook fireplace** N grande cheminée f à l'ancienne

inglorious [ɪnˈglɔːrɪəs] ADJ peu glorieux; (stronger) déshonorant, honteux

ingloriously [ɪnˈglɔːrɪəslɪ] ADV [*fall, slip*] piteusement ; [*fail*] lamentablement

ingoing [ˈɪnˌgəʊɪŋ] ADJ [*people, crowd*] qui entre ; [*tenant*] nouveau (nouvelle *f*)

ingot [ˈɪŋgət] N lingot *m*

ingrained [ˈɪnˈgreɪnd] ADJ a (= *deep-seated*) [*attitude, prejudice, hostility, distrust*] enraciné (**in sb** chez qn, **in sth** dans qch) ; [*habit*] invétéré b [*dirt, grime*] incrusté ; **~ with dirt** encrassé, incrusté de saleté

ingrate [ˈɪngreɪt] N ingrat(e) *m(f)*

ingratiate [ɪnˈgreɪʃɪeɪt] VT **to ~ o.s. with sb** se faire bien voir de qn, s'insinuer dans les bonnes grâces de qn

ingratiating [ɪnˈgreɪʃɪeɪtɪŋ] ADJ patelin, doucereux

ingratitude [ɪnˈgrætɪtjuːd] N ingratitude *f*

ingredient [ɪnˈgriːdɪənt] N (*Culin*) ingrédient *m* ; [*of character etc*] élément *m* ; (*on food packaging*) **~s** ingrédients *mpl*, composition *f*

ingress [ˈɪngres] N (*Jur*) entrée *f* ; **to have free ~** avoir le droit d'entrée

ingrowing [ˈɪnˌgrəʊɪŋ], **ingrown** (*US*) [ˈɪnˌgrəʊn] ADJ **~ nail** ongle *m* incarné

inguinal [ˈɪngwɪnl] ADJ inguinal

inhabit [ɪnˈhæbɪt] VT [+ *town, country*] habiter ; [+ *house*] habiter (dans) ; **~ed** habité

inhabitable [ɪnˈhæbɪtəbl] ADJ habitable

inhabitant [ɪnˈhæbɪtənt] N habitant(e) *m(f)*

inhalant [ɪnˈheɪlənt] N inhalant *m*

inhalation [ˌɪnhəˈleɪʃən] N (*gen, Med*) inhalation *f*

inhalator [ˈɪnhəleɪtər] N = **inhaler**

inhale [ɪnˈheɪl] 1 VT [+ *vapour, gas*] inhaler ; [+ *perfume*] respirer, humer ; [*smoker*] avaler 2 VI [*smoker*] avaler la fumée

inhaler [ɪnˈheɪlər] N inhalateur *m*

inharmonious [ˌɪnhɑːˈməʊnɪəs] ADJ inharmonieux, peu harmonieux

inhere [ɪnˈhɪər] VI (*frm*) être inhérent (**in** à)

inherent [ɪnˈhɪərənt] ADJ [*dangers, problems, contradictions, risks, weaknesses, rights*] inhérent, intrinsèque ; (*Jur*) propre (**in,** to à) ; **to be ~ to sb/sth** être inhérent à qn/qch ; **with all the ~ difficulties** avec toutes les difficultés qui s'y rattachent

inherently [ɪnˈhɪərəntlɪ] ADV [*involve, entail, dangerous, difficult*] par nature ; (*Philos*) par inhérence ; (*Jur*) en propre ; **there is nothing ~ wrong with the system** le système n'a rien de mauvais en soi ; **war is ~ a dirty business** la guerre est par nature une sale affaire

inherit [ɪnˈherɪt] 1 VT hériter de, hériter (*liter*) ; **she ~ed £10,000** elle a hérité de 10 000 livres ; **to ~ a house/fortune** hériter d'une maison/d'une fortune, hériter (*liter*) une maison/une fortune ; **to ~ a house/fortune from sb** hériter (*liter*) une maison/une fortune de qn ; **he ~ed the estate from his father** il a succédé à son père à la tête du domaine, il a hérité du domaine de son père ; **to ~ a title** succéder à un titre, hériter d'un titre ; **the new government has ~ed a weak economy** le nouveau gouvernement a hérité d'une économie en mauvaise santé ; **she ~ed her mother's beauty** elle a hérité de la beauté de sa mère ; **he ~s his patience/his red hair from his father** il tient sa patience/ses cheveux roux de son père ; (*hum*) **I've ~ed my brother's coat** j'ai hérité du manteau de mon frère → **inherited** 2 VI hériter ; **she is due to ~ on the death of her aunt** elle doit hériter à la mort de sa tante

inheritance [ɪnˈherɪtəns] 1 N a (*NonC*) succession *f* ; (*Jur*) **law of ~** droit *m* de succession b [*of individual, family*] héritage *m* ; [*of nation*] patrimoine *m* ; **to come into an ~** faire un héritage ; **an ~ of £10,000** un héritage de 10 000 livres ; **it's part of our cultural ~** cela fait partie de notre patrimoine culturel ; **our genetic ~** notre patrimoine génétique

2 COMP ► **inheritance tax** N droits *mpl* de succession

inherited [ɪnˈherɪtɪd] ADJ [*disease, defect*] héréditaire ; [*gene*] hérité ; **~ wealth/property** richesse *f*/propriété *f* dont on a hérité

inheritor [ɪnˈherɪtər] N (*lit, fig*) héritier *m*, -ière *f*

inhibit [ɪnˈhɪbɪt] VT a [+ *growth, development*] (= *slow down*) freiner ; (= *hinder*) entraver ; (= *prevent*) empêcher ; [*situation, sb's presence*] [+ *person*] gêner ; (*Psych*) inhiber ; **tablets which ~ the desire to eat** des pilules qui coupent la faim, des coupe-faim *mpl* ; **orthodox drugs can ~ the action of natural treatments** les médicaments traditionnels peuvent gêner l'action des traitements naturels ; **a drug that ~s the formation of blood clots** un médicament qui empêche la formation de caillots de sang ; **alcohol can ~ our ability to think logically** l'alcool peut diminuer nos facultés de raisonnement ; **stress can ~ a man's sexual performance** le stress peut diminuer *or* amoindrir les capacités sexuelles d'un homme ; **to ~ freedom of speech** entraver la liberté d'expression ; **to ~ sb from doing** (= *restrain*) retenir qn de faire ; (= *prevent*) empêcher qn de faire ; **his presence ~ed the discussion** (= *limited it*) sa présence gênait la discussion ; (= *prevented it*) sa présence empêchait toute discussion ; **he was greatly ~ed by his lack of education** (= *held back*) il était handicapé par son manque d'instruction ; (= *embarrassed*) il était très gêné par son manque d'instruction b (*Jur = prohibit*) interdire, défendre (**sb from doing** à qn de faire)

inhibited [ɪnˈhɪbɪtɪd] ADJ refoulé, inhibé ; **he is very ~** il a beaucoup d'inhibitions ; **to be sexually ~** être refoulé sexuellement

inhibiting [ɪnˈhɪbɪtɪŋ] ADJ inhibiteur (-trice *f*)

inhibition [ˌɪnhɪˈbɪʃən] N a (*gen*) complexe *m* ; (*Physiol, Psych*) inhibition *f* b (*Jur = prohibition*) interdiction *f*

inhibitory [ɪnˈhɪbɪtərɪ] ADJ a (*Physiol, Psych*) inhibiteur (-trice *f*) b (*Jur*) prohibitif

inhospitable [ˌɪnhɒsˈpɪtəbl] ADJ [*person, behaviour, reception*] inhospitalier, peu accueillant ; [*country, climate*] inhospitalier ; [*weather*] désagréable, inclément (*liter*)

inhospitably [ˌɪnhɒsˈpɪtəblɪ] ADV [*behave*] de façon *or* manière inhospitalière ; **to treat sb ~** se montrer inhospitalier envers qn ; **~ cold** [*region, climate*] d'un froid inhospitalier ; (*fig*) [*person*] d'une froideur glaciale

inhospitality [ˈɪnˌhɒspɪˈtælɪtɪ] N [*of person, country, climate*] inhospitalité *f* ; [*of weather*] inclémence *f* (*liter*)

inhuman [ɪnˈhjuːmən] ADJ (*lit, fig*) inhumain

inhumane [ˌɪnhjuːˈmeɪn] ADJ inhumain

inhumanity [ˌɪnhjuːˈmænɪtɪ] N inhumanité *f*

inhumation [ˌɪnhjuːˈmeɪʃən] N (*frm*) inhumation *f*

inimical [ɪˈnɪmɪkəl] ADJ (= *hostile*) hostile ; **~ to** défavorable à, (l')ennemi de

inimitable [ɪˈnɪmɪtəbl] ADJ inimitable

inimitably [ɪˈnɪmɪtəblɪ] ADV d'une façon inimitable

iniquitous [ɪˈnɪkwɪtəs] ADJ inique, profondément injuste

iniquitously [ɪˈnɪkwɪtəslɪ] ADV iniquement

iniquity [ɪˈnɪkwɪtɪ] N iniquité *f*

initial [ɪˈnɪʃəl] 1 ADJ a [*investment, cost, results, period, enthusiasm*] initial ; **after the ~ shock, I ...** après le choc initial, je ... ; **my ~ reaction was to refuse** ma première réaction *or* ma réaction initiale a été de refuser ; **~ reports suggest that hundreds of people have been wounded** selon les premiers rapports il y aurait des centaines de blessés ; **in the ~ stages** au début, dans un premier temps ; **~ expenses** [*of shop, firm etc*] frais *mpl* d'éta-

blissement b (*Phon*) initial c (*Typ*) **~ letter** initiale *f* 2 N (lettre *f*) initiale *f* ; **~s** initiales *fpl* ; (*as signature*) parafe or paraphe *m* 3 VT [+ *letter, document*] parafer *or* parapher ; (= *approve*) viser 4 COMP ► **Initial Teaching Alphabet** N (*Brit Scol*) alphabet phonétique d'apprentissage de la lecture

initialize [ɪˈnɪʃəˌlaɪz] VT (*Comput*) initialiser

initially [ɪˈnɪʃəlɪ] ADV d'abord, au départ ; **~, they were wary of him** au départ, ils se méfiaient de lui

initiate [ɪˈnɪʃɪeɪt] 1 VT a [+ *negotiations, discussion, action, reform*] engager, lancer ; [+ *enterprise, fashion*] lancer ; [+ *scheme, programme*] mettre en place ; **to ~ sex** prendre l'initiative de l'acte sexuel ; (*Jur*) **to ~ proceedings against sb** intenter un procès à qn b (*Rel etc*) [+ *person*] initier ; **to ~ sb into a science/a secret** initier qn à une science/un secret ; **to ~ sb into a society** admettre qn au sein d'une société (secrète) 2 [ɪˈnɪʃɪɪt] ADJ, N initié(e) *m(f)*

initiation [ɪˌnɪʃɪˈeɪʃən] 1 N a [*of negotiations, discussion, action, reform, enterprise, fashion*] lancement *m* ; [*of scheme, programme*] mise *f* en place b (*into society*) admission *f* (**into** dans), initiation *f* ; (*into knowledge, secret*) initiation *f* (**into** à) 2 COMP ► **initiation rite** N rite *m* d'initiation

initiative [ɪˈnɪʃətɪv] 1 N initiative *f* ; **to take the ~** prendre l'initiative (**in doing sth** de faire qch) ; **to use one's (own) ~** faire preuve d'initiative ; **on one's own ~** de sa propre initiative, par soi-même ; **he's got ~** il a de l'initiative ; **to have/lose the ~** avoir/perdre l'initiative ; **a new peace ~** une nouvelle initiative de paix 2 COMP ► **initiative test** N test *m* d'initiative

initiator [ɪˈnɪʃɪˌeɪtər] N auteur *m*, instigateur *m*, -trice *f*

inject [ɪnˈdʒekt] 1 VT a [+ *liquid, gas*] injecter (**into** dans) ; (*Med*) **to ~ sb with sth** injecter qch à qn, faire une piqûre *or* une injection de qch à qn ; **to ~ sb's arm with penicillin** ◊ **to ~ penicillin into sb's arm** faire une piqûre *or* injection de pénicilline dans le bras de qn ; **he ~s himself** [*diabetic etc*] il se fait ses piqûres ; **to ~ drugs** [*addict*] se piquer* ; **to ~ heroin** se piquer* à l'héroïne b (*fig*) **to ~ sb with enthusiasm** communiquer *or* insuffler de l'enthousiasme à qn ; **I wanted to ~ some humour into my speech** je voulais introduire un peu d'humour dans mon discours ; **they need to ~ some new life into their relationship** il faut qu'ils introduisent un peu de nouveauté dans leur relation ; **the government are trying to ~ some life into the economy** le gouvernement essaie de relancer l'économie ; **she ~ed some money/£5 million into the company** elle a injecté de l'argent/5 millions de livres dans la société 2 VI [*drug addict*] se piquer*

injection [ɪnˈdʒekʃən] N (*lit, fig, also Fin = process*) injection *f* ; (*Med, Brit Dentistry = shot*) injection *f*, piqûre *f* ; **to give medicine by ~** administrer un remède par injection ; **an ~ of new capital** une injection *or* un apport de capital frais ; **a £250 million cash ~** un apport de 250 millions de livres

injector [ɪnˈdʒektər] N (*Aut*) injecteur *m* → **fuel**

injudicious [ˌɪndʒuːˈdɪʃəs] ADJ peu judicieux, malavisé

injudiciously [ˌɪndʒuːˈdɪʃəslɪ] ADV peu judicieusement

injunction [ɪnˈdʒʌŋkʃən] N (*gen*) ordre *m*, recommandation *f* formelle ; (*Jur*) injonction *f* ; (= *court order*) ordonnance *f* (**to do** de faire, **against doing** de ne pas faire) ; **she plans to seek a court ~ to stop publication of the photographs** elle a l'intention de demander une ordonnance pour empêcher la publication des photos ; **an ~ banning the sale of the**

book une ordonnance interdisant la vente du livre ; **to give sb strict ~s to do** enjoindre formellement *or* strictement à qn de faire

injure ['ɪndʒəʳ] VT **a** (= *hurt physically*) [+ *person, limb*] blesser ; **to ~ o.s.** se blesser ; **to ~ one's leg** se blesser à la jambe ; **no one was ~d** il n'y a pas eu de blessés, personne n'a été blessé → **injured b** (*fig*) [+ *person*] (= *wrong*) faire du tort à, nuire à, léser ; (*Jur*) porter préjudice à, léser ; (= *offend*) blesser, offenser ; (= *damage*) [+ *reputation, sb's interests, chances, trade*] compromettre ; (*Comm*) [+ *cargo, goods*] avarier ; **to ~ sb's feelings** offenser qn ; **to ~ one's health** compromettre sa santé, se détériorer la santé → **injured**

injured ['ɪndʒəd] **1** ADJ **a** (*physically*) blessé ; (*in road accident*) accidenté ; [*limb*] blessé **b** (*fig*) [*person*] offensé ; [*look, voice*] blessé, offensé ; [*wife, husband*] outragé, trompé ; (*Jur*) **the ~ party** la partie lésée **2 the injured** NPL (*gen*) les blessés *mpl* ; (*in road accident etc*) les accidentés *mpl*, les blessés *mpl*

injurious [ɪn'dʒʊərɪəs] ADJ nuisible, préjudiciable (**to** à)

injury ['ɪndʒərɪ] **1** N **a** (*physical*) blessure *f* ; **to do sb an ~** blesser qn ; **you'll do yourself an ~!** tu vas te faire mal ! ; (*Sport*) **three players have injuries** il y a trois joueurs (de) blessés **b** (*fig* = *wrong*) (*to person*) tort *m*, préjudice *m* ; (*to reputation*) atteinte *f* ; (*Jur*) lésion *f*, préjudice *m* ; **to the ~ of sb** au détriment *or* au préjudice de qn **c** (*Comm, Naut*) avarie *f* **2** COMP ► **injury time** N (*Brit Ftbl*) arrêts *mpl* de jeu ; **to play ~ time** jouer les arrêts de jeu

injustice [ɪn'dʒʌstɪs] N injustice *f* ; **to do sb an ~** être *or* se montrer injuste envers qn

ink [ɪŋk] **1** N **a** encre *f* ; **written in ~** écrit à l'encre ► **Indian, invisible ~** [*of octopus, cuttlefish*] encre *f*, sépia *f* **2** VT **a** (*Typ*) [+ *roller*] encrer **b** (*US* * *fig* = *sign*) signer **3** COMP ► **ink bag** N (*Zool*) sac *m or* poche *f* d'encre ► **ink blot** N tache *f* d'encre, pâté *m* ► **ink blot test** N (*Psych*) test *m* de la tache d'encre, test *m* de Rorschach ► **ink bottle** N bouteille *f* d'encre ► **ink eraser** N gomme *f* à encre ► **ink-jet printer** N (*Comput*) imprimante *f* à jet d'encre ► **ink rubber** N = **ink eraser**

► **ink in** VT SEP repasser à l'encre

► **ink out** VT SEP raturer *or* barrer à l'encre

► **ink over** VT SEP = **ink in**

inkling ['ɪŋklɪŋ] N soupçon *m*, vague *or* petite idée *f* ; **I had no ~ that ...** je n'avais pas la moindre idée que ... ; **je ne me doutais pas du tout que ...** ; **he had no ~ of what was going on** il n'avait pas la moindre idée de ce qui se passait, il ne se doutait pas du tout de ce qui se passait ; **we had some ~ of their plan** nous avions une petite idée de leur plan ; **there was no ~ of the disaster to come** rien ne laissait présager le désastre qui allait se produire

inkpad ['ɪŋkpæd] N tampon *m* (encreur)

inkpot ['ɪŋkpɒt] N encrier *m*

inkstain ['ɪŋksteɪn] N tache *f* d'encre

inkstand ['ɪŋkstænd] N (grand) encrier *m* (de bureau)

inkwell ['ɪŋkwel] N encrier *m* (de pupitre *etc*)

inky ['ɪŋkɪ] ADJ **a** (*liter* = *dark*) [*colour*] très foncé ; [*sky*] noir *inv* d'encre *or* comme de l'encre ; **~ black** noir *inv* d'encre ; **~ blue** (d'un) bleu outremer foncé *inv* **b** (= *covered with ink*) [*finger, paper*] plein d'encre ; [*pad, rubber stamp*] encré

inlaid ['ɪn'leɪd] ADJ [*brooch, sword*] incrusté (**with** de) ; [*box, table*] marqueté ; [*metal*] damasquiné ; **ivory ~ with gold** ivoire *m* incrusté d'or ; **an ~ floor** un parquet ; **~ work** (= *jewels*) incrustation *f* ; (= *wood*) marqueterie *f*

inland ['ɪnlænd] **1** ADJ **a** (= *not coastal*) [*sea, town*] intérieur (-eure *f*) ; **~ navigation** navigation *f* fluviale ; **~ waterways** canaux *mpl* et rivières *fpl* **b** (*Brit* = *domestic*) [*mail, trade*] inté-

rieur (-eure *f*) **2** ['ɪn'lænd] ADV à l'intérieur ; **to go ~** aller dans l'arrière-pays **3** COMP ► **the Inland Revenue** N (= *organization, system*) le fisc ► **inland revenue** N (= *payments*) contributions *fpl* directes ► **Inland Revenue stamp** N timbre *m* fiscal

inlay ['ɪnleɪ] (*vb: pret, ptp* **inlaid**) **1** N [*of brooch, sword*] incrustation *f* ; [*of table, box*] marqueterie *f* ; [*of floor*] parquet *m* ; [*of metal*] damasquinage *m* **2** ['ɪn'leɪ] VT [+ *brooch, sword*] incruster (**with** de) ; [+ *table, box*] marqueter ; [+ *floor*] parqueter ; [+ *metal*] damasquiner → **inlaid**

inlet ['ɪnlet] **1** N **a** [*of sea*] crique *f*, anse *f* ; [*of river*] bras *m* de rivière **b** (*Tech*) arrivée *f*, admission *f* ; [*of ventilator*] prise *f* (d'air) **2** COMP ► **inlet pipe** N tuyau *m* d'arrivée → **valve**

in loco parentis [ɪn'ləʊkəʊpə'rentɪs] ADV en tant que substitut *or* à la place des parents

inmate ['ɪnmeɪt] N [*of prison*] détenu(e) *m(f)* ; [*of asylum*] interné(e) *m(f)* ; [*of hospital*] malade *mf*, hospitalisé(e) *m(f)*, pensionnaire* *mf*

inmost ['ɪnməʊst] ADJ [*thoughts*] le plus secret, le plus intime ; [*feelings*] le plus intime ; **in the ~ part of the temple** au plus profond *or* au cœur du temple ; **in one's ~ being** au plus profond de soi-même ; **in one's ~ heart** au fond de son cœur

inn [ɪn] **1** N (*small, wayside*) auberge *f* ; (*larger, wayside*) hostellerie *f* ; (*in town*) hôtel *m* ; († = *tavern*) cabaret† *m* **2** COMP ► **inn sign** N enseigne *f* d'auberge ► **the Inns of Court** NPL (*Brit Jur*) les (quatre) écoles *fpl* de droit (londoniennes)

innards* ['ɪnədz] NPL entrailles *fpl*, intérieurs* *mpl*

innate [ɪ'neɪt] ADJ [*ability, talent, wisdom, intelligence, conservatism*] inné ; [*dignity*] naturel ; [*distrust*] naturel ; **an ~ sense of sth** un sens inné de qch

innately [ɪ'neɪtlɪ] ADV **~ aggressive/generous** d'une agressivité/générosité innée, naturellement agressif/généreux

inner ['ɪnəʳ] **1** ADJ **a** [*room, court*] intérieur (-eure *f*) ; **on the ~ side** à l'intérieur ; **they formed an ~ circle within the society** ils formaient un petit noyau *or* un petit cercle (fermé) à l'intérieur de la société **b** (*fig*) [*emotions, thoughts*] intime ; [*life*] intérieur (-eure *f*) ; **the ~ meaning** le sens intime *or* profond ; **the ~ man** (= *spiritual self*) l'homme *m* intérieur ; (*hum* = *stomach*) l'estomac *m* ; **the discovery of the ~ self** la découverte de soi ; **trust your ~ self** suivez votre instinct

2 COMP ► **inner city** N quartiers *mpl* déshérités (à l'intérieur de la ville) ► **inner-city** ADJ [*buildings, problems, crime, renewal*] des quartiers déshérités ► **inner-city areas** NPL = **inner city** ► **inner-directed** ADJ (*esp US*) individualiste ► **inner dock** N (*Naut*) arrière-bassin *m* ► **inner ear** N (*Anat*) oreille *f* interne ► **inner harbour** N arrière-port *m* ► **inner sole** N [*of shoe*] semelle *f* (intérieure) ► **inner spring mattress** N (*US*) matelas *m* à ressorts ► **inner tube** N [*of tyre*] chambre *f* à air

INNER CITY

L'expression **inner city** *désigne initialement le centre des villes. Dans l'évolution des villes anglosaxonnes, les quartiers du centre, délaissés par les classes aisées, se caractérisent souvent par une grande pauvreté, un taux de chômage élevé, de très mauvaises conditions de logement et des tensions entre les groupes ethniques. En ce sens, la notion de* **inner city** *correspond en français aux banlieues à problèmes.*

innermost ['ɪnəməʊst] ADJ = **inmost**

inning ['ɪnɪŋ] N (*Baseball*) tour *m* de batte

innings ['ɪnɪŋz] N (*pl inv*) **a** (*Cricket*) tour *m* de batte **b** (*fig*) tour *m* ; **I've had a good ~** j'ai bien profité de l'existence

innit: ['ɪnɪt] EXCL (*Brit*) **~?** pas vrai ?*

innkeeper ['ɪnki:pəʳ] N (*wayside*) aubergiste *mf* ; (*in town*) hôtelier *m*, -ière *f*

innocence ['ɪnəsns] N (*gen, Jur*) innocence *f* ; (= *simplicity*) innocence *f*, naïveté *f* ; **in all ~** en toute innocence ; **in his ~ he believed it all** naïf comme il est (*or* était *etc*) il a tout cru, dans son innocence il a tout cru ; (*Jur*) **to protest one's ~** protester de son innocence

Innocent ['ɪnəsnt] N (= *Papal name*) Innocent *m*

innocent ['ɪnəsnt] **1** ADJ **a** (= *not guilty, not involved, naive*) [*person, victim, bystander*] innocent (**of sth** de qch) ; **to be found ~ of sth** être déclaré innocent de qch ; **as ~ as a newborn babe** innocent comme l'enfant qui vient de naître

b (= *harmless, not malicious*) [*question, remark, pastime*] innocent ; **it was the source of much ~ amusement** on s'en est beaucoup amusé mais il n'y avait aucune méchanceté là-dedans ; **an ~ mistake** une erreur commise en toute innocence ; (*Jur: of patent*) **~ infringement** contrefaçon *f* involontaire

c (*frm*) **~ of** (= *free from*) vierge de (*liter*), dépourvu de ; **a room ~ of all ornament** une pièce vierge de (*liter*) *or* dépourvue de tout ornement

2 N **he's one of Nature's ~s** ◊ **he's a bit of an ~*** c'est un grand innocent ; **he tried to come the ~ with me:** il a essayé de jouer aux innocents avec moi ; (*Rel*) **Massacre of the Holy Innocents** massacre *m* des (saints) Innocents ; **Holy Innocents' Day** jour *m* des saints Innocents

innocently ['ɪnəsntlɪ] ADV innocemment, en toute innocence

innocuous [ɪ'nɒkjʊəs] ADJ inoffensif

innovate ['ɪnəʊveɪt] VTI innover

innovation [ˌɪnəʊ'veɪʃən] N innovation *f* (**in sth** en (matière de) qch), changement *m* (**in sth** en (matière de) qch) ; **to make ~s in sth** apporter des innovations *or* des changements à qch ; **scientific/technical ~s** innovations *fpl* scientifiques/techniques

innovative ['ɪnəʊˌveɪtɪv] ADJ [*person, organization*] innovateur (-trice *f*), novateur (-trice *f*) ; [*idea, design*] novateur (-trice *f*) ; [*product*] original ; **we aim to be ~** nous cherchons à innover

innovator ['ɪnəʊveɪtəʳ] N innovateur *m*, -trice *f*, novateur *m*, -trice *f*

innovatory ['ɪnəʊˌveɪtərɪ] ADJ (*Brit*) = **innovative**

innuendo [ˌɪnjʊ'endəʊ] N (*pl* **innuendo(e)s**) insinuation *f*, allusion *f* (malveillante) ; **to make ~(e)s about sb** faire des insinuations (malveillantes) à l'égard de qn ; **to spread ~(e)s about sb** faire courir des bruits sur qn ; **sexual ~** allusions *fpl* grivoises

Innuit ['ɪnjuːɪt] = **Inuit**

innumerable [ɪ'njuːmərəbl] ADJ innombrable, sans nombre ; **there are ~ reasons** il y a une infinité de raisons ; **I've told you ~ times** je te l'ai dit cent fois ; **goals can be pursued in ~ ways** on peut poursuivre un but de cent manières différentes ; **she drank ~ cups of coffee** elle a bu un nombre incalculable de tasses de café

innumerate [ɪ'njuːmərɪt] ADJ qui n'a pas le sens de l'arithmétique ; **he's totally ~** il ne sait pas du tout compter

inoculate [ɪ'nɒkjʊleɪt] VT (*Med, Vet*) [+ *person, animal*] vacciner (**against sth** contre qch) ; **to ~ sb with sth** inoculer qch à qn

inoculation [ɪˌnɒkjʊ'leɪʃən] N (*Med, Vet*) inoculation *f*

inoffensive [ˌɪnə'fensɪv] ADJ inoffensif

inoperable [ɪnˈɒpərəbl] ADJ inopérable

inoperative [ɪnˈɒpərətɪv] ADJ inopérant

inopportune [ɪnˈɒpətjuːn] ADJ inopportun

inopportunely [ɪnˈɒpətjuːnlɪ] ADV inopportunément

inordinate [ɪˈnɔːdɪnɪt] ADJ [size, number, quantity] démesuré; [demands] immodéré, extravagant; [pride, pleasure] extrême; **an ~ amount of luggage/time/money** énormément de bagages/de temps/d'argent; **an ~ sum (of money)** une somme exorbitante or astronomique

inordinately [ɪˈnɔːdɪnɪtlɪ] ADV [hot, cold, difficult] excessivement; [proud] infiniment; **to be ~ fond of sth** aimer particulièrement qch

inorganic [ˌɪnɔːˈɡænɪk] ADJ **a** (= artificial) [fibre, material, fertilizer] inorganique **b** (Sci) minéral; **~ chemistry** chimie f inorganique or minérale

inpatient [ˈɪnpeɪʃənt] N malade mf hospitalisé(e)

input [ˈɪnpʊt] **1** N **a** (= contribution) contribution f, participation f; [of funds, labour] apport m; (= ideas) idées fpl; **we need a regular ~ of new ideas** nous avons besoin d'un flux or d'un apport constant de nouvelles idées; **artistic/creative ~** apport m artistique/créatif **b** (Econ) **~s** input m, intrants mpl; (Ind = materials, parts) consommations fpl intermédiaires **c** (Elec) énergie f, puissance f; (Tech) [of machine] consommation f **d** (Comput) (= data) input m; (= act of inputting) saisie f, entrée f (de données) **2** VT (Comput) saisir (**into** sur), entrer (**into sth** dans qch) **3** COMP ► **input data** N (Comput) données fpl en entrée ► **input/output** N (Comput) entrée-sortie f ► **input/output device** N (Comput) périphérique m entrée-sortie ► **input/output table** N (Econ) tableau m d'entrées-sorties

inquest [ˈɪnkwest] N (Jur) enquête f (criminelle) → **coroner**

inquietude [ɪnˈkwaɪətjuːd] N (liter) inquiétude f

inquire [ɪnˈkwaɪəʳ] **1** VI se renseigner (**about sth** sur qch), s'informer (**about, after** de); (= ask) demander; **to ~ after sb/sth** demander des nouvelles de qn/qch; **I'll go and ~** je vais demander; **~ at the office** demandez au bureau, renseignez-vous au bureau; **"~ within"** « renseignements ici », « s'adresser ici »; **"~ at the information desk"** « s'adresser aux renseignements », « s'adresser au bureau de renseignements »; **to ~ into** (subject) faire des recherches or des investigations sur; (possibilities) se renseigner sur; (Admin, Jur: event, situation) enquêter sur, faire une enquête sur **2** VT demander; **"is something wrong?" he ~d** « il y a quelque chose qui ne va pas? » a-t-il demandé; **he rang up to ~ how she was** il a téléphoné pour demander or savoir comment elle allait; **he ~d what she wanted** il a demandé ce qu'elle voulait; **I ~d whether my letter had arrived** j'ai demandé si ma lettre était arrivée; **he ~d his way to the cemetery** ◊ **he ~d how to get to the cemetery** il a demandé le chemin du cimetière

inquiring [ɪnˈkwaɪərɪŋ] ADJ [attitude, frame of mind] curieux; [look] interrogateur (-trice f)

inquiringly [ɪnˈkwaɪərɪŋlɪ] ADV [look] d'un air interrogateur; [say] d'un ton interrogateur

inquiry [ɪnˈkwaɪərɪ] **1** N **a** (from individual) demande f de renseignements; **to make inquiries (about sb/sth)** se renseigner (sur qn/qch), demander des renseignements (sur qn/qch) → **1b**; **on ~ he found that ...** renseignements pris il a découvert que ...; **a look of ~** un regard interrogateur; **he gave me a look of ~ il m'a interrogé du regard; "all inquiries to ..."** « pour tous renseignements s'adresser à ... » **b** (Admin, Jur) enquête f, investigation f; **to set up** or **open an ~ (into sth)** ouvrir une enquête (sur qch); **committee of ~** commission f d'enquête; **to hold an ~ (into sth)** enquêter or faire une enquête (sur qch); **to call for an ~ into sth** demander une enquête sur qch; **a murder ~** une enquête sur un meurtre; **they are pursuing a new line of ~** ils suivent une nouvelle piste; **the police are making inquiries** la police enquête → **help, officer c** (Telec, Rail etc) **the Inquiries** les renseignements mpl **2** COMP ► **inquiry agent** N détective m privé ► **inquiry desk, inquiry office** N (bureau m de) renseignements mpl

inquisition [ˌɪnkwɪˈzɪʃən] N investigation f, recherches fpl; (Jur) enquête f (judiciaire); (Rel) **the Inquisition** l'Inquisition f

inquisitive [ɪnˈkwɪzɪtɪv] ADJ curieux, inquisiteur (-trice f) (pej)

inquisitively [ɪnˈkwɪzɪtɪvlɪ] ADV avec curiosité; (pej) d'un air inquisiteur

inquisitiveness [ɪnˈkwɪzɪtɪvnɪs] N curiosité f; (pej) curiosité f indiscrète, indiscrétion f

inquisitor [ɪnˈkwɪzɪtəʳ] N (Jur) enquêteur m, -euse f; (Rel) inquisiteur m

inquisitorial [ɪnˌkwɪzɪˈtɔːrɪəl] ADJ inquisitorial

inquorate [ɪnˈkwɔːreɪt] ADJ (Admin) qui n'a pas le quorum, où le quorum n'est pas atteint

inroad [ˈɪnrəʊd] N (Mil) incursion f (**into** en, dans); (fig) **to make ~s on** or **into** (majority, numbers, supplies) entamer; (sb's rights) empiéter sur; **they have made significant ~s into the commercial aircraft market** ils ont fait une percée importante sur le marché de l'aéronautique commerciale

inrush [ˈɪnrʌʃ] N [of air, water, people] irruption f

ins. (ABBR = **inches**) → **inch**

insalubrious [ˌɪnsəˈluːbrɪəs] ADJ (gen) insalubre, malsain; [district] peu recommandable

insane [ɪnˈseɪn] **1** ADJ (Med) aliéné, dément; (gen) [person, desire] fou (folle f), insensé; [project] démentiel; **to become ~** perdre la raison; **to go ~** perdre la raison, devenir fou; **to drive sb ~** rendre qn fou; **he must be ~ to think of going** il faut qu'il soit fou pour envisager d'y aller; **you must be ~!** tu es fou!; (temporarily) pris d'une crise de folie; (US) **~ asylum** asile m d'aliénés → **certify 2 the insane** NPL (Med) les aliénés mpl

insanely [ɪnˈseɪnlɪ] ADV [behave] de façon insensée; **to laugh ~** (= hysterically) rire de façon hystérique; **~ possessive/expensive/fast** follement possessif/cher/rapide; **~ jealous** (on one occasion) fou de jalousie; (by nature) d'une jalousie maladive

insanitary [ɪnˈsænɪtərɪ] ADJ insalubre, malsain

insanity [ɪnˈsænɪtɪ] N (Med) aliénation f mentale, démence f; (gen) folie f, démence f

insatiable [ɪnˈseɪʃəbl] ADJ (lit, fig) insatiable (**for sth** de qch)

insatiably [ɪnˈseɪʃəblɪ] ADV **to be ~ hungry** avoir une faim insatiable; **to be ~ curious** être d'une curiosité insatiable

inscribe [ɪnˈskraɪb] VT **a** (in book etc) inscrire; (on monument etc) inscrire, graver; [+ surface] marquer, graver; (fig) [+ ideas] graver, inscrire, fixer; **to ~ a tomb with a name** or **a name on a tomb** graver un nom sur une tombe; **a watch ~d with his name** une montre gravée à son nom; **a watch, ~d "to Laura"** une montre portant l'inscription « à Laura »; (Fin) **~d stock** titres mpl nominatifs or inscrits **b** (= dedicate) [+ book] dédicacer

inscription [ɪnˈskrɪpʃən] N (on coin, monument etc) inscription f; (on cartoon) légende f; (= dedication) dédicace f

inscrutability [ɪnˌskruːtəˈbɪlɪtɪ] N impénétrabilité f

inscrutable [ɪnˈskruːtəbl] ADJ impénétrable (**to sb/sth** à qn/qch)

insect [ˈɪnsekt] **1** N insecte m **2** COMP ► **insect bite** N piqûre f d'insecte ► **insect eater** N insectivore m ► **insect powder** N poudre f insecticide ► **insect repellent** ADJ antimoustiques inv, insectifuge (frm) ◆ N (= cream, ointment etc) crème f (or lotion f etc) antimoustiques inv, insectifuge m (frm) ► **insect spray** N aérosol m or bombe f insecticide

insecticide [ɪnˈsektɪsaɪd] ADJ, N insecticide m

insectivorous [ˌɪnsekˈtɪvərəs] ADJ insectivore

insecure [ˌɪnsɪˈkjʊəʳ] ADJ **a** (= unsure of oneself) **to be ~** manquer d'assurance; (Psych) être anxieux or angoissé; **to feel ~** (gen) se sentir mal dans sa peau; (= afraid) ne pas se sentir en sécurité **b** (= uncertain) [future] incertain; [job, rights] précaire **c** (= unsafe, unprotected) [building, lock, door, window, district] peu sûr **d** (= not firm, badly fixed) [structure, ladder] qui n'est pas sûr; [rope, rope ladder, load] mal attaché

insecurity [ˌɪnsɪˈkjʊərɪtɪ] N (also Psych) insécurité f

inseminate [ɪnˈsemɪneɪt] VT inséminer

insemination [ɪnˌsemɪˈneɪʃən] N insémination f → **artificial**

insensate [ɪnˈsenseɪt] ADJ (frm) (= senseless) insensé; (= inanimate) inanimé, insensible; (= unfeeling) insensible

insensibility [ɪnˌsensəˈbɪlɪtɪ] N **a** (frm Med = unconsciousness) insensibilité f, inconscience f **b** (= unfeelingness) insensibilité f (**to sb/sth** à qn/qch), indifférence f (**to sb/sth** pour qn/qch)

insensible [ɪnˈsensəbl] ADJ **a** (frm = unconscious) inconscient, sans connaissance; **the blow knocked him ~** le coup lui fit perdre connaissance **b** (= unaware, impervious) insensible (**to sth** à qch); **~ to the cold/to shame/to ridicule** insensible au froid/à la honte/au ridicule

insensibly [ɪnˈsensəblɪ] ADV [change, grow] insensiblement, imperceptiblement

insensitive [ɪnˈsensɪtɪv] ADJ (lit, fig: physically or emotionally) [person] insensible (**to sth** à qch, **to sb** envers qn); [remark, act] indélicat; [policy] pas assez réfléchi; **policies which are ~ to the needs of ...** des mesures qui ne tiennent pas compte des besoins de ...

insensitivity [ɪnˌsensɪˈtɪvɪtɪ] N insensibilité f

inseparable [ɪnˈsepərəbl] ADJ inséparable (**from** de)

inseparably [ɪnˈsepərəblɪ] ADV inséparablement; **~ bound up with** or **linked with** inséparablement lié à

insert [ɪnˈsɜːt] **1** VT insérer (**in, into** dans, **between** entre); [+ paragraph, word] insérer, introduire (**in** dans), ajouter (**in** à); [+ knife, finger] introduire, enfoncer (**in** dans); [+ key] introduire, mettre (**in** dans); (Typ) [+ page, leaflet] encarter, insérer; [+ advertisement] insérer (**in** dans) **2** [ˈɪnsɜːt] N **a** (= extra pages) encart m; (in print = advertisement, note, word) insertion f **b** (Tech) pièce f insérée, ajout m; (Sewing) entre-deux m inv, incrustation f

insertion [ɪnˈsɜːʃən] **1** N **a** (NonC) insertion f, introduction f **b** = **insert 2a 2** COMP ► **insertion mark** N (Typ) signe m d'insertion

inset [ˈɪnset] (pret, ptp **inset**) **1** VT [+ jewel] insérer (**into** dans), incruster (**into** sur); [+ leaflet] encarter, insérer (**into** dans); (in typing, printing) [+ word, line] rentrer; (Sewing) **to ~ a panel into a skirt** rapporter un panneau sur une jupe; **to ~ a map into the corner of a larger one** insérer une carte en cartouche sur une plus grande [2] N (= *diagram*) schéma *m* en cartouche; (= *map*) carte *f* en cartouche; (= *portrait*) portrait *m* en cartouche; (*Typ* = *leaflet, pages*) encart *m*; (*Sewing*) entre-deux *m inv*, incrustation *f* [3] ADJ [*gem, pearl*] enchâssé, serti; **~ with** incrusté de

inshore ['ɪn'ʃɔːʳ] [1] ADJ [*area, fisherman, navigation, waters*] côtier; [*fishing boat*] côtier, caboteur; [*reefs*] près de la côte; **~ fishing** pêche *f* côtière; **~ lifeboat** canot *m* de sauvetage côtier; **~ wind** vent *m* de mer [2] ADV [*be, fish*] près de la côte; [*blow, flow, go*] vers la côte

inside ['ɪn'saɪd]

> When **inside** is an element in a phrasal verb, eg **step inside**, look up the verb.

[1] ADV [a] dedans, à l'intérieur; **~ and outside** au-dedans et au-dehors; **come** *or* **step ~!** entrez (donc)!; **it is warmer ~** il fait plus chaud à l'intérieur; **wait for me ~** attendez-moi à l'intérieur; **let's go ~** rentrons [b] (* = *in jail*) à l'ombre*, au frais* [2] PREP [a] (*of place*) à l'intérieur de, dans; **he was waiting ~ the house** il attendait à l'intérieur (de la maison) *or* dans la maison; **she was standing just ~ the gate** (*seen from inside*) elle était juste de ce côté-ci de la barrière; (*seen from outside*) elle était juste de l'autre côté de la barrière [b] (*of time*) en moins de; **he came back ~ three minutes** *or* (*US*) **~ of three minutes** il est revenu en moins de trois minutes; (*Sport*) **he was well ~ the record time** il avait largement battu le record [3] N [a] dedans *m*, intérieur *m*; [*of house, box, company*] intérieur *m*; **on the ~** à l'intérieur; **walk on the ~ of the pavement** *or* (*US*) **sidewalk** marchez sur le trottoir du côté maisons; **the door is bolted on** *or* **from the ~** la porte est fermée au verrou de l'intérieur; **I heard music coming from ~** j'ai entendu de la musique qui venait de l'intérieur [b] **your coat is ~ out** ton manteau est à l'envers; **her umbrella blew ~ out** son parapluie s'est retourné sous l'effet du vent; **I turned the bag ~ out** j'ai retourné le sac (entièrement); **he knows his subject ~ out** il connaît son sujet à fond; **he knows the district ~ out** il connaît le quartier comme sa poche; **we know each other ~ out** nous nous connaissons parfaitement; **war turns morality ~ out** la guerre met les valeurs morales sens dessus dessous [c] (* = *stomach: also* ~s) ventre *m*; **he felt the fear grip his ~s** il a senti la peur le prendre au ventre [4] ADJ [a] intérieur (-eure *f*), d'intérieur; **pocket** poche *f* intérieure; **~ seat** [*of plane*] place *f* côté fenêtre; (*fig*) **to get ~ information** obtenir des renseignements grâce à des complicités dans la place; (*Press*) **the ~ story** les dessous *mpl* de l'histoire; **it must have been an ~ job*** (*theft etc*) c'est un coup qui a dû être monté de l'intérieur *or* par quelqu'un de la maison [b] (*Aut*) [*wheel, headlight etc*] (*in Brit*) gauche; (*in US, Europe etc*) droit; **the ~ lane** (*in Brit*) la voie de gauche; (*in US, Europe etc*) ≈ la voie de droite; **to be on** *or* **hold the ~ track** (*Sport*) être à la corde, tenir la corde; (*fig*) être le mieux placé [5] COMP ► **inside-forward** N (*Sport*) intérieur *m*, inter* *m* ► **inside-left** N (*Sport*) intérieur *m* gauche ► **inside leg** N entrejambe *m* ► **inside leg measurement** N mesure *f* *or* hauteur *f* de l'entrejambe ► **inside-right** N (*Sport*) intérieur *m* droit

insider [ɪn'saɪdəʳ] [1] N (*gen*) quelqu'un qui connaît les choses de l'intérieur; (*in firm, organization*) quelqu'un qui est dans la place; (*esp sb with influence, knowledge, also St Ex*) initié(e) *m(f)* [2] COMP ► **insider dealing, insider trading** N (*Jur, Fin*) délit *m* d'initiés

insidious [ɪn'sɪdɪəs] ADJ insidieux
insidiously [ɪn'sɪdɪəslɪ] ADV insidieusement
insight ['ɪnsaɪt] N [a] (= *revealing glimpse*) aperçu *m*, idée *f* (**into** de, **about** sur); **to give sb an ~ into sth** donner à qn un aperçu de qch; **this gave us new ~s into what's been happening** cela nous a ouvert de nouvelles perspectives sur ce qui s'est passé; **that will give you an ~ into his reasons for doing it** cela vous éclairera sur les raisons qui l'ont poussé à le faire [b] (= *discernment*) pénétration *f*, perspicacité *f*
insightful ['ɪnsaɪtfʊl] ADJ pénétrant, perspicace
insignia [ɪn'sɪgnɪə] N (*pl* **insignias** *or* **insignia**) insigne *m*
insignificance [ˌɪnsɪg'nɪfɪkəns] N insignifiance *f* → **pale¹**
insignificant [ˌɪnsɪg'nɪfɪkənt] ADJ insignifiant; **not ~** non négligeable; **statistically ~** statistiquement non significatif
insincere [ˌɪnsɪn'sɪəʳ] ADJ [*person*] pas sincère, hypocrite; [*book, smile, remark*] faux (fausse *f*), hypocrite
insincerely [ˌɪnsɪn'sɪəlɪ] ADV [*speak, smile, promise*] sans sincérité, de façon hypocrite
insincerity [ˌɪnsɪn'serɪtɪ] N manque *m* de sincérité, hypocrisie *f*
insinuate [ɪn'sɪnjʊeɪt] VT [a] (= *hint, suggest*) insinuer; **to ~ that ...** insinuer que ...; **to ~ to sb that ...** insinuer à qn que ...; **what are you insinuating?** qu'est-ce que tu veux dire *or* insinuer par là? [b] **to ~ o.s. into sb's favour** s'insinuer dans les bonnes grâces de qn
insinuating [ɪn'sɪnjʊeɪtɪŋ] ADJ insinuant
insinuation [ɪnˌsɪnjʊ'eɪʃən] N [a] (= *suggestion*) insinuation *f*, allusion *f* [b] (*NonC*) insinuation *f*
insipid [ɪn'sɪpɪd] ADJ [*food, taste, entertainment, person*] insipide; [*colour*] fade
insipidity [ˌɪnsɪ'pɪdɪtɪ] N [*of food, taste, entertainment, person*] insipidité *f*; [*of colour*] fadeur *f*
▼ **insist** [ɪn'sɪst] [1] VI insister; **if you ~** si vous insistez, si vous y tenez; **I won't ~** je n'insisterai pas; **please don't ~** inutile d'insister; **if he refuses, I will ~** s'il refuse, j'insisterai; **to ~ on doing** insister pour faire, vouloir absolument faire; **I ~ on your coming** j'insiste pour que tu viennes, je tiens absolument à ce que tu viennes; **he ~ed on my waiting for him** il a insisté pour que je l'attende, il voulait absolument que je l'attende; **they ~ed on silence** ils ont exigé le silence; **he ~ed on his innocence** il a clamé son innocence, il protestait de son innocence; **they ~ on the right to defend themselves** ils revendiquent leur droit de se défendre eux-mêmes; **he ~ed on the need for dialogue** il a insisté sur le besoin de dialogue; **to ~ on a point in a discussion** insister sur un point dans une discussion [2] VT [a] (= *demand*) insister; **I must ~ that you let me help** j'insiste pour que tu me permettes d'aider; **she ~ed that I should come** elle a insisté pour que je vienne; **I ~ that you should come** j'insiste pour que tu viennes, je tiens absolument à ce que tu viennes [b] (= *affirm*) affirmer, soutenir; **he ~s that he has seen her before** il affirme *or* soutient l'avoir déjà vue; **"it's not that difficult", she ~ed** «ce n'est pas si difficile» a-t-elle affirmé *or* soutenu
insistence [ɪn'sɪstəns] N insistance *f*; **his ~ on coming with me** l'insistance qu'il met (*or* a mis *etc*) à vouloir venir avec moi; **their ~ on being involved** *or* **that they should be involved** leur insistance à vouloir être associé; **his ~ on his innocence** ses protestations d'innocence; **his ~ on secrecy made her uneasy** son insistance à exiger le secret la mettait mal à l'aise; **with ~** avec insistance; **I did it on** *or* **at his ~** je l'ai fait parce qu'il a insisté

insistent [ɪn'sɪstənt] ADJ [*person, tone, question, attitude, demands*] insistant; **she was (most) ~ (about it)** elle a (beaucoup) insisté (là-dessus)
insistently [ɪn'sɪstəntlɪ] ADV avec insistance
in situ [ɪn'sɪtjuː] ADV (*frm*) in situ, en place
insofar [ˌɪnsəʊ'fɑː] ADV **~ as** en ce sens que, dans la mesure où
insole ['ɪnˌsəʊl] N (*removable*) semelle *f* intérieure; (*part of shoe*) première *f*
insolence ['ɪnsələns] N (*NonC*) insolence *f* (**to** envers)
insolent ['ɪnsələnt] ADJ insolent (**to** *or* **with sb** avec qn)
insolently ['ɪnsələntlɪ] ADV insolemment
insolubility [ɪnˌsɒljʊ'bɪlɪtɪ] N insolubilité *f*
insoluble [ɪn'sɒljʊbl] ADJ insoluble
insolvable [ɪn'sɒlvəbl] ADJ insoluble
insolvency [ɪn'sɒlvənsɪ] N (*gen*) insolvabilité *f*; (= *bankruptcy*) faillite *f*
insolvent [ɪn'sɒlvənt] ADJ (*gen*) insolvable; (= *bankrupt*) en faillite, en état de cessation de paiement (*Jur*); **to become ~** [*trader*] tomber en *or* faire faillite; [*individual*] tomber en déconfiture; **to declare oneself ~** [*trader*] déposer son bilan; [*individual*] se déclarer insolvable
insomnia [ɪn'sɒmnɪə] N insomnie *f*
insomniac [ɪn'sɒmnɪæk] ADJ, N insomniaque *mf*
insomuch [ˌɪnsəʊ'mʌtʃ] ADV **~ that** à tel point *or* au point que; **~ as** d'autant que
insouciance [ɪn'suːsɪəns] N (*frm*) insouciance *f*
insouciant [ɪn'suːsɪənt] ADJ (*frm*) insouciant (**about sth** de qch)
insp. ABBR = **inspector**
inspect [ɪn'spekt] VT [a] (= *examine*) [+ *document, object*] examiner (avec attention *or* de près), inspecter; (*Brit*) [+ *ticket*] contrôler; (*Customs*) [+ *luggage*] visiter; [+ *machinery*] inspecter, vérifier; (*Mil, Pol*) [+ *weapon sites*] inspecter; [+ *school, teacher*] inspecter; (*Jur*) **right to ~ (sth)** droit *m* de regard (sur qch) [b] (*Mil*) [+ *troops*] (= *check*) inspecter; (= *review*) passer en revue
inspection [ɪn'spekʃən] [1] N [a] [*of document, object*] examen *m* (attentif); (*Brit*) [*of ticket*] contrôle *m*; [*of machinery*] inspection *f*, vérification *f*; [*of school*] (visite *f* d')inspection *f*; **close ~** (*gen*) examen *m* minutieux; (*for checking purposes*) inspection *f*; **customs ~** visite *f* de douane; **factory ~** inspection *f* d'usine; **to make an ~ of sth** effectuer une inspection *or* un contrôle de qch; **on ~ everything proved normal** une vérification a permis de s'assurer que tout était normal; **on closer ~** en regardant de plus près [b] (*Mil*) [*of troops*] (= *check*) inspection *f*; (= *review*) revue *f* [2] COMP ► **inspection pit** N (*Aut*) fosse *f* (de réparation)
inspector [ɪn'spektəʳ] [1] N [a] (*gen*) inspecteur *m*, -trice *f*; (*Brit: on bus, train*) contrôleur *m*, -euse *f*; **tax ~** ◊ **~ of taxes** (*Brit*) contrôleur *m* *or* inspecteur *m* des impôts [b] (*Brit: also* **police ~**) inspecteur *m* (de police) → **chief** [c] (*Brit Scol: also* **schools ~, ~ of schools**) (*secondary*) inspecteur *m*, -trice *f* d'académie; (*primary*) inspecteur *m*, -trice *f* primaire [2] COMP ► **inspector general** N (*pl* **inspectors general**) inspecteur *m* général → **1**
inspectorate [ɪn'spektərɪt] N (*esp Brit*) (= *body of inspectors*) corps *m* des inspecteurs, inspection *f*; (= *office*) inspection *f*
inspiration [ˌɪnspɪ'reɪʃən] N [a] (*NonC*) inspiration *f*; **to draw one's ~ from sth** s'inspirer de qch [b] **to be an ~ to sb** [*person, thing*] être une source d'inspiration; **you've been an ~ to us all** vous avez été notre source d'inspiration à tous; **to be the ~ for sth** servir d'inspiration pour qch; **the ~ behind the re-**

forms was a paper written in 1985 les réformes s'inspiraient d'un article écrit en 1985 [c] (= good idea) inspiration f; **to have a sudden ~** avoir une inspiration subite

inspirational [ˌɪnspəˈreɪʃənl] ADJ [teacher, leader] enthousiasmant, stimulant; [book, film] stimulant, inspirant; (Rel) édifiant

inspire [ɪnˈspaɪəʳ] VT [+ person, work of art, action, decision] inspirer (**to do** à faire); **the book was ~d by a real person** le livre s'inspirait d'un personnage réel; **to ~ confidence in sb** ◊ **to ~ sb with confidence** inspirer confiance à qn; **to ~ courage in sb** insuffler du courage à qn; **to ~ sb with an idea** inspirer une idée à qn; **her beauty ~d him to write the song** inspiré par sa beauté, il a écrit cette chanson; **what ~d you to offer to help?** qu'est-ce qui vous a donné l'idée de proposer votre aide?

inspired [ɪnˈspaɪəd] ADJ [a] [person, performance, idea, choice] inspiré; **that was an ~ guess** or **a piece of ~ guesswork!** bien deviné! [b] (= motivated) **politically/divinely/classically ~** d'inspiration politique/divine/classique

inspiring [ɪnˈspaɪərɪŋ] ADJ [a] (= edifying, impressive) [story, film, example] édifiant, inspirant; **the ~ tale of her fight against cancer** l'histoire édifiante de sa lutte contre le cancer; **it wasn't particularly ~** ce n'était pas terrible* [b] (= stimulating) [teacher, leader] enthousiasmant, stimulant; [book, film] stimulant, inspirant

inst. ADV (Comm) (ABBR = **instant**) courant; **the 16th ~** le 16 courant

instability [ˌɪnstəˈbɪlɪtɪ] N instabilité f

instal(l) [ɪnˈstɔːl] VT (gen, Rel) installer; **to ~ o.s. in** s'installer dans

installation [ˌɪnstəˈleɪʃən] N (all senses) installation f

instalment, installment (US) [ɪnˈstɔːlmənt] [1] N [a] (= payment) versement m (partiel or échelonné); (= down payment) acompte m; [of loan, investment, credit] tranche f, versement m; **to pay an ~** faire un versement (partiel); **to pay in** or **by ~s** payer en plusieurs versements or par traites échelonnées; **~ on account** acompte m provisionnel; **annual ~** versement m annuel, annuité f; **monthly ~** versement m mensuel, mensualité f [b] [of story, serial] épisode m; [of book] fascicule m, livraison f; (TV etc) **this is the first ~ of a six-part serial** voici le premier épisode d'un feuilleton qui en comportera six; **this story will appear in ~s over the next eight weeks** ce récit paraîtra par épisodes pendant les huit semaines à venir; **to publish a work in ~s** publier un ouvrage par fascicules

[2] COMP ► **installment plan** N (US) contrat m de vente à crédit or à tempérament; **to buy on the installment plan** acheter à crédit

▼ **instance** [ˈɪnstəns] [1] N [a] (= example) exemple m, cas m; (= occasion) circonstance f, occasion f; **for ~** par exemple; **in the present ~** dans le cas présent, dans cette circonstance; **in many ~s** dans bien des cas; **in the first ~** en premier lieu; **as an ~ of** comme exemple de; **let's take an actual ~** prenons un exemple or un cas concret; **this is an ~ of what I was talking about** c'est un exemple de ce dont je parlais; **a serious ~ of corruption** un cas sérieux de corruption [b] (Jur) **at the ~ of** sur or à la demande de, sur l'instance de [2] VT donner en exemple, citer en exemple, faire état de (more frm)

instant [ˈɪnstənt] [1] ADJ [a] [obedience, relief, response, effect] immédiat, instantané; [need] urgent, pressant; **this calls for ~ action** ceci nécessite des mesures immédiates; **~ camera/photography** appareil m (photo)/photographie f à développement instantané [b] (Culin) [coffee] soluble; [potatoes] déshydraté; [food] à préparation rapide; **~ soup** potage m (instantané) en poudre

[c] (Comm) courant; **your letter of the 10th ~** votre lettre du 10 courant

[2] N [a] (= moment) instant m, moment m; **come here this ~** viens ici tout de suite or à l'instant; **for an ~** pendant un instant, l'espace d'un instant; **on the ~** tout de suite, à l'instant; **the next ~** l'instant d'après; **I did it in an ~** je l'ai fait en un instant; **I'll be ready in an ~** je serai prêt dans un instant; **in** or **at the same ~** au même moment; **he left the ~ he heard the news** il est parti dès qu'il or aussitôt qu'il a appris la nouvelle

[b] (lottery = scratchcard) jeu instantané de grattage, ≈ Tac o Tac® m

[3] COMP ► **instant replay** N (TV) répétition immédiate d'une séquence; (= slow-motion) ralenti m

instantaneous [ˌɪnstənˈteɪnɪəs] ADJ [event, response] instantané; **I took an ~ dislike to him** je l'ai tout de suite or immédiatement détesté

instantaneously [ˌɪnstənˈteɪnɪəslɪ] ADV instantanément

instantly [ˈɪnstəntlɪ] ADV [die, be killed] sur le coup, instantanément; [know, recognize] immédiatement; [recognizable, identifiable, available] immédiatement; **~ likeable** [person] sympathique au premier abord; **the giant panda is ~ recognizable** or **identifiable by its black and white coat** le panda géant est immédiatement reconnaissable à son pelage noir et blanc; **~ forgettable** (= mediocre) sans aucun intérêt

instead [ɪnˈsted] ADV [a] plutôt, au contraire; **if you don't like orange juice, have some mineral water ~** si vous n'aimez pas le jus d'orange, prenez plutôt de l'eau minérale; **forget about dieting and eat normally ~** oubliez votre régime et mangez normalement; **his brother came ~ (of him)** son frère est venu à sa place; **I didn't go to the office, I went to the cinema ~** je ne suis pas allé au bureau, au lieu de cela je suis allé au cinéma [b] **~ of:** **~ of going to school** au lieu d'aller à l'école, plutôt que d'aller à l'école; **we decided to have dinner at 8 o'clock ~ of 7** nous avons décidé de dîner à 8 heures au lieu de 7; **~ of Louise** à la place de Louise; **this is ~ of a birthday present** c'est à la place d'un cadeau d'anniversaire

instep [ˈɪnstep] N [a] (Anat) cou-de-pied m; **to have a high ~** avoir le pied cambré [b] [of shoe] cambrure f

instigate [ˈɪnstɪɡeɪt] VT être l'instigateur de

instigation [ˌɪnstɪˈɡeɪʃən] N instigation f; **at sb's ~** à l'instigation de qn

instigator [ˈɪnstɪɡeɪtəʳ] N instigateur m, -trice f; [of riot, plot] auteur m

instil, instill (US) [ɪnˈstɪl] VT [+ courage, optimism] insuffler (**into sb** à qn); [+ knowledge, principles] inculquer (**into sb** à qn); [+ idea, fact] faire comprendre (**into sb** à qn); [+ fear] faire naître (**into sb** chez qn); **to ~ into sb that ...** faire pénétrer dans l'esprit de qn que ...

instinct [ˈɪnstɪŋt] [1] N instinct m; **by** or **from ~** d'instinct; **to have an ~ for business** or **a good business ~** avoir le sens des affaires [2] [ɪnˈstɪŋkt] ADJ (liter) **~ with** qui exhale or respire (liter), plein de

instinctive [ɪnˈstɪŋktɪv] ADJ instinctif

instinctively [ɪnˈstɪŋktɪvlɪ] ADV instinctivement

instinctual [ɪnˈstɪŋktʃʊəl] ADJ = **instinctive**

institute [ˈɪnstɪtjuːt] [1] VT [a] (= establish) [+ system, rules] instituer, établir; (= found) [+ society] fonder, constituer; **newly ~d** [post] récemment créé, de création récente; [organization] de fondation récente [b] (= set in motion) [+ inquiry] ouvrir; [+ action] entreprendre (**against sb** contre qn); **to ~ proceedings against sb** intenter un procès contre qn

[c] (Rel) investir [2] N [a] (gen) institut m; **Institute of Education** Institut m de formation des maîtres; **Institute of Linguistics** etc Institut m de linguistique etc [b] (US = course) stage m (d'études)

institution [ˌɪnstɪˈtjuːʃən] N [a] (= organization) institution f; **a religious/political ~** une institution religieuse/politique; **financial/ credit/educational ~** établissement m financier/de crédit/d'enseignement; **an academic ~** un établissement d'enseignement supérieur

[b] (= feature, custom) institution f; **democratic ~s** ◊ **the ~s of democracy** les institutions fpl démocratiques; **the ~ of marriage** l'institution f du mariage; **tea is a great British ~** le thé est une grande institution britannique; (hum) **he's been with the firm so long that he's now an ~** il fait partie de l'entreprise depuis si longtemps qu'il en est devenu une véritable institution

[c] (= hospital, mental home etc) institution f; **he has been in ~s all his life** il a passé toute sa vie en institution

[d] (NonC) [of system, practice] institution f; [of proceedings, inquiry] ouverture mf

[e] (Rel) [of priest] investiture f

institutional [ˌɪnstɪˈtjuːʃənl] ADJ [a] (= of institutions) [reform, structure] institutionnel; **~ care** soins mpl en institution [b] (Fin, Comm = of companies) [investors, funds, buying] institutionnel [c] (pej = reminiscent of institutions) [food] d'internat; [atmosphere] réglementé

institutionalize [ˌɪnstɪˈtjuːʃnəlaɪz] VT [a] [+ person] placer dans une institution [b] [+ procedure, custom, event etc] institutionnaliser, donner un caractère officiel à

institutionalized [ˌɪnstɪˈtjuːʃnəlaɪzd] ADJ [a] (= living in an institution) **~ people** personnes fpl vivant en institution [b] (= dependent) dépendant; **after all those years in prison, he's become totally ~** après toutes ces années en prison, il est désormais totalement dépendant or il a désappris à être autonome [c] (= ingrained) [racism etc] institutionnalisé; **to become ~** s'institutionnaliser, devenir une institution; (NonC) **~ religion** la religion institutionnalisée

instruct [ɪnˈstrʌkt] VT [a] (= teach) [+ person] instruire; **to ~ sb in sth** instruire qn en qch, enseigner or apprendre qch à qn; **to ~ sb in how to do sth** enseigner or apprendre à qn comment (il faut) faire qch [b] (= order, direct) [+ person] donner des instructions or des ordres à; **to ~ sb to do** charger qn de faire, donner pour instructions à qn de faire; (frm) **I am ~ed to inform you that ...** je suis chargé de or j'ai mission de vous informer que ...

[c] (Brit Jur) **to ~ a solicitor** donner ses instructions à un notaire; **to ~ counsel** constituer avocat; **to ~ the jury** [judge] donner des instructions au jury (**to do** pour qu'il fasse)

instruction [ɪnˈstrʌkʃən] [1] N [a] (NonC = teaching) instruction f, enseignement m; **to give ~ to sb (in sth)** instruire qn (en qch); **driving ~** leçons fpl de conduite [b] (gen pl) **~s** instructions fpl; (Mil) consigne f; (Comm, Pharm, Tech) indications fpl; **he gave me precise ~s on what to do if ...** il m'a donné des consignes précises or des instructions précises sur la conduite à tenir au cas où ...; **I gave ~s for him to be brought to me** j'ai donné des instructions pour qu'on or j'ai donné ordre qu'on me l'amène (subj); **he gave me ~s not to leave until ...** il m'a donné ordre de ne pas partir avant ...; **he was given strict ~s to avoid alcohol** on lui a rigoureusement interdit de boire de l'alcool; **to act according to ~s** se conformer aux instructions; (Mil) se conformer à la consigne; **"~s for use"** « mode d'emploi »; **the ~s are on the back of the box** le mode d'emploi est (indiqué) au dos de la boîte

---

➤ LANGUAGE IN USE: **instance** 26.2

2 COMP ► **instruction book** N (*Comm, Tech*) mode *m* d'emploi, notice *f* d'utilisation ► **instruction manual** N manuel *m* d'utilisation

instructive [ɪnˈstrʌktɪv] ADJ instructif

instructor [ɪnˈstrʌktər] N **a** (*Sport*) moniteur *m*, -trice *f*, professeur *m*; (*Mil*) instructeur *m* → **driving b** (*US Univ*) ≈ assistant *m*

instructress [ɪnˈstrʌktrɪs] N (*Sport*) monitrice *f*, professeur *m*

instrument [ˈɪnstrəmənt] **1** N (*gen, Med, Mus, Tech, fig*) instrument *m*; (*Jur*) instrument *m*, acte *m* juridique; (*Fin*) titre *m*, effet *m*; **to fly by** *or* **on ~s** naviguer aux instruments; **~ of government** instrument *m* du gouvernement → **blunt, wind¹ 2** [ˈɪnstrʊˈment] VT (*Mus*) orchestrer; (*Jur*) instrumenter **3** COMP (*Aviat*) [*flying, landing*] aux instruments (de bord) ► **instrument board**, **instrument panel** N (*Aut, Aviat*) tableau *m* de bord

instrumental [ˌɪnstrʊˈmentl] ADJ **a** [*role*] déterminant; **to be ~ in sth** jouer un rôle-clé dans qch; **he was ~ in setting up/launching the scheme** il a joué un rôle-clé dans la mise en place/le lancement du projet **b** (*Mus*) [*music, composition, arrangement, tuition, ensemble*] instrumental; [*recording, album*] de musique instrumentale; [*composer*] d'œuvres instrumentales; ► **performer** instrumentiste *mf*

instrumentalist [ˌɪnstrʊˈmentəlɪst] N (*Mus*) instrumentiste *mf*

instrumentation [ˌɪnstrʊmenˈteɪʃən] N (*Mus, Tech*) instrumentation *f*

insubordinate [ˌɪnsəˈbɔːdɪnɪt] ADJ insubordonné, indiscipliné

insubordination [ˈɪnsəˌbɔːdɪˈneɪʃən] N insubordination *f*, indiscipline *f*, désobéissance *f*

insubstantial [ˌɪnsəbˈstænʃəl] ADJ **a** (= *small*) [*sum, amount*] peu important; [*meal, work*] peu substantiel; (= *weak*) [*argument*] sans substance; [*evidence*] sans fondement; [*structure*] peu solide **b** (*liter* = *unreal*) [*vision, illusion*] chimérique

insufferable [ɪnˈsʌfərəbl] ADJ (*frm*) insupportable

insufferably [ɪnˈsʌfərəblɪ] ADV (*frm*) insupportablement; **it was ~ hot** il faisait une chaleur insupportable

insufficiency [ˌɪnsəˈfɪʃənsɪ] N insuffisance *f*

insufficient [ˌɪnsəˈfɪʃənt] ADJ insuffisant

insufficiently [ˌɪnsəˈfɪʃəntlɪ] ADV insuffisamment

insular [ˈɪnsjələr] ADJ **a** (*pej* = *parochial*) [*person, attitude, views, outlook*] borné (*pej*); [*community, existence*] coupé du monde extérieur **b** (*SPEC* = *relating to an island*) insulaire

insularity [ˌɪnsjʊˈlærɪtɪ] N insularité *f*; (*fig pej*) [*of person*] étroitesse *f* d'esprit; [*of community, existence*] fermeture *f* au monde extérieur; [*of outlook, views*] étroitesse *f*

insulate [ˈɪnsjʊleɪt] **1** VT **a** (*Elec*) isoler; (*against cold, heat*) [+ *room, roof*] isoler; [+ *water tank*] calorifuger; (*against sound*) [+ *room, wall*] insonoriser; **~d handle** manche *m* isolant; **~d pliers** pince *f* isolante; **insulating material** isolant *m* **b** (*fig*) [+ *person*] (= *separate*) séparer (**from** de); (= *protect*) protéger (**against** de) **2** COMP ► **insulating tape** N (ruban *m*) isolant *m*; (= *adhesive*) chatterton *m*

insulation [ˌɪnsjʊˈleɪʃən] N **a** (*NonC*) (*Elec*) isolation *f*; [*of house, room*] (*against cold*) isolation *f* (calorifuge); (*against sound*) insonorisation *f* **b** (*fig*) **they lived in happy ~ from brutal facts** ils vivaient heureux à l'abri de la réalité brutale **c** (*NonC* = *material*) isolant *m*

insulator [ˈɪnsjʊleɪtər] N (*Elec*) (= *device*) isolateur *m*; (= *material*) isolant *m*

insulin [ˈɪnsjʊlɪn] **1** N insuline *f* **2** COMP [*injection*] d'insuline ► **insulin shock** N (*Med*) choc *m* insulinique ► **insulin treat-**

-ment N insulinothérapie *f*, traitement *m* insulinique *or* à l'insuline

insult 1 [ɪnˈsʌlt] VT (*with words, gestures*) insulter, injurier; (= *offend*) faire (un) affront à, insulter; **she felt ~ed by his indifference** elle s'est sentie insultée par son indifférence **2** [ˈɪnsʌlt] N (= *remark*) insulte *f*, injure *f*; (= *action, affront*) affront *m*, insulte *f*; **to hurl ~s at sb** injurier qn, lancer des insultes à qn; **the book is an ~ to the reader's intelligence** le livre est une insulte à *or* fait affront à l'intelligence du lecteur; **these demands are an ~ to the profession** ces revendications sont un affront à la profession; **an ~ to sb's memory** une insulte à la mémoire de qn; **it was seen as an ~ to Islam** cela a été perçu comme un affront à l'islam → **add**

insulting [ɪnˈsʌltɪŋ] ADJ insultant, injurieux; **to be ~ to sb** [*remarks, comments etc*] être un affront à qn

insultingly [ɪnˈsʌltɪŋlɪ] ADV [*behave, talk*] de façon insultante; **~ dismissive** dédaigneux au point d'être insultant; **~ sexist** d'un sexisme insultant

insuperable [ɪnˈsuːpərəbl] ADJ insurmontable

insuperably [ɪnˈsuːpərəblɪ] ADV d'une façon insurmontable

insupportable† [ˌɪnsəˈpɔːtəbl] ADJ insupportable

insurable [ɪnˈʃʊərəbl] ADJ assurable

insurance [ɪnˈʃʊərəns] **1** N (*gen*) assurance *f* (**on** *or* **for sth** pour qch, **against** contre); (= *policy*) police *f* *or* contrat *m* d'assurances (**on** *or* **for sth** pour qch, **against sth** contre qch); (*fig*) garantie *f*; **he pays £300 a year in ~** il paie 300 livres (de primes) d'assurance par an; **~ on a building** assurance *f* sur le capital immobilier; **to take out ~** contracter une assurance; **to take out ~ against** s'assurer contre, se faire assurer contre; **what does your ~ cover?** que couvre votre police *or* contrat d'assurance?; **we must extend our ~** nous devons augmenter le montant pour lequel nous sommes assurés; **the ~ runs out on 5 July** l'assurance arrive à échéance le 5 juillet; (*fig*) **to do sth as an ~ against** faire qch comme garantie contre, faire qch pour se prémunir contre → **fire, life**

2 COMP ► **insurance adjuster** N (*US*) expert *m* en sinistres ► **insurance agent** N agent *m* d'assurances ► **insurance broker** N courtier *m* d'assurances ► **insurance certificate** N (*Aut*) attestation *f* d'assurance ► **insurance claim** N (déclaration *f* de) sinistre *m* ► **insurance company** N compagnie *f* *or* société *f* d'assurances ► **insurance policy** N police *f* d'assurance, assurances* *fpl* ► **insurance premium** N prime *f* (d'assurance) ► **insurance scheme** N régime *m* d'assurances ► **insurance stamp** N (*Brit Admin*) vignette *f* *or* timbre *m* de contribution à la sécurité sociale ► **insurance underwriter** N (*gen*) assureur *m*; (= *underwriting company*) réassureur *m*

insurant [ɪnˈʃʊərənt] N (*SPEC*) assuré(e) *m(f)*, souscripteur *m*, -trice *f*

insure [ɪnˈʃʊər] VT **a** [+ *car, house*] (faire) assurer; **he ~d his guitar for £1000** il a assuré sa guitare pour 1000 livres; **to ~ o.s.** *or* **one's life** s'assurer *or* se faire assurer sur la vie; **I am ~d against fire** je suis assuré contre l'incendie; (*fig*) **we ~d (ourselves) against possible disappointment** nous avons paré aux déceptions possibles; **in order to ~ against any delay ...** pour nous (*or* les *etc*) garantir contre tout retard ... **b** [+ *power, success*] assurer, garantir; **this will ~ that you will be notified when ...** grâce à ceci vous êtes assuré d'être avisé quand ...; **in order to ~ that terrorists do not enter the country** afin de s'assurer que les terroristes n'entrent pas dans le pays; **they want to ~ that their children will be educated properly** ils

veulent s'assurer *or* être sûrs que leurs enfants recevront une éducation correcte

insured [ɪnˈʃʊəd] ADJ, N assuré(e) *m(f)*

insurer [ɪnˈʃʊərər] N assureur *m*

insurgence [ɪnˈsɜːdʒəns], **insurgency** [ɪnˈsɜːdʒənsɪ] N insurrection *f*

insurgent [ɪnˈsɜːdʒənt] ADJ, N insurgé(e) *m(f)*

insurmountable [ˌɪnsəˈmaʊntəbl] ADJ insurmontable

insurrection [ˌɪnsəˈrekʃən] N **a** (*NonC*) insurrection *f*; **to rise in ~** se soulever, s'insurger **b** (= *uprising*) insurrection *f*, soulèvement *m*

insurrectionary [ˌɪnsəˈrekʃnərɪ] ADJ insurrectionnel

insurrectionist [ˌɪnsəˈrekʃənɪst] N insurgé(e) *m(f)*

int. ADJ, N (ABBR = **international**) international

intact [ɪnˈtækt] ADJ intact; **to remain** *or* **survive ~** rester intact

intake [ˈɪnteɪk] **1** N **a** (*NonC: Tech*) [*of water*] prise *f*, adduction *f*; [*of gas, steam*] adduction *f*, admission *f* → **air b** (*Scol, Univ*) admission(s) *f(pl)*, (nombre *m* des) inscriptions *fpl*; (*Mil*) contingent *m*, recrues *fpl*; **the latest ~ of young graduates into our company** le dernier contingent de jeunes diplômés recrutés dans notre société; **the US's annual ~ of immigrants** le contingent annuel d'immigrants arrivant aux États-Unis **c** [*of protein, liquid, alcohol etc*] consommation *f*; **food ~** ration *f* alimentaire **d** **she heard his ~ of breath** elle l'a entendu retenir sa respiration **2** COMP ► **intake valve** N (*Tech*) soupape *f* d'admission

intangible [ɪnˈtændʒəbl] **1** ADJ [*quality, presence*] intangible, impalpable **2** impondérable *m* **3** COMP ► **intangible assets** NPL (*Jur*) immobilisations *fpl* incorporelles ► **intangible property** N (*Jur*) biens *mpl* incorporels

integer [ˈɪntɪdʒər] N (nombre *m*) entier *m*

integral [ˈɪntɪɡrəl] **1** ADJ **a** [*part*] intégrant, constituant; **to be an ~ part of sth** ◊ **to be ~ to sth** faire partie intégrante de qch **b** (= *whole*) intégral, complet (-ète *f*), entier; **~ payment** paiement *m* intégral **c** (*Math*) intégral; **~ calculus** calcul *m* intégral **2** N (*Math, fig*) intégrale *f*

integrate [ˈɪntɪɡreɪt] **1** VT **a** (= *combine into a whole*) [+ *people, objects, ideas*] intégrer, incorporer (**in, into** dans); **b** (= *complete by adding parts*) compléter; (*Psych*) **an ~d personality** une personnalité bien intégrée **c** (= *combine, desegregate*) [+ *races, religions, ethnic groups etc*] intégrer; **to ~ Catholic and non-Catholic schools** intégrer les écoles catholiques et non catholiques; **to ~ a school** *etc* imposer la déségrégation dans un établissement scolaire *etc*; **~d school** établissement *m* scolaire où se pratique l'intégration **d** (*Math*) intégrer **2** VI **a** [*school, neighbourhood etc*] pratiquer l'intégration raciale **b** [*person, religious or ethnic group etc*] s'intégrer (**into** dans)

integrated [ˈɪntɪɡreɪtɪd] **1** ADJ intégré **2** COMP ► **integrated accounting package** N logiciel *m* intégré de comptabilité ► **integrated circuit** N (*Elec*) circuit *m* intégré ► **integrated course** N (*Brit Educ*) cours *m* de formation professionnelle (*pour apprentis*) ► **integrated day** N (*Brit Scol*) journée *f* sans emploi du temps structuré ► **Integrated Services Digital Network** N Réseau *m* numérique à intégration de services ► **integrated studies** NPL (*Brit Scol*) études *fpl* générales (*où les matières ne sont pas différenciées*)

integration [ˌɪntɪˈɡreɪʃən] N (*also Math, Psych*) intégration *f* (**into** dans); **racial/social/European ~** intégration *f* raciale/sociale/européenne

integrity [ɪnˈtegrɪtɪ] N **a** (= *honesty*) intégrité *f*, probité *f*; **a man of ~** un homme intègre **b** (= *totality*) intégrité *f*, totalité *f*; **in its ~** dans son intégrité, dans sa totalité; **territorial ~** l'intégrité *f* du territoire; **the ~ of the nation** l'intégrité *f* de la nation

integument [ɪnˈtegjʊmənt] N tégument *m*

intellect [ˈɪntɪlekt] N **a** (*NonC*) (= *reasoning power*) intellect *m*, intelligence *f*; (= *cleverness*) intelligence *f*, esprit *m*; **a man of (great) ~** un homme d'une grande intelligence **b** [*of person*] intelligence *f*, esprit *m*

intellectual [ˌɪntɪˈlektjʊəl] **1** ADJ (*gen*) intellectuel; [*group, family*] d'intellectuels; **~ property** propriété *f* intellectuelle **2** N intellectuel(le) *m(f)*

intellectualize [ˌɪntɪˈlektjʊəlaɪz] **1** VT intellectualiser **2** VI **you always have to ~** il faut toujours que tu intellectualises tout

intellectually [ˌɪntɪˈlektjʊəlɪ] ADV intellectuellement, sur le plan intellectuel; **~ satisfying/honest** *etc* intellectuellement satisfaisant/honnête *etc*

intelligence [ɪnˈtelɪdʒəns] **1** N **a** (*NonC*) intelligence *f*; **a man of little ~** un homme peu intelligent *or* de peu d'intelligence; **his book shows ~** son livre est intelligent **b** (= *information*) renseignement(s) *m(pl)*, information(s) *f(pl)*; (*Press*) **latest ~** informations *fpl* de dernière minute **c** **Military/Naval Intelligence** service *m* de renseignements de l'armée de Terre/de la Marine; **he was in Intelligence during the war** il était dans les services de renseignements pendant la guerre **2** COMP ► **intelligence agent** N agent *m* de renseignements, agent *m* secret ► **Intelligence Corps** N (*Brit Mil*) service de renseignements et de sécurité militaires ► **Intelligence officer** N (*Brit Pol*) officier *m* de renseignements ► **intelligence quotient** N quotient *m* intellectuel ► **Intelligence Service** N (*Brit Pol*) services *mpl* secrets *or* de renseignements ► **intelligence test** N test *m* d'aptitude intellectuelle ► **intelligence work** N **to do ~ work** être dans *or* travailler dans les services de renseignements

intelligent [ɪnˈtelɪdʒənt] ADJ (*gen*) intelligent; (*Comput*) **terminal** terminal *m* intelligent; **the search for ~ life on other planets** la recherche de formes de vie intelligente sur d'autres planètes

intelligently [ɪnˈtelɪdʒəntlɪ] ADV intelligemment

intelligentsia [ɪnˌtelɪˈdʒentsɪə] N (*collective sg*) **the ~** l'intelligentsia *f*, l'élite *f* intellectuelle

intelligibility [ɪnˌtelɪdʒəˈbɪlɪtɪ] N intelligibilité *f*

intelligible [ɪnˈtelɪdʒəbl] ADJ intelligible

intelligibly [ɪnˈtelɪdʒəblɪ] ADV intelligiblement

intemperance [ɪnˈtempərəns] N (= *lack of self-restraint*) intempérance *f*; (= *lack of moderation*) manque *m* de modération

intemperate [ɪnˈtempərɪt] ADJ (*frm*) [*attitude, comment*] immodéré; [*language*] sans retenue; [*person*] intempérant†; [*haste, zeal*] excessif

▼ **intend** [ɪnˈtend] VT avoir l'intention; [+ *gift etc*] destiner (**for** à); **to ~ to do** ◊ **to ~ doing** avoir l'intention de faire; **I ~ to go and see him** j'ai l'intention d'aller le voir; **I don't ~ to tell him about it** je n'ai pas l'intention de lui en parler; **I'm sure he didn't ~ that we should hear him** je suis sûr qu'il ne pensait pas que nous allions l'entendre; **I fully ~ to punish him** j'ai la ferme intention de le punir; **he ~s to be a doctor** il a l'intention de devenir médecin, il se destine à la médecine; **it was ~ed that he should become an accountant** il était prévu qu'il devienne comptable; **this scheme is ~ed to help the poor** ce projet est destiné à

venir en aide aux indigents; **~ed for** destiné à; **the money was ~ed for British families** l'argent était destiné aux familles britanniques; **hospital facilities which were ~ed for AIDS patients** des infrastructures hospitalières qui étaient destinées aux malades du sida; **the building was originally ~ed as a sports complex** le bâtiment devait initialement être un complexe sportif; **I ~ed it as a compliment** (dans mon esprit) cela voulait être un compliment; **he ~ed no harm** il l'a fait sans mauvaise intention; **to ~ marriage** avoir des intentions de mariage; **did you ~ that?** est-ce que vous avez fait cela exprès? → **intended**

intended [ɪnˈtendɪd] **1** ADJ **a** (= *desired, planned*) [*target*] visé; [*effect*] voulu; **the ~ victim (of the attack)** la victime visée (par l'attentat); **he stayed only ten days of his ~ six-month visit** il n'est resté que dix jours sur les six mois de visite qu'il avait prévus **b** (= *deliberate*) [*insult etc*] intentionnel, fait intentionnellement **2** N† **his ~** sa promise†, sa future (*hum*); **her ~** son promis†, son futur (*hum*)

intense [ɪnˈtens] ADJ **a** [*heat, cold, pain, light, colour, activity, fighting, speculation*] intense; [*fear, anger, hatred*] violent; [*interest, enthusiasm, competition*] très vif **b** (= *passionate*) [*person*] sérieux; [*relationship*] passionné; [*gaze, expression*] d'une grande intensité

intensely [ɪnˈtenslɪ] ADV **a** (= *very*) [*hot, cold, unpleasant*] extrêmement; [*moving, moved, irritated*] vivement **b** [*concentrate, look at*] intensément; [*hate*] de tout son être; **I dislike her ~** elle me déplaît profondément

intensification [ɪnˌtensɪfɪˈkeɪʃən] N [*of heat, light, pain, activity, fighting*] intensification *f*; [*of production*] accélération *f*, intensification *f*

intensifier [ɪnˈtensɪfaɪə] N (*Gram*) intensif *m*

intensify [ɪnˈtensɪfaɪ] **1** VT intensifier; **to ~ (one's) efforts to do sth** intensifier ses efforts pour faire qch **2** VI [*fighting, competition, speculation*] s'intensifier; [*heat, cold, pain, fear, anger, hatred, light, colour*] augmenter

intensity [ɪnˈtensɪtɪ] N [*of anger, hatred, love*] intensité *f*, force *f*; [*of cold, heat*] intensité *f*; [*of current, light, sound*] intensité *f*, puissance *f*; [*of tone*] véhémence *f*; **her ~ disturbs me** son côté sérieux me met mal à l'aise; **capital ~** intensité *f* capitalistique

intensive [ɪnˈtensɪv] **1** ADJ (*gen, Ling, Agr*) intensif; **an ~ course in French** un cours accéléré *or* intensif de français **2** COMP ► **intensive care** N **to be in ~ care** être en réanimation; **to need ~ care** demander des soins intensifs ► **intensive care unit** N (*Med*) service *m* de réanimation, unité *f* de soins intensifs ► **intensive farming** N agriculture *f* intensive

-intensive [ɪnˈtensɪv] ADJ (*in compounds*) à forte intensité de; **capital-intensive** à forte intensité de capital → **energy, labour**

intensively [ɪnˈtensɪvlɪ] ADV [*work, campaign, study, farm*] intensivement; **~ reared** [*meat*] provenant d'un élevage intensif

intent [ɪnˈtent] **1** N intention *f*; **it was not my ~ to do business with him** il n'était pas dans mes intentions de traiter avec lui, je n'avais pas l'intention de traiter avec lui; **to all ~s and purposes** pratiquement; **with good ~** dans une bonne intention; **to do sth with ~** faire qch de propos délibéré; (*Jur*) **with criminal ~** dans un but délictueux; **with ~ to do** dans l'intention de *or* le but de faire; (*Jur*) **he denied possessing a firearm with ~ to endanger life** il a nié avoir détenu une arme à feu dans le but d'intenter à la vie de quelqu'un; **he signed a letter of ~ to sell his assets** il a signé une lettre d'intention concernant la vente de ses biens → **loiter** **2** ADJ **a** (= *absorbed*) [*face, look, expression*] attentif; **~ on his work/on a jigsaw puzzle** absorbé par son travail/par un puzzle; **he was**

~ on what she was saying il écoutait attentivement ce qu'elle disait **b** (= *determined*) **to be ~ on doing sth** être résolu à faire qch; **~ on revenge** résolu à se venger; **they were ~ on his downfall** ils étaient résolus à provoquer sa perte; **he was so ~ on seeing her that ...** il avait l'esprit tellement occupé par l'idée de la voir que ...

▼ **intention** [ɪnˈtenʃən] N intention *f*; **it is my ~ to retire** j'ai l'intention de prendre ma retraite; **to have no ~ of doing** n'avoir aucune intention de faire; **he has every ~ of doing this** il a bien l'intention de le faire; **I haven't the least** *or* **slightest ~ of staying** je n'ai pas la moindre intention de rester ici, il n'est nullement dans mes intentions de rester ici; **with the ~ of doing** dans l'intention de *or* dans le but de faire; **with this ~** à cette intention, à cette fin; **with good ~s** avec de bonnes intentions; **with the best of ~s** avec les meilleures intentions (du monde); **what are your ~s?** quelles sont vos intentions?, que comptez-vous faire?; **I don't know what his ~s were when he did it** je ne sais pas quelles étaient ses intentions quand il l'a fait; **his ~s are honourable** il a des intentions honorables

intentional [ɪnˈtenʃənl] ADJ intentionnel; **how can I blame him? it wasn't ~** comment pourrais-je lui en vouloir? il ne l'a pas fait exprès *or* ce n'était pas intentionnel

intentionally [ɪnˈtenʃnəlɪ] ADV [*mislead, violate, discriminate etc*] intentionnellement; **the authorities consider him ~ homeless** l'administration considère qu'il a délibérément quitté son domicile; **~ vague/misleading** délibérément vague/trompeur

intently [ɪnˈtentlɪ] ADV [*listen, look, watch, stare*] intensément; **they were talking ~ about work** ils étaient absorbés à parler travail

intentness [ɪnˈtentnɪs] N intensité *f*; **~ of purpose** résolution *f*

inter [ɪnˈtɜː] VT enterrer, ensevelir

inter- [ˈɪntə] PREF (+ *nsg*) entre (+ *npl*), inter... (+ *adj*); **~company** entre compagnies; **~regional** interrégional → **inter-city**

interact [ˌɪntərˈækt] VI **a** [*substances*] (ré)agir l'un sur l'autre, interagir **b** (*Comput*) dialoguer (**with** avec); (*fig*) **we don't ~ very well** le courant passe mal (entre nous)

interaction [ˌɪntərˈækʃən] N interaction *f*

interactive [ˌɪntərˈæktɪv] **1** ADJ (*gen, Comput*) interactif; **~ computing** traitement *m* interactif, informatique *f* conversationnelle; **~ mode** mode *m* conversationnel *or* interactif **2** COMP ► **interactive television** N télévision *f* interactive ► **interactive video** N vidéo *f* interactive

interactively [ˌɪntərˈæktɪvlɪ] ADV (*Comput*) [*work*] en mode conversationnel *or* interactif

inter alia [ˌɪntərˈeɪlɪə] ADV (*frm*) notamment, entre autres

interbreed [ˈɪntəˈbriːd] (*pret, ptp* interbred [ˈɪntəˈbred]) **1** VT (+ *animals*) croiser **2** VI se croiser (**with** avec)

intercalate [ˌɪnˈtɜːkəleɪt] VT intercaler

intercalation [ɪnˌtɜːkəˈleɪʃən] N intercalation *f*

intercampus [ˌɪntəˈkæmpəs] ADJ (*US Univ*) interuniversitaire

intercede [ˌɪntəˈsiːd] VI intercéder (**with** auprès de, **for** pour, en faveur de)

intercensal [ˌɪntəˈsensl] ADJ intercensitaire

intercept [ˌɪntəˈsept] **1** VT [+ *message, light*] intercepter, capter; [+ *plane, suspect*] intercepter; [+ *person*] arrêter au passage **2** N interception *f*

interception [ˌɪntəˈsepʃən] N interception *f*

interceptor [ˌɪntəˈseptə] N (= *aircraft, missile*) intercepteur *m*

intercession [ˌɪntəˈseʃən] N intercession *f*

► LANGUAGE IN USE: **intend** 8 **intention** 8

interchange ['ɪntə.tʃeɪndʒ] **1** N **a** (NonC) (= exchange) échange m; (= alternation) alternance f **b** (on motorway) échangeur m **2** [.ɪntə'tʃeɪndʒ] VT **a** (= alternate) faire alterner (**with** avec); (= change positions of) changer de place, mettre à la place l'un de l'autre; (= exchange) [+ gifts, letters, ideas] échanger (**with sb** avec qn) **3** VI (= change position) changer de place (**with** avec); (= alternate) alterner (**with** avec)

interchangeable [.ɪntə'tʃeɪndʒəbl] ADJ interchangeable

interchangeably [.ɪntə'tʃeɪndʒəblɪ] ADV de façon interchangeable

inter-city [.ɪntə'sɪtɪ] **1** ADJ [travel] d'une grande ville à une autre; [communications] interurbain **2** N (Brit Rail: also **~ train**) rapide m

intercollegiate ['ɪntəkə'li:dʒɪɪt] ADJ entre collèges

intercom ['ɪntəkɒm] N interphone m; **over** or **on the ~** à l'interphone

intercommunicate [.ɪntəkə'mju:nɪkeɪt] VI communiquer (réciproquement)

intercommunication ['ɪntəkə.mju:nɪ'keɪʃən] N intercommunication f, communication f réciproque

intercommunion [.ɪntəkə'mju:nɪən] N (Rel) intercommunion f; (gen) intercommunication f

interconnect [.ɪntəkə'nekt] **1** VT (gen) connecter (entre eux or elles); (Comput) [+ systems] interconnecter; **~ed facts** faits mpl intimement or étroitement liés; **~ed rooms** pièces fpl communicantes **2** VI [rooms, tunnels] communiquer (entre eux or elles); [parts of a structure] être relié(e)s (les un(e)s aux autres); **~ing wall** mur m mitoyen

interconnection [.ɪntəkə'nekʃən] N (Elec) interconnexion f; (fig) lien m

intercontinental ['ɪntə.kɒntɪ'nentl] ADJ intercontinental; **~ ballistic missile** missile m balistique intercontinental

intercostal [.ɪntə'kɒstl] ADJ intercostal

intercourse ['ɪntəkɔ:s] N **a** (NonC) relations fpl, rapports mpl; **business/human/social ~** relations fpl commerciales/humaines/sociales **b** sexual ~ rapports mpl (sexuels); **anal ~** sodomie f; **to have ~** avoir des rapports (**with** avec)

intercut [.ɪntə'kʌt] VT (Cine) **to ~ sth with sth** entrecouper qch de qch

interdenominational ['ɪntədɪ.nɒmɪ'neɪʃənl] ADJ entre confessions, interconfessionnel

interdepartmental ['ɪntə.di:pɑːt'mentl] ADJ (within firm) entre services; (Univ) entre départements; (Pol) interministériel

interdependence [.ɪntədɪ'pendəns] N interdépendance f

interdependent [.ɪntədɪ'pendənt] ADJ interdépendant

interdict ['ɪntədɪkt] **1** VT **a** (Jur, frm) interdire, prohiber **b** (Rel) [+ priest, person] jeter l'interdit sur **2** N **a** (Jur) prohibition f, interdiction f **b** (Rel) interdit m

interdiction [.ɪntə'dɪkʃən] N (Jur, Rel) interdiction f

interdisciplinarity [.ɪntə.dɪsɪplɪ'nærɪtɪ] N interdisciplinarité f

interdisciplinary [.ɪntə'dɪsɪplɪnərɪ] ADJ interdisciplinaire

▼ **interest** ['ɪntrɪst] **1** N **a** (NonC: in sb/sth) intérêt m; **to take** or **have an ~ in sb** s'intéresser à qn; **to take** or **have an ~ in sth** s'intéresser à qch, prendre de l'intérêt à qch; **he took no further ~ in it** il ne s'y est plus intéressé; **to show an ~ in sb/sth** manifester or montrer de l'intérêt pour qn/qch; **to take a great ~ in sb/sth** s'intéresser vivement à qn/qch; **to arouse sb's ~** éveiller l'intérêt de qn; **that's of no ~ to me** ça ne m'intéresse pas, ça

a peu d'intérêt pour moi; **a subject of little ~** un sujet présentant peu d'intérêt; **questions of public ~** questions fpl d'intérêt public or qui intéressent le public → **1c**; **she doesn't really need to work - she's doing it just for ~** elle n'a pas vraiment besoin de travailler: elle le fait parce que ça l'intéresse; **it adds ~ to the story** ça ajoute un certain intérêt à l'histoire; **matters of vital ~** questions fpl d'un intérêt or d'une importance capital(e)
b (= hobby etc) **what are your ~s?** quelles sont les choses qui vous intéressent?, à quoi vous intéressez-vous?; **my main ~ is baroque architecture** mon principal centre d'intérêt est l'architecture baroque; **special ~ holidays** vacances fpl à thème
c (= advantage, well-being) intérêt m, avantage m; **in one's (own) ~(s)** dans son (propre) intérêt; **it is in your own ~ to do so** il est de votre intérêt d'agir ainsi, vous avez tout intérêt à agir ainsi; **to act in sb's ~(s)** agir dans l'intérêt de qn; **in the ~(s) of hygiene/safety** par souci d'hygiène/de sécurité; **in the ~(s) of peace/national security** dans l'intérêt de la paix/la sécurité nationale; **in the public ~** dans l'intérêt public, pour le bien public; **Washington has an ~ in helping Russia with its economy** c'est dans l'intérêt de Washington d'aider économiquement la Russie
d (Comm, Jur etc = share stake) intérêts mpl, participation f; **I have an ~ in a hairdressing business** j'ai des intérêts dans un salon de coiffure; **he has business ~s abroad** il a des intérêts commerciaux à l'étranger; **Switzerland is looking after British ~s** la Suisse défend les intérêts britanniques; **he has sold his ~ in the firm** il a vendu la participation or les intérêts qu'il avait dans l'entreprise → **vest²**
e (= interested parties) **the coal/oil ~(s)** (gros) intérêts mpl houillers/pétroliers; **shipping ~s** les intérêts mpl maritimes; **the landed ~s** les propriétaires mpl terriens
f (NonC: Fin) intérêt(s) m(pl); **simple/compound ~** intérêts mpl simples/composés; **~ on an investment** intérêts mpl d'un placement; **loan with ~** prêt m à intérêt; **to lend out money at ~** faire un prêt (or des prêts) à intérêt; **to bear ~** rapporter un intérêt; **to bear ~ at 8%** donner un intérêt de 8%, porter intérêt à 8%; **to carry ~** rapporter or produire des intérêts
2 VT **a** intéresser; **to be ~ed in sth/sb** s'intéresser à qch/qn; **I'm not ~ed in football** le football ne m'intéresse pas, je ne m'intéresse pas au football; **the company is ~ed in buying land** l'entreprise est intéressée par l'achat de terrains; **I'm ~ed in going** ça m'intéresse d'y aller; **I'm not ~ed!** ça ne m'intéresse pas!; **I'm not ~ed in your excuses!** tes excuses ne m'intéressent pas!; **I'd be ~ed to see what this man has to offer** je serais curieux de savoir or j'aimerais bien savoir or cela m'intéresserait de savoir ce que cet homme a à proposer; **they spent time trying to ~ customers in their product** ils ont passé du temps à essayer d'intéresser les clients à leurs produits; **can I ~ you in contributing to ...?** est-ce que cela vous intéresserait de contribuer à ...?; **can I ~ you in a new computer?** seriez-vous intéressé par un nouvel ordinateur?
b (= concern) intéresser, concerner; **the struggle against inflation ~s us all** la lutte contre l'inflation touche chacun d'entre nous or nous concerne tous
3 COMP ▸ **interest-bearing** ADJ (Fin) [loan] productif d'intérêt ▸ **interest-free** ADJ (Fin) sans intérêt ▸ **interest group** N groupe m d'intérêt ▸ **interest payment** (Fin) versement m d'intérêts ▸ **interest rate** N (Fin) taux m d'intérêt; **at an ~ rate of 10%** à un taux d'intérêt de 10%

interested ['ɪntrɪstɪd] ADJ **a** (= attentive) [expression] d'intérêt **b** (= involved, partial)

[person, motive] intéressé; **to be an ~ party** être une des parties intéressées; **the ~ parties** les intéressés mpl, les parties fpl intéressées (Jur) → **interest**

interesting ['ɪntrɪstɪŋ] ADJ [book, story, idea, person] intéressant; **the meeting was very ~ for me** cette réunion m'a beaucoup intéressé; **the ~ thing (about it) is that ...** ce qu'il y a d'intéressant (à ce propos), c'est que ...

interestingly ['ɪntrɪstɪŋlɪ] ADV de façon intéressante; **~ (enough), he ...** chose intéressante, il ...

interface ['ɪntəfeɪs] **1** N **a** (Comput, Phys, Chem) interface f; (Comput) **user ~** interface f utilisateur **b** (fig) interface f, point m de liaison or de contact **2** VI (Comput, Tech) faire interface **b** (fig) [person, organization] être en liaison or en contact (**with** avec) **3** VT (Tech) connecter (**with** avec)

interfacing ['ɪntəfeɪsɪŋ] N **a** (Sewing) entoilage m **b** (Comput) interfaçage m, interface f

interfere [.ɪntə'fɪə'] VI **a** (= intrude) **stop interfering!** ne vous mêlez pas de ce qui ne vous regarde pas!; **he's always interfering** il se mêle toujours de ce qui ne le regarde pas; **to ~ with sb's plans** [weather, accident, circumstances etc] contrarier or contrecarrer les projets de qn; **computer games can ~ with school work** les jeux électroniques peuvent perturber le travail scolaire; **tiredness ~s with your ability to study** la fatigue affecte l'aptitude à étudier; **alcohol can ~ with your sexual performance** l'alcool peut affecter votre puissance sexuelle **b** (sexually) **to ~ with sb** abuser de qn; **the child had been ~d with** on avait abusé de l'enfant **c** (= handle) **don't ~ with my camera*** ne touche pas à or ne tripote pas mon appareil, laisse mon appareil tranquille* **d** (Phys) interférer

interference [.ɪntə'fɪərəns] N (NonC) **a** (gen) ingérence f, intrusion f (**in** dans, **from** de); (Econ) **state ~** ingérence f de l'État; (Jur) unwarrantable ~ immixtion f **b** (Phys) interférence f; (Rad) parasites mpl, interférence f

interfering [.ɪntə'fɪərɪŋ] ADJ [person] importun; [neighbour] envahissant; **he's an ~ busybody** il se mêle toujours de ce qui ne le regarde pas

interferon [.ɪntə'fɪərɒn] N interféron m

intergalactic [.ɪntəgə'læktɪk] ADJ intergalactique

intergovernmental [.ɪntəgʌvn'mentl] ADJ intergouvernemental

interim ['ɪntərɪm] **1** N intérim m; **in the ~** dans l'intérim, entre-temps **2** ADJ [arrangement, report, payment, loan] provisoire; [post, postholder] par intérim, intérimaire; [government] intérimaire, provisoire; **the ~ period** l'intérim m **3** COMP ▸ **interim dividend** N (Fin) dividende m intérimaire ▸ **interim financing** N préfinancement m

interior [ɪn'tɪərɪə'] **1** ADJ intérieur (-eure f) **2** N **a** (of building, country) intérieur m; **Minister/Ministry of the Interior** ministre m/ministère m de l'Intérieur; (US) **Secretary/Department of the Interior** ministre/ministère de l'Environnement chargé des Parcs nationaux **b** (Art) [tableau m d'] intérieur m **3** COMP ▸ **interior angle** N (Math) angle m interne ▸ **interior decoration** N décoration f d'intérieur ▸ **interior decorator** N décorateur m, -trice f d'intérieur ▸ **interior design** N architecture f d'intérieur ▸ **interior designer** N architecte mf d'intérieur ▸ **interior sprung mattress** N matelas m à ressorts

interject [.ɪntə'dʒekt] VT [+ remark, question] placer; **"yes" he ~ed** « oui » dit-il soudain

interjection [.ɪntə'dʒekʃən] N interjection f

interlace [.ɪntə'leɪs] **1** VT entrelacer, entrecroiser **2** VI s'entrelacer, s'entrecroiser

interlard [.ɪntə'lɑːd] VT entrelarder, entremêler (**with** de)

interleave [ˌɪntəˈliːv] VT interfolier

interlibrary loan [ˈɪntəˌlaɪbrərɪˈləʊn] N prêt m interbibliothèque

interline [ˌɪntəˈlaɪn] VT [a] (Typ) interligner [b] (Sewing) mettre une triplure à

interlinear [ˌɪntəˈlɪnɪər] ADJ interlinéaire

interlining [ˌɪntəˈlaɪnɪŋ] N (Sewing) triplure f

interlink [ˌɪntəˈlɪŋk] [1] VI [parts of a structure] se rejoindre; [factors, problems, aspects] se lier; [bus, train services] interconnecter; **a transport network with bus and rail services ~ing** un réseau de transport avec interconnexion des services de bus et de train [2] VT **to be ~ed** [factors, problems, aspects] être lié (**with** à)

interlock [ˌɪntəˈlɒk] [1] VT (Tech) enclencher [2] VI (Tech) (= click into place) s'enclencher; (= join together) s'emboîter; (fig) [problems, ideas, projects] être étroitement lié; [groups] avoir des intérêts en commun

interlocutor [ˌɪntəˈlɒkjʊtər] N interlocuteur m, -trice f

interloper [ˈɪntələʊpər] N intrus(e) m(f); (Comm) commerçant m marron

interlude [ˈɪntəluːd] N intervalle m; (Theat) intermède m; **in the ~** (gen) dans l'intervalle, entre-temps; (Theat) pendant l'intermède; **musical ~** interlude m, intermède m musical

intermarriage [ˌɪntəˈmærɪdʒ] N (NonC) (within family, tribe etc) endogamie f; (between families, tribes etc) mariage m

intermarry [ˈɪntəˈmærɪ] VI (within one's own family, tribe etc) pratiquer l'endogamie; (with other family, tribe etc) se marier entre eux; **to ~ with** se marier avec

intermediary [ˌɪntəˈmiːdɪərɪ] ADJ, N intermédiaire mf

intermediate [ˌɪntəˈmiːdɪət] [1] ADJ [a] intermédiaire; (Econ) **~ goods** biens mpl intermédiaires; **~ stop** [of ship, plane] escale f; **the ~ stages of the project** les phases fpl or étapes fpl intermédiaires du projet [b] (Scol etc) moyen; **~ course/exam** cours m/examen m (de niveau) moyen [2] N [a] (Sport, Educ etc) niveau m intermédiaire; **language courses for ~s** des cours mpl de langue pour les étudiants de niveau intermédiaire [b] (US = intermediary) intermédiaire mf [c] (US = car) automobile f de taille moyenne [d] (= substance) substance f or produit m intermédiaire [3] COMP ► **intermediate-range ballistic missile**, **intermediate-range weapon** N (Mil) missile m à moyenne portée

interment [ɪnˈtɜːmənt] N enterrement m, inhumation f

intermezzo [ˌɪntəˈmetsəʊ] N (pl **intermezzos** or **intermezzi** [ˌɪntəˈmetsiː]) (Mus) intermezzo m

interminable [ɪnˈtɜːmɪnəbl] ADJ interminable, sans fin

interminably [ɪnˈtɜːmɪnəblɪ] ADV [talk, argue, continue] interminablement; **~ long** interminable

intermingle [ˌɪntəˈmɪŋgl] [1] VT entremêler (**with** de), mélanger [2] VI se mêler, se mélanger (**with** avec)

intermission [ˌɪntəˈmɪʃən] N [a] (gen) interruption f, pause f; (in hostilities, quarrel, work, session) trêve f; (frm) **without ~** sans arrêt, sans relâche [b] (Cine, Theat) entracte m [c] (Med) intermission f

intermittent [ˌɪntəˈmɪtənt] ADJ intermittent; (Aut) **~ wipe** essuie-glace m à balayage intermittent

intermittently [ˌɪntəˈmɪtəntlɪ] ADV par intermittence

intermodal [ɪntəˈməʊdəl] ADJ [transport] intermodal

intern [ɪnˈtɜːn] [1] VT (Pol, Mil) interner (pour raisons de sécurité) [2] [ˈɪntɜːn] N (US Med) interne mf

internal [ɪnˈtɜːnl] [1] ADJ [a] (Med) interne; **~ bleeding** hémorragie f interne; **~ examination** toucher m vaginal; **~ injuries** lésions fpl internes [b] (Math, Tech) interne [c] (Ind, Pol) [dispute, trouble, reorganization, security] intérieur (-eure f), interne; (Pol) **~ wars** guerres fpl civiles or intestines (liter); (Pol) **~ quarrels** querelles fpl intestines; **~ (phone) call** appel m or communication f interne; **~ candidate** candidat m interne; **~ mail** courrier m interne [d] (= intrinsic) [proof, evidence] intrinsèque [e] [hope] secret (-ète f); **~ conviction** conviction f intime [2] COMP ► **internal auditor** N (Fin) contrôleur m financier ► **internal combustion engine** N moteur m à explosion or à combustion interne ► **internal examiner** N (Univ) examinateur m, -trice f interne ► **internal market** N (in country) marché m intérieur or domestique; (in European Union) marché m intérieur; (in organization) marché m interne ► **internal medicine** N (US) médecine f interne ► **internal revenue** N (US) contributions fpl directes ► **Internal Revenue Service** N (US) ≈ fisc m

internalization [ɪnˌtɜːnəlaɪˈzeɪʃən] N intériorisation f

internalize [ɪnˈtɜːnəˌlaɪz] VT [+ skill, fact] intégrer; [+ problem] intérioriser; (Ling) intérioriser

internally [ɪnˈtɜːnəlɪ] ADV [a] (gen, Med) intérieurement; **to bleed ~** avoir des hémorragies internes; **~ coherent** qui a une cohérence interne; (Pharm) **"to be taken ~"** « à usage interne »; (Pharm) **"not to be taken ~"** « pour usage externe » [b] (Comm) **software developed ~ at IBM** un logiciel créé au sein d'IBM

international [ˌɪntəˈnæʃnəl] [1] ADJ international; **~ law** droit m international; **~ relations** fpl internationales → **road** [2] N [a] (Brit Sport) (= match) match m international; (= player) international(e) m(f) [b] (Pol) **International** Internationale f (association) [3] COMP ► **International Atomic Energy Agency** N Agence f internationale de l'énergie atomique ► **International Bank for Reconstruction and Development** N Banque f internationale pour la reconstruction et le développement ► **International Court of Justice** N Cour f internationale de Justice ► **International Date Line** N ligne f de changement de date or de changement de jour ► **International Labour Organization** N Organisation f internationale du travail ► **International Modernism** N = **International Style** ► **International Monetary Fund** N Fonds m monétaire international ► **International Olympic Committee** N Comité m international olympique ► **International Phonetic Alphabet** N alphabet m phonétique international ► **international reply coupon** N coupon-réponse m international ► **International Standards Organization** N Organisation f internationale de normalisation ► **International Style** N (Archit) style m international

Internationale [ˌɪntəˌnæʃəˈnɑːl] N Internationale f

internationalism [ˌɪntəˈnæʃnəlɪzəm] N internationalisme m

internationalist [ˌɪntəˈnæʃnəlɪst] N internationaliste mf

internationalize [ˌɪntəˈnæʃnəlaɪz] VT internationaliser

internationally [ˌɪntəˈnæʃnəlɪ] ADV [recognized] internationalement; [discussed, accepted, competitive] au niveau international; **~ renowned** de réputation internationale, réputé internationalement; **~ respected** respecté dans le monde entier; **to compete ~** [athlete etc] participer à des compétitions internationales; [company] être présent sur le marché international; **~, the situation is even worse** sur le plan international, la situation est encore pire

internecine [ˌɪntəˈniːsaɪn] ADJ (frm) [strife, warfare, feud] interne; **~ quarrels/battles** querelles fpl/luttes fpl internes or intestines (liter)

internee [ˌɪntɜːˈniː] N (Mil, Pol) interné(e) m(f)

Internet [ˈɪntəˌnet] [1] N **the ~** l'Internet m [2] COMP ► **Internet café** N cybercafé m

internist [ɪnˈtɜːnɪst] N (US Med) ≈ spécialiste mf de médecine interne, interniste mf

internment [ɪnˈtɜːnmənt] [1] N (Mil, Pol) internement m [2] COMP ► **internment camp** N camp m d'internement

internship [ˈɪntɜːnˌʃɪp] N (US Med) internat m; (Univ etc) stage m en entreprise

interoperability [ˈɪntəˌrɒpərəˈbɪlɪtɪ] N (Comput) interopérabilité f, interfonctionnement m

interpenetrate [ˈɪntəˈpenɪtreɪt] [1] VT imprégner [2] VI s'interpénétrer

interpersonal [ˌɪntəˈpɜːsnl] ADJ **~ skills/relationships** compétences fpl/relations fpl interpersonnelles

interplanetary [ˌɪntəˈplænɪtərɪ] ADJ [journey] interplanétaire; **~ vessel** vaisseau m spatial

interplay [ˈɪntəpleɪ] N (NonC) effet m réciproque, interaction f

Interpol [ˈɪntəˌpɒl] N Interpol m

interpolate [ɪnˈtɜːpəˌleɪt] VT (gen) interpoler (**into** dans); [+ text, manuscript] altérer par interpolation

interpolation [ɪnˌtɜːpəˈleɪʃən] N interpolation f

interpose [ˌɪntəˈpəʊz] [1] VT [+ remark] placer; [+ objection, veto] opposer; [+ obstacle] interposer; **to ~ o.s. between** s'interposer entre; **"he rang me just now", she ~d** « il vient de me téléphoner » dit-elle soudain [2] VI intervenir, s'interposer

▼ **interpret** [ɪnˈtɜːprɪt] [1] VT (all senses) interpréter [2] VI interpréter, servir d'interprète, faire l'interprète

interpretation [ɪnˌtɜːprɪˈteɪʃən] N (all senses) interprétation f; **she put quite a different ~ on the figures** elle a donné à ces chiffres une tout autre interprétation

interpretative [ɪnˈtɜːprɪtətɪv] ADJ [article, account] explicatif; [skills, grasp, problems] d'interprétation; **~ centre** centre m d'information

interpreter [ɪnˈtɜːprɪtər] N (= person: lit, fig) interprète mf; (Comput) interpréteur m

interpreting [ɪnˈtɜːprɪtɪŋ] N (= profession) interprétariat m, interprétation f

interpretive [ɪnˈtɜːprɪtɪv] ADJ = **interpretative**

interracial [ˌɪntəˈreɪʃəl] ADJ [marriage] mixte; [problems, violence] interracial

interregnum [ˌɪntəˈregnəm] N (pl **interregnums** or **interregna** [ˌɪntəˈregnə]) interrègne m

interrelate [ˌɪntərɪˈleɪt] [1] VT mettre en corrélation [2] VI [concepts] être en corrélation (**with** avec); **the way in which we ~ with others** la manière dont nous communiquons avec les autres; **the body and the mind ~** le corps et l'esprit sont étroitement liés

interrelated [ˌɪntərɪˈleɪtɪd] ADJ étroitement lié

interrelation [ˌɪntərɪˈleɪʃən], **interrelationship** [ˌɪntərɪˈleɪʃənˌʃɪp] N corrélation f, lien m étroit

interrogate [ɪnˈterəgeɪt] VT interroger, soumettre à une interrogation; (Police) soumettre à un interrogatoire; (Comput) interroger

interrogation [ɪnˌterəˈgeɪʃən] [1] N interrogation f; (Police) interrogatoire m [2] COMP ► **interrogation mark**, **interrogation point** N point m d'interrogation

► LANGUAGE IN USE: **interpret** 26.1

interrogative [ˌɪntəˈrɒgətɪv] **1** ADJ [look, tone] interrogateur (-trice f); (Ling) interrogatif **2** N (Ling) interrogatif m; **in the ~** à l'interrogatif

interrogatively [ˌɪntəˈrɒgətɪvlɪ] ADV d'un air or d'un ton interrogateur; (Ling) interrogativement

interrogator [ɪnˈterəgeɪtəʳ] N interrogateur m, -trice f

interrogatory [ˌɪntəˈrɒgətərɪ] ADJ interrogateur (-trice f)

interrupt [ˌɪntəˈrʌpt] VT [+ speech, traffic, circuit, holiday] interrompre; [+ communication] interrompre, couper; [+ person] (when talking) interrompre, couper la parole à; (when busy etc) interrompre; [+ view] gêner, boucher; **to ~ a private conversation** interrompre un tête-à-tête; **the match was ~ed by rain** la match a été interrompu par la pluie; **don't ~!** pas d'interruptions!; **I don't want to ~, but ...** je ne voudrais pas vous interrompre, mais ...

interruption [ˌɪntəˈrʌpʃən] N interruption f; **without ~** sans interruption, sans arrêt; **an ~ to her career** une interruption dans sa carrière

intersect [ˌɪntəˈsekt] **1** VT couper, croiser; (Math) intersecter; **the city is ~ed by three waterways** la ville est traversée par trois cours d'eau **2** VI [lines, wires, roads etc] se couper, se croiser; (Math) s'intersecter; (Math) **~ing arcs/lines** arcs mpl/lignes fpl intersecté(e)s; **their histories ~** leurs histoires se croisent; **historical events ~ with our lives** nos vies sont traversées par des événements historiques

intersection [ˌɪntəˈsekʃən] N (US = crossroads) croisement m, carrefour m; (Math) intersection f

interservice [ˌɪntəˈsɜːvɪs] ADJ (Mil) interarmes inv

intersperse [ˌɪntəˈspɜːs] VT semer, parsemer (**among, between** dans, parmi); **a book ~d with quotations** un livre parsemé or émaillé de citations; **a speech ~d with jokes** un discours émaillé de plaisanteries; **a rocky landscape ~d with lakes** un paysage de rochers et de lacs; **periods of tremendous heat ~d with sudden showers** des périodes de très forte chaleur entrecoupées de brusques averses

interstate [ˌɪntəˈsteɪt] (US) **1** ADJ [commerce etc] entre états **2** N (also **~ highway**) autoroute f (qui relie plusieurs États) **3** COMP ► **interstate highway** N → **2**; → ROADS

interstellar [ˌɪntəˈstelɑːʳ] ADJ interstellaire, intersidéral

interstice [ɪnˈtɜːstɪs] N interstice m

intertextuality [ˌɪntəˈtekstjuːˌælɪtɪ] N (Literat) intertextualité f

intertwine [ˌɪntəˈtwaɪn] **1** VT entrelacer; **their destinies are ~d** leurs destins sont inextricablement liés **2** VI s'entrelacer; **intertwining branches** branches fpl entrelacées; **her fate ~d with his** son destin était inextricablement lié au sien

interurban [ˌɪntəˈɜːbən] ADJ interurbain

interval [ˈɪntəvəl] N [a] (in time) intervalle m; **at ~s** par intervalles; **at frequent/regular ~s** à intervalles rapprochés/réguliers; **at rare ~s** à intervalles espacés, de loin en loin; **at fortnightly ~s** tous les quinze jours; **there was an ~ for discussion** il y eut une pause pour la discussion; (Med) **he has lucid ~s** il a des moments de lucidité; (Met) **showery ~s** averses fpl → **sunny** [b] (Theat) entracte m; (Sport) mi-temps f, pause f; (Scol) récréation f [c] (= space between objects) intervalle m, distance f; **at ~s of 2 metres** à 2 mètres d'intervalle, à 2 mètres de distance; **rest areas spaced at regular ~s along major roads** des aires de repos aménagées à intervalles réguliers sur les routes principales [d] (Mus) intervalle m;

second/third ~ intervalle m de seconde/de tierce

intervene [ˌɪntəˈviːn] **1** VI [a] [person] intervenir (**in** dans); **the government ~d to resolve the crisis** le gouvernement est intervenu pour résoudre la crise; **Europe would ~ with military force** l'Europe interviendrait militairement [b] [event, circumstances etc] survenir, arriver; [time] s'écouler, s'étendre (**between** entre); **war ~d** survint la guerre; **if nothing ~s** s'il n'arrive or ne se passe rien entre-temps; **you never know what might ~ between now and election day** on ne sait jamais ce qui pourrait se passer d'ici les élections **2** VT (= interrupt) **"I've told you he's not here", Irene ~d** « je vous ai dit qu'il n'était pas là » coupa Irene

intervening [ˌɪntəˈviːnɪŋ] ADJ [event] survenu; [period of time] intermédiaire; **the ~ years were happy** les années qui s'écoulèrent entre-temps furent heureuses, la période intermédiaire a été heureuse; **I had spent the ~ time in London** entre-temps j'étais resté à Londres; **they scoured the ~ miles of moorland** ils ont parcouru les kilomètres de lande qui séparaient les deux endroits

intervention [ˌɪntəˈvenʃən] N intervention f (**in** dans); (Econ) **~ price** prix m d'intervention

interventionist [ˌɪntəˈvenʃənɪst] N, ADJ interventionniste mf

▼ **interview** [ˈɪntəvjuː] **1** N [a] (for job, place on course etc) entretien m; (to discuss working conditions, pay rise etc) entrevue f; **to call** or **invite sb to (an) ~** convoquer qn à or pour un entretien; **to come to (an) ~** venir pour or se présenter à un entretien; **I had an ~ with the manager** j'ai eu un entretien or une entrevue avec le directeur; **the ~s will be held next week** les entretiens auront lieu la semaine prochaine [b] (Press, Rad, TV) interview f; **to give an ~** accorder une interview **2** VT [a] (for job, place on course etc) avoir un entretien avec; **he is being ~ed on Monday** on le convoque (pour) lundi; **she was ~ed for the job** elle a passé un entretien pour le poste [b] (Press, Rad, TV) interviewer [c] (Police) interroger; **he was ~ed by the police** il a été interrogé par les policiers; **the police want to ~ him** la police le recherche **3** VI **we shall be ~ing throughout next week** nous faisons passer des entretiens toute la semaine prochaine

interviewee [ˌɪntəvjuːˈiː] N (for job, place on course etc) candidat(e) m(f) (qui passe un entretien); (Press, Rad, TV) interviewé(e) m(f)

interviewer [ˈɪntəvjuːəʳ] N (Press, Rad, TV) interviewer m; (in market research, opinion poll) enquêteur m, -trice f; (for job etc) **the ~ asked me ...** la personne qui m'a fait passer l'entretien m'a demandé ...

inter vivos [ˈɪntəˈviːvɒs] ADJ (Jur) **~ gift** donation f entre vifs

intervocalic [ˌɪntəvəʊˈkælɪk] ADJ (Phon) intervocalique

interwar [ˈɪntəˈwɔːʳ] ADJ **the ~ period** or **years** l'entre-deux-guerres m

interweave [ˌɪntəˈwiːv] **1** VT [+ threads] tisser ensemble; [+ lines etc] entrelacer; (fig) [+ stories, subplots] entremêler **2** VI s'entrelacer, s'emmêler

intestate [ɪnˈtestɪt] **1** ADJ (Jur) intestat f inv; **to die ~** mourir ab intestat **2** COMP ► **intestate estate** N succession f ab intestat

intestinal [ɪnˈtestɪnl] ADJ intestinal; **~ blockage** occlusion f intestinale; (US fig) **to have ~ fortitude** avoir quelque chose dans le ventre*

intestine [ɪnˈtestɪn] N (Anat) intestin m; **small ~** intestin m grêle; **large ~** gros intestin m

inti [ˈɪntɪ] N inti m

intifada [ˌɪntɪˈfɑːdə] N intifada f

intimacy [ˈɪntɪməsɪ] N [a] (NonC) intimité f [b] (NonC: sexual) rapports mpl (intimes or sexuels) [c] **intimacies** familiarités fpl

intimate [ˈɪntɪmɪt] **1** ADJ [a] (= close) [friend, friendship, contact] intime; [link, bond] étroit; (sexually) intime; **to be on ~ terms (with sb)** (gen) être intime (avec qn), être très proche (de qn); (sexually) avoir des relations intimes (avec qn); (euph) **to be ~ with sb** (= have sex with) avoir des rapports intimes avec qn (euph) [b] (= private, cosy) [conversation, moment, details, restaurant, photo etc] intime; **an ~ atmosphere** une atmosphère intime or d'intimité; **an ~ candlelit dinner for two** un dîner aux chandelles en tête-à-tête [c] (= detailed) **to have an ~ knowledge of sth** avoir une connaissance intime or approfondie de qch **2** N intime mf, familier m, -ière f **3** [ˈɪntɪmeɪt] VT (frm) [a] (= hint) laisser entendre, donner à entendre [b] (= make known officially) annoncer (**that** que); **he ~d his approval** ◊ **he ~d that he approved** il a annoncé qu'il était d'accord

intimately [ˈɪntɪmɪtlɪ] ADV [know] intimement; [talk] en toute intimité; **~ concerned** intimement concerné; **to be ~ involved in** or **with a project** être très engagé dans un projet; **to be ~ involved with sb** (sexually) avoir des relations intimes avec qn; **~ linked** or **connected** étroitement lié; **to be ~ acquainted with sb/sth** connaître intimement qn/qch

intimation [ˌɪntɪˈmeɪʃən] N (= announcement) (gen) annonce f; [of death] avis m; [of birth, wedding] annonce f; (= notice) signification f, notification f; (= hint) suggestion f; (= sign) indice m, indication f; **this was the first ~ we had of their refusal** c'était la première fois qu'on nous notifiait leur refus; **this was the first ~ we had that the company was in financial difficulty** c'était la première fois que nous entendions parler des difficultés financières de l'entreprise; **he gave no ~ that he was going to resign** rien dans son comportement ne permettait de deviner qu'il allait démissionner

intimidate [ɪnˈtɪmɪdeɪt] VT intimider

intimidating [ɪnˈtɪmɪdeɪtɪŋ] ADJ [person, manner, presence, atmosphere] intimidant; [sight, figure] impressionnant, intimidant; [tactics] d'intimidation

intimidation [ɪnˌtɪmɪˈdeɪʃən] N (NonC) intimidation f; (Jur) menaces fpl

intimidatory [ɪnˌtɪmɪˈdeɪtərɪ] ADJ [tactics, telephone call] d'intimidation; [behaviour] intimidant

into [ˈɪntʊ]

When **into** is an element in a phrasal verb, eg **break into, enter into, look into, walk into**, look up the verb.

PREP (gen) dans; **to come** or **go ~ a room** entrer dans une pièce; **to go ~ town** aller en ville; **to get ~ a car** monter dans une voiture or en voiture; **he helped his mother ~ the car** il a aidé sa mère à monter dans la or en voiture; **she fell ~ the lake** elle est tombée dans le lac; **he went off ~ the desert** il est parti dans le désert; **to put sth ~ a box** mettre qch dans une boîte; **put the book ~ it** mets le livre dedans; **it broke ~ a thousand pieces** ça s'est cassé en mille morceaux; **to change traveller's cheques ~ francs/francs ~ pounds** changer des chèques de voyage contre des francs/des francs contre des livres sterling; **to translate** or **put sth ~ French** traduire qch en français; **he went further ~ the forest** il s'est enfoncé dans la forêt; **far ~ the night** tard dans la nuit; **it was ~ 1996** c'était déjà 1996, on était déjà en 1996; **it continued well ~** or **far ~ 1996** cela a continué pendant une bonne partie de

1996; **he's well ~ his fifties/sixties** il a une bonne cinquantaine/soixantaine d'années; **he's well ~ his seventies/eighties** il a soixante-dix/quatre-vingts ans bien tassés*; **let's not go ~ that again!** ne revenons pas là-dessus!; **we must go ~ this very carefully** nous devons étudier la question de très près; **4 ~ 12 goes 3** 12 divisé par 4 donne 3; **the children are ~ everything*** les enfants touchent à tout; (fig) **she's ~* health foods/jazz/buying antiques** les aliments naturels/le jazz/acheter des antiquités, c'est son truc*; (fig) **to be ~ drugs*** toucher à la drogue* → burst, get into, grow into

intolerable [ɪn'tɒlərəbl] ADJ (= unacceptable) intolérable; (= unbearable) insupportable, intolérable; **an ~ intrusion into his private life** une intrusion intolérable dans sa vie privée; **the heat was ~** la chaleur était insupportable or intolérable; **it is ~ that ...** il est intolérable or il n'est pas tolérable que ... (+ subj)

intolerably [ɪn'tɒlərəblɪ] ADV (frm) [a] [high, low, expensive, rude, arrogant etc] horriblement; **it was ~ hot** il faisait une chaleur intolérable or insupportable, il faisait horriblement chaud [b] (with vb) [annoy, disturb, behave] de façon intolérable

intolerance [ɪn'tɒlərəns] N (NonC: also Med) intolérance f

intolerant [ɪn'tɒlərənt] ADJ intolérant; **to be ~ of** (gen) ne pas supporter; (Med) [foodstuff, drug etc] présenter une intolérance à

intolerantly [ɪn'tɒlərəntlɪ] ADV avec intolérance

intonation [ˌɪntəʊ'neɪʃən] N (Ling, Mus) intonation f

intone [ɪn'təʊn] VT entonner; (Rel) psalmodier

intoxicant [ɪn'tɒksɪkənt] [1] ADJ enivrant [2] N (= alcohol) alcool m, boisson f alcoolisée; (= narcotic) stupéfiant m

intoxicate [ɪn'tɒksɪkeɪt] VT (lit, fig) enivrer

intoxicated [ɪn'tɒksɪkeɪtɪd] ADJ (frm = drunk) en état d'ivresse; **~ by or with success/victory etc** enivré par le succès/la victoire etc

intoxicating [ɪn'tɒksɪkeɪtɪŋ] ADJ [drink] alcoolisé; [effect, perfume] enivrant

intoxication [ɪnˌtɒksɪ'keɪʃən] N ivresse f; (Med) intoxication f (par l'alcool); (fig) ivresse f; (Jur) **in a state of ~** en état d'ivresse or d'ébriété

intra... ['ɪntrə] PREF intra...

intractability [ɪnˌtræktə'bɪlɪtɪ] N [a] (= difficulty) [of problem, dispute] insolubilité f (frm), caractère m insoluble [b] (= stubbornness) [of person, government] intransigeance f

intractable [ɪn'træktəbl] ADJ [problem] insoluble; [illness, pain] réfractaire (à tout traitement); [child, temper] intraitable, indocile

intramural [ˌɪntrə'mjʊərəl] [1] ADJ [studies, sports, competitions] à l'intérieur d'un même établissement [2] **intramurals** NPL (US Scol, Univ) matchs mpl entre élèves (or étudiants) d'un même établissement

intramuscular [ˌɪntrə'mʌskjʊlər] ADJ intramusculaire

intramuscularly [ˌɪntrə'mʌskjʊləlɪ] ADV par voie intramusculaire

intranet ['ɪntrənet] N intranet m

intransigence [ɪn'trænsɪdʒəns] N intransigeance f

intransigent [ɪn'trænsɪdʒənt] ADJ, N intransigeant(e) m(f)

intransitive [ɪn'trænsɪtɪv] ADJ, N (Gram) intransitif m

intrauterine [ˌɪntrə'juːtəraɪn] [1] ADJ [procedure, surgery, insemination, pregnancy] intra-utérin [2] COMP ▸ **intrauterine device** N stérilet m, dispositif m anticonceptionnel intra-utérin

---

intravenous [ˌɪntrə'viːnəs] [1] ADJ (injection, fluids, solution) intraveineux; [feeding] par voie intraveineuse; [line, tube, needle] pour voie intraveineuse; [drugs] administré par voie intraveineuse; (Drugs) **~ drug users/drug use** utilisateurs mpl/utilisation f de drogue par voie intraveineuse [2] COMP ▸ **intravenous drip** N perfusion f intraveineuse, goutte-à-goutte m ▸ **intravenous injection** N (injection f or piqûre f) intraveineuse f

intravenously [ˌɪntrə'viːnəslɪ] ADV par voie intraveineuse

intrepid [ɪn'trepɪd] ADJ intrépide

intrepidity [ˌɪntrɪ'pɪdɪtɪ] N intrépidité f

intrepidly [ɪn'trepɪdlɪ] ADV intrépidement

intricacy ['ɪntrɪkəsɪ] N [of problem, plot, pattern, mechanism] complexité f; **the intricacies of English law** les subtilités fpl du droit anglais

intricate ['ɪntrɪkɪt] ADJ [mechanism] complexe; [pattern, style] complexe, très élaboré; [plot, problem, situation] complexe; **all the ~ details** les détails dans toute leur complexité

intricately ['ɪntrɪkɪtlɪ] ADV **~ carved** finement sculpté; **~ designed** (in conception) de conception très élaborée; (elaborately drawn) au dessin or motif très élaboré; **~ patterned tiles** des carreaux aux motifs complexes or élaborés

intrigue [ɪn'triːg] [1] VI intriguer, comploter (with sb avec qn, to do pour faire) [2] VT intriguer; **she ~s me** elle m'intrigue; **go on, I'm ~d** continue, ça m'intrigue; **I'm ~d to hear what she's been saying** je suis curieux de savoir ce qu'elle a dit; **I was ~d with or by what you said about the case** ce que vous avez dit sur l'affaire m'a intrigué [3] N (= plot) intrigue f; (= love affair) intrigue f, liaison f; **political ~** intrigue f politique

intriguer [ɪn'triːgər] N intrigant(e) m(f)

intriguing [ɪn'triːgɪŋ] [1] ADJ fascinant [2] N (NonC) intrigues fpl

intriguingly [ɪn'triːgɪŋlɪ] ADV **~ different** étrangement différent; **~ of** une originalité fascinante; **~-titled** au titre fascinant; **~, this was never confirmed** très curieusement, ça n'a jamais été confirmé

intrinsic [ɪn'trɪnsɪk] ADJ intrinsèque; **the sculpture has no ~ value** cette sculpture n'a pas de valeur intrinsèque; **financial insecurity is ~ to capitalism** l'insécurité financière est une caractéristique intrinsèque du capitalisme

intrinsically [ɪn'trɪnsɪklɪ] ADV intrinsèquement; **~ linked** intrinsèquement lié

intro* ['ɪntrəʊ] N (ABBR = introduction) intro* f

intro... ['ɪntrəʊ] PREF intro...

introduce [ˌɪntrə'djuːs] VT [a] (= make acquainted) présenter; **he ~d me to his friend** il m'a présenté à son ami; **let me ~ myself** permettez-moi de me présenter; **I ~d myself to my new neighbour** je me suis présenté à mon nouveau voisin; **who ~d them?** qui les a présentés?; **we haven't been ~d** nous n'avons pas été présentés; (frm) **may I ~ Mr Smith?** puis-je (me permettre de) vous présenter M. Smith?; **he ~d me to the delights of skiing** il m'a initié aux plaisirs du ski; **I was ~d to Shakespeare at the age of 11** on m'a fait connaître Shakespeare quand j'avais 11 ans; **who ~d him to drugs?** qui est-ce qui lui a fait connaître la drogue? [b] (= announce etc) [+ speaker] présenter; [+ subject] présenter, aborder; (Rad, TV) [+ programme etc] présenter [c] (= adopt, bring in) [+ reform, new method, innovation] introduire, mettre en place; [+ practice] faire adopter, introduire; (= tackle) [+ subject, question] aborder; (Parl) introduire; **this ~d a note of irony into the conversation** ça a introduit une note d'ironie dans la conversation [d] (= put in place) introduire; [+ key etc] intro-

---

duire, insérer (into dans); **he ~d the tape recorder surreptitiously** il a introduit surrepticement le magnétophone; **when video cameras were first ~d into the courtroom** le jour où les caméras ont été autorisées pour la première fois dans les salles d'audience; (frm) **we were ~d into a dark room** on nous introduisit dans une pièce sombre; **I ~d him into the firm** je l'ai introduit or fait entrer dans l'entreprise; **privatization will ~ real competition into the telecommunications industry** la privatisation amènera une réelle concurrence dans l'industrie des télécommunications; **potatoes were ~d into Europe from America** la pomme de terre a été introduite d'Amérique en Europe

introduction [ˌɪntrə'dʌkʃən] [1] N [a] (= introducing, putting in place: gen) introduction f (into dans); [of system, legislation] mise f en place; **the ~ of new technology** l'introduction des technologies nouvelles; **his ~ to professional football** ses débuts dans le monde du football professionnel [b] présentation f (of sb to sb de qn à qn); **to give sb an ~ or a letter of ~ to sb** donner à qn une lettre de recommandation auprès de qn; **someone who needs no ~** une personne qu'il est inutile de présenter; **will you make or do* the ~s?** voulez-vous faire les présentations? [c] (to book etc) avant-propos m, introduction f [d] (= elementary course) introduction f (to à), manuel m élémentaire; **"an ~ to German"** « initiation à l'allemand » [2] COMP ▸ **introduction agency** N club m de rencontres

introductory [ˌɪntrə'dʌktərɪ] ADJ préliminaire, d'introduction; **a few ~ words** quelques mots d'introduction; **~ remarks** remarques fpl (préliminaires), préambule m; (Comm) **~ offer** offre f de lancement; **an ~ price of £2.99** un prix de lancement de 2,99 livres

introit ['ɪntrɔɪt] N introït m

introspection [ˌɪntrəʊ'spekʃən] N (NonC) introspection f

introspective [ˌɪntrəʊ'spektɪv] ADJ introspectif, replié sur soi-même

introspectiveness [ˌɪntrəʊ'spektɪvnɪs] N tendance f à l'introspection

introversion [ˌɪntrəʊ'vɜːʃən] N introversion f

introvert ['ɪntrəʊvɜːt] [1] N (Psych) introverti(e) m(f); **he's something of an ~** c'est un caractère plutôt fermé [2] ADJ introverti [3] VT (Psych) **to become ~ed** se replier sur soi-même

introverted ['ɪntrəʊvɜːtɪd] ADJ (Psych) introverti; (fig = inward-looking) [system, society] replié sur soi-même

intrude [ɪn'truːd] VI [person] être importun, s'imposer; **to ~ on sb's privacy** s'ingérer dans la vie privée de qn; **to ~ on sb's grief** ne pas respecter le chagrin de qn; **to ~ into sb's affairs** s'immiscer or s'ingérer dans les affaires de qn; **my family has been ~d upon by the press** la presse s'est immiscée dans la vie privée de ma famille; **I don't want to ~ on your meeting** je ne veux pas interrompre votre réunion; **don't let personal feelings ~** ne vous laissez pas influencer par vos sentiments; **don't let negative thoughts ~** écartez toute pensée négative; **am I intruding?** est-ce que je (vous) dérange?; (stronger) est-ce que je (vous) gêne? [2] VT introduire de force (into dans), imposer (into à); **to ~ one's views (on sb)** imposer ses idées (à qn)

intruder [ɪn'truːdər] [1] N (= person, animal) intrus(e) m(f); (Mil, Aviat = aircraft) avion pénétrant sans autorisation dans un espace aérien; **the ~ fled when he heard the car** l'intrus s'est enfui en entendant la voiture; **I felt like an ~** je me sentais étranger or de trop [2] COMP ▸ **intruder alarm** N alarme f anti-effraction

intrusion [ɪn'truːʒən] N intrusion f (into dans); **excuse this ~** excusez-moi de vous déranger

intrusive [ɪnˈtruːsɪv] ADJ [person, presence] indiscret (-ète f), importun ; (Ling) **~ consonant** consonne f d'appui ; (Ling) **the ~ "r"** le « r » ajouté en anglais en liaison abusive

intuit [ɪnˈtjuːɪt] VT **to ~ that ...** savoir intuitivement or par intuition que ... ; savoir par intuition que ... ; **he ~s your every thought** il connaît intuitivement toutes vos pensées

intuition [ˌɪntjuːˈɪʃən] N intuition f

intuitive [ɪnˈtjuːɪtɪv] ADJ intuitif

intuitively [ɪnˈtjuːɪtɪvlɪ] ADV intuitivement ; **the plan seemed ~ attractive** ce projet nous (or leur etc) a plu ; **~, the idea seems reasonable to me** intuitivement, je trouve cette idée raisonnable

Inuit [ˈɪnjuːɪt] [1] N Inuit mf ; **the ~(s)** les Inuit mfpl [2] ADJ inuit inv

inundate [ˈɪnʌndeɪt] VT (lit, fig) inonder (**with** de) ; **to be ~d with work** être débordé (de travail), être submergé de travail ; **to be ~d with visits** être inondé de visiteurs, être débordé de visites ; **to be ~d with letters** être submergé de lettres

inundation [ˌɪnʌnˈdeɪʃən] N inondation f

inure [ɪnˈjʊəʳ] VT **to be ~d to** [+ criticism, cold] être endurci contre ; [+ sb's charms] être insensible à ; [+ pressures] être habitué à

invade [ɪnˈveɪd] VT [a] (gen, Mil, fig) envahir ; **city ~d by tourists** ville f envahie par les touristes ; **he was suddenly ~d by doubts** il fut soudain envahi de doutes ; **cells that have been ~d by a virus** des cellules qui ont été envahies par un virus [b] [+ privacy] violer, s'ingérer dans ; **to ~ sb's rights** empiéter sur les droits de qn

invader [ɪnˈveɪdəʳ] N envahisseur m, -euse f ; **the immune system produces antibodies to neutralize the ~** le système immunitaire fabrique des anticorps afin de neutraliser l'envahisseur

invading [ɪnˈveɪdɪŋ] ADJ [army, troops] d'invasion ; **the ~ Romans** l'envahisseur romain

invalid¹ [ˈɪnvəlɪd] [1] N (= sick person) malade mf ; (with disability) invalide mf, infirme mf ; **chronic ~** malade mf chronique ; **to treat sb like an ~** traiter qn comme un handicapé [2] ADJ (= ill) malade ; (with disability) invalide, infirme [3] [ˈɪnvəliːd] VT (esp Brit Mil) **he was ~ed home from the front** il fut rapatrié du front pour blessures (or pour raisons de santé) [4] COMP ► **invalid car, invalid carriage** N (Brit) voiture f d'infirme or pour handicapé
► **invalid out** VT SEP (Mil) **to ~ sb out of the army** réformer qn (pour blessures or pour raisons de santé)

invalid² [ɪnˈvælɪd] ADJ (esp Jur) non valide, non valable ; [argument] nul (nulle f) ; **to become ~** [ticket] ne plus être valable, être périmé ; **to declare sth ~** déclarer qch nul

invalidate [ɪnˈvælɪdeɪt] VT invalider, annuler ; (Jur) [+ judgment] casser, infirmer ; [+ will] rendre nul et sans effet ; [+ contract] vicier ; [+ statute] abroger

invalidity [ˌɪnvəˈlɪdɪtɪ] N [a] (= disability) invalidité f ; (Brit Admin) **~ benefit** allocation f d'invalidité [b] [of argument] nullité f ; [of law, election] invalidité f

invaluable [ɪnˈvæljʊəbl] ADJ (lit, fig) inestimable, inappréciable ; **her help or she has been ~ to me** elle m'a été d'une aide inestimable or inappréciable

invariable [ɪnˈvɛərɪəbl] ADJ invariable

invariably [ɪnˈvɛərɪəblɪ] ADV invariablement

invariant [ɪnˈvɛərɪənt] ADJ, N invariant m

invasion [ɪnˈveɪʒən] N [a] (Mil, fig) invasion f ; **a tourist ~** une invasion de touristes [b] [of rights] empiétement m (**of** sur) ; [of privacy] (by journalist, police etc) intrusion f dans la vie privée ; **reading her diary was a gross ~ of pri-**vacy lire son journal intime était une intrusion choquante dans sa vie privée

invasive [ɪnˈveɪsɪv] ADJ (Med) [disease] (gen) qui gagne du terrain ; [cancer, carcinoma] invasif ; [surgery, treatment] agressif ; **the legislation has been criticized as being too ~** cette législation a été critiquée parce qu'elle porterait atteinte à la vie privée

invective [ɪnˈvektɪv] N (NonC) invective f ; **torrent** or **stream of ~** flot m d'invectives or d'injures ; **racist ~** injures fpl racistes

inveigh [ɪnˈveɪ] VI **to ~ against sb/sth** invectiver qn/qch ; (more violently) fulminer or tonner contre qn/qch

inveigle [ɪnˈviːgl] VT **to ~ sb into sth** entraîner or attirer qn dans qch (par la ruse) ; **to ~ sb into doing** entraîner or amener qn à faire (par la ruse)

invent [ɪnˈvent] VT (lit, fig) inventer

invention [ɪnˈvenʃən] N [a] invention f ; **the ~ of the telephone** l'invention f du téléphone ; **one of his most practical ~s** une de ses inventions les plus pratiques [b] (= falsehood) invention f, mensonge m ; **it was pure ~ on her part** c'était pure invention de sa part ; **it was (an) ~ from start to finish** c'était (une) pure invention du début à la fin

inventive [ɪnˈventɪv] ADJ inventif

inventiveness [ɪnˈventɪvnɪs] N (NonC) esprit m inventif or d'invention

inventor [ɪnˈventəʳ] N inventeur m, -trice f

inventory [ˈɪnvəntrɪ] [1] N inventaire m ; (US Comm) stock m ; **to draw up** or **make an ~ of sth** inventorier qch, faire or dresser un inventaire de qch ; **~ of fixtures** état m des lieux [2] VT inventorier [3] COMP
► **inventory control** N (US Comm) gestion f des stocks

inverse [ˈɪnvɜːs] [1] ADJ inverse ; **in ~ order** en sens inverse ; **in ~ proportion to** inversement proportionnel à ; **in ~ ratio (to)** en raison inverse (de) ; **an ~ relationship between ...** une relation inverse entre ... [2] N inverse m, contraire m

inversely [ɪnˈvɜːslɪ] ADV inversement

inversion [ɪnˈvɜːʃən] N (gen) inversion f ; [of values, roles etc] (also Mus) renversement m

invert [ɪnˈvɜːt] [1] VT [a] [+ elements, order, words] inverser, intervertir ; [+ roles] renverser, intervertir ; **to ~ a process** renverser une opération [b] [+ cup, object] retourner [2] [ˈɪnvɜːt] N (Psych) inverti(e) m(f) [3] COMP ► **inverted chord** N (Mus) accord m renversé ► **inverted commas** NPL (Brit) guillemets mpl ; **in ~ed commas** entre guillemets ► **inverted nipples** NPL mamelons mpl ombiliqués ► **inverted snobbery** N snobisme m à l'envers ► **invert sugar** N sucre m inverti

invertebrate [ɪnˈvɜːtɪbrɪt] ADJ, N invertébré m

invest [ɪnˈvest] [1] VT [a] (Fin) [+ money, capital, funds] investir, placer (**in** dans, en) ; **to ~ money** faire un or des placement(s), placer de l'argent ; **I have ~ed a lot of time in this project** j'ai consacré beaucoup de temps à ce projet ; **she ~ed a lot of effort in it** elle s'est beaucoup investie [b] (= endow) revêtir, investir (**sb with sth** qn de qch) ; **to ~ sb as** [+ monarch, president etc] élever qn à la dignité de ; **the buildings are ~ed with a nation's history** ces bâtiments sont empreints de l'histoire d'une nation [c] (Mil = surround) investir, cerner [2] VI investir ; **to ~ in shares/property** placer son argent or investir dans des actions/dans l'immobilier ; (hum) **I've ~ed in a new car** je me suis offert une nouvelle voiture

investigate [ɪnˈvestɪgeɪt] VT [+ question, possibilities] examiner, étudier ; [+ motive, reason] scruter, sonder ; [+ crime] enquêter sur, faire une enquête sur

investigation [ɪnˌvestɪˈgeɪʃən] N [a] (NonC) [of facts, question] examen m ; [of crime] enquête f (**of** sur) ; **to be under ~ for sth** faire l'objet d'une enquête pour qch ; **the matter under ~** la question à l'étude [b] [of researcher] investigation f, enquête f ; [of policeman] enquête f ; **his ~s led him to believe that ...** ses investigations l'ont amené à penser que ... ; **criminal ~** enquête f criminelle ; **to launch an ~** ouvrir une enquête ; **preliminary ~** enquête f or investigations fpl préalable(s) or préparatoire(s) ; **it calls for an immediate ~** cela demande une étude immédiate or à être étudié immédiatement ; **to call for an immediate ~ into sth** demander que l'on ouvre (subj) immédiatement une enquête sur qch ; **to order an ~ into of sth** ordonner une enquête sur qch ; **we have made ~s** nous avons fait une enquête or des recherches

investigative [ɪnˈvestɪgeɪtɪv] ADJ [journalism, reporter, team, method] d'investigation

investigator [ɪnˈvestɪgeɪtəʳ] N investigateur m, -trice f → **private**

investigatory [ɪnˈvestɪgeɪtərɪ] ADJ **~ group/ panel** groupe m/commission f d'enquête

investiture [ɪnˈvestɪtʃəʳ] N investiture f

investment [ɪnˈvestmənt] [1] N [a] (Fin) investissement m, placement m ; (fig, esp Psych) investissement m ; **by careful ~ of his capital** en investissant or plaçant soigneusement son capital ; **he regretted his ~ in the company** il regrettait d'avoir investi dans la firme ; **~ in shares** placement m en valeurs ; **in property** placement m or investissement m immobilier ; **we need a major ~ in new technology** il nous faut investir massivement dans les nouvelles technologies ; **foreign ~ in the region** les investissements mpl étrangers dans la région ; **~s** (= money invested) placements mpl, investissements mpl ; **return on one's ~s** retour m sur investissement ; **a portable TV is always a good ~** une télévision portable est toujours un bon investissement [b] (Mil) investissement m [c] = **investiture**
[2] COMP ► **investment analyst** N analyste mf en placements ► **investment bank** N (US Fin) banque f d'affaires or d'investissement ► **investment company** N société f de placement ► **investment income** N revenu m des placements or des investissements ► **investment management** N gestion f de portefeuille ► **investment manager** N gérant(e) m(f) de portefeuille ► **investment opportunities** NPL investissements mpl or placements mpl intéressants ► **investment trust** N société f d'investissement

investor [ɪnˈvestəʳ] N (gen) investisseur m ; (= shareholder) actionnaire mf ; **(the) big ~s** les gros actionnaires mpl ; **(the) small ~s** les petits actionnaires mpl, la petite épargne (NonC)

inveterate [ɪnˈvetərɪt] ADJ [gambler, smoker, liar] invétéré ; [traveller] insatiable ; [collector] impénitent ; [laziness, extravagance] incurable

invidious [ɪnˈvɪdɪəs] ADJ [decision, distinction, choice] injuste, propre à susciter la jalousie ; [comparison] blessant, désobligeant ; [task] ingrat, déplaisant

invigilate [ɪnˈvɪdʒɪleɪt] (Brit) [1] VI être de surveillance (à un examen) [2] VT [+ examination] surveiller

invigilator [ɪnˈvɪdʒɪleɪtəʳ] N (Brit) surveillant(e) m(f) (à un examen)

invigorate [ɪnˈvɪgəreɪt] VT [+ person] [drink, food, thought, fresh air] redonner des forces à, revigorer ; [climate, air] vivifier, tonifier ; [exercise] tonifier ; [+ campaign] animer ; **to feel ~d** se sentir revigoré or vivifié

invigorating [ɪnˈvɪgəreɪtɪŋ] ADJ [climate, air, walk] vivifiant, tonifiant ; [speech] stimulant

invincibility [ɪnˌvɪnsɪˈbɪlɪtɪ] N invincibilité f

invincible [ɪnˈvɪnsəbl] ADJ [a] (= unbeatable) invincible [b] (= unshakeable) [faith, belief, spirit] inébranlable

inviolability [ɪn͵vaɪələ'bɪlɪtɪ] N inviolabilité f
inviolable [ɪn'vaɪələbl] ADJ inviolable
inviolably [ɪn'vaɪələblɪ] ADV inviolablement
inviolate [ɪn'vaɪəlɪt] ADJ inviolé
invisibility [ɪn͵vɪzə'bɪlɪtɪ] N invisibilité f
invisible [ɪn'vɪzəbl] 1 ADJ ⓐ (lit) invisible ⓑ (fig = ignored) ignoré ; **to feel ~** se sentir ignoré 2 **invisibles** NPL invisibles mpl 3 COMP ► **invisible exports** NPL (Econ) exportations fpl invisibles ► **invisible ink** N encre f sympathique ► **invisible mending** N stoppage m
invisibly [ɪn'vɪzəblɪ] ADV invisiblement
▼ **invitation** [͵ɪnvɪ'teɪʃən] 1 N invitation f ; **~ to dinner** invitation f à dîner ; **the unions have not yet accepted the ~ to attend** les syndicats n'ont pas encore accepté de venir ; **their ~ to attend a July conference** leur invitation à participer à une conférence en juillet ; **he has refused an ~ to attend the inauguration ceremony** il a refusé d'assister à la cérémonie d'ouverture ; **at sb's ~** à or sur l'invitation de qn ; **by ~ (only)** sur invitation (seulement) ; **to send out ~s** envoyer des invitations ; (Fin) **to bid** avis m d'appel d'offres ; (iro) **this lock is an open ~ to burglars!** cette serrure est une véritable invite au cambriolage ! 2 COMP ► **invitation card** N (carte f or carton m d')invitation f
invitational [͵ɪnvɪ'teɪʃənl] ADJ (Sport) **~ tournament** tournoi m sur invitation
▼ **invite** [ɪn'vaɪt] 1 VT ⓐ (= ask) [+ person] inviter (**to do** à faire) ; **to ~ sb to dinner** inviter qn à dîner ; **he ~d him for a drink** il l'a invité à prendre un verre ; **I've never been ~d to their house** je n'ai jamais été invité chez eux ; **he was ~d to the ceremony** il a été invité (à assister) à la cérémonie ; **to ~ sb in/up** etc inviter qn à entrer/monter etc ; (iro) **that store ~s thieves** ce magasin est une invite au vol ⓑ (= ask for) [+ sb's attention, subscriptions etc] demander, solliciter ; **when he had finished he ~d questions from the audience** quand il eut fini il invita le public à poser des questions ; **he was ~d to give his opinion** on l'a invité à donner son avis ⓒ (= lead to) [+ confidences, questions, doubts, ridicule] appeler ; [+ discussion, step] inviter à ; [+ failure, defeat] chercher ; **I wouldn't walk home alone, it only ~s trouble** je ne rentrerais pas à pied tout seul, c'est vraiment chercher les ennuis
2 ['ɪnvaɪt] N* invitation f
► **invite out** VT SEP inviter (à sortir) ; **he has ~d her out several times** il l'a invitée plusieurs fois à sortir ; **I've been ~d out to dinner this evening** j'ai été invité à dîner ce soir
► **invite over** VT SEP ⓐ inviter (à venir) ; **they often ~ us over for a drink** ils nous invitent souvent à venir prendre un verre chez eux ; **let's ~ them over some time** invitons-les un de ces jours (à venir nous voir) ⓑ **he ~d me over to his table** il (m'appela et) m'invita à venir m'asseoir à sa table
inviting [ɪn'vaɪtɪŋ] ADJ [place, room, atmosphere] accueillant ; [dish, smell] alléchant, appétissant ; [prospect] engageant, tentant ; (for swimming) **the water looked very ~** l'eau était très tentante ; **it's not an ~ prospect** ce n'est pas une perspective engageante or tentante
invitingly [ɪn'vaɪtɪŋlɪ] ADV **to smile ~** sourire d'un air engageant ; **the soup steamed ~** la soupe fumait de façon appétissante ; **the chocolate sat ~ on his desk*** le chocolat était sur son bureau, tel une invitation à la gourmandise ; **the waters of the tropics are ~ clear** les eaux tropicales sont d'une limpidité engageante
in vitro [ɪn'viːtrəʊ] 1 ADJ, ADV in vitro 2 COMP ► **in vitro fertilization** N fécondation f in vitro
invocation [͵ɪnvə'keɪʃən] N invocation f

▼ **invoice** ['ɪnvɔɪs] 1 N facture f 2 VT [+ customer, goods] facturer ; **they will ~ us for the maintenance** ils vont nous facturer l'entretien 3 COMP ► **invoice clerk** N facturier m, -ière f
invoicing ['ɪnvɔɪsɪŋ] N (NonC) facturation f
invoke [ɪn'vəʊk] VT ⓐ (= call on) [+ God, Muse, mercy, precedent, law] invoquer ; [+ memories, atmosphere] évoquer ; **to ~ sb's help** invoquer or demander l'aide de qn ⓑ (= evoke) [+ spirits, the devil] évoquer
involuntarily [ɪn'vɒləntərɪlɪ] ADV involontairement
involuntary [ɪn'vɒləntərɪ] 1 ADJ involontaire 2 COMP ► **involuntary manslaughter** N (Jur) homicide m involontaire
involuted [͵ɪnvə'luːtɪd] ADJ compliqué
involve [ɪn'vɒlv] VT ⓐ (= implicate, associate) impliquer (**in** dans), mêler (**in** à) ; **we would prefer not to ~ Robert** nous ne préférerions ne pas mêler Robert à l'affaire or ne pas impliquer Robert dans l'affaire ; **don't try to ~ me in this scheme** n'essaie pas de me mêler à ce projet ; **he wasn't ~d in the plot** il n'était pour rien dans le complot, il n'était pas impliqué dans le complot or mêlé au complot ; **to be ~d in a quarrel** être mêlé à une querelle ; **to ~ sb in a quarrel** mêler qn à une querelle ; **to get ~d in sth** ◊ **to ~ o.s. in sth** (= get dragged into) se laisser entraîner dans qch ; (from choice) s'engager dans qch ; **she didn't want to ~ herself in this debate** elle ne voulait pas se laisser entraîner dans ce débat ; **she ~d herself** or **got ~d in the freedom movement** elle s'est engagée dans le mouvement pour la liberté ; **he was so ~d in politics that he had no time to ...** il était tellement engagé dans la politique qu'il n'avait pas le temps de ... ; **a riot involving a hundred prison inmates** une émeute à laquelle ont pris part cent détenus ; **the school likes to ~ parents in their children's education** l'école aime associer les parents à l'éducation de leurs enfants ; **this is going to ~ us in a lot of expense** cela va nous entraîner dans de grosses dépenses ; **how did you come to be ~d?** comment vous êtes-vous trouvé impliqué ? ; **we are all ~d** nous sommes tous concernés ; **she wasn't directly ~d** (= affected) elle n'était pas directement concernée ; (= taking part) elle n'était pas directement impliquée ; **the police became ~d** la police est intervenue ; **a question of principle is ~d** il s'agit d'une question de principe ; **the factors/forces/principles ~d** les facteurs mpl/ forces fpl/principes mpl en jeu ; **the vehicles ~d** les véhicules mpl en cause ; **the person ~d** l'intéressé(e) m(f) ; **to feel personally ~d** se sentir concerné ; **to get ~d with sb** (socially) se mettre à fréquenter qn ; (= fall in love with) avoir une liaison avec qn ; **she likes him but she doesn't want to get (too) ~d** elle l'aime bien, mais elle ne veut pas (trop) s'engager ⓑ (= entail) impliquer ; (= cause) occasionner ; (= demand) exiger ; **such an attack would inevitably ~ considerable loss of life** une telle attaque ferait inévitablement de très nombreuses victimes ; **such a project ~s considerable planning** un tel projet exige une organisation considérable ; **will the post ~ much foreign travel?** ce poste impliquera-t-il or exigera-t-il de nombreux déplacements à l'étranger ? ; **the job would ~ my moving to London** ce travail impliquerait or exigerait que je déménage (subj) à Londres ; **there will be a good deal of work ~d** cela demandera or entraînera beaucoup de travail ; **the charges against him ~ allegations of corruption** parmi les accusations portées contre lui, il y a des allégations de corruption
involved [ɪn'vɒlvd] ADJ [situation, relationship, question] compliqué, complexe ; [style] contourné, compliqué → **involve**

involvement [ɪn'vɒlvmənt] N (NonC) (= rôle) rôle m (**in** dans) ; (= participation) participation f (**in** à) ; **his ~ in the affair/plot** etc son rôle dans l'affaire/le complot etc ; **the increasing ~ of employees in decision-making processes** la participation de plus en plus importante des employés dans la prise de décisions ; **his ~ in politics** son engagement m dans la politique ; **his ~ in social work** son action f en matière sociale ; **we don't know the extent of her ~** nous ne savons pas dans quelle mesure elle est impliquée ; **we have no hard proof of his ~** nous n'avons aucune preuve concrète qu'il ait été impliqué ; **she denied any ~ in or with drugs** elle a nié toute implication dans des histoires de drogues ; **they were good friends but there was no romantic ~** ils étaient bons amis mais leur relation n'allait pas plus loin
invulnerability [ɪn͵vʌlnərə'bɪlɪtɪ] N invulnérabilité f
invulnerable [ɪn'vʌlnərəbl] ADJ invulnérable
inward ['ɪnwəd] 1 ADJ [movement] vers l'intérieur ; [happiness, peace] intérieur (-eure f) ; [thoughts, desire, conviction] intime, profond 2 ADV = **inwards** 3 COMP ► **inward investment** N (NonC: Comm) investissements mpl étrangers ► **inward-looking** ADJ replié sur soi(-même)
inwardly ['ɪnwədlɪ] ADV [groan, smile] intérieurement ; **she was ~ furious** en son for intérieur elle était furieuse
inwards ['ɪnwədz] ADV [move] vers l'intérieur ; **his thoughts turned ~** il devint songeur
in-your-face ‡, **in-yer-face** ‡ [͵ɪnjə'feɪs] ADJ cru
I/O [aɪ'əʊ] N (ABBR = **input/output**) E/S f
IOC [͵aɪəʊ'siː] N (ABBR = **International Olympic Committee**) CIO m
iodide ['aɪədaɪd] N iodure m
iodine ['aɪədiːn] N iode m
iodize ['aɪədaɪz] VT ioder
iodoform [aɪ'ɒdəfɔːm] N iodoforme m
IOM (ABBR = **Isle of Man**) → **isle**
ion ['aɪən] N ion m
Iona [aɪ'əʊnə] N (île f d')Iona f
Ionian [aɪ'əʊnɪən] ADJ ionien ; **the ~ Islands** les îles fpl Ioniennes ; **the ~ (Sea)** la mer Ionienne
Ionic [aɪ'ɒnɪk] ADJ (Archit) ionique
ionic [aɪ'ɒnɪk] ADJ (Chem, Phys) ionique
ionize [aɪ'ənaɪz] VT ioniser
ionizer ['aɪənaɪzə'] N ioniseur m
ionosphere [aɪ'ɒnəsfɪə'] N ionosphère f
iota [aɪ'əʊtə] N (= letter) iota m ; (fig = tiny amount) brin m, grain m ; (in written matter) iota m ; **he won't change an ~ of what he has written**) il refuse de changer un iota (à ce qu'il a écrit) ; **if he had an ~ of sense** s'il avait un grain de bon sens ; **not an ~ of truth** pas un brin de vérité, pas un mot de vrai ; **it won't make an ~ of difference** cela ne changera absolument rien ; **it won't affect us one ~** cela ne nous touchera absolument pas
IOU [͵aɪəʊ'juː] N (ABBR = **I owe you**) reconnaissance f de dette ; **he gave me an ~ for £20** il m'a signé un reçu de 20 livres
IOW (Brit) (ABBR = **Isle of Wight**) → **isle**
Iowa ['aɪəʊə] N l'Iowa m ; **in ~** dans l'Iowa
IPA [͵aɪpiː'eɪ] N (ABBR = **International Phonetic Alphabet**) API m
ipecac(uanha) [͵ɪpɪkæk(jʊ'ænə)] N ipéca(cuana) m
ipso facto ['ɪpsəʊ'fæktəʊ] ADJ, ADV ipso facto
IQ [͵aɪ'kjuː] N (ABBR = **intelligence quotient**) QI m
IR [͵aɪ'ɑː'] (Brit) (ABBR = **Inland Revenue**) ≈ fisc m
IRA [͵aɪɑːr'eɪ] N (ABBR = **Irish Republican Army**) IRA f
Irak [ɪ'rɑːk] N = **Iraq**
Iraki [ɪ'rɑːkɪ] = **Iraqi**

► LANGUAGE IN USE: invitation 25   invite 25.1, 25.2   invoice 20.6

Iran [ɪˈrɑːn] N l'Iran m; **in ~** en Iran

Irangate [ɪˈrɑːngeɪt] N, ADJ Irangate m

Iranian [ɪˈreɪnɪən] 1 ADJ iranien 2 a Iranien(ne) m(f) b (Ling) iranien m

Iraq [ɪˈrɑːk] N l'Irak or l'Iraq m; **in ~** en Irak

Iraqi [ɪˈrɑːkɪ] 1 ADJ irakien or iraqien 2 N Irakien(ne) or Iraqien(ne) m(f)

irascibility [ɪˌræsɪˈbɪlɪtɪ] N irascibilité f

irascible [ɪˈræsɪbl] ADJ irascible, coléreux

irascibly [ɪˈræsɪblɪ] ADV irasciblement

irate [aɪˈreɪt] ADJ furieux, courroucé (liter)

IRBM [ˌaɪɑːˌbiːˈem] (ABBR = intermediate range ballistic missile) → **intermediate**

ire [aɪə] N (liter) courroux m (liter); **to rouse sb's ~** provoquer le courroux de qn

Ireland [ˈaɪələnd] N l'Irlande f; **Republic of ~** la République d'Irlande → **northern**

irides [ˈɪrɪdiːz] NPL of **iris a**

iridescence [ˌɪrɪˈdesns] N [of prism, crystal] irisation f; [of plumage etc] chatoiement m

iridescent [ˌɪrɪˈdesnt] ADJ [prism, crystal] irisé, iridescent; [plumage] chatoyant

iridium [aɪˈrɪdɪəm] N iridium m

iridology [ˌɪrɪˈdɒlədʒɪ] N iridologie f

iris [ˈaɪərɪs] N a (pl **irides**) [of eye] iris m b (pl **irises**) (Bot) iris m

Irish [ˈaɪərɪʃ] 1 ADJ (gen) irlandais; [ambassador, embassy] d'Irlande; [teacher] d'irlandais 2 N (Ling) irlandais m 3 **the Irish** NPL les Irlandais mpl 4 COMP ► **Irish coffee** N café m irlandais, irish coffee m ► **Irish Free State** N (Hist) État m libre d'Irlande ► **Irish Sea** N (Hist) mer f d'Irlande ► **Irish stew** N ragoût m de mouton (à l'irlandaise) ► **Irish terrier** N irish-terrier m ► **Irish wolfhound** N lévrier m irlandais

Irishman [ˈaɪərɪʃmən] N (pl **-men**) Irlandais m

Irishwoman [ˈaɪərɪʃˌwʊmən] N (pl **-women**) Irlandaise f

irk [ɜːk] VT contrarier, ennuyer

irksome [ˈɜːksəm] ADJ [restriction, person] ennuyeux; [task] ingrat

iron [ˈaɪən] 1 N a (NonC = metal) fer m; **old or scrap ~** ferraille f (NonC); (fig) **a man of ~** (unyielding) un homme de fer; (cruel) un homme au cœur de pierre; **to strike while the ~ is hot** battre le fer pendant qu'il est chaud; (fig liter) **the ~ had entered his soul** il avait la mort dans l'âme, il était comme une âme en peine → **cast, pump, rod, wrought** b (= tool) fer m; (for laundry: also **flat ~**) fer m (à repasser); **electric ~** fer m électrique; **to give a dress an ~*** ◊ **to run the ~ over a dress** donner un coup de fer à une robe; (fig) **to have too many ~s in the fire** mener trop de choses or d'affaires de front; (fig) **she's got other ~s in the fire** elle a d'autres affaires en train → **fire, grapple, solder** c (Golf) fer m; **a number three ~** un fer trois d (NonC: Med) (sels mpl de) fer m e (= surgical appliance) appareil m orthopédique → **leg** 2 **irons** NPL (= fetters) fers mpl, chaînes fpl; **to put sb in ~s** mettre qn aux fers; (Naut) **to be in ~s** faire chapelle 3 VT [+ clothes etc] repasser; (more sketchily) donner un coup de fer à; **"~ under a damp cloth"** « repasser à la pattemouille » → **minimum, non-** 4 VI [person] repasser; [clothes etc] se repasser 5 COMP (lit) [tool, bridge] de or en fer; (fig) [determination] de fer, d'acier ► **the Iron Age** N l'âge m de fer ► **the iron and steel industry** N l'industrie f sidérurgique ► **the Iron Chancellor** N (Hist) le Chancelier de fer (Bismarck) ► **iron constitution** N **to have an ~ constitution** avoir une santé de fer ► **the Iron Curtain** N (Pol Hist) rideau m de fer; **the Iron Curtain countries** les pays mpl de l'Est, le bloc de l'Est ► **the Iron Duke** N (Brit Hist) le Duc

de fer (Wellington) ► **iron fist** N **an ~ fist in a velvet glove** une main de fer dans un gant de velours ► **iron foundry** N fonderie f de fonte ► **iron grey** ADJ gris inv de fer, gris fer inv; [hair] gris argenté ► **iron hand** N **to rule with an ~ hand** gouverner d'une main or poigne de fer → **iron fist** ► **the Iron Lady** N (Brit Pol) la Dame de fer (Margaret Thatcher) ► **iron lung** N (Med) poumon m d'acier ► **iron mask** N **the man in the ~ mask** l'homme m au masque de fer ► **iron ore** N minerai m de fer ► **iron oxide** N oxyde m de fer ► **iron pyrite** N pyrite f ► **iron rations** NPL vivres mpl or rations fpl de réserve ► **iron will** N volonté f de fer

► **iron out** VT SEP [+ creases] faire disparaître au fer; (fig) [+ difficulties] aplanir; [+ problems] régler; **the two sides were unable to ~ out their differences** les deux camps n'ont pas réussi à régler leurs différends

ironclad [ˈaɪənklæd] 1 N (Naut) cuirassé m 2 ADJ (lit) [warship] cuirassé; (fig) [argument, case, guarantee, promise, defence] en béton; [rule] strict

ironic(al) [aɪˈrɒnɪk(əl)] ADJ ironique

ironically [aɪˈrɒnɪkəlɪ] ADV ironiquement; **~, she never turned up** l'ironie de la chose, c'est qu'elle n'est pas venue du tout

ironing [ˈaɪənɪŋ] 1 N repassage m; **to do the ~** repasser, faire le repassage; **it doesn't need ~** cela n'a pas besoin d'être repassé 2 COMP ► **ironing board** N planche f à repasser

ironist [ˈaɪərənɪst] N maître mf de l'ironie; **the master ~** le maître de l'ironie

ironize [ˈaɪərənaɪz] 1 VI ironiser 2 VT **to ~ sb/sth** traiter qn/qch avec ironie

ironmonger [ˈaɪənˌmʌŋgəʳ] N (Brit) quincaillier m, -ière f; **~'s (shop)** quincaillerie f

ironmongery [ˈaɪənˌmʌŋgərɪ] N (Brit) quincaillerie f

ironstone [ˈaɪənstəʊn] N (also **~ china**) terre f de fer

ironwork [ˈaɪənwɜːk] N (NonC) [of gates, railings etc] ferronnerie f, serrurerie f; [of parts of construction] ferronnerie f, ferrures fpl; **heavy ~** grosse ferronnerie f or serrurerie f

ironworks [ˈaɪənwɜːks] N (pl inv) usine f sidérurgique

irony [ˈaɪərənɪ] N ironie f; **the ~ of the situation was not lost on her** l'ironie de la situation ne lui a pas échappé; **by some ~ of fate, she ...** l'ironie du sort a voulu qu'elle ...; **the ~ of it is that ...** l'ironie de la chose c'est que ...; **one of the great ironies of this story is that ...** le comble de l'ironie (dans cette histoire), c'est que ... → **dramatic**

Iroquois [ˈɪrəkwɔɪ] 1 ADJ iroquois 2 N (pl inv) a (also **~ Indian**) Iroquois(e) m(f) b (Ling) iroquois m

irradiate [ɪˈreɪdɪeɪt] VT a (Med, Nucl = expose to radiation) [+ food, population, tumour, patient] irradier; **~d foods** aliments mpl irradiés b (= illuminate: lit, fig) illuminer

irradiation [ɪˌreɪdɪˈeɪʃən] N (with radiation) [of person, food] irradiation f; (with light) illumination f

irrational [ɪˈræʃənl] ADJ [person] qui n'est pas rationnel; [conduct] irrationnel, déraisonnable; [fear] irraisonné, irrationnel; [hatred, idea, reaction] irrationnel; [thoughts] fou (folle f); (Math) irrationnel; **he had become quite ~ about it** c'était un sujet qu'il n'était plus capable d'aborder rationnellement

irrationality [ɪˌræʃəˈnælɪtɪ] N irrationalité f

irrationally [ɪˈræʃnəlɪ] ADV [act, behave] irrationnellement; [think, believe] en dépit du bon sens, irrationnellement; [angry] sans véritable raison; **~ jealous** d'une jalousie irraisonnée

irreconcilable [ɪˌrekənˈsaɪləbl] ADJ [differences, positions] inconciliable; [beliefs, opinions] inconciliable, incompatible (**with sth** avec

qch); [objectives] incompatible (**with sth** avec qch); [enemy, opponent] irréconciliable; [conflict] insoluble; [hatred] implacable

irrecoverable [ˌɪrɪˈkʌvərəbl] ADJ [object] irrécupérable; [loss] irréparable, irrémédiable; (Fin) irrécouvrable

irredeemable [ˌɪrɪˈdiːməbl] ADJ a [error] irréparable; [liar, thief] invétéré; [optimist] impénitent, incorrigible b (Fin) [loan] non amortissable, non remboursable; [bond] irremboursable

irredeemably [ˌɪrɪˈdiːməblɪ] ADV [lost, ruined, damaged] irrémédiablement; **~ evil/incompetent** d'une méchanceté/incompétence irrémédiable

irredentism [ˌɪrɪˈdentɪzəm] N (fig) irrédentisme m

irredentist [ˌɪrɪˈdentɪst] ADJ, N (fig) irrédentiste mf

irreducible [ˌɪrɪˈdjuːsəbl] ADJ irréductible

irrefutable [ˌɪrɪˈfjuːtəbl] ADJ [argument, evidence] irréfutable; [testimony] irrécusable

irregular [ɪˈregjʊləʳ] 1 ADJ a (gen, Math, Gram) [features, pulse, meals, hours] irrégulier; **at ~ intervals** à intervalles irréguliers; **he leads a very ~ life** il mène une vie très déréglée; **all this is most ~** (= against regulations) tout cela n'est pas du tout régulier; (= unorthodox) cela ne se fait pas; **he is ~ in his attendance at classes** il n'assiste pas régulièrement aux cours; (Med) **~ periods** règles fpl irrégulières b (= uneven) [surface] inégal c (Mil) [soldier] irrégulier 2 NPL (Mil) **the ~s** les irréguliers mpl

irregularity [ɪˌregjʊˈlærɪtɪ] N irrégularité f; (NonC) irrégularités fpl; (Jur, Admin: in procedure) vice m de forme

irregularly [ɪˈregjʊləlɪ] ADV irrégulièrement; **~-shaped** aux formes irrégulières

irrelevance [ɪˈreləvəns], **irrelevancy** [ɪˈreləvənsɪ] N a (NonC) manque m de pertinence (**to** par rapport à); **the ~ of nuclear weapons in this day and age** le fait que les armements nucléaires n'ont plus de raison d'être à l'heure actuelle b (= person, thing) **a report full of ~s** or **irrelevancies** un compte rendu qui s'écarte sans cesse du sujet; **the party is rapidly becoming a political ~** ce parti est de plus en plus coupé de la réalité politique; **she dismissed this idea as an ~** elle a écarté cette idée comme étant non pertinente

irrelevant [ɪˈreləvənt] ADJ [facts, details] non pertinent; [question, remark] hors de propos; **~ to** sans rapport avec; **that's ~ (to the subject)** ça n'a rien à voir, ça n'a aucun rapport; **written in the 1960s, his novels are largely ~ to the concerns of today** écrits dans les années 60, ses romans n'ont guère de rapport avec les préoccupations d'aujourd'hui; **many of these issues seem ~ to the younger generation** les jeunes ne se sentent pas concernés par beaucoup de ces questions

irrelevantly [ɪˈreləvəntlɪ] ADV [say, add, ask] hors de propos

irreligion [ˌɪrɪˈlɪdʒən] N irréligion f

irreligious [ˌɪrɪˈlɪdʒəs] ADJ irréligieux

irremediable [ˌɪrɪˈmiːdɪəbl] ADJ irrémédiable, sans remède

irremediably [ˌɪrɪˈmiːdɪəblɪ] ADV irrémédiablement

irremovable [ˌɪrɪˈmuːvəbl] ADJ [thing] immuable; [difficulty] invincible; [judge etc] inamovible

irreparable [ɪˈrepərəbl] ADJ [harm, wrong] irréparable; [loss] irréparable, irrémédiable

irreparably [ɪˈrepərəblɪ] ADV irréparablement, irrémédiablement

irreplaceable [ˌɪrɪˈpleɪsəbl] ADJ irremplaçable

irrepressible [ˌɪrɪˈpresəbl] ADJ [laughter] irrépressible; [person] débordant d'activité, exubérant

irrepressibly [ˌɪrɪ'presəblɪ] ADV [laugh] de façon irrépressible; **~ cheerful/optimistic** d'une gaieté/d'un optimisme à toute épreuve

irreproachable [ˌɪrɪ'prəʊtʃəbl] ADJ irréprochable

irresistible [ˌɪrɪ'zɪstəbl] ADJ irrésistible (**to sb** pour qn); **he is ~ to women** les femmes le trouvent irrésistible

irresistibly [ˌɪrɪ'zɪstəblɪ] ADV [attract, remind, impel, spread] irrésistiblement; **she found him ~ attractive** elle lui trouvait un charme irrésistible

irresolute [ɪ'rezəluːt] ADJ irrésolu, indécis, hésitant

irresolutely [ɪ'rezəˌluːtlɪ] ADV [hesitate, pause etc] d'un air irrésolu or indécis

irresoluteness [ɪ'rezəluːtnɪs] N irrésolution f, indécision f

irrespective [ˌɪrɪ'spektɪv] ADJ **~ of: they were all the same price, ~ of their quality** ils étaient tous au même prix, indépendamment de leur qualité or quelle que soit la qualité; **~ of race, creed or colour** sans distinction de race, de religion ou de couleur, indépendamment de la race, de la religion ou de la couleur; **~ of whether they are needed** que l'on en ait besoin ou non

irresponsibility [ˈɪrɪˌspɒnsə'bɪlɪtɪ] N [of person] irresponsabilité f (also Jur), légèreté f; [of act] légèreté f

irresponsible [ˌɪrɪs'pɒnsəbl] ADJ [person, behaviour, attitude, action] (also Jur) irresponsable; [remark] irréfléchi; **it was ~ of her to say that ◊ she was ~ to say that** c'était irresponsable de sa part de dire cela; **it would be ~ of me to encourage you** ce serait irresponsable de ma part si je t'encourageais; **it is ~ to drink and drive** c'est faire preuve d'irresponsabilité de conduire lorsqu'on a bu

irresponsibly [ˌɪrɪs'pɒnsəblɪ] ADV [act, behave] de façon irresponsable; **~ extravagant** d'une extravagance irresponsable

irretrievable [ˌɪrɪ'triːvəbl] ADJ [harm, damage, loss] irréparable; [object] irrécupérable; (Fin) [debt] irrécouvrable; **the ~ breakdown of a relationship** la rupture irrémédiable d'une relation; (Jur) **to divorce on grounds of ~ breakdown** divorcer pour rupture de la vie commune

irretrievably [ˌɪrɪ'triːvəblɪ] ADV irréparablement, irrémédiablement

irreverence [ɪ'revərəns] N irrévérence f

irreverent [ɪ'revərənt] ADJ irrévérencieux

irreverently [ɪ'revərəntlɪ] ADV irrévérencieusement

irreversible [ˌɪrɪ'vɜːsəbl] ADJ [damage, process, change, decline, disease, brain damage, operation] irréversible; [decision, judgment] irrévocable

irreversibly [ˌɪrɪ'vɜːsəblɪ] ADV [change] irréversiblement; [damage] de façon irréversible

irrevocable [ɪ'revəkəbl] ADJ irrévocable

irrevocably [ɪ'revəkəblɪ] ADV irrévocablement

irrigable [ɪ'rɪgəbl] ADJ irrigable

irrigate [ˈɪrɪgeɪt] VT (Agr, Med) irriguer

irrigation [ˌɪrɪ'geɪʃən] N (Agr, Med) irrigation f

irritability [ˌɪrɪtə'bɪlɪtɪ] N irritabilité f

irritable [ˈɪrɪtəbl] **1** ADJ [person] (= cross) irritable; (= irascible) irascible, coléreux; [look, mood] irritable; [temperament, nature] irascible; **to get** or **grow ~** devenir irritable **2** COMP **► irritable bowel syndrome** N syndrome m du côlon irritable, colopathie f spasmodique

irritably [ˈɪrɪtəblɪ] ADV avec irritation

irritant [ˈɪrɪtənt] **1** N **a** (= annoying noise, interference etc) source f d'irritation; (= contentious issue) point m épineux; **the issue**

has become a major ~ to the government cette question donne du fil à retordre au gouvernement **b** (= substance) irritant m **2** ADJ [substance, effect] irritant

irritate [ˈɪrɪteɪt] VT **a** (= annoy) irriter, agacer; **to get** or **become ~d** s'irriter **b** (Med) irriter

irritating [ˈɪrɪteɪtɪŋ] ADJ **a** (= annoying) irritant, agaçant **b** (Med) irritant

irritatingly [ˈɪrɪteɪtɪŋlɪ] ADV **~ slow/smug** d'une lenteur/d'une autosuffisance irritante or agaçante

irritation [ˌɪrɪ'teɪʃən] N **a** (NonC = annoyance) irritation f, agacement m **b** (= irritant) source f d'irritation

irruption [ɪ'rʌpʃən] N irruption f

IRS [ˌaɪɑː'res] N (US) (ABBR = **Internal Revenue Service**) **the ~** ≈ le fisc

is [ɪz] → **be**

Isaac [ˈaɪzək] N Isaac m

Isaiah [aɪ'zaɪə] N Isaïe m

ISBN [ˌaɪesbiː'en] N (ABBR = **International Standard Book Number**) ISBN m

ischium [ˈɪskɪəm] N (pl **ischia** [ˈɪskɪə]) ischion m

ISDN [ˌaɪesdiː'en] N (ABBR = **Integrated Services Digital Network**) RNIS m

ish* [ɪʃ] ADV (Brit) **hungry? ~** tu as faim? – un (petit) peu; **is it good? ~** est-ce que c'est bien? – pas mal*

...ish [ɪʃ] SUF **a** ...âtre; **blackish** plutôt noir, noirâtre (pej) **b** **she came at threeish** elle est venue vers 3 heures or sur les 3 heures; **it's coldish** il fait un peu froid or frisquet*; **she's fortyish** elle a dans les quarante ans*

isinglass [ˈaɪzɪŋglɑːs] N ichtyocolle f

Isis [ˈaɪsɪs] N (Myth) Isis f

Islam [ˈɪzlɑːm] N Islam m

Islamic [ɪz'læmɪk] ADJ islamique; **the ~ Republic of ...** la République islamique de ...

Islamicist [ɪz'læmɪsɪst] N islamiste mf

Islamism [ˈɪzləmɪzəm] N islamisme m

Islamist [ˈɪzləmɪst] N = **Islamicist**

island [ˈaɪlənd] **1** N (lit, fig) île f; (smaller) îlot m **2** COMP [people, community] insulaire **► island-hopping*** N **to go ~-hopping** aller d'île en île **♦** ADJ **~-hopping holiday** vacances passées à aller d'île en île

islander [ˈaɪləndəʳ] N insulaire mf, habitant(e) m(f) d'une île or de l'île

isle [aɪl] **1** N (liter) île f → **British 2** COMP **► the Isle of Man** N l'île f de Man **► the Isle of Wight** N l'île f de Wight

islet [ˈaɪlɪt] N îlot m

ism [ˈɪzəm] N doctrine f, idéologie f; **Marxism or any other ~** le marxisme ou tout autre doctrine or idéologie

...ism [ˈɪzəm] SUF ...isme

isn't [ˈɪznt] = **is not**; → **be**

ISO [ˌaɪes'əʊ] N (ABBR = **International Standards Organization**) ISO f

iso... [ˈaɪsəʊ] PREF iso...

isobar [ˈaɪsəʊbɑːʳ] N isobare f

Isobel [ˈɪzəʊbel] N Isabelle f

isogloss [ˈaɪsəʊglɒs] N isoglosse f

isolate [ˈaɪsəʊleɪt] VT (all senses) isoler (**from** de)

isolated [ˈaɪsəʊleɪtɪd] ADJ (gen, Chem, Med etc) isolé (**from sb/sth** de qn/qch); **to keep sb/sth ~ (from sb/sth)** tenir qn/qch à l'écart (de qn/qch)

isolation [ˌaɪsəʊ'leɪʃən] **1** N **a** (gen, Med) isolement m; **international ~** isolement m international; **to be (kept) in ~** [prisoner] être maintenu en isolement; **he was in ~ for three months** il a passé trois mois en isolement **b** **in ~** isolément; **my remarks should not be considered in ~** mes remarques ne devraient pas être considérées isolément or hors contexte; **taken in ~ these statements can be dangerously misleading** hors contexte ces dé-

clarations risquent d'être mal interprétées; **no social class can exist in ~** aucune classe sociale ne peut exister isolément; **to act in ~** agir seul; **to deal with sth in ~** traiter de qch à part **c** (Chem etc) (= action) isolation f; (= state) isolement m **2** COMP **► isolation hospital** N hôpital m de quarantaine **► isolation ward** N salle f de quarantaine

isolationism [ˌaɪsəʊ'leɪʃənɪzəm] N isolationnisme m

isolationist [ˌaɪsəʊ'leɪʃənɪst] ADJ, N isolationniste mf

Isolde [ɪ'zɒldə] N Iseult or Iseut f

isomer [ˈaɪsəməʳ] N isomère m

isometric [ˌaɪsəʊ'metrɪk] **1** ADJ isométrique **2** **isometrics** NPL exercices mpl musculaires isométriques

isomorphic [ˌaɪsəʊ'mɔːfɪk] ADJ isomorphe

isopluvial [ˌaɪsəʊ'pluːvɪəl] ADJ **~ map** carte f pluviométrique

isosceles [aɪ'sɒsɪliːz] ADJ isocèle

isotherm [ˈaɪsəʊθɜːm] N isotherme f

isotonic [ˌaɪsəʊ'tɒnɪk] ADJ [contraction, solution] isotonique

isotope [ˈaɪsəʊtəʊp] ADJ, N isotope m

I-spy [ˈaɪ'spaɪ] N (Brit) jeu où l'on essaie de faire deviner le nom d'un objet à partir de sa première lettre

Israel [ˈɪzreɪl] N Israël m; **in ~** en Israël

Israeli [ɪz'reɪlɪ] **1** ADJ (gen) israélien; [ambassador, embassy] d'Israël **2** N (pl **Israelis** or **Israeli**) Israélien(ne) m(f)

Israelite [ˈɪzrɪəlaɪt] N israélite mf

issue [ˈɪʃuː] **1** N **a** (= matter, question) question f; (= point) point m; (= problem) problème m; **it is a very difficult ~** c'est une question ou un problème très complexe; **she raised several new ~s** elle a soulevé plusieurs points nouveaux; **the priest raised the ~ of human rights** le prêtre a soulevé la question des droits de l'homme; **she raised the ~ of who was to control the budget** elle a posé la question de savoir qui contrôlerait le budget; **the ~ is whether ...** la question est de savoir si ...; **the main** or **key ~ is to discover if ...** la question centrale est de découvrir si ...; **that's the main** or **key ~** c'est la question principale or le problème principal; **it's not a political ~** ce n'est pas une question politique; **this needn't become an ~ between us** il ne faut pas que ça devienne un problème entre nous; **the real ~ was never addressed** le vrai problème or la vraie question n'a jamais été posé(e); **to face the ~** regarder le problème en face; **to evade** or **avoid the ~** éluder le problème, prendre la tangente; **he makes an ~ of every tiny detail** il fait une montagne du moindre détail; **I don't want to make an ~ of it but ...** je ne veux pas trop insister là-dessus mais ...; **to take** or **join ~ with sb** engager une controverse avec qn; **I feel I must take ~ with you on this** je me permets de ne pas partager votre avis là-dessus

b **at ~: the point at ~** le point controversé; **the question at ~** la question en jeu or qui fait problème; **the matter at ~** l'affaire f en jeu; **his integrity is not at ~** son intégrité n'est pas (mise) en doute or en cause; **his political future is at ~** son avenir politique est (mis) en question or en cause; **what is at ~ is whether/how ...** la question est de savoir si/comment ...; **they were at ~ over this** ils étaient en désaccord sur cela → **side**

c (= release) [of book] publication f, parution f, sortie f; [of goods, tickets] distribution f; [of passport, document] délivrance f; [of banknote, cheque, shares, stamp] émission f, mise f en circulation; [of proclamation] parution f; (Jur) [of warrant, writ, summons] lancement m; **there has been a new ~ of banknotes/stamps/shares** il y a eu une nouvelle émission de billets/de timbres/d'actions; **these coins are a new ~** ces pièces viennent d'être émises

[d] (= copy, number) [of newspaper, magazine] numéro m, livraison f; **in this ~** dans ce numéro

[e] (Med) écoulement m

[f] (NonC: Jur or liter = offspring) descendance f, progéniture f (liter); **without ~** sans descendance, sans progéniture (liter); **the king and his ~** le roi et sa descendance or ses descendants

[g] (frm = outcome) résultat m

[2] VT [+ book] publier, faire paraître; [+ order] donner; [+ goods, tickets] distribuer; [+ passport, document] délivrer; [+ banknote, cheque, shares, stamps] émettre, mettre en circulation; [+ proclamation] faire; [+ threat, ultimatum, warning, warrant, writ] lancer; [+ verdict] rendre; **to ~ a statement** faire une déclaration; (Jur) **to ~ a summons** lancer une assignation; (Fin) **~d to bearer** émis au porteur; **to ~ sth to sb** ◊ **to ~ sb with sth** fournir or donner qch à qn; **the children were ~d with pencils** on a fourni or distribué des crayons aux enfants

[3] VI (liter) **to ~ forth** [steam, liquid, people] jaillir; **to ~ from** sortir de; **blood issuing from his mouth, he ...** alors que du sang sortait de sa bouche, il ...

[4] COMP (esp Mil) [clothing etc] réglementaire, d'ordonnance ► **issue price** N (St Ex) prix m or cours m d'émission

issuer ['ɪʃʊə^r] N (Fin, St Ex) émetteur m, société f émettrice

Istanbul [ˌɪstæn'buːl] N Istanbul

isthmus ['ɪsməs] N (pl **isthmuses** or **isthmi** ['ɪsmaɪ]) isthme m

Istria ['ɪstrɪə] N l'Istrie f

IT ['aɪ'tiː] (ABBR = **information technology**) → **information**

it[1] [ɪt] PRON [a] (specific) (nominative) il, elle; (accusative) le, la; (before vowel) l'; (dative) lui; **where is the book? — it's on the table** où est le livre? — il est sur la table; **my machine is old but it works** ma machine est vieille mais elle marche; **here's the pencil — give it to me** voici le crayon — donne-le-moi; **if you find the watch give it to him** si tu trouves la montre, donne-la-lui; **he found the book and brought it to me** il a trouvé le livre et me l'a apporté; **let the dog in and give it a drink** fais entrer le chien et donne-lui à boire

[b] **of** or **from** or **about** or **for it** etc en; **he's afraid of it** il en a peur; **I took the letter out of it** j'en ai sorti la lettre; **I feel the better for it** ça m'a fait du bien; **I don't care about it** ça m'est égal, je m'en fiche*; **speak to him about it** parlez-lui-en; **he didn't speak to me about it** il ne m'en a pas parlé; (following French verbs with "de") **I doubt it** j'en doute

[c] **in** or **to** or **at it** etc y; **he fell in it** il y est tombé; **he'll be at it** (meeting etc) il y sera; **he agreed to it** il y a consenti; (following French verbs with "à") **taste it!** goûtez-y!; **don't touch it** n'y touche pas

[d] **above** or **over it** (au-)dessus; **below** or **beneath** or **under it** (au-)dessous, (en-)dessous; **there's the table and your book is on it** voilà la table et votre livre est dessus; **a table with a cloth over it** une table avec une nappe dessus; **he drew a house with a cloud above it** il a dessiné une maison avec un nuage au-dessus; **there is a fence but you can get under it** il y a une barrière mais vous pouvez passer (en-)dessous

[e] (weather, time) il; **it is raining** il pleut; **it's hot today** il fait chaud aujourd'hui; **it was a warm evening** il faisait doux ce soir-là; **it's 3 o'clock** il est 3 heures; **it's Wednesday 16 October** nous sommes (le) mercredi 16 octobre

[f] (impers: non-specific) **it all frightens me** tout cela m'effraie; **it's very pleasant here** c'est agréable or bien ici; **who is it?** qui est-ce?; **it's me** c'est moi; **what is it?** qu'est-ce que c'est?

what's it all about? qu'est-ce qui se passe?, de quoi s'agit-il?; **where is it?** où est-ce?, où est-ce que c'est?; **that's it!** (approval) c'est ça!; (agreement) exactement!, tout à fait!; (achievement) ça y est!, c'est fait!; (anger) ça suffit!; (dismay) ça y est!; **how was it?** comment ça s'est passé?, comment c'était?*; **what was that noise? — it was the cat** qu'est-ce que c'était que ce bruit? — c'était le chat; **it's no use trying to see him** ce n'est pas la peine de or ça ne sert à rien d'essayer de le voir; **it's difficult to understand** c'est difficile à comprendre; **it's difficult to understand why** il est difficile de comprendre pourquoi; **it's a pity** c'est dommage; **I considered it pointless to protest** j'ai jugé (qu'il était) inutile de protester; **it's fun to go for a swim** c'est amusant d'aller nager; **it was your father who phoned** c'est ton père qui a téléphoné; **it was Anne I gave it to** c'est à Anne que je l'ai donné; **it can't be helped** on n'y peut rien, on ne peut rien y faire; **the best of it is that ...** ce qu'il y a de mieux (là-dedans) c'est que ...; **he's not got it in him to do this job properly** il est incapable de faire ce travail comme il faut; **keep at it!** continuez!; **let's face it** regardons les choses en face; **he's had it** il est fichu*; **to be with it** être dans le vent* or à la page; **to get with it*** se mettre à la page*; **she's got it in for me** elle m'en veut, elle a une dent contre moi*

[g] (in games) **you're it!** c'est toi le chat!

[h] (* = something special) **she really thinks she's it** elle se prend vraiment pour le nombril du monde*; **she's got it** elle est sexy*

it[2] [ɪt] N (ABBR = **Italian**) gin and it vermouth-gin m

ITA [ˌaɪtiː'eɪ] (ABBR = **Initial Teaching Alphabet**) → **initial**

Italian [ɪ'tæljən] [1] ADJ (gen) italien; [ambassador, embassy] d'Italie; [teacher] d'italien [2] N [a] Italien(ne) m(f) [b] (Ling) italien m → **Switzerland**

Italianate [ɪ'tæljənɪt] ADJ [garden, landscape] à l'italienne; [building, architecture, singing] de style italien, italianisant

italic [ɪ'tælɪk] [1] ADJ (Typ) italique; **~ script** or **writing** écriture f italique [2] **italics** NPL italique m; **to put a word/to write in ~s** mettre un mot/écrire en italique; **"my ~s"** « c'est moi qui souligne »

italicize [ɪ'tælɪsaɪz] VT (Typ) mettre or imprimer en italique

Italo- [ɪ'tæləʊ] PREF italo-

Italy ['ɪtəlɪ] N l'Italie f

ITC [ˌaɪtiː'siː] N (Brit) (ABBR = **Independent Television Commission**) ≈ CSA m, organisme de contrôle de l'audiovisuel

itch [ɪtʃ] [1] N (lit) démangeaison f; **I've got an ~ in my leg/back** ma jambe/mon dos me démange, j'ai des démangeaisons à la jambe/dans le dos; (Med, Vet) **the ~** la gale; (fig) **I've got an ~*** for or to travel l'envie de voyager me démange; **the seven-year ~** le cap des sept ans de mariage

[2] VI [person] éprouver des démangeaisons; **his legs ~** ses jambes le or lui démangent; **my leg/back ~es** ma jambe/mon dos me démange, j'ai des démangeaisons à la jambe/dans le dos; **my eyes are ~ing** j'ai les yeux qui me piquent; **my skin ~es** j'ai la peau qui me gratte or me démange

[b] (* fig) **I was ~ing to get started** cela me démangeait de commencer; **I'm ~ing to tell him the news** la langue me démange de lui annoncer la nouvelle; **he's ~ing for a fight** ça le démange de se battre; **she was ~ing for her contract to end** elle avait hâte que son contrat se termine (subj); **the people are ~ing for change** les gens attendent un changement avec impatience

[3] VT démanger

itchiness ['ɪtʃɪnɪs] N démangeaisons fpl

itching ['ɪtʃɪŋ] [1] N démangeaison f [2] COMP ► **itching powder** N poil m à gratter

itchy ['ɪtʃɪ] ADJ **my eyes are ~** j'ai les yeux qui me piquent; **my skin is** or **feels ~** j'ai la peau qui me gratte or me démange; **my scalp is** or **feels ~** ◊ **I have an ~ scalp** j'ai le cuir chevelu qui me démange or qui me gratte; **a dry, ~ scalp** un cuir chevelu sec et irrité; **I have an ~ leg** j'ai la jambe qui me démange, j'ai des démangeaisons à la jambe; **I'm** or **I feel all ~** ça me démange de partout, ça me gratte partout; **the baby has an ~ rash** le bébé a des rougeurs qui le démangent; **this sweater is ~** ce pull me gratte; (esp Brit fig) **to have ~ feet*** avoir la bougeotte*; (fig) **to have ~ fingers*** (= be impatient to act) ne pas tenir en place; (= be likely to steal) être kleptomane sur les bords*; (fig, pej) **to have an ~ palm*** avoir les doigts crochus*; (fig) **to have an ~ trigger finger*** avoir la gâchette facile

it'd ['ɪtd] = **it had, it would**; → **have, would**

item ['aɪtəm] [1] N (Comm, Comput) article m; (in discussion: at meeting) question f, point m; (in variety show) numéro m; (in catalogue, newspaper) article m; (Jur: in contract) article m; (Accounts) poste m; **an ~ of clothing** un vêtement; **an ~ of food** ◊ **a food ~** un aliment; **an ~ of jewellery** ◊ **a jewellery ~** un bijou; **~s on the agenda** questions fpl à l'ordre du jour; **the first ~ on the programme** le premier numéro du programme; **the first ~ on the list** (gen) la première chose sur la liste; (on shopping list) le premier article sur la liste; (in discussion) la première question or le premier point sur la liste; (Rad, TV) **the main ~ in the news** ◊ **the main news ~** l'information f principale; **we have several ~s for discussion** nous avons plusieurs points à discuter; **they're an ~*** ils sont ensemble

[2] ADV item, en outre

[3] COMP ► **item veto** N (US Pol) veto m partiel (sur un projet de loi)

itemize ['aɪtəmaɪz] VT [+ bill etc] détailler

iterate ['ɪtəreɪt] VT (frm) réitérer

itinerant [ɪ'tɪnərənt] ADJ [preacher] itinérant; [actor, musician] ambulant; **~ (lace-)seller** colporteur m, -euse f (de dentelle); **an ~ lifestyle/childhood** un mode de vie/une enfance nomade; (US Scol) **~ teacher** professeur qui enseigne dans plusieurs établissements

itinerary [aɪ'tɪnərərɪ] N itinéraire m

it'll ['ɪtl] = **it will**; → **will**

ITN [ˌaɪtiː'en] N (Brit) (ABBR = **Independent Television News**) chaîne indépendante d'actualités télévisées

its [ɪts] [1] POSS ADJ son m (also f before vowel), sa f, ses pl [2] POSS PRON le sien, la sienne, les siens, les siennes

it's [ɪts] = **it is, it has**; → **be, have**

itself [ɪt'self] PRON [a] (emphatic) lui-même m, elle-même f; **the book ~ is not valuable** le livre (en) lui-même n'est pas de grande valeur; **the chair ~ was covered with ink** la chaise elle-même était couverte d'encre; **you've been kindness ~** vous avez été la gentillesse même; **she fainted in the theatre ~** elle s'est évanouie en plein théâtre or dans le théâtre même; **the door closes by ~** la porte se ferme d'elle-même or toute seule; **this by** or **in ~ is not bad** ceci n'est pas un mal en soi; **the involvement of the foreign ministers was ~ a sign of progress** l'engagement des ministres des affaires étrangères était en soi un signe encourageant; **in the town ~, the atmosphere remained calm** dans la ville même, le calme régnait; **no matter who's elected, the system ~ is not going to change** peu importe qui sera élu, le système en lui-même ne va pas changer; **the mere will to cooperate is by ~ not sufficient** la simple volonté de coopérer n'est pas suffisante en soi; **just reaching the**

semifinals has been an achievement in ~ arriver en demi-finale a déjà été un exploit en soi; **an end in ~** une fin en soi
b (*reflexive*) se; **the dog hurt ~** le chien s'est fait mal; **the computer can reprogram ~** l'ordinateur peut se reprogrammer tout seul; **a group which calls ~ the freedom movement** un groupe qui se donne le nom de mouvement pour la liberté

ITV [ˌaɪtiːˈviː] N (*Brit*) (ABBR = **Independent Television**) chaîne indépendante de télévision

IU(C)D [ˌaɪjuːsiːˈdiː] N (ABBR = **intrauterine (contraceptive) device**) DIU *m*

IV, **i.v.** [ˈaɪˈviː] (ABBR = **intravenous(ly)**) IV, iv

Ivan [ˈaɪvən] N Ivan *m*; ~ **the Terrible** Ivan le Terrible

I've [aɪv] = **I have**; → **have**

IVF [ˌaɪviːˈef] (ABBR = **in vitro fertilization**) FIV *f*

ivory [ˈaɪvərɪ] **1** N **a** (*NonC*) ivoire *m* **b** (= *object*) ivoire *m* **c** *ivories** (= *piano keys*) touches *fpl*; (= *dice*) dés *mpl*; (= *teeth*) dents *fpl* **2** COMP [*statue, figure*] en ivoire, d'ivoire; (*also* **~-coloured**) ivoire *inv* ► **the Ivory Coast** N la Côte-d'Ivoire ► **ivory tower** N (*fig*) tour *f* d'ivoire ► **ivory trade** N (= *selling*) commerce *m* de l'ivoire; (= *industry*) industrie *f* de l'ivoire

ivy [ˈaɪvɪ] **1** N lierre *m* **2** COMP ► **Ivy League** N (*US*) les huit grandes universités privées du nord-est ♦ ADJ ≈ BCBG*

ivyleaf geranium [ˌaɪvɪliːfdʒəˈreɪnɪəm] N géranium-lierre *m*

J

J, j [dʒeɪ] N (= letter) J, j m ; **J for Jack** ◊ **J for John** ◊ **J for Jig** (US) ≈ J comme Jean

jab [dʒæb] **1** VT [+ knife, stick] enfoncer, planter (**into** dans) ; **he ~bed his elbow into my side** il m'a donné un coup de coude dans les côtes ; **he ~bed the fabric with his needle** il a planté son aiguille dans l'étoffe ; **he ~bed a finger at the map** il a montré la carte du doigt **2** VI (Boxing) lancer un coup droit, envoyer un direct (**at** à) **3** N **a** coup m (donné avec un objet pointu) **b** (Brit*) = injection) piqûre f ; **I've had my ~** on m'a fait ma piqûre **c** (Boxing) coup m droit, direct m

jabber ['dʒæbəʳ] (pej) **1** VT (also ~ **out**) [+ excuse, explanation] bafouiller, bredouiller ; [+ foreign language] baragouiner ; [+ prayers] marmotter **2** VI **a** (= speak unintelligibly: also ~ **away**) baragouiner ; **they were ~ing (away) in Chinese** ils baragouinaient en chinois **b** (= chatter: also ~ **on**) jacasser, caqueter ; **he was ~ing (on) about his holidays** il parlait à n'en plus finir de ses vacances

jabbering ['dʒæbərɪŋ] N jacassement m, caquetage m

jacaranda [ˌdʒækəˈrændə] N jacaranda m

jack [dʒæk] **1** N **a** (Aut) cric m
b (Bowls) cochonnet m, bouchon* m
c (Cards) valet m
d (= flag) → **union**
e dim of **John**
f **Jack and the Beanstalk** Jack au pays des géants ; **before you could say Jack Robinson*** en moins de temps qu'il n'en faut pour le dire
g **every man ~** chacun ; **every man ~ of them** tous tant qu'ils sont (or étaient etc)
2 **jacks** NPL (= game) osselets mpl
3 COMP ► **Jack Frost** N (le) Bonhomme Hiver ► **jack-in-office** N (pej) rond-de-cuir qui joue les petits chefs ► **jack-in-the-box** N diable m (à ressort) ► **jack-knife** N (pl jack-knives) couteau m de poche ♦ VI **the lorry ~knifed** la remorque (du camion) s'est mise en travers ; **~knife dive** saut m carpé or de carpe ► **jack of all trades** N (pl jacks of all trades) **he's a ~ of all trades (and master of none)** c'est un touche-à-tout ► **jack-o'-lantern** N feu follet m ► **jack plug** N fiche f mâle, jack m ► **jack rabbit** N gros lièvre m (de l'Ouest américain) ► **jack shit**ⁱ N (US) que dalle⁑ ► **Jack Tar***, **jack tar*** N (Naut) marin m, matelot m ► **Jack-the-lad*** N (Brit) petit frimeur* m (pej)

► **jack in**ⁱ VT SEP (Brit) plaquer*

► **jack up** VT SEP **a** [+ car] soulever avec un cric ; **the car was ~ed up** la voiture était sur le cric **b** (* = raise) [+ prices, wages] faire grimper

jackal ['dʒækɔ:l] N chacal m

jackanapes† ['dʒækəneɪps] N polisson(ne) m(f)

jackass ['dʒækæs] N âne m, baudet* m ; (* fig) crétin* m → **laughing**

jackboot ['dʒækbu:t] **1** N **a** botte f cavalière **b** (fig = military dictatorship) régime m totalitaire ; **to live under the ~ of** vivre or être sous la botte de **2** ADJ [discipline, method] autoritaire, dictatorial

jackdaw ['dʒækdɔ:] N choucas m

jacket ['dʒækɪt] N **a** (straight, fitted style) (man's) veste f, veston m ; (woman's) veste f ; (padded or blouson style) blouson m → **life** **b** [of water boiler] enveloppe f calorifugée ; [of book] jaquette f ; [of record] pochette f ; (Brit) ~ **potatoes** ◊ **potatoes baked in their ~s** pommes fpl de terre cuites au four dans leur peau or en robe des champs

jackfruit ['dʒækfru:t] N (= tree) jaquier m ; (= fruit) jaque m

jackhammer ['dʒæk,hæməʳ] N (US) marteau-piqueur m

jackleg ['dʒækleg] ADJ (US) (= not qualified) [carpenter etc] amateur ; (= dishonest) [work] louche ; (= makeshift) [structure] de fortune

jackpot ['dʒækpɒt] N gros lot m, jackpot m ; (lit, fig) **to hit the ~** (= win prize) gagner le gros lot or le jackpot ; (= be successful) faire un malheur* or un tabac*

jackstraw ['dʒækstrɔ:] **1** N (fig) nullité f **2** COMP ► **jackstraws** NPL (= game) (jeu de) jonchets mpl

Jacob ['dʒeɪkəb] **1** N Jacob m **2** COMP ► **Jacob's ladder** N l'échelle f de Jacob

Jacobean [ˌdʒækəˈbiːən] ADJ jacobéen (-enne f) (de l'époque de Jacques Iᵉʳ d'Angleterre (1603-1625))

Jacobite ['dʒækəbaɪt] **1** N Jacobite mf **2** ADJ jacobite

Jacuzzi® [dʒəˈkuːzɪ] N jacuzzi® m, bain m à jet propulsé

jade¹ [dʒeɪd] **1** N jade m **2** ADJ (colour) (couleur de) jade inv **3** COMP ► **jade-green** ADJ vert jade inv

jade² [dʒeɪd] N (= horse) haridelle f, rossinante f ; († pej = prostitute) traînée⁑ f ; († = pert girl) coquine f

jaded ['dʒeɪdɪd] ADJ [person] las (lasse f) (with or about de), blasé ; [palate] blasé ; **his appetite was ~** il avait l'estomac fatigué

jag [dʒæg] **1** N **a** saillie f, aspérité f **b** (* fig) **a drinking ~** une cuite* ; **they were on a drinking ~ last night** ils se sont bien cuités* or ils ont pris une fameuse cuite* hier soir ; **a crying ~** une crise de larmes **c** (Scot) injection f, piqûre f **2** VT (= catch, tear) déchirer

jagged ['dʒægɪd] ADJ [rocks, edge, glass, metal] déchiqueté ; [tear] irrégulier, en dents de scie ; [hole] aux bords déchiquetés or irréguliers

jaguar ['dʒægjʊəʳ] N jaguar m

jai alai [ˈhaɪəˌlaɪ] N (US Sport) ≈ pelote f basque

jail [dʒeɪl] **1** N prison f ; **he is in ~** il est en prison ; **he was in ~ for five years** il a fait cinq ans de prison ; **to put sb in ~** mettre qn en prison ; **to send sb to ~** condamner qn à la prison ; **to send sb to ~ for five years** condamner qn à cinq ans de prison ; **to break ~** s'évader (de prison) **2** VT mettre en prison ; **to ~ sb for life** condamner qn (à la réclusion) à perpétuité ; **to ~ sb for theft/murder** condamner qn à la prison pour vol/meurtre **3** COMP ► **jail sentence** N peine f de prison ; **she got a three-year ~ sentence** elle a été condamnée à (une peine de) trois ans de prison

jailbait⁑ ['dʒeɪlbeɪt] N (US) mineure f ; (NonC) **she's ~** si tu touches à cette fille, tu te retrouves en taule⁑

jailbird ['dʒeɪlbɜːd] N récidiviste mf

jailbreak ['dʒeɪlbreɪk] N évasion f (de prison)

jailbreaker ['dʒeɪlbreɪkəʳ] N évadé(e) m(f)

jailer ['dʒeɪləʳ] N geôlier m, -ière f

jailhouse ['dʒeɪlhaʊs] N prison f

Jakarta [dʒəˈkɑːtə] N Djakarta or Jakarta

jakes [dʒeɪks] N **the ~** les cabinets mpl

jalop(p)y* [dʒəˈlɒpɪ] N vieux tacot* m, guimbarde f

jalousie [ˈʒæluːzɪ] N jalousie f (store)

jam¹ [dʒæm] **1** N **a** (= crush) [of vehicles] embouteillage m ; [of people] foule f, masse f → **log**¹, **traffic**
b (* = mess) pétrin m ; **to be in a ~** être dans le pétrin ; **to get into/out of a ~** se mettre dans le/se tirer du pétrin ; **to get sb into/out of a ~** mettre qn dans le/tirer qn du pétrin **c** (Climbing) coincement m, verrou m
2 VT **a** (= stuff) entasser ; (= thrust) fourrer, enfoncer ; **to ~ clothes into a suitcase** entasser des vêtements dans une valise ; **the prisoners were ~med into a small cell** les prisonniers ont été entassés dans une petite cellule ; **he ~med his hat on** il a enfoncé son chapeau sur sa tête ; **she ~med her hands into her pockets** elle a enfoncé or fourré ses mains dans ses poches ; **he ~med a handkerchief up his sleeve** il a fourré un mouchoir dans sa manche ; **to ~ one's foot on the brake** écraser le frein, enfoncer la pédale de frein
b (= wedge) [+ door etc] coincer ; **to be ~med between the wall and the door** être coincé entre le mur et la porte ; **he got his finger ~med in the door** ◊ **he ~med his finger in the door** il s'est coincé le doigt dans la porte ; **the coins got ~med in the machine** les pièces se sont coincées dans la machine ; **to ~ a door open/shut** coincer or bloquer une porte en position ouverte/fermée
c (= make unworkable: also ~ **up**) [+ lock] bloquer ; [+ mechanism] enrayer, coincer ; [+ gun, machine] enrayer ; [+ hinge] coincer ; [+ brake] bloquer, coincer
d (= block) [crowd, cars etc] [+ street, corridor] encombrer, embouteiller ; **a street ~med with cars** une rue embouteillée ; **the street was ~med with people** la rue était noire de monde ; **the entrance was ~med with people** des gens bouchaient l'entrée ; **spectators ~med the stadium for the match** les spectateurs se sont entassés dans le stade pour le match ; **the drain was ~med with rubbish** l'égout était bouché par des ordures
e [+ station, broadcast, transmission, radar sig-

nal] brouiller; (*Telec*) [+ *line*] encombrer; [+ *switchboard*] encombrer, saturer

[3] VI [a] (= *become stuck*) [*door, switch, lever, hinge*] se coincer; [*mechanism*] s'enrayer, se coincer; [*gun*] s'enrayer; [*brake*] se bloquer; **the key ~med in the lock** la clé s'est coincée dans la serrure [b] (= *press tightly*) **the crowd ~med into the courtroom** la foule s'est entassée dans la salle de tribunal

[4] COMP ▶ **jam-full, jam-packed** ADJ [*room*] comble, plein à craquer*; [*bus*] bondé, plein à craquer*; [*street, pavements*] noir de monde; [*container, suitcase*] plein à ras bord

▶**jam in** VT SEP [+ *people*] (= *pack in*) entasser; (= *trap, wedge*) coincer; [+ *cars, objects, fabric*] coincer; **to be ~med in by the crowd** être compressé *or* coincé par *or* dans la foule

▶**jam on** VT SEP [a] **to ~ on the brakes** écraser le frein, enfoncer la pédale de frein [b] **to ~ on one's hat** enfoncer son chapeau sur sa tête

jam² [dʒæm] [1] N (*esp Brit*) confiture f; **cherry ~** confiture f de cerises; (*Brit*) **you want ~ on it!** et quoi encore?; **to promise ~ tomorrow** promettre des jours meilleurs; **(it's a case of) ~ tomorrow** ça ira mieux demain → **money** [2] COMP [*tart*] à la confiture ▶ **jam jar, jam pot** N pot m à confiture ▶ **jam puff** N (*Brit*) feuilleté m à la confiture ▶ **jam roll** N (*Brit*) roulé m à la confiture

jam³ [dʒæm] (*Mus*) [1] N (*also* **~ session**) bœuf m, jam-session f [2] VI faire un bœuf*

Jamaica [dʒə'meɪkə] N la Jamaïque; **in ~** à la Jamaïque

Jamaican [dʒə'meɪkən] [1] ADJ jamaïquain; [*ambassador, embassy*] de la Jamaïque [2] N Jamaïquain(e) m(f)

jamb [dʒæm] N [*of door, window*] jambage m, montant m

jambalaya [ˌdʒʌmbə'laɪə] N *plat de la Louisiane à base de riz et de fruits de mer*

jamboree [ˌdʒæmbə'riː] N (= *gathering*) grand rassemblement m; (= *merrymaking*) festivités fpl; (*scouts*) jamboree m; (*fig*) réjouissances fpl

James [dʒeɪmz] N Jacques m

jamming ['dʒæmɪŋ] N (*Rad*) brouillage m; (*Telec*) encombrement m

jammy ['dʒæmɪ] ADJ [a] (*lit*) [*fingers, hands*] poisseux (*de confiture*) [b] (*Brit* = *lucky*) verni*; **that was pretty ~!** c'était un coup de veine* *or* de pot*!; **~ devil** *or* **so-and-so** veinard(e)* m(f)

JAN [ˌdʒeɪ'en] N (*US*) (ABBR = **Joint Army-Navy**) *organisation commune armée-marine*

Jan. ABBR = **January**

Jane [dʒeɪn] [1] N Jeanne f → **plain** [2] COMP ▶ **Jane Doe** N (*US Jur*) femme dont on ignore le nom

jangle ['dʒæŋgl] [1] VI [*bracelets, chains*] cliqueter; [*saucepans*] retentir avec un bruit de ferraille *or* de casserole; [*bells*] retentir; **his nerves were jangling** il avait les nerfs à vif [2] VT faire cliqueter; **~d nerves** nerfs mpl à vif [3] N cliquetis m

jangling ['dʒæŋglɪŋ] [1] ADJ [*keys, bracelets*] cliquetant; [*phone, music*] strident [2] N [*of keys*] cliquetis m; [*of phone*] sonnerie f stridente

janitor ['dʒænɪtər] N (= *doorkeeper*) portier m; (*US, Scot* = *caretaker*) concierge m, gardien m

Jansenism ['dʒænsəˌnɪzəm] N jansénisme m

Jansenist ['dʒænsənɪst] ADJ, N janséniste mf

January ['dʒænjʊərɪ] N janvier m; *for phrases see* **September**

Janus ['dʒeɪnəs] N Janus m

Jap [dʒæp] N (*pej*) (ABBR = **Japanese**) Japonais(e) m(f)

Japan [dʒə'pæn] N le Japon

japan [dʒə'pæn] [1] N laque f [2] VT laquer

Japanese [ˌdʒæpə'niːz] [1] ADJ (*gen*) japonais; [*ambassador, embassy*] du Japon; [*teacher*] de japonais [2] N [a] Japonais(e) m(f) [b] (*Ling*) ja-

ponais m [3] **the Japanese** NPL les Japonais mpl

jape† [dʒeɪp] N (= *trick*) farce f, tour m; (= *joke*) blague* f

jar¹ [dʒɑːr] [1] N (= *harsh sound*) son m discordant; (= *jolt: lit, fig*) secousse f, choc m; (*lit, fig*) **that gave him a nasty ~** cela l'a sérieusement ébranlé *or* secoué [2] VI [a] (= *sound discordant*) rendre un son discordant; (= *rattle, vibrate*) vibrer, trembler; **to ~ against sth** cogner sur qch *or* heurter qch (*avec un bruit discordant*) [b] (= *clash, be out of harmony*) [*note*] détonner; [*colours*] jurer (**with** avec); (*fig*) [*ideas, opinions*] se heurter; **what he says ~s a little** ce qu'il dit sonne faux [3] VT [+ *structure*] ébranler; [+ *person*] ébranler, secouer; (*fig*) commotionner, choquer; **the explosion ~red the whole building** l'explosion a ébranlé tout le bâtiment; **he was badly ~red by the blow** il a été sérieusement commotionné par le choc; **you ~red my elbow** tu m'as cogné le coude

▶**jar (up)on** VT FUS irriter, agacer; **this noise ~s (up)on my nerves** ce bruit me met les nerfs en boule* *or* me tape sur les nerfs; **her screams ~ (up)on my ears** ses cris m'écorchent *or* me percent les oreilles

jar² [dʒɑːr] N [a] (*of glass*) bocal m; (*of stone, earthenware*) pot m, jarre f → **jam²** [b] (*Brit* = *drink*) pot* m, verre m; **we had a few ~s** on a pris quelques verres

jargon ['dʒɑːgən] N (= *technical language*) jargon m; (= *pompous nonsense*) jargon m, charabia* m

jarring ['dʒɑːrɪŋ] ADJ [a] (= *discordant*) [*noise, voice, colours*] discordant; (*fig*) **to strike a ~ note** détonner [b] (= *jolting*) **~ shock** secousse f [c] (= *upsetting*) [*experience*] bouleversant

jasmine ['dʒæzmɪn] N jasmin m; **~ tea** thé m au jasmin

Jason ['dʒeɪsən] N Jason m

jasper ['dʒæspər] N jaspe m

jaundice ['dʒɔːndɪs] N (*Med*) jaunisse f

jaundiced ['dʒɔːndɪst] ADJ (*fig* = *bitter*) amer, aigri; **to look on sth with a ~ eye** ◊ **to take a ~ view of sth** voir qch d'un mauvais œil; **he has a fairly ~ view of things** il voit les choses en noir; **to give sb a ~ look** regarder qn d'un œil torve

jaunt [dʒɔːnt] N **to go for a ~** aller faire un tour *or* une virée*

jauntily ['dʒɔːntɪlɪ] ADV (= *cheerily*) [*say*] d'une voix enjouée; [*walk*] d'un pas leste

jauntiness ['dʒɔːntɪnɪs] N désinvolture f

jaunty ['dʒɔːntɪ] ADJ (= *cheery*) [*air, tone*] enjoué; [*step*] leste, vif; [*hat, clothes*] coquet; **a hat worn at a ~ angle** un chapeau incliné sur le côté de façon guillerette

Java ['dʒɑːvə] N Java f; **in ~** à Java

java* ['dʒɑːvə] N (*US* = *coffee*) café m

Javanese [ˌdʒɑːvə'niːz] [1] ADJ javanais [2] N [a] (*pl inv*) Javanais(e) m(f) [b] (*Ling*) javanais m

javelin ['dʒævlɪn] [1] N (*Sport*) javelot m; (*Mil*) javelot m, javeline f; **the ~** (= *competition*) le (lancer du) javelot [2] COMP ▶ **javelin thrower** N (*Sport*) lanceur m, -euse f de javelot ▶ **javelin throwing** N (*NonC*) le lancement *or* le lancer du javelot

jaw [dʒɔː] [1] N [a] (*Anat*) mâchoire f; [*of pincer, vice*] mâchoire f; **his ~ dropped (in astonishment)** il en est resté bouche bée; **his ~ was set in concentration** la concentration lui faisait serrer les mâchoires; **his ~ was set in an angry line** sa mâchoire serrée lui donnait un air furieux; (*liter*) **the ~s of death** les bras mpl *or* l'étreinte f (*liter*) de la mort; (*liter*) **the ~s of hell** les portes fpl de l'enfer → **lockjaw, lower** [b] (= *chat*) **we had a good old ~** on a bien

papoté* [2] VI* (= *chat*) papoter*, tailler une bavette*; (= *moralize*) faire un sermon*; **he was ~ing (on) about ...** il discourait sur ... (*pej*)

jawbone ['dʒɔːbəʊn] [1] N (os m) maxillaire m [2] VT (*US fig*) chercher à convaincre, exercer des pressions sur

jawboning ['dʒɔːbəʊnɪŋ] N (*US Pol*) pressions fpl gouvernementales

jawbreaker ['dʒɔːˌbreɪkər] N (*US*) (= *word*) mot m très difficile à prononcer; (= *sweet*) bonbon m à sucer

-jawed [dʒɔːd] ADJ (*in compounds*) au menton ...; **square-jawed** au menton carré

jawline ['dʒɔːlaɪn] N menton m

jay [dʒeɪ] N (*Orn*) geai m

Jayhawker ['dʒeɪˌhɔːkər] N (*US*) habitant(e) m(f) du Kansas; **the ~ State** le Kansas

jaywalk ['dʒeɪwɔːk] VI traverser la chaussée en dehors des clous

jaywalker ['dʒeɪˌwɔːkər] N piéton(ne) m(f) indiscipliné(e)

jaywalking ['dʒeɪˌwɔːkɪŋ] N (*gen*) indiscipline f des piétons; **to be accused of ~** être accusé d'avoir traversé la chaussée en dehors des clous

jazz [dʒæz] [1] N (*Mus*) jazz m; **and all that ~*** et tout le bataclan*, et tout ça → **hot** [2] VI (*US* = *exaggerate*) exagérer [3] COMP [*band, club, record*] de jazz ▶ **jazz ballet** N ballet m sur musique de jazz ▶ **jazz rock** N jazz-rock m

▶**jazz up** VT SEP [a] (*Mus*) **to ~ up the classics** mettre les classiques au goût du jour; **a ~ed-up version of the national anthem** une version de l'hymne national mise au goût du jour [b] [+ *occasion*] animer; **to ~ up a party** mettre de l'animation dans une soirée; **to ~ up an old dress** égayer *or* rajeunir une vieille robe; **she ~ed her outfit up with a scarf** elle a égayé sa tenue avec un foulard

jazzed* [dʒæzd] ADJ (*US*) **to be ~ for sth** être plein d'entrain à la pensée de qch

jazzman ['dʒæzmən] N (*pl* **-men**) jazzman m

jazzy ['dʒæzɪ] ADJ [a] (* = *showy*) [*clothes, product, car*] voyant, qui en jette* [b] (= *upbeat*) [*music*] vivant, gai; (= *jazz-like*) [*rhythm, beat*] de jazz

J.C. (ABBR = **Jesus Christ**) → **Jesus**

JCB® [ˌdʒeɪsiː'biː] N ABBR pelle f hydraulique automotrice

JCR [ˌdʒeɪsiː'ɑːr] N (*Brit Univ*) (ABBR = **Junior Common Room**) → **junior**

JCS [ˌdʒeɪsiː'es] N (*US Mil*) (ABBR = **Joint Chiefs of Staff**) → **joint**

jct., jctn ABBR = **junction**

JD [ˌdʒeɪ'diː] N (*US* = *Doctor of Laws*) ≈ doctorat m en droit

jealous ['dʒeləs] ADJ (= *envious*) [*person, nature, look*] jaloux (**of** de); **a ~ rage** une crise de jalousie; **~ feelings** jalousie f; **to keep a ~ watch over** *or* **a ~ eye on sb/sth** surveiller qn/qch d'un œil jaloux

jealously ['dʒeləslɪ] ADV [*watch*] d'un œil jaloux; [*guard, protect*] jalousement; **~ guarded** [*secret, privilege etc*] jalousement gardé

jealousy ['dʒeləsɪ] N jalousie f

Jean [dʒiːn] N Jeanne f

jeans [dʒiːnz] NPL (*also* **pair of ~**) jean m → **blue**

Jeep® [dʒiːp] N jeep® f

jeer [dʒɪər] [1] N (= *mocking remark*) raillerie f; (*from a crowd*) quolibet m, huée f [2] VI [*individual*] railler; [*crowd*] huer, conspuer (*frm*); **to ~ at sb** se moquer de qn, railler qn [3] VT huer, conspuer

jeering ['dʒɪərɪŋ] [1] ADJ railleur, moqueur [2] N (= *mocking remarks*) railleries fpl; [*of crowd*] huées fpl

jeeringly ['dʒɪərɪŋlɪ] ADV [*say*] d'un ton moqueur

Jeez‡ [dʒiːz] EXCL bon Dieu !‡, putain !‡

jehad [dʒɪˈhæd] N → **jihad**

Jehovah [dʒɪˈhəʊvə] **1** N Jéhovah m **2** COMP ► **Jehovah's Witness** N Témoin m de Jéhovah

jejune [dʒɪˈdʒuːn] ADJ (liter) (= naive) naïf (naïve f); (= dull) ennuyeux, plat

jejunum [dʒɪˈdʒuːnəm] N jéjunum m

Jekyll and Hyde [ˈdʒekələnˈhaɪd] N **a ~ (character)** une sorte de Docteur Jekyll et Mister Hyde

jell [dʒel] VI = **gel¹**

jellied [ˈdʒelɪd] ADJ [eels, meat] en gelée

Jell-O®, jello [ˈdʒeləʊ] N (US Culin) gelée f

jelly [ˈdʒelɪ] **1** N **a** (Brit: gen) gelée f; (US = jam) confiture f; **blackcurrant ~** gelée f de cassis → **petroleum b**‡ = **gelignite 2** COMP ► **jelly baby** N bonbon m à la gélatine (en forme de bébé) ► **jelly bean** N bonbon m à la gelée ► **jelly bear** N nounours m (bonbon) ► **jelly roll** N (US Culin) gâteau m roulé

jellyfish [ˈdʒelɪfɪʃ] N (pl **jellyfish** or **jellyfishes**) méduse f

jemmy [ˈdʒemɪ] (Brit) **1** N pince-monseigneur f **2** COMP ► **to ~ sth open** ouvrir qch à l'aide d'une pince-monseigneur

jeopardize [ˈdʒepədaɪz] VT mettre en danger, compromettre

jeopardy [ˈdʒepədɪ] N (NonC) péril m; **his life is in ~** sa vie est or ses jours sont en péril; **his happiness is in ~** son bonheur est menacé; **my business is in ~** mon affaire risque de couler

jerbil [ˈdʒɜːbɪl] N = **gerbil**

jerboa [dʒɜːˈbəʊə] N gerboise f

jeremiad [ˌdʒerɪˈmaɪəd] N jérémiade f

Jeremiah [ˌdʒerɪˈmaɪə] N Jérémie m

Jericho [ˈdʒerɪkəʊ] N Jéricho

jerk [dʒɜːk] **1** N **a** (= push, pull, twist etc) secousse f, saccade f; (Med) réflexe m tendineux, crispation f nerveuse; **the car moved along in a series of ~s** la voiture a avancé par saccades or par à-coups; **the train started with a series of ~s** le train s'est ébranlé avec une série de secousses or de saccades **b** (esp US‡ pej = person) pauvre type* m → **physical, soda 2** VT (= pull) tirer brusquement; (= shake) secouer (par saccades), donner une secousse à; **she ~ed her head up** elle a brusquement redressé la tête; **he ~ed the book out of my hand** il m'a brusquement arraché le livre que je tenais à la main; **he ~ed himself free** il s'est libéré d'une secousse; **to ~ out an apology** bafouiller une excuse **3** VI **a** **the car ~ed along** la voiture roulait en cahotant; **he ~ed away (from me)** il s'est brusquement écarté de moi **b** [person, muscle] se contracter, se crisper ► **jerk off**‡ VI se branler‡‡

jerkily [ˈdʒɜːkɪlɪ] ADV [move, walk] d'une démarche saccadée; [speak, say] d'une voix entrecoupée

jerkin [ˈdʒɜːkɪn] N gilet m; (Hist) justaucorps m, pourpoint m

jerkiness [ˈdʒɜːkɪnɪs] N [of walk] rythme m saccadé; [of journey] cahots mpl; [of style, delivery] caractère m haché

jerkwater town‡ [ˈdʒɜːkwɔːtəˈtaʊn] N (US pej) trou m perdu, bled* m

jerky [ˈdʒɜːkɪ] ADJ [motion, movement, rhythm] saccadé; [song] au rythme saccadé

jeroboam [ˌdʒerəˈbəʊəm] N jéroboam m

Jerry† [ˈdʒerɪ] N (Brit = German) Boche* m

jerry‡ [ˈdʒerɪ] **1** N (Brit = chamberpot) pot m (de chambre), Jules‡ m **2** COMP ► **jerry-building** N (NonC) construction f bon marché ► **jerry-built** ADJ [house] (construit) en carton-pâte; (fig) [agreement, plan] cousu de fil blanc ► **jerry can** N jerrycan m

Jersey [ˈdʒɜːzɪ] N **a** (Geog) (île f de) Jersey f; **in ~** à Jersey **b** (Zool) race f Jersey; **a ~ (cow)** une vache jersiaise or de Jersey

jersey [ˈdʒɜːzɪ] N (= pullover) chandail m; (= material) jersey m → **yellow**

Jerusalem [dʒəˈruːsələm] **1** N Jérusalem; **the New/Heavenly ~** la Jérusalem nouvelle/céleste **2** COMP ► **Jerusalem artichoke** N topinambour m

jest [dʒest] **1** N plaisanterie f; **in ~** pour rire, en plaisantant; **many a true word is spoken in ~** beaucoup de vérités se disent en plaisantant **2** VI plaisanter, se moquer

jester [ˈdʒestə'] N (Hist) bouffon m; (= joker) plaisantin m, farceur m, -euse f; **the King's ~** le fou du Roi

jesting [ˈdʒestɪŋ] **1** ADJ [remark] (fait) en plaisantant or pour plaisanter **2** N plaisanteries fpl

Jesuit [ˈdʒezjʊɪt] N, ADJ (Rel, fig) jésuite m

jesuitic(al) [ˌdʒezjʊˈɪtɪk(əl)] ADJ (Rel, fig) jésuitique

Jesus [ˈdʒiːzəs] **1** N Jésus m; **~ Christ** Jésus-Christ m; **~ (wept)!**‡ nom de Dieu !‡ → **society 2** ► **Jesus freak*** N chrétien(ne) m(f) militant(e) branché(e)* ► **Jesus Movement** N Jesus Movement m ► **Jesus sandals** NPL nu-pieds mpl

jet¹ [dʒet] **1** N **a** [of liquid] jet m, giclée f; [of gas] jet m **b** (Aviat: also = **plane**) avion m à réaction, jet m **c** (= nozzle) brûleur m; (Aut) gicleur m **2** VI* voyager en avion or en jet; **she's ~ting off to Spain next week** elle prend l'avion pour l'Espagne la semaine prochaine **3** COMP (Aviat) [travel] en jet ► **jet engine** N (Aviat) moteur m à réaction, réacteur m ► **jet fighter** N (Aviat) chasseur m à réaction ► **jet-foil** N hydroglisseur m ► **jet fuel** N kérosène m ► **jet lag** N fatigue f due au décalage horaire ► **jet-lagged** ADJ **to be ~-lagged** souffrir du décalage horaire ► **jet-propelled** ADJ à réaction ► **jet propulsion** N propulsion f par réaction ► **jet set** N jet-set m or f ► **jet-set** ADJ [travellers etc] du or de la jet-set ► **jet setter** N membre m du or de la jet-set ► **jet-setting** ADJ [lifestyle] du or de la jet-set; [person] qui fait partie du or de la jet-set ► **jet ski** N scooter m des mers, jet-ski m ► **jet-ski** VI faire du scooter des mers or du jet-ski ► **jet skiing** N (NonC) jet-ski m ► **jet stream** N (Met, Aviat) jet-stream m, courant-jet m

jet² [dʒet] **1** N jais m **2** COMP ► **jet-black** ADJ de jais, noir comme jais

jetliner [ˈdʒet,laɪnə'] N avion m de ligne

jetsam [ˈdʒetsəm] N **a** (NonC) jets mpl à la mer → **flotsam b** (fig = down-and-outs) épaves fpl (fig)

jettison [ˈdʒetɪsn] VT **a** (Naut) jeter par-dessus bord, se délester de **b** (Aviat) [+ bombs, fuel, cargo] larguer **c** (fig) [+ idea, system, plans] abandonner; [+ assets, product] se défaire de

jetty [ˈdʒetɪ] N (= breakwater) jetée f, digue f; (= landing pier) embarcadère m, débarcadère m; (of wood) appontement m

jetway [ˈdʒetweɪ] N (Aviat) passerelle f télescopique

Jew [dʒuː] **1** N juif or Juif m, juive or Juive f **2** COMP ► **Jew-baiting** N persécution f des juifs ► **Jew's harp** N guimbarde f

jewel [ˈdʒuːəl] **1** N **a** bijou m, joyau m; (= gem) pierre f précieuse; (Tech: in watch) rubis m **b** (fig) [object, work of art etc] bijou m, joyau m; (= person) perle f, trésor m; **the ~ in the crown of ...** le joyau de ..., le plus beau fleuron de ...; **his latest book is the ~ in his crown** son dernier livre est le couronnement de sa carrière **2** COMP ► **jewel case** N (also

jewel box: for jewels) coffret m à bijoux; (for CD) boîtier m de disque compact

jewelled, jeweled (US) [ˈdʒuːəld] ADJ orné de bijoux or de pierreries; [watch] monté sur rubis

jeweller, jeweler (US) [ˈdʒuːələ'] N bijoutier m; **~'s (shop)** bijouterie f

jewellery, jewelry (US) [ˈdʒuːəlrɪ] N (NonC) bijoux mpl; **a piece of ~** un bijou; (US) **jewelry store** bijouterie f

Jewess† [ˈdʒuːɪs] N (gen pej) Juive f

Jewish [ˈdʒuːɪʃ] ADJ juif

Jewishness [ˈdʒuːɪʃnɪs] N judaïté f, judéité f

Jewry [ˈdʒʊərɪ] N la communauté juive, les Juifs mpl

Jezebel [ˈdʒezə,bel] N Jézabel f

jib [dʒɪb] **1** N **a** (Naut) foc m; (fig) **the cut of his ~**† son allure **b** [of crane] flèche f **2** VI [person] rechigner (at sth à qch, at doing à faire); [horse] refuser d'avancer; **the horse ~bed at the fence** le cheval a refusé l'obstacle or a renâclé devant l'obstacle

jibe¹ [dʒaɪb] N = **gibe**

jibe²* [dʒaɪb] VI (US = agree) coller (fig)

jiffy [ˈdʒɪfɪ] **1** N **wait a ~** attends une minute or une seconde; **in a ~** en moins de deux* **2** COMP ► **Jiffy bag®** N enveloppe f matelassée

jig [dʒɪg] **1** N **a** (= dance) gigue f; (US fig) **the ~'s up** c'est cuit* **b** (Tech) calibre m, gabarit m **2** VI (also ~ **about, ~ around**) se trémousser, gigoter*; **to ~ up and down** sautiller

jigger¹ [ˈdʒɪgə'] N **a** (= whisky measure) mesure f d'une once et demie (= 42 ml) **b** (esp US* = thingummy) truc* m, machin* m

jigger² [ˈdʒɪgə'] N (= flea) chique f

jiggered* [ˈdʒɪgəd] ADJ (Brit) **a** (= astonished) étonné, baba* **f inv**; **well, I'll be ~!** nom d'un chien !* **b** (= exhausted) crevé*

jiggery-pokery‡ [ˈdʒɪgərɪˈpəʊkərɪ] N (NonC: Brit) magouilles* fpl, manigances fpl

jiggle [ˈdʒɪgl] VT secouer légèrement

jigsaw [ˈdʒɪg,sɔː] N **a** (also ~ **puzzle**) puzzle m **b** (= saw) scie f sauteuse

jihad [dʒɪˈhæd] N (Rel) djihad m

jilt [dʒɪlt] VT [+ lover, girlfriend, boyfriend] plaquer*, laisser tomber*; **~ed** abandonné, plaqué*; **he was ~ed at the altar** il a été plaqué* par sa fiancée le jour de son mariage

Jim [dʒɪm] **1** N (dim of James) Jim m **2** COMP ► **Jim Crow** N (US = policy) politique f raciste (envers les Noirs)

jimjams¹‡ [ˈdʒɪmdʒæmz] N **to have the ~** (from revulsion) avoir des frissons or la chair de poule; (from fear) avoir les chocottes*; (from drink) avoir une (or des) crise(s) de délirium tremens

jimjams²* [ˈdʒɪmdʒæmz] NPL (baby talk) pyjama m

Jimmy [ˈdʒɪmɪ] N (dim of James) Jimmy m

jimmy [ˈdʒɪmɪ] N (US) pince-monseigneur f

jimson weed [ˈdʒɪmsən,wiːd] N (US Bot) stramoine f, datura m

jingle [ˈdʒɪŋgl] **1** N **a** [of jewellery etc] (musical) tintement m; (clinking) cliquetis m **b** (= catchy verse) jingle m; **advertising ~** jingle m or sonal m publicitaire **2** VI (musically) tinter; (= clink) cliqueter **3** VT (musically) faire tinter; (= clink) faire cliqueter

jingo [ˈdʒɪŋgəʊ] N (pl **jingoes**) chauvin m; **by ~!*** ça alors !, nom d'une pipe !*

jingoism [ˈdʒɪŋgəʊɪzəm] N chauvinisme m

jingoistic [ˌdʒɪŋgəʊˈɪstɪk] ADJ chauvin

jink* [dʒɪŋk] VI (Brit = zigzag) zigzaguer; **he ~ed out of the way** il a fait un bond de côté

jinks [dʒɪŋks] NPL → **high**

jinx* [dʒɪŋks] **1** N **to put a ~ on sb** porter la poisse à qn; **to put a ~ on sth** jeter un sort à qch; **there's a ~ on this watch** on a jeté un sort à cette montre **2** VT [+ person] porter la guigne* or la poisse* à; **to be ~ed** [person] avoir la guigne* or la poisse*; **this project must be ~ed** un mauvais sort semble peser sur ce projet

jitney: ['dʒɪtnɪ] N (US) **a** pièce f de cinq cents **b** véhicule à itinéraire fixe et à prix modique

jitterbug ['dʒɪtəbʌg] **1** N **a** (= dance) danse acrobatique sur rythme de swing ou de boogie-woogie **b** (* = panicky person) froussard(e)* m(f), trouillard(e)* m(f) **2** VI (= dance) danser le jitterbug

jitters* ['dʒɪtəz] NPL frousse* f; **to have the ~** (gen) être nerveux or agité; (before performance) avoir le trac, avoir la frousse*; **to give sb the ~** rendre qn nerveux or agité, ficher la frousse à qn*

jittery* ['dʒɪtərɪ] ADJ nerveux, agité; **to be ~** avoir la frousse*

jiujitsu [dʒuːˈdʒɪtsuː] N = **jujitsu**

jive [dʒaɪv] **1** N **a** (= music, dancing) swing m **b** (esp US:) (= big talk) baratin* m; (= nonsense) fpl; **stop that ~** arrête de dire tes conneries; **c** (US = type of speech) argot m (des Noirs surtout) **2** VI (= dance) danser le swing

Jly ABBR = **July**

Jnr (Brit) ABBR = **junior**

Joan [dʒəʊn] N Jeanne f; **~ of Arc** Jeanne f d'Arc

Job [dʒəʊb] **1** N (Bible) Job m **2** COMP ▶ **Job's comforter** N piètre consolateur m, -trice f

job [dʒɒb] **1** N **a** (= piece of work, task) travail m, boulot* m; **I have a little ~ for you** j'ai un petit travail or un petit boulot* pour vous; **he has made a good ~ of it** ◊ **he has done a good ~ (on it)** or **a good ~ of work** il a fait du bon travail or du bon boulot*; **he has made a poor ~ of it** il n'a pas fait du bon travail or boulot*; **he has made a terrible ~ of it** il a saboté le travail, il a fait du sale boulot*; **the decorators made a terrible ~ of the kitchen** les peintres ont fait du sale boulot* dans la cuisine; **it's not ideal but it'll do the ~*** ce n'est pas l'idéal mais cela fera l'affaire; **we could have done a far better ~ of running the project than they have** on aurait pu gérer ce projet beaucoup mieux qu'eux; **she's done a fine ~ with her children** elle a bien élevé ses enfants → **chin, odd, nose**
b (= employment) travail m, emploi m, boulot* m; **to get a ~** trouver un travail or un emploi or un boulot*; **to look for a ~** chercher un travail or un emploi or un boulot*; **to have a ~** avoir un travail or un emploi; **to lose one's ~** perdre son travail or son emploi or son boulot*; **a ~ as a librarian** un poste or un emploi de bibliothécaire; **he's looking for a ~ as a teacher/secretary/manager** il cherche un poste or un emploi de professeur/secrétaire/directeur; **teaching/manufacturing ~s** emplois mpl dans l'enseignement/l'industrie; **nursing ~s** postes mpl d'infirmiers; **he has a ~ for the vacation** il a un travail or un boulot* or un job* pour les vacances; **to be out of a ~** être au chômage; (Ind, Press) **7,000 ~s lost** 7000 suppressions d'emplois; **on the ~** (= while working) [talk, sleep, learn] pendant le travail; **he fell asleep on the ~:** (= during sex) il s'est endormi en pleine action* (hum) or en faisant l'amour; **she's always on the ~:** (= always working) elle est toujours en train de travailler; **to stay or remain on the ~** rester à son poste; **on-the-~ training** (formal) formation f dans l'entreprise; (informal) formation f sur le tas; **off-the-~ training** formation f à l'extérieur; (Brit) **~s for the boys*** des boulots pour les (petits) copains* → **cushy, loss**
c (= duty, responsibility) travail m, boulot* m; **it's not my ~ to supervise him** ce n'est pas à moi or ce n'est pas mon travail de contrôler

ce qu'il fait; **he's got a ~ to do** ◊ **he's only doing his ~** il ne fait que son boulot*; **drinking a lot of water helps the kidneys do their ~** boire beaucoup d'eau facilite le travail des reins; **he knows his ~** il connaît son affaire; **that's not his ~** ce n'est pas de son ressort, ce n'est pas son boulot*; **I had the ~ of telling them** c'est moi qui ai dû le leur dire
d (= state of affairs) **it's a good ~ (that) he managed to meet you** c'est heureux or c'est une chance qu'il ait pu vous rencontrer; **and a good ~ too!** à la bonne heure!; **it's a bad ~** c'est une sale affaire; **to give sth/sb up as a bad ~** renoncer à qch/qn en désespoir de cause; (Brit) **this is just the ~*** c'est juste or exactement ce qu'il faut
e (= difficult time) **to have a ~ to do sth** or **doing sth** avoir du mal à faire qch; **I had a ~ to finish this letter** j'ai eu du mal à finir cette lettre; **it was a ~** or **an awful ~ to organize this party** ça a été un sacré* travail or tout un travail que d'organiser cette soirée; **it was a (terrible) ~ convincing him** or **to convince him** ça a été toute une affaire or ça n'a pas été une mince affaire pour le convaincre; **you'll have a ~ convincing him** or **to convince him!** vous aurez du mal à le convaincre!; **you've got a real ~ there!** tu n'es pas au bout de tes peines!
f (* = dishonest business) **to do a ~** faire un coup; **a put-up ~** un coup monté; **remember that bank ~?** tu te rappelles le coup de la banque?
g (:= thing) truc* m; **that red ~ over there** ce truc rouge là-bas
2 VI (= do casual work) faire des petits travaux; (St Ex) négocier, faire des transactions; (= profit from public position) magouiller*
3 VT (also ~ **out**) [+ work] sous-traiter
4 COMP ▶ **job action** N (US Ind) action f revendicative, (mouvement m de) grève f ▶ **job analysis** N (Ind) analyse f des tâches, analyse f statique or par poste de travail ▶ **job centre** N (Brit) ≈ ANPE f, ≈ Agence f nationale pour l'emploi ▶ **job club** N (Brit) club m d'entraide pour chômeurs ▶ **job control language** N (Comput) langage m de contrôle de travaux ▶ **job creation** N création f d'emplois ▶ **job creation scheme** N plan m de création d'emplois ▶ **job description** N description f de poste, profil m de l'emploi ▶ **job evaluation** N évaluation f des tâches ▶ **job-hop*** VI changer fréquemment d'emploi ▶ **job hopper*** N personne f qui change fréquemment d'emploi ▶ **job hunting** N chasse f à l'emploi ▶ **job lot** N lot m d'articles divers; **to sell/buy sth as a ~ lot** vendre/acheter qch par lots ▶ **job offer** N offre f d'emploi ▶ **job queue** N (Comput) file f d'attente des travaux ▶ **job rotation** N rotation f des tâches ▶ **job satisfaction** N satisfaction f au travail; **I get a lot of ~ satisfaction** je trouve beaucoup de satisfaction dans mon travail ▶ **job security** N sécurité f de l'emploi ▶ **job seeker** N (Brit Admin) demandeur f d'emploi ▶ **job seeker's allowance** N (Brit Admin) allocation f de demandeur d'emploi ▶ **job-share** (Brit) N partage m de poste ♦ VI partager un poste ▶ **job sharing** N partage m de poste ▶ **job title** N intitulé m de poste

jobber ['dʒɒbər] N (Brit St Ex) négociant m en valeurs (boursières); (also **stock ~**) contrepartiste mf; (= pieceworker) ouvrier m, -ière f à la tâche; (= dishonest person) magouilleur* m, -euse* f

jobbery ['dʒɒbərɪ] N (NonC: Brit) malversation f, magouillage m

jobbing ['dʒɒbɪŋ] **1** ADJ (Brit) (paid by the day) payé à la journée; (paid by the task) à la tâche, à façon **2** N (NonC: St Ex) transactions fpl boursières

jobholder ['dʒɒb,həʊldər] N (= employed per-

son) personne f qui travaille; (in specific post) employé(e) m(f)

jobless ['dʒɒblɪs] **1** ADJ sans emploi, au chômage **2** **the jobless** NPL les chômeurs mpl, les sans-emploi mpl; **the ~ figures** le nombre de chômeurs or sans-emploi, les chiffres mpl du chômage

joblessness ['dʒɒblɪsnɪs] N chômage m

jobsworth* ['dʒɒbz,wɜːθ] N (Brit) employé qui applique le règlement à la lettre

Jock* [dʒɒk] N (pej) Écossais m

jock [dʒɒk] N **a** = **jockstrap** **b** (US) sportif m

jockey ['dʒɒkɪ] **1** N jockey m **2** VI **to ~** se bousculer; (lit, fig) **to ~ for position** manœuvrer pour se placer avantageusement; **they were ~ing for office in the new government** ils manœuvraient pour obtenir des postes dans le nouveau gouvernement **3** VT **to ~ sb into doing** manœuvrer qn (habilement) pour qu'il fasse, amener adroitement qn à faire **4** COMP ▶ **Jockey club** N Jockey-Club m ▶ **Jockey Shorts®** NPL caleçon m

jockstrap ['dʒɒkstræp] N (Sport) slip m de sport; (Med) suspensoir m

jocose [dʒəˈkəʊs] ADJ (liter) (= merry) enjoué, jovial; (= jesting) facétieux

jocosely [dʒəˈkəʊslɪ] ADV (liter) [say] (= merrily) d'un ton enjoué; (= jestingly) facétieusement

jocular ['dʒɒkjʊlər] ADJ (= merry) enjoué, jovial; (= humorous) plaisant

jocularity [,dʒɒkjʊˈlærɪtɪ] N jovialité f

jocularly ['dʒɒkjʊləlɪ] ADV [say, ask, speak, discuss] en plaisantant

jocund ['dʒɒkənd] ADJ jovial, joyeux

jodhpurs ['dʒɒdpəz] NPL jodhpurs mpl, culotte f de cheval

Joe [dʒəʊ] **1** N (dim of Joseph) Jo m **2** COMP ▶ **Joe Bloggs*** (Brit), **Joe Blow*** (US) N Monsieur tout-le-monde m, l'homme m de la rue ▶ **Joe College*** N (US Univ) étudiant m type américain ▶ **Joe Public*** N (Brit) le public ▶ **Joe Soap*** N (Brit) Monsieur tout-le-monde m, l'homme m de la rue

Joel ['dʒəʊəl] N Joël m

jog [dʒɒg] **1** N **a** (Sport = run) jogging m, footing m; **to go for a ~** aller faire un jogging or un footing; **she begins the day with a ~ around the park** elle commence la journée en faisant son jogging or footing dans le parc **b** (also **~-trot**) petit trot m; **he set off at a ~ down the path** il s'est mis à descendre le sentier au petit trot; **to go along at a ~(-trot)** aller au petit trot **c** (= nudge, knock) légère poussée f; (with elbow) coup m de coude **2** VT (= shake) secouer, bringuebaler; (= nudge) pousser; **to ~ sb's elbow** pousser le coude de qn; **to ~ sb's memory** rafraîchir la mémoire de qn **3** VI **a** (Sport) faire du jogging, faire du footing **b** cahoter, bringuebaler; **the cart ~s along the path** la charrette cahote or bringuebale sur le chemin
▶ **jog about 1** VI sautiller **2** VT SEP remuer
▶ **jog along** VI (lit) [person, vehicle] aller son petit bonhomme de chemin, cheminer; (fig) [person] aller cahin-caha*; [piece of work, course of action] aller tant bien que mal
▶ **jog around** VTI = **jog about**
▶ **jog on** VI = **jog along**

jogger ['dʒɒgər] **1** N jogger m, joggeur m, -euse f **2** COMP ▶ **jogger's nipple*** N mamelon m du jogger

jogging ['dʒɒgɪŋ] **1** N (Sport) jogging m, footing m **2** COMP ▶ **jogging shoes** NPL chaussures fpl de jogging ▶ **jogging suit** N jogging m

joggle ['dʒɒgl] **1** VT secouer **2** VI bringuebaler, ballotter **3** N légère secousse f

Johannesburg [dʒəʊˈhænɪsˌbɜːg] N Johannesburg

John [dʒɒn] **1** N **a** Jean m **b** (*esp US = lavatory*) **the john*** les chiottes* *fpl* **c** (*US = prostitute's customer*) **john*** micheton* m **2** COMP ► **John Bull** N John Bull m (*Anglais de caricature*) ► **John Doe** N (*US Jur*) *homme dont on ignore le nom* ► **John Dory** N saint-pierre m *inv*, dorée f ► **John Hancock***, **John Henry*** N (*US fig = signature*) signature f, paraphe m ► **John of the Cross** N (*also* **Saint ~ of the Cross**) saint Jean m de la Croix ► **John Q. Public*** N (*US*) le public, le quidam (*hum*) ► **John the Baptist** N (*also* **Saint ~ the Baptist**) saint Jean m Baptiste

Johnny ['dʒɒnɪ] **1** N **a** *dim of* **John** **b** **johnny*** type* m **c** (*Brit†* = condom: also* **johnny, rubber johnny**) capote f (*anglaise*)* **2** COMP ► **Johnny-come-lately** N nouveau venu m; (= *upstart*) parvenu m

▼ **join** [dʒɔɪn] **1** VT **a** (= *attach*) attacher, relier; (= *assemble, put together*) [+ *parts*] assembler; [+ *broken pieces*] raccorder; (*with glue*) recoller; (*Elec*) [+ *batteries*] accoupler, connecter; **to ~ (together) two ends of a chain** attacher *or* relier les deux bouts d'une chaîne; (*in instructions*) **~ part A to part B** assemblez l'élément A avec l'élément B; **~ the panels (together) with screws** assemblez les panneaux à l'aide de vis; (*fig, pej*) **they are ~ed at the hip*** ils sont comme cul et chemise*, ils sont inséparables → **issue**

b (= *link*) relier (**to** à); **~ the dots (together) with a line** reliez les points par un trait; **the island was ~ed to the mainland by a bridge** l'île était reliée à la terre par un pont; **to ~ hands** se donner la main; **~ed in marriage** *or* **matrimony** unis par les liens du mariage

c (= *merge with*) [*river*] [+ *another river, the sea*] rejoindre, se jeter dans; [*road*] [+ *another road*] rejoindre; **this is where the river ~s the sea** c'est là que le fleuve se jette dans la mer

d (*Mil, fig*) **to ~ battle (with)** engager le combat (avec); **they ~ed forces** ils ont uni leurs forces; **to ~ forces (with sb) to do** s'unir (à qn) pour faire

e (= *become member of*) [+ *club, association, political party*] devenir membre de, adhérer à, s'affilier à; [+ *university*] entrer à, s'inscrire à; [+ *circus, religious order*] entrer dans; [+ *procession*] se joindre à; **to ~ NATO/the European Union** devenir membre de l'OTAN/l'Union européenne; (*Ftbl*) **he ~ed Liverpool** il a rejoint l'équipe de Liverpool; **to ~ the army** s'engager *or* s'enrôler dans l'armée; **to ~ a trade union** s'affilier à un syndicat, se syndiquer; (*fig*) **~ the club!*** tu es en bonne compagnie!

f [+ *person*] rejoindre, retrouver; **I'll ~ you in five minutes** je vous rejoins *or* retrouve dans cinq minutes; **Paul ~s me in wishing you ...** Paul se joint à moi pour vous souhaiter ...; **Moscow has ~ed Washington in condemning these actions** Moscou, comme Washington, a condamné ces actions; **she ~ed me in support of the idea** elle s'est jointe à moi pour défendre cette idée; **will you ~ us?** (= *come with us*) voulez-vous venir avec nous?; (= *be one of our number*) voulez-vous être des nôtres?; (*in restaurant etc*) voulez-vous vous asseoir à notre table?; (*in restaurant etc*) **may I ~ you?** je peux *or* puis-je m'asseoir avec vous?; **will you ~ me in a drink?** voulez-vous prendre un verre avec moi?; **to ~ one's regiment** rejoindre son régiment; **to ~ one's ship** rallier *or* rejoindre son bâtiment; **to ~ the queue** se mettre à la queue

2 VI **a** (= *connect*) [*pieces, parts, edges*] se raccorder (**with** à); [*ends*] s'attacher

b (= *link up*) [*lines*] se rejoindre, se rencontrer

c (= *merge*) [*roads, rivers*] se rejoindre; (= *become a member*) [*of political party, sports club, leisure club, class, group*] devenir membre; **to ~ in doing** [*people*] s'associer pour faire; **Moscow and Washington have ~ed in condemning these actions** Moscou et Washington ont toutes deux condamné ces actions

3 N (*in mended object*) ligne f de raccord; (*Sewing*) couture f

4 COMP ► **joined case** N (*Jur*) affaire f jointe ► **join-the-dots puzzle** N (*Brit*) jeu qui consiste à relier des points pour découvrir une figure

►**join in 1** VI participer, se mettre de la partie; (*in singing etc*) **~ in!** chantez *etc* avec nous! **2** VT FUS [+ *game, activity*] participer à; [+ *conversation*] prendre part à; [+ *protests, shouts*] joindre sa voix à; [+ *thanks, wishes*] se joindre à → **chorus**

►**join on 1** VI [*links, parts of structure*] se joindre (**to** à) **2** VT SEP fixer; (*by tying*) attacher

►**join together 1** VI = **join 2a 2** VT SEP = **join 1a, 1b**

►**join up 1** VI (*Mil*) entrer dans l'armée **2** VT SEP joindre, assembler; [+ *pieces of wood or metal*] abouter, rabouter; (*Elec*) [+ *wires*] connecter, raccorder

joinder ['dʒɔɪndər] N (*Jur*) jonction f

joiner ['dʒɔɪnər] N (*Brit = carpenter*) menuisier m

joinery ['dʒɔɪnərɪ] N (*Brit*) menuiserie f

joint [dʒɔɪnt] **1** N **a** (*Anat*) articulation f; **ankle/knee/elbow ~** articulation f de la cheville/du genou/du coude; **out of ~** [*knee, ankle, hip etc*] démis; (*fig*) de travers; **to put one's shoulder/wrist etc out of ~** se démettre l'épaule/le poignet *etc*; (*fig*) **his nose is out of ~** il est dépité; **that put his nose out of ~** ça l'a défrisé* → **ball**

b (*in wood, metal etc*) articulation f, jointure f; (*Geol: in rock*) diaclase f → **mitre, universal**

c (*Brit*) [*of meat*] rôti m; **a cut off the ~** une tranche de rôti

d * (= *night club*) boîte* f; (= *disreputable pub*) bistro(t)* m mal famé; (= *gambling den*) tripot m

e (*Drugs**) joint* m

2 ADJ [*statement, action, project, approach, meeting, control*] commun; [*research*] en commun; [*decision*] pris d'un commun accord; [*effort*] conjugué; (*in race, competition*) **to come ~ first/second** *etc* être classé premier/deuxième *etc* ex aequo; **to make** *or* **take a ~ decision to do sth** décider d'un commun accord de faire qch; **~ consultations** consultations *fpl* bilatérales; **~ obligation** cobligation f; **~ responsibility** coresponsabilité f; **in ~ names** [*sign*] conjointement

3 VT **a** (*Brit Culin*) découper (aux jointures)

b [+ *pipes*] joindre, raccorder

4 COMP ► **joint account** N (*Fin*) compte m joint ► **joint agreement** N (*Ind*) convention f collective ► **joint and several guarantee** N caution f solidaire ► **joint and several liability** N responsabilité f conjointe et solidaire ► **joint author** N coauteur m ► **Joint Chiefs of Staff** NPL (*US*) chefs *mpl* d'état-major (des armées) ► **joint committee** N (*gen*) commission f mixte; (*US Pol*) commission f interparlementaire ► **joint estate** N (*Jur*) biens *mpl* communs ► **joint favourite** N **the horses are ~ favourites** ces chevaux sont les deux favoris ► **joint financing** N cofinancement m ► **joint heir** N cohéritier m, -ière f ► **joint honours** N (*Brit Univ = degree*) ≈ licence f préparée dans deux matières (*ayant le même coefficient*) ► **joint manager** N codirecteur m, -trice f, cogérant(e) m(f) ► **joint mortgage** N emprunt m logement souscrit conjointement ► **joint ownership** N copropriété f ► **joint partner** N coassocié(e) m(f) ► **joint passport** N passeport m conjoint (*pour mari et femme*) ► **joint-stock company** N (*Fin*) société f par actions ► **joint venture** N (*gen*) entreprise f commune; (*Jur, Fin = company, operation*) joint-venture f

Collectivement, les **Joint Chiefs of Staff** *(c'est-à-dire les chefs d'état-major des trois corps d'armée) constituent un organe du ministère américain de la Défense ayant pour rôle de conseiller le Président, le Conseil national de sécurité et le ministre de la Défense en matière de défense nationale.*

jointed ['dʒɔɪntɪd] ADJ [*doll*] articulé; [*fishing rod, tent pole*] démontable

jointly ['dʒɔɪntlɪ] ADV conjointement (**with** avec); **to be ~ responsible** *or* **liable for sth** être conjointement responsable de qch; (*Jur*) **~ and severally** conjointement et solidairement

jointure ['dʒɔɪntʃər] N douaire m

joist [dʒɔɪst] N (*wooden*) solive f; (*metal*) poutrelle f

jojoba [həʊ'həʊbə] N jojoba m

joke [dʒəʊk] **1** N **a** (= *funny anecdote*) plaisanterie f, blague* f; **for a ~** pour rire, pour blaguer*; **to make a ~ about sb/sth** plaisanter sur qn/qch; **to make a ~ of sth** tourner qch à la plaisanterie; **he can't take a ~** il ne comprend pas *or* il prend mal la plaisanterie; **it's no ~!** (= *it's not easy*) ce n'est pas une petite affaire! (**doing** que de faire); (= *it's not enjoyable*) ce n'est pas drôle *or* marrant* (**doing** (que) de faire); (*gen, iro*) **what a ~!** ce que c'est drôle!; (*pej = useless*) **it's a ~!** c'est de la blague!; (*Brit*) **his behaviour is (getting) beyond a ~*** il a dépassé les bornes; **the situation is (getting) beyond a ~*** la situation devient alarmante; **the ~ is that ...** le plus drôle c'est que ..., ce qu'il y a de drôle *or* de marrant* c'est que ... → **see, standing**

b (= *trick*) tour m, farce f; **to play a ~ on sb** faire une farce à qn, jouer un tour à qn → **practical**

c (= *object of amusement*) risée f; **he is the ~ of the village** il est la risée du village

2 VI plaisanter, blaguer*; **you're joking!** vous voulez rire!, sans blague!*; **£100 for that? — you must be joking!** 100 livres pour ça? — vous n'êtes pas sérieux *or* vous voulez rire!; **I'm not joking** je ne plaisante pas; **I was only joking** ce n'était qu'une plaisanterie; **you mustn't ~ about his accent** il ne faut pas se moquer de son accent

joker ['dʒəʊkər] N **a** (* = *idiot*) rigolo* m; **some ~ will always start singing** il y aura toujours un rigolo* pour se mettre à chanter **b** (*Cards*) joker m; (*fig*) **the ~ in the pack** l'outsider m, le joker **c** = **jokester** **d** (*Jur*) clause f ambiguë

jokester ['dʒəʊkstər] N blagueur m, -euse f, plaisantin m

jokey* ['dʒəʊkɪ] ADJ (= *amusing*) rigolo* (-ote* f); (= *jocular*) blagueur, jovial; **in a ~ way** en plaisantant

joking ['dʒəʊkɪŋ] **1** ADJ [*tone*] de plaisanterie **2** N (*NonC*) plaisanterie f, blague* f; **~ apart** *or* **aside** plaisanterie *or* blague* à part

jokingly ['dʒəʊkɪŋlɪ] ADV en plaisantant, pour plaisanter; **she ~ referred to her son as "my little monster"** elle appelait son fils « mon petit monstre » pour plaisanter

jollification* [ˌdʒɒlɪfɪ'keɪʃən] N (*NonC*) réjouissances *fpl*

jollity ['dʒɒlɪtɪ] N [*of person, atmosphere*] gaieté f, joyeuse humeur f

jolly ['dʒɒlɪ] **1** ADJ (*esp Brit*) **a** (= *cheerful*) [*person, atmosphere, smile, mood*] jovial **b** (†* = *enjoyable*) amusant; **to have a ~ (old) time** bien s'amuser **2** ADV (*Brit** = *very*) [*good, decent*] drôlement*, rudement*; **you are ~ lucky** tu as une drôle de veine*; (*expressing approval*) **~ good!** très bien!; **you ~ well will go!** pas question que tu n'y ailles pas!; **I (should) ~ well hope** *or* **think so!** j'espère bien! **3** VT **to**

~ **sb along** enjôler qn; **they jollied him into joining them** ils l'ont convaincu (en douceur) de se joindre à eux **4** N (US) **to get one's jollies** prendre son pied; (from doing sth en faisant qch) **5** COMP ► **jolly boat** N (Naut) canot m ► **the Jolly Roger** N le pavillon noir

jolt [dʒəʊlt] **1** VI [vehicle] cahoter, tressauter; **to ~ along** avancer en cahotant; **to ~ to a stop** s'arrêter brutalement **2** VT (lit, fig) secouer, cahoter; **she was ~ed awake** elle s'est réveillée en sursaut; (fig) **to ~ sb into action/ into doing sth** pousser qn à agir/à faire qch; **she was ~ed back to reality** elle fut brutalement rappelée à la réalité; **it ~ed her out of her self-pity/depression** ça l'a tellement secouée qu'elle a arrêté de s'apitoyer sur son sort/qu'elle a arrêté de déprimer **3** N **a** (= jerk) [of vehicle etc] secousse f, à-coup m **b** (fig) choc m; **it gave me a ~** ça m'a fait un choc

jolting ['dʒəʊltɪŋ] **1** ADJ cahotant **2** N (NonC) cahots mpl

Jonah ['dʒəʊnə] N Jonas m; (fig) porte-malheur m inv, oiseau m de malheur

Jonas ['dʒəʊnəs] N Jonas m

Jonathan ['dʒɒnəθən] N Jonathan m

Joneses ['dʒəʊnzɪz] NPL **to try to keep up with the ~*** ne pas vouloir faire moins bien que le voisin

jonquil ['dʒɒŋkwɪl] **1** N jonquille f, narcisse m **2** ADJ jonquille inv

Jordan ['dʒɔːdn] N (= country) la Jordanie; **the river ~** le Jourdain

Jordanian [dʒɔːˈdeɪnɪən] **1** N Jordanien(ne) m(f) **2** ADJ jordanien; [ambassador, embassy, monarch] de Jordanie

Joseph ['dʒəʊzɪf] N Joseph m

Josephine ['dʒəʊzɪfiːn] N Joséphine f

josh* [dʒɒʃ] (esp US) **1** VT charrier*, mettre en boîte* **2** VI blaguer* **3** N mise f en boîte*

Joshua ['dʒɒʃjʊə] N Josué m

joss stick ['dʒɒsstɪk] N bâton m d'encens

jostle ['dʒɒsl] **1** VI **he ~d against me** il m'a bousculé; **to ~ through the crowd** se frayer un chemin (à coups de coudes) à travers la foule; (lit, fig) **to ~ for sth** jouer des coudes pour obtenir qch **2** VT bousculer **3** N bousculade f

jot [dʒɒt] **1** N brin m, iota m; **there is not a ~ of truth in this** il n'y a pas une once de vérité là-dedans; **not one ~ or tittle** pas un iota, pas un brin **2** VT noter, prendre note de
► **jot down** VT SEP noter, prendre note de; **to ~ down notes** prendre or griffonner des notes; **to ~ down a few points** prendre note de or noter quelques points

jotter ['dʒɒtər] N (Brit) (= exercise book) cahier m (de brouillon); (= pad) bloc-notes m

jottings ['dʒɒtɪŋz] NPL notes fpl

joual [ʒwɑːl] N (Can) joual m

joule [dʒuːl] N joule m

journal ['dʒɜːnl] **1** N **a** (= periodical) revue f; (= newspaper) journal m **b** (= diary) journal m **c** (Naut) livre m de bord; (Comm) livre m de comptes; (Jur) compte rendu m **2** COMP ► **journal bearing** N (Tech) palier m

journalese [ˌdʒɜːnəˈliːz] N (NonC: pej) jargon m journalistique

journalism ['dʒɜːnəlɪzəm] N journalisme m

journalist ['dʒɜːnəlɪst] N journaliste mf

journalistic [ˌdʒɜːnəˈlɪstɪk] ADJ [profession, community, experience, talent, cliché] de journaliste; [style, career] journalistique

journey ['dʒɜːnɪ] **1** N (gen) voyage m; (short or regular trip) trajet m; (distance covered) trajet m, parcours m; **to go on a ~** partir en voyage; **to set out on one's ~** se mettre en route; **a two days' ~** un voyage de deux jours; **it's a 50-minute train ~ from Glasgow to Edinburgh** le trajet Glasgow-Édimbourg en train est de or prend 50 minutes; **to reach one's ~'s end** arriver à destination; **the ~ from home to office** le trajet de la maison au bureau; **the return ~** ◊ **the ~ home** le (voyage or trajet de) retour; **a car ~** un voyage or trajet en voiture; **a long bus ~** un long trajet en autobus **2** VI voyager; **to ~ on** continuer son voyage **3** COMP ► **journey time** N durée f du trajet

journeyman ['dʒɜːnɪmən] **1** N (pl -men) artisan m **2** COMP ► **journeyman baker** N ouvrier m boulanger ► **journeyman joiner** N compagnon m charpentier

journo* ['dʒɜːnəʊ] N (ABBR = **journalist**) journaliste mf, journaleux* m (pej)

joust [dʒaʊst] **1** N joute f **2** VI (lit, fig) jouter

Jove [dʒəʊv] N Jupiter m; **by ~!**†* sapristi !*

jovial ['dʒəʊvɪəl] ADJ jovial

joviality [ˌdʒəʊvɪˈælɪtɪ] N jovialité f

jovially ['dʒəʊvɪəlɪ] ADV [say] jovialement; [laugh] gaiement

jowl [dʒaʊl] N (= jaw) mâchoire f; (= cheek) bajoue f → **cheek**

-jowled [dʒaʊld] ADJ (in compounds) **square-jowled** à la mâchoire carrée

jowly ['dʒaʊlɪ] ADJ aux joues flasques

joy [dʒɔɪ] **1** N **a** (NonC) joie f; **to my great ~** à ma grande joie **b** (= enjoyable thing) plaisir m; **the ~s of the seaside** les plaisirs or les charmes du bord de la mer; **the ~s of motherhood** les joies fpl or satisfactions fpl de la maternité; **it was a ~ to see him again** c'était un (vrai) plaisir de le revoir; **this car is a ~ to drive** c'est un (vrai) plaisir de conduire cette voiture; **his dancing was a ~ to watch** ◊ **it was a ~ to watch him dancing** c'était un (vrai) plaisir or délice de le regarder danser; **to be full of the ~s of spring** avoir le cœur joyeux; (iro) **I wish you ~ of it!** je vous souhaite bien du plaisir ! **c** (Brit* = success) **any ~?** alors, ça a marché ?*; **I got no ~ out of it** ça n'a pas marché, ça n'a rien donné; **I got no ~ out of him** avec lui ça n'a rien donné, je n'en ai rien tiré

joyful ['dʒɔɪfʊl] ADJ joyeux

joyfully ['dʒɔɪfəlɪ] ADV [greet, sing] joyeusement

joyfulness ['dʒɔɪfʊlnɪs] N (gen) joie f; **the ~ of the occasion** le caractère joyeux de l'événement

joyless ['dʒɔɪlɪs] ADJ [world] sans joie; [person, experience] triste

joyous ['dʒɔɪəs] ADJ (liter) joyeux

joyously ['dʒɔɪəslɪ] ADV (liter) (with vb) avec joie; (with adj) joyeusement

joyride ['dʒɔɪraɪd] **1** N **to go for a ~** faire une virée* dans une voiture volée **2** VI (also **go joyriding**) faire une virée* dans une voiture volée

joyrider ['dʒɔɪraɪdər] N jeune chauffard m au volant d'une voiture volée

joyriding ['dʒɔɪraɪdɪŋ] N **~ is on the increase** il y a de plus en plus de jeunes qui volent une voiture juste pour aller faire une virée

joystick ['dʒɔɪstɪk] N (Aviat) manche m à balai; (Comput) manche m à balai, manette f (de jeu)

JP [ˌdʒeɪˈpiː] N (Brit Jur) (ABBR = **Justice of the Peace**) → **justice**

Jr (US) (ABBR = **Junior**) Jr

JSA N (Brit Admin) (ABBR = **job seeker's allowance**) → **job**

jubilant ['dʒuːbɪlənt] ADJ [person, voice] débordant de joie; [face] épanoui, radieux; **he was ~** il jubilait

jubilation [ˌdʒuːbɪˈleɪʃən] **1** N (= emotion) allégresse f, jubilation f **2** jubilations NPL (= celebrations) fête f, réjouissance(s) f(pl)

jubilee ['dʒuːbɪliː] N jubilé m → **diamond**

Judaea [dʒuːˈdiːə] N la Judée

Judaeo-Christian, **Judeo-Christian** (US) [dʒuːˌdiːəʊˈkrɪstɪən] ADJ judéo-chrétien

Judah ['dʒuːdə] N Juda m

Judaic [dʒuːˈdeɪɪk] ADJ judaïque

Judaism ['dʒuːdeɪɪzəm] N judaïsme m

Judas ['dʒuːdəs] N **a** (= name) Judas m; **~ Iscariot** Judas m Iscariote **b** (= traitor) judas m **c** (= peephole) **judas** judas m

judder ['dʒʌdər] (Brit) **1** VI vibrer; (stronger) trépider; **to ~ to a halt** s'arrêter en trépidant **2** N vibration f, trépidation f

Jude [dʒuːd] N Jude m

judge [dʒʌdʒ] **1** N **a** (gen, Jur, Sport) juge m; (= member of judging panel) membre m du jury; (Bible) **(the book of) Judges** (le livre des) Juges mpl; (Brit Police) **the ~s' rules** la procédure criminelle avant un procès → **4** **b** (fig) connaisseur m, juge m; **to be a good ~ of character** être bon psychologue, savoir juger les gens; **to be a good ~ of wine** être bon juge en vins, s'y connaître en vins; **I'll be the ~ of that** c'est à moi de juger **2** VT **a** (= assess) [+ person, conduct, competition] juger; [+ qualities] apprécier **b** (= consider) juger, estimer (that que); **to ~ it necessary to do sth** juger or estimer nécessaire de faire qch ■ (PROV) **you can't ~ a book by its cover** il ne faut pas se fier aux apparences **3** VI juger, rendre un jugement; **to ~ for oneself** juger par soi-même; **as far as one can ~** ◊ **as far as can be ~d** autant qu'on puisse en juger; **judging by** or **from** à en juger par or d'après **4** COMP ► **judge advocate** N (pl **judge advocates**) (Mil, Jur) assesseur m (auprès d'un tribunal militaire) ► **judge of appeal** N (Jur) conseiller m à la cour d'appel

judg(e)ment ['dʒʌdʒmənt] **1** N **a** (Jur, Rel) jugement m; **to sit in ~ on** or **over** juger; **to give** or **pass ~ (on)** prononcer or rendre un jugement or un arrêt (sur) → **last[1]** **b** (= opinion) jugement m, avis m; **to give one's ~ (on)** donner son avis (sur); **in my ~** selon moi **c** (NonC = good sense) jugement m, discernement m; **to have (sound) ~** avoir du jugement **2** COMP ► **judg(e)ment call** N (esp US) **to make a ~ call** prendre une décision en s'en remettant à son jugement personnel ► **Judg(e)ment Day** N (Rel) le jour du Jugement (dernier)

judg(e)mental [dʒʌdʒˈmentəl] ADJ **he is very ~** il porte toujours des jugements catégoriques, il s'érige toujours en juge

judicature ['dʒuːdɪkətʃər] N **a** (= process of justice) justice f **b** (= body of judges) magistrature f **c** (= judicial system) système m judiciaire

judicial [dʒuːˈdɪʃəl] **1** ADJ **a** (Jur) [power, function] judiciaire; **~ and extrajudicial documents** actes mpl judiciaires et extrajudiciaires; **the ~ process** la procédure judiciaire; **~ appointments** nominations fpl judiciaires **b** (= wise) [mind] sage; **~ faculty** sens m critique **2** COMP ► **judicial inquiry** N enquête f judiciaire ► **judicial murder** N meurtre m légal ► **judicial proceedings** NPL poursuites fpl judiciaires ► **judicial review** N (Jur) (Brit) réexamen m d'une décision de justice (par une juridiction supérieure); (US) examen m de la constitutionnalité d'une loi ► **judicial sale** N vente f forcée or judiciaire

judicially [dʒuːˈdɪʃəlɪ] ADV judiciairement

judiciary [dʒuːˈdɪʃərɪ] **1** ADJ judiciaire **2** N **a** (= system) système m judiciaire **b** (= body of judges) magistrature f **c** (= branch of government) pouvoir m judiciaire

judicious [dʒuːˈdɪʃəs] ADJ (frm) judicieux

judiciously [dʒuːˈdɪʃəslɪ] ADV (frm) [use, say] judicieusement

Judith ['dʒu:dɪθ] N Judith f

judo ['dʒu:dəʊ] N judo m

judoka ['dʒu:dəʊ,kɑ:] N judoka m

Judy ['dʒu:dɪ] N *dim of* **Judith**; → **Punch**

jug [dʒʌg] **1** N **a** *(for water)* carafe f; *(for wine)* pichet m; *(round, heavy, jar-shaped)* cruche f; *(for milk)* pot m; *(for washing water)* broc m **b** (‡ = *prison*) taule* f or tôle* f, bloc* m; **in ~** en taule, au bloc* **2** VT **a** *(Culin)* cuire en civet; **~ged hare** civet m de lièvre **b** (‡ = *imprison*) coffrer* **3** COMP ► **jug band** N *(US)* orchestre m (de folk or de jazz) improvisé *(utilisant des ustensiles ménagers)*

juggernaut ['dʒʌgənɔ:t] N **a** *(Brit = truck)* gros poids lourd m, mastodonte m **b** *(fig = irresistible force)* **the media/military ~** le rouleau compresseur que représente(nt) les médias/l'armée; **the ~ of tradition/religion** l'influence écrasante de la tradition/religion *(Rel)* **Juggernaut** Jagannâth m

juggins‡ ['dʒʌgɪnz] N jobard(e) m(f), cruche* f

juggle ['dʒʌgl] **1** VI *(lit, fig)* jongler (**with** avec) **2** VT [+ *balls, plates, facts, figures*] jongler avec; [+ *one's time*] essayer de partager; **to ~ a career and a family** jongler pour concilier sa carrière et sa vie de famille

juggler ['dʒʌglə'] N jongleur m, -euse f

juggling ['dʒʌglɪŋ] **1** N *(NonC)* **a** *(lit: with balls, plates)* jonglerie f **b** *(fig = clever organization)* **combining career and family requires a lot of ~** il faut beaucoup jongler pour concilier sa carrière et sa famille; **with a bit of ~ I managed to pack everything into one suitcase** avec un peu d'astuce j'ai réussi à tout mettre dans une seule valise **c** (= *trickery*) tours mpl de passe-passe **2** COMP ► **juggling act** N *(fig)* **to do a ~** act tout mener de front; **to do a ~ act with sth** jongler avec qch *(fig)*

jughead‡ ['dʒʌghed] N *(US pej)* andouille* f

Jugoslav ['ju:gəʊ,slɑ:v] **1** ADJ yougoslave **2** N Yougoslave mf

Jugoslavia [,ju:gəʊ'slɑ:vɪə] N la Yougoslavie

jugular ['dʒʌgjʊlə'] **1** ADJ jugulaire **2** N *(veine f)* jugulaire f; **to go for the ~** frapper au point le plus faible

juice [dʒu:s] **1** N **a** [*of fruit, meat*] jus m; **orange ~** jus m d'orange **b** *(Physiol)* suc m; **digestive ~s** sucs mpl digestifs **c** *(US‡ = alcohol)* alcool m **d** (* = *electricity, gas etc*) jus* m; *(Brit = petrol)* essence f **2** COMP ► **juice extractor** N *(Brit)* centrifugeuse f électrique

► **juice up*** VT SEP **a** *(US Aut)* [+ *car*] gonfler le moteur de **b** (= *spice up*) [+ *occasion*] mettre de l'ambiance dans; [+ *image, brand*] donner du punch à*

juicehead‡ ['dʒu:shed] N *(US)* poivrot(e)* m(f), alcoolique mf

juicer ['dʒu:sə'] N centrifugeuse f électrique

juiciness ['dʒu:sɪnɪs] N juteux m

juicy ['dʒu:sɪ] ADJ **a** (= *succulent*) [*fruit, steak*] juteux **b*** (= *desirable*) [*role, part*] savoureux; [*deal*] juteux; (= *interesting*) [*story, scandal, details*] croustillant; **I heard some ~ gossip about him** j'ai entendu des histoires bien croustillantes à son sujet

jujitsu [dʒu:'dʒɪtsu:] N jiu-jitsu m

juju [dʒu:'dʒu:] N *culte africain proche du vaudou*

jujube ['dʒu:dʒu:b] N jujube m

jukebox ['dʒu:kbɒks] N juke-box m

Jul. ABBR = **July**

julep ['dʒu:lep] N boisson f sucrée, sirop m, julep m → **mint²**

Julian ['dʒu:lɪən] **1** N Julien m **2** ADJ julien

Juliet ['dʒu:lɪet] N Juliette f

Julius ['dʒu:lɪəs] N Jules m; **~ Caesar** Jules m César

July [dʒu:'laɪ] N juillet m; *for phrases see* **September**

jumble ['dʒʌmbl] **1** VT *(also ~* **up**) **a** *(lit)* [+ *objects, clothes, figures*] mélanger; **to ~ everything (up)** tout mélanger; **his clothes are all ~d up on his bed** ses vêtements sont pêle-mêle or en vrac sur son lit; **a ~d mass of wires** un amas de fils entortillés; *(in magazine etc)* **can you work out whose famous face has been ~d up in the picture?** pouvez-vous recomposer le visage du personnage célèbre qui figure sur cette image? **b** *(fig)* [+ *facts, details*] brouiller, embrouiller; **~d thoughts/memories** pensées fpl/souvenirs mpl confus(es)

2 N *(lit)* [*of objects*] fouillis m, méli-mélo* m; **a ~ of toys/papers** un tas de jouets/papiers en vrac; **in a ~** [*objects, papers, toys*] en vrac **b** *(fig)* **a ~ of words** une suite de mots sans queue ni tête; **a ~ of ideas/thoughts/memories** des idées fpl/pensées fpl/souvenirs mpl confus(es); **in a ~** [*ideas, thoughts*] confus **c** *(NonC: Brit = junk, goods at jumble sale)* bric-à-brac m

3 COMP ► **jumble sale** N *(Brit)* vente f d'objets d'occasion

jumbo ['dʒʌmbəʊ] **1** N* éléphant m **b** = **jumbo jet 2** COMP [*order, load, box, bottle, vegetable, prawn, egg*] géant ► **jumbo jet** N *(Aviat)* jumbo-jet m, avion m gros porteur ► **jumbo loan** N prêt m géant or jumbo ► **jumbo pack** N *(gen)* paquet m géant; [*of bottles, cans*] emballage m géant

jump [dʒʌmp] **1** N **a** *(gen)* saut m; *(of fear, nervousness)* sursaut m; **to give a ~** faire un saut, sauter; *(nervously)* sursauter; **at one ~** d'un *(seul)* bond; *(fig)* **to be one ~ ahead** avoir une longueur d'avance (**of** sur); *(US)* **to get a** or **the ~ on sb/sth** prendre une longueur d'avance sur qn/qch → **bungee jumping, high, parachute, running**

b *(fig = leap)* bond m; **a ~ in profits/sales/inflation** un bond des profits/des ventes/de l'inflation; **the ~ in prices** la hausse brutale des prix; **a 5% ~ in the unemployment figures** un bond de 5 % des chiffres du chômage; **it's a big ~ from medical student to doctor** il y a une grande différence entre être étudiant en médecine et devenir médecin, c'est un grand changement de passer d'étudiant en médecine à médecin

c *(Comput)* saut m

d *(Horse-riding)* obstacle m

2 VI **a** (= *leap*) sauter, bondir; **to ~ in/out/across** etc entrer/sortir/traverser etc d'un bond; **to ~ across a stream** franchir un ruisseau d'un bond; **to ~ into the river** sauter dans la rivière; **to ~ off a bus/train** sauter d'un autobus/d'un train; **to ~ off a wall** sauter (du haut) d'un mur; **to ~ over a wall/fence/ditch** sauter un mur/une barrière/un fossé; **he managed to ~ clear as the car went over the cliff** il a réussi à sauter hors de la voiture au moment où celle-ci passait par-dessus la falaise; **to ~ up and down** sauter; **to ~ up and down with excitement** bondir d'excitation; **to ~ up and down with anger** trépigner de colère

b *(from nervousness)* sursauter, tressauter; **to make sb ~** [*loud noise etc*] faire sursauter or tressauter qn; **it almost made him ~ out of his skin*** ça l'a fait sauter au plafond*; **his heart ~ed** *(with fear)* il a eu un coup au cœur; *(with happiness)* son cœur a bondi

c *(fig)* [*person*] sauter; **to ~ from one subject to another** sauter (sans transition) d'un sujet à un autre, passer du coq à l'âne; **she ~ed from kitchen assistant to chef** elle est passée directement de simple aide-cuisinière à chef de cuisine; **she ~ed from seventh place to second** elle est passée directement de la septième à la seconde place; **to ~ at** [+ *chance, suggestion, offer*] sauter sur; [+ *idea*] accueillir avec enthousiasme; **to ~ down sb's throat*** rembarrer qn; **to ~ to conclusions** tirer des conclusions hâtives; **he ~ed to the conclu-**

sion that ... il en a conclu hâtivement que ... ; **to ~ to sb's defence** s'empresser de prendre la défense de qn; **~ to it!*** et plus vite que ça !*, et que ça saute !*

d [*prices, shares, profits, costs*] monter en flèche, faire un bond; **her salary ~ed from £15,000 to £22,000** son salaire est passé brusquement or d'un seul coup de 15 000 à 22 000 livres; **losses ~ed to £4.1 million** les pertes ont subitement atteint les 4,1 millions de livres

3 VT **a** [*person, horse*] [+ *obstacle, ditch, fence*] sauter, franchir (d'un bond); **the horse ~ed a clear round** le cheval a fait un parcours d'obstacles sans faute; **the electric current ~s the gap between the two wires** sans que les fils se touchent, le courant électrique passe de l'un à l'autre; **to ~ 2 metres** sauter 2 mètres, faire un saut de 2 mètres

b [*rider*] [+ *horse*] faire sauter; **the jockey ~ed his horse over the fence** le jockey a fait sauter l'obstacle à son cheval; **she's ~ing three horses in this competition** [*jockey*] elle monte trois chevaux dans cette épreuve d'obstacles; [*owner*] elle engage trois chevaux dans cette épreuve d'obstacles

c (= *skip*) sauter; **the stylus ~ed a groove** la pointe de lecture a sauté un sillon; **the disease has ~ed a generation** cette maladie a sauté une génération; **the film then ~s ten years to 1996** le film fait alors un bond de dix ans pour arriver en 1996; **the company's shares ~ed £1.25/3%** les actions de la société ont fait un bond de 1,25 livres/de 3 %; *(Jur)* **to ~ bail** ne pas comparaître au tribunal; **to ~ a claim** s'emparer illégalement d'une concession minière; **to ~ the gun** *(Sport)* partir avant le départ; (* *fig*) agir prématurément; **to ~ the gun on sb** couper l'herbe sous le pied de qn; **to ~ the lights** or **a red light*** [*motorist etc*] brûler le feu rouge; *(Brit)* **to ~ the queue*** passer avant son tour, resquiller*; **to ~ the points** [*train*] dérailler à l'aiguillage; **to ~ the rails** *(lit)* [*train*] dérailler; *(esp Brit fig = go wrong)* déraper; **to ~ a train** (= *get on*) sauter dans un train en marche; (= *get off*) sauter d'un train en marche; **to ~ ship** *(lit)* déserter le navire; *(fig = join rival organization etc)* passer dans un autre camp; *(US)* **to ~ town*** quitter la ville

d (= *attack*) **to ~ sb*** sauter sur qn

4 COMP ► **jumped-up*** ADJ *(Brit pej)* (= *pushy*) parvenu; (= *cheeky*) effronté; (= *conceited*) prétentieux; **he is a ~ up-end clerk** ce n'est qu'un petit employé qui a monté en grade ► **jump-jet** N avion m à décollage vertical ► **jump jockey** N *(Brit Racing)* jockey m de steeple-chase ► **jump leads** NPL *(Brit Aut)* câbles mpl de démarrage *(pour batterie)* ► **jump-off** N *(Horse-riding)* (épreuve f) finale f *(d'un concours hippique)* ► **jump rope** N *(US)* corde f à sauter ► **jump seat** N *(Aut, Aviat)* strapontin m ► **jump-start** N → **jump-start** ► **jump suit** N *(gen)* combinaison(-pantalon) f, combinaison f de saut

► **jump about, jump around** VI sautiller

► **jump down** VI *(gen)* descendre d'un bond (**from** de); *(from wall, bicycle etc)* **~ down!** sautez!

► **jump in** VI sauter dedans; **he came to the river and ~ed in** arrivé à la rivière il a sauté dedans; **~ in!** *(into vehicle)* montez!; *(into swimming pool)* sautez!

► **jump off 1** VI sauter; **he ~ed off** il a sauté **2** ~ing-off ADJ → **jumping 3** ~-off N → **jump**

► **jump on 1** VI *(onto truck, bus)* **~ on!** montez!; **to ~ on(to) one's bicycle** sauter sur son vélo **2** VT FUS **a** **to ~ on(to) a bus** sauter dans un autobus **b** (* = *reprimand*) tomber sur

► **jump out** VI sauter (**of** de); **to ~ out of bed** sauter (à bas) du lit; **to ~ out of the window** sauter par la fenêtre; **to ~ out of a car/train** sauter d'une voiture/d'un train; *(from car etc)*

~ out! sortez!, descendez!; (fig) **the mistake ~ed out of the page at him** l'erreur dans la page lui a sauté aux yeux
► **jump up** ① VI se (re)lever d'un bond ② **~ed-up*** ADJ → **jump**

jumper ['dʒʌmpər] ① N [a] (Brit = sweater) pull(over) m [b] (US = dress) robe-chasuble f [c] (= one who jumps: person, animal) sauteur m, -euse f [d] (Comput) cavalier m ② COMP ► **jumper cables** NPL câbles mpl de démarrage (pour batterie)

jumping ['dʒʌmpɪŋ] ① N (gen) saut m; (= equitation) jumping m, concours m hippique ② ADJ (US* = lively) plein d'animation ③ COMP ► **jumping bean** N haricot m sauteur ► **jumping-off place, jumping-off point** N (fig) tremplin m; **they used the agreement as a ~-off place** or **point for further negotiations** ils se sont servis de l'accord comme d'un tremplin pour de plus amples négociations ► **jumping rope** N (US) corde f à sauter

jump-start ['dʒʌmpstɑ:t] ① VT [a] (Aut) **to ~ a car** (by pushing) faire démarrer une voiture en la poussant; (with jump-leads) faire démarrer une voiture en branchant sa batterie sur une autre [b] (fig) [+ negotiations, process, economy] relancer ② N [a] (Aut) **to give sb a ~** (by pushing) faire démarrer la voiture de qn en la poussant; (with jump leads) faire démarrer la voiture de qn en branchant sa batterie sur une autre [b] (fig) [of negotiations, process, economy] relance f

jumpy* ['dʒʌmpɪ] ADJ [person] nerveux; (St Ex) [market] instable

Jun. [a] ABBR = **June** [b] (ABBR = **Junior**) Jr

junction ['dʒʌŋkʃən] ① N [a] (NonC) jonction f [b] (Brit) (= meeting place) [of roads] bifurcation f; (= crossroads) carrefour m; [of rivers] confluent m; [of railway lines] embranchement m; [of pipes] raccordement m; (= station) gare f de jonction; **leave the motorway at ~ 13** prenez la sortie numéro 13 ② COMP ► **junction box** N (Elec) boîte f de dérivation

juncture ['dʒʌŋktʃər] N [a] (= joining place) jointure f, point m de jonction; (Ling) joncture f [b] (fig = state of affairs) conjoncture f; (fig = point) **at this ~** à ce moment

June [dʒu:n] ① N juin m; for phrases see **September** ② COMP ► **June bug** N hanneton m

Jungian [jʊŋɪən] ① N (= follower of Jung) jungien(ne) m(f) ② ADJ jungien

jungle ['dʒʌŋgl] ① N (lit, fig) jungle f ② COMP [animal, bird] de la jungle ► **jungle bunny** N (esp US pej) nègre m, négresse f, Noir(e) m(f) ► **jungle gym** N (in playground) cage f à poules or aux écureuils ► **jungle juice*** N gnôle* f ► **jungle warfare** N (NonC) combats mpl de jungle

junior ['dʒu:nɪər] ① ADJ [a] (in age) (plus) jeune, cadet; **John Smith, Junior** John Smith fils or junior → **3** [b] (in position) [employee, job] subalterne; **members of staff** les employés subalternes; **he is ~ to me in the business** il est au-dessous de moi dans l'entreprise; **people at the most ~ level in the company** les petits employés de l'entreprise → **3** [c] (Sport) [competition, team, title etc] (gen) junior; (= under 11) ≈ de poussins; (= 12 to 13) ≈ de benjamins; (= 14 to 15) ≈ de minimes; (= 16 to 17) ≈ de cadets; (= 18 to 19) ≈ de juniors; **to compete at ~ level** faire partie de l'équipe des poussins (or des benjamins etc) ② N [a] cadet(te) m(f); **he is two years my ~** ◊ **he is my ~ by two years** il est mon cadet de deux ans [b] (Brit Scol) petit(e) élève m(f) (de 7 à 11 ans); (US Scol) élève mf de classe de première; (US Univ) étudiant(e) m(f) de troisième année [c] (Sport) (gen) junior mf; (= under 11) ≈ poussin mf; (= 12 to 13) ≈ benjamin(e) m(f);

(= 14 to 15) ≈ minime mf; (= 16 to 17) ≈ cadet(te) m(f); (= 18 to 19) ≈ junior mf ③ COMP ► **junior class** N **the ~ classes** les petites classes fpl (de 7 à 11 ans) ► **junior clerk** N petit commis m ► **junior college** N (US) institut m universitaire (du premier cycle) ► **Junior Common Room** N (Brit Univ = room) salle f des étudiants; (= students) étudiants mpl ► **junior doctor** N interne m des hôpitaux ► **junior executive** N jeune cadre m ► **junior high school** N (US) ≈ collège m ► **Junior League** N [a] (US: for voluntary work) association locale féminine d'aide à la communauté [b] (Brit Sport) championnat m junior ► **junior minister** N (Parl) sous-secrétaire m d'État ► **junior miss†** N (Comm) fillette f (de 11 à 14 ans) ► **junior officer** N officier m subalterne ► **junior partner** N associé(-adjoint) m ► **junior rating** N (Brit Navy) matelot m ► **junior school** N (Brit) école f primaire (de 7 à 11 ans) ► **junior's license** N (US) permis spécial pour adolescents et autres apprentis conducteurs → DRIVING LICENCE, DRIVER'S LICENSE ► **junior technician** N (Brit Aviat) soldat m de première classe ► **junior training centre** N (Brit) centre m médico-éducatif ► **junior varsity sports** NPL (US Univ) sports pratiqués entre les équipes de deuxième division des établissements scolaires et universitaires

juniper ['dʒu:nɪpər] N genévrier m; **~ berry** baie f de genièvre; **~ berries** genièvre m

junk¹ [dʒʌŋk] ① N (NonC) (= discarded objects) bric-à-brac m inv, vieilleries fpl; (= metal) ferraille f; (* = bad quality goods) camelote* f; (* = worthless objects) pacotille f; (* = nonsense) âneries fpl; (Drugs*) came* f ② VT* bazarder*, balancer* ③ COMP ► **junk art** N junk art m (sculptures réalisées à l'aide de déchets) ► **junk bond** N junk bond m, obligation f à risque ► **junk dealer** N brocanteur m, -euse f ► **junk food*** N (NonC) **to eat ~ food** manger des cochonneries* ► **junk heap** N dépotoir m ► **junk mail** N (NonC) imprimés mpl publicitaires (envoyés par la poste) ► **junk market** N marché m aux puces ► **junk shop** N (boutique f de) brocante f

junk² [dʒʌŋk] N (= boat) jonque f

junket ['dʒʌŋkɪt] ① N [a] (Culin) (lait m) caillé m [b] (US = trip at public expense) voyage m aux frais de la princesse* ② VI faire bombance

junketing ['dʒʌŋkɪtɪŋ] N (NonC) (= merrymaking) bombance f, bringue* f; (US* = trip, banquet etc at public expense) voyage m or banquet m etc aux frais de la princesse*

junkie* ['dʒʌŋkɪ] N drogué(e) m(f), camé(e)* m(f); **a television ~** un accro* de la télé etc

junkyard ['dʒʌŋkjɑ:d] N entrepôt m de chiffonnier-ferrailleur

Juno ['dʒu:nəʊ] N Junon f

Junr (ABBR = **Junior**) Jr

junta ['dʒʌntə] N junte f

Jupiter ['dʒu:pɪtər] N (Myth) Jupiter m; (Astron) Jupiter f

Jura ['dʒʊərə] N (also **~ Mountains**) Jura m

Jurassic [dʒʊˈræsɪk] ADJ (Geol) [period] jurassique

juridical [dʒʊəˈrɪdɪkəl] ADJ juridique

jurisdiction [ˌdʒʊərɪsˈdɪkʃən] N (Jur) juridiction f; (Admin etc) compétence f; **it comes within our ~** (Jur) cela relève de notre juridiction; (Admin) cela relève de notre compétence or de nos attributions, c'est de notre ressort; **to be outside sb's ~** (Jur) ne pas relever de la juridiction de qn; (Admin) ne pas relever des compétences de qn, sortir des attributions de qn → **court**

jurisdictional [ˌdʒʊərɪsˈdɪkʃənl] ADJ (US) **~ dispute** conflit m d'attributions

jurisprudence [ˌdʒʊərɪsˈpru:dəns] N jurisprudence f → **medical**

jurist ['dʒʊərɪst] N juriste m

juror ['dʒʊərər] N juré m

jury ['dʒʊərɪ] ① N (Jur) jury m, jurés mpl; [of examination, exhibition, competition] jury m; **to be on the ~** faire partie du jury; **Ladies and Gentlemen of the ~** Mesdames et Messieurs les jurés; **the ~ is out** (lit) le jury s'est retiré pour délibérer; (fig) cela reste à voir; **the ~ is out on whether this is true** reste à voir si c'est vrai → **coroner, grand** ② COMP ► **jury box** N banc m des jurés ► **jury duty** N (US, Scot) = **jury service** ► **jury-rigging** N constitution d'un jury partisan ► **jury service** N **to do ~ service** faire partie d'un jury, être juré; **to be called for ~ service** être appelé à faire partie d'un jury ► **jury shopping** N (US Jur) recherche du jury idéal (par récusation de jurés) ► **the jury system** N le système de jugement par jury

jury² ['dʒʊərɪ] ADJ (Naut) de fortune, improvisé

juryman ['dʒʊərɪmən] N (pl **-men**) juré m

jurywoman ['dʒʊərɪwʊmən] N (pl **-women**) femme f juré

---

just¹ [dʒʌst]
ADVERB

[a] **= exactly** juste, exactement; **it's ~ 9 o'clock** il est 9 heures juste, il est exactement 9 heures; **you're ~ in time** vous arrivez juste à temps; **it took me ~ two hours** il m'a fallu exactement or juste deux heures; **it's ~ what I wanted** c'est exactement or juste ce que je voulais; **that's ~ what I thought** c'est exactement ce que je pensais; **that's ~ what I was going to say** c'est juste or exactement ce que j'allais dire; **~ how many came we don't know** nous ne savons pas exactement or au juste combien de personnes sont venues; **~ then** or **at that moment** à ce moment-là, juste à ce moment; **he has to have everything ~ so*** il faut que tout soit exactement comme il veut

Note the translations of the following examples, where **just** is used for emphasis:
~ what are you implying? qu'est-ce que tu veux dire au juste?; **~ what did they hope to achieve!** on se demande bien ce qu'ils s'imaginaient obtenir!; **I'm sure that's ~ what it was** c'était sûrement ça; **~ when everything was going so well!** dire que tout allait si bien!

♦ **just on** tout juste; **it cost ~ on 50 francs** ça a coûté tout juste 50 F; **it's ~ on 2 kilos** ça fait tout juste 2 kilos; **it's ~ on nine** il est tout juste 9 heures

[b] **indicating position** juste; **~ by the church** juste à côté de or tout près de l'église; **my house is ~ here** ma maison est juste ici; **it's ~ on the left as you go in** c'est tout de suite à gauche en entrant; **~ over there** là(, tout près); **~ past the station** juste après la gare; **it's ~ to the left of the bookcase** c'est juste à gauche de la bibliothèque

[c] **= at this or that moment** **we're ~ off** nous partons à l'instant; **I'm ~ coming!** j'arrive!; **it's okay, I was ~ leaving** ce n'est pas grave, je partais; **are you leaving?** — **not ~ yet** tu pars? — pas encore or pas tout de suite; **are you ready?** — **not ~ yet** tu es prêt? — pas tout à fait

[d] **referring to recent time** **~ last week** pas plus tard que la semaine dernière; **I saw him ~ last week** je l'ai vu pas plus tard que la semaine dernière; **this book is ~ out** ce livre vient de paraître

♦ **to have just done sth** venir de faire qch; **he had ~ left** il venait de partir; **I have only ~ heard about it** je viens juste de l'apprendre; **I've ~ this minute finished it** je viens de le finir à l'instant, je viens tout juste de le finir

[e] **= barely** **we (only) ~ caught the train** nous avons juste eu le temps de sauter dans le train; **I'll ~ catch the train if I hurry** j'aurai tout juste le temps d'attraper le train si je me dépêche; **his voice was ~ audible** sa voix était tout juste audible

♦ **only just** tout juste; **I will only ~ get there on time** j'arriverai tout juste à l'heure; **I have only ~ enough money** j'ai tout juste assez d'argent; BUT **we only ~ missed the train** nous avons raté le train de justesse; **he passed the exam but only ~** il a été reçu à l'examen mais de justesse *or* mais ça a été juste

f **= slightly** juste; **he got home ~ after 9 o'clock** il est rentré peu après *or* juste après 9 heures; **~ after he came** juste après son arrivée; **~ after this** juste après, tout de suite après; **~ before Christmas** juste avant Noël; **~ before it started to rain** juste avant qu'il ne commence à pleuvoir; **that's ~ over the kilo** cela fait juste un peu plus du kilo; BUT **~ over £10** un peu plus de 10 livres; **~ under £10** un peu moins de 10 livres; **it's ~ after 9 o'clock** il est un peu plus de 9 heures

g **= conceivably** **it may ~ be possible** ce n'est pas totalement exclu; **it's an old trick, but it could ~ work** c'est une vieille astuce mais avec un peu de chance ça pourrait marcher

h **= merely** juste, ne ... que; **it's ~ a suggestion** c'est juste une suggestion, ce n'est qu'une suggestion; **there will be ~ the two of us** il n'y aura que nous deux, il y aura juste nous deux; **~ a few** juste quelques-uns; **would you like some?** — **~ a little bit** tu en veux? — juste un petit peu; **~ a quick note to let you know that ...** juste un petit mot pour vous dire que ...; **he did it ~ for a laugh*** il l'a fait juste pour rigoler*; BUT **that's ~ your opinion** ça c'est ce que tu penses, ça c'est ton opinion

i **= simply** (tout) simplement; **I ~ told him to go away** je lui ai simplement dit de s'en aller; **I would ~ like to say this** je voudrais juste *or* seulement *or* simplement dire ceci; **don't take any notice of her, she's ~ jealous** ne fais pas attention à elle, elle est tout simplement jalouse

When **just** *is used in mitigation, or for emphasis, this is expressed in French in various ways.*
I was ~ wondering if you knew ... je me demandais si vous saviez ...; **I'm ~ phoning to remind you that ...** je te téléphone juste pour te rappeler que ...; **it's ~ one of those things*** c'est comme ça*, c'est la vie; **I ~ can't imagine what's happened to him** je n'arrive tout simplement pas à comprendre *or* j'ai du mal à imaginer ce qui a (bien) pu lui arriver; **you should ~ send it back** vous n'avez qu'à le renvoyer; **because YOU think so doesn't mean ...** ce n'est pas parce que tu le crois que ...

j **= specially** spécialement; **I did it ~ for you** je l'ai fait spécialement pour toi

k **= absolutely** absolument, tout simplement; **it was ~ marvellous!** c'était absolument *or* tout simplement merveilleux!; **she's ~ amazing!** elle est tout simplement *or* absolument stupéfiante!; BUT **that's ~ stupid!** c'est complètement *or* vraiment stupide; **we're managing ~ fine** on s'en sort (sans problème)

l **in imagination** **I can ~ see her face if I told her** j'imagine déjà la tête qu'elle ferait si je (le) lui disais; **I can ~ hear the roars of laughter** j'entends déjà les rires (que ça provoquerait)

m **in commands, requests, threats** **~ wait here a minute** attends une minute ici; **~ be reasonable** sois donc (un peu) raisonnable; **~ don't ask me to help** ne me demande surtout pas de t'aider; **~ a moment please** un instant s'il vous plaît; **~ imagine!*** rends-toi compte!, tu t'ima-

gines un peu!*; **~ look at that!** regarde-moi ça!*; **~ you do!*** ◊ **~ you try it!*** ◊ **~ you dare!*** essaie un peu pour voir!; **~ shut up!*** veux-tu te taire!, tu vas te taire!; **~ let me get my hands on him!*** celui-là, si je l'attrape!

n **in rejoinders** **~ that's it!** ◊ **that's ~ the point!** justement!; **~ so!** exactement!; **yes, but ~ the same ...** oui, mais tout de même ...; (Brit) **that's ~ ridiculous!** — **isn't it ~!** c'est ridicule! — ça tu peux le dire!; (Brit) **she made a real mess of it — didn't she ~!** elle a tout gâché — ça tu peux le dire!

o SET STRUCTURES

♦ **just about** (= approximately) à peu près; **it's ~ about 3 o'clock** il est à peu près 3 heures; **it's ~ about 5 kilos** ça pèse à peu près 5 kilos; BUT **I think that it was ~ about here that I saw him** je pense que c'est par ici que je l'ai vu; **have you finished?** — **~ about** avez-vous fini? — presque; **the incident ~ about ruined him** l'incident l'a ruiné ou presque *or* l'a quasiment ruiné; **I've had ~ about enough** *or* **about as much as I can stand!** j'en ai par-dessus la tête!*, j'en ai vraiment assez!

♦ **to be just about to do sth** être sur le point de faire qch; **we were ~ about to leave** on était sur le point de partir, on allait partir

♦ **just as: leave everything ~ as you find it** laissez tout exactement en l'état; **~ as we arrived it began to rain** juste au moment où nous arrivions, il s'est mis à pleuvoir; **come ~ as you are** venez comme vous êtes; **~ as you like** (c'est) comme vous voulez *or* voudrez; **~ as I thought!** c'est bien ce que je pensais!; **this one is ~ as good as the more expensive model** celui-ci est tout aussi bon que le modèle plus cher

♦ **just as well**: **I wasn't expecting much, which was ~ as well** je ne m'attendais pas à grand-chose, heureusement *or* et c'est tant mieux; **I was driving slowly, and ~ as well** heureusement que je roulais lentement; **we might ~ as well have stayed on a few days longer** on aurait très bien pu rester quelques jours de plus

♦ **just in case**: **~ in case it rains** juste au cas où il pleuvrait; **I'm taking a sleeping bag, ~ in case** j'emmène un sac de couchage, au cas où *or* pour le cas où

♦ **just like**: **he's ~ like his father** (physically) c'est le portrait de son père, c'est son père tout craché; (in behaviour) il est comme son père; **they have their problems ~ like the rest of us** eux aussi, ils ont leurs problèmes comme tout le monde; **that's ~ like Robert, always late** c'est bien Robert ça, toujours en retard; **I can't find £1,000 ~ like that** je ne peux pas trouver 1 000 livres comme ça

♦ **just now** (= a short time ago) à l'instant, tout à l'heure; **I saw him ~ now** je l'ai vu à l'instant *or* tout à l'heure; (= at the moment) **I'm busy ~ now** je suis occupé (pour l'instant); **he's on the phone ~ now** il est au téléphone

just² [dʒʌst] ADJ (= fair) juste (**to** *or* **towards sb** avec qn); **it is only ~ to point out that ...** il n'est que juste de faire remarquer que ... → **deserts**

justice ['dʒʌstɪs] N a (NonC: Jur) justice f; **to bring sb to ~** traduire qn en justice; (US) **Department of Justice** ministère m de la Justice → **poetic** b (NonC = fairness) justice f; **I must, in (all) ~, say (that) ...** pour être juste, je dois dire (que) ...; **in ~ to him he ...** ◊ **to do him ~ he ...** pour être juste envers lui, il ..., il faut lui

rendre cette justice qu'il ...; **this photograph doesn't do him ~** cette photo ne le flatte pas *or* ne l'avantage pas; **she never does herself ~** elle ne se montre jamais à sa juste valeur; **to do ~ to a meal** faire honneur à un repas c (= judge) (Brit) juge m; (US) juge m de la Cour Suprême; **Justice of the Peace** juge m de paix → **lord** d (= justness) [of cause etc] bien-fondé m; **to dispute the ~ of a claim** contester le bien-fondé d'une réclamation

justifiable [,dʒʌstɪ'faɪəbl] ADJ [action] justifié; [desire, emotion] légitime; [choice] défendable; (Jur) **~ homicide** homicide m justifiable (commis par qn dans l'exercice de ses fonctions)

justifiably [,dʒʌstɪ'faɪəblɪ] ADV à juste titre; **he was angry, and ~ so** il était en colère, à juste titre *or* et il y avait de quoi

justification [,dʒʌstɪfɪ'keɪʃən] N a (gen, also Rel) justification f (**of, for** de, à, pour); **as a ~ for his action** comme justification de *or* à son acte; **in ~ of** pour justifier; **to have some ~ for doing sth** avoir des raisons de faire qch; **he had no ~ for lying** il n'avait aucune raison valable de mentir b (Typ, Comput) [of text, page] justification f

justify ['dʒʌstɪfaɪ] VT a [+ behaviour, action] justifier; [+ decision] prouver le bien-fondé de; **to ~ o.s.** se justifier; **this does not ~ his being late** cela ne justifie pas son retard; **to be justified in doing sth** avoir de bonnes raisons de faire qch; **you're not justified in talking to her like that** rien ne vous autorise à lui parler de cette façon; **am I justified in thinking ...?** est-ce que j'ai raison de penser ...? b (Typ, Comput) [+ paragraph, text] justifier; **justified left/right** ◊ **left/right justified** justifié à gauche/à droite

justly ['dʒʌstlɪ] ADV a (= justifiably, deservedly) [proud, famous, claim, accuse etc] à juste titre b (= fairly, equitably) [treat, rule, govern, reward] justement

justness ['dʒʌstnɪs] N [of cause] justesse f

jut [dʒʌt] VI (also **~ out**) faire saillie, dépasser; **he saw a gun ~ting (out) from behind a wall** il a vu le canon d'un fusil dépasser de derrière un mur; **the cliff ~s (out) into the sea** la falaise avance dans la mer; **to ~ (out) over the street/the sea** surplomber la rue/la mer

Jute [dʒuːt] N Jute m

jute [dʒuːt] N jute m

Juvenal ['dʒuːvɪnəl] N Juvénal m

juvenile ['dʒuːvənaɪl] 1 N (human) adolescent(e) m(f), jeune mf; (bird, animal) jeune mf 2 ADJ a (= young) [animal] jeune b [violence, employment] des jeunes; [diabetes, arthritis] juvénile; **~ crime** délinquance f juvénile; **~ books** livres mpl pour enfants → 3; **~ lead** c (pej) [behaviour, attitude] puéril(e) m(f), juvénile 3 COMP ► **juvenile court** N (Jur) tribunal m pour enfants ► **juvenile delinquency** N délinquance f juvénile ► **juvenile delinquent** N délinquant(e) m(f) juvénile, jeune délinquant(e) m(f); **~ delinquents** l'enfance f *or* la jeunesse délinquante ► **juvenile offender** N (Jur) jeune délinquant(e) m(f)

juvenilia [,dʒuːvɪ'nɪlɪə] NPL (frm) œuvres fpl de jeunesse

juxtapose ['dʒʌkstəpəʊz] VT juxtaposer

juxtaposition [,dʒʌkstəpə'zɪʃən] N juxtaposition f; **to be in ~** se juxtaposer

K

K, k [keɪ] N **a** (= letter) K, k m ; **K for King** ≈ K comme Kléber **b** (= thousand) mille m ; **he earns 30K*** il gagne 30 000 livres **c** (Comput) **K** K m

kabala [kæˈbɑːlə] N cabale f

kabob [kəˈbɒb] N = **kebab**

kabuki [kəˈbuːkɪ] N kabuki m

Kabul [kəˈbʊl] N Kaboul

kaffeeklatsch [ˈkæfɪklætʃ] N (US) réunion de femmes qui se retrouvent régulièrement pour bavarder autour d'une tasse de café

Kaffir [ˈkæfəɪ] (pej) **1** N (pl **Kaffirs** or **Kaffir**) Cafre mf **2** ADJ cafre

Kafkaesque [ˌkæfkəˈesk] ADJ kafkaïen

kaftan [ˈkæftæn] N caf(e)tan m

kagoul(e) [kəˈguːl] N = **cagoule**

kail [keɪl] N = **kale**

Kaiser [ˈkaɪzəʳ] N Kaiser m

Kalahari [ˌkæləˈhɑːrɪ] N **~ (Desert)** (désert m du) Kalahari m

kalashnikov [kəˈlæʃnɪkɒf] N kalachnikov f

kale [keɪl] N chou m frisé

kaleidoscope [kəˈlaɪdəskəʊp] N (lit, fig) kaléidoscope m

kaleidoscopic [kəˌlaɪdəˈskɒpɪk] ADJ kaléidoscopique

Kamasutra [ˌkɑːməˈsuːtrə] N Kamasutra m

kamikaze [ˌkæmɪˈkɑːzɪ] **1** N kamikaze m **2** ADJ (lit, fig) kamikaze

Kampala [kæmˈpɑːlə] N Kampala

Kampuchea [ˌkæmpʊˈtʃɪə] N **~ (Democratic)** le Kampuchéa (démocratique)

Kampuchean [ˌkæmpʊˈtʃɪən] **1** N Kampuchéen(ne) m(f) **2** ADJ kampuchéen

Kan. ABBR = **Kansas**

Kanak [kəˈnæk] N canaque mf, kanak(e) m(f)

kangaroo [ˌkæŋgəˈruː] **1** N kangourou m ; (Austral) **to have ~s in one's top paddock*** débloquer* **2** COMP ► **kangaroo court** N (pej) tribunal m irrégulier

Kans. ABBR = **Kansas**

Kansas [ˈkænzəs] N le Kansas ; **in ~** dans le Kansas

Kantian [ˈkæntɪən] **1** N kantien(ne) m(f) **2** ADJ kantien

kaolin [ˈkeəlɪn] N kaolin m

kapok [ˈkeɪpɒk] **1** N (= material) kapok m ; (tree) fromager m **2** COMP [cushion] rembourré de kapok

Kaposi's sarcoma [kæˈpəʊsɪzəˈkəʊmə] N (Med) sarcome m de Kaposi

kaput* [kəˈpʊt] ADJ [watch, car] fichu*, kaput inv ; [plan] fichu*, foutu*:

karabiner [ˌkærəˈbiːnəʳ] N (Climbing) mousqueton m

karaoke [ˌkɑːrəˈəʊkɪ] **1** N karaoké m **2** COMP [competition, singer] de karaoké ► **karaoke bar** N bar m karaoké

karat [ˈkærət] N = **carat**

karate [kəˈrɑːtɪ] **1** N (NonC) karaté m

2 COMP ► **karate chop** N coup m de karaté (donné avec le tranchant de la main)

Kariba [kəˈriːbə] N **Lake ~** le lac Kariba

karma [ˈkɑːmə] N (Rel) karma m ; (fig) **good/ bad ~** bonnes/mauvaises vibrations fpl

kart [kɑːt] **1** N kart m **2** VI **to go ~ing** faire du karting

karting [ˈkɑːtɪŋ] N karting m

Kashmir [kæʃˈmɪəʳ] N le Cachemire

Kashmiri [kæʃˈmɪərɪ] **1** N **a** (= person) Cachemirien(ne) m(f) **b** (Ling) kashmiri m, cachemirien m **2** ADJ cachemirien

kat [kæt] N = **khat**

Kate [keɪt] N dim of **Katharine**

Katharine, Katherine [ˈkæθərɪn], **Kathleen** [ˈkæθliːn] N Catherine f

katydid [ˈkeɪtɪdɪd] N sauterelle f d'Amérique

katzenjammer* [ˈkætsənˌdʒæməʳ] N (US) **a** (= noise) tapage m **b** (= hangover) gueule f de bois*

kayak [ˈkaɪæk] N kayak m

Kazak(h) [kəˈzɑːk] **1** N **a** (= person) Kazakh(e) m(f) **b** (Ling) kazakh m **2** ADJ kazakh

Kazakhstan [ˌkɑːzɑːkˈstæn] N le Kazakhstan

kazoo [kəˈzuː] N mirliton m

KB (ABBR = **kilobyte**) Ko m

KBE [ˌkeɪbiːˈiː] N (Brit) (ABBR = **Knight of the British Empire**) titre honorifique

KC [keɪˈsiː] N **a** (Brit Jur) (ABBR = **King's Counsel**) → **counsel b** ABBR = **Kansas City**

kcal [ˈkeɪkæl] N (ABBR = **kilocalorie**) kcal

KCB [ˌkeɪsiːˈbiː] N (Brit) (ABBR = **Knight Commander of the Bath**) titre honorifique

KD [keɪˈdiː] ADJ (US Comm) (ABBR = **knocked down**) (livré) non monté

kebab [kəˈbæb] N (also **shish ~**) brochette f (de viande) ; (also **doner ~**) doner kebab m

kedge [kedʒ] (Naut) **1** N ancre f à jet **2** VT haler (sur une ancre à jet)

kedgeree [ˌkedʒəˈriː] N (Brit) kedgeree m (pilaf de poisson avec des œufs durs)

keel [kiːl] N (Naut) quille f ; **on an even ~** (Naut) dans ses lignes, à égal tirant d'eau ; (fig) stable ; (fig) **to keep sth on an even ~** maintenir qch en équilibre ; **to get back on an even ~** retrouver l'équilibre

► **keel over 1** VI **a** (Naut) chavirer **b** (* fig) [person] tourner de l'œil* **2** VT (Naut) (faire) chavirer

keelhaul [ˈkiːlhɔːl] VT (Naut) faire passer sous la quille (en guise de châtiment) ; (* fig) passer un savon à*

▼**keen¹** [kiːn] ADJ **a** (= eager) **to be ~ to do sth** or **on doing sth** tenir à faire qch ; **to be ~ for** [+ solution, referendum etc] avoir hâte de voir ; **she's ~ for a family** elle a envie d'avoir des enfants ; **he's not ~ on her coming** il ne tient pas tellement à ce qu'elle vienne ; **to be ~ for sb to do sth** or **that sb should do sth** tenir à ce que qn fasse qch ; **to await sth with ~ anticipation** attendre qch avec beaucoup d'impatience

b (= enthusiastic) [student, amateur] enthou-

siaste ; **a ~ gardener/photographer** un passionné de jardinage/de photo ; **a ~ advocate of sth** un fervent partisan de qch ; **he tried not to seem too ~** il a essayé de ne pas se montrer trop enthousiaste or de ne pas montrer trop d'enthousiasme ; **to be ~ on music/cycling** aimer beaucoup la musique/le vélo ; **to be ~ on an idea** être emballé* par une idée ; **to become** or **get ~ on sth** se passionner pour qch ; **I got quite ~ on the idea** l'idée m'a séduit ; (Brit) **to be (as) ~ as mustard*** ◊ **to be mustard ~*** déborder d'enthousiasme ; **to be mad ~ on sth*** être fou de qch

c (esp Brit*) **to be ~ on sb** être inspiré or branché* par qn, être attiré par qn ; (= sexually attracted) en pincer* pour qn ; **I'm not too ~ on him** il ne me plaît pas beaucoup

d (= acute) [desire, interest, disappointment, sense of humour, intellect, intelligence] vif ; [look, gaze, sight] perçant ; [hearing, sense of smell] fin ; **to have a ~ sense of** or **instinct for sth** avoir un sens aigu de qch ; (fig) **to have a ~ appetite for sth** avoir un vif intérêt pour qch ; **to have a ~ awareness of sth** être profondément conscient de qch, avoir une conscience vive de qch ; **to have a ~ eye** (= good eyesight) avoir la vue perçante ; **to have a ~ eye for detail** être minutieux ; **to have a ~ ear** (= good hearing) avoir l'oreille or ouïe fine ; **to have a ~ nose for sth** (= sense of smell) avoir le nez fin or du nez pour qch ; (fig) savoir flairer qch

e (= fierce) [competition] serré ; [fight] acharné **f** (= sharp) [blade, edge] tranchant ; [wind] pénétrant ; [frost] mordant ; [air] vif

g (esp Brit = competitive) [price] compétitif

h (US* = good) chouette* ; **he plays a ~ game of squash** il se défend bien au squash

keen² [kiːn] **1** N (= lament) mélopée f funèbre (irlandaise) **2** VI chanter une mélopée funèbre

keenly [ˈkiːnlɪ] ADV **a** (= intensely) [interested] vivement ; [aware] profondément ; **to feel sth ~** ressentir qch profondément **b** (= alertly) [listen, watch] très attentivement **c** (= eagerly) [awaited, anticipated] impatiemment, avec impatience **d** (= fiercely) [fight, debate] âprement ; **~ contested** vivement contesté **e** (= competitively) **~ priced** vendu à un prix compétitif

keenness [ˈkiːnnɪs] N **a** (= eagerness) volonté f ; (= haste) empressement m ; **the Government's ~ for economic reform** la volonté du gouvernement de mettre en place des réformes économiques ; **his ~ to leave** son empressement à partir **b** (= enthusiasm) [of student, supporter] enthousiasme m **c** (= acuteness) [of interest, pleasure, grief] intensité f ; [of pain] violence f, acuité f ; [of cold, wind] âpreté f ; [of hearing] finesse f ; [of intelligence, mind] finesse f, pénétration f ; **~ of sight** acuité f visuelle **d** (= sharpness) [of blade] tranchant m

keep [kiːp]

vb: pret, ptp **kept**

1 TRANSITIVE VERB	**4** COMPOUNDS
2 INTRANSITIVE VERB	**5** PHRASAL VERBS
3 NOUN	

1 TRANSITIVE VERB

When keep is part of a set combination, eg keep control/a promise/an appointment, look up the noun.

a = retain garder, conserver (*more frm*); **you can ~ this book** tu peux garder ce livre; **if that's what it costs, you can ~ it!*** à ce prix-là, vous pouvez le garder!; **you must ~ the receipt** il faut garder *or* conserver le reçu; **~ the change!** gardez la monnaie!; **to ~ one's job** garder *or* conserver son emploi; **this material will ~ its colour/softness** ce tissu garde ses couleurs/sa souplesse; **to ~ sth for o.s.** garder qch (pour soi); **I bought it for my niece but decided to ~ it for myself** je l'ai acheté pour ma nièce mais j'ai décidé de le garder (pour moi); **~ it to yourself*** garde-ça pour toi, ne le répète à personne; *BUT* **I can't ~ telephone numbers in my head** je n'arrive pas à retenir les numéros de téléphone

b = preserve, put aside garder, mettre de côté; **we're ~ing the best ones for Christmas** nous gardons *or* mettons de côté les meilleurs pour Noël; **you must ~ it in a cold place** il faut le garder *or* le conserver au froid; **I'm ~ing this champagne in case we have visitors** je garde cette bouteille de champagne (en réserve) au cas où nous aurions de la visite

c = have ready avoir; **I always ~ a blanket and a shovel in the car** j'ai toujours une couverture et une pelle dans la voiture

d Comm (= stock) faire, avoir; **we don't ~ that model any more** nous ne faisons plus *or* n'avons plus ce modèle

e = store, put ranger, mettre; **where does he ~ his passport?** où est-ce qu'il range *or* met son passeport?; **where do you ~ the sugar?** où est-ce que vous mettez *or* rangez le sucre?; **~ it somewhere safe** mettez-le en lieu sûr; *BUT* **she ~s her money under the mattress** elle cache son argent sous son matelas

f = detain retenir; **they kept him prisoner for two years** ils l'ont retenu *or* gardé prisonnier pendant deux ans; **what kept you?** qu'est-ce qui vous a retenu?; **I mustn't ~ you** je ne veux pas vous retenir *or* vous retarder; *BUT* **he was kept in hospital over night** il a dû passer une nuit à l'hôpital; **he was kept in prison for 20 years** il a passé 20 ans en prison; **they kept the prisoners in a dark room** les prisonniers étaient enfermés dans une salle sombre; **a nasty cold kept her in bed** un mauvais rhume l'a forcée à rester au lit *or* à garder le lit

g = have tenir, avoir; [+ *house, servant, dog*] avoir; [+ *pigs, bees, chickens*] élever; **he ~s a good cellar** il a une bonne cave

h = support subvenir aux besoins de; [+ *mistress*] entretenir; **you can't ~ a family on that** ça ne suffit pas pour subvenir aux besoins d'une famille *or* pour faire vivre une famille; **he kept a mistress in Manchester** il entretenait une maîtresse à Manchester; *BUT* **I have three children to ~** j'ai trois enfants à ma charge *or* à nourrir; **our garden ~s us in vegetables all summer** notre jardin nous fournit tout l'été les légumes dont nous avons besoin; **the money ~s me in beer and cigarettes** cet argent me permet d'acheter de la bière et des cigarettes

i = observe [+ *law*] observer, respecter; [+ *vow*] respecter; [+ *feast day*] célébrer; **to ~ Christmas** célébrer Noël

j [+ *accounts, diary*] tenir; **~ a note of this number, in case there's some problem** prends *or* note ce numéro, au cas où il y aurait un problème → count¹, track

k † = guard, protect protéger; **God ~ you!** que Dieu vous garde *or* protège!

l SET STRUCTURES

♦ **to keep sb at sth**: **they kept him at it all day** ils l'ont fait travailler toute la journée → keep at

♦ **to keep sth from sb** (= conceal) cacher qch à qn; **to ~ a piece of news from sb** cacher une nouvelle à qn; **I know he's ~ing something from**

me je sais qu'il me cache quelque chose

♦ **to keep sb from sth**: **the thought kept him from despair** cette pensée l'a empêché de sombrer dans le désespoir

♦ **to keep sb/sth from doing sth** (= prevent) empêcher qn/qch de faire qch; **his timidity kept him from making new friends** sa timidité l'empêchait de se faire de nouveaux amis; **a spot of oil will ~ it from going rusty** une goutte d'huile l'empêchera de rouiller; *BUT* **to ~ o.s. from doing sth** se retenir *or* s'abstenir de faire qch; **what can we do to ~ it from happening again?** que pouvons-nous faire pour que ça ne se reproduise pas?

♦ **to keep sb to sth**: **she kept him to his promise** elle l'a forcé à tenir sa promesse

♦ **to keep o.s. to o.s.** se tenir à l'écart; **she ~s herself to herself** elle n'est pas très sociable, elle ne se mêle pas aux autres; **they ~ themselves to themselves** [*group*] ils font bande à part, ils restent entre eux

♦ **to keep sb/sth** + *-ing*: **to ~ sb waiting** faire attendre qn; **he kept them working all night** il les a fait travailler toute la nuit; **~ him talking while I ...** fais-lui la conversation pendant que je ...; **we want to ~ customers coming back** nous voulons fidéliser notre clientèle; **she managed to ~ the conversation going** elle a réussi à entretenir la conversation; **he kept the engine running** il a laissé le moteur en marche

♦ **to keep ...** + *adjective*: **to ~ sth clean** tenir *or* garder qch propre; **cats ~ themselves clean** les chats sont toujours propres; **exercise will ~ you fit** l'exercice physique vous maintiendra en forme; **to ~ inflation as low as possible** maintenir l'inflation au plus bas niveau possible; **you must ~ your bedroom tidy** ta chambre doit toujours être bien rangée *or* en ordre; **~ me informed (of)** tenez-moi au courant (de); **she kept the plants watered for me** elle a arrosé mes plantes régulièrement

2 INTRANSITIVE VERB

a = continue continuer; **to ~ straight on** continuer *or* aller tout droit; **~ north till you get to ...** continuez vers le nord jusqu'à ce que vous arriviez (*subj*) à ...

b = remain rester; **she kept inside for three days** elle est restée enfermée chez elle *or* elle n'est pas sortie pendant trois jours; **~ there for a minute** restez là une minute; **to ~ in the middle of the road** rester au milieu de la route

c in health aller, se porter; **how are you ~ing?** comment allez-vous?, comment vous portez-vous?; **to ~ well** aller bien, se porter bien; **she's not ~ing very well** elle ne va pas très bien *or* elle ne se porte pas très bien

d food se garder, se conserver; **apples that ~ all winter** des pommes qui se gardent *or* se conservent tout l'hiver

e = wait attendre; **that letter will ~ until tomorrow** cette lettre peut attendre jusqu'à demain

f SET STRUCTURES

♦ **to keep** + *-ing*: **to ~ doing sth** (= continue) continuer à *or* de faire qch; (= do repeatedly) ne pas arrêter de faire qch, ne pas cesser de faire qch; **he kept walking** il a continué à *or* de marcher; **if you ~ complaining** si vous continuez à vous plaindre; **she ~s saying it was my fault** elle ne cesse de dire *or* n'arrête pas de dire que c'était de ma faute; **he kept interrupting us** il n'a pas arrêté *or* cessé de nous couper la parole; *BUT* **~ smiling!** gardez le sourire!

An adverb is often added to verbs such as oublier *and* espérer.

I ~ leaving things on the bus j'oublie constamment des choses dans le bus; **I ~ forgetting to pay the gas bill** j'oublie tout le temps de payer la facture de gaz; **I ~ hoping she'll come back** j'espère toujours qu'elle reviendra

♦ **to keep** + *preposition*: **she bit her lip to ~ from crying** elle s'est mordu la lèvre pour s'empê-

cher de pleurer; **he leaned against the wall to ~ from falling** il s'est appuyé contre le mur pour ne pas tomber; **he's promised to ~ off alcohol** il a promis de ne plus boire; **you'll save money if you ~ off the motorways** vous économiserez de l'argent si vous évitez d'utiliser les autoroutes; **"~ off the grass"** « défense de marcher sur les pelouses »; **~ on this road until you come to ...** suivez cette route jusqu'à ce que vous arriviez (*subj*) à ...; **~ to the left!** gardez votre gauche!; **to ~ to one's bed/one's room** garder le lit/la chambre; **she ~s to herself** elle n'est pas très sociable; **they ~ to themselves** [*group*] ils font bande à part, ils restent entre eux → 5

♦ **to keep** + *adjective*: **~ calm!** reste calme!; **to ~ fit** se maintenir en forme → 4; **to ~ silent** se taire, rester silencieux; **to ~ still** rester *or* se tenir tranquille

3 NOUN

a = livelihood, food **I got £30 a week and my ~** je gagnais 30 livres par semaine logé et nourri, je gagnais 30 livres par semaine plus le gîte et le couvert; **I need to give my parents money for my ~** je dois donner de l'argent à mes parents pour participer aux frais de la maison; **in a poem every word must earn its ~** dans un poème chaque mot doit avoir sa raison d'être

b of castle donjon *m*

c for ~s* pour toujours

4 COMPOUNDS

► **keep-fit** N (*Brit*) **she does ~-fit once a week** elle fait de la culture physique *or* de la gymnastique une fois par semaine; **~-fit (classes)** cours *mpl* de gymnastique; **~-fit exercises** culture *f* physique

5 PHRASAL VERBS

► **keep at** VT FUS **a** (= continue) continuer, poursuivre; (= work with persistence at) persévérer; **despite his problems he kept at his studies** malgré ses problèmes, il a poursuivi *or* continué ses études; **~ at it!** persévère!, ne baisse pas les bras!

b (= nag at) harceler; **I kept at them until they paid me** je les ai harcelés jusqu'à ce qu'ils me paient

► **keep away 1** VI (*lit*) ne pas s'approcher (from de); **~ away from the fire** ne t'approche pas du feu; **he promised to ~ away from drink** il a promis de ne plus toucher une goutte d'alcool; **~ away!** n'approchez pas!

2 VT SEP empêcher de s'approcher (from de); **the police kept the crowds away** la police a empêché la foule de s'approcher; **~ him away!** ne le laisse pas approcher!

► **keep back 1** VI ne pas approcher; **~ back!** n'approchez pas!, restez où vous êtes!

2 VT SEP **a** (= restrain) retenir; **he struggled to ~ back his tears** il retenait ses larmes à grand-peine

b (= save) mettre de côté; **~ back some of the parsley to garnish** mettez de côté *or* réservez une partie du persil pour la garniture

c (= conceal) cacher; [+ *secrets*] ne pas révéler, taire; **I'm sure he's ~ing something back** je suis sûr qu'il me (*or* nous *etc*) cache quelque chose

d [+ *crowd*] empêcher de s'approcher (from de)

► **keep down 1** VI rester à couvert; **~ down!** baissez-vous!, restez à couvert!

2 VT SEP **a** (= control) [+ *one's anger*] réprimer, contenir; [+ *dog*] retenir, maîtriser; **it's just a way to ~ women down** c'est une manière de cantonner les femmes à un statut inférieur; **you can't ~ her down** elle ne se laisse jamais abattre; **he's living proof that you can't ~ a good man down** il est la preuve vivante que quelqu'un qui en veut arrive toujours à s'en sortir!

b (= limit) [+ *inflation, costs*] maîtriser; [+ *number*] limiter; **to ~ prices down** empêcher les prix de monter; **could you ~ the noise down?** est-ce que vous pourriez faire un peu moins de bruit?

[c] (*Scol*) **to ~ a pupil down** faire redoubler une classe à un élève; **to be kept down** redoubler [d] (= *avoid vomiting*) **she drank some water but couldn't ~ it down** elle a bu de l'eau mais elle a tout vomi *or* rendu; **I can't ~ anything down** je ne peux rien garder

► **keep in** [1] VI **to ~ in with sb** rester en bons termes avec qn

[2] VT SEP [a] [+ *anger*] contenir

[b] (*Scol*) **to ~ a child in** garder un enfant en retenue, consigner un enfant; **I'm going to ~ her in till she is better** je vais la garder à la maison jusqu'à ce qu'elle soit rétablie

[c] **~ your tummy in!*** rentre le ventre!

► **keep off** [1] VI [*person*] rester à l'écart *or* à distance; **if the rain ~s off** s'il ne se met pas à pleuvoir

[2] VT SEP **cover it with cling film to ~ the flies off** recouvrez-le du film alimentaire pour le protéger des mouches; **they want to ~ young people off the streets** ils veulent qu'il n'y ait plus de jeunes qui traînent dans les rues; **~ your hands off!** pas touche!*; **he kept his hat off** il s'était découvert → **keep 2f**

► **keep on** [1] VI [a] (= *continue*) continuer; **if you ~ on like this you'll fail the exam** si tu continues comme ça, tu seras recalé à l'examen; **he kept on reading** il a continué à *or* de lire; **~ on past the church till you get to the school** continuez après l'église jusqu'à (ce que vous arriviez (*subj*) à) l'école; (*on phone*) **I'll ~ on trying** je rappellerai

[b] (*Brit* = *nag*) **don't ~ on!*** arrête donc un peu!, laisse-moi tranquille!

[2] VT SEP [a] [+ *servant, employee*] garder

[b] **to ~ one's hat on** garder son chapeau; [*man*] rester couvert → **keep 2f**

► **keep on about*** VT FUS (*Brit*) ne pas arrêter de parler de; **she ~s on about her important friends** elle n'arrête pas de parler de ses amis haut placés; **he kept on about me being selfish** il n'arrêtait pas de dire que j'étais égoïste

► **keep on at*** VT FUS (*Brit*) harceler; **she kept on at him to look for a job** elle le harcelait pour qu'il cherche du travail

► **keep out** [1] VI rester en dehors; **"~ out"** « défense d'entrer », « accès interdit »; **to ~ out of danger** rester *or* se tenir à l'abri du danger; **to ~ out of a quarrel** ne pas se mêler à une dispute; **~ out of this!** ◊ **you ~ out of it!** ne te mêle pas de ça!

[2] VT SEP [+ *person, dog*] ne pas laisser entrer, empêcher d'entrer; **that coat looks as if it will ~ out the cold** ce manteau doit bien protéger du froid

► **keep to** VT FUS [+ *promise*] tenir, être fidèle à; [+ *agreement, rules, schedule*] respecter; [+ *plan*] s'en tenir à; [+ *subject*] ne pas s'écarter de, rester dans; **his production/translation ~s close to the original text** sa mise en scène/ traduction reste fidèle au texte original; **to ~ to one's bed** garder le lit; **to ~ to a/one's diet** suivre scrupuleusement un/son régime, ne pas faire d'écart à un/son régime; **to ~ to one's ideal weight** rester *or* se maintenir à son poids idéal → **keep 1l** and **2f**

► **keep together** [1] VI [*people*] ne pas se séparer, rester ensemble; **~ together!** ne vous séparez pas, restez ensemble!

[2] VT SEP [+ *objects*] garder ensemble; (= *keep fixed together*) maintenir ensemble; [+ *team, group*] maintenir la cohésion de, souder; **it's been hard to ~ the team together** ça n'a pas été facile de souder l'équipe

► **keep under** VT SEP [+ *people, race*] assujettir; [+ *subordinates*] dominer; [+ *unruly pupils etc*] se faire obéir de, mater

► **keep up** [1] VI [a] [*prices*] se maintenir; **their spirits are ~ing up** ils ne se découragent pas, ils ne se laissent pas abattre; **I hope the good weather will ~ up** j'espère que le beau temps va

continuer *or* se maintenir; **they went so fast I couldn't ~ up** ils allaient si vite que je n'arrivais pas à suivre

[b] **to ~ up with sb** (*in race, walk etc*) aller aussi vite que qn; (*in work, achievement*) se maintenir au niveau de qn; (*in comprehension*) suivre qn; **he went so fast I couldn't ~ up with him** il allait si vite que je n'arrivais pas à le suivre; **I couldn't ~ up with what he was saying** je n'ai pas pu suivre ce qu'il disait; **to ~ up with the class** se maintenir au niveau de la classe; **the company has failed to ~ up with the times** la société n'a pas réussi à évoluer; **to ~ up with demand** parvenir à satisfaire la demande; **wage increases have not kept up with inflation** les hausses de salaires n'ont pas suivi le taux d'inflation → **Joneses**

[c] (= *stay friends with*) **to ~ up with sb** rester en relations avec qn, garder le contact avec qn

[2] VT SEP [a] [+ *pressure, standards, subscription*] maintenir; [+ *correspondence*] entretenir; [+ *study*] continuer; **I try to ~ up my German** j'essaie d'entretenir mon allemand; **I couldn't ~ the diet up for more than a week** je n'ai pas réussi à suivre ce régime pendant plus d'une semaine; **they can no longer ~ the payments up** ils n'arrivent plus à payer les traites; **they kept up a constant barrage of criticism** ils ont opposé un flot ininterrompu de critiques; **to ~ up a custom** maintenir *or* perpétuer une tradition; **~ it up!** continuez!

[b] (= *maintain*) [+ *house, paintwork*] entretenir, maintenir en bon état

keeper ['ki:pər] N (*in museum*) conservateur *m*, -trice *f*; (*in park, zoo*) gardien *m*; (*also* **keeper**) garde-chasse *m*; (*also* **goalkeeper**) gardien(ne) *m(f)* (de but); (*Bible*) **am I my brother's ~?** suis-je le gardien de mon frère?; (*fig*) **I'm not his ~** je ne suis pas responsable de lui → **beekeeper, goalkeeper, shopkeeper**

keeping ['ki:pɪŋ] N (*NonC*) [a] (= *care*) garde *f*; **to put sb in sb's ~** confier qn à (la garde de) qn; **to put sth in sb's ~** confier qch à qn → **safekeeping** [b] (= *observing*) [of *rule*] observation *f*; [of *festival etc*] célébration *f* [c] **to be in ~ with** [+ *regulation, law, image*] être conforme à, correspondre à; [+ *status, tradition*] être conforme à; [+ *character*] correspondre à; [+ *surroundings, area*] être en harmonie avec; **to be out of ~ with** [+ *image, character*] ne pas correspondre à; [+ *status, tradition*] ne pas être conforme à; [+ *surroundings, area*] détonner dans

keepsake ['ki:pseɪk] N souvenir *m* (*objet*)

keester: ['ki:stər] N = **keister**

keg [keg] N [a] (= *barrel*) [of *beer, brandy etc*] tonnelet *m*, baril *m*; [of *fish*] caque *f* [b] (*also* **~ beer**) bière *f* en tonneau

keister: ['ki:stər] N (*US*) (= *buttocks*) derrière *m*, postérieur* *m*; (= *case*) mallette *f*

keks: [keks] NPL (*Brit*) falzar* *m*

kelly-green ['kelɪ'gri:n] ADJ, N (*US*) vert pomme *m inv*

kelp [kelp] N (*NonC*) varech *m*

ken [ken] [1] N **that is beyond** *or* **outside my ~** ça dépasse mes capacités d'entendement [2] VT (*Scot*) = **know**

Ken. ABBR = **Kentucky**

kendo ['kendəʊ] N kendo *m*

kennel ['kenl] N [a] [of *dog*] niche *f*; (*fig pej*) chenil *m* (*fig*), tanière *f* (*fig*); **~s** (for *breeding*) élevage *m* (de chiens), chenil *m*; (for *boarding*) chenil *m*; **to put a dog in ~s** mettre un chien dans un chenil [b] [of *fox*] repaire *m*, tanière *f*

Kentucky [ken'tʌkɪ] N le Kentucky; **in ~** dans le Kentucky

Kenya ['kenjə] N le Kenya; **Mount ~** le mont Kenya

Kenyan ['kenjən] [1] N Kényan(ne) *m(f)* [2] ADJ kényan

kepi ['keɪpɪ] N képi *m*

kept [kept] VB (*pret, ptp of* **keep**) **a ~ man/ woman†** un homme/une femme entretenu(e)

keratin ['kerətɪn] N kératine *f*

kerb [kɜ:b] (*Brit*) [1] N [a] [of *pavement*] (bordure *f or* bord *m* du) trottoir *m*; **along the ~** le long du trottoir; **to pull into the ~** s'arrêter (le long du trottoir); **to hit the ~** [*car*] heurter le trottoir [b] (*St Ex*) **on the ~** en coulisse, après la clôture (*de la Bourse*) [2] COMP ► **kerb broker** N (*St Ex*) courtier *m* en valeurs mobilières ► **kerb crawler** N dragueur* *m* motorisé, conducteur *m* qui accoste les femmes sur le trottoir ► **kerb crawling** N (*NonC*) drague* *f* en voiture ► **kerb drill** N **to learn one's ~ drill** apprendre à traverser la rue (en toute sécurité) ► **kerb market** N (*St Ex*) marché *m* hors-cote, coulisse† *f*

kerbstone ['kɜ:bstəʊn] N bordure *f* de trottoir

kerchief† ['kɜ:tʃɪf] N fanchon *f*, fichu *m*

kerfuffle* [kə'fʌfl] N (*Brit*) histoire* *f*; **what a ~!** quelle histoire!*, que d'histoires!*

kernel ['kɜ:nl] N [a] [of *nut, fruit stone*] amande *f*; (= *seed*) grain *m*; (*fig*) **there's a ~ of truth in what he says** il y a un grain de vérité dans ce qu'il dit [b] (*Ling, Comput*) noyau *m*; (*Ling*) **~ sentence** phrase-noyau *f*

kerosene ['kerəsi:n] [1] N [a] (= *aircraft fuel*) kérosène *m* [b] (*US: for stoves, lamps*) pétrole *m* (lampant) [2] COMP ► **kerosene lamp** N lampe *f* à pétrole

kestrel ['kestrəl] N crécerelle *f*

ketch [ketʃ] N ketch *m*

ketchup ['ketʃəp] N ketchup *m*

kettle ['ketl] N [a] (for *water. US: also* **tea-kettle**) bouilloire *f*; **the ~'s boiling** l'eau bout (dans la bouilloire); **I'll just put the ~ on (for some tea)** je vais mettre l'eau à chauffer (pour le thé) [b] (*also* **fish ~**) poissonnière *f*; (*fig*) **that's a fine** *or* **a pretty ~ of fish** quel micmac!*; (*fig*) **that's another** *or* **a different ~ of fish** c'est une autre paire de manches*

kettledrum ['ketldrʌm] N (*Mus*) timbale *f*

key [ki:] [1] N [a] (for *lock*) clé *or* clef *f*; **to turn the ~ (in the door)** donner un tour de clé (dans la serrure); **leave the ~ in the door** laisse la clé sur la porte → **latchkey, lock¹, master** [b] [of *clock*] clé *f or* clef *f* (de pendule), remontoir *m*; [of *clockwork toy etc*] remontoir *m*; (*Tech*) clé *f* de serrage *or* à écrous [c] (*fig: to problem etc*) clé *f or* clef *f*; **he holds the ~ to the mystery** il détient la clé du mystère; **the ~ to understanding his behaviour is ...** la clé pour comprendre son comportement, c'est ..., l'explication de son comportement, c'est ...; **the ~ to ending this recession** la solution pour mettre fin à la récession [d] (= *answers*) solutions *fpl*; (*Scol*) corrigé *m*; (= *explanation*) (for *map, diagram etc*) légende *f*; (*to symbols, abbreviations*) liste *f* [e] [of *piano, computer, typewriter etc*] touche *f*; [of *wind instrument*] clé *f or* clef *f* → **function** [f] (*Mus*) ton *m*; **to be in/off ~** être/ne pas être dans le ton; **to go off ~** sortir du ton; **to sing in/off ~** chanter juste/faux; **to play in/off ~** jouer juste/faux; **that note was off ~** cette note était fausse; **in the ~ of C/D** *etc* en do/ré *etc*; **in the major ~** en mode majeur; **change of ~** changement *m* de ton → **low¹, minor**

[2] ADJ (= *crucial*) [*person, job, component, issue etc*] clé *inv*

[3] VT [a] (*Comput, Typ: also* **~ in** *or* **up**) [+ *text, data*] saisir

[b] **to ~ one's speech to** *or* **for one's audience** adapter son discours à son auditoire; **the colour scheme was ~ed to brown** les coloris s'harmonisaient autour du brun

[4] COMP ► **key money** N pas *m* de porte (*fig*) ► **key punch** N (*Comput*) perforatrice *f* à clavier ► **key ring** N porte-clés *m inv* ► **key**

signature N (Mus) armature f
► **key in** VT SEP (Comput, Typ) = **key 3a**
► **key up** VT SEP [a] = **key 3a** [b] (fig) (= excite) surexciter ; (= make tense) tendre ; **she was (all) ~ed up about the interview** elle était excitée or tendue à la perspective de l'entrevue

keyboard ['ki:bɔ:d] [1] N (of piano, computer, typewriter etc) clavier m [2] VT (Comput, Typ) saisir [3] **keyboards** NPL (Mus) (instrument m à) clavier m électronique, synthétiseur m ; **he's on ~s** il est aux claviers or au synthétiseur [4] COMP ► **keyboard instruments** NPL (Mus) instruments mpl à clavier ► **keyboard operator** N (Comput) = **keyboarder** ► **keyboard player** N (Mus) **he's a ~ player** il joue du piano (or clavecin etc) ► **keyboard skills** NPL (Comput) compétences fpl de claviste

keyboarder ['ki:bɔ:də'] N (Comput) opérateur m, -trice f de saisie, claviste mf

keyboardist ['ki:bɔ:dɪst] N (Mus) joueur m, -euse f de synthétiseur

keyhole ['ki:həʊl] [1] N trou m de serrure ; **through the ~** par le trou de la serrure [2] COMP ► **keyhole saw** N scie f à guichet ► **keyhole surgery** N (Med) chirurgie f endoscopique

keying ['ki:ɪŋ] N saisie f (de données)

keynote ['ki:nəʊt] [1] N (Mus) tonique f ; (fig = main theme) (of speech, policy) idée-force f [2] COMP ► **keynote speaker** N (Pol etc) orateur m principal ► **keynote speech** N discours-programme m

keynoter ['ki:nəʊtə'] N (US) = **keynote speaker** ; → **keynote**

keypad ['ki:pæd] N (Comput) pavé m numérique

keystone ['ki:stəʊn] [1] N (Archit, fig) clé f or clef f de voûte [2] COMP ► **the Keystone State** N (US) la Pennsylvanie

keystroke ['ki:strəʊk] N (Typ, Comput) frappe f

keyword ['ki:wɜ:d] N mot-clé m

Kg (ABBR = kilogram(s)) kg

KGB [keɪdʒi:'bi:] N (in former USSR) KGB m

khaki ['ka:kɪ] [1] ADJ kaki inv [2] N kaki m

Khartoum [ka:'tu:m] N Khartoum

khat [kæt] N qat m or khat m

Khmer [kmeə'] [1] ADJ khmer (khmère f) [2] N [a] Khmer m, Khmère f [b] (Ling) khmer m, cambodgien m [3] COMP ► **Khmer Republic** N République f khmère ► **Khmer Rouge** N Khmer m rouge

Khyber Pass [,kaɪbə'pɑ:s] N passe f de Khyber or Khaybar

kHz ABBR = kilohertz

kibbutz [kɪ'bʊts] N (pl **kibbutzim** [kɪ'bʊtsɪm]) kibboutz m

kibitz* ['kɪbɪts] VI (US) (Cards) regarder le jeu de quelqu'un par-dessus son épaule ; (fig) mettre son grain de sel*

kibitzer* ['kɪbɪtsə'] N (US) (Cards) spectateur m, -trice f (qui regarde le jeu de quelqu'un par-dessus son épaule) ; (= busybody) mouche f du coche ; (pej = disruptive wisecracker) petit malin m, petite maligne f

kibosh: ['kaɪbɒʃ] N **to put the ~ on sth** mettre le holà à qch

kick [kɪk] [1] N [a] (= action) coup m de pied ; **to give the door a ~** donner un coup de pied dans la porte ; **to get a ~ on the leg** recevoir un coup de pied à la jambe ; **to aim** or **take a ~ at sb/sth** lancer un coup de pied à qn/qch or dans la direction de qn/qch ; **he needs a ~ up the backside:** il a besoin d'un bon coup de pied au cul: ; **to give sb a ~ in the pants*** botter* le derrière à or de qn ; **this refusal was a ~ in the teeth for her** ce refus lui a fait l'effet d'une gifle ; **~-free**
[b] (* = thrill, excitement) **I get a ~ out of it** je trouve ça stimulant or excitant ; **she got quite a ~ out of seeing Paris** elle a été tout

émoustillée or excitée de voir Paris ; **he gets a ~ out of making his sister cry** il prend un malin plaisir à faire pleurer sa sœur ; **he did it for ~s** il l'a fait pour se marrer* or pour rigoler*
[c] (* = zest, punch) **a drink with plenty of ~ in it** une boisson qui vous donne un coup de fouet ; **an old man with plenty of ~ left in him** un vieil homme encore plein de punch*
[d] (of gun) recul m ; (Aut) **a ~ of the starting handle** un retour de manivelle
[e] (fig) **he's on a fishing ~ now** son truc* en ce moment c'est la pêche
[f] (Ftbl etc) **he's a good ~*** il a un bon dégagement

[2] VI [a] (person) donner or lancer un coup de pied ; (footballer etc) shooter ; (baby) (in womb) donner des coups de pied ; (after birth) gigoter* ; (horse) ruer ; **to ~ at sb/sth** (person) lancer un coup de pied à qn/qch or en direction de qn/qch ; (horse) lancer une ruade à qn/qch or en direction de qn/qch → **2b** ; (Rugby) **to ~ for touch** chercher la touche ; (fig) **to ~ against the pricks** regimber en pure perte ; (fig) **to ~ over the traces** ruer dans les brancards (fig)
[b] (* = object to sth) ruer dans les brancards, se rebiffer* ; **to ~ (out) at** or **against sth** se rebiffer contre qch*
[c] (gun) reculer

[3] VT [a] (person) (gen) donner un coup de pied à ; (+ ball) donner un coup de pied à, botter ; (horse) lancer une ruade à ; **she ~ed him in the face/head/shin/stomach** elle lui a donné un coup de pied au visage/à la tête/dans le tibia/dans le ventre ; **to ~ one's legs in the air** (baby) gigoter ; **to ~ sb's bottom** botter* le derrière or les fesses à or de qn ; (Ftbl etc) **to ~ a goal** marquer un but ; (Rugby) **to ~ the ball into touch** botter en touche ; **I could have ~ed myself*** je me serais giflé ; (fig) **to ~ sb in the teeth*** faire un coup vache* à qn ; (fig) **to ~ sb when he's (or she's) down*** frapper qn à terre ; **to ~ sb downstairs** (lit) faire descendre qn à coups de pied dans le derrière ; (fig) rétrograder qn ; **to ~ sb upstairs** (lit) faire monter qn à coups de pied dans le derrière ; (* fig) catapulter or bombarder* qn à un poste supérieur (pour s'en débarrasser) ; (Brit Pol*) catapulter qn à la Chambre des lords (un député dont on ne veut plus aux Communes) ; (esp US, fig) **I'm going to ~ (some) ass::** il y a des coups de pied au cul qui se perdent:: ; **to ~** (Brit) or **~ up** (US) **one's heels*** (= wait around) faire le pied de grue, poireauter* ; **to ~ the bucket:** (= die) casser sa pipe:
[b] (= stop) **to ~ the habit** (gen) arrêter ; (smoker) arrêter de fumer ; (drug addict) décrocher*

[4] COMP ► **kick boxing** N boxe f française ► **kick-off** N (Ftbl etc) coup m d'envoi ; (* fig = start) (of meeting, ceremony etc) démarrage* m ; (Ftbl) **the ~-off is at 3pm** le coup d'envoi est à 15 h ; (fig) **when's the ~-off?*** à quelle heure ça démarre ?* ; (fig) **for a ~-off*** d'abord, pour commencer ► **kick pleat** N (Sewing) pli m d'aisance ► **kick-stand** N (of motorcycle, bicycle) béquille f ► **kick-start** VT (+ motorcycle) démarrer au pied ; (fig) (+ economy) donner un coup de fouet à ; (+ negotiations, process) relancer ► **kick starter** N (of motorcycle) démarreur m au pied, kick m ► **kick turn** N (Ski) conversion f

► **kick about, kick around** [1] VI: (books, clothes etc) traîner ; (person) traîner, traînasser (pej) [2] VT SEP **to ~ a ball about** or **around** jouer au ballon, s'amuser avec un ballon ; (fig) **don't ~ that book about** or **around** ne maltraite pas ce livre ; (= mistreat) **to ~ sb around** traiter qn sans ménagement, malmener qn ; (fig) **to ~ an idea around*** (reflecting) tourner et retourner une idée ; (discussing) débattre une idée

► **kick away** VT SEP [a] (+ object on ground) repousser du pied [b] **he ~ed away the last part of the fence** il a démoli à coups de pied ce

qui restait de la clôture

► **kick back** [1] VI (engine) avoir un retour de manivelle [2] VT SEP [a] (+ ball etc) renvoyer (du pied) [b] (+ money) ristourner [3] **~back** N → **kickback**

► **kick down** VT SEP (+ door) enfoncer à coups de pied ; (+ hedge, barrier) démolir à coups de pied

► **kick in** [1] VT SEP [a] (+ door) enfoncer à coups de pied ; **to ~ sb's teeth in*** casser la figure* or la gueule: à qn [b] (US = contribute) cracher*, abouler: [2] VI (* = begin, take effect) (drug) commencer à agir ; (mechanism, generator) entrer en action

► **kick off** [1] VI (Ftbl) donner le coup d'envoi ; (* fig) démarrer* ; **the party ~ed off in great style** la soirée a démarré en beauté [2] VT SEP enlever (du pied or d'un coup de pied) [3] **~- off** N → **kick**

► **kick out** [1] VI (horse) ruer ; **the man ~ed out at his assailants** l'homme envoyait de grands coups de pied à ses assaillants ; (fig) **to ~ out against one's lot/society** etc se révolter contre son sort/la société etc → **kick 2b** [2] VT SEP (lit) chasser à coups de pied, flanquer* dehors ; (* fig) flanquer* dehors or à la porte

► **kick up** VT SEP (+ dust) faire voler ; (fig) **to ~ up a row*** or **a din*** or **a racket*** faire du chahut or du tapage or du boucan* ; **to ~ up a fuss*** faire des histoires or toute une histoire ; **he ~ed up a stink: about it** il en a fait tout un plat* or tout un foin:: → **kick 3a**

kickback* ['kɪkbæk] N (= reaction) réaction f, contrecoup m ; (= bribe) pot-de-vin m ; (= rebate on sale) ristourne f, rabais m

kicker ['kɪkə'] N (Rugby) botteur m

kicky* ['kɪkɪ] ADJ excitant, palpitant

kid [kɪd] [1] N [a] (= goat) chevreau m, chevrette f
[b] (NonC = leather) chevreau m (NonC)
[c] * (= child) gosse* mf, gamin(e)* m(f) ; (= teenager) (petit(e)) jeune m(f) ; **when I was a ~** quand j'étais gosse* ; **that's ~'s stuff** (= easy to do) un gamin* or un gosse* saurait faire ça ; (= suitable for children) c'est bon pour des gosses* ; **hi, ~!** salut mon vieux (or ma vieille) ! ; (US) **to be like a ~ in a candy store** être aux anges
[2] VT* **to ~ sb** faire marcher qn* ; **no ~ding!** sans blague !* ; **you can't ~ me** tu ne me la feras pas* ; **I ~ you not** je te jure ; **who are you trying to ~?** à qui tu veux faire croire ça ? ; **to ~ o.s.** se faire des illusions, se fourrer le doigt dans l'œil ; **to ~ o.s. that ...** s'imaginer que ...
[3] VI (*: also ~ on) raconter des blagues* ; **he's just ~ding (on)** il te (or nous etc) fait marcher* ; **I was only ~ding (on)** j'ai dit ça pour plaisanter or pour rigoler*
[4] COMP ► **kid brother*** N petit frère m ► **kid gloves** NPL gants mpl de chevreau ; (fig) **to handle with ~ gloves** (+ person) ménager, prendre des gants avec* ; (+ subject) traiter avec précaution ► **kid sister*** N petite sœur f
► **kid on** [1] VI = **kid 3** [2] VT SEP [a] **to ~ sb on** faire marcher qn*, raconter des blagues à qn* [b] (= pretend) **he was ~ding on that he was hurt** il faisait semblant d'être blessé

kiddy* ['kɪdɪ] N gosse* mf, gamin(e)* m(f)

kidnap ['kɪdnæp] VT kidnapper, enlever

kidnapper, kidnaper (US) ['kɪdnæpə'] N kidnappeur m, -euse f, ravisseur m, -euse f

kidnapping, kidnaping (US) ['kɪdnæpɪŋ] N enlèvement m, kidnapping m, rapt m

kidney ['kɪdnɪ] [1] N (Anat) rein m ; (Culin) rognon m ; (fig) **of the same ~** du même acabit [2] COMP (disease etc) rénal, de(s) reins ► **kidney bean** N haricot m rouge or de Soissons ► **kidney dish** N haricot m ► **kidney donor** N donneur m, -euse f de rein(s) ► **kidney machine** N (Med) rein m artificiel ; **to be on a ~ machine** être sous rein artificiel or en (hémo)dialyse ► **kidney-shaped** ADJ en forme de haricot ► **kidney**

specialist N néphrologue *mf* ► **kidney stone** N calcul *m* rénal ► **kidney transplant** N greffe *f* du rein, transplantation *f* rénale

kidology* [kɪˈdɒlədʒɪ] N (*Brit*) bluff *m*

Kiel [kiːl] N ~ **Canal** canal *m* de Kiel

kike⁝ [kaɪk] N (*esp US pej*) youpin(e)⁝ *m(f)* (*pej*)

Kilimanjaro [ˌkɪlɪmənˈdʒɑːrəʊ] N **Mount ~** le Kilimandjaro

kill [kɪl] **1** N **a** (*at bullfight, hunt*) mise *f* à mort; **the wolves gathered round for the ~** les loups se sont rassemblés pour tuer leur proie; **the tiger had made a ~** le tigre avait tué; **to move in for the ~** (*lit*) s'approcher pour la curée; (*fig*) guetter le dénouement; (*fig*) **to be in at the ~** = assister au dénouement; (*for unpleasant event*) assister au coup de grâce (*fig*) **b** (*NonC: Hunting = animals killed*) pièces *fpl* tuées, tableau *m* de chasse; **the lion dragged his ~ over to the trees** le lion a traîné (le cadavre de) sa proie sous les arbres

2 VT **a** (= *murder*) assassiner; (= *gun down*) abattre; [+ *animal*] tuer; (*Hunting, Shooting: also in slaughterhouse*) abattre; **the earthquake ~ed five people** le tremblement de terre a fait cinq morts; **the shock ~ed her** c'est le choc qui l'a tuée; **the frost has ~ed my trees** le gel a tué *or* a fait mourir mes arbres; **to be ~ed in action/battle** tomber au champ d'honneur/au combat; **thou shalt not ~** tu ne tueras point ∎ (*PROV*) **to ~ two birds with one stone** faire d'une pierre deux coups (*PROV*); (*hum*) **it was ~ or cure** c'était un remède de cheval* (*fig*)

b (*fig*) [+ *parliamentary bill*] couler; [+ *proposal, attempt*] faire échouer; (*Press etc*) [+ *paragraph, line*] (faire) supprimer; [+ *story*] interdire la publication de; [+ *rumour*] étouffer, mettre fin à; [+ *pain*] supprimer; [+ *feeling, hope*] détruire; [+ *flavour, smell*] tuer; [+ *sound*] étouffer; [+ *engine, motor*] arrêter; **to ~ time** tuer le temps; **to ~* a bottle of whisky** liquider* une bouteille de whisky

c * **to ~ o.s. with work** se tuer au travail; **to ~ sb with kindness** accabler qn de prévenances; **he certainly wasn't ~ing himself** le moins qu'on puisse dire c'est qu'il ne se surmenait pas; (*iro*) **don't ~ yourself!** surtout ne te surmène pas! (*iro*); **I'll do it (even) if it ~s me** je le ferai même si je dois y laisser ma peau; **this heat is ~ing me** cette chaleur me tue *or* me crève*; **my feet are ~ing me** j'ai un de ces* mal aux pieds; **she was ~ing herself (laughing)** elle était morte de rire, elle était pliée en deux de rire; **this will ~ you!** tu vas (mourir de) rire! → **dressed**

3 VI [*cancer, drugs, drink etc*] tuer

► **kill off** VT SEP [+ *people*] tuer; [+ *weeds, disease, bacteria, infection*] éliminer; [+ *parliamentary bill*] couler

killer [ˈkɪləʳ] **1** N tueur *m*, -euse *f*; (= *murderer*) assassin *m*, meurtrier *m*, -ière *f*; **diphtheria was once a ~** autrefois la diphtérie tuait; (*fig*) **it's a ~*** (= *hard work*) c'est tuant; (= *very funny*) c'est tordant*; (= *very impressive*) c'est terrible* *or* formidable → **ladykiller 2** COMP ► **killer disease** N (*gen*) maladie *f* mortelle; (= *epidemic*) maladie *f* meurtrière ► **killer instinct** N (*lit*) instinct *m* de meurtre; (*fig*) **he's got the ~ instinct** c'est un battant; **he lacks the ~ instinct** il manque d'agressivité ► **killer satellite** N (*Mil*) satellite-chasseur *m* ► **killer whale** N épaulard *m*, orque *f*

killing [ˈkɪlɪŋ] **1** N [*of person*] meurtre *m*; [*of people, group*] tuerie *f*, massacre *m*; [*of animal*] (*Hunting*) mise *f* à mort; (*at abattoir*) abattage *m*; **the ~ of stags is forbidden** il est interdit de tuer les cerfs; **the ~ sickened him of war** toute cette tuerie lui fit prendre la guerre en horreur; (*fig: in buying and selling*) **to make a ~** réussir un beau coup **2** ADJ **a** [*blow, disease,*

shot] meurtrier **b** (* = *exhausting*) [*work*] tuant, crevant* **3** COMP ► **killing fields** NPL charniers *mpl*

killingly [ˈkɪlɪŋlɪ] ADV ~ **funny** crevant*, tordant*; **it was ~ funny** c'était crevant* *or* tordant*, c'était à mourir de rire

killjoy [ˈkɪldʒɔɪ] N rabat-joie *mf inv*

kiln [kɪln] N four *m*; **pottery ~** four *m* céramique → **lime¹**

Kilner jar® [ˈkɪlnəˌdʒɑːʳ] N (*Brit*) bocal *m* à conserves

kilo [ˈkiːləʊ] N (ABBR = **kilogram(me)**) kilo *m*

kiloampère [ˈkɪləʊˌæmpeəʳ] N kiloampère *m*

kilobar [ˈkɪləˌbɑːʳ] N kilobar *m*

kilobyte [ˈkɪləʊˌbaɪt] N (*Comput*) kilo-octet *m*

kilocalorie [ˈkɪləʊˌkælərɪ] N kilocalorie *f*

kilocycle [ˈkɪləʊˌsaɪkl] N kilocycle *m*

kilogram(me) [ˈkɪləʊˌɡræm] N kilogramme *m*

kilohertz [ˈkɪləʊˌhɜːts] N (*pl inv*) kilohertz *m*

kilolitre, kiloliter (*US*) [ˈkɪləʊˌliːtəʳ] N kilolitre *m*

kilometre, kilometer (*US*) [ˈkɪləʊˌmiːtəʳ, kɪˈlɒmətəʳ] N kilomètre *m*; **it is 5 ~s to the nearest town** la ville la plus proche est à 5 kilomètres

kilometric [ˌkɪləʊˈmetrɪk] ADJ kilométrique

kiloton [ˈkɪləʊˌtʌn] N kilotonne *f*

kilovolt [ˈkɪləʊˌvəʊlt] N kilovolt *m*

kilowatt [ˈkɪləʊwɒt] **1** N kilowatt *m* **2** COMP ► **kilowatt-hour** N kilowattheure *m*

kilt [kɪlt] N kilt *m*

kilted [ˈkɪltɪd] ADJ [*man*] en kilt; **~ skirt** kilt *m*

kilter [ˈkɪltəʳ] N **out of ~** détraqué, déglingué*; **out of ~ with** déphasé par rapport à

kimono [kɪˈməʊnəʊ] N kimono *m*

kin [kɪn] N (*NonC*) parents *mpl*, famille *f* → **kith, next**

▼ **kind** [kaɪnd] **1** N **a** (= *class, variety, sort, type*) genre *m*, type *m*, sorte *f*; (= *make*) [*of car, coffee etc*] marque *f*; **this ~ of book** ce genre de livre; **books of all ~s** des livres de tous genres *or* de toutes sortes; **this ~ of thing** ce genre *or* ce type de chose; **what ~ of flour do you want? — the ~ you gave me last time** quelle sorte *or* quel type de farine voulez-vous? — celle que vous m'avez donnée la dernière fois; **what ~ do you want?** vous en voulez de quelle sorte?; **what ~ of car is it?** quelle marque de voiture est-ce?; **what ~ of dog is he?** qu'est-ce que c'est comme (race de) chien?; **what ~ of man is he?** quel genre *or* quel type d'homme est-ce?; **he is not the ~ of man to refuse** ce n'est pas le genre d'homme à refuser, il n'est pas homme à refuser; **he's not that ~ of person** ce n'est pas son genre; **I'm not that ~ of girl!*** (*gen*) ce n'est pas mon genre!; (*refusing sb's advances*) pour qui me prenez-vous?; **that's the ~ of person I am** c'est comme ça que je suis (fait); **what ~ of people does he think we are?** (mais enfin,) pour qui nous prend-il?; **what ~ of a fool does he take me for?** (non mais*,) il me prend pour un imbécile!; **what ~ of behaviour is this?** qu'est-ce que c'est que cette façon de se conduire?; **what ~ of an answer do you call that?** vous appelez ça une réponse?; **classical music is the ~ she likes most** c'est la musique classique qu'elle préfère; **and all that ~ of thing** et tout ça*; **you know the ~ of thing I mean** vous voyez (à peu près) ce que je veux dire; **I don't like that ~ of talk** je n'aime pas ce genre de propos; **he's the ~ that will cheat** il est du genre à tricher; **I know his ~!*** je connais ce genre de type; **your ~ never do any good*** il n'y a rien de bon à tirer de gens de votre espèce; **he's not my ~*** (*gen*) je n'aime pas les gens de son genre *or* de son espèce; (*sexually*) ce n'est pas mon genre d'homme; **it's my ~* of film** c'est le genre de film que j'aime *or* qui me plaît

b (*in phrases*) **something of the ~** quelque

chose de ce genre *or* d'approchant; **this is wrong — nothing of the ~!** c'est faux — pas le moins du monde *or* absolument pas!; **I shall do nothing of the ~!** je n'en ferai rien!, certainement pas!; **I will have nothing of the ~!** je ne tolérerai pas cela!; (*pej*) **it was beef of a ~** c'était quelque chose qui pouvait passer pour du bœuf; **it was an apology of a ~** ça pouvait ressembler à une excuse; **the cease-fire brought peace of a ~** le cessez-le-feu a introduit une certaine paix

c **a ~ of** une sorte *or* une espèce de, un genre de; **there was a ~ of box in the middle of the room** il y avait une sorte *or* une espèce de boîte au milieu de la pièce; **there was a ~ of tinkling sound** on entendait quelque chose qui ressemblait à un bruit de grelot; **in a ~ of way I'm sorry** d'une certaine façon je le regrette; **I had a ~ of fear that ...*** ◊ **I was ~ of frightened that ...*** j'avais comme peur que ... + ne (+ *subj*) je ne sais assez ça; **I ~ of* like that** j'aime assez ça; **I ~ of* thought that he would come** j'avais dans l'idée qu'il viendrait; **he was ~ of* worried-looking** il avait l'air un peu inquiet, il avait l'air comme qui dirait* inquiet; **it's ~ of* blue** c'est plutôt bleu; **aren't you pleased? — ~ of!*** tu n'es pas content? — si, assez!

d (= *race, species*) genre *m*, espèce *f*; **they differ in ~** ils sont de genres différents *or* de natures différentes; **they're two of a ~** ils sont du même genre; (*pej*) ils sont du même acabit; **this painting is perfect of/the only one of its ~** ce tableau est parfait dans/unique en son genre → **humankind, mankind**

e (*NonC = goods as opposed to money*) nature *f*; **to pay/payment in ~** payer/paiement *m* en nature; (*fig*) **I shall repay you in ~** (*after good deed*) je vous revaudrai ça; (*after bad deed*) je vous rendrai la monnaie de votre pièce

2 ADJ **a** (= *caring, helpful*) [*person, remark, smile*] gentil; [*gesture*] aimable; [*face, voice*] doux (douce *f*), affable; **to be ~ to sb** [*person*] être gentil avec qn; **to be ~ to sb/sth** [*photograph, lighting*] montrer qn/qch à son avantage; [*clothes*] avantager qn/qch; **to be ~ to animals** être bon avec les animaux; **that's very ~ of you** c'est très gentil *or* (*more frm*) aimable (à vous *or* de votre part); **life has been ~ to me** j'ai eu de la chance dans la vie, j'ai eu la vie belle; **life has not been ~ to me** la vie ne l'a pas gâtée; **to have a ~ heart** avoir bon cœur → **soul**

b (= *charitable*) [*person*] gentil; [*comments*] aimable; [*thought*] délicat, attentionné; **he was very ~ about me** il a dit des choses très gentilles *or* aimables sur moi; **the critics were not ~ to the film** les critiques n'ont pas été tendres avec le film; **the ~est thing that can be said about him is that ...** ce qu'on peut en dire de plus aimable, c'est que ...

c (*in polite formulae*) **he was ~ enough to write to me** il a eu la gentillesse de m'écrire; **please be ~ enough to ...** ◊ veuillez avoir la gentillesse de ... (*frm*); **would you be ~ enough to ...?** ◊ would you be so ~ as to ...? voudriez-vous avoir la gentillesse *or* l'amabilité de ...? (*frm*)

d (= *not harmful*) doux (douce *f*); **a washing-up liquid that is ~ to your hands** un produit à vaisselle qui n'abîme pas vos mains *or* qui est doux pour vos mains

3 COMP ► **kind-hearted** ADJ bon, qui a bon cœur ► **kind-heartedness** N bonté *f*, grand cœur *m*

kinda* [ˈkaɪndə] = **kind of**; → **kind**

kindergarten [ˈkɪndəˌɡɑːtn] N (*gen*) jardin *m* d'enfants; (*state-run*) (école *f*) maternelle *f*; **she's in ~ now** elle est en maternelle maintenant

kindle [ˈkɪndl] **1** VT [+ *fire*] allumer; [+ *wood*] enflammer; (*fig*) [+ *passion, desire*] allumer, enflammer; [+ *enthusiasm, interest*] susciter; [+ *heart*] enflammer **2** VI s'allumer, s'enflammer

---

►   LANGUAGE IN USE: **kind**   4, 22, 25.1

kindliness ['kaɪndlɪnɪs] N bienveillance f, bonté f

kindling ['kɪndlɪŋ] N (NonC = wood) petit bois m, bois m d'allumage

kindly ['kaɪndlɪ] **1** ADV **a** (= in a caring way) [say, speak, treat] avec bienveillance **b** (= generously) [offer, give, invite] gentiment, aimablement; **Mr Lea has ~ offered to help us** M. Lea nous a gentiment proposé son aide **c** (= please) ~ **be seated** veuillez vous asseoir; **would you ~ pass the salt?** auriez-vous la gentillesse de me passer le sel?; (annoyed) **will you ~ be quiet!** veux-tu te taire? **d** (= favourably) **to think ~ of sb** apprécier qn; **to look ~ (up)on sb/sth** considérer qn/qch avec bienveillance; **not to take ~ to sb/sth/to doing sth** ne pas apprécier qn/qch/de faire qch; **she didn't take it ~ when I said that** elle n'a pas apprécié quand j'ai dit cela → **disposed 2** ADJ [person, smile, words] bienveillant; [face, eyes] doux (douce f) → **soul**

kindness ['kaɪndnɪs] N **a** (NonC) gentillesse f, bonté f (**towards** pour, envers); **to treat sb with ~** ◊ **to show ~ to sb** être gentil avec or envers qn, faire preuve de bonté envers qn; **out of the ~ of his heart** par (pure) bonté d'âme → **kill b** (= act of kindness) gentillesse f, attention f; **to do sb a ~** rendre service à qn; **he thanked the teachers for all their ~es** il a remercié les professeurs pour toutes leurs petites attentions; **it would be a ~ to let him know** ce serait lui rendre service que de le lui dire

kindred ['kɪndrɪd] **1** N (NonC) (= relatives) parents mpl, famille f; (= relationship) parenté f **2** ADJ **a** (= related) [languages, tribes] apparenté, de la même famille **b** (= similar) similaire, semblable, analogue; **to have a ~ feeling for sb** sympathiser avec qn **3** COMP ▶ **kindred spirit** N âme f sœur

kinesiology [ˌkɪniːsɪˈɒlədʒɪ] N cinésiologie f, kinésiologie f

kinetic [kɪˈnetɪk] ADJ (Phys, Art) cinétique

kinetics [kɪˈnetɪks] N (NonC) cinétique f

kinfolk ['kɪnfəʊk] NPL = **kinsfolk**

king [kɪŋ] **1** N (lit, fig) roi m; **King David** le roi David; (Bible) (**the Book of**) **Kings** le livre des Rois; **the ~ of beasts** le roi des animaux; (fig) **it cost a ~'s ransom** ça a coûté des sommes fabuleuses; **an oil ~** un roi or un magnat du pétrole **b** (Cards, Chess) roi m; (Draughts) dame f **2** COMP ▶ **king cobra** N cobra m royal ▶ **king penguin** N manchot m royal ▶ **King's Bench** N (Brit Jur) cour f supérieure de justice ▶ **King's Counsel** N (Jur) avocat m de la Couronne ▶ **King's evidence** N (Jur) **to turn King's evidence** témoigner contre ses complices ▶ **the King's highway** (Jur) la voie publique ▶ **king-size bed** N grand lit m (de 1,95 m de large) ▶ **king-size(d)** ADJ (Comm) [cigarette] long (longue f); [packet] géant; **I've got a ~size(d) headache** j'ai un mal de crâne carabiné ▶ **King's Messenger** N courrier m diplomatique ▶ **King's speech** N (Brit) discours m du roi → QUEEN'S SPEECH, KING'S SPEECH

kingbolt ['kɪŋbəʊlt] N pivot m central, cheville f ouvrière

kingcup ['kɪŋkʌp] N (= buttercup) bouton m d'or; (= marsh marigold) souci m d'eau or des marais, populage m

kingdom ['kɪŋdəm] N royaume m; (Bot, Zool) règne m; **the plant ~** le règne végétal; **Kingdom of God** le royaume de Dieu; **the Kingdom of Heaven** le royaume des cieux, le royaume céleste; **he's gone to ~ come*** il est parti dans l'autre monde or dans un monde meilleur; **to send sb to ~ come*** envoyer qn dans l'autre monde or dans un monde meilleur or ad patres*; **till ~ come*** jusqu'à la fin des siècles ■ (PROV) **in the ~ of the blind**

(**the one-eyed man is king**) au royaume des aveugles, les borgnes sont rois (PROV) → **animal, united**

kingfish* ['kɪŋfɪʃ] N (US = leader) caïd* m

kingfisher ['kɪŋfɪʃər] N martin-pêcheur m

kingly ['kɪŋlɪ] ADJ (lit, fig) royal, de roi

kingmaker ['kɪŋmeɪkər] N personne f qui fait et défait les rois; (Pol fig) **the ~s** les gens mpl qui font et défont les hommes politiques

kingpin ['kɪŋpɪn] N (Tech) pivot m central, cheville f ouvrière; (fig) pilier m; (US = tenpin bowling, skittles) première quille f

kingship ['kɪŋʃɪp] N royauté f

kink [kɪŋk] **1** N (in rope, tube, wire) nœud m; (in paper) défaut m; (fig) **to work out** or **iron out the ~s** résoudre les problèmes; **her hair has a ~ in it** ses cheveux frisent légèrement **2** VI [rope, tube, wire] s'entortiller

kinky ['kɪŋkɪ] **1** ADJ **a** (*: sexually) [person] aux mœurs spéciales, pervers sur les bords*; [activity] spécial (euph); [underwear] d'un goût spécial; **~ sex** des pratiques sexuelles un peu spéciales; **~ black leather gear** un attirail en cuir noir d'un goût spécial **b** (* = eccentric) [person] farfelu* **c** (= curly) [hair] frisé **2** COMP ▶ **kinky boots** NPL bottes fpl de cuir (ajustées au-dessous du genou)

kinsfolk ['kɪnzfəʊk] NPL (NonC) parents mpl, famille f

kinship ['kɪnʃɪp] N (NonC) **a** (= blood relationship) parenté f **b** (fig = bond) affinité f; **to feel a deep ~ with sb** avoir de nombreuses affinités avec qn

kinsman ['kɪnzmən] N (pl -men) parent m

kinswoman ['kɪnzˌwʊmən] N (pl -women) parente f

kiosk ['kiːɒsk] N (for selling, also bandstand) kiosque m; (Brit Telec) cabine f téléphonique

kip* [kɪp] (Brit) **1** N (= bed) plumard* m, pieu* m; (= nap) roupillon* m; **to get some ~** piquer un roupillon*, pioncer* **2** VI (also ~ **down**) se pieuter*

kipper ['kɪpər] (Brit) **1** N hareng m fumé et salé, kipper m **2** VT [+ herring] fumer et saler **3** COMP ▶ **kipper tie** N large cravate f (des années 60)

kir [kɪər] N kir m

Kirbigrip®, kirbygrip ['kɜːbɪˌgrɪp] N pince f à cheveux

Kirg(h)iz ['kɜːgɪz] **1** ADJ kirghiz inv **2** N **a** (= person) Kirghiz(e) m(f) **b** (Ling) kirghiz m

Kirg(h)izstan [ˌkɜːgɪsˈtɑːn], **Kirg(h)izia** [ˌkɜːˈgɪzɪə] N le Kirghizstan

kirk [kɜːk] N (Scot) église f; **the Kirk** l'Église f presbytérienne (d'Écosse)

Kirsch ['kɪəʃ], **Kirschwasser** ['kɪəʃˌvɑːsər] N kirsch m

kiss [kɪs] **1** N baiser m; **to give sb a ~** donner un baiser à qn, embrasser qn; **give me a ~** embrasse-moi; (to child) fais-moi une bise*; (esp Brit Med) **~ of life** bouche-à-bouche m; (in letter) **"love and ~es"** « bons baisers », « grosses bises »*; (fig) **to give the ~ of death to ...** porter le coup fatal à ... → **blow¹ 2** VT **a** embrasser, donner un baiser à; **to ~ sb's cheek** embrasser qn sur la joue; **to ~ sb's hand** baiser la main de qn; (Diplomacy etc) **to ~ hands** être admis au baisemain (du roi or de la reine); **they ~ed each other** ils se sont embrassés; **to ~ sb good night/goodbye** embrasser qn en lui souhaitant bonne nuit/en lui disant au revoir, souhaiter bonne nuit/ dire au revoir à qn en l'embrassant; (to child) **I'll ~ it better** un petit bisou* et ça ira mieux; (esp US) **to ~ ass‡** faire de la lèche‡; (esp US) **to ~ sb's ass‡** lécher le cul à qn‡; (esp US) **~ my ass!‡** va chier!‡ → **goodbye b** (= touch lightly: also liter) frôler; **the ball ~ed the top of the crossbar** le ballon a frôlé la barre transversale

3 VI s'embrasser; **to ~ and make up** faire la paix; **to ~ and tell** raconter ses secrets d'alcôve **4** COMP ▶ **kiss-and-tell*** ADJ [story, memoirs] divulguant des secrets d'alcôve (avec une personnalité en vue) ▶ **kiss curl** N (Brit) accroche-cœur m ▶ **kiss-off*** N (US) **to give sb the ~-off** [+ employee] virer* qn; [+ girlfriend etc] plaquer* qn

▶ **kiss away** VT SEP **she ~ed away the child's tears** elle a séché les larmes de l'enfant en l'embrassant

▶ **kiss back** VT SEP [+ person] rendre un baiser à

kissagram ['kɪsəˌgræm] N baiser télégraphié

KISSAGRAM

Un **kissagram** est un « baiser télégraphié » adressé à une personne pour lui faire une surprise, par exemple à l'occasion de son anniversaire. Le message est remis par un porteur costumé, qui lit un petit texte et embrasse le destinataire devant tout le monde.

---

kisser‡ ['kɪsər] N gueule‡ f

kit [kɪt] **1** N **a** (NonC) (= equipment, gear) (for camping, skiing, climbing, photography etc) matériel m, équipement m; (Mil) fourniment m, fourbi* m; (= tools) outils mpl; **fishing** etc **~** matériel m or attirail m de pêche etc; (US) **the whole ~ and caboodle*** tout le bataclan*, tout le fourbi* **b** (NonC:*) (= belongings) affaires fpl; (= clothes) fringues* fpl; (for sports) affaires fpl; (= luggage) bagages mpl; **get your ~ off!‡** à poil!‡; **have you got your gym/football ~?** tu as tes affaires de gym/de football? **c** (= set of items) trousse f; **puncture-repair ~** trousse f de réparations; **first-aid ~** trousse f d'urgence or de premiers secours → **survival d** (= parts for assembly) kit m; **sold in ~ form** vendu en kit; **he built it from a ~** il l'a assemblé à partir d'un kit; **model aeroplane ~** maquette f d'avion (à assembler) **2** COMP ▶ **kit car** N voiture f en kit ▶ **kit inspection** N (Mil) revue f de détail

▶ **kit out, kit up** VT SEP (Brit) **a** (Mil) équiper (**with de**) **b to ~ sb out with sth** équiper qn de qch; **he arrived ~ted out in oilskins** il est arrivé équipé d'un ciré; **he had ~ted himself out in a bright blue suit** il avait mis un costume bleu vif

kitbag ['kɪtbæg] N (esp Brit) sac m (de voyage, de sportif, de soldat, de marin etc)

kitchen ['kɪtʃɪn] **1** N cuisine f → **thief 2** COMP [table, cutlery, scissors etc] de cuisine ▶ **kitchen cabinet** N buffet m de cuisine; (Pol fig) proches conseillers mpl du Premier ministre; (in US) proches conseillers mpl du Président → CABINET ▶ **kitchen-diner, kitchen-dinette** N cuisine f avec coin-repas ▶ **kitchen foil** N papier m d'aluminium or d'alu* ▶ **kitchen garden** N (jardin m) potager m ▶ **kitchen paper** N essuie-tout m inv ▶ **kitchen police** N (US Mil) (= work) corvée f de cuisine; (= soldiers) soldats mpl chargés de la corvée de cuisine ▶ **kitchen range** N fourneau m (de cuisine), cuisinière f ▶ **kitchen roll** N = **kitchen paper** ▶ **kitchen salt** N sel m de cuisine, gros sel m ▶ **kitchen scales** NPL balance f (de cuisine) ▶ **kitchen sink** N évier m; (fig) **I've packed everything but the ~ sink** j'ai tout emporté sauf les murs ▶ **kitchen-sink drama*** N (Theat) théâtre misérabiliste des années 50 et 60 ▶ **kitchen soap** N savon m de Marseille ▶ **kitchen unit** N élément m de cuisine ▶ **kitchen utensil** N ustensile m de cuisine ▶ **kitchen waste** N déchets mpl domestiques ▶ **kitchen wastes** NPL (US) = **kitchen waste**

kitchenette [ˌkɪtʃɪˈnet] N kitchenette f

kitchenmaid ['kɪtʃɪnmeɪd] N fille f de cuisine

kitchenware ['kɪtʃɪnwɛər] N (NonC) (= dishes)

vaisselle *f* or faïence *f* (de cuisine) ; (= *equipment*) ustensiles *mpl* de cuisine

kite [kaɪt] **1** N **[a]** (*Orn*) milan *m* ; (= *toy*) cerf-volant *m* → **fly³**, **high [b]** (*Fin**) (= *cheque*) chèque *m* en bois* ; (= *bill*) traite *f* en l'air* **2** COMP ► **kite balloon** N (*Mil*) ballon *m* d'observation, saucisse *f* ► **Kite mark** N (*Brit Comm*) label *m* de qualité (*délivré par l'Association britannique de normalisation*)

kith [kɪθ] N **~ and kin** amis *mpl* et parents *mpl*

kitsch [kɪtʃ] **1** N (*NonC*) kitsch *m*, art *m* kitsch or pompier **2** ADJ kitsch *inv*, pompier

kitten ['kɪtn] N chaton *m*, petit chat *m* ; (*Brit fig*) **to have ~s** piquer une crise*

kittenish ['kɪtənɪʃ] ADJ (*lit*) de chaton ; (*fig*) de chaton, mutin

kittiwake ['kɪtɪweɪk] N mouette *f* tridactyle

kitty ['kɪtɪ] **1** N **[a]** (*Cards etc*) cagnotte *f* ; (* *fig*) caisse *f*, cagnotte *f* ; **there's nothing left in the ~** il n'y a plus un sou dans la caisse or dans la cagnotte **[b]** (* = *cat*) minet* *m*, minou* *m* **2** COMP ► **Kitty Litter**® N (*US*) litière *f* pour chats

kiwi ['ki:wi:] N **[a]** (= *bird*) kiwi *m*, aptéryx *m* **[b]** (*also* **~ fruit**) kiwi *m* **[c]** (* = *New Zealander*) néo-zélandais(e) *m(f)*

KKK [,keɪkeɪ'keɪ] (*US*) ABBR = **Ku Klux Klan**

Klansman ['klænzmən] N (*US*) membre *m* du Ku Klux Klan

klaxon ['klæksn] N klaxon® *m*

Kleenex® ['kli:neks] N (*pl* **Kleenex** or **Kleenexes**) kleenex® *m*

kleptomania [,kleptəʊ'meɪnɪə] N kleptomanie *f*

kleptomaniac [,kleptəʊ'meɪnɪæk] ADJ, N kleptomane *mf*

klieg light ['kli:glaɪt] N (*esp US*) lampe *f* à arc

klutz [klʌts] N (*US*) empoté(e) *m(f)*, manche* *m*

klystron ['klɪstrɒn] N klystron *m*

km N (ABBR = **kilometre(s)**) km

kmh N (ABBR = **kilometres per hour**) km/h

knack [næk] N **[a]** (= *physical dexterity*) tour *m* de main ; **to learn** or **get the ~ of doing sth** prendre le tour de main pour faire qch ; **there's a ~ to it** il y a un tour de main à prendre ; **I've lost the ~** j'ai perdu la main **[b]** (= *talent*) **to have the ~ of doing sth** avoir le don pour faire qch ; (*iro*) avoir le chic pour faire qch ; **she's got a ~ of saying the wrong thing** elle a le chic pour dire ce qu'il ne faut pas ; **I never really got the ~ of it** je n'ai jamais compris le truc*

knacker ['nækər] (*Brit*) **1** N **[a]** [*of horses*] équarrisseur *m* ; **to send a horse to the ~'s yard** envoyer un cheval à l'équarrissage **[b]** [*of boats, houses*] entrepreneur *m* de démolition, démolisseur *m* **2** VT* **[a]** (= *tire*) crever* **[b]** (= *break*) bousiller*

knackered ['nækəd] ADJ (*Brit*) **[a]** (= *tired out*) crevé*, éreinté* **[b]** (= *broken, worn out*) nase*, foutu*

knapsack ['næpsæk] N sac *m* à dos, havresac *m*

knave [neɪv] N († *pej*) filou *m*, fripon† *m* ; (*Cards*) valet *m*

knavery ['neɪvərɪ] N (*NonC: pej*) filouterie *f*, friponnerie† *f*

knavish ['neɪvɪʃ] ADJ (*pej*) de filou, de fripon†

knead [ni:d] VT [+ *dough*] pétrir, travailler ; [+ *muscles*] malaxer

knee [ni:] **1** N genou *m* ; **he sank in up to the ~s** il s'est enfoncé jusqu'aux genoux ; **the trousers are worn at or have gone at the ~(s)** ce pantalon est usé aux genoux ; **to sit on sb's ~** s'asseoir sur les genoux de qn ; **to put a child over one's ~** donner une fessée à un enfant ; **to learn sth at one's mother's ~** apprendre qch dès son jeune âge ; **to go (down) on one's ~s** s'agenouiller, tomber or se mettre à genoux ;

to go down on one's ~s to sb (*lit*) tomber or se mettre à genoux devant qn ; (*fig*) se mettre à genoux devant qn, supplier qn à genoux ; **on bended ~(s)** à genoux ; (*fig*) **to bring sb to his ~s** forcer qn à capituler or à se soumettre ; (*fig*) **it will bring the country/the steel industry to its ~s** ça va mettre le pays/l'industrie sidérurgique à genoux

2 COMP ► **knee-bend** N (*gen*, *Ski*) flexion *f* (du genou) ► **knee breeches** NPL culotte *f* courte ► **knee-deep** ADJ **he was ~-deep in mud** la boue lui arrivait aux genoux, il était dans la boue jusqu'aux genoux ; **the water was ~-deep** l'eau arrivait aux genoux ; (*fig*) **to be ~-deep in paperwork*** être dans la paperasse jusqu'au cou ► **knee-high** ADJ à hauteur de genou ; **~-high to a grasshopper*** haut comme trois pommes ► **knee jerk** N réflexe *m* rotulien ► **knee-jerk** ADJ [*reaction, response*] réflexe ; **he's a ~-jerk conservative*** c'est un conservateur primaire ► **knee joint** N articulation *f* du genou ► **knee level** N **at ~ level** à (la) hauteur du genou ► **knee pants** NPL (*US*) bermuda *m* ► **knee reflex** N réflexe *m* rotulien ► **knees-up*** N (*pl* **knees-ups**) (*Brit*) pince-fesses* *m*, bringue* *f*

kneecap ['ni:kæp] **1** N (*Anat*) rotule *f* **2** VT tirer dans le genou de

kneecapping ['ni:,kæpɪŋ] N mutilation *f* en tirant dans le genou

kneel [ni:l] (*pret, ptp* **knelt** or **kneeled**) VI (*also* **~ down**) s'agenouiller, se mettre à genoux ; (= *be kneeling*) être agenouillé ; **he had to ~ on his case to shut it** il a dû se mettre à genoux sur sa valise pour la fermer ; (*lit, fig*) **to ~ (down) to** or **before sb** se mettre à genoux devant qn

kneepad ['ni:pæd] N genouillère *f*

kneeroom ['ni:rʊm] N espace *m* pour les jambes

knell [nel] N glas *m* ; **to sound** or **toll the (death) ~** sonner le glas

knelt [nelt] VB *pt, ptp of* **kneel**

Knesset ['knesɪt] N **the ~** la Knesset

knew [nju:] VB *pt of* **know**

knickerbocker ['nɪkə,bɒkər] **1** **knickerbockers** NPL (*knee-length*) knickers *mpl* ; (*longer*) culotte *f* de golf **2** COMP ► **knickerbocker glory** N (*Brit*) coupe glacée faite de glace, de gelée, de crème et de fruits

knickers ['nɪkəz] NPL **[a]** (*Brit: woman's*) culotte *f*, slip *m* (*de femme*) ; **~!*** (*annoyed*) mince !* ; (*disbelieving*) mon œil !* ; (*fig*) **to get one's ~ in a twist*** se mettre dans tous ses états **[b]**† = **knickerbockers** → **knickerbocker**

knick-knack ['nɪknæk] N bibelot *m*, babiole *f* ; (*on dress*) colifichet *m*

knife [naɪf] **1** N (*pl* **knives**) couteau *m* ; (*also* **pocket ~**) canif *m* ; (*fig*) **~, fork and spoon** couvert *m* ; (*fig*) **to turn** or **twist the ~ in the wound** retourner le couteau dans la plaie (*fig*) ; (*fig*) **he's got his ~ into me*** il s'acharne contre moi ; (*esp Brit fig*) **the knives are out*** c'est la guerre ouverte ; (*esp Brit fig*) **the knives are out for him*** on en a après lui ; (*fig*) **to put** or **stick the ~ into sb** blesser qn ; **it's war to the ~ between them** ils sont à couteaux tirés (*fig*) ; (*Med*) **(to go) under the ~*** (passer) sur le billard ; **before you could say ~*** en moins de temps qu'il n'en faut pour le dire

2 VT [+ *person*] donner un coup de couteau à ; **she had been ~d** elle avait reçu un coup (or des coups) de couteau ; (*to death*) elle avait été tuée à coups de couteau

3 COMP ► **knife edge** N fil *m* d'un couteau ; (*Tech*) couteau *m* ; (*fig*) **on a ~ edge** (= *tense, anxious*) sur des charbons ardents (*fig*) ; **the success of the scheme/the result was balanced on a ~ edge** la réussite du projet/le résultat ne tenait qu'à un fil ► **knife-edge(d)** ADJ [*blade*] tranchant, aiguisé ; [*crease*] bien marqué ► **knife-grinder** N rémouleur *m* ► **knife pleat** N pli *m* couché ► **knife**

point N **to hold sb at ~ point** menacer qn d'un couteau ► **knife rest** N porte-couteau *m* ► **knife-sharpener** N (*on wall, on wheel etc*) affiloir *m*, aiguisoir *m* ; (*long, gen with handle*) fusil *m* (à repasser les couteaux)

knifeman ['naɪfmən] N (*Brit*) agresseur *m* armé d'un couteau

knifing ['naɪfɪŋ] N attaque *f* au couteau

knight [naɪt] **1** N **[a]** chevalier *m* ; (*Chess*) cavalier *m* ; **a ~ in shining armour** (= *romantic figure*) un prince charmant ; (= *saviour*) un sauveur, un redresseur de torts **2** VT **[a]** (*Hist*) [+ *squire etc*] adouber, armer chevalier **[b]** (*Brit*) [*sovereign*] donner l'accolade (de chevalier) à, faire chevalier ; **he was ~ed for services to industry** il a été fait chevalier pour services rendus dans l'industrie **3** COMP ► **knight errant** N (*pl* **knights errant**) (*Hist*) chevalier *m* errant ► **knight-errantry** N (*NonC*) chevalerie *f* errante ► **Knight of the Garter** N chevalier *m* de (l'ordre de) la Jarretière ► **Knight Templar** N (*pl* **Knights Templars** or **Knights Templar**) chevalier *m* de l'ordre du Temple, Templier *m*

knighthood ['naɪthʊd] N **[a]** (= *knights collectively*) chevalerie *f* **[b]** (*Brit* = *rank*) titre *m* de chevalier ; **to get** or **receive a ~** être fait chevalier, recevoir le titre de chevalier

knightly ['naɪtlɪ] ADJ [*courtesy*] chevaleresque ; [*armour*] de chevalier

knit [nɪt] (*pret, ptp* **knitted** or **knit**) **1** VT **[a]** [+ *garment, blanket etc*] tricoter ; **"~ three, purl one"** « trois mailles à l'endroit, une maille à l'envers » ; **to ~ sth for sb** ◊ **to ~ sb sth** tricoter qch pour qn ; **~ted jacket** veste *f* tricotée or en tricot ; **~ted goods** *mpl*, articles *mpl* en maille → **close¹**, **thick [b] to ~ one's brows** froncer les sourcils **2** VI **[a]** tricoter **[b]** (*also* **~ together**, **~ up**) [*bone*] se souder **3** COMP ► **knit stitch** N maille *f* à l'endroit

► **knit together 1** VI = **knit 2b 2** VT SEP **[a] "~ two mailles"** « tricoter deux mailles ensemble » **[b]** (*fig*) [+ *family, community*] lier, unir ; [+ *team*] souder

► **knit up 1** VI **[a]** = **knit 2b [b]** **this wool ~s up very quickly** cette laine monte très vite **2** VT SEP [+ *jersey*] tricoter

knitter ['nɪtər] N tricoteur *m*, -euse *f*

knitting ['nɪtɪŋ] **1** N (*NonC*) **[a]** (*gen*) tricot *m* ; (*Ind*) tricotage *m* ; **where's my ~?** où est mon tricot ? → **double [b]** [*of bone*] consolidation *f*, soudure *f* **2** COMP ► **knitting bag** N sac *m* à tricot ► **knitting machine** N machine *f* à tricoter, tricoteuse *f* ► **knitting needle**, **knitting pin** N aiguille *f* à tricoter ► **knitting wool** N laine *f* à tricoter

knitwear ['nɪtweər] N (*NonC: Comm*) tricots *mpl*

knives [naɪvz] NPL *of* **knife**

knob [nɒb] N **[a]** [*of door, instrument*] bouton *m* ; [*of cane, walking stick*] pommeau *m* ; (= *small bump*) bosse *f*, protubérance *f* ; (*on tree*) nœud *m* ; (*fig*) **with ~s on*** et encore plus **[b]** (= *small piece*) [*of cheese etc*] petit morceau *m* ; (*Brit*) **~ of butter** noix *f* de beurre **[c]** (** = *penis*) zob** *m*, bitte** *f*

knobbly ['nɒblɪ], **knobby** ['nɒbɪ] ADJ noueux

knobkerrie ['nɒb,kerɪ] N massue *f*

knock [nɒk] **1** N **[a]** (= *blow*) coup *m* ; (= *collision*) heurt *m*, choc *m* ; (*in engine etc*) cognement *m* ; **he got a ~ (on the head etc)** il a reçu or pris* un coup (sur la tête etc) ; **he gave himself a nasty ~ (on the head etc)** il s'est cogné très fort (la tête etc) **[b]** (*at door*) **there was a ~ at the door** on a frappé (à la porte) ; **I heard a ~ (at the door)** j'ai entendu (quelqu'un) frapper (à la porte) ; **~, ~!** toc, toc, toc ! ; **I'll give you a ~ at 7 o'clock** je viendrai taper à la porte à 7 heures **[c]** (*fig*) (= *setback*) revers *m* ; (= *criticism*) **~s*** critiques *fpl* ; **to take a ~** [*person*] recevoir un coup (*fig*) ; **his pride/credibility has taken a ~**

son orgueil/sa crédibilité en a pris un coup; **his confidence has taken a ~** sa confiance a été sérieusement ébranlée; **her professional reputation took a very hard ~** sa réputation professionnelle en a pris un sacré* coup

[2] VT [a] (= hit, strike) [+ object] frapper; **to ~ a nail into a plank** planter or enfoncer un clou dans une planche; **to ~ a nail in (with a hammer/shoe etc)** enfoncer un clou (d'un coup or à coups de marteau/de chaussure etc); **he ~ed the ball into the hedge** il a envoyé la balle dans la haie; **she ~ed the knife out of his hand** elle lui a fait tomber le couteau des mains; **to ~ a glass off a table** faire tomber un verre d'une table; **she ~ed the cup to the floor** elle a fait tomber la tasse (par terre); **to ~ the bottom out of a box** défoncer (le fond d')une boîte; (fig) **to ~ the bottom out of an argument** démolir un argument; (St Ex) **this ~ed the bottom out of the market** cela a provoqué l'effondrement des cours; **to ~ holes in sth** faire des trous dans qch; (fig) **to ~ holes in an argument** battre un argument en brèche; **to ~ sb's confidence** ébranler la confiance de qn; (Brit) **that ~ed his plans on the head*** ça a flanqué* par terre or démoli ses projets; **it's time to ~ this idea on the head*** il est temps de faire rentrer à coups de pied* cette idée, or enfoncer à coups de pied* cette idée; **to ~ some sense into sb*** ramener qn à la raison (par la manière forte); **to ~ spots off sb*** battre qn à plate(s) couture(s); **to ~ spots off sth*** être beaucoup mieux que qch → **stuffing**

[b] (= hit, strike) [+ person] **to ~ sb to the ground** [person, explosion] jeter qn à terre, faire tomber qn; (= stun) assommer qn; **to ~ sb unconscious** or **cold** or **senseless** or **silly** assommer qn; **he ~ed the child out of the way** il a brusquement écarté l'enfant; **to ~ sb dead*** épater qn*, en mettre plein la vue à qn*; **go out there and ~ 'em dead!** montreleur de quoi tu es capable!; **to ~ sb on the head** frapper qn à la tête; (= stun) assommer qn; **to ~ sb into the middle of next week*** faire voir trente-six chandelles à qn*; (Brit) **his wife's death really ~ed him sideways*** (= shook him) la mort de sa femme l'a profondément ébranlé; (Brit) **confidence in the legal system has been ~ed sideways*** la confiance dans le système légal a été sérieusement ébranlée; (Brit) **to ~ sb for six*** [cold, flu] lessiver* qn; [news] faire un choc à qn

[c] (= collide with, strike) [person] cogner dans, heurter; [vehicle] heurter; **to ~ one's head on** or **against** se cogner la tête contre; **he ~ed his foot against the leg of the table** il a buté contre le pied de la table

[d] (Constr) **to ~ two rooms into one** abattre la cloison entre deux pièces

[e] (* = denigrate) [+ person, sb's work] débiner*; [+ plan, project, idea] dénigrer; **don't ~ it!** arrête de dénigrer!; **don't ~ it if you haven't tried it!** c'est pas la peine* de critiquer si tu n'as pas essayé!

[f] (Scot* = steal) piquer*

[3] VI [a] (= strike, hit) frapper; (more forcefully) cogner; **to ~ at the door/window** frapper à la porte/la fenêtre; **he ~ed on the table** il a frappé la table, il a cogné sur la table; **his knees were ~ing** il tremblait de peur, il avait les chocottes*

[b] (= bump, collide) **to ~ against** or **into sb/sth** se cogner contre qn/qch, heurter qn/qch; **his hand ~ed against the shelf** il s'est cogné la main contre l'étagère, il s'est cogné la main contre l'étagère; **he ~ed into the table** il s'est cogné dans or contre la table, il a heurté la table; **the car ~ed into the lamppost** la voiture a heurté le réverbère

[c] [car engine] cogner

[4] COMP ► **knocked down** ADJ (US Comm) [table, shed etc] (livré) non monté ► **knock-for-knock agreement** N (Insurance) convention f d'indemnisation directe de

l'assuré ► **knock-kneed** ADJ **to be ~-kneed** avoir les genoux cagneux ► **knock-knees** NPL **to have ~-knees** avoir les genoux cagneux ► **knock-on** N (Rugby) en-avant m inv ► **knock-on effect** N répercussions fpl ► **knock-out agreement** N (Jur, Fin) entente f entre enchérisseurs ► **knock-out drops*** NPL soporifique m ► **knock-up** N (Tennis) **to have a ~-up** faire des balles

► **knock about***, **knock around*** [1] VI [a] (= travel) vadrouiller*, bourlinguer* (fig); (= hang around) traîner, glander*; **he spent many years ~ing about in the provinces** il a passé de nombreuses années à vadrouiller* or bourlinguer* en province; **he has ~ed about a bit** il a beaucoup bourlingué*; **what are all these boxes ~ing about in the garage?** que font tous ces cartons dans le garage?; **who's he ~ing around with these days?** qui est-ce qu'il fréquente en ce moment? [2] VT FUS **to ~ about the world** vadrouiller* de par le monde; **he's ~ing about France somewhere*** il vadrouille* or il se balade* quelque part en France [3] VT SEP [a] (* = beat) taper sur, frapper; **he ~s her about** il lui tape dessus*; [b] [storm, waves] [+ boat] ballotter [c] **to ~ a ball about** taper dans le ballon* [4] **~about** N, ADJ → **knockabout**

► **knock back** [1] VI (lit) **he ~ed on the wall and she ~ed back** il a frappé au mur et elle a répondu de la même façon [2] VT SEP* [a] (fig) (= drink) s'enfiler*, s'envoyer*; (= eat) avaler, engloutir [b] (* = cost) coûter; **how much did it ~ you back?** ça vous a coûté combien?; **this watch ~ed me back £120** cette montre m'a coûté 120 livres [c] (fig = shock) sonner*; **the news ~ed her back a bit** la nouvelle l'a un peu sonnée*

► **knock down** [1] VT SEP [a] [+ object] (= topple) renverser; (= knock off shelf, table etc) faire tomber; [+ building, wall etc] abattre, démolir; [+ door] (= remove) démolir; (= kick in) défoncer, enfoncer; **he ~ed me down with one blow** il m'a jeté à terre d'un seul coup → **feather** [b] (= run over) [vehicle] [+ person] renverser; [+ lamppost] emboutir; [+ fence, wall] défoncer; **he got ~ed down by a bus** il a été renversé par un autobus [c] [+ price] baisser; **he ~ed the price down by 10%** il a baissé le prix de 10%, il a fait une remise de 10% sur le prix [d] (at auction) **to ~ down sth to sb** adjuger qch à qn; **it was ~ed down for £10** ça a été adjugé 10 livres [2] **~down** ADJ, N → **knockdown** [3] **~ed down** ADJ → **knock**

► **knock off** [1] VI* (= stop work) s'arrêter (de travailler); (= leave work) se casser*, se tirer*; (= strike) débrayer [2] VT SEP [a] (lit) [+ object on shelf etc] faire tomber; **I got ~ed off my bike** j'ai été renversé en vélo; **to ~ sb's block off*** casser la figure* à qn (= reduce price by) [+ percentage, amount] faire une remise de; **I'll ~ off £10/10%** je vous fais une remise de 10 livres/de 10%; **she ~ed 15 seconds off the world record** elle a battu le record du monde de 15 secondes [c]* [+ homework, correspondence, piece of work] expédier [d] (Brit* = steal) piquer* [e] (= stop) **~ it off!*** ça suffit! [f] (* = kill) liquider* [3] **~ing-off** ADJ → **knocking**

► **knock on** [1] VT SEP (Rugby) **to ~ the ball on** faire un en-avant [2] VT FUS **he's ~ing on for fifty*** il frise la cinquantaine [3] **~-on** N, ADJ → **knock**

► **knock out** [1] VT SEP [a] [+ nail etc] faire sortir (of de); **to ~ out one's pipe** débourrer or éteindre sa pipe; **to ~ a window out** [builder] enlever une fenêtre; [explosion, earthquake] souffler une fenêtre [b] (* = put out of action) [storm, earthquake, bomb] [+ power supply, electricity] couper; [missile] [+ target] détruire, bousiller* [c] (= stun) [person] assommer; (Boxing) mettre knock-out or k.-o.; [drug] sonner*, assommer; **to ~ o.s. out** s'assommer [d]* (= shock, overwhelm) sidérer*; (= exhaust) mettre à plat* [e] (from competition, contest) éliminer

(of de) [2] **~out** N, ADJ → **knockout**

► **knock over** VT SEP [a] [+ object] renverser [b] [vehicle] [+ pedestrian] renverser; [+ lamppost] emboutir; [+ fence] défoncer; **he was ~ed over by a taxi** il a été renversé par un taxi

► **knock together** [1] VI [glasses, knees] s'entrechoquer [2] VT SEP [a] (lit) [+ two objects] cogner l'un contre l'autre; **I'd like to ~ their heads together!*** ce sont deux têtes à claques [b]* = knock up 2c

► **knock up** [1] VI (Tennis) faire des balles [2] VT SEP [a] (lit) [+ handle, lever etc] faire lever d'un coup [b] (Brit = waken) réveiller (en frappant à la porte) [c] (* = make hurriedly) [+ meal] improviser; [+ shed, furniture] bricoler (en vitesse) [d] (Brit* = exhaust) [+ person] crever* [e] (‡ = make pregnant) engrosser‡ [3] **~-up** N → **knock**

knockabout ['nɒkə,baʊt] [1] N (esp US Naut) dériveur m, petit voilier m [2] ADJ (esp Brit = boisterous) [fun, humour, style] exubérant; (Theat) **~ comedy** (grosse) farce f

knockdown ['nɒkdaʊn] [1] ADJ [a] **a ~ blow** (lit) un coup à assommer un bœuf; (fig) un coup de boutoir [b] (Brit Comm) **~ price** prix m très avantageux or intéressant; (in posters, announcements) **"~ prices"** « prix sacrifiés »; **to sell at ~ prices** vendre pour une bouchée de pain [2] N (Boxing) knock-down m inv

knocker ['nɒkəʳ] N [a] (also **door-~**) marteau m (de porte), heurtoir m [b] **~s**‡ (= breasts) nichons‡ mpl, roberts‡ mpl

knocking ['nɒkɪŋ] [1] N (NonC) [a] coups mpl; **I can hear ~ at the door** j'entends frapper à la porte (in engine) cognement m [2] COMP ► **knocking copy** N (Advertising) publicité f comparative ► **knocking-off time*** N (Ind etc) heure f de la sortie ► **knocking shop**‡ N (Brit) bordel* m

knockout ['nɒkaʊt] [1] N [a] (Boxing) knockout m inv [b] (= overwhelming success) **to be a ~*** [person, record, achievement] être sensationnel* [c] (= competition) compétition f (avec épreuves éliminatoires); (TV: formerly) **"It's a Knockout"** ≈ « Jeux sans frontières » [2] ADJ [a] (Boxing etc) **he delivered** or **landed a ~ blow** or **punch** il a mis son adversaire K.-O.; **the ~ blow came in round six** il a été mis K.-O. au sixième round; (fig) **~ blow** coup m terrible [b] (Brit Sport) [competition, tournament] par élimination

knoll [nəʊl] N (= hillock) tertre m, monticule m

Knossos ['nɒsəs] N Cnossos

knot [nɒt] [1] N [a] nœud m; **to tie/untie a ~** faire/défaire un nœud; **the marriage ~** le lien du mariage; **to have a ~ in one's stomach (= feel tense)** avoir l'estomac noué, avoir un nœud à l'estomac → **granny, reef‡, slipknot, tie** [b] (Naut = unit of speed) nœud m; **to make 20 ~s** filer 20 nœuds → **rate**[1] [c] (in wood) nœud m; **a ~ of people** un petit groupe de gens [2] VT [a] [+ rope, scarf, tie, handkerchief] faire un nœud à, nouer; **he ~ted the piece of string to the rope** il a noué la ficelle à la corde; **get ~ted!‡** va te faire voir* or foutre‡! ► **knot together** VT SEP attacher, nouer

knothole ['nɒthəʊl] N (in wood) trou m (laissé par un nœud)

knotty ['nɒtɪ] ADJ [a] (lit) [wood, muscle, hand] noueux; [rope, hair] plein de nœuds [b] (fig = thorny) [problem, issue, question] épineux

knout [naʊt] N knout m

▼ **know** [nəʊ]

vb: pret **knew**, ptp **known**	
[1] TRANSITIVE VERB	[4] NOUN
[2] INTRANSITIVE VERB	[5] COMPOUNDS
[3] SET STRUCTURES	

[1] TRANSITIVE VERB

Look up set combinations such as **know the ropes**, **know the score** *at the noun.*

boxed-a = have knowledge of connaître; **to ~ the details/the results/the truth** connaître les détails/les résultats/la vérité; **I ~ the problem!** je connais le problème!; **to ~ one's business*** connaître son affaire, s'y connaître

savoir can often also be used.

to ~ the difference between connaître *or* savoir la différence entre; **to ~ French** savoir *or* connaître le français; **that's worth ~ing** c'est bon à savoir; **it was sure to cause trouble, as well he knew** ça allait sûrement faire des histoires et il le savait très bien; **I ~ the problems that arise when ...** je connais les problèmes qui surviennent lorsque ...

When **know** *is followed by a clause,* **savoir** *must be used. Unlike* **that**, **que** *can never be omitted.*

I ~ (that) you're wrong je sais que vous avez tort; **I ~ him to be a liar** je sais que c'est un menteur; **I would have you ~ that ...** sachez que ...; **to ~ how to do sth** savoir faire qch; **I ~ how you feel** je sais ce que tu ressens, je connais ça; **you don't ~ how glad/relieved I am to see you** vous ne pouvez pas savoir comme je suis content/soulagé de vous voir; **she ~s what it means to suffer** *or* **what suffering means** elle sait ce qu'est la souffrance; **he ~s what he's talking about** il sait de quoi il parle; **I don't ~ where to begin** je ne sais pas par où commencer; **do you ~ whether she's coming?** est-ce que tu sais si elle vient?; **I don't ~ why he reacted like that** je ne sais pas pourquoi il a réagi comme ça

boxed-b = be acquainted with [+ *person, place, book, author*] connaître; **I ~ him well** je le connais bien; **do you ~ Paris?** connaissez-vous Paris?; **to ~ sb by sight/by name/by reputation** connaître qn de vue/de nom/de réputation; **he ~s all his customers by name** il connaît tous ses clients par leur(s) nom(s); **I don't ~ her to speak to** je ne la connais que de vue; **everyone ~s him as Dizzy** on le connaît sous le nom de Dizzy; **most of us ~ him only as a comedian** la plupart d'entre nous ne le connaissons qu'en tant que comique; **he is ~n as a man of great charm** c'est un homme connu pour son charme, il passe pour un homme plein de charme; **civilisation as we ~ it** la civilisation telle que nous la connaissons

boxed-c = understand I **don't ~ how you can say that!** comment peux-tu dire une chose pareille!; **you ~ what I mean** tu vois ce que je veux dire

boxed-d = recognize reconnaître; **to ~ sb by his voice/his walk** reconnaître qn à sa voix/à sa démarche; **I knew him at once** je l'ai reconnu tout de suite; **I ~ real expertise when I see it!** je sais reconnaître un spécialiste quand j'en vois un!; *BUT* **she ~s a good thing when she sees it*** elle ne laisse pas passer les bonnes occasions; **he knew he was to blame** il se savait coupable

boxed-e = be certain I **don't ~ that it's made things any easier** je ne suis pas sûr que ça ait simplifié les choses; **I don't ~ if** *or* **that that is a very good idea** je ne suis pas sûr que ce soit une bonne idée; **I don't ~ if I can do it** je ne suis pas sûr de pouvoir le faire

boxed-f = exclamations **well, what do you ~!*** tiens, tiens!; **I ~ (what)*, let's leave it till tomorrow!** et si on remettait ça à demain?; **(do) you ~ what*, I think they did it!** tu sais quoi, je pense que c'est elle qui a fait ça!; **she's furious!** — **don't I ~ it!*** elle est furieuse! — à qui le dis-tu *or* je suis bien placé pour le savoir!; **not if I ~ it!*** ça m'étonnerait!; **that's all you ~ (about it)!*** c'est ce que tu crois!; **you ~ what you can do with it!*** tu peux te le mettre où je pense!*

boxed-2 INTRANSITIVE VERB

savoir; **who ~s?** qui sait?; **is she nice?** — **I don't ~** *or* **I wouldn't ~*** est-ce qu'elle est gentille? — je ne sais pas *or* je n'en sais rien; **how should I ~?** est-ce que je sais (moi)!*, comment veux-tu que je sache?; **it'll be expensive, you ~** ça va coûter cher, tu sais; **you**

~, that's not a bad idea tu sais, ce n'est pas une mauvaise idée; **as far as I ~** autant que je sache, à ma connaissance; **not as far as I ~** pas que je sache, pas à ma connaissance; **for all I ~** pour ce que j'en sais; **one never ~s** ◊ **you never ~** on ne sait jamais; *BUT* **and afterwards they just don't want to ~*** et après ça ils ne veulent plus en entendre parler

boxed-3 SET STRUCTURES

♦ **to know sth about sth/sb**: **to ~ a lot about sth/sb** en savoir long sur qch/qn; **I don't ~ much about it/him** je ne sais pas grand-chose à ce sujet/je ne le connais pas beaucoup; **I'd like to ~ more (about it)** je voudrais en savoir plus (à ce sujet); **it's no good lying, I ~ all about it** ce n'est pas la peine de mentir, je sais tout; **she ~s all about computers** elle s'y connaît en informatique; **I ~ nothing about music** je n'y connais rien en musique, je ne m'y connais pas du tout en musique; **I ~ nothing about it** je ne sais rien à ce sujet

♦ **to know about sth/sb**: **I didn't ~ about their quarrel** je ne savais pas qu'ils s'étaient disputés, je n'étais au courant de leur dispute; **I didn't ~ about the accident** je n'étais pas au courant de cet accident; **I didn't ~ about that** j'ignorais cela, je n'étais pas au courant; **he ~s about antiques** il s'y connaît en antiquités; **do you ~ about Paul?** tu es au courant pour Paul?; **I don't ~ about you, but I think it's terrible** je ne sais pas ce que tu en penses mais personnellement je trouve ça affreux; **so you're satisfied?** — **I don't ~ about that** alors tu es satisfait? — pas vraiment; **I'm not going to school tomorrow** — **I don't ~ about that!*** je ne vais pas à l'école demain — c'est à voir *or* c'est ce qu'on va voir!

♦ **to know of** (= *be acquainted with*) connaître; (= *be aware of*) savoir; (= *learn about*) apprendre; (= *have heard of*) entendre parler de; **do you ~ of a good hairdresser?** vous connaissez un bon coiffeur?; **I ~ of a nice little café** je connais un petit café sympathique; **I'd ~n of his death for some time** je savais depuis quelque temps qu'il était mort; **is he married?** — **not that I ~ of** il est marié? — pas que je sache *or* pas à ma connaissance; **I knew of his death through a friend** j'ai appris sa mort par un ami; **I ~ of you through your sister** j'ai entendu parler de vous par votre sœur; **I don't ~ him but I ~ of him** je ne le connais pas mais j'ai entendu parler de lui; **I ~ of no reason why he should have committed suicide** je ne lui connais aucune raison de se suicider; *BUT* **I ~ of no evidence for this claim** rien à ma connaissance ne permet de l'affirmer

♦ **to know sb/sth from sb/sth** (= *distinguish*) savoir distinguer qn/qch de qn/qch, savoir faire la différence entre qn/qch et qn/qch; **students may not ~ a pronoun from an adverb** les étudiants ne savent pas toujours distinguer un pronom d'un adverbe; **he doesn't ~ good wine from cheap plonk*** il ne sait pas faire la différence entre un bon vin et une piquette, il est incapable de distinguer un bon vin d'une piquette; *BUT* **he doesn't ~ one end of a horse/hammer from the other** c'est à peine s'il sait ce que c'est qu'un cheval/marteau

♦ **to know sb/sth** + *infinitive*: **I've never ~n him to smile** je ne l'ai jamais vu sourire; **I've never ~n her to be wrong** je dois dire qu'elle ne se trompe jamais; **I've ~n such things to happen before** ça s'est déjà produit auparavant; **well, it has been ~n (to happen)** enfin, ça c'est déjà vu; **I've never ~n it to rain like this in June** je n'ai jamais vu autant de pluie en juin

♦ **to know better**: **I ~ better than to offer advice** je me garde bien de donner des conseils; **he ~s better than to touch his capital** il est trop prudent pour entamer son capital; **you ought to ~ better than to listen to him** tu sais bien qu'il ne faut pas l'écouter; **you ought to have ~n better** tu aurais dû réfléchir; **he should ~**

better at his age à son âge il devrait avoir un peu plus de bon sens; **they re-used needles because they didn't ~ any better** ils réutilisaient les seringues par ignorance; **he says he didn't do it but I ~ better** il dit qu'il ne l'a pas fait mais je ne suis pas dupe

♦ **to know best**: **mother ~s best!** maman a toujours raison!; **you ~ best, I suppose!** bon, puisque tu le dis!

♦ **to get to know** [+ *fact*] apprendre; [+ *person*] faire plus ample connaissance avec, apprendre à connaître; **I'd like to see you again and get to ~ you better** j'aimerais vous revoir et faire plus ample connaissance avec vous *or* apprendre à mieux vous connaître

♦ **to let sb know**: **I'll let you ~** je vous le ferai savoir; **I'll let you ~ on Monday** je te dirai *or* te ferai savoir ça lundi; (*in advance*) **if you can't come, please let me ~** préviens-moi si tu ne peux pas venir

♦ **to let sb know sth** dire qch à qn; **I'll let you ~ the price as soon as possible** je te dirai combien ça coûte dès que possible; **let me ~ if I can help so I can help us être utile, dites-le-moi; *BUT* **he soon let me ~ what he thought of it** il n'a pas tardé à me faire savoir ce qu'il en pensait

boxed-4 NOUN

♦ **to be in the know*** être au courant *or* au parfum*

boxed-5 COMPOUNDS

▸ **know-all*** N (*Brit*) (Monsieur) je-sais-tout* m, (Madame *or* Mademoiselle) je-sais-tout* f

▸ **know-how*** N savoir-faire m; **they have the materials to make the missile but they haven't got the ~-how** ils ont le matériel nécessaire à la fabrication du missile mais ils n'ont pas le savoir-faire; **after years in the job he has acquired a lot of ~-how** après des années dans cet emploi il a acquis beaucoup de savoir-faire *or* de métier; **you need quite a bit of ~-how to operate this machine** il faut pas mal s'y connaître pour faire marcher cette machine

▸ **know-it-all*** N (*US*) = know-all

knowable ['nəʊəbəl] ADJ connaissable

knowing ['nəʊɪŋ] boxed-1 ADJ boxed-a (= *shrewd*) fin, malin (-igne f); (= *wise*) sage boxed-b (= *arch*) [*look, smile*] entendu boxed-2 N **there's no ~ what he might do** impossible de savoir ce qu'il va faire; **will he help us?** — **there's no ~** est-ce qu'il va nous aider? — on ne peut pas savoir

knowingly ['nəʊɪŋlɪ] ADV boxed-a (= *consciously*) sciemment, intentionnellement boxed-b (= *archly*) [*look, smile, nod*] d'un air entendu

▼**knowledge** ['nɒlɪdʒ] boxed-1 N (*NonC*) boxed-a (= *understanding, awareness*) connaissance f; **to have ~** avoir connaissance de; **to have no ~ of** ne pas savoir, ignorer; **to (the best of) my ~** à ma connaissance, pour autant que je sache; **not to my ~** pas à ma connaissance, pas que je sache; **they had never to her ~ complained before** à sa connaissance ils ne s'étaient jamais plaints auparavant; **without his ~** à son insu, sans qu'il le sache; **without the ~ of her mother** à l'insu de sa mère, sans que sa mère le sache; **to bring sth to sb's ~** porter qch à la connaissance de qn; **to bring to sb's ~ that ...** porter à la connaissance de qn le fait que ...; **it has come to my ~ that ...** j'ai appris que ...; **~ of the facts** la connaissance des faits; **it's common** *or* **public ~ that ...** il est de notoriété publique que ...

boxed-b (= *body of knowledge*) savoir m; (= *learning, facts learnt*) connaissances fpl; **his ~ will die with him** son savoir mourra avec lui; **my ~ of English is elementary** mes connaissances d'anglais sont élémentaires; **he has a thorough ~ of geography** il a de grandes connaissances en géographie, il possède la géographie à fond; **he has a working ~ of Japanese** il possède les éléments de base du japonais

> LANGUAGE IN USE: **knowledge** 19.2

2 COMP ► **knowledge-based system** N (*Comput*) système *m* expert ► **knowledge engineering** N (*Comput*) génie *m* cognitif

knowledgeable ['nɒlɪdʒəbl] ADJ [*person*] (*in general*) cultivé; (*in a given subject*) qui s'y connaît; **she's very ~ about cars** elle s'y connaît en voitures

knowledgeably ['nɒlɪdʒəblɪ] ADV de manière compétente

known [nəʊn] **1** N *ptp of* **know**
2 ADJ connu; **to be ~ for sth/for doing sth** être connu pour qch/pour faire qch; **she wishes to be ~ as Jane Beattie** elle veut se faire appeler Jane Beattie; **he is ~ to be unreliable** il est bien connu qu'on ne peut pas compter sur lui; **he is ~ to have been there/to be dishonest** on sait qu'il y a été/qu'il est malhonnête; **it soon became ~ that ...** on a bientôt su que ...; **to make sth ~ to sb** faire savoir qch à qn; **to make o.s. ~ to sb** se présenter à qn; **to make one's presence ~ to sb** manifester sa présence à qn; **~ to the Ancient Greeks** connu des Grecs de l'antiquité; **to let it be ~ that** faire savoir que; **it is a ~ fact that ...** c'est un fait établi que ...; **an internationally-~ expert** un expert reconnu au plan international; **he is a ~ quantity** on sait ce qu'il vaut; **the most dangerous snake ~ to man** le serpent le plus dangereux que l'homme connaisse

knuckle ['nʌkl] **1** N articulation *f or* jointure *f* du doigt; **to graze one's ~s** s'écorcher les articulations des doigts; **to be near the ~*** être limite* ► **rap 2** COMP ► **knuckle-bone** N (*Anat*) articulation *f* du doigt; (*Culin*) os *m* de jarret
► **knuckle down*** VI s'y mettre; **to ~ down to work** s'atteler au travail
► **knuckle under*** VI céder

knuckleduster ['nʌkl,dʌstər] N coup-de-poing *m* américain

knucklehead: ['nʌklhed] N crétin(e)* *m(f)*, nouille* *f*

knurl [nɜːl] **1** N (*in wood*) nœud *m*; (*Tech*) moletage *m* **2** VT (*Tech*) moleter

KO* ['keɪ'əʊ] ABBR = **knockout 1** N (*pl* **KO's**) (= *blow*) K.-O. *m* **2** VT (*vb: pret, ptp* **KO'd** ['keɪ'əʊd]) (*gen, Boxing*) mettre K.-O.

koala [kəʊ'ɑːlə] N (*also ~ bear*) koala *m*

kohl [kəʊl] **1** N khôl *m* **2** COMP ► **kohl pencil** N crayon *m* khôl

kohlrabi [kəʊl'rɑːbɪ] N (*pl* **kohlrabies**) chou-rave *m*

kook: [kuːk] N (*US*) dingue* *mf*

kookaburra ['kʊkə,bʌrə] N kookaburra *m*

kookie:, kooky: ['kuːkɪ] ADJ (*US*) dingue, cinglé

kopeck ['kəʊpek] N kopeck *m*

Koran [kɒ'rɑːn] N Coran *m*

Koranic [kɒ'rænɪk] ADJ coranique

Korea [kə'rɪə] N la Corée; **North/South ~** la Corée du Nord/du Sud

Korean [kə'rɪən] **1** ADJ coréen; **North/South ~** nord-/sud-coréen **2** a N Coréen(ne) *m(f)*; **North/South ~** Nord-/Sud-Coréen(ne) **b** (*Ling*) coréen *m*

korma ['kɔːmə] N *type de curry souvent préparé à la crème et à la noix de coco*

kosher ['kəʊʃər] ADJ **a** (*Rel*) casher *inv*, kasher *inv* **b** (* *fig*) **it's ~** c'est OK*; **there's something not quite ~ about him/it** il y a quelque chose de pas très catholique* en lui/là-dedans

Kosovo ['kɒsə,vəʊ] N le Kosovo

Kowloon Peninsula ['kaʊluːnpɪ'nɪnsjʊlə] N péninsule *f* de Kowloon

kowtow ['kaʊ'taʊ] VI se prosterner; **to ~ to sb** courber l'échine devant qn, faire des courbettes devant qn

KP [keɪ'piː] N **a** (*US Mil*) (ABBR = **kitchen police**) → **kitchen b** (*Med*) ABBR = **Kaposi's sarcoma**

kph [,keɪpiː'aɪtʃ] N (ABBR = **kilometres per hour**) km/h

kraal [krɑːl] N kraal *m*

Kraut: [kraʊt] N (*pej*) Boche: *mf*

Kremlin ['kremlɪn] N Kremlin *m*

kremlinologist ['kremlɪ'nɒlədʒɪst] N kreml-

nologue *mf*

kremlinology ['kremlɪ'nɒlədʒɪ] N kremlinologie *f*

krill [krɪl] N (*pl inv*) krill *m*

Krishna ['krɪʃnə] N (= *deity*) Krisna *or* Krishna; (= *river*) Krishna *m*, Kistna *m*

Krishnaism ['krɪʃnə,ɪzəm] N kris(h)naïsme *m*

krona ['krəʊnə] N couronne *f* (suédoise)

krone ['krəʊnə] N (*Danish*) couronne *f* (danoise); (*Norwegian*) couronne *f* (norvégienne)

Krugerrand ['kruːgə,rænd] N krugerrand *m*

Krum(m)horn ['krʌm,hɔːn] N (*Mus*) cromorne *m*

krypton ['krɪptɒn] N krypton *m*

KS ABBR = **Kansas**

Kt (*Brit*) ABBR = **knight**

kudos* ['kjuːdɒs] N (*NonC*) gloire *f*; **to have ~** avoir du prestige; **he got all the ~** c'est lui qui a récolté toute la gloire *or* tous les lauriers

Ku Klux Klan ['kuː'klʌks'klæn] N Ku Klux Klan *m*

kummel ['kɪməl] N kummel *m*

kumquat ['kʌmkwɒt] N kumquat *m*

kung fu ['kʌŋ'fuː] N kung-fu *m*

Kuomintang ['kwəʊ'mɪn'tæŋ] N Kuo-min-tang *m*

Kurd [kɜːd] N Kurde *mf*

Kurdish ['kɜːdɪʃ] ADJ kurde

Kurdistan [,kɜːdɪ'stɑːn] N le Kurdistan

Kuwait [kʊ'weɪt] N le Koweït

Kuwaiti [kʊ'weɪtɪ] **1** N Koweitien(ne) *m(f)* **2** ADJ koweitien

kvas(s) [kvɑːs] N kvas *or* kvass *m*

kvetch* [kvetʃ] VI (*US*) se plaindre (**about** de), râler*

kW (ABBR = **kilowatt**) kW

kwashiorkor [,kwɑːʃɪ'ɔːr] N kwashiorkor *m*

kWh (ABBR = **kilowatt-hour(s)**) kWh

KY ABBR = **Kentucky**

Kyrgyzstan [,kɜːgɪs'tɑːn] N = **Kirg(h)izstan**

L

L, l [el] [1] N [a] (= letter) L, l m; **L for London** ◊ **L for Love** (US) ≈ L comme Louis [b] (ABBR = **li-tre(s)**) l [c] (US) **the L*** le métro aérien [d] (Geog) (ABBR = **Lake**) L [e] (US) (ABBR = **left**) gauche [f] (ABBR = **large**) L [g] (pour indiquer la taille sur l'étiquette) [g] (Ling) ABBR = **Latin** [2] COMP ► **L-driver** N (Brit Aut) conducteur m, -trice f débutant(e) ► **L-plate** N (Brit Aut) plaque signalant la conduite accompagnée; [of driving school] plaque f d'auto-école ► **L-shaped** ADJ [room] en (forme de) L

LA¹ [el'eɪ] N = **Los Angeles**

LA² ABBR = **Louisiana**

La ABBR = **Lane**

La. ABBR = **Louisiana**

Lab (Brit Pol) ABBR = **Labour** [1] ADJ travailliste [2] N (NonC) le parti travailliste, les travaillistes mpl

lab* [læb] [1] N (ABBR = **laboratory**) labo* m [2] COMP [work, test] en laboratoire ► **lab book** N (Scol etc) cahier m de travaux pratiques ► **lab coat** N blouse f blanche ► **lab technician** N technicien(ne) m(f) de laboratoire

label ['leɪbl] [1] N (lit, fig, Ling) étiquette f; (= brand guarantee) label m; **an album on the Technix** ~ un album sorti chez Technix or sous le label Technix; **he was stuck with the ~ of "political activist"** il avait du mal à se défaire de l'étiquette d'« activiste politique » → **luggage** [2] VT [a] (+ parcel, bottle) coller une or des étiquette(s) sur; (Comm) (+ goods for sale) étiqueter; **all packets must be clearly ~led** tous les paquets doivent être clairement étiquetés; **the bottle was not ~led** il n'y avait pas d'étiquette sur la bouteille; **the bottle was ~led "poison"** sur la bouteille il y avait marqué « poison » [b] (fig) (+ person, group) étiqueter, cataloguer (pej) (**as** comme); **he was ~led a dissident** on l'a étiqueté or catalogué comme dissident [c] (Ling) marquer

labia ['leɪbɪə] N (pl of **labium**) lèvres fpl; **~ minora/majora** petites/grandes lèvres fpl

labial ['leɪbɪəl] [1] ADJ (Anat, Phon) labial [2] N (Phon) labiale f

labiodental [ˌleɪbɪəʊ'dentəl] [1] ADJ labiodental [2] N labiodentale f

labiovelar [ˌleɪbɪəʊ'viːlə'] ADJ, N labiovélaire f

labor ['leɪbə'] (US) = **labour**

laboratory [lə'bɒrətərɪ, (US) 'læbrətɔːrɪ] [1] N laboratoire m → **language** [2] COMP [experiment, instrument, product] de laboratoire ► **laboratory assistant** N assistant(e) m(f) de laboratoire, laborantin(e) m(f) ► **laboratory equipment** N équipement m de laboratoire ► **laboratory school** N (US) école f d'application ► **laboratory technician** N technicien(ne) m(f) de laboratoire

laborious [lə'bɔːrɪəs] ADJ laborieux

laboriously [lə'bɔːrɪəslɪ] ADV laborieusement

labour, labor (US) ['leɪbə'] [1] N [a] (= hard work, task) travail m; **~ of love** tâche f accomplie avec amour; **this biography is clearly a ~ of love** il est évident que cette bio-graphie a été écrite avec amour; **his involvement is more a ~ of love than a financial investment** il s'est engagé par passion, plus que par intérêt financier; **~s of Hercules** travaux mpl d'Hercule → **hard, manual**

[b] (NonC: Ind = workers) main-d'œuvre f; **Minister/Ministry of Labour** ◊ **Secretary/Department of Labour** (US) ministre m/ministère m du Travail → **management, skilled**

[c] (Pol) **Labour** le parti travailliste, les travaillistes mpl; **he votes Labour** il vote travailliste

[d] (Med) travail m; **in ~** en travail, en train d'accoucher; **to go into ~** commencer à avoir des contractions

[2] ADJ (Pol) **Labour** [leader, party] travailliste

[3] VI [a] (= work with effort) travailler dur (**at** à); (= work with difficulty) peiner (**at** sur); **to ~ to do** peiner pour faire; **to ~ up a slope** [person, car] gravir péniblement une pente [b] [engine, motor] peiner; [ship, boat] fatiguer [c] **to ~ under a delusion** être victime d'une illusion; **to ~ under the delusion** or **misapprehension that ...** s'imaginer que ...

[4] VT insister sur, s'étendre sur; **I won't ~ the point** je n'insisterai pas (lourdement) sur ce point, je ne m'étendrai pas là-dessus

[5] COMP (Ind) [dispute, trouble] ouvrier ► **labor union** N (US) syndicat m ► **labo(u)r agreement** N convention f collective ► **labo(u)r camp** N camp m de travail ► **Labo(u)r Day** N fête f du Travail (Brit: 1er mai; US, Can: premier lundi de septembre) ► **Labour Exchange** N (Brit: formerly) ≈ Bourse f de l'emploi†, ≈ Agence f pour l'emploi ► **labo(u)r force** N (Ind) main-d'œuvre f, travailleurs mpl ► **labo(u)r-intensive** ADJ intensif en main-d'œuvre ► **labo(u)r laws** NPL législation f or droit m du travail ► **labo(u)r market** N marché m du travail ► **labo(u)r movement** N (Pol) mouvement m ouvrier; **the Labo(u)r movement** le mouvement travailliste ► **labo(u)r pains** NPL (Med) douleurs fpl de l'accouchement ► **labo(u)r-saving** ADJ qui facilite le travail ► **labo(u)r-saving device** N (in household) appareil m ménager ► **labo(u)r shortage** N (Ind) pénurie f de main-d'œuvre ► **labo(u)r supply** N (Ind) main-d'œuvre f (disponible) ► **labo(u)r ward** N (Med) salle f d'accouchement or de travail

---

┌─────────────────┐
│ **LABOR DAY** │
└─────────────────┘

La fête du Travail aux États-Unis et au Canada est fixée au premier lundi de septembre. Instituée par le Congrès en 1894 après avoir été réclamée par les mouvements ouvriers pendant douze ans, elle a perdu une grande partie de son caractère politique pour devenir un jour férié assez ordinaire et l'occasion de partir pour un long week-end avant la rentrée des classes.

---

laboured, labored (US) ['leɪbəd] ADJ [a] (= involving effort) [movement] pénible; [debate, negotiations, process, task] laborieux; **~ breath-ing** respiration f pénible or difficile [b] (= clumsy) [joke, pun, rhyme, style] lourd, laborieux

labourer, laborer (US) ['leɪbərə'] N ouvrier m, travailleur m; (on farm) ouvrier m agricole; (on roads, building sites etc) manœuvre m ■ (PROV) **the ~ is worthy of his hire** l'ouvrier mérite son salaire → **dock¹**

labouring, laboring (US) ['leɪbərɪŋ] ADJ [class] ouvrier

labourite, laborite (US) ['leɪbəraɪt] N (Pol) travailliste mf

Labrador ['læbrə,dɔːr] N [a] (Geog) le Labrador [b] (= dog: also **labrador**) labrador m

laburnum [lə'bɜːnəm] N cytise m, faux ébénier m

labyrinth ['læbɪrɪnθ] N (lit, fig) labyrinthe m; **a ~ of streets** un dédale or un labyrinthe de rues

labyrinthine [ˌlæbɪ'rɪnθaɪn] ADJ labyrinthique, labyrinthien

lace [leɪs] [1] N [a] (NonC: Tex) dentelle f; **dress trimmed with ~** robe f bordée de dentelle(s); **a piece of ~** de la dentelle [b] (of shoe, corset) lacet m [2] VT [a] (also **~ up**) (+ shoe, corset) lacer; **to ~ one's fingers together** joindre les mains [b] **to ~ with** (+ alcohol) arroser de; **tea ~d with whisky** du thé arrosé de whisky; **coffee ~d with cyanide** du café dans lequel on a ajouté du cyanure; **her comments were ~d with sarcasm/humour** ses propos étaient empreints de sarcasme/d'humour [3] VI (also **~ up**) se lacer [4] COMP [collar, curtains] de or en dentelle ► **lace-ups*** NPL = **lace-up shoes** ► **lace-up shoes** NPL (Brit) chaussures fpl à lacets

lacemaker ['leɪsˌmeɪkə'] N dentellier m, -ière f

lacemaking ['leɪsˌmeɪkɪŋ] N fabrication f de la dentelle, dentellerie f

lacerate ['læsəreɪt] VT (lit) (+ face, skin, clothes) lacérer; (fig) (+ person) déchirer, fendre le cœur de

laceration [ˌlæsə'reɪʃən] N (= act) lacération f; (= tear: also Med) déchirure f

lacey ['leɪsɪ] ADJ = **lacy**

lachrymal ['lækrɪməl] ADJ lacrymal

lachrymose ['lækrɪməʊs] ADJ (liter) larmoyant

▼ **lack** [læk] [1] N manque m; **through** or **for ~** faute de, par manque de; **such was their ~ of confidence that ...** ils manquaient tellement de confiance que ...; **there was a complete ~ of interest in my proposals** mes suggestions se sont heurtées à une indifférence totale; **there was no ~ of applicants/customers** ce n'étaient pas les candidats/les clients qui manquaient → **try**

[2] VT (+ confidence, friends, strength, interest) manquer de; **we ~ the resources** nous manquons de ressources, nous n'avons pas les ressources nécessaires; **he doesn't ~ talent** ce n'est pas le talent qui lui manque or qui lui fait défaut

[3] VI [a] **to be ~ing** [food, money etc] manquer, faire défaut; **innovation has been sadly ~ing**

throughout this project l'innovation a fait cruellement défaut tout au long de ce projet **b to be ~ing in** ◊ **to ~ for** [person] manquer de

lackadaisical [ˌlækəˈdeɪzɪkəl] ADJ (= listless) nonchalant, apathique; (= lazy) indolent; [work] fait à la va-comme-je-te-pousse*

lackey [ˈlækɪ] N laquais m (also pej), larbin* m (pej)

lacking* [ˈlækɪŋ] ADJ (= stupid) simplet, demeuré*

lacklustre, lackluster (US) [ˈlækˌlʌstəʳ] ADJ terne, peu brillant

laconic [ləˈkɒnɪk] ADJ laconique

laconically [ləˈkɒnɪkəlɪ] ADV laconiquement

lacquer [ˈlækəʳ] **1** N (= substance: for wood, hair etc) laque f; (= object) laque m; **~ ware** laques mpl **2** VT [+ wood] laquer; (Brit) [+ hair] mettre de la laque sur

lacrosse [ləˈkrɒs] **1** N lacrosse m **2** COMP ► **lacrosse stick** N crosse f

lactase [ˈlækteɪs] N lactase f

lactate [ˈlækteɪt] **1** N (Chem) lactate m **2** VI produire du lait

lactation [lækˈteɪʃən] N lactation f

lacteal [ˈlæktɪəl] **1** ADJ lacté **2 lacteals** NPL veines fpl lactées

lactic [ˈlæktɪk] **1** ADJ lacté **2** COMP ► **lactic acid** N (Chem) acide m lactique

lactiferous [lækˈtɪfərəs] ADJ lactifère

lactogenic [ˌlæktəˈdʒenɪk] ADJ lactogène

lacto-ovo-vegetarian [ˌlæktəʊˌəʊvəʊˌvedʒɪˈtɛərɪən] N lacto-ovo-végétarien(ne) m(f)

lactose [ˈlæktəʊs] N lactose m

lacto-vegetarian [ˌlæktəʊˌvedʒɪˈtɛərɪən] N lactovégétarien(ne) m(f)

lacuna [ləˈkjuːnə] N (pl **lacunas** or **lacunae** [ləˈkjuːniː]) lacune f

lacustrine [ləˈkʌstraɪn] ADJ lacustre

lacy [ˈleɪsɪ] ADJ [underwear, shirt, cushion] (= made of lace) en dentelle; (= containing lace) avec des dentelles; (= resembling lace) **her tights had a ~ pattern** ses collants avaient un motif de dentelle; **the frost made a ~ pattern** il y avait une dentelle de givre

lad [læd] N (esp Brit) (= boy) garçon m, gars* m; (* = son) fiston* m; **when I was a ~** quand j'étais jeune, dans mon jeune temps; **he's only a ~** ce n'est qu'un gosse* ou un gamin*; (Brit) **I'm going for a drink with the ~s*** je vais boire un pot* avec les copains; **come on ~s!** allez les gars!*; (Brit) **he's one of the ~s*** il fait partie de la bande; (Brit) **he's a bit of a ~*** c'est un vrai mec* → **stable²**

ladder [ˈlædəʳ] **1** N **a** (lit, fig) échelle f; (fig) **to be at the top/bottom of the ~** être en haut/en bas de l'échelle; **the social ~** l'échelle f sociale; **to move up the social ~** monter dans l'échelle sociale; **to move up the career ~** monter dans la hiérarchie; **she has reached the top of the career ~** elle est au sommet de sa carrière; **to get on the housing ~** accéder à la propriété; **an evolutionary ~ from monkey to ape to man** l'échelle de l'évolution du singe au grand singe puis à l'homme → **rope, stepladder b** (Brit: in tights) échelle f, maille f filée; **to have a ~ in one's tights** avoir une échelle à son collant, avoir un collant filé **2** VT (Brit) [+ tights, stocking] filer, faire une échelle à **3** VI (Brit) [tights, stocking] filer

ladderproof [ˈlædəpruːf] ADJ (Brit) [tights, stockings] indémaillable

laddie* [ˈlædɪ] N (esp Scot and dial) garçon m, (petit) gars* m; **look here, ~!** dis donc, mon petit* or fiston*!

laddish* [ˈlædɪʃ] ADJ (Brit) macho* inv

lade [leɪd] (pret **laded**, ptp **laden**) VT charger

laden [ˈleɪdn] **1** VB ptp of **lade 2** ADJ chargé

(with de); **fully ~ truck/ship** camion m/navire m avec un plein chargement

la-di-da* [ˈlɑːdɪˈdɑː] (pej) **1** ADJ [person] chochotte*, [voice] maniéré, apprêté; [manner] affecté **2** ADV [talk, speak] de façon maniérée or affectée

lading [ˈleɪdɪŋ] N cargaison f, chargement m → **bill**

ladle [ˈleɪdl] **1** N louche f **2** VT [+ soup] servir (à la louche) ► **ladle out** VT SEP [+ soup] servir (à la louche); (* fig) [+ money, advice] prodiguer (à foison)

lady [ˈleɪdɪ] **1** N **a** (= woman) dame f; **she's a real ~** c'est une vraie dame; **she's no ~** elle n'a aucune classe; **a little old ~** une petite vieille*; **young ~** (married) jeune femme f; (unmarried) jeune fille f; **look here, young ~!** dites donc, jeune fille!; (in shop, restaurant etc) **this is the young ~ who served me** voilà la demoiselle qui m'a servi; **Ladies and Gentlemen!** Mesdames, Mesdemoiselles, Messieurs!; **good morning, ladies and gentlemen** bonjour mesdames, bonjour mesdemoiselles, bonjour messieurs; **listen here, ~*** écoutez, ma petite dame*; (Brit) **the ~ of the house** la maîtresse de maison → **first, leading b** († = wife) dame f; **the headmaster and his ~** le directeur et sa dame†; (hum) **your good ~** votre dame* (also hum); **his young ~*** (= girlfriend) sa petite amie; (= fiancée) sa fiancée **c** (in titles) **Lady Davenport** lady Davenport; **Sir John and Lady Smith** sir John Smith et lady Smith **d** (for ladies) **ladies' hairdresser** coiffeur m, -euse f pour dames; **~'s umbrella** parapluie m de dame or de femme; **he's a ladies' man** or a **~'s man** c'est un homme à femmes **e ladies** (also **ladies' room**) (= public lavatory) toilettes fpl (pour dames); **where is the ladies' room?** ◊ **where is the ladies?** où sont les toilettes (pour dames)?; (on sign) "**Ladies**" « Dames » **f** (Rel) **Our Lady** Notre-Dame f **2** COMP [engineer etc] femme (before n) ► **ladies' auxiliary** N (US Med) association de bénévoles s'occupant d'œuvres de bienfaisance dans un hôpital ► **Lady Bountiful** N généreuse bienfaitrice f ► **Lady Chapel** N (Rel) chapelle f de la (Sainte) Vierge ► **Lady Day** N (Brit) la fête de l'Annonciation ► **lady doctor** N femme f médecin ► **lady friend*** N amie f ► **lady-in-waiting** N (pl **ladies-in-waiting**) dame f d'honneur ► **lady-love** N († or hum) **his ~-love** sa bien-aimée†, la dame de ses pensées (hum) ► **Lady Mayoress** N (Brit) femme f du lord-maire ► **Lady Muck** N **she thinks she's Lady Muck*** ce qu'elle peut se croire!* ► **lady's finger** N (= biscuit) boudoir m; (= vegetable) gombo m ► **lady's maid** N femme f de chambre (attachée au service particulier d'une dame) ► **lady teacher** N femme f professeur

ladybird [ˈleɪdɪbɜːd] N (Brit) coccinelle f, bête f à bon Dieu

ladybug [ˈleɪdɪbʌg] N (US) = **ladybird**

ladyfinger [ˈleɪdɪˌfɪŋgəʳ] N (US Culin) boudoir m (biscuit)

ladykiller [ˈleɪdɪˌkɪləʳ] N don Juan m, bourreau m des cœurs (hum)

ladylike [ˈleɪdɪlaɪk] ADJ [person] bien élevé, distingué; [manners] raffiné; **it's not ~ to yawn** une jeune fille bien élevée or comme il faut ne bâille pas

ladyship [ˈleɪdɪʃɪp] N **Her/Your Ladyship** Madame f (la comtesse or la baronne etc)

lag¹ [læg] **1** N (= delay) retard m; (between two events) décalage m → **jet¹, time 2** VI rester en arrière, traîner; **he was ~ging behind the others** il était à la traîne; (physically) il traînait derrière les autres; **their country ~s behind ours in car exports** leur pays a du retard or est en retard sur le nôtre dans l'exportation automobile; **he now ~s ten points behind the**

leader il a maintenant un retard de dix points sur le leader ► **lag behind** VI rester en arrière, traîner; **the government is ~ging behind in the opinion polls** le gouvernement est à la traîne dans les sondages

lag² [læg] VT [+ pipes] calorifuger

lag³† [læg] N (esp Brit) **old ~** récidiviste mf, cheval m de retour

lager [ˈlɑːgəʳ] N lager f, ≈ bière f blonde; (Brit) **~ lout** jeune voyou m (porté sur la bière)

laggard [ˈlægəd] N traînard(e) m(f)

lagging [ˈlægɪŋ] N (NonC) [= material] calorifuge m; (= act) calorifugeage m

lagniappe [ˈlænjæp] N (US) prime f

lagoon [ləˈguːn] N (gen) lagune f; (coral) lagon m

Lagos [ˈleɪgɒs] N Lagos m

lah [lɑː] N (Mus) la m

lah-di-dah* [ˈlɑːdɪˈdɑː] = **la-di-da**

laicize [ˈleɪɪsaɪz] VT laïciser

laid [leɪd] **1** VB pt, ptp of **lay¹**; → **new 2** COMP ► **laid-back*** ADJ relax*, décontracté

lain [leɪn] VB ptp of **lie¹**

lair [lɛəʳ] N (lit, fig) tanière f, repaire m

laird [lɛəd] N (Scot) laird m, propriétaire m foncier

laity [ˈleɪɪtɪ] NPL **the ~** les laïcs or les laïques mpl

lake¹ [leɪk] **1** N lac m; (in Geog names) **Lake Michigan** le lac Michigan; **Lake Constance** le lac de Constance; **Lake Geneva** le lac Léman or de Genève **2** COMP ► **the Lake District** N (Brit Geog) la région des lacs ► **lake dwellers** NPL (Hist) habitants mpl d'un village (or d'une cité) lacustre ► **lake dwelling** N (Hist) habitation f lacustre ► **the Lake poets** NPL (Literat) les lakistes mpl ► **the Lakes** NPL (Brit Geog) = **the Lake District**

lake² [leɪk] N (Art) laque f

Lakeland [ˈleɪklænd] N (Brit Geog) = **the Lake District**; →**lake¹**

lakeside [ˈleɪksaɪd] **1** N bord m de lac **2** ADJ au bord du (or d'un) lac; **along the ~** le long du lac; **by** or **at the ~** au bord du lac

la-la land [ˈlɑːlɑːlænd] N (esp US) Los Angeles, et plus particulièrement Hollywood

Lallans [ˈlælənz] **1** N lallans m (forme littéraire du dialecte parlé dans les Basses Terres d'Écosse) **2** ADJ en lallans

lallygag* [ˈlælɪˌgæg] VI (US) = **lollygag**

lam¹* [læm] **1** VT tabasser* **2** VI **to ~ into sb** (= thrash) rentrer dans qn*; (= scold) engueuler qn*

lam²* [læm] N (US) **on the ~** en fuite, en cavale*; **to take it on the ~** filer, partir en cavale*

lama [ˈlɑːmə] N lama m (Rel)

lamaism [ˈlɑːməˌɪzəm] N (Rel) lamaïsme m

lamaist [ˈlɑːməˌɪst] ADJ, N (Rel) lamaïste mf

lamb [læm] **1** N (Culin, Zool) agneau m; (Rel) **Lamb of God** Agneau de Dieu; **my little ~!*** mon trésor!, mon ange!; **poor ~!*** pauvre petit(e)!; **he followed her like a ~** il l'a suivie sans broncher or sans protester; **like a ~ to the slaughter** comme un agneau que l'on mène à l'abattoir **2** VI agneler, mettre bas **3** COMP ► **lamb chop, lamb cutlet** N côtelette f d'agneau ► **lamb's lettuce** N mâche f, doucette f ► **lamb's wool** N = **lambswool**

lambada [læmˈbɑːdə] N lambada f

lambast [læmˈbæst], **lambaste** [læmˈbeɪst] VT (= scold) réprimander, (= criticize severely) éreinter, démolir; (= beat) rosser*

lambent [ˈlæmbənt] ADJ chatoyant

lambing [ˈlæmɪŋ] N agnelage m; **~ time** ◊ **~ season** (période f d')agnelage m

lambkin [ˈlæmkɪn] N jeune agneau m, agnelet m; **my little ~!*** mon trésor or ange!

lambrequin [ˈlæmbrɪkɪn] N lambrequin m

lambskin ['læmskɪn] [1] N (= skin itself) peau f d'agneau; (= material) agneau m (NonC) [2] ADJ en agneau, d'agneau

lambswool ['læmzwʊl] N (NonC) lambswool m, laine f d'agneau

lame [leɪm] [1] ADJ [a] (= disabled) [person] éclopé; [horse] boiteux; [leg] estropié; **to be ~ boiter**; **to be slightly ~** boitiller; **to go ~** [horse] se mettre à boiter; **this horse is ~ in one leg** ce cheval boite d'une jambe [b] (= feeble) [excuse] mauvais; [performance] piètre (before n); [joke] vaseux; [argument] boiteux [c] (Poetry) [metre] boiteux, faux (fausse f) [2] VT [+ person, animal] estropier [3] N (US⧺) personne f qui n'est pas dans le coup [4] COMP ► **lame duck** N (= failure) canard m boiteux; (US Pol) homme politique non réélu qui assure l'intérim en attendant l'entrée en fonction de son successeur

lamé ['lɑːmeɪ] [1] N lamé m [2] COMP en lamé; **gold ~ jacket** veste f lamée (d')or

lamebrain ['leɪmbreɪn] N crétin(e) m(f)

lamebrained ['leɪmbreɪnd] ADJ crétin

lamely ['leɪmlɪ] ADV [say, ask] sans conviction; **to argue ~ (that ...)** avancer des arguments boiteux (selon lesquels ...)

lameness ['leɪmnɪs] N (lit) claudication f (frm), boiterie f; (of excuse) faiblesse f

lament [lə'ment] [1] N [a] lamentation f [b] (= poem) élégie f; (= song) complainte f; (at funerals) chant m funèbre; (for bagpipes etc) lamentation f [2] VT [+ loss, lack] regretter; **to ~ sb's death** pleurer la mort de qn; **to ~ the fact that ...** regretter que ... (+ subj); **"she doesn't believe me!", he ~ed** « elle ne me croit pas! », gémit-il or se lamenta-t-il; **our (late) ~ed sister** notre sœur regrettée; **the late ~ed James Rose** le regretté James Rose [3] VI se lamenter (for sur); **to ~ over one's lost youth** pleurer sa jeunesse perdue

lamentable ['læməntəbl] ADJ [state, situation, performance] lamentable, déplorable; [incident] fâcheux, regrettable

lamentably ['læməntəblɪ] ADV lamentablement; **there are still ~ few women surgeons** il est déplorable qu'il y ait toujours aussi peu de femmes chirurgiens; **there are, ~, no set rules** il n'y a pas, on peut le déplorer, de règles établies

lamentation [,læmən'teɪʃən] N lamentation f; (Bible) **(the Book of) Lamentations** le livre des Lamentations

laminate ['læmɪneɪt] [1] VT [+ metal] laminer; [+ book jacket] plastifier [2] N stratifié m

laminated ['læmɪneɪtɪd] ADJ [metal] laminé; [glass] feuilleté; [windscreen] (en verre) feuilleté; [book, jacket] plastifié; **~ wood** contreplaqué m

lamp [læmp] [1] N [a] (= light) lampe f; (Aut) feu m → **blowlamp, safety, streetlamp** [b] (= bulb) ampoule f; **100-watt ~** ampoule f de 100 watts [2] COMP ► **lamp bracket** N applique f ► **lamp standard** N réverbère m

lampblack ['læmpblæk] N noir m de fumée or de carbone

lampern ['læmpən] N lamproie f de rivière

lamplight ['læmplaɪt] N **by ~** à la lumière de la (or d'une) lampe

lamplighter ['læmplaɪtər] N allumeur m de réverbères

lamplit ['læmplɪt] ADJ éclairé (par une lampe)

lampoon [læm'puːn] [1] N (gen) virulente satire f; (written) pamphlet m, libelle m; (spoken) diatribe f [2] VT [+ person, action, quality] railler, tourner en dérision, faire la satire de; (in song) chansonner

lampoonist [læm'puːnɪst] N (gen) satiriste m; (= writer) pamphlétaire m; (= singer) chansonnier m

lamppost ['læmppəʊst] N réverbère m; (fig)

between you, me and the ~* tout à fait entre nous, soit dit entre nous

lamprey ['læmprɪ] N lamproie f

lampshade ['læmpʃeɪd] N abat-jour m inv

lampstand ['læmpstænd] N pied m de lampe

LAN [læn] N (Comput) (ABBR = **local area network**) → **local**

lanai [lə'naɪ] N (US) véranda f

Lancaster ['læŋkəstər] N (Geog) Lancaster; (Hist) Lancastre

Lancastrian [læŋ'kæstrɪən] [1] ADJ (Geog) lancastrien, de Lancaster; (Hist) de Lancastre [2] N Lancastrien(ne) m(f), natif m, -ive f or habitant(e) m(f) de Lancaster; (Hist) Lancastrien(ne) m(f), natif m, -ive f or habitant(e) m(f) de Lancastre

lance [lɑːns] [1] N [a] (= weapon) lance f; (= soldier) lancier m [b] (Med) lancette f, bistouri m [2] VT [+ abscess] percer, ouvrir; [+ finger] ouvrir [3] COMP ► **lance corporal** N (Brit Mil) caporal m

lancer ['lɑːnsər] N (= soldier) lancier m

lancet ['lɑːnsɪt] [1] N (Med) lancette f, bistouri m [2] COMP ► **lancet window** N (Archit) fenêtre f en ogive

Lancs. [læŋks] N ABBR = **Lancashire**

land [lænd] [1] N [a] (NonC: as opposed to sea) terre f; **on ~** à terre; **over ~ and sea** sur terre et sur mer; **dry ~** terre f ferme; **on dry ~** sur la terre ferme; **to sight ~** apercevoir la terre; **to go by ~** voyager par voie de terre; **to make ~** toucher terre; (fig) **to see how the ~ lies** ◊ **to find out the lie** (Brit) **or the lay** (US) **of the ~** tâter le terrain, prendre le vent*; (US) **(for) ~'s sake!** juste ciel! (liter) [b] (NonC: Agr) terre f; (= countryside) campagne f; **many people have left the ~** beaucoup de gens ont quitté or déserté la campagne; **agricultural ~** terres fpl agricoles; **fertile ~** terre f fertile; **grazing ~** pâturage m; **to work (on) the ~** travailler la terre; **to live off the ~** vivre de la terre [c] (= property) (large) terre(s) f(pl); (smaller) terrain m; **she's bought a piece of ~** elle a acheté un terrain; **get off my ~!** sortez de mon terrain or de mes terres! [d] (= country, nation) pays m; **people of many ~s** des gens de nationalités diverses; **throughout the ~** dans tout le pays; **a ~ of contrasts** une terre de contrastes; **a ~ of opportunity** un pays où tout le monde a ses chances; **a ~ fit for heroes** un pays digne de ses héros; **to be in the ~ of the living** être encore de ce monde; **~ of milk and honey or flowing with milk and honey** pays m de cocagne; **in the Land of Nod** au pays des rêves → **law, native, promised**

[2] VT [a] [+ cargo] décharger, débarquer; [+ passengers] débarquer; [+ aircraft] poser; [+ fish] prendre; **to ~ a blow on sb's cheek/mouth** ◊ **to ~ sb a blow on the cheek/mouth** frapper qn sur la joue/bouche [b] (* = obtain) [+ job, contract, prize] décrocher* [c] (Brit* = cause to be) **to ~ sb in it** mettre qn dans de beaux draps or dans le pétrin; **that will ~ you in trouble** ça va vous attirer des ennuis; **to ~ sb in debt** endetter qn; **buying the house ~ed him in debt** en achetant la maison, il s'est endetté; **that's what ~ed him in jail** c'est comme ça qu'il s'est retrouvé en prison; **his outspoken comments ~ed him in court for slander** son franc-parler lui a valu un procès en diffamation [d] (Brit*) **to be ~ed with sth** (= left with) avoir qch or rester avec qch sur les bras; (= forced to take on) récolter qch*, devoir se coltiner qch*; **now we're ~ed with all this extra work** maintenant il faut qu'on se coltine* (subj) tout ce boulot* en plus; **I've got ~ed with this job** on m'a collé* ce travail; **being overdrawn could ~ you with big bank charges** avec un dé-

couvert, vous pourriez vous retrouver à payer d'importants frais bancaires

[3] VI [a] [aircraft] atterrir, se poser; (on sea) amerrir; (on ship's deck) apponter; **to ~ on the moon** [rocket, spacecraft] alunir, se poser sur la lune; [person] atterrir sur la lune; **we ~ed at Orly** nous sommes arrivés or nous avons atterri à Orly; **as the plane was coming in to ~** comme l'avion s'apprêtait à atterrir [b] [person, object] (gen) retomber; (= fall) tomber; [ski jumper, gymnast] retomber, se recevoir; **he slipped and ~ed heavily on his arm** il a glissé et est tombé lourdement sur le bras; **to ~ awkwardly** mal retomber; **to ~ on sth** [falling object] tomber sur qch; [person or animal jumping] retomber or atterrir* sur qch; [bird, insect] se poser sur qch; (lit, fig) **to ~ on one's feet** retomber sur ses pieds [c] (from boat) débarquer

[4] COMP [breeze] de terre; [prices] des terrains; [defences] terrestre; [law, policy, reform] agraire; [tax] foncier ► **land agent** N (= steward) régisseur m; (= estate agent) agent m immobilier ► **land army** N (Brit) travailleuses fpl agricoles (pendant les deux guerres mondiales) ► **land forces** NPL armée f de terre, forces fpl terrestres ► **land girl** N (Brit) travailleuse f agricole (pendant les deux guerres mondiales) ► **land grant college** N (US) établissement m d'enseignement supérieur (créé grâce à une donation foncière du gouvernement fédéral) ► **land line** N (Telec) ligne f terrestre ► **land mass** N bloc m continental ► **land-office** N (US fig) **to do a ~-office business** faire d'excellentes affaires ► **land ownership** N propriété f foncière ► **land patent** N (US) titre m (constitutif) de propriété foncière ► **land-poor farmer** N (US) fermier m riche en terre mais pauvre en disponibilités ► **land reform** N réforme f agraire ► **land registry** N (Brit) ≈ bureau m du cadastre ► **Land's End** N (Geog) Land's End (pointe sud-ouest de l'Angleterre) ► **land worker** N ouvrier m, -ière f agricole ► **land yacht** N char m à voile

► **land up*** VI atterrir*, (finir par) se retrouver; **to ~ up in Paris/in jail** atterrir* or finir par se retrouver à Paris/en prison; **the report ~ed up on my desk** le rapport a atterri* or a fini par arriver sur mon bureau; **we finally ~ed up in a small café** nous avons fini par échouer or nous retrouver dans un petit café

landau ['lændɔː] N landau m (véhicule)

landed ['lændɪd] [1] ADJ [proprietor] foncier, terrien; [property] foncier [2] COMP ► **landed gentry** N aristocratie f terrienne ► **landed price** N (Comm) prix m débarqué or au débarquement

landfall ['lændfɔːl] N terre f (aperçue d'un navire); **to make ~** (= see land) apercevoir la terre; (= make land) accoster

landfill ['lændfɪl] N enfouissement m des déchets; **~ site** site m d'enfouissement (des déchets)

landing¹ ['lændɪŋ] [1] N [a] [of aircraft, spacecraft etc] atterrissage m; (on sea) amerrissage m; (on moon) alunissage m; (on deck) appontage m → **crash, pancake, soft** [b] (from ship) débarquement m; (Mil Hist) **the Normandy ~s** le débarquement (du 6 juin 1944) [c] [of high jumper, ski jumper, gymnast] réception f

[2] COMP ► **landing card** N carte f de débarquement ► **landing craft** N (Mil) chaland m or navire m de débarquement ► **landing field** N terrain m d'aviation ► **landing force** N (Mil) troupes fpl de débarquement ► **landing gear** N (Aviat) train m d'atterrissage ► **landing ground** N terrain m d'atterrissage ► **landing lights** NPL (on aircraft) phares mpl d'atterrissage; (on ground) balises fpl (d'atterrissage) ► **landing net** N

(*Fishing*) épuisette *f* ► **landing party** N (*Naut*) détachement *m* de débarquement ► **landing stage** N (*Brit*) débarcadère *m*, appontement *m* ► **landing strip** N (*Aviat*) piste *f* d'atterrissage ► **landing wheels** NPL roues *fpl* du train d'atterrissage

landing² ['lændɪŋ] N (*between stairs*) palier *m*; (= *storey*) étage *m*

landlady ['læn,leɪdɪ] N [*of flat, house*] (*gen*) propriétaire *f*; (= *live-in owner*) logeuse *f*; (*Brit*) [*of pub, guest house*] patronne *f*

landless ['lændlɪs] ADJ sans terre

landlocked ['lændlɒkt] ADJ (= *totally enclosed*) [*country*] enclavé, sans accès à la mer; [*lake*] qui ne communique pas avec la mer; (= *almost totally enclosed*) entouré par les terres

landlord ['læn,lɔːd] N [*of flat, house*] (*gen*) propriétaire *m*; (= *live-in owner*) logeur *m*; (*Brit*) [*of pub, guest house*] patron *m*

landlubber* ['lænd,lʌbəʳ] N (*hum*) marin *m* d'eau douce (*pej*)

landmark ['lændmɑːk] N point *m* de repère; (*fig*) **a ~ in ...** un moment marquant de ..., un temps fort de ...

landmine ['lændmaɪn] N (*Mil*) mine *f* terrestre

landowner ['lændəʊnəʳ] N propriétaire *m* terrien

landowning ['lændəʊnɪŋ] ADJ [*family*] de propriétaires terriens; **the ~ class** les propriétaires *mpl* terriens

Land Rover® ['lændrəʊvəʳ] N Land Rover *f*, landrover *f*

landscape ['lænd,skeɪp] **1** N (= *land, view, picture*) paysage *m* **2** VT [+ *garden*] dessiner; [+ *bomb site, dirty place etc*] aménager **3** ADJ, ADV (*Comput*) en format paysage **4** COMP ► **landscape architect** N architecte *mf* paysagiste ► **landscape gardener** N jardinier *m*, -ière *f* paysagiste ► **landscape gardening** N jardinage *m* paysagiste, paysagisme *m* ► **landscape mode** N (*Comput*) **to print sth in ~ mode** imprimer qch en format paysage ► **landscape painter** N (peintre *m*) paysagiste *mf*

landscaping ['lænd,skeɪpɪŋ] N (*NonC*) aménagements *mpl* paysagers

landslide ['lænd,slaɪd] **1** N glissement *m* de terrain; [*of loose rocks etc*] éboulement *m*; (*fig Pol: also* **~ victory**) victoire *f* écrasante; **to win by a ~** ◊ **to win a ~ victory** remporter une victoire écrasante; **~ majority** majorité *f* écrasante; **2** N (*US Pol*) remporter une victoire électorale écrasante

landslip ['lændslɪp] N (*esp Brit*) glissement *m* de terrain; [*of loose rocks etc*] éboulement *m*

landward ['lændwəd] **1** ADJ (situé *or* dirigé) du côté de la terre; **~ breeze** brise *f* de mer; **~ side** côté *m* terre **2** ADV (*also* **~s**) vers *or* en direction de la terre, vers l'intérieur

lane [leɪn] **1** N **a** (*in country*) chemin *m*, petite route *f*; (*in town*) ruelle *f* **b** (*Aut*) (= *part of road*) voie *f*; (= *line of traffic*) file *f*; **"keep in ~"** ne changez pas de file; **"get in ~"** mettez-vous dans *or* sur la bonne file; (**to be in**) **the left-hand ~** (être *or* rouler sur) la voie de gauche; **three-~ road** route *f* à trois voies; **I'm in the wrong ~** je suis dans *or* sur la mauvaise file; **traffic was reduced to a single ~** on ne roulait plus que sur une seule file **c** (*for aircraft, ships, runners, swimmers*) couloir *m*; **air/shipping ~** couloir *m* aérien/de navigation **2** COMP ► **lane closure** N (*Aut*) fermeture *f* de voie(s) de circulation; **there'll be ~ closures on the M1** certaines voies seront fermées à la circulation sur la M1 ► **lane markings** NPL (*Aut*) signalisation *f* au sol des voies, signalisation *f* horizontale

langlauf ['lɑːŋ,laʊf] N (*Ski*) ski *m* de fond; **~ specialist** fondeur *m*, -euse *f*; **~ skier** skieur *m*, -euse *f* de fond

language ['læŋgwɪdʒ] **1** N **a** (= *particular tongue*) langue *f*; **the French ~** la langue française; **English has become the international ~ of business** l'anglais est devenu la langue internationale des affaires; **he's studying ~s** il fait des études de langues → **dead**, **source** **b** (*NonC* = *ability to talk*) langage *m*; **the faculty of ~** le langage; **animal ~** le langage des animaux; **the origin of ~** l'origine du langage; **how do children acquire ~?** comment se fait l'acquisition du langage chez les enfants?; **speaking is one aspect of ~** la parole est l'un des aspects du langage; **he's studying ~** il étudie les sciences du langage **c** (= *specialized terminology: also Comput*) langage *m*; **the formal ~ of official documents** le langage conventionnel des documents officiels; **scientific/legal ~** langage *m* scientifique/juridique; **the ~ of art/science/flowers** le langage de l'art/de la science/des fleurs; (*fig*) **we're not speaking the same ~ here** nous ne parlons pas le même langage; **to speak the ~ of diplomacy/violence** parler le langage de la diplomatie/violence → **machine**, **sign** **d** (*NonC* = *individual's manner of expression*) langage *m*; (**watch your**) **~!*** surveille ton langage!; **strong** *or* **bad** *or* **foul ~** gros mots *mpl*, grossièretés *fpl* **2** COMP [*studies, textbooks, department*] de langues; [*students, degree*] en langues; [*development*] langagier, linguistique; [*ability*] à s'exprimer ► **language barrier** N barrière *f* linguistique *or* de la langue ► **language laboratory**, **language lab*** N laboratoire *m* de langues; **~ lab training** *or* **practice** entraînement *m* en cabines

languid ['læŋgwɪd] ADJ languissant

languidly ['læŋgwɪdlɪ] ADV avec langueur; **~ graceful/elegant** d'une grâce/élégance langoureuse

languidness ['læŋgwɪdnɪs] N langueur *f*

languish ['læŋgwɪʃ] VI (*gen*) se languir (**for**, **over** après); (*in prison*) se morfondre, dépérir

languishing ['læŋgwɪʃɪŋ] ADJ languissant, langoureux

languor ['læŋgəʳ] N langueur *f*

languorous ['læŋgərəs] ADJ langoureux, alangui

lank [læŋk] ADJ [*hair*] raide et terne; [*grass, plant*] long (longue *f*) et grêle

lanky ['læŋkɪ] ADJ grand et maigre, dégingandé

lanolin ['lænəlɪn] N lanoline *f*

lantern ['læntən] **1** N (*all senses*) lanterne *f*; (*in paper*) lanterne *f* vénitienne, lampion *m* → **Chinese**, **magic** **2** COMP ► **lantern-jawed** ADJ aux joues creuses ► **lantern slide** N plaque *f* de lanterne magique

lanthanum ['lænθənəm] N lanthane *m*

lanyard ['lænjəd] N (*gen, Mil*) cordon *m*; (*Naut*) ride *f* (de hauban)

Lao [laʊ] N (*pl inv*) Lao *mpl*

Laos [laʊs] N le Laos

Laotian ['laʊʃən] **1** ADJ laotien **2** N **a** Laotien(ne) *m(f)* **b** (*Ling*) laotien *m*

Laotze, **Lao-tzu** ['laʊ'tzeɪ] N Laozi *m*, Lao-tseu *m*

lap¹ [læp] **1** N (= *knees*) genoux *mpl*, giron *m* (*gen hum*); **sitting on his mother's ~** assis sur les genoux de sa mère; **with her hands in her ~** les mains sur les genoux; (*fig*) **it fell right into his ~*** ça lui est tombé tout cuit dans le bec*; **they dropped the problem in his ~** ils lui ont laissé *or* collé* le problème (à résoudre); **it's in the ~ of the gods** c'est entre les mains des dieux; (**to live**) **in the ~ of luxury** (vivre) dans le plus grand luxe **2** COMP ► **lap and shoulder belt** N (*Aut*) ceinture *f* (de sécurité) trois points ► **lap dancing** N (*esp US*) numéro de strip-tease où une danseuse s'asseoit de ma-nière suggestive sur les genoux d'un client ► **lap robe** N (*US*) plaid *m* (*pour les genoux*)

lap² [læp] **1** N (*Sport*) tour *m* de piste; **to run a ~** faire un tour de piste; **ten-~ race** course *f* en *or* sur dix tours; **on the 10th ~** au 10ᵉ tour; (*esp Brit*) **~ of honour** tour *m* d'honneur; (*fig*) **we're on the last ~** on a fait le plus gros *or* le plus difficile, on tient le bon bout* **2** VT (*Sport*) [+ *runner, car*] prendre un tour d'avance sur **3** VI (*Racing*) **the car was ~ping at 200km/h** la voiture faisait le circuit à 200 km/h de moyenne

lap³ [læp] **1** VT [+ *milk*] laper **2** VI [*waves*] clapoter (**against** contre)

► **lap up** VT SEP **a** [+ *milk etc*] laper **b** (* *fig*) [+ *information, congratulations, compliments*] avaler, gober; [+ *attention*] se délecter de; **he ~s up everything you say** il gobe* tout ce qu'on lui dit; **he fairly ~ped it up** il buvait du petit-lait*; **the media are ~ping up this latest scandal** les médias se délectent de *or* font leurs choux gras* de ce dernier scandale

lap⁴ [læp] VT (= *wrap*) enrouler (**round** autour de), envelopper (**in** de)

► **lap over** VI [*tiles etc*] se chevaucher

laparoscopy [,læpə'rɒskəpɪ] N laparoscopie *f*, cœlioscopie *f*

laparotomy [,læpə'rɒtəmɪ] N laparotomie *f*

La Paz [læ'pæz] N La Paz

lapdog ['læpdɒg] N petit chien *m* d'appartement, chien *m* de manchon†

lapel [lə'pel] N revers *m* (*de veston etc*); **~ microphone** ◊ **~ mike*** micro *m* cravate

lapidary ['læpɪdərɪ] N (= *craftsman*) lapidaire *m*; (= *craft*) art *m* *or* métier *m* du lapidaire

lapin ['læpɪn] N (*US*) (fourrure *f* *or* peau *f* de) lapin *m*

lapis lazuli ['læpɪs'læzjʊlaɪ] N (= *stone*) lapis(-lazuli) *m*; (= *colour*) bleu *m* lapis(-lazuli)

Lapland ['læp,lænd] N la Laponie

Laplander ['læp,lændəʳ] N Lapon(ne) *m(f)*

Lapp [læp] **1** ADJ lapon **2** N **a** Lapon(ne) *m(f)* **b** (*Ling*) lapon *m*

lapping ['læpɪŋ] N [*of waves*] clapotis *m*

Lappish ['læpɪʃ] = **Lapp 1, 2b**

lapse [læps] **1** N **a** (= *fault*) faute *f* (légère), défaillance *f*; (= *in behaviour*) écart *m* (de conduite); **a ~ into bad habits** un retour à de mauvaises habitudes; **~s of (good) taste** des fautes *fpl* de goût; **a serious security ~** une grave défaillance des services de sécurité; **~s of judgement** des erreurs *fpl* de jugement; **~ of memory** ◊ **memory ~** trou *m* de mémoire; **~ from a diet** entorse *f* à un régime; **a momentary ~ of concentration** *or* **attention** un moment d'inattention **b** (= *passage of time*) intervalle *m*; **a ~ of time** ◊ **a time ~** un laps de temps; **after a ~ of ten weeks** au bout de dix semaines, après un intervalle de dix semaines **c** (= *falling into disuse*) [*of custom etc*] disparition *f*, oubli *m*; [*of right, privilege*] déchéance *f* **2** VI **a** (= *err*) faire un *or* des écart(s) **b** (*Rel*) cesser de pratiquer; **to ~ from grace** perdre l'état de grâce **c** **to ~ into bad habits** prendre de mauvaises habitudes *or* un mauvais pli; **to ~ into silence** se taire; **to ~ into unconsciousness** (re)perdre connaissance; **to ~ into a coma** tomber dans le coma; **he ~d into reverie** il s'est laissé aller à la rêverie; **he ~d into French** il est repassé au français, il s'est remis à parler français; **she ~d into legal jargon** elle s'est remise à parler le jargon juridique **d** [*act, law*] devenir caduc, tomber en désuétude; [*contract*] expirer, venir à expiration; [*ticket, passport*] se périmer; [*membership, subscription*] prendre fin, venir à expiration; **her insurance policy has ~d** sa police d'assurance est périmée *or* n'est plus valable

lapsed [læpst] ADJ [*contract, law*] caduc (-uque *f*); [*ticket, passport*] périmé; **a ~ Catholic** un(e) catholique qui ne pratique plus

laptop (computer) [ˈlæptɒpkəmˈpjuːtəʳ] N (ordinateur *m*) portable *m*

lapwing [ˈlæpwɪŋ] N vanneau *m*

larboard†† [ˈlɑːbəd] (*Naut*) ① N bâbord *m* ② ADJ de bâbord

larceny [ˈlɑːsənɪ] N (*Jur*) vol *m* simple; (*US Jur*) **to commit ~ by servant** commanditer un vol → **grand, petty**

larch [lɑːtʃ] N mélèze *m*

lard [lɑːd] ① N saindoux *m* ② VT (*Culin*) larder (**with** de); (*fig*) **a speech ~ed with quotations/references to ...** un discours bourré *or* truffé de citations/références à ...

larder [ˈlɑːdəʳ] N (= *cupboard*) garde-manger *m inv*; (= *small room*) cellier *m*

large [lɑːdʒ] ① ADJ [*area, town, house, garden, company, object, amount, problem*] grand; [*person, animal, hand, slice, piece*] gros (grosse *f*); [*dose*] fort; [*sum, share, proportion, group*] important; [*population*] nombreux, important; [*family, crowd*] nombreux; [*losses*] lourd, important; [*meal*] copieux, grand; **to get** *or* **grow ~(r)** [*stomach*] grossir; [*population, overdraft*] augmenter; **to make ~r** agrandir; (*Comm: on garment*) **"~"** L; (*of packet, tube*) **the ~ size** la grande modèle; (*of garment*) **the ~st size of this dress** la plus grande taille dans ce modèle de robe; **a ~ number of them refused** beaucoup d'entre eux ont refusé; **= numbers of people came** les gens sont venus nombreux *or* en grand nombre; **a ~ slice of his savings** une bonne partie de ses économies; **a ~ proportion of the business** une part importante des affaires; **to do sth on a ~ scale** faire qch sur une grande échelle *or* en grand → **large-scale**; **to a ~ extent** dans une grande mesure; **in (a) ~ measure** en grande partie, dans une large mesure; **in ~ part** en grande partie; **there he was (as) ~ as life** c'était bien lui; **~r than life** [*character*] plus vrai que nature

② **at ~** (= *at liberty*) en liberté; (*US Pol*) [*candidate, congressman*] non rattaché à une circonscription électorale; **the prisoner is still at ~** le prisonnier court toujours *or* est toujours en liberté; (= *as a whole*) **the country/population at ~** le pays/la population dans son ensemble → **ambassador**

③ ADV **by and ~** d'une façon générale, en gros; **taking it by and ~** à tout prendre → **loom**¹

④ COMP ► **large-handed** ADJ (*fig*) généreux ► **large-hearted** ADJ (*fig*) au grand cœur ► **large intestine** N (*Anat*) gros intestin *m* ► **large-minded** ADJ (*fig*) large d'esprit ► **large-mouth bass** N achigan *m* à grande bouche ► **large-print book** N livre *m* imprimé en gros caractères ► **large-scale** ADJ ⓐ (= *extensive*) [*production, attack, operation*] à grande échelle, [*unrest*] général; [*business activities, reforms, relations*] (fait) sur une grande échelle; [*powers*] étendu ⓑ [*Geog*] [*drawing, map*] à grande échelle ⓒ [*Comput*] **very ~-scale integration** intégration *f* à (très) grande échelle ► **large-size(d)** ADJ grand

largely [ˈlɑːdʒlɪ] ADV [*correct, responsible*] en grande partie; [*ignore*] largement

largeness [ˈlɑːdʒnɪs] N (= *size*) [*of person, body, object*] grande taille *f*; [*of number, amount*] importance *f*; (*fig* = *breadth*) largesse *f*

largesse [lɑːˈʒes] N (NonC = *generosity*) largesse *f*; (= *gifts*) largesses *fpl*

largish [ˈlɑːdʒɪʃ] ADJ assez grand; [*person, body, object*] assez gros (grosse *f*); [*amount, proportion*] assez important

largo [ˈlɑːɡəʊ] ADV, N largo *m inv*

lariat [ˈlærɪət] N (= *lasso*) lasso *m*; (= *tether*) longe *f*

lark¹ [lɑːk] N (*Orn*) alouette *f*; **to be up** *or* **rise with the ~** se lever au chant du coq → **happy, sing**

lark²†* [lɑːk] N blague *f*, niche† *f*; **we only did it for a ~** on l'a seulement fait pour rigoler*, on l'a seulement fait histoire de rigoler*; **what a ~!** quelle rigolade!*, la bonne blague!; **I don't believe in all this horoscope ~** je ne crois pas à ces histoires d'horoscope

► **lark about***, **lark around*** VI faire le fou*; **they were ~ing about with a ball/on their bikes** ils s'amusaient avec une balle/leurs vélos

larkspur [ˈlɑːkspɜːʳ] N (*Bot*) pied-d'alouette *m*

larky [ˈlɑːkɪ] ADJ espiègle

Larry [ˈlærɪ] N *dim of* **Laurence, Lawrence**; → **happy**

larva [ˈlɑːvə] N (pl **larvae** [ˈlɑːviː]) larve *f* (*Zool*)

larval [ˈlɑːvəl] ADJ larvaire (*Zool*)

laryngitis [ˌlærɪnˈdʒaɪtɪs] N laryngite *f*

larynx [ˈlærɪŋks] N (pl **larynxes** *or* **larynges** [ləˈrɪndʒiːz]) larynx *m*

lasagna, lasagne [ləˈzænjə] N lasagne *f inv*

lascivious [ləˈsɪvɪəs] ADJ lascif, luxurieux

lasciviously [ləˈsɪvɪəslɪ] ADV lascivement

lasciviousness [ləˈsɪvɪəsnɪs] N luxure *f*, lasciveté *or* lascivité *f*

laser [ˈleɪzəʳ] ① N laser *m* ② COMP ► **laser beam** N rayon *m* laser ► **laser disk** N disque *m* laser ► **laser-guided** ADJ (*Mil*) guidé par laser ► **laser printer** N (*Comput*) imprimante *f* laser ► **laser proof** N épreuve *f* laser ► **laser show** N spectacle *m* laser ► **laser surgery** N chirurgie *f* au laser ► **laser weapon** N arme *f* laser

lash [læʃ] ① N ⓐ (= *blow from whip*) coup *m* de fouet; **sentenced to ten ~es** condamné à dix coups de fouet; **to feel the ~ of sb's tongue** essuyer les propos cinglants de qn → **whiplash**

ⓑ (*also* **eyelash**) cil *m*

ⓒ (= *thong*) mèche *f*, lanière *f*

② VT ⓐ [*person*] (= *beat*) frapper (d'un grand coup de fouet), fouetter violemment; (= *flog*) flageller

ⓑ [*storm*] s'abattre sur; [*wind*] cingler, fouetter; [*waves*] fouetter; **the wind ~ed the sea into a fury** le vent a déchaîné la mer; **the storm has been ~ing the Bahamas with high winds and heavy rain** de violentes bourrasques de vent et de pluie se sont abattues sur les Bahamas; **the hailstones ~ed my face** la grêle me cinglait le visage; **to ~ sb with one's tongue** faire des remarques cinglantes à qn ⓒ **the crocodile ~ed its tail** le crocodile a donné de grands coups de queue; **the lion ~ed its tail** le lion a fouetté l'air de sa queue ⓓ (= *fasten*) attacher *or* fixer fermement; [+ *cargo*] arrimer; [+ *load*] attacher, amarrer; **to ~ sth to a post** attacher solidement qch à un piquet; **he ~ed himself to the life raft** il s'est attaché *or* amarré solidement au radeau de sauvetage

③ VI **the rain was ~ing against the window** la pluie fouettait *or* cinglait les carreaux

► **lash about** VI (*in bonds, in pain etc*) se débattre violemment

► **lash down** ① VI [*rain*] tomber avec violence ② VT SEP [+ *cargo*] arrimer

► **lash out** ① VI ⓐ **to ~ out at sb (with one's fists/a knife)** envoyer des coups de poing/de couteau à qn; **she ~ed out with her fists** elle s'est débattue à coups de poing; **she ~ed out with a knife** elle a brandi un couteau; (*fig: verbally*) **to ~ out at sb** se répandre en invectives contre qn, fustiger qn (*liter*) ⓑ (* = *spend a lot of money*) faire une folie*; **he ~ed out on a car** il a fait une folie* et s'est payé une voiture ② VT SEP* [+ *money*] lâcher*, allonger*

► **lash up** VT SEP (+ *person, dog*) attacher; [+ *boat*) attacher, amarrer

lashing [ˈlæʃɪŋ] N ⓐ (= *flogging*) flagellation *f*; **to give sb a ~** (*lit*) donner le fouet à qn; (*fig*:

verbally) réprimander sévèrement qn, tancer† vertement qn ⓑ (= *rope*) corde *f*; (*Naut*) amarre *f* ⓒ (*esp Brit**) **~s of cream/butter** avec une montagne *or* des tonnes de crème/beurre; **~s of mascara** des tonnes de mascara

lass [læs] N (*esp Scot and dial*) (= *girl*) jeune fille *f*; († = *sweetheart*) bonne amie† *f*

Lassa fever [ˈlæsəˈfiːvəʳ] N fièvre *f* de Lassa

lassie [ˈlæsɪ] N (*esp Scot and dial*) gamine* *f*, gosse* *f*

lassitude [ˈlæsɪtjuːd] N lassitude *f*

lasso [læˈsuː] ① N (pl **lassos** *or* **lassoes**) ⓐ (= *rope*) lasso *m* ⓑ [*Climbing*) = **lassoing** ② VT prendre au lasso

lassoing [læˈsuːɪŋ] N (*Climbing*) lancer *m* de corde

last¹ [lɑːst] ① ADJ ⓐ (= *final in series*) dernier (*before n*); **the ~ Saturday of the month** le dernier samedi du mois; **the ~ ten pages** les dix dernières pages; **~ but one** ◊ avant-dernier; **the ~ time but one** l'avant-dernière fois; **it's the ~ round but three** il ne reste plus que trois rounds (après celui-ci); **his office is the second ~** son bureau est l'avant-dernier; **the third and ~ point is that ...** le troisième et dernier point est que ...; **to fight to the ~ man** se battre jusqu'au dernier; **to make it through to the ~ four** (*in tournament*) atteindre les demi-finales; (*in race*) arriver dans les quatre premiers → **every**

ⓑ (= *past, most recent*) dernier (*gen after n*); **~ night** (= *evening*) hier soir; (= *night*) cette nuit, la nuit dernière; **~ week/year** la semaine/l'année *f* dernière; **~ month/summer** le mois/l'été *m* dernier; **~ Monday** ◊ **on Monday ~** lundi dernier; **for the ~ few days** ces derniers jours, ces jours-ci; **for the ~ few weeks** ces dernières semaines, depuis quelques semaines; **he hasn't been seen these ~ two years** on ne l'a pas vu ces deux dernières années *or* depuis deux ans; **for the ~ two years he has been ...** depuis deux ans il est ...; **the day before ~** avant-hier; **the night/morning before ~** avant-hier soir/matin; **the week before ~** l'avant-dernière semaine; **what did you do ~ time?** qu'avez-vous fait la dernière fois?; **he was ill (the) ~ time I saw him** il était malade la dernière fois que je l'ai vu; **this time ~ year** l'an dernier à la même époque

ⓒ (= *final*) [*chance, hope*] dernier; **this is my ~ pound** c'est ma dernière livre; **I'm down to my ~ pound** il ne me reste plus qu'une seule livre; **he took the ~ sandwich** il a pris le dernier sandwich; **at the ~ minute** à la dernière minute → **4**; **that was the ~ time I saw him** c'est la dernière fois que je l'ai vu; **that's the ~ time I lend you anything!** c'est la dernière fois que je te prête quelque chose!; **for the ~ time, shut up!** pour la dernière fois, tais-toi!; **~ thing (at night)** juste avant de se coucher; **I'll get it, if it's the ~ thing I do** je l'aurai coûte que coûte *or* même si ça doit me coûter la vie; (*lit, fig*) **to fight to the ~ ditch** se battre jusqu'au bout → **4**; **at one's ~ gasp** (= *dying*) sur le point de mourir, à l'agonie; (* = *exhausted*) à bout de force → **4**; **he was on his ~ legs*** il était à bout; **the company is on its ~ legs*** l'entreprise est au bord de la faillite; **the washing machine is on its ~ legs*** la machine à laver va bientôt nous lâcher, la machine à laver va bientôt rendre l'âme; **she always wants to have the ~ word** elle veut toujours avoir le dernier mot; **it's the ~ word in comfort** c'est ce que l'on fait de mieux *or* c'est le dernier cri en matière de confort → **first, laugh, stand, straw**

ⓓ (= *least likely or desirable*) dernier; **he's the ~ person to ask** c'est la dernière personne à qui demander; **that's the ~ thing to worry about** c'est le dernier *or* le moindre *or* le cadet de mes (*or* tes) soucis

ⓔ (*Rel*) **at the Last Judgement** au Jugement dernier; **the ~ rites** les derniers sacrements *mpl*; **the Last Supper** la Cène; **the ~ trump** or **trumpet** la trompette du Jugement dernier

2 ADV **a** (= *at the end*) en dernier; **she arrived ~** elle est arrivée en dernier *or* la dernière; **he arrived ~ of all** il est arrivé le tout dernier; **his horse came in ~** son cheval est arrivé (bon) dernier; **~ but not least** enfin et surtout; **~ in, first out** dernier entré, premier sorti; **to leave sth/sb till ~** placer qch/qn en dernier *or* à la fin

b (= *most recently*) la dernière fois; **when I ~ saw him** quand je l'ai vu la dernière fois, la dernière fois que je l'ai vu; (*Cards*) **who dealt ~?** qui a donné en dernier?

c (= *finally*) finalement, pour terminer; **~, I would like to say ...** pour terminer *or* enfin, je voudrais dire ...

3 N **a** dernier *m*, -ière *f*; **he was the ~ of the Tudors** ce fut le dernier des Tudor; **this is the ~ of the pears** (*one*) c'est la dernière poire; (*several*) ce sont les dernières poires, voici le reste des poires; **this is the ~ of the cider** c'est tout ce qui reste de *or* comme cidre; **the ~ but one** l'avant-dernier *m*, -ière *f*; **I'd be the ~ to criticize, but ...** ce n'est pas mon genre de critiquer, mais ...; **each one better than the ~** tous meilleurs les uns que les autres; (*fig*) **to stick to one's ~** s'en tenir à ce qu'on sait faire; (*liter*) **to look one's ~ on sth** jeter un ultime regard sur qch

b **the ~** (= *the end*): **we shall never hear the ~ of this** on n'a pas fini d'en entendre parler; **you haven't heard the ~ of this!** vous n'avez pas fini d'en entendre parler!; (*threatening*) vous aurez de mes nouvelles!; (*fig*); **the ~ I heard (of her), she was abroad** aux dernières nouvelles, elle était à l'étranger; **I shall be glad to see the ~ of this** je serai content de voir tout ceci terminé *or* de voir la fin de tout ceci; **we were glad to see the ~ of him** nous avons été contents de le voir partir *or* d'être débarrassés de lui; **that was the ~ I saw of him** c'est la dernière fois que je l'ai vu, je ne l'ai pas revu depuis; **to the ~** jusqu'au bout, jusqu'à la fin → **breathe**

c **at ~** enfin, à la fin; **at (long) ~** enfin; **at long ~ he came** il a enfin fini par arriver; **here he is! — at ~!** le voici! — enfin *or* ce n'est pas trop tôt!

4 COMP ► **last-chance saloon** N (*Brit*) **it's the ~-chance saloon for them** ◊ **they are drinking in the ~-chance saloon** c'est leur dernière chance ► **last-ditch, last-gasp** ADJ ultime, de dernière minute ► **last-minute** ADJ de dernière minute ► **last post** (*Brit*) (= *bugle call*) (sonnerie *f* de l')extinction *f* des feux; (*at funerals*) sonnerie *f* aux morts ► **the Last Supper** N (*Rel*) la Cène

last² [lɑːst] **1** VI **a** (= *continue*) [*pain, film, supplies etc*] durer; **it ~ed two hours** cela a duré deux heures; **it's too good to ~** c'est trop beau pour durer *or* pour que ça dure (*subj*); **will this good weather ~ till Saturday?** est-ce que le beau temps va durer *or* tenir jusqu'à samedi?

b (= *hold out*) tenir; **no one ~s long in this job** personne ne reste longtemps dans ce poste; **after he got pneumonia he didn't ~ long** après sa pneumonie il n'en a pas eu pour longtemps*; **that whisky didn't ~ long** ce whisky n'a pas fait long feu *or* n'a pas duré longtemps

c (= *remain usable*) durer; **made to ~** fait pour durer; **this table will ~ a lifetime** ce table vous fera toute une vie; **will this material ~?** ce tissu fera-t-il de l'usage?

2 VT durer; **this amount should ~ you (for) a week** cela vous durera *or* vous fera une semaine; **I have enough money to ~ me a lifetime** j'ai assez d'argent pour tenir jusqu'à la fin de mes jours; **she must have got enough chocolates to ~ her a lifetime** elle a dû recevoir assez de chocolats pour tenir jusqu'à la

fin de ses jours

► **last out** **1** VI [*person*] tenir (le coup); [*money*] suffire **2** VT SEP faire; **he won't ~ the winter out** il ne passera pas *or* ne fera pas l'hiver, il ne verra pas la fin de l'hiver; **my money doesn't ~ out the month** mon argent ne me fait pas le mois

last³ [lɑːst] N [*of cobbler*] forme *f*

Lastex® ['læsteks] N (*US*) Lastex® *m*

lasting ['lɑːstɪŋ] ADJ [*friendship, situation, benefit, impression, effect*] durable; **to cause ~ damage to sb/sth** affecter qn/qch de façon durable; **to his ~ shame** à sa plus grande honte

lastly ['lɑːstlɪ] ADV (= *as final point, item*) enfin, en dernier lieu; (= *as final action*) enfin

latch [lætʃ] **1** N clenche *f*, loquet *m*; **the door is on** *or* **off the ~** la porte n'est pas fermée à clé; **to leave the door on** *or* **off the ~** fermer la porte sans la verrouiller **2** VT fermer au loquet

► **latch on*** VI **a** (= *grab*) s'accrocher (**to** à) **b** (= *understand*) saisir, piger*

► **latch on to*** VT FUS **a** (= *get possession of*) prendre possession de; (= *catch hold of*) saisir; (*US* = *obtain*) se procurer; **he ~ed on to me as soon as I arrived** il n'a pas arrêté de me coller* depuis que je suis arrivé; **he ~es on to the slightest mistake** il ne laisse pas passer la moindre erreur **b** (= *understand*) saisir, piger*; (= *realize*) se rendre compte de, réaliser*; **when children ~ on to the idea that reading is fun** quand les enfants se rendent compte que la lecture est un plaisir

latchkey ['lætʃkiː] **1** N clé *f* (de la porte d'entrée) **2** COMP ► **latchkey child, latchkey kid*** N enfant qui rentre à la maison avant ses parents

late [leɪt] (*compar* **later**, *superl* **latest**) **1** ADJ **a** (= *delayed, after scheduled time*) **to be ~** [*person*] (*gen*) être en retard; (*arriving*) arriver en retard; **I'm ~** (*gen*) je suis en retard; (*menstrual period*) j'ai du retard* (*euph*), mes règles ont du retard; **to be ~ (in) arriving** arriver avec du retard *or* en retard; **she was ~ (in) returning from work** elle est rentrée du travail en retard; **to be ~ for an appointment** être *or* arriver en retard à un rendez-vous; **I was ~ for work** je suis arrivé au travail en retard; **hurry up, I'm ~ for work** dépêche-toi, je vais arriver en retard au travail; **to be ~ with sth** avoir du retard dans qch; **I was ~ with the rent** (*now paid*) j'avais payé mon loyer en retard; **the train is ~** le train est en retard *or* a du retard; **your essay is ~** vous rendez votre dissertation en retard; **too ~** trop tard; **to make sb ~** mettre qn en retard; **I apologized for my ~ arrival** je me suis excusé d'être arrivé en retard; **we apologize for the ~ arrival of flight XY 709** nous vous prions d'excuser le retard du vol XY 709; **~ arrivals will not be admitted** les retardataires ne seront pas admis; **his campaign got off to a ~ start** sa campagne a démarré tard; **both my babies were ~** mes deux bébés sont nés *or* arrivés après terme → **little**

b (*with time expressions*) **to be 20 minutes ~** avoir 20 minutes de retard; **it made me an hour ~** j'ai eu une heure de retard à cause de ça; **the train is 30 minutes ~** le train a 30 minutes de retard; **I'm/I was two hours ~ for work** je vais arriver/je suis arrivé au travail avec deux heures de retard; **a technical problem on the plane made us two hours ~** un problème technique dans l'avion nous a fait arriver avec deux heures de retard; **I'm a week ~** (*gen*) j'ai une semaine de retard*; (*menstrual period*) j'ai une semaine de retard* (*euph*), mes règles ont une semaine de retard

c (= *after usual time*) [*crop, flowers*] tardif; [*booking*] de dernière minute; **Easter is ~ this year** Pâques est *or* tombe tard cette année; **spring was ~** le printemps était en retard *or* était tardif

d (= *at advanced time of day*) tard; **it was very**

~ il était très tard; **it's getting ~ il se fait tard; **owing to the ~ hour** en raison de l'heure tardive; **at this ~ hour** à cette heure tardive; **to work ~ hours** finir son travail tard le soir, travailler tard le soir; **to keep ~ hours** être un(e) couche-tard* *inv*; **to have a ~ meal/lunch** manger/déjeuner tard; (*Cine*) **there's a ~ (-night) film on Saturdays** le samedi, il y a une séance supplémentaire le soir; (*TV*) **the ~ film tonight is ...** le film diffusé en fin de soirée est ...; (*Theat*) **there's a ~(-night) show on Saturdays** il y a une seconde représentation en soirée le samedi; (*Comm*) **~(-night) opening** nocturne *f*; **there's ~(-night) opening on Thursdays** les magasins ouvrent en nocturne *or* font nocturne* le jeudi; **~(-night) opening Fridays until 7pm** nocturne jusqu'à 19 heures le vendredi

e (= *near end of period or series*) **the ~st edition of the catalogue** la toute dernière édition du catalogue; **the subject of her ~r books is ...** le sujet de ses derniers livres est ...; **two ~ goals** deux buts en fin de match; **at this ~ stage** à ce stade avancé; **he was in his ~ thirties** il approchait de la quarantaine; **in the ~ afternoon** en fin d'après-midi; **she was enjoying the cool ~ evening** elle appréciait la fraîcheur de cette fin de soirée; **by ~ morning** à la fin de la matinée; **in ~ June/September** fin juin/septembre, à la fin (du mois de) juin/septembre; **in ~ spring** à la fin du printemps; **it was not until ~ 1989 that ...** ce n'est qu'à la fin de l'année 1989 que ...; **in the ~ 1980s** à la fin des années 80; **in the ~ 18th century** à la fin du 18ᵉ (siècle); **in the ~ Middle Ages** à la fin du moyen âge; **a ~ Victorian house** une maison de la fin de l'époque victorienne → **later, latest**

f (= *dead*) feu (*liter*); **the ~ queen** feu la reine; **the ~ Harry Thomas** feu Harry Thomas; **my ~ wife** ma pauvre *or* défunte (*frm*) femme; **our ~ colleague** notre regretté (*frm*) *or* défunt (*frm*) collègue

2 ADV **a** (= *after scheduled time*) [*arrive*] en retard; [*start, finish, deliver*] avec du retard; **to arrive ~ for sth** (*meeting, dinner, film*) arriver en retard à qch; **we're running ~ this morning** nous sommes en retard ce matin; **the baby was born ~** le bébé est né *or* arrivé après terme; **the baby was born two weeks ~** le bébé est né avec deux semaines de retard; **he turned up two hours ~** il est arrivé avec deux heures de retard; **we're running about 40 minutes ~** nous avons environ 40 minutes de retard; **work on the new motorway started two years ~** la construction de la nouvelle autoroute a commencé avec deux ans de retard; **too ~** trop tard; **later** → **better**

b (= *after usual time*) **to flower ~** fleurir tard; **her periods started very ~** elle a eu ses premières règles très tard; **they married ~ in life** ils se sont mariés sur le tard; **she had started learning German quite ~ in life** elle avait commencé à apprendre l'allemand assez tard; **she came ~ to acting** elle est devenue comédienne sur le tard; **he had come quite ~ to painting** il s'était mis à la peinture sur le tard

c (= *at advanced time of day*) [*work, get up, sleep, start, finish*] tard; **they stayed up talking until very ~** ils sont restés à parler jusque tard dans la nuit; **the chemist is open ~ on Thursdays** la pharmacie est ouverte tard *or* en nocturne le jeudi; **to stay up ~** veiller tard, se coucher tard; **to work ~ at the office** rester tard au bureau pour travailler; **~ at night** tard dans la nuit *or* la soirée; **~ that night** tard dans la nuit *or* la soirée; **~ last night** tard hier soir; **~ in the afternoon** en fin d'après-midi; **the previous evening** la veille, en fin de soirée; **it was ~ in the evening before I returned to Baker Street** il ne suis retourné à Baker Street qu'en fin de soirée; **~ into the night** tard dans la nuit; (*fig*) **it is rather ~ in the day**

to change your mind c'est un peu tard pour changer d'avis; (*fig*) **it was her intervention, ~ in the day, that saved the scheme** ce fut son intervention, assez tardive, qui sauva le projet

d (= *near end of period*) **~ in 1992** à la fin de l'année 1992, fin 1992; **~ in the year** en fin d'année; **~ last year** à la fin de l'année dernière; **~ in May** fin mai; **they scored ~ in the second half** ils ont marqué à la fin de la deuxième mi-temps; **symptoms appear only ~ in the disease** les symptômes n'apparaissent qu'à un stade avancé de la maladie; **very ~ in the proceedings*** tout à la fin, très tard; **it wasn't until relatively ~ in his career that ...** ce n'est que vers la fin de sa carrière que ...

e (= *recently*) **as ~ as last week** pas plus tard que la semaine dernière, la semaine dernière encore; **as ~ as 1950** en 1950 encore; **as ~ as the 1980s** jusque dans les années 80

f **of ~** (= *lately*) dernièrement, ces derniers temps; **we haven't seen much of him of ~** on ne l'a pas beaucoup vu ces derniers temps

g (*frm = formerly*) **Jane Burdon, ~ of Bristol** Jane Burdon, autrefois domiciliée à Bristol; **Carrington, ~ of the Diplomatic Service** Carrington, ancien membre du corps diplomatique

3 COMP ► **late developer** N he's a ~ developer il n'est pas précoce, il a mis du temps à sortir de l'enfance ► **late-night shopping** N there's ~-night shopping on Thursdays le magasin ouvre en nocturne *or* fait nocturne* le jeudi

latecomer ['leɪtkʌmə'] N **a** (*lit*) retardataire *mf*; (*frm*) **~s will not be admitted** les retardataires ne seront pas admis **b** (*fig*) **he is a ~ to politics** il est venu à la politique sur le tard

lateen [lə'tiːn] N (*also* **~ sail**) voile *f* latine

lately ['leɪtlɪ] ADV ces derniers temps, dernièrement; **till ~** jusqu'à ces derniers temps → **Johnny**

latency ['leɪtənsɪ] N (*Med*) latence *f*

lateness ['leɪtnɪs] N **a** (= *not being on time*) [*of person, train, flight*] retard *m*; **he apologized for his ~** il s'est excusé de son retard; **his boss became exasperated by his constant ~** ses retards perpétuels ont fini par exaspérer son patron **b** **a crowd had gathered despite the ~ of the hour** une foule s'était formée malgré l'heure tardive

latent ['leɪtənt] **1** ADJ [*tendency, talent, antagonism, racism, threat*] latent; [*meaning*] caché **2** ► **latent defect** N (*Jur*) vice *m* caché ► **latent heat** N (*Phys*) chaleur *f* latente ► **latent period** N (*Med*) période *f* de latence

later ['leɪtə'] *compar of* **late 1** ADV plus tard; **~ that night** plus tard (dans la soirée); **even ~** encore plus tard; **two years ~** deux ans plus tard; **~ on** (*in period of time, film*) plus tard; (*in book*) plus loin; **not** *or* **no ~ than ...** pas plus tard que ...; **essays must be handed in not ~ than Monday morning** les dissertations devront être remises lundi matin dernier délai *or* au plus tard; **~!** (*when interrupted etc*) tout à l'heure!; (*US* = *goodbye*) à plus!*; **see you ~!*** (= *in a few minutes*) à tout à l'heure!; (*longer*) à plus tard! → **soon**

2 ADJ **a** (= *subsequent, more recent*) [*chapter, date*] ultérieur (-eure *f*); **we'll discuss it at a ~ meeting** nous en discuterons au cours d'une réunion ultérieure *or* d'une autre réunion; **at a ~ meeting they decided ...** au cours d'une réunion ultérieure, ils ont décidé ...; **I decided to take a ~ train** j'ai décidé de prendre un autre train *or* de partir plus tard; **the ~ train** (*of two*) le train suivant; **a ~ edition** une édition postérieure; **this version is ~ than that one** (= *subsequent*) cette version est postérieure à celle-là **b** (*in period or series*) **at a ~ stage** plus tard; **at a ~ stage in the negotiations** lors d'une phase

ultérieure des négociations; **the ~ 18th century** la fin du 18ᵉ (siècle); **Beethoven's ~ symphonies** les dernières symphonies de Beethoven; **in ~ life** plus tard; **in his ~ years** vers la fin de sa vie

lateral ['lætərəl] **1** ADJ latéral (*also Phon*) **2** COMP ► **lateral thinking** N (*esp Brit*) la pensée latérale (*manière non conventionnelle d'aborder les problèmes*)

laterally ['lætərəlɪ] ADV (= *sideways*) latéralement; (= *originally*) **to think ~** pratiquer la pensée latérale, avoir une manière originale d'aborder les problèmes

latest ['leɪtɪst] *superl of* **late 1** ADJ **a** (= *most recent*) dernier; **his ~ film** son dernier film; **the ~ in a series of murders** le dernier en date d'une série de meurtres; **the ~ news** les dernières nouvelles *fpl*; (*Rad, TV*) **the ~ news (bulletin)** les dernières informations *fpl*; **his ~ statement** sa dernière déclaration (en date); **he is the ~ minister to resign** c'est le dernier ministre en date à démissionner; **the very ~ technology** la toute dernière technologie **b** (= *last possible*) limite; **what is the ~ date for applications?** quelle est la date limite de dépôt des candidatures?; **the ~ date he could do it was 31 July** la dernière date à laquelle il pouvait le faire était le 31 juillet; **the ~ possible date for the election** la date ultime pour les élections; **the ~ time you may come is 4 o'clock** l'heure limite à laquelle vous pouvez arriver est 4 heures; **the ~ time for doing it is April** il faut le faire en avril au plus tard; **at the ~ possible moment** au tout dernier moment

2 ADV (= *last*) **to arrive/get up (the) ~** être le dernier *or* la dernière à arriver/se lever; **to work ~** travailler plus tard que les autres; **to flower (the) ~** fleurir en dernier

3 N **a*** (= *latest version*) **it's the ~ in computer games** c'est le dernier cri* en matière de jeux électroniques; **the very ~ in technology** le dernier cri* de la technologie; (= *news*) **have you heard the ~?** tu connais la dernière?*; **what's the ~ on this affair?** qu'y a-t-il de nouveau sur cette affaire?; (*Rad, TV*) **for the ~ on the riots, over to Ian** pour les dernières informations sur les émeutes, à vous, Ian; (= *girlfriend*) **have you seen his ~?** tu as vu sa nouvelle?*; (= *joke*) **have you heard his ~?** tu connais sa dernière?*; (= *exploit*) **did you hear about his ~?** on t'a raconté son dernier exploit *or* sa dernière prouesse? **b** (= *latest time*) **when** *or* **what is the ~ you can come?** quand pouvez-vous venir, au plus tard?; **I'll be there by noon at the ~** j'y serai à midi au plus tard; **give me your essay by Monday at the ~** rendez-moi votre dissertation lundi dernier délai *or* au plus tard

latex ['leɪteks] N (*pl* **latexes** *or* **latices** ['læti,siːz]) latex *m*

lath [lɑːθ] N (*pl* **laths** [lɑːðz]) (*Constr*) latte *f*; **a ~-and-plaster wall** un mur fait en lattes et enduit de plâtre

lathe [leɪð] N (*Tech*) tour *m* → **capstan, power**

lather ['lɑːðə'] **1** N **a** [*of soap*] mousse *f* (de savon) **b** (= *sweat*) [*of horse*] écume *f*; **in a ~** [*horse*] couvert d'écume; (* *fig* = *nervous, anxious*) [*person*] agité, dans tous ses états; **to work o.s. up into a ~*** se mettre dans tous ses états; **what's he getting into such a ~ about?*** pourquoi se met-il dans un état pareil? **2** VT **to ~ one's face/hands** *etc* se savonner le visage/les mains *etc* **3** VI [*soap*] mousser

latices ['læti,siːz] NPL *of* **latex**

latifundia [,læti'fʊndɪə] NPL latifundia *mpl*

Latin ['lætɪn] **1** ADJ **a** (*Ling*) [*text, grammar, poet*] latin; [*lesson*] de latin **b** [*people, temperament, culture*] (*European*) latin; (*in US*) latino-américain **2** N (*Ling*) latin *m*; **late ~** bas latin *m*; **low ~** bas latin *m*; **vulgar ~** latin *m* vulgaire **b** Latin(e) *m(f)*; (*in US*) Latino-Américain(e) *m(f)* **3** COMP ► **Latin America**

N Amérique *f* latine ► **Latin-American** ADJ latino-américain, d'Amérique latine ♦ N Latino-Américain(e) *m(f)* ► **latin lover** N latin lover *m* ► **Latin quarter** N quartier *m* latin ► **Latin school** N (*US*) ≈ lycée *m* classique

Latinist ['lætɪnɪst] N latiniste *mf*

Latinization [,lætɪnaɪ'zeɪʃən] N latinisation *f*

Latinize ['lætɪnaɪz] VT latiniser

Latino [læ'tiːnəʊ] N (*pl* **Latinos**) (*in US*) Latino *mf*

Latino-American [læ'tiːnəʊə'merɪkən] **1** ADJ latino-américain **2** N (*US*) Latino-Américain(e) *m(f)*

latish* ['leɪtɪʃ] **1** ADJ [*hour*] assez avancé, assez tardif; **it's getting ~** il commence à se faire tard; **we had a ~ breakfast** nous avons pris notre petit déjeuner assez *or* plutôt tard **2** ADV assez tard, plutôt tard

latitude ['lætɪtjuːd] N **a** (*Geog*) latitude *f*; **at a ~ of 48° north** à par par 48° de latitude Nord; **in these ~s** sous ces latitudes **b** (*NonC* = *freedom*) latitude *f*; **to give** *or* **allow sb a certain amount of ~** laisser *or* accorder une certaine latitude à qn

latitudinal [,lætɪ'tjuːdɪnl] ADJ latitudinal

latrine [lə'triːn] N latrine(s) *f(pl)* (*gen pl*)

▼ **latter** ['lætə'] (*frm*) **1** ADJ **a** (= *second of two*) dernier, second; **the ~ proposition was accepted** cette dernière *or* la seconde proposition fut acceptée; **of the two, we prefer the ~ solution** nous préférons la seconde solution; **the ~ half** la seconde moitié; **the ~ half of the month** la seconde quinzaine du mois **b** (= *later*) **the ~ stages of the match produced some fine football** vers la fin du match, il y a eu du très bon football; **the college was destroyed in the ~ stages of the war/ the century** le collège a été détruit vers la fin de la guerre/du siècle; **in the ~ years of his life** ◊ **in his ~ years** les dernières années de sa vie, tard dans sa vie

2 N **the ~ is the more expensive of the two systems** ce dernier *or* second système est le plus coûteux des deux; **of these two books the former is expensive but the ~ is not** le premier de ces deux livres est cher mais le second ne l'est pas; **he visited his cousin and uncle - the ~ was ill** il a rendu visite à son cousin et à son oncle: ce dernier était souffrant; **of the two possible solutions, I prefer the ~** je préfère la seconde solution

3 COMP ► **latter-day** ADJ moderne, d'aujourd'hui ► **Latter-Day Saints** NPL (*Rel*) Saints *mpl* des derniers jours

latterly ['lætəlɪ] ADV (*frm*) (= *recently*) récemment, dernièrement; (= *towards end of life*) vers la fin de sa (*or leur etc*) vie; (= *towards end of period*) vers la fin; **he has lived abroad for many years, ~ in Rome** il a longtemps vécu à l'étranger, dernièrement il était à Rome

lattice ['lætɪs] **1** N treillis *m*; (= *fence*) treillage *m*, claire-voie *f*; (*also* **~ structure**) structure *f* réticulaire **2** COMP ► **lattice girder** N poutre *f* en treillis ► **lattice window** N fenêtre *f* treillissée

latticed ['lætɪst] ADJ [*window*] treillissé; [*fence, wall*] treillagé

latticework ['lætɪswɜːk] N treillis *m*

Latvia ['lætvɪə] N la Lettonie

Latvian ['lætvɪən] **1** ADJ lette, letton (on(n)e *f*) **2** N **a** Lette *mf*, Letton((n)e) *m(f)*, Latvien(ne) *m(f)* **b** (*Ling*) lette *m*, letton *m*

laud [lɔːd] VT (*liter*) louanger (*liter*); (*Rel*) louer, glorifier, chanter les louanges de

laudable ['lɔːdəbl] ADJ louable, digne de louanges

laudably ['lɔːdəblɪ] ADV [*behave*] de façon louable; **he was ~ calm** son calme était re-

marquable; a ~ objective article un article d'une louable objectivité

laudanum ['lɔ:dnəm] N laudanum *m*

laudatory ['lɔ:dətərɪ] ADJ (*frm*) élogieux

laugh [lɑ:f] 1 N a rire *m*; **he has a very distinctive ~** il a un rire très caractéristique; **with a ~** (*brief*) dans un éclat de rire; (*longer*) en riant; **with a scornful ~** avec un rire méprisant *or* dédaigneux; **to give a ~** rire; **to have a good ~ at sb/sth** bien rire de qn/qch; **his act didn't get a single ~** son numéro n'a fait rire personne; **that joke always gets a ~** cette plaisanterie fait toujours rire; **he had the last ~** finalement c'est lui qui a bien ri; **we'll see who has the last ~** on verra bien qui rira le dernier; **the ~ is on you*** c'est toi qui fais les frais de la plaisanterie; (*also iro*) **it was a ~ a minute!** c'était d'un drôle! (*also iro*) → **play, raise**

b (* = *amusement, amusing time*) **it was** *or* **we had a good ~** on s'est bien amusés, on a bien rigolé*; **if you want a ~ go to her German class!** si tu veux t'amuser *or* rigoler* va assister à son cours d'allemand!; **what a ~!** ça, c'est (*or* c'était *etc*) marrant!*; **just for a ~** *or* **for ~s** rien que pour rire, histoire de rire*; **he's always good for a ~** il nous fera toujours bien rire; **his films are always good for a ~** ses films sont toujours drôles; **he's a good ~** on rigole* bien avec lui

2 VI rire; **you may ~!** ◊ **it's easy for you to ~!** tu peux toujours rire!; (*philosophical*) **you've got to ~*** ◊ **you have to ~*** il vaut mieux en rire; **I didn't know whether to ~ or cry** je ne savais plus si je devais rire ou pleurer; **he ~ed until he cried** il pleurait de rire, il riait aux larmes; **to ~ about** *or* **over sth** rire de qch; **there's nothing to ~ about** il n'y a pas de quoi rire; **he never ~s at my jokes** mes plaisanteries ne le font jamais rire → **laugh at**; **she ~ed to herself** elle a ri dans sa barbe, elle a ri sous cape; **to ~ up one's sleeve** rire dans sa barbe, rire sous cape; **he makes me ~** il me fait rire; (*iro*) **don't make me ~*** (= *don't be silly*) laisse-moi rire, ne me fais pas rire ■ (*PROV*) **he who ~s last ~s longest** rira bien qui rira le dernier (*PROV*); **to ~ in sb's face** rire au nez de qn; **he'll soon be ~ing on the other side of his face** il n'aura bientôt plus envie de rire, il va bientôt rire jaune; **I'll make you ~ on the other side of your face!** je vais t'apprendre à rire!; **it's all right for him, he's ~ing*** lui il s'en fiche, il est peinard*; **once we get this contract signed we're ~ing*** une fois ce contrat signé, ce sera dans la poche*; **he's ~ing all the way to the bank*** il n'a pas de problèmes de compte en banque! → **burst out**

3 VT **he ~ed a jolly laugh** il eut un rire jovial; **"don't be silly," he ~ed** « ne sois pas idiot » dit-il en riant; **to be ~ed out of court** [*person, idea*] être tourné en ridicule; **they ~ed him to scorn** ils l'ont tourné en dérision; **he ~ed himself silly*** il a ri comme un bossu* *or* une baleine*

4 COMP ► **laugh track** N (*US Rad, TV*) (bande *f* sonore de) rires *mpl* préenregistrés

► **laugh at** VT FUS (*lit*) [+ *person, sb's behaviour*] rire de; (*unpleasantly*) se moquer de; (*fig*) [+ *difficulty, danger*] se rire de

► **laugh down** VT SEP **they ~ed the speaker down** leurs moqueries ont réduit l'orateur au silence

► **laugh off** VT SEP a **to ~ one's head off*** rire comme un bossu* *or* une baleine* b [+ *accusation*] écarter d'une plaisanterie *or* d'une boutade; **she managed to ~ it off** elle a réussi à tourner la chose en plaisanterie; **you can't ~ this one off** cette fois tu ne t'en tireras pas par la plaisanterie

laughable ['lɑ:fəbl] ADJ [*person, behaviour, idea, suggestion*] ridicule; [*offer, amount*] dérisoire; **it's ~ to compare him with Gandhi** il est ridicule de le comparer à Gandhi

laughably ['lɑ:fəblɪ] ADV ridiculement

laughing ['lɑ:fɪŋ] 1 ADJ a [*person, face, eyes*] riant, rieur b (= *light-hearted*) **this is no ~ matter** il n'y a pas de quoi rire; **I'm in no ~ mood** (= *angry*) je ne suis pas d'humeur à rire; (= *sad*) je n'ai pas le cœur à rire 2 COMP ► **laughing gas** N gaz *m* hilarant ► **laughing hyena** N (*Zool*) hyène *f* (tachetée) ► **laughing jackass** N (*Orn*) martin-pêcheur *m* géant ► **laughing stock** N **he was the ~ stock of the class** il était la risée de la classe; **he made himself a ~ stock** il s'est couvert de ridicule

laughingly ['lɑ:fɪŋlɪ] ADV a (= *amusedly*) [*say*] en riant b (= *ironically*) **this patch of lawn that I ~ call my garden** ce carré de gazon que j'appelle pour rire mon jardin; (= *risibly*) **what the government ~ calls its economic policy** ce que le gouvernement appelle sans rire sa politique économique

laughline ['lɑ:flaɪn] N (*US: on face*) ride *f* d'expression

laughter ['lɑ:ftər] 1 N (*NonC*) rire(s) *m(pl)*; **there was a little nervous ~** on entendit quelques rires nerveux; **there was loud ~ at this remark** cette remarque a provoqué des éclats de rire; **he said amid ~ that ...** il dit au milieu des rires que ...; **~ is good for you** cela fait du bien de rire; **their ~ could be heard in the next room** on les entendait rire dans la pièce à côté → **can²**, **roar** 2 COMP ► **laughter line** N (*Brit: on face*) ride *f* d'expression

launch [lɔ:ntʃ] 1 N a (= *motorboat*) (*for patrol etc*) vedette *f*; (*for pleasure*) bateau *m* de plaisance; **police ~** vedette *f* de la police b (= *boat carried by warship*) chaloupe *f* c (= *launching*) [*of ship, spacecraft, product*] lancement *m* → **window**

2 VT a [+ *ship, satellite, missile*] lancer; [+ *shore lifeboat etc*] faire sortir; [+ *ship's boat*] mettre à la mer b [+ *company, product, career, scheme, plan*] lancer; [+ *attack, offensive*] lancer, déclencher; [+ *inquiry, investigation*] ouvrir; (*Fin*) **to ~ a share issue** émettre des actions, faire une émission d'actions; **it was this novel that really ~ed her as a writer** c'est ce roman qui l'a vraiment lancée en tant qu'écrivain; **the film ~ed her as Hollywood's latest star** le film a fait d'elle la nouvelle star d'Hollywood

3 VI (*fig: also* ► **forth**) se lancer; [+ *speech, explanation, attack*] **to ~ into** se lancer dans

4 COMP ► **launch pad** N (*Space*) = **launching pad** ► **launch party** N (*Publishing etc*) réception *f* de lancement ► **launch vehicle** N (*Space*) fusée *f* de lancement

► **launch forth** VI = **launch 3**

► **launch out** VI [*business, company*] (= *diversify*) se diversifier; **to ~ out into sth** [*speaker, business*] se lancer dans qch

launcher ['lɔ:ntʃər] N (*Mil, Space*) lanceur *m* → **missile, rocket**

launching ['lɔ:ntʃɪŋ] 1 N a [*of new ship, missile, satellite*] lancement *m*; [*of shore lifeboat*] sortie *f*; [*of ship's boat*] mise *f* à la mer b [*of company, product, career*] lancement *m* 2 COMP ► **launching ceremony** N cérémonie *f* de lancement ► **launching pad** N (*Space*) rampe *f* de lancement ► **launching site** N (*Mil, Space*) aire *f* de lancement

launder ['lɔ:ndər] VT a [+ *clothes*] laver; **to send sth to be ~ed** envoyer qch à la blanchisserie *or* au blanchissage b [+ *money*] blanchir

Launderette® [,lɔ:ndə'ret] N (*Brit*) laverie *f* automatique

laundering ['lɔ:ndərɪŋ] N a [*of clothes*] blanchissage *m* b [*of money*] blanchiment *m*

laundress ['lɔ:ndrɪs] N blanchisseuse *f*

Laundromat® ['lɔ:ndrəmæt] N (*US*) = **Launderette**

laundry ['lɔ:ndrɪ] 1 N a (*NonC*) (= *clean clothes*) linge *m*; (= *dirty clothes*) linge *m* (sale); **to do the ~** faire la lessive, laver le linge b (= *place*) blanchisserie *f* 2 COMP ► **laundry basket** N panier *m* à linge ► **laundry list** N (*lit*) liste *f* de blanchissage; (*fig pej*) liste *f* interminable ► **laundry mark** N marque *f* de la blanchisserie *or* du blanchissage ► **laundry van** N camionnette *f* de la blanchisserie ► **laundry worker** N blanchisseur *m*, -euse *f* (*employé*)

laureate ['lɔ:rɪɪt] ADJ, N lauréat(e) *m(f)*; (*in Brit*) **(poet) ~** poète *m* lauréat

laurel ['lɒrəl] 1 N (*Bot, fig*) laurier *m*; **to rest on one's ~s** se reposer sur ses lauriers; **to win one's ~s** se couvrir de lauriers; **you must look to your ~s** ne t'endors pas sur tes lauriers 2 COMP ► **laurel wreath** N couronne *f* de lauriers

lav* [læv] N (ABBR = **lavatory**) cabinets *mpl*

lava ['lɑ:və] 1 N lave *f* 2 COMP ► **lava bed** N champ *m* de lave ► **lava flow** N coulée *f* de lave

lavalier(e) [,lævə'lɪər] N (*US*) pendentif *m*

lavatorial [,lævə'tɔ:rɪəl] ADJ scatologique

lavatory ['lævətrɪ] 1 N a (= *room*) toilettes *fpl*, W.-C. *mpl* b (*Brit* = *fitting*) (cuvette *f* et siège *m* de) W.-C. *mpl*; **to put sth down the ~** jeter qch dans les W.-C. *or* cabinets → **public** 2 COMP ► **lavatory bowl** N cuvette *f* de W.-C. ► **lavatory humour** N (*pej*) humour *m* scatologique ► **lavatory pan** N = **lavatory bowl** ► **lavatory paper** N papier *m* hygiénique ► **lavatory seat** N siège *m* de W.-C.

lavender ['lævɪndər] 1 N lavande *f* 2 COMP [*colour*] lavande *inv* ► **lavender bag** N sachet *m* de lavande ► **lavender-blue** ADJ bleu lavande *inv* ► **lavender water** N eau *f* de lavande

laver bread ['lɑ:vəbred] N gâteau *m* d'algues

lavish ['lævɪʃ] 1 ADJ a [*person*] prodigue (**of, with** de); **to be ~ with one's money** dépenser sans compter, se montrer prodigue b (= *generous*) [*expenditure*] très considérable; [*amount*] gigantesque; [*meal*] plantureux, copieux; [*helping, hospitality*] généreux; **to bestow ~ praise on sb** se répandre en éloges sur qn 2 VT prodiguer (**sth on sb** qch à qn)

lavishly ['lævɪʃlɪ] ADV [*illustrated, decorated*] somptueusement; [*equipped, furnished*] somptueusement, luxueusement; **to entertain ~** recevoir somptueusement; **to spend ~** dépenser sans compter; **to tip sb ~** donner un pourboire très généreux à qn

lavishness ['lævɪʃnɪs] N [*of spending*] extravagance *f*; [*of hospitality, helping*] générosité *f*; [*of meal*] luxe *m*

law [lɔ:] 1 N a (*NonC* = *set of laws, legislation*) loi *f*, législation *f*; **the ~** la loi; **it's the ~** c'est la loi; **the ~ as it stands** la législation en vigueur; **they're campaigning for a change in the ~** ils font campagne pour la modification de la loi; **according to French/European ~** selon la législation française/européenne; (*Parl*) **when a bill becomes ~** quand un projet de loi est voté; **to be above the ~** être au-dessus des lois; **it's against the ~** c'est contraire à la loi, c'est illégal; **by ~** conformément à la loi; **by** *or* **under French/international ~** selon la loi *or* la législation française/internationale; **to keep within the ~** rester dans (les limites de) la légalité; **to take the ~ into one's own hands** (se) faire justice soi-même; **the ~ of the land** la législation *or* les lois du pays; **the ~ of the jungle** la loi de la jungle; **the Law of Moses** la loi de Moïse; **~ and order** l'ordre *m* public → **2**; **forces of ~ and order** forces *fpl* de l'ordre; **to have the ~ on one's side** avoir la loi pour soi; **he's a ~ unto himself** il ne connaît d'autre loi que la sienne, il fait ce qu'il veut → **break, lay down, rule, word**

b (NonC = operation of the law) justice f; **the ~ report looks at how women are treated by the ~** ce rapport étudie la façon dont la justice traite les femmes; **court of ~** cour f de justice, tribunal m; **to go to ~** recourir à la justice; **to take a case to ~** porter une affaire devant les tribunaux; **to take sb to ~** faire un procès à qn; **I'll have the ~ on you!*** je vous traînerai devant les tribunaux!; (= the police) **here's the ~ arriving!*** voilà les flics!* → **arm¹**, **brush**, **officer**

c (NonC = system, science, profession) droit m; **civil/criminal** etc ~ le droit civil/criminel etc; **to study** or **read ~** faire son ou du droit; **to practise ~** [solicitor] être notaire m; [barrister] être avocat(e); (Univ) **Faculty of Law** faculté f de droit → **common, martial, point**

d (= regulation) loi f; **to pass a ~** voter une loi; **several ~s have been passed against pollution** plusieurs lois ont été votées pour combattre la pollution; **is there a ~ against it?** est-ce que c'est interdit par la loi?; **there should be a ~ against it!** ça devrait être interdit!; **there's no ~ against it!*** ce n'est pas défendu! → **framework** ~ loi-cadre f

e (= principle, rule) (also Phys) loi f; (Sport) règle f; **the ~ of averages** la loi des probabilités; **the ~ of diminishing returns** la loi des rendements décroissants; **the ~(s) of gravity** la loi de la chute des corps or de la pesanteur; **the ~s of nature** les lois fpl de la nature; **the ~(s) of supply and demand** la loi de l'offre et de la demande → **Murphy, Parkinson's law, sod²**

2 COMP ► **law-abiding** ADJ respectueux des lois ► **law-and-order issues** NPL questions fpl d'ordre public ► **law centre, law center** (US) N service de consultations juridiques gratuites ► **law clerk** N (US Jur) jeune juriste qui prépare le travail du juge ► **law court** N cour f de justice, tribunal m ► **Law Courts** NPL ≈ Palais m de justice ► **law enforcement agency** (US) N service chargé de faire respecter la loi ► **law enforcement officer** N (US) personne ayant des pouvoirs de police ► **Law Faculty** N (Univ) faculté f de droit ► **Law Lords** NPL (Brit) juges siégeant à la Chambre des lords ► **law school** N (Univ) faculté f de droit; **he's at ~ school** il fait son droit or du droit ► **law student** N étudiant(e) m(f) en droit

lawbreaker ['lɔːˌbreɪkər] N personne f qui enfreint la loi

law-breaking ['lɔːˌbreɪkɪŋ] **1** N (NonC) violation f de la loi **2** ADJ violant or enfreignant la loi

lawful ['lɔːfʊl] ADJ [action] légal; [marriage, child] légitime; [contract] valide; **it is not ~ to do that** il n'est pas légal de or il est illégal de faire cela; **to go about one's ~ business** vaquer à ses occupations

lawfully ['lɔːfəlɪ] ADV légalement

lawgiver ['lɔːˌɡɪvər] N (Brit) législateur m, -trice f

lawless ['lɔːlɪs] ADJ [country] sans loi; [period] d'anarchie; [person] sans foi ni loi; **~ behaviour** manque m de respect des lois; **we live in an increasingly ~ society** nous vivons dans une société où l'on respecte de moins en moins la loi

lawlessness ['lɔːlɪsnɪs] N [of person] non-respect m des lois; [of country, period] anarchie f

lawmaker ['lɔːˌmeɪkər] N (US) législateur m, -trice f

lawman ['lɔːmæn] N (pl **-men**) (US) policier m

lawn¹ [lɔːn] **1** N pelouse f **2** COMP ► **lawn tennis** N (on grass) tennis m sur gazon; (on hard surface) tennis m

lawn² [lɔːn] N (Tex) batiste f, linon m

lawnmower ['lɔːnˌməʊər] N tondeuse f (à gazon)

Lawrence ['lɒrəns] N ≈ Laurent m

lawrencium [lɔːˈrensɪəm] N lawrencium m

lawsuit ['lɔːsuːt] N (esp US) procès m; **to bring a ~ against sb** intenter un procès à qn, poursuivre qn en justice

lawyer ['lɔːjər] N **a** (= solicitor) (for sales, wills etc) notaire m; (in court for litigation) avocat m; (= barrister) avocat m; (in business firm etc) conseiller m juridique **b** (= person trained in law) juriste mf

┌─────────────┐
│ **LAWYER** │
└─────────────┘

Il existe deux catégories d'avocats en Grande-Bretagne : les « solicitors » et les « barristers » (appelés « advocates » en Écosse). Les premiers sont à la fois des notaires, qui traitent donc les transactions immobilières, les affaires de succession, etc, et des avocats habilités à plaider au civil dans les instances inférieures. Les seconds sont des avocats plus spécialisés, qui interviennent au pénal ou au civil dans les instances supérieures, y compris pour défendre des affaires dont ils sont saisis par des « solicitors ».

Aux États-Unis, les avocats sont appelés « attorneys ». Ils travaillent souvent selon le système dit « no win no fee » (c'est-à-dire que le client ne paie les honoraires que s'il a gain de cause), ce qui leur permet de défendre des clients pauvres dans des affaires importantes, avec la perspective d'obtenir des gains importants en cas de succès. Ainsi, les dommages et intérêts demandés dans les affaires civiles sont souvent beaucoup plus élevés qu'en Europe, et les Américains ont volontiers recours aux voies judiciaires pour régler leurs différends.

lax [læks] ADJ **a** [behaviour, discipline, morals] relâché; [person] négligent; [government] laxiste; [pronunciation] relâché; **to be ~ in doing sth** faire qch avec négligence or sans soin; **to be ~ about security/one's work/duties** négliger la sécurité/son travail/ses devoirs; **he's become ~ recently** il s'est beaucoup relâché récemment **b** (Med) [bowels] relâché **c** (Ling) [vowel] lâche

laxative ['læksətɪv] ADJ, N laxatif m

laxity ['læksɪtɪ], **laxness** ['læksnɪs] N [of behaviour, discipline, morals] relâchement m; [of person] négligence f; [of government] laxisme m

lay¹ [leɪ] (vb: pret, ptp **laid**) **1** N **a** [of countryside, district etc] disposition f, configuration f → **land**

b (‡ = sex) partie f de jambes-en-l'air; **it was a good ~** on a bien baisé‡‡; **she's an easy ~** elle couche* avec n'importe qui, c'est une fille facile; **he's/she's a good ~** il/elle baise bien‡‡, c'est un bon coup‡

2 VT **a** (= put, place) [+ cards, objects] mettre, poser; (= stretch out) [+ cloth etc] étendre; **he laid his briefcase on the table** il a posé or mis sa serviette à plat sur la table; **she laid her hand on my shoulder** elle a posé or mis la main sur mon épaule; **he laid his head on the table/the pillow** il a posé sa tête sur la table/l'oreiller; **I didn't ~ a finger on him** je ne l'ai pas touché; **if you so much as ~ a finger on me ...** si tu oses (seulement) lever la main sur moi ...; **I wish I could ~ my hands on a good dictionary** si seulement je pouvais mettre la main sur or dénicher un bon dictionnaire; **to ~ hands on a territory** etc (= seize) s'emparer d'un territoire etc; **to ~ a hand** or **hands on sb** (= strike) porter or lever la main sur qn; (Rel) **to ~ hands on sb** faire l'imposition des mains à qn; (fig) **to ~ it on the line*** y aller carrément, ne pas y aller par quatre chemins; (US fig = explain) **he laid it on me*** il m'a tout expliqué; (Brit) **to ~ one on sb‡** (= hit) coller un pain‡ à qn, flanquer une châtaigne* à qn; (= trick) jouer un sale tour à qn → **curse, eye, hand, rest, siege**

b (= put down, install) poser, mettre; [+ bricks, carpet, cable, pipe] poser; [+ mine] poser, mouiller; **to ~ a road** faire une route; **to ~ a floor with carpet** poser une moquette sur un sol → **foundation**

c [+ eggs] pondre; **this bird ~s its eggs in the sand** cet oiseau pond (ses œufs) dans le sable → **egg, new**

d (= prepare) [+ fire] préparer; [+ snare, trap] tendre, dresser (for à); [+ plans] élaborer; (Brit) **to ~ the table (for lunch)** mettre la table or le couvert (pour le déjeuner); **all our carefully-laid plans went wrong** tous nos projets si bien élaborés ont échoué; **even the best-laid plans can go wrong** même les projets les mieux élaborés peuvent échouer → **best**

e (with adjective) **to ~ bare one's innermost thoughts/feelings** mettre à nu or dévoiler ses pensées les plus profondes/ses sentiments les plus secrets; (liter) **to ~ bare one's soul** mettre son âme à nu; **the blow laid him flat** le coup l'étendit par terre or l'envoya au tapis; **the storm laid the town flat** la tempête a rasé la ville; **to be laid low** être immobilisé; **he was laid low with flu** il était immobilisé par la grippe, la grippe l'obligeait à garder le lit; **to ~ sb/o.s. open to criticism** etc exposer qn/s'exposer à la critique etc; **to ~ waste a town** ◊ **to ~ a town to waste** ravager or dévaster une ville

f (= impose, place) [+ tax] faire payer (**on sth** sur qch); [+ burden] imposer (**on sb** à qn) → **blame, emphasis, responsibility**

g (= wager) [+ money] parier, miser (**on** sur); **I'll ~ you (a fiver*) that ...** je te parie (5 livres) que ...; **to ~ a bet (on sth)** parier (sur qch)

h (= register, bring to sb's attention) [+ accusation, charge] porter; **we shall ~ the facts before him** nous lui exposerons les faits; **they laid their plan before him** ils lui ont soumis leur projet; (Jur) **to ~ a matter before the court** saisir le tribunal d'une affaire; **he laid his case before the commission** il a porté son cas devant or soumis son cas à la commission; (Jur) **to ~ a complaint** porter plainte (**against** contre, with auprès de); (Police) **to ~ information** (= inform authorities) donner des informations, servir d'indicateur → **claim**

i (= suppress) [+ ghost] exorciser, conjurer; [+ doubt, fear] dissiper; **to ~ the dust** faire tomber la poussière

j (‡ = have sex with) baiser‡‡; **to get laid** baiser‡‡, se faire sauter‡‡

3 VI [bird, fish, insect] pondre

4 COMP ► **lay-by** N (Brit Aut) (petite) aire f de stationnement (sur le bas-côté) ► **lay days** NPL (Naut) jours mpl de planche, estarie f ► **lay-off** N (Ind) licenciement m

► **lay about** VT FUS **to ~ about sb (with a stick)** rouer qn de coups (de bâton)

► **lay alongside** (Naut) VI, VT SEP accoster

► **lay aside** VT SEP **a** (= save) [+ money, supplies] mettre de côté **b** (= put away) [+ object] mettre de côté; **he laid aside his book to greet me** il a posé son livre pour me dire bonjour **c** (= relinquish) [+ prejudice, scruples] faire abstraction de; [+ differences, disagreements, doubts] faire taire; [+ principles] se départir de; [+ fears, anxieties, doubts] écarter; [+ plans, projects] abandonner

► **lay away** VT **1** VT SEP (US) = **lay aside a 2** ~**away** ADJ → **layaway plan**

► **lay back 1** VT SEP remettre (**on** sur) **2** ~**back** N → **layback**

► **lay by 1** VT SEP = **lay aside a 2** ~**-by** N → **lay¹**

► **lay down 1** VI (Cards) étaler son jeu or ses cartes **2** VT SEP **a** (= deposit) [+ object, parcel, burden] poser, déposer; **to ~ down one's cards** poser son jeu or ses cartes **b** [+ wine] mettre en cave **c** (= give up) **to ~ down one's arms** déposer ses or les armes; **to ~ down one's life for sb** sacrifier sa vie pour qn **d** (= establish, decide) [+ rule] établir, poser; (= condition, price) imposer, fixer; **he laid it down that ...** il décréta or stipula que ...; **it is laid down in the rules that ...** il est stipulé dans le règlement que ...; **to ~ down a policy** dicter une politique; (fig) **to ~ down the law (to sb) (about sth)** (essayer de) faire la loi (à qn) (sur qch); **in our house it's my mother who ~s down the law** c'est ma mère qui fait la loi à la maison; **stop ~ing down the law!** arrête de commander!

► **lay in** VT SEP [+ *goods, reserves*] faire provision de; (*in shop*) emmagasiner; **to ~ in provisions** faire des provisions; **I must ~ in some fruit** il faut que je m'approvisionne (*subj*) en fruits *or* que je fasse provision de fruits

► **lay into*** VT FUS (= *attack verbally*) prendre à partie; (= *scold*) passer un savon à*; (= *attack physically*) rentrer dans le chou *or* le lard de*, tomber à bras raccourcis sur; (*fig* = *devour*) **we really laid into the beer last night** on a descendu pas mal de bière hier soir*

► **lay off** **1** VT SEP (*Ind*) [+ *workers*] licencier, débaucher **2** VT FUS (* = *leave alone*) **you'd better ~ off the beer/running for a while** tu ferais mieux de t'abstenir de boire/courir pour le moment; **~ off (it)!** (= *stop*) tu veux t'arrêter?*; (= *don't touch*) pas touche!*, bas les pattes!*; **~ off him!** fiche-lui la paix!*; **I told him to ~ off (it)** je lui ai dit d'arrêter **3** **~-off** N → **lay¹**

► **lay on** VT SEP [a] [+ *tax*] mettre; **they ~ on an extra charge for tea** ils ajoutent à la note le prix du thé [b] (*Brit*) (= *install*) [+ *water, gas*] installer, mettre; (= *provide*) [+ *facilities, entertainment*] fournir; **a house with water/gas/electricity laid on** une maison qui a l'eau courante/le gaz/l'électricité; **I'll have a car laid on for you** je mettrai une voiture à votre disposition, je ferai en sorte que vous ayez une voiture à votre disposition; **everything will be laid on** il y aura tout ce qu'il faut; **it was all laid on (for us) so that we didn't have to buy anything** tout (nous) était fourni si bien qu'on n'a rien eu à acheter [c] [+ *varnish, paint*] étaler; (*fig*) **he laid it on thick** *or* **with a trowel*** il en a rajouté → **lay¹**

► **lay out** **1** VT SEP [a] (= *plan, design*) [+ *garden*] dessiner; [+ *house*] concevoir (le plan de); [+ *essay*] faire le plan de; **a well laid-out flat** un appartement bien conçu; (*Typ*) **to ~ out page 4** faire la mise en page de la (page) 4, monter la (page) 4 [b] (= *get ready, display*) [+ *clothes*] sortir, préparer; [+ *goods for sale*] disposer, étaler; **the meal that was laid out for them** le repas qui leur avait été préparé; **to ~ out a body** faire la toilette d'un mort [c] (= *present systematically*) [+ *reasons, events etc*] exposer systématiquement [d] (= *spend*) [+ *money*] débourser, dépenser (**on** pour) [e] (= *knock out*) mettre knock-out *or* KO [f] (= *make an effort*) **to ~ o.s. out to do sth** faire tout son possible pour faire qch, se mettre en quatre pour faire qch **2** **~out** N → **layout**

► **lay over** (*US*) **1** VI s'arrêter, faire une halte **2** **~over** N → **layover**

► **lay to** (*Naut*) **1** VI être en panne **2** VT SEP mettre en panne

► **lay up** VT SEP [a] [+ *store, provisions*] amasser, entasser; (*in shop*) emmagasiner; **to ~ up trouble for o.s.** se préparer des ennuis [b] [+ *car*] remiser; [+ *boat*] désarmer; **he is laid up (in bed) with flu** il est au lit avec la grippe

lay² [leɪ] VB pt of **lie¹**

lay³ [leɪ] N (*Mus, Poetry*) lai *m*

lay⁴ [leɪ] **1** ADJ [a] [*missionary, school, education*] laïque [b] (*fig*) **to the ~ mind** aux yeux du profane, pour le profane; **~ opinion on this** l'opinion des profanes sur la question **2** COMP ► **lay brother** N frère *m* convers *or* lai ► **lay person** N (*Rel*) laïc *m* [b] (*fig*) profane *mf*, non-initié(e) *m(f)* ► **lay reader** N prédicateur *m* laïque ► **lay sister** N sœur *f* converse

lay⁵ [leɪ] ADJ (*Art*) **~ figure** mannequin *m*

layabout* ['leɪəbaʊt] N (*Brit*) fainéant(e) *m(f)*, feignant(e)* *m(f)*

layaway plan ['leɪəweɪ,plæn] N (*US Comm*) vente *f* à livraison différée

► LANGUAGE IN USE: **lead** 26.3

layback ['leɪbæk] N (*Climbing*) dülfer *f*

layer ['leɪə'] **1** [a] [*of atmosphere, paint, dust, sand*] couche *f*; (*Geol*) couche *f*, strate *f*; **several ~s of clothing** plusieurs épaisseurs *fpl* de vêtements [b] (= *hen*) **a good ~** une bonne pondeuse [c] (*Hort*) marcotte *f* **2** VT [a] [+ *hair*] couper en dégradé [b] (*Hort*) marcotter **3** COMP ► **layer cake** N gâteau *m* fourré

layette [leɪ'et] N layette *f*

laying ['leɪɪŋ] **1** N [*of carpet*] pose *f*; (*ceremony*) **the ~ of wreaths** le dépôt de gerbes; (*Rel*) **the ~ on of hands** l'imposition *f* des mains **2** ADJ **~ hen** poule *f* pondeuse

layman ['leɪmən] N (*pl* **-men**) [a] (*Rel*) laïc *m* [b] (*fig*) profane *m*, non-initié *m*

layout ['leɪaʊt] N [*of house, school*] disposition *f*, agencement *m*; [*of garden*] plan *m*, dessin *m*, disposition *f*; [*of district*] disposition *f*; [*of essay*] plan *m*; [*of advertisement, newspaper article etc*] agencement *m*, mise *f* en page; (*Press etc*) **the ~ of page 4** la mise en page de la (page) 4; (*Cards*) **I don't like the ~ of my hand** je n'aime pas mon jeu

layover ['leɪ,əʊvə'] N (*US*) halte *f*

Lazarus ['læzərəs] N Lazare *m*

laze [leɪz] VI (*also* **~ about**, **~ around** = *be idle*) paresser, ne rien faire, traînasser (*pej*); **we ~d (about** *or* **around) in the sun for a week** nous avons passé une semaine au soleil à ne rien faire, nous avons eu une semaine de farniente au soleil; **stop lazing about** *or* **around and do some work!** cesse de perdre ton temps (à ne rien faire) et mets-toi au travail!

► **laze away** VT SEP **to ~ the time away** passer son temps à ne rien faire

lazily ['leɪzɪlɪ] ADV (= *idly, languidly*) [*stretch, get up, yawn, watch*] paresseusement; [*smile*] avec indolence; **to drift ~** [*smoke, cloud*] flotter mollement; [*snowflakes*] voleter légèrement

laziness ['leɪzɪnɪs] N paresse *f*, indolence *f*, fainéantise *f*

lazy ['leɪzɪ] **1** ADJ [a] (*pej* = *idle*) [*person*] paresseux; **I'm ~ about washing my vegetables** je suis trop paresseux pour laver mes légumes, je ne prends pas la peine de laver mes légumes; **to feel ~** être pris de paresse [b] (*pej* = *sloppy*) [*attitude*] nonchalant, paresseux; [*writing, work*] peu soigné; [*style*] relâché [c] (= *relaxed, languid*) [*gesture, smile*] nonchalant, indolent; [*river*] paresseux, lent; [*hour, day, afternoon*] de détente; [*lunch, dinner*] décontracté; **a ~ drawl** une voix traînante et nonchalante; **we had a ~ holiday on the beach** nous avons passé des vacances reposantes à la plage **2** COMP ► **lazy eye** N (*Med*) amblyopie *f* ► **lazy Susan** N (= *dish*) plateau *m* tournant

lazybones* ['leɪzɪbəʊnz] N (*NonC*) feignant(e)* *m(f)*

lb (ABBR = **libra**) = **pound¹**

LBO [,elbiː'əʊ] N (*Fin*) (ABBR = **leveraged buyout**) → **leverage**

lbw [,elbiː'dʌblju:] N (*Cricket*) (ABBR = **leg before wicket**) *faute du batteur qui met la jambe devant le guichet au moment où la balle arrive*

LC N (*in US*) (ABBR = **Library of Congress**) → **library**

lc (*Typ*) (ABBR = **lower case**) → **lower**

L/C (*Fin*) (ABBR = **letter of credit**) → **letter**

LCD [,elsiː'diː] N [a] (ABBR = **liquid crystal display**) → **liquid** [b] (ABBR = **lowest common denominator**) PPDC *m*

lcd [,elsiː'diː] N = **LCD b**

LCM, **lcm** [,elsiː'em] N (ABBR = **lowest common multiple**) PPCM *m*

Ld (*Brit*) ABBR = **Lord**

L-dopa [el'dəʊpə] N L-dopa *f*

LDS [,eldiː'es] N (ABBR = **Licentiate in Dental Surgery**) diplôme *m* de chirurgien dentiste

LEA [,eliː'eɪ] N (*Brit Educ*) (ABBR = **local education authority**) → **local**

lea [li:] N (*liter*) pré *m*

leach [li:tʃ] **1** VT [+ *liquid*] filtrer; [+ *particles*] lessiver **2** VI [*liquid*] filtrer (**from** de, **into** dans, **through** à travers)

▼ **lead¹** [li:d]

vb: pret, ptp **led**

1 NOUN	**4** INTRANSITIVE VERB
2 ADJECTIVE	**5** COMPOUNDS
3 TRANSITIVE VERB	**6** PHRASAL VERBS

1 NOUN

[a] **esp Sport** (= *front position*) tête *f*; (= *distance or time ahead*) avance *f*; **to be in the ~** (*in match*) mener; (*in race, league*) être en tête; **to go into** *or* **take the ~** (*in race*) prendre la tête; (*in match, league*) mener; **to have a three-point ~** avoir trois points d'avance; **to have a two-minute/ten-metre ~** avoir deux minutes/dix mètres d'avance sur qn [b] = **initiative** initiative *f*, exemple *m*; **to follow sb's ~** suivre l'exemple de qn; **to give the ~** donner le ton, montrer l'exemple; **to give sb a ~** montrer l'exemple à qn; **to take the ~ in doing sth** être le premier à faire qch; **thanks to his ~ the rest were able to ...** grâce à son initiative les autres ont pu ... [c] = **clue** piste *f*; **the police have a ~** la police tient une piste; **the footprints gave them a ~** les traces de pas les ont mis sur la piste [d] **Theat** rôle *m* principal; **to play the ~** tenir *or* jouer *or* avoir le rôle principal; **to sing the ~** chanter le rôle principal; **male/female ~** premier rôle *m* masculin/féminin; **juvenile ~** jeune premier *m* [e] = **leash** laisse *f*; **dogs must be kept on a ~** les chiens doivent être tenus en laisse [f] **Elec** (= *flex*) fil *m* [g] **Press** article *m* à la une; (= *editorial*) éditorial *m*; (= *headlines*) manchette *f*; **the financial crisis is the ~ (story) in this morning's papers** la crise financière fait les gros titres des journaux *or* est à la une des journaux ce matin [h] **Cards** whose ~ is it? à qui est-ce de jouer? [i] **Comm** **~s and lags** termaillage *m*, jeu *m* de termes de paiement

2 ADJECTIVE

= **leading** **~ guitarist** première guitare *f*; **~ vocalist** (*chanteur m*) leader *m*, (*chanteuse f*) leader *f*

3 TRANSITIVE VERB

[a] = **conduct, show the way to** [+ *person, horse*] conduire, mener (**to** à); [+ *procession, parade*] être à la tête de; **to ~ sb in/out/across etc** faire entrer/sortir/traverser *etc* qn; **they led him into the king's presence** on le conduisit devant le roi; **to ~ sb into a room** faire entrer qn dans une pièce; **the guide led them through the courtyard** le guide leur a fait traverser la cour *or* les a fait passer par la cour; **the first street on the left will ~ you to the church** la première rue à gauche vous mènera à l'église; **what led you to Venice?** qu'est-ce qui vous a amené à Venise?; **each clue led him to another** chaque indice le menait au suivant; **this ~s me to an important point** cela m'amène à un point important; **to ~ a team onto the field** conduire une équipe sur le terrain

♦ **to lead the way** (= *go ahead*) aller devant; (= *show the way*: *lit, fig*) montrer le chemin; **he led the way to the garage** il nous (*or* les *etc*) a menés jusqu'au garage; **will you ~ the way?** passez devant, nous vous suivons

[b] = **be leader of** [+ *government, movement, party, team*] être à la tête de, diriger; [+ *expedition*] être à la tête de, mener; [+ *regiment*] être à la tête de, commander; (*Ftbl etc*) [+ *league*] être en tête de; [+ *orchestra*] (*Brit*) être le premier violon de; (*US*) diriger; **we are looking for someone to ~ our new department** nous

cherchons quelqu'un pour assurer la direction de notre nouveau service

[c] [Sport, fig = be ahead of] they were ~ing us by 10 metres ils avaient une avance de 10 mètres sur nous ; (Sport, fig) to ~ the field venir or être en tête ; our country ~s the world in textiles notre pays est le leader mondial dans le domaine du textile

[d] [+ life, existence] mener ; they ~ a simple life ils mènent une vie simple

[e] [= induce, bring] porter, amener ; I am led to the conclusion that ... je suis amené à conclure que ...

♦ to lead sb to do sth : he led me to believe that he would help me il m'a amené à croire qu'il m'aiderait ; what led you to think that? qu'est-ce qui vous a amené à penser ça ? ; his financial problems led him to change his attitude ses problèmes financiers l'ont amené à changer d'attitude

[f] [Cards] jouer ; (Bridge etc: at first trick) attaquer de, entamer ; what is led? qu'est-ce qui est joué or demandé ?

4 INTRANSITIVE VERB

[a] [= be ahead: esp Sport] (in match) mener ; (in race) être en tête ; which horse is ~ing? quel est le cheval de tête ? ; to ~ by half a length/three points avoir une demi-longueur/trois points d'avance ; to ~ (by) four goals to three mener (par) quatre (buts) à trois

[b] [= go ahead] aller devant ; (= show the way) montrer le chemin ; you ~, I'll follow passez devant, je vous suis

[c] [Jur] to ~ for the defence être l'avocat principal de la défense

[d] [Dancing] mener, conduire

[e] [= go] [road, corridor] mener, conduire ; [door] mener (to à) s'ouvrir (to sur) ; (fig) mener (to à) ; where is all this ~ing? (trend, events) où cela va-t-il nous mener ? ; (questions, reasoning) où veut-il (or voulez-vous etc) en venir ? ; the streets that ~ into/from the square les rues qui débouchent sur/partent de la place → lead off

♦ to lead to sth : it led to war cela a conduit à la guerre ; it led to his arrest cela a abouti à son arrestation ; that will ~ to his undoing cela causera or sera sa perte ; it led to nothing ça n'a mené à rien ; this led to their asking to see the president cela les a amenés à demander à voir le président ; it could ~ to some confusion cela pourrait créer or occasionner une certaine confusion ; it led to a change in his attitude cela a provoqué un changement dans son attitude ; one story led to another une histoire en a amené une autre ; one thing led to another and we ... une chose en amenant une autre, nous ...

[f] [Cards] who is it to ~? c'est à qui de commencer ? ; (Bridge) south to ~ sud joue

5 COMPOUNDS

► **lead-in** N introduction f, entrée f en matière ► **lead story** N (Press) ► **1g** ► **lead time** N [of project, process] délais mpl (d'exécution or de réalisation) ; [of stock] délais mpl (de réapprovisionnement) ; [of new product] délais mpl (de démarrage or de mise en production) ► **lead-up** N préparation f (to sth de qch)

6 PHRASAL VERBS

► **lead away** VT SEP emmener ; he was led away by the soldiers il a été emmené par les soldats ; they led him away to the cells ils l'ont conduit en cellule

► **lead back** VT SEP ramener, reconduire ; they led us back to the office ils nous ont ramenés or reconduits au bureau ; this street ~s you back to the town hall cette rue vous ramène à l'hôtel de ville

► **lead off** [1] VI (= begin) commencer

[2] VT FUS [corridor, path] partir de ; a passage ~ing off the foyer un couloir qui part du

foyer ; the rooms which ~ off the corridor les pièces qui donnent sur le couloir

[3] VT SEP = lead away

► **lead on** [1] VI (= lead the way) marcher devant ; (hum) ~ on(, Macduff)! allez-y, je vous suis !

[2] VT SEP [a] (= tease) taquiner, faire marcher* ; (= fool) duper, avoir* ; (= raise hopes in) donner de faux espoirs à ; (sexually) allumer* [b] (= induce) amener ; they led him on to talk about his experiences ils l'ont amené à parler de son expérience ; this led him on to say that ... cela l'amena à dire que ...

► **lead up** VI [a] [path etc] conduire ; this road ~s up to the castle cette route conduit or mène au château ; this staircase ~s up to the roof cet escalier conduit au or donne accès au toit [b] (= precede) précéder ; the years that led up to the war les années qui ont précédé la guerre ; the events that led up to the revolution les événements qui ont conduit à la révolution [c] (= lead on) he led up carefully to his proposal il a soigneusement amené sa proposition ; what are you ~ing up to? où voulez-vous en venir ? ; what's all this ~ing up to? (= what's he trying to say?) où veut-il en venir ?

---

lead² [led] [1] N [a] (NonC = metal) plomb m ; (hum) they filled or pumped him full of ~* ils l'ont criblé de balles, ils l'ont transformé en écumoire* → red

[b] (NonC: also black ~) mine f de plomb [c] [of pencil] mine f ; [of fishing line] plomb m ; (for sounding) plomb m (de sonde) ; (Aut: for wheel balancing) masselotte f ; (Brit hum) that'll put ~ in your pencil ‡ ça va te donner de la vigueur (virile) → swing [d] (Brit) ~s [of roof] couverture f de plomb ; (window) ~s plombures fpl

[2] COMP [object, weight etc] de or en plomb ► **lead acetate** N acétate m de plomb ► **lead balloon*** it went down like a ~ balloon c'est tombé à plat, ça a foiré‡ ► **lead crystal** N cristal m au plomb ► **lead-crystal** ADJ [decanter, bowl] en cristal (au plomb) ► **lead-free** ADJ sans plomb ► **lead oxide** N oxyde m de plomb ► **lead paint** N peinture f à base de carbonate de plomb ► **lead pencil** N crayon m à papier ► **lead pipe** N tuyau m de plomb ► **lead piping** N tuyauterie f de plomb ► **lead poisoning** N saturnisme m, coliques fpl de plomb ► **lead shot** N (NonC) grenaille f de plomb

leaded ['ledid] ADJ [a] ~ window fenêtre f à petits carreaux ; ~ lights petits carreaux mpl [b] [petrol] au plomb, qui contient du plomb

leaden ['ledn] [1] ADJ [a] († = made of lead) de or en plomb [b] (liter: in colour) [sky, clouds] de plomb, plombé [c] (= heavy) [footsteps, atmosphere] lourd, pesant ; [silence] de mort ; [translation, dialogue] lourd [d] (pej = stodgy) [food] bourratif* [2] COMP ► **leaden-eyed** ADJ aux yeux ternes ► **leaden-limbed** ADJ to feel ~-limbed se sentir des membres de plomb

leader ['li:dəʳ] [1] N [a] [of expedition, gang, tribe] chef m ; [of club] dirigeant(e) m(f) ; (= guide) guide m ; (Climbing) premier m (de cordée) ; [of riot, strike] meneur m, -euse f ; (Mil) commandant m ; (Pol) dirigeant(e) m(f), leader m ; (Pol) the ~ of the Socialist Party le leader or le chef (du parti) socialiste ; political ~s leaders mpl or chefs mpl politiques ; one of the ~s of the trade union movement un des dirigeants or chefs de file or leaders du mouvement syndical ; he's a born ~ il est né pour commander ; the ~ of the orchestra (Brit) le premier violon ; (US) le chef d'orchestre ; one of the ~s in the scientific field une des sommités du monde scientifique ; they're the (world) ~s in the cosmetics industry ce sont les leaders mondiaux de l'industrie cosméti-

que ; (Jur) the ~ for the defence l'avocat m principal de la défense → follow, youth, world [b] (Sport) (in race) (= runner) coureur m de tête ; (= horse) cheval m de tête ; (in league) leader m ; he managed to stay up with the ~s il a réussi à rester dans les premiers or dans le peloton de tête [c] (Press) article m principal ; (= editorial) éditorial m ; (Brit) ~ writer éditorialiste mf [d] (Mus) (= principal violinist) premier violon m ; (US = director) chef m d'orchestre [e] (Recording: also ~ tape) amorce f [f] (Fishing) bas m de ligne [g] (Comm: also loss ~) produit m d'appel [h] (St Ex) ~s valeurs fpl vedettes [2] COMP ► **Leader of the House** N (Brit Parl) président m de la Chambre (des communes ou des lords)

┌─────────────────────────┐
│ **LEADER OF THE HOUSE** │
└─────────────────────────┘

Leader of the House désigne le président de la Chambre des communes ou celui de la Chambre des lords. Ils ont pour fonction de préparer les débats parlementaires et d'en assurer le bon déroulement. L'un et l'autre occupent une place importante au sein de l'équipe gouvernementale.

leadership ['li:dəʃɪp] N [a] (NonC) (= position) direction f, leadership m ; (= action) direction f ; during or under his ~ sous sa direction ; to take over the ~ of the country prendre la succession à la tête du pays ; they were rivals for the party ~ ils étaient candidats rivaux à la direction du parti ; to resign the party ~ démissionner de la tête du parti ; he has ~ potential il a l'étoffe d'un chef ; he praised her ~ during the crisis il a loué la manière dont elle a géré la crise ; the company is suffering from poor ~ la société est mal gérée [b] (= leaders collectively) dirigeants mpl ; the union ~ has or have agreed to arbitration les dirigeants du syndicat ont accepté l'arbitrage

leading¹ ['li:dɪŋ] [1] ADJ [a] (= important) important ; a ~ industrialist un industriel de premier plan ; a ~ industrial nation une des principales nations industrialisées ; a ~ advocate of economic sanctions un des principaux partisans des sanctions économiques [b] (= most important) principal ; Britain's ~ car manufacturer le premier or le principal constructeur automobile britannique ; one of the ~ figures of the twenties un personnage marquant des années vingt ; one of our ~ industries l'une de nos principales industries ; one of the country's ~ writers un des écrivains les plus importants or les plus en vue du pays [c] (Theat, Cine) [role, part] principal ; to play the ~ part or role (in a film/play) être la vedette (d'un film/d'une pièce) ; (fig) to play or take a ~ part or role in sth jouer un rôle majeur or prépondérant dans qch [d] (= in foremost position) [car, aircraft, battalion] de tête [e] (= winning) (in race) [runner, driver, car] en tête de course ; (in league) [competitor, club, team] en tête de classement

[2] COMP ► **leading aircraft(s)man** (pl leading aircraft(s)men), **leading aircraft(s)woman** (pl leading aircraft(s)women) N (Brit Aviat) ≈ soldat m (de l'armée de l'air) ► **leading article** N (Press) (Brit) éditorial m ; (US) article m de tête ► **leading case** N (Jur) précédent m ► **leading counsel** N (Brit Jur) avocat commis sur une affaire ► **leading edge** N [a] (Aviat) the ~ edge le bord d'attaque [b] (fig) to be at or on the ~ edge of technology être à la pointe de la technologie ; to invest in the ~ edge of technology investir dans les technologies de pointe ► **leading lady** N (Cine) actrice f principale ; his ~ lady in that film was Gill Page sa partenaire principale dans ce film était Gill Page ; (Theat) the ~ lady was Mary Dodd c'est Mary Dodd qui tenait le premier rôle féminin ► **leading light** N he is

one of the ~ **lights in the campaign** c'est un des personnages les plus en vue de la campagne; **she was one of the ~ lights in the local drama society** c'était une des étoiles du groupe d'art dramatique local; **one of the ~ lights in the economic field** une des sommités or lumières en matière d'économie ► **leading man** N (pl **leading men**) (Cine) acteur m principal; **her ~ man in that film was Will Preston** son partenaire principal dans ce film était Will Preston; (Theat) **the ~ man was David Penn** c'est David Penn qui tenait le premier rôle masculin ► **leading note** N (Mus) note f sensible ► **leading question** N (Jur, fig: pej) question f tendancieuse ► **leading rating** N (Brit Navy) quartier-maître m de 1ère classe ► **leading rein** N (Horse-riding) longe f

leading² ['ledɪŋ] N (NonC: Typ) interligne f, blanc m

leadworks ['ledwɜːks] N fonderie f de plomb

leaf [liːf] (pl **leaves**) ① N a [of tree, plant] feuille f; **the leaves** les feuilles fpl, le feuillage; **in ~** en feuilles; **to come into ~** se couvrir de feuilles; **to shake like a ~** trembler comme une feuille → **fig** b [of book] feuillet m, page f; **you should take a ~ out of his book** vous devriez prendre exemple sur lui; (fig) **to turn over a new ~** changer de conduite → **flyleaf** c [of table] (on hinges) rabat m, abattant m; (in groove, removable) rallonge f d (NonC) [of metal] feuille f → **gold** ② COMP ► **leaf bud** N bourgeon m à feuilles ► **leaf mould, leaf mold** (US) N (NonC) terreau m de feuilles ► **leaf tobacco** N tabac m en feuilles

► **leaf through** VT FUS [+ book] feuilleter, parcourir

leafless ['liːflɪs] ADJ sans feuilles, dénudé

leaflet ['liːflɪt] ① N a (= publication) prospectus m; (Pol, Rel) tract m; (for publicity) dépliant m, prospectus m; (Comm etc = instruction sheet) notice f explicative, mode m d'emploi b (Bot) foliole f ② VI distribuer des prospectus or des tracts etc ③ VT [+ area, street] distribuer des prospectus or des tracts etc dans

leafy ['liːfɪ] ADJ [branch] couvert de feuilles; [tree, plant] touffu; [garden] luxuriant; [lane] bordé d'arbres (feuillus); [suburb] vert; **green ~ vegetables** les légumes mpl verts à feuilles

league¹ [liːg] ① N a (= association) ligue f; **to form a ~ against** se liguer contre; **to be in ~ (with sb)** être de connivence (avec qn) b (Ftbl) championnat m; (Baseball) division f; (Baseball) **major/minor ~** première/deuxième division f → **rugby** c (fig = class) classe f, catégorie f; **they're in a different** or **not in the same ~** ils ne sont pas du même calibre; **in the big ~** dans le peloton de tête, parmi les premiers; **this is way out of your ~!** tu ne fais pas le poids!, tu n'es pas de taille! ② COMP ► **league champions** NPL (Brit Ftbl) vainqueurs mpl du championnat; **they were the ~ champions last year** ils ont remporté le championnat l'année dernière ► **league championship** N championnat m ► **league leaders** NPL **they are the ~ leaders now** pour le moment ils sont en tête du championnat ► **league match** N (Brit Ftbl) match m de championnat ► **League of Nations** N Société f des Nations ► **league table** N (Ftbl) classement m du championnat

league² [liːg] N lieue f; **seven-~ boots** bottes fpl de sept lieues

leak [liːk] ① N a (in bucket, pipe, roof, bottle, pen) fuite f; (in boat) voie f d'eau; (in shoe) trou m; **to spring a ~** [bucket, pipe] se mettre à fuir; [boat] commencer à faire eau; **the ship sprang a ~ in the bow** une voie d'eau s'est déclarée à l'avant du navire; **a gas ~** une fuite de gaz b [of information] fuite f; (fig) **a Cabinet ~** une fuite ministérielle; **budget/security ~** fuite f concernant le budget/la sécurité c (‡ = urinate) **to take a ~** pisser‡; **to go for a ~** aller pisser‡ ② VI a [bucket, pen, pipe, bottle] fuir; [ship] faire eau; [shoe] prendre l'eau; **the roof ~s** le toit fuit, il y a des fuites dans le toit b [gas, liquid] fuir, s'échapper; **the acid ~ed (through) onto the carpet** l'acide a filtré jusque dans le tapis c [cabinet, ministry etc] **the Cabinet has been ~ing** il y a eu des fuites au sein du cabinet ③ VT a [+ liquid] répandre, faire couler; **the tanker had ~ed its contents into the river/all over the road** le contenu du camion-citerne s'était répandu dans la rivière/sur la route b [+ information] divulguer; [+ story, document] divulguer (à la presse)

► **leak in** VI [spilt liquid] filtrer; [water] s'infiltrer; **the water is ~ing in through the roof** l'eau s'infiltre par le toit

► **leak out** VI [gas, liquid] fuir, s'échapper; [secret, news] filtrer, être divulgué; **it finally ~ed out that ...** on a fini par apprendre que ...

leakage ['liːkɪdʒ] N (= leak) [of gas, liquid, information] fuite f; (= amount lost) perte f

leakproof ['liːkpruːf] ADJ étanche

leaky ['liːkɪ] ADJ [roof, pipe, bucket] qui fuit; [boat] qui fait eau; [shoe] qui prend l'eau

lean¹ [liːn] (pret, ptp **leaned** or **leant**) ① VI a (= slope) [wall, construction etc] pencher; (fig) **I ~ towards the belief that ...** je tends à or j'incline à croire que ...; **to ~ towards sb's opinion** tendre à partager l'opinion de qn; (Pol) **to ~ towards the left** avoir des sympathies pour la gauche or à gauche b (= support o.s., rest) [person] s'appuyer ((up) against contre, à, on sur), prendre appui ((up) against contre, à, on sur); (with one's back) s'adosser ((up) against à), s'appuyer ((up) against contre, à); (with elbows) s'accouder (on à); **to be ~ing** être appuyé or adossé or accoudé; **to be ~ing (up) against the wall** [ladder, cycle etc] être appuyé contre le mur; [person] être appuyé contre le mur, être adossé au mur; **to ~ on one's elbows** s'appuyer or prendre appui sur les coudes; **to ~ on sb for help** or **support** s'appuyer sur qn; **to ~ (heavily) on sb for advice** compter (beaucoup) sur qn pour ses conseils c (* = apply pressure) faire pression (on sur), forcer la main (on à); **they ~ed on him for payment** ils ont fait pression sur lui pour qu'il paie (subj); **the editor was ~ing on him for the article** le rédacteur en chef le pressait pour qu'il remette son article ② VT [+ ladder, cycle etc] appuyer ((up) against contre); **to ~ one's elbows on the table/one's head on sb's shoulder** poser ses coudes sur la table/sa tête sur l'épaule de qn; **she ~ed her weight on the door** elle s'appuya de tout son poids contre la porte ③ N inclinaison f ④ COMP ► **lean-to** N (pl **lean-tos**) appentis m; ~**to garage/shed** etc garage m/cabane f etc en appentis

► **lean back** ① VI se pencher en arrière; **to ~ back in an armchair** se laisser aller en arrière dans un fauteuil; **to ~ back against sth** s'adosser contre or à qch ② VT SEP [+ chair] pencher en arrière; **to ~ one's head back** pencher la tête en arrière, renverser la tête (en arrière)

► **lean forward** ① VI se pencher en avant ② VT SEP pencher en avant

► **lean out** ① VI se pencher au dehors; **to ~ out of the window** se pencher par la fenêtre; "**do not ~ out**" « ne pas se pencher au dehors » ② VT SEP pencher au dehors; **he leant his head out of the window** il a passé la tête par la fenêtre

► **lean over** VI [person] (= forward) se pencher en avant; (= sideways) se pencher sur le côté; [object, tree] pencher, être penché; **to ~ over**

backwards se pencher en arrière
► **lean up** VI, VT SEP → **lean¹** 1b, 2

lean² [liːn] ① ADJ a (= slim) [person, body] mince; [animal] svelte; **to have a ~ build** être mince b (= fatless) [meat, beef] maigre c (= poor) [harvest] maigre, pauvre; ~ **diet** régime m maigre; ~ **years** années fpl de vaches maigres; **there are ~ times ahead in the property market** le marché de l'immobilier connaîtra une période difficile; **we had a ~ time of it** on a mangé de la vache enragée; **to go through a ~ patch** traverser une période difficile d (Comm) [company] dégraissé c [of meat] maigre m ③ COMP ► **lean-burn engine** N moteur m à carburant maigre

leaning ['liːnɪŋ] ① N (= liking) penchant m (towards pour); (= tendency) tendance f (towards à); **I always had a ~ towards sport** j'ai toujours été attiré par le sport; **he has artistic ~s** il a une prédisposition pour les arts, il a des tendances artistiques; **what are his political ~s?** quelles sont ses tendances politiques? ② ADJ [wall, building] penché ③ COMP ► **the Leaning Tower of Pisa** N la tour penchée de Pise

leanness ['liːnnɪs] N maigreur f

leant [lent] VB pt, ptp of **lean¹**

leap [liːp] (vb: pret, ptp **leaped** or **leapt**) ① N a (lit) saut m, bond m; **to take a ~** bondir, sauter; **at one ~** d'un bond b (fig) bond m; **a ~ in profits/inflation** un bond dans les profits/l'inflation; **there has been a ~ of 13% in profits/sales** les profits/les ventes ont fait un bond de 13%; **Russia's ~ into the market economy** le passage de la Russie à l'économie de marché; **the film takes a ~ into fantasy** le film plonge dans le fantastique; **to make the ~ from singer to actor** réussir à passer de la chanson au cinéma (or au théâtre); **in** or **by ~s and bounds** à pas de géant; **a ~ in the dark** un saut dans l'inconnu; **a big** or **great ~ forward** un grand bond en avant; **a giant ~ for mankind** un pas de géant pour l'humanité; (Rel, fig) (**to take** or **make**) **a ~ of faith** (faire) un acte de foi; **to make a ~ of the imagination** or **an imaginative ~** faire preuve de beaucoup d'imagination; **you're making a ~ of logic here that I can't follow** je n'arrive pas à suivre votre logique

② VI a [person, animal, fish] sauter, bondir; [flames] jaillir; **to ~ in/out** etc entrer/sortir etc d'un bond; **to ~ to one's feet** se lever d'un bond; **he leapt into/out of the car** il sauta dans/de la voiture; **he leapt out of bed** il sauta du lit; **he leapt over to the window** il se précipita à la fenêtre; **to ~ off a bus/train** sauter d'un bus/train; **to ~ over a ditch** franchir un fossé d'un bond, sauter (par-dessus) un fossé; **he leapt into the air** il fit un bond (en l'air); **the flames leapt into the air** les flammes ont jailli or se sont élevées dans les airs; **to ~ to attention** se mettre vivement au garde-à-vous; **he leapt for joy** il a sauté or bondi de joie; **the word leapt out at him** or **leapt off the page (at him)** le mot lui a sauté aux yeux b (fig) [profits, sales, prices, unemployment] faire un bond; **the shares leapt from 125p to 190p** les actions ont fait un bond de 125 à 190 pence; **the shares leapt (by) 21p to 370p** les actions ont fait un bond de 21 pence pour atteindre la cote de 370 pence; **her heart leapt** son cœur a bondi dans sa poitrine; **my heart leapt at the sight of her** j'ai eu un coup au cœur en la voyant; **to ~ at sth** [+ chance, suggestion, offer] sauter sur qch; [+ idea] accueillir qch avec enthousiasme; **to ~ to the conclusion that ...** conclure hâtivement que ...; **you mustn't ~ to conclusions** il ne faut pas tirer de conclusions hâtives; **to ~ to sb's defence** s'empresser de prendre la défense de qn → **look**

③ VT a [+ stream, hedge etc] sauter (par-dessus), franchir d'un bond

b [+ horse] faire sauter
c (fig) **to ~ a generation** [disease, illness, trait] sauter une génération
4 COMP ▶ **leap year** N année f bissextile
▶**leap about** VI gambader; **to ~ about with excitement** sauter de joie
▶**leap up** VI a (lit) (off ground) sauter en l'air; (to one's feet) se lever d'un bond; [flame] jaillir; **the dog leapt up at him** le chien lui a sauté dessus; **he leapt up indignantly** il a bondi d'indignation b (fig) [profits, sales, prices, unemployment] faire un bond

leapfrog ['li:p,frɒg] 1 N saute-mouton m 2 VI **to ~ over** (lit) [+ person] sauter à saute-mouton par-dessus; [+ stool, object] franchir à saute-mouton; (fig) dépasser 3 VT (fig) dépasser

leapt [lept] VB pt, ptp of **leap**

learn [lɜːn] (pret, ptp **learned** or **learnt**) 1 VT a (by study) [+ language, lesson, musical instrument] apprendre; **to ~ (how) to do sth** apprendre à faire qch; (fig) **he's learnt his lesson** il a compris la leçon; (fig) **I've learnt a lot since then** je sais à quoi m'en tenir maintenant, maintenant j'ai compris
b (= find out) [+ facts, news, results etc] apprendre; **I was sorry to ~ (that) you had been ill** j'ai appris avec regret que vous aviez été malade; **we haven't yet ~ed whether he recovered** nous ne savons toujours pas s'il est guéri
c (Psych = acquire) [behaviour, reaction] acquérir; **a ~ed reaction** une réaction acquise; **~ed behaviour** comportement m acquis
d (: = teach) apprendre; **I'll ~ you!** je vais t'apprendre, moi!*; **that'll ~ you!** ça t'apprendra!*
2 VI a apprendre; **it's never too late to ~** il n'est jamais trop tard pour apprendre, on apprend à tout âge; (fig iro) **he'll ~!** un jour il comprendra; **we are ~ing about the Revolution at school** on étudie la Révolution en classe; **to ~ from experience** apprendre par l'expérience; **to ~ from one's mistakes** tirer la leçon de ses erreurs → **live¹**
b (= hear) **I was sorry to ~ of** or **about your illness** j'ai appris avec regret votre maladie
▶**learn off** VT SEP apprendre par cœur
▶**learn up** VT SEP (= revise) [+ maths etc] travailler, bûcher*; [+ new facts] apprendre; **she ~ up all she could about the district** elle a appris tout ce qu'elle a pu sur la région

learned ['lɜːnɪd] ADJ (= erudite) [person, journal, society, essay] savant; [profession] intellectuel; (Brit Jur) **my ~ friend** mon éminent confrère

learnedly ['lɜːnɪdlɪ] ADV avec érudition, savamment

learner ['lɜːnəʳ] 1 N apprenant(e) m(f); (Brit Aut) **~ (driver)** apprenti(e) conducteur m, -trice f; **you are a quick ~** vous apprenez vite; **a ~'s dictionary** un dictionnaire pour apprenants; **language ~** étudiant(e) m(f) en langues; **a ~ of English** un apprenant d'anglais 2 COMP ▶ **learner-centred**, **learner-centered** (US) ADJ centré sur l'apprenant ▶ **learner's license** N (US) permis spécial pour apprentis conducteurs →
DRIVING LICENCE, DRIVER'S LICENSE

learning ['lɜːnɪŋ] 1 N (NonC) a (= fund of knowledge) érudition f, savoir m; **a man of ~** (in humanities) un érudit; (in sciences) un savant ■ (PROV) **a little ~ is a dangerous thing** mieux vaut être ignorant qu'à demi-savant → **seat**
b (= act) apprentissage m, étude f (**of** de); **language etc ~** apprentissage m or étude f des langues etc; **children who are behind in their ~** des enfants qui ont du retard à l'école; **~ develops the memory** apprendre développe la mémoire; **a place of ~** un lieu d'étude → **distance**, **rote**
2 COMP ▶ **learning curve** N courbe f d'apprentissage ▶ **learning difficulties**, **learn-**

ing **disabilities** NPL difficultés fpl d'apprentissage ▶ **learning-disabled** ADJ (US Scol) ayant des difficultés d'apprentissage ▶ **learning resources centre** N (Educ) centre m de documentation et d'information

learnt [lɜːnt] VB (esp Brit) pt, ptp of **learn**

lease [liːs] 1 N a (Jur = contract, duration) bail m; **long ~** bail m à long terme; **99-year ~** bail m de 99 ans; **to take a house on ~** prendre une maison à bail, louer une maison b (fig) **to take on a new ~ of** (Brit) or **on** (US) **life** [person] reprendre goût à la vie, retrouver un second souffle, repartir pour un tour*; **the heart transplant has given him a new ~ of** or **on life** sa greffe du cœur lui a donné un regain de vitalité; **their renovations have given the old farmhouse a new ~ of** or **on life** leurs travaux de rénovation ont donné une nouvelle jeunesse à la vieille ferme; **printing can give old T-shirts a new ~ of** or **on life** l'impression d'un motif peut donner une nouvelle jeunesse à de vieux tee-shirts 2 VT [+ house, car etc] louer à bail 3 COMP ▶ **lease-lend** N (Econ) prêt-bail m

leaseback ['liːsbæk] N cession-bail f; **~ scheme** or **contract** contrat m de cession-bail

leasehold ['liːshəʊld] 1 N (= contract) bail m emphytéotique; (= property) propriété f louée à bail 2 ADJ [property, building, land] loué à bail 3 ADV [buy] à bail 4 COMP ▶ **leasehold reform** N révision f du bail

leaseholder ['liːshəʊldəʳ] N ≈ locataire mf emphytéotique

leash [liːʃ] N (for dog) laisse f; **to keep a dog on a ~** tenir un chien en laisse; (fig) **to hold** or **keep sb on a short** or **tight ~** tenir la bride haute à qn; (esp US) **to give sb a longer ~** laisser la bride sur le cou à qn

leasing ['liːsɪŋ] N crédit-bail m

▼**least** [liːst] superl of **little²** 1 ADJ (= smallest amount of) le moins de; (= smallest) le moindre, la moindre, le plus petit, la plus petite; **he has (the) ~ money** c'est lui qui a le moins d'argent; **the ~ thing upsets her** la moindre chose or la plus petite chose la contrarie; **the principle of ~ effort** le principe du moindre effort; (Math) **the ~ common denominator** le plus petit dénominateur commun; **with the ~ possible expenditure** avec le moins de dépenses possible(s); **that's the ~ of our worries** c'est le moindre or le cadet de nos soucis → **resistance**
2 PRON a le moins; **you've given me the ~** c'est à moi que tu en as donné le moins; **it's the ~ I can do** c'est le moins que je puisse faire, c'est la moindre des choses; **it's the ~ one can expect** c'est la moindre des choses; **what's the ~ you are willing to accept?** quel prix minimum êtes-vous prêt à accepter?
b (in phrases) **at ~** (with quantity, comparison) au moins; (parenthetically) du moins, tout au moins; **it costs £5 at ~** cela coûte au moins 5 livres; **there were at ~ eight books** il y avait au moins huit livres; **he's at ~ as old as you** il a au moins votre âge; **he eats at ~ as much as I do** il mange au moins autant que moi; **at ~ it's not raining** au moins il ne pleut pas; **you could at ~ have told me!** tu aurais pu au moins me le dire!; **I can at ~ try** je peux toujours essayer; **he's ill, at ~ that's what he says** il est malade, du moins c'est ce qu'il dit; **at the very ~** au moins, au minimum; **it will cost £100 at the very ~** cela coûtera 100 livres au minimum or au bas mot; **not in the ~!** pas du tout!; **he was not in the ~ tired** or **not the ~ bit tired** or **not tired in the ~** il n'était pas le moins du monde fatigué; **it didn't surprise me in the ~** ◊ **I wasn't the ~ bit surprised** cela ne m'a pas surpris le moins du monde; **it doesn't matter in the ~** cela n'a pas la moindre importance ■ (PROV) **~ said soonest mended** moins on en dit mieux on se porte, moins on en dit et mieux ça vaut; **that's the ~ of it!**

s'il n'y avait que ça!, ça, ce n'est rien!; **I was annoyed, to say the ~ (of it)** j'étais mécontent, c'est le moins qu'on puisse dire; **she was not very wise, to say the ~** elle était pour le moins imprudente; **it wasn't a very good meal, to say the ~ of it** c'était un repas assez médiocre pour ne pas dire plus
3 ADV le moins; **the ~ expensive** le moins cher; **the ~ expensive car** la voiture la moins chère; **he did it ~ easily of all** (= least easily of all he did) c'est ce qu'il a eu le plus de mal à faire; (= least easily of all people involved) c'est lui qui l'a fait le moins facilement de tous; **she is ~ able to afford it** elle est la dernière à pouvoir se l'offrir; **when you are ~ expecting it** quand vous vous y attendez le moins; **he deserves it ~ of all** c'est lui qui le mérite le moins de tous; **nobody seemed amused, ~ of all John** cela ne semblait amuser personne et surtout pas John; **~ of all would I wish to offend him** je ne voudrais surtout pas le froisser; **all countries, not ~ the USA** tous les pays, et en particulier les USA; **not ~ because** ... notamment or entre autres parce que ...

leastways* ['liːstweɪz], **leastwise*** ['liːstwaɪz] ADV du moins, ou plutôt

least-worst* ['liːstwɜːst] ADJ le moins pire:, le moins mauvais

leather ['leðəʳ] 1 N a (NonC) cuir m → **hell**, **patent** b (also **wash ~**) peau f de chamois → **chamois** c (US: = wallet) portefeuille m 2 **leathers** NPL (= suit) cuir* m; (= trousers) pantalon m en cuir 3 VT (* = beat) tanner le cuir à:* 4 COMP [boots, jacket, seat] de or en cuir ▶ **leather bar*** N bar m cuir* (à clientèle sado-masochiste et homosexuelle) ▶ **leather goods** NPL (gen) articles mpl en cuir; (fancy goods) maroquinerie f

leatherbound ['leðəbaʊnd] ADJ [book] relié (en) cuir

Leatherette® [,leðə'ret] N similicuir m, skaï® m

leathering* ['leðərɪŋ] N **to give sb a ~** tanner le cuir à qn:*

leatherjacket ['leðə,dʒækɪt] N (Zool) larve f de la tipule

leathern ['leðən] ADJ (= of leather) de or en cuir; (= like leather) tanné

leatherneck: ['leðənek] N (US) marine m, fusilier m marin américain

leathery ['leðərɪ] ADJ [meat, substance] coriace; [skin] parcheminé, tanné

leave [liːv] (vb: pret, ptp **left**) 1 N a (NonC = consent) permission f; **to ask ~ (from sb) to do sth** demander (à qn) la permission de faire qch; **by** or **with your ~** avec votre permission → **by**
b (= holiday) (gen) congé m; (Mil) permission f; **how much ~ do you get?** vous avez droit à combien de jours de congé (or de jours de permission)?; **six weeks' ~** permission f or congé m de six semaines; **to be on ~** être en congé or en permission; **on ~ of absence** en congé exceptionnel; (Mil) en permission spéciale → **absent**, **French**, **sick**
c (= departure) congé m; **to take (one's) ~ (of sb)** prendre congé (de qn); **I must take my ~** il faut que je prenne congé; (fig) **have you taken ~ of your senses?** avez-vous perdu la tête or la raison?
2 VT a (= go away from) [+ town] quitter, partir de; (permanently) quitter; [+ room, building] sortir de, quitter; [+ person, job, one's husband, wife] quitter; [+ one's children] abandonner; **he left Paris in 1994** il a quitté Paris en 1994; **we left Paris at 6 o'clock** nous sommes partis de Paris or nous avons quitté Paris à 6 heures; **I must ~ you** il faut que je vous quitte (subj); (frm) **you may ~ us** vous pouvez vous retirer (frm); **they were left to die/to starve** on les a laissés mourir/mourir de faim; **he has left this address** il n'habite plus

▶ LANGUAGE IN USE: **least** 3.1, 7.5, 26.3

à cette adresse ; **he left home in 1989** il a quitté la maison en 1989 ; **I left home at 6 o'clock** je suis sorti de chez moi or j'ai quitté la maison à 6 heures ; **to ~ hospital** sortir de or quitter l'hôpital ; **the ship left port** le navire a quitté le port ; **to ~ prison** sortir de prison ; **the car left the road** la voiture a quitté la route ; **to ~ the room** (= go out) sortir de la pièce ; (euph = go to toilet) sortir (euph) ; **he left school in 1996** (Brit) il a quitté l'école en 1996 ; (US) il a terminé ses études en 1996 ; (US = gave up studies) il a arrêté ses études en l996 ; **he left school at 4pm** il est sorti de l'école or il a quitté l'école à 16 heures ; **the train left the station** le train est sorti de or a quitté la gare, (Rail) **to ~ the table** se lever de table, quitter la table ; (Rail) **to ~ the track** dérailler → **love, lurch²**

b (= forget) [+ object, keys, umbrella] laisser, oublier ; **he left his umbrella on the train** il a laissé or oublié son parapluie dans le train

c (= deposit, put) laisser ; **I'll ~ the book for you with my neighbour** je laisserai le livre pour vous chez mon voisin ; **has the postman left anything?** est-ce que le facteur a apporté or laissé quelque chose ? ; **can I ~ my camera with you?** ◊ **can I ~ you my camera?** puis-je vous confier mon appareil-photo ? ; **he left the children with a neighbour** il a laissé or confié les enfants à un voisin ; **he ~s a widow and one son** il laisse une veuve et un orphelin ; **to ~ a message for sb** laisser un message à qn ; **to ~ the waiter a tip** laisser un pourboire au garçon ; **to ~ word** laisser un mot or un message (with sb for sb à qn pour qn, that que) ; **he left word for Paul to go and see him** il a fait dire à Paul d'aller le voir ; **he left word with me for Paul to go and see him** il m'a chargé de dire à Paul d'aller le voir

d (= allow to remain) laisser ; **~ it where it is** laisse-le là où il est ; **he left half his meal** il a laissé la moitié de son repas ; (Typ etc) **to ~ a space** laisser un blanc or un espace ; **to ~ the door open/the phone off the hook** laisser la porte ouverte/le téléphone décroché ; **to ~ two pages blank** laisser deux pages blanches ; **it left me free for the afternoon** cela m'a laissé l'après-midi de libre, cela m'a libéré pour l'après-midi ; **this deal has left me in debt** cette affaire m'a laissé des dettes ; **he was left a widower** il est devenu veuf ; **he left it lying on the floor** il l'a laissé traîner par terre ; **don't ~ that letter lying around** ne laissez pas traîner cette lettre ; **to ~ sb on his own** or **to himself** laisser qn tout seul ; **to ~ sb in peace** or **to himself** laisser qn tranquille ; **left to himself, he'd never have finished** (tout) seul, il n'aurait jamais fini ; **to ~ it to sb to decide** je te laisse le soin de décider ; **I('ll) ~ you to judge** je vous laisse juger ; **I'll ~ the matter in your hands** je vous laisse le soin occuper de l'affaire, je vous laisse le soin d'arranger cela ; **shall we go via Paris? — I'll ~ it to you** et si on passait par Paris ? — je m'en remets à vous or je vous laisse décider ; **~ it to me!** laissez-moi faire !, je m'en charge ! ; **I'll ~ you to it*** je vous laisse (à vos occupations) ; **I wanted to ~ myself (with) at least £80 a week** je voulais garder or qu'il me reste (subj) au moins 80 livres par semaine ; **let's ~ it at that** tenons-nous-en là ; **let's ~ it at that for today** restons-en là pour aujourd'hui ; **it left a good impression on me** cela m'a fait bonne impression ; **to ~ sb in charge of a house/shop** etc laisser à qn la garde d'une maison/d'une boutique etc ; **the boss is out and he's left me in charge** le patron est sorti et m'a laissé la charge de tout ; **take it or ~ it** c'est à prendre ou à laisser ; (fig) **I can take it or ~ it** cela ne me fait ni chaud ni froid → **alone, baby, chance, cold, desire, device, go, shelf, stand, stone, unsaid**

e (Math) **three from six ~s three** six moins trois égalent trois ; **if you take four from seven, what are you left with?** si tu enlèves quatre de sept, qu'est-ce qui te reste ?

f (in will) [+ money] laisser (to à) ; [+ object, property] laisser, léguer (to à)

g **to be left** rester ; **what's left?** qu'est-ce qui reste ? ; **who's left?** qui est-ce qui reste ? ; **there'll be none left** il n'en restera pas ; **how many are (there) left?** combien est-ce qu'il en reste ? ; **there are three cakes left** il reste trois gâteaux ; **are there any left?** est-ce qu'il en reste ? ; **nothing was left for me but to sell the house** il ne me restait plus qu'à vendre la maison ; **I was left with a lot of stock I couldn't sell** je me suis retrouvé avec un gros stock que je ne pouvais pas écouler ; **I've got £6 left** il me reste six livres ; **I've got a half left** il m'en reste la moitié ; **I'll have nothing left** il ne me restera plus rien ; **I've no money left** il ne me reste plus d'argent, je n'ai plus d'argent ; **have you got any left?** est-ce qu'il vous en reste ?

③ VI (= go away) [person, train, ship etc] partir, s'en aller ; (= resign) partir, démissionner ; **to ~ for Paris** [person, train] partir pour Paris ; [ship] partir or appareiller pour Paris ; **it's time we left** ◊ **it's time for us to ~** il est l'heure de partir or que nous partions (subj) ; **the train ~s at 4 o'clock** le train part à 4 heures ; **he's just left** il vient de partir ; **his wife has left** (permanently) sa femme est partie

►**leave about, leave around** VT SEP [+ clothes, possessions etc] laisser traîner

►**leave aside** VT SEP laisser de côté

►**leave behind** VT SEP a (= not take) [+ person] laisser, ne pas emmener ; [+ object] laisser, ne pas emporter ; **he left the children behind in Paris** il a laissé les enfants à Paris ; **you'll get left behind if you don't hurry up** on va te laisser là si tu ne te dépêches pas b (= outdistance) [+ opponent in race] distancer ; [+ fellow students etc] dépasser c (= forget) [+ gloves, umbrella etc] laisser, oublier

►**leave in** VT SEP [+ paragraph, words etc] garder, laisser ; [+ plug] laisser, ne pas enlever ; (in oven) **~ the cake in for 50 minutes** laisser cuire le gâteau pendant 50 minutes

►**leave off** ① VI (* = stop) s'arrêter ; (in work, reading) **where did we ~ off?** où nous sommes-nous arrêtés ? ; **~ off!** arrête !, ça suffit !* ② VT SEP a (* = stop) arrêter (doing de faire) b [+ lid] ne pas remettre ; [+ clothes] (= not put back on) ne pas remettre ; (= stop wearing) cesser de porter, abandonner ; (= not put on) ne pas mettre c [+ gas, heating, tap] laisser fermé ; [+ light] laisser éteint d (= not add to list) (deliberately) exclure ; (accidentally) oublier, omettre

►**leave on** VT SEP a [+ one's hat, coat etc] garder, ne pas enlever ; [+ lid] ne pas enlever, laisser b [+ gas, heating, tap] laisser ouvert ; [+ light] laisser allumé

►**leave out** VT SEP a (= omit) (accidentally) oublier, omettre ; (deliberately) exclure ; [+ line in text] (also Mus) [+ name] sauter ; **they left him out** ils l'ont tenu or laissé à l'écart ; **I'm feeling left out** j'ai l'impression d'être tenu à l'écart ; **~ it out!:** arrête !* b (= not put back) laisser sorti, ne pas ranger ; (= leave visible) [+ food, note, etc] laisser ; **I left the box out on the table** j'ai laissé la boîte sortie sur la table ; **to ~ sth out in the rain** laisser qch dehors sous la pluie ; **to ~ sb out in the cold** (lit) laisser qn dans le froid ; (fig) laisser qn à l'écart

►**leave over** ① VT SEP a **this is all the meat that was left over** c'est toute la viande qui reste ; **there's nothing left (over)** il ne reste plus rien ; **there's anything left over** il n'y a rien de restes ; **after each child has three there are two left over** quand chaque enfant en a pris trois, il en reste deux ; **if there's any money left over** s'il reste de l'argent b (= postpone) remettre (à plus tard) ; **let's ~ this over till tomorrow** remettons cela à demain ② **leftovers** NPL → **leftover**

-leaved [liːvd] ADJ (in compounds) **small-leaved**

à petites feuilles ; **round-leaved** à feuilles rondes ; **five-leaved stem** tige f à cinq feuilles

leaven ['levn] ① N levain m ② VT (lit) faire lever ; **his speech was ~ed by a few witty stories** son discours était agrémenté de quelques anecdotes spirituelles ③ COMP ► **leavened bread** N pain m au levain

leavening ['levnɪŋ] N (lit, fig) levain m

leaves [liːvz] NPL of **leaf**

leavetaking ['liːvˌteɪkɪŋ] N adieux mpl

leaving ['liːvɪŋ] ① N départ m ② COMP ► **leaving present** N cadeau m de départ

leavings ['liːvɪŋz] NPL restes mpl

Lebanese [ˌlebə'niːz] ① ADJ libanais ② N (pl inv) Libanais(e) m(f) ③ **the Lebanese** NPL les Libanais mpl

Lebanon ['lebənən] N le Liban → **cedar**

lech* [letʃ] ① VI **to ~ after sb** (= desire) désirer qn ; (= behave lecherously) courir après qn ② N = **lecher**

lecher ['letʃər] N coureur m de jupons

lecherous ['letʃərəs] ADJ lubrique, libidineux (hum) ; [look] lascif

lecherously ['letʃərəslɪ] ADV lubriquement, lascivement

lechery ['letʃərɪ] N (NonC) luxure f, lubricité f

lectern ['lektən] N lutrin m

lector ['lektɔːr] N (Univ) lecteur m, -trice f

lecture ['lektʃər] ① N a (gen single occurrence) conférence f ; (Univ etc: gen one of a series) cours m (magistral) ; **to give a ~** faire or donner une conférence, faire un cours (on sur) ; **I went to the ~s on French poetry** j'ai suivi les cours de poésie française ; **inaugural ~** b (fig = reproof) réprimande f, sermon m (pej) ; **to give** or **read sb a ~** sermonner qn (about au sujet de) ② VI faire or donner une conférence (to à, on sur), faire un cours (to à, on sur) ; **he ~s at 10 o'clock** il fait son cours à 10 heures ; **he ~s at Bristol** il enseigne dans le supérieur à Bristol ; **he ~s in law** il est professeur de droit ; **she ~s on Keats** elle fait cours sur Keats ③ VT (= reprove) réprimander (for having done pour avoir fait), sermonner (pej) ; **he ~d me for my clumsiness** il m'a réprimandé pour ma maladresse ④ COMP ► **lecture course** N (Univ) cours m magistral ► **lecture hall** N amphithéâtre m ► **lecture notes** NPL notes fpl de cours ► **lecture room, lecture theatre** N (gen) salle f de conférences ; (Univ) amphithéâtre m

lecturer ['lektʃərər] N a (= speaker) conférencier m, -ière f b (Brit Univ) ≈ enseignant(e) m(f) du supérieur ; **senior ~** ≈ maître m de conférences

lectureship ['lektʃəʃɪp] N (Brit Univ) ≈ poste m d'enseignant(e) du supérieur ; **senior ~** ≈ poste m de maître de conférences ; **he's got a ~ in English at Birmingham University** il enseigne l'anglais à l'université de Birmingham

LED [ˌeliː'diː] ① N (ABBR = **light-emitting diode**) (diode f) LED f ② COMP ► **LED display** N affichage m LED

led [led] VB pt, ptp of **lead¹**

ledge [ledʒ] N (on wall) rebord m, saillie f ; (also **window ~**) rebord m (de la fenêtre) ; (on mountain) saillie f ; (Climbing) vire f ; (under sea) (= ridge) haut-fond m ; (= reef) récif m

ledger ['ledʒər] ① N (Accounts) grand livre m ② COMP ► **ledger line** N (Mus) ligne f supplémentaire

lee [liː] ① N côté m sous le vent ; **in** or **under the ~ of …** à l'abri de … ② ADJ [side of ship, shore] sous le vent

leech [liːtʃ] N (lit, also fig pej) sangsue f ; **he clung like a ~ to me all evening** il est resté pendu à mes basques* toute la soirée

leek [liːk] N poireau m

leer [lɪər] **1** VI lorgner; **to ~ at sb** lorgner qn **2** N (*evil*) regard *m* mauvais; (*lustful*) regard *m* concupiscent

leery* [ˈlɪərɪ] ADJ (*esp US, Can*) **to be ~ about sth** se méfier de qch

lees [liːz] NPL [*of wine*] lie *f* (*NonC*)

leeward [ˈliːwəd] (*esp Naut*) **1** ADJ, ADV sous le vent **2** N côté *m* sous le vent; **to ~** sous le vent **3** COMP ► **the Leeward Islands** NPL (*Geog*) les îles *fpl* Sous-le-Vent

leeway [ˈliːweɪ] N **a** (*Naut*) dérive *f* **b** (*fig = freedom*) liberté *f*; **he gives his children/his staff too much ~** il donne trop de liberté à ses enfants/à son personnel; **that allows** or **gives him a certain (amount of) ~** cela lui donne une certaine liberté d'action or marge de manœuvre; **we had ten minutes' ~ to catch the train** nous avions une marge (de sécurité) de dix minutes pour attraper le train; **they want more ~ to make decisions** ils veulent davantage de latitude or de liberté pour prendre des décisions; **we had little ~ in our choice of hotel** or **in choosing a hotel** nous n'étions pas vraiment libres de choisir notre hôtel; **he has some ~ in deciding how much money to spend** il dispose d'une certaine liberté or marge de manœuvre pour les dépenses

left¹ [left] **1** VB *pt, ptp* of **leave 2** COMP ► **left luggage** N (*Brit*) bagages *mpl* en consigne ► **left-luggage locker** N (casier *m* à) consigne *f* automatique ► **left-luggage office** N consigne *f* ► **left-over** ADJ → **leftover**

left² [left] **1** ADJ gauche; **my ~ arm/foot** mon bras/pied gauche; (*Aut*) **~ hand down!** braquez à gauche!; **to have two ~ feet*** être maladroit de ses pieds; (*esp US*) **to be (way) out in ~ field*** être (tout à fait) saugrenu; (*esp US*) **to come out of ~ field*** être totalement inattendu → **4**

2 ADV [*turn, look*] à gauche; **go** or **bear** or **turn ~ at the church** tournez or prenez à gauche à l'église; (*Mil*) **eyes ~!** tête gauche! → **right**

3 N **a** gauche *f*; **on your ~** à or sur votre gauche; **on the ~** sur la gauche, à gauche; **the door on the ~** la porte de gauche; **to drive on the ~** conduire à gauche; **to the ~** à gauche; (*Aut*) **to keep to the ~** se tenir sa gauche; **turn it to the ~** tournez-le vers la gauche or à gauche **b** (*Pol*) **the Left** la gauche; **he's further to the Left than I am** il est plus à gauche que moi; **the parties of the Left** les partis *mpl* de gauche **c** (*Boxing*) gauche *m*; **he threw a ~ to the jaw** il a porté un direct du gauche à la mâchoire; **he hit him with his ~** il l'a frappé du gauche

4 COMP ► **left back** N (*Sport*) arrière *m* gauche ► **left-footed** ADJ [*shot*] du pied gauche; [*player*] gaucher ► **left half** N (*Sport*) demi *m* gauche ► **left-hand** ADJ à or de gauche; **the ~-hand door/page** *etc* la porte/page *etc* de gauche; **~-hand drive car** conduite *f* à gauche (*véhicule*); **this car is a ~-hand drive** cette voiture a la conduite à gauche; **on the ~-hand side** à gauche; **a ~-hand turn** un virage à gauche ► **left-handed** ADJ [*person*] gaucher; [*screw*] fileté à gauche, avec pas à gauche; [*scissors etc*] pour gaucher; (*fig*) **~-handed compliment** (= *insincere*) compliment *m* hypocrite; (= *ambiguous*) compliment *m* ambigu ► **left-hander** N (= *person*) gaucher *m*, -ère *f*; (* = *blow*) gifle *f* or claque* *f* (assenée de la main gauche) ► **left-of-centre** ADJ (*Pol*) de centre gauche ► **left wing** N (*Mil, Sport*) aile *f* gauche; (*Pol*) gauche *f* ► **left-wing** ADJ [*newspaper, view*] de gauche; **he's very ~-wing** il est très à gauche ► **left-winger** N (*Pol*) homme *m* or femme *f* de gauche; (*Sport*) ailier *m* gauche

leftie* [ˈleftɪ] N **a** (*esp Brit: Pol, pej*) gaucho* *mf* (*pej*), gauchiste *mf* **b** (*US = left-handed person*) gaucher *m*, -ère *f*

leftish [ˈleftɪʃ] ADJ = **leftist 2**

leftism [ˈleftɪzəm] N (*NonC*) gauchisme *m*

leftist [ˈleftɪst] (*Pol*) **1** N gauchiste *mf* **2** ADJ de gauche

leftover [ˈleftˌəʊvər] **1** N (= *throwback*) vestige *m* (*from* de); **a ~ from the days when ...** un vestige des jours or de l'époque où ... **2** ► **leftovers** NPL (*after meal*) restes *mpl* **3** ADJ restant, qui reste; **a bottle with some ~ wine in it** une bouteille avec un restant de vin; **a ~ bottle of wine** une bouteille de vin qui reste (or restait *etc*)

leftward(s) [ˈleftwəd(z)] (*Pol, lit*) **1** ADJ orienté vers la gauche **2** ADV vers la gauche

lefty* [ˈleftɪ] N = **leftie**

leg [leg] **1** N **a** [*of person, horse*] jambe *f*; [*of other animal, bird, insect*] patte *f*; **my ~s won't carry me any further!** je ne tiens plus sur mes jambes!; **to stand on one ~** se tenir sur un pied or une jambe; **to give sb a ~ up** (*lit*) faire la courte échelle à qn; (* *fig*) donner un coup de pouce à qn; (*fig*) **he hasn't got a ~ to stand on** il ne peut s'appuyer sur rien, il n'a aucun argument valable; (*esp US*) **it's got ~s*** [*idea, plan, story*] ça tient debout; (*fig*) **to pull sb's ~** (= *hoax*) faire marcher qn; (= *tease*) taquiner qn; (*Brit*) **to get one's ~ over*** s'envoyer en l'air → **fast¹, hind², last¹**
b (*Culin*) [*of lamb*] gigot *m*; [*of beef*] gîte *m*; [*of veal*] sous-noix *f*; [*of pork, chicken, frog*] cuisse *f*; [*of venison*] cuissot *m*
c [*of table etc*] pied *m*; [*of trousers, tights etc*] jambe *f* → **inside**
d (= *stage*) [*of journey*] étape *f*; (*Ftbl etc*) **first ~** match *m* aller; **second** or **return ~** match *m* retour; (*Sport: in relay*) **to run/swim the first ~** courir/nager la première distance or le premier relais

2 VT **to ~ it*** (= *run*) cavaler*; (= *flee*) se barrer*; (= *walk*) aller à pied, faire le chemin à pied

3 COMP ► **leg bone** N tibia *m* ► **leg iron** N (*Med*) appareil *m* (orthopédique) ► **leg muscle** N muscle *m* de la jambe, muscle *m* jambier (*frm*) ► **leg-of-mutton sleeve** N manche *f* gigot *inv* ► **leg-pull*** N canular *m* ► **leg-pulling*** N mise *f* en boîte* ► **leg shield** N protège-jambe *m* ► **leg-warmers** NPL jambières *fpl*

legacy [ˈlegəsɪ] **1** N (*Jur*) legs *m* (*de biens mobiliers*); (*fig*) legs *m*, héritage *m*; **to leave a ~ to sb** (*Jur*) faire un legs or un héritage à qn; (*fig*) laisser un héritage à qn; **they have left us a ~ of bureaucracy and red tape** ils nous ont légué leur bureaucratie et leur paperasserie; **we are left with the ~ of 40 years of environmental disaster** nous héritons de 40 ans de désastre écologique; **the ~ of the past** l'héritage *m* or le legs du passé; **the tragedy left a ~ of bitterness** cette tragédie a laissé un profond sentiment d'amertume; **this law is a ~ from medieval times** cette loi est un héritage de l'époque médiévale; **the economic ~ of Thatcherism/Communism** l'héritage *m* économique du thatchérisme/du communisme; (*hum*) **this vase is a ~ from the previous tenants** on a hérité ce vase des précédents locataires

2 COMP ► **legacy duty, legacy tax** (*US*) N droits *mpl* de succession

legal [ˈliːgəl] **1** ADJ **a** (= *concerning the law*) [*error, protection*] judiciaire; [*question, battle, services, framework*] juridique; [*status*] légal, judiciaire; **to take ~ action against sb** intenter un procès à qn, poursuivre qn en justice; **I am considering taking ~ action** j'envisage d'intenter une action; **to take ~ advice** (**on** or **about** or **over sth**) consulter un juriste or un avocat (à propos de qch); **~ loophole** vide *m* juridique; **it's a ~ matter** c'est une question juridique or de droit; **in ~ matters** en matière de droit; **to have a fine ~ mind** être un excellent juriste; **to the ~ mind the issue is quite clear** pour un juriste ce problème est tout à fait clair; **for ~ reasons** pour des raisons légales
b (= *lawful*) [*act, decision, right, obligation, requirement*] légal

2 COMP ► **legal adviser** N conseiller *m*, -ère *f* juridique ► **legal aid** N aide *f* judiciaire ► **legal costs** NPL frais *mpl* de justice ► **legal currency** N (*Fin*) monnaie *f* légale; **this note is no longer ~ currency** ce billet n'a plus cours ► **legal department** N [*of bank, firm*] service *m* du contentieux ► **legal document** N (*concerning the law*) document *m* juridique; (*legally valid*) document *m* légal ► **legal eagle*** N as* *m* du barreau ► **legal entity** N personne *f* morale ► **legal fees** NPL frais *mpl* de justice ► **legal fiction** N fiction *f* juridique ► **legal holiday** N (*US*) jour *m* férié ► **the legal limit** N la limite légale ► **legal offence** N infraction *f* à la loi ► **legal opinion** N avis *m* juridique ► **legal proceedings** NPL procès *m*, poursuites *fpl*; **to begin** or **start ~ proceedings against sb** engager des poursuites contre qn, intenter un procès à qn ► **the legal process** N la procédure (judiciaire) ► **the legal profession** N (= *lawyers*) les gens *mpl* de loi; (= *occupation*) **to go into the ~ profession** faire une carrière juridique ► **legal redress** N réparation *f* en justice ► **legal representation** N représentation *f* en justice ► **legal successor** N ayant cause *m* ► **legal system** N système *m* juridique ► **legal tender** N (*Fin*) monnaie *f* légale; **is this ~ tender?** [*banknote*] ce billet a-t-il cours?; [*coin*] cette pièce a-t-elle cours?

legalese* [ˌliːgəˈliːz] N (*pej*) jargon *m* des juristes

legalism [ˈliːgəˌlɪzəm] N (*pej*) **a** (*word, point, rule etc*) arguitie *f* juridique **b** (*turn of mind*) juridisme *m*, légalisme *m*

legalistic [ˌliːgəˈlɪstɪk] ADJ (*pej*) légaliste

legalistically [ˌliːgəˈlɪstɪkəlɪ] ADV (*frm*) d'un point de vue purement juridique

legality [lɪˈgælɪtɪ] N légalité *f*

legalization [ˌliːgəlaɪˈzeɪʃən] N légalisation *f*

legalize [ˈliːgəlaɪz] VT légaliser

legally [ˈliːgəlɪ] ADV (*gen*) légalement; **to acquire sth ~** acquérir qch légalement or par des moyens légaux; **~, the whole issue is a nightmare** du point de vue juridique, toute cette question est un cauchemar

legate [ˈlegɪt] N légat *m*

legatee [ˌlegəˈtiː] N légataire *mf*

legation [lɪˈgeɪʃən] N légation *f*

legator [ˌlegəˈtɔːr] N testateur *m*, -trice *f*

legend [ˈledʒənd] N (*all senses*) légende *f*; **a ~ in his own lifetime** ◊ **a living ~** une légende de son vivant

legendary [ˈledʒəndərɪ] ADJ (*gen*) légendaire; **to achieve ~ status** devenir légendaire

-legged [ˈlegɪd] ADJ (*in compounds*) **four-legged** à quatre pattes, quadrupède (*frm*); **bare-legged** aux jambes nues → **three**

leggings [ˈlegɪŋz] NPL (*for woman*) caleçon *m*, leggings *mpl*; (= *legwarmers*) jambières *fpl*; (*for baby*) petit pantalon *m*; (*protective: for walker, farmer*) cuissardes *fpl*; **waterproof ~** jambières *fpl* or guêtres *fpl* imperméables

leggo* [leˈgəʊ] EXCL = **let go**; → **go 1b**

leggy* [ˈlegɪ] ADJ [*person*] aux longues jambes; (*slightly pej*) [*youth etc*] tout en jambes; [*animal*] aux longues pattes, haut sur pattes; **a gorgeous ~ blonde** une magnifique blonde aux longues jambes

Leghorn [ˈlegˌhɔːn] N (*Geog*) Livourne

legibility [ˌledʒɪˈbɪlɪtɪ] N lisibilité *f*

legible [ˈledʒəbl] ADJ lisible

legibly [ˈledʒəblɪ] ADV de façon lisible

legion [ˈliːdʒən] **1** N (*lit, fig*) légion *f* → **foreign 2** ADJ légion *inv*; **books on the**

subject are ~ les ouvrages sur ce sujet sont légion

LEGION

La **British Legion** *est un organisme d'aide aux anciens combattants et à leurs familles. Comptant de nombreux clubs locaux, elle organise des collectes au profit des associations caritatives de l'armée le jour anniversaire de l'armistice de la Première Guerre mondiale. C'est le « Poppy Day Appeal ».*

*L'*American Legion *remplit des fonctions similaires et aide à la réinsertion des anciens combattants. D'autre part, elle fait pression auprès du Congrès pour défendre leurs intérêts et milite en faveur d'une forte défense nationale. Elle compte également de nombreux clubs locaux où ses membres peuvent se retrouver.*

legionary [ˈliːdʒənəri] **1** N légionnaire *m* **2** ADJ de la légion

legionella [ˌliːdʒəˈnelə] N légionellose *f*

legionnaire [ˌliːdʒəˈneəʳ] **1** N légionnaire *m* **2** COMP ► **legionnaire's disease** N (*Med*) maladie *f* du légionnaire

legislate [ˈledʒɪsleɪt] VI légiférer, faire des lois ; **to ~ against** faire des lois contre ; **the government's decision to ~ for immigration control** la décision du gouvernement de légiférer sur le contrôle de l'immigration ; **we can't ~ for people doing that** ça ne servirait à rien d'interdire aux gens de le faire

legislation [ˌledʒɪsˈleɪʃən] N **a** (= *body of laws*) législation *f* ; (= *single law*) loi *f* ; **a piece of ~** une loi ; **to bring in** or **introduce ~** faire des lois ; **the government is considering ~ against ...** le gouvernement envisage de légiférer contre ... ; **we are in favour of ~ to abolish ...** nous sommes partisans d'une législation qui abolirait ... ; **under the present ~** sous la législation actuelle **b** (*NonC*) (= *making laws*) élaboration *f* des lois ; (= *enacting*) promulgation *f* des lois

legislative [ˈledʒɪslətɪv] ADJ (*frm*) [*reform, assembly, powers, process*] législatif ; [*session*] parlementaire ; [*programme*] de lois ; [*proposals*] de loi ; **the ~ body** le (corps) législatif ; (*US*) **a ~ agenda** un programme de lois ; (*US*) **~ drafting** rédaction *f* des projets de loi

legislator [ˈledʒɪsleɪtəʳ] N législateur *m*, -trice *f*

legislature [ˈledʒɪslətʃəʳ] N (corps *m*) législatif *m*

legist [ˈliːdʒɪst] N légiste *mf*

legit [ləˈdʒɪt] ADJ [*business, deal*] réglo* ; **to go ~** faire les choses dans les règles

legitimacy [lɪˈdʒɪtɪməsɪ] N légitimité *f*

legitimate [lɪˈdʒɪtɪmɪt] **1** ADJ **a** (= *lawful*) [*action, government, business, child*] légitime ; (= *valid*) [*reason, excuse, argument, conclusion*] valable ; [*complaint*] fondé ; [*target*] admissible ; **for ~ purposes** dans un but légitime, pour des motifs valables ; **he has a ~ claim to the property** il a légitimement droit à cette propriété ; **it's ~ for the international community to intervene** il est légitime que la communauté internationale intervienne ; **it's perfectly ~ to raise objections** il est parfaitement légitime de soulever des objections **b** (*Theat*) **the ~ stage** or **theatre** (*gen*) le théâtre sérieux ; (*as opposed to cinema*) le théâtre **2** [lɪˈdʒɪtɪmeɪt] VT légitimer

legitimately [lɪˈdʒɪtɪmɪtlɪ] ADV [*act, claim, argue, expect*] légitimement ; **a ~ elected government** un gouvernement élu légitimement ; **one might ~ believe/ask ...** on est en droit de croire/de demander ...

legitim(iz)ation [lɪˌdʒɪtɪm(aɪˈz)eɪʃən] N légitimation *f*

legitimize [lɪˈdʒɪtɪmaɪz] VT légitimer

legless [ˈleglɪs] ADJ **a** (*lit*) sans jambes, cul-de-jatte **b** (*Brit* * *fig* = *drunk*) bourré*, rond*

legman * [ˈlegmæn] N (*pl* -**men**) (*Press*) reporter *m* débutant (qui enquête sur le terrain) ; (*gen*) garçon *m* de courses

Lego® [ˈlegəʊ] **1** N Lego® *m* **2** COMP ► **Lego brick** N bloc *m* de Lego®

legroom [ˈlegrʊm] N place *f* pour les jambes

legume [ˈlegjuːm] N (*gen*) (= *plant*) légumineuse *f* ; (= *pod*) gousse *f*

leguminous [leˈgjuːmɪnəs] ADJ légumineux

legwork * [ˈlegwɜːk] N [*of reporter, investigator etc*] travail *m* sur le terrain ; (*gen*) **I had to do all the ~** c'est moi qui ai dû me déplacer

Leibnitzian [laɪbˈnɪtsɪən] ADJ leibnizien

Leics. ABBR = **Leicestershire**

Leipzig [ˈlaɪpsɪg] N Leipzig

leisure [ˈleʒəʳ, (*US*) ˈliːʒəʳ] **1** N (*NonC*) loisir *m*, temps *m* libre ; **he had the ~ in which to go fishing** il avait le loisir d'aller à la pêche ; (*hum*) **she's a lady of ~** elle est rentière (*fig hum*) ; **a life of ~** une vie pleine de loisirs, une vie oisive (*pej*) ; **in my moments** or **hours of ~** à mes moments perdus, pendant mes loisirs ; **do it at your ~** prenez tout votre temps ; **think about it at (your) ~** réfléchissez-y à tête reposée ; **a park where the public can stroll at ~** un parc où l'on peut flâner à sa guise ; **he is not often at ~** il n'a pas souvent de temps libre **2** COMP [*pursuits, activities*] de loisirs ; [*sector*] des loisirs ► **leisure centre** N (*Brit*) centre *m* de loisirs ► **leisure complex** N complexe *m* de loisirs ► **the leisure industry** N l'industrie *f* des loisirs ► **leisure occupations** N loisirs *mpl* ► **leisure suit** N costume *m* sport, tenue *f* décontractée ► **leisure time** N loisirs *mpl*, temps *m* libre ► **leisure wear** N (*NonC: Comm*) vêtements *mpl* décontractés

leisured [ˈleʒəd] ADJ [*person, life, existence*] oisif ; [*meal*] tranquille ; **the ~ classes** les classes *fpl* oisives

leisurely [ˈleʒəlɪ] **1** ADJ [*pace, stroll, meal, occupation*] tranquille ; **to adopt a ~ approach to sth** aborder qch avec décontraction ; **to have a ~ bath** prendre tranquillement un bain **2** ADV tranquillement, sans se presser

leitmotif, leitmotiv [ˈlaɪtməʊˌtiːf] N (*Mus, fig*) leitmotiv *m*

lem [lem] N (*Space*) lem *m*, module *m* lunaire

lemma [ˈlemə] N (*pl* **lemmas** or **lemmata** [ˈlemətə]) (*Ling: gen*) vocable *m* ; (*Comput Ling*) lemme *m*

lemmatization [ˌleməˌtaɪˈzeɪʃən] N lemmatisation *f*

lemmatize [ˈlemətaɪz] VT lemmatiser

lemming [ˈlemɪŋ] N lemming *m*

lemon [ˈlemən] **1** N **a** (= *fruit, drink*) citron *m* ; (= *tree*) citronnier *m* ; (= *colour*) citron *m* → **bitter**

b * (= *idiot*) cruche* *f*, imbécile *mf* ; (= *defective object*) cochonnerie* *f* ; **I stood there like a ~** j'étais là comme un imbécile or une cruche* **2** ADJ (*in colour*) citron *inv* **3** COMP ► **lemon balm** N citronnelle *f*, eau *f* de mélisse ► **lemon cheese, lemon curd** N (*Brit*) crème *f* au citron ► **lemon drink** N citronnade *f* ► **lemon drop** N bonbon *m* (acidulé) au citron ► **lemon grass** N lemon-grass *m inv* ► **lemon grove** N plantation *f* de citronniers ► **lemon juice** N jus *m* de citron ; (= *drink*) citron *m* pressé ► **lemon soda** N (*esp US*) limonade *f* ► **lemon sole** N (*Brit*) limande-sole *f* ► **lemon squash** N ≃ citronnade *f* ► **lemon squeezer** N presse-citron *m*, presse-agrumes *m inv* ► **lemon tea** N thé *m* au citron ► **lemon tree** N citronnier *m* ► **lemon yellow** ADJ, N jaune citron *m inv*

lemonade [ˌleməˈneɪd] N (*still*) citronnade *f* ; (*fizzy*) limonade *f*

lemur [ˈliːməʳ] N maki *m*, lémur *m*

lend [lend] (*pret, ptp* **lent**) **1** VT **a** [+ *money, possessions*] prêter ; **to ~ sb sth** ◊ **to ~ sth to sb** prêter qch à qn ; **to ~ money at 10%** prêter de l'argent à 10 % → **lease**

b (*fig*) [+ *importance*] prêter, accorder (**to** à) ; [+ *dignity, mystery*] donner, conférer (**to** à) ; **to**

~ credibility to sth donner or conférer une certaine crédibilité à qch ; **to ~ authority to sth** conférer une certaine autorité à qch ; **to ~ an ear (to sb)** prêter l'oreille (à qn), écouter (qn) → **ear** ; **to ~ one's name to ...** prêter son nom à ..., accorder son patronage à ...

c (*reflexive*) **to ~ itself** (or **o.s.**) **to ...** se prêter à ... ; **the novel doesn't ~ itself to being filmed** ce roman ne se prête pas à une adaptation cinématographique ; **the programme doesn't really ~ itself to radio** cette émission ne se prête pas vraiment à la radio ; **these problems don't ~ themselves to quick solutions** ces problèmes ne se prêtent pas à des solutions rapides ; **he refused to ~ himself to such a dishonest scheme** il a refusé de cautionner un plan aussi malhonnête, il a refusé de se laisser impliquer dans une affaire aussi malhonnête → **hand, support, weight**

2 COMP ► **lend-lease** N (*US*) = **lease-lend** → **lease**

► **lend out** VT SEP [+ *object, book*] prêter

lender [ˈlendəʳ] N prêteur *m*, -euse *f* → **money-lender**

lending [ˈlendɪŋ] **1** N prêt *m* ; **bank ~** le prêt bancaire **2** COMP ► **lending library** N bibliothèque *f* de prêt ► **lending limit** N (*Fin*) plafond *m* de crédit ► **lending policy** N (*Fin*) politique *f* de prêt ► **lending rate** N (*Fin*) taux *m* de prêt, taux *m* d'intérêt débiteur

length [leŋ(k)θ] **1** N **a** (*NonC: in space*) longueur *f* ; **its ~ was 6 metres** ◊ **it was 6 metres in ~** il faisait 6 mètres de long, sa longueur était de 6 mètres ; **what is the ~ of the field?** ◊ **what ~ is the field?** quelle est la longueur du champ ? ; **along the whole ~ of the river** tout le long or sur toute la longueur de la rivière ; **what ~ do you want?** quelle longueur vous faut-il ?, il vous en faut combien (de long) ? ; **what ~ (of cloth) did you buy?** quel métrage (de tissu) as-tu acheté ? ; **the ship turns in its own ~** le navire vire sur place ; (*fig*) **over the ~ and breadth of England** dans toute l'Angleterre ; **to fall full ~** ◊ **to go** or **measure one's ~** tomber or s'étaler* de tout son long → **full** ; → **arm'**

b (*NonC: in time etc*) durée *f* ; [*of book, essay, letter, film, speech*] longueur *f* ; **what ~ is the film?** ◊ **what's the ~ of the film?** quelle est la durée du film ? ; **~ of** durée *f* de vie ; **for the whole ~ of his life** pendant toute la durée de sa vie ; **for what ~ of time?** pour combien de temps ?, pour quelle durée ? ; **for some ~ of time** pendant un certain temps, pendant quelque temps ; **the ~ of time he took to do it** le temps qu'il a mis à le faire ; **~ of service** ancienneté *f* ; **4,000 words in ~** (*essay, book*) de 4 000 mots

c **at ~** (= *at last*) enfin, à la fin ; **at (great) ~** (= *for a long time*) fort longuement ; (= *in detail*) dans le détail, en long et en large

d **to go to the ~/to ... ~s: he went to the ~ of asking my advice** il est allé jusqu'à me demander conseil ; **I've gone to great ~s to get it finished** je me suis donné beaucoup de mal pour le terminer ; **he would go to any ~(s) to succeed** il ne reculerait devant rien pour réussir ; **I didn't think he would go to such ~s to get the job** je n'aurais pas cru qu'il serait allé jusque-là pour avoir le poste

e (*Sport*) longueur *f* ; **to win by a ~** gagner d'une longueur ; **he was two ~s behind** il avait deux longueurs de retard ; **the race will be swum over six ~s** la course se nagera sur six longueurs ; **four ~s of the pool** quatre longueurs de piscine ; **he was about three car ~s behind me** il était à trois longueurs de voiture derrière moi

f (*Phon*) [*of vowel*] quantité *f* ; [*of syllable*] longueur *f*

g (= *section*) [*of rope, wire*] morceau *m*, bout *m* ; [*of wallpaper*] lé *m*, laize *f* ; [*of cloth*] métrage *m*, pièce *f* ; [*of tubing*] morceau *m*, bout *m* ; [*of track*] tronçon *m* ; **cut into metre ~s** coupé en morceaux d'un mètre ; **I bought several ~s of dress material** j'ai acheté plusieurs métrages de tissu de confection ; (*Sewing*) **dress/ skirt ~** hauteur *f* de robe/de jupe [2] COMP ► **length mark** N (*Ling*) signe *m* diacritique de longueur

-length [leŋ(k)θ] ADJ (*in compounds*) **ankle-length skirt** jupe *f* qui descend jusqu'aux chevilles ; **elbow-length sleeve** manche *f* mi-longue → **shoulder**

lengthen [ˈleŋ(k)θən] [1] VT [+ *object*] allonger, rallonger ; [+ *visit, life*] prolonger ; (*Phon*) [+ *vowel*] allonger ; **to ~ one's stride** allonger le pas [2] VI [*object, process, cycle, shadows, queue*] s'allonger ; [*visit, silence*] se prolonger ; [*skirts*] rallonger ; **the days/nights are ~ing** les jours/nuits rallongent ; **the intervals between his visits were ~ing** ses visites s'espaçaient

lengthily [ˈleŋ(k)θɪlɪ] ADV longuement

lengthways [ˈleŋ(k)θweɪz], **lengthwise** [ˈleŋ(k)θwaɪz] [1] ADV dans le sens de la longueur [2] ADJ longitudinal

lengthy [ˈleŋ(k)θɪ] ADJ très long (longue *f*) ; **delays on the M8** de très forts ralentissements sur la M8 ; **for a ~ period of time** pendant très longtemps ; **patients who have a ~ wait for treatment** les patients qui doivent attendre très longtemps pour être soignés

lenience [ˈliːnɪəns], **leniency** [ˈliːnɪənsɪ] N [*of parent, teacher, treatment, view*] indulgence *f* ; [*of government, judge, sentence*] clémence *f*

lenient [ˈliːnɪənt] ADJ [*parent, teacher, treatment, view*] indulgent (**with sb** avec qn) ; [*government, judge, sentence*] clément

leniently [ˈliːnɪəntlɪ] ADV [*treat*] avec indulgence

Lenin [ˈlenɪn] N Lénine *m*

Leningrad [ˈlenɪngræd] N Leningrad

Leninism [ˈlenɪˌnɪzəm] N léninisme *m*

Leninist [ˈlenɪnɪst] ADJ, N léniniste *mf*

lens [lenz] [1] N (*for magnifying*) lentille *f* ; [*of camera*] objectif *m* ; [*of spectacles*] verre *m* ; (*also* **contact ~**) lentille *f*, verre *m* de contact ; [*of eye*] cristallin *m* → **contact, telephoto, wide** [2] COMP ► **lens cap** N bouchon *m* d'objectif ► **lens field** N angle *m* de couverture ► **lens holder** N porte-objectif *m inv* ► **lens hood** N pare-soleil *m inv*

Lent [lent] N (*Rel*) le carême ; **in** *or* **during ~** pendant le carême ; **to keep ~** observer le carême, faire carême ; **I gave it up for ~** j'y ai renoncé pour le carême

lent [lent] VB *pt, ptp of* **lend**

Lenten [ˈlentən] ADJ de carême

lentil [ˈlentl] N (*Bot, Culin*) lentille *f* ; **~ soup** soupe *f* aux lentilles

Leo [ˈliːəʊ] N (*Astron*) le Lion ; (*Astrol*) **I'm (a) ~** je suis (du) Lion

Leonard [ˈlenəd] N Léonard *m*

Leonardo (da Vinci) [ˌliːəˈnɑːdəʊ(dəˈvɪntʃɪ)] N Léonard de Vinci

Leonian [liːˈəʊnɪən] N **to be a ~** être (du) Lion

leonine [ˈliːənaɪn] ADJ léonin

leopard [ˈlepəd] N léopard *m* ▪ (*PROV*) **the ~ cannot change its spots** on ne peut pas changer sa nature, chassez le naturel, il revient au galop

leopardess [ˈlepədes] N léopard *m* femelle

leopardskin [ˈlepədskɪn] N peau *f* de léopard

leotard [ˈliːətɑːd] N justaucorps *m*

leper [ˈlepəʳ] N (*Med, fig*) lépreux *m*, -euse *f* ; **~ colony** léproserie *f*

lepidoptera [ˌlepɪˈdɒptərə] NPL lépidoptères *mpl*

lepidopterist [ˌlepɪˈdɒptərɪst] N lépidoptériste *mf*

leprechaun [ˈleprəkɔːn] N lutin *m*, farfadet *m*

leprosy [ˈleprəsɪ] N lèpre *f*

leprous [ˈleprəs] ADJ lépreux

lesbian [ˈlezbɪən] [1] ADJ [*woman, activist, feminist*] lesbien ; [*couple*] de lesbiennes ; [*relationship, affair*] homosexuel (*entre femmes*) ; **~ sex** rapports *mpl* homosexuels entre femmes ; **~ and gay community** communauté *f* lesbienne et gay ; **~ and gay issues** questions *fpl* concernant les lesbiennes et les gays ; **~ and gay movement/rights** mouvement *m*/ droits *mpl* des lesbiennes et des gays ; **~ and gay people** les lesbiennes *fpl* et les gays *mpl* [2] N lesbienne *f*

lesbianism [ˈlezbɪənɪzəm] N lesbianisme *m*, homosexualité *f* féminine

lesion [ˈliːʒən] N lésion *f*

Lesotho [lɪˈsuːtu] N le Lesotho

less [les] *compar of* **little²** [1] ADJ, PRON [a] (*in amount, size, degree*) moins (de) ; **~ butter** moins de beurre ; **even ~** encore moins ; **even** *or* **still ~ butter** encore moins de beurre ; **much ~ milk** beaucoup moins de lait ; **a little ~ cream** un peu moins de crème ; **~ and ~** de moins en moins ; **~ and ~ money** de moins en moins d'argent ; (*fig*) **he couldn't have done ~ if he'd tried** il aurait pu difficilement (en) faire moins ; **of ~ importance** de moindre importance, de moins d'importance ; **I have ~ time for reading** j'ai moins le temps de lire, j'ai moins de temps pour lire ; **can't you let me have it for ~?** vous ne pouvez pas me faire un prix ? ; **~ of your cheek!*** ça suffit ! ; **~ noise please!** moins de bruit s'il vous plaît ! ; **~ of that** *or* **it!** assez !, ça suffit ! ; **with ~ trouble** avec moins de mal ; **he knows little German and ~ Russian** il ne connaît pas bien l'allemand et encore moins le russe ; **he has little but I have ~** il n'a pas grand-chose mais j'en ai encore moins ; **we must see ~ of her** il faut que nous la voyions (*subj*) moins souvent [b] **~ than** moins que ; (*before a number*) moins de ; **I have ~ than you** j'en ai moins que vous ; **I need ~ than that** il m'en faut moins que cela ; **I have ~ money than you** j'ai moins d'argent que vous ; **it costs ~ than the export model** il coûte moins cher que le modèle d'exportation ; **it was ~ money than I expected** c'était moins (d'argent) que je n'escomptais ; **~ than half the audience** moins de la moitié de l'assistance ; **I got ~ out of it than you did** j'en ai tiré moins de profit que toi ; **it took ~ time than I expected** cela a pris moins de temps que je ne pensais ; **we eat ~ bread than we used to** nous mangeons moins de pain qu'avant ; **he did ~ to help them than his brother did** il a moins fait *or* fait moins pour les aider que son frère ; **it is ~ than perfect** on ne peut pas dire que ce soit parfait ; **in ~ than a month** en moins d'un mois ; **in ~ than no time*** en un rien de temps, en moins de deux* ; **not ~ than one kilo** pas moins d'un kilo ; **a sum ~ than 10 francs** une somme de moins de 10 F ; **it's ~ than you think** c'est moins que vous ne croyez ; **I won't sell it for ~ than £10** je ne le vendrai pas à *or* pour moins de 10 livres [c] (*in phrases*) **with no ~ skill than enthusiasm** avec non moins d'habileté que d'enthousiasme ; **no ~ a person than the Prime Minister** rien moins que le Premier ministre ; **he's bought a car, no ~*** il s'est payé une voiture, rien que ça* ; **I was told the news by the bishop, no ~*** c'est l'évêque en personne, s'il vous plaît*, qui m'a appris la nouvelle ; **he has no ~ than four months' holiday a year** il a au moins quatre mois de vacances par an ; **it costs no ~ than £100** ça ne coûte pas moins de 100 livres ; **I think no ~ of him** *or* **I think none the ~ of him** *or* **I don't think any (the) ~ of him for that** il n'est pas descendu dans mon estime pour autant ; **there will be so much the ~ to pay** cela fera autant de moins à payer ; **the ~ said about it the better** mieux vaut ne pas en parler ; **the ~ you buy the ~ you spend** moins vous achetez, moins vous dépensez ; **nothing ~ than** rien moins que, tout simplement ; **he's nothing ~ than a thief** c'est tout simplement un voleur, ce n'est qu'un voleur ; **nothing ~ than a bomb would move them** il faudrait au moins une bombe pour les faire bouger ; **nothing ~ than a public apology will satisfy him** il ne lui faudra rien moins que des excuses publiques pour le satisfaire ; **it's nothing ~ than disgraceful** le moins qu'on puisse dire c'est que c'est une honte [2] ADV [a] moins ; **you must eat ~** vous devez moins manger, il faut que vous mangiez (*subj*) moins ; **I must see you ~** il faut que je vous voie moins souvent ; **to grow ~** diminuer ; **that's ~ important** c'est moins important, ça n'est pas si important ; **~ and ~** de moins en moins ; **still ~** ◊ **much** ~ ◊ **even ~** encore moins ; **~ regularly/often** moins régulièrement/souvent ; **it's ~ expensive than you think** c'est moins cher que vous ne croyez ; **whichever is (the) ~ expensive** le moins cher des deux ; **he is ~ well known** il est moins (bien) connu ; **he was ~ hurt than frightened** il a eu plus de peur que de mal ; **the problem is ~ one of capital than of personnel** ce n'est pas tant *or* c'est moins un problème de capital qu'un problème de personnel [b] (*in phrases*) **the ~ he works the ~ he earns** moins il travaille, moins il gagne ; **the ~ you worry about it the better** moins vous vous ferez du souci à ce sujet, mieux ça vaudra ; **he was (all) the ~ pleased as he'd refused to give his permission** il était d'autant moins content qu'il avait refusé son autorisation ; **he wasn't expecting me but he was none the ~ pleased to see me** il ne m'attendait pas mais il n'en était pas moins content de me voir ; **she is no ~ intelligent than you** elle n'est pas moins intelligente que vous ; **he criticized the director no ~ than the caretaker** il a critiqué le directeur tout autant que le concierge ; **he was ~ annoyed than amused** il était moins fâché qu'amusé ; **it is ~ a short story than a novel** c'est moins une nouvelle qu'un roman → **more** [3] PREP moins ; **~ 10% discount** moins 10% de remise ; **in a year ~ four days** dans un an moins quatre jours

...less [lɪs] SUF **hatless** sans chapeau ; **childless** sans enfants

lessee [leˈsiː] N preneur *m*, -euse *f* (à bail)

lessen [ˈlesn] [1] VT (*gen*) diminuer ; [+ *cost*] réduire ; [+ *anxiety, pain*] atténuer ; [+ *effect, shock*] amortir ; (*Pol*) [+ *tension*] relâcher [2] VI diminuer, s'amoindrir ; [*pain*] s'atténuer ; [*tension*] se relâcher

lessening [ˈlesnɪŋ] N (*NonC*) diminution *f*, amoindrissement *m* ; (*Pol*) **~ of tension** détente *f*

lesser [ˈlesəʳ] [1] ADJ [a] moindre ; **to a ~ degree** *or* **extent** à un moindre degré, à un degré moindre ; **the ~ of two evils** le moindre de deux maux ; (*hum*) **we mortals*** *or* **beings*** nous (autres) simples mortels (*hum*) [b] (*Bot, Zool, Geog*) petit [2] COMP ► **the Lesser Antilles** NPL les Petites Antilles *fpl* ► **lesser celandine** N ficaire *f* ► **lesser panda** N petit panda *m*

lesson [ˈlesn] [1] N [a] (*gen*) leçon *f* ; (*in school, college etc*) leçon *f*, cours *m* ; **a French/ geography** *etc* **~** une leçon *or* un cours de français/de géographie *etc* ; **swimming/driving ~** leçon *f* de natation/de conduite ; **to have** *or* **take ~s in** prendre des leçons de ; **to give ~s in** donner des leçons de ; **we have ~s from nine to midday** nous avons classe *or* cours de 9 heures à midi ; **~s start at 9 o'clock** la classe commence *or* les cours commencent à 9 heures ; (*fig*) **let that be a ~ to you!** que cela te serve de leçon ! → **private, teach** [b] (*Rel*) leçon *f* → **read¹** [2] COMP ► **lesson plans** NPL (*Scol*) dossier *m* pédagogique

lessor [le'sɔːr] N bailleur m, -eresse f

lest [lest] CONJ (liter) de peur or de crainte de (+ infin), de peur or de crainte que (+ ne) (+ subj); **he took the map ~ he should get lost** il a pris la carte de peur or crainte de se perdre, il a pris la carte au cas où il se perdrait; **I gave him the map ~ he should get lost** je lui ai donné la carte de peur or de crainte qu'il (ne) se perde, je lui ai donné la carte au cas où il se perdrait; **anyone had forgotten, may I remind you that ...** au cas où certains auraient oublié, permettez-moi de vous rappeler que ...; **I was afraid ~ he should** or **might fall** je craignais qu'il ne tombe (subj) or ne tombât (subj) (frm); (on war memorial etc) "**~ we forget**" «in memoriam »

▼ **let¹** [let] (pret, ptp **let**) ① VT ⓐ (= allow) laisser; **to ~ sb do sth** laisser qn faire qch; **he wouldn't ~ us** il n'a pas voulu; **she wanted to help but her mother wouldn't ~ her** elle voulait aider mais sa mère ne l'a pas laissée faire; **I won't ~ you be treated like that** je ne permettrai pas qu'on vous traite (subj) de cette façon; **I won't ~ it be said that ...** je ne permettrai pas que l'on dise que ...; **to ~ sb into a secret** révéler un secret à qn; **don't ~ it get you down*** ne te laisse pas démoraliser pour autant*; **don't ~ me forget** rappelle-le-moi, tu m'y feras penser; **don't ~ the fire go out** ne laisse pas s'éteindre le feu; **~ me have a look** faites voir; **~ me help you** laissez-moi vous aider; **~ me give you some advice** permettez-moi de vous donner un conseil; **~ me take your coat** laissez-moi vous débarrasser de votre manteau; **~ me tell you ...** que je vous dise ... or raconte (subj) ...; **when can you ~ me have it?** quand est-ce que je pourrai l'avoir or le prendre?; **~ him have it!** (= give) donnez-le-lui!; (‡ = shoot, strike etc) règle-lui son compte!*; **~ him be!** laisse-le (tranquille)!; **(just you) ~ me catch you stealing again!*** que je t'attrape (subj) or t'y prenne encore à voler!; **the hunted man ~ himself be seen** l'homme traqué s'est laissé repérer; **I ~ myself be persuaded** je me suis laissé convaincre → **alone, drop, fall, fly³, go, know, lie**

ⓑ (used to form imperative of 1st person) **~ us** or **~'s go for a walk** allons nous promener; **~'s go!** allons-y!; **~'s get out of here!** filons!, fichons le camp (d'ici)!*; **don't ~'s*** or **~'s not start yet** ne commençons pas tout de suite; **don't ~ me keep you** que je ne vous retienne pas; **don't ~ me see you doing that again** que je ne t'y reprenne pas, que je ne te revois pas faire ça; **~ us pray** prions; **~ me see (now) ...** ◊ **~'s see (now) ...** voyons ...; **~ me think** laissez-moi réfléchir → **say**

ⓒ (used to form imperative of 3rd person) **if he wants the book, ~ him come and get it himself** s'il veut le livre, qu'il vienne le chercher lui-même or il n'a qu'à venir le chercher lui-même; **~ him say what he likes, I don't care** qu'il dise ce qu'il veut, ça m'est égal; **~ no one believe that I will change my mind** que personne ne s'imagine (subj) que je vais changer d'avis; **~ that be a warning to you** que cela vous serve d'avertissement; **~ there be light** que la lumière soit; **just ~ them try!** qu'ils essaient (subj) un peu!; (frm) **~ it be done at once** que cela soit fait tout de suite; (Math) **~ x equal two** soit x égal à deux

ⓓ (Med) **to ~ blood** tirer du sang, faire une saignée

ⓔ **to ~ a window/door into a wall** percer or ouvrir une fenêtre/porte dans un mur

ⓕ (esp Brit = hire out) [+ house etc] louer, mettre en location; **"flat to ~"** «appartement à louer »; **"to ~"** ◊ **"to be ~"** « à louer »

② N [of house etc] location f; **I'm looking for a long/short ~ for my villa** je cherche à louer ma villa pour une longue/brève période

③ COMP ► **let alone** CONJ → **alone** e ► **let-down*** N déception f; **what a ~-down!**

quelle déception!; **the film was a ~-down after the book** le film était décevant par rapport au livre ► **let-out** N (Brit) échappatoire f, issue f ► **let-up** N (= decrease) diminution f; (= stop) arrêt m; (= respite) relâchement m, répit m; **if there is a ~-up in the rain** si la pluie s'arrête un peu; **he worked five hours without (a) ~-up** il a travaillé cinq heures d'affilée or sans s'arrêter; **there will be no ~-up in my efforts** je ne relâcherai pas mes efforts

► **let away** VT SEP (= allow to leave) laisser partir; **the headmaster ~ the children away early today** le directeur a laissé partir or a renvoyé les enfants tôt aujourd'hui; (fig) **you can't ~ him away with that!** tu ne peux pas le laisser s'en tirer comme ça!

► **let down** ① VT SEP ⓐ [+ window] baisser; [+ one's hair] dénouer, défaire; [+ dress] rallonger; [+ tyre] dégonfler; (on rope etc) [+ person, object] descendre; **to ~ down a hem** défaire un ourlet (pour rallonger un vêtement); (fig) **he ~ me down gently** (in giving bad news) il me l'a dit or il m'a traité avec ménagement; (in punishing etc) il n'a pas été trop sévère avec moi → **hair**

ⓑ (= disappoint, fail) faire faux bond à, décevoir; **we're expecting you on Sunday, don't ~ us down** nous vous attendons dimanche, nous comptons sur vous or ne nous faites pas faux bond; **he's ~ me down several times** il m'a déçu plusieurs fois or à plusieurs reprises; **that shop has ~ me down before** j'ai déjà été déçu par cette boutique; **the car ~ me down** la voiture m'a joué des tours; **my watch never ~s me down** ma montre est toujours à l'heure; **you've ~ the team down** tu as façon de jouer a beaucoup déçu or desservi l'équipe; (fig) **you've ~ the side down** tu ne nous (or leur) as pas fait honneur; **the weather ~ us down** le beau temps n'a pas été de la partie

② **~-down*** N → **let¹**

► **let in** VT SEP ⓐ [+ person, cat] faire entrer, laisser entrer, ouvrir (la porte) à; **can you ~ him in?** pouvez-vous lui ouvrir (la porte)?; **the maid ~ him in** la bonne lui a ouvert la porte or l'a fait entrer; **he pleaded with us to ~ him in** il nous a suppliés de le laisser entrer or de lui ouvrir (la porte); **they wouldn't ~ me in** ils ne voulaient pas me laisser entrer; **he ~ himself in with a key** il a ouvert (la porte) or il est entré avec une clé; **to ~ in water** [shoes, tent] prendre l'eau; [roof] laisser entrer or passer la pluie; **the curtains ~ the light in** les rideaux laissent entrer la lumière; **this camera ~s the light in** cet appareil-photo laisse passer la lumière; (Aut) **to ~ the clutch in** embrayer

ⓑ (* = involve, commit) **see what you've ~ me in for now!** tu vois dans quelle situation tu me mets maintenant!; **if I'd known what you were ~ting me in for I'd never have come** si j'avais su dans quoi tu allais m'entraîner je ne serais jamais venu; **you're ~ting yourself in for trouble** tu te prépares des ennuis; **you don't know what you're ~ting yourself in for** tu ne sais pas à quoi tu t'engages; **I ~ myself in for doing the washing-up** je me suis laissé coincer pour la corvée de vaisselle; **I got ~ in for a £5 donation** j'ai dû donner cinq livres

ⓒ **to ~ sb in on a secret/a plan** mettre qn au courant d'un secret/d'un plan; **can't we ~ him in on it?** ne peut-on pas le mettre au courant?

► **let off** VT SEP ⓐ (= cause to explode, fire etc) [+ bomb] faire éclater; [+ firework] tirer, faire partir; [+ firearm] faire partir

ⓑ (= release) dégager, lâcher; **to ~ off steam** [boiler, engine] lâcher or dégager de la vapeur; (* fig) [person] [+ anger] décharger sa bile; [+ excitement] se défouler*

ⓒ (= allow to leave) laisser partir; **they ~ the children off early today** aujourd'hui ils ont laissé partir or renvoyé les enfants de bonne heure; **will you please ~ me off at 3 o'clock?**

pourriez-vous s'il vous plaît me laisser partir à 3 heures?

ⓓ (= excuse) dispenser; **to ~ sb off (doing) sth** dispenser qn de (faire) qch; **if you don't want to do it, I'll ~ you off** si tu ne veux pas le faire, je t'en dispense

ⓔ (= not punish) ne pas punir, faire grâce à; **he ~ me off** il ne m'a pas puni; **I'll ~ you off this time** je vous fais grâce or je ferme les yeux pour cette fois; **the headmaster ~ him off with a warning** le directeur lui a seulement donné un avertissement; **he was ~ off with a fine** il s'en est tiré avec une amende, il en a été quitte pour une amende; **to ~ sb off lightly** laisser qn s'en tirer à bon compte

ⓕ (= rooms etc) louer; **the house has been ~ off in flats** la maison a été louée en plusieurs appartements

► **let on** ① VI (= tell) **I won't ~ on** je ne dirai rien, je garderai ça pour moi; **they knew the answer but they didn't ~ on** ils connaissaient la réponse mais ils n'ont pas pipé; **don't ~ on!** motus!; **don't ~ on about what they did** ne va pas raconter or dire ce qu'ils ont fait; **she didn't ~ on that she'd seen me** elle n'a pas dit qu'elle m'avait vu ② VT SEP ⓐ (= admit, acknowledge) dire, aller raconter (**that** que)

ⓑ (= pretend) prétendre, raconter (**that** que)

► **let out** ① VI **to ~ out at sb** (with fists, stick etc) envoyer des coups à qn; (= abuse) injurier qn; (= speak angrily to) attaquer qn; (= scold) réprimander qn sévèrement

② VT SEP ⓐ (= allow to leave) [+ person, cat] faire or laisser sortir; (= release) [+ prisoner] relâcher; [+ sheep, cattle] faire sortir (**of** de); [+ caged bird] lâcher; **~ me out!** laissez-moi sortir!; **I'll ~ you out** je vais vous ouvrir la porte or vous reconduire; **the watchman ~ me out** le veilleur m'a fait sortir; **he ~ himself out quietly** il est sorti sans faire de bruit, il a ouvert la porte sans faire de bruit; **I'll ~ myself out** pas besoin de me reconduire; **they are ~ out of school at 4** on les libère à 16 heures; **to ~ the air out of a tyre** dégonfler un pneu; **to ~ the water out of the bath** vider l'eau de la baignoire → **cat**

ⓑ [+ fire, candle] laisser s'éteindre

ⓒ (= reveal) [+ secret, news] laisser échapper, révéler; **don't ~ it out that ...** ne va pas raconter que ...

ⓓ [+ shout, cry] laisser échapper; **to ~ out a laugh** faire entendre un rire

ⓔ [+ dress] élargir; **to ~ one's belt out by two holes** desserrer sa ceinture de deux crans; **to ~ out a seam** défaire une couture (pour agrandir un vêtement)

ⓕ (= remove suspicion from) disculper, mettre hors de cause; (= exclude) exclure, éliminer; **his alibi ~s him out** son alibi le met hors de cause; **if it's a bachelor you need that ~s me out** si c'est un célibataire qu'il vous faut je ne peux pas faire votre affaire

ⓖ (esp Brit) [+ house etc] louer

③ **~-out** N → **let¹**

► **let past** VT SEP [+ person, vehicle, animal, mistake] laisser passer

► **let through** VT SEP [+ vehicle, person, light] laisser passer

► **let up** ① VI [rain] diminuer; [cold weather] s'adoucir; **he didn't ~ up until he'd finished** il ne s'est accordé aucun répit avant d'avoir fini; **she worked all night without ~ting up** elle a travaillé toute la nuit sans relâche; **what a talker she is, she never ~s up!** quelle bavarde, elle n'arrête pas! **to ~ up on sb*** lâcher la bride à qn ② VT SEP (= allow to rise) **to ~ sb up** permettre à qn de se lever ③ **~-up*** N → **let¹**

let² [let] N ⓐ (Tennis) let m, balle f à remettre; **to play a ~** jouer un let, remettre le service; **~ ball** balle f de let; **~!** net!, let! ⓑ (Jur) **without ~ or hindrance** librement, sans empêchement aucun

letch* [letʃ] VI = **lech**

➤ LANGUAGE IN USE: **let** 3.1, 9.3, 9.4, 26.1

lethal ['liːθəl] ADJ (= causing death) [poison, chemical, gas, effect, injection, dose] mortel ; [attack, blow] fatal ; [weapon, explosion] meurtrier ; **(by) ~ injection** (par) injection f (d'une dose) mortelle ; **a ~ combination** or **cocktail (of ...)** [of drink, drugs etc] un mélange fatal (de ...) ; (fig) [of ignorance, fear, poverty etc] un mélange explosif or détonant (de ...) ; (Pol, Mil) **~/non-~ aid** aide f militaire/humanitaire ; (hum: coffee, beer etc) **that stuff is ~!*** c'est infect !

lethargic [lɪˈθɑːdʒɪk] ADJ [a] (= tired) [person] léthargique ; [movement] indolent ; **to feel ~** avoir une sensation de léthargie [b] (Comm, St Ex) léthargique ; **trading was ~** les affaires étaient moroses

lethargy ['leθədʒɪ] N léthargie f

let's [lets] = **let us** ; →**let¹**

Lett [let] N Latvian

letter ['letəʳ] [1] N [a] (of alphabet) lettre f ; **the ~ L** la lettre L ; **it was printed in ~s 15cm high** c'était écrit en lettres de 15 cm de haut ; (fig) **the ~ of the law** la lettre de la loi ; **he followed the instructions to the ~** il a suivi les instructions à la lettre or au pied de la lettre ; **to have a lot of ~s after** (Brit) **or behind** (US) **one's name** être bardé de diplômes → **block, capital, red**
[b] (= written communication) lettre f ; **I wrote her a ~** je lui ai écrit une lettre ; **thank you for your ~ of 1 June 1996** je vous remercie pour votre lettre du 1ᵉʳ juin 1996 ; **were there any ~s for me?** y avait-il du courrier or des lettres pour moi ? ; **to write a ~ of complaint/support/apology/protest** écrire une lettre de réclamation/de soutien/d'excuse/de protestation ; **she apologized/complained by ~** elle a envoyé une lettre d'excuse/de réclamation ; **he was invited by ~** il a reçu une invitation écrite ; **his appointment to the post was confirmed by ~** il a reçu une lettre confirmant sa nomination ; **the news came in a ~ from her brother** une lettre de son frère annonçait la nouvelle ; **"The Letters of Virginia Woolf"** « La correspondance de Virginia Woolf », « Les lettres de Virginia Woolf » → **covering, love, open**
[c] (= literature) **~s** (belles-)lettres fpl ; **man of ~s** homme m de lettres
[d] (US Scol) distinctions fpl (pour succès sportifs)
[2] VT [a] (= put letter on) **I've ~ed the packets according to the order they arrived in** j'ai inscrit des lettres sur les paquets selon leur ordre d'arrivée ; **she ~ed the envelopes from A to M** elle a marqué les enveloppes de A à M
[b] (= add lettering to) **the book cover was ~ed in gold** la couverture du livre portait une inscription en lettres d'or ; **the case is ~ed with my initials** l'étui est gravé à mes initiales, mes initiales sont gravées sur l'étui
[3] COMP ► **letter bomb** N lettre f piégée ► **letter-card** N (Brit) carte-lettre f ► **letter of acknowledgement** N (Comm) lettre f accusant réception ► **letter of attorney** N (Jur) procuration f ► **letter of credence** N = **letters of credence** ► **letter of credit** N (Fin) lettre f de crédit ► **letter of intent** N lettre f d'intention ► **letter of introduction** N lettre f de recommandation ► **letter of request** N (Jur) commission f rogatoire ► **letter opener** N coupe-papier m inv ► **letter paper** N papier m à lettres ► **letter-perfect** ADJ (US) **to be ~-perfect in sth** connaître qch sur le bout des doigts ► **letter quality** N (Comput) qualité f « courrier » ► **letter rogatory** N = **letter of request** ► **letters of credence** NPL (Diplomacy) lettres fpl de créance ► **letter patent** NPL lettres fpl patentes ► **letter-writer** N **he's a good/bad ~-writer** c'est un bon/mauvais correspondant or épistolier (hum)

letterbox ['letəbɒks] N (esp Brit) boîte f aux or à lettres

lettered ['letəd] ADJ [person] lettré → **letter**

letterhead ['letəhed] N en-tête m (de lettre)

lettering ['letərɪŋ] N (NonC) (= engraving) gravure f ; (= letters) caractères mpl

letterpress ['letəpres] N (Typ) (= method) typographie f ; (= text) texte m imprimé

letting ['letɪŋ] N [a] [of flat etc] location f [b] → **bloodletting**

lettuce ['letɪs] N (as plant, whole) laitue f ; (leaves, as salad) salade f

leucocyte, leukocyte (esp US) ['luːkəˌsaɪt] N leucocyte m

leucotomy, leukotomy (esp US) [luːˈkɒtəmɪ] N leucotomie f, lobotomie f cérébrale

leukaemia, leukemia (esp US) [luːˈkiːmɪə] N leucémie f

leukocyte ['luːkəˌsaɪt] N (esp US) = **leucocyte**

leukotomy [luːˈkɒtəmɪ] N (esp US) = **leucotomy**

Levant [lɪˈvænt] N Levant m

Levantine ['levəntaɪn] [1] ADJ levantin [2] N (Hist) Levantin(e) m(f)

levee¹ ['levɪ] N (= raised riverside of silt) levée f naturelle ; (= man-made embankment) levée f, digue f ; (= ridge surrounding field) digue f ; (= landing place) quai m

levee² [leˈveɪ] N (Hist) réception f royale (pour hommes) ; (at royal bedside) lever m (du roi) ; (US) **a presidential ~** une réception présidentielle

level ['levl] [1] N [a] (lit = height) niveau m, hauteur f ; **the water reached a ~ of 10 metres** l'eau a atteint un niveau or une hauteur de 10 mètres ; **water finds its own ~** l'eau trouve son niveau ; **at roof ~** au niveau du toit ; **the top of the tree was on a ~ with the roof** la cime de l'arbre arrivait au niveau or à la hauteur du toit ; **she bent down until her eyes were on a ~ with mine** elle s'est baissée pour que ses yeux soient au même niveau que les miens → **eye, knee, sea**
[b] (fig: in intellect, achievement) niveau m ; **the child will find his own ~** l'enfant trouvera son niveau ; **intellectual ~** niveau m intellectuel ; **he's far above my ~** il est d'un niveau bien supérieur au mien ; **the teacher came down to their ~** le professeur s'est mis à leur niveau ; **I'm not on his ~ at all** je ne suis pas du tout à son niveau ; **his reading/writing is on a ~ with that of his brother** il a le même niveau que son frère en lecture/écriture ; **that dirty trick is on a ~ with the other one he played** ce mauvais coup est (bien) à la hauteur du or vaut le précédent
[c] (fig: in hierarchy) niveau m, échelon m ; **social ~** niveau m social ; **at a higher/lower ~** (in company) à un échelon supérieur/inférieur ; [talks, negotiations] à un niveau or échelon supérieur/inférieur ; **at local/national/international ~** au niveau local/national/international ; **at departmental ~** à l'échelon départemental ; **there were redundancies at all ~s of the organization** il y a eu des licenciements à tous les niveaux or échelons de l'organisation
[d] (= rate, degree) [of inflation, unemployment, radiation] niveau m, taux m ; [of income, noise, difficulty, violence] niveau m ; **the ~ of hormones/insulin in the blood** le taux d'hormones/d'insuline dans le sang ; **the ~ of alcohol in the blood** le taux d'alcoolémie ; **cholesterol ~(s)** ◊ **~(s) of cholesterol** taux m de cholestérol ; (Med) **~ of consciousness** état m de conscience ; **a higher ~ of consciousness** un niveau de conscience supérieur ; **the idea attracted a high ~ of interest** cette idée a suscité beaucoup d'intérêt ; **the ~ of support for the government is high/low** beaucoup/peu de gens soutiennent le gouvernement ; **the ~ of violence in those societies is very high** il y a énormément de violence dans ces sociétés ; **the strike received a fairly low ~ of support** la grève n'a pas vraiment été suivie ; **the ~ of public interest in the scheme remains low** le public continue à manifester peu d'intérêt pour ce projet ; **these polls do not reflect the true ~ of support for Green policies** ces sondages ne reflètent pas la popularité réelle des mesures écologiques ; **the rising ~ of violence** la montée de la violence ; **the rising ~ of inflation/unemployment** l'augmentation f de l'inflation/du chômage ; **there has been a falling/rising ~ of support for their policies** de moins en moins/de plus en plus de gens soutiennent leur politique
[e] (= floor) niveau m ; **the house is on four ~s** la maison est sur or la maison a quatre niveaux
[f] (Nucl Ind) **high-/intermediate-/low-~ waste** déchets mpl de haute/moyenne/faible activité
[g] (Aut, Rail) palier m ; **speed on the ~** vitesse f en palier ; (fig) **I'm telling you on the ~*** je te le dis franchement ; (fig) **is this on the ~?*** est-ce que c'est réglo ?* ; (fig) **is he on the ~?*** est-ce qu'il joue franc-jeu ?, est-ce qu'il est fair-play ?
[h] (also **spirit ~**) niveau m à bulle
[i] (= flat place) terrain m plat
[2] ADJ [a] (= flat, not bumpy, not sloping) [surface] plat, plan, uni ; **~ ground** terrain m plat or plan ; **it's dead ~** c'est parfaitement plat ; **the tray must be absolutely ~** il faut que le plateau soit parfaitement horizontal ; **hold the stick ~** tiens le bâton horizontal or à l'horizontale ; **a ~ spoonful** une cuillerée rase ; (fig) **a ~ playing field** une situation équitable pour tout le monde ; **a ~ playing field for all companies** une situation équitable pour toutes les entreprises ; **to compete on a ~ playing field** être sur un pied d'égalité ; **to do one's ~ best (to do sth)*** faire tout son possible or faire de son mieux (pour faire qch)
[b] (= equal) (at same standard) à égalité ; (at same height) à la même hauteur ; **the two contestants are dead ~** les deux participants sont exactement à égalité ; **hold the two sticks absolutely ~ (with each other)** tiens les deux bâtons exactement à la même hauteur ; **keep your shoulders ~ throughout the exercise** gardez vos épaules à la même hauteur tout au long de l'exercice ; **he knelt down so that their eyes were ~** il s'est agenouillé afin que leurs yeux soient au même niveau ; **the dining room is ~ with the garden** la salle à manger est de plain-pied avec le jardin ; **~ with the ground** au niveau du sol, à ras du sol ; **to be ~ with sb** (in race) être à la hauteur de qn ; (in league) être à égalité avec qn, avoir le même nombre de points que qn ; (in one's studies, achievements etc) être au niveau de or au même niveau que qn ; (in salary, rank) être à l'échelon de or au même échelon que qn, être au même niveau que qn ; **to be ~ in seniority with** avoir la même ancienneté que, être au même niveau d'ancienneté que ; (esp Brit) **to draw ~ with sb** (in race) arriver à la hauteur de or à la même hauteur que qn ; (in league) arriver dans la même position que qn, arriver au même score que qn ; (in one's studies, achievements etc) arriver au niveau de or au même niveau que qn ; (in salary, rank) arriver au niveau de or au même niveau que qn, arriver au même échelon que qn ; **she slowed down a little to let the car draw ~ (with her)** elle a ralenti un peu afin de permettre à la voiture d'arriver à sa hauteur
[c] (= steady) [voice, tones] calme ; **she gave him a ~ stare** elle l'a dévisagé calmement ; **to keep a ~ head** garder tout son sang-froid → **5**
[d] (US* = honest) [person, deal] honnête, régulier
[3] VT [a] (= make level) [+ site, ground] niveler, aplanir ; [+ quantities] répartir également ; (in competition, league etc) **to ~ the score** égaliser ; (Tennis) **Graf ~led the score to one set all** Graf

a égalisé à un set partout

b (= *demolish*) [+ *building, town*] raser; **to ~ sth to the ground** raser qch

c (= *aim*) **to ~ a blow at sb** allonger un coup de poing à qn; **to ~ a gun at sb** braquer *or* pointer un pistolet sur qn; **to ~ an accusation at sb** lancer *or* porter une accusation contre qn; **to ~ criticism at** *or* **against sb** formuler des critiques à l'encontre de qn; (*Jur*) **to ~ charges at** *or* **against sb** porter des accusations contre qn

4 VI **I'll ~ with you** je vais être franc avec vous; **you're not ~ling with me about how much it cost** tu ne me dis pas combien ça a coûté

5 COMP ► **level crossing** N (*Brit Rail*) passage *m* à niveau ► **level-headed** ADJ équilibré, pondéré ► **level-pegging** ADJ (*Brit*) **they were ~-pegging** ils étaient à égalité
► **level down** **1** VT SEP (*lit*) [+ *surface*] aplanir, raboter; (*fig*) [+ *standards*] niveler par le bas **2** ~**ling down** N → **levelling**
► **level off** **1** VI [*statistics, results, prices etc*] se stabiliser; [*curve on graph*] s'aplatir; [*aircraft*] amorcer le vol en palier; **output has ~led off over recent months** la production s'est stabilisée ces derniers mois **2** VT SEP (= *make flat*) [+ *heap of sand etc*] égaliser, niveler **3** ~**ling off** N → **levelling**
► **level out** **1** VI [*statistics, results, prices etc*] se stabiliser; [*curve on graph*] s'aplatir; [*road etc*] s'aplanir **2** VT SEP niveler, égaliser

leveling ['levlɪŋ] (*US*) = **levelling**

leveller, leveler (*US*) ['levlə'] N **poverty is a great ~** tous les hommes sont égaux dans la misère ■ (*PROV*) **death is the great ~** nous sommes tous égaux devant la mort

levelling, leveling (*US*) ['levlɪŋ] **1** N (*NonC: lit, fig*) nivellement *m* **2** ADJ (*fig*) [*process, effect*] de nivellement **3** COMP ► **levelling down** N nivellement *m* par le bas ► **levelling off** N (*gen*) égalisation *f*, nivellement *m*; (*Econ, Fin*) stabilisation *f*, tassement *m* ► **levelling rod, levelling staff** N mire *f*, jalon-mire *m* ► **levelling up** N nivellement *m* par le haut

levelly ['levlɪ] ADV (= *evenly*) [*look at, say*] posément

lever ['liːvə'] **1** N (*gen, also fig*) levier *m*; (*small: on machine etc*) manette *f*; (*fig*) **he used it as a ~ to get what he wanted** cela lui a servi de marchepied pour arriver à ses fins → **gear 2** VT **to ~ sth into position** mettre qch en place (à l'aide d'un levier); **to ~ sth out/open** extraire/ouvrir qch (au moyen d'un levier); **they had ~ed open the door with a crowbar** ils avaient ouvert la porte à l'aide d'un levier; (*hum*) **he ~ed himself out of the chair** il s'est extirpé* du fauteuil; (*fig*) **to ~ sb into a post** pistonner qn pour un poste; **to ~ sb out** déloger qn
► **lever up** VT SEP soulever au moyen d'un levier; (*fig*) **he ~ed himself up on one elbow** il s'est soulevé sur un coude; (*fig*) **to ~ up the bank rate** relever le taux d'escompte officiel

leverage ['liːvərɪdʒ] **1** N (*lit*) force *f* (de levier); (*fig* = *influence*) influence *f*, prise *f* (**on** *or* **with sb** sur qn); (*US Fin*) effet *m* de levier **2** VT (*Fin*) [+ *company*] augmenter le ratio d'endettement de; ~**d buyout** rachat *m* d'entreprise financé par l'endettement

leveret ['levərɪt] N levraut *m*

leviathan [lɪ'vaɪəθən] N (*Bible*) Léviathan *m*; (*fig* = *ship/organization etc*) navire *m*/organisme *m* etc géant

Levi's® ['liːvaɪz] NPL Levi's® *m*

levitate ['levɪteɪt] **1** VI se soulever *or* être soulevé par lévitation **2** VT soulever *or* élever par lévitation

levitation [ˌlevɪ'teɪʃən] N lévitation *f*

Leviticus [lɪ'vɪtɪkəs] N Lévitique *m*

levity ['levɪtɪ] N (= *frivolity*) manque *m* de sérieux, légèreté *f*

levy ['levɪ] **1** N **a** (*gen*) prélèvement *m* (**on** sur); (= *tax*) impôt *m*, taxe *f* (**on** sur); (= *amount, act of taxing*) taxation *f*; **import ~** prélèvement *m* à l'importation; (*in Brit*) **the political ~** cotisation des membres d'un syndicat au parti travailliste; **training ~** ≈ taxe *f* d'apprentissage → **capital b** (*Mil*) (= *act*) levée *f*, enrôlement *m*; (= troops) troupes *fpl* enrôlées, levée *f* **2** VT **a** (= *impose*) [+ *tax*] prélever (**on sth** sur qch); [+ *fine*] infliger, imposer (**on sb à** qn); **b** (= *collect*) [+ *taxes, contributions*] lever, percevoir **c** (*Mil*) **to ~ troops/an army** lever des troupes/une armée; **to ~ war (on** *or* **against)** faire la guerre (à)
► **levy on** VT FUS (*Jur*) **to ~ on sb's property** saisir (les biens de) qn

lewd [luːd] ADJ [*comment, picture, gesture, joke*] obscène; **to have a ~ expression on one's face** avoir un air lubrique

lewdly ['luːdlɪ] ADV de façon obscène

lewdness ['luːdnɪs] N [*of person*] lubricité *f*; [*of object, drawing*] obscénité *f*

lexeme ['leksiːm] N lexème *m*

lexical ['leksɪkəl] ADJ lexical; **~ item** unité *f* lexicale, item *m* lexical

lexicalize ['leksɪkəˌlaɪz] VT lexicaliser

lexicographer [ˌleksɪ'kɒɡrəfə'] N lexicographe *mf*

lexicographical [ˌleksɪkəʊ'ɡræfɪkəl] ADJ lexicographique

lexicography [ˌleksɪ'kɒɡrəfɪ] N lexicographie *f*

lexicologist [ˌleksɪ'kɒlədʒɪst] N lexicologue *mf*

lexicology [ˌleksɪ'kɒlədʒɪ] N lexicologie *f*

lexicon ['leksɪkən] N **a** (*Ling* = *wordlist, lexis*) lexique *m* **b** (*fig* = *terminology, language*) vocabulaire *m*; **the word "perestroika" has entered the political ~** le mot « perestroïka » fait désormais partie du vocabulaire politique

lexis ['leksɪs] N (*Ling*) lexique *m*

LI ABBR = **Long Island**

liability [ˌlaɪə'bɪlɪtɪ] **1** N **a** (*NonC*) responsabilité *f*; **don't admit ~ for the accident** n'acceptez pas la responsabilité de l'accident; **his ~ for the company's debts was limited to £50,000** il n'était responsable qu'à hauteur de 50 000 livres des dettes de la société **b** (*NonC*) **~ for tax/for paying tax** assujettissement *m* à l'impôt/au paiement de l'impôt; **~ for military service** obligations *fpl* militaires **c** (*Fin*) **liabilities** (= *debts*) dettes *fpl*, passif *m*; **assets and liabilities** actif *m* et passif *m*; **to meet one's liabilities** rembourser ses dettes; **current ~** dettes *fpl* à court terme; **non-current ~** dettes *fpl* à moyen et long terme **d** (= *handicap*) **this car is a ~ (for us)** on n'arrête pas d'avoir des problèmes avec cette voiture; **he's a real ~** il ne fait que nous attirer des ennuis; **this issue has become a political ~** cette question constitue maintenant un handicap politique
2 COMP ► **liability insurance** N assurance *f* responsabilité civile → **joint, limited, strict**

liable ['laɪəbl] ADJ **a to be ~ to do sth** (= *be likely to*) avoir des chances de faire qch; (= *risk*) risquer de faire qch; **he's ~ to refuse to do it** il risque de refuser de le faire; **he is ~ not to come** il y a des chances (pour) qu'il ne vienne pas, il y a peu de chances qu'il vienne; **we are ~ to get shot at** on risque de se faire tirer dessus; **we are ~ to be in London next week** nous pourrions bien être *or* nous serons probablement à Londres la semaine prochaine; **it's ~ to be hot there** il peut faire très chaud là-bas
b (= *subject*) **to be ~ to sth** être sujet à qch; **the programme is ~ to alteration without notice** la direction se réserve le droit d'apporter sans préavis des modifications à ce pro-

gramme; **to be ~ to imprisonment/a fine** être passible d'emprisonnement/d'une amende; **to be ~ to** *or* **for prosecution** s'exposer à des poursuites; **to be ~ to** *or* **for duty** [*goods*] être assujetti à des droits; [*person*] avoir à payer des droits; **to be ~ to** *or* **for tax** [*person*] être imposable; [*thing*] être assujetti à la taxation; **every man of 20 is ~ for military service** tout homme de 20 ans est astreint au service militaire; **he is not ~ for military service** il a été exempté du service militaire
c (*Jur* = *responsible*) (civilement) responsable (**for sb/sth** de qn/qch); **jointly and severally ~** responsable conjointement et solidairement; **to be ~ for sb's debts** répondre des dettes de qn; **he is still ~ for interest on the loan** il est toujours redevable d'intérêts sur cet emprunt; **~ for damages** tenu de verser des dommages et intérêts; **you could be ~ for hefty damages** on serait en droit de vous demander des dommages et intérêts importants; **to be held ~ (for sth)** être tenu (pour) responsable (de qch); **to be ~ in law** *or* **under the law** être responsable devant la loi; **to be ~ in law** *or* **under the law to do sth** être tenu, de par la loi, de faire qch, être tenu par la loi de faire qch

liaise [liː'eɪz] VI (*Brit*) se contacter; **to ~ with** (= *cooperate with*) se concerter avec; (= *act as go-between*) assurer la liaison avec; **to ~ between** assurer la liaison entre

liaison [liː'eɪzɒn] **1** N (*gen, Mil, Phon*) liaison *f* **2** COMP ► **liaison committee** N comité *m* de liaison ► **liaison officer** N (*Mil, gen*) officier *m* de liaison

liana [liː'ɑːnə] N liane *f*

liar ['laɪə'] N menteur *m*, -euse *f*

Lib [lɪb] ADJ, N (*Brit Pol*) (ABBR = **Liberal**) libéral(e) *m(f)*

lib: [lɪb] N ABBR = **liberation**

libation [laɪ'beɪʃən] N libation *f*

libber* ['lɪbə'] N = **liberationist**

libel ['laɪbəl] **1** N (*Jur*) (= *act*) diffamation *f* (par écrit); (= *document*) écrit *m* diffamatoire; **to sue sb for ~ ◊ to bring an action for ~ against sb** intenter un procès en diffamation à qn; (*fig*) **that's (a) ~!** c'est une calomnie! **2** VT (*Jur*) diffamer (par écrit); (*gen*) calomnier, médire de **3** COMP ► **libel laws** NPL (*Jur*) lois *fpl* sur la diffamation ► **libel proceedings** NPL ► **libel suit** ► **libel suit** N procès *m* en diffamation

libellous, libelous (*US*) ['laɪbələs] ADJ diffamatoire

liberal ['lɪbərəl] **1** ADJ **a** (= *broad-minded*) [*education, régime, society*] libéral; [*ideas, views*] progressiste; [*person*] large d'esprit **b** (= *broad*) [*interpretation*] libre **c** (= *generous*) [*amount, helping, contribution, offer*] généreux; [*person*] prodigue (**with** de), généreux; [*supply*] ample, abondant; **a ~ amount of** beaucoup de; **she made ~ use of the hairspray** elle a utilisé beaucoup de laque; **she made ~ use of her sister's make-up and clothes** elle se servait abondamment du maquillage et des vêtements de sa sœur; **because of the ~ use of weedkillers and pesticides these days** parce que les herbicides et les pesticides sont utilisés abondamment de nos jours; **the artist's ~ use of black** la dominante noire dans l'œuvre de ce peintre **d** (*Brit Pol*) **Liberal** libéral
2 N (*Pol*) **Liberal** libéral(e) *m(f)*
3 COMP ► **liberal arts** NPL arts *mpl* libéraux ► **liberal democracy** N démocratie *f* libérale ► **Liberal Democrat** N (*Pol*) libéral(e)-démocrate *m(f)* ► **the Liberal Democrat Party** N (*Brit*) le parti démocrate-libéral ► **liberal-minded** ADJ = **1a** ► **liberal studies** NPL (*Scol etc*) ≈ programme *m* de culture générale

liberalism ['lɪbərəlɪzəm] N (gen, Pol) libéralisme m

liberality [ˌlɪbə'rælɪtɪ] N (= broad-mindedness) libéralisme m; (= generosity) libéralité f, générosité f

liberalization [ˌlɪbərəlaɪ'zeɪʃən] N libéralisation f

liberalize ['lɪbərəlaɪz] VT libéraliser

liberally ['lɪbərəlɪ] ADV [a] (= generously) généreusement [b] (= indulgently) [treat] libéralement

liberate ['lɪbəreɪt] VT [+ prisoner, slave] libérer; [+ women etc] libérer, émanciper; (Chem) [+ gas] libérer, dégager; (Fin) [+ capital] dégager

liberated ['lɪbəreɪtɪd] ADJ libéré

liberation [ˌlɪbə'reɪʃən] [1] N libération f; (Fin) dégagement m [2] COMP ► **liberation theology** N (Rel) théologie f de la libération

liberationist [ˌlɪbə'reɪʃənɪst] N (active) membre m d'un (or du) mouvement de libération; (sympathiser) partisan m de la libération (des femmes etc)

liberator ['lɪbəreɪtəʳ] N libérateur m, -trice f

Liberia [laɪ'bɪərɪə] N le Libéria or Liberia

Liberian [laɪ'bɪərɪən] [1] ADJ (gen) libérien; [ambassador, embassy] du Libéria [2] N Libérien(ne) m(f)

libertarian [ˌlɪbə'tɛərɪən] [1] ADJ [person, attitude, view, policy, politics] libertaire [2] N libertaire mf

libertarianism [ˌlɪbə'tɛərɪənɪzəm] N (= philosophy) doctrine f libertaire; (= sb's characteristic) idées fpl libertaires

libertinage ['lɪbətɪnɪdʒ] N libertinage m

libertine ['lɪbətiːn] ADJ, N libertin(e) m(f)

liberty ['lɪbətɪ] [1] N [a] (= freedom) liberté f; individual/political ~ liberté f individuelle/politique; ~ of the press liberté f de la presse; ~ of conscience liberté f de conscience; at ~ (= not detained) en liberté; (= not busy) libre; the escaped prisoner remains at ~ le prisonnier évadé est toujours en liberté; to set sb at ~ mettre qn en liberté; to set or leave sb at ~ to do sth permettre à qn à faire qch; you are at ~ to choose vous êtes libre de choisir, libre à vous de choisir; I am not at ~ to reveal that information je n'ai pas le droit de révéler ces informations → civil [b] (= presumption) liberté f; to take liberties (with sb) prendre or se permettre des libertés (avec qn); to take the ~ of doing prendre la liberté or se permettre de faire; that was rather a ~ on his part il ne s'est pas gêné; what a ~! quel toupet!* [2] COMP ► **liberty bodice**† N ≈ chemise f américaine ► **liberty cap** N (Hist) bonnet m phrygien ► **liberty hall** N (fig hum) it's ~ hall here* ici tout est permis

libidinal [lɪ'bɪdɪnl] ADJ libidinal

libidinous [lɪ'bɪdɪnəs] ADJ (frm) libidineux (liter or hum)

libido [lɪ'biːdəʊ] N libido f

Lib-Lab* ['lɪb,læb] ADJ (Brit Pol Hist) (ABBR = Liberal-Labour) ~ **pact** pacte m libéral-travailliste

Libra ['liːbrə] N (Astron) la Balance; (Astrol) I'm (a) ~ je suis (de la) Balance

Libran ['liːbrən] N to be a ~ être (de la) Balance

librarian [laɪ'brɛərɪən] N bibliothécaire mf

librarianship [laɪ'brɛərɪənʃɪp] N (= job) poste m de bibliothécaire; (esp Brit) (= science) bibliothéconomie f; (= knowledge) connaissances fpl de bibliothécaire; to do or study ~ faire des études de bibliothécaire or de bibliothéconomie

library ['laɪbrərɪ] [1] N [a] (= building, room) bibliothèque f → mobile, public, reference [b] (= collection, also Comput) bibliothèque f; (= published series) collection f, série f [2] COMP ► **library book** N livre m de bibliothèque ► **library card** N = library ticket ► **library edition** N édition f de luxe ► **Library of Congress** N (US) Bibliothèque f du Congrès ► **library pictures** NPL (TV) images fpl d'archives ► **library science** N bibliothéconomie f ► **library software** N (Comput) répertoire m de macro-instructions ► **library ticket** N carte f de lecteur or de bibliothèque

librettist [lɪ'bretɪst] N librettiste mf

libretto [lɪ'bretəʊ] N (pl librettos or libretti [lɪ'bretiː]) libretto m, livret m

Librium® ['lɪbrɪəm] N Librium® m

Libya ['lɪbɪə] N la Libye

Libyan ['lɪbɪən] [1] N Libyen(ne) m(f) [2] ADJ (gen) libyen; [ambassador, embassy] de Libye; ~ **Arab Jamahiriya** Jamahiriya f arabe libyenne; **the ~ Desert** le désert de Libye

lice [laɪs] NPL of **louse**

licence, license (US) ['laɪsəns] [1] N [a] (= permit) (gen) autorisation f, permis m; (for manufacturing, trading etc) licence f; (Aut) (for driver) permis m; (for car) vignette f; (for radio, TV) redevance f; (= document itself) fiche f de redevance; (Brit) driving ~ permis m de conduire; export/import ~ permis m d'exporter/d'importer; pilot's ~ brevet m de pilote; have you got a ~ for this television? est-ce que vous avez payé votre redevance pour cette télévision?; they were married by special ~ ils se sont mariés avec dispense (de bans); to manufacture sth under ~ fabriquer qch sous licence → marriage, off [b] (NonC) (= freedom) licence f, liberté f; (= excess) licence f; you can allow some ~ in translation on peut tolérer une certaine licence or liberté dans la traduction → poetic [2] COMP ► **licence fee** N (Brit TV) redevance f ► **licence number** N (Aut) [of licence] numéro m de permis de conduire; [of car] numéro m minéralogique or d'immatriculation ► **licence plate** N plaque f minéralogique or d'immatriculation

license ['laɪsəns] [1] N (US) = licence [2] VT [a] (= give licence to) donner une licence à; [+ car] [licensing authority] délivrer la vignette pour; [owner] acheter la vignette de or pour; is that gun ~d? avez-vous un permis pour ce revolver?; the shop is ~d to sell tobacco le magasin détient une licence de bureau de tabac; the shop is ~d for the sale of alcoholic liquor le magasin détient une licence de débit de boissons; (Brit Jur) ~d victualler patron m or gérant m d'un pub; (Brit) (on) ~d premises (dans un) établissement ayant une licence de débit de boissons; (Jur) ~d product produit m sous licence; (US) ~d practical nurse infirmier m, -ière f auxiliaire [b] (frm = permit) autoriser (sb to do qn à faire), permettre (sb to do à qn de faire) [3] COMP ► **license plate** N (US) = licence plate

licensee [ˌlaɪsən'siː] N concessionnaire mf d'une licence, licencié m; (Brit) [of pub] patron(ne) m(f)

licenser ['laɪsənsəʳ] N = licensor

licensing ['laɪsənsɪŋ] [1] ADJ the ~ authority l'organisme m or le service délivrant les permis (or les licences etc) [2] COMP ► **licensing agreement** N (Comm) accord m de licence ► **licensing hours** NPL (Brit) heures fpl d'ouverture légales (des débits de boisson) ► **licensing laws** NPL (Brit) lois fpl réglementant la vente d'alcool

licensor ['laɪsənsəʳ] N (Jur) bailleur m or bailleresse f de licence

licentiate [laɪ'senʃɪɪt] N diplômé(e) m(f) (pour pratiquer une profession libérale)

licentious [laɪ'senʃəs] ADJ (frm) licencieux

licentiousness [laɪ'senʃəsnɪs] N (frm) licence f

lichee [ˌlaɪ'tʃiː] N = lychee

lichen ['laɪkən] N lichen m

lichgate ['lɪtʃgeɪt] N porche m de cimetière

licit ['lɪsɪt] ADJ licite

lick [lɪk] [1] N [a] coup m de langue; the cat gave me a ~ le chat m'a donné un coup de langue; the cat gave my hand a ~ le chat m'a léché la main; give me or let me have a ~ je peux goûter?; to give o.s. a ~ and a promise* faire un (petit) brin de toilette; a ~ of paint un (petit) coup de peinture; he didn't do a ~ of work* il n'a rien fichu* [b] (* = speed) vitesse f; at a fair or a good or one hell of a ~ en quatrième vitesse*, à toute blinde‡ [c] (Mus*) riff m [2] VT [a] [person, animal, flames] lécher; she ~ed the cream off her fingers elle a léché la crème qu'elle avait sur les doigts; the cat ~ed her hand le chat lui a léché la main; the cat ~ed its paws le chat s'est léché les pattes; to ~ sth clean nettoyer qch à coups de langue; to ~ the bowl out or clean lécher le saladier; to ~ one's lips (lit) se lécher les lèvres; (fig) se frotter les mains; to ~ one's chops* se lécher les babines*; (fig) se frotter les mains, s'en lécher les babines*; to ~ sb's boots lécher les bottes à qn*, jouer les lèche-bottes* avec qn; to ~ sb's arse‡ lécher le cul à qn‡; (fig) to ~ one's wounds panser ses blessures (fig) [b] * (= defeat) écraser*, battre à plate(s) couture(s); (= outdo, surpass) battre; (= thrash) flanquer une correction à, tabasser*; I've got it ~ed [+ problem, puzzle etc] j'ai trouvé la solution; [+ bad habit] j'ai réussi à m'arrêter; it's got me ~ed [problem etc] cela me dépasse → shape
► **lick off** VT SEP enlever à coups de langue, lécher; ~ it off! lèche-le!
► **lick up** VT SEP lécher; [cat] laper

lickety-split* ['lɪkɪtɪ'splɪt] ADV (US) à fond de train

licking* ['lɪkɪŋ] N (= whipping) rossée* f, raclée* f; (= defeat) déculottée‡ f

lickspittle ['lɪk,spɪtl] N (pej) lèche-botte* mf

licorice ['lɪkərɪs] N (US) = liquorice

lid [lɪd] N [a] [of pan, box, jar, piano] couvercle m; (fig) the newspaper articles took or blew the ~ off his illegal activities les articles de presse ont étalé au grand jour ses activités illégales; that puts the (tin) ~ on it!† (= that's the end) ça c'est un comble or le pompon!*; to keep the ~ on sth [+ scandal, affair] étouffer qch; [+ *crime*] contenir qch; **to keep a ~ on prices** enrayer la hausse des prix b (*also* **eye-lid**) paupière *f*

lidded ['lɪdɪd] ADJ [*container, jar*] à couvercle; **heavily ~ eyes** yeux *mpl* aux paupières lourdes

lido ['liːdəʊ] N (= *resort*) complexe *m* balnéaire; (*Brit* = *swimming pool*) piscine *f* (*en plein air*)

lie¹ [laɪ] (*pret* **lay**, *ptp* **lain**) 1 VI a [*person etc*] (= *lie down*) s'allonger, s'étendre; (*state* = *be lying*) être allongé or étendu; (*in grave etc*) être enterré; **go and ~ on the bed** allez vous allonger or vous étendre sur le lit; **don't ~ on the grass** ne t'allonge pas sur l'herbe; **he was lying on the floor** (*resting etc*) il était allongé or étendu par terre; (*unable to move*) il était étendu or il gisait par terre; **she lay in bed until 10 o'clock** elle est restée or a traîné (*pej*) au lit jusqu'à 10 heures; **she was lying in bed** elle était au lit; **she was lying on her bed** elle était allongée or étendue sur son lit; **she was lying in bed reading** elle lisait au lit; **~ on your side** couche-toi or allonge-toi sur le côté; **she was lying face downwards** elle était (allongée or étendue) à plat ventre; **he was lying asleep** il était allongé et il dormait, il était allongé endormi; **he lay asleep on the bed** il dormait allongé or étendu sur le lit; **he lay dead** il était étendu mort; **he lay dead at her feet** il était étendu mort à ses pieds, il gisait à ses pieds; **he lay helpless on the floor** il était étendu or il gisait par terre sans pouvoir rien faire; **he was lying still** il était étendu immobile; **~ still!** ne bouge pas!, reste tranquille!; **his body was lying on the ground** son corps gisait sur le sol; **he ~s in the churchyard** il repose dans le or est enterré au cimetière; **the corpse lay in the coffin/the tomb** le corps reposait or était dans le cercueil/la tombe; **to ~ in state** être exposé solennellement; (*on tombstone*) **here ~s** or **lieth**† ... ci-gît ...; (*fig*) **to ~ low** (= *hide*) se cacher, rester caché; (= *stay out of limelight*) ne pas se faire remarquer, se tenir à carreau* → **ambush, sleeping, wait**

b [*object*] être; [*place, road*] se trouver, être; [*land, sea etc*] s'étendre; (= *remain*) rester, être; **the book lay on the table** le livre était sur la table; **the book lay unopened all day** le livre est resté fermé toute la journée; **the book lay open on the table** le livre était ouvert sur la table; **his food lay untouched while he told us the story** il n'a pas touché à son assiette pendant qu'il nous racontait l'histoire; **his clothes were lying on the floor** ses vêtements étaient par terre; **the contents of the box lay scattered on the carpet** le contenu de la boîte était éparpillé sur le tapis; **our road lay along the river** notre route longeait la rivière; **the road ~s over the hills** la route traverse les collines; **the British team is lying third** l'équipe britannique est troisième or en troisième position; **to ~ at anchor** [*ship*] être à l'ancre, avoir mouillé; **obstacles ~ in the way** la route est semée d'embûches; **the money is lying (idle) in the bank** l'argent dort à la banque; **the factory lay idle** personne ne travaillait dans l'usine; **the machines lay idle** les machines étaient arrêtées; **the snow lay two metres deep** il y avait deux mètres de neige; **the snow lay thick** or **deep on the ground** il y avait une épaisse couche de neige sur le sol; **this snow will not ~** la neige ne tiendra pas; **the town lay in ruins** la ville était en ruines; **the meal lay heavy on his stomach** le repas lui pesait sur l'estomac; **the crime lay heavy on his conscience** ce crime lui pesait sur la conscience; **the valley/lake/sea lay before us** la vallée/le lac/la mer s'étendait devant nous; **Stroud ~s to the west of Oxford** Stroud est situé à l'ouest d'Oxford; **the years that ~ before us** les années à venir; **a brilliant future ~s before you** vous avez devant vous un brillant avenir; (*fig: in future*) **what ~s before him** ce que lui réserve l'avenir; (*fig*) **what ~s ahead** ce qui reste à venir, ce que réserve l'avenir; (*fig*)

the (whole) world lay at her feet toutes les portes lui étaient ouvertes; (*fig*) **to let it** or **things ~** laisser les choses comme elles sont → **land**

c (*with abstract subject*) être, résider; **he knows where his interests ~** il sait où sont or résident ses intérêts; **what ~s behind his refusal?** quelle est la véritable raison de son refus?; **the real cause that lay behind the rise in divorce** la vraie cause de la hausse du nombre des divorces; **the trouble ~s in the engine** le problème vient du moteur; **the trouble ~s in his inability to be strict** le problème provient de or réside dans son incapacité d'être sévère; **the difference ~s in the fact that ...** la différence vient de ce que ...; **the real solution ~s in education** la véritable solution réside dans l'éducation; **the blame ~s with you** c'est vous qui êtes à blâmer, c'est à vous que la faute est imputable; **a curse lay on the family** une malédiction pesait sur la famille; **it does not ~ within my power to decide** il n'est pas en mon pouvoir de décider; **it ~s with you to decide** il vous appartient de décider, c'est à vous (qu'il incombe) de décider; (*liter, frm*) **as far as in me ~s** au mieux de mes possibilités, du mieux que je peux

d (*Jur*) [*evidence, appeal*] être recevable

2 N a (*Golf*) [*of ball*] position *f* b [*of land*] configuration *f* → **land**

3 COMP ► **lie-abed**† N flemmard(e)* *m(f)* (qui traîne au lit) ► **lie-down** N (*Brit*) **to have a ~-down** s'allonger, se reposer ► **lie-in** N (*Brit*) **to have a ~-in** faire la grasse matinée

► **lie about, lie around** VI a [*objects, clothes, books*] traîner; **don't leave that money lying about** ne laissez pas traîner cet argent b [*person*] traîner, traînasser* (*pej*); **don't just ~ about all day!** tâche de ne pas traîner or traînasser* (*pej*) toute la journée!

► **lie back** VI (*in chair, on bed*) se renverser (en arrière); (*fig*) **just ~ back and enjoy yourself!** laisse-toi (donc) vivre!

► **lie down** 1 VI [*person, animal*] s'allonger, s'étendre; **she lay down for a while** elle s'est allongée quelques instants; **when I arrived she was lying down** quand je suis arrivé elle était allongée; (*to dog*) **~ down!** couché!; **to ~ down on the job*** tirer au flanc*, flemmarder*; (*fig*) **to take sth lying down*** encaisser qch* sans broncher, accepter qch sans protester; **he won't take that lying down** il va se rebiffer*, il ne va pas se laisser faire; **I won't take it lying down*** ça ne va pas se passer comme ça, je ne vais pas me laisser faire; **he's not one to take things lying down*** il n'est pas du genre à tout encaisser sans rien dire 2 **~-down*** N → **lie¹**

► **lie in** 1 VI a (= *stay in bed*) rester au lit, faire la grasse matinée b (†: *in childbirth*) être en couches 2 **~-in*** N → **lie¹**

► **lie off** VI (*Naut*) rester au large

► **lie over** VI (= *be postponed*) être ajourné, être remis (à plus tard)

► **lie to** VI (*Naut*) être or se tenir à la cape

► **lie up** VI a (= *stay in bed*) garder le lit or la chambre b (= *hide*) se cacher, rester caché

lie² [laɪ] (*vb: pret, ptp* **lied**) 1 N mensonge *m*; **to tell ~s** mentir, dire des mensonges; **I tell a ~*** je mens, je dis une bêtise; **that's a ~!** vous mentez!, c'est un mensonge!; **to give the ~ to** [+ *person*] accuser de mentir; [+ *claim, account*] démentir, contredire → **pack, still²** 2 VI mentir; **he's lying through** or **in his teeth*** il ment effrontément or comme un arracheur de dents 3 VT **he tried to ~ his way out of it** il a essayé de s'en sortir par des mensonges; **he managed to ~ his way into the director's office** il a réussi à s'introduire dans le bureau du directeur sous un prétexte mensonger; **he ~d his way into the job** il a obtenu le poste grâce à des mensonges 4 COMP ► **lie detector** N détecteur *m* de mensonges

Liechtenstein ['lɪktən,staɪn] 1 N le Liechtenstein; **native** or **inhabitant of ~** Liechtensteinois(e) *m(f)* 2 ADJ liechtensteinois

lied [liːd] N (*pl* **lieder** ['liːdəʳ]) lied *m*

lief†† [liːf] ADV **I would as ~ die as tell a lie** j'aimerais mieux mourir que mentir

liege [liːdʒ] N (*Hist*) a (*also* **~ lord**) seigneur *m*, suzerain *m*; **yes, my ~!** oui, Sire! b (*also* **~ man**) vassal *m* (lige)

lien [lɪən] N (*Jur*) privilège *m*, droit *m* de gage; **to have a ~ on the estate of a debtor** avoir un privilège sur les biens d'un débiteur

lienee [lɪə'niː] N débiteur-gagiste *m*

lienor ['lɪənəʳ] N créancier-gagiste *m*

lieu [luː] N **in ~ of** au lieu de, à la place de; **one month's notice or £2,400 in ~** un mois de préavis ou bien 2 400 livres

Lieut. (ABBR = **Lieutenant**) (*on envelope*) **~ J Smith** le lieutenant J. Smith

lieutenant [lef'tenənt, (*US*) luː'tenənt] 1 N a (*Brit Army*) lieutenant *m*; (*Brit, US Navy*) lieutenant *m* de vaisseau; (*US Army*) **first ~** lieutenant *m* → **lord** b (*US Police*) (*uniformed*) officier *m* de paix; (*plain clothes*) inspecteur *m* de police 2 COMP ► **lieutenant colonel** N (*Brit, US Army, also US Air Force*) lieutenant-colonel *m* ► **lieutenant commander** N (*Navy*) capitaine *m* de corvette ► **lieutenant general** N (*Brit, US Army*) général *m* de corps d'armée; (*US Air Force*) général *m* de corps aérien ► **lieutenant-governor** N (*Can*) lieutenant-gouverneur *m*

life [laɪf] 1 N (*pl* **lives**) a (*in general*) vie *f*; **is there (a) ~ after death?** y a-t-il une vie après la mort?; **I don't believe in ~ after death** je ne crois pas à la vie après la mort; **a matter of ~ and death** une question de vie ou de mort; **loss of ~** perte *f* de vies humaines; **to be tired of ~** être las de vivre; **he came to ~ again** il a repris conscience, **to lose one's ~** perdre la vie; **how many lives were lost?** combien de vies cela a-t-il coûté?; **many lives were lost** beaucoup ont trouvé la mort; **no lives were lost** il n'y a eu aucun mort or aucune victime; **to take one's (own) ~** se donner la mort, **to take sb's ~** donner la mort à qn; **when is it acceptable to take a ~?** quand devient-il acceptable de tuer quelqu'un?; **to take one's ~ in one's hands** jouer sa vie; **to bring sb back to ~** ranimer qn; **his interpretation brings the character to ~** son interprétation fait vivre le personnage; (*liter*) **to lay down one's ~ (for sb)** sacrifier sa vie (pour qn), donner sa vie (pour qn); **to be on trial for one's ~** risquer la peine capitale; **he ran for his ~** il a pris ses jambes à son cou, il s'est sauvé à toutes jambes; **run for your lives!** sauve qui peut!; **I couldn't for the ~ of me tell you his name*** je ne pourrais absolument pas vous dire son nom; **I couldn't for the ~ of me understand ...*** je n'arrivais absolument pas à comprendre ... → **large, still²**

b (= *living things*) vie *f*; **is there ~ on Mars?** la vie existe-t-elle sur Mars?; **bird ~** les oiseaux *mpl*; **insect ~** les insectes *mpl*; **animal and plant ~** vie *f* animale et végétale

c (= *existence*) vie *f*; **~ went on uneventfully** la vie poursuivit son cours paisible; **~ goes on ◊ ~ must go on** la vie continue; **he lived in France all his ~** il a vécu toute sa vie en France; **~ begins at forty** la vie commence à quarante ans; **she began ~ as a teacher** elle a débuté comme professeur; (*on tombstone etc*) **departed this ~, 27th February 1997** enlevé(e) (*liter*) aux siens le 27 février 1997; **in early ~ ◊ early in ~** de bonne heure, tôt dans la vie; **in her early ~** dans sa jeunesse; **in later ~** plus tard (dans la vie); **in his later ~** plus tard dans sa vie; **late in ~** sur le tard, à un âge avancé; **they married late in ~** ils se sont mariés sur le tard; **in the next ~** dans l'autre vie; **~ isn't worth living** la vie ne vaut pas la peine d'être vécue ; **cats have nine lives** le chat a neuf vies → **afterlife, claim, danger, fight, risk, rose²**, **save, working**

d (= *way of living*) vie *f* ; **which do you prefer, town or country ~?** que préférez-vous, la vie à la ville ou (la vie) à la campagne ? ; **his ~ was very unexciting** sa vie n'avait rien de passionnant ; **to lead a busy ~** avoir une vie bien remplie ; **to lead a charmed ~** avoir la chance avec soi ; **the good ~** (= *pleasant*) la belle vie ; (*Rel*) la vie d'un saint, une vie sainte ; **it's a good ~** c'est la belle vie ; **to live one's own ~** vivre sa vie ; **to make a new ~ for o.s.** ◊ **to start a new ~** commencer une nouvelle vie ; **to lead a quiet ~** mener une vie tranquille ; **to have another ~ or a ~ of one's own** avoir sa propre vie ; **I do have a ~ outside of work, you know!** il n'y a pas que le travail dans ma vie, vous savez ! → **live¹, married, nightlife, private, see¹**

e (= *liveliness*) **there isn't much ~ in our village** notre village n'est pas très vivant or est plutôt mort ; **she brought the party to ~** elle a animé la soirée ; **the town came to ~ when the sailors arrived** la ville s'éveillait à l'arrivée des marins ; (*hum*) **there's ~ in the old dog yet*** le bonhomme a encore du ressort ; **to be full of ~** elle est plein de vie ; **you need to put a bit of ~ into it** il faut y mettre plus d'ardeur, il faut y aller avec plus d'entrain ; **it put new ~ into me** ça m'a fait revivre, ça m'a ragaillardi ; **he's the ~ and soul of the party** c'est un boute-en-train, c'est lui qui met l'ambiance

f (*in exclamations*) **that's ~!** ◊ **such is ~!** c'est la vie ! ; **get a ~!*** bouge-toi un peu !* ; **how's ~?** comment (ça) va ? ; **not on your ~!*** jamais de la vie ! ; **this is the ~!*** voilà comment je comprends la vie ! ; **upon my ~!** † seigneur !, diantre !† ; **what a ~!** quelle vie !

g (= *lifespan*) vie *f* ; [*of car, ship, government, battery etc*] durée *f* de vie ; [*of licence*] validité *f* ; **for the first time in my ~** pour la première fois de ma vie ; **never in (all) my ~ have I seen such stupidity** jamais de ma vie je n'ai vu une telle stupidité ; **it will last you for ~** or (**for**) **all your ~** cela vous durera toute votre vie ; **for the rest of his ~** pour le restant de ses jours, pour le reste de sa vie ; **at my time of ~** être condamné à perpétuité or à la prison à vie ; **friends for ~** amis pour toujours ; **a job for ~** un emploi pour la vie ; **my car's nearing the end of its ~** ma voiture a fait son temps

h (*Art*) **a portrait taken from ~** un portrait d'après nature ; **it was Paul to the ~** c'était Paul tout craché*

i (= *biography*) vie *f*, biographie *f* ; **a ~ of Henry VIII** une biographie d'Henri VIII, la vie d'Henri VIII ; **the lives of the Saints** la vie des saints

j (* = *life imprisonment*) **he got ~** il a été condamné à perpétuité or à perpète* ; **he's doing ~ (for murder)** il a été condamné à perpétuité or à perpète* (pour meurtre)

k (*US: of prostitute*) **she's in the ~*** elle fait le trottoir

2 COMP [*subscription etc*] à vie ► **life-and-death struggle** N combat *m* à mort, lutte *f* désespérée ► **life annuity** N rente *f* viagère ► **life assurance** N (*esp Brit*) assurance *f* vie, assurance-vie *f* ► **life class** N (*Art*) cours *m* de dessin d'après modèle ► **life cycle** N cycle *m* de (la) vie ► **life-enhancing** ADJ revigorant ► **life expectancy** N espérance *f* de vie ; **~ expectancy table** table *f* de survie ► **the life force** N la force vitale ► **life form** N forme *f* de vie ► **life-giving** ADJ vivifiant ► **Life Guards** NPL (*Brit Mil*) régiment *m* de cavalerie de la garde royale ► **life history** N **her ~ history** l'histoire *f* de sa vie ; (*Bio*) **the ~ history of the salmon** la vie du saumon ► **life imprisonment** N réclusion *f* à perpétuité, réclusion *f* à perpétuité ► **life insurance** N = **life assurance** ► **life interest** N (*Jur*) usufruit *m* ► **life**

jacket N gilet *m* de sauvetage ; (*Navy*) brassière *f* (de sauvetage) ► **life member** N membre *m* à vie ► **life membership** N carte *f* de membre à vie ; **to be given ~ membership** être nommé or fait membre à vie ► **life-or-death struggle** N = **life-and-death struggle** ► **life peer** N (*Brit*) pair *m* à vie ► **life peerage** N (*Brit*) pairie *f* à vie ► **life preserver** N (*US = life jacket*) gilet *m* de sauvetage ; (*Navy*) brassière *f* (de sauvetage) ; (*Brit** *= bludgeon*) matraque *f* ► **life president** N président(e) *m(f)* à vie ► **life raft** N radeau *m* de sauvetage ► **life-saver** N (= *person*) maître *m* nageur (*surveillant un lieu de baignade*) ; (*fig*) **that money was a ~-saver** cet argent m'a sauvé la vie ► **life-saving** N (= *rescuing*) sauvetage *m* ; (= *first aid*) secourisme *m* ♦ ADJ de sauvetage ► **the life sciences** NPL les sciences *fpl* de la vie ► **life sentence** N (*Jur*) condamnation *f* à perpétuité ► **life-size(d)** ADJ grandeur nature *inv* ► **life span** N durée *f* or espérance *f* de vie ► **life story** N biographie *f* ; **his ~ story** sa biographie, l'histoire *f* de sa vie ; **he started telling me his ~ story*** il a commencé à me raconter sa vie ► **life support machine** N (*Space*) équipements *mpl* de vie ; (*Med*) respirateur *m* artificiel ; (*Med*) **he's on a ~ support machine** il est sous assistance respiratoire ; (*Med*) **to switch off the ~ support machine** débrancher le respirateur artificiel ► **life's work** N œuvre *f* de toute une (*or* ma *or* sa *etc*) vie ► **life tenancy** N **to hold a ~ tenancy of a house** être locataire d'une maison à vie ► **life-threatening** ADJ [*disease, emergency*] extrêmement grave ► **life-vest** ADJ (*US*) = **life jacket**

lifebelt ['laɪfbelt] N bouée *f* de sauvetage

lifeblood ['laɪfblʌd] N (*fig*) élément *m* vital or moteur, âme *f*

lifeboat ['laɪfbəʊt] N (*from shore*) bateau *m* or canot *m* de sauvetage ; (*from ship*) chaloupe *f* de sauvetage ; **~ station** centre *m* or poste *m* de secours en mer

lifeboatman ['laɪfbəʊtmən] N (*pl* **-men**) sauveteur *m* (en mer)

lifebuoy ['laɪfbɔɪ] N bouée *f* de sauvetage

lifeguard ['laɪfɡɑːd] N (*on beach*) maître nageur *m* ; (*Mil = bodyguard*) garde *m* du corps

lifeless ['laɪflɪs] ADJ **a** (= *dead*) [*person, eyes*] sans vie ; [*animal*] mort ; [*body*] sans vie, inanimé **b** (= *inanimate*) [*object*] inanimé **c** (= *not supporting life*) [*lake*] stérile ; [*planet*] sans aucune forme de vie **d** (*pej = dull, feeble*) [*style, novel, description*] plat ; [*voice*] terne ; [*team, player, performer*] sans énergie

lifelessness ['laɪflɪsnɪs] N (*lit*) absence *f* de vie ; (*fig*) manque *m* de vigueur or d'entrain

lifelike ['laɪflaɪk] ADJ qui semble vivant or vrai

lifeline ['laɪflaɪn] N **a** (*on ship*) main *f* courante ; (*for diver*) corde *f* de sécurité ; (*fig*) **it was his ~** c'était vital pour lui **b** (*in palmistry*) ligne *f* de vie

lifelong ['laɪflɒŋ] ADJ [*ambition*] de toute ma (*or* sa *etc*) vie ; [*friend, friendship*] de toujours ; **it is a ~ task** c'est le travail de toute une vie

lifer* ['laɪfə'] N condamné(e) *m(f)* à perpète*

lifestyle ['laɪfstaɪl] N style *m* or mode *m* de vie ; **a ~ change** un changement de mode de vie

lifetime ['laɪftaɪm] N **a** (*of person*) vie *f* ; **it won't happen in** or **during my ~** je ne verrai pas cela de mon vivant ; **it was the chance/ holiday of a ~** c'était la chance/c'étaient les plus belles vacances de ma (*or* sa *etc*) vie ; **the experience of a ~** une expérience inoubliable ; **once in a ~** une fois dans la *or* une vie ; **the work of a ~** l'œuvre de toute une vie ; **a ~'s experience/work** l'expérience/le travail de toute une vie → **last²** **b** (*fig = eternity*) éternité *f* ; **an hour that seemed (like) a ~** une heure qui semblait une éternité **c** [*of battery, ma-*

chine etc] (durée *f* de) vie *f* ; [*of nuclear reactor*] durée *f* de vie

LIFO ['laɪfəʊ] (ABBR = **last in, first out**) DEPS

lift [lɪft] **1** N **a** (*Brit*) (= *elevator*) ascenseur *m* ; (*for goods*) monte-charge *m inv* → **service** **b** (*Ski*) téléski *m*, tire-fesses* *m*, remontée *f* mécanique **c** **give the box a ~** soulève la boîte ; **can you give me a ~ up, I can't reach the shelf** soulève-moi, s'il te plaît, je n'arrive pas à atteindre l'étagère → **airlift, face d** (= *transport*) **can I give you a ~?** est-ce que je peux vous déposer quelque part ? ; **I gave him a ~ to Paris** je l'ai pris en voiture or je l'ai emmené jusqu'à Paris ; **we didn't get any ~s** personne ne s'est arrêté pour nous prendre ; **he stood there hoping for a ~** il était là (debout) dans l'espoir d'être pris en stop → **hitch e** (*NonC: Aviat*) portance *f* **f** (*fig = boost*) **it gave us a ~** cela nous a remonté le moral or nous a encouragés

2 VT **a** (= *raise*) lever, soulever ; (*Agr*) [+ *potatoes etc*] arracher ; **to ~ sth into the air** lever qch en l'air ; **to ~ sb/sth onto a table** soulever qn/qch et le poser or pour le poser sur une table ; **to ~ sb/sth off a table** descendre qn/qch d'une table ; **to ~ sb over a wall** faire passer qn par-dessus un mur ; **this suitcase is too heavy for me to ~** cette valise est trop lourde pour que je la soulève (*subj*) ; (*Sport*) **to ~ weights** faire de l'haltérophilie or des haltères ; **he ~ed his fork to his mouth** il a porté la fourchette à sa bouche ; **"~ here"** « soulever ici » → **face, finger**

b (= *repeal*) [+ *restrictions*] supprimer, abolir ; [+ *ban, blockade, siege*] lever ; **to ~ the prohibition on sth** lever l'interdiction de qch **c** (* = *steal*) piquer*, chiper* → **shoplift d** (= *copy*) [+ *quotation, passage*] prendre, voler ; **he ~ed that idea from Sartre** il a volé or pris cette idée à Sartre, il a plagié Sartre

3 VI [*lid etc*] se soulever ; [*fog*] se lever

4 COMP ► **lift attendant** N (*Brit*) liftier *m*, -ière *f* ► **lift cage** N (*Brit*) cabine *f* d'ascenseur ► **lift-off** N (*Space*) décollage *m* ; **we have ~-off!** décollage ! ► **lift operator** N = **lift attendant** ► **lift shaft** N (*Brit*) cage *f* d'ascenseur

► **lift down** VT SEP [+ *box, person*] descendre ; **to ~ sth down from a shelf** descendre qch d'une étagère

► **lift off 1** VI (*Space*) décoller **2** VT SEP [+ *lid*] enlever ; [+ *person*] descendre **3** **~-off** N → **lift**

► **lift out** VT SEP [+ *object*] sortir ; (*Mil*) [+ *troops*] (*by plane*) évacuer par avion, aéroporter ; (*by helicopter*) héliporter, évacuer par hélicoptère ; **he ~ed the child out of his playpen** il a sorti l'enfant de son parc

► **lift up 1** VI [*drawbridge etc*] se soulever, basculer **2** VT SEP [+ *object, carpet, skirt, person*] soulever ; **to ~ up one's eyes** lever les yeux ; **to ~ up one's head** lever or redresser la tête ; (*liter*) **he ~ed up his voice** il a élevé la voix

liftboy ['lɪftbɔɪ] N (*Brit*) liftier *m*, garçon *m* d'ascenseur

liftgate ['lɪftɡeɪt] N (*esp US Aut*) hayon *m*

liftman ['lɪftmæn] N (*pl* **-men**) (*Brit*) = **liftboy**

lig* [lɪɡ] VI (*Brit*) (*at party*) s'inviter ; (*at concert etc*) resquiller*

ligament ['lɪɡəmənt] N ligament *m*

ligature ['lɪɡətʃə'] N (*Surg, Typ = act, object*) ligature *f* ; (*Mus*) coulé *m*, liaison *f*

ligger* ['lɪɡə'] N (*Brit*) (*at party*) personne qui s'invite ; (*at concert etc*) resquilleur* *m*, -euse* *f*

ligging* ['lɪɡɪŋ] N (*Brit*) (*at party*) fait *m* de s'inviter ; (*at concert etc*) resquille* *f*

▼ **light¹** [laɪt] (*vb: pret, ptp* **lit** or **lighted**) **1** N **a** (*gen*) lumière *f* ; (*from lamp*) lumière *f*, éclairage *m* ; (*from sun*) lumière *f* ; (*also day-light*) lumière *f*, jour *m* ; **we saw several ~s on the horizon** nous avons vu plusieurs lumières à l'horizon ; **by the ~ of a candle/the fire/a**

► LANGUAGE IN USE: **light** 26.3

torch à la lumière or lueur d'une bougie/du feu/d'une lampe de poche; **there were ~s on in several of the rooms** il y avait de la lumière dans plusieurs pièces; (*fig hum*) **the ~s are on but nobody's (at) home*** il (*or elle etc*) est complètement dans les nuages; **~s out at 9 o'clock** extinction des feux à 21 heures; **~s out!** extinction des feux!, on éteint!; **at first ~** au point du jour; **the ~ was beginning to fail** le jour commençait à baisser; **the ~ isn't good enough to take photographs** il ne fait pas assez clair or il n'y a pas assez de lumière pour prendre des photos; (*Art, Phot*) **~ and shade** ombre *f* et lumière *f*; (*fig*) **there's no ~ and shade in their life** leur vie est très monotone; **you're holding it against the ~** vous le tenez à contre-jour; **to stand sth in the ~** mettre qch à la lumière; **to be** or **stand in one's own ~** se faire de l'ombre; **you're in my** or **the ~** (*daylight*) vous me cachez le jour; (*electric*) vous me cachez la lumière; **she was sitting with her back to the ~** elle tournait le dos à la lumière → **firelight, go out, hide¹, electric, moonlight**

b (*fig*) **in a good/bad ~** sous un jour favorable/défavorable; **the incident revealed him in a new ~** l'incident l'a montré sous un jour nouveau; **to see sb/sth in a different ~** voir qn/qch sous un autre jour or un jour différent; **to shed** or **cast a new ~ on a subject** jeter un jour nouveau sur un sujet; **can you throw any ~ on this question?** pouvez-vous éclaircir cette question?; **to bring to ~** mettre en lumière, révéler; **to come to ~** être dévoilé or découvert; **new facts have come to ~** on a découvert des faits nouveaux; **in (the) ~ of what you say** à la lumière de ce que vous dites; **I don't see things in that ~** je ne vois pas les choses sous cet angle-là or sous ce jour-là; **in the cold ~ of day** à tête reposée; **to see the ~** (= *understand*) comprendre; (= *see error of one's ways: also Rel*) trouver son chemin de Damas; **to see the ~ (of day)** (= *be born*) venir au monde; (= *be published etc*) paraître; **there is (a)** or **one can see the ~ at the end of the tunnel** on entrevoit la lumière au bout du tunnel

c (*in eyes*) lueur *f*; **with the ~ of battle in his eyes** (avec) une lueur belliqueuse dans le regard

d (= *lamp etc*) lampe *f*; **desk ~** lampe *f* de bureau

e (*of motor vehicle*) (*gen*) feu *m*; (= *headlight*) phare *m*; (*of cycle*) feu *m*; **have you got your ~s on?** as-tu mis tes phares (*or* tes feux)? → **parking, sidelight**

f **the ~s** (= *traffic lights*) les feux *mpl* (de circulation); **the ~s aren't working** les feux sont en panne; **the ~s were (at) red** le feu était (au) rouge; **he stopped at the ~s** il s'est arrêté au feu (rouge) → **red**

g (*for cigarette etc*) feu *m*; **have you got a ~?** avez-vous du feu?; (*Brit*) **to set ~ to sth** mettre le feu à qch → **pilot, strike**

h (*Archit* = *window*) fenêtre *f*, ouverture *f* → **fan¹, leaded, skylight**

2 ADJ **a** (*in brightness*) (*evening, room*) clair; **it was growing** or **getting ~** il commençait à faire jour; **while it's still ~** pendant qu'il fait encore jour

b (*in colour*) (*hair*) clair, blond; (*colour, complexion, skin*) clair; **~ green** vert clair *inv*; **~ blue** bleu clair *inv*

3 VT **a** (= *set fire to*) (+ *candle, cigarette, gas*) allumer; **to ~ a match** frotter or gratter une allumette; **a ~ed match** une allumette enflammée; **he lit the fire** il a allumé le feu; **he lit a fire** il a fait du feu; (*esp US fig*) **to ~ a fire under sb** mettre la pression sur qn

b (= *illuminate*) éclairer; **lit by electricity** éclairé à l'électricité; **this torch will ~ your way** or **the way for you** cette lampe de poche vous éclairera le chemin

4 VI **a** (*match*) s'allumer; (*coal, wood*) prendre (feu)

b **to ~ into sb*** tomber sur qn (à bras raccourcis)

5 COMP ► **light bulb** N (*Elec*) ampoule *f* ► **light-coloured** ADJ clair, de couleur claire ► **light effects** NPL effets *mpl* or jeux *mpl* de lumière ► **light-emitting diode** N diode *f* électroluminescente ► **light fitting** N appareil *m* d'éclairage ► **light-haired** ADJ blond ► **light meter** N (*Phot*) posemètre *m* ► **light pen, light pencil** N (*Comput*) photostyle *m*, crayon *m* optique ► **light pollution** N pollution *f* lumineuse ► **light-sensitive** ADJ photosensible ► **light show** N éclairages *mpl* ► **lights-out** N (*NonC*) extinction *f* des feux ► **light switch** N interrupteur *m* ► **light wave** N onde *f* lumineuse ► **light-year** N année-lumière *f*; **3000 ~-years away** à 3 000 années-lumière; (*fig*) **that's ~-years away** c'est à des années-lumière

► **light out** †‡ VI partir à toute vitesse (**for** pour), se barrer*

► **light up** **1** VI **a** (*lamp*) s'allumer; (*fig*) s'allumer, s'éclairer; **her eyes/face lit up** son regard/visage s'est éclairé **b** (* = *start to smoke*) allumer une cigarette or une pipe *etc* **2** VT SEP (= *illuminate*) éclairer; (*fig*) **a smile lit up her face** un sourire a éclairé or illuminé son visage **3** **lit up** ADJ → **lit** **4** **~ing-up** N → **lighting**

light² [laɪt] **1** ADJ **a** (= *not heavy*) (*parcel, weapon, clothes, sleep, meal, wine, soil*) léger; **~er than air** plus léger que l'air; **as ~ as a feather** léger comme une plume; **to be ~ on one's feet** (*gen*) avoir le pas léger or la démarche légère; (*of boxer*) avoir un très bon jeu de jambes; (*of dancer*) être aérien; **to be a ~ sleeper** avoir le sommeil léger

b (*fig*) (= *not serious*) (*play, music, breeze, punishment, shower*) léger; (*rain*) petit, fin; (*work, task*) (= *easy*) facile; (= *not strenuous*) peu fatigant; **it is no ~ matter** c'est sérieux, ça n'est pas une plaisanterie; **a ~ fall of snow** une légère chute de neige; **with a ~ heart** le cœur léger; **"woman wanted for ~ work"** «on demande employée de maison pour travaux légers»; **to make ~ work of sth** faire qch aisément or sans difficulté; **to make ~ of sth** prendre or traiter qch à la légère

2 ADV **to sleep ~** avoir le sommeil léger; **to travel ~** voyager avec peu de bagages

3 **lights** NPL (= *meat*) mou *m* (*abats*)

4 COMP ► **light aircraft** N petit avion *m* ► **light ale** N (*Brit*) sorte de bière blonde légère ► **light beer** N (*US*) bière *f* basses calories ► **light comedy** N comédie *f* légère ► **light entertainment** N (*NonC: Rad, TV*) variétés *fpl* ► **light-fingered** ADJ **to be ~-fingered** être chapardeur ► **light-footed** ADJ (*gen*) au pas léger, à la démarche légère; (*dancer*) aérien ► **light-headed** ADJ (= *dizzy*) étourdi, pris de vertige; (= *unable to think clearly*) étourdi, hébété; (= *excited*) exalté, grisé; (= *thoughtless*) étourdi, écervelé ► **light-hearted** ADJ (*person*) gai, aimable, enjoué; (*laugh*) joyeux, gai; (*atmosphere*) joyeux, gai, plaisant; (*discussion*) enjoué; (*question, remark*) plaisant, peu sérieux ► **light-heartedly** ADV (= *happily*) joyeusement, allégrement; (= *jokingly*) en plaisantant; (= *cheerfully*) de bon cœur, avec bonne humeur ► **light heavyweight** ADJ, N (*Boxing*) (poids *m*) mi-lourd *m* ► **light industry** N industrie *f* légère ► **light infantry** N (*Mil*) infanterie *f* légère ► **light middleweight** ADJ, N (*Boxing*) (poids *m*) superwelter *m* or super-mi-moyen *m* ► **light opera** N opérette *f* ► **light railway** N transport *m* urbain sur rail ► **light reading** N lecture *f* distrayante ► **light vehicles** NPL véhicules *mpl* légers ► **light verse** N poésie *f* légère ► **light welterweight** ADJ, N (*Boxing*) (poids *m*) super-léger *m*

light³ [laɪt] (*pret, ptp* **lighted** *or* **lit**) VI **to ~ (up)on sth** trouver qch par hasard, tomber par chance sur qch; **his eyes lit upon the jewels** son regard est tombé sur les bijoux

lighten¹ [ˈlaɪtn] **1** VT **a** (= *light up*) (+ *darkness, face*) éclairer, illuminer **b** (= *make lighter*) (+ *colour, hair*) éclaircir **2** VI **a** (*sky*) s'éclaircir **b** (*Met: of lightning*) **it is ~ing** il fait or il y a des éclairs

lighten² [ˈlaɪtn] **1** VT **a** (= *make less heavy*) (+ *cargo, burden*) alléger; (+ *tax*) alléger, réduire **b** (*fig*) (+ *atmosphere*) détendre; (+ *discussion*) rendre plus léger; **to ~ sb's mood** dérider qn; **the sunshine did nothing to ~ his mood** malgré le soleil, il ne s'est pas déridé **2** VI (*load*) se réduire; **her heart ~ed at the news** la nouvelle lui a enlevé le poids qu'elle avait sur le cœur or lui a ôté un grand poids

► **lighten up*** VI se relaxer, se détendre

lighter¹ [ˈlaɪtəʳ] **1** N (*for gas cooker*) allume-gaz *m inv*; (*also* **cigarette ~**) briquet *m*; (*Aut: on dashboard*) allume-cigare *m inv*, allume-cigarette *m inv* → **cigar, firelighter, lamplighter 2** COMP ► **lighter flint** N pierre *f* à briquet ► **lighter fuel** N gaz *m* (or essence *f*) à briquet

lighter² [ˈlaɪtəʳ] N (*Naut*) (= *barge*) péniche *f*, chaland *m*; (= *for unloading ships*) allège *f*

lighterage [ˈlaɪtərɪdʒ] N (transport *m* par) ac(c)onage *m*; (= *fee*) droit *m* d'ac(c)onage

lighthouse [ˈlaɪthaʊs] **1** N phare *m* **2** COMP ► **lighthouse keeper** N gardien(ne) *m(f)* de phare

lighting [ˈlaɪtɪŋ] **1** N (*NonC*) **a** (*Elec*) éclairage *m*; (*Theat*) éclairages *mpl* **b** (= *act*) (*of lamp, candle etc*) allumage *m* **2** COMP ► **lighting effects** NPL effets *mpl* or jeux *mpl* d'éclairage, éclairages *mpl* ► **lighting engineer** N éclairagiste *mf* ► **lighting fixture** N appareil *m* d'éclairage ► **lighting-up time** N (*Brit Aut*) heure à laquelle les automobilistes sont tenus d'allumer leurs phares

lightly [ˈlaɪtlɪ] ADV **a** (= *gently*) (*walk*) légèrement; (*stroke*) doucement, délicatement; (*brush*) délicatement; **she touched his brow ~ with her hand** elle lui a effleuré le front de la main; **bring to the boil and season ~ with pepper** faire bouillir et assaisonner légèrement de poivre; **~ boiled egg** ≈ œuf *m* mollet; **~ cooked** pas trop cuit; **to kiss sb ~** donner un petit baiser à qn; **he kissed me ~ on the lips** il a déposé un petit baiser sur mes lèvres **b** (= *light-heartedly*) (*speak*) légèrement, à la légère; (*laugh*) légèrement; (*remark, say*) d'un ton dégagé; **if this deadline is not met, they will not take it ~** si ce délai n'est pas respecté, ils ne le prendront pas à la légère; **to get off ~** s'en tirer à bon compte

lightness¹ [ˈlaɪtnɪs] N (= *brightness*) clarté *f*

lightness² [ˈlaɪtnɪs] N (*in weight, Culin*) légèreté *f*

lightning [ˈlaɪtnɪŋ] **1** N (= *flash*) éclair *m*; (= *phenomenon*) foudre *f*; **we saw ~** nous avons vu un éclair or des éclairs; **there was a lot of ~** il y avait beaucoup d'éclairs; **a flash of ~** un éclair; **struck by ~** frappé par la foudre, foudroyé ■ (*PROV*) **~ never strikes twice in the same place** la foudre ne frappe or ne tombe jamais deux fois au même endroit; **like ~*** avec la rapidité de l'éclair or à la vitesse de l'éclair → **forked, grease, sheet 2** COMP (*attack*) foudroyant; (*Ind*) (*strike*) surprise *inv*; (*visit*) éclair *inv* ► **lightning bug** N (*US*) luciole *f* ► **lightning conductor, lightning rod** (*US*) N paratonnerre *m*

lightship [ˈlaɪtʃɪp] N bateau-phare *m*, bateau-feu *m*

lightweight [ˈlaɪtweɪt] **1** ADJ (*jacket, shoes*) léger; (*Boxing*) poids léger *inv* **2** N (*Boxing*) poids *m* léger; **European ~ champion/championship** champion *m*/championnat *m* d'Europe des poids légers

ligneous [ˈlɪgnɪəs] ADJ ligneux
lignite [ˈlɪgnaɪt] N lignite *m*
lignum vitae [ˈlɪgnəmˈviːtaɪ] N a (= *tree*) gaïac *m* b (= *wood*) bois *m* de gaïac
Liguria [lɪˈgjʊərɪə] N la Ligurie
Ligurian [lɪˈgjʊərɪən] ADJ ligurien
likable [ˈlaɪkəbl] ADJ = likeable

▼ **like** [laɪk]

1 ADJECTIVE	5 NOUN
2 PREPOSITION	6 PLURAL NOUN
3 ADVERB	7 TRANSITIVE VERB
4 CONJUNCTION	8 COMPOUNDS

1 ADJECTIVE
= similar de ce type *or* genre, analogue; **this technique detects sugar and other ~ substances** cette technique permet de détecter le sucre et d'autres substances de ce type *or* analogues; **in ~ manner** de la même manière; **they are as ~ as two peas (in a pod)** ils se ressemblent comme deux gouttes d'eau

2 PREPOSITION
a = in the manner of comme; **he spoke ~ an aristocrat** il parlait comme un aristocrate; **he spoke ~ the aristocrat he was** il parlait comme l'aristocrate qu'il était; **he behaved ~ a fool** il s'est conduit comme un imbécile; **~ the fool he is, he ...** imbécile comme il l'est, il ...; **~ an animal in a trap he ...** comme *or* telle une bête prise au piège, il ...; **an idiot ~ you** un imbécile comme toi; **she was ~ a sister to me** elle était comme une sœur pour moi; **the news spread ~ wildfire** la nouvelle s'est répandue comme une traînée de poudre; **to tell it ~ it is*** dire les choses comme elles sont

• **like that** comme ça; **don't do it ~ that** ne fais pas comme ça; **some people are ~ that** il y a des gens comme ça; **his father is ~ that** son père est comme ça; **it wasn't ~ that at all** ce n'est pas comme ça que ça s'est passé; **people ~ that can't be trusted** on ne peut pas se fier à des gens pareils *or* à des gens comme ça

• **like this** comme ceci, comme ça; **you do it ~ this** tu fais comme ceci *or* ça; **it happened ~ this ...** voici comment ça s'est passé ...; **it was ~ this, I'd just got home ...** voilà, je venais juste de rentrer chez moi ...; **I'm sorry I didn't come but it was ~ this ...** je m'excuse de ne pas être venu mais c'est que ...

b in comparisons comme; **to be ~ sb/sth** ressembler à qn/qch; **they are very (much) ~ one another** ils se ressemblent beaucoup; **he is ~ his father** il ressemble à son père, il est comme son père; **he's just ~ anybody else** il est comme tout le monde; **the portrait is not ~ him** le portrait ne lui ressemble pas *or* n'est pas ressemblant; **his work is rather ~ Van Gogh's** son œuvre est un peu dans le style de Van Gogh; **your writing is rather ~ mine** vous avez un peu la même écriture que moi, votre écriture ressemble un peu à la mienne; **a house ~ mine** une maison comme la mienne; **a hat rather** *or* **something ~ yours** un chapeau un peu comme le vôtre *or* dans le genre du vôtre; **I found one ~ it** j'en ai trouvé un pareil, j'ai trouvé le même; **I never saw anything ~ it!** je n'ai jamais rien vu de pareil!; **we heard a noise ~ a car backfiring** on a entendu comme une pétarade de voiture

c in descriptions **what's he ~?** comment est-il?; **you know what she's ~*** vous savez comment elle est; **what's he ~ as a teacher?** comment est-il *or* que vaut-il comme professeur?; **what was the film ~?** comment as-tu trouvé le film?; **what's the weather ~ in Paris?** quel temps fait-il à Paris?; **that's more ~ it!*** voilà qui est mieux!, il y a du progrès!

♦ **something/nothing like: it cost something ~ £100** cela a coûté dans les 100 livres, cela a coûté quelque chose comme 100 livres; **he's called Middlewick** *or* **something ~ that** il s'appelle Middlewick ou quelque chose

comme ça *or* quelque chose d'approchant; **I was thinking of giving her something ~ a necklace** je pensais lui offrir un collier ou quelque chose dans ce genre-là *or* quelque chose comme ça; **that's something ~ a steak!*** voilà ce que j'appelle *or* ce qui s'appelle un bifteck!; **there's nothing ~ real silk** rien de tel que la soie véritable, rien ne vaut la soie véritable; **that's nothing ~ it!** ça n'est pas du tout ça!

d = typical of **that's just ~ him!** c'est bien de lui!; **it's not ~ him to be late** ça ne lui ressemble pas *or* ça n'est pas son genre d'être en retard; **that's just ~ a woman!** voilà bien les femmes!

e = in the same way as comme, de même que; **~ me, he is fond of Brahms** comme moi, il aime Brahms; **he, ~ me, thinks that ...** comme moi, il pense que ...; **he thinks ~ us*** il pense comme nous; **do it ~ me*** fais comme moi; **can't you just accept it ~ everyone else?** tu ne peux pas simplement l'accepter comme tout le monde? ■ (*PROV*) **~ father, ~ son** tel père, tel fils (*PROV*)

f = such as comme, tel que; **the things she prefers, ~ reading and music** les activités qu'elle préfère, telles que la lecture et la musique *or* comme la lecture et la musique

3 ADVERB
a = likely **(as) ~ as not ◊ ~ enough*** probablement

b = near **that record's nothing ~ as good as this one** ce disque-là est loin d'être aussi bon que celui-ci; **she's more ~ 30 than 25** elle a plutôt 30 ans que 25, elle est plus près de 30 ans que de 25; **he asked her to do it — ordered her, more ~!*** il lui a demandé de le faire — il le lui a ordonné, plutôt!

c ⁂ conversational filler **he felt tired ~ ◊ he felt ~ tired** (*US*) il se sentait comme qui dirait* fatigué; **I had a fortnight's holiday, ~, so I did a bit of gardening** j'avais quinze jours de vacances, alors comme ça* j'ai fait un peu de jardinage

4 CONJUNCTION
a ⁂ = as comme; **he did it ~ I did** il l'a fait comme moi; **he can't play poker ~ his brother can** il ne sait pas jouer au poker comme *or* aussi bien que son frère; **~ we used to** comme nous en avions l'habitude; **it's just ~ I say** c'est comme je vous le dis

b ⁂ = as if comme si; **he behaved ~ he was afraid** il se conduisait comme s'il avait peur; **it's not ~ she's poor, or anything** ce n'est pas comme si elle était pauvre

5 NOUN
= similar thing oranges, lemons and the ~ les oranges, les citrons et autres fruits de ce genre; **the ~ of which we'll never see again** comme on n'en reverra plus jamais; **did you ever see the ~ (of it)?*** a-t-on jamais vu une chose pareille?; **I've never known his ~ for ...** il n'a pas son pareil pour ...; **we'll never see his ~ again** nous ne verrons plus jamais quelqu'un comme lui *or* son pareil; **the ~s of him*** les gens comme lui *or* de son acabit (*pej*)

6 **likes** NPL goûts *mpl*, préférences *fpl*; **he knows all my ~s and dislikes** il sait tout ce que j'aime et (tout) ce que je n'aime pas

7 TRANSITIVE VERB
a + person aimer bien; **I ~ him** je l'aime bien; **I don't ~ him** je ne l'aime pas beaucoup, il me déplaît; **I've come to ~ him** il m'est devenu sympathique, maintenant je l'aime bien; **he is well ~d here** on l'aime bien ici, on le trouve sympathique ici; **how do you ~ him?** comment le trouvez-vous?; **I don't ~ the look of him** son allure ne me dit rien qui vaille

b + object, food, activity aimer (bien); **I ~ that hat** j'aime bien ce chapeau, ce chapeau me plaît; **which do you ~ best?** lequel préfères-tu?; **this plant doesn't ~ sunlight** cette plante ne se plaît pas à la lumière du soleil; **I ~ oysters but they don't ~ me*** j'aime bien les

huîtres mais elles ne me réussissent pas; **I ~ music/Beethoven/football** j'aime bien la musique/Beethoven/le football; **I ~ to have a rest after lunch** j'aime (bien) me reposer après déjeuner; **he ~s to be obeyed** il aime être obéi *or* qu'on lui obéisse; **I ~ people to be punctual** j'aime que les gens soient à l'heure, j'aime qu'on soit ponctuel; **I don't ~ it when he's unhappy** je n'aime pas ça quand il est malheureux; (*iro*) **well, I ~ that!*** ah ça, par exemple!; (*iro*) **I ~ your cheek!*** tu as quand même du toupet!*; **how do you ~ Paris?** que pensez-vous de Paris?, est-ce que Paris vous plaît?; **how do you ~ it here?** (est-ce que) vous vous plaisez ici?; **your father won't ~ it** cela ne plaira pas à ton père, ton père ne sera pas content; **whether he ~s it or not** que cela lui plaise ou non

c = want, wish aimer (bien), vouloir; **I'd ~ to go home** j'aimerais (bien) *or* je voudrais (bien) rentrer chez moi; **I'd have ~d to be there** j'aurais (bien) aimé être là; **I didn't ~ to disturb you** je ne voulais pas vous déranger; **I thought of asking him but I didn't ~ to** j'ai bien pensé (à) le lui demander mais j'étais gêné; **would you ~ a drink?** voulez-vous boire quelque chose?; **I would ~ more time** je voudrais plus de temps; **which one would you ~?** lequel voudriez-vous *or* aimeriez-vous?; **I would ~ you to speak to him** je voudrais que tu lui parles (*subj*); **would you ~ me to go and get it?** veux-tu que j'aille le chercher?; **would you ~ to go to Paris?** aimerais-tu aller à Paris?; **how would you ~ to go to Paris?** est-ce que cela te plairait *or* te dirait* d'aller à Paris?; **how would you ~ your steak: rare, medium or well done?** vous le voulez comment, votre bifteck: saignant, à point ou bien cuit?; **how would you ~ a steak?** est-ce que ça te dirait* de manger un bifteck?; **I can do it when/where/as much as/how I ~** je peux le faire quand/où/autant que/comme je veux; **when would you ~ breakfast?** à quelle heure voulez-vous votre petit déjeuner?; **whenever you ~** quand vous voudrez; **"As You Like It"** « Comme il vous plaira »; **don't think you can do as you ~** ne croyez pas que vous pouvez *or* puissiez faire comme vous voulez *or* comme bon vous semble; **I'll go out as much as I ~** je sortirai autant qu'il me plaira; **come on Sunday if you ~** venez dimanche si vous voulez; **if you ~** si tu veux, si vous voulez; **she can do what(ever) she ~s with him** elle fait tout ce qu'elle veut de lui; **(you can) shout as much as you ~, I won't open the door** crie tant que tu veux *or* voudras, je n'ouvrirai pas la porte; **he can say** *or* **let him say what he ~s, I won't change my mind** il peut dire ce qu'il veut, je ne changerai pas d'avis

8 COMPOUNDS
▸ **like-minded** ADJ de même sensibilité; **it was nice to be with ~-minded individuals** c'était agréable d'être en compagnie de gens de même sensibilité

...like [laɪk] SUF **childlike** enfantin; **statesman-like** d'homme d'État → **catlike**
likeable [ˈlaɪkəbl] ADJ sympathique, agréable
likeableness [ˈlaɪkəblnɪs] N caractère *m* sympathique *or* agréable

likelihood [ˈlaɪklɪhʊd] N probabilité *f*, chance *f*; **there is little ~ of his coming** *or* **that he will come** il y a peu de chances *or* il est peu probable qu'il vienne; **there is a strong ~ of his coming** *or* **that he will come** il y a de fortes chances (pour) qu'il vienne, il est très probable qu'il viendra; **there is no ~ of that** cela ne risque pas d'arriver; **in all ~ she ...** selon toute probabilité elle ..., il est fort probable qu'elle ...

▼ **likely** [ˈlaɪklɪ] 1 ADJ a (= *probable*) [*outcome, result, consequences*] probable; **~ developments in the region** les développements que la région va probablement connaître; **what is the likeliest time to find him at home?** à quelle heure a-t-on le plus de chances de le trouver chez lui?; **it is ~ that ...** il est probable que ... (+ subj), il y a des chances (pour) que ... (+ subj); **it is not ~ that ...** il est peu probable que ... (+ subj), il y a peu de chances que ... (+ subj); **it is very ~ that ...** il est tout à fait possible que ... (+ subj), il y a de grandes chances (pour) que ... (+ subj); **it's hardly ~ that ...** il n'est guère probable que ... (+ subj); **is it ~ that he would forget?** se peut-il qu'il oublie (subj)?; **is it ~ that I'd forget?** comment aurais-je pu oublier? [b] **he/it is ~ to ...** il est bien possible qu'il/que cela ... (+ subj); (with pleasant outcome) **to be ~ to win/succeed** [person] avoir de fortes chances de gagner/réussir; (with unpleasant outcome) **to be ~ to fail/refuse** [person] risquer d'échouer/de refuser; (pleasant) **it is ~ to sell well/to improve** [thing] il y a de fortes chances (pour) que cela se vende bien/que cela s'améliore; (unpleasant) **it is ~ to break/make a loss** [thing] cela risque de se casser/de ne pas être rentable; **she is ~ to arrive at any time** (gen) elle va probablement arriver d'une minute à l'autre; (unwelcome) elle risque d'arriver d'une minute à l'autre; **she is not ~ to come** il est peu probable or il y a peu de chances qu'elle vienne; **this trend is ~ to continue** (gen) cette tendance va probablement se poursuivre; (unpleasant) cette tendance risque de se poursuivre; **he is not ~ to succeed** il a peu de chances de réussir; **the man most ~ to succeed** l'homme qui a le plus de chances de réussir; **this incident is ~ to cause trouble** cet incident pourrait bien créer or risque de créer des problèmes; **that is not ~ to happen** cela a peu de chances de se produire; **they were not ~ to forget it** ils n'étaient pas près de l'oublier [c] (= plausible) [explanation] plausible, vraisemblable; (iro) **a ~ story** or **tale!** elle est bonne, celle-là! (iro); **a ~ excuse!** belle excuse! (iro) [d] (= promising) **he's a ~ candidate/recruit** c'est un candidat/une nouvelle recrue qui promet; **a ~ candidate to become** or **for Prime Minister** quelqu'un qui a de fortes chances de devenir Premier ministre; **I asked six ~ people** j'ai demandé à six personnes susceptibles de convenir or qui me semblaient pouvoir convenir; **he's a ~ young man** c'est un jeune homme qui promet; **it's not a very ~ place for a film festival** (surprising choice) ce n'est pas vraiment l'endroit auquel on penserait pour un festival du cinéma; **he glanced round for a ~-looking person to help him** il chercha des yeux une personne susceptible de l'aider; **a ~ place for him to be hiding** un endroit où il pouvait être caché

[2] ADV [a] **very** or **most ~** très probablement; **it will very** or **most ~ rain** il va très probablement pleuvoir; **as ~ as not** sans doute [b] (US) probablement; **some prisoners will ~ be released soon** certains prisonniers seront probablement bientôt libérés [c] (esp Brit:*) **not ~!** sûrement pas!*; **are you going? — not ~!** tu y vas? — sûrement pas or ça risque pas!

liken ['laɪkən] VT comparer (**to** à); **to ~ sb to a fox/bird/hamster** comparer qn à un renard/un oiseau/un hamster; **he ~ed the situation to a time bomb** il a comparé la situation à une bombe à retardement; **he ~ed himself to the former president** il se comparait à l'ancien président; **X can be ~ed to Y** on peut comparer X et Y

likeness ['laɪknɪs] N [a] (= resemblance) ressemblance f (**to** avec); **I can't see much ~ between them** je ne vois guère de ressemblance entre eux, je ne trouve pas qu'ils se ressemblent (subj) beaucoup; **a strong family ~** un air de famille très marqué; **to bear a ~ to sb/sth** ressembler à qn/qch [b] **in the ~ of ...** sous la forme or l'aspect de ... [c] (= portrait)

---

to draw sb's ~ faire le portrait de qn; **to have one's ~ taken** se faire faire son portrait; **it is a good ~** c'est très ressemblant; (Art, Phot) **to catch a ~** saisir une ressemblance

likewise ['laɪkwaɪz] ADV [a] (= similarly) de même; (= also) également, aussi; (= moreover) de plus, en outre; **in Italy football is the national sport, ~ in Britain** en Italie, le football est le sport national; **il en est, de même en Grande-Bretagne**; **I can talk to him about anything. Likewise with my brother** je peux lui parler de tout; c'est la même chose avec mon frère or il en est de même avec mon frère; **overtures from the Right have ~ been rejected** des ouvertures de la part de la droite ont de même or ont également été rejetées; **my wife is well, the children ~** ma femme va bien, les enfants aussi or également; **and ~, it cannot be denied that ...** et on ne peut pas nier non plus que ... [b] (with vb) **to do ~** faire de même [c] (in replies) **nice to talk to you — ~** ça m'a fait plaisir de parler avec vous — moi de même

liking ['laɪkɪŋ] N (for person) sympathie f, affection f (**for** pour); (for thing) goût m (**for** pour), penchant m (**for** pour); **to take a ~ to sb** se prendre d'amitié pour qn; **to take a ~ to (doing) sth** se mettre à aimer (faire) qch; **to have a ~ for sb** tenir qn en affection, avoir de la sympathie pour qn; **to have a ~ for sth** avoir un penchant or du goût pour qch, aimer qch; **a ~ for work** le goût du travail; **to your ~ ◊ for your ~** à votre goût

lilac ['laɪlək] [1] N (= bush, colour, flower) lilas m; **a bunch of white ~** un bouquet de lilas blanc [2] ADJ (in colour) lilas inv

Lilliputian [ˌlɪlɪˈpjuːʃən] [1] ADJ lilliputien [2] N Lilliputien(ne) m(f)

Lilo® ['laɪləʊ] N matelas m pneumatique

lilt [lɪlt] N [of speech, song] rythme m, cadence f; **a song with a ~ to it** une chanson bien rythmée; **her voice had a pleasant ~ (to it)** sa voix avait des inflexions mélodieuses

lilting ['lɪltɪŋ] ADJ [song] cadencé; [voice] aux intonations mélodieuses; [movement] cadencé

lily ['lɪlɪ] [1] N lis m; **~ of the valley** muguet m → **water** [2] COMP ► **lily-livered** ADJ poltron ► **lily pad** N feuille f de nénuphar ► **lily-white** ADJ (lit) d'une blancheur de lis; (fig = innocent) blanc (blanche f) comme neige; (US: for Whites only) excluant totalement les Noirs

Lima ['liːmə] [1] N Lima [2] COMP ► **Lima bean** N haricot m de Lima

limb [lɪm] N (Anat, Zool, also fig) membre m; [of tree] grosse branche f; [of cross] bras m; **to tear ~ from** [+ person] mettre en pièces; [+ animal] démembrer; (fig) **to be out on a ~** (= isolated) être isolé; (= vulnerable) être dans une situation délicate; (fig) **to go out on a ~** prendre des risques; **~ of Satan** suppôt m de Satan → **risk**

-limbed [lɪmd] ADJ (in compounds) long-limbed aux membres longs; **strong-limbed** aux membres forts

limber¹ ['lɪmbər] ADJ [person] leste; [thing] souple, flexible

► **limber up** VI (Sport etc) se dégourdir, faire des exercices d'assouplissement; (fig) se préparer, se mettre en train; **~ing-up exercises** exercices mpl d'assouplissement

limber² ['lɪmbər] N [of gun carriage] avant-train m

limbic ['lɪmbɪk] ADJ limbique

limbless ['lɪmlɪs] ADJ **~ man** (= no limbs) homme m sans membres, homme m tronc; (= limb missing) homme m estropié, homme m à qui il manque un bras or une jambe; (after amputation) amputé m (d'un membre); **~ ex-servicemen** ≈ (grands) mutilés mpl de guerre

limbo¹ ['lɪmbəʊ] N **in ~** (= forgotten) tombé dans l'oubli; (= still undecided) encore dans les limbes mpl (liter); (Rel) dans les limbes; **in legal/social ~** dans un vide juridique/social

---

limbo² ['lɪmbəʊ] N (= dance) limbo m; **~ dancer** danseur m, -euse f de limbo

lime¹ [laɪm] [1] N [a] (Chem) chaux f → **quicklime** [b] (also **birdlime**) glu f [2] [+ ground] chauler [b] [+ twig] engluer; [+ bird] prendre à la glu, engluer [3] COMP ► **lime kiln** N four m à chaux

lime² [laɪm] [1] N [a] (= fruit) citron m vert, lime f [b] (= tree) lime f [c] (= drink) jus m de citron vert; **vodka/lager and ~** vodka f/bière f citron vert [2] COMP ► **lime cordial** N sirop m de citron vert ► **lime green** N vert m jaune inv ► **lime juice** N jus m de citron vert

lime³ [laɪm] N (= linden: also **~ tree**) tilleul m

limelight ['laɪmlaɪt] N (Theat) feux mpl de la rampe; (fig) **to be in the ~** être en vedette or au premier plan; **to keep out of the ~** ne pas se faire remarquer

limerick ['lɪmərɪk] N limerick m

limestone ['laɪmstəʊn] N calcaire m

Limey* ['laɪmɪ] N (US, Austral) Anglais(e) m(f), Anglicke mf

limit ['lɪmɪt] [1] N (= furthest point) [of territory, experience, vision etc] limite f; (fig) limite f, borne f; (= restriction on amount, number etc) limitation f, restriction f; (= permitted maximum) limite f; **the city ~s (of Baghdad)** les limites de la ville (de Bagdad); **we must set a ~ to the expense** il faut limiter or restreindre les dépenses; **his anger knows no ~s** sa colère ne connaît pas de limites, sa colère est sans borne(s); **to go to the ~ to help sb** faire tout son possible pour aider qn; (= speed limit) **the 60km/h ~** la limitation de vitesse de 60 km/h; **there is a 60km/h ~ on this road** la vitesse est limitée à 60 km/h sur cette route → **speed**; **that's the ~!*** c'est le comble!, ça dépasse les bornes!; **he's the ~!*** (= goes too far) il dépasse les bornes!; (= amusing) il est impayable!*; **there are ~s!** quand même il y a des limites!, il y a des limites à tout!; **he is at the ~ of his patience/endurance** il est à bout de patience/de forces; **off ~s** [area, district] d'accès interdit; (on sign) « accès interdit »; **there is no ~ on the amount you can import** la quantité que l'on peut importer n'est pas limitée; **outside the ~s of ...** en dehors des limites de ...; **over the ~** (of lorry in weight) en surcharge, surchargé; (of driver on Breathalyser) qui excède le taux maximal légal d'alcoolémie; **he was three times over the ~** [driver] son taux d'alcoolémie était trois fois plus élevé que le maximum légal; **there is a ~ to my patience** ma patience a des limites or des bornes; **there is a ~ to what one can do** il y a une limite à ce que l'on peut faire, on ne peut (quand même) pas faire l'impossible; **within the ~s of** dans les limites de; **within a 5-mile ~** dans un rayon de 8 kilomètres; **it is true within ~s** c'est vrai dans une certaine limite or mesure; **without ~** sans limitation, sans limite → **stretch**

[2] VT [a] (= restrict) [+ speed, time] limiter (**to** à); [+ expense, power] limiter, restreindre (**to** à); [+ person] limiter; **he ~ed questions to 25 minutes** il a limité les questions à 25 minutes; **he ~ed questions to those dealing with education** il a accepté seulement les questions portant sur l'éducation; **to ~ o.s.** to a few remarks se borner à (faire) quelques remarques; **to ~ o.s. to ten cigarettes a day** se limiter à dix cigarettes par jour; **we are ~ed in what we can do** nous sommes limités dans ce que nous pouvons faire

b (= *confine*) limiter; **Neo-Fascism is not ~ed to Europe** le néofascisme ne se limite pas à l'Europe; **our reorganization plans are ~ed to Africa** nos projets de réorganisation se limitent à *or* ne concernent que l'Afrique; **the government's attempts to ~ unemployment to 2.5 million** les efforts du gouvernement pour empêcher le chômage de dépasser la barre des 2,5 millions

limitation [ˌlɪmɪˈteɪʃən] N **a** (= *restriction*) limitation *f*, restriction *f*; **the ~ on imports** la limitation *or* la restriction des importations; **there is no ~ on the amount of currency you may take out** il n'y a aucune restriction sur les devises que vous pouvez emporter; **he has/knows his ~s** il a/connaît ses limites **b** (*Jur*) prescription *f*

limited [ˈlɪmɪtɪd] **1** ADJ **a** (= *restricted*) [*number, resources, choice, means, amount, range*] limité; [*intelligence, person*] borné, limité; **for a ~ period only** seulement pendant une période limitée; **to a ~ extent** jusqu'à un certain point, dans une certaine mesure seulement **b** (*esp Brit Comm, Jur*) **Smith and Sons Limited** ≈ Smith et fils, SA **2** COMP ► **limited bus** N (*US*) = **limited-stop bus** ► **limited company** N (*esp Brit Jur*) (*also* **private ~ company**) ≈ société *f* à responsabilité limitée; (*also* **public ~ company**) ≈ société *f* anonyme ► **limited edition** N [*of book*] édition *f* à tirage limité; [*of poster, print*] tirage *m* limité; [*of record*] pressage *m* limité; [*of car*] série *f* limitée ► **limited liability** N (*Brit Jur*) responsabilité *f* limitée; **~ liability company** société *f* à responsabilité limitée ► **limited partnership** N société *f* en commandite simple ► **limited-stop bus** N autobus *m* semi-direct

limiting [ˈlɪmɪtɪŋ] ADJ restrictif, contraignant

limitless [ˈlɪmɪtlɪs] ADJ [*power*] sans borne(s), illimité; [*opportunities*] illimité

limo* [ˈlɪməʊ] N (ABBR = **limousine**) limousine *f*

limousine [ˈlɪməziːn] **1** N (*gen*) limousine *f*; (*US: from airport etc*) (voiture-)navette *f* **2** COMP ► **limousine liberal*** N (*US*) libéral *m* de salon

limp¹ [lɪmp] **1** ADJ **a** (= *not firm*) [*hand, handshake, hair, penis*] mou (molle *f*); [*lettuce, flowers*] plus frais (fraîche *f*); **to go ~** devenir mou; **his body went ~** tous les muscles de son corps se sont relâchés; **to let one's body go ~** laisser son corps se relâcher; **let your arm go ~** laissez aller votre bras; **his arms hung ~ by his sides** il avait les bras ballants; **he was ~ with exhaustion** il était épuisé; **I feel very ~ in this hot weather** je me sens tout ramolli *or* avachi par cette chaleur; (*fig*) **to have a ~ wrist*** (= *be effeminate*) avoir des manières efféminées **b** (*fig* = *feeble*) [*excuse*] faible; [*style*] mou (molle *f*) **c** (*Publishing*) **~ cover(s)** reliure *f* souple **2** COMP ► **limp-wristed** ADJ (*pej* = *effeminate*) efféminé

limp² [lɪmp] **1** VI [*person*] boiter; (*fig*) [*vehicle etc*] marcher tant bien que mal; **to ~ in/out etc** entrer/sortir *etc* en boitant; **to ~ along** avancer en boitant, aller clopin-clopant*; **he ~ed to the door** il est allé à la porte en boitant, il a clopiné jusqu'à la porte; (*fig*) **the plane managed to ~ home** l'avion a réussi à regagner sa base tant bien que mal **2** N claudication *f*, boiterie *f*; **to have a ~** ◊ **to walk with a ~** boiter, clopiner

limpet [ˈlɪmpɪt] N **a** (*Zool*) patelle *f*, bernique *f*; (*fig* = *person*) crampon *m*; **to cling** *or* **stick to sth like a ~** s'accrocher à qch comme une moule au rocher **b** (*Mil: also* **~ mine**) mine-ventouse *f*

limpid [ˈlɪmpɪd] (*liter*) ADJ limpide

limply [ˈlɪmplɪ] ADV **a** (*lit*) mollement; **his arms hung ~ by his side** il avait les bras ballants; **the flag hung ~ from the mast** le dra-

peau pendait mollement **b** (*fig*) [*say, express*] mollement

limpness [ˈlɪmpnɪs] N **a** (*lit*) mollesse *f* **b** (*fig*) [*of style*] mollesse *f*; [*of excuse*] faiblesse *f*

limy [ˈlaɪmɪ] ADJ **a** (= *chalky*) [*soil, water*] calcaire **b** (*also* **~ green**) vert avec acide

linage [ˈlaɪnɪdʒ] **1** N (*Press*) lignage *m*, nombre *m* de lignes; **advertising ~** nombre *m* de lignes de publicité **2** COMP ► **linage advertisement** N petite annonce *f* ordinaire (*sans encadrement*)

linchpin [ˈlɪntʃˌpɪn] N (*Aut*) esse *f*; (*fig*) pivot *m*, charnière *f*

Lincs. [lɪŋks] ABBR = **Lincolnshire**

linctus [ˈlɪŋktəs] N (*pl* **linctuses**) sirop *m* (contre la toux)

linden [ˈlɪndən] N (*also* **~ tree**) tilleul *m*

▼**line¹** [laɪn]

| **1** NOUN | **3** COMPOUNDS |
| **2** TRANSITIVE VERB | **4** PHRASAL VERBS |

1 NOUN

a = **mark** ligne *f*, trait *m*; (*Math, TV, Sport*) ligne *f*; (= *pen stroke*) trait *m*; (*on palm*) ligne *f*; **a straight ~** une (ligne) droite; **a curved ~** une (ligne) courbe; **to put a ~ through sth** barrer *or* rayer qch; **the teacher put a red ~ through my translation** le professeur a barré *or* rayé ma traduction au stylo rouge; **to draw a ~ under sth** (*in exercise book*) tirer un trait sous qch; (*fig: episode, event*) tirer un trait sur qch; **~ by ~** ligne par ligne; (*Bridge*) **above the ~** (marqué) en points d'honneur; (*Bridge*) **below the ~** (marqué) en points de marche; (*Accounts*) hors bilan; (*Mus*) **on the ~** sur la ligne → **bottom, dotted, draw, state**

b = **boundary** frontière *f*; **there's a thin** *or* **fine ~ between genius and madness** il n'y a qu'un pas du génie à la folie, peu de choses séparent génie et folie

c Geog **the Line** (= *equator*) la ligne

d = **wrinkle** ride *f*; **the ~s on her face were now deeper** les rides de son visage s'étaient creusées

e = **shape** **the rounded ~s of this car** les contours *mpl* arrondis de cette voiture; **clothes that follow the ~s of the body** des vêtements *mpl* moulants *or* qui épousent les contours du corps

f = **rope** corde *f*; (= *wire*) fil *m*; (*Fishing*) ligne *f*, fil *m*; [*of diver*] corde *f* (de sûreté); (*also* **clothes ~, washing ~**) corde *f* (à linge); **they threw a ~ to the man in the sea** ils ont lancé une corde à l'homme qui était tombé à la mer

g = **pipe** tuyau *m*; (*larger: esp for oil, gas*) pipeline *m*

h Telec, also Elec = **cable** ligne *f*; "**663-1111 five ~s**" « 663.11.11 cinq lignes groupées »; **it's a bad ~** la ligne est mauvaise; **the ~'s gone dead** (*during conversation*) on nous a coupés; (*before dialling*) la ligne est en dérangement; **the ~s are down** les lignes ont été coupées; **the ~ is engaged** *or* (*US*) **busy** la ligne est occupée, c'est occupé; **Mr Smith is on the ~ (for you)** j'ai M. Smith à l'appareil (pour vous); **he's on the ~ to the manager** il est en ligne avec le directeur; **the ~s are open from 6 o'clock onwards** on peut téléphoner *or* appeler à partir de 6 heures

i of print, writing ligne *f*; [*of poem*] vers *m*; (* = *letter*) mot *m*; **page 20, ~ 18** page 20, ligne 18; (*in dictation*) **new ~** à la ligne; **a six-~ stanza** une strophe de six vers; **it's one of the best ~s in "Hamlet"** c'est l'un des meilleurs vers de « Hamlet »; **drop me a ~** envoyez-moi un (petit) mot; **to read between the ~s** lire entre les lignes; (*Scol* = *punishment*) **~s** lignes *fpl* à copier; (*Theat*) **to learn/forget one's ~s** apprendre/oublier son texte

j = **queue** esp US file *f*, queue *f*; **to form a ~** faire la queue; **to stand** *or* **wait in ~** faire la queue

k = **row, column** [*of trees, parked cars, hills*] rangée *f*; [*of cars in traffic jam*] file *f*; [*of people*] (*side by side*) rang *m*, rangée *f*; (*one behind another*) file *f*, colonne *f*; (*also* **assembly ~**) chaîne *f*; **the new recruits marched in a ~** les nouvelles recrues avançaient en file; **they sat in a ~ in front of him** ils se sont assis en rang devant lui; (*lit, fig*) **to fall into ~** s'aligner; (*fig*) **to fall into ~ with sb** se ranger *or* se conformer à l'avis de qn; **a ~ of winning numbers** une série de numéros gagnants; **the first ~ of defence** le premier moyen de défense; **the first ~ of treatment** le premier traitement à suivre

l = **succession** série *f*; (= *descent*) ligne *f*, lignée *f*; **the latest in a long ~ of tragedies** la dernière d'une longue série de tragédies; **in a direct ~ from** en droite ligne de, en ligne directe de; **he comes from a long ~ of artists** il est issu d'une longue lignée d'artistes; **the royal ~** la lignée royale; **succession passes through the male ~** la succession se fait par les hommes

m (*also* **shipping ~**) (= *company*) compagnie *f* maritime; (= *route*) ligne *f* (maritime); **the Cunard Line** la compagnie Cunard; **the New York-Southampton ~** la ligne New York-Southampton

n Rail etc (= *route*) ligne *f* (de chemin de fer); [*of underground*] ligne *f* (de métro); [*of bus*] ligne *f*; (= *track*) voie *f*; **the Brighton ~** la ligne de Brighton; **the ~ was blocked for several hours** la voie a été bloquée plusieurs heures; **cross the ~ by the footbridge** empruntez la passerelle pour traverser la voie; **the train left the ~** le train a déraillé

o = **direction** **the main** *or* **broad ~s** [*of story, plan*] les grandes lignes *fpl*; **~ of argument** raisonnement *m*; **the next chapter continues this ~ of thinking** le chapitre suivant développe cet argument; **~ of research** ligne *f* de recherche; **you're on the right ~s** vous êtes sur la bonne voie; **on ethnic/geographical ~s** selon des critères ethniques/géographiques → **inquiry, resistance**

p = **stance** position *f*; (= *argument*) argument *m*; **they voted against the government ~** ils ont voté contre la position adoptée par le gouvernement; **they came out with their usual ~** ils ont sorti leur argument habituel; **to take a strong ~ on ...** se montrer ferme sur ...

q * = **field** **~ of business** *or* **work** activité *f*; **you must be very aware of that in your ~ of business** vous devez en être très conscient dans votre métier; **what's your ~ (of business** *or* **work)?** que faites-vous dans la vie?; (*of companies*) **we're in the same ~ (of business)** nous sommes dans la même branche; **most kids can do something in the art ~** la plupart des gosses ont un certain don artistique; **cocktail parties are not (in) my ~** les cocktails ne sont pas mon genre; **fishing's more (in) my ~ (of country)** la pêche est davantage mon truc*; **he's got a nice ~ in rude jokes** il connaît plein d'histoires cochonnes*

r = **product** **this lager is the shop's best selling ~** cette bière blonde est ce qui se vend le mieux (dans le magasin)

s = **course** **in the ~ of duty** dans l'exercice de ses (*or* mes *etc*) fonctions; (*fig*) **it's all in the ~ of duty*** ça fait partie du boulot*

t * = **idea** **... but I really don't have a ~ on what's going to happen** ... mais je n'ai vraiment aucune idée de ce qui va se passer; **we've got a ~ on where he's gone to** nous croyons savoir où il est allé

u = **spiel** **to give sb a ~*** baratiner* qn; **to feed** *or* **hand sb a ~ about sth*** raconter des bobards* à qn sur qch

v Mil ligne *f*; (*Mil, fig*) **in the front ~** en première ligne; **behind (the) enemy ~s** derrière les lignes ennemies; **~ of battle** ligne *f* de combat; (*Brit Mil*) regiment of the ~ ≈ régiment *m* d'infanterie; (*Navy*) ~ **abreast** ligne *f* de front; (*Navy*) ~ **astern** ligne *f* de file; **ship of the** ~ vaisseau *m* de ligne, navire *m* de haut bord; (*fig*) **the (battle)** ~**s are drawn** les hostilités *fpl* sont engagées

w Drugs [*of cocaine etc*] ligne *f*

x SET STRUCTURES

♦ **along the line**: somewhere along the ~ he got an engineering degree je ne sais pas exactement quand, il a décroché son diplôme d'ingénieur; all along the ~ (= *constantly*) toujours; (= *everywhere*) partout; didn't I tell you that all along the ~? c'est ce que je n'ai pas arrêté de te dire; they've been involved all along the ~ ils ont participé depuis le début; the effects will be felt all along the ~ les effets en seront ressentis à tous les niveaux

♦ **all (the way)** or **right down the line** = all along the line

♦ **along those/the same** etc **lines**: he'd already said something along those ~s il avait déjà dit quelque chose du même genre; we are all thinking along the same ~s nous pensons tous de la même façon, nous sommes tous d'accord or du même avis; several projects were suggested, all along the same ~s plusieurs projets avaient été suggérés et tous étaient du même genre; I hope we'll continue along the same ~s j'espère que nous continuerons sur cette lancée; along or on political/racial ~s [*decide, divide*] selon des critères politiques/raciaux; [*organize, plan*] dans une optique politique/raciale; factories now work along Japanese ~s les usines emploient maintenant des méthodes japonaises

♦ **in line**: to keep sb in ~ faire tenir qn tranquille; if the Prime Minister fails to keep the rebels in ~ si le Premier ministre ne réussit pas à maîtriser les éléments rebelles; to be in ~ for a job être sur les rangs pour un emploi; public sector pay is in ~ to rise les salaires des fonctionnaires vont augmenter; Earth was in ~ with Venus and the Sun la Terre était alignée avec Vénus et le Soleil; the law is now in ~ with most medical opinion la loi va maintenant dans le sens de l'avis de la plupart des médecins; our system is broadly in ~ with that of other countries notre système correspond plus ou moins à celui d'autres pays

♦ **into line**: to come or fall or step into ~ [*person, group*] se conformer (with à); to come or fall into ~ [*plans, proposals*] concorder (with avec); (*lit, fig*) to bring sth into ~ with sth aligner qch sur qch; attempts to bring the system into ~ with that of Germany des tentatives pour aligner le système sur celui de l'Allemagne

♦ **on line** (= *on computer*) en ligne; they can order their requirements on ~ ils peuvent passer leurs commandes en ligne; (= *in or into service*) to come on ~ [*power station, machine*] entrer en service

♦ **on the line** (* = *at stake*) en jeu; my reputation/job is on the ~ ma réputation/mon emploi est en jeu; to put one's reputation/job on the ~ mettre sa réputation/son emploi en jeu; to put o.s. on the ~ prendre de gros risques; to put one's neck* or (*US*) ass** on the ~ risquer sa peau

♦ **out of line*** (= *unreasonable*) to be out of ~: he was completely out of ~ to suggest that ... il n'aurait vraiment pas dû suggérer que ...; (= *in conflict*) he is out of ~ with his own party il est en conflit avec son parti; their debts are completely out of ~ with their incomes leurs dettes sont tout à fait disproportionnées par rapport à leurs revenus; this result is out of ~ with the trend ce résultat ne s'inscrit pas dans la tendance générale

2 TRANSITIVE VERB

= mark [+ *face*] rider, marquer; his face was ~d with exhaustion il avait le visage marqué par la fatigue; ~d paper papier *m* réglé

3 COMPOUNDS

► **line dancing** N *danse de style country*
► **line drawing** N (*Art*) dessin *m* (au trait)
► **line feed** N (*Comput*) saut *m* or changement *m* de ligne ► **line fishing** N (*Sport*) pêche *f* à la ligne ► **line judge** N (*Tennis*) juge *m* de ligne ► **line manager** N (*Brit Ind*) supérieur *m* hiérarchique or direct ► **line of attack** N (*Mil*) plan *m* d'attaque; (*fig*) plan *m* d'action ► **line of communication** N ligne *f* de communication; to keep the ~s of communication open with sb ne pas rompre le dialogue avec qn ► **line of descent** N (*lit, fig*) lignée *f*; (*lit*) an ancient family who trace their ~ of descent back more than a thousand years une vieille famille dont les origines remontent à plus de mille ans; (*fig*) in a direct ~ of descent from sth dans la lignée directe de qch ► **line of fire** N (*Mil*) ligne *f* de tir; right in the ~ of fire en plein dans la ligne de tir or de feu ► **line of flight** N [*of bird etc*] ligne *f* de vol; [*of object*] trajectoire *f* ► **line of latitude** N ligne *f* de latitude ► **line of longitude** N ligne *f* de longitude ► **line of sight** N (*Mil*) ligne *f* de visée ► **line of vision** N champ *m* de vue ► **line-out** N (*Rugby*) touche *f* ► **line printer** N (*Comput*) imprimante *f* ligne par ligne ► **line spacing** N (*Typ, Comput*) interligne *m* ► **line storm** N (*US*) ouragan *m* ► **line-up** N [*of people etc*] (= *row*) file *f*; (*Police* = *identity parade*) séance *f* d'identification (d'un suspect); (*Ftbl etc*) (composition *f* de l'équipe *f*; (*fig, Pol etc*) the new ~-up la nouvelle composition du Parlement (or du Congrès *etc*); the President chose his ~-up le Président a choisi son équipe or ses collaborateurs; (*fig, Pol*) the ~-up of African powers le front des puissances africaines

4 PHRASAL VERBS

► **line up** **1** VI **a** (= *stand in row*) se mettre en rang(s), s'aligner; (= *stand in queue*) faire la queue; the teams ~d up and waited for the whistle les équipes se sont alignées et ont attendu le coup de sifflet

b (*fig = align o.s.*) to ~ up against sb/sth se liguer contre qn/qch; to ~ up behind sth se rallier à qch; most senators ~d up in support of the president la plupart des sénateurs se sont ralliés au président; black people have ~d up on both sides of the issue les Noirs se sont ralliés aux deux camps; to ~ up with or behind or alongside sb se ranger du côté de qn

2 VT SEP **a** [+ *people, objects*] aligner, mettre en ligne; ~ them up against the wall alignez-les contre le mur; they were ~d up and shot on les a alignés pour les fusiller; to be all ~d up* (= *ready*) être fin prêt (**for** pour, **to do** pour faire)

b * (= *organize*) [+ *party, trip*] organiser; (= *find*) trouver; we must ~ up a chairman for the meeting il faut que nous trouvions un président pour la réunion; to have sth ~d up avoir prévu qch; to have sb ~d up avoir qn en vue; have you got something ~d up for this evening? est-ce que tu as prévu quelque chose pour ce soir?; have you got someone ~d up? avez-vous quelqu'un en vue?; I wonder what he's got ~d up for us je me demande ce qu'il nous prépare

line² [laɪn] VT [+ *clothes, bag, box*] doubler (with de); [*bird*] [+ *nest*] garnir, tapisser; (*Tech*) revêtir, chemiser; (*fig: esp pej*) to ~ one's pockets se remplir les poches; eat something to ~ your stomach ne reste pas l'estomac vide; the walls were ~d with books and pictures les murs étaient couverts or tapissés de livres et de tableaux; the streets were ~d with cheering crowds les rues étaient bordées d'une (double) haie de spectateurs enthousiastes; cheering crowds ~d the route une foule enthousiaste faisait la haie tout le long du

parcours; the road was ~d with trees la route était bordée d'arbres → **wool**

lineage ['lɪnɪdʒ] N **a** (= *ancestry*) lignage† *m*, famille *f*; (= *descendants*) lignée *f*; she can trace her ~ back to the 17th century sa famille remonte au 17ᵉ siècle **b** ['laɪnɪdʒ] = **linage**

lineal ['lɪnɪəl] ADJ en ligne directe

lineament ['lɪnɪəmənt] N (*liter*) (= *feature*) trait *m*, linéament *m* (*liter*); (= *characteristic*) ~s caractéristiques *fpl*, particularités *fpl*

linear ['lɪnɪəʳ] **1** ADJ linéaire **2** COMP ► **linear accelerator** N (*Phys*) accélérateur *m* linéaire ► **linear equation** N (*Math*) équation *f* linéaire ► **linear perspective** N (*Art*) perspective *f* linéaire ► **linear programming** N (*Econ, Math*) programmation *f* linéaire

lineman ['laɪnmən] N (*pl* **-men**) (*US*) (*Rail*) poseur *m* de rails; (*Telec*) ouvrier *m* de ligne

linen ['lɪnɪn] **1** N **a** (*NonC: Tex*) (toile *f* de) lin *m* **b** (*collective n*) (= *sheets, tablecloths etc: also* ~s: *esp US*) linge *m* (de maison); (= *underwear*) linge *m* (de corps); dirty or soiled ~ linge *m* sale → **household, wash** **2** COMP [*sheet*] de fil, pur fil; [*suit, thread*] de lin ► **linen basket** N panier *m* à linge ► **linen closet, linen cupboard** N armoire *f* or placard *m* à linge ► **linen paper** N papier *m* de lin

liner ['laɪnəʳ] **1** N **a** (*Naut*) paquebot *m* de grande ligne, liner *m* → **airliner, Atlantic** **b** (*also* **dustbin** ~) sac *m* à poubelle **c** → **eyeliner** **d** (*US*) [*of record*] pochette *f* **2** COMP ► **liner note** N (*US*) texte *m* (sur pochette de disque)

linesman ['laɪnzmən] N (*pl* **-men**) (*Sport, Tennis*) juge *m* de ligne; (*Ftbl, Rugby*) juge *m* de touche

ling¹ [lɪŋ] N (= *heather*) bruyère *f*

ling² [lɪŋ] N (*pl* **ling** or **lings**) **a** (= *sea fish*) lingue *f*, julienne *f* **b** (= *freshwater fish*) lotte *f* de rivière

linger ['lɪŋgəʳ] VI (*also* ~ **on**) [*person*] (= *wait behind*) s'attarder, rester (en arrière); (= *take one's time*) prendre son temps; (= *dawdle*) traîner, lambiner*; [*smell, pain*] persister; [*tradition, memory*] persister, subsister; [*doubt*] subsister; the others had gone, but he ~ed (on) les autres étaient partis, lui restait en arrière or s'attardait; after the accident he ~ed (on) for several months (*before dying*) après l'accident il a traîné quelques mois avant de mourir; he always ~s behind everyone else il est toujours derrière tout le monde, il est toujours à la traîne; don't ~ about or around ne lambine pas*, ne traîne pas; to ~ over a meal rester longtemps à table, manger sans se presser; I let my eye ~ on the scene j'ai laissé mon regard s'attarder sur la scène; to ~ on a subject s'attarder or s'étendre sur un sujet

lingerie ['lænʒəriː] N (*NonC*) lingerie *f*

lingering ['lɪŋgərɪŋ] ADJ [*look*] long (longue *f*), insistant; [*doubt*] qui subsiste (encore); [*hope*] faible; [*death*] lent

lingo* ['lɪŋgəʊ] N (*pl* **lingoes**) (*pej*) (= *language*) langue *f*; (= *jargon*) jargon *m*; I had a hard time in Spain because I don't speak the ~ j'ai eu du mal en Espagne parce que je ne cause* pas la langue

lingua franca ['lɪŋgwə'fræŋkə] N (*pl* **lingua francas** or **linguae francae** ['lɪŋgwiː'frænsiː]) langue *f* véhiculaire, lingua franca *f inv*

linguist ['lɪŋgwɪst] N linguiste *mf*; I'm no great ~ je ne suis pas vraiment doué pour les langues

linguistic [lɪŋ'gwɪstɪk] **1** ADJ linguistique **2** COMP ► **linguistic atlas** N atlas *m* linguistique ► **linguistic borrowing** N (= *item borrowed*) emprunt *m*; (= *process*) emprunts *mpl* ► **linguistic geography** N géographie *f* linguistique ► **linguistic philosophy** N philosophie *f* linguistique

linguistically [lɪŋ'gwɪstɪkəlɪ] ADV linguistiquement

linguistics [lɪŋ'gwɪstɪks] [1] N (NonC) linguistique f → **comparative** [2] COMP [book, degree, professor] de linguistique; [student] en linguistique

liniment ['lɪnɪmənt] N liniment m

lining ['laɪnɪŋ] N [of clothes, bag, box] doublure f; (Tech) revêtement m; [of brakes] garniture f; [of stomach] paroi f; ~ **paper** papier m d'apprêt; (for drawers) papier m à tapisser → **silver**

▼ **link** [lɪŋk] [1] N [a] [of chain] maillon m
[b] (= connection) lien m, liaison f; (= interrelation) rapport m, lien m; (= bonds) lien m, relation f; **a new rail** ~ une nouvelle liaison ferroviaire; **there must be a** ~ **between the two phenomena** il doit y avoir un lien or un rapport entre ces deux phénomènes; **he served as** ~ **between management and workers** il a servi de lien or d'intermédiaire entre la direction et les ouvriers; **cultural** ~**s** liens mpl culturels, relations fpl culturelles; ~**s of friendship** liens mpl d'amitié; **he broke off all** ~**s with his friends** il a cessé toutes relations avec ses amis, il a rompu tous les liens avec ses amis → **cufflink, missing, weak**
[2] VT [a] (physically) lier; **to** ~ **arms** se donner le bras
[b] (= establish communication between) relier; (fig) téléphone; ~**ed by rail/by telephone** reliés par (la) voie ferrée/par téléphone; ~**ed (together) in friendship** liés d'amitié; **the two companies are now** ~**ed (together)** ces deux sociétés sont maintenant liées or associées
[c] (= establish logical connection between) établir un lien or rapport entre; **to** ~ **sth with sb** établir un lien entre qch et qn; **the police are not** ~**ing him with the murder** la police n'a établi aucun rapport entre lui et le meurtre; **this is closely** ~**ed to our sales figures** ceci est étroitement lié à nos chiffres de vente; **smoking and lung cancer are closely** ~**ed** le tabac et le cancer des poumons sont étroitement liés
[3] COMP ► **linking consonant** N (Phon) consonne f de liaison ► **linking verb** N (Ling) verbe m copulatif, copule f ► **link road** N (Brit) route f de jonction ► **link-up** N (gen) lien m, rapport m; (Rad, TV) (= connection) liaison f; (= programme) émission f en duplex; (Space) jonction f; **there is no apparent** ~**-up between the two cases** il n'y a pas de rapport apparent or de lien apparent entre les deux affaires; **is there any** ~**-up between our company and theirs?** y a-t-il un lien entre notre entreprise et la leur?
► **link together** [1] VI s'unir, se rejoindre [2] VT SEP [+ two objects] unir, joindre; (by means of a third) relier → **link 2b**
► **link up** [1] VI [persons] se rejoindre; [firms, organizations etc] s'associer; [spacecraft] opérer l'arrimage; [roads, railway lines] se rejoindre, se rencontrer; **they** ~**ed up with the other group** ils ont rejoint l'autre groupe [2] VT SEP [a] (Rad, Telec, TV) relier, assurer la liaison entre [b] [+ spacecraft] opérer l'arrimage de [3] ~**-up** → **link**

linkage ['lɪŋkɪdʒ] N [a] (= connection) lien m, relation f [b] (Tech) tringlerie f, transmission f par tringlerie [c] (Bio) linkage m

linkman ['lɪŋkmæn] N (pl **-men**) (esp US TV, Rad) présentateur m

links [lɪŋks] NPL (terrain m de) golf m, links mpl

linnet ['lɪnɪt] N linotte f

lino* ['laɪnəʊ] N (Brit) (ABBR = **linoleum**) lino m; ~ **cut** gravure f sur linoléum

linoleum [lɪ'nəʊlɪəm] N linoléum m

Linotype® ['laɪnəʊtaɪp] N linotype f

linseed ['lɪnsiːd] N (NonC) graines fpl de lin; ~ **oil** huile f de lin

lint [lɪnt] N (NonC) [a] (Med) tissu m ouaté (pour pansements); **a small piece of** ~ une compresse, un petit pansement ouaté [b] (US

= fluff) peluches fpl; **a piece** or **speck of** ~ une peluche

lintel ['lɪntl] N linteau m

Linus ['laɪnəs] N (esp US) ~ **blanket*** couverture f sécurisante (pour jeune enfant)

lion ['laɪən] [1] N lion m; (fig = person) personnage m en vue, célébrité f; (Astrol, Astron) **the Lion** le Lion; **to get** or **take the** ~**'s share** se tailler la part du lion; (fig) **to put one's head in the** ~**'s mouth** se jeter or se précipiter dans la gueule du loup; (fig) **to throw sb to the** ~**s** abandonner qn à son sort, jeter or livrer qn en pâture → **beard, mountain, Richard** [2] COMP ► **lion cub** N lionceau m ► **lion-hearted** ADJ d'un courage de lion ► **lion-hunter** N (fig) **she is a** ~**-hunter*** elle cherche toujours à avoir des célébrités comme invités ► **lion-tamer** N dompteur m, -euse f de lions

lioness ['laɪənɪs] N lionne f

lionize ['laɪənaɪz] VT [+ person] aduler, stariser*

lip [lɪp] [1] N [a] (Anat) lèvre f; [of dog etc] babine f; (fig) **on every** ~ or **everyone's** ~**s** sur toutes les lèvres
[b] (= edge) [of jug] bec m; [of cup, saucer] rebord m; [of crater] bord m; [of wound] bord m, lèvre f
[c] (* = insolence) culot* m, insolences fpl; **less of your** ~! ne sois pas insolent! → **bite, button, stiff**
[2] COMP ► **lip balm** N (esp US) = **lip salve** ► **lip gloss** N brillant m à lèvres ► **lip pencil** N crayon m à lèvres ► **lip-read** VT lire sur les lèvres ► **lip-reading** N lecture f sur les lèvres ► **lip salve** N (Brit) pommade f rosat, baume m pour les lèvres ► **lip service** N **he pays** ~ **service to socialism but ...** à l'écouter on dirait qu'il est socialiste mais ...; **he only pays** ~ **service to socialism** il n'est socialiste qu'en paroles; **that was merely** ~ **service on his part** il ne l'a dit que pour la forme, il l'a dit du bout des lèvres ► **lip-smacking*** ADJ [pleasure, satisfaction, relish] vif

lipase ['laɪpeɪs] N lipase f

lipid ['laɪpɪd] N lipide m

liposuction ['lɪpəʊ,sʌkʃən] N lipo-aspiration f, liposuccion f

-lipped [lɪpt] ADJ (in compounds) dry-lipped aux lèvres sèches → **thick**

lippy* ['lɪpɪ] ADJ insolent

lipstick ['lɪpstɪk] N (NonC) (= substance) rouge m à lèvres; (= stick) (bâton m or tube m de) rouge m à lèvres

lip-sync(h) ['lɪp,sɪŋk] [1] VI (= sing) chanter en play-back; (= speak) doubler des films [2] VT (= sing) chanter en play-back; (= speak) doubler; **to** ~ **sb's words** doubler qn [3] N play-back m

liquefaction [,lɪkwɪ'fækʃən] N liquéfaction f

liquefied ['lɪkwɪfaɪd] ADJ liquéfié; ~ **natural gas** gaz m naturel liquéfié

liquefy ['lɪkwɪfaɪ] [1] VT liquéfier [2] VI se liquéfier

liqueur [lɪ'kjʊə] [1] N liqueur f [2] COMP ► **liqueur brandy** N fine (champagne) f ► **liqueur chocolates** NPL chocolats mpl à la liqueur ► **liqueur glass** N verre m à liqueur

liquid ['lɪkwɪd] [1] ADJ [a] (= not solid etc) [substance] liquide; [container] pour (les) liquides; ~ **air/oxygen** air m/oxygène m liquide; ~ **ammonia** ammoniaque m (liquide); (Comput) ~ **crystal** cristal m liquide; ~ **crystal display** affichage m à cristaux liquides; ~ **diet** régime m (exclusivement) liquide; (hum) **to have a** ~ **lunch** faire de l'alcool en guise de déjeuner; ~ **measure** mesure f de capacité pour les liquides; (for corrections) **Liquid Paper**® correcteur m liquide; (Pharm) ~ **paraffin** huile f de paraffine or de vaseline; ~ **petroleum gas** GPL m, gaz m de pétrole liquéfié [b] (fig) [eyes, sky]

limpide, clair; [sound, voice] limpide, harmonieux; (Phon) liquide; (Fin) ~ **assets** liquidités fpl, disponibilités fpl [2] N (= fluid) liquide m; (Ling) liquide f

liquidate ['lɪkwɪdeɪt] VT [a] (Fin, Jur) liquider; (Jur) ~**d damages** dommages-intérêts mpl préalablement fixés (par les parties) [b] (* = kill) liquider*

liquidation [,lɪkwɪ'deɪʃən] N (Fin, Jur) liquidation f; [of debt] remboursement m; **to go into** ~ déposer son bilan

liquidator ['lɪkwɪ,deɪtə] N (Jur) ≈ liquidateur m

liquidity [lɪ'kwɪdɪtɪ] N (Econ) liquidité f; (Fin) disponibilités fpl de trésorerie [2] COMP ► **liquidity cushion** N (Fin) volant m de trésorerie

liquidize ['lɪkwɪdaɪz] VT liquéfier; (Culin) passer au mixer or mixeur

liquidizer ['lɪkwɪdaɪzə] N (Brit Culin) mixer m, mixeur m

liquor ['lɪkə] [1] N [a] (esp US) (= alcoholic drink) boissons fpl alcoolisées; (= spirits) spiritueux m, alcool m; (US) **to be the worse for** ~ être soûl or ivre; **he can't hold his** ~ il ne supporte pas l'alcool [b] (Culin) liquide m [2] COMP ► **liquor license** N (US) licence f de débit de boissons ► **liquor store** N (US) magasin m de vins et spiritueux → LICENSING LAWS
► **liquor up*** (US) [1] VI se pinter* [2] VT SEP **to** ~ **sb up** faire trop boire qn, soûler* qn

liquorice ['lɪkərɪs] (Brit) [1] N (Bot) réglisse f; (= sweet) réglisse m [2] COMP ► **liquorice all-sorts** NPL (gen Brit) bonbons mpl assortis au réglisse ► **liquorice root** N bois m de réglisse ► **liquorice stick** N bâton m de réglisse

lira ['lɪərə] N (pl **lire** ['lɪərɪ]) lire f

Lisbon ['lɪzbən] N Lisbonne

lisp [lɪsp] [1] VI zézayer, zozoter* [2] VT (also ~ out) dire en zézayant; **"please don't say that," she** ~**ed coyly** «s'il vous plaît, ne dites pas cela» dit-elle en minaudant [3] N zézaiement m; **... she said with a** ~ ... dit-elle en zézayant; **to speak with** or **have a** ~ zézayer, zozoter*, avoir un cheveu sur la langue*

lissom(e) ['lɪsəm] ADJ souple, agile

list[1] [lɪst] [1] N liste f; (Comm) catalogue m; **your name isn't on the** ~ votre nom ne figure pas sur la liste; **you can take me off the** ~ vous pouvez me rayer de la liste; (lit) **you're (at the) top/bottom of the** ~ vous êtes en tête/en fin de liste; **that's at the top of my** ~ je le ferai en priorité → **active, civil, danger**
[2] VT (= make list of) faire or dresser la liste de; (= write down) inscrire; (= produce list of: Comput) lister; (= enumerate) énumérer; **your name isn't** ~**ed** votre nom n'est pas inscrit, votre nom n'est pas sur la liste; (Comm) **it isn't** ~**ed** cela ne figure pas au catalogue; **an airgun is** ~**ed as a weapon** les fusils à air comprimé sont classés parmi les armes; **"airgun" is** ~**ed under "air"** « airgun » se trouve sous « air »; (St Ex) **the shares are** ~**ed at 85 francs** les actions sont cotées 85 F; (St Ex) ~**ed on the Stock Exchange** coté en Bourse
[3] COMP ► **listed building** N (Brit) monument m classé or historique ► **listed company** N société f cotée en Bourse ► **listed securities** NPL (St Ex) valeurs fpl inscrites or admises à la cote officielle, valeurs fpl cotées en Bourse ► **list price** N (Comm) prix m catalogue

list[2] [lɪst] [1] VI (= lean) donner de la bande, gîter; **the ship is** ~**ing badly** le bateau gîte dangereusement; **to** ~ **to port** gîter or donner de la bande sur bâbord; ~**ing** inclinaison f; **to have a** ~ gîter; **to have a** ~ **of 20°** gîter de 20°, donner 20° de gîte or de bande

listen ['lɪsn] 1 VI a écouter; ~ to me écoute-moi → b; ~! écoute!; you never ~ to a word I say! tu n'écoutes jamais ce que je dis!; to ~ to the radio écouter la radio; you are ~ing to the BBC vous êtes à l'écoute de la BBC; to ~ for [+ voice, remark, sign] guetter; [+ footsteps] guetter le bruit de; ~ for the telephone while I'm out réponds au téléphone pendant mon absence → half b (= heed) écouter; ~ to your father écoute ton père; (as threat) ~ to me! écoute-moi bien!; ~*, I can't stop to talk now but ... écoute, je n'ai pas le temps de parler tout de suite mais ...; he wouldn't ~ to reason il n'a pas voulu entendre raison; when I asked him to stop, he would not ~ quand je lui ai demandé d'arrêter, il n'a rien voulu entendre 2 N to have a ~* écouter (to sth qch).

▸ **listen in** VI a (Rad†) être à l'écoute, écouter b (= eavesdrop) écouter; (secretly) to ~ in on sth or to sth écouter qch secrètement; I should like to ~ in to your discussion j'aimerais assister à votre discussion
▸ **listen out for** VT FUS [+ voice, remark, sign] guetter; [+ footsteps] guetter le bruit de
▸ **listen up** VI (esp US) écouter

listener ['lɪsnər] N (gen) personne f qui écoute; (to speaker, radio etc) auditeur m, -trice f; the ~s l'auditoire m, le public; she's a good ~ elle sait écouter

listening ['lɪsnɪŋ] 1 N écoute f; good ~ is good parenting il faut savoir écouter ses enfants; he did all the talking, I did all the ~ il a monopolisé la parole et moi, je me suis contenté d'écouter 2 COMP ▸ listening device N dispositif m d'écoute ▸ listening post N (Mil) poste m d'écoute

listeria [lɪ'stɪərɪə] N listéria f

listeriosis [lɪ,stɪərɪ'əʊsɪs] N listériose f

listing ['lɪstɪŋ] 1 N (gen, also Comput) listage m; (St Ex) inscription f à la cote officielle; the TV ~s les programmes mpl de télévision 2 COMP ▸ listings magazine N (gen) guide m des spectacles et distractions; (TV) magazine m de télévision

listless ['lɪstlɪs] ADJ (= without energy) sans énergie, mou (molle f); to feel ~ se sentir sans énergie or ressort; the heat made him ~ la chaleur lui enlevait son énergie; a day of ~ trading on the world's stock markets une journée morose sur les marchés financiers mondiaux

listlessly ['lɪstlɪslɪ] ADV [say, behave] avec apathie

listlessness ['lɪstlɪsnɪs] N manque m d'énergie

lists [lɪsts] NPL (Hist) lice f; (lit, fig) to enter the ~ entrer en lice

lit [lɪt] 1 VB pt, ptp of light¹ 2 ADJ éclairé, illuminé; the street was very badly ~ la rue était très mal éclairée; ~ up* (= drunk) parti*, paf* inv

lit.¹·* [lɪt] N a ABBR = literature b (ABBR = literary) littér

lit.² (ABBR = literal(ly)) lit

litany ['lɪtənɪ] N litanie f; (Rel) the Litany les litanies

litchi ['laɪ'tʃiː] N = lychee

liter ['liːtər] N (US) = litre

literacy ['lɪtərəsɪ] 1 N [of person] fait m de savoir lire et écrire; [of population] degré m d'alphabétisation; his ~ was not in doubt personne ne doutait du fait qu'il savait lire et écrire; universal ~ is one of the principal aims l'un des buts principaux est de donner à tous la capacité de lire et d'écrire; there is a high/low degree of ~ in that country le degré d'alphabétisation est élevé/bas dans ce pays; many adults have problems with ~ de nombreux adultes ont du mal à lire et à écrire 2 COMP ▸ literacy campaign N campagne f d'alphabétisation or contre l'illettrisme

▸ **literacy project**, **literacy scheme** N projet m d'alphabétisation ▸ **literacy test** N test m mesurant le niveau d'alphabétisation

literal ['lɪtərəl] 1 ADJ a (= basic) [meaning] littéral; in the ~ sense (of the word) au sens propre du terme b (= verbatim) [translation] littéral, mot pour mot; [interpretation] littéral; to be very ~ about sth prendre qch au pied de la lettre → literal-minded c (= absolute) the ~ truth l'entière or la pure vérité; it was a ~ fact c'était un fait; the drought has meant ~ starvation for millions la sécheresse a réduit littéralement à la famine des millions de gens 2 COMP ▸ literal-minded ADJ prosaïque, sans imagination ▸ literal-mindedness N manque m d'imagination

literally ['lɪtərəlɪ] ADV [translate, believe, understand] littéralement; to take sb/sth ~ prendre qn/qch au pied de la lettre; he interpreted the message ~ il a interprété le message au pied de la lettre or dans son sens littéral; I'm ~* dumbstruck by the news je suis littéralement* assommé par cette nouvelle

literary ['lɪtərərɪ] 1 ADJ littéraire; a ~ man un lettré; ~ types* amateurs mpl de littérature 2 COMP ▸ literary agent N agent m littéraire ▸ literary critic N critique mf littéraire ▸ literary criticism N critique f littéraire ▸ literary editor N rédacteur m, -trice f littéraire ▸ literary theory N théorie f littéraire

literate ['lɪtərɪt] ADJ a (= able to read etc) qui sait lire et écrire; (= educated) instruit; (= cultured) cultivé; few of them are ~ peu d'entre eux savent lire et écrire; highly ~ très instruit or cultivé b (fig = competent) to be economically/scientifically etc ~ avoir des connaissances de base en économie/sciences etc → computer

literati [lɪtə'rɑːtiː] NPL gens mpl de lettres, lettrés mpl

literature ['lɪtərɪtʃər] N (NonC) a (= literary works) littérature f; 18th-century French ~ la littérature française du 18e siècle; the ~ of ornithology la littérature or la bibliographie de l'ornithologie b (= documentation) documentation f; travel/educational ~ documentation f sur les voyages/pédagogiques; sales ~ brochures fpl publicitaires

lithe [laɪð] ADJ [person, body, movement] souple, agile

lithium ['lɪθɪəm] N lithium m

litho* ['laɪθəʊ] N (ABBR = lithograph) litho* f

lithograph ['lɪθəʊɡrɑːf] 1 N lithographie f (estampe) 2 VT lithographier

lithographer [lɪ'θɒɡrəfər] N lithographe mf

lithographic [ˌlɪθə'ɡræfɪk] ADJ lithographique

lithography [lɪ'θɒɡrəfɪ] N (NonC) lithographie f (procédé)

Lithuania [ˌlɪθjʊ'eɪnɪə] N la Lituanie

Lithuanian [ˌlɪθjʊ'eɪnɪən] 1 ADJ lituanien 2 N a Lituanien(ne) m(f) b (Ling) lituanien m

litigant ['lɪtɪɡənt] N (Jur) plaideur m, -euse f

litigate ['lɪtɪɡeɪt] 1 VI plaider 2 VT mettre en litige, contester

litigation [ˌlɪtɪ'ɡeɪʃən] N litige m

litigator ['lɪtɪɡeɪtər] N (Jur) avocat-conseil m

litigious [lɪ'tɪdʒəs] ADJ (Jur) litigieux; [person] (= given to litigation) procédurier, chicaneur; (= argumentative etc) chicanier

litmus ['lɪtməs] 1 N (Chem) tournesol m; ~ (paper) papier m de tournesol 2 COMP ▸ litmus test N (lit) réaction f au (papier de) tournesol; (fig) test m décisif

litre, liter (US) ['liːtər] N litre m; ~ bottle (bouteille f d')un litre m

litter ['lɪtər] 1 N a (NonC) (= rubbish) détritus mpl; (dirtier) ordures fpl; (= papers) vieux papiers mpl; (left after picnic etc) papiers mpl gras; (on basket etc) "~" « papiers (SVP) »; (on

notice) "(leave) no ~" « prière de ne pas laisser de détritus » b (= untidy mass) fouillis m; a ~ of books un fouillis or un fatras de livres c (Zool = offspring) portée f d (Agr = bedding) litière f e (= stretcher) civière f; (= couch) litière f f cat ~ litière f (pour chats) 2 VT a [person] [+ room] mettre du désordre dans, mettre en désordre; [+ countryside] laisser des détritus dans; he ~ed the floor with all his football gear il a éparpillé ses affaires de football par terre b (gen pass) [rubbish, papers] joncher (with de); the floor was ~ed with paper des papiers jonchaient le sol; glass from broken bottles ~ed the pavements ◊ the pavements were ~ed with glass from broken bottles les trottoirs étaient jonchés de tessons de bouteilles; ~ed with mistakes bourré de fautes; the desk was ~ed with books le bureau était couvert or encombré de livres; the streets were ~ed with corpses les rues étaient jonchées de cadavres; the road is ~ed with obstacles cette route est parsemée d'obstacles; a field ~ed with mines un champ truffé de mines 3 VI (Zool) mettre bas 4 COMP ▸ litter basket, litter bin N (Brit) poubelle f ▸ litter box N (US) = litter tray ▸ litter tray N (esp Brit) caisse f à litière

litterbug* ['lɪtəbʌɡ], **litter-lout*** ['lɪtəlaʊt] N (pej) personne qui jette des détritus par terre; ~s should be fined on devrait mettre à l'amende ces cochons* qui jettent des détritus n'importe où; all these ~s who foul up camp sites tous ces cochons* qui jettent leurs détritus dans les campings

little¹ ['lɪtl] 1 ADJ petit; a ~ present un petit cadeau; a ~ cat un petit chat; when I was ~ quand j'étais petit; she had a ~ girl yesterday elle a eu une petite fille hier; here's a ~ something for yourself* voilà un petit quelque chose* pour vous; a ~ old woman une petite vieille; poor ~ thing! pauvre petit(e)!; (patronizing) she's a dear ~ thing c'est une jolie petite fille; what an annoying ~ man! ce qu'il est agaçant, ce type!; the ~ ones (= children) les petits mpl; (hum, gen patronizing) the ~ woman (= wife) ma (or ta etc) petite femme; it's always the ~ man who suffers (= small trader) ce sont toujours les petits (commerçants) qui patient; he's quite a or the ~ gentleman! qu'il est bien élevé ce petit!; we went for a ~ holiday nous sommes partis quelques jours (en vacances); I'll pay you a ~ visit je passerai rapidement te voir; (pej) who knows what's going on in his ~ mind qui sait ce qui se passe dans son esprit; all his dirty ~ jokes toutes ses plaisanteries cochonnes*

2 COMP ▸ little auk N (Orn) mergule m (nain) ▸ little end N (Aut) pied m de bielle ▸ Little Englander N (Brit) a (Hist) Anglais opposé à l'expansion de l'empire britannique b (= chauvinistic) Anglais(e) m(f) chauvin(e) et insulaire; (= anti-European) Anglais(e) m(f) anti-européen(ne) ▸ little finger N petit doigt m, auriculaire m ▸ little green men* NPL (hum = aliens) petits hommes mpl verts, extraterrestres mpl ▸ little hand N [of clock] petite aiguille f ▸ Little League N (US Sport) championnat de baseball pour les moins de 12 ans ▸ little owl N (Orn) (chouette f) chevêche f ▸ the little people NPL (Ir = fairies) les fées fpl, les lutins mpl ▸ little toe N petit orteil m

little² ['lɪtl]

compar less, superl least
| 1 ADJECTIVE | 3 ADVERB |
| 2 PRONOUN | 4 SET STRUCTURES |

1 ADJECTIVE
= not much peu de; there is ~ hope of finding

survivors il y a peu d'espoir de retrouver des survivants; **I have very ~ money** j'ai très peu d'argent; **he gave me too ~ money** il m'a donné trop peu d'argent; **I have ~ money left** il me reste peu d'argent, il ne me reste pas beaucoup d'argent; **so ~ time** si peu de temps; **I have ~ time for reading** je n'ai pas beaucoup *or* je n'ai guère le temps de lire; **with no ~ trouble/difficulty/satisfaction** avec beaucoup de mal/difficulté/satisfaction

♦ **a little ...** (= *some*) un peu de ...; **I have a ~ money left** il me reste un peu d'argent; **would you like a ~ milk in your tea?** voulez-vous une goutte de lait dans votre thé?; **a ~ bit (of)** un peu (de); **we're having a ~ (bit of) trouble** nous avons un petit problème *or* quelques difficultés

2 PRONOUN

a = not much peu, pas grand-chose; **he reads ~** il lit peu; **so ~ of what he says is true** il y a si peu de vrai dans ce qu'il dit; **he lost weight because he ate so ~** il a perdu du poids parce qu'il mangeait si peu; **so ~ of the population is literate** une proportion si infime de la population est alphabétisée, la population est si peu alphabétisée; **I know too ~ about him to have an opinion** je le connais trop mal pour me former une opinion; **there was ~ anyone could do** il n'y avait pas grand-chose à faire; **he did ~ to help** il n'a pas fait grand-chose pour aider; **he did very ~** il n'a vraiment pas fait grand-chose; **he had ~ to say** il n'avait pas grand-chose à dire; **I had ~ to do with it** je n'ai pas eu grand-chose à voir là-dedans; **that has very ~ to do with it!** ça n'a pas grand-chose à voir!; **however ~ you give, we'll be grateful** même si vous ne donnez pas grand-chose, nous vous serons reconnaissants; **I see ~ of her nowadays** je ne la vois plus beaucoup; **he had ~ or nothing to say about it** il n'avait pratiquement rien à dire là-dessus

b = small amount the **~ I have seen is excellent** le peu que j'en ai vu est excellent; **I did what ~ I could** j'ai fait ce que j'ai pu; **every ~ helps** (= *gift*) tous les dons sont les bienvenus; **it's all I can do — every ~ helps!** c'est tout ce que je peux faire — c'est toujours ça!

♦ **a little** (= *a certain amount*) un peu; **give me a ~** donne-m'en un peu; **I'd like a ~ of everything** je voudrais un peu de tout; **I know a ~ about stamp collecting** je m'y connais un peu en philatélie; (= *a certain time*) **they'll have to wait a ~** ils vont devoir attendre un moment; **after/for a ~** (*time* *or* *while*) au bout d'un/pendant un moment

3 ADVERB

a = hardly, scarcely, not much they spoke very **~ on the way home** ils n'ont pas dit grand-chose sur le chemin du retour; **it's ~ better now he's rewritten it** ça n'est pas beaucoup *or* ça n'est guère mieux maintenant qu'il l'a réécrit; **it's ~ short of folly** ça frise la folie; **~ more than a month ago** il y a à peine plus d'un mois; **a ~-known work by Corelli** un morceau peu connu de Corelli; **his work is ~ performed these days** on ne joue plus beaucoup ses œuvres aujourd'hui; **however ~ you like it** you'll have to go même si ça ne te plaît pas, il va falloir que tu y ailles

♦ **a little ...** (= *slightly, somewhat*) un peu ...; **she is a ~ tired** elle est un peu fatiguée; **a ~ too big** un peu trop grand; **a ~ more** un peu plus, encore un peu; **a ~ less** un peu moins; **a ~ more slowly** un peu plus lentement; **a ~ later** un peu plus tard; **a ~ more/less cream** un peu plus de/moins de crème; (*frm* *or* *hum*) **he was not a ~ surprised** il a été pour le moins surpris; **he spoke a ~ harshly** il a eu des propos un peu trop durs; **she reacted a ~ unreasonably** elle ne s'est pas montrée très raisonnable

b = not at all he **~ imagined that ...** il était loin de s'imaginer que ...; **~ did he think that ...** il était loin de se douter que ...

c = rarely rarement, peu souvent; **I see him/it happens very ~** je le vois/cela arrive très rarement *or* très peu souvent; **I watch television very ~ nowadays** je ne regarde plus beaucoup *or* plus très souvent la télévision

4 SET STRUCTURES

♦ **as little as**: **as ~ as possible** le moins possible; **you could get one for as ~ as £20** on peut en trouver un pour (seulement) 20 livres; **you can eat well for as ~ as 50 francs** on peut bien manger pour 50 francs; **I like him as ~ as you do** je ne l'aime pas plus que toi; **(as) ~ as I like him, I must admit that ...** bien que je ne l'aime pas beaucoup, je dois admettre que ...

♦ **little by little** petit à petit, peu à peu

♦ **to make little of sth** (= *accomplish easily*) faire qch sans aucun mal; (= *play down*) minimiser; (= *underestimate*) sous-estimer; **the sailors made ~ of loading the huge boxes** les marins chargeaient les énormes caisses sans aucun mal; **it's hard work, but the scouts make ~ of it** c'est dur mais les scouts ne s'arrêtent pas à ça; **government spokesmen have made ~ of the latest setback** les porte-parole du gouvernement ont minimisé les implications de ce dernier revers; **we've made ~ of the link between women's health and work** nous avons sous-estimé le lien entre la santé et le travail des femmes; (= *fail to exploit*) **he made ~ of his opportunities** il n'a pas tiré parti des possibilités qu'il avait

♦ **to say little for sb/sth** (= *reflect badly on*) **it says (very) ~ for him** cela n'est pas vraiment à son honneur; **it says ~ for his honesty** cela en dit long sur son honnêteté (*iro*)

littleness ['lɪtlnɪs] N petitesse *f*

littoral ['lɪtərəl] ADJ, N littoral *m*

liturgical [lɪ'tɜːdʒɪkəl] ADJ liturgique

liturgy ['lɪtədʒɪ] N liturgie *f*

livable ['lɪvəbl] ADJ [*climate, life*] supportable; [*pain*] supportable, tolérable; [*house*] habitable; **this house is not ~ (in)*** cette maison est inhabitable; **he is/is not ~ (with)*** il est facile à vivre/insupportable *or* invivable*; **her life is not ~** elle mène une vie impossible *or* insupportable

live¹ ['lɪv] **1** VI **a** (= *be alive*) vivre; (= *survive*) survivre; (*after illness, accident*) s'en sortir; **she has only six months to ~** il ne lui reste plus que six mois à vivre; **she'll never ~ to see it** elle ne vivra pas assez longtemps pour le voir; **the doctor said she would ~** le docteur a dit qu'elle s'en sortirait; **nothing could ~ in such a hostile environment** rien ne pourrait survivre dans un environnement si hostile; **he didn't ~ long after his wife died** il n'a pas survécu longtemps à sa femme; **he won't ~ long** (*general*) il n'en a plus pour longtemps; [*young person*] il ne fera pas de vieux os; **as long as I ~ I shall never leave you** je ne te quitterai pas tant que je vivrai; **I shall remember it as long as I ~** je m'en souviendrai jusqu'à mon dernier jour; **he was still living when his daughter got married** il était encore en vie quand sa fille s'est mariée; **are your parents still living?** vous avez encore vos parents?; **while his uncle ~d** du vivant de son oncle; **to ~ to be 90** vivre jusqu'à (l'âge de) 90 ans; **you'll ~ to be a hundred** vous serez centenaire; (*hum, iro*) **you'll ~!*** tu n'en mourras pas!; **she only ~s for her children/her work** elle ne vit que pour ses enfants/son travail; **he is living for the day when he will see his son again** il ne vit que pour le jour où il reverra son fils; **he just ~d for football** il ne vivait que pour le football, il n'y avait que le football dans sa vie; **I've got nothing left to ~ for** je n'ai plus de raison de vivre; **you must learn to ~ with it** il faut que tu t'y fasses *or* que tu t'en accommodes (*subj*); **he will have to ~ with that awful memory all his life** il lui faudra vivre avec cet horrible souvenir

jusqu'à la fin de ses jours; **people living with HIV and AIDS** ceux qui vivent avec la séropositivité et le sida

b (*fig* = *live on*) **her voice will ~ with me forever** je garderai toujours le souvenir de sa voix; **this night will ~ in history** cette nuit fera date (dans l'histoire)

c (= *have lifestyle*) vivre; **to ~ honestly** vivre honnêtement, mener une vie honnête; **to ~ in luxury** vivre dans le luxe; **to ~ like a king** *or* **a lord** mener grand train; **to ~ by an ideal/a principle** *etc* vivre en accord avec un idéal/un principe *etc*; **to ~ in fear/terror (of)** vivre dans la peur/la terreur (de); **you** *or* **we ~ and learn** on apprend à tout âge ■ (*PROV*) **~ and let ~** il faut se montrer tolérant; **let's ~ a little!** il faut profiter de la vie!; **if you haven't been to London you haven't ~d!*** si tu n'as pas vu Londres, tu n'as rien vu!; **you haven't ~d until you've tried real Italian spaghetti*** il n'y a rien de meilleur que de véritables spaghettis italiens → **hand, hope, style, well**

d (= *earn one's living*) gagner sa vie; **to ~ by journalism** gagner sa vie en tant que *or* comme journaliste; **to ~ by buying and selling used cars** gagner sa vie en achetant et vendant des voitures d'occasion

e (= *reside*) habiter, vivre; **where do you ~?** où habitez-vous?; **to ~ in London** habiter (à) Londres, vivre à Londres; **to ~ in a flat** habiter un appartement; **she ~s in Station Road** elle habite (dans) Station Road; **this is a nice place to ~** il fait bon vivre ici; **he ~s with his mother** il vit *or* habite avec sa mère; (*in her house*) il vit chez sa mère; **he's living with Ann** (*as man and wife*) il vit avec Ann; **he's not an easy person to ~ with** il n'est pas facile à vivre; **a house fit for a queen to ~ in** une maison princière → **fit, unfit**; **to ~ under occupation** être occupé → **sin**

2 VT vivre, mener; **to ~ a life of luxury/crime** vivre dans le luxe/le crime; **to ~ a healthy life** mener une vie saine; **to ~ a life of ease** avoir une vie facile; **to ~ life to the full** vivre pleinement sa vie, profiter au maximum de la vie; **he has ~d and breathed football since he was seven** il ne vit que pour le football depuis qu'il a sept ans; **to ~ a lie** vivre dans le mensonge; (*Theat, fig*) **to ~ the part** entrer dans la peau du personnage → **life**

3 COMP ► **lived-in** ADJ (*lit* = *inhabited*) [*house, flat etc*] habité; (*fig* = *well-worn*) [*face*] marqué par le temps ► **live-in** ADJ (*gen*) [*housekeeper etc*] à demeure; **~-in lover** petit(e) ami(e) *m(f)* avec qui l'on vit; **~-in partner** compagnon *m*, compagne *f*

► **live down** VT SEP [+ *disgrace, scandal*] faire oublier (avec le temps); **you'll never ~ it down!** jamais tu ne feras oublier ça!

► **live in** **1** VI [*servant*] être logé et nourri; [*student, doctor*] être interne **2** **~d-in** ADJ → **live¹ 3** **~-in** ADJ → **live¹**

► **live off** VT FUS **a** [+ *fruit, rice*] vivre de, se nourrir de; **to ~ off the land** vivre des ressources naturelles **b** = **live on 2c**

► **live on** **1** VI [*person*] continuer à vivre; [*tradition, memory*] rester, survivre **2** VT FUS **a** (= *feed on*) [+ *fruit, rice*] vivre de, se nourrir de; **you can't ~ on air*** on ne vit pas de l'air du temps; **she absolutely ~s on chocolate*** elle se nourrit exclusivement de chocolat; **to ~ on hope** vivre d'espérance **b** (= *subsist on*) **to ~ on £10,000 a year** vivre avec 10 000 livres par an; **we have just enough to ~ on** nous avons juste de quoi vivre; **what does he ~ on?** de quoi vit-il?, qu'est-ce qu'il a pour vivre?; **to ~ on one's salary** vivre de son salaire; **to ~ on one's capital** vivre de *or* manger son capital; **to ~ on borrowed time** être en sursis (*fig*) **c** (= *depend financially on*) [+ *person*] vivre aux dépens *or* aux crochets de

► **live out** **1** VI [*servant*] ne pas être logé; [*student, doctor*] être externe **2** VT SEP passer; **she won't ~ the year out** elle ne passera pas l'année; **he ~d out the war in the country** il a passé la durée de la guerre à la campagne ③ VT FUS (*frm*) [+ *one's destiny*] accomplir, réaliser; [+ *one's beliefs*] mettre en pratique, vivre en accord avec

▶**live through** VT FUS ⓐ (= *experience*) vivre, voir; **she has ~d through two world wars** elle a vu deux guerres mondiales; **the difficult years he has ~d through** les années difficiles qu'il a vécues ⓑ (= *survive*) supporter; **he can't ~ through the winter** il ne passera pas l'hiver; **I couldn't ~ through another day like that** je ne pourrais pas supporter *or* passer une deuxième journée comme ça

▶**live together** VI (*as man and wife*) vivre ensemble; (*as flatmates*) partager un appartement

▶**live up** VT SEP **to ~ it up*** (= *live in luxury*) mener la grande vie; (= *have fun*) mener une vie de bâton de chaise

▶**live up to** VT FUS ⓐ (= *be true to*) [+ *one's principles*] vivre en accord avec, vivre selon; [+ *one's promises*] être fidèle à, respecter ⓑ (= *be equal to*) être *or* se montrer à la hauteur de; (= *be worthy of*) répondre à, se montrer digne de; **to ~ up to sb's expectations** être *or* se montrer à la hauteur des espérances de qn; **the holiday didn't ~ up to expectations** les vacances n'ont pas été ce qu'on avait espéré; **sales have not ~d up to expectations this year** les ventes ont été décevantes cette année; **his brother's success will give him something to ~ up to** la réussite de son frère lui servira de modèle

live² [laɪv] ① ADJ ⓐ [*person, animal*] vivant, en vie; (*fig*) dynamique; **a ~ birth** une naissance vivante; (*Fishing*) **bait** vif *m* (*appât*); **a real ~ spaceman** un astronaute en chair et en os ⓑ (*Rad, TV*) (transmis *or* diffusé) en direct; **the programme was ~** cette émission était (transmise *or* diffusée) en direct; **performed before a ~ audience** joué en public; **they're a great ~ act** ils font un excellent numéro sur scène; **a CD featuring ~ recordings from her New York concert** un CD avec des morceaux du concert qu'elle a donné à New York; **"recorded ~"** « enregistré en public » ⓒ [*coal*] ardent; [*ammunition, shell, cartridge*] de combat; (= *unexploded*) non explosé ⓓ (*Elec*) **that's ~!** c'est branché!; **the switch/hair-dryer was ~** l'interrupteur/le séchoir à cheveux était mal isolé (et dangereux) → **3** ② ADV (*Rad, TV*) en direct; (= *on stage*) **to play ~** jouer sur scène; **it was broadcast ~** c'était (transmis *or* diffusé) en direct; **the match is brought to you ~ from ...** le match vous est transmis en direct depuis ...; **here, ~ from New York, is our reporter Guy Pugh** voici, en direct de New York, notre envoyé spécial Guy Pugh; (*Brit*) **to go ~** prendre l'antenne ③ COMP ▶**live rail** N (*Elec*) rail *m* conducteur ▶**live wire** N (*Elec*) fil *m* sous tension; (*fig*) **he's a (real) ~ wire*** il a un dynamisme fou ▶**live yoghurt** N yaourt *m* fermenté

liveable ['lɪvəbl] ADJ = **livable**

livelihood ['laɪvlɪhʊd] N (*NonC*) moyens *mpl* d'existence, gagne-pain *m inv*; **to earn a** *or* **one's ~** gagner sa vie; **his ~ depends on ...** son gagne-pain dépend de ...; **their principal ~ is tourism/rice** leur principale source de revenu est le tourisme/la culture du riz

liveliness ['laɪvlɪnɪs] N ⓐ (= *lively nature*) [*of person, animal, mind, language*] vivacité *f*, vitalité *f*; [*of eyes*] éclat *m*; [*of voice*] enjouement *m* ⓑ (= *lively mood*) [*of party, bar, street, debate*] animation *f*; [*of mind*] entrain *m*; [*of song, tune*] gaieté *f*

livelong ['laɪvlɒŋ] ADJ (*liter*) **all the ~ day** tout au long du jour (*liter*), toute la journée

lively ['laɪvlɪ] ADJ ⓐ (*by nature*) [*person, animal, personality*] vif, plein de vitalité; [*mind, imagi-*

nation] vif; **she took a ~ interest in everything** elle manifestait un vif intérêt pour tout ⓑ (*in mood*) [*party, bar, street, atmosphere, debate*] animé; [*person*] plein d'entrain; [*description, language, style*] vivant; [*song, tune*] entraînant, gai; **the meeting promises to be a ~ affair** la réunion va sûrement être mouvementée; (*hum*) **things were getting quite ~** ça commençait à chauffer*; **at a ~ pace** *or* **speed** à vive allure ⓒ **to look ~!** se remuer*; **come on, look ~!** allez, remue-toi!*

liven ['laɪvn] ① VT **to ~ up** [+ *person*] égayer; [+ *evening, discussion, party etc*] animer; **a bit of paint should ~ the room up** un peu de peinture égayerait la pièce ② VI **to ~ up** s'animer; **things are beginning to ~ up** ça commence à s'animer

liver ['lɪvəʳ] ① N (*Anat, Culin*) foie *m* → **lily** ② COMP ▶**liver complaint** N problème *m* de foie ▶**liver fluke** N (*Vet*) douve *f* du foie ▶**liver paste** N pâté *m* de foie ▶**liver pâté** N pâté *m* de foie ▶**liver salts** NPL ≈ Alka-Seltzer® *m* ▶**liver sausage** N saucisse *f* au pâté de foie ▶**liver spot** N (*Med*) tache *f* brune *or* de vieillesse

liveried ['lɪvərɪd] ADJ en livrée

liverish ['lɪvərɪʃ] ADJ ⓐ (= *bilious*) qui a mal au foie ⓑ (= *irritable*) de mauvais poil*, grincheux

Liverpudlian [ˌlɪvəˈpʌdlɪən] ① N **he's a ~** il est de Liverpool ② ADJ de Liverpool

liverwort ['lɪvəwɜːt] N (*Bot*) hépatique *f*, herbe *f* de la Trinité

liverwurst ['lɪvəwɜːst] N (*esp US*) = **liver sausage**; → **liver**

livery ['lɪvərɪ] ① N ⓐ [*of servant*] livrée *f* ⓑ [*of company, product*] couleurs *fpl* ⓒ **to keep a horse at ~** avoir un cheval en pension *or* en garde ② COMP ▶**livery company** N (*Brit*) corporation *f* londonienne ▶**livery man** N (*pl* **livery men**) (*in London*) membre *m* d'une corporation; (†† = *retainer*) serviteur *m* ▶**livery stable** N (*boarding*) pension *f* pour chevaux; (*hiring out*) écurie *f* de louage

lives [laɪvz] NPL *of* **life**

livestock ['laɪvstɒk] N (*NonC*) bétail et animaux de basse-cour

livid ['lɪvɪd] ADJ ⓐ (* = *furious*) [*person, expression, glare*] furieux (**at** *or* **about sth** à propos de qch); **to be ~ at** *or* **about having to do sth** être furieux de devoir faire qch; **to be ~ that ...** être furieux que ... ⓑ (= *purple*) [*bruise, scar*] violet; [*shade, hue*] livide (*liter*); [*sky*] plombé, de plomb; **~ red** rouge plombé ⓒ (*liter* = *pale, greyish*) [*face*] livide, blême; **to be ~ with rage (at sth)** être livide *or* blême de rage (contre qch)

living ['lɪvɪŋ] ① ADJ [*person*] vivant, en vie; [*language, example, faith*] vivant; [*water*] vif; **~ or dead** mort ou vif; **the (world's) greatest ~ pianist** le plus grand pianiste vivant; **a ~ death** un enfer, un calvaire; **"the Living Desert"** « le désert vivant »; **the ~ rock** le roc; **carved out of the ~ rock** taillé à même le roc *or* dans le roc; **~ fossil** fossile *m* vivant; (*fig*) **a ~ skeleton** un cadavre ambulant; **in** *or* **within ~ memory** de mémoire d'homme; (*fig*) **it's the ~ end*** c'est super* → **daylight, image, proof, soul** ② N ⓐ (= *livelihood*) vie *f*; **to earn** *or* **make a ~ by painting portraits/as an artist** gagner sa vie en peignant des portraits/en tant qu'artiste; **to work for one's ~** travailler pour gagner sa vie; **what does he do for a ~?** que fait-il dans la vie?; **he thinks the world owes him a ~** il croit que tout lui est dû → **cost** ⓑ (*NonC* = *way of life*) vie *f*; **gracious ~** vie *f* élégante *or* raffinée; **healthy ~** vie *f* saine; **~ was not easy in those days** la vie n'était pas facile en ce temps-là → **loose, standard** ⓒ (*Brit Rel*) cure *f*, bénéfice *m* ③ **the living** NPL les vivants *mpl* → **land**

④ COMP ▶**living conditions** NPL conditions *fpl* de vie ▶**the living dead** NPL (*Occultism*) les morts *mpl* vivants; (*fig*) les morts *mpl* en sursis ▶**living expenses** NPL frais *mpl* de subsistance ▶**living quarters** NPL quartiers *mpl*, logement(s) *m(pl)* ▶**living room** N salon *m*, salle *f* de séjour ▶**living space** N espace *m* vital ▶**living standards** NPL niveau *m* de vie ▶**living wage** N **they were asking for a ~ wage** ils demandaient un salaire décent; **£50 a week isn't a ~ wage** on ne peut pas vivre avec 50 livres par semaine ▶**living will** N testament *m* de vie

Livorno [lɪˈvɔːnəʊ] N Livourne

Livy ['lɪvɪ] N Tite-Live *m*

Lizard ['lɪzəd] N (*Brit Geog*) **the ~** le cap Lizard

lizard ['lɪzəd] ① N lézard *m*; (*also* **~skin**) (peau *f* de) lézard *m* ② COMP [*bag etc*] en lézard

llama ['lɑːmə] N lama *m* (*Zool*)

LLB [ˌelelˈbiː] N (ABBR = **Legum Baccalaureus**) (= *Bachelor of Laws*) ≈ licence *f* de droit

LLD [ˌelelˈdiː] N (ABBR = **Legum Doctor**) (= *Doctor of Laws*) ≈ doctorat *m* de droit

LM [elˈem] N (ABBR = **lunar module**) → **lunar**

LMS [ˌelemˈes] N (ABBR = **local management of schools**) → **local**

LMT [ˌelemˈtiː] N (*US*) (ABBR = **local mean time**) heure *f* locale

LNG N (ABBR = **liquefied natural gas**) → **liquefy**

lo [ləʊ] EXCL (*liter or hum*) regardez!; **... when lo and behold, in he walked!** ... et c'est alors qu'il est entré!; **lo and behold the result!** et voilà le résultat!

loach [ləʊtʃ] N loche *f* (de rivière)

load [ləʊd] ① N ⓐ (= *cargo, weight*) [*of person, animal, washing machine*] charge *f*; [*of lorry*] chargement *m*, charge *f*; [*of ship*] cargaison *f*; (= *weight*) (gros) poids *m*; (= *pressure*) poids *m*, pression *f*; **he was carrying a heavy ~** il était lourdement chargé; **the ~ slipped off the lorry** le chargement *or* la charge a glissé du camion; **the lorry had a full ~** le camion avait un chargement complet; **the ship had a full ~** le navire avait une cargaison complète; **under (full) ~** chargé (à plein); **I had three ~s of coal (delivered) last autumn** on m'a livré trois fois du charbon l'automne dernier; **I put another ~ in the washing machine** j'ai mis une autre charge de linge dans la machine à laver; **he was buckling under the ~ of his rucksack** il pliait sous le poids de son sac à dos ⓑ (*fig* = *burden*) fardeau *m*, charge *f*; (= *mental strain*) poids *m*; **supporting his brother's family was a heavy ~ for him** c'était pour lui une lourde charge (que) de faire vivre la famille de son frère; **he finds his new responsibilities a heavy ~** il trouve ses nouvelles responsabilités pesantes *or* lourdes; **to take a ~ off sb's mind** débarrasser qn de ce qui lui pèse (*fig*); **that's a ~ off my mind!** c'est un poids en moins!, quel soulagement! → **busload, payload, shed², work** ⓒ (*Constr, Elec, Tech, also of firearm*) charge *f* ⓓ (* *fig*) **a ~ of** un tas de, des masses de*; **~s of** des tas de*, des masses de*; **that's a ~ of rubbish!** tout ça c'est de la blague!*; **we've got ~s of time** on a tout notre temps, on a largement le temps; **he's got ~s of money** il est plein de fric*; **we've got ~s (of them) at home** nous en avons des tas* *or* des tonnes* à la maison; **there were ~s of people there** il y avait des tas de gens*; **get a ~ of this!‡** (= *look*) vise‡ un peu ça!, regarde voir!*; (= *listen*) écoute un peu ça!, écoute voir!* ② VT ⓐ [+ *lorry, ship, washing machine etc*] charger (**with** de); [+ *person*] charger; (= *overwhelm*) accabler; **the branch was ~ed (down) with pears** la branche était chargée de poires, la branche ployait sous les poires; **she was ~ed (down) with shopping** elle pliait sous le poids de ses achats; **his pockets were ~ed with sweets and toys** ses poches étaient

bourrées de bonbons et de jouets; **they ar-rived ~ed (down) with presents for us** ils sont arrivés chargés de cadeaux pour nous; **to ~ sb (down)** couvrir qn de cadeaux; **to ~ sb with honours** combler or couvrir qn d'honneurs; **we are ~ed (down) with debts** nous sommes couverts or criblés de dettes; **~ed (down) with cares** accablé de soucis; **a heart ~ed (down) with sorrow** un cœur lourd or accablé de chagrin; **the whole business is ~ed with problems** toute cette affaire présente d'énormes difficultés
b (= take on cargo of) [ship etc] **to ~ coal/grain etc** charger du charbon/du grain etc
c (= refill) [+ gun, camera, computer, file, disk] charger (**with** de, avec)
d (= weight) [+ cane etc] plomber; [+ dice] piper; **to ~ the dice against sb** défavoriser qn; **his lack of experience ~s the dice against him** son manque d'expérience joue contre lui → **loaded**
e [+ insurance premium] majorer
3 VI [lorry, ship, camera, gun] (also Comput) se charger
4 COMP ► **load-bearing** ADJ (Constr) [beam, structure] porteur ► **load factor** N (Elec) facteur m d'utilisation; (Aviat) coefficient m de remplissage ► **load line** N (Naut) ligne f de charge ► **load-shedding** N (Elec) délestage m
► **load down** VT SEP charger (**with** de) → **load 2a**
► **load up 1** VI [ship, lorry] se charger; [person] charger, ramasser son chargement; **to ~ up with sth** charger qch; (Comput) **to ~ up with or on:** [+ food, drink] se bourrer de* **2** VT SEP [+ truck, animal, person] charger (**with** de, avec)

...load [ləʊd] N (in compounds) → **carload, planeload**

loaded [ˈləʊdɪd] ADJ **a** (= full) [lorry, shelf, gun, camera] chargé (**with sth** de qch); **she was ~ (down) with parcels** elle avait les bras chargés de colis; (Comput) **~ software** logiciel m chargé → **load b** (= rich) **to be ~:** (**with money**) être plein aux as* **c** (‡ = drunk) bourré*; (through drugs) défoncé* **d** (= tendentious) [word, term, statement] lourd de sens; **that's a ~ question!** c'est une question tendancieuse! **e** (= weighted) [cane etc] plombé; [dice] pipé; (lit, fig) **the dice were ~** les dés étaient pipés; **the dice were ~ against him** il avait peu de chances de réussir; **the dice were ~ in his favour** tout jouait en sa faveur; **the situation is ~ in our favour** les faits jouent en notre faveur **f** (US Baseball) [bases] occupé

loader [ˈləʊdər] N (= person, instrument) chargeur m; (Constr) chargeuse f → **low¹**

loading [ˈləʊdɪŋ] **1** N chargement m; (street sign) **"no ~ or unloading"** «interdiction de charger et de décharger» **2** COMP ► **loading bay** N aire f de chargement

loadstar [ˈləʊdstɑːr] N = **lodestar**

loadstone [ˈləʊdstəʊn] N = **lodestone**

loaf¹ [ləʊf] **1** N (pl **loaves**) **a** (also **~ of bread**) pain m; (= round loaf) pain m rond, miche f de pain ■ (PROV) **half a ~ is better than no bread** faute de grives on mange des merles (PROV); (Brit) **use your ~!:** réfléchis un peu!, fais marcher tes méninges!* → **cottage, sandwich, slice b** sugar ~ pain m de sucre → **meat 2** COMP ► **loaf pan** N (US) = **loaf tin** ► **loaf sugar** N sucre m en pain ► **loaf tin** N moule m à pain

loaf² [ləʊf] VI (also **~ about, ~ around**) traîner, fainéanter

loafer [ˈləʊfər] N **a** (= person) flemmard(e)* m(f), tire-au-flanc* m inv **b** (= shoe) mocassin m

loam [ləʊm] N (NonC) **a** (= soil) terreau m **b** (for moulds) terre f de moulage

loamy [ˈləʊmɪ] ADJ [soil] riche en terreau

loan [ləʊn] **1** N **a** (= money) (lent) prêt m; (borrowed) emprunt m; **can I ask you for a ~?** pouvez-vous m'accorder un prêt?; (Banking) **~s and deposits** emplois mpl et ressources fpl → **raise**
b prêt m; **this picture is on ~** or **is a ~ from the city museum** ce tableau est prêté par le or est un prêt du musée municipal; **I have a car on ~ from the company** la compagnie me prête une voiture or met une voiture à ma disposition; **my assistant is on ~ to another department at the moment** mon assistant est détaché dans un autre service en ce moment; (in library) **the book is out on ~** le livre est sorti; **I have this book out on ~ from the library** j'ai emprunté ce livre à la bibliothèque; **I asked Barbara for a ~ of her car** j'ai demandé à Barbara de me prêter sa voiture; **may I have the ~ of your lawnmower?** pouvez-vous me prêter votre tondeuse à gazon?; **I can give you the ~ of it for a few days** je peux vous le prêter pour quelques jours; **he had offered the ~ of his villa at Cavalaire** il avait offert de prêter sa villa à Cavalaire
2 VT prêter (**sth to sb** qch à qn)
3 COMP ► **loan agreement** N (Fin) convention f de prêt ► **loan capital** N capital m d'emprunt ► **loan collection** N (Art etc) collection f de tableaux (or d'objets etc) en prêt ► **loan investment** N (Fin) investissement m sous forme de prêt ► **loan office** N bureau m de prêt ► **loan officer** N [of bank] gestionnaire mf de crédit ► **loan shark*** N (pej) usurier m, -ière f ► **loan translation** N (Ling) calque m ► **loan word** N (Ling) (mot m d')emprunt m

loath [ləʊθ] ADJ (frm) **to be (very) ~ to do sth** répugner à faire qch; **he was ~ to see her again** il n'était pas du tout disposé à la revoir; **I am ~ to add to your difficulties but ...** je ne voudrais surtout pas ajouter à vos difficultés mais ...; **nothing ~** très volontiers

▼ **loathe** [ləʊð] VT [+ person] détester, haïr; [+ thing] avoir en horreur; **to ~ doing sth** avoir horreur de faire qch; **he ~s being criticized** il a horreur d'être critiqué

loathing [ˈləʊðɪŋ] N (NonC) dégoût m, répugnance f; **he/it fills me with ~** il/cela me répugne or dégoûte

loathsome [ˈləʊðsəm] ADJ détestable

loathsomeness [ˈləʊðsəmnɪs] N caractère m répugnant, nature f détestable or écœurante

loaves [ləʊvz] NPL of **loaf**

lob [lɒb] **1** VT [+ stone etc] lancer (haut or en chandelle); (Tennis) **to ~ a ball** faire un lob, lober; **he ~bed the book (over) to me** il m'a lancé or balancé* le livre; (Ftbl) **to ~ the goalkeeper** lober le gardien de but **2** VI (Tennis) lober, faire un lob **3** N (Tennis) lob m

lobby [ˈlɒbɪ] **1** N **a** (= entrance hall) [of hotel] hall m; (smaller) vestibule m, entrée f; [of private house] vestibule m, entrée f; [of theatre] foyer m (des spectateurs) **b** (Brit Parl) [where MPs meet public] hall m (de la Chambre des communes où les députés rencontrent le public), ≈ salle f des pas perdus; (where MPs vote: also **division ~**) vestibule m (où les députés se répartissent pour voter) **c** (Pol = pressure group) groupe m de pression, lobby m; **the anti-vivisection ~** le groupe de pression or le lobby antivivisection **2** VT (Parl, also gen) [+ person] faire pression sur; (esp US) [+ proposal, cause] faire pression en faveur de, soutenir activement **3** VI (Pol) **to ~ for sth** faire pression pour obtenir qch **4** COMP ► **lobby correspondent** N (Brit Press) journaliste mf parlementaire

lobbyer [ˈlɒbɪər] N (US) = **lobbyist**

lobbying [ˈlɒbɪɪŋ] N (Pol) sollicitations fpl (d'un groupe de pression), pressions fpl

lobbyism [ˈlɒbɪɪzəm] N (US) = **lobbying**

lobbyist [ˈlɒbɪɪst] N (Pol) membre m d'un groupe de pression (**for** en faveur de) → **lobby**

lobe [ləʊb] N lobe m

lobelia [ləʊˈbiːlɪə] N lobélie f

lobotomize [ləʊˈbɒtəmaɪz] VT lobotomiser

lobotomy [ləʊˈbɒtəmɪ] N lobotomie f

lobster [ˈlɒbstər] **1** N (pl **lobsters** or **lobster**) homard m **2** COMP ► **lobster nets** NPL filets mpl à homards ► **lobster pot** N casier m à homards

lobule [ˈlɒbjuːl] N lobule m

local [ˈləʊkəl] **1** ADJ [custom, saying, weather forecast, newspaper, currency, train, branch, fog] local; [shops, library] du or de quartier; [wine, speciality] du pays, local; (Med) [pain] localisé; **he's a ~ man** il est du pays or du coin*; **the ~ doctor** (gen) le médecin le plus proche; (in town) le médecin du quartier; **what is the ~ situation?** (here) quelle est la situation ici?; (there) quelle est la situation là-bas?; **it adds a bit of ~ colour** ça met un peu de couleur locale; **of ~ interest** d'intérêt local; (Telec) **a ~ call** une communication locale; (Brit) **~ management of schools** gestion f des établissements scolaires par les administrations locales
2 N **a** (* = person) personne f du pays or du coin*; **the ~s** les gens du pays or du coin*; **he's one of the ~s** il est du pays or du coin* **b** (Brit* = pub) café m du coin, bistro(t)* m du coin; **my ~** le café du coin, le pub où je vais **c** (US Rail) (train m) omnibus m **d** * = **local anaesthetic e** (US = trade union branch) section f syndicale
3 COMP ► **local anaesthetic** N anesthésie f locale ► **local area network** N (Comput) réseau m local ► **local authority** N autorité f locale ♦ ADJ des autorités locales ► **local education authority** N autorité locale chargée de l'enseignement ► **local government** N administration f locale; **~ government elections** élections fpl municipales ► **local government officer, local government official** N ≈ fonctionnaire mf (de l'administration locale) ► **local radio** N radio f locale; **she works in ~ radio** elle travaille dans une radio locale ► **local time** N heure f locale

locale [ləʊˈkɑːl] N endroit m

locality [ləʊˈkælɪtɪ] N **a** (= neighbourhood) environs mpl, voisinage m; (= district) région f; **in the ~** dans les environs, dans la région; **in the immediate ~ of** tout près de **b** (= place, position) lieu m; **the ~ of the murder** le lieu du meurtre → **bump**

localize [ˈləʊkəlaɪz] VT localiser; **~d pain** douleur f localisée

locally [ˈləʊkəlɪ] ADV (gen) localement; **to live ~** habiter dans le coin; **both nationally and ~** à l'échelon tant national que local; **to be available ~** être disponible sur place; **to produce/buy sth ~** produire/acheter qch sur place; **~ grown** cultivé localement; **we deliver free ~** nous livrons gratuitement dans les environs; **this is Cirencester, known ~ as "Ciren"** c'est Cirencester, que l'on appelle ici « Ciren »; **an ugly concrete building known ~ as "the Gulag"** un bâtiment en béton très laid que les gens du coin surnomment « le goulag »

locate [ləʊˈkeɪt] **1** VT **a** (= find) [+ place, person] repérer, trouver; [+ noise, leak, cause] localiser; **I can't ~ the school on this map** je n'arrive pas à repérer or à trouver l'école sur cette carte; **have you ~d the briefcase I left yesterday?** avez-vous retrouvé la serviette que j'ai oubliée hier?; **the doctors have ~d the cause of the pain/the source of the infection** les médecins ont localisé la cause de la douleur/la source de l'infection

► **LANGUAGE IN USE:** **loathe** 7.3

b (= *situate*) [+ *factory, school etc*] situer ; **they decided to ~ the factory in Manchester** ils ont décidé d'implanter *or* de construire leur usine à Manchester ; **where is the hospital to be ~d?** où va-t-on construire l'hôpital ? ; **the college is ~d in London** le collège est situé *or* se trouve à Londres

c (= *assume to be*) situer, placer ; **many scholars ~ the Garden of Eden there** c'est là que de nombreux érudits situent *or* placent le Paradis terrestre

d (*US* = *have place to live*) **to be ~d** être installé

2 VI (*US**) s'installer

location [ləʊˈkeɪʃən] **1** N **a** (= *position*) emplacement *m* ; **a hotel set in a beautiful ~** un hôtel situé dans un endroit magnifique ; **what's your ~?** où vous trouvez-vous ? **b** (*Cine*) extérieur *m* ; **to film in foreign ~s** tourner en extérieur à l'étranger ; **on ~** en extérieur **c** (*NonC* = *finding*) [*of person, object*] repérage *m* **2** COMP (*Cine*) [*scene, shot*] en extérieur

locative [ˈlɒkətɪv] ADJ, N locatif *m*

loch [lɒx] N (*Scot*) lac *m*, loch *m* ; **Loch Lomond** le loch Lomond → **sea**

loci [ˈləʊsaɪ] NPL of **locus**

lock¹ [lɒk] **1** N **a** [*of door, box etc*] serrure *f* ; (*on steering wheel, bicycle, motorbike*) antivol *m* ; **under ~ and key** [*possessions*] sous clé ; [*prisoner*] sous les verrous ; **to put/keep sth under ~ and key** mettre/garder qch sous clé ; **to put sb under ~ and key** enfermer qn à clé ; [*prisoner*] mettre qn sous les verrous ; **to keep sb under ~ and key** garder qn enfermé à clé ; [*prisoner*] garder qn sous les verrous → **combination, pick**

b [*of gun*] (*also* **safety ~**) cran *m* de sûreté ; (*also* **gunlock**) percuteur *m* ; (*fig*) **he sold the factory ~, stock and barrel** il a vendu l'usine en bloc ; **they rejected the proposals ~, stock and barrel** ils ont rejeté les suggestions en bloc *or* toutes les suggestions sans exception ; **he has moved out ~, stock and barrel** il a déménagé en emportant tout son fourbi*

c (*Comput*) verrouillage *m*

d [*of canal*] écluse *f* → **airlock**

e (*Wrestling*) immobilisation *f* ; **to hold sb in a ~** immobiliser qn

f (*Aut*) rayon *m* de braquage ; **this car has a good ~** cette voiture braque bien *or* a un bon rayon de braquage ; **3.5 turns from ~ to ~** 3,5 tours d'une butée à l'autre

g (*Rugby*: *also* **~ forward**) (avant *m* de) deuxième ligne *f*

2 VT **a** (= *fasten*) [+ *door, suitcase, car, safe*] fermer à clé, verrouiller ; **behind ~ed doors** à huis clos ; **to ~ the stable door after the horse has bolted** prendre ses précautions trop tard ; **to ~ horns** (*lit*) [*animals*] se mettre à lutter cornes contre cornes ; (*fig*) se disputer ; **to ~ horns with sb** avoir une prise de bec avec qn

b [+ *person*] enfermer (**in** dans) ; **he got ~ed in the bathroom** il s'est trouvé enfermé dans la salle de bains

c (= *prevent use of*) [+ *mechanism*] bloquer ; (*Comput*) verrouiller ; **he ~ed the steering wheel on his car** il a bloqué la direction de sa voiture (en mettant l'antivol) ; (*Aut*: by braking*) **to ~ the wheels** bloquer les roues

d (= *grip*, *also fig*) [+ *person*] étreindre, serrer ; **she was ~ed in his arms** elle était serrée dans ses bras ; **they were ~ed in a close embrace** ils étaient unis dans une étreinte passionnée ; **the two armies were ~ed in combat** les deux armées étaient aux prises

3 VI **a** [*door*] fermer à clé **b** [*wheel, elbow, knee*] se bloquer

4 COMP ► **lock gate** N porte *f* d'écluse ► **lock keeper** N éclusier *m*, -ière *f* ► **lockup** N (*Brit* = *garage*) box *m* ; (*Brit* = *shop*) boutique *f* (*sans logement*) ; (*US** = *prison*) prison *f*,

lieu *m* de détention provisoire ; (** = *cell*) cellule *f* provisoire

► **lock away** **1** VT SEP [+ *object, jewels*] mettre sous clé ; [+ *criminal*] mettre sous les verrous ; [+ *mental patient etc*] enfermer **2** ► **~away** N → **lockaway**

► **lock in** VT SEP **a** [+ *person, dog*] enfermer (à l'intérieur) ; **to ~ o.s. in** s'enfermer (à l'intérieur) **b** (*Fin*) [+ *assets, loans*] engager (à plus d'un an)

► **lock on** VI [*spacecraft*] s'arrimer (**to** à) ; **to ~ on to sth** [*radar*] capter qch

► **lock out** **1** VT SEP **a** [+ *person*] (*deliberately*) mettre à la porte, (*by mistake*) enfermer dehors, laisser dehors (sans clé) ; **to find o.s. ~ed out** (*by mistake*) se trouver enfermé dehors, se retrouver à la porte ; (*as punishment*) se trouver mis à la porte ; **to ~ o.s. out** s'enfermer dehors ; **to ~ o.s. out of one's car** fermer la voiture en laissant les clés à l'intérieur **b** (*Ind*) [+ *workers*] fermer l'usine à, lock-outer **2** ► **~out** N → **lockout**

► **lock up** **1** VI fermer (toutes les portes) à clé ; **will you ~ up when you leave?** voulez-vous tout fermer en partant ? ; **to ~ up for the night** tout fermer pour la nuit **2** VT SEP **a** [+ *object, jewels*] enfermer, mettre sous clé ; [+ *house*] fermer (à clé) ; [+ *criminal*] mettre sous les verrous *or* en prison ; [+ *mental patient etc*] enfermer ; **you ought to be ~ed up!*** on devrait t'enfermer !, il faut te faire soigner ! **b** [+ *capital, funds*] immobiliser, bloquer (**in** dans) **3** ► **~-up** N → **lock¹**

lock² [lɒk] N [*of hair*] mèche *f* ; (= *ringlet*) boucle *f* ; **his ~s** sa chevelure, ses cheveux *mpl* ; **her curly ~s** ses boucles *fpl*

lockaway [ˈlɒkəˌweɪ] N (*Fin*) titre *m* à long terme

locker [ˈlɒkəʳ] **1** N casier *m* (*fermant à clé*) ; **the left-luggage ~s** la consigne (automatique) **2** COMP ► **locker-room** N vestiaire *m* ♦ ADJ (*fig*) [*joke etc*] de corps de garde, paillard

locket [ˈlɒkɪt] N médaillon *m* (*bijou*)

locking [ˈlɒkɪŋ] **1** ADJ [*door, container, cupboard*] qui ferme à clé, verrouillable ; (*Aut*) **~ petrol cap** bouchon *m* antivol (*pour réservoir*) **2** N (*gen, Comput*) verrouillage *m* ; (*Aut*) [*of door*] verrouillage *m*, condamnation *f*

lockjaw [ˈlɒkdʒɔː] N (*Med*) tétanos *m*

locknut [ˈlɒknʌt] N (= *washer*) contre-écrou *m* ; (*self-locking*) écrou *m* autobloquant

lockout [ˈlɒkaʊt] N (*Ind*) lock-out *m inv*

locksmith [ˈlɒksmɪθ] N serrurier *m*

loco¹* [ˈləʊkəʊ] ADJ (*esp US*) dingue*

loco²* [ˈləʊkəʊ] N (ABBR = **locomotive**) loco† *f*, locomotive *f*

locomotion [ˌləʊkəˈməʊʃən] N locomotion *f*

locomotive [ˌləʊkəˈməʊtɪv] **1** N (*Rail*) locomotive *f* **2** ADJ [*engine, power*] locomotif ; [*muscle*] locomoteur (-trice *f*) **3** COMP ► **locomotive driver, locomotive engineer** N mécanicien *m* ► **locomotive shed** N hangar *m* à locomotives ► **locomotive workshop** N (= *factory*) usine *f* de construction de locomotives ; (*for repairs*) atelier *m* de réparation de locomotives

locoweed [ˌləʊkəʊˈwiːd] N (*Bot*) sorte d'astragale

locum [ˈləʊkəm] N (*also* **~ tenens** ; *esp Brit*) suppléant(e) *m(f)* (*de prêtre ou de médecin etc*)

locus [ˈləʊkəs] N (*pl* **loci**) lieu *m*, point *m* ; (*Math*) lieu *m* géométrique

locust [ˈləʊkəst] **1** N locuste *f*, sauterelle *f* **2** COMP ► **locust bean** N caroube *f* ► **locust tree** N caroubier *m*

locution [ləˈkjuːʃən] N locution *f*

lode [ləʊd] N (*Miner*) filon *m*, veine *f*

lodestar [ˈləʊdstɑːʳ] N **a** (*Astron*) étoile *f* polaire **b** (*fig*) principe *m* directeur

lodestone [ˈləʊdstəʊn] N magnétite *f*, aimant *m* naturel

lodge [lɒdʒ] **1** N (= *small house in grounds*) maison *f* *or* pavillon *m* de gardien ; (= *porter's room in building*) loge *f* ; (*Freemasonry*) loge *f* ; (*US Ind*) section *f* syndicale ; [*of beaver*] abri *m*, gîte *m* → **hunting** **2** VT **a** [+ *person*] héberger **b** [+ *bullet*] loger **c** (*Admin, Jur*) (= *leave*) [+ *money*] déposer ; [+ *statement, report*] présenter (**with sb** à qn), déposer (**with sb** chez qn) ; (*Jur*) **to ~ an appeal** interjeter appel, se pourvoir en cassation ; **to ~ a complaint against** porter plainte contre ; (*Jur*) **documents ~d by the parties** pièces *fpl* versées aux débats par les parties **3** VI [*person*] être logé, être en pension (**with** chez) ; [*bullet*] se loger

lodger [ˈlɒdʒəʳ] N (*Brit*) (*room only*) locataire *mf* ; (*room and meals*) pensionnaire *mf* ; **to take (in) ~s** (*room only*) louer des chambres ; (*room and meals*) prendre des pensionnaires

lodging [ˈlɒdʒɪŋ] **1** N **a** (*NonC* = *accommodation*) logement *m*, hébergement *m* ; **they gave us a night's ~** ils nous ont logés *or* hébergés une nuit → **board** **b** **lodgings** NPL (= *room*) chambre *f* ; (= *flatlet*) logement *m* ; **he took ~s with Mrs Smith†** (*with meals*) il a pris pension chez Mme Smith ; (*without meals*) il a pris une chambre *or* un logement chez Mme Smith ; **he's in ~s** il vit en meublé *or* en garni† ; **to look for ~s** (*room*) chercher une chambre meublée ; (*flatlet*) chercher un logement meublé ; (*with meals*) chercher à prendre pension ; **we took him back to his ~s** nous l'avons ramené chez lui **3** COMP ► **lodging house** N pension *f*

loess [ˈləʊɪs] N lœss *m*

loft [lɒft] **1** N **a** [*of house, stable, barn*] grenier *m* → **hayloft, pigeon** **b** [*of church, hall*] galerie *f* → **organ** **2** VT **a** (*Golf*) [+ *ball*] lancer en chandelle **b** (= *send very high*) lancer très haut **3** COMP ► **loft conversion** N (*Brit*) (= *accommodation*) grenier *m* aménagé ; (*NonC* = *process, activity*) aménagement *m* de grenier

loftily [ˈlɒftɪlɪ] ADV [*say, declare, look at*] avec hauteur ; **his ~ dismissive attitude** son attitude hautaine et dédaigneuse ; **to be ~ indifferent to sb/sth** être d'une indifférence hautaine vis-à-vis de qn/qch

loftiness [ˈlɒftɪnɪs] N **a** (= *great height*) hauteur *f* **b** (*fig* = *nobility*) noblesse *f* **c** (*pej* = *haughtiness*) hauteur *f*

lofty [ˈlɒftɪ] ADJ **a** (= *high*) [*building, ceiling, mountain*] haut ; [*room*] haut de plafond ; **to rise to a ~ position in government** atteindre un poste élevé au gouvernement **b** (= *noble*) [*aim, ideal, idea*] noble **c** (*pej* = *haughty*) hautain **d** (= *elevated*) [*style, rhetoric*] élevé, noble

log¹ [lɒg] **1** N **a** (= *felled tree trunk*) rondin *m* ; (*for fire*) bûche *f* → **sleep** **b** (*Naut* = *device*) loch *m* **c** (= *book*) (*Aviat, Naut*) journal *m* de bord ; [*of lorry driver etc*] carnet *m* de route ; (*gen*) registre *m* ; **to keep the ~** tenir le journal de bord ; **to write up the ~** rédiger le journal de bord

2 VT **a** [+ *trees*] tronçonner, débiter *or* tailler en rondins

b (= *record*) (*gen*) noter, consigner ; (*Aviat, Naut*: *also* **~ up**) inscrire au journal de bord ; **details of the crime are ~ged in the computer** les données concernant le crime sont entrées dans l'ordinateur

c (*speeds*) **the ship was ~ging 18 knots** le navire filait 18 nœuds ; **the plane was ~ging 300mph** l'avion volait à 500 km/h

d (= *clock up*: *also* **~ up**) **he has ~ged 5,000 hours' flying time** il a à son actif *or* il compte 5 000 heures de vol ; **sailors often ~ 5,000 sea miles in a year** les marins font souvent 5 000 milles marins par an ; **I ~ged eight hours' work each day** j'ai travaillé huit heures par jour

3 COMP ▶ **log cabin** N cabane f en rondins ▶ **log fire** N feu m de bois ▶ **log jam** N (lit) train m de flottage bloqué; (fig) impasse f (fig) ▶ **log-rolling** N (Sport) sport de bûcheron, consistant à faire tourner avec les pieds, sans tomber, un tronc d'arbre flottant; (fig pej) échange de concessions ou de faveurs

▶**log in** (Comput) = **log on**
▶**log off** (Comput) **1** VI sortir **2** VT SEP déconnecter
▶**log on** (Comput) **1** VI entrer **2** VT SEP connecter, faire entrer dans le système
▶**log out** (Comput) = **log off**
▶**log up** VT SEP → **log¹ 2b, 2d**

log² [lɒg] N (Math) (ABBR = **logarithm**) log* m; ~ **tables** tables fpl de logarithmes

loganberry ['ləʊgənbərɪ] N framboise f de Logan

logarithm ['lɒgərɪθəm] N logarithme m

logbook ['lɒgbʊk] N **a** (Aviat, Naut etc) = **log¹ 1c** **b** (Brit Aut) ≈ carte f grise

loge [ləʊʒ] N (Theat) loge f

logger ['lɒgəʳ] N (US) bûcheron m

loggerheads ['lɒgəhedz] NPL **to be at ~ (with)** être en désaccord or à couteaux tirés (avec)

loggia ['lɒdʒɪə] N (pl **loggias** or **loggie** ['lɒdʒe]) loggia f

logging ['lɒgɪŋ] N exploitation f du bois

logic ['lɒdʒɪk] **1** N logique f; **I can't see the ~ of it** ça ne me paraît pas rationnel; (Brit fig) **to chop ~** discutailler (pej), ergoter (**with sb** avec qn) **2** COMP ▶ **logic-chopping** N (Brit fig) ergoterie f, ergotage m ▶ **logic circuit** N (Comput) circuit m logique

logical ['lɒdʒɪkəl] **1** ADJ logique; **capable of ~ thinking** capable de penser logiquement **2** COMP ▶ **logical positivism** N positivisme m logique, logicopositivisme m ▶ **logical positivist** N logicopositiviste mf

logically ['lɒdʒɪkəlɪ] ADV (possible, consistent) logiquement; (consider, examine, discuss) rationnellement; **it follows ~ (from this) that ...** il s'ensuit logiquement que ...; **the keyboard is laid out ~** le clavier est logiquement conçu or conçu avec logique; **~, I should have taken this into consideration** logiquement, j'aurais dû en tenir compte

logician [lɒ'dʒɪʃən] N logicien(ne) m(f)

logistic [lɒ'dʒɪstɪk] **1** ADJ logistique **2** **logistics** NPL logistique f

logistical [lɒ'dʒɪstɪkəl] ADJ = **logistic 1**

logistically [lɒ'dʒɪstɪkəlɪ] ADV sur le plan logistique

logo ['ləʊgəʊ] N logo m

logy* ['ləʊgɪ] ADJ (US) apathique, léthargique

loin [lɔɪn] N **a** (Culin: gen) filet m; (of veal, venison) longe f; (of beef) aloyau m **2** **loins** NPL **a** (= lower back) reins mpl, lombes mpl **b** (= groin) aine f; (euph = genitals) bas-ventre m (euph) → **gird 3** COMP ▶ **loin chop** N (Culin) côte f première

loincloth ['lɔɪnklɒθ] N pagne m (d'étoffe)

Loire [lwaʳ] N Loire f; **the ~ Valley** la vallée de la Loire; (between Orléans and Tours) le Val de Loire

loiter ['lɔɪtəʳ] VI **a** (also ~ **about** = stand around) traîner; (suspiciously) rôder **b** (Jur) **to ~ with intent** ≈ commettre un délit d'intention; (Jur) **to be charged with ~ing with intent** être accusé d'un délit d'intention
▶**loiter away** VT SEP **to ~ away one's time/days** passer son temps/ses journées à ne rien faire

loll [lɒl] VI (person) se prélasser; (head) pendre
▶**loll about, loll around** VI fainéanter, flâner
▶**loll back** VI (person) se prélasser; (head) pendre en arrière; **to ~ back in an armchair** se prélasser dans un fauteuil
▶**loll out 1** VI (tongue) pendre **2** VT SEP (+ tongue) laisser pendre

lollapalooza: [ˌlɒləpə'luːzəʳ], **lollapaloosa:**

[ˌlɒləpə'luːsəʳ] N (US) (amazing) truc* m génial; (large) truc m maous*

Lollards ['lɒlədz] NPL (Hist) Lollards mpl

lollipop ['lɒlɪpɒp] **1** N sucette f (bonbon) **2** COMP ▶ **lollipop lady***, **lollipop man*** (pl **lollipop men**) (Brit) personne chargée d'aider les écoliers à traverser la rue

LOLLIPOP LADY, LOLLIPOP MAN

On appelle **lollipop lady** et **lollipop man** une femme ou un homme placé à proximité d'une école et chargé d'aider les écoliers à traverser la rue. Vêtues d'un manteau blanc ou jaune fluorescent, ces personnes arrêtent la circulation à l'aide d'un grand panneau rond indiquant « stop » et qui rappelle par sa forme les sucettes appelées « lollipops ».

lollop ['lɒləp] VI (animal) galoper; (person) courir gauchement or à grandes enjambées maladroites; **to ~ in/out** etc entrer/sortir etc à grandes enjambées maladroites

lolly ['lɒlɪ] N **a** (Brit)* sucette f → **ice b** (NonC:* = money) fric* m, pognon* m

lollygag: ['lɒlɪgæg] VI (US) **a** (= waste time) glander: **b** (= kiss and cuddle) se peloter:

Lombard ['lɒmbəd] **1** N Lombard(e) m(f) **2** ADJ lombard

Lombardy ['lɒmbədɪ] **1** N la Lombardie **2** COMP ▶ **Lombardy poplar** N peuplier m d'Italie

London ['lʌndən] **1** N Londres **2** COMP (life) londonien, à Londres; (person, accent, street) londonien, de Londres; (taxi) londonien ▶ **London Bridge** N pont m de Londres ▶ **London pride** N (Bot) saxifrage f ombreuse, désespoir m des peintres

Londoner ['lʌndənəʳ] N Londonien(ne) m(f)

lone [ləʊn] **1** ADJ (gunman) isolé; (piper, rider) solitaire; (survivor) unique; **a ~ figure** une silhouette solitaire; **to fight a ~ battle for sth** être seul à se battre pour qch; **she was a ~ voice** elle était la seule à être de cet avis **2** COMP ▶ **lone father** N père m célibataire ▶ **lone mother** N mère f célibataire ▶ **lone parent** N père ou mère qui élève seul ses enfants ▶ **lone-parent family** N (Brit) famille f monoparentale ▶ **the lone star state** N (US) le Texas ▶ **lone wolf** N **he's a ~ wolf** c'est un (loup) solitaire

loneliness ['ləʊnlɪnɪs] N (of person, atmosphere, life) solitude f; (of house, road) (= isolated position) isolement m

lonely ['ləʊnlɪ] **1** ADJ (person, time, life, journey, job) solitaire; (village, house) isolé; (road) peu fréquenté; **it's ~ at the top** le pouvoir isole; **to feel ~** se sentir seul; **you might find London a ~ place** il se peut que vous sentiez seul or que vous souffriez de solitude à Londres **2** COMP ▶ **lonely hearts ad*** N petite annonce f de rencontre ▶ **lonely hearts club*** N club m de rencontres (pour personnes seules) ▶ **lonely hearts column*** N petites annonces fpl de rencontres

loner ['ləʊnəʳ] N solitaire mf

lonesome ['ləʊnsəm] **1** ADJ (esp US) = **lonely 2** N **all on my** (or **your** etc) **~*** tout seul, toute seule

long¹ [lɒŋ]

1 ADJECTIVE	**3** NOUN	
2 ADVERB	**4** COMPOUNDS	

1 ADJECTIVE
a in size (dress, hair, rope, distance, journey, book etc) long (longue f); **the wall is 10 metres ~** le mur fait or a 10 mètres de long; **a wall 10 metres ~** un mur de 10 mètres de long; **how is the swimming pool?** quelle est la longueur de la piscine?; **to get ~er** (queue) s'allonger; (hair) pousser; **the document is ~ on generalities and short on practicalities** le document fait une large place aux généralités et ne donne

pas beaucoup de détails pratiques; **the cooking wasn't exactly ~ on imagination*** la cuisine n'était pas très originale; (fig) **to have a ~ arm** avoir le bras long; **they were eventually caught by the ~ arm of the law** ils ont fini par être rattrapés par la justice; **a string of degrees as ~ as your arm*** (= masses of degrees) des diplômes à n'en plus finir; (fig) **to have a ~ face** avoir la mine allongée, faire triste mine; **to make** or **pull a ~ face** faire la grimace; **to be ~ in the leg** (of person) avoir de longues jambes; (of trousers) être trop long; **he's getting a bit ~ in the tooth*** il n'est plus tout jeune, il n'est plus de la première jeunesse; **not by a ~ chalk** or **shot*** loin de là; (fig) **it's a ~ shot but we might be lucky** c'est très risqué mais nous aurons peut-être de la chance; (fig) **it was just a ~ shot** il y avait peu de chances pour que cela réussisse → 4

b in distance **it's a ~ way** c'est loin; **it's a ~ way to the shops** les magasins sont loin; **we walked a ~ way** nous avons beaucoup marché; **it was a ~ 3 miles to the nearest pub** le pub le plus proche était à 5 bons kilomètres

c in time (visit, wait, weekend, look, film) long (longue f); (delay) important; **I find the days very ~** je trouve les jours bien longs; **the days are getting ~er** les jours rallongent; **to be six months ~** durer six mois; **at ~ last** enfin; **he took a ~ drink of water** il a bu beaucoup d'eau → 4; **it will be a ~ job** ça va prendre du temps; **to have a ~ memory** ne pas oublier vite; **in the ~ run** à la longue; **in the ~ term** à long terme → **long-term**; **~ time no see!*** tiens, un revenant!*, ça fait une paye!*; **to take the ~ view** penser à l'avenir; **he's not ~ for this world*** il n'en a plus pour longtemps; **the reply was not ~ in coming** la réponse n'a pas tardé à venir

◆ **a long time** longtemps; **a ~ time ago** il y a longtemps; **that was a ~, ~ time ago** il y a bien longtemps de cela; **what a ~ time you've been!** tu en as mis du temps!*; **it will be a ~ time before I see her again** je ne la reverrai pas de si tôt or pas avant longtemps; **it will be remembered for a ~ time to come** on s'en souviendra longtemps; **it'll be a ~ time before I do that again!** je ne recommencerai pas de si tôt!; **for a ~ time I had to stay in bed** j'ai dû longtemps garder le lit; **have you been studying English for a ~ time?** il y a longtemps que vous étudiez l'anglais?; **it's a ~ time since I last saw him** ça fait longtemps que je ne l'ai pas vu; **he has not been seen for a ~ time** on ne l'a pas vu depuis longtemps, cela fait longtemps qu'on ne l'a pas vu; **for a ~ time now he has been unable to work** voilà longtemps qu'il est dans l'incapacité de travailler; **you took a ~ time to get here** or **getting here** tu as mis longtemps pour or à venir; **it takes a ~ time for the drug to act** ce médicament met du temps à agir; **it took a ~ time for the truth to be accepted** les gens ont mis très longtemps à accepter la vérité

d Ling (vowel) long (longue f)

2 ADVERB
a (= a long time) longtemps; **they didn't stay ~** ils ne sont pas restés longtemps; **he didn't live ~ after that** il n'a pas survécu longtemps; **he hasn't been gone ~** il n'y a pas longtemps qu'il est parti; **it didn't take him ~ to realize that ...** il n'a pas mis longtemps à se rendre compte que ...; **are you going away for ~?** vous partez pour longtemps?; **not for ~** pas pour longtemps; **not for much ~er** plus pour très longtemps; **will you be ~?** tu en as pour longtemps?; **I won't be ~** je n'en ai pas pour longtemps; **don't be ~** dépêche-toi; **he hasn't ~ to live** il n'en a plus pour longtemps; **women live ~er than men** les femmes vivent plus longtemps que les hommes; **this method has ~ been used in industry** cette méthode est employée depuis longtemps dans l'industrie; **have you been here/been waiting ~?** vous êtes ici/vous attendez depuis longtemps?, il y a longtemps que vous êtes ici/que vous

attendez?; **these are ~-needed changes** ce sont des changements qui s'imposent depuis longtemps; **his ~-awaited reply** sa réponse (si) longtemps attendue; **I have ~ wished to say ...** il y a longtemps que je souhaite dire ...; **~ may this situation continue** espérons que cela continuera; **~ live the King!** vive le roi!; **I only had ~ enough to buy a paper** je n'ai eu que le temps d'acheter un journal; **six months at (the) ~est** six mois au plus; **so ~!** à bientôt!

b = **through all night ~** toute la nuit; **all summer ~** tout l'été; **his whole life ~** toute sa vie

c SET STRUCTURES

♦ **before long** (+ *future*) sous peu, dans peu de temps; (+ *past*) peu après

♦ **how long?** (*in time*) **how ~ will you be?** ça va te demander combien de temps?, tu vas mettre combien de temps?; **how ~ did they stay?** combien de temps sont-ils restés?; **how ~ is it since you saw him?** cela fait combien de temps que tu ne l'as pas vu?; **how ~ are the holidays?** les vacances durent combien de temps?

In the following **depuis** + *present/imperfect translates English perfect/pluperfect continuous.*

how ~ have you been learning Greek? depuis combien de temps apprenez-vous le grec?; **how ~ had you been living in Paris?** depuis combien de temps viviez-vous à Paris?, cela faisait combien de temps que vous viviez à Paris?

♦ **long ago** il y a longtemps; **how ~ ago was it?** il y a combien de temps de ça?; **as ~ ago as 1930** déjà en 1930; **of ~ ago** d'il y a longtemps; **not ~ ago** il n'y a pas longtemps, il y a peu de temps; **he arrived not ~ ago** il n'y a pas longtemps qu'il est arrivé, il vient d'arriver

♦ **long after** longtemps après; **~ after he died** longtemps après sa mort; **he died ~ after his wife** il est mort longtemps après sa femme

♦ **long before**: **~ before the war** bien avant la guerre; **~ before his wife's death** bien avant la mort de sa femme, bien avant que sa femme ne meure; **his wife had died ~ before** sa femme était morte depuis longtemps, il y avait longtemps que sa femme était morte; **you should have done it ~ before** now vous auriez dû le faire il y a longtemps; **not ~ before the war** peu (de temps) avant la guerre; **not ~ before his wife died** peu (de temps) avant la mort de sa femme, peu avant que sa femme ne meure; **she had died not ~ before** elle était morte peu de temps avant *or* auparavant

♦ **long since**: **it's not ~ since he died** ◊ **he died not ~ since*** il est mort il y a peu *or* il n'y a pas longtemps; **~ since** il y a longtemps; **he thought of friends ~ since dead** il a pensé à des amis morts depuis longtemps

♦ **any/no/a little longer**: **I can't stay any ~er** je ne peux pas rester plus longtemps; **she no ~er wishes to do it** elle ne veut plus le faire; **he is no ~er living there** il n'y habite plus; **wait a little ~er** attendez encore un peu

♦ **as long as** (*conditional*) à condition que (+ *subj*); **you can borrow it as ~ as** *or* **so ~ as John doesn't mind** vous pouvez l'emprunter à condition que John n'y voie pas d'inconvénient; (*relating to time*) **as ~ as necessary** le temps qu'il faudra; **stay (for) as ~ as you like** restez autant que *or* aussi longtemps que vous voulez; **as** *or* **so ~ as this crisis lasts** tant que durera cette crise; **as** *or* **so ~ as the war lasted** tant que dura la guerre

3 NOUN

a **the ~ and the short of it is that ...** le fin mot de l'histoire, c'est que ...

b = **syllable, beat** longue *f*

4 COMPOUNDS

▶ **long-acting** ADJ [*drug*] à effet lent et à action longue ▶ **long-chain** ADJ (*Chem*) à chaîne longue ▶ **long-dated** ADJ (*Fin*) à longue échéance ▶ **long-distance** ADJ [*race, runner*] de fond; (*Telec*) **~-distance call** appel *m*

LANGUAGE IN USE: **look** 16.2

(à) longue distance; **~-distance flight** vol *m* long-courrier; (*Brit*) **~-distance lorry driver** routier *m*; **~-distance skier** fondeur *m*, -euse *f* ♦ ADV **to call sb ~-distance** appeler qn à longue distance ▶ **long division** N (*Math*) division *f* écrite complète (*avec indication des restes partiels*) ▶ **long-drawn-out** ADJ interminable, qui n'en finit pas ▶ **long drink** N long drink *m* ▶ **long-eared** ADJ aux longues oreilles ▶ **long-established** ADJ [*business, company*] qui existe depuis longtemps; [*habit*] vieux (vieille *f*) ▶ **long fin tuna, long fin tunny** N thon *m* blanc ▶ **long-forgotten** ADJ oublié depuis longtemps ▶ **long-grain rice** N riz *m* long ▶ **long green*** N (*US* = *money*) argent *m*, fric* *m* ▶ **long-haired** ADJ [*person*] aux cheveux longs; [*animal*] à longs poils ▶ **long-haul** N transport *m* à longue distance; **~-haul airline/flight** ligne *f*/vol *m* long-courrier ▶ **long-headed** ADJ (*fig*) avisé, perspicace, prévoyant ▶ **long johns*** NPL caleçon *m* long ▶ **long jump** N (*Sport*) saut *m* en longueur ▶ **long jumper** N sauteur *m*, -euse *f* en longueur ▶ **long-lasting** ADJ durable; **to be longer-lasting** *or* **more ~-lasting** durer plus longtemps ▶ **long-legged** ADJ [*person, horse*] aux jambes longues; [*other animal, insect*] à longues pattes ▶ **long-life** ADJ [*milk*] longue conservation; [*batteries*] longue durée ▶ **long-limbed** ADJ aux membres longs ▶ **long-lived** ADJ d'une grande longévité; **women are longer-lived** *or* **more ~-lived than men** les femmes vivent plus longtemps que les hommes ▶ **long-lost** ADJ [*person*] perdu de vue depuis longtemps; [*thing*] perdu depuis longtemps ▶ **long-nosed** ADJ au nez long ▶ **long play** N (*US*) = **long-playing record** ▶ **long-playing record** N 33 tours *m* inv ▶ **long-range** ADJ [*missile, rocket, gun*] à longue portée; [*planning etc*] à long terme; **~-range plane** (*Mil*) avion *m* à grand rayon d'action; (*civil*) long-courrier *m*; **~-range weather forecast** prévisions *fpl* météorologiques à long terme ▶ **long-running** ADJ [*play*] qui tient l'affiche depuis longtemps; [*TV programme*] qui est diffusé depuis longtemps; (*TV*) **~-running series** série-fleuve *f*; [*dispute*] qui dure depuis longtemps ▶ **long shot** N (*Cine*) plan *m* général *or* d'ensemble → **1a** ▶ **long-sighted** ADJ (*Brit*) (*lit*) hypermétrope; (*in old age*) presbyte; (*fig*) [*person*] prévoyant, qui voit loin; [*decision*] pris avec prévoyance; [*attitude*] prévoyant ▶ **long-sightedness** N (*lit*) hypermétropie *f*; (*in old age*) presbytie *f*; (*fig*) prévoyance *f* ▶ **long-sleeved** ADJ à manches longues ▶ **long-standing** ADJ de longue date ▶ **long-stay car park** N parking *m* *or* parc *m* de stationnement de longue durée ▶ **long stop** N (*fig*) garde-fou *m* ▶ **long-suffering** ADJ très patient, d'une patience à toute épreuve ▶ **long-tailed** ADJ à longue queue; **~-tailed tit** mésange *f* à longue queue ▶ **long-term** ADJ → **long-term** ▶ **long-time** ADJ de longue date, vieux (vieille *f*) ▶ **long trousers** NPL (*as opposed to shorts*) pantalon *m*; **when I was old enough to wear ~ trousers** quand j'ai passé l'âge des culottes courtes ▶ **the long vacation, the long vac*** N (*Brit Univ*) les grandes vacances *fpl* ▶ **long wave** N (*Rad*) grandes ondes *fpl*; **on (the) ~ wave** sur les grandes ondes ▶ **long-winded** ADJ [*person*] intarissable, prolixe; [*speech*] interminable ▶ **long-windedly** ADV intarissablement ▶ **long-windedness** N prolixité *f*

long² [lɒŋ] VI **to ~ to do sth** (= *hope to*) avoir très envie de faire qch; (= *dream of*) rêver de faire qch; **I'm ~ing to meet her** j'ai très envie de la rencontrer; **to ~ for sth** (= *hope for*) avoir très envie de qch; (= *dream of*) rêver de qch; **the ~ed-for news** la nouvelle tant attendue; **to ~ for sb to do sth** mourir d'envie que qn

fasse qch; **she ~ed for her friends** ses amis lui manquaient beaucoup *or* terriblement

longboat ['lɒŋbəʊt] N (grande) chaloupe *f*

longbow ['lɒŋbəʊ] N arc *m* (anglais)

longevity [lɒn'dʒevɪtɪ] N longévité *f*

longhair* ['lɒŋheəʳ] N (*US*) intello* *m*

longhand ['lɒŋhænd] **1** N écriture *f* normale *or* courante; **in ~** (*not shorthand*) en clair; (*not typed*) à la main **2** ADJ en clair

longhorn cattle ['lɒŋhɔːnˈkætl] N (*NonC*) bovins *mpl* longhorn *inv* *or* à longues cornes

longing ['lɒŋɪŋ] **1** N **a** (= *urge*) désir *m*, envie *f* (**for sth** de qch); (= *craving*: for food etc) envie *f*; **to have a sudden ~ to do sth** avoir un désir soudain *or* une envie soudaine de faire qch **b** (= *nostalgia*) nostalgie *f*; **his ~ for the happy days of his childhood** la nostalgie qu'il avait des jours heureux de son enfance **2** ADJ [*look, glance*] (*for sth*) plein d'envie; (*for sb*) plein de désir

longingly ['lɒŋɪŋlɪ] ADV **to look ~ at sb** regarder qn d'un air énamouré; **to look ~ at sth** regarder qch avec convoitise, dévorer qch des yeux; **to think ~ of sb** penser amoureusement à qn; **to think ~ of sth** penser avec envie à qch

longish ['lɒŋɪʃ] ADJ [*hair, period, distance*] assez long (longue *f*); [*book, play*] assez long (longue *f*), longuet* (*slightly pej*); **(for) a ~ time** assez longtemps

longitude ['lɒŋgɪtjuːd] N longitude *f*; **at a ~ of 48°** par 48° de longitude

longitudinal [ˌlɒŋgɪ'tjuːdɪnl] ADJ longitudinal

longitudinally [ˌlɒŋgɪ'tjuːdɪnəlɪ] ADV longitudinalement

longship ['lɒŋʃɪp] N (*Vikings*) drakkar *m*

longshoreman ['lɒŋʃɔːmən] N (*pl* **-men**) (*US*) débardeur *m*, docker *m*

longshoring ['lɒŋʃɔːrɪŋ] N (*US*) débardage *m*

long-term ['lɒŋ'tɜːm] **1** ADJ [*loan, policy, investment, effects, solution, view, interests, future*] à long terme; **he's in a ~ relationship** (*going out together*) il sort avec la même personne depuis longtemps; (*living together*) il vit avec la même personne depuis longtemps; **they're in a ~ relationship** (*going out*) ils sortent ensemble depuis longtemps; (*living together*) ils vivent ensemble depuis longtemps **2** COMP ▶ **long-term care** N prise *f* en charge de longue durée ▶ **long-term car park** N parc *m* de stationnement (*avec forfait à la journée/à la semaine etc*) ▶ **long-term health care** N = **long-term care** ▶ **the long-term unemployed** NPL les chômeurs *mpl* de longue durée → **long¹**

longways ['lɒŋweɪz] ADV en longueur, en long; **~ on** dans le sens de la longueur

loo* [luː] N (*Brit*) toilettes *fpl*, W.-C. *mpl*; **he's in the ~** il est au petit coin* *or* aux toilettes

loofah ['luːfəʳ] N luffa *m*, loofa *m*

▼ **look** [lʊk]

1 NOUN	**4** TRANSITIVE VERB
2 PLURAL NOUN	**5** COMPOUNDS
3 INTRANSITIVE VERB	**6** PHRASAL VERBS

1 NOUN

a **at sth, sb do you want a ~?** tu veux regarder *or* jeter un coup d'œil?; **and now for a quick ~ at the papers** et maintenant, les grands titres de vos journaux

♦ **to have/take a look**: **let me have a ~** (= *may I*) fais voir; (= *I'm going to*) je vais voir; **let me have another ~** (= *may I*) je peux regarder encore une fois?; **to have** *or* **take a ~ at sth** regarder qch, jeter un coup d'œil à qch; **take** *or* **have a ~ at this!** regarde-moi ça!, regarde!; **to take another** *or* **a second ~ at sth** examiner qch de plus près; **to take a good ~ at sth** bien regarder qch; **to take a good ~ at sb** regarder qn avec attention; **take a good ~!** regarde bien!; **to take a long ~ at sb** regarder longuement qn, bien regarder qn; (fig) to take a long hard ~ at sth examiner qch de près; (fig) to take a long (hard) ~ at o.s. faire son autocritique; to have a ~ round the house visiter la maison; I just want to have a ~ round (in town) je veux simplement faire un tour; (in a shop) est-ce que je peux regarder?; have a ~ through the telescope regarde dans le télescope

b = **expression** regard m; **an inquiring ~** un regard interrogateur; **with a nasty ~ in his eye** avec un regard méchant; **he gave me a furious ~** il m'a jeté un regard furieux, il m'a regardé d'un air furieux; **we got some very odd ~s** les gens nous ont regardé d'un drôle d'air; **I told her what I thought and if ~s could kill*, I'd be dead** je lui ai dit ce que je pensais et elle m'a fusillé or foudroyé du regard → **black, dirty, long**[1]

c = **search** **to have a ~ for sth** chercher qch; **have another ~!** cherche bien!; **I've had a good ~ for it already** je l'ai déjà cherché partout

d = **appearance** air m; **there was a sad ~ about him** il avait l'air plutôt triste, son allure avait quelque chose de triste; **I like the ~ of her*** je trouve qu'elle a l'air sympathique or qu'elle a une bonne tête*; **I don't like the ~(s) of him*** il a une tête qui ne me revient pas*; **he had the ~ of a sailor** (about him) il avait l'air d'un marin; **she has a ~ of her mother** (about her) elle a quelque chose de sa mère; **by the ~(s) of him*** à le voir; **by the ~(s) of it** or **things*** de toute évidence; **you can't go by ~s** il ne faut pas se fier aux apparences (PROV); **I don't like the ~ of this at all*** ça ne me dit rien qui vaille

e Fashion = **style** look m; **I need a new ~** il faut que je change (subj) de look

2 looks* NPL beauté f; **~s aren't everything** la beauté n'est pas tout; **she has kept her ~s** elle est restée belle; **she's losing her ~s** elle n'est plus aussi belle qu'autrefois, sa beauté se fane

3 INTRANSITIVE VERB

a = **see, glance** regarder; **~ over there!** regarde là-bas!; **~!** regarde!; **just ~!** regarde un peu!; **~ and see if he's still there** regarde s'il est encore là; **~ what a mess you've made!** regarde le gâchis que tu as fait!; **~ who's here!*** regarde qui est là!; **let me ~** (= may I) fais voir; (= I'm going to) je vais voir; **to ~ the other way** (lit = avert one's eyes) détourner le regard; (fig) fermer les yeux (fig) ■ (PROV) **~ before you leap** il faut réfléchir avant d'agir

◆ **to look** + adverb/preposition: **he ~ed around him for an ashtray** il a cherché un cendrier des yeux; **to ~ down one's nose at sb*** regarder qn de haut; **she ~s down her nose at*** romantic novels elle méprise les romans à l'eau de rose; **to ~ down the list** parcourir la liste; **~ here*, we must discuss it first** écoutez, il faut d'abord en discuter; **~ here*, that isn't what I said!** dites donc, ce n'est pas ça que j'ai dit!; **she ~ed into his eyes** (gen) elle l'a regardé droit dans les yeux; (romantically) elle a plongé son regard dans le sien; (you must) **~ on the bright side** (of life) il faut être optimiste, il faut voir le bon côté des choses; **to ~ over sb's shoulder** (lit) regarder par-dessus l'épaule de qn; (fig) être constamment sur le dos de qn, surveiller qn constamment; (fig) **to be ~ing over one's shoulder** être sur ses gardes; (fig) **he ~ed right through me*** il a fait comme s'il ne me voyait pas

b = **face** [building] donner; **the house ~s east** la maison donne à l'est; **the house ~s onto the main street** la maison donne sur la rue principale

c = **search** chercher; **you should have ~ed more carefully** tu aurais dû chercher un peu mieux; **you can't have ~ed far** tu n'as pas dû beaucoup chercher

d = **seem** avoir l'air; **he doesn't ~ himself** ◊ **he's not ~ing himself** il n'a pas l'air dans

son assiette, il n'a pas l'air en forme; **he ~s about 40** il doit avoir la quarantaine; **he ~s about 75 kilos/1 metre 80** il doit faire environ 75 kilos/1 mètre 80; **she's tired and it ~s it** elle est fatiguée et ça se voit; **he's 50 and he ~s it** il a 50 ans et il les fait; **how did she ~?** (health) elle avait l'air en forme?; (on hearing news) quelle tête elle a fait?; **how do I ~?** comment me trouves-tu?; **how does it ~ to you?** qu'en pensez-vous?

◆ **to look as if**: **try to ~ as if you're glad to see them!** essaie d'avoir l'air content de les voir!; **it ~s as if it's going to snow** on dirait qu'il va neiger; **it ~s as if he isn't coming** ◊ **it doesn't ~ as if he's coming** on dirait qu'il ne va pas venir; **it ~s to me as if he isn't coming** ◊ **it doesn't ~ to me as if he's coming** j'ai l'impression qu'il ne va pas venir

◆ **to look** + adjective/noun: **she ~s her age** elle fait son âge; **~ alive** or **lively!*** remue-toi!*; **it will ~ bad** ça va faire mauvais effet; **she ~s her best in blue** c'est le bleu qui lui va le mieux; **you must ~ your best for this interview** il faut que tu présentes bien pour cet entretien; **he just does it to ~ big*** il fait ça uniquement pour se donner de l'importance; **they made me ~ foolish** or **a fool** ils m'ont ridiculisé; **he ~s good in uniform** l'uniforme lui va bien; **that dress ~s good** or **well on her** cette robe lui va bien; **that hat/necklace ~s good on you** ce chapeau/collier te va bien; **that pie ~s good** cette tarte a l'air bonne; **how are you getting on with your autobiography? - it's ~ing good** comment avance ton autobiographie? - elle avance bien; **it ~s good on paper** c'est très bien en théorie or sur le papier; **that story ~s interesting** cette histoire a l'air intéressante or semble intéressante; **that hairstyle makes her ~ old** cette coiffure la vieillit; **it makes him ~ ten years older/younger** ça le vieillit/rajeunit de dix ans; **he ~s older than that** il a l'air plus âgé que ça; (fig) **to ~ the part** avoir le physique or avoir la tête de l'emploi*; **how pretty you ~!** comme vous êtes jolie!; **it ~s promising** c'est prometteur; **it doesn't ~ right** il y a quelque chose qui ne va pas; **it ~s all right to me** ça m'a l'air d'aller; (fig) **to make sb ~ small** rabaisser qn, diminuer qn; **she ~s tired** elle a l'air fatigué(e); **you ~** or **you're ~ing well** vous avez bonne mine; **she doesn't ~ well** elle n'a pas bonne mine, elle a mauvaise mine

◆ **to look like** (= be in appearance) **what does he ~ like?** comment est-il?; **you can see what the house used to ~ like** on voit comment était la maison; (= resemble) **he ~s like his father** il ressemble à son père; **the picture doesn't ~ like him at all** on ne le reconnaît pas du tout sur cette photo; **he ~s like a soldier** il a l'air d'un soldat; (pej) **she ~ed like nothing on earth*** (ill, depressed) elle avait une tête épouvantable; (= seem) **it ~s like salt** on dirait du sel; **this ~s to me like the right shop** cela m'a l'air d'être le bon magasin; **it ~s like rain*** on dirait qu'il va pleuvoir; **the rain doesn't ~ like stopping** la pluie n'a pas l'air de (vouloir) s'arrêter; **it certainly ~s like it** ça m'en a tout l'air; **the evening ~ed like being interesting** la soirée promettait d'être intéressante

4 TRANSITIVE VERB

a = **look at** regarder; **to ~ sb in the face** or in **the eye(s)** regarder qn en face or dans les yeux; **I could never ~ him in the face** or in **the eye(s) again** je ne pourrais plus le regarder en face; **to ~ sb up and down** toiser qn

b = **pay attention to** regarder, faire attention à; **~ where you're going!** regarde où tu vas!; **~ what you've done now!** regarde ce que tu as fait!

5 COMPOUNDS

▶ **look-alike** N sosie m; **a Churchill ~-alike** un sosie de Churchill ▶ **looked-for** ADJ [result] attendu, prévu; [effect] escompté, recherché ▶ **look-in** N (= visit) **to give sb a ~-in**

passer voir qn, faire une visite éclair or un saut chez qn; (Brit = chance) **with such competition we won't get a ~-in** avec de tels concurrents nous n'avons pas la moindre chance; **our team didn't have** or **get a ~-in** notre équipe n'a jamais eu le moindre espoir or la moindre chance de gagner ▶ **look-out** N → look-out ▶ **look-see**: N **to have** or **to take a ~-see** jeter un coup d'œil, jeter un œil* ▶ **look-up** (Comput) N consultation f ♦ ADJ [list etc] à consulter

6 PHRASAL VERBS

▶ **look about** VI regarder autour de soi; **to ~ about for sb/sth** chercher qn/qch (des yeux)

▶ **look after** VT FUS **a** (= take care of) [+ invalid, animal, plant] s'occuper de; [+ one's possessions] prendre soin de; [+ finances] gérer; **she doesn't ~ after herself properly** elle se néglige; **~ after yourself!*** prends soin de toi!, fais bien attention à toi!*; **she's quite old enough to ~ after herself** elle est assez grande pour se débrouiller* toute seule; **he certainly ~s after his car** il bichonne sa voiture; **we're well ~ed after here** on s'occupe bien de nous ici, on nous soigne ici

b (= mind) [+ child] garder, s'occuper de; [+ shop, business] s'occuper de; [+ luggage, house] (= watch over) surveiller; (= keep temporarily) garder (**sth for sb** qch pour qn); **to ~ after one's own interests** protéger ses propres intérêts

▶ **look ahead** VI (= in front) regarder devant soi; (= to future) penser à l'avenir; **I'm ~ing ahead to what might happen** j'essaie d'imaginer ce qui pourrait se passer

▶ **look around** VI = look about

▶ **look at** VT FUS **a** (= observe) [+ person, object] regarder; **to ~ hard at** [+ person] dévisager; [+ thing] regarder or examiner de très près; **just ~ at this mess!** regarde un peu ce fouillis!; **just ~ at you!*** regarde de quoi tu as l'air!, regarde-toi!; **to ~ at him you would never think (that) ...** à le voir, on n'imaginerait pas que ...; **it isn't much to ~ at*** ◊ **it's nothing to ~ at*** ça ne paie pas de mine

b (= consider) [+ situation, problem] examiner; **let's ~ at the facts** considérons or examinons les faits; **they wouldn't ~ at my proposal** ils n'ont même pas pris ma proposition en considération, ils ont d'emblée rejeté ma proposition; **he now ~ed at her with new respect** il commença à la considérer avec respect; **that's one way of ~ing at it** c'est un point de vue, mais pas le mien; **it depends (on) how you ~ at it** tout dépend comment on voit or envisage la chose; **just ~ at him now!** (what's become of him) regarde où il en est aujourd'hui!

c (= check) vérifier; (= see to) s'occuper de; **will you ~ at the carburettor?** pourriez-vous vérifier le carburateur?; **I'll ~ at it tomorrow** je m'en occuperai demain

d (* = have in prospect) **you're ~ing at a minimum of £65** ça va vous coûter 65 livres au minimum; **they are ~ing at savings of £3m** il s'agit d'économies qui pourraient atteindre 3 millions de livres

▶ **look away** VI (lit) détourner les yeux or le regard (**from** de); (fig) fermer les yeux

▶ **look back** VI **a** (lit) regarder derrière soi; **she ~ed back at Marie and smiled** elle se retourna pour regarder Marie et lui sourit

b (fig: in memory) revenir sur le passé; **after that he never ~ed back*** après, ça n'a fait qu'aller de mieux en mieux pour lui; **there's no point ~ing back** ça ne sert à rien de revenir sur le passé; **~ing back, I'm surprised I didn't suspect anything** rétrospectivement or avec le recul, je suis étonné de n'avoir rien soupçonné; **to ~ back on** or at or over sth (= remember, evaluate) repenser à qch; **when they ~ back on** or at this match ... lorsqu'ils repenseront à ce match ...; **we can ~ back on** or over **20 years of happy marriage** nous avons derrière nous 20 ans de bonheur conjugal

► **look behind** VI regarder en arrière

► **look down** VI baisser les yeux ; **to ~ down at the ground** regarder par terre ; **don't ~ down or you'll fall** ne regarde pas en bas, sinon tu vas tomber ; **he ~ed down at** or **on the town from the hilltop** il a regardé la ville du haut de la colline

► **look down on** VT FUS [a] (= *despise*) mépriser ; **to ~ down on sb** regarder qn de haut, mépriser qn
[b] (= *overlook*) dominer ; **the castle ~s down on the valley** le château domine la vallée

► **look for** VT FUS [a] (= *seek*) [+ *object, work*] chercher ; **to be ~ing for trouble*** chercher les ennuis
[b] (= *expect*) [+ *praise, reward*] attendre, espérer

► **look forward to** VT FUS [+ *event, meal, trip, holiday*] attendre avec impatience ; **I'm ~ing forward to seeing them** j'ai hâte de les voir ; (*frm*) **I ~ forward to meeting you on the 5th** je vous verrai donc le 5 ; (*in letter*) **~ing forward to hearing from you** en espérant avoir bientôt de vos nouvelles, dans l'attente de votre réponse (*frm*) ; **I ~ forward to the day when ...** j'attends avec impatience le jour où ... ; **are you ~ing forward to your birthday?** tu attends ton anniversaire avec impatience ? ; **we'd been ~ing forward to it for weeks** on attendait ça depuis des semaines ; **I'm really ~ing forward to it** je m'en fais déjà une fête, je m'en réjouis à l'avance ; **they are ~ing forward to an increase in sales** ils anticipent une augmentation des ventes

► **look in** VI [a] (*lit*) regarder à l'intérieur ; **to ~ in at the window** regarder par la fenêtre
[b] (* = *pay visit*) passer ; **we ~ed in at Robert's** nous sommes passés chez Robert, nous avons fait un saut chez Robert ; **to ~ in on sb** passer voir qn ; **the doctor will ~ in again tomorrow** le docteur repassera demain

► **look into** VT FUS (= *examine*) [+ *possibility, problem, situation*] examiner, étudier ; **they are going to ~ into other possibilities** ils vont examiner d'autres solutions ; **there's obviously been a mistake, I'll ~ into it** il y a dû y avoir une erreur. Je vais m'en occuper ; **we must ~ into what happened to the money** il va falloir que nous enquêtions pour voir ce qu'est devenu cet argent

► **look on** [1] VI regarder (faire) ; **they just ~ed on while the raiders escaped** quand les bandits se sont enfuis, ils se sont contentés de regarder ; **he wrote the letter while I ~ed on** il a écrit la lettre tandis que je le regardais faire
[2] VT FUS considérer ; **many ~ on him as a hero** beaucoup le considèrent comme un héros ; (*frm*) **to ~ kindly (up)on sth/sb** approuver qch/qn ; (*frm*) **I do not ~ on the matter in that way** je ne vois or n'envisage pas la chose de cette façon(-là)

► **look out** [1] VI [a] (*lit* = *look outside*) regarder dehors ; **to ~ out of the window** regarder par la fenêtre
[b] (= *take care*) faire attention, prendre garde ; **I told you to ~ out!** je t'avais bien dit de faire attention ! ; **~ out!** attention !
[2] VT SEP (*Brit*) (= *look for*) chercher ; (= *find*) trouver ; **I'll ~ out some old magazines** je vais essayer de trouver or vais chercher des vieux magazines ; **I've ~ed out the minutes of the meeting** j'ai trouvé le procès-verbal de la réunion

► **look out for** VT FUS [a] (= *look for*) chercher, être à la recherche de ; (= *watch out for*) [+ *sth good*] essayer de repérer ; [+ *danger*] se méfier de, faire attention à ; **~ out for special deals** soyez à l'affût des bonnes affaires ; **~ out for ice on the road** méfiez-vous du or faites attention au verglas
[b] (* = *look after*) [+ *person*] s'occuper de ; **to ~ out for oneself** se débrouiller tout seul ; **we ~ out for each other** on se tient les coudes

► **look over** VT SEP [+ *document, list*] parcourir ; [+ *goods, produce*] inspecter ; [+ *town, building*] visiter ; [+ *person*] (*quickly*) jeter un coup d'œil à ; (*slowly*) regarder de la tête aux pieds, toiser

► **look round** [1] VI [a] (= *glance about*) regarder (autour de soi) ; (*in shop*) **we're just ~ing round** on regarde
[b] (= *search*) chercher ; **I ~ed round for you after the concert** je vous ai cherché après le concert ; **I'm ~ing round for an assistant** je cherche un assistant, je suis à la recherche d'un assistant
[c] (= *look back*) se retourner ; **I ~ed round to see where he was** je me suis retourné pour voir où il était ; **don't ~ round!** ne vous retournez pas !
[2] VT FUS [+ *town, factory*] visiter, faire le tour de

► **look through** VT FUS [a] (= *scan*) [+ *mail*] regarder ; (*thoroughly*) [+ *papers, book*] examiner ; (*briefly*) [+ *papers*] parcourir ; [+ *book*] parcourir, feuilleter
[b] (= *revise*) [+ *lesson*] réviser, repasser ; (= *reread*) [+ *notes*] relire
[c] (= *ignore*) **he just ~ed right through me*** il a fait comme s'il ne me voyait pas

► **look to** VT FUS [a] (= *seek help from*) se tourner vers ; **many sufferers ~ to alternative therapies** de nombreux malades se tournent vers les médecines parallèles ; **I ~ to you for help** je compte sur votre aide
[b] (= *think of*) penser à ; **to ~ to the future** penser à l'avenir
[c] (= *seek to*) chercher à ; **they are ~ing to make a profit** ils cherchent à réaliser un bénéfice

► **look up** [1] VI [a] (= *glance upwards*) regarder en haut ; (*from reading etc*) lever les yeux
[b] (* = *improve*) [*prospects, weather*] s'améliorer ; [*business*] reprendre ; **things are ~ing up** ça va mieux, ça s'améliore ; **oil shares are ~ing up** les actions pétrolières remontent or sont en hausse
[2] VT SEP [a] (* = *seek out*) [+ *person*] passer voir ; **~ me up the next time you are in London** venez or passez me voir la prochaine fois que vous serez à Londres
[b] (*in reference book*) [+ *name, word*] chercher ; **to ~ up a word in the dictionary** chercher un mot dans le dictionnaire ; **you'll have to ~ that one up** [+ *word*] il va falloir que tu cherches (*subj*) dans le dictionnaire
[3] VT FUS [+ *reference book*] consulter, chercher dans or vérifier dans

► **look upon** VT FUS = look on 2

► **look up to** VT FUS (= *admire*) admirer

looker ['lʊkəʳ] [1] N* **she's a (real) ~** c'est une belle plante*, elle est vraiment canon* ; **he's a (real) ~** c'est un beau mec* [2] COMP
► **looker-on** N badaud(e) m(f)

-looking ['lʊkɪŋ] (*in compounds*) **ugly-looking** laid (d'aspect) ; **sinister-looking** à l'air sinistre → **good**

looking-glass† ['lʊkɪŋɡlɑːs] N glace f, miroir m

look-out ['lʊkaʊt] [1] N [a] (= *observation*) surveillance f, guet m ; **to keep a ~** ◊ **to be on the ~** faire le guet, guetter ; **to keep a** or **be on the ~ for sb/sth** guetter qn/qch ; **to be on the ~ for bargains** être à l'affût des bonnes affaires ; **to be on the ~ for danger** être sur ses gardes ; **to be on ~ (duty)** (*Mil*) être au guet ; (*Naut*) être en vigie → **sharp**
[b] (= *observer*) (*gen*) guetteur m ; (*Mil*) homme m de guet, guetteur m ; (*Naut*) homme m de veille or de vigie, vigie f
[c] (= *observation post*) (*gen, Mil*) poste m de guet ; (*Naut*) vigie f
[d] (*esp Brit** = *outlook*) perspective f ; **it's a poor ~ for cotton** les perspectives pour le coton ne sont pas brillantes ; **it's a grim ~ for people like us** la situation or ça s'annonce mal pour les gens comme nous ; **that's your ~!** cela vous regarde !, c'est votre affaire !
[2] COMP [*tower*] d'observation ► **look-out post** N (*Mil*) poste m de guet or d'observation

loom[1] [luːm] VI (*also* **~ up** = *appear*) [*building, mountain*] apparaître indistinctement, se dessiner ; [*figure, ship*] surgir ; (*fig*) [*danger, crisis*] menacer ; [*event*] être imminent ; **the ship ~ed (up) out of the mist** le navire a surgi de or dans la brume ; **the dark mountains ~ed (up) in front of us** les sombres montagnes sont apparues or se sont dressées menaçantes devant nous ; **the possibility of defeat ~ed (up) before him** la possibilité de la défaite s'est présentée à son esprit ; **a recession is ~ing in the United States** une récession menace sérieusement les États-Unis ; **the threat of war ~s ahead** la guerre menace d'éclater ; **the threat of an epidemic ~ed large in their minds** la menace d'une épidémie était au premier plan de leurs préoccupations ; **the exams are ~ing large** les examens sont dangereusement proches

loom[2] [luːm] N (*Tex: for weaving*) métier m à tisser

loon [luːn] N [a] (* = *fool*) imbécile m, idiot m
[b] (*US Orn*) plongeon m arctique, huard m or huart m

loon pants ['luːnpænts], **loons** [luːnz] NPL *pantalon moulant à taille basse et pattes d'éléphant*

loony* ['luːnɪ] [1] N timbré(e)* m(f), cinglé(e)* m(f) [2] ADJ timbré*, cinglé* [3] COMP
► **loony bin** N maison f de fous, asile m ; **in the ~ bin** chez les fous ► **loony left*** (*Brit Pol: pej*) **the ~ left** l'aile extrémiste du parti travailliste ♦ ADJ de l'aile extrémiste du parti travailliste

loop [luːp] [1] N [a] (*in string, ribbon, writing*) boucle f ; (*in river*) méandre m, boucle f ; **the string has a ~ in it** la ficelle fait une boucle ; **to put a ~ in sth** faire une boucle à qch ; (*esp US*) **to knock** or **throw sb for a ~*** sidérer* qn
[b] (*Elec*) circuit m fermé ; (*Comput*) boucle f ; (*Rail: also* **line**) voie f d'évitement ; (*by motorway etc*) bretelle f [c] (*Med* = *contraceptive*) **the ~** le stérilet [d] (*curtain fastener*) embrasse f
[2] VT [+ *string etc*] faire une boucle à, boucler ; **he ~ed the rope round the post** il a passé la corde autour du poteau ; (*Aviat*) **to ~ the loop** faire un looping, boucler la boucle [3] VI former une boucle

► **loop back** [1] VI [*road, river*] former une boucle ; (*Comput*) se reboucler [2] VT SEP [+ *curtain*] retenir or relever avec une embrasse

► **loop up** VT SEP = loop back 2

loophole ['luːphəʊl] N (*Archit*) meurtrière f ; (*fig: in law, argument, regulations*) point m faible, lacune f ; (*fig*) **we must try to find a ~** il faut que nous trouvions une échappatoire or une porte de sortie*

loopy* ['luːpɪ] ADJ cinglé* ; **to go ~** perdre les pédales*

loose [luːs] [1] ADJ [a] (= *not tied up*) [*animal*] (= *free*) en liberté ; (= *escaped*) échappé ; (= *freed*) lâché ; [*hair*] dénoué, flottant ; (= *not attached*) [*page from book*] détaché ; (*on roadway*) ~ **chippings** gravillons mpl ; (*Brit: of furniture*) ~ **covers** housses fpl ; **write it on a ~ sheet of paper** écrivez-le sur une feuille volante ; (*to pupil*) écrivez-le sur une (feuille de) copie ; **the ~ end of a rope** le bout libre d'une corde ; (*fig*) **to be at a ~ end** ne pas trop savoir quoi faire, ne pas savoir quoi faire de sa peau* ; (*fig*) **to tie up (the) ~ ends** régler les détails qui restent ; **to get ~** [*animal*] s'échapper ; **to have come ~** [*page*] s'être détaché ; [*hair*] s'être dénoué ; **to let** or **set** or **turn an animal ~** libérer or lâcher un animal ; **to let the dogs ~ on sb** lâcher les chiens sur qn ; **we can't let him ~ on that class** on ne peut pas le lâcher dans cette classe ; **to tear (o.s.) ~** se dégager ; **to tear sth ~** détacher qch (en déchirant); (*Naut*) **to cut ~** couper les amarres; (*fig*) **he cut ~ (from his family)** il a coupé les amarres (avec sa famille) → **break, hell**

b (= *not firmly in place*) [*screw*] desserré, qui a du jeu; [*stone, brick*] branlant; [*tooth*] qui branle, qui bouge; [*knot, shoelace*] qui se défait, desserré; **one of your buttons is very ~** l'un de tes boutons va tomber *or* se découd; (*Elec*) **a ~ connection** un mauvais contact; **to be coming** *or* **getting** *or* **working ~** [*knot*] se desserrer, se défaire; [*screw*] se desserrer, avoir du jeu; [*stone, brick*] branler; [*tooth*] branler, bouger; [*page*] se détacher; [*hair*] se dénouer, se défaire; **to have come ~** [*knot*] s'être défait; [*screw*] s'être desserré; [*stone, brick*] branler; [*tooth*] branler, bouger; **the reins hung ~** les rênes n'étaient pas tenues *or* tendues, les rênes étaient sur le cou *or* lâches; **hang** *or* **stay ~!**‡ relax !* → **screw**

c (*Comm* = *not pre-packed*) [*biscuits, carrots etc*] en vrac; [*butter, cheese*] au poids; **the potatoes were ~ in the bottom of the basket** les pommes de terre étaient à même au fond du panier; **just put them ~ into the basket** mettez-les à même *or* tels quels dans le panier

d (= *not tight*) [*skin*] flasque, mou (molle *f*); [*coat, dress*] (= *not close-fitting*) vague, ample; (= *not tight enough*) lâche, large; [*collar*] lâche; **these trousers are too ~ round the waist** ce pantalon est trop large *or* lâche à la taille; **~ clothes are better for summer wear** l'été il vaut mieux porter des vêtements amples *or* pas trop ajustés; **the rope round the dog's neck was quite ~** la corde passée au cou du chien était toute lâche; **a ~ weave** un tissu lâche → **4**; (*Med*) **his bowels are ~** ses intestins sont relâchés → **play**

e (= *not strict*) [*discipline*] relâché; [*organization*] peu structuré; [*translation*] approximatif, assez libre; [*style*] lâche, relâché; (= *vague*) [*reasoning, thinking*] imprécis; [*association, link*] vague; **a ~ interpretation of the rules** une interprétation peu rigoureuse du règlement; **there is a ~ connection between the two theories** il y a un vague lien entre les deux théories

f (*pej*) (= *dissolute*) [*woman*] facile, de mœurs légères; [*morals*] relâché, douteux; **to lead a ~ life** mener une vie dissolue; **~ living** vie *f* dissolue *or* de débauche; (= *careless*) **~ talk** propos *mpl* inconsidérés

g (= *available*) [*funds*] disponible, liquide

h (= *not compact*) [*soil*] meuble; (*Rugby*) **~ scrum** mêlée *f* ouverte

2 N (*of prisoner*) **on the ~*** en cavale; **there was a crowd of kids on the ~* in the town** il y avait une bande de jeunes qui traînait dans les rues sans trop savoir quoi faire; **a gang of hooligans on the ~*** une bande de voyous déchaînés; (*Rugby*) **in the ~** dans la mêlée ouverte

3 VT **a** (= *undo*) défaire, délier, dénouer; [+ *screw etc*] desserrer; (= *free*) [+ *animal*] lâcher; [+ *prisoner*] relâcher, mettre en liberté; **to ~ a boat (from its moorings)** démarrer une embarcation, larguer les amarres; **they ~d the dogs on him** ils ont lâché les chiens après *or* sur lui

b (*also* **~ off**) [+ *gun*] décharger (**on** *or* **at sb** sur qn); [+ *arrow*] tirer (**on** *or* **at sb** sur qn); [+ *violence etc*] déclencher (**on** contre); (*fig*) **to ~ (off) a volley of abuse at sb** déverser un torrent *or* lâcher une bordée d'injures sur qn

4 COMP ► **loose box** N (*Brit: for horses*) box *m* ► **loose cannon*** N franc-tireur *m* ► **loose change** N petite *or* menue monnaie *f* ► **loose-fitting** ADJ ample, vague ► **loose-leaf** ADJ à feuilles volantes, à feuilles *or* feuillets mobiles ► **loose-leaf binder** N classeur *m* (à feuilles mobiles) ► **loose-leafed** ADJ = **loose-leaf** ► **loose-limbed** ADJ agile ► **loose-weave** ADJ [*material*] lâche; [*curtains*] en tissu lâche

► **loose off 1** VI (= *shoot*) tirer (**at sb** sur qn) **2** VT SEP = **loose 3b**

loosely ['luːslɪ] **1** ADV **a** (= *not tightly*) [*hold*] sans serrer; [*tie*] lâchement; **stand with your arms hanging ~ by your sides** tenez-vous debout, les bras relâchés le long du corps; **a ~ woven mesh** des mailles lâches **b** (= *imprecisely, not strictly*) [*translated*] librement; [*connected*] vaguement; **~ defined** mal défini; **~ organized** peu structuré; **~ knit** [*association, grouping*] peu structuré; **a character ~ based on Janis Joplin** un personnage librement inspiré de Janis Joplin; **~ speaking** grosso modo; **that word is ~ used to mean ...** on emploie couramment ce mot pour dire ... **2** COMP ► **loosely-knit** ADJ aux mailles lâches

loosen ['luːsn] **1** VT **a** (= *slacken*) [+ *screw, belt, knot*] desserrer; [+ *rope*] détendre, relâcher; (= *untie*) [+ *knot, shoelace*] défaire; (*fig*) [+ *emotional ties*] distendre; [+ *laws, restrictions*] assouplir; **first ~ the part then remove it gently** il faut d'abord dégager la pièce puis l'enlever doucement; **to ~ one's grip (on sth)** (*lit*) desserrer sa prise *or* son étreinte (sur qch); (*fig* = *be less strict with*) perdre son emprise (sur qch); (*fig*) **to ~ sb's tongue** délier la langue à qn **b** (*Agr*) [+ *soil*] rendre meuble, ameublir; (*Med*) **to ~ the bowels** relâcher les intestins **2** VI [*fastening*] se défaire; [*screw*] se desserrer, jouer; [*knot*] (= *slacken*) se desserrer; (= *come undone*) se défaire; [*rope*] se détendre

► **loosen up 1** VI **a** (= *limber up*) faire des exercices d'assouplissement; (*before race etc*) s'échauffer **b** (= *become less shy*) se dégeler, perdre sa timidité **c** (= *become less strict with*) **to ~ up on sb*** se montrer plus coulant* *or* moins strict envers qn **2** VT SEP **to ~ up one's muscles** faire des exercices d'assouplissement; (*before race etc*) s'échauffer

looseness ['luːsnɪs] N **a** (= *immorality*) [*of behaviour*] immoralité *f*; [*of morals*] relâchement *m* **b** [*of translation*] imprécision *f*; [*of style*] manque *m* de rigueur *or* de précision **c** [*of soil*] ameublissement *m*; (*Med*) **~ of the bowels** relâchement *m* des intestins *or* intestinal

loot [luːt] **1** N **a** (= *plunder*) butin *m* **b** (‡ *fig* = *prizes, gifts etc*) butin *m*; (= *money*) pognon‡ *m*, fric‡ *m* **2** VT [+ *town*] piller, mettre à sac; [+ *shop, goods*] piller **3** VI **to go ~ing** se livrer au pillage

looter ['luːtə'] N pillard *m*

looting ['luːtɪŋ] N pillage *m*

lop [lɒp] VT [+ *tree*] tailler; [+ *branch*] couper

► **lop off** VT SEP [+ *branch, piece*] couper; [+ *head*] trancher

lope [ləʊp] VI courir en bondissant; **to ~ along/in/out** *etc* avancer/entrer/sortir *etc* en bondissant

lop-eared ['lɒp,ɪəd] ADJ aux oreilles pendantes

lopsided ['lɒp'saɪdɪd] ADJ **a** (= *not straight*) de travers, de guingois*; [*smile*] de travers; (= *asymmetric*) disproportionné **b** (*fig* = *unequal*) [*contest etc*] inégal

loquacious [lə'kweɪʃəs] ADJ loquace, bavard

loquacity [lə'kwæsɪtɪ] N loquacité *f*, volubilité *f*

lord [lɔːd] **1** N **a** seigneur *m*; **~ of the manor** châtelain *m*; (*hum*) **and master** seigneur *m* et maître *m* (*hum*); (*Brit*) **Lord (John) Smith** lord (John) Smith; **the (House of) Lords** la Chambre des lords; **my Lord Bishop of Tooting** (Monseigneur) l'évêque de Tooting; **my Lord** Monsieur le baron (*or* comte *etc*); (*to judge*) Monsieur le Juge; (*to bishop*) Monseigneur, Excellence → **law, live¹, sea** **b** (*Rel*) **the Lord** le Seigneur; **Our Lord** Notre Seigneur; **the Lord Jesus** le Seigneur Jésus; **the Lord's supper** l'Eucharistie *f*, la sainte Cène; **the Lord's prayer** le Notre-Père; **the Lord's day** le jour du Seigneur; **good Lord!*** mon Dieu !, bon sang !*; **oh Lord!*** Seigneur !,

zut !*; **Lord knows* (what/who** *etc*) Dieu sait (quoi/qui *etc*)

2 VT* **to ~ it** vivre en grand seigneur, mener la grande vie; **to ~ it over sb** traiter qn avec arrogance *or* de haut

3 COMP ► **Lord Advocate** N (*Scot Jur*) ≈ procureur *m* de la République ► **Lord Chamberlain** N (*Brit*) grand chambellan *m* ► **Lord Chancellor** N = **Lord High Chancellor** ► **Lord Chief Justice (of England)** N (*Jur*) président *m* de la Haute Cour de justice ► **Lord High Chancellor** N (*Jur, Parl*) grand chancelier *m* d'Angleterre ► **Lord High Commissioner** N représentant de la Couronne à l'Assemblée générale de l'église d'Écosse ► **Lord Justice of Appeal** N (*Jur*) juge *m* à la cour d'appel ► **Lord Lieutenant** N représentant de la Couronne dans un comté ► **Lord Mayor** N lordmaire *m* (*titre du maire des principales villes anglaises et galloises*) ► **Lord of Appeal (in Ordinary)** N (*Jur*) juge *m* de la Cour de cassation (*siégeant à la Chambre des lords*) ► **Lord President of the Council** N (*Parl*) président *m* du Conseil privé de la reine ► **Lord Privy Seal** N (*Parl*) lord *m* du Sceau privé ► **Lord Provost** N titre du maire des principales villes écossaises ► **lords-and-ladies** N (*Bot*) pied-de-veau *m* ► **Lord spiritual** N (*Brit Parl*) membre ecclésiastique de la Chambre des lords ► **Lord temporal** N (*Brit Parl*) membre laïque de la Chambre des lords

lordliness ['lɔːdlɪnɪs] N (*frm*) **a** (*pej* = *haughtiness*) morgue *f* (*liter*) **b** (= *dignity*) [*of person, bearing*] dignité *f*; (= *impressiveness*) [*of mansion, palace*] magnificence *f*

lordly ['lɔːdlɪ] ADJ (*frm*) **a** (*pej* = *haughty*) [*person, expression, sneer*] hautain, arrogant; [*behaviour, indifference*] souverain **b** (= *dignified*) [*person*] noble, digne; [*bearing*] noble, majestueux **c** (= *impressive*) [*mansion, palace*] seigneurial

lordship ['lɔːdʃɪp] N (= *rights, property*) seigneurie *f*; (= *power*) autorité *f* (**over** sur); **your Lordship** Monsieur le comte (*or* le baron *etc*); (*to judge*) Monsieur le Juge; (*to bishop*) Monseigneur, Excellence

lore [lɔː'] N (*NonC*) **a** (= *traditions*) tradition(s) *f(pl)*, coutumes *fpl*, usages *mpl* → **folklore** **b** (= *knowledge: gen in compounds*) **his bird/wood ~** sa (grande) connaissance des oiseaux/de la vie dans les forêts

Lorenzo [lə'renzəʊ] N **~ the Magnificent** Laurent *m* le Magnifique

lorgnette [lɔː'njet] N (= *eyeglasses*) face-à-main *m*; (= *opera glasses*) lorgnette *f*, jumelles *fpl* de spectacle

Lorraine [lɒ'reɪn] N la Lorraine; **Cross of ~** croix *f* de Lorraine

lorry ['lɒrɪ] (*Brit*) **1** N camion *m*, poids *m* lourd; **to transport sth by ~** transporter qch par camion, camionner qch; (*Brit euph, hum*) **it fell off the back of a ~*** ça sort pas d'un magasin*, c'est de la fauche* → **articulate** **2** COMP ► **lorry driver** N camionneur *m*, conducteur *m* de poids lourd; (*long-distance*) routier *m* ► **lorry load** N chargement *m* (de camion)

Los Angeles [lɒs'ændʒɪ,liːz] N Los Angeles

lose [luːz] (*pret, ptp* **lost**) **1** VT **a** (= *mislay, fail to find*) [+ *object*] perdre, égarer; **some of our boxes got lost in the move** nous avons perdu quelques cartons pendant le déménagement; **to get lost in the post** être égaré par la poste; **he got lost in the wood** il s'est perdu *or* égaré dans la forêt; **I lost him in the crowd** je l'ai perdu dans la foule; **you've lost me there*** je ne vous suis plus, je n'y suis plus; **get lost!**‡ (= *go away*) barre-toi !‡; (= *forget it*) va te faire voir !‡

b (= *not win*) [+ *game, match, money, bet*] perdre; (*in gambling etc*) **how much did you ~?** combien avez-vous perdu ?

c (= *be deprived of*) [+ *person, money, possessions, job, one's sight, limb, enthusiasm*] perdre; **he lost £1,000 on that deal** il a perdu 1 000 livres dans cette affaire; **7,000 jobs lost** 7 000 suppressions *fpl* d'emploi; **they lost 100 planes in one battle** ils ont perdu 100 avions en une seule bataille; **he's lost his licence** [*driver*] on lui a retiré or il s'est fait retirer son permis de conduire; **I lost my father when I was ten** j'ai perdu mon père à l'âge de dix ans; **to ~ a patient** [*doctor*] perdre un malade; **100 men were lost** 100 hommes ont perdu la vie, 100 hommes ont péri (*liter*); **to be lost at sea** [*person*] être perdu en mer, périr (*liter*) en mer; **the ship was lost with all hands** le navire a disparu or a sombré corps et biens; **to ~ one's life** perdre la vie; **20 lives were lost in the explosion** 20 personnes ont trouvé la mort or ont péri (*liter*) dans l'explosion; **to ~ one's breath** s'essouffler; **to have lost one's breath** être hors d'haleine, être à bout de souffle; **he didn't ~ any sleep over it** il n'en a pas perdu le sommeil pour autant, ça ne l'a pas empêché de dormir; **don't ~ any sleep over it!** ne vous en faites pas!, dormez sur vos deux oreilles!; **to ~ one's voice** (*because of a cold*) avoir une extinction de voix; **to have lost one's voice** avoir une extinction de voix, être aphone; **she's lost her figure** elle a perdu sa ligne; **she's losing her looks** elle n'est plus aussi belle qu'autrefois, sa beauté se fane; **to ~ interest in sth** se désintéresser de qch; **to ~ the use of an arm** perdre l'usage d'un bras; **the poem ~s a lot in translation** la traduction n'a pas su rendre les subtilités de ce poème; **you've got nothing to ~ (by it)** tu n'as rien à perdre; **you've got nothing to ~ by helping him** tu n'as rien à perdre à l'aider → **lost**; → **balance, consciousness, cool, heart**

d (= *miss, waste*) [+ *opportunity*] manquer, perdre; **he said was lost in the applause** ses paroles se sont perdues dans les applaudissements; **this was not lost on him** cela ne lui a pas échappé; **there's no time to ~** or **to be lost** il n'y a pas de temps à perdre; **there's not a minute to ~** il n'y a pas une minute à perdre

e [*watch, clock*] **to ~ ten minutes a day** retarder de dix minutes par jour

f (= *get rid of*) [+ *unwanted object*] renoncer à, se débarrasser de; (= *shake off*) [+ *competitors, pursuers*] distancer, semer; **to ~ weight** perdre du poids, maigrir; **I lost 2 kilos** j'ai maigri de or j'ai perdu 2 kilos; **they had to ~ 100 workers** ils ont dû licencier 100 employés; **he managed to ~ the detective who was following him** il a réussi à semer le détective qui le suivait; **try to ~ him* before you come to see us** essaie de le semer avant de venir nous voir

g (= *cause to lose*) faire perdre, coûter; **that will ~ you your job** cela va vous faire perdre or vous coûter votre place; **that lost us the war/the match** cela nous a fait perdre la guerre/le match

2 VI **a** [*player, team*] perdre; (*Ftbl etc*) **they lost 6-1** ils ont perdu or ils se sont fait battre 6 à 1; **they lost to the new team** ils se sont fait battre par la nouvelle équipe; **our team is losing today** notre équipe est en train de perdre aujourd'hui

b (*fig*) **he lost on the deal** il a été perdant dans l'affaire; **you can't ~!*** tu n'as rien à perdre (mais tout à gagner); **it ~s in translation** cela perd à la traduction; **the story did not ~ in the telling** l'histoire n'a rien perdu à être racontée

c [*watch, clock*] retarder

► **lose out** VI être perdant; **to ~ out on a deal** être perdant dans une affaire; **he lost out on it** il y a été perdant

loser ['lu:zə^r] N **a** (*Sport etc*) perdant(e) *m(f)*; **good/bad ~** bon/mauvais joueur *m*, bonne/mauvaise joueuse *f*; **to come off the ~** être

perdant; **he is the ~ by it** il y perd **b** (* *pej*) loser* or looser* *m*; **he's a born ~** c'est un loser* or looser* → **back**

losing ['lu:zɪŋ] **1** ADJ [*team, party, candidate*] perdant; (*fig*) **(to fight) a ~ battle** (livrer) une bataille perdue d'avance; **to be on the ~ side** être du côté des perdants; **(to be on) a ~ streak*** (être dans) une période de déveine*; (*Brit fig*) **to be on a ~ wicket*** ne pas être en veine* **2** **losings** NPL (= *money losses*) pertes *fpl*

▼ **loss** [lɒs] **1** N **a** (*gen*) perte *f*; **a ~ of confidence/control/interest** une perte de confiance/de contrôle/d'intérêt; **the ~ of a limb/one's eyesight** la perte d'un membre/de la vue; **our sadness at the ~ of a loved one** notre tristesse après la perte d'un être aimé; **after the ~ of his wife, he ...** après avoir perdu sa femme, il ...; **it was a comfort to her in her great ~** c'était un réconfort pour elle dans son grand malheur or sa grande épreuve; **his death was a great ~ to the company** sa mort a été or a représenté une grande perte pour la société; **he's no great ~*** ce n'est pas une grande or une grosse perte; **to feel a sense of ~** éprouver un sentiment de vide; **~es amounting to £2 million** des pertes qui s'élèvent (or s'élevaient etc) à 2 millions de livres; **to suffer heavy ~es** subir des pertes importantes or de lourdes pertes; (*Mil*) **enemy ~es were high** l'ennemi avait subi de lourdes pertes; (*Pol: in election*) **Conservative ~es in the North** les sièges perdus par les conservateurs dans le nord; **to sell at a ~** [*salesman*] vendre à perte; [*goods*] se vendre à perte; **to cut one's ~es** faire la part du feu, sauver les meubles*

b **~ of appetite** ◊ **appetite ~** perte *f* d'appétit; **~ of blood** ◊ **blood ~** perte *f* de sang; (*more serious*) hémorragie *f*; **hair ~** perte *f* de cheveux; **weight ~** ◊ **~ of weight** perte *f* de poids; **there was great ~ of life** il y a eu beaucoup de victimes or de nombreuses victimes; **the coup succeeded without ~ of life** le coup (d'État) a réussi sans faire de victimes; **~ of heat** ◊ **heat ~** perte *f* de chaleur; **~ of earnings** or **income** perte *f* de revenus; **job ~es** suppressions *fpl* d'emploi; **the factory closed with the ~ of 300 jobs** l'usine a fermé et 300 emplois ont été supprimés; **without ~ of time** sans perte or sans perdre de temps; **to suffer a ~ of face** perdre la face → **dead, profit**

c **to be at a ~** être perplexe or embarrassé; **to be at a ~ to explain sth** être incapable d'expliquer qch, être embarrassé pour expliquer qch; **we are at a ~ to know why he did it** nous ne savons absolument pas pourquoi il l'a fait; **to be at a ~ for words** chercher or ne pas trouver ses mots; **he's never at a ~ for words** il a toujours quelque chose à dire

2 COMP ► **loss adjuster** N (*Brit Insurance*) expert *m* en sinistres ► **loss leader** N (*Comm*) article *m* pilote (*vendu à perte pour attirer les clients*) ► **loss maker** N (*Comm*) (= *product*) article *m* vendu à perte; (= *firm*) entreprise *f* en déficit chronique ► **loss-making** ADJ (*Comm*) [*product*] vendu à perte; [*firm*] déficitaire ► **loss ratio** N (*Insurance*) ratio *m* sinistres-pertes

lost [lɒst] **1** VB *pt, ptp* of **lose**

2 ADJ **a** (= *mislaid, not found*) perdu, égaré; **several ~ children were reported** on a signalé plusieurs cas d'enfants qui s'étaient perdus or égarés; (*Rel*) **the ~ sheep** la brebis égarée

b (= *bewildered, uncomprehending*) perdu; **it was too difficult for me, I was ~** c'était trop compliqué pour moi, j'étais perdu; **after his death I felt ~** après sa mort j'étais complètement perdu or désorienté; **he had a ~ look in his eyes** or **a ~ expression on his face** il avait l'air complètement perdu or désorienté; **to be ~ for words** chercher or ne pas trouver ses mots

c (= *gone, disappeared, departed*) [*person, job,*

limb, enthusiasm, interest] perdu; **to give sb/sth up for ~** considérer qn/qch comme perdu; **the ~ generation** la génération perdue; **songs that reminded him of his ~ youth** des chansons qui lui rappelaient sa jeunesse passée; **a mother mourning for her ~ child** une mère pleurant son enfant (disparu); **he was ~ to British science forever** ses dons ont été perdus à jamais pour la science britannique; **to regain one's ~ confidence** retrouver confiance en soi

d (= *beyond hope*) **~ cause** cause *f* perdue; (*Rel fig*) **a ~ soul** une âme en peine; **all is not ~!** tout n'est pas perdu!; **he is ~ to all finer feelings** tous les sentiments délicats le dépassent

e (= *wasted*) [+ *opportunity*] manqué, perdu; **my advice was ~ on him** il n'a pas écouté mes conseils, mes conseils ont été en pure perte; **modern music is ~ on me** (= *don't understand it*) je ne comprends rien à la musique moderne; (= *don't enjoy it*) la musique moderne me laisse froid; **the remark was ~ on him** il n'a pas compris la remarque; **to make up for ~ time** rattraper le temps perdu

f (= *absorbed*) perdu, plongé (**in** dans), absorbé (**in** par); **to be ~ in one's reading** être plongé dans sa lecture, être absorbé par sa lecture; **he was ~ in thought** il était perdu dans or absorbé par ses pensées; **she is ~ to the world*** elle est ailleurs, plus rien n'existe pour elle

3 COMP ► **lost and found** N (*US*) = **lost property** ► **lost-and-found columns** NPL (*Press*) (page *f* des) objets *mpl* perdus et trouvés ► **lost-and-found department** N (*US*) = **lost property office** ► **lost property** N objets *mpl* trouvés ► **lost property office** N (bureau *m* des) objets *mpl* trouvés

Lot [lɒt] N (*Bible*) Lot(h) *m*

lot¹ [lɒt] **1** N **a ~** (= *a great deal*) beaucoup; **I'd give a ~ to know ...** je donnerais cher pour savoir ...; **there wasn't a ~ we could do/say** nous ne pouvions pas faire/dire grand-chose; **a ~ of** beaucoup de; **a ~ of time/money** beaucoup de temps/d'argent; **there were a ~ of people** il y avait beaucoup de monde; **a ~ of people think that ...** beaucoup de gens pensent que ...; **quite a ~ of** [*of people, cars*] un assez grand nombre de, pas mal de; [*of honey, cream*] une assez grande quantité de, pas mal de; **such a ~ of ...** tellement de ..., tant de ...; **what a ~!** quelle quantité!; **what a ~ of people!** que de monde or de gens!; **what a ~ of time you take to get dressed!** tu en mets du temps à t'habiller!; **we don't go out a ~** nous ne sortons pas beaucoup or pas souvent; **we see a ~ of her** nous la voyons souvent or beaucoup; **things have changed quite a ~** les choses ont beaucoup or pas mal changé; **he cries such a ~** il pleure tellement; **he's a ~ better** il va beaucoup or bien mieux; **that's a ~ better** c'est beaucoup or bien mieux; (*iro*) **a ~ you care!*** comme si ça te faisait quelque chose!; (*iro*) **a ~ that'll help!*** la belle avance!; **thanks a ~!*** merci beaucoup!; (*iro*) merci (bien)! (*iro*) → **awful, fat**

2 **lots*** NPL (= *plenty*) beaucoup, des tas*; **~s of** beaucoup de, plein de*; **~s and ~s (of)** [*of people, cars*] des tas* (de); [*of flowers*] des masses* (de); [*of butter, honey*] des tonnes* (de); **I've got ~s** j'en ai plein*; **there's ~s (of it)** il y en a plein*; **there were ~s (of them)** il y en avait plein*; **~s better/bigger/easier** bien mieux/plus grand/plus facile

lot² [lɒt] N **a** (= *destiny*) sort *m*, lot *m* (*liter*); **the hardships that are the ~ of the poor** la dure vie qui est le lot des pauvres; (*liter*) **it is the common ~** c'est le sort or le lot commun; **she is content with her ~** elle est contente de son sort; **a woman's/soldier's ~ is not always a happy one** ce n'est pas toujours facile d'être une femme/d'être soldat; **her ~ (in life) had not been a happy one** elle n'avait pas eu une vie heureuse; **it was not his ~ to make a fortune**, il n'était pas destiné à faire fortune, le sort n'a pas voulu qu'il fasse fortune; **it fell to my ~ to break the news to her** il m'incomba de or il me revint de lui annoncer la nouvelle; **to improve one's ~** améliorer sa condition; **to throw in** or **cast in one's ~ with sb** partager (volontairement) le sort de qn, unir sa destinée à celle de qn

b (= *random selection*) tirage *m* au sort, sort *m*; **by ~** par tirage au sort; **to draw** or **cast ~s** tirer au sort

c (= *batch*) [*of goods*] lot *m*; [*of shares*] paquet *m*; **there was only one ~ of recruits still to arrive** il ne manquait plus qu'un lot de recrues; (*at auction*) **~ no. 69 is an antique table** le lot no. 69 est une table ancienne; **are you coming, you ~?*** bon vous venez, vous autres?; **us ~‡ should stick together** il faut qu'on se serre (*subj*) les coudes; **he's a bad ~*** il ne vaut pas cher*; **you rotten ~!*** vous êtes vaches!‡ → **job**

d (*noun phrase*) **the ~*** (= *everything*) (le) tout*; (= *everyone*) tous *mpl*, toutes *fpl*; **that's the ~** c'est tout, tout y est; **here are some apples, take the (whole) ~** voici des pommes, prends-les toutes; **here's some money, just take the ~** voici de l'argent, prends tout; **the (whole) ~ cost me £1** ça m'a coûté une livre en tout; **big ones, little ones, the ~!** les grands, les petits, tous!; **the ~ of you** vous tous; **they went off, the whole ~ of them** ils sont tous partis, ils sont partis tous tant qu'ils étaient

e (*esp US*) (= *plot of land*) lot *m* (de terrain), parcelle *f*; (= *film studio*) enceinte *f* des studios; **building ~** terrain *m* à bâtir; **vacant** or **empty ~** terrain *m* disponible; **parking*** (*US*) **all over the ~*** (= *everywhere*) partout; (= *in confusion*) en désordre, bordélique*

loth [ləʊθ] ADJ = **loath**

Lothario [ləʊˈθɑːrɪˌəʊ] N (*liter* or *hum*) don Juan *m*

lotion [ˈləʊʃən] N lotion *f* → **hand**

lotos [ˈləʊtəs] N = **lotus**

lottery [ˈlɒtərɪ] N (*lit*, *fig*) loterie *f*; **~ ticket** billet *m* de loterie

lotto [ˈlɒtəʊ] N loto *m*

lotus [ˈləʊtəs] **1** N lotus *m* **2** COMP ► **lotus-eater** N (*Myth*) mangeur *m*, -euse *f* de lotus, lotophage *m* ► **lotus position** N (*Yoga*) position *f* du lotus

louche [luːʃ] ADJ [*person, place*] louche

loud [laʊd] **1** ADJ **a** (= *noisy*) [*voice*] fort, sonore; [*laugh*] bruyant, sonore; [*noise, cry*] sonore, grand; [*music*] bruyant, sonore; [*thunder*] fracassant; [*protests*] vigoureux; (*pej*) [*behaviour*] tapageur; **the orchestra is too ~** l'orchestre joue trop fort; **the music is too ~** la musique est trop bruyante; **in a ~ voice** d'une voix forte; **... he said in a ~ whisper** ... chuchota-t-il bruyamment; **this remark was greeted by ~ applause** un tonnerre d'applaudissements a accueilli cette remarque; **to be ~ in one's support/condemnation of sth** soutenir/condamner qch avec force et virulence; (*Mus*) **~ pedal** pédale *f* forte

b (*pej* = *gaudy*) [*colour*] voyant, criard; [*clothes*] voyant, tapageur

2 ADV [*speak etc*] fort, haut; **turn the radio up a little ~er** mets la radio un peu plus fort, augmente le volume (de la radio); **out ~** tout haut; **to laugh out ~** rire tout haut; (*Telec*) **I am reading** or **receiving you ~ and clear** je vous reçois cinq sur cinq; (*fig*) **the president's message was received ~ and clear** le message du président a été reçu cinq sur cinq; **we could hear it ~ and clear** nous l'entendions clairement

3 COMP ► **loud-mouth*** N (*pej*) grande gueule‡ *f* ► **loud-mouthed** ADJ (*pej*) braillard, fort en gueule

loudhailer [ˌlaʊdˈheɪlə] N (*Brit*) porte-voix *m inv*, mégaphone *m*

loudly [ˈlaʊdlɪ] ADV **a** (= *noisily, in a loud voice*) [*say*] d'une voix forte; [*talk, speak, shout*] fort; [*laugh, clear one's throat, knock, applaud, quarrel, complain*] bruyamment; [*proclaim*] haut et fort **b** (*fig* = *vociferously*) [*complain, protest*] vigoureusement **c** (*pej* = *garishly*) [*dress*] d'une façon voyante or tapageuse

loudness [ˈlaʊdnɪs] N [*of voice, tone, music, thunder*] force *f*; [*of applause*] bruit *m*; [*of protests*] vigueur *f*

loudspeaker [ˌlaʊdˈspiːkə] N (*for PA system, musical instruments*) haut-parleur *m*, enceinte *f*; [*of stereo*] baffle *m*, enceinte *f*

lough [lɒx] N (*Ir*) lac *m*; **Lough Corrib** le lough Corrib

Louis [ˈluːɪ] N Louis *m*; **~ XIV** Louis XIV

louis [ˈluːɪ] N (*pl inv*) louis *m* (d'or)

Louisiana [luːˌiːzɪˈænə] N la Louisiane; **in ~** en Louisiane

lounge [laʊndʒ] **1** N (*esp Brit*) [*of house, hotel*] salon *m* → **airport, arrival, departure, sun, television 2** VI (= *recline*) (*on bed, chair*) se prélasser; (*pej* = *sprawl*) être allongé paresseusement; **to ~ against a wall** s'appuyer paresseusement contre un mur **3** COMP ► **lounge bar** N [*of pub*] ≈ salon *m*; [*of hotel*] ≈ bar *m* ► **lounge jacket** N (*US*) veste *f* d'intérieur or d'appartement ► **lounge lizard**†* N (*pej*) salonnard *m* (*pej*) ► **lounge suit** N (*Brit*) complet(-veston) *m*; (*US*) tenue *f* d'intérieur (de femme); (*Brit: on invitation*) **"~ suit"** « tenue de ville »

► **lounge about, lounge around** VI paresser, flâner, flemmarder*

► **lounge back** VI **to ~ back in a chair** se prélasser dans un fauteuil

lounger [ˈlaʊndʒə] N **a** (= *bed*) lit *m* de plage **b** (*pej* = *person*) fainéant(e) *m(f)*, flemmard(e)* *m(f)*

louse [laʊs] N (*pl* **lice**) **a** (= *insect*) pou *m* **b** (‡ *pej* = *person*) salaud‡ *m*, (peau *f* de) vache‡ *f* (« *louse* » dans ce sens est utilisé au singulier seulement)

► **louse up*** VT SEP [+ *deal, event*] bousiller*, foutre en l'air‡

lousy [ˈlaʊzɪ] ADJ **a** (* = *terrible*) [*car, day, weather*] pourri*; [*idea, film, book, pay*] nul, minable; [*food*] infect, dégueulasse‡; [*headache*] fichu* (*before n*); [*mood*] massacrant; **to be a ~ secretary/teacher** être nul en tant que secrétaire/professeur; **she's a ~ driver** elle conduit comme un pied*; **to be a ~ lover** être nul au lit; **to be ~ at sth** être nul en qch; **she's been having a ~ time lately** la vie n'est pas drôle pour elle en ce moment; **we had a ~ time on holiday** nos vacances ont été un vrai cauchemar; **to be ~ to sb** être infect avec qn **b** (*: *expressing displeasure*) **fifty ~ pounds!** 50 malheureuses livres!; **a ~ trick** une vacherie*; **you can keep your ~ job, I don't want it!** votre boulot minable or votre boulot de merde‡, je n'en veux pas! **c** (= *ill*) **to feel ~*** être mal fichu* **d** (*esp US:** = *teeming*) **this place is ~ with cops** c'est infesté de flics* ici; **he is ~ with money** il est bourré de fric* **e** (= *infested with lice*) [*person, blanket*] pouilleux

lout [laʊt] N rustre *m*, butor *m* → **litterbug**

loutish [ˈlaʊtɪʃ] ADJ [*manners*] de rustre, de butor; **his ~ behaviour** la grossièreté de sa conduite

louvre, louver (*US*) [ˈluːvə] N (*in roof*) lucarne *f*; (*on window*) persienne *f*, jalousie *f*

louvred door, louvered door (*US*) [ˈluːvədɔː] N porte *f* à claire-voie

lovable [ˈlʌvəbl] ADJ [*person*] très sympathique; [*child, animal*] adorable

▼ **love** [lʌv] **1** N **a** (*for person*) amour *m* (**of** de, **for** pour); (*for country, music, horses*) amour *m* (**of** de, **for** pour); (*stronger*) passion *f*

(**of** de, **for** pour); **her ~ for** or **of her children** son amour pour ses enfants, l'amour qu'elle porte (or portait *etc*) à ses enfants; **her children's ~ (for her)** l'amour que lui portent (or portaient *etc*) ses enfants; **I feel no ~ for** or **towards him any longer** je n'éprouve plus d'amour pour lui; **for ~ of her son** ◊ **out of ~ for her son** par amour pour son fils; **for the ~ of God** pour l'amour de Dieu → **god**; → **Mike**; **don't give me any money, I'm doing it for ~** ne me donnez pas d'argent, je le fais gratuitement or pour l'amour de l'art; **to marry for ~** faire un mariage d'amour; **he studies history for the ~ of it** il étudie l'histoire pour son or le plaisir; **they are in ~ (with each other)** ils s'aiment; **she's in ~** elle est amoureuse; **to be/fall in ~ with** être/tomber amoureux de; **it was ~ at first sight** ça a été le coup de foudre; **there's no ~ lost between them** ils ne peuvent pas se sentir*; **to make ~** faire l'amour (**with** avec, **to** à); **I won't do it for ~ nor money** je ne le ferai pour rien au monde; **it wasn't to be had for ~ nor money** c'était introuvable, on ne pouvait se le procurer à aucun prix → **brotherly, labour, lady**

b (*in formulae: in letter*) **(with) ~ (from) Jim** affectueusement, Jim; **all my ~, Jim** bises, Jim; **give her my ~** dis-lui bien des choses de ma part; (*stronger*) embrasse-la pour moi; **~ and kisses** bisous *mpl*, grosses bises *fpl*; **he sends (you) his ~** il t'envoie ses amitiés; (*stronger*) il t'embrasse

c (= *object of affections*) [*of thing, object*] passion *f*; [*of person*] amour *m*; **the theatre was her great ~** le théâtre était sa grande passion; **he's a little ~!*** il est adorable!; **his first ~ was football** sa première passion a été le football; **he thought of his first ~** il pensait à son premier amour; **he/she is the ~ of my life** c'est l'homme/la femme de ma vie; **football is the ~ of her life** le football est sa grande passion

d (*Brit*: term of address: in shop etc*) (*to man*) monsieur; (*to woman*) ma jolie*; (*to child*) mon petit, ma petite; **(my) ~** (*to man*) mon chéri; (*to woman*) ma chérie

e (*Tennis etc*) rien *m*, zéro *m*; **~ 30** rien à 30, zéro 30

2 VT **a** (= *feel affection for*) [+ *partner, spouse, child*] aimer; [+ *relative, friend*] aimer (beaucoup); **he didn't just like her, he ~d her** il ne l'aimait pas d'amitié, mais d'amour; **they each other** ils s'aiment ■ (*PROV*) **~ me, ~ my dog** qui m'aime aime mon chien; **I must ~ you and leave you*** malheureusement, il faut que je vous quitte; (*Bible*) **~ thy neighbour as thyself** tu aimeras ton prochain comme toi-même; (*counting etc*) **she ~s me, she ~s me not** elle m'aime, un peu, beaucoup, passionnément, à la folie, pas du tout

b (= *appreciate, enjoy*) [+ *music, food, activity, place*] aimer (beaucoup); (*stronger*) adorer; **to ~ to do** or **doing sth** aimer (beaucoup) or adorer faire qch; **he ~s reading/knitting/photography** il est passionné de lecture/tricot/photographie, il aime or adore lire/tricoter/la photographie; **she ~s singing/swimming** elle aime or adore chanter/nager; **I'd ~ to come** j'aimerais beaucoup venir, je serais enchanté or ravi de venir; (*in answer to question*) **I'd ~ to!** avec plaisir!; **I'd ~ to but unfortunately ...** j'aimerais bien, malheureusement ...; **I ~ the way she smiles** j'adore son sourire; (*iro*) **she's going to ~ you!** elle va te bénir! (*iro*); (*iro*) **she's going to ~ that!** elle va être ravie! (*iro*)

3 COMP ► **love affair** N (*lit*) liaison *f* (amoureuse); (*fig*) passion *f* (**with** pour) ► **love apple**† N (= *tomato*) pomme *f* d'amour† ► **love child** N enfant *mf* de l'amour, enfant *mf* illégitime or naturel(le) ► **loved ones** NPL êtres *mpl* chers; **my ~d ones** les être qui me sont chers ► **love feast** N (*among early Christians*) agape *f*; (= *banquet*) banquet *m*; (*iro*) agapes *fpl* ► **love game** N (*Tennis*) jeu *m* blanc ► **love handles*** NPL poignées *fpl* d'amour* ► **love-hate relationship** N rapport *m* amour-haine; **they have a ~hate relationship** ils s'aiment et se détestent à la fois ► **love-in-a-mist** N (*Bot*) nigelle *f* de Damas ► **love-knot** N lacs *mpl* d'amour ► **love letter** N lettre *f* d'amour, billet *m* doux (*often hum*) ► **love life*** N how's your ~ **life (these days)?** comment vont les amours?; **his ~ life is bothering him** il a des problèmes de cœur *or* sentimentaux ► **love match** N mariage *m* d'amour ► **love nest*** N nid *m* d'amoureux *or* d'amour ► **love scene** N scène *f* d'amour ► **love seat** N causeuse *f* (*siège*) ► **love story** N histoire *f* d'amour ► **love token** N gage *m* d'amour ► **love triangle** N triangle *m* amoureux

lovebirds ['lʌvbɜːdz] NPL [a] (*Orn*) perruches *fpl* inséparables [b] (*fig* = *lovers*) tourtereaux *mpl*

lovebite ['lʌvbaɪt] N suçon *m*

-loved [-lʌvd] ADJ (*in compounds*) **much-loved** adoré; **best-loved** préféré

loveless ['lʌvlɪs] ADJ [*life, family, marriage*] sans amour; [*person*] (= *unloved*) qui manque d'affection; (= *unloving*) incapable d'aimer

loveliness ['lʌvlɪnɪs] N beauté *f*, charme *m*

lovelorn ['lʌv.lɔːn] ADJ († *or hum*) qui languit d'amour

lovely ['lʌvlɪ] [1] ADJ [a] (= *beautiful*) [*woman, place, clothes, flower*] ravissant; [*baby, animal, picture, voice*] beau (belle *f*); **you look ~** tu es ravissant; **this dress looks ~ on you** cette robe te va à ravir [b] (= *pleasant*) [*person*] charmant; [*day, weekend, flavour, meal, surprise*] merveilleux; [*weather, holiday*] beau (belle *f*), merveilleux; [*food, smell*] délicieux; [*idea, suggestion*] excellent; **~!** formidable!; (= *fine*) **thanks, that's ~*** merci, c'est très bien comme ça; **it's ~ to see you again** ça me fait bien plaisir de te revoir; **it's been ~ seeing** *or* **to see you** j'ai été vraiment content de vous voir; **we had a ~ time** nous nous sommes bien amusés; **he made a ~ job of it** il a fait du bon travail; **the water's ~ and warm** l'eau est bonne; **it was ~ and hot outside** il faisait agréablement chaud dehors; **we're ~ and early*** c'est bien, on est en avance [2] N (* = *girl*) belle fille *f*, beau brin *m* de fille, mignonne *f*; **my ~** ma jolie, ma mignonne

lovemaking ['lʌv.meɪkɪŋ] N (*NonC*) amour *m*, rapports *mpl* (sexuels); **after ~** après l'amour

lover ['lʌvə'] [1] N [a] amant *m*; († = *suitor*) amoureux *m*; **~s' vows** promesses *fpl* d'amoureux; **they are ~s** ils ont une liaison, ils couchent* ensemble; **they have been ~s for two years** leur liaison dure depuis deux ans; **she took a ~** elle a pris un amant; **Casanova was a great ~** Casanova fut un grand séducteur [b] [*of hobby, wine etc*] amateur *m*; **he's a ~ of good food** il est grand amateur de bonne cuisine, il aime beaucoup la bonne cuisine; **he's a great ~ of Brahms** *or* **a great Brahms ~** c'est un fervent de Brahms, il aime beaucoup (la musique de) Brahms; **art/theatre ~** amateur *m* d'art/de théâtre; **music ~** amateur *m* de musique, mélomane *mf*; **he's a nature ~** il aime la nature, c'est un amoureux de la nature; **football ~s everywhere** tous les amateurs *or* passionnés de football [2] COMP ► **lover boy*** N (*hum or iro* = *womanizer*) don Juan *m*, tombeur* *m*; **come on ~ boy!** allez, beau gosse!*

lovesick ['lʌvsɪk] ADJ amoureux, qui languit d'amour

lovesong ['lʌvsɒŋ] N chanson *f* d'amour

lovey-dovey* ['lʌvɪ'dʌvɪ] ADJ (*hum*) (trop) tendre

loving ['lʌvɪŋ] [1] ADJ [*person, child, couple, relationship*] affectueux; [*marriage*] heureux; [*wife, husband, parent*] aimant; [*family*] uni; [*kiss*] tendre; [*smile*] plein de tendresse; **~ kindness** bonté *f*, charité *f*; **with ~ care** avec le plus grand soin; **"from your ~ son, Martin"** « ton fils qui t'aime, Martin » [2] COMP ► **loving cup** N coupe *f* de l'amitié

-loving ['lʌvɪŋ] ADJ (*in compounds*) **art-loving** qui aime l'art, qui est amateur d'art; **money-loving** qui aime l'argent

lovingly ['lʌvɪŋlɪ] ADV [a] [*look at*] (= *with affection*) tendrement, avec tendresse; (= *with love*) amoureusement [b] (= *carefully*) [*restored, maintained*] avec amour

low¹ [ləʊ] [1] ADJ [a] [*wall, shelf, seat, ceiling, level, tide*] bas (basse *f*); **a dress with a ~ neck** une robe décolletée; **to make a ~ bow** saluer bien bas; (*Met*) **~ cloud** nuages *mpl* bas; **fog on ~ ground** brouillard *m* à basse altitude; **the ~ ground near the sea** les basses terres *fpl* près de la mer; **the house/town is on ~ ground** la maison/ville est bâtie dans une dépression; **the river is very ~ just now** la rivière est très basse en ce moment; **the sun is ~ in the sky** le soleil est bas dans le ciel *or* bas sur l'horizon; **at ~ tide** à marée basse; **~ water** marée *f* basse, basses eaux *fpl*; (*fig*) **the ~ point** [*of sb's career*] le creux de la vague → 4, **lower¹**; → **ebb** [b] [*voice*] (= *soft*) bas (basse *f*); (= *deep*) bas (basse *f*); (*Mus*) [*note*] bas (basse *f*); **in a ~ voice** (= *softly*) à voix basse; (= *in deep tones*) d'une voix basse *or* profonde; **a ~ murmur** un murmure sourd *or* étouffé; **they were talking in a ~ murmur** ils chuchotaient; **he gave a ~ groan** il a gémi faiblement, il a poussé un faible gémissement; **it's a bit ~** [*radio etc*] on n'entend pas, ce n'est pas assez fort → 4 [c] [*wage, rate*] bas (basse *f*), faible; [*price*] bas (basse *f*), modéré; **people on ~ incomes** les gens à faibles revenus; (*Comm*) **at the ~est price** au meilleur prix [d] [*latitude, number, frequency*] bas (basse *f*); (*Scol*) [*mark*] bas (basse *f*), faible; (*Chem, Phys*) [*density*] faible; [*temperature*] bas (basse *f*), peu élevé; [*speed*] petit (*before n*); [*lights*] faible, bas (basse *f*); [*visibility*] mauvais, limité; (*Aut*) **in ~ gear** en première *or* en seconde (vitesse); **the temperature never falls below 20° at the ~est** la température ne tombe jamais en dessous de 20°; **the temperature is in the ~ thirties** il fait entre 30 et 35 degrés; **the fire is getting ~ /is ~** le feu baisse/est bas; (*Culin*) **at** *or* **on a ~ heat** à feu doux; **cook in a ~ oven** cuire au four à feu doux [e] [*standard*] bas (basse *f*), faible; [*quality*] inférieur (-eure *f*); **activity is at its ~est in the summer** c'est en été que l'activité est particulièrement réduite; **people of ~ intelligence** les gens peu intelligents; **to have a ~ opinion of sb** ne pas avoir bonne opinion de qn, avoir une piètre opinion de qn; **to have a ~ opinion of sth** ne pas avoir bonne opinion de qch; (*Comm etc*) **their stock of soap was very ~** leur stock de savon était presque épuisé; **supplies are getting** *or* **running ~** les provisions diminuent → 4, **lower¹**; → **profile** [f] **~ in fat** à faible teneur en matières grasses; **~ in nitrogen** contenant peu d'azote; **we're a bit ~ on petrol** nous n'avons plus beaucoup *or* il ne nous reste plus beaucoup d'essence; **they were ~ on water** ils étaient à court d'eau; **I'm ~ on funds*** je suis à court (d'argent) [g] (*Cards*) **a ~ card** une basse carte; **a ~ diamond** un petit carreau [h] (= *feeble*) [*person*] faible, affaibli; [*health*] mauvais, (= *depressed*) déprimé; **to be in ~ spirits ◊ to be** *or* **feel ~** être déprimé, ne pas avoir le moral; **the patient is very ~** le malade est bien bas → 4 [i] (*Bio, Zool* = *primitive*) inférieur (-eure *f*), peu

évolué; **the ~ forms of life** les formes *fpl* de vie inférieures *or* les moins évoluées [j] (= *humble*) [*rank, origin*] bas (basse *f*); (= *vulgar*) [*company, taste*] mauvais; [*character*] grossier, bas (basse *f*); [*café etc*] de bas étage; (= *shameful*) [*behaviour*] ignoble, odieux; **the ~est of the ~** le dernier des derniers; **that's a ~ trick** c'est un sale tour*; **with ~ cunning** avec une ruse ignoble → 4, **lower¹** [2] ADV [a] (= *in low position*) [*aim, fly*] bas; **to bow ~** saluer bien bas; **a dress cut ~ in the back** une robe très décolletée dans le dos; **she is rather ~ down in that chair** elle est bien bas dans ce fauteuil, elle est assise bien bas; **~er down the wall/the page** plus bas sur le mur/la page; **~er down the hill** plus bas sur la colline, en contrebas; **the plane came down ~ over the town** l'avion est descendu et a survolé la ville à basse altitude; **the plane flew ~ over the town** l'avion a survolé la ville à basse altitude; **to fall** *or* **sink ~** tomber bien bas; **I wouldn't stoop so ~ as to do that** je ne m'abaisserais pas à faire cela → **lay¹, lie¹** [b] (= *at low volume, intensity, cost*) **to turn the heating/lights/music/radio down ~** baisser le chauffage/la lumière/la musique/la radio; **the fire was burning ~** le feu était bas; **to speak ~** parler à voix basse *or* doucement; **to sing ~** chanter bas; **the song is pitched too ~ for me** le ton de cette chanson est trop bas pour moi; (*in singing*) **I can't get as ~ as that** ma voix ne descend pas si bas; (*St Ex*) **to buy ~** acheter quand le cours est bas; (*Cards*) **to play ~** jouer une basse carte [3] N [a] (*Met*) dépression *f* [b] (*Aut*) = **low gear** → **1d** [c] (= *low point: esp Fin*) minimum *m*; **prices/temperatures have reached a new ~** *or* **an all-time ~** les prix/les températures ont atteint leur niveau le plus bas *or* n'ont jamais été aussi bas(ses); **the pound has sunk** *or* **fallen to a new ~** la livre a atteint son niveau le plus bas; **this is really a new ~ in vulgarity** cela bat tous les records de vulgarité [4] COMP ► **low-alcohol** ADJ [*lager, wine, beer*] à faible teneur en alcool, peu alcoolisé ► **low-angle shot** N (*Phot*) contre-plongée *f* ► **low blow** N (*Boxing, fig*) coup *m* bas ► **low-budget** ADJ [*film, project*] à petit budget; [*car etc*] pour les petits budgets ► **low-calorie, low-cal*** ADJ [*food, diet*] à basses calories, hypocalorique ► **Low Church** N tendance évangéliste de l'Église anglicane ► **low-cost** ADJ (à) bon marché, pas cher; (*NonC*) **~cost housing** habitations *fpl* à loyer modéré, HLM *mpl* ► **the Low Countries** NPL les Pays-Bas *mpl* ► **low-cut** ADJ [*dress etc*] décolleté ► **low-down** → **low-down** ► **lowest common denominator** N (*Math*) plus petit commun dénominateur *m*; (*fig*) **teachers have to go at the pace of the ~est common denominator** les professeurs doivent suivre le rythme des éléments les moins doués ► **lowest common multiple** N (*Math*) plus petit commun multiple *m* ► **low-fat** ADJ [*diet*] pauvre en matières grasses; [*milk, cheese etc*] allégé ► **low-flying** ADJ volant à basse altitude ► **low flying** N (*NonC*) vol(s) *m(pl)* à basse altitude ► **Low German** N bas allemand *m* ► **low-grade** ADJ de qualité *or* de catégorie inférieure ► **low-heeled** ADJ à talon(s) plat(s), plat ► **low-key** ADJ discret (-ète *f*); **it was a ~key operation** l'opération a été conduite de façon très discrète; **to keep sth ~key** faire qch de façon discrète ► **Low Latin** N bas latin *m* ► **low-level** ADJ (*gen*) bas (basse *f*); [*job*] subalterne; [*talks, discussions*] à bas niveau; (*Aviat*) **~level flying** vol *m* *or* navigation *f* à basse altitude; (*Comput*) **~level language** langage *m* de bas niveau; (*Nucl Phys*) **~level waste** déchets *mpl* de faible activité ► **low-loader** N (*Aut*) semi-remorque *f* à plateforme surbaissée; (*Rail*) wagon *m* (de marchandises) à plateforme surbaissée ► **low-lying** ADJ à basse altitude ► **Low Mass** N (*Rel*) messe *f* basse ► **low-**

minded ADJ vulgaire, grossier ► **low-necked** ADJ décolleté ► **low-paid** ADJ [*job*] mal payé, qui paie mal; [*worker*] mal payé, qui ne gagne pas beaucoup; **the ~-paid** les petits salaires *mpl*, les petits salariés *mpl* → **lower¹** ► **low-pitched** ADJ [*ball*] bas (basse *f*); [*sound*] bas (basse *f*), grave ► **low-powered** ADJ de faible puissance ► **low-pressure** ADJ à or de basse pression ► **low-priced** ADJ à bas prix, (à) bon marché *inv* ► **low-principled** ADJ sans grands principes ► **low-profile** ADJ (*gen*) au profil bas; (*Aut*) **~-profile tyre** pneu *m* taille basse ► **low-quality** ADJ [*goods*] de qualité inférieure ► **low-rent** ADJ [*housing, flat*] à loyer modéré; (*fig*) de bas étage ► **low-rise** ADJ (*Archit*) à or de hauteur limitée, bas (basse *f*) ► **low-scoring** ADJ *où peu de points ou buts sont marqués* ► **low season** N (*esp Brit*) basse or morte-saison *f* ♦ ADJ [*rates, holiday*] pendant la basse or morte-saison ► **low-slung** ADJ [*chair*] bas (basse *f*); [*sports car*] surbaissé ► **low-spirited** ADJ déprimé, démoralisé ► **low-start mortgage** N (*Brit*) *emprunt hypothécaire à faibles remboursements initiaux* ► **Low Sunday** N dimanche *m* de Quasimodo ► **low-tar** ADJ [*cigarette*] à faible teneur en goudron ► **low-tech** ADJ [*machinery*] rudimentaire; [*design*] sommaire ► **low-tension** ADJ à basse tension ► **low vowel** N (*Ling*) voyelle *f* basse ► **low-water mark** N (*lit*) laisse *f* de basse mer; (*fig*) **their morale had reached ~-water mark** leur moral était on ne peut plus bas, ils avaient le moral à zéro*; **sales had reached ~-water mark** les ventes n'avaient jamais été aussi mauvaises

low² [ləʊ] VI [*cattle*] meugler, beugler, mugir

lowborn ['ləʊbɔːn] ADJ de basse extraction

lowboy ['ləʊbɔɪ] N (*US*) commode *f* basse

lowbrow* ['ləʊbraʊ] **1** N (= *person*) personne *f* peu intellectuelle or sans prétentions intellectuelles **2** ADJ [*person, book, film, programme*] sans prétentions intellectuelles

low-down* ['ləʊdaʊn] **1** ADJ (*esp US pej*) [*person*] méprisable; **a ~ trick** un sale tour **2** N **to get the ~ on sb/sth** se renseigner sur qn/qch; **to give sb the ~ on sth** mettre au courant or au parfum* de qch

lower¹ ['ləʊəʳ] *compar of* **low¹** **1** ADJ inférieur (-eure *f*); **the ~ half of the body** le bas du corps; **Annapurna is the ~ of the two** l'Annapurna est la moins haute (des deux); **the ~ shelf** l'étagère *f* du bas → **low¹**; → **reach**

2 COMP ► **the lower abdomen** N le bas-ventre ► **the lower animals** NPL les animaux *mpl* inférieurs ► **the lower back** N le bas du dos ► **lower-back pain** N douleurs *fpl* lombaires ► **lower case** N (*Typ*) bas *m* de casse; **in ~ case** en bas de casse ► **lower-case** ADJ minuscule ► **the lower chamber** N (*Parl*) la Chambre basse ► **lower class** N classes *fpl* inférieures, classe *f* populaire; **~-class family** famille *f* prolétarienne or ouvrière ► **lower classes** NPL = **lower class** ► **lower court** N (*Jur*) instance *f* inférieure ► **lower deck** N [*of bus*] plate-forme *f* inférieure; (*Naut*) (= *part of ship*) pont *m* inférieur; (= *personnel*) **the ~ deck*** les sous-officiers *mpl* et les matelots *mpl* ► **Lower Egypt** N la Basse-Égypte ► **the Lower House** N (*Parl*) (*gen*) la Chambre basse; (*Brit*) la Chambre basse, la Chambre des communes ► **lower-income** ADJ [*group, family*] économiquement faible ► **lower jaw** N mâchoire *f* inférieure ► **the lower leg** N la partie inférieure de la jambe ► **lower limbs** NPL membres *mpl* inférieurs ► **lower lip** N lèvre *f* inférieure ► **the lower mammals** NPL les mammifères *mpl* inférieurs ► **lower middle class** N petite bourgeoisie *f*, (petite) classe *f* moyenne; **a ~ middle-class family** une famille de la classe moyenne or de la petite bourgeoisie; **a ~ middle-class background** un milieu petit bourgeois ► **the lower paid** NPL les personnes *fpl* à faible revenu ► **the lower ranks** NPL (*Mil*) les grades *mpl* inférieurs; (*fig*) les rangs *mpl* inférieurs ► **the Lower Rhine** N le Bas-Rhin ► **Lower Saxony** N la Basse-Saxe ► **the lower school** N ≈ le collège ► **lower sixth (form)** N (*Brit Scol*) ≈ classe *f* de première ► **the lower vertebrates** NPL (*Zool*) les vertébrés *mpl* inférieurs → **second¹**

lower² ['ləʊəʳ] **1** VT **a** [+ *blind, window, construction*] baisser, abaisser; [+ *sail, flag*] abaisser, amener; [+ *boat, lifeboat*] mettre à la mer; **to ~ the boats** mettre les embarcations à la mer; **to ~ sb/sth on a rope** (faire) descendre qn/descendre qch au bout d'une corde; **to ~ one's guard** (*Boxing*) baisser sa garde; (*fig*) ne plus être sur ses gardes; (*fig*) **to ~ the boom on sb** serrer la vis* à qn
b (*fig*) [+ *pressure, heating, price, voice*] baisser; (*Med*) **to ~ sb's resistance** diminuer la résistance de qn; **to ~ sb's morale** démoraliser qn, saper le moral de qn; **~ your voice!** baisse la voix!, (*parle*) moins fort!; **he ~ed his voice to a whisper** il a baissé la voix jusqu'à en chuchoter, il s'est mis à chuchoter; **to ~ o.s. to do sth** s'abaisser à faire qch; **I refuse to ~ myself** je refuse de m'abaisser or de m'avilir ainsi **2** VI (*lit*) baisser; [*pressure, price etc*] baisser, diminuer

lower³ ['laʊəʳ] VI [*sky*] se couvrir, s'assombrir; [*clouds*] être menaçant; [*person*] prendre un air sombre or menaçant; **to ~ at sb** jeter un regard menaçant à qn, regarder qn de travers

lowering¹ ['ləʊərɪŋ] **1** N **a** [*of window, flag*] abaissement *m*; [*of boat*] mise *f* à la mer **b** [*of temperature*] baisse *f*, abaissement *m*; [*of price, value*] baisse *f*, diminution *f*; [*of pressure*] baisse *f*; (*Med*) [*of resistance*] diminution *f*; **the ~ of morale** la baisse du moral, la démoralisation **2** ADJ abaissant, dégradant, humiliant

lowering² ['laʊərɪŋ] ADJ [*look, sky*] sombre, menaçant

lowing ['ləʊɪŋ] N [*of cattle*] meuglement *m*, beuglement *m*, mugissement *m*

lowland ['ləʊlənd] **1** N plaine *f*; **the Lowlands (of Scotland)** la Basse Écosse, les Basses-Terres *fpl* (d'Écosse) **2** COMP (*in Scot*) [*town, people, culture*] de Basse-Écosse ► **Lowland Scots** N (*Ling*) = **Lallans 1**

lowlander ['ləʊləndəʳ] N (*gen*) habitant(e) *m(f)* de la (or des) plaine(s); (*in Scot*) **Lowlander** habitant(e) *m(f)* or originaire *mf* de la Basse-Écosse

lowlife* ['ləʊlaɪf] ADJ (*esp US*) **his ~ friends** les voyous qu'il fréquente

lowlights ['ləʊlaɪts] NPL **a** (*Hairdressing*) mèches *fpl* sombres **b** (*hum*) **one of the ~* of the sporting season** un des moments les moins glorieux de la saison sportive

lowliness ['ləʊlɪnɪs] N humilité *f*

lowly ['ləʊlɪ] ADJ humble

lowness ['ləʊnɪs] N (*in height*) manque *m* de hauteur; [*of price, wages*] modicité *f*; [*of temperature*] peu *m* d'élévation; **the ~ of the ceiling made him stoop** la maison était si basse de plafond qu'il a dû se baisser

lox [lɒks] N (*US*) saumon *m* fumé

loyal ['lɔɪəl] ADJ [*friend, ally, supporter*] loyal, fidèle; [*wife, customer, reader*] fidèle; [*employee, servant*] fidèle, dévoué; **he has a ~ following** il a des partisans fidèles; **the Queen's ~ subjects** les loyaux sujets de la reine; (*Brit*) **the ~ toast** le toast porté au souverain; **to be/remain or stay ~ to sb/sth** être/rester fidèle à qn/qch

loyalist ['lɔɪəlɪst] ADJ, N loyaliste *mf*

loyally ['lɔɪəlɪ] ADV [*serve, support*] fidèlement; [*say*] en toute loyauté

loyalty ['lɔɪəltɪ] **1** N (*to person*) loyauté *f* (**to** envers); (*to cause*) dévouement *m* (**to** à); (*to political party*) loyauté *f*, loyalisme *m* (**to** envers); **my first ~ is to my family** ma famille passe avant tout; **to pledge one's ~ to sb/sth** promettre d'être loyal envers qn/d'être dé-

voué à qch; **to decide where one's loyalties lie** choisir son camp; **to suffer from** or **have divided loyalties** être partagé, se sentir écartelé; **a man of fierce loyalties** un homme d'une loyauté farouche **2** COMP ► **loyalty card** N (*Brit Comm*) carte *f* de fidélité

lozenge ['lɒzɪndʒ] N **a** (*Med*) pastille *f* **b** (*Her, Math*) losange *m*

LP [el'piː] N (*Mus*) (ABBR = **long-playing (record)**) → **long**

LPN [elpiː'en] N (*US Med*) (ABBR = **Licensed Practical Nurse**) → **license**

LRAM [elɑːreɪ'em] N (*Brit*) (ABBR = **Licentiate of the Royal Academy of Music**) *diplôme d'un des Conservatoires de musique*

LRCP [elɑːsiː'piː] N (*Brit*) (ABBR = **Licentiate of the Royal College of Physicians**) ≈ agrégation *f* de médecine

LRCS [elɑːsiː'es] N (*Brit*) (ABBR = **Licentiate of the Royal College of Surgeons**) ≈ agrégation *f* de médecine (opératoire)

LSAT [eleseɪ'tiː] N (*US Univ*) (ABBR = **Law School Admission Test**) *examen d'entrée à une faculté de droit*

LSD [eles'diː] N (*Drugs*) (ABBR = **lysergic acid diethylamide**) LSD *m*

L.S.D. [eles'diː] N (*Brit*) (ABBR = **librae, solidi, denarii**) (= *pounds, shillings and pence*) *ancien système monétaire britannique*

LSE [,eles'iː] N (*Brit*) ABBR = **London School of Economics**

LT [el'tiː] (*Elec*) (ABBR = **low tension**) → **low¹**

Lt (ABBR = **Lieutenant**) (*on envelope etc*) **~ J. Smith** Lieutenant J. Smith; **~-Col** (ABBR = **Lieutenant-Colonel**) → **lieutenant**; **~-Gen** (ABBR = **Lieutenant-General**) → **lieutenant**

Ltd (*Brit Comm etc*) (ABBR = **Limited (Liability)**) **Smith & Co. ~** Smith & Cie SA or Ltée (*Can*)

lube* [luːb] **1** N huile *f* de graissage **2** VT graisser, lubrifier

lubricant ['luːbrɪkənt] ADJ, N lubrifiant *m*; (*fig*) **alcohol is a great (social) ~** l'alcool facilite beaucoup les contacts

lubricate ['luːbrɪkeɪt] **1** VT **a** (*lit*) lubrifier; (*Aut*) graisser **b** (*fig = facilitate*) faciliter **2** COMP ► **lubricating oil** N huile *f* (de graissage), lubrifiant *m*

lubricated: ['luːbrɪkeɪtɪd] ADJ (*hum = drunk*) paf* *inv*, beurré*

lubrication [,luːbrɪ'keɪʃən] N lubrification *f*; (*Aut*) graissage *m*

lubricator ['luːbrɪkeɪtəʳ] N (= *person, device*) graisseur *m*

lubricious [luː'brɪʃəs] ADJ (*frm = lewd*) lubrique

lubricity [luː'brɪsɪtɪ] N (*frm = lewdness*) lubricité *f*

lucerne [luː'sɜːn] N (*esp Brit*) luzerne *f*

lucid ['luːsɪd] **1** ADJ **a** (= *clear*) [*style, explanation, account*] clair **b** (= *clear-headed*) [*person*] lucide; [*moment, interval*] de lucidité **c** (*liter = bright*) [*air, light*] lucide† (*also liter*) **2** COMP ► **lucid dream** N (*Psych*) rêve *m* lucide ► **lucid dreamer** N (*Psych*) rêveur *m*, -euse *f* lucide ► **lucid dreaming** N (*Psych*) rêverie *f* lucide

lucidity [luː'sɪdɪtɪ] N **a** (= *clarity*) [*of style, explanation, book*] clarté *f* **b** (= *clear-headedness*) [*of mind*] lucidité *f* **c** (*liter = brightness*) éclat *m*

lucidly ['luːsɪdlɪ] ADV [*explain, write, argue*] clairement; [*think*] lucidement, avec lucidité

Lucifer ['luːsɪfəʳ] N Lucifer *m*

▼ luck [lʌk] N **a** (= *chance, fortune*) chance *f*, hasard *m*; **good ~** (bonne) chance *f*, bonheur *m*, veine* *f*, pot* *m*; **bad ~** malchance *f*, malheur *m*, déveine* *f*; **it's good/bad ~ to see a black cat** voir un chat porte bonheur/malheur de voir un chat noir; **to bring (sb) good/bad** or **ill ~** porter bonheur/malheur (à qn); **it brought us nothing but bad ~** cela ne nous a vraiment

pas porté chance; **good ~!** bonne chance!; **bad** *or* **hard** *or* **tough ~!** manque de pot!*, pas de veine!*; **better ~ next time!** ça ira mieux la prochaine fois!; **any ~?*** (*gen*) alors (ça a marché)?*; (*= did you find it?*) tu as trouvé?*; **no ~?*** (*gen*) ça n'a pas marché?*; (*= didn't you find it?*) tu n'as pas trouvé?*; **worse ~!*** malheureusement!; **to have the good/bad ~ to do sth** avoir la chance *or* la bonne fortune/la malchance *or* la mauvaise fortune de faire qch; **~ favoured him ◊ ~ was with him ◊ ~ was on his side** la chance lui souriait; **as ~ would have it** comme par hasard; **don't push your ~** vas-y doucement; **he's pushing his ~*** il y va un peu fort, il charrie*; (*fig*) **it's the ~ of the draw** c'est une question de chance; **(it's) just my ~!** c'est bien ma chance *or* ma veine!*; **it was just his ~* to meet the boss** par malchance *or* par malheur il a rencontré le patron, il a eu la malchance *or* le malheur de rencontrer le patron; **to be down on one's ~*** (*= be unlucky*) avoir la déveine* *or* la poisse*; (*= go through bad patch*) traverser une mauvaise passe → **beginner**, **chance**
(b) (*= good fortune*) (bonne) chance *f*, bonheur *m*, veine* *f*, pot* *m*; **you're in ~* ◊ your ~'s in*** tu as de la chance *or* de la veine* *or* du pot*; **you're out of ~* ◊ your ~'s out*** tu n'as pas de chance *or* de veine* *or* de pot*; **that's a bit of a stroke of ~!** quelle veine!*, coup de pot!*; **he had the ~ to meet her in the street** il a eu la chance de la rencontrer dans la rue; **here's (wishing you) ~!** bonne chance!; **no such ~!*** ç'aurait été trop beau!, penses-tu!; **with any ~ ...** avec un peu de chance *or* de veine* ...; **to keep a horseshoe for ~** avoir un fer à cheval comme porte-bonheur; (*iro*) **and the best of (British) ~!** je vous (*or* leur *etc*) souhaite bien du plaisir!* (*iro*) **he's got the ~ of the devil*** ◊ **he's got the devil's own ~*** il a une veine de cocu*

▶**luck out*** VI (*US*) avoir de la veine* *or* du pot*

luckily ['lʌkɪlɪ] ADV heureusement; **~ for me ...** heureusement pour moi ...

luckless ['lʌklɪs] (*liter*) ADJ [*person, journey*] infortuné (*liter*); [*week, year*] d'infortune (*liter*)

lucky ['lʌkɪ] **1** ADJ **a** [*person*] (*= having luck*) (*always*) qui a de la chance, chanceux; (*on one occasion*) qui a de la chance; **we were ~ with the weather** on a eu de la chance avec le temps; **he is ~ to be alive** il a de la chance d'être en vie; **he's ~ that I didn't run him over** il a eu de la chance, j'aurais pu l'écraser; **it was ~ that you got here in time** heureusement que vous êtes arrivé à temps; **it was ~ for him that he got out of the way** heureusement (pour lui), il s'est écarté; **to be ~ in life** avoir de la chance dans la vie; **to be ~ in love** être heureux en amour; **I'm ~ in having an excellent teacher** j'ai la chance d'avoir un excellent professeur; **to count o.s. ~** s'estimer heureux; **some people are born ~** il y a des gens qui ont de la chance; **~ winner** heureux gagnant *m*, heureuse gagnante *f*; (*hum*) **who's the ~ man/woman?** comment s'appelle l'heureux élu/l'heureuse élue?; **(you) ~ thing*** *or* **devil*** *or* **dog*!** veinard(e)!*; **he's a ~ thing*** *or* **devil*** *or* **dog*!** quel veinard!*; **~ (old) you!** tu en as de la veine!*; **~ old Thomson!** quel veinard!, ce Thomson!; **if you're ~** avec un peu de chance; **you'll be ~!** (*= not likely*) tu peux toujours courir!*; **you'll be ~* if you get any breakfast** tu pourras t'estimer heureux si tu as un petit déjeuner; **you'll be ~* to get £5 for that** tu auras du mal à en tirer 5 livres; **I should be so ~!** tu parles!*, ce serait trop beau!*; **to get ~* (with sb)** (*= be allowed sex*) arriver à ses fins (avec qn) → **strike, third**
b (*= fortunate, resulting from luck*) [*coincidence, shot*] heureux; **how ~!** ◊ **that was ~!** quelle chance!; **to have a ~ escape** l'échapper belle, s'en tirer de justesse; **a ~ chance** un coup de chance; **a ~ break*** un coup de bol*; **how did**

you know? — **it was just a ~ guess** comment as-tu deviné? — par hasard *or* j'ai dit ça au hasard; **it's your ~ day*** c'est ton jour de chance
c (*= bringing luck*) [*number, horseshoe*] porte-bonheur *inv*; **a ~ charm** un porte-bonheur; **a ~ rabbit's foot** une patte de lapin porte-bonheur → **star**
2 COMP ▶ **lucky bag** N pochette-surprise *f* ▶ **lucky dip** N (*Brit: at fair*) ≈ pêche *f* à la ligne; (*fig*) loterie *f* (*fig*)

lucrative ['lu:krətɪv] ADJ lucratif

lucre ['lu:kər] N **a** (*NonC: pej = gain*) lucre *m* **b** (* *hum = money: also* **filthy ~**) fric* *m*

Lucretia [lu:'kri:ʃɪə] N Lucrèce *f*

Lucretius [lu:'kri:ʃəs] N Lucrèce *m*

Lucy ['lu:sɪ] N Lucie *f*

Luddite ['lʌdaɪt] ADJ, N luddite *mf*

ludic ['lʌdɪk] ADJ (*liter*) ludique

ludicrous ['lu:dɪkrəs] ADJ ridicule

ludicrously ['lu:dɪkrəslɪ] ADV ridiculement

ludo ['lu:dəʊ] N (*Brit*) jeu *m* des petits chevaux

luff [lʌf] (*Naut*) **1** N aulof(f)ée *f* **2** VI lofer, venir au lof

luffa ['lʌfə] N (*US*) = **loofah**

lug¹ [lʌg] N **a** (*Constr*) tenon *m*; [*of dish, saucepan etc*] oreille *f* (*d'une casserole etc*) **b** (*Brit*: *= ear*) oreille *f*, portugaise* *f*

lug²* [lʌg] VT traîner, tirer; **to ~ sth up/down** monter/descendre qch en le traînant; **to ~ sth out** traîner qch dehors; **why are you ~ging that parcel around?** pourquoi est-ce que tu trimballes* ce paquet?; (*fig*) **they ~ged him off to the theatre** ils l'ont traîné *or* embarqué* au théâtre (malgré lui)

luge [lu:ʒ] **1** N luge *f* **2** VI faire de la luge

luggage ['lʌgɪdʒ] **1** N (*NonC*) bagages *mpl*; (*Rail*) **~ in advance** bagages *mpl* non accompagnés → **hand, left¹, piece 2** COMP ▶ **luggage boot** N (*Brit Aut*) coffre *m* ▶ **luggage carrier** N porte-bagages *m inv* ▶ **luggage handler** N (*at airport etc*) bagagiste *m* ▶ **luggage insurance** N assurance *f* bagages ▶ **luggage label** N étiquette *f* à bagages ▶ **luggage locker** N (casier *m* de) consigne *f* automatique ▶ **luggage rack** N (*Rail*) porte-bagages *m inv*, filet *m*; (*Aut*) galerie *f* ▶ **luggage van** N (*esp Brit Rail*) fourgon *m* (à bagages)

lugger ['lʌgər] N lougre *m*

lughole* ['lʌghəʊl] N (*Brit* = *ear*) oreille *f*, portugaise* *f*

lugubrious [lʊ'gu:brɪəs] ADJ (*liter*) lugubre

lugubriously [lʊ'gu:brɪəslɪ] ADV (*liter*) lugubrement

lugworm ['lʌgwɜːm] N arénicole *f*

Luke [lu:k] N Luc *m*

lukewarm ['lu:kwɔːm] ADJ **a** (*in temperature*) tiède **b** (*= unenthusiastic*) [*response, reception, applause*] peu enthousiaste; **to be ~ about sb/sth** ne pas être enthousiasmé par qn/qch; **to be ~ about (doing) sth** ne pas être très chaud pour (faire) qch

lull [lʌl] **1** N [*of storm*] accalmie *f*; [*of hostilities, shooting*] arrêt *m*; [*of conversation*] arrêt *m*, pause *f* **2** VT [*+ person, fear*] apaiser, calmer; **to ~ a child to sleep** endormir un enfant en le berçant; **to be ~ed into a false sense of security** s'endormir dans une fausse sécurité

lullaby ['lʌləbaɪ] N berceuse *f*; **~ my baby** dors (mon) bébé, dors

lulu* ['lu:lu:] N (*esp US*) **it's a ~!** c'est super!*; (*iro*) c'est pas de la tarte!*

lumbago [lʌm'beɪgəʊ] N lumbago *m*

lumbar ['lʌmbər] **1** ADJ lombaire **2** COMP ▶ **lumbar puncture** N ponction *f* lombaire

lumber¹ ['lʌmbər] **1** N (*NonC*) **a** (*= wood*) bois *m* de charpente **b** (* *= junk*) bric-à-brac *m inv* **2** VT **a** (*Brit* = *burden*) **to ~ sb with sth** coller* *or* flanquer* qch à qn; **he got ~ed with**

the job of making the list il s'est tapé* *or* appuyé* *or* farci* le boulot de dresser la liste; **I got ~ed with the girl for the evening** j'ai dû me coltiner* *or* m'appuyer* la fille toute la soirée; **now (that) we're ~ed with it ...** maintenant qu'on a ça sur les bras *or* qu'on nous a collé* ça ... **b** (*US Forestry*) (*= fell*) abattre; (*= saw up*) débiter **3** COMP ▶ **lumber jacket** N grosse veste *f* (de bûcheron) ▶ **lumber mill** N scierie *f* ▶ **lumber room** N (*Brit*) (cabinet *m* de) débarras *m* ▶ **lumber yard** N dépôt *m* de bois d'œuvre et de construction

lumber² ['lʌmbər] VI (*also* **~ about, ~ along**) [*person, animal*] marcher pesamment; [*vehicle*] rouler pesamment; **to ~ in/out** *etc* [*person*] entrer/sortir *etc* d'un pas pesant *or* lourd

lumbering¹ ['lʌmbərɪŋ] N (*US*) débit *m* *or* débitage *m* *or* tronçonnage *m* de bois

lumbering² ['lʌmbərɪŋ] ADJ [*step*] lourd, pesant; [*person*] mal dégrossi

lumberjack ['lʌmbədʒæk] **1** N bûcheron *m* **2** COMP ▶ **lumberjack shirt** N épaisse chemise *f* à carreaux

lumberman ['lʌmbəmən] N (*pl* **-men**) = **lumberjack**

luminary ['lu:mɪnərɪ] N (*= person*) lumière *f*, sommité *f*

luminescence [,lu:mɪ'nesns] N luminescence *f*

luminosity [,lu:mɪ'nɒsɪtɪ] N luminosité *f*

luminous ['lu:mɪnəs] ADJ lumineux; **my watch is ~** le cadran de ma montre est lumineux

lumme†* ['lʌmɪ] EXCL (*Brit*) = **lummy**

lummox ['lʌməks] N (*US*) lourdaud(e) *m(f)*

lummy†* ['lʌmɪ] EXCL (*Brit*) ça alors!, sapristi!*

lump¹ [lʌmp] **1** N **a** (*= piece*) (*gen*) morceau *m*; (*larger*) gros morceau *m*, masse *f*; [*of metal, rock, stone*] morceau *m*, masse *f*; [*of coal, cheese, sugar*] morceau *m*; [*of clay, earth*] motte *f*; (*in sauce etc*) grumeau *m*; **after the explosion there were large ~s of rock everywhere** après l'explosion il y avait de gros éclats de pierre partout
b (*Med*) grosseur *f*; (*= swelling*) protubérance *f*; (*from bump etc*) bosse *f*; (*fig*) **to have a ~ in one's throat** avoir une boule dans la gorge, avoir la gorge serrée
c (* *pej = person*) lourdaud(e) *m(f)*, empoté(e)* *m(f)*; **fat ~!** gros lourdaud!, espèce d'empoté(e)!*
2 VT (*also* **~ together**) [*+ books, objects*] réunir, mettre en tas; [*+ persons*] réunir; [*+ subjects*] réunir, considérer en bloc
3 COMP ▶ **lump sugar** N sucre *m* en morceaux ▶ **lump sum** N (*Fin etc*) montant *m* forfaitaire; (*= payment*) paiement *m* unique; **he was working for a ~ sum** il travaillait à forfait; (*Insurance etc*) **to pay a ~ sum** verser un capital

▶**lump together** VT SEP réunir; (*fig*) [*+ people, cases*] mettre dans la même catégorie *or* dans le même sac* (*pej*), considérer en bloc → **lump¹**

lump²* [lʌmp] VT (*Brit* = *endure*) (*if you don't like it*) **you'll just have to ~ it** que ça te plaise ou pas, t'as pas le choix*; **like it or ~ it*, you'll have to** que tu le veuilles ou non *or* que ça te plaise ou non il faudra que tu y ailles

lumpectomy [lʌm'pektəmɪ] N ablation *f* d'une tumeur mammaire

lumpen ['lʌmpən] ADJ (*esp Brit*) **a** (*liter* = *shapeless*) informe **b** (*= dull*) [*person*] terne

lumpenproletariat [,lʌmpənprəʊlə'tɛərɪət] N sous-prolétariat *m*, lumpenprolétariat *m*

lumpfish ['lʌmpfɪʃ] N (*pl* **lumpfish** *or* **lumpfishes**) lump *m*, lompe *m*; **~ roe** œufs *mpl* de lump

lumpish ['lʌmpɪʃ] ADJ **a** (*= clumsy*) gauche, maladroit, pataud; (*= stupid*) idiot, godiche* **b** (*= shapeless*) [*mass, piece*] informe

lumpsucker ['lʌmp,sʌkər] N lump *m*, lompe *m*

lumpy ['lʌmpɪ] ADJ [mattress, bed] plein de bosses ; [gravy, sauce, mixture] grumeleux, plein de grumeaux ; [person, face, thighs] plein de bourrelets ; [surface, ground] plein de bosses, inégal ; (Culin) **to become** or **go ~** faire des grumeaux

lunacy ['lu:nəsɪ] N (Med) aliénation f mentale, folie f, démence f ; (Jur) démence f ; (fig) folie f, démence f ; **that's sheer ~!** c'est de la pure folie !, c'est dément or de la démence !

lunar ['lu:nə'] **1** ADJ [month, rock, year] lunaire ; [eclipse] de lune **2** COMP ▶ **lunar landing** N (Space) alunissage m ▶ **lunar module** N (Space) module m lunaire ▶ **lunar orbit** N (Space) **in ~ orbit** en orbite lunaire or autour de la lune

lunatic ['lu:nətɪk] **1** N (Med) fou m, folle f, aliéné(e) m(f), dément(e) m(f) ; (Jur) dément(e) m(f) ; (fig) fou m, folle f, cinglé(e)* m(f) ; **he's a ~!** il est fou à lier !, il est cinglé !* **2** ADJ (Med) [person] (also fig) fou (folle f), dément ; [idea, action] absurde, extravagant, démentiel ; **~ asylum** asile m d'aliénés ; **the ~ fringe** les enragés* mpl, les extrémistes mpl fanatiques

lunch [lʌntʃ] **1** N déjeuner m ; **light/quick ~** déjeuner m léger/rapide ; **we're having pork for ~** nous allons manger or nous avons du porc pour déjeuner or à midi ; **to have ~** déjeuner ; **he is at** or **out to ~** (= away from office etc) il est parti déjeuner ; (Brit = having lunch) il est en train de déjeuner ; (fig, hum) **to be out to ~‡** débloquer‡ ; **come to** or **for ~ on Sunday** venez déjeuner dimanche ; **we had him to ~ yesterday** il est venu déjeuner (chez nous) hier → **school, working 2** VI déjeuner ; **we ~ed on sandwiches** nous avons déjeuné de sandwiches, nous avons eu des sandwiches pour déjeuner ; **to ~ out** déjeuner à l'extérieur or en ville **3** COMP ▶ **lunch break** N pause f de midi, heure f du déjeuner ▶ **lunch hour** N **it's his ~ hour just now** c'est l'heure à laquelle il déjeune, c'est l'heure de son déjeuner ; **during one's ~ hour** à l'heure du déjeuner → **lunchtime**

lunchbox ['lʌntʃbɒks] N mallette f à pique-nique

luncheon ['lʌntʃən] **1** N (frm) déjeuner m **2** COMP ▶ **luncheon basket** N panier-repas m ▶ **luncheon meat** N viande de porc en conserve ▶ **luncheon voucher** N (in Brit) chèque-repas m, ticket-repas m, ticket-restaurant m

luncheonette [,lʌntʃə'net] N (US) ≈ snack-bar m

lunchpail ['lʌntʃpeɪl] N (US) = lunchbox

lunchtime ['lʌntʃtaɪm] N **it's his ~ just now** c'est l'heure à laquelle il déjeune, c'est l'heure de son déjeuner ; **it's ~** c'est l'heure de déjeuner ; **at ~** à l'heure du déjeuner

lung [lʌŋ] **1** N poumon m ; (fig) **at the top of one's ~s** à pleins poumons, à tue-tête → **iron 2** COMP [disease, infection] pulmonaire ▶ **lung cancer** N cancer m du poumon ▶ **lung specialist** N pneumologue mf ▶ **lung transplant** N greffe f du poumon

lunge [lʌndʒ] **1** N **a** (= thrust) (brusque) coup m or mouvement m en avant ; (Fencing) botte f **b** (also **~ rein**) longe f **2** VI **a** (= move: also **~ forward**) faire un mouvement brusque en avant ; (Fencing) se fendre **b** (= attack) **to ~ at sb** envoyer or assener un coup à qn ; (Fencing) porter or allonger une botte à qn **3** VT [+ horse] mener à la longe

lunula ['lu:njulə] N (pl **lunulae** ['lu:nju,li:]) (Anat) lunule f

lupin ['lu:pɪn] N lupin m

lurch¹ [lɜ:tʃ] **1** N **a** [of person] écart m brusque, vacillement m ; [of car, ship] embardée f ; **to give a ~** [car, ship] faire une embardée ; [person] vaciller, tituber ; (from disgust, sickness) **my stomach gave a ~** j'ai eu

un haut-le-cœur ; (from misery) **my heart gave a ~** mon cœur s'est serré ; (from fear) **my heart** or **stomach gave a ~** mon sang n'a fait qu'un tour **b** (fig: Pol) **the party's ~ to the right** le virage à droite du parti ; **they fear a ~ into recession** ils craignent que l'on ne sombre (subj) dans la récession **2** VI **a** [person] vaciller, tituber ; [car, ship] faire une embardée ; **to ~ in/out/along** etc [person] entrer/sortir/avancer etc en titubant ; **the car ~ed along** or **forwards** la voiture avançait en faisant des embardées ; **the ship ~ed from side to side** le bateau se mit à rouler violemment ; **he ~ed to his feet** il s'est levé en titubant ; (from disgust, sickness) **my stomach ~ed** j'ai eu un haut-le-cœur ; (from misery) **my heart** or **stomach ~ed** mon sang n'a fait qu'un tour **b** (fig) **to ~ towards crisis/into turmoil** sombrer dans la crise/le chaos ; **the government ~es from one crisis to the next** le gouvernement navigue entre les écueils

lurch² [lɜ:tʃ] N **to leave sb in the ~** faire faux bond à qn, planter là qn*, laisser qn le bec dans l'eau

lure [ljuə'] **1** N **a** (NonC) (= charm) [of sea, travel etc] attrait m, charme m ; (fig = false attraction) **the ~ of money/drugs** l'attrait m exercé par l'argent/la drogue ; **the ~ of profit** l'appât m du gain **b** (Hunting = decoy) leurre m **2** VT tromper, attirer or persuader par la ruse ; **to ~ sb in/out** etc persuader qn par la ruse d'entrer/de sortir etc ; **clever advertising to ~ customers in** de la publicité accrocheuse pour faire entrer les clients ; **to ~ sb into a trap** attirer qn dans un piège ; **to ~ sb into a house** attirer qn dans une maison ▶ **lure away** VT SEP **to ~ sb away from the house** éloigner qn or faire sortir qn de la maison par la ruse ; **to ~ customers away from one's competitors** attirer les clients de ses concurrents ▶ **lure on** VT SEP entraîner par la ruse, séduire

lurex ['luəreks] N lurex m

lurgy‡ ['lɜ:gɪ] N (Brit hum) **to have the (dreaded) ~** (= cold, flu) avoir la crève* ; (= infectious illness) avoir chopé* un microbe

lurid ['ljuərɪd] ADJ **a** (= graphic, sensational) [story] horrible, cru ; [image, photo] horrible ; [headlines] à sensation ; [scandal, rumour] épouvantable ; **in ~ detail** avec un luxe de détails choquants ; **~ details of their relationship** les détails les plus scabreux de leur liaison **b** (= garish) [colour] criard ; [shirt, skirt] aux couleurs criardes **c** (= glowing) [sky, sunset] empourpré ; [glow] sanglant **d** (liter = pallid) [light] blafard

luridly ['ljuərɪdlɪ] ADV (= garishly) [lit] de façon tapageuse ; **~ coloured** (one colour) criard ; (two or more colours) aux couleurs criardes

lurk [lɜ:k] VI [person] se cacher (dans un but malveillant), se tapir ; [danger] menacer ; [doubt] persister ; **he was ~ing behind the bush** il se cachait or il était tapi derrière le buisson ; **there's someone ~ing (about) in the garden** quelqu'un rôde dans le jardin, il y a un rôdeur dans le jardin

lurking ['lɜ:kɪŋ] ADJ [fear, doubt] vague ; **a ~ idea** une idée de derrière la tête

luscious ['lʌʃəs] ADJ **a** (* = beautiful) [woman, blonde, lips] pulpeux ; [fabrics] somptueux **b** (= delicious) [food, wine] succulent

lush [lʌʃ] **1** ADJ **a** (= luxuriant) [field, vegetation] luxuriant ; [pasture] riche ; **~ green meadows** de luxuriantes prairies fpl **b** (= opulent) [hotel, surroundings, fabric] luxueux **c** (Mus) [harmonies, sound] riche **2** N (* = alcoholic) alcoolo* m, poivrot(e)* m(f)

lushness ['lʌʃnɪs] N [of vegetation] luxuriance f **b** (= opulence) luxe m

lust [lʌst] N (sexual) désir m (sexuel) ; (Rel = one of the seven sins) luxure f ; (for fame, power etc) soif f (for de) ; **the ~ for life** la soif or la rage de vivre ▶ **lust after, lust for** VT FUS [+ woman] désirer, convoiter ; [+ revenge, power] avoir soif de ; [+ riches] convoiter

luster ['lʌstə'] N (US) = lustre

lustful ['lʌstfʊl] ADJ (= lecherous) lascif

lustfully ['lʌstfəlɪ] ADV lascivement

lustfulness ['lʌstfʊlnɪs] N lubricité f, lasciveté f

lustily ['lʌstɪlɪ] ADV vigoureusement

lustre, luster (US) ['lʌstə'] **1** N (= gloss) lustre m, brillant m ; (= substance) lustre m ; (fig = renown) éclat m **2** VT lustrer

lustreless ['lʌstəlɪs] ADJ (liter) terne

lustreware ['lʌstəweə'] N poterie f mordorée

lustrous ['lʌstrəs] ADJ (= shining) [material] lustré, brillant ; [eyes] brillant ; [pearls] chatoyant ; (fig = splendid) splendide, magnifique

lusty ['lʌstɪ] ADJ (= healthy) [person, infant] vigoureux, robuste ; (= hearty) [cheer, voice] vigoureux, vif

lute [lu:t] N luth m

Lutetia [lu:'ti:ʃə] N Lutèce f

lutetium [lʊ'ti:ʃɪəm] N lutécium m

Luther ['lu:θə'] N Luther m

Lutheran ['lu:θərən] **1** N Luthérien(ne) m(f) **2** ADJ luthérien

Lutheranism ['lu:θərənɪzəm] N luthéranisme m

luv* [lʌv] (Brit) = **love**

luvvie‡ ['lʌvɪ] N (Brit) **a** (term of address = darling) chéri(e) m(f) **b** (hum, gen pej = actor, actress) acteur m (prétentieux), actrice f (prétentieuse)

Luxemb(o)urg ['lʌksəmbɜ:g] N le Luxembourg ; **the Grand Duchy of ~** le grand-duché de Luxembourg ; **the ~ Embassy** ◊ **the Embassy of ~** l'ambassade f du Luxembourg

Luxemb(o)urger ['lʌksəmbɜ:gə'] N Luxembourgeois(e) m(f)

Luxor ['lʌksɔ:'] N Louxor m

luxuriance [lʌg'zjuərɪəns] N **a** [of foliage, garden] luxuriance f ; [of hair] abondance f **b** (fig) [of style, language] exubérance f

luxuriant [lʌg'zjuərɪənt] ADJ **a** (= lush) [foliage, leaves] luxuriant, touffu ; [garden, countryside, forest, flowers] luxuriant ; [plants, beard] touffu ; [hair, moustache] abondant **b** (fig = rich) [style, imagery] exubérant

luxuriantly [lʌg'zjuərɪəntlɪ] ADV **a** (= in profusion) **to grow ~** [flowers, hair] pousser en abondance ; [tropical vegetation] pousser avec exubérance ; **his ~ silky beard** sa barbe épaisse et soyeuse **b** (= richly) **poetic writing** des écrits d'une poésie exubérante

luxuriate [lʌg'zjuərɪeɪt] VI **a** (= revel) **to ~ in sth** s'abandonner or se livrer avec délices à qch **b** (= grow profusely) pousser avec exubérance or à profusion

luxurious [lʌg'zjuərɪəs] ADJ **a** (= comfortable) [hotel, surroundings] luxueux, somptueux ; [car, fabric, lifestyle] luxueux ; [tastes] de luxe **b** (= sensuous) [sigh, yawn] voluptueux

luxuriously [lʌg'zjuərɪəslɪ] ADV **a** (= comfortably) [furnished, appointed, decorated] luxueusement ; **to live ~** vivre dans le luxe **b** (= sensuously) [sigh, yawn, stretch] voluptueusement

luxuriousness [lʌg'zjuərɪəsnɪs] N [of hotel, car, surroundings] luxe m

luxury ['lʌkʃərɪ] **1** N **a** (NonC) luxe m ; **to live in luxury** vivre dans le luxe → **lap¹ b** (= luxurious item) luxe m ; **beef is becoming a ~** le bœuf devient un (produit de) luxe ; **it's quite a ~ for me to go to the theatre** c'est du luxe pour moi que d'aller au théâtre ; **what a ~ to have** or **take a bath at last!** quel luxe de pouvoir enfin prendre un bain! [2] ADJ [*goods, article, item*] de luxe; [*flat, hotel*] de grand luxe, de grand standing; **a ~ car** une voiture de luxe

LV (ABBR = **luncheon voucher**) → **luncheon**

LW (*Rad*) (ABBR = **long wave**) GO *fpl*

lycanthropy [laɪˈkænθrəpɪ] N lycanthropie *f*

lyceum [laɪˈsiːəm] N ≈ maison *f* de la culture

lychee [ˈlaɪtʃiː] N litchi *or* letchi *m*

lychgate [ˈlɪtʃgeɪt] N = **lichgate**

Lycra® [ˈlaɪkrə] [1] N Lycra® *m* [2] COMP en Lycra

lye [laɪ] N lessive *f* (*substance*)

lying¹ [ˈlaɪɪŋ] [1] N (*NonC*) mensonge(s) *m(pl)*; **~ will get you nowhere** ça ne te servira à rien de mentir [2] ADJ [*person*] menteur; [*statement, story*] mensonger; **you ~ bastard!**‡ sale menteur!*

lying² [ˈlaɪɪŋ] [1] N [*of body*] **~ in state** exposition *f* (solennelle) [2] COMP ▶ **lying-in**† N (*pl* **lyings-in**) (*Med*) accouchement *m*, couches

fpl ▶ **lying-in ward** N salle *f* de travail *or* d'accouchement

lymph [lɪmf] [1] N (*Anat*) lymphe *f* [2] COMP ▶ **lymph gland**† N = **lymph node** ▶ **lymph node** N ganglion *m* lymphatique

lymphatic [lɪmˈfætɪk] ADJ lymphatique

lymphocyte [ˈlɪmfəʊˌsaɪt] N lymphocyte *m*

lymphoid [ˈlɪmfɔɪd] ADJ lymphoïde

lymphoma [lɪmˈfəʊmə] N lymphome *m*

lymphosarcoma [ˌlɪmfəʊsɑːˈkəʊmə] N lymphosarcome *m*

lynch [lɪntʃ] [1] VT (= *hang*) exécuter sommairement (*par pendaison*); (= *kill*) lyncher [2] COMP ▶ **lynch law** N loi *f* de Lynch ▶ **lynch mob** N lyncheurs *mpl*

lynching [ˈlɪntʃɪŋ] N (= *action, result*) lynchage *m*

lynchpin [ˈlɪntʃpɪn] N = **linchpin**

lynx [lɪŋks] [1] N (*pl* **lynxes** *or* **lynx**) lynx *m inv* [2] COMP ▶ **lynx-eyed** ADJ aux yeux de lynx

Lyons [ˈlaɪənz] N Lyon

lyophilize [laɪˈɒfɪˌlaɪz] VT lyophiliser

lyre [ˈlaɪəʳ] N lyre *f*

lyrebird [ˈlaɪəbɜːd] N oiseau-lyre *m*, ménure *m*

lyric [ˈlɪrɪk] [1] N [a] (= *poem*) poème *m* lyrique [b] (= *words of song*) **~(s)** paroles *fpl* [2] ADJ [*poem, poet*] lyrique [3] COMP ▶ **lyric writer** N parolier *m*, -ière *f*

lyrical [ˈlɪrɪkəl] ADJ [a] (*Poetry*) lyrique [b]* → **wax²**

lyrically [ˈlɪrɪkəlɪ] ADV (= *poetically*) [*speak, write, describe*] avec lyrisme; **~ beautiful** d'une beauté lyrique

lyricism [ˈlɪrɪsɪzəm] N lyrisme *m*

lyricist [ˈlɪrɪsɪst] N (= *poet*) poète *m* lyrique; (= *song-writer*) parolier *m*, -ière *f*

lysergic [laɪˈsɜːdʒɪk] [1] ADJ lysergique [2] COMP ▶ **lysergic acid** N acide *m* lysergique

M

M, m [em] N [a] (= *letter*) M, m *m*; **M for Mike** ◇ **M for Mother** ≈ M comme Marie [b] (*Brit*) (ABBR = **motorway**) **on the M6** sur l'autoroute M6, ≈ sur l'A6 [c] (ABBR = **million(s)**) → **million** [d] (ABBR = **medium**) moyen [e] (ABBR = **metre(s)**) m [f] (ABBR = **mile(s)**) → **mile**

MA [ˌemˈeɪ] [a] (*Univ*) (ABBR = **Master of Arts**) **to have an MA in French** ≈ avoir une maîtrise de français → **master**; → DEGREE [b] ABBR = **Massachusetts** [c] (*US*) (ABBR = **Military Academy**) → **military**

ma* [maː] N maman *f*; (*pej*) **Ma Smith** la mère Smith

ma'am [mæm] N (ABBR = **madam**) (*gen: esp US*) Madame *f*, Mademoiselle *f*; (*to royalty*) Madame *f*

Maastricht Treaty [ˈmaːstrɪkˈtriːtɪ] N **the ~** le traité de Maastricht

mac [mæk] N [a] (*Brit**) (ABBR = **mackintosh**) imperméable *m*, imper* *m* [b] (*esp US*: form of address*) **hurry up Mac!** hé! dépêchez-vous!; (*to friend*) dépêche-toi mon vieux *or* mon pote!*

macabre [məˈkaːbrə] ADJ macabre

macadam [məˈkædəm] [1] N macadam *m* → **tar**[1] [2] COMP [*surface*] en macadam; [*road*] macadamisé

macadamize [məˈkædəmaɪz] VT macadamiser

macaroni [ˌmækəˈrəʊnɪ] [1] N (*pl* **macaronis** *or* **macaronies**) macaroni(s) *m(pl)* [2] COMP ► **macaroni cheese** N gratin *m* de macaroni(s)

macaronic [ˌmækəˈrɒnɪk] [1] ADJ macaronique [2] N vers *m* macaronique

macaroon [ˌmækəˈruːn] N macaron *m*

macaw [məˈkɔː] N ara *m*

Mace® [meɪs] [1] N (= *gas*) gaz *m* incapacitant, mace *m* [2] VT attaquer au gaz incapacitant *or* au mace

mace¹ [meɪs] N (*NonC* = *spice*) macis *m*

mace² [meɪs] N (= *weapon*) massue *f*; (= *ceremonial staff*) masse *f*

macebearer [ˈmeɪsbɛərər] N massier *m*

Macedonia [ˌmæsɪˈdəʊnɪə] N la Macédoine

Macedonian [ˌmæsɪˈdəʊnɪən] [1] ADJ macédonien [2] N (= *person*) Macédonien(ne) *m(f)*

macerate [ˈmæsəreɪt] VTI macérer

Mach [mæk] N (*Aviat: also* **~ number**) (nombre *m* de) Mach *m*; **to fly at ~ 2** voler à Mach 2

machete [məˈʃetɪ] N machette *f*

Machiavelli [ˌmækɪəˈvelɪ] N Machiavel *m*

Machiavellian [ˌmækɪəˈvelɪən] ADJ machiavélique

machination [ˌmækɪˈneɪʃən] N machination *f*, intrigue *f*, manœuvre *f*

machine [məˈʃiːn] [1] N [a] (*gen, Tech, Theat*) machine *f*; **adding/bread-making/cigarette-making** *etc* **~** machine *f* à calculer/à fabriquer du pain/à fabriquer des cigarettes *etc*; **shredding ~** broyeur *m*, broyeuse *f*; **milking ~** trayeuse *f*; **by ~** à la machine → **flying, knitting, washing**

[b] (*fig*) machine *f*; **the company is a real money-making ~** cette société est une vraie machine à fabriquer de l'argent; **the military ~** la machine *or* l'appareil *m* militaire; **publicity/propaganda ~** appareil *m* publicitaire/de propagande; **the political ~** la machine *or* l'appareil *m* politique; (*US Pol*) **the Democratic ~** la machine administrative *or* l'appareil *m* du parti démocrate → **party** [c] (*pej* = *soulless person*) machine *f*, automate *m*

[2] VT (*Tech*) façonner à la machine, usiner; (*Sewing*) coudre à la machine, piquer (à la machine)

[3] COMP (*gen*) de la machine, des machines; (*Comput*) machine ► **machine age** N siècle *m* de la machine *or* des machines ► **machine-assisted translation** N traduction *f* assistée par ordinateur ► **machine code** N (*Comput*) code *m* machine ► **machine error** N erreur *f* technique ► **machine gun** N mitrailleuse *f* ► **machine-gun** VT mitrailler ► **machine gunner** N mitrailleur *m* ► **machine-gunning** N mitraillage *m* ► **machine intelligence** N intelligence *f* artificielle ► **machine language** N langage *m* machine ► **machine-made** ADJ fait à la machine ► **machine operator** N (*Ind*) opérateur *m*, -trice *f* (sur machines); (*Comput*) opérateur *m*, -trice *f* ► **machine-readable** ADJ (*Comput*) exploitable par un ordinateur; **in ~-readable form** sous (une) forme exploitable par ordinateur ► **machine shop** N atelier *m* d'usinage ► **machine stitch** N point *m* (de piqûre) à la machine ► **machine-stitch** VT piquer à la machine ► **machine time** N temps *m* d'opération (d'une machine) ► **machine tool** N machine-outil *f* ► **~-tool operator** N opérateur *m* sur machine-outil, usineur *m* ► **machine translation** N traduction *f* automatique ► **machine-washable** ADJ lavable à la *or* en machine

machinery [məˈʃiːnərɪ] N (*NonC*) [a] (= *machines collectively*) machinerie *f*, machines *fpl*; (= *parts of machine*) mécanisme *m*, rouages *mpl*; **a piece of ~** un mécanisme; **to get caught in the ~** être pris dans la machine; **agricultural ~** machines *fpl* agricoles; **electrical ~** appareils *mpl* électriques; **industrial ~** équipements *mpl* industriels [b] (*fig*) **the ~ of government** l'appareil *m* étatique; (*fig*) **the ~ to enforce this legislation simply doesn't exist** aucun dispositif d'application n'a été mis en place pour cette législation

machinist [məˈʃiːnɪst] N machiniste *mf*, opérateur *m*, -trice *f* (sur machine); (*on sewing, knitting machines*) mécanicienne *f*

machismo [mæˈtʃɪzməʊ] N (*NonC*) machisme *m*, phallocratie *f*

macho [ˈmætʃəʊ] [1] N macho *m*, phallocrate *m* [2] ADJ macho *inv*

mackerel [ˈmækrəl] [1] N (*pl* **mackerel** *or* **mackerels**) maquereau *m* [2] COMP ► **mackerel sky** N ciel *m* pommelé

Mackinaw [ˈmækɪˌnɔː] N (*US*) (*also* **~ coat**) grosse veste *f* de laine à carreaux; (*also* **~ blanket**) grosse couverture *f* de laine à carreaux

mackintosh [ˈmækɪntɒʃ] N imperméable *m*

macramé [məˈkraːmɪ] [1] N macramé *m* [2] COMP [*plant holder etc*] en macramé

macro [ˈmækrəʊ] N [a] (*Comput*) macro *f* [b] (*Phot*) **~ lens** objectif *m* macro

macro... [ˈmækrəʊ] PREF macro...; **~molecule** macromolécule *f* → **macrobiotic**

macrobiotic [ˌmækrəʊbaɪˈɒtɪk] ADJ macrobiotique

macrobiotics [ˌmækrəʊbaɪˈɒtɪks] N (*NonC*) macrobiotique *f*

macrocosm [ˈmækrəʊkɒzəm] N macrocosme *m*

macroeconomics [ˌmækrəʊˌiːkəˈnɒmɪks] N (*NonC*) macroéconomie *f*

macro-instruction [ˌmækrəʊɪnˈstrʌkʃən] N macro-instruction *f*

macrolinguistics [ˌmækrəʊlɪŋˈgwɪstɪks] N (*NonC*) macrolinguistique *f*

macromarketing [ˌmækrəʊˈmaːkɪtɪŋ] N macromarketing *m*

macron [ˈmækrɒn] N macron *m*

macrophotography [ˌmækrəʊfəˈtɒgrəfɪ] N macrophotographie *f*

macroscopic [ˌmækrəˈskɒpɪk] ADJ macroscopique

MAD [ˌemeɪˈdiː] N (*US Mil*) (ABBR = **mutual(ly) assured destruction**) → **mutual**

mad [mæd] [1] ADJ [a] [*person*] (= *deranged*) fou (folle *f*); (= *rash, crazy*) fou (folle *f*), insensé; [*hope, plan, idea*] insensé; [*race, gallop*] effréné; [*bull*] furieux, [*dog*] enragé; **to go ~** devenir fou; **this is idealism gone ~** c'est de l'idéalisme qui dépasse les bornes; (*stronger*) c'est de l'idéalisme qui vire à la folie; (*lit, fig*) **to drive sb ~** rendre qn fou → **b**; **as ~ as a hatter** *or* **a March hare** ◇ (*stark*) **raving ~*** ◇ **stark staring ~*** fou à lier; **~ with grief** fou de chagrin; **that was a ~ thing to do** il fallait être fou pour faire cela; **you're ~ to think of it!** tu es fou d'y songer!; **are you ~?** ça ne va pas?* (*iro*); **you must be ~!** ça ne va pas, non!*; **you must be ~ to cycle in this weather!** ◇ **you must be ~, cycling in this weather!** il faut vraiment que tu sois fou pour faire du vélo par ce temps!, tu es fou de faire du vélo par ce temps!; **to pedal/push** *etc* **like ~*** pédaler/appuyer *etc* comme un fou; **to run like ~*** courir comme un fou *or* un dératé; **to cry like ~*** pleurer comme une Madeleine; **to laugh like ~*** rire comme une baleine*; **the phone has been ringing like ~* all morning** le téléphone n'a pas arrêté de sonner ce matin; **to work/shout like ~*** travailler/crier comme un fou *or* un forcené; **this plant grows like ~*** cette plante pousse comme du chiendent; **we had a ~ dash for the bus** nous avons dû foncer* pour attraper le bus; **I'm in a ~ rush*** je suis à la bourre*

[b] (*esp US** = *angry*) furieux; **to be ~ at** *or* **with**

sb être furieux contre qn ; **to get ~ at** or **with sb** s'emporter contre qn ; **don't get ~ at** or **with me!** ne te fâche pas contre moi! ; **he was ~ at** or **with me for spilling the tea** il était furieux contre moi pour avoir renversé le thé ; **he was really ~ about my mistake** mon erreur l'a mis hors de lui ; **he makes me ~!** ce qu'il peut m'agacer or m'énerver! ; **to drive sb ~** faire enrager qn, mettre qn en fureur ; **he's hopping** or **spitting ~** il est fou furieux ; (US) **as a hornet*** furibard*

[c] (* = enthusiastic: also **~ keen**) **to go ~ on sth** devenir dingue* de qch ; **~ on** or **about sth** mordu* or dingue* de qch ; **to be ~ on** or **about sb** être fou de qn ; **I'm not ~ on** or **about him** je ne l'aime pas trop ; **to be ~ on** or **about swimming/football/computers** ◊ **to be swimming-/football-/computer-~** être mordu* or dingue* de natation/ de football/d'informatique ; **I'm not ~ about it** ça ne m'emballe pas*

[d] (* = excited) **the audience went ~** la folie a gagné le public ; **the dog went ~ when he saw his master** le chien est devenu comme fou quand il a vu son maître ; **I went ~ and finished everything in an hour** sur un coup de tête or de folie, j'ai tout fini en une heure

[2] COMP ▶ **mad cow disease** N maladie f de la vache folle ▶ **mad money*** N (NonC: US) **this is my ~ money** cet argent-là, c'est pour mes petits plaisirs

Madagascan [ˌmædəˈgæskən] [1] ADJ malgache [2] N (= person) Malgache mf

Madagascar [ˌmædəˈgæskə] N (= island) Madagascar f ; (= country) Madagascar m ; **the Democratic Republic of ~** la République démocratique de Madagascar ; **in ~** à Madagascar

madam [ˈmædəm] N (pl **madams** or **mesdames** [ˈmeɪdæm]) [a] madame f ; (unmarried) mademoiselle f ; (in letters) **Dear Madam** Madame, Mademoiselle ; (frm) **Madam Chairman** Madame la Présidente [b] (Brit) **she's a little ~*** c'est une petite pimbêche or mijaurée [c] (= brothelkeeper) sous-maîtresse f, tenancière f de maison close

madcap [ˈmædkæp] ADJ, N écervelé(e) m(f)

madden [ˈmædn] VT rendre fou ; (= infuriate) exaspérer ; **~ed by pain** fou de douleur

maddening [ˈmædnɪŋ] ADJ exaspérant

maddeningly [ˈmædnɪŋlɪ] ADV (say, smile) d'une façon exaspérante ; **to be ~ cautious/ slow** être d'une prudence/lenteur exaspérante

made [meɪd] [1] VB pt, ptp of **make** [2] COMP ▶ **made-to-measure** ADJ (fait) sur mesure ▶ **made-to-order** ADJ (fait) sur commande ▶ **made-up** ADJ (= invented) (story) inventé, fabriqué ; (pej) faux (fausse f) ; (with cosmetics) (face, eyes) maquillé ; (nails) fait ; **she is too ~-up** elle est trop maquillée

Madeira [məˈdɪərə] [1] N (Geog) (l'île f de) Madère f ; (= wine) (vin m de) madère m [2] COMP ▶ **Madeira cake** N ≈ quatre-quarts m ▶ **Madeira sauce** N sauce f madère

madhouse* [ˈmædhaʊs] N (lit, fig) maison f de fous

Madison Avenue [ˈmædɪsənˈævənjuː] N (US) le monde de la publicité

madly [ˈmædlɪ] ADV [a] (scream, grin) comme un fou ; **to be/fall ~ in love with sb** être/ tomber éperdument amoureux de qn ; **to love sb ~** aimer qn à la folie ; (= furiously) **we were ~ rushing for the train** c'était la course pour attraper le train ; **I was ~ trying to open it** j'essayais désespérément de l'ouvrir [b] (attractive, exciting) follement ; (irritating) extrêmement ; **~ impatient** piaffant d'impatience ; **~ jealous** fou de jalousie

madman [ˈmædmən] N (pl **-men**) fou m

madness [ˈmædnɪs] N (gen, Med) folie f ; (in animals = rabies) rage f ; (= rashness) folie f, démence f ; **it is sheer ~ to say so** c'est de la

pure folie or de la démence de le dire ; **what ~!** c'est de la pure folie!, il faut être fou!

Madonna [məˈdɒnə] [1] N (Rel) Madone f ; (fig) madone f [2] COMP ▶ **Madonna lily** N lis m blanc

Madras [məˈdrɑːs] N (Geog) Madras

madras [məˈdrɑːs] [a] (Culin = curry) curry très épicé ; **beef/chicken ~** curry de bœuf/poulet très épicé [b] (Tex: also **~ cotton**) madras m

Madrid [məˈdrɪd] N Madrid

madrigal [ˈmædrɪgəl] N madrigal m

madwoman [ˈmædwʊmən] N (pl **-women**) folle f

maelstrom [ˈmeɪlstrəm] N (lit, fig) tourbillon m, maelström m

maestro [ˈmaɪstrəʊ] N (pl **maestros** or **maestri** [ˈmaɪstrɪ]) maestro m

Mae West †* [ˈmeɪˈwest] N gilet m de sauvetage (gonflable)

MAFF N (Brit) (ABBR = **Ministry of Agriculture, Fisheries and Food**) ministère m de l'Agriculture, de la Pêche et de l'Alimentation

mafia [ˈmæfɪə] N (lit, fig) mafia f ; **it's a real ~** c'est une véritable mafia ; **a literary ~** une coterie littéraire

mafioso [ˌmæfɪˈəʊsəʊ] N maf(f)ioso m

mag* [mæg] N (ABBR = **magazine**) revue f, magazine m

magazine [ˌmægəˈziːn] N [a] (Press) revue f, magazine m ; (Rad, TV: also **~ programme**) magazine m [b] (Mil = store) magasin m (du corps) [c] (in gun = compartment) magasin m ; (= cartridges) chargeur m ; (in slide projector etc) magasin m

Magellan [məˈgelən] N Magellan m ; **~ Strait** détroit m de Magellan

magenta [məˈdʒentə] [1] N magenta m [2] ADJ magenta inv

Maggie [ˈmægɪ] N (dim of **Margaret**) Maguy f

Maggiore [ˌmædʒɪˈɔːrɪ] N **Lake ~** le lac Majeur

maggot [ˈmægət] N ver m, asticot m

maggoty [ˈmægətɪ] ADJ (fruit) véreux

Maghreb [ˈmʌgreb] N Maghreb m

Magi [ˈmeɪdʒaɪ] NPL (rois mpl) mages mpl

magic [ˈmædʒɪk] [1] N (NonC) magie f, enchantement m ; **as if by** ◊ **like ~** comme par enchantement or magie ; **the ~ of that moment** la magie de cet instant [2] ADJ [a] (= supernatural) magique, enchanté ; (fig) merveilleux, prodigieux ; **to say the ~ word** prononcer la formule magique ; **the Magic Flute** la Flûte enchantée [b] (esp Brit* = brilliant) super*, génial* [3] COMP ▶ **magic bullet** N (Med) médicament m miracle ; (US* = solution) solution f miracle ▶ **magic carpet** N tapis m volant ▶ **magic circle** N cercle m magique ▶ **magic lantern** N lanterne f magique ▶ **magic realism** N (Art, Literat) réalisme m magique ▶ **magic spell** N sort m, sortilège m ▶ **magic square** N carré m magique

▶**magic away** VT SEP faire disparaître comme par enchantement

▶**magic up** VT SEP faire apparaître comme par enchantement

magical [ˈmædʒɪkəl] [1] ADJ [a] (= supernatural) (powers, properties) magique [b] (= wonderful) (story, tale, experience) merveilleux ; (place, moment) magique [2] COMP ▶ **magical mystery tour** N voyage m enchanté ▶ **magical realism** N = **magic realism** → **magic**

magically [ˈmædʒɪkəlɪ] ADV (disappear, transform, produce) comme par magie or enchantement

magician [məˈdʒɪʃən] N (lit, fig) magicien(ne) m(f) ; (Theat etc) illusionniste mf

magisterial [ˌmædʒɪsˈtɪərɪəl] ADJ (lit) de magistrat ; (fig) magistral, formidable

magisterially [ˌmædʒɪsˈtɪərɪəlɪ] ADV magistralement

magistracy [ˈmædʒɪstrəsɪ] N (NonC) magistrature f

magistrate [ˈmædʒɪstreɪt] N magistrat m, juge m ; **~s' court** ≈ tribunal m d'instance

magma [ˈmægmə] N (pl **magmas** or **magmata** [ˈmægmətə]) magma m

Magna C(h)arta [ˌmægnəˈkɑːtə] N (Brit Hist) Grande Charte f

magna cum laude [ˈmægnəkʌmˈlaʊdeɪ] ADV (US Univ) **to graduate ~** ≈ obtenir la mention très bien

magnanimity [ˌmægnəˈnɪmɪtɪ] N magnanimité f

magnanimous [mægˈnænɪməs] ADJ (person, gesture) magnanime (**to sb** envers qn) ; **to be ~ in victory** se montrer magnanime dans la victoire, être un vainqueur magnanime

magnanimously [mægˈnænɪməslɪ] ADV magnanimement

magnate [ˈmægneɪt] N magnat m, roi m ; **industrial/financial ~** magnat m de l'industrie/de la finance ; **oil ~** magnat m or roi m du pétrole

magnesia [mægˈniːʃə] N magnésie f → **milk**

magnesium [mægˈniːzɪəm] N magnésium m

magnet [ˈmægnɪt] N (lit, fig) aimant m

magnetic [mægˈnetɪk] [1] ADJ (lit, fig) magnétique [2] COMP ▶ **magnetic card reader** N lecteur m de cartes magnétiques ▶ **magnetic disk** N disque m magnétique ▶ **magnetic field** N champ m magnétique ▶ **magnetic needle** N aiguille f aimantée ▶ **magnetic north** N nord m magnétique ▶ **magnetic resonance imager** N imageur m à résonance magnétique ▶ **magnetic resonance imaging** N imagerie f par résonance magnétique ▶ **magnetic storm** N orage m magnétique ▶ **magnetic strip, magnetic stripe** N (on credit card etc) piste f magnétique ▶ **magnetic tape** N bande f magnétique

magnetically [mægˈnetɪkəlɪ] ADV [a] (Phys) (attach) magnétiquement [b] (fig) **to be ~ drawn to sb/sth** être attiré par qn/qch comme par un aimant

magnetism [ˈmægnɪtɪzəm] N (lit, fig) magnétisme m

magnetize [ˈmægnɪtaɪz] VT (lit) aimanter, magnétiser ; (fig) magnétiser

magneto [mægˈniːtəʊ] N magnéto f

magneto... [mægˈniːtəʊ] PREF magnéto...

magnetometer [ˌmægnɪˈtɒmɪtə] N magnétomètre m

magnetosphere [mægˈniːtəʊˌsfɪə] N magnétosphère f

Magnificat [mægˈnɪfɪˌkæt] N (Rel) Magnificat m inv

magnification [ˌmægnɪfɪˈkeɪʃən] [1] N [a] (Opt) grossissement m ; **under ~** au microscope [b] (fig = amplification) exagération f [c] (Rel) glorification f [2] COMP ▶ **magnification factor** N coefficient m de grossissement

magnificence [mægˈnɪfɪsəns] N magnificence f, splendeur f, somptuosité f

magnificent [mægˈnɪfɪsənt] ADJ (gen) magnifique ; (food, meal) splendide

magnificently [mægˈnɪfɪsəntlɪ] ADV magnifiquement

magnify [ˈmægnɪfaɪ] [1] VT [a] (+ image) grossir ; (+ sound) amplifier ; (+ incident etc) exagérer, grossir ; **to ~ sth four times** grossir qch quatre fois [b] (Rel = praise) glorifier [2] COMP ▶ **magnifying glass** N loupe f, verre m grossissant

magnitude [ˈmægnɪtjuːd] N ampleur f ; (Astron) magnitude f ; (fig) **of the first ~** de première grandeur

magnolia [mægˈnəʊlɪə] [1] N [a] (also **~ tree**) magnolia m, magnolier m [b] (= colour) rose m pâle [2] ADJ rose pâle *inv* [3] COMP ► **the Magnolia State** N (*US*) le Mississippi

magnox ['mægnɒks] N magnox *m*; **~ reactor** réacteur *m* au magnox

magnum ['mægnəm] [1] N (*pl* **magnums**) magnum *m* [2] COMP ► **magnum opus** N (*Art, Literat, fig*) œuvre *f* maîtresse

magpie ['mægpaɪ] N [a] (*Orn*) pie *f*; **to chatter like a ~** jacasser comme une pie, être un vrai moulin à paroles* [b] (*fig* = *collector*) **he's a real ~** c'est un collectionneur invétéré

Magyar ['mægjɑːʳ] [1] ADJ magyar [2] N Magyar(e) *m(f)*

maharaja(h) [ˌmɑːhəˈrɑːdʒə] N maharaja *m*

maharanee, maharani [ˌmɑːhəˈrɑːniː] N maharani *f*

maharishi [ˌmɑːhɑːˈriːʃi] N maharishi *m*

mahatma [məˈhɑːtmə] N mahatma *m*

mahjong(g) [ˌmɑːˈdʒɒŋ] N ma(h)-jong *m*

mahogany [məˈhɒgənɪ] [1] N acajou *m* [2] COMP (= *made of mahogany*) en acajou; (= *mahogany-coloured*) acajou *inv*

Mahomet [məˈhɒmɪt] N Mahomet *m*

Mahometan† [məˈhɒmɪtən] [1] ADJ mahométan [2] N mahométan(e) *m(f)*

Mahometanism† [məˈhɒmɪtənɪzəm] N mahométisme *m*

mahout [məˈhaʊt] N cornac *m*

maid [meɪd] [1] N [a] (= *servant*) domestique *f*; (*in hotel*) femme *f* de chambre → **barmaid, housemaid, lady** [b]†† (= *young girl*) jeune fille *f*; (= *virgin*) vierge *f*; (*Hist*) **the Maid (of Orleans)** la Pucelle (d'Orléans) → **old** [2] COMP ► **maid-of-all-work** N bonne *f* à tout faire ► **maid of honour** N (*esp US*) demoiselle *f* d'honneur

maiden [meɪdn] [1] N (*liter*) (= *girl*) jeune fille *f*; (= *virgin*) vierge *f* [2] COMP [*flight, voyage*] premier (*before n*), inaugural ► **maiden aunt** N tante *f* célibataire, tante *f* restée vieille fille (*pej*) ► **maiden lady** N († *or hum*) demoiselle *f* ► **maiden name** N nom *m* de jeune fille ► **maiden over** N (*Cricket*) série de six balles où aucun point n'est marqué ► **maiden speech** N (*Parl*) premier discours *m* (*d'un député etc*)

maidenhair ['meɪdnhɛəʳ] N (*Bot: also* ~ **fern**) capillaire *m*, cheveu-de-Vénus *m*

maidenhead ['meɪdnhɛd] N [a] (*Anat*) hymen *m* [b] (= *virginity*) virginité *f*

maidenhood ['meɪdnhʊd] N virginité *f*

maidenly ['meɪdnlɪ] ADJ de jeune fille, virginal, modeste

maidservant† ['meɪdsɜːvənt] N servante *f*

mail[1] [meɪl] [1] N [a] (*NonC* = *postal system*) poste *f*; **by ~** par la poste [b] (*NonC* = *letters*) courrier *m*; **here's your ~** voici votre courrier [c] (*Comput: also* **e-~, electronic ~**) courrier *m* électronique, e-mail *m*; **to send sb a ~** envoyer un message à qn (*par courrier électronique*), envoyer un courrier électronique *or* un e-mail à qn [2] VT [a] (*esp US* = *post*) envoyer *or* expédier (par la poste), poster [b] (*Comput: also* **e-~**) [+ *message, memo etc*] envoyer par courrier électronique; **to ~ sb** envoyer un message à qn (*par courrier électronique*), envoyer un courrier électronique à qn (**about** à propos de) [3] COMP ► **mail bomb** N (*US*) colis *m* piégé ► **mail car** N (*US Rail*) wagon *m* postal ► **mail carrier** N (*US*) facteur *m*, préposé(e) *m(f)* ► **mail clerk** N (employé(e) *m(f)*) préposé(e) *m(f)* au courrier ► **mail coach** N (*Rail*) wagon-poste *m*; (*horse-drawn*) malle-poste *f* ► **mailing list** N (*Comm*) liste *f* d'adresses ► **mail-merge** N (*Comput*) publipostage *m* ► **mail order** N vente *f* par correspondance; **we got it by ~ order** nous l'avons acheté par correspondance ► **mail-order** ADJ **~-order**

catalogue catalogue *m* de vente par correspondance; **~-order firm** ◊ **~-order house** maison *f* de vente par correspondance ► **mail room** N (*esp US*) service *m* courrier ► **mail slot** N (*US*) fente *f* de la *or* d'une boîte aux lettres ► **mail train** N train *m* postal ► **mail truck** N (*US*) camionnette *f or* fourgon *m* des postes ► **mail van** N (*Brit*) (*Aut*) camionnette *f or* fourgon *m* des postes; (*Rail*) wagon *m* postal

mail[2] [meɪl] N (*NonC*) mailles *fpl*; **coat of ~** cotte *f* de mailles; (*fig*) **the ~ed fist** la manière forte → **chain**

mailbag ['meɪlbæg] N sac *m* postal

mailboat ['meɪlbəʊt] N paquebot(-poste) *m*

mailbox ['meɪlbɒks] N (*Comput, US Post*) boîte *f* aux lettres

Mailgram® ['meɪlgræm] N (*US*) télégramme *m* (*distribué avec le courrier*)

mailing ['meɪlɪŋ] [1] N publipostage *m*, mailing *m*; **~ list** fichier *m or* liste *f* d'adresses [2] COMP ► **mailing address** N (*US*) adresse *f* postale

mailman ['meɪlmæn] N (*pl* **-men**) (*US*) facteur *m*, préposé *m*

mailshot ['meɪlʃɒt] N (*Brit*) mailing *m*, publipostage *m*

maim [meɪm] VT estropier, mutiler; **to be ~ed for life** être estropié pour la vie *or* à vie

Main [meɪn] N (*Geog*) Main *m*

main [meɪn] [1] ADJ [a] [*door, entrance, shop, feature, idea, objective*] principal; [*pipe, beam*] maître (maîtresse *f*); **the ~ body of the army/ the crowd** le gros de l'armée/de la foule; **one of his ~ ideas was ...** une de ses principales idées *or* idées maîtresses consistait à ...; **my ~ idea was to establish ...** mon idée directrice était d'établir ...; **the ~ point of his speech** le point fondamental de son discours; **the ~ point** *or* **object** *or* **objective of the meeting** l'objet principal de cette réunion; **the ~ thing is to keep quiet** l'essentiel est de se taire; **the ~ thing to remember is ...** ce qu'il ne faut surtout pas oublier c'est ...; **to have an eye to the ~ chance** tirer profit de toutes les situations → **3**; → **drag, eye, issue** [b] **by ~ force** de vive force

[2] N [a] (= *principal pipe, wire*) canalisation *f or* conduite *f* maîtresse; **(electricity) ~ conductor** *m* principal; **(gas) ~** (*in street*) conduite *f* principale; (*in house*) conduite *f* de gaz; **~ (sewer)** (égout *m*) collecteur *m*; (*in street or house*) **(water) ~** conduite *f* d'eau de la ville; **the water in this tap comes from the ~s** l'eau de ce robinet vient directement de la conduite; (*Elec*) **the ~s** le secteur; **connected to the ~s** branché sur (le) secteur; **this radio works by battery or from the ~s** ce poste de radio marche sur piles ou sur (le) secteur; **to turn off the electricity/gas/water at the ~(s)** couper le courant/le gaz/l'eau au compteur [b] **in the ~** dans l'ensemble, en général → **might** [c] (*liter*) **the ~** (= *sea*) l'océan *m*, le (grand) large → **Spanish**

[3] COMP ► **main beam** N (*Archit*) poutre *f* maîtresse ► **main bearing** N (*Aut etc*) palier *m* ► **main clause** N (*Gram*) proposition *f* principale ► **main course** N (*Culin*) plat *m* principal ► **main deck** N (*Naut*) pont *m* principal ► **main door (flat)** N (*Brit*) appartement *m* avec porte d'entrée particulière sur la rue ► **main line** N (*Rail*) grande ligne *f* ► **main man*** N (*pl* **main men**) (*US*) meilleur pote* *m* ► **main memory** N (*Comput*) mémoire *f* centrale ► **main office** N (*Comm etc*) bureau *m* principal; [*of political party, newspaper, agency etc*] siège *m* (social) ► **main road** N grande route *f*, route *f* à grande circulation; **the ~ road** la grand-route; **it is one of the ~ roads into Edinburgh** c'est une des grandes voies d'accès à

Édimbourg ► **main sheet** N (*Naut*) écoute *f* de (la) grand-voile ► **mains set** N (*radio, tape recorder etc*) appareil *m* fonctionnant sur secteur ► **mains supply** N **to be on the ~s supply** (*for electricity/gas/water*) être raccordé au réseau (de distribution) d'électricité/de gaz/d'eau ► **main street** N grand-rue *f*, rue *f* principale ► **mains water** N eau *f* de la ville

mainbrace ['meɪnbreɪs] N (*Naut*) bras *m* (de grand-vergue) → **splice**

Maine [meɪn] N le Maine; **in ~** dans le Maine

mainframe ['meɪnfreɪm] N (*also* ~ **computer**) (= *central computer*) unité *f* centrale, processeur *m* central; (= *large computer*) gros ordinateur *m*

mainland ['meɪnlænd] [1] N continent *m* (*opposé à une île*); **the ~ of Greece** ◊ **the Greek ~** la Grèce continentale; (*Brit*) **the Mainland** (*not Northern Ireland*) la Grande-Bretagne (l'Angleterre, l'Écosse et le Pays de Galles); (*not Hong Kong*) la Chine continentale [2] ['meɪnlənd] ADJ continental; **~ Greece** la Grèce continentale

mainline ['meɪnlaɪn] [1] ADJ [a] (= *principal*) → **mainstream** [b] [*station, train*] de grande ligne [2] VI (*Drugs**) se shooter [3] VT (= *inject*) **to ~ heroin*** se shooter* à l'héroïne

mainliner* ['meɪnlaɪnəʳ] N (*Drugs*) junkie *mf* qui se shoote*

mainly ['meɪnlɪ] ADV surtout, principalement; **~ because** surtout parce que

mainmast ['meɪnmɑːst] N (*Naut*) grand mât *m*

mainsail ['meɪnseɪl] N (*Naut*) grand-voile *f*

mainspring ['meɪnsprɪŋ] N [*of clock etc*] ressort *m* principal; (*fig*) mobile *m* principal

mainstay ['meɪnsteɪ] N (*Naut*) étai *m* (de grand mât); (*fig*) soutien *m*, point *m* d'appui; **he was the ~ of the organization** c'était lui le pilier *or* le pivot de l'organisation

mainstream ['meɪnstriːm] [1] ADJ [*political party, denomination*] grand, dominant; [*media*] principal; [*press*] traditionnel; [*culture*] grand public *inv*; [*film, music*] conventionnel, mainstream*; [*audience*] moyen; **fascism has never been part of ~ politics in Britain** le fascisme n'a jamais fait partie des grands courants politiques en Grande-Bretagne [2] N [*of politics etc*] courant *m* dominant [3] VT (*US Scol*) intégrer dans la vie scolaire normale

mainstreaming ['meɪnstriːmɪŋ] N (*US*) intégration (*d'enfants retardés ou surdoués*) dans la vie scolaire normale

▼ **maintain** [meɪnˈteɪn] [1] VT [a] (= *continue, keep up*) [+ *rate, level, order, progress, stability, sanctions, temperature, speed, value, standard, quality*] maintenir; [+ *friendship, correspondence, diplomatic relations*] entretenir; [+ *silence*] garder; [+ *attitude, advantage*] conserver, garder; **to ~ the status quo** maintenir le statu quo; **to ~ sth at a constant temperature** maintenir qch à une température constante; **to ~ radio silence** maintenir le silence radio; **to ~ control** garder le contrôle; **~ the pressure on the wound** continuez à comprimer la blessure; **to ~ one's living standards** maintenir son niveau de vie; **the government has failed to ~ standards of health care in this country** le gouvernement n'a pas réussi à maintenir la qualité des soins médicaux dans notre pays; **pupils who manage to ~ their high standards throughout their school career** des élèves qui arrivent à rester parmi les meilleurs pendant toute leur scolarité; **he ~ed his opposition to ...** il continua à s'opposer à ...; **if the improvement is ~ed** si l'on (*or* s'il *etc*) continue à faire des progrès; **products which help to ~ healthy skin and hair** des produits qui aident à garder une peau et des cheveux en bonne santé; **to ~ one's weight (at the same level)** garder le même poids; **he wants to ~ his weight at 150 pounds** il veut rester à 68 kilos

► LANGUAGE IN USE: **maintain** 26.2

b (= *support, finance*) [+ *family, wife, child, army*] entretenir

c (= *assure upkeep of*) [+ *road, building, car, machine*] entretenir

d (= *assert*) [+ *opinion, fact*] soutenir, maintenir; **to ~ one's innocence** clamer son innocence; **I ~ that ...** je soutiens or maintiens que ...

2 COMP ► **maintained school** N (*Brit*) école *f* publique

maintenance ['meɪntɪnəns] **1** N (*NonC*) **a** (= *continuation, preservation*) [of *rate, level, order, progress, stability, sanctions, temperature, speed, value, standard, quality*] maintien *m*

b (= *upkeep*) [of *road, building, car, machine*] entretien *m*, maintenance *f* (*Tech*); **car ~** mécanique *f* (auto)

c (= *financing*) [of *family, wife, child, army*] entretien *m*

d (*Jur*) pension *f* alimentaire; **he pays £50 per week ~** il verse une pension alimentaire de 50 livres par semaine

2 COMP ► **maintenance allowance** N [of *student*] bourse *f* (d'études); [of *worker away from home*] indemnité *f* (pour frais) de déplacement ► **maintenance contract** N contrat *m* d'entretien ► **maintenance costs** NPL frais *mpl* d'entretien ► **maintenance crew** N équipe *f* d'entretien ► **maintenance grant** N = **maintenance allowance** ► **maintenance man** (*pl* **maintenance men**) (*Tech etc*) employé *m* chargé de l'entretien ► **maintenance order** N (*Jur*) ordonnance *f* de versement de pension alimentaire

maisonette [ˌmeɪzə'net] N (*esp Brit*) (appartement *m* en) duplex *m*

maître d'hôtel [ˌmetrədəʊ'tel] N (*pl* **maîtres d'hôtel**) (*also* **maître d'**) maître *m* d'hôtel

maize [meɪz] N (*Brit*) maïs *m*; **~ field** champ *m* de maïs

Maj. (ABBR = **Major**) (*on envelope*) **~ J. Smith** Monsieur le Major J. Smith

majestic [mə'dʒestɪk] ADJ majestueux

majestically [mə'dʒestɪkəlɪ] ADV majestueusement

majesty ['mædʒɪstɪ] N majesté *f*; **His Majesty the King** Sa Majesté le Roi; **Your Majesty** Votre Majesté; (*Brit*) **His** or **Her Majesty's Government** le gouvernement britannique; (*Brit*) **on His** or **Her Majesty's service** au service du gouvernement britannique; (*Brit*) **His** or **Her Majesty's Stationery Office** ≈ l'Imprimerie *f* nationale → **ship**

major ['meɪdʒə^r] **1** ADJ (*gen, Jur, Mus, Philos etc*) majeur; **of ~ importance** d'une importance majeure or exceptionnelle; **of ~ interest** d'intérêt majeur; (*Mus*) **~ key** ton *m* majeur; **in the ~ key** en majeur; **the ~ portion** la majeure partie; (*Med*) **a ~ operation** une grosse opération; **~ repairs** grosses réparations *fpl*, gros travaux *mpl*; (*US*) **~ road** route *f* principale; **it was a ~ success** cela a eu un succès considérable; (*Cards*) **~ suit** majeure *f*; (*Brit Scol*) **Smith Major** Smith aîné

2 N **a** (*Mil, also US Air Force*) commandant *m*; [of *cavalry*] chef *m* d'escadron; [of *infantry*] chef *m* de bataillon

b (*US Univ*) majeur(e) *m(f)*

c (*US Univ*) matière *f* principale

d (*esp US Univ*) **music/psychology** etc **~** étudiant(e) *m(f)* en musique/psychologie etc

3 VI (*US Univ*) **to ~ in chemistry** se spécialiser en chimie

4 COMP ► **major-general** N (*Mil*) général *m* de division; (*US Air Force*) général *m* de division aérienne ► **major league** N (*US Sport*) première division *f*

Majorca [mə'jɔːkə] N Majorque *f*; **in ~** à Majorque

Majorcan [mə'jɔːkən] **1** ADJ majorquin **2** N Majorquin(e) *m(f)*

---

majordomo [ˌmeɪdʒə'dəʊməʊ] N majordome *m*

majorette [ˌmeɪdʒə'ret] N majorette *f*

majority [mə'dʒɒrɪtɪ] **1** N **a** (= *greater part*) majorité *f*; **to be in the** or **a ~** être majoritaire or en majorité; **elected by a ~ of nine** élu avec une majorité de neuf voix; **a four-fifths ~** une majorité des quatre cinquièmes; **in the ~ of cases** dans la majorité or la plupart des cas; **the ~ of people think that ...** la plupart or la majorité des gens pensent que ...; **the vast ~ of them believe ...** dans leur immense majorité ils croient ... → **silent b** (*in age*) majorité *f*; **the age of ~** l'âge *m* de la majorité; **to reach one's ~** atteindre sa majorité **2** COMP (*Pol*) [*government, rule*] majoritaire ► **majority opinion** N (*US Jur*) arrêt *m* rendu à la majorité (*des votes des juges*) ► **majority verdict** N (*Jur*) verdict *m* majoritaire or rendu à la majorité

---

make [meɪk]

> *vb: pret, ptp* **made**
>
> | | |
> |---|---|
> | **1** TRANSITIVE VERB | **4** COMPOUNDS |
> | **2** INTRANSITIVE VERB | **5** PHRASAL VERBS |
> | **3** NOUN | |

1 TRANSITIVE VERB

> *When* **make** *is part of a set combination, eg* **make a case, make an attempt, make a bow, make sure, make bold,** *look up the other word.*

a **= create, produce** [+ *bed, cake, clothes, coffee, fire, noise, remark, one's will*] faire; [+ *shelter*] construire; [+ *toys, tools, machines*] fabriquer, faire; **I'm going to ~ a cake** je vais faire un gâteau; **he made it himself** il l'a fait lui-même; **two and two ~ four** deux et deux font or égalent quatre; **how much does that ~ (altogether)?** combien ça fait (en tout)?; **that ~s the third time I've rung him** ça fait la troisième fois or trois fois que je l'appelle; BUT **to ~ a payment** effectuer or faire un paiement; **God made Man** Dieu a créé l'homme; **he's as clever as they ~ 'em*** il est malin comme pas un*, il est malin comme tout*

- **to make the/a total:** **I ~ the total 70 francs** selon mes calculs ça fait 70 F; **that ~s a total of 18 points** ça fait 18 points en tout

- **to make sth into sth else** transformer qch en qch

- **made** + *preposition*: **they were made for each other** ils étaient faits l'un pour l'autre; **her shoes weren't made for walking** elle n'avait pas les chaussures adaptées pour la marche; (*on label*) **made in France** fabriqué en France, « made in France »; **the frames are made of plastic** la monture est en plastique; **to show what one is made of** montrer ce dont on est capable; **this car wasn't made to carry eight people** cette voiture n'est pas faite pour transporter huit personnes

b **= earn** [+ *money*] [*person*] gagner, se faire; [*company, firm*] réaliser un bénéfice net de; [*product, deal*] rapporter; **he ~s £400 a week** il gagne or se fait 400 livres par semaine; **how much do you ~?** combien gagnez-vous?; **how much do you stand to ~?** combien pensez-vous pouvoir gagner?; **the company made 1.4 million pounds last year** la société a réalisé un bénéfice net de 1,4 millions de livres l'année dernière; **the film made millions** le film a rapporté des millions; **the deal made him £500** cette affaire lui a rapporté 500 livres; **what did you ~ by** or **on it?** combien est-ce que ça t'a rapporté?

c **= score** marquer; **Lara made a hundred** Lara a marqué cent points

d **= reach, attain** [+ *destination*] arriver à; (= *catch*) [+ *train, plane*] attraper, avoir; **will we ~ Paris before lunch?** est-ce que nous arriverons à Paris avant le déjeuner?; BUT **we made good time** (*on foot*) nous avons bien marché;

(*in vehicle*) nous avons bien roulé; **he made the list of ...*** son nom a figuré sur la liste de ...

> **réussir à/arriver à** + *infinitive are used in the following to translate* **make** + *noun*:

do you think he'll ~ (it to) university? croyez-vous qu'il arrivera à entrer à l'université?; **the novel made the bestseller list** le roman a réussi à se placer sur la liste des best-sellers; **he made (it into) the first team** il a réussi à être sélectionné dans l'équipe première

e **= force** obliger, forcer; **you can't ~ me!** tu ne peux pas m'y forcer or obliger! → **j**

f **= reckon** **how many do you ~ it?** combien en comptes-tu?; **I ~ it 100km from here to Paris** d'après moi or selon moi il y a 100 km d'ici à Paris; **what time do you ~ it?** quelle heure as-tu?

g **= ensure success of** **the beautiful pictures ~ the book** ce livre doit beaucoup à ses magnifiques images; **that film made her** ce film l'a consacrée; **he was made for life*** son avenir était assuré; **you're made!*** ton avenir est assuré, tu n'as pas de soucis à te faire pour ton avenir!; **he's got it made*** son avenir est assuré, il n'a pas à s'en faire pour son avenir; **to ~ or break sb** assurer ou briser la carrière de qn; **his visit made my day!*** sa visite m'a fait un plaisir fou*!; (*iro*) **go ahead, ~ my day!*** vas-y, qu'est-ce que tu attends?

h **= be, constitute** faire; **he'll ~ a good footballer** il fera un bon joueur de football; **he'll ~ somebody a good husband** il fera un bon mari; (*in game*) **to ~ a fourth** faire le quatrième; **I made one of their group** je faisais partie de leur groupe; **they ~ good cooking apples** ce sont or elles font de bonnes pommes à cuire; BUT **she made him a good wife** elle a été une bonne épouse pour lui; **they ~ a handsome pair** ils forment un beau couple; **these books ~ a set** ces livres forment une collection; **the latest report doesn't ~ pleasant reading** le dernier compte-rendu n'est pas très réjouissant

i Cards **to ~ the cards** battre les cartes; **to ~ a trick** faire un pli; **he made ten and lost three (tricks)** il a fait dix plis et en a perdu trois; (*Bridge*) **to bid and ~ three hearts** demander et faire trois cœurs; **he managed to ~ his queen of diamonds** il a réussi à faire un pli avec sa dame de carreau

j SET STRUCTURES

- **to make sb do sth** (= *cause to*) faire faire qch à qn; (= *force*) obliger or forcer qn à faire qch, faire faire qch à qn; **to ~ sb laugh** faire rire qn; **what made you believe that ...?** qu'est-ce qui vous a fait croire que ...?; **the author ~s him die in the last chapter** l'auteur le fait mourir au dernier chapitre; **I was made to wait for an hour** on m'a fait attendre une heure; **they made him tell them the password** ils l'ont obligé or forcé à leur dire le mot de passe; BUT **I don't know what ~s him do it** je ne sais pas ce qui le pousse à faire ça

- **to make sb sth** (= *choose as*) **to ~ sb king** mettre qn sur le trône; **he made John his assistant** il a fait de John son assistant; **he made her his wife** il l'a épousée; **this actor ~s the hero a tragic figure** cet acteur fait du héros un personnage tragique

- **to make of**: **what did you ~ of the film?** que penses-tu de ce film?; **what do you ~ of him?** qu'est-ce que tu penses de lui?; **I don't know what to ~ of it all** je ne sais pas quoi penser de tout ça; **I can't ~ anything of this letter** ◊ **I can ~ nothing of this letter** je ne comprends rien à cette lettre

- **to make ...** + *adjective*: **to ~ o.s. useful/ill** se rendre utile/malade; **to ~ sb happy/unhappy** rendre qn heureux/malheureux; **~ yourself comfortable** mettez-vous à l'aise

> *Look up other combinations, eg* **to make sb thirsty, to make o.s. ridiculous,** *at the adjective.*

- **to make believe** (= *pretend*) faire semblant; (= *imagine*) imaginer; **he made believe** he couldn't understand il a fait semblant de ne pas comprendre; **let's ~ believe we're on a desert island** imaginons que nous sommes sur une île déserte

♦ **to make do** (= *manage*) se débrouiller; **I'll ~ do with what I've got** je vais me débrouiller avec ce que j'ai; **she had to ~ do and mend for many years** elle a dû se débrouiller pendant des années avec ce qu'elle avait; (= *be satisfied*) **he can't come, you'll have to ~ do with me** il ne peut pas venir, tu vas devoir te contenter de moi

♦ **to make it** (= *come*) venir; (= *arrive*) arriver; (= *succeed*) réussir, y parvenir, y arriver; **sorry, I can't ~ it** désolé, je ne peux pas venir; **he made it just in time** il est arrivé juste à temps; **you've got the talent to ~ it** tu as tout pour réussir; **he tried for months to get into the team and eventually made it** il a essayé pendant des mois d'intégrer l'équipe et a fini par y parvenir *or* y arriver; [BUT] **can you ~ it by 3 o'clock?** est-ce que tu peux y être pour 3 heures?

♦ **to make it with sb** (⁑ *= be accepted*) être accepté par qn; (⁑ *= have sex with*) s'envoyer⁑ *or* se taper⁑ qn; **he'll never ~ it with them⁑** il ne réussira jamais à se faire accepter d'eux; **they're making it (together)⁑** ils couchent* ensemble

♦ **to make it** + *time, date, amount*: **let's ~ it 5 o'clock/£30** si on disait 5 heures/30 livres?; **I'm coming tomorrow — okay, can you ~ it the afternoon?** je viendrai demain — d'accord, mais est-ce que tu peux venir dans l'après-midi?

[2] INTRANSITIVE VERB
[a] **= act**

♦ **to make as if** ◊ **to make like**⁕: **he made as if to strike me** il fit mine de me frapper; **she made as if to protest, then hesitated** elle parut sur le point de protester, puis hésita; **he was making like he didn't have any money** il faisait mine de ne pas avoir d'argent

[b] [*tide, flood*] monter

[3] NOUN
[a] **Comm** (= *brand*) marque *f*; (= *manufacture*) fabrication *f*; **it's a good ~** c'est une bonne marque; **the cars were mainly of French ~** les voitures étaient pour la plupart de fabrication française; **what ~ of car do you drive?** qu'est-ce que vous avez comme (marque de) voiture?; [BUT] **these are our own ~** (*industrial products*) ceux-là sont fabriqués par nous; (*confectionery, food*) ceux-là sont faits maison; **it's my own ~** je l'ai fait moi-même

[b]

♦ **to be on the make** (⁕: *pej*) [*person*] (= *trying to make money*) chercher à se remplir les poches; (= *trying to get power*) avoir une ambition dévorante; (*US*) [*person, thing*] (= *to be successful*) avoir du succès; [*tide*] (= *to be rising*) monter; **some politicians are on the ~** certains hommes politiques cherchent à se remplir les poches; **a brilliant young man on the ~** un jeune homme brillant à l'ambition dévorante; **it's on the ~** ça a du succès; **the tide is on the ~** la marée monte

[4] COMPOUNDS
► **make-believe** N **to play at ~-believe** jouer à faire semblant; **the land of ~-believe** le pays des chimères; **theatre is a world of ~-believe** le théâtre est un monde d'illusions ♦ ADJ **his story is pure ~-believe** son histoire est de l'invention pure *or* (de la) pure fantaisie; **they were on a ~-believe island** ils faisaient semblant d'être sur une île; **the child made a ~-believe boat out of the chair** l'enfant faisait de la chaise un bateau imaginaire ► **make-or-break**⁕ ADJ décisif (**for sb/sth** pour qn/qch) ► **make-up** N → make-up

[5] PHRASAL VERBS
► **make after** VT FUS se lancer à la poursuite de; **they made after him** ils se sont lancés à sa poursuite

► **make at** VT FUS se jeter sur; **he made at me with a knife** il s'est jeté sur moi avec un cou-

teau

► **make away** VI = make off

► **make away with** VT FUS (= *murder*) supprimer; **to ~ away with o.s.** se supprimer

► **make for** VT FUS [a] (= *go to*) **where are you making for?** où allez-vous?; **he made for the door** il se dirigea vers la porte; **the ship is making for Cyprus** le navire fait route vers Chypre; **to ~ for home** rentrer (chez soi)

[b] (= *produce*) produire; (= *contribute to*) contribuer à; **controversy ~s for eye-catching headlines** toute controverse produit des gros titres accrocheurs; **a good education system ~s for a successful economy** un bon système éducatif contribue à la prospérité de l'économie; **happy parents ~ for a happy child** quand les parents sont heureux, l'enfant l'est aussi, à parents heureux, enfant heureux

► **make off** VI se tirer⁕; **to ~ off with sth** se tirer* avec qch

► **make out** [1] VI [a] (⁕ *= manage*) se débrouiller; **they're making out fairly well** ils se débrouillent assez bien; **how are you making out?** comment ça marche?, comment te débrouilles-tu?; **how are you making out with your research?** comment avancent tes recherches?; **the firm is making out all right** l'entreprise marche bien [b] (*US*⁑ *= have sex*) s'envoyer⁑ en l'air⁑; **to ~ out with sb** s'envoyer⁑ qn

[2] VT SEP [a] (= *draw up, write*) [+ *list, bill*] faire, dresser; [+ *cheque*] libeller; [+ *will*] faire, rédiger; **cheques made out to ...** chèques *mpl* libellés à l'ordre *or* au nom de ...; **who shall I ~ it out to?** je le fais à l'ordre de qui?, c'est à quel ordre?

[b] (= *put forward*) **he made out a good case for not doing it** il a présenté de bons arguments pour ne pas le faire

[c] (= *see, distinguish*) [+ *object, person*] discerner, distinguer; (= *hear*) distinguer, comprendre; (= *understand*) comprendre; (= *decipher*) [+ *handwriting*] déchiffrer; **I could just ~ out three figures in the distance** j'arrivais tout juste à discerner *or* distinguer trois silhouettes au loin; **I can't ~ it out at all** je n'y comprends rien; **how do you ~ that out?** qu'est-ce qui vous fait penser cela?; **I can't ~ out what he wants/why he is here** je n'arrive pas à comprendre ce qu'il veut/pourquoi il est ici

[d] (= *claim, pretend*) prétendre (**that** que); (= *portray as*) présenter comme; **he's not as stupid as he ~s out** il n'est pas aussi stupide qu'il le prétend; **he isn't as rich as people ~ out** il n'est pas aussi riche que les gens le prétendent; **the programme made her out to be naïve** l'émission la présentait comme une femme naïve; **the biography ~s her out to be ruthless** cette biographie la décrit comme une femme impitoyable; **they made him out to be a fool** ils disaient que c'était un imbécile; **he made out that he was a doctor** il se faisait passer pour (un) médecin

► **make over** VT SEP [a] (= *assign*) [+ *money, land*] céder, transférer (**to** à)

[b] (= *remake*) [+ *garment, story*] reprendre; (= *convert*) [+ *building*] convertir; **she made the jacket over to fit her son** elle a repris la veste pour (qu'elle aille à) son fils

► **make up** [1] VI [a] (= *become friends again*) se réconcilier, se rabibocher*

[b] (= *apply cosmetics*) se maquiller; (*Theat*) se maquiller; (*heavily*) se grimer

[2] VT SEP [a] (= *invent*) [+ *story, excuse, explanation*] inventer, fabriquer; **you're making it up!** tu l'inventes (de toutes pièces)!

[b] (= *put together*) [+ *packet, parcel*] faire; [+ *dish, medicine, solution*] préparer; [+ *garment*] assembler; [+ *list*] faire, dresser; **to ~ sth up into a bundle** faire un paquet de qch; (*Typ*) **to ~ up a page** mettre un livre en pages; (*Pharm*) **to ~ up a prescription** exécuter *or* préparer une ordonnance; **she made up a bed for him on the sofa** elle lui a fait *or* préparé un lit sur le canapé; **have you made up the beds?** as-tu fait les

lits?; **customers' accounts are made up monthly** les relevés de compte des clients sont établis chaque mois; **they sell material and also ~ up clothes** ils vendent du tissu et font aussi des vêtements; **"customers' own material made up"** « travail à façon »

[c] (= *counterbalance, replace*) [+ *loss, deficit*] combler, compenser; [+ *sum of money, numbers, quantity, total*] compléter; **to ~ up the difference** mettre la différence; **they made up the number with five amateurs** ils ont complété l'équipe en faisant appel à cinq amateurs; **he made it up to £100** il a complété les 100 livres; **to ~ up lost time** rattraper le temps perdu; **to ~ up lost ground** regagner le terrain perdu; **to ~ up ground on sb** gagner du terrain sur qn

[d] (= *repay*) **to ~ sth up to sb** ◊ **to ~ it up to sb for sth** revaloir qch à qn; **I'll ~ it up to you I promise** je te revaudrai ça, je te le promets; **I must ~ it up to him for my stupid mistake** je dois me faire pardonner auprès de lui pour mon erreur stupide

[e] (= *settle*) [+ *dispute*] mettre fin à; [+ *differences*] régler; **to ~ up one's quarrel** ◊ **to ~ it up** se réconcilier, se rabibocher*; **let's ~ it up** faisons la paix

[f] (= *apply cosmetics to*) [+ *person*] maquiller; (*Theat*) maquiller; (*heavily*) grimer; **to ~ o.s. up** ◊ **to ~ up one's face** se maquiller; (*Theat*) se maquiller; (*heavily*) se grimer; **she was making up her eyes** elle se maquillait les yeux

[g] (= *compose, form*) composer, constituer; (= *represent*) constituer, représenter; **the group was made up of six teachers** le groupe était composé *or* constitué de six professeurs; **how many people ~ up the team?** combien y a-t-il de personnes dans l'équipe?; **they ~ up 6% of ...** ils représentent *or* constituent 6 % de ...

► **make up for** VT FUS compenser; **he has made up for last year's losses** il a comblé les pertes de l'année dernière; **money can't ~ up for what we've suffered** l'argent ne peut compenser ce que nous avons souffert; **he tried to ~ up for all the trouble he'd caused** il essaya de se faire pardonner les ennuis qu'il avait causés; **he made up for all the mistakes he'd made** il s'est rattrapé pour toutes les erreurs qu'il avait commises; **she said that nothing could ~ up for her husband's death** elle dit que rien ne la consolerait de la mort de son mari; **to ~ up for lost time** rattraper le temps perdu

► **make up on** VT FUS (= *catch up with*) rattraper

► **make up to**⁕ VT FUS (= *curry favour with*) passer de la pommade⁕ à qn

makefast ['meɪkfɑːst] N (*US*) point *m* d'amarre

makeover ['meɪkəʊvər] N (*lit, fig*) changement *m* de look*

Maker ['meɪkər] N (*Rel*) **our ~** le Créateur; (*hum*) **he's gone to meet his ~** il est allé ad patres (*hum*)

-maker ['meɪkər] N (*in compounds*) [a] (= *manufacturer: gen*) fabricant(e) *m(f)* de ...; **tyre/furniture-maker** fabricant *m* de pneus/de meubles; **film-maker** cinéaste *mf* → watchmaker [b] (= *machine*) **coffee-maker** cafetière *f* électrique; **yoghurt-maker** yaourtière *f*

makeshift ['meɪkʃɪft] [1] N expédient *m*, moyen *m* de fortune [2] ADJ de fortune

make-up ['meɪkʌp] [1] N [a] (*NonC* = *nature*) [*of object, group etc*] constitution *f*; [*of person*] tempérament *m*, caractère *m* [b] (*NonC* = *cosmetics*) maquillage *m*; **she wears too much ~** elle se maquille trop, elle est trop maquillée [c] (*US Scol etc*⁕) examen *m* de rattrapage [2] COMP ► **make-up artist** N maquilleur *m*, -euse *f* ► **make-up bag** N trousse *f* de maquillage ► **make-up base** N base *f* (de maquillage) ► **make-up case** N nécessaire *m* *or* boîte *f* de maquillage ► **make-up class** N (*US Scol*) cours *m* de rattrapage ► **make-up girl** N maquilleuse *f* ► **make-up man** N (*pl*

make-up men) maquilleur *m* ► **make-up remover** N démaquillant *m*

makeweight ['meɪkweɪt] N a (*lit* = *weight, object*) tare *f* b (*fig* = *person*) bouche-trou *m*

making ['meɪkɪŋ] 1 N a (*NonC*) (*Comm, gen*) fabrication *f*; [*of dress*] façon *f*, confection *f*; [*of machines*] fabrication *f*, construction *f*; [*of food*] (*Ind: by machine*) fabrication *f*; **rennet is used in the ~ of cheese** on utilise la présure dans la fabrication du fromage; (*Ind*) **bread-/cheese-/wine-** *etc* ~ fabrication *f* du pain/du fromage/du vin *etc*; **she does her own wine-~** elle fait son vin elle-même; **all his troubles are of his own ~** tous ses ennuis sont de sa faute; **decision-~** prise *f* de décisions; **he wrote a book on the ~ of the film** il a écrit un livre sur la genèse de ce film; (*Ind*) **the ~ of the film took three months** ◊ **the film was three months in the ~** il a fallu trois mois pour faire ce film; **a new system/society is in the ~** un nouveau système/une nouvelle société est en train de se créer; **a compromise may be in the ~** il se peut que l'on soit sur le point d'arriver à un compromis; **a genius/star in the ~** un génie/une star en herbe; **a dictator/criminal in the ~** de la graine de dictateur/criminel; **it's a disaster in the ~** ça risque de tourner au désastre; **it's history in the ~** c'est l'histoire en train de se faire; **it's still in the ~** [*product, film*] c'est encore en chantier b (= *forming*) **it was the ~ of him** (*gen*) c'est ce qui a formé son caractère; (= *made him successful*) son succès est parti de là 2 **makings** NPL éléments *mpl* essentiels; **he has the ~s of a footballer** il a l'étoffe d'un footballeur; **the situation has the ~s of a civil war** cette situation laisse présager une guerre civile; **we have all the ~s of a great movie** il y a tous les ingrédients pour faire un grand film

Malachi ['mælə,kaɪ] N Malachie *m*

malachite ['mælə,kaɪt] N malachite *f*

maladjusted [,mælə'dʒʌstɪd] ADJ a (*Psych*) inadapté b (*Tech*) mal ajusté, mal réglé

maladjustment [,mælə'dʒʌstmənt] N a (*Psych*) inadaptation *f* b (*Tech*) mauvais ajustement *m*

maladministration ['mæləd,mɪnɪs'treɪʃən] N mauvaise gestion *f*

maladroit [,mælə'drɔɪt] ADJ (*frm*) inhabile, maladroit

maladroitly [,mælə'drɔɪtlɪ] ADV (*frm*) maladroitement

maladroitness [,mælə'drɔɪtnɪs] N (*frm*) maladresse *f*

malady ['mælədɪ] N (*frm*) maladie *f*, mal *m*

Malagasy ['mælə'gɑːzɪ] 1 N a Malgache *mf* b (*Ling*) malgache *m* 2 ADJ (*Hist*) malgache; **the ~ Republic** la République malgache

malaise [mæ'leɪz] N (*frm*) malaise *m*

malapropism ['mæləprɒpɪzəm] N impropriété *f* (de langage)

malaria [mə'lɛərɪə] N paludisme *m*, malaria *f*

malarial [mə'lɛərɪəl] ADJ [*parasite*] du paludisme; [*mosquito*] porteur de paludisme; [*region*] impaludé; **~ fever** paludisme *m*, malaria *f*

malark(e)y [mə'lɑːkɪ] N (*NonC*) âneries *fpl*

Malawi [mə'lɑːwɪ] N le Malawi

Malawian [mə'lɑːwɪən] 1 N Malawien(ne) *m(f)* 2 ADJ malawien

Malay [mə'leɪ] 1 ADJ [*language, community, culture*] malais; **the ~ mainland** la Malaisie continentale 2 N a (= *person*) Malais(e) *m(f)* b (*Ling*) malais *m* 3 COMP ► **the Malay Archipelago** N l'archipel *m* malais ► **the Malay Peninsula** la péninsule malaise

Malaya [mə'leɪə] N la Malaisie occidentale

Malayan [mə'leɪən] = **Malay**

Malaysia [mə'leɪzɪə] N la Malaisie, la Malaysia

Malaysian [mə'leɪzɪən] 1 ADJ malais 2 N Malais(e) *m(f)*

malcontent ['mælkən,tent] ADJ, N mécontent(e) *m(f)*

Maldives ['mɔːldaɪvz] NPL Maldives *fpl*

male [meɪl] 1 ADJ (*Anat, Bio, Tech etc*) mâle; (*fig = manly*) mâle, viril (virile *f*); **~ child** enfant *m* mâle; **the ~ sex** le sexe masculin → **chauvinist, menopause, model** 2 N (= *animal*) mâle *m*; (= *man*) homme *m* 3 COMP ► **male bonding** N fraternisation *f* masculine ► **male-dominated** ADJ dominé par les hommes ► **male-voice choir** N chœur *m* d'hommes, chœur *m* de voix mâles

malediction [,mælɪ'dɪkʃən] N malédiction *f*

malefactor ['mælɪfæktəʳ] N malfaiteur *m*, -trice *f*

maleness ['meɪlnɪs] N (= *being male*) fait *m* d'être mâle; (= *masculinity*) masculinité *f*

malevolence [mə'levələns] N malveillance *f* (**towards** envers)

malevolent [mə'levələnt] ADJ malveillant

malevolently [mə'levələntlɪ] ADV avec malveillance

malformation [,mælfɔː'meɪʃən] N malformation *f*, difformité *f*

malformed [,mæl'fɔːmd] ADJ [*baby*] malformé; **to have a ~ heart/foot** avoir une malformation cardiaque/du pied

malfunction [,mæl'fʌŋkʃən] 1 N mauvais fonctionnement *m*, défaillance *f* 2 VI mal fonctionner

Mali ['mɑːlɪ] N le Mali

Malian ['mɑːlɪən] 1 N Malien(ne) *m(f)* 2 ADJ malien

malice ['mælɪs] N méchanceté *f*, malice† *f* (*also liter*); (*stronger*) malveillance *f*; **to bear sb ~** vouloir du mal à qn; (*Jur*) **with ~ aforethought** avec préméditation, avec intention criminelle *or* délictueuse

malicious [mə'lɪʃəs] 1 ADJ [*person*] méchant; [*talk, rumour, attack, phone call*] malveillant; [*smile*] mauvais; **~ gossip** médisances *fpl*; **with ~ intent** avec l'intention de nuire 2 COMP ► **malicious falsehood** N (*Jur*) diffamation *f* ► **malicious wounding** N (*Jur*) ≈ coups *mpl* et blessures *fpl* volontaires

maliciously [mə'lɪʃəslɪ] ADV [*say, smile*] méchamment; (*stronger*) avec malveillance; (*Jur*) avec préméditation, avec intention criminelle

malign [mə'laɪn] 1 ADJ pernicieux 2 VT calomnier, diffamer; **you ~ me** vous me calomniez

malignancy [mə'lɪgnənsɪ] N a malveillance *f*, malfaisance *f* b (*Med*) malignité *f*

malignant [mə'lɪgnənt] ADJ a (= *malevolent*) [*influence, effect*] nocif; [*plot, look, person*] malveillant b (*Med*) malin (-igne *f*)

malignantly [mə'lɪgnəntlɪ] ADV [*speak, say*] avec malveillance

malignity [mə'lɪgnɪtɪ] N = **malignancy**

malinger [mə'lɪŋgəʳ] VI faire le (*or* la) malade

malingerer [mə'lɪŋgərəʳ] N faux malade *m*, fausse malade *f*; (*Admin, Mil etc*) simulateur *m*, -trice *f*; **he's a ~** il se fait passer pour malade

mall [mɔːl, mæl] N a (*gen*) allée *f*, mail *m* b (*US*) (= *pedestrianized street*) rue *f* piétonnière; (*also* **shopping ~**) centre *m* commercial

mallard ['mælɑːd] N (*pl* **mallard(s)**) (*also* **~ duck**) colvert *m*

malleability [,mælɪə'bɪlɪtɪ] N malléabilité *f*

malleable ['mælɪəbl] ADJ a (*lit*) [*material*] malléable b (*fig*) [*person*] malléable, influençable

mallet ['mælɪt] N maillet *m*

malleus ['mælɪəs] N (*pl* **mallei** ['mælɪ,aɪ]) marteau *m*

mallow ['mæləʊ] N (*Bot*) mauve *f* → **marshmallow**

malnourished [,mæl'nʌrɪʃt] ADJ [*person*] qui souffre de malnutrition

malnutrition [,mælnjʊ'trɪʃən] N malnutrition *f*

malodorous [mæl'əʊdərəs] ADJ (*liter*) malodorant

malpractice [,mæl'præktɪs] 1 N (= *wrongdoing*) faute *f* professionnelle; (= *neglect of duty*) négligence *f* *or* incurie *f* professionnelle 2 COMP ► **malpractice suit** N (*US Jur*) procès *m* pour faute professionnelle; **to bring a ~ suit against sb** poursuivre qn pour faute professionnelle

malt [mɔːlt] 1 N malt *m* 2 VT malter 3 COMP [*vinegar*] de malt ► **malt extract** N extrait *m* de malt ► **malt liquor** N (*US*) bière *f* ► **malt whisky** N (whisky *m*) pur malt *m*

Malta ['mɔːltə] N (*island*) Malte *f*; (*state*) Malte *m*; **in ~** à Malte

maltase ['mɔːlteɪz] N maltase *f*

malted ['mɔːltɪd] 1 ADJ malté 2 COMP ► **malted barley** N orge *f* maltée ► **malted milk** N lait *m* malté

Maltese [,mɔːl'tiːz] 1 ADJ maltais; **~ cross** croix *f* de Malte; **~ fever** fièvre *f* de Malte 2 N a (*pl inv*) Maltais(e) *m(f)* b (*Ling*) maltais *m* 3 **the Maltese** NPL les Maltais *mpl*

Malthus ['mælθəs] N Malthus *m*

Malthusianism [mæl'θjuːzɪə,nɪzəm] N malthusianisme *m*

maltreat [mæl'triːt] VT maltraiter, malmener

maltreatment [,mæl'triːtmənt] N mauvais traitement *m*

mam* [mæm] N (*Brit dial*) maman *f*; **my ~** maman

mama ['mæmɑː] N (*esp US*) mère *f*, maman *f*; (*pej*) **he's a mam(m)a's boy** c'est un fils à sa mère (*pej*)

mamba ['mæmbə] N (*Zool*) mamba *m*; **black/green ~** mamba *m* noir/vert

mamma [mə'mɑː] N = **mama**

mammal ['mæməl] N mammifère *m*

mammalian [mæ'meɪlɪən] ADJ mammalien

mammary ['mæmərɪ] 1 ADJ mammaire 2 COMP ► **mammary gland** N glande *f* mammaire

mammogram ['mæməgræm] N (*Med*) mammographie *f*

mammography [mæ'mɒgrəfɪ] N mammographie *f*

Mammon ['mæmən] N le dieu Argent, Mammon *m*

mammoth ['mæməθ] 1 N mammouth *m* 2 ADJ colossal

mammy ['mæmɪ] N a* maman *f* b (*US* = *Black nurse*) nourrice *f* noire

man [mæn] 1 N (*pl* **men**) (*gen*) homme *m*; (= *servant*) domestique *m*; (*in factory etc*) ouvrier *m*; (*in office, shop etc*) employé *m*; (*Sport* = *player*) joueur *m*, équipier *m*; (= *husband*) homme *m*; **men and women** les hommes *mpl* et les femmes *fpl*; **he's a nice ~** c'est un homme sympathique; **an old ~** un vieil homme, un vieillard; **a blind ~** un aveugle; **a medical ~** un docteur; **a ~ of God** un homme de Dieu; **I don't like the ~** je n'aime pas cet homme *or* ce type*; **the ~'s an idiot** c'est un imbécile; **that ~ Smith** ce (type*) Smith; **the ~ Jones**† le dénommé *or* le nommé Jones; **the ~ in the moon** le visage que l'on peut imaginer en regardant la lune; **as one ~** (= *in unison*) comme un seul homme; **as one ~ to another** d'homme à homme; **they're communists to a ~ or to the last ~** ils sont tous communistes sans exception; **they perished to a ~** pas un seul d'entre eux n'a survécu; **he's been with this firm ~ and boy for 30 years** cela fait 30 ans qu'il est entré tout jeune encore dans la maison; (*also* **~ and wife**) **the employers and the men** les patrons *mpl* et les ouvriers *mpl*; **~ and wife** mari *m* et femme *f*; **to live as ~ and wife** vivre maritalement; **her ~*** son homme; **my old ~*** (= *father*) mon paternel*; (= *husband*) mon homme; **her young ~†*** son amoureux†, son futur (hum); **it will make a ~ of him** cela fera de lui un homme; **be a ~!** sois un homme!; **he took it like a ~** il a pris ça vaillamment; **he was ~ enough to apologize** il a eu le courage de s'excuser; **he's his own ~ again** (= not subordinate to anyone) il est redevenu son propre maître; (= in control of his emotions etc) il est de nouveau maître de lui → **best, estate, jack**

[b] (Mil) homme m (de troupe), soldat m; (Naut) homme m (d'équipage), matelot m; **officers and men** (Aviat, Mil) officiers mpl et soldats mpl, officiers mpl et hommes mpl de troupe; (Naut) officiers mpl et matelots mpl; **the corporal and his men** le caporal et ses hommes; **they fought to the last ~** ils se sont battus jusqu'au dernier

[c] (= sort, type) **I'm not a drinking ~** je ne bois pas (beaucoup); **I'm not a gambling ~** je ne suis pas joueur; **he's not a football ~** ce n'est pas un amateur de football; **I'm a whisky ~ myself** personnellement, je préfère le whisky; **a leg/tit*/bum*** ~ un homme attiré par les belles jambes/les beaux nichons*/les belles fesses; **he's a man's ~** c'est un homme qui est plus à l'aise avec les hommes; **he's a Leeds ~** (= native) il est or vient de Leeds; (= football supporter) c'est un supporter de Leeds; **he's not the ~ to fail** il n'est pas homme à échouer; **he's not the ~ for that** il n'est pas fait pour cela; **he's the ~ for the job** c'est l'homme qu'il nous (or leur etc) faut; **if you're looking for someone to help you, then I'm your ~** si vous cherchez quelqu'un pour vous aider, je suis votre homme; **the ~ in the street** l'homme m de la rue, Monsieur Tout-le-monde; **a ~ of the world** un homme d'expérience; **a ~ about town** un homme du monde; **the ~ of the hour or the moment** le héros du jour, l'homme m du moment → **destiny, idea, lady, letter, local, property**

[d] (in compounds) **the ice-cream ~** le marchand de glaces; **the TV ~** l'installateur m (or le dépanneur) de télé; **the gas ~** l'employé m du gaz; (Brit Aut) **it's the green/red ~** le feu pour les piétons est au vert/au rouge → **repair¹**

[e] (= humanity in general) **Man** l'homme m; **that's no use or good to ~ (n)or beast** cela ne sert strictement à rien ■ (PROV) **Man proposes, God disposes** l'homme propose et Dieu dispose (PROV)

[f] (= person) homme m; **all men must die** tous les hommes sont mortels, nous sommes tous mortels; **men say that ...** on dit que ..., certains disent que ...; **any ~ would have done the same** n'importe qui aurait fait de même; **no ~ could blame him** personne ne pouvait le lui reprocher; **what else could a ~ do?** qu'est-ce qu'on aurait pu faire d'autre?

[g] (in direct address) **hurry up, ~!*** dépêchez-vous!, magnez-vous donc!*; (to friend etc) magne-toi, mon vieux!*; **~*, was I terrified!** quelle frousse* j'ai eue!; **look here young ~!** dites donc, jeune homme!; **(my) little ~!** mon grand!; **old ~†*** mon vieux*; **my (good) ~†** mon brave†; **good ~!** bravo!

[h] (Chess) pièce f; (Draughts) pion m

[i] (US) **the Man*** (= white man) le blanc; (= boss) le patron; (= police) les flics* mpl

[2] VT [a] (= provide staff for) assurer une permanence à; (= work at) être de service à; **they haven't enough staff to ~ the office every day** ils n'ont pas assez de personnel pour assurer une permanence au bureau tous les jours; **who will ~ the enquiry desk?** qui sera de service au bureau des renseignements?; **the telephone is ~ned twelve hours per day** il y a une permanence téléphonique douze heures par jour

[b] (Mil) **to ~ a ship** équiper un navire en personnel; **the ship was ~ned mainly by Chinese** l'équipage était composé principalement de Chinois; **the troops who ~ned the**

look-out posts les troupes qui tenaient les postes d'observation; **the soldiers ~ning the fortress** les soldats qui étaient en garnison dans la forteresse; (Naut) **to ~ the boats** armer les bateaux; (Mil) **to ~ the guns** servir les canons; **to ~ the pumps** armer les pompes → **manned**

[3] COMP ► **man-at-arms** N (pl men-at-arms) homme m d'armes, cuirassier m ► **man-child** N (liter) enfant m mâle ► **man-day** N (Comm, Ind etc) jour-homme m, jour m de travail ► **man-eater** N (= animal) mangeur m d'hommes; (= cannibal) cannibale m, anthropophage m; (fig hum = woman) dévoreuse f d'hommes, mante f religieuse ► **man-eating** ADJ [animal] mangeur d'hommes; [tribe etc] anthropophage ► **man Friday** N (in Robinson Crusoe) Vendredi m; (fig) (= retainer) fidèle serviteur m; (= assistant) aide m de bureau ► **man-hater** N **to be a ~hater** [woman] avoir les hommes en horreur ► **man-hour** N (Comm, Ind etc) heure-homme f, heure f de travail ► **man-made** ADJ [fibre, fabric] synthétique; [lake, barrier] artificiel ► **man management** N he's not very good at ~ **management** il ne sait pas très bien diriger une équipe; ~ **management is an important skill** savoir bien diriger une équipe ► **man-of-war, man-o'-war** N (pl men-of-war) (Naut) vaisseau m or navire m or bâtiment m de guerre → **Portuguese** ► **man-sized*** ADJ (fig) grand, de taille, de grande personne* ► **man-to-man** ADJ, ADV d'homme à homme ► **man-to-man marking** N (Brit Ftbl) marquage m individuel

manacle ['mænəkl] [1] N (gen pl) menottes fpl [2] VT mettre les menottes à; **~d** les menottes aux poignets

▼ **manage** ['mænɪdʒ] [1] VT [a] (= direct) [+ business, estate, theatre, restaurant, hotel, shop, time, capital] gérer; [+ institution, organization] administrer, diriger; [+ football team, boxer etc] être le manager de; [+ actor, singer etc] être le manager or l'imprésario de; [+ farm] exploiter

[b] (= handle, deal with) [+ boat, vehicle] manœuvrer, manier; [+ animal, person] savoir s'y prendre avec; **you ~d the situation very well** tu as très bien géré la situation

[c] (= succeed, contrive) **to ~ to do sth** réussir or arriver à faire qch; **how did you ~ to do it?** comment as-tu réussi à le faire?, comment y es-tu arrivé?; **how did you ~ not to spill it?** comment as-tu fait pour ne pas le renverser?; **he ~d not to get his feet wet** il a réussi à ne pas se mouiller les pieds; (iro) **he ~d to annoy everybody** il a trouvé le moyen de mécontenter tout le monde; **you'll ~ it next time!** tu réussiras or tu y arriveras la prochaine fois!; **will you come? — I can't ~ (it) just now** tu viendras? — je ne peux pas pour l'instant

[d] (= manage to do, pay, eat etc) **how much will you give? — I can ~ 50 francs** combien allez-vous donner? — je peux aller jusqu'à 50 F or je peux mettre 50 F; **surely you could ~ another biscuit?** tu mangeras bien encore un autre biscuit?; **I couldn't ~ another thing!** je n'en peux plus!; **can you ~ the suitcases?** pouvez-vous porter les valises?; **can you ~ 8 o'clock?** 8 heures, ça vous convient?; **can you ~ two more in the car?** peux-tu encore en prendre deux or as-tu de la place pour deux de plus dans la voiture?; **I ~d a smile/a few words of greeting** etc j'ai quand même réussi à sourire/à dire quelques mots de bienvenue etc

[2] VI (= succeed, get by) se débrouiller; **can you ~?** tu y arrives or arriveras?; **thanks, I can ~ merci**, ça va; **I can ~ without him** je peux me débrouiller sans lui; **she ~s on her pension/on £60 a week** elle se débrouille avec seulement sa retraite/avec seulement 60 livres par semaine; **how will you ~?** comment allez-vous faire or vous débrouiller?

[3] COMP ► **managed competition** N (US Ind) concurrence f réglementée or encadrée ► **managed economy** N économie f dirigée ► **managed forests** NPL forêts fpl gérées ► **managed funds** NPL (Fin) fonds mpl gérés ► **managed trade** N (Ind) commerce m dirigé

manageable ['mænɪdʒəbl] ADJ [size, amount, number, proportions] raisonnable; [problem] soluble; [task] faisable; [person] souple; [child, animal] docile; [hair] facile à coiffer; [vehicle, boat] maniable; **the situation is ~** la situation est gérable

management ['mænɪdʒmənt] [1] N [a] (NonC = managing) [of company, estate, theatre] gestion f; [of institution, organization] administration f, direction f; [of farm] exploitation f; **his skilful ~ of his staff** l'habileté avec laquelle il dirige son personnel

[b] (= people in charge) [of business, hotel, theatre etc] direction f; **by order of the ~** par ordre de la direction; **the ~ and the workers** la direction et les travailleurs; (Ind) ~ **and labour or unions** les partenaires mpl sociaux; **he's (one of the) ~ now** il fait partie des cadres (supérieurs) maintenant; **"under new ~"** « changement de propriétaire »

[2] COMP ► **management accounting** N comptabilité f de gestion ► **management buyout** N rachat m d'une entreprise par ses cadres or sa direction ► **management chart** N organigramme m ► **management committee** N comité m de direction ► **management company** N société f de gestion ► **management consultancy** N (= business) cabinet m de conseil; (= advice) conseil m en gestion d'entreprise ► **management consultant** N conseiller m en gestion (d'entreprise) ► **management information system** N système m intégré de gestion ► **management selection procedures** NPL (procédure f de) sélection f des cadres ► **management studies** NPL (Educ) (études fpl de) gestion f ► **management style** N mode m de gestion ► **management trainee** N cadre m stagiaire

manager ['mænɪdʒər] N [of company, business] directeur m, administrateur m; [of theatre, cinema] directeur m; [of restaurant, hotel, shop] gérant m; [of farm] exploitant m; [of actor, singer, boxer etc] manager m; [of sports team] manager m; (Fin) chef m de file; (Brit) **school ~** ≈ membre m du conseil d'établissement; **general ~** directeur m général; **to be a good ~** être bon gestionnaire → **business, sale**

manageress [ˌmænɪdʒə'res] N [of hotel, café, shop] gérante f; [of theatre, cinema] directrice f

managerial [ˌmænə'dʒɪərɪəl] ADJ [responsibilities, staff] d'encadrement; [job, position] d'encadrement, de cadre; (Ftbl) [career] de directeur sportif; **the ~ class** les cadres mpl (supérieurs); **proven ~ skills** des compétences fpl confirmées en matière de gestion; **his ~ style** son style de gestion; **a ~ decision** une décision de la direction

managership ['mænɪdʒəʃɪp] N directorat m

managing ['mænɪdʒɪŋ] [1] ADJ (Brit = bossy) autoritaire [2] COMP ► **managing bank** N banque f chef de file ► **managing director** N (Brit) directeur m général, PDG m ► **managing editor** N directeur m de la rédaction

manatee [ˌmænə'tiː] N lamantin m

Manchu [mæn'tʃuː] [1] N [a] (= person) Mandchou(e) m(f) [b] (Ling) mandchou m [2] ADJ mandchou

Manchuria [mæn'tʃʊərɪə] N la Mandchourie

Manchurian [mæn'tʃʊərɪən] [1] ADJ mandchou [2] N Mandchou(e) m(f)

Mancunian [mæn'kjuːnɪən] [1] N **he's a ~** il est de Manchester [2] ADJ de Manchester

mandala ['mændələ] N mandala m

► LANGUAGE IN USE: **manage** 15.4, 16.4

Mandarin ['mændərɪn] N (also ~ **Chinese**) Mandarin m

mandarin ['mændərɪn] N [a] (= person: lit, fig) mandarin m [b] (also ~ **orange**) mandarine f [c] (also ~ **duck**) canard m mandarin

mandate ['mændeɪt] [1] N [a] (= authority) mandat m; **they have no ~ to govern** ils n'ont pas le mandat du peuple; **with such a small majority, how can the government claim to have a ~?** avec une majorité si infime, le gouvernement ne peut pas prétendre avoir reçu le mandat du peuple; **the union has a ~ to ...** le syndicat est mandaté pour ...; **the ICRC's ~ is to provide impartial assistance to victims of conflict** le CICR a pour mandat de fournir une assistance impartiale aux victimes de conflits [b] (= country) pays m sous mandat; **under French ~** sous mandat français
[2] VT [a] (= give authority to) donner mandat (**sb to do sth** à qn de faire qch) [b] (US) (= make obligatory) rendre obligatoire; (= entail) [act, decision] entraîner, comporter [c] (= place under mandate) [+ territory] mettre sous le mandat (**to** de)

mandatory ['mændətərɪ] ADJ [a] (= obligatory) obligatoire (**for sb/sth** pour qn/qch); **to be ~ (for sb) to do sth** être obligatoire (pour qn) de faire qch; **the ~ retirement age** l'âge m de la retraite obligatoire [b] (Jur = not discretionary) [life sentence, death penalty, ban, fine] automatique [c] (Pol) [state, functions] mandataire; **to be a ~ power** être une puissance mandataire; **to have ~ powers** avoir des pouvoirs conférés par mandat

mandible ['mændɪbl] N [of bird, insect] mandibule f; [of mammal, fish] mâchoire f (inférieure)

mandolin(e) ['mændəlɪn] N mandoline f

mandrake ['mændreɪk], **mandragora** [mæn'drægərə] N mandragore f

mandrill ['mændrɪl] N mandrill m

mane [meɪn] N (lit, fig) crinière f

maneuver etc [mə'nu:vər] (US) = **manoeuvre** etc

manful ['mænfʊl] ADJ [attempt] vaillant

manfully ['mænfəlɪ] ADV [struggle, battle, cope] vaillamment

manga ['mæŋgə] N (pl **manga**) manga m

manganese [,mæŋgə'ni:z] [1] N manganèse m [2] COMP ▶ **manganese bronze** N bronze m au manganèse ▶ **manganese oxide** N oxyde m de manganèse ▶ **manganese steel** N acier m au manganèse

mange [meɪndʒ] N gale f

mangel(-wurzel) ['mæŋgl(,wɜ:zl)] N betterave f fourragère

manger ['meɪndʒər] N (Agr) mangeoire f; (Rel) crèche f → **dog**

mangetout ['mɒnʒ'tu:] N (pl inv: also ~ **pea**) mange-tout m inv

mangle¹ ['mæŋgl] [1] N (for wringing) essoreuse f à rouleaux; (for smoothing) calandre f [2] VT essorer, calandrer

mangle² ['mæŋgl] VT (also ~ **up**) [+ object, body] déchirer, mutiler; (fig) [+ text] mutiler; [+ quotation] estropier; [+ message] estropier, mutiler

mango ['mæŋgəʊ] [1] N (pl **mango(e)s**) (= fruit) mangue f; (= tree) manguier m [2] COMP ▶ **mango chutney** N condiment m à la mangue

mangold(-wurzel) ['mæŋgəld(,wɜ:zl)] N = **mangel(-wurzel)**

mangosteen ['mæŋgə,sti:n] N mangoustan m

mangrove ['mæŋgrəʊv] [1] N palétuvier m, manglier m [2] COMP ▶ **mangrove swamp** N mangrove f

mangy ['meɪndʒɪ] ADJ [a] (= diseased) [animal] galeux [b]* (= shabby) [coat, wig, rug, blanket] miteux; **what a ~ trick!** quel tour de cochon!*

manhandle ['mæn,hændl] VT (= treat roughly)

malmener; (esp Brit = move by hand) [+ goods etc] manutentionner

Manhattan [mæn'hætən] N [a] (Geog) Manhattan [b] (= drink) manhattan m (cocktail de whisky et de vermouth doux)

manhole ['mænhəʊl] [1] N bouche f d'égout [2] COMP ▶ **manhole cover** N plaque f d'égout

manhood ['mænhʊd] N [a] (= age, state) âge m d'homme, âge m viril; **to reach ~** atteindre l'âge d'homme; **during his early ~** quand il était jeune homme [b] (= manliness) virilité f; **a threat to his ~** une menace pour sa virilité [c] (= men collectively) hommes mpl [d] (euph or hum = penis) membre m viril

manhunt ['mænhʌnt] N chasse f à l'homme

mania ['meɪnɪə] N (Psych, fig) manie f; **persecution ~** manie f or folie f de la persécution; **to have a ~ for (doing) sth*** avoir la manie de (faire) qch

...mania ['meɪnɪə] SUF ...manie f

maniac ['meɪnɪæk] [1] N (Psych) maniaque mf; * fou m, folle f; (Jur) dément(e) m(f); **a self-confessed golf ~*** un mordu* du golf, de son propre aveu; **he drives like a ~*** il conduit comme un fou; **he's a ~!*** il est fou à lier!, il est bon à enfermer! [2] ADJ (Psych) maniaque; * fou (folle f); (Jur) dément

maniacal [mə'naɪəkəl] ADJ [person] maniaque; [laughter] hystérique; [expression, eyes] de fou (folle f)

maniacally [mə'naɪəkəlɪ] ADV [grin] comme un(e) dément(e); **he laughed ~** il a ri d'un rire hystérique

manic ['mænɪk] [1] ADJ (Psych) [person] maniaque; (fig) [person] survolté*; [activity, energy] frénétique; [grin, smile] de dément(e); [laughter] hystérique [2] COMP ▶ **manic depression** N psychose f maniacodépressive, cyclothymie f ▶ **manic-depressive** ADJ, N maniacodépressif m, -ive f, cyclothymique mf

Manich(a)ean [,mænɪ'ki:ən] ADJ, N manichéen(ne) m(f); **the ~ heresy** l'hérésie f manichéenne

Manich(a)eism ['mænɪki:,ɪzəm] N (Hist, fig) manichéisme m

manicure ['mænɪ,kjʊər] [1] N (= act) soin m des mains, manucure f; **to have a ~** se faire faire les mains, se faire manucurer; **to give sb a ~** faire les mains à qn, manucurer qn [2] VT [+ person] faire les mains à, manucurer; [+ sb's nails] faire; **to ~ one's nails** se faire les ongles [3] COMP ▶ **manicure case** N trousse f à ongles or de manucure ▶ **manicure scissors** NPL ciseaux mpl de manucure or à ongles ▶ **manicure set** N = **manicure case**

manicured ['mænɪkjʊəd] ADJ [nails, hands] manucuré; [person] aux mains manucurées; (fig) [lawn, garden] impeccable

manicurist ['mænɪ,kjʊərɪst] N manucure mf

manifest ['mænɪfest] [1] ADJ manifeste [2] VT manifester [3] N (Aviat, Naut) manifeste m [4] COMP ▶ **Manifest Destiny** N (US Hist) destinée f manifeste

┌─────────────────────────┐
│ **MANIFEST DESTINY** │
└─────────────────────────┘
Au 19ᵉ siècle, les Américains estimaient que les États-Unis avaient pour « destinée manifeste », voulue par Dieu, d'étendre leur territoire et leur influence à travers le continent nord-américain. Ce principe a servi à justifier l'avance des colons vers le Mexique ainsi que la guerre hispano-américaine de 1898, à l'issue de laquelle les États-Unis ont annexé Porto Rico et les Philippines. Rarement évoqué aujourd'hui, ce sentiment demeure sous-jacent chez beaucoup d'Américains qui trouvent naturelle la suprématie de leur pays en Amérique et sur le pourtour de l'Océan pacifique.

manifestation [,mænɪfes'teɪʃən] N manifestation f

manifestly ['mænɪfestlɪ] ADV (frm) manifestement

manifesto [,mænɪ'festəʊ] N (pl manifesto(e)s) (Pol etc) manifeste m

manifold ['mænɪfəʊld] [1] ADJ (frm) [difficulties, benefits] multiple; [effects] divers; [shortcomings, duties] nombreux; [collection] divers, varié; **in ~ forms** sous diverses formes; **~ wisdom** sagesse f infinie [2] N (Aut etc) **inlet/exhaust ~** collecteur m or tubulure f d'admission/d'échappement

manikin ['mænɪkɪn] N = **mannikin**

Manila [mə'nɪlə] N Manille, Manila

mani(l)la envelope [mə,nɪlə'enveləʊp] N enveloppe f en papier kraft

mani(l)la paper [mə,nɪlə'peɪpə] N papier m kraft

manioc ['mænɪɒk] N manioc m

manipulate [mə'nɪpjʊleɪt] VT [a] [+ tool etc] manipuler; **they use computers to ~ images** ils utilisent l'ordinateur pour manipuler des images [b] (pej) [+ facts, figures, accounts] tripoter, trafiquer*; [+ events] agir sur; [+ person] manipuler, manœuvrer; **to ~ a situation** faire son jeu des circonstances; **to ~ sb into doing sth** manipuler qn pour lui faire faire qch

manipulation [mə,nɪpjʊ'leɪʃən] N (gen, Med) manipulation f; (Fin) **market ~** manœuvre(s) f(pl) boursière(s)

manipulative [mə'nɪpjʊlətɪv] ADJ [a] (pej = controlling) [person, behaviour, film, speech] manipulateur (-trice f) [b] (Physiotherapy) **~ therapy** or **treatment** (traitement m par) manipulations fpl; **~ therapist** thérapeute mf qui soigne par manipulations

manipulator [mə'nɪpjʊleɪtə] N manipulateur m, -trice f

Manitoba [,mænɪ'təʊbə] N le Manitoba

mankind [mæn'kaɪnd] N (NonC) (= the human race) le genre humain, l'humanité f; (= the male sex) les hommes mpl

manky* ['mæŋkɪ] (Brit) ADJ cradingue*

manlike ['mænlaɪk] ADJ [form, figure, qualities] humain; (pej) [woman] hommasse (pej)

manliness ['mænlɪnɪs] N virilité f, caractère m viril

manly ['mænlɪ] ADJ [man, boy, chest, shoulders, sport] viril (virile f); [pride, virtue] mâle

manna ['mænə] N **~ from heaven** manne f tombée du ciel or providentielle

manned [mænd] ADJ [spacecraft, flight] habité; [mission] habité, humain → **man**

mannequin ['mænɪkɪn] N mannequin m

manner ['mænə] [1] N [a] (= mode, way) manière f, façon f; **the ~ in which he did it** la manière or façon dont il l'a fait; (frm) **in such a ~ that ...** de telle sorte que ... (+ indic (actual result) or + subj (intended result)); **in this ~** ◊ **after this ~** (frm) de cette manière or façon; **in or after the ~ of Van Gogh** à la manière de Van Gogh; **in the same ~** ◊ **in like ~** (frm) de la même manière; **in a (certain) ~** en quelque sorte; **in such a ~ as to ...** de façon à ...; **in a ~ of speaking** pour ainsi dire; **it's a ~ of speaking** c'est une façon de parler; **~ of payment** mode m de paiement; **(as) to the ~ born** comme s'il (or elle etc) avait cela dans le sang [b] (= behaviour, attitude) attitude f, comportement m; **his ~ to his mother** son attitude envers sa mère, sa manière de se conduire avec sa mère; **I don't like his ~** je n'aime pas son attitude; **there's something odd about his ~** il y a quelque chose de bizarre dans son comportement [c] (= class, sort, type) sorte f, genre m; **all ~ of birds** toutes sortes d'oiseaux; **no ~ of doubt** aucun doute → **means**
[2] **manners** NPL [a] (= social behaviour) manières fpl; **good ~s** bonnes manières fpl, savoir-vivre m; **bad ~s** mauvaises manières

fpl ; **it's good/bad ~s (to do that)** ça se fait/ne se fait pas (de faire ça) ; **he has no ~s** ◊ **his ~s are terrible** il a de très mauvaises manières, il n'a aucun savoir-vivre ; *(to child)* **aren't you forgetting your ~s?** est-ce que c'est comme ça qu'on se tient ? ; **road ~s** politesse *f* au volant **b** (= *social customs*) mœurs *fpl*, usages *mpl* ; **novel of ~s** roman *m* de mœurs → **comedy**

mannered ['mænəd] ADJ **a** *(pej* = *affected)* [*voice, gesture, writing, painting*] maniéré ; [*style*] maniéré, précieux **b** (= *polite)* [*person*] bien élevé ; [*society*] civilisé ; **beautifully** *or* **impeccably ~** qui a des manières exquises

-mannered ['mænəd] ADJ *(in compounds)* **rough-mannered** aux manières rudes → **bad**, **mild-mannered**, **well**

mannerism ['mænərɪzəm] N **a** (= *habit, trick of speech etc)* trait *m* particulier ; *(pej)* tic *m*, manie *f* **b** *(NonC: Art, Literat etc)* maniérisme *m*

mannerist ['mænərɪst] ADJ, N maniériste *mf*

mannerliness ['mænəlɪnɪs] N (= *civility)* savoir-vivre *m*

mannerly ['mænəlɪ] ADJ bien élevé

mannikin ['mænɪkɪn] N **a** *(Art, Dressmaking)* mannequin *m (objet)* **b** (= *dwarf etc)* homoncule *m*, nabot *m*

manning ['mænɪŋ] N *(Mil)* armement *m* ; *(Ind)* effectifs *mpl* ; **~ levels** niveau *m* des effectifs

mannish ['mænɪʃ] ADJ [*woman*] masculin, hommasse *(pej)* ; [*behaviour, clothes*] masculin ; **in a ~ way** comme un homme, d'une façon masculine

mannishly ['mænɪʃlɪ] ADV [*dress*] comme un homme

manoeuvrability, **maneuverability** *(US)* [mə,nu:vrə'bɪlɪtɪ] N manœuvrabilité *f*, maniabilité *f*

manoeuvrable, **maneuverable** *(US)* [mə'nu:vrəbl] ADJ [*car, ship*] maniable, manœuvrable

manoeuvre, **maneuver** *(US)* [mə'nu:və'] **1** N *(all senses)* manœuvre *f* ; *(Mil etc)* **to be on ~s** faire des *or* être en manœuvres ; *(fig)* **it doesn't leave much room for ~** cela ne laisse pas une grande marge de manœuvre **2** VT *(all senses)* manœuvrer ; **to ~ sth out/in/through** *etc* faire sortir/entrer/traverser *etc* qch en manœuvrant ; **they ~d the gun into position** ils ont manœuvré le canon pour le mettre en position ; **he ~d the car through the gate** il a pu à force de manœuvres faire passer la voiture par le portail ; **to ~ sb into doing sth** manœuvrer qn pour qu'il fasse qch ; **the government tried to ~ itself into a stronger position** le gouvernement a essayé de manœuvrer pour renforcer ses positions **3** VI *(all senses)* manœuvrer

manoeuvring [mə'nu:vərɪŋ] N *(NonC: pej* = *scheming)* magouille* *f*

manometer [mæ'nɒmɪtə'] N manomètre *m*

manor ['mænə'] N **a** *(also ~ house)* manoir *m*, gentilhommière *f* **b** *(Hist* = *estate)* domaine *m* seigneurial → **lord** **c** *(Brit Police etc:*)* fief *m*

manorial [mə'nɔ:rɪəl] ADJ seigneurial

manpower ['mæn,pauə'] **1** N *(NonC)* **a** (= *workers available)* (*gen, Ind*) main-d'œuvre *f* ; *(Mil etc)* effectifs *mpl* ; **the shortage of skilled ~** la pénurie de main-d'œuvre qualifiée **b** (= *physical exertion)* force *f* physique **2** COMP **► Manpower Services Commission** N *(Brit: formerly)* ≈ Agence *f* nationale pour l'emploi

mansard ['mænsɑ:d] N *(also ~ roof)* mansarde *f*, comble *m* brisé

manse [mæns] N presbytère *m* *(d'un pasteur presbytérien)*

manservant ['mænsɜ:vənt] N *(pl* **menservants** *or* **manservants**) valet *m* de chambre

mansion ['mænʃən] N **1** *(in town)* hôtel *m* particulier ; *(in country)* château *m*, manoir *m*

2 COMP **► the Mansion House** N résidence officielle du Lord Mayor de Londres

manslaughter ['mænslɔ:tə'] N *(Jur)* homicide *m (involontaire* or *par imprudence)*

**mansuetude†† ** ['mænswɪtju:d] N mansuétude *f*, douceur *f*

mantel ['mæntl] N **a** *(also ~piece, ~shelf)* (*dessus m* or *tablette f de*) cheminée *f* **b** (= *structure round fireplace)* manteau *m*, chambranle *m (de cheminée)*

mantes ['mænti:z] NPL *of* **mantis**

mantilla [mæn'tɪlə] N mantille *f*

mantis ['mæntɪs] N *(pl* **mantises** *or* **mantes** mante *f* → **praying**

mantle ['mæntl] **1** N **a† ** (= *cloak)* cape *f* ; *[of lady]* mante†† *f* ; *(liter)* **~ of snow** manteau *m* de neige *[of gas lamp]* manchon *m* → **gas** **c** *(Geol: of earth)* manteau *m* **2** VT *(liter)* (re)couvrir

mantra ['mæntrə] N **a** *(lit)* mantra *m* **b** *(fig)* litanie *f*

mantrap ['mæntræp] N piège *m* à hommes

manual ['mænjuəl] **1** ADJ [*work, worker, lens, method, dexterity, gearbox*] manuel ; [*transmission, typewriter*] mécanique ; [*pump*] à main ; **~ labour** main-d'œuvre *f* ; **~ controls** commandes *fpl* manuelles **2** N **a** (= *book)* manuel *m* **b** *[of organ]* clavier *m*

manually ['mænjuəlɪ] ADV à la main, manuellement ; **~ operated** à main, manuel

manufacture [,mænju'fæktʃə'] **1** N *(NonC)* fabrication *f* ; *[of clothes]* confection *f* **2** **manufactures** NPL produits *mpl* manufacturés **3** VT *(Ind)* fabriquer ; [+ *clothes*] confectionner ; *(fig)* [+ *story, excuse*] fabriquer ; **~d goods** produits *mpl* manufacturés

manufacturer [,mænju'fæktʃərə'] **1** N fabricant *m* **2** COMP **► manufacturers' recommended price** N prix *m* public

manufacturing [,mænju'fæktʃərɪŋ] **1** N fabrication *f* **2** COMP [*town, city, job, output, sector*] industriel ; [*industry*] de transformation **► manufacturing base** N base *f* industrielle **► manufacturing company** N manufacture *f* **► manufacturing plant** N usine *f*

manure [mə'njuə'] **1** N *(NonC)* *(also farmyard ~)* fumier *m* ; *(also artificial ~)* engrais *m* ; **liquid ~** *(organic)* purin *m*, lisier *m* ; *(artificial)* engrais *m* liquide **2** VT *(with farmyard manure)* fumer ; *(with artificial manure)* répandre des engrais sur **3** COMP **► manure heap** N *(tas de)* fumier *m*

manuscript ['mænjuskrɪpt] **1** N manuscrit *m* ; **in ~** (= *not yet printed)* sous forme de manuscrit ; (= *handwritten)* écrit à la main **2** ADJ manuscrit, écrit à la main

Manx [mæŋks] **1** ADJ de l'île de Man, mannois **2** N *(Ling)* mannois *m* **3** **the Manx** NPL les Mannois *mpl* **4** COMP **► Manx cat** N chat *m* de l'île de Man

Manxman ['mæŋksmən] N *(pl* **-men**) Mannois *m*

Manxwoman ['mæŋkswumən] N *(pl* **-women**) Mannoise *f*

many ['menɪ] **1** ADJ, PRON *(compar* **more**, *superl* **most**) **a** *(gen)* beaucoup (de), un grand nombre (de) ; **~ books** beaucoup de livres, un grand nombre de livres ; **very ~ books** un très grand nombre de livres, de très nombreux livres ; **~ of those books** un grand nombre de ces livres ; **~ of them** un grand nombre d'entre eux, beaucoup d'entre eux ; **a good ~ of those books** (un) bon nombre de ces livres ; **~ people** beaucoup de gens *or* de monde, bien des gens ; **~ came** beaucoup sont venus ; **~ believe that to be true** bien des gens croient que c'est vrai ; *(liter)* **the ~** (= *the masses)* la multitude, la foule ; **the ~ who admire him** le grand nombre de gens qui l'admirent ; **~ times** bien des fois ; **~ a time** ◊ **~'s the time* ** maintes fois, souvent ; **I've lived here for ~ years** j'habite ici

depuis des années ; **he lived there for ~ years** il vécut là de nombreuses années *or* de longues années ; **people of ~ kinds** des gens de toutes sortes ; **a good *or* great ~ things** beaucoup de choses ; **in ~ cases** dans bien des cas, dans de nombreux cas ; **~ a man would be grateful** il y en a plus d'un qui serait reconnaissant ; **a woman of ~ moods** une femme d'humeur changeante ; **a man of ~ parts** un homme qui a des talents très divers ; **~ happy returns (of the day)!** bon *or* joyeux anniversaire !

b *(in set structures)* **I have as ~ problems as you** j'ai autant de problèmes que vous ; **I have as ~ as you** j'en ai autant que vous ; **as ~ as wish to come** tous ceux qui désirent venir ; **as ~ as 100 people are expected** on attend jusqu'à 100 personnes ; **how ~?** combien ? ; **how ~ people?** combien de gens ? ; **how ~ there are!** qu'ils sont nombreux ! ; **however ~ books you have** quel que soit le nombre de livres que vous ayez ; **however ~ there may be** quel que soit leur nombre ; **so ~ have said it** il y en a tant qu'ils l'ont dit ; **I've got so ~ already (that ...)** j'en ai déjà tant (que ...) ; **there were so ~ (that ...)** il y en avait tant (que ...) ; **so ~ dresses** tant de robes ; **ever so ~ times* ** je ne sais combien de fois, tant de fois ; **they ran away like so ~ sheep** ils se sont sauvés comme un troupeau de moutons ; **he did not say that in so ~ words** il n'a pas dit cela explicitement ; **there were too ~** il y en avait trop ; **too ~ cakes** trop de gâteaux ; **three too ~** trois de trop ; **20 would not be too ~** il n'y en aurait pas trop de 20 ; *(fig)* **he's had one too ~* ** il a bu un coup de trop ; **I've got too ~ already** j'en ai déjà trop ; **there are too ~ of you** vous êtes trop nombreux ; **too ~ of these books** trop de ces livres ; **too ~ of us know that ...** nous sommes trop (nombreux) à savoir que ...

2 COMP **► many-coloured**, **many-hued** ADJ *(liter)* multicolore **► many-sided** ADJ [*object*] qui a de nombreux côtés ; *(fig)* [*person*] aux intérêts *(or* talents) variés *or* multiples ; [*problem*] complexe, qui a de nombreuses facettes

Maoism ['mauɪzəm] N maoïsme *m*

Maoist ['mauɪst] ADJ, N maoïste *mf*

Maori ['maurɪ] **1** ADJ maori **2** N **a** (= *person)* Maori(e) *m(f)* **b** *(Ling)* maori *m*

Mao (Tse Tung) ['mau(tseɪ'tuŋ)] N Mao (Tsé-Tung) *m*

map [mæp] **1** N *(gen)* carte *f* ; *[of town, bus, tube, subway]* plan *m* ; **geological/historical/linguistic ~** carte *f* géologique/historique/linguistique ; **~ of Paris/the Underground** plan *m* de Paris/du métro ; **~ of France** carte *f* de la France ; *(fig)* **this will put Bishopbriggs on the ~** cela fera connaître Bishopbriggs ; **the whole town was wiped off the ~** la ville entière a été rayée de la carte ; *(fig)* **off the ~* ** (= *unimportant)* perdu ; (= *distant)* à l'autre bout du monde **2** VT [+ *country, district etc*] faire *or* dresser la carte *(or* le plan) de ; [+ *route*] tracer **3** COMP **► map-reading** N lecture *f* des cartes

► map out VT SEP [+ *route, plans*] tracer ; [+ *book, essay*] établir les grandes lignes de ; [+ *one's time, career, day*] organiser ; [+ *strategy, plan*] élaborer ; **he hasn't yet ~ped out what he will do** il n'a pas encore de plan précis de ce qu'il va faire

maple ['meɪpl] **1** N érable *m* **2** COMP **► maple leaf** N *(pl* **maple leaves**) feuille *f* d'érable **► maple sugar** N sucre *m* d'érable **► maple syrup** N sirop *m* d'érable

mapmaker ['mæpmeɪkə'] N cartographe *mf*

mapmaking ['mæpmeɪkɪŋ] N cartographie *f*

mapping ['mæpɪŋ] **1** N *(Math)* application *f* ;

(*Comput*) mappage *m* [2] COMP ► **mapping pen** N plume *f* de dessinateur *or* à dessin

mar [mɑːʳ] VT gâter, gâcher ; **to make or ~ sth** assurer le succès ou l'échec de qch

Mar. ABBR = **March**

maracas [məˈrækəz] NPL maracas *mpl*

maraschino [ˌmærəsˈkiːnəʊ] [1] N marasquin *m* [2] COMP ► **maraschino cherry** N cerise *f* au marasquin

Marathon [ˈmærəθən] N (*Geog, Hist*) Marathon

marathon [ˈmærəθən] [1] N (*Sport, fig*) marathon *m* [2] ADJ [a] (*Sport*) [*runner*] de marathon [b] (*fig = very long*) marathon *inv* ; **a ~ session** une séance-marathon

maraud [məˈrɔːd] VI marauder, être en maraude ; **to go ~ing** aller à la maraude

marauder [məˈrɔːdəʳ] N maraudeur *m*, -euse *f*

marauding [məˈrɔːdɪŋ] [1] ADJ en maraude [2] N maraude *f*

marble [ˈmɑːbl] [1] N [a] (= *stone, sculpture*) marbre *m* [b] (= *toy*) bille *f* ; **to play ~s** jouer aux billes ; (*fig*) **to lose one's ~s*** perdre la boule* ; (*US*) **to pick up one's ~s and go home*** reprendre ses billes [2] VT marbrer [3] COMP [*staircase, statue*] de or en marbre ; [*industry*] marbrier ► **marble cake** N gâteau *m* marbré ► **marble quarry** N marbrière *f*

March [mɑːtʃ] N mars *m* → **mad** ; *for phrases see* **September**

march [mɑːtʃ] [1] N [a] (*Mil etc*) marche *f* ; **on the ~** en marche ; **quick/slow ~** marche *f* rapide/lente ; **a day's ~** une journée de marche ; **a 10km ~** or ◊ **a ~ of 10km** une marche de 10 km ; **the ~ on Rome** la marche sur Rome ; (*fig*) **the ~ of time/progress** la marche du temps/progrès → **forced, route, steal** [b] (= *demonstration*) manifestation *f* (**against** contre, **for** pour) [c] (*Mus*) marche *f* → **dead** [2] VI [a] (*Mil etc*) marcher au pas ; **the army ~ed in/out** l'armée entra/sortit (au pas) ; **to ~ into battle** marcher au combat ; **to ~ past** défiler ; **to ~ past sb** défiler devant qn ; **~!** marche ! → **forward, quick** [b] (*walk in/out/up etc* (*briskly*) entrer/sortir/monter *etc* d'un pas énergique ; (*angrily*) entrer/sortir/monter *etc* d'un air furieux ; **he ~ed up to me** il s'est approché de moi d'un air décidé ; **to ~ up and down the room** faire les cent pas dans la pièce, arpenter la pièce [c] (= *demonstrate*) manifester (**against** contre, **for** pour) [3] VT [a] (*Mil*) faire marcher (au pas) ; **to ~ troops in/out** *etc* faire entrer/faire sortir *etc* des troupes (au pas) [b] (*fig*) **to ~ sb in/out/away** faire entrer/faire sortir/emmener qn tambour battant ; **to ~ sb off to prison*** embarquer qn en prison* [4] COMP ► **march-past** N (*Mil etc*) défilé *m*

marcher [ˈmɑːtʃəʳ] N (*in demo etc*) manifestant(e) *m(f)*

marches [ˈmɑːtʃɪz] NPL (= *border*) frontière *f* ; (= *borderlands*) marches *fpl*

marching [ˈmɑːtʃɪŋ] [1] N marche *f* [2] COMP ► **marching band** N (*US*) orchestre *m* d'école (avec majorettes) ► **marching orders** NPL (*Mil*) feuille *f* de route ; (*fig*) **to give sb his ~ orders*** flanquer* qn à la porte, envoyer promener* qn ; (*fig*) **to get one's ~ orders*** se faire mettre à la porte ► **marching song** N chanson *f* de route

marchioness [ˈmɑːʃənɪs] N marquise *f* (*personne*)

Marco Polo [ˈmɑːkəʊˈpəʊləʊ] N Marco Polo

Marcus Aurelius [ˈmɑːkəsɔːˈriːliəs] N Marc Aurèle *m*

Mardi Gras [ˈmɑːdɪˈgrɑː] N mardi gras *m inv*, carnaval *m*

mare [mɛəʳ] N jument *f* ; (*fig*) **his discovery**

turned out to be a **~'s nest** sa découverte s'est révélée très décevante

marg* [mɑːdʒ] N (*Brit*) ABBR = **margarine**

Margaret [ˈmɑːgərɪt] N Marguerite *f*

margarine [ˌmɑːdʒəˈriːn] N margarine *f*

margarita [ˌmɑːgəˈriːtə] N margarita *f*

marge* [mɑːdʒ] N (*Brit*) ABBR = **margarine**

margin [ˈmɑːdʒɪn] N [*of book, page*] marge *f* ; [*of river, lake*] bord *m* ; [*of wood*] lisière *f* ; (*fig : Comm, Econ, gen*) marge *f* ; **notes in the ~** notes en marge or marginales ; **do not write in the ~** n'écrivez rien dans la marge ; (*Typ*) **wide/narrow ~** grande/petite marge *f* ; (*fig*) **to win by a wide/narrow ~** gagner de loin/de peu ; **elected by a narrow ~** élu de justesse *or* avec peu de voix de majorité ; **on the ~(s) of society** en marge de la société ; **to allow a ~ for ...** laisser une marge pour ... ; **to allow for a ~ of error** prévoir une marge d'erreur ; **profit ~** ◊ **~ of profit** marge *f* (bénéficiaire) ; **~ of safety** marge *f* de sécurité

marginal [ˈmɑːdʒɪnl] [1] ADJ [a] (= *unimportant*) [*importance, significance, role, writer, business*] marginal (**to sth** par rapport à qch) ; [*existence*] de marginal(e) ; [*issue*] insignifiant ; [*benefit*] minime ; [*improvement*] négligeable ; **a ~ case** un cas limite ; **the effect will be ~** l'effet sera négligeable [b] (*Brit Parl*) [*seat, constituency*] très disputé [c] (*Sociol*) [*people, groups*] marginal [d] (*Agr*) [*land*] à faible rendement [e] (= *written in margin*) [*comments, notes*] en marge, marginal [2] N (*Brit Parl*) siège *m* à faible majorité

MARGINAL SEAT

En Grande-Bretagne, siège de député obtenu à une faible majorité et qui ne peut donc être considéré comme solidement acquis à un parti, contrairement au « safe seat » (siège sûr). Les circonscriptions à faible majorité appelées « marginal constituencies », intéressent particulièrement les médias en cas d'élection partielle, car elles constituent un bon baromètre de la popularité du parti au pouvoir.

---

marginalize [ˈmɑːdʒɪnəlaɪz] VT marginaliser

marginally [ˈmɑːdʒɪnəlɪ] ADV légèrement

marguerita [ˌmɑːgəˈriːtə] N = **margarita**

marguerite [ˌmɑːgəˈriːt] N marguerite *f*

Maria [məˈraɪə] N Marie *f* → **black**

marigold [ˈmærɪgəʊld] N (*Bot*) souci *m*

marijuana, marihuana [ˌmærɪˈhwɑːnə] N marihuana *f or* marijuana *f*

marimba [məˈrɪmbə] N marimba *m*

marina [məˈriːnə] N marina *f*

marinade [ˌmærɪˈneɪd] [1] N marinade *f* [2] VT mariner

marinate [ˈmærɪneɪt] VT mariner

marine [məˈriːn] [1] ADJ (= *in the sea*) [*plant, animal*] marin ; (= *from the sea*) [*products*] de la mer ; (= *by the sea*) [*vegetation, forces*] maritime [2] N [a] (*Naut*) **mercantile** *or* **merchant ~ marine** *f* marchande [b] (*Mil*) fusilier *m* marin ; (*US*) marines *mpl* (américains) ; **the Marines** (*Brit*) ◊ **the Marine Corps** (*US*) les fusiliers *mpl* marins, les marines *mpl* ; **tell that to the ~s!*** à d'autres !* [3] COMP ► **marine biologist** N océanographe *mf* biologiste ► **marine biology** N océanographie *f* biologique ► **marine engineer** N ingénieur *m* du génie maritime ► **marine engineering** N génie *m* maritime ► **marine insurance** N assurance *f* maritime ► **marine life** N vie *f* marine ► **marine science** N sciences *fpl* marines *or* de la mer ► **marine underwriter** N assureur *m* maritime

mariner [ˈmærɪnəʳ] [1] N (*liter*) marin *m* [2] COMP ► **mariner's compass** N boussole *f*, compas *m* → **master**

Mariolatry [ˌmɛərɪˈɒlətrɪ] N (*Rel : pej*) vénération *f* excessive de la Vierge

Mariology [ˌmɛərɪˈɒlədʒɪ] N mariologie *f*

marionette [ˌmærɪəˈnet] N marionnette *f*

marital [ˈmærɪtl] [1] ADJ [a] (= *relating to marriage*) conjugal ; **~ breakdown** rupture *f* des rapports conjugaux ; **to commit ~ rape** violer son épouse [b] (= *relating to husband*) marital [2] COMP ► **marital relations** NPL rapports *mpl* conjugaux ► **marital status** N (*frm*) situation *f* de famille, état *m* civil

maritime [ˈmærɪtaɪm] [1] ADJ maritime [2] COMP ► **maritime law** N droit *m* maritime ► **the Maritime Provinces** NPL (*Can*) les provinces *fpl* maritimes

marjoram [ˈmɑːdʒərəm] N marjolaine *f*

Mark [mɑːk] N Marc *m* ; **~ Antony** Marc-Antoine *m*

mark[1] [mɑːk] N (= *currency*) mark *m*

mark[2] [mɑːk] [1] N [a] (= *physical marking*) marque *f* ; (= *stain*) marque *f*, tache *f* ; (= *written symbol on paper, cloth etc*) signe *m* ; (*as signature*) marque *f*, croix *f* ; (= *footprint, animal track, tyre track etc*) empreinte *f* ; (= *marking*) (*on animal, bird*) tache *f* ; **that will leave a ~** (*gen*) cela laissera une marque ; (= *stain*) cela laissera une tache ; (*as signature*) **to make one's ~** faire une marque *or* une croix → **d** ; **he was found without a ~ on his body** quand on l'a trouvé, son corps ne portait aucune trace de blessure ; **the ~s of violence were visible everywhere** on voyait partout des marques *or* traces de violence ; **the city still bears the ~s of occupation** la ville porte encore les marques *or* traces de son occupation → **c** ; → **finger, punctuation** [b] (*fig = sign*) signe *m* ; **a ~ of strength/success** un signe de force/de réussite (sociale) ; **the tendency to drink in secret is a ~ of addiction** la propension à boire en cachette est un signe d'alcoolisme ; **a ~ of shame** un objet de honte ; **as a ~ of protest/defiance** en signe de protestation/défi ; **as a ~ of respect** en signe de respect ; **as a ~ of my gratitude** en témoignage de ma gratitude ; **as a ~ of his confidence in/disapproval of ...** pour marquer sa confiance en/sa désapprobation de ... [c] (*fig = hallmark*) marque *f* ; **it bears the ~(s) of genius** cela porte la marque du génie ; **the attack bore the ~s of a terrorist organization** cet attentat portait la marque d'une organisation terroriste ; **it is the ~ of a good teacher** c'est le signe d'un bon professeur ; **the ~ of a true teacher/architect is the ability to ...** on reconnaît le véritable professeur/architecte à sa capacité à ... ; **to react the way he did was the ~ of a true hero** il s'est montré *or* révélé un véritable héros en réagissant comme il l'a fait [d] (*fig = lasting impression*) **to leave one's ~ on sth** laisser son empreinte sur qch ; **he has certainly made his ~** il s'est certainement imposé ; **he has certainly made a** *or* **his ~ in British politics** il a certainement marqué la politique britannique de son empreinte ; **to make one's ~ as a politician** s'imposer comme homme politique ; **to make one's ~ as a poet/writer** se faire un nom en tant que poète/qu'écrivain [e] (*Scol*) (= *grade : in exam, essay, overall assessment*) note *f* ; (= *point*) point *m* ; **good/bad ~** bonne/mauvaise note *f* ; **she got a good ~** or **good ~s in French** elle a eu une bonne note en français ; (*Brit*) **~s for effort/conduct** *etc* note *f* d'application/de conduite *etc* ; **the ~ is out of 20** c'est une note sur 20 ; **you need 50 ~s to pass** il faut avoir 50 points pour être reçu ; **to fail by two ~s** échouer à deux points près ; (*Brit Scol*) **he got full ~s** il a eu dix sur dix (*or* vingt sur vingt *etc*) ; (*Brit : fig*) **he deserves full ~s** il mérite vingt sur vingt ; (*Brit : fig*) **full ~s to him for achieving so much** on ne peut que le féliciter de tout ce qu'il a accompli ; **(I give him) full ~s for trying** c'est bien d'avoir essayé ; **full ~s for honesty** bravo pour l'honnêteté ! ; (*hum*) **there are no ~s* for guessing his name** il n'y a pas besoin d'être un génie pour savoir de qui je parle

[f] (= *target*) cible *f*; **to hit the ~** (*lit*) faire mouche; (*fig*) faire mouche, mettre dans le mille; **to be right on the ~** [*comment, observation*] être très pertinent; **she's normally right on the ~** d'habitude, ses observations sont très pertinentes; (*lit*) **to miss the ~** manquer le but; (*fig*) **to miss the ~ ◊ to be wide of the ~** *or* **off the ~** *or* **far from the ~** être loin de la vérité; **it's way off the ~*** [*forecast, estimate*] c'est complètement à côté de la plaque*; (*pej*) **to be an easy ~** être une cible facile → **overshoot, overstep**

[g] (*Sport*) ligne *f* de départ; (*Rugby*) arrêt *m* de volée; **on your ~s! get set! go!** à vos marques! prêts! partez!; **to get off the ~** démarrer; (*fig*) **to be quick off the ~** (= *quick on the uptake*) avoir l'esprit vif; (= *quick in reacting*) avoir des réactions rapides; (*fig*) **to be quick off the ~ in doing sth** ne pas perdre de temps pour faire qch; (*fig*) **to be slow off the ~** être lent (à la détente*); (*fig*) **I don't feel up to the ~** je ne suis pas dans mon assiette, je ne suis pas en forme; (*fig*) **he isn't up to the ~ for this job** il n'est pas à la hauteur de ce travail; (*fig*) **it's way off the ~ ◊ his work doesn't come up to the ~** son travail n'est pas satisfaisant, son travail laisse à désirer; (*fig*) **this film came well up to the ~** ce film ne m'a pas déçu

[h] (*Econ* = *level, point*) barre *f*; **the number of unemployed has reached the 2 million ~/fallen below the 2 million ~** le chiffre du chômage a atteint la barre des 2 millions/est descendu en dessous de la barre des 2 millions

[i] (*Comm* = *brand name*) marque *f*

[j] (*Mil, Tech* = *model, type*) série *f*; **Concorde Mark 1** Concorde *m* première série

[k] (*Culin* = *oven temperature*) **(gas) ~ 6** thermostat *m* 6

[2] VT [a] (= *make a mark on*) marquer, mettre une marque à *or* sur; [+ *paragraph, item, linen, suitcase*] marquer; (= *stain*) tacher, marquer; **I hope your dress isn't ~ed** j'espère que ta robe n'est pas tachée; (*lit*) **to ~ the cards** marquer les cartes

[b] [*animal, bird*] **a bird ~ed with red** un oiseau tacheté de rouge

[c] (*fig* = *scar*) marquer; **the accident ~ed him for life** l'accident l'a marqué pour la vie; **suffering had ~ed him** la douleur l'avait marqué; **his reign was ~ed by civil wars** son règne fut marqué par des guerres civiles

[d] (= *indicate*) marquer; [+ *price etc*] marquer, indiquer; (*St Ex*) coter; (*Sport*) [+ *score*] marquer; **this flag ~s the frontier** ce drapeau marque la frontière; **they ~ed his grave with a cross** ils ont mis une croix sur sa tombe; **it ~s a change of policy** cela indique un changement de politique; **in order to ~ the occasion** pour marquer l'occasion; **this ~s him as a future manager** ceci fait présager pour lui une carrière de cadre; **to ~ time** (*Mil*) marquer le pas; (*fig*) (= *wait*) faire du sur place, piétiner; (*by choice, through doing sth*) attendre son heure → **X**; → **marked**

[e] (*Scol etc*) [+ *essay, exam*] corriger, noter; [+ *candidate*] noter, donner une note à; **to ~ sth right/wrong** marquer qch juste/faux

[f] (= *note, pay attention to*) bien écouter; **(you) ~ my words!** crois-moi!; (*predicting*) tu verras!; **~ you, he may have been right** remarquez qu'il avait peut-être raison; **~ him well††** écoutez bien ce qu'il dit

[g] (*Sport*) [+ *opposing player*] marquer

[3] VI se tacher

[4] COMP ► **mark reader** N lecteur *m* optique ► **mark reading** N lecture *f* optique ► **mark scanner** N lecteur *m* de marques ► **mark scanning** N lecture *f* de marques ► **mark-up** N (*Comm*) (= *increase*) hausse *f*, majoration *f* de prix; (= *profit margin*) bénéfice *m*; **~-up on a bill** majoration *f* sur une facture; **there's a 50% ~-up on this product** ils ont une marge

or ils font un bénéfice de 50% sur ce produit

► **mark down** [1] VT SEP [a] (= *write down*) inscrire, noter [b] (= *reduce*) [+ *price*] baisser; [+ *goods*] démarquer, baisser le prix de; **all these items have been ~ed down for the sales** tous ces articles ont été démarqués pour les soldes; (*St Ex*) **to be ~ed down** s'inscrire en baisse, reculer [c] (*Scol*) [+ *exercise, pupil*] baisser la note de [d] (= *single out*) [+ *person*] désigner, prévoir (**for** pour) [2] **~down** N → **markdown**

► **mark off** VT SEP [a] (= *separate*) séparer, distinguer (**from** de) [b] (*Surv etc* = *divide by boundary*) délimiter; [+ *distance*] mesurer; [+ *road, boundary*] tracer [c] [+ *items on list etc*] cocher; **he ~ed the names off as the people went in** il cochait les noms (sur la liste) à mesure que les gens entraient

► **mark out** VT SEP [a] [+ *zone etc*] délimiter, tracer les limites de; [+ *field*] borner; [+ *route, footpath*] baliser; (*with stakes*) jalonner; **to ~ out a tennis court** tracer les lignes d'un court de tennis; **the route is ~ed out with flags** l'itinéraire est jalonné de drapeaux [b] (= *single out*) désigner, distinguer; **to ~ sb out for promotion** désigner qn pour l'avancement; **he was ~ed out long ago for that job** il y a longtemps qu'on l'avait prévu pour ce poste; **his red hair ~ed him out from the others** ses cheveux roux le distinguaient des autres

► **mark up** [1] VT SEP [a] (*on board, wall etc*) [+ *price, score*] marquer [b] (*Comm* = *put a price on*) indiquer *or* marquer le prix de; **these items have not been ~ed up** le prix n'est pas marqué sur ces articles [c] (= *increase*) [+ *price*] majorer; [+ *goods*] majorer le prix de; **all these chairs have been ~ed up** toutes ces chaises ont été augmenté; (*St Ex*) **to be ~ed up** s'inscrire en hausse, avancer [d] (*Scol*) [+ *exercise, pupil*] surnoter, gonfler la note de [2] **~up** N → **mark²**

markdown ['mɑːkdaʊn] N (*Comm*) remise *f*, réduction *f*

marked [mɑːkt] ADJ [a] (= *noticeable*) [*improvement, increase, decline, change, effect*] sensible; [*lack*] net; [*preference, tendency, difference*] net, marqué; [*reluctance*] vif, marqué; [*contrast*] frappant; [*bias*] manifeste; [*accent*] prononcé; **it is becoming more ~** cela s'accentue; **in ~ contrast (to ...)** en contraste frappant (avec ...) [b] **to be a ~ man** être un homme marqué [c] [*signposted*] [*path, trail*] balisé [d] (*Ling*) marqué; **~ form** forme *f* marquée; **to be ~ for number/gender** porter la marque du nombre/du genre [e] (*St Ex*) **~ shares** actions *fpl* estampillées

markedly ['mɑːkɪdlɪ] ADV [*improve, differ, contrast, change*] sensiblement; **to be ~ better/worse** être nettement mieux/moins bien

marker ['mɑːkər] N [a] (*also* **~ pen**) marqueur *m* indélébile; (*for laundry etc*) marquoir *m* [b] (= *flag, stake*) marque *f*, jalon *m*; (= *light etc*) balise *f* [c] (= *bookmark*) signet *m* [d] (*Sport etc* = *person*) marqueur *m*, -euse *f*; (*Ftbl*) **to lose** *or* **shake off one's ~** se démarquer [e] (*Scol* = *person*) correcteur *m*, -trice *f* [f] (*Tech: showing sth is present*) indicateur *m* (**for sth** de qch) [g] (*Ling*) marqueur *m*

market ['mɑːkɪt] [1] N [a] (= *trade, place, also St Ex*) marché *m*; **to go to ~** aller au marché; **the wholesale ~** le marché de gros; **cattle ~** marché *m* or foire *f* aux bestiaux; **the sugar ~ ◊ the ~ in sugar** le marché du sucre; **the world coffee ~** le marché mondial du *or* des café(s); **free ~** marché *m* libre; (*St Ex*) **a dull/lively ~** un marché lourd/actif; (*St Ex*) **the ~ is rising/falling** les cours *mpl* sont en hausse/en baisse; (*St Ex*) **the company intends to go to the ~** la société a l'intention d'entrer en Bourse → **black, buyer, common** [b] (*fig*) marché *m*; **home/overseas/world ~** marché *m* intérieur/d'outre-mer/mondial; **to have a good ~ for sth** avoir une grosse de-

mande pour qch; **to find a ready ~ for sth** trouver facilement un marché *or* des débouchés pour qch; **there is a ready ~ for small cars** les petites voitures se vendent bien; **there's no ~ for pink socks** les chaussettes roses ne se vendent pas; **this appeals to the French ~** cela plaît à la clientèle française, cela se vend bien en France; **our competitors control 72% of the ~** nos concurrents contrôlent 72% du marché; **to be in the ~ for sth** être acheteur de qch; **to put sth/to be on the ~** mettre qch/être en vente *or* dans le commerce *or* sur le marché; **it's the dearest car on the ~** c'est la voiture la plus chère sur le marché; **on the open ~** en vente libre → **flood**

[2] VT (= *promote*) commercialiser; (= *sell*) vendre; (= *find outlet for*) trouver un *or* des débouché(s) pour

[3] VI (*esp US: also* **to go ~ing**) aller faire des commissions

[4] COMP ► **market analysis** N analyse *f* de marché ► **market cross** N croix *f* sur la place du marché ► **market day** N jour *m* de *or* du marché; (*St Ex*) jour *m* de bourse ► **market economy** N économie *f* de marché ► **market forces** NPL forces *fpl* du marché ► **market garden** N (*Brit*) jardin *m* maraîcher ► **market gardener** N (*Brit*) maraîcher *m*, -ère *f* ► **market gardening** N (*Brit*) culture *f* maraîchère ► **market leader** N company, product) leader *m* du marché ► **market opportunity** N créneau *m* ► **market place** N (*lit*) place *f* du marché; **in the ~ place** (*lit*) au marché; (*fig: Econ*) sur le marché ► **market price** N (*Comm*) prix *m* marchand *or* du marché; **at ~ price** au cours, au prix courant; (*St Ex*) **~ prices** cours *m* du marché ► **market rates** NPL taux *m* du cours libre ► **market research** N étude *f* de marché (**in** de); **to do some ~ research** faire une étude de marché; **I work in ~ research** je travaille pour un consultant en études de marché *or* une société de marketing; **~ research institute** *or* **organization** institut *m* de marketing ► **market researcher** N enquêteur *m*, -trice *f* (*qui fait des études de marché*) ► **market share** N part *f* du marché ► **market square** N place *f* du marché ► **market trader** N (*Brit*) commerçant(e) *m(f)* (*qui vend sur les marchés*) ► **market trends** NPL (*St Ex*) tendances *fpl* du marché ► **market value** N valeur *f* marchande

marketability [,mɑːkɪtəˈbɪlɪtɪ] N possibilité *f* de commercialisation

marketable ['mɑːkɪtəbl] ADJ [a] [*commodity, product, skill*] facilement commercialisable; (*St Ex*) [*securities*] négociable; **of ~ quality** d'une bonne qualité marchande [b] (*fig*) [*person*] coté

marketeer [,mɑːkɪˈtɪər] N [a] → **black** [b] (*Brit Pol*) (**pro-)Marketeers** ceux qui sont en faveur du Marché commun; **anti-Marketeers** ceux qui s'opposent au Marché commun

marketing ['mɑːkɪtɪŋ] [1] N [a] [*of product, goods*] commercialisation *f*, marketing *m* [b] (= *field of activity*) marketing *m*, mercatique *f* [c] (= *department*) service *m* du marketing, département *m* marketing [2] COMP [*concept, plan*] de commercialisation ► **marketing arrangement** N accord *m* de commercialisation ► **marketing department** N service *m* du marketing, département *m* marketing ► **marketing intelligence** N informations *fpl* commerciales ► **marketing manager** N directeur *m*, -trice *f* du marketing ► **marketing mix** N marketing mix *m*, plan *m* de marchéage ► **marketing people** NPL **one of our ~ people** l'un de nos commerciaux ► **marketing strategy** N stratégie *f* marketing

marking ['mɑːkɪŋ] [1] N [a] (*NonC*) [*of animals, trees, goods*] marquage *m* [b] (*Brit Scol*) (*gen* =

correcting) correction *f* (des copies) ; (= *giving of marks*) attribution *f* de notes, notation *f* ; (= *marks given*) notes *fpl* [c] (*also* **~s**) (*on animal*) marques *fpl*, taches *fpl* ; (*on road*) signalisation *f* horizontale [d] (*Ftbl*) marquage *m* (d'un joueur) [2] COMP ► **marking ink** N encre *f* indélébile ► **marking scheme** N barème *m*

marksman ['mɑ:ksmən] N (*pl* **-men**) tireur *m* ; (*Police*) tireur *m* d'élite

marksmanship ['mɑ:ksmənʃɪp] N adresse *f* au tir

marl [mɑ:l] (*Geol*) [1] N marne *f* [2] VT marner

marlin ['mɑ:lɪn] N [a] (*pl* **marlin** *or* **marlins**) (= *fish*) marlin *m*, makaire *m* [b] = **marline**

marline ['mɑ:lɪn] N (*Naut*) lusin *m*

marlin(e) spike ['mɑ:lɪnspaɪk] N (*Naut*) épissoir *m*

marly ['mɑ:lɪ] ADJ marneux

marmalade ['mɑ:məleɪd] [1] N confiture *f or* marmelade *f* d'oranges (*or de citrons etc*) [2] COMP ► **marmalade orange** N orange *f* amère, bigarade *f*

Marmara, **Marmora** ['mɑ:mərə] N **the Sea of ~** la mer de Marmara

marmoreal [mɑ:'mɔ:rɪəl] ADJ (*liter*) marmoréen

marmoset ['mɑ:məʊzet] N ouistiti *m*

marmot ['mɑ:mət] N marmotte *f*

maroon[1] [mə'ru:n] ADJ (= *colour*) bordeaux *inv*

maroon[2] [mə'ru:n] N (= *distress signal*) fusée *f* de détresse

maroon[3] [mə'ru:n] VT (*lit*) [+ *castaway*] abandonner (sur une île or une côte déserte) ; (*fig*) [*sea, traffic, strike etc*] bloquer ; (*fig*) **to be ~ed** être abandonné *or* délaissé

marque [mɑ:k] N (= *brand*) marque *f*

marquee [mɑ:'ki:] N [a] (*esp Brit*) (= *tent*) grande tente *f* ; (*in circus*) chapiteau *m* [b] (= *awning*) auvent *m* ; (*US*) [*of theatre, cinema*] marquise *f*, fronton *m*

Marquesas Islands [mɑ:'keɪsæs'aɪləndz] NPL îles *fpl* Marquises

marquess ['mɑ:kwɪs] N marquis *m*

marquetry ['mɑ:kɪtrɪ] [1] N marqueterie *f* [2] COMP [*table etc*] de *or* en marqueterie

marquis ['mɑ:kwɪs] N = **marquess**

Marrakesh, **Marrakech** [mə'rækeʃ, mærə'keʃ] N Marrakech

▼ **marriage** ['mærɪdʒ] [1] N mariage *m* ; (*fig*) mariage *m*, alliance *f* ; **to give sb in ~** donner qn en mariage ; **to take sb in ~**† (*gen*) épouser qn ; (*in actual wording of service*) prendre qn comme époux (*or épouse*) ; **civil ~** mariage *m* civil, **~ of convenience** mariage *m* de convenance ; **aunt by ~** tante *f* par alliance ; **they are related by ~** ils sont parents par alliance → **offer, shotgun**

[2] COMP ► **marriage bed** N lit *m* conjugal ► **marriage bonds** NPL liens *mpl* conjugaux ► **marriage broker** N agent *m* matrimonial ► **marriage bureau** N agence *f* matrimoniale ► **marriage ceremony** N (cérémonie *f* de) mariage *m* ► **marriage certificate** N (extrait *m* d')acte *m* de mariage ► **marriage customs** NPL coutumes *fpl* matrimoniales ► **marriage guidance** N consultation *f* conjugale ► **marriage guidance counsellor** N conseiller *m*, -ère *f* conjugal(e) ► **marriage licence** N certificat *m* de publication des bans ► **marriage lines** NPL (*Brit*) = **marriage certificate** ► **marriage partner** N conjoint(e) *m(f)* ► **marriage rate** N taux *m* de nuptialité ► **marriage settlement** N ≈ contrat *m* de mariage ► **marriage vows** NPL vœux *mpl* de mariage

marriageable† ['mærɪdʒəbl] ADJ [*person*] mariable ; **of ~ age** en âge de se marier ; **he's very ~** c'est un très bon parti

married ['mærɪd] [1] ADJ [a] (= *wedded*) [*person, couple*] marié (**to** à, avec) ; **twice-~** marié deux fois ; **"just ~"** « jeunes mariés » ; **the**

newly ~ **couple** les (nouveaux) mariés *mpl* ; **he is a ~ man** c'est un homme marié ; **to be happily ~** être heureux en ménage ; **~ life** vie *f* conjugale [b] (*fig*) **to be ~ to one's job** *or* **work** ne vivre que pour son travail [2] COMP ► **married name** N nom *m* de femme mariée ► **married quarters** NPL (*Mil*) quartiers *mpl* des personnes mariées → **marry**

marrow ['mærəʊ] N [a] [*of bone*] moelle *f* ; (*fig*) essence *f* ; **to be chilled** *or* **frozen to the ~** être gelé jusqu'à la moelle des os [b] (*Brit* = *vegetable*) courge *f* ; **baby ~** courgette *f*

marrowbone ['mærəʊbəʊn] N os *m* à moelle

marrowfat ['mærəʊfæt] N (*also* **~ pea**) pois de grande taille

▼ **marry** ['mærɪ] [1] VT [a] (= *take in marriage*) épouser, se marier avec ; **will you ~ me?** veux-tu *or* voulez-vous m'épouser ? ; **to get** *or* **be married** se marier ; **they've been married for ten years** ils sont mariés depuis dix ans ; **to ~ money** faire un riche mariage, épouser une grosse fortune [b] (= *give or join in marriage*) [*priest, parent*] marier ; **he has three daughters to ~ (off)** il a trois filles à marier ; **she married (off) her daughter to a lawyer** elle a marié sa fille avec *or* à un avocat [2] VI se marier ; **to ~ for money/love** faire un mariage d'argent/d'amour ; **to ~ into a family** s'allier à une famille par le mariage, s'apparenter à une famille ; **to ~ into money** épouser une grosse fortune ; **to ~ beneath o.s.**† se mésallier, faire une mésalliance ; **to ~ again** se remarier

► **marry off** VT SEP [*parent etc*] marier → **marry 1b**

► **marry up** VT SEP [*pattern etc*] faire coïncider

Mars [mɑ:z] N (*Myth*) Mars *m* ; (*Astron*) Mars *f*

Marseillaise [,mɑ:sə'leɪz] N Marseillaise *f*

Marseilles [mɑ:'seɪlz] N Marseille

marsh [mɑ:ʃ] [1] N marais *m*, marécage *m* → **salt** [2] COMP ► **marsh fever** N paludisme *m*, fièvre *f* des marais ► **marsh gas** N gaz *m* des marais ► **marsh marigold** N renoncule *f* des marais ► **marsh warbler** N rousserolle *f*

marshal ['mɑ:ʃəl] [1] N [a] (*Mil etc*) maréchal *m* ; (*Brit*) **Marshal of the Royal Air Force** maréchal de la RAF → **air, field** [b] (*Brit: at demonstration, sports event etc*) membre *m* du service d'ordre [c] (*in US*) (*in police/fire department*) ≈ capitaine *m* de gendarmerie/des pompiers ; (= *law officer*) marshal *m* (*magistrat et officier de police fédérale*) [d] (*in Brit: at Court etc*) chef *m* du protocole [2] VT [a] (*Mil, Police*) [+ *troops, forces*] rassembler ; [+ *crowd, traffic*] canaliser ; (*Rail*) [+ *wagons*] trier ; **the police ~led the procession into the town** la police a fait entrer le cortège en bon ordre dans la ville [b] (*fig*) [+ *facts*] organiser ; [+ *evidence*] rassembler ; [+ *resources*] mobiliser ; [+ *support*] obtenir, rallier ; **to ~ one's thoughts** rassembler ses idées

marshalling ['mɑ:ʃəlɪŋ] [1] N [a] [*of crowd, demonstrators*] maintien *m* de l'ordre (**of** parmi) [b] (*Rail*) triage *m* [2] COMP ► **marshalling yard** N gare *f* or centre *m* de triage

marshland ['mɑ:ʃlænd] N région *f* marécageuse, marécage *m*

marshmallow [mɑ:ʃ'mæləʊ] N [a] (*Bot*) guimauve *f* [b] (= *sweet*) marshmallow *m*

marshy ['mɑ:ʃɪ] ADJ marécageux

marsupial [mɑ:'su:pɪəl] ADJ, N marsupial *m*

mart [mɑ:t] N (*esp US*) (= *trade centre*) centre *m* commercial ; (= *market*) marché *m* ; (= *auction room*) salle *f* des ventes → **property**

marten ['mɑ:tɪn] N (*pl* **martens** *or* **marten**) martre *f or* marte *f*

Martha ['mɑ:θə] N Marthe *f*

martial ['mɑ:ʃəl] [1] ADJ [*music*] militaire ; [*spirit*] guerrier ; [*behaviour*] martial → **court martial** [2] COMP ► **martial art** N art *m* martial ► **martial artist** N expert *m* en arts martiaux ► **martial law** N loi *f* martiale ; **to be under ~**

law être soumis à la loi martiale ► **martial rule** N domination *f* militaire

Martian ['mɑ:ʃən] [1] N martien(ne) *m(f)* [2] ADJ martien

martin ['mɑ:tɪn] N (*Orn*) **house ~** hirondelle *f* de fenêtre ; **sand ~** hirondelle *f* de rivage

martinet [,mɑ:tɪ'net] N **to be a (real) ~** être impitoyable *or* intraitable en matière de discipline

martingale ['mɑ:tɪŋɡeɪl] N (*Horse-riding, Gambling*) martingale *f*

Martini® [mɑ:'ti:nɪ] N Martini® *m* ; (*US* = *cocktail*) Martini *m* américain ; **sweet ~** Martini *m* rouge

Martinique [,mɑ:tɪ'ni:k] N la Martinique ; **in ~** à la Martinique

Martinmas ['mɑ:tɪnməs] N la Saint-Martin

martyr ['mɑ:tər] [1] N (*Rel, fig*) martyr(e) *m(f)* (**to** de) ; **a ~'s crown** la couronne du martyre ; **he is a ~ to migraine(s)** ses migraines lui font souffrir le martyre ; **don't be such a ~!** ◊ **stop acting like a ~!** arrête de jouer les martyrs ! [2] VT (*Rel, fig*) martyriser

martyrdom ['mɑ:tədəm] N (*NonC*) (*Rel*) martyre *m* ; (*fig*) martyre *m*, calvaire *m*

martyrize ['mɑ:tɪraɪz] VT (*Rel, fig*) martyriser

marvel ['mɑ:vəl] [1] N (= *thing*) merveille *f* ; (= *wonder*) prodige *m*, miracle *m* ; **the ~s of modern science** les prodiges *mpl* de la science moderne ; **plastics were hailed as a ~ of modern science** on a salué les matières plastiques comme un prodige de la science moderne ; **the cathedral is a ~ of Gothic architecture** la cathédrale est un joyau de l'architecture gothique ; **if he gets there it will be a ~** ce sera (un) miracle s'il y arrive ; **she's a ~*** c'est une perle ; **it's a ~ to me* how he does it** je ne sais vraiment pas comment il y arrive ; **it's a ~ to me* that ...** cela me paraît un miracle que ... (+ *subj*), je n'en reviens pas que ... (+ *subj*) ; **it's a ~ that ...** c'est un miracle que ... (+ *subj*) → **work** [2] VI s'émerveiller, s'étonner (**at** de) [3] VT s'étonner (**that** de ce que + *indic or* + *subj*)

marvellous, **marvelous** (*US*) ['mɑ:vələs] ADJ merveilleux ; (*iro*) **(isn't it) ~!** c'est vraiment extraordinaire ! ; (*iro*) **to have a ~ time** s'amuser énormément ; **it's ~ to see you** je suis si content de te voir

marvellously, **marvelously** (*US*) ['mɑ:vələslɪ] ADV merveilleusement

Marxian ['mɑ:ksɪən] ADJ marxien

Marxism ['mɑ:ksɪzəm] [1] N marxisme *m* [2] COMP ► **Marxism-Leninism** N marxisme-léninisme *m*

Marxist ['mɑ:ksɪst] [1] ADJ, N marxiste *mf* ; **with ~ tendencies** marxisant [2] COMP ► **Marxist-Leninist** ADJ, N marxiste-léniniste *mf*

Mary ['mɛərɪ] N Marie *f* ; **~ Magdalene** Marie-Madeleine *f* ; **~ Queen of Scots** ◊ **~ Stuart** Marie Stuart(, reine d'Écosse) ; (*Drugs*) **~ Jane*** marie-jeanne* *f*, marijuana *f* → **bloody**

Maryland ['mɛərɪlænd] N le Maryland ; **in ~** dans le Maryland

marzipan ['mɑ:zɪpæn] [1] N pâte *f* d'amandes, massepain *m* [2] COMP [*sweet etc*] à la pâte d'amandes

masc. ABBR = **masculine**

mascara [mæs'kɑ:rə] N mascara *m*

mascaraed [mæs'kɑ:rəd] ADJ maquillé (au mascara)

mascot ['mæskət] N mascotte *f*

masculine ['mæskjʊlɪn] [1] ADJ masculin [2] N (*Gram*) masculin *m* ; **in the ~** au masculin

masculinist ['mæskjʊlɪnɪst], **masculist** ['mæskjʊlɪst] ADJ masculin ; (*pej*) phallocrate, machiste

masculinity [,mæskjʊ'lɪnɪtɪ] N masculinité *f*

masculinize ['mæskjʊlɪnaɪz] VT masculiniser

masculist ['mæskjʊlɪst] N = **masculinist**
maser ['meɪzər] N maser *m*
MASH [mæʃ] **1** N (US) (ABBR = **mobile army surgical hospital**) unité *f* chirurgicale mobile de campagne **2** COMP ► **MASH team** N équipe *f* chirurgicale mobile de campagne ► **MASH unit** N unité *f* chirurgicale mobile de campagne
mash [mæʃ] **1** N **a** (= *pulp*) pulpe *f* **b** (*Brit Culin** = *potatoes*) purée *f* (de pommes de terre) → **banger c** (*Agr*) (for pigs, hens etc) pâtée *f*; (for horses) mash *m* **d** (*Brewing*) pâte *f* **2** VT **a** (= *crush*) (*also* ~ **up**) écraser, broyer; (*Culin*) (*potatoes, bananas*) faire une purée de; **~ed potatoes** purée *f* de pommes de terre **b** (= *injure, damage*) écraser **c** (*Brewing*) brasser
masher ['mæʃər] N (*Tech*) broyeur *m*; (in kitchen) presse-purée *m inv*
mashie ['mæʃɪ] N (*Golf*) mashie *m*
mask [mɑːsk] **1** N (gen) masque *m*; (for eyes: in silk or velvet) masque *m*, loup *m*; (*Comput*) masque *m* de saisie → **death, gasmask, iron** **2** VT **a** (+ *person, face*) masquer **b** (= *hide*) (+ *object, truth, fact, differences*) masquer, cacher; (+ *motives, pain*) cacher, dissimuler; (+ *taste, smell*) masquer; (fig) **to ~ sth from sb** cacher qch à qn **4** COMP ► **masked ball** N bal *m* masqué ► **masking tape** N ruban *m* de masquage
masochism ['mæsəʊkɪzəm] N masochisme *m*
masochist ['mæsəʊkɪst] N masochiste *mf*
masochistic [,mæsəʊ'kɪstɪk] ADJ masochiste
mason ['meɪsn] **1** N **a** (= *stoneworker*) maçon *m* → **monumental b** (*also* **freemason**) (franc-)maçon *m* **2** COMP ► **the Mason-Dixon Line** N (*US Hist*) la ligne Mason-Dixon ► **Mason jar** N (US) bocal *m* à conserves (étanche)

──── **MASON-DIXON LINE** ────
La **ligne** *Mason-Dixon est la frontière symbolique (longue de 375 km) qui, au 18ᵉ siècle, séparait le nord du sud des États-Unis, c'est-à-dire les États esclavagistes des États anti-esclavagistes. L'expression est encore utilisée de nos jours. De même, les chanteurs de musique country parlent souvent avec nostalgie de traverser la* **ligne** *Mason-Dixon pour évoquer leur désir de rentrer chez eux dans le Sud.*

masonic [mə'sɒnɪk] ADJ (franc-)maçonnique
Masonite® ['meɪsənaɪt] N (US) aggloméré *m*
masonry ['meɪsənrɪ] N (*NonC*) **a** (= *stonework*) maçonnerie *f* **b** (*also* **freemasonry**) (franc-)maçonnerie *f*
masque [mɑːsk] N (*Theat*) mascarade *f*, comédie-masque *f*
masquerade [,mæskə'reɪd] **1** N (lit, fig) mascarade *f* **2** VI **to ~ as ...** se faire passer pour ...
mass¹ [mæs] **1** N **a** (*NonC: Art, Phys*) masse *f* **b** (of matter, dough, rocks, air, snow, water etc) masse *f*; **a ~ of daisies** une multitude de pâquerettes; **the garden was a (solid) ~ of colour** le jardin n'était qu'une profusion de couleurs; **he was a ~ of bruises** il était couvert de bleus; **in the ~** dans l'ensemble; **the great ~ of people** la (grande) masse des gens, la (grande) majorité des gens **c** (= *people*) **the ~(es)** les masses (populaires); **Shakespeare for the ~es** Shakespeare à l'usage des masses **2 masses*** NPL **~es (of ...)** des masses* (de ...), des tas* (de ...); **I've got ~es** j'en ai plein* **3** ADJ **a** (= *en masse*) [support, unemployment, opposition, destruction] massif; [rally] massif, de masse; [resignations, desertions, sackings] en masse; [hysteria, hypnosis] collectif; **~ executions** exécutions *fpl* systématiques **b** (= *for the masses*) [culture, civilization, move-

ment, magazine] (*also* Comput) [memory] de masse; (= *relating to the masses*) [psychology, education] des masses
4 VT **~ed bands/troops** fanfares *fpl*/troupes *fpl* regroupées
5 VI [troops, people] se masser; [clouds] s'amonceler
6 COMP ► **mass cult*** N (US) culture *f* populaire or de masse ► **mass funeral** N obsèques *fpl* collectives ► **mass grave** N charnier *m* ► **mass mailing** N publipostage *m* ► **mass-market** ADJ grand public *inv* ► **mass marketing** N commercialisation *f* de masse ► **mass media** NPL (mass-)médias *mpl* ► **mass meeting** N grand rassemblement *m* ► **mass murder** N tuerie *f*, massacre *m* ► **mass murderer** N (lit, fig) boucher *m* ► **mass noun** N (*Ling*) nom *m* massif ► **mass-produce** VT (*Ind*) fabriquer en série ► **mass production** N production *f* or fabrication *f* en série
mass² [mæs] N (*Rel, Mus*) messe *f*; **to say ~** dire la messe; **to go to ~** aller à la messe → **black**
Mass. ABBR = **Massachusetts**
Massachusetts [,mæsə'tʃuːsɪts] N le Massachusetts; **in ~** dans le Massachusetts
massacre ['mæsəkər] **1** N (lit, fig) massacre *m*; **a ~ on the roads** une hécatombe sur les routes **2** VT (lit, fig) massacrer
massage ['mæsɑːʒ] **1** N massage *m*; (euph) massage *m* thaïlandais **2** VT masser; (fig) (+ *figures*) manipuler **3** COMP ► **massage parlour** N institut *m* de massage (spécialisé)
masseur [mæ'sɜːr] N masseur *m*
masseuse [mæ'sɜːz] N masseuse *f*
massicot ['mæsɪkɒt] N massicot *m*
massif [mæ'siːf] **1** N massif *m* **2** COMP ► **the Massif Central** N le Massif central
massive ['mæsɪv] ADJ **a** (= *imposing, solid*) [features, physique, building, furniture, rock face] massif **b** (= *large-scale*) [dose, explosion, increase] massif; [majority] écrasant; [heart attack, stroke] foudroyant; **on a ~ scale** à très grande échelle **c** (* = *huge*) [suitcase, car, house etc] énorme, gigantesque; **he weighs in at a ~ 100 kilos** il fait le poids imposant de 100 kilos, c'est un colosse de 100 kilos
massively ['mæsɪvlɪ] ADV [invest, borrow, increase] massivement; [reduce] énormément; [successful, popular] extrêmement; **~ overloaded** beaucoup trop chargé; **~ overweight** obèse
massiveness ['mæsɪvnɪs] N **a** (of building, features, dose, increase) aspect *m* or caractère *m* massif; [of majority] ampleur *f* **b*** [of suitcase, car, house etc] taille *f* gigantesque
mast¹ [mɑːst] N (on ship, also flagpole) mât *m*; (for radio) pylône *m*; **the ~s of a ship** la mâture d'un navire; (*Naut*) **to sail before the ~** servir comme simple matelot
mast² [mɑːst] N (*Bot*) → **beechmast**
mastectomy [mæ'stektəmɪ] N mastectomie *f*
-masted ['mɑːstɪd] ADJ (in compounds) **three-masted** à trois mâts
master ['mɑːstər] **1** N **a** [of household, institution, animal] maître *m*; **the ~ of the house** le maître de maison; **to be ~ in one's own house** être maître chez soi; **the ~ is not at home†** Monsieur n'est pas là ■ (*PROV*) **like ~ like man** tel maître tel valet (*PROV*); (*Art*) **old ~s** (= *pictures*) tableaux *mpl* de maître; **I am the ~ now** c'est moi qui commande or qui donne les ordres maintenant; (fig) **he has met his ~** il a trouvé son maître; **to be ~ of o.s./of the situation** être maître de soi/de la situation; **to be (the) ~ of one's own** ~ être son (propre) maître; **to be ~ of one's destiny or fate** être maître de sa destinée; **he is a ~ of the violin** c'est un virtuose du violon; (*Bible*) **the Master** le Seigneur → **old, past** **b** († *also* **schoolmaster**) (in secondary school) professeur *m*; (in primary school) instituteur *m*,

maître *m*; **music ~** (in school) professeur *m* de musique; (private tutor) professeur *m* or maître *m* de musique → **fencing**
c (*Naut*) [of ship] capitaine *m*; [of liner] (capitaine) commandant *m*; [of fishing boat] patron *m*
d (*Univ*) **Master of Arts/Science** etc ≈ titulaire *mf* d'une maîtrise en lettres/sciences etc → **DEGREE**; **a ~'s (degree)** ≈ une maîtrise; (US) **~'s essay** or **paper** or **thesis** ≈ mémoire *m* (de maîtrise)
e (*Brit Univ*) [of Oxbridge college etc] ≈ directeur *m*, ≈ principal *m*
f (*Brit: title for boys*) monsieur *m*
g = **master tape, master disk**
h (*Golf*) **the (US) Masters** les Masters *mpl*
2 VT (+ *person*) mater; (+ *animal*) dompter; (+ *emotion*) maîtriser; (+ *difficulty, crisis, problem*) gérer, surmonter; (+ *situation*) se rendre maître de
b (= *understand, learn*) (+ *theory*) saisir; (+ *language, skill*) maîtriser; **he has ~ed Greek** il connaît or possède le grec à fond; **he'll never ~ the violin** il ne saura jamais bien jouer du violon; **he has ~ed the trumpet** il est devenu très bon trompettiste or un trompettiste accompli; **it's so difficult that I'll never ~ it** c'est si difficile que je n'y parviendrai jamais
3 COMP [beam] maître (maîtresse *f*); [control, cylinder, switch] principal ► **master-at-arms** N (*pl* **masters-at-arms**) (*Naut*) capitaine *m* d'armes ► **master baker** N maître *m* boulanger ► **master bedroom** N chambre *f* principale ► **master builder** N entrepreneur *m* en bâtiment ► **master butcher** N maître *m* boucher ► **master card** N (*Cards, fig*) carte *f* maîtresse ► **master chief petty officer** N (*US Naut*) major *m* ► **master class** N cours *m* de (grand) maître ► **master copy** N original *m* ► **master cylinder** N (*Aut*) maître cylindre *m* ► **master disk** N (*Comput*) disque *m* d'exploitation ► **master file** N (*Comput*) fichier *m* maître or permanent ► **master hand** N (= *expert*) maître *m*; **to be a ~ hand at (doing) sth** être passé maître dans l'art de (faire) qch; **the work of a ~ hand** un travail exécuté de main de maître ► **master key** N passe-partout *m inv* ► **master mariner** N (*Naut*) (foreign-going) ≈ capitaine *m* au long cours; (home trade) ≈ capitaine *m* de la marine marchande ► **master of ceremonies** N maître *m* des cérémonies; (*TV etc*) animateur *m* ► **master of (fox)hounds** N grand veneur *m* ► **Master of the Rolls** N (*Brit Jur*) ≈ premier président *m* de la Cour de cassation ► **master plan** N schéma *m* directeur ► **master print** N (*Cine*) copie *f* étalon ► **master race** N race *f* supérieure ► **master sergeant** N (US) adjudant *m*; (US Aviat) ≈ sergent-chef *m* ► **master stroke** N coup *m* magistral or de maître ► **master tape** N bande *f* mère
MasterCard® ['mɑːstəkɑːd] N MasterCard® *f*
masterful ['mɑːstəfʊl] ADJ **a** (= *dominant*) [person] à l'autorité naturelle **b** (= *skilful*) [performance, job, display] magistral; **to be ~ at doing sth** réussir remarquablement à faire qch
masterfully ['mɑːstəfəlɪ] ADV **a** (= *imperiously*) [act, decide] en maître; [speak, announce] d'un ton décisif, sur un ton d'autorité **b** (= *expertly*) magistralement, de main de maître
masterly ['mɑːstəlɪ] ADJ [performance, analysis] magistral; [actor, player, politician] de grande classe; **in ~ fashion** avec maestria; **to say sth with ~ understatement** dire qch avec un art consommé de la litote
mastermind ['mɑːstəmaɪnd] **1** N (= *genius*) génie *m*, cerveau *m*; [of plan, crime etc] cerveau *m* **2** VT (+ *operation etc*) diriger, organiser
masterpiece ['mɑːstəpiːs] N chef-d'œuvre *m*
masterwork ['mɑːstəwɜːk] N chef-d'œuvre *m*

mastery ['mɑːstərɪ] N (gen) maîtrise f (of de); **to gain ~ over** [+ person] avoir le dessus sur, l'emporter sur; [+ animal] dompter; [+ nation, country] s'assurer la domination de; [+ the seas] s'assurer la maîtrise de

masthead ['mɑːsthed] N [of ship] tête f de mât; [of newspaper] (= title) titre m; (= staff etc) ours* m (Press)

mastic ['mæstɪk] N (= resin, adhesive) mastic m

masticate ['mæstɪkeɪt] VTI mastiquer, mâcher

mastiff ['mæstɪf] N mastiff m

mastitis [mæ'staɪtɪs] N mastite f

mastodon ['mæstədɒn] N mastodonte m (lit)

mastoid ['mæstɔɪd] [1] ADJ mastoïdien [2] N (= bone) apophyse f mastoïde

mastoiditis [ˌmæstɔɪ'daɪtɪs] N mastoïdite f

masturbate ['mæstəbeɪt] [1] VI se masturber [2] VT masturber

masturbation [ˌmæstə'beɪʃən] N masturbation f

masturbatory [ˌmæstə'beɪtərɪ] ADJ masturbatoire, masturbateur (-trice f)

MAT [ˌemeɪ'tiː] N (ABBR = machine-assisted translation) TAO f

mat¹ [mæt] [1] N a (for floors etc) (petit) tapis m, carpette f; [of straw etc] natte f; (at door) paillasson m; (in car, gymnasium) tapis m; (fig) **to have sb on the ~*** passer un savon à qn*; **a ~ of hair** des cheveux emmêlés; (US) **to go to the ~ for sb/to do sth** monter au créneau pour qn/pour faire qch → **rush²** b (on table) (heat-resistant) dessous-de-plat m inv; (decorative) set m (de table); (embroidered linen) napperon m → **drip**, **place** [2] VI (= become matted) [hair etc] s'emmêler; [woollens] (se) feutrer → **matted**

mat² [mæt] ADJ = **matt(e)**

matador ['mætədɔː] N matador m

match¹ [mætʃ] N allumette f; **box/book of ~es** boîte f/pochette f d'allumettes; **have you got a ~?** avez-vous une allumette ou du feu?; **to strike** or **light a ~** gratter or frotter ou faire craquer une allumette; **to put** or **set a ~ to sth** mettre le feu à qch → **safety**

match² [mætʃ] [1] N a (Sport) match m; (esp Brit = game) partie f; **to play a ~ against sb** disputer un match contre qn, jouer contre qn; **international ~** match m international, rencontre f internationale; **~ abandoned** match m suspendu → **away**, **home**, **return** b (= equal) égal(e) m(f); **to meet one's ~ (in sb)** trouver à qui parler (avec qn), avoir affaire à forte partie (avec qn); **he's a ~ for anybody** il est de taille à faire face à n'importe qui; **he's no ~ for Paul** il n'est pas de taille à lutter contre Paul, il ne fait pas le poids contre Paul; **he was more than a ~ for Simon** Simon n'était pas à sa mesure or ne faisait pas le poids contre lui c **to be a good ~** [clothes, colours etc] aller bien ensemble, s'assortir bien; **I'm looking for a ~ for these curtains** je cherche quelque chose pour aller avec ces rideaux d (= comparison) adéquation f; **a poor ~ between our resources and our objectives** une mauvaise adéquation entre nos ressources et nos objectifs e († = marriage) mariage m; **he's a good ~ for her** c'est un bon parti (pour elle); **they're a good ~** ils sont bien assortis → **love** [2] VT a (= be equal to: also **~ up to**) égaler, être l'égal de; **his essay didn't ~ (up to) Jason's in originality** sa dissertation n'égalait pas or ne valait pas celle de Jason en originalité; **she doesn't ~ (up to) her sister in intelligence** elle n'a pas l'intelligence de sa sœur; **the result didn't ~ (up to) our hopes** le résultat a déçu nos espérances b (= produce equal to) **to ~ sb's offer/proposal** faire une offre/une proposition équivalente à celle de qn; **I can ~ any offer** je peux offrir autant que n'importe qui; **to ~ sb's price/**

terms offrir le même prix/des conditions aussi favorables que qn; **this is ~ed only by ...** cela n'a d'égal que ...

c [clothes, colours etc] (intended as a set) être assorti à; (a good match) aller bien avec; **his tie doesn't ~ his shirt** sa cravate ne va pas avec sa chemise

d (= find similar piece etc to: also **~ up**) **can you ~ (up) this material?** (exactly same) avez-vous du tissu identique à celui-ci?; (going well with) avez-vous du tissu assorti à celui-ci?

e (= pair off) **to ~ sb against sb** opposer qn à qn; **she ~ed her wits against his strength** elle opposait son intelligence à sa force; **evenly ~ed** de force égale; **they are well ~ed** [opponents] ils sont de force égale; [married couple etc] ils sont bien assortis

[3] VI [colours, materials] être bien assortis, aller bien ensemble; [cups] être appareillés; [gloves, socks] faire la paire; [two identical objects] se faire pendant; **with (a) skirt to ~** avec (une) jupe assortie

[4] COMP ► **match day** N (Brit Sport) jour m de match ► **match-fit** ADJ (Brit Sport) en état de jouer (un match) ► **match fitness** N (Brit Sport) **to regain ~ fitness** retrouver la forme pour jouer (un match) ► **match point** N (Tennis) balle f de match

► **match up** [1] VI [colours etc] aller bien ensemble, être assortis [2] VT SEP = **match² 2d**
► **match up to** VT FUS = **match² 2a**

matchbook ['mætʃbʊk] (esp US) N pochette f d'allumettes

matchbox ['mætʃbɒks] N boîte f d'allumettes

matching ['mætʃɪŋ] ADJ [clothes, accessories, earrings, curtains] assorti; **he was dressed in a smart grey suit and ~ tie** il était vêtu d'un élégant costume gris avec une cravate assortie; **her ~ blue sweater and skirt** son pull bleu et sa jupe assortie; **a ~ pair** une paire

matchless ['mætʃlɪs] ADJ (liter) sans égal

matchmake* ['mætʃmeɪk] VI jouer les entremetteurs

matchmaker ['mætʃmeɪkə] N entremetteur m, -euse f, marieur* m, -euse* f; **she is a great ~** elle aime jouer les entremetteuses

matchstick ['mætʃstɪk] [1] N allumette f [2] COMP (= thin) [limbs, body] filiforme

matchwood ['mætʃwʊd] N (for matches) bois m d'allumettes; (= debris) **to smash sth to ~** réduire qch en miettes, pulvériser qch

mate¹ [meɪt] [1] N a (at work) camarade mf b (Brit* = friend) copain* m, copine* f; **he's a good ~** c'est un bon copain; **cheers ~!** merci, mon vieux!* → **classmate**, **playmate**, **workmate** c (= assistant) aide mf; **plumber's ~** aide-plombier m [2] [of animal] mâle m, femelle f; (* hum) [of human] (= spouse etc) compagnon m, compagne f e (Brit Merchant Navy) ≈ second m (capitaine m); (US Naut) maître m (dans la marine) → **first** [2] VT accoupler (**with** à) [3] VI s'accoupler (**with** à, avec)

mate² [meɪt] (Chess) [1] N mat m → **checkmate**, **stalemate** [2] VT mettre échec et mat, mater

material [mə'tɪərɪəl] [1] ADJ (esp Jur) a (= physical) matériel(le); **~ evidence** preuves fpl matérielles b (= relevant) pertinent (**to sth** pour qch); **~ information** informations fpl pertinentes; **~ witness** témoin m de fait [2] N a (= substance) substance f, matière f; **chemical/dangerous ~s** substances fpl or matières fpl chimiques/dangereuses → **waste** b (= cloth, fabric) tissu m; **dress ~** tissu m pour robes c (esp Ind = substance from which product is made) matériau m; **building ~s** matériaux mpl de construction; (fig) **he's officer ~** il a l'étoffe d'un officier; **he's not university ~** il n'est pas capable d'entreprendre des études supérieu-

res → **raw**

d (= necessary tools, supplies) (gen) matériel m; **the desk held all his writing ~s** le bureau contenait tout son matériel nécessaire pour écrire; **have you got any writing ~s?** avez-vous de quoi écrire?; **reading ~** (gen) de quoi lire, de la lecture; (for studies) des ouvrages mpl (et des articles mpl) à consulter; **play ~s** le matériel pour le jeu; (Scol etc) **teaching** or **course ~(s)** matériel m pédagogique

e (NonC = facts, data) matériaux mpl; **they had all the ~ required for a biography** ils avaient tous les matériaux or toutes les données nécessaires pour une biographie; **I had all the ~ I needed for my article** j'avais tout ce qu'il me fallait pour mon article; **the amount of ~ to be examined** la quantité de matériaux or de documents à examiner; **all the background ~** toute la documentation d'appui; **reference ~** ouvrages mpl de référence

f (NonC = sth written, composed etc) **all his ~ is original** tout ce qu'il écrit (or chante etc) est original; **an album of original ~** un album de titres inédits; **she has written some very funny ~** elle a écrit des choses très amusantes; **we cannot publish this ~** nous ne pouvons pas publier ce texte; **in my version of the story, I added some new ~** dans ma version de l'histoire, j'ai ajouté des éléments nouveaux; (Comm) **publicity ~** matériel m publicitaire or promotionnel; **video ~** enregistrements mpl vidéo; **30% of the programme was recorded ~** 30 % de l'émission avait été préenregistrée

materialism [mə'tɪərɪəlɪzəm] N matérialisme m

materialist [mə'tɪərɪəlɪst] ADJ, N matérialiste mf

materialistic [mə,tɪərɪə'lɪstɪk] ADJ (pej) matérialiste

materialize [mə'tɪərɪəlaɪz] [1] VI a (= take shape) [plan, wish] se matérialiser, se réaliser; [offer, loan etc] se concrétiser, se matérialiser; [idea] prendre forme b (= appear, happen) **the promised cash didn't ~** l'argent promis ne s'est pas concrétisé or matérialisé; **a rebellion by radicals failed to ~** il n'y a pas eu de rébellion de radicaux; **none of the anticipated difficulties ~d** les difficultés auxquelles on s'attendait ne se sont pas présentées c (Spiritualism etc) prendre une forme matérielle, se matérialiser; (hum) **Derek ~d at her side** Derek est soudain apparu à ses côtés [2] VT matérialiser, concrétiser

materially [mə'tɪərɪəlɪ] ADV matériellement

maternal [mə'tɜːnəl] [1] ADJ maternel; **~ smoking can damage the unborn child** en fumant, les femmes enceintes risquent de compromettre la santé de leur bébé [2] COMP ► **maternal death** N mort f en couches ► **maternal deprivation** N (Psych) dépression f anaclitique ► **maternal health care** N soins mpl aux jeunes mères ► **maternal instinct** N instinct m maternel

maternity [mə'tɜːnɪtɪ] [1] N maternité f [2] COMP [services etc] obstétrique; [clothes] de grossesse ► **maternity allowance**, **maternity benefit** N (Brit) allocation f de maternité ► **maternity dress** N robe f de grossesse ► **maternity home**, **maternity hospital** N maternité f; (private) clinique f d'accouchement ► **maternity leave** N congé m de maternité ► **maternity pay** N (Brit) salaire versé pendant le congé de maternité ► **maternity ward** N (service m de) maternité f

matey ['meɪtɪ] (Brit) [1] ADJ* [person] copain* (copine* f) (**with sb** avec qn); [tone] copain-copain* (f inv); [charm] familier [2] N (as term of address) **sorry, ~!** désolé, mon vieux!*

math* [mæθ] N (US) (ABBR = **mathematics**) math(s)* fpl

mathematical [ˌmæθə'mætɪkəl] ADJ [formula, equation, model, calculations] mathématique;

[skills, ability] en mathématiques; **I'm not ~*** je ne suis pas un matheux*, je n'ai pas la bosse* des maths; **I haven't got a ~ mind** je n'ai pas l'esprit mathématique; **she was a ~ genius** c'était une mathématicienne de génie, c'était un génie en mathématiques

mathematically [ˌmæθə'mætɪkəlɪ] ADV (gen) mathématiquement; **~ gifted** doué en mathématiques; (fig) **~ precise** avec une précision mathématique; **to be ~ inclined** or **minded** avoir l'esprit mathématique

mathematician [ˌmæθəmə'tɪʃən] N mathématicien(ne) m(f)

mathematics [ˌmæθə'mætɪks] N (NonC) mathématiques fpl; **I don't understand the ~ of it** je ne vois pas comment on arrive à ce chiffre or à ce résultat

maths* [mæθs] N (Brit) (ABBR = **mathematics**) math(s)* fpl

Matilda [mə'tɪldə] N Mathilde f

matinée ['mætɪneɪ] **1** N (Theat) matinée f **2** COMP ► **matinée coat** N (Brit) veste f (de bébé) ► **matinée idol** N idole f du public féminin ► **matinée jacket** N = **matinée coat**

mating ['meɪtɪŋ] **1** N [of animals] accouplement m **2** COMP ► **mating call** N appel m du mâle ► **mating season** N saison f des amours

matins ['mætɪnz] N (Rel) matines fpl

matri... ['meɪtrɪ] PREF matri...

matriarch ['meɪtrɪɑːk] N matrone f, femme f chef de tribu or de famille

matriarchal ['meɪtrɪ'ɑːkl] ADJ matriarcal

matriarchy ['meɪtrɪɑːkɪ] N matriarcat m

matric* [mə'trɪk] N (Brit Scol: formerly) ABBR = **matriculation 1b**

matrices ['meɪtrɪsiːz] NPL of **matrix**

matricide ['meɪtrɪsaɪd] N (= crime) matricide m; (= person) matricide mf

matriculate [mə'trɪkjʊleɪt] VI **[a]** s'inscrire, se faire immatriculer **[b]** (Brit Scol: formerly) être reçu à l'examen de « matriculation »

matriculation [mə,trɪkjʊ'leɪʃən] **1** N **[a]** (Univ) inscription f, immatriculation f **[b]** (Brit Scol: formerly) examen donnant droit à l'inscription universitaire **2** COMP (Univ) [card, fee] d'inscription

matrimonial [ˌmætrɪ'məʊnɪəl] ADJ (frm) [bed, problems] matrimonial; [law] sur le mariage; **the ~ home** le domicile conjugal

matrimony ['mætrɪmənɪ] N (NonC) mariage m → **holy**

matrix ['meɪtrɪks] N (pl **matrixes** or **matrices**) matrice f

matron ['meɪtrən] **1** N **[a]** († = woman) matrone† f **[b]** (Med) [of hospital] surveillante f générale; (in school) infirmière f; [of orphanage, old people's home etc] directrice f; **yes ~** oui madame (or mademoiselle) **2** COMP ► **matron of honour** N dame f d'honneur

matronly ['meɪtrənlɪ] ADJ [figure] imposant; [manner, clothes] de matrone; **a ~ woman** une matrone

matt(e) [mæt] **1** ADJ mat **2** COMP ► **matt emulsion** N peinture f mate ► **matt finish** N finition f mate ► **matt paint** N peinture f mate

matted ['mætɪd] ADJ [hair, beard, fur] emmêlé; [fibres, wool] feutré; **to become ~** [hair, beard, fur] s'emmêler; [fibres, wool] feutrer; **~ together** emmêlé; **~ with blood/mud** mêlé de sang/boue, collé par le sang/la boue

▼ matter ['mætə^r] **1** N **[a]** (NonC) (= physical substance) matière f, substance f; (Philos, Phys) matière f; (Typ) matière f, copie f; (Med = pus) pus m; **vegetable/inanimate ~** matière f végétale/inanimée; **colouring ~** substance f colorante; **advertising ~** publicité f, réclames fpl → **grey, mind, reading**

[b] (NonC = content) [of book etc] fond m, contenu m; **~ and form** le fond et la forme; **the ~ of his essay was good but the style poor** le contenu de sa dissertation était bon mais le style laissait à désirer

[c] (= affair, concern) affaire f, question f; **the ~ in hand** l'affaire en question; **the ~ is closed** l'affaire est close or classée; **she placed the ~ in the hands of her solicitor** elle a remis l'affaire entre les mains de son avocat; **it's a small ~** c'est un détail; **in this ~** à cet égard; **in the ~ of ...** en matière de ..., en ce qui concerne ...; **he doesn't see this as a resigning ~** il n'y a pas là, selon lui, de quoi démissionner; **this is no joking ~** c'est très sérieux → **laughing**; **it will be no easy ~** cela ne sera pas une mince affaire; **for that ~** d'ailleurs; **there's the ~ of my expenses** il y a la question de mes frais; **there's the small ~ of that £200 I lent you** il y a le petit problème des 200 livres que je vous ai prêtées; **in all ~s of education** pour tout ce qui touche à or concerne l'éducation; **it is a ~ of great concern** c'est extrêmement inquiétant; **it's a ~ of habit** c'est une question or une affaire d'habitude; **it took a ~ of days** cela a été l'affaire de quelques jours; **in a ~ of ten minutes** en l'espace de dix minutes; **it's a ~ of £200 or so** il s'agit de quelque 200 livres; **as a ~ of course** automatiquement; **as a ~ of fact** à vrai dire, en fait → **matter-of-fact**; **it's a ~ of life and death** c'est une question de vie ou de mort; **that's a ~ of opinion!** c'est discutable!; **it is only a ~ of time** ce n'est qu'une question de temps; **it is only a ~ of time before the bridge collapses** le pont va s'écrouler, ce n'est qu'une question de temps

[d] (= importance) **no ~!** peu importe!, tant pis!; (liter) **what ~ (if ...)?** qu'importe (si ...)?; **(it is of) no ~ whether ...** peu importe si ...; **it is (of) no great ~** c'est peu de chose, cela n'a pas grande importance; **get one, no ~ how** débrouille-toi (comme tu peux) pour en trouver un; **it must be done, no ~ how** cela doit être fait par n'importe quel moyen; **ring me no ~ how late** téléphonez-moi même tard or à n'importe quelle heure; **no ~ how you use it** peu importe comment vous l'utilisez; **no ~ when he comes** quelle que soit l'heure à laquelle il arrive; **no ~ how big it is** aussi grand qu'il soit; **no ~ what he says** quoi qu'il dise; **no ~ where/who** où/qui que ce soit

[e] (NonC = difficulty, problem) **what's the ~?** qu'est-ce qu'il y a?, qu'y a-t-il?; **what's the ~ with him?** qu'est-ce qu'il a?, qu'est-ce qui lui prend?; **what's the ~ with your hand?** qu'est-ce que vous avez à la main?; **what's the ~ with my hat?** qu'est-ce qu'il a, mon chapeau?; **what's the ~ with trying to help him?** quel inconvénient or quelle objection y a-t-il à ce qu'on l'aide (subj)?; **is anything the ~?** quelque chose ne va pas?; **there's something the ~ with my arm** j'ai quelque chose au bras; **there's something the ~ with the engine** il y a quelque chose qui ne va pas dans le moteur; **as if nothing was the ~** comme si de rien n'était; **nothing's the ~*** il n'y a rien; **there's nothing the ~ with me!** moi, je vais tout à fait bien!; **there's nothing the ~ with the car** la voiture marche très bien; **there's nothing the ~ with that idea** il n'y a rien à redire à cette idée

2 VI importer (**to** à); **it doesn't ~** ça n'a pas d'importance, ça ne fait rien; **it doesn't ~ whether ...** peu importe que ... (+ subj), cela ne fait rien si ...; **it doesn't ~ who/where** etc peu importe qui/où etc; (frm) **it ~s little** peu importe; **what does it ~?** qu'est-ce que cela peut faire?; **what does it ~ to you (if ...)?** qu'est-ce que cela peut bien vous faire (si ...)?; **why should it ~ to me?** pourquoi est-ce que cela me ferait quelque chose?; **some things ~ more than others** il y a des choses qui importent plus que d'autres; **nothing else ~s** le reste n'a aucune importance

3 COMP ► **matter-of-fact** ADJ → **matter-of-fact**

Matterhorn ['mætəhɔːn] N **the ~** le Cervin

matter-of-fact [ˌmætərəv'fækt] ADJ [tone, voice] neutre; [style] prosaïque; [attitude, person] terre à terre or terre-à-terre; [assessment, account] neutre, qui se limite aux faits

matter-of-factly [ˌmætərəv'fæktlɪ] ADV [say, explain] d'un ton neutre

Matthew ['mæθjuː] N Matthieu m

matting ['mætɪŋ] N (NonC) sparterie f, pièces fpl de natte → **rush²**

mattins ['mætɪnz] N = **matins**

mattock ['mætək] N pioche f

mattress ['mætrɪs] **1** N matelas m **2** COMP ► **mattress cover** N alèse f

maturation [ˌmætjʊə'reɪʃən] N maturation f

mature [mə'tjʊə^r] **1** ADJ [age, reflection, plan] mûr; [person] (gen) mûr; (Psych) mature; (euph = old) d'âge mûr; [wine] qui est arrivé à maturité; [cheese] fait; (Fin) [bill] échu; **he's got much more ~ since then** il a beaucoup mûri depuis **2** VT faire mûrir **3** VI [person] mûrir; [wine, cheese] se faire; (Fin) venir à échéance, échoir **4** COMP ► **mature student** N (gen) étudiant(e) m(f) plus âgé(e) que la moyenne; (Brit Admin) étudiant(e) m(f) de plus de 26 ans (ou de 21 ans dans certains cas)

maturely [mə'tjʊəlɪ] ADV [think, behave] en adulte

maturity [mə'tjʊərɪtɪ] N maturité f; (Fin) **date of ~** échéance f

matzo ['mɒtsə] **1** N pain m azyme **2** COMP ► **matzo balls** NPL boulettes fpl de pain azyme ► **matzo cracker** N cracker m de pain azyme ► **matzo meal** N farine f de pain azyme

maudlin ['mɔːdlɪn] ADJ larmoyant; **to get ~ about sth** devenir excessivement sentimental à propos de qch

maul [mɔːl] **1** VT **[a]** (= attack) [tiger etc] mutiler, lacérer; (fatally) déchiqueter **[b]** (= manhandle) malmener **[c]** (* = paw at: sexually) tripoter; **stop ~ing me!** arrête de me tripoter! **2** N (Rugby) maul m

mauling ['mɔːlɪŋ] N **to get a ~** [player, team] être battu à plate(s) couture(s); [author, book] être éreinté par la critique

maulstick ['mɔːlstɪk] N appuie-main m

maunder ['mɔːndə^r] VI (= talk) divaguer; (= move) errer; (= act) agir de façon incohérente

Maundy money [ˌmɔːndɪ'mʌnɪ] N (Brit) aumône f royale du jeudi saint

Maundy Thursday ['mɔːndɪ'θɜːzdɪ] N le jeudi saint

Mauritania [ˌmɔːrɪ'teɪnɪə] N la Mauritanie

Mauritanian [ˌmɔːrɪ'teɪnɪən] **1** ADJ mauritanien **2** N Mauritanien(ne) m(f)

Mauritian [mə'rɪʃən] **1** ADJ (gen) mauricien; [ambassador, embassy] de l'île Maurice **2** N Mauricien(ne) m(f)

Mauritius [mə'rɪʃəs] N (l'île f) Maurice f; **in ~** à (l'île) Maurice

mausoleum [ˌmɔːsə'lɪəm] N (pl **mausoleums** or **mausolea** [ˌmɔːsə'lɪə]) mausolée m

mauve [məʊv] ADJ, N mauve m

maverick ['mævərɪk] **1** N **[a]** (= unmarked calf) veau m non marqué **[b]** (fig = person) franc-tireur m (fig), indépendant(e) m(f) **2** ADJ dissident, non-conformiste

maw [mɔː] N (= mouth: lit, fig) gueule f

mawkish ['mɔːkɪʃ] ADJ (= sentimental) mièvre

mawkishness ['mɔːkɪʃnɪs] N [of film, poem] mièvrerie f

max [mæks] ABBR = **maximum** **1** ADV **a couple**

of weeks, ~: quinze jours, pas plus [2] N max
m; **to do sth to the ~:** faire qch à fond

maxi* ['mæksɪ] [1] N (= *coat/skirt*) (manteau m/
jupe f) maxi m [2] COMP ► **maxi single** N
disque m double durée

maxilla [mæk'sɪlə] N (pl **maxillae** mæk'sɪliː)
(Anat) maxillaire m

maxillary [mæk'sɪlərɪ] ADJ (Anat) maxillaire

maxim ['mæksɪm] N maxime f

maxima ['mæksɪmə] NPL of **maximum**

maximization [,mæksɪmaɪ'zeɪʃən] N maxima-
lisation f, maximisation f; ~ **of profits** maxi-
malisation or maximisation f des bénéfices

maximize ['mæksɪmaɪz] VT maximiser, porter
au maximum; **to ~ the advantages of sth** tirer
le maximum de qch

maximum ['mæksɪməm] [1] N (pl **maximums** or
maxima) maximum m; **a ~ of £8** un maximum de 8 livres, 8 livres au maximum; **at
the ~** au maximum; **to the ~** au maximum, à
fond [2] ADJ maximum; ~ **prices** prix mpl
maximums or maxima; ~ **security jail** or
prison prison f de haute sécurité → **security**
(Aut etc) ~ **speed** (= *highest permitted*) vitesse f
limite, vitesse f maximale autorisée; (=
highest possible) plafond m; (on truck) ~ **load**
charge f limite; ~ **temperatures** températures
fpl maximales [3] ADV (au) maximum; **twice
a week ~** deux fois par semaine (au) maximum

May [meɪ] [1] N mai m; (liter) **the merry month
of ~** le joli mois de mai → **September**
[2] COMP ► **May beetle, May bug** N hanneton m ► **May Day** N le Premier Mai (fête du
Travail) ► **May queen** N reine f de mai

▼ **may¹** [meɪ] MODAL AUX VB (pret, cond **might**)
[a] (indicating possibility) **he ~ arrive** il arrivera
peut-être; **he might arrive** il se peut qu'il arrive (subj), il pourrait arriver; **I said that he
might arrive** j'ai dit qu'il arriverait peut-être;
you ~ or might be making a big mistake tu fais
peut-être or tu es peut-être en train de faire
une grosse erreur; **might they have left already?** se peut-il qu'ils soient déjà partis?; **I
might have left it behind** il se peut que je l'aie
oublié, je l'ai peut-être bien oublié; **you
might have killed me!** tu aurais pu me tuer!; **I
might have known** j'aurais dû m'en douter;
that's as ~ be but ... ◊ **that ~ well be but ...**
peut-être bien or c'est bien possible mais ...;
as soon as ~ be aussitôt que possible; (frm) **be
that as it ~** quoi qu'il en soit; **one might well
ask whether ...** on est en droit de demander si
...; **what might your name be?** (abrupt) et vous,
comment vous appelez-vous?; (polite) puis-je
savoir votre nom?; **who might you be?** qui
êtes-vous sans indiscrétion?; **how old might
he be, I wonder?** je me demande quel âge il
peut bien avoir
[b] (indicating permission) ~ **I have a word with
you?** — **yes, you ~** puis-je vous parler un
instant? — mais oui or bien sûr; ~ **I help
you?** puis-je or est-ce que je peux vous
aider?; (in shop) vous désirez (quelque chose)?; **might I see it?** est-ce que je pourrais le
voir?, vous permettez que je le voie?; **might I
suggest that ...?** puis-je me permettre de
suggérer que ...?; **if I ~ say so** si je puis me
permettre; ~ **I tell her now?** — **you ~ or might
as well** est-ce que je peux le lui dire maintenant? — après tout pourquoi pas?; ~ **I sit
here?** vous permettez que je m'assoie ici?; ~
I? vous permettez?; **you ~ go now** (permission,
also polite order) vous pouvez partir; (to subordinate) vous pouvez disposer; **he said I
might leave** il a dit que je pouvais partir, il
m'a permis de partir
[c] (indicating suggestion: with "might" only) (polite) **you might try writing to him** tu pourrais
toujours lui écrire; **you might give me a lift
home if you've got time** tu pourrais peut-être
me ramener si tu as le temps; **mightn't it be
an idea to go and see him?** on ferait (or tu fe-

rais etc) peut-être bien d'aller le voir; (abrupt)
you might have told me you weren't coming!
tu aurais (tout de même) pu me prévenir que
tu ne viendrais pas!; **you might at least say
thank you** tu pourrais au moins dire merci
[d] (phrases) **one might as well say £5 million**
autant dire 5 millions de livres; **we might as
well not buy that newspaper at all since no
one ever reads it** je me demande bien
pourquoi nous achetons ce journal puisque
personne ne le lit; **I ~ or might as well tell you
all about it** après tout je peux bien vous le raconter, je ferais aussi bien de tout vous dire;
**you ~ or might as well leave now as wait any
longer** vous feriez aussi bien de partir tout de
suite plutôt que d'attendre encore; **they
might (just) as well not have gone** ils auraient
tout aussi bien pu ne pas y aller, ce n'était
pas la peine qu'ils y aillent; **she blushed, as
well she might!** elle a rougi, et pour cause!;
try as he might, he couldn't do it il a eu beau
essayer, il n'y est pas arrivé
[e] (frm or liter: subj use) ~ **God bless you!**
(que) Dieu vous bénisse!; ~ **he rest in peace**
qu'il repose (subj) en paix; **much good ~ it do
you!** grand bien vous fasse!; **O Lord, grant
that we ~ always obey** Seigneur, accorde-nous
or donne-nous de toujours obéir; **lest he ~ or
might be anxious** de crainte qu'il n'éprouve
(subj) de l'anxiété; **in order that they ~ or
might know** afin qu'ils sachent

may² [meɪ] [1] N (= *hawthorn*) aubépine f
[2] COMP [branch etc] d'aubépine ► **may tree**
N (Brit) aubépine f

Mayan ['maɪən] (in South America) [1] ADJ maya
[2] N [a] Maya mf [b] (Ling) maya m

▼ **maybe** ['meɪbiː] ADV peut-être; ~ **he'll be there**
peut-être qu'il sera là, il sera peut-être là; ~,
not peut-être que oui, peut-être que non;
that's as ~ peut-être bien

mayday ['meɪdeɪ] N SOS m

Mayfair ['meɪˈfeə] N (Brit) Mayfair (le quartier le
plus chic de Londres)

mayfly ['meɪflaɪ] N éphémère mf

mayhem ['meɪhem] N [a] (Jur††, also US) mutilation f du corps humain [b] (= *havoc*) grabuge* m; (= destruction) destruction f

mayn't [meɪnt] = **may not**; → **may¹**

mayo* ['meɪəʊ] N (US) ABBR = **mayonnaise**

mayonnaise [,meɪə'neɪz] N mayonnaise f

mayor ['meə] N maire m; **Mr/Madam Mayor**
Monsieur/Madame le maire → **lord**

mayoral ['meərəl] ADJ de (or du) maire; **the ~
residence/limousine** etc la résidence/
limousine etc du maire

mayoralty ['meərəltɪ] N mandat m de maire

mayoress ['meəres] N (esp Brit) [a] (= *female
mayor*) maire m [b] (= wife of mayor) femme f
du maire → **lady**

maypole ['meɪpəʊl] N mât m enrubanné

maze [meɪz] N labyrinthe m, dédale m; (fig) **a
~ of little streets** un labyrinthe or un dédale
de ruelles

mazuma* [mə'zuːmə] N (US = money) fric* m,
pognon* m

mazurka [mə'zɜːkə] N mazurka f

MB [em'biː] N [a] (Comput) (ABBR = **megabyte**)
Mo [b] (Brit Univ) (ABBR = **Bachelor of Medicine**) diplôme de médecine

MBA ['embiː'eɪ] N (Univ) (ABBR = **Master of Business Administration**) mastère de gestion

MBBS, MBChB (Univ) (ABBR = **Bachelor of
Medicine and Surgery**) diplôme de chirurgie

MBE [,embiː'iː] N (Brit) (ABBR = **Member of the
Order of the British Empire**) titre honorifique →
HONOURS LIST

MBO [,embiː'əʊ] N (Fin) (ABBR = **management
buyout**) RES m

MC [em'siː] N [a] (ABBR = **Master of Ceremonies**)
→ **master** [b] (US) (ABBR = **Member of**

Congress) → **member** [c] (Brit Mil) (ABBR = **Military Cross**) ≈ Croix f de la valeur militaire

MCAT N (US Univ) (ABBR = **Medical College Admissions Test**) → **medical**

McCarthyism [mə'kɑːθɪˌɪzəm] N (US Pol: gen
pej) maccarthysme m

MCP* [,emsiː'piː] N (ABBR = **male chauvinist pig**)
→ **chauvinist**

MD [em'diː] N [a] (Univ) (ABBR = **Doctor of Medicine**) → **medicine** [b] (US) **the MD*** le médecin
[c] (Brit) (ABBR = **Managing Director**) PDG m
[d] ABBR = **Maryland**

Md. ABBR = **Maryland**

MDT [,emdiː'tiː] (US) (ABBR = **Mountain Daylight
Time**) → **mountain**

ME [,em'iː] N [a] (Med) (ABBR = **myalgic encephalomyelitis**) SFC m, syndrome m de la fatigue chronique, encéphalomyélite f myalgique [b] ABBR = **Maine**

me¹ [miː] PERS PRON [a] (direct) (unstressed) me;
(before vowel) m'; (stressed) moi; **he can see
me** il me voit; **he saw me** il m'a vu; **you don't
like jazz? Me, I love it*** tu n'aimes pas le jazz?
Moi, j'adore [b] (indirect) me, moi; (before
vowel) m'; **he gave me the book** il me donna
or m'a donné le livre; **give it to me** donnez-
le-moi; **he was speaking to me** il me parlait
[c] (after prep etc) moi; **without me** sans moi;
I'll take it with me je l'emporterai avec moi;
it's me c'est moi; **it's me he's speaking to** c'est
à moi qu'il parle; **you're smaller than me** tu es
plus petit que moi; **if you were me** à ma place; **poor (little) me!** pauvre de moi!; **dear
me!*** mon Dieu!, oh là là!*

me² [miː] N (Mus) mi m

Me. ABBR = **Maine**

mead¹ [miːd] N (= *drink*) hydromel m

mead² [miːd] N (liter = *meadow*) pré m, prairie f

meadow ['medəʊ] N pré m, prairie f → **water**

meadowlark ['medəʊlɑːk] N sturnelle f

meadowsweet ['medəʊswiːt] N reine f des
prés

meagre, meager (US) ['miːgə] ADJ maigre
(before n); **he eked out a ~ existence (as a labourer)** il gagnait péniblement sa vie (en tant
qu'ouvrier); **his salary is a ~ £350 a month** il
gagne un salaire de misère: 350 livres par
mois

meal¹ [miːl] [1] N repas m; **to have a ~** prendre
un repas, manger; **to have** or **get a good ~**
bien manger; **to have one ~ a day** manger
une fois par jour; **we had a ~ at the Sea Crest
Hotel** nous avons déjeuné (or dîné) au Sea
Crest Hotel; **midday ~** déjeuner m; **evening ~**
dîner m; **that was a lovely ~!** nous avons très
bien déjeuné (or dîné)!; **he made a ~ of bread
and cheese** il a déjeuné (or dîné) de pain et
de fromage; (fig) **to make a ~ of sth*** faire tout
un plat de qch* → **square** [2] COMP ► **meals
on wheels** NPL repas livrés à domicile aux
personnes âgées ou handicapées ► **meal ticket**
N (lit) ticket-repas m, coupon-repas m; (* fig)
(= job) gagne-pain m inv; (= person) **(don't forget) she's your ~ ticket** (n'oublie pas que)
sans elle tu crèverais de faim

meal² [miːl] N (NonC = *flour etc*) farine f (d'avoine, de seigle, de maïs etc) → **oatmeal,
wheatmeal**

mealie meal ['miːlɪmiːl] N (in South Africa) farine f de maïs, maïzena® f

mealies ['miːlɪz] NPL maïs m

mealtime ['miːltaɪm] N heure f du repas; **at ~s**
aux heures des repas

mealworm ['miːlwɜːm] N ver m de farine

mealy ['miːlɪ] [1] ADJ [substance, mixture, texture, potato] farineux; [complexion] blême
[2] COMP ► **mealy-mouthed** ADJ **to be ~-
mouthed** ne pas s'exprimer franchement,
tourner autour du pot*

▼ **mean¹** [miːn] (pret, ptp **meant**) VT [a] (= *signify*)
vouloir dire, signifier; (= *imply*) vouloir dire;

➤ LANGUAGE IN USE: **may** 9.1, 15.3   **maybe** 15.3   **mean** 26.3

what does "media" ~? ◊ what is meant by "media"? que veut dire or que signifie « media » ?; "homely" ~s something different in America « homely » a un sens différent en Amérique; what do you ~ (by that)? que voulez-vous dire (par là)?, qu'entendez-vous par là?; is he honest? — how or what do you ~, honest? est-il honnête? — que voulez-vous dire or qu'entendez-vous par « honnête » ?; see what I ~?* tu vois ce que je veux dire?; this is John, I ~ Jim voici John, pardon (je veux dire) Jim; the name ~s nothing to me ce nom ne me dit rien; the play didn't ~ a thing to her la pièce n'avait aucun sens pour elle; what does this ~? qu'est-ce que cela signifie or veut dire?; it ~s he won't be coming cela veut dire qu'il ne viendra pas; this ~s war c'est la guerre à coup sûr; it ~s trouble cela nous annonce des ennuis; it will ~ a lot of expense cela entraînera beaucoup de dépenses; catching the train ~s getting up early pour avoir ce train il faut se lever tôt; a pound ~s a lot to him une livre représente une grosse somme pour lui; holidays don't ~ much to me les vacances comptent peu pour moi; I can't tell you what your gift has meant to me! je ne saurais vous dire à quel point votre cadeau m'a touché!; don't I ~ anything to you at all? je ne suis donc rien pour toi?; you ~ everything to me, darling tu es tout pour moi, mon amour; what it ~s to be free! quelle belle chose que la liberté!; money doesn't ~ happiness l'argent ne fait pas le bonheur; (= fully intend) you don't really ~ that? vous n'êtes pas sérieux?, vous plaisantez?; I really ~ it je ne plaisante pas, je suis sérieux; he said it as if he meant it il a dit cela d'un air sérieux or sans avoir l'air de plaisanter; I always ~ what I say quand je dis quelque chose c'est que je le pense; (as conversational filler) I ~, it's not difficult* après tout, ce n'est pas difficile → know 1, world 1b
[b] (= intend, purpose) avoir l'intention (to do de faire), compter (to do faire); (= intend, destine) [+ gift etc] destiner (for à); [+ remark] adresser (for à); I meant to come yesterday j'avais l'intention de or je comptais venir hier; what does he ~ to do now? qu'a-t-il l'intention de faire maintenant?, que compte-t-il faire maintenant?; I didn't ~ to break it je n'ai pas fait exprès de le casser, je ne l'ai pas cassé exprès; I didn't ~ to! je ne l'ai pas fait exprès!; I touched it without ~ing to je l'ai touché sans le vouloir; I ~ to succeed j'ai bien l'intention de réussir; despite what he says I ~ to go je partirai quoi qu'il dise; I ~ you to leave ◊ I ~ for you to leave (US) je veux que vous partiez (subj); I'm sure he didn't ~ it je suis sûr que ce n'était pas intentionnel or délibéré; he didn't ~ anything by it il l'a fait (or dit) sans penser à mal; I meant it as a joke j'ai dit (or fait) cela par plaisanterie or pour rire; we were meant to arrive at six nous étions censés arriver or nous devions arriver à six heures; she ~s well ce qu'elle fait (or dit etc) part d'un bon sentiment, elle est pleine de bonnes intentions; he ~s trouble* il cherche la bagarre; he looks as if he ~s trouble* il a une mine qui n'annonce rien qui vaille or de bon; do you ~ me? (= are you speaking to me) c'est à moi que vous parlez?; (= are you speaking about me) c'est de moi que vous parlez?; he meant you when he said ... c'est vous qu'il visait or c'est à vous qu'il faisait allusion lorsqu'il disait ...; I meant the book for Douglas je destinais le livre à Douglas; that book is meant for children ce livre est destiné aux enfants or s'adresse aux enfants; perhaps you're not meant to be a doctor peut-être n'êtes-vous pas fait pour être médecin; it was meant to be le destin en avait décidé ainsi; this cupboard was never meant to be or meant for a larder ce placard n'a jamais été conçu pour servir de garde-manger or n'a jamais été censé être un garde-manger; this portrait is meant to be Anne ce portrait est censé être

celui d'Anne or représenter Anne → business, harm, offence
[c] (modal usage in passive) it's meant to be good (= considered to be) on dit que c'est bien; (= supposed to be) c'est censé être bien

mean² [miːn] [1] N (= middle term) milieu m, moyen terme m; (Math) moyenne f; the golden or happy ~ le juste milieu → geometric(al), means [2] ADJ (= average) [distance, temperature, price] moyen; (Phys) ~ life vie f moyenne

mean³ [miːn] [1] ADJ [a] (Brit = stingy) avare, mesquin; ~ with one's time/money avare de son temps/argent; don't be so ~! ne sois pas si radin!*
[b] (= unpleasant, unkind) [person, behaviour] mesquin, méchant; a ~ trick un sale tour, une crasse*; you ~ thing!* chameau!*; (to a child) méchant!; you were ~ to me tu n'as vraiment pas été chic* or sympa* avec moi; that was ~ of them c'était bien mesquin de leur part, ce n'était pas chic* de leur part; to feel ~ about sth avoir un peu honte de qch, ne pas être très fier de qch
[c] (US* = vicious) [horse, dog etc] méchant, vicieux
[d] (= inferior, poor) [appearance, existence] misérable, minable; the ~est citizen le dernier des citoyens; the ~est intelligence l'esprit le plus borné; he is no ~ scholar c'est un grand savant; he's no ~ singer c'est un chanteur de talent; it was no ~ feat cela a été un véritable exploit, ce n'a pas été un mince exploit; to have no ~ opinion of o.s. avoir une (très) haute opinion de soi-même
[e] (‡ = excellent) super*; she plays a ~ game of tennis elle joue super* bien au tennis
[2] COMP ► mean-spirited ADJ mesquin ► mean-spiritedness N mesquinerie f

meander [mɪˈændə] [1] VI [a] [river] faire des méandres, serpenter [b] [person] (= aimlessly) errer, vagabonder; (= leisurely) flâner [2] N méandre m

meandering [mɪˈændərɪŋ] ADJ [a] (= winding) [river, stream, road, path, route] sinueux [b] (pej = rambling) [speech, account, article] plein de méandres

meanie* [ˈmiːnɪ] N [a] (Brit = stingy person) radin(e)* m(f), pingre m [b] (US = unpleasant person) sale type m, mégère f

meaning [ˈmiːnɪŋ] [1] N [of word] sens m, signification f; [of phrase, action] signification f; (Ling) signification f; with a double ~ à double sens; literal ~ sens m propre or littéral; what is the ~ of this word? quel est le sens de ce mot?, que signifie ce mot?; (fig) he doesn't know the ~ of the word "fear" il ne sait pas ce que le mot « peur » veut dire, il ignore le sens du mot « peur »; she doesn't know the ~ of love/kindness elle ne sait pas ce qu'est l'amour/la gentillesse; (in anger, disapproval etc) what is the ~ of this? qu'est-ce que cela signifie?; (Jur) within the ~ of this Act au sens de la présente loi; ... if you get my ~* ... vous voyez ce que je veux dire?; look/gesture full of ~ regard m/geste m éloquent; "really?" he said with ~ son « vraiment ? » était éloquent
[2] ADJ [look etc] éloquent, expressif → well²

meaningful [ˈmiːnɪŋfʊl] ADJ [a] (= worthwhile) [relationship, discussion, dialogue] sérieux; [experience] riche; [role] important; (= contribution) important, significatif; a ~ life une vie qui a (or avait) un sens [b] (= comprehensible, not spurious) [response, results, statement, gesture] significatif; [explanation] sensé [c] (= eloquent) [look, glance, smile] éloquent [d] (Ling) [phrase] sémantique

meaningfully [ˈmiːnɪŋfʊlɪ] ADV [a] (= eloquently, pointedly) [say] d'un ton qui en dit (or disait) long; he looked/smiled at her ~ il lui jeta un regard éloquent/fit un sourire qui en disait long [b] (= usefully) [participate, spend

time] utilement [c] (= comprehensibly) [explain] clairement

meaningless [ˈmiːnɪŋlɪs] ADJ [a] (= without meaning) [words, song, action, gesture] dénué de sens; [distinction] insignifiant; to be ~ (to sb) ne pas avoir de sens (pour qn), ne rien vouloir dire (pour qn) [b] (= futile) [life, existence, victory] futile, vain; [waste, suffering] insensé

meanly [ˈmiːnlɪ] ADV [a] (= spitefully) méchamment [b] (= stingily) mesquinement

meanness [ˈmiːnnɪs] N [a] (= stinginess) [of person] avarice f [b] (= unkindness) [of person] méchanceté f; ~ of spirit mesquinerie f [c] (US = viciousness) [of animal] comportement m sauvage [d] (= wretchedness) [of place] misère f

means [miːnz] [1] N [a] (= method, way) moyen(s) m(pl); to find the ~ to do or of doing trouver le(s) moyen(s) de faire; to find (a) ~ of doing trouver moyen de faire; the only ~ of contacting him is ... le seul moyen de le joindre, c'est ...; there's no ~ of getting in il n'y a pas moyen d'entrer; the ~ to an end le moyen d'arriver à ses fins; by illegal/political/military ~ par des moyens illégaux/politiques/militaires; (Rel) the ~ of salvation les voies fpl du salut; come in by all ~! je vous en prie, entrez!; by all ~! (= of course) mais certainement!, bien sûr!; read them if you like, by all ~ vous pouvez les lire si vous voulez; by all ~ consult your physician about this vous pouvez en parler à votre médecin si vous voulez; by all manner of ~ par tous les moyens; the military collapse is not imminent by any ~ la débâcle militaire est loin d'être imminente; I'm not a country person by any (manner of) ~ je ne suis vraiment pas attiré par la (vie à la) campagne; I don't think we're leading the field by any (manner of) ~ je suis loin de penser que nous sommes les leaders dans ce domaine; by no ~ nullement, pas le moins du monde; she is by no ~ stupid elle est loin d'être stupide; they were by no ~ the poorest residents of their neighbourhood ils étaient loin d'être les plus pauvres de leur quartier; by some ~ or (an)other d'une façon ou d'une autre; by this ~ de cette façon → fair¹
[b] by ~ of ... (gen) au moyen de ...; by ~ of a penknife/binoculars au moyen d'un or à l'aide d'un canif/au moyen de or à l'aide de jumelles; by ~ of the telephone/a ballot par le moyen du téléphone/du scrutin; he taught English by ~ of play il enseignait l'anglais par le jeu or par le biais du jeu; by ~ of hard work à force de travail
[c] (= wealth) moyens mpl, ressources fpl; he is a man of ~ il a une belle fortune or de gros moyens*; to live within/beyond one's ~ vivre selon ses moyens/au-dessus de ses moyens; to have private ~ avoir une fortune personnelle; slender ~ ressources fpl très modestes
[2] COMP ► means test N (Admin) examen m des ressources (d'une personne qui demande une aide pécuniaire) ► means-test VT (Admin) to ~-test sb examiner les ressources de qn (avant d'accorder certaines prestations sociales); the grant is not ~-tested cette allocation ne dépend pas des ressources familiales (or personnelles)

meant [ment] VB pt, ptp of mean¹

meantime [ˈmiːntaɪm], **meanwhile** [ˈmiːnwaɪl] ADV (in the) ~ en attendant, pendant ce temps, dans l'intervalle

meany* [ˈmiːnɪ] N = meanie

measles [ˈmiːzlz] N rougeole f → German

measly* [ˈmiːzlɪ] ADJ misérable; a ~ £5! 5 misérables livres!

measurable [ˈmeʒərəbl] ADJ mesurable

measure [ˈmeʒə] [1] N [a] (= system, unit) mesure f; (fig) mesure f; [of alcohol] dose f; to give good or full ~ faire bonne mesure or bon poids; **to give short ~** voler or rogner sur la quantité; (*fig*) **for good ~** pour faire bonne mesure; **suit made to ~** complet *m* fait sur mesure; **liquid ~** mesure *f* de capacité pour les liquides; **a pint ~** ≈ une mesure d'un demi-litre; **happiness beyond ~** bonheur *m* sans bornes; **in some ~** dans une certaine mesure, jusqu'à un certain point; **in great** or **large ~** dans une large mesure, en grande partie; **the audience laughed and cried in equal ~** le public a ri autant qu'il a pleuré; (*fig*) **to take the ~ of sth** évaluer qch; **I've got his ~**† je sais ce qu'il vaut; **it had a ~ of success** cela a eu un certain succès

[b] (*sth for measuring*) (= *ruler*) règle *f*; (*folding*) mètre *m* pliant; (= *tape*) (*steel*) mètre *m* à ruban; (*fabric*) centimètre *m*; (= *jug, glass*) verre *m* gradué or mesureur; (= *post*) toise *f*; (*fig*) **to be the ~ of sth** donner la mesure de qch; (*fig*) **this exam is just a ~ of how you're getting on** cet examen sert simplement à évaluer votre progression → **tape**

[c] (= *step*) mesure *f*, démarche *f*; (*Parl*) (= *bill*) projet *m* de loi; (= *act*) loi *f*; **strong/drastic ~s** mesures *fpl* énergiques/draconiennes; **precautionary/preventive ~s** mesures *fpl* de précaution/de prévention; **temporary** or **interim ~s** mesures *fpl* temporaires or provisoires; **to take ~s against** prendre des mesures contre; **~s aimed at building confidence between states** des mesures *fpl* visant à créer un climat de confiance entre États

[d] (*Mus, Poetry etc*) mesure *f*

[2] VT (*lit*) [+ *child, length, time*] mesurer; (*fig*) [+ *strength, courage*] mesurer; [+ *success, performance*] évaluer, juger; **to ~ the height of sth** mesurer or prendre la hauteur de qch; **to be ~d for a dress** faire prendre ses mesures pour une robe; **what does it ~?** quelles sont ses dimensions?; **the room ~s 4 metres across** la pièce fait or mesure 4 mètres de large; **the carpet ~s 3 metres by 2** le tapis fait or mesure 3 mètres sur 2; (*fig*) **to be ~d against** être comparé avec or à; (*fig*) **to ~ one's strength against sb** se mesurer à qn → **length**

► **measure off** VT SEP [+ *lengths of fabric etc*] mesurer

► **measure out** VT SEP [a] [+ *ingredients, piece of ground*] mesurer [b] (= *issue*) distribuer

► **measure up** [1] VT SEP [+ *wood*] mesurer; (*fig*) [+ *sb's intentions*] jauger; [+ *person*] évaluer, jauger [2] VI (*fig*) [*person*] être à la hauteur

► **measure up to** VT FUS [+ *task*] être au niveau de, être à la hauteur de; [+ *person*] être l'égal de

measured ['meʒəd] ADJ [a] [*amount, dose, distance, time*] mesuré; **over a ~ kilometre** sur un kilomètre exactement [b] (= *even, calm*) [*look, gaze*] posé; [*pace, words, language, statement*] modéré, mesuré; **to make a ~ response to sth** réagir de façon modérée à qch; **with ~ steps** à pas comptés or mesurés; **to speak in ~ tones** parler d'un ton mesuré

measureless ['meʒəlɪs] ADJ (*liter*) incommensurable

measurement ['meʒəmənt] N [a] (= *dimension: gen pl*) **~s** mesures *fpl*, dimensions *fpl*; [*of piece of furniture etc*] encombrement *m* au sol; **to take the ~s of a room** prendre les mesures d'une pièce; **what are your ~s?** quelles sont vos mesures? [b] (*NonC* = *activity*) mesurage *m* [c] (*Comm*) [*of freight*] cubage *m*; **to pay by ~ for freight** payer la cargaison au cubage

measuring ['meʒərɪŋ] [1] N (*NonC*) mesurage *m*, mesure *f* [2] COMP ► **measuring chain** N chaîne *f* d'arpenteur ► **measuring device** N appareil *m* de mesure or de contrôle ► **measuring glass** N verre *m* gradué or mesureur ► **measuring jug** N pot *m* gradué ► **measuring rod** N règle *f*, mètre *m* ► **measuring spoon** N cuiller *f* à mesurer

► **measuring tape** N (*fabric*) centimètre *m*; (*steel*) mètre *m* (à) ruban

meat [mi:t] [1] N [a] (= *fresh*) viande *f*; (†† = *food*) nourriture *f*, aliment *m*; **cold ~** viande *f* froide; **cold ~ platter** assiette *f* anglaise; **~ and two veg*** de la viande avec des pommes de terre et un légume; **remove the ~ from the bone** ôter la chair de l'os; (*lit*) **~ and drink** de quoi manger et boire; (*fig*) **this is ~ and drink to them** c'est une aubaine pour eux; (*US fig*) **that's my ~!**‡ ça me botte vachement!‡ ■ (*PROV*) **one man's ~ is another man's poison** le malheur des uns fait le bonheur des autres (*PROV*)

[b] (*fig*) substance *f*; **there's not much ~ in his book** son livre n'a pas beaucoup de substance

[2] COMP ► **meat ax** N (*US*) = **meat axe** ► **meat axe** N couperet *m* ► **meat cleaver** N = **meat axe** ► **meat diet** N régime *m* carné ► **meat-eater** N (= *animal*) carnivore *m*; **he's a big ~-eater** c'est un gros mangeur de viande ► **meat-eating** ADJ carnivore ► **meat extract** N concentré *m* de viande ► **meat hook** N crochet *m* de boucherie, allonge *f* ► **meat loaf** N pain *m* de viande ► **meat market** N [a] (*for animals*) halle *f* aux viandes [b] (* *pej: for people*) lieu *m* de drague* ► **meat pie** N (sorte *f* de) pâté *m* en croûte ► **meat products** NPL produits *mpl* carnés ► **meat safe** N (*Brit*) garde-manger *m inv*

meatball ['mi:tbɔ:l] N boulette *f* de viande

meathead‡ ['mi:thed] N (*US*) andouille‡ *f*

meatless ['mi:tlɪs] ADJ sans viande

meatpacker ['mi:tpækə'] N (*US Comm*) ouvrier *m*, -ière *f* d'abattoir

meatpacking ['mi:tpækɪŋ] N (*US Comm*) abattage *m*

meatus [mɪ'eɪtəs] N (*pl* **meatus** or **meatuses**) (*Anat*) conduit *m*, méat *m*

meaty ['mi:tɪ] ADJ [a] (= *like meat*) [*flavour*] de viande; [*soup*] plein de viande; **a ~ sauce** une sauce qui contient beaucoup de viande; **to have a ~ texture** avoir la consistance de la viande; **shark is a ~ fish** la chair du requin ressemble à de la viande [b] (* = *containing meat, meat-based*) [*diet*] carné; [*sauce, stock*] à base de viande; **nothing ~ for me, thanks** pas de viande pour moi, merci [c] (= *fleshy*) [*hands*] épais (-aisse *f*); [*arms, legs*] gros (grosse *f*) (*before n*); [*lips*] charnu [d] (* = *satisfying, chewy*) **~ chunks** gros morceaux *mpl*; **a nice ~ steak** un bon steak bien épais; **a ~ wine** un vin qui a du corps [e] (* = *substantial*) [*story, report, book*] où il y a de quoi lire; [*role*] substantiel

Mecca ['mekə] N (*Geog*) La Mecque; (*fig*) **a ~ for Japanese tourists** la Mecque des touristes japonais

Meccano® [mɪ'kɑ:nəʊ] N (*Brit*) Meccano® *m*

mechanic [mɪ'kænɪk] N mécanicien *m*; **motor ~** mécanicien *m* garagiste

mechanical [mɪ'kænɪkəl] [1] ADJ [a] [*device, means, problem, process*] mécanique; **a ~ failure** une panne (mécanique) [b] (= *mechanically minded*) **to be ~** avoir le sens de la mécanique [c] (= *unthinking*) [*behaviour, action, reply*] machinal, mécanique [d] (= *stilted*) [*style, painting*] qui manque de naturel; **his dancing is ~** il danse d'une manière guindée [2] COMP ► **mechanical digger** N pelleteuse *f*, pelle *f* mécanique ► **mechanical drawing** N dessin *m* à l'échelle ► **mechanical engineer** N ingénieur *m* mécanicien ► **mechanical engineering** N (= *theory*) mécanique *f*; (= *practice*) construction *f* mécanique ► **mechanical shovel** N pelle *f* mécanique

mechanically [mɪ'kænɪkəlɪ] ADV [a] [*operate, work, harvest*] mécaniquement; **to be ~ minded** or **inclined** avoir le sens de la mécanique [b] (= *unthinkingly*) [*eat, drink, say, reply,*

shake hands] machinalement, mécaniquement

mechanics [mɪ'kænɪks] [1] N (*NonC* = *science*) mécanique *f* [2] NPL [a] (= *technical aspect*) mécanisme *m*, processus *m*; (= *mechanism, working parts*) mécanisme *m*, mécanique *f*; (*fig*) **the ~ of running an office** le processus or l'aspect *m* pratique de la gestion d'un bureau; **the ~ of government** les mécanismes *mpl* du gouvernement

mechanism ['mekənɪzəm] N (*all senses*) mécanisme *m*; **defence ~** mécanisme *m* de défense → **safety**

mechanistic [ˌmekə'nɪstɪk] ADJ mécaniste

mechanization [ˌmekənaɪ'zeɪʃən] N mécanisation *f*

mechanize ['mekənaɪz] VT [+ *process, production*] mécaniser; [+ *army*] motoriser; **~d industry** industrie *f* mécanisée; **~d troops** troupes *fpl* motorisées

MEd [em'ed] N (*Univ*) (ABBR = **Master of Education**) ≈ CAPES *m*

Med* [med] N (ABBR = **Mediterranean Sea**) **the ~** la Méditerranée [b] (= *region*) région *f* méditerranéenne

med. ADJ ABBR = **medium**

medal ['medl] N (*Mil, Sport, gen*) médaille *f*; **swimming/athletics ~** médaille *f* de natation/d'athlétisme; (*in US*) (**Congressional) Medal of Honor** Médaille *f* d'honneur (*la plus haute décoration militaire*)

medalist ['medəlɪst] N (*US*) = **medallist**

medallion [mɪ'dælɪən] N (*gen, Archit*) médaillon *m*

medallist, medalist (*US*) ['medəlɪst] N **he's a gold/silver ~** il a eu la médaille d'or/d'argent; **the three ~s on the podium** les trois médaillés *mpl* or vainqueurs *mpl* sur le podium

meddle ['medl] VI [a] (= *interfere*) se mêler, s'occuper (**in** de), s'ingérer (*frm*) (**in** dans); **stop meddling!** cesse de t'occuper or de te mêler de ce qui ne te regarde pas! [b] (= *tamper*) toucher (**with** à)

meddler ['medlə'] N [a] (= *busybody*) **he's a compulsive ~** il faut toujours qu'il fourre son nez partout [b] (*touching things*) touche-à-tout *m inv*

meddlesome ['medlsəm], **meddling** ['medlɪŋ] ADJ (*pej*) [*person*] qui fourre son nez partout

medevac ['medɪˌvæk] N (= *helicopter*) hélicoptère *m* sanitaire de l'armée

media ['mi:dɪə] [1] NPL of **medium the ~** les médias *mpl*; **the ~ is state-controlled** les médias sont étatisés; **the ~ has welcomed her visit** les médias ont salué sa visite; **the government's restrictions on the ~** les restrictions que le gouvernement a imposées aux médias; **they issued a statement to the ~** ils ont fait une déclaration à l'intention des journalistes qui attendaient à l'extérieur

[2] COMP [*attention, reaction*] des médias; [*event, coverage*] médiatique ► **media circus*** N (*pej* = *event*) cirque *m* médiatique ► **media man** N (*pl* **media men**) (*Press, Rad, TV*) journaliste *m*, reporter *m*; (*Advertising*) publicitaire *m* ► **media person** N (*Press, Rad, TV*) journaliste *mf*; (*Advertising*) publicitaire *mf* ► **media-shy** ADJ qui n'aime pas être interviewé ► **media star** N vedette *f* des médias ► **media studies** NPL (*Univ etc*) études *fpl* de communication

mediaeval *etc* [ˌmedɪ'i:vəl] = **medieval**

medial ['mi:dɪəl] [1] ADJ [a] (= *middle*) (*gen*) médian; (*Phon*) médial, médian [b] (= *midpoint*) moyen [2] N (*Phon*) médiane *f*

median ['mi:dɪən] [1] ADJ (= *mid value*) médian; **~ income** revenu *m* médian [2] N [a] (*Math, Stat*) médiane *f* [b] (*US Aut: also ~ strip*) terre-plein *m* central [3] COMP ► **me-**

dian nerve N (*Anat*) nerf *m* médian ► **median strip** N (*US Aut*) terre-plein *m* central

mediant ['miːdɪənt] N médiante *f*

mediate ['miːdɪeɪt] [1] VI servir d'intermédiaire (**between** entre, **in** dans) [2] VT [a] (= *arbitrate*) [+ *peace, settlement*] obtenir par médiation ; [+ *dispute*] arbitrer [b] (*frm, lit* = *change*) modifier (légèrement)

mediating ['miːdɪeɪtɪŋ] ADJ médiateur (-trice *f*)

mediation [ˌmiːdɪ'eɪʃən] N médiation *f* ; **through the ~ of sb** par l'entremise *f* de qn

mediator ['miːdɪeɪtəʳ] N médiateur *m*, -trice *f*

Medibank ['medɪbæŋk] N (*Austral*) Sécurité sociale australienne

medic* ['medɪk] N (ABBR = **medical**) (= *student*) carabin* *m* ; (= *doctor*) toubib* *m*

Medicaid® ['medɪˌkeɪd] N (*US Med*) Medicaid *m*

┌─────────────────────────┐
│ **MEDICAID, MEDICARE** │
└─────────────────────────┘

Medicaid *est un organisme américain, administré conjointement par le gouvernement fédéral et par les États, qui prend en charge les traitements hospitaliers et les soins médicaux des personnes de moins de 65 ans vivant en dessous du seuil de pauvreté officiel. Les critères pour bénéficier de ces soins gratuits varient selon les États.*

    Medicare *est un régime d'assurance maladie, financé par le gouvernement fédéral, qui prend en charge une partie des coûts d'hospitalisation et de traitement des personnes âgées de plus de 65 ans, des insuffisants rénaux et de certains handicapés. Les bénéficiaires de ce régime paient une cotisation mensuelle et doivent se faire soigner dans certains hôpitaux et par certains médecins agréés. Il existe parallèlement une assurance complémentaire privée appelée « Medigap ». Toute personne non couverte par* **Medicare** *ou* **Medicaid** *doit prendre en charge personnellement ses soins de santé par le biais d'une assurance maladie privée.*

medical ['medɪkəl] [1] ADJ [*subject, certificate, treatment*] médical [2] N (*also* ~ **examination**) (*in hospital, school, army etc*) visite *f* médicale ; (*private*) examen *m* médical [3] COMP ► **medical board** N commission *f* médicale, conseil *m* de santé ; (*Mil*) conseil *m* de révision ► **medical care** N soins *mpl* médicaux ► **Medical College Admissions Test** N (*US Univ*) examen d'entrée en faculté de médecine ► **medical doctor** N docteur *m* en médecine ► **medical examination** N = **medical 2** ► **medical examiner** N (*US Med*) médecin *m* légiste ► **medical history** N [a] [*of person*] (= *record*) dossier *m* médical ; (= *background*) antécédents *mpl* médicaux [b] (= *history of medicine*) histoire *f* de la médecine ► **medical insurance** N assurance *f* maladie ► **medical jurisprudence** N médecine *f* légale ► **medical librarian** N (*US*) bibliothécaire *mf* médical(e) ► **medical man*** N (*pl* **medical men**) médecin *m* ► **medical officer** N (*Ind*) médecin *m* du travail ; (*Mil*) médecin-major *m* (*or* -colonel *etc*) ► **Medical Officer of Health** N directeur *m* de la santé publique ► **medical practitioner** N médecin *m* (de médecine générale), généraliste *mf* ► **the medical profession** N (= *career*) la carrière médicale ; (= *personnel*) le corps médical ► **the Medical Research Council** N (*Brit*) organisme d'aide à la recherche médicale ► **medical school** N (*Univ*) école *f* or faculté *f* de médecine ► **medical social worker** N (*Brit*) assistant(e) *m(f)* social(e) (dans un hôpital) ► **medical student** N étudiant(e) *m(f)* en médecine ► **medical studies** NPL études *fpl* de médecine *or* médicales ► **medical technician** N technicien(ne) *m(f)* de laboratoire ► **medical unit** N service *m* de médeci-

ne générale ► **medical ward** N salle *f* de médecine générale

medically ['medɪkəlɪ] ADV [*treat*] médicalement ; [*prove, explain, recognize*] d'un point de vue médical ; **to examine sb ~** faire subir un examen médical à qn ; **to be ~ fit for sth** être en état de faire qch ; **to be ~ qualified** être diplômé en médecine ; **to be ~ safe** être sans danger pour la santé ; **to be ~ trained** avoir suivi une formation médicale

medicament [me'dɪkəmənt] N médicament *m*

Medicare® ['medɪkeəʳ] N (*US*) Medicare *m* → MEDICAID, MEDICARE

medicate ['medɪkeɪt] VT [+ *patient*] traiter avec des médicaments ; [+ *substance*] ajouter une substance médicinale à

medicated ['medɪkeɪtɪd] ADJ [*soap*] médical ; [*shampoo*] traitant ; **~ sweet** pastille *f* médicamenteuse

medication [ˌmedɪ'keɪʃən] N médication *f*

Medici ['medɪtʃɪ] NPL Médicis *mpl*

medicinal [me'dɪsɪnl] ADJ [*plant, herb, value*] médicinal ; [*property, quality*] thérapeutique ; **~ drug** médicament *m* ; (*lit*) **for ~ purposes** *or* **use** à des fins thérapeutiques ; **"~ use only"** « pour usage médical »

medicinally [me'dɪsɪnəlɪ] ADV [*use, prescribe*] comme médicament

medicine ['medsn, 'medɪsn] [1] N [a] (*NonC* = *science*) médecine *f* ; **to study ~** faire (sa) médecine ; (*Univ*) **Doctor of Medicine** docteur *m* en médecine → **forensic** [b] (= *drug etc*) médicament *m* ; **it's a very good ~ for colds** c'est un remède souverain contre les rhumes ; **to take one's ~** (*lit*) prendre son médicament ; (*fig*) avaler la pilule ; **let's give him a taste or dose of his own ~** on va lui rendre la monnaie de sa pièce → **patent** [2] COMP ► **medicine ball** N médecine-ball *m* ► **medicine box** N pharmacie *f* (portative) ► **medicine cabinet** N (armoire *f* à) pharmacie *f* ► **medicine chest** N (= *box*) pharmacie *f* (portative) ; (= *cupboard*) (armoire *f* à) pharmacie *f* ► **medicine cupboard** N = **medicine cabinet** ► **medicine man** N (*pl* **medicine men**) sorcier *m*

medico* ['medɪkəʊ] N = **medic**

medieval [ˌmedɪ'iːvəl] [1] ADJ [a] (*Hist*) [*period, building, town, streets, art, architecture, manuscript*] médiéval ; [*knight, lady, peasant*] du Moyen Âge ; [*atmosphere, charm*] moyenâgeux ; **~ Europe/England** l'Europe *f*/l'Angleterre *f* médiévale *or* du Moyen Âge ; **German literature** la littérature allemande médiévale ; **in ~ times** à l'époque médiévale [b] (*pej* = *primitive*) [*plumbing, facilities*] moyenâgeux (*pej*) [2] COMP ► **Medieval History** N histoire *f* médiévale ► **Medieval Latin** N latin *m* médiéval ► **medieval studies** NPL études *fpl* médiévales

medievalism [ˌmedɪ'iːvəlɪzəm] N médiévisme *m*

medievalist [ˌmedɪ'iːvəlɪst] N médiéviste *mf*

Medina [me'diːnə] N (*Geog, Rel*) Médine

mediocre [ˌmiːdɪ'əʊkəʳ] ADJ médiocre

mediocrity [ˌmiːdɪ'ɒkrɪtɪ] N médiocrité *f*

meditate ['medɪteɪt] [1] VT méditer (**sth** qch, **doing** de faire) [2] VI méditer (**on, about** sur), réfléchir (**on, about** à)

meditation [ˌmedɪ'teɪʃən] N méditation *f* (**on, about** sur) ; **the fruit of long ~** le fruit de longues méditations ; (*Literat, Rel etc*) **~s** méditations *fpl* (**on** sur)

meditative ['medɪtətɪv] ADJ [*person, mood, techniques, music*] méditatif ; [*exercises, state*] de méditation ; **the ~ calm of churches** le calme des églises qui incite à la méditation

meditatively ['medɪtətɪvlɪ] ADV d'un air méditatif

Mediterranean [ˌmedɪtə'reɪnɪən] [1] ADJ [*country, town, coast, culture, climate, diet, species*] méditerranéen ; [*island*] de la Méditerranée ; [*holiday*] au bord de la Méditerranée ; [*cruise*] en Méditerranée ; **the ~ Sea** la mer Méditerranée ; **~ people** les Méditerranéens *mpl* ; **the ~ type** le type méditerranéen [2] N **the ~** (= *sea*) la Méditerranée ; (= *region*) la région méditerranéenne

medium ['miːdɪəm] [1] N (*pl* **media**) [a] (*Bio, Chem, gen*) milieu *m* ; (*fig*) moyen *m*, véhicule *m* ; (*fig*) **through the ~ of the press** par voie de presse ; **advertising** ~ organe *m* de publicité ; **an artist's ~** (*painting, sculpture etc*) la discipline d'un artiste ; (*oils, bronze etc*) le matériau d'un artiste ; **language is the ~ of thought** le langage est le véhicule de la pensée ; **television is the best ~ for this type of humour** c'est à la télévision que ce genre d'humour passe le mieux, la télévision est le meilleur véhicule pour ce genre d'humour → **culture** [b] (= *mid-point*) milieu *m* ; **the happy ~** le juste milieu [c] (*pl* **mediums**) (*Spiritualism*) médium *m* [2] ADJ (*gen*) moyen ; [*pen*] à pointe moyenne ; (*on garment labels*) **"~"** « moyen » → **3** [3] COMP ► **medium close shot** N (*Cine*) plan *m* américain ► **medium-dry** ADJ [*wine, sherry, cider*] demi-sec ► **medium-fine pen** N stylo *m* or feutre *m* à pointe moyenne ► **medium-priced** ADJ à un (*or* des) prix intéressant(s) *or* raisonnable(s) ► **medium range missile** N missile *m* à moyenne portée ► **medium rare** ADJ (*of steaks*) à point ► **medium-sized** ADJ de grandeur *or* de taille moyenne ► **medium-sweet** ADJ [*wine, sherry, cider*] demi-doux ► **medium-term** ADJ à moyen terme ► **medium-wave** ADJ (*Rad*) sur ondes moyennes ; **on ~ wave** sur les ondes moyennes

mediumship ['miːdɪəmʃɪp] N médiumnité *f*

medlar ['medləʳ] N (= *fruit*) nèfle *f* ; (*also* ~ **tree**) néflier *m*

medley ['medlɪ] N mélange *m* ; (*Mus*) pot-pourri *m* ; (*Sport*) **400 metres ~** le 4 x 100 mètres quatre nages

medulla [me'dʌlə] N (*pl* **medullas** *or* **medullae** [me'dʌliː]) (*Anat*) moelle *f* ; (= *part of brain*) bulbe *m* rachidien

Medusa [mɪ'djuːzə] N Méduse *f*

meek [miːk] [1] ADJ [*person*] docile, bonasse (*pej*) ; [*voice*] doux (douce *f*) ; **~ and mild** doux et docile ; **as ~ as a lamb** doux comme un agneau [2] **the meek** NPL (*Bible*) les débonnaires *mpl*

meekly ['miːklɪ] ADV [*listen, accept, sit, stand*] docilement ; [*say*] humblement

meekness ['miːknɪs] N humilité *f*

meerschaum ['mɪəʃəm] N [a] (*NonC* = *clay*) écume *f* (de mer) [b] (= *pipe*) pipe *f* en écume (de mer)

meet¹ [miːt] (*pret, ptp* **met**) [1] VT [a] [+ *person*] (*by chance*) rencontrer, tomber sur ; (*coming in opposite direction*) croiser ; (*by arrangement*) retrouver ; (= *go to meet*) aller chercher ; (= *come to meet*) venir chercher ; **to arrange to ~ sb at 3 o'clock** donner rendez-vous à qn pour 3 heures ; **I am ~ing the chairman at the airport** je vais chercher le président à l'aéroport ; **I am being met at the airport** on doit venir me chercher à l'aéroport ; **I'll ~ you outside the cinema** je te *or* on se retrouve devant le cinéma ; **don't bother to ~ me** ne prenez pas la peine de venir me chercher ; **he went to ~ them** il est allé à leur rencontre, il est allé audevant d'eux ; **she came down the steps to ~ me** elle a descendu les escaliers et est venue à ma rencontre, elle a descendu les escaliers pour venir à ma rencontre ; **candidates will be required to ~ the committee** les candidats devront se présenter devant les membres du comité → **halfway, match²**

b [+ *river, sea*] rencontrer; **the bus for Aix ~s the 10 o'clock train** l'autobus d'Aix assure la correspondance avec le train de 10 heures; **a car met his train at King's Cross** une voiture l'attendait à l'arrivée de son train en gare de King's Cross; **I'm due back at 10 o'clock, can you be there to ~ my plane?** mon avion doit arriver à 10 heures, peux-tu venir me chercher à l'aéroport?

c (= *make acquaintance of*) rencontrer, faire la connaissance de; **~ Mr Martin** je vous présente M. Martin; **I am very pleased to ~ you** enchanté de faire votre connaissance; **glad** *or* **pleased to ~ you!** enchanté!

d (= *encounter*) [+ *opponent, opposing team, obstacle*] rencontrer; (= *face*) [+ *enemy, danger*] faire face à, affronter; (*in duel*) se battre avec; **he met his death** *or* **his end in 1880** il trouva la mort en 1880; **to ~ death calmly** affronter la mort avec calme *or* sérénité → **halfway**

e (= *satisfy, settle*) [+ *expenses, bill*] régler, payer; [+ *responsibilities, debt*] faire face à, s'acquitter de; [+ *deficit*] combler; [+ *goal, aim*] atteindre; [+ *demand, need, want*] satisfaire, répondre à; [+ *condition, stipulation*] remplir; [+ *charge, objection*] réfuter; (*Comm*) [+ *orders*] satisfaire, assurer; **to ~ the cost of sth** prendre en charge les frais de qch; **he offered to ~ the full cost of the repairs** il a proposé de payer la totalité des réparations; **this will ~ the case** ceci fera l'affaire; **to ~ payments** faire face à ses obligations financières; **to ~ the payments on a washing machine** payer les traites d'une machine à laver; **this ~s our requirements** cela correspond à nos besoins; **it did not ~ our expectations** nous n'en avons pas été satisfaits

f (*seeing, hearing*) **the sound which met his ears** le bruit qui frappa ses oreilles; **the sight which met my eye(s)** le spectacle qui s'offrit à mes yeux; **I met his eye** mon regard rencontra le sien, nos regards se croisèrent; **I dared not** *or* **couldn't ~ her eye** je n'osais pas la regarder en face; **there's more to this than ~s the eye** (*sth suspicious*) on ne voit pas ce on ne connaît pas les dessous de cette affaire; (*more difficult than it seems*) c'est moins simple que cela n'en a l'air

2 VI **a** [*people*] (*by chance*) se rencontrer; (*by arrangement*) se retrouver; (*more than once*) se voir; (= *become acquainted*) se rencontrer, faire connaissance; **to ~ again** se revoir; **until we ~ again!** au revoir!, à la prochaine fois!; **keep it until we ~ again** *or* **until we next ~** garde-le jusqu'à la prochaine fois; **have you met before?** vous vous connaissez déjà?; **they arranged to ~ at 10 o'clock** ils se sont donné rendez-vous pour 10 heures

b [*Parliament etc*] se réunir, tenir séance; [*committee, society etc*] se réunir; **the class ~s in the art room** le cours a lieu dans la salle de dessin

c [*armies*] se rencontrer, s'affronter; [*opposing teams*] se rencontrer

d [*lines, roads etc*] (= *join*) se rencontrer; (= *cross*) se croiser; [*rivers*] se rencontrer, confluer; **our eyes met** nos regards se croisèrent → **end**

3 N **a** (*Brit Hunting*) rendez-vous *m* de chasse (*au renard*); (= *huntsmen collectively*) chasse *f*

b (*Sport etc*) meeting *m*

▶**meet up** VI (*by chance*) se rencontrer; (*by arrangement*) se retrouver; **to ~ up with sb** (*by chance*) rencontrer qn; (*by arrangement*) retrouver qn; **this road ~s up with the motorway** cette route rejoint l'autoroute

▶**meet with** VT FUS **a** [+ *difficulties, resistance, obstacles*] rencontrer; [+ *refusal, losses, storm, gale*] essuyer; [+ *welcome, reception*] recevoir; **he met with an accident** il lui est arrivé un accident; **to ~ with failure** essuyer un (*or* des) échec(s); **to ~ with success** obtenir *or* remporter un (*or* des) succès; **this suggestion**

was met with angry protests de vives protestations ont accueilli cette suggestion; **this met with no response** (*in writing*) il n'y a pas eu de réponse; (*in person*) il (*or* elle) n'a pas réagi; (*frm*) **we hope our offer ~s with your approval** nous espérons que notre proposition vous conviendra **b** (*US*) [+ *person*] (*by chance*) rencontrer, tomber sur; (*coming in opposite direction*) croiser; (*by arrangement*) retrouver

meet²†† [miːt] ADJ (= *fitting*) convenable, séant†

meeting ['miːtɪŋ] **1** N **a** (*of group of people, political party, club etc*) réunion *f*; (*large, formal*) assemblée *f*; (*Pol, Sport*) meeting *m*; **business ~** réunion *f* d'affaires *or* de travail; **he's in a ~** il est en réunion; **I've got ~s all afternoon** je suis pris par des réunions tout l'après-midi; **to call a ~ of shareholders** convoquer les actionnaires; **to call a ~ to discuss sth** convoquer une réunion pour débattre qch; **to address a ~** prendre la parole à une réunion (*or* un meeting) → **annual, mass†, open**

b (*between individuals*) rencontre *f*; (*arranged*) rendez-vous *m*; (*formal*) entrevue *f*; **the minister had a ~ with the ambassador** le ministre s'est entretenu avec l'ambassadeur, le ministre a eu une entrevue avec l'ambassadeur; **a ~ of minds** une entente profonde

c (*Quakers*) culte *m*; **to go to ~** aller au culte

2 COMP ▶ **meeting house** N (*also* **Quakers' ~ house**) temple *m* (des Quakers) ▶ **meeting place** N lieu *m* de réunion

meg* [meg] N (*pl* **meg** *or* **megs**) (*Comput* = *megabyte*) méga* *m*; (= *megahertz*) mégahertz *m*

mega* [ˈmegə] ADJ hypergénial*

mega... [ˈmegə] PREF méga...; **~star** mégastar *f*

megabuck* [ˈmegə,bʌk] N **a** (*US* = *million dollars*) million *m* de dollars **b** (*fig*) **~s** des sommes astronomiques; **it's worth ~s** ça vaut la peau des fesses*

megabyte [ˈmegə,baɪt] N (*Comput*) méga-octet *m*, Mo *m*

megacycle [ˈmegə,saɪkl] N mégacycle *m*

megadeath [ˈmegə,deθ] N million *m* de morts

megahertz [ˈmegə,hɜːts] N (*pl* **megahertz**) mégahertz *m*

megalith [ˈmegəlɪθ] N mégalithe *m*

megalithic [ˌmegəˈlɪθɪk] ADJ mégalithique

megalomania [ˌmegələʊˈmeɪnɪə] N mégalomanie *f*

megalomaniac [ˌmegələʊˈmeɪnɪæk] ADJ, N mégalomane *mf*

megalopolis [ˌmegəˈlɒpəlɪs] N mégalopole *f*

megaphone [ˈmegəfəʊn] N porte-voix *m inv*

megaton [ˈmegətʌn] N mégatonne *f*; **a five-~ bomb** une bombe de cinq mégatonnes

megavolt [ˈmegəvɒlt] N mégavolt *m*

megawatt [ˈmegəwɒt] N mégawatt *m*

megillah* [məˈgɪlə] N (*US*) grand laïus *m*, longues explications *fpl*; **the whole ~** tout le tremblement*

meiosis [maɪˈəʊsɪs] N (*pl* **meioses** [maɪˈəʊˌsiːz]) **a** (*Bio*) méiose *f* **b** (*Literat*) litote *f*

Mekong [ˌmiːˈkɒŋ] **1** N Mékong *m* **2** COMP ▶ **Mekong Delta** N delta *m* du Mékong

melamine [ˈmeləmiːn] **1** N mélamine *f* **2** COMP [*cup, surface*] de *or* en mélamine ▶ **melamine-coated, melamine-faced** ADJ mélaminé

melancholia [ˌmelənˈkəʊlɪə] N (*Psych*) mélancolie *f*

melancholic† [ˌmelənˈkɒlɪk] ADJ [*person, nature, mood, song*] mélancolique; (*Med*) **the ~ temperament** le tempérament mélancolique

melancholically [ˌmelənˈkɒlɪklɪ] ADV mélancoliquement

melancholy [ˈmelənkəlɪ] **1** N (*NonC*) mélancolie *f* **2** ADJ [*person, place, look, smile, thoughts, sound, song*] triste; [*news, event, duty*] triste; **to be in a ~ mood** être d'humeur mélancolique; **the ~ truth** la triste vérité

Melanesia [ˌmeləˈniːzɪə] N la Mélanésie

Melanesian [ˌmeləˈniːzɪən] **1** ADJ mélanésien **2** N **a** (= *person*) Mélanésien(ne) *m(f)* **b** (*Ling*) mélanésien *m*

melange, mélange [meɪˈlɑːnʒ] N (*esp liter*) mélange *m*

melanic [məˈlænɪk] ADJ mélanique

melanin [ˈmelənɪn] N mélanine *f*

melanism [ˈmelənɪzəm] N mélanisme *m*

melanoma [ˌmeləˈnəʊmə] N (*pl* **melanomas** *or* **melanomata** [ˌmeləˈnəʊmətə]) (*Med*) mélanome *m*

melatonin [ˌmeləˈtəʊnɪn] N mélatonine *f*

Melba toast [ˈmelbəˈtəʊst] N (*Culin*) biscotte *f* très fine

Melbourne [ˈmelbən] N Melbourne

melee, mêlée [ˈmeleɪ] N mêlée *f*

mellifluous [meˈlɪflʊəs] ADJ mélodieux

mellow [ˈmeləʊ] **1** ADJ **a** (= *soft, smooth*) [*light, colour, music, voice*] doux (douce *f*); [*brick, stone*] patiné; [*wine, flavour, cheese, fruit*] moelleux; [*brandy, whisky*] velouté **b** (= *genial, serene*) [*person*] serein **c** (* = *relaxed*) [*person, mood, feeling*] relax **2** VT [+ *wine*] rendre moelleux, donner du bouquet à; [+ *voice, sound*] adoucir, rendre plus moelleux; [+ *colour*] fondre, velouter; [+ *person, character*] adoucir; **the years have ~ed him** les angles de son caractère se sont arrondis avec l'âge, il s'est adouci *or* assagi avec les années **3** VI [*fruit*] mûrir; [*wine*] se velouter; se patiner; [*voice*] prendre du moelleux, se velouter; [*person, character*] s'adoucir

mellowing [ˈmeləʊɪŋ] **1** N [*of fruit, wine*] maturation *f*; [*of voice, colours, person, attitude*] adoucissement *m* **2** ADJ [*effect etc*] adoucissant

mellowness [ˈmeləʊnɪs] N [*of light, colour, music, voice*] douceur *f*; [*of wine, flavour, cheese, fruit*] moelleux *m*; [*of brick, stone*] patine *f*

melodic [mɪˈlɒdɪk] **1** ADJ **a** (= *melodious*) [*music, song, voice*] mélodieux **b** (*Mus*) [*line, theme, structure, invention*] mélodique **2** COMP ▶ **melodic minor (scale)** N (*Mus*) gamme *f* mineure mélodique

melodically [mɪˈlɒdɪklɪ] ADV mélodiquement

melodious [mɪˈləʊdɪəs] ADJ mélodieux

melodiously [mɪˈləʊdɪəslɪ] ADV mélodieusement

melodrama [ˈmeləʊˌdrɑːmə] N (*lit, fig*) mélodrame *m*

melodramatic [ˌmeləʊdrəˈmætɪk] **1** ADJ mélodramatique **2** **melodramatics** NPL mélo* *m*; **I've had enough of your ~s** j'en ai assez de ton cinéma*

melodramatically [ˌmeləʊdrəˈmætɪklɪ] ADV d'une façon mélodramatique

melody [ˈmelədɪ] N mélodie *f*

melon [ˈmelən] N **a** (*Bot, Culin*) melon *m*; (*US fig*) **to cut a ~*** se partager le gâteau → **watermelon** **b** **~s*** (= *breasts*) roberts* *mpl*

melt [melt] **1** VI **a** [*ice, butter, metal*] fondre; [*solid in liquid*] fondre, se dissoudre; **these cakes ~ in the mouth** ces pâtisseries fondent dans la bouche; (*fig*) **he looks as if butter wouldn't ~ in his mouth** on lui donnerait le bon Dieu sans confession* → **melting**
b (*fig*) [*colours, sounds*] se fondre, s'estomper (**into** dans); [*person*] se laisser attendrir; [*anger*] tomber; [*resolution, determination*] fléchir, fondre; **to ~ into tears** fondre en larmes; **her heart ~ed with pity** son cœur a fondu de pitié; **night ~ed into day** la nuit a

fait insensiblement place au jour; **one colour ~ed into another** les couleurs se fondaient les unes dans les autres; **the thief ~ed into the crowd** le voleur s'est fondu *or* a disparu dans la foule **c** (= *be too hot*) **to be ~ing*** fondre, être en nage **2** VT [+ *ice, butter*] (faire) fondre; [+ *metal*] fondre; (*fig*) **to ~ sb's heart** attendrir *or* émouvoir (le cœur de) qn; (*Culin*) **~ed butter** beurre *m* fondu → **melting**

▶ **melt away** VI **a** [*ice etc*] fondre complètement, disparaître **b** (*fig*) [*money, savings*] fondre; [*anger*] se dissiper, tomber; [*confidence*] disparaître; [*fog*] se dissiper; [*crowd*] se disperser; [*person*] se volatiliser

▶ **melt down** **1** VT SEP fondre; [+ *scrap iron, coins*] remettre à la fonte **2** **~down** N → **meltdown**

meltdown ['meltdaʊn] N (*Nucl Phys*) fusion *f* (*du cœur d'un réacteur nucléaire*)

melting ['meltɪŋ] **1** ADJ [*snow*] fondant; (*fig*) [*voice, look*] attendri; [*words*] attendrissant **2** N [*of snow*] fonte *f*; [*of metal*] fusion *f*, fonte *f* **3** COMP ▶ **melting point** N point *m* de fusion ▶ **melting pot** N (*fig*) melting-pot *m*; **the country was a ~ pot of many nationalities** ce pays fut un melting-pot *or* fut un creuset ethnique; (*Brit*) **the scheme was back in the ~ pot** le projet a été remis en question une fois de plus; (*Brit*) **it's still all in the ~ pot** c'est encore en pleine discussion *or* au stade des discussions

member ['membər] **1** N **a** [*of society, political party etc*] membre *m*, adhérent(e) *m(f)*; [*of family, tribe*] membre *m*; (*on notice etc*) **"~s only"** « réservé aux adhérents »; **a ~ of the audience** un membre de l'assistance; (= *hearer*) un auditeur; (= *spectator*) un spectateur; (*US Pol*) **Member of Congress** membre *m* du Congrès, ≈ député *m*; **a ~ of the congress** un(e) congressiste; **they treated her like a ~ of the family** ils l'ont traitée comme si elle faisait partie de *or* était de la famille; (*Brit Pol*) **Member of Parliament** ≈ député *m*; **the Member (of Parliament) for Woodford** le député de Woodford; (*Brit*) **Member of the European Parliament** député *m* européen; **a ~ of the public** un simple particulier, un(e) simple citoyen(ne); **a ~ of the staff** (*of firm, organization*) un(e) employé(e); (*Scol, Univ*) **a ~ of staff** un professeur → **full, honorary, private** **b** (*Anat, Bot, Math etc*) membre *m*; (= *penis*) **(male) ~** membre *m* (viril) **2** COMP ▶ **member countries, member nations, member states** NPL États *mpl* or pays *mpl* membres

membership ['membəʃɪp] **1** N **a** adhésion *f*, appartenance *f*; **Britain's ~ of the EU** l'appartenance de la Grande-Bretagne à l'UE; **when I applied for ~ of the club** quand j'ai fait ma demande d'adhésion au club; **he has given up his ~ of the party** il a rendu sa carte du parti; **~ carries certain privileges** l'adhésion donne droit à certains privilèges, les membres jouissent de certains privilèges **b** (= *number of members*) **this society has a ~ of over 800** cette société a plus de 800 membres **2** COMP ▶ **membership card** N carte *f* d'adhérent *or* de membre ▶ **membership fee** N cotisation *f*, droits *mpl* d'inscription ▶ **membership qualifications** NPL conditions *fpl* d'adhésion

membrane ['membreɪn] N membrane *f*

membranous [mem'breɪnəs] ADJ membraneux

memento [mə'mentəʊ] N (*pl* **mementos** *or* **mementoes**) (= *keepsake*) souvenir *m*; (= *note, mark etc*) mémento *m*; (= *scar*) souvenir *m*; **as a ~ of** en souvenir de

memo ['meməʊ] **1** N (ABBR = **memorandum**) note *f* (de service) **2** COMP ▶ **memo pad** N bloc-notes *m*

memoir ['memwɑː] N (= *essay*) mémoire *m*, étude *f* (**on** sur); (= *short biography*) notice *f* biographique; **~s** (*autobiographical*) mémoires *mpl*; [*of learned society*] actes *mpl*

memorabilia [,memərə'bɪliə] N souvenirs *mpl* (*objets*)

memorable ['memərəbl] ADJ mémorable; **one of his more ~ films** un de ses films dont on se souvient mieux

memorably ['memərəblɪ] ADV mémorablement

memorandum [,memə'rændəm] N (*pl* **memorandums** *or* **memoranda** [,memə'rændə]) **a** (= *reminder, note*) note *f*; **to make a ~ of sth** prendre note de qch, noter qch **b** (= *communication within company etc*) note *f* (de service); **he sent a ~ round about the drop in sales** il a fait circuler une note *or* il a fait passer une circulaire à propos de la baisse des ventes **c** (*Diplomacy*) mémorandum *m* **d** (*Jur*) sommaire *m* des articles d'un contrat; (*Jur*) **~ of agreement** protocole *m* d'accord

memorial [mɪ'mɔːrɪəl] **1** ADJ [*plaque*] commémoratif **2** N **a** (= *sth serving as reminder*) **this scholarship is a ~ to John F. Kennedy** cette bourse d'études a été créée en mémoire de John F. Kennedy **b** (= *monument*) monument *m* (commémoratif), mémorial *m*; (*over grave*) monument *m* (funéraire); **a ~ to the victims** un monument aux victimes **c** (*also* **war ~**) monument *m* aux morts **d** (*Hist*) **~s** (= *chronicles*) chroniques *fpl*, mémoires *mpl*, mémorial *m* **e** (*Admin etc* = *petition*) pétition *f*, requête *f* (officielle) **3** COMP ▶ **Memorial Day** N (*US*) le jour des morts au champ d'honneur (*dernier lundi de mai*) ▶ **memorial park** N (*US* = *cemetery*) cimetière *m* ▶ **memorial service** N ≈ messe *f* de souvenir

memorialize [mɪ'mɔːrɪəlaɪz] VT commémorer

memorize ['meməraɪz] VT [+ *facts, figures, names*] mémoriser, retenir; [+ *poem, speech*] apprendre par cœur

memory ['memərɪ] **1** N **a** (= *faculty: also Comput*) mémoire *f*; **to have a good/bad ~** avoir (une) bonne/mauvaise mémoire; **to have a ~ for faces** avoir la mémoire des visages, être physionomiste *mf*; **to play/quote from ~** jouer/citer de mémoire; **to have a long ~** ne pas oublier facilement; **to commit to ~** [+ *poem*] apprendre par cœur; [+ *facts, figures*] mémoriser, retenir; **to the best of my ~** autant que je m'en souvienne; **loss of ~** perte *f* de mémoire; (*Med*) amnésie *f*; **additional** *or* **back-up ~** mémoire *f* auxiliaire → **fresh, living** **b** (= *recollection*) souvenir *m*; **childhood memories** souvenirs *mpl* d'enfance; **he had happy memories of his father** il avait de bons souvenirs de son père; **"Memories of a country childhood"** « Souvenirs d'une enfance à la campagne »; **the ~ of the accident remained with him all his life** il a conservé toute sa vie le souvenir de l'accident, le souvenir de l'accident est resté gravé dans sa mémoire toute sa vie; **to keep sb's ~ alive** *or* **green** garder vivant le souvenir de qn, entretenir la mémoire de qn; **in ~ of** en souvenir de, à la mémoire de; **sacred to the ~ of** à la mémoire de; **of blessed ~** de glorieuse mémoire **2** COMP ▶ **memory bank** N bloc *m* de mémoire ▶ **memory capacity** N (*Comput*) capacité *f* de mémoire ▶ **memory card** N (*Comput*) carte *f* d'extension mémoire ▶ **memory chip** N (*Comput*) puce *f* mémoire ▶ **memory lane** N (*fig*) **it was a trip down ~ lane** c'était un retour en arrière *or* un retour aux sources ▶ **memory typewriter** N machine *f* à écrire à mémoire

memsahib ['mem,sɑːhɪb] N Madame *f* (*aux Indes*)

men [men] **1** NPL *of* **man** (*hum*) **that'll separate the ~ from the boys** cela fera la différence

(entre les hommes et les mauviettes*) **2** COMP ▶ **men's room** N (*US*) toilettes *fpl* pour hommes

menace ['menɪs] **1** N menace *f*; **he drives so badly he's a ~ to the public** il conduit si mal qu'il est un danger public; **that child/dog/motorbike is a ~*** cet enfant/ce chien/cette moto est une plaie*; (*Brit Jur*) **to demand money with ~s** extorquer de l'argent **2** VT menacer

menacing ['menɪsɪŋ] ADJ menaçant

menacingly ['menɪsɪŋlɪ] ADV [*act*] d'un air menaçant; [*say*] d'un ton menaçant

ménage [me'nɑːʒ] N (*pej*) ménage *m*; **~ à trois** ménage *m* à trois

menagerie [mɪ'nædʒərɪ] N ménagerie *f*

mend [mend] **1** VT **a** (= *repair*) [+ *watch, wall, vehicle, shoes etc*] réparer; (= *darn*) [+ *sock, stocking*] repriser; (= *darn*) [+ *clothes etc*] raccommoder; [+ *laddered stocking*] remmailler → **fence** **b** [+ *marriage*] sauver; **to ~ relations with sb** renouer de bonnes relations avec qn; **that won't ~ matters** cela ne va pas arranger les choses; **to ~ one's ways** ◊ **to ~ one's manners** s'amender → **least** **2** VI (= *darn etc*) faire le raccommodage **b*** **to be on the mend**; → **3b** **3** N **a** (*on clothes*) raccommodage *m*; (= *patch*) pièce *f*; (= *darn*) reprise *f* **b** **to be on the ~** [*invalid*] être en voie de guérison, aller mieux; [*business, sales*] reprendre, s'améliorer; [*conditions, situation, weather*] s'améliorer

mendacious [men'deɪʃəs] ADJ (*frm*) [*statement, report*] mensonger; [*person*] menteur

mendacity [men'dæsɪtɪ] N **a** (*NonC*) (*habit*) fausseté *f*, habitude *f* de mentir; (*tendency*) propension *f* au mensonge; [*of report*] caractère *m* mensonger **b** (= *lie*) mensonge *m*

mendelevium [,mendɪ'liːvɪəm] N mendélévium *m*

Mendelian [men'diːlɪən] ADJ mendélien

Mendelism ['mendəlɪzəm] N mendélisme *m*

mendicancy ['mendɪkənsɪ] N mendicité *f*

mendicant ['mendɪkənt] ADJ, N mendiant(e) *m(f)*

mendicity [men'dɪsɪtɪ] N mendicité *f*

mending ['mendɪŋ] N (= *act*) raccommodage *m*; (= *clothes to be mended*) vêtements *mpl* à raccommoder → **invisible**

Menelaus [,menɪ'leəs] N Ménélas *m*

menfolk ['menfəʊk] NPL **the ~** les hommes *mpl*

menhir ['menhɪə] N menhir *m*

menial ['miːnɪəl] **1** ADJ [*person*] servile; [*task*] de domestique, inférieur (-eure *f*); [*position*] subalterne **2** N domestique *mf*, laquais *m* (*pej*)

meninges [mɪ'nɪndʒiːs] NPL méninges *fpl*

meningitis [,menɪn'dʒaɪtɪs] N méningite *f*

meniscus [mɪ'nɪskəs] N (*pl* **meniscuses** *or* **menisci** [mɪ'nɪsaɪ]) ménisque *m*

menopausal ['menəʊpɔːzəl] ADJ [*symptom*] de la ménopause; [*woman*] ménopausé

menopause ['menəʊpɔːz] N ménopause *f*; **the male ~** l'andropause *f*

Menorca [mɪ'nɔːkə] N Minorque *f*; **in ~** à Minorque

menorrhagia [,menɔː'reɪdʒɪə] N ménorragie *f*

Mensa ['mensə] N Mensa *f* (*association de personnes ayant un QI supérieur à la moyenne*)

mensch* [menʃ] N (*US*) (= *man*) type *m* vraiment bien; (= *woman*) fille *f* vraiment bien; **be a ~!** comporte-toi en adulte!

menses ['mensiːz] NPL menstrues *fpl*

Menshevik ['menʃɪvɪk] N, ADJ menchevik *m*

menstrual ['menstrʊəl] **1** ADJ menstruel **2** COMP ▶ **menstrual cramps** NPL dysménorrhée *f*, règles *fpl* douloureuses ▶ **menstrual cycle** N cycle *m* (menstruel) ▶ **menstrual period** N règles *fpl*, menstruation *f*

menstruate ['menstrʊeɪt] VI avoir ses règles

menstruation [,menstrʊ'eɪʃən] N menstruation f

mensuration [,mensjʊə'reɪʃən] N (also Math) mesurage m

menswear ['menzweəʳ] N (NonC: Comm) (= clothing) habillement m masculin; (= department) rayon m hommes

mental ['mentl] [1] ADJ [a] (= not physical) mental; **I made a ~ note of her phone number** j'ai noté mentalement son numéro de téléphone; **I made a ~ note to get petrol** je me suis dit que je devais faire le plein [b] (* = mad) cinglé*; **to go ~** perdre la boule* [2] COMP ► **mental age** N âge m mental ► **mental arithmetic** N calcul m mental ► **mental block** N blocage m (psychologique) ► **mental cruelty** N (Jur) cruauté f mentale ► **mental defective** N débile mf mental(e) ► **mental deficiency** N débilité f or déficience f mentale ► **mental disability, mental handicap** N handicap m mental ► **mental healing** N (US Med) thérapeutique f par la suggestion ► **mental health** N (of person) santé f mentale; (= activity, profession) psychiatrie f ► **mental home** N clinique f psychiatrique ► **mental hospital** N hôpital m psychiatrique ► **mental illness** N maladie f mentale ► **mental institution** N institution f psychiatrique ► **mental patient** N malade mf mental(e) ► **mental powers** NPL facultés fpl intellectuelles ► **mental reservation** N restriction f mentale ► **mental retardation** N arriération f mentale ► **mental strain** N (= tension) tension f nerveuse; (= overwork) surmenage m (intellectuel); **she's been under a great deal of ~ strain** ses nerfs ont été mis à rude épreuve

mentality [men'tælɪtɪ] N mentalité f

mentally ['mentlɪ] ADV [calculate, formulate] mentalement; **~ handicapped** handicapé mental; **a ~ handicapped son/child** un fils/enfant handicapé mental; **he is ~ handicapped** c'est un handicapé mental; **~ ill** or **sick** malade mental; **a ~ ill** or **sick person** un(e) malade mental(e); **the ~ ill** les malades mpl mentaux; **~ retarded†** débile mental; **~ subnormal†** débile léger; **~ disturbed** or **disordered** or **unstable** or **unbalanced** déséquilibré; **~ defective** or **deficient†** mentalement déficient

menthol ['menθɒl] [1] N menthol m [2] COMP ► **menthol cigarettes** NPL cigarettes fpl mentholées

mentholated ['menθəleɪtɪd] ADJ mentholé

▼**mention** ['menʃən] [1] VT (gen) mentionner; [+ dates, figures] citer; **he ~ed to me that you were coming** il m'a dit que vous alliez venir; **I'll ~ it to him** je lui en toucherai un mot, je le lui signalerai; **I've never heard him ~ his father** je ne l'ai jamais entendu parler de son père; **to ~ sb in one's will** coucher qn sur son testament; **he didn't ~ the accident** il n'a pas fait mention de l'accident, il n'a pas soufflé mot de l'accident; **just ~ my name** dites que c'est de ma part; **he ~ed several names** il a cité plusieurs noms; **without ~ing any names** sans nommer or citer personne; **I ~ this fact only because ...** je relève ce fait uniquement parce que ...; **they are too numerous to ~** ils sont trop nombreux pour qu'on les mentionne (subj) or cite (subj) tous; **don't ~ it!** il n'y a pas de quoi!, je vous en prie!; **I need hardly ~ that ...** il va sans dire que ...; **not to ~ ...** sans compter ...; **it is not worth ~ing** cela ne vaut pas la peine d'en parler; **I have no jazz records worth ~ing** je n'ai pour ainsi dire pas de disques de jazz → **dispatch** [2] N mention f; (frm) **to make ~ of sth** faire mention de qch, signaler qch; **honourable ~** mention f honorable; **it got a ~ in the news** on en a parlé or on l'a mentionné aux informations

► LANGUAGE IN USE: **mention** 26.2, 26.3

mentor ['mentɔːʳ] N mentor m

menu ['menjuː] [1] N (in restaurant etc) menu m; (printed, written) menu m, carte f; (Comput) menu m; **on the ~** au menu → **fixed** [2] COMP ► **menu-driven** ADJ (Comput) dirigé or piloté par menu

meow [miːˈaʊ] = **miaow**

MEP [,emiːˈpiː] N (Brit) (ABBR = **Member of the European Parliament**) → **member**

Mephistopheles [,mefɪsˈtɒfɪliːz] N Méphistophélès m

mephistophelian [,mefɪstəˈfiːlɪən] ADJ méphistophélique

mercantile ['mɜːkəntaɪl] [1] ADJ [a] [class, tradition, navy, vessel] marchand; [nation] commerçant; [firm, establishment, court] de commerce [b] (pej) [person, attitude] mercantile [2] COMP ► **mercantile law** N droit m commercial ► **mercantile marine** N (Brit) marine m marchande

mercantilism ['mɜːkəntɪlɪzəm] N (Econ, also pej) mercantilisme m

mercantilist ['mɜːkəntɪlɪst] ADJ, N (Econ) mercantiliste m

Mercator [mɜːˈkeɪtəʳ] N ~ **projection** projection f de Mercator

mercenary ['mɜːsɪnərɪ] [1] ADJ [a] (pej) [person, attitude] intéressé, mercenaire [b] (Mil) mercenaire [2] N (Mil) mercenaire m

mercer ['mɜːsəʳ] N (Brit) marchand m de tissus

merchandise ['mɜːtʃəndaɪz] [1] N (NonC) marchandises fpl [2] VI commercer, faire du commerce [3] VT promouvoir la vente de

merchandizer ['mɜːtʃəndaɪzəʳ] N spécialiste mf du marchandisage or merchandising

merchandizing ['mɜːtʃəndaɪzɪŋ] N marchandisage m, merchandising m

merchant ['mɜːtʃənt] [1] N (= trader, dealer) négociant m; (= wholesaler) marchand m en gros, grossiste m; (= retailer) marchand m au détail, détaillant m; (= shopkeeper) commerçant m; **builders'/plumbers' ~** fournisseur m de or en matériaux de construction/en sanitaires; **timber/cloth/spice ~** marchand m de bois/de tissu/d'épices; "**The Merchant of Venice**" « le Marchand de Venise »; **a doom-and-gloom ~** un oiseau de mauvais augure; **a rip-off ~** un arnaqueur* → **coal, speed, wine** [2] COMP ► **merchant bank** N (Brit) banque f d'affaires ► **merchant banker** N (Brit) banquier m d'affaires ► **merchant marine** N (US) = **merchant navy** ► **merchant navy** N (Brit) marine f marchande ► **merchant seaman** N (pl **merchant seamen**) marin m de la marine marchande ► **merchant ship** N navire m marchand or de commerce ► **merchant shipping** N (NonC) navires mpl marchands or de commerce ► **merchant vessel** N navire m marchand or de commerce

merchantability ['mɜːtʃəntəˈbɪlɪtɪ] N (Comm) valeur f commerciale; (Jur) qualité f loyale et marchande

merchantable ['mɜːtʃəntəbl] ADJ [a] (Comm) commercialisable, vendable [b] (Jur: also **of ~ quality**) d'une bonne qualité marchande

merchantman ['mɜːtʃəntmən] N (pl -men) (Naut) = **merchant ship; → merchant**

merciful ['mɜːsɪfʊl] ADJ [a] (= compassionate) [person, judge, court] clément (**to** or **towards sb** envers qn); [God] miséricordieux (**to** or **towards sb** envers qn) [b] (= welcome) **death came as a ~ release** la mort fut une délivrance; **his death came with ~ suddenness** heureusement pour lui, la mort a été rapide

mercifully ['mɜːsɪfəlɪ] ADV [a] [judge, act] (person) avec clémence; (God) miséricordieusement [b] (= fortunately) **~ it didn't rain** Dieu merci or par bonheur il n'a pas plu

merciless ['mɜːsɪlɪs] ADJ [person, attack, treatment] impitoyable (**towards sb** envers

qn); [sun, heat, rain, scrutiny] implacable; **to be a ~ critic of sb/sth** critiquer qn/qch impitoyablement

mercilessly ['mɜːsɪlɪslɪ] ADV [behave, attack, treat, criticize] impitoyablement, sans pitié; **the sun beat down ~** le soleil était implacable

mercurial [mɜːˈkjʊərɪəl] ADJ [a] (liter) (= changeable) [person, temperament, nature] versatile, lunatique (pej); [moods] changeant; (= lively) [wit] vif [b] (Chem) mercuriel

mercury ['mɜːkjʊrɪ] N [a] (Chem) mercure m [b] **Mercury** (Myth) Mercure m; (Astron) Mercure f

mercy ['mɜːsɪ] [1] N [a] (gen) miséricorde f; (= clemency) clémence f; (= pity) pitié f; **God in his ~** Dieu en sa miséricorde; **to have ~ on sb ◊ to show ~ to sb†** faire preuve de clémence envers qn, avoir pitié de qn; **have ~ on me!** ayez pitié de moi!; **to beg for ~** demander grâce; (Jur) **with a recommendation to ~** avec avis en faveur d'une commutation de peine; **a cruelty without ~** une cruauté impitoyable; **he was beaten without ~** il a été battu impitoyablement; **no ~ was shown to them** ils furent impitoyablement traités or traités sans merci; (liter) **to throw o.s. on sb's ~** s'en remettre à la merci de qn; **at the ~ of sb/the weather** etc à la merci de qn/du temps etc; (iro) **to leave sb to the ~ of** or **to the tender mercies of ...** livrer qn à ..., abandonner qn à la merci de ...; **(me)!†** Seigneur!, miséricorde!; **for ~'s sake!†** par pitié! → **errand** [b] (= piece of good fortune) **it's a ~ that ...** heureusement que ... (+ indic), c'est une chance que ... (+ subj); **his death was a ~** sa mort a été une délivrance [2] COMP [flight, journey] de secours, d'urgence (humanitaire) ► **mercy killing** N euthanasie f

mere¹ [mɪəʳ] N étang m, (petit) lac m

mere² [mɪəʳ] ADJ [a] (= least, even) simple (before n); **the ~ mention of sth** le simple fait de mentionner qch; **the ~ existence of neo-Nazis is an outrage** le simple fait que les néo-nazis existent est un scandale, la simple existence des néonazis constitue un scandale; **the ~ possibility of rain was enough to put him off** le fait qu'il risquait de pleuvoir a suffi à le décourager; **the ~ sight of him makes me shiver** sa seule vue me fait frissonner, rien qu'à le voir je frissonne; **the ~st suggestion of sth** (= mention) le simple fait d'évoquer qch; **the ~st hint** or **suspicion of sth** le moindre soupçon de qch [b] (= simple, slight) [coincidence, formality] simple (before n); **a ~ mortal** un(e) simple mortel(le); **he's a ~ clerk** c'est un simple employé de bureau; **I was a ~ child when I married him** je n'étais qu'une enfant quand je l'ai épousé; **by a ~ chance** par pur hasard; **he's a ~ nobody** c'est un moins que rien; **a ~ nothing** trois fois rien; **they quarrelled over a ~ nothing** ils se sont disputés pour une vétille; **his voice was the merest whisper** sa voix n'était qu'un murmure; **it's a ~ kilometre away** ce n'est qu'à un kilomètre (de distance); **in a ~ 17 minutes** en 17 minutes seulement; **a ~ £45** 45 livres seulement

merely ['mɪəlɪ] ADV simplement; **I ~ said that she was coming** j'ai tout simplement dit or je n'ai fait que dire qu'elle arrivait; **he ~ nodded** il se contenta de faire un signe de tête; **he's a ~ clerk** c'est un simple employé de bureau; **I did it ~ to please her** je ne l'ai fait que pour lui faire plaisir; **~ to look at him makes me shiver** rien que de le regarder me fait frissonner; **it's a ~ formality** c'est une simple formalité; **it's not ~ dirty, it's filthy** ce n'est pas seulement sale, c'est dégoûtant

meretricious [,merɪˈtrɪʃəs] ADJ (frm) [charm, attraction] factice; [style] ampoulé

merge [mɜːdʒ] [1] VI [a] [colours, shapes] se mêler (**into, with** à), se fondre (**into, with** dans);

[sounds] se mêler (**into, with** à), se perdre (**into, with** dans) ; [roads] se rencontrer (**with** avec), se joindre (**with** à) ; [river] confluer (**with** avec) ; (also fig) **to ~ into** [+ darkness, background etc] se fondre dans [b] (Comm, Fin) fusionner (**with** avec) [2] VT [a] unifier ; **the states were ~d (into one) in 1976** ces États se sont unifiés en 1976, l'unification de ces États s'est réalisée en 1976 [b] (Comm, Fin) fusionner ; (Comput) fusionner ; **the firms were ~d** les entreprises ont fusionné ; **they decided to ~ the companies into a single unit** ils décidèrent de fusionner les deux sociétés

merger ['mɜːdʒəʳ] N (Comm, Fin) fusion f, fusionnement m

meridian [mə'rɪdɪən] [1] N (Astron, Geog) méridien m ; (fig) apogée m, zénith m [2] ADJ méridien

meridional [mə'rɪdɪənl] [1] ADJ méridional [2] N (= person) méridional(e) m(f)

meringue [mə'ræŋ] N meringue f

merino [mə'riːnəʊ] N mérinos m

▼ **merit** ['merɪt] [1] N mérite m, valeur f ; **people of ~** gens mpl de valeur or de mérite ; **a work of great ~** un travail de grande valeur ; **the great ~ of this scheme** le grand mérite de ce projet ; **there is little ~ in doing so** il y a peu de mérite à le faire ; **he sees little ~ in ...** il ne voit pas vraiment l'intérêt de ... ; **to treat sb according to his ~s** traiter qn selon ses mérites ; **to judge sth on its own ~s** juger qch en fonction de ses mérites ; **to judge sb on their own ~s** juger qn selon ses mérites ; **to take** or **judge each case on its own ~s** décider au cas par cas ; **they went into the ~s of the new plan** ils ont discuté le pour et le contre de ce nouveau projet ; **certificate of ~** prix m [2] VT mériter ; **this ~s fuller discussion** ceci mérite plus ample discussion [3] COMP ► **merit list** N (Scol etc) tableau m d'honneur ; **to get one's name on the ~ list** être inscrit au tableau d'honneur ► **merit system** N (US Admin) système m de recrutement et de promotion par voie de concours

meritocracy [,merɪ'tɒkrəsɪ] N méritocratie f

meritocrat ['merɪtəʊkræt] N membre m de la méritocratie

meritocratic [,merɪtəʊ'krætɪk] ADJ méritocratique

meritorious [,merɪ'tɔːrɪəs] ADJ (frm) [performance, victory, work, deed] méritoire ; [person] méritant ; **for ~ conduct** pour conduite exemplaire

meritoriously [,merɪ'tɔːrɪəslɪ] ADV d'une façon méritoire

Merlin ['mɜːlɪn] N (Myth) Merlin m l'Enchanteur

merlin ['mɜːlɪn] N (Orn) émerillon m

mermaid ['mɜːmeɪd] N (Myth) sirène f

merman ['mɜːmæn] N (pl -**men**) (Myth) triton m

Merovingian [,merəʊ'vɪndʒɪən] [1] ADJ mérovingien [2] N Mérovingien(ne) m(f)

merrie† ['merɪ] ADJ **Merrie England** l'Angleterre f du bon vieux temps

merrily ['merɪlɪ] ADV [a] (= jovially) [laugh, say] gaiement, joyeusement [b] (= cheeringly) [burn, boil, bubble, ring] gaiement [c] (* = obliviously, inconsiderately) gaiement ; **I was chattering away ~, without realizing that ...** je bavardais gaiement sans me rendre compte que ...

merriment ['merɪmənt] N (NonC) gaieté or gaîté f, joie f ; (= laughter) hilarité f ; **this remark caused a lot of ~** cette remarque a provoqué l'hilarité générale

▼ **merry** ['merɪ] [1] ADJ [a] (= cheerful) [laughter, mood, face, sound, tune] joyeux ; [eyes] rieur ; **Merry Christmas** Joyeux Noël ; **a Merry Christmas to all our readers** Joyeux Noël à tous nos lecteurs ; **Robin Hood and his ~ men** Robin des Bois et ses joyeux compagnons ; (liter) **to**

---

make ~ se divertir → **May, more** [b] (pej, iro) **to go on one's ~ way** poursuivre son petit bonhomme de chemin ; (Brit) **to lead sb a ~ dance**† donner du fil à retordre à qn → **hell** [c] (Brit*: euph = tipsy) éméché, gris* ; **to get ~** être éméché* [2] COMP ► **merry-go-round** N (in fairground) manège m ; (fig) tourbillon m

merrymaker ['merɪmeɪkəʳ] N fêtard m

merrymaking ['merɪmeɪkɪŋ] N (NonC) réjouissances fpl

mesa ['meɪsə] N (US) mesa f, plateau m

mescaline ['meskəlɪn] N mescaline f

mesh [meʃ] [1] N [a] (of net, sieve etc) (= space) maille f ; (fig = network) réseau m, rets mpl ; (= snare) rets mpl, filets mpl ; **netting with a 5cm ~** filet m à mailles de 5 cm ; **~es** (= threads) mailles fpl ; [of spider's web] fils mpl, toile f ; **a ~ of lies** un tissu de mensonges ; **caught in the ~es of the law** pris dans les mailles de la justice ; **the ~(es) of intrigue** le réseau d'intrigues → **micromesh stockings** [b] (NonC = fabric) tissu m à mailles ; **nylon ~** tulle m de nylon® ; **wire ~** treillis m, grillage m ; **a belt of fine gold ~** une ceinture tressée de fils d'or [c] [of gears etc] engrenage m ; **in ~** en prise [2] VI [wheels, gears] s'engrener ; [dates, plans] concorder, cadrer ; (fig) [two people, their characters etc] avoir des affinités [3] VT [+ fish etc] prendre au filet [4] COMP ► **mesh bag** N filet m (à provisions) ► **mesh stockings** NPL (non-run) bas mpl indémaillables ; (in cabaret, circus etc) bas mpl résille

meshug(g)a, meshuggah [mɪ'ʃʊgə] ADJ (US) cinglé*, maboul‡

mesmeric [mez'merɪk] ADJ (lit, fig) hypnotique, magnétique

mesmerism ['mezmərɪzəm] N mesmérisme m

mesmerize ['mezməraɪz] VT (lit, fig) hypnotiser, magnétiser ; [snake] fasciner ; (fig) **I was ~d** je ne pouvais pas détourner mon regard, j'étais comme hypnotisé

mesomorph ['mesəʊ,mɔːf] N mésomorphe mf

meson ['miːzɒn] N (Phys) méson m

Mesopotamia [,mesəpə'teɪmɪə] N la Mésopotamie

Mesozoic [,mesəʊ'zəʊɪk] ADJ, N mésozoïque m

mess [mes] [1] N [a] (= confusion of objects etc) pagaille* f, pagaïe* f, fouillis m ; (= dirt) saleté f ; (= muddle) **what a ~ the children have made!** les enfants ont mis une de ces pagailles* or un de ces fouillis ! ; **what a ~ your room is in!** quelle pagaille* or quel fouillis il y a dans ta chambre ! ; **get this ~ cleared up at once!** range-moi ce fouillis tout de suite ! ; **the result is a political/legal** etc **~** politiquement/juridiquement etc on aboutit à un vrai gâchis ; **a financial/an administrative ~** une pagaille* financière/administrative ; **what a ~ it all is!** quel gâchis ! ; **this page is a ~, rewrite it** cette page est un vrai torchon, recopiez-la ; **you look a ~** ◊ **you're a ~** tu n'es pas présentable ; **he's a ~*** (emotionally, psychologically) il est complètement déboussolé* ; (US = no use) il n'est bon à rien ; **to get (o.s.) out of a ~** se sortir d'un mauvais pas, se dépatouiller* ; **to get sb out of a ~** sortir qn d'un mauvais pas [b] **in a ~: the house was in a terrible ~** (= untidy) la maison était dans un désordre épouvantable ; (= dirty) la maison était d'une saleté épouvantable ; (after bombing etc) la maison était dans un état épouvantable ; **the toys were in a ~** les jouets étaient en pagaille* or en désordre ; **they left everything in a ~** ils ont tout laissé en désordre ; (after fight, accident etc) **his face was in a dreadful ~** il avait le visage dans un état épouvantable ; (fig = difficulties) **to be/get (o.s.) in a ~** être/se mettre dans de beaux draps ; **his life is in a ~** sa vie est un vrai gâchis [c] **to make a ~: she made a ~ of her new skirt**

(= dirtied it) elle a sali or tout taché sa jupe neuve ; (= damaged it) elle a déchiré sa jupe neuve ; **the dog has made a ~ of the flowerbeds** le chien a saccagé les plates-bandes ; **your boots have made an awful ~ on the carpet** tu as fait des saletés sur le tapis avec tes bottes ; (euph) **the cat has made a ~ in the kitchen** le chat a fait des saletés dans la cuisine ; (fig) **to make a ~ of** [+ one's life, career] gâcher ; **to make a ~ of things*** tout bousiller*, tout gâcher

[d] (Mil) (= place) mess m, cantine f ; (Naut) carré m, gamelle f ; (= food) ordinaire m, gamelle f ; (= members collectively) mess m

[e] (= animal food) pâtée f ; (†† = dish) mets m, plat m ; (Bible) **a ~ of pottage** un plat de lentilles

[2] VT salir, souiller

[3] VI (Mil etc) manger au mess, manger en commun (**with** avec) ; (fig) **no ~ing!*** sans blague !*

[4] COMP ► **mess deck** N (Naut) poste m d'équipage ► **mess dress**, **mess gear*** (Brit) N (Mil etc) tenue f de soirée ► **mess hall** N (US) = **mess room** ► **mess jacket** N (Mil etc) veston m de tenue de soirée ; [of civilian waiter] veste f courte ► **mess kit** N (US) gamelle f ; (Brit*) tenue f de soirée ► **mess mate** N (Mil) camarade mf de mess ► **mess room** N (Mil) mess m ; (Naut) carré m ► **mess tin** N (Mil) gamelle f ► **mess-up*** N gâchis m

► **mess about*** [1] VI [a] (= play in water, mud) patouiller* ; (= act the fool) faire l'imbécile or le fou ; **we were ~ing about playing with paint** on faisait les fous en jouant avec de la peinture ; **stop ~ing about!** arrête tes bêtises ! ; (= have fun) **I love ~ing about in boats** j'aime (m'amuser à) faire du bateau [b] (= waste time) gaspiller or perdre son temps ; (= dawdle) lambiner, lanterner ; **he was ~ing about with his friends** il traînait avec ses copains ; **what were you doing? — just ~ing about** que faisais-tu ? — rien de particulier or de spécial [2] VT SEP (Brit = disturb, upset) [+ person] créer des complications à, embêter* ; [+ plans, arrangements] chambarder*, chambouler* ; **stop ~ing me about** arrête de me traiter pardessus la jambe* comme ça

► **mess about with*** VT FUS [a] (= fiddle with) [+ pen etc] s'amuser avec, tripoter [b] (= amuse o.s. with) **they were ~ing about with a ball** ils s'amusaient à taper dans un ballon [c] = **mess about 2** [d] (sexually) peloter*

► **mess around** = **mess about**

► **mess around with*** VT FUS = **mess about with**

► **mess together** VI (Mil etc) manger ensemble au mess ; (* gen) faire popote* ensemble

► **mess up** [1] VT SEP [+ clothes] salir, gâcher ; [+ room] mettre en désordre, semer la pagaille dans* ; [+ hair] ébouriffer ; [+ task, situation, plans, life etc] gâcher ; **to ~ sb's hair up** décoiffer qn ; **that's ~ed everything up!** ça a tout gâché ! ; (fig) **to ~ sb up*** (psychologically) perturber or traumatiser qn ; (US = beat up) abîmer le portrait de qn* [2] ~**up** N = **mess**

► **mess with*** VT FUS [+ people] se frotter à* ; [+ drugs, drinks etc] toucher à* ; (threatening) **if you ~ with me ...** si tu m'embêtes ...

▼ **message** ['mesɪdʒ] N [a] (= communication) message m ; **telephone ~** message m téléphonique ; **to leave a ~ (for sb)** laisser un message (pour or à qn) ; **would you give him this ~?** voudriez-vous lui transmettre ce message ? ; **I'll give him the ~** je lui ferai la commission ; **to send sb a ~** envoyer un message à qn ; **the President's ~ to Congress** le message du Président au Congrès [b] (= meaning) [of prophet, writer, artist, book etc] message m ; **to get the ~*** comprendre, saisir* ; **to get the** or **one's ~ across to sb** se faire comprendre de qn ; **I get the ~!** (c'est) compris !, je pige !* [c] (Scot = errand) course f, commission f ; **to** go on a ~ for sb faire une course pour qn ; **to go for** *or* **get the ~s** faire les courses *or* les commissions [2] COMP ► **message bag** N (*Scot*) sac *m* à provisions ► **message-boy** N garçon *m* de courses ► **message switching** N (*Comput*) commutation *f* des messages

messaging ['mesɪdʒɪŋ] N (*Comput*) messagerie *f*

messenger ['mesɪndʒəʳ] [1] N messager *m*, -ère *f* ; (*in office*) commissionnaire *m*, coursier *m* ; (*in hotel etc*) chasseur *m*, coursier *m* ; (*Post*) (petit) télégraphiste *m* → **king** [2] COMP ► **messenger boy** N garçon *m* de courses

Messiah [mɪ'saɪə] N Messie *m*

messiah [mɪ'saɪə] N messie *m*

messianic [,mesɪ'ænɪk] ADJ messianique

messily ['mesɪlɪ] ADV [*play, eat, work*] salement, de manière peu soignée ; **my parents divorced very ~** le divorce de mes parents a été très pénible *or* difficile

Messrs ['mesəz] NPL (*Brit*) (ABBR = **Messieurs**) MM., messieurs *mpl* ; **~ Smith & Co** MM. Smith & Cie

messy ['mesɪ] ADJ [a] (= *producing mess*) [*person*] désordonné ; [*activity, meal*] salissant ; **to be ~** [*animal*] salir ; **to be a ~ eater** manger salement [b] (= *dirty*) [*nappy*] sale [c] (= *untidy*) [*place, room, desk*] en désordre ; [*clothes*] négligé ; [*hair*] en bataille ; [*work, job*] bâclé ; [*handwriting*] peu soigné [d] (= *complicated, awkward*) [*situation, business, compromise*] embrouillé ; [*process*] délicat ; [*dispute, relationship, love affair*] compliqué ; **he had been through a ~ divorce** son divorce a été difficile

mestizo [mes'tiːzəʊ] N (*pl* **mestizos** *or* **mestizoes**) (*US*) métis(se) *m(f)* (né d'un parent espagnol ou portugais et d'un parent indien)

Met* [met] N **the ~** [a] (*US*) = **Metropolitan Opera Company**) principal opéra de New York [b] (*US*) (ABBR = **Metropolitan Museum of Art**) principal musée d'art de New York [c] (*Brit*) (ABBR = **Metropolitan Police**) → **metropolitan**

met¹ [met] VB *pt, ptp* of **meet¹**

met² [met] [1] ADJ (*Brit*) (ABBR = **meteorological**) météo *inv* [2] COMP ► **the Met Office** N (*Brit*) ≈ la Météorologie nationale ► **met report** N bulletin *m* (de la) météo

meta... ['metə] PREF mét(a)...

metabolic [,metə'bɒlɪk] [1] ADJ [*process, activity*] métabolique ; [*disorder*] du métabolisme [2] COMP ► **metabolic rate** N métabolisme *m* basal *or* de base

metabolically [,metə'bɒlɪklɪ] ADV métaboliquement

metabolism [me'tæbəlɪzəm] N métabolisme *m*

metabolize [me'tæbəlaɪz] VT métaboliser

metacarpal [,metə'kɑːpl] ADJ, N métacarpien *m*

metacarpus [,metə'kɑːpəs] N (*pl* **metacarpi** [,metə'kɑːpaɪ]) métacarpe *m*

metal ['metl] [1] N [a] (*Chem, Miner*) métal *m* [b] (*Brit*) (*for road*) empierrement *m*, cailloutis *m* ; (*for railway*) ballast *m* → **mettle** [2] VT [a] (= *cover with metal*) métalliser [b] (*Brit*) [+ *road*] empierrer, caillouter [3] COMP de métal, en métal ► **metal detector** N détecteur *m* de métaux ► **metal fatigue** N fatigue *f* du métal ► **metal polish** N produit *m* d'entretien (*pour métaux*)

metalanguage ['metəlæŋgwɪdʒ] N (*Ling*) métalangue *f*, métalangage *m*

metalinguistic [,metəlɪŋ'gwɪstɪk] ADJ (*Ling*) métalinguistique

metalinguistics [,metəlɪŋ'gwɪstɪks] N (*NonC*) (*Ling*) métalinguistique *f*

metallic [mɪ'tælɪk] ADJ [*object, element, mineral, sound, colour, taste*] métallique ; [*paint, finish*] métallisé ; [*dish*] en métal ; **a ~ blue Ford** une Ford bleu métallisé

metallurgic(al) [,metə'lɜːdʒɪk(əl)] ADJ métallurgique

metallurgist [me'tælədʒɪst] N métallurgiste *m*

metallurgy [me'tælədʒɪ] N métallurgie *f*

metalwork ['metlwɜːk] N (*NonC*) [a] (= *structure, articles*) ferronnerie *f* ; [*of car*] carrosserie *f* [b] (= *craft: also* **~ing**) travail *m* des métaux [c] (*Scol*) travail *m* des métaux

metalworker ['metlwɜːkəʳ] N ferronnier *m* ; (*Ind*) (ouvrier *m*) métallurgiste *m*

metamorphic [,metə'mɔːfɪk] ADJ métamorphique

metamorphism [,metə'mɔːfɪzəm] N [a] (*Geol*) métamorphisme *m* [b] (= *metamorphosis*) métamorphose *f*

metamorphose [,metə'mɔːfəʊz] [1] VT métamorphoser, transformer (**into** en) [2] VI se métamorphoser (**into** en)

metamorphosis [,metə'mɔːfəsɪs] N (*pl* **metamorphoses** [,metə'mɔːfə,siːz]) métamorphose *f*

metamorphous [,metə'mɔːfəs] ADJ = **metamorphic**

metaphor ['metəfəʳ] N métaphore *f* → **mix, mixed**

metaphorical [,metə'fɒrɪkəl] ADJ [*language*] métaphorique ; **to talk** *or* **speak in ~ terms** parler par métaphores ; **to express sth in ~ terms** exprimer qch en termes métaphoriques

metaphorically [,metə'fɒrɪkəlɪ] ADV [*speak*] métaphoriquement ; **~ speaking** métaphoriquement

metaphysical [,metə'fɪzɪkəl] ADJ métaphysique ; **the Metaphysical poets** les poètes *mpl* métaphysiques

metaphysics [,metə'fɪzɪks] N (*NonC*) métaphysique *f*

metastasis [mɪ'tæstəsɪs] N (*pl* **metastases** [mɪ'tæstə'siːz]) métastase *f*

metatarsal [,metə'tɑːsəl] ADJ, N métatarsien *m*

metatarsus [,metə'tɑːsəs] N (*pl* **metatarsi** [,metə'tɑːsaɪ]) métatarse *m*

metathesis [me'tæθəsɪs] N (*pl* **metatheses** [me'tæθə,siːz]) métathèse *f*

metazoan [,metə'zəʊən] N, ADJ métazoaire *m*

mete [miːt] VT **to ~ out** [+ *punishment*] infliger, donner ; [+ *reward*] décerner ; **to ~ out justice** rendre la justice

meteor ['miːtɪəʳ] [1] N météore *m* [2] COMP ► **meteor crater** N cratère *m* météorique ► **meteor shower** N averse *f* météorique

meteoric [,miːtɪ'ɒrɪk] ADJ [a] (= *rapid*) [*career*] fulgurant ; **his ~ rise to power/to fame** sa fulgurante ascension au pouvoir/à la célébrité [b] (*Astron*) [*dust, impact*] météorique

meteorite ['miːtɪəraɪt] N météorite *m or f*

meteorological [,miːtɪərə'lɒdʒɪkəl] [1] ADJ [*conditions, data, station, centre*] météorologique [2] COMP ► **the Meteorological Office** N *office météorologique britannique*, ≈ la Météorologie nationale

meteorologically [,miːtɪərə'lɒdʒɪklɪ] ADV météorologiquement

meteorologist [,miːtɪə'rɒlədʒɪst] N météorologiste *mf*, météorologue *mf*

meteorology [,miːtɪə'rɒlədʒɪ] N météorologie *f*

meter ['miːtəʳ] [1] N [a] (*gen* = *measuring device*) compteur *m* ; **electricity/gas/water ~** compteur *m* d'électricité/à gaz/à eau ; **to turn water/gas/electricity off at the ~** fermer l'eau/le gaz/l'électricité au compteur → **light¹** [b] (*also* **parking ~**) parcmètre *m* [c] (*US*) = **metre** [2] COMP ► **meter maid*** N (*Aut*) contractuelle *f* ► **meter reader** N releveur *m* de compteurs

meterage ['miːtərɪdʒ] N métrage *m*

methadone ['meθədəʊn] N méthadone *f*

methamphetamine [,meθæm'fetəmiːn] N méthamphétamine *f*

methane ['miːθeɪn] N (*also* **~ gas**) méthane *m*

methanol ['meθənɒl] N méthanol *m*

methinks [mɪ'θɪŋks] (*pret* **methought**) VB (†† *or hum*) ce me semble

method ['meθəd] [1] N [a] (*NonC* = *orderliness*) méthode *f*, ordre *m* ; **lack of ~** manque *m* de méthode ; **there's ~ in his madness** il n'est pas si fou qu'il en a l'air [b] (= *manner, fashion*) méthode *f* ; **his ~ of working** sa méthode de travail ; **there are several ~s of doing this** il a plusieurs méthodes pour faire cela ; (*Scol etc*) **~ of assessment** modalités *fpl* de contrôle ; **teaching ~s** la didactique [c] (*Cine, Theat*) **the Method** le système *or* la méthode de Stanislavski [2] COMP ► **method acting** N (*Cine, Theat*) système *m or* méthode *f* de Stanislavski ► **method actor, method actress** N (*Cine, Theat*) adepte *mf* du système *or* de la méthode de Stanislavski

methodical [mɪ'θɒdɪkəl] ADJ méthodique

methodically [mɪ'θɒdɪkəlɪ] ADV méthodiquement

Methodism ['meθədɪzəm] N méthodisme *m*

Methodist ['meθədɪst] ADJ, N méthodiste *mf*

methodological [,meθədə'lɒdʒɪkəl] ADJ méthodologique

methodologically [,meθədə'lɒdʒɪkəlɪ] ADV méthodologiquement

methodology [,meθə'dɒlədʒɪ] N méthodologie *f*

methought †† [mɪ'θɔːt] VB *pret of* **methinks**

meths* [meθs] (*Brit*) [1] N ABBR = **methylated spirit(s)** [2] COMP ► **meths drinker** N alcoolo* *mf* (*qui se soûle à l'alcool à brûler*)

Methuselah [mə'θuːzələ] N (*Bible*) Mathusalem *m* ; **he's as old as ~** il est vieux comme Mathusalem

methyl ['meθɪl] N méthyle *m* ; **~ acetate/bromide/chloride** acétate *m*/bromure *m*/chlorure *m* de méthyle

methylated spirit(s) ['meθɪleɪtɪd'spɪrɪt(s)] N(PL) alcool *m* à brûler *or* dénaturé

methylene ['meθɪliːn] N méthylène *m*

meticulous [mɪ'tɪkjʊləs] ADJ méticuleux ; **to be ~ about sth** apporter un soin méticuleux à qch ; **~ attention to detail** souci *m* minutieux du détail

meticulously [mɪ'tɪkjʊləslɪ] ADV méticuleusement ; **to be ~ clean** être d'une propreté méticuleuse ; **~ precise** d'une exactitude scrupuleuse

meticulousness [mɪ'tɪkjʊləsnɪs] N soin *m* méticuleux

métier ['meɪtɪeɪ] N [a] (= *calling*) métier *m* [b] (= *strong point*) point *m* fort

metonymy [mɪ'tɒnɪmɪ] N métonymie *f*

metre ['miːtəʳ] N (*Measure, Poetry*) mètre *m* ; (*Mus*) mesure *f*

metric ['metrɪk] [1] ADJ [*measurement, weights and measures*] du système métrique ; [*equivalent, size*] dans le système métrique ; **Britain went ~* in 1971** la Grande-Bretagne a adopté le système métrique en 1971 [2] COMP ► **the metric system** N le système métrique ► **metric ton, metric tonne** N tonne *f*

metrical ['metrɪkəl] [1] ADJ (*Literat, Mus*) métrique [2] COMP ► **metrical psalm** N psaume *m* versifié

metricate ['metrɪkeɪt] VT convertir au système métrique

metrication [,metrɪ'keɪʃən] N conversion *f* au *or* adoption *f* du système métrique

metrics ['metrɪks] N (*NonC*) métrique *f*

metro ['metrəʊ] N métro *m*

metrological [,metrə'lɒdʒɪkəl] ADJ métrologique

metrology [mɪ'trɒlədʒɪ] N métrologie *f*

metronome ['metrənəʊm] N métronome *m*

metronomic [ˌmetrəˈnɒmɪk] ADJ métronomique

metropolis [mɪˈtrɒpəlɪs] N (pl **metropolises**) métropole f (ville)

metropolitan [ˌmetrəˈpɒlɪtən] ①️ ADJ (Geog, Rel) métropolitain ②️ N (Rel) métropolitain m; (in Orthodox Church) métropolite m ③️ COMP ► **the Metropolitan Police** N (Brit) la police de Londres

mettle [ˈmetl] N [of person] courage m; [of horse] fougue f; **to be on one's ~** être prêt à donner le meilleur de soi-même; **to prove** or **show one's ~** montrer de quoi on est capable, faire ses preuves; **to test sb's ~** mettre qn à l'épreuve; **to be a test of sb's ~** être un test pour qn

mettlesome [ˈmetlsəm] ADJ ardent, fougueux

mew [mjuː] ①️ N [of cat etc] (also **~ing**) miaulement m ②️ VI miauler

mewl [mjuːl] VI vagir

mews [mjuːz] (Brit) ①️ N ④️ (= small street) ruelle f, venelle f ⑤️ (= stables) écuries fpl ②️ COMP ► **mews flat** N petit appartement aménagé dans une ancienne écurie, remise etc

Mexican [ˈmeksɪkən] ①️ ADJ (gen) mexicain; [ambassador, embassy] du Mexique ②️ N Mexicain(e) m(f) ③️ COMP ► **Mexican jumping bean** N fève f sauteuse ► **Mexican standoff** N (US fig) impasse f ► **Mexican wave** N hola f (vague déferlante produite dans un stade par les spectateurs qui se lèvent tour à tour)

Mexico [ˈmeksɪkəʊ] ①️ N le Mexique ②️ COMP ► **Mexico City** N Mexico

mezcaline [ˈmezkəlɪn] N = **mescaline**

mezzanine [ˈmezəniːn] N ④️ (= floor) entresol m ⑤️ (Theat) (Brit) dessous m de scène; (US) mezzanine f, corbeille f

mezzo(-soprano) [ˈmetsəʊ(səˈprɑːnəʊ)] N (= voice) mezzo-soprano m; (= singer) mezzo(-soprano) f

mezzotint [ˈmetsəʊtɪnt] N mezzo-tinto m inv

MF [emˈef] N (ABBR = **medium frequency**) OM

MFA [ˌemefˈeɪ] N (US Univ) (ABBR = **Master of Fine Arts**) diplôme des beaux-arts

MFH [ˌemefˈeɪtʃ] N (Brit) (ABBR = **Master of Foxhounds**) → **master**

mfrs. (Comm) (ABBR = **manufacturers**) → **manufacturer**

mg N (ABBR = **milligram(s)**) mg

Mgr ABBR = **Monseigneur** or **Monsignor**

mgr ABBR = **manager**

MHR [ˌemeɪtʃˈɑːʳ] N (in US) (ABBR = **Member of the House of Representatives**) ≈ député m

MHz (Rad etc) (ABBR = **megahertz**) MHz

MI N ④️ ABBR = **Michigan** ⑤️ (ABBR = **machine intelligence**) IA f

mi [miː] N (Mus) mi m

MI5 [ˌemaɪˈfaɪv] N (Brit) (ABBR = **Military Intelligence 5**) service britannique chargé de la surveillance du territoire, ≈ DST f

MI6 [ˌemaɪˈsɪks] N (Brit) (ABBR = **Military Intelligence 6**) services britanniques d'espionnage et de contre-espionnage, ≈ DGSE f

MIA [ˌemaɪˈeɪ] (Mil) (ABBR = **missing in action**) → **missing**

miaow [miːˈaʊ] ①️ N miaulement m, miaou m; **~!** miaou! ②️ VI miauler

miasma [mɪˈæzmə] N (pl **miasmas** or **miasmata** [mɪˈæzmətə]) miasme m

mica [ˈmaɪkə] ①️ N mica m ②️ COMP ► **micaschist** N micaschiste m

mice [maɪs] NPL of **mouse**

Mich. ABBR = **Michigan**

Michael [ˈmaɪkl] N Michel m

Michaelmas [ˈmɪklməs] ①️ N (also **~ Day**) la Saint-Michel ②️ COMP ► **Michaelmas daisy** N aster m d'automne ► **Michaelmas term** N (Brit Jur, Univ) trimestre m d'automne

Michelangelo [ˌmaɪkəlˈændʒɪləʊ] N Michel-Ange m

Michigan [ˈmɪʃɪgən] N le Michigan; **in ~** dans le Michigan; **Lake ~** le lac Michigan

Mick [mɪk] N ④️ dim of **Michael** ⑤️ (‡ pej) Irlandais m ⑥️ (Brit) **to take the ~*** se moquer; **to take the ~ out of sb*** se payer la tête de qn

Mickey [ˈmɪkɪ] ①️ N dim of **Michael** ②️ COMP ► **Mickey Finn** N boisson f droguée ► **Mickey Mouse** N (= cartoon character) Mickey m ◊ ADJ (* pej: also **mickey-mouse**) [car, penknife, regulations] à la noix*; [job, courses] pas sérieux, enfantin; [degree] sans valeur, à la noix*

mickey [ˈmɪkɪ] ①️ N (Brit) **to take the ~* out of sb** se payer la tête de qn; **he's always taking the ~*** il n'arrête pas de se payer la tête des gens ②️ COMP ► **mickey finn** N = **Mickey Finn**; → **Mickey** ► **mickey-mouse** ADJ → **Mickey**

micra [ˈmaɪkrə] NPL of **micron**

micro* [ˈmaɪkrəʊ] N ABBR = **microcomputer**

micro... [ˈmaɪkrəʊ] PREF micro...

microanalysis [ˌmaɪkrəʊəˈnælɪsɪs] N microanalyse f

microanalytical [ˌmaɪkrəʊˌænəˈlɪtɪkl] ADJ microanalytique

microbe [ˈmaɪkrəʊb] N microbe m

microbial [maɪˈkrəʊbɪəl], **microbian** [maɪˈkrəʊbɪən], **microbic** [maɪˈkrəʊbɪk] ADJ microbien

microbiological [ˌmaɪkrəʊbaɪəˈlɒdʒɪkəl] ADJ microbiologique

microbiologist [ˌmaɪkrəʊbaɪˈɒlədʒɪst] N microbiologiste mf

microbiology [ˌmaɪkrəʊbaɪˈɒlədʒɪ] N microbiologie f

microbus [ˈmaɪkrəʊˌbʌs] N (US Aut) microbus m

microcapsule [ˈmaɪkrəʊˌkæpsjʊl] N microcapsule f

microcassette [ˈmaɪkrəʊkəˈset] N microcassette f

microcephalic [ˌmaɪkrəʊsɪˈfælɪk] ADJ microcéphale

microcephaly [ˌmaɪkrəʊˈsefəlɪ] N microcéphalie f

microchip [ˈmaɪkrəʊˌtʃɪp] N puce f (électronique)

microcircuit [ˈmaɪkrəʊˌsɜːkɪt] N microcircuit m

microcircuitry [ˈmaɪkrəʊˈsɜːkətrɪ] N microcircuit m

microclimate [ˈmaɪkrəʊklaɪmɪt] N microclimat m

micrococcus [ˌmaɪkrəʊˈkɒkəs] N microcoque m

microcomputer [ˈmaɪkrəʊkəmˈpjuːtəʳ] N micro-ordinateur m

microcomputing [ˈmaɪkrəʊkəmˈpjuːtɪŋ] N micro-informatique f

microcopy [ˈmaɪkrəʊˌkɒpɪ] ①️ N microcopie f ②️ VT microcopier

microcosm [ˈmaɪkrəʊˌkɒzəm] N microcosme m; **a ~ of ...** un microcosme de ...; **in ~** en microcosme

microcosmic [ˌmaɪkrəʊˈkɒzmɪk] ADJ microcosmique

microcrystal [ˌmaɪkrəʊˈkrɪstəl] N microcristal m

microcrystalline [ˈmaɪkrəʊˈkrɪstəˌlaɪn] ADJ microcristallin

microculture [ˈmaɪkrəʊˌkʌltʃəʳ] N microculture f

microdissection [ˈmaɪkrəʊdɪˈsekʃən] N microdissection f

microdot [ˈmaɪkrəʊˌdɒt] N microcopie f

microeconomic [ˈmaɪkrəʊˌiːkəˈnɒmɪk] ADJ microéconomique

microeconomics [ˈmaɪkrəʊˌiːkəˈnɒmɪks] N (NonC) microéconomie f

microelectrode [ˈmaɪkrəʊɪˈlektrəʊd] N microélectrode f

microelectronic [ˈmaɪkrəʊɪlekˈtrɒnɪk] ADJ microélectronique

microelectronically [ˈmaɪkrəʊɪlekˈtrɒnɪklɪ] ADV microélectroniquement

microelectronics [ˈmaɪkrəʊɪlekˈtrɒnɪks] N (NonC) microélectronique f

microenvironment [ˈmaɪkrəʊɪnˈvaɪərənmənt] N microenvironnement m

microfauna [ˈmaɪkrəʊˌfɔːnə] N microfaune f

microfiche [ˈmaɪkrəʊˌfiːʃ] ①️ N microfiche f ②️ COMP ► **microfiche reader** N microlecteur m (pour microfiches)

microfilm [ˈmaɪkrəʊˌfɪlm] ①️ N microfilm m ②️ VT microfilmer ③️ COMP ► **microfilm reader** N microlecteur m

microflora [ˈmaɪkrəʊˌflɔːrə] N microflore f

microform [ˈmaɪkrəʊˌfɔːm] N microforme f

microgram [ˈmaɪkrəʊˌgrɑːm] N microgramme m

micrographic [ˌmaɪkrəʊˈgræfɪk] ADJ micrographique

micrographically [ˌmaɪkrəʊˈgræfɪklɪ] ADV micrographiquement

micrographics [ˌmaɪkrəʊˈgræfɪks] N (NonC) micrographie f

micrography [maɪˈkrɒgrəfɪ] N micrographie f

microgravity [ˈmaɪkrəʊˈgrævɪtɪ] N (Phys) microgravité f

microgroove [ˈmaɪkrəʊˌgruːv] N microsillon m

microhabitat [ˈmaɪkrəʊˈhæbɪtæt] N microhabitat m

microlight [ˈmaɪkrəʊˌlaɪt] N (Aviat) ULM m, ultra-léger-motorisé m

microlinguistics [ˈmaɪkrəʊlɪŋˈgwɪstɪks] N (NonC) microlinguistique f

microlitre, microliter (US) [ˈmaɪkrəʊˈliːtəʳ] N microlitre m

micromesh stockings [ˈmaɪkrəʊmeʃˈstɒkɪŋz] NPL bas mpl superfins

micrometeorite [ˈmaɪkrəʊˈmiːtɪə,raɪt] N micrométéorite f or m

micrometeorologist [ˈmaɪkrəʊmiːtɪəˈrɒlədʒɪst] N micrométéorologue mf

micrometeorology [ˈmaɪkrəʊmiːtɪəˈrɒlədʒɪ] N micrométéorologie f

micrometer [maɪˈkrɒmɪtəʳ] N ④️ (= instrument) micromètre m ⑤️ (US = unit) micromètre m

micrometry [maɪˈkrɒmɪtrɪ] N micrométrie f

microminiature [ˌmaɪkrəʊˈmɪnɪtʃəʳ] N microminiature f

microminiaturization [ˈmaɪkrəʊˌmɪnɪtʃəraɪˈzeɪʃən] N microminiaturisation f

microminiaturize [ˈmaɪkrəʊˈmɪnɪtʃəraɪz] VT microminiaturiser

micron [ˈmaɪkrɒn] N (pl **microns** or **micra** [ˈmaɪkrə]) micron m

microorganism [ˈmaɪkrəʊˈɔːgəˌnɪzəm] N micro-organisme m

microphone [ˈmaɪkrəfəʊn] N microphone m

microphotograph [ˈmaɪkrəʊˌfəʊtəˌgrɑːf] ①️ N microphotographie f ②️ VT microphotographier

microphotographic [ˈmaɪkrəʊˌfəʊtəˈgræfɪk] ADJ microphotographique

microphotography [ˈmaɪkrəʊfəˈtɒgrəfɪ] N microphotographie f

microphotometer [ˈmaɪkrəʊfəˈtɒmɪtəʳ] N microphotomètre m

microphotometric ['maɪkrəʊfəʊtə'metrɪk] ADJ microphotométrique

microphotometry ['maɪkrəʊ'tɒmɪtrɪ] N microphotométrie f

microphysical ['maɪkrəʊ'fɪzɪkəl] ADJ microphysique

microphysicist ['maɪkrəʊ'fɪzɪsɪst] N microphysicien(ne) m(f)

microphysics ['maɪkrəʊ,fɪzɪks] N (NonC) microphysique f

microprism ['maɪkrəʊ,prɪzəm] N microprisme m

microprobe ['maɪkrəʊ,prəʊb] N microsonde f

microprocessor [,maɪkrəʊ'prəʊsesər] N microprocesseur m

microprogram ['maɪkrəʊ,prəʊgræm] N microprogramme m

microprogramming ['maɪkrəʊ,prəʊgræmɪŋ] N (Comput) microprogrammation f

microreader ['maɪkrəʊ,ri:dər] N lecteur m de microforme, microlecteur m

microreproduction ['maɪkrəʊ,ri:prə'dʌkʃən] N microreproduction f

microscope ['maɪkrəʊskəʊp] N microscope m ; **under the ~** au microscope

microscopic [,maɪkrə'skɒpɪk] ADJ [a] (= visible with, using microscope) [cell, fibre, particle, organism] microscopique ; [examination, analysis] au microscope ; **~ section** coupe f histologique [b] (= minute) [amount] minuscule ; [writing] microscopique, minuscule ; **to be ~ in size** être d'une taille microscopique or minuscule [c] (= meticulous) **with ~ care** avec un soin minutieux ; **with ~ precision** avec une précision minutieuse

microscopical [,maɪkrə'skɒpɪkəl] ADJ = **microscopic**

microscopically [,maɪkrə'skɒpɪkəlɪ] ADV [a] (= with microscope) [examine, detect] au microscope [b] (= minutely) **~ small** microscopique

microscopy [maɪ'krɒskəpɪ] N microscopie f

microsecond ['maɪkrəʊ,sekənd] N microseconde f

microstructural [,maɪkrəʊ'strʌktʃərəl] ADJ microstructurel

microstructure ['maɪkrəʊ,strʌktʃər] N microstructure f

microsurgery ['maɪkrəʊ,sɜ:dʒərɪ] N microchirurgie f

microsurgical ['maɪkrəʊ'sɜ:dʒɪkəl] ADJ microchirurgical

microtransmitter [,maɪkrəʊtrænz'mɪtər] N microémetteur m

microvolt ['maɪkrəʊ,vəʊlt] N microvolt m

microwatt ['maɪkrəʊ,wɒt] N microwatt m

microwave ['maɪkrəʊ,weɪv] [1] N [a] (Phys, Rad) micro-onde f [b] (also **~ oven**) (four m à) micro-ondes m [2] VT faire cuire au micro-ondes [3] COMP ► **microwave spectroscopy** N spectroscopie f à ondes courtes

micturate ['mɪktjʊəreɪt] VI uriner

micturition [,mɪktjʊə'rɪʃən] N miction f

mid¹ [mɪd] PREF ► **May** la mi-mai ; **in ~ May** à la mi-mai, au milieu (du mois) de mai ; **in ~ morning** au milieu de la matinée ; **~-morning coffee break** pause-café f du matin ; **in ~ course** à mi-course ; **in ~ ocean** en plein océan, au milieu de l'océan ; **in ~ Atlantic** en plein Atlantique, au milieu de l'Atlantique ; **a ~-Channel collision** une collision au milieu de la Manche ; **in ~ discussion** etc au beau milieu de la discussion etc ; **she's in her ~ forties** elle a dans les quarante-cinq ans ; **Mid Wales** la région centrale du pays de Galles → **midday, midstream, mid-Victorian**

mid² [mɪd] PREP (liter) = **amid**

midair [,mɪd'eər] [1] N (lit) **in ~** en plein ciel ; (fig) **to leave sth in ~** laisser qch en suspens [2] ADJ [collision etc] en plein ciel

Midas ['maɪdəs] N Midas m ; **to have the ~ touch** avoir le don de tout transformer en or

mid-Atlantic [,mɪdət'læntɪk] ADJ [accent] mi-britannique, mi-américain

midbrain ['mɪd,breɪn] N mésencéphale m

midday [,mɪd'deɪ] [1] N midi m ; **at ~** à midi [2] ['mɪddeɪ] COMP [sun, heat] de midi

midden ['mɪdn] N (= dunghill) fumier m ; (= refuse-heap) tas m d'ordures ; **this place is (like) a ~!** c'est une vraie écurie or porcherie ici !, on se croirait dans une écurie or porcherie ici !

middie ['mɪdɪ] N = **middy**

middle ['mɪdl] [1] ADJ [chair, period etc] du milieu ; **the ~ button of his jacket** le bouton du milieu de sa veste ; **she's in her ~ forties** elle a dans les quarante-cinq ans ; (fig) **the ~ way** (= compromise) la solution intermédiaire ; (= happy medium) le juste milieu ; **to take the ~ course** choisir le moyen terme or la solution intermédiaire ; **he was of (less than) ~ height** il était d'une taille (inférieure à la) moyenne ; **I'm the ~ child of three** je suis la deuxième de trois enfants ; **the ~ fortnight in May** les deuxième et troisième semaines de mai → 3 [2] N [a] milieu m ; **in the ~ of the morning/year/century** au milieu de la matinée/de l'année/du siècle ; **in the ~ of the room** au milieu de la pièce ; **in the very ~ (of ...)** ◊ **right in the ~ (of ...)** au beau milieu (de ...) ; **the shot hit him in the ~ of his chest** le coup de feu l'a atteint en pleine poitrine ; **in the ~ of June** au milieu (du mois) de juin, à la mi-juin ; **by the ~ of the 19th century** vers le milieu du 19ᵉ siècle ; **they are all due to leave by the ~ of next year** ils doivent tous partir d'ici le milieu de l'année prochaine ; **it's in the ~ of nowhere** c'est dans un bled perdu* or en pleine brousse* ; **a village in the ~ of nowhere** un petit trou perdu* ; **I was in the ~ of my work** j'étais en plein travail ; **I'm in the ~ of reading it** je suis justement en train de le lire → **split** [b] (* = waist) taille f ; **he wore it round his ~** il le portait à la taille or autour de la taille ; **in the water up to his ~** dans l'eau jusqu'à mi-corps or la ceinture or la taille [3] COMP ► **middle age** N ≈ la cinquantaine ; **he's reached ~ age** il a la cinquantaine ; **during his ~ age** lorsqu'il avait la cinquantaine ► **middle-aged** ADJ [person] d'âge moyen ; [outlook, attitude] vieux jeu inv ► **the Middle Ages** NPL le Moyen Âge or moyen âge ► **Middle America** N les Américains mpl moyens ► **middle C** N (Mus) do m du milieu du piano ► **middle class** N **the ~ class(es)** les classes fpl moyennes, la classe moyenne ► **middle-class** ADJ des classes moyennes ► **middle distance** N **in the ~ distance** (Art etc) au second plan ; (gen) à mi-distance ► **middle-distance race** N (Sport) course f de demi-fond ► **middle-distance runner** N (Sport) coureur m, -euse f de demi-fond ► **middle ear** N (Anat) oreille f moyenne ► **Middle East** N Moyen-Orient m ► **Middle Eastern** ADJ du Moyen-Orient ► **Middle England** N (Brit fig) l'Angleterre f moyenne ► **Middle English** N (Ling) moyen anglais m ► **middle finger** N majeur m, médius m ► **Middle French** N (Ling) moyen français m ► **middle-grade manager** N (US) cadre m moyen ► **middle ground** N terrain m d'entente ► **Middle High German** N (Ling) moyen haut allemand m ► **the Middle Kingdom** N (Hist) (of Egypt) le Moyen Empire ; (of China) l'Empire m du Milieu ► **middle management** N (NonC) cadres mpl intermédiaires or moyens ; **to be in ~ management** être cadre intermédiaire or moyen ► **middle manager** N cadre m intermédiaire or moyen ► **middle name** N deuxième prénom m ; (Brit fig) **his ~ name is Scrooge** c'est un vieil Harpagon ; **discretion is my ~ name** la discrétion est ma plus grande

vertu or qualité ► **middle-of-the-road** ADJ (fig) [politics, approach, group] modéré, centriste ; [solution] moyen, du juste milieu ; [music] grand public inv ; [fashion] passe-partout inv ► **middle-of-the-roader** N modéré(e) m(f), centriste mf, partisan(e) m(f) du juste milieu ► **middle school** N ≈ premier cycle m du secondaire ► **middle-sized** ADJ [tree, building] de grandeur moyenne ; [parcel] de grosseur moyenne ; [person] de taille moyenne ► **middle voice** N (Ling) voix f moyenne ► **the Middle West** N (US) le Middle West, le Midwest

middlebrow* ['mɪdlbrəʊ] [1] N personne f sans grandes prétentions intellectuelles [2] ADJ intellectuellement moyen

middleman ['mɪdlmæn] N (pl -men) (gen) intermédiaire m ; (Comm) intermédiaire m, revendeur m ; **to cut out the ~** se passer d'intermédiaire

middlemost ['mɪdlməʊst] ADJ = **midmost**

middleweight ['mɪdlweɪt] (Boxing) [1] N (poids m) moyen m [2] ADJ [championship, boxer] de poids moyen

middling* ['mɪdlɪŋ] [1] ADJ [performance, result] moyen, passable ; [success] moyen ; **business is only ~** les affaires vont comme ci comme ça or moyennement ; **how are you?** — **comment ça va?** — **couci-couça** → **fair¹** [2] ADV* assez, moyennement ; **~ well** assez bien ; **~ big** assez grand

Middx ABBR = **Middlesex**

middy* ['mɪdɪ] N (Naut) (ABBR = **midshipman**) midship* m

Mideast [mɪd'i:st] (US) [1] N **the ~** le Moyen-Orient [2] ADJ du Moyen-Orient

midfield ['mɪd,fi:ld] N (Ftbl = place, player) milieu m de terrain

midfielder [mɪd'fi:ldər] N (Ftbl) milieu m de terrain

midge [mɪdʒ] N moucheron m

midget ['mɪdʒɪt] [1] N nain(e) m(f) ; (fig) puce f [2] ADJ minuscule

MIDI ['mɪdɪ] ABBR = **musical instrument digital interface** [1] N interface f MIDI [2] ADJ MIDI inv [3] COMP ► **MIDI system** N chaîne f (hi-fi) MIDI

midi ['mɪdɪ] N (= skirt) jupe f mi-longue

midland ['mɪdlənd] [1] N (Brit Geog) **the Midlands** les Midlands (les comtés du centre de l'Angleterre) [2] COMP du centre (du pays) ► **midland regions** NPL régions fpl centrales (de l'Angleterre)

midlife ['mɪd,laɪf] [1] ADJ de la cinquantaine [2] ADV autour de la cinquantaine [3] **in ~** autour de la cinquantaine [4] N COMP ► **midlife crisis** N crise f de la cinquantaine

midmost ['mɪdməʊst] ADJ le plus proche du milieu or centre

midnight ['mɪdnaɪt] [1] N minuit m ; **at ~** à minuit [2] COMP de minuit ► **midnight blue** N bleu m nuit ► **midnight-blue** ADJ bleu nuit inv ► **midnight oil** N **to burn the ~ oil** travailler très tard dans la nuit ; **his essay smells of the ~ oil*** on dirait qu'il a passé la moitié de la nuit sur sa dissertation ► **midnight sun** N soleil m de minuit

midpoint ['mɪdpɔɪnt] N milieu m ; **at ~ course**, à mi-parcours

midriff ['mɪdrɪf] N [of person] ventre m ; [of dress] taille f ; **dress with a bare ~** robe f découpée à la taille, robe f (deux-pièces) laissant voir le ventre

mid-sentence [,mɪd'sentəns] N **in ~** au beau milieu d'une phrase

midshipman ['mɪdʃɪpmən] N (pl -men) (Naut) midshipman m, ≈ enseigne m de vaisseau de deuxième classe, ≈ aspirant m

midships ['mɪdʃɪps] ADV = **amidships**

midsize ['mɪd,saɪz] ADJ de taille moyenne

midst [mɪdst] [1] N **in the ~ of** (= *in the middle of*) au milieu de; (= *surrounded by*) entouré de; (= *among*) parmi; (= *during*) pendant, au milieu de; **we are in the ~ of an economic crisis** nous sommes en pleine crise économique; **he's in the ~ of revising for his exams** il est en plein dans ses révisions; **in our ~** parmi nous; (*liter*) **in the ~ of plenty** dans l'abondance; **in the ~ of life** au milieu de la vie [2] PREP (*liter*) = **amidst**

midstream ['mɪd'striːm] [1] N **in ~** (*lit*) au milieu du courant; (*fig*) en plein milieu; (*when speaking*) au beau milieu d'une phrase; **to change course in ~** (*fig*) changer d'avis en cours de route *or* à mi-parcours; (*Sport*) changer de tactique en milieu de match → **horse** [2] ADV = **in midstream**; → **1**

midsummer ['mɪd,sʌmər] [1] N (= *height of summer*) milieu *m or* cœur *m* de l'été; (= *solstice*) solstice *m* d'été; **in ~** au cœur de l'été, en plein été; **at ~** à la Saint-Jean; (*Literat*) **"A Midsummer Night's Dream"** «le Songe d'une nuit d'été» [2] COMP [*heat, weather, storm etc*] estival, de plein été ► **Midsummer Day** N la Saint-Jean ► **midsummer madness** N **it's ~ madness** c'est de la folie pure

midterm ['mɪd'tɜːm] [1] N [a] le milieu du trimestre [b] (*also* ~ **holiday**) ≈ vacances *fpl* de (la) Toussaint (*or* de février *or* de Pentecôte) [2] COMP ► **midterm elections** NPL ≈ élections *fpl* législatives (*intervenant au milieu du mandat présidentiel*) ► **midterm exams** NPL examens *mpl* de milieu de trimestre

midtown ['mɪdtaʊn] (*US*) [1] N centre-ville *m* [2] ADJ du centre-ville

mid-Victorian ['mɪdvɪk'tɔːrɪən] ADJ (*Brit*) du milieu de l'époque victorienne

midway [,mɪd'weɪ] [1] ADJ [*place*] (situé à) mi-chemin [2] ADV [*stop, pause*] à mi-chemin, à mi-route; **~ between** à mi-chemin entre [3] N (*US: in fair*) (centre *m* de la) fête foraine

midweek [,mɪd'wiːk] [1] ADJ [*flight, performance, match*] en milieu de semaine; (*Rail*) **~ return (ticket)** (billet *m*) aller et retour *m* en semaine (*meilleur marché*) [2] ADV en milieu de semaine

Midwest [,mɪd'west] N (*in US*) **the ~** le Middle West, le Midwest

Midwestern [,mɪd'westən] ADJ du Middle West, du Midwest

Midwesterner [mɪd'westənər] N natif *m*, -ive *f or* habitant(e) *m(f)* du Middle West

midwife ['mɪdwaɪf] N (*pl* -**wives**) sage-femme *f*, maïeuticien *m*

midwifery ['mɪdwɪfərɪ] N (*NonC* = *profession*) profession *f* de sage-femme; **she's studying ~** elle fait des études de sage-femme

midwinter [,mɪd'wɪntər] [1] N (= *heart of winter*) milieu *m or* fort *m* de l'hiver; (= *solstice*) solstice d'hiver; **at ~** au solstice d'hiver, en plein hiver [2] COMP [*cold, snow, temperature*] hivernal, de plein hiver

mien [miːn] N (*frm, liter*) contenance *f*, air *m*, mine *f*

miff* [mɪf] [1] N (= *quarrel*) fâcherie *f*; (= *sulks*) bouderie *f* [2] VT fâcher, mettre en boule*; **to be ~ed about** *or* **at sth** être fâché *or* vexé de qch

▼ **might**[1] [maɪt] [1] MODAL AUX VB → **may**[1] [2] COMP ► **might-have-been** N ce qui aurait pu être, espoir *m* déçu, vœu *m* non comblé; (= *person*) raté(e) *m(f)*, fruit *m* sec

might[2] [maɪt] N (*NonC*) puissance *f*, force(s) *f(pl)* ■ (*PROV*) **~ is right** la force prime le droit; **with ~ and main** ◊ **with all one's ~** de toutes ses forces

mightily ['maɪtɪlɪ] ADV [a] († = *greatly*) considérablement; **to deem sth ~ important** donner une importance considérable à qch [b] (*liter* = *powerfully*) [*strike, hit*] vigoureusement

mightiness ['maɪtɪnɪs] N puissance *f*, pouvoir *m*, grandeur *f*

mightn't ['maɪtnt] = **might not**; → **may**[1]

mighty ['maɪtɪ] [1] ADJ (*liter*) [*nation, king, river, effort, blow, bang*] puissant; [*oak, redwood*] imposant, majestueux; [*power*] formidable; **the ~ ocean** le vaste océan → **high** [2] ADV (*esp US**) vachement* **the mighty** NPL les puissants *mpl*; (*Bible*) **how are the ~ fallen** ils sont tombés les héros

mignonette [,mɪnjə'net] N (*Bot*) réséda *m*

migraine ['miːgreɪn] N (*Med*) migraine *f*; **it gives me a ~** ça me donne la migraine; **to get** *or* **suffer from ~s** souffrir de migraines

migrant ['maɪgrənt] [1] ADJ [a] (*Agr, Ind*) [*worker, labour*] (*gen*) itinérant; (= *immigrant*) immigré; (= *seasonal*) saisonnier; [*family, child*] (*gen*) itinérant; (= *nomadic*) nomade; (= *immigrant*) d'immigrés [b] (*Zool*) migrateur (-trice *f*) [2] N [a] (= *bird, animal*) migrateur *m*; (= *person*) migrant(e) *m(f)* [b] (*also* ~ **worker**) (*gen*) travailleur *m* itinérant; (*immigrant*) travailleur *m* immigré; (*seasonal*) travailleur *m* saisonnier → **economic**

migrate [maɪ'greɪt] VI migrer

migration [maɪ'greɪʃən] N migration *f*

migratory ['maɪgrətərɪ] ADJ [a] (*Zool*) [*bird, animal, fish, locust*] migrateur (-trice *f*); [*habits, movement, journey*] migratoire [b] (*Ind, Agr*) [*labour*] (*gen*) itinérant; (= *immigrant*) immigré; (= *seasonal*) saisonnier; [*population*] (*gen*) itinérant; (= *nomadic*) nomade; (= *immigrant*) d'immigrés; **~ pressures** les pressions *fpl* qui obligent les gens à migrer

mikado [mɪ'kɑːdəʊ] N mikado *m*

Mike [maɪk] N [a] *dim of* **Michael** [b] **for the love of ~**! pour l'amour du ciel!

mike* [maɪk] N (ABBR = **microphone**) micro *m*

milady † ['mɪleɪdɪ] N madame la comtesse *etc*

Milan [mɪ'læn] N Milan

Milanese [,mɪlə'niːz] ADJ (*gen, also Culin*) milanais

milch cow ['mɪltʃkaʊ] N [a] (*Agr*†) vache *f* laitière [b] (*fig*) vache *f* à lait

mild [maɪld] [1] ADJ [*climate, winter, voice, flavour, cheese, soap, shampoo*] doux (douce *f*); [*tobacco, reproach, punishment*] léger; [*exercise, effect, protest*] modéré; [*sauce*] peu épicé *or* relevé; [*medicine*] bénin (-igne *f*), anodin; [*illness*] bénin (-igne *f*); **it's ~ today** il fait doux aujourd'hui; (*Met*) **a ~ spell** (*gen*) une période clémente; (*after frost*) un redoux; **he had a ~ form of polio** il a eu la poliomyélite sous une forme bénigne *or* atténuée; **a ~ sedative** un sédatif léger; (*Culin*) **a ~ curry** un curry pas trop fort *or* pimenté [2] N (*Brit: also* ~ **ale**) bière brune faiblement alcoolisée

mildew ['mɪldjuː] [1] N (*NonC*) (*gen*) moisissure *f*; (*on wheat, roses etc*) rouille *f*; (*on vine*) mildiou *m* [2] VT [+ *plant*] piquer de rouille; [+ *vine*] frapper de mildiou; [+ *paper, cloth*] piquer d'humidité [3] VI [*roses, wheat etc*] se rouiller; [*vine*] devenir mildiousé, être attaqué par le mildiou; [*paper, cloth*] se piquer

mildewed ['mɪl,djuːd] ADJ [*carpet, mattress, wallpaper, wall, wood*] moisi; [*cloth, paper*] piqué (par l'humidité); [*wheat, roses*] piqué de rouille; [*vine*] mildiousé

mildly ['maɪldlɪ] ADV [a] (= *gently*) [*say, reply, ask*] doucement, avec douceur; **to protest ~** protester faiblement *or* timidement; (= *euphemistically*) **that's putting it ~** c'est le moins que l'on puisse dire; **to call him naïve is putting it ~** le qualifier de naïf est un euphémisme [b] (= *moderately*) [*interested, amusing*] modérément; [*surprised, irritated, encouraging*] légèrement; **to be ~ critical of sb/sth** critiquer légèrement qn/qch

mild-mannered [,maɪld'mænəd] ADJ doux (douce *f*), d'un naturel doux

mildness ['maɪldnɪs] N [*of person, manner, response, weather, soap*] douceur *f*; [*of flavour, food, tobacco, cigarette*] légèreté *f*; [*of punishment, sentence*] clémence *f*; (*Med*) [*of illness*] bénignité *f*

mile [maɪl] N [a] mile *m* (= 1 609,33 m); (*also* **nautical ~**) mille *m*; **a 50-~ journey** ≈ un trajet de 80 km; **it's 12 ~s to Manchester** ≈ il y a vingt kilomètres d'ici à Manchester; (*Aut*) **30 ~s per gallon** ≈ huit litres aux cent; **50 ~s per hour** ≈ 80 kilomètres à l'heure; **there was nothing but sand for ~s and ~s** il n'y avait que du sable sur des kilomètres (et des kilomètres); **they live ~s away** ils habitent à cent lieues d'ici; **we've walked (for) ~s!** on a marché pendant des kilomètres!, on a fait des kilomètres! (IMPERIAL SYSTEM); (*fig*) **not a million ~s from here** sans aller chercher bien loin; **you could see/smell it a ~ off** ça se voyait/se sentait à un kilomètre; **you were ~s off (the) target*** vous n'étiez pas près de toucher la cible, vous étiez bien loin du but; **sorry, I was ~s away*** (= *day-dreaming*) désolé, j'étais ailleurs; **the President is willing to go the extra ~ for peace** *or* **to achieve peace** le président est prêt à faire un effort supplémentaire pour ramener la paix [b] **~s*** (= *lots*): **she's ~s better than I am at maths** elle est bien plus calée que moi en maths*; **he's ~s bigger than you** il est bien plus grand que toi

mileage ['maɪlɪdʒ] [1] N [a] (*Aut etc* = *distance covered*) distance *f or* parcours *m* en milles, ≈ kilométrage *m*; **the indicator showed a very low ~** le compteur marquait peu de kilomètres; **the car had a low ~** la voiture avait peu roulé *or* avait peu de kilomètres; **what ~ has this car done?** quel est le kilométrage de cette voiture?, combien de kilomètres a cette voiture?; **most of our ~ is in and around town** nous roulons surtout en ville et dans les alentours [b] (*Aut etc* = *miles per gallon or litre*) ≈ consommation *f* (de carburant) aux cent (km); **for a car of that size the ~ was very good** pour une voiture aussi puissante elle consommait peu; **you'll get a better ~ from this car** vous consommerez moins (d'essence) avec cette voiture → **gas** [c] (* *fig* = *potential, profit*) **he got a lot of ~ out of it** (*of idea, story, event*) il en a tiré le maximum; (*of coat, gadget etc*) ça lui a fait de l'usage; **there's still some ~ left in it** (*idea etc*) on peut encore en tirer quelque chose; (*coat etc*) ça peut encore faire de l'usage; **he decided there was no ~ in provoking a row with his boss** il a décidé que cela ne servirait à rien de se disputer avec son patron [2] COMP ► **mileage allowance** N (*Admin etc*) ≈ indemnité *f* kilométrique ► **mileage indicator** N (*Aut*) ≈ compteur *m* kilométrique

mileometer [maɪ'lɒmɪtər] N = **milometer**

milepost ['maɪlpəʊst] N ≈ borne *f* kilométrique

miler* ['maɪlər] N (= *person, horse*) athlète ou cheval qui court le mile

milestone ['maɪlstəʊn] N (*lit*) borne *f* (milliaire), ≈ borne *f* kilométrique; (*fig: in life, career etc*) jalon *m*, événement *m* marquant *or* déterminant

milieu ['miːljɜː] N (*pl* **milieus**) (*frm*) milieu *m* (social)

militancy ['mɪlɪtənsɪ] N militantisme *m*

militant ['mɪlɪtənt] [1] ADJ militant [2] N (*all senses*) militant(e) *m(f)* [3] COMP ► **Militant Tendency** N (*Brit Pol*) ex-faction trotskiste du parti travailliste britannique

militantly ['mɪlɪtəntlɪ] ADV [*act*] de façon militante; **to be ~ opposed to sb/sth** s'opposer activement à qn/qch; **~ nationalist/Catholic** d'un nationalisme/catholicisme militant

► LANGUAGE IN USE: **might** 15.3

militarily [‚mɪlɪtərɪlɪ] ADV [significant, useful, sensitive, effective] d'un point de vue militaire; [strong, powerful] militairement; **to intervene/ respond ~** intervenir/répondre militairement

militarism [‚mɪlɪtərɪzəm] N militarisme m

militarist [‚mɪlɪtərɪst] ADJ, N militariste mf

militaristic [‚mɪlɪtə'rɪstɪk] ADJ (pej) militariste

militarize [‚mɪlɪtəraɪz] VT militariser

military [‚mɪlɪtərɪ] 1 ADJ [government, life, uniform] militaire; [family] de militaires; (US) ~ **academy** école f (spéciale) militaire; **of ~ age** en âge de faire son service (militaire or national); ~ **attaché** attaché m militaire; ~ **band** musique f militaire; ~ **police** police f militaire; ~ **policeman** agent m de la police militaire; ~ **superiority** supériorité f militaire; ~ **training** préparation f militaire; **to do one's ~ service** faire son service (militaire or national) 2 **the military** NPL l'armée f, le(s) militaire(s) m(pl) 3 COMP ► **military-industrial complex** N complexe m militaro-industriel

militate [‚mɪlɪteɪt] VI militer (**against** contre, **for, in favour of** pour)

militia [mɪ'lɪʃə] COLLECTIVE N (gen) milice(s) f(pl); (US) **the ~** la réserve (territoriale) → **state**

militiaman [mɪ'lɪʃəmən] N (pl **-men**) milicien m

milk [mɪlk] 1 N (also Cosmetics) lait m; **coconut ~** lait m de coco; **moisturising ~** lait m hydratant; (fig) **the ~ of human kindness** le lait de la tendresse humaine; (fig) **a land flowing with ~ and honey** un pays de cocagne; (hum) **he came home with the ~*** il est rentré avec le jour or à potron-minet*; **he dismissed the report as ~ and water** il a déclaré que le rapport n'était ni fait ni à faire → **cleansing, condense, cry, skim**
2 VT a [+ cow] traire
b (fig = rob) dépouiller (**of** de), exploiter; **his son ~ed him of all his savings** son fils l'a dépouillé de toutes ses économies; **it ~ed (him of) his strength** cela a sapé or miné ses forces; **to ~ sb of ideas/information** soutirer des idées/des renseignements à qn; **to ~ sb dry** exploiter qn à fond, épuiser les forces créatrices de qn
3 VI **to go ~ing** (s'en) aller traire ses vaches
4 COMP ► **milk-and-water** ADJ (fig pej) [talk] manque* ► **milk bar** N milk-bar m ► **milk can** N pot m à lait; (larger) bidon m à lait ► **milk chocolate** N chocolat m au lait ► **milk churn** N bidon m à lait ► **milk diet** N régime m lacté ► **milk duct** N (Anat) canal m galactophore ► **milk fever** N fièvre f lactée ► **milk float** N (Brit) voiture f de laitier ► **milk gland** N (Anat) glande f galactogène ► **milk jug** N (petit) pot m à lait ► **milk of magnesia** N lait m de magnésie, magnésie f hydratée ► **milk pan** N petite casserole f pour le lait ► **milk powder** N lait m en poudre ► **milk products** NPL produits mpl laitiers ► **milk pudding** N entremets m au lait ► **milk round** N (Brit) tournée f (du laitier); (Brit Univ) tournée f de recrutement dans les universités; **to do a ~ round** [child etc] livrer le lait ► **milk run*** N (Aviat) vol m sans accroc ► **milk saucepan** N petite casserole f pour le lait ► **milk shake** N milk-shake m ► **milk stout** N (Brit) bière f brune douce ► **milk tooth** N dent f de lait ► **the milk train** N (fig hum) le tout premier train (du matin) ► **milk-white** ADJ (liter) d'une blancheur de lait, blanc (blanche f) comme le or du lait, laiteux

milking [‚mɪlkɪŋ] 1 N traite f 2 COMP [pail, stool] à traire ► **milking machine** N trayeuse f (mécanique) ► **milking time** N heure f de la traite

milkmaid [‚mɪlkmeɪd] N trayeuse f (personne)

milkman [‚mɪlkmən] N (pl **-men**) laitier m

milksop* [‚mɪlksɒp] N chiffe f molle* (fig), lavette* f (fig), mollusque* m (fig)

milkweed [‚mɪlkwiːd] N (Bot) laiteron m

milky [‚mɪlkɪ] 1 ADJ a (in colour) [liquid, mist, haze, blue, green] laiteux; [eyes] plein d'opacités blanchâtres b (Culin) [drink] à base de lait; [coffee, tea] avec beaucoup de lait 2 COMP ► **the Milky Way** N la Voie lactée ► **milky-white** ADJ [skin, sap] d'un blanc laiteux

mill [mɪl] 1 N a (also **windmill** or **water ~**) moulin m; (Ind: for grain) minoterie f; (small: for coffee etc) moulin m; **pepper-~** moulin m à poivre; (fig) **to go through the ~** passer par de dures épreuves, en voir de dures*; (fig) **to put sb through the ~** mettre qn à l'épreuve, en faire voir de dures à qn* → **coffee, run, windmill**
b (= factory) (gen) usine f, fabrique f; (also **spinning ~**) filature f; (also **weaving ~**) tissage m; (also **steel ~**) aciérie f; **paper ~** papeterie f; **cotton ~** filature f de coton → **sawmill**
2 VT a [+ flour, coffee, pepper] moudre
b (Tech) [+ screw, nut] moleter; [+ wheel, edge of coin] créneler; **~ed edge** [of coin] tranche f cannelée
3 VI **to ~ round sth** [crowd etc] grouiller autour de qch
4 COMP ► **mill girl** N (Ind) ouvrière f des filatures (or des tissages or des aciéries) ► **mill owner** N (Ind) industriel m ► **mill race** N bief m d'amont or de moulin ► **mill stream** N courant m du bief ► **mill wheel** N roue f de moulin ► **mill worker** N (Ind) ouvrier m, -ière f des filatures (or des tissages or des aciéries)
► **mill about, mill around** VI [crowd] grouiller, fourmiller; [cattle etc] tourner sur place or en rond

millboard [‚mɪlbɔːd] N carton m pâte

millenarian [‚mɪlə'nɛərɪən] ADJ, N millénariste mf

millenary [mɪ'lenərɪ], **millennial** [mɪ'lenɪəl] ADJ, N millénaire m

millennium [mɪ'lenɪəm] N (pl **millenniums** or **millennia** [mɪ'lenɪə]) millénaire m; (Rel, also fig) **the ~** le millénium

millepede [‚mɪlɪpiːd] N = **millipede**

miller [‚mɪlər] N meunier m; (Ind: large-scale) minotier m

millet [‚mɪlɪt] N (NonC) millet m

millhand [‚mɪlhænd] N (Ind) = **mill worker**; → **mill**

milli... [‚mɪlɪ] PREF milli...

milliard [‚mɪlɪɑːd] N (Brit) milliard m

millibar [‚mɪlɪbɑːr] N millibar m

milligram(me) [‚mɪlɪgræm] N milligramme m

millilitre, milliliter (US) [‚mɪlɪ‚liːtər] N millilitre m

millimetre, millimeter (US) [‚mɪlɪ‚miːtər] N millimètre m

milliner [‚mɪlɪnər] N modiste f, chapelier m, -ière f

millinery [‚mɪlɪnərɪ] N (NonC) chapellerie f féminine

milling [‚mɪlɪŋ] 1 N (NonC) [of flour etc] mouture f; [of screw etc] moletage m; [of coin] crénelage m 2 ADJ [crowd, people] grouillant

million [‚mɪljən] N million m; **a ~ men** un million d'hommes; **he's one in a ~*** c'est la crème des hommes or la perle des hommes; **it's a chance etc in a ~** c'est une occasion etc unique; (fig) **~s of ...*** des milliers de ...; **thanks a ~!*** merci mille fois!; **to feel (like) a ~ dollars** or (esp US) **bucks*** se sentir dans une forme époustouflante*; **she looked (like) a ~ dollars** or (esp US) **bucks in her new outfit*** elle était absolument superbe dans sa nouvelle tenue

millionaire [‚mɪljə'nɛər] N millionnaire m, ≈ milliardaire m

millionairess [‚mɪljə'nɛərɪs] N millionnaire f

millionth [‚mɪljənθ] 1 ADJ millionième 2 N millionième mf; (= fraction) millionième m

millipede [‚mɪlɪpiːd] N mille-pattes m inv

millisecond [‚mɪlɪ‚sekənd] N milliseconde f

millpond [‚mɪlpɒnd] N bief m or retenue f d'un moulin; **the sea was like a ~** c'était une mer d'huile

Mills bomb [‚mɪlz‚bɒm] N grenade f à main

millstone [‚mɪlstəʊn] N (lit) meule f; (fig) **it's a ~ round his neck** c'est un boulet qu'il traîne avec lui

millwright [‚mɪlraɪt] N constructeur m or installateur m de moulins

milometer [maɪ'lɒmɪtər] N (Brit) compteur m de miles, ≈ compteur m kilométrique

milord [mɪ'lɔːd] N milord m

milt [mɪlt] N laitance f, laite f

mime [maɪm] 1 N a (= skill, classical play) mime m; (= modern play) mimodrame m; (fig = gestures etc) mimique f b (= actor) mime m 2 VTI mimer; **to ~ to a tape** (= sing etc) chanter etc en play-back 3 COMP ► **mime artist** N mime mf

mimeo [‚mɪmɪəʊ] ABBR = **mimeograph** 1 N ronéo® f 2 VT ronéoter*

Mimeograph® [‚mɪmɪəgrɑːf] 1 N (= machine) ronéo® f; (= copy) polycopié m 2 VT **mimeograph** ronéotyper, ronéoter*

mimetic [mɪ'metɪk] ADJ mimétique

mimic [‚mɪmɪk] 1 N imitateur m, -trice f 2 ADJ a (= imitating) imitateur (-trice f) b (= sham) factice, simulé 3 VT (= copy) imiter; (= burlesque) imiter, singer; **computers that ~ human intelligence** des ordinateurs qui cherchent à reproduire l'intelligence humaine

mimicry [‚mɪmɪkrɪ] N (NonC) imitation f; (Zool) mimétisme m

mimosa [mɪ'məʊzə] N a (= tree) mimosa m b (US = cocktail) mimosa m (champagne-jus d'orange)

Min. (Brit) ABBR = **Ministry**

min. a (ABBR = **minute¹**) min. b (ABBR = **minimum**) min.

mina [‚maɪnə] N = **mynah**

minaret [‚mɪnəret] N minaret m

minatory [‚mɪnətərɪ] ADJ (frm) [silence, place] menaçant

mince [mɪns] 1 N (Brit Culin) bifteck m haché, hachis m de viande 2 VT a [+ meat, vegetables] hacher; **~d beef** bœuf m haché b (fig) **he didn't ~ (his) words** il n'a pas mâché ses mots, il n'y est pas allé par quatre chemins; **never one to ~ words, he ...** n'ayant pas l'habitude de mâcher ses mots, il ... 3 VI (in talking) parler du bout des lèvres; (in walking) marcher en minaudant; **to ~ in/out** entrer/sortir en minaudant 4 COMP ► **mince pie** N (Culin) tartelette f de Noël (aux fruits secs)
► **mince up** VT SEP (Culin etc) hacher

mincemeat [‚mɪnsmiːt] N a (Culin) hachis de fruits secs, de pommes et de graisse, (US) = **mince** 1; (fig) **to make ~ of** [+ opponent, enemy] battre à plate(s) couture(s)*, pulvériser; [+ theories, arguments] pulvériser

mincer [‚mɪnsər] N hachoir m (appareil)

mincing [‚mɪnsɪŋ] 1 ADJ (pej) [steps, gait, voice] affecté 2 COMP ► **mincing machine** N hachoir m

mincingly [‚mɪnsɪŋlɪ] ADV (pej) [say, walk] en minaudant

▼ **mind** [maɪnd]

1 NOUN	4 COMPOUNDS
2 TRANSITIVE VERB	5 PHRASAL VERBS
3 INTRANSITIVE VERB	

1 NOUN
a = **brain** esprit m; **a logical/an analytical/a creative ~** un esprit logique/d'analyse/créateur or créatif; **he is one of the great ~s of**

the century c'est un des grands esprits de son siècle ■ (*PROV*) **great ~s think alike** les grands esprits se rencontrent; **he has the ~ of a five-year-old** il a cinq ans d'âge mental; **~ over matter** victoire de l'esprit sur la matière; **his ~ went blank** il a eu un trou *ou* un passage à vide; **his ~ is going** il n'a plus toute sa tête; **at the back of my ~ I had the feeling that ...** je sentais confusément que ...; **of sound ~** sain d'esprit; **to be of unsound ~** ne plus avoir toutes ses facultés (mentales); **that's a load** *or* **a weight off my ~!** c'est un gros souci de moins, cela m'ôte un poids; **what's on your ~?** qu'est-ce qui vous préoccupe *or* vous tracasse?; **it came (in)to** *or* **entered my ~ that ...** il m'est venu à l'esprit que ..., l'idée m'est venue que ...; **to come** *or* **spring to ~** venir à l'esprit; **she wanted to get into the ~ of this woman** elle voulait se mettre dans la peau de cette femme; **I can't get it out of my ~** je ne peux pas m'empêcher d'y penser; **you can put that right out of your ~!** tu peux faire une croix dessus!; **try to put it out of your ~** essayez de ne plus y penser; **to let one's ~ run on sth** se laisser aller à penser à qch; **to read** *or* **see into sb's ~** lire dans les pensées de qn; **to set** *or* **put sb's ~ at ease** *or* **rest** rassurer qn

[b] = **attention, concentration** **to have one's ~ on sth** être préoccupé par qch; **to have one's ~ on something else** avoir la tête ailleurs; **to let one's ~ wander** relâcher son attention; **it went quite** *or* **right** *or* **clean* out of my ~** ça m'est complètement sorti de la tête*; **to bring one's ~ to bear on sth** porter *ou* concentrer son attention sur qch; **to give one's ~ to sth** bien réfléchir à qch; **I haven't had time to give my ~ to it** je n'ai pas eu le temps de bien y réfléchir; **he can't give his whole ~ to his work** il n'arrive pas à se concentrer sur son travail; **to keep one's ~ on sth** se concentrer sur qch; **to put** *or* **set one's ~ to a problem** s'attaquer à un problème; **you can do it if you put** *or* **set your ~ to it** tu peux le faire si tu le veux vraiment; **this will take her ~ off her troubles** cela lui changera les idées

[c] = **opinion** avis *m*, idée *f*; **to my ~** à mon avis; **to have a closed ~ (on** *or* **about sth)** avoir des idées *ou* opinions arrêtées (sur *or* au sujet de qch); **to have a ~ of one's own** [*person*] avoir ses idées; [*machine*] avoir des caprices; **they were of one ~** *or* **like** *or* **the same ~** ils étaient d'accord *ou* du même avis; **I'm still of the same ~** je n'ai pas changé d'avis; **they thought with one ~** ils étaient unanimes; **to know one's own ~** savoir ce que l'on veut; **to make up one's ~ to do sth** décider de faire qch; **we can't make up our ~s about the house** nous ne savons pas quelle décision prendre pour la maison; **I can't make up my ~ about him** je ne sais pas vraiment que penser de lui

[d] = **inclination, intention** envie *f*; **you can do it if you have a ~ (to)** vous pouvez le faire si vous en avez envie; **I have no ~ to offend him†** je n'ai aucune envie de l'offenser; **I've a good ~ to do it** j'ai bien envie de le faire; **I've a good ~ to tell him everything!** j'ai bien envie de tout lui dire!; **I've half a ~ to do it*** j'ai presque envie de le faire; **nothing is further from my ~!** (bien) loin de moi cette pensée!; **nothing was further from my ~ than going to see her** je n'avais nullement l'intention d'aller la voir; **I was of a ~ to go and see him** j'avais l'intention d'aller le voir; **to set one's ~ on doing sth** avoir fermement l'intention de faire qch

[e] = **memory** **to bear sth in ~** (= *take account of*) tenir compte de qch; (= *remember*) ne pas oublier qch; **bear it in ~!** songez-y bien!; **I'll bear you in ~** je songerai *ou* penserai à vous; **to bring** *or* **call sth to ~** rappeler qch; **to keep sth in ~** ne pas oublier qch; **we must keep in ~ that ...** n'oublions pas que ...; (*liter*) **to pass out of**

~ tomber dans l'oubli; **that puts me in ~ of ...** cela me rappelle ...; **to stick in sb's ~** rester gravé dans la mémoire de qn

[f] SET STRUCTURES

♦ **in + mind**: **it's all in the ~** tout ça, c'est dans la tête*; **have you (got) anything particular in ~?** avez-vous quelque chose de particulier en tête?; **do you have somebody in ~ for the job?** vous avez quelqu'un en vue pour ce poste?; **to have (it) in ~ to do sth** penser faire qch; **to be in two ~s about doing sth** hésiter à faire qch; **I'm in two ~s about it** j'hésite, je me tâte*; **I'm not clear in my own ~ about it** je ne sais pas qu'en penser moi-même; **to be easy in one's ~ (about sth)** avoir l'esprit tranquille (à propos de qch); **to be uneasy in one's ~ (about sth)** être inquiet (au sujet de qch); **to be in one's right ~** avoir toute sa raison *ou* sa tête; **nobody in their right ~ would do that** aucun être sensé ne ferait cela; **in one's ~'s eye** en imagination

♦ **out of one's mind**: **to be out of one's ~* (with worry/jealousy)** être fou (d'inquiétude/de jalousie); **to go out of one's ~ with worry/jealousy** devenir fou d'inquiétude/de jalousie; **he's out of his ~!** il est complètement fou!; **you must be out of your ~!** tu es complètement fou!, ça ne va pas?!*; **he went out of his ~** il a perdu la tête *ou* la raison

2 TRANSITIVE VERB

[a] = **pay attention to** faire *or* prêter attention à; (= *beware of*) prendre garde à; (*US* = *listen to*) écouter; **~ what you're doing!** (fais) attention à ce que tu fais!; **~ you don't fall!** prenez garde de ne pas tomber!; **~ what I say!** écoute bien ce que je te dis!, fais bien attention à ce que je te dis!; **~ the step!** attention à la marche!; **~ your head!** attention à votre tête!; **~ your backs!** gare à vous!, dégagez!*; **~ yourself!** ◊ **~ your eye!** prends garde!, fais gaffe!*; **~ your language/ your manners!** surveille ton langage/tes manières!; **~ how you go*** prends bien soin de toi; **don't ~ him!** ne t'occupe pas de lui!, ne fais pas attention à lui!; (*iro*) **don't ~ me!*** ne vous gênez surtout pas (pour moi)!* (*iro*)

[b] = **dislike, object to** **I don't ~ ironing/ travelling alone** ça ne me dérange pas de faire le repassage/de voyager seul; **I don't ~ wet weather** la pluie ne me dérange pas; **I don't ~ him but she's awful!*** lui, passe encore *ou* lui, ça va, mais elle, je la trouve vraiment horrible!; **I wouldn't ~ a cup of coffee*** une tasse de café ne serait pas de refus*, je prendrais bien une tasse de café*; **~ you** (*frm*) *or* **me saying (so)** si je puis me permettre; **I don't ~ telling you*, I was shocked** inutile de dire que j'ai été vraiment choqué; **I don't ~ going with you** je veux bien vous accompagner; **cigarette? — I don't ~ if I do** une cigarette? — ce n'est pas de refus!*

♦ **would you mind** + *gerund*: **would you ~ opening the door?** cela vous ennuierait d'ouvrir la porte?; **would you ~ coming with me?** cela vous dérangerait de m'accompagner?; (*abruptly*) suivez-moi, s'il vous plaît

[c] = **care** **I don't ~ what people say** je me moque du qu'en-dira-t-on; **I don't ~ where we go** peu importe où nous allons

[d] = **take charge of** [+ *children, animals*] garder; [+ *shop, business*] garder, tenir; (*fig*) **to ~ the shop*** *or* (*US*) **the store*** veiller au grain

[e] **dial** = **remember** **I ~ the day when ...** je me rappelle le jour où ...

3 INTRANSITIVE VERB

[a] = **object** **if you don't ~** si cela ne vous fait rien; (*iro*: *indignantly*) **if you don't ~!** non, mais!; **do you ~ if I take this book?** *or* **I don't ~ at all** ça ne vous ennuie pas que je prenne ce livre? — mais non, je vous en prie; **I'm sure they won't ~ if you don't come** je suis sûre

qu'ils ne seront pas trop contrariés si tu ne viens pas

[b] = **care** **which do you want? — I don't ~** lequel voulez-vous? — ça m'est égal

♦ **never mind** (= *don't worry*) ne t'en fais pas!, ne t'inquiète pas!; (= *it makes no odds*) ça ne fait rien!, peu importe!; **never ~ that now!** (*soothingly*) n'y pense plus!; (*irritably*) ça peut très bien attendre!; **he can't walk, never ~* run** il ne peut pas marcher, encore moins courir; **never you ~!*** ça ne te regarde pas!, ce ne sont pas tes oignons!*

[c] = **be sure** **~ you tell her!** n'oubliez pas de lui dire!; **~ and come to see us!*** n'oublie pas de venir nous voir!; **be there at ten, ~*** sois là à 10 heures sans faute

♦ **mind you***: **~ you, I didn't know he was going to Paris** remarquez, je ne savais pas qu'il allait à Paris; **~ you, it won't be easy** mais ce ne sera pas facile pour autant; **~ you, he could be right** ◊ **he could be right, ~ you** peut-être qu'il a raison après tout; **I got substantial damages. It took two years, ~ you** je me suis fait largement dédommager mais ça a quand même pris deux ans

4 COMPOUNDS

► **mind-bender*** N (*US*) révélation *f* ► **mind-bending***, **mind-blowing*** ADJ [*drug*] hallucinogène; [*experience, news, scene*] hallucinant ► **mind-boggling*** ADJ époustouflant*, ahurissant ► **mind-expanding** ADJ [*drug etc*] hallucinogène ► **mind game** N manœuvre *f* psychologique; **to play ~ games with sb** chercher à manœuvrer qn psychologiquement ► **mind-numbing*** ADJ ennuyeux à mourir ► **mind-numbingly*** ADV **~ numbingly boring** ennuyeux à mourir; **~ numbingly simple** d'une simplicité enfantine; **~-numbingly banal** d'une banalité affligeante ► **mind reader** N (*lit*) télépathe *mf*; (*fig*) **he's a ~ reader!** il lit dans la pensée des gens!; **I'm not a ~ reader!*** je ne suis pas devin!* ► **mind reading** N télépathie *f* ► **mind-set** N mentalité *f*

5 PHRASAL VERBS

► **mind out*** VI faire attention, faire gaffe*; **~ out!** attention!; **~ out of the way!** ôtez-vous de là!, dégagez!*; **~ out or you'll break it** fais attention de ne pas le casser

---

minded ['maɪndɪd] ADJ (*frm*) **if you are so ~** si le cœur vous en dit; **to be ~ to do sth** être disposé à faire qch

-minded ['maɪndɪd] ADJ (*in compounds*) **[a]** (*describing mental faculties*) qui est ... d'esprit; **feeble-minded** faible d'esprit → **high, strong-minded** **[b]** (*describing interests*) qui s'intéresse à ...; **business-minded** qui a le sens des affaires; **he's become very ecology-minded** il est devenu très sensible aux problèmes écologiques; **an industrially-minded nation** une nation tournée vers l'industrie; **a romantically-minded girl** une jeune fille aux idées romantiques → **family, like**

minder ['maɪndə] N **[a]** (*Brit: also* **baby-~, child-~**) gardienne *f* **[b]** (* = *bodyguard etc*) ange *m* gardien (*fig*)

mindful ['maɪndfʊl] ADJ (*frm*) **to be ~ of sth** être attentif à qch; **to be ~ that ...** être attentif au fait que ...; **I am ever ~ of how much I am indebted to you** je n'oublie pas à quel point je vous suis obligé; **be ~ of what I said** songez à ce que j'ai dit

mindless ['maɪndlɪs] ADJ **[a]** (*Brit* = *senseless*) [*violence, brutality, vandalism, killing*] gratuit **[b]** (= *stupid*) [*work, routine, film, entertainment*] bêtifiant; [*person*] stupide; **a ~ idiot** un(e) idiot(e) fini(e) **[c]** (*frm* = *unmindful*) **to be ~ of sth** être oublieux *or* insouciant de qch

mine¹ [maɪn] **1** POSS PRON le mien, la mienne, les miens *mpl*, les miennes *fpl*; **that book is ~** ce livre m'appartient *or* est à moi; **this poem is ~** ce poème est de moi; **will you**

be ~?† voulez-vous m'épouser?; **the house became** ~ la maison est devenue (la) mienne; **no advice of** ~ **could prevent him** aucun conseil de ma part ne pouvait l'empêcher; **no it's** ~ non, c'est à moi *or* le mien; **which dress do you prefer, hers or** ~? quelle robe préférez-vous, la sienne ou la mienne?; **a friend of** ~ un de mes amis, un ami à moi; **I think that cousin of** ~* **is responsible** je pense que c'est mon cousin qui est responsable; **it's no fault of** ~ ce n'est pas (de) ma faute; **what is** ~ **is yours** ce qui est à moi est à toi, ce qui m'appartient t'appartient; (*frm*) **it is not** ~ **to decide** ce n'est pas à moi de décider, il ne m'appartient pas de décider; ~ **is a specialized department** le service où je suis est spécialisé

[2] POSS ADJ†† mon, ma, mes → **host¹**

mine² [maɪn] [1] N [a] (*Min*) mine *f*; **coalmine** mine *f* de charbon; **to go down the** ~(**s**) travailler *or* descendre à la mine; **to work a** ~ exploiter une mine

[b] (*fig = rich source*) **a (real)** ~ **of information** une véritable mine de renseignements, une source inépuisable de renseignements; **she's a** ~ **of celebrity gossip** elle connaît tous les potins sur les célébrités

[c] (*Mil, Naut = bomb*) mine *f*; **to lay a** ~ mouiller *or* poser une mine; **to clear a beach of** ~**s** déminer une plage → **landmine**

[2] VT [a] (*Min*) [+ *coal, ore*] extraire [b] (*Mil, Naut etc*) [+ *sea, beach*] miner, semer de mines; [+ *ship, tank*] miner

[3] VI exploiter un gisement; **to** ~ **for coal** extraire du charbon, exploiter une mine (de charbon)

[4] COMP ▶ **mine-clearing** N (*Mil, Naut*) déminage *m* ▶ **mine detector** N (*Mil*) détecteur *m* de mines ▶ **mine disposal** N (*Mil, Naut*) déminage *m* ▶ **mine-sweeping** N (*Mil, Naut*) dragage *m* de mines, déminage *m*

minefield ['maɪnfiːld] N [a] (*Mil, Naut*) champ *m* de mines [b] (*fig = problematic area*) **it's a legal/political** ~ c'est un terrain politiquement/juridiquement miné

minehunter ['maɪnhʌntəʳ] N (*Mil, Naut*) chasseur *m* de mines

minelayer ['maɪnleɪəʳ] N (*Mil, Naut*) mouilleur *m* de mines

minelaying ['maɪnleɪɪŋ] N (*Mil, Naut*) mouillage *m* de mines

miner ['maɪnəʳ] N mineur *m*; **the** ~**s' strike** la grève des mineurs; ~**'s lamp** lampe *f* de mineur

mineral ['mɪnərəl] [1] N (*Geol*) minéral *m* [2] **minerals** NPL (*Brit = soft drinks*) boissons *fpl* gazeuses [3] ADJ minéral [4] COMP ▶ **mineral deposits** NPL gisements *mpl* miniers ▶ **the mineral kingdom** N le règne minéral ▶ **mineral oil** N (*Brit*) huile *f* minérale; (*US*) huile *f* de paraffine ▶ **mineral rights** NPL droits *mpl* miniers ▶ **mineral water** N eau *f* minérale

mineralogical [,mɪnərə'lɒdʒɪkl] ADJ minéralogique

mineralogist [,mɪnə'rælədʒɪst] N minéralogiste *m*

mineralogy [,mɪnə'rælədʒɪ] N minéralogie *f*

Minerva [mɪ'nɜːvə] N Minerve *f*

mineshaft ['maɪnʃɑːft] N puits *m* de mine

minestrone [,mɪnɪ'strəʊnɪ] N minestrone *m*

minesweeper ['maɪnswiːpəʳ] N (*Mil, Naut*) dragueur *m* de mines

mingle ['mɪŋɡl] [1] VT mêler, mélanger (**with** avec) [2] VI (= *mix*) se mêler, se mélanger; (*at party etc*) se mêler aux invités *or* à la fête; (= *become indistinguishable*) se confondre (**with** avec); **to** ~ **with the crowd** se mêler à la foule; **he** ~**s with all sorts of people** il fraye avec toutes sortes de gens; **guests ate and** ~**d** les invités ont mangé et ont discuté les uns avec les

autres; **she** ~**d for a while and then sat down with her husband** elle s'est mêlée aux autres invités pour discuter puis s'est assise avec son mari

mingy* ['mɪndʒɪ] ADJ (*Brit*) [a] (= *mean*) [*person*] radin* (**about sth** en ce qui concerne qch) [b] (= *measly*) [*amount*] misérable

Mini® ['mɪnɪ] N (= *car*) Mini (Cooper)® *f*

mini ['mɪnɪ] [1] N (= *fashion*) mini *f* [2] ADJ ~ **system** (= *hi-fi*) chaîne *f* (hi-fi) mini

mini... ['mɪnɪ] PREF mini...; **he's a kind of ~-dictator*** c'est une sorte de minidictateur

miniature ['mɪnɪtʃəʳ] [1] N [a] (*Art*) miniature *f*; (*lit, fig*) **in** ~ en miniature [b] (*of whisky etc*) mignonnette *f* [2] ADJ [*rose, railway, car, camera, version*] miniature; [*dog, tree*] nain; ~ **submarine** sous-marin *m* de poche; ~ **bottle of whisky** mignonnette *f* de whisky [3] COMP ▶ **miniature golf** N minigolf *m* ▶ **miniature poodle** N caniche *m* nain

miniaturist ['mɪnɪtʃərɪst] N miniaturiste *mf*

miniaturization [,mɪnɪtʃərаɪ'zeɪʃən] N miniaturisation *f*

miniaturize ['mɪnɪtʃəraɪz] VT miniaturiser

minibar ['mɪnɪbɑːʳ] N (= *fridge*) minibar *m*

mini-boom ['mɪnɪbuːm] N miniboom *m*

minibudget ['mɪnɪˌbʌdʒɪt] N (*Pol*) collectif *m* budgétaire

minibus ['mɪnɪˌbʌs] N minibus *m*

minicab ['mɪnɪˌkæb] N (*Brit*) taxi *m* (*qu'il faut commander par téléphone*)

minicalculator† ['mɪnɪˈkælkjʊˌleɪtəʳ] N calculette *f*, calculatrice *f* de poche

minicar ['mɪnɪˌkɑːʳ] N toute petite voiture *f*

minicomputer ['mɪnɪkəmˈpjuːtəʳ] N miniordinateur *m*

mini-course ['mɪnɪˌkɔːs] N (*US Scol*) cours *m* extrascolaire

minidress ['mɪnɪˌdres] N minirobe *f*

minim ['mɪnɪm] [1] N [a] (*Brit Mus*) blanche *f* [b] (*Measure* = 0.5ml) ≈ goutte *f* [2] COMP ▶ **minim rest** N demi-pause *f*

minima ['mɪnɪmə] NPL of **minimum**

minimal ['mɪnɪml] [1] ADJ [*risk, role, resources, effect, change*] minime; [*level, requirements*] minimal, minimum; **the money saved is** ~ la somme d'argent économisée est minime; ~ **publicity/disruption** un minimum de publicité/perturbation; **a** ~ **amount of effort** un minimum d'effort, un effort minime; **to have** ~ **impact on sth** n'avoir qu'un très faible impact sur qch; **damage was** ~ les dégâts étaient minimes; ~ **loss of life** des pertes minimums en vies humaines; **at** ~ **cost** pour un coût minimum; **with** ~ **effort** avec un minimum d'effort [2] COMP ▶ **minimal art** N art *m* minimal ▶ **minimal free form** N (*Ling*) forme *f* libre minimale ▶ **minimal pair** N (*Ling*) paire *f* minimale

minimalism ['mɪnɪməlɪzəm] N (*Art etc*) minimalisme *m*

minimalist ['mɪnɪməlɪst] ADJ, N (*Art etc*) minimaliste *mf*

minimally ['mɪnɪməlɪ] ADV à peine

minimarket ['mɪnɪˌmɑːkɪt], **minimart** ['mɪnɪˌmɑːt] N supérette *f*

minimize ['mɪnɪmaɪz] VT [a] (= *reduce to minimum*) [+ *amount, risk, losses*] réduire au minimum [b] (= *play down*) [+ *risk, losses, sb's contribution, help*] minimiser

minimum ['mɪnɪməm] [1] N (*pl* **minimums** *or* **minima**) minimum *m*; **a** ~ **of £100** un minimum de 100 livres; **to reduce to a** *or* **the** ~ réduire au minimum; **keep interruptions to a** *or* **the** ~ limitez les interruptions autant que possible; **to keep costs to a** ~ maintenir les coûts au plus bas; **with a** ~ **of commonsense one could ...** avec un minimum de bon sens on pourrait ... [2] ADJ minimum (*f inv*), minimal; **with** ~ **effort** avec un minimum d'effort;

at ~ **cost** pour un coût minimum [3] COMP ▶ **minimum iron fabric** N tissu *m* ne demandant qu'un repassage minimum ▶ **minimum lending rate** N (*Econ*) taux *m* de base bancaire ▶ **minimum wage** N (*Econ, Ind*) salaire *m* minimum, ≈ SMIC *m*

mining ['maɪnɪŋ] [1] N (*NonC*) [a] (*Min*) exploitation *f* minière [b] (*Mil, Naut*) pose *f or* mouillage *m* de mines [2] COMP [*village, company, industry, rights*] minier; [*family*] de mineurs ▶ **mining area** N région *f* (*d'industrie*) minière ▶ **mining engineer** N ingénieur *m* des mines ▶ **mining engineering** N génie *m* minier; **to study** ~ **engineering** ≈ faire des études à l'école des Mines

minion ['mɪnɪən] N (*lit* = *servant*) laquais *m*; (*fig, hum*) sous-fifre* *m*; **she delegated the job to one of her** ~**s** elle a donné ce travail à l'un de ses sous-fifres*

minipill ['mɪnɪpɪl] N minipilule *f*

miniscule ['mɪnɪˌskjuːl] ADJ = **minuscule**

miniseries ['mɪnɪsɪərɪz] N (*TV*) minifeuilleton *m*

mini-ski ['mɪnɪˌskiː] N (*Ski*) miniski *m*

miniskirt ['mɪnɪˌskɜːt] N minijupe *f*

minister ['mɪnɪstəʳ] [1] N [a] (*Brit Govt*) ministre *m* [b] (*Rel: also* ~ **of religion**) pasteur *m*, ministre *m* [2] VI **to** ~ **to sb's needs** pourvoir aux besoins de qn; **to** ~ **to sb** secourir qn; (*Rel*) **to** ~ **to a parish** desservir une paroisse [3] COMP ▶ **ministering angel** N (*fig*) ange *m* de bonté ▶ **Minister of Health** N ministre *m* de la Santé ▶ **Minister of State** N (*Brit Govt*) ≈ secrétaire *m* d'État; (*gen*) ministre *m* ▶ **minister plenipotentiary** N ministre *m* plénipotentiaire ▶ **minister resident** N ministre *m* résident → **defence**, **foreign**

ministerial [,mɪnɪs'tɪərɪəl] ADJ [a] (*Govt*) [*meeting, team, reshuffle, approval, decision*] ministériel; [*post, career, duties*] de ministre; [*resignation*] d'un ministre; **the** ~ **benches** le banc des ministres; **a** ~ **colleague** un(e) collègue ministre; **the rules governing** ~ **conduct** le règlement régissant la conduite des ministres; **at** ~ **level** à niveau ministériel; **to hold** ~ **office** occuper des fonctions ministérielles [b] (*Rel*) **his** ~ **duties** les obligations de son ministère; **a** ~ **friend of his in Glasgow** un de ses amis, ministre du culte à Glasgow

ministration [,mɪnɪs'treɪʃən] N [a] ~**s** (= *services, help*) soins *mpl* [b] (*Rel*) ministère *m*

ministry ['mɪnɪstrɪ] N [a] (= *government department*) ministère *m*; **Ministry of Health/ Defence** ministère *m* de la Santé/Défense; (*Parl*) **to form a** ~ former un ministère *or* un gouvernement; **the coalition** ~ **lasted two years** le ministère de coalition a duré deux ans [b] (= *period of office*) ministère *m* [c] (= *clergy*) **the** ~ le saint ministère; **to go into** *or* **enter the** ~ devenir *or* se faire pasteur *or* ministre

minium ['mɪnɪəm] N minium *m*

miniver ['mɪnɪvəʳ] N menu-vair *m*

mink [mɪŋk] [1] N (*pl* **mink** *or* **minks**) (= *animal, fur*) vison *m* [2] COMP [*coat etc*] de vison

minke ['mɪŋkɪ] N ~ (**whale**) baleine *f* minke

Minn. ABBR = **Minnesota**

minneola [,mɪnɪ'əʊlə] N minnéola *m*

Minnesota [,mɪnɪ'səʊtə] N le Minnesota; **in** ~ dans le Minnesota

minnow ['mɪnəʊ] N (*pl* **minnow** *or* **minnows**) [a] (*Zool*) vairon *m*; (= *any small fish*) fretin *m* [b] (*fig = unimportant person*) menu fretin *m* (*pl inv*)

Minoan [mɪ'nəʊən] ADJ minoen

minor ['maɪnəʳ] [1] ADJ [*change, consideration, defect*] (*also Jur, Mus, Philos, Rel*) mineur (-eure *f*); [*detail, expenses, repairs*] petit, menu; [*importance, interest, position, role*] secondaire, mineur; ~ **poet** poète *m* mineur; ~ **problem/ worry** problème *m*/souci *m* mineur; (*Mus*) **G** ~

sol mineur; (*Mus*) **~ key** ton *m* mineur; **in the ~ key** en mineur; (*Jur*) **~ offence** ≈ délit *m* mineur; (*Med*) **~ operation** opération *f* bénigne; (*Theat, fig*) **to play a ~ part** jouer un rôle accessoire *or* un petit rôle; **~ planet** petite planète *f*, astéroïde *m*; (*Cards*) **~ suit** (couleur *f*) mineure *f*; (*Brit Scol*) **Smith ~** Smith junior ② N ⓐ (*Jur*) mineur(e) *m(f)* ⓑ (*US Univ*) matière *f* secondaire ③ VI (*US Univ*) **to ~ in chemistry** étudier la chimie comme matière secondaire *or* sous-dominante

Minorca [mɪˈnɔːkə] N Minorque *f*; **in ~** à Minorque

minority [maɪˈnɒrɪtɪ] ① N (*also Jur*) minorité *f*; **in a** *or* **the ~** en minorité; (*hum*) **you are in a ~ of one** vous êtes le seul à penser ainsi, personne ne partage vos vues *or* votre opinion; **the reforms will affect only a small ~ of the population** les réformes ne toucheront qu'une petite minorité de la population ② COMP [*party, opinion, government*] minoritaire ▶ **minority president** N (*US Pol*) président n'ayant pas la majorité absolue au Congrès ▶ **minority programme** N (*Rad, TV*) émission *f* destinée à un public restreint ▶ **minority report** N (*Admin*) rapport *m* soumis par un groupe minoritaire

Minos [ˈmaɪnɒs] N Minos *m*

Minotaur [ˈmaɪnətɔːʳ] N Minotaure *m*

minster [ˈmɪnstəʳ] N cathédrale *f*; [*of monastery*] église *f* abbatiale; **York Minster** cathédrale *f* d'York

minstrel [ˈmɪnstrəl] ① N (*Hist etc*) ménestrel *m* ② COMP ▶ **minstrel gallery** N (*Archit*) tribune *f* des musiciens ▶ **minstrel show** N (*Theat*) spectacle *m* de chanteurs et musiciens blancs déguisés en noirs

minstrelsy [ˈmɪnstrəlsɪ] N (*NonC*) (= *art*) art *m* du ménestrel *or* trouvère *or* troubadour; (= *songs*) chants *mpl*

mint¹ [mɪnt] ① N ⓐ (*also Brit: also* **Royal Mint**) Monnaie *f*, hôtel *m* de la Monnaie ⓑ (*fig* = *large sum*) une *or* des somme(s) folle(s); **to make a ~ (of money)** faire fortune; **he made a ~ in oil*** il a fait fortune dans le pétrole ② VT [+ *coins*] battre; [+ *gold*] monnayer (**into** pour obtenir); (*fig*) [+ *word, expression*] forger, inventer; (*fig*) **he ~s money*** il fait des affaires d'or, il ramasse l'argent à la pelle ③ COMP ▶ **mint condition** N **in ~ condition** à l'état (de) neuf, en parfaite condition ▶ **mint stamp** N (*Philat*) timbre *m* non oblitéré

mint² [mɪnt] ① N (*Bot, Culin*) menthe *f*; (= *sweet*) bonbon *m* à la menthe ② COMP [*chocolate, sauce*] à la menthe ▶ **mint julep** N (*US*) whisky *m etc* glacé à la menthe ▶ **mint sauce** N sauce *f* à la menthe ▶ **mint tea** N (= *herbal tea*) infusion *f* de menthe; (= *tea with mint*) thé *m* à la menthe

-minted [ˈmɪntɪd] ADJ (*in compounds*) **newly-minted** [*coin*] tout neuf

minuet [ˌmɪnjʊˈet] N menuet *m*

minus [ˈmaɪnəs] ① PREP ⓐ (*Math*) moins; **five ~ three equals two** cinq moins trois égale(nt) deux; (*Scol*) **A/B ~** ≈ A/B moins ⓑ (* = *without*) sans, avec ... en *or* de moins; **he arrived ~ his coat** il est arrivé sans son manteau; **they found his wallet ~ the money** ils ont retrouvé son portefeuille mais sans l'argent; **~ a finger** avec un doigt en *or* de moins ② N (*Math*) (= *sign*) moins *m*; (= *amount*) quantité *f* négative; (*fig: of situation etc*) **the ~es** les inconvénients *mpl*; **the ~es far outweigh any possible gain** les inconvénients l'emportent largement sur les avantages éventuels; **the plusses and ~es were about equal** les avantages et les inconvénients s'équilibraient plus ou moins ③ COMP ▶ **minus quantity** N (*Math*) quantité *f* négative; (*: *fig*) quantité *f* négligeable ▶ **minus sign** N (*Math*) (signe *m*) moins *m*

minuscule [ˈmɪnəˌskjuːl] ADJ minuscule

minute¹ [ˈmɪnɪt] ① N ⓐ (*fig, of time*) minute *f*; **it is 23 ~s past 2** il est 2 heures 23 (minutes); **at 4 o'clock to the ~** à 4 heures pile *or* tapant(es); **we got the train without a ~ to spare** une minute de plus et nous manquions le train; **I'll do it in a ~** je le ferai dans une minute; **I'll do it the ~ he comes** je le ferai dès qu'il arrivera; **do it this ~!** fais-le tout de suite *or* à la minute!; **he went out this (very) ~*** il vient tout juste de sortir; **I've just this ~ heard of it*** je viens de l'apprendre à la minute; **at any ~** à tout moment, d'une minute *or* d'un instant à l'autre; **any ~ now*** d'une minute à l'autre; **at the last ~** à la dernière minute; **to leave things till the last ~** tout faire à la dernière minute; **I'll just be a ~ ◊ I shan't be a ~*** j'en ai pour deux secondes; **it won't take five ~s** ce sera fait en un rien de temps; **it's a few ~s' walk from the station** c'est tout près de la gare; **wait a ~ ◊ just a ~** attendez une minute *or* un instant *or* un moment; (*indignantly*) minute!; **half a ~!** une petite minute!; **up to the ~** [*equipment*] dernier modèle *inv*; [*fashion*] dernier cri *inv*; [*news*] de (la) dernière heure; **there's one born every ~!*** il faut vraiment le faire!* ⓑ (*Geog, Math* = *part of degree*) minute *f* ⓒ (= *official record*) compte rendu *m*, procès-verbal *m*; (*Comm etc* = *memorandum*) note *f*; **to take the ~s of a meeting** rédiger le procès-verbal *or* le compte rendu d'une réunion; **who will take the ~s?** qui se charge du compte rendu? ② VT ⓐ (= *note etc*) [+ *fact, detail*] prendre note de; [+ *meeting*] rédiger le compte rendu de, dresser le procès-verbal de ⓑ (= *send minute to*) [+ *person*] faire passer une note à (**about** au sujet de) ③ COMP ▶ **minute book** N (*Admin, Comm etc*) registre *m* des délibérations ▶ **minute hand** N [*of clock etc*] grande aiguille *f* ▶ **minute steak** N (*Culin*) entrecôte *f* minute

minute² [maɪˈnjuːt] ADJ (= *tiny*) [*object, amount, variation, trace*] minuscule; (= *detailed*) [*examination, analysis*] minutieux; **in ~** *or* **the ~st detail** jusque dans les moindres *or* plus infimes détails

minutely [maɪˈnjuːtlɪ] ADV ⓐ (= *in detail*) [*examine, describe*] minutieusement, dans les moindres détails; **a ~ detailed account** un compte rendu extrêmement détaillé *or* circonstancié ⓑ (= *slightly*) [*move, change, differ*] très légèrement; **anything ~ resembling a fish** quelque chose ayant très vaguement l'apparence d'un poisson ⓒ (= *very small*) [*write, fold*] en tout petit

minutiae [maɪˈnjuːʃiiː] NPL menus détails *mpl*, minuties *fpl*

minx [mɪŋks] N (petite) espiègle *f*, friponne *f*

Miocene [ˈmaɪəˌsiːn] ADJ, N miocène *m*

MIPS, mips [mɪps] N (ABBR = **millions of instructions per second**)

miracle [ˈmɪrəkl] ① N miracle *m*; **by a ~ ◊ by some ~** par miracle; **it is a ~ of ingenuity** c'est un miracle *or* une merveille d'ingéniosité; **it is a ~ that ...** c'est miracle que ... (+ *subj*); **it will be a ~ if ...** ce sera (un) miracle si ... ② COMP ▶ **miracle cure, miracle drug** N remède *m* miracle ▶ **miracle-man** N (*pl* **miracle-men**) faiseur *m* de miracles ▶ **miracle play** N (*Rel, Theat*) miracle *m* ▶ **miracle worker** N (*fig*) **I'm not a ~ worker!*** je ne sais pas faire de miracles!

miraculous [mɪˈrækjʊləs] ADJ (*Rel, fig*) miraculeux; **to make a ~ escape** en réchapper miraculeusement; **to make a ~ recovery** guérir miraculeusement; **to be little** *or* **nothing short of ~** être tout bonnement miraculeux

miraculously [mɪˈrækjʊləslɪ] ADV ⓐ (= *as if by miracle*) [*survive, escape, transform*] miraculeusement, par miracle; **to be ~ intact/unharmed**

être miraculeusement intact/indemne; **~ the baby appeared to be unhurt** par miracle, il semblait que le bébé était indemne ⓑ (= *extremely*) [*beautiful*] merveilleusement

mirage [ˈmɪrɑːʒ] N (*lit, fig*) mirage *m*

MIRAS [ˈmaɪræs] N (*Brit Fin*) (ABBR = **mortgage interest relief at source**) exonération fiscale à la source sur les intérêts d'emprunts hypothécaires

mire [ˈmaɪəʳ] N (*liter*) (= *mud*) fange *f* (*liter*); (= *swampy ground*) bourbier *m*; (*fig*) **to drag sb's name through the ~** traîner (le nom de) qn dans la fange *or* la boue

mired [ˈmaɪəd] ADJ (*esp liter*) ⓐ (= *dirtied*) **~ in mud** [*vehicle*] embourbé; [*road*] recouvert de boue ⓑ (= *involved*) **~ in debt** endetté jusqu'au cou; **~ in scandal** fortement compromis dans un scandale

mirror [ˈmɪrəʳ] ① N miroir *m*, glace *f*; (*Aut*) rétroviseur *m*; (*fig*) miroir *m*; **hand ~** miroir *m* à main; **pocket ~** miroir *m* de poche; **to look at o.s. in the ~** se regarder dans le miroir *or* dans la glace; (*fig*) **it holds a ~ (up) to ...** cela reflète ... ② VT (*lit, fig*) refléter; (*lit, fig*) **to be ~ed in** *or* **by sth** se refléter dans qch ③ COMP ▶ **mirror image** N image *f* inversée ▶ **mirror writing** N écriture *f* en miroir

mirth [mɜːθ] N (*NonC*) hilarité *f*; **this remark caused some ~** cette remarque a déclenché une certaine hilarité

mirthful [ˈmɜːθfʊl] ADJ (*liter*) gai, joyeux

mirthless [ˈmɜːθlɪs] ADJ sans joie

mirthlessly [ˈmɜːθlɪslɪ] ADV sans joie

MIRV [mɜːv] (ABBR = **Multiple Independently Targeted Re-entry Vehicle**) MIRV *m*

miry [ˈmaɪərɪ] ADJ (*liter*) fangeux (*liter*), bourbeux

MIS [ˌeməˈes] N (ABBR = **management information system**) SIG *m*

misadventure [ˌmɪsədˈventʃəʳ] N mésaventure *f*; (*less serious*) contretemps *m*; (*Jur*) **death by ~** mort *f* accidentelle

misalignment [ˌmɪsəˈlaɪnmənt] N mauvais alignement *m*; **the dollar ~** le mauvais alignement du dollar

misalliance [ˌmɪsəˈlaɪəns] N mésalliance *f*

misanthrope [ˈmɪzənθrəʊp] N misanthrope *mf*

misanthropic [ˌmɪzənˈθrɒpɪk] ADJ [*person*] misanthrope; [*feeling, mood, view*] de misanthrope

misanthropist [mɪˈzænθrəpɪst] N misanthrope *mf*

misanthropy [mɪˈzænθrəpɪ] N misanthropie *f*

misapplication [ˌmɪsæplɪˈkeɪʃən] N [*of knowledge*] usage *m* impropre; [*of funds*] détournement *m*

misapply [ˈmɪsəˈplaɪ] VT [+ *discovery, knowledge*] mal employer, mal appliquer; [+ *abilities, intelligence*] mal employer; [+ *money, funds*] détourner

misapprehend [ˈmɪsˌæprɪˈhend] VT mal comprendre, se faire une idée fausse de *or* sur

misapprehension [ˈmɪsˌæprɪˈhenʃən] N malentendu *m*, méprise *f*; **there seems to be some ~** il semble y avoir malentendu *or* méprise

misappropriate [ˈmɪsəˈprəʊprɪeɪt] VT [+ *money, funds*] détourner

misappropriation [ˈmɪsəˌprəʊprɪˈeɪʃən] N détournement *m*

misbegotten [ˈmɪsbɪˈɡɒtn] ADJ ⓐ (*lit: liter*) illégitime, bâtard ⓑ (*fig* = *misguided*) [*plan, scheme*] mal conçu, malencontreux

misbehave [ˈmɪsbɪˈheɪv] VI se conduire mal; [*child*] ne pas être sage, se tenir mal

misbehaviour, misbehavior (*US*) [ˈmɪsbɪˈheɪvjəʳ] N [*of person, child*] mauvaise conduite *f* or tenue *f*; (*stronger*) inconduite *f*

misbelief [ˈmɪsbɪˈliːf] N (*Rel*) croyance *f* fausse

misbeliever ['mɪsbɪ'liːvəʳ] N (Rel) mécréant(e) m(f)

misc. ADJ (ABBR = **miscellaneous**) divers

miscalculate ['mɪs'kælkjʊleɪt] 1 VT mal calculer 2 VI (fig) se tromper

miscalculation ['mɪs‚kælkjʊ'leɪʃən] N (lit, fig) erreur f de calcul, mauvais calcul m

miscall ['mɪs'kɔːl] VT mal nommer, appeler à tort

miscarriage ['mɪs'kærɪdʒ] N a [of plan etc] insuccès m, échec m; [of letter, goods] perte f; **~ of justice** erreur f judiciaire b (Med) fausse couche f; **to have a ~** faire une fausse couche

miscarry [‚mɪs'kærɪ] VI a [plan, scheme] échouer, avorter; [letter, goods] s'égarer, ne pas arriver à destination b (Med) faire une fausse couche

miscast ['mɪs'kɑːst] (pret, ptp **miscast**) VT (Cine, Theat etc) **the play has been ~** la distribution est mauvaise; **he was ~** on n'aurait pas dû lui donner or attribuer ce rôle

miscegenation [‚mɪsɪdʒɪ'neɪʃən] N croisement m entre races (humaines)

miscellaneous [‚mɪsɪ'leɪnɪəs] 1 ADJ [people, objects, writings, costs] divers; [collection] hétéroclite; **categorized** or **classified as "~"** classé « divers » or (on agenda) « ~ » « divers » 2 COMP ► **miscellaneous expenses** NPL frais mpl divers ► **miscellaneous items** NPL (Comm) articles mpl divers; (Press) faits mpl divers

miscellany [mɪ'selənɪ] N [of objects etc] collection f hétéroclite; (Literat) sélection f, anthologie f; (Rad, TV) sélection f, choix m; (Literat) **miscellanies** miscellanées fpl, (volume m de) mélanges mpl

mischance [‚mɪs'tʃɑːns] N mésaventure f, malchance f; **by (a) ~** par malheur

mischief ['mɪstʃɪf] 1 N a (NonC) (= roguishness) malice f, espièglerie f; (= naughtiness) sottises fpl, polissonerie f; (= maliciousness) méchanceté f; **he's up to (some) ~** [child] il (nous) prépare une sottise; [adult] (in fun) il (nous) prépare une farce or niche; (from malice) il médite un mauvais tour or coup; **he's always up to some ~** il trouve toujours une sottise or niche à faire; **to get into ~** [child only] faire des sottises, faire des siennes; **to keep sb out of ~** empêcher qn de faire des sottises or des bêtises, garder qn sur le droit chemin (hum); **the children managed to keep out of ~** les enfants sont arrivés à ne pas faire de sottises, les enfants ont même été sages; **he means ~** [child] il va sûrement faire une sottise; [adult] (in fun) il va sûrement faire une farce; (from malice) il est mal intentionné; **out of sheer ~** (for fun) par pure espièglerie; (from malice) par pure méchanceté; **full of ~** espiègle, plein de malice; **bubbling over with ~** pétillant de malice; **to make ~ (for sb)** créer des ennuis (à qn); **to make ~ between two people** semer la zizanie or la discorde entre deux personnes b (* = child) polisson(ne) m(f), petit(e) vilain(e) m(f) c (= injury, damage) mal m; (to ship, building etc) dommage m(pl); **to do sb a ~*** faire mal à qn; **to do o.s. a ~*** se faire mal 2 COMP ► **mischief-maker** N semeur m, -euse f de discorde, faiseur m, -euse f d'histoires; (esp gossip) mauvaise langue f

mischievous ['mɪstʃɪvəs] ADJ a (= impish) [person, nature, smile, glance] malicieux; (= naughty) [child, trick] vilain; [kitten, behaviour] espiègle b (= malicious) [person, behaviour, attempt, suggestion, rumour] malveillant

mischievously ['mɪstʃɪvəslɪ] ADV a (= impishly) [say, smile] malicieusement; (= naughtily) [behave] mal b (= maliciously) [suggest, claim, attempt] avec malveillance

mischievousness ['mɪstʃɪvəsnɪs] N (= roguishness) malice f, espièglerie f; (= naughtiness) polissonerie f

misconceive ['mɪskən'siːv] 1 VT mal comprendre, mal interpréter 2 VI se tromper, se méprendre (**of** sur)

misconceived [‚mɪskən'siːvd] ADJ [policy, plan, approach] peu judicieux; [idea] faux (fausse f), erroné

misconception ['mɪskən'sepʃən] N a (= wrong idea/opinion) idée f/opinion f fausse or erronée b (= misunderstanding) malentendu m, méprise f

misconduct [‚mɪs'kɒndʌkt] 1 N a (= bad behaviour) mauvaise conduite f; (Jur: sexual) adultère m; (Sport) mauvaise conduite f; **to be sacked for ~** être licencié pour faute professionnelle; **gross ~** faute f (professionnelle) grave; **professional ~** faute f professionnelle; **allegations of police ~** des allégations fpl selon lesquelles la police aurait commis des abus b (= bad management) [of business etc] mauvaise administration f or gestion f 2 [‚mɪskən'dʌkt] N [+ business] mal diriger, mal gérer; **to ~ o.s.†** se conduire mal

misconstruction ['mɪskən'strʌkʃən] N (= misinterpretation) fausse interprétation f; **words open to ~** mots qui prêtent à méprise or confusion

misconstrue ['mɪskən'struː] VT [+ acts, words] mal interpréter

miscount ['mɪs'kaʊnt] 1 N (gen) mécompte m; (Pol: during election) erreur f de comptage or dans le décompte des voix 2 VTI mal compter

miscreant ['mɪskrɪənt] N (frm) scélérat(e) m(f), gredin(e) m(f)

misdeal ['mɪs'diːl] (vb: pret, ptp **misdealt**) (Cards) 1 N maldonne f 2 VTI **to ~ (the cards)** faire maldonne

misdeed ['mɪs'diːd] N méfait m, mauvaise action f; (stronger) crime m

misdemeanour, **misdemeanor** (US) [‚mɪsdɪ'miːnəʳ] N a (= misdeed) incartade f, écart m de conduite; (more serious) méfait m b [mɪsdɪ'miːnəʳ] (Brit) infraction f, contravention f; (US) délit m

misdescribe [‚mɪsdɪ'skraɪb] VT [+ goods for sale] décrire de façon mensongère

misdiagnose ['mɪsdaɪəgnəʊz] VT a (Med) [+ illness] faire une erreur de diagnostic au sujet de; [+ patient] faire une erreur de diagnostic sur b (= analyse wrongly) [+ problem, situation] faire une erreur d'analyse quant à

misdiagnosis [‚mɪsdaɪəg'nəʊsɪs] N (pl **misdiagnoses** [‚mɪsdaɪəg'nəʊsiːz]) a (Med) [of illness] erreur f de diagnostic b (= wrong analysis) [of problem, situation] erreur f d'analyse

misdirect ['mɪsdɪ'rekt] VT [+ letter etc] mal acheminer; [+ person] mal renseigner, fourvoyer; [+ blow, efforts] mal diriger, mal orienter; [+ operation, scheme] mener mal; (Jur) **to ~ the jury** mal instruire le jury

misdirection ['mɪsdɪ'rekʃən] N [of letter etc] erreur f d'acheminement; [of blow, efforts] mauvaise orientation f; [of operation, scheme] mauvaise conduite f

miser ['maɪzəʳ] N avare mf, grippe-sou m

miserable ['mɪzərəbl] ADJ a (= unhappy) [person, face, look, experience] malheureux; **to feel ~** (= unhappy) ne pas avoir le moral; (= unwell) être mal en point; **to make sb's life ~ ◊ to make life ~ for sb** [person] mener la vie dure à qn; [illness] gâcher la vie à qn; **don't look so ~!** ne fais pas cette tête!; **she's been having a ~ time recently** la vie n'est pas drôle pour elle en ce moment; **we had a ~ time on holiday** nos vacances ont été un vrai cauchemar b **~ weather*** (= awful) un temps affreux, un très sale temps; (= depressing, overcast) un temps maussade c (= wretched, abject) [person, place, conditions, life, existence] misérable; [sight] lamentable, déplorable; [failure] lamentable d (= paltry) [number, amount] dérisoire; [offer] minable; [salary] dérisoire, de misère; [meal] piteux; [gift] miteux; **a ~ 50 francs** la somme dérisoire de 50 F

miserably ['mɪzərəblɪ] ADV a (= unhappily) [say, look, smile, nod] d'un air malheureux; **a ~ unhappy family** une famille des plus misérables et malheureuses; **it was ~ cold and wet** il faisait désagréablement froid et humide b (= wretchedly, horribly) [live] misérablement; [perform, fail] lamentablement; **a ~ low wage** un salaire de misère; **they played ~** ils ont été minables, ils ont joué d'une façon minable

misère [mɪ'zɛəʳ] N (Cards) misère f

miserliness ['maɪzəlnɪs] N avarice f

miserly ['maɪzəlɪ] ADJ a (= mean) [person] avare (**with sth** de qch) b (= parsimonious) [sum, amount, offer] dérisoire; **a ~ 8 dollars** 8 malheureux dollars

misery ['mɪzərɪ] 1 N a (= unhappiness) tristesse f, douleur f; (= suffering) souffrances fpl, supplice m; (= wretchedness) misère f, détresse f; **the miseries of mankind** la misère de l'homme; **a life of ~** une vie de misère; **to make sb's life a ~** [person] mener la vie dure à qn; [illness] gâcher la vie de qn; **to put an animal out of its ~** achever un animal; **put him out of his ~*** abrégez son supplice et donnez-lui les résultats b (Brit* = gloomy person) (child) pleurnicheur m, -euse f; (adult) grincheux m, -euse f; **what a ~ you are!** ce que tu peux être grincheux or rabat-joie! 2 COMP ► **misery-guts** N râleur* m, -euse* f, rabat-joie m inv

misfire ['mɪs'faɪəʳ] VI [gun] faire long feu, rater; [plan] rater, foirer*; [joke] tomber à plat; [car engine] avoir des ratés

misfit ['mɪsfɪt] N a (Dress) vêtement m mal réussi or qui ne va pas bien b (fig = person) inadapté(e) m(f); **he's always been a ~ here** il ne s'est jamais intégré ici, il n'a jamais su s'adapter ici → **social**

misfortune [mɪs'fɔːtʃən] N (single event) malheur m; (NonC = bad luck) malchance f, infortune f (liter); **~s never come singly** un malheur n'arrive jamais seul; (liter) **~ dogs his footsteps** il joue de malchance; **he'd had more than his fair share of ~** il avait eu plus que sa part de malheur; **companion in ~** compagnon m or compagne f d'infortune; **it is his ~ that he is deaf** pour son malheur il est sourd; **I had the ~ to meet him** par malheur or par malchance je l'ai rencontré; **that's your ~!** tant pis pour toi!

misgiving [mɪs'gɪvɪŋ] N appréhension f; **not without some ~(s)** non sans appréhension; **I had ~s about the scheme** j'avais des doutes quant au projet

misgovern ['mɪs'gʌvən] VTI mal gouverner, mal administrer

misgovernment ['mɪs'gʌvənmənt] N mauvaise gestion f

misguided ['mɪs'gaɪdɪd] ADJ [person] dans l'erreur; [attempt] peu judicieux; [patriotism, idealism] fourvoyé; [belief, view, policy] erroné; **to be ~ in sth/in doing sth** faire erreur en ce qui concerne qch/en faisant qch; **it would be ~ to do that** ce serait une erreur de faire cela

misguidedly ['mɪs'gaɪdɪdlɪ] ADV malencontreusement, peu judicieusement, à mauvais escient

mishandle ['mɪs'hændl] VT a (= treat roughly) [+ object] manier or manipuler sans précaution b (= mismanage) [+ person] mal prendre, mal s'y prendre avec; [+ problem] mal traiter, mal aborder; **he ~d the whole situation** il a mal géré l'ensemble de la situation

mishap ['mɪshæp] N mésaventure f; **slight ~** contretemps m, anicroche f; **without ~** sans encombre ; **he had a ~** il lui est arrivé une (petite) mésaventure

mishear ['mɪs'hɪə'] (pret, ptp **misheard** ['mɪs'hɜːd]) VT mal entendre

mishit ['mɪs'hɪt] 1 N coup m manqué 2 VT [+ ball] mal jouer

mishmash* ['mɪʃmæʃ] N méli-mélo* m

misinform ['mɪsɪn'fɔːm] VT mal renseigner

misinformation [,mɪsɪnfə'meɪʃən] N désinformation f

misinterpret ['mɪsɪn'tɜːprɪt] VT mal interpréter, prendre à confusion

misinterpretation ['mɪsɪn,tɜːprɪ'teɪʃən] N interprétation f erronée (**of** de), contresens m ; **open to ~** qui prête à confusion

misjudge ['mɪs'dʒʌdʒ] VT [+ amount, numbers, time] mal évaluer ; (= underestimate) sousestimer ; [+ person] méjuger, se méprendre sur le compte de

misjudg(e)ment [,mɪs'dʒʌdʒmənt] N [of person, situation, mood, attitude] appréciation f erronée ; [of time, distance, speed, amount] mauvaise évaluation f ; **the government's economic ~s** les erreurs de jugement du gouvernement en matière d'économie

miskick [,mɪs'kɪk] 1 VT **to ~ the ball** rater son coup de pied 2 N coup m de pied raté

mislay [,mɪs'leɪ] (pret, ptp **mislaid**) VT égarer

mislead [,mɪs'liːd] (pret, ptp **misled**) VT (accidentally) induire en erreur, tromper ; (deliberately) tromper, fourvoyer

misleading [,mɪs'liːdɪŋ] ADJ [information, report, statement] trompeur ; **~ advertising** publicité f mensongère ; **it would be ~ to suggest that ...** il serait trompeur de suggérer que ...

misleadingly [,mɪs'liːdɪŋlɪ] ADV [describe] de façon trompeuse

misled [,mɪs'led] VB pt, ptp of **mislead**

mislike† [mɪs'laɪk] VT ne pas aimer, détester

mismanage [mɪs'mænɪdʒ] VT [+ business, estate, shop] mal gérer, gérer en dépit du bon sens ; [+ institution, organization] mal administrer ; **the whole situation has been ~d** l'affaire a été mal gérée d'un bout à l'autre

mismanagement ['mɪs'mænɪdʒmənt] N mauvaise gestion f or administration f

mismatch [mɪs'mætʃ] N [of objects] disparité f ; [of colours, styles] dissonance f

mismatched [mɪs'mætʃt] ADJ [people, things] mal assortis

misname ['mɪs'neɪm] VT donner un nom inexact or impropre à, mal nommer

misnomer [mɪs'nəʊmə'] N terme m impropre ; **that is a ~** c'est un terme qui ne convient guère

misogamist [mɪ'sɒgəmɪst] N misogame mf

misogamy [mɪ'sɒgəmɪ] N misogamie f

misogynist [mɪ'sɒdʒɪnɪst] 1 N misogyne mf 2 ADJ (= misogynistic) misogyne

misogynistic [mɪ,sɒdʒɪ'nɪstɪk] ADJ misogyne

misogyny [mɪ'sɒdʒɪnɪ] N misogynie f

misplace ['mɪs'pleɪs] VT a [+ object, word] mal placer, ne pas mettre où il faudrait ; [+ affection, trust] mal placer b (= lose) égarer

misplaced ['mɪs'pleɪst] ADJ [remark, humour] déplacé, hors de propos

misprint ['mɪsprɪnt] 1 N faute f d'impression or typographique, coquille f 2 [,mɪs'prɪnt] VT imprimer mal or incorrectement

mispronounce ['mɪsprə'naʊns] VT prononcer de travers, écorcher

mispronunciation ['mɪsprə,nʌnsɪ'eɪʃən] N prononciation f incorrecte (**of** de), faute(s) f(pl) de prononciation

misquotation ['mɪskwəʊ'teɪʃən] N citation f inexacte

misquote ['mɪs'kwəʊt] VT citer faussement or inexactement ; **he was ~d in the press** la presse a déformé ses propos ; **he was ~d as**

having said ... on lui a incorrectement fait dire que ... ; **he said that he had been ~d** il a dit qu'on avait déformé ses propos

misread ['mɪs'riːd] (pret, ptp **misread** ['mɪs'red]) VT a (lit) [+ word] mal lire ; **he misread "bat" as "rat"** il s'est trompé et a lu « rat » au lieu de « bat » b (fig = misinterpret) [+ sb's reply, signs etc] mal interpréter, se tromper sur ; **he misread the statements as promises of ...** il s'est mépris sur les déclarations en y voyant des promesses de ..., il a vu à tort dans ces déclarations des promesses de ... ; **he misread the whole situation** il a interprété la situation de façon tout à fait incorrecte

misrepresent ['mɪs,reprɪ'zent] VT [+ facts] dénaturer, déformer ; [+ person] présenter sous un faux jour, donner une impression incorrecte de ; **he was ~ed in the press** (= wrongly portrayed) la presse a donné de lui une image inexacte ; (= misquoted) la presse a déformé ses propos

misrepresentation ['mɪs,reprɪzen'teɪʃən] N déformation f, présentation f déformée

misrule ['mɪs'ruːl] 1 N a (= bad government) mauvaise administration f b (= disorder) désordre m, anarchie f 2 VT gouverner mal

miss[1] [mɪs] 1 N a (shot etc) coup m manqué or raté ; (* = omission) manque m, lacune f ; (* = mistake) erreur f, faute ■ (PROV) **a ~ is as good as a mile** rater c'est rater (même de justesse) → **hit, near** b (= failure) four m, bide* m (fig) ; **they voted the record a ~*** le disque a été jugé minable* c **to give sth a ~*** se passer de qch ; **to give a concert/a lecture/the Louvre a ~*** se passer d'aller à un concert/à une conférence/au Louvre ; **I'll give the wine a ~ this evening*** je m'abstiendrai de boire du vin or je me passerai de vin ce soir ; **I'll give my evening class a ~ this week*** tant pis pour mon cours du soir cette semaine ; **oh give it a ~!*** ça suffit !, en voilà assez !, arrête !

2 VT a (= fail to hit) [+ target, goal] manquer ; **the shot just ~ed me** la balle m'a manqué de justesse or d'un cheveu ; **the plane just ~ed the tower** l'avion a failli toucher la tour b (= fail to find, catch, use etc) [+ vocation, opportunity, appointment, train, person to be met, cue, road, turning] manquer, rater ; [+ house, thing looked out for, solution] ne pas trouver, ne pas voir ; [+ meal] sauter ; [+ class, lecture] manquer ; (iro) **you haven't ~ed much!** n'avez pas manqué or perdu grand-chose ! ; **we ~ed the tide** nous avons manqué la marée ; (fig) **to ~ the boat*** or **the bus*** louper le coche* (fig) ; **to ~ one's cue** (Theat) manquer sa réplique ; (fig) rater l'occasion, manquer le coche* ; **to ~ one's footing** glisser ; **she doesn't ~ much** or **a trick*** rien ne lui échappe ; **to ~ one's way** perdre son chemin, s'égarer ; **you can't ~ our house** vous trouverez tout de suite notre maison ; **you mustn't ~ (seeing) this film** ne manquez pas (de voir) or ne ratez pas ce film, c'est un film à ne pas manquer or rater ; **don't ~ the Louvre** ne manquez pas d'aller au Louvre ; **if we go that way we'll ~ Bourges** si nous prenons cette route nous ne verrons pas Bourges ; **I ~ed him at the station by five minutes** je l'ai manqué or raté de cinq minutes à la gare ; **to ~ a payment (on sth)** sauter un versement (pour qch) ; **I've never ~ed a payment on my mortgage** je n'ai jamais sauté de versement pour mon emprunt logement c [+ remark, joke, meaning] (= not hear) manquer, ne pas entendre ; (= not understand) ne pas comprendre, ne pas saisir ; **I ~ed what you said** je n'ai pas entendu ce que vous avez dit ; **I ~ed that** je n'ai pas entendu, je n'ai pas compris ; **I ~ed the point of that joke** je n'ai pas compris ce que ça avait de drôle, je n'ai pas saisi l'astuce ; **you've ~ed the whole point!** vous n'avez rien compris !, vous avez laissé passer l'essentiel !

d (= escape, avoid) [+ accident, bad weather] échapper à ; **he narrowly ~ed being killed** il a manqué or il a bien failli se (faire) tuer e (= long for) [+ person] regretter (l'absence de) ; **I do ~ Paris** Paris me manque beaucoup ; **we ~ you very much** nous regrettons beaucoup ton absence, tu nous manques beaucoup ; **are you ~ing me?** est-ce que je te manque ? ; **they're ~ing one another** ils se manquent l'un et l'autre ; **he will be greatly ~ed** on le regrettera beaucoup ; **he won't be ~ed** personne ne le regrettera, bon débarras ; **I ~ the old trams** je regrette les vieux trams ; **I ~ the sunshine/the freedom** le soleil/la liberté me manque f (= notice loss of) [+ money, valuables] remarquer l'absence or la disparition de ; **I suddenly ~ed my wallet** tout d'un coup je me suis aperçu que je n'avais plus mon portefeuille ; **I'm ~ing 8 dollars*** il me manque 8 dollars ; **here's your hat back — I hadn't even ~ed it!** je vous rends votre chapeau — je ne m'étais même pas aperçu or n'avais même pas remarqué que je ne l'avais plus ! ; **you can keep that pen, I won't ~ it** vous pouvez garder ce stylo, je n'en aurai pas besoin

3 VI [shot, person] manquer son coup, rater ; (fig) **you can't ~!** vous ne pouvez pas ne pas réussir ! → **missing**

▶ **miss out** 1 VT SEP (esp Brit) a (accidentally) [+ name, word, line of verse, page] sauter, oublier ; (in distributing sth) [+ person] sauter, oublier b (on purpose) [+ course at meal] ne pas prendre, sauter ; [+ name on list] omettre ; [+ word, line of verse, page] laisser de côté, sauter ; [+ concert, lecture, museum] ne pas aller à ; (in distributing sth) [+ person] omettre 2 VI (= lose out) ne pas obtenir son dû

▶ **miss out on*** VT FUS a (= fail to benefit from) [+ opportunity, bargain] rater, louper* ; [+ one's share] ne pas recevoir, perdre ; **he ~ed out on several good deals** il a raté or loupé* plusieurs bonnes affaires b (= come off badly) **he ~ed out on the deal** il n'a pas obtenu tout ce qu'il aurait pu de l'affaire ; **make sure you don't ~ out on anything** vérifie que tu reçois ton dû

miss[2] [mɪs] 1 N a Mademoiselle f ; **Miss Smith** Mademoiselle Smith, Mlle Smith ; **the Misses Smith**† les demoiselles fpl Smith ; (on letter) Mesdemoiselles Smith ; (in letter) **Dear Miss Smith** Chère Mademoiselle ; **yes Miss Smith** oui, Mademoiselle ; **yes, ~*** oui, Mademoiselle ; **Miss France 1998** Miss France 1998 b †* petite or jeune fille f ; **the modern ~** la jeune fille moderne ; **she's a cheeky little ~** c'est une petite effrontée

Miss. ABBR = **Mississippi**

missal ['mɪsəl] N missel m

misshapen ['mɪs'ʃeɪpən] ADJ difforme

missile ['mɪsaɪl] 1 N (Mil) missile m ; (= stone etc thrown) projectile m → **ballistic, ground**[1], **guided** 2 COMP ▶ **missile base** N base f de missiles (or fusées) ▶ **missile launcher** N lance-missiles m inv

missing ['mɪsɪŋ] 1 ADJ a (= lost) **to be ~** [person, object] avoir disparu (**from sth** de qch) ; **to go ~** disparaître ; **there is one plate ~ one plate has gone** or **is ~** il manque une assiette ; **~ luggage** bagages mpl égarés b (= lacking) **to be ~** [person, object, details, information] manquer (**from sth** à qch) ; **two pieces are ~** il manque deux pièces ; **how many are ~?** combien en manque-t-il ? ; **there's nothing ~** il ne manque rien, tout y est ; **there's a button ~ on** or **from my jacket** il manque un bouton à ma veste ; **he had a tooth ~** il lui manquait une dent, il avait une dent en moins ; **fill in the ~ words** trouvez les mots manquants or qui manquent c (Mil, Aviat, Naut) [serviceman, fisherman, plane] porté disparu ; **~ in action** (adj) porté disparu ♦ (n) soldat m etc porté disparu ; **~ (and) presumed dead** ◊ **~ believed killed** or **presumed dead** ◊ **reported ~** porté disparu ;

one of our aircraft is ~ un de nos avions n'est pas rentré
[2] COMP ► **the missing link** N (Anthropology, Zool) le chaînon manquant; (detail) l'élément m manquant ► **missing person** N personne f disparue; ~ **persons file** fichier m des personnes disparues ► **Missing Persons*** N (US) = **Missing Persons Bureau** ► **Missing Persons Bureau** N service de police enquêtant sur les personnes disparues

mission ['mɪʃən] [1] N (all senses) mission f; (Rel) **foreign ~s** missions fpl étrangères; **to send sb on a ~ to sb** envoyer qn en mission auprès de qn; **his ~ in life is to help others** il s'est donné pour mission d'aider autrui [2] COMP ► **mission control** N (Space etc) centre m de contrôle ► **mission controller** N ingénieur m du centre de contrôle → **trade**

missionary ['mɪʃənrɪ] [1] N missionnaire mf [2] COMP [work, duties] missionnaire; (society) de missionnaires ► **missionary position** N (sex) position f du missionnaire

missis‡ ['mɪsɪz] N **the/my ~** (= wife) la/ma bourgeoise‡; **~** (= boss) la patronne‡; **hey ~!** eh, Madame !*

Mississippi [,mɪsɪ'sɪpɪ] N (= state, river) le Mississippi; **in ~** dans le Mississippi; **the ~ Delta** le delta du Mississippi

missive ['mɪsɪv] N missive f

Missouri [mɪ'zʊərɪ] N (= state, river) le Missouri; **in ~** dans le Missouri; (US fig) **I'm from ~*** je veux des preuves

misspell ['mɪs'spel] (pret, ptp **misspelled** or **misspelt**) VT mal écrire, mal orthographier

misspelling ['mɪs'spelɪŋ] N [a] (= mistake) faute f d'orthographe [b] (= mistakes) fautes fpl d'orthographe

misspend ['mɪs'spend] (pret, ptp **misspent**) VT [+ money] dépenser à mauvais escient, gaspiller; [+ time, strength, talents] mal employer, gaspiller

misspent ['mɪs'spent] [1] VB pret, ptp of **misspend** [2] ADJ **~ youth** folle jeunesse f

misstate ['mɪs'steɪt] VT rapporter incorrectement

misstatement ['mɪs'steɪtmənt] N rapport m inexact

missus‡ ['mɪsɪz] N = **missis**

missy†* ['mɪsɪ] N ma petite demoiselle*

mist [mɪst] [1] N (Met) brume f; (on glass) buée f; (before eyes) brouillard m; [of perfume, dust etc] nuage m; [of ignorance, tears] voile m; **morning/sea ~** brume f matinale/de mer; (fig liter) **lost in the ~s of time** perdu dans la nuit des temps → **Scotch** [2] VT (also ~ **over, ~ up**) [+ mirror, windscreen, eyes] embuer [3] VI (also ~ **over, ~ up**) [scene, landscape, view] se couvrir de brume, devenir brumeux; [mirror, windscreen, eyes] s'embuer

mistakable ['mɪs'teɪkəbl] ADJ facile à confondre (**with, for** avec)

▼**mistake** [mɪs'teɪk] (vb: pret **mistook**, ptp **mistaken**) [1] N (= error) erreur f, faute f; (= misunderstanding) méprise f; **there be no ~ about it** qu'on ne s'y méprenne pas or ne s'y trompe (subj) pas; **it was a ~ to do that** c'était une erreur de faire cela; **my ~ was to do ... or in doing ...** mon erreur a été de faire ...; **my ~!** c'est (de) ma faute !, mea culpa !; **there must be some ~** il doit y avoir erreur; **by ~** par erreur; **I took his keys in ~ for mine** j'ai pris ses clés par erreur or en croyant prendre les miennes; **they arrested him in ~ for his brother** ils l'ont pris pour son frère or l'ont confondu avec son frère et l'ont arrêté; **that's a surprise and no ~!** pour une surprise c'est une surprise !; **she told him what she thought about it and no ~** elle lui a dit son opinion là-dessus sans y aller par quatre chemins; **to make a ~** faire une erreur or une faute, (= misunderstand) se tromper; **you're making a big ~** tu fais une grave or lourde

erreur; **she doesn't want her daughters to make the same ~s she did** elle ne veut pas que ses filles fassent les mêmes erreurs qu'elle; **to make the ~ of thinking/doing** faire l'erreur de penser/faire; **to make a ~ in a calculation** faire une erreur de calcul; **to make a ~ in a dictation** faire une faute dans une dictée; **I made a ~ about the book/about him** je me suis trompé sur le livre/sur son compte; **I made a ~ about or over the dates** je me suis trompé de dates; **I made a ~ about the** or **over the** or **which road to take** je me suis trompé de route; **make no ~ about it** ne vous y trompez pas [2] VT [+ meaning] mal comprendre, mal interpréter; [+ intentions] se méprendre sur; [+ time, road] se tromper de; **there's no mistaking her voice** il est impossible de ne pas reconnaître sa voix; **there's no mistaking that ...** il est indubitable que ...; **there's no mistaking it, he ...** il ne faut pas s'y tromper, il ...; **to ~ A for B** prendre A pour B, confondre A avec B → **mistaken**

▼**mistaken** [mɪs'teɪkən] [1] VB ptp of **mistake** [2] ADJ [a] (= wrong) **to be ~ (about sb/sth)** se tromper (à propos de qn/qch); **to be ~ in thinking that ...** se tromper en croyant que ...; **I knew I wasn't ~!** je savais bien que je ne me trompais pas!; **unless I'm (very much) ~** ◊ if I'm **not (very much) ~** si je ne me trompe, sauf erreur de ma part; **if they think that, then they are very much ~** si c'est ce qu'ils croient, eh bien ils se trompent lourdement; **that's just where you're ~!** c'est là que vous vous trompez! [b] (= erroneous) [belief, idea, opinion, conclusion] erroné; **to do sth in the ~ belief that ...** faire qch en croyant à tort que ...; **to be under** or **have the ~ impression that ...** avoir l'impression fausse que ... → **identity**

mistakenly [mɪs'teɪkənlɪ] ADV [a] (= wrongly) [believe, think, assume] à tort [b] (= accidentally) [kill, attack] par erreur

mister ['mɪstə^r] N [a] (gen shortened to Mr) monsieur m; **Mr Smith** Monsieur Smith, M. Smith; **yes Mr Smith** oui, Monsieur; **Mr Chairman** monsieur le président; (fig) **Mister Big*** le caïd‡, le gros bonnet*; (fig) **Mister Right*** l'homme idéal or de ses (or mes etc) rêves [b] **hey ~!**‡ eh, Monsieur !*

mistime ['mɪs'taɪm] VT [+ act, blow, kick] mal calculer; **~d remark** remarque f inopportune; **he ~d it** il a choisi le mauvais moment; **he ~d his entrance** [actor] il a raté son entrée; **to ~ one's arrival** (= arrive inopportunely) arriver au mauvais moment; (= miscalculate time) se tromper sur or mal calculer son (heure d')arrivée

mistiming [,mɪs'taɪmɪŋ] N **the ~ of his arrival** son arrivée malencontreuse; **the ~ of the announcement** le moment mal choisi de cette annonce

mistiness ['mɪstɪnɪs] N [of morning etc] bruine f, état m brumeux; (on mirror, window pane) buée f

mistlethrush ['mɪsl̩θrʌʃ] N draine f or drenne f

mistletoe ['mɪsltəʊ] N (NonC) gui m

mistook [mɪs'tʊk] VB pt of **mistake**

mistranslate ['mɪstrænz'leɪt] VT mal traduire, faire un (or des) contresens en traduisant

mistranslation ['mɪstrænz'leɪʃən] N [a] erreur f de traduction, contresens m [b] (NonC) [of text etc] mauvaise traduction f, traduction f inexacte

mistreat [,mɪs'triːt] VT maltraiter

mistreatment [,mɪs'triːtmənt] N mauvais traitement m

mistress ['mɪstrɪs] N [a] (= lover) maîtresse f; (†† = sweetheart) amante† [b] [of household, institution etc] maîtresse f; (to servant) **is your** or **the ~ at home?**† Madame est-elle là?; **to be one's own ~** être sa propre maîtresse, être indépendante [c] (Brit‡ = teacher) (in primary

school) maîtresse f, institutrice f; (in secondary school) professeur m; **the English ~** le professeur d'anglais [d] (†† : term of address) madame f

mistrial [,mɪs'traɪəl] N (Brit, US Jur) procès m entaché d'un vice de procédure; (US) procès m ajourné pour défaut d'unanimité dans le jury

mistrust ['mɪs'trʌst] [1] N méfiance f, défiance f (**of** à l'égard de) [2] VT [+ person, sb's motives, suggestion] se méfier de, se défier de (liter); [+ abilities] douter de, ne pas avoir confiance en

mistrustful ['mɪs'trʌstfʊl] ADJ [person, look, glance] méfiant; **to be ~ of sb/sth** se méfier de qn/qch

mistrustfully ['mɪs'trʌstfəlɪ] ADV avec méfiance; [look, say] d'un air méfiant

misty ['mɪstɪ] [1] ADJ [weather] brumeux; [day] de brume, brumeux; [mirror, windowpane] embué; (fig) [eyes, look] embrumé, embué; (fig) [outline, recollection, idea] nébuleux, flou; **~ blue/grey/green** bleu/gris/vert vaporeux or fondu [2] COMP ► **misty-eyed** ADJ (= near tears) qui a les yeux embués de larmes; (= sentimental) qui a la larme à l'œil

misunderstand ['mɪsʌndə'stænd] (pret, ptp **misunderstood**) VT [+ words, action, reason] mal comprendre, comprendre de travers; **you – me** vous m'avez mal compris; **she was misunderstood all her life** toute sa vie elle est restée incomprise or méconnue

misunderstanding ['mɪsʌndə'stændɪŋ] N malentendu m, méprise f; **there must be some ~** il doit y avoir méprise or une erreur; (= disagreement) **they had a slight ~** il y a eu un léger malentendu entre eux

misunderstood ['mɪsʌndə'stʊd] VB pt, ptp of **misunderstand**

misuse [,mɪs'juːs] [1] N [of power, authority] abus m; [of word, tool] usage m impropre or abusif; [of money, resources, energies, one's time] mauvais emploi m; (Jur) **~ of funds** détournement m de fonds [2] ['mɪs'juːz] VT [+ power, authority] abuser de; [+ word] employer improprement or abusivement; [+ tool, money, resources, energies, one's time] mal employer; [+ funds] détourner

MIT [,emaɪ'tiː] N (US Univ) ABBR = **Massachusetts Institute of Technology**

mite [maɪt] N [a] (= ancient coin) denier m; (as contribution) obole f; **the widow's ~** le denier de la veuve; **he gave his ~ to the collection** il a apporté son obole à la souscription [b] (= small amount) **there's not a ~ of bread left** il ne reste plus une miette de pain; **not a ~ of truth** pas une parcelle or un atome de vérité; **a ~ of consolation** une toute petite consolation; **well, just a ~ then** bon, mais alors un tout petit peu seulement; **we were a ~ surprised*** nous avons été un tantinet or un rien surpris [c] (= small child) petit(e) m(f); **poor little ~** (le) pauvre petit [d] (Zool) mite f; **cheese ~** mite f du fromage

miter ['maɪtə^r] (US) = **mitre**

Mithraic [mɪθ'reɪk] ADJ mithriaque

Mithras ['mɪθræs] N Mithra m

mitigate ['mɪtɪgeɪt] VT [+ punishment, sentence, suffering, sorrow] alléger, atténuer; [+ effect, evil] atténuer; **mitigating circumstances** circonstances fpl atténuantes

mitigation [,mɪtɪ'geɪʃən] N [a] (Jur) [of sentence] réduction f, allègement m [b] (= excuse for crime, behaviour) circonstances fpl atténuantes (**for** pour); **in ~** en guise de circonstances atténuantes; **to tender a plea in ~** plaider les circonstances atténuantes [c] (= alleviation) [of problem, illness, suffering] atténuation f [of situation] apaisement m

mitral ['maɪtrəl] ADJ mitral; **~ valve** valvule f mitrale

mitre, miter (US) ['maɪtə^r] [1] N (Rel) mitre f; (Carpentry) onglet m [2] VT (Carpentry) (= join)

[+ *frame etc*] assembler à *or* en onglet ; (= *cut*) [+ *corner, end*] tailler à onglet ③ COMP ▶ **mitre box** N (*Carpentry*) boîte *f* à onglets ▶ **mitre joint** N (assemblage *m* à) onglet *m*

mitt [mɪt] N ⓐ = **mitten** ⓑ (*Baseball: also* **catcher's** ~) gant *m* de baseball ⓒ (‡ = *hand*) patte* *f*, paluche* *f*

mitten ['mɪtn] N (*with cut-off fingers*) mitaine *f* ; (*with no separate fingers*) moufle *f* ; (*Boxing* *) gant *m*, mitaine* *f*

mix [mɪks] ① N ⓐ (= *combination*) [*of styles, types, cultures, emotions*] mélange *m* ; **a ~ of modern and traditional styles** un mélange de styles modernes et traditionnels ; **the company's product ~** les différents articles produits par l'entreprise ; **a real ~ of people** toutes sortes de gens ; **schools which have an ethnic or religious ~** des écoles qui ont des élèves d'origines ethniques ou religieuses variées ; **the broad racial ~ in this country** le melting-pot *or* le brassage des races dans ce pays ; **the candidate with the correct ~ of skills for this job** le candidat possédant la diversité des compétences requises pour cet emploi ; **pupils study a broad ~ of subjects at this school** les élèves étudient des matières diverses dans cette école ; **a ~ of plants including roses and lavender** un assortiment de plantes comprenant (notamment) des roses et des lavandes ; **shirt in a linen and cotton ~** chemise *f* en mélange lin et coton ; **a wool ~ pullover** un pullover en laine mélangée ⓑ (*Culin etc*) (**packet**) **cake/bread/pizza ~** préparation *f* pour gâteau/pain/pizza ; **cement ~** mortier *m* ⓒ (*Mus*) (= *track*) version *f* mixée ; (= *mixing process*) mixage *m*

② VT ⓐ [+ *liquids, ingredients, colours*] mélanger (**with** avec, à) ; [+ *small objects*] mêler, mélanger (**with** avec, à) ; [+ *metals*] allier, amalgamer ; [+ *cement, mortar*] malaxer, préparer ; [+ *cake, sauce*] préparer, faire ; [+ *salad*] remuer, retourner ; **to ~ one thing with another** mélanger une chose à *or* avec une autre ; **to ~ sth to a smooth paste** (bien) mélanger qch pour obtenir une pâte homogène ; **~ the eggs into the sugar** incorporez les œufs au sucre ; **he ~ed the drinks** il a préparé les boissons ; **can I ~ you a drink?** je vous sers un verre ? ; **never ~ your drinks!** évitez toujours les mélanges ! ; **to ~ business and *or* with pleasure** mélanger le travail et l'agrément, joindre l'utile à l'agréable ; **to ~ one's metaphors** faire des métaphores incohérentes ; **to ~ and match** mélanger différents types de ⓑ (*Mus*) [+ *track, album*] mixer ⓒ (*Brit fig*) **to ~ it*** (= *cause trouble*) causer des ennuis ; (= *quarrel, fight*) se bagarrer*

③ VI ⓐ [*liquids, ingredients, colours*] se mélanger ; **oil and water don't ~** (*lit*) l'huile et l'eau ne se mélangent pas ; (*fig*) l'eau et le feu ne se marient pas ; **these colours just don't ~** ces couleurs ne s'harmonisent pas *or* ne vont pas bien ensemble ; **to ~ and match** faire des mélanges ⓑ (*socially*) **he ~es with all kinds of people** il fréquente toutes sortes de gens ; **he doesn't ~ well** il est peu sociable ; **children from different social backgrounds don't often ~** les enfants d'origines sociales différentes ne se fréquentent *or* ne se mélangent pas souvent ; **they don't ~ (with each other) socially** [*work colleagues*] ils ne se voient pas en dehors du bureau

④ COMP ▶ **mix-and-match** ADJ composite ▶ **mix-up** N (= *confusion*) confusion *f* ; (= *trouble*) démêlé *m* ; **there was a ~-up over tickets** il y a eu confusion en ce qui concerne les billets ; **we got in a ~-up over the dates** nous nous sommes embrouillés dans les dates ; **he got into a ~-up with the police** il a eu un démêlé avec la police

▶ **mix in** ① VI **he doesn't want to ~ in** il préfère rester à l'écart ; **you must try to ~ in** il faut

essayer de vous mêler un peu aux autres ② VT SEP **~ in the eggs with ...** incorporez les œufs à ... ; **the producer used archive news footage ~ed in with interviews** le producteur a combiné documents d'archives et interviews

▶ **mix round** VT SEP mélanger, remuer

▶ **mix together** VT SEP mélanger, amalgamer

▶ **mix up** ① VT SEP ⓐ (= *prepare*) [+ *drink, medicine*] préparer ⓑ (= *put in disorder*) [+ *documents, garments*] mêler, mélanger ⓒ (= *confuse*) [+ *two objects, two people*] confondre ; **he ~ed her up with Jane** il l'a confondue avec Jane ⓓ **to ~ sb up in sth** impliquer qn dans qch ; **to be/get ~ed up in an affair** être/se trouver mêlé à une affaire ; **don't get ~ed up in it!** restez à l'écart ! ; **he is/he has got ~ed up with a lot of criminals** il fréquente/il s'est mis à fréquenter un tas de malfaiteurs*, (*US*) **to ~ it up*** (= *cause trouble*) causer des ennuis ; (= *quarrel, fight*) se bagarrer* ⓔ (= *muddle*) [+ *person*] embrouiller ; **to be ~ed up** [*person*] être tout désorienté *or* déboussolé* ; [*account, facts*] être embrouillé *or* confus ; **I'm all ~ed up about it** je ne sais plus où j'en suis, je ne m'y reconnais plus ; **you've got me all ~ed up** vous m'avez embrouillé ② **~-up** N → **mix** ③ **~ed-up** ADJ → **mixed**

mixed [mɪkst] ① ADJ ⓐ (*gen*) [*school, education, bathing*] mixte ; [*neighbourhood*] mélangé, hétérogène ; [*vegetables, herbs, biscuits*] assorti ; **a man/woman of ~ blood** un/une sang-mêlé ; **in ~ company** en présence d'hommes et de femmes ; **you shouldn't swear in ~ company** tu ne devrais pas jurer devant des dames ; **~ nuts** noix *fpl* et noisettes *fpl* assorties ; **to be of ~ parentage** être issu d'un mariage mixte ⓑ (= *varying*) [*reviews, emotions, messages, signals*] contradictoire ; [*results, reaction*] inégal ; [*weather*] inégal, variable ; [*success, reception*] mitigé ; [*year*] avec des hauts et des bas ; **she had ~ feelings about it** elle était partagée à ce sujet ; **to have had ~ fortunes** avoir connu un sort inégal ; **to have ~ motives** ne pas être complètement désintéressé

② COMP ▶ **mixed ability** N (*Scol*) **a class of ~ ability** une classe sans groupes de niveau ; **~-ability group** classe *f* sans groupes de niveau ; **~-ability teaching** enseignement *m* sans groupes de niveau ▶ **mixed bag** N **to be a ~ bag (of sth)** être un mélange (de qch) ; **the students are a bit of a ~ bag** il y a un peu de tout parmi les étudiants ; **it's very much a ~ bag of activities** c'est tout un pot-pourri d'activités, c'est tout un mélange d'activités ▶ **mixed blessing** N **to be a ~ blessing** avoir du bon et du mauvais ; **children can be a ~ blessing!** les enfants, ça peut avoir du bon et du mauvais ! ▶ **mixed bunch** N **a ~ bunch** [*of people*] un groupe hétérogène *or* disparate ; [*of products*] un ensemble hétéroclite ; [*of flowers*] un bouquet composé ▶ **mixed doubles** NPL (*Sport*) double *m* mixte ▶ **mixed economy** N (*Pol, Econ*) économie *f* mixte ▶ **mixed farm** N exploitation *f* en polyculture et élevage ▶ **mixed farming** N polyculture *f* et élevage *m* ▶ **mixed grill** N (*Brit*) assortiment *m* de grillades, mixed-grill *m* ▶ **mixed marriage** N mariage *m* mixte ▶ **mixed media** ADJ multimédia ▶ **mixed metaphor** N mélange *m* de métaphores ▶ **mixed race** N **to be of ~ race** être métis ; **people of ~ race** des métis ▶ **mixed-race** ADJ [*couple, neighbourhood*] mixte ; [*child*] métis (-isse *f*) ; **a ~-race marriage** un mariage interracial ▶ **mixed spice** N mélange *m* d'épices ▶ **mixed-up** ADJ [*person*] désorienté, déboussolé ; [*report etc*] embrouillé, confus ; **he's a ~-up kid*** c'est un gosse* qui a des problèmes

mixer ['mɪksər] ① N ⓐ (*Culin*) **hand ~** batteur *m* à main ; **electric ~** batteur *m* électrique, mixer *or* mixeur *m* ⓑ [*of cement, mortar etc*] malaxeur *m* ; [*of industrial liquids*] agitateur *m* ; **cement ~** bétonnière *f*, malaxeur *m* à béton ⓒ (*Cine etc: also* **sound ~**) (= *person*) ingénieur

m du son ; (= *machine*) mélangeur *m* de signaux, mixeur *m* ⓓ (*socially*) **he's a good ~** il est très sociable *or* liant ⓔ (*US* = *social gathering*) soirée-rencontre *f*, réunion-rencontre *f* ⓕ (*Brit** = *troublemaker*) fauteur *m* de troubles ⓖ (= *drink*) boisson *f* gazeuse (*servant à couper un alcool*) ② COMP ▶ **mixer tap** N (*Brit*) (robinet *m*) mélangeur *m*

mixing ['mɪksɪŋ] ① N ⓐ (*gen*) [*of ingredients, substances, sexes, generations, races*] mélange *m* ; [*of cocktails, cake, sauce*] préparation *f* ; [*of cement, mortar*] malaxage *m* ; **the ~ of charcoal with clay** le mélange de charbon de bois et d'argile ; **the ~ of the eggs into the flour** l'incorporation *f* des œufs dans la farine ; **colour ~** mélange *m* de couleurs ⓑ (*Cine, Audio, Video*) mixage *m* ; **audio ~** mixage *m* audio ② COMP ▶ **mixing bowl** N (*Culin*) saladier *m* (de cuisine) ▶ **mixing faucet** N (*US*) (robinet *m*) mélangeur *m*

mixture ['mɪkstʃər] N ⓐ (= *combination*) [*of colours, flavours, ingredients, styles, types, reasons, emotions*] mélange *m* ; **they spoke in a ~ of French, Italian and English** ils parlaient un mélange de français, d'italien et d'anglais ; **the family is an odd ~** cette famille est un mélange bizarre *or* curieux ; **a ~ of people** toutes sortes de gens ; **the course offers a ~ of subjects** le cours propose des matières diverses ; (*fig*) **it's just the ~ as before** c'est toujours la même chose, il n'y a rien de nouveau ⓑ (*Med*) préparation *f*, mixture *f* ; (*Culin: for cake, dough, batter etc*) mélange *m* ; **fold the eggs into the cheese ~** incorporez les œufs dans le mélange à base de fromage → **cough**

miz(z)en ['mɪzn] N (*Naut*) artimon *m*

miz(z)enmast ['mɪznmɑːst] N (*Naut*) mât *m* d'artimon

mizzle* ['mɪzl] (*also dial*) ① VI bruiner ② N bruine *f*

mk (ABBR = **mark**) DM *m*

ml N (ABBR = **millilitre(s)**) ml

MLitt ['em'lɪt] N (ABBR = **Master of Literature** *or* **Master of Letters**) ≈ doctorat *m* de troisième cycle

MLR [ˌemel'ɑːr] N (ABBR = **minimum lending rate**) → **minimum**

MLS [ˌemel'es] N (*US Univ*) (ABBR = **Master of Library Science**) diplôme supérieur de bibliothécaire

M'lud [məˈlʌd] N (*Brit Jur*) (ABBR = **My Lord**) Monsieur le Juge

mm¹ [əm] EXCL mmm !

mm² (ABBR = **millimetre(s)**) mm

MMC [ˌemem'siː] N (ABBR = **Monopolies and Mergers Commission**) → **monopoly**

MME [ˌemem'iː] N (*US Univ*) ⓐ (ABBR = **Master of Mechanical Engineering** ⓑ ABBR = **Master of Mining Engineering**)

MN ['em'en] N ⓐ (*Brit*) (ABBR = **Merchant Navy**) → **merchant** ⓑ ABBR = **Minnesota**

mnemonic [nɪˈmɒnɪk] ADJ, N mnémotechnique *f*, mnémonique *f*

mnemonics [nɪˈmɒnɪks] N (*NonC*) mnémotechnique *f*

MO ['em'əʊ] N ⓐ (ABBR = **medical officer**) → **medical** ⓑ ABBR = **Missouri** ⓒ (*esp US**) (ABBR = **modus operandi**) méthode *f*, truc* *m*

Mo. ABBR = **Missouri**

mo'* [məʊ] N (ABBR = **moment**) moment *m*, instant *m* ; **half** *or* **just a ~!** un instant ! ; (*interrupting*) minute !*

m.o. ['em'əʊ] N (ABBR = **money order**) → **money**

moan [məʊn] ① N (= *groan*) gémissement *m*, plainte *f* ; (= *complaint*) **I'm fed up with all your ~s*** j'en ai marre de tes récriminations *or* de t'entendre râler* ; **one of my biggest ~s is that ...** une des choses qui me fait le plus râler*, c'est que ... ② VI (= *groan*) gémir, geindre ; [*wind etc*] gémir ; (* = *complain*) récriminer, râler* ③ VT dire en gémissant

moaner* ['məʊnə'] N rouspéteur* m, -euse* f, râleur* m, -euse* f

moaning ['məʊnɪŋ] **1** N gémissements mpl, plainte(s) f(pl); (* = complaints) récriminations fpl **2** ADJ gémissant; (* = complaining) rouspéteur*, râleur*

moat [məʊt] N douves fpl, fossés mpl

moated ['məʊtɪd] ADJ [castle etc] entouré de douves or de fossés

mob [mɒb] **1** N **a** (= crowd) foule f; **they went in a ~ to the town hall** ils se rendirent en foule or en masse à la mairie; **the embassy was set on fire by the ~** la foule a incendié l'ambassade; **an angry ~** une foule en colère **b** (* = group) bande f, clique f (pej); **Paul and his ~** Paul et sa bande, Paul et sa clique (pej) **c** (= gang) [of criminals, bandits etc] gang m **d** (= Mafia) **the Mob*** la Maf(f)ia **e** (pej) **the ~** (= the common people) la populace **2** VT **b** [+ person] (= surround) faire foule autour de; (= attack) assaillir; [+ place] assiéger; **the shops were ~bed*** les magasins étaient bondés* **3** COMP ► **mob hysteria** N hystérie f collective ► **mob oratory** N éloquence f démagogique ► **mob rule** N (pej) la loi de la populace or de la rue ► **mob violence** N violence f collective

mobcap ['mɒbkæp] N charlotte f (bonnet)

mobile ['məʊbaɪl] **1** ADJ (gen, also Sociol) mobile; (fig) **I'm not ~ this week*** je ne suis pas motorisé* cette semaine → **shop, upwardly mobile 2** N (also ~ **phone**) portable m **b** (Art, toy) mobile m **3** COMP ► **mobile canteen** N (cuisine f) roulante f ► **mobile data system** N système m de données mobile ► **mobile home** N mobile home m ► **mobile library** N bibliobus m ► **mobile phone** N (téléphone m) portable m ► **mobile police unit** N unité f mobile de police ► **mobile studio** N (Rad, TV) car m de reportage

mobility [məʊ'bɪlɪtɪ] **1** N mobilité f **2** COMP ► **mobility allowance** N allocation f or indemnité f de transport (pour handicapés) → **upward**

mobilization [ˌməʊbɪlaɪ'zeɪʃən] N (all senses) mobilisation f

mobilize ['məʊbɪlaɪz] VTI (gen, also Mil) mobiliser; **to ~ sb into doing** mobiliser qn pour faire; **they were ~d into a group which ...** on les a mobilisés pour constituer un groupe qui ...

mobster ['mɒbstə'] N membre m du milieu, truand m

moccasin ['mɒkəsɪn] N mocassin m

mocha ['mɒkə] N moka m

mock [mɒk] **1** N **to make a ~ of sth/sb** tourner qch/qn en ridicule **2 mocks*** NPL (Brit Scol) examens mpl blancs **3** ADJ **a** (= imitation) [leather etc] faux (fausse f) (before n), imitation inv (before n), simili- inv **b** (= pretended) [anger, modesty] simulé, feint; **a ~ battle/trial** un simulacre de bataille/de procès **c** (Literat) burlesque → **6 4** VT **a** (= ridicule) ridiculiser; (= scoff at) se moquer de, railler; (= mimic, burlesque) singer, parodier **b** (liter = defy) [+ sb's plans, attempts] narguer **5** VI se moquer (**at** de) **6** COMP ► **mock examination** N examen m blanc ► **mock-heroic** ADJ (gen) burlesque; (Literat) héroïcomique, burlesque ► **mock orange** N (Bot) seringa(t) m ► **mock-serious** ADJ à demi sérieux ► **mock turtle soup** N consommé m à la tête de veau ► **mock-up** N maquette f

► **mock up 1** VT SEP faire la maquette de **2** ~**-up** N → **mock**

mocker ['mɒkə'] N moqueur m, -euse f

mockers* ['mɒkəz] NPL **to put the ~ on sth*** ficher qch en l'air*

mockery ['mɒkərɪ] N **a** (= mocking) moquerie f, raillerie f; (= person, thing) sujet m de moquerie or de raillerie, objet m de risée; **to**

make a ~ of sb/sth tourner qn/qch en dérision, bafouer qn/qch; **he had to put up with a lot of ~** il a dû endurer beaucoup de railleries or de persiflages **b** (= travesty) **it is a ~ of justice** c'est une parodie de justice; **a ~ of a trial** une parodie or une caricature de procès; **what a ~ it was!** c'était grotesque!

mocking ['mɒkɪŋ] **1** N (NonC) moquerie f, raillerie f **2** ADJ (gen) moqueur, railleur; (maliciously) narquois

mockingbird ['mɒkɪŋ,bɜːd] N moqueur m (oiseau)

mockingly ['mɒkɪŋlɪ] ADV (say) (gen) d'un ton moqueur or railleur; (= maliciously) d'un ton narquois; (smile) (gen) d'une façon moqueuse; (= maliciously) d'une façon narquoise

MOD [ˌeməʊ'diː] N (Brit) (ABBR = **Ministry of Defence**) → **defence**

mod[1] [mɒd] ABBR = **modern 1** ADJ (Brit) ~ **cons*** = **modern conveniences**; → **modern 2 mods** NPL mods* mpl

mod[2] [mɒd] N (Scot) concours m de musique et de poésie (en gaélique)

modal ['məʊdl] ADJ (Ling, Mus etc) modal; ~ **verb** auxiliaire m modal

modality [məʊ'dælɪtɪ] N modalité f

mode [məʊd] N **a** (= way, manner) mode m, façon f, manière f; ~ **of life** façon f or manière f de vivre, mode m de vie **b** (Comput, Ling, Mus, Philos etc) mode m; (Comput) **in interactive** etc ~ en mode conversationnel etc

model ['mɒdl] **1** N **a** (= small-scale representation) [of boat etc] modèle m (réduit); (Archit, Tech, Town Planning etc) maquette f → **scale**[1] **b** (= standard, example) modèle m, exemple m; **he was a ~ of discretion** c'était un modèle de discrétion; **on the ~ of** sur le modèle de, à l'image de; **to take sb/sth as one's ~** prendre modèle or exemple sur qn/qch; **to hold sb out** or **up as a ~** citer or donner qn en exemple **c** (= person) (Art, Phot, Sculp etc) modèle m; (Fashion) mannequin m; **male ~** mannequin m masculin **d** (Comm) modèle m; **the latest ~s** (= garments, hats) les derniers modèles mpl; (Aut) **a 1978 ~** un modèle 1978; (Aut) **sports ~** modèle m sport; **four-door ~** version f quatre portes; **factory ~** modèle m de fabrique **e** (Ling) modèle m **2** ADJ **a** (= exemplary, designed as model) modèle **b** (= miniature) [railway, theatre, village] miniature; ~ **aeroplane/boat/train** maquette f d'avion/de bateau/de train, modèle m réduit d'avion/de bateau/de train; ~ **car** modèle m réduit de voiture **3** VT **a** (= make model of) modeler (**in** en) **b** (= base) **to ~ sth on sth** modeler qch sur qch; **to ~ o.s. on sb** se modeler sur qn, prendre modèle or exemple sur qn **c** (Fashion) **to ~ clothes** être mannequin, présenter les modèles de collection; **she was ~ling swimwear** elle présentait les modèles de maillots de bain **d** (= describe, map out) [+ system, process] modéliser **4** VI (Art, Phot, Sculp) poser (**for** pour); (Fashion) être mannequin (**for** chez)

modeller, modeler (US) ['mɒdlə'] N modeleur m, -euse f

modelling, modeling (US) ['mɒdlɪŋ] **1** N **a** (Art etc) modelage m; **she does ~** (fashion) elle travaille comme mannequin; (for artist) elle travaille comme modèle **b** [of system, process] modélisation f **2** COMP ► **modelling clay** N pâte f à modeler

modem ['məʊdem] N modem m

Modena ['mɔːdena] N Modène

moderate ['mɒdərɪt] **1** ADJ **a** (also Pol = not extreme) [person, behaviour, views, demands]

modéré; [language, terms] mesuré; **he was ~ in his demands** ses exigences étaient raisonnables or n'avaient rien d'excessif; **to be a ~ drinker** boire modérément; **to take ~ exercise** faire de l'exercice avec modération **b** (= average, middling) [size] moyen, modéré; [amount, appetite, speed] modéré; [improvement, reduction, success, benefit] léger; [price] modéré, raisonnable; (Culin) **over a ~ heat** à or sur feu moyen; **in a ~ oven** à four moyen **c** [climate] tempéré **2** N (esp Pol) modéré(e) m(f) **3** ['mɒdəreɪt] VT **a** (= restrain, diminish) modérer; **moderating influence** influence f modératrice **b** (= preside over) présider **4** VI [storm, wind etc] se modérer, se calmer **5** ['mɒdəreɪt] COMP ► **moderate-sized** ADJ de grandeur or de grosseur or de taille moyenne

moderately ['mɒdərɪtlɪ] ADV **a** [wealthy, pleased, expensive, difficult] relativement, moyennement; **to make a ~ good attempt to do sth** essayer tant bien que mal de faire qch; ~ **priced** d'un prix raisonnable; ~ **quickly** assez or relativement vite; **to be ~ successful** réussir moyennement; **she did ~ well in her exams** elle s'en est relativement bien tirée à ses examens **b** [increase, decline] quelque peu; **the dollar has gained ~ against the yen** le dollar a enregistré une hausse modérée par rapport au yen **c** [act] avec modération; [eat, drink] modérément, avec modération; **to exercise ~** faire de l'exercice avec modération

moderation [ˌmɒdə'reɪʃən] N (NonC) modération f, mesure f; **in ~** [eat, drink, exercise] avec modération, modérément; **it's all right in ~** c'est très bien à petites doses or à condition de ne pas en abuser; **with ~** avec mesure or modération; **to advise ~ in drinking** conseiller la modération en matière de consommation d'alcool, conseiller de boire modérément or avec modération

moderator ['mɒdəreɪtə'] N **a** (Rel) **Moderator** président m (de l'Assemblée générale de l'Église presbytérienne) **b** (in assembly, council, discussion) président(e) m(f) **c** (Brit Univ = examiner) examinateur m, -trice f **d** (Phys, Tech) modérateur m

modern ['mɒdən] **1** ADJ moderne; **house with all ~ conveniences** maison f tout confort; **it has all ~ conveniences** il y a tout le confort (moderne); ~ **languages** langues fpl vivantes; **in ~ times** dans les temps modernes, à l'époque moderne; ~**-day** les temps modernes **2** N (= artist, poet etc) moderne mf

modernism ['mɒdənɪzəm] N **a** (NonC: Art, Rel) modernisme m **b** (= word) néologisme m

modernist ['mɒdənɪst] ADJ, N moderniste mf

modernistic [ˌmɒdə'nɪstɪk] ADJ [building, room, architecture, design] moderniste

modernity [mɒ'dɜːnɪtɪ] N modernité f

modernization [ˌmɒdənaɪ'zeɪʃən] N modernisation f

modernize ['mɒdənaɪz] **1** VT moderniser **2** VI se moderniser

modest ['mɒdɪst] ADJ **a** (= not boastful) [person] modeste; **to be ~ about sth** être modeste à propos de qch; **to be ~ about one's achievements** ne pas se faire gloire de ses réussites or exploits **b** (= small, unostentatious) [amount, size, house, income, proposal, ambition] modeste; **his ~ beginnings/origins** ses modestes débuts/origines; **a family of ~ means** une famille aux moyens modestes; **he was ~ in his demands** ses exigences étaient modestes; **on a ~ scale** à une échelle modeste; **the book was a ~ success** le livre a eu un succès modeste **c** (= decorous) [person] pudique; [clothes] décent

modestly ['mɒdɪstlɪ] ADV **a** (= in moderation) [gamble] avec modération; [drink] modérément, avec modération; **to live ~** vivre simplement; **~ furnished** modestement meublé; **~ priced** d'un prix raisonnable; **~ sized** de taille modeste; **his ~ successful paintings** ses tableaux au succès modeste [b] (= *not boastfully*) [*talk, smile*] modestement, avec modestie [c] (= *decorously*) [*behave*] pudiquement; [*dress*] avec pudeur

modesty ['mɒdɪstɪ] N [a] (*gen*) modestie *f*; († = *chasteness*) pudeur *f*, modestie *f*; **false ~** fausse modestie *f*; **may I say with all due ~ ...** soit dit en toute modestie ... [b] [*of request etc*] modération *f*; [*of sum of money, price*] modicité *f*

modicum ['mɒdɪkəm] N **a ~ of ...** un minimum de ...

modifiable ['mɒdɪfaɪəbl] ADJ modifiable

modification [ˌmɒdɪfɪ'keɪʃən] N modification *f* (**to, in** à); **to make ~s (in** or **to)** faire or apporter des modifications (à)

modifier ['mɒdɪfaɪə'] N modificateur *m*; (*Gram*) modificatif *m*

modify ['mɒdɪfaɪ] VT [a] (= *change*) [+ *plans, design*] modifier, apporter des modifications à; [+ *customs, society*] transformer, modifier; (*Gram*) modificatif [b] (= *make less strong*) modérer; **he'll have to ~ his demands** il faudra qu'il modère (*subj*) ses exigences; **he modified his statement** il modéra les termes de sa déclaration

modifying ['mɒdɪfaɪɪŋ] [1] N modification *f* [2] ADJ [*note, term*] modificatif (*also Gram*); [*factor*] modifiant

modish ['məʊdɪʃ] ADJ à la mode

modishly ['məʊdɪʃlɪ] ADV à la mode

modiste [məʊ'diːst] N modiste *f*

Mods* [mɒdz] N (*at Oxford university*) (ABBR = **moderations**) *premier examen du cursus universitaire*

modular ['mɒdjʊlə'] ADJ [a] (*Constr*) modulaire [b] (*esp Brit Univ*) [*course, programme, curriculum*] par modules or unités de valeur; **the course is ~ in structure** l'enseignement est organisé en modules or unités de valeur; **a six-week ~ course** une unité de valeur or un module de six semaines; **~ degree** licence *f* (*par modules ou unités de valeur*)

modulate ['mɒdjʊleɪt] [1] VT (*all senses*) moduler [2] VI (*Mus*) moduler

modulation [ˌmɒdjʊ'leɪʃən] N modulation *f*; **amplitude ~** modulation *f* d'amplitude; **frequency ~** modulation *f* de fréquence

module ['mɒdjuːl] N (*gen*) module *m*; (*esp Brit Univ*) module *m*, ≈ unité *f* de valeur, ≈ UV *f*; (*US*) **learning ~** enseignement *m* par groupes de niveaux → **lunar**

modulus ['mɒdjʊləs] N (*pl* **moduli** ['mɒdjʊ,laɪ]) (*Math, Phys*) module *m*, coefficient *m*

modus ['məʊdəs] N **~ operandi** modus operandi *m inv*; **~ vivendi** modus vivendi *m inv*

moggie*, **moggy*** ['mɒgɪ] N (*Brit* = *cat*) minou* *m*

Mogul ['məʊgəl] [1] ADJ mog(h)ol [2] N Mog(h)ol *m*

mogul ['məʊgəl] N [a] (*fig* = *powerful person*) nabab *m*; **a ~ of the film industry** un nabab du cinéma [b] (*Ski*) bosse *f*

MOH [ˌeməʊ'eɪtʃ] N (*Brit*) (ABBR = **Medical Officer of Health**) → **medical**

mohair ['məʊhɛə'] [1] N mohair *m* [2] COMP = en or de mohair

Mohammed [məʊ'hæmed] N Mohammed *m*, Mahomet *m*

Mohammedan† [məʊ'hæmɪdən] [1] ADJ mahométan [2] N mahométan(e) *m(f)*

Mohammedanism† [məʊ'hæmɪdənɪzəm] N mahométisme *m*

Mohican [məʊ'hiːkən] N (*pl* **Mohicans** or **Mohican**) (*also* **~ Indian**) Mohican *mf*; **mohican (hairdo)** iroquoise *f*

moire [mwɑː] N moire *f*

moiré ['mwɑːreɪ] ADJ, N moiré(e) *m(f)*

moist [mɔɪst] ADJ [*air, atmosphere, heat, skin*] (*gen*) humide; (*unpleasantly*) moite; [*place, climate, soil, eyes*] humide; [*cake, texture*] moelleux; **a plant which likes ~ conditions** une plante qui aime l'humidité; **~ with tears** mouillé de larmes

moisten ['mɔɪsn] [1] VT humecter, mouiller légèrement; (*Culin*) mouiller légèrement; **to ~ one's lips** s'humecter les lèvres [2] VI devenir humide or moite

moistness ['mɔɪstnɪs] N [*of air, atmosphere, heat, skin*] (*gen*) humidité *f*; (*unpleasant*) moiteur *f*; [*of soil*] humidité *f*; [*of cake, texture*] moelleux *m*; **she tried to hide the ~ in her eyes** elle essaya de cacher ses yeux embués de larmes

moisture ['mɔɪstʃə'] N humidité *f*; (*on glass etc*) buée *f*

moisturize ['mɔɪstʃəraɪz] VT [+ *skin*] hydrater; [+ *air, atmosphere*] humidifier

moisturizer ['mɔɪstʃəraɪzə'] N crème *f* hydratante, lait *m* hydratant

moke: [məʊk] N (*Brit*) bourricot *m*, baudet *m*

molar ['məʊlə'] [1] N (= *tooth*) molaire *f* [2] ADJ (*Dentistry, Phys*) molaire

molasses [məʊ'læsɪz] N (*NonC*) mélasse *f*; (*US*) **to be as slow as ~ in winter*** être lent comme une tortue

mold [məʊld] (*US*) = **mould**

Moldavia [mɒl'deɪvɪə] N (*formerly*) la Moldavie

Moldavian [mɒl'deɪvɪən] (*formerly*) [1] N Moldave *mf* [2] ADJ moldave

Moldova [mɒl'dəʊvə] N la Moldova

Moldovan [mɒl'dəʊvən] [1] ADJ moldave [2] N Moldave *mf*

mole[1] [məʊl] [1] N taupe *f* (*also fig*) [2] COMP ▶ **mole-catcher** N taupier *m*

mole[2] [məʊl] N (*on skin*) grain *m* de beauté

mole[3] [məʊl] N (= *breakwater*) môle *m*, digue *f*

molecular [məʊ'lekjʊlə'] [1] ADJ [*structure*] moléculaire [2] COMP ▶ **molecular biologist** N biologiste *mf* moléculaire ▶ **molecular biology** N biologie *f* moléculaire ▶ **molecular geneticist** N chercheur *m* en génétique moléculaire ▶ **molecular genetics** N (*NonC*) génétique *f* moléculaire

molecule ['mɒlɪkjuːl] N molécule *f*

molehill ['məʊlhɪl] N taupinière *f* → **mountain**

moleskin ['məʊlskɪn] [1] N (*lit*) (peau *f* de) taupe *f*; (*Brit Tex*) moleskine *f* [2] ADJ (*lit*) de or en (peau de) taupe; (*Brit Tex*) de or en moleskine

molest [məʊ'lest] VT (= *attack*) attaquer; (*Jur: sexually*) attenter à la pudeur de; [*dog*] s'attaquer à; († = *trouble*) importuner, harceler

molestation [ˌməʊles'teɪʃən] N [a] (*Jur*) brutalités *fpl*; **child ~** maltraitance *f* à enfant; **sexual ~** agression *f* sexuelle [b] († (= *annoyance*) importunité† *f*; **I was allowed to work without hindrance or ~** on m'a laissé travailler sans me gêner ni m'importuner

molester [məʊ'lestə'] N satyre *m*

Moley ['məʊlɪ] → **holy**

moll* [mɒl] N (*pej*) nana: *f* (*de gangster*)

mollify ['mɒlɪfaɪ] VT apaiser, calmer; **~ing remarks** propos *mpl* lénifiants

mollusc, mollusk (*US*) ['mɒləsk] N mollusque *m*

mollycoddle ['mɒlɪkɒdl] VT (*gen*) élever dans du coton, chouchouter*; [+ *pupil*] materner

mollycoddling ['mɒlɪkɒdlɪŋ] N (*pej*) chouchoutage *m*, maternage *m*

Molotov ['mɒlətɒf] N **~ cocktail** cocktail *m* Molotov

molt [məʊlt] (*US*) = **moult**

molten ['məʊltən] ADJ en fusion

Molucca [məʊ'lʌkə] N **the ~ Islands** or **the ~s** les Moluques *fpl*

Moluccan [məʊ'lʌkən] N → **south**

molybdenum [mɒ'lɪbdɪnəm] N molybdène *m*

mom* [mɒm] N (*US*) maman *f*; **~ and pop store*** petite boutique *f* familiale, petit commerce *m*

moment ['məʊmənt] N [a] moment *m*, instant *m*; **man of the ~** homme *m* du moment; **the psychological ~** le moment psychologique; **wait a ~!** ◊ **just a ~!** ◊ **one ~!** ◊ **half a ~!*** (attendez) un instant or une minute!; (*objecting to sth*) minute!, pas si vite!*; **I shan't be a ~** ◊ **I'll just** or **only be a ~** j'en ai pour un instant; **a ~ ago** il y a un instant; **a ~ later** un instant plus tard; **that very ~** à cet instant or ce moment précis; **the ~ he arrives** dès or aussitôt qu'il arrivera; **the ~ he arrived** dès or aussitôt qu'il arriva, dès son arrivée; **do it this ~!** fais-le à l'instant or tout de suite!; **I've just this ~ heard of it** je viens de l'apprendre à l'instant (même); **it won't take a ~** c'est l'affaire d'un instant; **at the (present) ~** ◊ **at this ~ in time** en ce moment (même), à l'heure qu'il est; **at that ~** à ce moment(-là); **(at) any ~** d'un moment or instant à l'autre; **at every ~** à chaque instant, à tout moment; **at the right ~** au bon moment, à point nommé; **at the last ~** au dernier moment; **to leave things till the last ~** attendre le dernier moment; **for a ~** un instant; **for a brief ~** l'espace d'un instant; **not for a ~!** jamais de la vie!; **I don't think for a** or **one ~ (that) he believed my story** je ne crois or pense pas un (seul) instant qu'il ait cru mon histoire; **for the ~** pour le moment; **that's enough for the ~** ça suffit pour le moment; **from the ~ I saw him** dès l'instant où je l'ai vu; **from that ~** dès ce moment, dès cet instant; **I'll come in a ~** j'arrive dans un instant; **it was all over in a ~** ça n'a duré qu'un instant; **the ~ of truth** la minute or l'heure *f* de vérité; (*fig*) **he has his ~s** il a ses bons côtés; **it has its ~s** (*of film*) il y a de bons moments; (*of book*) il y a de bons passages; (*of essay*) il y a de bonnes choses → **spur** [b] († = *importance*) importance *f*; **of little ~** de peu d'importance; **of (great) ~** de grande or haute importance [c] (*Tech*) moment *m*; **~ of inertia** moment *m* d'inertie

momentarily ['məʊməntərɪlɪ] ADV [a] (= *temporarily*) [*distracted, blinded*] momentanément; **I had ~ forgotten** j'avais momentanément oublié; **to be ~ lost for words** ne pas savoir quoi dire pendant un moment; **to pause ~** s'arrêter un instant [b] (*US* = *shortly*) dans un instant

momentary ['məʊməntərɪ] ADJ [*lapse, lull, weakness, silence*] momentané; [*feeling, relief, panic, hesitation*] passager; **I caught a ~ glimpse of him** je l'ai entrevu rapidement or l'espace d'un instant; **a ~ lapse of concentration** un moment d'inattention; **she experienced a ~ loss of confidence** elle perdit momentanément confiance

momentous [məʊ'mentəs] ADJ [*event, occasion, day*] de grande importance; [*decision, change*] capital

momentousness [məʊ'mentəsnɪs] N (*NonC*) importance *f* capitale, portée *f*

momentum [məʊ'mentəm] N (*pl* **momentums** or **momenta** [məʊ'mentə]) (*gen*) vitesse *f* (acquise); (*Phys etc*) moment *m* (*des quantités de mouvement*); [*of political movement etc*] dynamisme *m*; **to gain** or **gather ~** [*spacecraft, car etc*] prendre de la vitesse; (*fig*) gagner du terrain; (*Aut, Space etc, also fig*) **to lose ~** être en perte de vitesse; **to have ~** [*politician, party etc*] avoir le vent en poupe; **the Reagan ~** la dynamique or l'effet *m* Reagan

momma* ['mɒmə] N (*US*) = **mom**

mommy* ['mɒmɪ] N (*US*) = **mom**

Mon. ABBR = Monday

Monacan [mɒˈnɑːkən] [1] ADJ monégasque [2] N Monégasque mf

Monaco [ˈmɒnəkəʊ] N Monaco m; **in** ~ à Monaco

monad [ˈmɒnæd] N (Chem, Philos) monade f

Mona Lisa [ˌməʊnəˈliːzə] N **the** ~ la Joconde

monarch [ˈmɒnək] N (lit, fig) monarque m

monarchic(al) [mɒˈnɑːkɪk(əl)] ADJ monarchique

monarchism [ˈmɒnəkɪzəm] N monarchisme m

monarchist [ˈmɒnəkɪst] ADJ, N monarchiste mf

monarchy [ˈmɒnəkɪ] N monarchie f

monastery [ˈmɒnəstərɪ] N monastère m

monastic [məˈnæstɪk] ADJ [a] (Rel) [life] monacal, monastique; [community, building, vows] monastique [b] (= austere) [life, existence] monacal; [room] austère

monasticism [məˈnæstɪsɪzəm] N monachisme m

monaural [ˌmɒnˈɔːrəl] ADJ [instrument] monophonique, monaural; [hearing] monauriculaire

Monday [ˈmʌndɪ] [1] N lundi m → **Easter**, **Whit**; for phrases see **Saturday** [2] COMP ▶ **Monday-morning** ADJ (fig) that ~**-morning feeling** la déprime* du lundi matin; (US fig) ~**-morning quarterback** spécialiste mf du je-vous-l'avais-bien-dit

Monegasque [mɒnəˈgæsk] [1] ADJ monégasque [2] N Monégasque mf

monetarism [ˈmʌnɪtərɪzəm] N monétarisme m

monetarist [ˈmʌnɪtərɪst] ADJ, N monétariste mf

monetary [ˈmʌnɪtərɪ] ADJ [cooperation, policy, control, value] monétaire; [gain] financier; **economic and ~ union** union f économique et monétaire; **~ school** école f monétaire or monétariste → **international**

money [ˈmʌnɪ] [1] N [a] (NonC) argent m; (Fin) monnaie f; **French/Swedish ~** argent m français/suédois; **paper ~** papier-monnaie m, monnaie f de papier (often pej); **to make ~** [person] gagner de l'argent; [business etc] rapporter, être lucratif → **1b; he made his ~ by dealing in cotton** il s'est enrichi avec le coton; **the government's answer to the problem has been to throw ~ at it** le gouvernement n'a pas trouvé d'autre solution pour résoudre le problème que d'y injecter de l'argent; **to come into ~** (by inheritance) hériter (d'une somme d'argent); (gen) recevoir une somme d'argent; **I paid** or **gave good ~ for it** ça m'a coûté de l'argent; **he's earning good ~** il gagne bien sa vie → **1b; he's earning big ~** il gagne gros; **that's big ~** c'est une grosse somme; **the deal involves big ~** de grosses sommes sont en jeu dans cette transaction → **1b; he gets his ~ on Fridays** il touche son argent or sa paie le vendredi, il est payé le vendredi; **when do I get my ~?** quand est-ce que j'aurai mon argent?; (lit, fig) **to get one's ~'s worth** en avoir pour son argent; **to get one's ~ back** se faire rembourser; (with difficulty) récupérer son argent; **I want my ~ back!** remboursez!; **to put ~ into sth** placer son argent dans qch; **is there ~ in it?** est-ce que ça rapporte?, est-ce que c'est lucratif?; **it was ~ well spent** j'ai (or nous avons etc) fait une bonne affaire → **coin**, **counterfeit**, **ready** [b] (phrases) **it's a bargain for the ~!** à ce prix-là c'est une occasion!; **that's the one for my ~!** c'est juste ce qu'il me faut!; **that's the team for my ~** je serais prêt à parier pour cette équipe; **for my ~ we should do it now** à mon avis nous devrions le faire maintenant; (Brit) **it's ~ for jam*** or **old rope*** c'est de l'argent vite gagné or gagné sans peine, c'est être payé à ne rien faire; **he's made of ~*** ◊ **he's rolling in ~*** ◊ he has pots of ~* il est cousu d'or, il

roule sur l'or*; **he's got ~ to burn** il a de l'argent à ne savoir qu'en faire or à jeter par la fenêtre; **we're in the ~ now!** nous roulons sur l'or* maintenant; **he's in the big ~*** il récolte un fric fou‡ ■ (PROV) ~ **makes** ~ l'argent attire l'argent ■ (PROV) ~ **is the root of all evil** l'argent est la racine de tous les maux ■ (PROV) ~ **talks** l'argent est roi; ~ **doesn't grow on trees** l'argent ne tombe pas du ciel; **to put one's ~ where one's mouth is** joindre l'acte à la parole (en déboursant une somme d'argent); **to throw** or **send good ~ after bad** dépenser de l'argent pour rien; **bad ~ drives out good** les capitaux douteux font fuir les investissements sains; **your ~ or your life!** la bourse ou la vie!; ~ **runs through his fingers like water** ◊ **he spends** ~ **like water** l'argent lui fond dans les mains; (US fig) **it's ~ from home*** c'est du tout cuit*; (US) **his analysis was right on the** ~ son analyse était tout à fait juste → **even²** [c] (Jur) ~**s** ◊ **monies** sommes fpl d'argent; ~**s paid out** versements mpl; ~**s received** recettes fpl, rentrées fpl; **public** ~**s** deniers mpl publics

[2] COMP [difficulties, problems, questions] d'argent, financier ▶ **money belt** N ceinture-portefeuille f ▶ **money expert** N expert m en matières financières ▶ **money-loser** N affaire f non rentable or qui perd de l'argent ▶ **money market** N (Econ) marché m monétaire ▶ **money matters** NPL questions fpl d'argent or financières ▶ **money order** N (US) mandat m postal, mandat-poste m ▶ **money spider** N araignée f porte-bonheur inv ▶ **money spinner*** N (Brit) mine f d'or (fig) ▶ **money-spinning*** ADJ (Brit) [idea] qui peut rapporter de l'or ▶ **money supply** N (Econ) masse f monétaire

moneybag [ˈmʌnɪbæg] N sac m d'argent; **he's a ~s**‡ il est plein aux as‡

moneybox [ˈmʌnɪbɒks] N tirelire f

moneychanger [ˈmʌnɪˌtʃeɪndʒə²] N (= person) changeur m; (= change machine) distributeur m de monnaie, monnayeur m

moneyed [ˈmʌnɪd] ADJ riche, aisé; **the ~ classes** les classes fpl possédantes, les nantis mpl

moneygrubber [ˈmʌnɪgrʌbə²] N (pej) grippe-sou m

moneygrubbing [ˈmʌnɪgrʌbɪŋ] [1] N (pej) thésaurisation f, rapacité f [2] ADJ rapace, grippe-sou inv

moneylender [ˈmʌnɪlendə²] N prêteur m, -euse f sur gages

moneylending [ˈmʌnɪlendɪŋ] [1] N prêt à intérêt [2] ADJ prêteur

moneymaker [ˈmʌnɪmeɪkə²] N **to be a ~** [scheme] être une affaire lucrative; [person] gagner beaucoup d'argent

moneymaking [ˈmʌnɪmeɪkɪŋ] [1] N acquisition f d'argent [2] ADJ lucratif, qui rapporte

moneyman* [ˈmʌnɪmæn] N (pl -men) (US) financier m

moneywort [ˈmʌnɪwɜːt] N (Bot) souci m d'eau, lysimaque f

...monger [ˈmʌŋgə²] SUF marchand m de ... → **fishmonger**, **scandalmonger**, **warmonger**

Mongol [ˈmɒŋgɒl] [1] ADJ (Geog, Ling) mongol [2] N [a] Mongol(e) m(f) [b] (Ling) mongol m

mongol† [ˈmɒŋgɒl] [1] ADJ (= with/of Down's syndrome) mongolien; [2] N (= person with Down's syndrome) mongolien(ne) m(f)

Mongolia [mɒŋˈgəʊlɪə] N la Mongolie

Mongolian [mɒŋˈgəʊlɪən] [1] N Mongol(e) m(f) [2] ADJ mongol; **the ~ People's Republic** la République populaire de Mongolie

mongolism† [ˈmɒŋgəlɪzəm] N (= Down's syndrome) mongolisme m

Mongoloid [ˈmɒŋgəˌlɔɪd] ADJ, N = **Mongol 1 and 2a, mongol 2**

mongoose [ˈmɒŋguːs] N (pl **mongooses**) mangouste f

mongrel [ˈmʌŋgrəl] [1] N (= dog) (chien m) bâtard m; (= animal, plant) hybride m, métis(se) m(f) [2] ADJ hybride, bâtard, (de race) indéfinissable

monied [ˈmʌnɪd] ADJ = **moneyed**

monies [ˈmʌnɪz] NPL of **money 1c**

moniker [ˈmɒnɪkə²] N (= name) nom m; (= nickname) surnom m

monitor [ˈmɒnɪtə²] [1] N [a] (= device: Comput, Med, Tech, TV etc) moniteur m; **heart rate ~** moniteur m cardiaque [b] (= person: Rad) rédacteur m, -trice f d'un service d'écoute [c] (Scol) ≈ chef m de classe [2] VT [a] (+ person, pupil, work, progress, system] suivre de près; [+ equipment etc] contrôler (les performances de); [+ machine] contrôler; **a nurse ~s the patient's progress** une infirmière suit de près or surveille l'évolution de l'état du malade; **a machine ~s the patient's progress** une machine contrôle l'évolution de l'état du malade; **to ~ the situation** surveiller l'évolution des choses [b] (Rad) [+ foreign broadcasts, station] être à l'écoute de

monitoring [ˈmɒnɪtərɪŋ] N (gen) (by person) surveillance f; (by machine) contrôle m; (Med, Tech) monitorage m; (Univ, Scol) contrôle m continu (des connaissances) [b] (Rad) (service m d')écoute f

monitory [ˈmɒnɪtərɪ] ADJ monitoire, d'admonition

monk [mʌŋk] N moine m, religieux m

monkey [ˈmʌŋkɪ] [1] N singe m; (fig = child) galopin(e) m(f), polisson(ne) m(f); (Brit‡ = £500) cinq cents livres; **female ~** guenon f; **to make a ~ out of sb** tourner qn en ridicule; (US Drugs) **to have a ~ on one's back*** être esclave de la drogue; (Brit) **I don't give a ~'s**‡ or a **~'s cuss**†‡ **(about football)** je n'en ai rien à foutre‡ (du football); (Brit) **as clever as a cartload** or **barrel (load) of ~s**†* malin comme un singe

[2] COMP ▶ **monkey bars** NPL (for climbing on) cage f à poules ▶ **monkey business*** N (fig) (dishonest) affaire f louche, combine(s) f(pl); (mischievous) singeries fpl; **no ~ business now!*** pas de blagues!* ▶ **monkey house** N cage f des singes, singerie f ▶ **monkey jacket** N (Naut) vareuse f ajustée ▶ **monkey nut** N (Brit) cacahouète or cacahuète f ▶ **monkey puzzle** N (= tree) araucaria m ▶ **monkey suit*** N (esp US: pej) costume m de pingouin*, smoking m ▶ **monkey tricks*** NPL (fig) (dishonest) manœuvres fpl, combine(s) f(pl); (mischievous) singeries fpl; **no ~ tricks now!*** pas de blagues!* ▶ **monkey wrench** N clé f anglaise or à molette; (US fig) **to throw a ~ wrench into the works*** flanquer la pagaille* ▶ **monkey about***, **monkey around***, VI [a] (= waste time) perdre son temps; **stop ~ing about and get on with your work** cesse de perdre ton temps et fais ton travail [b] (= play the fool) faire l'idiot or l'imbécile; **to ~ about with sth** tripoter qch, faire l'imbécile avec qch

monkeyshines* [ˈmʌŋkɪʃaɪnz] NPL (US) pitreries fpl

monkfish [ˈmʌŋkfɪʃ] N (pl **monkfish** or **monkfishes**) (= angler fish) lotte f; (= angel fish) ange m de mer

monkish [ˈmʌŋkɪʃ] ADJ de moine

monkshood [ˈmʌŋkshʊd] N (Bot) aconit m

mono [ˈmɒnəʊ] [1] ADJ (ABBR = **monophonic**) mono inv [2] N [a] **recorded in ~** enregistré en mono [b] (also ~ **record**) disque m mono

mono... [ˈmɒnəʊ] PREF mon(o)...

monobasic [mɒnəʊˈbeɪsɪk] ADJ monobasique

monochromatic [mɒnəʊkrəʊˈmætɪk] ADJ monochromatique

monochrome [ˈmɒnəkrəʊm] [1] N (gen, also Art) camaïeu m; (Phot, TV) noir m et blanc m;

landscape in ~ paysage *m* en camaïeu [2] ADJ (*gen*) monochrome; (*Art*) en camaïeu; (*Phot, TV*) en noir et blanc

monocle ['mɒnəkl] N monocle *m*

monocled ['mɒnəkld] ADJ qui porte un monocle

monocoque ['mɒnəkɒk] [1] ADJ monocoque [2] N (= *car*) monocoque *f*; (= *boat, bicycle*) monocoque *m*

monocracy [mɒ'nɒkrəsɪ] N monocratie *f*

monocrat ['mɒnəkræt] N monocrate *m*

monocratic [mɒnə'krætɪk] ADJ monocratique

monocular [mɒ'nɒkjʊləʳ] ADJ monoculaire

monoculture ['mɒnəʊkʌltʃəʳ] N monoculture *f*

monocyte ['mɒnəʊsaɪt] N monocyte *m*

monody ['mɒnədɪ] N monodie *f*

monogamist [mə'nɒgəmɪst] N monogame *mf*

monogamous [mə'nɒgəməs] ADJ monogame

monogamy [mə'nɒgəmɪ] N monogamie *f*

monogenetic [mɒnəʊdʒɪ'netɪk] ADJ monogénétique

monogram ['mɒnəgræm] [1] N monogramme *m* [2] VT marquer de son (*or mon etc*) monogramme *or* de son (*or mon etc*) chiffre

monogrammed ['mɒnəgræmd] ADJ portant un (*or son etc*) monogramme, à son (*or mon etc*) chiffre

monograph ['mɒnəgræf] N monographie *f*

monogynous [mɒ'nɒdʒɪnəs] ADJ monogame

monogyny [mɒ'nɒdʒɪnɪ] N monogamie *f*

monohull ['mɒnəʊhʌl] N monocoque *m* (*Naut*)

monokini [mɒnəʊki:nɪ] N monokini *m*

monolingual [mɒnəʊ'lɪŋgwəl] ADJ monolingue

monolith ['mɒnəlɪθ] N [a] (*lit* = *stone*) monolithe *m* [b] (*fig* = *organization etc*) mastodonte *m*

monolithic [mɒnə'lɪθɪk] ADJ [*system, structure, state, party*] monolithique; [*building*] colossal; (*Archeol*) monolithe

monolog ['mɒnəlɒg] N (*US*) = **monologue**

monologist ['mɒnəlɒgɪst] N monologueur *m*

monologue, monolog (*also US*) ['mɒnəlɒg] N monologue *m*

monomania [mɒnəʊ'meɪnɪə] N monomanie *f*

monomaniac [mɒnəʊ'meɪnɪæk] N, ADJ monomane *mf*, monomaniaque *mf*

monometallism [mɒnəʊ'metəlɪzəm] N monométallisme *m*

monometer [mɒ'nɒmɪtəʳ] N monomètre *m*

monomial [mɒ'nəʊmɪəl] [1] N monôme *m* [2] ADJ de *or* en monôme

monomorphic [mɒnəʊ'mɔ:fɪk] ADJ monomorphe

monomorphism [mɒnəʊ'mɔ:fɪzəm] N monomorphisme *m*

mononuclear [mɒnəʊ'nju:klɪəʳ] ADJ mononucléaire

mononucleosis [mɒnəʊnju:klɪ'əʊsɪs] N mononucléose *f*

monophonic [mɒnəʊ'fɒnɪk] ADJ monophonique, monaural

monophony [mɒ'nɒfənɪ] N monophonie *f*

monophthong ['mɒnəfθɒŋ] N monophthongue *f*

monoplane ['mɒnəʊpleɪn] N monoplan *m*

monopolist [mə'nɒpəlɪst] N monopoliste *mf*

monopolistic [mənɒpə'lɪstɪk] ADJ monopolistique

monopolization [mənɒpəlaɪ'zeɪʃən] N monopolisation *f*

monopolize [mə'nɒpəlaɪz] VT (*Comm*) monopoliser, avoir le monopole de; (*fig*) monopoliser, accaparer

monopoly [mə'nɒpəlɪ] [1] N [a] monopole *m* (**of, in** de) [b] (= *game*) **Monopoly**® Monopo-

ly® *m* [2] COMP ► **Monopolies and Mergers Commission** N (*Brit*) Commission *f* d'enquête sur les monopoles, Commission *f* de la concurrence ► **Monopoly money*** N (*NonC*) (= *large amount*) somme *f* mirobolante*; (*pej* = *foreign currency*) ≈ monnaie *f* de singe

monorail ['mɒnəʊreɪl] N monorail *m*

monoski ['mɒnəʊski:] N monoski *m*

monosodium glutamate [mɒnəʊ'səʊdɪəm'glu:təmeɪt] N glutamate *m* (de sodium)

monosyllabic ['mɒnəʊsɪ'læbɪk] ADJ [*word, reply*] monosyllabique; **she was** ~ elle ne s'exprimait que par monosyllabes; **his English was fairly** ~ son anglais était plutôt rudimentaire

monosyllable ['mɒnə,sɪləbl] N monosyllabe *m*; **to answer in ~s** répondre par monosyllabes

monotheism ['mɒnəʊ,θi:ɪzəm] N monothéisme *m*

monotheist ['mɒnəʊ,θi:ɪst] N monothéiste *mf*

monotheistic [,mɒnəʊθi:'ɪstɪk] ADJ monothéiste

monotone ['mɒnətəʊn] N (= *voice/tone etc*) voix *f*/ton *m* etc monocorde; **to speak in a ~** parler sur un ton monocorde

monotonous [mə'nɒtənəs] ADJ monotone

monotonously [mə'nɒtənəslɪ] ADV [*predictable*] de façon monotone; **the rain dripped ~ from the trees** la pluie ruisselait des arbres avec monotonie; **the sky was ~ grey** le ciel était d'un gris monotone

monotony [mə'nɒtənɪ] N monotonie *f*

monotype ['mɒnətaɪp] N (*Art, Engraving*) monotype *m*; (*Typ* = *machine*) **Monotype**® Monotype® *f*

monoxide [mɒ'nɒksaɪd] N monoxyde *m*

Monroe doctrine [mən'rəʊ'dɒktrɪn] N doctrine *f* de Monroe

monseigneur [,mɒnsen'jɜ:ʳ] N monseigneur *m*

monsignor [mɒn'si:njəʳ] N (*pl* **monsignors** *or* **monsignori**) (*Rel*) monsignor *m*

monsoon [mɒn'su:n] N mousson *f*; **the ~s** la mousson; **the ~ season** la mousson d'été

mons pubis ['mɒnz'pju:bɪs] N (*pl* **montes pubis** ['mɒnti:z'pju:bɪs]) mont *m* de Vénus, pénil *m* (*chez l'homme*)

monster ['mɒnstəʳ] [1] N (*all senses*) monstre *m* [2] ADJ* colossal, monstre*

monstrance ['mɒnstrəns] N ostensoir *m*

monstrosity [mɒn'strɒsɪtɪ] N (= *thing*) monstruosité *f*; (= *person*) monstre *m*

monstrous ['mɒnstrəs] ADJ monstrueux; **it is ~ that ...** c'est monstrueux que ... (+ *subj*)

monstrously ['mɒnstrəslɪ] ADV monstrueusement

mons veneris ['mɒnz'venərɪs] N (*pl* **montes veneris** ['mɒnti:z'venərɪs]) mont *m* de Vénus

Mont. ABBR = **Montana**

montage [mɒn'tɑ:ʒ] N (*Cine, Phot*) montage *m*

Montana [mɒn'tænə] N le Montana; **in ~** dans le Montana

Mont Blanc [mɔ̃blɑ̃] N le mont Blanc

monte* ['mɒntɪ] N = **monty**

Monte Carlo ['mɒntɪ'kɑ:ləʊ] N Monte-Carlo

Montenegrin [,mɒntɪ'ni:grɪn], **Montenegran** [,mɒntɪ'ni:grən] [1] ADJ monténégrin [2] N Monténégrin(e) *m(f)*

Montenegro [,mɒntɪ'ni:grəʊ] N le Monténégro

Montezuma [mɒntɪ'zu:mə] N Montezuma *m*, Moctezuma II *m*; (*fig*) **~'s revenge*** turista *f*

month [mʌnθ] N mois *m*; **it went on for ~s or for ~ after ~** cela a duré des mois (et des mois); **the ~ of May** au mois de mai, en mai; **to be paid by the ~** être payé au mois, être mensualisé; **every ~** [*happen*] tous les

mois; [*pay*] mensuellement; **which day of the ~ is it?** le combien sommes-nous?; **at the end of this ~** à la fin du *or* de ce mois; (*Comm*) **at the end of the current ~** fin courant*; **he owes his landlady two ~s' rent** il doit deux mois à sa propriétaire; **six ~s pregnant** enceinte de six mois; **he'll never do it in a ~ of Sundays*** il le fera la semaine des quatre jeudis* *or* à la saint-glinglin* → **calendar, lunar**

monthly ['mʌnθlɪ] [1] ADJ mensuel; **on a ~ basis** [*pay*] par mensualités; [*happen, do sth*] tous les mois; **~ payment** *or* **instalment** mensualité *f*; (*Med*) **~ period** règles *fpl*; **~ ticket** carte *f* (d'abonnement) mensuelle [2] N (*Press*) mensuel *m* [3] ADV [*publish*] mensuellement; [*pay*] au mois; [*happen*] tous les mois; **~ paid staff** employés *mpl* mensualisés

Montreal [,mɒntrɪ'ɔ:l] N Montréal

monty* ['mɒntɪ] N (*Brit*) **the full ~** la totale*

monument ['mɒnjʊmənt] N (*all senses*) monument *m* (**to, of** à); **Monty Python films are a ~ to British eccentricity** les films de Monty Python sont un monument d'excentricité britannique

monumental [,mɒnjʊ'mentl] [1] ADJ [a] (= *huge*) [*object, task, achievement, blunder*] monumental; [*effort, success*] prodigieux; **on a ~ scale** [*build*] sur une très grande *or* une vaste échelle; **he was stupid on a ~ scale** il était d'une bêtise monumentale [b] (*to do with monuments*) funéraire [2] COMP ► **monumental mason** N marbrier *m* (*funéraire*)

monumentally [,mɒnjʊ'mentəlɪ] ADV [*dull, boring*] prodigieusement; **~ important** d'une importance capitale *or* monumentale; **it was ~ successful** ça a eu un succès foudroyant

moo [mu:] [1] N meuglement *m*; **~!** meuh!; **silly ~** pauvre cloche* *f* [2] VI meugler [3] COMP ► **moo-cow** N (*baby talk*) meuh-meuh *f* (*baby talk*)

mooch* [mu:tʃ] [1] VT (*US* = *cadge*) **to ~ sth from sb** taper qn de qch* [2] VI **to ~ in/out** *etc* entrer/sortir *etc* en traînant

► **mooch about*, mooch around*** VI traînasser, flemmarder*

mood [mu:d] [1] N [a] humeur *f*, disposition *f*; **to be in a good/bad ~** être de bonne/mauvaise humeur, être de bon/mauvais poil*; **to be in an ugly ~** [*person*] être d'une humeur massacrante *or* exécrable; [*crowd*] être menaçant; **to be in a forgiving ~** être en veine de générosité *or* d'indulgence; **I'm in the ~ for dancing** je danserais volontiers, j'ai envie de danser; **I'm not in the ~** *or* **I'm in no ~ for laughing** je ne suis pas d'humeur à rire, je n'ai aucune envie de rire; **I'm in no ~ to listen to him** je ne suis pas d'humeur à l'écouter; **are you in the ~ for chess?** une partie d'échecs ça vous dit?; **he plays well when he's in the ~** quand il veut *or* quand ça lui chante* il joue bien; **I'm not in the ~** ça ne me dit rien; **as the ~ takes him** selon son humeur, comme ça lui chante*; **that depends on his ~** cela dépend de son humeur; **he's in one of his ~s** il est encore mal luné; **she has ~s** elle a des sautes d'humeur, elle est lunatique; **the ~ of the meeting** l'état d'esprit de l'assemblée → **good, ugly** [b] (*Ling, Mus*) mode *m*

[2] COMP ► **mood music** N musique *f* d'ambiance ► **mood swing** N saute *f* d'humeur

moodily ['mu:dɪlɪ] ADV (= *bad-temperedly*) [*reply*] d'un ton maussade, maussadement; (= *gloomily*) [*stare at*] d'un air morose

moodiness ['mu:dɪnɪs] N (= *sulkiness*) humeur *f* maussade; (= *changeability*) humeur *f* changeante

moody ['mu:dɪ] ADJ [a] (= *sulky*) [*person*] de mauvaise humeur (**with sb** avec qn); **Elvis's ~ looks** la beauté ténébreuse d'Elvis [b] (=

temperamental) [*person*] d'humeur changeante, lunatique; **to be ~** être lunatique [c] (= *atmospheric*) [*music, film, picture*] sombre

moola(h)‡ ['muːlɑː] N (*US* = *money*) pèze‡ *m*, fric‡ *m*

moon [muːn] [1] N lune *f*; **there was no ~** c'était une nuit sans lune; **there was a ~ that night** il y avait clair de lune cette nuit-là; **when the ~ is full** à la pleine lune; **by the light of the ~** à la clarté de la lune, au clair de lune; **the ~s of Jupiter** les lunes de Jupiter; (*hum*) **many ~s ago** il y a de cela bien longtemps; (*fig*) **to ask for the ~** demander la lune; **he's over the ~*** (**about it**) il est aux anges → **blue, half, land, man, new, shoot** [2] VI (‡ = *exhibit buttocks*) montrer son cul*‡ [3] COMP ► **moon buggy** N jeep® *f* lunaire ► **moon landing** N alunissage *m* ► **moon rock** N roche *f* lunaire ► **moon shot** N (*Space*) lancement *m* d'une fusée lunaire ► **moon walk** N marche *f* sur la lune

► **moon about, moon around** VI musarder en rêvassant

► **moon over** VT FUS **to ~ over sb** soupirer pour qn

moonbeam ['muːnbiːm] N rayon *m* de lune

moonboots ['muːnbuːts] NPL moonboots *fpl*

mooncraft ['muːnkrɑːft] N (*Space*) module *m* lunaire

moonfaced ['muːnfeɪst] ADJ au visage rond

Moonie ['muːnɪ] N mooniste *mf*, adepte *mf* de la secte Moon

moonless ['muːnlɪs] ADJ sans lune

moonlight ['muːnlaɪt] [1] N clair *m* de lune; **by ~** ◊ **in the ~** au clair de lune [2] VI (* = *work extra*) travailler au noir [3] COMP [*walk, encounter*] au clair de lune ► **moonlight flit** N (*Brit fig*) **to do a ~ flit** déménager à la cloche de bois ► **moonlight night** N nuit *f* de lune

moonlighting* ['muːnlaɪtɪŋ] N (*NonC*) travail *m* au noir

moonlit ['muːnlɪt] ADJ éclairé par la lune; **a ~ night** une nuit de lune

moonrise ['muːnraɪz] N lever *m* de (la) lune

moonscape ['muːnskeɪp] N paysage *m* lunaire

moonshine* ['muːnʃaɪn] N (*fig* = *nonsense*) sornettes *fpl*; (*US* = *illegal spirits*) alcool *m* de contrebande

moonshiner ['muːnʃaɪnər] N (*US*) (= *distiller*) bouilleur *m* de cru clandestin; (= *smuggler*) contrebandier *m* d'alcool

moonshining ['muːnʃaɪnɪŋ] N (*US*) distillation *f* clandestine

moonship ['muːnʃɪp] N (*Space*) module *m* lunaire

moonstone ['muːnstəʊn] N pierre *f* de lune

moonstruck ['muːnstrʌk] ADJ **he's ~** il n'a pas toute sa tête

moony* ['muːnɪ] ADJ dans la lune

Moor [mʊər] N Maure *m* or More *m*, Mauresque *f* or Moresque *f*

moor[1] [mʊər] N (*esp Brit*) lande *f*

moor[2] [mʊər] [1] VT [+ *ship*] amarrer [2] VI mouiller

moorhen ['mʊəhen] N poule *f* d'eau

mooring ['mʊərɪŋ] N (*Naut*) (= *place*) mouillage *m*; (= *ropes etc*) amarres *fpl*; **at her ~s** sur ses amarres; **~ buoy** coffre *m* (d'amarrage), bouée *f* de corps-mort

Moorish ['mʊərɪʃ] ADJ [*person, culture, influence, invasion*] maure; [*architecture*] mauresque

moorland ['mʊələnd] N lande *f*; (*boggy*) terrain *m* tourbeux

moose [muːs] N (*pl inv*) (*in Canada*) orignal *m*; (*in Europe*) élan *m*

moot [muːt] [1] ADJ [*question*] discutable, controversé; **it's a ~ point** c'est discutable [2] VT [+ *question*] soulever, mettre sur le ta-

pis; **it has been ~ed that ...** on a suggéré que ... [3] COMP ► **moot case** N (*Jur*) hypothèse *f* d'école ► **moot court** N (*US*) tribunal fictif permettant aux étudiants de s'exercer

mop [mɒp] [1] N [a] (*for floor*) balai *m* à franges; (*for dishes*) lavette *f* (à vaisselle); (*Naut*) faubert *m* [b] (*also* **~ of hair**) tignasse *f*; **~ of curls** crinière* *f* bouclée [2] VT [+ *floor, surface*] essuyer; **to ~ one's brow** s'éponger le front [3] COMP ► **mopping-up operation, mop-up** N (*Mil*) (opération *f* de) nettoyage *m*

► **mop down** VT SEP passer un coup de balai à

► **mop up** [1] VT SEP [a] [+ *liquid*] éponger; [+ *floor, surface*] essuyer; **she ~ped up the sauce with a piece of bread** elle a saucé son assiette avec un morceau de pain [b] (*fig*) [+ *profits*] rafler, absorber [c] (*Mil*) [+ *terrain*] nettoyer; [+ *remnants of enemy*] éliminer [2] **~ping-up** ADJ → **mop**

mopboard ['mɒpbɔːd] N (*US*) plinthe *f*

mope [məʊp] VI se morfondre, avoir le cafard* *or* des idées noires; **she ~d about it all day** toute la journée elle a broyé du noir en y pensant

► **mope about, mope around** VI passer son temps à se morfondre, traîner son ennui

moped ['məʊped] N (*esp Brit*) vélomoteur *m*, mobylette® *f*

moppet* ['mɒpɪt] N chéri(e) *m(f)*

moquette [mɒˈket] N moquette *f* (*étoffe*)

MOR ADJ (*Mus*) (ABBR = **middle-of-the-road**) grand public *inv*

moraine [mɒˈreɪn] N moraine *f*

moral ['mɒrəl] [1] ADJ (*all senses*) moral; **it is a ~ certainty** c'est une certitude morale; **to be under** *or* **have a ~ obligation to do** être moralement obligé de faire, être dans l'obligation morale de faire; **~ support** soutien *m* moral; **I'm going along as ~ support for him** j'y vais pour le soutenir moralement; (*US Pol*) **the Moral Majority** les néoconservateurs *mpl* (américains); **~ philosopher** moraliste *mf*; **~ philosophy** la morale, l'éthique *f*; (*Rel*) **Moral Rearmament** Réarmement *m* moral; **to raise ~ standards** relever le niveau moral; **~ standards are falling** le sens moral se perd; **~ suasion** pression *f* morale; **a ~ victory** une victoire morale

[2] N [*of story*] morale *f*; **to point the ~** tirer la morale

[3] **morals** NPL [*of person, act, attitude*] moralité *f*; **of loose ~s** de mœurs relâchées; **he has no ~s** il est sans moralité

morale [mɒˈrɑːl] [1] N (*NonC*) moral *m*; **high ~** bon moral; **his ~ was very low** il avait le moral très bas *or* à zéro; **to raise sb's ~** remonter le moral à qn; **to lower** *or* **undermine sb's ~** démoraliser qn [2] COMP ► **morale booster** N **to be a ~ booster for sb** remonter le moral de qn

moralist ['mɒrəlɪst] N moraliste *mf*

moralistic [ˌmɒrəˈlɪstɪk] ADJ (*pej*) moralisateur (-trice *f*) (*pej*)

morality [məˈrælɪtɪ] N [a] (*NonC*) moralité *f* [b] (*Theat: also* **~ play**) moralité *f*

moralize ['mɒrəlaɪz] [1] VI moraliser (**about** sur), faire le moraliste [2] VT moraliser, faire la morale à

moralizing ['mɒrəlaɪzɪŋ] [1] ADJ moralisateur (-trice *f*) [2] N leçons *fpl* de morale

morally ['mɒrəlɪ] ADV [a] (= *ethically*) moralement; **~ wrong** contraire à la morale; **~ right** conforme à la morale; **she was ~ right** elle avait raison d'un point de vue moral; **~ the situation is a minefield** d'un point de vue moral la situation est épineuse [b] (*frm* = *virtually*) **~ certain** pratiquement sûr

morass [məˈræs] N marais *m*, marécage *m*; (*fig*) **a ~ of problems** des problèmes à ne plus s'y retrouver *or* à ne plus s'en sortir; **a ~ of fig-**

ures un fatras de chiffres; **a ~ of paperwork** de la paperasserie, un monceau de paperasserie

moratorium [ˌmɒrəˈtɔːrɪəm] N (*pl* **moratoriums** *or* **moratoria** [ˌmɒrəˈtɔːrɪə]) moratoire *m*, moratorium *m*

Moravia [məˈreɪvɪə] N la Moravie

Moravian [məˈreɪvɪən] [1] ADJ morave; **the ~ Church** l'Église *f* morave [2] N Morave *mf*

moray eel [mɒˈreɪˈiːl] N murène *f*

morbid ['mɔːbɪd] [1] ADJ (= *ghoulish*) [*person, thoughts, interest*] morbide; [*fear, dislike*] maladif; **don't be so ~!** cesse donc de broyer du noir! [2] COMP ► **morbid anatomy** N anatomie *f* pathologique

morbidity [mɔːˈbɪdɪtɪ] [1] N (*also Med*) morbidité *f* [2] COMP ► **morbidity rate** N taux *m* de morbidité

morbidly ['mɔːbɪdlɪ] ADV **to be ~ curious about sb/sth** être animé d'une curiosité malsaine pour qn/qch; **to be ~ fascinated by sb/sth** avoir une fascination malsaine pour qn/qch; **to be ~ obsessed by sth** avoir la hantise de qch

morbidness ['mɔːbɪdnɪs] N = **morbidity**

mordacious [mɔːˈdeɪʃəs] ADJ mordant, caustique

mordacity [mɔːˈdæsɪtɪ] N mordacité *f* (*liter*), causticité *f*

mordant ['mɔːdənt] ADJ (*frm*) mordant

mordent ['mɔːdənt] N (*Mus*) (**lower**) **~** mordant *m*, pincé *m*; **upper** *or* **inverted ~** pincé *m* renversé

▼ **more** [mɔːr] *compar of* **many**, **much** [1] ADJ, PRON [a] (= *greater in number etc*) plus (de), davantage (de); (= *additional*) encore (de); (= *other*) d'autres; **many came but ~ stayed away** beaucoup de gens sont venus mais davantage *or* un plus grand nombre se sont abstenus; **many ~** *or* **a lot ~ books/time** beaucoup plus de livres/de temps; **I need a lot ~** il m'en faut beaucoup plus *or* bien davantage; **I need a few ~ books** il me faut encore quelques livres *or* quelques livres de plus; **some were talking and a few ~ were reading** il y en avait qui parlaient et d'autres qui lisaient; **a little ~** un peu plus (de); **several ~ days** quelques jours de plus, encore quelques jours; **I'd like (some) ~ meat** je voudrais encore de la viande; **there's no ~ meat** il n'y a plus de viande; **is there (any) ~ wine?** y a-t-il encore du vin?, est-ce qu'il reste du vin?; **have some ~ ice cream** reprenez de la glace; **has she any ~ children?** a-t-elle d'autres enfants?; **no ~ shouting!** assez de cris!, arrêtez de crier!; **I've got no ~** ◊ **I haven't any ~** je n'en ai plus, il ne m'en reste plus; **I've no ~ time** je n'ai plus le temps; **he can't afford ~ than a small house** il ne peut se payer qu'une petite maison; **I shan't say any ~** ◊ **I shall say no ~** je n'en dirai pas davantage; (*threat*) tenez-le-vous pour dit; **have you heard any ~ about him?** avez-vous d'autres nouvelles de lui?; **I've got ~ like these** j'en ai d'autres comme ça; **you couldn't ask for ~** on ne peut guère en demander plus *or* davantage; **we must see ~ of her** il faut que nous la voyions (*subj*) davantage *or* plus souvent; **I want to know ~ about it** je veux en savoir plus long, je veux en savoir davantage; **there's ~ where that came from** ce n'est qu'un début; **the ~ the merrier** plus on est de fous plus on rit (*PROV*); **and what's ~ ...** et qui plus est ...; **his speech, of which ~ later, ...** son discours, sur lequel nous reviendrons, ...; **let's say no ~ about it** n'en parlons plus; **I shall have ~ to say about that** je reviendrai sur ce sujet (plus tard); **I've nothing ~ to say** je n'ai rien à ajouter; **nothing ~** rien de plus; **something ~** autre chose, quelque chose d'autre *or* de plus → **meet**[1]

[b] **~ than** plus que; (*before a number*) plus de; **I've got ~ money/books than you** j'ai plus d'argent/de livres que vous; **he's got ~ than**

you il en a plus que vous; **~ people than seats/than usual/than we expected** plus de gens que de places/que de coutume/que prévu; **it cost ~ than I expected** c'était plus cher que je ne pensais; **~ than half the audience** plus de la moitié de l'assistance or des auditeurs; **not ~ than a kilo** pas plus d'un kilo; **than 20 came** plus de 20 personnes sont venues; **no ~ than a dozen** une douzaine au plus; **~ than enough** plus que suffisant, amplement or bien suffisant

2 ADV a (forming compar of adjs and advs) plus; **~ difficult** plus difficile; **~ easily** plus facilement; **~ and ~ difficult** de plus en plus difficile; **even ~ difficult** encore plus difficile b [exercise, sleep etc] plus, davantage; **you must rest ~** vous devez vous reposer davantage; **he talks ~ than I do** il parle plus or davantage que moi; **she talks even ~ than he does** elle parle encore plus or davantage que lui; **he sleeps ~ and** il dort de plus en plus; **I like apples ~ than oranges** je préfère les pommes aux oranges c (in phrases) **~ amused than annoyed** plus amusé que fâché; **he was ~ frightened than hurt** il a eu plus de peur que de mal; **each ~ beautiful than the next** or **the other** tous plus beaux les uns que les autres; **it's ~ a short story than a novel** c'est une nouvelle plus qu'un roman; **he's no ~ a duke than I am** il n'est pas plus duc que moi; **he could no ~ pay me than fly in the air*** il ne pourrait pas plus me payer que devenir pape*; **no** or **nothing ~ than ...** rien (de plus) que ...; **not much ~ than ...** pas beaucoup plus que ...; **~ or less** plus ou moins; **no ~ and no less** ni plus ni moins; **neither ~ nor less (than ...)** ni plus ni moins (que ...); **it will ~ than cover the cost** cela couvrira largement or amplement les frais; **the house is ~ than half built** la maison est plus qu'à moitié bâtie; **I had ~ than kept my promise** j'avais fait plus que tenir ma promesse; **I can't bear him! — no ~**† **can I!** je ne peux pas le souffrir! — ni moi non plus!; **I shan't go there again! — no ~**† **you shall** je ne veux pas y retourner! — c'est entendu d **the ~: the ~ you rest the quicker you'll get better** plus vous vous reposerez plus vous vous rétablirez rapidement; **the ~ I think of it the ~ ashamed I feel** plus j'y pense plus j'ai honte; **he is all the ~ happy** il est d'autant plus heureux (**as** que); (**all**) **the ~ so as** or **because ...** d'autant plus que ...; **... only ~ so ...** mais encore plus e (= again etc) **I won't do it any ~** je ne le ferai plus; **don't do it any ~!** ne recommence pas!; **he doesn't live here any ~** il n'habite plus ici; **I can't stay any ~** je ne peux pas rester plus longtemps or davantage; (liter) **we shall see him no ~** nous ne le reverrons jamais plus or plus jamais; (liter) **he is no ~** il n'est plus; **once ~** une fois de plus, encore une fois; **only once ~** une dernière fois → **never**

moreish* ['mɔːrɪʃ] ADJ **these cakes are very ~** ces gâteaux ont un goût de revenez-y*

▼ **moreover** [mɔː'rəʊvəʳ] ADV (frm) de plus, en outre

mores ['mɔːreɪz] NPL mœurs fpl

morganatic [,mɔːgə'nætɪk] ADJ morganatique

morganatically [,mɔːgə'nætɪkəlɪ] ADV morganatiquement

morgue [mɔːg] N (= mortuary) morgue f; (*: of newspaper) archives fpl (d'un journal)

MORI ['mɔːrɪ] N ABBR (= Market and Opinion Research Institute) ~ **poll** sondage m d'opinion

moribund ['mɒrɪbʌnd] ADJ (frm: lit, fig) moribond

Mormon ['mɔːmən] 1 N mormon(e) m(f) 2 ADJ mormon

Mormonism ['mɔːmənɪzəm] N mormonisme m

morn [mɔːn] N (liter) (= morning) matin m; (= dawn) aube f

morning ['mɔːnɪŋ] 1 N (= point in time) matin m; (= duration) matinée f; **on the ~ of 23 January** le 23 janvier au matin, le matin du 23 janvier; **during (the course of) the ~** pendant la matinée; **I was busy all ~** j'ai été occupé toute la matinée; **good ~!** (= hello) bonjour!; († = goodbye) au revoir!; **he came in the ~** il est arrivé dans la matinée; **I'll do it in the ~** je le ferai le matin or dans la matinée; (= tomorrow) je le ferai demain matin; **it happened first thing in the ~** c'est arrivé tout au début de la matinée; **I'll do it first thing in the ~** je le ferai demain à la première heure; **at 7 (o'clock) in the ~** à 7 heures du matin; **in the early ~** au (petit) matin; **to get up very early in the ~** se lever de très bonne heure or très tôt le matin, se lever de bon or de grand matin; **I work in the ~(s)** je travaille le matin; **she's working ~s** or **she's on ~s* this week** elle travaille le matin, cette semaine; **a ~'s work** une matinée de travail; **she's got the ~ off (today)** elle a congé ce matin; **I have a ~ off every week** j'ai un matin or une matinée (de) libre par semaine; **what a beautiful ~!** quelle belle matinée!; **this ~** ce matin; **tomorrow ~** demain matin; **the ~ before** la veille au matin; **yesterday ~** hier matin; **the next** or **following ~** ◊ **the ~ after** le lendemain matin; **the ~ after (the night before)*** un lendemain de cuite*; **every Sunday ~** tous les dimanches matin; **one summer ~** (par) un matin d'été → **Monday**

2 ADJ [walk, swim] matinal, du matin; **a ~ train** un train le matin or dans la matinée; **the ~ train** le train du matin

3 COMP ► **morning-after pill** N (= contraceptive) pilule f du lendemain ► **morning coat** N jaquette f ► **morning coffee** N pause-café f (dans la matinée); **we have ~ coffee together** nous prenons un café ensemble le matin ► **morning dress** N jaquette f (et pantalon m rayé) ► **morning-glory** N (= flower) belle-de-jour f ► **morning paper** N journal m (du matin) ► **morning prayer(s)** N(PL) prière(s) f(pl) du matin ► **morning room**† N petit salon m (conçu pour recevoir le soleil le matin) ► **morning service** N office m du matin ► **morning sickness** N nausée f (du matin), nausées fpl matinales ► **morning star** N étoile f du matin ► **morning watch** N (Naut) premier quart m du jour

Moroccan [mə'rɒkən] 1 ADJ (gen) marocain; [ambassador, embassy] du Maroc 2 N Marocain(e) m(f)

Morocco [mə'rɒkəʊ] N a le Maroc b **morocco (leather)** maroquin m; **morocco-bound** relié en maroquin

moron ['mɔːrɒn] N (* = idiot) crétin(e) m(f); (Med) débile m léger, débile f légère

moronic [mə'rɒnɪk] ADJ crétin

morose [mə'rəʊs] ADJ morose

morosely [mə'rəʊslɪ] ADV [look at] d'un air morose; [say] d'un ton morose

morph [mɔːf] N (Ling) morphe m

morpheme ['mɔːfiːm] N (Ling) morphème m

morphemics [mɔː'fiːmɪks] N (NonC: Ling) morphématique f

Morpheus ['mɔːfɪəs] N Morphée m → **arm¹**

morphia ['mɔːfɪə] N = **morphine**

morphine ['mɔːfiːn] 1 N morphine f 2 COMP ► **morphine addict** N morphinomane mf ► **morphine addiction** N morphinomanie f

morphing ['mɔːfɪŋ] N (Cine, Comput) morphing m

morphological [,mɔːfə'lɒdʒɪkəl] ADJ morphologique

morphologically [,mɔːfə'lɒdʒɪkəlɪ] ADV morphologiquement

morphologist [mɔː'fɒlədʒɪst] N morphologue mf

morphology [mɔː'fɒlədʒɪ] N morphologie f

morphophonemics [,mɔːfəʊfəʊ'niːmɪks] N (NonC) morphophonémique f

morphophonology [,mɔːfəʊfəʊ'nɒlədʒɪ] N morphophonologie f

morphosyntax [,mɔːfəʊ'sɪntæks] N morphosyntaxe f

morris dance ['mɒrɪsdɑːns] N (Brit) danse folklorique anglaise

morris dancers ['mɒrɪsdɑːnsəz] NPL danseurs de « morris dance » → **morris dance**

morris dancing ['mɒrɪsdɑːnsɪŋ] N danse folklorique anglaise

morris men ['mɒrɪsmen] NPL = **morris dancers**

morrow ['mɒrəʊ] N († or liter) (= morning) matin m; (= next day) lendemain m

Morse [mɔːs] 1 N morse m 2 COMP ► **Morse alphabet** N alphabet m morse ► **Morse Code** N morse m ► **Morse signals** NPL signaux mpl en morse

morsel ['mɔːsl] N (gen) (petit) bout m; **she ate only a ~ of fish** elle n'a mangé qu'une bouchée de poisson; **choice ~** morceau m de choix

mortadella [,mɔːtə'delə] N mortadelle f

mortal ['mɔːtl] 1 ADJ [life, hatred, enemy, fear] mortel; [injury] mortel, fatal; **~ combat** combat m à mort; **~ remains** dépouille f mortelle; **~ sin** péché m mortel; **it's no good to him*** cela ne lui sert strictement à rien 2 N mortel(le) m(f)

mortality [mɔː'tælɪtɪ] N mortalité f; **infant ~** (taux m de) mortalité f infantile

mortally ['mɔːtəlɪ] ADV [wounded, offended] mortellement; [embarrassed] horriblement; **~ ill** condamné; **~ afraid** mort de peur

mortar ['mɔːtəʳ] N (Constr, Mil, Pharm) mortier m

mortarboard ['mɔːtəbɔːd] N toque portée par les enseignants et les étudiants pendant la cérémonie de remise de diplômes universitaires

mortgage ['mɔːgɪdʒ] 1 N (in house buying etc) emprunt m logement; (= second loan etc) hypothèque f; **to take out** or **raise a ~** obtenir un emprunt logement (**on, for** pour), prendre une hypothèque; **to pay off** or **clear a ~** rembourser un emprunt logement, purger une hypothèque; **to carry a ~** être grevé d'une hypothèque 2 VT [+ house, one's future] hypothéquer 3 COMP ► **mortgage broker** N courtier m en prêts hypothécaires ► **mortgage payment** N remboursement m d'un emprunt-logement ► **mortgage rate** N taux m d'emprunt hypothécaire ► **mortgage relief** N (Brit) exonération fiscale sur les emprunts logement

mortgageable ['mɔːgədʒɪbl] ADJ hypothécable

mortgagee [,mɔːgə'dʒiː] N créancier m, -ière f hypothécaire

mortgagor [,mɔːgə'dʒɔːʳ] N débiteur m, -trice f hypothécaire

mortice ['mɔːtɪs] N = **mortise**

mortician [mɔː'tɪʃən] N (US) entrepreneur m de pompes funèbres

mortification [,mɔːtɪfɪ'keɪʃən] N (gen) grande honte f; (Rel) mortification f

mortified ['mɔːtɪfaɪd] ADJ **I was ~ to learn that ...** j'ai été morte de honte en apprenant que ...

mortify ['mɔːtɪfaɪ] VT (gen) faire honte à, rendre honteux; (Rel) mortifier; **to ~ the flesh** se mortifier, mortifier sa chair

mortifying ['mɔːtɪfaɪɪŋ] ADJ très gênant (**to sb** pour qn)

mortise ['mɔːtɪs] 1 N mortaise f 2 VT mortaiser 3 COMP ► **mortise and tenon joint** N assemblage m à tenon et mortaise ► **mortise lock** N serrure f encastrée

---

► LANGUAGE IN USE: **moreover** 26.2, 26.3

mortuary ['mɔːtjʊərɪ] ① N morgue f, dépôt m mortuaire ② ADJ mortuaire

Mosaic [məʊˈzeɪɪk] ADJ (*Bible Hist*) mosaïque, de Moïse

mosaic [məʊˈzeɪɪk] ① N mosaïque f ② COMP en mosaïque

Moscow ['mɒskəʊ] N Moscou; **the ~ team** l'équipe f moscovite

Moselle [məʊˈzel] N ⓐ (*Geog*) Moselle f ⓑ (= *wine*) (vin m de) Moselle m

Moses ['məʊzɪz] ① N Moïse m; **Holy ~!*** mince alors!* ② COMP ► **Moses basket** N moïse m

mosey ['məʊzɪ] (*US*) ① VI **to ~ along** (se) baguenauder*, aller *or* marcher sans (trop) se presser; **they ~ed over to Joe's** ils sont allés faire un tour chez Joe; **I'll just ~ on down** je vais y aller doucement ② **to have a ~ round somewhere** faire une balade* *or* un tour quelque part

Moslem ['mɒzləm] = **Muslim**

mosque [mɒsk] N mosquée f

mosquito [mɒsˈkiːtəʊ] ① N (*pl* **mosquito(e)s**) moustique m ② COMP ► **mosquito bite** N piqûre f de moustique ► **mosquito net** N moustiquaire f ► **mosquito netting** N mousseline f *or* gaze f pour moustiquaire

moss [mɒs] ① N mousse f (*Bot*) → **rolling** ② COMP ► **moss green** ADJ vert mousse *inv* ♦ N vert m mousse *inv* ► **moss rose** N rose f mousseuse ► **moss stitch** N (*Knitting*) point m de riz

Mossad ['mɒsæd] N Mossad m

mossback* ['mɒsbæk] N (*US fig*) conservateur m à tout crin

mossy ['mɒsɪ] ADJ [*wall, stone*] moussu; **~ green** (*adj*) vert mousse *inv* ♦ (*n*) vert m mousse

▼**most** [məʊst] *superl of* **many, much** ① ADJ, PRON ⓐ (= *greatest in amount etc*) le plus (de), la plus grande quantité (de), le plus grand nombre (de); **he earns (the) ~ money** c'est lui qui gagne le plus d'argent; **I've got (the) ~ records** c'est moi qui ai le plus (grand nombre) de disques; **(the) ~ le plus, le maximum; who has got (the) ~?** qui en a le plus?; **do the ~ you can** fais-en le plus que tu pourras; **at (the) ~** ◊ **at the very ~** au maximum, (tout) au plus; **to make the ~ of** [+ *one's time*] ne pas perdre, bien employer; [+ *respite, opportunity, sunshine, sb's absence*] profiter (au maximum) de; [+ *one's talents, business offer, money*] tirer le meilleur parti de; [+ *one's resources, remaining food*] utiliser au mieux, faire durer; **make the ~ of it!** profitez-en bien!, tâchez de bien en profiter!; **he certainly made the ~ of the story** il a vraiment exploité cette histoire à fond; **to make the ~ of o.s.** se faire valoir, se mettre en valeur; **they're the ~!*** ils sont champions!*

ⓑ (= *largest part*) la plus grande partie (de), la majeure *or* la meilleure partie (de); (= *greatest number*) la majorité (de), la plupart (de); **~ (of the) people/books** etc la plupart *or* la majorité des gens/des livres etc; **~ honey is expensive** le miel en général coûte cher, la plupart des marques de miel coûtent cher; **~ of the butter** presque tout le beurre; **~ of the money** la plus grande *or* la majeure partie de l'argent, presque tout l'argent; **~ of it** presque tout; **~ of them** la plupart d'entre eux; **~ of the day** la plus grande *or* la majeure partie de la journée; **~ of the time** la plupart du temps; **for the ~ part** pour la plupart, en général; **in ~ cases** dans la plupart *or* la majorité des cas

② ADV ⓐ (*forming superl of adjs and advs*) le plus; **the ~ intelligent boy** le garçon le plus intelligent; **the ~ beautiful woman of all** la plus belle femme *or* la femme la plus belle de toutes; **~ easily** le plus facilement

ⓑ [*work, sleep etc*] le plus; **he talked ~** c'est lui qui a le plus parlé *or* parlé le plus; **what he** →

wants ~ (of all) ce qu'il désire le plus *or* par-dessus tout *or* avant tout; **the book he wanted ~ (of all)** le livre qu'il voulait le plus *or* entre tous; **that's what annoyed me ~ (of all)** c'est ce qui m'a contrarié le plus *or* par-dessus tout

ⓒ (= *very*) bien, très, fort; **~ likely** très probablement; **a ~ delightful day** une journée on ne peut plus agréable *or* des plus agréables *or* bien agréable; **you are ~ kind** vous êtes (vraiment) très aimable; **it's a ~ useful gadget** c'est un gadget des plus utiles *or* tout ce qu'il y a de plus utile; **the Most High** le Très-Haut; **Most Reverend** révérendissime

ⓓ (*US* * = *almost*) presque

...most [məʊst] SUF le plus; **northernmost** le plus au nord → **foremost, innermost**

mostly ['məʊstlɪ] ADV ⓐ (= *chiefly*) principalement, surtout; **he now works ~ in Hollywood** à présent, il travaille principalement *or* surtout à Hollywood; **the human body is ~ water** le corps humain est presque entièrement composé d'eau; **it is ~ a book about nature** c'est avant tout un livre sur la nature ⓑ (= *almost all*) pour la plupart; **the men were ~ fairly young** les hommes étaient, pour la plupart, assez jeunes; **more than one hundred people, ~ women** plus de cent personnes, pour la plupart des femmes ⓒ (= *usually*) en général; **he ~ comes on Mondays** il vient en général le lundi

MOT [ˌeməʊˈtiː] (*Brit*) ① N ⓐ ABBR = **Ministry of Transport** ⓑ (*Aut: also* **~ test**) ≈ contrôle m technique; **the car has passed/failed its ~ (test)** la voiture a obtenu/n'a pas obtenu le certificat de contrôle technique; **the ~ (certificate) runs out in April** le certificat de contrôle technique expire en avril ② VT **to get one's car ~'d** faire passer sa voiture au contrôle technique; **car for sale, ~'d till June** voiture à vendre, certificat de contrôle technique valable jusqu'en juin

mote [məʊt] N atome m; [*of dust*] grain m; (*Bible*) **the ~ in thy brother's eye** la paille dans l'œil de ton frère

motel [məʊˈtel] N motel m

motet [məʊˈtet] N motet m

moth [mɒθ] ① N papillon m de nuit, phalène m *or* f; (*also* **clothes-~**) mite f; **to be attracted like a ~ to a flame** être irrésistiblement attiré ② COMP ► **moth-eaten** ADJ mangé par les mites, mité; (* *fig*) mangé aux mites*; **to become ~-eaten** se miter ► **moth-hole** N trou m de mite

mothball ['mɒθbɔːl] ① N boule f de naphtaline; (*fig*) **in ~s*** [*object*] au placard (*hum*); [*ship*] en réserve; (*fig*) **to put sth in ~s** [+ *project*] mettre *or* remiser qch au placard ② VT [+ *ship*] mettre en réserve; [+ *factory*] fermer provisoirement; (*fig*) [+ *project*] mettre *or* remiser au placard

mother ['mʌðər] ① N ⓐ (*lit, fig*) mère f; (*as form of address*) **yes, Mother** oui, mère; **she was (like) a ~ to me** elle était une vraie mère pour moi; **a ~ of three** une mère de trois enfants; (*Rel*) **the Reverend Mother** la Révérende Mère; **she's her ~'s daughter** c'est (bien) la fille de sa mère; **every ~'s son of them*** tous sans exception; (*Brit hum*) **shall I be ~?** (= *shall I serve*) je fais le service *or* la mère de famille? → **foster, housemother, necessity, single**

ⓑ * **the ~ of all battles** une bataille homérique *or* sans précédent; **the ~ of all controversies/confrontations** une controverse/une confrontation homérique *or* sans précédent; **the ~ of all traffic jams** un énorme bouchon

ⓒ († *or liter*) **old Mother Jones** la mère Jones → **3**

ⓓ (*US**) = **motherfucker**

② VT (= *act as mother to*) s'occuper de; (= *indulge, protect*) dorloter, chouchouter; (*Psych*) materner; (†† = *give birth to*) donner

naissance à; **she always ~s her lodgers** c'est une vraie mère pour ses locataires; **why do men so often want their girlfriends to ~ them?** pourquoi les hommes veulent-ils si souvent être maternés par leur petite amie?

③ COMP ► **Mother Church** N **our Mother Church** notre sainte mère l'Église ► **mother country** N mère patrie f ► **mother craft** N (*Space*) vaisseau m amiral ► **Mother Earth** N notre mère f la terre, la Terre mère ► **Mother Goose** N ma Mère l'Oye ► **mother hen** N mère f poule ► **mother-in-law** N (*pl* **mothers-in-law**) belle-mère f ► **mother love** N amour m maternel ► **mother-naked** ADJ nu comme un ver ► **Mother Nature** N Dame Nature f ► **Mother of God** N Marie, mère f de Dieu ► **mother-of-pearl** N nacre f (*de perle*) ► **mother-of-thousands** N (*Bot*) chlorophytum m ► **Mother's Day** N la fête des Mères ► **mother's help, mother's helper** (*US*) N aide f maternelle ► **mother ship** N (*Naut*) ravitailleur m ► **Mother Superior** N (*pl* **Mother Superiors** *or* **Mothers Superior**) (*Rel*) Mère f supérieure ► **mother-to-be** N (*pl* **mothers-to-be**) future maman f ► **mother tongue** N langue f maternelle ► **mother wit** N bon sens m inné

motherboard ['mʌðəbɔːd] N (*Comput*) carte f mère

mothercraft ['mʌðəkrɑːft] N puériculture f

motherfucker‡ ['mʌðəfʌkəʳ] N (*esp US*) (= *person*) enfoiré(e)‡ m(f), enculé(e)‡ m(f); (= *thing*) saloperie‡ f

motherfucking‡ ['mʌðəfʌkɪŋ] ADJ (*esp US*) **that ~ car!** cette putain de bagnole!‡; **get your ~ ass in gear!** magne-toi le cul!*‡; **you ~ son-of-a-bitch!** espèce de fils de pute!‡

motherhood ['mʌðəhʊd] N maternité f

mothering ['mʌðərɪŋ] ① N soins mpl maternels; (*fig*) maternage m; **he needs ~** il a besoin d'être materné ② COMP ► **Mothering Sunday** N (*Brit*) la fête des Mères

motherland ['mʌðəlænd] N patrie f

motherless ['mʌðəlɪs] ADJ sans mère

motherly ['mʌðəlɪ] ADJ maternel

mothproof ['mɒθpruːf] ① ADJ traité à l'antimite ② VT traiter à l'antimite

motif [məʊˈtiːf] N (*Art, Mus*) motif m

motion ['məʊʃən] ① N ⓐ (*NonC*) mouvement m, marche f; (*Mus*) mouvement m; **perpetual ~** mouvement m perpétuel; **to be in ~** [*vehicle*] être en marche; [*machine*] être en mouvement *or* en marche; **to set in ~** [+ *machine*] mettre en mouvement *or* en marche; [+ *vehicle*] mettre en marche; (*fig*) [+ *process etc*] mettre en branle; (*fig: of process etc*) **to put** *or* **set the wheels in ~** lancer le processus, mettre les choses en branle; **the ~ of the car made him ill** le mouvement de la voiture l'a rendu malade

ⓑ (= *gesture etc*) mouvement m, geste m; **he made a ~ to close the door** il a esquissé le geste d'aller fermer la porte; (*fig*) **to go through the ~s of doing sth** (*mechanically*) faire qch machinalement *or* en ayant l'esprit ailleurs; (*insincerely*) faire mine *or* semblant de faire qch

ⓒ (*at meeting etc*) motion f; (*Parl*) proposition f; **~ carried/rejected** motion f adoptée/rejetée; (*Admin, Jur*) **meeting convened of its own ~** réunion f convoquée d'office

ⓓ (*Brit: also* **bowel ~**) selles fpl; **to have** *or* **pass a ~** aller à la selle

ⓔ [*of watch*] mouvement m

② VTI **to ~ (to) sb to do** faire signe à qn de faire; **he ~ed me in/out/up to a chair** il m'a fait signe d'entrer/de sortir/de m'asseoir

③ COMP ► **motion picture** N (*esp US Cine*) film m (*de cinéma*); **~-picture camera** caméra f; **the ~-picture industry** l'industrie f cinématographique, le cinéma ► **motion sickness**

N mal *m* des transports ► **motion study** N (*Ind etc*) étude *f* des cadences

motionless ['məʊʃənlɪs] ADJ [*person, body*] immobile; **to remain ~** rester immobile; **to stand/sit/lie ~** rester debout/assis/étendu sans bouger

motivate ['məʊtɪveɪt] VT [+ *act, decision*] motiver; [+ *person*] pousser, inciter (**to do** à faire)

motivated ['məʊtɪveɪtɪd] ADJ motivé (**to do sth** pour faire qch); **to keep sb ~** faire en sorte que qn reste (*subj*) motivé; **highly ~** extrêmement motivé; **he's not very politically ~** il ne s'intéresse pas beaucoup à la politique; **the violence was racially ~** c'est le racisme qui a motivé les violences

motivation [,məʊtɪ'veɪʃən] 1 N motivation *f*; **he lacks ~** il n'est pas assez motivé, il manque de motivation (**to do** pour faire) 2 COMP ► **motivation research** N études *fpl* de motivation

motivational research [,məʊtɪ'veɪʃənəl rɪ'sɜːtʃ] N = **motivation research**; → **motivation**

motive ['məʊtɪv] 1 N a (= *reason*) intention *f*, raison *f*; (= *motivation*) [*of person*] motivations *fpl*; (*for action*) motifs *mpl*; (*Jur*) mobile *m*; **I did it from the best ~s** je l'ai fait avec les meilleures intentions *or* avec les motifs les plus louables; **his ~ for saying that** la raison pour laquelle il a dit cela; **what were his ~s?** quelles étaient ses motivations?; **what was the ~ for his behaviour?** quels étaient les motifs de sa conduite?; **he had no ~ for killing her** il l'a tuée sans raison(s) *or* sans mobile; **what was the ~ for the murder?** quel était le mobile du meurtre?; **the only suspect with a ~** le seul suspect à avoir un mobile → **profit**; **ulterior** b = **motif** 2 ADJ moteur (-trice *f*); **~ power** force *f* motrice

motiveless ['məʊtɪvlɪs] ADJ [*act, crime*] immotivé, gratuit

motley ['mɒtlɪ] 1 ADJ a (*pej* = ill-assorted) [*collection, assortment*] disparate; **what a ~ crew!** en voilà une belle équipe!* b (= multi-coloured: *also* **~ coloured**) bariolé 2 N (= garment) habit *m* bigarré (*du bouffon*)

motocross ['məʊtəkrɒs] N moto-cross *m*

motor ['məʊtə'] 1 N a (= engine) moteur *m* b (*Brit*) voiture *f*, bagnole* *f* 2 ADJ [*muscle, nerve*] moteur (-trice *f*) → **5** 3 VI† aller en auto; **to go ~ing** faire de l'auto; **to ~ away/back** *etc* partir/revenir *etc* en auto; (*in boat*) **we ~ed downriver** nous avons descendu la rivière en bateau à moteur 4 VT (*Brit*) conduire en auto; **to ~ sb away/back** *etc* emmener/ramener *etc* qn en auto 5 COMP [*accident*] de voiture ► **motor-assisted** ADJ à moteur ► **motor bus**† N autobus *m* ► **motor coach** N (*Brit*) car *m* ► **motor drive** N (*Tech*) entraînement *m* par moteur ► **motor-driven** ADJ à entraînement par moteur ► **motor home** N (*US*) camping-car *m* ► **motor industry** N industrie *f* automobile ► **motor inn** N (*US*) = **motor lodge** ► **motor insurance** N assurance-automobile *f* ► **motor launch** N (*Naut*) vedette *f* ► **motor lodge** N (*US*) motel *m* ► **motor lorry** N (*Brit*) = **motor truck** ► **motor mechanic** N mécanicien *m* garagiste ► **motor mower** N tondeuse *f* (à gazon) à moteur ► **motor neuron disease** N (*Med*) sclérose *f* latérale amyotrophique ► **motor oil** N huile *f* (de graissage) ► **motor racing** N (*NonC*) course *f* automobile ► **motor road**† N route *f* carrossable ► **motor scooter** N scooter *m* ► **motor ship** N = **motor vessel** ► **motor show** N exposition *f* de voitures; (*Brit*) **the Motor Show** le Salon de l'automobile ► **motor torpedo boat** N vedette *f* lance-torpilles ► **the motor trade** N (le secteur de) l'automobile *f* ► **motor truck** N camion *m* ► **motor vehicle** N véhicule *m* automobile ► **motor vessel** N

(*Naut*) navire *m* à moteur (diesel), motorship *m*

motorail ['məʊtəreɪl] N train *m* auto-couchettes

motorbike ['məʊtəbaɪk] N moto *f*; **~ gang** bande *f* de motards*

motorboat ['məʊtəbəʊt] N canot *m* automobile, bateau *m* à moteur

motorcade ['məʊtəkeɪd] N cortège *m* de voitures

motorcar ['məʊtəkɑː'] N (*Brit*) automobile *f*, voiture *f*

motorcycle ['məʊtəsaɪkl] 1 N moto(cyclette) *f* 2 COMP ► **motorcycle club** N club *m* de moto ► **motorcycle combination** N (motocyclette *f* à) side-car *m* ► **motorcycle engine** N moteur *m* de moto

motorcycling ['məʊtəsaɪklɪŋ] N motocyclisme *m*

motorcyclist ['məʊtəsaɪklɪst] N motocycliste *mf*

-motored ['məʊtəd] ADJ (*in compounds*) **four-motored** quadrimoteur (-trice *f*)

motoring ['məʊtərɪŋ] 1 N les promenades *fpl* en automobile 2 COMP [*accident*] de voiture, d'auto; [*holiday*] en voiture, en auto ► **motoring correspondent** N (*Brit Press*) chroniqueur *m* automobile ► **motoring magazine** N (*Press*) revue *f* automobile ► **motoring public** N automobilistes *mpl* ► **motoring school** N auto-école *f*

motorist ['məʊtərɪst] N automobiliste *mf*

motorization [,məʊtəraɪ'zeɪʃən] N motorisation *f*

motorize ['məʊtəraɪz] VT (*esp Mil*) motoriser; **~d bicycle** *or* **bike*** cyclomoteur *m*

motorman ['məʊtəmæn] N (*pl* **-men**) (*US*) conducteur *m*; [*of train*] conducteur *m*, mécanicien *m*

motormouth: ['məʊtəmaʊθ] N moulin *m* à paroles*

motorway ['məʊtəweɪ] (*Brit*) 1 N autoroute *f* → ROADS 2 COMP [*bridge, exit, junction*] d'autoroute

Motown ['məʊtaʊn] N (*US*) a Detroit b (*Mus*) Motown *m*

mottle ['mɒtl] VT marbrer (**with** de)

mottled ['mɒtld] ADJ [*leaf, skin, colour, porcelain*] marbré (**with** de qch); [*horse*] moucheté; [*sky*] pommelé; [*material*] chiné; **~ complexion** teint *m* brouillé; **~ blue and white** marbré de bleu et de blanc

motto ['mɒtəʊ] N (*pl* **mottoes** *or* **mottos**) a [*of family, school etc*] devise *f* b (*in cracker*) (= riddle) devinette *f*; (= joke) blague *f* c (*Mus*) **~ theme** leitmotiv *m*

mould¹, mold¹ (*US*) [məʊld] 1 N (*Art, Culin, Metal, Tech etc*) (= container, core, frame) moule *m*; (= model for design) modèle *m*, gabarit *m*; (*Culin*) **rice ~** gâteau *m* de riz; **to cast metal in a ~** couler *or* jeter du métal dans un moule; **to cast a figure in a ~** jeter une figure en moule, mouler une figure; (*fig*) **to break the ~** (= reorganize) rompre avec la tradition; **they broke the ~ when they made him** il n'y a pas deux comme lui; **cast in a heroic ~** de la trempe des héros; **cast in the same ~** fait sur *or* coulé dans le même moule; **men of his ~** des hommes de sa trempe *or* de son calibre* 2 VT (= cast) [+ *metals*] fondre, mouler; [+ *plaster, clay*] mouler; (= fashion) [+ *figure etc*] modeler (**in, out of** en); (*fig*) [+ *sb's character, public opinion etc*] former, façonner

mould², mold² (*US*) [məʊld] 1 N (= fungus) moisissure *f* 2 VI moisir

mould³, mold³ (*US*) [məʊld] N (= soil) humus *m*, terreau *m* → **leaf**

moulder, molder (*US*) ['məʊldə'] VI (*gen*) moisir; (*also* **~ away**) [*building*] tomber en poussière, se désagréger; (* *fig*) [*person, object*] moisir

moulding, molding (*US*) ['məʊldɪŋ] 1 N a (*Archit*) moulure *f* b (*Aut*) baguette *f* c (*Metal* = object) objet *m* moulé, moulage *m*; (= process: gen) moulage *m*; [*of metal*] coulée *f*; [*of statue*] coulage *m* d (*NonC* = influencing) [*of character, public opinion*] formation *f* 2 COMP ► **moulding machine** N machine *f* à moulures ► **moulding process** N procédé *m* de moulage ► **moulding technique** N technique *f* de moulage

mouldy, moldy (*US*) ['məʊldɪ] ADJ a (= with mould) [*food, mattress, wallpaper, clothes*] moisi; **to go ~** moisir; **to smell ~** sentir le moisi; **to taste ~** avoir goût de moisi b (*Brit** = paltry) minable; **all he gave me was a ~ £5** il m'a juste refilé un malheureux billet de 5 livres

moult, molt (*US*) [məʊlt] 1 N mue *f* 2 VI [*bird*] muer; [*dog, cat*] perdre ses poils 3 VT [+ *feathers, hair*] perdre

mound [maʊnd] N a [*of earth*] (*natural*) monticule *m*; (*artificial*) levée *f* de terre, remblai *m*; (*Archeol: also* **burial ~**) tumulus *m* b (= pile) tas *m*, monceau *m*

mount [maʊnt] 1 N a (*liter*) mont *m*, montagne *f*; **Mount Carmel** le mont Carmel; **the Mount of Olives** le mont des Oliviers → **sermon** b (= horse) monture *f* c (= support) [*of machine*] support *m*; [*of jewel, lens, specimen*] monture *f*; [*of microscope slide*] lame *f*; [*of transparency*] cadre *m*; [*of painting, photo*] carton *m* de montage; [*of stamp in album*] charnière *f* 2 VT a (= climb on *or* up) [+ *hill, stairs*] monter; (with effort) gravir; [+ *horse, ladder*] monter à *or* sur; [+ *cycle*] monter sur, enfourcher; [+ *platform, throne*] monter sur; **the car ~ed the pavement** la voiture est montée sur le trottoir b [*male animal*] monter c [+ *machine, specimen, jewel*] monter (**on, in** sur); [+ *map*] monter, enrouler; [+ *picture, photo*] monter *or* coller sur un carton; [+ *exhibit*] fixer sur un support; [+ *gun*] mettre en position; **to ~ stamps in an album** coller *or* mettre des timbres dans un album; (*Phot*) **~ing press** colleuse *f* d (= stage, orchestrate) [+ *play, demonstration, plot, campaign, rescue operation etc*] monter; (*Mil*) **to ~ guard** monter la garde (**on** sur, **over** auprès de); **to ~ an offensive** monter une attaque; **she ~ed a challenge to the Prime Minister's leadership** elle s'est posée en successeur du Premier ministre, en contestant son autorité; **she ~ed a title challenge to the reigning World Champion** elle a essayé de ravir son titre au champion du monde; **they ~ed a legal challenge to the directive** ils ont essayé de contester cette directive devant les tribunaux e (= provide with horse) → **mounted** 3 VI a [*prices, temperature*] monter, augmenter; [*pressure, tension*] monter; [*concern*] grandir, monter; [*debts, losses*] augmenter; **the death toll has ~ed to 8,000** le nombre de morts se monte maintenant à 8 000; **opposition to the treaty is ~ing** l'opposition au traité grandit *or* prend de l'ampleur; **pressure is ~ing on him to resign** la pression s'accentue sur lui pour qu'il démissionne; **evidence is ~ing that ...** il y a de plus en plus de raisons de penser que ...; **speculation was ~ing that she was about to resign** on se perdait en conjectures sur sa démission éventuelle b (= get on horse) se mettre en selle

► **mount up** VI (= increase) monter, s'élever; (= accumulate) s'accumuler; **it all ~s up** tout cela finit par chiffrer

mountain ['maʊntɪn] 1 N montagne *f*; **to go to/live in the ~s** aller à/habiter la montagne; **to make a ~ out of a molehill** (se) faire une montagne d'une taupinière; (*Econ*) **beef/**

butter ~ montagne f de bœuf/de beurre; **faith can move ~s** la foi soulève des montagnes; (*esp Brit fig*) **we have a ~ to climb** nous allons devoir soulever des montagnes; **if Mohammed won't go to the ~, the ~ must come to Mohammed** si la montagne ne vient pas à Mahomet, Mahomet ira à la montagne; (*fig*) **a ~ of** une montagne de; **a ~ of dirty washing** un monceau de linge sale; **a ~ of work** un travail fou *or* monstre

[2] COMP [*tribe, people*] montagnard; [*animal, plant*] de(s) montagne(s); [*air*] de la montagne; [*path, scenery, shoes, chalet*] de montagne ► **mountain ash** N sorbier *m* (des oiseleurs) ► **mountain bike** N VTT *m*, vélo *m* tout terrain ► **mountain cat** N puma *m*, couguar *m* ► **mountain chain** N chaîne f de montagnes ► **mountain climber** N grimpeur *m*, alpiniste *mf* ► **Mountain Daylight Time** N (*US*) heure f d'été des montagnes Rocheuses ► **mountain dew*** N whisky *m* (*gén illicitement distillé*) ► **mountain goat** N chèvre f de montagne ► **mountain guide** N (*Climbing*) guide *m* de montagne ► **mountain lion** N (*US*) = **mountain cat** ► **mountain pass** N col *m* ► **mountain range** N chaîne f de montagnes ► **mountain sickness** N mal *m* des montagnes ► **Mountain Standard Time** N (*US*) heure f d'hiver des montagnes Rocheuses ► **the Mountain State** N (*US*) la Virginie occidentale ► **Mountain Time** N (*US*) heure f des montagnes Rocheuses ► **mountain top** N sommet *m* de la (*or* d'une) montagne, cime f

mountaineer [ˌmaʊntɪˈnɪəʳ] [1] N alpiniste *mf* [2] VI faire de l'alpinisme

mountaineering [ˌmaʊntɪˈnɪərɪŋ] N alpinisme *m*

mountainous [ˈmaʊntɪnəs] ADJ [a] (= *hilly*) montagneux [b] (= *immense*) colossal [c] [*seas*] démonté; [*waves*] énorme

mountainside [ˈmaʊntɪnsaɪd] N flanc *m* or versant *m* d'une (*or* de la) montagne

mountebank [ˈmaʊntɪbæŋk] N charlatan *m*

mounted [ˈmaʊntɪd] [1] ADJ [*soldiers, troops*] à cheval [2] COMP ► **mounted police** N police f montée ► **mounted policeman** N (*pl* **mounted policemen**) policier *m* à cheval

Mountie* [ˈmaʊntɪ] N (*Can*) membre *m* de la police montée; **the ~s** la police montée

mounting [ˈmaʊntɪŋ] N = **mount 2c**

mourn [mɔːn] [1] VI pleurer; **to ~ for sb** pleurer qn; **to ~ for sth** pleurer la perte de qch [2] VT [+ *person*] pleurer; [*sth gone*] pleurer la perte de; (*sth dead*) déplorer (*the loss of*); **he was still ~ing the loss of his son** il pleurait encore son fils; **he is still ~ing the break-up of his relationship** il ne s'est pas encore remis de leur rupture

mourner [ˈmɔːnəʳ] N parent(e) *m(f)* or ami(e) *m(f)* du défunt; **the ~s** le convoi *or* le cortège funèbre; **to be the chief ~** mener le deuil

mournful [ˈmɔːnfʊl] ADJ [*person, face, voice, sound, music*] mélancolique; [*howl*] lugubre; [*occasion*] triste

mournfully [ˈmɔːnfəlɪ] ADV mélancoliquement

mournfulness [ˈmɔːnfʊlnɪs] N [*of person*] tristesse f, mélancolie f

mourning [ˈmɔːnɪŋ] [1] N deuil *m*; (= *clothes*) vêtements *mpl* de deuil; **in deep ~** en grand deuil; **to be in ~ (for sb)** porter le deuil (de qn); **to go into/come out of ~** prendre/quitter le deuil [2] COMP ► **mourning band** N crêpe *m* ► **mourning clothes** NPL habits *mpl* de deuil

mouse [maʊs] [1] N (*pl* **mice**) souris f; (*fig*) timide *mf*, souris f → **fieldmouse** [b] (*Comput*) souris f [2] ADJ [*hair*] châtain terne *inv*; **~ brown** brun terne *inv* [3] VI chasser les souris [4] COMP ► **mouse mat, mouse pad** N (*Comput*) tapis *m* (pour souris)

mousehole [ˈmaʊshəʊl] N trou *m* de souris

mouser [ˈmaʊsəʳ] N souricier *m*

mousetrap [ˈmaʊstræp] N souricière f; (*pej*) ~ **(cheese)*** fromage *m* ordinaire

mousy [ˈmaʊsɪ] ADJ = **mousy**

moussaka [mʊˈsɑːkə] N moussaka f

mousse [muːs] N (*Culin*) mousse f; **chocolate ~** mousse f au chocolat; (*for hair*) **(styling) ~** mousse f coiffante or de coiffage

moustache [məsˈtɑːʃ], **mustache** (*US*) [ˈmʌstæʃ] N moustache(s) f(pl); **man with a ~** homme *m* moustachu *or* à moustache

moustachio [məsˈtɑːʃɪəʊ] N moustache f à la gauloise

moustachioed [məsˈtɑːʃɪəʊd] ADJ moustachu

mousy [ˈmaʊsɪ] ADJ (*pej*) (= *nondescript*) [*person*] effacé; (= *brownish*) [*hair*] châtain terne *inv*; ~ **brown** brun terne *inv*

mouth [maʊθ] [1] N (*pl* **mouths** [maʊðz]) [a] [*of person, horse, sheep, cow*] bouche f; [*of dog, cat, lion, tiger, bear, snake, whale*] gueule f; (*Pharm*) **to be taken by ~** à prendre par voie orale; **with one's ~ wide open** la bouche grand ouverte; (*lit, fig*) **it makes my ~ water** cela me met l'eau à la bouche; **she didn't dare open her ~** elle n'a pas osé ouvrir la bouche; **he never opened his ~ all evening** il n'a pas ouvert la bouche *or* il n'a pas desserré les dents de la soirée; **he kept his ~ shut (about it)** il n'a pas soufflé mot; **keep your ~ shut about this!** n'en parle à personne!, garde-le pour toi!; **shut your ~!*** ferme-la!*, boucle-la!*; (*fig*) **to shut sb's ~ (for him)*** (= *silence*) clouer le bec à qn*; (= *kill*) supprimer qn; **he's a big ~*** c'est un fort en gueule*, c'est une grande gueule*; **(you've got a) big ~!** tu ne pouvais pas te la fermer!*; **me and my big ~!*** j'ai encore perdu une occasion de me taire!; (*US*) **to speak** *or* **talk out of both sides of one's ~** retourner sa veste sans arrêt; (*Brit*) **he's all ~*** c'est un fort en gueule*; **watch your ~!*** sois poli!, surveille ton langage! → **down**[1], **feed, heart, word**

[b] [*of river*] embouchure f; [*of bag*] ouverture f; [*of hole, cave, harbour*] entrée f; [*of bottle*] goulot *m*; [*of cannon, gun*] bouche f, gueule f; [*of well*] trou *m*; [*of volcano*] bouche f; [*of letterbox*] ouverture f, fente f

[2] [maʊð] VT [a] (*soundlessly: gen*) articuler en silence, dire sans un son; (*during spoken voice-over*) faire semblant de prononcer; (*during singing*) faire semblant de chanter; **"go away!" she ~ed at him** [*hair*] « va-t-en! » lui dit-elle en remuant les lèvres silencieusement [b] (*insincerely*) [+ *platitudes, slogans, rhetoric*] débiter; **to ~ apologies/promises** se répandre en plates excuses/en fausses promesses

[3] COMP ► **mouth organ** N (*esp Brit*) harmonica *m* ► **mouth-to-mouth (resuscitation)** N bouche-à-bouche *m inv* ► **mouth ulcer** N aphte *m* ► **mouth-watering** ADJ appétissant, alléchant

► **mouth off*** VI (= *talk boastfully*) en avoir plein la bouche* (**about** de); (*US* = *talk insolently*) dégoiser*

-mouthed [maʊðd] ADJ (*in compounds*) **wide-mouthed** [*person*] qui a une grande bouche; [*river*] à l'embouchure large; [*cave*] avec une vaste entrée; [*bottle*] au large goulot → **loud, mealy**

mouthful [ˈmaʊθfʊl] N [*of food*] bouchée f; [*of drink*] gorgée f; **he swallowed it in one ~** [+ *food*] il n'en a fait qu'une bouchée; [+ *drink*] il l'a avalé d'un trait; (*fig*) **it's a real ~ of a name!** quel nom à coucher dehors!; (*fig*) **you said a ~!*** c'est vraiment le cas de le dire!; (*fig*) **to give sb a ~*** passer un savon* à qn, enguirlander* qn

mouthpiece [ˈmaʊθpiːs] N [*of wind instrument, brass instrument*] embouchoir *m*; [*of recorder*] bec *m*; [*of telephone*] microphone *m*; (*fig* = *spokesman*) porte-parole *m inv*

mouthwash [ˈmaʊθwɒʃ] N bain *m* de bouche; (*for gargling*) gargarisme *m*

mouthy* [ˈmaʊθɪ] ADJ **to be ~** être grande gueule*

movable [ˈmuːvəbl] [1] ADJ mobile; (*Rel*) **feast** fête f mobile; (*fig*) **it's a ~ feast** il n'y a pas de date fixe [2] **movables** NPL (*Jur*) effets *mpl* mobiliers, biens *mpl* meubles

move [muːv]

[1] **NOUN**	[3] **INTRANSITIVE VERB**
[2] **TRANSITIVE VERB**	[4] **PHRASAL VERBS**

[1] NOUN

[a] mouvement *m*

♦ **to be on the move** [*troops, army*] être en marche *or* en mouvement; (= *moving around*) **he's on the ~ the whole time** il se déplace constamment, il est sans arrêt en déplacement; **to be always on the ~** (= *gipsies etc*) se déplacer continuellement, être sans cesse par monts et par vaux; [*military or diplomatic personnel etc*] être toujours en déplacement; [*child, animal*] ne pas tenir en place; (* = *be busy*) ne jamais (s')arrêter; **the circus is on the ~ again** le cirque a repris la route; **the police were after him and he had to stay on the ~** recherché par la police, il était obligé de se déplacer constamment *or* de déménager constamment; (*fig*) **it's a country on the ~** c'est un pays en marche

♦ **to make a move** (= *leave*) manifester l'intention de partir; (= *act*) faire quelque chose, agir; **it's time we made a ~** (= *that we left*) il est temps que nous partions; (= *acted, did sth*) il est temps que nous fassions quelque chose; **it was midnight and no one had made a ~** il était minuit et personne n'avait manifesté l'intention de partir; **he made a ~ towards the door** il esquissa un mouvement vers la porte; **get a ~ on!*** remue-toi!*, grouille-toi!*

[b] = **change** (*of house*) déménagement *m*; (*of job*) changement *m* d'emploi; **it's our third ~ in two years** c'est notre troisième déménagement en deux ans; **it's time he had a ~** il a besoin de changer d'air *or* d'horizon

[c] **Chess, Draughts etc** [*of chessman etc*] coup *m*; (= *player's turn*) tour *m*; (*fig*) pas *m*, démarche f, manœuvre f, mesure f; **knight's ~** marche f du cavalier; **that was a silly ~** (*in game*) c'était un coup stupide; (*fig*) c'était une démarche *or* une manœuvre stupide; **it's your ~** (c'est) à vous de jouer; **to have the first ~** jouer en premier; (*Chess, Draughts*) avoir le trait; (*fig*) **he knows every ~ in the game** il connaît toutes les astuces; **his first ~ after his election was to announce ...** la première mesure qu'il a prise après son élection a été d'annoncer ...; **what's our** *or* **the next ~?** et maintenant, qu'est-ce qu'on fait?; **let him make the first ~** laisse-lui faire les premiers pas; **we must watch his every ~** il nous faut surveiller tous ses faits et gestes; **there was a ~ to defeat the proposal** on a tenté de faire échec à la proposition

[d] **Climbing** (= *step etc*) pas *m*; (= *section of pitch*) passage *m*

[2] TRANSITIVE VERB

[a] = **change position of** [+ *object, furniture*] déplacer; [+ *limbs*] remuer; [+ *troops, animals*] transporter; **you've ~d the stick!** tu as bougé le bâton!; **he hadn't ~d his chair** il n'avait pas déplacé sa chaise *or* changé sa chaise de place; **~ your chair nearer the fire** approchez votre chaise du feu; **~ your books over here** mets tes livres par ici; **can you ~ your fingers?** pouvez-vous remuer vos doigts?; **he ~d his family out of the war zone** il a évacué sa famille hors de la zone des conflits; **they ~d the crowd off the grass** ils ont fait dégager la foule de la pelouse; **~ your feet off the table** enlève tes pieds de la table; **the wind ~s the leaves** le vent agite *or* fait remuer les feuilles; (*Brit*) **to ~ house** déménager; **to ~ one's job** changer d'emploi; **his**

firm want to ~ him son entreprise veut l'envoyer ailleurs; (*Admin*) son entreprise veut le muter; he's asked to be ~d to London/ to a new department/to an easier job il a demandé à être muté à Londres/affecté à *or* muté à dans un autre service/affecté à un emploi plus facile; (*fig*) to ~ heaven and earth to do sth remuer ciel et terre pour faire qch, se mettre en quatre pour faire qch; (*Chess*) to ~ a piece jouer une pièce

b = change timing of   to ~ sth (forward/back) [+ *event, date*] avancer/reculer qch

c = remove   [+ *stain, mark*] enlever, faire partir

d Med   to ~ one's bowels aller à la selle

e Comm   [+ *stock*] écouler

f emotionally   émouvoir, attendrir; she's easily ~d elle est facilement émue *or* attendrie; this did not ~ him ceci n'a pas réussi à l'émouvoir *or* à l'attendrir; to ~ sb to tears émouvoir qn jusqu'aux larmes; to ~ sb to laughter faire rire qn; to ~ sb to anger mettre qn en colère; to ~ sb to pity apitoyer qn

g = stimulate, persuade   pousser, inciter (sb to do sth qn à faire qch); I am ~d to ask why ... je suis incité à demander pourquoi ...; if I feel ~d to do it ◊ if the spirit ~s me (*hum*) si le cœur m'en dit; he won't be ~d il est inébranlable; even this did not ~ him même ceci n'a pas réussi à l'ébranler

h Admin, Parl etc = propose   proposer; to ~ a resolution proposer une motion; to ~ that sth be done proposer que qch soit fait; he ~d the adjournment of the meeting *or* that the meeting be adjourned il a proposé que la séance soit levée

3 INTRANSITIVE VERB

a person, animal   (= *stir*) bouger, remuer; (= *go*) aller, se déplacer; [*limb, lips, trees, leaves, curtains, door*] bouger, remuer; [*clouds*] passer, avancer; [*vehicle, ship, plane, procession*] aller, passer; [*troops, army*] se déplacer; don't ~! ne bougez pas!; she ~s well elle a de l'aisance dans ses mouvements; troops are moving near the frontier il y a des mouvements de troupes près de la frontière; the procession ~d slowly out of sight petit à petit la procession a disparu; I saw something moving over there j'ai vu quelque chose bouger là-bas; keep moving! (*to keep warm etc*) ne restez pas sans bouger!; (= *pass along there*) circulez!; to ~ freely [*mechanical part*] jouer librement; [*people, cars*] circuler aisément; [*traffic*] être fluide; to keep the traffic moving assurer la circulation ininterrompue des véhicules; the car in front isn't moving la voiture devant nous est à l'arrêt; do not get out while the bus is moving ne descendez pas de l'autobus en marche, attendez l'arrêt complet de l'autobus pour descendre; the coach was moving at 30km/h le car faisait du 30 km/h *or* roulait à 30 (km) à l'heure; (*fig*) to ~ in high society fréquenter la haute société; he was certainly moving! il ne traînait pas!; that horse can certainly ~ quand il s'agit de foncer ce cheval se défend!*; you can't ~ for books in that room* on ne peut plus se retourner dans cette pièce tellement il y a de livres

♦ **to move** + *preposition*: they ~d rapidly **across** the lawn ils ont traversé la pelouse rapidement; I'll not ~ **from** here je ne bougerai pas d'ici; he has ~d **into** another class il est passé dans une autre classe; let's ~ **into** the garden passons dans le jardin; the car ~d **round** the corner la voiture a tourné au coin de la rue; he ~d slowly **towards** the door il se dirigea lentement vers la porte

b = depart   it's time we were moving il est temps que nous partions (*subj*), il est temps de partir; let's ~! partons!, en route!

c = move house etc   [*person, family*] déménager; [*office, shop, business*] être transféré; to ~ to a bigger house emménager dans une mai-

son plus grande; to ~ to the country aller habiter (à) la campagne, aller s'installer à la campagne

d = progress   [*plans, talks etc*] progresser, avancer; things are moving at last! enfin ça avance *or* ça progresse!; he got things moving avec lui ça a bien démarré *or* c'est bien parti

e = act, take steps   agir; the government won't ~ until ... le gouvernement ne bougera pas *or* ne fera rien tant que ...; we must ~ first nous devons prendre l'initiative; we'll have to ~ quickly if we want to avoid ... il nous faudra agir sans tarder si nous voulons éviter ...; the committee ~d to stop the abuse le comité a pris des mesures pour mettre fin aux abus

f in games   [*player*] jouer; [*chesspiece*] avancer, se déplacer; it's you to ~ (c'est) votre tour de jouer; (*Chess*) white ~s les blancs jouent; (*Chess*) the knight ~s like this le cavalier avance *or* se déplace comme cela

g Comm   [*goods*] se vendre

4 PHRASAL VERBS

▶ **move about** **1** VI (*gen*) se déplacer; (= *fidget*) remuer; (= *travel*) voyager; he can ~ about only with difficulty il ne se déplace qu'avec peine; stop moving about! tiens-toi tranquille!; (= *change residence*) we've ~d about a good deal nous ne sommes jamais restés longtemps au même endroit, nous avons souvent déménagé

2 VT SEP [+ *person, furniture, employee*] déplacer

▶ **move along** **1** VI [*people or vehicles in line*] avancer, circuler; ~ along there! (*on bus*) avancez un peu, ne restez pas près des portes!; (*policeman*) circulez!; (*on bench etc*) can you ~ along a few places? pouvez-vous vous pousser un peu?

2 VT SEP [+ *crowd*] faire circuler, faire avancer; [+ *animals*] faire avancer

▶ **move around** = move about

▶ **move away** **1** VI **a** (= *depart*) partir, s'éloigner (**from** de)

b (= *move house*) déménager; they've ~d away from here ils n'habitent plus ici

2 VT SEP [+ *person, object*] éloigner, écarter (**from** de)

▶ **move back** **1** VI **a** (= *withdraw*) reculer

b (*to original position*) (= *go back*) retourner; (= *come back*) revenir; he ~d back to the desk il retourna au bureau

c (= *move house*) (= *gone back*) ils sont retournés habiter (à) Londres; (= *come back*) ils sont revenus habiter (à) Londres

2 VT SEP **a** (*backwards*) [+ *person, crowd, animals*] faire reculer; [+ *troops*] replier; [+ *object, furniture*] reculer

b (*to original position*) [+ *person*] faire revenir *or* retourner; [+ *object*] remettre; his firm ~d him back to London (= *go back*) son entreprise l'a fait retourner à Londres; (= *come back*) son entreprise l'a fait revenir à Londres; ~ the table back to where it was before remets la table là où elle était

▶ **move down** **1** VI **a** [*person, object, lift*] descendre; he ~d down from the top floor il est descendu du dernier étage; (*on bench etc*) can you ~ down a few places? pouvez-vous vous pousser un peu?

b (*Sport: in league*) reculer; (*Scol*) he has had to ~ down one class il a dû descendre d'une classe

2 VT SEP **a** [+ *person*] faire descendre; [+ *object*] descendre

b (= *demote*) [+ *pupil*] faire descendre (dans une classe inférieure); [+ *employee*] rétrograder

▶ **move forward** **1** VI [*person, animal, vehicle*] avancer; [*troops*] se porter en avant

2 VT SEP [+ *person, vehicle*] faire avancer; [+ *troops*] porter en avant; [+ *object, chair*] avancer

▶ **move in** **1** VI **a** (= *approach*) [*police etc*]

avancer, intervenir

b (*to a house*) emménager

2 VT SEP [+ *person*] faire entrer; [+ *furniture etc*] rentrer, mettre *or* remettre à l'intérieur; (*on removal day*) installer

▶ **move in on*** VT FUS (= *advance on*) (*Mil etc*) marcher sur, avancer sur; [*police*] faire une descente dans; (= *attempt takeover of*) [+ *firm*] essayer de mettre la main sur; to ~ in on sb (for the night) se faire héberger par qn (pour la nuit)

▶ **move off** **1** VI [*person*] s'en aller, partir; [*car*] démarrer; [*train, army, procession*] s'ébranler, partir

2 VT SEP [+ *object*] enlever

▶ **move on** **1** VI [*person, vehicle*] avancer; (*after stopping*) se remettre en route; [*time*] passer, s'écouler; the gipsies ~d on to another site les gitans sont allés s'installer plus loin; (*policeman etc*) ~ on (now) please! circulez s'il vous plaît!; (*in discussion etc*) moving on now to ... passons maintenant à ...

2 VT SEP [+ *person, onlookers*] faire circuler; [+ *clock*] avancer

▶ **move out** **1** VI (*of house, office, room etc*) déménager; to ~ out of a flat déménager d'un appartement, quitter un appartement

2 VT SEP [+ *person, animal*] faire sortir; [+ *troops*] retirer; [+ *object, furniture*] sortir; (*on removal day*) déménager

▶ **move over** **1** VI s'écarter, se pousser; ~ over! pousse-toi!; (*in job*) if he can't do the job he should ~ over and let someone else who can s'il n'est pas capable de faire ce travail, il n'a qu'à céder la place à quelqu'un de plus compétent; (= *change over*) to ~ over to sth new adopter qch de nouveau

2 VT SEP [+ *object*] déplacer

▶ **move up** **1** VI **a** [*person, flag etc*] monter; can you ~ up a few seats? pouvez-vous vous pousser un peu *or* vous décaler de quelques sièges?; I want to ~ up nearer the stage je veux m'approcher de la scène

b [*employee*] avoir de l'avancement; (*Sport: in league*) progresser dans le classement; to ~ up a class [*pupil*] passer dans la classe supérieure

2 VT SEP **a** [+ *person*] faire monter; [+ *object*] monter

b (= *promote*) [+ *pupil*] faire passer dans une classe supérieure; [+ *employee*] donner de l'avancement à

moveable ['muːvəbl] ADJ = movable

movement ['muːvmənt] N **a** [*of person, troops, army, population, vehicles, goods, capital*] mouvement m; (= *gesture*) mouvement m, geste m; he lay without ~ il était étendu sans mouvement; massage the skin using small circular ~s massez la peau en faisant de petits mouvements circulaires; hand ~s mouvements mpl *or* gestes mpl de la main; (*during sleep*) eye ~s mouvements mpl oculaires; her eye ~s were furtive and suspicious elle jetait des coups d'œil furtifs et soupçonneux; there was a ~ towards the exit il y eut un mouvement vers la sortie, on se dirigea vers la sortie; the accident disrupted the ~ of traffic l'accident a perturbé la circulation; the free ~ of labour, capital and goods la libre circulation de la main-d'œuvre, des capitaux et des marchandises

b ~s (= *comings and goings*) allées fpl et venues fpl; the police know very little about the suspect's ~s la police ne sait pas grand-chose sur les allées et venues du suspect

c (= *action, impetus*) [*of prices, shares, market, situation*] mouvement m; the film lacks ~ le film manque de mouvement, le rythme du film est trop lent; an upward/downward ~ in the economy une progression/régression économique; an upward/downward ~ in share prices un mouvement *or* une tendance à la

hausse/à la baisse du prix des actions ; **there has been little ~ in the political situation** la situation politique demeure à peu près inchangée ; **there has been some ~ towards fewer customs restrictions** il semble que l'on aille vers une réduction des restrictions douanières ; **a ~ towards multimedia products** un intérêt grandissant pour les produits multimédia
[d] (Pol = group, party) mouvement m ; **peace ~** mouvement m en faveur de la paix ; **separatist/resistance ~** mouvement m séparatiste/de résistance
[e] (Mus) [of symphony, concerto etc] mouvement m ; **in four ~s** en quatre mouvements
[f] (= mechanism) [of machine, clock, watch etc] mouvement m
[g] (Med: also **bowel ~**) selles fpl ; **to have a (bowel) ~** aller à la selle

mover ['muːvər] N [a] (Admin, Parl etc) [of motion] motionnaire mf, auteur m d'une motion → **prime** [b] (US = removal person) déménageur m [c] **she's a lovely ~*** elle a une chouette façon de danser (or de marcher etc)* [d] **the ~s and shakers*** les personnages mpl influents

movie ['muːvɪ] (esp US) [1] N film m (de cinéma) ; **the ~s*** le ciné* ; **to go to the ~s*** aller au ciné* [2] COMP ► **movie actor** N acteur m de cinéma ► **movie actress** N actrice f de cinéma ► **movie camera** N caméra f ► **movie-going** N la fréquentation des salles de cinéma ► **movie house** N cinéma m (salle) ► **the movie industry** N l'industrie f cinématographique, le cinéma ► **movie maker** N (US) cinéaste mf ► **movie rating** N (US) système de classification des films ► **movie star** N star f or vedette f (de cinéma) ► **movie theater** N (US) cinéma m (salle)

┌─────────────────────────────┐
│ **MOVIE RATING, FILM RATING** │
└─────────────────────────────┘

En Grande-Bretagne, l'organisme chargé d'autoriser la diffusion des films et vidéos est le British Board of Classification. Le système de classification adopté est le suivant : « U » (Universal) : pour tous publics ; « PG » (Parental Guidance) : certaines scènes peuvent heurter les jeunes enfants ; « 12 », « 15 » ou « 18 » : interdiction aux moins de 12, 15 ou 18 ans ; « Restricted 18 » : pour adultes seulement, le film ne pouvant être diffusé que dans des salles disposant d'une licence spéciale.

Aux États-Unis, ces fonctions de contrôle sont assumées par la Motion Picture Association of America, et la classification est la suivante : « G » (General) : pour tous publics ; « PG » (Parental Guidance) : certaines scènes peuvent heurter la sensibilité des jeunes enfants ; « PG13 » : certaines scènes sont déconseillées aux moins de 13 ans ; « R » (Restricted) : toute personne de moins de 17 ans doit être accompagnée d'un adulte ; « NC-17 » ou « X » : strictement interdit aux moins de 17 ans.

moviegoer ['muːvɪɡəʊər] N (gen) amateur m de cinéma, cinéphile mf ; **I'm an occasional ~** je vais de temps en temps au cinéma

movieland* ['muːvɪlænd] N le (monde du) cinéma

moving ['muːvɪŋ] [1] ADJ [a] (= in motion) [vehicle, train] en marche ; [object, crowd] en mouvement ; [picture, image, graphics] animé ; (in machine) **~ part** pièce f mobile ; **~ target** cible f mouvante or mobile ; **~ traffic** circulation f [b] (emotionally) [sight, plea] émouvant, touchant ; [book, film, story, account] émouvant ; **it was a deeply ~ moment** c'était un moment vraiment très émouvant [c] (= motivating) **he was the ~ force** or **spirit in the whole affair** il était l'âme de toute l'affaire [2] COMP ► **moving belt** N tapis m roulant ► **the moving party** N (Jur) la partie demanderesse ► **moving pavement** N trottoir m roulant ► **moving picture†** N (Cine) film m (de cinéma) ► **moving sidewalk** N (US) trottoir m

roulant ► **moving staircase** N escalier m mécanique or roulant ► **moving walkway** N trottoir m roulant

movingly ['muːvɪŋlɪ] ADV d'une manière émouvante or touchante

mow [məʊ] (pret **mowed**, ptp **mowed** or **mown**) VT [+ corn] faucher ; **to ~ the lawn** tondre le gazon
► **mow down** VT SEP (fig) [+ people, troops] faucher

mower ['məʊər] N [a] (= machine) (Agr) faucheuse f ; (also **lawnmower**) tondeuse f (à gazon) → **motor** [b] (= person) faucheur m, -euse f

mowing ['məʊɪŋ] N (Agr) fauchage m ; **~ machine** (Agr) faucheuse f ; (in garden) tondeuse f (à gazon)

mown [məʊn] VB ptp of **mow**

Mozambican [ˌməʊzæmˈbiːkən] [1] ADJ mozambicain [2] N Mozambicain(e) m(f)

Mozambique [ˌməʊzəmˈbiːk] N le Mozambique

Mozart ['məʊtsɑːt] N Mozart m

Mozartian [məʊˈtsɑːtɪən] ADJ mozartien

mozzarella [ˌmɒtsəˈrelə] N (= cheese) mozzarella f

MP [ˈemˈpiː] N [a] (Brit) (ABBR = **Member of Parliament**) → **member** [b] (ABBR = **Military Police**) → **military** [c] (Can) (ABBR = **Mounted Police**) → **mounted**

mpg [ˌempiːˈdʒiː] N (ABBR = **miles per gallon**) → **mile**

mph [ˌempiːˈeɪtʃ] N (ABBR = **miles per hour**) ≈ km/h

MPhil [ˌemˈfɪl] N (Univ) (ABBR = **Master of Philosophy**) diplôme de fin de deuxième cycle universitaire en lettres, ≈ DEA m

MPS [ˌempiːˈes] N (Brit) (ABBR = **Member of the Pharmaceutical Society**) diplôme de pharmacie

MPV [ˌempiːˈviː] N (ABBR = **multipurpose vehicle**) → **multipurpose**

Mr ['mɪstər] N (pl **Messrs**) M., Monsieur → **mister**

MRC [ˌemɑːˈsiː] N (Brit) (ABBR = **Medical Research Council**) → **medical**

MRCP [ˌemɑːsiːˈpiː] N (Brit) (ABBR = **Member of the Royal College of Physicians**) diplôme supérieur de médecine générale

MRCS [ˌemɑːsiːˈes] N (Brit) (ABBR = **Member of the Royal College of Surgeons**) diplôme supérieur de chirurgie

MRCVS [ˌemɑːsiːviːˈes] N (Brit) (ABBR = **Member of the Royal College of Veterinary Surgeons**) diplôme de médecine vétérinaire

MRI [ˌemɑːˈraɪ] N (ABBR = **magnetic resonance imaging**) IRM f, imagerie f par résonance magnétique

MRP [ˌemɑːˈpiː] N (ABBR = **manufacturers' recommended price**) → **manufacturer**

Mrs ['mɪsɪz] [1] N (pl inv) Mme [2] COMP ► **Mrs Mop*** N (Brit hum) femme f de ménage

MS [ˌemˈes] N [a] (also **ms**) (ABBR = **manuscript**) [b] (ABBR = **multiple sclerosis**) → **multiple** [c] (US Univ) (ABBR = **Mississippi**) [d] (US Univ) (ABBR = **Master of Science**) maîtrise de sciences → DEGREE

Ms [mɪz, məz] N ≈ Mme

┌──────┐
│ **MS** │
└──────┘

Ms est un titre utilisé à la place de « Mrs » (Mme) ou de « Miss » (Mlle) pour éviter la distinction traditionnelle entre femmes mariées et femmes non mariées. Il se veut ainsi l'équivalent du « Mr » (M.) pour les hommes. Souvent tourné en dérision à l'origine comme étant l'expression d'un féminisme exacerbé, ce titre est aujourd'hui couramment utilisé.

MSA [ˌemesˈeɪ] N (US Univ) (ABBR = **Master of Science in Agriculture**) diplôme d'ingénieur agronome

MSC N (Brit: formerly) (ABBR = **Manpower Services Commission**) → **manpower**

MSc [ˌemesˈsiː] N (Brit Univ) (ABBR = **Master of Science**) **to have an ~ in Biology** avoir une maîtrise de biologie → **master** ; → DEGREE

MSF N (Brit) (ABBR = **Manufacturing, Science, Finance**) syndicat

MSG [ˌemesˈdʒiː] N (ABBR = **monosodium glutamate**)

Msgr ABBR = **monsignor**

MSS, mss NPL ABBR = **manuscripts**

MST [ˌemesˈtiː] N (US) (ABBR = **Mountain Standard Time**) → **mountain**

MT [ˈemˈtiː] N [a] (ABBR = **machine translation**) → **machine** [b] (ABBR = **Montana**) [c] (US) (ABBR = **Mountain Time**) → **mountain**

Mt (Geog) (ABBR = **Mount**) Mt ; **Mt Pelat** Mt Pelat ; **Mt Everest** l'Everest m

mth ABBR = **month**

MTV [ˌemtiːˈviː] N (ABBR = **music television**) MTV

much [mʌtʃ]

┌──┐
│ compar **more**, superl **most** │
│ [1] PRONOUN   [3] ADVERB │
│ [2] ADJECTIVE │
└──┘

[1] PRONOUN
[a] **= a great deal, a lot** **~ has happened since then** beaucoup de choses se sont passées depuis ; **~ will depend on the state of the economy** cela va dépendre en grande partie de l'état de l'économie ; **we have ~ to be thankful for** nous avons tout lieu d'être reconnaissants ; **does it cost ~?** est-ce que ça coûte cher ? ; **is it worth ~?** est-ce que ça a de la valeur ?
♦ **much of** (= a large part of) une bonne partie de ; **~ of the town/night** une bonne partie de la ville/de la nuit ; **~ of what you say** une bonne partie de ce que vous dites
♦ **to make much of sth** (= emphasize) faire grand cas de qch, attacher beaucoup d'importance à qch ; **he made ~ of the fact that ...** il a fait grand cas du fait que ..., il a attaché beaucoup d'importance au fait que ... ; **he made too ~ of it** il y attachait trop d'importance ; (= understand) **I couldn't make ~ of what he was saying** je n'ai pas bien compris or saisi ce qu'il disait
[b] **in negative sentences**
♦ **not ... much** (= a small amount) pas grand-chose, pas beaucoup

┌───┐
│ When the sense is **not much of it**, en is required │
│ with **pas beaucoup**, but not with **pas grand-** │
│ **chose**. │
└───┘

I haven't got ~ left il ne m'en reste pas beaucoup, il ne me reste pas grand-chose ; **what was stolen? — nothing ~** qu'est-ce qui a été volé ? — pas grand-chose ; **he hadn't ~ to say about it** il n'avait pas grand-chose à en dire ; **there's not ~ anyone can do about it** personne n'y peut grand-chose ; **I haven't heard ~ of him lately** je n'ai pas eu beaucoup de nouvelles de lui ces derniers temps ; **we don't see ~ of each other** nous ne nous voyons pas beaucoup ; [BUT] **he's/it's not ~ to look at** il/ça ne paie pas de mine ; **it isn't up to ~*** ce n'est pas terrible* ; **she won but there wasn't ~ in it** elle a gagné mais de justesse

┌───┐
│ Constructions with **valoir** are often used when as- │
│ sessing value or merit. │
└───┘

I don't think ~ of that film à mon avis ce film ne vaut pas grand-chose, je ne trouve pas ce film très bon ; **there isn't ~ to choose between them** ils se valent plus ou moins ; (in choice, competition) **there isn't ~ in it** ça se vaut

[2] ADJECTIVE
beaucoup de ; **~ money** beaucoup d'argent ; **~ crime goes unreported** beaucoup de crimes ne sont pas signalés ; **he hasn't (very) ~ time** il n'a pas beaucoup de temps ; **~ "antique" furniture is not genuine** beaucoup de or bien des meubles

dits «anciens» ne le sont pas; BUT without ~ money avec peu d'argent; (iro) and ~ good may it do you grand bien t'en fasse; it's a bit ~!* c'est un peu fort!

3 ADVERB

a = to a great degree beaucoup; he hasn't changed ~ il n'a pas beaucoup changé; she doesn't go out ~ elle ne sort pas beaucoup or pas souvent; ~ bigger beaucoup plus grand; more easily beaucoup plus facilement; ~ the cleverest de beaucoup or de loin le plus intelligent; it doesn't ~ matter ça n'a pas grande importance; BUT he ~ regrets that ... (frm) il regrette beaucoup or vivement que ...; he was ~ displeased (frm) il était très mécontent; ~ to my amazement à ma grande stupéfaction

♦ **very much**: thank you very ~ merci beaucoup; I very ~ hope that ... j'espère de tout cœur que ...; something was very ~ the matter quelque chose n'allait pas du tout; this is very ~ the case c'est tout à fait le cas

b = more or less it's (very or pretty) ~ the same c'est presque la même chose; the town is (pretty) ~ the same as it was ten years ago la ville n'a pas beaucoup changé en dix ans; they are (very or pretty) ~ of an age ils sont à peu près du même âge

c SET STRUCTURES

♦ **as much** (= that quantity) as ~ again encore autant; twice as ~ deux fois plus or autant; half as ~ again la moitié de plus; (= that) I thought as ~! c'est bien ce que je pensais!, je m'y attendais!; it was his fault, and he admitted as ~ later c'était de sa faute et il l'a admis par la suite

♦ **as much as** (in comparisons of equality) as ~ as possible autant que possible; as ~ time as ... autant de temps que ...; I've got as ~ as you j'en ai autant que toi; I need it as ~ as you do j'en ai autant besoin que toi; I love him as ~ as ever je l'aime toujours autant; twice as ~ money as ... deux fois plus d'argent que ...; I didn't enjoy it as ~ as all that je ne l'ai pas aimé tant que ça; it's as ~ as he can do to stand up c'est tout juste s'il peut se lever

♦ **as much as** + amount: you could pay as ~ as 200 francs for that ça va chercher jusqu'à 200 francs; they hope to raise as ~ as £5 million ils espèrent collecter près de or jusqu'à 5 millions de livres

♦ **however much**: however ~ you protest ... on a beau protester ...; however ~ you like him ... quelle que soit votre affection pour lui, ...

♦ **how much ...?** combien?; how ~ does it cost? combien ça coûte?; how ~ money have you got? combien d'argent as-tu?

♦ **much as**: ~ as I like him, I don't trust him ce n'est pas que je ne l'aime pas mais je ne lui fais pas confiance; ~ as I dislike doing this, ... bien que je n'aime pas du tout faire cela, ...

♦ **much less** (= and even less) he couldn't understand the question, ~ less answer it il ne pouvait pas comprendre la question et encore moins y répondre

♦ **much though**: ~ though she loves them both bien qu'elle les aime (subj) tous deux profondément

♦ **not much of a*** (= not a great) he is not ~ of a writer ce n'est pas un très bon écrivain, comme écrivain il y a mieux; I'm not ~ of a drinker je ne bois pas beaucoup; it wasn't ~ of an evening ce n'était pas une soirée très réussie

♦ **so much** (= a lot) tellement, tant; he'd drunk so ~ that ... il avait tellement or tant bu que ...; so ~ of what he says is untrue il y a tellement or tant de mensonges dans ce qu'il dit; so ~ pleasure tant de plaisir; you spend so ~ of your time worrying that ... tu passes tellement de temps à te faire du souci que ...; BUT he beat me by so ~ il m'a battu de ça; do you want water in your whisky? — about so ~ vous voulez de l'eau dans votre whisky? — à peu

près comme ça; so ~ so that ... à tel point que ...; without so ~ as a word sans même (dire) un mot

♦ **not so much ... as**: the problem is not so ~ one of money as of staff il ne s'agit pas tant d'un problème d'argent que d'un problème de personnel; I think of her not so ~ as a doctor as a friend je la considère plus comme une amie que comme un médecin

♦ **so much for**: so ~ for the producers, what of the consumers? nous avons examiné le cas des producteurs mais qu'en est-il des consommateurs?; so ~ for his help! c'est ça qu'il appelle aider!; so ~ for his promises! voilà ce que valaient ses promesses!; so ~ for that! tant pis!

♦ **so much the** + comparative: so ~ the better! tant mieux!; that leaves us so ~ the less to do c'est toujours ça de moins à faire

♦ **this/that much**: this ~? (ça ira) comme ça?; it's that ~ too long c'est trop long de ça; he was at least this ~ taller than me il était plus grand que moi d'au moins ça; I can't carry this ~ je ne peux pas porter (tout) ceci; I know this ~ je sais tout au moins ceci; this ~ we do know: ... tout au moins nous savons ceci: ...; he has left, this ~ we do know il est parti, ça nous le savons déjà; this ~ is certain ... un point est acquis ...; this ~ is true il y a ceci de vrai

♦ **too much** trop; I've eaten too ~ j'ai trop mangé; he talks too ~ il parle trop; £500 is too ~ 500 livres, c'est trop; that was too ~ for me il en était trop pour moi; too ~ sugar trop de sucre; that's too ~! (lit) c'est trop!; (protesting) (ça) c'est trop fort!; BUT too ~!* c'est dingue*!; he was too ~ for his opponent il était trop fort pour son adversaire; the stress was too ~ for me je n'arrivais plus à supporter le stress; (disapproving) that film was really too ~ or a bit ~ for me j'ai trouvé que le film dépassait vraiment or un peu les bornes

muchness* ['mʌtʃnɪs] N they're much of a ~ c'est blanc bonnet et bonnet blanc

mucilage ['mjuːsɪlɪdʒ] N mucilage m

mucilaginous [ˌmjuːsɪˈlædʒɪnəs] ADJ mucilagineux

muck [mʌk] **1** N **a** (= dirt) saletés fpl; (= mud) boue f, gadoue f ■ (PROV) where there's ~ there's brass* l'argent n'a pas d'odeur → lady **b** (= excrement) [of dog] crotte f; [of horse] crottin m; [of cow] bouse f; [of bird] fiente f; (= manure) fumier m **c** (fig: describing food, film, book, conversation etc) saleté(s) f(pl), cochonnerie(s)* f(pl) **d** (= bungle) to make a ~* of sth saloper* qch **2** COMP ► **muck heap** N tas m de fumier or d'ordures ► **muck-up***‡ N (= bungle) gâchis m

► **muck about*, muck around*** (Brit) **1** VI **a** (= spend time aimlessly) perdre son temps; stop ~ing about and get on with your work cesse de perdre ton temps et fais ton travail **b** (= potter around) he enjoys ~ing about in the garden il aime bricoler dans le jardin **c** (= play the fool) faire l'idiot or l'imbécile; to ~ about with sth (= fiddle with) jouer avec qch, tripoter qch **2** VT SEP [+ person] traiter par-dessus la jambe*

► **muck in*** VI (Brit) (= share money etc) faire bourse commune (with avec); (= share room) to ~ in with sb crécher* avec qn; everyone ~s in here tout le monde met la main à la pâte* ici

► **muck out** VT SEP (Brit) [+ stable] nettoyer, curer

► **muck up*** (Brit) **1** VT SEP **a** (= ruin) [+ task] saloper*; [+ plans, deal] chambouler*; [+ life] gâcher; [+ mechanism] bousiller*; he's really ~ed things up! c'est vraiment tout flanqué par terre!* **b** (= make untidy) [+ room] semer la pagaille* dans; [+ hair] emmêler; [+ hairstyle] abîmer; (= make dirty) [+ room, clothes] salir **2** ~-up N → muck

muckiness ['mʌkɪnɪs] N saleté f, malpropreté f

muckraker ['mʌkreɪkər] N (fig) fouineur m, -euse f (qui déterre des scandales), fouille-merde* mf

muckraking ['mʌkreɪkɪŋ] N mise f au jour de scandales

mucky* ['mʌkɪ] ADJ (Brit) **a** (= dirty) [person, animal, place, object] boueux; [job] crasseux; to get ~ se salir; to get sth ~ salir qch; (hum) keep your ~ paws off! touche pas avec tes pattes sales!; (hum) you ~ pup! petit(e) cochon(ne)! **b** (= smutty) [book, magazine, film] cochon **c** (= unpleasant) [weather] sale

mucous ['mjuːkəs] ADJ muqueux; ~ membrane (membrane f) muqueuse f

mucus ['mjuːkəs] N mucus m, mucosités fpl

mud [mʌd] **1** N boue f; (in river, sea) boue f, vase f; (in swamp) boue f, bourbe f; car stuck in the ~ voiture f embourbée; (fig) to drag sb's (good) name through the ~ or drag sb through the ~ calomnier qn; (fig) to throw or sling ~ at sb couvrir qn de boue; (esp Brit) ~ sticks il est difficile de se laver de tout soupçon; (hum) here's ~ in your eye!* à la tienne Étienne!* (hum) → clear, name, stick **2** COMP ► **mud-caked** ADJ tout crotté ► **mud flap** N (Aut: gen) pare-boue m inv; [of truck] bavette f ► **mud flat(s)** N(PL) laisse f de vase ► **mud hut** N hutte f de terre ► **mud pie** N pâté m (de sable, de terre) ► **mud-slinging** N (NonC) médisance f, dénigrement m ► **mud wrestling** N catch m dans la boue (généralement féminin)

mudbank ['mʌdbæŋk] N banc m de vase

mudbath ['mʌdbɑːθ] N bain m de boue

muddle ['mʌdl] **1** N (= disorder) désordre m; (= tangle of objects) fouillis m; (fig) confusion f; the ~ of notebooks and papers on her desk le fouillis de bloc-notes et de papiers sur son bureau; her office was a ~ of files and papers il y avait un vrai fouillis de dossiers et de papiers dans son bureau; there's been a ~ over the seats il y a eu confusion en ce qui concerne les places; a legal/financial/bureaucratic ~ un imbroglio juridique/financier/bureaucratique; what a ~! (= disorder) quel fouillis!; (= mix-up) quelle confusion!, quelle pagaille!*; to be in a ~ [room, books, clothes] être en désordre, être sens dessus dessous; [person] ne plus s'y retrouver (over sth dans qch); [ideas] être embrouillé or confus; [plans, arrangements] être confus or incertain; to get into a ~ [person] s'embrouiller (over sth dans qch, au sujet de qch); [ideas] s'embrouiller; the files have got into a real ~ les dossiers sont sens dessus dessous

2 VT (also ~ up) **a** to ~ (up) A and or with B confondre A avec B **b** (= perplex) [+ person] embrouiller; [+ sb's ideas] brouiller, embrouiller; to be ~d (up) être embrouillé; he was ~d by the whisky le whisky lui avait brouillé l'esprit; I got rather ~d by her explanation son explication m'a plutôt embrouillé; to get ~d (up) [person, ideas] s'embrouiller → muddled **c** [+ facts, story, details] brouiller, embrouiller → muddled

3 COMP ► **muddle-headed** ADJ [person] aux idées confuses, brouillon; [plan, ideas] confus ► **muddle-up** N confusion f, embrouillamini* m

► **muddle along** VI se débrouiller tant bien que mal

► **muddle on** VI se débrouiller tant bien que mal

► **muddle through** VI se tirer d'affaire or s'en sortir tant bien que mal; I expect we'll ~ through je suppose que nous nous en sortirons d'une façon ou d'une autre

► **muddle up** **1** VT SEP = muddle 2 **2** ~-up N → muddle

muddled ['mʌdəld] ADJ [message, effort, attempt, situation, storyline] confus

muddler ['mʌdlə'] N esprit m brouillon (personne)

muddy ['mʌdɪ] [1] ADJ [a] (= dirty) [clothes, object] boueux, couvert de boue; [person] couvert de boue [b] (= dull) [colour] terne; [skin, complexion] terreux; [liquid] trouble; ~ **brown** brun terne [c] (= confused) [ideas, thinking] confus [2] VT [+ hands, clothes, shoes] crotter, salir; [+ road] rendre boueux; [+ water, river] troubler; (fig) **to ~ the waters** brouiller les pistes

mudflat ['mʌdflæt] N = mud flat; → mud

mudguard ['mʌdgɑːd] N (Brit) [of car etc] pare-boue m inv; [of bicycle] garde-boue m inv

mudlark† ['mʌdlɑːk] N gamin(e) m(f) des rues

mudpack ['mʌdpæk] N masque m (de beauté) à l'argile

mudslide ['mʌdslaɪd] N coulée f de boue

muesli ['mju:zlɪ] N muesli m

muezzin [mu:'ezɪn] N muezzin m

muff [mʌf] [1] N (Dress, Tech) manchon m [2] VT* rater, louper*; (Sport) [+ ball, shot] rater, louper*; [+ chance, opportunity] rater, laisser passer; (Theat) **to ~ one's lines** se tromper dans son texte; **to ~ it*** rater son coup [3] VI* rater son coup

muffin ['mʌfɪn] N (Brit) muffin m (petit pain rond et plat); (US) petit gâteau au chocolat ou aux fruits

muffle ['mʌfl] VT [a] [+ sound, noise] assourdir, étouffer, amortir; [+ noisy thing, bell, drum] assourdir; **to ~ the oars** assourdir les avirons; **in a ~d voice** d'une voix sourde or voilée or étouffée [b] (also ~ **up** = wrap up) [+ object] envelopper; [+ person] emmitoufler; **~d (up) in a blanket** enveloppé or emmitouflé dans une couverture; **to ~ o.s. (up)** s'emmitoufler; **he was all ~d up** il était emmitouflé des pieds à la tête

► **muffle up** [1] VI s'emmitoufler [2] VT SEP = muffle b

muffler ['mʌflə'] N [a] (= scarf) cache-nez m inv, cache-col m inv [b] (US Aut) silencieux m

mufti ['mʌftɪ] N [a] (Brit*) tenue f civile; **in ~** en civil, en pékin* (Mil) [b] (Muslim) mufti or muphti m

mug [mʌg] [1] N [a] (= cup) tasse f (américaine), grande tasse f; (= glass: for beer etc) chope f; (= amount) **a ~ of coffee** un grand café [b] (‡ = face) bouille* f, bille* f; **ugly ~** sale gueule f [c] (Brit‡ = fool) andouille* f, poire* f; **what sort of a ~ do you take me for?** tu me prends pour une andouille ?‡; **they're looking for a ~ to help** ils cherchent une bonne poire* pour aider; **it's a ~'s game** c'est un piège à con‡ [2] VT (= assault) agresser [3] VI* [a] (= pull faces) faire des grimaces [b] (= overact, act up) charger son rôle [4] COMP ► **mug shot*** N (Police) photo f d'identité judiciaire; (gen) photo f d'identité

► **mug up*** [1] VT SEP [a] (Brit = swot up) bûcher*, potasser* [b] (US) faire des grimaces [2] VI (Brit) **to ~ up for an exam** bûcher* pour un examen

mugger ['mʌgə'] N agresseur m

mugging ['mʌgɪn] N [a] (= assault) agression f [b] (= overacting) jeu m forcé

muggins‡ ['mʌgɪnz] N (Brit) idiot(e) m(f), niais(e) m(f); (= oneself) **~ had to pay for it** c'est encore ma pomme* qui a payé

muggy ['mʌgɪ] ADJ [weather, air, heat] lourd; [climate] chaud et humide; [summer, day, evening] lourd, chaud et humide; **it's very ~ today** il fait très lourd aujourd'hui

mugwump ['mʌgwʌmp] N (US Pol) non-inscrit m, indépendant m

mujaheddin, mujahedeen [ˌmu:dʒəhə'di:n] NPL **the ~** les moudjahiddin mpl

mulatto [mju:'lætəʊ] [1] N (pl **mulattos** or **mulattoes**) mulâtre(sse) m(f) [2] ADJ mulâtre (f inv)

mulberry ['mʌlbərɪ] N (= fruit) mûre f; (also ~ **tree**) mûrier m

mulch [mʌltʃ] [1] N paillis m, mulch m [2] VT pailler, couvrir

mulct [mʌlkt] [1] N (= fine) amende f [2] VT [a] (= fine) frapper d'une amende [b] (by fraud etc) **to ~ sb of sth** ◊ **to ~ sth from sb** extorquer qch à qn

mule¹ [mju:l] [1] N [a] mulet m; (female) mule f; (= person) mule f; **obstinate** or **stubborn as a ~** têtu comme une mule or un mulet [b] (Spinning) renvideur m [c] (Drugs* = courier) fourmi* f [2] COMP ► **mule driver, mule skinner*** (US) N muletier m, -ière f ► **mule track** N chemin m muletier

mule² [mju:l] N (= slipper) mule f

muleteer [ˌmju:lɪ'tɪə'] N muletier m, -ière f

mulish ['mju:lɪʃ] ADJ (pej) [person] têtu; [look] buté, têtu; [attitude] buté

mulishness ['mju:lɪʃnɪs] N entêtement m

mull [mʌl] VT [+ wine, ale] chauffer et épicer → **mulled**

► **mull over** VT SEP retourner dans sa tête

mullah ['mʌlə] N mollah m

mulled [mʌld] ADJ **(a glass of) ~ wine** (un) vin chaud

mullet ['mʌlɪt] N **grey ~** mulet m; **red ~** rouget m

mulligan stew‡ ['mʌlɪgən stju:] N (US) ragoût m grossier

mulligatawny [ˌmʌlɪgə'tɔ:nɪ] N soupe f au curry

mullion ['mʌlɪən] N meneau m; **~ed window** fenêtre f à meneaux

multi... ['mʌltɪ] PREF multi...; (often translated by "plusieurs") **~-family accommodation** résidence f pour or destinée à plusieurs familles; **~-journey ticket** abonnement m (pour un nombre déterminé de trajets); **~-person vehicle** véhicule m pour plusieurs personnes; **~-stage rocket** fusée f à plusieurs étages

multi-access [ˌmʌltɪ'ækses] N (Comput) multivoie f; **~ system** système m à multivoie

multicellular [ˌmʌltɪ'seljʊlə'] ADJ multicellulaire

multichannel [ˌmʌltɪ'tʃænl] ADJ **~ TV** télévision f à canaux multiples

multicoloured, multicolored (US) [ˈmʌltɪˌkʌləd] ADJ multicolore

multicultural [ˌmʌltɪ'kʌltʃərəl] ADJ multiculturel, pluriculturel

multiculturalism [ˌmʌltɪ'kʌltʃərəlɪzəm] N multiculturalisme m, pluriculturalisme m

multidimensional [ˌmʌltɪdaɪ'menʃənl] ADJ multidimensionnel

multidirectional [ˌmʌltɪdɪ'rekʃənl] ADJ multidirectionnel

multidisciplinary [ˌmʌltɪ'dɪsɪplɪnərɪ] ADJ pluridisciplinaire, multidisciplinaire; **~ system** pluridisciplinarité f

multifaceted [ˌmʌltɪ'fæsɪtɪd] ADJ (fig) qui présente de nombreux aspects, à multiples facettes

multifarious [ˌmʌltɪ'fɛərɪəs] ADJ (frm) multiple

multiflora [ˌmʌltɪ'flɔːrə] ADJ [rose etc] multiflore

multiform ['mʌltɪfɔːm] ADJ multiforme

multi-function [ˌmʌltɪ'fʌŋkʃən] ADJ multifonctionnel, polyvalent

multigym ['mʌltɪˌdʒɪm] N banc m de musculation

multihull ['mʌltɪhʌl] N multicoque m

multilateral [ˌmʌltɪ'lætərəl] ADJ multilatéral

multilateralist [ˌmʌltɪ'lætərəlɪst] (Pol) [1] ADJ en faveur des accords multilatéraux sur le désarmement nucléaire [2] N partisan(e) m(f) des accords multilatéraux sur le désarmement nucléaire

multi-level ['mʌltɪˌlevl] ADJ (US) à plusieurs niveaux

multilingual [ˌmʌltɪ'lɪŋgwəl] ADJ [person] polyglotte; [society, country, dictionary] multilingue, plurilingue; [pamphlet, announcement, sign] en plusieurs langues

multilingualism [ˌmʌltɪ'lɪŋgwəlɪzəm] N multilinguisme m, plurilinguisme m

multimedia ['mʌltɪ'mi:dɪə] ADJ [product, system, market, CD] multimédia (f inv)

multimillion ['mʌltɪ'mɪljən] ADJ **a ~ pound deal** une affaire qui vaut plusieurs millions de livres; **a ~ dollar investment** un investissement de plusieurs millions de dollars

multimillionaire [ˌmʌltɪˌmɪljə'nɛə'] N multimillionnaire mf, multimilliardaire mf

multi-nation ['mʌltɪ'neɪʃən] ADJ [treaty, agreement] multinational

multinational [ˌmʌltɪ'næʃənl] [1] N multinationale f [2] ADJ multinational

multipack ['mʌltɪpæk] N pack m

multiparous [mʌl'tɪpərəs] ADJ multipare

multipartite [ˌmʌltɪ'pɑːtaɪt] ADJ divisé en plusieurs parties

multiparty [ˌmʌltɪ'pɑːtɪ] ADJ (Pol) pluripartite

multiple ['mʌltɪpl] [1] N (Math) multiple m; **low~** [2] ADJ multiple; (Aut) **~ crash** or **pileup** carambolage m [3] COMP ► **multiple choice** N (Scol, Univ) (also **~-choice exam** or **test**) QCM m, questionnaire m à choix multiple; (also **~-choice question**) question f à choix multiple ► **multiple-entry visa** N visa autorisant à entrer plusieurs fois dans un pays ► **multiple exposure** N (Phot) exposition f multiple ► **multiple ownership** N multipropriété f ► **multiple personality** N (Psych) dédoublement m de la personnalité ► **multiple-risk insurance** N assurance f multirisque ► **multiple sclerosis** N (Med) sclérose f en plaques ► **multiple store** N (Brit) grand magasin m à succursales multiples

multiplex ['mʌltɪpleks] [1] ADJ multiplex; **~ cinema** complexe m multisalle [2] N multiplex m; (Cine) multisalle m [3] VT communiquer en multiplex

multiplexer ['mʌltɪpleksə'] N multiplexeur m

multiplexing ['mʌltɪpleksɪŋ] N multiplexage m

multipliable ['mʌltɪˌplaɪəbl], **multiplicable** ['mʌltɪˌplɪkəbl] ADJ multipliable

multiplicand [ˌmʌltɪplɪ'kænd] N multiplicande m

multiplication [ˌmʌltɪplɪ'keɪʃən] [1] N multiplication f [2] COMP ► **multiplication sign** N signe m de multiplication ► **multiplication tables** NPL tables fpl de multiplication

multiplicative ['mʌltɪplɪˌkeɪtɪv] ADJ (Math, Gram) multiplicatif

multiplicity [ˌmʌltɪ'plɪsɪtɪ] N multiplicité f

multiplier ['mʌltɪplaɪə'] [1] N multiplicateur m [2] COMP ► **multiplier effect** N effet m multiplicateur

multiply ['mʌltɪplaɪ] [1] VT multiplier (**by** par) [2] VI se multiplier

multiplying ['mʌltɪplaɪɪŋ] ADJ multiplicateur (-trice f), multiplicatif

multipolar ['mʌltɪ'pəʊlə'] ADJ multipolaire

multiprocessing [ˌmʌltɪ'prəʊsesɪŋ] N (Comput) multitraitement m

multiprocessor [ˌmʌltɪ'prəʊsesə'] N (Comput) multiprocesseur m

multiprogramming [ˌmʌltɪ'prəʊgræmɪŋ] N (Comput) multiprogrammation f

multipurpose ['mʌltɪ'pɜːpəs] [1] ADJ polyvalent, à usages multiples [2] COMP ► **multipurpose vehicle** N (= off-roader) tout-terrain m; (= people-carrier) monospace m

multiracial [ˌmʌltɪˈreɪʃəl] ADJ multiracial

multirisk [ˌmʌltɪˈrɪsk] ADJ (*Insurance*) multirisque

multisensory [ˌmʌltɪˈsensərɪ] ADJ multisensoriel

multistandard [ˌmʌltɪˈstændəd] ADJ (*TV*) [*set, video etc*] multistandard *inv*

multistorey [ˌmʌltɪˈstɔːrɪ], **multistoreyed**, **multistoried** (*US*) [ˌmʌltɪˈstɔːrɪd] ADJ à étages; **~ car park** parking *m* à étages *or* à niveaux multiples

multitasking [ˌmʌltɪˈtɑːskɪŋ] N (*Comput*) traitement *m* multitâche

multitrack [ˌmʌltɪˈtræk] ADJ à plusieurs pistes

multitude [ˈmʌltɪtjuːd] N multitude *f*; **the ~** la multitude, la foule; **for a ~ of reasons** pour une multitude *or* une foule de raisons; **that covers** *or* **hides a ~ of sins** c'est un véritable cache-misère

multitudinous [ˌmʌltɪˈtjuːdɪnəs] ADJ innombrable

multiuser [ˌmʌltɪˈjuːzəʳ] ADJ (*Comput*) **~ system** configuration *f* multiposte

multivalence [ˌmʌltɪˈveɪləns] N polyvalence *f*

multivalent [ˌmʌltɪˈveɪlənt] ADJ polyvalent

multivitamin [ˌmʌltɪˈvɪtəmɪn] N complexe *m* vitaminé; **~ tablet** comprimé *m* de multivitamines

mum¹* [mʌm] N (*Brit* = *mother*) maman *f*

mum² [mʌm] ADJ **to keep ~ (about sth)** ne pas piper mot (de qch), ne pas souffler mot (de qch); **~'s the word!** motus!, bouche cousue!

mum³* [mʌm] N (ABBR = **chrysanthemum**) **~s** chrysanthèmes *mpl*

mumble [ˈmʌmbl] **1** VI marmotter; **stop mumbling!** arrête de marmotter *or* de parler entre tes dents! **2** VT marmonner, marmotter; **to ~ one's words** manger ses mots; **to ~ an answer** répondre entre ses dents, marmonner une réponse **3** N marmonnement *m*, marmottement *m*; **... he said in a ~** ... dit-il entre ses dents

mumbo jumbo [ˌmʌmbəʊˈdʒʌmbəʊ] N (= *nonsense*) baragouin* *m*, charabia* *m*; (= *pretentious words*) jargon *m* obscur; (= *pretentious ceremony etc*) tralala* *m*, salamalecs* *mpl*

mummer [ˈmʌməʳ] N (*Theat*) mime *mf*

mummery [ˈmʌmərɪ] N (*Theat, fig*) momerie *f*

mummification [ˌmʌmɪfɪˈkeɪʃən] N momification *f*

mummify [ˈmʌmɪfaɪ] VT momifier

mummy¹ [ˈmʌmɪ] N (= *embalmed*) momie *f*

mummy²* [ˈmʌmɪ] N (*Brit* = *mother*) maman *f*; (*pej*) **~'s boy** fils *m* à sa maman*

mump [mʌmp] VI grogner, grommeler

mumps [mʌmps] N (*NonC*) oreillons *mpl*

munch [mʌntʃ] VTI (*gen*) croquer; (= *chew noisily*) mastiquer bruyamment; **to ~ (away) on** *or* **at sth** dévorer qch à belles dents

Münchhausen's syndrome [ˌmʌntʃaʊzənzˈsɪndrəʊm] N (*Med*) syndrome *m* de Münchhausen

munchies [ˈmʌntʃɪz] NPL **a** (= *snack*) quelque chose à grignoter **b to have the ~** (= *be hungry*) avoir un creux

mundane [ˌmʌnˈdeɪn] ADJ [*matter, issue, problem, object*] banal; [*task*] courant; [*explanation, concern*] terre-à-terre; **on a more ~ level** au niveau pratique

mung bean [ˈmʌŋbiːn] N haricot *m* mung

Munich [ˈmjuːnɪk] N Munich

municipal [mjuːˈnɪsɪpəl] **1** ADJ municipal **2** COMP ► **municipal court** N (*US Jur*) tribunal local de première instance

municipality [mjuːˌnɪsɪˈpælɪtɪ] N municipalité *f*

munificence [mjuːˈnɪfɪsns] N munificence *f*

munificent [mjuːˈnɪfɪsnt] ADJ (*frm*) munificent (*liter*)

muniments [ˈmjuːnɪmənts] NPL (*Jur*) titres *mpl* (*concernant la propriété d'un bien-fonds*)

munitions [mjuːˈnɪʃənz] **1** NPL munitions *fpl* **2** COMP ► **munitions dump** N dépôt *m* de munitions ► **munitions factory** N fabrique *f* de munitions

muon [ˈmjuːɒn] N (*Phys*) muon *m*

mural [ˈmjʊərəl] **1** ADJ mural **2** N peinture *f* murale; (*in Modern Art*) mural *m*

murder [ˈmɜːdəʳ] **1** N **a** (*gen*) meurtre *m*; (*Jur*) meurtre *m*; (*premeditated*) assassinat *m*; **four ~s in one week** quatre meurtres en une semaine; **~!** au meurtre!, à l'assassin! ▪ (*PROV*) **~ will out** tôt ou tard la vérité se fait jour; (*fig*) **he was screaming** *or* **shouting blue ~*** il criait comme un putois *or* comme si on l'écorchait; (*fig*) **she lets the children get away with ~*** elle passe tout aux enfants; (*fig*) **they get away with ~*** ils peuvent tout se permettre **b** (* *fig*) **the noise/heat in here is ~** le bruit/la chaleur ici est infernal(e); **the exam was ~** l'examen était épouvantable *or* coton*; **did you have a good holiday? — no, it was ~** avez-vous passé de bonnes vacances? — non, c'était l'enfer; **the roads were ~** les routes étaient un cauchemar **2** VT [+ *person*] assassiner; (*fig*) [+ *song, music, language*] massacrer; [+ *opponent, team*] battre à plates coutures, écraser; **the ~ed man** (*or* **woman** *etc*) la victime **3** COMP ► **murder case** N (*Jur*) procès *m* pour meurtre; (*Police*) affaire *f* de meurtre ► **murder hunt** N chasse *f* à l'homme pour retrouver le (*or* un) meurtrier ► **Murder Squad** N (*Police*) ≈ brigade *f* criminelle (de la police judiciaire) ► **murder trial** N ≈ procès *m* pour homicide ► **murder weapon** N arme *f* du crime

murderer [ˈmɜːdərəʳ] N meurtrier *m*, assassin *m*

murderess [ˈmɜːdərɪs] N meurtrière *f*

murderous [ˈmɜːdərəs] ADJ **a** (= *homicidal*) meurtrier; **a ~-looking individual** un individu à tête d'assassin **b** (* = *awful*) [*heat*] effroyable

murk [mɜːk], **murkiness** [ˈmɜːkɪnɪs] N obscurité *f*

murky [ˈmɜːkɪ] ADJ [*room, street, day, sky*] sombre; [*fog, night, darkness*] épais (épaisse *f*); [*water, depths*] trouble; [*colour*] terne, terreux; **~ brown/green** brun *inv*/vert *inv* sale; **the room was ~ with smoke** la pièce était obscurcie par la fumée; **his ~ past** son passé trouble; **the ~ world of the arms trade** le monde trouble des trafiquants d'armes

murmur [ˈmɜːməʳ] **1** N **a** [*of voice(s)*] murmure *m*; [*of bees, traffic etc*] bourdonnement *m*; (*fig* = *protest*) murmure *m*; **there wasn't a ~ in the classroom** il n'y avait pas un murmure dans la classe; **to speak in a ~** parler à voix basse, chuchoter; **a ~ of conversation** un bourdonnement de voix; **there were ~s of disagreement** il y eut des murmures de désapprobation; **he agreed without a ~** il accepta sans murmure **b** (*Med*) **a heart ~** un souffle au cœur **2** VT murmurer **3** VI [*person, stream*] murmurer; (= *complain*) murmurer (**against, about** contre)

murmuring [ˈmɜːmərɪŋ] **1** N [*of people, stream*] (*also fig*) [*of protests*] murmures *mpl*; [*of bees etc*] bourdonnement *m* **2** ADJ [*stream*] murmurant, qui murmure

Murphy [ˈmɜːfɪ] **1** N (*US, Ir** = *potato*) pomme *f* de terre **2** COMP ► **Murphy bed** N (*US*) lit *m* escamotable ► **Murphy's law** N (*hum*) loi *f* de l'emmerdement* maximum

MusBac N (ABBR = **Bachelor of Music**) diplôme *m* d'études musicales

muscat [ˈmʌskət] N **a** (*also* **~ grape**) (raisin *m*) muscat *m* **b** (= *wine*) (vin *m*) muscat *m*

muscatel [ˌmʌskəˈtel] N (= *grape, wine*) muscat *m*

muscle [ˈmʌsl] **1** N **a** (*Anat*) muscle *m*; (*fig*) **he didn't move a ~** il n'a pas levé *or* remué le petit doigt (**to help** *etc* pour aider *etc*); (= *didn't flinch*) il n'a pas bronché, il n'a pas sourcillé; (*fig* = *energy*) **put some ~ into it*** vas-y avec un peu plus de nerf* *or* de force **b** (= *power*) pouvoir *m* effectif, impact *m*; **political ~** pouvoir *m* politique effectif, moyens *mpl* politiques; **this union hasn't much ~** ce syndicat n'a pas beaucoup d'impact *or* de poids **2** COMP ► **muscle-bound** ADJ (*lit*) aux muscles hypertrophiés

► **muscle in*** VI **a** (*Brit*: *into group etc*) intervenir, s'immiscer; **to ~ (one's way) in on a group/a discussion** essayer de s'imposer dans un groupe/une discussion; **stop muscling in!** occupe-toi de tes oignons!* **b** (*US* = *force one's way inside*) entrer violemment

muscleman [ˈmʌslmæn] N (*pl* **-men**) (= *strong man*) hercule *m*; (= *gangster etc*) homme *m* de main, sbire *m*

muscl(e)y [ˈmʌsəlɪ] ADJ musclé

Muscovite [ˈmʌskəvaɪt] **1** ADJ moscovite **2** N Moscovite *mf*

muscular [ˈmʌskjʊləʳ] **1** ADJ **a** (= *brawny*) musclé; **to be of ~ build** être musclé **b** (*Med, Physiol*) musculaire **2** COMP ► **muscular dystrophy** N dystrophie *f* musculaire, myopathie *f* musculaire progressive

musculature [ˈmʌskjʊlətjʊəʳ] N musculature *f*

MusDoc N (ABBR = **Doctor of Music**) ≈ doctorat *m* de musique

muse [mjuːz] **1** VI méditer (**on, about, over** sur), songer, réfléchir (**on, about, over** à) **2** VT **"they might accept," he ~d** « il se pourrait qu'ils acceptent » dit-il d'un ton songeur; (= *thought*) « il se pourrait qu'ils acceptent » songeait-il **3** N (*Myth, fig: also* **Muse**) muse *f*

museum [mjuːˈzɪəm] **1** N musée *m* **2** COMP ► **museum piece** N (*lit, fig*) pièce *f* de musée

mush¹ [mʌʃ] N (*NonC*) bouillie *f*; (*fig*) sentimentalité *f* de guimauve *or* à l'eau de rose

mush²* [mʌʃ] N (*Brit*) **a** (= *face*) tronche* *f* **b** (= *person*) hey, **~!** hé, machin!*

mushroom [ˈmʌʃrʊm] **1** N champignon *m* (comestible); **to spring up** *or* **sprout like ~s** pousser comme des champignons **2** VI **a** (= *grow quickly*) [*town*] pousser comme un champignon; [*sales, debts, investment*] augmenter rapidement; [*market*] connaître une expansion rapide; [*population*] connaître une croissance rapide; **the village ~ed into a town** le village est rapidement devenu ville; **the dispute ~ed into a serious political crisis** le contentieux a pris de l'ampleur et s'est vite transformé en une grave crise politique; **unemployment has ~ed** le chômage monte en flèche; **his debts have ~ed into thousands of dollars** ses dettes se montent maintenant à des milliers de dollars **b** (= *appear, spring up*) apparaître un peu partout; (= *multiply*) proliférer, se multiplier; **shops ~ed all over the place** des magasins ont proliféré un peu partout **c** (= *gather mushrooms*) **to go ~ing** aller aux champignons **3** COMP [*soup, omelette*] aux champignons; [*flavour*] de champignons; (= *colour*) [*carpet etc*] beige rosé *inv* ► **mushroom cloud** N champignon *m* atomique ► **mushroom growth** N poussée *f* soudaine ► **mushroom town** N ville *f* champignon *inv*

mushrooming [ˈmʌʃrʊmɪŋ] **1** N **a** (= *picking mushrooms*) cueillette *f* des champignons → **mushroom 2c b** (*fig* = *growth*) [*of town etc*] poussée *f* rapide; [*of sales, debts, investment*] montée *f* en flèche; [*of market*] expansion *f* or essor *m* rapide; (= *proliferation*) **the ~ of new shopping centres in the suburbs** la prolifération des centres commerciaux en périphérie des villes [2] ADJ (= *fast-growing*) [*unemployment*] qui monte en flèche; [*problem*] de plus en plus présent; [*number*] croissant; [*growth*] très rapide; [*population*] qui connaît une croissance rapide

mushy ['mʌʃɪ] [1] ADJ [a] (= *soft*) [*vegetables, fish*] en bouillie; [*fruit*] blet; [*snow*] à demi fondu; **to become** or **get** or **go** ~ se ramollir [b] (*pej* = *sentimental*) [*film, book, sentimentality*] à l'eau de rose [2] COMP ► **mushy peas** NPL (*Brit*) purée f de petits pois

music ['mjuːzɪk] [1] N (*all senses*) musique f; **to set to** ~ mettre en musique; (*fig*) **it was** ~ **to his ears** c'était doux à son oreille; (*Univ*) **the Faculty of Music** la faculté de musique → **ear¹, face, pop²** [2] COMP [*teacher, lesson, exam*] de musique ► **music box** N boîte f à musique ► **music case** N porte-musique m inv ► **music centre** N (= *equipment*) chaîne f (stéréo); (= *shop*) magasin m de hi-fi ► **music critic** N (*Press*) critique m musical ► **music director** N directeur m musical ► **music festival** N festival m de musique ► **music hall** (*Brit*) N music-hall m ♦ ADJ de music-hall ► **music lover** N mélomane mf ► **music paper** N papier m à musique ► **music stand** N pupitre m à musique ► **music stool** N tabouret m (de musicien) ► **music video** N (*for single*) vidéoclip m; (*for album*) série f de vidéoclips; (*for concert*) concert m en vidéo

musical ['mjuːzɪkəl] [1] ADJ (*lit, fig*) [*voice, sound, criticism, studies*] musical; [*family, person*] musicien; **he comes from a** ~ **family** ils sont très musiciens dans sa famille; **she's very** ~ (= *gifted*) elle est musicienne, elle est très douée pour la musique; (= *fond of it*) elle est mélomane [2] N (*Cine, Theat*) comédie f musicale [3] COMP ► **musical box** N boîte f à musique ► **musical chairs** NPL chaises fpl musicales; (*fig*) **they were playing at** ~ **chairs** ils changeaient tout le temps de place ► **musical comedy** N comédie f musicale, opérette f ► **musical director** N directeur m musical ► **musical evening** N soirée f musicale ► **musical instrument** N instrument m de musique

musically ['mjuːzɪkəlɪ] ADV musicalement; [*develop*] du point de vue musical; (*melodiously*) **she laughed** ~ elle a eu un rire mélodieux; **I'm** ~ **illiterate** j'ai pris des leçons de musique; **there's a lot going on** ~ **in London** il se passe beaucoup de choses d'un point de vue musical à Londres; ~ (**speaking**) **this piece is beautiful** musicalement parlant, ce morceau est magnifique

musician [mjuː'zɪʃən] N musicien(ne) m(f)

musicianship [mjuː'zɪʃənʃɪp] N maestria f (de musicien), sens m de la musique

musicologist [ˌmjuːzɪ'kɒlədʒɪst] N musicologue mf

musicology [ˌmjuːzɪ'kɒlədʒɪ] N musicologie f

musing ['mjuːzɪŋ] [1] ADJ songeur, pensif [2] N songerie f; **idle ~s** rêvasseries fpl

musingly ['mjuːzɪŋlɪ] ADV d'un air songeur, pensivement

musk [mʌsk] [1] N musc m [2] COMP ► **musk ox** N bœuf m musqué ► **musk rose** N rose f muscade

muskeg ['mʌskeɡ] N (*US* = *bog*) tourbière f

musket ['mʌskɪt] N mousquet m

musketeer [ˌmʌskɪ'tɪəʳ] N mousquetaire m; **the Three Musketeers** les Trois Mousquetaires

musketry ['mʌskɪtrɪ] [1] N tir m (au fusil *etc*) [2] COMP [*range, training*] de tir (au fusil *etc*)

muskmelon ['mʌskmelən] N cantaloup m

muskrat ['mʌskræt] N rat m musqué, ondatra m

musky ['mʌskɪ] ADJ musqué

Muslim ['mʊzlɪm] [1] N (*pl* **Muslims** or **Muslim**) musulman(e) m(f) → **black** [2] ADJ musulman

muslin ['mʌzlɪn] [1] N mousseline f [2] COMP de or en mousseline

musquash ['mʌskwɒʃ] [1] N (= *animal*) rat m musqué, ondatra m; (= *fur*) rat m d'Amérique, ondatra m [2] COMP [*coat*] d'ondatra

muss* [mʌs] VT (*also* ~ **up**) [+ *dress, clothes*] chiffonner, froisser; **to** ~ **sb's hair** décoiffer qn

mussel ['mʌsl] N moule f; ~ **bed** parc m à moules, moulière f

▼ **must¹** [mʌst] [1] MODAL AUX VB [a] (*indicating obligation*) **you** ~ **leave now** vous devez partir or il faut que vous partiez (*subj*) maintenant; (*on notice*) **"the windows** ~ **not be opened"** « défense d'ouvrir les fenêtres »; **I (absolutely)** ~ **see him!** il faut absolument que je le voie!; **you mustn't touch it** il ne faut pas or tu ne dois pas y toucher, c'est défendu d'y toucher; **what** ~ **we do now?** que faut-il or que devons-nous faire à présent?; **why** ~ **you always be so rude?** pourquoi faut-il toujours que tu sois si grossier?; (*frm*) **you** ~ **know that ...** il faut que vous sachiez que ...; **I** ~ **ask you not to touch that** je dois vous prier or je vous prie de ne pas toucher à cela; (*Comm: in letters*) **we** ~ **ask you to send us ...** nous nous trouvons dans l'obligation de vous demander de nous envoyer ...; **if you** ~ **leave then go at once** s'il faut vraiment que vous partiez (*subj*), partez tout de suite; (**well**), **if I** ~ eh bien, s'il le faut vraiment; **sit down if you** ~ asseyez-vous si c'est indispensable or si vous y tenez; **if you** ~ **know ...** si tu tiens vraiment à le savoir ..., si tu veux vraiment le savoir ...; **I** ~ **away ††** je dois partir, il faut que je parte; **I** ~ **say, he's very irritating** il n'y a pas à dire or franchement il est très agaçant; **you look well, I** ~ **say!** je dois dire que or vraiment tu as très bonne mine!; (*iro*) **that's brilliant, I** ~ **say!** pour être réussi, c'est réussi (je dois dire)! (*iro*); **well I** ~ **say!*** eh bien vraiment!, ça alors!*; **what** ~ **he do but bang the door just when ...** ◊ **he** ~ **bang the door just when ...** il a fallu qu'il claque (*subj*) la porte juste au moment où ...

[b] (*indicating certainty*) **he** ~ **be wrong** il doit se tromper, il se trompe certainement; **I realized he** ~ **be wrong** j'ai compris qu'il devait se tromper or qu'il se trompait certainement; **he** ~ **be clever, mustn't he?** il doit être intelligent, n'est-ce pas?, il doit être drôlement intelligent; **he** ~ **be mad!** il est (complètement) fou!; **is he mad? — he** ~ **be!** est-ce qu'il est fou? — on pourrait le croire!; **I** ~ **have made a mistake** j'ai dû me tromper; **you** ~ **be joking!** vous plaisantez!; **you** ~ **know my aunt** vous devez connaître ma tante, vous connaissez sans doute ma tante; **that** ~ **be Paul** ça doit être Paul

[2] N* chose f indispensable, must* m; **a** ~ **for all housewives!** un must* pour toutes les ménagères!, indispensable pour toutes les ménagères!; **this concert is a** ~ **for all Barry Manilow fans** ce concert est un must* pour tous les fans de Barry Manilow; **this book is a** ~ c'est un livre à lire absolument; **a car is a** ~ **in the country** une voiture est absolument indispensable à la campagne

must² [mʌst] N [*of fruit*] moût m

must-* [mʌst] PREF **a ~see movie** un film à ne pas manquer; **a ~read** un livre à lire absolument; **the ~have fashion item of the season** le must* de la saison; **it was a ~win match** c'était un match qu'ils devaient gagner

mustache ['mʌstæʃ] N (*US*) = **moustache**

mustang ['mʌstæŋ] N mustang m

mustard ['mʌstəd] [1] N (*Bot, Culin*) moutarde f; (*fig*) **to cut the ~** faire le poids, être à la hauteur → **keen¹** [2] ADJ moutarde [3] COMP ► **mustard and cress** N salade de cresson alénois et de pousses de moutarde blanche ► **mustard bath** N bain m sinapisé or à la moutarde ► **mustard gas** N ypérite f, gaz m

moutarde ► **mustard plaster** N sinapisme m, cataplasme m sinapisé ► **mustard pot** N moutardier m, pot m à moutarde ► **mustard powder** N farine f de moutarde

muster ['mʌstəʳ] [1] N (= *gathering*) assemblée f; (*Mil, Naut: also* ~ **roll**) rassemblement m; (= *roll-call*) appel m; (*fig: gen*) **to pass** ~ (pouvoir) passer, être acceptable [2] VT [a] (= *assemble, collect*) [+ *helpers, number, sum*] réunir; (*also* ~ **up**) [+ *strength, courage, energy*] rassembler; **I couldn't** ~ **(up) enough energy to protest** je n'ai pas trouvé l'énergie de protester; **they could only** ~ **five volunteers** ils n'ont trouvé que cinq volontaires; **the club can only** ~ **20 members** le club ne compte que 20 membres [b] (= *call roll of*) battre le rappel de [3] VI (= *gather, assemble*) se réunir, se rassembler [4] COMP ► **muster station** N (*on ship*) point m de rassemblement

mustiness ['mʌstɪnɪs] N (= *stale taste*) goût m de moisi; (= *stale smell*) odeur f de renfermé; (= *damp smell*) odeur f de moisi

mustn't ['mʌsnt] = **must not**; → **must**

musty ['mʌstɪ] ADJ [a] [*taste*] de moisi; [*smell*] (= *stale*) de renfermé; (= *damp*) de moisi; [*book, clothes*] moisi; **to grow** ~ moisir; **to smell** ~ [*room*] sentir le renfermé; [*book, clothes*] avoir une odeur de moisi [b] (= *hackneyed*) [*ideas, methods*] suranné

mutability [ˌmjuːtə'bɪlɪtɪ] N mutabilité f

mutable ['mjuːtəbl] ADJ sujet à mutation; [*virus, gene*] mutable; (*Ling*) sujet à la mutation

mutagen ['mjuːtədʒən] N mutagène m

mutagenic [ˌmjuːtə'dʒenɪk] ADJ mutagène

mutant ['mjuːtənt] ADJ, N mutant m

mutate [mjuː'teɪt] [1] VI [a] (*lit* = *undergo mutation*) subir une mutation [b] (*fig* = *change*) se transformer (**into sth** en qch) [2] VT faire subir une mutation à

mutation [mjuː'teɪʃən] N (*gen, Ling*) mutation f

mutatis mutandis [muː'tɑːtɪsmuː'tændɪs] ADV mutatis mutandis

mute [mjuːt] [1] ADJ [a] [*person, reproach*] muet; [*consent*] tacite; ~ **with admiration** ◊ **in** ~ **admiration** muet d'admiration; **he turned to her in** ~ **appeal** il lui lança un regard suppliant; **to be** or **bear** ~ **testimony** or **witness to sth** être un témoin silencieux or muet de qch [b] (*Ling*) **H** ~ **H** muet; (*Ling*) ~ **"e"** « e » muet [2] N [a] (*Med†* = *deaf person*) muet(te) m(f) → **deaf** [b] (*Mus*) sourdine f [3] VT [a] (*Mus*) [+ *trumpet, violin etc*] mettre la sourdine à [b] [+ *sound*] assourdir, rendre moins sonore; [+ *colour*] adoucir, atténuer [c] [+ *feelings, emotions, enthusiasm*] tempérer, modérer; **to** ~ **one's criticism of sth** tempérer or modérer ses critiques de qch [4] COMP ► **mute swan** N cygne m tuberculé or muet

muted ['mjuːtɪd] ADJ [*voice, sound*] sourd, assourdi; [*colour*] sourd; (*Mus*) [*violin*] en sourdine; [*criticism, protest, feelings, emotions, enthusiasm*] tempéré

mutilate ['mjuːtɪleɪt] VT [+ *person, limb*] mutiler, estropier; [+ *object*] mutiler, dégrader; (*fig*) [+ *text*] mutiler, tronquer

mutilation [ˌmjuːtɪ'leɪʃən] N mutilation f

mutineer [ˌmjuːtɪ'nɪəʳ] N (*Mil, Naut*) mutiné m, mutin m

mutinous ['mjuːtɪnəs] ADJ [*crew, soldiers*] prêt à se mutiner, mutin; [*workers, prisoners*] rebelle; [*feelings*] de rébellion; [*attitude, mood*] rebelle; [*look*] de défi; **the children were already fairly** ~ les enfants regimbaient déjà

mutiny ['mjuːtɪnɪ] [1] N (*Mil, Naut*) mutinerie f; (*fig*) révolte f [2] VI se mutiner; (*fig*) se révolter

mutt‡ [mʌt] N [a] (= *fool*) corniaud* m, crétin(e)* m(f) [b] (= *dog*) clebs* m, corniaud m

mutter ['mʌtəʳ] [1] N marmonnement m; (= *grumbling*) grommellement m [2] VT [+ *word,* *excuse, threat, prayer*] marmonner, marmotter; [+ *curses, obscenities*] marmonner, grommeler; **"no", he ~ed** « non » marmonna-t-il *or* dit-il entre ses dents; **he ~ed something to himself** il a marmonné *or* marmotté quelque chose entre ses dents; **a ~ed conversation** une conversation à voix basse **3** VI marmonner, murmurer; (= *grumble*) grommeler, grogner; **to ~ to oneself** (*talking*) marmonner *or* marmotter entre ses dents; (*complaining*) grommeler entre ses dents; **she was ~ing about the bad weather** elle maugréait contre le mauvais temps; **to ~ about doing sth** parler de faire qch; **the man who dared to say what others only ~ed about** l'homme qui osait dire tout haut ce que les autres pensaient tout bas

muttering ['mʌtərɪŋ] N grommellement *m*

mutton ['mʌtn] **1** N (*Culin*) mouton *m*; **leg of ~** gigot *m*; **shoulder of ~** épaule *f* de mouton; (*fig, hum*) **she's ~ dressed (up) as lamb*** elle s'habille trop jeune pour son âge.→ **dead, leg** **2** COMP ► **mutton chop** N (*Culin*) côtelette *f* de mouton ► **mutton chops*** NPL (= *whiskers*) favoris *mpl* (*bien fournis*), rouflaquettes *fpl*

muttonhead* ['mʌtnhed] N cornichon* *m*

mutual ['mjuːtjʊəl] **1** ADJ **a** (= *reciprocal*) [*support, hatred, respect, need, destruction*] mutuel; **~ aid** entraide *f*, aide *f* mutuelle; **I didn't like him and the feeling was ~** je ne l'aimais pas et c'était réciproque **b** (= *common*) [*interest, friend*] commun; **it is to our ~ benefit** *or* **advantage** c'est dans notre intérêt commun; **by ~ consent** par consentement mutuel **2** COMP ► **mutual assured destruction** N (*US Mil*) destruction *f* mutuelle assurée ► **mutual fund (company)** N (*US*) société *f* d'investissement (*de type SICAV*) ► **mutual insurance (company)** N mutuelle *f* ► **mutual masturbation** N masturbation *f* mutuelle ► **mutual society** N mutuelle *f*

mutuality [,mjuːtjʊˈælɪtɪ] N mutualité *f*

mutually ['mjuːtjʊəlɪ] **1** ADV [*convenient, acceptable, beneficial*] mutuellement; **a ~ agreed goal** un objectif convenu; **~ contradictory** contradictoire; **the two things are not ~ exclusive** ces deux choses ne sont pas incompatibles **2** COMP ► **mutually assured destruction** N = mutual assured destruction; → **mutual**

Muzak® ['mjuːzæk] N musique *f* (d'ambiance) enregistrée

muzzle ['mʌzl] **1** N **a** [*of dog, fox etc*] museau *m*; [*of gun*] bouche *f*, gueule *f* **b** (= *anti-biting device*) muselière *f*; (*fig*) muselière *f*, bâillon *m* **2** VT [+ *dog*] museler; (*fig*) museler, bâillonner **3** COMP ► **muzzle loader** N arme *f* qu'on charge par le canon ► **muzzle velocity** N vitesse *f* initiale

muzzy ['mʌzɪ] ADJ (*Brit*) **a** (= *groggy, confused*) [*brain*] brouillé; [*feeling*] de confusion; [*ideas*] confus, nébuleux; **to be** *or* **feel ~** [*person*] avoir le cerveau brouillé **b** (= *blurred*) [*TV picture*] flou; [*outline*] estompé, flou

MVP N (*US Sport*) (ABBR = **most valuable player**) (= *person*) meilleur joueur *m*, meilleure joueuse *f*; (= *title*) titre *m* de meilleur joueur

MW N **a** (*Rad*) (ABBR = **medium wave**) PO **b** (*Elec*) (ABBR = **megawatt(s)**) MW

my [maɪ] **1** POSS ADJ mon, ma, mes; **my book** mon livre; **my table** ma table; **my friend** mon ami(e); **my clothes** mes vêtements; **MY book** mon livre à moi; **I've broken my leg** je me suis cassé la jambe **2** EXCL **(oh) my!*** ◊ **my, my!*** ça, par exemple!

myalgia [maɪˈældʒə] N myalgie *f*

myalgic encephalomyelitis [maɪˈældʒɪken,sefələʊmaɪəˈlaɪtɪs] N (*Med*) encéphalomyélite *f* myalgique

Myanmar ['maɪənmɑːr] N le Myanmar

mycology [maɪˈkɒlədʒɪ] N mycologie *f*

mycosis [maɪˈkəʊsɪs] N mycose *f*

mynah ['maɪnə] N (*also* **~ bird**) mainate *m*

myocardial infarction ['maɪəʊ,kɑːdɪəlɪn'fɑːkʃən] N (*Med*) infarctus *m* du myocarde

myopia [maɪˈəʊpɪə] N myopie *f*

myopic [maɪˈɒpɪk] ADJ (*Opt*) myope; (*fig*) [*attitude*] peu prévoyant, à courte vue; **this is a somewhat ~ view** c'est une vision à court terme

myriad ['mɪrɪəd] **1** N myriade *f* **2** ADJ (*liter*) innombrable, sans nombre

myrmidon ['mɜːmɪdən] N (*pej hum*) sbire *m*

myrrh [mɜːr] N myrrhe *f*

myrtle ['mɜːtl] N myrte *m*

myself [maɪˈself] PERS PRON (*reflexive: direct and indirect*) me; (*emphatic*) moi-même; (*after prep*) moi; **I've hurt ~** je me suis blessé; **I said to ~** je me suis dit; **I spoke to him ~** je lui ai parlé moi-même; **people like ~** des gens comme moi; **I've kept one for ~** j'en ai gardé un pour moi; **he asked me for a photo of ~** il m'a demandé une photo de moi; **I told him ~** je le lui ai dit moi-même; **all by ~** tout seul; **I'm not ~ today** je ne suis pas dans mon assiette aujourd'hui

mysterious [mɪsˈtɪərɪəs] ADJ [*person, object, disappearance, illness, power*] mystérieux; [*smile*] mystérieux, énigmatique; **why are you being so ~?** pourquoi tous ces mystères?; **God moves in ~ ways** les voies du Seigneur sont impénétrables

mysteriously [mɪsˈtɪərɪəslɪ] ADV mystérieusement

mystery ['mɪstərɪ] **1** N **a** (*gen, Rel*) mystère *m*; **there's no ~ about it** ça n'a rien de mystérieux; **it's a ~ to me how he did it** je n'arrive pas à comprendre comment il l'a fait; **to make a great ~ of sth** faire grand mystère de qch **b** (*Theat: also ~ play*) mystère *m* **c** (*Literat: also ~ story*) roman *m* à énigmes **2** COMP [*ship, man*] mystérieux ► **mystery play** N (*Theat*) mystère *m* ► **mystery tour** N (*in coach etc*) voyage *m* surprise (*dont on ne connaît pas la destination*)

mystic ['mɪstɪk] **1** ADJ (*Rel*) mystique; [*power*] occulte; [*rite*] ésotérique; [*truth*] surnaturel; [*formula*] magique **2** N mystique *mf*

mystical ['mɪstɪkəl] ADJ mystique

mysticism ['mɪstɪsɪzəm] N mysticisme *m*

mystification [,mɪstɪfɪˈkeɪʃən] N **a** (= *bewilderment*) perplexité *f* **b** [*of issue, subject*] mystification *f*; **why all the ~?** pourquoi tout ce mystère?

mystify ['mɪstɪfaɪ] VT rendre *or* laisser perplexe; (= *deliberately deceive*) mystifier

mystique [mɪsˈtiːk] N mystique *f*

myth [mɪθ] N (*lit, fig*) mythe *m*

mythic ['mɪθɪk] ADJ (*Myth, fig*) [*figure, symbol, status*] mythique; [*proportions*] fabuleux

mythical ['mɪθɪkəl] ADJ (*Myth*) [*beast, creature, figure*] mythique; (= *unreal*) [*world*] fictif, mythique

mythological [,mɪθəˈlɒdʒɪkəl] ADJ mythologique

mythology [mɪˈθɒlədʒɪ] N mythologie *f*

myxomatosis [,mɪksəʊməˈtəʊsɪs] N myxomatose *f*

N

N, n [en] N [a] (= letter) N, n m; **N for Nancy** ≈ N comme Noémie [b] (Math) **to the nth (power)** à la puissance n; (fig) **to the nth degree** à la puissance mille; **I told him for the nth time*** **to stop talking** je lui ai dit pour la énième fois de se taire; **there are n ways of doing it** il y a mille or des tas de* façons de le faire [c] (ABBR = **north**) N [d] (Elec) (ABBR = **neutral**) N

'n': [ən] CONJ = **and**

n/a [a] (ABBR = **not applicable**) ne s'applique pas [b] (Banking) (ABBR = **no account**) pas de compte

NAACP [enei,eisi:'pi:] N (US) (ABBR = **National Association for the Advancement of Colored People**) défense des droits civiques des Noirs

NAAFI ['næfi] N (Brit Mil) (ABBR = **Navy, Army and Air Force Institute**) coopérative f militaire

nab* [næb] VT [a] (= catch in wrongdoing) pincer*, choper*; [b] (= catch to speak to etc) attraper, coincer* [c] (= take) [+ sb's pen, chair etc] accaparer

nabob ['neɪbɒb] N (lit, fig) nabab m

nacelle [næ'sel] N (Aviat) nacelle f

nacho ['nɑ:tʃəʊ] N (pl **nachos**) (Culin) nacho m

nacre ['neɪkə] N nacre f

nacred ['neɪkəd], **nacreous** ['neɪkrɪəs] ADJ nacré

Naderism ['neɪdərɪzəm] N consumérisme m, défense f du consommateur

nadir ['neɪdɪə] N (Astron) nadir m; (fig) point m le plus bas; **in the ~ of despair** dans le plus profond désespoir; **his fortunes reached their ~ when ...** il atteignit le comble de l'infortune quand ...

naevus, nevus (US) ['ni:vəs] N (pl **naevi, (US) nevi** ['ni:vaɪ]) nævus m

naff [næf] (Brit) ADJ tarte*, ringard*
► **naff off:** VI foutre le camp*

naffing: ['næfɪŋ] ADJ (Brit) foutu*

NAFTA ['næftə] N (ABBR = **North American Free Trade Agreement**) ALENA f

nag¹ [næg] [1] VT (also **~ at**) [person] harceler, asticoter*; [worries] harceler, accabler; [doubt] harceler, assaillir; [anxiety] tenailler; **he was ~ging (at) me to tidy my room** il me harcelait or m'asticotait* pour que je range (subj) ma chambre; **to ~ sb into doing sth** harceler or asticoter* qn jusqu'à ce qu'il fasse qch; **to ~ sb about sth** embêter* qn avec qch; **to ~ sb to do sth** or **about doing sth** harceler or asticoter* qn pour qu'il fasse qch; **she ~ged him about never being home** elle lui reprochait de ne jamais être à la maison; **his conscience was ~ging (at) him** sa conscience le travaillait; **~ged by doubts** rongé par le doute

[2] VI [person] (= scold) ne pas arrêter de faire des remarques; [pain, doubts] être harcelant; **to ~ at sb** = **to nag sb**; → **1**

[3] N **he's a dreadful ~*** (scolding) il n'arrête pas de faire des remarques; (pestering) il n'arrête pas de nous (or le etc) harceler

nag²: [næg] N (= horse) cheval m; (pej) canasson* m (pej)

Nagasaki [,nɑ:gə'sɑ:kɪ] N Nagasaki

nagger ['nægə] N = **nag¹ 3**

nagging ['nægɪŋ] [1] ADJ [a] [doubt, feeling, fear, worry, question] persistant; [pain] tenace [b] [wife] qui n'arrête pas de faire des remarques, acariâtre; [voice] insistant [2] N (NonC) remarques fpl continuelles

NAHT [,eneɪtʃ'ti:] N (Brit) (ABBR = **National Association of Head Teachers**) association nationale des chefs d'établissements

Nahum ['neɪhəm] N Nahum m

naiad ['naɪæd] N (pl **naiads** or **naiades** ['naɪədi:z]) naïade f

nail [neɪl] [1] N [a] (Anat) ongle m → **bite, fingernail, toenail, tooth** [b] (Tech) clou m; **to pay on the ~** payer rubis sur l'ongle; **to demand cash on the ~** demander à être payé rubis sur l'ongle; (fig) **that decision was a** or **another ~ in his coffin** cette décision a été un nouveau coup dur pour lui; (fig) **to be as hard** or **tough as ~s** (= resilient) être coriace; (towards other people) être impitoyable → **bed, hit**

[2] VT [a] (= fix with nails) clouer; **to ~ the lid on(to) a crate** clouer le couvercle d'une caisse; (fig) **to be ~ed to the spot** or **ground** rester cloué sur place; (fig) **to ~ one's colours to the mast** proclamer une fois pour toutes sa position; **the Prime Minister has ~ed his colours firmly to the European mast** le Premier ministre a proclamé une fois pour toutes qu'il était proeuropéen; (US) **it's like trying to ~ Jell-O® to the wall*** autant essayer de vider la mer avec une petite cuiller

[b] (= put nails into) clouter; **~ed shoes** chaussures fpl cloutées

[c] * (= catch in crime etc) [+ person] pincer*, choper*; (= expose) [+ lie] démasquer; [+ rumour] démentir

[d] * (= hit with shot etc) descendre*, abattre

[3] COMP ► **nail-biting** N habitude f de se ronger les ongles ♦ ADJ [film] à suspense, angoissant; [finish, match] serré ► **nail bomb** N ≈ bombe f de fabrication artisanale ► **nail clippers** NPL coupe-ongles m inv, pince f à ongles ► **nail enamel** N (US) = **nail lacquer** ► **nail lacquer, nail polish** N vernis m à ongles ► **nail polish remover** N dissolvant m ► **nail scissors** NPL ciseaux mpl à ongles ► **nail varnish** N (Brit) = **nail polish** ► **nail varnish remover** N (Brit) = **nail polish remover**

► **nail down** VT SEP [a] [+ lid] clouer [b] (fig) [+ hesitating person] obtenir une décision de; [+ agreement, policy] établir, arrêter; **I ~ed him down to coming at 6 o'clock** je l'ai réduit or contraint à accepter de venir à 6 heures

► **nail up** VT SEP [a] [+ picture etc] fixer par des clous [b] [+ door, window] condamner (en clouant) [c] [+ box, crate] clouer; **to ~ up goods in a crate** empaqueter des marchandises dans une caisse clouée

nailfile ['neɪlfaɪl] N lime f à ongles

Nairobi [naɪ'rəʊbɪ] N Nairobi

naïve, naive [naɪ'i:v] ADJ [a] (pej = unrealistic) [person, belief, optimism] naïf (naïve f); **politically ~** naïf sur le plan politique; **it is ~ to think that ...** il faut être naïf pour croire que ... [b] (= innocent) [person; charm] ingénu [c] (Art) [painting, style] naïf (naïve f)

naïvely, naively [naɪ'i:vlɪ] ADV [think, assume, expect, believe] naïvement; **to be ~ idealistic** être d'un idéalisme naïf

naïveté, naiveté [naɪ'i:vteɪ], **naïvety, naivety** [naɪ'i:vtɪ] N naïveté f, ingénuité f

naked ['neɪkɪd] ADJ [a] [person, body, flesh, animal, light bulb, sword] nu; [wire] dénudé; **to go ~** être (tout) nu; **to sunbathe ~** se bronzer (tout) nu, faire du bronzage intégral; **~ to the waist** torse nu; **~ except for his socks** tout nu à part ses chaussettes, avec ses chaussettes pour seul vêtement; (fig) **to feel ~ without sth** se sentir nu sans qch; (as) **~ as the day he/she was born** nu/nue comme un ver, en costume d'Adam/d'Ève; **to see sth with the ~ eye** voir qch à l'œil nu; **visible/invisible to the ~ eye** visible/invisible à l'œil nu; **a ~ flame** une flamme (nue) → **stark, strip** [b] (= pure) [hatred] non déguisé; [greed] éhonté; [attempt] flagrant; [ambition, aggression] pur; [facts] brut; **the ~ truth** la vérité toute nue [c] (liter = defenceless) [person] sans défense

nakedly ['neɪkɪdlɪ] ADV ouvertement; **he was ~ ambitious** il ne cachait pas son ambition

nakedness ['neɪkɪdnɪs] N nudité f

NALGO ['nælgəʊ] N (Brit: formerly) (ABBR = **National and Local Government Officers Association**) ancien syndicat

namby-pamby* ['næmbɪ'pæmbɪ] (pej) [1] N gnangnan* mf [2] ADJ gnangnan* inv

name [neɪm] [1] N [a] nom m; **what's your ~?** comment vous appelez-vous?; **my ~ is Robert** je m'appelle Robert; **I'll do it or my ~'s not Robert Smith!*** je le ferai, foi de Robert Smith!; **I haven't a ha'penny** or **a penny to my ~*** je n'ai pas un sou vaillant, je suis sans le sou; **what ~ are they giving the child?** comment vont-ils appeler l'enfant?; **they married to give the child a ~** ils se sont mariés pour que l'enfant soit légitime; **what ~ shall I say?** (on telephone) c'est de la part de qui?; (announcing arrival) qui dois-je annoncer?; **please fill in your ~ and address** prière d'inscrire vos nom, prénom et adresse; **to take sb's ~ and address** noter le nom et l'adresse or les coordonnées de qn; **to put one's ~ down for a job** poser sa candidature à un poste; **to put one's ~ down for a competition/for a class** s'inscrire à un concours/à un cours; **I'll put my ~ down for a company car** je vais faire une demande pour avoir une voiture de fonction; (Ftbl etc) **to have one's ~ taken** recevoir un avertissement; **this man, Smith by ~** or **by the ~ of Smith** cet homme, qui répond au nom de Smith; **he goes by the ~ of ...** il est connu sous le nom de ...; **we know him by the ~ of ...** on le connaît sous le nom de ...; **to go by** or **under the ~ of ...** se faire appeler ...; **he writes under the ~ of John Smith** il écrit sous le pseudonyme de John Smith ; **but his real ~ is Piers Knight** mais il s'appelle Piers Knight de son vrai nom, mais son vrai nom est Piers Knight ; **she's the boss in all but ~** elle est le patron sans en avoir le titre ; **to refer to sb by ~** désigner qn par son nom ; **in ~ only** or **alone** de nom seulement ; **to exist in ~ only** or **in ~ alone** n'exister que de nom ; [power, rights] être nominal ; **a marriage in ~ only** or **in ~ alone** un mariage qui n'en est pas un ; **he is king in ~ only** il n'est roi que de nom, il n'a de roi que le nom ; **to name ~s** donner des noms ; **to name** or **mention no ~s** ◊ **naming** or **mentioning no ~s** pour ne nommer personne ; **without mentioning any ~s** sans nommer or citer personne ; **that's the ~ of the game** (= that's what matters) c'est ce qui compte ; (= that's how it is) c'est comme ça ; (lit, fig) **in the ~ of ...** au nom de ... ; **in God's ~** pour l'amour du ciel or de Dieu ; **in the king's ~** au nom du roi, de par le roi ; **what in the ~ of goodness*** or **in Heaven's*** or **God's* ~ are you doing?** mais qu'est-ce que tu fais, pour l'amour du ciel ? ; **what in Heaven's*** or **God's* ~ does that mean?** mais qu'est-ce que ça peut bien vouloir dire ? ; **all the great** or **big ~s were there** toutes les célébrités étaient là ; **he's one of the big ~s in show business** c'est un des grands noms du show-business → **first**, **know**, **maiden**, **pet¹**

b (= reputation) réputation f, renom m ; **he has a ~ for honesty** il est réputé honnête, il a la réputation d'être honnête ; **he has a ~ for stubbornness** il a la réputation d'être têtu ; **to protect one's (good) ~** protéger sa réputation ; **this firm has a good ~** cette maison a (une) bonne réputation ; **to have a bad ~** avoir (une) mauvaise réputation ; **to get a bad ~** se faire une mauvaise réputation ; **my ~ is mud*** in this place je ne suis pas en odeur de sainteté ici, je suis grillé* ici ; **if I do that my ~ will be mud* in the office** si je fais ça, c'en est fini de ma réputation or je suis grillé* au bureau ; **to make one's ~** se faire un nom ; **this book made his ~** ce livre l'a rendu célèbre ; **to make a ~ for o.s. (as)** se faire une réputation or un nom (comme or en tant que) ; **he made his ~ as a singer** il s'est fait un nom en tant que chanteur → **dog**, **vain**

c (= insult) **to call sb ~s** injurier qn, traiter qn de tous les noms ; **he called me ~s!** il m'a traité de tous les noms ! ; **~s can't hurt me** les injures ne me touchent pas

d (Fin: also **Lloyd's ~**) membre de la Lloyd's

2 VT **a** (= call by a name, give a name to) nommer, appeler ; [+ ship] baptiser ; [+ comet, star, mountain] donner un nom à ; **a person ~d Smith** un(e) nommé(e) Smith ; **the child was ~d Isobel** on a appelé l'enfant Isobel ; **to ~ a child after** or **for sb** donner à un enfant le nom de qn ; **the child was ~d after his father** l'enfant a reçu le nom de son père ; **they ~d him Winston after Churchill** ils l'ont appelé Winston en souvenir de Churchill ; **tell me how plants are ~d** expliquez-moi l'appellation des plantes

b (= give name of) nommer ; (= list) nommer, citer ; (= fix) [+ date, price] fixer ; **he was ~d for the chairmanship** son nom a été avancé pour la présidence ; **he ~d his son (as) his heir** il a désigné son fils comme héritier ; **he refused to ~ his accomplices** il a refusé de nommer ses complices or de révéler les noms de ses complices ; **my collaborators are ~d in the preface** mes collaborateurs sont mentionnés dans l'avant-propos ; **~ the presidents** donnez le nom des présidents, nommez les présidents ; **~ the chief works of Shakespeare** citez les principaux ouvrages de Shakespeare ; **~ your price** fixez votre prix ; (for wedding) **to ~ the day** fixer la date du mariage ; **you ~ it, they have it!** [shop] ils ont tous les produits possibles et imaginables ; [family] ils ont tous les gadgets ; **he was ~d as chairman** il a été

nommé président ; **he has been ~d as the leader of the expedition** on l'a désigné pour diriger l'expédition ; **he was ~d as the thief** on a dit que c'était lui le voleur ; **they have been ~d as witnesses** ils ont été cités comme témoins

3 COMP ► **name-calling** N injures fpl ► **name day** N fête f ► **name-drop** VI émailler sa conversation de noms de gens en vue ► **name-dropper*** N **he's a dreadful ~-dropper** il émaille toujours sa conversation de noms de gens en vue, à l'entendre il connaît la terre entière ► **name-dropping*** N **there was so much ~-dropping in his speech** son discours était truffé de noms de gens en vue ► **name part** N (Theat) rôle-titre m ► **name tape** N marque f (sur du linge ou des vêtements)

-named [neɪmd] ADJ (in compounds) **the first-named** le premier, la première ; **the last-named** ce dernier, cette dernière

nameless ['neɪmlɪs] ADJ **a** (= unnamed) [person, grave] anonyme ; [baby, town, island] sans nom ; (= anonymous) **to remain ~** garder l'anonymat ; **a certain person, who shall be** or **remain ~** une certaine personne, que je ne nommerai pas **b** (= indefinable) [terror, sensation, emotion] indéfinissable ; (= unmentionable) [vice, crime] innommable

namely ['neɪmlɪ] ADV à savoir ; **two of them, ~ Emma and Harry** deux d'entre eux, (à savoir) Emma and Harry ; **~ that ...** à savoir que ...

nameplate ['neɪmpleɪt] N (on door etc) plaque f ; (on manufactured goods) plaque f du fabricant or du constructeur

namesake ['neɪmseɪk] N homonyme m

Namibia [nɑːˈmɪbɪə] N la Namibie

Namibian [nɑːˈmɪbɪən] **1** ADJ namibien **2** N Namibien(ne) m(f)

nan¹ [nɑːn] N (also **~ bread**) nan m (pain indien)

nan²* [næn], **nana*** ['nænə] N (Brit = grandmother) mamie f, mémé f

nance* [næns], **nancy*** ['nænsɪ], **nancy-boy*** ['nænsɪbɔɪ] N (Brit pej) tante* f (pej), tapette* f (pej)

nankeen [næn'kiːn] N (Tex) nankin m

nanny ['nænɪ] **1** N **a** (= live-in carer) bonne f d'enfants, nurse f ; (= daytime carer) garde f d'enfants, nourrice f ; **yes ~** oui nounou (baby talk) **b** (* = grandmother) mamie f, mémé f **2** COMP ► **nanny-goat** N chèvre f, bique* f ► **nanny state** N (esp Brit) État-providence m

nannying ['nænɪŋ] **1** N **a** (= job) garde f d'enfants **b** (pej = mollycoddling) maternage m (excessif)

nano... ['nænəʊ] PREF nano...

nanometre ['nænəʊˌmiːtəʳ] N nanomètre m

nanotechnology [ˌnænəʊtekˈnɒlədʒɪ] N nanotechnologie f

Naomi ['neɪəmɪ] N Noémi f

nap¹ [næp] **1** N (= sleep) petit somme m ; **afternoon ~** sieste f ; **to have** or **take a ~** faire un petit somme ; (after lunch) faire la sieste **2** VI faire un (petit) somme, sommeiller ; (fig) **to catch sb ~ping** (= unawares) prendre qn à l'improviste or au dépourvu ; (= in error etc) surprendre qn en défaut

nap² [næp] N (Tex) poil m ; **cloth that has lost its ~** tissu m râpé or élimé ; (on sewing pattern) **with/without ~** avec/sans sens

nap³ [næp] N (Cards) ≈ manille f aux enchères

nap⁴ [næp] VT (Brit Racing) **to ~ the winner** donner le cheval gagnant

napalm ['neɪpɑːm] **1** N napalm m **2** VT attaquer au napalm **3** COMP ► **napalm bomb** N bombe f au napalm ► **napalm bombing** N bombardement m au napalm

nape [neɪp] N (also **~ of the neck**) nuque f

naphtha ['næfθə] N (gen) naphte m ; **petroleum ~** naphta m

naphthalene ['næfθəliːn] N naphtaline f

napkin ['næpkɪn] **1** N **a** serviette f (de table) **b** (Brit: for babies) couche f **2** COMP ► **napkin ring** N rond m de serviette

Naples ['neɪplz] N Naples

Napoleon [nəˈpəʊlɪən] N **a** Napoléon m **b** (= coin) napoleon napoléon m **c** (US = pastry) napoleon millefeuille m

Napoleonic [nəˌpəʊlɪˈɒnɪk] ADJ napoléonien

napper†* ['næpəʳ] N (= head) caboche* f

nappy ['næpɪ] (Brit) **1** N couche f **2** COMP ► **nappy liner** N protège-couche m ► **nappy rash** N érythème m (fessier) (Med, frm) ; (gen) **to have ~ rash** avoir les fesses rouges

narc [nɑːk] N (US) (ABBR = **narcotics agent**) agent m de la brigade des stupéfiants, stup* m

narcissi [nɑːˈsɪsaɪ] NPL of **narcissus**

narcissism [nɑːˈsɪsɪzəm] N narcissisme m

narcissist [nɑːˈsɪˌsɪst] N narcissique mf

narcissistic [ˌnɑːsɪˈsɪstɪk] **1** ADJ [person] narcissique **2** COMP ► **narcissistic personality disorder** N (Psych) névrose f narcissique

narcissus [nɑːˈsɪsəs] N (pl **narcissi** or **narcissuses**) **a** (= flower) narcisse m **b** **Narcissus** Narcisse m

narcolepsy ['nɑːkəʊlepsɪ] N (Med) narcolepsie f

narcosis [nɑːˈkəʊsɪs] N narcose f

narco-terrorism [ˌnɑːkəʊˈterəˌrɪzəm] N narco-terrorisme m

narcotic [nɑːˈkɒtɪk] **1** ADJ **a** (Med) [effect] narcotique ; **~ drug** narcotique m **b** (esp US Drugs) [industry] des stupéfiants **2** N **a** (Med) narcotique m **b** (esp US Drugs) stupéfiant m **3** COMP ► **narcotics agent** N agent m de la brigade des stupéfiants ► **narcotics charge** N **to be on a ~s charge** être mis en examen pour une affaire de stupéfiants ► **Narcotics Squad** N brigade f des stupéfiants

narcotism ['nɑːkəˌtɪzəm] N narcotisme m

narcotize ['nɑːkətaɪz] VT donner or administrer un narcotique à, narcotiser

nark* [nɑːk] **1** VT **a** (Brit = infuriate) ficher en boule*, foutre en rogne* → **narked** **b** **to ~ it** arrêter (de faire qch) ; **~ it!** suffit !*, écrase !* **2** VI (Brit = inform police) moucharder* **3** N **a** (Brit: also **copper's ~**) indic* m, mouchard* m **b** (US) = **narc**

narked* [nɑːkt] ADJ de mauvais poil* ; **to get ~** se mettre or se foutre* en rogne* (**about** à propos de)

narky* ['nɑːkɪ] ADJ (Brit) grognon(ne), mal embouché ; (on one occasion) de mauvais poil*, en rogne*

narrate [nəˈreɪt] VT raconter, narrer (liter)

narration [nəˈreɪʃən] N narration f

narrative ['nærətɪv] **1** N **a** (= story, account) récit m, narration f ; (NonC) narration f ; **he has a gift for ~** il est doué pour la narration **2** ADJ [poem, painting, structure, style] narratif ; [skill] de conteur ; **Jane Austen's ~ voice** le ton narratif de Jane Austen

narrator [nəˈreɪtəʳ] N narrateur m, -trice f ; (Mus) récitant(e) m(f)

narrow ['nærəʊ] **1** ADJ **a** [road, path] étroit ; [valley] étroit, encaissé ; [passage] étranglé ; [garment] étroit, étriqué ; [boundary, limits] restreint, étroit ; **within a ~ compass** dans d'étroites limites, dans un champ restreint ; **to grow** or **become ~(er)** se rétrécir, se resserrer **b** (fig) [mind] étroit, borné ; [outlook] restreint, borné ; [existence] limité, circonscrit ; [scrutiny] serré, poussé ; [means, resources, income] limité, juste (fig) ; [majority] faible, petit ; [advantage] petit ; **in the ~est sense (of the word)** au sens le plus restreint (du terme) ; **a ~ victory** une victoire remportée de justesse ; **to have a ~ escape** s'en tirer de justesse, l'échapper belle ; **that was a ~ shave*** *or* **squeak!*** on l'a échappé belle !, il était moins une !* ; (*Ling*) **~ vowel** voyelle *f* tendue

[2] **narrows** NPL passage *m* étroit ; [*of harbour*] passe *f*, goulet *m* ; [*of river*] pertuis *m*, étranglement *m*

[3] VI [a] [*road, path, river, valley*] se rétrécir ; **his eyes ~ed** il plissa les yeux

[b] (*fig*) [*majority*] s'amenuiser, se rétrécir ; **the search has now ~ed (down) to Soho** les recherches se concentrent maintenant sur Soho ; **the choice has ~ed (down) to five candidates** il ne reste maintenant que cinq candidats en lice ; **the field of inquiry has ~ed (down) to five people** ils concentrent maintenant leurs recherches sur cinq personnes ; **the question ~s (down) to this** la question se ramène *or* se réduit à ceci ; **his outlook has ~ed considerably since then** son horizon s'est beaucoup restreint *or* rétréci depuis lors ; **Britain's trade deficit ~ed a little last month** le déficit commercial de la Grande-Bretagne s'est légèrement réduit le mois dernier ; **the gap between Labour and the Conservatives is ~ing** l'écart entre les travaillistes et les conservateurs se réduit

[4] VT [a] (= *make narrower*) [+ *road, piece of land*] rétrécir, réduire la largeur de ; [+ *skirt*] rétrécir, resserrer ; **with ~ed eyes** en plissant les yeux

[b] (*fig*) [+ *choice*] réduire, restreindre ; [+ *ideas*] rétrécir ; [+ *differences*] réduire ; **they decided to ~ the focus of their investigation** ils ont décidé de restreindre le champ de leur enquête ; **to ~ the field (down)** restreindre le champ ; **they are hoping to ~ the gap between rich and poor nations** ils espèrent réduire l'écart entre pays riches et pays pauvres

[5] COMP ► **narrow boat** N (*Brit*) péniche *f* ► **narrow-gauge line, narrow-gauge track** N (*Rail*) voie *f* étroite ► **narrow-minded** ADJ [*person*] à l'esprit étroit, borné ; [*ideas, outlook*] étroit, borné ► **narrow-mindedness** N étroitesse *f* d'esprit ► **narrow-shouldered** ADJ étroit de carrure

► **narrow down** [1] VI [a] [*road, path, valley*] se rétrécir [b] (*fig*) = **narrow 4b** [2] VT SEP [+ *choice*] réduire, restreindre ; [+ *meaning, interpretation*] restreindre, limiter → **narrow 4**

narrowcasting ['næɾəʊ,kæstɪŋ] N (*Telec, TV*) câblodistribution *f* (*sur une zone réduite*)

narrowing ['næɾəʊɪŋ] N (*NonC*) (*lit*) rétrécissement *m* ; (*fig* = *reduction*) réduction *f*

narrowly ['næɾəʊlɪ] ADV [a] (= *barely*) [*escape, avoid, defeat*] de justesse ; [*miss, fail*] de peu [b] [*defined*] (= *strictly*) rigoureusement ; (= *restrictively*) d'une manière restrictive ; [*technical, vocational*] strictement ; **a ~ based curriculum** un programme d'enseignement restreint ; **to focus too ~ on sth** trop se focaliser sur qch ; **to interpret a rule ~** interpréter une règle de manière restrictive, donner une interprétation restrictive d'une règle [c] (= *closely*) [*look at, watch*] de près

narrowness ['næɾəʊnɪs] N étroitesse *f*

narwhal ['nɑːwəl] N narval *m*

NAS [enei'es] N (*US*) (ABBR = **National Academy of Sciences**) académie *f* des sciences

NASA ['næsə] N (*US*) (ABBR = **National Aeronautics and Space Administration**) NASA *f*

nasal ['neɪzəl] [1] ADJ (*Anat*) nasal ; (*Ling*) [*sound, vowel, pronunciation*] nasal ; [*accent*] nasillard ; **to speak with a ~ voice** parler du nez, nasiller [2] N (*Ling*) nasale *f*

nasality [neɪ'zælɪtɪ] N nasalité *f*

nasalization [,neɪzəlaɪ'zeɪʃən] N nasalisation *f*

nasalize ['neɪzəlaɪz] VT nasaliser

nasally ['neɪzəlɪ] ADV [*whine, complain*] d'une voix nasillarde ; **to speak ~** nasiller

nascent ['næsnt] ADJ [a] (*frm* = *developing*) [*democracy, science, industry*] naissant [b] (*Chem*) naissant

Nassau ['næsɔː] N (*Bahamas*) Nassau

nastily ['nɑːstɪlɪ] ADV [a] (= *spitefully*) [*say, laugh*] méchamment [b] (= *badly*) [*injured*] gravement ; **to cough ~** avoir une vilaine toux ; **her marriage ended rather ~** son mariage s'est mal terminé

nastiness ['nɑːstɪnɪs] N [a] (= *unpleasantness*) [*of war, crime*] horreur *f*, laideur *f* ; [*of taste, smell*] caractère *m* désagréable ; [*of substance*] nocivité *f* [b] (= *spitefulness*) [*of person, behaviour, remark*] méchanceté *f*

nasturtium [nəs'tɜːʃəm] N (*Bot*) capucine *f* ; **climbing/dwarf ~** capucine *f* grimpante/naine

nasty ['nɑːstɪ] [1] ADJ [a] (= *unkind, spiteful*) [*person, remark, joke*] méchant ; **to get** *or* **turn ~** [*person*] devenir méchant ; **to be ~ to sb** être méchant avec qn ; **to be ~ about sb/sth** dire du mal de qn/qch ; **she never said a ~ word about anybody** elle n'a jamais dit de mal de personne ; **a ~ little man** un type* désagréable ; **he's/she's a ~ piece of work** c'est un sale type*/une sale bonne femme* ; **to have a ~ look in one's eye** avoir une lueur mauvaise dans le regard ; **to have a ~ temper** avoir un sale caractère ; **to have a ~ mind** toujours voir le mal partout ; **a ~ trick** un sale tour`

[b] (= *unpleasant*) [*habit, rumour*] vilain ; [*bend, corner*] dangereux ; [*smell, taste, moment*] mauvais (*before n*), désagréable ; [*feeling, situation, experience*] désagréable ; [*problem*] épineux ; [*weather*] affreux, vilain ; [*book, story*] ignoble ; [*life*] dur ; **a ~ business** une sale affaire ; **a ~ job** un sale travail ; **what a ~ mess!** (*lit*) quel pagaille épouvantable ! ; (*fig*) quel gâchis ! ; **a ~ shock** *or* **surprise** une mauvaise surprise ; **to turn ~** [*situation*] mal tourner ; [*weather*] se gâter ; **events took a ~ turn** les choses ont mal tourné ; **to smell ~** sentir mauvais, avoir une mauvaise odeur ; **to taste ~** avoir un goût désagréable → **taste** ; **he had a ~ time of it!** (*short spell*) il a passé un mauvais quart d'heure ! ; (*longer period*) il a traversé une période très éprouvante !

[c] (= *serious*) [*accident, disease*] grave ; [*fall, wound*] vilain, mauvais ; **a ~ cold** un gros rhume ; **a ~ bout of flu** une mauvaise grippe ; **a ~ case of food poisoning** une grave intoxication alimentaire

[2] **nasties*** NPL (= *nasty things*) saletés *fpl*, saloperies* *fpl* → **video**

NAS/UWT [enei'es,juː'dʌblJʊ'tiː] (*Brit*) (ABBR = **National Association of Schoolmasters/Union of Women Teachers**) syndicat

Natal [nə'tæl] N le Natal

natal ['neɪtl] ADJ natal ; (*liter*) **~ day** jour *m* de (la) naissance → **antenatal, postnatal**

natality [nə'tælɪtɪ] N natalité *f*

natch* [nætʃ] EXCL (ABBR = **naturally**) nature*, naturellement

NATFHE [,eneɪ'tiː,efef'iː] N (*Brit*) (ABBR = **National Association of Teachers in Further and Higher Education**) syndicat

nation ['neɪʃən] [1] N nation *f* ; **the French ~** la nation française ; **people of all ~s** des gens de toutes les nationalités ; **the voice of the ~** la voix de la nation *or* du peuple ; **in the service of the ~** au service de la nation ; **the whole ~ watched while he did it** il l'a fait sous les yeux de la nation tout entière → **league¹, united** [2] COMP ► **nation-state** N État-nation *m*

national ['næʃənl] [1] ADJ [a] (= *of one nation*) national [b] (= *nationwide*) [*campaign, survey, network, TV, radio, broadcast*] national ; [*election, referendum*] à l'échelon national ; **on a ~ scale** à l'échelon national ; **there was ~ opposition to ...** la nation (entière) s'est opposée à ... ; **~ strike of miners** grève *f* des mineurs touchant l'ensemble du pays ; (*Press*) **the ~ and local papers** la presse nationale et la presse locale ; **they won 20% of the ~ vote** ils ont obtenu 20 % des voix à l'échelle nationale

[2] N [a] (= *person*) ressortissant(e) *m(f)* ; **he's a French ~** il est de nationalité française, c'est un ressortissant français ; **foreign ~s** ressortissants *mpl* étrangers

[b] (*Brit Racing*) **the (Grand) National** le Grand National (*course d'obstacles qui se tient annuellement à Liverpool*)

[c] (*also ~* **newspaper**) quotidien *m* national

[3] COMP ► **National Aeronautics and Space Administration** N (*US Admin*) Agence *f* nationale de l'aéronautique et de l'espace ► **national anthem** N hymne *m* national ► **National Assembly** N Assemblée *f* nationale ► **National Assistance** N (*Brit Admin: formerly*) ≈ Sécurité *f* sociale ► **national bank** N (*US*) banque *f* fédérale ► **national costume** N = **national dress** ► **National Curriculum** N (*Brit*) programme *m* d'enseignement obligatoire ► **national debt** N dette *f* publique *or* nationale ► **national dress** N costume *m* national *or* du pays ► **National Economic Development Council** N (*Brit: formerly*) ≈ Agence *f* nationale d'information économique ► **National Enterprise Board** N (*Brit*) ≈ Institut *m* de développement industriel ► **National Executive Committee** N bureau *m* exécutif *or* national ► **National Extension College** N (*Brit Scol*) ≈ Centre *m* national d'enseignement par correspondance ► **national flag** N drapeau *m* national ; (*Naut*) pavillon *m* national ► **National Foundation of the Arts and the Humanities** N (*US*) ≈ ministère *m* de la Culture ► **National Front** N (*Brit Pol*) parti britannique d'extrême-droite ► **national government** N (= *not local*) gouvernement *m* (central) ; (= *coalition*) gouvernement *m* de coalition ► **national grid** N (*Brit Elec*) réseau *m* national ► **National Guard** N (*US*) garde *f* nationale (*milice de volontaires intervenant en cas de catastrophe naturelle et pouvant prêter main forte à l'armée en cas de crise*) ► **National Guardsman** N (*pl* **National Guardsmen**) (*US*) membre *m* de la garde nationale → **National Guard** ► **National Health** N **I got it on the National Health*** je l'ai eu par la Sécurité sociale, ≈ çà m'a été remboursé par la Sécurité sociale ► **National Health Service** N (*Brit*) ≈ Sécurité *f* sociale → NHS ; NATIONAL INSURANCE ► **national holiday** N fête *f* nationale ► **National Hunt racing** N (*NonC: Brit*) courses *fpl* d'obstacles ► **national income** N revenu *m* national ► **National Insurance** N (*Brit*) ≈ Sécurité *f* sociale ► **National Insurance benefits** NPL (*Brit*) ≈ prestations *fpl* de la Sécurité sociale ► **National Insurance contributions** NPL (*Brit*) ≈ cotisations *fpl* de Sécurité sociale ► **National Insurance number** N (*Brit*) ≈ numéro *m* de Sécurité sociale ► **National Labor Relations Board** N (*US Admin*) commission d'arbitrage du ministère du travail ► **National League** N (*US Sport*) l'une des deux principales divisions de base-ball aux États-Unis ► **national liberation front** N front *m* de libération nationale ► **the National Lottery** N (*Brit*) ≈ la Loterie nationale ► **national monument** N monument *m* national ► **national park** N parc *m* national ► **National Rifle Association** N (*US*) organisation américaine militant pour le droit du port d'armes → GUN CONTROL ► **National Safety Council** N (*Brit*) Protection *f* civile ► **National Savings** N (*Brit*) épargne *f* nationale ► **National Savings Bank** N ≈ Caisse *f* nationale d'épargne ► **National Savings Certificate** N (*Brit*) bon *m* d'épargne ► **National Security Council** N (*US Pol*) Conseil *m* national de sécurité ► **national service** N (*Brit Mil*) service *m* national *or* militaire ; **to do one's ~ service** faire son service national *or* militaire ► **national serviceman** N (*pl* **national servicemen**) (*Brit Mil*) appelé *m*, conscrit *m* ► **National Socialism** N national-socialisme *m* ► **national status** N

nationalité *f* ► **National Trust** N (*Brit*) ≈ Caisse *f* nationale des monuments historiques et des sites

---
NATIONAL CURRICULUM

Le **National Curriculum** *est le programme d'enseignement obligatoire pour tous les élèves des écoles en Angleterre, au Pays de Galles et en Irlande du Nord. Il comprend les matières suivantes : anglais, mathématiques, sciences, technologie, histoire, géographie, musique, art, éducation physique et une langue vivante étrangère (et le gallois dans les écoles du pays de Galles). Tous les établissements primaires et secondaires doivent dispenser un enseignement religieux, et les écoles secondaires une éducation sexuelle, mais les parents sont libres, s'ils le veulent, d'en dispenser leurs enfants.*

NATIONAL INSURANCE

La **National Insurance** *est le régime de sécurité sociale britannique auquel cotisent les salariés, leurs employeurs et les travailleurs indépendants. Une partie de ces contributions finance l'assurance maladie (National Health Service), mais l'essentiel sert à payer les pensions de retraite, l'assurance chômage et les allocations de veuvage, d'invalidité et de maternité. Pour avoir droit à ces dernières prestations, il faut avoir cotisé à la* **National Insurance** *pendant un certain nombre d'années.* → [NHS]

---

nationalism ['næʃnəlɪzəm] N nationalisme *m* → **Scottish**

nationalist ['næʃnəlɪst] ADJ, N nationaliste *mf*; **Nationalist China** la Chine nationaliste → **Scottish**

nationalistic [,næʃnə'lɪstɪk] ADJ (*esp pej*) nationaliste, chauvin

nationality [,næʃə'nælɪtɪ] N nationalité *f* → **dual**

nationalization [,næʃnəlaɪ'zeɪʃən] N [a] (*Ind, Pol*) nationalisation *f* [b] (*of person*) = **naturalization a**

nationalize ['næʃnəlaɪz] VT [a] (*Ind, Pol*) nationaliser [b] [+ *person*] = **naturalize 1a**

nationally ['næʃnəlɪ] ADV [*distribute, make available*] dans l'ensemble du pays; [*broadcast*] sur l'ensemble du pays; [*organize*] à l'échelon national; **a ~ recognized qualification** une qualification reconnue dans tout le pays

nationhood ['neɪʃənhʊd] N nationalité *f* (*existence en tant que nation*)

nationwide ['neɪʃənwaɪd] [1] ADJ [*strike, protest etc*] à l'échelle nationale, national [2] ADV à l'échelle nationale; **there was a ~ search for the killers** on a organisé une chasse à l'homme dans tout le pays pour retrouver les assassins

native ['neɪtɪv] [1] ADJ [a] (= *original*) [*country, town*] natal; [*language*] maternel; **~ land** pays *m* natal, patrie *f*; **French ~ speaker** personne *f* de langue maternelle française, francophone *mf*; (*Ling*) **you should ask a ~ speaker** il faudrait (le) demander à un locuteur natif; (*fig*) **~ son** enfant *m* du pays → **informant** [b] (= *innate*) [*charm, talent, ability*] inné, naturel; **~ wit** bon sens *m* inné [c] (= *indigenous*) [*plant, animal*] indigène; [*product, resources*] (= *of country*) du pays; (= *of region*) de la région; **plant/animal ~ to ...** plante *f*/animal *m* originaire de ... [d] (= *of the natives*) [*customs, costume*] du pays; [*matters, rights, knowledge*] du pays, des autochtones; **Minister of Native Affairs** ministre *m* chargé des Affaires indigènes; **Ministry of Native Affairs** ministère *m* des Affaires indigènes; **~ labour** main-d'œuvre *f* indigène; **~ quarter** quartier *m* indigène; **to go ~*** adopter le mode de vie indigène

[2] N [a] (= *person*) autochtone *mf*; (*esp of colony*) indigène *mf*; **a ~ of France** un(e) Français(e) de naissance; **he is a ~ of Bourges** il est originaire de *or* natif de Bourges; **she speaks French like a ~** elle parle français comme si c'était sa langue maternelle; (*hum or pej*) **the ~s** les autochtones *mpl*, les indigènes *mpl* [b] (*Bot, Zool*) indigène *mf*; **this plant/animal is a ~ of Australia** cette plante/cet animal est originaire d'Australie

[3] COMP ► **Native American** N Indien(ne) *m(f)* d'Amérique, Amérindien(ne) *m(f)* ♦ ADJ amérindien ► **native-born** ADJ **he's a ~-born Scot** il est écossais de naissance

---
NATIVE AMERICAN

Aux États-Unis, l'expression **Native Americans** *désigne les populations autochtones, par opposition aux Américains d'origine européenne, africaine ou asiatique. On peut aussi parler d'« American Indian » (Indien d'Amérique), mais l'on évite les dénominations « Red Indian » ou « redskin » (Peau-Rouge), considérées comme méprisantes ou insultantes.*

---

nativism ['neɪtɪ,vɪzəm] N (*US*) hostilité *f* aux immigrants

nativity [nə'tɪvɪtɪ] [1] N [a] (*Rel*) **Nativity** Nativité *f* [b] (*Astrol*) horoscope *m* [2] COMP ► **nativity play** N pièce *f* représentant la Nativité

NATO ['neɪtəʊ] N (ABBR = **North Atlantic Treaty Organization**) OTAN *f*

NATSOPA [næt'səʊpə] N (*Brit*) (ABBR = **National Society of Operative Printers, Graphical and Media Personnel**) syndicat

natter* ['nætə] (*Brit*) [1] VI (= *chat*) causer, bavarder; (= *chatter*) bavarder, jacasser; **we ~ed (away) for hours** nous avons bavardé pendant des heures; **she does ~!** elle n'arrête pas de jacasser! [2] N [a] (= *chat*) causerie *f*, causette* *f*; **we had a good ~** nous avons bien bavardé, nous avons taillé une bonne bavette* [b] (= *chatterbox*) moulin *m* à paroles*

natterer* ['nætərə] N = **natter 2b**

natty* ['nætɪ] ADJ [a] (= *smart*) [*person*] chic *inv*; **to be a ~ dresser** être toujours bien sapé*; **to look ~** être très chic [b] (= *handy*) [*gadget*] pratique

natural ['nætʃrəl] [1] ADJ [a] (= *normal*) naturel, normal; **it's only ~** c'est tout naturel, c'est bien normal; **it seems quite ~ to me** ça me semble tout à fait naturel *or* normal; **there's a perfectly ~ explanation for the sound** le bruit s'explique tout à fait naturellement; **it is ~ for this animal to hibernate** il est dans la nature de cet animal d'hiberner, il est naturel *or* normal que cet animal hiberne (*subj*); **it is ~ for you to think ...** ◊ **it is ~ that you should think ...** il est naturel *or* normal que vous pensiez (*subj*) ...; (*in television programme*) **~ break** interruption *f* normale; (*Jur*) **death from ~ causes** mort *f* naturelle; (*Jur*) **to die of** *or* **from ~ causes** mourir de mort naturelle; **to die a ~ death** mourir de sa belle mort; (*Jur*) **for (the rest of) his ~ life** à vie; **~ size** grandeur *f* nature [b] (= *of* or *from nature*) naturel; **~ resources** ressources *fpl* naturelles; **her hair is a ~ blonde** ses cheveux sont naturellement blonds [c] (= *inborn*) inné, naturel; **to have a ~ talent for** être naturellement doué pour, avoir un don (inné) pour; **he's a ~** *or* (*US*) **~-born painter** c'est un peintre né [d] (= *unaffected*) [*person, manner*] simple, naturel [e] (*Mus*) naturel; **B ~** si *m* naturel; **~ horn** cor *m* d'harmonie; **~ key** ton *m* naturel; **~ trumpet** trompette *f* naturelle [f] (= *biological*) [*parents, child*] biologique [g] (†† = *illegitimate*) [*child*] naturel

[2] ADV* **playing the piano comes ~ to her** elle est naturellement douée pour le piano; **try to act ~!** essaie d'avoir l'air naturel!, fais comme si de rien n'était!

[3] N [a] (*Mus*) (= *sign*) bécarre *m*; (= *note*) note *f* naturelle [b] (* = *ideal*) **he's a ~ for this part** il est fait pour ce rôle; **did you hear her play the piano? she's a ~!** est-ce que vous l'avez entendue jouer? c'est une pianiste née!; (*US*) **it's a ~** ça coule de source [c] († = *simpleton*) idiot(e) *m(f)* (de naissance), demeuré(e) *m(f)*

[4] COMP ► **natural (child)birth** N accouchement *m* sans douleur ► **natural disaster** N catastrophe *f* naturelle ► **natural gas** N gaz *m* naturel ► **natural history** N histoire *f* naturelle ► **natural justice** N (*NonC*) principes *mpl* élémentaires du droit ► **natural language** N langage *m* naturel ► **natural language processing** N (*Comput*) traitement *m* automatique de la langue, traitement *m* de la langue naturelle ► **natural law** N loi *f* naturelle *or* de la nature ► **natural logarithm** N logarithme *m* népérien *or* naturel ► **natural monopoly** N (*Econ*) monopole *m* naturel ► **natural number** N (*Math*) nombre *m* naturel ► **natural philosopher** N physicien(ne) *m(f)* ► **natural philosophy** N physique *f* ► **natural science** N (*NonC*) sciences *fpl* naturelles ► **natural selection** N sélection *f* naturelle ► **natural theology** N théologie *f* naturelle, théodicée *f* ► **natural wastage** N (*Ind*) départs *mpl* naturels; (*esp Brit*) **to reduce the staff by ~ wastage** réduire le personnel par départs naturels

naturalism ['nætʃrəlɪzəm] N naturalisme *m*

naturalist ['nætʃrəlɪst] ADJ, N naturaliste *mf*

naturalistic [,nætʃrə'lɪstɪk] ADJ (*Art, Literat*) [*artist, writer, novel, painting*] naturaliste; (= *simulating nature*) **a ~ environment** un environnement qui reproduit les conditions naturelles

naturalization [,nætʃrəlaɪ'zeɪʃən] [1] N [a] [*of person*] naturalisation *f* [b] [*of plant, animal*] acclimatation *f* [2] COMP ► **naturalization papers** NPL (*Brit*) déclaration *f* de naturalisation

naturalize ['nætʃrəlaɪz] [1] VT [a] [+ *person*] naturaliser; **to be ~d** se faire naturaliser [b] [+ *animal, plant*] acclimater; [+ *word, sport*] naturaliser [2] VI [*plant, animal*] s'acclimater

naturally ['nætʃrəlɪ] ADV [a] (= *as is normal*) [*happen, develop, follow from, lead to, give birth*] naturellement; [*die*] de mort naturelle [b] (= *of course*) naturellement; **~, I understand your feelings** naturellement, je comprends vos sentiments; **~, I'll do all I can to help you** je ferai naturellement tout mon possible pour vous aider, il va de soi que je ferai tout mon possible pour vous aider; **~ enough** bien naturellement [c] (= *unaffectedly*) [*behave, talk, smile*] avec naturel, naturellement [d] (= *by nature*) [*cautious, cheerful, lazy*] de nature; **her hair is ~ blond** c'est une vraie blonde; **her hair is ~ curly** elle frise naturellement; **a ~ optimistic person** un(e) optimiste né(e); **to do what comes ~ (to one)** faire ce qui (vous) semble naturel; **caution comes ~ to him** il est prudent de nature; **cynicism doesn't come ~ to her** elle n'est pas du genre cynique; **playing the piano comes ~ to her** elle a un don (inné) pour le piano

naturalness ['nætʃrəlnɪs] N naturel *m*

nature ['neɪtʃə] [1] N [a] (*NonC: also* **Nature**) nature *f*; **he loves ~** il aime la nature; **~ versus nurture** l'inné *m* et l'acquis *m*; **let ~ take its course** laissez faire la nature; **a freak of ~** un caprice de la nature; **to paint from ~** peindre d'après nature; **against ~** contre nature; **~ abhors a vacuum** la nature a horreur du vide; (*hum*) **in a state of ~** à l'état naturel, dans le costume d'Adam*; **to go back** or **return to ~** [*person*] retourner à la nature; [*land*] retourner à la nature or l'état sauvage; **a return to ~** [*of garden, land*] un retour à la nature or l'état sauvage; [*of person*] un retour à la nature → **law, mother**

b (= *character*) [*of person, animal*] nature *f*, naturel *m*; **by** ~ de nature, par tempérament → **c**; **he has a nice ~** c'est quelqu'un de très gentil; **it is in the ~ of human beings to contradict themselves** la contradiction est le propre de l'homme; **it is in the ~ of young people to want to travel** il est naturel de vouloir voyager quand on est jeune; **it is not in his ~ to lie** il n'est pas de or dans sa nature de mentir; **that's very much in his ~** c'est tout à fait dans sa nature; **the ~ of the soil** la nature du sol; **it is in the ~ of things** c'est dans l'ordre des choses, c'est dans la nature des choses; **the true ~ of things** l'essence des choses; **in the ~ of this case it is clear that ...** vu la nature de ce cas il est clair que ...; **cash is, by its (very) ~, easy to steal** l'argent est, par nature or de par sa nature, facile à voler; (*fig*) **that's the ~ of the beast** ça fait partie (des règles) du jeu → **better¹, good, human, second¹**

c (= *type, sort*) nature *f*, genre *m*; **things of this ~** ce genre de chose; **I will have nothing to do with anything of that ~** je refuse d'être mêlé à ce genre de chose; **his comment was in the ~ of a compliment** sa remarque était en quelque sorte un compliment; **something in the ~ of an apology** une sorte d'excuse, une vague excuse; **ceremonies of a religious/solemn** etc ~ cérémonies *fpl* religieuses/solennelles etc

2 COMP ► **nature conservancy** N protection *f* de la nature ► **Nature Conservancy Board** N (*Brit*) ≈ Direction *f* générale de la protection de la nature et de l'environnement ► **nature cure** N (*NonC: Med*) naturopathie *f* ► **nature lover** N amoureux *m*, -euse *f* de la nature ► **nature reserve** N réserve *f* naturelle ► **nature study** N histoire *f* naturelle, (*Scol*) sciences *fpl* naturelles ► **nature trail** N sentier *m* de découverte de la nature ► **nature worship** N adoration *f* de la nature

-natured ['neɪtʃəd] ADJ (*in compounds*) de nature; **jealous-natured** jaloux de nature, d'un naturel jaloux → **good, ill**

naturism ['neɪtʃərɪzəm] N (*esp Brit*) naturisme *m*

naturist ['neɪtʃərɪst] N (*esp Brit*) naturiste *mf*

naturopath ['neɪtʃərə,pæθ] N naturopathe *mf*

naturopathy [,neɪtʃə'rɒpəθɪ] N naturopathie *f*

naught [nɔːt] N **a** (*esp Brit Math*) zéro *m*; (*Brit*) **~s and crosses** ≈ morpion *m* (*jeu*) **b** († or liter = nothing) rien *m*; **to bring sth to ~** faire échouer qch, faire avorter qch; **to come to ~** échouer, n'aboutir à rien; **to care ~ for** ◊ **to set at ~** ne faire aucun cas de, ne tenir aucun compte de

naughtily ['nɔːtɪlɪ] ADV **a** [*say, remark*] avec malice; **to behave ~** se conduire mal; [*child*] être vilain **b** (= *suggestively*) d'une manière osée

naughtiness ['nɔːtɪnɪs] N **a** [*of child etc*] désobéissance *f*, mauvaise conduite *f*; **it was just a young boy's natural ~** il était désobéissant, comme tous les enfants de son âge **b** (= *suggestiveness*) [*of story, joke, play*] grivoiserie *f*; **a writer who shocked the bourgeoisie with his sexual ~** un écrivain qui a choqué la bourgeoisie avec ses grivoiseries

naughty ['nɔːtɪ] **1** ADJ **a** (= *badly behaved*) **a ~ boy/girl** un vilain garçon/une vilaine (petite) fille; **(you) ~ boy/girl!** vilain/vilaine!; **he's ~** c'est un vilain garçon; **girls, you're being very ~** les filles, vous êtes très vilaines; **that was a ~ thing to do!** c'est vilain d'avoir fait ça! **b** (*esp Brit hum = slightly immoral*) [*person*] culotté*; **it was ~ of us, but it solved the**

---

problem on n'aurait peut-être pas dû, mais ça a résolu le problème; **a wonderfully ~ chocolate cake** un gâteau au chocolat à se mettre à genoux devant* **c** (*Brit = suggestive*) [*joke*] grivois, leste; [*book, magazine, story*] osé **2** COMP ► **naughty bits** NPL (*euph = genitals*) parties *fpl* intimes ► **the Naughty Nineties** NPL (*Brit*) ≈ la Belle Époque ► **naughty word** N (*esp baby talk*) vilain mot *m*

nausea ['nɔːsɪə] N (*lit*) nausée *f*; (*fig*) dégoût *m*, écœurement *m*; **she looked at the plate with a feeling of ~** l'assiette de nourriture lui soulevait le cœur

nauseate ['nɔːsɪeɪt] VT (*lit, fig*) écœurer

nauseating ['nɔːsɪeɪtɪŋ] ADJ (*lit, fig*) écœurant

nauseatingly ['nɔːsɪeɪtɪŋlɪ] ADV d'une façon dégoûtante or écœurante; **she was ~ beautiful/thin** elle était d'une beauté/minceur écœurante

nauseous ['nɔːsɪəs] ADJ **a** (= *queasy*) **to be** or **feel ~ at (the sight/thought of sth)** avoir la nausée (à la vue/pensée de qch); **to make sb (feel) ~** donner la nausée à qn **b** (= *nauseating*) [*smell*] écœurant

nautical ['nɔːtɪkəl] **1** ADJ [*chart*] nautique, marin; [*theme, look, feel*] marin; [*term*] de marine; [*uniform*] de marin; [*book*] sur la navigation maritime; **he's a ~ man** c'est un marin **2** COMP ► **nautical almanac** N almanach *m* marin ► **nautical mile** N mille *m* marin or nautique

nautilus ['nɔːtɪləs] N (*pl* **nautiluses** or **nautili** ['nɔːtɪ,laɪ]) (*Zool*) nautile *m*

Navaho ['nævəhəʊ] N (*also ~ Indian*) Navaho or Navajo *mf*

naval ['neɪvl] **1** ADJ [*battle, blockade, operation, unit*] naval; [*affairs, matters*] de la marine; [*commander*] de marine; **~ forces** forces *fpl* navales; **to have a ~ presence in a region** avoir des forces navales dans une région; **~ warfare** combats *mpl* navals **2** COMP ► **naval air station** N station *f* aéronavale ► **naval architect** N (*gen*) ingénieur *m* en construction navale; (*Navy*) ingénieur *m* du génie maritime ► **naval architecture** N construction *f* navale ► **naval aviation** N aéronavale *f* ► **naval barracks** NPL caserne *f* maritime ► **naval base** N base *f* navale ► **naval college** N école *f* navale ► **naval dockyard** N arsenal *m* (maritime) ► **naval hospital** N hôpital *m* maritime ► **naval officer** N officier *m* de marine ► **naval station** N = **naval base** ► **naval stores** NPL entrepôts *mpl* maritimes

Navarre [nə'vɑː] N la Navarre

nave¹ [neɪv] N [*of church*] nef *f*

nave² [neɪv] **1** N [*of wheel*] moyeu *m* **2** COMP ► **nave plate** N (*Aut*) enjoliveur *m*

navel ['neɪvl] **1** N (*Anat*) nombril *m*, ombilic *m* **2** COMP ► **navel-gazing** N (*pej*) nombrilisme* *m* ► **navel orange** N (orange *f*) navel *f inv*

navigable ['nævɪɡəbl] ADJ [*river, canal, channel*] navigable; [*missile, balloon, airship*] dirigeable

navigate ['nævɪɡeɪt] **1** VI naviguer; (*in car*) **you drive, I'll ~** tu prends le volant, moi je lis la carte (or le plan); **the Government is trying to ~ through its present difficulties** le gouvernement essaie actuellement de naviguer entre les écueils **2** VT **a** (= *plot course of*) **to ~ a ship** (or **a plane**) naviguer **b** (= *steer*) [+ *boat*] être à la barre de; [+ *aircraft*] piloter; [+ *missile*] diriger; **he ~d the ship through the dangerous channel** il a dirigé le navire dans ce dangereux chenal **c** (= *sail*) [+ *seas, ocean*] naviguer sur **d** (*fig*) **he ~d his way through to the bar** il s'est frayé un chemin jusqu'au bar; **he ~d the maze of back streets** il a réussi à retrouver son chemin dans le dédale des petites rues

---

navigation [,nævɪ'ɡeɪʃən] **1** N navigation *f* → **coastal 2** COMP ► **navigation laws** NPL code *m* maritime ► **navigation lights** NPL feux *mpl* de bord

navigational [,nævɪ'ɡeɪʃənl] ADJ [*instrument, techniques*] de navigation; **it is a ~ hazard** c'est un danger pour la navigation

navigator ['nævɪɡeɪtə] **a** N (*Aut, Aviat, Naut*) navigateur *m* **b** (= *sailor-explorer*) navigateur *m*, marin *m*

navvy ['nævɪ] N (*Brit*) terrassier *m*

navy ['neɪvɪ] **1** N **a** marine *f* (militaire or de guerre); **he's in the ~** il est dans la marine; (*US*) **Department of the Navy** ◊ **Navy Department** ministère *m* de la Marine; (*US*) **Secretary for the Navy** ministre *m* de la Marine; **to serve in the ~** servir dans la marine → **merchant, royal b** (= *colour*) = **navy-blue 2** ADJ = **navy-blue 3** COMP ► **navy bean** N (*US*) haricot *m* blanc ► **navy-blue** N, ADJ bleu marine *m inv* ► **Navy Register** N (*US*) liste *f* navale ► **navy yard** N (*US*) arsenal *m* (maritime)

nay [neɪ] (†† or liter) **1** PARTICLE non; **do not say me ~** ne me dites pas non → **yea 2** ADV ou plutôt; **surprised, ~ astonished** surpris, ou plutôt abasourdi

naysayer ['neɪseɪə] N (*US*) opposant(e) *m(f)* systématique

Nazareth ['næzərɪθ] N Nazareth

Nazi ['nɑːtsɪ] **1** N Nazi(e) *m(f)* **2** ADJ nazi

Nazism ['nɑːtsɪzəm] N nazisme *m*

NB [en'biː] (ABBR = **nota bene**) NB

NBA [,enbiː'eɪ] N **a** (*US*) (ABBR = **National Basketball Association**) association nationale de basket-ball **b** (*Brit*) (ABBR = **Net Book Agreement**) → **net²**

NBC [,enbiː'siː] N (*US*) (ABBR = **National Broadcasting Company**) NBC *f* (chaîne de télévision américaine)

NC a (*Comm etc*) (ABBR = **no charge**) gratuit **b** ABBR = **North Carolina**

NCB [,ensiː'biː] N (*Brit: formerly*) (ABBR = **National Coal Board**) Charbonnages *mpl* de Grande-Bretagne

NCCL [,ensiːsiː'el] N (*Brit*) (ABBR = **National Council for Civil Liberties**) ≈ ligue *f* des droits de l'homme

NCO [,ensiː'əʊ] N (*Mil*) (ABBR = **non-commissioned officer**) sous-officier *m*

ND ABBR = **North Dakota**

NDP [,endiː'piː] N (ABBR = **net domestic product**) → **net²**

NE a (ABBR = **north-east**) N-E **b** ABBR = **Nebraska**

Neanderthal [nɪ'ændətɑːl] **1** N **a** (*lit: Geog*) Neandertal or Néandertal *m* **b** (*fig*) (= *unreconstructed male*) primaire *m* (*pej*), primate* *m* (*pej*); (= *brute*) brute *f* épaisse **2** ADJ **a** (= *primitive*) [*age, times*] de Neandertal or de Néandertal; [*skeleton, grave*] de l'époque de Neandertal or de Néandertal **b** (*pej = primitive*) [*person, attitude, approach*] primitif (*pej*); [*system, method*] primitif, archaïque **c** (*hum = brutish*) [*person, grunt, conversation*] fruste; [*appearance*] simiesque **3** COMP ► **Neanderthal man** N (*pl* **Neanderthal men**) homme *m* de Neandertal or de Néandertal

neap [niːp] **1** N (*also ~tide*) marée *f* de morte-eau **2** COMP ► **neap season** N (*also ~tide season*) époque *f* des mortes-eaux

Neapolitan [nɪə'pɒlɪtən] **1** ADJ napolitain; **a ~ ice (cream)** une tranche napolitaine **2** N Napolitain(e) *m(f)*

near [nɪə] **1** ADV **a** (*in space*) tout près, à proximité; (*in time*) près, proche; **he lives quite ~** il habite tout près; **~ at hand** [*object*] à portée de (la) main; [*event*] tout proche; **the shops are ~** el les magasins sont tout près; **to draw** or **come ~ (to)** s'approcher (de); **to draw** or **bring sth ~er** rapprocher qch; **it was drawing** or **getting ~ to Christ-**

mas ◊ **Christmas was drawing** or **getting ~** Noël approchait; **the ~er it gets to the election, the more they look like losing** plus les élections approchent, plus leur défaite semble certaine; **it was ~ to 6 o'clock** il était près de or presque 6 heures; **~ to where I had seen him** près de l'endroit où je l'avais vu; **she was ~ to tears** elle était au bord des larmes; **so ~ and yet so far!** on était pourtant si près du but!

b (also ~**ly**: in degree) presque; **this train is nowhere ~ full** ce train est loin d'être plein

c (= close) **as ~ as I can judge** pour autant que je puisse en juger; **you won't get any ~er than that to what you want** vous ne trouverez pas mieux; **that's ~ enough*** ça pourra aller; **there were 60 people, ~ enough*** il y avait 60 personnes à peu près or grosso modo; **as ~ as dammit*** ou presque, ou c'est tout comme*

d (Naut) près du vent, en serrant le vent; **as ~ as she can** au plus près

2 PREP **a** (in space) près de, auprès de; (in time) près de, vers; **~ here/there** près d'ici/de là; **~ the church** près de l'église; **he was standing ~ the table** il se tenait près de la table; **regions ~ the Equator** les régions fpl près de or avoisinant l'équateur; **stay ~ me** restez près de moi; **don't come ~ me** ne vous approchez pas de moi; **the sun was ~ to setting** le soleil était près or sur le point de se coucher; **the passage is ~ the end of the book** le passage se trouve vers la fin du livre; **her birthday is ~ mine** son anniversaire est proche du mien; (fig) **he won't go ~ anything illegal** il ne se risquera jamais à faire quoi que ce soit d'illégal

b (= on the point of) près de, sur le point de; **~ tears** au bord des larmes; **~ death** près de or sur le point de mourir

c (= on the same level, in the same degree) au niveau de, près de; **to be ~ sth** se rapprocher de qch; (fig) ressembler à qch; **French is ~er Latin than English is** le français ressemble plus au latin or est plus près du latin que l'anglais; **it's the same thing or ~ it** c'est la même chose ou presque; **it was of a quality as ~ perfection as makes no difference** c'était d'une qualité proche de la perfection; **nobody comes anywhere ~ him at swimming** personne ne lui arrive à la cheville en natation; **that's ~er it** ◊ **that's ~er the thing** voilà qui est mieux → **nowhere**

3 ADJ **a** (= close in space) [building, town, tree] proche, voisin; [neighbour] proche; **these glasses make things look ~er** ces lunettes rapprochent les objets; (Math) **to the ~est decimal place** à une place décimale près; **to the ~est pound** à une livre près; **the ~est route** l'itinéraire le plus court or le plus direct → **5**

b (= close in time) proche, prochain; **the hour is ~ (when ...)** l'heure est proche (où ...); **in the ~ future** dans un proche avenir, dans un avenir prochain; **these events are still very ~** ces événements sont encore très proches or très rapprochés de nous

c (fig) [relative] proche; [race, contest, result] serré; **my ~est and dearest*** les êtres qui me sont chers; **the ~est equivalent** ce qui s'en rapproche le plus; **his ~est rival/challenger** son plus dangereux rival/challenger; **a ~ miss** (Aviat) une quasi-collision; (Mil) [of shot] un tir très près du but; **that was a ~ miss** or **a ~ thing** il s'en est fallu de peu or d'un cheveu; [of shot] c'est passé très près; (of election, race etc result) **it was a ~ thing** ça a été très juste; **we had a ~ miss with that truck** on a frôlé l'accident or on l'a échappé belle avec ce camion; **the translation is fairly ~** la traduction est assez fidèle; **that's the ~est thing to a compliment** ça pourrait passer pour un compliment, de sa etc part c'est un compliment → **5, offer**

d = **nearside**

e (* = mean) radin*, pingre

4 VT [+ place] approcher de; [+ person] approcher, s'approcher de; **to be ~ing one's goal** toucher au but; **my book is ~ing completion** mon livre est près d'être achevé; **the book is ~ing publication** la date de publication du livre approche; **the country is ~ing disaster** le pays est au bord de la catastrophe; **to be ~ing one's end** (= dying) toucher à or être près de sa fin

5 COMP ► **near beer** N (US) bière f légère ► **near-death experience** N état m de mort imminente ► **the Near East** N le Proche-Orient ► **near gold** N similor m ► **near letter quality** N qualité f pseudo-courrier ♦ ADJ de qualité pseudo-courrier ► **near money** N (Fin) quasi-monnaie f ► **near-nudity** N nudité f presque totale, quasi-nudité f ► **near-sighted** ADJ (esp US) **to be ~-sighted** être myope, avoir la vue basse ► **near-sightedness** N (esp US) myopie f ► **near silk** N soie f artificielle

nearby [ˌnɪəˈbaɪ] **1** ADV tout près, à proximité **2** ADJ voisin; **the house is ~** la maison est tout près; **a ~ house** une maison voisine

nearly [ˈnɪəlɪ] **1** ADV **a** (= almost) presque; **it's ~ complete** c'est presque terminé; **~ black** presque noir; **I've ~ finished** j'ai presque fini; **we are ~ there** nous sommes presque arrivés; **it's ~ 2 o'clock** il est près de or presque 2 heures; **it's ~ time to go** il est presque l'heure de partir; **she is ~ 60** elle a près de 60 ans, elle va sur ses 60 ans; **their marks are ~ the same** leurs notes sont à peu près les mêmes; **~ all my money** presque tout mon argent, la presque totalité de mon argent; **he ~ laughed** il a failli rire; **I very ~ lost my place** j'ai bien failli perdre ma place; **she was ~ crying** elle était sur le point de pleurer, elle était au bord des larmes; **it's the same or very ~ so** c'est la même chose ou presque

b **not ~** loin de; **she is not ~ so old as you** elle est loin d'être aussi âgée que vous; **that's not ~ enough** c'est loin d'être suffisant; **it's not ~ good enough** c'est loin d'être satisfaisant

c (= closely) près, de près; **this concerns me very ~** cela me touche de très près

2 COMP ► **nearly-new** ADJ [clothes] d'occasion (en bon état) ► **nearly-new shop** N (Brit) magasin m d'articles d'occasion

nearness [ˈnɪənɪs] N **a** (in time, place) proximité f; [of relationship] intimité f; [of translation] fidélité f; [of resemblance] exactitude f **b** (* = meanness) parcimonie f, radinerie* f

nearside [ˈnɪəˌsaɪd] (Aut, Horse-riding etc) N **1** N (in Brit) côté m gauche; (in France, US etc) côté m droit **2** ADJ (in Brit) de gauche; (in France, US etc) de droite

neat [niːt] ADJ **a** (= ordered) [house, room, desk] bien rangé; [garden] bien entretenu; [hair] bien coiffé; [handwriting, clothes, notes, work, appearance, sewing, stitches] soigné; **everything was ~ and tidy** tout était bien rangé; **she put her clothes in a ~ pile** elle a soigneusement empilé ses vêtements; **in ~ rows** en rangées régulières; **a ~ hairstyle** une coiffure nette; **a ~ little suit** un petit tailleur bien coupé; **she is very ~ in her dress** elle est toujours impeccable or tirée à quatre épingles; **he is a ~ worker** il est soigneux dans son travail

b (= trim) [waist, waistline, ankles] fin; [legs] bien fait; **she has a ~ figure** elle est bien faite; **a ~ little car** une jolie petite voiture

c (= skilful and effective) [solution] ingénieux; [plan] habile, ingénieux; [division, category] net, bien défini; [explanation] (= clever) astucieux; (= devious) habile; [phrase] bien tourné; **to make a ~ job of sth** bien faire qch, réussir qch

d (US* = good) [car, apartment, idea] super*; **he's a really ~ guy** c'est un mec super*; **it**

would be ~ to do that ce serait chouette* (de faire ça)

e (= undiluted) [whisky, brandy, vodka] sec (sèche f), sans eau

neaten [ˈniːtn] VT [+ dress] ajuster; [+ desk] ranger; **to ~ one's hair** se recoiffer

'neath [niːθ] PREP (liter) = **beneath 1**

neatly [ˈniːtlɪ] ADV **a** (= carefully) [write, type, dress, fold] soigneusement; **to put sth away ~** ranger qch soigneusement or avec soin **b** (= skilfully) [summarize] habilement; **he avoided the question very ~** il a éludé la question très habilement; **as you so ~ put it** comme vous le dites si bien; **a ~ turned sentence** une phrase bien tournée or joliment tournée; **you got out of that very ~** vous vous en êtes très habilement tiré **c** (= conveniently) [fit, work out] parfaitement

neatness [ˈniːtnɪs] N **a** (= tidiness) [of person, clothes, house] netteté f, belle ordonnance f; [of garden, sewing] aspect m soigné; **the ~ of her work/appearance** le soin qu'elle apporte à son travail/sa tenue soignée, le soin qu'elle apporte à son travail/à sa tenue **b** [of ankles] finesse f; [of figure] sveltesse f **c** (= skilfulness) adresse f, habileté f

NEB [ˌniːiːˈbiː] N **a** (Brit) = **National Enterprise Board**) → **national** **b** (ABBR = **New English Bible**) → **new³**

nebbish: [ˈnebɪʃ] **1** ADJ (US) empoté*; **your ~ brother** ton empoté de frère **2** N ballot* m, empoté(e) m(f)

Nebraska [nɪˈbræskə] N le Nebraska; **in ~** dans le Nebraska

Nebuchadnezzar [ˌnebjʊkədˈnezəʳ] N Nabuchodonosor m

nebula [ˈnebjʊlə] N (pl **nebulas** or **nebulae** [ˈnebjʊliː]) nébuleuse f

nebulizer [ˈnebjʊlaɪzəʳ] N (Med) nébuliseur m

nebulous [ˈnebjʊləs] ADJ (= vague) [notion, concept] nébuleux, vague; (Astron) nébuleux

NEC [ˌeniːˈsiː] N (ABBR = **National Executive Committee**) → **national**

▼ **necessarily** [ˈnesɪsrɪlɪ] ADV **a** (= automatically) **not ~** pas forcément; **this is not ~ the case** ce n'est pas forcément le cas; **you don't ~ have to believe it** vous n'êtes pas forcé or obligé de le croire; **he was lying, of course — not ~** bien entendu, il mentait — pas forcément **b** (= inevitably) [slow, short] forcément, nécessairement; **at this stage the plan ~ lacks detail** à ce stade, le plan n'est forcément pas très détaillé

▼ **necessary** [ˈnesɪsərɪ] **1** ADJ **a** (= required) [skill, arrangements] nécessaire, requis (to, for sth à qch); **all the qualifications ~ for this job** toutes les qualifications requises pour ce poste; **if ~** le cas échéant, si nécessaire; **when** or **where ~** lorsque c'est nécessaire; **to do more than is ~** en faire plus qu'il n'est nécessaire; **to do no more than is strictly ~** ne faire que le strict nécessaire; **to do whatever is** or **everything ~ (for)** faire le nécessaire (pour); **to make it ~ for sb to do sth** mettre qn dans la nécessité de faire qch; **it is ~ to do this** il est nécessaire de le faire; **it is ~ for him to do this** il est nécessaire qu'il le fasse; **it is ~ that ...** il est nécessaire que ... (+ subj)

b (= inevitable) [consequence] inéluctable; [corollary] nécessaire; [result] inévitable; **there is no ~ connection between ...** il n'y a pas nécessairement de rapport entre ...; **a ~ evil** un mal nécessaire

2 N **a** **to do the ~*** faire le nécessaire **b** (= money) **the ~*** le fric* **c** (Jur) **necessaries** (= necessities) les choses fpl nécessaires

necessitate [nɪˈsesɪteɪt] VT nécessiter, rendre nécessaire; **the situation ~d his immediate return** la situation l'a obligé à revenir immédiatement, la situation a nécessité son retour immédiat

necessitous [nɪˈsɛsɪtəs] ADJ (frm) nécessiteux ; **in ~ circumstances** dans le besoin, dans la nécessité

necessity [nɪˈsɛsɪtɪ] N [a] (NonC) (= compelling circumstances) nécessité f ; (= need, compulsion) besoin m, nécessité f ; **the ~ of doing** le besoin or la nécessité de faire ; **she realized the ~ of going to see him** elle a compris qu'il était nécessaire d'aller le voir or qu'il fallait aller le voir ; **she questioned the ~ of buying a brand new car** elle mettait en doute la nécessité d'acheter une voiture neuve ; **she regretted the ~ of making him redundant** elle regrettait d'avoir à le licencier ; **is there any ~?** est-ce nécessaire ? ; **there's no ~ for tears/apologies** il n'est pas nécessaire de pleurer/s'excuser ; **there is no ~ for you to do that** il n'est pas nécessaire que vous fassiez cela ; **from** or **out of ~** par nécessité, par la force des choses ; **of ~** par nécessité ; **to be born of ~** être dicté par les circonstances ; (frm) **to be under the ~ of doing sth** être dans la nécessité or dans l'obligation de faire qch ; **a case of absolute ~** un cas de force majeure ; **in case of ~** au besoin, en cas de besoin ■ (PROV) **~ knows no law** nécessité fait loi (PROV) ■ (PROV) **~ is the mother of invention** la nécessité rend ingénieux, nécessité est mère d'invention† → **virtue**

[b] (NonC = poverty) besoin m, nécessité† f

[c] (= necessary object etc) chose f indispensable ; **a dishwasher is a ~ nowadays** un lave-vaisselle est indispensable de nos jours, de nos jours, il est indispensable d'avoir un lave-vaisselle ; (= product) **a basic ~** un produit de première nécessité ; **water is a basic ~ of life** l'eau est indispensable à la vie ; **a political/economic ~** un impératif politique/économique → **bare**

neck [nɛk] [1] N [a] cou m ; [of horse, cow, swan] encolure f ; **to have a sore ~** avoir mal au cou ; **to fling one's arms round sb's ~** ◊ **to fall on sb's ~** (liter) se jeter or sauter au cou de qn ; (Racing) **to win by a ~** gagner d'une encolure ; **I don't want (to have) him (hanging) round my ~** je ne veux pas l'avoir sur le dos ; **to risk one's ~** risquer sa vie or sa peau* ; (in crime, plot, conspiracy) **he's up to his ~ in it*** il est mouillé jusqu'au cou* ; **to be up to one's ~ in work** être débordé (de travail) ; **he's up to his ~ in debt*** il est endetté jusqu'au cou ; **he's up to his ~ in drug dealing** il est mouillé jusqu'au cou dans des affaires de trafic de stupéfiants ; **the government is up to its ~ in new allegations of corruption*** le gouvernement a fort à faire avec ces nouvelles allégations de corruption ; (fig) **he got it in the ~:** (= got told off) il en a pris pour son grade* ; (= got beaten up) il a dérouillé‡ ; (= got killed) il s'est fait descendre* ; **to stick one's ~ out** se mouiller* ; **to throw sb out ~ and crop** jeter qn dehors avec violence ; (Brit) **it's ~ or nothing*** il faut jouer or risquer le tout pour le tout → **breakneck, breathe, pain, save†, stiff**

[b] (Culin) **~ of mutton** collet m or collier m de mouton ; **~ of beef** collier m de bœuf ; **best end of ~** côtelettes fpl premières

[c] [of dress, shirt etc] encolure f ; **high ~** col m montant ; **square ~** col m carré ; **a dress with a low ~** une robe décolletée ; **a shirt with a 38cm ~** une chemise qui fait 38 cm d'encolure or de tour de cou → **polo-neck, roll**

[d] [of bottle] col m, goulot m ; [of vase] col m ; [of tooth, screw] collet m ; [of land] isthme m ; [of guitar, violin] manche m ; [of uterus, bladder] col m ; **in our** or **this ~ of the woods** par ici ; **she's from your ~ of the woods** elle vient du même coin que vous → **bottleneck**

[e] (Brit* = impertinence) toupet* m, culot* m

[2] VI (esp US*) [couple] se peloter* ; **to ~ with sb** peloter* qn

[3] COMP ► **neck and neck** ADJ à égalité

neckband [ˈnɛkbænd] N (= part of garment) col m ; (= choker) tour m de cou

-necked [nɛkt] ADJ (in compounds) → **low¹, round, stiff**

neckerchief [ˈnɛkətʃiːf] N (= scarf) foulard m, tour m de cou ; (on dress) fichu m

necking* [ˈnɛkɪŋ] N (esp US) pelotage* m

necklace [ˈnɛklɪs] [1] N collier m ; (long) sautoir m ; **ruby/pearl ~** collier m de rubis/de perles ; **diamond ~** collier m or rivière f de diamants [2] VT (* = kill with burning tyre) faire subir le supplice du collier à [3] COMP ► **necklace killing** N supplice m du collier

necklacing [ˈnɛklɪsɪŋ] N = **necklace killing** ; → **necklace**

necklet [ˈnɛklɪt] N collier m

neckline [ˈnɛklaɪn] N encolure f

neckshot [ˈnɛkʃɒt] N ≈ balle f dans la nuque

necktie [ˈnɛktaɪ] N (esp US) cravate f

necrological [ˌnɛkrəʊˈlɒdʒɪkəl] ADJ nécrologique

necrologist [neˈkrɒlədʒɪst] N nécrologue m

necrology [neˈkrɒlədʒɪ] N nécrologie f

necromancer [ˈnɛkrəʊmænsəʳ] N nécromancien(ne) m(f)

necromancy [ˈnɛkrəʊmænsɪ] N nécromancie f

necrophile [ˈnɛkrəʊˌfaɪl] N nécrophile mf

necrophilia [ˌnɛkrəʊˈfɪlɪə] N nécrophilie f

necrophiliac [ˌnɛkrəʊˈfɪlɪˌæk] N nécrophile mf

necrophilic [ˌnɛkrəʊˈfɪlɪk] ADJ nécrophile

necrophilism [neˈkrɒfɪlɪzəm] N = **necrophilia**

necrophobe [ˈnɛkrəʊˌfəʊb] N nécrophobe mf

necrophobia [ˌnɛkrəʊˈfəʊbɪə] N nécrophobie f

necrophobic [ˌnɛkrəʊˈfəʊbɪk] ADJ nécrophobe

necropolis [neˈkrɒpəlɪs] N (pl necropolises or necropoleis [neˈkrɒpəˌleɪs]) nécropole f

necrosis [neˈkrəʊsɪs] N nécrose f

necrotising fasciitis, necrotizing fasciitis (US) [ˈnɛkrəʊtaɪzɪnfæsɪˈaɪtɪs] N (Med) fasciite f nécrosante or gangreneuse

nectar [ˈnɛktəʳ] N nectar m

nectarine [ˈnɛktərɪn] N (= fruit) brugnon m, nectarine f ; (= tree) brugnonier m

ned: [nɛd] N (esp Scot) voyou m

NEDC [ˌɛniːdiːˈsiː] N (Brit: formerly) (ABBR = **National Economic Development Council**) → **national**

Neddy* [ˈnɛdɪ] N (Brit: formerly) (ABBR = **National Economic Development Council**) → **national**

née [neɪ] ADJ née ; **Mrs Gautier, ~ Buchanan** Mme Gautier, née Buchanan

▼**need** [niːd] [1] N [a] (NonC = necessity, obligation) besoin m ; **if ~ be** si besoin est, s'il le faut ; **in case of ~** en cas de besoin ; **there is no ~ for tears** ce n'est pas la peine de pleurer ; **there's no ~ to hurry** il n'y a pas besoin or lieu de se dépêcher ; **no ~ to rush!** il n'y a pas le feu ! ; **no ~ to worry!** inutile de s'inquiéter ! ; **no ~ to tell him** pas besoin de lui dire ; **there's no ~ for you to come** vous n'avez pas besoin or vous n'êtes pas obligé de venir ; **to have no ~ to do sth** ne pas avoir besoin de faire qch ; **I can't see the ~ for it** je n'en vois pas la nécessité

[b] (NonC) (= want, lack) besoin m ; (= poverty) besoin m ; **there is much ~ of food** il y a un grand besoin de vivres ; **when the ~ arises** quand le besoin se présente or s'en fait sentir ; **to have ~ of** ◊ **to be in ~ of** avoir besoin de ; **to be badly** or **greatly in ~ of** avoir grand besoin de ; **I have no ~ of advice** je n'ai pas besoin de conseils ; **I'm in ~ of a drink** j'ai besoin de prendre un verre ; **the house is in ~ of repainting** la maison a besoin d'être repeinte ; **those most in ~ of help** ceux qui ont le plus besoin d'aide ; **your ~ is greater than mine** vous êtes plus dans le besoin que moi ; (* hum) vous en avez plus besoin que moi → **serve**

[c] (NonC) (= misfortune) adversité f, difficulté

f ; (= poverty) besoin m ; **in times of ~** aux heures or aux moments difficiles ; **do not fail me in my hour of ~** ne m'abandonnez pas dans l'adversité ; **to be in ~** être dans le besoin → **friend**

[d] (= thing needed) besoin m ; **to supply sb's ~s** subvenir aux besoins de qn ; **his ~s are few** il a peu de besoins ; **give me a list of your ~s** donnez-moi une liste de ce dont vous avez besoin or de ce qu'il vous faut ; **the greatest ~s of industry** ce dont l'industrie a le plus besoin

[2] VT [a] (= require) [person, thing] avoir besoin de ; **they ~ one another** ils ont besoin l'un de l'autre ; **I ~ money** j'ai besoin d'argent, il me faut de l'argent ; **I ~ more money** il me faut plus d'argent ; **I ~ it** j'en ai besoin ; **do you ~ more time?** avez-vous besoin qu'on vous accorde (subj) plus de or davantage de temps ? ; **have you got all that you ~?** vous avez tout ce qu'il vous faut ? ; **it's just what I ~ed** c'est tout à fait ce qu'il me fallait ; **I ~ two more to complete the series** il m'en faut encore deux pour compléter la série ; **he ~ed no second invitation** il n'a pas eu besoin qu'on lui répète (subj) l'invitation ; **the house ~s repainting** or **to be repainted** la maison a besoin d'être repeinte ; **her hair ~s brushing** or **to be brushed** ses cheveux ont besoin d'un coup de brosse ; **a visa is ~ed** il faut un visa ; **a much ~ed holiday** des vacances dont on a (or j'ai etc) grand besoin ; **I gave it a much ~ed wash** je l'ai lavé, ce dont il avait grand besoin ; **it ~ed a war to alter that** il a fallu une guerre pour changer ça ; **it** or **he doesn't ~ me to tell him** il n'a pas besoin que je le lui dise ; **she ~s watching** or **to be watched** elle a besoin d'être surveillée ; **he ~s to have everything explained to him in detail** il faut tout lui expliquer en détail ; **you will hardly ~ to be reminded that ...** vous n'avez sûrement pas besoin qu'on (or que je etc) vous rappelle (subj) que ... ; **you only ~ed to ask** tu n'avais qu'à demander ; (fig) **who ~s it?** on s'en fiche !* ; (fig) **who ~s politicians (anyway)?*** (de toutes façons) les hommes politiques, à quoi ça sert* or qu'est-ce qu'on en a à faire ?* → **hole**

[b] (= demand) demander ; **this book ~s careful reading** ce livre demande à être lu attentivement or nécessite une lecture attentive ; **this coat ~s to be cleaned regularly** ce manteau doit être nettoyé régulièrement ; **this plant ~s care** il faut prendre soin de cette plante ; **the situation ~s detailed consideration** la situation doit être considérée dans le détail ; **this will ~ some explaining** il va falloir fournir de sérieuses explications là-dessus ; **it shouldn't ~ a famine to make us realize that ...** nous ne devrions pas avoir besoin d'une famine pour nous apercevoir que ...

[3] MODAL AUX VB [a] (indicating obligation) **~ he go?** ◊ **does he ~ to go?** a-t-il besoin or est-il obligé d'y aller ?, faut-il qu'il y aille ? ; **you needn't wait** vous n'avez pas besoin or vous n'êtes pas obligé d'attendre ; **you needn't bother to write to me** ce n'est pas la peine or ne vous donnez pas la peine de m'écrire ; **I told her she needn't reply** or **she didn't ~ to reply** je lui ai dit qu'elle n'était pas obligée or forcée de répondre ; **we needn't have hurried** ce n'était pas la peine de nous presser ; **~ I finish the book now?** faut-il que je termine (subj) le livre maintenant ? ; **~ we go into all this now?** est-il nécessaire de or faut-il discuter de tout cela maintenant ? ; **I ~ hardly say that ...** je n'ai guère besoin de dire que ..., inutile de dire que ... ; **~ I say more?** ai-je besoin d'en dire plus (long) ? ; **you needn't say any more** inutile d'en dire plus (long) ; **there ~ be no questions asked** si on fait attention personne ne demandera rien ; **no one ~ go** or **~s to go hungry nowadays** de nos jours personne ne devrait souffrir de la faim ; **why ~ you always remind me of that?** ◊ **why do you always ~ to**

remind me of that? pourquoi faut-il toujours que tu me rappelles (*subj*) cela ? **b** (*indicating logical necessity*) ▶ **that be true?** est-ce nécessairement vrai ? ; **that needn't be the case** ce n'est pas nécessairement *or* forcément le cas ; **it ~ not follow that they are all affected** il ne s'ensuit pas nécessairement *or* forcément qu'ils soient tous affectés

needful ['ni:dfʊl] **1** ADJ nécessaire ; **to do what is ~** faire ce qui est nécessaire, faire le nécessaire ; **as much as is ~** autant qu'il en faut **2** N **to do the ~** faire ce qu'il faut

neediness ['ni:dɪnɪs] N indigence *f*

needle ['ni:dl] **1** N **a** aiguille *f* ; **knitting/ darning** *etc* ~ aiguille f à tricoter/à repriser *etc* ; **record-player** ~ pointe *f* de lecture, saphir *m* ; **gramophone** ~ aiguille *f* de phonographe ; (*Bot*) **pine** ~ aiguille *f* de pin ; **it's like looking for a ~ in a haystack** autant chercher une aiguille dans une botte de foin ; (*Drugs*) **to be on the ~**‡ se shooter‡ → **pin, sharp**
b (*Brit*‡ *fig*) **he gives me the ~** (= *teases me*) il me charrie‡ ; (= *annoys me*) il me tape sur les nerfs* *or* sur le système* ; **to get the ~** se ficher en boule‡

2 VT **a** * (= *annoy*) asticoter, agacer ; (= *sting*) piquer *or* toucher au vif ; (= *nag*) harceler ; **she was ~d into replying sharply** touchée au vif *or* agacée elle a répondu avec brusquerie
b (*US*) **to ~ a drink**‡ corser une boisson

3 COMP ▶ **needle book, needle case** N porte-aiguilles *m inv* ▶ **needle exchange** N (= *needle swapping*) échange *m* de seringues ; (= *place*) centre *m* d'échange de seringues ▶ **needle match** N (*Brit Sport*) règlement *m* de comptes ▶ **needle-sharp** ADJ (*fig*) (= *alert*) malin (-igne *f*) comme un singe ; (= *penetrating*) perspicace

needlecord ['ni:dlkɔ:d] N velours *m* mille-raies

needlecraft ['ni:dlkrɑ:ft] N travaux *mpl* d'aiguille

needlepoint ['ni:dlpɔɪnt] N tapisserie *f* (à l'aiguille)

needless ['ni:dlɪs] ADJ [*death, suffering, sacrifice, repetition*] inutile ; [*cruelty, destruction*] gratuit ; [*expense, risk*] inutile, [*remark, sarcasm, rudeness*] déplacé ; **~ to say, ...** inutile de dire que ..., il va sans dire que ...

needlessly ['ni:dlɪslɪ] ADV [*repeat, prolong*] inutilement ; [*die*] en vain ; [*suffer*] pour rien ; **you're worrying quite ~** vous vous inquiétez sans raison ; **he was ~ rude** il a été d'une impolitesse tout à fait déplacée

needlessness ['ni:dlɪsnɪs] N inutilité *f* ; [*of remark*] inopportunité *f*

needlestick injury ['ni:dlstɪk'ɪndʒərɪ] N (*Med*) blessure *f* causée par une seringue

needlewoman ['ni:dlwʊmən] N (*pl* **-women**) **she is a good ~** elle est douée pour les travaux d'aiguille

needlework ['ni:dlwɜ:k] N (*gen*) travaux *mpl* d'aiguille ; (= *mending etc: also Scol*) couture *f* ; **bring your ~ with you** apportez votre ouvrage

needn't ['ni:dnt] = **need not** ; → **need 3**

needs [ni:dz] ADV (*liter*) **I must ~ leave tomorrow** il me faut absolument partir demain, je dois de toute nécessité partir demain ; **if ~ must** s'il le faut absolument, si c'est absolument nécessaire ■ (*PROV*) ▶ **must when the devil drives** nécessité fait loi (*PROV*)

needy ['ni:dɪ] **1** ADJ [*person*] indigent, dans le besoin ; [*area*] sinistré ; (*emotionally*) **he's very ~ at the moment** il a besoin de beaucoup d'attention en ce moment **2** **the needy** NPL les nécessiteux *mpl*

neep [ni:p] N (*Scot*) rutabaga *m*

ne'er [nɛəʳ] **1** ADV (*liter*) = **never 1 2** COMP ▶ **ne'er-do-well** N bon(ne) *m(f)* *or* propre *mf* à rien ♦ ADJ bon *or* propre à rien

ne'ertheless ['nɛəðəles] ADV (*liter*) = **nevertheless**

nefarious [nɪ'fɛərɪəs] ADJ (*frm*) vil (vile *f*) (*liter*)

nefariousness [nɪ'fɛərɪəsnɪs] N (*frm*) scélératesse *f*

neg. (ABBR = **negative**) nég.

negate [nɪ'geɪt] VT (*frm*) (= *nullify*) annuler ; (= *deny truth of*) nier la vérité de ; (= *deny existence of*) nier (l'existence de) ; **this ~d all the good that we had achieved** cela a réduit à rien tout le bien que nous avions fait

negation [nɪ'geɪʃən] N (*all senses*) négation *f*

negative ['negətɪv] **1** ADJ (*gen, Elec, Ling, Phys etc*) négatif (**about sb/sth** à l'égard de qn/qch) ; (= *harmful*) [*effect, influence*] néfaste ; **he's a very ~ person** c'est quelqu'un de très négatif
2 N **a** réponse *f* négative ; **his answer was a curt ~** il a répondu par un non fort sec ; **the answer was in the ~** la réponse était négative ; **to answer in the ~** répondre négativement *or* par la négative, faire une réponse négative ; (*as answer*) **"~"** (*gen*) « négatif » ; (*computer voice*) « réponse négative »
b (*Ling*) négation *f* ; **double ~** double négation *f* ; **two ~s make a positive** deux négations équivalent à une affirmation ; **in(to) the ~** à la forme négative
c (*Phot*) négatif *m*, cliché *m*
d (*Elec*) (pôle *m*) négatif *m*
3 VT **a** (= *veto*) rejeter, repousser ; **the amendment was ~d** l'amendement fut repoussé
b (= *contradict, refute*) [+ *statement*] contredire, réfuter
c (= *nullify*) [+ *effect*] neutraliser
4 COMP ▶ **negative campaigning** N (*NonC: Pol*) campagne *f* négative ▶ **negative charge** N (*Phys*) charge *f* négative ▶ **negative equity** N moins-value *f* ▶ **negative feedback** N (*NonC*) **a** (= *criticism*) réactions *fpl* négatives ; **to give sb/get ~ feedback (about sb/sth)** faire part à qn de ses/recevoir des réactions négatives (au sujet de qn/qch) **b** (*Elec*) contre-réaction *f* ▶ **negative income tax** N impôt *m* négatif ▶ **negative number** N nombre *m* négatif ▶ **negative particle** N (*Ling*) particule *f* négative ▶ **negative pole** N (*Phys*) pôle *m* négatif ▶ **negative sign** N (*Math*) signe *m* moins ▶ **negative tax** N = **negative income tax**

negatively ['negətɪvlɪ] ADV [*respond*] négativement ; [*affect*] d'une manière défavorable ; **to look at things ~** voir les choses de façon négative

Negev Desert ['negev'dezət] N désert *m* du Néguev

neglect [nɪ'glekt] **1** VT [+ *person, animal*] négliger, délaisser ; [+ *garden, house, car, machinery*] ne pas entretenir ; [+ *rule, law*] ne tenir aucun compte de, ne faire aucun cas de ; [+ *duty, obligation, promise*] manquer à ; [+ *business, work, hobby*] négliger ; [+ *opportunity*] laisser passer ; [+ *one's health*] négliger ; [+ *advice*] ne tenir aucun compte de, ne faire aucun cas de (*frm*) ; **to ~ o.s.** *or* **one's appearance** se négliger ; **to ~ to do** négliger *or* omettre de faire → **neglected**
2 N (*NonC*) [*of duty, obligation*] manquement *m* (**of** à) ; [*of work*] manque *m* d'intérêt *m* (**of** pour) ; **~ of one's appearance** manque *m* de soins apportés à son apparence ; **his ~ of his promise** son manquement à sa promesse, le fait de ne pas tenir sa promesse ; **his ~ of his children** la façon dont il a négligé *or* délaissé ses enfants ; **his ~ of his house/garden/car** le fait qu'il ne s'occupe pas de sa maison/de son jardin/de sa voiture ; **the garden was in a state of ~** le jardin était mal tenu *or* était à l'abandon ; **children left in utter ~** enfants *mpl* complètement délaissés

neglected [nɪ'glektɪd] ADJ **a** (= *uncared-for*) [*person, district*] délaissé ; [*house, garden*] mal entretenu ; [*appearance*] négligé **b** (= *forgotten*) [*play*] méconnu, ignoré ; **a ~ area of scientific research** un domaine négligé de la recherche scientifique

neglectful [nɪ'glektfʊl] ADJ négligent ; **to be ~ of sth** négliger qch

neglectfully [nɪ'glektfəlɪ] ADV avec négligence

négligé, negligee ['neglɪʒeɪ] N négligé *m*, déshabillé *m*

negligence ['neglɪdʒəns] N (*NonC*) négligence *f*, manque *m* de soins *or* de précautions ; **through ~** par négligence ; (*Rel*) **sin of ~** faute *f* *or* péché *m* d'omission → **contributory**

negligent ['neglɪdʒənt] **1** ADJ **a** (= *careless*) négligent ; **he was ~ in his work** il a fait preuve de négligence dans son travail ; **to be ~ in doing sth** faire preuve de négligence en faisant qch ; **to be ~ of sth** négliger qch **b** (= *nonchalant*) nonchalant **2** COMP ▶ **negligent homicide** N (*US*) ≈ homicide *m* involontaire

negligently ['neglɪdʒəntlɪ] ADV **a** (= *carelessly*) **to behave ~** faire preuve de négligence **b** (= *nonchalantly, offhandedly*) négligemment ; **... she answered ~** ... répondit-elle négligemment

negligible ['neglɪdʒəbl] ADJ [*amount, effect*] négligeable ; [*risk, impact*] négligeable, insignifiant ; [*support, cost*] insignifiant

negotiable [nɪ'gəʊʃəbl] **1** ADJ **a** (*esp Fin*) [*price, salary*] à débattre ; [*rates, conditions, contract, bonds*] négociable ; **not ~** non négociable **b** (= *passable*) [*road, valley*] praticable ; [*mountain, obstacle*] franchissable ; [*river*] (= *can be sailed*) navigable ; (= *can be crossed*) franchissable **2** COMP ▶ **negotiable securities** NPL fonds *mpl* négociables

negotiant [nɪ'gəʊʃɪənt] N négociateur *m*, -trice *f*

negotiate [nɪ'gəʊʃɪeɪt] **1** VT **a** [+ *sale, loan, settlement, salary*] négocier **b** [+ *obstacle, hill*] franchir ; [+ *river*] (= *sail on*) naviguer ; (= *cross*) franchir, traverser ; [+ *rapids, falls*] franchir ; [+ *bend in road*] prendre, négocier ; [+ *difficulty*] surmonter, franchir **c** [+ *bill, cheque, bond*] négocier **2** VI négocier, traiter (**with sb for sth** avec qn pour obtenir qch) ; **they are negotiating for more pay** ils sont en pourparler(s) *or* ils ont entamé des négociations pour obtenir des augmentations

negotiation [nɪ,gəʊʃɪ'eɪʃən] N (= *discussion*) négociation *f* ; **to begin ~s with** engager *or* entamer des négociations *or* des pourparlers avec ; **to be in ~ with** être en pourparlers avec ; **~s are proceeding** des négociations *or* des pourparlers sont en cours ; **to solve sth by ~** résoudre qch par la négociation

negotiator [nɪ'gəʊʃɪeɪtəʳ] N négociateur *m*, -trice *f*

Negress ['ni:gres] N Noire *f*

Negro ['ni:grəʊ] **1** ADJ noir ; (*Anthropology*) négroïde → **spiritual 2** N (*pl* **Negroes**) Noir *m*

Negroid ['ni:grɔɪd] ADJ négroïde

Nehemiah [ni:ɪ'maɪə] N Néhémie *m*

neigh [neɪ] **1** VI hennir **2** N hennissement *m*

neighbour, neighbor (*US*) ['neɪbəʳ] **1** N voisin(e) *m(f)* ; (*Bible etc*) prochain(e) *m(f)* ; **she is my ~** c'est ma voisine ; **she is a good ~** c'est une bonne voisine ; (*US Pol*) **Good Neighbor Policy** politique *f* de bon voisinage ; **Britain's nearest ~ is France** la France est la plus proche voisine de la Grande-Bretagne → **next door 2** VI (*US*) **to neighbor with sb** se montrer bon voisin envers qn **3** COMP ▶ **neighbor states** NPL (*US*) États *mpl* voisins

neighbourhood, neighborhood (*US*) ['neɪbəhʊd] **1** N (= *district*) quartier *m* ; (= *area nearby*) voisinage *m*, environs *mpl* ; **all the**

children of the ~ tous les enfants du voisinage or du quartier; **it's not a nice** ~ c'est un quartier plutôt mal famé; **the whole** ~ **knows him** tout le quartier le connaît; **the soil in this** ~ **is very rich** la terre de cette région est très riche; **the cinema is in his** ~ le cinéma est près de or à proximité de chez lui; **in the** ~ **of the church** dans le voisinage de l'église, du côté de l'église; **(something) in the** ~ **of £100** dans les 100 livres, environ 100 livres; **anyone in the** ~ **of the crime** toute personne se trouvant dans les parages du crime

[2] ADJ [doctor, shops] du quartier; [café] du coin; (fig, often iro) **our/your friendly** ~ **dentist** le gentil dentiste de notre/votre quartier

[3] COMP ► **neighbourhood TV** N télévision f locale ► **neighbourhood watch** N système de surveillance assuré par les habitants d'un quartier

neighbouring, neighboring (US) ['neɪbərɪŋ] ADJ [country, area, building] voisin, avoisinant; [state, town] voisin; **in** ~ **Italy** dans l'Italie voisine

neighbourliness, neighborliness (US) ['neɪbəlɪnɪs] N **(good)** ~ rapports mpl de bon voisinage

neighbourly, neighborly (US) ['neɪbəlɪ] ADJ [person] aimable **(to sb** avec qn), amical; [feeling] amical; [behaviour, gesture] de bon voisin; **they are** ~ **people** ils sont bons voisins; ~ **relations** rapports mpl de bon voisinage; **to behave in a** ~ **way** se conduire en bon voisin; **that's very** ~ **of you** c'est très aimable (de votre part)

neighing ['neɪɪŋ] [1] N hennissement(s) m(pl) [2] ADJ hennissant

neither ['naɪðəʳ, 'niːðəʳ] [1] ADV ni; ~ ... **nor** ni ... ni (+ ne before vb); **she described the hotel as** ~ **good nor bad** elle a dit que l'hôtel n'était ni bon ni mauvais; **I've seen** ~ **him nor her** je ne les ai vus ni l'un ni l'autre; **he can** ~ **read nor write** il ne sait ni lire ni écrire; **the house has** ~ **water nor electricity** la maison n'a ni eau ni électricité; ~ **you nor I know** ni vous ni moi ne (le) savons; **he** ~ **knows nor cares** il n'en sait rien et ça lui est égal; **that's** ~ **here nor there** ce n'est pas la question; **the fact that she needed the money for her children is** ~ **here nor there, it's still stealing** peu importe qu'elle ait besoin de cet argent pour ses enfants, il n'en reste pas moins que c'est du vol; **an extra couple of miles is** ~ **here nor there** on n'en est pas à deux ou trois kilomètres près

[2] CONJ [a] **if you don't go,** ~ **shall I** si tu n'y vas pas je n'irai pas non plus; **I'm not going** — ~ **am I** je n'y vais pas — moi non plus; **he didn't do it** — ~ **did his brother** il ne l'a pas fait — son frère non plus

[b] (liter = moreover ... not) d'ailleurs ... ne ... pas; **I can't go,** ~ **do I want to** je ne peux pas y aller et d'ailleurs je n'en ai pas envie

[3] ADJ ~ **story is true** ni l'une ni l'autre des deux histoires n'est vraie, aucune des deux histoires n'est vraie; ~ **candidate got the job** les candidats n'ont eu le poste ni l'un ni l'autre; **in** ~ **way** ni d'une manière ni de l'autre; **in** ~ **case** ni dans un cas ni dans l'autre

[4] PRON aucun(e) m(f), ni l'un(e) ni l'autre (+ ne before vb); ~ **of them knows** ni l'un ni l'autre ne le sait, ils ne le savent ni l'un ni l'autre; **I know** ~ **of them** je ne (les) connais ni l'un ni l'autre; **which (of the two) do you prefer?** — ~ lequel (des deux) préférez-vous? — ni l'un ni l'autre

Nelly ['nelɪ] N (dim of **Helen, Ellen**) Hélène f, Éléonore f; **not on your** ~! jamais de la vie!

nelson ['nelsən] N (Wrestling) **full** ~ nelson m; **half-** ~ clef f du cou; (fig) **to put a half-** ~ **on sb*** attraper qn (pour l'empêcher de faire qch)

nematode ['nemətəʊd] N (also ~ **worm**) nématode m

---

nem. con. (ABBR = **nemine contradicente**) (= no one contradicting) à l'unanimité

nemesia [nɪ'miːʒə] N némésia m (fleur)

Nemesis ['nemɪsɪs] N (pl **Nemeses**) [a] (Myth) Némésis f [b] (also **nemesis**) némésis f, instrument m de vengeance; **it's** ~ c'est un juste retour des choses; (esp US) **she's my** ~ je suis vaincu d'avance avec elle

neo... ['niːəʊ] PREF néo...

Neocene ['niːə,siːn] N néogène m

neoclassical [,niːəʊ'klæsɪkəl] ADJ néoclassique

neoclassicism [,niːəʊ'klæsɪ,sɪzəm] N néoclassicisme m

neocolonial [,niːəʊkə'ləʊnɪəl] ADJ néocolonial

neocolonialism [,niːəʊkə'ləʊnɪəlɪzəm] N néocolonialisme m

neodymium [,niːəʊ'dɪmɪəm] N néodyme m

neofascism [,niːəʊ'fæʃɪzəm] N néofascisme m

neofascist [,niːəʊ'fæʃɪst] ADJ, N néofasciste mf

Neogene ['niːə,dʒiːn] N néogène m

neolith ['niːəlɪθ] N (Archeol) pierre f polie

neolithic [,niːəʊ'lɪθɪk] [1] ADJ [site, tomb] néolithique; [person] du néolithique [2] COMP ► **the Neolithic Age, the Neolithic Period** N le néolithique

neological [,nɪə'lɒdʒɪkəl] ADJ néologique

neologism [nɪ'ɒlə,dʒɪzəm] N néologisme m

neologize [nɪ'ɒlədʒaɪz] VI faire un (or des) néologisme(s)

neology [nɪ'ɒlədʒɪ] N = **neologism**

neomycin [,niːəʊ'maɪsɪn] N néomycine f

neon ['niːɒn] [1] N (gaz m) néon m [2] COMP [lamp, lighting] au néon ► **neon sign** N enseigne f (lumineuse) au néon

neonatal [,niːəʊ'neɪtl] ADJ néonatal

neonate ['niːəʊ,neɪt] N (frm) nouveau-né m

neonazi [,niːəʊ'nɑːtsɪ] ADJ, N néonazi(e) m(f)

neophyte ['niːəʊ,faɪt] N néophyte mf

neoplasm ['niːəʊ,plæzəm] N néoplasme m

Neo-Platonic, neoplatonic [,niːəʊplə'tɒnɪk] ADJ néoplatonicien

Neo-Platonism, neoplatonism [,niːəʊ'pleɪtə,nɪzəm] N néoplatonisme m

Neo-Platonist, neoplatonist [,niːəʊ'pleɪtə,nɪst] N néoplatonicien(ne) m(f)

Neozoic [,niːəʊ'zəʊɪk] ADJ néozoïque

Nepal [nɪ'pɔːl] N le Népal

Nepalese [,nepɔː'liːz], **Nepali** [nɪ'pɔːlɪ] [1] ADJ népalais [2] N [a] (pl inv) Népalais(e) m(f) [b] (Ling) népalais m

nephew ['nevjuː, (esp US) 'nefjuː] N neveu m

nephralgia [nɪ'frældʒɪə] N néphralgie f

nephrectomy [nɪ'frektəmɪ] N néphrectomie f

nephritic [ne'frɪtɪk] ADJ néphrétique

nephritis [ne'fraɪtɪs] N néphrite f

nephrology [nɪ'frɒlədʒɪ] N néphrologie f

nephrosis [nɪ'frəʊsɪs] N néphrose f

nephrotomy [nɪ'frɒtəmɪ] N néphrotomie f

nepotism ['nepətɪzəm] N népotisme m

Neptune ['neptjuːn] N (Myth) Neptune m; (Astron) Neptune f

neptunium [nep'tjuːnɪəm] N neptunium m

nerd* [nɜːd] N pauvre mec* m, ringard* m

nerdish* ['nɜːdɪʃ], **nerdy*** ['nɜːdɪ] ADJ ringard*

nereid ['nɪərɪɪd] N (Myth, Zool) néréide f

Nero ['nɪərəʊ] N Néron m

nerve [nɜːv] [1] N [a] (Anat, Dentistry) nerf m; (Bot) nervure f; **to kill the** ~ **of a tooth** dévitaliser une dent; **his speech touched** or **struck a (raw)** ~ son discours a touché un point sensible

[b] (NonC: fig) sang-froid m; **it was a test of** ~ **and stamina for the competitors** le sang-froid et l'endurance des concurrents furent mis à l'épreuve; **to hold** or **keep one's** ~ garder son

---

sang-froid; (Sport) **he held his** ~ **to win the race** il a gardé son sang-froid et il a gagné la course; **he never got his** ~ **back** or **never regained his** ~ il n'a jamais repris confiance en lui; **I haven't the** ~ **to do that** je n'ai pas le courage or le cran* de faire ça; **did you tell him?** — **I didn't/wouldn't have the** ~! je lui as-tu dit? — je n'en ai pas eu/je n'en aurais pas le courage!; **his** ~ **failed him** ◊ **he lost his** ~ le courage lui a manqué, il s'est dégonflé*

[c] (* = cheek) toupet* m, culot* m; **you've got a** ~! tu es gonflé!*, tu as du culot* or du toupet*!; (Brit) **you've got a bloody:** ~! tu charries!:; **what a** ~! ◊ **of all the** ~! ◊ **the** ~ **of it!** quel toupet!*, quel culot!*; **he had the** ~ **to say that ...** il a eu le toupet* or le culot* de dire que ...

[2] **nerves** NPL (fig = nervousness) nerfs mpl, nervosité f; **her** ~**s are bad** ◊ **she suffers from** ~**s** elle a les nerfs fragiles; (before performance, exam etc) **to have a fit** or **an attack of** ~**s** avoir le trac*; **it's only** ~**s** c'est de la nervosité; **to be all** ~**s** ◊ **to be a bundle of** ~**s** être un paquet de nerfs; **he was in a state of** ~**s** ◊ **his** ~**s were on edge** il était sur les nerfs, il avait les nerfs tendus or à vif; **the noise gets on my** ~**s** il/ce bruit me tape sur les nerfs* or me*; **to live on one's** ~**s** vivre sur les nerfs; **to have** ~**s of steel** avoir les nerfs solides or des nerfs d'acier; **war of** ~**s** guerre f des nerfs → **strain**[1]

[3] VT **to** ~ **o.s. to do sth** prendre son courage à deux mains or s'armer de courage pour faire qch; **I can't** ~ **myself to do it** je n'ai pas le courage de le faire

[4] COMP ► **nerve cell** N cellule f nerveuse ► **nerve centre** N (Anat) centre m nerveux; (fig) centre m d'opérations [2] ► **nerve ending** N terminaison f nerveuse ► **nerve gas** N gaz m neurotoxique ► **nerve-racking** ADJ angoissant, très éprouvant pour les nerfs ► **nerve specialist** N neurologue mf ► **nerve-wracking** ADJ = **nerve-racking**

nerveless ['nɜːvlɪs] ADJ [a] (= weak) [fingers, hands] inerte; **the dagger fell from his** ~ **grasp** sa main inerte a lâché le poignard [b] (= brave) intrépide; (= calm, collected) impassible [c] (pej = cowardly) lâche, dégonflé*; **he's** ~ c'est un dégonflé* [d] (Anat) peu innervé; (Bot) sans nervures

nervelessness ['nɜːvlɪsnɪs] N (fig) [a] (= calmness) sang-froid m [b] (= cowardice) lâcheté f

nerviness* ['nɜːvɪnɪs] N [a] nervosité f [b] (US = cheek) culot* m, toupet* m

nervous ['nɜːvəs] [1] ADJ [a] [person] (= tense) nerveux, tendu; (by nature) nerveux; **to be** ~ **about sth** appréhender qch; **I was** ~ **about him** or **on his account** j'étais inquiet pour lui; **to be** ~ **of sth** appréhender qch; **to be** ~ **of** or **about doing sth** hésiter à faire qch; **don't be** ~, **it'll be all right** ne t'inquiète pas, tout se passera bien; **people of a** ~ **disposition** les personnes sensibles; **to feel** ~ être nerveux; (before performance, exam etc) avoir les nerfs or le trac*; **he makes me (feel)** ~! il m'intimide [b] (Med) [disorder, tension] nerveux; **on the verge of** ~ **collapse** au bord de la dépression nerveuse

[2] COMP ► **nervous breakdown** N dépression f nerveuse; **to have a** ~ **breakdown** avoir or faire* une dépression nerveuse ► **nervous energy** N vitalité f, énergie f ► **nervous exhaustion** N fatigue f nerveuse; (serious) surmenage m mental ► **nervous Nellie*** (esp US) timoré(e) m(f), trouillard(e)* m(f) ► **nervous system** N système m nerveux ► **nervous wreck*** N **to be a** ~ **wreck** être à bout de nerfs; **to turn sb into** or **make sb a** ~ **wreck** pousser qn à bout

nervously ['nɜːvəslɪ] ADV nerveusement

nervousness ['nɜːvəsnɪs] N nervosité f

nervy* ['nɜːvɪ] ADJ a (= *nervous*) nerveux; **to be in a ~ state** avoir les nerfs à vif b (*US = cheeky*) **to be ~** avoir du toupet* *or* du culot*

...ness [nɪs] SUF **greatness** grandeur *f*; **selfishness** égoïsme *m*; **weariness** lassitude *f*

nest [nest] 1 N a [*of birds, mice, turtles, ants etc*] nid *m*; (= *contents*) nichée *f*; (*lit, fig*) **to leave** *or* **fly the ~** quitter le nid → **hornet, love** b (*fig*) nid *m*; **~ of spies/machine guns** nid d'espions/de mitrailleuses c [*of boxes etc*] jeu *m*; **~ of tables** tables *fpl* gigognes 2 VI a [*bird etc*] (se) nicher, faire son nid b **to go (bird) ~ing** aller dénicher les oiseaux *or* les œufs c [*boxes etc*] s'emboîter 3 COMP ▶ **nest egg** N (*fig*) pécule *m*

nested ['nestɪd] ADJ a [*tables*] gigognes b (*Gram*) emboîté

nesting ['nestɪŋ] N a [*of birds*] nidification *f*; **~ box** nichoir *m*; (*gen: for hens*) pondoir *m* b (*Gram*) emboîtement *m*

nestle ['nesl] VI [*person*] se blottir, se pelotonner (**up to, against** contre); [*house etc*] se nicher; **to ~ down in bed** se pelotonner dans son lit; **to ~ against sb's shoulder** se blottir contre l'épaule de qn; **a house nestling among the trees** une maison nichée parmi les arbres *or* blottie dans la verdure

nestling ['nestlɪŋ] N oisillon *m*

net[1] [net] 1 N a (*gen, Ftbl, Tennis etc*) filet *m*; (*Tennis*) **to come up to the ~** monter au filet; (*Ftbl etc*) **the ball's in the ~!** c'est un but! b (*fig*) filet *m*; **to slip through the ~** passer à travers les mailles du filet; **to be caught in the ~** être pris au piège; **to walk into the ~** donner *or* tomber dans le panneau; **to cast one's ~ wider** élargir son horizon *or* ses perspectives → **butterfly, hairnet, mosquito, safety** c (*NonC: Tex*) tulle *m*, voile *m* d (*Comput*) **the Net** (= *Internet*) le net 2 VT a (= *catch*) [+ *fish, game*] prendre au filet; (*fig*) **the police ~ted several wanted men** un coup de filet de la police a permis d'arrêter plusieurs personnes recherchées b [+ *river*] tendre des filets dans; [+ *fruit bushes*] poser un filet sur c (*Sport*) **to ~ the ball** envoyer la balle dans le filet; **to ~ a goal** marquer un but 3 COMP ▶ **net cord** N (*Tennis*) bande *f* du filet ▶ **net curtains** NPL voilage *m*; (*half-length*) brise-bise *m inv* ▶ **net fishing** N pêche *f* au filet ▶ **net play** N (*Tennis etc*) jeu *m* au filet ▶ **Net surfer** N (*Comput*) internaute *mf*

net[2] [net] 1 ADJ a [*income, assets, worth, price, loss*] net; **the price is £15 ~** le prix net est de 15 livres; **"terms strictly ~"** « prix nets » b [*result, effect*] final 2 VT [*business deal etc*] rapporter *or* produire net; [*person*] gagner *or* toucher net 3 COMP ▶ **the Net Book Agreement** N (*Brit: formerly*) *accord de maintien des prix publics des livres (entre les éditeurs et les libraires)* ▶ **net domestic product** N produit *m* intérieur net ▶ **net national product** N produit *m* national net ▶ **net present value** N valeur *f* actuelle nette ▶ **net profit** N bénéfice *m* net ▶ **net realizable value** N valeur *f* nette réalisable ▶ **net weight** N poids *m* net

netball ['netbɔːl] N (*Brit*) netball *m*

nether†† ['neðə'] ADJ ▶ **lip** lèvre *f* inférieure; (*also hum*) **~ garments** sous-vêtements *mpl*; **the ~ regions** (= *Hell*) les enfers *mpl*; (*hum euph = genitals*) les parties *fpl* intimes; (*hum*) **the ~ regions of the company** les coulisses *fpl* de l'entreprise; **the ~ world** les enfers *mpl*

Netherlander ['neðə‚lændə'] N Néerlandais(e) *m(f)*

Netherlands ['neðələndz] 1 NPL **the ~** les Pays-Bas *mpl*; **in the ~** aux Pays-Bas 2 ADJ néerlandais

nethermost†† ['neðəməʊst] ADJ le plus bas, le plus profond

netiquette ['netɪket] N (*Comput*) netiquette *f*

nett [net] = **net**[2]

netting ['netɪŋ] N (*NonC*) a (= *nets*) filets *mpl*; (= *mesh*) mailles *fpl*; (*for fence etc*) treillis *m* métallique; (*Tex*) voile *m*, tulle *m* (*pour rideaux*) → **mosquito, wire** b (= *net-making*) fabrication *f* de filets c (= *action: Fishing*) pêche *f* au filet

nettle ['netl] 1 N a (*Bot*) ortie *f*; **stinging ~** ortie *f* brûlante *or* romaine; **dead ~** ortie *f* blanche; (*Brit fig*) **to grasp the ~** prendre le taureau par les cornes 2 VT (*fig*) agacer, irriter; **he was ~d into replying sharply** agacé, il a répondu avec brusquerie 3 COMP ▶ **nettle sting** N piqûre *f* d'ortie

nettlerash ['netlræʃ] N urticaire *f*

nettlesome ['netlsəm] ADJ (= *annoying*) irritant; (= *touchy*) susceptible

network ['netwɜːk] 1 N (*gen, also Comput, Elec, Rad, TV*) réseau *m*; **rail ~** réseau *m* ferré *or* ferroviaire *or* de chemin de fer; **road ~** réseau *m or* système *m* routier; **a ~ of narrow streets** un lacis (*liter*) *or* enchevêtrement de ruelles; **~ of veins** réseau *m or* lacis *m* de veines; **a ~ of spies/contacts/salesmen** un réseau d'espions/ de relations/de représentants; (*Rad, TV*) **the programme went out over the whole ~** le programme a été diffusé sur l'ensemble du réseau; (*TV*) **the ~s** les chaînes *fpl* → **old** 2 VT (*Rad, TV*) diffuser sur l'ensemble du réseau; (*Comput*) interconnecter 3 COMP ▶ **Network Standard** N (*US Ling*) américain *m* standard → ENGLISH

networking ['net‚wɜːkɪŋ] N (*Comm*) maillage *m* de réseau; (*Comput*) gestion *f* de réseau

neural ['njʊərəl] 1 ADJ [*tube*] neural; [*system*] nerveux 2 COMP ▶ **neural cell** N cellule *f* nerveuse, neurone *m* ▶ **neural network** N (*Comput*) réseau *m* neuronal

neuralgia [njʊˈrældʒə] N névralgie *f*

neuralgic [njʊˈrældʒɪk] ADJ névralgique

neurasthenia [‚njʊərəsˈθiːnɪə] N neurasthénie *f*

neurasthenic [‚njʊərəsˈθenɪk] ADJ, N neurasthénique *mf*

neuritis [njʊəˈraɪtɪs] N névrite *f*

neuro... ['njʊərəʊ] PREF neuro..., névro...

neurogenic [‚njʊərəʊˈdʒenɪk] ADJ neurogène

neurolinguistic programming ['njʊərəʊ‚lɪŋˈgwɪstɪk'prəʊɡræmɪŋ] N programmation *f* neurolinguistique

neurological [‚njʊərəˈlɒdʒɪkəl] ADJ [*disease, disorder, damage*] neurologique; **~ surgeon** neurochirurgien *m*; **~ department** (service *m* de) neurologie *f*

neurologist [njʊəˈrɒlədʒɪst] N neurologue *mf*

neurology [njʊəˈrɒlədʒɪ] N neurologie *f*

neuroma [njʊəˈrəʊmə] N (*pl* **neuromas** *or* **neuromata** [njʊəˈrəʊmətə]) névrome *m*, neurome *m*

neuromuscular [‚njʊərəʊˈmʌskjʊlə'] ADJ neuromusculaire

neuron ['njʊərɒn] N neurone *m*

neuropath ['njʊərəpæθ] N névropathe *mf*

neuropathic [‚njʊərəˈpæθɪk] ADJ névropathique

neuropathology [‚njʊərəʊpəˈθɒlədʒɪ] N neuropathologie *f*

neuropathy [njʊəˈrɒpəθɪ] N névropathie *f*

neurophysiological [‚njʊərəʊ‚fɪzɪəˈlɒdʒɪkəl] ADJ neurophysiologique

neurophysiologist [‚njʊərəʊ‚fɪzɪˈɒlədʒɪst] N neurophysiologiste *mf*

neurophysiology [‚njʊərəʊ‚fɪzɪˈɒlədʒɪ] N neurophysiologie *f*

neuropsychiatric [‚njʊərəʊ‚saɪkɪˈætrɪk] ADJ neuropsychiatrique

neuropsychiatrist [‚njʊərəʊsaɪˈkaɪətrɪst] N neuropsychiatre *mf*

neuropsychiatry [‚njʊərəʊsaɪˈkaɪətrɪ] N neuropsychiatrie *f*

neurosis [njʊˈrəʊsɪs] N (*pl* **neuroses** [njʊˈrəʊsiːz]) (*Psych, fig*) névrose *f*

neurosurgeon [‚njʊərəʊˈsɜːdʒən] N neurochirurgien(ne) *m(f)*

neurosurgery [‚njʊərəʊˈsɜːdʒərɪ] N neurochirurgie *f*

neurosurgical [‚njʊərəʊˈsɜːdʒɪkəl] ADJ neurochirurgique

neurotic [njʊˈrɒtɪk] 1 ADJ a (*Psych*) [*person*] névrosé; [*behaviour, personality, disorder*] névrotique b (*pej = unreasonably anxious*) [*person*] parano*; [*obsession*] maladif; **he's getting ~ about the whole business** toute cette histoire le rend complètement parano* 2 N (*Psych*) névrosé(e) *m(f)*; (*fig pej*) parano* *mf*

neurotically [njʊˈrɒtɪkəlɪ] ADV de façon obsessionnelle, jusqu'à la névrose

neuroticism [njʊˈrɒtɪsɪzəm] N tendances *fpl* à la névrose

neurotomy [njʊˈrɒtəmɪ] N neurotomie *f*

neurotransmitter [‚njʊərəʊˈtrænzˈmɪtə'] N neurotransmetteur *m*

neurovascular ['njʊərəʊˈvæskʊlə'] ADJ neurovasculaire

neuter ['njuːtə'] 1 ADJ a neutre b (*Bot, Zool*) neutre; (*Zool = castrated*) châtré 2 N a (*Gram*) neutre *m*; **in the ~** au neutre b (*Zool*) animal *m* châtré 3 VT a (*Vet*) châtrer b (*esp Brit fig = render ineffective*) neutraliser

neutral ['njuːtrəl] 1 ADJ neutre; **let's meet on ~ territory** rencontrons-nous en terrain neutre; **let's try to find some ~ ground** essayons de trouver un terrain d'entente; **~ policy** politique *f* neutraliste *or* de neutralité 2 N a (*Pol*) habitant(e) *m(f)* d'un pays neutre b (*Aut*) point *m* mort; **in ~** au point mort

neutralism ['njuːtrəlɪzəm] N neutralisme *m*

neutralist ['njuːtrəlɪst] ADJ, N neutraliste *mf*

neutrality [njuːˈtrælɪtɪ] N (*gen, Chem, Pol etc*) neutralité *f* → **armed**

neutralization [‚njuːtrəlaɪˈzeɪʃən] N neutralisation *f*

neutralize ['njuːtrəlaɪz] VT (*also Chem*) neutraliser

neutrino [njuːˈtriːnəʊ] N neutrino *m*

neutron ['njuːtrɒn] 1 N neutron *m* 2 COMP ▶ **neutron bomb** N bombe *f* à neutrons ▶ **neutron number** N nombre *m* de neutrons ▶ **neutron star** N étoile *f* à neutrons

Nevada [nɪˈvɑːdə] N le Nevada; **in ~** dans le Nevada

never ['nevə'] 1 ADV a ne ... jamais; **I ~ eat it** je n'en mange jamais; **I have ~ seen him** je ne l'ai jamais vu; **I've ~ seen him before** je ne l'ai jamais vu (jusqu'à aujourd'hui); **I'd ~ seen him before** je ne l'avais jamais vu auparavant; **~ before had there been such a disaster** jamais on n'avait connu tel désastre; **he will ~ come back** il ne reviendra jamais *or* plus (jamais); **~ again** *or* (*liter*) **more** (ne ...) plus jamais, (ne ...) jamais plus; **~ again!** plus jamais!, jamais plus!; **~ say that again** ne répète jamais ça; **we shall ~ see her again** on ne la reverra (plus) jamais; **I have ~ yet been able to find ...** je n'ai encore jamais pu trouver ..., jusqu'ici je n'ai jamais pu trouver ...; **~ in all my life** jamais de ma vie; **I ~ heard such a thing!** je n'ai jamais entendu une chose pareille! → **now** b (*emphatic*) **that will ~ do!** c'est inadmissible!; **I ~ slept a wink** je n'ai pas fermé l'œil; **he ~ so much as smiled** il n'a pas même souri; **he ~ said a word** ◊ **he said ~ a word** (*liter*) il n'a pas pipé mot; **~ a one** pas un seul; **~ was a child more loved** jamais enfant ne fut plus aimé; **(surely) you've ~ left it behind!**∗ ne me dites pas que vous l'avez oublié!; **I've left it behind! — ~!** je l'ai oublié! — ça n'est pas vrai or pas possible!; **you must ~ ever come here again** tu ne dois jamais plus revenir ici; **well I ~ (did)!**∗ ça par exemple!∗, ça alors!∗; **~ mind!** ça ne fait rien!, ne vous en faites pas!; **~ fear!** n'ayez pas peur!, soyez tranquille!

2 COMP ► **never-ending** ADJ interminable ► **never-failing** ADJ [*method*] infaillible; [*source, spring*] inépuisable, intarissable ► **never-never**∗ N (*Austral = outback*) régions désertiques d'Australie; (*Brit*) **to buy on the ~-~** acheter à crédit or à tempérament ► **never-never land** N pays m imaginaire ► **never-outs** NPL (*Comm*) articles mpl toujours en stock ► **never-to-be-forgotten** ADJ inoubliable, qu'on n'oubliera jamais

nevermore ['nevəmɔːʳ] ADV ne ... plus jamais, ne ... jamais plus; **~!** jamais plus!, plus jamais!

▼ **nevertheless** [ˌnevəðə'les] ADV néanmoins; **it wasn't my fault. Nevertheless, I felt guilty** ce n'était pas ma faute; néanmoins or cependant, je me suis senti coupable; **it is ~ true that ...** cependant, il est vrai que ..., il est néanmoins vrai que ...; **I shall go ~** j'irai néanmoins or malgré tout; **he is ~ my brother** il n'en reste pas moins mon frère; **she has had no news, (yet) ~ she goes on hoping** elle n'a pas eu de nouvelles, et pourtant or et malgré tout elle continue d'espérer

nevus ['niːvəs] N (*US*) = **naevus**

new [njuː] 1 ADJ a (= *not previously known etc*) nouveau (nouvelle f), nouvel (m before vowel); (*also* **brand-~**) neuf (neuve f); (= *different*) nouveau (nouvelle f), nouvel (m before vowel), autre; **I've got a ~ car** (= *different*) j'ai une nouvelle or une autre voiture; (= *brand-new*) j'ai une voiture neuve; **he has written a ~ book/article** il a écrit un nouveau livre/un nouvel article; **this is Juliette's ~ book** c'est le nouveau or dernier livre de Juliette; **I've got a ~ library book** j'ai emprunté un nouveau livre à la bibliothèque; **~ carrots** carottes fpl de primeur or nouvelles; **there are several ~ plays on in London** on donne plusieurs nouvelles pièces à Londres; **~ fashion** dernière or nouvelle mode f; **a ~ theory/invention** une nouvelle théorie/invention; **the ~ moon** la nouvelle lune; **there's a ~ moon tonight** c'est la nouvelle lune ce soir; **I need a ~ notebook** il me faut un nouveau carnet or un carnet neuf; **don't get your ~ shoes wet** ne mouille pas tes chaussures neuves; **dressed in ~ clothes** vêtu or habillé de neuf; **as good as ~** comme neuf, à l'état de neuf; **he made the bike as good as ~** il a remis le vélo à neuf; **"as ~"** « état neuf »; **I don't like all these ~ paintings** je n'aime pas tous ces tableaux modernes; **I've got several ~ ideas** j'ai plusieurs idées nouvelles or neuves; **this idea is not ~** ce n'est pas une idée nouvelle or neuve; **the ~ nations** les pays mpl neufs; **this is a completely ~ subject** c'est un sujet tout à fait neuf; **this sort of work is ~ to me** ce genre de travail est (quelque chose de) nouveau pour moi; **I'm ~ to this kind of work** je n'ai jamais fait ce genre de travail, je suis novice dans ce genre de travail; **he came ~ to the firm last year** il est arrivé (dans l'entreprise) l'an dernier; **he's ~ to the trade** il est nouveau dans le métier; **he's quite ~ to the town** il est tout nouvellement arrivé dans la ville; **she's ~ to this game**∗ elle fait ses premières armes; **the ~ people at number five** les gens qui viennent d'emménager au numéro cinq; **~ recruit** nouvelle recrue f, bleu∗ m; **the ~ students** les nouveaux mpl, les nouvelles fpl; (*Scol*) **a ~ boy** un nouveau; (*Scol*) **a ~ girl** une nouvelle; **she's ~, poor thing** elle est nouvelle, la pauvre; **are you ~ here?** (*gen*) vous venez d'arriver ici?; (*in school, firm etc*) vous êtes nouveau ici?; **the ~ woman** la femme moderne; (*Pol*)

etc) **a ~ deal** une nouvelle donne; **the ~ diplomacy** la diplomatie nouvelle manière or moderne; **~ style** nouveau style m → 3; (*Pol*) **the New Left** la nouvelle gauche; **the ~ rich** les nouveaux riches mpl; **bring me a ~ glass, this one is dirty** apportez-moi un autre verre, celui-ci est sale; **there was a ~ waiter today** il y avait un autre or un nouveau serveur aujourd'hui; (*fig*) **he's a ~ man since he remarried** il est transformé or c'est un autre homme depuis qu'il s'est remarié → 3; ▪ (*PROV*) **there's nothing ~ under the sun** il n'y a rien de nouveau sous le soleil (*PROV*); **that's nothing ~!** ce or ça n'est pas nouveau!, il n'y a rien de neuf là-dedans!; **that's a ~ one on me!**∗ première nouvelle!∗, on en apprend tous les jours! (*iro*); **that's something ~!** ça c'est nouveau!; **what's ~?**∗ quoi de neuf?∗ → 3; → **brand, broom, leaf, split**

b (= *fresh*) [*bread*] frais (fraîche f); [*milk*] frais (fraîche f), fraîchement trait; [*cheese*] frais (fraîche f), pas (encore) fait; [*wine*] nouveau (nouvelle f), nouvel (m before vowel), jeune

2 ADV (*gen in compounds*) nouvellement; **he's ~ out of college** il est frais émoulu du collège, il sort tout juste du collège → 3

3 COMP ► **New Age** N New Age m ♦ ADJ New Age *inv* ► **New Ager**∗ N adepte mf du New Age ► **New Age travellers** NPL voyageurs mpl New Age ► **New Brunswick** N le Nouveau-Brunswick ► **New Caledonia** N la Nouvelle-Calédonie ► **New Caledonian** N Néo-Calédonien(ne) *m(f)* ► **New Delhi** N New Delhi ► **New England** N la Nouvelle-Angleterre ► **New Englander** N habitant(e) *m(f)* de la Nouvelle-Angleterre ► **New English Bible** N traduction moderne de la Bible en anglais ► **new face** N nouveau visage m ► **new-fangled** ADJ (*pej*) ultramoderne ► **new-found** ADJ [*happiness etc*] de fraîche date ► **New Guinea** N la Nouvelle-Guinée ► **New Hampshire** N le New Hampshire; **in New Hampshire** dans le New Hampshire ► **the New Hebrides** NPL les Nouvelles-Hébrides fpl ► **New Jersey** N le New Jersey; **in New Jersey** dans le New Jersey ► **New Jerusalem** N la Nouvelle Jérusalem ► **New Lad**∗ N (*Brit*) macho m nouvelle manière ► **new-laid egg** N œuf m du jour or tout frais (pondu) ► **New Latin** N latin m moderne ► **new look** N new-look m ► **new-look** ADJ new-look *inv* ► **New Man** N (*Brit*) ≈ homme m moderne (*qui partage les tâches ménagères, s'occupe des enfants etc*) ► **new maths** N mathématiques fpl or maths∗ fpl modernes ► **New Mexico** N le Nouveau-Mexique ► **new-mown** ADJ [*grass*] frais coupé; [*hay*] frais fauché ► **New Orleans** N La Nouvelle-Orléans ► **new potato** N pomme f (de terre) nouvelle ► **new product development** N (*Comm*) développement m de nouveaux produits ► **New Scotland Yard** N Scotland Yard m ► **New South Wales** N la Nouvelle-Galles du Sud ► **new-speak** N (*Pol*) langue f de bois; (*Literat*) novlangue f ► **the new-style calendar** N le nouveau calendrier, le calendrier grégorien ► **New Testament** N Nouveau Testament m ► **new town** N (*Brit*) ville f nouvelle ► **New Wave** ADJ [*film*] nouvelle vague; [*music*] New Wave *inv* ♦ N (*Cine*) nouvelle vague f; (*Mus*) New Wave f ► **the New World** N le Nouveau Monde; (*Mus*) **the New World Symphony** ◊ **the Symphony from the New World** la Symphonie du Nouveau Monde ► **New Year** N → **New Year** ► **New Year's**∗ N (*US*) = **New Year's Day, New Year's Eve** → **New Year** ► **New York** N (= *state*) (l'État m de) New York m; (= *city*) New York; **in New York (State)** dans l'État de New York ♦ ADJ newyorkais ► **New Yorker** N New-Yorkais(e) *m(f)* ► **New Zealand** N la Nouvelle-Zélande ♦ ADJ néo-zélandais ► **New Zealander** N Néo-Zélandais(e) *m(f)*

newborn ['njuːbɔːn] 1 ADJ a (*lit*) [*child, animal*] nouveau-né; **a ~ babe** un(e) nouveau-né(e) *m(f)* b (*fig*) [*nation, organization*] tout jeune 2 the newborn NPL les nouveaux-nés mpl 3 N nouveau-né(e) *m(f)* → **innocent**

newcomer ['njuːkʌməʳ] N nouveau venu m, nouvelle venue f; **they are ~s to this town** ils viennent d'arriver dans cette ville

newel ['njuːəl] N noyau m (d'escalier)

Newfoundland ['njuːfəndlənd] 1 N Terre-Neuve f 2 ADJ terre-neuvien; **~ fisherman** terre-neuvas m 3 COMP ► **Newfoundland dog** N chien m de Terre-Neuve, terre-neuve m inv

Newfoundlander [njuːˈfaundləndəʳ] N habitant(e) *m(f)* de Terre-Neuve, Terre-Neuvien(ne) *m(f)*

newish ['njuːɪʃ] ADJ assez neuf (neuve f)

newly ['njuːlɪ] 1 ADV nouvellement; **the ~-elected members** les membres nouvellement élus; **her ~-awakened curiosity** sa curiosité récemment éveillée; **~ arrived** récemment arrivé; **~ rich** nouveau riche; **~ shaved** rasé de frais; **a ~-dug grave** une tombe fraîchement creusée or ouverte; **a ~-formed friendship** une amitié de fraîche date; **his ~-found happiness** son bonheur tout neuf; **~-made wine** vin m qu'on vient de faire; **her ~-made friends** ses nouveaux amis; **when I was ~ married** quand j'étais jeune marié 2 COMP ► **newly industrialized country, newly industrializing country** N nouveau pays m industrialisé, pays m nouvellement industrialisé ► **newly-weds** NPL jeunes or nouveaux mariés mpl

newness ['njuːnɪs] N [*of fashion, ideas etc*] nouveauté f; [*of clothes etc*] état m (de) neuf; [*of bread*] fraîcheur f; [*of cheese*] manque m de maturité; [*of wine*] jeunesse f

news [njuːz] 1 N (*NonC*) a nouvelle(s) *f(pl)*; **a piece** or **an item of ~** (*gen*) une nouvelle; (*Press*) une information; **have you heard the ~?** tu es au courant?; **have you heard the ~ about Paul?** vous savez ce qui est arrivé à Paul?; **have you any ~ of him?** (= *heard from him*) avez-vous de ses nouvelles?; **I have no ~ of her** je ne sais pas ce qu'elle est devenue; **do let me have your ~** surtout donnez-moi de vos nouvelles; **what's your ~?** quoi de neuf or de nouveau (chez vous)?; **is there any ~?** y a-t-il du nouveau?; **I've got ~ for you!** j'ai du nouveau à vous annoncer!; **this is ~ to me!**∗ première nouvelle!∗, on en apprend tous les jours! (*iro*); **it will be ~ to him**∗ **that we are here** ça va le surprendre de nous savoir ici; **good ~** bonnes nouvelles fpl; **bad** or **sad ~** mauvaises or tristes nouvelles fpl; **he's/it's bad ~**∗ on a toujours des ennuis avec lui/ça; **she/it made ~** on a parlé d'elle/on en a parlé dans le journal; **bad ~ travels fast** les malheurs s'apprennent vite ▪ (*PROV*) **no ~ is good ~!** pas de nouvelles, bonnes nouvelles!; **when the ~ broke** quand on a su la nouvelle; **"dog bites man" isn't ~** « un homme mordu par un chien » n'est pas (ce qu'on peut appeler) une nouvelle; (*fig*) **he's in the ~ again** le voilà qui refait parler de lui → **break**

b (*Press, Rad*) informations fpl; (*TV*) informations fpl, journal m télévisé; **official ~** communiqué m officiel; **financial/sporting etc ~** chronique f or rubrique f financière/sportive etc; (*Press*) **"~ in brief"** « nouvelles brèves »

2 COMP ► **news agency** N agence f de presse ► **news analyst** N (*US Rad, TV*) commentateur m ► **news blackout** N black-out m ► **news broadcast, news bulletin** N (bulletin m d')informations fpl, journal m télévisé ► **news conference** N conférence f de presse ► **news desk** N service m des informations ► **news editor** N rédacteur m ► **news film** N film m d'actualités ► **news flash** N flash m (d'information)

► **news gathering** N (NonC) collecte f des informations ► **news headlines** NPL titres mpl de l'actualité ► **news item** N (Press etc) information f ► **news magazine** N magazine m d'actualités ► **news photographer** N reporter m photographe ► **news pictures** NPL reportage m photographique ► **news release** N (esp US) communiqué m de presse ► **news service** N agence f de presse ► **news sheet** N feuille f d'informations ► **news stand** N kiosque m (à journaux) ► **news theatre** N cinéma m or salle f d'actualités ► **news value** N **to have ~ value** présenter un intérêt pour le public ► **news weekly** N hebdomadaire m d'actualités

newsagent ['nju:z,eɪdʒənt] **1** N (Brit) marchand(e) m(f) de or dépositaire mf de journaux **2** COMP ► **newsagent's (shop)** N (Brit) maison f de la presse

newsboy ['nju:zbɔɪ] N vendeur m or crieur m de journaux

newsbreak ['nju:zbreɪk] N (US) nouvelle f digne d'intérêt

newscast ['nju:zka:st] N (US) (bulletin m d')informations fpl

newscaster ['nju:zka:stər] N (Rad, TV) présentateur m, -trice f (de journal télévisé)

newsclip ['nju:zklɪp] N (US Press) coupure f de journal

newsdealer ['nju:zdi:lər] N (US) = **newsagent**

newsgroup ['nju:zgru:p] N (Comput: on Internet) forum m de discussion

newshound ['nju:zhaʊnd], **newshawk** ['nju:zhɔ:k] N reporter m; (pej) **there was a crowd of ~s around him** il était aux prises avec une meute de journalistes

newsletter ['nju:zletər] N bulletin m (d'une entreprise)

newsmaker ['nju:zmeɪkər] N (US) (= event) sujet m d'actualité; (= person) vedette f de l'actualité

newsman ['nju:zmən] N (pl -men) journaliste m

newsmonger ['nju:zmʌngər] N (pej) pipelette* f, commère f

newspaper ['nju:z,peɪpər] **1** N journal m; **daily ~** quotidien m; **weekly ~** hebdomadaire m; **he works for or on a ~** il travaille pour un journal **2** COMP ► **newspaper advertising** N publicité-presse f ► **newspaper clipping**, **newspaper cutting** N coupure f de journal or de presse ► **newspaper office** N (bureaux mpl de la) rédaction f ► **newspaper photographer** N reporter m photographe ► **newspaper report** N reportage m

newspaperman ['nju:z,peɪpəmæn] N (pl -men) journaliste m

newspaperwoman ['nju:z,peɪpəwʊmən] N (pl -women) journaliste f

newsprint ['nju:zprɪnt] N (NonC) (= paper) papier m (journal); (= ink) encre f d'imprimerie

newsreader ['nju:zri:dər] N (Brit Rad, TV) présentateur m, -trice f (de journal télévisé)

newsreel ['nju:zri:l] N actualités fpl (filmées)

newsroom ['nju:zrʊm] N salle f de rédaction

newsvendor ['nju:zvendər] N vendeur m de journaux

newsworthy ['nju:zwɜ:ðɪ] ADJ **to be ~** valoir la peine d'être publié

newsy* ['nju:zɪ] ADJ (= full of news) [letter] plein de nouvelles

newt [nju:t] N triton m

newton ['nju:tən] N (Phys) newton m

Newtonian [nju:'təʊnɪən] ADJ newtonien

▼ **New Year** ['nju:'jɪər] **1** N nouvel an m, nouvelle année f; **to bring in** or **see in the ~** réveillonner (à la Saint-Sylvestre), fêter le nouvel an; **Happy ~!** bonne année!; **to wish sb a happy ~** souhaiter une or la bonne année à qn **2** COMP ► **New Year gift** N étrennes fpl

► **New Year resolution** N bonne résolution f (de nouvel an) ► **New Year's Day** N jour m or premier m de l'an, nouvel an m ► **New Year's Eve** N la Saint-Sylvestre ► **New Year's Honours List** N (Brit) = Honours List; → honour; → HONOURS LIST

next [nekst] **1** ADJ **a** (in time) (in future) prochain; (in past) suivant; **come back ~ week/month** revenez la semaine prochaine/le mois prochain; **he came back the ~ week** il est revenu la semaine suivante or d'après; **he came back the ~ day** il est revenu le lendemain or le jour suivant; **the ~ day but one** le surlendemain; **during the ~ five days he did-not go out** il n'est pas sorti pendant les cinq jours qui ont suivi; **I will finish this in the ~ five days** je finirai ceci dans les cinq jours qui viennent or à venir; **the ~ morning** le lendemain matin; **(the) ~ time I see him** la prochaine fois que je le verrai; **the ~ time I saw him** la première fois où or que je l'ai revu, quand je l'ai revu; **I'll come back ~ week and the ~ again** je reviendrai la semaine prochaine et la suivante; **this time ~ week** d'ici huit jours; **the ~ moment** l'instant d'après; **from one moment to the ~** d'un moment à l'autre; **the year after ~** dans deux ans; **~ Wednesday ◊ Wednesday ~*** mercredi prochain; **~ March** en mars prochain; **~ year** l'année prochaine, l'an prochain

b (in series, list etc) (= following) [page, case] suivant; (= which is to come) prochain; **he got off at the ~ stop** il est descendu à l'arrêt suivant; **you get off at the ~ stop** vous descendez au prochain arrêt; **who's ~?** à qui le tour?, c'est à qui?; **you're ~** c'est votre tour, c'est à vous (maintenant); **~ please!** au suivant!; **I was the ~ person** or **I was ~ to speak** ce fut ensuite à mon tour de parler → **4a**; **I'll ask the very ~ person I see** je vais demander à la première personne que je verrai; **in the ~ place** ensuite; **on the ~ page** à la page suivante; **"continued in the ~ column"** « voir colonne ci-contre »; **the ~ thing to do is ...** la première chose à faire maintenant est de ...; **he saw that the ~ thing to do was ...** il a vu que ce qu'il devait faire ensuite (c')était ...; **(the) ~ thing I knew, he had gone*** et tout d'un coup, il a disparu; **I'll try the ~ size up** je vais essayer la taille au-dessus; **the ~ size down** la taille au-dessous

c (= immediately adjacent) [house, street, room] d'à côté

2 ADV **a** ensuite, après; **~ we had lunch** ensuite or après nous avons déjeuné; **what shall we do ~?** qu'allons-nous faire maintenant?; **when you ~ come to see us** la prochaine fois que vous viendrez nous voir; **when I ~ saw him ◊ when ~ I saw him** (frm) quand je l'ai revu (la fois suivante); **when shall we meet ~?** quand nous reverrons-nous?; **a new dress! what(ever) ~?** une nouvelle robe! et puis quoi encore?

b (with superl) **the ~ best thing would be to speak to his brother** à défaut le mieux serait de parler à son frère; **she's my ~ best friend** à part une autre c'est ma meilleure amie; **this is my ~ oldest daughter after Marie** c'est la plus âgée de mes filles après Marie; **she's the ~ youngest** elle suit (par ordre d'âge); **who's the ~ tallest (boy)?** qui est le plus grand après?

c **~ to** (= beside) à côté de; (= almost) presque; **his room is ~ to mine** sa chambre est à côté de la mienne; **the church stands ~ to the school** l'église est à côté de l'école; **he was sitting ~ to me** il était assis à côté de moi; **to wear wool ~ to the skin** porter de la laine à même la peau; (fig) **the thing ~ to my heart** la chose qui me tient le plus à cœur; **~ to France, what country do you like best?** après la France, quel est votre pays préféré?; (US) **to get ~ to sb** se mettre bien avec qn; **the ~ to last row** l'avant-dernier or le pénultième

rang; **he was ~ to last** il était avant-dernier; **~ to nothing*** presque rien; **I got it for ~ to nothing*** je l'ai payé trois fois rien; **~ to no-body*** presque personne; **there's ~ to no news*** il n'y a presque rien de neuf; **the ~ to top/bottom shelf** le deuxième rayon (en partant) du haut/du bas

3 PREP (Brit †) à côté de → **2c**

4 N prochain(e) m(f); **the ~ to speak is Paul** c'est Paul qui parle ensuite, c'est Paul qui est le prochain à parler; **the ~ to arrive was Robert** c'est Robert qui est arrivé ensuite or le suivant; (= baby) **I hope my ~* will be a boy** j'espère que mon prochain (enfant) sera un garçon; (= edition) **to be continued in our ~** suite au prochain numéro

5 COMP ► **next door** N, ADV → **next door** ► **next of kin** N (on forms etc) «nom et prénom de votre plus proche parent»; **who is your ~ of kin?** qui est votre plus proche parent?; **the police will inform the ~ of kin** la police préviendra la famille

next door ['neks'dɔ:r] **1** N la maison (or l'appartement etc) d'à côté; **it's the man from ~** c'est le monsieur d'à côté or qui habite à côté

2 ADV **a** (= in or to next house, room) [live, go] à côté; **she lived ~ to me** elle habitait à côté de chez moi; **we live ~ to each other** nous sommes voisins; **he has the room ~ to me at the hotel** il a la chambre à côté de la mienne à l'hôtel; **the house ~** la maison d'à côté; (lit) **the boy/girl ~** le garçon/la fille d'à côté; (fig) **he's the boy ~ type** c'est quelqu'un de très simple; (fig) **she married the boy ~** elle s'est mariée avec un bon gars*; **at the table ~*** à la table d'à côté

b (* fig = almost) **that is ~ to madness** cela frise la folie; **if he isn't mad he's ~ to it** s'il n'est pas fou il s'en faut de peu or c'est tout comme*; **we were ~ to being ruined** nous avons été au bord de la ruine, nous avons frôlé la ruine

3 **next-door** ADJ [neighbour, building, room, table] d'à côté

nexus ['neksəs] N (pl inv) (= connection) lien m; (= series of connections) liaison f

NF [en'ef] N (Brit Pol) (ABBR = **National Front**) → national

n/f (Banking) (ABBR = **no funds**) défaut m de provision

NFL [enef'el] N (US) (ABBR = **National Football League**) Fédération f américaine de football

NFU [,enef'ju:] N (Brit) (ABBR = **National Farmers' Union**) syndicat

NG [en'dʒi:] N (US) (ABBR = **National Guard**) → national

NGA [,endʒi:'eɪ] N (Brit: formerly) (ABBR = **National Graphical Association**) ancien syndicat

NGO [,endʒi:'əʊ] N ABBR = **non-governmental organization**

NH ABBR = **New Hampshire**

NHL [,eneɪtʃ'el] N (US) (ABBR = **National Hockey League**) Fédération f américaine de hockey sur glace

NHS [,eneɪtʃ'es] N (Brit) (ABBR = **National Health Service**) ≈ Sécurité f sociale

┌─ **NHS** ─────────────────────┐

Le **National Health Service**, ou **NHS**, est la branche maladie du régime de sécurité sociale, qui, depuis 1948, assure des soins médicaux gratuits à toute personne résidant en Grande-Bretagne. Le NHS est essentiellement financé par l'impôt, mais aussi par les charges et les cotisations sociales et, enfin, par la quote-part à la charge de l'assuré sur les médicaments prescrits. Les soins dentaires ne sont pas gratuits. → PRESCRIPTION CHARGE

└────────────────────────────┘

NI **a** (ABBR = **Northern Ireland**) → northern

► LANGUAGE IN USE: **New Year** 23.2

b (Brit) (ABBR = **National Insurance**) → **national**

niacin ['naɪəsɪn] N acide m nicotinique

Niagara [naɪ'ægrə] **1** N Niagara m **2** COMP ► **Niagara Falls** NPL les chutes fpl du Niagara

nib [nɪb] N **a** [of pen] (bec m de) plume f; **fine ~** plume f fine or à bec fin; **broad ~** grosse plume f, plume f à gros bec **b** [of tool] pointe f

-nibbed [nɪbd] ADJ (in compounds) **fine-nibbed** à plume fine; **gold-nibbed** à plume en or

nibble ['nɪbl] **1** VTI [person] [+ food] grignoter; [+ pen, finger, ear] mordiller; [sheep, goats etc] brouter; [fish] mordre, mordiller; **to ~ (at) one's food** chipoter; **she was nibbling (at) some chocolate** elle grignotait un morceau de chocolat; **he was nibbling (at) her ear** il lui mordillait l'oreille; **she ~d (on) her pencil** elle mordillait son crayon; (fig) **to ~ at an offer** se montrer tenté par une offre **2** N **a** (Fishing) touche f **b** (= snack) **I feel like a ~*** je grignoterais bien quelque chose ici; **nibbles** NPL amuse-gueule(s) m(pl)

niblick ['nɪblɪk] N (Golf) niblick m

nibs [nɪbz] N (hum) **his ~:** Son Altesse (iro), sézigue*

NIC [,enar'si:] N **a** (ABBR = **newly industrialized** or **industrializing country**) NPI m **b** (Brit) (ABBR = **National Insurance Contribution**) → **national**

NICAM ['naɪkæm] (ABBR = **near-instantaneous companded audio multiplex**) NICAM

Nicaragua [,nɪkə'rægjʊə] N le Nicaragua

Nicaraguan [,nɪkə'rægjʊən] **1** ADJ nicaraguayen **2** N Nicaraguayen(ne) m(f)

nice [naɪs] **1** ADJ **a** (= pleasant, likeable) [person] sympathique; [place, manners] agréable; [view] beau (belle f); [holiday] beau (belle f), agréable; [smell, taste] bon, agréable; [meal, idea] bon; [dress, face, voice, smile, ring, photo] joli; [car] (to look at) beau (belle f); (to drive) bon; **he seems like a ~ person** il a l'air sympathique; **it's ~ here** on est bien ici; **to smell ~** sentir bon; **to taste ~** avoir bon goût; **you look very ~** tu es très bien; **you look ~ in that dress** cette robe te va bien; **a ~ little house** une jolie petite maison; **it would be ~ if ...** ce serait bien si ...; **it would be ~ to know what they intend to do** j'aimerais bien savoir ce qu'ils ont l'intention de faire; **(it's) ~ to see you** ça fait plaisir de vous voir; **(it's been) ~ meeting you** or **to have met you** ça m'a fait plaisir de faire votre connaissance; **to meet you!** enchanté!; **a ~ cup of coffee** un bon petit café; (Brit) **~ one!** ◊ **~ work!*** (lit) bien joué!*; (also iro) bravo!; **have a ~ day!** bonne journée!; **we had a ~ evening** nous avons passé une bonne soirée or une soirée agréable; **did you have a ~ time at the party?** vous vous êtes bien amusés à la soirée ? **b** (= kind, friendly) [person] gentil (**to sb** avec qn), aimable (**to sb** envers qn); **he was perfectly ~ about it** il a bien pris la chose; **that wasn't ~ of you** ce n'était pas gentil à vous or de votre part; **it's ~ of you to do that** c'est gentil à vous de faire cela; **to say ~ things about sb/sth** dire du bien de qn/sur qch; **to be as ~ as pie* (to sb)** être gentil comme tout (avec qn); **to be as ~ as pie* about sth** très bien prendre qch; (hum) **no more Mr Nice Guy!*** finis les ronds de jambe! **c** (often iro = respectable, refined) [person, behaviour, expression, book, film] convenable, comme il faut; **not ~** peu convenable, pas comme il faut; **that's not ~!** ça ne se fait pas!; **~ girls don't do that** les filles bien élevées ne font pas ce genre de chose **d** (= fine) [weather, day] beau (belle f); **~ weather we're having!** beau temps, n'est-ce pas ? **e** (*: used as intensifier) **to get up ~ and early** se lever de bonne heure; **we'll take it ~ and easy** on va y aller doucement; **it's so ~ and**

2 COMP ► **nice-looking** ADJ joli, beau (belle f); **he's ~-looking** il est joli or beau garçon

nicely ['naɪslɪ] ADV **a** (= well) [manage, function, work, progress] bien; **to dress ~** être bien habillé; **~ done** bien fait; **that will do ~** c'est parfait!; **to be doing very ~ (for oneself)*** s'en sortir très bien; **to be coming along ~*** bien se présenter; **to be ~ placed to do sth** être bien placé pour faire qch **b** (= politely) [eat, thank] poliment; [ask] gentiment, poliment; **a ~ behaved child** un enfant bien élevé **c** (frm = subtly) [differentiated] subtilement

Nicene ['naɪsi:n] ADJ **the ~ Creed** le Credo or le symbole de Nicée

niceness ['naɪsnɪs] N **a** (= pleasantness) [of person] gentillesse f, amabilité f; [of place, thing] agrément m, caractère m agréable **b** (frm = subtlety) délicatesse f; [of distinction, point, taste etc] subtilité f

nicety ['naɪsɪtɪ] N **a** (of one's judgement) justesse f, précision f; **to a ~** à la perfection **b** **niceties** (= subtleties, fine details) [of system, process, legislation, diplomacy] subtilités fpl; (= refinements) [of clothes, fashion etc] raffinements mpl; **legal/diplomatic niceties** subtilités fpl légales/diplomatiques; **social niceties** mondanités fpl; **the niceties of dinner party conversation** les mondanités qui s'échangent lors des dîners

niche [ni:ʃ] **1** N (gen) niche f; (Comm) créneau m; (fig) **to find one's ~ (in life)** trouver sa voie (dans la vie) **2** COMP ► **niche marketing** N (Comm) marketing m du créneau

Nicholas ['nɪkələs] N Nicolas m

Nick [nɪk] N **a** dim of **Nicholas** **b** **Old ~*** le diable, le malin

nick [nɪk] **1** N **a** (in wood) encoche f; (in blade, dish) ébréchure f; (on face, skin) (petite) coupure f; (fig) **in the ~ of time** juste à temps **b** (Brit*) **to be in the ~** être en taule* **c** (Brit* = condition) état m, condition f; **in good ~** en bon état; **in bad ~** en mauvais état, nase*; **his car's in better ~ than mine** sa voiture est en meilleur état que la mienne **2** VT **a** [+ plank, stick] faire une or des encoche(s) sur; [+ blade, dish] ébrécher; [+ cards] biseauter; **he ~ed his chin while shaving** il s'est fait une (petite) coupure au menton en se rasant **b** (Brit* = arrest) pincer*, choper*; **to get ~ed** se faire pincer* or choper*; **to ~ sb for sth** pincer* qn pour qch; **all right mate, you're ~ed!** allez, mon gars, tu es fait!* **c** (Brit* = steal) piquer*, faucher* **d** (US) **how much did they ~ you for that suit?*** tu t'es fait avoir* de combien pour or sur ce costume ?

nickel ['nɪkl] **1** N **a** (NonC = metal) nickel m **b** (in Can, US = coin) pièce f de cinq cents **2** VT nickeler **3** COMP ► **nickel-and-dime*** ADJ (US = cheap and nasty) de camelote, au rabais ► **nickel-in-the-slot machine†** N (US) machine f à sous ► **nickel-plated** ADJ

nickelé ► **nickel-plating** N nickelage m ► **nickel silver** N argentan m, maillechort m

nickelodeon [,nɪkə'ləʊdɪən] N (US) (= cinema) cinéma m à cinq sous; (= jukebox) juke-box m

nicker ['nɪkər] **1** VI **a** [horse] hennir doucement **b** (= snigger) ricaner **2** N (pl inv: Brit*) livre f

nickname ['nɪkneɪm] **1** N surnom m; (esp humorous or malicious) sobriquet m; (= short form of name) diminutif m **2** VT surnommer, donner un sobriquet à; **John, ~d "Taffy"** John, surnommé « Taffy »; **they ~d their teacher "Goggles"** ils ont donné leur professeur « Goggles », ils ont donné à leur professeur le sobriquet de « Goggles »

Nicodemus [,nɪkə'di:məs] N Nicodème m

Nicosia [,nɪkə'si:ə] N Nicosie f

nicotiana [nɪ,kəʊʃɪ'ɑ:nə] N nicotiana m

nicotine ['nɪkəti:n] **1** N nicotine f **2** COMP ► **nicotine patch** N patch m de nicotine, timbre m à la nicotine or antitabac ► **nicotine poisoning** N nicotinisme m ► **nicotine-stained** ADJ jauni or taché de nicotine

nicotinic [nɪkə'tɪnɪk] ADJ **~ acid** acide m nicotinique

nicotinism [nɪkəti:,nɪzəm] N nicotinisme m, tabagisme m

niece [ni:s] N nièce f

Nielsen rating ['ni:lsənreɪtɪŋ] N (TV) ≈ audimat® m

Nietzschean ['ni:tʃɪən] ADJ nietzschéen

niff [nɪf] N (Brit) puanteur f; **what a ~!** ce que ça cocotte* or (s)chlingue!

niffy* ['nɪfɪ] ADJ (Brit) puant; **it's ~ in here** ça cocotte* or (s)chlingue! ici!

nifty* ['nɪftɪ] ADJ **a** (= excellent) [person, place, idea, gadget, car] chouette* **b** (= skilful) [player] habile; **he's pretty ~ with a screwdriver** il manie drôlement bien le tournevis **c** (= quick) **you'd better be ~ about it!** tu as intérêt à te magner!* **d** (= stylish) [outfit] coquet, chic inv

Niger ['naɪdʒər] **1** N **a** (= country) le Niger **b** (= river) Niger m **2** COMP nigérien; [embassy, capital] du Niger

Nigeria [naɪ'dʒɪərɪə] N le Nigeria

Nigerian [naɪ'dʒɪərɪən] **1** N Nigérian(e) m(f) **2** ADJ (gen) nigérian; [ambassador, embassy] du Nigéria

niggardliness ['nɪgədlɪnɪs] N avarice f, pingrerie f

niggardly ['nɪgədlɪ] **1** ADJ [person] pingre, avare; [amount, portion] mesquin, piètre; [salary] piètre; **a ~ £50** 50 malheureuses livres **2** ADV chichement, mesquinement

nigger ['nɪgər] **1** N (* pej) nègre m, négresse f; (fig) **there's a ~ in the woodpile** il se trame quelque chose; (Brit fig) **to be the ~ in the woodpile** faire le trouble-fête **2** COMP ► **nigger brown†** ADJ (Brit) tête-de-nègre inv

niggle ['nɪgl] **1** VI [person] (= go into detail) couper les cheveux en quatre; (= find fault) trouver toujours à redire **2** VT **his conscience was niggling him** sa conscience le travaillait **3** N (= doubt, query) **your report is excellent, I just have one little ~*** votre rapport est excellent, j'ai juste une petite remarque

niggling ['nɪglɪŋ] **1** ADJ (= trivial but annoying) [doubt, suspicion] obsédant; (= finicky) [person] tatillon; (= petty) [details] insignifiant; **a ~ injury** une vieille blessure qui se réveille de temps en temps; **a ~ little pain** une petite douleur tenace; **I've got a ~ worry about it** il y a quelque chose qui me tracasse (là-dedans) **2** N (NonC) chicanerie f

nigh [naɪ] ADV (liter) **near 1, 2, 3**

night [naɪt] **1** N **a** (= night-time) nuit f; **~ after ~** des nuits durant; **~ and day** nuit et jour; **all ~ (long)** toute la nuit; **to sit up all ~ talking** passer la nuit (entière) à bavarder; **at**

~ ◊ in the ~ la nuit ; **by ~ ◊ in the ~** de nuit ; **during the ~ ◊ in the ~** pendant la nuit ; **far into the ~** jusqu'à une heure avancée de la nuit, (très) tard dans la nuit ; **to spend the ~ (with sb)** passer la nuit (avec qn) ; **to have a good/bad ~** bien/mal dormir, passer une bonne/mauvaise nuit ; **I've had several bad ~s in a row** j'ai mal dormi plusieurs nuits de suite ; **he needs a good ~'s sleep** il a besoin d'une bonne nuit de sommeil ; **a ~'s lodging** un toit or un gîte pour la nuit ; **he's on ~s this week** il est de nuit cette semaine ; **to work ~s** travailler de nuit ; (US) **I can't sleep (at) ~s** je ne peux pas dormir la nuit → **Arabian**, **early**, **goodnight**

b (= evening) soir m ; **6 o'clock at ~** 6 heures du soir ; **to have a ~** sortir le soir ; **a ~ at the opera** une soirée à l'opéra ; **to make a ~ of it*** prolonger la soirée ; **I've had too many late ~s** je me suis couché tard trop souvent ; **she's used to late ~s** elle a l'habitude de se coucher tard

c (specifying) **last ~** (= night-time) la nuit dernière, cette nuit ; (= evening) hier soir ; **to-morrow ~** demain soir ; **the ~ before** la veille au soir ; **the ~ before last** avant-hier soir m ; **Monday ~** lundi soir ; (= night-time) dans la nuit de lundi à mardi

d (NonC = darkness) nuit f ; **~ is falling** la nuit or le soir tombe ; **he went out into the ~** il partit dans la nuit ; **he's afraid of the ~** il a peur du noir ; (lit, fig) **a creature of the ~** une créature de la nuit

e (Theat) soirée f, représentation f ; **the last three ~s of ...** les trois dernières (représentations) de ... ; **Mozart ~** soirée f (consacrée à) Mozart → **first**

2 COMP [clothes, flight] de nuit ► **night-bird** N (lit) oiseau m de nuit, nocturne m ; (fig) couche-tard mf inv, noctambule mf (hum) ► **night-blind** ADJ héméralope ► **night blindness** N héméralopie f ► **night editor** N (Press) secrétaire mf de rédaction de nuit ► **night-fighter** N (Aviat) chasseur m de nuit ► **night letter** N (US) télégramme à tarif réduit, livré le lendemain matin ► **night light** N (child's) veilleuse f ; (Naut) feu m de position ► **night-night*** EXCL (= goodnight) bonne nuit ► **night nurse** N infirmier m, -ière f de nuit ► **night owl*** N (fig) couche-tard mf inv, noctambule mf (hum) ► **night porter** N gardien m de nuit, concierge mf de service la nuit ► **night safe** N coffre m de nuit ► **night school** N cours mpl du soir ► **night shelter** N asile m de nuit ► **night shift** N (= workers) équipe f de nuit ; (= work) poste m de nuit ; **to be** or **to work on (the) ~ shift** être (au poste) de nuit ► **the night sky** N (gen) le ciel la nuit ; (liter) la voûte céleste ► **night soil**† N selles fpl (nocturnes) ► **night stand** N (US) table f de nuit ► **night stick** N (US Police) matraque f (d'agent de police) ► **night storage heater** N radiateur m par accumulation (fonctionnant au tarif de nuit) ► **night storage heating** N chauffage m par accumulation (fonctionnant au tarif de nuit) ► **night table** N table f de nuit ► **night-time** N (NonC) nuit f ; **at ~time** la nuit ; **in the ~time** pendant la nuit, de nuit ► **night vision** N vision f nocturne ► **night-vision** ADJ [equipment, goggles] pour la vision nocturne ► **night watch** N (= activity, period of time) veille f or garde f de nuit ; (= group of guards) équipe f des veilleurs or gardiens de nuit ; (one man) ► **night watchman** N (pl **night watchmen**) veilleur m or gardien m de nuit ► **night work** N travail m de nuit → **black**, **deadly**, **woody**

nightcap ['naɪtkæp] N **a** (= hat) bonnet m de nuit **b** (= drink) boisson f (généralement alcoolisée, prise avant le coucher) ; **would you like a ~?** voulez-vous boire quelque chose avant d'aller vous coucher ?

nightclothes ['naɪtkləʊðz] NPL vêtements mpl de nuit

nightclub ['naɪtklʌb] N boîte f de nuit, nightclub m

nightclubber ['naɪtklʌbəʳ] N **he's a real ~** il adore sortir en boîte

nightclubbing ['naɪtklʌbɪŋ] N sorties fpl en boîte (de nuit)

nightdress ['naɪtdres] N (esp Brit) chemise f de nuit

nightfall ['naɪtfɔːl] N tombée f du jour or de la nuit ; **at ~** à la tombée du jour, à la nuit tombante

nightgown ['naɪtgaʊn] N chemise f de nuit

nighthawk ['naɪthɔːk] N **a** (= bird) engoulevent m (d'Amérique) **b** (US fig = person) couche-tard mf inv, noctambule mf (hum)

nightie* ['naɪtɪ] N chemise f de nuit

nightingale ['naɪtɪŋgeɪl] N rossignol m

nightjar ['naɪtdʒɑːʳ] N engoulevent m (d'Europe)

nightlife ['naɪtlaɪf] N vie f nocturne ; **the Parisian/Roman ~** la vie nocturne à Paris/Rome

nightlong ['naɪtlɒŋ] ADJ (gen) de toute une nuit ; [festivities, vigil] qui dure toute la nuit

nightly ['naɪtlɪ] **1** ADJ **muggings are a ~ occurrence** les agressions nocturnes sont devenues quotidiennes ; (Theat) **~ performance** représentation f tous les soirs **2** ADV (= every evening) tous les soirs ; (= every night) toutes les nuits ; (Theat) **performances ~** représentations fpl tous les soirs

nightmare ['naɪtmeəʳ] **1** N (lit, fig) cauchemar m ; **what a ~!*** quel cauchemar ! ; **to be sb's worst ~** être la pire hantise de qn **2** COMP ► **nightmare scenario** N scénario m catastrophe

nightmarish ['naɪtmeərɪʃ] ADJ de cauchemar, cauchemardesque

nightshirt ['naɪtʃɜːt] N chemise f de nuit

nightspot* ['naɪtspɒt] N = **nightclub**

nightwear ['naɪtweəʳ] N (NonC) vêtements mpl de nuit

nihilism ['naɪɪlɪzəm] N nihilisme m

nihilist ['naɪɪlɪst] N nihiliste m

nihilistic [ˌnaɪɪˈlɪstɪk] ADJ nihiliste

Nikkei index [nɪˌkeɪˈɪndeks], **Nikkei average** [nɪˌkeɪˈævərɪdʒ] N (Fin) indice m Nikkei

nil [nɪl] **1** N (Sport) zéro → ZERO ; (in form-filling etc) néant ; **my morale was ~** j'avais le moral à zéro ; **his motivation was ~*** il n'était pas du tout motivé ; (in hospital) **"~ by mouth"** « à jeun »

Nile [naɪl] N Nil m ; (Hist) **the Battle of the ~** la bataille d'Aboukir

nimbi ['nɪmbaɪ] NPL of **nimbus**

nimble ['nɪmbl] **1** ADJ [person, fingers, feet] agile ; [mind] vif ; [car] maniable **2** COMP ► **nimble-fingered** ADJ aux doigts agiles ► **nimble-footed** ADJ au pied léger ► **nimble-minded**, **nimble-witted** ADJ à l'esprit vif

nimbleness ['nɪmblnɪs] N [of person, fingers, limbs etc] agilité f ; [of mind] vivacité f

nimbly ['nɪmblɪ] ADV [move, jump] lestement

nimbostratus [ˌnɪmbəʊˈstreɪtəs] N (pl **nimbostrati** [ˌnɪmbəʊˈstreɪtaɪ]) nimbostratus m

nimbus ['nɪmbəs] N (pl **nimbi** or **nimbuses**) **a** (= halo) nimbe m, halo m **b** (= cloud) nimbus m

Nimby* ['nɪmbɪ] N (ABBR = **not in my back yard**) riverain(e) m(f) contestataire (s'opposant à toute installation gênante près de chez lui)

nincompoop†* ['nɪŋkəmpuːp] N cornichon* m, gourde* f

nine [naɪn] **1** ADJ neuf inv ; **~ times out of ten** neuf fois sur dix ; **cats have ~ lives** un chat retombe toujours sur ses pattes ; (hum) **he's got**

~ lives [person] un ange gardien veille sur lui **2** N neuf m inv ; **dressed (up) to the ~s*** sur son trente et un ; for other phrases see **six 3** PRON neuf ; **there are ~** il y en a neuf **4** COMP ► **nine-day wonder** N merveille f d'un jour ► **nine-hole** ADJ **~-hole golf course** (parcours m de) neuf trous ► **nine-to-five*** ADJ **~-to-five job** travail m de bureau ; **he's got a ~-to-five mentality** or **attitude** il a une mentalité de fonctionnaire

ninepins ['naɪnpɪnz] NPL (jeu m de) quilles fpl ; **they went down like ~** ils sont tombés comme des mouches

nineteen ['naɪn'tiːn] **1** ADJ dix-neuf inv **2** N dix-neuf m inv ; (Brit) **he talks ~ to the dozen*** c'est un vrai moulin à paroles ; **they were talking ~ to the dozen*** ils jacassaient à qui mieux mieux ; for other phrases see **six 3** PRON dix-neuf ; **there are ~** il y en a dix-neuf

nineteenth ['naɪn'tiːnθ] **1** ADJ dix-neuvième ; (Golf hum) **the ~ (hole)** le bar, la buvette **2** N dix-neuvième mf ; (= fraction) dix-neuvième m ; for phrases see **sixth**

ninetieth ['naɪntɪɪθ] **1** ADJ quatre-vingt-dixième **2** N quatre-vingt-dixième mf ; (= fraction) quatre-vingt-dixième m ; for phrases see **sixth**

ninety ['naɪntɪ] **1** ADJ quatre-vingt-dix inv **2** N quatre-vingt-dix m inv ; **~-one** quatre-vingt-onze ; **~-nine** quatre-vingt-dix-neuf ; **~-nine times out of a hundred** quatre-vingt dix-neuf fois sur cent ; **to be in one's nineties** être nonagénaire, avoir passé quatre-vingt-dix ans ; (at doctor's) **"say ~-nine!"** ≈ « dites trente-trois ! » ; (hum) for other phrases see **sixty 3** PRON quatre-vingt-dix ; **there are ~** il y en a quatre-vingt-dix

ninny* ['nɪnɪ] N cornichon* m, serin(e)* m(f), gourde* f

ninth [naɪnθ] **1** ADJ neuvième **2** N neuvième mf ; (= fraction) neuvième m ; for phrases see **sixth**

niobium [naɪˈəʊbɪəm] N niobium m

Nip* [nɪp] N (pej) Nippon m, -on(n)e f, Jap* m (pej)

nip¹ [nɪp] **1** N (= pinch) pinçon m ; (= bite) morsure f ; **the dog gave him a ~** le chien lui a donné un (petit) coup de dent ; (= chill) **there's a ~ in the air today** il fait frisquet aujourd'hui

2 VT (= pinch) pincer ; (= bite) donner un (petit) coup de dent à ; [cold, frost] [+ plants] brûler ; (= prune) [+ bud, shoot] pincer ; (fig) [+ plan, ambition] faire échec à ; **the cold air ~ped our faces** l'air froid nous piquait or pinçait le or au visage ; (fig) **to ~ sth in the bud** faire avorter qch, tuer or écraser qch dans l'œuf

3 VI (Brit*) **to ~ up/down/out** etc monter/descendre/sortir etc en courant ; **he ~ped into the café** il a fait un saut au café

4 COMP ► **nip and tuck*** ADV (= neck and neck) **it was ~ and tuck** (race) la course a été serrée, ils sont arrivés dans un mouchoir de poche ◊ N (= plastic surgery) lifting m

► **nip along*** VI (Brit) [person] aller d'un bon pas ; [car] filer ; **~ along to Anne's house** cours vite or fais un saut chez Anne

► **nip in*** **1** VI (Brit) entrer en courant, entrer un instant ; **I've just ~ped in for a minute** je ne fais qu'entrer et sortir ; **to ~ in and out of the traffic** se faufiler entre les voitures **2** VT SEP (Sewing) faire une (or des) pince(s) à ; **dress ~ped in at the waist** robe f pincée à la taille

► **nip off*** **1** VI (Brit*) filer*, se sauver* **2** VT SEP [+ bud, shoot] pincer ; [+ top of sth] couper

nip² [nɪp] N (= drink) goutte f, petit verre m ; **to take a ~** boire une goutte or un petit verre ; **have a ~ of whisky!** une goutte de whisky ?

nipper ['nɪpəʳ] N **a** (Brit*) gosse mf, mioche* mf **b** (= tool) **(pair of) ~s** pince f, tenaille(s) f(pl) **c** (Zool) pince f

nipple ['nɪpl] N a (Anat) mamelon m, bout m de sein b [of baby's bottle] tétine f; (Geog) mamelon m c (for grease etc) graisseur m

Nippon ['nɪpɒn] N (= Japan) le Japon

Nipponese [,nɪpə'niːz] 1 ADJ nippon (-on(n)e f) 2 N Nippon m, -on(n)e f

nippy* ['nɪpɪ] ADJ a (= chilly) [weather, wind] frisquet; **it's a bit ~ today** il fait frisquet aujourd'hui; **a ~ autumn day** une fraîche journée d'automne b (Brit = brisk) [person] rapide; **a ~ little car** une petite voiture rapide et nerveuse c (US = piquant) [cheese, flavour] piquant

NIREX ['naɪreks] (ABBR = **Nuclear Industry Radioactive Waste Executive**) → **nuclear**

nirvana [nɪə'vɑːnə] N nirvana m

Nisei ['niːseɪ] N (pl **Nisei** or **Niseis**) (US) Américain né d'immigrants japonais

nisi ['naɪsaɪ] ADJ → **decree**

Nissen hut ['nɪsn,hʌt] N hutte f préfabriquée (en tôle, en forme de tunnel)

nit [nɪt] 1 N a (= louse-egg) lente f b (Brit = fool) crétin(e)* m(f) 2 COMP ► **nit-pick*** VI **he's always ~-picking** il est très tatillon ► **nit-picker*** N tatillon m, -onne f

niter ['naɪtə] N (US) = **nitre**

nitrate ['naɪtreɪt] N nitrate m

nitration [naɪ'treɪʃən] N nitration f

nitre, niter (US) ['naɪtə'] N nitre m, salpêtre m

nitric ['naɪtrɪk] 1 ADJ nitrique 2 COMP ► **nitric acid** N acide m nitrique ► **nitric oxide** N oxyde m nitrique

nitrite ['naɪtraɪt] N nitrite m

nitro* ['naɪtrəʊ] N ABBR = **nitroglycerin(e)**

nitro... ['naɪtrəʊ] PREF nitro...

nitrogen ['naɪtrədʒən] 1 N azote m 2 COMP ► **nitrogen cycle** N cycle m de l'azote ► **nitrogen dioxide** N dioxyde m d'azote ► **nitrogen gas** N (gaz m) azote m

nitrogenous [naɪ'trɒdʒɪnəs] ADJ azoté

nitroglycerin(e) ['naɪtrəʊ'glɪsəriːn] N nitroglycérine f

nitrous ['naɪtrəs] 1 ADJ nitreux, d'azote 2 COMP ► **nitrous acid** N acide m nitreux ► **nitrous oxide** N oxyde m d'azote

nitty-gritty* ['nɪtɪ'grɪtɪ] 1 N **to get down to the ~** passer aux choses sérieuses; (= hard facts) **the ~ of life** la dure réalité; **the ~ of motherhood** (les difficultés de) la vie quotidienne d'une mère de famille; **the ~ of everyday politics** la dure réalité quotidienne de la vie politique 2 ADJ [details] pratique; [problems] concret

nitwit* ['nɪtwɪt] N crétin(e) m(f)

nix [nɪks] 1 N (esp US* = nothing) que dalle* 2 VT (US) mettre son veto à

nixie mail* ['nɪksɪmeɪl] N (US) courrier difficile à faire parvenir en raison d'une adresse illisible, incomplète etc

NJ ABBR = **New Jersey**

NLF ['enel'ef] N (ABBR = **National Liberation Front**) FLN m

NLP [,enel'piː] N (ABBR = **neurolinguistic programming**) PNL f

NLQ [,enel'kjuː] (ABBR = **near letter quality**) → **near**

NM, N.Mex. ABBR = **New Mexico**

NMR [,enem'ɑː] N (ABBR = **nuclear magnetic resonance**) RMN f

no [nəʊ] 1 PARTICLE non; **oh no!** mais non!; **to say/answer no** dire/répondre non; **the answer is no** la réponse est non or négative; **I won't take no for an answer*** j'insiste; **I wouldn't do it, no not for £1000** je ne le ferais pas, même pas pour 1000 livres; **no to nuclear power!** non au nucléaire! 2 N (pl **noes**) non m inv; **the noes have it** les non l'emportent, les voix contre l'em-

portent; **there were seven noes** il y avait sept non or sept voix contre → **ay(e)**

3 ADJ a (= not any) pas de (used with ne), aucun (used with ne); **she had no coat** elle n'avait pas de manteau; **I have no idea** je n'ai aucune idée; **I have no more money** je n'ai plus d'argent; **no man could do more** aucun homme ne pourrait faire davantage; **no one man could do it** aucun homme ne pourrait le faire (à lui) seul; **no two men would agree on this** il n'y a pas deux hommes qui seraient d'accord là-dessus; **no two are alike** il n'y en a pas deux pareils; **no sensible man would have done that** un homme sensé n'aurait pas fait ça, aucun homme sensé n'aurait fait ça; **no Frenchman would say that** aucun Français ne dirait ça, un Français ne dirait jamais ça; **there's no whisky like Scotch whisky** il n'y a pas de meilleur whisky que le whisky écossais; **there's no Catholic like a converted Catholic** il n'y a pas plus catholique qu'un catholique converti; **it's of no interest** ça n'a aucun intérêt, c'est sans intérêt; **a man of no intelligence** un homme sans intelligence, un homme dénué d'intelligence; (US) **no win no fee** le client ne paie les honoraires que s'il a gain de cause; **no way!*** ◊ **no go!*** pas question!* → 5; **it's no good waiting for him** cela ne sert à rien or ce n'est pas la peine de l'attendre; **it's no wonder (that ...)** (ce n'est) pas étonnant (que ... (+ subj) or si ... (+ indic)); **no wonder!*** pas étonnant!*

b (emphatic) **by no means** pas du tout, absolument pas; **he's no friend of mine** il n'est pas de mes amis; **he's no genius** ce n'est certes pas un génie, il n'a rien d'un génie; **this is no place for children** ce n'est pas un endroit pour les enfants; **in no time (at all)** en un rien de temps; (frm) **it's no small matter** ce n'est pas rien; **headache or no headache, you'll have to do it*** migraine ou pas (migraine), tu vas devoir le faire; **theirs is no easy task** ils n'ont pas la tâche facile, leur tâche n'est pas facile; **there's no such thing** cela n'existe pas → **end, mistake**

c (forbidding) **no smoking** défense de fumer; **no entry** entrée f interdite, défense d'entrer; **no parking** stationnement m interdit; **no surrender!** on ne se rend pas!; **no nonsense!** pas d'histoires!, pas de blagues!* → 5

d (with gerund) **there's no saying or knowing what he'll do next** impossible de dire ce qu'il fera après; **there's no pleasing him** (quoi qu'on fasse) il n'est jamais satisfait

4 ADV a non; **whether he comes or no** qu'il vienne ou non; **hungry or no, you'll eat your soup** que tu aies faim ou non, tu vas manger ta soupe

b (with compar) ne ... pas; **the patient is no better** le malade ne va pas mieux; **I can go no further** je ne peux pas aller plus loin, je n'en peux plus; **I can bear it no longer** je ne peux plus le supporter, je n'en peux plus; **she took no less than four weeks to do it** il lui a fallu pas moins de quatre semaines pour le faire; **he returned with a bottle of champagne, no less!** il est revenu avec une bouteille de champagne, excusez du peu!*; **no sooner said than done** aussitôt dit aussitôt fait

5 COMP ► **no-account*** ADJ, N (US) bon(ne) m(f) à rien ► **no ball** N (Cricket) balle f nulle ► **no-claim(s) bonus** N (Insurance) bonus m ► **no-fault divorce** N (Jur) ≈ divorce m par consentement mutuel (sans torts prononcés) ► **no-fault insurance** N (esp US Jur) assurance f automobile à remboursement automatique ► **no-fly zone** N zone f d'exclusion aérienne ► **no-frills** ADJ avec service (réduit au strict) minimum or simplifié ► **no-go** ADJ **it's no-go*** ça ne marche pas; **no-go area** zone f interdite ► **no-good*** ADJ nul (nulle f), propre or bon à rien ♦ N propre mf à rien ► **no-holds-barred** ADJ (lit, fig) où tous les coups

sont permis → **hold** ► **no-hoper*** N raté(e) m(f), nullard(e)* m(f), zéro* m ► **no jump** N (Sport) saut m annulé ► **no-knock raid** N (US) perquisition-surprise f ► **no-man's-land** N (Mil) no man's land m; (= wasteland) terrain m vague; (= indefinite area) zone f mal définie ► **no-no*** N **it's a no-no** (= forbidden) ça ne se fait pas; (= impossible) c'est impossible ► **no-nonsense** ADJ [approach, attitude] raisonnable, plein de bon sens ► **no one** N = **nobody 1** ► **no place*** ADV (esp US) = **nowhere** ► **no sale** N (Comm) non-vente f ► **no-show** N (esp US: on plane/at show etc) passager m/spectateur m etc qui ne se présente pas ► **no throw** N (Sport) lancer m annulé ► **no-trump(s)** N ADJ m inv; **to call no-trump(s)** annoncer sans-atout; **three tricks in no-trump(s)** trois sans-atout ► **no-win situation** N impasse f

no. (ABBR = **number**) n°

Noah ['nəʊə] N Noé m; **~'s ark** l'arche f de Noé

nob[1]* [nɒb] N (esp Brit) aristo* mf, richard(e)* m(f) (pej); **the ~s** (les gens de) la haute*, les rupins* mpl

nob[2]* [nɒb] N (= head) caboche* f, fiole* f

nobble* ['nɒbl] VT (Brit) a (= corrupt) [+ person, jury etc] (by bribery) acheter, soudoyer; (by intimidation) intimider b [+ horse, dog] droguer (pour l'empêcher de gagner) c (= thwart) [+ plan etc] contrecarrer d (= obtain dishonestly) [+ votes etc] acheter e (= catch) [+ wrongdoer] pincer*, choper*; **the reporters ~d him as he left his hotel** les reporters l'ont happé or lui ont mis la main dessus au moment où il quittait son hôtel

Nobel [nəʊ'bel] N **~ prize** prix m Nobel; **~ prizewinner** or **laureate** (lauréat(e) m(f) du) prix m Nobel

nobelium [nəʊ'biːliəm] N nobélium m

nobility [nəʊ'bɪlɪtɪ] N (NonC) a (= nobles) (haute) noblesse f b (= quality) noblesse f; **~ of mind** grandeur f d'âme, magnanimité f

noble ['nəʊbl] 1 ADJ a (= aristocratic, admirable) [person, family, cause, attempt, sentiment] noble; [wine] grand, noble; [brandy] grand; [monument, edifice] majestueux, imposant; **to be of ~ birth** être de naissance noble; **the noble art** le noble art, la boxe → 3 b (* = unselfish) généreux, magnanime; **I was very ~ and gave her my share** dans un geste magnanime je lui ai donné ma part, je lui ai généreusement donné ma part; **it's very ~ of you to give up your day off to help** c'est très généreux de ta part de te priver de ton jour de congé pour aider c (Chem) [metal] noble → 3 2 N noble mf 3 COMP ► **noble gas** N (Chem) gaz m noble ► **noble-minded** ADJ magnanime, généreux ► **noble savage** N bon sauvage m

nobleman ['nəʊblmən] N (pl **-men**) noble m, aristocrate m

nobleness ['nəʊblnɪs] N [of person, birth] noblesse f; [of spirit, action etc] noblesse f, magnanimité f, générosité f; [of animal, statue etc] belles proportions fpl, noblesse f de proportions; [of building etc] majesté f; **~ of mind** grandeur f d'âme, magnanimité f

noblewoman ['nəʊblwʊmən] N (pl **-women**) aristocrate f, noble f

nobly ['nəʊblɪ] ADV a (= aristocratically, admirably) [behave] noblement; **~ born** de naissance noble b (* = selflessly) [volunteer, offer] généreusement; **he ~ did the washing up** généreux, il a fait la vaisselle c (= imposingly) [stand, rise] majestueusement

nobody ['nəʊbədɪ] 1 PRON personne (+ ne before vb); **I saw ~** je n'ai vu personne; **~ knows** personne or nul ne le sait; **~ spoke to me** personne ne m'a parlé; **who saw him?** — **~** qui l'a vu? — personne; **~ knows better than I** personne ne sait mieux que moi; **~ (that was) there will ever forget ...** personne parmi ceux qui étaient là n'oubliera jamais ...; **it is ~'s**

business cela ne regarde personne ; **it's ~'s business what I do** ◊ **what I do is ~'s business** ce que je fais ne regarde personne ; **like ~'s business:** [run etc] à toutes jambes, comme un dératé* ; [work etc] d'arrache-pied, sans désemparer ; **he's ~'s fool** il n'est pas né d'hier, c'est loin d'être un imbécile

[2] N moins que rien mf inv, rien du tout m ; **he's a mere ~** ◊ **he's just a ~** c'est un moins que rien or un rien du tout ; **they are nobodies** ce sont des moins que rien or des riens du tout ; **I worked with him when he was ~** j'ai travaillé avec lui alors qu'il était encore inconnu

nocturnal [nɒk'tɜːnl] [1] ADJ [animal, activity, habits] nocturne ; [raid] de nuit [2] COMP ► **nocturnal emission**† N (Med) pollutions fpl nocturnes

nocturne ['nɒktɜːn] N (Mus) nocturne m

nod [nɒd] [1] N [a] signe m (affirmatif) or inclination f de (la) tête ; **he gave me a ~** (gen) il m'a fait un signe de (la) tête ; (in greeting) il m'a salué de la tête ; (signifying "yes") il m'a fait signe que oui de la tête ; **he rose with a ~ of agreement** il s'est levé, signifiant son accord d'un signe de (la) tête ; **to answer with a ~** répondre d'un signe de (la) tête ; **to get the ~*** [project etc] avoir le feu vert ; (Brit) **on the ~*** [pass, approve] sans discussion, d'un commun accord ; **a ~ and a wink*** un clin d'œil entendu ; **to give sb a ~ and a wink*** faire un clin d'œil entendu à qn ■ (PROV) **a ~ is as good as a wink (to a blind horse)** l'allusion est claire [b] **Land of Nod** → land

[2] VI [a] (= move head) faire un signe de (la) tête, incliner la tête ; (as sign of assent) hocher la tête, faire signe que oui ; **to ~ to sb** faire un signe de tête à qn ; (in greeting) saluer qn d'un signe de tête, saluer qn de la tête ; **"does it work?" he asked, ~ding at the piano** «est-ce qu'il marche ?» demanda-t-il, montrant le piano d'un signe de (la) tête ; **he ~ded to me to go** de la tête il m'a fait signe de m'en aller ; **we're on ~ding terms** ◊ **we have a ~ding acquaintance** nous nous disons bonjour, nous nous saluons ; (fig) **he has a ~ding acquaintance with German/Montaigne** il connaît vaguement l'allemand/Montaigne

[b] (= doze) sommeiller, somnoler ; **he was ~ding over a book** il dodelinait de la tête or il somnolait sur un livre ; (fig) **to catch sb ~ding** prendre qn en défaut

[c] [flowers, plumes] se balancer, danser

[3] VT **to ~ one's head** (= move head down) faire un signe de (la) tête, incliner la tête ; (as sign of assent) faire un signe de tête affirmatif ; **to ~ one's agreement/approval** manifester son assentiment/son approbation par un or d'un signe de tête ; **they ~ded goodnight to Jane** ils ont dit bonsoir à Jane d'un signe de tête ; (Ftbl) **Taylor leapt up to ~ the ball home** Taylor a bondi pour marquer un but de la tête

► **nod off*** VI s'endormir ; **I ~ded off for a moment** je me suis endormi un instant

nodal ['nəʊdl] ADJ nodal

noddle†* ['nɒdl] N (= head) caboche* f, fiole* f

Noddy* ['nɒdɪ] ADJ (Brit = very easy, childish) d'une simplicité enfantine

node [nəʊd] N (gen, Astron, Geom, Ling, Phys) nœud m ; (Bot) nœud m, nodosité f ; (Anat) nodus m, nodosité f

nodular ['nɒdjʊlə'] ADJ nodulaire

nodule ['nɒdjuːl] N (Anat, Bot, Geol) nodule m

Noel ['nəʊəl] N Noël m

noggin ['nɒgɪn] N [a] (= container) (petit) pot m ; (= amount) quart m (de pinte) ; (Brit = drink) **let's have a ~** allons boire or prendre un pot [b] (US* = head) caboche* f, tête f

nohow* ['nəʊhaʊ] ADV (esp US = no way) pas du tout

noise [nɔɪz] [1] N [a] (= sound) bruit m ; **I heard a small ~** j'ai entendu un petit bruit ; **the ~ of the traffic** le bruit de la circulation ; **to make a ~** faire du bruit ; **stop that ~!** arrêtez(-moi) tout ce bruit ! ; **~s in the ears** bourdonnements mpl (d'oreilles) ; **a hammering ~** un martèlement ; **a clanging ~** un bruit métallique ; (Theat) **~s off** bruits mpl dans les coulisses

[b] (fig) **to make reassuring/placatory ~s** tenir des propos rassurants/apaisants ; **to make (all) the right ~s*** se montrer complaisant ; **the book made a lot of ~ when it came out** le livre a fait beaucoup de bruit quand il est sorti ; **to make a lot of ~ about sth*** faire du tapage autour de qch ; **she made ~s* about wanting to go home early** elle a laissé entendre qu'elle voulait rentrer tôt → **big**

[c] (NonC) (Rad, TV) interférences fpl, parasites mpl ; (on phone) friture f ; (Comput) bruit m

[2] VT (frm) **to ~ sth about** or **abroad** ébruiter qch

[3] COMP ► **noise abatement** N lutte f anti-bruit ; **~-abatement campaign/society** campagne f/ligue f antibruit or pour la lutte contre le bruit ► **noise pollution** N nuisances fpl sonores ► **noise prevention** N mesure f antibruit or contre le bruit

noiseless ['nɔɪzlɪs] ADJ [person, machine] silencieux

noiselessly ['nɔɪzlɪslɪ] ADV sans bruit

noiselessness ['nɔɪzlɪsnɪs] N silence m, absence f de bruit

noisily ['nɔɪzɪlɪ] ADV bruyamment

noisiness ['nɔɪzɪnɪs] N caractère m bruyant ; [of child] turbulence f

noisome ['nɔɪsəm] ADJ (liter) [a] (= malodorous) [smell, odour, vapours] méphitique (liter) [b] (= unpleasant) [person] immonde ; (= harmful) [environment] néfaste

noisy ['nɔɪzɪ] ADJ [a] (= loud) bruyant ; **to be ~** [person, car] être bruyant, faire beaucoup de bruit [b] (= garish) [colour] criard, voyant

nomad ['nəʊmæd] N nomade mf

nomadic [nəʊ'mædɪk] ADJ (lit, fig) nomade

nomadism ['nəʊmædɪzəm] N nomadisme m

nom de plume† ['nɒmdə'pluːm] N (pl **noms de plume**) (Literat) pseudonyme m

nomenclature [nəʊ'menklətʃə'] N nomenclature f

nomenklatura [ˌnəʊmenklə'tʊərə] N (Pol: formerly in Eastern Europe) **the ~** la nomenklatura

nominal ['nɒmɪnl] [1] ADJ [a] (= in name only) [agreement, power, rights, control, leader, value] nominal ; **he's a ~ socialist/Christian** il n'a de socialiste/chrétien que le nom [b] (= minimal) [fee, charge, sum] minimal, insignifiant ; [wage, salary, rent] insignifiant ; [fine, penalty] symbolique ; (Jur) **~ damages** dommages-intérêts mpl symboliques, ≈ franc m symbolique [c] (Gram) [clause] nominal [2] N (Gram) expression f nominale

nominalism ['nɒmɪnəlɪzəm] N nominalisme m

nominalist ['nɒmɪnəlɪst] N, ADJ nominaliste mf

nominalization [ˌnɒmɪnəlaɪ'zeɪʃən] N (Ling) nominalisation f

nominalize ['nɒmɪnəlaɪz] VT (Ling) nominaliser

nominally ['nɒmɪnəlɪ] ADV [independent] théoriquement, en théorie ; **~ in charge** théoriquement responsable ; **~, they are on the same side, but ...** en principe, ils sont du même bord, mais ... ; **~ socialist/Christian** qui n'a de socialiste/chrétien que le nom

nominate ['nɒmɪneɪt] VT [a] (= appoint) nommer, désigner ; **he was ~d chairman** ◊ **he** was ~d to the chairmanship il a été nommé président ; **~d and elected members of a committee** membres mpl désignés et membres élus d'un comité [b] (= propose) proposer, présenter ; **he was ~d for the presidency** il a été proposé comme candidat à la présidence ; **they ~d Mr Lambotte for mayor** ils ont proposé M. Lambotte comme candidat à la mairie ; **to ~ sb for an Oscar** proposer or nominer qn pour un Oscar

nomination [ˌnɒmɪ'neɪʃən] [1] N [a] (= appointment) nomination f (to à) [b] (for job, political office etc) proposition f de candidat ; **~s must be received by ...** toutes propositions de candidats doivent être reçues avant ... [c] (Cine: for award) nomination f [2] COMP ► **nomination paper** N (Pol) feuille f de candidature, nomination f

nominative ['nɒmɪnətɪv] [1] ADJ (gen) nominatif ; [ending] du nominatif [2] N nominatif m ; **in the ~** au nominatif, au cas sujet

nominator ['nɒmɪneɪtə'] N présentateur m

nominee [ˌnɒmɪ'niː] N (for post) personne f désignée or nommée ; (in election) candidat(e) m(f) désigné(e) ; (for annuity etc) personne f dénommée ; (St Ex) mandataire mf ; (St Ex) **~ company** société f prête-nom

non- [nɒn] [1] PREF non- ; **strikers and ~strikers** grévistes mpl et non-grévistes mpl ; **believers and ~believers** ceux qui croient et ceux qui ne croient pas, (les) croyants mpl et (les) non-croyants mpl

[2] COMP ► **non-absorbent** ADJ non absorbant ► **non-accidental injury** N (NonC) maltraitance f ► **non-accountable** ADJ non responsable ► **non-achievement** N échec m ► **non-achiever** N personne f qui ne réussit pas ► **non-addictive** ADJ qui ne crée pas de dépendance ► **non-affiliated** ADJ [business] non affilié ; [industry] non confédéré ► **non-aggression** N non-agression f ; **~aggression pact** or **treaty** pacte m de non-agression ► **non-alcoholic** ADJ non alcoolisé, sans alcool ► **non-aligned** ADJ (Pol) non aligné ► **non-alignment** N (Pol) non-alignement m ; **~alignment policy** politique f de non-alignement ► **non-appearance** N (Jur) non-comparution f ► **non-arrival** N non-arrivée f ► **non-assertive** ADJ qui manque d'assurance, qui ne se met pas en avant ► **non-attendance** N absence f ► **non-availability** N non-disponibilité f ► **non-believer** N (Rel) incroyant(e) m(f) ► **non-biological** ADJ sans enzymes ► **non-Catholic** ADJ, N non catholique mf ► **non-Christian** ADJ non chrétien ► **non-classified** ADJ qui n'est pas classé secret ► **non-collegiate** ADJ [student] qui n'appartient à aucun collège ; **~collegiate university** université f qui n'est pas divisée en collèges ► **non-com*** N (ABBR = **non-commissioned officer**) (US Mil) sous-off* m ► **non-communication** N manque m de communication ► **non-completion** N [of work] non-achèvement m ; [of contract] non-exécution f ► **non-compliance** N refus m d'obéissance (with à) ► **non compos mentis** ADJ qui n'a pas toute sa raison ► **non-contagious** ADJ non contagieux ► **non-contributory** ADJ **~contributory pension scheme** régime m de retraite sans retenues or cotisations ► **non-controversial** ADJ = **uncontroversial** ► **non-conventional** ADJ non conventionnel ► **non-cooperation** N refus m de coopérer, non-coopération f ► **non-cooperative** ADJ peu coopératif ► **non-crush(able)** ADJ infroissable ► **non-cumulative** ADJ non cumulatif ► **non-custodial** ADJ (Jur) **~custodial sentence** peine f non privative de liberté ► **non-dairy** ADJ qui n'est pas à base de lait ► **non-degradable** ADJ qui n'est pas biodégradable ► **non-democratic** ADJ non démocratique ► **non-denominational** ADJ œcuménique

► **non-drinker** N personne f qui ne boit pas d'alcool ► **non-drip** ADJ [paint] qui ne coule pas ► **non-driver** N (Aut) personne f qui n'a pas le permis de conduire ► **non-EU** ADJ [citizens, passports] des pays qui n'appartiennent pas à l'UE; [imports] hors Union européenne ► **non-greasy** ADJ [ointment, lotion] qui ne graisse pas; [skin, hair] normal, qui n'est pas gras (grasse f) ► **non-hero** N antihéros m ► **non-interference** N non-intervention f ► **non-iron** ADJ qui ne nécessite aucun repassage; (on label) **"~iron"** « ne pas repasser » ► **non-Jew** N non-juif m, -ive f ► **non-Jewish** ADJ non juif ► **non-league** ADJ (Brit Sport) hors division ► **non-manual worker** N col m blanc ► **non-Muslim** ADJ non musulman ♦ N non-musulman(e) m(f) ► **non-negotiable** ADJ (Comm) non négociable; [decision etc] qui n'est pas négociable ► **non-nuclear** ADJ [weapon] conventionnel; [country] non nucléaire ► **non-nutritious** ADJ sans valeur nutritive ► **non-party** ADJ (Pol) [vote, decision] indépendant, neutre ► **non-penetrative** ADJ [sex] sans pénétration ► **non-person** N (= stateless etc) personne f sans identité juridique ► **non-practising** ADJ [Christian, Muslim etc] non pratiquant ► **non-productive** ADJ non productif ► **non-professional** ADJ [player etc] amateur; **~professional conduct** manquement m aux devoirs de sa profession ♦ N (Sport etc) amateur mf ► **non-punitive** ADJ dont l'intention n'est pas de punir ► **non-racial** ADJ non racial ► **non-refillable** ADJ [pen, bottle] non rechargeable ► **non-reflective** ADJ [glass] non réfléchissant, antireflet f inv ► **non-religious** ADJ non croyant ► **non-resident** ADJ (gen) non résident; **~resident course** stage m sans hébergement; **~resident doctor** attaché(e) m(f) de consultations; (US Univ Admin) **~resident student** étudiant(e) d'une université d'État dont le domicile permanent est situé en dehors de cet État ♦ N non-résident(e) m(f); (Brit: in hotel) client(e) m(f) de passage (qui n'a pas de chambre) ► **non-sexist** ADJ qui n'est pas sexiste, non sexiste ► **non-student** N non-étudiant(e) m(f) ► **non-threatening** ADJ qui n'est pas menaçant ► **non-traditional** ADJ non traditionnel ► **non-union** ADJ (Ind) [company, organization] qui n'emploie pas de personnel syndiqué ► **non-unionized** ADJ = **non-union** ► **non-white** N personne f de couleur ♦ ADJ de couleur

nonacademic [ˌnɒnækəˈdemɪk] ADJ **a** (= extra-curricular) extrascolaire **b** (= non-educational) [staff] non enseignant; [career] en dehors de l'enseignement **c** (= not academically gifted) [child, pupil] peu doué pour les études

nonage [ˈnəʊnɪdʒ] N (Jur) minorité f

nonagenarian [ˌnɒnədʒɪˈnɛərɪən] ADJ, N nonagénaire mf

nonbreakable [ˌnɒnˈbreɪkəbl] ADJ incassable

nonce [nɒns] **1** N **a** **for the ~** pour la circonstance, pour l'occasion **b**; pointeur* m **2** COMP ► **nonce-bashing*** N chasse f aux pointeurs*

nonchalance [ˈnɒnʃələns] N nonchalance f

nonchalant [ˈnɒnʃələnt] ADJ nonchalant; **to be ~ about sth** prendre qch avec nonchalance

nonchalantly [ˈnɒnʃələntlɪ] ADV nonchalamment, avec nonchalance

noncombatant [ˌnɒnˈkɒmbətənt] ADJ, N non-combattant(e) m(f)

noncombustible [ˌnɒnkəmˈbʌstɪbl] ADJ non combustible

noncommercial [ˌnɒnkəˈmɜːʃəl] ADJ sans but lucratif

noncommissioned [ˌnɒnkəˈmɪʃənd] ADJ (Mil) non breveté, sans brevet; **~ officer** sous-officier m

noncommittal [ˌnɒnkəˈmɪtl] ADJ [person] qui ne s'engage pas; [letter, statement] qui n'engage à rien, évasif; [grunt] évasif; [expression, attitude] réservé; **he gave a ~ answer** il fit une réponse évasive or qui ne l'engageait pas; **I'll be very ~** je ne m'engagerai pas; **he was very ~ about it** il ne s'est pas prononcé là-dessus

noncommittally [ˌnɒnkəˈmɪtlɪ] ADV [say, answer] évasivement, sans s'engager

noncommunicant [ˌnɒnkəˈmjuːnɪkənt] ADJ, N (Rel) non-communiant(e) m(f)

nonconductor [ˈnɒnkənˈdʌktər] N (Phys) non-conducteur m, mauvais conducteur m; [of heat] isolant m, calorifuge m; (Elec) isolant m

nonconformism [ˈnɒnkənˈfɔːmɪzəm] N non-conformisme m

nonconformist [ˈnɒnkənˈfɔːmɪst] **1** N non-conformiste mf **2** ADJ non conformiste

Nonconformity [ˈnɒnkənˈfɔːmɪtɪ] N (Rel) non-conformité f

nondazzle [ˈnɒnˈdæzl] ADJ antiéblouissant

nondescript [ˈnɒndɪskrɪpt] ADJ [person, face, building] quelconque; [appearance] insignifiant, quelconque; [colour] indéfinissable

nondestructive [ˌnɒndɪsˈtrʌktɪv] ADJ (Tech) [testing] non destructeur

nondetachable [ˌnɒndɪˈtætʃəbl] ADJ [handle etc] fixe, indémontable; [lining, hood] non détachable

nondirectional [ˌnɒndɪˈrekʃənl] ADJ omnidirectionnel

nondirective therapy [ˌnɒndɪˌrektɪvˈθerəpɪ] N (Psych) psychothérapie f non directive, non-directivisme m

nondistinctive [ˌnɒndɪsˈtɪŋktɪv] ADJ (Ling) non distinctif

none [nʌn] **1** PRON **a** (= nothing) aucun(e) m(f) (+ ne before vb); **~ of these problems should affect us** aucun de ces problèmes ne devrait nous toucher; **~ of the books** aucun livre, aucun des livres; **~ of the money was used to build houses** on n'a pas utilisé un centime de cet argent pour construire des maisons; **~ of this** rien de ceci; **~ of that!** pas de ça!; **I want ~ of your excuses!** vos excuses ne m'intéressent pas!; **he would have ~ of it** il ne or n'en voulait rien savoir; **I need money but have ~ at all** j'ai besoin d'argent mais je n'en ai pas du tout; **there was no evidence, ~ at all** il n'y a eu aucune preuve, absolument aucune; **we had no notice of it, ~ at all** nous n'en avons pas été prévenus à l'avance, absolument pas; **is there any bread left? — ~ at all** y a-t-il encore du pain? — pas une miette; **~ of this money** pas un centime de cet argent; **~ of this cheese** pas un gramme de ce fromage; **~ of this milk** pas une goutte de ce lait; **~ of this land** pas un mètre carré or pas un pouce de ce terrain; **there's ~ left** il n'en reste plus **b** (= nobody) personne, aucun(e) m(f) (both + ne before vb); **~ of us knew how to change a wheel** aucun de nous or d'entre nous ne savait changer une roue; **~ can tell** personne or nul ne peut le dire; **~ of them** aucun d'entre eux; **~ of us** aucun de nous or d'entre nous, personne parmi nous; (frm) **~ but you can do it** vous seul êtes capable de le faire; (frm) **I have told ~ but you** je ne l'ai dit à personne d'autre or à nul autre que vous; (frm) **~ but a fool would do it** il n'y a qu'un imbécile pour le faire; **I know, ~ better, that ...** je sais mieux que personne que ...; **their guest was ~ other than the president himself** leur invité n'était autre que le président en personne **c** (in form-filling) néant m

2 ADV **he's ~ the worse for it** il ne s'en porte pas plus mal; **she's looking ~ the worse for her ordeal** cette épreuve ne semble pas l'avoir trop marquée; **I like him ~ the worse for it** je ne l'en aime pas moins pour cela; **the house would be ~ the worse for a coat of paint** une couche de peinture ne ferait pas de mal à cette maison; **he was ~ the wiser** il n'en savait pas plus pour autant, il n'était pas plus avancé; **it's ~ too warm** il ne fait pas tellement chaud; **and ~ too soon either!** et ce n'est pas trop tôt!; **at last he arrived and ~ too soon** il arriva enfin et ce n'était pas trop tôt; **I was ~ too sure that he would come** j'étais loin d'être sûr qu'il viendrait; **she was ~ too happy about it** elle était loin d'être contente; **he was ~ too pleased at being disturbed** ça ne l'a pas enchanté qu'on le dérange

nonedible [nɒˈnedɪbl] ADJ non comestible

nonentity [nɒˈnentɪtɪ] N personne f insignifiante or sans intérêt; **he's a complete ~** c'est une nullité

nonessential [ˌnɒnɪˈsenʃl] **1** ADJ non essentiel, accessoire **2** **nonessentials** NPL accessoires mpl; **the ~s** l'accessoire m

nonestablished [ˌnɒnɪsˈtæblɪʃt] ADJ [church] non établi

nonesuch [ˈnɒnsʌtʃ] N = **nonsuch**

nonet [nɒˈnet] N (Mus) nonet m

nonetheless [ˌnɒnðəˈles] ADV = **nevertheless**

nonevent* [ˈnɒnɪˈvent] N non-événement m

nonexamination course [ˌnɒnɪgˈzæmɪˈneɪʃənkɔːs] N (Scol etc) études fpl non sanctionnées par un examen

nonexecutive director [ˌnɒnɪgˈzekjutɪvdɪˈrektər] N administrateur m

nonexistence [ˈnɒnɪgˈzɪstəns] N non-existence f

nonexistent [ˈnɒnɪgˈzɪstənt] ADJ inexistant

nonexplosive [ˈnɒnɪkˈspləʊsɪv] ADJ [gas] non explosif

nonfactual [ˌnɒnˈfæktjʊəl] ADJ qui n'est pas fondé sur des faits

nonfat [ˈnɒnfæt] ADJ [cooking, diet] sans corps gras or matière grasse; [meat] maigre

nonfattening [ˌnɒnˈfætnɪŋ] ADJ qui ne fait pas grossir

nonferrous [ˌnɒnˈferəs] ADJ non ferreux

nonfiction [ˌnɒnˈfɪkʃən] N littérature f non romanesque; **he only reads ~** il ne lit jamais de romans

nonfinite [ˌnɒnˈfaɪnaɪt] ADJ **~ verb** verbe m au mode impersonnel; **~ forms** modes mpl impersonnels

nonflammable [ˌnɒnˈflæməbl] ADJ = **noninflammable**

nonfulfilment [ˌnɒnfʊlˈfɪlmənt] N non-exécution f, inexécution f

nonglare [ˌnɒnˈgleər] ADJ antiéblouissant

nongovernmental [ˌnɒngʌvənˈmentl] ADJ non gouvernemental

nongrammatical [ˌnɒngrəˈmætɪkəl] ADJ non grammatical

non grata* [ˌnɒnˈgrɑːtə] ADJ **he felt rather ~** il avait l'impression d'être un intrus → **persona**

nonillion [nəʊˈnɪljən] N (esp Brit = 10^54) nonillion m; (esp US = 10^30) quintillion m

noninfectious [ˌnɒnɪnˈfekʃəs] ADJ non contagieux

noninflammable [ˌnɒnɪnˈflæməbl] ADJ ininflammable

nonintervention [ˌnɒnɪntəˈvenʃən] N (Pol etc) non-intervention f, laisser-faire m

noninterventionist [ˌnɒnɪntəˈvenʃənɪst] **1** ADJ non interventionniste **2** N (Pol etc) non-interventionniste mf

noninvolvement [ˌnɒnɪnˈvɒlvmənt] N (in war, conflict) non-engagement m, neutralité f; (in negotiations etc) non-participation f; (Psych) détachement m

nonjudg(e)mental [ˌnɒndʒʌdʒˈmentəl] ADJ qui ne porte pas de jugement, neutre

nonladdering [ˌnɒnˈlædərɪŋ] ADJ = **nonrun**

nonlinear [ˌnɒnˈlɪnɪər] ADJ non linéaire

nonlinguistic [ˌnɒnlɪŋˈgwɪstɪk] ADJ [communication etc] non verbal

nonliterate [ˌnɒnˈlɪtərɪt] ADJ [tribe, culture] sans écriture

nonmalignant [ˌnɒnməˈlɪgnənt] ADJ [tumour] bénin (-igne f)

nonmaterial [ˌnɒnməˈtɪərɪəl] ADJ immatériel

nonmember [ˌnɒnˈmembə^r] N [of club etc] personne f étrangère (au club etc); **open to ~s** ouvert au public

nonmetal [ˈnɒnmetl] N (Chem) non-métal m, métalloïde m

nonmetallic [ˌnɒnmɪˈtælɪk] ADJ (= relating to nonmetals) métalloïdique; (= not of metallic quality) non métallique

nonmilitant [ˌnɒnˈmɪlɪtənt] ADJ non militant

nonmilitary [ˌnɒnˈmɪlɪtərɪ] ADJ non militaire

nonobservance [ˌnɒnəbˈzɜːvəns] N (gen) non-observation f, inobservation f; (Rel) non-observance f

non obst. PREP (ABBR = **non obstante**) (= notwithstanding) nonobstant

nonoperational [ˌnɒnɒpəˈreɪʃənl] ADJ non opérationnel

nonpareil [ˈnɒnpərəl] (liter) 1 N personne f or chose f sans pareille 2 ADJ incomparable, sans égal

nonpartisan [ˈnɒnˌpɑːtɪˈzæn] ADJ impartial

nonpaying [ˌnɒnˈpeɪɪŋ] ADJ [visitor etc] qui ne paie pas, admis à titre gracieux

nonpayment [ˈnɒnˈpeɪmənt] N non-paiement m (**of** de)

nonplus [ˈnɒnˈplʌs] VT déconcerter, dérouter; **I was utterly ~sed** j'étais complètement déconcerté or dérouté

nonpolitical [ˈnɒnpəˈlɪtɪkəl] ADJ apolitique

nonpolluting [ˈnɒnpəˈluːtɪŋ] ADJ non polluant

nonprofitmaking [ˈnɒnˈprɒfɪtmeɪkɪŋ], **nonprofit** (US) [ˈnɒnˈprɒfɪt] ADJ à but non lucratif

nonproliferation [ˈnɒnprəˌlɪfəˈreɪʃən] N non-prolifération f; **~ treaty** traité m de non-prolifération

nonpunitive [ˈnɒnˈpjuːnɪtɪv] ADJ dont l'intention n'est pas de punir

nonreceipt [ˈnɒnrɪˈsiːt] N [of letter etc] non-réception f

nonrecurring expenses [ˈnɒnrɪˈkɜːrɪŋɪkˈspensɪz] NPL dépenses fpl d'équipement

nonreturnable [ˈnɒnrɪˈtɜːnəbl] ADJ [bottle etc] non consigné

nonrun [ˈnɒnrʌn] ADJ indémaillable

nonrunner [ˈnɒnˈrʌnə^r] N non-partant m

nonscheduled [ˈnɒnˈʃedjuːld] ADJ [plane, flight] spécial

nonsectarian [ˈnɒnsekˈtɛərɪən] ADJ non confessionnel

nonsegregated [ˈnɒnˈsegrɪgeɪtɪd] ADJ sans ségrégation

nonsense [ˈnɒnsəns] 1 N (NonC) absurdités fpl, idioties fpl; **to talk ~** dire n'importe quoi; **that's a piece of ~!** c'est une absurdité!, n'importe quoi!; **that's (a lot of) ~** tout ça ce sont des absurdités; **but that's ~!** mais c'est absurde!, mais c'est n'importe quoi!; **oh, ~!** oh, ne dis pas n'importe quoi!; **I'm putting on weight — ~!** je grossis — penses-tu!; **all this ~ about them not being able to pay** toutes ces histoires idiotes comme quoi* or selon lesquelles ils seraient incapables de payer; **it is ~ to say ...** il est absurde or idiot de dire ...; **he will stand no ~ from anybody** il ne se laissera pas faire par qui que ce soit, il ne se laissera marcher sur les pieds par personne; **he won't stand any ~ about that** il ne plaisante pas là-dessus; **I've had enough of this ~!** j'en ai assez de ces histoires or idioties!; **stop this ~!** ◊ no more of your ~! arrête tes idioties!; **there's no ~ about him** c'est un homme très

carré; **to knock the ~ out of sb*** ramener qn à la raison; **to make (a) ~ of** [+ project, efforts, pledge] rendre inutile; [+ claim] invalider; **it is an economic ~ to ...** c'est absolument absurde d'un point de vue économique que de ... → **stuff**

2 COMP ► **nonsense verse** N vers mpl amphigouriques ► **nonsense word** N mot m inventé de toutes pièces

nonsensical [nɒnˈsensɪkəl] ADJ [idea, action] absurde, dénué de sens; [person, attitude, rule, lyrics] absurde

nonsensically [nɒnˈsensɪkəlɪ] ADV absurdement

non sequitur [ˌnɒnˈsekwɪtə^r] N **it's a ~** ça manque de suite

nonshrink [ˈnɒnˈʃrɪŋk] ADJ irrétrécissable

nonsinkable [ˈnɒnˈsɪŋkəbl] ADJ insubmersible

nonsked* [ˈnɒnˈsked] N (US) avion m spécial

nonskid [ˈnɒnˈskɪd] ADJ antidérapant

nonskilled [ˈnɒnˈskɪld] ADJ = **unskilled**

nonslip [ˈnɒnˈslɪp] ADJ [shoe sole, ski] antidérapant

nonsmoker [ˈnɒnˈsməʊkə^r] N (= person) non-fumeur m, -euse f, personne f qui ne fume pas; **he is a ~** il ne fume pas

nonsmoking [ˈnɒnˈsməʊkɪŋ] ADJ [flight, seat, compartment, area] non-fumeurs (inv); [office, restaurant] où il est interdit de fumer; [person] qui ne fume pas, non fumeur; **the ~ population** ceux mpl qui ne fument pas, les non-fumeurs mpl

nonsolvent [ˈnɒnˈsɒlvənt] ADJ (Chem) non dissolvant

nonspecialist [ˈnɒnˈspeʃəlɪst] 1 N (gen) non-spécialiste mf; (Med) généraliste mf 2 ADJ [knowledge, dictionary] général

nonspecific [ˈnɒnspəˈsɪfɪk] 1 ADJ a (Med) non spécifique b (= imprecise) général 2 COMP ► **nonspecific urethritis** N (Med) urétrite f

nonstandard [ˈnɒnˈstændəd] ADJ (Ling) non standard inv

nonstarter [ˈnɒnˈstɑːtə^r] N a (= horse) non-partant m b (= person) nullité f c (= idea) **it is a ~** c'est voué à l'échec

nonstick [ˈnɒnˈstɪk] ADJ [coating] antiadhésif; [saucepan] qui n'attache pas

nonstop [ˌnɒnˈstɒp] 1 ADJ [flight] sans escale; [train] direct; [journey] sans arrêt; [music] ininterrompu; (Ski) non-stop; **the movie's two hours of ~ action** les deux heures d'action ininterrompue du film 2 ADV [talk, work, rain] sans interruption, sans arrêt; (Ski) non-stop; **to fly ~ from London to Chicago** faire Londres-Chicago sans escale

nonsuch [ˈnʌnsʌtʃ] N (liter) personne f or chose f sans pareille

nonsuit [ˈnɒnˈsuːt] 1 N (Jur) (gen) ordonnance f de non-lieu; (on the part of the plaintiff) cessation f de poursuites, retrait m de plainte; **to direct a ~** rendre une ordonnance de non-lieu 2 VT† débouter; **to be ~ed** être débouté (de sa demande)

nonsupport [ˈnɒnsəˈpɔːt] N (US Jur) défaut m de pension alimentaire

nonswimmer [ˈnɒnˈswɪmə^r] N personne f qui ne sait pas nager

nontaxable [ˈnɒnˈtæksəbl] ADJ non imposable

nonteaching staff [ˈnɒnˈtiːtʃɪŋstɑːf] N (Scol etc) personnel m non enseignant

nontoxic [ˈnɒnˈtɒksɪk] ADJ non toxique

nontransferable [ˈnɒnᵗrænsˈfɜːrəbl] ADJ [ticket] non transmissible; [share] nominatif; [pension] non réversible

nonverbal [ˈnɒnˈvɜːbəl] ADJ non verbal

nonviable [ˈnɒnˈvaɪəbl] ADJ non viable

nonviolence [ˈnɒnˈvaɪələns] N non-violence f

nonviolent [ˈnɒnˈvaɪələnt] ADJ non violent

nonvocational [ˈnɒnvəˈkeɪʃənl] ADJ [courses] non professionnel

nonvoluntary [ˈnɒnˈvɒləntərɪ] ADJ [work] rémunéré

nonvoter [ˈnɒnˈvəʊtə^r] N (US Pol) abstentionniste mf

nonvoting share [ˈnɒnˈvəʊtɪŋʃɛə^r] N (Fin) action f sans droit de vote

nonworker [ˈnɒnˈwɜːkə^r] N personne f sans activité professionnelle

nonworking [ˈnɒnˈwɜːkɪŋ] ADJ sans emploi, qui ne travaille pas

nonwoven [ˈnɒnˈwəʊvən] ADJ non tissé

noodle [ˈnuːdl] 1 a (Culin) **~s** nouilles fpl; **~ soup** potage m au vermicelle b (* = silly person) nouille* f, nigaud(e) m(f) c (US, Can* = head) caboche* f, tête f

nook [nʊk] N (= corner) coin m, recoin m; (= remote spot) retraite f; **~s and crannies** coins mpl et recoins mpl; **breakfast ~** coin-repas m; **a shady ~** une retraite ombragée, un coin ombragé

nookie‡**, nooky**‡ [ˈnʊkɪ] N (Brit: esp hum) la fesse‡; **to have a bit of ~** avoir une partie de jambes en l'air‡

noon [nuːn] N midi m; **at/about ~** à/vers midi → **high**

noonday [ˈnuːndeɪ], **noontide**†† [ˈnuːntaɪd], **noontime** (esp US) [ˈnuːntaɪm] 1 N midi m; (fig, liter) **at the ~ of his fame** à l'apogée de sa gloire 2 ADJ de midi

noose [nuːs] 1 N a nœud m coulant; (in animal trapping) collet m; [of cowboy] lasso m; [of hangman] corde f; (fig) **to put one's head in the ~** ◊ **to put a ~ round one's neck** se jeter dans la gueule du loup 2 VT a [+ rope] faire un nœud coulant à b (in trapping) prendre au collet; [cowboy] prendre or attraper au lasso

nope‡ [nəʊp] PARTICLE non

nor [nɔː^r] CONJ a (following "neither") ni; **neither you ~ I can do it** ni vous ni moi (nous) ne pouvons le faire; **she neither eats ~ drinks** elle ne mange ni ne boit; **neither here ~ elsewhere does he stop working** ici comme ailleurs il ne cesse pas de travailler → **neither** b (= and not) [don't know, ~ do I care] je ne sais pas et d'ailleurs je m'en moque; **that's not funny, ~ is it true** ce n'est ni drôle ni vrai; **that's not funny, ~ do I believe it's true** cela n'est pas drôle et je ne crois pas non plus que ce soit vrai; **I shan't go and ~ will you** je n'irai pas et toi non plus; **I don't like him — do I** je ne l'aime pas — moi non plus; **~ was this all** et ce n'était pas tout; **~ will I deny that ...** et je ne nie pas non plus que ... (+ subj); **~ was he disappointed** et il ne fut pas déçu non plus → **yet**

nor' [nɔː^r] ADJ (Naut: in compounds) = **north**; **~east** etc = **north-east**; → **north**

noradrenalin(e) [ˈnɔːrəˈdrenəlɪn, -iːn] N noradrénaline f

Nordic [ˈnɔːdɪk] 1 ADJ nordique 2 COMP ► **Nordic skier** N skieur m, -euse f nordique ► **Nordic skiing** N ski m nordique

norm [nɔːm] N norme f

normal [ˈnɔːməl] 1 ADJ a (gen) normal; (= usual) habituel; **traffic was ~ for a bank holiday weekend** la circulation était normale pour un long week-end; **a higher than ~ risk of infection** un risque d'infection plus élevé que la normale; **it's perfectly ~ to feel that way** il est tout à fait normal de ressentir cela; **it was quite ~ for him to be late** c'était tout à fait dans ses habitudes d'arriver en retard; **as ~** comme d'habitude; **it's ~ practice to do that** il est normal de faire cela; **to buy sth for half the ~ price** acheter qch à moitié prix; (TV) **~ service will be resumed as soon as possible** nous vous prions de nous excuser pour

cette interruption momentanée de l'image ; **the factory is back to ~ working** le travail a repris normalement à l'usine
[b] (*Math*) normal, perpendiculaire
[c] (*Chem*) neutre

[2] N [a] normale *f* ; **above/below ~** au-dessus/en dessous de la normale ; **temperatures below ~** des températures au-dessous de la normale ; **to return** or **get back to ~** revenir à la normale
[b] (*Math*) normale *f*, perpendiculaire *f*
[3] COMP ► **normal school** N (*US: formerly*) institut universitaire de formation des maîtres, ≈ école *f* normale

normality [nɔːˈmælɪtɪ], **normalcy** (*esp US*) [ˈnɔːməlsɪ] N normalité *f*

normalization [ˌnɔːməlaɪˈzeɪʃən] N normalisation *f*

normalize [ˈnɔːməlaɪz] [1] VT normaliser, régulariser [2] VI se normaliser, se régulariser

normally [ˈnɔːməlɪ] ADV (= *usually*) généralement, d'habitude ; (= *as normal*) normalement ; **he ~ arrives at about 10 o'clock** d'habitude il arrive vers 10 heures ; **the trains are running ~** les trains circulent normalement

Norman [ˈnɔːmən] [1] ADJ normand ; (*Archit*) roman ; **the ~ Conquest** la conquête normande ; (*Ling*) **~ French** anglo-normand *m* [2] N Normand(e) *m(f)*

Normandy [ˈnɔːməndɪ] N la Normandie → **landing**[1]

normative [ˈnɔːmətɪv] ADJ normatif

Norse [nɔːs] [1] ADJ (*Hist*) nordique, scandinave ; **~man** Scandinave *m* [2] N (*Ling*) nordique *m*, norrois *m* ; **Old ~** vieux norrois *m*

north [nɔːθ] [1] N nord *m* ; **magnetic ~** nord *m* or pôle *m* magnétique ; **to the ~ of ...** au nord de ... ; **house facing the ~** maison *f* exposée au nord ; **to veer to the ~** ◊ **to go into the ~** [*wind*] tourner au nord, anordir (*Naut*) ; **the wind is in the ~** le vent est au nord ; **the wind is (coming** or **blowing) from the ~** le vent vient or souffle du nord ; **to live in the ~** habiter dans le nord ; **in the ~ of Scotland** dans le nord de l'Écosse ; (*US Hist*) **the North** les États *mpl* antiesclavagistes or du nord
[2] ADJ [*side, coast, slope, end*] nord *inv* ; [*region, area*] septentrional (*frm*) ; **~ wind** vent *m* du nord ; **(in) ~ Wales/London** (dans) le nord du pays de Galles/de Londres ; **on the ~ side** du côté nord ; **studio with a ~ light** atelier *m* exposé au nord ; **a ~ aspect** une exposition au nord ; **room with a ~ aspect** pièce *f* exposée au nord ; **~ wall** mur *m* (exposé au) nord ; (*Archit*) **~ transept/door** transept *m*/portail *m* nord → **4**
[3] ADV [*lie, be*] au nord (**of** de) ; [*go*] vers le nord, en direction du nord ; **further ~** plus au nord ; **~ of the island** au nord de l'île ; **the town lies ~ of the border** la ville est (située) au nord de la frontière ; **we drove ~ for 100km** nous avons roulé pendant 100 km en direction du nord or vers le nord ; **go ~ till you get to Oxford** allez en direction du nord or vers le nord jusqu'à Oxford ; **to sail due ~** aller droit vers le nord ; (*Naut*) avoir le cap au nord ; **~ by ~-east** nord quart nord-est
[4] COMP ► **North Africa** N l'Afrique *f* du Nord ► **North African** ADJ nord-africain, d'Afrique du Nord ◊ N Africain(e) *m(f)* du Nord, Nord-Africain(e) *m(f)* ► **North America** N l'Amérique *f* du Nord ► **North American** ADJ nord-américain, d'Amérique du Nord ◊ N Nord-Américain(e) *m(f)* ► **the North Atlantic** N l'Atlantique *m* nord ► **North Atlantic Drift** N dérive *f* nord-atlantique ► **North Atlantic Treaty Organization** N Organisation *f* du traité de l'Atlantique nord ► **North Carolina** N la Caroline du Nord ; **in North Carolina** en Caroline du Nord ► **the North Country** N (*Brit*) le Nord de l'Angleterre ► **north-country** ADJ du Nord (de l'An-

gleterre) ► **North Dakota** N le Dakota du Nord ; **in North Dakota** dans le Dakota du Nord ► **north-east** N nord-est *m* ◊ ADJ (du or au) nord-est *inv* ◊ ADV vers le nord-est ► **north-easter** N nordet *m* (*Naut*), vent *m* du nord-est ► **north-easterly** ADJ [*wind, direction*] du nord-est ; [*situation*] au nord-est ◊ ADV vers le nord-est ► **north-eastern** ADJ (du) nord-est *inv* ► **north-eastward(s)** ADV vers le nord-est ► **north-facing** ADJ exposé au nord ► **North Island** N (*of New Zealand*) l'île *f* du Nord (*de la Nouvelle-Zélande*) ► **North Korea** N la Corée du Nord ► **North Korean** ADJ nord-coréen ◊ N Nord-Coréen(ne) *m(f)* ► **north-north-east** N nord-nord-est *m* ◊ ADJ (du or au) nord-nord-est *inv* ◊ ADV vers le nord-nord-est ► **north-north-west** N nord-nord-ouest *m* ◊ ADJ (du or au) nord-nord-ouest *inv* ◊ ADV vers le nord-nord-ouest ► **North Pole** N pôle *m* Nord ► **North Sea** N mer *f* du Nord ► **North Sea gas** N (*Brit*) gaz *m* naturel de la mer du Nord ► **North Sea oil** N pétrole *m* de la mer du Nord ► **North Star** N étoile *f* polaire ► **North Vietnam** N le Vietnam du Nord ► **North Vietnamese** ADJ nord-vietnamien ◊ N Nord-Vietnamien(ne) *m(f)* ► **north-wall hammer** N (*Climbing*) marteau-piolet *m* ► **north-west** N nord-ouest *m* ◊ ADJ (du or au) nord-ouest *inv* ◊ ADV vers le nord-ouest ► **north-wester** N noroît *m* (*Naut*), vent *m* du nord-ouest ► **north-westerly** ADJ [*wind, direction*] du nord-ouest ; [*situation*] au nord-ouest ◊ ADV vers le nord-ouest ► **north-western** ADJ (du) nord-ouest *inv* ► **North-West Frontier** N frontière *f* du Nord-Ouest ► **North-West Passage** N passage *m* du Nord-Ouest ► **north-westward(s)** ADV vers le nord-ouest

Northants [nɔːˈθænts] ABBR = **Northamptonshire**

northbound [ˈnɔːθbaʊnd] ADJ [*traffic*] en direction du nord ; [*vehicle*] qui va vers le nord ; [*carriageway*] nord *inv*

Northd ABBR = **Northumberland**

northerly [ˈnɔːðəlɪ] [1] ADJ [*wind*] du nord ; [*situation*] au nord ; [*direction*] vers le nord ; **~ latitudes** latitudes *fpl* boréales ; **~ aspect** exposition *f* au nord ; **in a ~ direction** en direction du nord, vers le nord [2] ADV vers le nord

northern [ˈnɔːðən] [1] ADJ [*province, state, neighbour*] du nord ; [*border, suburbs*] nord *inv* ; **the ~ coast** le littoral nord or septentrional ; **house with a ~ outlook** maison *f* exposée au nord ; **~ wall** mur *m* exposé au nord ; **in ~ Spain** dans le nord de l'Espagne ; **~ hemisphere** hémisphère *m* nord or boréal ; **in the town of Lille** à Lille, dans le nord [2] COMP ► **Northern Ireland** N l'Irlande *f* du Nord ► **Northern Irish** ADJ d'Irlande du Nord ◊ NPL Irlandais *mpl* du Nord ► **northern lights** NPL aurore *f* boréale ► **the Northern Territory** N (*of Australia*) le Territoire du Nord

northerner [ˈnɔːðənə] [1] N [a] homme *m* or femme *f* du Nord, habitant(e) *m(f)* du Nord ; **he is a ~** il vient du Nord ; **the ~s** les gens *mpl* du Nord, les septentrionaux *mpl* [b] (*US Hist*) Nordiste *mf*

northernmost [ˈnɔːðənməʊst] ADJ le plus au nord, à l'extrême nord

Northlands [ˈnɔːθləndz] NPL pays *mpl* du Nord

Northman [ˈnɔːθmən] N (*pl* **-men**) (*Hist*) Viking *m*

Northumb ABBR = **Northumberland**

Northumbria [nɔːˈθʌmbrɪə] N la Northumbrie

Northumbrian [nɔːˈθʌmbrɪən] [1] ADJ de Northumbrie [2] N habitant(e) *m(f)* or natif *m*, -ive *f* de Northumbrie

northward [ˈnɔːθwəd] [1] ADJ au nord [2] ADV (*also* **~s**) vers le nord

Northwest Territories [ˌnɔːθwestˈterɪtərɪz] NPL (*Can*) (Territoires *mpl* du) Nord-Ouest *m*

Northwest Territory [ˌnɔːθwestˈterɪtərɪ] N (*US Hist*) Territoire *m* du Nord-Ouest

Norway [ˈnɔːweɪ] N la Norvège

Norwegian [nɔːˈwiːdʒən] [1] ADJ (*gen*) norvégien ; [*ambassador, embassy*] de Norvège [2] N [a] (= *person*) Norvégien(ne) *m(f)* [b] (*Ling*) norvégien *m*

nos. NPL (ABBR = **numbers**) n°

nose [nəʊz] [1] N [a] [*of person, animal*] nez *m* ; [*of dog, cat*] museau *m* ; **he has a nice ~** il a un joli nez ; **his ~ was bleeding** il saignait du nez ; **the horse won by a ~** le cheval a gagné d'une demi-tête ; **to speak through one's ~** nasiller, parler du nez
[b] (= *sense of smell*) odorat *m*, nez *m* ; **to have a good ~** avoir l'odorat or le nez fin
[c] (= *instinct*) **to have a (good) ~ for sth** savoir flairer qch ; **he's got a (good) ~ for a bargain/ for danger/for a story** il sait flairer les bonnes affaires/le danger/les scoops
[d] [*of wine etc*] arôme *m*, bouquet *m*
[e] (*in phrases: fig*) **with one's ~ in the air** d'un air hautain ; **she's always got her ~ in a book*** elle a toujours le nez fourré dans un livre* ; **it was there under his very ~** or **right under his ~** all the time c'était là juste or en plein sous son nez ; **she did it under his very ~** or **right under his ~** elle l'a fait à sa barbe or sous son nez ; **to look down one's ~ at sb/sth** prendre qn/qch de haut ; **he can't see beyond** or **further than (the end of) his ~** il ne voit pas plus loin que le bout de son nez ; **to turn one's ~ up (at sth)** faire le dégoûté (devant qch) ; **to keep one's ~ out of sth** ne pas se mêler de qch ; **to poke** or **stick one's ~ into sth** mettre or fourrer son nez dans qch ; **you'd better keep your ~ clean*** il vaut mieux que tu te tiennes à carreau* ; **to lead sb by the ~** mener qn par le bout du nez ; **it gets up my ~*** ça me pompe l'air*, ça me tape sur les nerfs* ; (*US*) **right on the ~*** en plein dans le mille → **blow[1], end, follow, grindstone, joint, pay, rub, thumb**
[2] VT [a] (= *smell*) flairer, renifler
[b] **a van ~d its way past** or **through** une camionnette est passée lentement
[3] VI [*ship, vehicle*] avancer lentement
[4] COMP ► **nose cone** N [*of missile*] ogive *f* ► **nose drops** NPL gouttes *fpl* nasales, gouttes *fpl* pour le nez ► **nose job*** N (*plastic surgery*) **to have a ~ job** se faire refaire le nez ► **nose ring** N anneau *m* de nez ► **nose wheel** N (*Aviat*) roue *f* avant du train d'atterrissage

► **nose about*, nose around*** VI fouiner*, fureter
► **nose at** VT FUS flairer, renifler
► **nose in** VI [a] [*car*] se glisser dans une file [b]* [*person*] s'immiscer or s'insinuer (dans un groupe)
► **nose out** [1] VI [*car*] déboîter prudemment [2] VT SEP [a] [*dog*] flairer [b] **to ~ out a secret** découvrir or flairer un secret ; **to ~ sb out** dénicher or dépister qn

nosebag [ˈnəʊzbæg] N musette *f*

noseband [ˈnəʊzbænd] N [*of horse*] muserolle *f*

nosebleed [ˈnəʊzbliːd] N saignement *m* de nez ; **to have a ~** saigner du nez

-nosed [nəʊzd] ADJ (*in compounds*) au nez ... ; **red-nosed** au nez rouge → **long[1], snub[2]**

nosedive [ˈnəʊzdaɪv] [1] N [a] (*Aviat*) piqué *m* [b] (*fig*) [*of stocks, prices*] chute *f* libre, plongeon *m* ; **to take a ~** = **2b** [2] VI [a] [*plane*] descendre en piqué [b] (*fig*) [*stocks*] baisser rapidement ; [*prices, sales*] chuter ; [*career*] s'effondrer

nosegay [ˈnəʊzgeɪ] N petit bouquet *m*

nosepiece ['nəʊzpiːs] N (on spectacles) pont m; (on microscope) porte-objectif m

nosey* ['nəʊzɪ] ADJ fouineur*, curieux; **to be ~** mettre or fourrer* son nez partout; **don't be (so) ~!** mêlez-vous de vos affaires or de ce qui vous regarde!; (pej) **Nosey Parker** fouineur* m, -euse f

nosh*: [nɒʃ] **1** N **a** (Brit = food) bouffe* f; **to have some ~** boulotter*, bouffer*; **b** (US = snack) casse-croûte m **2** VI **a** (Brit = eat) boulotter*, bouffer*; **b** (US = have a snack) manger or grignoter entre les repas **3** COMP ► **nosh-up** N (Brit) bouffe* f; **to have a ~-up** bouffer*, bâfrer*

nosily* ['nəʊzɪlɪ] ADV indiscrètement

nosiness* ['nəʊzɪnɪs] N curiosité f

nosing ['nəʊzɪŋ] N (of stair) rebord m

nosography [nɒ'sɒɡrəfɪ] N nosographie f

nosological [ˌnɒsə'lɒdʒɪkəl] ADJ nosologique

nosologist [nɒ'sɒlədʒɪst] N nosologiste mf

nosology [nɒ'sɒlədʒɪ] N nosologie f

nostalgia [nɒs'tældʒɪə] N nostalgie f

nostalgic [nɒs'tældʒɪk] ADJ nostalgique; **to be ~ for** or **about sth** avoir la nostalgie de qch

nostalgically [nɒs'tældʒɪkəlɪ] ADV avec nostalgie

Nostradamus [ˌnɒstrə'dɑːməs] N Nostradamus m

nostril ['nɒstrəl] N [of person, dog etc] narine f; [of horse etc] naseau m

nostrum ['nɒstrəm] N (= patent medicine, also fig) panacée f, remède m universel; (= quack medicine) remède m de charlatan

nosy* ['nəʊzɪ] ADJ = nosey

not [nɒt] ADV **a** (with vb) ne ... pas; **he is ~ here** il n'est pas ici; **he has ~** or **hasn't come** il n'est pas venu; **he will ~** or **won't stay** (prediction) il ne restera pas; (refusal) il ne veut pas rester; **is it ~?** or **isn't it?** non?, n'est-ce pas?; **you have got it, haven't you?** vous l'avez (bien), non or n'est-ce pas?; **~ only ... but also ...** non seulement ... mais également ...; **he told me ~ to come** il m'a dit de ne pas venir; **~ to mention ...** sans compter ..., pour ne pas parler de ...; **~ wanting to be heard, he removed his shoes** ne voulant pas qu'on l'entende, il ôta ses chaussures
b (as substitute for clause) non; **is he coming? — I believe ~** est-ce qu'il vient? — je crois que non; **is it going to rain? — I hope ~** va-t-il pleuvoir?; **I'espère que non; it would appear ~** il semble que non; **I am going whether he comes or ~** j'y vais qu'il vienne ou non; **believe it or ~, she has gone** le croiriez-vous, elle est partie
c (elliptically) **are you cold? — ~ at all** avez-vous froid? — pas du tout; **thank you very much — ~ at all** merci beaucoup — je vous en prie or de rien or il n'y a pas de quoi; **~ in the least** pas du tout, nullement; (frm) **I wish it were ~ so** je voudrais bien qu'il ne soit autrement; **for the young and the ~ so young** pour les jeunes et les moins jeunes; **big, ~ to say enormous** gros pour ne pas dire énorme; **~ that I care** non pas que cela me fasse quelque chose; **~ that I know of** pas (autant) que je sache; **~ that they haven't been useful** on ne peut pas dire qu'ils or ce n'est pas qu'ils n'aient pas été utiles; **will he come? — as likely as ~** est-ce qu'il viendra? — ça se peut; **as likely as ~** comme il y a une chance sur deux or il y a des chances (pour) qu'il vienne; **why ~?** pourquoi pas?
d (understatement) **~ a few ...** bien des ..., pas mal de ...; **~ without reason** non sans raison; **~ without some regrets** non sans quelques regrets; **I shall ~ be sorry to ...** je ne serai pas mécontent de ...; **it is ~ unlikely that ...** il n'est pas du tout impossible que ...; **a ~ inconsiderable number of ...** un nombre non négligeable de ...
e (with pron etc) **~ me** or (frm) **I!** moi pas!, pas

moi!; **~ one book** pas un livre; **~ one man knew** pas un (homme) ne savait; **~ everyone can do that** tout le monde n'en est pas capable, ce n'est pas donné à tout le monde; **~ any more** plus (maintenant); **~ yet** pas encore
f (with adj) non, pas; **~ guilty** non coupable; **~ negotiable** non négociable

notability [ˌnəʊtə'bɪlɪtɪ] N **a** (NonC) [of quality] prééminence f **b** [of person] notabilité f, notable m

notable ['nəʊtəbl] **1** ADJ [designer, philosopher, example] éminent; [fact] notable, remarquable; [success] remarquable; **with a few ~ exceptions** à quelques notables exceptions près; **to be ~ for sth** se distinguer par qch; **it is ~ that ...** il est remarquable que ... (+ subj) **2** N notable m

▼ **notably** ['nəʊtəblɪ] ADV **a** (= in particular) notamment **b** (= noticeably) notablement; **~, she failed to mention ...** il est significatif or intéressant qu'elle n'ait pas mentionné ...

notarial [nəʊ'tɛərɪəl] ADJ [seal] notarial; [deed] notarié; [style] de notaire

notarize ['nəʊtəˌraɪz] VT (US) [notary] authentifier, certifier conforme

notary ['nəʊtərɪ] N (also ~ **public**) notaire m; **before a ~** par-devant notaire

notate [nəʊ'teɪt] VT (Mus) noter, transcrire

notation [nəʊ'teɪʃən] N (Mus, Ling, Math) notation f

notch [nɒtʃ] **1** N (in wood, stick etc) entaille f, encoche f; (in belt etc) cran m; (in wheel, board etc) dent f, cran m; (in saw) dent f; (in blade) ébréchure f; (US Geog) défilé m; (Sewing) cran m; **he pulled his belt in one ~** il a resserré sa ceinture d'un cran **2** VT [+ stick etc] encocher; [+ wheel etc] cranter, denteler; [+ blade] ébrécher; (Sewing) [+ seam] cranter
► **notch together** VT SEP (Carpentry) assembler à entailles
► **notch up** VT SEP [+ score, point, win, success] marquer

notchback ['nɒtʃbæk] N (US = car) tricorps f, trois-volumes f

▼ **note** [nəʊt] **1** N **a** (= short record of facts, things to do etc) note f; **to take** or **make a ~ of sth** prendre qch en note, prendre note de qch; **I must make a mental ~ to buy some more** il faut que je me souvienne d'en racheter; **to take** or **make ~s** [student, policeman, secretary etc] prendre des notes; **lecture ~s** notes fpl de cours; **to speak from ~s** parler en consultant ses notes; **to speak without ~s** parler sans notes or papiers → compare
b (= short commentary) note f, annotation f; **author's ~** note f de l'auteur; **translator's ~** (= footnotes etc) remarques fpl or notes fpl du traducteur; (= foreword) préface f du traducteur; **"Notes on Molière"** « Notes sur Molière »; **~s on a literary work** commentaire m sur un ouvrage littéraire; **to put ~s into a text** annoter un texte
c (= informal letter) mot m; (to secretary) **take a ~ to Mr Jones** je vais vous dicter un mot pour M. Jones; **just a quick ~ to tell you ...** un petit mot à la hâte or en vitesse pour te dire ...
d (Diplomacy) note f; **diplomatic ~** note f diplomatique, mémorandum m; **official ~ from the government** note f officielle du gouvernement
e (Mus) note f; [of piano] touche f; [of bird] note f; **to hold a ~** tenir or prolonger une note; **to play a false ~** ◊ **to sing a false ~** faire une fausse note
f (fig = tone) note f; **on an optimistic/positive ~** sur une note optimiste/positive; **on a personal/practical ~** d'un point de vue personnel/pratique; **if I could add just a personal ~** si je peux me permettre une remarque personnelle; **on a more positive ~ ...** pour continuer sur une note plus optimiste ...; **peace talks ended on a high/a more posi-**

tive **~** les pourparlers de paix se sont terminés sur une note optimiste/plus positive; **on a more serious ~ ...** plus sérieusement or pour passer aux choses sérieuses ...; (fig) **the talks began on a friendly ~** les négociations ont débuté sur une note amicale; **his speech struck the right/wrong ~** son discours était bien dans la note/n'était pas dans la note; **several speakers struck a pessimistic ~** plusieurs orateurs se sont montrés pessimistes
g (= quality, implication) note f, accent m; **with a ~ of anxiety in his voice** avec une note d'anxiété dans la voix; **his voice held a ~ of desperation** sa voix avait un accent de désespoir; **a ~ of nostalgia** une note or touche nostalgique; **a ~ of warning** un avertissement discret
h (Brit: also **banknote**) billet m (de banque); **ten-pound ~** billet m de dix livres (sterling)
i (Comm) (= promise to pay) effet m, billet m; (= voucher) bon m; **~ of hand** reconnaissance f (de dette); (Fin) **~s payable** effets mpl à payer → **advice, promissory note**
j (NonC; frm = notability) **a man of ~** un homme éminent or de marque; **a family of ~** une famille éminente; **all the people of ~** toutes les personnes importantes; **nothing of ~** rien d'important
k (NonC = notice) **to take ~ of** prendre (bonne) note de, remarquer; **take ~!** prenez bonne note!; **the critics took ~ of the book** les critiques ont remarqué le livre; **they will take ~ of what you say** ils feront or prêteront attention à ce que vous dites; (frm) **worthy of ~** remarquable, digne d'attention
2 VT **a** (gen) noter, prendre (bonne) note de (frm); (Jur) prendre acte de; **to ~ a fact** (gen) prendre note d'un fait; (Jur) prendre acte d'un fait; (Jur) **which fact is duly ~d** dont acte; **we have ~d your remarks** nous avons pris (bonne) note de vos remarques
b (= notice) constater; **to ~ an error** constater une erreur; **I ~ that ...** je constate que ...; **that the matter is not yet closed** notez bien que l'affaire n'est pas encore close
c (also ~ **down**) noter; **let me ~ it (down)** laissez-moi le noter; **to ~ (down) sb's remarks** noter les remarques de qn; **to ~ (down) an appointment in one's diary** noter un rendez-vous dans son agenda
3 COMP ► **note-case** N (Brit) portefeuille m, porte-billets m inv ► **note issue** N émission f fiduciaire
► **note down** VT SEP = note 2c

notebook ['nəʊtbʊk] N **a** (= notepad) carnet m, calepin m; (Scol) cahier m; [tear-off] bloc-notes m **b** (Comput: also ~ **computer**) notebook m

noted ['nəʊtɪd] ADJ [historian, writer] éminent, célèbre; [thing, fact] célèbre; **to be ~ for sth/ for doing sth** être connu pour qch/pour avoir fait qch; (iro) **a man not ~ for his generosity** un homme qui ne passe pas pour être particulièrement généreux

notelet ['nəʊtlɪt] N carte-lettre f

notepad ['nəʊtpæd] N bloc-notes m

notepaper ['nəʊtpeɪpə'] N papier m à lettres

noteworthiness ['nəʊtwɜːðɪnɪs] N importance f

noteworthy ['nəʊtwɜːðɪ] ADJ (frm) remarquable, notable; **it is ~ that ...** il convient de noter que ...

nothing ['nʌθɪŋ] **1** N **a** rien m (+ ne before vb); **I saw ~** je n'ai rien vu; **~ happened** il n'est rien arrivé, il ne s'est rien passé; **to eat ~** ne rien manger; **~ to eat/read** rien à manger/à lire; **he's had ~ to eat yet** il n'a encore rien mangé; **~ could be easier** rien de plus simple; **~ pleases him** rien ne le satisfait, il n'est jamais content
b (+ adj) rien de; **~ new/interesting** etc rien de nouveau/d'intéressant etc
c (in phrases) **he's five foot ~*** il ne fait qu'un

(petit) mètre cinquante deux; **~ on earth** rien au monde; **you look like ~ on earth!** regarde l'allure que tu as! **as if ~ had happened** comme si de rien n'était; **fit for ~** bon à rien; **to say ~ of ...** sans parler de ...; **I can do ~ (about it)** je n'y peux rien; **he is ~ if not polite** il est avant tout poli; **for ~** (= in vain) en vain, inutilement; (= without payment) pour rien, gratuitement; (= for no reason) sans raison; **he was working for ~** il travaillait gratuitement or sans se faire payer; **he got ~ out of it** il n'en a rien retiré, il n'y a rien gagné; **all his fame counted for ~** ◊ **all his fame counted for ~** toute sa gloire ne comptait pour rien; (hum) **I'm not Scottish for ~*** ce n'est pas pour rien que je suis écossais; **~ of the kind!** absolument pas!, (mais) pas du tout!; **to think ~ of doing sth** (= consider normal) trouver naturel de faire qch; (= do without thinking) n'attacher aucune importance à faire qch; (= do unscrupulously) n'avoir aucun scrupule à faire qch; **think ~ of it!** (= don't thank me) mais je vous en prie!, mais pas du tout!; **don't apologize, it's ~** ne vous excusez pas, ce n'est rien; **that is ~ to you** (= it's easy for you) pour vous ce n'est rien; **£500 is ~ to her** 500 livres, c'est une bricole pour elle, elle n'en est pas à 500 livres près; **she is** or **means ~ to him** elle n'est rien pour lui; **it's** or **it means ~ to me whether he comes or not** il m'est indifférent qu'il vienne ou non; **her secretarial skills are ~ compared with** or **to her sister's** elle est beaucoup moins bonne secrétaire que sa sœur; **that's ~ to what is to come** ce n'est rien à côté de ce qui nous attend; **I can make ~ of it** je n'y comprends rien; **to have ~ on** (= be naked) être nu; (= have no plans) être libre; **I have ~ on (for) this evening** je suis libre ce soir, je n'ai rien de prévu ce soir; **the police have ~ on him** la police n'a rien pu retenir contre lui; (fig) **he has ~ on her*** (= isn't as good as) il n'arrive pas à la cheville; **there's ~ in it** (= not interesting) c'est sans intérêt; (= not true) ce n'est absolument pas vrai; (= no difference) c'est du pareil au même; (in contest = very close) c'est très serré; **there's ~ in these rumours** il n'y a rien de vrai or pas un grain de vérité dans ces rumeurs; **there's ~ in it* for us** nous n'avons rien à y gagner; **Oxford is leading, but there's ~ in it** Oxford est en tête, mais c'est très serré; **there's ~ to it*** c'est facile (comme tout*); **I love swimming, there's ~ like it!** j'adore la natation, il n'y a rien de tel or de mieux!; **there's ~ like exercise for keeping you fit** il n'y a rien de tel que l'exercice pour garder la forme ■ (PROV) **~ venture(d) ~ gain(ed)** qui ne risque rien n'a rien (PROV); **you get ~ for ~** on n'a rien pour rien; **to come to ~** ne pas aboutir, ne rien donner, faire fiasco; **to be reduced to ~** être réduit à néant; **~ much** pas grand-chose; **~ but** rien que; **he does ~ but eat** il ne fait que manger; **he does ~ but complain** il ne fait que se plaindre, il n'arrête pas de se plaindre; **I get ~ but complaints all day** je n'entends que des plaintes à longueur de journée; (Brit) **there's ~ for it but to go** il n'y a qu'à or il ne nous reste qu'à partir; **~ less than ...** rien moins que ...; **~ more** rien de plus; **~ else** rien d'autre; **there's ~ else for it** c'est inévitable; **we could do ~ else** (= nothing more) nous ne pouvions rien faire de plus; (= no other thing) nous ne pouvions rien faire d'autre; **that has ~ to do with us** nous n'avons rien à voir là-dedans; **I've got ~ to do with it** je n'y suis pour rien; **have ~ to do with it!** ne vous en mêlez pas!; **that has ~ to do with it** cela n'a rien à voir; **there is ~ to laugh at** il n'y a pas de quoi rire; **I've got ~ to say** je n'ai rien à dire; **he had ~ to say for himself** (= no explanation) il ne trouvait aucune excuse; (= no conversation) il n'avait pas de conversation; **I've got ~ more to say** je n'ai rien à ajouter; **I have ~ against him/the idea** je n'ai rien contre

lui/cette idée; **there was ~ doing* at the club so I went home** il ne se passait rien d'intéressant au club, alors je suis rentré; **~ doing!*** (refusing) pas question!; (reporting lack of success) pas moyen!; **in ~ flat*** (= very quickly) en un rien de temps, en cinq sec* → **something, wrong**

d (Math*) zéro m

e (NonC = nothingness) néant m, rien m

f (= person) nullité f; (= thing) vétille f, rien m; **it's a mere ~ compared with what he spent last year** ça n'est rien en comparaison de ce qu'il a dépensé l'an dernier; **he's a ~** c'est une nullité

2 ADV aucunement, nullement; **~ less than** rien moins que; **it was ~ like as big as we thought** c'était loin d'être aussi grand qu'on avait cru; **~ daunted, he ...** nullement or aucunement découragé, il ..., sans se (laisser) démonter, il ... → **loath**

3 ADJ (US* pej) minable, de rien du tout

nothingness [ˈnʌθɪŋnɪs] N (NonC) néant m

notice [ˈnəʊtɪs] **1** N **a** (NonC) (= warning, intimation) avis m, notification f; (Jur = official personal communication) mise f en demeure; (= period) délai m; (= end of work contract) (by employer) congé m; (by employee) démission f; **I must have (some) ~ of what you intend to do** il faut que je sois prévenu or avisé à l'avance de ce que vous avez l'intention de faire; **we require six days' ~** nous demandons un préavis de six jours; **a week's ~** une semaine de préavis, un préavis d'une semaine; **I must have at least a week's ~ if you want to ...** il faut me prévenir or m'avertir au moins une semaine à l'avance si vous voulez ...; **we had no ~ (of it)** nous n'avons pas été prévenus à l'avance; **advance** or **previous ~** préavis m; **final ~** dernier avertissement m; (from job) **to get one's ~** recevoir son congé, être licencié; **to give ~ to** [+ tenant] donner congé à; [+ landlord etc] donner un préavis de départ à; **to give ~ that ...** faire savoir que ...; (Admin etc: officially) donner acte que ...; **to give ~ of sth** annoncer qch; **~ is hereby given that ...** il est porté à la connaissance du public par la présente que ...; **to give sb ~ of sth** avertir or prévenir qn de qch; (Admin etc: officially) donner acte à qn de qch; **to give sb ~ that ...** aviser qn que ..., faire savoir à qn que ...; **he gave her ~ to ...** il l'a avisée qu'elle devait ...; **to give sb ~ (of dismissal)** [+ employee] licencier qn, renvoyer qn; [+ servant etc] donner son congé à qn, congédier qn; **to give in** or **hand in one's ~** [professional or office worker] donner sa démission; [servant] donner ses huit jours; **to serve ~ on sb that ...** aviser qn que ..., faire savoir à qn que ...

b (Jur) **~ to appear** assignation f (à comparaître); (Jur, Fin) **~ of calls** (avis m d')appel m de fonds; **~ to pay** avis m d'avoir à payer; (to tenant etc) **~ to quit** congé m; (Comm) **~ of receipt** avis m de réception; (Jur) **~ of termination** avis m de clôture (d'une procédure)

c **at short ~** (Fin) à court terme; **he rang me up at short ~** il m'a téléphoné à la dernière minute; **you must be ready to leave at very short ~** il faut que vous soyez prêt à partir dans les plus brefs délais; **at a moment's ~** sur-le-champ, immédiatement; **at three days' ~** dans un délai de trois jours; (from job) **he's under ~ (to leave)** il a reçu son congé; **until further ~** jusqu'à nouvel ordre; (Admin frm) **without ~ (previous)** sans préavis, sans avis préalable; **he was dismissed without (any) ~** il a été renvoyé sans préavis

d (= announcement) avis m, annonce f; (in newspaper) (= advert etc) annonce f; (= short article) entrefilet m; (= poster) affiche f, placard m; (= sign) pancarte f, écriteau m; **birth/ marriage/death ~** annonce f de naissance/ mariage/décès; **public ~** avis m au public; **to put a ~ in the paper** mettre or faire insérer une annonce dans le journal; (Press) **I saw a ~**

in the paper about the concert j'ai vu une annonce or un entrefilet dans le journal à propos du concert; **the ~ says "keep out"** l'écriteau porte l'inscription « défense d'entrer »; **the ~ of the meeting was published in ...** l'annonce de la réunion a été publiée dans ...

e (= review) [of book, film, play etc] compte rendu m, critique f; **the book/film/play got good ~s** le livre/le film/la pièce a eu de bonnes critiques

f (NonC = attention) **to take ~ of sb/sth** tenir compte de qn/qch, faire or prêter attention à qn/qch; **to take no ~ of sb/sth** ne tenir aucun compte de qn/qch, ne pas faire attention à qn/qch; **take no ~!** ne faites pas attention!; **he took no ~ of her remarks** il n'a absolument pas tenu compte de ses remarques; **he took no ~ of her** il n'a absolument pas fait attention à elle; (iro) **a lot of ~ he takes of me!*** pour lui c'est comme si je n'existais pas!; **I wasn't taking much ~ at the time** je ne faisais pas très attention à ce moment-là; **it escaped his ~ that ...** il ne s'est pas aperçu que ..., il n'a pas remarqué que ...; **to attract ~ se faire remarquer**; (deliberately = show off) s'afficher (pej); **it has attracted a lot of ~** cela a suscité un grand intérêt; **to avoid ~** (essayer de) passer inaperçu; **to bring sth to sb's ~** faire observer or remarquer qch à qn, porter qch à la connaissance de qn; (frm) **it has come** or **it has been brought to my ~ that ...** il a été porté à ma connaissance que ..., on m'a signalé que ... → **sit up, slip**

2 VT **a** (= perceive) s'apercevoir de, remarquer; (= heed) faire attention à; **I ~d a tear in his coat** j'ai remarqué un accroc dans son manteau; **when he ~d me he called out to me** quand il m'a vu, il m'a appelé; **to ~ a mistake** remarquer une faute, s'apercevoir d'une faute; **without my noticing it** sans que je le remarque (subj) or que je m'en aperçoive; **I'm afraid I didn't ~** malheureusement je n'ai pas remarqué; **I never ~ such things** je ne remarque jamais ce genre de chose; **I ~d her hesitating** j'ai remarqué or je me suis aperçu qu'elle hésitait; **I ~ you have a new dress** je vois que vous avez une nouvelle robe; **yes, so I've ~d!** je m'en suis aperçu!, j'ai remarqué!

b (= review) [+ book, film, play] faire le compte rendu or la critique de

3 COMP ► **notice board** N (esp Brit) (printed or painted sign) écriteau m, pancarte f; (for holding announcements) panneau m d'affichage

▼ **noticeable** [ˈnəʊtɪsəbl] ADJ [effect, difference, improvement] visible, sensible; [lack] évident, sensible; **it isn't really ~** ça ne se voit pas vraiment; **it is ~ that ...** on voit bien que ...; **to be ~ by one's absence** briller par son absence

noticeably [ˈnəʊtɪsəblɪ] ADV [better, worse, higher, lower] nettement; **to be ~ absent** briller par son absence; **~ lacking** manquant visiblement; **to improve ~** s'améliorer sensiblement; **he shuddered ~** il frissonna de façon visible

notifiable [ˈnəʊtɪfaɪəbl] ADJ (frm: Admin) [disease] à déclarer obligatoirement; [offence] à signaler; **all changes of address are ~ immediately** tout changement d'adresse doit être signalé immédiatement aux autorités

notification [ˌnəʊtɪfɪˈkeɪʃən] N (NonC) avis m; (Jur, Admin) notification f; [of marriage, engagement] annonce f; [of birth, death] déclaration f; (Press) **written ~** notification f écrite

notify [ˈnəʊtɪfaɪ] VT **to ~ sth to sb** signaler or notifier qch à qn; **to ~ sb of sth** aviser or avertir qn de qch; **any change of address must be notified** tout changement d'adresse doit être signalé or notifié; **you will be notified later of the result** on vous communiquera le résultat ultérieurement or plus tard

notion ['nəʊʃən] [1] N [a] (= thought, project) idée f; **I've got a ~ for a play** j'ai l'idée d'une pièce; **I hit (up)on the ~ of going to see her** tout à coup l'idée m'est venue d'aller la voir; **the ~ never entered my head!** cette idée ne m'est jamais venue à l'esprit or ne m'a jamais effleuré!; **he got the ~ (into his head)** or **he somehow got hold of the ~ that she wouldn't help him** il s'est mis en tête (l'idée) qu'elle ne l'aiderait pas; **where did you get the ~** or **what gave you the ~ that I couldn't come?** qu'est-ce qui t'a fait penser que je ne pourrais pas venir?; **to put ~s into sb's head*** or **to give sb ~s*** mettre or fourrer* des idées dans la tête de qn; **that gave me the ~ of inviting her** c'est ce qui m'a donné l'idée de l'inviter; **I'd had a few ~s about being a journalist** j'avais songé à devenir journaliste

[b] (= opinion) idée f, opinion f; (= way of thinking) façon f de penser; **he has some odd ~s** il a de drôles d'idées; **she has some odd ~s about how to bring up children** elle a de drôles d'idées sur la façon d'élever les enfants; **according to his ~** selon sa façon de penser; **if that's your ~ of fun ...** si c'est ça que tu appelles t'amuser ...; **it wasn't my ~ of a holiday** ce n'était pas ce que j'appelle des vacances

[c] (= vague knowledge) idée f, notion f; **I've got some ~ of physics** j'ai quelques notions de physique; **have you any ~ of what he meant to do?** avez-vous la moindre idée de ce qu'il voulait faire?; **I haven't the least†** or **slightest** or **foggiest*** je n'en ai pas la moindre idée; **I have a ~ that he was going to Paris** j'ai dans l'idée qu'il allait à Paris; **I had no ~ they knew each other** je n'avais aucune idée or j'ignorais absolument qu'ils se connaissaient; **he has no ~ of time** il n'a pas la notion du temps

[2] **notions** NPL (US = ribbons, thread etc) (articles mpl de) mercerie f

notional ['nəʊʃənl] ADJ [a] (= hypothetical) [value, profit, amount] théorique, hypothétique; [time, line] imaginaire [b] (Philos) notionnel, conceptuel [c] (Ling) [grammar] notionnel; **~ word** mot m plein [d] (US = whimsical) [person] capricieux, fantasque

notionally ['nəʊʃənəlɪ] ADV (= hypothetically) théoriquement

notoriety [ˌnəʊtəˈraɪətɪ] N [a] (NonC) (triste) notoriété f, triste réputation f [b] (= person) individu m au nom tristement célèbre

notorious [nəʊˈtɔːrɪəs] ADJ [criminal, liar, womaniser, meanness, brothel] notoire; [crime, case] célèbre; [person, prison] tristement célèbre; **the ~ Richard** le tristement célèbre Richard; **to be ~ for one's meanness** être d'une mesquinerie notoire; **to be ~ for one's racism** être bien connu pour ses idées racistes; **he's as a womanizer** c'est un coureur de jupons notoire; **he's ~ for murdering his wife** il est tristement célèbre pour avoir assassiné sa femme; **it is ~ that ...** il est notoire que ...

notoriously [nəʊˈtɔːrɪəslɪ] ADV [slow, unreliable, fickle] notoirement; **~ cruel/inefficient** d'une cruauté/incompétence notoire; **it is ~ difficult to do that** chacun sait à quel point c'est difficile à faire

Notts ABBR = **Nottinghamshire**

notwithstanding [ˌnɒtwɪθˈstændɪŋ] [1] PREP malgré, en dépit de [2] ADV néanmoins, malgré tout [3] CONJ (also **~ that**) quoique (+ subj), bien que (+ subj)

nougat ['nuːgɑː, 'nʌgət] N nougat m

nought [nɔːt] N = **naught**; → ZERO

noun [naʊn] [1] N nom m, substantif m [2] COMP ► **noun clause** N proposition f ► **noun phrase** N syntagme m nominal

nourish ['nʌrɪʃ] VT [+ person] nourrir (**with** de); [+ leather etc] entretenir; (fig) [+ hopes etc] nourrir, entretenir → **ill, undernourish, well²**

nourishing ['nʌrɪʃɪŋ] ADJ (= nutritious) [food] nourrissant, nutritif; (Cosmetics) [cream] qui nourrit la peau

nourishment ['nʌrɪʃmənt] N (NonC = food) nourriture f, aliments mpl; (frm) **to take ~** se nourrir, s'alimenter; (frm) **he has taken (some)** il s'est alimenté; **sugar provides no real ~** ◊ **there's no real ~ in sugar** le sucre n'est pas vraiment nourrissant

nous* [naʊs] N (NonC: Brit) bon sens m; **he's got a lot of ~** il a du plomb dans la cervelle*

Nov. ABBR = **November**

nova ['nəʊvə] N (pl **novas** or **novae** ['nəʊviː]) nova f

Nova Scotia ['nəʊvəˈskəʊʃə] N la Nouvelle-Écosse

Nova Scotian ['nəʊvəˈskəʊʃən] [1] ADJ néo-écossais [2] N Néo-Écossais(e) m(f)

novel ['nɒvəl] [1] N (Literat) roman m [2] ADJ original

novelette [ˌnɒvəˈlet] N (Literat) nouvelle f; (trivial) roman m de quatre sous (pej); (= love story) roman m à l'eau de rose

novelist ['nɒvəlɪst] N romancier m, -ière f

novella [nəʊˈvelə] N (pl **novellas** or **novelle** [nəʊˈveleɪ]) roman m court

novelization [ˌnɒvəlaɪˈzeɪʃən] N novélisation f

novelty ['nɒvəltɪ] N [a] (NonC) (= newness) nouveauté f; (= unusualness) étrangeté f; **once** or **when the ~ has worn off** une fois passée la nouveauté [b] (= idea, thing) innovation f; **it was quite a ~** c'était une innovation or du nouveau or de l'inédit [c] (Comm) (article m de) nouveauté f, fantaisie f

November [nəʊˈvembər] N novembre m; for phrases see **September**

novena [nəʊˈviːnə] N (pl **novenae** [nəʊˈviːniː]) neuvaine f

novice ['nɒvɪs] [1] N [a] (= beginner) novice mf, débutant(e) m(f); **to be a ~ at sth** être novice en qch; **he's a ~ in politics** ◊ **he's a political ~** c'est un novice or débutant en politique; **he's no ~** il n'est pas novice, il n'en est pas à son coup d'essai [b] (Sport) (= person) débutant(e) m(f) (sportif qui n'a pas remporté de titre important); (= racehorse) cheval qui n'a pas remporté suffisamment de courses [c] (Rel) novice m [2] ADJ [worker, writer etc] novice, débutant

noviciate, novitiate [nəʊˈvɪʃɪɪt] N [a] (Rel) (= novice) (temps m du) noviciat m; (= place) maison f des novices, noviciat m [b] (fig) noviciat m, apprentissage m

Novocain(e)® ['nəʊvəʊkeɪn] N novocaïne f

NOW [naʊ] (in US) ABBR = **National Organization for Women** organisation féministe

now [naʊ] [1] ADV [a] (= at this time) maintenant; (= these days, at the moment) actuellement, en ce moment; (= at that time) alors, à ce moment-là; **~ I'm ready** je suis prêt maintenant; **~ is the best time to go to Scotland** c'est maintenant le meilleur moment pour aller en Écosse; **she's a widow ~** elle est maintenant veuve; **the couple, who ~ have three children ...** ce couple, qui a maintenant trois enfants ...; **they won't be long ~** ils ne vont plus tarder (maintenant); **what are you doing ~?** qu'est-ce que tu fais actuellement or en ce moment?; **strawberries are in season ~** c'est la saison des fraises; **he ~ understood why she had left him** alors il comprit or il comprit alors pourquoi elle l'avait quitté; **~ is the time to do it** c'est le moment de le faire; **I'll do it (right) ~** je vais le faire dès maintenant or à l'instant; **I am doing it (right) ~** je suis (justement) en train de le faire, je le fais à l'instant même; **~ for the question of your expenses** et maintenant en ce qui concerne la question de vos dépenses; **how can I believe you ~?** comment puis-je te croi-

re maintenant?; **(every) ~ and again** ◊ **(every) ~ and then** de temps en temps, de temps à autre; **it's ~ or never!** c'est le moment ou jamais!; **even ~ there's time to change your mind** il est encore temps (maintenant) de changer d'avis; **even ~ he doesn't believe me** il ne me croit toujours pas; **people do that even ~** les gens font ça encore aujourd'hui or maintenant; **even ~ we have no rifles** encore actuellement or à l'heure actuelle nous n'avons pas de fusils

[b] (with prep) **you should have done that before** vous auriez déjà dû l'avoir fait; **before ~ people thought that ...** auparavant les gens pensaient que ...; **you should have finished long before** il y a longtemps que vous auriez dû avoir fini; **long before ~ it was realized that ...** il y a longtemps déjà, on comprenait que ...; **between ~ and next Tuesday** d'ici (à) mardi prochain; **they should have arrived by ~** ils devraient être déjà arrivés, ils devraient être arrivés à l'heure qu'il est; **haven't you finished by ~?** vous n'avez toujours pas fini?, vous n'avez pas encore fini?; **by ~ it was clear that ...** dès lors, il était évident que ...; **that will do for ~** ça ira pour l'instant or pour le moment; **from ~ on(wards)** (with present tense) à partir de maintenant; (with future tense) à partir de maintenant, dorénavant, désormais; (with past tense) dès lors, dès ce moment-là; **(in) three weeks from ~** dans trois semaines; **from ~ until then** d'ici là; **till ~** ◊ **until ~** ◊ **up to ~** (= till this moment) jusqu'à présent, jusqu'ici; (= till that moment) jusque-là

[c] (showing alternation) **~ walking, ~ running** tantôt (en) marchant tantôt (en) courant; **~ here, ~ there** tantôt par ici tantôt par là

[d] (without temporal implication) **~!** bon!, alors!; **~, ~!** allons, allons!; (warning) **~, Simon!** allons, Simon!; **come ~!** allons!; **well, ~!** eh bien!; **~ then, let's start!** bon, commençons!; **~ then, what's all this?** alors, qu'est-ce que c'est que ça?; **~, they had been looking for him all morning** or, ils avaient passé toute la matinée à sa recherche; **~, he was a fisherman** or, il était pêcheur; **~ do be quiet for a minute** allons, taisez-vous une minute

[2] CONJ maintenant que; **~ (that) you've seen him** maintenant que vous l'avez vu

[3] ADJ [a] (esp US = present) actuel; **the ~ president** le président actuel [b] * (= exciting and new) [clothes] du dernier cri; (= interested in new things) [people] branché*, dans le vent

[4] N → **here**

nowadays ['naʊədeɪz] ADV (in contrast to past years) de nos jours, aujourd'hui; (in contrast to recently) ces jours-ci; **rents are very high ~** les loyers sont très élevés de nos jours; **why don't we ever see Jim ~?** pourquoi ne voit-on plus jamais Jim ces jours-ci?

noway(s) ['nəʊweɪ(z)] ADV (US) (after request for favour) pas question; (= not at all) pas du tout

nowhere ['nəʊwɛər], **nowheres*** (US) ['nəʊwɛəz] ADV (lit = no place) nulle part; **they have ~ to go** ils n'ont nulle part où aller; **there was ~ to hide** il n'y avait aucun endroit où se cacher; **from (out of) ~** de nulle part; **there's ~ I'd rather be** je me sens vraiment bien ici; **there is ~ more romantic than Paris** il n'y a pas d'endroit plus romantique que Paris; **~ else** nulle part ailleurs; **she had ~ else to go** c'est le seul endroit où elle pouvait aller; **it's ~ you know** ce n'est pas un endroit que tu connais; **it's ~ you'll ever find it** tu n'arriveras jamais à le trouver; **where are you going? — ~ special** or **~ in particular** où vas-tu? — nulle part; **~ was ~ to be found** elle était introuvable; **he was ~ in sight** or **~ to be seen** il avait disparu → **middle**

[b] (fig) **without him I would be ~** sans lui, je ne serais arrivé à rien; (Sport) **to come ~***

n'arriver à rien; **he came from ~ to take the lead from Coe** contre toute attente, il a dépassé Coe; **he came from ~ to win the election** cet outsider a remporté l'élection; **the enquiry was getting ~** l'enquête piétinait; **threatening me will get you ~** vous n'obtiendrez rien en me menaçant; **lying will get you ~** ça ne te servira à rien de mentir; **we're getting** *or* **this is getting us ~ (fast)*** ça ne nous mène à rien, on tourne en rond; **to be going ~ (fast)*** [person] n'arriver à rien; [talks] être dans l'impasse; **to get ~ with sb** n'arriver à rien avec qn; **a fiver goes ~ these days** on ne va pas loin avec un billet de cinq livres (or dollars) aujourd'hui
□ **~ near: his house is ~ near the church** sa maison n'est pas près de l'église du tout; **you are ~ near the truth** vous êtes à mille lieues de la vérité; **you're ~ near it!** ◊ **you're ~ near right!** tu n'y es pas du tout!; **we're ~ near finding a cure** nous sommes loin d'avoir trouvé un traitement; **she is ~ near as clever as he is** elle est nettement moins intelligente que lui; **£10 is ~ near enough** 10 livres sont loin de suffire → **near 1b**

nowise ['nəʊwaɪz] ADV (US) = **noway(s)**

nowt [naʊt] N (Brit dial) = **nothing**

noxious ['nɒkʃəs] ADJ (= toxic) [gas, substance] nocif; (= unpleasant) [smell] infect, nauséabond; (= repugnant) [attitude, behaviour] odieux; [influence, habit] nocif; **to have a ~ effect on** avoir un effet nocif sur

nozzle ['nɒzl] N □ [of hose etc] ajutage m, jet m; [of syringe] canule f; [for icing] douille f; [of bellows] bec m; [of vacuum cleaner] suceur m; [of flamethrower] ajutage m □ (‡ = nose) pif‡ m, blair‡ m

NPD [ˌenpiː'diː] N (Comm) (ABBR = **new product development**) → **new**

NPV [ˌenpiː'viː] N (Fin) (ABBR = **net present value**) VAN f

nr PREP ABBR = **near**

NRA [ˌenɑːr'eɪ] N □ (US) (ABBR = **National Rifle Association**) → **national** □ (Brit) (ABBR = **National Rivers Authority**) administration nationale des cours d'eau

NRV [ˌenɑːr'viː] N (Fin) (ABBR = **net realizable value**) → **net²**

NS ABBR = **Nova Scotia**

n/s □ N ABBR = **nonsmoker** □ ADJ ABBR = **nonsmoking**

NSB [ˌenes'biː] N (Brit) (ABBR = **National Savings Bank**) → **national**

NSC [ˌenes'siː] N □ (US Pol) (ABBR = **National Security Council**) → **national** □ (Brit) (ABBR = **National Safety Council**) → **national**

NSPCC [ˌenespiː'siː'siː] N (Brit) (ABBR = **National Society for the Prevention of Cruelty to Children**) société pour la protection de l'enfance

NSU [ˌenes'juː] N (Med) (ABBR = **nonspecific urethritis**) → **nonspecific**

NSW (Geog) (ABBR = **New South Wales**) → **new**

NT □ (Bible) (ABBR = **New Testament**) → **new** □ (Brit) (ABBR = **National Trust**) → **national**

nth [enθ] ADJ → **N b**

NUAAW N (Brit) (ABBR = **National Union of Agricultural and Allied Workers**) syndicat

nuance ['njuːɑːns] □ N nuance f □ VT nuancer

nub [nʌb] N (= small lump) petit morceau m; (fig) **the ~ of the matter** l'essentiel m; **to get to the ~ of the matter** entrer dans le vif du sujet

Nubia ['njuːbɪə] N la Nubie

Nubian ['njuːbɪən] □ ADJ nubien □ N Nubien(ne) m(f)

nubile ['njuːbaɪl] ADJ (frm or hum) [young woman] nubile

nubility [njuː'bɪlɪtɪ] N nubilité f

nuclear ['njuːklɪər] □ ADJ (Phys, Mil) [charge, weapons, missile, war, arsenal] nucléaire; **to go ~** [country] acquérir l'arme nucléaire, se nucléariser; [conflict] dégénérer en guerre nucléaire; (esp Brit*) [person] piquer une crise*, exploser*
□ COMP ► **nuclear bomb** N bombe f atomique or nucléaire ► **nuclear capability** N capacité f nucléaire ► **nuclear deterrent** N force f de dissuasion nucléaire ► **nuclear disarmament** N désarmement m nucléaire ► **nuclear energy** N énergie f nucléaire ► **nuclear family** N (Sociol) famille f nucléaire ► **nuclear fission** N fission f nucléaire ► **nuclear-free** ADJ [zone, world] dénucléarisé ► **nuclear fuel** N combustible m nucléaire ► **nuclear fusion** N fusion f nucléaire ► **nuclear industry** N industrie f nucléaire ► **Nuclear Industry Radioactive Waste Executive** N (Brit) organisme de décision en matière de politique concernant les déchets radioactifs ► **nuclear magnetic resonance** N résonance f magnétique nucléaire ► **nuclear medicine** N médecine f nucléaire ► **the Nuclear Non-Proliferation Treaty** N le Traité de non-prolifération des armes nucléaires ► **nuclear physicist** N physicien(ne) m(f) nucléaire ► **nuclear physics** N physique f nucléaire ► **nuclear plant** N centrale f nucléaire ► **nuclear power** N puissance f nucléaire ► **nuclear-powered** ADJ (à propulsion) nucléaire ► **nuclear power station** N centrale f nucléaire ► **nuclear reaction** N réaction f nucléaire ► **nuclear reactor** N réacteur m nucléaire ► **nuclear reprocessing plant** N usine f de retraitement des déchets nucléaires ► **nuclear scientist** N chercheur m en physique nucléaire ► **nuclear submarine** N sous-marin m nucléaire ► **nuclear test** N essai m nucléaire ► **nuclear testing** N essais mpl nucléaires ► **nuclear umbrella** N parapluie m nucléaire ► **nuclear warhead** N ogive f or tête f nucléaire ► **nuclear waste** N déchets mpl nucléaires ► **nuclear weapon** N arme f nucléaire ► **nuclear winter** N hiver m nucléaire

nuclei ['njuːklɪaɪ] NPL of **nucleus**

nucleic acid [njuː'kliːɪk'æsɪd] N acide m nucléique

nucleo... ['njuːklɪəʊ] PREF nucléo...

nucleotide ['njuːklɪəˌtaɪd] N nucléotide m

nucleus ['njuːklɪəs] N (pl nuclei or nucleuses) (Astron, Phys, Ling) noyau m; (Bio) [of cell] nucléus m, noyau m; **atomic ~** noyau m atomique; (fig) **the ~ of a library/university/crew** les principaux éléments mpl d'une bibliothèque/d'une université/d'un équipage; **these three great footballers form the ~ of the side** ces trois grands footballeurs forment la base de l'équipe; **this group could be the ~ of a future centrist party** ce groupe pourrait servir de base à un futur parti centriste

nude [njuːd] □ ADJ [person, body] nu; [photograph] de nu; **to bathe ~** se baigner nu; **to sunbathe ~** bronzer nu; (Cine) **~ scene** scène f déshabillée; (Art) **~ figures** or **studies** nus mpl □ N □ (Art) nu m; **a Goya ~** un nu de Goya □ **in the ~** nu

nudge [nʌdʒ] □ VT □ (lit) pousser du coude, donner un (petit) coup de coude à; **she ~d him forward** elle l'a (légèrement) poussé en avant □ (fig = approach) **she's nudging fifty** elle approche de la cinquantaine; **the temperature was nudging 35°C** la température approchait or frôlait les 35° □ (= encourage) encourager; **to ~ sb into doing sth** amener qn à faire qch; **to ~ sb's memory** rafraîchir la mémoire à qn □ N □ (lit) coup m de coude; (fig) coup m de pouce; **to give sb a ~** a) [friend] a donner un coup de coude à; b) [government] encourager; **a ~ and a wink** un clin d'œil; **she made me an offer I couldn't refuse, ~~ wink-wink (say no more)!**‡ elle m'a fait une proposition très intéressante, si vous voyez ce que je veux dire

► **nudge up** VT SEP [+ prices] donner un coup de pouce à

nudie* ['njuːdɪ] ADJ **~ calendar** calendrier m avec des photos de femmes nues; **~ magazine** (gen) magazine m de charme; (= pornographic) revue f porno*

nudism ['njuːdɪzəm] N nudisme m

nudist ['njuːdɪst] □ N nudiste mf □ COMP ► **nudist camp** N camp m de nudistes ► **nudist colony** N colonie f de nudistes

nudity ['njuːdɪtɪ] N nudité f

nudnik‡ ['n(j)ʊdnɪk] N (US) casse-pieds mf inv

nugatory ['njuːgətərɪ] ADJ (frm) (= worthless) futile, sans valeur; (= trivial) insignifiant; (= ineffectual) inefficace, inopérant; (= not valid) non valable

nugget ['nʌgɪt] N pépite f; **gold ~** pépite f d'or

NUGMW N (Brit) (ABBR = **National Union of General and Municipal Workers**) syndicat

nuisance ['njuːsns] □ N □ (= annoying thing or event) **what a ~ he can't come** comme c'est ennuyeux or embêtant qu'il ne puisse pas venir; **it's a ~ having to shave** c'est agaçant d'avoir à se raser; **the ~ of having to shave each morning** la corvée de devoir se raser tous les matins; **these weeds are a ~** ces mauvaises herbes sont une vraie plaie*, quel fléau, ces mauvaises herbes; **these mosquitoes are a ~** ces moustiques sont un vrai fléau or une plaie*; **what a ~!** c'est vraiment ennuyeux!, quelle barbe!*
□ (= annoying person) peste f, fléau m; **that child is a ~** cet enfant est une peste or un fléau; **what a ~ you are!** ce que tu peux être agaçant or casse-pieds*!; **he could be a bit of a ~ when he was drunk** il pouvait être un peu casse-pieds* quand il était ivre; **you're being a ~** tu es agaçant; **sorry to be a ~** désolé de vous déranger or importuner; **to make a ~ of o.s.** embêter le monde*, être une peste or un fléau → **public**
□ (Jur) infraction f simple, dommage m simple → **public**
□ COMP ► **nuisance call** N appel m anonyme ► **nuisance caller** N auteur m d'un appel anonyme ► **nuisance value** N **it has a certain ~ value** cela sert à gêner or embêter* le monde

NUJ [ˌenjuː'dʒeɪ] N (Brit) (ABBR = **National Union of Journalists**) syndicat

nuke* [njuːk] □ VT (= attack) [+ city] lancer une bombe atomique sur; [+ nation, enemy] lancer une attaque nucléaire contre; (= destroy) détruire à l'arme atomique or nucléaire □ N □ (= weapon) arme f atomique or nucléaire; (slogan) **"no ~s!"*** «à bas les armes nucléaires!», «non au nucléaire!» □ (US = power station) centrale f nucléaire

null [nʌl] □ ADJ □ (Jur) [act, decree] nul (nulle f), invalide; [legacy] caduc (-uque f); **~ and void** nul et non avenu; **to render ~** annuler, frapper de nullité □ (= ineffectual) [person] insignifiant; [influence] inexistant □ COMP ► **null hypothesis** N hypothèse f nulle

nullification [ˌnʌlɪfɪ'keɪʃən] N □ infirmation f, invalidation f □ (US Hist) invalidation f par un État d'une loi fédérale

nullify ['nʌlɪfaɪ] VT infirmer, invalider

nullity ['nʌlɪtɪ] □ N (NonC: Jur) [of act, decree] nullité f, invalidité f; [of legacy] caducité f □ COMP ► **nullity suit** N (Jur) demande f en nullité de mariage

NUM [ˌenjuː'em] N (Brit) (ABBR = **National Union of Mineworkers**) syndicat

numb [nʌm] □ ADJ □ (= without sensation) [person, limb, face, lip] engourdi; **to go ~** s'engourdir; **~ with cold** [person, body] transi, engourdi par le froid; [face, hands, feet] engourdi par le froid □ (= stunned) [person] hébété; **~ with disbelief** figé d'incrédulité; **~ with fright** paralysé par la peur, transi or glacé de peur; **~ with grief** muet de douleur; **numb with shock** abasourdi par le choc [2] VT engourdir; *(fig)* *[fear etc]* transir, glacer; **~ed with grief** muet de douleur; **~ed with fear** paralysé par la peur, transi *or* glacé de peur; **it ~s the pain** cela endort la douleur

▼ number ['nʌmbəʳ] [1] N [a] *(gen)* nombre *m*; *(= actual figure: when written etc)* chiffre *m*; **even/odd/whole/cardinal/ordinal ~** nombre *m* pair/impair/entier/cardinal/ordinal; *(Bible)* **(the Book of) Numbers** les Nombres *mpl*; **to paint by ~s** peindre selon des indications chiffrées; *(fig)* **to do sth by ~s** *or (US)* **by the ~s** faire qch mécaniquement *or* bêtement; *(US Gambling)* **to play the ~s** *or* **the ~s game** *or* **the ~s racket*** faire des paris clandestins, jouer à une loterie clandestine → **lucky, round**

[b] *(= quantity, amount)* nombre *m*, quantité *f*; **a ~ of people** de nombreuses personnes; **large ~s of people** un grand nombre de personnes; **a great ~ of books/chairs** une grande quantité de livres/chaises; **in a small ~ of cases** dans un petit nombre de cas; **on a ~ of occasions** à plusieurs occasions, à maintes occasions; **there were a ~ of faults in the machine** la machine avait un (certain) nombre de défauts; **there are a ~ of things which ...** il y a un certain nombre de choses *or* pas mal* de choses qui ...; **a fair ~** un assez grand nombre, un nombre assez important; **boys and girls in equal ~s** garçons et filles en nombre égal; **~s being equal ...** à nombre égal ...; **ten in ~** au nombre de dix; **they were ten in ~** ils étaient (au nombre de) dix; **to the ~ of some 200** au nombre de 200 environ; **few in ◊ in small ~s** en petit nombre; **many in ◊ in large ~s** en grand nombre; **to swell the ~ of ...** grossir le nombre de ...; **he was brought in to swell the ~s** on l'a amené pour grossir l'effectif; **without** *or* **beyond ~** innombrable, sans nombre; **times without ~** à maintes reprises, mille et mille fois; **any ~ can play** le nombre de joueurs est illimité; **there were any ~ of* cards in the box** il y avait une quantité *or* un tas* de cartes dans la boîte; **I've told you any ~ of* times** je te l'ai dit mille fois; **they are found in ~s in Africa** on les trouve en grand nombre en Afrique; **they came in their ~s** ils sont venus en grand nombre; **there were flies in such ~s that ...** les mouches étaient en si grand nombre que ...; **the power of ~s** le pouvoir du nombre; **to win by force of ~s** *or* **by sheer ~s** l'emporter par le nombre *or* par la force du nombre; **one of their ~** un d'entre eux; **one of our ~** un des nôtres; **he was of our ~** il était des nôtres, il était avec nous

[c] *(in series)* *(Telec)* numéro *m*; *(Telec)* **wrong ~** faux numéro; **to get a wrong ~** se tromper de numéro; *(Telec)* **that's the wrong ~** ce n'est pas le bon numéro; **at ~ four** au (numéro) quatre; *(Brit Pol)* **Number 10** 10 Downing Street *(résidence du Premier ministre)* → DOWNING STREET **reference ~** numéro *m* de référence; *(Aut, Mil)* **(registration) ~** (numéro *m* d')immatriculation, numéro *m* minéralogique; **to take a car's ~** relever le numéro d'une voiture; *(fig)* **I've got his ~!** je l'ai repéré!; **their ~ came up*** ça a été leur tour d'y passer*, il a fallu qu'ils y passent* aussi; **his ~'s up*** il est fichu*, son compte est bon; **that bullet had his ~ on it!*** cette balle était pour lui!; **he only thinks of ~ one*** il ne pense qu'à lui *or* qu'à sa pomme*; **to look after** *or* **take care of ~ one*** penser avant tout à soi; *(Mus)* **to be ~ one (in the charts)** être numéro un (au hit-parade); **the ~ one English player** le meilleur *or* premier joueur anglais; **he's the ~ one there** c'est lui qui dirige tout là-dedans; **he's my ~ two*** il est mon second → **opposite**

[d] *(= model, issue)* *[of manufactured goods, clothes, car]* modèle *m*; *[of newspaper, journal]* numéro *m*; *(Press)* **the January ~** le numéro de janvier; **this car's a nice little ~*** c'est une

chouette* petite voiture; **this wine is a nice little ~*** c'est un bon petit vin; *(= dress)* **a little ~ in black** une petite robe noire (toute simple); **she's a pretty little ~*** c'est une jolie fille, c'est une belle nénette* → **back**

[e] *[of music hall, circus]* numéro *m*; *[of pianist, dance band]* morceau *m*; *[of singer]* chanson *f*; *[of dancer]* danse *f*; **there were several dance ~s on the programme** le programme comprenait plusieurs numéros de danse; *(singer)* **my next ~ will be ...** je vais maintenant chanter ...

[f] *(NonC: Gram)* nombre *m*; **~ is one of the basic concepts** le nombre est un des concepts de base; **to agree in ~** s'accorder en nombre

[g] *(Mus)* rythme *m*; **~s** *(Poetry)* vers *mpl*, poésie *f*; *(Mus)* mesures *fpl*

[2] VT [a] *(= give a number to)* numéroter; **they are ~ed from one to ten** ils sont numérotés de un à dix; **the houses are not ~ed** les maisons n'ont pas de numéro; **~ed (bank) account** compte *m* (en banque) numéroté

[b] *(= include)* compter, comprendre; **the library ~s 30,000 volumes** la bibliothèque compte *or* comporte 30 000 volumes; **I ~ him among my friends** je le compte parmi mes amis; **to be ~ed with the heroes** compter au nombre des *or* parmi les héros

[c] *(= amount to)* compter; **the crew ~s 50 men** l'équipage compte 50 hommes; **they ~ed 700** leur nombre s'élevait *or* se montait à 700, ils étaient au nombre de 700

[d] *(= count)* compter; *(fig)* **his days were ~ed** ses jours étaient comptés; **your chances of trying again are ~ed** il ne reste plus beaucoup d'occasions de tenter ta chance; **he was ~ing the hours till the attack began** il comptait les heures qui le séparaient de l'assaut

[3] VI *(Mil etc: also ~ off)* se numéroter; **to ~ (off) from the right** se numéroter en partant de la droite

[4] COMP ► **number-cruncher*** N *(= machine)* calculatrice *f*; **he's the ~-cruncher*** c'est le comptable, c'est le préposé aux chiffres *(hum)* ► **number-crunching*** N calcul *m* ► **number plate** N *(Brit Aut)* plaque *f* minéralogique *or* d'immatriculation *or* de police; **a car with French ~ plates** une voiture immatriculée en France ► **numbers game** N *(US Gambling: also ~s racket)* = **number 1a** [b] *(= focusing on numbers)* usage trompeur de chiffres; **to play the ~s game** jouer sur les chiffres ► **number theory** N théorie *f* des nombres

numbering ['nʌmbərɪŋ] [1] N *(NonC)* *[of houses, seats etc]* numérotage *m* [2] COMP ► **numbering machine** N machine *f* à numéroter

numberless ['nʌmbəlɪs] ADJ *(liter)* innombrable

numbhead* ['nʌmhed] N *(US)* imbécile *mf*, gourde* *f*

numbly ['nʌmlɪ] ADV *[say, look at]* d'un air hébété; *[walk]* l'air hébété

numbness ['nʌmnɪs] N *[of hand, finger, senses]* engourdissement *m*; *[of mind]* torpeur *f*, engourdissement *m*

numbskull* ['nʌmskʌl] N imbécile *mf*, gourde* *f*

numerable ['nju:mərəbl] ADJ nombrable, dénombrable

numeracy ['nju:mərəsɪ] N *(NonC)* notions *fpl* de calcul, capacités *fpl* au calcul

numeral ['nju:mərəl] [1] N chiffre *m*, nombre *m*; **Arabic/Roman ~** chiffre *m* arabe/romain [2] ADJ numéral

numerate ['nju:mərɪt] ADJ *[child, graduate]* qui sait compter; **he is barely ~** il sait à peine compter

numeration [,nju:mə'reɪʃən] N *(Math)* numération *f*

numerator ['nju:məreɪtəʳ] N *(Math)* numérateur *m*; *(= instrument)* numéroteur *m*

numerical [nju:'merɪkəl] ADJ *[value, data, superiority, strength]* numérique; *[majority]* en nombre; **in ~ order** dans l'ordre numérique

numerically [nju:'merɪkəlɪ] ADV numériquement

numeric keypad [nju:'merɪk'ki:pæd] N pavé *m* numérique

numerological [,nju:mərə'lɒdʒɪkəl] ADJ numérologique

numerology [,nju:mə'rɒlədʒɪ] N numérologie *f*

numerous ['nju:mərəs] ADJ nombreux

numinous ['nju:mɪnəs] ADJ *(liter)* *[power, symbol]* sacré

numismatic [,nju:mɪz'mætɪk] ADJ numismatique

numismatics [,nju:mɪz'mætɪks] N *(NonC)* numismatique *f*

numismatist [nju:'mɪzmətɪst] N numismate *mf*

numpkin* ['nʌmpkɪn], **numpty*** ['nʌmptɪ] N *(Brit)* tête *f* de linotte

numskull ['nʌmskʌl] N imbécile *mf*, gourde* *f*

nun [nʌn] N religieuse *f*, bonne sœur* *f*; **to become a ~** entrer en religion, prendre le voile

nunciature ['nʌnsɪətjʊəʳ] N nonciature *f*

nuncio ['nʌnsɪəʊ] N nonce *m* → **papal**

nunnery† ['nʌnərɪ] N couvent *m*

NUPE ['nju:pɪ] N *(Brit: formerly)* (ABBR = **National Union of Public Employees**) *ancien syndicat*

nuptial ['nʌpʃəl] *(liter or hum)* [1] ADJ nuptial; **the ~ day** le jour des noces [2] **nuptials** NPL noce *f*

NUR [,enju:'ɑːʳ] N *(Brit: formerly)* (ABBR = **National Union of Railwaymen**) *ancien syndicat*

nurd* [nɜːd] N = **nerd**

nurse [nɜːs] [1] N [a] *(in hospital)* infirmier *m*, -ière *f*; *(at home)* infirmier *m*, -ière *f*, garde-malade *f*; **(male) ~** infirmier *m*, garde-malade *m*; *(US Med)* **~'s aide** aide-soignant(e) *m(f)*; *(US Med)* **~ station** bureau *m* des infirmières; **the ~s' strike** la grève du personnel soignant *or* des infirmiers → **night**

[b] *(† = children's nurse)* nurse *f*, bonne *f* d'enfants; **yes ~** oui, nounou

[c] *(†: also wet-~)* nourrice *f*

[2] VT [a] *(Med)* *[+ person, illness, injury]* soigner; **she ~d him through pneumonia** elle l'a soigné pendant sa pneumonie; **she ~d him back to health** il a guéri grâce à ses soins; **to ~ a cold** soigner un rhume

[b] *[+ baby]* *(= suckle)* nourrir, allaiter; *(Brit = cradle in arms)* bercer (dans ses bras)

[c] *(fig)* *[+ hope, one's wrath etc]* nourrir, entretenir; *[+ ambition]* nourrir; *[+ plan, plot]* mijoter, couver; *[+ horse, car engine]* ménager; *[+ a fire]* entretenir; **to ~ one's wounded pride** lécher ses plaies; *(Brit Pol)* **to ~ a constituency** soigner les électeurs; **Jane still ~s the pain of rejection** Jane souffre toujours d'avoir été rejetée; **to ~ the business along** (essayer de) maintenir la compagnie à flot; **to ~ a drink all evening** faire durer un verre toute la soirée

nurseling ['nɜːslɪŋ] N = **nursling**

nursemaid ['nɜːsmeɪd] N nurse *f*, bonne *f* d'enfants

nursery ['nɜːsərɪ] [1] N [a] *(= room)* nursery *f*, chambre *f* d'enfants; **night ~** chambre *f* des enfants *or* d'enfants → **day** [b] *(= institution)* *(daytime only)* crèche *f*, garderie *f*; *(daytime or residential)* pouponnière *f* [c] *(Agr)* pépinière *f* [d] *(fig)* pépinière *f*; **a ~ of talent** une pépinière de talents [2] COMP ► **nursery education** N enseignement *m* de l'école maternelle ► **nursery nurse** N puéricultrice *f* ► **nursery rhyme** N comptine *f* ► **nursery school** N *(state-run)* école *f* maternelle; *(gen private)* jardin *m* d'enfants; **~ school teacher** *(state-run)* professeur *m* d'école maternelle; *(private)* jardinière *f* d'enfants ► **nursery**

► **LANGUAGE IN USE:** **number** 27

slopes NPL (*Brit Ski*) pentes *fpl or* pistes *fpl* pour débutants

nurseryman ['nɜːsərɪmən] N (*pl* **-men**) pépiniériste *m*

nursing ['nɜːsɪŋ] **1** ADJ **a** ~ **mother** mère *f* qui allaite; **room for ~ mothers** salle *f* réservée aux mères qui allaitent

b **the ~ staff** [*of hospital*] le personnel soignant *or* infirmier; (*all female*) les infirmières *fpl*; (*male and female*) les infirmiers *mpl*

2 N **a** (= *profession of nurse*) profession *f* d'infirmière; (= *care of invalids*) soins *mpl*; **she's going in for ~** elle va être infirmière **b** (= *suckling*) allaitement *m*

3 COMP ► **nursing auxiliary** N (*Brit*) aide-soignant(e) *m(f)* ► **nursing bra** N soutien-gorge *m* d'allaitement ► **nursing home** N (*esp Brit*) (*for medical, surgical cases*) clinique *f*, polyclinique *f*; (*for mental cases, disabled etc*) maison *f* de santé; (*for convalescence/rest cure*) maison *f* de convalescence/de repos; (*for old people*) maison *f* de retraite ► **nursing officer** N (*Brit Med*) surveillant *m(f)* général(e) ► **nursing orderly** N (*Brit Mil*) infirmier *m* (militaire) ► **nursing sister** N (*Brit Med*) infirmière *f* chef ► **nursing studies** NPL études *fpl* d'infirmière *or* d'infirmier

nursling ['nɜːslɪŋ] N (*liter*) nourrisson *m*

nurture ['nɜːtʃəʳ] **1** N (*frm: lit, fig*) nourriture *f* → **nature 2** VT (*lit, fig*) (= *rear*) élever, éduquer; (= *feed*) nourrir (**on** de)

NUS [,enjuːˈes] N (*Brit*) **a** (ABBR = **National Union of Students**) syndicat **b** (*formerly*) (ABBR = **National Union of Seamen**) *ancien syndicat*

NUT [,enjuːˈtiː] N (*Brit*) (ABBR = **National Union of Teachers**) *syndicat*

nut [nʌt] **1** N **a** (*Bot: no generic term in French*) (= *hazelnut*) noisette *f*; (= *walnut*) noix *f*; (= *almond*) amande *f*; **this chocolate has got ~s in it** c'est du chocolat aux noisettes (*or* aux amandes *etc*); **a bag of mixed ~s** un sachet de noisettes, cacahouètes, amandes *etc* panachées; **~s and raisins** mendiants *mpl*; (*fig*) **he's a tough ~** c'est un dur à cuire*; (*fig*) **that's a hard ~ to crack*** ce n'est pas un petit problème*; **he's a hard ~ to crack*** c'est un dur à cuire*; **he can't paint for ~s:** il peint comme un pied: → **beechnut, nuts, pistachio**

b (*Tech*) écrou *m*; (*Climbing*) coinceur *m*; (*fig*) **the ~s and bolts of ...** les détails *mpl* pratiques de ... → **2**

c (*coal*) ~**s** ◊ ~ **coal** noix *fpl*, tête(s)-de-moineau *f(pl)* *or* tête(s) de moineau *f(pl)*; **anthracite ~s** noix *fpl or* tête(s)-de-moineau *f(pl)* d'anthracite

d (*Culin*) → **ginger**

e (: = *head*) caboche* *f*; **use your ~!** réfléchis donc un peu!, creuse-toi un peu les méninges:; **to be off one's ~** être tombé sur la tête*, être cinglé*; **you must be off your ~!**

mais ça (ne) va pas!*, mais tu es tombé sur la tête!*; **to go off one's ~** perdre la boule:; (*Brit*) **to do one's ~** piquer une crise*

f (= *mad person*) **he's a real ~:** il est cinglé* *or* toqué*

g (= *enthusiast*) **a movie/football ~:** un(e) dingue* de cinéma/football

h * **~s!** des clous!:; **~s to you!** va te faire fiche!*

i ~**s:** (= *testicles*) couilles:* *fpl*, roubignoles:* *fpl* → **nuts**

2 COMP (*Culin*) [*cutlet, rissoles, roast etc*] à base de cacahouètes (*or* noisettes *etc*) hachées ► **nut-brown** ADJ [*eyes*] noisette *inv*; [*complexion*] brun; [*hair*] châtain ► **nut chocolate** N chocolat *m* aux noisettes (*or* aux amandes *etc*) ► **nuts-and-bolts*** ADJ (*fig* = *practical*) avant tout pratique; **~s-and-bolts education** enseignement *m* axé sur les matières fondamentales

nutcase: ['nʌtkeɪs] N dingue* *mf*, cinglé(e)* *m(f)*; **he's a ~** il est bon à enfermer*, il est dingue*

nutcracker(s) ['nʌtkrækə(z)] **1** N(PL) casse-noix *m inv*, casse-noisette(s) *m*; (*Mus*) **The Nutcracker** Casse-noisette *m* **2** COMP ► **nutcracker chin** N menton *m* en galoche *or* en casse-noisette

nuthatch ['nʌthætʃ] N (*Orn*) sittelle *f*, grimpereau *m*

nuthouse: ['nʌthaʊs] N asile *m*; **he's in the ~** il est à l'asile

nutmeg ['nʌtmeg] **1** N (= *nut*) (noix *f*) muscade *f*; (= *tree*) muscadier *m* **2** COMP ► **nutmeg-grater** N râpe *f* à muscade ► **the Nutmeg State** N (*US*) le Connecticut

Nutrasweet® ['njuːtrəswiːt] N (= *artificial sweetener*) édulcorant *m*; (*for tea, coffee*) sucrette® *f*

nutrient ['njuːtrɪənt] **1** ADJ nutritif **2** N substance *f* nutritive, nutriment *m*

nutriment ['njuːtrɪmənt] N élément *m* nutritif

nutrition [njuːˈtrɪʃən] N nutrition *f*, alimentation *f*

nutritional [njuːˈtrɪʃənl] ADJ [*information, advice*] nutritionnel; [*value, content, requirements, deficiencies*] nutritif

nutritionist [njuːˈtrɪʃənɪst] N nutritionniste *mf*

nutritious [njuːˈtrɪʃəs] ADJ nourrissant, nutritif

nutritiousness [njuːˈtrɪʃəsnɪs] N caractère *m* nutritif

nutritive ['njuːtrɪtɪv] ADJ nutritif

nuts: [nʌts] ADJ dingue*, cinglé*; **to go ~** perdre la boule*; **to be ~ about sb/sth** être dingue* de qn/qch → **nut**

nutshell ['nʌtʃel] N coquille *f* de noix *or* de noisette *etc*; (*fig*) **in a ~ ...** en un mot ...; (*fig*)

to put the matter in a ~ résumer l'affaire en un mot

nutter: ['nʌtəʳ] N (*Brit*) cinglé(e)* *m(f)*, dingue* *mf*

nutty ['nʌtɪ] **1** ADJ **a** (*no generic term in French*) (*with hazelnuts*) aux noisettes; (*with almonds*) aux amandes; (*with walnuts*) aux noix; [*flavour, taste, smell*] de noisette *etc* **b** (* = *mad*) [*idea*] dingue*; [*person*] cinglé*, dingue*; (*hum*) **to be (as) ~ as a fruitcake** être complètement dingue*; (= *enthusiastic*) **to be ~ about sb/sth** être dingue* de qn/qch **2** COMP ► **nutty professor*** N professeur Tournesol *m* ► **nutty slack** N (*Brit Min*) déclassés *mpl* des gros

nuzzle ['nʌzl] VI (*pig*) fouiller du groin, fouiner; **the dog ~d up to my leg** le chien est venu fourrer son nez contre ma jambe; **she ~d up to me** elle est venue se blottir contre moi

NV ABBR = **Nevada**

NVQ [,enviːˈkjuː] N (ABBR = **National Vocational Qualification**) ≈ CAP *m*

NVQ

Les **National Vocational Qualifications**, *ou* **NVQ**, *sont un système de qualifications à la fois théoriques et pratiques destinées essentiellement aux personnes occupant déjà un emploi. Toutefois, certains établissements secondaires préparent à ces examens, en plus ou à la place des examens traditionnels («* GCSE *» ou «* A levels *»). Ce système existe en Angleterre, au pays de Galles et en Irlande du Nord; en Écosse, il existe une filière comparable qui porte le nom de «* Scottish Vocational Qualifications *» ou «* SVQ *».*

NW (ABBR = **north-west**) N-O

NY [en'waɪ] N (ABBR = **New York**) → **new**

NYC [enwaɪ'siː] N ABBR = **New York City**

Nyasaland [nɪ'æsə,lænd] N le Nyas(s)aland

nylon ['naɪlɒn] **1** N (*NonC*) nylon® *m* **2** ADJ [*stockings etc*] de *or* en nylon® **3 nylons** NPL bas *mpl* (*or* collant *m*) de *or* en nylon®

nymph [nɪmf] N nymphe *f*; (*also* **water ~**) naïade *f*; (*also* **wood ~**) (hama)dryade *f*; (*also* **sea ~**) néréide *f*; (*also* **mountain ~**) oréade *f*

nymphet [nɪm'fet] N nymphette *f*

nympho: ['nɪmfəʊ] ADJ, N ABBR = **nymphomaniac**

nymphomania [,nɪmfəʊ'meɪnɪə] N nymphomanie *f*

nymphomaniac [,nɪmfəʊ'meɪnɪæk] ADJ, N nymphomane *f*

NYSE [,enwaɪes'iː] N (*US*) (ABBR = **New York Stock Exchange**) *Bourse de New York*

NZ, N. Zeal (ABBR = **New Zealand**) → **new**

O

O, o¹ [əʊ] ① N ⓐ (= letter) O, o m; **O for Orange** ≈ O comme Oscar → **OK** ⓑ (= number: Telec etc) zéro m ② COMP ► **O Grade** N (Scot Educ: formerly) ≈ matière f présentée au brevet; **to do an O Grade in French** ≈ passer l'épreuve de français au brevet ► **O level** N (Brit Educ: formerly) ≈ matière f présentée au brevet; **to do an O level in French** ≈ passer l'épreuve de français au brevet; **O levels** ≈ brevet m ► **O-shaped** ADJ en forme de O or de cercle

O² [əʊ] EXCL (liter) ô

O' [əʊ] PREP (ABBR = of) de → **o'clock**

oaf [əʊf] N (awkward) balourd* m; (bad-mannered) malotru(e) m(f), mufle m

oafish [ˈəʊfɪʃ] ADJ (pej) [person] mufle; [behaviour, remark] de mufle

oak [əʊk] ① N (= wood, tree) chêne m; **light/dark ~** chêne m clair/foncé; **great ~s from little acorns grow** les petits ruisseaux font les grandes rivières ② COMP (= made of oak) de or en (bois de) chêne; (= oak-coloured) (couleur) chêne inv ► **oak apple** N noix f de galle, galle f du chêne ► **oak leaf cluster** N (US) ≈ barrette f (portée sur le ruban d'une médaille)

oaken [ˈəʊkən] ADJ (liter) de or en chêne

oakum [ˈəʊkəm] N étoupe f; **to pick ~** faire de l'étoupe

oakwood [ˈəʊkwʊd] N ⓐ (= forest) chênaie f, forêt f de chênes ⓑ (NonC = material) (bois m de) chêne

O & M [əʊənˈem] (ABBR = organization and methods) → **organization**

OAP [ˌəʊeɪˈpiː] (Brit) (ABBR = old age pension or pensioner) → **old**

oar [ɔːʳ] ① N ⓐ (gen) rame f; (Sport) aviron m; **he always puts or sticks* or shoves* his ~ in** il faut toujours qu'il se mêle (subj) de tout or qu'il vienne mettre son grain de sel* → **rest, ship** ⓑ (= person) rameur m, -euse f

-oared [ɔːd] ADJ (in compounds) **four-oared** à quatre avirons

oarlock [ˈɔːlɒk] N dame f (de nage), tolet m

oarsman [ˈɔːzmən] N (pl **-men**) rameur m, nageur m (SPEC)

oarsmanship [ˈɔːzmənʃɪp] N (= art of rowing) art m de ramer; (= skill as rower) qualités fpl de rameur

oarswoman [ˈɔːzwʊmən] N (pl **-women**) rameuse f, nageuse f (SPEC)

OAS [ˌəʊeɪˈes] N ⓐ (US) (ABBR = Organization of American States) OEA f ⓑ (Hist: in Algeria) (ABBR = Organisation de l'armée secrète) OAS f

oasis [əʊˈeɪsɪs] N (pl **oases** [əʊˈeɪsiːz]) (lit, fig) oasis f; **an ~ of peace** un havre or une oasis de paix

oast [əʊst] ① N four m à (sécher le) houblon ② COMP ► **oast-house** N sécherie f or séchoir m à houblon

oat [əʊt] N (= plant, food) **~s** avoine f (NonC); (Brit) **to get one's ~s:** tirer son coup:; (US) **to feel one's ~s*** (= feel high-spirited) avoir la pê-

che; (= feel important) faire l'important → **rolled, wild**

oatcake [ˈəʊtkeɪk] N biscuit m or galette f d'avoine

oath [əʊθ] ① N (pl **oaths** [əʊðz]) ⓐ serment m; **he took or swore an ~ promising to uphold the country's laws** il a fait le serment or il a juré de faire respecter les lois du pays; **he took or swore an ~ of loyalty to the government** il a juré loyauté au gouvernement; **he swore on his ~ that he had never been there** il jura n'y avoir jamais été or qu'il n'y avait jamais été; **I'll take my ~ on it!** je vous le jure! ⓑ (Jur) **to take the ~** prêter serment; **on or under ~** sous serment; **witness on or under ~** témoin m assermenté; **to put sb on or under ~ ◊ to administer the ~ to sb** faire prêter serment à qn; **to put sb on or under ~ to do sth** faire promettre à qn sous serment de faire qch → **allegiance** ⓒ (= bad language) juron m; **to let out or utter an ~** lâcher or pousser un juron ② COMP ► **oath-taking** N (Jur etc) prestation f de serment

oatmeal [ˈəʊtmiːl] ① N (NonC) (= cereal) flocons mpl d'avoine; (US = porridge) bouillie f d'avoine, porridge m ② COMP (in colour) [dress, fabric] beige, grège

OAU [ˌəʊeɪˈjuː] N (ABBR = Organization of African Unity) OUA f

OB N (Brit) (ABBR = outside broadcast) → **outside**

Obadiah [ˌəʊbəˈdaɪə] N Abdias m

obbligato [ˌɒblɪˈɡɑːtəʊ] (Mus) ① ADJ obligé ② (pl **obbligatos** or **obbligati** [ˌɒblɪˈɡɑːtiː]) partie f obligée

obduracy [ˈɒbdjʊrəsɪ] N (frm) ⓐ (pej = stubbornness) [of person] obstination f, entêtement m; **the ~ of his behaviour** son comportement obstiné; **the ~ of his silence** son silence obstiné ⓑ (= difficulty) [of problem, situation] insolubilité f

obdurate [ˈɒbdjʊrɪt] ADJ (frm, pej) [person] obstiné, entêté; **her look of ~ stubbornness** son air obstiné et inflexible; **to remain ~** s'obstiner, rester inflexible; **they were ~ in their refusal** ils s'obstinaient dans leur refus

obdurately [ˈɒbdjʊrɪtlɪ] ADV (frm) (= stubbornly) obstinément, opiniâtrement; (= unyieldingly) inflexiblement

OBE [ˌəʊbiːˈiː] N (ABBR = Officer of the Order of the British Empire) titre honorifique → [HONOURS LIST]

obedience [əˈbiːdɪəns] N (NonC) obéissance f (to à); (Rel) obédience f (to à); **in ~ to the law/his orders** conformément à la loi/ses ordres; (frm) **to owe ~ to sb** devoir obéissance à qn; **to show ~ to sb/sth** obéir à qn/qch; **to command ~ (from)** savoir se faire obéir (de) → **blind**

obedient [əˈbiːdɪənt] ADJ [person, child] obéissant; [dog] obéissant, docile; **to be ~ to sb** être obéissant avec qn, obéir à qn; **to be ~ to sb's wishes** obéir aux désirs de qn; (in

letters) **your ~ servant**† votre très obéissant serviteur† m

obediently [əˈbiːdɪəntlɪ] ADV docilement

obeisance [əʊˈbeɪsəns] N (frm) ⓐ (NonC = homage) hommage m ⓑ (= bow) révérence f, salut m cérémonieux

obelisk [ˈɒbɪlɪsk] N ⓐ (Archit) obélisque m ⓑ (Typ†) obel m or obèle m

obese [əʊˈbiːs] ADJ obèse

obeseness [əʊˈbiːsnɪs], **obesity** [əʊˈbiːsɪtɪ] N obésité f

obey [əˈbeɪ] ① VT [+ person, instinct, order] obéir à; [+ the law] se conformer à, obéir à; [+ instructions] se conformer à, observer; (Jur) [+ summons, order] obtempérer à; **the plane's engine refused to ~ the computer's commands** le moteur de l'avion refusait de répondre aux commandes de l'ordinateur ② VI obéir

obfuscate [ˈɒbfəskeɪt] VT (frm) [+ mind, judgement] obscurcir; [+ person] dérouter, déconcerter

obfuscation [ˌɒbfəˈskeɪʃən] N obscurcissement m

obit* [ˈəʊbɪt] N (= obituary) notice f nécrologique, nécrologie f

obituarist [əˈbɪtjʊərɪst] N nécrologue mf

obituary [əˈbɪtjʊərɪ] ① N (also **~ notice**) notice f nécrologique, nécrologie f ② COMP [announcement] nécrologique ► **obituary column** N nécrologie f, rubrique f nécrologique

▼ **object** ① N ⓐ (= thing in general) objet m, chose f; (pej) **what is this ~?** quelle est cette chose? (pej)
ⓑ (= focus) **~ of pity/ridicule** objet m de pitié/de risée; **the ~ of one's love** l'objet m aimé
ⓒ (= aim) but m; (Philos) objet m; **he has no ~ in life** il n'a aucun but dans la vie; **with this ~ (in view or in mind)** dans ce but, à cette fin; **with the ~ of doing** dans le but de faire; **with the sole ~ of doing** à seule fin or dans le seul but de faire; **what ~ is there in or what's the ~ of doing that?** à quoi bon faire cela?; **money is no ~** le prix importe peu → **defeat**
ⓓ (Gram) complément m (d'objet); **direct/indirect ~** complément m (d'objet) direct/indirect
ⓔ **~ of virtu** objet m d'art, curiosité f
② [əbˈdʒekt] VI s'élever une objection (**to sb/sth** contre qn/qch); **I ~!** je proteste!; **I ~ most strongly!** je proteste catégoriquement or énergiquement!; **if you don't ~** si cela ne vous fait rien, si vous n'y voyez pas d'inconvénient or d'objection; **he didn't ~ when ...** il n'a élevé or formulé aucune objection quand ...; **I ~ to that remark** je proteste or je m'élève contre cette remarque; **I ~ to your rudeness** votre grossièreté est inadmissible; **he ~s to her drinking** cela l'ennuie qu'elle boive; **do you ~ to my smoking?** cela vous ennuie que je fume (subj)?, est-ce que cela vous gêne si je fume?; **she ~s to all this noise** elle se plaint de tout ce bruit;

I don't ~ to helping you je veux bien vous aider ; **to ~ to sb** élever des objections contre qn ; **I would ~ to Paul but not to Robert as chairman** je ne voudrais pas que Paul soit président mais je n'ai rien contre Robert ; **they ~ed to him because he was too young** ils lui ont objecté son jeune âge ; (*Jur*) **to ~ to a witness** récuser un témoin ; **I wouldn't ~ to a bite to eat*** je mangerais bien un morceau

3 [əb'dʒekt] VT **to ~ that ...** objecter que ..., faire valoir que ...

4 COMP ► **object clause** N (*Gram*) proposition *f* complément d'objet, complétive *f* d'objet ► **object language** N (*Ling*) langage-objet *m* ► **object lesson** N (*fig*) **it was an ~ lesson in how not to drive a car** c'était une illustration de ce que l'on ne doit pas faire au volant ; **it was an ~ lesson in good manners** c'était une démonstration de bonnes manières

▼ **objection** [əb'dʒekʃən] N objection *f* ; **I have no ~(s)** je n'ai pas d'objection, je ne m'y oppose pas ; **if you have no ~(s)** si cela ne vous fait rien, si vous n'y voyez pas d'inconvénient or d'objection ; **I have no ~ to him** je n'ai rien contre lui ; **I have a strong ~ to dogs in shops** je ne supporte pas les chiens dans les magasins ; **have you any ~ to my smoking?** cela ne vous ennuie pas que je fume (*subj*) ?, est-ce que cela vous gêne si je fume ? ; **I have no ~ to the idea/to his leaving** je ne vois pas d'objection or je ne m'oppose pas à cette idée/à ce qu'il parte ; **there is no ~ to our leaving** il n'y a pas d'obstacle or d'inconvénient à ce que nous partions (*subj*) ; **to make** or **raise an ~** soulever or formuler une objection ; (*Jur*) **to make ~ to an argument** récuser un argument ; **~!** (*Jur*) objection ! ; (*gen*) je proteste ! ; (*Jur*) **~ overruled!** objection rejetée !

objectionable [əb'dʒekʃnəbl] ADJ [*smell*] nauséabond ; [*behaviour, attitude*] répréhensible ; [*language*] choquant ; [*remark*] désobligeant ; **I find him thoroughly ~** il me déplaît souverainement ; **I find your tone highly ~** je trouve votre ton tout à fait désagréable ; **the language used in the programme was ~ to many viewers** le langage utilisé au cours de l'émission a choqué de nombreux téléspectateurs

objective [əb'dʒektɪv] **1** ADJ **a** (= *impartial*) [*person, report, view*] objectif, impartial ; [*evidence, facts, criteria*] objectif ; **to take an ~ look at sth** examiner qch d'une manière objective ; **he is very ~ in his reporting** ses reportages sont très objectifs **b** (*Philos*) objectif **c** (*Gram*) [*pronoun*] complément d'objet ; [*genitive*] objectif ; **~ case** (*cas m*) accusatif *m*, cas *m* régime **2** N (*gen, also Phot*) objectif *m* ; **to reach** or **attain one's ~** atteindre le but qu'on s'était fixé or son objectif **b** (*Gram*) accusatif *m*

objectively [əb'dʒektɪvlɪ] ADV objectivement

objectivism [əb'dʒektɪvɪzəm] N objectivisme *m*

objectivity [ˌɒbdʒɪk'tɪvɪtɪ] N objectivité *f*, impartialité *f*

objector [əb'dʒektər] N opposant(e) *m(f)* ; **the ~s to this scheme** les opposants au projet, les adversaires du projet → **conscientious**

objet d'art ['ɒbʒeɪ'dɑː] N (*pl* **objets d'art**) objet *m* d'art

objet de vertu ['ɒbʒeɪdə'vɜːtjuː] N (*pl* **objets de vertu**) objet *m* d'art, curiosité *f*

objurgate ['ɒbdʒɜːgeɪt] VT (*frm*) réprimander ; (*stronger*) accabler de reproches

objurgation [ˌɒbdʒɜː'geɪʃən] N (*frm*) objurgation *f*, réprimande *f*

oblate ['ɒbleɪt] **1** N (*Rel*) oblat(e) *m(f)* **2** ADJ (*Geom*) aplati aux pôles

oblation [əʊ'bleɪʃən] N (*Rel*) (= *act*) oblation *f* ; (= *offering: also* **~s**) oblats *mpl*

---

obligate ['ɒblɪgeɪt] VT obliger, contraindre (**sb to do** qn à faire) ; **to be ~d to do** être obligé de or contraint à faire

obligation [ˌɒblɪ'geɪʃən] N **a** (= *duty*) obligation *f* ; **to be under an ~ to do** être tenu de faire, être dans l'obligation de faire ; **I'm under no ~ to do it** rien ne m'oblige à le faire ; **to lay** or **put sb under an ~** créer une obligation à qn ; **to put** or **lay an ~ on sb to do sth** mettre qn dans l'obligation de faire qch ; **it is your ~ to see that ...** il vous incombe de veiller à ce que ... (+ *subj*) ; **"without ~"** (*in advert*) « sans engagement » ; **"no ~ to buy"** (*in advert*) « aucune obligation d'achat » ; (*in shop*) « entrée libre »

b (= *commitment*) obligation *f*, engagement *m* ; **to meet one's ~s** respecter ses obligations or ses engagements ; **to fail to meet one's ~s** manquer à ses obligations or à ses engagements ; **to be under an ~ to sb** devoir de la reconnaissance à qn ; **to be under an ~ to sb for sth** être redevable à qn de qch

c (= *debt*) devoir *m*, dette *f* (de reconnaissance) ; **to repay an ~** acquitter une dette de reconnaissance

▼ **obligatory** [ɒ'blɪgətərɪ] ADJ **a** (= *compulsory*) [*attendance*] obligatoire ; **it is not ~ to attend** il n'est pas obligatoire d'y assister ; **it is ~ for you to attend** vous êtes dans l'obligation or vous êtes tenu d'y assister ; **to make it ~ for sb to do sth** obliger qn à faire qch **b** (= *customary*) [*smile, kiss*] de rigueur ; **she was wearing the ~ sweater and pearl necklace** elle portait le pull et le collier de perles de rigueur

▼ **oblige** [ə'blaɪdʒ] **1** VT **a** (= *compel*) obliger (**sb to do** qn à faire) ; **to be ~d to do** être obligé de faire

b (= *do a favour to*) rendre service à, obliger (*liter*) ; **he did it to ~ us** il l'a fait pour nous rendre service ; (*frm*) **can you ~ me with a pen?** auriez-vous l'amabilité or l'obligeance de me prêter un stylo ? ; **he's always ready to ~ journalists with information** il est toujours prêt à communiquer des informations aux journalistes ; (*Comm*) **to be ~d to sb for sth** être reconnaissant or savoir gré à qn de qch ; **I am much ~d to you** je vous remercie infiniment ; **I would be ~d if you would read it to us** je vous serais reconnaissant de bien vouloir nous le lire ; **thanks, I'd be ~d** merci, ce serait très gentil (de votre part) ; **much ~d!** merci beaucoup !, merci mille fois ! ; **much ~d for your assistance!** merci beaucoup or merci mille fois de votre aide !

2 VI **she is always ready** or **willing to ~** elle est toujours prête à rendre service ; **anything to ~!*** à votre service ! ; **he asked for more time and they ~d by delaying their departure** il a demandé un délai et ils se sont pliés à ses désirs en retardant leur départ ; **we asked him the way and he ~d with directions** nous lui avons demandé notre chemin et il nous a très gentiment donné des indications ; (*Comm†*) **a prompt answer will ~** une réponse rapide nous obligerait

obligee [ˌɒblɪ'dʒiː] N (*Jur*) obligataire *m*, créancier *m*

obliging [ə'blaɪdʒɪŋ] ADJ obligeant, serviable ; **it is very ~ of them** c'est très gentil or aimable de leur part

obligingly [ə'blaɪdʒɪŋlɪ] ADV obligeamment

obligor [ˌɒblɪ'gɔːr] N (*Jur*) obligé *m*

oblique [ə'bliːk] **1** ADJ **a** (= *indirect*) [*approach, reference, angle*] indirect **b** (= *slanting*) [*line, plane, cut*] oblique ; [*look*] en biais, oblique ; [*view*] de biais ; (*Math*) [*angle*] aigu ; (= *obtuse*) obtus ; **it lies at an ~ angle to the coastline** c'est en biais par rapport à la côte **c** (*Gram*) **~ case** cas *m* oblique **2** N **a** (*Anat*) oblique *f* **b** (*Brit Typ: also* **~ stroke**) trait *m* oblique, oblique *f*

obliquely [ə'bliːklɪ] ADV **a** (= *indirectly*) [*refer

---

to, answer, approach] indirectement **b** (= *diagonally*) [*cut*] obliquement, en biais

obliqueness [ə'bliːknɪs], **obliquity** [ə'blɪkwɪtɪ] N **a** [*of approach, reference*] caractère *m* indirect **b** [*of line*] obliquité *f*

obliterate [ə'blɪtəreɪt] VT **a** (= *destroy*) détruire, anéantir **b** [+ *writing etc*] (= *erase*) effacer, enlever ; (= *obscure*) rendre illisible ; (*by progressive wear*) oblitérer (*frm*) ; (*fig*) [+ *memory, impressions*] oblitérer (*frm*) ; [+ *the past*] faire table rase de **c** (*Post*) [+ *stamp*] oblitérer

obliteration [ə,blɪtə'reɪʃən] N **a** (= *destruction*) [*of person, object, country*] anéantissement *m* ; [*of rainforest*] destruction *f* **b** (= *erasure*) rature *f*, biffure *f* ; (*fig*) [*of memory*] effacement *m*

oblivion [ə'blɪvɪən] N (état *m* d')oubli *m* ; **to sink** or **fall into ~** tomber dans l'oubli

oblivious [ə'blɪvɪəs] ADJ (= *unaware*) inconscient (**of** or **to sb/sth** de qn/qch) ; (= *forgetful*) oublieux (**of** or **to sb/sth** de qn/qch)

oblong ['ɒblɒŋ] **1** ADJ (= *rectangular*) oblong (oblongue *f*) ; (= *elongated*) allongé ; **an ~ dish** un plat rectangulaire **2** N rectangle *m*

obloquy ['ɒbləkwɪ] N opprobre *m*

obnoxious [əb'nɒkʃəs] ADJ [*person*] odieux ; [*child, dog, behaviour*] odieux, détestable ; [*smell*] nauséabond ; **stop being so ~!** arrête d'être odieux !

obnoxiously [əb'nɒkʃəs] ADV odieusement

o.b.o. [əʊbiː'əʊ] (ABBR = *or best offer*) à déb., à débattre → **offer**

oboe ['əʊbəʊ] **1** N hautbois *m* **2** COMP ► **oboe d'amore** N hautbois *m* d'amour

oboist ['əʊbəʊɪst] N hautboïste *mf*

obscene [əb'siːn] **1** ADJ [*act, gesture, language, remark, phone call*] obscène ; [*profit, salary*] indécent **2** COMP ► **obscene publication** N (*Jur*) publication *f* obscène ► **Obscene Publications Act** N (*Brit*) loi *f* sur les publications obscènes ► **Obscene Publications Squad** N (*Brit*) brigade de répression des publications obscènes

obscenely [əb'siːnlɪ] ADV [*fat etc*] monstrueusement ; **to talk ~** dire des obscénités ; **~ rich** d'une richesse indécente ; **she earns ~ large amounts of money** elle gagne tellement d'argent que c'en est indécent ; **an ~ expensive house** une maison tellement chère que c'en est indécent

obscenity [əb'senɪtɪ] N (*gen, also Jur*) obscénité *f* ; (= *moral outrage*) infamie *f* ; **the ~ laws** les lois *fpl* sur l'obscénité

obscurantism [ˌɒbskjʊə'ræntɪzəm] N obscurantisme *m*

obscurantist [ˌɒbskjʊə'ræntɪst] ADJ, N obscurantiste *mf*

obscure [əb'skjʊər] **1** ADJ **a** (= *not straightforward, not obvious*) [*word, reference, reason, origins*] obscur **b** (= *not well-known*) [*writer, artist, book*] obscur, mal connu ; [*village*] peu connu, perdu **c** (= *indistinct*) [*shape*] indistinct **2** VT **a** (= *hide*) [+ *sun*] (*partly*) voiler ; (*completely*) cacher ; [+ *view*] cacher, masquer ; (*fig*) [+ *argument, idea*] rendre obscur ; **to ~ the issue** embrouiller la question

obscurely [əb'skjʊəlɪ] ADV obscurément

obscurity [əb'skjʊərɪtɪ] N **a** (= *darkness*) obscurité *f*, ténèbres *fpl* (*liter*) **b** (*fig*) [*of argument, idea*] obscurité *f*

obsequies ['ɒbsɪkwɪz] NPL (*frm*) obsèques *fpl*, funérailles *fpl*

obsequious [əb'siːkwɪəs] ADJ (*pej*) [*person, manner*] obséquieux, servile (**to sb** devant qn) ; [*smile*] obséquieux ; **their ~ treatment of the film star** leur obséquiosité *f* à l'égard de la vedette

obsequiously [əb'siːkwɪəslɪ] ADV (*pej*) obséquieusement

obsequiousness [əb'siːkwɪəsnɪs] N obséquiosité f, servilité f

observable [əb'zɜːvəbl] ADJ [facts, phenomena, pattern] observable; [benefits, consequences, effect] observable, visible; (Astron) **the ~ universe** l'univers m observable

observably [əb'zɜːvəblɪ] ADV visiblement

observance [əb'zɜːvəns] N a [of rule, law] observation f, respect m; [of rite, custom, Sabbath] observance f; [of anniversary] célébration f b (= rite, ceremony) observance f; **religious ~s** observances fpl religieuses

observant [əb'zɜːvənt] ADJ [person, eye] observateur (-trice f)

observation [ˌɒbzə'veɪʃən] 1 N a (NonC) observation f; **~ of birds/bats** observation f des oiseaux/des chauves-souris; **his powers of ~** ses facultés fpl d'observation; **careful ~ of the movement of the planets** une observation attentive du mouvement des planètes; **to keep sb under ~** (Med) garder qn en observation; (Police) surveiller qn; **they kept the house under ~** ils surveillaient la maison; **to be under ~** (Med) être en observation; (Police) être sous surveillance; (Police) **he came under ~ when ...** on s'est mis à le surveiller quand ... b (= remark) observation f, remarque f; **this book contains ~s about the causes of addictions** ce livre contient diverses observations or remarques sur les causes des dépendances; **his ~s on "Hamlet"** ses réflexions fpl sur « Hamlet »

2 COMP ► **observation balloon** N ballon m d'observation ► **observation car** N (Rail) wagon m or voiture f panoramique ► **observation deck** N terrasse f panoramique ► **observation post** N (Mil) poste m d'observation, observatoire m ► **observation satellite** N satellite m d'observation ► **observation tower** N mirador m, tour f de guet ► **observation ward** N (Med) salle f d'observation

observational [ˌɒbzə'veɪʃənl] ADJ (frm) [skills, faculties, test, device] d'observation; [evidence, data, study] basé sur l'observation

observatory [əb'zɜːvətrɪ] N observatoire m

▼**observe** [əb'zɜːv] VT a (= obey) [+ rule, custom, ceasefire] observer, respecter; [+ silence] garder, observer; (Jur) **failure to ~ the law** inobservation f de la loi b (= celebrate) [+ anniversary] célébrer; [+ the Sabbath] observer; **to ~ Christmas/May Day** fêter Noël/le premier mai c (= take note of) observer, remarquer; (= study) observer; **to ~ sth closely** observer qch attentivement, scruter qch; **I'm only here to ~** je ne suis ici qu'en tant qu'observateur d (= say, remark) (faire) remarquer, faire observer; **he ~d that the weather was cold** il a fait observer or remarquer qu'il faisait froid; **as I was about to ~ ...** comme j'allais le dire or le faire remarquer ...; **I ~d to him that ...** je lui ai fait remarquer or observer que ...; **"he's a handsome young man", she ~d** « c'est un beau jeune homme », remarqua-t-elle; **... as Elliot ~d ...** comme l'a remarqué or relevé Elliot

observer [əb'zɜːvəʳ] N a (= person watching) observateur m, -trice f, spectateur m, -trice f; **the ~ may note ...** les observateurs or spectateurs remarqueront ...; **a casual ~ would have assumed they were friends** un simple observateur aurait pensé qu'ils étaient amis b (= official: at meeting etc) observateur m, -trice f; **UN ~s will attend the conference** les observateurs de l'ONU assisteront à la conférence c (Pol etc = analyst, commentator) spécialiste mf, expert m; **an ~ of Soviet politics** un spécialiste de la politique soviétique; **political ~s believe that ...** les observateurs politiques pensent que ...

obsess [əb'ses] VT obséder; **~ed by** obsédé par

obsession [əb'seʃən] N (= state) obsession f; (= fixed idea) obsession f, idée f fixe; (of sth un-

pleasant) hantise f; **sport is an ~ with him** c'est un obsédé de sport; **he has an ~ about cleanliness** c'est un obsédé de la propreté, il a l'obsession de la propreté; **his ~ with her** la manière dont elle l'obsède; **his ~ with death** (= fascination) son obsession de la mort; (= fear) sa hantise de la mort

obsessional [əb'seʃənl] ADJ [behaviour, love, hatred] obsessionnel; **to be ~** [person] souffrir d'une obsession or d'obsessions; **to be ~ about tidiness/cleanliness** etc être un maniaque de l'ordre/de la propreté etc

obsessionally [əb'seʃənəlɪ] ADV de façon obsessionnelle; **~ tidy** obsédé par l'ordre, maniaque de l'ordre; **to be ~ jealous of sb** éprouver une jalousie obsessionnelle vis-à-vis de qn

obsessive [əb'sesɪv] 1 ADJ [behaviour, need, desire, love, interest, secrecy] obsessionnel; [memory, thought] obsédant; **to be ~** [person] souffrir d'une obsession or d'obsessions; **to be ~ about tidiness/cleanliness** etc être un maniaque de l'ordre/de la propreté etc; **an ~ gambler** un(e) obsédé(e) du jeu; **his ~ tidiness was driving her crazy** son obsession de l'ordre la rendait folle 2 COMP ► **obsessive compulsive disorder** N (Psych) troubles mpl obsessionnels compulsifs

obsessively [əb'sesɪvlɪ] ADV [work, love, hate] de façon obsessionnelle; **she is ~ tidy** c'est une maniaque de l'ordre; **to be ~ in love with sb** aimer qn d'un amour obsessionnel; **he's worried about her** il se fait tellement de souci pour elle que ça tourne à l'obsession

obsidian [əb'sɪdɪən] N obsidienne f

obsolescence [ˌɒbsə'lesns] 1 N [of machinery, goods, words] obsolescence f; (Bio) atrophie f, myopathie f; (Comm) **planned or built-in ~** obsolescence f calculée 2 COMP ► **obsolescence clause** N (Insurance) clause f de vétusté

obsolescent [ˌɒbsə'lesnt] ADJ [machinery, weapon] obsolescent; [word] qui tombe en désuétude; (Bio) [organ] en voie d'atrophie

obsolete ['ɒbsəliːt] ADJ [weapon, equipment, machine] obsolète; [system, attitude, idea, process, practice] dépassé; [word] obsolète, tombé en désuétude; [law] caduc (caduque f), tombé en désuétude; (Bio) atrophié

obstacle ['ɒbstəkl] 1 N (lit, fig) obstacle m; **to be an ~ to sth** être un obstacle à qch; **overcrowding remains a serious ~ to improving living conditions** le surpeuplement reste un obstacle important à l'amélioration des conditions de vie; **the main ~ in negotiations is ...** le principal obstacle dans les négociations est ...; **to put an ~ in the way of sth/in sb's way** faire obstacle à qch/qn 2 COMP ► **obstacle course** N parcours m du combattant ► **obstacle race** N (Sport) course f d'obstacles

obstetric(al) [ɒb'stetrɪk(əl)] ADJ [techniques etc] obstétrical; [clinic] obstétrique

obstetrician [ˌɒbstə'trɪʃən] N obstétricien(ne) m(f), (médecin m) accoucheur m

obstetrics [ɒb'stetrɪks] N (NonC) obstétrique f

obstinacy ['ɒbstɪnəsɪ] N [of person] obstination f (**in doing** à faire); [of illness] persistance f; [of resistance, refusal] obstination f

obstinate ['ɒbstɪnɪt] ADJ a (= stubborn) [person, refusal, silence, resistance] obstiné; **to have an ~ streak** être du genre obstiné; **he's very ~ about it** il n'en démord pas b (= persistent) [weeds, stain, cough] rebelle; [pain, illness] persistant

obstinately ['ɒbstɪnɪtlɪ] ADV [refuse, insist, struggle] obstinément; **to be ~ uncooperative** refuser obstinément de coopérer; **he was ~ silent** il restait obstinément silencieux; **unemployment figures are remaining ~ high** le taux de chômage reste obstinément élevé; **"no" he said** « non » répondit-il d'un air obstiné; **he**

tried ~ to do it by himself il s'est obstiné or entêté à le faire tout seul

obstreperous [əb'strepərəs] ADJ [person, behaviour] tapageur; **the crowd grew ~** la foule s'est mise à faire du tapage

obstreperously [əb'strepərəslɪ] ADV (= noisily) bruyamment, tapageusement; (= rebelliously) avec force protestations, en rouspétant*

obstruct [əb'strʌkt] 1 VT a (= block) [+ road] obstruer (**with** de); [+ pipe] engorger; (Med) [+ artery, windpipe] obstruer; [+ view] boucher, cacher b (= halt) [+ traffic] bloquer; [+ progress] arrêter, entraver c (= hinder) [+ progress, traffic plan] entraver; [+ person] gêner, entraver; (Sport) [+ player] faire obstruction à; (Pol) **to ~ (the passage of) a bill** faire de l'obstruction parlementaire; (Jur) **to ~ a policeman in the execution of his duty** gêner or entraver un agent de police dans l'exercice de ses fonctions 2 VI (Sport) faire de l'obstruction

obstruction [əb'strʌkʃən] N a (to plan, progress, view) obstacle m; (in pipe) bouchon m; (in artery, windpipe) obstruction f, occlusion f; **to remove an ~ from a chimney** enlever un objet qui obstrue une cheminée; **the country's ~ of the UN inspection process** l'obstruction du pays au processus d'inspection de l'ONU; **legal ~s** obstacles mpl juridiques; **a bowel ~** une occlusion intestinale; **an ~ of the Fallopian tubes** une obturation des trompes de Fallope; **to cause an ~** (Jur, gen) encombrer or obstruer la voie publique; (to traffic) bloquer la circulation; (Jur) **~ of justice** entrave f à la justice; **he was charged with ~ of the police in the course of their duties** il a été inculpé pour entrave à l'action de la police dans l'exercice de ses fonctions b (Sport) obstruction f

obstructionism [əb'strʌkʃənɪzəm] N obstructionnisme m

obstructionist [əb'strʌkʃənɪst] ADJ, N obstructionniste mf; **to adopt ~ tactics** faire de l'obstruction, pratiquer l'obstruction

obstructive [əb'strʌktɪv] ADJ a (= troublesome) [bureaucracy] qui vous met des bâtons dans les roues; **he's intent on being ~** il fait de l'obstruction systématique b (Parl) [person, behaviour, policy, tactics, measures] obstructionniste c (Med) obstructif, obstruant

obstructiveness [əb'strʌktɪvnɪs] N tendance f à dresser des obstacles or à faire obstacle

obtain [əb'teɪn] 1 VT (gen) obtenir; [+ goods] procurer (**for sb** à qn); (for o.s.) se procurer; [+ information, job, money] obtenir, (se) procurer; [+ votes] obtenir, recueillir; [+ prize] obtenir, remporter; (Fin) [+ shares] acquérir; **this gas is ~ed from coal** on obtient ce gaz à partir du charbon; **these goods may be ~ed from any large store** on peut se procurer ces articles dans tous les grands magasins 2 VI (frm) [rule, custom etc] avoir cours, être en vigueur; [fashion] être en vogue; [method] être courant

obtainable [əb'teɪnəbl] ADJ [product] qu'on peut se procurer, disponible; **the form is ~ from** or **at post offices** on peut se procurer ce formulaire dans les bureaux de poste

obtrude [əb'truːd] (frm) 1 VT imposer (**sth on sb** qch à qn) 2 VI (object) gêner; [person] s'imposer, imposer sa présence; **the author's opinions do not ~** l'auteur n'impose pas ses opinions

obtrusion [əb'truːʒən] N intrusion f

obtrusive [əb'truːsɪv] ADJ [person] envahissant, qui s'impose; [object, building] trop en évidence; [presence] gênant, envahissant; [music, smell] gênant, envahissant

obtrusively [əb'truːsɪvlɪ] ADV [leave, walk out] ostensiblement; [stare] de façon importune

obtuse [əb'tjuːs] ADJ a [person] obtus; **are you just being deliberately ~?** faites-vous ex-

> LANGUAGE IN USE: **observe** 26.2, 26.3

près de ne pas comprendre? **b** (Math) [angle] obtus

obtuseness [əb'tjuːsnɪs] N stupidité f

obverse ['ɒbvɜːs] **1** N [of coin] face f, côté m face; [of statement, truth] contrepartie f, contre-pied m **2** ADJ **a** [side of coin etc] de face, qui fait face; (fig) correspondant, faisant contrepartie **b** (in shape) [leaf] renversé, plus large au sommet qu'à la base

obviate ['ɒbvɪeɪt] VT [+ difficulty] obvier à, parer à; [+ need, necessity] éviter; [+ danger, objection] prévenir

▼ **obvious** ['ɒbvɪəs] **1** ADJ [question, solution, danger, reason, disadvantage] évident (**to sb** pour qn); [good faith] évident, incontestable; [remark] prévisible; [lie] flagrant; **an ~ injustice** une injustice manifeste or patente; **he was the ~ choice for the role** il était tout désigné pour ce rôle; **~ statement** truisme m, lapalissade f; **it's the ~ thing to do** c'est la chose à faire, cela s'impose; **the ~ thing to do is to leave** la chose à faire c'est évidemment de partir; **that's the ~ one to choose** c'est bien évidemment celui-là qu'il faut choisir; **we mustn't be too ~ about it** il ne faut pas dévoiler notre jeu; **it's ~ that ...** il est évident que ... **2** N **you are merely stating the ~** c'est une lapalissade or un truisme, vous enfoncez une porte ouverte*

▼ **obviously** ['ɒbvɪəslɪ] ADV [angry, upset, happy, pregnant] visiblement; **it's ~ true that ...** il est manifeste or notoire que ...; **that's ~ true!** c'est la vérité!; **he was not ~ drunk** de toute évidence, il n'était pas ivre; **he was not ~ drunk** à le voir, on ne pouvait pas dire s'il était ivre; **she ~ adores her big sister** il est évident qu'elle adore sa grande sœur; **~ I am delighted** je suis bien entendu ravi; **~!** bien sûr!, évidemment!; **~ not!** apparemment non!

OC ['əʊ'siː] N ABBR = **Officer Commanding**

ocarina [ˌɒkə'riːnə] N ocarina m

Occam ['ɒkəm] N Occam m; **~'s razor** le rasoir d'Occam

occasion [ə'keɪʒən] **1** N **a** (= particular time, date, occurrence etc) occasion f; **on the ~ of ...** à l'occasion de ...; **(on) the first ~ (that) it happened** la première fois que cela s'est passé; **on that ~** à cette occasion, cette fois-là; **on several ~s** à plusieurs occasions or reprises; **on rare ~s** en de rares occasions; **on just such an ~** dans une occasion tout à fait semblable; **on great ~s** dans les grandes occasions; **on a previous or former ~** précédemment; **I'll do it on the first possible ~** je le ferai à la première occasion (possible) or dès que l'occasion se présentera; **on ~(s)** à l'occasion, quand l'occasion se présente (or se présentait etc); **should the ~ arise** le cas échéant; **should the ~ so demand** si les circonstances l'exigent; **as the ~ requires** selon le cas; **he has had few ~s to speak Italian** il n'a pas eu souvent l'occasion de parler italien; **he took (the) ~ to say ...** il en a profité pour dire ...; **he was waiting for a suitable ~ to apologize** il attendait une occasion favorable pour or l'occasion de présenter ses excuses; **this would be a good ~ to try it out** c'est l'occasion tout indiquée pour l'essayer; **to rise to or be equal to the ~** être à la hauteur de la situation

b (= event, function) événement m, occasion f; **a big ~** un grand événement, une grande occasion; **it was quite an ~** cela n'a pas été une petite affaire or un petit événement; **play/music written for the ~** pièce f spécialement écrite/musique f spécialement composée pour l'occasion

c (= reason) motif m; **there is no ~ for alarm or to be alarmed** il n'y a pas lieu de s'alarmer, il n'y a pas de quoi s'inquiéter; **there was no ~ for it** ce n'était pas nécessaire; **I have no ~ for complaint** je n'ai pas motif à or sujet de

me plaindre; **you had no ~ to say that** vous n'aviez aucune raison de dire cela; (frm) **I had ~ to reprimand him** j'ai eu l'occasion de or j'ai eu à le réprimander

d (frm) **to go about one's lawful ~s** vaquer à ses occupations

2 VT (frm) occasionner, causer

occasional [ə'keɪʒənl] **1** ADJ **a** (= infrequent) [meeting, event] qui a (or avait) lieu de temps en temps or de temps à autre; [rain, showers] intermittent; **I have the ~ drink** je prends un verre de temps en temps; **she made ~ visits to England** elle allait de temps en temps en Angleterre; **they had passed an ~ car on the road** ils avaient croisé quelques rares voitures **b** (frm: Literat, Mus) [poem, essay, music] de circonstance **2** COMP ► **occasional table** N (Brit) table f d'appoint

occasionally [ə'keɪʒnəlɪ] ADV [do, say, think etc] à l'occasion, occasionnellement; [rude, silly, angry etc] parfois; **(only) very ~** très rarement, exceptionnellement

occident ['ɒksɪdənt] N (liter) occident m, couchant m; **the Occident** l'Occident m

occidental [ˌɒksɪ'dentl] ADJ (liter) occidental

occipita [ɒk'sɪpɪtə] NPL of **occiput**

occipital [ɒk'sɪpɪtl] ADJ occipital

occiput ['ɒksɪpʌt] N (pl **occiputs** or **occipita**) occiput m

occlude [ɒ'kluːd] **1** VT (all senses) occlure **2** VI (Dentistry) s'emboîter **3** COMP ► **occluded front** N (Met) front m occlus

occlusion [ɒ'kluːʒən] N (all senses) occlusion f

occlusive [ɒ'kluːsɪv] **1** ADJ (also Ling) occlusif **2** N (Phon) (consonne f) occlusive f

occult [ɒ'kʌlt] **1** ADJ occulte **2** N **the ~** le surnaturel; **to study the ~** étudier les sciences occultes

occultism ['ɒkəltɪzəm] N occultisme m

occultist [ɒ'kʌltɪst] N occultiste mf

occupancy ['ɒkjʊpənsɪ] N occupation f (d'une maison etc)

occupant ['ɒkjʊpənt] N [of house] occupant(e) m(f), habitant(e) m(f); (= tenant) locataire mf; [of land, vehicle etc] occupant(e) m(f); [of job, post] titulaire mf

occupation [ˌɒkjʊ'peɪʃən] **1** N **a** (NonC) [of house etc] occupation f; (Jur) prise f de possession; **unfit for ~** impropre à l'habitation; **the house is ready for ~** la maison est prête à être habitée; **we found them already in ~** nous les avons trouvés déjà installés **b** (NonC: Mil, Pol) occupation f; **army of ~** armée f d'occupation; **under (military) ~** sous occupation (militaire); **during the Occupation** pendant or sous l'Occupation **c** (= trade) métier m; (= profession) profession f; (= work) emploi m, travail m; (= activity, pastime) occupation f, passe-temps m inv; **he's a plumber by ~** il est plombier de son métier; **he needs some ~ for his spare time** il lui faut une occupation or de quoi occuper ses loisirs; **his only ~ was helping his father** sa seule occupation était or il avait pour seule occupation d'aider son père; **parachuting is a dangerous ~** le parachutisme est un passe-temps dangereux

2 COMP [troops] d'occupation

occupational [ˌɒkjʊ'peɪʃənl] **1** ADJ [training, group] professionnel; [disease, accident] du travail; [safety] au travail; [risk] professionnel, du métier

2 COMP ► **occupational hazard** N [of job] risque m professionnel or du métier; [of skiing/sailing etc] risque m encouru par ceux qui font du ski/de la voile etc; **it's an ~ hazard of or in this job** c'est un des risques de ce métier ► **occupational health** N santé f au travail; **~ health service or department** service m de médecine du travail ► **occupational pension** N retraite f complémentaire

► **occupational psychologist** N psychologue mf du travail ► **occupational psychology** N psychologie f du travail ► **Occupational Safety and Health Administration** N (US) ≈ inspection f du travail ► **occupational therapist** N ergothérapeute mf ► **occupational therapy** N ergothérapie f; **~ therapy department** service m d'ergothérapie

occupationally [ˌɒkjʊ'peɪʃnəlɪ] ADV [acquired, received] dans l'exercice de sa (or leur etc) profession; **an ~ induced disease** une maladie professionnelle

occupied ['ɒkjʊpaɪd] **1** ADJ **a** (= inhabited) [house] habité **b** (= busy, taken) [toilet, room] occupé; [seat, bed] occupé, pris **c** (Mil) occupé; **Nazi-~ Budapest** Budapest sous l'occupation nazie → **occupy 2** COMP ► **the Occupied Territories** NPL (in Middle East) les territoires mpl occupés

occupier ['ɒkjʊpaɪəʳ] N [of house] occupant(e) m(f), habitant(e) m(f); (= tenant) locataire mf; [of land] occupant(e) m(f) → **owner**

occupy ['ɒkjʊpaɪ] VT **a** (= inhabit) [+ house] résider dans, habiter; (= fill) [+ post] occuper **b** [troops, demonstrators] occuper → **occupied c** (= take up) [+ attention, mind, person, time, space] occuper; **occupied with the thought of ...** absorbé par la pensée de ...; **to be occupied in or with doing** être occupé à faire; **to ~ o.s. or one's time (with or by doing)** s'occuper (à faire); **how do you ~ your time/your days?** comment occupez-vous votre temps/vos journées?; **how do you keep occupied all day?** qu'est-ce que vous faites pour occuper vos journées?; **to keep one's mind occupied** s'occuper l'esprit

occur [ə'kɜːʳ] VI **a** [event] se produire, arriver; [word] se rencontrer, se trouver; [difficulty, opportunity] se présenter; [change] s'opérer; [disease, error] se produire, se rencontrer; [plant etc] se trouver; **if a vacancy ~s** en cas de poste vacant; **should the case ~** le cas échéant

b (= come to mind) se présenter or venir à l'esprit (**to sb** de qn); **an idea ~red to me** une idée m'est venue à l'esprit; **it ~red to me that he might be wrong** il m'a traversé l'esprit qu'il pouvait avoir tort; **it ~red to me that we could ...** j'ai pensé or je me suis dit que nous pourrions ...; **it didn't ~ to him to refuse** il n'a pas eu l'idée de refuser; **the thought would never ~ to me** ça ne me viendrait jamais à l'idée or à l'esprit; **did it never ~ to you to ask?** il ne t'est jamais venu à l'esprit de demander?, tu n'as jamais eu l'idée de demander?

occurrence [ə'kʌrəns] N **a** (= event) événement m, circonstance f; **an everyday ~** un fait journalier; **this is a common ~** ceci arrive or se produit souvent; **terrorist attacks have become a daily ~** les attentats terroristes sont devenus une réalité quotidienne **b** fait m de se produire or d'arriver; **chemicals which are used to prevent the ~ of algae** les produits chimiques utilisés pour empêcher l'apparition d'algues; **the greatest ~ of heart disease is in those over 65** c'est chez les plus de 65 ans que l'on trouve or observe le plus grand nombre de cas de maladies cardiaques; **to be of frequent ~** se produire or arriver souvent

ocean ['əʊʃən] **1** N (lit, fig) océan m; (fig) **~s of*** énormément de*; **it's a drop in the ~** c'est une goutte d'eau dans la mer **2** COMP [climate, region] océanique; [cruise] sur l'océan ► **ocean bed** N (of sea) m(pl) sous-marin(s) ► **ocean-going** ADJ de haute mer; **~-going ship** navire m de haute mer ► **ocean liner** N paquebot m ► **the Ocean State** N (US) le Rhode Island

oceanarium [ˌəʊʃə'nɛərɪəm] N (pl **oceanariums** or **oceanaria** [ˌəʊʃə'nɛərɪə]) parc m océanographique

Oceania [ˌəʊʃɪˈeɪnɪə] N l'Océanie f
Oceanian [ˌəʊʃɪˈeɪnɪən] **1** ADJ océanien **2** N Océanien(ne) m(f)
oceanic [ˌəʊʃɪˈænɪk] **1** ADJ océanique **2** COMP ▸ **the oceanic feeling** N (Psych) le sentiment océanique ▸ **oceanic ridge** N dorsale f océanique ▸ **oceanic trench** N fosse f océanique
oceanographer [ˌəʊʃəˈnɒgrəfəʳ] N océanographe mf
oceanographic [ˌəʊʃənəˈgræfɪk] ADJ océanographique
oceanography [ˌəʊʃəˈnɒgrəfɪ] N océanographie f
ocelot [ˈəʊsɪlɒt] N ocelot m
och [ɒx] EXCL (Scot) oh!
ochre, ocher (US) [ˈəʊkəʳ] N (= substance) ocre f; (= colour) ocre m
ochreous [ˈəʊkrɪəs] ADJ ocreux
o'clock [əˈklɒk] ADV **it is one** ~ il est une heure; **it's 4 ~ in the morning** il est 4 heures du matin; **at 5 ~** à 5 heures; **at exactly 9 ~** à 9 heures précises or justes; **at 12 ~** (= midday) à midi; (= midnight) à minuit; **the 12 ~ train** (= midday) (gen) le train de midi; (over loudspeaker) le train de 12 heures; (= midnight) (gen) le train de minuit; (over loudspeaker) le train de 0 heure; **the 6 ~** (bus/train etc) le bus/train etc de 6 heures; **the Nine O'Clock News** le journal de 21 heures; (Aviat, Mil: direction) **aircraft approaching at 5 ~** avion à 5 heures → **five**
OCR [ˌəʊˌsiːˈɑːʳ] (Comput) (ABBR = **optical character reader, optical character recognition**) → **optical**
Oct. ABBR = **October**
octagon [ˈɒktəgən] N octogone m
octagonal [ɒkˈtægənl] ADJ octogonal
octahedron [ˌɒktəˈhiːdrən] N (pl **octahedrons** or **octahedra** [ˈɒktəˈhiːdrə]) octaèdre m
octal [ˈɒktl] N, ADJ (Comput) ~ **(notation)** octal
octane [ˈɒkteɪn] **1** N octane m; **high-~ petrol** carburant m à indice d'octane élevé **2** COMP d'octane ▸ **octane number, octane rating** N indice m d'octane
octave [ˈɒktɪv] N (gen, Mus, Rel, Fencing) octave f; (Poetry) huitain m
octavo [ɒkˈteɪvəʊ] N (pl **octavos**) in-octavo m
octet [ɒkˈtet] N (Mus) octuor m; (Poetry) huitain m
octillion [ɒkˈtɪljən] N (Brit) 10⁴⁸; (US) 10²⁷
October [ɒkˈtəʊbəʳ] **1** N octobre m; for phrases see **September** **2** COMP ▸ **the October Revolution** N (Russian Hist) la Révolution d'octobre
octogenarian [ˌɒktəʊdʒɪˈnɛərɪən] ADJ, N octogénaire mf
octopus [ˈɒktəpəs] (pl **octopuses**) **1** N (Zool) pieuvre f; (Culin) poulpe m; (Brit Aut: for luggage etc) fixe-bagages m inv **2** COMP [organization] ramifié, à ramifications (multiples)
octoroon [ˌɒktəˈruːn] N octavon(ne) m(f)
octosyllabic [ˌɒktəʊsɪˈlæbɪk] **1** ADJ octosyllabique **2** N octosyllabe m, vers m octosyllabique
octosyllable [ˌɒktəʊˈsɪlæbl] N (= line) octosyllabe m, vers m octosyllabique; (= word) mot m octosyllabique
ocular [ˈɒkjʊləʳ] ADJ, N oculaire m
oculist [ˈɒkjʊlɪst] N oculiste m
OD: [əʊˈdiː] **1** ABBR = **overdose** **1** N (lit) surdose f, overdose f **2** VI **a** (lit) (gen) faire une overdose; (fatally) mourir d'une surdose or d'une overdose; **to OD on sth** prendre une surdose de qch **b** (fig, hum) **to OD on TV** etc faire une overdose de télé etc; **to OD on chocolate** forcer* sur le chocolat
odalisque [ˈəʊdəlɪsk] N odalisque f

odd [ɒd] **1** ADJ **a** (= strange) bizarre, étrange; **(how)** ~! bizarre!, étrange!; **how ~ that we should meet him** comme c'est étrange que nous l'ayons rencontré; **what an ~ thing for him to do!** c'est bizarre qu'il ait fait cela!; **he says/does some very ~ things** il dit/fait de drôles de choses parfois; **the ~ thing about it is ...** ce qui est bizarre or étrange à ce sujet c'est ...; **he's got rather ~ lately** il est bizarre depuis quelque temps
b (Math) [number] impair
c (= extra, left over) qui reste(nt); (from pair, set) [shoe, sock] dépareillé; **I've got it all but the ~ penny** il me manque un penny pour avoir le compte; **£5 and some ~ pennies** 5 livres et quelques pennies; **any ~ piece of wood** un morceau de bois quelconque; **an ~ scrap of paper** un bout de papier; **a few ~ bits of paper** deux ou trois bouts de papier; (Brit) **this is an ~ size that we don't stock** c'est une taille peu courante que nous n'avons pas (en stock); **to be the ~ one over** être en surnombre; **the ~ man out** ◊ **the ~ one out** l'exception f → **2, odds**
d (* = and a few more) **sixty-~** soixante et quelques, **forty-~ years** une quarantaine d'années, quarante et quelques années; **£20-~** 20 et quelques livres, 20 livres et quelques
e (= occasional, not regular) **in ~ moments he ...** à ses moments perdus, il ...; **at ~ times** de temps en temps; **in ~ corners all over the house** dans les coins et recoins de la maison; ~ **jobs** travaux mpl divers, petits travaux mpl → **2**; **I did a lot of ~ jobs before becoming an actor** j'ai fait beaucoup de petits boulots* or j'ai touché un peu à tout avant d'être acteur; **to do ~ jobs about the house** (= housework) faire des travaux domestiques divers; (= do-it-yourself) bricoler dans la maison; **he does ~ jobs around the garden** il fait des petits travaux de jardinage; **I've got one or two ~ jobs for you (to do)** j'ai deux ou trois choses or bricoles* à te faire faire; **he has written the ~ article** il a écrit un ou deux articles; **I get the ~ letter from him** de temps en temps je reçois une lettre de lui; **tomorrow will be mainly sunny with the ~ shower** la journée de demain sera ensoleillée avec quelques averses éparses
2 COMP ▸ **odd-jobber, odd-job man** homme m à tout faire ▸ **odd-looking** ADJ à l'air bizarre ▸ **odd lot** N (St Ex) lot m fractionné (au nombre de titres inférieur à 100)
oddball* [ˈɒdbɔːl] **1** N excentrique mf **2** ADJ excentrique
oddbod: [ˈɒdbɒd] N **he's a bit of an** ~ c'est un drôle d'oiseau*
oddity [ˈɒdɪtɪ] N **a** (= strangeness) = **oddness** **b** (= odd person) personne f bizarre, excentrique mf; (= odd thing) curiosité f; (= odd trait) singularité f; **he's a real** ~ il a vraiment un genre très spécial; **one of the oddities of the situation** un des aspects insolites de la situation
oddly [ˈɒdlɪ] ADV curieusement, bizarrement; **they sound ~ like the Beatles** leur style ressemble curieusement à celui des Beatles; **an ~ shaped room** une pièce aux formes bizarres; ~ **enough ...** chose curieuse ..., curieusement ...
oddment [ˈɒdmənt] N (Brit Comm) fin f de série; (one of a pair or collection) article m dépareillé; [of cloth] coupon m
oddness [ˈɒdnɪs] N (NonC) bizarrerie f, étrangeté f
odds [ɒdz] **1** NPL **a** (Betting) cote f; **he gave him ~ of 5 to 1 (for Jupiter)** il lui a donné une cote de 5 contre 1 (sur Jupiter); **he gave him ~ of 5 to 1 that he would fail his exams** il lui a parié à 5 contre 1 qu'il échouerait à ses examens; **I got good/short/long ~ on** on m'a donné une bonne/faible/forte cote; **the ~ on** or **against a horse** la cote d'un cheval; **the ~ are 7 to 2 against Lucifer** Lucifer est à 7 contre 2,

la cote de Lucifer est de 7 contre 2; **the ~ are 6 to 4 on** la cote est à 4 contre 6; **the ~ are 6 to 4 against** la cote est à 6 contre 4; **what ~ will you give me?** quelle est votre cote?; (fig) **the ~ are 10 to 1 in favour of his** or **him* going** il y a 9 chances sur 10 (pour) qu'il y aille; (Brit fig) **over the ~** plus que nécessaire; **I got £30 over the ~ for it** on me l'a payé 30 livres de plus que je ne demandais (or ne m'y attendais etc)
b (fig = balance of advantage) chances fpl (for pour, against contre), avantage m; **all the ~ are against you** nous n'avez pratiquement aucune chance d'y arriver, c'est pratiquement perdu d'avance; **the ~ are against his** or **him coming** il est pratiquement certain qu'il ne viendra pas, il y a gros à parier qu'il ne viendra pas; **the ~ against another attack are very high** une nouvelle attaque est hautement improbable; **the ~ are on him coming** or **that he will come** il y a gros à parier qu'il viendra, il y a de fortes chances (pour) qu'il vienne; **the ~ are even that he will come** il y a cinquante pour cent de chances qu'il vienne; **to fight against heavy** or **great ~** avoir affaire à plus fort que soi, combattre or lutter contre des forces supérieures; **he managed to succeed against overwhelming ~** or **against all the ~** il a réussi alors que tout était contre lui; **the ~ are too great** le succès est trop improbable; **by all the ~** (= unquestionably) sans aucun doute; (= judging from past experience) à en juger par l'expérience, d'après ce que l'on sait → **stack**
c (= difference) **it makes no ~** cela n'a pas d'importance, ça ne fait rien*; **it makes no ~ to me** ça m'est complètement égal, ça ne me fait rien; **what's the ~?*** qu'est-ce que ça peut bien faire?
d **to be at ~ (with sb over sth)** être en désaccord (avec qn sur qch); **to be at ~ with the world** (= discontented) en vouloir au monde entier; **to be at ~ with o.s.** être mal dans sa peau; **his pompous tone was at ~ with the vulgar language he used** son ton pompeux ne cadrait pas avec son langage vulgaire; **to set two people at ~** brouiller deux personnes, semer la discorde entre deux personnes
2 COMP ▸ **odds and ends** NPL (gen) des petites choses fpl qui restent; [of cloth] bouts mpl; [of food] restes mpl; **there were a few ~ and ends lying about the house** quelques objets traînaient çà et là dans la maison; (fig) **we still have a few ~ and ends to settle** il nous reste encore quelques points à régler ▸ **odds-on** ADJ (Racing) grand favori m; (fig) **he's the ~-on favourite for the job** c'est le grand favori pour le poste; **it's ~-on that he'll come** il y a toutes les chances qu'il vienne, il y a gros à parier qu'il viendra
ode [əʊd] N ode f (**to** à, **on** sur)
odious [ˈəʊdɪəs] ADJ [person] détestable, odieux; [behaviour, crime] odieux
odiously [ˈəʊdɪəslɪ] ADV odieusement
odiousness [ˈəʊdɪəsnɪs] N [of person] caractère m détestable or odieux; [of crime] caractère m odieux
odium [ˈəʊdɪəm] N (NonC) réprobation f générale, anathème m
odometer [ɒˈdɒmɪtəʳ] N (US) odomètre m
odont(o)... [ɒˈdɒnt(əʊ)] PREF odont(o)...
odontological [ɒˌdɒntəˈlɒdʒɪkəl] ADJ odontologique
odontologist [ˌɒdɒnˈtɒlədʒɪst] N odontologiste mf
odontology [ˌɒdɒnˈtɒlədʒɪ] N odontologie f
odor [ˈəʊdəʳ] N (US) = **odour**
odoriferous [ˌəʊdəˈrɪfərəs] ADJ odoriférant, parfumé
odorless [ˈəʊdəlɪs] ADJ (US) = **odourless**
odorous [ˈəʊdərəs] ADJ (liter) (gen) odorant; (pleasantly) parfumé

odour, odor (US) ['əʊdə'] N odeur f; (pleasant) odeur f (agréable), parfum m; (unpleasant) (mauvaise) odeur f; (fig) trace f, parfum m (liter); (fig) **to be in good/bad ~ with sb** être/ne pas être en faveur auprès de qn, être bien/mal vu de qn; **~ of sanctity** odeur f de sainteté

odourless, odorless (US) ['əʊdəlɪs] ADJ inodore

Odysseus [ə'di:sɪəs] N Ulysse m

Odyssey ['ɒdɪsɪ] N (Myth) Odyssée f; (gen) **odyssée** odyssée f

OE N (Ling) (ABBR = **Old English**) → **old**

OECD ['əʊ,i:si:'di:] N (ABBR = **Organization for Economic Cooperation and Development**) OCDE f

oecology [i'kɒlədʒɪ] N = **ecology**

oecumenical [,i:kju:'menɪkəl] ADJ = **ecumenical**

oedema [ɪ'di:mə] N (pl **oedemata** [ɪ'di:mətə]) (Brit) œdème m

Oedipal ['i:dɪpəl] ADJ œdipien

Oedipus ['i:dɪpəs] [1] N Œdipe m [2] COMP ► **Oedipus complex** N (Psych) complexe m d'Œdipe

oenological [,i:nə'lɒdʒɪkəl] ADJ œnologique

oenologist [i:'nɒlədʒɪst] N œnologue mf

oenology [i:'nɒlədʒɪ] N œnologie f

o'er ['əʊə'] (liter) = **over**

oesophagus [i:'sɒfəgəs] N = **esophagus**

oestrogen ['i:strəʊdʒən] N œstrogène m

oestrone ['i:strəʊn] N œstrone f

oestrous ['i:strəs] ADJ œstral; **~ cycle** cycle m œstral

oestrus ['i:strəs] N œstrus m

œuvre ['ɜ:vrə] N œuvre f

of [ɒv,əv] PREP [a] (possession) de; **the wife of the doctor** la femme du médecin; **a painting of the queen's** un tableau de la reine or qui appartient à la reine; **a friend of ours** (l')un de nos amis, un ami à nous; **that funny nose of hers** son drôle de nez, ce drôle de nez qu'elle a; **of it** en; **the tip of it is broken** le bout en est cassé

[b] (objective genitive) de, pour; (subjective) de; **his love of his father** son amour pour son père, l'amour qu'il porte (or portait etc) à son père; **love of money** amour de l'argent; **a painting of the queen** un tableau de la reine or qui représente la reine; **a leader of men** un meneur d'hommes; **writer of legal articles** auteur m d'articles de droit

[c] (partitive) de, entre; **the whole of the house** toute la maison; **how much of this do you want?** combien or quelle quantité en voulez-vous?; **there were six of us** nous étions six; **he asked the six of us to lunch** il nous a invités tous les six à déjeuner; **of the ten only one was absent** sur les dix un seul était absent; **he is not one of us** il n'est pas des nôtres; **the 2nd of June** le 2 juin; **today of all days** ce jour entre tous; **you of all people ought to know** vous devriez le savoir mieux que personne; (liter) **he is the bravest of the brave** c'est un brave entre les braves; (liter) **he drank of the wine** il but du vin → **best, first, most, some**

[d] (concerning, in respect of) de; **what do you think of him?** que pensez-vous de lui?; **what of it?** et alors? → **bachelor, capable, hard, warn, year**

[e] (separation in space or time) de; **south of Paris** au sud de Paris; **within a month/a kilometre of ...** à moins d'un mois/d'un kilomètre de ...; (US) **a quarter of six** six heures moins le quart

[f] (origin) de; **of noble birth** de naissance noble; **of royal origin** d'origine royale; **a book of Dante's** un livre de Dante

[g] (cause) de; **to die of hunger** mourir de faim; **because of** à cause de; **for fear of** de peur de → **ashamed, choice, necessity**

[h] (material) de, en; **dress (made) of wool** robe f en or de laine

[i] (descriptive) de; **a man of courage** un homme courageux; **a girl of ten** une petite fille de dix ans; **a question of no importance** une question sans importance; **the city of Paris** la ville de Paris; **town of narrow streets** ville f aux rues étroites; **fruit of his own growing** fruits mpl qu'il a cultivés lui-même; **that idiot of a doctor** cet imbécile de docteur; **he has a real palace of a house** c'est un véritable palais que sa maison → **extraction, make, name**

[j] (agent etc) de; **beloved of all** bien-aimé de tous; **it was nasty of him to say so** c'était méchant de sa part de dire cela → **old**

[k] (in temporal phrases) **of late** depuis quelque temps; (dial) **it was often fine of a morning** il faisait souvent beau le matin → **old**

[l] → **free, irrespective, rid, short, smell, taste**

---

off [ɒf]

[1]	PREPOSITION	[5]	INTRANSITIVE VERB
[2]	ADVERB	[6]	TRANSITIVE VERB
[3]	ADJECTIVE	[7]	COMPOUNDS
[4]	NOUN		

When **off** is the second element in a phrasal verb, eg **get off, keep off, take off**, look up the verb. When it is part of a set combination, eg **off duty/work, far off**, look up the other word.

[1] PREPOSITION

[a] = **from** de

de + le = **du**, de + les = **des**

he fell/jumped ~ the wall il est tombé/a sauté du mur; **the orange fell ~ the table** l'orange est tombée de la table; **he cut a piece ~ the steak and gave it to the dog** il a coupé un morceau du steak et l'a donné au chien; BUT **he was balancing on the wall and fell ~** il était en équilibre sur le mur et il est tombé

Note the French prepositions used in the following:

he took the book ~ the table il a pris le livre sur la table; **we ate ~ paper plates** nous avons mangé dans des assiettes en papier

[b] = **missing from** **there are two buttons ~ my coat** il manque deux boutons à mon manteau; **the lid was ~ the tin** le couvercle n'était pas sur la boîte

[c] = **away from** de; **the helicopter was just a few metres ~ the ground** l'hélicoptère n'était qu'à quelques mètres du sol; BUT **he ran towards the car and was 5 yards ~ it when ...** il a couru vers la voiture et n'en était plus qu'à 5 mètres lorsque ...; **we want a house ~ the main road** nous cherchons une maison en retrait de la route principale

[d] = **near** près de; **a flat just ~ the high street** un appartement près de la rue principale; BUT **it's ~ Baker Street** c'est une rue qui donne dans Baker Street, c'est dans une rue perpendiculaire à Baker Street; **a street (leading) ~ the square** une rue qui part de la place

[e] Naut au large de; **~ Portland Bill** au large de Portland Bill; **~ the coast of Brittany** c'est au large de la Bretagne

[f] * = **not taking, avoiding** **I'm ~ coffee at the moment** je ne bois pas de café en ce moment; **I'm ~ smoking** je ne fume plus; **he's ~ drugs** il ne touche plus à la drogue → **go off**

[2] ADVERB

[a] = **away** **the house is 5km ~** la maison est à 5 km; **the power station is visible from miles ~** la centrale électrique est visible à des kilomètres à la ronde; **my holiday is a week ~** je suis en vacances dans une semaine

♦ **to be off*** (= going) partir; **we're ~ to France today** nous partons pour la France aujourd'hui; (Sport) **they're ~!** les voilà partis!, ils sont partis!; **Dave's not here, he's ~ fishing** Dave n'est pas ici, il est parti pêcher or il est allé à la pêche; BUT **I must be ~** ◊ **it's time I was ~** il faut que je file* or me sauve*; **be ~ with**

you! ◊ **~ you go!** va-t-en!, file!*; **where are you ~ to?** où allez-vous?; **I'm ~ fishing** je vais à la pêche; **he's ~ on his favourite subject** le voilà lancé sur son sujet favori

[b] = **as holiday** **to take a day ~** prendre un jour de congé; **I've got this afternoon ~** je ne travaille pas cet après-midi; **he gets two days ~ each week** il a deux jours de congé or de repos par semaine; **he gets one week ~ a month** il a une semaine de congé par mois

[c] = **removed** **he had his coat ~** il avait enlevé son manteau; **the lid was ~** le couvercle n'était pas mis; **the handle is ~** or **has come ~** la poignée s'est détachée; **there are two buttons ~** il manque deux boutons; **~ with those socks!** enlève ces chaussettes!; **~ with his head!** qu'on lui coupe (subj) la tête!

[d] = **as reduction** **10% ~** 10% de remise or de réduction; **I'll give you 10% ~** je vais vous faire une remise or une réduction de 10%

[e] * : **referring to time**

♦ **off and on** par intermittence; **I'm still working as a waitress ~ and on** je travaille toujours comme serveuse par intermittence or de temps à autre; **they lived together ~ and on for six years** ils ont vécu six ans ensemble par intermittence

[3] ADJECTIVE

[a] = **absent from work** **he's ~ sick** il est malade or en congé de maladie; **several teachers were ~ sick** plusieurs enseignants étaient malades; **10% of the workforce were ~ sick** 10% des effectifs or du personnel étaient absents pour cause de maladie; **he's been ~ for three weeks** cela fait trois semaines qu'il est absent

[b] = **off duty** **she's ~ at 4 o'clock today** elle termine à 4 heures aujourd'hui; **he's ~ on Tuesdays** il n'est pas là le mardi, il ne travaille pas le mardi

[c] = **not functioning, connected, flowing** [brake] desserré; [machine, light] éteint; [engine, gas at main, electricity, water] coupé; [tap] fermé; **make sure the gas is ~** n'oubliez pas de fermer le gaz; **the light/TV/radio is ~** la lumière/la télé/la radio est éteinte; **the switch was in the ~ position** l'interrupteur était en position « arrêt » or n'était pas enclenché

[d] = **cancelled** [meeting, trip, match] annulé; **the party is ~** la soirée est annulée; **their engagement is ~** ils ont rompu leurs fiançailles; (in restaurant) **the lasagne is ~** il n'y a plus de lasagnes

[e] Brit = **bad** [fish, meat] avarié; [milk] tourné; [butter] rance; [taste] mauvais

[f] indicating wealth, possession **they are comfortably ~** ils sont aisés; **they are badly ~** (financially) ils sont dans la gêne; **how are you ~ for bread?** qu'est-ce que vous avez comme pain?

[g] = **not right**

♦ **a bit off***: **it was a bit ~, him leaving like that** ce n'était pas très bien de sa part de partir comme ça; **that's a bit ~!** ce n'est pas très sympa!*; **the timing seems a bit ~, seeing that an election is imminent** le moment est mal choisi étant donné l'imminence des élections

[h] Brit = **offside 2a**

[4] NOUN

* = **start** **they're ready for the ~** ils sont prêts à partir; **from the ~** dès le départ

[5] INTRANSITIVE VERB

esp US* = **leave** ficher le camp*

[6] TRANSITIVE VERB

US* = **kill** buter*, tuer

[7] COMPOUNDS

► **off air** ADV (TV, Rad) hors antenne; **to go ~ air** [broadcast] rendre l'antenne; [station] cesser d'émettre; **to take sb ~ air** reprendre l'antenne à qn; **to take sth ~ air** arrêter la diffusion de qch ► **off-air** ADJ (TV, Rad) hors antenne ► **off-balance-sheet reserve** N (Fin) réserve f hors bilan ► **off-beam*** ADJ [statement, person] à côté de la plaque*

► **off-Broadway** ADJ (*US Theat*) d'avant-garde, off ► **off-camera** ADJ (*TV, Cine*) hors champ ► **off-campus** ADJ (*Univ*) en dehors de l'université or du campus ► **off-centre** ADJ (*gen*) désaxé, décentré; [+ *construction*] en porte-à-faux; (*fig*) [+ *assessment etc*] pas tout à fait exact ► **off chance** N **I came on the ~ chance of seeing her** je suis venu avec l'espoir de la voir; **he bought it on the ~ chance that it would come in useful** il l'a acheté pour le cas où cela pourrait servir; **I did it on the ~ chance*** je l'ai fait à tout hasard or au cas où* ► **off-colour** ADJ (*Brit*) **he's ~colour today** il est mal fichu* or il n'est pas dans son assiette* aujourd'hui; **an ~colour*** story une histoire osée or scabreuse ► **off day** N **he was having an ~ day** il n'était pas en forme ce jour-là, ce n'était pas son jour; (*US = holiday*) jour *m* de congé ► **off-key** (*Mus*) ADJ faux (fausse *f*) ♦ ADV [*sing*] faux ► **off-label store** N (*US*) magasin *m* de (vêtements) dégriffés ► **off-licence** N (*Brit*) (= *shop*) magasin *m* de vins et spiritueux; (= *permit*) licence *f* (*permettant la vente de boissons alcoolisées à emporter*) ► **off-limits** ADJ (*US Mil*) **~limits to troops** interdit au personnel militaire ► **off-line** (*Comput*) ADJ autonome ♦ ADV **to go ~line** [*computer*] se mettre en mode autonome; **to put the printer ~line** mettre l'imprimante en mode manuel ► **off-load** VT [+ *goods*] décharger, débarquer; [+ *passengers*] débarquer; [+ *task, responsibilities*] se décharger de (**on** or **onto sb** sur *qn*) ► **off-off-Broadway** ADJ (*US Theat*) résolument expérimental → OFF-BROADWAY ► **off-peak** ADJ → off-peak ► **off-piste** ADJ, ADV (*Ski*) hors-piste ► **off-putting** ADJ [*task*] rebutant; [*food*] peu ragoûtant; [*person, manner*] rébarbatif, peu engageant ► **off-road** ADJ [*driving, racing, cycling*] off-road *inv* ► **off-road vehicle** N véhicule *m* tout terrain ► **off-sales** N (*Brit*) (= *sales*) vente *f* de boissons alcoolisées (à emporter); (= *shop*) ≈ marchand *m* de vins; (= *counter*) comptoir *m* des vins et spiritueux ► **off screen** ADV (*Cine, TV*) dans le privé, hors écran ► **off-screen** ADJ (*Cine, TV*) hors écran; **an ~-screen romance** une aventure sentimentale à la ville ► **off-season** ADJ hors saison ♦ N morte-saison *f*; **in the ~-season** en morte-saison ► **off site** ADV à l'extérieur du site ► **off-site** ADJ hors site ► **off-street parking** N place *f* de parking; **a flat with ~-street parking** un appartement avec une place de parking ► **off-the-cuff** ADJ [*remark*] impromptu; [*speech*] impromptu, au pied levé ► **cuff** ► **off-the-job training** N → job 1b ► **off-the-peg**, **off-the-rack** (*US*) ADJ de confection → peg, rack† ► **off-the-record** ADJ (= *unofficial*) officieux; (= *confidential*) confidentiel → record ► **off-the-shelf** ADJ (*Econ*) [*goods, item*] disponible dans le commerce ♦ ADV **to buy sth ~-the-shelf** acheter qch dans le commerce → shelf ► **off-the-shoulder** ADJ [*dress*] sans bretelles ► **off-the-wall*** ADJ bizarre, dingue* ► **off-white** ADJ blanc cassé *inv* ► **off year** N (*US Pol*) année sans élections importantes → offbeat, offhand, offset, offshore

---

offal ['ɒfəl] N (*NonC*) a (*Culin*) abats *mpl* (*de boucherie*) b (= *refuse, rubbish*) ordures *fpl*; (= *waste or by-product*) déchets *mpl*

offbeat ['ɒfbiːt] 1 ADJ a (* = *unusual*) [*film, book, comedy, approach*] original; [*person, behaviour, clothes*] excentrique; **his ~ sense of humour** son sens de l'humour cocasse b (*Mus*) à temps faible 2 N (*Mus*) temps *m* faible

offcut ['ɒfkʌt] N [*of fabric*] chute *f*; [*of wood*] copeau *m*; [*of meat, fish*] (*for human consumption*) parures *fpl*; (*for animals*) déchets *mpl*

offence, offense (*US*) [ə'fens] N a (*Jur*) délit *m* (**against** contre), infraction *f* (**against** à); (*Rel* = *sin*) offense *f*, péché *m*; (*Jur*) **it is an ~ to do that** il est contraire à la loi or il est illégal de faire cela; **first ~** premier délit *m*; **further ~** récidive *f*; **political ~** délit *m* or crime *m* politique; **capital ~** crime *m* capital; **to commit an ~** commettre un délit, commettre une infraction (à la loi); **~s against national security** atteintes *fpl* à la sécurité nationale; **he was charged with four ~s of indecent assault** il a été inculpé de quatre attentats à la pudeur; **~ against God** offense *f* faite à Dieu; **an ~ against common decency** un outrage aux bonnes mœurs; (*fig*) **it is an ~ to the eye** cela choque or offense la vue → **indictable** b (*NonC* = *insult*) **to give** or **cause ~ to sb** froisser or offenser qn; **to take ~ (at)** s'offenser (de), s'offusquer (de); **no ~ meant** il n'y a pas de mal!; **no ~ meant (but ...)!** je ne voulais pas vous offenser or froisser (mais ...)!; **no ~ to the Welsh, of course!** sans vouloir offenser les Gallois, bien sûr! c (*NonC*) (*Mil: as opposed to defence*) attaque *f*; (*US Sport*) **the ~** les attaquants *mpl* → **weapon**

offend [ə'fend] 1 VT [+ *person*] offenser; [+ *ears, eyes*] offusquer, choquer; [+ *reason*] choquer, heurter; **to be** or **become ~ed** (*at*) s'offenser (de), s'offusquer (de); **she was ~ed by** or **at my remark** mon observation l'a offensée or vexée; **you mustn't be ~ed** or **don't be ~ed if I say ...** sans vouloir vous offenser or vous vexer, je dois dire ...; **it ~s my sense of justice** cela va à l'encontre de or cela choque mon sens de la justice 2 VI a (*gen*) choquer; **scenes that may ~** des scènes qui peuvent choquer b (*Jur*) commettre un délit or une infraction; **girls are less likely to ~ than boys** les filles ont moins tendance que les garçons à commettre des délits or infractions

► **offend against** VT FUS [+ *law, rule*] enfreindre, violer; [+ *good taste*] offenser; [+ *common sense*] être une insulte or un outrage à; **this bill ~s against good sense** ce projet de loi est une insulte au bon sens

offender [ə'fendər] N a (= *lawbreaker*) délinquant(e) *m(f)*; (*against traffic regulations etc*) contrevenant(e) *m(f)*; (*Jur*) **first ~** délinquant(e) *m(f)* primaire; **previous ~** récidiviste *mf*; **persistent** or **habitual ~** récidiviste *mf*; **sex ~** délinquant *m* sexuel; **young ~** jeune délinquant *m*; **carbon dioxide is one of the main environmental ~s** le dioxyde de carbone est l'un des principaux responsables de la dégradation de l'environnement; **small firms are the worst ~s when it comes to ...** les petites entreprises sont les plus coupables quand il s'agit de ... b (= *insulter*) offenseur *m*; (= *aggressor*) agresseur *m*

offending [ə'fendɪŋ] ADJ (*hum*) **the ~ word/object** *etc* le mot/l'objet *etc* incriminé

offense [ə'fens] N (*US*) = offence

offensive [ə'fensɪv] 1 ADJ a (= *shocking*) offensant, choquant; (= *hurtful*) blessant, vexant; (= *disgusting*) repoussant; (= *insulting*) grossier, injurieux; (= *rude, unpleasant*) déplaisant; **to be ~ to sb** [*person*] insulter or injurier qn; [*joke*] choquer qn; [*remark*] offenser qn; **~ language** propos *mpl* choquants, grossière-

tés *fpl*; **they found his behaviour very ~** sa conduite les a profondément choqués; **an ~ smell** une odeur repoussante b (*Mil, Sport*) [*action, tactics*] offensif 2 N (*Mil, Pol, Sport, Comm*) offensive *f*; **to be on the ~** avoir pris l'offensive; **to go on the ~** passer à l'offensive; **to take the ~** prendre l'offensive; **a sales/an advertising ~** une offensive commerciale/publicitaire; (*Pol*) **they mounted an ~ on the government** ils ont lancé une offensive contre le gouvernement; **a diplomatic ~** une offensive diplomatique → **peace** 3 COMP ► **offensive weapon** N (*Jur*) arme *f* offensive

offensively [ə'fensɪvlɪ] ADV a (= *abusively*) [*behave*] de manière offensante; [*shout*] de manière injurieuse; **~ rude** d'une impolitesse outrageante; **~ sexist** d'un sexisme offensant; **an ~ anti-German article** un article injurieux contre les Allemands b (= *unpleasantly*) [*loud, bland*] désagréablement; **to smell ~** sentir (très) mauvais c (*Mil, Sport*) [*use, deploy, play*] de manière offensive; (*Sport*) **to be good/poor ~** être bon/mauvais en attaque

▼ **offer** ['ɒfər] 1 N (*gen, Comm*) offre *f* (**of** de, **for** pour, **to do** de faire), proposition *f* (**of** de); [*of marriage*] demande *f* (en mariage); **to make a peace ~** faire une proposition or offre de paix; **make me an ~!** faites-moi une proposition or offre!; **I'm open to ~s** je suis ouvert à toute proposition; **it's my best ~** c'est mon dernier mot; **~s over/around £90,000** offres *fpl* au-dessus/autour de 90 000 livres; **he's had a good ~ for the house** on lui a fait une offre avantageuse or une proposition intéressante pour la maison; (*in advertisement*) **£50 or near(est) offer** or **best ~** 50 livres à débattre; (*lit, fig*) **he made me an ~ I couldn't refuse** il m'a fait une offre que je ne pouvais pas refuser; (*Comm*) **this brand is on ~** cette marque est en promotion; (*Comm*) **"on ~ this week"** ◊ **"this week's special ~"** « promotion de la semaine » 2 VT a [+ *job, gift, prayers, entertainment, food, friendship etc*] offrir (**to** à); [+ *help, money*] proposer (**to** à), offrir (**to** à); **to ~ to do** or **proposer de faire**; **he ~ed me a sweet** il m'a offert un bonbon; **she ~ed me her house for the holidays** elle m'a proposé sa maison pour les vacances; **to ~ o.s. for a mission** être volontaire or se proposer pour exécuter une mission; **to have a lot to ~** avoir beaucoup à offrir; (*Rel*) **to ~ a sacrifice** offrir un sacrifice, faire l'offrande d'un sacrifice; (*Mil*) **to ~ one's flank to the enemy** présenter le flanc à l'ennemi b (*fig*) [+ *apology, difficulty, opportunity, view, advantage*] offrir, présenter; [+ *remark*] suggérer; [+ *opinion*] émettre; [+ *facilities, guarantee, protection*] offrir → **resistance** 3 VI [*opportunity*] s'offrir, se présenter 4 COMP ► **offer of cover** N (*Fin*) promesse *f* de garantie ► **offer price** N (*St Ex*) prix *m* d'émission

► **offer up** VT SEP (*liter*) [+ *prayers*] offrir; [+ *sacrifice*] offrir, faire l'offrande de

offeree [ɒfə'riː] N (*Jur, Fin*) destinataire *m* de l'offre

offering ['ɒfərɪŋ] N (= *act, also thing offered*) offre *f*; (= *suggestion*) suggestion *f*; (*Rel*) offrande *f*, sacrifice *m* → **burnt, peace, thank**

offeror ['ɒfərər] N (*Jur, Fin*) auteur *m* de l'offre, offrant *m*

offertory ['ɒfətərɪ] 1 N (*Rel*) (= *part of service*) offertoire *m*, oblation *f*; (= *collection*) quête *f* 2 COMP ► **offertory box** N tronc *m*

offhand [ɒf'hænd] 1 ADJ (*also* **~ed**) a (= *casual*) [*person, manner*] désinvolte, sans-gêne *inv*; [*tone*] désinvolte b (= *curt*) brusque 2 ADV de but en blanc; **I can't say ~** je ne peux pas vous le dire comme ça*; **do you happen to know ~?** est-ce que vous pouvez me le dire de but en blanc?; **do you know ~**

whether ...? est-ce que vous pouvez me dire de but en blanc or comme ça* si ... ?

offhanded ['ɒf'hændɪd] ADJ = **offhand 1**

offhandedly ['ɒf'hændɪdlɪ] ADV [a] (= *casually*) avec désinvolture [b] (= *curtly*) avec brusquerie

offhandedness ['ɒf'hændɪdnɪs] N [a] (= *casualness*) désinvolture f, sans-gêne m [b] (= *curtness*) brusquerie f

office ['ɒfɪs] [1] N [a] (= *place, room*) bureau m ; (= *part of organization*) service m ; **lawyer's ~** étude f de notaire ; (*US*) **doctor's ~** cabinet m (médical) ; **our London ~** notre siège or notre bureau de Londres ; **the sales ~** le service des ventes ; **he works in an ~** il travaille dans un bureau, il est employé de bureau ; (*esp Brit*) **"usual ~s"** [*of house etc*] «sanitaires» → **box office, foreign, head, home, newspaper** [b] (= *function*) fonction f, charge f ; (= *duty*) fonctions fpl, devoir m ; (*frm*) **it is my ~ to ensure ...** j'ai charge d'assurer ..., il m'incombe d'assurer ... ; **he performs the ~ of treasurer** il fait fonction de trésorier ; **to hold ~** ◊ **to hold ~** [*mayor, chairman*] être en fonction, occuper sa charge ; [*government, minister*] détenir or avoir un portefeuille ; [*political party*] être au pouvoir or au gouvernement ; **to take or come into ~** [*chairman, mayor, government, minister*] entrer en fonction, prendre ses fonctions ; [*political party*] arriver au or prendre le pouvoir ; **he took ~ as prime minister in January** il est entré dans ses fonctions de premier ministre au mois de janvier ; **to go out of ~** [*mayor, chairman, minister*] quitter ses fonctions ; [*political party, government*] perdre le pouvoir ; **public ~** fonctions fpl officielles ; **to be in or hold public ~** occuper des fonctions officielles, être en fonction ; **to be disqualified from (holding) public ~** être révoqué → **jack, sweep** [c] **~s** offices mpl ; **through his good ~s** par ses bons offices ; **through the ~s of ...** par l'entremise de ... ; (*frm*) **to offer one's good ~s** offrir ses bons offices [d] (*Rel*) office m ; **Office for the Dead** office m funèbre or des morts → **divine[1]**

[2] COMP [*staff, furniture, work*] de bureau ► **office automation** N bureautique f ► **office bearer** N [*of club, society*] membre m du bureau or comité directeur ► **office block** N (*Brit*) immeuble m de bureaux ► **office boy** N garçon m de bureau ► **office building** N = **office block** ► **office holder** N = **office bearer** ► **office hours** NPL heures fpl de bureau ; **to work ~ hours** avoir des heures de bureau ► **office job** N **he's got an ~ job** il travaille dans un bureau ► **office junior** N employé(e) m(f) de bureau ► **office manager** N chef m de bureau ► **Office of Fair Trading** N ≈ Direction f générale de la concurrence, de la consommation et de la répression des fraudes ► **Office of Management and Budget** N (*US*) organisme chargé de gérer les ministères et de préparer le budget ► **office party** N fête f au bureau ► **office politics** N (*esp pej*) politique f interne ► **office space** N **"~ space to let"** «bureaux à louer» ; **100m² of ~ space** 100 m² de bureaux ► **office worker** N employé(e) m(f) de bureau

officer ['ɒfɪsə'] [1] N [a] (*Aviat, Mil, Naut*) officier m → **commission, man, petty** [b] (= *official*) [*of company, institution, organization, club*] membre m du bureau or comité directeur ; (*Admin, Jur*) **the Committee shall elect its ~** le comité désigne son bureau ; (*Jur*) **duly authorized ~** représentant m dûment habilité → **local** [c] **police ~** policier m ; **~ of the law** fonctionnaire m de police ; **the ~ in charge of the inquiry** l'inspecteur chargé or le fonctionnaire de police chargé de l'enquête ; (*to policeman*) **yes ~** oui, monsieur l'agent

[2] VT (*Mil*) (= *command*) commander ; (= *provide with officers*) pourvoir d'officiers or de cadres

[3] COMP ► **officer of the day** N (*Mil*) officier m or service m de jour ► **officer of the watch** N (*Naut*) officier m de quart ► **officers' mess** N mess m (des officiers) ► **Officers' Training Corps** N (*Brit Mil*) corps m volontaire de formation d'officiers

official [ə'fɪʃəl] [1] ADJ (*gen*) officiel ; [*uniform*] réglementaire ; **it's not yet ~** ce n'est pas encore officiel ; **~ biography/biographer** biographie f/biographe mf officiel(le) ; **he learned of her death through ~ channels** il a appris sa mort par des sources officielles ; **to apply for sth through ~ channels** faire la demande de qch par les voies officielles ; **"for ~ use only"** «réservé à l'administration»

[2] N (*gen, Sport etc* = *person in authority*) officiel m ; [*of civil service*] fonctionnaire mf ; [*of railways, post office etc*] employé(e) m(f) ; **the ~ in charge of ...** le (or la) responsable de ... ; **information/personnel ~** responsable mf de l'information/du personnel ; **town hall ~** employé(e) m(f) de mairie ; **local government ~** ≈ fonctionnaire mf (de l'administration locale) ; **government ~** fonctionnaire mf (de l'Administration) ; **an ~ of the Ministry** un représentant officiel du ministère → **elect**

[3] COMP ► **Official Receiver** N (*Brit Fin*) administrateur m judiciaire ► **the Official Secrets Act** N (*Brit*) loi relative aux secrets d'État

officialdom [ə'fɪʃəldəm] N (*NonC*) administration f, bureaucratie f (*also pej*)

officialese [ə,fɪʃə'liːz] N (*NonC: pej*) jargon m administratif

officially [ə'fɪʃəlɪ] ADV [a] (= *formally*) officiellement, à titre officiel ; (*Post*) **"may be opened ~"** «peut être ouvert d'office» [b] (= *theoretically*) en principe ; **~, she shares the flat with another girl** en principe, elle partage l'appartement avec une autre fille

officiate [ə'fɪʃɪeɪt] VI (= *arbitrate: at competition, sports match etc*) arbitrer ; (*Rel*) officier ; **to ~ as** remplir or exercer les fonctions de ; **to ~ at** assister à titre officiel à ; **to ~ at a wedding** célébrer un mariage

officious [ə'fɪʃəs] ADJ (*pej*) [*person, behaviour, manner*] trop empressé, zélé ; **to be ~** être trop empressé, faire du zèle

officiously [ə'fɪʃəslɪ] ADV (*pej*) avec un empressement or un zèle excessif

officiousness [ə'fɪʃəsnɪs] N (*pej*) excès m d'empressement or de zèle

offing ['ɒfɪŋ] N **in the ~** (*Naut*) au large ; (*fig*) en perspective

off-peak [ɒf'piːk] (*Brit*) [1] ADJ [*period, time*] creux ; [*train, service, journey, electricity*] en période creuse ; [*telephone call*] à tarif réduit (*aux heures creuses*) ; **~ rates or charges** tarif m réduit (*aux heures creuses*) ; (*Comm, Transport etc*) **~ hours** heures fpl creuses ; (*Rail etc*) **~ ticket** billet m au tarif réduit heures creuses [2] ADV [*travel, cost*] (*outside of rush hour*) en dehors des heures de pointe ; (*outside of holiday season*) en période creuse

offprint ['ɒfprɪnt] N (*Typ*) tirage m or tiré m à part ; **I'll send you an ~ of my article** je vous enverrai une copie de mon article

offset ['ɒfset] (*vb: pret, ptp* offset) [1] N [a] (= *counterbalancing factor*) compensation f ; **as an ~ to sth** pour compenser qch [b] (*Typ*) (= *process*) offset m ; (= *smudge etc*) maculage m [c] (*Bot*) rejeton m ; (*in pipe etc*) coude m, courbure f

[2] VT [a] (= *counteract, compensate for*) compenser ; **loans can be ~ against corporation tax** les emprunts peuvent venir en déduction de l'impôt sur les sociétés ; **the increase in pay costs was ~ by higher productiv**ity l'augmentation des coûts salariaux a été compensée par une amélioration de la productivité ; **they'll receive a large shipment of food to help ~ winter shortages** ils recevront une importante cargaison de nourriture pour compenser les pénuries de l'hiver [b] (= *weigh up*) **to ~ one factor against another** mettre en balance deux facteurs [c] (*Typ*) (= *print*) imprimer en offset ; (= *smudge*) maculer

[3] COMP ► **offset lithography** N (*Typ*) = **offset printing** ► **offset paper** N papier m offset ► **offset press** N presse f offset ► **offset printing** N offset m

offshoot ['ɒfʃuːt] N [*of plant, tree*] rejeton m ; [*of organization*] ramification f, antenne f ; [*of scheme, discussion, action*] conséquence f ; **a firm with many ~s** une société aux nombreuses ramifications

offshore [ɒf'ʃɔːr] [1] ADJ [a] (= *out at sea*) [*rig, platform*] offshore inv ; [*drilling, well*] en mer ; **Britain's ~ oil industry** l'industrie pétrolière offshore la Grande-Bretagne ; **~ worker** ouvrier m travaillant sur une plateforme offshore [b] (= *near land*) [*reef, island*] proche du littoral ; [*waters*] côtier, proche du littoral ; [*fishing*] côtier [c] (= *from land*) [*wind, breeze*] de terre [d] (*Fin*) [*investment, fund, banking, account*] offshore inv, extraterritorial ; **~ orders** commandes fpl d'outre-mer [2] ADV [a] (= *near coast*) [*lie, anchor, fish*] au large ; (*nearer*) en vue des côtes ; **20 miles ~** à 20 milles de la côte [b] (= *away from coast*) [*sail*] vers le large [c] (*Fin*) **to invest ~** faire des investissements offshore or extraterritoriaux ; **to move one's operations ~** se délocaliser

offside ['ɒf'saɪd] [1] N [a] (*Sport*) hors-jeu m inv [b] (*Aut*) (*in Brit*) côté m droit ; (*in France, US etc*) côté m gauche [2] ADJ [a] (*Sport*) **to be ~** être hors jeu ; **the ~ rule** la règle du hors-jeu [b] (*Aut*) (*in Brit*) de droite ; (*in France, US etc*) de gauche

offspring ['ɒfsprɪŋ] N (*pl inv*) progéniture f (*NonC*) ; (*fig*) fruit m, résultat m ; (*hum*) **how are your ~?*** comment va votre progéniture ?*, comment vont vos rejetons ?*

offstage ['ɒf'steɪdʒ] ADV, ADJ (*Theat*) dans les coulisses

Ofgas ['ɒfgæs] N (*Brit*) organisme de contrôle des réseaux de distribution du gaz

Oflot ['ɒflɒt] N (*Brit*) organisme de contrôle de la loterie nationale

Ofsted ['ɒfsted] N (*Brit*) organisme de contrôle des établissements scolaires

OFT N (*Brit*) (ABBR = **Office of Fair Trading**) ≈ DGCCRF f

oft [ɒft] ADV (*liter*) maintes fois, souvent ; **many a time and ~** maintes et maintes fois

oft- [ɒft] PREF **~repeated** souvent répété ; **~quoted** souvent cité ; **~times**†† souventes fois†

Oftel ['ɒftel] N (*Brit*) organisme de contrôle des réseaux de télécommunication

often ['ɒfən, 'ɒftən] ADV souvent ; **(all) too ~** trop souvent ; **it cannot be said too ~ that ...** on ne dira or répétera jamais assez que ... ; **once too ~** une fois de trop ; **every so ~** (*in time*) de temps en temps, de temps à autre ; (*in spacing, distance*) çà et là ; **as ~ as he did it** chaque fois or toutes les fois qu'il la fait ; **as ~ as not** ◊ **more ~ than not** la plupart du temps ; **how ~ have I warned you about him?** combien de fois t'ai-je dit de te méfier de lui ? ; **how ~ do the boats leave?** tous les bateaux partent les combien ? ; **how ~ she had asked herself that very question!** combien de fois elle s'était justement posé cette question !

Ofwat ['ɒfwɒt] N (*Brit*) organisme de contrôle des réseaux de distribution d'eau

ogival [əʊ'dʒaɪvəl] ADJ ogival, en ogive

ogive ['əʊdʒaɪv] N ogive f (*Archit*)

ogle* ['əʊgl] VT reluquer*, lorgner

ogre ['əʊgə'] N ogre *m*
ogress ['əʊgrɪs] N ogresse *f*
OH ABBR = **Ohio**
oh [əʊ] EXCL [a] oh!, ah!; **oh dear!** oh là là!, (oh) mon Dieu!; **oh what a waste of time!** quelle perte de temps!; **oh for some fresh air!** si seulement on pouvait avoir un peu d'air frais!; **oh to be in France!** si seulement je pouvais être en France!; **oh really?** ce n'est pas vrai!; **he's going with her — oh is he!** (neutral) il y a avec elle — tiens, tiens *or* ah bon!; (surprise) il y a avec elle — vraiment!; (disapproval) il y a avec elle — je vois!; **oh no you don't! — oh yes I do!** ah mais non! — ah mais si *or* oh que si!; **oh, just a minute ...** euh, une minute ... [b] (cry of pain) aïe!
Ohio [əʊ'haɪəʊ] N l'Ohio *m*; **in ~** dans l'Ohio
ohm [əʊm] N ohm *m*
OHMS [əʊeɪtʃem'es] (Brit) (ABBR = **On His** *or* **Her Majesty's Service**) → **majesty**
OHP N (ABBR = **overhead projector**) → **overhead**
oi(c)k♯ [ɔɪk] N (Brit) péquenaud♯ *m*
oil [ɔɪl] [1] [a] (NonC: Geol, Ind etc) pétrole *m*; **to find** *or* **strike ~** (lit) trouver du pétrole; (fig) trouver le filon; (fig) **to pour ~ on troubled waters** ramener le calme → **crude** [b] (Art) huile *f*; **painted in ~s** peint à l'huile; **to paint in ~s** faire de la peinture à l'huile; **an ~ by Picasso** une huile de Picasso [c] (Aut) huile *f*; **to check the ~** vérifier le niveau d'huile; **to change the ~** faire la vidange [d] (Culin, Pharm etc) huile *f*; **fried in ~** frit à l'huile; **~ and vinegar dressing** vinaigrette *f* → **hair, palm², midnight** [2] VT [+ machine] graisser, lubrifier; (fig) **to ~ the wheels** *or* **works** mettre de l'huile dans les rouages; (fig) **to be well ~ed♯** (= drunk) être beurré♯, être paf♯ *inv* → **oiled** [3] COMP [industry, shares] pétrolier; [prices, king, magnate, millionaire] du pétrole ► **oil-based paint** N peinture *f* glycérophtalique *or* à l'huile ► **oil-burning** ADJ [lamp] à pétrole, à huile; [stove] [paraffin] à pétrole; (fuel oil) à mazout; [boiler] à mazout ► **oil change** N (Aut) vidange *f* ► **oil colour** N peinture *f* à l'huile ► **oil-cooled** ADJ à refroidissement par huile ► **oil deposits** NPL gisements *mpl* pétrolifères *or* de pétrole ► **oil drill** N trépan *m* ► **oil drum** N baril *m* de pétrole ► **oil filter** N (Aut) filtre *m* à huile ► **oil find** N (Geol) découverte *f* de pétrole ► **oil-fired** ADJ [boiler] à mazout; [central heating] au mazout ► **oil gauge** N jauge *f* de niveau d'huile ► **oil industry** N industrie *f* pétrolière, secteur *m* pétrolier ► **oil installation** N installation *f* pétrolière ► **oil lamp** N lampe *f* à huile *or* à pétrole ► **oil level** N (Aut) niveau *m* d'huile ► **oil men** NPL pétroliers *mpl* ► **oil of cloves** N essence *f* de girofle ► **oil paint** N peinture *f* à l'huile; (Art) couleur *f* à l'huile ► **oil painting** N (= picture, occupation) peinture *f* à l'huile; (fig) **she's no ~ painting** ce n'est vraiment pas une beauté ► **oil pipeline** N oléoduc *m*, pipe-line *m* ► **oil platform** N plateforme *f* pétrolière ► **oil pollution** N pollution *f* due aux hydrocarbures ► **oil pressure** N pression *f* d'huile ► **oil producers, oil-producing countries** NPL pays *mpl* producteurs de pétrole ► **oil refinery** N raffinerie *f* (de pétrole) ► **oil rig** N (on land) derrick *m*; (at sea) plateforme *f* pétrolière ► **oil sheik** N émir *m* du pétrole ► **oil slick** N (at sea) nappe *f* de pétrole; (on beach) marée *f* noire ► **oil spill** N (Naut, Road Transport etc) déversement *m* accidentel de pétrole ► **oil storage tank** N (Ind) réservoir *m* de stockage de pétrole; (for central heating) cuve *f* à mazout ► **oil stove** N (paraffin) poêle *m* à pétrole; (fuel oil) poêle *m* à mazout ► **oil tank** N (Ind) réservoir *m* de pétrole; (for central heating) cuve *f* à mazout ► **oil tanker** N (= ship) pétrolier *m*, tanker *m*; (= truck) camion-citerne *m* (à pétrole) ► **oil ter-**

minal N port *m* d'arrivée *or* de départ pour le pétrole ► **oil well** N puits *m* de pétrole
oilcake ['ɔɪlkeɪk] N tourteau *m* (pour bétail)
oilcan ['ɔɪlkæn] N (for lubricating) burette *f* d'huile *or* de graissage; (for storage) bidon *m* d'huile
oilcloth ['ɔɪlklɒθ] N toile *f* cirée
oiled [ɔɪld] ADJ [a] [cloth, paper] huilé [b] (♯ = drunk: also **well ~**) beurré♯, soûl*
oiler ['ɔɪlə'] [1] N (= ship) pétrolier *m*; (= can) burette *f* à huile *or* de graissage; (= person) graisseur *m* [2] **oilers** NPL (US = clothes) ciré *m*
oilfield ['ɔɪlfiːld] N gisement *m* pétrolifère *or* de pétrole, champ *m* de pétrole
oiliness ['ɔɪlɪnɪs] N [a] [of liquid, consistency, stain] aspect *m* huileux; [of cooking, food] aspect *m* gras; (= greasiness) [of skin, hair] aspect *m* gras [b] (pej) [of manners, tone etc] onctuosité *f*
oilpan ['ɔɪlpæn] N (US Aut) carter *m*
oilpaper ['ɔɪlpeɪpə'] N papier *m* huilé
oilseed rape ['ɔɪlsiːd'reɪp] N (Bot) colza *m*
oilskin ['ɔɪlskɪn] [1] N toile *f* cirée [2] **oilskins** NPL (Brit = clothes) ciré *m* [3] ADJ en toile cirée
oilstone ['ɔɪlstəʊn] N pierre *f* à aiguiser (lubrifiée avec de l'huile)
oily ['ɔɪlɪ] [1] ADJ [a] (= greasy) [skin, hair, food, cooking] gras (grasse *f*); [hands] graisseux, gras (grasse *f*); [rag, clothes] graisseux; [stain] d'huile; [liquid, consistency, substance, flavour] huileux; [road] couvert d'huile; [beach] mazouté [b] (pej = smarmy) [person, manner, voice, tone] onctueux, mielleux [2] COMP ► **oily fish** N (Culin) poisson *m* gras
oink [ɔɪŋk] [1] VI [pig] grogner [2] N grognement *m*
ointment ['ɔɪntmənt] N onguent *m*, pommade *f*
OK¹ ABBR = **Oklahoma**
OK²♯ ['əʊ'keɪ] (vb: pret, ptp **OK'd**) [1] EXCL d'accord!, O.K.* *or* OK*!; **OK, OK!** (= don't fuss) ça va, ça va!; **OK, the next subject on the agenda is ...** bon, le point suivant à l'ordre du jour est ... [2] ADJ [a] (= agreed) parfait, très bien; (= in order) en règle; (on draft etc: as approval) (lu et) approuvé; **I'm coming too, OK?** je viens aussi, d'accord *or* O.K.*?; **leave me alone, OK?** tu me laisses tranquille, compris* *or* O.K.*? [b] (= acceptable) **it's OK by me** *or* **with me!** (je suis) d'accord!, ça me va!, O.K.!*; **is it OK with you if I come too?** ça ne vous ennuie pas si je vous accompagne?; **this car is OK but I prefer the other one** cette voiture n'est pas mal mais je préfère l'autre [c] (= no problem) **everything's OK** tout va bien; **it's OK(, it's not your fault)** ce n'est pas grave, ce n'est pas de ta faute; **can I help? — it's OK, I'm sure I'll manage** je peux vous aider? — ne vous en faites pas, ça va aller; **thanks! — that's OK** merci! — de rien [d] (= undamaged, in good health) **are you OK?** (gen) tu vas bien?; (after accident) tu n'as rien?; **I'm OK** (gen) je vais bien, ça va (bien); (after accident) je n'ai rien; **he's OK, he's only bruised** il n'a rien de grave, seulement quelques bleus; **the car is OK** (= undamaged) la voiture est intacte *or* n'a rien; (= repaired, functioning) la voiture marche *or* est en bon état [e] (= likeable) **he's OK** ◊ **he's an OK guy** c'est un type bien* [f] (= well provided for) **another drink? — no thanks, I'm OK (for now)** un autre verre? — non merci, ça va (pour le moment); **are you OK for cash/work?** question argent/travail etc, ça va *or* tu n'as pas de problème? [3] ADV (recovering from illness, operation) **she's doing OK** elle va bien; (socially, financially, in career) **she's doing OK (for herself)** elle se dé-

brouille *or* se défend bien; **we managed OK for the first year** nous nous sommes bien débrouillés la première année
[4] VT [+ document, plan] approuver; **his doctor wouldn't OK the trip** son docteur ne voulait pas donner son accord pour le voyage
[5] N (gen) **to give the** *or* **one's OK** donner son accord (to à); **to give** *or* **one's OK to a plan** donner le feu vert à un projet; **I'm free to start work as soon as I get the OK** je suis prêt à commencer à travailler dès que j'aurai reçu le feu vert
okapi [əʊ'kɑːpɪ] N (pl **okapis** *or* **okapi**) okapi *m*
okay♯ ['əʊ'keɪ] = **OK²**
okey-doke(y)♯ ['əʊkɪ'dəʊk(ɪ)] EXCL d'ac!*, O.K.* *or* OK*!
Okie ['əʊkiː] N (US) travailleur *m* agricole migrant
Okla ABBR = **Oklahoma**
Oklahoma [əʊklə'həʊmə] N l'Oklahoma *m*; **in ~** dans l'Oklahoma
okra ['əʊkrə] N gombo *m*, okra *m*
ol'♯ [əʊl] ADJ (esp US) = **old**
old [əʊld] [1] ADJ [a] (= aged, not young) vieux (vieille *f*), vieil (*m* before vowel), âgé; **an ~ man** un vieil homme, un vieillard; **an ~ lady** une vieille dame; **an ~ woman** une vieille femme; **he's a real ~ woman** il a des manies de petite vieille; **a poor ~ man** un pauvre vieillard, un pauvre vieux*; **~ people** ◊ **~ folk*** ◊ **~ folks*** les personnes *fpl* âgées; (disrespectful) les vieux *mpl*; **the ~er generation** la génération antérieure *or* précédente; **~er people** les personnes *fpl* d'un certain âge; **it will appeal to ~ and young (alike)** cela plaira aux vieux comme aux jeunes, cela plaira à tous les âges; **to have an ~ head on young shoulders** être mûr pour son âge, faire preuve d'une maturité précoce; **~ for his age** *or* **his years** mûr pour son âge; **to be/grow ~ before one's time** être vieux/vieillir avant l'âge; **to grow** *or* **get ~(er)** vieillir; **he's getting ~** il vieillit; **that dress is too ~ for you** cette robe te vieillit, cette robe fait trop vieux pour toi; **~ Mr Smith** le vieux M. Smith; **~ Smith*** ◊ **~ man Smith*** le vieux Smith, le (vieux) père Smith* → **4**; → **fogey, Methuselah, ripe, salt** [b] (*: as term of affection) **~ Paul here** ce bon vieux Paul; **he's a good ~ dog** c'est un brave (vieux) chien; **you ~ scoundrel!** sacré vieux!; **I say, ~ man** *or* **~ fellow** *or* **~ chap** *or* **~ boy†** dites donc, mon vieux*; **my** *or* **the ~ man♯** (= husband) le patron*; (= father) le *or* mon paternel♯, le *or* mon vieux♯; **my** *or* **the ~ woman♯** *or* **lady♯** (= wife) la patronne*, ma bourgeoise*; (= mother) la *or* ma mater♯, la *or* ma vieille♯ [c] (of specified age) **how ~ are you?** quel âge as-tu?; **he is ten years ~** il a dix ans; **at ten years ~** à (l'âge de) dix ans; **a six-year-~ boy** ◊ **a boy (of) six years ~** un garçon (âgé de) six ans; **a three-year-~** (= child) un(e) enfant de trois ans; (= horse) un cheval de trois ans; (gen) **for 10 to 15-year-~s** destiné aux 10-15 ans; **the firm is 80 years ~** la compagnie a 80 ans; **too ~ for that sort of work** trop vieux *or* âgé pour ce genre de travail; **I didn't know he was as ~ as that** je ne savais pas qu'il avait cet âge-là; **if I live to be as ~ as that** si je vis jusqu'à cet âge-là; (to child) **when you're ~er** quand tu seras plus grand; **if I were ~er** si j'étais plus âgé; **if I were ten years ~er** si j'avais dix ans de plus; **he is ~er than you** il est plus âgé que toi; **he's six years ~er than you** il a six ans de plus que toi; **~er brother/son** frère *m*/fils *m* aîné; **his ~est son** son fils aîné; **she's the ~est** elle est *or* c'est elle la plus âgée, elle est l'aînée; **he is ~ enough to dress himself** il est assez grand pour s'habiller tout seul; **they are ~ enough to vote** ils sont en âge de voter; **you're ~ enough to know better!** à ton âge tu devrais avoir plus de bon sens!;

she's ~ enough to be his mother! elle a l'âge d'être sa mère!, elle pourrait être sa mère! **d** (= *not new*) vieux (vieille *f*), vieil (*m before vowel*); (*with antique value*) ancien (*after n*); (= *of long standing*) vieux (vieille *f*), vieil (*m before vowel*); **an ~ building** un vieil immeuble, un immeuble ancien; **~ wine** vin *m* vieux; **that's an ~ one!** [*story, joke*] elle n'est pas nouvelle!, elle est connue!; [*trick etc*] ce n'est pas nouveau!; **the ~ part of Nice** le vieux Nice; **we're ~ friends** nous sommes de vieux amis *or* des amis de longue date; **an ~ family** une vieille famille, une famille de vieille souche → **4**; → **Adam, brigade, hand, hill, lag³, school¹**

e (= *former*) [*school, mayor, home*] ancien (*before n*); (*Brit Scol*) **~ boy** ancien élève *m* → **4**; (*Brit Scol*) **~ girl** ancienne élève *f*; **this is the ~ way of doing it** c'est comme ça que l'on faisait autrefois; (*Mil*) **~ campaigner** vétéran *m*; **in the ~ days** dans le temps, autrefois, jadis; **they chatted about ~ times** ils ont causé du passé; **just like ~ times!** comme au bon vieux temps!; **in the good ~ days** *or* **times** au bon vieux temps; **those were the good ~ days** c'était le bon vieux temps → **4**; → **school¹, soldier**

f (**: as intensifier*) **any ~ how/where** *etc* n'importe comment/où *etc*; **any ~ thing** n'importe quoi; **we had a great ~ time** on s'est vraiment bien amusé; (*fig*) **it's the same ~ story** c'est toujours la même histoire; **it isn't (just) any ~ painting, it's a Rembrandt** ce n'est pas n'importe quel tableau, c'est un Rembrandt

2 N **(in days) of ~** autrefois, (au temps) jadis; **the men of ~** les hommes *mpl* du temps jadis; **I know him of ~** je le connais depuis longtemps

3 **the old** NPL les vieux *mpl*, les vieillards *mpl*

4 COMP ► **old age** N vieillesse *f*; **in his ~ age** dans sa vieillesse, sur ses vieux jours ► **old age pension** N (pension *f* de) retraite *f* (*de la sécurité sociale*) ► **old age pensioner** N (*Brit*) retraité(e) *m(f)* ► **Old Bailey** N (*Brit Jur*) cour d'assises de Londres ► **(the) Old Bill** N (*Brit*) les poulets *mpl*, la rousse; ► **the old boy network** N (*Brit*) le réseau de relations des anciens élèves des écoles privées; **he heard of it through the ~ boy network** il en a entendu parler par ses relations ► **the old country** N la mère patrie ► **the Old Dominion** N (*US*) la Virginie ► **Old English** N (*Ling*) vieil anglais *m* ► **Old English sheepdog** N *m* ► **old-established** ADJ ancien (*after n*), établi (depuis longtemps) ► **old-fashioned** ADJ → **old-fashioned** ► **Old folks' home** ► **old people's home** ► **Old French** N (*Ling*) ancien *or* vieux français *m* ► **Old Glory** N (*US*) la bannière étoilée (*drapeau des États-Unis*) ► **old gold** ADJ (= *colour*) vieil *or* inv ► **old guard** N → **guard** ► **old hat** N (*fig*) **that's ~ hat!*** c'est vieux!, c'est dépassé! ► **old-line** ADJ (*Pol etc*) ultraconservateur (-trice *f*), ultratraditionaliste ► **old-looking** ADJ qui a un vieil air ► **old maid** N (*pej*) vieille fille *f* ► **old-maidish** ADJ (*pej*) [*habits*] de vieille fille; **she's very ~-maidish** elle fait très vieille fille ► **Old Man River** N (*US*) le Mississippi ► **old master** N (*Art*) (= *artist*) grand peintre *m*, grand maître *m* (de la peinture); (= *painting*) tableau *m* de maître ► **old money** N vieilles fortunes *fpl* ► **old people's home** N maison *f* de retraite ► **old school tie** N (*Brit*) (*lit*) cravate *f* aux couleurs de son ancienne école; (*fig*) réseau *m* des relations; (*fig*) **it's the ~ school tie** c'est l'art de faire marcher ses relations ► **the Old South** N (*US Hist*) le vieux Sud (*d'avant la guerre de Sécession*) ► **old stager** N vétéran *m*, vieux routier *m* ► **old-style** ADJ à l'ancienne (mode) ► **Old Testament** N Ancien Testament *m* ► **old-time** ADJ du temps jadis; (*older*) ancien (*before n*); **~-time**

dancing danses *fpl* d'autrefois ► **old-timer*** N (*US*) vieillard *m*, ancien *m*; (*as term of address*) le vieux, l'ancien *m* ► **old wives' tale** N conte *m* de bonne femme ► **old-womanish** ADJ (*pej*) [*behaviour, remark*] de petite vieille; **she's very ~-womanish** on dirait vraiment une petite vieille ► **the Old World** N le Vieux *or* l'Ancien Monde *m* ► **old-world** ADJ → **old-world**

olde†† [ˈəʊldɪ] ADJ d'antan (*liter*)

olden [ˈəʊldən] ADJ (*liter*) **~ days** *or* **times** le temps jadis; **the quaint customs of ~ times** les curieuses coutumes d'antan; **in (the) ~ days** dans le temps jadis; **in ~ times** jadis, autrefois

olde-worlde [ˈəʊldˈwɜːldɪ] ADJ (*hum or pej*) (*genuinely*) vieillot (-otte *f*); (*pseudo*) faussement ancien (*after n*)

old-fashioned [ˈəʊldˈfæʃnd] **1** ADJ **a** (= *not modern*) démodé; (= *traditional*) traditionnel; **to look ~** faire vieux jeu; **a good ~ love story** une bonne vieille histoire d'amour; **she is a good ~ kind of teacher** c'est un professeur de la vieille école; **good ~ discipline** la bonne (vieille) discipline d'autrefois; **good ~ home cooking** la bonne (vieille) cuisine à l'ancienne **b** (= *not progressive*) [*person, attitude, ideas, values, virtues*] vieux jeu *inv*, dépassé **c** (*Brit = disapproving*) **to give sb an ~ look†** regarder qn de travers **2** N (*US = cocktail*) old-fashioned *m* (*cocktail à base de whisky*)

oldie* [ˈəʊldɪ] N (= *film, song*) vieux succès* *m*; (= *person*) croulant(e)* *m(f)*; (= *joke*) bonne vieille blague *f* → **golden**

oldish [ˈəʊldɪʃ] ADJ assez vieux (vieille *f*), assez vieil (*m before vowel*)

oldster* [ˈəʊldstə^r] N (*US*) ancien *m*, vieillard *m*

old-world [ˈəʊldˈwɜːld] ADJ **a** (= *traditional*) [*charm, atmosphere*] suranné, désuet (-ète *f*); [*village, cottage*] de l'ancien temps; **an ~ interior** un intérieur de style ancien; **Stratford is very ~** Stratford est une ville au charme suranné **b** (*Geog*) [*country*] du vieux monde *or* continent

OLE [ˈəʊelˈiː] N (*Comput*) (ABBR = **object linking and embedding**) liaison *f* OLE

ole* [əʊl] ADJ (*esp US: often hum*) = **old**

oleaginous [ˌəʊlɪˈædʒɪnəs] ADJ oléagineux

oleander [ˌəʊlɪˈændə^r] N laurier-rose *m*

olefine [ˈəʊlɪfiːn] N oléfine *f*

oleo* [ˈəʊlɪəʊ] N (*US*) ABBR = **oleomargarine**

oleo... [ˈəʊlɪəʊ] PREF olé(i)..., olé(o)...

oleomargarine [ˌəʊlɪəʊˈmɑːdʒəriːn] N (*US*) margarine *f*

olfactory [ɒlˈfæktərɪ] ADJ olfactif

oligarchic(al) [ˌɒlɪˈgɑːkɪk(əl)] ADJ oligarchique

oligarchy [ˈɒlɪgɑːkɪ] N oligarchie *f*

Oligocene [ˈɒlɪgəʊsiːn] ADJ, N oligocène *m*

oligopoly [ˌɒlɪˈgɒpəlɪ] N oligopole *m*

olive [ˈɒlɪv] **1** N **a** olive *f*; (*also* **~ tree**) olivier *m*; (*also* **~ wood**) (bois *m* d')olivier *m* → **mount b** (= *colour*) (vert *m*) olive *m* **2** ADJ (*also* **~-coloured**) [*paint, cloth*] (vert) olive *inv*; [*complexion, skin*] olivâtre **3** COMP ► **olive branch** N (*fig*) **to hold out the ~ branch to sb** tendre à qn le rameau d'olivier ► **olive drab** (*US*) ADJ gris-vert (olive) *inv* ♦ N toile *f* de couleur gris-vert (olive) (*utilisée pour les uniformes de l'armée des USA*) ► **olive-green** ADJ (vert) olive *inv* ♦ N (vert *m*) olive *m* ► **olive grove** N olivaie *f* *or* oliveraie *f* ► **olive oil** N huile *f* d'

Oliver [ˈɒlɪvə^r] N Olivier *m*

Olympia [əˈlɪmpɪə] N **a** (*in Greece*) Olympie *f* **b** (*Brit*) nom du palais des expositions de Londres

Olympiad [əˈlɪmpɪæd] N olympiade *f*

Olympian [əˈlɪmpɪən] **1** ADJ (*Myth, fig*) olympien **2** N (*Myth*) dieu *m* de l'Olympe, Olympien *m*; (*Sport*) athlète *mf* olympique

Olympic [əˈlɪmpɪk] **1** ADJ olympique **2** **the Olympics** NPL les Jeux *mpl* olympiques **3** COMP ► **the Olympic flame** N la flamme olympique ► **the Olympic Games** NPL les Jeux *mpl* olympiques ► **the Olympic torch** N le flambeau olympique

Olympus [əˈlɪmpəs] N (*Geog, Myth: also* **Mount ~**) le mont Olympe, l'Olympe *m*

OM [əʊˈem] (*Brit*) (ABBR = **Order of Merit**) → **order**

Oman [əʊˈmɑːn] N **(the Sultanate of) ~** (le Sultanat d')Oman *m*

Omani [əʊˈmɑːnɪ] **1** N Omanais(e) *m(f)* **2** ADJ omanais

Omar Khayyám [ˈəʊmɑːkaɪˈɑːm] N Omar Khayam *m*

OMB [əʊemˈbiː] N (*US*) (ABBR = **Office of Management and Budget**) organisme chargé de gérer les ministères et de préparer le budget

ombudsman [ˈɒmbʊdzmən] N (*pl* **-men**) médiateur *m*, ombudsman *m* (*Admin*), protecteur *m* du citoyen (*Can*)

omega [ˈəʊmɪgə] N oméga *m*

omelet(te) [ˈɒmlɪt] N omelette *f*; **cheese ~** omelette *f* au fromage ■ (*PROV*) **you can't make an ~ without breaking eggs** on ne fait pas d'omelette sans casser des œufs (*PROV*)

omen [ˈəʊmən] N présage *m*, augure *m*; **it is a good ~ that ...** il est de bon augure *or* c'est un bon présage que ... (+ *subj*); **of ill** *or* **bad ~** de mauvais augure *or* présage → **bird**

omentum [əʊˈmentəm] N (*pl* **omenta** [əʊˈmentə]) épiploon *m*; **lesser/greater ~** petit/grand épiploon *m*

ominous [ˈɒmɪnəs] ADJ [*sign, development, event*] de mauvais augure; [*warning, tone, look, clouds*] menaçant; [*sound*] sinistre, inquiétant; **there was an ~ silence** il y eut un silence qui ne présageait rien de bon; **to look/sound ~** ne rien présager de bon

ominously [ˈɒmɪnəslɪ] ADV [*say*] d'un ton sinistre; [*loom, creak*] de façon sinistre *or* inquiétante; **he was ~ quiet** son silence ne présageait rien de bon; **this sounded ~ like a declaration of war** ceci ressemblait de façon inquiétante à une déclaration de guerre; **the deadline was drawing ~ close** l'heure limite s'approchait de façon inquiétante; **more ~, the government is talking of reprisals** fait plus inquiétant, le gouvernement parle de représailles

omission [əʊˈmɪʃən] N (= *thing omitted*) omission *f*, lacune *f*; (*Typ*) (= *words omitted*) bourdon *m*; (= *act of omitting*) omission *f*, oubli *m*; **it was an ~ on my part** c'est un oubli de ma part → **sin**

omit [əʊˈmɪt] VT (*accidentally*) omettre, oublier (**to do** de faire); (*deliberately*) omettre, négliger (**to do** de faire); **to ~ any reference to sth** passer qch sous silence

omni... [ˈɒmnɪ] PREF omni...

omnibus [ˈɒmnɪbəs] **1** N **a** († = *bus*) omnibus‡ *m* **b** = **omnibus edition c** (= *book*) recueil *m* **2** ADJ [*device*] à usage multiple **3** COMP ► **omnibus bill** N (*US Pol*) projet *m* de loi fourre-tout ► **omnibus edition** N (*Publishing*) gros recueil *m*; (*Brit TV, Rad*) récapitulation des épisodes de la semaine ou du mois

omnidirectional [ˌɒmnɪdɪˈrekʃənl] ADJ omnidirectionnel

omnipotence [ɒmˈnɪpətəns] N omnipotence *f*, toute-puissance *f*

omnipotent [ɒmˈnɪpətənt] **1** ADJ [*God, person, figure*] omnipotent; [*power*] absolu **2** N **the Omnipotent** le Tout-Puissant

omnipresence [ˌɒmnɪˈprezəns] N omniprésence *f*

omnipresent [ˈɒmnɪˈprezənt] ADJ omniprésent

omniscience [ɒmˈnɪsɪəns] N omniscience *f*

omniscient [ɒmˈnɪsɪənt] ADJ omniscient

omnivore [ˈɒmnɪvɔːʳ] N omnivore *m*

omnivorous [ɒmˈnɪvərəs] ADJ [*animal, person, diet*] omnivore ; (*fig*) [*reader*] vorace

---

on [ɒn]

1	ADVERB	3	ADJECTIVE
2	PREPOSITION	4	COMPOUNDS

1 ADVERB

When **on** *is the second element in a phrasal verb, eg* **have on**, **get on**, **go on**, **look up** *the verb. When it is part of a set combination, such as* **broadside on**, **farther on**, *look up the other word.*

a = in place the lid is on le couvercle est mis ; it was not on properly ça avait été mal mis ; on with your pyjamas! allez, mets ton pyjama !

b in time expressions from that time on à partir de ce moment-là ; it was well on in the night il était tard dans la nuit ; it was well on into September septembre était déjà bien avancé ; early on in the pregnancy au début de la grossesse ; the vital goal came late on le but décisif a été marqué en fin de partie

c indicating continuation let's drive on a bit continuons un peu (*en voiture*) ; if you read on, you'll see that ... si tu continues (à lire), tu verras que ...

d SET STRUCTURES

♦ **on and off*** par intermittence ; I'm still working as a waitress on and off je travaille toujours comme serveuse, par intermittence ou de temps à autre ; they lived together on and off for six years ils ont vécu six ans ensemble par intermittence

♦ **on and on**: they talked on and on for hours ils n'ont pas arrêté de parler pendant des heures ; the list goes on and on la liste n'en finit plus

♦ **to be on about sth*** (= talk) I don't know what you're on about qu'est-ce que tu racontes ?* → **go on**

♦ **to be on at sb*** (= nag) he is always on at me il est toujours après moi*

♦ **to be on to sb*** (= speak to) parler à qn ; he's been on to me about the broken window il m'a parlé de la fenêtre cassé ; I've been on to him on the phone je lui ai parlé ou je l'ai eu au téléphone → **get on to**

♦ **to be on to sb/sth*** (= have found out about) the police are on to him la police est sur sa piste ; I'm on to something je suis sur une piste intéressante ; archeologists knew they were on to something big les archéologues savaient qu'ils allaient faire une découverte importante ; she's on to the fact that we met yesterday elle a découvert ou elle a su que nous nous étions vus hier ; he's on to a good thing il a trouvé le filon*

2 PREPOSITION

When **on** *occurs in a set combination, eg* **on the right**, **on occasion**, **on the dole**, **to swear on**, **to lecture on**, *look up the other word.*

a indicating place, position sur, à

à *is not used in relation to a horizontal surface.*

on the pavement sur le trottoir ; a house on the main road une maison sur la route principale ; he threw it on (to) the table il l'a jeté sur la table ; I have no money on me je n'ai pas d'argent sur moi ; he climbed (up) on (to) the wall il a grimpé sur le mur ; there was mould on the bathroom walls il y avait de la moisissure sur les murs de la salle de bain ; there were posters on the wall il y avait des posters sur le mur ou au mur ; he hung his jacket on the hook il a suspendu sa veste à la patère ; what page are we on? à quelle page sommes-nous ? ; she had sandals on her feet elle avait des sandales aux pieds ; *BUT* the ring on her finger la bague

qu'elle avait au doigt ; on the other side of the road de l'autre côté de la route

on it *and* on them, (when them *refers to things*), are not translated by preposition + noun:
you can't wear that shirt, there's a stain on it tu ne peux pas porter cette chemise, il y a une tache dessus ; bottles with no labels on them des bouteilles sans étiquette ; envelopes with no stamps on them des enveloppes non affranchies

b with name of place on the continent of Europe sur le continent européen ; on an island dans ou sur une île ; on the island of ... à ou dans ou sur l'île de ... ; on Malta à Malte

c with street names dans ; I live on Main Street j'habite (dans) Main Street ; a house on North Street une maison dans North Street

d = on board dans ; there were a lot of people on the train/bus/plane il y avait beaucoup de monde dans le train/le bus/l'avion ; on the boat dans ou sur le bateau

♦ **to go/come on the train/bus**: I went on the train/bus j'ai pris le train/le bus ; he came on the train/bus il est venu en train/bus

e = at the time of

♦ **on** + noun: on my arrival home à mon arrivée à la maison ; on the death of his son à la mort de son fils ; on my refusal to go away devant mon refus de partir

♦ **on** + -ing: on hearing this en entendant cela ; on completing the course, she got a job in an office à la fin de son stage elle a trouvé un emploi dans un bureau

f with day, date on Sunday dimanche ; on Sundays le dimanche ; on 1 December le 1ᵉʳ décembre ; on the evening of 3 December le 3 décembre au soir ; on or about the 20th vers le 20 ; on or before 9 November le 9 novembre au plus tard ; on and after the 20th à partir ou à dater du 20 ; on Easter Day le jour de Pâques

g with number (score) avec ; (phone number) à ; Smith is second on 21, but Jones is top on 23 Smith est second avec 21, mais Jones le bat avec 23 points ; you can get me on 329 3065 tu peux m'appeler au 329 30 65

h Rad, TV à ; (name of channel) sur ; on the radio/TV à la radio/la télé* ; on the BBC à la BBC ; on Radio 3/Channel 4 sur Radio 3/ Channel 4 ; you're on air vous êtes en direct ou à l'antenne

i = earning, getting he's on £19,000 a year il gagne 19 000 livres par an ; how much are you on? combien gagnez-vous ? ; a student on a grant un boursier ou une boursière de l'enseignement supérieur

j = taking, using I'm back on cigarettes je me suis remis à fumer ; to be on drugs se droguer ; he's on heroin il se drogue à l'héroïne ; to be on the pill prendre la pilule ; (*rhetorical question*) what is he on?* à quoi il carbure ?* ; the doctor put her on antibiotics/Valium® le médecin l'a mise sous antibiotiques/Valium®

k = playing with Louis Armstrong on trumpet avec Louis Armstrong à la trompette ; he played it on the piano il l'a joué au piano

l = about, concerning sur ; a lecture/book on medical ethics un cours/livre sur l'éthique médicale ; an essay on this subject une dissertation sur ce sujet ; a decision on this project une décision sur ce projet ; *BUT* we've read Jones on Marx nous avons lu ce que Jones a écrit sur Marx ; have you heard him on VAT? vous l'avez entendu parler de la TVA ? ; while we're on the subject pendant que nous y sommes

m = doing he's on a course il suit un cours ; (away from office, home) il fait un stage ; he was away on an errand il était parti faire une course ; I'm on a new project je travaille à ou sur un nouveau projet

n = at the expense of we had a drink on the house nous avons bu un verre aux frais du patron ou de la maison ; this round's on me

c'est ma tournée ; the tickets are on me je vous paie le billet ; it's on me c'est moi qui paie

o indicating membership to be on the team/ committee faire partie de l'équipe/du comité ; he is on the "Evening News" il travaille à l'« Evening News »

3 ADJECTIVE

a = functioning, operative [machine, engine] en marche ; [radio, TV, electrical apparatus, light] allumé ; [handbrake] mis ; [electricity] branché ; [water tap, gas tap, gas main] ouvert ; leave the tap on laisse le robinet ouvert ; is the water on? est-ce que l'arrivée d'eau est ouverte ? ; don't leave the lights on! ne laisse pas les lumières allumées ; don't leave the lights on in the kitchen ne laisse pas la lumière allumée dans la cuisine ; the gas is still on le gaz est toujours allumé ; are you sure the handbrake is on? est-ce que tu as bien mis le frein à main ? ; the "on" switch l'interrupteur *m* ; the switch is in the "on" position l'interrupteur est enclenché ou en position « marche »

b = taking place there's a marvellous match on at Wimbledon at the moment il y a un très bon match à Wimbledon en ce moment ; while the meeting was on pendant la réunion ; is the party still on? est-ce que la fête a bien ou toujours lieu ? ; the search for a new Tory leader is on again le Parti conservateur est de nouveau en quête d'un leader

c = being performed, shown it's on in London [play] ça se joue à Londres ; [film] ça passe à Londres ; it's on for three nights [play] il y a trois représentations ; [film] ça passe trois soirs de suite ; it's still on [play, film] ça se joue encore, c'est encore à l'affiche ; what's on? (Theat, Cine) qu'est-ce qu'on joue ? ; (Rad, TV) qu'est-ce qu'il y a à la radio/à la télé ? ; (Rad, TV) "Eastenders"/Clive James is on tonight il y a « Eastenders »/Clive James ce soir ; (Rad, TV, Theat) you're on now! à vous (maintenant) ! ; you're on in five minutes c'est à vous dans cinq minutes

d = on duty I'm on every Saturday je travaille tous les samedis ; which doctor is on this morning? qui est le médecin de garde ce matin ? ; she's not on till 6 o'clock elle n'arrive pas avant 6 heures

e = available: in restaurant are the chops still on? il y a encore des côtelettes ?

f indicating agreement you're on!* d'accord ! ; are you on for dinner over here tonight?* est-ce que vous pouvez venir dîner ici ce soir ?

♦ **it's not on*** (Brit) (= not acceptable) c'est inadmissible ; (= not feasible) ce n'est pas concevable

♦ **you're not on!*** (= no way!) pas question !

4 COMPOUNDS

▶ **on-campus** ADJ (Univ) sur le campus, à l'université ▶ **on-costs** NPL (Brit Comm) frais *mpl* généraux ▶ **on day** N* he's having an on day today!* c'est son jour aujourd'hui !, il est dans un forme olympique aujourd'hui ! ▶ **on-glide** N (Phon) catastase *f* ▶ **on-line** (Comput) ADJ en ligne ♦ ADV to go on-line [computer] se mettre en mode interactif ; to put the printer on-line connecter l'imprimante ▶ **on-off** ADJ on-off switch interrupteur *m* marche-arrêt ; it's an on-off affair* [relationship, plan etc] c'est une affaire qui évolue en dents de scie ▶ **on screen** ADV (Cine, TV, Comput) à l'écran ▶ **on-screen** ADJ (Cine, TV, Comput) à l'écran ; their on-screen romance leur aventure sentimentale à l'écran ▶ **on-site** ADJ sur place ▶ **on-street parking** N stationnement *m* dans la rue ▶ **on-the-job** ADJ → **job 1b**

---

onanism [ˈəʊnənɪzəm] N onanisme *m*

ONC [ˌəʊenˈsiː] N (Brit Educ) (ABBR = **Ordinary National Certificate**) → **ordinary**

once [wʌns] **1** ADV **a** (= on one occasion) une fois ; he walked away without looking back ~ il est parti sans regarder une seule fois en arrière; **you ~ said you'd never do that** vous avez dit un jour que vous ne le feriez jamais; **only ~ ◊ ~ only** une seule fois → **3**; **he visited them only ~** il ne leur a rendu visite qu'une seule fois; **~ or twice** une ou deux fois, une fois ou deux; **more than ~** plus d'une fois; **never ~ ◊ not ~** pas une seule fois; **~ again ◊ ~ more** encore une fois, une fois de plus; **~ before** une fois déjà; **~ a week** tous les huit jours, une fois par semaine; **~ a month ◊ ~ every month** une fois par mois; **~ every fortnight/two days** une fois tous les quinze jours/tous les deux jours; **~ in a while** or **way** (une fois) de temps en temps, de temps à autre; **for ~** pour une fois, (**just) this ~** juste pour cette fois-ci, (juste) pour une fois; **~ and for all** une fois pour toutes; **~ a thief, always a thief** qui a volé volera; **~ a smoker, always a smoker** qui a été fumeur le restera toute sa vie

b (= *ever*) jamais; **if ~ you begin to hesitate** si jamais vous commencez à hésiter

c (= *formerly*) autrefois; **Texas was ~ ruled by Mexico** le Texas était autrefois gouverné par le Mexique; **a ~ powerful nation** une nation autrefois or jadis puissante; (*in children's stories*) **~ upon a time there were three little pigs** il était une fois trois petits cochons; (*historically*) **~ upon a time you could be hanged for stealing a sheep** autrefois or jadis, on pouvait être pendu pour avoir volé des moutons

d **at ~** (= *immediately*) immédiatement; (= *simultaneously*) en même temps; **all at ~** (= *simultaneously*) tous (toutes *fpl*) en même temps or à la fois; (= *suddenly*) tout à coup, soudain

2 CONJ une fois que; **~ she'd seen him she left** l'ayant vu or après l'avoir vu or une fois qu'elle l'eut vu elle s'en alla; **~ you give him the chance** si jamais on lui en donne l'occasion

3 COMP ► **once-only** ADJ **a ~-only offer** une offre unique ► **once-over*** N (= *quick look*) **to give sb the ~-over** jauger qn d'un coup d'œil; **to give sth the ~-over** vérifier qch très rapidement, jeter un coup d'œil rapide à qch; (= *quick clean*) **I gave the room a quick ~-over with the duster** j'ai donné or passé un coup (de chiffon) dans la pièce

oncologist [ɒŋˈkɒlədʒɪst] N oncologiste *mf*
oncology [ɒŋˈkɒlədʒɪ] N oncologie *f*
oncoming [ˈɒnkʌmɪŋ] **1** ADJ [*traffic, vehicle*] venant en sens inverse; [*headlights, troops*] qui approche (or approchait); [*winter, night*] qui arrive (or arrivait); [*danger*] imminent **2** N [*of winter etc*] approche *f*, arrivée *f*

OND [ˌəʊenˈdiː] N (*Brit Educ*) (ABBR = **Ordinary National Diploma**) → **ordinary**

one [wʌn] **1** ADJ **a** (*numerical*) un, une; **~ woman out of** or **in two** une femme sur deux; **~ or two people** une ou deux personnes; **a girl was pretty, the other was ugly** une des filles était jolie, l'autre était laide; **~ hundred and twenty** cent vingt; **God is ~** Dieu est un; **that's ~ way of doing it** c'est une façon (entre autres) de le faire, on peut aussi le faire comme ça; **she is ~ (year old)** elle a un an; **it's ~ o'clock** il est une heure; **for ~ thing I've got no money** d'abord or pour commencer je n'ai pas d'argent; **as ~ man** comme un seul homme; **as ~ woman** toutes ensemble; **with ~ voice** d'une seule voix

b (*indefinite*) un, une; **~ day** un jour; **~ Sunday morning** un (certain) dimanche matin; **~ hot summer afternoon she went ...** par un chaud après-midi d'été elle partit ...; **~ moment she's laughing, the next she's in tears** une minute elle rit, l'autre elle pleure

c (= *sole*) seul(e), unique; **the ~ man who could do it** le seul qui pourrait or puisse le faire; **no ~ man could do it** un homme ne pourrait le faire (à lui) seul; **my ~ and only pleasure** mon seul et unique plaisir; **the ~ and only Charlie Chaplin!** le seul, l'unique Charlot!

d (= *same*) (le/la) même, identique; **they all went in the ~ car** ils sont tous partis dans la même voiture; **they are ~ (and the same) person** ils sont une seule et même personne; **it's ~ and the same thing** c'est exactement la même chose

2 N **a** (= *numeral*) un(e) *m(f)*; **~, two, three** un(e), deux, trois; **twenty-~** vingt et un; **there are three ~s in her phone number** il y a trois un dans son numéro de téléphone; **~ of them** (*people*) l'un d'eux, l'une d'elles; (*things*) (l')un(e); **any ~ of them** (*people*) n'importe lequel d'entre eux, n'importe laquelle d'entre elles; (*things*) n'importe lequel, n'importe laquelle; **the last but ~** l'avant-dernier *m*, -ière *f*; **chapter ~** chapitre *m* un; (*Comm*) **price of ~** prix *m* à la pièce; **these items are sold in ~s** ces articles se vendent à la pièce

b (*phrases*) **I for ~ don't believe it** pour ma part je ne le crois pas; **who doesn't agree? — I for ~!** qui n'est pas d'accord? — moi par exemple or pour commencer!; **never (a) ~** pas un (seul); **~ by ~** un à un, un par un; **by** or **in ~s and twos** par petits groupes; **~ after the other** l'un après l'autre; **~ and all** tous tant qu'ils étaient, tous sans exception; **it's all ~** c'est tout un; **it's all ~ to me** cela m'est égal or indifférent; **~ and sixpence ††** un shilling et six pence; **he's president and secretary (all) in ~** il est à la fois président et secrétaire; **it's made all in ~** c'est fait d'une seule pièce or tout d'une pièce; **to be** or **have/go** or **get ~ up (on sb)*** avoir/prendre l'avantage (sur qn) → **4**; **to go ~ better than sb** faire mieux que qn; **he's had ~ too many*** il a bu un coup de trop* → **number, road**

3 PRON **a** (*indefinite*) un(e) *m(f)*; **would you like ~?** en voulez-vous (un)?; **have you got ~?** en avez-vous (un)?; **the problem is ~ of money** c'est une question d'argent; **~ of these days** un de ces jours; **he's ~ of my best friends** c'est un de mes meilleurs amis; **she's ~ of the family** elle fait partie de la famille; **he's ~ of us** il est des nôtres, il est un des nôtres; **the book is ~ which** or **that I've never read** c'est un livre que je n'ai jamais lu; **he's a teacher and I want to be ~ too** il est professeur et je veux l'être aussi; **every ~ of the boys/books** tous les garçons/les livres sans exception; **you can't have ~ without the other** on ne peut avoir l'un sans l'autre; **sit in ~ or other of the chairs** asseyez-vous sur l'une des chaises → **anyone, no, someone**

b (*specific*) **this ~** celui-ci, celle-ci; **these ~s** ceux-ci, celles-ci; **that ~** celui-là, celle-là; **those ~s** ceux-là, celles-là; **which ~?** lequel?, laquelle?; **which ~s?** lesquels?, lesquelles?; **which is the ~ you want?** lequel voulez-vous?; **the ~ who** or **that** celui qui, celle qui; **the ~ whom** or **that** celui que, celle que; **the ~ that** or **which is lying on the table** celui or celle qui se trouve sur la table; **the ~ on the floor** celui or celle qui est par terre; **here's my brother's ~*** voici celui or celle de mon frère; **he's the ~ with brown hair** c'est celui qui a les cheveux bruns; **he hit her ~ on the nose*** il lui a flanqué un coup sur le nez*; **I want the red ~/the grey ~s** je veux le rouge/les gris; **this grey ~ will do** ce gris-ci fera l'affaire; **mine's a better ~** le mien or la mienne est meilleur(e); **you've taken the wrong ~** vous n'avez pas pris le bon; **that's a difficult ~!** (= *question*) ça c'est difficile! → **eye, quick**

c (= *person*) **they thought of the absent ~** ils ont pensé à l'absent; **the little ~s** les petits *mpl*; **my dearest ~** mon chéri, ma chérie; **our dear ~s** ceux qui nous sont chers; († or *frm*) **~ John Smith** un certain or un nommé John Smith; **he's a clever ~** c'est un malin; **to sing as ~** chanter en chœur; **for ~ who claims to know the language, he ...** pour quelqu'un qui prétend connaître la langue, il ...; **he looked like ~ who had seen a ghost** il avait l'air de

quelqu'un qui aurait vu un fantôme; **to ~ who can read between the lines ...** à celui qui sait lire entre les lignes ...; **he's never** or **not ~ to agree to that sort of thing** il n'est pas de ceux qui acceptent ce genre de choses; **he's a great ~ for chess** c'est un mordu* des échecs; **I'm not ~** or **much of a ~* for sweets** je ne suis pas (grand) amateur de bonbons; **you are a ~!†*** tu en as de bonnes!* → **fine²**

d **~ another** = **each other**; → **each**

e (*impersonal*) (*subject*) on; (*object*) vous; **~ must try to remember** on doit or il faut se souvenir; **it tires ~ too much** cela vous fatigue trop; **~ likes to see one's friends happy** on aime voir ses amis heureux, on aime que ses amis soient heureux

4 COMP ► **one-...** ADJ d'un/une (seul(e)) ..., à un/une seul(e) ..., à ... unique ► **one-acter***, **one-act play** N pièce *f* en un acte ► **one-arm bandit** N = **one-armed bandit** ► **one-armed** ADJ manchot ► **one-armed bandit*** N machine *f* à sous, ≈ jackpot *m* ► **one-day** ADJ [*seminar, course*] d'une journée ► **one-dimensional** ADJ (*Math*) unidimensionnel; (*fig*) [*character*] d'une pièce, carré, [*story*] simpliste ► **one-eyed** ADJ [*person*] borgne; [*animal etc*] qui n'a qu'un œil ► **one-handed** ADJ [*person*] manchot, qui a une (seule) main; [*tool*] utilisable d'une (seule) main ♦ ADV d'une (seule) main ► **one-horse place*** N bled* *m*, trou* *m* ► **one-horse race** N (*fig*) **it's a ~-horse race** c'est couru d'avance ► **one-horse town*** N = **one-horse place** ► **one-legged** ADJ unijambiste ► **one-line message** N message *m* d'une (seule) ligne ► **one-liner** N (= *joke*) bon mot *m*; (* = *letter*) note *f*, mot *m* ► **one-man** ADJ → **one-man** ► **one-night stand** N (*Theat*) soirée *f* or représentation *f* unique; (*sex*) liaison *f* sans lendemain ► **one-off*** ADJ, N (*Brit*) → **one-off** ► **one-one, one-one** ADJ, ADV (*US*) = **one-to-one** ► **one-owner** ADJ (*Aut etc*) qui n'a eu qu'un propriétaire ► **one-parent family** N famille *f* monoparentale ► **one-party system** N (*Pol*) système *m* à parti unique ► **one-piece** (*Dress*) ADJ une pièce *inv*, d'une seule pièce ♦ N (*also* **~-piece swimsuit**) maillot *m* une pièce ► **one-reeler** N (*US Cine*) court-métrage *m*, film *m* d'une bobine ► **one-room(ed) apartment** N (*US*) = **one-room(ed) flat** ► **one-room(ed) flat** N (*Brit*) studio *m*, appartement *m* d'une pièce ► **one-shot*** ADJ, N (*US*) → **one-off** ► **one-sided** ADJ [*decision*] unilatéral; [*contest, game*] inégal; [*judgement, account*] partial; [*bargain, contract*] inéquitable ► **one-sidedness** N [*of account, presentation*] partialité *f*; [*of bargain*] caractère *m* inéquitable ► **one-size** ADJ taille unique *inv* ► **one-stop shopping** N concentration *f* des achats sur un seul point de vente ► **one-time** ADJ ancien (*before n*) ► **one-to-one** ADJ, ADV (*Brit*) → **one-to-one** ► **one-track** ADJ (*Rail*) à voie unique; (*fig*) **to have a ~-track mind** n'avoir qu'une idée en tête ► **one-two** N **a** (*Boxing*) gauche-droite *m inv* **b** (*Ftbl*) une-deux *m inv* **c** (*in race*) arrivée où le gagnant est suivi d'un coéquipier ► **one-up*** VT (*US*) **to ~-up sb** marquer un point sur qn ► **one-upmanship*** N (*hum*) art *m* de faire mieux que les autres ► **one-way** ADJ [*street*] à sens unique; [*traffic*] en sens unique; [*transaction*] unilatéral; [*bottle*] non consigné; (*fig*) [*friendship, emotion etc*] non partagé; **~-way mirror** miroir *m*; **~-way trip** (voyage *m*) aller *m*; **a ~-way ticket** un aller simple; **it's a ~-way ticket to disaster** c'est la catastrophe assurée; **she knew the job was a ~-way ticket to nowhere*** elle savait que ce boulot* ne mènerait à rien ► **one-woman** ADJ [*business, office*] que fait marcher une seule femme; **~-woman show** (*Art*) exposition *f* consacrée à une seule artiste; (*Rad, Theat, TV*) one woman show *m*; **he's a ~-woman man** c'est l'homme d'une seule femme

one-man ['wʌn'mæn] [1] ADJ [a] (= *solo*) [*business, company*] individuel; [*rule, government*] d'une seule personne [b] (= *designed, suitable for one*) [*canoe*] monoplace; [*job*] pour une seule personne [c] (= *monogamous*) **a ~ woman** la femme d'un seul homme [2] COMP ▶ **one-man band** N (*Mus*) homme-orchestre *m*; (*fig*) **the company is a ~ band** il (*or* elle) fait marcher l'affaire à lui (*or* elle) tout seul (*or* toute seule) ▶ **one-man show** N (*Rad, Theat, TV*) one man show *m*; (*Art*) exposition *f* consacrée d'un seul artiste; (*fig*) **this company is a ~ show*** il (*or* elle) fait marcher l'affaire à lui (*or* elle) tout seul (*or* toute seule)

oneness ['wʌnnɪs] N unité *f*; (= *sameness*) identité *f*; (= *agreement*) accord *m*, entente *f*

one-off* ['wʌnɒf] (*Brit*) [1] ADJ [*object, building*] unique; [*event*] exceptionnel [2] N **it's a ~** (= *extraordinary*) il n'y en a qu'un comme ça; (= *not part of series*) [*TV programme etc*] ça ne fait pas partie d'une série; [*event*] ça ne va pas se reproduire *or* se répéter

onerous ['ɒnərəs] ADJ (*frm*) [*duty, restrictions*] pénible; [*task*] pénible, lourd; [*responsibility*] lourd

oneself [wʌn'self] PRON (*reflexive*) se, soi-même; (*after prep*) soi(-même); (*emphatic*) soi-même; **to hurt ~** se blesser; **to speak to ~** se parler (à soi-même); **to be sure of ~** être sûr de soi(-même); **one must do it ~** il faut le faire soi-même; **(all) by ~** (tout) seul; **to have sth (all) to ~** avoir qch pour soi (tout) seul

one-to-one [wʌntə'wʌn], **one-on-one** (*US*) [wʌnɒn'wʌn] [1] ADJ [a] (= *involving two people*) [*conversation*] en tête-à-tête, seul à seul; [*talks*] en tête-à-tête; [*training, therapy, counselling*] individuel; **on a ~ basis** [*discuss etc*] seul à seul, en tête-à-tête; **to teach sb on a ~ basis** donner des leçons particulières à qn; **she has a ~ relationship with her pupils** elle connaît bien chacun de ses élèves; **to have a ~ meeting with sb** voir qn en tête-à-tête *or* seul à seul; **a ~ session** (*gen*) une réunion seul à seul *or* en tête-à-tête; (*Psych*) un face à face; **~ tuition** leçons *fpl* particulières [b] (= *corresponding exactly*) [*correspondence*] biunivoque; [*ratio, rate*] de un pour un [2] ADV [a] (= *person-to-person*) [*talk, discuss*] seul à seul [b] (= *in exact correspondence*) [*convert*] au taux de un pour un

ongoing ['ɒngəʊɪŋ] ADJ (*gen*) [*debate, process, research*] en cours; [*crisis, situation*] actuel; **they have an ~ relationship** ils ont des relations suivies

onion ['ʌnjən] [1] N oignon *m*; (*Brit*) **to know one's ~s†*** connaître son affaire, s'y connaître → **cocktail, spring** [2] COMP [*soup, pie*] à l'oignon; [*stew*] aux oignons ▶ **onion dome** N (*Archit*) bulbe *m* ▶ **onion johnny** N vendeur *m* d'oignons (ambulant) ▶ **onion ring** N (*Culin*) rondelle *f* d'oignon en beignet ▶ **onion-shaped** ADJ bulbeux ▶ **onion skin** N pelure *f* d'oignon

onlooker ['ɒnlʊkə'] N **the ~s** les spectateurs *mpl*, l'assistance *f*

only ['əʊnlɪ] [1] ADJ seul, unique; **~ child** enfant *mf* unique; **you're the ~ one to think of that** vous êtes le seul à y avoir pensé, vous seul y avez pensé; **I'm tired! — you're not the ~ one!*** je suis fatigué! — vous n'êtes pas le seul *or* il n'y a pas que vous; **it's the ~ one left** c'est le seul qui reste (*subj*); **he is not the ~ one here** il n'est pas le seul ici, il n'y a pas que lui ici; **the ~ book he has** le seul livre qu'il ait; **his ~ friend** was his dog son chien était son seul ami; **his ~ answer was to sigh deeply** pour toute réponse il a poussé un profond soupir; **your ~ hope is to find another one** votre unique espoir est d'en trouver un autre; **the ~ thing is that it's too late** seulement *or* malheureusement il est trop tard;

that's the **~ way to do it** c'est la seule façon de le faire, on ne peut pas le faire autrement → **one, pebble**

[2] ADV [a] seulement, ne ... que; **he's ~ ten** il n'a que dix ans; **there are ~ two people who know that** il n'y a que deux personnes qui savent *or* sachent cela; **~ Paul can come** Paul seul peut venir, il n'y a que Paul qui puisse venir; **~ time will tell** c'est l'avenir qui le dira; **I'm ~ the secretary** je ne suis que le secrétaire; **a ticket for one person** ~ un billet pour une seule personne; **"ladies ~"** «réservé aux dames»; **he can ~ wait** il ne peut qu'attendre; **God ~ knows!** Dieu seul le sait!; **I can ~ say how sorry I am** tout ce que je peux dire c'est combien je suis désolé; **that ~ makes matters worse** cela ne fait qu'aggraver les choses; **I will ~ say that ...** je me bornerai à dire *or* je dirai simplement que ...; **it will ~ take a minute** ça ne prendra qu'une minute; **I ~ looked at it** je n'ai fait que le regarder; **you've ~ to ask** vous n'avez qu'à demander; **~ think of the situation!** imaginez un peu la situation!; **~ to think of it** rien que d'y penser; **it's ~ that I thought he might ...** c'est que je pensais qu'il pourrait ...

[b] (*phrases*) **he was ~ too pleased to come** il n'a été que trop content de venir, il ne demandait pas mieux que de venir; **it's ~ too true** ce n'est que trop vrai; **not ~ A but also B** non seulement A mais aussi B; **not ~ was it dark, but it was also foggy** non seulement il faisait noir, mais il y avait aussi du brouillard; **~ yesterday** hier encore, pas plus tard qu'hier; **it seems like ~ yesterday** il semble que c'était hier; **he has ~ just arrived** il vient tout juste d'arriver; **but I've ~ just bought it!** mais je viens seulement de l'acheter!; **I caught the train but ~ just** j'ai eu le train mais (c'était) de justesse

[3] CONJ seulement, mais; **I would buy it, ~ it's too dear** je l'achèterais bien, seulement *or* mais il est trop cher; **he would come too, ~ he's ill** il viendrait bien aussi, si ce n'est qu'il est malade *or* seulement il est malade; **if ~** si seulement; **~ if** seulement si

o.n.o. [əʊɛn'əʊ] (ABBR = **or near(est) offer**) à déb., à débattre → **offer**

onomasiology [ɒnəʊ,meɪsɪ'ɒlədʒɪ] N [a] (*Ling*) onomasiologie *f* [b] = **onomastics**

onomastic [ɒnəʊ'mæstɪk] ADJ onomastique

onomastics [ɒnə'mæstɪks] N (*NonC*) onomastique *f*

onomatopoeia [ˌɒnəʊmætəʊ'piːə] N onomatopée *f*

onomatopoeic [ˌɒnəʊmætəʊ'piːɪk] ADJ, **onomatopoetic** [ˌɒnəʊmætəʊpəʊ'etɪk] ADJ onomatopéique

onrush ['ɒnrʌʃ] N [*of people*] ruée *f*; [*of water*] torrent *m*

onrushing ['ɒn,rʌʃɪŋ] ADJ [*vehicle*] qui arrive à toute allure; [*water*] qui arrive à flots

onset ['ɒnset] N [a] (= *attack*) attaque *f*, assaut *m* [b] (= *beginning*) [*of illness, winter etc*] début *m*, commencement *m*; **at the ~** d'emblée

onshore ['ɒn'ʃɔː'] [1] ADJ [a] (= *towards land*) [*wind, breeze*] de mer, du large [b] (= *on, near land*) [*oilfield, facilities, job, work*] à terre [2] ADV (*also* **on shore**) [a] (= *towards land*) **to wash up ~** être rejeté sur le rivage; **the wind was blowing ~** le vent venait du large [b] (= *on land*) [*build, work*] à terre

onside [ɒn'saɪd] ADJ (*Ftbl etc*) **to be ~** ne pas être hors jeu

onslaught ['ɒnslɔːt] N attaque *f*; **their relentless ~ against the government's plans** leurs attaques implacables contre les projets du gouvernement; **the constant ~ of adverts on TV** le matraquage publicitaire constant à la télé

onstage ['ɒnsteɪdʒ] [1] ADV en scène [2] ADJ **her ~ presence** sa présence en scène

Ont. ABBR = **Ontario**

Ontario [ɒn'teərɪəʊ] N l'Ontario *m*; **Lake ~** le lac Ontario

onto ['ɒntʊ] PREP = **on to**; → **on 1d**

ontogenesis [ˌɒntə'dʒenɪsɪs] N ontogenèse *f*

ontogeny [ɒn'tɒdʒənɪ] N ontogénie *f*

ontological [ˌɒntə'lɒdʒɪkəl] ADJ ontologique

ontology [ɒn'tɒlədʒɪ] N ontologie *f*

onus ['əʊnəs] N (*pl* **onuses**) (= *responsibility*) responsabilité *f*; (= *duty*) charge *f*; **the ~ of proof rests with him** la charge de la preuve lui incombe; **the ~ is on him to do it** il lui incombe de le faire; **the ~ is on the manufacturers** c'est la responsabilité des fabricants

onward ['ɒnwəd] [1] ADJ [a] (*Transport, Comm*) **~ flight** *or* **connection** correspondance *f*; **"British Airways would like to wish you a safe ~ journey"** «British Airways vous souhaite de poursuivre agréablement votre voyage»; **a flight to Mykonos, with an ~ boat journey to Paros** un vol jusqu'à Mykonos suivi d'une traversée en bateau jusqu'à Paros; **goods delivered to Staverton for ~ movement by rail** des marchandises livrées à Staverton d'où elles seront transportées par chemin de fer [b] (= *developing*) **~ progress** avancée *f*; **the ~ march of sth** la marche en avant de qch [2] ADV (*esp Brit*) = **onwards**

onwards ['ɒnwədz] ADV [a] (*in direction*) **to continue** (*or* **walk** *or* **sail** *etc*) **~** avancer; **to journey ~** poursuivre son voyage; **~! en avant!** [b] (*in development*) **to move ~** aller de l'avant; **the plot moves breathlessly ~** l'intrigue se déroule à un rythme haletant [c] (*in time*) **from then ~** ◊ **from that time ~** depuis, depuis lors; **from now ~** désormais, dorénavant; **from today ~** à partir d'aujourd'hui; **from Saturday/September/1960 ~** à partir de samedi/septembre/1960

onyx ['ɒnɪks] [1] N onyx *m* [2] COMP en onyx, d'onyx

oodles* ['uːdlz] NPL un tas*, des masses* *fpl*; **~ of** un tas* de, des masses* de

ooh* [uː] [1] EXCL oh! [2] VI **to ~ and aah** pousser des oh! et des ah!

oohing* ['uːɪŋ] N **there was a lot of ~ and aahing** on entendait fuser des oh! et des ah!

oolite ['əʊəlaɪt] N oolithe *m*

oolitic [ˌəʊə'lɪtɪk] ADJ oolithique

oompah ['uːmpɑː] N flonflon *m*

oomph* [ʊmf] N (= *energy*) punch* *m*, dynamisme *m*; **a pill designed to put the ~ back into your sex life** un médicament conçu pour redonner du tonus à votre vie sexuelle

oophorectomy [ˌəʊəfə'rektəmɪ] N ovariectomie *f*

oophoritis [ˌəʊəfə'raɪtɪs] N ovarite *f*

oops* [ʊps] EXCL houp!; **~-a-daisy!** hop-là!

oosphere ['əʊəsfɪə'] N oosphère *f*

oospore ['əʊəspɔː'] N oospore *f*

ooze [uːz] [1] N vase *f*, limon *m* [2] VI [*water, pus, walls etc*] suinter; [*resin, gum*] exsuder; **she was oozing with confidence** elle débordait d'assurance [3] VT **his wounds ~d pus** le pus suintait de ses blessures; (*pej*) **she was oozing charm/complacency** le charme/la suffisance lui sortait par tous les pores
▶ **ooze away** VI [*liquids*] s'en aller, suinter; [*strength, courage, enthusiasm*] disparaître, se dérober; **his strength** *etc* **was oozing away** ses forces *etc* l'abandonnaient
▶ **ooze out** VI [*liquids*] sortir, suinter

op¹* [ɒp] N (*Med, Mil*) ABBR = **operation 1b, 1c**

op² [ɒp] ADJ (*in compounds*) **op art** op art *m*; **op artist** artiste *mf* op art

op. (ABBR = **opus**) O

opacity [əʊ'pæsɪtɪ] N [*of material*] opacité *f*; [*of meaning etc*] obscurité *f*

opal ['əʊpəl] [1] N opale *f* [2] COMP [*ring, necklace*] d'opale; (*also* **~-coloured**) opalin

opalescence [ˌəʊpəˈlesns] N opalescence f

opalescent [ˌəʊpəˈlesnt] ADJ (liter) [light, sky, glass, colour] opalescent (liter) ; [eyes] d'opale

opaque [əʊˈpeɪk] ① ADJ [glass, liquid, darkness, language] opaque ; [plan, intention] obscur ; **black tights/stockings** collants mpl/bas mpl noirs opaques ② COMP ► **opaque projector** N (US Opt) épiscope m

op. cit. [ˈɒpˈsɪt] (ABBR = **opere citato**) op. cit.

OPEC [ˈəʊpek] N (ABBR = **Organization of Petroleum-Exporting Countries**) OPEP f

Op-Ed [ˈɒpˈed] N, ADJ (US Press) (ABBR = **opposite editorial**) ~ **(page)** page contenant les chroniques et commentaires (en face des éditoriaux)

open [ˈəʊpən] ① ADJ ⓐ (= not closed) [shop, road, door, box, bottle, book, shirt, grave, wound, eyes, flower] ouvert ; **the shops are ~** les magasins sont ouverts ; **the house is not ~ to visitors** la maison n'est pas ouverte au public ; **to welcome sb/sth with ~ arms** accueillir qn/qch à bras ouverts ; **the door was slightly ~** la porte était entrouverte or entrebâillée ; **the window flew ~** la fenêtre s'ouvrit brusquement ; **he is an ~ book** c'est un homme transparent, on lit en lui comme dans un livre ouvert → **5** ; → **break, cut, eye, mouth, throw**

ⓑ [river, water, canal] ouvert à la navigation ; [road] dégagé ; [pipe] ouvert ; [pores] dilaté ; **the way to Paris lay ~** la route de Paris était libre ; **the ~ air** le plein air ; **in the ~ air** [eat] en plein air ; [live, walk] au grand air ; [sleep] à la belle étoile → **5** ; **the ~ sea** la haute mer, le large ; **on the ~ sea(s)** en haute mer, au large ; **in ~ country** en rase campagne ; (outside of town) à la campagne ; (Mil) **when you reach ~ country** or **~ ground** quand vous arriverez en rase campagne ; (between trees) **patch of ~ ground** clairière f ; **beyond the woods there were ~ fields** au-delà des bois, il y avait des champs ; **the speed permitted on the ~ road** la vitesse autorisée en dehors des agglomérations ; **an ~ space for public use** un espace vert à l'usage du public ; **the (wide) ~ spaces** les grands espaces mpl ; **~ view** or **aspect** vue f dégagée ; **have your bowels been ~ this morning?** est-ce que vous êtes allé à la selle ce matin ?

ⓒ (= not enclosed) [car, carriage] découvert ; [boat] non ponté ; [drain, sewer] à ciel ouvert ; (in town) ~ **market** marché m en plein air → **5**

ⓓ (= unrestricted) [meeting, trial, discussion] public (-ique f) ; [economy, city] ouvert ; (Jur) **in ~ court** en audience publique ; **to keep ~ house** tenir table ouverte ; **we had an ~ invitation (to visit anytime)** on nous avait invités à venir quand nous voulions ; (Sport) **~ tournament** tournoi m open ; **jobs are advertised and filled by ~ competition** le recrutement se fait par voie de presse

ⓔ (= exposed) ouvert ; **(wide) ~ to the winds/the elements** ouvert à tous les vents or aux quatre vents

ⓕ (fig: to advice, question etc) **I'm ~ to advice** je suis ouvert à toutes les suggestions ; **it is ~ to doubt whether ...** on peut douter que ... (+ subj) ; **it is ~ to question** or **debate if** or **whether ...** (il) reste à savoir si ... → **abuse, attack, correction, criticism, lay**[1], **offer, persuasion**

ⓖ (= available) [post, job] vacant ; **this post is still ~** ce poste est encore vacant ; **the offer is still ~** cette proposition tient toujours ; **the number of jobs ~ to women is limited** le nombre de postes ouverts aux femmes or auxquels les femmes peuvent postuler est limité ; **membership is not ~ to women** l'adhésion n'est pas ouverte aux femmes, les femmes ne peuvent pas être membres ; **the course is not ~ to men** ce cours n'est pas ouvert aux hommes or est réservé aux femmes ; **it is ~ to you to refuse** libre à vous de refuser ; **several methods/choices were ~ to them** plusieurs méthodes/choix s'offraient or se présentaient à eux

ⓗ (= frank) [person, character, face, manner,

hostility] ouvert ; (= declared) [admiration, envy, attempt] non dissimulé ; **in ~ revolt (against)** en rébellion ouverte (contre) ; **I'm going to be completely ~ with you** je vais être tout à fait franc avec vous ; **you're not being very ~ with me** tu me caches quelque chose

ⓘ (= undecided) **they left the matter ~** ils n'ont pas tranché la question, ils ont laissé la question en suspens ; **let's leave the date/arrangements ~** attendons avant de fixer une date/avant de prendre ces dispositions ; **to keep an ~ mind on sth** réserver son jugement or son opinion sur qch ; **I've got an ~ mind about it** je n'ai pas encore formé d'opinion à ce sujet → **5** ; **it's an ~ question whether he will come** (il) reste à voir s'il viendra ; **how effective those sanctions are is an ~ question** (il) reste à voir si ces sanctions seront vraiment efficaces ; **the legality of these sales is still an ~ question** la légalité de ces ventes n'a pas encore été clairement établie → **option**

② N ⓐ (outside) **(out) in the ~** (= out of doors) dehors, en plein air ; (= in the country) au grand air ; (= not secretly) au grand jour ; **to sleep (out) in the ~** dormir à la belle étoile ; **why can't we do it out in the ~?** (= not secretly) pourquoi ne pouvons-nous pas le faire ouvertement ? ; **that swindle is now in the ~** cette escroquerie est maintenant sur la place publique ; **to come out into the ~** [fact] apparaître au grand jour ; [scandal] éclater au grand jour ; **to come out into the ~ about sth** [person] s'exprimer au grand jour sur qch ; **he came (out) into the ~ about what had been going on** il s'est exprimé au grand jour sur ce qui s'était passé ; **why don't you come into the ~ about it?** pourquoi ne le dites-vous pas ouvertement ? ; **to bring a dispute (out) into the ~** révéler des différends au grand jour

ⓑ (Golf, Tennis) **the Open** l'open m, le tournoi open ; **the French Open** (le tournoi de) Roland Garros ; **the California Open** l'Open m de Californie

③ VT ⓐ (gen) ouvrir ; [+ pores] dilater ; [+ wound] (r)ouvrir ; [+ legs] écarter ; **it ~s the way for new discoveries** cela ouvre la voie à de nouvelles découvertes ; **he ~ed his heart to me** il m'a ouvert son cœur ; **to ~ sb's mind (to sth)** ouvrir l'esprit de qn (à qch) ; **have you ~ed your bowels?** êtes-vous allé à la selle ? ; **to ~ wide** ouvrir grand ; (mouth) **wide!** ouvrez grand ! ; **to ~ slightly** (door, window, eyes) entrouvrir ; **to ~ again** rouvrir → **eye, mouth**

ⓑ [+ make] tracer ; [+ hole] percer ; [+ gulf] creuser ; **this ~ed a gulf between father and son** cela a creusé un fossé entre le père et le fils ; **he ~ed his way through the bushes** il s'est frayé un chemin à travers les buissons

ⓒ (= begin, inaugurate, found) [+ meeting, debate, exhibition, trial] ouvrir ; [+ account, conversation] commencer, entamer ; [+ new building, institution] inaugurer ; [+ negotiations] ouvrir, engager ; **he had ~ed the conversation by telling her that ...** il avait commencé par lui dire que ...

ⓓ (Bridge) **to ~ (with) two hearts** ouvrir de deux cœurs

④ VI ⓐ [door, book, eyes, flower] s'ouvrir ; [shop, museum, bank] ouvrir ; [crack] se former ; **the door ~ed** la porte s'est ouverte ; **the door ~ed slightly** la porte s'est entrouverte or s'est entrebâillée ; **to ~ again** [door] se rouvrir ; [shops etc] rouvrir ; **there's a door that ~s onto the garden** il y a une porte qui donne sur le jardin ; **the kitchen ~s into the dining room** la cuisine donne sur la salle à manger ; **the two rooms ~ into one another** les deux pièces communiquent

ⓑ (= begin) commencer ; (Bridge) ouvrir ; **to ~ with sth** [debate, meeting, trial] s'ouvrir sur qch, commencer par qch ; [class, book, play] commencer par qch ; **the trial ~ed with the testimony of the victim** le procès s'est ouvert sur or a commencé par le témoignage de la

victime ; **he ~ed with a warning about inflation** il a commencé par lancer un avertissement sur l'inflation ; **the play/film ~ next week** la première (de la pièce/du film) a lieu la semaine prochaine

⑤ COMP ► **open-air** ADJ [games, activities] de plein air ; [swimming pool] découvert ; [market, meeting] en plein air, à ciel ouvert ; **~-air theatre** théâtre m en plein air ► **open-and-shut** ADJ (fig) **it's an ~-and-shut case** la solution est évidente or crève les yeux ► **open-cast** ADJ (Brit Min) à ciel ouvert ► **open cheque** N (Brit Banking) chèque m non barré ► **open circuit** N (Elec) circuit m ouvert ► **open-cut** ADJ (US Min) = **open-cast** ► **open day** N (Brit) journée f portes ouvertes ► **open door** (Econ) politique f d'ouverture ♦ ADJ [policy, approach etc] d'ouverture ► **open-ended, open-end** (US) ADJ [tube] ouvert ; [discussion, meeting] sans limite de durée ; [ticket] sans réservation de retour ; [contract] à durée indéterminée ; [question] ouvert ; [commitment] inconditionnel ► **open-eyed** ADJ (lit) les yeux ouverts ; **to be ~-eyed about sth** garder les yeux ouverts sur qch ► **open-faced sandwich** N (US) tartine f ► **open government** N (NonC) politique f de transparence (pratiquée par un gouvernement) ► **open-handed** ADJ **to be ~-handed** être généreux, avoir le cœur sur la main ► **open-hearted** ADJ franc (franche f), sincère ► **open-heart surgery** N (Med) chirurgie f à cœur ouvert ► **open learning** N (gen) enseignement universitaire à la carte, notamment par correspondance ; (= distance learning) téléenseignement m ► **open letter** N lettre f ouverte ► **open market** N (Econ) marché m libre ► **open marriage** N mariage m libre ► **open-minded** ADJ à l'esprit ouvert or large ; **to be very ~-minded** avoir l'esprit très ouvert ► **open-mindedness** N ouverture f d'esprit ► **open-mouthed** ADJ, ADV (fig) bouche bée ; **in ~-mouthed disbelief/amazement** bouche bée ; **in ~-mouthed admiration** béat d'admiration ► **open-necked** ADJ (not buttoned up) à col ouvert ; (low-cut) échancré ► **open-plan** ADJ (Archit) [design] qui élimine les cloisons ; [house, school] sans cloison ; **~-plan office** bureau m paysager ► **open primary** N (US Pol) élection primaire ouverte aux non-inscrits d'un parti ► **open prison** N prison f ouverte ► **open sandwich** N tartine f ► **open scholarship** N (Scol etc) bourse décernée par un concours ouvert à tous ► **open season** N (Hunting) saison f de la chasse ► **open secret** N secret m de Polichinelle ; **it's an ~ secret that ...** ce n'est un secret pour personne que ... ► **open shop** N (Ind) atelier m ouvert aux non-syndiqués ► **open station** N gare f avec libre accès aux quais ► **open string** N (Mus) corde f à vide ► **open ticket** N billet m open ► **open-top(ped)** ADJ [bus] à impériale découverte ; [car] découvert ► **the Open University** N (Brit) ≈ le Centre national d'enseignement par correspondance, **an Open University course** un cours universitaire par correspondance ► **open verdict** N (Jur) verdict m de décès sans cause déterminée ► **open vowel** N (Ling) voyelle f ouverte

► **open out** ① VI ⓐ [view] **soon a wonderful view ~ed out** bientôt une vue magnifique s'offrit à nous ; **as he left the town the countryside ~ed out** à la sortie de la ville, la campagne s'offrit à ses yeux ⓑ (= widen) [passage, tunnel, street] s'élargir ; **to ~ out** or **out on to** déboucher sur ⓒ [person] (= become less shy) s'ouvrir ; [team, player etc] s'affirmer ② VT SEP ouvrir ; [+ map, newspaper] ouvrir, déplier

► **open up** ① VI ⓐ [new shop, business] s'ouvrir ; [new career] commencer ; [opportunity] se présenter

ⓑ (= start shooting) ouvrir le feu ; **they ~ed up with machine guns** ils ont ouvert le feu à la mitrailleuse

[c] [*flower*] s'ouvrir

[d] (= *confide*) s'ouvrir (**to sb** à qn) ; **I couldn't get him to ~ up at all** je ne suis pas arrivé à le faire parler ; **he finds it difficult to ~ up** il a de la peine à s'ouvrir *or* à se confier

[e] (*Sport*) [*match*] s'animer

[f] (= *develop*) [*gulf*] se creuser ; [*split*] se former ; **a gulf has ~ed up between the countries involved** un fossé s'est creusé entre les pays concernés

[2] VT SEP [a] [+ *box, building, shop, wound, business, branch*] ouvrir ; [+ *map, newspaper*] ouvrir, déplier ; **to ~ up again** rouvrir

[b] [+ *oilfield, mine, road, area*] ouvrir ; [+ *possibilities*] offrir ; [+ *virgin country*] défricher ; [+ *blocked road*] dégager ; [+ *blocked pipe*] déboucher ; **they ~ed up the way for other women** elles ont ouvert la voie à d'autres femmes ; **they ~ed up new paths in transplantation** ils ont ouvert de nouvelles voies en matière de transplantation ; **she ~ed up a lead of almost four minutes** elle était en tête avec près de quatre minutes d'avance ; **Deng decided to ~ up China for foreign investors** Deng décida d'ouvrir la Chine aux investisseurs étrangers

---

OPEN UNIVERSITY

L'Open University est une université ouverte à tous et fonctionnant essentiellement sur le principe du téléenseignement : cours par correspondance et émissions de radio et de télévision diffusées par la BBC. Ces enseignements sont complétés par un suivi pédagogique et par des stages, qui se tiennent généralement en été.

---

opener ['əʊpnər] N [a] (*esp in compounds*) personne ou dispositif qui ouvre → **bottle, eye, tin** [b] (*Theat*) (= *artiste*) artiste *mf* en lever de rideau ; (= *act*) lever *m* de rideau [c] (*Bridge*) ouvreur *m* [d] (*fig*) **for ~s*** pour commencer, tout d'abord

opening ['əʊpnɪŋ] [1] N [a] ouverture *f* ; (*in wall*) brèche *f* ; [*of door, window*] embrasure *f* ; (*in trees*) trouée *f* ; (*in forest, roof*) percée *f* ; (*in clouds*) éclaircie *f* ; [*of tunnel*] entrée *f*
[b] (= *beginning*) [*of meeting, debate, play, speech*] ouverture *f* ; [*of negotiations*] ouverture *f*, amorce *f*
[c] (*NonC = act of opening*) [*of door, road, letter*] ouverture *f* ; [*of shooting, war*] déclenchement *m* ; [*of flower*] éclosion *f* ; (*Jur*) exposition *f* des faits ; (*Cards, Chess*) ouverture *f* ; [*of ceremony, exhibition*] inauguration *f* ; (*Brit*) **the Opening of Parliament** l'ouverture *f* de la session parlementaire
[d] (= *opportunity*) occasion *f* (**to do** de faire, pour faire) ; (= *trade outlet*) débouché *m* (**for** pour) ; **to give one's opponent/the enemy an ~** prêter le flanc à son adversaire/à l'ennemi
[e] (= *work: gen*) débouché *m* ; (= *specific job, or work in specific firm*) poste *m* ; **there are a lot of ~s in computing** il y a beaucoup de débouchés dans l'informatique ; **we have an ~ for an engineer** nous avons un poste (vacant) d'ingénieur ; **an ~ with HarperCollins** un poste vacant chez HarperCollins
[2] ADJ [*ceremony, speech*] d'inauguration, inaugural ; [*remark*] préliminaire ; (*St Ex*) [*price*] d'ouverture ; **~ gambit** (*Chess*) gambit *m* ; (*fig*) manœuvre *f or* ruse *f* (stratégique) ; (*in conversation*) **his favourite ~ gambit is ...** sa remarque préférée pour entamer une conversation, c'est ... ; **~ hours** heures *fpl* d'ouverture ; **~ lines** [*of play*] premières répliques *fpl* ; [*of poem*] premiers vers *mpl* ; **~ night** (*Theat*) première *f* ; [*of festival etc*] soirée *f* d'ouverture ; **~ shot** (*in battle etc*) premier coup *m* de feu ; (*fig*) [*of campaign etc*] coup *m* d'envoi ; (*Brit*) **~ time** l'heure *f* d'ouverture des pubs

openly ['əʊpənlɪ] ADV [*admit, acknowledge, talk about*] ouvertement ; **to be ~ critical of sb/sth** critiquer qn/qch ouvertement ; **she wept ~**

elle n'a pas caché ses larmes ; **he is ~ gay** il ne cache pas son homosexualité

openness ['əʊpnnɪs] N [a] (= *candour*) franchise *f* ; **~ of mind** largeur *f* d'esprit [b] [*of land, countryside*] aspect *m* découvert *or* exposé

openwork ['əʊpənwɜːk] [1] N (*Sewing*) jours *mpl* ; (*Archit*) claire-voie *f*, ajours *mpl* [2] COMP [*stockings etc*] ajouré ; (*Archit*) à claire-voie

opera ['ɒpərə] [1] N [a] opéra *m* → **comic, grand, light²** [b] *pl of* **opus** [2] COMP ► **opera bouffe** N opéra *m* bouffe ► **opera company** N troupe *f or* compagnie *f* d'opéra ► **opera glasses** NPL jumelles *fpl* de théâtre ► **opera-goer** N amateur *m* d'opéra ► **opera hat** N (*chapeau m*) claque *m*, gibus *m* ► **opera house** N opéra *m* (*édifice*) ► **opera-lover** N amateur *m* d'opéra ► **opera singer** N chanteur *m*, -euse *f* d'opéra

operable ['ɒpərəbl] ADJ opérable

operand ['ɒpərænd] N opérande *m*

operate ['ɒpəreɪt] [1] VI [a] [*machine, vehicle*] marcher, fonctionner ; [*system, sb's mind*] fonctionner ; [*law*] jouer ; **he believes that a conspiracy is operating to discredit his good name** il pense qu'il se trame un complot visant à le discréditer ; **several factors are operating to moderate wage rises** plusieurs facteurs jouent pour freiner les hausses de salaires
[b] [*drug, medicine, propaganda*] opérer, faire effet (**on, upon** sur)
[c] [*fleet, regiment, thief etc*] opérer ; (*St Ex*) faire des opérations (de bourse), spéculer ; **they can't ~ efficiently on so little money** le manque d'argent les empêche d'opérer *or* de procéder avec efficacité ; **this allowed commercial banks to ~ in the country** cela a permis aux banques commerciales d'opérer dans ce pays
[d] (*Med*) opérer ; **he was ~d on for appendicitis** il a été opéré de l'appendicite ; **he ~d for appendicitis** [*surgeon*] il l'a opéré de l'appendicite ; **to ~ on sb's eyes** opérer qn aux *or* des yeux, opérer les yeux de qn ; **he has still not been ~d on** il n'a pas encore été opéré

[2] VT [a] [+ *person machine, tool, vehicle, switchboard, telephone, brakes etc*] faire marcher, faire fonctionner ; **a machine ~d by electricity** une machine qui marche à l'électricité ; **this switch ~s a fan** ce bouton commande *or* actionne un ventilateur
[b] [+ *business, factory*] diriger, gérer ; [+ *coalmine, oil well, canal, quarry*] exploiter, faire valoir
[c] [+ *system*] pratiquer ; **the government constantly ~d embargoes against them** le gouvernement les frappait constamment d'embargo

operatic [ˌɒpəˈrætɪk] [1] ADJ [*aria, role, piece of music*] d'opéra ; **Verdi's Requiem is often criticised for being too ~** on reproche souvent au Requiem de Verdi d'être trop opératique ; **an ~ society** une association d'amateurs d'art lyrique [2] N (**amateur**) **~s** opéra *m* d'amateurs

operating ['ɒpəreɪtɪŋ] [1] ADJ (*Comm, Ind*) [*cost, deficit, expenses etc*] d'exploitation [2] COMP ► **operating cash** N trésorerie *f* d'exploitation ► **operating cycle** N cycle *m* d'exploitation ► **operating instructions** NPL mode *m or* notice *f* d'emploi ► **operating manual** N manuel *m* d'utilisation ► **operating profit** N bénéfice *m* d'exploitation ► **operating room** N (*US*) = **operating theatre** ► **operating system** N (*Comput*) système *m* d'exploitation ► **operating table** N (*Med*) table *f* d'opération ► **operating theatre** N (*Brit*) salle *f* d'opération

operation [ˌɒpəˈreɪʃən] [1] N [a] (*NonC*) [*of machine, vehicle*] marche *f*, fonctionnement *m* ; [*of mind, digestion*] fonctionnement *m* ; [*of*

drug etc] action *f* (**on** sur) ; [*of business*] gestion *f* ; [*of mine, oil well, quarry, canal*] exploitation *f* ; [*of system*] application *f* ; **to be in ~** [*machine*] être en service ; [*business etc*] fonctionner ; [*mine etc*] être en exploitation ; [*law, system*] être en vigueur ; **in full ~** [*machine*] fonctionner à plein (rendement) ; [*business, factory etc*] en pleine activité ; [*mine etc*] en pleine exploitation ; **to come into ~** [*law, system*] entrer en vigueur ; [*machine*] entrer en service ; [*business*] se mettre à fonctionner ; **to put into ~** [*machine*] mettre en service ; [*law*] mettre *or* faire entrer en vigueur ; [*plan*] mettre en application
[b] (= *enterprise, action*: Comm, Fin, Ind, Math, Mil, Pol etc) opération *f* ; **that was an expensive ~** l'opération a été coûteuse ; (*Comm, Ind*) **our ~s in Egypt** (*trading company*) nos opérations *or* nos activités en Égypte ; (*oil, mining*) nos exploitations en Égypte ; **rebuilding ~s began at once** les opérations de reconstruction ont commencé immédiatement ; (*Mil*) **Operation Overlord** opération *f* Overlord
[c] (*Med*) opération *f*, intervention *f* (chirurgicale) ; **to have an ~** se faire opérer (**for** de) ; **a lung/heart/kidney ~** une opération des poumons/du cœur/des reins ; **to perform an ~ on sb (for sth)** opérer qn (de qch)

[2] COMP ► **operation code** N (*Comput*) code *m* d'opération ► **operations research** N recherche *f* opérationnelle ► **operations room** N (*Mil, Police*) centre *m* d'opérations

operational [ˌɒpəˈreɪʃənl] ADJ [*staff, troops, vehicle, plan, system, service*] opérationnel ; [*cost, expenses, profit*] d'exploitation ; [*problems*] de fonctionnement ; **to have ~ control** avoir le contrôle des opérations ; **at an ~ level** au niveau opérationnel ; **for ~ reasons** pour des raisons opérationnelles ; **~ research** recherche *f* opérationnelle ; (*Police*) **on ~ duties** en service ; (*Fin, Econ*) **~ strategy** stratégie *f* d'intervention

operative ['ɒpərətɪv] [1] ADJ [a] (= *functioning*) [*scheme, plan, system, service*] opérationnel ; (*Jur*) **the ~ part of the text** le dispositif [b] **the ~ word** le mot clé, le mot qui compte [c] (*Med*) [*report*] d'opération ; [*risk*] opératoire [2] N (= *worker*) ouvrier *m*, -ière *f* ; (= *machine operator*) opérateur *m*, -trice *f* ; (= *detective*) détective *m* (privé) ; (= *spy*) espion(ne) *m(f)* ; (= *secret agent*) agent *m* secret ; (*US Pol* = *campaign worker*) membre *m* de l'état-major (d'un candidat) ; **the steel ~s** la main-d'œuvre des aciéries

operator ['ɒpəreɪtər] N [a] (= *person*) [*of machine, computer etc*] opérateur *m*, -trice *f* ; (*Cine*) opérateur *m*, -trice *f* (de prise de vues) ; [*telephones*] téléphoniste *mf*, standardiste *mf* ; [*of business, factory*] dirigeant(e) *m(f)*, directeur *m*, -trice *f* ; **~s in this section of the industry** ceux qui travaillent dans ce secteur de l'industrie ; (= *criminal*) **a big-time ~** un escroc d'envergure → **smooth, tour** [b] (*Math*) opérateur *m*

operetta [ˌɒpəˈretə] N opérette *f*

ophthalmia [ɒfˈθælmɪə] N ophtalmie *f*

ophthalmic [ɒfˈθælmɪk] [1] ADJ [*clinic, hospital, surgery*] ophtalmologique ; [*surgeon*] ophtalmologue ; [*nerve, vein*] ophtalmique [2] COMP ► **ophthalmic optician** N opticien(ne) *m(f)* optométriste ; (*prescribing*) oculiste *mf* ; (*dispensing*) opticien(ne) *m(f)*

ophthalmologist [ˌɒfθælˈmɒlədʒɪst] N ophtalmologiste *mf*, ophtalmologue *mf*

ophthalmology [ˌɒfθælˈmɒlədʒɪ] N ophtalmologie *f*

ophthalmoscope [ɒfˈθælməskəʊp] N ophtalmoscope *m*

ophthalmoscopy [ˌɒfθælˈmɒskəpɪ] N ophtalmoscopie *f*

opiate ['əʊpɪɪt] [1] N opiat *m* ; (*fig*) soporifique *m* [2] ADJ opiacé

opine [əʊˈpaɪn] VT (frm) (= think) être d'avis (**that** que); (= say) émettre l'avis (**that** que)

▼ **opinion** [əˈpɪnjən] **1** N (= point of view) avis m, opinion f; (= belief, judgement) opinion f; (= professional advice) avis m; **in my ~** à mon avis, d'après moi; **in the ~ of** d'après, selon; **that's my ~ for what it's worth** c'est mon humble avis; **it's a matter of ~ whether ...** c'est (une) affaire d'opinion pour ce qui est de savoir si ...; **I'm entirely of your ~** je suis tout à fait de votre avis or opinion, je partage tout à fait votre opinion; **to be of the ~ that ...** être d'avis que ..., estimer que ...; **political ~s** opinions fpl politiques; **she's in a position to influence ~** elle occupe une position d'influence; **what is your ~ of this book?** quel est votre point de vue sur ce livre?; **her already favourable ~ of him** l'opinion favorable qu'elle avait déjà de lui; **I haven't much of an ~ of him** ◊ **I've got a low ~ of him** j'ai mauvaise opinion or une piètre opinion de lui; (Jur) **to take counsel's ~** consulter un avocat; (Jur) **~ of the court** jugement m rendu par le tribunal → **legal, public, second¹, strong**

2 COMP ▶ **opinion poll** N sondage m d'opinion

opinionated [əˈpɪnjəneɪtɪd] ADJ (pej) [person] qui a des opinions très arrêtées; **you're so ~** tu as des opinions tellement arrêtées

opium [ˈəʊpɪəm] **1** N opium m **2** COMP ▶ **opium addict** N opiomane mf ▶ **opium den** N fumerie f d'opium

opossum [əˈpɒsəm] N (pl **opossums** or **opossum**) opossum m, sarigue f

opp. ABBR = **opposite**

opponent [əˈpəʊnənt] N (Mil, Sport, in election) adversaire mf; (in discussion, debate) antagoniste mf; (of government, ideas etc) adversaire mf, opposant(e) m(f) (de); **he has always been an ~ of nationalization** il a toujours été contre les nationalisations, il s'est toujours opposé aux nationalisations

opportune [ˈɒpətjuːn] ADJ [action, remark] à propos, opportun; **to happen/arrive at an ~ time** or **moment (for sb/sth)** tomber/arriver au moment opportun (pour qn/qch); **you have come at an ~ moment** vous arrivez à point nommé, vous tombez bien

opportunely [ˈɒpətjuːnlɪ] ADV opportunément, à propos

opportuneness [ˈɒpətjuːnnɪs] N opportunité f

opportunism [ˌɒpəˈtjuːnɪzəm] N opportunisme m

opportunist [ˌɒpəˈtjuːnɪst] ADJ, N opportuniste mf

opportunistic [ˌɒpətjuːˈnɪstɪk] ADJ opportuniste

opportunity [ˌɒpəˈtjuːnɪtɪ] N **a** (= occasion, chance) occasion f; **a trip to London is a great ~ for shopping** un voyage à Londres est une excellente occasion de faire du shopping; **to have the** or **an ~ to do** or **of doing** avoir l'occasion de faire; **to take the ~ of doing** or **to do** profiter de l'occasion pour faire; **you really missed your ~ there!** tu as vraiment laissé passer ta chance or l'occasion!; **at the first** or **earliest ~** à la première occasion, dès que l'occasion se présentera; **when the ~ presents itself** or **arises** à l'occasion; **if the ~ should present itself** or **arise** si l'occasion se présente; **if you get the ~** si vous en avez l'occasion

b (= possibility for action) chance f; (in career etc) perspective f d'avenir; **equality of ~** égalité f des chances; **to make the most of one's opportunities** profiter pleinement de ses chances; **this job offers great opportunities** ce poste offre d'excellentes perspectives d'avenir; **I want to see more opportunities for young people** je veux que les jeunes aient da-

vantage de perspectives d'avenir → **equal, every**

oppose [əˈpəʊz] VT **a** [+ person, argument, opinion, decision, plan] s'opposer à; [+ sb's will, desires, suggestion] s'opposer à, faire opposition à; [+ motion, resolution] (Pol) faire opposition à; (in debate) parler contre; **the government ~s a lifting of the embargo** le gouvernement s'oppose à une levée de l'embargo; **the President ~s sending the refugees back** le président s'oppose au renvoi des réfugiés; **he ~d it** il s'y est opposé **b** (= set against) opposer (**sth to sth else** qch à qch d'autre)

▼ **opposed** [əˈpəʊzd] ADJ [aims, attitudes, viewpoints] opposé; **to be ~ to sth** être opposé à qch; **I'm ~ to your marrying him** je ne veux pas que tu l'épouses (subj); **as ~ to** par opposition à; **as ~ to that, there is the question of ...** par contre, il y a la question de ...

opposing [əˈpəʊzɪŋ] ADJ [factions, forces, views] opposé; (Jur) adverse; **to be on ~ sides** ne pas être du même bord; **the ~ team** l'équipe f adverse; **the ~ votes** les voix fpl contre

opposite [ˈɒpəzɪt] **1** ADJ [house etc] d'en face; [bank, side, end] opposé, autre; [direction, pole] opposé; (fig) [attitude, point of view] opposé, contraire; **"see map on ~ page"** « voir plan ci-contre »; **the ~ sex** l'autre sexe m; **we take the ~ view (to his)** nous pensons le contraire (de ce qu'il pense), notre opinion est diamétralement opposée (à la sienne); **his ~ number** son homologue mf

2 ADV (d')en face; **the house ~** la maison d'en face; **the house is immediately ~** directly **~** la maison est directement en face; **~ to** en face de

3 PREP en face de; **the house is ~ the church** la maison est en face de l'église; **the house and the church are ~ one another** la maison et l'église sont en vis-à-vis; **they sat ~ one another** ils étaient assis face à face or en vis-à-vis; **they live ~ us** ils habitent en face de chez nous; (Cine, Theat etc) **to play ~ sb** partager la vedette avec qn; (Naut) **~ Calais** à la hauteur de Calais

4 N contraire m, inverse m; **quite the ~!** bien au contraire!; **he told me just the ~** or **the exact ~** il m'a dit exactement l'inverse or le contraire; **he says the ~ of everything I say** il prend le contre-pied de tout ce que je dis, il faut toujours qu'il me contredise; **what's the ~ of white?** quel est le contraire de blanc?

Opposition [ˌɒpəˈzɪʃən] (Brit Pol) **1** N **the ~** l'opposition f; **the leader of the ~** le chef de l'opposition **2** COMP [speaker, member, motion, party] de l'opposition ▶ **the Opposition benches** NPL (les bancs mpl de) l'opposition f

opposition [ˌɒpəˈzɪʃən] **1** N **a** opposition f (also Astron, Pol); **his ~ to the scheme** son opposition au projet; **in ~ (to)** en opposition (avec); (Pol) **the party in ~** le parti de l'opposition; (Pol) **to be in ~** être dans l'opposition; **the ~** (= opposing team, rival political faction) l'adversaire m; (= business competitors) la concurrence **b** (Mil etc) opposition f, résistance f; **they put up** or **offered considerable ~** ils opposèrent une vive résistance; **the army met with little or no ~** l'armée a rencontré peu sinon point de résistance **2** COMP ▶ **opposition hold** N (Climbing) opposition f

oppositionist [ˌɒpəˈzɪʃənɪst] N (Pol) opposant(e) m(f) (systématique)

oppress [əˈpres] VT **a** (Mil, Pol etc) opprimer **b** [anxiety, heat etc] oppresser, accabler

oppression [əˈpreʃən] N (all senses) oppression f

oppressive [əˈpresɪv] ADJ **a** (Mil, Pol) [system, regime, law] oppressif **b** (= uncomfortable) [air, heat, silence, mood] oppressant; [weather]

lourd; **the little room was ~** on étouffait dans cette petite pièce

oppressively [əˈpresɪvlɪ] ADV **a** (Mil, Pol) [rule] de manière oppressive **b** (= uncomfortably) **the room was ~ hot** on étouffait dans cette pièce; **~ humid** d'une humidité oppressante; **it's ~ hot today** il fait très lourd aujourd'hui; **~ drab** or **grey** d'un gris sinistre

oppressor [əˈpresəʳ] N oppresseur m

opprobrious [əˈprəʊbrɪəs] ADJ (frm) chargé d'opprobre (liter)

opprobrium [əˈprəʊbrɪəm] N opprobre m

opt [ɒpt] VI **to ~ for sth** opter pour qch; **to ~ to do** choisir de faire
▶ **opt in** VI choisir de participer (**to** à)
▶ **opt out** VI choisir de ne pas participer (**of** à); [hospital, school] choisir l'autonomie par rapport aux autorités locales; [dentist] choisir de ne plus être conventionné par la Sécurité sociale; (Sociol) s'évader de or rejeter la société (de consommation); (Brit: pension) choisir une caisse de retraite privée (par opposition au système de la Sécurité sociale); **he ~ed out of going** il a choisi de ne pas y aller; **you can always ~ out** tu peux toujours te retirer or te récuser → **opt-out**

optative [ˈɒptətɪv] ADJ, N optatif m

optic [ˈɒptɪk] **1** ADJ optique **2** N (Brit: in bar) bouchon m doseur **3** **optics** NPL optique f **4** COMP ▶ **optic nerve** N nerf m optique

optical [ˈɒptɪkəl] **1** ADJ [microscope, telescope, system, glass, lens] optique; [instrument] d'optique, optique **2** COMP ▶ **optical brightener** N agent m éclaircissant ▶ **optical character reader** N lecteur m optique de caractères ▶ **optical character recognition** N reconnaissance f optique de caractères ▶ **optical disc, optical disk** N (Comput) disque m optique ▶ **optical fibre** N fibre f optique ▶ **optical illusion** N illusion f d'optique ▶ **optical scanner** N (Comput) lecteur m optique ▶ **optical scanning** N (Comput) lecture f optique

optician [ɒpˈtɪʃən] N opticien(ne) m(f); (prescribing) oculiste mf

optima [ˈɒptɪmə] NPL of **optimum**

optimal [ˈɒptɪml] ADJ optimal

optimism [ˈɒptɪmɪzəm] N optimisme m

optimist [ˈɒptɪmɪst] N optimiste mf

optimistic [ˌɒptɪˈmɪstɪk] ADJ optimiste (**about sth** quant à qch); **she was ~ of success** or **that she would succeed** elle avait bon espoir de réussir; **to be cautiously ~** être d'un optimisme prudent

optimistically [ˌɒptɪˈmɪstɪklɪ] ADV avec optimisme

optimization [ˌɒptɪmaɪˈzeɪʃən] N optimisation f

optimize [ˈɒptɪmaɪz] VT optimiser, optimaliser

optimum [ˈɒptɪməm] **1** ADJ [level, number, time] optimum, optimal; **~ conditions** conditions fpl optimales; **exercise three times a week for ~ health** faites de l'exercice trois fois par semaine pour être au mieux de votre forme **2** N (pl **optimums** or **optima**) optimum m

option [ˈɒpʃən] N **a** (gen) choix m, option f; (Comm, Fin) option f (**on** sur); **to take up the ~** lever l'option; **at the ~ of the purchaser** au gré de l'acheteur; (Comm, Fin) **~ taker** optant m; (Jur) **the buyer shall have the ~ to decide** l'acheteur aura la faculté de décider; (Jur) **six months with/without the ~ of a fine** six mois avec/sans substitution d'amende; **I have no ~** je n'ai pas le choix; **he had no ~ but to come** il n'a pas pu faire autrement que de venir; **you have the ~ of remaining here** vous pouvez rester ici si vous voulez; **the military ~** l'option f militaire; (fig) **he left** or **kept his ~s open** il n'a pas voulu s'engager (irrévocable-

➤ LANGUAGE IN USE: **opinion** 1.1, 2.1, 2.2, 6, 26.2   **opposed** 8.3, 9.3, 12, 14 ment); **to give sb the ~ of doing sth** donner à qn la possibilité de faire qch; **children are given the ~ of learning French or German** les enfants peuvent choisir entre le français et l'allemand [b] (*Brit Scol = subject/course etc*) (matière *f*| cours *m etc*) à option *f*; **programme offering ~s** programme *m* optionnel

optional ['ɒpʃənl] ADJ [*course, subject*] (*Scol*) facultatif; (*Univ*) en option; [*accessories*] en option; **a medical with ~ eye test** un contrôle médical avec examen de la vue en option; **~ extra** option *f*; **dress ~** tenue *f* de soirée facultative

optometrist [ɒp'tɒmətrɪst] N optométriste *mf*

optometry [ɒp'tɒmətrɪ] N optométrie *f*

opt-out ['ɒptaʊt] [1] ADJ (*Brit*) [*school, hospital*] qui a choisi l'autonomie par rapport aux autorités locales [2] N [a] (*Brit*) [*of school, hospital*] choix d'autonomie par rapport aux autorités locales [b] (*esp Brit: also ~ clause*) (*Jur, Comm*) clause *f* de sortie; (*from treaty*) clause *f* d'exemption

opulence ['ɒpjʊləns] N [*of person, lifestyle*] opulence *f*; [*of palace*] somptuosité *f*, opulence *f*; [*of room*] somptuosité, richesse *f*; [*of clothes, furnishings*] somptuosité *f*; [*of material, voice*] richesse *f*; **a life of ~** une vie opulente; (*Cine, Theat*) **the ~ of the production** la somptuosité de la production

opulent ['ɒpjʊlənt] ADJ [*person, lifestyle*] opulent; [*building, room, costume, film, production*] somptueux; **silk curtains give the room an ~ feel** des rideaux de soie rendent la pièce plus somptueuse

opulently ['ɒpjʊləntlɪ] ADV [*furnish etc*] avec opulence; [*live*] dans l'opulence

opus ['əʊpəs] N (*pl* **opuses** *or* **opera**) opus *m* → **magnum**

opuscule [ɒ'pʌskjuːl] N opuscule *m*

OR ABBR = **Oregon**

or [ɔː'] CONJ ou; (*with neg*) ni; **red or black?** rouge ou noir?; **or else** ou bien; **do it or else!*** fais-le, sinon (tu vas voir)!; **without tears or sighs** sans larmes ni soupirs; **he could not read or write** il ne savait ni lire ni écrire; **an hour or so** environ une heure, à peu près une heure; **botany, or the science of plants** la botanique, ou la science des plantes *or* autrement dit la science des plantes → **either**

oracle ['ɒrəkl] N (*Hist, fig*) oracle *m*; (*fig*) **the government managed to work the ~ and be re-elected** le gouvernement a réussi l'exploit d'être réélu

oracular [ɒ'rækjʊlə'] ADJ (*frm*) (= *prophetic*) [*guidance, utterance*] prophétique; (= *mysterious*) [*person, tone, pronouncement*] sibyllin; **~ shrine** oracle *m*

oral ['ɔːrəl] [1] ADJ [a] [*examination, teaching methods*] oral; [*testimony, message, account*] oral, verbal [b] (*Anat*) [*cavity*] buccal, oral; (*Pharm etc*) [*dose*] par voie orale [2] N oral *m* [3] COMP ► **oral examiner** N (*Scol etc*) examinateur *m*, -trice *f* à l'oral ► **oral history** N la tradition orale ► **oral hygiene** N hygiène *f* buccale *or* buccodentaire ► **oral hygienist** N hygiéniste *mf* dentaire ► **oral sex** N (= *fellatio*) fellation *f*; (= *cunnilingus*) cunnilingus *m* ► **oral society** N société *f* à tradition orale ► **oral tradition** N la tradition orale ► **oral vowel** N (*Ling*) voyelle *f* orale

orally ['ɔːrəlɪ] ADV [a] (= *verbally*) [*express, promise, pass down*] oralement; [*testify, communicate*] oralement, de vive voix [b] (*Med*) [*take, administer*] par voie orale [c] (= *with mouth*) **to stimulate sb ~** stimuler qn avec la bouche *or* par des caresses bucco-génitales

orange ['ɒrɪndʒ] [1] N [a] (*fruit*); (*also ~ tree*) oranger *m*; (= *colour*) orange *m*, orangé *m*; **"~s and lemons"** chanson et jeu d'enfants → **blood** [2] ADJ [a] (*in colour*) [*dress, shirt, glow*] orange *inv*; **bright ~** orange vif *inv*

[b] (*in taste*) [*drink, liqueur*] à l'orange; [*flavour*] d'orange [3] COMP ► **orange blossom** N fleur(s) *f(pl)* d'oranger ► **orange box**, **orange crate** (*US*) N caisse *f* à oranges ► **Orange Day** N (*Ir*) le 12 juillet (*procession annuelle des orangistes*) ► **orange flower water** N eau *f* de fleur d'oranger ► **Orange Free State** N État *m* libre d'Orange ► **orange grove** N orangeraie *f* ► **orange juice** N jus *m* d'orange ► **orange marmalade** N confiture *f* d'orange ► **orange peel** N (*gen*) peau *f* *or* écorce *f* d'orange; (*Culin*) zeste *m* d'orange; (*Med*) **~ peel effect** peau *f* d'orange ► **orange squash** N ≈ orangeade *f* ► **orange stick** N bâtonnet *m* (*pour manucure etc*) ► **orange tree** N oranger *m*

orangeade ['ɒrɪndʒeɪd] N orangeade *f*

Orangeman ['ɒrɪndʒmən] N (*pl* **-men**) orangiste *m*

orangery ['ɒrɪndʒərɪ] N orangerie *f*

orangewood ['ɒrɪndʒwʊd] N (bois *m* d')oranger *m*

orangey ['ɒrɪndʒɪ] ADJ [*colour*] orangé; [*taste, flavour*] d'orange; **~-red** rouge orangé *inv*

orang-outang [ɔː,ræŋuː'tæŋ], **orang-utan** [ɔː,ræŋuː'tæn] N orang-outan(g) *m*

orate [ɒ'reɪt] [1] VI discourir, faire un discours; (*pej*) pérorer [2] VT déclamer

oration [ɒ'reɪʃən] N discours *m* solennel → **funeral**

orator ['ɒrətə'] N orateur *m*, -trice *f*

oratorical [,ɒrə'tɒrɪkəl] ADJ oratoire

oratorio [,ɒrə'tɔːrɪəʊ] N (*pl* **oratorios**) oratorio *m*

oratory[1] ['ɒrətərɪ] N (= *art*) art *m* oratoire; (= *what is said*) éloquence *f*, rhétorique *f*; **brilliant piece of ~** brillant discours *m*

oratory[2] ['ɒrətərɪ] N (*Rel*) oratoire *m*

orb [ɔːb] N [a] (= *sphere*) globe *m*, sphère *f*; (*in regalia*) globe *m* [b] (*liter = eye*) œil *m* [c] (*liter = celestial body*) orbe *m*

orbit ['ɔːbɪt] [1] N (*Anat, Astron*) orbite *f*; **to be in/go into/put into ~ (around)** être/entrer/mettre en *or* sur orbite (autour de); **countries within the communist ~** pays *mpl* dans l'orbite communiste [2] VT graviter autour de, décrire une *or* des orbite(s) autour de [3] VI orbiter, être *or* rester en *or* sur orbite (**round** autour de)

orbital ['ɔːbɪtl] ADJ [a] (*Brit*) [*road, motorway*] périphérique [b] (*Space*) orbital [c] (*Anat*) orbitaire

orbiter ['ɔːbɪtə'] N (*Space*) orbiteur *m*

Orcadian [ɔː'keɪdɪən] [1] ADJ des (îles) Orcades [2] N habitant(e) *m(f)* des (îles) Orcades

orchard ['ɔːtʃəd] N verger *m*; **cherry ~** champ *m* de cerisiers, cerisaie *f*

orchestra ['ɔːkɪstrə] [1] N [a] (*Mus*) orchestre *m* → **leader**, **string** [b] (*US Theat*) (fauteuils *mpl* d')orchestre *m* [2] COMP ► **orchestra pit** N (*Theat*) fosse *f* d'orchestre ► **orchestra stalls** NPL (fauteuils *mpl* d')orchestre *m*

orchestral [ɔː'kestrəl] ADJ [*music*] orchestral, d'orchestre; [*playing*] de l'orchestre; [*concert*] d'orchestre; [*piece, work, arrangement*] pour orchestre; **~ score** orchestration *f*

orchestrate ['ɔːkɪstreɪt] VT orchestrer

orchestration [,ɔːkɪs'treɪʃən] N orchestration *f*, instrumentation *f*

orchid ['ɔːkɪd] N orchidée *f*; **wild ~** orchis *m*

orchis ['ɔːkɪs] N orchis *m*

ordain [ɔː'deɪn] VT [a] [*God, fate*] décréter (**that** que); [*law*] décréter (**that** que), prescrire (**that** que + *subj*); [*judge*] ordonner (**that** que + *subj*); **it was ~ed that he should die young** il était destiné à mourir jeune, le sort *or* le destin a voulu qu'il meure jeune [b] (*Rel*) [+ *priest*] ordonner; **he was ~ed (priest)** il a reçu l'ordination, il a été ordonné prêtre

ordeal [ɔː'diːl] N [a] rude épreuve *f*, supplice *m*; **they suffered terrible ~s** ils ont subi d'atroces épreuves; **speaking in public was an ~ for him** il était au supplice quand il devait parler en public, parler en public le mettait au supplice; **the painful ~ of the last eight months** l'épreuve pénible qu'ont été ces huit derniers mois [b] (*Hist Jur*) ordalie *f*; **~ by fire** épreuve *f* du feu

▼ **order** ['ɔːdə']

[1] NOUN		[4] COMPOUNDS	
[2] TRANSITIVE VERB		[5] PHRASAL VERBS	
[3] INTRANSITIVE VERB			

[1] NOUN

[a] NonC = *disposition, sequence* ordre *m*; **word ~** ordre *m* des mots; **what ~ should these documents be in?** dans quel ordre faut-il classer ces documents?; **to be in ~** être en ordre; **to put in(to) ~** mettre en ordre; **the cards were out of ~** les cartes n'étaient pas en ordre; **the files have got all out of ~** les dossiers sont sens dessus dessous; **in ~ of merit/precedence** par ordre de mérite/préséance; **"cast in ~ of appearance:"** (*Theat*) « avec par ordre d'entrée en scène: »; (*Cine*) « avec par ordre d'apparition: »

[b] NonC: *also* **good ~** ordre *m*; **he's got no sense of ~** il n'a aucun (sens de l')ordre; **in ~** [*room etc*] en ordre; [*passport, documents*] en règle; **to put one's room/one's affairs in ~** mettre de l'ordre dans sa chambre/ses affaires, mettre sa chambre/ses affaires en ordre; (*US*) **in short ~** sans délai, tout de suite; **to be in running or working ~** être en état de marche; **in good ~** (= *in good condition*) en bon état; **the machine is out of ~** la machine est en panne *or* détraquée; (*on sign*) **"out of ~"** « hors service »; (*Telec*) **the line is out of ~** la ligne est en dérangement

[c] *expressing purpose*

◆ **in order to** pour, afin de; **I did it in ~ to clarify matters** je l'ai fait pour *or* afin de clarifier la situation

◆ **in order that** afin que (+ *subj*), pour que (+ *subj*); **in ~ that there should be no misunderstanding** afin *or* pour qu'il n'y ait pas de malentendu, pour éviter tout malentendu

[d] = *correct procedure* (*Parl etc*) ordre *m*; **~, ~!** silence!; **to call sb to ~** rappeler qn à l'ordre; **he intervened on a point of ~** il a soulevé un point de procédure; **"(on a) point of ~, Mister Chairman ..."** « j'aimerais soulever un point de procédure ... »; **to be in ~** (*gen*) [*action, request etc*] être dans les règles; **that's quite in ~** je n'y vois aucune objection; **is it in ~ to do that?** est-ce que ça se fait?; **would it be in ~ for me to speak to her?** pourrais-je lui parler?; **it's quite in ~ for him to do that** rien ne s'oppose à ce qu'il le fasse; **reforms are clearly in ~** il est évident que des réformes s'imposent; **a drink seems in ~** un verre s'impose; **congratulations are surely in ~!** recevez toutes nos (*or* mes *etc*) félicitations!; **it seems a celebration is in ~!** on va devoir fêter ça!; (*on a*) **point of ~:** [*remark*] déplacé; **that was well out of ~!** ◊ **you're way out of ~!** ça se fait pas!*

[e] = *peace, control* ordre *m*; **to keep ~** [*police*] faire régner l'ordre, maintenir l'ordre; [*teacher*] faire régner la discipline; **she can't keep her class in ~** elle n'arrive pas à tenir sa classe; **keep your dog in ~!** surveillez votre chien!

[f] = *category, class* (*Bio*) ordre *m*; (= *social position*) classe *f*; (= *kind*) ordre *m*; (= *social rank*) **the lower/higher ~s** les classes *fpl* inférieures/supérieures; (*fig*) **of a high ~** de premier ordre; **~ of magnitude** ordre *m* de grandeur; **something in the ~ of 3,000 francs** ◊ **something of the ~ of 3,000 francs** (*Brit*) ◊ **something on the ~ of 3,000 francs** (*US*) quelque chose de l'ordre de 3 000 francs; **the present crisis is of a (very) dif-**

➤ LANGUAGE IN USE: **order** 20.3, 27.7

ferent ~ la crise actuelle est d'un (tout) autre ordre

g = the way things are ordre *m*; **it is in the ~ of things** c'est dans l'ordre des choses; **the old ~ is changing** le monde change; **a new world** un nouvel ordre mondial; **a new social/ political ~** un nouvel ordre social/politique; **strikes were the ~ of the day** les grèves étaient à l'ordre du jour

h Rel ordre *m*; **the Benedictine Order** l'ordre *m* des bénédictins; **to be in/take (holy) ~s** être/entrer dans les ordres

i = command ordre *m*, consigne *f* (*Mil*); **to obey ~s** obéir aux ordres, observer *or* respecter la consigne (*Mil*); **~s are ~s** les ordres sont les ordres, la consigne c'est la consigne; **that's an ~!** c'est un ordre!; **on the ~s of ...** sur l'ordre de ...; **by ~ of ...** par ordre de ...; **till further ~s** jusqu'à nouvel ordre; **to give sb ~s to do sth** ordonner à qn de faire qch; **he gave the ~ for it to be done** il a ordonné qu'on le fasse, il a donné l'ordre de le faire; **you can't give me ~s!** ◊ **I don't take ~s from you!** je ne suis pas à vos ordres!, ce n'est pas à vous de me donner des ordres!; **I don't take ~s from anyone** je n'ai d'ordres à recevoir de personne; **to be under the ~s of** être sous les ordres de; **to be under ~s to do sth** avoir (reçu) l'ordre de faire qch; **sorry, I'm under ~s** désolé, j'ai (reçu) des ordres; (*Brit Parl*) **Order in Council** ordonnance *f* prise en Conseil privé, ≈ décret-loi *m*

j Jur **judge's ~** ordonnance *f*; **~ of bankruptcy** déclaration *f* de faillite; **~ of the Court** injonction *f* de la cour; **deportation ~** arrêté *m* d'expulsion

k Comm commande *f*; **made to ~** fait sur commande; **to give an ~ to sb (for sth)** ◊ **to place an ~ with sb (for sth)** passer une commande (de qch) à qn; **we have received your ~ for ...** nous avons bien reçu votre commande de ...; **we have the shelves on ~ for you** vos étagères sont commandées; (*Comm, fig*) **to do sth to ~** faire qch sur commande

l = warrant, permit permis *m*; **~ to view** permis *m* de visiter

m Fin **pay to the ~ of ...** payer à l'ordre de ...; **pay John Smith or ~** payez John Smith ou à son ordre

n in café etc portion *f*; **an ~ of French fries** une portion de frites

o Archit ordre *m*

2 TRANSITIVE VERB

a = command ordonner à, donner l'ordre à; **to ~ sb to do sth** ordonner à qn de faire qch, donner l'ordre à qn de faire qch; (*frm*) **he ~ed that the army should advance** il a donné l'ordre à l'armée d'avancer; **he was ~ed to be quiet** on lui a ordonné de se taire; **to ~ sb in/out/up** *etc* ordonner à qn d'entrer/de sortir/de monter *etc*; **to ~ a player off** renvoyer un joueur; **to ~ a regiment abroad** envoyer un régiment à l'étranger; **the regiment was ~ed to Berlin** le régiment a reçu l'ordre d'aller à Berlin

b = ask for [+ *goods, meal*] commander; [+ *taxi*] faire venir; **to ~ more wine** redemander du vin; **I didn't ~ this!** ce n'est pas ce que j'ai commandé!

c = put in sequence classer, ranger; **they are ~ed by date/size** ils sont classés *or* rangés dans l'ordre chronologique/par ordre de grandeur

d = put in good order [+ *one's affairs etc*] régler

3 INTRANSITIVE VERB

in restaurant etc passer sa commande; **are you ready to ~?** vous avez choisi?

4 COMPOUNDS

► **order book** N (*Comm, Ind*) carnet *m* de commandes; (*Ind*) **the company's ~ books were full** les carnets de commandes de l'entreprise étaient pleins ► **order form** N (*Comm*)

bulletin *m or* bon *m* de commande ► **order mark** N (*Brit Scol*) avertissement *m* ► **the Order of Merit** N (*Brit*) l'ordre *m* du mérite ► **Order of Service** N (*Rel*) ordre *m* de cérémonie ► **the Order of the Bath** N (*Brit*) l'ordre *m* du Bain ► **the Order of the Garter** N (*Brit*) l'ordre *m* de la Jarretière ► **order paper** N (*Brit Parl*) ordre *m* du jour

5 PHRASAL VERBS

► **order about**, **order around** VT SEP commander; **he likes ~ing people about** il aime donner des ordres (à droite et à gauche); **I won't be ~ed about by him!** je ne suis pas à ses ordres!, je n'ai pas d'ordres à recevoir de lui!

ordered [ˈɔːbɪd] ADJ (*also* **well ~**) [*world, society, universe*] ordonné

ordering [ˈɔːdərɪŋ] N (*Comm*) passation *f* de commandes

orderliness [ˈɔːdəlɪnɪs] N (*NonC*) (habitudes *fpl* d')ordre *m*

orderly [ˈɔːdəlɪ] **1** ADJ [*person*] (= *tidy*) ordonné; (= *methodical*) méthodique; (= *disciplined*) discipliné; [*mind, system*] méthodique; [*life*] rangé, réglé; [*room, queue*] ordonné; [*row*] régulier; [*school*] où règne la discipline; **in an ~ fashion** *or* **manner** avec ordre **2** N **a** (*Mil*) planton *m*, ordonnance *f* **b** (*Med*) garçon *m* de salle → **nursing 3** COMP ► **orderly officer** N (*Mil*) officier *m* de service ► **orderly room** N (*Mil*) salle *f* de rapport

ordinal [ˈɔːdɪnl] **1** ADJ [*number*] ordinal **2** N (*nombre m*) ordinal *m*

ordinance [ˈɔːdɪnəns] N ordonnance *f*, arrêté *m*

ordinand [ˈɔːdɪnænd] N ordinand *m*

ordinarily [ˈɔːdnrɪlɪ] ADV **more than ~** polite/ honest d'une politesse/honnêteté qui sort de l'ordinaire; **the car would ~ cost more** cette voiture coûterait normalement plus; **~, I would have disbelieved him** normalement, je ne l'aurais pas cru

ordinary [ˈɔːdnrɪ] **1** ADJ **a** (= *usual, day-to-day*) ordinaire, normal; **it has 25 calories less than ~ ice cream** elle a 25 calories de moins que les glaces ordinaires; **in ~ use** d'usage *or* d'emploi courant; **my ~ grocer's** mon épicerie habituelle; **the heat made ~ life impossible** la chaleur rendait impossible la routine habituelle; **in the ~ way†** en temps normal, d'ordinaire

b (= *average, not outstanding*) [*person, day*] ordinaire, comme les autres; [*intelligence, knowledge, reader etc*] moyen; **a perfectly ~ Monday morning** un lundi matin comme les autres; **mine was a fairly ~ childhood** j'ai eu une enfance normale *or* assez ordinaire; **I'm just an ~ fellow** je suis un homme comme les autres; **~ people** le commun des mortels; **~ Germans** *etc* l'Allemand *etc* moyen; **it's not what you would call an ~ present** c'est vraiment un cadeau peu ordinaire *or* peu banal; **it was no ~ bar** ce n'était pas un bar ordinaire *or* comme les autres; **she's no ~ woman** ce n'est pas une femme ordinaire *or* comme les autres; **this is no ~ novel, this is a masterpiece** ce n'est pas un roman comme les autres, c'est un chef-d'œuvre

c (*pej*) [*person, meal etc*] ordinaire, quelconque

2 N ordinaire *m*; **out of the ~** hors du commun, qui sort de l'ordinaire; **above the ~** au-dessus du commun *or* de l'ordinaire

b (*Rel*) **the ~ of the mass** l'ordinaire *m* de la messe

3 COMP ► **ordinary degree** N (*Brit Univ*) ≈ licence *f* ► **Ordinary grade** N (*Scot*) = **Ordinary level** ► **Ordinary level** N (*Brit Educ: formerly*) examen passé à l'âge de 16 ans dans le cadre des études secondaires ► **Ordinary National Certificate** N (*Brit Educ*) ≈ brevet *m* de

technicien ► **Ordinary National Diploma** N (*Brit Educ*) ≈ brevet *m* de technicien supérieur ► **ordinary seaman** N (*pl* **ordinary seamen**) (*Brit Navy*) matelot *m* non breveté ► **ordinary share** N (*St Ex*) action *f* ordinaire

ordination [ˌɔːdɪˈneɪʃən] N (*Rel*) ordination *f*

ordnance [ˈɔːdnəns] (*Mil*) **1** N (= *guns*) (pièces *fpl* d')artillerie *f*; (= *unit*) service *m* du matériel et des dépôts **2** COMP ► **Ordnance Corps** N Service *m* du matériel ► **ordnance factory** N usine *f* d'artillerie ► **Ordnance Survey** N (*in Brit*) service *m* cartographique de l'État; **Ordnance Survey map** ≈ carte *f* d'état-major

Ordovician [ˌɔːdəʊˈvɪʃən] ADJ ordovicien

ordure [ˈɔːdjʊə] N ordure *f*

ore [ɔːʳ] N minerai *m*; **iron ~** minerai *m* de fer

Ore(g). ABBR = **Oregon**

oregano [ˌɒrɪˈɡɑːnəʊ, (*US*) əˈreɡənəʊ] N origan *m*

Oregon [ˈɒrɪɡən] N l'Oregon *m*; **in ~** dans l'Oregon

Oreo® [ˈɔːriəʊ] N (*US*) **a** (= *food*) gâteau sec au chocolat fourré à la vanille **b** (ⵀ: *fig, hum* = *person*) Noir(e) *m(f)* qui imite les Blancs

Orestes [ɒˈrestiːz] N Oreste *m*

organ [ˈɔːɡən] **1** N **a** (*Mus*) orgue *m*, orgues *fpl*; **grand ~** grandes orgues *fpl* → **barrel**, **mouth**

b (*Anat*) organe *m*; (= *penis*) sexe *m*; **vocal ~s** ◊ **~s of speech** organes *mpl* vocaux, appareil *m* vocal; **reproductive** *or* **sex(ual) ~s** organes *mpl* génitaux *or* sexuels; **the male ~** le sexe masculin

c (*fig* = *instrument*) organe *m*; **the chief ~ of the administration** l'organe principal de l'administration

d (*Press* = *mouthpiece*) organe *m*, porte-parole *m inv*

2 COMP ► **organ bank** N (*Med*) banque *f* d'organes ► **organ-builder** N facteur *m* d'orgues ► **organ donor** N donneur *m*, -euse *f* d'organe(s) ► **organ-grinder** N joueur *m*, -euse *f* d'orgue de Barbarie; (*pej*) **I want to talk to the ~-grinder, not the (~-grinder's) monkey*** je veux parler au responsable ► **organ loft** N tribune *f* d'orgue ► **organ pipe** N tuyau *m* d'orgue ► **organ screen** N jubé *m* ► **organ stop** N jeu *m* d'orgue ► **organ transplant** N greffe *f* *or* transplantation *f* d'organe

organdie, organdy (*US*) [ˈɔːɡəndɪ] **1** N organdi *m* **2** COMP en organdi, d'organdi

organic [ɔːˈɡænɪk] **1** ADJ **a** (*Chem*) [*matter, waste, fertiliser compound*] organique **b** (*Agr, Culin* = *non-chemical*) [*farm, farming, methods, produce, food*] biologique, bio* *inv*; [*farmer*] biologique; [*meat, poultry*] sans hormones; **~ restaurant** restaurant *m* diététique **c** (*frm* = *integral*) [*society, state, community*] organique; [*part*] fondamental; **~ whole** tout *m* systématique; **~ law** loi *f* organique **2** COMP ► **organic chemistry** N chimie *f* organique ► **organic disease** N maladie *f* organique

organically [ɔːˈɡænɪkəlɪ] ADV **a** (*Agr, Culin* = *not chemically*) [*farm, grow, produce*] biologiquement, sans engrais chimiques; **~ grown vegetables** légumes *mpl* biologiques; **an ~ rich soil** un sol riche en composés organiques **b** (= *naturally*) [*develop, integrate*] naturellement **c** (= *physically*) [*weak*] physiquement

organism [ˈɔːɡənɪzəm] N organisme *m* (*Bio*)

organist [ˈɔːɡənɪst] N organiste *mf*

organization [ˌɔːɡənaɪˈzeɪʃən] **1** N **a** (*gen*) organisation *f*; (= *statutory body*) organisme *m*, organisation *f*; (= *society*) organisation *f*, association *f*; **youth ~** organisation *f or* organisme *m* de jeunesse; **she belongs to several ~s** elle est membre de plusieurs organisations *or* associations; **a charitable ~** une œuvre *or* une association de bienfaisance → **travel**

b (= *executives etc*) [*of business firm, political party*] cadres *mpl* **c** (*NonC*) organisation *f*;

his work lacks ~ son travail manque d'organisation

2 COMP ► **organization and methods** N (Comm, Admin) organisation f scientifique du travail, OST f ► **organization chart** N organigramme m ► **organization expenses** NPL (Fin) frais mpl d'établissement ► **organization man** N (pl **organization men**) (pej) cadre qui s'identifie complètement à son entreprise

organizational [ˌɔːɡənaɪˈzeɪʃənl] ADJ [skill, ability] d'organisateur; [problems] d'organisation, organisationnel; [support, goals, links, structure] organisationnel; [experience] de l'organisation; [framework] structurel, organisationnel; (Jur, Comm) **~ change** changement m structurel, modification f structurelle; **at an ~ level** au niveau organisationnel or de l'organisation

organize [ˈɔːɡənaɪz] **1** VT **a** [+ meeting, scheme, course, visit, elections, strike, campaign, protest] organiser; **they ~d (it) for me to go to London** ils ont organisé mon départ pour Londres; **I'll ~ something to eat for us*** ◊ **I'll ~ us something to eat*** (= buy food) je vais prévoir quelque chose à manger pour nous; (= prepare food) je vais nous préparer un petit quelque chose; **can you ~ the food for us?** vous pouvez vous occuper de la nourriture ?; **she's always organizing people*** elle veut toujours tout organiser; **to ~ one's thoughts** ◊ **to get one's thoughts ~d** mettre de l'ordre dans ses idées; **to get (o.s.) ~d** s'organiser → **organized** **b** (Ind: into trade union) syndiquer → **organized** **2** VI (Ind) se syndiquer

organized [ˈɔːɡənaɪzd] **1** ADJ organisé **2** COMP ► **organized chaos*** N (hum) désordre m organisé ► **organized crime** N crime m organisé ► **organized labour** N (Ind) main-d'œuvre f syndiquée ► **organized religion** N religion f en tant qu'institution

organizer [ˈɔːɡənaɪzəʳ] N **a** [of event, activity] organisateur m, -trice f; **the ~s apologize for ...** les organisateurs vous prient de les excuser pour ... **b** **to be a good/bad ~** être un bon/mauvais organisateur **c** (= diary) **personal ~** Filofax® m, organiseur m personnel; **electronic ~** agenda m électronique

organizing [ˈɔːɡənaɪzɪŋ] **1** N [of event, activity etc] organisation f; **she loves ~** elle adore organiser **2** ADJ [group, committee] (qui est) chargé de l'organisation

organo... [ˈɔːɡənəʊ] PREF organo...

organophosphate [ɔːˌɡænəʊˈfɒsfeɪt] N organophosphoré m

organza [ɔːˈɡænzə] N organza m

orgasm [ˈɔːɡæzəm] N orgasme m

orgasmic [ɔːˈɡæzmɪk] ADJ **a** [person, state] orgasmique **b** (* = enjoyable) [experience, pleasure] jouissif

orgiastic [ˌɔːdʒɪˈæstɪk] ADJ orgiaque

orgy [ˈɔːdʒɪ] N (lit, fig) orgie f; **an ~ of killing/destruction** une orgie de tueries/destruction

oriel [ˈɔːrɪəl] N (also **~ window**) (fenêtre f en) oriel m

orient [ˈɔːrɪənt] **1** N (liter) orient m, levant m; **the Orient** l'Orient **2** VT (lit, fig) orienter → **oriented**

oriental [ˌɔːrɪˈentəl] **1** ADJ [peoples, civilization, design] oriental; [carpet] d'Orient **2** N **Oriental**† Oriental(e) m(f)

orientalist [ˌɔːrɪˈentəlɪst] N orientaliste mf

orientate [ˈɔːrɪənteɪt] VT = **orient 2**; → **oriented**

orientated [ˈɔːrɪənteɪtɪd] ADJ = **oriented**

orientation [ˌɔːrɪənˈteɪʃən] N (gen) orientation f; (US Univ) **~ week** semaine f d'accueil des étudiants

oriented [ˈɔːrɪəntɪd] ADJ **~ to** or **towards** (= giving priority to, influenced by) axé sur; (= specially for needs of) adapté aux besoins de; **the film is**

~ to the British audience ce film s'adresse en premier lieu au public britannique; **their policies are ~ to(wards) controlling inflation** leurs politiques ont pour objet de or visent à juguler l'inflation; **a defence-~ budget** un budget axé sur la défense, un budget qui privilégie la défense; **a strongly export-~ economy** une économie fortement axée sur l'exportation; **industry-~ research** recherche f axée sur les besoins de l'industrie; **user-/pupil- etc ~** adapté aux besoins de or spécialement conçu pour l'usager/l'élève etc; **politically ~** orienté (politiquement); **he's not very family-~** il n'est pas très famille; **it's still a very male-~ job** cela demeure un emploi essentiellement masculin

orienteering [ˌɔːrɪənˈtɪərɪŋ] N (Sport) exercice m d'orientation sur le terrain

orifice [ˈɒrɪfɪs] N orifice m

origami [ˌɒrɪˈɡɑːmɪ] N origami m

origan [ˈɒrɪɡən] N origan m

origin [ˈɒrɪdʒɪn] N (= parentage, source) origine f; [of manufactured goods etc] origine f, provenance f; **the ~ of this lies in ...** l'origine en est ...; **to have humble ~s** ◊ **to be of humble ~** être d'origine modeste, avoir des origines modestes; **his family's ~s are in France** sa famille est d'origine française; **country of ~** pays m d'origine

original [əˈrɪdʒɪnl] **1** ADJ **a** (= first, earliest) [meaning] originel; [inhabitant, member] premier; [purpose, suggestion] initial, premier; [shape, colour] primitif; [edition] original, princeps inv; (Fin, Comm) **~ cost** coût m d'acquisition; (US Jur) **~ jurisdiction** juridiction f de première instance; **~ sin** le péché originel **b** (= not copied etc) [painting, idea, writer] original; [play] inédit, original **c** (= unconventional, innovative) [character, person] original; **he's an ~ thinker** ◊ **he's got an ~ mind** c'est un esprit original **2** N **a** [of painting, language, document] original m; **to read Dante in the ~ (Italian)** lire Dante dans le texte **b** (* = person) original(e) m(f), phénomène* m

originality [əˌrɪdʒɪˈnælɪtɪ] N originalité f

originally [əˈrɪdʒnəlɪ] ADV **a** (= initially) [intend, plan] au départ, à l'origine; **he's ~ from Armenia** il est originaire d'Arménie; **it was ~ a hit for Janis Joplin** au départ, c'était un tube de Janis Joplin **b** (= unconventionally, innovatively) [dress] de façon originale; **to think ~** avoir des idées novatrices or originales

originate [əˈrɪdʒɪneɪt] **1** VT [person] être l'auteur de, être à l'origine de; [event etc] donner naissance à; **originating bank** banque f émettrice **2** VI **to ~ from** [person] être originaire de; [goods] provenir de; **to ~ from sb** [suggestion, idea] émaner de qn; **to ~ in** [stream, custom etc] prendre naissance or sa source dans

origination fee [əˌrɪdʒɪˈneɪʃənˌfiː] N frais mpl de constitution de dossier

originator [əˈrɪdʒɪneɪtəʳ] N auteur m, créateur m, -trice f; [of plan etc] initiateur m, -trice f

Orinoco [ˌɒrɪˈnəʊkəʊ] N Orénoque m

oriole [ˈɔːrɪəʊl] N loriot m → **golden**

Orion [əˈraɪən] N (Astron) Orion f; (Myth) Orion m

Orkney [ˈɔːknɪ] N **the ~ Islands** ◊ **the ~s** les Orcades fpl

Orlon® [ˈɔːlɒn] **1** N orlon® m **2** COMP en orlon®

ormer [ˈɔːməʳ] N (Zool) ormeau m

ormolu [ˈɔːməluː] **1** N similor m, chrysocale m **2** COMP en similor, en chrysocale

ornament [ˈɔːnəmənt] **1** N **a** (on building, ceiling, dress etc) ornement m **b** (= ornamental object) objet m décoratif, bibelot m; (fig, liter = person, quality) ornement m (fig, liter); **a row of**

~s on the shelf une rangée de bibelots sur l'étagère **c** (NonC = ornamentation) ornement m; **rich in ~** richement orné **d** (Mus) ornement m **2** [ˈɔːnəment] VT [+ style] orner, embellir (**with** de); [+ room, building, ceiling] décorer, ornementer (**with** de); [+ dress] agrémenter, orner (**with** de)

ornamental [ˌɔːnəˈmentl] ADJ **a** (= decorative) [plant, shrub] ornemental, décoratif; [garden, pond, lake] d'agrément; [design] décoratif **b** (*: pej hum) [person, role] décoratif (pej)

ornamentation [ˌɔːnəmenˈteɪʃən] N (NonC) (gen) ornementation f, décoration f; (Mus) ornements mpl

ornate [ɔːˈneɪt] ADJ très orné

ornately [ɔːˈneɪtlɪ] ADV [carved, decorated] richement

ornery* [ˈɔːnərɪ] ADJ (US) [person] (= bad-tempered) désagréable; (= nasty) méchant; (= stubborn) entêté

ornithological [ˌɔːnɪθəˈlɒdʒɪkəl] ADJ ornithologique

ornithologist [ˌɔːnɪˈθɒlədʒɪst] N ornithologiste mf, ornithologue mf

ornithology [ˌɔːnɪˈθɒlədʒɪ] N ornithologie f

orogeny [ɒˈrɒdʒɪnɪ] N orogénie f, orogénèse f

orphan [ˈɔːfən] **1** N orphelin(e) m(f) **2** ADJ orphelin **3** VT **to be ~ed** devenir orphelin(e); **the children were ~ed by** or **in the accident** les enfants ont perdu leurs parents dans l'accident

orphanage [ˈɔːfənɪdʒ] N orphelinat m

Orpheus [ˈɔːfjuːs] N Orphée m; (Mus) **~ in the Underworld** Orphée aux enfers

Orphic [ˈɔːfɪk] ADJ orphique

ortho... [ˈɔːθəʊ] PREF ortho...

orthodontic [ˌɔːθəʊˈdɒntɪk] ADJ orthodontique

orthodontics [ˌɔːθəʊˈdɒntɪks] N (NonC) orthodontie f

orthodontist [ˌɔːθəʊˈdɒntɪst] N orthodontiste mf

orthodox [ˈɔːθədɒks] **1** ADJ (gen, Rel) [person, view, method] orthodoxe; (Med) [doctor, practitioner] exerçant la médecine traditionnelle; [medicine] traditionnel; **~ Jews/Communists** juifs mpl/communistes mpl orthodoxes **2** COMP ► **the Orthodox Church** N (also **the Eastern Orthodox Church**) les Églises fpl orthodoxes

orthodoxy [ˈɔːθədɒksɪ] N orthodoxie f

orthogonal [ɔːˈθɒɡənl] ADJ orthogonal

orthographic(al) [ˌɔːθəˈɡræfɪk(əl)] ADJ orthographique

orthography [ɔːˈθɒɡrəfɪ] N orthographe f

orthopaedic, orthopedic (US) [ˌɔːθəʊˈpiːdɪk] **1** ADJ [ward, shoes] orthopédique; [patient] en traitement orthopédique **2** COMP ► **orthopaedic bed** N (specially firm) lit m à sommier anatomique, lit m orthopédique ► **orthopaedic mattress** N sommier m anatomique ► **orthopaedic surgeon** N chirurgien m orthopédiste ► **orthopaedic surgery** N chirurgie f orthopédique

orthopaedics, orthopedics (US) [ˌɔːθəʊˈpiːdɪks] N (NonC) orthopédie f

orthopaedist, orthopedist (US) [ˌɔːθəʊˈpiːdɪst] N orthopédiste mf

orthopaedy, orthopedy (US) [ˈɔːθəʊpiːdɪ] N = **orthopaedics**

ortolan [ˈɔːtələn] N ortolan m

Orwellian [ɔːˈwelɪən] ADJ (Literat etc) d'Orwell

oryx [ˈɒrɪks] N (pl **oryxes** or **oryx**) oryx m

OS [ˌəʊˈes] **a** (Brit Navy) (ABBR = **Ordinary Seaman**) → **ordinary** **b** (in Brit) (ABBR = **Ordnance Survey**) → **ordnance** **c** ABBR = **outsize**

os [ɒs] **1** N (Anat) os m **2** COMP ► **os coxae** N os m iliaque or coxal

Oscar ['ɒskəʳ] N (Cine) oscar m; **~-winning** qui a remporté un oscar (or des oscars)

oscillate ['ɒsɪleɪt] [1] VI (gen, Elec, Phys etc) osciller; (fig) [ideas, opinions] fluctuer, varier; [person] osciller, balancer (**between** entre) [2] VT faire osciller

oscillation [,ɒsɪ'leɪʃən] N oscillation f

oscillator ['ɒsɪleɪtəʳ] N oscillateur m

oscillatory ['ɒsɪleɪtərɪ] ADJ oscillatoire

oscilloscope [ɒ'sɪləskəʊp] N oscilloscope m

osculate ['ɒskjʊleɪt] (hum) [1] VI s'embrasser [2] VT embrasser

OSHA ['əʊeseɪtʃ'eɪ] N (US) (ABBR = **Occupational Safety and Health Administration**) → **occupational**

osier ['əʊʒəʳ] [1] N osier m [2] COMP [branch] d'osier; [basket] en osier, d'osier

Osiris [əʊ'saɪrɪs] N Osiris m

Oslo ['ɒzləʊ] N Oslo

osmium ['ɒzmɪəm] N osmium m

osmosis [ɒz'məʊsɪs] N (Phys, fig) osmose f; (lit, fig) **by ~** par osmose

osmotic [ɒz'mɒtɪk] ADJ osmotique

osprey ['ɒspreɪ] N (Orn) balbuzard m (pêcheur)

osseous ['ɒsɪəs] ADJ [a] (Anat, Zool) osseux [b] = **ossiferous**

ossicle ['ɒsɪkl] N osselet m

ossiferous [ɒ'sɪfərəs] ADJ ossifère

ossification [,ɒsɪfɪ'keɪʃən] N ossification f

ossify ['ɒsɪfaɪ] (lit, fig) [1] VT ossifier [2] VI s'ossifier

ossuary ['ɒsjʊərɪ] N ossuaire m

Ostend [ɒs'tend] N Ostende

ostensible [ɒs'tensəbl] ADJ (frm) prétendu (before n)

ostensibly [ɒs'tensəblɪ] ADV (frm) [independent, innocuous etc] prétendument; **he was ~ a student** il était soi-disant étudiant; **he went out, ~ to telephone** il est sorti soi-disant or prétendument pour téléphoner; **the road is closed, ~ because of landslides** la route est barrée, soi-disant à cause d'éboulements

ostensive [ɒ'stensɪv] ADJ [a] (Ling etc) ostensif [b] = **ostensible**

ostentation [,ɒsten'teɪʃən] N (NonC) ostentation f

ostentatious [,ɒsten'teɪʃəs] ADJ [a] (pej = extravagant) [car, clothes] tape-à-l'œil inv; [surroundings] prétentieux [b] (pej = flamboyant) [person] prétentieux; [manner] prétentieux, ostentatoire (liter) [c] (= exaggerated) [gesture, dislike, concern, attempt] exagéré, ostentatoire (liter)

ostentatiously [,ɒsten'teɪʃəslɪ] ADV (pej = extravagantly) [decorate, live] avec ostentation; [dress] de façon voyante [b] (= exaggeratedly) [try, yawn] avec ostentation; **he looked ~ at his watch** il a regardé sa montre avec ostentation

osteo... ['ɒstɪəʊ] PREF ostéo...

osteoarthritis ['ɒstɪəʊɑː'θraɪtɪs] N ostéoarthrite f

osteoblast ['ɒstɪəʊblɑːst] N ostéoblaste m

osteogenesis [,ɒstɪəʊ'dʒenɪsɪs] N ostéogenèse f, ostéogénie f

osteology [,ɒstɪ'ɒlədʒɪ] N ostéologie f

osteomalacia [,ɒstɪəʊmə'leɪʃɪə] N ostéomalacie f

osteomyelitis [,ɒstɪəʊmaɪɪ'laɪtɪs] N ostéomyélite f

osteopath ['ɒstɪəpæθ] N ostéopathe mf

osteopathy [,ɒstɪ'ɒpəθɪ] N ostéopathie f

osteophyte ['ɒstɪəfaɪt] N ostéophyte m

osteoplasty ['ɒstɪəplæstɪ] N ostéoplastie f

osteoporosis [,ɒstɪəʊpɔː'rəʊsɪs] N ostéoporose f

osteotomy [,ɒstɪ'ɒtəmɪ] N ostéotomie f

ostler†† ['ɒsləʳ] N (esp Brit) valet m d'écurie

ostracism ['ɒstrəsɪzəm] N ostracisme m

ostracize ['ɒstrəsaɪz] VT frapper d'ostracisme

ostrich ['ɒstrɪtʃ] N (pl **ostriches** or **ostrich**) autruche f

OT [əʊ'tiː] [a] (Bible) (ABBR = **Old Testament**) → **old** [b] (Med) (ABBR = **occupational therapy**) → **occupational**

OTB [,əʊtiː'biː] N (US) (ABBR = **off-track betting**) ≈ PMU m

OTC [,əʊtiː'siː] N (Brit Mil) (ABBR = **Officers' Training Corps**) → **officer**

OTE [,əʊtiː'iː] (ABBR = **on-target earnings**) → **target**

other ['ʌðəʳ] [1] ADJ autre; **the ~ one** l'autre mf; **the ~ five** les cinq autres mfpl; **~ people have done it** d'autres l'ont fait; **~ people's property** la propriété d'autrui; **it always happens to ~ people** ça arrive toujours aux autres; (fig) **the ~ world** l'au-delà m, l'autre monde m; **~ worldly** → **day/week** l'autre jour m/semaine f; **come back some ~ time** revenez un autre jour; (esp Brit: Mil) **~ ranks** ≈ sous-officiers mpl et soldats mpl; **I wouldn't wish things ~ than they are** les choses sont très bien comme elles sont; **some writer or ~ said that ...** je ne sais quel écrivain a dit que ..., un écrivain, je ne sais plus lequel, a dit que ...; **some fool or ~** un idiot quelconque; **there must be some ~ way of doing it** on doit pouvoir le faire d'une autre manière → **every, hand, time, word**

[2] PRON autre mf; **and these five ~s** et ces cinq autres; **there are some ~s** il y en a d'autres; **several ~s have mentioned it** plusieurs autres l'ont mentionné; **one after the ~** l'un après l'autre; **~s have spoken of him** il y en a d'autres qui ont parlé de lui; **he doesn't like hurting ~s** il n'aime pas faire de mal aux autres or à autrui; **some like flying, ~s prefer the train** les uns aiment prendre l'avion, les autres préfèrent le train; **some do, ~s don't** il y en a qui le font, d'autres qui ne le font pas; **one or ~ of them will come** il y en aura bien un qui viendra; **somebody or ~ suggested that ...** je ne sais qui a suggéré que ..., quelqu'un, je ne sais qui, a suggéré que ...; **they concentrated on one problem to the exclusion of all ~s** ils se sont concentrés sur un problème, à l'exclusion de tous les autres; **you and no ~** vous et personne d'autre; **no ~ than** nul autre que → **each, none**

[3] ADV [a] (= otherwise) autrement; **he could not have acted ~ than he did** il n'aurait pas pu agir autrement; **I wouldn't wish him ~ than he is** il est très bien comme il est; **I've never seen her ~ than with her husband** je ne l'ai jamais vue (autrement) qu'avec son mari; (frm) **I couldn't do ~ than come** ◊ **I could do nothing ~ than come** je ne pouvais faire autrement que de venir, je ne pouvais pas ne pas venir [b] **~ than ...** (= apart from) à part ...; **~ than that, I said nothing** à part ça, je n'ai rien dit, je n'ai rien dit d'autre; **no one ~ than a member of the family** nul autre qu'un membre de la famille → **somehow**

[4] COMP ► **other-directed** ADJ (US Psych) conformiste

otherness ['ʌðənɪs] N altérité f

otherwise ['ʌðəwaɪz] [1] ADV [a] (= in another way) autrement; **I could not do ~ than agree** je ne pouvais faire autrement que de consentir; **it cannot be ~** il ne peut en être autrement; **until proved ~** jusqu'à preuve du contraire; **he was ~ engaged** il était occupé à (faire) autre chose; **except where ~ stated** sauf indication contraire; **whether sold or ~** vendu ou non; (frm) **should it be ~** dans le cas contraire; **Montgomery ~ (known as) Monty** Montgomery autrement (dit or appelé) Monty [b] (= in other respects) autrement, à part cela; **~ it's a very good car** autrement or à

part ça c'est une excellente voiture; **an ~ excellent essay** une dissertation par ailleurs excellente [2] CONJ autrement

otherworldly [,ʌðə'wɜːldlɪ] ADJ [attitude] détaché des contingences; [person] détaché du monde

otiose ['əʊʃɪəʊs] ADJ (frm) (= idle) oisif; (= useless) oiseux

otitis [əʊ'taɪtɪs] N otite f

OTT* [,əʊtiː'tiː] (ABBR = **over the top**) → **top**

Ottawa ['ɒtəwə] N (= city) Ottawa; (= river) Ottawa f, Outaouais m

otter ['ɒtəʳ] N (pl **otters** or **otter**) loutre f → **sea**

Otto ['ɒtəʊ] N (Hist) Othon m or Otton m

Ottoman ['ɒtəmən] [1] ADJ ottoman [2] N Ottoman(e) m(f)

ottoman ['ɒtəmən] N (pl **ottomans**) ottomane f

OU [əʊ'juː] (Brit Educ) [a] (ABBR = **Open University**) → **open** [b] ABBR = **Oxford University**

ouch [aʊtʃ] EXCL aïe !

▼**ought**[1] [ɔːt] (pret **ought**) MODAL AUX VB [a] (indicating obligation, advisability, desirability) **I ~ to do it** je devrais le faire, il faudrait or il faut que je le fasse; **I really ~ to go and see him** je devrais bien aller le voir; **he thought he ~ to tell you** il a pensé qu'il devait vous le dire; **if they behave as they ~** s'ils se conduisent comme ils le doivent, s'ils se conduisent correctement; **this ~ to have been finished long ago** cela aurait dû être terminé il y a longtemps; **oughtn't you to have left by now?** est-ce que vous n'auriez pas dû déjà être parti ? [b] (indicating probability) **they ~ to be arriving soon** ils devraient bientôt arriver; **he ~ to have got there by now I expect** je pense qu'il est arrivé or qu'il a dû arriver (à l'heure qu'il est); **that ~ to do** ça devrait aller; **that ~ to be very enjoyable** cela devrait être très agréable

ought[2] [ɔːt] N = **aught**

Ouija®, **ouija** ['wiːdʒə] N ► **board** oui-ja m inv

ounce [aʊns] N [a] (= measurement) once f (= 28,35 grammes); (fig) [of truth, malice, sense, strength etc] once f, gramme m [b] (Zool) once f

our ['aʊəʳ] POSS ADJ notre (nos pl); **~ book** notre livre m; **~ table** notre table f; **~ clothes** nos vêtements mpl; (Rel) **Our Father/Lady** Notre Père m/Dame f; (emphatic) **that's OUR car** c'est notre voiture à nous

ours ['aʊəz] POSS PRON le nôtre, la nôtre, les nôtres; **this car is ~** cette voiture est à nous or nous appartient or est la nôtre; **a friend of ~** un de nos amis (à nous), un ami à nous*; **I think it's one of ~** je crois que c'est un des nôtres; **your house is better than ~** votre maison est mieux que la nôtre; **it's no fault of ~** ce n'est pas de notre faute (à nous); (pej) **that car of ~** notre fichue* voiture; **that stupid son of ~** notre idiot de fils; **the house became ~** la maison est devenue la nôtre; **no advice of ~ could prevent him** aucun conseil de notre part ne pouvait l'empêcher; (frm) **it is not ~ to decide** ce n'est pas à nous de décider, il ne nous appartient pas de décider; **~ is a specialized department** nous sommes un service spécialisé

ourself [,aʊə'self] PERS PRON (frm, liter: of royal or editorial "we") nous-même

ourselves [,aʊə'selvz] PERS PRON (reflexive: direct and indirect) nous; (emphatic) nous-mêmes; (after prep) nous; **we enjoyed ~** nous nous sommes bien amusés; **we said to ~** nous nous sommes dit, on s'est dit*; **we saw it ~** nous l'avons vu nous-mêmes; **we've kept three for ~** nous nous en sommes réservé trois; **people like ~** des gens comme nous; **we were talking amongst ~** nous discutions entre nous; **(all) by ~** tout seuls, toutes seules

➤ **LANGUAGE IN USE:** **ought** 1.1

oust [aʊst] VT évincer (**sb from sth** qn de qch); **they ~ed him from the chairmanship** ils l'ont évincé de à l'extérieur; ils l'ont forcé à démissionner; **she soon ~ed him as the teenagers' idol** elle eut vite fait de lui prendre sa place d'idole des jeunes

out [aʊt]

1 ADVERB	4 NOUN
2 ADJECTIVE	5 TRANSITIVE VERB
3 PREPOSITION	6 COMPOUNDS

When **out** *is the second element in a phrasal verb, eg* **get out, go out, speak out,** *look up the verb. When* **out** *is part of a set combination, eg* **day out, voyage out,** *look up the noun.*

1 ADVERB

a = **outside** dehors; **it's hot ~** il fait chaud dehors *or* à l'extérieur; *BUT* **~ you go!** sortez!, filez!*; (*above exit*) **"~"** «sortie»

b **person** **to be ~** (= *to have gone out*) être sorti; (= *to go out*) sortir; **Paul is ~** Paul est sorti *or* n'est pas là; **he's ~ a good deal** il sort beaucoup, il n'est pas souvent chez lui; **he's ~ fishing** il est (parti) à la pêche

out, when followed by a preposition, is not usually translated.

he's ~ in the garden il est dans le jardin; **when he was ~ in Iran** lorsqu'il était en Iran; **he's ~ to dinner** il est sorti dîner; **he went ~ to China** il est parti en Chine → **out of**

c **homosexual** **to be ~*** assumer publiquement son homosexualité

d **Tennis** (**the ball is**) **~!** (la balle est) out!

e **tide** **when the tide is ~** à marée basse

f **expressing distance** **five days ~ from Liverpool** à cinq jours (de voyage) de Liverpool; **the boat was 10 miles ~** (**to sea**) le bateau était à 10 milles de la côte; **their house is 10km ~** (**of town**) leur maison est à 10 km de la ville; **to be ~ at sea** être en mer

g **SET STRUCTURES**

♦ **to be out and about: you should be ~ and about!** ne restez donc pas enfermé!; **to be ~ and about again** être de nouveau sur pied
♦ **out here** ici; **come in! — no, I like it ~ here** entrez! — non, je suis bien ici; **she doesn't know how to get on with the people ~ here** elle a du mal à sympathiser avec les gens d'ici
♦ **out there** (= *in that place*) là; (*further away*) là-bas; **look ~ there** regardez là-bas
♦ **out with it!*** vas-y, parle!

2 ADJECTIVE

a = **extinguished** [*light, fire, gas*] éteint

b = **available** en vente; **the video is ~ now** la vidéo est maintenant en vente; *BUT* **a new edition is ~ this month** une nouvelle édition sort ce mois-ci

c = **unavailable** (*for lending, renting*) **that book is ~** ce livre est sorti; **the video I wanted was ~** la cassette vidéo que je voulais était sortie

d = **revealed** **the secret is ~** le secret n'en est plus un

e = **unconscious** évanoui, sans connaissance; **he was ~ for 30 seconds** il est resté évanoui *or* sans connaissance pendant 30 secondes

f = **wrong, incorrect** **their timing was five minutes ~** ils s'étaient trompés de cinq minutes; **you were ~ by 20cm** ◊ **you were 20cm ~** vous vous êtes trompé *or* vous avez fait une erreur de 20 cm; **you're not far ~** tu ne te trompes pas de beaucoup, tu n'es pas tombé loin*

g = **unacceptable** [*idea, suggestion*] **that's right ~, I'm afraid** il n'en est malheureusement pas question

h = **defeated** (*in cards, games*) **you're ~** tu es éliminé; (*politically*) **the socialists are ~** les socialistes sont battus

i = **finished** **before the month was ~** avant la fin du mois

j = **striking** **the steelworkers are ~** (**on strike**) les ouvriers des aciéries sont en grève

k = **unfashionable** passé de mode, out *inv*; **long skirts are ~** les jupes longues sont passées de mode *or* out; **romance is making a come-back, reality is ~** les histoires d'amour font leur come-back, le réalisme est passé de mode *or* out

l **in society** [*girl*] **is your sister ~?†** est-ce que votre sœur a fait son entrée dans le monde?

m **flowers, sun, moon** *etc* **the roses are ~** les rosiers sont en fleur(s); **the trees were ~** les arbres étaient verts; **the sun was ~** le soleil brillait; **the moon was ~** la lune s'était levée, il y avait clair de lune; **the stars were ~** les étoiles brillaient

n **SET STRUCTURES**

♦ **to be out to do sth*** (= *seeking to do*) chercher à faire qch; **they're just ~ to make a quick profit** ils ne cherchent qu'à se remplir les poches; *BUT* **they were ~ to get him** ils voulaient sa peau*
♦ **to be out for sth*** (= *seeking*) **he's ~ for all he can get** il cherche à profiter au maximum de la situation; **she was just ~ for a good time** elle ne cherchait qu'à s'amuser

3 out of PREPOSITION

When **out of** *is part of a phrasal verb, eg* **come out of, run out of,** *look up the verb. When it is part of a set combination, eg* **out of danger, out of the way, out of bounds,** *look up the noun.*

a = **outside** en dehors de, hors de; **he lives ~ of town** il habite en dehors de la ville; **the town was ~ of range of their missiles** la ville était hors d'atteinte de leurs missiles

♦ **out of it*** (= *escaped from situation*) **I was glad to be ~ of it** j'étais bien content d'y avoir échappé; **you're well ~ of it** tu n'as rien à regretter; (= *excluded*) **I felt rather ~ of it at the party** je me sentais un peu exclu à cette fête; (= *drunk, drugged*) **he's ~ of it** il est dans les vapes*

b **expressing distance** **they were 100km ~ of Paris** ils étaient à 100 km de Paris; **it's 15km ~ of town** c'est à 15 km du centre-ville

c = **absent from** **the boss is ~ of town this week** le patron est en déplacement cette semaine; **he's ~ of the office at the moment** il n'est pas au bureau actuellement

d = **through** par; **~ of the window** par la fenêtre; **he went ~ of the back door** il est sorti par la porte de derrière

e = **from** **only one chapter ~ of the novel** un seul chapitre du roman; **a model made ~ of matchsticks** un modèle réduit construit avec des allumettes; **one chapter ~ of a long novel** ce n'est qu'un chapitre tiré d'un long roman; **he had made the table ~ of a crate** il avait fabriqué la table avec une caisse; **it was like something ~ of a nightmare** c'était cauchemardesque; **he looked like something ~ of "Star Trek"** il semblait sorti tout droit de «Star Trek»

In the following **dans** *describes the original position of the thing being moved:*

to take sth ~ of a drawer prendre qch dans un tiroir; **to drink ~ of a glass** boire dans un verre; **they ate ~ of the same plate** ils mangeaient dans la même assiette; **he copied the poem ~ of a book** il a copié le poème dans un livre

f = **because of** par; **~ of curiosity/necessity** par curiosité/nécessité

g = **from among** sur; **in nine cases ~ of ten** dans neuf cas sur dix; **one ~ of five smokers** un fumeur sur cinq

h = **without** **we are ~ of bread/money** nous n'avons plus de pain/d'argent; **we were ~ of petrol** nous n'avions plus d'essence, nous étions en panne d'essence

i = **sheltered from** à l'abri de; **~ of the wind** à l'abri du vent

j = **eliminated from** éliminé de; **~ of the World Cup** éliminé de la coupe du monde

k **Racing** **Lexicon by Hercules ~ of Alphabet** Lexicon issu d'Hercule et d'Alphabet

4 NOUN

a ***** = **means of escape** **this gives them an ~, a chance to change their minds** cela leur laisse une porte de sortie, une occasion de changer d'avis

♦ **to want out: the cat wants ~** le chat veut sortir; **he wants ~ but he doesn't know what he can do instead** il veut partir mais il ne sait pas trop ce qu'il pourrait faire d'autre; **he wants ~ of his contract** il veut résilier son contrat

b **US** **on the ~s with sb‡** brouillé avec qn

5 TRANSITIVE VERB

= **expose as a homosexual** révéler l'homosexualité de

6 COMPOUNDS

► **out-of-body experience** N *expérience au cours de laquelle on se projette hors des limites de son corps* ► **out-of-bounds** ADJ [*place*] interdit; (*US Ftbl*) [*ball*] sorti ► **out-of-date** ADJ [*passport, ticket*] périmé; [*custom*] suranné, désuet (-ète *f*); [*clothes*] démodé; [*theory, concept*] périmé, démodé; [*word*] vieilli ► **out-of-doors** ADV = **outdoors** ► **out-of-pocket expenses** NPL débours *mpl*, frais *mpl* ► **out-of-sight‡** ADJ (*US fig*) formidable, terrible* ► **out-of-the-body experience** N = **out-of-body experience** ► **out-of-the-ordinary** ADJ [*theory, approach, film, book*] insolite, qui sort de l'ordinaire ► **out-of-the-way** ADJ (= *remote*) [*spot*] isolé, perdu; (= *unusual*) = **out-of-the-ordinary** ► **out-of-this-world*** ADJ (*fig*) sensationnel*, fantastique* ► **out-tray** N corbeille *f* de départ

outa‡ ['aʊtə] (*esp US*) ABBR = **out of I'm ~ here** (= *I'm going*) moi, je me tire‡; **get ~ here!** (= *go away*) fiche le camp!*; (= *you're joking*) tu me fais marcher?*

outage ['aʊtɪdʒ] N **a** (= *break in functioning*) interruption *f* de service; (*Elec*) coupure *f* de courant **b** (= *amount removed: gen*) quantité *f* enlevée; (*Cine* = *cut from film*) film *m* (*rejeté au montage*); (= *amount lost: gen*) quantité *f* perdue; (*Comm: during transport*) déchet *m* de route *or* de freinte

out-and-out ['aʊtəndaʊt] ADJ [*lie*] pur et simple; [*liar*] fieffé, fini; [*cheat, fool, crook*] fini; [*racist, fascist*] à tout crin; [*winner*] incontestable; [*success, victory, defeat*] total

out-and-outer* [aʊtən'daʊtə] N (*esp US*) jusqu'au-boutiste *mf*

outasite‡ [aʊtə'saɪt] ADJ (*US* = *out of sight*) formidable, terrible*

outback ['aʊtbæk] N **a** (*in Austral*) intérieur *m* du pays (*plus ou moins inculte*) **b** (= *back country*) campagne *f* isolée *or* presque déserte, cambrousse* *f*

outbid [aʊt'bɪd] (*pret* **outbid** *or* **outbade** [aʊt'bɪd], *ptp* **outbidden** *or* **outbid**) **1** VT enchérir sur **2** VI surenchérir

outbidding [aʊt'bɪdɪŋ] N (*Fin*) surenchères *fpl*

outboard ['aʊtbɔːd] ADJ, N = **(motor)** (moteur *m*) hors-bord *m*

outbound ['aʊtbaʊnd] ADJ [*passengers, train*] en partance

outbox [aʊt'bɒks] VT boxer mieux que

outbreak ['aʊtbreɪk] N [*of war, fighting*] début *m*, déclenchement *m*; [*of violence*] éruption *f*; [*of emotion*] débordement *m*; [*of fever, disease*] accès *m*; [*of spots*] éruption *f*, poussée *f*; [*of demonstrations*] vague *f*; [*of revolt*] déclenchement *m*; **at the ~ of the disease** lorsque la maladie se déclara; **at the ~ of war** lorsque la guerre éclata; **the ~ of hostilities** l'ouverture *f* des hostilités

outbuilding ['aʊtbɪldɪŋ] N dépendance f; (*separate*) appentis m, remise f; **the ~s** les communs mpl, les dépendances fpl

outburst ['aʊtbɜːst] N (*gen*) emportement m passager, (= *anger*) explosion f, accès m; (= *energy*) accès m; **he was ashamed of his ~** il avait honte de l'éclat or de la scène qu'il venait de faire

outcast ['aʊtkɑːst] N exclu(e) m(f), paria m; **their government's attitude has made them international ~** l'attitude de leur gouvernement les a mis au ban de la communauté internationale; **this has made him an ~ from his own family** à cause de cela, il a été rejeté par sa propre famille; **social ~** exclu(e) m(f), paria m

outclass [aʊt'klɑːs] VT (*gen*) surclasser, surpasser; (*Sport*) surclasser

outcome ['aʊtkʌm] N [*of meeting, work, discussion*] issue f, résultat m; [*of decision etc*] conséquence f

outcrop ['aʊtkrɒp] (*Geol*) 1 N affleurement m 2 [aʊt'krɒp] VI affleurer

outcry ['aʊtkraɪ] N (= *protest*) tollé m (général); (= *raised voices*) huées fpl; **there was a general ~ against ...** un tollé général s'éleva contre ...; **to raise an ~ about sth** crier haro sur qch, ameuter l'opinion sur qch

outdated [aʊt'deɪtɪd] ADJ [*technology, equipment*] périmé; [*clothes*] démodé; [*method, system, concept, theory, idea, notion, practice*] dépassé, démodé; [*custom*] suranné, désuet (-ète f)

outdid [aʊt'dɪd] VB pt of **outdo**

outdistance [aʊt'dɪstəns] VT distancer

outdo [aʊt'duː] (*pret* **outdid**, *ptp* **outdone** [aʊt'dʌn]) VT l'emporter sur (**sb in sth** qn en qch); **but he was not to be outdone** mais il refusait de s'avouer vaincu or battu; **and I, not to be outdone, said that ...** et moi, pour ne pas être en reste, j'ai dit que ...

outdoor ['aʊtdɔːr] ADJ [*activities, pursuits, sports, games*] de plein air; [*work, swimming pool, tennis court*] en plein air; [*toilet*] à l'extérieur; [*market*] à ciel ouvert; [*shoes*] de marche; (*Sport*) **~ clothing** vêtements mpl sport inv; **~ centre** centre m aéré; **for ~ use** pour usage extérieur; **to lead an ~ life** vivre au grand air; **he likes the ~ life** il aime la vie au grand air or en plein air; **~ living** vie f au grand air; **she's the** or **an ~ type** elle aime le grand air et la nature

outdoors ['aʊt'dɔːz] 1 ADV (*also* **out-of-doors**) [*stay, play, exercise, bathe*] dehors; [*live*] au grand air; [*sleep*] dehors, à la belle étoile; **to be ~** être dehors; **to go ~** sortir; **~, there are three heated swimming pools** il y a trois piscines chauffées à l'extérieur 2 N **the great ~** le grand air 3 ADJ = **outdoor**

outer ['aʊtər] 1 ADJ [*layer, surface, skin, shell, wall, edge*] extérieur (-eure f); [*door*] qui donne sur l'extérieur; **~ garments** vêtements mpl de dessus; **the ~ harbour** avant-port m; **the ~ suburbs** la grande banlieue; **the ~ world** le monde extérieur; **the ~ reaches of the solar system** les confins mpl du système solaire 2 COMP ► **Outer London** N la grande banlieue londonienne ► **Outer Mongolia** N la Mongolie-Extérieure ► **outer office** N (*reception area*) réception f ► **outer space** N espace m

outermost ['aʊtəməʊst] ADJ [*layer, rim*] extérieur (-eure f); [*edge*] extrême; **the ~ planet** la planète la plus éloignée; **the ~ suburbs** la grande banlieue; **the ~ limits of ...** les extrémités fpl de ...

outerwear ['aʊtəweər] N (*NonC: US*) vêtements mpl d'extérieur (*pardessus, manteaux, vestes etc*)

outface [aʊt'feɪs] VT (= *stare out*) dévisager; (*fig*) faire perdre contenance à

outfall ['aʊtfɔːl] N [*of river*] embouchure f; [*of sewer*] déversoir m

outfield ['aʊtfiːld] N (*Baseball, Cricket*) champ m or terrain m extérieur

outfielder ['aʊtfiːldər] N (*Baseball, Cricket*) joueur m, -euse f de champ or de terrain extérieur

outfit ['aʊtfɪt] 1 a (= *set of clothes*) tenue f; **did you see the ~ she was wearing?** (*in admiration*) avez-vous remarqué sa toilette?; (*pej*) avez-vous remarqué son accoutrement or comment elle était accoutrée?; **she's got a new spring ~** elle s'est achetée une nouvelle tenue pour le printemps; **travelling/skiing ~** tenue f de voyage/de ski; **cowboy ~** panoplie f de cowboy b (= *clothes and equipment*) équipement m; (= *tools*) matériel m, outillage m; **puncture repair ~** trousse f de réparation (de pneus) c (※ = *company, organization, sports team etc*) équipe f; **when I joined this ~** quand je suis entré dans cette boîte*; **I wouldn't want to work for that ~** je ne voudrais pas travailler pour cette boîte* 2 VT (*esp US*) équiper

outfitter ['aʊtfɪtər] N (*Brit*) **gents' ~** magasin m d'habillement or de confection pour hommes; **sports ~'s** magasin m de sports

outflank [aʊt'flæŋk] VT (*Mil*) déborder; (*fig*) déjouer les manœuvres de

outflow ['aʊtfləʊ] N [*of water*] écoulement m, débit m; [*of emigrants etc*] exode m; [*of capital*] exode m, sortie(s) f(pl)

outfox [aʊt'fɒks] VT se montrer plus futé que

out-front* [aʊt'frʌnt] ADJ (*US* = *frank*) ouvert, droit

outgeneral [aʊt'dʒenərəl] VT (*Mil*) surpasser en tactique

outgoing ['aʊtgəʊɪŋ] 1 ADJ a (= *departing*) [*president, director, tenant*] sortant; [*flight, mail*] en partance; [*tide*] descendant; [*Telec*] **"~ calls only"** « appels sortants uniquement »; b (= *extrovert*) [*person, personality, nature*] extraverti 2 **outgoings** NPL (*Brit*) dépenses fpl, débours mpl

outgrow [aʊt'grəʊ] (*pret* **outgrew** [aʊt'gruː], *ptp* **outgrown** [aʊt'grəʊn]) VT a [*+ clothes*] devenir trop grand pour b (*fig*) **to ~ sth** [*hobby, sport*] ne plus s'intéresser à qch en grandissant; [*habit, defect*] perdre or se défaire de qch en prenant de l'âge; [*opinion, way of life*] abandonner en prenant de l'âge; **we've ~n all that now** nous avons dépassé ce stade, nous n'en sommes plus là; **to ~ one's friends** se détacher de ses amis en grandissant

outgrowth ['aʊtgrəʊθ] N (*Geol*) excroissance f; (*fig*) développement m, conséquence f

outguess [aʊt'ges] VT (= *outwit*) se montrer plus rapide que

outgun [aʊt'gʌn] VT a (= *surpass in fire power*) avoir une puissance de feu supérieure à b (= *surpass in shooting*) tirer mieux que c (* = *outperform*) éclipser

out-Herod [aʊt'herəd] VT **to ~ Herod** dépasser Hérode en cruauté

outhouse ['aʊthaʊs] N a appentis m, remise f; (*gen*) **the ~s** les communs mpl, les dépendances fpl b (*US* = *outdoor lavatory*) cabinets mpl extérieurs

outing ['aʊtɪŋ] N a (= *excursion*) sortie f, excursion f; **the school ~** la sortie annuelle de l'école; **the annual ~ to Blackpool** l'excursion f annuelle à Blackpool; **let's go for an ~ tomorrow** faisons une sortie demain; **to go for an ~ in the car** partir faire une randonnée or un tour en voiture; **a birthday ~ to the theatre** une sortie au théâtre pour (fêter) un anniversaire b (*NonC*: ※ = *exposing as homosexual*) [*of public figure*] révélation f de l'homosexualité

outlandish [aʊt'lændɪʃ] ADJ (*pej*) [*clothes*] excentrique; [*idea, claim*] excentrique, farfelu

outlast [aʊt'lɑːst] VT survivre à

outlaw ['aʊtlɔː] 1 N hors-la-loi m 2 VT [+ person] mettre hors la loi; [+ activity, organisation] proscrire, déclarer illégal

outlay ['aʊtleɪ] N (= *spending*) dépenses fpl; (= *investment*) mise f de fonds; **national ~ on education** dépenses fpl nationales pour l'éducation

outlet ['aʊtlet] 1 a (*for water etc*) issue f, sortie f; (*US Elec*) prise f de courant; [*of lake*] dégorgeoir m, déversoir m; [*of river, stream*] embouchure f; [*of tunnel*] sortie f b (*for talents etc*) débouché m; (*for energy, emotions*) exutoire m (**for** à) c (*Comm*) débouché m → **retail** 2 COMP (*Tech*) [*pipe*] d'échappement, d'écoulement; [*valve*] d'échappement ► **outlet point** N [*of pipe*] point m de sortie

outline ['aʊtlaɪn] 1 N a (= *profile, silhouette*) [*of object*] contour m, configuration f; [*of building, tree etc*] profil m, silhouette f; [*of face*] profil m; **he drew the ~ of the house** il traça le contour de la maison; **to draw sth in ~** dessiner qch au trait; (*Art*) **rough ~** premier jet m, ébauche f b (= *plan, summary*) plan m; (*less exact*) esquisse f, idée f; **~s** (= *main features*) grandes lignes fpl, grands traits mpl; **rough ~ of an article** canevas m d'un article; **to give the broad** or **main** or **general ~s of sth** décrire or exposer qch à grands traits; **in broad ~ the plan is as follows** dans ses grandes lignes or en gros, le plan est le suivant; **I'll give you a quick ~ of what we mean to do** je vous donnerai un aperçu de ce que nous avons l'intention de faire; (*as title*) **"Outlines of Botany"** « Éléments de botanique » 2 VT a délinéer, tracer le contour de; **she ~d her eyes with a dark pencil** elle a souligné or dessiné le contour de ses yeux avec un crayon foncé; **the mountain was ~d against the sky** la montagne se profilait or se dessinait or se découpait sur le ciel b (= *summarize*) [+ theory, plan, idea] exposer les grandes lignes de; [+ book, event] faire un compte rendu de; [+ facts, details] passer brièvement en revue; **to ~ the situation** brosser un tableau or donner un aperçu de la situation 3 COMP ► **outline drawing** N dessin m au trait ► **outline map** N tracé m des contours (d'un pays), carte f muette ► **outline planning permission** N (*Brit: for building*) avant-projet m (*valorisant le terrain*) ► **outline specifications** NPL (*Comm*) devis m préliminaire

outlive [aʊt'lɪv] VT (= *survive*) [+ person, era, war, winter] survivre à; **he ~d her by ten years** il lui a survécu dix ans; **to have ~d one's usefulness** [person, object, scheme] avoir fait son temps

outlook ['aʊtlʊk] N a (= *view*) vue f (**on, over** sur), perspective f (**on, over** de) b (*fig* = *prospect*) perspective f (d'avenir), horizon m (*fig*); **the ~ for June is wet** on annonce or prévoit de la pluie pour juin; **the economic ~** les perspectives fpl or les horizons mpl économiques; **the ~ for the wheat crop is good** la récolte de blé s'annonce bonne; **the ~ (for us) is rather rosy*** les choses se présentent or s'annoncent assez bien (pour nous); **it's a grim** or **bleak ~** l'horizon est sombre or bouché, les perspectives sont fort sombres c (= *point of view*) attitude f (**on** à l'égard de), point m de vue (**on** sur), conception f (**on** de); **he has a pessimistic ~** il voit les choses en noir

outlying ['aʊtlaɪɪŋ] ADJ [*area*] écarté; **the ~ villages/islands** les villages mpl/îles fpl les plus éloigné(e)s; **the ~ suburbs** la grande banlieue

outmanoeuvre, **outmaneuver** (*US*) [ˌaʊtmə'nuːvər] VT (*Mil*) dominer en manœuvrant plus habilement; (*fig*) déjouer les plans de; **domestic car manufacturers are ~d by foreign competitors** les constructeurs automobiles du pays sont surclassés par leurs concurrents étrangers

outmoded [aʊt'məʊdɪd] ADJ [attitude, clothes] démodé; [concept, theory, system] dépassé, démodé; [custom] suranné, désuet (-ète f); [equipment] périmé; [industry] obsolète

outnumber [aʊt'nʌmbə'] VT surpasser en nombre, être plus nombreux que; **we were ~ed five to one** ils étaient cinq fois plus nombreux que nous

out-of-towner* [,aʊtə'taʊnə'] N (US) étranger m, -ère f à la ville

outpace [aʊt'peɪs] VT devancer, distancer

outpatient ['aʊtpeɪʃənt] N malade mf en consultation externe; **~s (department)** service m de consultation externe

outperform [,aʊtpə'fɔːm] VT [person, machine, company] être plus performant que; [product] donner de meilleurs résultats que; (Fin, St Ex) [shares etc] réaliser mieux que; **this car ~s its competitors on every score** cette voiture l'emporte sur ses concurrentes sur tous les plans

outplacement [aʊt'pleɪsmənt] N outplacement m (aide à la réinsertion professionnelle des cadres au chômage)

outplay [aʊt'pleɪ] VT (Sport) dominer par son jeu

outpoint [aʊt'pɔɪnt] VT (gen) l'emporter sur; (in game) avoir plus de points que

outpost ['aʊtpəʊst] N (Mil) avant-poste m; [of firm, organization] antenne f; (fig) avant-poste m

outpourings ['aʊtpɔːrɪŋz] NPL (fig) épanchement(s) m(pl), effusion(s) f(pl)

output ['aʊtpʊt] (vb: pret, ptp **output**) 1 N a [of factory, mine, oilfield, writer] production f; (Agr) [of land] rendement m, production f; [of machine, factory worker] rendement m; **~ fell/rose** le rendement or la production a diminué/augmenté; **this factory has an ~ of 600 radios per day** cette usine débite 600 radios par jour; (Ind, Econ) **gross ~** production f brute b (Comput) sortie f, restitution f; (also **~ data**) données fpl de sortie c (Elec) puissance f fournie or de sortie 2 VT a (Comput) sortir; **to ~ sth to a printer** imprimer qch b [factory etc] sortir, débiter 3 VI (Comput) sortir les données or les informations; **to ~ to a printer** imprimer 4 COMP ► **output device** N (Comput) unité f périphérique de sortie

outrage ['aʊtreɪdʒ] 1 N a (= act, event) atrocité f; (during riot etc) acte m de violence; (= public scandal) scandale m; **the prisoners suffered ~s at the hands of ...** les prisonniers ont été atrocement maltraités par ...; **it's an ~ against humanity** c'est un crime contre l'humanité; **an ~ against justice** un outrage à la justice; **several ~s occurred** or **were committed in the course of the night** plusieurs actes de violence ont été commis au cours de la nuit; **bomb ~** attentat m au plastic or à la bombe; **it's an ~!** c'est un scandale! b (= emotion) (sentiment m d')intense indignation f 2 VT [aʊt'reɪdʒ] [+ morals, sense of decency] outrager, faire outrage à

outraged ['aʊtreɪdʒd] ADJ [person] outré (about, at, by sth de qch), indigné; [protest, letter, tone] indigné; [dignity, pride] offensé

outrageous [aʊt'reɪdʒəs] ADJ a (= scandalous) [behaviour, act, conduct] scandaleux; [prices] exorbitant; **that's ~!** c'est scandaleux!; **he's ~!** il dépasse les bornes! b (= unconventional, flamboyant) [remark] outrancier; [story, claim, clothes, idea] extravagant; [sense of humour] outré

outrageously [aʊt'reɪdʒəslɪ] ADV [expensive, high, funny, exaggerated] outrageusement; [behave] effrontément; [dress] de manière extravagante; **to flirt/lie ~** flirter/mentir effrontément or de façon outrancière

outrank [aʊt'ræŋk] VT (Mil) avoir un grade supérieur à

outré ['uːtreɪ] ADJ outré, outrancier

outreach worker ['aʊtriːtʃ,wɜːkə'] N travailleur social effectuant un travail d'information sur le terrain auprès des groupes défavorisés

outrider ['aʊt,raɪdə'] N (on motorcycle) motocycliste mf, motard* m; (on horseback) cavalier m; **there were four ~s** il y avait une escorte de quatre motocyclistes (or cavaliers etc)

outrigger ['aʊt,rɪgə'] N (Naut) outrigger m

outright [aʊt'raɪt] 1 ADV a (= openly) [say, tell] carrément, tout net; [laugh] franchement b (= completely) [win] haut la main; [reject, refuse, deny] catégoriquement; **he won the prize ~** il a gagné le prix haut la main; (Comm) **to be owned ~ by sb** appartenir entièrement or complètement à qn; **to buy sth ~** (= buy and pay immediately) acheter qch au comptant; (= buy all of sth) acheter qch en totalité c (= instantly) **to be killed ~** être tué sur le coup 2 ADJ [aʊt'raɪt] a (= undisguised) [lie, fraud, selfishness, arrogance] pur; [hostility] franc (franche f); [condemnation, denial, refusal, rejection] catégorique; [support, supporter] inconditionnel b (= absolute) [victory] total, complet (-ète f); [independence] total; [majority, ban] absolu; [winner] incontesté; (Comm) (= full) [owner, ownership] à part entière; [grant] sans conditions; [sale, purchase] (= paying immediately) au comptant; (= selling all of sth) en totalité; **to be an ~ opponent of sth** s'opposer catégoriquement à qch

outrival [,aʊt'raɪvəl] VT surpasser

outrun [aʊt'rʌn] (pret, ptp **outrun**) VT a [+ opponent, pursuer] distancer b (fig) [+ resources, abilities] excéder, dépasser

outsell [,aʊt'sel] VT [company] obtenir de meilleurs résultats que; [product] mieux se vendre que

outset ['aʊtset] N début m, commencement m; **at the ~** au début; **from the ~** dès le début

outshine [aʊt'ʃaɪn] (pret, ptp **outshone** [aʊt'ʃɒn]) VT (fig) éclipser, surpasser

outside ['aʊt'saɪd] 1 ADV a (gen) à l'extérieur, dehors; **~ in the corridor** dehors dans le couloir; **the car was clean ~ but filthy inside** la voiture était propre à l'extérieur mais dégoûtante à l'intérieur; **the difficulties of life ~ for ex-prisoners** les difficultés de la vie en liberté pour les anciens détenus; (lit, fig) **seen from ~** vu du dehors or de l'extérieur b (= outdoors) dehors; **to go ~** sortir (dehors); **he left the car ~** il a laissé la voiture dans la rue; (Cine) **the scene was shot ~** cette scène a été tournée en extérieur 2 PREP (also **~ of***) a [+ building] (= on the exterior of) à l'extérieur de, hors de; (= in front of) devant; **store flammable substances ~ the house** conservez les produits inflammables à l'extérieur de or hors de la maison; **the noise was coming from ~ the house** le bruit venait de dehors; **a man was standing ~ the house** un homme se tenait devant la maison; **the street ~ his house** la rue devant sa maison; **a crowd had gathered ~ the building** une foule s'était rassemblée à l'extérieur du bâtiment or devant le bâtiment; **they chose to live ~ London** ils ont choisi de vivre à l'extérieur de or hors de Londres; **they have 45 shops, 38 ~ the UK** ils possèdent 45 magasins dont 38 à l'extérieur du Royaume-Uni or hors du Royaume-Uni; **countries ~ Europe** pays mpl non européens; **he was waiting ~ the door** il attendait à la porte; **don't go ~ the garden** ne sors pas du jardin; **the ball landed ~ the line** la balle a atterri de l'autre côté de la ligne; **~ the harbour** au large du port; **this fish can live for several hours ~ water** ce poisson peut vivre plusieurs heures hors de l'eau; **women who work ~ the home** les femmes qui travaillent à l'extérieur; **visitors from ~ the area** les visiteurs mpl étrangers à la région

b (fig = beyond, apart from) en dehors de, hors de; **investments ~ Europe** investissements mpl en dehors de l'Europe or hors d'Europe; **their reluctance to get involved militarily ~ NATO** leur réticence à intervenir militairement en dehors du cadre or hors du cadre de l'OTAN; **~ the festival proper** en dehors du or en marge du festival à proprement parler; **~ office hours** en dehors des heures de bureau; **it's ~ the normal range** ça ne fait pas partie de la gamme habituelle; **that falls ~ the committee's terms of reference** ceci n'est pas du ressort de la commission; **she doesn't see anyone ~ her immediate family** elle ne voit personne en dehors de ses proches parents; **babies born ~ marriage** naissances fpl hors mariage, bébés mpl nés hors mariage; **sex ~ marriage** relations fpl sexuelles hors (du) mariage; **to marry ~ one's religion** se marier avec une personne d'une autre confession; **to marry ~ the Church** (= with non-Christian) se marier avec un(e) non-chrétien(e)

3 N [of house, car, object] extérieur m, dehors m; (= appearance) aspect m extérieur, apparence f; (fig) [of prison, convent etc] (monde m) extérieur m; **on the ~ of** sur l'extérieur de; (= beyond) à l'extérieur de, hors de, en dehors de; **he opened the door from the ~** il a ouvert la porte du dehors; **there's no window on to the ~** aucune fenêtre ne donne sur l'extérieur; **the box was dirty on the ~** la boîte était sale à l'extérieur; **the ~ of the box was dirty** l'extérieur or le dehors de la boîte était sale; **~ in = inside out**; → **inside**; (lit, fig) **to look at sth from the ~** regarder qch de l'extérieur or du dehors; (fig) **(judging) from the ~** à en juger par les apparences; **he passed the car on the ~** (in Brit) il a doublé la voiture sur la droite; (in US, Europe etc) il a doublé la voiture sur la gauche; **at the (very) ~** (= at most) (tout) au plus, au maximum; **life on the ~** [of prison] la vie en liberté or à l'air libre

4 ADJ a (= outdoor) [temperature, aerial, staircase] extérieur (-eure f); [toilet] à l'extérieur; **~ swimming pool/running track** piscine f/piste f en plein air

b (= outer) [wall, edge, measurements] extérieur (-eure f); **the ~ lane** (of road) (in Brit) la voie de droite; (in US, Europe etc) la voie de gauche; (Sport) la piste extérieure

c (Telec) **~ call** appel m extérieur; **~ line** ligne f extérieure

d (= from elsewhere) [world, community, influence] extérieur (-eure f); [consultant, investor] externe; (Scol, Univ) **~ examiner** examinateur m, -trice f externe; **to need ~ help** avoir besoin d'aide extérieure; **without ~ help** sans aide extérieure; **to get an ~ opinion** demander l'avis d'un tiers

e (= beyond usual environment) **~ commitments** autres responsabilités fpl; **~ work** (in addition to main job) autre travail m; (outside the home) travail m à l'extérieur; **~ interests** (= hobbies) passe-temps mpl inv

f (= faint) **there is an ~ chance or possibility that he will come** il y a une petite chance qu'il vienne; **he has an ~ chance of a medal** il a une petite chance de remporter une médaille, il n'est pas impossible qu'il remporte (subj) une médaille

5 COMP ► **outside broadcast** N (Rad, TV) émission f réalisée en extérieur ► **outside broadcasting unit, outside broadcasting van** N (Rad, TV) car m de reportage ► **outside-left** N (Ftbl) ailier m gauche ► **outside-right** N (Ftbl) ailier m droit

outsider ['aʊt'saɪdə'] N a (= stranger) étranger m, -ère f; **we don't want some ~ coming in and telling us what to do** ce n'est pas quelqu'un de l'extérieur qui va nous dire ce qu'il faut faire; (pej) **he is an ~** il n'est pas des nôtres b (= horse or person unlikely to win) outsider m

outsize ['aʊtsaɪz] ADJ a (also **~d** = exceptionally large) [spectacles, scissors, bed] énorme; [photograph] géant; [ego] démesuré b (Dress) [clothes] grande taille inv; **~ shop** magasin m spécialisé dans les grandes tailles c (Transport) **~ load** convoi m exceptionnel

outskirts ['aʊtskɜːts] NPL [of town] périphérie f, banlieue f; [of forest] orée f, lisière f

outsmart* [aʊt'smɑːt] VT être or se montrer plus malin que

outsource ['aʊtsɔːs] VT (Ind) externaliser, sous-traiter

outsourcing ['aʊtsɔːsɪŋ] N (Ind) externalisation f, sous-traitance f; **the ~ of components** l'externalisation de la fabrication de composants

outspend [aʊt'spend] (pret, ptp **outspent** [aʊt'spend]) VT **to ~ sb** dépenser plus que qn

outspoken [aʊt'spəʊkən] ADJ [person, criticism, comment, answer] franc (franche f); [critic, opponent] qui ne mâche pas ses mots; [attack] cinglant; [views] tranché; **to be ~** avoir son franc-parler, ne pas mâcher ses mots

outspokenly [aʊt'spəʊkənlɪ] ADV franchement, carrément

outspokenness [aʊt'spəʊkənnɪs] N franc-parler m, franchise f

outspread ['aʊt'spred] ADJ [wings] déployé; [fingers] écarté; [arms] grand ouvert

outstanding [aʊt'stændɪŋ] 1 ADJ a (= exceptional) [person, work, service, talent, success, achievement] remarquable, exceptionnel; [example, event] remarquable; [importance] exceptionnel; [feature] dominant; [exception] notable; (in Brit) **an area of ~ natural beauty** une zone naturelle protégée b (= remaining) [debt, balance, bill, account] impayé; [loan] non remboursé; [interest] à échoir; [work] en suspens, en souffrance; [issue, problem] non résolu; **a lot of work is still ~** beaucoup de travail reste à faire; (Fin, Comm) **~ amount** montant m dû; (Jur, Fin) **claims** sinistres mpl en cours; (Banking) **~ item** suspens m; (Jur, Fin) **~ share** action f en circulation 2 N (Banking) encours m

outstandingly [aʊt'stændɪŋlɪ] ADV [good, beautiful] exceptionnellement; [play] magnifiquement; **to be ~ successful** réussir remarquablement; **~ well** exceptionnellement bien

outstare [,aʊt'steəʳ] VT = **stare out**

outstation ['aʊtsteɪʃən] N (in remote area) poste m éloigné; (Comput) terminal m

outstay [aʊt'steɪ] VT [+ person] rester plus longtemps que; **I hope I haven't ~ed my welcome** j'espère que je n'ai pas abusé de votre hospitalité; **I know when I've ~ed my welcome** je sais reconnaître quand je deviens indésirable

outstretched ['aʊtstretʃt] ADJ [arm, hand, leg] tendu; [wings] déployé

▼ **outstrip** [aʊt'strɪp] VT (Sport, fig) devancer (**in** en)

outtake ['aʊtteɪk] N (Cine, TV) chute f

outturn ['aʊttɜːn] N (US) [of factory] production f; [of machine, worker] rendement m

outvote [aʊt'vəʊt] VT [+ person] mettre en minorité, battre; **his project was ~d** son projet a été mis en minorité

outward ['aʊtwəd] 1 ADJ a (= from a place) [flight] à l'aller; [ship, freight] en partance; [movement] vers l'extérieur; **the ~ journey/voyage** ◊ **the ~ leg of the trip** l'aller m, le voyage (d')aller b (= external) [appearance, display, sign] extérieur (-eure f); [calm] apparent; **to make a ~ show of concern** faire mine de s'inquiéter 2 ADV a (esp Brit) = **outwards** b (Naut) **~ bound (for/from)** en partance (pour/de) 3 COMP ► **outward-looking** ADJ ouvert sur l'extérieur

outwardly ['aʊtwədlɪ] ADV a (= externally) [calm, unattractive] extérieurement; [respectable] apparemment; **~ he appeared calm and confident** extérieurement, il paraissait calme et confiant; **~ I showed not the faintest sign of anger** extérieurement, je n'ai pas donné le moindre signe de colère b (in direction) [point, direct, curve] vers l'extérieur

outwards ['aʊtwədz] ADV [move, spread, face, open] vers l'extérieur; [look] au loin; **the journey/voyage ~** l'aller m, le voyage (d')aller

outweigh [aʊt'weɪ] VT (= be more important than) (gen) l'emporter sur; [figures, balance etc] dépasser; (= compensate for) compenser

outwit [aʊt'wɪt] VT (gen) se montrer plus malin or spirituel que [+ pursuer] dépister, semer*

outwith [,aʊt'wɪθ] PREP (Scot) = **outside 2b**

outwork ['aʊtwɜːk] N travail m (fait) à domicile

outworker ['aʊtwɜːkəʳ] N travailleur m, -euse f à domicile, ouvrier m, -ière f à domicile

outworn [aʊt'wɔːn] ADJ [custom, superstition] qui n'a plus cours; [idea, concept] périmé

ouzo ['uːzəʊ] N ouzo m

ova ['əʊvə] NPL of **ovum**

oval ['əʊvəl] 1 ADJ oval 2 N ovale m 3 COMP ► **the Oval Office** N (US Pol) (lit) le bureau ovale (bureau du président à la Maison-Blanche); (fig) la présidence (des États-Unis)

ovarian [əʊ'veərɪən] ADJ ovarien

ovariectomy [əʊ,veərɪ'ektəmɪ] N ovariectomie f

ovariotomy [əʊ,veərɪ'ɒtəmɪ] N ovariotomie f

ovaritis [əʊvə'raɪtɪs] N ovarite f

ovary ['əʊvərɪ] N (Anat, Bot) ovaire m

ovate ['əʊveɪt] ADJ ové

ovation [əʊ'veɪʃən] N ovation f, acclamations fpl; **to give sb an ~** ovationner qn, faire une ovation à qn → **standing**

oven ['ʌvn] 1 N (Culin) four m; (Tech) four m, étuve f; (Culin) **in the ~** au four; **in a hot ~** à four vif or chaud; **in a cool** or **slow ~** à four doux; **the room/the town was like an ~** la pièce/la ville était une fournaise or une étuve → **Dutch, gas** 2 COMP ► **oven cleaner** N nettoyant m pour four ► **oven glove** N (Brit) gant m de cuisine, manique f ► **oven-ready** ADJ prêt à cuire

ovenproof ['ʌvnpruːf] ADJ allant au four

ovenware ['ʌvnweəʳ] N (NonC) plats mpl allant au four

---

over ['əʊvəʳ]

1	ADVERB	4	PREFIX
2	ADJECTIVE	5	NOUN
3	PREPOSITION		

When over is the second element in a phrasal verb, eg come over, go over, turn over, look up the verb.

1 ADVERB

a = **above** dessus; **this one goes ~ and that one goes under** celui-ci passe dessus et celui-là dessous; **where do you want it, under or ~?** où est-ce que tu veux le mettre, dessus ou dessous?

b = **here, there** I'll be **~ at 7 o'clock** je serai là à 7 heures; **when you're next ~ this way** la prochaine fois que vous passerez par ici; **they were ~ for the day** ils sont venus passer la journée

♦ **to have sb over** (= invite) inviter qn chez soi; **I must have them ~ some time** il faut que je les invite (subj) chez moi un de ces jours; **we had them ~ to dinner last week** ils sont venus dîner chez nous la semaine dernière

c with preposition/adverb

When followed by a preposition or adverb, over is not usually translated.

they're ~ from Canada for the summer ils sont venus du Canada pour passer ici l'été; ~ here ici; they're ~ in France ils sont en France; ~ there là-bas; he drove us ~ to the other side of town il nous a conduits de l'autre côté de la ville; (Rad, TV) and now ~ to our Birmingham studio et nous passons maintenant l'antenne à notre studio de Birmingham

♦ **over against** contre; ~ against the wall contre le mur; the issue of quality ~ against economy le problème de l'opposition entre les exigences de la qualité et les contraintes de l'économie

d Telec ~ (to you)! à vous!; ~ and out! terminé!

e = **more** plus; if it is 2 metres or ~, then ... si ça fait 2 mètres ou plus, alors ...; those aged 65 and ~ les personnes âgées de 65 ans et plus; balances of £50,000 and ~ les comptes créditeurs de 50 000 livres et plus; children of eight and ~ les enfants de huit ans et plus, les enfants à partir de huit ans

f = **in succession** he did it five times ~ il l'a fait cinq fois de suite

♦ **over and over (again)**: he played the same tune ~ and ~ (again) il a joué le même air je ne sais combien de fois; I got bored doing the same thing ~ and ~ again je m'ennuyais à refaire toujours la même chose; all directors make the same film ~ and ~ again tous les réalisateurs ne font qu'un seul film, qu'ils déclinent à l'infini; they have fallen into this trap ~ and ~ again ils sont tombés dans ce piège maintes et maintes fois or à maintes reprises

g = **remaining**

Note the impersonal use of il reste:

if there is any meat (left) ~ s'il reste de la viande; there are three ~ il en reste trois; four into twenty-nine goes seven and one ~ vingt-neuf divisé par quatre font sept et il reste un; BUT there were two slices each and one ~ il y avait deux tranches pour chacun et une en plus; when they've paid the bills there's nothing ~ for luxuries une fois qu'ils ont payé les factures, ils n'ont pas de quoi faire des folies

2 ADJECTIVE

= **finished** after the war was ~ après la guerre; when this is (all) ~ quand tout cela sera fini; when the exams/holidays are ~ après les examens/vacances, quand les examens/vacances seront fini(e)s; our troubles are ~ voilà la fin de nos ennuis

♦ **over and done with** fini et bien fini; I'll be glad when it's all ~ and done with je serai content lorsque tout sera fini et bien fini; as far as we were concerned the incident was ~ and done with pour nous, l'incident était clos; to get sth ~ and done with en finir avec qch

3 PREPOSITION

When over occurs in a set combination, eg over the phone, an advantage over, look up the noun. When over is used with a verb such as jump, trip, step, look up the verb.

a = **on top of** sur; she put an apron on ~ her dress elle a mis un tablier sur sa robe; BUT I spilled coffee ~ it/them j'ai renversé du café dessus

b = **above** au-dessus de; the water came ~ his knees l'eau lui arrivait au-dessus du genou; he's ~ me in the firm il est au-dessus de moi dans l'entreprise; a washbasin with a mirror ~ it un lavabo surmonté d'une glace

c = **across** de l'autre côté de; it's just ~ the river c'est juste de l'autre côté de la rivière; the noise came from ~ the wall le bruit venait de l'autre côté du mur; BUT the bridge ~ the river le pont qui traverse la rivière; ~ the road or way en face; there is a café ~ the road il y a un café en face; the house ~ the way or the road la maison d'en face

d = **during** ~ the summer pendant l'été; ~ Christmas pendant les fêtes de Noël; a fare which doesn't require a stay ~ **Saturday night** un tarif qui n'impose pas de passer sur place la nuit du samedi ; **the meetings take place ~ several days** les réunions se déroulent sur plusieurs jours ; **~ a period of** sur une période de ; **~ the last few years** ces dernières années

[e] **= about** : **they fell out ~ money** ils se sont brouillés pour une question d'argent ; **the two sides disagreed ~ how much should be spent** les deux côtés n'arrivaient pas à se mettre d'accord sur la somme à dépenser

[f] **= more than** : plus de ; **they stayed for ~ three hours** ils sont restés plus de trois heures ; **she is ~ 60** elle a plus de 60 ans ; **(the) ~-18s/-21s** les plus de 18/21 ans ; **women ~ 21** les femmes de plus de 21 ans ; **the boat is ~ 10 metres long** le bateau fait plus de 10 mètres de long ; **well ~ 200 people** bien plus de 200 personnes ; BUT **all numbers ~ 20** tous les chiffres au-dessus de 20 ; **an increase of 5% ~ last year's total** une augmentation de 5% par rapport au total de l'année dernière

♦ **over and above** : **this was ~ and above his normal duties** cela dépassait le cadre de ses fonctions or attributions ; **spending has gone up by 7% ~ and above inflation** les dépenses ont augmenté de 7%, hors inflation ; ~ **above the fact that ...** sans compter que ... ; **yes, but ~ and above that, we must ...** oui, mais en plus nous devons ...

[g] **= on** : **I spent a lot of time ~ that report** j'ai passé beaucoup de temps sur ce rapport ; **he took hours ~ the preparations** il a consacré des heures à ces préparatifs

[h] **= while having** : **they talked ~ a cup of coffee** ils ont bavardé autour d'une tasse de café ; **we met ~ a meal in the canteen** nous nous sommes vus autour d'un repas à la cantine

[i] **= recovered from**

♦ **to be over sth** [+ illness, bad experience] s'être remis de qch ; **I was heartbroken when she left but I'm ~ it now** j'ai eu le cœur brisé lorsqu'elle est partie mais je m'en suis remis, **hoping you'll soon be ~ your cold** en espérant que tu te remettras vite de ton rhume ; **we're ~ the worst now** ça devrait aller mieux maintenant

[4] PREFIX
overabundant surabondant ; overabundance surabondance f → **overachieve, overanxious, overmuch** etc

[5] NOUN
Cricket série f de six balles

overachieve [,əʊvərə'tʃiːv] VI [pupil, student] réussir mieux que prévu ; [executive] être un bourreau de travail

overachiever [,əʊvərə'tʃiːvər] N (Educ) élève ou étudiant(e) qui réussit mieux que prévu ; (Comm) bourreau m de travail

overact [əʊvər'ækt] VI (Theat) charger son rôle, en faire trop*

overactive [əʊvər'æktɪv] ADJ trop actif ; [imagination] débordant ; (Med) **to have an ~ thyroid** souffrir d'hyperthyroïdie f

overage ['əʊvərɪdʒ] N (US Comm) excédent m (de marchandises etc)

overall ['əʊvərɔːl] [1] ADJ [length, width, height, capacity, loss, gain] total ; [effect, impression] d'ensemble ; [improvement, increase, trend] global ; [study, survey] global, d'ensemble ; (Sport) [winner, leader, victory] au classement général ; **no party holds ~ control of the council** aucun parti n'a la majorité absolue dans la municipalité ; **an ~ majority** une majorité absolue ; **a satisfactory ~ performance** une performance globalement satisfaisante ; **he has ~ responsibility** il a la responsabilité d'ensemble ; (Aut) ~ **measurements** encombrement m, dimensions fpl hors tout ; (Sport) ~ **placings** le classement général, le combiné ; (Sport) **to be in ~ lead** être en tête du classement général

[2] [,əʊvər'ɔːl] ADV [view, survey] en général ; [measure] d'un bout à l'autre, hors tout ; [cost] en tout ; (Sport) **he came first ~** il a gagné le combiné ; **~, it was disappointing** dans l'ensemble, ça a été décevant

[3] ['əʊvərɔːl] N (Brit: shirt-type) blouse f

[4] **overalls** NPL [of mechanic etc] bleu m (de travail) ; (= dungarees) salopette f

overanxious [əʊvər'æŋkʃəs] ADJ (= worried) trop inquiet (-ète f), trop anxieux ; (= zealous) trop zélé ; **~ parents** des parents mpl hyper-anxieux ; **I'm not ~ to go** (= not keen) je n'ai pas trop or tellement envie d'y aller ; (= not in a hurry) je ne suis pas trop pressé d'y aller

overarching ['əʊvərɑːtʃɪŋ] ADJ [question] que se pose tout le monde ; [desire] partagé par tout le monde

overarm ['əʊvərɑːm] ADV, ADJ (esp Brit) par en dessus

overate [əʊvər'eɪt] VB pt of **overeat**

overawe [əʊvər'ɔː] VT [person] intimider, impressionner, troubler ; [sight etc] impressionner

overbade [əʊvə'beɪd] VB pt of **overbid**

overbalance [,əʊvə'bæləns] [1] VI [person] perdre l'équilibre, basculer ; [object] se renverser, basculer [2] VT [+ object, boat] (faire) basculer, renverser ; [+ person] faire perdre l'équilibre à

overbearing [əʊvə'bɛərɪŋ] ADJ (pej) dominateur (-trice f)

overbid [əʊvə'bɪd] (pret **overbid** or **overbade**, ptp **overbid** or **overbidden**) (at auction) [1] VT enchérir sur [2] VI surenchérir

overblown [əʊvə'bləʊn] ADJ [flower] trop ouvert ; [woman] plantureux ; [style] ampoulé

overboard ['əʊvəbɔːd] ADV [fall, jump] par-dessus bord, **man ~!** un homme à la mer ! ; **to throw sth ~** (lit) jeter qch par-dessus bord ; (* fig) ne faire aucun cas de qch ; (fig) **to go ~*** aller trop loin ; **to go ~ about sth*** s'emballer* pour qch ; **to go ~ about sb*** s'emballer* pour qn ; **don't go ~ with the sugar*** vas-y mollo* avec le sucre → **wash**

overbold [əʊvə'bəʊld] ADJ [person, remark] impudent ; [action] trop audacieux

overbook [əʊvə'bʊk] VTI [hotel, airline] surréserver

overbooking [əʊvə'bʊkɪŋ] N [of hotel, flight] surréservation f, surbooking m

overburden [əʊvə'bɜːdn] VT (lit) surcharger ; (fig) surcharger, accabler (**with** de)

overburdened [əʊvə'bɜːdnd] ADJ [person] (with work) surchargé ; (with problems) accablé ; [system] surchargé ; **~ with** or **by sth** surchargé or accablé de qch

overcame [əʊvə'keɪm] VB pt of **overcome**

overcast ['əʊvəkɑːst] (vb: pret, ptp **overcast**) [1] ADJ [sky] couvert, sombre ; [weather, conditions] couvert ; [day] au temps couvert ; **it is ~** le temps est couvert ; **it/the weather grew ~** ça/le temps s'est couvert [2] N (Sewing: also **stitch**) point m de surjet [3] [,əʊvə'kɑːst] VT (Sewing) surjeter

overcautious [əʊvə'kɔːʃəs] ADJ trop prudent, trop circonspect

overcautiously [əʊvə'kɔːʃəslɪ] ADV avec un excès de prudence or de circonspection

overcautiousness [əʊvə'kɔːʃəsnɪs] N excès m de prudence or de circonspection

overcharge [,əʊvə'tʃɑːdʒ] [1] VT **a to ~ sb for sth** faire payer qch trop cher à qn, surfacturer qch à qn [b] [+ electric circuit] surcharger [2] VI **he ~d for it** il le lui a (or il me l'a etc) fait payer trop cher

overcoat ['əʊvəkəʊt] N pardessus m

overcome [əʊvə'kʌm] (pret **overcame**, ptp **overcome**) [1] VT [+ enemy] vaincre, triompher de ; [+ difficulty, obstacle, temptation] surmonter ; [+ one's rage, disgust, dislike etc] maîtriser, dominer ; [+ opposition] triompher

de ; **to be ~ by temptation/remorse/grief** succomber à la tentation/au remords/à la douleur ; **sleep overcame him** il a succombé au sommeil ; **~ with fear** paralysé par la peur, transi de peur ; **~ with cold** transi (de froid) ; **she was quite ~** elle fut saisie, elle resta muette de saisissement [2] VI **we shall ~!** nous vaincrons !

overcommit [,əʊvəkə'mɪt] [1] VI trop s'engager [2] VT **to ~ o.s.** trop s'engager ; **to be ~ted** (financially) avoir des charges financières excessives ; (= have too much work) s'être engagé à faire trop de travail

overcompensate [əʊvə'kɒmpənseɪt] VI (gen) faire de la surcompensation ; (Psych) surcompenser (**for sth** qch)

overcompensation [,əʊvə,kɒmpən'seɪʃən] N (gen, Psych) surcompensation f

overcompress [əʊvəkəm'pres] VT surcomprimer

overconfidence [əʊvə'kɒnfɪdəns] N (= assurance) suffisance f, présomption f ; (= trust) confiance f aveugle (**in** en)

overconfident [əʊvə'kɒnfɪdənt] ADJ (= assured) suffisant, présomptueux ; (= trusting) trop confiant (**in** en)

overconsumption [,əʊvəkən'sʌmpʃən] N (Comm, Econ) surconsommation f

overcook [əʊvə'kʊk] VT trop (faire) cuire

overcritical [əʊvə'krɪtɪkəl] ADJ trop critique

overcrowded [əʊvə'kraʊdɪd] ADJ [city, prison, house] surpeuplé ; [classroom] surchargé ; [train, bus, office] bondé ; **they live in ~ conditions** ils vivent dans des conditions de surpeuplement

overcrowding [əʊvə'kraʊdɪŋ] N (in housing, prison, town, district) surpeuplement m ; (in classroom) effectif(s) m(pl) surchargé(s) ; (in bus etc) encombrement m

overdependence [,əʊvədɪ'pendəns] N dépendance f excessive (**on** envers, à l'égard de)

overdependent [,əʊvədɪ'pendənt] ADJ trop dépendant (**on** de)

overdevelop [,əʊvədɪ'veləp] VT (Econ) surdévelopper

overdeveloped [əʊvədɪ'veləpt] ADJ (gen, Phot) trop développé ; (Econ) surdéveloppé

overdevelopment [,əʊvədɪ'veləpmənt] N (Econ) surdéveloppement m

overdo [,əʊvə'duː] (pret **overdid** [,əʊvə'dɪd], ptp **overdone**) VT [a] (= exaggerate) [+ attitude, accent, concern, interest] exagérer ; (= eat or drink to excess) abuser de, forcer sur* ; **don't ~ the beer** ne bois pas trop de bière, ne force* pas sur la bière ; **she rather overdoes the perfume** elle force* un peu sur le parfum, elle y va un peu fort* avec le parfum ; **he rather overdoes the devoted husband bit*** il en rajoute* dans le rôle du mari dévoué ; **to ~ it ◊ to ~ things** (= push o.s. too hard) s'épuiser ; (= go too far: in comments, description etc) exagérer ; **he's overdone it a bit on the sunbed** il y a été un peu fort* avec les UV [b] (= overcook) trop cuire

overdone [,əʊvə'dʌn] [1] VB ptp of **overdo** [2] ADJ [a] (= exaggerated) excessif, outré [b] (= overcooked) trop cuit

overdose ['əʊvədəʊs] [1] N [a] (lit) surdose f, overdose f ; **to take an ~** faire une overdose ; **to take an ~ of sth** prendre une surdose de qch ; **he died from an ~ (of heroin)** il est mort d'une overdose or d'une surdose (d'héroïne) [b] (fig, hum) overdose f ; **I had an ~ of TV last week** j'ai fait une overdose de télé la semaine dernière [2] VI (a) (lit) (gen) faire une overdose ; (fatally) mourir d'une surdose or d'une overdose ; **to ~ on sth** prendre une surdose de qch [b] (fig, hum) **to ~ on TV** etc faire une overdose de télé etc ; **to ~ on chocolate** forcer* sur le chocolat

overdraft ['əʊvədrɑːft] (Banking) [1] N découvert m ; **I've got an ~** mon compte est à découvert, j'ai un découvert à la banque [2] COMP ► **overdraft facility** N découvert *m* autorisé, autorisation *f* de découvert ► **overdraft interest** N intérêts *mpl* débiteurs, agios *mpl*

overdraw [ˌəʊvəˈdrɔː] (*pret* **overdrew**, *ptp* **overdrawn**) (*Banking*) [1] VI mettre son compte à découvert, dépasser son crédit [2] VT [+ *one's account*] mettre à découvert

overdrawn [ˌəʊvəˈdrɔːn] [1] VB *ptp of* **overdraw** [2] ADJ [*person, account*] à découvert ; **I'm £500 ~** ◊ **my account is £500 ~** j'ai un découvert de 500 livres ; **I'm ~/my account is ~ by £500** je suis à découvert/mon compte est à découvert de 500 livres

overdress [ˈəʊvədres] [1] N robe-chasuble *f* [2] [ˌəʊvəˈdres] VI (*also* **to be ~ed**) être trop habillé

overdrew [ˌəʊvəˈdruː] VB *pt of* **overdraw**

overdrive [ˈəʊvədraɪv] N (*Aut*) (vitesse *f*) surmultipliée *f* ; (*Aut*) **in ~** en surmultipliée ; (*fig*) **to go into ~*** mettre les bouchées doubles

overdue [ˌəʊvəˈdjuː] ADJ [*train, bus*] en retard ; [*reform*] qui tarde (à être réalisé) ; [*acknowledgement, recognition, apology*] tardif ; [*account*] impayé, en souffrance ; **the plane is 20 minutes ~** l'avion a 20 minutes de retard ; **that change is long ~** ce changement se fait attendre depuis longtemps ; **she's (a week) ~** (*menstrual period*) elle est en retard (d'une semaine) ; (*baby*) elle a dépassé le terme (d'une semaine), elle aurait déjà dû accoucher (il y a une semaine) ; **the baby is (a week) ~** l'enfant aurait déjà dû naître (il y a une semaine) ; **my books are (a week) ~** je suis en retard (d'une semaine) pour rendre mes livres

overeager [ˌəʊvərˈiːgəʳ] ADJ trop zélé, trop empressé ; **he was not ~ to leave** (= *not keen*) il n'avait pas une envie folle de partir ; (= *not in a hurry*) il n'était pas trop pressé de partir

overeat [ˌəʊvərˈiːt] (*pret* **overate**, *ptp* **overeaten**) VI (*on one occasion*) trop manger ; (*regularly*) trop manger, se suralimenter

overeating [ˌəʊvərˈiːtɪŋ] N excès *mpl* de table

over-egg* [ˌəʊvərˈeg] VT (*Brit fig*) **to ~ the pudding** exagérer

overelaborate [ˌəʊvərɪˈlæbərɪt] ADJ [*design, plan*] trop compliqué ; [*style, excuse*] contourné ; [*dress*] trop recherché

overemphasis [ˌəʊvərˈemfəsɪs] N **to put an ~ on sth** accorder trop d'importance à qch

overemphasize [ˌəʊvərˈemfəsaɪz] VT accorder trop d'importance à ; **the importance of education cannot be ~d** on n'insistera jamais assez sur *or* on ne soulignera jamais assez l'importance de l'éducation

overemphatic [ˌəʊvərɪmˈfætɪk] ADJ trop catégorique

overemployment [ˌəʊvərɪmˈplɔɪmənt] N suremploi *m*

overenthusiastic [ˌəʊvərɪnˌθuːzɪˈæstɪk] ADJ trop enthousiaste

overenthusiastically [ˌəʊvərɪnˌθuːzɪˈæstɪkəlɪ] ADV avec trop d'enthousiasme

overestimate [ˌəʊvərˈestɪmeɪt] VT [+ *price, costs, importance*] surestimer ; [+ *strength*] trop présumer de ; [+ *danger*] exagérer

overexcite [ˌəʊvərɪkˈsaɪt] VT surexciter

overexcited [ˌəʊvərɪkˈsaɪtɪd] ADJ surexcité ; **to get ~** se mettre dans un état de surexcitation, devenir surexcité ; **don't get ~!** ne vous excitez pas !

overexcitement [ˌəʊvərɪkˈsaɪtmənt] N surexcitation *f*

overexert [ˌəʊvərɪgˈzɜːt] VT **to ~ o.s.** se surmener, s'éreinter

overexertion [ˌəʊvərɪgˈzɜːʃən] N surmenage *m*

overexpose [ˌəʊvərɪksˈpəʊz] VT (*Phot*) surexposer

overexposure [ˌəʊvərɪksˈpəʊzəʳ] N (*Phot, also fig*) surexposition *f*

overextended [ˌəʊvərɪkˈstendɪd] ADJ [*person*] qui a trop d'activités ; [*organization*] qui a trop diversifié ses activités

overfamiliar [ˌəʊvəfəˈmɪljəʳ] ADJ trop familier

overfeed [ˌəʊvəˈfiːd] [1] VT (*pret, ptp* **overfed** [ˌəʊvəˈfiːd]) suralimenter, donner trop à manger à [2] VI se suralimenter, trop manger

overfeeding [ˌəʊvəˈfiːdɪŋ] N suralimentation *f*

overfill [ˌəʊvəˈfɪl] VT trop remplir

overfish [ˌəʊvəˈfɪʃ] VT surexploiter

overfishing [ˌəʊvəˈfɪʃɪŋ] N surpêche *f*

overflew [ˌəʊvəˈfluː] VB *pt of* **overfly**

overflight [ˈəʊvəflaɪt] N (*authorized*) survol *m* de l'espace aérien ; (*unauthorized*) violation *f* de l'espace aérien

overflow [1] N [ˈəʊvəfləʊ] [a] (= *pipe, outlet*) [of *bath, sink etc*] trop-plein *m* ; [of *canal, reservoir etc*] déversoir *m*, dégorgeoir *m* [b] (= *flooding*) inondation *f* ; (= *excess liquid*) débordement *m*, trop-plein *m* [c] (= *excess*) [of *people, population*] excédent *m* ; [of *objects*] excédent *m*, surplus *m* [2] [ˌəʊvəˈfləʊ] VT [+ *container*] déborder de ; **the river has ~ed its banks** la rivière a débordé *or* est sortie de son lit [3] [ˌəʊvəˈfləʊ] VI [a] [*liquid, river etc*] déborder ; **the river ~ed into the fields** la rivière a inondé les champs [b] (*fig*) [*people, objects*] déborder ; **the crowd ~ed into the next room** la foule a débordé dans la pièce voisine [c] [*container*] déborder (**with** de) ; [*room, vehicle*] regorger (**with** de) ; **to be full to ~ing** [*cup, jug*] être plein à ras bords *or* à déborder ; [*room, vehicle*] être plein à craquer ; **to fill a cup to ~ing** remplir une tasse à ras bords [d] (*fig* = *be full of*) déborder, regorger (**with** de), abonder (**with** en) ; **the town was ~ing with visitors** la ville regorgeait de visiteurs ; **his heart was ~ing with love** son cœur débordait d'amour ; **he was ~ing with optimism** il débordait d'optimisme ; **he ~ed with suggestions** il abondait en suggestions [4] [ˈəʊvəˌfləʊ] COMP [*pipe*] d'écoulement

overfly [ˌəʊvəˈflaɪ] (*pret* **overflew**, *ptp* **overflown** [ˌəʊvəˈfləʊn]) VT survoler

overfond [ˌəʊvəˈfɒnd] ADJ **she is not ~ of ...** elle ne raffole pas de ...

overfull [ˌəʊvəˈfʊl] ADJ trop plein (**of** de)

overgenerous [ˌəʊvəˈdʒenərəs] ADJ [*person*] prodigue (**with** de) ; [*amount, helping*] excessif

overground [ˌəʊvəˈgraʊnd] ADJ (*Transport*) à l'air libre

overgrown [ˈəʊvəˌgraʊn] ADJ **the path is ~ (with grass)** le chemin est envahi par l'herbe ; **~ with weeds** recouvert de mauvaises herbes ; **a wall ~ with ivy/moss** un mur recouvert *or* tapissé de lierre/de mousse ; **the garden is very ~** le jardin est une vraie forêt vierge *or* est complètement envahi (par la végétation) ; **he's just an ~ schoolboy** il a gardé une mentalité d'écolier

overhand [ˈəʊvəhænd] (*US*) [1] ADV [a] (*Sport etc*) [*throw, serve*] par en dessus [b] (*Sewing*) à points de surjet [2] VT (*Sewing*) coudre à points de surjet

overhang [ˌəʊvəˈhæn] (*pret, ptp* **overhung**) [1] VT [*tree, branch, rocks, balcony*] surplomber ; [*mist, smoke*] planer sur ; [*danger etc*] menacer [2] VI [*tree, branch, cliff, balcony*] être en surplomb [3] [ˈəʊvəˌhæn] N [of *cliff, rock, balcony, building*] surplomb *m*

overhanging [ˌəʊvəˈhæŋɪŋ] ADJ [*rock, cliff, eaves*] en surplomb, en saillie ; [*tree, branch*] en surplomb

overhastily [ˌəʊvəˈheɪstɪlɪ] ADV trop hâtivement, de façon trop précipitée

overhasty [ˌəʊvəˈheɪstɪ] ADJ trop précipité *or* hâtif ; **to be ~ in doing sth** faire qch de façon

trop précipitée ; **he was ~ in his condemnation of ...** il a été trop hâtif en condamnant ...

overhaul [ˈəʊvəhɔːl] [1] N [of *vehicle, machine*] révision *f* (complète) ; [of *ship*] radoub *m* ; (*fig*) [of *system, programme*] refonte *f*, remaniement *m* [2] [ˌəʊvəˈhɔːl] VT [a] (= *check, repair*) [+ *vehicle, machine*] réviser, remettre en état ; [+ *ship*] radouber ; (*fig*) [+ *system, programme*] remanier [b] (= *catch up with*) rattraper, gagner de vitesse ; (= *overtake*) dépasser

overhead [1] [ˌəʊvəˈhed] ADV (= *up above*) au-dessus (de nos *or* vos *etc* têtes) ; (= *in the sky*) dans le ciel ; (= *on the floor above*) (à l'étage) au-dessus, en haut [2] [ˈəʊvəhed] ADJ [a] [*wires, cables, railway*] aérien [b] (*Comm*) **~ charges** *or* **costs** *or* **expenses** frais *mpl* généraux [3] (*US*) = **overheads** [4] **overheads** NPL (*Brit*) frais *mpl* généraux [5] COMP ► **overhead light** N plafonnier *m* ► **overhead lighting** N éclairage *m* au plafond ► **overhead projection** N rétroprojection *f* ► **overhead projector** N rétroprojecteur *m* ► **overhead valve** N (*Aut*) soupape *f* en tête

overhear [ˌəʊvəˈhɪəʳ] (*pret, ptp* **overheard** [ˌəʊvəˈhɜːd]) VT surprendre, entendre (par hasard) ; **he was overheard to say that ...** on l'a entendu dire *or* on l'a surpris à dire que ... ; **I overheard your conversation** j'ai entendu ce que vous disiez, j'ai surpris votre conversation

overheat [ˌəʊvəˈhiːt] [1] VT surchauffer [2] VI (*gen*) devenir surchauffé ; [*engine, brakes*] chauffer

overheated [ˌəʊvəˈhiːtɪd] ADJ [*room*] surchauffé ; [*brakes, engine, computer*] qui chauffe ; [*economy, market*] en état de surchauffe ; **to get ~** (*lit*) [*person, animal*] avoir trop chaud ; (*fig*) [*person*] s'emporter

overheating [ˌəʊvəˈhiːtɪŋ] N (*Econ*) surchauffe *f*

overhung [ˌəʊvəˈhʌŋ] VB *pt, ptp of* **overhang**

overimpressed [ˌəʊvərɪmˈprest] ADJ **I'm not ~ with him** il ne m'impressionne pas vraiment ; **I'm not ~ with his work** je ne suis pas vraiment impressionné par son travail

overindulge [ˌəʊvərɪnˈdʌldʒ] [1] VI abuser (**in** de) ; **I rather ~d last night** j'ai un peu forcé *or* abusé* hier soir, je me suis laissé aller à des excès hier soir [2] VT [+ *person*] trop gâter, satisfaire tous les caprices de ; [+ *passion, appetite*] céder trop facilement à

overindulgence [ˌəʊvərɪnˈdʌldʒəns] N indulgence *f* excessive (**of/towards sb** des/envers les caprices de qn), abus *m* (**in sth** de qch)

overindulgent [ˌəʊvərɪnˈdʌldʒənt] ADJ trop indulgent (**to, towards** envers)

overinvestment [ˌəʊvərɪnˈvestmənt] N (*Econ*) surinvestissement *m*

overjoyed [ˌəʊvəˈdʒɔɪd] ADJ [*person*] ravi, enchanté ; **I can't say I'm ~** je ne peux pas dire que je sois enchanté ; **~ at** *or* **about** *or* **with sth** ravi *or* enchanté de qch ; **to be ~ to see sb** être ravi *or* enchanté de voir qn ; **to be ~ that ...** être ravi *or* enchanté que ... (+ *subj*)

overkill [ˈəʊvəkɪl] N [a] (*Mil*) surarmement *m* [b] (*fig*) **that was a bit of an ~!*** c'était un peu exagéré ! ; **such security measures may well be ~** de telles mesures de sécurité sont peut-être exagérées *or* excessives ; **her new fitness régime quickly reached ~** elle a vite dépassé la mesure avec son nouveau programme de mise en forme ; **every time I switch on the TV, there's football. It's ~** chaque fois que j'allume la télévision, il y a du football : trop, c'est trop ; **an ~ in negative propaganda** trop de propagande hostile

overladen [ˌəʊvəˈleɪdn] ADJ (*gen, also Elec*) surchargé

overlaid [ˌəʊvəˈleɪd] VB *pt, ptp of* **overlay**

overland ['əʊvəlænd] ① ADJ par voie de terre (**to** pour aller à); **by an ~ route** par voie de terre ② ADV par voie de terre

overlap ['əʊvəlæp] ① N empiètement *m*, chevauchement *m*; [*of tiles*] chevauchement *m* ② [,əʊvə'læp] VI (*also* **~ each other**) se recouvrir partiellement; [*teeth, boards, tiles*] se chevaucher; (*fig*) se chevaucher; **his work and ours ~** son travail et le nôtre se chevauchent or se recoupent; **our holidays ~** nos vacances coïncident en partie or (se) chevauchent ③ [,əʊvə'læp] VT [+ *tiles, slates*] enchevaucher; [+ *edges*] dépasser, déborder de; (*fig*) recouper; **to ~ each other → 2**

overlay [,əʊvə'leɪ] (*pret, ptp* **overlaid**) ① VT (re)couvrir (**with** de) ② ['əʊvə,leɪ] N revêtement *m*

overleaf ['əʊvəliːf] ADV au verso; **see ~** voir au verso

overlie [,əʊvə'laɪ] VT recouvrir

overload ① ['əʊvələʊd] N surcharge *f* ② [,əʊvə'ləʊd] VT [+ *circuit, truck, animal*] surcharger (**with** de); [+ *engine*] surmener

overlook [,əʊvə'lʊk] VT ⓐ (= *have a view over*) [*house, balcony etc*] donner sur, avoir vue sur; [*window, door*] s'ouvrir sur, donner sur; [*castle etc*] dominer; **our garden is not ~ed** personne n'a vue sur notre jardin ⓑ (= *accidentally miss*) [+ *fact, detail*] oublier, laisser échapper; [+ *problem, difficulty*] oublier, négliger; **I ~ed that** j'ai oublié cela, cela m'a échappé; **it is easy to ~ the fact that ...** on oublie facilement que ...; **this plant is so small that it is easily ~ed** cette plante est si petite qu'il est facile de ne pas la remarquer ⓒ (= *deliberately allow to pass, ignore*) [+ *mistake*] passer sur, fermer les yeux sur; **we'll ~ it this time** nous passerons là-dessus cette fois-ci, nous fermerons les yeux (pour) cette fois ⓓ (= *supervise*) surveiller

overlord ['əʊvəlɔːd] N (*Hist*) suzerain *m*; (= *leader*) chef *m* suprême; (*fig*) **the steel/coal etc ~** le grand patron de la sidérurgie/des charbonnages etc

overly ['əʊvəlɪ] ADV trop

overmanned [,əʊvə'mænd] ADJ en sureffectif

overmanning [,əʊvə'mænɪŋ] N sureffectif *m*, effectif *m* pléthorique

overmuch [,əʊvə'mʌtʃ] ① ADV excessivement, à l'excès; **I don't like it ~** je ne l'aime pas trop ② ADJ excessif

overnice [,əʊvə'naɪs] ADJ [*person*] trop pointilleux, trop scrupuleux; [*distinction*] trop subtil

overnight [,əʊvə'naɪt] ① ADV (= *during the night*) (pendant) la nuit; (= *until next day*) jusqu'au lendemain; (= *suddenly*) du jour au lendemain; **to stay ~ with sb** passer la nuit chez qn; **we drove ~** nous avons roulé de nuit; **will it keep ~?** est-ce que cela se gardera jusqu'à demain?; **the town had changed ~** la ville avait changé du jour au lendemain ② ['əʊvə,naɪt] ADJ [*stay*] d'une nuit; [*journey*] de nuit; (*fig*) **there had been an ~ change of plans** les plans avaient changé du jour au lendemain ③ COMP ► **overnight bag** N nécessaire *m* de voyage

overpaid [,əʊvə'peɪd] VB *pt, ptp of* **overpay**

overpass ['əʊvəpɑːs] N (*US Aut*) (*gen*) pont *m* autoroutier; (*at flyover*) autopont *m*

overpay [,əʊvə'peɪ] (*pret, ptp* **overpaid**) VT [+ *person, job*] trop payer, surpayer; **he was overpaid by £50** on lui a payé 50 livres de trop

overpayment [,əʊvə'peɪmənt] N ⓐ **~ (of wages)** surpaye *f*, rémunération *f* excessive ⓑ **~ (of tax)** trop-perçu *m*; **refund of ~** remboursement *m* du trop-perçu

overplay [,əʊvə'pleɪ] VT (*fig*) **to ~ one's hand** trop présumer de sa situation

overpopulated [,əʊvə'pɒpjʊleɪtɪd] ADJ surpeuplé

overpopulation [,əʊvəpɒpjʊ'leɪʃən] N surpopulation *f* (**in** dans), surpeuplement *m* (**of** de)

overpower [,əʊvə'paʊə'] VT (= *defeat*) vaincre, subjuguer; (= *subdue physically*) dominer, maîtriser; (*fig* = *overwhelm*) accabler, terrasser

overpowering [,əʊvə'paʊərɪŋ] ADJ [*desire, urge, need, strength*] irrésistible; [*feeling*] irrépressible; [*force*] impérieux; [*smell, scent, flavour*] envahissant; [*noise*] assourdissant; [*heat*] accablant; [*colour*] tapageur; [*decoration*] oppressant; [*person, manner*] dominateur (-trice *f*)

overpraise [,əʊvə'preɪz] VT faire des éloges excessifs de

overprescribe [əʊvəprɪs'kraɪb] (*Pharm, Med*) ① VI prescrire trop de médicaments ② VT prescrire en trop grande quantité

overprice [,əʊvə'praɪs] VT [+ *goods*] vendre trop cher, demander un prix excessif pour

overpriced [,əʊvə'praɪst] ADJ excessivement cher

overprint [,əʊvə'prɪnt] (*Typ*) ① VT surcharger; **the price had been ~ed with the word "sale"** les mots « en solde » avaient été imprimés sur l'ancien prix ② ['əʊvə,prɪnt] N surcharge *f*

overproduce [əʊvəprə'djuːs] VT (*Ind*) surproduire

overproduction [əʊvəprə'dʌkʃən] N (*Ind*) surproduction *f*

overprotect [əʊvəprə'tekt] VT [+ *child*] protéger excessivement, surprotéger

overprotective [əʊvəprə'tektɪv] ADJ protecteur (-trice *f*) à l'excès

overqualified [əʊvə'kwɒlɪfaɪd] ADJ trop qualifié

overran [əʊvə'ræn] VB *pt of* **overrun**

overrate [əʊvə'reɪt] VT surévaluer, faire trop de cas de

overrated [əʊvə'reɪtɪd] ADJ surfait, qui ne mérite pas sa réputation

overreach [əʊvə'riːtʃ] ① VT **to ~ o.s.** (vouloir) trop entreprendre ② VI [*person*] tendre le bras trop loin; (*fig*) aller trop loin

overreact [əʊvə'ækt] VI (*gen, Psych*) réagir de manière exagérée or excessive; **observers considered that the government had ~ed** les observateurs ont trouvé excessive la réaction gouvernementale; **she's always ~ing** elle exagère toujours, elle dramatise toujours tout

overreaction [,əʊvəriː'ækʃən] N réaction *f* exagérée or excessive or disproportionnée

overreliance [,əʊvərɪ'laɪəns] N (= *dependence*) dépendance *f* excessive (**on** vis-à-vis de); (= *trust*) confiance *f* excessive (**on** en)

override [,əʊvə'raɪd] (*pret* **overrode**, *ptp* **overridden** [,əʊvə'rɪdn]) VT [+ *law, duty, sb's rights*] fouler aux pieds; [+ *order, instructions*] outrepasser; [+ *decision*] annuler, casser; [+ *opinion, objection, protests, sb's wishes, claims*] passer outre à, ne pas tenir compte de; [+ *person*] passer outre aux désirs de; **this fact ~s all others** ce fait l'emporte sur tous les autres; **this ~s what we decided before** ceci annule ce que nous avions décidé auparavant

overrider ['əʊvəraɪdə'] N (*Aut: of bumper*) tampon *m* (de pare-chocs)

overriding [,əʊvə'raɪdɪŋ] ADJ [*need, consideration, objective, principle, issue*] primordial; [*concern, impression, feeling*] premier; [*factor*] prépondérant; (*Jur*) [*act, clause*] dérogatoire; **of ~ importance** d'une importance primordiale; **his ~ desire was to leave as soon as possible** sa seule envie était de partir le plus vite possible

overripe [,əʊvə'raɪp] ADJ [*fruit*] trop mûr, blet (blette *f*); [*cheese*] trop fait

overrode [,əʊvə'rəʊd] VB *pt of* **override**

overrule [,əʊvə'ruːl] VT [+ *judgement, decision*] annuler, casser; [+ *claim, objection*] rejeter; **he was ~d by the chairman** la décision du président a prévalu contre lui → **objection**

overrun [,əʊvə'rʌn] (*pret* **overran**, *ptp* **overrun**) ① VT ⓐ [*rats, weeds*] envahir, infester; [*troops, army*] se rendre maître de, occuper; **the town is ~ by or with tourists** la ville est envahie par les touristes or de touristes ⓑ [+ *line, edge etc*] dépasser, aller au-delà de; (*Rail*) **to ~ a signal** brûler un signal; **the train overran the platform** le train s'est arrêté au-delà du quai ⓒ **to ~ one's time (by ten minutes)** [*speaker*] dépasser le temps alloué (de dix minutes); [*programme, concert etc*] dépasser l'heure prévue (de dix minutes) ② VI **to ~ (by ten minutes)** [*speaker*] dépasser le temps alloué (de dix minutes); [*programme, concert etc*] dépasser l'heure prévue (de dix minutes)

oversaw [əʊvə'sɔː] VB *pt of* **oversee**

overscrupulous [əʊvə'skruːpjʊləs] ADJ trop pointilleux, trop scrupuleux

overseas [əʊvə'siːz] ① ADV outre-mer; (= *abroad*) à l'étranger; **he's back from ~** il revient de l'étranger; **visitors from ~** visiteurs *mpl* (venus) d'outre-mer, étrangers *mpl* ② ADJ [*colony, market*] d'outre-mer; [*trade*] extérieur (-eure *f*); [*visitor*] (venu) d'outre-mer, étranger; [*aid*] aux pays étrangers; (*Admin, Ind etc*) **he got an ~ posting** il a été détaché à l'étranger or outre-mer; (*Brit*) **Minister/Ministry of Overseas Development** ≈ ministre *m*/ministère *m* de la Coopération ③ COMP ► **overseas cap** N (*US*) calot *m*, bonnet *m* de police

oversee [əʊvə'siː] (*pret* **oversaw**, *ptp* **overseen**) VT surveiller

overseer ['əʊvəsiːə'] N (*in factory, on roadworks etc*) contremaître *m*, chef *m* d'équipe; (*in coalmine*) porion *m*; [*of prisoners, slaves*] surveillant(e) *m(f)*

oversell [əʊvə'sel] (*pret, ptp* **oversold**) VT ⓐ (*lit*) **the match/show was oversold** on a vendu plus de billets qu'il n'y avait de places pour le match/le spectacle ⓑ (*fig*) faire trop valoir, mettre trop en avant

oversensitive [əʊvə'sensɪtɪv] ADJ trop sensible, trop susceptible

oversew [əʊvə'səʊ] (*pret* **oversewed**, *ptp* **oversewed** or **oversewn**) VT coudre à points de surjet

oversexed [əʊvə'sekst] ADJ très porté sur le sexe or sur la chose

overshadow [əʊvə'ʃædəʊ] VT [*leaves etc*] ombrager; [*clouds*] obscurcir; [*tree, building*] dominer; (*fig* = *cloud, spoil*) [+ *person, period of time*] assombrir; (= *eclipse*) [+ *person, sb's achievement*] éclipser; **her childhood was ~ed by her mother's death** son enfance a été assombrie par la mort de sa mère

overshoe ['əʊvəʃuː] N (*gen*) galoche *f*; (*made of rubber*) caoutchouc *m*

overshoot [,əʊvə'ʃuːt] (*pret, ptp* **overshot** [,əʊvə'ʃɒt]) VT dépasser, aller au-delà de; **the plane overshot the runway** l'avion a dépassé la piste d'atterrissage; (*lit, fig*) **to ~ the mark** dépasser le but

oversight ['əʊvəsaɪt] N ⓐ (= *omission*) omission *f*, oubli *m*; **by** or **through an ~** par mégarde, par inadvertance ⓑ (= *supervision*) surveillance *f*; (*frm*) **under the ~ of** sous la surveillance de

oversimplification [,əʊvə,sɪmplɪfɪ'keɪʃən] N simplification *f* excessive

oversimplify [əʊvə'sɪmplɪfaɪ] VT trop simplifier, simplifier à l'extrême

oversize(d) [əʊvə'saɪz(d)] ADJ ⓐ (= *too big*) trop grand; (*Scol*) [*class*] trop nombreux, pléthorique; [*family*] trop nombreux ⓑ (= *huge*) gigantesque, énorme

oversleep [əʊvə'sliːp] (*pret, ptp* **overslept** [,əʊvə'slept]) VI (= *wake up too late*) ne pas se réveiller à l'heure; (= *sleep too long*) dormir trop; **I overslept** (= *woke too late*) je me suis réveillé trop tard

oversold [əʊvə'səʊld] VB *pt, ptp of* **oversell**

overspend [əʊvə'spend] (*pret, ptp* **overspent**)
[1] VT [+ *allowance, resources*] dépenser au-
dessus de *or* au-delà de [2] VI trop dépenser ;
to ~ by £10 dépenser 10 livres de trop [3] N
dépassement *m* de budget

overspending [əʊvə'spendɪŋ] N (*gen*) dépenses *fpl* excessives ; (*Econ, Admin etc*) dépassements *mpl* de crédits, dépassements *mpl*
budgétaires

overspent [əʊvə'spent] VB *pt, ptp of* **overspend**

overspill ['əʊvəspɪl] (*Brit*) [1] N excédent *m* de
population ; **the London ~** l'excédent *m* de la
population de Londres [2] COMP ▶ **overspill
town** N ville *f* satellite

overstaffed [əʊvə'stɑːft] ADJ en sureffectif

overstaffing [əʊvə'stɑːfɪn] N effectif *m* pléthorique, sureffectif *m*

overstate [əʊvə'steɪt] VT exagérer

overstatement [əʊvə'steɪtmənt] N exagération *f*

overstay [əʊvə'steɪ] VT **to ~ one's leave** (*Mil*)
excéder la durée fixée de sa permission ; (*gen*)
excéder la durée fixée de son congé ; **I hope I
haven't ~ed my welcome** j'espère que je n'ai
pas abusé de votre hospitalité ; **I know when
I've ~ed my welcome** je sais reconnaître
quand je deviens indésirable

oversteer [əʊvə'stɪər] VI trop braquer

overstep [əʊvə'step] VT [+ *limits*] dépasser, outrepasser ; **to ~ one's authority** abuser de son
autorité ; (*Pol*) outrepasser son mandat ; (*fig*)
to ~ the line *or* **mark** exagérer (*fig*), dépasser la
mesure *or* les bornes

overstocked [əʊvə'stɒkt] ADJ [*pond, river*] surchargé de poissons ; [*farm*] qui a un excès de
cheptel ; [*shop, market*] surapprovisionné

overstrain [əʊvə'streɪn] VT [+ *person*] surmener ; [+ *heart*] fatiguer ; [+ *strength*] abuser de ;
[+ *horse, metal*] forcer ; [+ *resources, reserves*]
surexploiter ; **to ~ o.s.** se surmener

overstretch [əʊvə'stretʃ] [1] VT [a] (*lit*) [+ *muscles, legs*] trop étirer [b] (*fig*) [+ *budget, finances*]
grever ; [+ *resources*] surexploiter ; [+ *abilities*]
trop pousser ; **to ~ o.s.** (= *do too much*) se
surmener ; (*financially*) dépasser les limites de
son budget [2] VI [*person, muscles, legs*] s'étirer
de trop

overstretched [əʊvə'stretʃt] ADJ [*person*] débordé ; **my budget is ~** mon budget est extrêmement serré

overstrung [əʊvə'strʌŋ] ADJ [*piano*] à cordes
croisées

overstuffed [əʊvə'stʌft] ADJ [*chair*] rembourré

oversubscribed [əʊvəsəb'skraɪbd] ADJ (*St Ex*)
sursouscrit ; (*gen*) **this outing was ~** il y a eu
trop d'inscriptions pour cette sortie

overt [əʊ'vɜːt] ADJ [*hostility, interference*] manifeste ; [*criticism*] franc (franche *f*) ; [*discrimination, racism*] déclaré ; [*sexuality*] non réprimé ;
[*message*] évident ; (*Mil, Pol*) **~ and covert operations** opérations *fpl* à découvert et secrètes

overtake [əʊvə'teɪk] (*pret* **overtook**, *ptp*
overtaken) [1] VT [a] (= *pass*) [+ *car*] (*Brit*)
doubler, dépasser ; [+ *competitor, runner*] devancer, dépasser
[b] (*fig* = *take the lead over*) [+ *competitor, rival*]
devancer, dépasser ; **they have ~n Britain as
the world's fifth largest economy** ils ont dépassé la Grande-Bretagne et sont devenus la
cinquième puissance économique mondiale ;
**lung cancer has ~n breast cancer as the main
cause of death for women** le cancer des poumons a remplacé le cancer du sein comme
principale cause de mortalité chez les
femmes
[c] (*fig* = *overwhelm*) [*storm, night*] surprendre ;
the terrible fate that has ~n them le terrible
sort qui s'est abattu sur eux *or* qui les a
frappés ; **~n by fear** frappé d'effroi ; **to be ~n
by events** être dépassé par les événements ;

his fear was quickly ~n by anger sa peur a vite
cédé la place à la colère
[2] VI (*Brit Aut*) doubler, dépasser ; **"no overtaking"** « interdiction de dépasser *or* doubler » ;
to ~ on the inside dépasser du mauvais côté

overtax [əʊvə'tæks] VT [a] (*Fin*) surimposer
[b] [+ *person*] surmener ; **to ~ one's strength**
abuser de ses forces, se surmener ; **a singer
who has ~ed his voice** un chanteur qui a trop
poussé sa voix ; **such a project might ~ the
skills of our workforce** un tel projet risque de
mettre les compétences de notre main-
d'œuvre à trop rude épreuve

over-the-counter [əʊvəðə'kaʊntər] [1] ADJ
[a] (*Pharm*) [*drugs, medicine*] vendu sans
ordonnance → **counter** [b] (*St Ex*) [*securities,
transactions*] hors cote [2] COMP ▶ **over-the-
counter market** N (*St Ex*) marché *m* hors
cote *m*, hors-cote *m*

overthrow [əʊvə'θrəʊ] (*pret* **overthrew**
[əʊvə'θruː], *ptp* **overthrown** [əʊvə'θrəʊn])
[1] VT [+ *enemy, country, empire*] vaincre
(définitivement) ; [+ *dictator, government,
system*] renverser [2] ['əʊvəθrəʊ] N [*of enemy
etc*] défaite *f* ; [*of empire, government, system*]
chute *f*, renversement *m*

overtime ['əʊvətaɪm] [1] N [a] (*at work*) heures
fpl supplémentaires ; **I am on ~** ◊ **I'm doing** *or*
working ~ je fais des heures supplémentaires ;
£300 per week with ~ 300 livres par semaine
heures supplémentaires comprises ; **to work ~**
(*lit*) faire des heures supplémentaires ; (*fig*)
mettre les bouchées doubles ; (*fig*) **his imagination was working ~** il s'était laissé emporter
par son imagination [b] (*US Sport*) prolongation *f* [2] COMP ▶ **overtime pay** N (rémunération *f* pour) heures *fpl* supplémentaires
▶ **overtime work(ing)** N heures *fpl* supplémentaires

overtired [əʊvə'taɪəd] ADJ (*gen*) surmené ;
[*baby, child*] énervé ; **don't get ~** ne te surmène pas, ne te fatigue pas trop

overtly [əʊ'vɜːtlɪ] ADV [*political, sexual*] ouvertement

overtone ['əʊvətəʊn] N [a] (*Mus*) harmonique
m or f [b] (*fig* = *hint*) note *f*, accent *m* ; **there
were ~s** *or* **there was an ~ of hostility in his
voice** on sentait une note *or* des accents
d'hostilité dans sa voix ; **to have political ~s**
avoir des connotations *or* des sous-entendus
politiques

overtook [əʊvə'tʊk] VB *pt of* **overtake**

overtrick ['əʊvətrɪk] N (*Bridge*) levée *f* de
mieux

overtrump [əʊvə'trʌmp] VT (*Cards*) surcouper

overture ['əʊvətjʊər] N [a] (*Mus*) ouverture *f* ;
the 1812 Overture l'Ouverture *f* solennelle
[b] (*fig*) ouverture *f*, avance *f* ; **to make ~s to
sb** faire des ouvertures à qn ; **peace ~s** ouvertures *fpl* de paix ; **friendly ~s** avances *fpl*
amicales

overturn [əʊvə'tɜːn] [1] VT [a] [+ *car, chair*]
renverser ; [+ *boat*] faire chavirer *or* capoter
[b] (*fig*) [+ *government, plans*] renverser ; [+ *decision, judgement*] annuler [2] VI [*chair*] se
renverser ; [*car, boat*] se retourner, capoter ;
[*railway coach*] se retourner, verser ; [*boat*] chavirer, capoter

overtype ['əʊvətaɪp] VT taper par-dessus

overuse [əʊvə'juːz] VT [+ *object, product*] abuser
de ; **the word is ~d** c'est un mot galvaudé

overvalue [əʊvə'væljuː] VT (*gen*) surestimer ;
(*Econ*) [+ *currency*] surévaluer

overview ['əʊvəvjuː] N [a] (*lit*) vue *f* d'ensemble, panorama *m* [b] (*fig*) [*of situation etc*] vue *f*
d'ensemble

overweening [əʊvə'wiːnɪŋ] ADJ (*frm*) [*pride,
arrogance, ambition, self-confidence, power*] démesuré ; [*person*] outrecuidant (*liter*) ; [*organization, bureaucracy*] présomptueux

overweight [əʊvə'weɪt] [1] ADJ **to be ~**
[*person*] avoir des kilos en trop ; **to be 5 kilos
~** peser 5 kilos de trop ; **to be medically ~**
avoir une surcharge pondérale ; **your luggage
is ~** vous avez un excédent de bagages
[2] ['əʊvə,weɪt] N poids *m* en excès ; [*of person*]
(*gen*) surpoids *m* ; (*Med*) surcharge *f* pondérale

overwhelm [əʊvə'welm] VT [a] (*lit*) [*flood,
waves, sea*] [+ *land, person, ship*] submerger, engloutir ; [*earth, lava, avalanche*] engloutir,
ensevelir ; [+ *one's enemy, opponent*] écraser
[b] (*fig*) [*emotions*] accabler, submerger ;
[*misfortunes*] atterrer, accabler ; [*shame, praise,
kindness*] confondre, rendre confus ; [*letters,
phone calls*] submerger, inonder ; **to ~ sb with
questions** accabler qn de questions ; **to ~ sb
with favours** combler qn de faveurs ; **I am ~ed
by his kindness** je suis tout confus de sa
gentillesse ; **to be ~ed with work** être débordé
or accablé de travail ; **we have been ~ed with
offers of help** nous avons été submergés *or*
inondés d'offres d'aide ; **Venice quite ~ed me**
Venise m'a bouleversé ; **to be ~ed with joy**
être au comble de la joie ; **to be ~ed with grief**
être accablé (par la douleur) ; **to be ~ed with
feelings of inadequacy** avoir le sentiment
accablant de ne pas être à la hauteur

overwhelming [əʊvə'welmɪŋ] ADJ [*victory,
majority, defeat*] écrasant ; [*desire, power, pressure*] irrésistible ; [*success*] énorme ; [*evidence,
misfortune, sorrow, heat*] accablant ; [*bad news*]
affligeant, atterrant ; [*good news*] extrêmement réjouissant ; [*welcome, reception*] extrêmement chaleureux ; [*response*] enthousiaste,
qui dépasse toute espérance ; **to give ~ support for sb/sth** soutenir qn/qch sans réserves
or à fond ; **one's ~ impression is that ...** l'impression dominante est que ... ; **an ~ vote in
favour of the plan** une majorité écrasante en
faveur du projet ; **he felt an ~ sense of relief** il
a ressenti un immense soulagement ; **they
won the competition despite ~ odds** ils ont
remporté le concours alors que tout était
contre eux ; **the odds against this happening
are ~** tout laisse à penser que cela ne se fera
pas ; **the ~ military superiority of the enemy** la
supériorité militaire écrasante de l'ennemi ;
for fear of an ~ military response par crainte
d'une riposte militaire fulgurante

overwhelmingly [əʊvə'welmɪŋlɪ] ADV [a] (=
overpoweringly) [*tired, anxious, lucky*] extraordinairement [b] (= *predominantly*) [*vote, approve,
reject*] à une écrasante majorité ; [*white, male,
positive, negative*] en très grande majorité

overwinter [əʊvə'wɪntər] [1] VI [*person, animal,
plant*] passer l'hiver [2] VT [+ *animal, plant*] faire passer l'hiver à

overwork [əʊvə'wɜːk] [1] N surmenage *m* ; **to
be ill from ~** être malade d'avoir trop travaillé
or de s'être surmené [2] VT [a] [+ *person*]
surmener, surcharger de travail ; [+ *horse*]
forcer ; **to ~ o.s.** se surmener [b] (= *make too
elaborate*) [+ *speech*] trop travailler ; **to ~ one's
written style** écrire dans un style trop affecté
[3] VI trop travailler, se surmener

overwrite [əʊvə'raɪt] VT (*Comput*) écraser

overwrought [əʊvə'rɔːt] ADJ [a] (= *upset*)
[*person*] à bout, sur les nerfs [b] (= *overelaborate*) [*poem, song*] tarabiscoté

overzealous [əʊvə'zeləs] ADJ trop zélé ; **to be
~** faire de l'excès de zèle, faire du zèle

Ovid ['ɒvɪd] N Ovide *m*

oviduct ['əʊvɪdʌkt] N oviducte *m*

oviform ['əʊvɪfɔːm] ADJ ovoïde

ovine ['əʊvaɪn] ADJ ovin

oviparous [əʊ'vɪpərəs] ADJ ovipare

ovoid ['əʊvɔɪd] [1] ADJ ovoïde [2] N forme *f*
ovoïde

ovulate ['ɒvjʊleɪt] VI ovuler

ovulation [ˌɒvjʊ'leɪʃən] N ovulation *f*

ovule ['ɒvjuːl] N (*Bot, Zool*) ovule *m*

ovum ['əʊvəm] N (pl **ova**) (Bio) ovule m

ow [aʊ] EXCL = **ouch**

owe [əʊ] VT ⓐ [+ money etc] devoir (**to sb à qn**); **he ~s me £5** il me doit 5 livres; **I'll ~ it to you** je vous le devrai; **I still ~ him for the meal** je lui dois toujours le (prix du) repas; **I ~ you a lunch** je vous dois un déjeuner ⓑ (fig) [+ respect, obedience, one's life] devoir (**to sb à qn**); **to ~ sb a grudge** garder rancune à qn, en vouloir à qn (**for** de); **I ~ you thanks for your help** je tiens à vous remercier de m'avoir aidé or pour votre aide, je ne vous ai pas encore remercié de m'avoir aidé or pour votre aide; **I ~ my family my grateful thanks for their understanding** je suis profondément reconnaissant à ma famille de sa compréhension; **you ~ him nothing** vous ne lui devez rien; **he ~s his talent to his father** il tient son talent de son père; **he ~s his failure to his own carelessness** il doit son échec à sa propre négligence; (frm) **to what do I ~ the honour of ...?** que me vaut l'honneur de ...?; **they ~ it to you that they succeeded** ils vous doivent leur succès or d'avoir réussi; **I ~ it to him to do that** je lui dois bien de faire cela; **you ~ it to yourself to make a success of it** vous vous devez de réussir

▼ **owing** ['əʊɪŋ] ① ADJ dû; **the amount ~ on the house** ce qui reste dû sur le prix de la maison; **a lot of money is ~ to me** on me doit beaucoup d'argent; **the money still ~ to me** la somme qu'on me doit encore, la somme qui m'est redue (Comm) ② **~ to** PREP en raison de, à cause de

owl [aʊl] N chouette f; (with ear tufts) hibou m; (fig = person) **a wise old ~** un vieux sage → **barn, tawny**

owlet ['aʊlɪt] N chouette f; (with ear tufts) jeune hibou m

owlish ['aʊlɪʃ] ADJ [man] qui a l'air d'un hibou; [woman] qui a l'air d'une chouette; (of appearance) [man] de hibou; [woman] de chouette; **his ~ spectacles** ses lunettes qui lui donnent (or donnaient) l'air d'un hibou; **he gave me an ~ stare** il m'a regardé fixement comme un hibou

owlishly ['aʊlɪʃlɪ] ADV [peer, stare] avec des yeux de hibou

own [əʊn] ① ADJ propre (before n); **his ~ car** sa (propre) voiture, sa voiture à lui; **it's her ~ company** c'est sa (propre) société; **this is my ~ book** ce livre est à moi, c'est mon livre à moi; **my very ~ book** c'est mon livre à moi; **I saw it with my ~ eyes** je l'ai vu de mes propres yeux; **but your ~ brother said so** mais c'est votre frère qui l'a dit; **all my ~ work!** c'est moi qui ai fait tout le travail!; **it was his ~ idea** c'était son idée à lui; **he's his ~ man** il est son propre maître; **he is his ~ worst enemy** son pire ennemi, c'est lui-même; **he does his ~ cooking** il fait la cuisine lui-même; **the house has its ~ garage** la maison a son garage particulier; **my ~ one** mon chéri, ma chérie; (in house-selling) **"~ garden"** « jardin privatif »; (Brit Ftbl) **~ goal** but m contre son camp; **he scored an ~ goal** (Ftbl) il a marqué un but contre son camp; (fig) ça s'est retourné contre lui; (fig) **to do one's ~ thing*** s'éclater; → **accord, sake¹, sweet, thing**

② PRON ⓐ **that's my ~** c'est à moi; **those are his ~** ceux-là sont à lui; **my time is my ~** je suis libre de mon temps, je fais ce que je veux quand il me plaît; **my time's not my ~** je n'ai pas une minute à moi; **I'm so busy I can scarcely call my time my ~** je suis si occupé que je n'ai pas une minute à moi; **I haven't a minute** or **a moment to call my ~** je n'ai pas une minute à moi; **it's all my ~** c'est tout à moi; **a style all his ~** un style bien à lui; **it has a charm all (of) its ~** or **of its ~** cela possède un charme tout particulier or qui lui est propre, cela a un charme bien à soi; **for reasons of his**

~ **pour des raisons personnelles** or qui lui sont propres; **a copy of your ~** votre propre exemplaire; **can I have it for my very ~?** puis-je l'avoir pour moi tout seul?; **it's my very ~** c'est à moi tout seul; **a house of your very ~** une maison bien à vous; **she wants a room of her ~** elle veut sa propre chambre or sa chambre à elle; **I have money of my ~** j'ai de l'argent à moi or des ressources personnelles; **he gave me one of his ~** il m'a donné un des siens; **Streep made the role her ~** ce rôle est définitivement associé à l'interprétation qu'en a donnée Streep

ⓑ (phrases) **to be on one's ~** être tout seul; **to look after one's ~** s'occuper des siens; **did you do it (all) on your ~?** est-ce que vous l'avez fait tout seul?; **if I can get him on his ~** si je réussis à le voir seul à seul; **each to his ~** chacun ses goûts; (fig) **you're on your ~ now!** à toi de jouer (maintenant)!; **he's got nothing to call** or **nothing that he can call his ~** il n'a rien à lui; **to come into one's ~** montrer de quoi on est capable; **to get one's ~ back (on sb for sth)** prendre sa revanche (sur qn de qch) → **hold**

③ VT ⓐ (= possess: gen) posséder; **who ~s this pen/house/paper?** à qui appartient ce stylo/cette maison/ce journal?; **he acts as if he ~s the place*** il se comporte comme en pays conquis ⓑ (frm = acknowledge) reconnaître, avouer (**that** que); **I ~ it** je le reconnais, je l'avoue; **he ~ed his mistake** il a reconnu or avoué son erreur; **he ~ed himself defeated** il s'est avoué vaincu; **he ~ed the child as his** il a reconnu l'enfant

④ VI (frm) **to ~ to a mistake** avouer or reconnaître avoir commis une erreur; **he ~ed to debts of £750** il a avoué or reconnu avoir 750 livres de dettes; **he ~ed to having done it** il a avoué l'avoir fait or qu'il l'avait fait

⑤ COMP ► **own-brand, own-label** ADJ (Comm) **their ~-brand** or **~-label peas etc** leur propre marque f de petits pois etc

► **own up** VI avouer; **to ~ up to sth** admettre qch; **he ~ed up to having stolen it** il a avoué d'avoir volé or qu'il l'avait volé; **come on, ~ up!** allons, avoue!

owner ['əʊnər] ① N (gen) propriétaire mf; (Jur: in house-building) maître m d'ouvrage; **he is the proud ~ of ...** il est l'heureux propriétaire de ...; **the ~ of car number ...** le propriétaire de la voiture immatriculée ...; **as ~s of this dictionary know, ...** comme les possesseurs de ce dictionnaire le savent, ...; **all dog ~s will agree that ...** tous ceux qui ont un chien conviendront que ...; **who is the ~ of this book?** à qui appartient ce livre?; (Comm) **at ~'s risk** aux risques du client → **landowner** ② COMP ► **owner-driver** N conducteur m propriétaire ► **owner-occupied house** N maison f occupée par son propriétaire ► **owner-occupier** N (Brit) propriétaire m occupant

ownerless ['əʊnəlɪs] ADJ sans propriétaire

ownership ['əʊnəʃɪp] N possession f; (Comm) **"under new ~"** « changement de propriétaire »; **under his ~ business was good** du temps où il était propriétaire, les affaires étaient bonnes; **his ~ of the vehicle was not in dispute** on ne lui contestait pas la propriété du véhicule; **to establish ~ of the estate** faire établir un droit de propriété sur le domaine

ownsome* ['əʊnsəm], **owny-o*** ['əʊnɪəʊ] N (hum) **on one's ~** tout seul

owt [aʊt] N (Brit dial) quelque chose

ox [ɒks] N (pl **oxen**) N bœuf m; **as strong as an ox** fort comme un bœuf; (pej) **he's a big ox*** c'est un gros balourd

oxalic [ɒk'sælɪk] ADJ oxalique

oxblood ['ɒksblʌd] ADJ (in colour) rouge sang inv

oxbow ['ɒksbəʊ] ① N (in river) méandre m ② COMP ► **oxbow lake** N bras m mort

Oxbridge ['ɒksbrɪdʒ] (Brit) ① N l'université d'Oxford ou de Cambridge (ou les deux) ② COMP [education] à l'université d'Oxford ou de Cambridge; [accent, attitude] typique des universitaires or des anciens d'Oxford ou de Cambridge

┌─ **OXBRIDGE** ─┐

Oxbridge désigne collectivement les universités d'Oxford et de Cambridge, notamment lorsque l'on veut souligner le côté élitiste de ces deux prestigieuses institutions britanniques. En effet, beaucoup des étudiants de ces universités se retrouvent ensuite aux postes clés de la politique, de l'industrie et de la diplomatie.

oxcart ['ɒkskɑːt] N char m à bœufs

oxen ['ɒksən] NPL of **ox**

oxeye daisy ['ɒksaɪ'deɪzɪ] N marguerite f (Bot)

Oxfam ['ɒksfæm] N (Brit) (ABBR = **Oxford Committee for Famine Relief**) association caritative d'aide au tiers-monde

┌─ **OXFAM** ─┐

Oxfam, acronyme de « Oxford Committee for Famine Relief » est une association caritative d'aide aux pays du tiers monde; elle cherche en particulier à y favoriser l'usage des technologies douces et l'utilisation des énergies renouvelables. Les magasins à l'enseigne d'Oxfam vendent des vêtements d'occasion et des objets artisanaux fabriqués dans les ateliers et coopératives gérés par l'association dans les pays du tiers-monde.

Oxford ['ɒksfəd] ① N Oxford ② COMP ► **the Oxford Movement** N (Brit Rel) le Mouvement d'Oxford

oxhide ['ɒkshaɪd] N cuir m de bœuf

oxidase ['ɒksɪdeɪs] N oxydase f

oxidation [ˌɒksɪ'deɪʃən] N oxydation f

oxide ['ɒksaɪd] N oxyde m

oxidize ['ɒksɪdaɪz] ① VT oxyder ② VI s'oxyder

Oxon ['ɒksən] ABBR = **Oxfordshire**

Oxon. ['ɒksən] (Brit) (ABBR = **Oxoniensis**) d'Oxford

Oxonian [ɒk'səʊnɪən] ① ADJ oxonien, oxfordien ② N Oxonien(ne) m(f), Oxfordien(ne) m(f)

oxtail ['ɒksteɪl] ① N queue f de bœuf ② COMP ► **oxtail soup** N soupe f à la queue de bœuf

oxter ['ɒkstər] N (Scot) aisselle f

oxyacetylene ['ɒksɪə'setɪliːn] ① ADJ oxyacétylénique ② COMP ► **oxyacetylene burner, oxyacetylene lamp, oxyacetylene torch** N chalumeau m oxyacétylénique ► **oxyacetylene welding** N soudure f (au chalumeau) oxyacétylénique

oxygen ['ɒksɪdʒən] ① N oxygène m ② COMP ► **oxygen bottle, oxygen cylinder** N bouteille f d'oxygène ► **oxygen mask** N masque m à oxygène ► **oxygen tank** N ballon m d'oxygène ► **oxygen tent** N tente f à oxygène

oxygenate ['ɒksɪdʒəneɪt] VT oxygéner

oxygenation [ˌɒksɪdʒə'neɪʃən] N oxygénation f

oxymoron [ˌɒksɪ'mɔːrɒn] N (pl **oxymora** [ˌɒksɪ'mɔːrə]) oxymore m

oyez [əʊ'jez] EXCL oyez! (cri du crieur public ou d'un huissier)

oyster ['ɔɪstər] ① N huître f; (fig) **the world is his ~** le monde est à lui ② COMP [industry] ostréicole, huîtrier; [knife] à huître ► **oyster bed** N banc m d'huîtres, huîtrière f ► **oyster cracker** N (US Culin) petit biscuit m salé ► **oyster farm** N établissement m ostréicole

► **oyster farming** N ostréiculture *f*
► **oyster shell** N coquille *f* d'huître
► **oyster stew** N (*US Culin*) soupe *f* aux huîtres
oystercatcher [ˈɔɪstəkætʃəʳ] N (*Orn*) huîtrier *m*

Oz: [ɒz] ABBR = **Australia**
OZ ABBR = **ounce(s)**
ozone [ˈəʊzəʊn] 1 N (*Chem*) ozone *m* 2 COMP ► **ozone depletion** N diminution *f* de la couche d'ozone ► **ozone-friendly** ADJ qui préserve la couche d'ozone

► **ozone hole** N trou *m* d'ozone ► **ozone layer** N couche *f* d'ozone ► **ozone-safe** ADJ sans danger pour la couche d'ozone
ozonosphere [əʊˈzəʊnə‚sfɪə] N couche *f* d'ozone

P

P¹, p [piː] [1] N [a] (= *letter*) P, p *m*; **to mind** *or* **watch one's Ps and Qs*** se surveiller; **P for Peter** ≈ P comme Pierre [b] (ABBR = **penny** *or* **pence**) penny *m*, pence *mpl*; **10p** 10 pence [c] (ABBR = **page**) p [2] COMP ► **P45** N (*Brit*) *attestation de fin de contrat de travail* ► **p and p** N (ABBR = **post(age) and packing**) → **post³**

┌─ **P45** ─┐

En Grande-Bretagne, le **P45** *est l'attestation délivrée à tout employé à la fin de son contrat de travail; elle indique la rémunération globale versée par l'employeur pendant la période considérée ainsi que les impôts et les cotisations sociales payés par l'employé. Le* **P45** *doit être présenté à tout nouvel employeur.*

L'expression « to get one's **P45** *» s'utilise dans le sens propre ou figuré de « être licencié ». Ainsi, on pourra dire du sélectionneur d'une équipe sportive qu'il « risque de recevoir son* **P45** *» si ses joueurs ne sont pas à la hauteur lors d'un match important.*

P² ABBR = **parking**

P. ABBR = **President, Prince**

PA [piːˈeɪ] [a] (ABBR = **personal assistant**) → **personal** [b] (ABBR = **public-address system**) (*also* **PA system**) (système *m* de) sonorisation *f*, sono* *f*; **it was announced over the PA that ...** on a annoncé par haut-parleur que ... [c] ABBR = **Pennsylvania**

pa* [pɑː] N papa *m*

Pa. ABBR = **Pennsylvania**

p.a. (ABBR = **per annum**) par an

pabulum [ˈpæbjʊləm] N [a] (*US* = *nonsense*) niaiseries *fpl* [b] (*rare* = *food*) aliment *m* semi-liquide

PAC N (*US*) (ABBR = **political action committee**) → **political**

pace¹ [peɪs] [1] N [a] (= *measure*) pas *m*; **20 ~s away** ◊ **at 20 ~s** à 20 pas; **to take two ~s forward** faire deux pas en avant

[b] (= *speed*) (*lit*) [*of movement, walking*] pas *m*; (*running*) allure *f*; (*fig*) [*of action*] rythme *m*; **to go at a quick** *or* **good** *or* **smart ~** [*walker*] aller d'un bon pas; [*runner, cyclist*] aller à vive allure; **to quicken one's ~** [*walker*] presser or hâter le pas; [*runner, cyclist*] presser or accélérer l'allure; **to go at a slow ~** [*walker*] marcher lentement *or* à pas lents; [*runner, cyclist*] aller à (une) petite allure; **to gather ~** (*lit*) prendre de la vitesse; (*fig*) [*campaign etc*] prendre de l'ampleur; **the ~ of life remains slow there** le rythme de vie y reste assez lent; **to speed up the ~ of reform** accélérer le rythme des réformes; **their snail-like ~ in implementing the programme** leur extrême lenteur dans la mise en œuvre du programme; **to set the ~** (*Sport*) mener le train, donner l'allure; (*fig*) donner le ton; **to keep ~ with sb** (*lit*) aller à la même allure que qn; (*fig*) suivre le rythme de qn; **earnings have not kept ~ with inflation** les salaires n'ont pas suivi le rythme de l'inflation; **he can't keep ~ with things** il est dépassé par les événements; (*fig*) **to do sth at one's own ~** faire qch à son rythme; (*fig*) **he can't stand** *or* **stay the ~** il n'arrive pas à tenir le rythme [c] **one's ~s: to put a horse through its ~s** faire parader un cheval; (*fig*) **to go through** *or* **show one's ~s** montrer ce dont on est capable; (*fig*) **to put sb through his ~s** mettre qn à l'épreuve, demander à qn de montrer ce dont il est capable

[2] VI marcher à pas mesurés; **to ~ up and down** faire les cent pas, marcher de long en large; **to ~ round a room** faire les cent pas dans une pièce, arpenter une pièce

[3] VT [a] (+ *room, floor, street*) arpenter [b] (*Sport*) (+ *runner*) régler l'allure de; (*lit, fig*) **to ~ o.s.** se ménager, ménager ses forces

[4] COMP ► **pace bowler** N (*Cricket*) *lanceur qui envoie des balles très rapides*

► **pace out** VT SEP (+ *distance*) mesurer en comptant ses pas

pace² [ˈpeɪsɪ] PREP (*frm*) n'en déplaise à; **~ your advisers** n'en déplaise à vos conseillers

-paced [peɪst] ADJ (*in compounds*) **fast-paced** au rythme rapide; **well-paced** au rythme soutenu

pacemaker [ˈpeɪsˌmeɪkər] N [a] (*Med*) stimulateur *m* (cardiaque), pacemaker *m* [b] (*Sport*) (= *person*) **to be (the) ~** mener le train

pacer [ˈpeɪsər] N (*US Sport*) meneur *m*, -euse *f* (de train)

pacesetter [ˈpeɪsˌsetər] N = **pacemaker b**

pacey [ˈpeɪsɪ] ADJ [*production, style, book*] au rythme enlevé

pachyderm [ˈpækɪdɜːm] N pachyderme *m*

pacific [pəˈsɪfɪk] [1] ADJ [*intentions, disposition*] pacifique *m* [2] Pacific = **Pacific Ocean** [3] COMP ► **Pacific Daylight Time** N (*US*) heure *f* d'été du Pacifique ► **the Pacific Islands** NPL les îles *fpl* du Pacifique ► **the Pacific Ocean** N le Pacifique, l'océan *m* Pacifique ► **Pacific Standard Time** N (*US*) heure *f* (normale) du Pacifique

pacifically [pəˈsɪfɪkəlɪ] ADV [*say*] pour calmer les esprits

pacification [ˌpæsɪfɪˈkeɪʃən] N [*of country, territory, population*] pacification *f*

pacifier [ˈpæsɪfaɪər] N [a] (*US* = *baby's dummy*) tétine *f*, sucette *f* [b] (= *person*) pacificateur *m*, -trice *f*

pacifism [ˈpæsɪfɪzəm] N pacifisme *m*

pacifist [ˈpæsɪfɪst] ADJ, N pacifiste *mf*

pacifistic [ˈpæsɪfɪst] ADJ pacifiste

pacify [ˈpæsɪfaɪ] VT (+ *person, fears*) calmer, apaiser; (+ *country, creditors*) pacifier

pack [pæk] [1] N [a] (= *packet*) [*of goods, cereal*] paquet *m*; [*of cotton, wool*] balle *f*; [*of pedlar*] ballot *m*; [*of horse, mule*] charge *f*; (*Mil*) paquetage *m*; (*also* **backpack**) sac *m* à dos; **a ~ of cigarettes** (= *individual packet*) un paquet de cigarettes; (= *carton*) une cartouche de cigarettes

[b] (= *group*) [*of hounds*] meute *f*; [*of wolves, thieves*] bande *f*; [*of brownies, cubs*] meute *f*; [*of runners, cyclists*] peloton *m*; (*Comm* = *set, lot*) pack *m*, lot *m*; **the yoghurt is sold in ~s of four** le yaourt se vend par packs or lots de quatre (pots); **a four-/six-~ (of beer)** un pack de quatre/six bières; **a ~ of lies** un tissu de mensonges; **a ~ of fools*** un tas* *or* une bande* d'imbéciles; **they're behaving like a ~ of kids!** ils se comportent comme de vrais gamins!; (*fig*) **to stay ahead of the ~** maintenir *or* conserver son avance [c] (*esp Brit*) [*of cards*] jeu *m* [d] (*Rugby*) (= *forwards*) pack *m*; (= *scrum*) mêlée *f* [e] (*Med*) **cold/wet ~** compresse *f* froide/humide

[2] VT [a] (= *parcel up*) (*into box, container*) empaqueter, emballer; (*into suitcase*) mettre dans une valise, emballer; **to ~ one's things** faire ses bagages; **~ fragile objects in newspaper** emballez les objets fragiles dans du papier journal; **they come ~ed in dozens** ils sont conditionnés en paquets de douze [b] (= *fill tightly*) (+ *trunk, box*) remplir (**with** de); (*fig*) (+ *mind, memory*) bourrer (**with** de); **to ~ one's case** *or* **suitcase** faire sa valise; **to ~ one's bags** (*lit*) faire ses bagages *or* ses valises; (*fig*) plier bagage, faire ses paquets *or* son balluchon*; (*fig*) **they ~ed the hall to see him** ils se pressaient *or* se sont entassés dans la salle pour le voir; (*Theat*) **to ~ the house** [*player, play*] faire salle comble; **the book is ~ed with information and photos** le livre est bourré de renseignements et de photos → **packed** [c] (= *crush together*) (+ *earth, objects*) [*person*] tasser (**into** dans); [*machine*] damer (**into** dans); (*Ski*) (+ *snow*) damer; (+ *people*) entasser (**into** dans) → **packed** [d] (*pej*) **to ~ a jury** composer un jury favorable; **he had ~ed the committee with his own supporters** il avait noyauté le comité en y plaçant ses partisans [e] (= *contain*) (+ *power etc*) **he ~s a lot of force in that small frame of his** tout menu qu'il soit, il a énormément de force; **this machine ~s enough power to ...** cette machine a assez de puissance pour ...; **he ~s a good punch** ◊ **he ~s quite a wallop*** il a un sacré punch*; **a film that still ~s real punch*** un film qui est toujours aussi fort; (*US*) **to ~ a gun:** porter un revolver

[3] VI [a] (= *do one's luggage*) faire ses bagages *or* sa valise → **send** [b] (= *fit*) **these books ~ easily into that box** ces livres tiennent bien dans cette boîte [c] (= *cram*) **they ~ed into the stadium to hear him** ils se sont entassés dans le stade pour l'écouter; **the crowd ~ed round him** la foule se pressait autour de lui

[4] COMP ► **pack animal** N bête *f* de somme ► **pack drill** N (*Mil*) marche *f* forcée avec paquetage; (*fig*) **no names, no ~ drill, but ...** je ne veux citer personne, mais ... ► **pack ice** N (*NonC*) banquise *f*, pack *m* ► **pack trail** N sentier *m* muletier

► **pack away** VT SEP ranger

► **pack in*** [1] VI (*fig* = *break down, stop working*)

[*machine, car, watch etc*] tomber en panne, rendre l'âme* [2] VT SEP (*Brit*) [+ *person, job*] plaquer* ; **to ~ it all in** tout lâcher, tout plaquer* ; (*Brit*) **~ it in!** (= *stop doing sth*) laisse tomber!* ; (= *stop talking*) écrase!* ; (*Brit*) **let's ~ it in for the day** assez or on arrête pour aujourd'hui ; (*fig*) **it's ~ing them in** [*film, play etc*] ça attire les foules

► **pack off*** VT SEP (= *dismiss*) envoyer promener* ; **to ~ a child off to bed** expédier or envoyer un enfant au lit ; **they ~ed John off to London** ils ont expédié* John à Londres

► **pack up** [1] VI [a] (= *do one's luggage*) faire sa valise or ses bagages ; (*moving house, business etc*) faire ses cartons [b] (* = *give up and go*) (*permanently*) plier bagage ; (*on one occasion*) **I think I'll ~ up and go home now** bon, je crois que je vais m'arrêter là et rentrer chez moi [c] (*Brit** = *break down, stop working*) [*machine, car, watch etc*] tomber en panne, rendre l'âme* [2] VT SEP [a] [+ *object, book*] emballer, empaqueter ; **he ~ed up his bits and pieces** il a rassemblé ses affaires ; **she ~ed up her few belongings** elle a mis ses quelques affaires dans une valise (or dans un sac etc) → **bag** [b] (‡ = *give up*) [+ *work, school*] laisser tomber* ; **~ it up now!** laisse tomber!*, arrête !

package ['pækɪdʒ] [1] N [a] (= *parcel*) paquet *m*, colis *m* [b] (*fig: group*) (= *items for sale*) marché *m* global ; (= *contract*) contrat *m* global ; (= *purchase*) achat *m* forfaitaire ; (*Comput*) progiciel *m* ; (*Pol*) **a ~ of measures** un train de mesures ; **an aid ~** un programme d'aide ; **a good financial ~ for those taking voluntary redundancy** une offre financière intéressante en cas de départ volontaire ; (*Comput*) **payroll/inventory/management ~** progiciel *m* de paie/de stock or inventaire/de gestion ; (*fig*) **the president wants his economic plan passed as a ~** le président veut que son plan économique soit accepté en bloc ; **the plan will be voted on as a ~** le plan sera soumis au vote en bloc [c] = **package holiday**
[2] VT (*Comm*) emballer ; (*fig*) présenter ; **how are they going to ~ the proposal?** comment vont-ils présenter cette proposition ?
[3] COMP ► **package deal** N (= *agreement*) accord *m* global ; (= *contract*) contrat *m* global ; (= *purchase*) achat *m* forfaitaire ► **package holiday** N voyage *m* organisé ► **package policy** N (*Insurance*) police *f* multirisque ► **package store** N (*US*) magasin *m* de vins et spiritueux → LICENSING LAWS ► **package tour** N voyage *m* organisé

packager ['pækɪdʒəʳ] N (*Publishing*) packager or packageur *m*

packaging ['pækɪdʒɪŋ] N (*Comm*) [*of goods*] conditionnement *m* ; (= *wrapping materials*) emballage *m* ; (*Publishing*) packaging *m*

packed [pækt] [1] ADJ [a] [*room*] (*with people*) comble, bondé ; (*with furniture etc*) bourré (**with** *sth*) ; [*bus*] bondé ; (*Brit: also* **~ out**) [*theatre, hall*] comble ; **the bus was ~** (*with people*) le bus était bondé ; **the lecture was ~** il y avait foule à la conférence ; (*with people*) **to be ~ solid** or **tight** être plein à craquer or archiplein* ; **the car park was ~ solid** le parking était archiplein* [b] (*with luggage ready*) **I'm ~ and ready to leave** j'ai fait mes bagages et je suis prêt à partir [c] (= *compressed*) [*snow, soil*] tassé ; **the snow was ~ hard** la neige était bien tassée [2] COMP ► **packed lunch** N (*Brit*) panier-repas *m*

-packed [pækt] ADJ (*in compounds*) **a fun-packed holiday** des vacances *fpl* pleines de distractions ; **a thrill-packed evening** une soirée pleine de or riche en péripéties → **action**

packer ['pækəʳ] N [a] (= *person*) emballeur *m*, -euse *f* [b] (= *device*) emballeuse *f*

packet ['pækɪt] [1] N [a] (= *parcel*) paquet *m* ; (= *paper bag*) pochette *f* ; **to earn a ~*** gagner des sommes folles ; **to cost a ~*** coûter une

somme folle ; (*Brit*) **that must have cost a ~!** cela a dû coûter les yeux de la tête ! [b] [*of sweets*] sachet *m* ; [*of cigarettes, seeds, biscuits, crisps, needles*] paquet *m* [c] (*Naut: also* **~ boat**) paquebot *m*, malle *f* ; **the Dover ~** la malle de Douvres [2] COMP ► **packet soup** N soupe *f* en sachet

packhorse ['pækhɔːs] N cheval *m* de bât

packing ['pækɪŋ] [1] N [a] [*of parcel, goods etc*] emballage *m*, empaquetage *m* ; **to do one's ~** faire sa valise or ses bagages ; (*Comm*) **meat ~** conserverie *f* de viande (*industrie*) [b] (= *act of filling*) [*of space*] remplissage *m* [c] (*Tech*) [*of piston, joint*] garniture *f* [d] (= *padding*) (fournitures *fpl* or matériaux *mpl* pour) emballage *m* ; (*Tech*) (matière *f* pour) garnitures *fpl* [2] COMP ► **packing case** N caisse *f* d'emballage ► **packing density** N (*Comput*) densité *f* d'implantation

packsaddle ['pæk,sædl] N bât *m*

pact [pækt] N pacte *m* ; **France made a ~ with England** la France conclut or signa un pacte avec l'Angleterre ; **we made a ~ to share the profits** nous nous sommes mis d'accord pour partager les bénéfices

pacy ['peɪsɪ] ADJ = **pacey**

pad [pæd] [1] N [a] (*to prevent friction, damage*) coussinet *m*, tampon *m* (*amortisseur*) [b] (*Ftbl*) protège-cheville *m inv* ; (*Hockey etc*) jambière *f* ; (*Fencing*) plastron *m* [c] (= *block of paper*) bloc *m* ; (*also* **writing ~**) bloc *m* (de papier à lettres) ; (*also* **notepad**) bloc-notes *m* → **blot** [d] (*for inking*) tampon *m* encreur [e] [*of rabbit*] patte *f* ; [*of cat, dog*] coussin *m* charnu ; [*of human fingers, toes*] pulpe *f* ; **a ~ of fat** un bourrelet de graisse [f] (*Space: also* **launch ~**) rampe *f* (de lancement) [g] [*of water lily*] feuille *f* de nénuphar [h] (* = *sanitary towel*) serviette *f* hygiénique [i] (‡ = *flat*) piaule* *f*, appart* *m* [j] (*US*) **to be on the ~‡** [*policeman*] toucher des pots-de-vin, palper*
[2] VI **to ~ along** [*person, animal*] marcher à pas de loup or à pas feutrés ; **to ~ about** aller et venir à pas de loup or à pas feutrés
[3] VT [a] [+ *cushion, shoulders*] rembourrer ; [+ *clothing*] matelasser ; [+ *furniture, door*] matelasser, capitonner ; **~ your puppy's bed with something soft** garnissez le panier de votre chiot avec quelque chose de doux ; **to ~ with cotton wool** ouater [b] (*Fin*) [+ *expenses*] gonfler

► **pad out** VT SEP [a] [+ *clothes, shoulders*] rembourrer [b] (*fig*) [+ *meal*] rendre plus copieux (**with** *sth* en ajoutant qch) ; [+ *speech, essay*] étoffer ; (*pej*) délayer

padded ['pædɪd] [1] ADJ [*garment*] matelassé, ouatiné ; [*chair*] rembourré ; [*bedhead*] capitonné, matelassé ; [*envelope*] matelassé [2] COMP ► **padded bra** N soutien-gorge *m* rembourré ► **padded cell** N cellule *f* capitonnée ► **padded shoulders** NPL épaules *fpl* rembourrées

padding ['pædɪŋ] N [a] (= *action*) rembourrage *m* [b] (= *material*) bourre *f*, ouate *f* ; (*fig: in book, speech*) délayage *m*, remplissage *m* ; (*fig*) **there's too much ~ in this essay** il y a trop de remplissage or de délayage dans cette dissertation

paddle ['pædl] [1] N [a] [*of canoe*] pagaie *f* ; [*of waterwheel, paddle boat*] aube *f*, palette *f* ; [*of mixer, fan*] pale *f*, palette *f* [b] **to have** or **go for a ~** (= *aller*) barboter or faire trempette [c] (*US* = *table tennis bat*) raquette *f* de ping-pong [2] VT [a] **to ~ a canoe** faire avancer un canoë à la pagaie ; (*fig*) **to ~ one's own canoe** se débrouiller tout seul (*US* = *spank*) donner une fessée à [3] VI [a] (*in boat, canoe*) **to ~ up/down the river** remonter/descendre la rivière en pagayant or à la pagaie [b] (= *walk*) (*in water*) [*person*] barboter, faire trempette ; [*dog,*

duck] barboter ; (*in mud*) patauger [4] COMP ► **paddle boat**, **paddle steamer** (*Brit*) N bateau *m* à aubes or à roues ► **paddle wheel** N roue *f* à aubes or à palettes ► **paddling pool** N (*Brit*) pataugeoire *f*

► **paddle along** VI [a] (*in boat*) pagayer [b] (= *walk in water*) barboter, faire trempette

paddock ['pædək] N enclos *m* (*pour chevaux*) ; (*Racing*) paddock *m*

Paddy ['pædɪ] N [a] dim of **Patrick** [b] (‡ *esp pej*) surnom des Irlandais

paddy[1] ['pædɪ] [1] N paddy *m*, riz *m* non décortiqué [2] COMP ► **paddy field** N rizière *f*

paddy[2]* ['pædɪ] N (= *anger*) rogne* *f* ; **to be in a ~** être en rogne

paddy waggon‡ ['pædɪ,wægən] N (*US*) panier *m* à salade*

padlock ['pædlɒk] [1] N [*of door, chain*] cadenas *m* ; [*of cycle*] antivol *m* [2] VT [+ *door*] cadenasser ; [+ *cycle*] mettre un antivol à

padre ['pɑːdrɪ] N [a] (*Mil, Naut etc*) aumônier *m* [b] (* = *clergyman*) (*Catholic*) curé *m*, prêtre *m* ; (*Protestant*) pasteur *m*

Padua ['pædjuə] N Padoue

paean ['piːən] N péan *m* ; **~s of praise** des éloges *mpl* dithyrambiques ; **the film is a ~ to nature** ce film est un hymne à la nature

paederast ['pedəræst] N = **pederast**

paediatric [,piːdɪ'ætrɪk] [1] ADJ [*department*] de pédiatrie ; [*illness, medicine, surgery*] infantile [2] COMP ► **paediatric nurse** N infirmier *m*, -ière *f* en pédiatrie ► **paediatric nursing** N puériculture *f*

paediatrician [,piːdɪə'trɪʃən] N pédiatre *mf*

paediatrics [,piːdɪ'ætrɪks] N (*NonC*) pédiatrie *f*

paedophile ['piːdəʊfaɪl] N pédophile *m*

paedophilia [,piːdəʊ'fɪlɪə] N pédophilie *f*

paedophiliac [,piːdəʊ'fɪlɪæk] ADJ pédophile

paella [paɪ'ɛlə] N paella *f*

pagan ['peɪgən] ADJ, N (*lit, fig*) païen(ne) *m(f)*

paganism ['peɪgənɪzəm] N paganisme *m*

page[1] ['peɪdʒ] [1] N (*lit, fig*) page *f* ; **on ~ 10** (à la) page 10 ; **continued on ~ 20** suite (en) page 20 ; (*in newspaper*) **the sports ~s** les pages *fpl* sportives ; **a magazine with ~ upon ~ of adverts** un magazine bourré de publicité ; (*US*) **to be on the same ~** (= *in agreement*) être d'accord [2] VT [+ *book*] paginer ; [+ *printed sheets*] mettre en pages [3] COMP ► **page break** N (*Comput*) saut *m* de page ► **page proofs** NPL (*Typ*) épreuves *fpl* en pages ► **page three** N (*Brit fig*) la page des pin up

PAGE THREE

Depuis de nombreuses années, les lecteurs du journal « The Sun » - le quotidien populaire le plus vendu en Grande-Bretagne - découvrent en page trois la photo pleine page d'une jeune femme posant seins nus. Ce genre de pin up est appelée « page three girl », et l'expression page three s'est étendue aujourd'hui à toutes les photos de modèles aux seins nus publiées dans les tabloïdes.

page[2] [peɪdʒ] [1] N [a] (*also* **~boy**) (*in hotel*) groom *m*, chasseur *m* ; (*at court*) page *m* [b] (*US: Congress*) jeune huissier *m* [c] (*US*) = **pageboy b** [2] VT (= *call for*) [+ *person*] faire appeler ; [*person calling*] appeler ; **they're paging Mr Smith** on appelle M. Smith ; **paging Mr Smith!** on demande M. Smith !

pageant ['pædʒənt] N (*historical*) spectacle *m* or reconstitution *f* historique ; (*fig*) spectacle *m* fastueux ; **Christmas ~** spectacle *m* de Noël

pageantry ['pædʒəntrɪ] N apparat *m*, pompe *f*

pageboy ['peɪdʒbɔɪ] N [a] (*also* **~ hairstyle**) (coupe *f* au) carré *m* [b] (*Brit: at wedding*) garçon *m* d'honneur [c] = **page**[2] **1a**

pager ['peɪdʒəʳ] N bip* *m*, Alphapage® *m*

paginate ['pædʒɪneɪt] VT paginer

pagination [ˌpædʒɪ'neɪʃən] N pagination f

paging ['peɪdʒɪŋ] N (Comput, also in book) pagination f

pagoda [pə'gəʊdə] N pagode f

pah † [pæ] EXCL pouah!

paid [peɪd] [1] VB pt, ptp of **pay** [2] ADJ [staff, employee] salarié; [work] rémunéré, salarié; [holidays] payé; **to be in ~ employment** avoir un emploi rémunéré or salarié; **highly ~** [person, job] très bien payé; **~ gunman** tueur m à gages; **a ~ hack** un nègre (fig) [3] COMP ▶ **paid-in** ADJ (Fin) [moneys] encaissé ▶ **paid-up ~~-up member** membre m à jour de sa cotisation; **fully/partly ~~-up shares** actions fpl entièrement/non entièrement libérées → **pay**

pail [peɪl] N seau m; **a ~ or ~ful of water** un seau d'eau

paillasse ['pælɪæs] N paillasse f

pain [peɪn] [1] N [a] (NonC) (physical) douleur f, souffrance f; (mental) peine f; (stronger) douleur f, souffrance f; **to be in (great) ~** souffrir (beaucoup); **to cause ~ to** (physically) faire mal à, faire souffrir; (mentally) faire de la peine à, peiner; **a cry of ~** un cri de douleur; **no ~, no gain** on n'a rien sans rien [b] (localized) douleur f; **I have a ~ in my shoulder** j'ai une douleur à l'épaule; **chest ~** douleurs fpl dans la poitrine; **stomach ~s** maux mpl d'estomac; **he suffers from back ~** il a mal au dos; **can you tell me where the ~ is?** pouvez-vous me dire où vous avez mal? [c] (* = nuisance) **to be a (real) ~** [person, situation] être enquiquinant* or embêtant*; **he's a ~ in the neck** il est enquiquinant* or casse-pieds*; **he's a ~ in the arse¦** (Brit) or **the ass¦** (esp US) c'est un emmerdeur¦ fini [d] **~s** (= trouble) peine f; **to take ~s or to be at ~s or to go to great ~s (not) to do sth** se donner beaucoup de mal pour (ne pas) faire qch; **to take ~s over sth** se donner beaucoup de mal pour (faire) qch; **to spare no ~s** ne pas ménager ses efforts (**to do** pour faire); **for one's ~s** pour sa peine, pour toute récompense [e] (†† = punishment) peine f, punition f; (frm) **on** or **under ~ of death** sous peine de mort [2] VT faire de la peine à, peiner; (stronger) faire souffrir; **it ~s him that she's unhappy** cela lui fait de la peine qu'elle soit malheureuse; **it ~s me to think that he's unhappy** cela me fait de la peine de penser qu'il est malheureux [3] COMP ▶ **pain barrier** N (Sport) **to go through the ~ barrier** vaincre la douleur ▶ **pain clinic** N service de consultation pour le traitement de la douleur

pained [peɪnd] ADJ [smile, expression, voice] peiné, froissé

painful ['peɪnfʊl] ADJ [a] (= causing physical pain) [wound etc] douloureux; **my hand is ~** j'ai mal à la main [b] (= distressing) [sight, duty] pénible; **it is ~ to see her now** maintenant elle fait peine à voir [c] (= laborious) [climb, task] pénible, difficile

painfully ['peɪnfəlɪ] ADV [a] (= in pain) [throb] douloureusement; [move, walk] péniblement; **~ swollen** enflé et douloureux [b] (= laboriously) [write, climb] péniblement, à grand-peine [c] (= agonizingly) [learn, realize, understand] de façon douloureuse; [shy, sensitive, thin, slow] terriblement; **my ignorance was ~ obvious** mon ignorance n'était que trop évidente; **it was ~ clear that ...** il n'était que trop évident que ...; **to be ~ aware of/that ...** être douloureusement conscient de/que ...

painkiller ['peɪnˌkɪləʳ] N calmant m, analgésique m

painkilling ['peɪnˌkɪlɪŋ] ADJ calmant, analgésique

painless ['peɪnlɪs] ADJ [operation] indolore, sans douleur; (fig) [experience] indolore; **a quick and ~ death** une mort rapide et sans souffrance; **a ~ way of paying one's taxes** un moyen indolore de payer ses impôts; (fig) **it's a ~ way of learning Chinese** de cette façon, on peut apprendre le chinois sans peine; **the exam was fairly ~*** l'examen n'avait rien de bien méchant*

painlessly ['peɪnlɪslɪ] ADV (lit = without pain) sans douleur; (fig = without problems) sans peine

painstaking ['peɪnzˌteɪkɪŋ] ADJ [person, work] minutieux, méticuleux

painstakingly ['peɪnzˌteɪkɪŋlɪ] ADV minutieusement, méticuleusement

paint [peɪnt] [1] N [a] (NonC) peinture f → **coat, wet** [b] **~s** couleurs fpl; **a box of ~s** une boîte de couleurs [2] VT [a] [+ wall etc] peindre; **to ~ a wall red** peindre un mur en rouge; **plates ~ed with flowers** des assiettes avec des motifs à fleurs; **to ~ sth again** repeindre qch; **to ~ one's nails** se vernir les ongles; (gen, pej) **to ~ one's face** se peinturlurer le visage; **they ~ed the children's faces** ils ont peint le visage des enfants; **to ~ one's lips** se mettre du rouge à lèvres; (fig) **to ~ the town red** faire la bringue*, faire la noce*; **to ~ sb into a corner** pousser qn dans ses derniers retranchements; **to ~ o.s. into a corner** se mettre dans une impasse [b] (Art) [+ picture, portrait] peindre; (Theat) **to ~ the scenery** brosser les décors; (fig) **she ~ed a vivid picture of the moment she escaped** elle a décrit son évasion avec beaucoup de vivacité; **he ~ed the situation in very black colours** il brossa un tableau très sombre de la situation [c] (Med) [+ throat, wound] badigeonner [3] VI (Art) peindre, faire de la peinture; **to ~ in oils** peindre à l'huile, faire de la peinture à l'huile; **to ~ in watercolours** faire de l'aquarelle [4] COMP ▶ **paint gun** N pistolet m à peinture ▶ **paint remover** N décapant m (pour peinture) ▶ **paint roller** N rouleau m à peinture ▶ **paint spray** N pulvérisateur m (de peinture); (Aut: for repairs) bombe f de peinture or de laque ▶ **paint stripper** N (= chemical) décapant m; (= tool) racloir m
▶ **paint in** VT SEP peindre
▶ **paint out** VT SEP faire disparaître sous une couche de peinture
▶ **paint over** VT SEP [+ slogan, graffiti] couvrir de peinture

paintballing ['peɪntˌbɔːlɪŋ] N jeu guerrier où les projectiles sont des capsules de peinture

paintbox ['peɪntbɒks] N boîte f de couleurs

paintbrush ['peɪntbrʌʃ] N pinceau m, brosse f

painted ['peɪntɪd] [1] ADJ [wall, furniture, room] peint [2] COMP ▶ **painted lady** N (= butterfly) belle-dame f, vanesse f; (pej: also **~ woman**) femme f trop fardée, cocotte* f (pej)

painter¹ ['peɪntəʳ] N [a] (Art) peintre m → **landscape, portrait** [b] (also **housepainter**) peintre m (en bâtiments); **~ and decorator** peintre m décorateur

painter² ['peɪntəʳ] N (Naut) amarre f

painterly ['peɪntəlɪ] ADJ (lit) [talents, skill, eye] de peintre; (fig) [film] très pictural; [account] pittoresque

painting ['peɪntɪŋ] N [a] (NonC: lit, fig) peinture f; **~ in oils** peinture f à l'huile; **to study ~** étudier la peinture [b] (= picture) tableau m, toile f

paintpot ['peɪntpɒt] N pot m de peinture (lit)

paintwork ['peɪntwɜːk] N (NonC) peinture f

pair [pɛəʳ] [1] N [a] (= two) [of shoes, socks, scissors, earrings, eyes, spectacles] paire f; **these gloves make or are a ~** ces gants vont ensem-ble; **these socks are not a ~** ces chaussettes sont dépareillées; **a ~ of scissors** une paire de ciseaux; **a ~ of pyjamas** un pyjama; **a ~ of tweezers** une pince à épiler; **I've only got one ~ of hands!** je ne peux pas tout faire à la fois!; **to be or have a safe ~ of hands** être fiable; **she's got a great ~ of legs*** elle a de belles jambes; **John won with a ~ of aces** John a gagné avec une paire d'as; **the children were shown ~s of words** on a montré aux enfants des mots deux par deux; **in ~s** (= two together) [work etc] à deux; (= by twos) [enter etc] par deux [b] [of animals] paire f; (= mated) couple m → **carriage** [c] (= two people) paire f; **you two are a right ~!*** vous faites vraiment la paire tous les deux!; **~s of identical twins** paires fpl de vrais jumeaux [d] (Brit Parl) un de deux députés de partis opposés qui se sont entendus pour s'absenter lors d'un vote [2] VT [+ socks] appareiller [b] [+ animals] accoupler, apparier; (in competition etc) **to be ~ed with/against sb** avoir qn comme partenaire/comme adversaire [3] VI [a] [gloves etc] aller ensemble; **to ~ with** aller avec [b] [animals] s'accoupler, s'apparier [4] COMP ▶ **pair bond** N (Zool etc: also **~-bonding**) union f monogame ▶ **pairs champions** NPL champions mpl par couple ▶ **pairs championship** N championnat m en double ▶ **pairs skaters** NPL patineurs mpl par couple en double ▶ **pairs tournament** N tournoi m en double
▶ **pair off** [1] VI [a] [people] s'arranger deux par deux; **to ~ off with sb** se mettre avec qn [b] (Brit Parl) s'entendre avec un adversaire pour s'absenter lors d'un vote [2] VT SEP mettre par paires; **John was ~ed off with her at the dance** on lui a attribué John comme cavalier
▶ **pair up** VI [people] former un tandem, faire équipe; **he ~ed up with his friend for the race** il a fait équipe avec son ami pour la course

pairing ['pɛərɪŋ] N [a] (= pair) [of footballers, rugby players, cricketers] association f; [of tennis players] équipe f de double; [of ice-skaters] couple m; [of golfers] camp m; (Cine, Theat) **the ~ of Laurel and Hardy** le duo or le tandem Laurel et Hardy [b] (NonC = action) **the ~ of Dixon with Winterburn was a success** l'association Dixon-Winterburn a été un succès [c] (Orn) appariement m

paisley ['peɪzlɪ] [1] N (= fabric) laine f à motif cachemire; (= design: also **~ pattern**) motif m or dessin m cachemire [2] COMP ▶ **paisley shawl** N châle m (à motif) cachemire

pajamas [pə'dʒɑːməz] NPL (US) = **pyjamas**

Paki ['pækɪ] (Brit pej) ABBR = **Pakistani** [1] N Pakistanais(e) m(f) [2] ADJ pakistanais(e) [3] COMP ▶ **Paki-basher** N personne qui participe à des attaques racistes contre des immigrés pakistanais ▶ **Paki-bashing** N attaques racistes contre des immigrés pakistanais

Pakistan [ˌpɑːkɪs'tɑːn] N le Pakistan

Pakistani [ˌpɑːkɪs'tɑːnɪ] [1] ADJ pakistanais [2] N Pakistanais(e) m(f)

pakora [pə'kɔːrə] N (pl pakora or pakoras) (Culin) pakora m (petit beignet indien)

PAL [pæl] N (TV) (ABBR = **phase alternation line**) PAL m

pal* [pæl] N copain* m, copine* f; (form of address) mon vieux*; **they're great ~s** ils sont très copains*, ce sont de grands copains*; **be a ~!** sois sympa!*
▶ **pal up*** VI devenir copain(s)* (or copine(s)*) (**with** avec)

palace ['pælɪs] [1] N palais m; **the Palace** (= the Queen's entourage) le Palais (de Buckingham); **bishop's ~** évêché m, palais m épiscopal; **royal ~** palais m royal; **presidential ~** palais *m* présidentiel [2] COMP ► **palace revolution** N (*fig*) révolution *f* de palais

paladin ['pælədɪn] N paladin *m*

palaeo... ['pælɪəʊ] PREF = **paleo...**

Palaeozoic [ˌpælɪəʊˈzəʊɪk] ADJ, N (*Geol*) paléozoïque *m*

palais ['pæleɪ] N (*Brit: also* **~ de danse**†) dancing *m*, salle *f* de danse *or* de bal

palatable ['pælətəbl] ADJ [*food*] agréable au goût ; (*fig*) [*fact etc*] acceptable

palatal ['pælətl] [1] ADJ palatal ; (*Ling*) **~ l** mouillé [2] N palatale *f*

palatalize ['pælətəlaɪz] VT palataliser, mouiller

palate ['pælɪt] N (*Anat*) palais *m* ; **to have a discriminating ~** avoir le palais fin ; **too sweet for my ~** trop sucré à mon goût → **hard, soft**

palatial [pəˈleɪʃəl] ADJ **the house is ~** la maison est un véritable palais ; **a ~ hotel** un palace ; **the ~ splendour of the building** la splendeur palatiale de cet édifice

palatinate [pəˈlætɪnɪt] N palatinat *m*

palaver [pəˈlɑːvəʳ] [1] N [a] (*lit = discussion*) palabre *f* [b] (* = *fuss*) palabres *fpl* ; **what a ~!** quelle histoire pour si peu ! ; **to make a lot of ~ about** *or* **over sth** faire toute une histoire à propos de qch [2] VI palabrer

pale¹ [peɪl] [1] ADJ [*face, person*] (*naturally*) pâle ; (*from sickness, fear*) blême ; [*colour*] pâle ; [*dawn, moonlight*] blafard ; **~ grey/pink** gris/rose pâle ; **to grow ~** (*gen*) pâlir ; (*from sickness, emotion*) blêmir, pâlir ; **he looked ~** il était pâle *or* blême ; **~ blue eyes** yeux *mpl* bleu pâle [2] VI [*person*] (*gen*) (*from shock, emotion*) pâlir ; (*from sickness*) blêmir ; (*from fear*) blêmir ; **to ~ with fear** pâlir *or* blêmir de peur ; (*fig*) **it ~s in comparison with ...** ◊ **it ~s into insignificance beside ...** cela paraît dérisoire par rapport *or* comparé à ... ; **her beauty ~d beside her mother's** sa beauté était éclipsée par celle de sa mère [3] COMP ► **pale ale** N (*Brit*) pale-ale *f* (*sorte de bière blonde légère*) ► **pale-faced** ADJ (*= not tanned*) au teint pâle ; (*from sickness, fear etc*) pâle, blême ► **pale-skinned** ADJ à la peau claire

pale² [peɪl] N (*= stake*) pieu *m* ; **to be beyond the ~** [*behaviour, ideas, beliefs*] être inadmissible *or* inacceptable ; [*person*] dépasser les bornes

paleface ['peɪlfeɪs] N Visage pâle *mf*

paleness ['peɪlnɪs] N pâleur *f*

paleo... ['pælɪəʊ] PREF paléo...

paleographer [ˌpælɪˈɒɡrəfəʳ] N paléographe *mf*

paleography [ˌpælɪˈɒɡrəfɪ] N paléographie *f*

paleolithic [ˌpælɪəʊˈlɪθɪk] ADJ paléolithique ; **the ~ age** le paléolithique

paleontologist [ˌpælɪɒnˈtɒlədʒɪst] N paléontologue *mf*

paleontology [ˌpælɪɒnˈtɒlədʒɪ] N paléontologie *f*

Palermo [pəˈlɛəməʊ] N Palerme

Palestine ['pælɪstaɪn] N la Palestine

Palestinian [ˌpælɪsˈtɪnɪən] [1] ADJ palestinien [2] N Palestinien(ne) *m(f)*

palette ['pælɪt] [1] N (*Art, Comput*) palette *f* [2] COMP ► **palette knife** N (*pl* **palette knives**) (*Art*) couteau *m* (à palette) ; (*for cakes*) pelle *f* (à tarte) ; (*for cooking*) spatule *f*

palfrey ['pɔːlfrɪ] N palefroi *m*

palimony* ['pælɪmənɪ] N pension *f* alimentaire (*versée à un(e) ex-concubin(e)*)

palimpsest ['pælɪmpsest] N palimpseste *m*

palindrome ['pælɪndrəʊm] N palindrome *m*

paling ['peɪlɪŋ] N (*= fence*) palissade *f* ; (*= stake*) palis *m*

palisade [ˌpælɪˈseɪd] N [a] palissade *f* [b] (*US Geol*) ligne *f* de falaises abruptes

pall¹ [pɔːl] VI perdre son charme (**on sb** pour qn) ; **the job was beginning to ~ for him** il commençait à se lasser de ce poste

pall² [pɔːl] N drap *m* mortuaire ; (*Rel*) pallium *m* ; (*fig*) [*of smoke*] voile *m* ; [*of snow*] manteau *m* ; (*= depressing atmosphere*) atmosphère *f* lugubre ; **to cast a ~ over** [+ *event, celebration*] assombrir

Palladian [pəˈleɪdɪən] ADJ (*Archit*) palladien

palladium [pəˈleɪdɪəm] N (*Chem*) palladium *m*

pallbearer N **to be a ~** porter le cercueil

pallet ['pælɪt] [1] N [a] (*= mattress*) paillasse *f* ; (*= bed*) grabat *m* [b] (*for handling goods*) palette *f* [c] = **palette** [2] COMP ► **pallet loader** N palettiseur *m* ► **pallet truck** N transpalette *m*

palletization [ˌpælɪtaɪˈzeɪʃən] N palettisation *f*

palletize ['pælɪtaɪz] VT palettiser

palliasse ['pælɪæs] N = **paillasse**

palliate ['pælɪeɪt] VT (*Med, fig*) pallier ; **palliating drugs** médicaments *mpl* palliatifs

palliative ['pælɪətɪv] ADJ, N palliatif *m*

pallid ['pælɪd] ADJ [*person, complexion*] pâle, blafard ; [*light*] blafard ; (*fig = insipid*) [*person, entertainment*] insipide

pallidness ['pælɪdnɪs], **pallor** ['pæləʳ] N pâleur *f* ; [*of face*] teint *m* blafard, pâleur *f*

pally* ['pælɪ] ADJ (*très*) copain* (copine* *f*) (**with avec**)

palm¹ [pɑːm] [1] N [*of hand*] paume *f* ; **she placed the money in his ~** elle lui mit l'argent dans le creux de la main ; **to read sb's ~** lire *or* faire les lignes de la main à qn ; **to cross sb's ~ with silver** donner la pièce à qn ; (*fig*) **to have sb in the ~ of one's hand** faire de qn ce qu'on veut ; (*fig*) **he had the audience in the ~ of his hand** il avait le public dans sa poche* ; (*fig*) **to grease** *or* **oil sb's ~** graisser la patte* à qn [2] VT (*= conceal*) cacher au creux de la main ; (*= pick up*) subtiliser, escamoter ; **to ~ sb sth** ◊ **to ~ sth to sb** glisser qch *or* faire passer qch à qn

► **palm off** VT SEP [+ *sth worthless*] refiler* (**on, onto** à) ; **to ~ sb off** se débarrasser de qn ; **they ~ed the children off on me** ils m'ont refilé les enfants*

palm² [pɑːm] [1] N (*also* **~ tree**) palmier *m* ; (*= branch*) palme *f* ; (*Rel*) rameau *m* ; (*Rel = straw cross*) rameaux *mpl* ; (*fig*) **to carry off the ~** remporter la palme [2] COMP ► **palm court** ADJ (*Brit*) [*music, orchestra etc*] ≈ de thé dansant ► **palm grove** N palmeraie *f* ► **palm oil** N huile *f* de palme ► **Palm Sunday** N (dimanche *m* des) Rameaux *mpl*

palmate ['pælmeɪt] ADJ (*Bot, Zool*) palmé

palmcorder ['pɑːmkɔːdəʳ] N caméscope *m* de paume

palmetto [pælˈmetəʊ] [1] N (*pl* **palmettos** *or* **palmettoes**) palmier *m* nain [2] COMP ► **the Palmetto State** N (*US*) la Caroline du Sud

palmist ['pɑːmɪst] N chiromancien *m(f)*

palmistry ['pɑːmɪstrɪ] N chiromancie *f*

palmtop computer ['pɑːmtɒpkəmˈpjuːtəʳ] N ordinateur *m* de poche

palmy ['pɑːmɪ] ADJ (*fig*) heureux ; [*era*] florissant, glorieux

palomino [ˌpæləˈmiːnəʊ] N (*pl* **palominos**) alezan *m* doré à crins blancs

palooka* [pəˈluːkə] N (*US pej*) pauvre type* *m*, type* *m* fini

palpable ['pælpəbəl] ADJ (*lit*) palpable ; (*fig*) [*tension, fear, unease, frustration, enthusiasm*] palpable ; [*error*] manifeste

palpably ['pælpəblɪ] ADV manifestement, d'une façon évidente

palpate ['pælpeɪt] VT (*Med*) palper

palpitate ['pælpɪteɪt] VI palpiter

palpitating ['pælpɪteɪtɪŋ] ADJ palpitant

palpitation [ˌpælpɪˈteɪʃən] N palpitation *f*

palsied† ['pɔːlzɪd] ADJ (*Med*) (*= paralyzed*) paralysé, paralytique ; (*= trembling: also fig*) tremblotant

palsy† ['pɔːlzɪ] N (*Med*) (*= trembling*) paralysie *f* agitante ; (*= paralysis*) paralysie *f*

palsy-walsy* [ˌpælzɪˈwælzɪ] ADJ (*Brit*) = **pally**

paltry ['pɔːltrɪ] ADJ [a] (*= tiny, insignificant*) [*amount*] misérable, dérisoire [b] (*= petty*) [*behaviour*] mesquin ; [*excuse*] piètre

paludism ['pæljʊdɪzəm] N paludisme *m*

pampas ['pæmpəs] [1] NPL pampa(s) *f(pl)* [2] COMP ► **pampas grass** N herbe *f* des pampas

pamper ['pæmpəʳ] VT [+ *person, pet*] bichonner, dorloter ; **she ~s her husband with small gifts** elle bichonne *or* dorlote son mari en lui offrant de petits cadeaux ; **~ your skin with ...** offrez à votre peau ... ; **to ~ o.s.** se faire plaisir ; **she ~s herself with luxury beauty products** elle se bichonne avec des produits de beauté de luxe ; **go on, ~ yourself!** allez, faites-vous plaisir !

pamphlet ['pæmflɪt] N brochure *f* ; (*Literat*) opuscule *m* ; (*= scurrilous tract*) pamphlet *m*

pamphleteer [ˌpæmflɪˈtɪəʳ] N auteur *m* de brochures *or* d'opuscules ; [*of tracts*] pamphlétaire *mf*

Pan [pæn] [1] N Pan *m* [2] COMP ► **Pan pipes** NPL flûte *f* de Pan

pan¹ [pæn] [1] N [a] (*Culin*) casserole *f* ; **roasting ~** plat *m* à rôtir → **frying, pot¹** [b] [*of scales*] plateau *m* ; [*of lavatory*] cuvette *f* ; (*Miner*) batée *f* ; (*fig*) **to go down the ~:** tomber à l'eau* → **brain, flash, salt** [c] (*US* = *face*) binette* *f*, bille *f* (de clown): → **deadpan** [2] VT [a] [+ *sand*] laver à la batée [b] (* = *criticize harshly*) [+ *film, book*] éreinter, démolir ; **his work was ~ned by his boss** son patron a descendu en flammes son travail [3] VI **to ~ for gold** laver le sable aurifère (à la batée) [4] COMP ► **pan-fry** VT (*Culin*) faire sauter ► **pan scrubber** N tampon *m* à récurer

► **pan out** VI (*= turn out*) tourner, se passer ; (*= turn out well*) bien tourner, bien se goupiller* ; **it all ~ned out in the long run** ça s'est (bien) goupillé* en fin de compte ; **things didn't ~ out as he'd planned** les choses ne se sont pas goupillées* comme il l'avait prévu

pan² [pæn] [1] VI (*Cine, TV*) [*camera*] faire un panoramique, panoramiquer (**to** sur) ; **the camera ~ned across the lawn** la caméra a fait un panoramique *or* a panoramiqué sur le gazon [2] VT **to ~ the camera** panoramiquer

pan... [pæn] PREF pan...

panacea [ˌpænəˈsɪə] N panacée *f*

panache [pəˈnæʃ] N panache *m*

Pan-African ['pænˈæfrɪkən] ADJ panafricain

Pan-Africanism ['pænˈæfrɪkənɪzəm] N panafricanisme *m*

Panama ['pænəˌmɑː] [1] N [a] le Panama [b] (*also* **~ hat**) panama *m* [2] COMP ► **the Panama Canal** N le canal de Panama

Panamanian [ˌpænəˈmeɪnɪən] [1] ADJ panaméen [2] N Panaméen(ne) *m(f)*

Pan-American ['pænəˈmerɪkən] [1] ADJ panaméricain [2] COMP ► **Pan-American Highway** N route *f* panaméricaine ► **Pan-American Union** N Union *f* panaméricaine

Pan-Americanism ['pænəˈmerɪkənɪzəm] N panaméricanisme *m*

Pan-Asian ['pænˈeɪʃən] ADJ panasiatique

Pan-Asianism ['pænˈeɪʃənɪzəm] N panasiatisme *m*

pancake ['pænkeɪk] [1] N [a] (*Culin*) crêpe *f* → **flat¹** [b] (*Aviat: also* **~ landing**) atterrissage *m* à plat [c] (*= make-up*) pancake make-up [2] VI (*Aviat*) se plaquer, atterrir à plat [3] COMP ► **pancake coil** N (*Elec*) galette *f* ► **Pancake Day** N (*Brit*) mardi *m* gras ► **pancake make-up** N (*= powder compact*) maquillage *m* compact; (*pej*) tartine *f* de maquillage ► **pancake roll** N (*Brit*) ≈ rouleau *m* de printemps ► **Pancake Tuesday** N = **Pancake Day**

panchromatic ['pænkrəʊ'mætɪk] ADJ panchromatique

pancreas ['pæŋkrɪəs] N pancréas *m*

pancreatic [ˌpæŋkrɪ'ætɪk] ADJ pancréatique

panda ['pændə] **1** N panda *m* **2** COMP ► **panda car** N (*Brit*) voiture *f* pie *inv* (*de la police*)

pandemic [pæn'demɪk] **1** ADJ universel **2** N pandémie *f*

pandemonium [ˌpændɪ'məʊnɪəm] N tohu-bohu *m*, chahut *m* (monstre); **it's sheer ~!** c'est un véritable charivari!, quel tohu-bohu!; **~ broke loose** il y eut un chahut monstre *or* un véritable tohu-bohu; **scenes of ~** des scènes de désordre indescriptible

pander ['pændəʳ] VI **to ~ to** [+ *person*] se prêter aux exigences de; [+ *whims, desires*] se plier à; [+ *tastes, weaknesses*] flatter

p & h [ˌpiːən'deɪtʃ] N (*US*) (ABBR = **postage and handling**) port et manutention *f*

P & L (*Comm*) (ABBR = **profit and loss**) → **profit**

Pandora [pæn'dɔːrə] **1** N Pandore *f* **2** COMP ► **Pandora's box** N boîte *f* de Pandore

p & p [ˌpiːən'piː] N (ABBR = **postage and packing**) → **postage**

pandrop ['pændrɒp] N grosse pastille *f* de menthe

pane [peɪn] N vitre *f*, carreau *m*

panegyric [ˌpænɪ'dʒɪrɪk] ADJ, N panégyrique *m*

panel ['pænəl] **1** N **a** [*of door, wall*] panneau *m*; [*of ceiling*] caisson *m*
b (*Aut, Aviat: also* **instrument ~**) tableau *m* de bord
c (*Dress*) pan *m*
d (*Jur*) (= *list*) liste *f* (*des jurés*); (= *jury*) jury *m*; (*Admin, Scol etc*) **~ of examiners** jury *m* (d'examinateurs)
e (*also* **interviewing ~**) jury *m* d'entretien
f (*Brit Med: formerly*) **to be on a doctor's ~** être inscrit sur le registre d'un médecin conventionné
g (*Rad, TV etc*) (*gen*) invités *mpl*; (*for game*) jury *m*; **a ~ of experts** un groupe d'experts, un panel (d'experts)
h (*in inquiry*) commission *f* d'enquête; (= *committee*) comité *m*; [*of negotiators etc*] table *f* ronde
2 VT [+ *surface*] plaquer; [+ *room, wall*] recouvrir de panneaux *or* de boiseries, lambrisser; **~led door** porte *f* à panneaux; **oak-~led** lambrissé de chêne, garni de boiseries de chêne
3 COMP ► **panel-beater** N (*Aut*) carrossier *m*, tôlier *m* ► **panel-beating** N (*Aut*) tôlerie *f* ► **panel discussion** N (*Rad, TV etc*) débat *m*, table *f* ronde (*qui a lieu devant un public*) ► **panel doctor** N (*Brit: formerly*) médecin *m* conventionné ► **panel game** N (*Rad, TV*) jeu *m* radiophonique (*or* télévisé) (*avec des équipes d'invités*) ► **panel patient** N (*Brit: formerly*) malade *mf* assuré(e) social(e) ► **panel pin** N pointe *f*, clou *m* à tête homme ► **panel truck, panel van** N (*US Aut*) camionnette *f*

panelling, paneling (*US*) ['pænəlɪŋ] N (*NonC*) panneaux *mpl*, lambris *m*, boiseries *fpl*

panellist, panelist (*US*) ['pænəlɪst] N (*Rad, TV*) invité(e) *m(f)* (*d'une émission*)

Pan-European ['pænˌjʊərə'piːən] ADJ paneuropéen

pang [pæŋ] N serrement *m or* pincement *m* de cœur; **a ~ of jealousy/regret** une pointe de jalousie/de regret; **a ~ of conscience** un accès de mauvaise conscience, des remords *mpl*; **he saw her go without a ~** il l'a vue partir sans regret, cela ne lui a fait ni chaud ni froid* de la voir partir; **hunger ~s ◊ ~s of hunger** tiraillements *mpl* d'estomac

panhandle ['pænhændl] **1** N **a** (*lit*) manche *m* (de casserole) **b** (*US = strip of land*) bande *f* de terre; **the Texas ~** la partie septentrionale du Texas **2** VI (*US: = beg*) faire la manche* **3** VT (*US: = beg from*) mendigoter* auprès de **4** COMP ► **the Panhandle State** N (*US*) la Virginie occidentale

panhandler: ['pænhændləʳ] N (*US = beggar*) mendiant(e) *m(f)*

panic ['pænɪk] **1** N (*NonC*) panique *f*; **to throw a crowd into a ~** semer la panique dans une foule; **to get into a ~** paniquer*; **to throw sb into a ~** paniquer* qn; **in a ~** complètement affolé *or* paniqué; **(there's) no ~*, it can wait** pas de panique* *or* il n'y a pas le feu*, ça peut attendre
2 VI être pris de panique, paniquer*; **she's ~king about the future of our relationship** elle est prise de panique *or* elle panique* quand elle pense à l'avenir de notre relation; **industry is ~king about the recession** l'industrie panique* à cause de la récession; **don't ~!** pas d'affolement!, pas de panique!
3 VT [+ *crowd*] jeter *or* semer la panique dans; [+ *person*] faire paniquer*; **he was ~ked by his wife's strange behaviour** le comportement étrange de sa femme le faisait paniquer*; **they were ~ked by the prospect of ...** ils étaient pris de panique *or* ils paniquaient* à la perspective de ...; **she was ~ked into burning the letter** dans un moment d'affolement, elle brûla la lettre
4 COMP [*fear*] panique; [*decision*] pris dans un moment de panique ► **panic attack** N crise *f* de panique ► **panic button** N (*fig*) signal *m* d'alarme; **to hit** *or* **push the ~ button** paniquer* ► **panic buying** N achats *mpl* de précaution ► **panic selling** N (*St Ex*) vente *f* d'actions sous l'effet de la panique ► **panic stations*** NPL **it was ~ stations** ça a été la panique générale* ► **panic-stricken** ADJ [*person, crowd*] affolé, pris de panique; [*look*] affolé

panicky ['pænɪkɪ] ADJ [*report, newspaper*] alarmiste; [*decision, action*] de panique; **to feel ~** être pris de panique

panjandrum [pæn'dʒændrəm] N grand ponte* *m*, grand manitou*

pannier ['pænɪəʳ] N panier *m*, corbeille *f*; [*of pack animal*] panier *m* de bât; (*on cycle, motorcycle: also* **~ bag**) sacoche *f*

panoply ['pænəplɪ] N panoplie *f*

panorama [ˌpænə'rɑːmə] N panorama *m*

panoramic [ˌpænə'ræmɪk] **1** ADJ panoramique **2** COMP ► **panoramic screen** N (*Cine*) écran *m* panoramique ► **panoramic view** N vue *f* panoramique

pansy ['pænzɪ] N **a** (*Bot*) pensée *f* **b** (: *pej* = *homosexual*) tante: *f*, tapette: *f*

pant [pænt] **1** VI (= *gasp*) [*person*] haleter; [*animal*] battre du flanc, haleter; **to ~ for breath** chercher (à reprendre) son souffle; **the boy/the dog ~ed along after him** le garçon/le chien le suivait, essoufflé; **he ~ed up the hill** il grimpa la colline en haletant **2** VT (*also* **~ out**) [+ *words, phrases*] dire d'une voix haletante, dire en haletant **3** N halètement *m*
► **pant for:** VT FUS [+ *cigarette, drink*] mourir d'envie de

pantaloon [ˌpæntə'luːn] N **a** (*a pair of*) **~s** une culotte **b** (*Theat*) **Pantaloon** Pantalon *m*

pantechnicon [pæn'teknɪkən] N (*Brit*) (= *van*) grand camion *m* de déménagement; (= *warehouse*) entrepôt *m* (*pour meubles*)

pantheism ['pænθiːɪzəm] N panthéisme *m*

pantheist ['pænθiːɪst] N panthéiste *mf*

pantheistic [ˌpænθiː'ɪstɪk] ADJ panthéiste

pantheon ['pænθɪən] N panthéon *m*

panther ['pænθəʳ] N (*pl* **panthers** *or* **panther**) panthère *f* → **black**

panties* ['pæntɪz] NPL slip *m* (*de femme*)

pantihose ['pæntɪˌhəʊz] NPL (*esp US*) (**a pair of**) ~ un collant, des collants *mpl*

pantile ['pæntaɪl] N tuile *f* imbriquée

panting ['pæntɪŋ] N essoufflement *m*, halètement *m*

panto* ['pæntəʊ] N (*Brit Theat*) ABBR = **pantomime 1a**

pantograph ['pæntəɡrɑːf] N (*Rail, Tech*) pantographe *m*

pantomime ['pæntəmaɪm] **1** N **a** (*Brit Theat*) (= *show*) spectacle de Noël pour enfants **b** (= *mime*) pantomime *f*, mime *m*; **in ~** en mimant **c** (*Brit fig pej* = *fuss*) pantomime *f*, comédie *f*; **the whole thing was a ~** toute cette affaire n'était qu'une pantomime *or* une comédie; **the government should abandon this ~ of secrecy** le gouvernement devrait abandonner cette comédie du secret **2** COMP ► **pantomime dame** N (*Brit*) rôle travesti de femme dans un spectacle de Noël

---
PANTOMIME

La **pantomime** *ou* **panto** *est un spectacle de théâtre pour enfants monté au moment de Noël. Le sujet en est un conte de fées ou une histoire populaire (par ex. Cendrillon ou Aladin), généralement présenté sous la forme d'une comédie bouffonne avec des chansons, des costumes fantaisistes et des décors féeriques. Les acteurs font beaucoup appel à la participation du public. Les principaux rôles masculins et féminins sont souvent interprétés par des acteurs du sexe opposé.*

---

pantry ['pæntrɪ] N (*in hotel, mansion*) office *f*; (*in house*) garde-manger *m inv*

pants [pænts] NPL **a** (*Brit = underwear*) (**a pair of**) ~ un slip **b** (*esp US* = *trousers*) (**a pair of**) ~ (un) pantalon; **short ~** culottes *fpl* courtes; **long ~** pantalon *m* (long); **she's the one who wears the ~*** c'est elle qui porte la culotte*; **to be caught with one's ~ down*** être pris au dépourvu; **to bore the ~ off sb*** barber qn*, raser qn*; **to charm the ~ off sb*** séduire qn; **to beat the ~ off sb*** (= *defeat*) mettre une raclée* à qn

pantsuit ['pæntsuːt] N (*esp US*) tailleur-pantalon *m*

panty girdle ['pæntɪˌɡɜːdl] N gaine-culotte *f*

pantyhose ['pæntɪhəʊz] N = **pantihose**

panty liner ['pæntɪˌlaɪnəʳ] N protège-slip *m*

panzer ['pænzəʳ] **1** N panzer *m* **2** COMP ► **panzer division** N division *f* blindée (allemande)

pap¹ [pæp] N (*Culin*) bouillie *f*; (*fig pej*) niaiseries *fpl*

pap²†† [pæp] N (= *nipple*) mamelon *m*

papa ['pɑːpɑː] N papa *m*

papacy ['peɪpəsɪ] N papauté *f*

papadum ['pæpədəm] N poppadum *m*

papal ['peɪpəl] **1** ADJ [*throne, mass, guards*] pontifical; [*legate, election, visit*] du Pape **2** COMP ► **papal bull** N bulle *f* papale ► **papal cross** N croix *f* papale ► **papal infallibility** N infaillibilité *f* pontificale ► **papal nuncio** N nonce *m* du Pape ► **Papal States** NPL États *mpl* pontificaux *or* de l'Église

Papanicolaou smear [ˌpæpə'nɪkəluːsmɪəʳ], **Papanicolaou test** [ˌpæpə'nɪkəluːtest] N = **Pap smear**

paparazzo [ˌpæpə'rætsəʊ] N (*pl* **paparazzi** [ˌpæpə'rætsiː]) paparazzi *m inv*

papaya [pə'paɪə] N (= *fruit*) papaye *f*; (= *tree*) papayer *m*

paper ['peɪpəʳ] **1** N **a** (*NonC*) papier *m*; (*pej* = *piles of paper*) paperasses *fpl*; **a piece of ~** (= *odd bit*) un bout *or* un morceau de papier; (= *sheet*) une feuille de papier; **he was asked to put his suggestions down on ~** on lui a demandé de mettre ses suggestions par écrit *or*

sur papier; **the project looks impressive enough on ~** sur le papier, le projet semble assez impressionnant → **brown, carbon, rice**
[b] (*also* **newspaper**) journal *m*; **to write for the ~s** faire du journalisme; **it was in the ~s yesterday** c'était dans les journaux hier; **I saw it in the ~** je l'ai vu dans le journal → **illustrate**
[c] (*Scol, Univ*) (= *set of exam questions*) épreuve *f* (écrite); (= *student's written answers*) copie *f*; **a geography ~** une épreuve de géographie; **she did a good ~ in French** elle a rendu une bonne copie de français
[d] (= *scholarly work*) (*printed*) article *m*; (*spoken*) communication *f*, intervention *f*; (*in seminar: by student etc*) exposé *m*; **to write a ~ on** écrire un article sur
[e] (= *government publication*) livre *m* → **white, green**
[f] (*also* **wallpaper**) papier *m* peint
[g] (*Comm*) effet *m*; **commercial ~** effet *m* de commerce
[h] (*US* = *money*) fric* *m*
[2] **papers** NPL (= *documents*) papiers *mpl*; **show me your (identity) ~s** montrez-moi vos papiers (d'identité); (*Mil*) **call-up ~s** ordre *m* d'appel; **ship's ~s** papiers *mpl* de bord; **voting ~s** bulletin *m* de vote
[3] VT [a] [+ *room, walls*] tapisser; (*fig*) **they ~ed the walls of the cafe with notices about ...** ils ont tapissé *or* complètement recouvert le mur du café d'affiches concernant ...
[b] (*US fig = fill theatre*) **to ~ the house*** remplir la salle d'invités
[4] COMP [*doll, towel*] en papier, de papier; (*fig pej*) [*diploma etc*] sans valeur, bidon‡ *inv*; [*profits*] sur le papier, théorique ► **paper bag** N sac *m* en papier; (*small*) poche *f* de papier; **they couldn't fight their way out of a ~ bag*** ils sont complètement nuls* ► **paper chain** N chaîne *f* en papier ► **paper chase** N jeu *m* de piste ► **paper cup** N gobelet *m* en carton ► **paper currency** N billets *mpl* (de banque) ► **paper dart** N avion *m* en papier ► **paper fastener** N attache *f* métallique (*à tête*); (*clip*) trombone *m* ► **paper handkerchief** N mouchoir *m* en papier ► **paper industry** N industrie *f* du papier ► **paper knife** N (*pl* **paper knives**) coupe-papier *m inv* ► **paper lantern** N lampion *m* ► **paper loss** N (*Fin*) perte *f* comptable ► **paper mill** N (usine *f* de) papeterie *f* ► **paper money** N papier-monnaie *m*, monnaie *f* fiduciaire ► **paper plate** N assiette *f* en papier ► **paper qualifications** NPL diplômes *mpl* ► **paper round** N tournée *f* de distribution des journaux ► **paper shop** N (*Brit*) marchand *m* de journaux ► **paper-shredder** N broyeur *m* (*pour papiers*) ► **paper tape** N (*Comput*) bande *f* perforée, ruban *m* perforé ► **paper-thin** ADJ [*slice*] extrêmement fin; [*wall*] fin comme du papier à cigarettes; **to cut sth into ~-thin slices** émincer finement qch ► **paper tiger** N (*fig*) tigre *m* de papier ► **paper trail** N (*esp US*) traces *fpl* écrites

► **paper over** VT FUS [+ *crack in wall etc*] recouvrir de papier; (*fig*) [+ *differences, disagreements*] passer sur; (*fig*) **to ~ over the cracks** dissimuler les problèmes *or* les failles

paperback ['peɪpəbæk] [1] N livre *m* broché; (*smaller*) livre *m* de poche; **it exists in ~** ça existe en (édition de) poche [2] ADJ **~(ed) edition** édition *f* brochée; (*smaller*) édition *f* de poche

paperbound ['peɪpəbaʊnd] ADJ = **paperbacked**; → **paperback**

paperboy ['peɪpəbɔɪ] N (*delivering*) livreur *m* de journaux; (*selling*) vendeur *m* *or* crieur *m* de journaux

paperclip ['peɪpəklɪp] N trombone *m*; (= *bulldog clip*) pince *f*

papergirl ['peɪpəgɜːl] N (*delivering*) livreuse *f* de journaux; (*selling*) vendeuse *f* de journaux

paperhanger ['peɪpəˌhæŋəʳ] N (*Brit* = *decorator*) tapissier-décorateur *m*; (*US‡* = *crook*) passeur *m* de faux billets (*or* de chèques falsifiés)

paperless ['peɪpəlɪs] ADJ **the ~ office** le bureau informatisé *or* zéro papier

paperweight ['peɪpəweɪt] N presse-papiers *m inv*

paperwork ['peɪpəwɜːk] N (*gen*) tâches *fpl* administratives; (*pej*) paperasserie *f*; **we need two more people to deal with the ~** il nous faut deux personnes de plus pour s'occuper des tâches administratives; **he brings home ~ every night** il rapporte du travail à la maison tous les soirs

papery ['peɪpərɪ] ADJ (*gen*) (*fin*) comme du papier; [*skin*] parcheminé

papier-mâché [ˌpæpjeɪˈmæʃeɪ] N papier *m* mâché

papilla [pəˈpɪlə] N (*pl* **papillae** [pəˈpɪliː]) papille *f*

papist ['peɪpɪst] (*pej*) [1] N papiste *mf* (*pej*) [2] ADJ de(s) papiste(s) (*pej*)

papistry ['peɪpɪstrɪ] N (*pej*) papisme *m* (*pej*)

papoose [pəˈpuːs] N [a] (= *baby*) bébé *m* amérindien [b] (= *baby sling*) sac *m* kangourou, porte-bébé *m*

pappus ['pæpəs] N aigrette *f* (*Bot*)

pappy* ['pæpɪ] N (*US dial*) papa *m*

paprika ['pæprɪkə] N paprika *m*

Pap smear ['pæpsmɪəʳ], **Pap test** ['pæptest] N frottis *m* (vaginal)

Papuan ['pæpjʊən] [1] ADJ papou [2] N [a] Papou(e) *m(f)* [b] (*Ling*) papou *m*

Papua New Guinea ['pæpjʊənjuːˌgɪnɪ] [1] N la Papouasie-Nouvelle-Guinée [2] ADJ papou

Papua-New-Guinean ['pæpjʊənjuːˌgɪnɪən] N Papou(e) *m(f)*

papyrus [pəˈpaɪərəs] N (*pl* **papyruses** *or* **papyri** [pəˈpaɪəraɪ]) papyrus *m inv*

par¹ [pɑːʳ] [1] N [a] (= *equality of value*) égalité *f*, pair *m*; (*Fin*) [*of currency*] pair *m*; **to be on a ~ with** être comparable à; **an environmental disaster on a ~ with Chernobyl** une catastrophe écologique comparable à celle de Tchernobyl; **to put sb on a ~ with** (= *compare with*) comparer qn avec; (= *consider as equal*) considérer qn comme l'égal de; (= *make level with*) mettre qn sur le même plan que; (*Fin*) **above/below ~** au-dessus/au-dessous du pair; (*Fin*) **at ~ pair**
[b] (= *average*) moyenne *f*; **his work isn't up to ~** ◊ **his work is below** *or* **under ~** son travail laisse à désirer; (*fig*) **to feel below** *or* **under ~** ne pas se sentir en forme
[c] (*Golf*) par *m*, normale *f* du parcours; **~ three** par trois; **a ~ three (hole)** un par trois; **four over ~** quatre coups au-dessus du par; (*fig*) **that's ~ for the course** c'est typique, il fallait (*or* faut *etc*) s'y attendre; **his behaviour was ~ for the course** il a eu un comportement typique
[2] COMP ► **par value** N (*Fin*) valeur *f* au pair
par²* [pɑːʳ] N (*Press*) ABBR = **paragraph**
para* ['pærə] N [a] ABBR = **paragraph 1a** [b] (*Brit Mil*) ABBR = **paratrooper**) para* *m*; **the ~s** les paras* *mpl* [c] (*Mil*) ABBR = **parachutist**) **the ~s** les paras* *mpl*; **he's in the ~s** il est para*
para... ['pærə] PREF para...

parable ['pærəbl] N parabole *f*; **to speak in ~s** parler par paraboles

parabola [pəˈræbələ] N parabole *f* (*Math*)

parabolic [ˌpærəˈbɒlɪk] ADJ parabolique

paraboloid [pəˈræbəlɔɪd] N paraboloïde *m*

Paracelsus [pærəˈselsəs] N Paracelse *m*

paracetamol [pærəˈsiːtəmɒl] N paracétamol *m*

parachute ['pærəʃuːt] [1] N parachute *m* [2] VI descendre en parachute; **to ~ behind enemy lines** se faire parachuter derrière les lignes

ennemies; (*Sport*) **to go parachuting** faire du parachutisme [3] VT [+ *person, supplies*] parachuter; **food supplies were ~d into the mountains** on a parachuté des vivres dans les montagnes [4] COMP [*cords*] de parachute
► **parachute drop** N parachutage *m*
► **parachute jump** N saut *m* en parachute
► **parachute regiment** N régiment *m* de parachutistes

parachutist ['pærəʃuːtɪst] N parachutiste *mf*

Paraclete ['pærəkliːt] N **the ~** Le Paraclet

parade [pəˈreɪd] [1] N [a] (*gen, Mil*) (= *procession*) défilé *m*; (= *ceremony*) parade *f*, revue *f*; (*drilling*) **to be on ~** (= *drilling*) être à l'exercice; (*for review*) défiler
[b] (*fig*) **~ of** (= *exhibition of*) [+ *wares, goods*] étalage *m* de; (= *procession, series of*) défilé *m* de; **an endless ~ of advertisements** des publicités à n'en plus finir; **the dockers' ~ of support for their union leader** (*gen*) la manifestation de soutien des dockers à leur leader syndical; (*pej*) le soutien que les dockers font mine d'apporter au leader de leur syndicat
[c] (*esp Brit* = *road*) boulevard *m* (*souvent au bord de la mer*)
[d] (*Mil: also* **~ ground**) terrain *m* de manœuvres
[2] VT [+ *troops*] faire défiler; (*fig* = *display*) [+ *one's wealth, possessions*] faire étalage de, afficher; **she never ~d her knowledge** elle ne faisait jamais étalage de ses connaissances; (*pej*) **these reforms were ~d as progress** ces réformes ont été présentées comme un progrès
[3] VI (*Mil*) défiler
► **parade about*, parade around*** VI se balader*, circuler*; **don't ~ about with nothing on!** ne te promène pas *or* ne te balade* pas tout nu!

paradigm ['pærədaɪm] N paradigme *m*

paradigmatic [ˌpærədɪgˈmætɪk] ADJ paradigmatique

paradisaic [ˌpærədɪˈseɪɪk] ADJ = **paradisiacal**

paradise ['pærədaɪs] N paradis *m*; (*fig*) **an earthly ~** un paradis terrestre; (*fig*) **it's a nature-lover's** *etc* **~** c'est un paradis pour les amoureux de la nature *etc*; (*euph*) **to go to ~** (= *die*) aller au ciel → **fool¹, bird**

paradisiacal [ˌpærədɪˈsaɪəkəl] ADJ paradisiaque

paradox ['pærədɒks] N paradoxe *m*

paradoxical [ˌpærəˈdɒksɪkəl] ADJ paradoxal

paradoxically [ˌpærəˈdɒksɪkəlɪ] ADV paradoxalement

paraffin ['pærəfɪn] [1] N (*Chem*) paraffine *f*; (*Brit* = *fuel: also* **~ oil**) pétrole *m* (lampant); (*Med*) **liquid ~** huile *f* de paraffine [2] COMP
► **paraffin heater** N poêle *m* à mazout *or* à pétrole ► **paraffin lamp** N lampe *f* à pétrole
► **paraffin wax** N paraffine *f*

paraglider ['pærəˌglaɪdəʳ] N [a] (= *person*) parapentiste *mf* [b] (= *object*) parapente *m*

paragliding ['pærəˌglaɪdɪŋ] N (*NonC*) parapente *m*

paragon ['pærəgən] N modèle *m*, parangon *m*; **a ~ of virtue** un modèle *or* parangon de vertu

paragraph ['pærəgrɑːf] [1] N [a] paragraphe *m*; **"new ~"** «à la ligne»; **to begin a new ~** aller à la ligne [b] (*newspaper item*) entrefilet *m* [2] VT diviser en paragraphes [3] COMP
► **paragraph mark** N (*Typ*) pied *m* de mouche

Paraguay ['pærəgwaɪ] N le Paraguay

Paraguayan [ˌpærəˈgwaɪən] [1] ADJ paraguayen [2] N Paraguayen(ne) *m(f)*

parakeet ['pærəkiːt] N perruche *f* (ondulée)

paralanguage ['pærəˌlæŋgwɪdʒ] N (*Ling*) paralangage *m*

paralegal ['pærəˌliːgəl] N (*esp US*) [1] N *auxi-*

liaire juridique [2] ADJ [*secretary, assistant*] juridique

paralinguistic [ˈpærəˌlɪŋgwɪstɪk] ADJ (*Ling*) paralinguistique

parallactic [ˌpærəˈlæktɪk] ADJ parallactique

parallax [ˈpærəlæks] N parallaxe f

parallel [ˈpærəlel] [1] ADJ [a] (*Geom, Math etc*) parallèle (**with**, to à); **the road runs ~ to the railway** la route est parallèle à la voie de chemin de fer
[b] (*fig*) [*situation, process, event, operation*] analogue; [*development*] parallèle (**with**, to à); [*talks, negotiations*] en parallèle; **a ~ universe** un univers parallèle; **in a ~ step, they ...** de la même manière, ils ...
[c] (*Ski*) parallèle
[2] ADV parallèlement (**to** à)
[3] N [a] (*Geog*) parallèle m; **the 22nd** ~ le 22ᵉ parallèle
[b] (*Math*) (ligne f) parallèle f
[c] (*fig*) parallèle m, comparaison f; **to draw a ~ between** établir or faire un parallèle or une comparaison entre; **an event without ~ in the modern era** un événement sans précédent à l'époque moderne; **this wooded landscape is almost without ~ (anywhere else)** ce paysage sylvestre est (pratiquement) unique; **he/she is without ~** il/elle est sans pareil(le); **to happen** *etc* **in ~ with sth** arriver *etc* parallèlement à or en parallèle avec qch
[4] VT (*Math*) être parallèle à; (*fig*) (= *find equivalent to*) trouver un équivalent à; (= *be equal to*) égaler; **a superb performance that no-one (else) could ~** une magnifique performance que personne ne pourrait égaler; **the increase in the number of smokers has been ~ed by an increase in lung cancers** l'augmentation du nombre des fumeurs s'est accompagnée d'une augmentation des cas de cancer du poumon; **his success here has not been ~ed by recognition in his home country** le succès qu'il remporte ici n'a pas trouvé d'équivalent dans son pays d'origine
[5] COMP ► **parallel bars** NPL barres fpl parallèles ► **parallel-park** VI (*Aut*) faire un créneau ► **parallel processing** N (*Comput*) traitement m en parallèle ► **parallel turn** N virage m parallèle

parallelepiped [ˌpærəˌleləˈpaɪped] N parallélépipède m

parallelism [ˈpærəlelɪzəm] N (*Math, fig*) parallélisme m

parallelogram [ˌpærəˈleləʊgræm] N parallélogramme m

Paralympic [ˌpærəˈlɪmpɪk] [1] ADJ paralympique [2] **Paralympics** NPL = Paralympic Games [3] COMP ► **Paralympic Games** NPL Jeux mpl paralympiques

paralysis [pəˈræləsɪs] N (*pl* **paralyses** [pəˈræləsiːz]) [a] (*Med*) paralysie f → **creeping, infantile** [b] (*fig*) [*of country, government, trade, talks*] paralysie f; [*of traffic etc*] immobilisation f; **political ~** immobilisme m politique

paralytic [ˌpærəˈlɪtɪk] [1] ADJ [a] (*Med*) paralytique [b] (*Brit*‡ = *drunk*) ivre mort [2] N paralytique mf

paralyzation [ˌpærəlaɪˈzeɪʃən] N immobilisation f

paralyze [ˈpærəlaɪz] VT [a] (*Med*) paralyser; **his arm is ~d** il est paralysé du bras; **~d from the waist/neck down** paralysé des membres inférieurs/des quatre membres [b] (*fig*) [+ *person, traffic, communications*] paralyser; **~d with fear** paralysé or transi de peur; **paralyzing cold** froid m paralysant; **paralyzing fear/loneliness** peur f/solitude f pétrifiante; **paralyzing shyness** timidité f maladive

paramedic [ˌpærəˈmedɪk] N auxiliaire mf médical(e)

paramedical [ˌpærəˈmedɪkəl] ADJ paramédical

parament [ˈpærəmənt] N (*pl* **paraments** or **paramenta** [ˌpærəˈmentə]) parement m

parameter [pəˈræmɪtər] N [a] (*Math*) paramètre m [b] (*fig* = *criterion, principle*) critère m, paramètre m; **to define** or **establish** or **set the ~s of** or **for sth** définir les critères or paramètres de qch; **to fall within certain ~s** respecter certains critères; **within the ~s of ...** dans les limites de ...; **the technical ~s of the system** les caractéristiques techniques de ce système; **the ~s of their energy policy** les orientations principales de leur politique énergétique

parametric [ˌpærəˈmetrɪk] ADJ paramétrique

paramilitary [ˌpærəˈmɪlɪtərɪ] [1] ADJ [*organization, group, operation*] paramilitaire [2] N (= *member*) membre m d'une force paramilitaire; **the paramilitaries** les forces fpl paramilitaires [3] **the paramilitary** NPL (= *organizations*) les forces fpl paramilitaires

paramnesia [ˌpærəmˈniːzɪə] N paramnésie f

paramount [ˈpærəmaʊnt] ADJ primordial; **of ~ importance** d'une importance primordiale, de la plus haute importance; **the interests of the child are ~** les intérêts de l'enfant sont primordiaux or passent avant tout

paramour [ˈpærəmʊər] N (*liter*) amant m, maîtresse f

paranoia [ˌpærəˈnɔɪə] N paranoïa f

paranoi(a)c [ˌpærəˈnɔɪɪk] ADJ, N paranoïaque mf

paranoid [ˈpærənɔɪd] [1] ADJ [a] (*Psych*) paranoïde [b] (*fig*) parano* [2] N paranoïaque mf

paranoidal [ˌpærəˈnɔɪdl] ADJ paranoïde

paranormal [ˌpærəˈnɔːməl] [1] ADJ paranormal [2] **the ~** les phénomènes mpl paranormaux

parapet [ˈpærəpɪt] N [a] [*of bridge, roof etc*] parapet m, garde-fou m; **to put** or **stick* one's head above the ~** se mouiller*, prendre un risque; **to keep one's head below the ~** ne pas se mouiller*, ne pas prendre de risques [b] (*Mil*) parapet m

paraph [ˈpærəf] N paraphe m or parafe m

paraphernalia [ˌpærəfəˈneɪlɪə] N (*pl inv*) [a] (= *belongings: also for hobbies, sports etc*) attirail m [b] (* = *bits and pieces*) bazar* m

paraphrase [ˈpærəfreɪz] [1] N paraphrase f [2] VT paraphraser

paraphrastic [ˌpærəˈfræstɪk] ADJ paraphrastique

paraplegia [ˌpærəˈpliːdʒə] N paraplégie f

paraplegic [ˌpærəˈpliːdʒɪk] [1] ADJ (*gen*) paraplégique; [*games*] pour les paraplégiques [2] N paraplégique mf

paraprofessional [ˌpærəprəˈfeʃənl] ADJ, N paraprofessionnel(le) mf

parapsychological [ˌpærəsaɪkəˈlɒdʒɪkəl] ADJ parapsychologique, parapsychique

parapsychologist [ˌpærəsaɪˈkɒlədʒɪst] N parapsychologue mf

parapsychology [ˌpærəsaɪˈkɒlədʒɪ] N parapsychologie f

Paraquat® [ˈpærəkwɒt] N paraquat® m

parasailing [ˈpærəseɪlɪŋ] N (*NonC*) parachutisme m ascensionnel

parascending [ˈpærəsendɪŋ] N (*Sport*) parachutisme m ascensionnel; **to go ~** faire du parachute ascensionnel

parasite [ˈpærəsaɪt] N (*Bot, Zool, fig*) parasite m

parasitic(al) [ˌpærəˈsɪtɪk(əl)] ADJ [a] (*lit, fig*) parasite (**on** de) [b] (*Med*) [*disease*] parasitaire

parasiticidal [ˌpærəˌsɪtɪˈsaɪdl] ADJ parasiticide

parasiticide [ˌpærəˈsɪtɪsaɪd] N parasiticide m

parasitism [ˈpærəsɪtɪzəm] N parasitisme m

parasitologist [ˌpærəsɪˈtɒlədʒɪst] N parasitologue mf

parasitology [ˌpærəsɪˈtɒlədʒɪ] N parasitologie f

parasitosis [ˌpærəsɪˈtəʊsɪs] N parasitose f

parasol [ˈpærəsɒl] N (*hand-held*) ombrelle f; (*over table etc*) parasol m

parasuicide [ˌpærəˈsuːɪsaɪd] N faux suicide m

parasympathetic [ˌpærəsɪmpəˈθetɪk] [1] ADJ parasympathique [2] COMP ► **parasympathetic nervous system** N système m parasympathique

parataxis [ˌpærəˈtæksɪs] N parataxe f

parathyroid [ˌpærəˈθaɪrɔɪd] [1] ADJ parathyroïdien [2] N (*also* ~ **gland**) parathyroïde f

paratrooper [ˈpærətruːpər] N parachutiste mf (*soldat*)

paratroops [ˈpærətruːps] NPL (*unités* fpl de) parachutistes mpl

paratyphoid [ˌpærəˈtaɪfɔɪd] [1] ADJ paratyphique; **~ fever** paratyphoïde f [2] N paratyphoïde f

parboil [ˈpɑːbɔɪl] VT (*Culin*) faire bouillir or faire cuire à demi

parcel [ˈpɑːsəl] [1] N [a] (= *package*) colis m, paquet m [b] (= *portion*) [*of land*] parcelle f; [*of shares*] paquet m; [*of goods*] lot m → **part** [c] (*esp Brit fig*) **a ~ of lies** un tas* or un tissu de mensonges; **it's a ~ of nonsense** c'est des inepties; **a ~ of fools** un tas* or une bande* d'idiots [2] VT (*also ~ up*) [+ *object, purchases*] emballer, empaqueter [3] COMP ► **parcel bomb** N colis m piégé ► **parcel net** N filet m à bagages ► **parcel post** N service m de colis postaux, service m de messageries; **to send sth (by) ~ post** envoyer qch par colis postal ► **parcel shelf** N (*Aut*) plage f arrière ► **parcels office** N bureau m des messageries

► **parcel out** VT SEP [+ *money, jobs, privileges etc*] distribuer; [+ *inheritance*] partager; [+ *land*] lotir; [+ *tasks, duties*] répartir

parch [pɑːtʃ] VT [+ *crops, land*] dessécher, brûler

parched [pɑːtʃt] ADJ [*lips, soil, plants*] desséché; **I'm ~!** je meurs de soif!*

parchment [ˈpɑːtʃmənt] N parchemin m; **~ paper** papier-parchemin m

pardner* [ˈpɑːdnər] N (*US*) camarade m; **so long, ~!** au revoir, mon pote!*

pardon [ˈpɑːdn] [1] N [a] (*NonC*) pardon m → **beg**
[b] (*Rel*) indulgence f
[c] (*Jur*) **(free) ~** grâce f; **letter of ~** lettre f de grâce; **general ~** amnistie f; **royal ~** grâce f royale; **to grant sb a posthumous ~** réhabiliter la mémoire de qn
[2] VT [a] [+ *mistake, person*] (*gen*) pardonner; (*Rel*) absoudre; **to ~ sb for sth** pardonner qch à qn; **to ~ sb for doing sth** pardonner à qn d'avoir fait qch; **~ me** (*apologizing for sth*) excusez-moi, désolé; (*disagreeing politely*) excusez-moi; (*interrupting*) excusez-moi, pardonnez-moi; (*US*) **~ me?** comment?, pardon?; **~ me for troubling you** excusez-moi de vous déranger; **~ my asking, but ...** excusez-moi de vous poser cette question, mais ...; (*hum: after swearing*) **~ my French!*** passez-moi or pardonnez-moi l'expression!; **if you'll ~ the expression** si vous me pardonnez l'expression
[b] (*Jur*) [+ *criminal*] gracier; (= *grant amnesty to*) amnistier; (*posthumously*) réhabiliter la mémoire de
[3] EXCL (*apologizing*) pardon!, excusez-moi!; (*not hearing*) **~?** comment?, pardon?

pardonable [ˈpɑːdnəbl] ADJ [*mistake*] pardonnable; (*Jur*) graciable

pardonably [ˈpɑːdnəblɪ] ADV de façon bien excusable or bien pardonnable

pare [pɛər] VT [a] [+ *fruit*] peler, éplucher; [+ *nails*] rogner, couper [b] (= *reduce: also ~ down*) [+ *expenses*] réduire

parent ['pɛərənt] [1] N (= *father*) père m ; (= *mother*) mère f ; **his ~s** ses parents mpl ; **to be born of Scottish ~s** être né de parents écossais ; **the ~ birds/animals** les parents mpl de l'oiseau/l'animal [2] COMP [*interest, involvement etc*] parental, des parents ► **parent company** N (*Comm, Fin*) maison f or société f mère ► **parent power*** N (*Scol*) influence f des parents d'élèves ► **parents' evening** N (*Scol*) réunion f d'information avec les parents (d'élèves) ► **parent-teacher association** N (*Scol*) association f de parents d'élèves et de professeurs ► **parent tree** N souche f

parentage ['pɛərəntɪdʒ] N **of Scottish ~** (*mother and father*) (né) de parents écossais ; **of unknown ~** de parents inconnus ; **children of (racially) mixed ~** les enfants issus de couples mixtes ; **there was some confusion about his ~** on ne savait pas exactement qui étaient ses parents ; **genetic techniques that provide proof of ~** des techniques génétiques qui permettent de prouver les liens de parenté

parental [pə'rɛntl] ADJ [*choice*] des parents, parental ; [*involvement, cooperation, responsibility*] parental ; [*rights, attitudes*] des parents ; **~ consent** le consentement des parents ; **~ control** or **authority** l'autorité f parentale ; **~ responsibility** la responsabilité des parents ; **~ rights over a child** (*gen*) les droits mpl des parents sur leur enfant ; (*Jur*) la tutelle d'un enfant

parenthesis [pə'rɛnθɪsɪs] N (*pl* **parentheses** [pə'rɛnθɪsiːz]) parenthèse f ; **in ~** or **parentheses** entre parenthèses

parenthetic(al) [ˌpærən'θɛtɪk(əl)] ADJ entre parenthèses

parenthetically [ˌpærən'θɛtɪkəlɪ] ADV entre parenthèses

parenthood ['pɛərənthʊd] N condition f de parent(s), paternité f (*or* maternité f) ; **the joys of ~** les joies fpl de la maternité (*or* paternité) ; **the responsibilities of ~** les responsabilités fpl des parents or que l'on a quand on a des enfants ; **she doesn't feel ready for ~** elle ne se sent pas mûre pour avoir des enfants

parenting ['pɛərəntɪŋ] N éducation f des enfants ; **~ is a full-time occupation** l'éducation d'un enfant or élever un enfant est un travail à plein temps ; **shared ~** partage m de l'éducation des enfants

parer ['pɛərə'] N épluche-légumes m inv

pariah [pə'raɪə] N paria m

parietal [pə'raɪɪtl] [1] ADJ pariétal [2] N (*Anat*) pariétal m [3] **parietals** NPL (*US Univ*) heures fpl de visite (*du sexe opposé dans les chambres d'étudiants*)

paring ['pɛərɪŋ] N [a] **~s** [*of fruit, vegetable*] épluchures fpl, pelures fpl ; [*of nails*] bouts mpl d'ongles ; [*of metal*] rognures fpl (de métal), cisaille f ; **potato ~s** épluchures fpl de pommes de terre [b] action f d'éplucher or de peler etc ; **~ knife** couteau m à éplucher, épluchoir m → **cheeseparing**

pari passu [ˈpærɪˈpæsuː] ADV (*frm*) de pair

Paris ['pærɪs] [1] N Paris → **plaster** [2] ADJ [*society, nightlife, metro etc*] parisien ; **~ fashions** la mode de Paris, la mode parisienne ; **~ people** les Parisiens mpl

parish ['pærɪʃ] [1] N (*Rel*) paroisse f ; (*Brit: civil*) commune f ; (*US: in Louisiana*) ≈ comté m [2] COMP ► **parish church** N église f paroissiale ► **parish council** N ≈ conseil m municipal (*d'une petite commune rurale, en Angleterre*) ► **parish hall** N salle f paroissiale or municipale ► **parish priest** N (*Catholic*) curé m ; (*Protestant*) pasteur m ► **parish-pump** ADJ (*Brit pej*) [*subject*] d'intérêt purement local ; [*attitude*] borné ; **~-pump mentality/politics/rivalries** esprit m/politique f/rivalités fpl de clocher ► **parish register** N registre m paroissial ► **parish school†** N école f communale

parishioner [pə'rɪʃənə'] N paroissien(ne) m(f)

Parisian [pə'rɪzɪən] [1] ADJ [*district, theatre, street*] parisien, de Paris ; [*habit, personality, society*] parisien [2] N Parisien(ne) m(f)

parity ['pærɪtɪ] N [a] [*of rights, currencies*] parité f ; (*in arms race*) équilibre m ; **they want ~ with their colleagues in the private sector** ils veulent une parité des salaires et des conditions de travail avec leurs collègues du secteur privé [b] (*Fin*) parité f ; **at ~ (with)** à parité (avec) ; **exchange at ~** change m au pair or à (la) parité [c] (*US Agr*) taux m de parité

park [pɑːk] [1] N [a] (= *public garden*) jardin m public, parc m ; (= *garden of country house*) parc m → **car, national, retail, safari** [b] (*Brit Sport = field*) terrain m [2] VT [a] [+ *car etc*] garer ; **to ~ the car** garer la voiture, se garer ; **don't ~ the car in the street** ne laisse pas la voiture dans la rue ; **a line of ~ed cars** une rangée de voitures en stationnement ; **he was ~ed near the theatre** il était stationné or garé près du théâtre [b] (* = *leave*) **to ~ a child with sb** laisser un enfant chez qn ; **I ~ed granddad in an armchair** j'ai installé pépé dans un fauteuil ; **she ~ed herself on the sofa/at our table** elle s'est installée sur le canapé/à notre table [3] VI stationner, se garer ; **I was ~ing when I caught sight of him** j'étais en train de me garer quand je l'aperçus ; **do not ~ here** ne stationnez pas ici [4] COMP ► **park-and-ride** N *stationnement en périphérie d'agglomération combiné à un système de transport en commun* ► **park bench** N banc m de parc ► **park keeper** N (*Brit*) gardien(ne) m(f) de parc ► **park ranger** N (*in national park*) gardien(ne) m(f) de parc national ; (*in forest*) garde m forestier ; (*in game reserve*) garde-chasse m ► **park-ride** N = **park-and-ride** ► **park warden** N = **park keeper**

parka ['pɑːkə] N parka f

parkin ['pɑːkɪn] N gâteau m à l'avoine et au gingembre

parking ['pɑːkɪŋ] [1] N stationnement m ; **"~"** « parking », « stationnement autorisé » ; **"no ~"** « défense de stationner », « stationnement interdit » ; **~ is very difficult** il est très difficile de trouver à se garer ; **there's plenty of ~ (space)** il y a de la place pour se garer [2] COMP ► **parking attendant** N gardien m de parking, gardien m de parc de stationnement ► **parking bay** N emplacement m (*sur un parking*) ► **parking brake** N (*US*) frein m à main ► **parking garage** N (*US*) parking m (couvert) ► **parking lights** NPL (*US*) feux mpl de position ► **parking lot** N (*US*) parking m, parc m de stationnement ► **parking meter** N parcmètre m ► **parking place, parking space** N place f de stationnement ; **I couldn't find a ~ place** or **space** je n'ai pas pu trouver à me garer ► **parking ticket** N P.-V.* m, contravention f

parkinsonism ['pɑːkɪnsənɪzəm] N parkinsonisme m

Parkinson's disease ['pɑːkɪnsənzdɪˌziːz] N maladie f de Parkinson

Parkinson's law ['pɑːkɪnsənzlɔː] N loi f de Parkinson (*principe humoristique selon lequel toute tâche finit par occuper l'intégralité du temps qu'on a alloué à son accomplissement*)

parkland ['pɑːklænd] N espace(s) m(pl) vert(s)

parkway ['pɑːkweɪ] N (*US*) route f (à plusieurs voies) bordée d'espaces verts

parky* ['pɑːkɪ] ADJ (*Brit*) **it's a bit ~!** il fait frisquet !*

parlance ['pɑːləns] N langage m, parler m ; **in common ~** en langage courant ; **in medical/legal ~** en langage médical/juridique

parlay ['pɑːlɪ] (*US*) [1] VT (*Betting*) réemployer (*les gains d'un précédent pari et le pari originel*) ;

(*fig*) [+ *talent, inheritance*] faire fructifier [2] VI (*fig*) faire fructifier de l'argent

parley ['pɑːlɪ] [1] N pourparlers mpl [2] VI (*also Mil*) parlementer (**with** avec) ; (*more frm*) entrer or être en pourparlers (**with** avec)

parliament ['pɑːləmənt] N [a] (= *institution, building*) parlement m ; (*Brit Hist*) Parliament Parlement m ; **the London** or **Westminster Parliament** le Parlement de Londres or Westminster ; **in Parliament** au Parlement ; **to go into** or **enter Parliament** entrer au Parlement ; **the Queen opened Parliament** la reine a ouvert la session parlementaire → **house, member** [b] (= *period between elections*) législature f ; **during the life of this ~** au cours de cette législature

parliamentarian [ˌpɑːləmɛn'tɛərɪən] [1] N [a] (*Brit Parl = MP*) parlementaire mf, membre m du Parlement [b] (*Brit Hist*) parlementaire mf [c] (= *expert*) spécialiste mf des procédures parlementaires [2] ADJ (*Brit Hist*) parlementaire

parliamentary [ˌpɑːlə'mɛntərɪ] [1] ADJ [*debate, session, business, language, majority*] parlementaire ; **~ candidate** candidat m au Parlement [2] COMP ► **parliamentary agent** N agent m parlementaire ► **Parliamentary Commissioner** N (*Brit*) médiateur m, -trice f ► **parliamentary democracy** N démocratie f parlementaire ► **parliamentary election** N élections fpl législatives ► **parliamentary government** N (*NonC*) gouvernement m parlementaire ► **Parliamentary Labour Party** N (*Brit*) députés mpl du parti travailliste ► **parliamentary private secretary** N (*Brit*) *parlementaire attaché à un ministre assurant la liaison avec les autres parlementaires* ► **parliamentary privilege** N (*Brit*) immunité f parlementaire ► **parliamentary secretary** N (*Brit*) (parlementaire mf faisant fonction de) sous-secrétaire mf d'État

parlour, parlor (*US*) ['pɑːlə'] [1] N (†: *in house*) petit salon m ; (*in convent*) parloir m ; (†: *in bar*) arrière-salle f → **beauty, funeral** [2] COMP ► **parlor car** N (*US Rail*) pullman m ► **parlour game** N jeu m de société

parlourmaid ['pɑːləmeɪd] N servante f

parlous ['pɑːləs] ADJ (*frm*) alarmant

Parma ['pɑːmə] [1] N Parme [2] COMP ► **Parma ham** N jambon m de Parme ► **Parma violet** N violette f de Parme

Parmesan [ˌpɑːmɪ'zæn] N (*also* **~ cheese**) parmesan m

Parnassian [pɑː'næsɪən] ADJ parnassien

Parnassus [pɑː'næsəs] N le Parnasse ; (**Mount**) **~** le mont Parnasse

parochial [pə'rəʊkɪəl] [1] ADJ (*Rel*) paroissial ; (*fig pej*) [*attitude, outlook*] borné ; **they're very ~** ils ont vraiment l'esprit de clocher, ils ne sont pas très ouverts sur le monde [2] COMP ► **parochial school** N (*US*) école f catholique

parochialism [pə'rəʊkɪəlɪzəm] N esprit m de clocher

parodist ['pærədɪst] N parodiste mf

parody ['pærədɪ] [1] N (*lit, fig*) parodie f [2] VT parodier

parole [pə'rəʊl] [1] N [a] (*Jur*) (= *period of release*) liberté f conditionnelle ; (= *act of release*) mise f en liberté conditionnelle ; **on ~** en liberté conditionnelle ; **to release sb on ~** mettre qn en liberté conditionnelle ; **to break ~** se rendre coupable d'un délit entraînant la révocation de la libération conditionnelle ; **ten years without ~** dix ans de prison sans possibilité de libération conditionnelle [b] (*Mil etc*) parole f d'honneur ; **on ~** sur parole [c] (*Ling*) parole f [2] VT [+ *prisoner*] mettre or placer en liberté conditionnelle [3] COMP ► **parole board** N (*Brit*) comité m de probation et d'assistance aux prisonniers mis en liberté conditionnelle ► **parole officer**

N (*US*) contrôleur *m* judiciaire (*chargé de surveiller un prisonnier en liberté conditionnelle*)

paroquet ['pærəkɪt] N = **parakeet**

paroxysm ['pærəksɪzəm] N [a] (*Med*) paroxysme *m* [b] (*fig*) **a ~ of tears/laughter/rage** une crise de larmes/rire/colère; **a ~ of coughing** une violente quinte de toux; **~s of rage** des transports *mpl* (*liter*) de colère; **in a ~ of grief/rage** au paroxysme de la douleur/de la colère; **in a ~ of delight** dans un transport de joie; **the news sent her into ~s of delight** la nouvelle l'a transportée de joie

parquet ['pɑːkeɪ] [1] N [a] (*also* **~ flooring**) parquet *m* [b] (*US Theat*) parterre *m* [2] VT parqueter

parquetry ['pɑːkɪtrɪ] N parquetage *m*, parqueterie *f*

parricidal ['pærɪsaɪdl] ADJ parricide

parricide ['pærɪsaɪd] N [a] (= *act*) parricide *m* [b] (= *person*) parricide *mf*

parrot ['pærət] [1] N (*Orn, fig*) perroquet *m*; (*Brit hum*) **she was sick as a ~**: il en était malade* [2] VT (= *repeat*) [+ *words, speech*] répéter comme un perroquet; (= *copy*) [+ *behaviour, actions*] imiter servilement [3] COMP ► **parrot cry** N (*pej*) slogan *m* ► **parrot disease** N psittacose *f* ► **parrot-fashion** ADV comme un perroquet ► **parrot fever** N = **parrot disease** ► **parrot fish** N (*pl* **parrot fish** *or* **fishes**) poisson *m* perroquet ► **parrot phrase** N = **parrot cry**

parry ['pærɪ] [1] VT [+ *blow, attack*] parer; [+ *question*] éluder; [+ *difficulty*] tourner, éviter [2] N (*Fencing*) parade *f*

parse [pɑːz] VT faire l'analyse grammaticale de

parsec ['pɑːsek] N parsec *m*

Parsee ['pɑːsiː] ADJ, N parsi(e) *m(f)*

parser ['pɑːzər] N (*Comput*) analyseur *m* syntaxique

parsimonious [ˌpɑːsɪ'məʊnɪəs] ADJ parcimonieux

parsimoniously [ˌpɑːsɪ'məʊnɪəslɪ] ADV avec parcimonie, parcimonieusement

parsimony ['pɑːsɪmənɪ] N parcimonie *f*

parsing ['pɑːzɪŋ] N (*Ling, Scol*) analyse *f* grammaticale

parsley ['pɑːslɪ] [1] N persil *m* [2] COMP ► **parsley sauce** N sauce *f* persillée

parsnip ['pɑːsnɪp] N panais *m*

parson ['pɑːsn] [1] N (= *parish priest*) pasteur *m* [2] COMP ► **parson's nose*** N (*Culin*) croupion *m* ► **Parsons table** N (*US*) table *f* (*en plastique*)

parsonage ['pɑːsənɪdʒ] N presbytère *m*

part [pɑːt] [1] N [a] (= *section, division*) partie *f*; **he spent ~ of his childhood in Wales** il a passé une partie de son enfance au pays de Galles; **he lost ~ of his foot in the accident** il a perdu une partie de son pied lors de l'accident; **in ~** en partie, partiellement; **the delay was due in ~ to the postal strike** le retard était dû en partie à une grève de la poste; **the play is good in ~s** ◊ **~s of the play are good** il y a de bons passages dans la pièce; **the funny ~ of it is that ...** le plus drôle dans l'histoire c'est que ... ; **~ of him wanted to call her, ~ of him wanted to forget about her** il était partagé entre le désir de l'appeler et l'envie de l'oublier; **it's all ~ of growing up** c'est normal quand on grandit; **to him, it's just ~ of the job** pour lui, ça fait partie du travail; **respect is an important ~ of any relationship** le respect est un élément important de toute relation; **an important ~ of her work is ...** une part importante de son travail consiste à ... ; **his Catholicism was an integral ~ of him** sa foi catholique faisait partie intégrante de lui-même; **she never really felt like ~ of the team** elle n'a jamais vraiment eu l'impression de faire partie de l'équipe; **for the most ~** dans l'ensemble, en général; **to be ~ and parcel of sth** faire partie

(*intégrante*) de qch; **a penny is the hundredth ~ of a pound** le penny est le centième de la livre; (*liter*) **a man of (many) ~s** (= *gifted*) un homme très doué; (= *versatile*) un homme qui a plusieurs cordes à son arc → **moving, private**

[b] (= *episode, instalment*) [*of book, play*] partie *f*; (*Publishing*) livraison *f*, fascicule *m*; (*Press, Rad, TV: of serial*) épisode *m*; **a six-~ serial** ◊ **a serial in six ~s** un feuilleton en six épisodes

[c] (*Tech*) pièce *f*; **you can't get the ~s for this model** on ne trouve pas de pièces pour ce modèle; **moving ~s** pièces *fpl* mobiles; **spare ~s** pièces *fpl* détachées, pièces *fpl* de rechange

[d] (*esp Culin* = *measure*) mesure *f*; **three ~s water to one ~ milk** trois mesures d'eau pour une mesure de lait

[e] (*Gram*) [*of verb*] **principal ~s** temps *mpl* principaux → **5**

[f] (= *share, involvement*) participation *f*, rôle *m*; (*Cine, Theat*) rôle *m*; **he was just right for the ~** il était parfait pour ce rôle; **we all have our ~ to play** nous avons tous notre rôle à jouer; **you can't get the ~s for this model** on ne trouve pas de pièces pour ce modèle; **to take ~ (in sth)** participer (à qch); **he had a large ~ in the organization of ...** il a joué un grand rôle dans l'organisation de ... ; **she had some ~ in it** elle y était pour quelque chose; **he had no ~ in it** il n'y était pour rien; **I'll have** *or* **I want no ~ in it** ◊ **I don't want any ~ of it** je ne veux pas m'en mêler → **act, play**

[g] (= *side, behalf*) parti *m*, part *f*; (*in quarrel*) **to take sb's ~** prendre le parti de qn, prendre parti pour qn; **for my ~** pour ma part, quant à moi; **an error on the ~ of his secretary** une erreur de la part de sa secrétaire; **to take sth in good ~**† prendre qch du bon côté

[h] (*Mus*) partie *f*; [*of song, fugue*] voix *f*; (= *sheet of music*) partition *f*; **the violin ~** la partie de violon; **the alto ~** la partie alto; **two-~ song** chant *m* à deux voix

[i] (= *place*) **in foreign ~s** à l'étranger; **in these ~s** ◊ **in this ~ of the world*** dans le coin*, par ici; **in my ~ of the world*** dans mon pays, chez moi

[j] (*US* = *parting: in hair*) raie *f*

[2] ADV (= *partly*) en partie; **she is ~ French** elle a des origines françaises; **the animal was ~ dog, ~ wolf** cet animal était moitié chien, moitié loup; **this novel is ~ thriller, ~ ghost story** ce roman est à la fois un thriller et une histoire de fantômes; **she was ~ fascinated, ~ horrified by the story** cette histoire provoqua chez elle un mélange de fascination et d'horreur

[3] VT [a] [+ *crowd*] ouvrir un passage dans; [+ *people, boxers*] séparer; [+ *curtains*] ouvrir, écarter; [+ *legs*] écarter; **they were ~ed during the war years** ils sont restés séparés pendant la guerre

[b] **to ~ one's hair** se faire une raie; **he ~s his hair at the side/in the centre** ◊ **his hair is ~ed at the side/in the centre** il porte *or* a la raie sur le côté/au milieu

[c] **to ~ company with sb** (= *leave*) fausser compagnie à qn, quitter qn; (= *disagree*) ne plus être d'accord avec qn; **they ~ed company** (*lit*) ils se quittèrent; (*fig*) ils se trouvèrent en désaccord; (*hum*) **the trailer ~ed company with the car** la remorque a faussé compagnie à la voiture

[4] VI (*gen*) [a] (= *take leave of each other*) se quitter; (= *break up*) [*couple, boxers*] se séparer; (= *open up*) [*crowd, lips, clouds, waters*] s'ouvrir; **to ~ from sb** quitter qn; (*permanently*) se séparer de qn; **to ~ with** [+ *money*] débourser; [+ *possessions*] se défaire de, renoncer à; [+ *employee etc*] se séparer de; **they ~ed friends** ◊ **they ~ed amicably** (*lovers, friends*) ils se sont quittés bons amis; (*business partners*) ils se sont séparés à l'amiable

[b] (= *break*) [*rope*] se rompre

[5] COMP ► **part exchange** N (*Brit*) reprise *f* (*en compte*); **to take a car etc in ~ exchange** reprendre une voiture *etc* (en compte)

► **part of speech** N partie *f* du discours, catégorie *f* grammaticale; **what ~ of speech is "of"?** à quelle catégorie grammaticale est-ce que «of» appartient? ► **part owner** N copropriétaire *mf* ► **part payment** N (= *exchange*) règlement *m* partiel; (= *deposit*) arrhes *fpl* ► **part song** N chant *m* à plusieurs voix *or* polyphonique ► **parts per million** NPL parties *fpl* par million ► **part-time** → **part-time** ► **part-timer** N travailleur *m*, -euse *f* *or* employé(e) *m(f)* à temps partiel ► **part work** N (*Brit*) fascicule *m*

partake [pɑː'teɪk] (*pret* **partook**, *ptp* **partaken**) VI (*frm*) **to ~ in** prendre part à, participer à; **to ~ of** [+ *meal, refreshment*] prendre; (*fig*) tenir de, avoir quelque chose de

parthenogenesis ['pɑːθɪnəʊ'dʒenɪsɪs] N parthénogenèse *f*

parthenogenetic [ˌpɑːθɪnəʊdʒɪ'netɪk] ADJ parthénogénétique

parthenogenetically [ˌpɑːθɪnəʊdʒɪ'netɪkəlɪ] ADV parthénogénétiquement

Parthenon ['pɑːθənɒn] N Parthénon *m*

Parthian ['pɑːθɪən] ADJ **~ shot** flèche *f* du Parthe

partial ['pɑːʃəl] ADJ [a] (= *in part*) [*success, solution, explanation, withdrawal, eclipse, paralysis*] partiel [b] (= *biased*) [*person, viewpoint*] partial (**to, towards** envers), injuste [c]* **to be ~ to sth** avoir un faible pour qch, être porté sur qch; **to be ~ to doing sth** aimer bien faire qch; **she is not (too) ~ to being disturbed** elle n'aime pas trop qu'on la dérange

partiality [ˌpɑːʃɪ'ælɪtɪ] N [a] (= *bias*) partialité *f* (**for** pour, **towards** envers), favoritisme *m* [b] (= *liking*) prédilection *f*, penchant *m*, faible *m* (**for** pour)

partially ['pɑːʃəlɪ] [1] ADV [a] (= *partly*) en partie (*after vb*); **~ hidden by the trees** caché en partie par les arbres; **the driver was ~ responsible for the accident** le conducteur était en partie responsable de l'accident; **he was only ~ successful** il n'a eu qu'un succès mitigé; **~ clothed** à moitié nu; **~, they were afraid of reprisals** une des raisons est qu'ils avaient peur des représailles; **~ because he was embarrassed** en partie parce qu'il était gêné [b] (= *with bias*) avec partialité, partialement [2] COMP ► **partially-sighted** ADJ **to be ~-sighted** être malvoyant → **disabled** ► **the partially-sighted** NPL les malvoyants *mpl*

participant [pɑː'tɪsɪpənt] N participant(e) *m(f)* (**in** à)

participate [pɑː'tɪsɪpeɪt] VI participer, prendre part (**in** à)

participation [pɑːˌtɪsɪ'peɪʃən] N participation *f* (**in** à)

participative [pɑː'tɪsɪpətɪv], **participatory** [pɑːtɪsɪ'peɪtərɪ] ADJ participatif

participial [ˌpɑːtɪ'sɪpɪəl] ADJ participial

participle ['pɑːtɪsɪpl] N participe *m*; **past/present ~** participe *m* passé/présent

particle ['pɑːtɪkl] [1] N [a] (= *small piece*) (*gen, Phys*) particule *f*; (*fig*) parcelle *f*, grain *m*; **dust ~s** ◊ **~s of dust** grains *mpl* de poussière; **food ~s** quantités *fpl* infimes de nourriture; **sub-atomic ~** particule *f* subatomique; **a ~ of truth/of sense** une parcelle de vérité/de bon sens; **not a ~ of evidence** pas l'ombre d'une preuve, pas la moindre preuve [b] (*Ling*) particule *f* [2] COMP ► **particle accelerator** N (*Phys*) accélérateur *m* de particules ► **particle board** N (*US*) panneau *m* de particules ► **particle physics** N physique *f* des particules élémentaires

parti-coloured, **parti-colored** (*US*) ['pɑːtɪˌkʌləd] ADJ bariolé

particular [pə'tɪkjʊlər] [1] ADJ [a] (= *specific, distinct*) particulier; **in this ~ case** dans ce cas particulier *or* précis; **there seemed to be no ~ reason for his outburst** son emportement passager ne semblait pas avoir de raison

particulière; **for no ~ reason** sans raison précise *or* bien définie; **that ~ brand** cette marque-là; **his ~ chair** son fauteuil à lui; **her ~ type of humour** son genre particulier d'humour, son humour personnel; **my ~ choice** mon choix personnel; (= *specific*) **the report moves from the ~ to the general** le rapport va du particulier au général
⌐b¬ (= *special*) particulier, spécial; **nothing ~ happened** rien de particulier *or* de spécial n'est arrivé; **he took ~ care over it** il y a mis un soin (tout) particulier; **to be of ~ interest to sb** intéresser qn (tout) particulièrement; **this is of ~ concern to us** ceci nous préoccupe tout particulièrement; **to pay ~ attention to sth** faire bien *or* particulièrement attention à qch; **a ~ friend of his** un de ses meilleurs amis, un de ses amis intimes; **she didn't say anything ~** elle n'a rien dit de spécial
⌐c¬ (= *fussy*) exigeant; **she is ~ about whom she talks to** elle ne parle pas à n'importe qui; **he is ~ about his food** il est exigeant *or* difficile pour la nourriture, il ne mange pas n'importe quoi; **which do you want? — I'm not ~** lequel voulez-vous? — cela m'est égal *or* je n'ai pas de préférence
⌐d¬ († = *exact, detailed*) [*account*] détaillé, circonstancié
⌐2¬ N ⌐a¬ **in ~** en particulier; **anything/anybody in ~** quelque chose/quelqu'un en particulier; **nothing/nobody in ~** rien de/personne en particulier; (*in shop*) **are you looking for anything in ~?** vous cherchez quelque chose en particulier?
⌐b¬ (= *detail*) détail *m*; **in every ~** en tout point; **he is wrong in one ~** il se trompe sur un point
⌐3¬ **particulars** NPL (= *information*) détails *mpl*, renseignements *mpl*; (= *description*) description *f*; [*of person*] (= *description*) signalement *m*; (= *name, address etc*) nom *m* et adresse *f*, coordonnées *fpl*; (*for official document etc*) caractéristiques *fpl* signalétiques; **full ~s** tous les détails, tous les renseignements; **for further ~s apply to ...** pour de plus amples renseignements s'adresser à ...

particularity [pə,tɪkjʊ'lærɪtɪ] N particularité *f*

particularize [pə'tɪkjʊlaraɪz] ⌐1¬ VT préciser, individualiser ⌐2¬ VI préciser

particularly [pə'tɪkjʊləlɪ] ADV ⌐a¬ (= *especially*) [*good, bad, well, badly etc*] particulièrement; [*specify, insist etc*] (tout) particulièrement; **I ~ told you not to do that** je t'ai bien dit de ne pas faire cela, j'ai bien insisté pour que tu ne fasses pas cela; **it's dangerous for children, ~ young ones** c'est dangereux pour les enfants, surtout *or* en particulier *or* notamment les tout jeunes; **not ~** pas particulièrement ⌐b¬ (= *very carefully*) méticuleusement, avec grand soin

parting ['pɑːtɪŋ] ⌐1¬ N ⌐a¬ séparation *f*; [*of waters*] partage *m*; (*lit, fig*) **the ~ of the ways** la croisée des chemins ⌐b¬ (*Brit*) [*of hair*] raie *f*; [*of mane*] épi *m*; **to have a side/centre ~** porter *or* avoir la raie sur le côté/au milieu ⌐2¬ ADJ [*gift*] d'adieu; **~ words** paroles *fpl* d'adieu; (*fig*) **~ shot** flèche *f* du Parthe (*liter*), pointe *f*; **he paused to deliver a or his ~ shot** il s'est arrêté pour lancer la flèche du Parthe (*liter*) *or* une dernière pointe

partisan [,pɑːtɪ'zæn] ⌐1¬ N (= *supporter, fighter*) partisan *m* ⌐2¬ ADJ [*politics, debate*] partisan; [*warfare*] de partisans; (*Pol etc*) **~ spirit** esprit *m* de parti

partisanship [,pɑːtɪ'zænʃɪp] N esprit *m* de parti, partialité *f*; (= *membership*) appartenance *f* à un parti

partita [pɑː'tiːtə] N (*pl* **partitas** *or* **partite** [pɑː'tiːteɪ]) (*Mus*) partita *f*

partition [pɑː'tɪʃən] ⌐1¬ N ⌐a¬ (*also* **~ wall**) cloison *f*; **a glass ~** une cloison vitrée ⌐b¬ (= *dividing*) [*of property*] division *f*; [*of country*] partition *f*, partage *m*; [*of estate*] morcellement *m*

⌐2¬ VT [+ *property*] diviser, partager; [+ *country*] partager; [+ *estate*] morceler; [+ *room*] cloisonner
▶**partition off** VT SEP [+ *room, part of room*] cloisonner

partitive ['pɑːtɪtɪv] ADJ, N partitif *m*

partly ['pɑːtlɪ] ADV en partie; **~ blue, ~ green** moitié bleu, moitié vert

partner ['pɑːtnəʳ] ⌐1¬ N ⌐a¬ (*gen*) partenaire *mf*; (*Comm, Fin, Jur, Med etc*) associé(e) *m(f)*; **our European ~s** nos partenaires européens; **~s in crime** complices *mpl* → **senior, sleeping, trading** ⌐b¬ (*Sport*) partenaire *mf*; (= *co-driver*) coéquipier *m*, -ière *f*; (*Dancing*) cavalier *m*, -ière *f*; **take your ~s for a waltz** choisissez vos partenaires pour la valse ⌐c¬ (*in relationship*) compagnon *m*, compagne *f*; (*Admin: cohabiting*) concubin(e) *m(f)*; **sexual ~** partenaire *mf* sexuel; **bring your ~ along** venez avec votre conjoint ⌐2¬ VT (*Comm, Fin etc*) être l'associé (de), s'associer à; (*Motor Racing*) être le coéquipier de; (*Dancing*) (*gen*) être le cavalier (*or* la cavalière) de; (*in competitions*) être le (*or* la) partenaire de

partnership ['pɑːtnəʃɪp] N (*gen*) association *f*; (*Comm, Fin, Jur*) ≈ société *f* en nom collectif; (*Comm, Fin*) **limited ~** (société *f* en) commandite *f*; **to be in ~** être en association (**with** avec), être associé (**with** à, avec); **to enter** *or* **go into ~** s'associer (**with** à, avec); **to take sb into ~** prendre qn comme associé; **a doctors' ~** un cabinet de groupe (*médical*), une association de médecins → **general, working**

partook [pɑː'tʊk] VB *pret* de **partake**

partridge ['pɑːtrɪdʒ] N (*pl* **partridges** *or* **partridge**) perdrix *f*; (*young bird, also Culin*) perdreau *m*

part-time ['pɑːt'taɪm] ⌐1¬ ADJ ⌐a¬ [*work, employment*] à temps partiel; (= *half-time*) à mi-temps; **to do ~ work** ◊ **to have a ~ job** travailler à temps partiel *or* à mi-temps; **on a ~ basis** à temps partiel ⌐b¬ [*employee, staff, student*] à temps partiel ⌐2¬ N (*Ind*) **to be on ~*** être au chômage partiel ⌐3¬ ADV [*work, study*] à temps partiel

parturition [,pɑːtjʊə'rɪʃən] N parturition *f*

partway [,pɑːt'weɪ] ADV **~ along** (*or* **through** *or* **there**) à mi-chemin

party ['pɑːtɪ] ⌐1¬ N ⌐a¬ (*Pol etc*) parti *m*; **political/Conservative/Labour ~** parti *m* politique/conservateur/travailliste ⌐b¬ (= *group*) [*of travellers*] groupe *m*, troupe* *f*; [*of workmen*] équipe *f*, brigade *f*; (*Mil*) détachement *m*, escouade *f* → **boarding, rescue, working** ⌐c¬ (= *celebration*) fête *f*; (*in the evening*) soirée *f*; (*formal*) réception *f*; **to give** *or* **have** *or* **throw* a ~** organiser une fête, inviter des amis; (*more formal gathering*) donner une réception *or* une soirée; **birthday ~** fête *f* d'anniversaire; **farewell ~** fête *f* d'adieu; **retirement ~** cocktail *m* *or* pot *m* de départ; **launch ~** lancement *m*; **children's ~** goûter *m* d'enfants; **private ~** réception *f* privée; (*fig*) **what does he bring to the ~?** quelle contribution apporte-t-il? → **bottle, Christmas, dinner, garden, tea** ⌐d¬ (*Jur etc*) partie *f*; **all parties concerned** toutes les parties concernées, tous les intéressés; **to be ~ to a suit** être en cause; **to become a ~ to a contract** signer un contrat; **injured ~** ◊ **aggrieved** partie *f* lésée, victime *f*; **innocent ~ innocent(e)** *m(f)*; **I will not be (a) ~ to any dishonesty** je ne me ferai le (*or* la) complice d'aucune malhonnêteté; **to be (a) ~ to a crime/to treachery** être complice d'un crime/d'une trahison; **the government insists it will never become a ~ to this conflict** le gouvernement affirme catégoriquement qu'il ne prendra jamais part à ce conflit; **they refused to be ~ to the negotiations** ils ont refusé de prendre part *or* participer aux négociations → **guilty, moving, prevailing, third**

⌐e¬ († *hum* = *person*) individu *m*
⌐f¬ (*Telec*) correspondant *m*; **your ~ is on the line** votre correspondant est en ligne
⌐2¬ VI* faire la fête; **let's ~!** faisons la fête!; **I'm not a great one for ~ing** je ne suis pas fêtard(e)*
⌐3¬ COMP [*politics, leader*] de parti, du parti; [*disputes*] de partis ▶ **party animal*** N fêtard(e)* *m(f)* ▶ **party dress** N robe *f* habillée; (= *evening dress*) robe *f* de soirée ▶ **party hat** N chapeau *m* de cotillon ▶ **party line** N (*Pol*) politique *f* *or* ligne *f* du parti; (*Telec*) ligne *f* commune à plusieurs abonnés; (*Pol*) **to follow** *or* **toe the ~ line** suivre la ligne du parti, être dans la ligne du parti → **toe** ▶ **party list** N scrutin *m* de liste ▶ **party machine** N (*Pol*) machine *f* *or* administration *f* du parti ▶ **party manners*** NPL **his ~ manners were terrible** sa façon de se tenir en société était abominable; **the children were on their ~ manners** les enfants se sont conduits de façon exemplaire ▶ **party piece*** N **to do one's ~ piece** faire son numéro* ▶ **party plan** N (= *system*) vente *f* par réunions; (= *party*) réunion *f* de vente à domicile ▶ **party political** ADJ (*Rad, TV*) **~ political broadcast** *émission réservée à un parti politique*; **this is not a ~ political question** cette question ne relève pas de la ligne du parti ▶ **party politics** N politique *f* de parti; (*pej*) politique *f* politicienne ▶ **party pooper*** N rabat-joie *m inv*, trouble-fête *mf* ▶ **party spirit** N (*Pol*) esprit *m* de parti; (* = *gaiety*) entrain *m* ▶ **party wall** N mur *m* mitoyen

partygoer ['pɑːtɪ,gəʊəʳ] N (*gen*) habitué(e) *m(f)* des réceptions; (*on specific occasion*) invité(e) *m(f)*

PASCAL, Pascal [pæs'kæl] N Pascal *m*

paschal ['pɑːskəl] ⌐1¬ ADJ (*Rel*) pascal ⌐2¬ COMP ▶ **the Paschal Lamb** N l'agneau *m* pascal

pasha ['pæʃə] N pacha *m*

pass [pɑːs] ⌐1¬ N ⌐a¬ (= *permit*) [*of journalist, worker etc*] coupe-file *m*, laissez-passer *m inv*; (*Rail etc*) carte *f* d'abonnement; (*Theat*) billet *m* de faveur; (*to museum etc*) laissez-passer *m*; (*Naut*) lettre *f* de mer; (*Mil etc* = *safe conduct*) sauf-conduit *m*
⌐b¬ (*in mountains*) col *m*, défilé *m* → **sell**
⌐c¬ (*in exam*) moyenne *f*, mention *f* passable; **did you get a ~?** avez-vous eu la moyenne?, avez-vous été reçu?; **to get a ~ in history** être reçu en histoire
⌐d¬ (* = *state*) **things have come to a pretty ~ when ...** il faut que les choses aillent bien mal pour que ...; **things have reached such a ~ that ...** les choses en sont arrivées à un tel point que ...
⌐e¬ (*Ftbl etc*) passe *f*; (*Fencing*) botte *f*, attaque *f*
⌐f¬ (= *sexual advance*) **to make a ~* at sb** faire du plat* à qn
⌐2¬ VI ⌐a¬ (= *come, go*) passer (**through** par); [*procession*] défiler; (*Aut* = *overtake*) dépasser, doubler; **to let sb ~** laisser passer qn; **to ~ behind/in front of** passer derrière/devant; **the procession ~ed down the street** la procession a descendu la rue; **to ~ out of sight** disparaître; **letters ~ed between them** ils ont échangé des lettres; **a knowing look ~ed between them** ils ont échangé un regard complice; **the virus ~es easily from one person to another** le virus se transmet facilement d'une personne à l'autre; **to ~ into history/legend** entrer dans l'histoire/la légende; **the word has ~ed into the language** le mot est entré dans la langue ⌐b¬ [*time*] (se) passer, s'écouler; **three hours/days/years had ~ed** trois heures/jours/années s'étaient écoulé(e)s; **the afternoon ~ed pleasantly** l'après-midi a passé *or* s'est passé agréablement; **how time ~es!** comme le temps passe!; **I'm very conscious of time ~ing** j'ai une conscience aiguë du temps qui passe ⌐c¬ (*esp Chem* = *change*) se transformer (**into** en)

d (*esp Jur* = *transfer*) passer, être transmis; **the estate ~ed to my sister** la propriété est revenue à ma sœur; **the land has now ~ed into private hands** le terrain appartient désormais à un propriétaire privé

e (= *go away*) [*pain, crisis*] passer; [*danger*] disparaître; [*memory*] s'effacer, disparaître; [*storm*] cesser; **to let an opportunity ~** laisser passer une occasion; **the deadline ~ed this morning** le délai a expiré ce matin

f (*in exam*) être reçu (**in** en)

g (= *take place*) se passer, avoir lieu; **all that ~ed between them** tout ce qui s'est passé entre eux; (*liter*) **to bring sth to ~** accomplir qch, réaliser qch; (*liter*) **it came to ~ that** ... il advint que ...

h (= *be accepted*) [*coins*] avoir cours; [*behaviour*] convenir, être acceptable; [*project*] passer; **to ~ under the name of ...** être connu sous le nom de ...; **he tried to ~ for a doctor** il a essayé de se faire passer pour (un) médecin; **what ~es for** *or* **as law and order in this country** ce que l'on appelle l'ordre public dans ce pays; **a cup of something that ~ed for coffee** une tasse d'un breuvage auquel ils donnaient le nom de café; **she would ~ for 20** on lui donnerait 20 ans; **will this do? — oh, it'll ~*** est-ce que ceci convient? — oh, ça peut aller; (*of insult*) **let it ~!*** laisse tomber!*; **that's not exactly right, but let it ~** ce n'est pas exactement ça, mais passons *or* ça ne fait rien; **he let it ~** il l'a laissé passer, il ne l'a pas relevé; **he couldn't let that ~** il ne pouvait pas laisser passer ça

i (*Cards*) passer; **(I) ~!** (*in games*) (je) passe!; (*fig*) aucune idée!; (*fig*) **I'll have to ~ on that one*** (= *can't answer*) là je donne ma langue au chat; **I'll ~ on that one*** (= *no thanks*) je m'en passerai; (*in discussion*) je passe mon tour

j (*Sport*) faire une passe (**to** à); **to ~ forward/back** faire une passe avant/arrière

3 VT **a** (= *go past*) [+ *building, person*] passer devant; [+ *barrier, frontier, customs*] passer; (*in car* = *overtake*) dépasser, doubler; (*Sport* = *go beyond*) dépasser; **when you have ~ed the town hall** ... quand vous aurez dépassé la mairie ...; (*Sport*) **to ~ the finishing line** passer la ligne d'arrivée; **they ~ed each other on the way** ils se sont croisés en chemin; **no word ~ed his lips** il ne souffla *or* ne dit un mot; **no meat has ~ed my lips for 20 years** il y a 20 ans que je n'ai plus mangé de viande

b (= *get through*) [+ *exam*] être reçu à *or* admis à, réussir; **the film ~ed the censors** le film a reçu le visa de la censure → **muster**

c [+ *time*] passer; **just to ~ the time** pour passer le temps; **to ~ the evening reading** passer la soirée à lire → **time**

d (= *hand over*) (faire) passer; **please ~ the salt** faites passer le sel s'il vous plaît; **to ~ a dish round the table** faire passer un plat autour de la table; **~ me the box** passez-moi la boîte; **to ~ sth down the line** faire passer qch (de main en main); **~ the word that it's time to go** faites passer la consigne que c'est l'heure de partir; **we should ~ this information to the police** nous devrions passer *or* transmettre ces informations à la police → **buck**

e (*on phone*) passer

f (= *accept, allow*) [+ *candidate*] recevoir, admettre; (*Parl*) [+ *bill*] voter, faire passer; **the censors ~ed the film** le film a reçu le visa de censure; (*Scol, Univ*) **they didn't ~ him** ils l'ont recalé; **the doctor ~ed him fit for work** le docteur l'a déclaré apte à reprendre le travail; (*Publishing*) **to ~ the proofs (for press)** donner le bon à tirer

g (= *utter*) **to ~ comment (on sth)** faire un commentaire (sur qch); **to ~ remarks about sb/sth** faire des observations sur qn/qch; (*Jur, fig*) **to ~ judgement** prononcer *or* rendre un jugement (**on** sur); (*Jur*) **to ~ sentence** pro-

noncer une condamnation (**on sb** contre qn) → **sentence**

h (= *move*) passer; **he ~ed his hand over his brow** il s'est passé la main sur le front; **he ~ed his handkerchief over his face** il a passé son mouchoir sur son visage; **to ~ a rope through a ring** passer une corde dans un anneau; **to ~ a cloth over a table** donner *or* passer un coup de chiffon à une table; **to ~ a knife through sth** enfoncer un couteau dans qch; (*Culin*) **to ~ sth through a sieve** passer qch (au tamis); (*Mil, fig*) **to ~ in review** passer en revue

i (*Sport*) [+ *ball*] passer

j [+ *forged money*] (faire) passer, écouler; [+ *stolen goods*] faire passer

k (= *surpass*) **to ~ comprehension** dépasser l'entendement; **to ~ belief** être incroyable

l (*Med* = *excrete*) **to ~ water** uriner; **to ~ blood** avoir du sang dans les urines; **to ~ a stone** évacuer un calcul

4 COMP ► **pass degree** N (*Univ*) ≈ licence *f* obtenue sans mention ► **pass mark** N (*Scol, Univ*) moyenne *f*; **to get a ~ mark** avoir la moyenne ► **pass-the-parcel** N (= *way to play* **~ the-parcel**) ≈ jouer au furet ► **pass-through** N (*US*) passe-plat *m*

► **pass along** **1** VI passer, circuler, passer son chemin **2** VT SEP **a** (*lit*) [+ *object, book etc*] faire passer (de main en main) **b** = **pass on 2**

► **pass away** VI (*euph* = *die*) s'éteindre (*euph*), décéder (*frm or euph*)

► **pass back** VT SEP [+ *object*] rendre, retourner; (*Rad, TV*) **I will now ~ you back to the studio** je vais rendre l'antenne au studio

► **pass by** **1** VI passer (à côté); [*procession*] défiler; **I saw him ~ing by** je l'ai vu passer; (*fig*) **to ~ by on the other side** (= *fail to help*) détourner les yeux **2** VT SEP **life has ~ed me by** je n'ai pas vraiment vécu; **the war seemed to ~ them by** la guerre ne semblait pas les toucher; **fashion just ~es him by** la mode le laisse froid

► **pass down** **1** VI [*inheritance etc*] être transmis, revenir (**to** à) **2** VT SEP transmettre; **to ~ sth down (in a family)** transmettre qch par héritage (dans une famille); **~ed down from father to son/from mother to daughter** transmis de père en fils/de mère en fille

► **pass in** VT SEP (faire) passer; **she ~ed the parcel in through the window** elle a passé *or* fait passer le colis par la fenêtre

► **pass off** **1** VI **a** (= *subside*) [*faintness, headache etc*] passer, se dissiper **b** (= *take place*) [*events*] se passer, se dérouler; **the demonstration ~ed off peacefully/without incident** la manifestation s'est déroulée pacifiquement/ sans incident **2** VT SEP faire passer, faire prendre; **to ~ someone off as someone else** faire passer une personne pour une autre; **to ~ something off as something else** faire passer une chose pour une autre; **to ~ o.s. off as a doctor** se faire passer pour (un) médecin; **to ~ sth off on sb** repasser *or* refiler* qch à qn

► **pass on** **1** VI **a** (*euph* = *die*) s'éteindre (*euph*), décéder (*frm or euph*) **b** (= *continue one's way*) passer son chemin, ne pas s'arrêter; (*fig*) **to ~ on to a new subject** passer à un nouveau sujet **2** VT SEP (= *hand on*) [+ *object*] (faire) passer (**to** à); [+ *news*] faire circuler, faire savoir; [+ *message*] transmettre; **take it and ~ it on** prends-le et fais passer; **to ~ on old clothes to sb** repasser de vieux vêtements à qn; **you've ~ed your cold on to me** tu m'as passé ton rhume; **to ~ on a tax to the consumer** répercuter un impôt sur le consommateur

► **pass out** **1** VI **a** (= *faint*) s'évanouir, perdre connaissance, tomber dans les pommes*; (*from drink*) tomber ivre mort; (= *fall asleep*) s'endormir comme une masse **b** (*Brit* = *complete training*) (*Police*) finir son entraînement (*avec succès*); (*Mil*) finir ses classes (*avec succès*) **2** VT SEP [+ *leaflets etc*] distribuer

► **pass over** **1** VI (*euph* = *die*) = **pass away** **2** VT SEP [+ *person, event, matter*] (= *fail to mention*) ne pas mentionner; (= *fail to take into consideration*) ne pas prendre en considération; **the good work they have done is ~ed over in this article** le bon travail qu'ils ont fait n'est même pas mentionné dans cet article; **to ~ sth over in silence** passer qch sous silence; **he was ~ed over in favour of his brother** on lui a préféré son frère; **they ~ed over Paul in favour of Robert** ils ont donné la préférence à Robert au détriment de Paul; **she was ~ed over for promotion** on ne lui a pas accordé la promotion qu'elle attendait **3** VT FUS (= *ignore*) passer sous silence, ne pas relever

► **pass round** VT SEP [+ *bottle*] faire passer; [+ *sweets, leaflets*] distribuer; (*fig*) **to ~ the hat round*** faire la quête

► **pass through** **1** VI passer; **I can't stop, I'm only ~ing through** je ne peux pas rester, je ne fais que passer **2** VT FUS [+ *country, area, substance, net*] traverser; [+ *hardships*] subir, endurer; **this thread is too coarse to ~ through the needle** ce fil est trop gros pour passer dans l'aiguille

► **pass up** VT SEP **a** (*lit*) passer **b** (* = *forego*) [+ *chance, opportunity*] laisser passer; **she ~ed him up for promotion** on ne lui a pas accordé la promotion qu'il attendait; **he was ~ed up for the job** on a pris quelqu'un d'autre que lui pour cet emploi; **she ~ed the film up for a rôle in a theatre play** elle a décliné un rôle dans ce film pour jouer dans une pièce de théâtre

passable ['pɑːsəbl] ADJ **a** (= *tolerable*) passable, assez bon; **he spoke ~ French** il parlait assez bien (le) français **b** [*road*] praticable, carrossable; [*river*] franchissable

passably ['pɑːsəbli] ADV assez; **he spoke ~ good French** il parlait assez bien (le) français; **she was doing ~ at school** elle avait d'assez bons résultats à l'école

passage ['pæsɪdʒ] N **a** (= *passing*) (*lit*) passage *m*; [*of bill, law*] adoption *f*; (*fig*) passage *m*, transition *f* (**from ... to** de ... à); **with the ~ of time he understood** avec le temps il finit par comprendre; (*fig, liter*) **~ of** *or* **at arms** passe *f* d'armes → **bird, rite, safe** **b** (*Naut*) voyage *m*, traversée *f*; **he worked his ~ to Australia** il a travaillé pour se payer la traversée *or* son voyage en Australie **c** (= *way through:* also **~way**) passage *m*; **to force a ~ through sth** frayer un passage *or* un chemin à travers qch; **to leave a ~** laisser un passage, laisser le passage libre **d** (*also* **~way**) (*indoors*) couloir *m*, corridor *m*; (*outdoors*) ruelle *f*, passage *m* **e** (*Mus*) passage *m*; [*of text*] passage *m*; (*Literat*) **selected ~s** morceaux *mpl* choisis

passageway ['pæsɪdʒweɪ] N = **passage 1c, 1d**

passbook ['pæsbʊk] N (= *bank book*) livret *m* (bancaire)

passé ['pæseɪ] ADJ [*play, book, person*] vieux jeu *inv*, démodé, dépassé*; [*woman*] défraîchi, fané

passel ['pæsəl] N (*US*) **a ~ of** ... une ribambelle de ..., un tas* de ...

passenger ['pæsndʒəʳ] **1** N (*in train*) voyageur *m*, -euse *f*; (*in boat, plane, car*) passager *m*, -ère *f*; (*fig pej*) **he's just a ~** il n'est vraiment qu'un poids mort

2 COMP ► **passenger car** N (*US*) = **passenger coach** ► **passenger cell** N (*Aut*) habitacle *m* ► **passenger coach** N (*Rail*) voiture *f* *or* wagon *m* de voyageurs ► **passenger door** N [*of car*] portière *f* avant côté passager ► **passenger enquiries** NPL (*Aviat, Rail:* also **~ service enquiries**) renseignements *mpl* ► **passenger ferry** N ferry *m* ► **passenger jet** N avion *m* de ligne ► **passenger list** N (*Aviat, Naut*) liste *f* des passagers ► **passenger mile** N (*Aviat*) ≈ kilomètre-passager *m*; (*Rail etc*) ≈ kilomètre-voyageur *m*

► **passenger seat** N [of car] (in front) siège m du passager; (in back) siège m arrière ► **passenger ship** N navire m à passagers ► **passenger station** N (Rail) gare f de voyageurs ► **passenger train** N train m de voyageurs

passe-partout ['pæspɑːtuː] N [a] (= master key) passe-partout m inv (clé), passe m [b] (Art) ~ (frame) (encadrement m en) sous-verre m

passer-by ['pɑːsə'baɪ] N (pl **passers-by**) passant(e) m(f)

passim ['pæsɪm] ADV passim

passing ['pɑːsɪŋ] [1] ADJ [a] (= moving by) [person, car] qui passe (or passait etc) [b] (= brief) éphémère, passager; **a ~ desire** un désir fugitif; **a ~ interest in sth/sb** un intérêt éphémère pour qch/qn, un intérêt passager pour qch/qn; **a ~ acquaintance** une vague connaissance; **to have a ~ acquaintance with sb/sth** connaître vaguement qn/qch; **a ~ remark** une remarque en passant; **to bear only a ~ resemblance to sb/sth** ne ressembler que vaguement à qn/qch; **to bear more than a ~ resemblance to sb/sth** ressembler beaucoup à qn/qch; **with each** or **every ~ day** de jour en jour; **with each** or **every ~ year** d'année en année, année après année [2] ADV (†† or liter) extrêmement; **~ fair** de toute beauté [3] N [a] **with the ~ of time** avec le temps; **in ~** en passant [b] [of train, car] passage m; (in car = overtaking) dépassement m [c] (euph = death) mort f, trépas m (liter) [4] COMP ► **passing bell** N glas m ► **passing note** N (Mus) note f de passage ► **passing-out parade** N (Mil) défilé m de promotion ► **passing place** N (in road) aire f de croisement ► **passing shot** N (Tennis) passing-shot m, tir m passant

passion ['pæʃən] [1] N [a] (= love) passion f (for sth); **to have a ~ for music** avoir la passion de la musique, adorer la musique; **I have a ~ for strong colours** j'adore les couleurs vives [b] (= burst of anger) colère f; (stronger) rage f; **fit of ~** accès m de rage; **to be in a ~** être furieux → **fly**³ [c] (= strong emotion) passion f, émotion f violente [d] (Rel, Mus) **Passion** Passion f; **the St John/St Matthew Passion** la Passion selon saint Jean/saint Matthieu [2] COMP ► **passion fruit** N (Bot) fruit m de la passion, maracuja m ► **Passion play** N (Rel) mystère m de la Passion (représentation théâtrale) ► **Passion Sunday** N (Rel) dimanche m de la Passion ► **Passion Week** N (Rel) semaine f de la Passion

passionate ['pæʃənɪt] ADJ [person, plea, love, embrace] passionné; [speech] véhément

passionately ['pæʃənɪtlɪ] ADV [argue, kiss, make love] avec passion; [believe] passionnément; [convinced, concerned] passionnément; [opposed] farouchement; **to be ~ fond of sth** adorer qch; **to be ~ in love with sb** aimer passionnément qn; **a ~-held opinion** une opinion défendue or soutenue avec passion

passionflower ['pæʃən,flaʊə'] N (Bot) passiflore f, fleur f de la Passion

passionless ['pæʃənlɪs] ADJ sans passion

passive ['pæsɪv] [1] ADJ [a] [person] (= motionless) passif, inerte; (= unresponsive) passif, soumis; [role, attitude] passif; **his response was ~** il n'a pas vraiment réagi [b] (Ling) [vocabulary, understanding] passif [c] (Gram) [tense, voice etc] passif [2] N (Gram) passif m; **in the ~** au passif [3] COMP ► **passive balance of trade** N balance f commerciale déficitaire ► **passive disobedience** N (Pol) désobéissance f passive ► **passive resistance** N (Pol) résistance f passive ► **passive restraint** N (Aut) dispositif m de sécurité passive ► **passive smoker** N non-fumeur m, -euse f affecté(e) par le taba-

gisme passif ► **passive smoking** N tabagisme m passif

passively ['pæsɪvlɪ] ADV passivement; (Gram) au passif

passiveness ['pæsɪvnɪs], **passivity** [pæ'sɪvɪtɪ] N passivité f

passkey ['pɑːskiː] N passe-partout m inv, passe* m

Passover ['pɑːsəʊvə'] N pâque f (juive)

passport ['pɑːspɔːt] [1] N passeport m; **a British/American/French etc ~** un passeport britannique/américain/français etc; (Brit) **visitor's ~** passeport m temporaire; (fig) **~ to success** clé f de la réussite; **the lottery could be your ~ to riches** la loterie pourrait vous ouvrir les portes de la fortune [2] COMP ► **passport control** N contrôle m des passeports ► **passport holder** N titulaire mf de passeport; **are you a British ~ holder?** avez-vous un passeport britannique? ► **passport office** N (= building) bureau m du contrôle des passeports; (= organization) service m du contrôle des passeports

password ['pɑːswɜːd] N (also Comput) mot m de passe

past [pɑːst] [1] N [a] passé m; **in the ~** (gen) dans le passé; (longer ago) autrefois; **several times in the ~** plusieurs fois dans le passé; **in the ~, many of these babies would have died** autrefois, beaucoup de ces bébés seraient morts; **all the happy times in the ~** tous les moments heureux du passé; **events in the recent ~ have demonstrated that ...** certains événements récents ont montré que ...; **as in the ~** comme par le passé; **she lives in the ~** elle vit dans le passé; **it's a thing of the ~** cela appartient au passé; **new vaccines could make these illnesses a thing of the ~** de nouveaux vaccins pourraient faire disparaître ces maladies; **I thought you'd quarrelled? — that's a thing of the ~** or **that's all in the ~** or **that's ancient history** je croyais que vous vous étiez disputés? — c'est de l'histoire ancienne; **we have to learn the lessons of the ~** il nous faut tirer les leçons du passé; **do you know about his ~?** vous connaissez son passé?; **a woman with a ~** une femme au passé chargé [b] (Gram) passé m; **in the ~** au passé [2] ADJ [a] (gen) passé; **for some time ~** depuis quelque temps; **in times ~** autrefois, (au temps) jadis; **in ~ centuries** pendant les siècles passés; **the ~ week** la semaine dernière or passée; **the ~ few days/years** ces derniers jours/dernières années; **she's been out of work for the ~ three years** elle est au chômage depuis trois ans; **all that is now ~** tout cela c'est du passé; **the time for recriminations is ~** le temps des récriminations est révolu; **president** ancien président m [b] (Gram: gen) passé; [verb] au passé; [form, ending] du passé [3] PREP [a] (beyond in time) plus de; **it is ~ 11 o'clock** il est plus de 11 heures, il est 11 heures passées; (Brit) **half ~ three** trois heures et demie; (Brit) **(a) quarter ~ three** trois heures et quart; (Brit) **at 20 ~ three** à 3 heures 20; (Brit) **the train goes at five ~*** le train part à cinq*; **she is ~ 60** elle a plus de 60 ans, elle a 60 ans passés [b] (= beyond in space) au delà de, plus loin que; ~ **it** au delà, plus loin; **just ~ the post office** un peu plus loin que la poste, juste après la poste; **I think we've gone ~ it** (= missed it) je pense que nous l'avons dépassé; **he stared straight ~ me** il a fait comme s'il ne me voyait pas [c] (= in front of) devant; **he goes ~ the house every day** tous les jours il passe devant la maison; **he rushed ~ me** il est passé devant moi à toute allure; (= overtook me) il m'a dépassé à toute allure [d] (= beyond limits of) au delà de; ~ **endurance** insupportable; **it is ~ all understanding**

cela dépasse l'entendement; **I'm ~ caring** je ne m'en fais plus, j'ai cessé de m'en faire; **he's ~ work** il n'est plus en état de travailler; **I'm long ~ being surprised at anything he does** il y a longtemps que je ne m'étonne plus de ce qu'il peut (encore) inventer; **he's a bit ~ it (now)*** il n'est plus dans la course*; **that cake is ~ its best** ce gâteau n'est plus très frais; **I wouldn't put it ~ her** to have done it je le crois capable d'avoir fait ça; **I wouldn't put it ~ him** cela ne m'étonnerait pas de lui

[4] ADV

> When **past** is an element in a phrasal verb, eg **let past**, **run past**, **squeeze past**, look up the verb.

auprès, devant; **to go** or **walk ~** passer → **march**

[5] COMP ► **past anterior** N passé m antérieur ► **past definite** N = **past historic** ► **past historic** N passé m simple ► **past master** N (fig) **to be a ~ master at** or **of sth** être expert en qch; **to be a ~ master at doing sth** avoir l'art de faire qch ► **past participle** N participe m passé ► **past perfect** N plus-que-parfait m ► **past tense** N passé m, forme f passée; **in the ~ tense** au passé

pasta ['pæstə] N (NonC: Culin) pâtes fpl

paste [peɪst] [1] N [a] (Culin = spread etc) (meat) pâté m; (fish) beurre m, mousse f; (vegetable, fruit) purée f; **mix the butter and flour into a ~** travaillez le beurre et la farine pour en faire une pâte; **liver ~** pâté m or crème f de foie; **tomato ~** concentré m or purée f de tomate; **garlic ~** purée f d'ail; **almond ~** pâte f d'amandes [b] (= glue) colle f; **wallpaper ~** colle f pour papier peint [c] (jewellery) strass m [2] VT [a] coller; [+ wallpaper] enduire de colle; **to ~ photos into an album** coller des photos dans un album [b] (Comput) coller, insérer; **to ~ text into a document** insérer du texte dans un document [c]‡ (= thrash) flanquer une raclée à*; (= defeat) flanquer une déculottée à*; (= criticize) descendre en flammes* [3] COMP [jewellery] en strass ► **paste-up** N (Comput) collage m; (Typ) montage m

► **paste up** [1] VT SEP [+ notice, list] afficher; [+ photos etc] coller; (Typ) monter [2] ~**-up** N → **paste**

pasteboard ['peɪstbɔːd] N [a] (= card) carton m [b] (US: also **pastry board**) planche f à pâtisserie

pastel ['pæstəl] N [a] (= pencil) (crayon m) pastel m [b] (= drawing) (dessin m au) pastel m [c] (also ~ **colour**) ton m pastel inv

pastern ['pæstən] N paturon m

pasteurization [,pæstərai'zeɪʃən] N pasteurisation f

pasteurize ['pæstəraɪz] VT pasteuriser

pasteurized ['pæstəraɪzd] ADJ pasteurisé

pastiche [pæs'tiːʃ] N pastiche m

pastille ['pæstɪl] N pastille f

pastime ['pɑːstaɪm] N passe-temps m inv, divertissement m, distraction f

pasting: ['peɪstɪŋ] N (= thrashing) raclée* f; (= defeat) déculottée* f; **to give sb a ~** (physically) flanquer une raclée à qn*; (= defeat) flanquer une déculottée à qn*; (= criticize) descendre qn en flammes*

pastor ['pɑːstə'] N pasteur m

pastoral ['pɑːstərəl] [1] ADJ [a] (= rural) pastoral, champêtre; (Agr) de pâture; (Literat) pastoral; (fig, liter) bucolique, champêtre; ~ **land** pâturages mpl [b] (Rel) pastoral; ~ **letter** lettre f pastorale [c] (Educ etc) [role, duties] de conseiller; **in a ~ capacity** dans un rôle de conseiller [2] (Literat, Rel) pastorale f [3] COMP ► **pastoral care system** N (Educ) tutorat m

pastrami [pə'strɑːmɪ] N bœuf fumé très épicé

pastry ['peɪstrɪ] [1] N [a] (NonC) pâte f → **puff**, **short** [b] (= cake) pâtisserie f [2] COMP ► **pastry board** N planche f à pâtisserie

► **pastry brush** N pinceau *m* à pâtisserie ► **pastry case** N croûte *f*; **in a ~ case** en croûte ► **pastry chef**, **pastry cook** N pâtissier *m*, -ière *f* ► **pastry cutter** N (*Culin: gen*) coupe-pâte *m inv*; (*for shapes*) emporte-pièce *m*

pasturage ['pɑːstjʊrɪdʒ] N pâturage *m*

pasture ['pɑːstʃə] 1 N (*Agr*) pré *m*, pâturage *m*; **to put out to ~** (*lit*) mettre au pré ou au pâturage; (*fig*) mettre à la retraite; (*fig*) **to move on to ~s new** changer d'horizon or d'air; **to seek ~s new** chercher de nouveaux horizons, chercher à changer d'air or d'horizon; **greener ~s** cieux *mpl* plus cléments 2 VI paître 3 VT faire paître, pacager 4 COMP ► **pasture land** N herbage *m*, pâturage(s) *m(pl)*

pasty[1] ['peɪstɪ] ADJ pâteux; (*pej*) [*face, complexion*] terreux; (*pej*) **~-faced** au teint terreux; **you look a bit ~** vous avez une mine de papier mâché

pasty[2] ['pæstɪ] N (*Brit Culin*) ≈ petit pâté *m* en croûte (*contenant généralement de la viande, des oignons et des pommes de terre*)

Pat [pæt] [a] *dim* of **Patrick** or **Patricia** [b] surnom des Irlandais

pat[1] [pæt] 1 VT [+ *object*] tapoter, donner une tape à; [+ *animal*] flatter; **he ~ted my hand** il me tapota la main; **to ~ one's stomach** se frotter le ventre; **to ~ sb on the back** (*lit*) tapoter qn dans le dos; (*fig*) complimenter qn, congratuler qn; **to ~ o.s. on the back** s'envoyer des fleurs, s'applaudir 2 N [a] (= *tap*) coup *m* léger, petite tape *f*; (*on animal*) petite tape *f*; **to give sb a ~ on the back** (*lit*) tapoter qn dans le dos; (*fig*) complimenter qn, congratuler qn; **give yourselves** or **you deserve a ~ on the back** s'envoyer des fleurs, s'applaudir [b] (*also* **~ of butter**) (*individual*) plaquette *f* (individuelle) de beurre; (*larger*) plaque *f* de beurre

pat[2] [pæt] 1 ADV [a] (= *exactly suitable*) à propos, à point; **to answer ~** (= *immediately*) répondre sur-le-champ; (= *with repartee*) répondre du tac au tac; **he had his explanation ~** il avait son explication toute prête [b] (= *perfectly*) [*learn*] par cœur; **to know sth off ~** savoir qch sur le bout du doigt; **she had all the answers off ~** elle a pu répondre du tac au tac [c] (= *firm, unmoving*) [*remain*] inflexible; (*US*) **to stand ~*** ne rien faire, refuser de bouger 2 ADJ [*example, answer, remark*] tout prêt

Patagonia [ˌpætə'gəʊnɪə] N la Patagonie

Patagonian [ˌpætə'gəʊnɪən] 1 ADJ patagonien 2 N Patagonien(ne) *m(f)*

patch [pætʃ] 1 N [a] (*for clothes*) pièce *f*; (*for inner tube, airbed*) rustine® *f*; (*over eye*) cache *m*; (*cosmetic: on face*) mouche *f*; (*Med: nicotine, HRT etc*) patch *m*, timbre *m* [b] (= *small area*) [*of colour*] tache *f*; [*of sky*] pan *m*, coin *m*; [*of land*] parcelle *f*; [*of vegetables*] carré *m*; [*of ice*] plaque *f*; [*of mist*] nappe *f*; [*of water*] flaque *f*; (*on dog's back etc*) tache *f*; **a damp ~ on the wall/sheet** une tache d'humidité sur le mur/drap; **he's got a bald ~** il a le crâne un peu dégarni; **a man with a bald ~** un homme à la calvitie naissante ou au crâne un peu dégarni [c] (*fig*) **a bad** or **rough** or **sticky* ~** un moment difficile, une mauvaise passe; **to hit** or **strike a bad ~** entrer dans une mauvaise passe; **to go through a rough ~** traverser une mauvaise passe; **good in ~es** bon par moments; **it isn't a ~ on ...** ça ne soutient pas la comparaison avec ...; **he's not a ~ on our old boss*** il est loin de valoir notre ancien patron; (*stronger*) il n'arrive pas à la cheville de notre ancien patron* [d] (*Comput*) correction *f* (de programme) [e] (*Brit**) [*of policeman, social worker etc*] secteur *m*; **they're off my ~ now** ils ont quitté mon secteur

2 VT [+ *clothes*] rapiécer; [+ *tyre*] réparer, poser une rustine® à

3 COMP ► **patch pocket** N poche *f* appliquée or plaquée ► **patch test** N (*Med*) test *m* cutané

► **patch together** VT SEP [+ *garment*] rapiécer; (*hum*) [+ *old car etc*] retaper*; **a new government was hastily ~ed together** un gouvernement de fortune a été mis sur pied à la hâte

► **patch up** VT SEP [+ *clothes*] rapiécer; [+ *machine*] rafistoler*;* [+ *injured person*] rafistoler*; **to ~ up a quarrel** se rabibocher*, se raccommoder*; **they soon ~ed up their differences** ils se sont vite rabibochés* or raccommodés*

patchwork ['pætʃwɜːk] 1 N (*lit, fig*) patchwork *m* 2 COMP [*quilt*] en patchwork; [*landscape*] bigarré; (*pej = lacking in unity*) fait de pièces et de morceaux, fait de bric et de broc

patchy ['pætʃɪ] ADJ (*lit, also fig pej*) inégal

pate [peɪt] N tête *f*; **a bald ~** un crâne chauve

pâté ['pæteɪ] N (*NonC: Culin*) pâté *m*

patella [pə'telə] N (*pl* **patellae** [pə'teliː]) rotule *f*

paten ['pætən] N patène *f*

patent ['peɪtənt] 1 ADJ [a] (*frm = obvious*) [*fact, dishonesty*] patent, manifeste; **it was a ~ impossibility** c'était manifestement impossible [b] [*invention*] breveté; **~ medicine** spécialité *f* pharmaceutique [c] (*also* **~ leather**) cuir *m* verni; **~ (leather) shoes** chaussures *fpl* vernies ou en cuir verni 2 N (= *licence*) brevet *m* d'invention; (= *invention*) invention *f* brevetée; **to take out a ~ (on sth)** déposer un brevet (pour qch); **"~(s) applied for"** « demande de brevet déposée »; **"~ pending"** « brevet en cours d'homologation »; **to come out of** or (*US*) **come off ~** tomber dans le domaine public 3 VT faire breveter 4 COMP ► **patent agent** N (*Jur*) conseil *m* en propriété industrielle ► **Patent and Trademark Office** N (*US*) = **Patent Office** ► **patent attorney** N (*US*) = **patent agent** ► **patent engineer** N conseil *m* en brevets d'invention ► **patent holder** N détenteur *m*, -trice *f* or titulaire *mf* d'un brevet d'invention ► **patent leather** N → **1c** ► **Patent Office** N (*Brit*) ≈ Institut *m* national de la propriété industrielle ► **patent right** N propriété *f* industrielle ► **Patent Rolls** NPL (*Brit*) registre *m* des brevets d'invention ► **patent still** N alambic dans lequel la distillation est ininterrompue

patentable ['peɪtəntəbl] ADJ (*Jur etc*) brevetable

patentee [ˌpeɪtən'tiː] N breveté(e) *m(f)*

patently ['peɪtntlɪ] ADV (*frm*) manifestement, de toute évidence; **~ obvious** tout à fait évident, absolument évident

patentor ['peɪtəntə'] N (*Jur etc*) personne ou organisme délivrant des brevets d'invention

pater[†]‡ ['peɪtə'] N (*esp Brit*) pater‡ *m*, paternel‡ *m*

paterfamilias [ˌpeɪtəfə'mɪlɪæs] N (*pl* **patresfamilias** [ˌpɑːtreɪzfə'mɪlɪæs]) paterfamilias *m*

paternal [pə'tɜːnl] ADJ paternel

paternalism [pə'tɜːnəlɪzəm] N paternalisme *m*

paternalist [pə'tɜːnəlɪst] ADJ paternaliste

paternalistic [pətɜːnə'lɪstɪk] ADJ (*pej*) (trop) paternaliste

paternalistically [pətɜːnə'lɪstɪklɪ] ADV (*pej*) de façon (trop) paternaliste

paternally [pə'tɜːnəlɪ] ADV paternellement

paternity [pə'tɜːnɪtɪ] 1 N (*lit, fig*) paternité *f* 2 COMP ► **paternity leave** N congé *m* parental (*pour le père*) ► **paternity order** N (*Jur*) (ordonnance *f* de) reconnaissance *f* de pa-

ternité ► **paternity suit** N (*Jur*) action *f* en recherche de paternité

paternoster [ˌpætə'nɒstə'] N [a] (*Rel*) Pater *m*; **the Paternoster** le Pater, le Notre Père [b] (= *elevator*) pater noster *m*

path[1] [pɑːθ] 1 N [a] (*also* **~way**) (*in woods etc*) sentier *m*, chemin *m*; (*in garden*) allée *f*; (*also* **footpath**: *beside road*) sentier *m* (pour les piétons); **to clear a ~ through the woods** ouvrir un sentier or un chemin dans les bois; (*fig*) **to beat a ~ to sb's door** accourir en foule chez qn → **primrose** [b] (*trajectory, route*) [*of river*] cours *m*; [*of sun*] route *f*; [*of bullet, missile, spacecraft, planet, hurricane*] trajectoire *f*; [*of advancing person*] chemin *m*; **to cross sb's ~** se trouver sur le chemin de qn; **to destroy everything in one's ~** [*person, storm etc*] tout détruire sur son chemin or son passage; **he found his ~ barred** il trouva le chemin or le passage barré; **he stepped off the kerb into the ~ of a car** il est descendu du trottoir au moment où une voiture arrivait [c] (*fig = way*) voie *f*; (*fig*) **she criticized the ~ the government was taking** elle a critiqué la voie suivie par le gouvernement; **the ~ to success** la voie or le chemin du succès; **the ~ towards peace/independence** la voie menant à la paix/l'indépendance; (*esp US*) **to break a new ~** montrer une voie nouvelle 2 COMP ► **path-breaking** ADJ (*esp US*) révolutionnaire ► **path name** N (*Comput*) nom *m* d'accès

path[2]* [pɑːθ] 1 N ABBR = **pathology** 2 COMP ► **path lab** N laboratoire *m* or labo* *m* d'analyses

Pathan [pə'tɑːn] 1 ADJ pathan 2 N Pathan(e) *m(f)*

pathetic [pə'θetɪk] ADJ [a] (= *very sad*) [*sight, grief*] pitoyable, navrant; **a ~ attempt** une tentative désespérée; **it was ~ to see it** cela faisait peine à voir, c'était un spectacle navrant [b] (* = *feeble*) [*person, piece of work, performance*] pitoyable, minable [c] (*Literat*) (**the**) **~ fallacy** l'anthropomorphisme *m*

pathetically [pə'θetɪklɪ] ADV [a] (= *pitifully*) [*behave, moan, weep*] d'une façon pitoyable, pitoyablement; **~ thin/shy** d'une maigreur/timidité pitoyable; **she was ~ glad to see him** elle était terriblement heureuse de le voir [b] (*pej* = *feebly*) lamentablement; **I wimped out, ~** je me suis lamentablement dégonflé*

pathfinder ['pɑːθfaɪndə'] N (*gen*) pionnier *m*, -ière *f*; (*Aviat*) avion *m* éclaireur

pathogen ['pæθədʒən] N (*Med*) agent *m* pathogène

pathogenic [ˌpæθə'dʒenɪk] ADJ pathogène

pathological [ˌpæθə'lɒdʒɪkəl] ADJ pathologique

pathologically [ˌpæθə'lɒdʒɪkəlɪ] ADV [*jealous, violent*] pathologiquement

pathologist [pə'θɒlədʒɪst] N pathologiste *mf*

pathology [pə'θɒlədʒɪ] N pathologie *f*

pathos ['peɪθɒs] N pathétique *m*; **the ~ of the situation** ce que la situation a (or avait etc) de pathétique; **told with great ~** raconté d'une façon très émouvante or très pathétique; **a film full of ~** un film très pathétique

patience ['peɪʃəns] N [a] patience *f*; **to have ~** prendre patience, savoir patienter; **she doesn't have much ~ with children** elle n'est pas très patiente or elle n'a pas beaucoup de patience avec les enfants; **I have no ~ with these people** ces gens m'exaspèrent; **to lose (one's) ~** perdre patience (**with sb/sth** avec qn/qch), s'impatienter (**with sb/sth** contre qn/qch); **my ~ is wearing thin** ma patience a des limites; **I am out of ~** ◊ **my ~ is exhausted** ma patience est à bout, je suis à bout de patience; **the ~ of Job** une patience d'ange → **possess**, **tax**, **try** [b] (*Brit Cards*) réussite *f*; **to play ~** faire des réussites

patient ['peɪʃənt] [1] ADJ patient (**with** avec); **(you must) be ~!** patientez!, (un peu de) patience!*; **I've been ~ long enough!** j'ai assez patienté or attendu!, ma patience a des limites! [2] N (gen) patient(e) m(f); (post-operative) opéré(e) m(f); **a doctor's ~s** (undergoing treatment) les patients or les malades d'un médecin; (on his/her list) les clients mpl d'un médecin; **psychiatric ~** malade mf psychiatrique; **cancer ~** cancéreux m, -euse f; **heart ~** cardiaque mf → **in, outpatient**

patiently ['peɪʃəntlɪ] ADV patiemment, avec patience

patina ['pætɪnə] N [a] (on surface) patine f [b] (= small amount) vernis m, aura f

patio ['pætɪəʊ] [1] N patio m [2] COMP ► **patio doors** NPL (esp Brit) portes-fenêtres fpl (donnant sur un patio)

Patna ['pætnə] [1] N Patna f [2] COMP ► **Patna rice** N riz à grain long

patois ['pætwɑː] N (pl **patois**) patois m

pat. pend. (ABBR = **patent pending**) → **patent**

patriarch ['peɪtrɪɑːk] N patriarche m

patriarchal [,peɪtrɪ'ɑːkəl] ADJ patriarcal

patriarchy [,peɪtrɪ'ɑːkɪ] N patriarcat m, gouvernement m patriarcal

Patricia [pə'trɪʃə] N Patricia f

patrician [pə'trɪʃən] ADJ, N patricien(ne) m(f)

patricide ['pætrɪsaɪd] N (= crime) parricide m; (= person) parricide mf

Patrick ['pætrɪk] N Patrice m, Patrick m

patrimony ['pætrɪmənɪ] N [a] patrimoine m, héritage m [b] (Rel) biens-fonds mpl (d'une église)

patriot ['peɪtrɪət] N patriote mf

patriotic [,pætrɪ'ɒtɪk] [1] ADJ [deed, speech] patriotique; [person] patriote [2] COMP ► **the Patriotic Front** N (Pol) le Front patriote

patriotically [,pætrɪ'ɒtɪkəlɪ] ADV patriotiquement, en patriote

patriotism ['pætrɪətɪzəm] N patriotisme m

patrol [pə'trəʊl] [1] N [a] (NonC) patrouille f; **to go on ~** aller en patrouille, faire une ronde; **to be on ~** être de patrouille [b] [of troops, police, scouts, guides etc] patrouille f; (= ship, aircraft on patrol) patrouilleur m; (= police officer) agent m de police ► **border, immigration, customs** [2] VT [police, troops etc] patrouiller dans, faire une patrouille dans [3] VI [troops, police] patrouiller; (fig = walk about) **to ~ up and down** faire les cent pas [4] COMP [helicopter, vehicle] de patrouille ► **patrol car** N (Police) voiture f de police ► **patrol leader** N (Mil, scouts, guides) chef mf de patrouille ► **patrol wagon** N (US) voiture f or fourgon m cellulaire

patrolboat [pə'trəʊlbəʊt] N (Naut) patrouilleur m

patrolman [pə'trəʊlmən] N (pl **-men**) [a] (US) agent m de police; **Patrolman Jim Sheppe** l'agent m Jim Sheppe [b] (Aut) agent m (d'une société de dépannage)

patrolwoman [pə'trəʊl,wʊmən] N (pl **-women**) (US) femme f agent de police; **Patrolwoman Jill Brown** l'agent m Jill Brown

patron ['peɪtrən] [1] N [a] [of artist] protecteur m, -trice f; [of a charity] patron(ne) m(f) [b] (= customer) [of hotel, shop] client(e) m(f); **our ~s** (Comm) notre clientèle f; (Theat) notre public m; **"parking for ~s only"** « stationnement réservé à la clientèle »; **"~s are reminded that ..."** « nous rappelons à notre aimable clientèle que ... » [c] **= patron saint** [2] COMP ► **patron of the arts** N protecteur m, -trice f des arts, mécène m ► **patron saint** N saint(e) patron(ne) m(f)

patronage ['pætrənɪdʒ] N [a] (gen) (= support) [of artist etc] patronage m; (= financial backing) parrainage m, sponsoring m; **under the ~ of ...** sous le patronage de ..., sous les auspices de

...; **~ of the arts** mécénat m, protection f des arts [b] (Rel) droit m de disposer d'un bénéfice; (Pol) droit m de présentation [c] (Pol pej) népotisme m; (US) **to give out ~ jobs** nommer ses amis politiques à des postes de responsabilité, attribuer des postes aux petits copains*

patroness† ['peɪtrənes] N [of artist] protectrice f

patronize ['pætrənaɪz] VT [a] (pej) traiter avec condescendance [b] (Comm) [+ shop, firm] donner or accorder sa clientèle à, se fournir chez; [+ dress shop] s'habiller chez; [+ bar, cinema, club] fréquenter

patronizing ['pætrənaɪzɪŋ] ADJ [person] condescendant; [look, tone, smile, manner] condescendant, de condescendance

patronizingly ['pætrənaɪzɪŋlɪ] ADV [speak] d'un ton condescendant, avec condescendance; [behave, bow, pat, laugh] de façon condescendante; [smile] d'un air condescendant

patronymic [,pætrə'nɪmɪk] [1] N patronyme m, nom m patronymique [2] ADJ patronymique

patsy: ['pætsɪ] N (US) pigeon* m, gogo* m, victime f

patter[1] ['pætə'] [1] N [of comedian, conjurer] bavardage m, baratin* m; [of salesman etc] boniment m, baratin* m [2] VI (also **~ away, ~ on**) jacasser, baratiner*

patter[2] ['pætə'] [1] N [of rain, hail] crépitement m, bruit m; **a ~ of footsteps** un petit bruit de pas pressés; (hum) **we'll soon be hearing the ~ of tiny feet** on attend un heureux événement [2] VI [footsteps] trottiner; [rain] tambouriner (**on** contre); [hail] crépiter [3] COMP ► **patter song** N (Mus) ≈ ritournelle f
► **patter about, patter around** VI trottiner çà et là

pattern ['pætən] [1] N [a] (= design: on material, wallpaper etc) dessin(s) m(pl), motif m; **a floral ~** un motif floral or à fleurs; **a ~ of small dots on the page** un motif de petits points sur la page; **the torches made ~s of light on the walls** la lumière des torches dessinait des formes sur les murs; **the ~ on a tyre** les sculptures fpl d'un pneu [b] (= style) style m; **various ~s of cutlery** différents modèles de couverts; **dresses of different ~s** des robes de styles différents [c] (Sewing: also **paper ~**) patron m; (also **knitting ~**) modèle m [d] (fig = model) exemple m, modèle m; (fig) **~ of living** mode m de vie; **on the ~ of ...** sur le modèle de ...; **this set a** or **the ~ for future meetings** cela a institué un modèle pour les réunions suivantes [e] (= standard, coherent behaviour etc) **eating ~s** habitudes fpl alimentaires; **behaviour ~s of teenagers** les types mpl de comportement chez les adolescents; **my sleep(ing) ~s became very disturbed** mes habitudes de sommeil se sont trouvées très perturbées; **his sleep(ing) ~s have returned to normal** il s'est remis à dormir comme avant; **the earth's weather ~s** les tendances fpl climatiques de la terre; **I began to notice a ~ in their behaviour/reactions etc** j'ai commencé à remarquer certaines constantes dans leur conduite/leurs réactions etc; **to be part of a ~** faire partie d'un tout; **it followed the usual ~** [meeting, interview, crime, epidemic, drought, storm] cela s'est passé selon le scénario habituel; [timetable, schedule] cela suivait le schéma habituel; **a clear ~ emerges from these statistics** un schéma très net ressort or se dégage de ces statistiques; **the disease followed the same ~ everywhere** la maladie a présenté partout les mêmes caractéristiques; **this week's violence follows a sadly familiar ~** les actes de violence de cette semaine suivent un scénario trop familier; **these strikes/attacks all followed the same ~**

ces grèves/attaques se sont toutes déroulées de la même manière; (Econ) **the ~ of trade** la structure ou la physionomie des échanges [f] (= sample) [of material etc] échantillon m [g] (Ling) modèle m; [of sentence] structure f; **on the ~ of ...** sur le modèle de ... [2] VT [a] (= model) modeler (**on** sur); **to ~ o.s. on sb** prendre modèle sur qn [b] (= decorate) orner de motifs [3] COMP ► **pattern book** N (material, wallpaper etc) album m d'échantillons; (Sewing) catalogue m or album m de patrons ► **pattern maker** N (Metal) modeleur m

patterned ['pætənd] ADJ [material, fabric, china] à motifs

patterning ['pætənɪŋ] N (NonC) [a] (= markings) [of creature] (motifs mpl de la) livrée f; **the ~ of the bird's winter/summer plumage** la livrée de cet oiseau pendant l'hiver/l'été [b] (Psych = conditioning) conditionnement m

patty ['pætɪ] [1] N rondelle f (de viande hachée) [2] COMP ► **patty pan** N petit moule m ► **patty shell** N croûte f feuilletée

paucity ['pɔːsɪtɪ] N [of crops, coal, oil] pénurie f; [of money] manque m; [of news, supplies, water] disette f; [of ideas] indigence f, disette f

Paul [pɔːl] N Paul m

Pauline[1] ['pɔːliːn] N Pauline f

Pauline[2] ['pɔːlaɪn] ADJ (Rel = relating to St Paul) paulinien

paulownia [pɔː'ləʊnɪə] N paulownia m

paunch [pɔːntʃ] N [of person] ventre m, panse f, bedaine* f; [of ruminants] panse f

paunchy ['pɔːntʃɪ] ADJ ventripotent

pauper ['pɔːpə'] N indigent(e) m(f), pauvre(sse) m(f); **~'s grave** fosse f commune

pauperism ['pɔːpərɪzəm] N paupérisme m

pause [pɔːz] [1] N [a] pause f; (Mus) point m d'orgue; (Poetry) césure f; **to give sb ~ for thought** ◊ **to give ~ to sb** (frm) faire hésiter qn, donner à réfléchir à qn; **a ~ in the conversation** un petit or bref silence (dans la conversation); **after a ~, he added ...** il marqua une pause et ajouta ...; **he continued speaking without a ~** il continua sur sa lancée or dans la foulée; **there was a ~ for discussion/for refreshments** on s'arrêta pour discuter/pour prendre des rafraîchissements; **they ~d for lunch** ils ont fait une pause pour le déjeuner or une pause-déjeuner [2] VI [a] (in work, activity) marquer un temps d'arrêt, (for a rest) faire une pause; **to ~ for breath** s'arrêter pour reprendre haleine [b] (in speaking) marquer une pause, marquer un temps d'arrêt; **to ~ for thought** prendre le temps de réfléchir; **without pausing to consider the consequences** sans prendre le temps de réfléchir aux conséquences [c] (= linger over) s'arrêter (**on** sur) [3] VT **to ~ a video/tape** appuyer sur la touche « pause » d'un magnétoscope/magnétophone; **can you ~ it there?** pouvez-vous appuyer sur la touche « pause »?

pavane [pə'vɑːn] N pavane f

pave [peɪv] VT [+ street] paver; [+ yard] carreler, paver; (fig) **~d with gold** pavé d'or; (fig) **to ~ the way (for)** ouvrir la voie (à)

pavement ['peɪvmənt] [1] N [a] (Brit) trottoir m [b] (= road surface) (of stone, wood) pavé m, pavage m; (stone slabs) dallage m; (ornate) pavement m [c] (US = roadway) chaussée f [2] COMP ► **pavement artist** N (Brit) artiste mf de rue ► **pavement café** N (Brit) café m avec terrasse (sur le trottoir)

pavilion [pə'vɪlɪən] N [a] (= tent, building) pavillon m (tente, construction) [b] (Brit Sport) pavillon m des vestiaires

paving ['peɪvɪŋ] [1] N [a] (material) (= stone) pavé m; (= flagstones) dalles fpl; (= tiles) carreaux mpl [b] (= paved ground) pavage m,

dallage *m*, carrelage *m* → **crazy** 2 COMP
► **paving stone** N pavé *m*

Pavlovian [pævˈləʊvɪən] ADJ pavlovien

paw [pɔː] 1 N a [*of animal*] patte *f* b (: =
hand) patte* *f*; **keep your ~s off!** bas les
pattes!* 2 VT a (*also* ~ **at**) [*animal*] donner
un coup de patte à; **to ~ the ground** [*horse*]
piaffer b (: *pej*) [*person*] tripoter*; (*amorously*)
tripoter*, peloter:

pawky [ˈpɔːkɪ] ADJ (*Scot*) narquois

pawl [pɔːl] N cliquet *m*

pawn[1] [pɔːn] N a (*Chess*) pion *m* b (*fig*) **to
be sb's ~** être le jouet de qn, se laisser manœuvrer par qn; **he is a mere ~ in the** (game)
il n'est qu'un pion sur l'échiquier

pawn[2] [pɔːn] 1 VT [+ *one's watch etc*] mettre
en gage *or* au mont-de-piété *or* au clou* 2 N
a (= *thing pledged*) gage *m*, nantissement *m*
b (*NonC*) **in ~** en gage, au mont-de-piété, au
clou*; **to get sth out of ~** dégager qch du
mont-de-piété 3 COMP ► **pawn ticket** N reconnaissance *f* du mont-de-piété

pawnbroker [ˈpɔːnˌbrəʊkə*] N prêteur *m*,
-euse *f* sur gages; **~'s** = **pawnshop**

pawnshop [ˈpɔːnʃɒp] N bureau *m* de prêteur
sur gages, mont-de-piété *m*

pawpaw [ˈpɔːpɔː] N papaye *f*

pax [pæks] 1 EXCL (*Brit*†*: during game*) pouce!
2 N (*Rel*) paix *f*; (*Hist*) **Pax Romana** pax *f* romana; (*Pol*) **Pax Americana/Britannica** pax *f*
americana/britannica

▼ **pay** [peɪ] (*vb: pret, ptp* **paid**) 1 N (*gen*) salaire
m; (*esp of manual worker*) paye *or* paye *f*; (*Mil,
Naut*) solde *f*, paie *f*; **three weeks' ~** trois semaines de salaire *or* paie; **to be on half/full ~**
toucher la moitié/l'intégralité de son salaire
or de sa paie; **in the ~ of ...** à la solde de ...;
(*pej*), aux gages de ...; **the ~'s not very good** ce
n'est pas très bien payé; **holidays with ~**
congés *mpl* payés; **time off without ~** congé *m*
sans solde → **equal, half, holiday, take**

2 VT a [+ *person*] payer (**to do** à faire, **for
doing** pour faire); [+ *tradesman, bill, fee*] payer,
régler; **to ~ sb £20** payer qn 20 livres; **he
paid them for the book/the ticket** il les a
payés pour le livre/le billet; **he paid £20 for
the book/the ticket** il leur a acheté le
livre/le billet pour 20 livres; **he paid them
£20 for the work** il les a payés 20 livres pour
ce travail; **he paid me for my trouble** il m'a
dédommagé de mes peines; **I don't ~ you to
ask questions** je ne vous paie pas pour poser
des questions; **we're not paid for that** on n'est
pas payé pour cela, on n'est pas payé pour*;
that's what you're paid for c'est pour cela
qu'on vous paie; **I get paid on Fridays** je touche ma paie *or* mon salaire le vendredi; **I am
paid on a monthly basis** *or* **by the month** je
suis payé au mois
b [+ *instalments, money*] payer; [+ *deposit*]
verser; [+ *debt*] acquitter, s'acquitter de, régler; [+ *loan*] rembourser; **he paid £20 for the
ticket** il a payé le billet 20 livres; **the company paid a high premium for Mr Peter's services**
la société a payé cher pour obtenir les services de M. Peter; **he paid a lot for his suit** son
costume lui a coûté cher, il a payé son costume très cher; **they ~ good wages** ils paient
bien; **to ~ cash (down)** payer comptant; **to ~
money into an account** verser de l'argent à un
compte
c (*Fin*) [+ *interest*] rapporter; [+ *dividend*] distribuer; **shares that ~ 5%** des actions qui
rapportent 5%; (*fig*) **his generosity paid dividends** sa générosité a porté ses fruits; **... but
it paid him in the long run** ... mais il y a gagné
en fin de compte; **it would ~ you to be nice
to him** vous gagneriez à être aimable avec lui;
it won't ~ him to tell the truth il ne gagnera
rien à dire la vérité
d (*fig*) **he's paid his dues** (*for achievement*) il
en a bavé*; (*for crime, error*) il a payé sa dette
(*fig*); **he's paid his debt to society** il a payé sa

dette envers la société; **the business is ~ing
its way now** l'affaire couvre ses frais maintenant; **he likes to ~ his (own) way** il préfère
payer sa part *or* son écot; **to ~ the price (for
sth)** subir *or* payer les conséquences (de qch);
to ~ the price of fame/success payer le prix de
la célébrité/du succès; **the city is still ~ing the
price of war** la ville souffre encore des conséquences de la guerre; **they've paid a high
price for their obstinacy/for being so naïve** ils
ont payé très cher leur entêtement/leur naïveté; **to put paid to sb's hopes/chances/plans**
ruiner les espoirs/chances/projets de qn; **I'll
soon put paid to him!*** j'aurai vite fait de lui
régler son compte; ▪(*PROV*) **he who ~s the
piper calls the tune** celui qui paie a le droit de
décider comment sera dépensé son argent →
3b

e **to ~ sb a visit** rendre visite à qn; **we paid a
visit to Paris on our way south** nous avons fait
un petit tour à Paris en descendant vers le
sud; (*euph*) **to ~ a visit*** *or* a **call*** aller au petit
coin*; **to ~ one's last respects to sb** rendre
un dernier hommage à qn

3 VI a payer; **his job ~s well** son travail
paie bien; (*on bus*) **"~ on entry"** « paiement à
l'entrée »; **I offered to ~ for my mother** j'ai
proposé de payer pour ma mère; **to ~ for the
meal** payer le repas; (*fig*) **he paid dearly for it**
il l'a payé cher; **to ~ through the nose for
sth*** payer le prix fort pour qch; **we'll have to
~ through the nose for it*** ça va nous coûter
les yeux de la tête*; (*fig*) **you'll ~ for this!** vous
(me) le payerez!; (*fig*) **I'll make him ~ for that**
je lui ferai payer ça; (*fig: for achievement*) **he's
had to ~ for it** il en a bavé*; **he made a mistake and he's had to ~ for it** il a fait une
erreur et il l'a payée cher → **cash, instalment,
nail**

b (= *be profitable*) [*business, deal*] rapporter,
être rentable; **does it ~?** est-ce que ça
rapporte?, c'est rentable?; **we need to sell
600 copies to make it ~** nous devons vendre
600 exemplaires pour rentrer dans nos frais
or pour que ce soit rentable; **crime doesn't ~**
le crime ne paie pas; **it ~s to advertise** la publicité rapporte; **it always ~s to ask an expert's opinion** on a toujours intérêt à demander l'avis d'un expert; **it doesn't ~ to be
polite these days** on ne gagne rien à être *or*
cela ne paie pas d'être poli de nos jours; **it
doesn't ~ to tell lies** cela ne sert à rien de
mentir, on ne gagne rien à mentir

4 COMP [*dispute, negotiation*] salarial ► **pay-
and-display** ADJ (*Brit*) [*car park*] à horodateur
► **pay as you earn, pay-as-you-go** (*US*) N
retenue *f* à la source de l'impôt sur le revenu
► **pay award** N augmentation *f* de salaire
collective ► **pay bargaining** N (*NonC*) négociations *fpl* salariales ► **pay bed** N (*Brit*) lit *m*
(d'hôpital) payant (*par opposition aux soins gratuits du système de Sécurité sociale britannique*)
► **Pay Board** N Commission *f* des salaires
► **pay-cable channel** N (*TV*) chaîne *f* câblée
payante ► **pay check** N (*US*) = **pay cheque**
► **pay cheque** N (*Brit*) salaire *m*, paie *or* paye
f ► **pay day** N jour *m* de paie; (*Sport*) **to have
a big ~ day** décrocher le gros lot ► **pay desk**
N caisse *f*; (*Theat*) caisse *f*, guichet *m* ► **pay
dirt**: N (*Min*) **to hit** *or* **strike ~ dirt** (*lit*)
découvrir un filon; (*fig*) trouver le filon
► **pay envelope** N (*US*) enveloppe *f* de paie
► **pay increase** N = **pay rise** ► **pay(ing)-in
slip, pay(ing)-in voucher** N (*Banking*) bordereau *m* de versement ► **pay packet** N (*Brit*)
enveloppe *f* de paie; (*fig*) salaire *m*
► **pay-per-view** N pay per view *m*, télévision *f* à la carte ◆ ADJ **~-per-view television** le
pay per view, la télévision à la carte; **~-per-
view channel** (chaîne *f* de) télévision *f* en pay
per view *or* à la carte; **~-per-view programme**
émission *f* en pay per view *or* à la carte; **on a
~-per-view basis** en pay per view, à la carte
► **pay phone** N téléphone *m* public ► **pay**

raise N (*US*) = **pay rise** ► **pay rise** N (*Brit*)
augmentation *f* de salaire ► **pay station** N
(*US*) téléphone *m* public ► **pay structure** N
(*Ind*) barème *m* des salaires ► **pay-TV** N télévision *f* payante

► **pay back** 1 VT SEP a [+ *stolen money*] rendre, restituer; [+ *loan*] rembourser; [+ *person*]
rembourser; **I paid my brother back the £10 I
owed him** j'ai remboursé à mon frère les 10 livres que je lui devais b (*fig* = *get even with*)
to ~ sb back for doing sth faire payer à qn
qch qu'il a fait; **I'll ~ you back for that!** je
vous le revaudrai! 2 **~back** N → **payback**

► **pay down** VT SEP **he paid £10 down** (*as deposit*) il a versé un acompte de 10 livres;
(*whole amount in cash*) il a payé 10 livres
comptant

► **pay in** VT SEP verser (**to** à); **to ~ in money at
the bank** verser de l'argent sur son compte,
créditer son compte (bancaire); **to ~ a sum in
to an account** verser une somme sur un
compte; **to ~ in a cheque** déposer un chèque

► **pay off** 1 VI [*risk, trick, scheme, work*] être
payant; [*decision*] être valable *or* payant;
[*perseverance, patience*] être récompensé; **his
patience paid off in the long run** finalement il
a été récompensé de sa patience *or* sa patience a été récompensée 2 VT SEP a [+
debts] s'acquitter de, régler; [+ *bill*] régler;
[+ *creditor, loan*] rembourser; (= *bribe*) **to ~ sb
off** donner des pots-de-vin à qn, acheter qn;
(*fig*) **to ~ off an old score** régler un vieux
compte; (*fig*) **to ~ off a grudge** satisfaire un
désir de vengeance b (= *discharge*) [+ *worker,
staff*] licencier; [+ *servant*] donner son
compte à, congédier; (*Naut*) [+ *crew*] débarquer 3 **~off** N → **payoff**

► **pay out** 1 VI [*fruit machine etc, insurance policy*] rembourser 2 VT SEP a [+ *rope*] laisser
filer b [+ *money*] (= *spend*) débourser, dépenser; **they paid out a large sum of money
on new equipment** ils ont dépensé beaucoup
d'argent pour acheter de nouveaux équipements

► **pay up** 1 VI payer; **~ up!** payez! 2 VT FUS
[+ *amount*] payer, verser; **~ up what you owe
me!** payez-moi *or* remboursez-moi ce que
vous me devez → **paid**

payable [ˈpeɪəbəl] ADJ (= *due, owed*) payable;
~ in/over three months payable dans/en trois
mois; (*Comm, Fin, Jur*) **~ when due** payable à
l'échéance; **~ to bearer/on demand/at sight**
payable au porteur/sur présentation/à vue;
to make a cheque ~ to sb faire un chèque à
l'ordre de qn; **please make cheques ~ to
...** ◊ **cheques should be made ~ to ...** les chèques doivent être libellés à l'ordre de ...; **the
interest ~ on the loan** les intérêts à payer sur
le prêt

payback [ˈpeɪˌbæk] N [*of investment*] retour *m*,
bénéfice *m*; [*of debt*] remboursement *m*

PAYE [ˌpiːeɪwaɪˈiː] (*Brit*) (ABBR = **pay as you earn**)
→ **pay**

payee [peɪˈiː] N [*of cheque*] bénéficiaire *mf*; [*of
postal order*] destinataire *mf*, bénéficiaire *mf*

payer [ˈpeɪə*] N payeur *m*, -euse *f*; [*of cheque*]
tireur *m*, -euse *f*; **to be a bad ~** être un mauvais payeur; **late ~s** personnes *fpl* qui paient
avec du retard

paying [ˈpeɪɪŋ] 1 ADJ a (= *who pays*) payant;
~ guest pensionnaire *mf*, hôte *m* payant
b (= *profitable*) [*business*] rémunérateur (-trice
f), qui rapporte, rentable; [*scheme*] rentable;
it's not a ~ proposition ce n'est pas (une proposition) rentable 2 N [*of debt*] règlement *m*,
acquittement *m*; [*of creditor*] remboursement
m; [*of money*] paiement *m*, versement *m*
3 COMP ► **paying-in book** N (*Banking*) carnet *m* de bordereaux de versement
► **paying-in slip** N (*Banking*) bordereau *m* de
versement

payload [ˈpeɪləʊd] N (= *cargo*) charge *f*; [*of ve-*

hicle, boat, spacecraft] charge f utile ; (= explosive energy) [of warhead, bomb load] puissance f

paymaster ['peɪˌmɑːstəʳ] [1] N (gen) intendant m, caissier m, payeur m ; (Naut) commissaire m ; (Mil) trésorier m [2] COMP ► **Paymaster General** N (Brit) trésorier-payeur de l'Échiquier

▼ **payment** ['peɪmənt] [1] N [a] (= money) (gen) paiement m ; (to creditor) remboursement m ; (into account) versement m ; (= monthly repayment) mensualité f ; **to make (a)** ~ faire or effectuer un paiement ; **method of** ~ mode m de paiement ; **£150, in monthly** ~**s of £10** 150 livres, payables en mensualités de 10 livres ; **prompt/late** ~ paiement m rapide/en retard ; **without** ~ à titre gracieux ; **we demand** ~ **in full** nous exigeons le paiement intégral ; ~ **by instalments** paiement m par traites or à tempérament ; ~ **by results** prime f au rendement ; ~ **in kind** paiement m en nature ; **to make** ~ **in kind** payer en nature ; **on** ~ **of a supplement/a deposit/£50** moyennant un supplément/une caution/la somme de 50 livres ; **the car will be yours on** ~ **of the balance** la voiture vous appartiendra une fois que vous aurez réglé le solde ; **as** or **in** ~ **for ...** en règlement or paiement de ... ; **as** or **in** ~ **for a debt** en règlement d'une dette ; **most major credit cards are accepted in** ~ les principales cartes de crédit sont acceptées comme moyen de paiement ; **as** or **in** ~ **for your help** pour vous remercier de votre aide ; **cash** ~ (= not credit) paiement m comptant ; (= in cash) paiement m en liquide → **balance, down¹, easy, exgratia, interest, miss, mortgage, nonpayment, part, redundancy, stop**
[b] (fig: for favour) récompense f ; **those who fought alongside the conquistadors were granted land in** ~ ceux qui combattaient aux côtés des conquistadors recevaient une terre en récompense ; **travelling minstrels provided entertainment and were given food and lodging in** ~ les ménestrels offraient un spectacle et recevaient le gîte et le couvert en échange
[2] COMP ► **payment card** N carte f de paiement ► **payment date** N date f de paiement ; **your first** ~ **date will be ...** la date de votre premier remboursement est le ... ► **payment system** N système m de paiement or de règlement ► **payment terms** NPL modalités fpl de paiement

payoff ['peɪɒf] N [a] [of person] remboursement m (total) ; [of debt etc] règlement m (total) ; (* = reward) récompense f ; (* = bribe) pot-de-vin m [b] (* = outcome) résultat m final ; (= climax) comble m, bouquet* m [c] (= punch line) chute f

payola* [peɪˈəʊlə] N (NonC: US) pots-de-vin mpl

payout ['peɪaʊt] N (in competition) prix m ; (from insurance) dédommagement m

payroll ['peɪrəʊl] [1] N (Ind) (= list) registre m du personnel ; (= money) masse f salariale ; (= all the employees) personnel m, effectifs mpl ; **the factory has 60 people on the** ~ or **a** ~ **of 60** l'usine compte 60 employés or salariés ; **to be on a firm's** ~ être employé par une société [2] COMP ► **payroll tax** N taxe f sur les traitements et salaires

payslip ['peɪslɪp] N feuille f or bulletin m de paie

PB N (Sport) (ABBR = **personal best**) → **personal**

PBS [ˌpiːbiːˈes] N (US) ABBR = **Public Broadcasting Service**

PBX [ˌpiːbiːˈeks] N (Brit Telec) (ABBR = **private branch exchange**) PBX m, commutateur m privé

PC [piːˈsiː] [1] N [a] (ABBR = **personal computer**) PC m [b] (ABBR = **Police Constable**) → **police** ; → **plod** [c] (ABBR = **Privy Councillor**) → **privy** [2] ADJ* (ABBR = **politically correct**) → **politically** ; → POLITICALLY CORRECT

pc [piːˈsiː] N ABBR = **postcard**

p.c. (ABBR = **per cent**) → **per**

p/c N [a] (ABBR = **prices current**) prix mpl courants [b] (ABBR = **petty cash**) → **petty**

PCB [ˌpiːsiːˈbiː] N [a] (ABBR = **polychlorinated biphenyl**) PCB m [b] (ABBR = **printed circuit board**) → **printed**

pcm ADV (ABBR = **per calendar month**) par mois ; **2,000 francs** ~ 2 000 F/m, 2 000 F par mois

PCP [ˌpiːsiːˈpiː] N [a] ® (Drugs) (ABBR = **phencyclidine**) PCP® f, phencyclidine f [b] (Med) ABBR = **pneumocystis carinii pneumonia**

PD [piːˈdiː] N (US) (ABBR = **police department**) → **police**

pd (ABBR = **paid**) payé

pdq* [ˌpiːdiːˈkjuː] ADV (ABBR = **pretty damn quick**) en vitesse*

PDSA [ˌpiːdiːesˈeɪ] N (Brit) (ABBR = **People's Dispensary for Sick Animals**) → **people**

PDT [ˌpiːdiːˈtiː] (US) (ABBR = **Pacific Daylight Time**) → **pacific**

PE [piːˈiː] N (Scol) (ABBR = **physical education**) → **physical**

pea [piː] [1] N (Bot, Culin) pois m ; **garden** or **green** ~**s** petits pois mpl ; (fig) **they are as like as two** ~**s (in a pod)** ils se ressemblent comme deux gouttes d'eau → **process¹, shell, split, sweet** [2] COMP ► **pea green** N vert m inv pomme ► **pea-green** ADJ vert pomme inv ► **pea jacket** N (Naut) caban m ► **pea soup** N soupe f aux pois ; (from split peas) soupe f aux pois cassés

peace [piːs] [1] N [a] (NonC) (= not war) paix f ; (= treaty) (traité m de) paix f ; **a lasting** ~ une paix durable ; **after a long (period of)** ~ **war broke out** après une longue période de paix la guerre éclata ; **to be at** ~ être en paix ; **to come in** ~ venir en ami(s) ; **to live in** or **at** ~ **with ...** vivre en paix avec ... ; **to make** ~ faire la paix ; **to make** ~ **with ...** signer or conclure la paix avec ... ; (fig) **to make (one's)** ~ **with sb** se réconcilier avec qn
[b] (= calm) paix f, tranquillité f ; **to be at** ~ **with oneself** avoir la conscience tranquille or en paix ; **to live at** ~ **with the world** avoir une vie paisible ; **to be at** ~ **with the world** ne pas avoir le moindre souci ; ~ **of mind** tranquillité f d'esprit ; **to disturb sb's** ~ **of mind** troubler l'esprit de qn ; **leave him in** ~ laisse-le tranquille, fiche-lui la paix* ; **to sleep in** ~ dormir tranquille ; **he gives them no** ~ il ne les laisse pas en paix ; **anything for the sake of** ~ **and quiet** n'importe quoi pour avoir la paix ; **I need a bit of** ~ **and quiet** j'ai besoin d'un peu de calme ; **to hold** or **keep one's** ~† garder le silence, se taire → **rest**
[c] (Jur etc = civil order) paix f, ordre m public ; **to disturb** or **break the** ~ troubler l'ordre public ; **to keep the** ~ [citizen] ne pas troubler l'ordre public ; [police] veiller à l'ordre public ; (fig = stop disagreement) maintenir le calme or la paix → **breach, justice**
[2] COMP (Pol) [poster, march, meeting, demonstration] pour la paix ► **peace campaign** N campagne f pour la paix ; (for nuclear disarmament) campagne f pour le désarmement nucléaire ► **peace campaigner** N militant(e) m(f) pour la paix ; (for nuclear disarmament) militant(e) m(f) pour le désarmement nucléaire ► **peace conference** N conférence f de paix ► **Peace Corps** N (US) organisation américaine de coopération et d'aide aux pays en développement ► **peace dividend** N économies sur le budget militaire réalisées depuis la fin d'une guerre et notamment de la guerre froide ► **peace initiative** N initiative f de paix ► **peace lobby** N lobby m pour la paix ; (for nuclear disarmament) lobby m pour le désarmement nucléaire ► **peace-loving** ADJ pacifique ► **Peace Movement** N Mouvement m pour la paix ; (for nuclear disarmament) Mouvement m pour le désarmement nucléaire ► **peace offensive** N offensive f de paix

► **peace offering** N (Rel = sacrifice) offrande f propitiatoire ; (fig) cadeau m or gage m de réconciliation ► **peace pipe** N calumet m de la paix ► **the peace process** N le processus de paix ► **peace studies** NPL (Educ) études fpl sur la paix ► **peace talks** NPL pourparlers mpl de paix ► **peace treaty** N (traité m de) paix f

peaceable ['piːsəbl] ADJ paisible, pacifique

peaceably ['piːsəblɪ] ADV [say, speak, agree] pacifiquement ; [gather, assemble, behave] de manière pacifique

peaceful ['piːsful] ADJ [a] (= quiet) [place, countryside, atmosphere, reign, period] paisible ; [life, place, sleep] paisible, tranquille ; [meeting] calme [b] (= not quarrelsome) [person, disposition, nation] pacifique, paisible ; (= non-violent) [demonstration] non violent ; [solution] pacifique ; ~ **coexistence** coexistence f pacifique ; **to do sth by** or **through** ~ **means** faire qch en utilisant des moyens pacifiques ; **the** ~ **uses of atomic energy** l'utilisation pacifique de l'énergie nucléaire ; **for** ~ **purposes** à des fins pacifiques

peacefully ['piːsfəlɪ] ADV [demonstrate, disperse] paisiblement, dans le calme ; [live, sleep, lie] paisiblement, tranquillement ; [die] paisiblement ; **the demonstration passed off** ~ la manifestation s'est déroulée dans le calme or paisiblement

peacefulness ['piːsfulnɪs] N paix f, tranquillité f, calme m

peacekeeper ['piːsˌkiːpəʳ] N (Mil) soldat m de la paix

peacekeeping ['piːsˌkiːpɪŋ] [1] N maintien m de la paix [2] COMP [operation, policy] de maintien de la paix ► **peacekeeping force** N (Mil) force f de maintien de la paix

peacemaker ['piːsˌmeɪkəʳ] N pacificateur m, -trice f, conciliateur m, -trice f ; (esp international politics) artisan m de la paix

peacemaking ['piːsˌmeɪkɪŋ] [1] N (NonC) négociations fpl de paix [2] ADJ [efforts] de conciliation ; [role] de conciliateur ; **the** ~ **process** le processus de paix

peacenik* ['piːsnɪk] N (pej) pacifiste mf

peacetime ['piːstaɪm] [1] N **in** or **during** ~ en temps de paix [2] ADJ en temps de paix

peach¹ [piːtʃ] [1] N [a] (Bot) pêche f ; (also ~ **tree**) pêcher m [b] (‡ = beauty) **she's a** ~! elle est jolie comme un cœur !* ; (Sport) **that was a** ~ **of a shot!** quel beau coup ! ; **what a** ~ **of a dress!** quel amour* de robe ! [2] ADJ (couleur) pêche inv [3] COMP ► **peach blossom** N fleur f de pêcher ► **peaches-and-cream complexion** N teint m de pêche ► **peach melba** N pêche f Melba ► **the Peach State** N (US) la Géorgie ► **peach stone** N noyau m de pêche

peach*² [piːtʃ] VTI (Prison) **to** ~ **(on) sb** moucharder qn*

peachy ['piːtʃɪ] ADJ [a] (in colour) [complexion] de pêche [b] (esp US:* = excellent) super* ; **how's it going? — just** ~! ça va ? — ça roule !

peacock ['piːkɒk] [1] N (pl peacocks or peacock) paon m [2] COMP ► **peacock blue** N bleu m paon ► **peacock-blue** ADJ bleu paon inv ► **peacock butterfly** N paon m de jour → **proud**

peahen ['piːhen] N paonne f

peak [piːk] [1] N [a] (= summit) [of mountain] cime f, sommet m ; (= mountain itself) pic m [b] [of cap] visière f
[c] (fig = high point) (on graph) sommet m ; [of career] sommet m, apogée m ; **the** ~ **of perfection** la perfection absolue ; **when the Empire was at its** ~ quand l'Empire était à son apogée ; (Comm) **when demand was at its** ~ quand la demande était à son maximum ; **business was at its** ~ **in 1985** les affaires ont atteint un point culminant en 1985 ; **at the** ~ **of his fame** à l'apogée or au sommet de sa gloire ; **to**

bureau *m* ministre *inv* ▶ **pedestal table** N
guéridon *m*

pedestrian [pɪ'destrɪən] **1** N piéton *m* **2** ADJ
(*fig* = *prosaic*) [*style, speech*] prosaïque, plat
3 COMP ▶ **pedestrian crossing** N (*Brit*)
passage *m* pour piétons, passage *m* clouté
▶ **pedestrian precinct** N (*Brit*) zone *f* piétonne *or* piétonnière ▶ **pedestrian traffic** N
piétons *mpl*; **~ traffic is increasing here** les
piétons deviennent de plus en plus nombreux ici; **"~ traffic only"** « réservé aux piétons » ▶ **pedestrian zone** N (*US*) = **pedestrian precinct**

pedestrianization [pɪ,destrɪənaɪ'zeɪʃən] N
transformation *f* en zone piétonne *or* piétonnière (**of** de), création *f* d'une *or* de
zone(s) piétonne(s) *or* piétonnière(s)

pedestrianize [pɪ'destrɪə,naɪz] VT [+ *area*]
transformer en zone piétonne *or* piétonnière

pediatric [,piː dɪ'ætrɪk] = **paediatric**

pedicab ['pedɪkæb] N cyclopousse *m* (à deux
places)

pedicure ['pedɪkjʊəʳ] N pédicurie *f*; **to have a
~** se faire soigner les pieds (*par un pédicure*)

pedigree ['pedɪgriː] **1** N **a** (= *lineage*) [*of
animal*] pedigree *m*; [*of person*] ascendance *f*,
lignée *f* **b** (= *genealogy*) [*of person, animal*] arbre *m* généalogique **c** (= *document*) [*of dogs,
horses etc*] pedigree *m*; [*of person*] pièce *f* or document *m* généalogique **2** COMP [*dog, cattle
etc*] de (pure) race

pediment ['pedɪmənt] N fronton *m*

pedlar ['pedləʳ] N (*door to door*) colporteur *m*;
(*in street*) camelot *m*

pedological [,piːdə'lɒdʒɪkl] ADJ pédologique

pedologist [pɪ'dɒlədʒɪst] N pédologue *mf*

pedology [pɪ'dɒlədʒɪ] N pédologie *f*

pedometer [pɪ'dɒmɪtəʳ] N podomètre *m*

pedophile ['piːdəʊfaɪl] N = **paedophile**

pee: [piː] **1** VI pisser*, faire pipi* **2** N pisse*
f, pipi* *m*

peek [piːk] **1** N coup *m* d'œil (furtif); **to take
a ~ at sb/sth** jeter un coup d'œil (furtif) à *or*
sur qn/qch **2** VI jeter un coup d'œil (furtif)
(**at** sur, à); **no ~ing!** on ne regarde pas!
3 COMP ▶ **peek-a-boo*** EXCL coucou!
▶ **peek-a-boo blouse*** N (*US*) corsage *m*
semi-transparent

peel [piːl] **1** N [*of apple, potato*] pelure *f*, épluchure *f*; [*of orange*] écorce *f*, peau *f*; (*Culin*)
zeste *m* **2** VT [+ *fruit*] peler, éplucher; [+ *potato*] éplucher; [+ *stick*] écorcer; [+ *shrimps*] décortiquer, éplucher; **to keep one's eyes ~ed***
faire attention, ouvrir l'œil*; **keep your eyes
~ed* for a signpost!** ouvre l'œil* et tâche
d'apercevoir un panneau! **3** VI [*fruit*] se peler; [*paint*] s'écailler; [*skin, part of body*] peler
▶ **peel away 1** VI [*skin*] peler; [*paint*] s'éca-
quamer; [*paint*] s'écailler; [*wallpaper*] se décoller **2** VT SEP [+ *rind, skin*] peler; [+ *film, covering*] détacher, décoller
▶ **peel back** VT SEP [+ *film, covering*] détacher,
décoller
▶ **peel off 1** VI **a** = **peel away 1 b** (= *leave
formation, group etc*) [*plane*] se détacher de la
formation; [*motorcyclists etc*] se détacher du
groupe (or du cortège etc) en virant; **to ~ off
from** s'écarter de, se détacher en virant de
2 VT SEP **a** = **peel away 2 b** (* fig) [+ *garment*] enlever, ôter; **to ~ off one's clothes** enlever ses vêtements, se déshabiller

peeler ['piːləʳ] N **a** (= *gadget*) (couteau-)
éplucheur *m*; (*electric*) éplucheur *m* électrique
b (*Brit*††† = *policeman*) sergent *m* de ville

peelie-wally* ['piːlɪ'wælɪ] ADJ (*Scot*) chétif,
souffreteux

peeling ['piːlɪŋ] **1** N **~s** [*of fruit, vegetables*]
pelures *fpl*, épluchures *fpl*; **potato ~s** épluchures *fpl* de pommes de terre **2** ADJ [*skin*]
qui pèle; [*wallpaper*] qui se décolle; [*paint*] qui
s'écaille

peep¹ [piːp] **1** N **a** (= *peek*) coup *m* d'œil,
regard *m* furtif; **have a ~!** jette un coup
d'œil!; **to have** *or* **take a ~ at sth** jeter un
coup d'œil à *or* sur qch, regarder qch furtivement *or* à la dérobée; **she had a ~ at her present** elle a jeté un (petit) coup d'œil à son cadeau; **to get** *or* **have a ~ at the exam papers**
jeter un (petit) coup d'œil discret sur les sujets d'examen
b [*of gas*] veilleuse *f*, (toute) petite flamme *f*;
a ~ of light showed through the curtains un
rayon de lumière filtrait entre les rideaux
2 VI jeter un coup d'œil, regarder furtivement; **to ~ at sth** jeter un coup d'œil à qch,
regarder qch furtivement; **she ~ed into the
box** elle a jeté un coup d'œil *or* elle a regardé
furtivement à l'intérieur de la boîte; **he was
~ing at us from behind a tree** il nous regardait
furtivement *or* à la dérobée de derrière un arbre; **to ~ over a wall** regarder furtivement
par-dessus un mur, passer la tête par-dessus
un mur; **to ~ through a window** regarder furtivement *or* jeter un coup d'œil par la fenêtre
3 COMP ▶ **peep-bo*** EXCL coucou!
▶ **Peeping Tom** N voyeur *m* ▶ **peep show**
N (= *box*) visionneuse *f*; (= *pictures*) vues *fpl*
stéréoscopiques; (= *event*) peep-show *m*

▶ **peep out 1** VI **a** (= *peek*) **she was ~ing out
from behind the curtains** elle passait le nez de
derrière les rideaux; **the sun ~ed out from behind the clouds** le soleil s'est montré entre les
nuages **b** (= *appear*) [*gun, petticoat etc*] dépasser (**from** de) **2** VT **she ~ed her head out**
elle a passé la tête

peep² [piːp] **1** N [*of bird*] pépiement *m*, piaulement *m*; [*of mouse*] petit cri *m* aigu; (*fig*)
one ~ out of you and I'll send you to bed!* si
tu ouvres la bouche je t'envoie te coucher!;
there wasn't a ~ of protest about this il n'y a
pas eu la moindre protestation à ce sujet
2 VI [*bird*] pépier, piauler; [*mouse*] pousser
de petits cris aigus

peepers: ['piːpəz] NPL quinquets* *mpl*

peephole ['piːphəʊl] N (*gen*) trou *m* (*pour
épier*); (*in front door etc*) judas *m*

peeptoe ['piːptəʊ] ADJ **~ sandal/shoe** sandale
f/chaussure *f* à bout découpé

peer¹ [pɪəʳ] VI (= *look*) **to ~ at sb** regarder qn;
(*inquiringly/doubtfully/anxiously*) regarder qn
d'un air interrogateur/dubitatif/inquiet;
(*short-sightedly*) regarder qn avec les yeux de
myope; **to ~ at a book/photograph** scruter
(du regard) un livre/une photographie; **she
~ed into the room** elle regarda dans la pièce
d'un air interrogateur *or* dubitatif *etc*; **to ~
out of the window/over the wall** regarder par
la fenêtre/par-dessus le mur d'un air interrogateur *etc*; **to ~ into sb's face** regarder qn
d'un air interrogateur *etc*, dévisager qn; **she
~ed around over her spectacles** elle regarda
autour d'elle par-dessus ses lunettes

peer² [pɪəʳ] **1** N **a** (= *social equal*) pair *m*; ac-
cepted by his ~s accepté par ses pairs **b** (*liter:
in achievement etc*) égal(e) *m(f)*; **as a musician
he has no ~** comme musicien il est hors pair
or il n'a pas son pareil **c** (= *noble: also* **~ of
the realm**) pair *m* (du royaume) **2** COMP ▶ **hereditary,
life 3** COMP ▶ **peer group** N (*Sociol*) pairs
mpl ▶ **peer pressure** N pressions *fpl*
exercées par l'entourage *or* par les autres

peerage ['pɪərɪdʒ] N (= *rank*) pairie *f*; (*collective
= the peers*) pairs *mpl*, noblesse *f*; (= *list of
peers*) nobiliaire *m*; **to inherit a ~** hériter
d'une pairie; **to be given a ~** être anobli →
life

peeress ['pɪərɪs] N pairesse *f*

peerless ['pɪəlɪs] ADJ hors pair, sans pareil

peeve* [piːv] **1** VT mettre en rogne* **2** N **pet
~** bête *f* noire (*fig*)

peeved* [piːvd] ADJ irrité, en rogne*

peevish ['piːvɪʃ] ADJ grincheux, maussade;
[*child*] grognon, de mauvaise humeur

peevishly ['piːvɪʃlɪ] ADV d'un air maussade,
avec (mauvaise) humeur

peevishness ['piːvɪʃnɪs] N maussaderie *f*,
mauvaise humeur *f*

peewee* ['piːwiː] (*US*) **1** ADJ minuscule **2** N
(= *child*) petit bout de chou*, enfant *m* haut
comme trois pommes*

peewit ['piːwɪt] N vanneau *m*

peg [peg] **1** N **a** (*wooden*) cheville *f*; (*metal*)
fiche *f*; (*for coat, hat*) patère *f*; (= *tent peg*) piquet *m*; (*Climbing*) piton *m*; [*of violin*] cheville
f; [*of cask*] fausset *m*; (*Croquet*) piquet *m*; (*Brit
= clothes peg*) pince *f* à linge; (*Brit*) **to buy a
dress off the ~** acheter une robe de prêt-à-
porter *or* de confection; **I bought this off the
~** c'est du prêt-à-porter, j'ai acheté ça tout fait
→ **off**; **to take sb down a ~** *or* **two** remettre qn
à sa place, rabattre le caquet à qn; (*fig*) **a ~ to
hang a complaint on** un prétexte de plainte,
un prétexte *or* une excuse pour se plaindre →
level, square
b (*Brit*) **a ~ of whisky** un whisky-soda
2 VT **a** (*gen*) fixer à l'aide de fiches (*or* de
piquets *etc*); (*Tech*) cheviller; **to ~ a tent
down** fixer une tente avec des piquets; **to ~
clothes (out) on the line** étendre du linge sur
la corde
b (*Econ*) [+ *prices, wages*] stabiliser, bloquer;
to ~ prices to sth lier les prix à qch; **they
~ged their currencies to the dollar** ils ont fixé
le cours de leurs monnaies par rapport au
dollar
c (*US* = *categorize*) **to have sb ~ged as an
extremist/a delinquent** cataloguer qn comme
extrémiste/délinquant
d (*Climbing*) pitonner
3 COMP ▶ **peg pants** NPL (*US*) ≈ pantalon
m fuseau

▶ **peg away*** VI bosser*, bûcher*; **he's ~ging
away at his maths** il bosse* *or* bûche* ses
maths

▶ **peg out 1** VI (‡ = *die*) casser sa pipe‡,
clamser‡ **2** VT SEP [+ *piece of land*] piqueter,
délimiter → **peg 2a**

Pegasus ['pegəsəs] N Pégase *m*

pegboard ['pegbɔːd] N (*Games*) plateau *m*
perforé (*utilisé dans certains jeux*)

pegleg* ['pegleg] N jambe *f* de bois

pejoration [,piːdʒə'reɪʃən] N péjoration *f*

pejorative [pɪ'dʒɒrətɪv] ADJ péjoratif

peke* [piːk] N ABBR = **pekin(g)ese**

Pekin [piː'kɪn], **Peking** [piː'kɪŋ] N Pékin *m*

Pekin(g)ese [,piːkɪ'niːz] N (*pl inv*) (= *dog*) pékinois *m*

Pekinologist [,piːkə'nɒlədʒɪst] N (*Pol*) sinologue *mf*

pekoe ['piːkəʊ] N (*thé m*) pekoe *m*

pelagic [pɪ'lædʒɪk] ADJ pélagique

pelargonium [,pelə'gəʊnɪəm] N pélargonium
m

pelf [pelf] N (*pej*) lucre *m* (*pej*), richesses *fpl*

pelican ['pelɪkən] **1** N pélican *m* **2** COMP
▶ **pelican crossing** N (*Brit*) passage *m* pour
piétons (*avec feux de circulation*)

pellagra [pə'leɪgrə] N pellagre *f*

pellet ['pelɪt] N [*of paper, bread*] boulette *f*; (*for
gun*) (grain *m* de) plomb *m*; (*Med*) pilule *f*; [*of
owl etc*] boulette *f* (de résidus regorgés); [*of
chemicals*] pastille *f*

pell-mell ['pel'mel] ADV **a** (= *in a jumble*)
[*throw, heap*] pêle-mêle; **the puppies tumbled
~ into their basket** les chiots se sont précipités pêle-mêle dans leur panier **b** (= *full tilt*)
[*run, dash, drive*] comme un fou; **she ran ~ to
the hospital** elle a couru comme une folle à
l'hôpital

pellucid [pe'luːsɪd] ADJ pellucide (*liter*),
transparent; (*fig*) [*style*] clair, limpide; [*mind*]
lucide, clair

pelmet ['pelmɪt] N (*esp Brit*) (*wooden*) lambrequin *m*; (*cloth*) cantonnière *f*

Peloponnese [ˌpeləpə'niːs] N **the ~** le Péloponnèse

Peloponnesian [ˌpeləpə'niːʃən] ADJ péloponnésien; **the ~ War** la guerre du Péloponnèse

pelota [pɪ'ləʊtə] N pelote f basque

pelt¹ [pelt] [1] VT bombarder (**with** de); **they were ~ed with stones/tomatoes** on les a bombardés de pierres/de tomates [2] VI [a] **the rain is** or **it's ~ing down*** ◊ **it's ~ing with rain*** il tombe des cordes*, il pleut à torrents or à seaux; **~ing rain** pluie f battante [b] (= run) **to ~ down the street** descendre la rue à toutes jambes; **she ~ed out of the house** elle est sortie de la maison en trombe or comme une flèche [3] N (**at**) **full ~** à toute vitesse, à fond de train

pelt² [pelt] N (= skin) peau f; (= fur) fourrure f

pelves ['pelviːz] NPL of **pelvis**

pelvic ['pelvɪk] [1] ADJ pelvien [2] COMP ▶ **pelvic floor** N plancher m pelvien ▶ **pelvic girdle** N ceinture f pelvienne

pelvis ['pelvɪs] N (pl **pelvises** or **pelves**) bassin m, pelvis m

pem(m)ican ['pemɪkən] N pemmican m

pen¹ [pen] [1] N stylo m; (= ball-point) stylo m à bille; (= felt-tip) (crayon m) feutre m; (= fountain-pen) stylo m à plume; **to put ~ to paper** prendre la plume, écrire; **a new novel from the ~ of ...** un nouveau roman de ...; **to live by one's ~** vivre de sa plume → **quill** [2] VT [+ letter] écrire; [+ article] rédiger [3] COMP ▶ **pen-and-ink drawing** N dessin m à la plume ▶ **pen friend** N (Brit) correspondant(e) m(f) ▶ **pen name** N pseudonyme m, nom m de plume ▶ **pen nib** N plume f (de stylo) ▶ **pen pal*** N = **pen friend**

pen² [pen] (vb: pret **penned**, ptp **penned** or **pent**) [1] N [of animals] parc m, enclos m; (also **playpen**) parc m (d'enfant); (also **submarine ~**) abri m de sous-marins [2] VT (also **~ in, ~ up**) [+ animals] parquer; [+ people] enfermer, parquer (pej)

pen³ [pen] N (Orn) cygne m femelle

pen⁴* [pen] N (US) (ABBR = **penitentiary**) taule‡ f or tôle‡ f, trou‡ m

penal ['piːnl] [1] ADJ [a] [law, clause, policy] pénal; [offence] punissable; **~ reform** réforme f du système pénal [b] (= harsh) [rate, charges] écrasant [2] COMP ▶ **penal code** N code m pénal ▶ **penal colony** N colonie f pénitentiaire ▶ **penal servitude** N (Jur) ~ **servitude (for life)** travaux mpl forcés (à perpétuité) ▶ **penal settlement** N = **penal colony**

penalization [ˌpiːnəlaɪ'zeɪʃən] N pénalisation f

penalize ['piːnəlaɪz] VT [a] (= punish) [+ person] pénaliser; [+ action, mistake] réprimer; **he was ~d for refusing (to ...)** il a été pénalisé pour avoir refusé (de ...); (Sport) **to be ~d for a foul** être pénalisé pour une faute [b] (= work against) pénaliser, défavoriser; **a law that ~s single mothers** une loi qui pénalise or défavorise les mères célibataires; **the rail strike ~s those who haven't got a car** la grève des chemins de fer pénalise ceux qui n'ont pas de voiture

penalty ['penltɪ] [1] N (= punishment) peine f; (= fine) pénalité f, amende f; (Sport) pénalisation f; (Ftbl etc) penalty m; **the ~ for murder is death** le meurtre est passible de la peine de mort; **"no smoking: maximum ~ £500"** « interdiction de fumer: jusqu'à 500 livres d'amende en cas d'infraction »; (in games) **a five-point ~ for a wrong answer** cinq points de pénalité pour chaque erreur; **on ~ of** sous peine de; **under ~ of death** sous peine de mort; **he has paid the ~ for neglecting his responsibilities** il n'a pas assumé ses responsabilités et en a subi les conséquences; **he has paid the ~ for (his) success** il a payé la rançon du succès

[2] COMP ▶ **penalty area, penalty box** N (Ftbl) surface f de réparation ▶ **penalty clause** N (Jur) clause f pénale ▶ **penalty goal** N (Rugby etc) but m sur pénalité ▶ **penalty kick** N (Ftbl) penalty m; (Rugby) coup m de pied de pénalité ▶ **penalty point** N (Aut, Jur, Sport) point m de pénalité ▶ **penalty shoot-out** N (Ftbl) (épreuve f des) tirs mpl au but ▶ **penalty spot** N (Ftbl) point m de penalty or de réparation

penance ['penəns] N (Rel, fig) pénitence f (**for** de, pour); (Rel) **to give (sb) ~** [priest] donner une pénitence (à qn); **to do ~ for sth** faire pénitence pour qch

pence [pens] NPL of **penny**

penchant ['pɑ̃ʃɑ̃] N penchant m (**for** pour), inclination f (**for** pour)

pencil ['pensl] [1] N [a] crayon m; **to write/draw in ~** écrire/dessiner au crayon; **a coloured ~** un crayon de couleur → **lead²**, **propel** [b] (= thin beam) **a ~ of light shone from his torch** sa lampe de poche projetait un pinceau lumineux [2] VT [+ note] crayonner, écrire au crayon [3] COMP [note, line, mark] au crayon ▶ **pencil box** N plumier m ▶ **pencil case** N trousse f (d'écolier) ▶ **pencil drawing** N dessin m au crayon, crayonnage m ▶ **pencil pusher*** N (US pej) gratte-papier* m, rond-de-cuir* m ▶ **pencil rubber** N gomme f (à crayon) ▶ **pencil sharpener** N taille-crayon m

▶ **pencil in** VT SEP [a] (lit) [+ note] crayonner, écrire au crayon; **to ~ in one's eyebrows** se faire les sourcils au crayon [b] (fig) [+ date, meeting] fixer provisoirement; **we had three dates pencilled in** nous avions fixé trois dates possibles, nous avions retenu provisoirement trois dates; **I've pencilled you in for Thursday** j'ai marqué votre nom provisoirement pour jeudi

pendant ['pendənt] N (on necklace) pendentif m; (= earring) pendant m (d'oreille); (= ceiling lamp) lustre m; (on chandelier etc) pendeloque f

pendency ['pendənsɪ] N (Jur) **during the ~ of the action** en cours d'instance

pending ['pendɪŋ] [1] ADJ [business, question] pendant, en suspens, en souffrance; (Jur) [case] pendant, en instance; **the ~ tray** le casier des affaires en souffrance; **other matters ~ will be dealt with next week** les affaires en suspens seront réglées la semaine prochaine [2] PREP en attendant

pendulous ['pendjʊləs] ADJ [a] (= hanging) [lips, cheeks, nest] [flowers] pendant, qui retombe [b] (= swinging) [movement] de balancement, oscillant

pendulum ['pendjʊləm] N [a] (gen) pendule m; [of clock] balancier m → **swing** [b] (Climbing) pendule m

Penelope [pə'neləpɪ] N Pénélope f

peneplain, peneplane ['piːnɪpleɪn] N pénéplaine f

penes ['piːniːz] NPL of **penis**

penetrable ['penɪtrəbl] ADJ pénétrable

penetrate ['penɪtreɪt] [1] VT [a] [+ area, region, territory] pénétrer dans; **rescue workers are penetrating this remote region** les sauveteurs pénètrent dans cette région isolée; **to ~ enemy territory** pénétrer en or entrer en territoire ennemi; **to ~ the enemy's defences/lines** pénétrer or percer les défenses ennemies/le front ennemi; **the bullet ~d his heart** la balle lui a perforé le cœur; **the knife ~d his heart** le couteau lui est entré dans le cœur; **the car's lights ~d the darkness** les phares de la voiture perçaient l'obscurité; **sunlight cannot ~ the thick foliage** la lumière du soleil ne peut pas passer à travers cette épaisse végétation; **to ~ a mystery/sb's mind** pénétrer or comprendre un mystère/les pensées de qn; **to ~ sb's disguise** percer le déguisement de qn; (Pol) sub-

versive elements have **~d the party** des éléments subversifs se sont infiltrés dans le parti; (Comm) **they managed to ~ the foreign market** ils ont réussi à pénétrer le marché étranger [b] (during sex) pénétrer

[2] VI **to ~ into** [+ area, region, territory] pénétrer dans; [light, water] pénétrer (dans), filtrer dans; **to ~ through** traverser; **the noise ~d into the lobby** le bruit est parvenu or est arrivé jusque dans le hall

penetrating ['penɪtreɪtɪŋ] ADJ [a] [wind, rain] pénétrant; [cold] pénétrant, mordant; [sound, voice, look] pénétrant, perçant [b] (= acute, discerning) [mind, remark] pénétrant, perspicace; [person, assessment] clairvoyant, perspicace

penetratingly ['penɪtreɪtɪŋlɪ] ADV [a] (= piercingly) [speak, shriek] d'une voix perçante [b] (= acutely, discerningly) [assess, observe] avec pénétration, avec perspicacité

penetration [ˌpenɪ'treɪʃən] N (NonC) pénétration f

penetrative ['penɪtrətɪv] ADJ pénétrant; **~ sex** (relations fpl sexuelles avec) pénétration f

penguin ['peŋgwɪn] N (Orn) manchot m

penholder ['pen,həʊldər] N porte-plume m

penicillin [ˌpenɪ'sɪlɪn] N pénicilline f

penile ['piːnaɪl] ADJ pénien

peninsula [pɪ'nɪnsjʊlə] N péninsule f

peninsular [pɪ'nɪnsjʊlər] [1] ADJ péninsulaire [2] COMP ▶ **the Peninsular War** N la guerre d'Espagne (napoléonienne)

penis ['piːnɪs] [1] N (pl **penises** or **penes**) pénis m [2] COMP ▶ **penis envy** N (Psych) envie f du pénis

penitence ['penɪtəns] N pénitence f, repentir m

penitent ['penɪtənt] ADJ, N pénitent(e) m(f)

penitential [ˌpenɪ'tenʃəl] [1] ADJ contrit; (Rel) **~ psalm** psaume m de la pénitence or pénitentiel [2] N [code] pénitentiel m

penitentiary [ˌpenɪ'tenʃərɪ] N [a] (US = prison: also state ~) prison f, (maison f) centrale f [b] (Rel) (= cleric) pénitencier m; (= tribunal) pénitencerie f

penitently ['penɪtəntlɪ] ADV d'un air or d'un ton contrit

penknife ['pennaɪf] N (pl **-knives**) canif m

penmanship ['penmənʃɪp] N calligraphie f

Penn(a) ABBR = **Pennsylvania**

pennant ['penənt] N (Sport etc, also on car, bicycle) fanion m; (Naut) flamme f, guidon m

penniless ['penɪlɪs] ADJ sans le sou, sans ressources; **he's quite ~** il n'a pas le sou, il est sans le sou or sans ressources

Pennine ['penaɪn] **the ~s** ou **the ~ ◊ the ~ Range** les Pennines fpl, la chaîne Pennine

pennon ['penən] N flamme f, banderole f; (Naut) flamme f, guidon m

penn'orth† ['penəθ] N (Brit) = **pennyworth**

Pennsylvania [ˌpensɪl'veɪnɪə] [1] N la Pennsylvanie; **in ~** en Pennsylvanie [2] COMP ▶ **Pennsylvania Dutch** NPL (= people) Allemands mpl de Pennsylvanie ♦ N (= language) dialecte des Allemands de Pennsylvanie

penny ['penɪ] [1] N (value) (pl **pence**) (coins) (pl **pennies**) penny m; **one old/new ~** un ancien/un nouveau penny; **it costs 50 pence** cela coûte 50 pence; **I have five pennies** j'ai cinq pennies, j'ai cinq pièces de un penny; **one ~ in the pound** ≈ un centime le franc; (fig) **they're two** or **ten a ~** on en trouve partout; **he hasn't a ~ to his name** ◊ **he hasn't got two pennies to rub together** il est sans le sou, il n'a pas un sou vaillant; **he didn't get a ~ (out of it)** il n'en a pas tiré un sou; **I'll pay you back every ~** je te rembourserai ce que je te dois jusqu'au dernier sou; **(a) ~ for your thoughts!*** à quoi penses-tu?; **the ~ dropped***

ça a fait tilt!*; (fig) **to count** or **watch the pennies** regarder à la dépense; (fig) **he keeps turning up like a bad ~** pas moyen de se débarrasser de lui ■ (PROV) **a ~ saved is a ~ gained** un sou est un sou ■ (PROV) **in for a ~ in for a pound** (au point où on en est) autant faire les choses jusqu'au bout ■ (PROV) **look after the pennies and the pounds will look after themselves** les petits ruisseaux font les grandes rivières (PROV), il n'y a pas de petites économies → **honest, pretty, spend, worth**

[2] COMP [book, pencil] de quatre sous ► **penny-a-liner*** N pigiste mf, journaliste mf à la pige or à deux sous la ligne ► **penny arcade** N (US) salle f de jeux (avec machines à sous) ► **Penny Black** N (Hist, Philat) penny m noir (premier timbre-poste britannique) ► **penny dreadful**†* N (Brit) (pl **penny dreadfuls**) roman m à quatre sous, roman m à sensation ► **penny-farthing** N (Brit) vélocipède m ► **penny-in-the-slot machine** N (for amusements) machine f à sous; (for selling) distributeur m automatique ► **penny loafer** N (US) mocassin m ► **penny-pincher** N pingre mf, radin(e)* m(f) ► **penny-pinching** N économies fpl de bouts de chandelle ♦ ADJ [person] pingre, radin* ► **penny whistle** N flûteau m ► **penny-wise** ADJ **to be ~-wise and pound-foolish** économiser un franc et en prodiguer mille

pennyweight ['penɪweɪt] N gramme m et demi

pennyworth ['penəθ] N **I want a ~ of sweets** je voudrais pour un penny de bonbons

penologist [piːˈnɒlədʒɪst] N pénologue mf

penology [piːˈnɒlədʒɪ] N pénologie f

penpusher ['penˌpʊʃəʳ] N (esp Brit pej) grattepapier* m, rond-de-cuir* m

penpushing ['penˌpʊʃɪŋ] N (esp Brit pej) travail m de gratte-papier*

pension ['penʃən] [1] N [a] (= state payment) pension f; (old age) ~ pension f de retraite; **retirement ~** (pension f de) retraite f; **war/ widow's/disability ~** pension f de guerre/de veuve/d'invalidité or ◆ **eligible** [b] (Ind: from company etc) retraite f; **to get a ~** toucher une retraite or une pension (de retraite); **it is possible to retire on a ~ at 55** il est possible de toucher une retraite à partir de 55 ans [c] (= allowance: to artist, former servant etc) pension f [2] COMP ► **pension book** N ≈ titre m de pension ► **pension fund** N caisse f or fonds m de retraite, assurance f vieillesse ► **pension plan** N plan m de retraite ► **pension scheme** N régime m de retraite ► **pension off** VT SEP mettre à la retraite

pensionable ['penʃnəbl] ADJ **to be of ~ age** avoir atteint l'âge de la retraite; **this is a ~ job** c'est un emploi qui donne droit à une retraite

pensioner ['penʃənəʳ] N (also **old age ~**) retraité(e) m(f); (any kind of pension) pensionné(e) m(f); (also **war ~**) militaire m retraité; (disabled) invalide m de guerre

pensive ['pensɪv] ADJ pensif, songeur

pensively ['pensɪvlɪ] ADV pensivement, d'un air pensif

pent [pent] [1] VB ptp of **pen²** [2] ADJ (liter) emprisonné [3] COMP ► **pent-up** ADJ [emotions, rage] refoulé, réprimé; [energy] refoulé, contenu; **she was very ~-up** elle était sur les nerfs or très tendue

pentacle ['pentəkl] N pentacle m

Pentagon ['pentəgən] N (US) **the ~** le Pentagone

pentagon ['pentəgən] N pentagone m

pentagonal [pen'tægənl] ADJ pentagonal

pentagram ['pentəgræm] N pentagramme m

pentahedron [ˌpentəˈhiːdrən] N (pl **pentahedrons** or **pentahedra** [ˌpentəˈhiːdrə]) pentaèdre m

pentameter [pen'tæmɪtəʳ] N pentamètre m → **iambic**

Pentateuch ['pentətjuːk] N Pentateuque m

pentathlete [pen'tæθliːt] N pentathlonien(ne) m(f)

pentathlon [pen'tæθlən] N (also **modern ~**) pentathlon m

pentatonic [ˌpentəˈtɒnɪk] ADJ pentatonique

Pentecost ['pentɪkɒst] N Pentecôte f

Pentecostal [ˌpentɪˈkɒstl] ADJ de (la) Pentecôte; [church, beliefs] pentecôtiste

Pentecostalism [ˌpentɪˈkɒstlɪzəm] N pentecôtisme m

Pentecostalist [ˌpentɪˈkɒstlɪst] ADJ, N pentecôtiste mf

penthouse ['penthaʊs] N [a] (also **flat or apartment**) appartement m de grand standing (construit sur le toit d'un immeuble) [b] (Archit = lean-to) auvent m, abri m extérieur; **~ roof** appentis m, toit m en auvent

penultimate [prˈnʌltɪmɪt] [1] ADJ avant-dernier, pénultième [2] N (Ling) pénultième f, avant-dernière syllabe f

penumbra [prˈnʌmbrə] N (pl **penumbras** or **penumbrae** [prˈnʌmbriː]) (Astron) pénombre f

penurious [prˈnjʊərɪəs] ADJ (frm) [a] (= poor) indigent, misérable [b] (= mean) parcimonieux, ladre

penury ['penjʊrɪ] N misère f, indigence f; **in ~** dans la misère or l'indigence

penwiper ['penˌwaɪpəʳ] N essuie-plume m inv

peon ['piːən] N péon m

peony (rose) ['piːənɪ(ˌrəʊz)] N pivoine f

people ['piːpl] [1] NPL [a] (= persons) gens pl (preceding adj gen fem), personnes fpl; **clever ~** les gens mpl intelligents; **all these good ~** toutes ces bonnes gens, tous ces braves gens; **old ~** les personnes fpl âgées; (less respectful) les vieux mpl; **young ~** les jeunes mpl; **~ are more important than animals** les gens or les êtres humains sont plus importants que les animaux; **a lot of ~** beaucoup de gens or de monde; **what a lot of ~!** que de monde!; **the place was full of ~** il y avait beaucoup de monde, il y avait un monde fou*; **she doesn't know many ~** elle ne connaît pas grand monde; **several ~ said ...** plusieurs personnes ont dit ...; **some ~ might prefer to wait** il y a peut-être des gens qui préféreraient attendre, certains préféreraient peut-être attendre; **how many ~?** combien de personnes?; **there were 120 ~ at the lecture** il y avait 120 personnes à la conférence; **they're strange ~** ce sont de drôles de gens; **why ask me of all ~?** pourquoi me le demander à moi?; **what do you ~* think?** qu'est-ce que vous en pensez, vous (tous) or vous autres? → **little¹, other**
[b] (in general) **what will ~ think?** que vont penser les gens?, que va-t-on penser?; **~ say ... on dit ...; don't tell ~ about that!** n'allez pas raconter ça (aux gens)!; **~ get worried when they see that** on s'inquiète quand on voit cela, les gens s'inquiètent quand ils voient cela
[c] (= inhabitants, natives) [of a country] peuple m, population f; [of district, town] habitants mpl, population f; **country ~** les gens mpl de la campagne; **town ~** les habitants mpl des villes, les citadins mpl; **Liverpool ~ are friendly** à Liverpool les gens sont gentils, les habitants de Liverpool sont gentils; **the ~ of France** les Français mpl; **English/French ~** les Anglais mpl/Français mpl
[d] (Pol) **the ~** le peuple; **government by the ~** gouvernement m par le peuple; **~ of the Republic!** citoyens!; **the ~ at large** le grand public; **the minister must tell the ~ the truth** le ministre doit dire la vérité au pays; **a man of the ~** un homme du peuple; **the ~'s army** l'armée f populaire; **~'s democracy** démocratie f populaire; (in country's name) **People's**

Democratic Republic (of ...) République f populaire (de ...); **the ~'s war** la guerre du peuple; (US) **'s park** jardin m public → **common**
[e] (* = family) famille f, parents mpl; **how are your ~?** comment va votre famille?, comment ça va chez vous?*
[f] (* = employees, workers) **the marketing ~** les gens mpl du marketing; **the TV ~** les gens mpl de la télé; **I'll get my ~ to look into it** je vais demander à mon personnel d'examiner cela
[2] N (sg = nation, race etc) peuple m, nation f, race f; **the Jewish ~** le peuple juif; **the ~s of the East** les nations de l'Orient
[3] VT peupler (**with** de)
[4] COMP ► **people-carrier** N (Brit Aut) monospace m ► **People's Dispensary for Sick Animals** N (Brit) association qui dispense des soins vétérinaires gratuits

PEP [pep] N (Brit Fin) (ABBR = **personal equity plan**) ≈ CEA m

pep* [pep] N (NonC) entrain m, punch* m; **to be full of ~** avoir la pêche* or la frite* [2] COMP ► **pep pill*** N excitant m, stimulant m ► **pep rally** N (US Scol) réunion des élèves (ou des étudiants) avant un match interscolaire, pour encourager leur équipe ► **pep talk*** N discours m or paroles fpl d'encouragement

► **pep up*** [1] VI [person] s'animer, être ragaillardi; [business, trade] reprendre, remonter [2] VT SEP [+ person] remonter le moral à, ragaillardir; [+ one's social life, love life] redonner du piment à; [+ party, conversation] animer; [+ drink, plot] corser

┌─── **PEP RALLY** ───┐

Aux États-Unis, un **pep rally** est une réunion de lycéens ou d'étudiants qui souhaitent stimuler le moral de leur équipe sportive avant un match. La manifestation comprend des discours d'encouragement mais aussi un défilé de l'orchestre de l'école (ou de l'université) avec ses majorettes. Le terme est parfois utilisé pour les meetings politiques ou les séminaires d'entreprise ayant pour but de motiver les militants ou les employés.

peplos, peplus ['peplǝs] N (pl **peploses**) péplum m

pepper ['pepǝʳ] [1] N [a] (= spice) poivre m; **white/black ~** poivre m blanc/gris or noir [b] (= vegetable) poivron m; **red/green ~** poivron m rouge/vert [2] VT [a] (Culin) poivrer [b] (fig) **to ~ sb with shot** cribler qn de plombs; **to ~ a speech with quotations** émailler or truffer un discours de citations; **the minister was ~ed with questions** le ministre a été assailli or bombardé de questions [3] COMP ► **pepper-and-salt** ADJ [cloth] chiné noir et blanc inv; [beard, hair] poivre et sel inv ► **pepper gas** N gaz m poivre ► **pepper mill** N moulin m à poivre ► **pepper shaker** N = **pepperpot**

peppercorn ['pepəkɔːn] [1] N grain m de poivre [2] COMP ► **peppercorn rent** N (Brit) loyer m très modique

peppermint ['pepəmɪnt] [1] N [a] (= sweet) pastille f de menthe [b] (= plant) menthe f poivrée [2] ADJ (also **~-flavoured**) à la menthe

pepperoni [ˌpepəˈrəʊnɪ] N saucisson sec de porc et de bœuf très poivré

pepperpot ['pepəpɒt] N poivrier m, poivrière f

peppery ['pepərɪ] ADJ [food, taste] poivré; (fig) [person] irascible, emporté; [speech] irrité

peppy* ['pepɪ] ADJ (US) [person] (= energetic) énergique; (= lively) plein d'entrain; [car] nerveux

pepsin ['pepsɪn] N pepsine f

peptic ['peptɪk] [1] ADJ digestif [2] COMP ► **peptic ulcer** N (Med) ulcère m de l'estomac; **he has a ~ ulcer** il a un ulcère à l'estomac

peptone ['peptəʊn] N peptone f

per [pɜːʳ] **1** PREP **a** par; **~ head** par tête, par personne; **~ head of population** par habitant; **30 miles ~ gallon** ≈ 8 litres aux cent (km); **to drive at 100km ~ hour** rouler à 100 (km) à l'heure; **she is paid 85 francs ~ hour** elle est payée 85 francs (de) l'heure; **30 francs ~ kilo** 30 francs le kilo **b** (Comm) **~ post** par la poste; **as ~ invoice** suivant facture; **as ~ normal*** or **usual*** comme d'habitude; (Jur) **~ pro** (ABBR = per procurationem) [= by proxy] p.p. **2** COMP ► **per annum** ADV par an ► **per capita** ADV par personne ► **per capita income** N (Econ) revenu m par habitant ► **per cent** ADV pour cent; **a ten ~ cent discount/increase** un rabais/une augmentation de dix pour cent ► **per day, per diem** ADV par jour; (US) **a ~ diem of 100 dollars** une indemnité journalière de 100 dollars ► **per se** ADV en soi

peradventure [ˌpərədˈventʃəʳ] ADV (liter) par hasard, d'aventure (liter)

perambulate [pəˈræmbjʊleɪt] (frm) **1** VT parcourir (un terrain, surtout en vue de l'inspecter) **2** VI marcher, faire les cent pas

perambulation [pəˌræmbjʊˈleɪʃən] N (frm) marche f, promenade(s) f(pl), déambulation f

perambulator† [ˈpræmbjʊleɪtəʳ] N (Brit) voiture f d'enfant, landau m

perborate [pəˈbɔːreɪt] N perborate m

perceive [pəˈsiːv] VT **a** (= see, hear) [+ sound, light] percevoir **b** (= notice) remarquer, apercevoir; (= realize) s'apercevoir de; **he ~d that ...** il a remarqué or s'est aperçu que ... **c** (= view, regard) [+ person, situation] percevoir; **she was ~d as a threat** elle était perçue comme une menace; **the things children ~ as being important** les choses que les enfants perçoivent comme étant importantes; **they ~ themselves as rebels** ils se considèrent comme des rebelles **d** (= understand) [+ implication, meaning] percevoir, saisir

perceived [pəˈsiːvd] ADJ **~ problems** ce que les gens perçoivent comme des problèmes, ce qui constitue un problème aux yeux des gens; **the ~ threat of nuclear weapons** la menace que constituent les armes nucléaires aux yeux des gens; **the president's ~ failure to deal with these problems** le fait qu'aux yeux du public le président n'ait pas réussi à régler ces problèmes

percent [pəˈsent] ADV = **per cent**; → **per**

percentage [pəˈsentɪdʒ] **1** N **a** (= proportion) proportion f; (Math) pourcentage m; **the figure is expressed as a ~** le chiffre est exprimé or donné en pourcentage; **a high ~ were girls** les filles représentaient un fort pourcentage, il y avait une forte proportion de filles; **few foods have such a high ~ of protein** peu d'aliments contiennent autant de protéines (* = share, profit) **to get a ~ on sth** recevoir or toucher un pourcentage sur qch; (fig) **there's no ~ in getting angry with him** ça ne sert à rien de se mettre en colère contre lui **2** COMP ► **percentage distribution** N (Econ) ventilation f en pourcentage ► **percentage point** N point m; **ten points** dix pour cent, dix points

percentile [pəˈsentaɪl] **1** N centile m; **she is in the top earning ~** elle est dans la catégorie des hauts salaires; **he's in the lowest 10th ~ for reading and writing** il est dans la tranche des 10% les moins bons en lecture et en écriture **2** COMP ► **percentile ranking** N classement m par pourcentage

perceptible [pəˈseptəbl] ADJ [sound, movement] perceptible; [difference, increase] perceptible, sensible, appréciable

perceptibly [pəˈseptɪblɪ] ADV (gen) sensiblement; (= visibly) visiblement; **to improve ~** s'améliorer sensiblement; **the weather was ~ warmer** il faisait sensiblement plus chaud; **he brightened ~** il s'égaya visiblement

perception [pəˈsepʃən] N **a** [of sound, sight etc] (also Psych) perception f; **visual ~** la perception visuelle; **one's powers of ~ decrease with age** la faculté de perception diminue avec l'âge **b** (= insight) perspicacité f; **a person of extraordinary ~** une personne d'une extraordinaire perspicacité; **his powers of ~** sa grande perspicacité **c** (= impression, opinion) **the public's ~ of the police/the Conservative party** l'image f de la police/du parti conservateur; **our ~ of the situation is that these problems are due to ...** d'après notre analyse de la situation, ces problèmes sont dus à ...; **the President has been giving his ~ of the situation** le président a donné son analyse de la situation; **consumers have a rather different ~ of the situation** les consommateurs se font une idée assez différente de la situation; **there is a popular ~ that she ...** beaucoup de gens imaginent qu'elle ... **d** (Admin, Comm) [of rents, taxes, profits] perception f

perceptive [pəˈseptɪv] ADJ **a** (= perspicacious) [analysis, assessment] pénétrant; [person] perspicace; **how very ~ of you!** vous êtes très perspicace! **b** [faculty] percepteur (-trice f), de (la) perception

perceptively [pəˈseptɪvlɪ] ADV avec perspicacité

perceptiveness [pəˈseptɪvnɪs] N = **perception b**

perceptual [pəˈseptjʊəl] ADJ [capacity, system, process, error] de perception; (Med, Psych) **~ distortion** troubles mpl de la perception

perch¹ [pɜːtʃ] N (pl **perch** or **perches**) (= fish) perche f

perch² [pɜːtʃ] **1** N **a** [of bird] perchoir m, juchoir m; (fig) **to knock sb off his ~*** faire dégringoler qn de son perchoir*; (Brit hum = die) **to fall** or **drop** or **topple off one's ~*** casser sa pipe* **b** (= measure) perche f **2** VI [bird] (se) percher; [person] se percher, se jucher; **she ~ed on the arm of my chair** elle se percha or se jucha sur le bras de mon fauteuil; (fig) **the tower ~es on the edge of the cliff** la tour est perchée or juchée au bord de la falaise **3** VT [+ object, child, building etc] percher, jucher

perchance [pəˈtʃɑːns] ADV (†† or hum) d'aventure (liter)

percipient [pəˈsɪpɪənt] **1** ADJ [faculty] percepteur (-trice f); [person] fin, perspicace; [choice] éclairé **2** N personne f qui perçoit

percolate [ˈpɜːkəleɪt] **1** VT **to ~ the coffee** passer le café; **~d coffee** café m fait dans une cafetière à pression **2** VI [coffee, water] passer (**through** par); (fig) **the news ~d through from the front** la nouvelle a filtré du front

percolation [ˌpɜːkəˈleɪʃən] N percolation f

percolator [ˈpɜːkəleɪtəʳ] N cafetière f à pression; (in café) percolateur m; **electric ~** cafetière f électrique

percussion [pəˈkʌʃən] **1** N **a** (= impact, noise) percussion f, choc m **b** (Mus) percussion f; **the ~ (section)** les percussions fpl **2** COMP ► **percussion bullet** N balle f explosive ► **percussion cap** N capsule f fulminante ► **percussion drill** N perceuse f à percussion ► **percussion instrument** N (Mus) instrument m à percussion ► **percussion player** N percussionniste mf

percussionist [pəˈkʌʃənɪst] N percussionniste mf

percussive [pəˈkʌsɪv] ADJ percutant

perdition [pəˈdɪʃən] N perdition f, ruine f, perte f; (Rel) perdition f, damnation f

peregrination† [ˌperɪɡrɪˈneɪʃən] N (frm) pérégrination f; **~s** voyage m, pérégrinations fpl

peregrine falcon [ˌperɪɡrɪnˈfɔːlkən] N faucon m pèlerin

peremptorily [pəˈremptərɪlɪ] ADV [speak] d'un ton péremptoire; [behave, gesture] de manière péremptoire, péremptoirement

peremptory [pəˈremptərɪ] ADJ [instruction, order] péremptoire, formel; [argument] décisif, sans réplique; [tone] tranchant, péremptoire

perennial [pəˈrenɪəl] **1** ADJ **a** (= long-lasting, enduring) perpétuel, éternel; (= perpetual, recurrent) perpétuel, continuel **b** (Hort) [plant] vivace, pluriannuel **2** N (Hort) (plante f) vivace f, plante f pluriannuelle → **hardy**

perennially [pəˈrenɪəlɪ] ADV (= always) perpétuellement, constamment; **~ popular** éternellement populaire

perestroika [ˌperəˈstrɔɪkə] N perestroïka f

perfect [ˈpɜːfɪkt] **1** ADJ **a** (= ideal) parfait; **no one is ~** personne n'est parfait, la perfection n'est pas de ce monde; **in a ~ world** dans un monde parfait; **she speaks ~ English** son anglais est parfait or impeccable; **his Spanish is far from ~** son espagnol est loin d'être parfait; **it was the ~ moment to speak to him about it** c'était le moment idéal pour lui en parler; **I've got the ~ solution!** j'ai trouvé la solution idéale! → **word b** (emphatic = complete) véritable, parfait; **he's a** or **the ~ gentleman** c'est le parfait gentleman; **he's a ~ stranger** personne ne le connaît; **he's a ~ stranger to me** il m'est complètement inconnu; **I am a ~ stranger in this town** je ne connais absolument rien de cette ville; **a ~ pest** un véritable fléau; **a ~ fool** un parfait imbécile, un imbécile fini; **I have a ~ right to be here** j'ai tout à fait le droit d'être ici; **it makes ~ sense to me** cela me paraît tout à fait évident **2** N (Gram) parfait m; **in the ~** au parfait **3** [pəˈfekt] VT [+ technique, skill, work of art] parfaire; [+ methods] mettre au point, perfectionner; [+ plan] mettre au point; [+ product, design] perfectionner; **to ~ one's French** se perfectionner en français **4** COMP ► **perfect pitch** N (Mus) **to have ~ pitch** avoir l'oreille absolue ► **perfect tense** N (Gram) parfait m

perfectibility [pəˌfektɪˈbɪlɪtɪ] N perfectibilité f

perfectible [pəˈfektɪbl] ADJ perfectible

perfection [pəˈfekʃən] **1** N **a** (= faultlessness) perfection f; **physical ~** perfection f physique; **to ~** à la perfection **b** (NonC = process of perfecting) perfectionnement m; **the ~ of production methods** le perfectionnement des méthodes de production

perfectionism [pəˈfekʃənɪzəm] N perfectionnisme m

perfectionist [pəˈfekʃənɪst] N perfectionniste mf

perfective [pəˈfektɪv] (Gram) **1** ADJ perfectif **2** N (= aspect) aspect m perfectif **b** (= verb) verbe m perfectif

perfectly [ˈpɜːfɪktlɪ] ADV **a** (= to perfection) parfaitement **b** (= completely) parfaitement, tout à fait; **but it's a ~ good car!** mais il n'y a aucun problème avec cette voiture!, mais cette voiture marche parfaitement!; **you know ~ well!** tu le sais parfaitement bien!; **to be ~ honest, I hate classical music** pour être parfaitement or tout à fait honnête, je déteste la musique classique; **it was ~ horrible**† c'était parfaitement horrible

perfidious [pɜːˈfɪdɪəs] ADJ (liter) perfide, traître (traîtresse f); **~ Albion** la perfide Albion

perfidiously [pɜːˈfɪdɪəslɪ] ADV (liter) perfidement, traîtreusement; [act] en traître, perfidement

perfidy [ˈpɜːfɪdɪ] N (liter) perfidie f

perforate [ˈpɜːfəreɪt] VT [+ paper, metal] perforer, percer; [+ ticket] perforer, poinçonner; (Comput) **~d tape** bande f perforée; **"tear along the ~d line"** « détachez suivant le pointillé »

perforation [ˌpɜːfəˈreɪʃən] N perforation f

perforce† [pəˈfɔːs] ADV (frm) nécessairement, forcément

perform [pəˈfɔːm] **1** VT **a** [+ task] exécuter, accomplir; [+ duty] accomplir, s'acquitter de; [+ function] remplir; [+ miracle] accomplir; [+ rite, ceremony] célébrer; [+ cunnilingus, fellatio] pratiquer; (Jur) [+ contract] exécuter; **to ~ an operation** (gen) accomplir or exécuter une opération; (Med) pratiquer une opération, opérer; **to ~ an abortion** pratiquer un avortement

b (Mus, Theat etc) [+ play, ballet, opera, symphony etc] interpréter; **to ~ a part** interpréter un rôle

2 VI **a** [person] se produire; [actor, musician] jouer; [singer] chanter; [dancer] danser; [clown, acrobat, trained animal] exécuter un or des numéro(s); **he's ~ing at the Vic tonight** [actor] il joue ce soir au Vic; **to ~ on the violin** jouer du violon, exécuter un morceau au violon; **he ~ed brilliantly as Hamlet** il a brillamment interprété Hamlet; (Theat) **when we ~ed in Edinburgh** quand nous avons donné une or des représentation(s) à Édimbourg, quand nous avons joué à Édimbourg; **the clowns ~ed well** les clowns ont bien exécuté leur numéro → **performing**

b [machine, vehicle] marcher, fonctionner; **the car is not ~ing properly** la voiture ne marche pas bien

c (Econ) **to ~ well/badly** [economy, industry, factory] avoir de bons/mauvais résultats; **their shares are ~ing strongly** leurs actions se comportent très bien

performance [pəˈfɔːməns] **1** N **a** (= session, show) (gen) spectacle m; (Theat, Mus) interprétation f, représentation f; (at circus, variety show) séance f; **"no ~ tonight"** «ce soir relâche»; **what a ~!*** (= rigmarole) quelle affaire!, quelle histoire!*; (= fuss about nothing) quel cinéma!*

b (= rendering) [of composition] interprétation f; [of one's act] numéro m; **her ~ as or of Desdemona** son interprétation de Desdémone, son jeu dans le rôle de Desdémone; **the pianist gave a splendid ~** le pianiste a joué de façon magnifique; **Kingsley gives an Oscar-winning ~ as Gandhi** l'interprétation de Kingsley dans le rôle de Gandhi lui a valu un oscar

c (= record, success) [of racehorse, athlete, team] performance f; [of economy, business, factory] résultats mpl; [of currency] tenue f; (Comm) [of product] comportement m; (Fin) [of investment] rentabilité f, rendement m; **their ~ in the election/in the exam/in maths** leurs résultats aux élections/à l'examen/en maths; **his ~ in the debate** sa prestation lors du débat; **economic/financial/academic ~** résultats mpl économiques/financiers/universitaires; **drinking too much can affect your sexual ~** l'excès d'alcool peut affecter vos performances sexuelles; **on past ~, an England victory seems unlikely** si l'on se réfère au passé or d'après ses résultats passés, l'Angleterre semble avoir peu de chances de gagner

d [of engine, vehicle] performance f → **high**

e (NonC = carrying out) [of task, duty] exécution f; [of miracle] accomplissement m; [of ritual] célébration f (**of** de); **in the ~ of my/his duties** dans l'exercice de mes/ses fonctions

f (Ling) performance f

2 COMP ► **performance anxiety** N trac m ► **performance art** N art m performance ► **performance artist** N performer m (artiste pratiquant l'art performance) ► **performance bond** N (Ind) garantie f de bonne fin or de bonne exécution ► **performance bonus** N (Comm, Fin) prime f de rendement ► **performance car** N voiture f à hautes performances ► **performance-enhancing drug** N dopant m ► **performance-related pay** N (Econ) salaire m au rendement

performative [pəˈfɔːmətɪv] (Ling) ADJ, N ~ **(verb)** (verbe m) performatif m

performer [pəˈfɔːmər] N (Mus, Theat etc) artiste mf, interprète mf

performing [pəˈfɔːmɪŋ] ADJ **the ~ arts** les arts mpl du spectacle; **~ artists** les gens mpl du spectacle; **~ seals/dogs** phoques mpl/chiens mpl savants; **~ flea** puce f savante

perfume ['pɜːfjuːm] **1** N parfum m
2 [pəˈfjuːm] VT parfumer

perfumery [pəˈfjuːmərɪ] N parfumerie f

perfunctorily [pəˈfʌŋktərɪlɪ] ADV [bow, greet, kiss] négligemment; [answer, agree, examine, check] pour la forme

perfunctory [pəˈfʌŋktərɪ] ADJ [nod, bow, greeting] négligent, pour la forme; [agreement] superficiel, fait pour la forme

pergola ['pɜːgələ] N pergola f

▼ **perhaps** [pəˈhæps, præps] ADV peut-être; **~ he is right** il a peut-être raison, peut-être qu'il a raison, peut-être a-t-il raison (frm); **coincidence? ~ (so)** coïncidence? peut-être (que oui); **should he have resigned? ~ he should** aurait-il dû démissionner? peut-être (que oui); **the worst prime minister of the century? ~ not, but ...** le pire Premier ministre du siècle? peut-être pas or peut-être que non, mais ...; **is there no hope left? ~ there is** n'y a-t-il plus d'espoir? peut-être que si

perianth ['perɪænθ] N (Bot) périanthe m

pericardium [perɪˈkɑːdɪəm] N (pl **pericardia** [perɪˈkɑːdɪə]) péricarde m

pericarp ['perɪkɑːp] N (Bot) péricarpe m

peridot ['perɪdɒt] N péridot m

perigee ['perɪdʒiː] N périgée m

periglacial [perɪˈgleɪʃəl] ADJ périglaciaire

peril ['perɪl] N (esp liter) péril m, danger m; **he is in great ~** il court un grand péril; **to be in ~ of annihilation** risquer d'être anéanti; **he's in ~ of his life** sa vie est en danger; **the cliff is in ~ of collapsing** la falaise risque de s'effondrer; **at the ~ of** au péril de; **at your ~** à vos risques et périls; (Insurance) **insured ~** risque m assuré

perilous ['perɪləs] ADJ périlleux

perilously ['perɪləslɪ] ADV périlleusement; **~ close** terriblement proche; **to be/come ~ close to disaster/death** etc frôler or friser la catastrophe/la mort etc; **I came ~ close to telling her everything** il s'en est fallu d'un cheveu que je ne lui dise tout

perimeter [pəˈrɪmɪtər] **1** N périmètre m
2 COMP ► **perimeter fence** N périmètre m enclos, clôture f d'enceinte

perinatal [perɪˈneɪtl] ADJ périnatal

perinea [perɪˈnɪə] NPL of **perineum**

perineal [perɪˈniːəl] ADJ périnéal

perineum [perɪˈniːəm] N (pl **perinea**) périnée m

period ['pɪərɪəd] **1** N **a** (= epoch) période f, époque f; (Geol) période f; (= stage: in career, development etc) époque f, moment m; (= length of time) période f; **the classical ~** la période classique; **costumes/furniture of the ~** costumes mpl/meubles mpl de l'époque; **Picasso's blue ~** la période bleue de Picasso; **the ~ from 1600 to 1750** la période entre 1600 et 1750; **the post-war ~** (la période de) l'après-guerre m; **during the whole ~ of the negotiations** pendant toute la période or durée des négociations; **at a later ~** à une époque ultérieure, plus tard; **at that ~ in or of his life** à cette époque or à ce moment de sa vie; **a ~ of social upheaval** une période or une époque de bouleversements sociaux; **the magazine was forced to close down for a ~** le magazine a dû interrompre sa publication pendant quelque temps or un certain temps; **the factory will be closed for an indefinite ~** l'usine sera fermée pour une durée indéterminée; **after a short ~ in hospital** après un court séjour à l'hôpital; **he had several ~s of illness** il a été malade à plusieurs reprises; **the holiday ~** la période des vacances; **bright/rainy ~s** périodes fpl ensoleillées/de pluie; **in the ~ of a year** en l'espace d'une année; **it must be done within a three-month ~** il faut le faire dans un délai de trois mois → **safe**

b (Scol = lesson) ≈ heure f; **first ~** la première heure; **a double ~ of French** ≈ deux heures de français

c (US = full stop) point m; **I won't do it, ~** je ne veux pas le faire or je ne le ferai pas, un point c'est tout

d (= menstruation) règles fpl

e (Phys, Math = reciprocal of frequency) période f

2 COMP ► **period costume**, **period dress** N costume m d'époque ► **period furniture** N (genuine) meuble m d'époque; (copy) meuble m de style ancien ► **period of revolution** or **rotation** N (Astron) période f de rotation ► **period pains** NPL (Med) règles fpl douloureuses ► **period piece** N (fig) curiosité f

periodic [pɪərɪˈɒdɪk] **1** ADJ périodique
2 COMP ► **periodic table** N classification f périodique des éléments

periodical [pɪərɪˈɒdɪkəl] **1** ADJ périodique
2 N (journal m) périodique m, publication f périodique

periodically [pɪərɪˈɒdɪkəlɪ] ADV périodiquement

periodicity [pɪərɪəˈdɪsɪtɪ] N périodicité f

periodontal [perɪˈdɒntl] ADJ parodontal

periosteum [perɪˈɒstɪəm] N (pl **periostea** [perɪˈɒstɪə]) périoste m

peripatetic [perɪpəˈtetɪk] ADJ (= itinerant) ambulant; (Brit) [teacher] qui exerce sur plusieurs établissements; (Philos) péripatétique

peripheral [pəˈrɪfərəl] **1** ADJ périphérique
2 N (Comput) périphérique m

periphery [pəˈrɪfərɪ] N périphérie f; (lit, fig) **on the ~ (of)** en marge (de)

periphrasis [pəˈrɪfrəsɪs] N (pl **periphrases** [pəˈrɪfrəsiːz]) périphrase f, circonlocution f

periscope ['perɪskəʊp] N périscope m

perish ['perɪʃ] **1** VI **a** (liter = die) périr, mourir (from de); **they ~ed in the attempt** ils y ont laissé la vie; **~ the thought!** jamais de la vie!, loin de moi cette pensée!; **if, ~ the thought, you should die suddenly** si par malheur or si, Dieu nous en préserve, vous veniez à mourir subitement **b** [rubber, material, leather] se détériorer, s'abîmer; [food] se détériorer, s'abîmer **2** VT [+ rubber, food] abîmer, détériorer

perishable ['perɪʃəbl] **1** ADJ périssable
2 **perishables** NPL denrées fpl périssables

perished ['perɪʃt] ADJ **a** [rubber] détérioré, abîmé **b** (esp Brit = cold) **to be ~**†* être frigorifié*, crever* de froid

perisher‡ ['perɪʃər] N (Brit) enquiquineur* m, -euse* f; **you little ~!** petite peste!

perishing ['perɪʃɪŋ] ADJ **a** (= very cold) très froid; **outside in the ~ cold** dehors dans le froid glacial or intense; **it was ~* (cold)** il faisait un froid de loup or de canard*; **to be ~*** [person] être frigorifié*, crever* de froid → **perish b** (Brit†‡) sacré* (before n), damné* (before n); **it's a ~ nuisance!** c'est vraiment enquiquinant!*

peristalsis [perɪˈstælsɪs] N (pl **peristalses** [perɪˈstælsiːz]) péristaltisme m

peristyle ['perɪstaɪl] N péristyle m

peritoneum [perɪtəˈnɪəm] N (pl **peritoneums** or **peritonea** [perɪtəˈnɪə]) péritoine m

peritonitis [perɪtəˈnaɪtɪs] N péritonite f

periwig ['perɪwɪg] N (Hist) perruque f

periwinkle ['perɪwɪŋkl] N (Bot) pervenche f; (Zool) bigorneau m

perjure ['pɜːdʒər] VT **to ~ o.s.** se parjurer; (Jur)

► LANGUAGE IN USE: **perhaps** 1, 2.2, 3.2, 15.3, 26.3

faire un faux serment; (*Jur*) **~d evidence** faux serment *m*, faux témoignage *m* (volontaire)

perjurer ['pɜːdʒərər] N parjure *mf*

perjury ['pɜːdʒərɪ] N (*Jur*) faux serment *m*; **to commit ~** se parjurer; (*Jur*) faire un faux serment

perk¹ [pɜːk] 1 VI **to ~ up** (= *cheer up*) se ragaillardir; (*after illness*) se remonter, se retaper*; (= *show interest*) s'animer, dresser l'oreille; (*lit, fig*) **his ears ~ed up** il a dressé l'oreille 2 VT **to ~ sb up** ragaillardir qn, retaper qn*; **she ~ed up her outfit with a bright scarf** elle a égayé sa tenue avec une écharpe de couleur vive

perk²* [pɜːk] N (ABBR = **perquisite**) (= *benefit*) à-côté *m*, avantage *m* annexe; **it's one of the ~s of the job** c'est l'un des avantages *or* des à-côtés du métier; **one of the ~s of being a student is ...** l'un des avantages à être étudiant est ...

perk³* [pɜːk] VI (ABBR = **percolate**) [*coffee*] passer

perkily ['pɜːkɪlɪ] ADV [*speak*] d'un ton guilleret; [*move*] vivement, avec vivacité; **a bow pinned ~ to her cap** un nœud coquin attaché à son chapeau

perkiness* ['pɜːkɪnɪs] N entrain *m*

perky* ['pɜːkɪ] ADJ (= *cheerful*) guilleret, gai; (= *lively*) vif, éveillé, plein d'entrain

perm¹ [pɜːm] 1 N (*esp Brit*) (ABBR = **permanent**) permanente *f*; **to have a ~** se faire faire une permanente 2 VT **to ~ sb's hair** faire une permanente à qn; **to have one's hair ~ed** se faire faire une permanente

perm²* [pɜːm] 1 N ABBR = **permutation** 2 VTI ABBR = **permutate**

permafrost ['pɜːməfrɒst] N permafrost *m*, pergélisol *m*

permanence ['pɜːmənəns] N permanence *f*

permanency ['pɜːmənənsɪ] N [a] → **permanence** [b] (*job*) emploi *m* permanent, poste *m* fixe

permanent ['pɜːmənənt] 1 ADJ permanent, **we cannot make any ~ arrangements** nous ne pouvons pas prendre de dispositions permanentes; **I'm not ~ here** je ne suis pas ici à titre définitif; **~ address** résidence *f or* adresse *f* fixe; **appointment to the ~ staff** nomination *f* à titre définitif; **a ~ fixture** (= *feature, object*) une constante; **a ~ fixture of government** une constante dans le gouvernement; **he's a ~ fixture*** il fait partie des meubles*; **he's no longer a ~ fixture* on the political scene** il n'est plus le personnage omniprésent *or* incontournable qu'il a été sur la scène politique

2 N (*US†: for hair*) permanente *f*

3 COMP ► **permanent-press** ADJ [*trousers*] à pli permanent; [*skirt*] indéplissable ► **Permanent Secretary** N (*Brit Admin*) secrétaire *m* général (de ministère) ► **permanent wave**† N (*Brit Rail*) voie *f* ferrée ► **permanent way** N (*Brit Rail*) voie *f* ferrée

permanently ['pɜːmənəntlɪ] ADV [a] [*change, live*] définitivement; [*damage*] de façon permanente [b] [*open, closed*] en permanence; [*tired, angry, unhappy etc*] éternellement, constamment

permanganate [pɜːˈmæŋɡənɪt] N permanganate *m*

permeability [ˌpɜːmɪəˈbɪlɪtɪ] N perméabilité *f*

permeable ['pɜːmɪəbl] ADJ perméable, pénétrable

permeate ['pɜːmɪeɪt] 1 VT [*liquid*] pénétrer, filtrer à travers; [*ideas*] pénétrer dans *or* parmi, se répandre dans *or* parmi; (*lit, fig*) **~d with** saturé de, imprégné de 2 VI (= *pass through*) pénétrer, s'infiltrer; (*fig = spread*) se répandre, pénétrer

Permian ['pɜːmɪən] N, ADJ (*Geol*) permien *m*

▼ **permissible** [pəˈmɪsɪbl] ADJ [*action etc*] permis; [*behaviour, attitude, level, limit*] acceptable; **it is ~ to refuse** il est permis de refuser; **would it be ~ to say that ...?** serait-il acceptable de dire que ...?; **the degree of ~ error is 2%** la marge d'erreur acceptable *or* tolérable est de 2 %

▼ **permission** [pəˈmɪʃən] N permission *f*; (*official*) autorisation *f*; **without ~** sans permission, sans autorisation; **with your ~** avec votre permission; **"by kind ~ of ..."** « avec l'aimable autorisation de ... »; **no ~ is needed** il n'est pas nécessaire d'avoir une autorisation; **he gave ~ for the body to be exhumed** il a autorisé l'exhumation du corps; **she gave ~ for her daughter's marriage** elle a consenti au mariage de sa fille; **she gave her daughter ~ to marry** elle a autorisé sa fille à se marier; **~ is required in writing from the committee** il est nécessaire d'obtenir l'autorisation écrite du comité; **who gave you ~ to do that?** qui vous a autorisé à *or* qui vous a permis de faire cela?; **you have my ~ to do that** je vous permets de *or* vous autorise à faire cela, je vous accorde la permission *or* l'autorisation de faire cela; **you have my ~ to leave** je vous autorise à partir; **to ask (sb's) ~ to do sth** demander (à qn) la permission *or* l'autorisation de faire qch; **to ask ~ for sb to do sth** demander que qn ait la permission de faire qch

permissive [pəˈmɪsɪv] ADJ (= *tolerant*) [*person, parent*] permissif; **the ~ society** la société permissive

permissively [pəˈmɪsɪvlɪ] ADV de façon permissive

permissiveness [pəˈmɪsɪvnɪs] N permissivité *f*

permit ['pɜːmɪt] 1 N autorisation *f* écrite; (*for specific activity*) permis *m*; (*for entry*) laissez-passer *m inv*; (*for goods at Customs*) passavant *m*; **fishing ~** permis *m* de pêche; **building ~** permis *m* de construire; **you need a ~ to go into the laboratory** pour entrer dans le laboratoire il vous faut une autorisation écrite *or* un laissez-passer → **entry**

2 [pəˈmɪt] VT (*gen*) permettre (**sb to do** à qn de faire), autoriser (**sb to do** qn à faire); **he was ~ted to leave** on lui a permis de partir, on l'a autorisé à partir; **camping is ~ted here** il est permis de camper ici; **is it ~ted to smoke?** est-il permis de fumer?; **it is not ~ted to smoke** il n'est pas permis *or* il est interdit de fumer; **we could never ~ that to happen** nous ne pourrions jamais permettre que cela se produise, nous ne pourrions jamais laisser cela se produire; **I won't ~ it** je ne le permettrai pas; **her mother will never ~ the sale of the house** sa mère n'autorisera jamais la vente de la maison; **her mother will not ~ her to sell the house** sa mère ne lui permet pas de *or* ne l'autorise pas à vendre la maison; **the law ~s the sale of this substance** la loi autorise la vente de cette substance; **the vent ~s the escape of gas** l'orifice permet l'échappement du gaz; (*frm*) **~ me to help you** permettez-moi de vous aider; **to ~ o.s. sth** se permettre qch

3 [pəˈmɪt] VI permettre; **weather ~ting ◇ if the weather ~s** si le temps le permet; **if time ~s** si j'ai (*or* nous avons *etc*) le temps; (*frm*) **to ~ of sth** permettre qch; **it does not ~ of doubt** cela ne permet pas le moindre doute

permutate ['pɜːmjuːteɪt] VTI permuter

permutation [ˌpɜːmjuːˈteɪʃən] N permutation *f*

permute [pəˈmjuːt] VT permuter

pernicious [pɜːˈnɪʃəs] 1 ADJ (*gen, also Med*) pernicieux 2 COMP ► **pernicious anaemia** N anémie *f* pernicieuse

perniciously [pɜːˈnɪʃəslɪ] ADV pernicieusement

pernickety* [pəˈnɪkɪtɪ] ADJ (= *fussy about*) pointilleux, formaliste; (= *hard to please*)

difficile; [*job*] délicat, minutieux; **he's very ~** il est très pointilleux, il cherche toujours la petite bête, il est très difficile; **he's very ~ about what he wears/about his food** il est très difficile pour ses vêtements/pour sa nourriture

peroration [ˌperəˈreɪʃən] N péroraison *f*

peroxide [pəˈrɒksaɪd] N (*Chem*) peroxyde *m*; (*for hair*) eau *f* oxygénée; **~ blonde*** blonde *f* décolorée *or* oxygénée* → **hydrogen**

perpendicular [ˌpɜːpənˈdɪkjʊləʳ] 1 ADJ (*also Archit, Math*) perpendiculaire (**to** à); [*cliff, slope*] à pic 2 N perpendiculaire *f*; **to be out of ~** être hors d'aplomb, sortir de la perpendiculaire 3 COMP ► **perpendicular Gothic** ADJ (*Archit*) gothique *m* perpendiculaire anglais

perpendicularly [ˌpɜːpənˈdɪkjʊləlɪ] ADV perpendiculairement

perpetrate ['pɜːpɪtreɪt] VT [+ *crime*] perpétrer, commettre; [+ *blunder, hoax*] faire

perpetration [ˌpɜːpɪˈtreɪʃən] N perpétration *f*

perpetrator ['pɜːpɪtreɪtəʳ] N auteur *m*; **~ of a crime** auteur *m* d'un crime

perpetual [pəˈpetjʊəl] ADJ [*movement, calendar, rain, sunshine, flower*] perpétuel; [*nuisance, worry*] perpétuel, constant; [*noise, questions, complaints*] perpétuel, continuel; [*snows*] éternel; **he's a ~ nuisance** il ne cesse d'embêter le monde

perpetually [pəˈpetjʊəlɪ] ADV perpétuellement, continuellement, sans cesse

perpetuate [pəˈpetjʊeɪt] VT perpétuer

perpetuation [pəˌpetjʊˈeɪʃən] N perpétuation *f*

perpetuity [ˌpɜːpɪˈtjuːɪtɪ] N perpétuité *f*; **in** *or* **for ~** à perpétuité

perplex [pəˈpleks] VT (= *puzzle*) plonger dans la perplexité, rendre perplexe

perplexed [pəˈplekst] ADJ [*person*] embarrassé, perplexe; [*tone, glance*] perplexe; **to look ~** avoir l'air perplexe *or* embarrassé

perplexedly [pəˈpleksɪdlɪ] ADV avec perplexité, d'un air *or* d'un ton perplexe, d'un air embarrassé

perplexing [pəˈpleksɪŋ] ADJ [*matter, question*] embarrassant, compliqué; [*situation*] embarrassant, confus

perplexity [pəˈpleksɪtɪ] N (= *puzzlement*) perplexité *f*

perquisite ['pɜːkwɪzɪt] N (*frm*) avantage *m* annexe; (*in money*) à-côté *m*, gratification *f*

perry ['perɪ] N poiré *m*

persecute ['pɜːsɪkjuːt] VT (= *harass, oppress*) [+ *minorities etc*] persécuter; (= *annoy*) harceler (**with** de), tourmenter, persécuter

persecution [ˌpɜːsɪˈkjuːʃən] N persécution *f*; **to have a ~ complex** avoir la manie *or* le délire de la persécution

persecutor ['pɜːsɪkjuːtəʳ] N persécuteur *m*, -trice *f*

Persephone [pəˈsefənɪ] N Perséphone *f*

Perseus ['pɜːsjuːs] N Persée *m*

perseverance [ˌpɜːsɪˈvɪərəns] N persévérance *f*

persevere [ˌpɜːsɪˈvɪəʳ] VI persévérer (**in sth** dans qch, **at doing sth** à faire qch)

persevering [ˌpɜːsɪˈvɪərɪŋ] ADJ persévérant

perseveringly [ˌpɜːsɪˈvɪərɪŋlɪ] ADV avec persévérance

Persia ['pɜːʃə] N la Perse

Persian ['pɜːʃən] 1 ADJ (*Antiq*) perse; (*from 7th century onward*) persan 2 N [a] (= *person*) Persan(e) *m(f)*; (*Antiq*) Perse *mf* [b] (*Ling*) persan *m* 3 COMP ► **Persian carpet** N tapis *m* de Perse ► **Persian cat** N chat *m* persan ► **Persian Gulf** N golfe *m* Persique ► **Persian lamb** N astrakan *m*, agneau *m* rasé

persiflage [ˌpɜːsɪˈflɑːʒ] N persiflage *m*, ironie *f*, raillerie *f*

➤ LANGUAGE IN USE: **permissible** 9.4 **permission** 9.2

persimmon [pɜːˈsɪmən] N (= tree) plaqueminier m de Virginie or du Japon, kaki m; (= fruit) kaki m

persist [pəˈsɪst] VI [person] persister, s'obstiner (**in sth** dans qch, **in doing** à faire); [pain, opinion] persister

persistence [pəˈsɪstəns], **persistency** [pəˈsɪstənsɪ] N (NonC) [of person] (= perseverance) persévérance f; (= obstinacy) obstination f; [of pain] persistance f; **as a reward for her ~** pour la récompenser de sa persévérance; **his ~ in seeking out the truth** son obstination à rechercher la vérité

persistent [pəˈsɪstənt] ① ADJ ⓐ [person] (= persevering) persévérant; (= obstinate) obstiné ⓑ (= continual) [smell, chemical substance] persistant; [warnings, complaints, interruptions] continuel, répété; [noise, nuisance] continuel, incessant; [pain, fever, cough] persistant, tenace; [fears, doubts] continuel, tenace ② COMP ► **persistent offender** N (Jur) multirécidiviste mf ► **persistent vegetative state** N état m végétatif persistant or permanent

persistently [pəˈsɪstəntlɪ] ADV ⓐ (= determinedly, obstinately) obstinément; **those who ~ break the law** ceux qui persistent à enfreindre la loi ⓑ (= constantly) constamment; **~ high unemployment** un taux de chômage qui demeure élevé

persnickety* [pəˈsnɪkɪtɪ] ADJ (US) = **pernickety**

person [ˈpɜːsn] N ⓐ personne f, individu m (often pej); (Jur) personne f; **I know no such ~** (= no one of that name) je ne connais personne de ce nom; (= no one like that) je ne connais personne de ce genre; **I like him as a ~, but not as a politician** je l'aime bien en tant que personne mais pas comme homme politique; **in ~** [go, meet, appear, speak etc] en personne; **give it to him in ~** remettez-le-lui en mains propres; **in the ~ of** dans or en la personne de; **I'm not the kind of ~ to ...** je ne suis pas du genre à ...; **I'm not much of a city ~** je n'aime pas beaucoup la ville; **she likes dogs, but I'm more of a cat ~** elle aime les chiens mais personnellement je préfère les chats; (Telec) **a ~ to ~ call** communication (téléphonique) avec préavis; (Jur) **he had a knife concealed on** or **about his ~** il avait un couteau caché sur lui; **acting with ~** or **~s unknown** (agissant) de concert or en complicité avec un ou des tiers non identifiés → **displace, private** ⓑ (Gram) personne f; **in the first ~ singular** à la première personne du singulier

persona [pɜːˈsəʊnə] N (pl **personae**) ⓐ (Literat, Psych etc) personnage m ⓑ **~ grata/non grata** persona grata/non grata

personable [ˈpɜːsnəbl] ADJ qui présente bien, de belle prestance

personae [pɜːˈsəʊniː] NPL of **persona**

personage [ˈpɜːsnɪdʒ] N (Theat, gen) personnage m

personal [ˈpɜːsnl] ① ADJ (= private) [opinion, matter] personnel; (= individual) [style] personnel, particulier; [liberty] personnel, individuel; (= for one's own use) [luggage, belongings] personnel; (= to do with the body) [habits] intime; (= in person) [call, visit] personnel; [application] (fait) en personne; (Gram) personnel; (= indiscreet) [remark, question] indiscret (-ète f); **my ~ belief is ...** personnellement or pour ma part je crois ...; **I have no ~ knowledge of this** personnellement je ne sais rien à ce sujet; **a letter marked "~"** une lettre marquée « personnel »; **his ~ interests were at stake** ses intérêts personnels étaient en jeu; **his ~ appearance leaves much to be desired** son apparence (personnelle) or sa tenue laisse beaucoup à désirer; **to make a ~ appearance** apparaître en personne; **I will give the matter my ~ attention** je m'occuperai personnellement de cette affaire; **these chil-** dren need the ~ attention of trained carers ces enfants ont besoin d'éducateurs spécialisés qui s'occupent individuellement de chacun; **the conversation/argument grew ~** la conversation/la discussion prit un ton or un tour personnel; **don't be ~!*** ne sois pas si blessant!; **don't let's get ~!*** abstenons-nous d'allusions personnelles!; **his ~ life** sa vie privée; **for ~ reasons** pour des raisons personnelles; **the president believes his ~ safety is at risk** le président craint pour sa sécurité personnelle; **to give sth the ~ touch** ajouter une note personnelle à qch

② N (US Press) (= article) entrefilet m mondain; (= ad) petite annonce f personnelle

③ COMP ► **personal accident insurance** N assurance f individuelle contre les accidents ► **personal ad*** N petite annonce f personnelle ► **personal allowance** N (Tax) abattement m personnel ► **personal assistant** N secrétaire mf particulier (-ière) ► **personal best** N (Sport) record m personnel ► **personal call** N (Brit Telec) (= person to person) communication f (téléphonique) avec préavis; (= private) appel m personnel ► **personal chair** N (Brit Univ) **to have a ~ chair** être professeur à titre personnel ► **personal cleanliness** N hygiène f intime ► **personal column** N (Press) annonces fpl personnelles ► **personal computer** N ordinateur m individuel or personnel ► **personal details** NPL (= name, address etc) coordonnées* fpl ► **personal effects** NPL effets mpl personnels ► **personal estate** N (Jur) biens mpl personnels ► **personal friend** N ami(e) m(f) intime ► **personal hygiene** = **personal cleanliness** ► **personal identification number** N code m personnel ► **personal insurance** N assurance f personnelle ► **personal loan** N (Banking) prêt m personnel ► **personal organizer** N (= Filofax) agenda m (personnel), Filofax® m; (electronic) agenda m électronique ► **personal pronoun** N (Gram) pronom m personnel ► **personal property** N = **personal estate** ► **personal space** N espace m vital ► **personal stationery** N papier m à lettres à en-tête personnel ► **personal stereo** N baladeur m, Walkman® m ► **personal trainer** N entraîneur m personnel ► **personal tuition** N cours mpl particuliers (in de)

personality [ˌpɜːsəˈnælɪtɪ] ① N ⓐ (NonC: also Psych) personnalité f; **you must allow him to express his ~** il faut lui permettre d'exprimer sa personnalité; **she has a pleasant/strong ~** elle a une personnalité sympathique/forte; **he has a lot of ~** il a beaucoup de personnalité; **cats all have their own personalities** les chats ont tous leur personnalité propre; **the house seemed to have a ~ of its own** la maison semblait avoir une personnalité propre → **dual, split**

ⓑ (= celebrity) personnalité f, personnage m connu; **a well-known television ~** une vedette de la télévision or du petit écran; (election etc) **it was more about personalities than about politics** c'était plus une confrontation de personnalités que d'idées politiques

② COMP (gen, Psych) [problems] de personnalité ► **personality cult** N culte m de la personnalité ► **personality disorder** N troubles mpl de la personnalité ► **personality test** N test m de personnalité, test m projectif (SPEC)

personalize [ˈpɜːsənəˌlaɪz] VT personnaliser

personalized [ˈpɜːsənəˌlaɪzd] ① ADJ personnalisé ② COMP ► **personalized number plate** N (Brit) plaque f d'immatriculation personnalisée | *VANITY PLATE*

▼ **personally** [ˈpɜːsnəlɪ] ADV personnellement; **~ I disapprove of gambling** personnellement

je désapprouve les jeux d'argent; **I like him ~ but not as an employer** je l'apprécie en tant que personne, mais pas comme patron; **that's something you would have to raise with the director ~** il faudrait en parler au directeur en personne; **I spoke to him ~** je lui ai parlé en personne; **to be ~ responsible** or **liable (for sth)** être personnellement responsable (de qch); **I hold you ~ responsible (for this)** je vous en tiens personnellement responsable; **I'm sorry, I didn't mean it ~** excusez-moi, je ne vous visais pas personnellement; **don't take it ~!** ne le prenez pas pour vous!

personalty [ˈpɜːsnltɪ] N (Jur) biens mpl personnels

personate [ˈpɜːsəneɪt] VT ⓐ (Theat) incarner (le rôle de) ⓑ (= personify) personnifier ⓒ (Jur = impersonate) se faire passer pour

personification [pɜːˌsɒnɪfɪˈkeɪʃən] N (all senses) personnification f; **she's the ~ of good taste** elle est la personnification or l'incarnation f du bon goût

personify [pɜːˈsɒnɪfaɪ] VT personnifier; **she's kindness personified** c'est la bonté personnifiée or en personne; **he's fascism personified** il est le fascisme personnifié

personnel [ˌpɜːsəˈnel] ① N personnel m ② COMP ► **personnel agency** N agence f pour l'emploi, bureau m de placement ► **personnel carrier** N (Mil) véhicule m de transport de troupes ► **personnel department** N service m du personnel ► **personnel management** N gestion f or direction f du personnel ► **personnel manager** N chef mf du (service du) personnel ► **personnel officer** N responsable mf (de la gestion) du personnel

perspective [pəˈspektɪv] N ⓐ (Archit, Art, Surv, gen) perspective f; **in/out of ~** en perspective/qui ne respecte pas la perspective ⓑ (fig = viewpoint) point m de vue, perspective f; **to see things from a different ~** voir les choses d'un point de vue différent or sous un angle différent or sous un jour différent; **in a historical ~** dans une perspective or une optique historique; **the reconstruction of history from a feminist ~** la reconstitution de l'histoire d'un point de vue féministe; **the book is written from the ~ of a parent** le livre est écrit du point de vue d'un parent; **the report gave a distorted ~ of the case** le rapport donnait une image déformée de l'affaire; **a child's ~ of the world** l'image f que se fait un enfant du monde; **let me put this case in (its proper) ~** je vais replacer cette affaire dans son contexte; **let's keep this in ~** ne perdons pas or gardons le sens des proportions

Perspex® [ˈpɜːspeks] N (esp Brit) plexiglas® m

perspicacious [ˌpɜːspɪˈkeɪʃəs] ADJ [person] perspicace; [analysis] pénétrant

perspicacity [ˌpɜːspɪˈkæsɪtɪ] N perspicacité f, clairvoyance f

perspicuity [ˌpɜːspɪˈkjuːɪtɪ] N ⓐ = **perspicacity** ⓑ [of explanation, statement] clarté f, netteté f

perspicuous [ˌpɜːˈspɪkjʊəs] ADJ clair, net

perspiration [ˌpɜːspəˈreɪʃən] N transpiration f; **bathed in** or **dripping with ~** en nage

perspire [pəsˈpaɪəʳ] VI transpirer

persuadable* [pəˈsweɪdəbl] ADJ qui peut être persuadé

persuade [pəˈsweɪd] VT (= urge) persuader (**sb of sth** qn de qch, **sb that** qn que); (= convince) convaincre (**sb of sth** qn de qch); **it doesn't take much to ~ him** il n'en faut pas beaucoup pour le persuader or le convaincre; **I am (quite) ~d that he is wrong** je suis (tout à fait) persuadé qu'il a tort; **I'm not ~d of the benefits of your approach** je ne suis pas convaincu des avantages de votre approche; **to ~ sb to do sth** persuader qn de faire qch;

to ~ **sb not to do sth** persuader qn de ne pas faire qch, dissuader qn de faire qch ; **I wanted to help but they ~d me not to** je voulais aider mais on m'en a dissuadé ; **to ~ sb into doing sth*** persuader qn de faire qch ; **they ~d me that I ought to see him** ils m'ont persuadé que je devais le voir ; **to ~ o.s. that ...** se persuader que ... ; **to ~ sb of the need for sth** persuader qn de la nécessité de qch ; **she is easily ~d** elle se laisse facilement persuader *or* convaincre

persuasion [pə'sweɪʒən] N 〔a〕 (*NonC*) persuasion *f* ; **he needed a lot of ~** il a fallu beaucoup de persuasion pour le convaincre ; **I don't need much ~ to stop working** il n'en faut pas beaucoup pour me persuader de m'arrêter de travailler ; **he is open to ~** il est prêt à se laisser convaincre 〔b〕 (= *belief, conviction*) (*gen*) croyance *f* ; (*religious*) confession *f* ; (*political*) conviction *f* politique ; **people of all religious/political ~s** des gens de toutes les religions *or* confessions/de toutes les convictions politiques ; **I am not of that ~ myself** personnellement je ne partage pas cette croyance

persuasive [pə'sweɪsɪv] ADJ [*person, voice*] persuasif ; [*evidence, argument*] convaincant

persuasively [pə'sweɪsɪvlɪ] ADV 〔a〕 (= *convincingly*) [*argue, write, speak*] de façon persuasive 〔b〕 (= *attempting to persuade*) **he smiled ~** il eut un sourire qui cherchait à convaincre ; **"oh go on, you know you want to", he said ~** « allons, tu sais que tu en as envie » dit-il en cherchant à le (*or* la) convaincre

persuasiveness [pə'sweɪsɪvnɪs] N pouvoir *m or* force *f* de persuasion

pert [pɜːt] ADJ 〔a〕 (= *coquettish*) [*person*] coquin ; **a ~ little hat** un petit chapeau coquin 〔b〕 (= *neat, firm*) [*bottom, buttocks, breasts*] ferme ; [*nose*] mutin

pertain [pɜː'teɪn] VI 〔a〕 (*frm* = *relate*) **to ~ to** se rapporter à, se rattacher à ; **documents ~ing to the case** documents se rapportant à *or* relatifs à l'affaire 〔b〕 (*Jur etc*) [*land*] appartenir (**to** à)

pertinacious [ˌpɜːtɪ'neɪʃəs] ADJ (*frm*) (= *stubborn*) entêté, obstiné ; (*in opinions etc*) opiniâtre

pertinaciously [ˌpɜːtɪ'neɪʃəslɪ] ADV (*frm*) [*maintain position*] obstinément ; [*argue*] avec persistance

pertinacity [ˌpɜːtɪ'næsɪtɪ] N (*frm*) opiniâtreté *f*

pertinence ['pɜːtɪnəns] N justesse *f*, à-propos *m*, pertinence *f* ; (*Ling*) pertinence *f*

pertinent ['pɜːtɪnənt] ADJ pertinent ; **to be ~ to sth** se rapporter à qch

pertinently ['pɜːtɪnəntlɪ] ADV pertinemment, avec justesse, à propos

pertly ['pɜːtlɪ] ADV (= *cheekily*) avec effronterie, avec impertinence

pertness ['pɜːtnɪs] N (= *cheek*) effronterie *f*, impertinence *f*

perturb [pə'tɜːb] VT perturber, inquiéter, agiter

perturbation [ˌpɜːtɜː'beɪʃən] N (*frm*) perturbation *f*, agitation *f*

perturbed [pə'tɜːbd] ADJ perturbé, inquiet (-ète *f*) ; **I was ~ to hear that ...** j'ai appris avec inquiétude que ...

perturbing [pə'tɜːbɪŋ] ADJ troublant, inquiétant

pertussis [pə'tʌsɪs] N coqueluche *f*

Peru [pə'ruː] N le Pérou

Perugia [pə'ruːdʒə] N Pérouse

perusal [pə'ruːzəl] N (*frm*) lecture *f* ; (*thorough*) lecture *f* attentive

peruse [pə'ruːz] VT lire ; (*thoroughly*) lire attentivement

Peruvian [pə'ruːvɪən] 〔1〕 ADJ péruvien 〔2〕 N Péruvien(ne) *m(f)*

perv* [pɜːv] N ABBR = **pervert**

pervade [pɜː'veɪd] VT [*smell*] se répandre dans ; [*influence*] s'étendre dans ; [*ideas*] s'insinuer dans, pénétrer dans ; [*gloom*] envahir ; [*problem*] sévir dans ; **this atmosphere ~s the whole book** tout le livre baigne dans cette atmosphère

pervading [pɜː'veɪdɪŋ] ADJ [*uncertainty, influence*] sous-jacent(e) ; **there is a ~ atmosphere of doom and gloom in the film** tout le film baigne dans une atmosphère sinistre ; **throughout the book there is a ~ sense of menace** tout au long du roman on ressent comme une menace sourde ; **the ~ feeling is that economic recovery is near** le sentiment général est que la reprise (économique) est proche → **all**

pervasive [pɜː'veɪsɪv] ADJ [*smell, ideas*] pénétrant ; [*gloom*] envahissant ; [*influence*] qui se fait sentir un peu partout

perverse [pə'vɜːs] ADJ 〔a〕 (= *twisted*) [*pleasure, desire, humour*] pervers 〔b〕 (= *stubborn*) têtu, entêté ; (= *contrary*) contrariant ; **how ~ of him!** qu'il est contrariant ! ; **what ~ behaviour!** quel esprit de contradiction ! ; **it would be ~ to refuse** ce serait faire preuve d'esprit de contradiction que de refuser

perversely [pə'vɜːslɪ] ADV 〔a〕 (= *determinedly*) obstinément ; (= *in order to annoy*) par esprit de contradiction 〔b〕 (= *paradoxically*) paradoxalement ; **~ enjoyable/engaging/appropriate** paradoxalement agréable/engageant/approprié

perverseness [pə'vɜːsnɪs] N = **perversity**

perversion [pə'vɜːʃən] N (*also Psych*) perversion *f* ; [*of facts*] déformation *f*, travestissement *m* ; **sexual ~s** perversions *fpl* sexuelles ; (*Med*) **~ of a function** perversion *f or* altération *f* d'une fonction ; **a ~ of justice** (*gen*) un travestissement de la justice ; (*Jur*) un déni de justice ; **a ~ of the truth** un travestissement de la vérité

perversity [pə'vɜːsɪtɪ] N 〔a〕 (= *wickedness*) perversité *f*, méchanceté *f* 〔b〕 (= *stubbornness*) obstination *f*, entêtement *m* ; (= *contrariness*) caractère *m* contrariant, esprit *m* de contradiction

pervert [pə'vɜːt] 〔1〕 VT [+ *person*] pervertir, dépraver ; (*Psych*) pervertir ; (*Rel*) détourner de ses croyances ; [+ *habits etc*] dénaturer, dépraver ; [+ *fact*] fausser, travestir ; [+ *sb's words*] dénaturer, déformer ; [+ *justice, truth*] travestir ; **to ~ the course of justice** entraver le cours de la justice 〔2〕 ['pɜːvɜːt] N (*Psych: also* **sexual ~**) pervers *m* sexuel, pervertie *f* sexuelle

perverted [pə'vɜːtɪd] ADJ (*frm*) pervers

pervious ['pɜːvɪəs] ADJ perméable, pénétrable ; (*fig*) accessible (**to** à)

peseta [pə'seɪtə] N peseta *f*

pesky* ['peskɪ] ADJ (*esp US*) sale* (*before n*), empoisonnant*

peso ['peɪsəʊ] N peso *m*

pessary ['pesərɪ] N pessaire *m*

pessimism ['pesɪmɪzəm] N pessimisme *m*

pessimist ['pesɪmɪst] N pessimiste *mf*

pessimistic [ˌpesɪ'mɪstɪk] ADJ pessimiste (*about* au sujet de, sur) ; **I'm very ~ about it** je suis très pessimiste à ce sujet *or* là-dessus ; **they are ~ about making a profit** ils n'ont pas grand espoir de faire des bénéfices

pessimistically [ˌpesɪ'mɪstɪkəlɪ] ADV avec pessimisme

pest [pest] 〔1〕 N 〔a〕 (= *insect*) insecte *m* nuisible ; (= *animal*) animal *m* nuisible ; **rabbits are classed as a ~ in Australia** en Australie le lapin est considéré comme un (animal) nuisible 〔b〕 (* = *person*) casse-pieds* *mf inv*, enquinuineur* *m*, -euse* *f* ; **you little ~!** que tu es enquinuinant !* ; (*to girl*) espèce de petite peste ! ; **a sex ~** un vicieux *or* une vicieuse (*qui harcèle qn sexuellement*) 〔2〕 COMP ► **pest control** N [*of insects*] désinsectisation *f*, lutte *f*

contre les insectes ; [*of rats*] dératisation *f* ; (*Admin*) **~ control officer** préposé(e) *m(f)* à la lutte antiparasitaire

pester ['pestə*r*] VT harceler ; **to ~ sb with questions** harceler qn de questions ; **she has been ~ing me for an answer** elle n'arrête pas de me réclamer une réponse ; **he ~ed me to go to the cinema with him** il n'a pas arrêté d'insister *or* il m'a cassé les pieds* pour que j'aille au cinéma avec lui ; **he ~ed me into going to the cinema with him** il n'a pas arrêté d'insister *or* il m'a cassé les pieds* pour que j'aille au cinéma avec lui, et j'ai fini par l'accompagner ; **he ~ed his father into lending him the car** à force d'insister auprès de son père, il a fini par se faire prêter la voiture ; **he ~s the life out of me*** il me casse les pieds* ; **stop ~ing me!** laisse-moi tranquille !, fiche-moi la paix !* ; **stop ~ing me about your bike** fiche-moi la paix* avec ton vélo ; **is this man ~ing you?** est-ce que cet homme vous importune ?

pesticidal [ˌpestɪ'saɪdl] ADJ pesticide

pesticide ['pestɪsaɪd] N (*gen*) pesticide *m*

pestiferous [pes'tɪfərəs] ADJ = **pestilent**

pestilence ['pestɪləns] N peste *f* (*also fig*)

pestilent ['pestɪlənt], **pestilential** [ˌpestɪ'lenʃəl] ADJ 〔a〕 (= *causing disease*) pestilentiel ; (= *pernicious*) nuisible 〔b〕 (* = *annoying*) fichu* (*before n*), sacré✱ (*before n*)

pestle ['pesl] N pilon *m*

pesto ['pestəʊ] N pesto *m*

pet¹ [pet] 〔1〕 N 〔a〕 (= *animal*) animal *m* domestique *or* familier *or* de compagnie ; **do you have any ~s?** avez-vous des animaux domestiques *or* familiers *or* de compagnie ? ; (*said by or to child*) avez-vous des animaux chez vous *or* à la maison ? ; **she keeps a goldfish as a ~** en fait d'animal elle a un poisson rouge ; **"no ~s (allowed)"** « les animaux sont interdits » 〔b〕 (* = *favourite*) chouchou(te)* *m(f)* ; **the teacher's ~** le chouchou* du professeur ; **to make a ~ of sb** chouchouter qn* 〔c〕 (*: *term of affection*) **be a ~ and fetch my slippers** sois un chou* *or* sois gentil, va chercher mes chaussons ; **he's a real ~** c'est un chou*, il est adorable ; **come here ~** viens ici mon chou* *or* mon lapin*

〔2〕 ADJ 〔a〕 [*lion, snake*] apprivoisé ; **he's got a ~ rabbit/dog** il a un lapin/chien ; **Jean-François has a ~ alligator** Jean-François a un alligator comme animal de compagnie *or* un alligator apprivoisé 〔b〕 (* = *favourite*) [*theory, project, charity, theme*] favori(te) *m(f)* ; **~ aversion** *or* **hate** bête *f* noire ; **it's his ~ subject** c'est sa marotte, c'est son dada* ; **once he gets onto his ~ subject ...** quand il enfourche son cheval de bataille *or* son dada* ...

〔3〕 VT (= *indulge*) chouchouter* ; (= *fondle*) câliner ; (*: *sexually*) caresser, peloter✱

〔4〕 VI (*: *sexually*) se caresser, se peloter✱

〔5〕 COMP ► **pet food** N aliments *mpl* pour animaux ► **pet name** N petit nom *m* (d'amitié) ► **pet shop** N boutique *f* d'animaux

pet²* [pet] N **to be in a ~** être de mauvais poil*

petal ['petl] N pétale *m* ; **~-shaped** en forme de pétale

petard [pɪ'tɑːd] N pétard *m* → **hoist**

Pete [piːt] N 〔a〕 *dim of* Peter 〔b〕 **for ~'s sake!*** mais enfin !, bon sang !*

Peter ['piːtə*r*] N Pierre *m* ; (*Rel*) **~'s pence** denier *m* de saint Pierre ; **~ Pan** Peter Pan *m* → **blue, rob**

peter¹ ['piːtə*r*] VI **to ~ out** [*supplies*] s'épuiser ; [*stream, conversation*] tarir ; [*plans*] tomber à l'eau ; [*story, plot, play, book*] tourner court ; [*fire, flame*] mourir ; [*road*] se perdre

peter²** ['piːtə*r*] N (*US* = *penis*) bite✱* *f*

pethidine ['peθɪdiːn] N (*Med*) péthédine *f*, mépéridine *f*

petite [pə'tiːt] ADJ [*woman*] menue

petit-four ['petɪ'fɔːʳ] N (pl **petits-fours**) petit-four m

petition [pə'tɪʃən] [1] N [a] (= list of signatures) pétition f; **to get up a ~ against/for sth** organiser une pétition contre/en faveur de qch [b] (= prayer) prière f; (= request) requête f, supplique f [c] (Jur) requête f, pétition f; **a ~ for divorce** une demande de divorce; **a ~ for** or **in bankruptcy** une demande de mise en liquidation judiciaire; **right of ~** droit m de pétition → **file²** [2] VT [a] (= address petition to) adresser une pétition à, pétitionner; **they ~ed the king for the release of the prisoner** ils ont adressé une pétition au roi pour demander la libération du prisonnier [b] (frm = request) implorer, prier (**sb to do** qn de faire) [c] (Jur) **to ~ the court** adresser or présenter une pétition en justice [3] VI adresser une pétition, pétitionner; (Jur) **to ~ for divorce** faire une demande de divorce; **to ~ for bankruptcy** faire une demande de mise en liquidation judiciaire

petitioner [pə'tɪʃnəʳ] N pétitionnaire mf; (Jur) requérant(e) m(f), pétitionnaire mf; (in divorce) demandeur m, -deresse f (en divorce)

petit jury [,petɪ'dʒʊərɪ] N (US) jury m (de jugement)

petit mal [peti'mæl] N (NonC: Med) petit mal m

petits pois [peti'pwɑː] NPL petits-pois mpl

petnapping* ['petnæpɪŋ] N (US) vol m d'animaux familiers (pour les revendre aux laboratoires)

Petrarch ['petrɑːk] N Pétrarque m

petrel ['petrəl] N pétrel m → **stormy**

Petri dish ['piːtrɪdɪʃ] N boîte f de Petri

petrifaction [,petrɪ'fækʃən] N (lit, fig) pétrification f

petrified ['petrɪfaɪd] ADJ [a] (lit = turned to stone) pétrifié [b] (fig = terrified) pétrifié or paralysé de peur; **I was absolutely ~!** j'étais terrifié!, j'étais pétrifié de peur!

petrify ['petrɪfaɪ] [1] VT [a] (lit = turn to stone) pétrifier [b] (fig = terrify) pétrifier or paralyser de peur, clouer (sur place) de peur [2] VI se pétrifier (lit)

petro... ['petrəʊ] PREF pétro...

petrochemical [,petrəʊ'kemɪkəl] [1] N produit m pétrochimique [2] ADJ pétrochimique

petrocurrency ['petrəʊ,kʌrənsɪ] N pétrodevise f

petrodollar ['petrəʊ,dɒləʳ] N pétrodollar m

petrographic(al) [,petrə'græfɪk(əl)] ADJ pétrographique

petrography [pe'trɒgrəfɪ] N pétrographie f

petrol ['petrəl] (Brit) [1] N essence f; **my car's very heavy on ~** ma voiture consomme beaucoup (d'essence); **this car runs on ~** cette voiture roule à l'essence → **star** [2] COMP ► **petrol bomb** N cocktail m Molotov ► **petrol can** N bidon m à essence ► **petrol cap** N = **petrol filler cap** ► **petrol-driven** ADJ à essence ► **petrol engine** N moteur m à essence ► **petrol filler cap** N bouchon m de réservoir d'essence ► **petrol gauge** N (Aut) jauge f d'essence ► **petrol pump** N (on forecourt, in engine) pompe f à essence ► **petrol rationing** N rationnement m de l'essence ► **petrol station** N station-service f, poste m d'essence ► **petrol tank** N réservoir m (d'essence) ► **petrol tanker** N (= ship) pétrolier m, tanker m; (= truck) camion-citerne m (transportant de l'essence)

petroleum [pɪ'trəʊlɪəm] [1] N pétrole m [2] COMP ► **petroleum jelly** N Vaseline® f

petroliferous [,petrə'lɪfərəs] ADJ pétrolifère

petrology [pe'trɒlədʒɪ] N pétrologie f

petticoat ['petɪkəʊt] N (= underskirt) jupon m; (= slip) combinaison f

pettifogging ['petɪfɒgɪŋ] ADJ (= trifling) [details] insignifiant; [objections] chicanier

pettily ['petɪlɪ] ADV avec mesquinerie, de façon mesquine

pettiness ['petɪnɪs] N (NonC) [a] (= small-mindedness) [of person, behaviour] mesquinerie f [b] (= triviality) [of detail, complaint] insignifiance f

petting* ['petɪŋ] [1] N (NonC) caresses fpl; **heavy ~** pelotage*; **to indulge in heavy ~** peloter* [2] COMP ► **petting zoo** N (esp US) zoo ou partie d'un zoo où sont réunis des animaux, souvent jeunes, que les enfants peuvent caresser

pettish ['petɪʃ] ADJ [person] de mauvaise humeur, irritable; [remark] maussade; [child] grognon

pettishly ['petɪʃlɪ] ADV avec mauvaise humeur, d'un air or d'un ton maussade

petty ['petɪ] [1] ADJ [a] (= small-minded) [person, behaviour] mesquin [b] (= trivial) [detail, complaint] insignifiant, sans importance; **~ annoyances** désagréments mpl mineurs, tracasseries fpl; **~ regulations** règlement m tracassier [c] (Naut) **~ officer** ≈ maître m; (US Navy) **~ officer third class** quartier-maître m de première classe [2] COMP ► **petty cash** N petite caisse f, caisse f de dépenses courantes ► **petty crime** N [a] (NonC = illegal activities) petite délinquance f [b] (= illegal act) délit m mineur ► **petty criminal** N petit malfaiteur m, malfaiteur m à la petite semaine ► **petty expenses** NPL menues dépenses fpl ► **petty larceny** N (Jur) larcin m ► **petty official** N fonctionnaire mf subalterne, petit fonctionnaire m ► **Petty Sessions** NPL (Brit Jur) sessions fpl des juges de paix

petulance ['petjʊləns] N mauvaise humeur f

petulant ['petjʊlənt] ADJ (by nature) irritable, irascible; (on one occasion) irrité; [expression, gesture] irrité; **in a ~ mood** de mauvaise humeur; **~ behaviour** irritabilité f, irascibilité f; (on one occasion) mauvaise humeur f

petulantly ['petjʊləntlɪ] ADV avec humeur

petunia [pɪ'tjuːnɪə] N pétunia m

pew [pjuː] N (Rel) banc m (d'église); (hum) **take a ~*** prenez donc un siège

pewter ['pjuːtəʳ] [1] N étain m; **to collect ~** collectionner les étains [2] COMP [pot etc] en étain, d'étain

peyote [peɪ'əʊtɪ] N peyotl m

PFC [,piːef'siː] N (US Mil) (ABBR = **Private First Class**) → **private**

pfennig ['fenɪg] N pfennig m

PFLP [,piːefel'piː] N (ABBR = **Popular Front for the Liberation of Palestine**) FPLP m

PG [piː'dʒiː] [1] (Cine: film censor's rating) (ABBR = **Parental Guidance**) certaines scènes peuvent heurter la sensibilité des jeunes enfants [2] N (ABBR = **paying guest**) → **paying**

PGA [,piːdʒiː'eɪ] N (ABBR = **Professional Golfers' Association**) PGA f

PGCE [,piːdʒiːsiː'iː] N (Brit) (ABBR = **Postgraduate Certificate in Education**) diplôme de troisième cycle en pédagogie

PH [piː'eɪtʃ] (US Mil) (ABBR = **Purple Heart**) → **purple**

pH [piː'eɪtʃ] N pH m

Phaedra ['fiːdrə] N Phèdre f

phaeton ['feɪtən] N phaéton m

phagocyte ['fægəsaɪt] N phagocyte m

phagocytosis [,fægəsaɪ'təʊsɪs] N phagocytose f

phalangeal [fə'lændʒɪəl] ADJ phalangien

phalanx ['fælæŋks] N (pl **phalanges** [fæ'lændʒiːz]) (gen, Mil, Hist, Anat) phalange f

phalarope ['fælə,rəʊp] N phalarope m

phalli ['fælaɪ] NPL of **phallus**

phallic ['fælɪk] [1] ADJ phallique [2] COMP ► **phallic symbol** N symbole m phallique

phallus ['fæləs] N (pl **phalluses** or **phalli**) phallus m

phantasm ['fæntæzəm] N fantasme m

phantasmagoria [,fæntæzmə'gɔːrɪə] N fantasmagorie f

phantasmagoric(al) [,fæntæzmə'gɒrɪk(əl)] ADJ fantasmagorique

phantasmal [fæn'tæzməl] ADJ fantomatique

phantasy ['fæntəzɪ] N = **fantasy**

phantom ['fæntəm] [1] N (= ghost) fantôme m; (= vision) fantasme m; (hum) **the ~ pencil thief strikes again!** le voleur de crayons masqué a encore frappé! [2] COMP ► **phantom pregnancy** N grossesse f nerveuse

Pharaoh ['feərəʊ] N pharaon m; (as name) Pharaon m

Pharisaic(al) [,færɪ'seɪɪk(əl)] ADJ pharisaïque

Pharisee ['færɪsiː] N pharisien(ne) m(f)

pharmaceutical [,fɑːmə'sjuːtɪkəl] [1] ADJ pharmaceutique [2] **pharmaceuticals** NPL médicaments mpl, produits mpl pharmaceutiques

pharmacist ['fɑːməsɪst] N (= person) pharmacien(ne) m(f); (Brit: also **~'s**) pharmacie f

pharmacological [,fɑːməkə'lɒdʒɪkəl] ADJ pharmacologique

pharmacologist [,fɑːmə'kɒlədʒɪst] N pharmacologue mf

pharmacology [,fɑːmə'kɒlədʒɪ] N pharmacologie f

pharmacopoeia [,fɑːməkə'piːə] N pharmacopée f

pharmacy ['fɑːməsɪ] N pharmacie f

pharynges [fæ'rɪndʒiːz] NPL of **pharynx**

pharyngitis [,færɪn'dʒaɪtɪs] N pharyngite f, angine f; **to have ~** avoir une pharyngite

pharynx ['færɪŋks] N (pl **pharynxes** or **pharynges**) pharynx m

phase [feɪz] [1] N [a] (= stage in process) phase f, période f; **a critical ~ in the negotiations** une phase or un stade critique des négociations; **the first ~ of the work** la première tranche des travaux; **the ~s of a disease** les phases fpl d'une maladie; **the ~s of the moon** les phases fpl de la lune; **every child goes through a difficult ~** tout enfant passe par une phase or une période difficile; **a passing ~** (gen) un état passager; (= fad) une passade; **it's just a ~ - he's going through** ça lui passera [b] (Astron, Chem, Elec, Phys etc) phase f; (Elec, fig) **in ~** en phase; (Elec, fig) **out of ~** déphasé [2] VT [+ innovations, developments] introduire graduellement; [+ execution of plan] procéder par étapes à; **the modernization of the factory was ~d over three years** la modernisation de l'usine s'est effectuée en trois ans par étapes; **the changes were ~d carefully so as to avoid unemployment** on a pris soin d'introduire les changements graduellement afin d'éviter le chômage; **we must ~ the various processes so as to lose as little time as possible** nous devons arranger or organiser les diverses opérations de façon à perdre le moins de temps possible; **~d changes** changements mpl organisés de façon progressive; **a ~d withdrawal of troops** un retrait progressif des troupes [3] COMP ► **phase-out** N suppression f progressive

► **phase in** VT SEP [+ new machinery, measures etc] introduire progressivement or graduellement

► **phase out** [1] VT SEP [+ machinery] retirer progressivement; [+ jobs] supprimer graduellement; [+ techniques, differences] éliminer progressivement [2] **~-out** N → **phase**

phatic ['fætɪk] ADJ phatique

PhD [,piːeɪtʃ'diː] N (Univ) (ABBR = **Doctor of Philosophy**) (= qualification) doctorat m; (=

person) ≈ titulaire *mf* d'un doctorat ; **to have a ~ in ...** avoir un doctorat de ...

pheasant ['feznt] N faisan *m* ; **cock ~** faisan *m* ; **hen ~** poule *f* faisane

phencyclidine [fen'sɪklɪ,di:n] N phencyclidine *f*

phenix ['fi:nɪks] N (*US*) = **phoenix**

phenobarbitone ['fi:nəʊ'bɑ:bɪtəʊn] N phénobarbital *m*

phenol ['fi:nɒl] N phénol *m*

phenomena [fɪ'nɒmɪnə] NPL of **phenomenon**

phenomenal [fɪ'nɒmɪnl] ADJ (*lit, fig*) phénoménal

phenomenally [fɪ'nɒmɪnəlɪ] ADV [*good, popular, well, quickly etc*] phénoménalement ; [*rise, increase*] de façon phénoménale ; **she has been ~ successful** elle a eu un succès phénoménal

phenomenological [fənɒmənə'lɒdʒɪkəl] ADJ phénoménologique

phenomenologist [fənɒmə'nɒlədʒɪst] N phénoménologue *mf*

phenomenology [fənɒmə'nɒlədʒɪ] N phénoménologie *f*

phenomenon [fɪ'nɒmɪnən] N (*pl* **phenomenons** or **phenomena**) (*lit, fig*) phénomène *m*

pheromone ['ferə,məʊn] N phéromone *f*

phew [fju:] EXCL (*relief*) ouf ! ; (*heat*) pfff ! ; (*disgust*) pouah ! ; (*surprise*) oh !

phial ['faɪəl] N fiole *f*

Phi Beta Kappa ['faɪ'beɪtə'kæpə] N (*US Univ*) *association élitiste d'anciens étudiants très brillants, ou membre de cette association*

┌──── **PHI BETA KAPPA** ────┐

Le **Phi Beta Kappa** *est le club estudiantin le plus ancien et le plus prestigieux des États-Unis. Fondé en 1776, il est réservé aux étudiants les plus brillants dont l'adhésion se fait par élection des membres au cours de la troisième ou de la quatrième année d'études universitaires. Le nom du club vient de l'expression grecque « philosophia biou kybernetes » (la philosophie pour diriger la vie), qui lui sert de devise. Un membre du club est un* **phi beta kappa**.

Phil ABBR = **Philadelphia**

Philadelphia [fɪlə'delfɪə] N Philadelphie

philander [fɪ'lændər] VI courir après les femmes, faire la cour aux femmes

philanderer [fɪ'lændərər] N coureur *m* (de jupons), don Juan *m*

philandering [fɪ'lændərɪŋ] N (*NonC*) flirts *mpl*, liaisons *fpl*

philanthropic [fɪlən'θrɒpɪk] ADJ philanthropique

philanthropist [fɪ'lænθrəpɪst] N philanthrope *mf*

philanthropy [fɪ'lænθrəpɪ] N philanthropie *f*

philatelic [fɪlə'telɪk] ADJ philatélique

philatelist [fɪ'lætəlɪst] N philatéliste *mf*

philately [fɪ'lætəlɪ] N philatélie *f*

...phile [faɪl] SUF ...phile ; **francophile** (*adj, n*) francophile *mf*

Philemon [faɪ'li:mɒn] N Philémon *m*

philharmonic [fɪlɑ:'mɒnɪk] ADJ philharmonique

philhellene [fɪl'heli:n] N, ADJ philhellène *mf*

philhellenic [fɪlhe'li:nɪk] ADJ philhellène

philhellenism [fɪl'helɪnɪzəm] N philhellénisme *m*

...philia [fɪlɪə] SUF ...philie *f* ; **francophilia** francophilie *f*

Philip ['fɪlɪp] N Philippe *m*

Philippi ['fɪlɪpaɪ] N Philippes

Philippians [fɪ'lɪpɪənz] NPL Philippiens *mpl*

philippic [fɪ'lɪpɪk] N (*liter*) philippique *f*

Philippine ['fɪlɪpi:n] [1] **Philippines** NPL = **the Philippine Islands** [2] COMP ► **the Philippine Islands** NPL les Philippines *fpl*

philistine ['fɪlɪstaɪn] [1] ADJ [a] (*fig*) béotien [b] **Philistine** philistin [2] N [a] (*Bible*) **Philistine** Philistin *m* [b] (*fig*) philistin *m*, béotien(ne) *m(f)*

philistinism ['fɪlɪstɪ,nɪzəm] N philistinisme *m*

Phillips® ['fɪlɪps] COMP **~ screw** vis *f* cruciforme ; **~ screwdriver** tournevis *m* cruciforme

philodendron [fɪlə'dendrən] N (*pl* **philodendrons** or **philodendra** [fɪlə'dendrə]) philodendron *m*

philological [fɪlə'lɒdʒɪkəl] ADJ philologique

philologist [fɪ'lɒlədʒɪst] N philologue *mf*

philology [fɪ'lɒlədʒɪ] N philologie *f*

philosopher [fɪ'lɒsəfər] [1] N philosophe *mf* ; (*fig*) **he is something of a ~** il est du genre philosophe [2] COMP ► **philosopher's stone** N pierre *f* philosophale

philosophic(al) [fɪlə'sɒfɪk(əl)] ADJ [a] (= *relating to philosophy*) [*subject, debate, discussion, tradition*] philosophique [b] (= *calm, resigned*) philosophe ; **in a ~ tone** d'un ton philosophe ; **to be ~ about sth** prendre qch avec philosophie

philosophically [fɪlə'sɒfɪkəlɪ] ADV [a] (= *with resignation*) avec philosophie [b] **~ important/disputable** *etc* philosophiquement important/disputable *etc*, important/discutable *etc* sur le plan philosophique ; **to be ~ inclined** or **minded** avoir l'esprit philosophique ; **he's ~ opposed to war** il est, par philosophie, opposé à la guerre

philosophize [fɪ'lɒsəfaɪz] VI philosopher (**about, on** sur)

philosophy [fɪ'lɒsəfɪ] N philosophie *f* ; **his ~ of life** sa philosophie, sa conception de la vie → **moral, natural**

philtre, philter (*US*) ['fɪltər] N philtre *m*

phiz: [fɪz], **phizog:** [fɪ'zɒg] N (ABBR = **physiognomy**) binette* *f*, bouille* *f*

phlebitis [flɪ'baɪtɪs] N phlébite *f*

phlebology [flɪ'bɒlədʒɪ] N phlébologie *f*

phlebotomist [flɪ'bɒtəmɪst] N phlébotomiste *mf*

phlebotomy [flɪ'bɒtəmɪ] N phlébotomie *f*

phlegm [flem] N [a] (= *mucus*) mucosité *f* [b] (= *equanimity*) flegme *m*

phlegmatic [fleg'mætɪk] ADJ flegmatique

phlegmatically [fleg'mætɪkəlɪ] ADV flegmatiquement, avec flegme

phlox [flɒks] N (*pl* **phlox** or **phloxes**) phlox *m inv*

Phnom-Penh ['nɒm'pen] N Phnom-Penh

...phobe [fəʊb] SUF ...phobe ; **francophobe** (*adj, n*) francophobe *mf*

phobia ['fəʊbɪə] N phobie *f* ; **I've got a ~ about ...** j'ai la phobie de ...

...phobia ['fəʊbɪə] SUF ...phobie *f* ; **anglophobia** anglophobie *f*

phobic ['fəʊbɪk] ADJ, N phobique *mf*

phoenix, phenix (*US*) ['fi:nɪks] N phénix *m* ; **like a ~ from the ashes** comme le phénix qui renaît de ses cendres

phonatory ['fəʊnətərɪ] ADJ phonateur (-trice *f*), phonatoire

▼ **phone**[1] [fəʊn] ABBR = **telephone** [1] N [a] (= *telephone*) téléphone *m* ; (*gen*) **on** or **over the ~** au téléphone ; (*Brit*) **to be on the ~** (= *be a subscriber*) avoir le téléphone ; (= *be speaking*) être au téléphone ; **I've got Jill on the ~** j'ai Jill au téléphone or au bout du fil* [b] (*Brit* = *phone call*) **to give sb a ~*** passer un coup de fil* à qn [2] VT (*also* **~ up**) téléphoner à, appeler, passer un coup de fil à* [3] VI téléphoner

[4] COMP ► **phone bill** N facture *f* de téléphone ► **phone book** N annuaire *m* (de téléphone) ► **phone booth** N [a] (*in station, hotel etc*) téléphone *m* public [b] (*US: in street*) cabine *f* téléphonique ► **phone box** N (*Brit*) cabine *f* téléphonique ► **phone call** N coup *m* de téléphone or de fil*, appel *m* téléphonique ; **to make a ~ call** passer un coup de téléphone or de fil*, téléphoner ► **phone-in (programme)** N (*Brit Rad, TV*) émission où les auditeurs ou téléspectateurs sont invités à intervenir par téléphone pour donner leur avis ou pour parler de leurs problèmes ► **phone number** N numéro *m* de téléphone ► **phone tapping** N mise *f* sur écoutes téléphoniques

► **phone back** [1] VT SEP (*returning call*) rappeler ; (*calling again*) rappeler, retéléphoner à [2] VI (= *return call*) rappeler ; (= *call again*) rappeler, retéléphoner

phone[2] [fəʊn] N (*Ling*) phone *m*

phonecard ['fəʊnkɑ:d] N (*Brit Telec*) télécarte® *f*

phoneme ['fəʊni:m] N phonème *m*

phonemic [fəʊ'ni:mɪk] ADJ phonémique

phonemics [fəʊ'ni:mɪks] N (*NonC*) phonémique *f*, phonématique *f*

phonetic [fəʊ'netɪk] [1] ADJ phonétique [2] COMP ► **phonetic alphabet** N alphabet *m* phonétique ► **phonetic law** N loi *f* phonétique

phonetically [fəʊ'netɪkəlɪ] ADV [*spell, learn*] phonétiquement ; **~ speaking** phonétiquement parlant

phonetician [fəʊnɪ'tɪʃən] N phonéticien(ne) *m(f)*

phonetics [fəʊ'netɪks] [1] N (*NonC* = *subject, study*) phonétique *f* ; **articulatory/acoustic/auditory ~** phonétique *f* articulatoire/acoustique/auditive [2] NPL (= *symbols*) transcription *f* phonétique ; **the ~ are wrong** la transcription phonétique est fausse [3] COMP [*teacher, student, exam, degree, textbook, laboratory*] de phonétique

phoney* ['fəʊnɪ] (*esp US*) [1] ADJ [*name*] faux (fausse *f*) ; [*jewels*] faux (fausse *f*), en toc ; [*emotion*] factice, simulé ; [*excuse, story, report*] bidon* *inv*, à la noix* ; [*person*] pas franc (franche *f*), poseur ; **this diamond is ~** ce diamant est faux ; **apparently he was a ~ doctor** il paraît que c'était un charlatan or un médecin marron ; **a ~ company** une société bidon* ; **it sounds ~** cela a l'air d'être de la frime* or de la blague* [2] N (*pl* **phoneys**) (= *person*) charlatan *m*, poseur *m*, faux jeton* *m* ; **that diamond is a ~** ce diamant est faux [3] COMP ► **the phoney war*** N (*Brit Hist: in 1939*) la drôle de guerre

phonic ['fɒnɪk] ADJ phonique

phono... ['fəʊnəʊ] PREF phono...

phonograph† ['fəʊnəgrɑ:f] N électrophone *m*, phonographe† *m*

phonological [fəʊnə'lɒdʒɪkəl] ADJ phonologique

phonologically [fəʊnə'lɒdʒɪklɪ] ADV phonologiquement

phonologist [fə'nɒlədʒɪst] N phonologue *mf*

phonology [fəʊ'nɒlədʒɪ] N phonologie *f*

phony* ['fəʊnɪ] = **phoney**

phooey* ['fu:ɪ] EXCL (*scorn*) peuh !, pfft !

phosgene ['fɒzdʒi:n] N phosgène *m*

phosphate ['fɒsfeɪt] N (*Chem*) phosphate *m* ; (*Agr*) **~s** phosphates *mpl*, engrais *mpl* phosphatés

phosphene ['fɒsfi:n] N phosphène *m*

phosphide ['fɒsfaɪd] N phosphure *m*

phosphine ['fɒsfi:n] N phosphine *f*

phosphoresce [fɒsfə'res] VI être phosphorescent

phosphorescence [fɒsfə'resns] N phosphorescence *f*

┌─────────────────────────────┐
│ ► LANGUAGE IN USE: **phone** 27.2, 27.3, 27.7 │
└─────────────────────────────┘

phosphorescent [ˌfɒsfəˈresnt] ADJ phosphorescent

phosphoric [fɒsˈfɒrɪk] ADJ phosphorique

phosphorous [ˈfɒsfərəs] ADJ phosphoreux

phosphorus [ˈfɒsfərəs] N phosphore m

photo [ˈfəʊtəʊ] 1 N (pl **photos**) (ABBR = **photograph**) photo f → **photograph** 2 COMP
► **photo album** N album m de photos
► **photo booth** N photomaton® m
► **photo finish** N (Sport) photo-finish m
► **photo opportunity** N séance f photo or de photos (pour la presse); **it is a great ~ opportunity** il y a de bonnes photos à prendre
► **photo session** N séance f photo or de photos

photo... [ˈfəʊtəʊ] PREF photo...

photocall [ˈfəʊtəʊˌkɔl] N (Brit Press) séance f de photos pour la presse

photocell [ˈfəʊtəʊˌsel] N photocellule f

photochemical [ˌfəʊtəʊˈkemɪkəl] ADJ photochimique

photochemistry [ˌfəʊtəʊˈkemɪstrɪ] N photochimie f

photocompose [ˌfəʊtəʊkəmˈpəʊz] VT photocomposer

photocomposer [ˌfəʊtəʊkəmˈpəʊzər] N photocomposeuse f

photocomposition [ˌfəʊtəʊkɒmpəˈzɪʃən] N photocomposition f

photocopier [ˈfəʊtəʊˌkɒpɪər] N photocopieur m, photocopieuse f

photocopy [ˈfəʊtəʊˌkɒpɪ] 1 N photocopie f 2 VT photocopier

photodisintegration [ˌfəʊtəʊdɪˌsɪntɪˈɡreɪʃən] N photodissociation f

photodisk [ˈfəʊtəʊˌdɪsk] N (Comput) photodisque m

photoelectric(al) [ˌfəʊtəʊɪˈlektrɪk(əl)] ADJ photo-électrique; **~ cell** cellule f photo-électrique

photoelectricity [ˌfəʊtəʊɪlekˈtrɪsɪtɪ] N photoélectricité f

photoelectron [ˌfəʊtəʊɪˈlektrɒn] N photoélectron m

photoengrave [ˌfəʊtəʊɪnˈɡreɪv] VT photograver

photoengraving [ˌfəʊtəʊɪnˈɡreɪvɪŋ] N photogravure f

Photofit® [ˈfəʊtəʊˌfɪt] N (Brit: also ~ **picture**) portrait-robot m

photoflash [ˈfəʊtəʊˌflæʃ] N flash m

photoflood [ˈfəʊtəʊˌflʌd] N projecteur m

photogenic [ˌfəʊtəˈdʒenɪk] ADJ photogénique

photogeology [ˌfəʊtəʊdʒɪˈɒlədʒɪ] N photogéologie f

photograph [ˈfəʊtəɡræf] 1 N photo f, photographie† f; **to take a ~ of sb/sth** prendre une photo de qn/qch, prendre qn/qch en photo; **he takes good ~s** il fait de bonnes photos; **he takes a good ~*** (= is photogenic) il est photogénique, il est bien en photo*; **in** or **on the ~** sur la photo → **aerial, colour** 2 VT photographier, prendre en photo 3 VI **to ~ well** être photogénique, être bien en photo* 4 COMP ► **photograph album** N album m de photos or de photographies†

photographer [fəˈtɒɡrəfər] N (also Press etc) photographe mf; **press ~** photographe mf de la presse, reporter m photographe; **street ~** photostoppeur m; **he's a keen ~** il est passionné de photo

photographic [ˌfəʊtəˈɡræfɪk] 1 ADJ photographique; **~ library** photothèque f 2 COMP ► **photographic memory** N mémoire f photographique

photographically [ˌfəʊtəˈɡræfɪkəlɪ] ADV photographiquement

photography [fəˈtɒɡrəfɪ] N (NonC) photographie f (NonC) → **colour, trick**

photogravure [ˌfəʊtəʊɡrəˈvjʊər] N photogravure f, héliogravure f

photojournalism [ˌfəʊtəʊˈdʒɜːnəlɪzəm] N photojournalisme m, photoreportage m

photojournalist [ˌfəʊtəʊˈdʒɜːnəlɪst] N photojournaliste mf, journaliste mf photographe

photokinesis [ˌfəʊtəʊkɪˈniːsɪs] N photokinésie f

photokinetic [ˌfəʊtəʊkɪˈnetɪk] ADJ photokinétique

photolitho [ˌfəʊtəʊˈlaɪθəʊ] N ABBR = **photolithography**

photolithograph [ˌfəʊtəʊˈlɪθəˌɡrɑːf] N gravure f photolithographique

photolithography [ˌfəʊtəʊlɪˈθɒɡrəfɪ] N photolithographie f

photolysis [fəʊˈtɒlɪsɪs] N photolyse f

photomachine [ˌfəʊtəʊməˈʃiːn] N photomaton® m

photomap [ˈfəʊtəʊˌmæp] N photoplan m

photomechanical [ˌfəʊtəʊmɪˈkænɪkl] ADJ photomécanique

photometer [fəʊˈtɒmɪtər] N photomètre m

photometric [ˌfəʊtəˈmetrɪk] ADJ photométrique

photometry [fəʊˈtɒmɪtrɪ] N photométrie f

photomontage [ˌfəʊtəʊmɒnˈtɑːʒ] N photomontage m

photomultiplier [ˌfəʊtəʊˈmʌltɪˌplaɪər] N photomultiplicateur m

photon [ˈfəʊtɒn] N photon m

photo-offset [ˌfəʊtəʊˈɒfˌset] N (Typ) offset m (processus)

photoperiodic [ˌfəʊtəʊˌpɪərɪˈɒdɪk] ADJ photopériodique

photoperiodism [ˌfəʊtəʊˈpɪərɪədɪzəm] N photopériodisme m

photophobia [ˌfəʊtəʊˈfəʊbɪə] N photophobie f

photorealism [ˌfəʊtəʊˈrɪəˌlɪzəm] N photoréalisme m

photoreconnaissance [ˌfəʊtəʊrɪˈkɒnɪsəns] N reconnaissance f photographique

photosensitive [ˌfəʊtəʊˈsensɪtɪv] ADJ photosensible

photosensitivity [ˌfəʊtəʊsensɪˈtɪvɪtɪ] N photosensibilité f

photosensitize [ˌfəʊtəʊˈsensɪˌtaɪz] VT photosensibiliser

photosensor [ˈfəʊtəʊˌsensər] N dispositif m photosensible

photoset [ˈfəʊtəʊˌset] VT photocomposer

Photostat® [ˈfəʊtəʊˌstæt] 1 N photostat m 2 VT photocopier

photosynthesis [ˌfəʊtəʊˈsɪnθɪsɪs] N photosynthèse f

photosynthesize [ˌfəʊtəʊˈsɪnθɪˌsaɪz] VT photosynthétiser

photosynthetic [ˌfəʊtəʊsɪnˈθetɪk] ADJ photosynthétique

phototelegram [ˌfəʊtəʊˈteleˌɡræm] N phototélégramme m

phototelegraphy [ˌfəʊtəʊtɪˈleɡrəfɪ] N phototélégraphie f

phototropic [ˌfəʊtəʊˈtrɒpɪk] ADJ phototropique

phototropism [ˌfəʊtəʊˈtrɒpɪzəm] N phototropisme m

phototype [ˈfəʊtəʊˌtaɪp] N (= process) phototypie f

phototypesetting [ˌfəʊtəʊˈtaɪpˌsetɪŋ] N (US Typ) photocomposition f

phototypography [ˌfəʊtəʊtaɪˈpɒɡrəfɪ] N phototypographie f

phrasal [ˈfreɪzl] 1 ADJ syntagmatique 2 COMP ► **phrasal verb** N verbe m à particule

phrase [freɪz] 1 N a (= saying) expression f; **as the ~ is** or **goes** comme on dit, selon l'expression consacrée; **to use Mrs Thatcher's ~ ...** comme dirait Mme Thatcher ...; **in Marx's famous ~ ...** pour reprendre la célèbre formule de Marx ...; **that's exactly the ~ I'm looking for** voilà exactement l'expression que je cherche → **set, turn** b (Ling: gen) locution f; (Gram) syntagme m; **noun/verb ~** syntagme m nominal/verbal c (Mus) phrase f 2 VT a [+ thought] exprimer; [+ letter] rédiger; **a neatly ~d letter** une lettre bien tournée; **can we ~ it differently?** peut-on exprimer or tourner cela différemment?; **she ~d her question carefully** elle a très soigneusement formulé sa question b (Mus) phraser 3 COMP ► **phrase marker** N (Ling) marqueur m syntagmatique ► **phrase structure** N (Ling) structure f syntagmatique ♦ ADJ [rule, grammar] syntagmatique

phrasebook [ˈfreɪzbʊk] N guide m de conversation

phraseology [ˌfreɪzɪˈɒlədʒɪ] N phraséologie f

phrasing [ˈfreɪzɪŋ] N a [of ideas] expression f; [of text] rédaction f, phraséologie f; **the ~ is unfortunate** les termes sont mal choisis b (Mus) phrasé m

phrenetic [frɪˈnetɪk] ADJ = **frenetic**

phrenic [ˈfrenɪk] ADJ (Anat) phrénique

phrenologist [frɪˈnɒlədʒɪst] N phrénologue mf, phrénologiste mf

phrenology [frɪˈnɒlədʒɪ] N phrénologie f

phthisis [ˈθaɪsɪs] N phtisie f

phut: [fʌt] ADV **to go ~** [machine, object] péter:, rendre l'âme*; [scheme, plan] tomber à l'eau

phycology [faɪˈkɒlədʒɪ] N phycologie f

phyla [ˈfaɪlə] NPL of **phylum**

phylactery [fɪˈlæktərɪ] N phylactère m

phylactic [fɪˈlæktɪk] ADJ phylactique

phyletic [faɪˈletɪk] ADJ phylogénique

phylloxera [ˌfɪlɒkˈsɪərə] N phylloxéra m

phylogenesis [ˌfaɪləʊˈdʒenɪsɪs] N phylogenèse f

phylogenetic [ˌfaɪləʊdʒɪˈnetɪk] ADJ phylogénique

phylum [ˈfaɪləm] N (pl **phyla**) phylum m

physic†† [ˈfɪzɪk] N médicament m

physical [ˈfɪzɪkəl] 1 ADJ a (= of the body) physique; **~ contact** contact m physique; **~ cruelty** brutalité f, sévices mpl; **it's a ~ impossibility for him to get there on time** il lui est physiquement or matériellement impossible d'arriver là-bas à l'heure b (= sexual) [love, relationship] physique; **~ attraction** attirance f physique c [geography, properties, sciences] physique; [world, universe, object] matériel d (* = tactile) [person] qui aime les contacts physiques 2 N (Med*) examen m médical, bilan m de santé, check-up* m inv; **to go for a ~** aller passer une visite médicale 3 COMP ► **physical activity** N activité f physique ► **physical education** N (Scol) éducation f physique ► **physical examination** N examen m médical, bilan m de santé ► **physical exercise** N exercice m physique ► **physical fitness** N forme f physique ► **physical handicap** N handicap m physique ► **physical jerks**†* NPL (Brit Scol) exercices mpl d'assouplissement, gymnastique f ► **physical therapist** N (US Med) physiothérapeute mf, kinésithérapeute mf ► **physical therapy** N (US Med) physiothérapie f, kinésithérapie f; **to have ~ therapy** faire de la rééducation ► **physical training**† N (Scol) éducation f physique

physically [ˈfɪzɪkəlɪ] ADV [restrain] de force; [violent, attractive, demanding, separate] physiquement; [*possible, impossible*] matériellement; **to be ~ fit** être en bonne forme physique; **to be ~ capable/incapable of (doing) sth** être physiquement capable/incapable de faire qch; **to be ~ sick** vomir; **to feel ~ sick** avoir envie de vomir; **he is ~ handicapped** or **disabled** or **challenged** c'est un handicapé physique, il a un handicap physique; **to abuse sb ~** [+ *partner*] battre qn; [+ *child*] maltraiter qn; **she was abused ~ but not sexually** elle a été brutalisée mais pas violée

physician [fɪˈzɪʃən] N médecin *m*

physicist [ˈfɪzɪsɪst] N physicien(ne) *m(f)*; **experimental/theoretical ~** physicien(ne) *m(f)* de physique expérimentale/théorique → **atomic**

physics [ˈfɪzɪks] N (*NonC*) physique *f*; **experimental/theoretical ~** physique *f* expérimentale/théorique → **atomic, nuclear**

physio* [ˈfɪzɪəʊ] N (*Brit*) a ABBR = **physiotherapy** b ABBR = **physiotherapist**

physio... [ˈfɪzɪəʊ] PREF physio...

physiognomy [ˌfɪzɪˈɒnəmɪ] N (*gen*) physionomie *f*; (* *hum* = *face*) bobine* *f*, bouille* *f*

physiological [ˌfɪzɪəˈlɒdʒɪkəl] ADJ physiologique

physiologically [ˌfɪzɪəˈlɒdʒɪkəlɪ] ADV physiologiquement

physiologist [ˌfɪzɪˈɒlədʒɪst] N physiologiste *mf*

physiology [ˌfɪzɪˈɒlədʒɪ] N physiologie *f*

physiotherapist [ˌfɪzɪəˈθerəpɪst] N physiothérapeute *mf*, ≈ kinésithérapeute *mf*

physiotherapy [ˌfɪzɪəˈθerəpɪ] N physiothérapie *f*, ≈ kinésithérapie *f*

physique [fɪˈziːk] N physique *m*; **he has the ~ of a footballer** il est bâti comme un footballeur; **he has a fine/poor ~** il est bien/mal bâti

phytogeography [ˌfaɪtəʊdʒɪˈɒɡrəfɪ] N phytogéographie *f*

phytology [faɪˈtɒlədʒɪ] N phytobiologie *f*

phytopathology [ˌfaɪtəʊpəˈθɒlədʒɪ] N phytopathologie *f*

phytoplankton [ˌfaɪtəˈplæŋktən] N phytoplancton *m*

PI [piːˈaɪ] N (ABBR = **private investigator**) → **private**

pi¹* [paɪ] ADJ (*Brit pej*) (ABBR = **pious**) [*person*] satisfait de soi, suffisant; [*expression*] suffisant, béat; (= *sanctimonious*) bigot

pi² [paɪ] N (*pl* **pis**) (*Math*) pi *m*

pianissimo [pɪəˈnɪsɪˌməʊ] ADJ, ADV pianissimo

pianist [ˈpɪənɪst] N pianiste *mf*

piano [ˈpjɑːnəʊ] 1 N (*pl* **pianos**) piano *m* → **baby, grand, upright** 2 ADV (*Mus*) piano 3 COMP ► **piano-accordion** N accordéon *m* à clavier ► **piano concerto** N concerto *m* pour piano ► **piano duet** N morceau *m* pour quatre mains ► **piano lesson** N leçon *f* de piano ► **piano music** N **I'd like some ~ music** je voudrais de la musique pour piano; **I love ~ music** j'adore écouter de la musique pour piano, j'adore le piano ► **piano organ** N orgue *m* mécanique ► **piano piece** N morceau *m* pour piano ► **piano stool** N tabouret *m* de piano ► **piano teacher** N professeur *m* de piano ► **piano tuner** N accordeur *m* (de piano)

pianoforte [ˌpjɑːnəʊˈfɔːtɪ] N (*frm*) = **piano 1**

Pianola® [pɪəˈnəʊlə] N piano *m* mécanique, pianola® *m*

piazza [pɪˈætsə] N a (= *square*) place *f*, piazza *f* b (*US*) véranda *f*

pibroch [ˈpiːbrɒx] N pibroch *m*

pica [ˈpaɪkə] N (*Typ*) douze *m*, cicéro *m*

picador [ˈpɪkədɔːʳ] N picador *m*

Picardy [ˈpɪkədɪ] N Picardie *f*

picaresque [ˌpɪkəˈresk] ADJ picaresque

picayune* [ˌpɪkəˈjuːn] ADJ (*US*) insignifiant, mesquin

piccalilli [ˈpɪkəˌlɪlɪ] N (espèce *f* de) pickles *mpl*

piccaninny [ˈpɪkəˌnɪnɪ] N négrillon(ne) *m(f)*

piccolo [ˈpɪkələʊ] N (*pl* **piccolos**) piccolo *m*

pick [pɪk] 1 N a (= *tool*) pioche *f*, pic *m*; (*Climbing: also* **ice ~**) piolet *m*; [*of mason*] smille *f*; [*of miner*] rivelaine *f* → **ice, toothpick** b (= *choice*) choix *m*; **to have one's ~ of sth** avoir le choix de qch; **she could have had her ~ of any man in the room** aucun des hommes de l'assistance n'aurait pu lui résister, elle aurait pu jeter son dévolu sur n'importe quel homme dans l'assistance; **children living closest to the school get first ~*** les enfants qui vivent le plus près de l'école sont prioritaires; **squatters get first ~* of all these empty flats** les squatters ont la priorité pour choisir parmi tous ces appartements vides; **to take one's ~** faire son choix; **take your ~** choisissez, vous avez le choix c (= *best*) meilleur; **the ~ of the bunch*** or **the crop** le meilleur de tous

2 VT a (= *choose*) choisir; **to ~ sb to do sth** choisir qn pour faire qch; **~ a card, any card** choisissez une carte; (*Sport*) **to ~ (the) sides** former or sélectionner les équipes; (*Sport*) **she was ~ed for England** elle a été sélectionnée pour être dans l'équipe d'Angleterre; (*Racing*) **he ~ed the winner** il a pronostiqué le (cheval) gagnant; (*Racing*) **I'm not very good at ~ing the winner** je ne suis pas très doué pour choisir le gagnant; (*fig*) **they certainly ~ed a winner in Colin Smith** avec Colin Smith ils ont vraiment tiré le bon numéro b **to ~ one's way through/among** avancer avec précaution à travers/parmi; **to ~ a fight (with sb)** (*physical*) chercher la bagarre* (avec qn); **to ~ a fight** or **a quarrel with sb** chercher noise or querelle à qn c (= *pluck*) [+ *fruit, flower*] cueillir; [+ *mushrooms*] ramasser; (*at fruit farm*) **"~ your own"** « cueillette à la ferme » d (= *pick at, fiddle with*) [+ *spot, scab*] gratter, écorcher; **to ~ one's nose** se mettre les doigts dans le nez; **to ~ a splinter from one's hand** s'enlever une écharde de la main; **to ~ a bone** (*with teeth*) ronger un os; [*bird*] nettoyer un os → **bone**; **to ~ one's teeth** se curer les dents; **you've ~ed a hole in your jersey** à force de tirer sur un fil tu as fait un trou à ton pull; **to ~ holes in an argument** relever les défauts or les failles d'un raisonnement; **their lawyers ~ed holes in the evidence** leurs avocats ont relevé des failles dans le témoignage; **to ~ sb's brains*** faire appel aux lumières de qn; **I need to ~ your brains about something*** j'ai besoin de vos lumières à propos de quelque chose; **to ~ a lock** crocheter une serrure; **to ~ pockets** pratiquer le vol à la tire; **I've had my pocket ~ed** on m'a fait les poches

3 VI a (= *choose*) choisir; (= *be fussy*) faire la fine bouche; **to ~ and choose** faire le (or la) difficile; **I haven't got time to ~ and choose** je n'ai pas le temps de faire la fine bouche; **you can afford to ~ and choose** tu peux te permettre de faire la fine bouche or de faire le difficile; **you can ~ and choose from the menu** vous pouvez choisir ce que vous voulez dans le menu; **consumers can ~ and choose from among the many telephone companies** les consommateurs peuvent choisir or ont le choix entre les nombreuses compagnies de téléphone b (= *poke, fiddle*) **to ~ at one's food** manger du bout des dents, chipoter*; **the bird ~ed at the bread** l'oiseau picorait le pain; **don't ~!** (*at food*) ne chipote pas!; (*at spot, scab*) ne gratte pas!; **don't ~ at your spots!** ne gratte pas tes boutons!

4 COMP ► **pick-me-up*** N remontant *m*

► **pick at*** VT FUS (*US*) = **pick on a**

► **pick off** VT SEP a [+ *paint*] gratter, enlever; [+ *flower, leaf*] cueillir, enlever b (= *kill*) **he ~ed off the sentry** il a visé soigneusement et a abattu la sentinelle; **he ~ed off the three sentries** il a abattu les trois sentinelles l'une après l'autre; **the lions ~ off any stragglers** les lions éliminent les traînards

► **pick on** VT FUS a (* = *nag, harass*) harceler, s'en prendre à*; **he's always ~ing on Robert** il s'en prend toujours à Robert*, c'est toujours après Robert qu'il en a*; **~ on someone your own size!** ne t'en prends pas à un plus petit que toi! b (= *choose*) choisir; (= *single out*) choisir, désigner; **why did they ~ on Venice for their holiday?** pourquoi ont-ils choisi Venise comme destination de vacances?; **the teacher ~ed on him to collect the books** le professeur le choisit or le désigna pour ramasser les livres; **why ~ on me? All the rest did the same** pourquoi t'en (or s'en) prendre à moi? Les autres ont fait la même chose

► **pick out** VT SEP a (= *choose*) choisir; **~ out two or three you would like to keep** choisissez-en deux ou trois que vous aimeriez garder; **she ~ed two apples out of the basket** elle choisit deux pommes dans le panier; **he had already ~ed out his successor** il avait déjà choisi son successeur b (= *distinguish*) repérer, distinguer; (*in identification parade*) identifier; **I couldn't ~ out anyone I knew in the crowd** je ne pouvais repérer or distinguer personne de ma connaissance dans la foule; **can you ~ out the melody in this passage?** pouvez-vous repérer or distinguer la mélodie dans ce passage?; **can you ~ me out in this photo?** pouvez-vous me reconnaître sur cette photo?; **to ~ out a tune on the piano** (= *play*) retrouver un air au piano c (= *highlight*) **to ~ out a colour** rehausser or mettre en valeur une couleur; **letters ~ed out in gold on a black background** caractères rehaussés d'or sur fond noir; **the bright light ~ed out all her grey hairs** la lumière crue faisait ressortir tous ses cheveux gris

► **pick over** VT SEP (= *examine, sort through*) [+ *fruit, lentils, rice*] trier; [+ *events, details, evidence*] décortiquer; **she was ~ing over the shirts in the sale** elle examinait les chemises en solde les unes après les autres; **it's no good ~ing over the past** cela ne sert à rien de ressasser le passé

► **pick through** VT FUS = **pick over**

► **pick up** 1 VI a (= *improve*) [*conditions, programme, weather*] s'améliorer; [*prices, wages*] remonter; [*trade, business*] reprendre; [*invalid*] se rétablir, se remettre; **business has ~ed up recently** les affaires ont repris récemment; **his support has ~ed up recently** sa cote de popularité a remonté récemment; (*Comm, Fin*) **the market will ~ up soon** le marché va bientôt remonter; **things are ~ing up a bit*** ça commence à aller mieux b (= *resume*) continuer, reprendre; **to ~ up (from) where one had left off** reprendre là où on s'était arrêté; **so, to ~ up where I left off, ...** alors je reprends là où je m'étais arrêté ...

2 VT SEP a (= *lift*) [+ *sth dropped, book, clothes etc*] ramasser; (*after fall*) **to ~ o.s. up** se relever, se remettre debout; **he ~ed up the child** (*gen*) il a pris l'enfant dans ses bras; (*after fall*) il a relevé l'enfant; **he ~ed up the phone and dialled a number** il a décroché (le téléphone) et a composé un numéro; **~ up all your clothes before you go out!** ramasse tous tes vêtements avant de sortir!; **to ~ up the pieces** (*lit*) ramasser les morceaux; (*fig*) recoller les morceaux; **she's trying to ~ up the pieces of her career/her marriage** elle essaie de recoller les morceaux de sa carrière/de son couple; **to ~ up the threads of one's life** se reprendre en main b (= *collect*) (*passer*) prendre; **can you ~ up my coat from the cleaners?** pourrais-tu (passer) prendre mon manteau chez le

teinturier?; **I'll ~ up the books next week** je passerai prendre les livres la semaine prochaine
c [+ *passenger, hitch-hiker*] (*in bus, car etc*) prendre; (*in taxi*) charger; **I'll ~ you up at 6 o'clock** je passerai vous prendre à 6 heures, je viendrai vous chercher à 6 heures
d [+ *girl, boy*] ramasser; **he ~ed up a girl at the cinema** il a ramassé une fille au cinéma
e (= *buy, obtain*) dénicher; **she ~ed up a secondhand car for just £800** elle a déniché une voiture d'occasion pour seulement 800 livres; **it's a book you can ~ up anywhere** c'est un livre que l'on peut trouver partout; **to ~ up a bargain in the sales** trouver une bonne affaire dans les soldes
f (= *acquire, learn*) [+ *language, skill*] apprendre; [+ *habit*] prendre; **he ~ed up French very quickly** il n'a pas mis longtemps à apprendre le français; **I've ~ed up a bit of German** j'ai appris quelques mots d'allemand; **you'll soon ~ it up** tu t'y mettras rapidement, ça viendra vite; **you'll soon ~ it up again** tu t'y remettras rapidement, ça reviendra vite; **to ~ up an accent** prendre un accent; **to ~ up bad habits** prendre de mauvaises habitudes; **to ~ up a bit of news about him today** j'ai appris quelque chose sur lui aujourd'hui; **see what you can ~ up about their export scheme** essayez d'avoir des renseignements *or* des tuyaux* sur leur plan d'exportations; **our agents have ~ed up something about it** nos agents ont appris *or* découvert quelque chose là-dessus; **the papers ~ed up the story** les journaux se sont emparés de l'affaire
g (= *detect*) [*security camera etc*] [+ *person, object, sound*] détecter; [*Rad, Telec*] [+ *station, signal, programme, message*] capter; **the dogs immediately ~ed up the scent** les chiens ont tout de suite détecté l'odeur; **the cameras ~ed him up as he left the hall** en sortant du hall il est entré dans le champ des caméras
h (= *rescue*) recueillir; (*from sea*) recueillir, repêcher; **the helicopter/lifeboat ~ed up ten survivors** l'hélicoptère/le canot de sauvetage a recueilli dix survivants
i (* = *take in*) [+ *suspect*] interpeller, cueillir*; **they ~ed him up for questioning** on l'a interpellé pour l'interroger
j (= *notice*) [+ *sb's error etc*] relever, ne pas laisser passer; **he ~ed up ten misprints** il a relevé *or* repéré dix fautes d'impression; **he ~ed up every mistake** il n'a pas laissé passer une seule erreur
k (= *reprimand*) faire une remarque *or* une observation à, reprendre; **she ~ed me up for this mistake** elle m'a repris sur cette erreur
l (= *gain*) **to ~ up speed** [*car, boat*] prendre de la vitesse; (*Sport*) **he managed to ~ up a few points in the later events** il a réussi à gagner *or* rattraper quelques points dans les épreuves suivantes; **he ~ed up a reputation as a womanizer** il s'est fait une réputation de coureur de jupons
3 VT FUS* (= *earn*) gagner, toucher*; (= *pay*) **to ~ up the bill** *or* **tab** payer la note *or* l'addition
4 **~up → pickup**
5 **~-me-up* → pick**

pickaback ['pɪkəbæk] = **piggyback 1, 2, 3a**
pick-and-mix ['pɪkən,mɪks] ADJ = **pick 'n' mix**
pickaninny ['pɪkə,nɪnɪ] N = **piccaninny**
pickaxe, pickax (*US*) ['pɪkæks] N pic *m*, pioche *f*
picker ['pɪkər] N (*gen in compounds*) cueilleur *m*, -euse *f*; **apple-~** cueilleur *m*, -euse *f* de pommes → **cherry**
picket ['pɪkɪt] **1** N **a** (*Ind, Pol*) (*during strike*) piquet *m* de grève; (*at civil demonstrations*) piquet *m* (de manifestants) **b** (*Mil*) (= *group of soldiers*) détachement *m* (de soldats); (= *sentry*) factionnaire *m*; **fire ~** piquet *m* d'incendie **c** (= *stake*) pieu *m*, piquet *m* **2** VT **a** (*Ind,*

Pol) **to ~ a factory** mettre un piquet de grève aux portes d'une usine; **the demonstrators ~ed the embassy** les manifestants ont formé un cordon devant l'ambassade **b** [+ *field*] clôturer **3** VI [*strikers*] organiser un piquet de grève **4** COMP ► **picket duty** N (*Ind*) **to be on ~ duty** faire partie d'un piquet de grève ► **picket fence** N palissade *f* ► **picket line** N piquet *m* de grève; **to cross a ~ line** traverser un piquet de grève
picketing ['pɪkɪtɪŋ] N (*NonC*) piquets *mpl* de grève; **there was no ~** il n'y a pas eu de piquet de grève → **secondary**
picking ['pɪkɪŋ] **1** N [*of object from group*] choix *m*; [*of candidate, leader*] choix *m*, sélection *f*; [*of fruit, vegetables*] cueillette *f*; [*of lock*] crochetage *m*; (= *careful choosing*) triage *m* **2** **pickings** NPL **a** (*of food*) restes *mpl* **b** (*fig = profits etc*) **there are rich ~s to be had** ça pourrait rapporter gros; **easy ~s for thieves** butin *m* facile pour des voleurs
pickle ['pɪkl] **1** N **a** (*NonC: Culin*) (= *brine*) saumure *f*; (= *wine, spices*) marinade *f*; (= *vinegar*) vinaigre *m* **b** **~(s)** pickles *mpl* (*petits légumes macérés dans du vinaigre*) **c** (* = *awkward situation*) **to be in a (pretty** *or* **fine) ~** être dans de beaux draps, être dans le pétrin; **I'm in rather a ~** je suis plutôt dans le pétrin **2** VT (*in brine*) conserver dans de la saumure; (*in vinegar*) conserver dans du vinaigre **3** COMP ► **pickling onions** NPL petits oignons *mpl*
pickled ['pɪkld] ADJ **a** [*cucumber, herring, cabbage*] conservé *or* macéré dans du vinaigre **b** (* = *drunk*) bourré*, ivre
picklock ['pɪklɒk] N **a** (= *key*) crochet *m*, rossignol *m* **b** (= *thief*) crocheteur *m*
pick 'n' mix* ['pɪkən,mɪks] ADJ [*approach, selection, collection*] hétéroclite; [*morality, politics*] qui réunit sélectivement des éléments hétéroclites
pickpocket ['pɪk,pɒkɪt] N pickpocket *m*, voleur *m*, -euse *f* à la tire
pickup ['pɪkʌp] **1** N **a** [*of record-player*] pick-up *m inv*, lecteur *m*
b (*Aut = passenger*) passager *m*, -ère *f* ramassé(e) en route; **the bus made three ~s** l'autobus s'est arrêté trois fois pour prendre *or* laisser monter des passagers
c (* = *casual lover*) partenaire *mf* de rencontre
d (= *collection*) **to make a ~** [*truck driver*] s'arrêter pour charger (des marchandises); [*drug runner, drug dealer*] aller chercher de la marchandise; **~ point** (*for people*) point *m* de rendez-vous; (*for goods*) point de collecte
e (*NonC: Aut = acceleration*) reprise(s) *f(pl)*
f (= *recovery*) (*Med*) rétablissement *m*; (*in trade etc*) reprise *f* (d'activité)
g (*: also* **pick-me-up**) remontant *m*
h = **pickup truck**
2 ADJ (*Sport*) [*game*] impromptu, improvisé; **~ side** équipe *f* de fortune
3 COMP ► **pickup truck, pickup van** N (*Brit*) camionnette *f* (découverte), pick-up *m*
picky* ['pɪkɪ] ADJ difficile (à satisfaire)
picnic ['pɪknɪk] (*vb: pret, ptp* **picnicked**) **1** N pique-nique *m*; (*fig*) **it's no ~*** ce n'est pas une partie de plaisir, c'est pas de la tarte*; **it's no ~* bringing up children on your own** ce n'est pas une partie de plaisir d'élever seul des enfants **2** VI pique-niquer, faire un pique-nique **3** COMP ► **picnic basket** N panier *m* à pique-nique ► **picnic ham** N (*US*) ≈ jambonneau *m* ► **picnic hamper** N = picnic basket
picnicker ['pɪknɪkər] N pique-niqueur *m*, -euse *f*
pics* [pɪks] NPL ABBR = **pictures a** (= *films*) ciné *m* **b** (= *photos*) photos *fpl*
Pict [pɪkt] N Picte *mf*
Pictish ['pɪktɪʃ] ADJ picte
pictogram ['pɪktə,græm] N pictogramme *m*

pictograph ['pɪktəgrɑːf] N **a** (= *record, chart etc*) pictogramme *m* **b** (*Ling*) (= *symbol*) idéogramme *m*; (= *writing*) idéographie *f*
pictorial [pɪk'tɔːrɪəl] **1** ADJ [*magazine, calendar*] illustré; [*record*] en images; [*work*] pictural; [*masterpiece*] pictural, de peinture **2** N illustré *m*
pictorially [pɪk'tɔːrɪəlɪ] ADV en images, au moyen d'images, à l'aide d'images
picture ['pɪktʃər] **1** N **a** (*gen*) image *f*; (= *illustration*) image *f*, illustration *f*; (= *photograph*) photo *f*; (*TV*) image *f*; (= *painting*) tableau *m*, peinture *f*; (= *portrait*) portrait *m*; (= *engraving*) gravure *f*; (= *reproduction*) reproduction *f*; (= *drawing*) dessin *m*; **a ~ by David Hockney** un tableau de David Hockney; **a ~ of David Hockney** un tableau *or* un dessin représentant David Hockney, un portrait de David Hockney; **a ~ of David Hockney's** (= *owned by him*) un tableau appartenant à David Hockney; **~s made by reflections in the water** images *fpl* produites par les reflets sur l'eau; (*TV*) **we have the sound but no ~** nous avons le son mais pas l'image; **to paint/draw a ~** faire un tableau/un dessin; **to paint/draw a ~ of sth** peindre/dessiner qch ■ (*PROV*) **every ~ tells a story** chaque image raconte une histoire ■ (*PROV*) **a ~ is worth a thousand words** une image en dit plus que de longs discours (*PROV*) → **pretty**
b (*fig = description*) (*spoken*) tableau *m*; (= *mental image*) image *f*, représentation *f*; **he gave us a ~ of the scenes at the front line** il nous brossa *or* nous fit un tableau de la situation au front; **to paint a gloomy/optimistic ~ of sth** brosser un sombre tableau/un tableau optimiste de qch; **eye witness accounts painted a ~ of anarchy** les récits des témoins oculaires (nous) ont donné l'image d'une situation anarchique; (*fig*) **to form a ~ of sth** se faire une idée de qch; **I have a clear ~ of him as he was when I saw him last** je le revois clairement *or* je me souviens très bien de lui tel qu'il était la dernière fois que je l'ai vu; **I have no very clear ~ of the room** je ne me représente pas très bien la pièce; **these figures give the general ~** ces chiffres donnent un tableau général de la situation; **(do you) get the ~?*** tu vois le tableau?*, tu piges?*; **OK, I get the ~*** ça va, j'ai compris *or* pigé*; **to be/put sb/keep sb in the ~** être/mettre qn/tenir qn au courant; **to be left out of the ~** être mis sur la touche *or* éliminé de la scène
c (*fig phrases*) **she was a ~ in her new dress** elle était ravissante dans sa nouvelle robe; **the garden is (like) a ~ in June** le jardin est magnifique en juin; **he is the** *or* **a ~ of health/happiness** il respire la santé/le bonheur; **he is** *or* **looks the ~ of misery** c'est la tristesse incarnée; **the other side of the ~** le revers de la médaille; **his face was a ~!*** son expression en disait long!, si vous aviez vu sa tête!*
d (*Cine*) film *m*; **they made a ~ about it** on en a fait *or* tiré un film; (*esp Brit*) **to go to the ~s†** aller au cinéma, aller voir un film; (*esp Brit*) **what's on at the ~s?†** qu'est-ce qui passe *or* qu'est-ce qu'on donne au cinéma? → **motion**
2 VT **a** (= *imagine*) s'imaginer, se représenter; **I can just ~ the consequences** je m'imagine très bien les conséquences; **can you ~ him as a father?** tu l'imagines père?; **I can't quite ~ it somehow** j'ai du mal à imaginer ça; **~ yourself as a father/lying on the beach** imaginez-vous dans le rôle de père/étendu sur la plage
b (= *describe*) dépeindre, décrire
c (*by drawing etc*) représenter; **the photo ~d her crossing the finishing line** la photo la représentait en train de franchir la ligne d'arrivée
3 COMP ► **picture book** N livre *m* d'images ► **picture card** N (*Cards*) figure *f* ► **picture**

desk N (*Brit Press*) service *m* photo (*d'un journal*) ► **picture editor** N (*Press*) directeur *m*, -trice *f* du service photo (*d'un journal*) ► **picture frame** N cadre *m* ► **picture-framer** N encadreur *m*, -euse *f* ► **picture-framing** N encadrement *m* ► **picture gallery** N (*public*) musée *m* (de peinture); (*private*) galerie *f* (de peinture) ► **picture hat** N capeline *f* ► **picture house**† N cinéma *m* ► **picture-in-picture** N (*NonC: TV, Comput*) insertion *f* d'image ► **picture postcard** N carte *f* postale (illustrée) ► **picture rail** N cimaise *f* ► **picture tube** N (*TV*) tube *m* cathodique ► **picture window** N fenêtre *f* panoramique ► **picture writing** N écriture *f* pictographique

picturegoer ['pɪktʃə,gəʊəʳ] N cinéphile *mf*, amateur *m* de cinéma

picturesque [,pɪktʃə'resk] ADJ pittoresque

picturesquely [,pɪktʃə'resklɪ] ADV pittoresquement; **a cliff ~ known as the Black Ladders** une falaise surnommée de façon pittoresque les Échelles Noires

picturesqueness [,pɪktʃə'resknɪs] N pittoresque *m*

piddle: ['pɪdl] VI faire pipi*

piddling* ['pɪdlɪŋ] ADJ (= *insignificant*) insignifiant, futile; (= *small*) négligeable, de rien

pidgin ['pɪdʒɪn] N [a] (*NonC: also ~* **English**) pidgin-english *m* [b] (*Ling*° = *improvised language*) sabir *m* [c] (*fig pej* = *illiterate language*) charabia *m*, jargon *m*; **~ English/French** mauvais anglais *m*/français *m* [d]* = **pigeon 1b**

pie [paɪ] [1] N [*of fruit, fish, meat with gravy etc*] tourte *f*; (*with compact filling*) pâté *m* en croûte; **apple ~** tourte *f* aux pommes; **rabbit/chicken ~** tourte *f* au lapin/au poulet; **pork ~** pâté *m* en croûte; **it's (all) ~ in the sky*** ce sont des promesses en l'air *or* de belles promesses (*iro*); (*fig*) **they want a piece of the ~** ils veulent leur part du gâteau; **Robert has a finger in the** *or* **that ~** (*gen*) il y a du Robert là-dessous, Robert y est pour quelque chose; (*financially*) Robert a des intérêts là-dedans *or* dans cette affaire; **he's got a finger in every ~** il se mêle de tout, il est mêlé à tout; (*US fig*) **that's ~ to him*** pour lui, c'est du gâteau* → **humble, mud** [2] COMP ► **pie chart** N (*Math*) graphique *m* circulaire, camembert* *m* ► **pie dish** N plat *m* allant au four, terrine *f* ► **pie-eyed** ADJ beurré*, rond* ► **pie plate** N moule *m* à tarte, tourtière *f*

piebald ['paɪbɔːld] [1] ADJ [*horse*] pie *inv* [2] N cheval *m* *or* jument *f* pie

---

piece [piːs]

1 NOUN	**3** PHRASAL VERBS
2 COMPOUNDS	

1 NOUN

[a] = **bit, portion** morceau *m*; [*of cloth, chocolate, glass, paper*] morceau *m*, bout *m*; [*of bread, cake*] morceau *m*, tranche *f*; [*of wood*] bout *m*, morceau *m*; (*large*) pièce *f*; [*of ribbon, string*] bout *m*; (= *broken or detached part*) morceau *m*, fragment *m*; (*Comm, Ind* = *part*) pièce *f*; (= *item, section, also Chess*) pièce *f*; (*Draughts*) pion *m*; **a ~ of silk/paper** *etc* un morceau de soie/de papier *etc*; **a ~ of land** (*for agriculture*) une pièce *or* parcelle de terre; (*for building*) un lotissement; **a ~ of meat** un morceau *or* une pièce de viande; (*left over*) un morceau *or* un bout de viande; **a ~ of beef** j'ai acheté un beau morceau de bœuf; **a sizeable ~ of beef** une belle pièce de bœuf; **I've got a ~ of grit in my eye** j'ai une poussière *or* une escarbille dans l'œil; **a ~ of clothing** un vêtement; **a ~ of fabric** un morceau de tissu; **a ~ of fruit** (= *whole fruit*) un fruit; (= *segment: of orange, grapefruit etc*) un quartier de fruit; **a ~ of furniture** un meuble; **a ~ of software** un logiciel; **a 30-~ tea set** un service à thé de 30 pièces; **three ~s of luggage** trois bagages; **how many ~s of luggage have you got?** qu'est-ce que vous avez comme bagages?; **~ by ~** morceau par morceau; **there's a ~ missing** (*of jigsaw, game*) il y a une pièce qui manque; **to put** *or* **fit together the ~s of a mystery** résoudre un mystère en rassemblant les éléments

♦ **in one piece**: the vase is still in one ~ le vase ne s'est pas cassé *or* est intact; **he had a nasty fall but he's still in one ~*** il a fait une mauvaise chute mais il est entier* *or* indemne; **we got back in one ~*** nous sommes rentrés sains et saufs

♦ **(all) of a piece**: the back is (all) of a ~ with the seat le dossier et le siège sont d'un seul tenant; **this latest volume is all of a ~ with her earlier poetry** ce dernier volume est dans l'esprit de ses poèmes précédents

♦ **by the piece** (*Comm*) sold by the ~ vendu à la pièce *or* au détail; (*Ind*) paid by the ~ payé à la pièce

♦ **in pieces** (= *broken*) en pièces, en morceaux; (= *not yet assembled: furniture etc*) en pièces détachées

♦ **to come/fall/go** *etc* **to pieces**: it comes *or* takes to ~s c'est démontable; **it just came to ~s** c'est parti en morceaux *or* en pièces détachées (*hum*); **the chair comes to ~s if you unscrew the screws** la chaise se démonte si on desserre les vis; **to cut sth to ~s** couper qch en morceaux; **it fell to ~s** c'est tombé en morceaux; **to take sth to ~s** démonter qch, désassembler qch; **to smash sth to ~s** briser qch en mille morceaux, mettre qch en miettes; **the boat was smashed to ~s** le bateau vola en éclats; (*fig*) **to go to ~s*** [*person*] (= *collapse*) s'effondrer; (*emotionally*) lâcher pied (*fig*); [*team etc*] se désintégrer; **his confidence is shot to ~s*** il a perdu toute confiance en lui; **the economy is shot to ~s*** l'économie est ruinée → **pull, tear**¹

[b] with abstract nouns a ~ of information un renseignement; **a ~ of advice** un conseil; **a ~ of news** une nouvelle; **a ~ of research** une recherche; **a good ~ of work** du bon travail; (*fig*) **he's a nasty ~ of work*** c'est un sale type*; **it's a ~ of folly** c'est de la folie; **a ~ of nonsense** une absurdité, une bêtise; **what a ~ of nonsense!** quelle absurdité!, quelle bêtise!; **that was a ~ of luck!** c'était un coup de chance!; **to give sb a ~ of one's mind*** dire ses quatre vérités à qn, dire son fait à qn

[c] (*Mus*) (= *passage*) morceau *m*; **a piano ~** ◊ **~ of piano music** un morceau pour piano; **a ~ by Grieg** un morceau de Grieg; (= *instrument, player*) **ten-~ band** orchestre *m* de dix exécutants

[d] = **poem** poème *m*, (pièce *f* de) vers *mpl*; (= *passage, excerpt*) passage *m*; (= *article*) article *m*; **a ~ of poetry** un poème, une poésie, une pièce de vers (*liter*); **a good ~ of writing** un bon texte; **read me a ~ out of "Ivanhoe"** lisez-moi un passage *or* un extrait d'« Ivanhoé »; **there's a ~ in the newspaper about ...** il y a un article dans le journal sur ...

[e] (*Mil*) (*also ~ of artillery*) pièce *f* (d'artillerie)

[f] : = **handgun** calibre* *m*, flingue* *m*; **he was packing a ~** il avait un calibre* *or* flingue*

[g] = **coin** pièce *f*; **a 5-franc ~** une pièce de 5 francs; **~ of eight** dollar *m* espagnol

[h] = **girl** she's a nice ~*: c'est un beau brin de fille

2 COMPOUNDS

► **piece rate** N (*Ind*) tarif *m* à la pièce ► **piece to camera** N (*TV, Cine*) **to do a ~ to camera** faire face à la caméra (*pour s'adresser directement au public*)

3 PHRASAL VERBS

► **piece together** VT SEP [+ *broken object*] rassembler; [+ *jigsaw*] assembler; (*fig*) [+ *story*] reconstituer; [+ *facts*] rassembler, faire concorder; **I managed to ~ together what had happened from what he said** à partir de ce qu'il a dit, j'ai réussi à reconstituer les événements

---

piecemeal ['piːsmiːl] [1] ADV (= *bit by bit*) [*construct*] petit à petit, par morceaux; (= *haphazardly*) sans (véritable) plan d'ensemble, au coup par coup; [*tell, explain, recount*] par bribes; **the railway system developed ~** le système ferroviaire s'est développé sans plan d'ensemble *or* au coup par coup; **he tossed the books ~ into the box** il jeta les livres en vrac dans la caisse [2] ADJ (= *bit by bit*) en plusieurs étapes; (= *haphazard*) au coup par coup; (= *unstructured*) décousu; **technology developed in a rapid and ~ fashion** la technologie s'est développée rapidement et au coup par coup; **the castle was built in ~ fashion** le château a été construit en plusieurs étapes, le château date de plusieurs époques; **the structure of the company has evolved in a ~ way** la structure de la société a évolué par étapes; **he gave me a ~ description of it** il m'en a fait une description fragmentaire *or* décousue; **a ~ argument** une argumentation décousue

piecework ['piːswɜːk] N travail *m* à la pièce; **to be on** ◊ **to do ~** travailler à la pièce

pieceworker ['piːs,wɜːkəʳ] N ouvrier *m*, -ière *f* payé(e) à la pièce

piecrust ['paɪkrʌst] N croûte *f* de *or* pour pâté

pied [paɪd] [1] ADJ bariolé, bigarré; [*animal*] pie *inv* [2] COMP ► **the Pied Piper** N le joueur de flûte d'Hamelin

pied-à-terre [,pjeɪdɑː'teəʳ] N (*pl* **pieds-à-terre** [,pjeɪdɑː'teəʳ]) pied-à-terre *m inv*

Piedmont ['piːdmɒnt] N [a] (*Geog*) le Piémont [b] (*Geol*) **piedmont** piémont *m*; **piedmont glacier** glacier *m* de piémont

Piedmontese [,piːdmɒn'tiːz] [1] ADJ (*Geog*) piémontais [2] N [a] (= *person*) Piémontais(e) *m(f)* [b] (*Ling*) piémontais *m*

pier [pɪəʳ] [1] N [a] (*with amusements etc*) jetée *f* (*promenade*); (= *landing stage*) appontement *m*, embarcadère *m*; (= *breakwater*) brise-lames *m*; (*in airport*) jetée *f* d'embarquement (*or de débarquement*) [b] (*Archit*) (= *column*) pilier *m*, colonne *f*; [*of bridge*] pile *f*; (= *brickwork*) pied-droit *or* piédroit *m* [2] COMP ► **pier glass** N (glace *f* de) trumeau *m*

pierce [pɪəs] VT [a] (= *make hole in, go through*) percer, transpercer; **the arrow ~d his armour** la flèche perça son armure; **the bullet ~d his arm** la balle lui transperça le bras; **to have** *or* **get one's ears/nose** *etc* **~d** se faire percer les oreilles/le nez *etc*; **to have ~d ears** avoir les oreilles percées; **~d earrings*** **earrings for ~d ears** boucles *fpl* d'oreilles pour oreilles percées [b] [*sound, light*] percer; [*cold, wind*] transpercer; (*liter*) **the words ~d his heart** ces paroles lui percèrent le cœur

piercing ['pɪəsɪŋ] [1] ADJ [*sound, voice*] aigu (-guë *f*), perçant; [*look*] perçant; [*cold, wind*] glacial, pénétrant; **~ blue eyes** yeux *mpl* bleus perçants [2] N (*also* **body ~**) piercing *m*; **to get a ~ (done)** se faire faire un piercing

piercingly ['pɪəsɪŋlɪ] ADV [*scream*] d'une voix perçante; [*look*] d'un œil perçant; **~ blue eyes** yeux *mpl* bleus perçants

pierhead ['pɪəhed] N musoir *m*

pierrot ['pɪərəʊ] N pierrot *m*

pietism ['paɪ,tɪzəm] N piétisme *m*

pietist ['paɪtɪst] ADJ, N piétiste *mf*

piety ['paɪətɪ] [1] N piété *f* [2] **pieties** NPL (*gen pej*) platitudes *fpl* pieuses

piezoelectric [paɪ,iːzəʊɪ'lektrɪk] ADJ piézoélectrique

piezoelectricity [paɪ,iːzəʊɪlek'trɪsɪtɪ] N piézo-électricité *f*

piezometer [,paɪ'zɒmɪtəʳ] N piézomètre *m*

piffle†* ['pɪfl] N balivernes *fpl*, fadaises *fpl*

piffling ['pɪflɪŋ] ADJ (= *trivial*) futile, frivole; (= *worthless*) insignifiant

pig [pɪg] **1** N **a** cochon *m*, porc *m*; **they were living like ~s** ils vivaient comme des porcs *or* dans une (vraie) porcherie; (fig) **it was a ~* to do** c'était vachement* difficile à faire; **to buy a ~ in a poke** acheter chat en poche; **~s might fly!*** ce n'est pas demain la veille!*, quand les poules auront des dents!; (Brit) **to be as happy as a ~ in muck*** *or* **shit**** être dans son élément; (Brit) **he was as sick as a ~*** il en était malade*; (Brit) **to make a ~'s ear* of sth** cochonner qch*; (US *fig*) **in a ~'s eye!** jamais de la vie!, mon œil!* → **Guinea, sucking pig** **b** (* *pej* = *person*) (*mean*) vache* *f*; (*dirty*) cochon(ne)* *m(f)*; (*greedy*) goinfre *m*; **to make a ~ of o.s.** manger comme un goinfre, se goinfrer* **c** (* *pej* = *policeman*) flicard* *m*, poulet* *m*; **the ~s** la flicaille* **2** VI [*sow*] mettre bas, cochonner **3** VT **to ~ o.s.*** se goinfrer (**on** de); **to ~ it*** vivre comme un cochon* (*or* des cochons) **4** COMP ▶ **pig breeding** N élevage *m* porcin ▶ **pig farmer** N éleveur *m*, -euse *f* de porcs ▶ **pig-ignorant*** ADJ d'une ignorance crasse ▶ **pig industry** N industrie *f* porcine ▶ **pig in the middle** N (= *game*) jeu où deux enfants se lancent un ballon tandis qu'un troisième, placé au milieu, essaie de l'intercepter; (fig) **he's the ~ in the middle** il est impliqué dans des disputes qui ne le concernent pas ▶ **pig iron** N saumon *m* de fonte ▶ **Pig Latin** N ≈ javanais* *m* ▶ **pig-swill** N pâtée *f* pour les porcs

▶ **pig out*** VI s'empiffrer* (**on** de)

pigeon ['pɪdʒən] **1** N **a** (*also Culin*) pigeon *m* → **carrier, clay, homing, woodpigeon** **b*** affaire *f*; **that's not my ~** ça n'est pas mes oignons* **2** COMP ▶ **pigeon-chested** ADJ à la poitrine bombée ▶ **pigeon fancier** N colombophile *mf* ▶ **pigeon house, pigeon loft** N pigeonnier *m* ▶ **pigeon post** N by ~ post par pigeon voyageur ▶ **pigeon shooting** N tir *m* aux pigeons ▶ **pigeon-toed** ADJ **to be ~-toed** avoir *or* marcher les pieds tournés en dedans

pigeonhole ['pɪdʒɪn,həʊl] **1** N (*in desk*) case *f*, casier *m*; (*on wall etc*) casier *m* **2** VT **a** (= *store away*) [+ *papers*] classer, ranger **b** (= *shelve*) [+ *project, problem*] enterrer provisoirement; (US *Pol*) **to ~ a bill** enterrer un projet de loi **c** (= *classify*) [+ *person*] étiqueter, cataloguer (**as** comme)

piggery ['pɪgərɪ] N porcherie *f*

piggish* ['pɪgɪʃ] ADJ (*pej*) (*in manners*) sale, grossier; (= *greedy*) goinfre; (= *stubborn*) têtu

piggy ['pɪgɪ] **1** N (*baby talk*) cochon *m* **2** ADJ [*eyes*] porcin, comme un cochon **3** COMP ▶ **piggy in the middle** N = **pig in the middle**; → **pig**

piggyback ['pɪgɪ,bæk] **1** ADV [*ride, be carried*] sur le dos; (fig) **the space shuttle rides ~ on the rocket** la navette spatiale est transportée sur le dos de la fusée **2** ADJ [*ride etc*] sur le dos **3 to give sb a ~** porter qn sur son dos; **give me a ~, Daddy!** fais-moi faire un tour (à dada) sur ton dos, Papa! **b** (US *Rail*) ferroutage *m* **4** VT **a** (= *carry on one's back*) porter sur son dos **b** (US *Rail*) ferrouter **c** (fig) [+ *plan etc*] englober, couvrir **5** VI [*plan, expenditure etc*] être couvert, être pris en charge

piggybank ['pɪgɪbæŋk] N tirelire *f* (*surtout en forme de cochon*)

pigheaded [,pɪg'hedɪd] ADJ (*pej*) entêté, obstiné

pigheadedly [,pɪg'hedɪdlɪ] ADV (*pej*) obstinément, avec entêtement

pigheadedness [,pɪg'hedɪdnɪs] N (*pej*) entêtement *m*, obstination *f*

piglet ['pɪglɪt] N porcelet *m*, petit cochon *m*

---

pigman ['pɪgmən] N (*pl* **-men**) porcher *m*

pigment ['pɪgmənt] N pigment *m*

pigmentation [,pɪgmən'teɪʃən] N pigmentation *f*

pigmented [pɪg'mentɪd] ADJ pigmenté

pigmy ['pɪgmɪ] = **pygmy**

pigpen ['pɪgpen] N (US) porcherie *f*

pigskin ['pɪgskɪn] **1** N **a** (= *leather*) peau *f* de porc **b** (US *Ftbl*) ballon *m* (*de football américain*) **2** COMP [*briefcase, gloves, book-binding etc*] en (peau de) porc

pigsty ['pɪgstaɪ] N (*lit, fig*) porcherie *f*; **your room is like a ~!** ta chambre est une vraie porcherie!

pigtail ['pɪgteɪl] N [*of hair*] natte *f*; **to have** *or* **wear one's hair in ~s** porter des nattes

pike[1] [paɪk] N (= *weapon*) pique *f*

pike[2] [paɪk] N (*pl* **pike** *or* **pikes**) (= *fish*) brochet *m*

pike[3] [paɪk] N **a** = **turnpike** **b** (US) **to come down the ~** faire son apparition

pikeman ['paɪkmən] N (*pl* **-men**) (Hist) piquier *m*

pikeperch ['paɪkpɜːtʃ] N (*pl* **pikeperch** *or* **pikeperches**) sandre *m*

piker* ['paɪkər] N (US) (= *small gambler*) thunard* *m*; (= *small speculator*) boursicoteur *m*, -euse *f*; (= *stingy person*) pingre *mf*; (= *contemptible person*) minable *mf*

pikestaff ['paɪkstɑːf] N → **plain**

pilaf(f) ['pɪlæf] N pilaf *m*

pilaster [pɪ'læstər] N pilastre *m*

Pilate ['paɪlət] N Pilate *m*

pilau [pɪ'laʊ] N = **pilaff**

pilchard ['pɪltʃəd] N pilchard *m*, sardine *f*

pile[1] [paɪl] **1** N **a** (*Constr etc*) pieu *m* de fondation; (*in water*) pilotis *m*; [*of bridge*] pile *f* **b** (= *pointed stake*) pieu *m* **2** VT [+ *land*] enfoncer des pieux *or* des pilotis dans **3** COMP ▶ **pile driver** N (*Constr*) sonnette *f*, hie *f*, mouton *m* ▶ **pile dwelling** N (Hist) maison *f* sur pilotis

pile[2] [paɪl] **1** N **a** (= *neat stack*) pile *f*; (= *heap*) tas *m*; **the linen was in a neat ~** le linge était rangé en une pile bien nette; **his clothes lay in a ~** ses vêtements étaient en tas; **the magazines were in an untidy ~** les magazines étaient entassés pêle-mêle; **to make a ~ of books ◊ to put books in a ~** empiler des livres, mettre des livres en tas *or* en pile; (fig) **to be at the top/bottom of the ~** être en haut/en bas de l'échelle; (fig) **companies at the bottom of the ~** des entreprises ayant très peu de poids d'un point de vue financier **b** (* = *fortune*) fortune *f*; **to make one's ~** faire son beurre*, faire fortune; **he made a ~ on this deal** il a ramassé un joli paquet* avec cette affaire; **~s of** [+ *butter, honey*] beaucoup de, des masses de*; [+ *cars, flowers*] beaucoup de, un tas de*; **to have/make a ~ of** *or* **~s of money** avoir/faire beaucoup d'argent *or* un argent fou **c** (*Phys*) pile *f* → **atomic** **d** (*liter or hum* = *imposing building*) édifice *m* **2 piles** NPL (Med) hémorroïdes *fpl* **3** VT **a** (= *stack up*) empiler; **he ~d the plates onto the tray** il a empilé les assiettes sur le plateau; **he ~d the books (up) one on top of the other** il a empilé les livres les uns sur les autres; **a table ~d up** *or* **high with books** une table couverte de piles de livres **b** (= *pack in*) **he ~d the books into the box** il a empilé *or* entassé les livres dans la caisse; **I ~d the children into the car*** j'ai entassé les enfants dans la voiture; **to ~ coal on the fire ◊ to ~ the fire up with coal** rajouter du charbon dans le feu **4** VI* **we all ~d into the car** nous nous sommes tous entassés *or* empilés* dans la voiture; **we ~d off the train** nous nous sommes des-

---

cendus du train en nous bousculant; **they ~d through the door** ils sont entrés *or* sortis en se bousculant

▶ **pile in*** VI [*people*] s'entasser; **the taxi arrived and we all ~d in** le taxi est arrivé et nous nous sommes tous entassés dedans*; **~ in!** entassez-vous* là-dedans!

▶ **pile off*** VI [*people*] descendre en désordre

▶ **pile on*** **1** VT SEP **to ~ it on** exagérer, en rajouter*; **he does tend to ~ it on** il faut toujours qu'il en rajoute (*subj*); **to ~ on the pressure** mettre toute la gomme*; **to ~ on weight** *or* **the pounds** prendre kilo sur kilo, grossir **2** VI **the bus/train arrived and we all ~d on** l'autobus/le train est arrivé et nous nous sommes tous entassés *or* empilés* dedans

▶ **pile out*** VI sortir en désordre *or* en se bousculant

▶ **pile up** **1** VI **a** (= *accumulate*) [*snow, leaves*] s'amonceler; [*work, bills, debts, problems, reasons*] s'accumuler; [*letters, papers, rubbish*] s'entasser, s'accumuler; **the evidence ~d up against him** les preuves s'amoncelaient *or* s'accumulaient contre lui **b** (* = *crash*) **ten cars ~d up on the motorway** dix voitures se sont carambolées sur l'autoroute; **the ship ~d up on the rocks** le bateau s'est fracassé sur les rochers **2** VT SEP **a** (*lit*) → **pile**[2] **3a** **b** [+ *evidence, reasons, debts, losses*] accumuler **c** (* = *crash*) **he ~d up the car/the motorbike last night** hier soir il a bousillé* la voiture/la moto **3** ~**up** N → **pileup**

pile[3] [paɪl] N (*Tex*) poils *mpl*; **the ~ of a carpet** les poils *mpl* d'un tapis; **a carpet with a deep ~** un tapis de haute laine

pileup ['paɪlʌp] N (Aut) carambolage *m*; **there was a ten-car ~ on the motorway** dix voitures se sont carambolées sur l'autoroute

pilfer ['pɪlfər] **1** VT chaparder* **2** VI se livrer au chapardage*

pilferage ['pɪlfərɪdʒ] N chapardage* *m*, coulage *m*

pilferer ['pɪlfərər] N chapardeur* *m*, -euse* *f*

pilfering ['pɪlfərɪŋ] N chapardage* *m*

pilgrim ['pɪlgrɪm] **1** N pèlerin *m*; **the ~s to Lourdes** les pèlerins de Lourdes; **"Pilgrim's Progress"** « Le Voyage du Pèlerin » **2** COMP ▶ **the Pilgrim Fathers** NPL (Hist) les (Pères *mpl*) pèlerins *mpl*

┌─────────────────────────────────┐
PILGRIM FATHERS

Les « Pères pèlerins » sont un groupe de puritains qui quittèrent l'Angleterre en 1620 pour fuir les persécutions religieuses. Ayant traversé l'Atlantique à bord du « Mayflower », ils fondèrent New Plymouth en Nouvelle-Angleterre, dans ce qui est aujourd'hui le Massachusetts, et inaugurèrent ainsi le processus de colonisation anglaise de l'Amérique. Ces Pères pèlerins sont considérés comme les fondateurs des États-Unis, et l'on commémore chaque année, le jour de « Thanksgiving », la réussite de leur première récolte. → THANKSGIVING
└─────────────────────────────────┘

pilgrimage ['pɪlgrɪmɪdʒ] N pèlerinage *m*; **to make** *or* **go on a ~** faire un pèlerinage

piling ['paɪlɪŋ] N (NonC), **pilings** ['paɪlɪŋz] NPL (for bridge) piles *fpl*; (for building) pilotis *m*

pill [pɪl] **1** N **a** (Med, *fig*) pilule *f*; (fig) **to coat** *or* **sugar** *or* **sweeten the ~** dorer la pilule (**for sb** à qn) → **bitter b** (*also* **Pill, contraceptive ~**) pilule *f*; **to be on the ~** prendre la pilule **2** COMP ▶ **pill popper*** N personne qui se gave de pilules

pillage ['pɪlɪdʒ] **1** N pillage *m*, saccage *m* **2** VT piller, saccager, mettre à sac **3** VI se livrer au pillage *or* au saccage

pillar ['pɪlər] **1** N **a** (*Archit*) pilier *m*, colonne *f*; (Min, *also Climbing*) pilier *m*; (Geog) **the Pillars of Hercules** les Colonnes *fpl* d'Hercule; (Bible) **a ~ of salt** une statue de sel; **a ~ of smoke** une colonne de fumée; **a ~ of water**

une trombe d'eau; **he was sent from ~ to post** on se le renvoyait de l'un à l'autre; **after giving up his job he went from ~ to post until ...** après avoir quitté son emploi il a erré à droite et à gauche jusqu'au jour où ... **[b]** (*fig = mainstay*) pilier *m*; **he was a ~ of the Church/ the community** c'était un pilier de l'Église/de la communauté; **he was a ~ of strength** il a vraiment été d'un grand soutien **[2]** COMP ▶ **pillar-box** N (*Brit*) boîte *f* aux *or* à lettres (*publique*); **~-box red** rouge vif *m inv*

pillbox ['pɪlbɒks] N (*Med*) boîte *f* à pilules; (*Mil*) casemate *f*, blockhaus *m inv*; (= *hat*) toque *f*

pillion ['pɪljən] **[1]** N (*of motorcycle*) siège *m* arrière, tansad *m*; (*of horse*) selle *f* de derrière; **~ passenger** passager *m*, -ère *f* de derrière **[2]** ADV **to ride ~** (*on horse*) monter en croupe; (*on motorcycle*) monter derrière

pillock ['pɪlək] N (*Brit*) con‡ *m*

pillory ['pɪlərɪ] **[1]** N pilori *m* **[2]** VT (*Hist, fig*) mettre au pilori

pillow ['pɪləʊ] **[1]** N **[a]** oreiller *m*; **a ~ of moss** un coussin de mousse **[b]** (*Tech: also* **lace ~**) carreau *m* (de dentellière) **[2]** VT [+ *head*] reposer; **she ~ed her head in her arms** elle a reposé sa tête sur ses bras **[3]** COMP ▶ **pillow fight** N bataille *f* d'oreillers *or* de polochons* ▶ **pillow lace** N guipure *f* ▶ **pillow slip** N = **pillowcase**

pillowcase ['pɪləʊkeɪs] N taie *f* d'oreiller

pillowtalk ['pɪləʊtɔːk] N confidences *fpl* sur l'oreiller

pilot ['paɪlət] **[1]** N **[a]** (*Aviat, Naut*) pilote *m*; **airline/fighter ~** pilote *m* de ligne/de chasse → **automatic [b]** (*Rad, TV: also* **~ episode**) épisode *m* pilote **[2]** VT (*Aviat, Naut*) piloter; **she ~ed the country through the difficult postwar period** elle a guidé *or* dirigé le pays à travers les difficultés de l'après-guerre; (*Parl*) **to ~ a bill through the House** assurer le passage d'un projet de loi **[3]** COMP ▶ **pilot boat** N bateau-pilote *m* ▶ **pilot film** N (*TV*) film-pilote *m* ▶ **pilot fish** N (*pl* **pilot fish** *or* **fishes**) poisson *m* pilote ▶ **pilot house** N poste *m* de pilotage ▶ **pilot jacket** N blouson *m* d'aviateur ▶ **pilot light** N veilleuse *f* (*de cuisinière, de chauffe-eau etc*) ▶ **pilot officer** N sous-lieutenant *m* (de l'armée de l'air) ▶ **pilot production** N (*Ind*) présérie *f* ▶ **pilot scheme** N projet *m* pilote, projet *m* expérimental ▶ **pilot study** N étude *f* pilote

Pils [pɪls, pɪlz] N bière *f* Pils

pimento [pɪ'mentəʊ] N (*pl* **pimentos**) piment *m*

pimp [pɪmp] **[1]** N souteneur *m*, maquereau‡ *m*, marlou‡ *m* **[2]** VI être souteneur, faire le maquereau‡

pimpernel ['pɪmpənəl] N mouron *m* → **scarlet**

pimple ['pɪmpl] N bouton *m* (*Med*); **to come out in ~s** avoir une poussée de boutons

pimply ['pɪmplɪ] ADJ [*face, person*] boutonneux

PIN [pɪn] N ABBR = **personal identification number**; **~ (number)** code *m* confidentiel *or* personnel

pin [pɪn] **[1]** N **[a]** (*Sewing: also for paper, hair, tie etc*) épingle *f*; (*Brit: also* **drawing ~**) punaise *f*; (= *badge*) badge *m*; (= *lapel badge*) pin *m*; (*also* **hatpin**) épingle *f* à chapeau; (**as**) **clean as a new ~** propre comme un sou neuf; **the room was as neat as a new ~** la pièce était impeccable; **you could have heard a ~ drop** on aurait entendu voler une mouche; **I've got ~s and needles (in my foot)** j'ai des fourmis (au pied); (*US*) **to be (sitting) on ~s and needles** être sur des charbons ardents; **for two ~s* I'd hand in my resignation** je suis à deux doigts de démissionner, il s'en faudrait d'un rien pour que je démissionne (*subj*) → **rolling, safety [b]** (*Tech*) goupille *f*, goujon *m*; [*of hand gre-*

nade] goupille *f*; [*of pulley*] essieu *m*; (*Elec*) fiche *f* or broche *f* (de prise de courant); (*Med: in limb*) broche *f*; (*Elec*) **three-~ plug** prise *f* à trois fiches *or* broches **[c]** (*Bowling*) quille *f*; (*Golf*) drapeau *m* de trou **[2] pins:** NPL (= *legs*) guibol(l)es* *fpl*, quilles* *fpl*; **he's not very steady on his ~s** il ne tient pas sur ses guibolles* **[3]** VT **[a]** (= *put pin in*) [+ *dress*] épingler; [+ *papers*] (*together*) attacher avec une épingle; (*to wall etc*) fixer avec une punaise; **he ~ned the medal to his uniform** il a épinglé la médaille sur son uniforme; **he ~ned the calendar on** *or* **to the wall** il a fixé le calendrier au mur (avec une punaise) **[b]** (= *trap*) clouer; **to ~ sb against a wall/tree** clouer qn contre un mur/arbre; **to ~ sb to the floor/ground** clouer qn au plancher/sol; **his arms were ~ned to his sides** il avait les bras collés au corps **[c]** (*fig = attach*) **to ~ (all) one's hopes on sth/sb** mettre tous ses espoirs dans qch/en qn; **you can't ~ it** *or* **the blame on me*** tu ne peux pas me mettre ça sur le dos; **they tried to ~ the crime on him*** ils ont essayé de lui mettre le crime sur le dos *or* de lui faire endosser le crime **[d]** (*Tech*) cheviller, goupiller **[e]** (*US: as sign of love*) **to ~ a girl*** offrir à une jeune fille son insigne de confrérie en gage d'affection **[4]** COMP ▶ **pin money*** N argent *m* de poche ▶ **pin table** N = **pinball machine;** → **pinball**

▶ **pin back** VT SEP retenir (avec une épingle); **~ back your ears!*** ouvre grand les oreilles!; **she had her ears ~ned back* listening for the baby's crying** elle ouvrait grand les oreilles pour entendre le bébé pleurer; (*US*) **to ~ sb's ears back*** (= *scold*) passer un savon* à qn; (= *beat up*) ficher une raclée à qn

▶ **pin down** VT SEP **[a]** (= *secure*) attacher *or* fixer avec une épingle *or* une punaise **[b]** (= *trap*) immobiliser, coincer; **to be ~ned down by a fallen tree** être immobilisé *or* coincé sous un arbre tombé; **the battalion had been ~ned down by guerillas** le bataillon avait été bloqué par des guérilleros **[c]** (*fig*) **to ~ sb down to a promise** obliger qn à tenir sa promesse; **I couldn't ~ her down to a date** je n'ai pas réussi à lui faire fixer une date; **see if you can ~ him down to naming a price** essaie de lui faire dire un prix **[d]** (= *define*) [+ *problem*] définir précisément, mettre le doigt sur; [+ *feeling, meaning, quality*] définir précisément; [+ *facts*] déterminer exactement

▶ **pin on** VT SEP attacher avec une punaise *or* une épingle, épingler

▶ **pin together** VT SEP épingler

▶ **pin up** **[1]** VT SEP [+ *notice*] fixer (au mur) avec une punaise, punaiser, afficher; [+ *hem*] épingler; [+ *hair*] relever avec des épingles **[2] ~up** N, ADJ → **pinup**

piña colada [ˌpiːnəkə'lɑːdə] N pinacolada *f*

pinafore ['pɪnəfɔːr] N (= *apron*) tablier *m*; (= *overall*) blouse *f* (de travail); **~ dress** robe *f* chasuble

pinball ['pɪnbɔːl] N (= *game*) flipper *m*; **~ machine** flipper *m*, billard *m* électrique

pince-nez [ˌpɪnts'neɪ] N (*pl inv*) pince-nez *m inv*

pincer ['pɪnsər] **[1]** N **[a]** (*of crab*) pince *f* **[b]** (= *tool*) **~s** tenailles *fpl* **[2]** COMP ▶ **pincer movement** N (*fig, Mil*) mouvement *m* de tenailles

pinch [pɪntʃ] **[1]** N **[a]** (= *action*) pincement *m*; (= *mark*) pinçon *m*; **to give sb a ~ (on the arm)** pincer qn (au bras); **we're feeling the ~* (of the latest tax increases)** (à cause des dernières augmentations d'impôts) nous sommes juste *or* financièrement très serrés; **at a ~* in a ~** (*US*) à la limite, à la rigueur; **it'll do at a ~** cela fera l'affaire à la rigueur *or* faute de mieux; **if**

it comes to the ~ ... si la situation devient critique ... **[b]** (= *small amount*) [*of salt*] pincée *f*; [*of snuff*] prise *f*; (*fig*) **you have to take his remarks with a ~ of salt** il ne faut pas prendre ses remarques pour argent comptant *or* au pied de la lettre **[2]** VT **[a]** (= *squeeze*) pincer; [*shoes*] serrer; **she ~ed me on the arm ◊ she ~ed my arm** elle m'a pincé le bras *or* au bras **[b]** (* = *steal*) piquer*, faucher*; **I had my car ~ed** on m'a fauché* *or* piqué* ma voiture; **he ~ed that idea from Shaw** il a chipé* *or* piqué* cette idée à Shaw; **Robert ~ed John's girlfriend** Robert a piqué* sa petite amie à John **[c]** (* = *arrest*) pincer*; **to get ~ed** se faire pincer*; **he got ~ed for speeding** il s'est fait pincer* pour excès de vitesse **[3]** VI **[a]** [*shoe*] être étroit, serrer **[b]** **to ~ and scrape** rogner sur tout, se serrer la ceinture* **[4]** COMP ▶ **pinch-hit** VI → **pinch-hit**

▶ **pinch back**, **pinch off** VT SEP [+ *bud*] épincer, pincer

pinchbeck ['pɪntʃbek] **[1]** N **[a]** (= *metal*) chrysocale *m*, similor *m* **[b]** (= *sth sham*) toc *m* **[2]** ADJ **[a]** (*lit*) en chrysocale, en similor **[b]** (= *sham*) en toc, de pacotille

pinched [pɪntʃt] ADJ **[a]** (= *drawn*) **to look ~** avoir les traits tirés; **to look ~ with cold/with hunger** avoir l'air transi de froid/tenaillé par la faim **[b]** **~ for money/time** à court d'argent/ de temps; **~ for space** à l'étroit

pinch-hit ['pɪntʃhɪt] VI (*US Baseball*) jouer en remplaçant; (*US fig*) **to ~ for sb** assurer le remplacement de qn au pied levé

pinch-hitter ['pɪntʃˌhɪtər] N remplaçant *m*, substitut *m*

pinchpenny ['pɪntʃˌpenɪ] ADJ grippe-sou

pincushion ['pɪnˌkʊʃən] N pelote *f* à épingles

Pindar ['pɪndər] N Pindare *m*

Pindaric [pɪn'dærɪk] ADJ pindarique

pindling* ['pɪndlɪŋ] ADJ (*US*) chétif, malingre

pine¹ [paɪn] **[1]** N (*also* **~ tree**) pin *m* **[2]** COMP ▶ **pine cone** N pomme *f* de pin ▶ **pine grove** N pinède *f* ▶ **pine kernel** N pigne *f*, pignon *m* ▶ **pine marten** N martre *f* ▶ **pine needle** N aiguille *f* de pin ▶ **pine nut** N = **pine kernel** ▶ **the Pine Tree State** N (*US*) le Maine

pine² [paɪn] VI se languir (**for** de); **he's pining (for his girlfriend)** il se languit (de sa petite amie); **an exile pining for home** un exilé qui se languit de son pays *or* qui se languit, loin de son pays; **after six months in London she began to ~ for home** après six mois passés à Londres elle commençait à avoir le mal du pays

▶ **pine away** VI languir, dépérir

pineal body ['pɪnɪəlˌbɒdɪ], **pineal gland** ['pɪnɪəlˌglænd] N glande *f* pinéale, épiphyse *f*

pineapple ['paɪnˌæpl] **[1]** N ananas *m* **[2]** COMP [*flavour, ice cream*] à l'ananas ▶ **pineapple juice** N jus *m* d'ananas

pinewood ['paɪnwʊd] N **[a]** (= *grove*) bois *m* de pins, pinède *f* **[b]** (*NonC = material*) pin *m*

ping [pɪŋ] **[1]** N bruit *m* métallique; [*of bell, clock*] tintement *m*; (*US Aut*) cliquetement *m* **[2]** VI faire un bruit métallique; [*bell, clock*] tinter; (*US Aut*) cliqueter **[3]** COMP ▶ **Ping-Pong®** N ping-pong *m*; **~-pong ball** balle *f* de ping-pong; **~-pong player** pongiste *mf*, joueur *m*, -euse *f* de ping-pong

pinging ['pɪŋɪŋ] N (*US Aut*) cliquetement *m*

pinhead ['pɪnhed] N **[a]** (*lit*) tête *f* d'épingle **[b]** (‡ *pej = idiot*) imbécile *mf*, andouille‡ *f*

pinhole ['pɪnhəʊl] N trou *m* d'épingle (*Phot*) sténopé *m*

pinion¹ ['pɪnjən] **[1]** N [*of bird*] aileron *m* **[2]** VT [+ *person*] lier; **to ~ sb's arms** (= *hold*) tenir les bras de qn; (= *tie up*) lier les

pinion¹ ... she ~ed his arms behind his back (= hold) elle lui a tenu les bras derrière le dos ; (= tie up) elle lui a lié les bras derrière le dos ; he was ~ed against the wall (by person) il était plaqué contre le mur ; (by object) il était coincé contre le mur **b** [+ bird] rogner les ailes à

pinion² ['pɪnjən] **1** N (Tech) pignon m → **rack¹** **2** COMP ▶ **pinion wheel** N roue f à pignon

pink¹ [pɪŋk] **1** N **a** (= colour) rose m → **hunting, salmon b*** to be in the ~ se porter comme un charme ; in the ~ of condition en excellente or pleine forme **c** (Bot) œillet m, mignardise f **2** ADJ **a** [cheek, clothes, paper] rose ; the petals turn ~ les pétales rosissent ; he turned ~ with embarrassment il rougit de confusion ; (fig) to be seeing ~ elephants* voir des éléphants roses → **strike, tickle b** (Pol) gauchisant **3** COMP ▶ **pink eye** N (Med) conjonctivite f aiguë contagieuse ▶ **pink gin** N cocktail m de gin et d'angustura ▶ **pink lady** N (= cocktail) cocktail m à base de gin, cognac, jus de citron et grenadine ▶ **the pink pound*** N le pouvoir d'achat de la communauté gay ▶ **pink slip** N (US: terminating employment) avis m de licenciement ▶ **pink-slip*** VT (US = dismiss) licencier ▶ **pink-slipped** ADJ (US = dismissed) [worker] licencié

┌─ **PINK SLIP** ─┐

*Aux États-Unis, la « feuille rose » (**pink slip**) désigne familièrement l'avis de licenciement. Cette expression est en usage depuis les années 20, où l'on glissait dans l'enveloppe de paie d'un employé licencié la copie carbone de couleur rose qui lui notifiait son renvoi. Elle s'utilise aussi comme verbe ou adjectif : ainsi, on dira « they **pink-slipped** him » (ils l'ont licencié), ou « a **pink-slipped** worker » (un ouvrier licencié).*

pink² [pɪŋk] **1** VT **a** (Sewing) denteler **b** (= put holes in) perforer **c** (= pierce) percer **2** COMP ▶ **pinking scissors, pinking shears** NPL ciseaux mpl à denteler

pink³ [pɪŋk] VI (Brit) [car engine etc] cliqueter

pinkie ['pɪŋkɪ] N petit doigt m, auriculaire m

pinking ['pɪŋkɪŋ] N (Brit Aut) cliquettement m

pinkish ['pɪŋkɪʃ] ADJ **a** rosé, rosâtre ; ~ red/orange/grey etc rouge/orange/gris etc tirant sur le rose ; ~ brown brun rosâtre **b** (Pol) gauchisant

pinko* ['pɪŋkəʊ] ADJ, N (pl **pinkos** or **pinkoes**) (esp US Pol pej) gauchisant(e) m(f)

pinnace ['pɪnɪs] N chaloupe f

pinnacle ['pɪnəkl] N (Archit) pinacle m ; (= mountain peak) pic m, cime f ; (Climbing) gendarme m ; (fig) apogée m, sommet m, pinacle m

pinny* ['pɪnɪ] N (Brit) (ABBR = **pinafore**) tablier m

Pinocchio [pɪ'nəʊkjəʊ] N Pinocchio m

pinochle ['pi:nʌkəl] N (US) (sorte f de) belote f

pinpoint ['pɪnpɔɪnt] **1** N (lit) pointe f d'épingle **2** VT [+ place] localiser avec précision ; [+ problem] mettre le doigt sur

pinprick ['pɪnprɪk] N piqûre f d'épingle ; (fig) a ~ of light un rai de lumière

pinstripe ['pɪnstraɪp] N rayure f très fine ; black material with a white ~ tissu m noir finement rayé de blanc ; ~ suit costume m rayé

pinstriped ['pɪnstraɪpt] ADJ rayé

pint [paɪnt] **1** N **a** pinte f, ≈ demi-litre m (Brit = 0,57 litre, US = 0,47 litre) IMPERIAL SYSTEM **b** (Brit* = beer) pinte f (de bière) ; let's go for a ~ allons prendre un pot* ; she had a few ~s* elle a bu quelques bières ; he likes his ~ il aime son verre de bière **2** COMP ▶ **pint-size(d)*** ADJ minuscule

pinta* ['paɪntə] N (Brit) (ABBR = **pint of milk**) ≈ demi-litre m de lait

pinto ['pɪntəʊ] **1** ADJ [horse] pie inv **2** N cheval m or jument f pie **3** COMP ▶ **pinto bean** N haricot m bicolore (du sud-ouest des États-Unis)

pinup* ['pɪnʌp] N (= girl) pin up* f ; (= photo) photo f de pin up*

pioneer [ˌpaɪə'nɪə] **1** N (gen) pionnier m, -ière f ; (= early settler) pionnier m, -ière f, colon m ; (Mil) pionnier m, sapeur m ; (= explorer) explorateur m, -trice f ; [of scheme, science, method] pionnier m, -ière f, précurseur m ; she was one of the ~s in this field elle a été l'une des pionnières or l'un des précurseurs dans ce domaine ; one of the ~s of aviation/scientific research l'un des pionniers de l'aviation/de la recherche scientifique ; a medical ~ un pionnier dans le domaine médical **2** VT ▶ to ~ the study of sth être l'un des premiers (or l'une des premières) à étudier qch ; she ~ed research in this field elle a été à l'avant-garde de la recherche or une pionnière de la recherche dans ce domaine ; he ~ed the use of this drug il a été l'un des premiers à utiliser ce médicament, il a lancé l'usage de ce médicament → **pioneering** **3** COMP [research, study] complètement nouveau (nouvelle f) ▶ **pioneer work** N (NonC) he did ~ work in the development of ... il a été le premier à développer ...

pioneering [ˌpaɪə'nɪərɪŋ] ADJ [work, research, study] complètement nouveau (nouvelle f) or original

pious ['paɪəs] ADJ **a** (= religious) pieux **b** (pej = sanctimonious) hypocrite ; a ~ hope un vœu pieux ; not ~ intentions, but real actions pas de bonnes intentions, mais des actes

piously ['paɪəslɪ] ADV **a** (= with piety) avec piété, pieusement **b** (= sanctimoniously) d'un air sentencieux, avec componction

pip¹ [pɪp] N **a** [of fruit] pépin m **b** [of card, dice] point m **c** (Brit Mil: on uniform) ≈ galon m **d** (Telec) top m ; the ~s* le bip-bip* ; put more money in when you hear the ~s* introduisez des pièces supplémentaires quand vous entendrez le bip-bip ; at the third ~ it will be 6.49 and 20 seconds au troisième top il sera exactement 6 heures 49 minutes 20 secondes **e** (on radar) spot m

pip² [pɪp] N (Vet) pépie f ; (Brit) he gives me the ~*† il me hérisse le poil*

pip³* [pɪp] VT **a** (= hit) atteindre d'une balle **b** (Brit) to be ~ped at or to the post se faire coiffer au poteau ; a woman ~ped him for the job/for second place c'est une femme qui lui a soufflé* le poste/la seconde place, il s'est vu souffler* le poste/la seconde place par une femme

pipe [paɪp] **1** N **a** (for water) tuyau m, conduite f ; (smaller) tube m ; (for gas) tuyau m ; to lay water ~s poser des conduites d'eau or une canalisation d'eau ; sewage ~ égout m → **drainpipe, windpipe** **b** (for smoking) pipe f ; he smokes a ~ il fume la pipe ; he smoked a ~ before he left il fuma une pipe avant de partir ; to fill a ~ bourrer une pipe ; a ~(ful) of tobacco une pipe de tabac ; put that in your ~ and smoke it!* si ça ne te plaît pas, c'est le même prix !*, mets ça dans ta poche et ton mouchoir par-dessus ! → **peace c** (Mus) pipeau m, chalumeau m ; [of organ] tuyau m ; (boatswain's) sifflet m ; (also **bagpipes**) ~s cornemuse f → **Pan 2** VT **a** (Agr, Comm etc) [+ liquid] amener par tuyau or conduite or canalisation etc ; water is ~d to the farm l'eau est amenée jusqu'à la ferme par une canalisation ; hot water is ~d to all the rooms l'eau chaude est amenée par conduites dans toutes les pièces ; to ~ oil across the desert transporter du pétrole à tra-vers le désert par pipeline or oléoduc ; to ~ oil into a tank verser or faire passer du pétrole dans un réservoir à l'aide d'un tuyau ; (hum) to ~ music into a room* passer de la musique dans une pièce **b** (Mus) [+ tune] jouer (sur un pipeau etc) ; (Naut) [+ order] siffler ; to ~ all hands on deck rassembler l'équipage sur le pont (au son du sifflet) ; to ~ sb in/out saluer l'arrivée/le départ de qn (au son du sifflet) ; the commander was ~d aboard le commandant a reçu les honneurs du sifflet en montant à bord **c** (Sewing) passepoiler, garnir d'un passepoil ; ~d with blue passepoilé de bleu, garni d'un passepoil bleu **d** (Culin) to ~ cream onto a cake décorer un gâteau avec de la crème chantilly (à l'aide d'une douille) **e** (= say) dire d'une voix flûtée ; (= sing) chanter d'une voix flûtée ; "it's for you", he ~d « c'est pour toi » dit-il d'une voix flûtée **3** VI **a** (Mus) (flute) jouer du pipeau (or du chalumeau) ; (bagpipes) jouer de la cornemuse **b** (Naut) donner un coup de sifflet **4** COMP ▶ **pipe bomb** N bombe f artisanale (fabriquée à partir d'un morceau de tuyau) ▶ **pipe cleaner** N cure-pipe m ▶ **piped music** N musique f d'ambiance enregistrée ▶ **pipe dream** N projet m chimérique ▶ **pipe organ** N grandes orgues fpl ▶ **pipe rack** N râtelier m à pipes ▶ **pipe smoker** N fumeur m de pipe ▶ **pipe tobacco** N tabac m à pipe

▶ **pipe down*** VI se taire ; ~ down! mets-la en sourdine !*

▶ **pipe up*** VI se faire entendre

pipeclay ['paɪpkleɪ] N terre f de pipe

pipefitter ['paɪpˌfɪtə'] N tuyauteur m

pipeline ['paɪplaɪn] N **a** (gen) pipeline m ; (for oil) oléoduc m ; (for natural gas) gazoduc m ; (for milk) lactoduc m **b*** in the ~ (= planned or about to happen) prévu ; (= begun or about to be completed) en cours de réalisation ; there are redundancies in the ~ des licenciements sont prévus ; they've got a pay increase in the ~ il est prévu qu'ils reçoivent or ils doivent recevoir une augmentation de salaire ; there's a new model in the ~ un nouveau modèle est en cours de réalisation, on est en train de développer un nouveau modèle

piper ['paɪpə'] N **a** (= flautist) joueur m, -euse f de pipeau (or de chalumeau) **b** (also **bagpiper**) cornemuseur m → **pay**

pipette [pɪ'pet] N pipette f

pipework ['paɪpwɜ:k] N (NonC) tuyauterie f

piping ['paɪpɪŋ] **1** N (NonC) **a** (in house) tuyauterie f, canalisation f **b** (Mus) (of flute) son m du pipeau or du chalumeau ; (of bagpipes) son m de la cornemuse **c** (Sewing) passepoil m **d** (on cake) décorations fpl (appliquées) à la douille **2** ADJ [voice, tone] flûté **3** ADV ~ hot tout chaud, tout bouillant **4** COMP ▶ **piping cord** N ganse f

pipit ['pɪpɪt] N (Orn) pipit m

pipkin ['pɪpkɪn] N poêlon m (en terre)

pippin ['pɪpɪn] N (pomme f) reinette f

pipsqueak† ['pɪpskwi:k] N foutriquet† m

piquancy ['pi:kənsɪ] N (flavour) goût m piquant ; [of story] sel m, piquant m

piquant ['pi:kənt] ADJ [flavour, story] piquant

piquantly ['pi:kəntlɪ] ADV d'une manière piquante

pique [pi:k] **1** VT **a** [+ person] froisser ; (stronger) piquer au vif **b** [+ sb's curiosity, interest] piquer, exciter **2** N ressentiment m, dépit m ; in a fit of ~ dans un accès de dépit ; to do sth out of ~ faire qch par dépit

piquet [pɪ'ket] N piquet m (jeu de cartes)

piracy ['paɪərəsɪ] N (NonC) **a** piraterie f ; a tale of ~ une histoire de pirates **b** (fig) [of *book, film, tape, video*] piratage *m*; [*of idea*] pillage *m*, vol *m*; (*Comm*) contrefaçon *f*; **video/computer/software** ► piratage *m* vidéo/ informatique/de logiciels

piranha [pɪˈrɑːnjə] N piranha *m*

pirate [ˈpaɪərɪt] **1** N **a** (*Hist*) pirate *m*, corsaire *m*, flibustier *m* **b** (*Comm: gen*) contrefacteur *m*; [*of book, tape, film, video*] pirate *m*; [*of ideas*] voleur *m*, -euse *f* **2** VT [+ *book, tape, film, video, software, product, invention, idea*] pirater **3** COMP [*flag, ship*] de pirates ► **pirate copy** N copie *f* pirate ► **pirate radio** N radio *f* pirate

pirated [ˈpaɪərɪtɪd] ADJ [*book, tape, film, video*] pirate; [*edition*] édition *f* pirate

piratical [paɪˈrætɪkəl] ADJ [*band, family*] de pirates; [*appearance*] de pirate

pirating [ˈpaɪərɪtɪŋ] N piratage *m*

pirouette [ˌpɪruˈet] **1** N pirouette *f* **2** VI faire la pirouette, pirouetter

Pisa [ˈpiːzə] N Pise *f*

Piscean [ˈpaɪsɪən] N **to be a ~** être Poisson(s)

Pisces [ˈpaɪsiːz] N (*Astron*) les Poissons *mpl*; (*Astrol*) **I'm (a) ~** je suis Poisson(s)

piss [pɪs] **1** N pisse *f*; (*Brit*) **it's ~ easy** or a **piece of ~** c'est fastoche‡; **to go for** or **have** or **take a ~** pisser un coup‡; **to take the ~** charrier; (*Brit*) **to take the ~ out of sb** se foutre de la gueule de qn‡‡; (*Brit*) **he took the ~ out of my accent** il s'est foutu‡ de moi à cause de mon accent; (*Brit*) **to go out on the ~** (= *go drinking*) aller se soûler la gueule‡ dans les bars **2** VI pisser‡; (*Brit fig* = *raining*) **it's ~ing down** or **with rain** il pleut comme vache qui pisse* **3** VT **to ~ one's pants** or **o.s.** (= *urinate*) pisser‡ dans sa culotte; (*Brit*) **to ~ o.s. (laughing)** pisser de rire‡ **4** COMP ► **piss artist** N (*Brit*) soûlographe* *mf*, poivrot(e)* *m(f)* ► **piss easy** ADJ (*Brit*) → **1** ► **piss-poor** ADJ nullard*, minable* ► **piss-take**‡ N mise *f* en boîte* ► **piss-up**‡ N (*Brit*) soûlerie *f*, beuverie* *f*; (*Brit*) **he couldn't organize a ~up in a brewery** il est complètement nul*, c'est un vrai nullard*

► **piss about**, **piss around**‡ **1** VI (*Brit* = *waste time*) glandouiller‡; **to ~ about with sth** déconner‡ avec qch; **to ~ about with sb** se foutre de la gueule de qn‡‡ **2** VT (*Brit*) [+ *person*] se foutre de la gueule de‡‡

► **piss off**‡ **1** VI foutre le camp‡; **~ off!** fous(- moi) le camp‡! **2** VT [*person, situation*] [+ *person*] faire chier‡; **she ~es me off sometimes** il y a des moments où elle me fait chier‡; **I'm ~ed off** j'en ai ras le bol* or le cul‡‡

pissed‡ [pɪst] ADJ **a** (*Brit* = *drunk*) bituré*, bourré*; **to get ~** se soûler la gueule‡; **~ as a newt** or **a fart** ◊ = *out of one's mind* complètement bituré* or bourré* **b** (*US*) **pissed off**; → **piss off 2**

pisshead‡ [ˈpɪshed] N (*Brit*) poivrot(e)* *m(f)*, soûlard(e)* *m(f)*

pistachio [pɪsˈtɑːʃɪəʊ] **1** N (*pl* **pistachios**) **a** (= *nut*) pistache *f*; (= *tree*) pistachier *m* **b** (= *colour*) (vert *m*) pistache *inv* **2** COMP ► **pistachio ice cream** N glace *f* à la pistache

piste [piːst] N (*Ski*) piste *f*; **off ~** hors piste

pisted [ˈpiːstɪd] ADJ (*Ski*) **it's well ~ down** c'est bien damé *f*

pistil [ˈpɪstɪl] N pistil *m*

pistol [ˈpɪstl] **1** N pistolet *m*; (*Sport: also* **starter's ~**) pistolet *m* (de starter) **2** COMP ► **pistol point** N **at ~ point** sous la menace du pistolet ► **pistol shot** N coup *m* de pistolet ► **pistol-whip** VT frapper avec un pistolet

piston [ˈpɪstən] **1** N piston *m* **2** COMP ► **piston engine** N moteur *m* à pistons ► **piston-engined** ADJ à moteur à pistons ► **piston pin** N (*US*) goupille *f* ► **piston ring** N segment *m* (de pistons) ► **piston rod** N tige *f* de piston

---

pit¹ [pɪt] **1** N **a** (= *large hole*) fosse *f*, trou *m*; (*on moon's surface etc*) cratère *m*, dépression *f*; (*also* **coalpit**) mine *f*, puits *m* de mine; (*as game trap etc*) trappe *f*, fosse *f*; (= *quarry*) carrière *f*; (*in garage*) fosse *f*; **chalkpit** carrière *f* à chaux; (*Min*) **to go down the ~** (*gen*) descendre au fond de la mine; (= *start work there*) aller travailler à la mine; **he works in the ~s** il travaille à la mine, il est mineur (de fond) **b** (*liter* = *hell*) **the ~** l'enfer *m* **c** (= *small depression*) (*in metal, glass*) petit trou *m*; (*on face*) (petite) marque *f* or cicatrice *f* **d** [*of stomach*] creux *m*; **he felt sick to the ~ of his stomach** il en était malade* → **armpit e** (*Brit Theat*) (fauteuils *mpl* d')orchestre *m*; (*for cock fighting*) arène *f*; (*US St Ex*) parquet *m* de la Bourse; (*US St Ex*) **the wheat ~** la Bourse du blé **f** (*Motor Racing*) **the ~s** le stand de ravitaillement; (*fig*) **it's the ~s!**‡ c'est merdique!‡

2 VT **a to ~ sb against** (= *make opponent of*) opposer qn à; (= *make enemy of*) dresser qn contre; **to ~ o.s. against sb** se mesurer à qn; **to ~ one's strength against sb** se mesurer à qn; **to be ~ted against sb** avoir qn comme or pour adversaire; **to ~ one's wits against** jouer au plus fin avec, se mesurer avec **b** [+ *metal*] trouer, piqueter; [+ *face, skin*] (*smallpox*) grêler; (*acne*) marquer; **a car ~ted with rust** une voiture piquée de rouille; **his face was ~ted with smallpox/acne scars** son visage était grêlé (par la variole)/par l'acné; **the ~ted surface of the glass** la surface piquetée du verre; **a ~ted road surface** une route pleine de nids-de-poule

3 COMP ► **pit bull terrier** N pit-bull *m* ► **pit pony** N (*Min*) cheval *m* de mine ► **pit prop** N (*Min*) poteau *m* or étai *m* de mine ► **pit stop** N (*Motor Racing*) arrêt *m* au stand ► **pit worker** N (*Min*) mineur *m* de fond

pit² [pɪt] **1** N (= *fruit-stone*) noyau *m* **2** VT dénoyauter; **~ted prunes/cherries** etc pruneaux *mpl*/cerises *fpl* etc dénoyauté(e)s

pita [ˈpiːtə], **pita bread** N (*US*) = **pitta**

pitapat [ˈpɪtəˈpæt] ADV **to go ~** [*feet*] trottiner; [*heart*] palpiter, battre; [*rain*] crépiter

pitch¹ [pɪtʃ] **1** N **a** (= *throw*) acte *m* de lancer, lancement *m*; **the ball went full ~ over the fence** le ballon a volé par-dessus la barrière **b** (= *degree*) degré *m*; **he had worked himself up to such a ~ of indignation that ...** il était parvenu à un tel degré d'indignation que ...; **things have reached such a ~ that ...** les choses en sont arrivées à un point tel que ...; **excitement was at fever ~** l'excitation était à son comble **c** (*Mus*) [*of instrument, voice*] ton *m*; [*of note, sound*] hauteur *f*; (*Phon*) hauteur *f* → **concert, perfect d** (*Brit Sport* = *ground*) terrain *m*; **football/cricket** etc **~** terrain *m* de football/de cricket etc **e** (*Brit*) [*of trader*] place *f* (habituelle) → **queer f** (= *sales talk*) baratin* *m*, boniment *m*; (*fig*) **to make a ~ for sth** (= *support*) [+ *plan, suggestion, sb's point of view*] préconiser qch → **sale g** [*of roof*] degré *m* de pente **h** (= *movement of boat*) tangage *m* **i** (*Aviat, Naut*) [*of propeller*] pas *m*; **variable ~ propeller** hélice *f* à pas variable **j** (*Climbing*) longueur *f* (de corde)

2 VT **a** (= *throw*) [+ *ball*] (*also Baseball*) lancer; [+ *object*] jeter, lancer; (*Agr*) [+ *hay*] lancer avec une fourche; (= *discard*) jeter; **~ it over here!** jette-le or lance-le par ici!; **to ~ sth over/through/under** etc lancer or jeter qch par-dessus/à travers/par-dessous etc; **the horse ~ed him off** le cheval l'a jeté à bas or à terre; (*US*) **~ it!**‡ balance-le‡!; (*fig*) **the inci-**

---

dent **~ed him into the political arena** cet incident l'a propulsé dans l'arène politique; **this could ~ the government into confrontation with the unions** cela pourrait précipiter le gouvernement dans un conflit avec les syndicats

b (*Mus*) [+ *note*] donner; [+ *melody*] donner le ton de or à; **she can't ~ a note properly** elle ne sait pas trouver la note juste (*lit*); **I'll ~ you a note** je vous donne une note pour commencer; **to ~ the voice higher/lower** hausser/baisser le ton de la voix; **this song is ~ed too low** cette chanson est dans un ton trop bas; **the prices of these cars are ~ed extremely competitively** le prix de ces voitures est très compétitif; **to ~ one's aspirations too high** aspirer or viser trop haut, placer ses aspirations trop haut; **it is ~ed in rather high-flown terms** c'est exprimé en des termes assez ronflants; **the speech must be ~ed at the right level for the audience** le ton du discours doit être adapté au public; (*fig*) **you're ~ing it a bit high!** or **strong!** tu exagères un peu!, tu y vas un peu fort!; **he ~ed me a story about having lost his wallet*** il m'a débité or m'a sorti* une histoire comme quoi il avait perdu son portefeuille

c (= *set up*) **to ~ a tent** dresser une tente; **to ~ camp** établir un camp

d (*Comm etc*)* (= *promote, propose*) [+ *product*] promouvoir, faire du battage pour; [+ *plan, idea*] présenter; **she ~ed the plan to business leaders** elle a présenté le plan à des chefs d'entreprise

3 VI **a** (= *fall*) tomber; (= *be jerked*) être projeté; [*ball*] rebondir, tomber; **she slipped and ~ed forward** elle a glissé et est tombée le nez en avant or et a piqué du nez; **he ~ed forward as the bus stopped** il a été projeté en avant quand l'autobus s'est arrêté; **he ~ed head first into the lake** il est tombé la tête la première dans le lac; **to ~ off a horse** tomber de cheval; **the aircraft ~ed into the sea** l'avion a plongé dans la mer; **he ~ed over (backwards)** il est tombé (à la renverse)

b (*Naut*) tanguer; **the ship ~ed and tossed** le navire tanguait

c (*Baseball*) lancer la balle; (*US fig*) **he's in there ~ing*** il est solide au poste

4 COMP ► **pitch-and-putt** N (*Golf*) pitch-and-putt *m* (*jeu de golf limité à deux clubs*) ► **pitch-and-toss** N sorte de jeu de pile ou face ► **pitch invasion** N (*Brit Sport*) invasion *f* du terrain; **there was a ~ invasion** les spectateurs ont envahi le terrain ► **pitch pipe** N (*Mus*) diapason *m* (en forme de sifflet)

► **pitch in** VI s'atteler or s'attaquer au boulot*, s'y coller*; **they all ~ed in to help him** ils s'y sont tous mis or collés* pour l'aider; **come on, ~ in all of you!** allez, mettez-vous-y or collez-vous-y* tous!

► **pitch into*** VT FUS **a** (= *attack*) tomber sur; (*fig* = *criticize*) [*reviewer, critic, journalist*] [+ *author, work*] éreinter; **the boss ~ed into me** le patron s'en est pris à moi or m'est tombé dessus* **b** s'attaquer à; **they ~ed into the work** ils se sont attaqués or collés* au travail; **they ~ed into the meal** ils se sont attaqués au repas, ils y sont allés d'un bon coup de fourchette

► **pitch on** VT FUS arrêter son choix sur

► **pitch out** VT SEP (= *get rid of*) [+ *person*] expulser, éjecter*, vider*; [+ *thing*] jeter, bazarder*; **the car overturned and the driver was ~ed out** la voiture a fait un tonneau et le conducteur a été éjecté

► **pitch upon** VT FUS = **pitch on**

pitch² [pɪtʃ] **1** N (= *tar*) poix *f*, brai *m*; **mineral ~** asphalte *m* minéral, bitume *m*; **as black as ~** = **pitch-black 2** VT brayer, enduire de poix or de brai **3** COMP ► **pitch-black** ADJ (*gen*) noir comme du charbon or comme de la suie; **it's ~black outside** il fait noir comme dans un four dehors ► **pitch blackness** N noir *m* absolu *or* complet ► **pitch-dark** ADJ **it's ~-dark** il fait noir comme dans un four; **it's a ~-dark night** il fait nuit noire ► **pitch darkness** N = **pitch blackness** ► **pitch pine** N (= *wood*) pitchpin *m*

pitchblende [ˈpɪtʃblend] N pechblende *f*

pitched [pɪtʃt] **1** ADJ **~ battle** (*Mil*) bataille *f* rangée; (*fig*) véritable bataille *f* **2** COMP ► **pitched roof** N toit *m* en pente

pitcher[1] [ˈpɪtʃər] N (*esp US*) cruche *f*; (*bigger*) broc *m*

pitcher[2] [ˈpɪtʃər] N (*Baseball*) lanceur *m*

pitchfork [ˈpɪtʃfɔːk] **1** N fourche *f* (à foin) **2** VT **a** (*Agr*) fourcher, lancer avec une fourche (*: fig*) **I was ~ed into this** j'ai dû faire cela du jour au lendemain; **he was ~ed into the job** il a été parachuté* à ce poste

pitchman* [ˈpɪtʃmən] N (*pl* **-men**) (*US*) (= *street seller*) camelot *m*; (*TV*) présentateur *m* de produits

piteous [ˈpɪtɪəs] ADJ (*esp liter*) pitoyable; **a ~ sight** un spectacle pitoyable *or* à faire pitié

piteously [ˈpɪtɪəslɪ] ADV [*say, complain*] d'un ton pitoyable, pitoyablement; [*look at, weep*] d'un air pitoyable, pitoyablement; [*howl, whine, meow*] d'une manière pitoyable, pitoyablement

pitfall [ˈpɪtfɔːl] N **a** (*lit*) trappe *f*, piège *m* **b** (*fig*) piège *m*, embûche *f*; **the ~s of English** les pièges de l'anglais; **there are many ~s ahead** de nombreuses embûches nous (*or* les *etc*) guettent

pith [pɪθ] **1** N **a** [*of bone, plant*] moelle *f*; [*of orange*] peau *f* blanche **b** (*fig*) (= *essence*) essence *f*, moelle *f* (*fig*); (= *force*) force *f*, vigueur *f* **2** COMP ► **pith helmet** N casque *m* colonial

pithead [ˈpɪthed] N (*Min*) carreau *m* de mine

pithecanthropine [ˌpɪθɪˈkænθrəʊˌpaɪn] **1** ADJ pithécanthropien **2** N pithécanthrope *m*

pithecanthropus [ˌpɪθɪkænˈθrəʊpəs] N (*pl* **pithecanthropi** [ˌpɪθɪkænˈθrəʊˌpaɪ]) pithécanthrope *m*

pithiness [ˈpɪθɪnɪs] N [*of style*] vigueur *f*, concision *f*

pithy [ˈpɪθɪ] ADJ (= *forceful*) nerveux, vigoureux; (= *terse*) concis; (= *pointed*) savoureux, piquant; **a ~ saying** une remarque piquante

pitiable [ˈpɪtɪəbl] ADJ [*hovel*] pitoyable; [*income*] misérable, de misère; [*appearance*] piteux, minable; [*attempt*] piteux; **a ~ situation** une situation pitoyable *or* navrante

pitiably [ˈpɪtɪəblɪ] ADV = **pitifully**

pitiful [ˈpɪtɪfʊl] ADJ **a** (= *touching*) [*appearance, sight, person*] pitoyable **b** (= *deplorable*) [*cowardice*] lamentable, déplorable; **his ~ efforts to speak French** ses lamentables efforts pour parler français

pitifully [ˈpɪtɪfəlɪ] ADV [*say, complain, weep*] d'un ton pitoyable, pitoyablement; [*look at*] d'un air pitoyable, pitoyablement; [*howl, whine, meow*] d'une manière pitoyable, pitoyablement; **~ thin/poor/inadequate** d'une maigreur/pauvreté/insuffisance affligeante; **a ~ bad play** une pièce lamentable; **a ~ small army** une armée si petite qu'elle fait (*or* faisait *etc*) pitié

pitiless [ˈpɪtɪlɪs] ADJ sans pitié, impitoyable

pitilessly [ˈpɪtɪlɪslɪ] ADV impitoyablement, sans pitié

pitman [ˈpɪtmən] N (*pl* **-men**) (*Brit*) mineur *m*

piton [ˈpiːtɒn] N (*Climbing*) piton *m*

pitta [ˈpɪtə], **pitta bread** N pain *m* grec (*plat et de forme ovale*)

pittance [ˈpɪtəns] N (*pej*) (= *sum*) somme *f* dérisoire; (= *income*) maigre revenu *m*; (= *wage*) salaire *m* de misère; **she's living on a ~** elle n'a presque rien pour vivre; **they're offering a mere ~** ils offrent un salaire de misère

---

pitter-pat [ˈpɪtəˈpæt] ADV = **pitapat**

pitter-patter [ˈpɪtəˈpætə] **1** ADV = **pitapat** **2** N = **patter**[1]

pituitary [pɪˈtjuːɪtərɪ] **1** ADJ pituitaire **2** COMP ► **pituitary gland** N glande *f* pituitaire, hypophyse *f*

▼ **pity** [ˈpɪtɪ] **1** N **a** (= *mercy, compassion*) pitié *f*; **for ~'s sake** par pitié, de grâce; **to have ~ on sb** avoir pitié de qn; **have ~ on him!** ayez pitié de lui!; **to take ~ on sb** avoir pitié de qn, prendre en pitié; **to feel ~ for sb** avoir pitié de qn, s'apitoyer sur qn; **to move sb to ~** exciter la compassion de qn, apitoyer qn; **out of ~ (for him)** par pitié (pour lui)
b (= *misfortune*) dommage *m*; **it is a (great) ~** c'est (bien) dommage; **it's a ~ about the job** c'est dommage pour le travail; **it would be a ~ if he lost** *or* **were to lose this job** cela serait dommage qu'il perde *or* s'il perdait ce travail; (*liter*) **it is a thousand pities that ...** il est mille fois *or* extrêmement dommage que ... (+ *subj*); **it's a ~ (that) you can't come** il est *or* quel dommage que vous ne puissiez (pas) venir; **it would be a ~ to waste the opportunity** cela serait dommage de rater cette occasion; **what a ~!** quel dommage!; **more's the ~!** c'est bien dommage!; **the ~ of it is that ...** le plus malheureux c'est que ...
2 VT [+ *person*] plaindre; [+ *sb's fate, sb's situation*] s'apitoyer sur; **you don't deserve to be pitied!** tu ne mérites pas que l'on te plaigne!

pitying [ˈpɪtɪɪŋ] ADJ **a** (= *compassionate*) compatissant, plein de pitié **b** (= *contemptuous*) méprisant

pityingly [ˈpɪtɪɪŋlɪ] ADV avec pitié

Pius [ˈpaɪəs] N Pie *m*

pivot [ˈpɪvət] **1** N (*Mil, Tech*) pivot *m*; (*fig*) centre *m*; **their daughter was the ~ of their lives** leur vie tournait autour de leur fille; **the ~ of his argument is that ...** son argument repose sur l'idée que ...
2 VT (= *turn*) faire pivoter; (= *mount on pivot*) monter sur pivot
3 VI (*Tech*) pivoter, tourner; **she ~ed round and round** elle tournoyait sans s'arrêter; **he ~ed on his heel** il a tourné sur ses talons; **his argument ~s on** *or* **around the fact that ...** son argument repose sur le fait que ...
4 COMP ► **pivot joint** N diarthrose *f* rotatoire

pivotal [ˈpɪvətl] **1** ADJ essentiel, central **2** **pivotals** NPL (*St Ex*) valeurs *fpl* essentielles *or* clés

pix* [pɪks] NPL (ABBR = **pictures**) (= *films*) ciné* *m*; (= *photos*) photos *fpl*

pixel [ˈpɪksəl] N pixel *m*

pixelate [ˈpɪksəleɪt] VT (*TV etc*) pixéliser

pixie [ˈpɪksɪ] **1** N lutin *m*, fée *f* **2** COMP ► **pixie hat**, **pixie hood** N bonnet *m* pointu

pixil(l)ated* [ˈpɪksɪleɪtɪd] ADJ farfelu

pizza [ˈpiːtsə] **1** N pizza *f* **2** COMP ► **pizza base** N pizza *f* à garnir ► **pizza delivery service** N service *m* de livraison de pizzas (à domicile) ► **pizza oven** N four *m* à pizzas ► **pizza parlour** N pizzeria *or* pizzéria *f*

piz(z)azz* [pɪˈzæz] N (*gen*) énergie *f*, vigueur *f*; (*US: in car*) allure *f*; (*pej = garishness*) tape-à-l'œil *m*

pizzeria [ˌpiːtsəˈriːə] N pizzeria *or* pizzéria *f*

pizzicato [ˌpɪtsɪˈkɑːtəʊ] ADJ, ADV pizzicato

pkt (ABBR = **packet**) paquet *m*

Pl. ABBR = **Place**

placard [ˈplækɑːd] **1** N (*gen*) affiche *f*, placard *m*; (*at demo etc*) pancarte *f* **2** VT [+ *wall*] placarder; [+ *announcement*] afficher

placate [pləˈkeɪt] VT calmer, apaiser

---

placating [pləˈkeɪtɪŋ], **placatory** [pləˈkeɪtərɪ] ADJ apaisant

---

place [pleɪs]

1 NOUN		**3** INTRANSITIVE VERB	
2 TRANSITIVE VERB		**4** COMPOUNDS	

1 NOUN

a gen endroit *m*; **we came to a place where ...** nous sommes arrivés à un endroit où ...; **this is no place for children** ce n'est pas un endroit pour les enfants; **can't you put it a safer place?** tu ne peux pas le mettre dans un endroit plus sûr?; **can you find a place for this bag?** pouvez-vous trouver un endroit où mettre ce sac?; **this isn't a very nice place for a picnic** ce n'est pas l'endroit idéal pour pique-niquer; **from place to place** d'un endroit à l'autre; *BUT* **the time and place of the crime** l'heure et le lieu du crime; **I can't be in two places at once!*** je ne peux pas être partout à la fois!, je n'ai pas le don d'ubiquité!; **this is the place** c'est ici; **any place will do** n'importe où fera l'affaire; **to find/lose one's place in a book** trouver/perdre sa page dans un livre; **to take place** avoir lieu

◆ **any/some/no place*** (*US*) **I couldn't find it any place** je ne l'ai trouvé nulle part; **some place** quelque part; **it must be some place in the house** ça doit être quelque part dans la maison; **some place else** quelque part ailleurs; **the kids* have no place to go** les gosses* n'ont pas d'endroit *or* n'ont nulle part oùaller

◆ **place of** + *noun* (*frm*) **place of birth/residence/work** lieu *m* de naissance/de résidence/de travail; **place of refuge** refuge *m*; **he is at his place of business** il est sur son lieu de travail; **place of worship** lieu *m* de culte; (*Phon*) **place of articulation** lieu *m* *or* point *m* d'articulation

b = geographical location endroit *m*; **the train doesn't stop at that place any more** le train ne s'arrête plus à cet endroit *or* ne s'y arrête plus; *BUT* **the train doesn't stop at many places** le train ne fait pas beaucoup d'arrêts

A more specific word is often used to translate place:
it's a small place (= *village*) c'est un village; **it's just a little country place** ce n'est qu'un petit village de campagne; **Venice is a lovely place** Venise est une très belle ville *or* un endroit charmant; **Brighton is a good place to live** Brighton est une ville où il fait bon vivre; **we found some excellent places to eat** nous avons trouvé d'excellents restaurants

Note adjective + place *translated by adjective alone:*
the Atlantic coast is a fine place for yachting la côte atlantique est parfaite pour la voile; **the museum is a huge place** le musée est immense; **it's a small place** c'est tout petit

◆ **to go places*** (*US* = *travel*) voyager, voir du pays; **we like to go places at weekends** le week-end, nous aimons faire un tour *or* bouger*; (*fig* = *make good*) **he'll go places all right!** il ira loin!; **he's going places** il fait son chemin; (= *make progress*) **we're going places at last** nous avançons enfin

c * = house **we were at Anne's place** nous étions chez Anne; **come over to our place** passez à la maison; **your place or mine?** on va chez moi ou chez toi?; **he has a place in the country** il a une maison de campagne; **his family is growing, he needs a bigger place** sa famille s'agrandit, il lui faut quelque chose de plus grand; **the house is a vast great place** la maison est immense; **his business is growing, he needs a bigger place** son affaire s'agrandit, il lui faut quelque chose de plus grand *or* des locaux plus grands

d = seat, space (*laid at table*) couvert *m*; **a car park with 200 places** un parking de 200 places; **keep a place for me** gardez-moi une place; (*Scol*) **go back to your places** retournez à *or* reprenez vos places; **to lay** *or* **set**

---

an extra place (at table) mettre un couvert supplémentaire

e = position place f; [of star, planet] position f; put the book back in its place remets le livre à sa place; the key wasn't in its place la clé n'était pas à sa place; a place for everything and everything in its place une place pour chaque chose et chaque chose à sa place; (if I were) in your place ... (si j'étais) à votre place ...; to keep/lose one's place in the queue garder/perdre sa place dans la queue; to give place to ... céder la place à ...; to go back or fall back into place se remettre en place; to take the place of sb/sth prendre la place de qn/qch, remplacer qn/qch; BUT to take or fill sb's place remplacer qn; (fig) to fall or fit or click into place (= become clear) devenir clair; the moment I changed jobs everything fell into place (= turned out well) il a suffi que je change de travail pour que tout s'arrange

f in competition, hierarchy Paul won the race with Robert in second place Paul a gagné la course et Robert est arrivé deuxième; (Racing) to back a horse for a place jouer un cheval placé; Sweden took second place in the championships la Suède s'est classée deuxième aux championnats; he took second place in history/in the history exam il a été deuxième en histoire/à l'examen d'histoire; my personal life has had to take second place to my career ma vie privée a dû passer après ma carrière; the team was in third place l'équipe était en troisième position; he has risen to second place in the opinion polls il occupe maintenant la deuxième place dans les sondages; I know my place je sais rester à ma place; people in high places les gens haut placés; to put sb in his place remettre qn à sa place

g = job poste m, place f; places for 500 workers des places fpl or des emplois mpl pour 500 ouvriers; we have a place for a receptionist nous avons un poste de réceptionniste; we will try to find a place for him on va essayer de lui trouver une place or un poste

h in school place f; a few private schools give free places quelques écoles privées offrent des places gratuites; (Univ) I've got a place to do sociology j'ai réussi à m'inscrire en sociologie; (in team) he's got a place in the first team il a été admis dans l'équipe première

i = role it's not your place to criticize ce n'est pas à vous de critiquer, ce n'est pas votre rôle de critiquer

j = room, scope there is no place for racism in the Party le parti ne peut tolérer le racisme; there is a place for this sort of counselling ce genre d'assistance aurait son utilité

k SET STRUCTURES

♦ all over the place* (= everywhere) partout; I've looked for him all over the place je l'ai cherché partout; his clothes were all over the place ses vêtements traînaient partout or étaient éparpillés un peu partout; (= confused) he was careful and diligent, I was all over the place il soigneux et appliqué, moi j'étais complètement désorganisé

♦ to be in place [object] être à sa place; [measure, policy, elements] être en place; [conditions] être rassemblé; [law, legislation] être en vigueur

♦ in places (= here and there) par endroits; the snow is very deep in places la neige est très profonde par endroits

♦ in place of à la place de, au lieu de; Lewis came onto the field in place of Jenkins Lewis est entré sur le terrain à la place de Jenkins

♦ in the first place (= firstly) en premier lieu, premièrement; in the first place, it will be much cheaper en premier lieu or premièrement, ça sera beaucoup moins cher; (= to start with) he shouldn't have been there in the first place et d'abord il n'aurait pas dû être là, il n'aurait même pas dû être là; the Latvians never agreed

to join the Soviet Union in the first place d'ailleurs, les Lettons n'ont jamais voulu être rattachés à l'Union soviétique; we need to consider why so many people are in prison in the first place nous devons commencer par chercher à comprendre pourquoi tant de gens sont en prison; what brought you here in the first place? qu'est-ce qui vous a amené ici?

♦ in the second place en second lieu, deuxièmement; in the second place, it's not worth the money en second lieu or deuxièmement, c'est trop cher

♦ out of place [object, remark] déplacé; such remarks were out of place at a funeral de telles remarques étaient déplacées lors d'un enterrement; dahlias look out of place in a formal garden les dahlias détonnent or ne vont pas bien dans un jardin à la française; I feel rather out of place here je ne me sens pas à ma place ici

2 TRANSITIVE VERB

a = put mettre; she placed a roll on each plate elle a mis or posé un petit pain sur chaque assiette; to place an advertisement in the paper mettre or passer une annonce dans le journal; events have placed the president in a difficult position les événements ont mis le président en mauvaise posture; BUT to place confidence in sb/sth placer sa confiance en qn/qch; to place a book with a publisher faire accepter un livre par un éditeur

♦ to be placed: the picture is placed rather high up le tableau est un peu trop haut; the house is well placed la maison est bien située; the shop is awkwardly placed le magasin est mal situé or mal placé; we are now well placed to ... nous sommes maintenant bien placés pour ...; we are better placed than we were a month ago notre situation est meilleure qu'il y a un mois; I am rather awkwardly placed at the moment je suis dans une position délicate en ce moment

b = rank (in exam) placer, classer; (in race) placer; he wasn't placed in the race il n'a pas été placé dans la course; my horse wasn't placed mon cheval n'a pas été placé; to be placed first/second se classer or se placer premier/second; he places good health among his greatest assets il considère sa (bonne) santé comme l'un de ses meilleurs atouts; BUT our team is well placed in the league notre équipe est en bonne position or est bien classé; to place local interests above or before or over those of central government faire passer les intérêts locaux avant ceux du gouvernement central

c = classify classer; the authorities have placed the drug in Class A les autorités ont classé cette drogue dans la catégorie A

d = make [+ order, contract] passer; [+ bet] engager; thousands of people placed bets with Ladbrokes des milliers de personnes ont engagé des paris chez Ladbrokes; I'd like to place an overseas call je voudrais téléphoner à l'étranger

e = invest [+ money] placer, investir

f = find job for trouver une place or un emploi pour; we have so far placed 28 people in permanent jobs jusqu'à présent nous avons réussi à trouver des emplois permanents à 28 personnes; the agency is trying to place him with a building firm l'agence essaie de lui trouver une place or de le placer dans une entreprise de construction

g = find home for older children are difficult to place il est difficile de placer les enfants plus âgés

h = identify situer; he looked familiar, but I couldn't immediately place him sa tête me disait quelque chose mais je n'arrivais pas à le situer

3 INTRANSITIVE VERB
US Racing être placé

4 COMPOUNDS
► place card N carte placée sur la table pour marquer la place des convives ► place kick N (Rugby) coup m de pied placé ► place mat N set m (de table) ► place-name N nom m de lieu; (as study, as group) place-names toponymie f ► place setting N couvert m

placebo [plə'si:bəu] **1** N (pl placebos or placeboes) (Med, fig) placebo m **2** COMP ► placebo effect N (Med, fig) effet m placebo

placeman ['pleɪsmən] N (pl -men) (Brit: pej) fonctionnaire qui doit son poste à ses obédiences politiques et en tire profit

placement ['pleɪsmənt] **1** N (Fin) placement m, investissement m; (Univ etc: during studies) stage m **2** COMP ► placement office N (US Univ) (for career guidance) centre m d'orientation; (for jobs) bureau m de placement pour étudiants ► placement test N (US Scol etc) test m de niveau

placenta [plə'sentə] N (pl placentas or placentae [plə'senti:]) placenta m

placer ['pleɪsə'] N (US Geol) sable m or gravier m aurifère

placid ['plæsɪd] ADJ [person, smile] placide, calme, serein; [waters] tranquille, calme

placidity [plə'sɪdɪtɪ] N placidité f, calme m, tranquillité f

placidly ['plæsɪdlɪ] ADV avec placidité, placidement

placing ['pleɪsɪŋ] N [of money, funds] placement m, investissement m; [of ball, players] position f

placings ['pleɪsɪŋz] NPL (in competition) classement m

placket ['plækɪt] N double patte f

plagal ['pleɪgəl] ADJ (Mus) plagal

plagiarism ['pleɪdʒərɪzəm] N plagiat m, démarquage m

plagiarist ['pleɪdʒərɪst] N plagiaire mf, démarqueur m, -euse f

plagiarize ['pleɪdʒəraɪz] VT plagier, démarquer

plague [pleɪg] **1** N **a** (Med) peste f; to avoid sb/sth like the ~ fuir qn/qch comme la peste → bubonic

b (= scourge) fléau m; (= annoying person) plaie f; a ~ of rats/locusts/ants une invasion de rats/de sauterelles/de fourmis; we're suffering from a ~ of car thefts at the moment nous avons affaire à une vague de vols de voitures en ce moment; he's the ~ of my life! il m'empoisonne la vie!

2 VT [person, fear etc] harceler; (stronger) tourmenter; to ~ sb with questions harceler qn de questions; they ~d me to tell them ... ils m'ont cassé les pieds* pour que je leur dise ...; my illness has ~d me for 12 years cette maladie m'a empoisonné la vie or m'a tourmenté pendant 12 ans; to be ~d by injury/kidney trouble souffrir de blessures à répétition/de problèmes de reins chroniques; to be ~d by bad luck jouer de malchance; ~d by or with [+ doubts, fears, remorse] rongé par; [+ nightmares] hanté par; [+ mosquitoes] tourmenté par

3 COMP ► plague-ridden, plague-stricken ADJ [region, household] frappé par la peste; [person] pestiféré

plaguey††* ['pleɪgɪ] ADJ fâcheux, assommant

plaice [pleɪs] N (pl plaice or plaices) carrelet m, plie f

plaid [plæd] **1** N **a** (NonC: esp US = cloth, pattern) tissu m écossais **b** (over shoulder) plaid m **2** ADJ (en tissu) écossais

plain [pleɪn] **1** ADJ **a** (= obvious) clair, évident; the path is quite ~ la voie est clairement tracée; in ~ view à la vue de tous; the tower was in ~ **view** on voyait parfaitement la tour; **it must be ~ to everyone that ...** il doit être clair pour tout le monde que ..., il ne doit échapper à personne que ...; **the facts are quite ~** les faits parlent d'eux-mêmes; **it's as ~ as a pikestaff** or **as the nose on your face*** c'est clair comme le jour or comme de l'eau de roche; **it is ~ from his comments that ...** ses remarques montrent clairement que ...; **the reason for their success is ~ to see** la raison de leur succès est évidente; **a ~ case of jealousy** un cas manifeste or évident de jalousie; **I must make it ~ that ...** vous devez bien comprendre que ...; **he made his feelings ~** il ne cacha pas ce qu'il ressentait or pensait; **he made it quite ~ that he would never agree** il a bien fait comprendre qu'il n'accepterait jamais; **to make sth ~ to sb** faire comprendre qch à qn

|b| (= *unambiguous*) clair, franc (franche *f*); [*statement, assessment*] clair; **~ talk** ◊ **~ speaking** (*gen*) propos *mpl* sans équivoque; **I like ~ speaking** j'aime le franc-parler or la franchise; **to be a ~ speaker** avoir son franc-parler; **it's a ~ statement of fact** ce sont les faits, ni plus ni moins; **to use ~ language** parler sans ambages; **in ~ words** or **in ~ English, I think you made a mistake** je vous le dis or pour vous le dire carrément, je pense que vous vous êtes trompé; **I explained it all in ~ words** or **in ~ English** j'ai tout expliqué très clairement; **I gave him a ~ answer** je lui ai répondu carrément or sans détours or sans ambages; **the ~ truth of the matter is (that) ...** à dire vrai ..., à la vérité ...; **let me be quite ~ with you** je serai franc avec vous; **do I make myself ~?** est-ce que je me fais bien comprendre?

|c| (= *sheer, utter*) pur (et simple); **it's ~ folly** c'est de la pure folie

|d| (= *simple, unadorned*) [*dress, style, diet, food*] simple; (= *in one colour*) [*fabric, suit, background, paper*] uni; [*envelope*] ordinaire; **~ white walls** murs *mpl* blancs unis; **~ living** mode *m* de vie tout simple or sans luxe; **I like good ~ cooking** j'aime la cuisine simple; **don't worry about "Mr Furness-Gibbon", just call me "Simon"** ne vous embêtez pas avec « Monsieur Furness-Gibbon », appelez-moi « Simon » tout court; (*Knitting*) **~ stitch** (= *one stitch*) maille *f* à l'endroit; (= *technique*) point *m* mousse; (*Knitting*) **one ~, one purl** une maille à l'endroit, une maille à l'envers; **a row of ~** ◊ **a ~ row** un rang à l'endroit; **to send sth under ~ cover** envoyer qch sous pli discret; **~ flour** farine *f* (*sans levure*); **~ yoghurt** yaourt *m* nature; **~ chocolate** chocolat *m* à croquer; (*fig*) **it's ~ sailing from now on** maintenant tout va marcher comme sur des roulettes

|e| (= *not pretty*) quelconque (*pej*); **she's very ~** elle n'a rien d'une beauté, elle est tout à fait quelconque; **she's rather a ~ Jane*** ce n'est pas une beauté

|2| ADV |a| (= *clearly*) **I can't put it ~er than this** je ne peux pas m'exprimer plus clairement que cela or en termes plus explicites |b| (* = *simply*) tout bonnement; **she's just ~ shy** elle est tout bonnement timide; **it's (just) ~ wrong** c'est tout simplement faux; **(just) ~ stupid** tout simplement idiot

|3| N plaine *f*; (*US*) **the (Great) Plains** les Prairies *fpl*, la Grande Prairie

|4| COMP ▶ **plain clothes** NPL **in ~ clothes** en civil ▶ **plain-clothes** ADJ **a ~-clothes policeman** un policier en civil; (*Police*) **~-clothes officers** personnel *m* en civil ▶ **plain-spoken** ADJ qui a son franc-parler, qui appelle les choses par leur nom

plainchant ['pleɪntʃɑːnt] N plain-chant *m*

plainly ['pleɪnlɪ] ADV |a| (= *obviously*) manifestement; **there has ~ been a mistake** il y a manifestement erreur, il est clair qu'il y a erreur; **~, these new techniques are a great improvement** à l'évidence, ces nouvelles

techniques représentent un grand progrès |b| (= *unambiguously, distinctly*) [*speak, explain*] clairement; [*see, hear*] distinctement; **~ visible** bien visible |c| (= *simply*) [*dressed, furnished*] simplement, sans recherche

plainness ['pleɪnnɪs] N |a| (= *simplicity*) [*of food, décor, dress, language*] simplicité *f*, sobriété *f* |b| (= *lack of beauty*) manque *m* de beauté

plainsman ['pleɪnzmən] N (*pl* **-men**) habitant *m* de la plaine

plainsong ['pleɪnsɒŋ] N = **plainchant**

plaint [pleɪnt] N (*liter*) plainte *f*

plaintiff ['pleɪntɪf] N (*Jur*) demandeur *m*, -deresse *f*, plaignant(e) *m(f)*

plaintive ['pleɪntɪv] ADJ [*voice, cry, question, expression*] plaintif

plaintively ['pleɪntɪvlɪ] ADV [*ask, say*] plaintivement, d'un ton plaintif; [*howl, whine, meow*] plaintivement

plait [plæt] |1| N (*esp Brit*) [*of hair*] natte *f*, tresse *f*; **she wears her hair in ~s** elle porte des tresses |2| VT (*esp Brit*) [+ *hair, string*] natter, tresser; [+ *basket, wicker*] tresser; [+ *straw*] ourdir

▼ **plan** [plæn] |1| N |a| (= *drawing, map*) [*of building, estate, district etc*] plan *m* → **seating** |b| (= *project, intention*) plan *m*, projet *m*; **her ~ for union reform** son plan or projet de réforme syndicale; **~ of action** plan *m* d'action; **~ of campaign** plan *m* de campagne; **development ~** plan *m* or projet *m* de développement; **to draw up a ~** dresser un projet; **everything is going according to ~** tout se passe selon les prévisions or comme prévu; **to make ~s** faire des projets; **to upset** or **spoil sb's ~s** déranger les projets de qn; **to change one's ~s** changer d'idée, prendre d'autres dispositions; **the best ~ would be to leave tomorrow** le mieux serait de partir demain; **the ~ is to come back here after the show** notre idée est or nous prévoyons de revenir ici après le spectacle; **what ~s do you have for the holidays/for your retirement?** quels sont vos projets pour les vacances/pour votre retraite?; **I haven't any particular ~s** je n'ai aucun projet précis; **have you got any ~s for tonight?** est-ce que vous avez prévu quelque chose pour ce soir?; **there are ~s to modernize the building** on projette de moderniser l'immeuble; **the government said they had no ~s to increase taxes** le gouvernement a dit qu'il n'avait pas l'intention d'augmenter les impôts

|2| VT |a| [+ *research, project, enterprise*] (= *devise and work out*) élaborer, préparer; (= *devise and schedule*) planifier; **to ~ the future of an industry** planifier l'avenir d'une industrie → **planned**; → **obsolescence**

|b| (= *make plans for*) [+ *house, estate, garden etc*] concevoir, dresser les plans de; [+ *programme, holiday, journey, crime*] préparer à l'avance, organiser; [+ *essay*] faire le plan de; (*Mil*) [+ *campaign, attack*] organiser; **who ~ned the house/garden?** qui a dressé les plans de la maison/du jardin?; **a well-~ned house** une maison bien conçue; **to ~ one's day** organiser sa journée; **they ~ned the attack together** ils ont concerté l'attaque; **he has got it all ~ned** il a tout prévu, il a pensé à tout; **that wasn't ~ned** cela n'était pas prévu; **we shall go on as ~ned** nous continuerons comme prévu; **couples can now ~ their families** les couples peuvent maintenant choisir quand avoir des enfants → **planned**

|c| (= *intend*) [+ *visit, holiday*] projeter; **to ~ to do** ◊ **to ~ on doing** projeter de or avoir l'intention de faire; **how long do you ~ to be away (for)?** combien de temps avez-vous l'intention de vous absenter or pensez-vous être absent?; **will you stay for a while? — I wasn't ~ning to** resterez-vous un peu? — ce n'était pas dans mes intentions; **she's ~ning a career in law** elle envisage une carrière de juriste

|3| VI faire des projets; **one has to ~ months ahead** il faut s'y prendre des mois à l'avance; **we are ~ning for the future/the holidays** *etc* nous faisons des projets or nous prenons nos dispositions pour l'avenir/les vacances *etc*; **we didn't ~ for** or **on such a large number of visitors** nous n'avions pas prévu un si grand nombre de visiteurs

▶ **plan on** VT FUS |a| (= *intend*) **to ~ on (taking) a trip** avoir l'intention de partir en voyage; **I'm ~ning on a hot bath and an early night** j'ai l'intention de prendre un bain bien chaud et d'aller me coucher tôt; **to ~ on doing sth** avoir l'intention de faire qch, compter faire qch; **she ~s on staying in London** elle a l'intention de or elle compte rester à Londres |b| (= *foresee, reckon with*) prévoir; **he hadn't ~ned on the bad weather** il n'avait pas prévu qu'il ferait mauvais temps; **I hadn't ~ned on being paid for my help** je n'avais pas prévu d'être dédommagé, je n'escomptais pas être dédommagé

▶ **plan out** VT SEP préparer or organiser dans tous les détails

planchette [plɑːnˈʃet] N planchette *f* (*spiritisme*)

plane¹ [pleɪn] |1| N (ABBR = **aeroplane** or **airplane**) avion *m*; **by ~** par avion |2| COMP ▶ **plane crash** N accident *m* d'avion ▶ **plane journey** N voyage *m* en avion ▶ **plane ticket** N billet *m* d'avion

plane² [pleɪn] (*Carpentry*) |1| N rabot *m* |2| VT (*also* **~ down**) raboter

plane³ [pleɪn] N (*also* **~ tree**) platane *m*

plane⁴ [pleɪn] |1| N (*Archit, Art, Math, fig*) plan *m*; **horizontal ~** plan *m* horizontal; **the physical/spiritual ~** le plan physique/spirituel; **a higher ~ of consciousness** un niveau de conscience supérieur; **he seems to exist on another ~ altogether** il semble vivre dans un autre monde or univers |2| ADJ (*gen, Math*) plan; **~ geometry** géométrie *f* plane

plane⁵ [pleɪn] VI [*bird, glider, boat*] planer; [*car*] faire de l'aquaplanage

▶ **plane down** VI [*bird, glider*] descendre en vol plané

planeload ['pleɪnləʊd] N **~s of tourists** ◊ **tourists by the ~** des cargaisons *fpl* de touristes

planet ['plænɪt] N planète *f*

planetarium [ˌplænɪˈtɛərɪəm] N (*pl* **planetariums** or **planetaria** [ˌplænɪˈtɛərɪə]) planétarium *m*

planetary ['plænɪtərɪ] ADJ planétaire

planetology [ˌplænɪˈtɒlədʒɪ] N planétologie *f*

plangent ['plændʒənt] ADJ (*liter*) retentissant

planisphere ['plænɪsfɪər] N [*of world*] planisphère *m*; [*of stars*] planisphère *m* céleste

plank [plæŋk] |1| N planche *f*; (*fig: of policy, argument*) article *m*, point *m*; **to walk the ~** subir le supplice de la planche (*sur un bateau de pirates*) |2| VT (*: *also* **~ down**) déposer brusquement, planter

planking ['plæŋkɪŋ] N (*NonC*) planchéiage *m*; (*Naut*) planches *fpl*, bordages *mpl*, revêtement *m*

plankton ['plæŋktən] N (*NonC*) plancton *m*

planned [plænd] ADJ (*Econ, Pol, Ind, Comm* = *organized*) planifié; **~ economy** économie *f* planifiée; **~ parenthood** planning *m* familial, contrôle *m* or régulation *f* des naissances; **~ pregnancies** grossesses *fpl* programmées |b| (= *premeditated*) [*crime etc*] prémédité |c| (= *proposed, intended*) prévu

planner ['plænər] N |a| (*also* **town ~**) urbaniste *mf* |b| (*Econ*) planificateur *m*, -trice *f*

planning ['plænɪŋ] |1| N |a| (= *organizing*) planification *f*; **forward ~** planification *f* à long terme; **we must do some ~ for the holidays** on va devoir organiser nos vacances; (*Comm, Admin*) **financial ~** gestion *f* prévisionnelle des dépenses [b] (*also* **town** *or* **urban ~**) urbanisme *m* → **family, town** [2] COMP ► **planning board, planning committee** N (*Econ, Ind*) service *m or* bureau *m* de planification ; (*in local government*) ≈ service *m* de l'urbanisme ► **planning department** N service *m* de l'urbanisme ► **planning permission** N permis *m* de construire ► **planning stage** N **it's still at the ~ stage** c'est encore à l'état d'ébauche

plant [plɑːnt] [1] N [a] (*Bot*) plante *f*
[b] (*NonC: Ind, Tech*) (= *machinery, equipment*) matériel *m*, biens *mpl* d'équipement ; (*fixed*) installation *f* ; (= *equipment and buildings*) bâtiments *mpl* et matériel ; **the heating ~** l'installation *f* de chauffage ; **he had to hire the ~ to do it** il a dû louer le matériel *or* l'équipement pour le faire ; **heavy ~** engins *mpl* « **"heavy ~ crossing"** « sortie d'engins »
[c] (= *factory*) usine *f*, fabrique *f* ; **a steel ~** une aciérie → **nuclear**
[d] (*Theat** = *stooge*) acolyte *m*, complice *mf* ; (= *infiltrator, mole*) taupe* *f*, agent *m* infiltré
[2] VT [a] (+ *seeds, plants, bulbs*] planter ; (+ *field etc*] planter (**with** en) ; **a field ~ed with wheat** un champ planté de *or* en blé
[b] (= *place*) (+ *flag, stick etc*] planter, enfoncer ; (+ *bomb*] poser ; (+ *spy, informer*] introduire ; **he ~ed his chair next to hers** il a planté sa chaise à côté de la sienne ; **to ~ a kiss on sb's cheek** planter un baiser sur la joue de qn ; **he ~ed his fist in my guts** il m'a planté son poing dans le ventre ; **to ~ o.s. in front of sb/sth** se planter devant qn/qch ; **to ~ an idea in sb's mind** mettre une idée dans la tête de qn ; **to ~ doubts in sb's mind** semer le doute dans l'esprit de qn ; **to ~ drugs/ evidence on sb** dissimuler de la drogue/des preuves sur qn (pour l'incriminer) ; **the drugs were ~ed!** quelqu'un a dissimulé la drogue dans mes (*or* ses *etc*) affaires !
[3] COMP ► **plant breeder** N phytogénéticien(ne) *m(f)* ► **plant food** N engrais *m* ► **plant-hire firm** N (*Ind, Tech*) entreprise *f* de location de matériel industriel ► **the plant kingdom** N (*Bot*) le règne végétal ► **plant life** N flore *f* ► **plant louse** N puceron *m* ► **plant pot** N pot *m* de fleurs
► **plant down** VT SEP planter, camper
► **plant out** VT SEP (+ *seedlings*] repiquer

Plantagenet [plæn'tædʒɪnɪt] N Plantagenêt *m*

plantain ['plæntɪn] N [a] (= *plant*) plantain *m*
[b] (= *fruit*) banane *f* plantain

plantar ['plæntə'] ADJ plantaire

plantation [plæn'teɪʃən] N (*all senses*) plantation *f* ; **coffee/rubber ~** plantation *f* de café/de caoutchouc

planter ['plɑːntə'] N (= *person*) planteur *m* ; (= *machine*) planteuse *f* ; (= *plant pot*) pot *m* ; (*bigger, decorative*) jardinière *f* ; **coffee/rubber ~** planteur *m* de café/de caoutchouc

planting ['plɑːntɪŋ] N plantations *fpl* ; **autumn ~** les plantations d'automne

plaque [plæk] N [a] (= *plate*) plaque *f*
[b] (*NonC: on teeth*) plaque *f* dentaire

plash [plæʃ] [1] N [of *waves*] clapotis *m*, clapotement *m* ; [of *object falling into water*] floc *m*
[2] VI clapoter, faire floc *or* flac

plasm ['plæzəm] N protoplasme *m*

plasma ['plæzmə] N plasma *m* → **blood**

plaster ['plɑːstə'] [1] N [a] (*Constr*) plâtre *m*
[b] (*Med: for broken bones*) plâtre *m* ; **he had his leg in ~** il avait la jambe dans le plâtre *or* la jambe plâtrée
[c] (*Brit Med: also* **adhesive** *or* **sticking ~**) sparadrap *m* ; **a (piece of) ~** un pansement adhésif → **mustard**
[2] VT [a] (*Constr, Med*) plâtrer
[b] (*fig* = *cover, stick*) couvrir (**with** de) ; (*fig*) **~ed with** couvert de ; **to ~ a wall with posters, to ~ posters over a wall** couvrir *or* tapisser un mur d'affiches ; **the story was ~ed***

all over the front page/all over the newspapers l'histoire s'étalait sur toute la première page/ à la une de tous les journaux ; **his fringe was ~ed to his forehead** sa frange était plaquée sur son front ; **to ~ one's face with make-up** se maquiller outrageusement
[c] (* = *bash up*) tabasser*, battre comme plâtre*
[3] COMP (*model, figure, moulding*] de *or* en plâtre ► **plaster cast** N (*Med*) plâtre *m* ; (*Sculp*) moule *m* (en plâtre) ► **plaster of Paris** N plâtre *m* à mouler ► **plaster work** N (*NonC: Constr*) plâtre(s) *m(pl)*
► **plaster down** VT to ~ **one's hair down** se plaquer les cheveux
► **plaster on*** VT SEP (+ *butter, hair cream, make- up etc*] étaler *or* mettre une couche épaisse de
► **plaster over, plaster up** VT SEP (+ *crack, hole*] boucher

plasterboard ['plɑːstəbɔːd] N (*NonC*) Placoplâtre® *m*

plastered ['plɑːstəd] ADJ (* = *drunk*) beurré*, bourré* ; **to get ~** se saouler (la gueule*)

plasterer ['plɑːstərə'] N plâtrier *m*

plastering ['plɑːstərɪŋ] N (*Constr*) plâtrage *m*

plastic ['plæstɪk] [1] N [a] (= *substance*) plastique *m*, matière *f* plastique ; **~s** matières *fpl* plastiques
[b] (*NonC*:* = *credit cards*) cartes *fpl* de crédit
[2] ADJ [a] (= *made of plastic*) [toy, *box, dish*] en (matière) plastique → **3**
[b] (*: *fig, pej*) [food, *coffee etc*] synthétique ; **actresses with ~ smiles** des actrices *fpl* aux sourires artificiels
[c] (*Art*) plastique ; (= *flexible*) plastique, malléable
[3] COMP ► **plastic bag** N sac *m* en plastique ► **plastic bomb** N bombe *f* au plastic ; ~ **bomb attack** attentat *m* au plastic, plastiquage *m* ► **plastic bullet** N balle *f* de plastique ► **plastic explosive** N plastic *m* ► **plastic foam** N mousse *f* de plastique ► **plastic money** N carte(s) *f(pl)* de crédit ► **plastics industry** N industrie *f* (des) plastique(s) ► **plastic surgeon** N spécialiste *mf* de chirurgie esthétique ► **plastic surgery** N chirurgie *f* esthétique

plasticated ['plæstɪˌkeɪtɪd] ADJ (*lit*) plastifié ; (*fig*) synthétique

Plasticine® ['plæstɪsiːn] N (*NonC*) pâte *f* à modeler

plasticity [plæs'tɪsɪtɪ] N plasticité *f*

Plate [pleɪt] N **the River ~** le Rio de la Plata

plate [pleɪt] [1] N [a] (*Culin*) assiette *f* ; (= *platter*) plat *m* ; (*in church*) plateau *m* de quête ; **a ~ of soup/sandwiches** une assiette de soupe/de sandwichs ; (*fig*) **to hand** *or* **give sth to sb on a ~*** apporter qch à qn sur un plateau ; (*fig*) **to have a lot** *or* **enough on one's ~*** (*things to do*) avoir déjà beaucoup à faire ; (*problems*) avoir déjà beaucoup de problèmes ; (*fig*) **he's got too much on his ~ already*** il ne sait déjà plus où donner de la tête → **dinner, soup, tea**
[b] (*NonC*) (*gold dishes*) orfèvrerie *f*, vaisselle *f* d'or ; (*silver dishes*) argenterie *f*, vaisselle *f* d'argent
[c] (= *flat metal*) plaque *f* ; (= *metal coating*) placage *m* ; (= *coated metal*) plaqué *m* ; **it's not silver, it's only ~** ce n'est pas de l'argent massif, ce n'est que du plaqué
[d] (*on wall, door, in battery, armour*) plaque *f* ; (*Aut: also* **pressure ~**) plateau *m* d'embrayage ; (*Aut: also* **number ~**) plaque *f* d'immatriculation, plaque *f* minéralogique → **clutch, hotplate, number**
[e] (*Geol: also* **tectonic ~**) plaque *f*
[f] (*Phot*) plaque *f* ; (*Typ*) cliché *m* ; (*for engraving*) planche *f* ; (= *illustration: in book*) planche *f* ; (*in book*) **full-page ~** gravure *f* horstexte, planche *f* → **fashion**
[g] (*Dentistry: also* **dental ~**) dentier *m* ; (*Med:*

repairing fracture etc) broche *f*
[h] (*Racing* = *prize, race*) coupe *f*
[i] (*Sci: for microscope*) lamelle *f*
[2] VT [a] (*gen: with metal*) plaquer ; (*with gold*) dorer ; (*with silver*) argenter ; (*with nickel*) nickeler → **armour**
[b] (+ *ship etc*] blinder
[3] COMP ► **plate armour** N (*NonC*) blindage *m* ► **plate glass** N (*NonC*) verre *m* à vitre ► **plate-glass window** N baie *f* vitrée ► **plate rack** N (*for drying*) égouttoir *m* ; (*for storing*) range-assiettes *m inv* ► **plate tectonics** N (*NonC: Geol*) tectonique *f* des plaques ► **plate warmer** N chauffe-assiette(s) *m*

plateau ['plætəʊ] [1] N (*pl* **plateaus** *or* **plateaux** ['plætəʊz]) (*Geog*) plateau *m* ; (*fig*) palier *m*
[2] VI atteindre un palier, se stabiliser

plateful ['pleɪtfʊl] N assiettée *f*, assiette *f*

platelayer ['pleɪtˌleɪə'] N (*Brit Rail*) poseur *m* de rails

platelet ['pleɪtlɪt] N plaquette *f*

platen ['plætən] N [of *printing press*] platine *f* ; [of *typewriter*] rouleau *m*

platform ['plætfɔːm] [1] N [a] (*on oil rig, bus, scales, in scaffolding etc*) plateforme *f* ; (*for band, in hall*) estrade *f* ; (*at meeting etc*) tribune *f* ; (*Rail*) quai *m* ; (*Rail*) **~ (number) six** quai *m* (numéro) six ; **he was on the ~ at the last meeting** il était sur l'estrade *or* il était à la tribune (d'honneur) lors de la dernière réunion ; **he campaigned on a socialist ~** il a adopté une plateforme socialiste pour sa campagne électorale ; **they campaigned on a ~ of national sovereignty** le thème principal de leur campagne électorale était la souveraineté de l'État ; **this gave him a ~ for his views** cela lui a fourni une tribune pour exprimer ses opinions → **diving**
[b] **~s*** (= *shoes*) = **platform shoes**
[2] COMP ► **the platform party** N (*at meeting*) la tribune ► **platform scales** NPL (balance *f* à) bascule *f* ► **platform shoes, platform soles*** NPL chaussures *fpl* à semelles compensées ► **platform ticket** N (*Brit Rail*) billet *m* de quai

plating ['pleɪtɪŋ] N [a] (*Metal*) placage *m* ; **tin-/ aluminium-/copper-~** *etc* placage *m* (à l'étain/ (à l'aluminium/(au) cuivre *etc* → **chromium, silver** [b] (*Naut, Mil*) [of *ship*] bordé *m* ; [of *armoured vehicle*] blindage *m* ; **hull ~** bordé *m* → **armour**

platinum ['plætɪnəm] [1] N (*NonC*) platine *m*
[2] COMP (*jewellery*] en *or* de platine ► **platinum-blond** ADJ (*hair*] blond platiné *or* platine ; (*person*) (aux cheveux) blond platiné *or* platine ► **platinum blond(e)** N blond(e) *m(f)* platiné(e) *or* platine ► **platinum disc** N (= *award*) disque *m* de platine

platitude ['plætɪtjuːd] N platitude *f*, lieu *m* commun

platitudinize [ˌplætɪ'tjuːdɪnaɪz] VI débiter des platitudes *or* des lieux communs

platitudinous [ˌplætɪ'tjuːdɪnəs] ADJ banal, d'une grande platitude, rebattu

Plato ['pleɪtəʊ] N Platon *m*

Platonic [plə'tɒnɪk] ADJ [a] (*philosophy*] platonicien [b] **platonic** (*relationship, love*] platonique

Platonism ['pleɪtənɪzəm] N platonisme *m*

Platonist ['pleɪtənɪst] ADJ, N platonicien(ne) *m(f)*

platoon [plə'tuːn] [1] N (*Mil*) section *f* ; [of *policemen, firemen etc*] peloton *m* [2] COMP ► **platoon sergeant** N (*US Mil*) adjudant *m*

platter ['plætə'] N [a] (*esp US* = *large dish*) plat *m* ; (*fig*) **on a (silver) ~** sur un plateau (d'argent) ; (*fig*) **she was handed it on a ~** on le lui a offert *or* apporté sur un plateau [b] (= *meal, course*) assiette *f* ; **seafood ~** assiette *f* de fruits de mer [c] (*US*:* = *record*) disque *m*

platypus ['plætɪpəs] N ornithorynque *m*

plaudits ['plɔːdɪts] NPL applaudissements *mpl*, acclamations *fpl*, ovations *fpl*

plausibility [ˌplɔːzəˈbɪlɪtɪ] N [*of argument, excuse*] plausibilité *f*; [*of person*] crédibilité *f*; **her ~ as party leader** sa crédibilité en tant que chef du parti

plausible ['plɔːzəbl] ADJ [*argument, excuse*] plausible, vraisemblable; [*person*] convaincant

plausibly ['plɔːzəblɪ] ADV de façon plausible

play [pleɪ]

1	NOUN	4	COMPOUNDS
2	TRANSITIVE VERB	5	PHRASAL VERBS
3	INTRANSITIVE VERB		

1 NOUN

a gen, Sport, fig jeu *m*; **there was some good ~ in the second half** on a assisté à du beau jeu pendant la deuxième mi-temps; **that was a clever piece of ~** c'était finement *or* astucieusement joué; **~ starts at 11 o'clock** le match commence à 11 heures; **ball in ~** ballon *m or* balle *f* en jeu; **ball out of ~** ballon *m or* balle *f* hors jeu; **the children were at ~** les enfants jouaient; **children learn through ~** les enfants apprennent par le jeu *or* en jouant; **to say sth in ~** dire qch en plaisantant; **the ~ of light on water** le jeu de la lumière sur l'eau

♦ **to be at play** (*fig*) entrer en jeu
♦ **to bring sth into play** mettre qch en œuvre
♦ **to call sth into play** faire entrer qch en jeu
♦ **to come into play** entrer en jeu
♦ **to make a play for sb** faire des avances à qn
♦ **to make a play for sth** s'efforcer d'obtenir qch

b Tech, fig = movement jeu *m*; **there's too much ~ in the clutch** il y a trop de jeu dans l'embrayage; **to give full *or* free ~ to one's imagination/emotions** donner libre cours à son imagination/à ses sentiments; **the ~ of different forces** le jeu des différentes forces; **the free ~ of market forces** le libre jeu du marché; **the ~ of ideas in the film is fascinating** l'interaction *f* des idées dans ce film est fascinante

c Theat jeu pièce *f* (de théâtre); **the ~s of Molière** les pièces *fpl or* le théâtre de Molière; **radio ~** pièce *f* radiophonique; **television ~** dramatique *f*; **the ~ ends at 10.30** la pièce se termine à 22 h 30; **a ~ by Pinter** ◊ **a Pinter ~** une pièce de Pinter; **to be in a ~** [*actor*] jouer dans une pièce; (*Brit: fig*) **the customs officers made (a) great ~ of examining our papers** les douaniers ont examiné nos papiers en prenant un air important

2 TRANSITIVE VERB

a + game, sport jouer à; **to ~ chess/bridge** jouer aux échecs/au bridge; **to ~ football** jouer au football; **will you ~ tennis with me?** voulez-vous faire une partie de tennis avec moi?; **to ~ a match against sb** disputer un match avec qn; **the match will be ~ed on Saturday** le match aura lieu samedi; (*in hockey, football etc*) **what position does she ~?** à quelle place joue-t-elle?; **to ~ centre-forward** *etc* jouer avant-centre *etc*; **the boys were ~ing soldiers** les garçons jouaient aux soldats; **the children were ~ing a game in the garden** les enfants jouaient dans le jardin; **to ~ a game** (*board game etc*) jouer à un jeu; (*of tennis etc*) faire une partie; (*fig: trickery*) jouer (*fig*); **don't ~ games with me!** ne vous moquez pas de moi!; (*Ftbl*) **to ~ the ball** jouer le ballon; (*fig*) **to ~ ball with sb** coopérer avec qn; (*fig*) **he won't ~ ball** il refuse de jouer le jeu; (*fig*) **England will be ~ing Smith** (*in the team*) l'Angleterre a sélectionné Smith (pour jouer dans l'équipe)

♦ **to play the game** (*fig = play fair*) (*gen*) jouer le jeu; (*in sports match, race etc*) jouer selon les règles

♦ **to play the field** * papillonner; **he gave up ~ing the field and married a year ago** il a cessé de papillonner et s'est marié il y a un an

b + opponent, opposing team jouer contre; **England are ~ing Scotland on Saturday** l'Angleterre joue *or* rencontre l'Écosse samedi; **I'll ~ you for the drinks** jouons la tournée

c = move [+ *chesspiece*] jouer; (*Tennis*) **he ~ed the ball into the net** il a mis *or* envoyé la balle dans le filet

d Cards **to ~ cards** jouer aux cartes; **to ~ a card** jouer une carte; **to ~ hearts/trumps** jouer cœur/atout; **he ~ed a heart** il a joué (un) cœur; (*fig*) **to ~ one's best/last card** jouer sa meilleure/dernière carte; (*fig*) **to ~ one's cards well *or* right** bien jouer; **he ~ed his ace** (*lit*) il a joué son as; (*fig*) il a joué sa carte maîtresse

e St Ex **to ~ the market** jouer à la Bourse

f Theat etc [+ *part*] jouer, interpréter; [+ *play*] [*actors*] jouer; [*director, producer, theatre*] présenter, donner; **they ~ed it as a comedy** ils en ont donné une interprétation comique, ils l'ont joué en comédie; **let's ~ it for laughs** jouons-la en farce; **we ~ed Brighton last week** nous avons joué à Brighton la semaine dernière; **he ~ed (the part of) Macbeth** il a joué (le rôle de) Macbeth; **what (part) did you ~ in "Macbeth"?** quel rôle jouiez-vous *or* interprétiez-vous dans « Macbeth »?; **he ~ed Macbeth as a well-meaning fool** il a fait de Macbeth un sot bien intentionné; (*lit, fig*) **to ~ one's part well** bien jouer; (*fig*) **he was only ~ing a part** il jouait la comédie; (*fig*) **to ~ a part in sth** [*person*] prendre part à qch, contribuer à qch; [*quality, object*] contribuer à qch; (*fig*) **he ~ed no part in it** il n'y était pour rien; (*fig*) **to ~ the peacemaker/the devoted husband** jouer les conciliateurs/les maris dévoués; **to ~ it cautious** ne prendre aucun risque; **to ~ it cool*** garder son sang-froid, ne pas s'énerver; **to ~ (it) safe** ne prendre aucun risque; (*fig*) **we could have ~ed it differently** nous aurions pu agir différemment

g Mus [+ *instrument*] jouer de; [+ *note, tune, concerto*] jouer; [+ *record, CD*] passer, jouer*; **to ~ the piano/the clarinet** jouer du piano/de la clarinette; **they were ~ing Beethoven** ils jouaient du Beethoven

h = direct [+ *hose, searchlight*] diriger (**on**, **onto** sur); **they ~ed the searchlights over the front of the building** ils ont promené les projecteurs sur la façade du bâtiment

3 INTRANSITIVE VERB

a gen, Cards, Sport etc jouer; [*lambs, puppies, kittens*] s'ébattre, folâtrer; **it's your ~** *or* **your turn to ~** c'est votre tour (de jouer); **is Paul coming out to ~?** est-ce que Paul vient jouer?; **what are you doing? — just ~ing** que faites-vous? — rien, on joue *or* s'amuse; **to ~ fair** (*Sport etc*) jouer franc jeu, jouer selon les règles; (*fig*) jouer le jeu, être loyal → **fast**, **hard**, **dirty**

♦ **play** + preposition: **England is ~ing against Scotland** (*in the semi-final*) l'Angleterre joue contre l'Écosse (en demi-finale); **to ~ at soldiers/chess/bridge** jouer aux soldats/aux échecs/au bridge; **the little girl was ~ing at being a lady** la petite fille jouait à la dame; (*fig*) **he just ~s at being a soldier** il ne prend pas au sérieux son métier de soldat; (*iro*) **they're ~ing at happy families for the sake of the children** ils jouent les familles unies pour les enfants; (*fig*) **what's he ~ing at?*** à quoi il joue?; **what do you think you're ~ing at!*** qu'est-ce que tu fabriques*?; **to ~ for money/matches** jouer de l'argent/des allumettes; **he ~s for Manchester** il joue dans l'équipe de Manchester; (*lit, fig*) **to ~ for high stakes** jouer gros (jeu); **to ~ for time** essayer de gagner du temps; (*Sport*) **to ~ in defence/in goal** jouer en défense/dans les buts; (*Golf*) **he ~ed into the trees** (= *hit, shoot*) il a envoyé sa balle dans les arbres; (*fig*) **she ~ed into the back of the net** elle a envoyé le ballon au fond des filets; (*fig*) **to ~ into sb's**

hands faire le jeu de qn; **to ~ to one's strengths** exploiter ses points forts; **to ~ with** [+ *object, pencil, toy*] jouer avec; (*euph*) **to ~ with o.s.*** se masturber; **to ~ with fire/words** jouer avec le feu/les mots; **how much time/money do we have to ~ with?*** combien de temps/d'argent avons-nous?; **it's not a question to be ~ed with** ce n'est pas une question qui se traite à la légère; **he's not a man to be ~ed with** ce n'est pas un homme avec qui on plaisante; **he's just ~ing with you** il te fait marcher; **to ~ with an idea** caresser une idée

b light, fountain jouer (on sur); **a smile ~ed on *or* over his lips** un sourire s'ébauchait sur ses lèvres

c Mus [*person, organ, orchestra*] jouer; **to ~ on the piano** jouer du piano; **will you ~ for us?** (= *perform*) voulez-vous nous jouer quelque chose?; (= *accompany*) voulez-vous nous accompagner?; **there was music ~ing** il y avait de la musique; (*as background music*) **a record was ~ing in the background** un disque passait en fond sonore

d Theat, Cine = act jouer; **he ~ed in a film with Greta Garbo** il a joué dans un film avec Greta Garbo; **we have ~ed all over the South** nous avons joué partout dans le Sud; **the film now ~ing at the Odeon** le film qui passe actuellement à l'Odéon; (*fig*) **to ~ dead** faire le mort

4 COMPOUNDS

► **play box** N coffre *m* à jouets ► **play-by-play** ADJ [*account etc*] (*Sport*) suivi; (*fig*) circonstancié ► **play clothes** NPL vêtements *mpl* qui ne craignent rien (*pour jouer*) ► **play-off** N (*Sport*) (*after a tie*) ≈ match *m* de barrage (*départageant des concurrents à égalité*); (*US: for championship*) match *m* de qualification (*de coupe or de championnat*) ► **play on words** N jeu *m* de mots, calembour *m* ► **play reading** N lecture *f* d'une pièce de théâtre

5 PHRASAL VERBS

► **play about** VI **a** [*children etc*] jouer, s'amuser
b (= *toy, fiddle*) jouer, s'amuser (**with** avec); **he was ~ing about with the gun when it went off** il s'amusait *or* jouait avec le fusil quand le coup est parti; **stop ~ing about with that watch** arrête de tripoter cette montre, laisse cette montre tranquille; **he's just ~ing about with you*** il te fait marcher, il se moque de toi

► **play along** **1** VI (*fig*) **to ~ along with sb** entrer dans le jeu de qn
2 VT SEP (*fig*) **to ~ sb along** tenir qn en haleine

► **play around** VI **a** **to ~ around with an idea** retourner une idée dans sa tête
b (* = *sleep around*) coucher à droite et à gauche
c = play about

► **play back** VT SEP [+ *tape*] réécouter, repasser

► **play down** VT SEP (= *minimize importance of*) [+ *decision, effect*] minimiser; [+ *situation, attitude*] dédramatiser; [+ *opinion, dissent*] mettre une sourdine à; [+ *language*] atténuer; [+ *policy*] mettre en sourdine

► **play in** VT SEP **a** **to ~ o.s. in** (*esp Cricket*) s'habituer aux conditions de jeu; (*fig*) s'acclimater
b **the band ~ed the procession in** le défilé entra au son de la fanfare

► **play off** VT SEP **a** [+ *person*] **to ~ off A against B** jouer A contre B (*pour en tirer profit*)
b (*Sport*) **to ~ a match off** jouer la belle

► **play on** VT FUS [+ *sb's emotions, credulity, good nature*] jouer sur, miser sur; **to ~ on words** jouer sur les mots; **the noise began to ~ on her nerves** le bruit commençait à l'agacer *or* à lui taper sur les nerfs*

► **play out** VT SEP **a** **the band ~ed the procession out** le cortège sortit au son de la fanfare
b **to be ~ed out*** [*person*] être éreinté* *or* vanné*; [*argument*] être périmé, avoir fait son

temps
[c] [+ *fantasies, roles, scenes*] jouer
► **play over, play through** VT SEP [+ *piece of music*] jouer
► **play up** [1] VI [a] (*Sport*) bien jouer; ~ **up!**† allez-y!
[b] (*esp Brit** = *give trouble*) **the engine is ~ing up** le moteur fait des siennes *or* ne tourne pas rond; **his rheumatism/his leg is ~ing up** ses rhumatismes/sa jambe le tracasse(nt); **the children have been ~ing up all day** les enfants ont été insupportables *or* ont fait des leurs toute la journée
[c] (= *curry favour*) **to ~ up to sb*** chercher à se faire bien voir de qn, faire de la lèche à qn**:**
[2] VT SEP [a] (*esp Brit:** = *give trouble to*) **his rheumatism/his leg is ~ing him up** ses rhumatismes/sa jambe le tracasse(nt); **that boy ~s his father up** ce garçon en fait voir à son père
[b] (= *magnify importance of*) insister sur (l'importance de)
► **play upon** VT FUS = **play on**

playact ['pleɪækt] VI (*lit*) jouer la comédie, faire du théâtre; (*fig*) jouer la comédie, faire du cinéma*

playacting ['pleɪˌæktɪŋ] N (*fig*) **it's only ~** c'est de la comédie *or* du cinéma*

playactor ['pleɪˌæktər] N (*fig*) **he's a ~** c'est un vrai comédien, il joue continuellement la comédie

playback ['pleɪbæk] N (*Recording*) enregistrement *m*; (*function*) (touche *f* de *or* position *f*) lecture *f*

playbill ['pleɪbɪl] N affiche *f* (de théâtre); (*US Theat*) **Playbill**® programme *m*

playboy ['pleɪbɔɪ] N playboy *m*

player ['pleɪər] [1] N [a] (*Sport*) joueur *m*, -euse *f*; **football ~** joueur *m*, -euse *f* de football; **he's a very good ~** il joue très bien, c'est un excellent joueur [b] (*Theat*) acteur *m*, -trice *f* [c] (*Mus*) musicien(ne) *m(f)*, exécutant(e) *m(f)*; **flute ~** joueur *m*, -euse *f* de flûte, flûtiste *mf*; **he's a good ~** c'est un bon musicien, il joue bien [d] (*esp Comm* = *party involved*) protagoniste *mf*; **one of the main** *or* **major ~s in ...** un des principaux protagonistes de ... [2] COMP ► **player piano** N piano *m* mécanique

playfellow† ['pleɪˌfeləu] N = **playmate**

playful ['pleɪfʊl] ADJ [*mood, tone, remark*] badin, enjoué; [*person*] enjoué, taquin; [*child, puppy etc*] espiègle; **he's only being ~** il fait ça pour s'amuser, c'est de l'espièglerie

playfully ['pleɪfəlɪ] ADV [*nudge, tickle*] par jeu; [*remark, say*] en plaisantant; [*joke*] d'un ton taquin

playfulness ['pleɪfʊlnɪs] N (*gen*) caractère *m* badin *or* enjoué; [*of person*] enjouement *m*; [*of child, puppy etc*] espièglerie *f*

playgoer ['pleɪˌgəuər] N amateur *m* de théâtre; **he is a regular ~** il va régulièrement au théâtre

playground ['pleɪgraund] N cour *f* de récréation

playgroup ['pleɪgru:p] N ≈ garderie *f*

playhouse ['pleɪhaus] N [a] (*Theat*) théâtre *m* [b] (*for children*) maison *f* (pliante)

playing ['pleɪɪŋ] [1] N (*NonC*) [a] (*Sport*) jeu *m*; **there was some good ~ in the second half** il y a eu du beau jeu à la deuxième mi-temps [b] (*Mus*) interprétation *f*; **the orchestra's ~ of the symphony was uninspired** l'orchestre manquait d'inspiration dans l'interprétation de la symphonie; **there was some fine ~ in the violin concerto** il y a eu des passages bien joués dans le concerto pour violon [2] COMP ► **playing card** N carte *f* à jouer ► **playing field** N terrain *m* de jeu *or* de sport

playlet ['pleɪlət] N courte pièce *f* (de théâtre)

playlist ['pleɪlɪst] N (*Rad, Mus*) playlist *f*

playmaker ['pleɪˌmeɪkər] N (*Ftbl*) meneur *m*, -euse *f* de jeu

playmate ['pleɪmeɪt] N camarade *mf* de jeu, (petit) copain *m*, (petite) copine *f*

playpen ['pleɪpen] N parc *m* (*pour bébés*)

playroom ['pleɪrum] N salle *f* de jeux

playschool ['pleɪsku:l] N = **playgroup**

playsuit ['pleɪsu:t] N ensemble *m* short

plaything ['pleɪθɪŋ] N (*lit, fig*) jouet *m*

playtime ['pleɪtaɪm] N (*Scol*) récréation *f*

playwright ['pleɪraɪt] N dramaturge *m*, auteur *m* dramatique

plaza ['plɑːzə] N [a] (= *public square*) place *f*, grand-place *f* [b] (*US*) (= *motorway services*) aire *f* de service (*sur une autoroute*); (= *toll*) péage *m* (d'autoroute) [c] (*US: for parking etc*) aire *f* de stationnement

PLC, plc [pi:el'si:] (*Brit*) (ABBR = **public limited company**) SARL *f*; **Smith & Co. ~** Smith et Cie SARL

plea [pli:] [1] N [a] (= *entreaty*) appel *m* (**for** à), supplication *f*; **to make a ~ for mercy** implorer la clémence
[b] (*Jur*) (= *allegation*) argument *m* (**that** selon lequel); (= *answer, defence*) défense *f* (**that** selon laquelle); **to put forward** *or* **make a ~ of self-defence** plaider la légitime défense; **to enter a ~ of guilty/not guilty** plaider coupable/non coupable
[c] (= *excuse*) excuse *f*; **on the ~ of ...** en alléguant ..., en invoquant ...; **on the ~ that ...** en alléguant *or* en invoquant que ...
[2] COMP ► **plea agreement, plea bargain** N (*Jur*) accord entre le procureur et l'avocat de la défense pour revoir à la baisse les chefs d'inculpation ► **plea-bargain** VI (*Jur*) négocier pour parvenir à un accord en vue de revoir à la baisse les chefs d'inculpation ► **plea bargaining** N (*Jur*) négociations entre le procureur et l'avocat de la défense visant à revoir à la baisse les chefs d'inculpation

pleached ['pli:tʃd] ADJ [*tree*] taillé

plead [pli:d] (*pret, ptp* **pleaded** *or* (*esp US and Scot*) **pled**) [1] VI [a] **to ~ with sb to do** supplier *or* implorer qn de faire; **he ~ed for help** il a imploré *or* supplié qu'on l'aide (*subj*); **he ~ed with them for help** il a imploré leur aide; **to ~ for mercy** implorer la clémence; **he ~ed for mercy for his brother** il a imploré la clémence pour son frère; **to ~ for a scheme/programme etc** plaider pour un projet/un programme etc
[b] (*Jur*) plaider (**for** pour, en faveur de, **against** contre); **to ~ guilty/not guilty** plaider coupable/non coupable; **how do you ~?** plaidez-vous coupable ou non coupable?
[2] VT [a] (*Jur etc* = *argue*) plaider; (*Jur, fig*) **to ~ sb's case** ◊ **to ~ sb's cause** plaider la cause de qn (*Jur, fig*)
[b] (= *give as excuse*) alléguer, invoquer; (*Jur*) plaider; **to ~ ignorance** alléguer *or* invoquer son ignorance; **he ~ed poverty as a reason for ...** il a invoqué la pauvreté pour expliquer ...; (*Jur*) **to ~ insanity** plaider la démence → **fifth**

pleading ['pli:dɪŋ] [1] N [a] (*NonC*) prières *fpl* (**for sb** en faveur de qn), intercession *f* (*liter*)
[b] (*Jur*) plaidoirie *f*, plaidoyer *m*; **~s** conclusions *fpl* (*des parties*) [2] ADJ implorant, suppliant

pleadingly ['pli:dɪŋlɪ] ADV [*say*] d'un ton suppliant; [*look at*] d'un air suppliant

▼ **pleasant** ['pleznt] ADJ [a] (= *pleasing*) [*house, town, surroundings, voice*] agréable; [*smell, taste*] agréable, bon; [*weather, summer*] agréable, beau (belle *f*); [*surprise*] agréable, bon; **they had a ~ time** ils se sont bien amusés; **they spent a ~ afternoon** ils ont passé un après-midi très agréable; **it's very ~ here** on est bien ici; **Barcombe is a ~ place** Barcombe est un endroit agréable; **~ dreams!** fais de beaux rê-

ves! [b] (= *polite, genial*) aimable; **try and be a bit more ~ to your sister** essaie d'être un peu plus aimable avec ta sœur; **he was very ~ to** *or* **with us** il s'est montré très aimable avec nous; **he has a ~ manner** il est (d'un abord) charmant

pleasantly ['plezntlɪ] ADV [*behave, smile, answer*] aimablement; **to be ~ surprised** être agréablement surpris; **the weather was ~ warm/cool** il faisait une chaleur/fraîcheur agréable

pleasantness ['plezntnɪs] N [*of person, manner, welcome*] amabilité *f*; [*of place, house*] agrément *m*, attrait *m*, charme *m*

pleasantry ['plezntrɪ] N [a] (= *joke*) plaisanterie *f* [b] **pleasantries** (= *polite remarks*) civilités *fpl*, propos *mpl* aimables

▼ **please** [pli:z] [1] ADV s'il vous (*or* te) plaît; **yes ~, merci**; **would you like some cheese? — yes ~** voulez-vous du fromage? — volontiers *or* oui, merci; **~ come in** ◊ **come in ~** entrez, je vous prie; (*frm*) **~ be seated** veuillez vous asseoir (*frm*); **~ do not smoke** (*on notice*) prière de ne pas fumer; (*spoken*) ne fumez pas s'il vous plaît, je vous prie de ne pas fumer; **~ let me know if I can help you** ne manquez pas de me faire savoir si je peux vous aider; **may I smoke? — ~ do!** je peux fumer? — faites donc *or* je vous en prie *or* mais bien sûr!; **shall I tell him? — ~ do!** je le lui dis? — mais oui dites-le-lui *or* mais oui bien sûr *or* mais oui allez-y!*; **~!** (*entreating*) s'il vous plaît!; (*protesting*) (ah non!) je vous en prie *or* s'il vous plaît!; **~ don't!** ne faites pas ça s'il vous plaît!; (*in prayer*) **~ let him be all right** mon Dieu, faites qu'il ne lui soit rien arrivé
[2] VI [a] (*frm* = *think fit*) **I shall do as I ~** je ferai comme il me plaira *or* comme je veux; **do as you ~!** faites comme vous voulez *or* comme bon vous semble!; **as you ~!** comme vous voulez!, à votre guise!; **you may take as many as you ~** vous pouvez en prendre autant qu'il vous plaira; (*frm*) **if you ~** (= *please*) s'il vous plaît; (*iro*) **he wanted £50 if you ~!** il voulait 50 livres, rien que ça *or* s'il vous plaît!
[b] (= *satisfy, give pleasure*) plaire, faire plaisir; (*esp Comm*) **our aim is to ~** nous ne cherchons qu'à satisfaire; **he is very anxious to ~** il est très désireux de plaire; **a gift that is sure to ~** un cadeau qui ne peut que faire plaisir *or* que plaire
[3] VT [a] (= *give pleasure to*) plaire à, faire plaisir à; (= *satisfy*) satisfaire, contenter; **the gift ~d him** le cadeau lui a plu *or* lui a fait plaisir; **I did it just to ~ you** je ne l'ai fait que pour te faire plaisir; **that will ~ him** ça va lui faire plaisir, il va être content; **he is easily ~d/hard to ~** il est facile/difficile à contenter *or* à satisfaire; **there's no pleasing him*** il n'y a jamais moyen de le contenter *or* de le satisfaire; **you can't ~ all (of) the people all (of) the time** on ne saurait contenter tout le monde; **music that ~s the ear** musique *f* plaisante à l'oreille *or* qui flatte l'oreille; (*frm*) **it ~d him to** *or* **he was ~d to refuse permission** il a trouvé bon de ne pas consentir
[b] **to ~ oneself** faire comme on veut; **~ yourself!** comme vous voulez!, à votre guise!; **you must ~ yourself whether you do it or not** c'est à vous de décider si vous voulez le faire ou non; (*liter*) **~ God he comes!** plaise à Dieu qu'il vienne!

pleased [pli:zd] ADJ content, heureux (**with** de); **as ~ as Punch*** heureux comme un roi, aux anges; **he looked very ~ at the news** la nouvelle a eu l'air de lui faire grand plaisir; **he was ~ to hear that ...** il a été heureux *or* content d'apprendre que ...; **~ to meet you!*** enchanté!; **I am ~ that you can come** je suis heureux *or* content que vous puissiez venir; (*frm*) **we are ~ to inform you that ...** nous avons le plaisir de *or* (*more frm*) l'honneur de vous faire savoir que ...; **to be ~ with o.s./sb/**

sth être content de soi/qn/qch; **they were anything but ~ with the decision** la décision était loin de leur faire plaisir → **graciously**

pleasing ['pli:zɪŋ] ADJ [*personality*] sympathique, aimable, plaisant; [*sight, news, results, effect*] plaisant, qui fait plaisir; **it was very ~ to him** cela lui a fait grand plaisir

pleasingly ['pli:zɪŋlɪ] ADV agréablement

pleasurable ['pleʒərəbl] ADJ (très) agréable

pleasurably ['pleʒərəblɪ] ADV (*with vb*) avec plaisir; (*with adj*) agréablement

▼ **pleasure** ['pleʒə^r] ① N ⓐ (*NonC = enjoyment, satisfaction*) plaisir *m*; **to do sth for ~** faire qch pour le plaisir; **sexual ~** plaisir *m* (sexuel); **toys which can give children hours of ~** des jouets avec lesquels les enfants peuvent s'amuser pendant des heures; **has he gone to Paris on business or for ~?** est-il allé à Paris pour affaires ou pour son plaisir?; **to get ~ from** *or* **out of doing sth** prendre plaisir à faire qch; **he gets a lot of ~ out of his hobby** son passe-temps lui apporte beaucoup de plaisir; **I no longer get much ~ from my work** mon travail ne me plaît plus vraiment; **if it gives you any ~** si ça peut vous faire plaisir; (*frm*) **it gave me much ~ to hear that ...** cela m'a fait grand plaisir d'apprendre que ...; **to take great ~ in doing sth** prendre beaucoup de plaisir à faire qch; **he finds** *or* **takes great ~ in reading/music** il prend beaucoup de plaisir à lire/écouter de la musique; **she takes ~ in the simple things in life** elle apprécie les choses simples; **they took great ~ in his success** ils se sont réjouis de son succès; **it takes all the ~ out of it** ça vous gâche le plaisir; **to listen/read/remember** *etc* **with ~** écouter/lire/se rappeler *etc* avec plaisir

ⓑ (= *source of enjoyment*) plaisir *m*; **one of my greatest ~s** un de mes plus grands plaisirs, une de mes plus grandes joies; **she has very few ~s in life** elle a très peu de plaisirs dans la vie; **it's her only real ~ in life** c'est son seul véritable plaisir dans la vie; **the film was a ~ to watch** j'ai eu beaucoup de plaisir à regarder ce film; **the book was a ~ to read** c'était un plaisir que de lire ce livre; **the children's singing was a ~ to hear** c'était un plaisir que d'écouter les enfants chanter; **it's always a ~ talking to her** *or* **to talk to her** ◊ **she's always a ~ to talk to** c'est toujours un plaisir (que) de parler avec elle; **it's a ~ to work with him** ◊ **he's a ~ to work with** c'est un plaisir (que) de travailler avec lui

ⓒ (*in polite phrases*) **it's a ~!** ◊ **my ~!** ◊ **the ~ is mine!** je vous en prie!; **it's a ~ to see you again!** quel plaisir de vous revoir!; **it has been a ~ meeting you** *or* **to meet you** j'ai été enchanté de vous rencontrer; **with ~** (= *willingly*) [*do, agree, help*] avec plaisir, volontiers; **would you care to join us?** — **with ~!** voudriez-vous vous joindre à nous?; — avec plaisir *or* volontiers!; **would you mind helping me with this?** — **with ~!** pourriez-vous m'aider? — avec plaisir *or* volontiers!; (*frm: at dance*) **may I have the ~?** voulez-vous m'accorder cette danse?; (*frm*) **may we have the ~ of your company at dinner?** voulez-vous nous faire le plaisir de dîner avec nous?; (*frm*) **I have ~ in accepting ...** j'ai l'honneur d'accepter ...; **it is my very great ~ to introduce to you ...** j'ai l'honneur de vous présenter ...; (*frm*) **Mrs Torrance requests the ~ of Mr Simmonds's company at dinner** Mme Torrance prie M. Simmonds de lui faire l'honneur de venir dîner; (*frm*) **Mr and Mrs Brewis request the ~ of your company at the marriage of their daughter Katherine** M. et Mme Brewis sont heureux de vous faire part du mariage de leur fille Katherine et vous prient d'assister à la bénédiction nuptiale

ⓓ (*NonC = will, desire*) bon plaisir *m*, volonté *f*; **at ~** à volonté; **at your ~** à votre gré; (*Jur*) **at** *or* **during His** *or* **Her Majesty's ~** aussi longtemps qu'il plaira à Sa Majesté; (*Comm*)

we await your ~ nous sommes à votre entière disposition

② COMP ► **pleasure boat** N bateau *m* de plaisance ► **pleasure craft** NPL bateaux *mpl* de plaisance ► **pleasure cruise** N croisière *f*; (*short*) promenade *f* en mer *or* en bateau ► **pleasure-loving** ADJ qui aime le(s) plaisir(s) ► **the pleasure principle** N (*Psych*) le principe de la recherche du plaisir ► **pleasure-seeker** N hédoniste *mf* ► **pleasure-seeking** ADJ hédoniste ► **pleasure steamer** N vapeur *m* de plaisance ► **pleasure trip** N excursion *f*

pleat [pli:t] ① N pli *m* ② VT plisser

pleb* [pleb] N (*Brit pej*) plébéien(ne) *m(f)*, roturier *m*, -ière *f*; **the ~s** le commun (des mortels)

plebe* [pli:b] N (*US*) élève *mf* de première année (*d'une école militaire ou navale*)

plebeian [plɪ'bi:ən] ADJ, N plébéien(ne) *m(f)*

plebiscite ['plebɪsɪt] N plébiscite *m*; **to hold a ~** faire un plébiscite

plectron ['plektrən], **plectrum** ['plektrəm] N (*pl* **plectrons** *or* **plectra** ['plektrə]) plectre *m*

pled* [pled] VB (*esp US and Scot*) pt, ptp of **plead**

pledge [pledʒ] ① N ⓐ (= *security, token: also in pawnshop*) gage *m*; **as a ~ of his love** en gage *or* témoignage de son amour

ⓑ (= *promise*) promesse *f*, engagement *m*; (= *agreement*) pacte *m*; **I give you this ~** je vous fais cette promesse; **he made a ~ of secrecy** il a promis de *or* il s'est engagé à garder le secret; **to be under a ~ of secrecy** avoir promis de ne rien dire; **it was told me under a ~ of secrecy** on me l'a raconté contre la promesse de ne rien dire; **the government did not honour its ~ to cut taxes** le gouvernement n'a pas honoré son engagement *or* n'a pas tenu sa promesse de réduire les impôts; **an election ~** une promesse électorale; **a ~ on pay rises** un engagement concernant les augmentations de salaires; **the countries signed a ~ to help each other** les pays ont signé un pacte d'aide mutuelle; **to sign** *or* **take the ~** faire vœu de tempérance

ⓒ (*US Univ*) (= *promise*) promesse d'entrer dans une confrérie; (= *student*) étudiant(e) qui accomplit une période d'essai avant d'entrer dans une confrérie

ⓓ (= *toast*) toast *m* (**to** à)

② COMP ► **Pledge of Allegiance** N (*US*) Serment *m* d'allégeance

③ VT ⓐ (= *pawn*) engager, mettre en gage

ⓑ (= *promise*) [+ *one's help, support, allegiance*] promettre; **to ~ (o.s.) to do** (*gen*) promettre de faire, s'engager à faire; (*solemnly*) faire vœu de faire; **to ~ sb to secrecy** faire promettre le secret à qn; **he is ~d to secrecy** il a promis de garder le secret; **to ~ one's word (that ...)** donner sa parole (que ...)

ⓒ (*US Univ: into fraternity*) coopter; **to be ~d to a fraternity** accomplir une période d'essai avant d'entrer dans une confrérie

ⓓ (= *toast*) boire à la santé de

> **☐ PLEDGE OF ALLEGIANCE**

*Le Serment d'allégeance (**Pledge of Allegiance**) date de 1892; il est prononcé chaque jour par les élèves des écoles primaires américaines, qui, debout devant le drapeau des États-Unis, la main sur le cœur, proclament: « Je jure allégeance au drapeau des États-Unis d'Amérique et à la république qu'il représente, une nation placée sous la protection de Dieu, indivisible et garantissant liberté et justice pour tous ».*

Pleiades ['plaɪədi:z] NPL Pléiades *fpl*

Pleistocene ['plaɪstəsi:n] ADJ, N pléistocène *m*

plena ['pleɪnə] NPL of **plenum**

plenary ['pli:nərɪ] ① ADJ [*power*] absolu; [*assembly*] plénier; (*Rel*) plénier; (**in**) **~ session** (en) séance plénière; **~ meeting** réunion *f* plé-

nière, plenum *m* ② N (*also* **~ session**) séance *f* plénière, plenum *m*

plenipotentiary [ˌplenɪpə'tenʃərɪ] ADJ, N plénipotentiaire *mf*; **ambassador ~** ambassadeur *m* plénipotentiaire

plenitude ['plenɪtju:d] N (*liter*) plénitude *f*

plenteous ['plentɪəs], **plentiful** ['plentɪfʊl] ADJ [*harvest, food*] abondant; [*meal, amount*] copieux; **a ~ supply of** une abondance *or* une profusion de

plentifully ['plentɪfəlɪ] ADV abondamment

plenty ['plentɪ] ① N ⓐ (*NonC = abundance*) abondance *f*; **it grows here in ~** cela pousse en abondance *or* à foison ici; **he had friends in ~** il ne manquait pas d'amis; **to live in ~** vivre dans l'abondance; **land of ~** pays *m* de cocagne → **horn** ⓑ **I've got ~** j'en ai bien assez; **I've got ~ to do** j'ai largement de quoi m'occuper; **~ of** (*bien*) assez de; **he's got ~ of friends** il ne manque pas d'amis; **he's got ~ of money** il n'est pas pauvre; **ten is ~** dix suffisent (largement *or* amplement); **that's ~** ça suffit (amplement); (*clues etc*) **there's ~ to go on** nous avons toutes les données nécessaires pour le moment ② ADJ (*: or dial*) **plenty of**; → **1b** ③ ADV* assez; **it's ~ big enough!** c'est bien assez grand!; (*US*) **it sure rained ~!** qu'est-ce qu'il est tombé!*

plenum ['pli:nəm] N (*pl* **plenums** *or* **plena**) plenum *m*, réunion *f* plénière

pleonasm ['pli:ənæzəm] N pléonasme *m*

pleonastic [pli:ə'næstɪk] ADJ pléonastique

plethora ['pleθərə] N pléthore *f*, surabondance *f* (**of** de); (*Med*) pléthore *f*

plethoric [ple'θɒrɪk] ADJ pléthorique

pleura ['plʊərə] N (*pl* **pleurae** ['plʊəri:]) plèvre *f*

pleurisy ['plʊərɪsɪ] N (*NonC*) pleurésie *f*; **to have ~** avoir une pleurésie

pleuritic [plʊə'rɪtɪk] ADJ pleurétique

Plexiglas® ['pleksɪglɑ:s] N (*US*) plexiglas® *m*

plexus ['pleksəs] N (*pl* **plexuses** *or* **plexus**) plexus *m* → **solar**

pliability [ˌplaɪə'bɪlɪtɪ] N ⓐ [*of material*] flexibilité *f* ⓑ [*of character, person*] malléabilité *f*

pliable ['plaɪəbl], **pliant** ['plaɪənt] ADJ [*material*] flexible; [*character, person*] malléable

pliers ['plaɪəz] NPL (*also* **pair of ~**) pince(s) *f(pl)*, tenaille(s) *f(pl)*

plight[1] [plaɪt] N situation *f* critique, état *m* critique; **the country's economic ~** la crise *or* les difficultés *fpl* économique(s) du pays; **in a sad** *or* **sorry ~** dans un triste état; **what a dreadful ~ (to be in)!** quelles circonstances désespérées!, quelle situation lamentable!

plight[2]†† [plaɪt] VT (*liter*) **to ~ one's word** engager sa parole; (*also hum*) **to ~ one's troth** engager sa foi†, se fiancer

plimsoll ['plɪmsəl] ① N (*Brit*) (chaussure *f* de) tennis *m* ② COMP ► **Plimsoll line**, **Plimsoll mark** N (*Naut*) ligne *f* de flottaison en charge

plink [plɪŋk] (*US*) ① VI ⓐ (= *sound*) tinter ⓑ (= *shoot*) canarder* ② VT ⓐ (= *sound*) faire tinter ⓑ (= *shoot at*) canarder*

plinth [plɪnθ] N [*of column, pedestal*] plinthe *f*; [*of statue, record player*] socle *m*

Pliny ['plɪnɪ] N Pline *m*

Pliocene ['plaɪəʊsi:n] ADJ, N pliocène *m*

PLO [pi:el'əʊ] N (ABBR = **Palestine Liberation Organization**) OLP *f*

plod [plɒd] ① VI ⓐ (= *trudge: also* **~ along**) avancer d'un pas lourd *or* pesant; **to ~ in/out** *etc* entrer/sortir *etc* d'un pas lourd *ou* pesant ⓑ (* *fig*) **he was ~ding through his maths** il bûchait* ses maths; **I'm ~ding through his book** je lis son livre mais c'est laborieux; **I've already ~ded through 900 pages of this!** je me suis déjà tapé* 900 pages de ce pavé! ② VT **we ~ded the streets for another hour** nous avons continué à errer dans la rue pendant une heure ③ N ⓐ (= *trudge*) they went at a steady ~ ils marchaient pesamment, d'un pas égal; **I heard the ~ of his footsteps behind me** j'entendais son pas lourd derrière moi [b] (‡ = *policeman*) poulet* *m*; **PC Plod** ◊ **Policeman Plod** *agent de police*

▶ **plod along** VI → **plod 1a**

▶ **plod on** VI (*lit*) continuer *or* poursuivre son chemin; (*fig*) persévérer *or* progresser (laborieusement)

plodder ['plɒdər] N travailleur *m*, -euse *f* assidu(e), bûcheur* *m*, -euse* *f*

plodding ['plɒdɪŋ] ADJ [*step*] lourd, pesant; [*student, worker*] bûcheur

plonk [plɒŋk] [1] N [a] (= *sound*) plouf *m*, floc *m* [b] (* = *cheap wine*) vin *m* ordinaire, pinard* *m* [2] ADV (*esp Brit*) **it fell ~ in the middle of the table** c'est tombé au beau milieu de la table [3] VT (*esp Brit*: also ~ **down**) poser (bruyamment); **he ~ed the book (down) on to the table** il a posé (bruyamment) *or* a flanqué* le livre sur la table; **he ~ed himself (down) into the chair** il s'est laissé tomber dans le fauteuil

plonker ['plɒŋkər] N (*Brit*) imbécile* *mf*, con‡ *m*

plop [plɒp] [1] N ploc *m*, floc *m* [2] ADV **it went ~ into the water*** c'est tombé dans l'eau (en faisant ploc *or* floc) [3] VT [*stone*] faire ploc *or* floc; [*single drop*] faire floc; [*raindrops*] faire flic flac; **to ~ down*** [*person*] s'asseoir lourdement, s'affaler [4] VT **to ~ o.s. down*** [*person*] s'asseoir lourdement, s'affaler

plosive ['pləʊsɪv] (*Ling*) [1] ADJ occlusif [2] N consonne *f* occlusive

plot [plɒt] [1] N [a] [*of ground*] (lot *m* de) terrain *m*, lotissement *m*; **~ of grass** gazon *m*; **building ~** terrain *m* à bâtir; **the vegetable ~** le coin des légumes [b] (= *plan, conspiracy*) complot *m*, conspiration *f* (**against** contre, **to do** pour faire) [c] (*Literat, Theat*) intrigue *f*, action *f*; (*fig*) **the ~ thickens** l'affaire *or* ça se corse!; **to lose the ~*** perdre l'objectif de vue [2] VT [a] (= *mark out: also* ~ **out**) (*Aviat, Naut etc* [+ *course, route*]) déterminer; [+ *graph, curve, diagram*] tracer point par point; [+ *progress, development*] faire le graphique de; [+ *boundary, piece of land*] relever; (*Naut*) **to ~ one's position on the map** pointer la carte [b] [+ *sb's death, ruin etc*] comploter; **to ~ to do** comploter de faire [3] VI (= *conspire*) comploter, conspirer (**against** contre)

plotless ['plɒtlɪs] ADJ (*pej*) [*play, film etc*] sans intrigue

plotter¹ ['plɒtər] N (= *conspirator*) conspirateur *m*, -trice *f*; (*against the government*) conjuré(e) *m(f)*

plotter² ['plɒtər] N (*Comput etc*) traceur *m* (de courbes)

plotting ['plɒtɪŋ] [1] N (*NonC*) complots *mpl*, conspirations *fpl* [2] COMP ▶ **plotting board, plotting table** N (*Comput etc*) table *f* traçante

plotzed [plɒtst] ADJ (*US* = *drunk*) bourré‡, ivre

plough, plow (*US*) [plaʊ] [1] N (*Agr*) charrue *f*; (*Astron*) **the Plough** la Grande Ourse, le Grand Chariot → **snowplough**
[2] VT (*Agr*) [+ *field*] labourer; [+ *furrow*] creuser, tracer; (*fig*) **to ~ a lonely furrow** travailler dans son coin; **she didn't want to ~ the same furrow as her brother** elle ne voulait pas suivre la même voie que son frère; **to ~ money into sth** investir gros dans qch; **we've ~ed millions into this project** nous avons investi des millions dans ce projet; (*fig*) **to ~ one's way →** **3b**
[3] VI [a] (*Agr*) labourer [b] (*fig: also* ~ **one's** *or* **its way**) **to ~ through the mud/snow** avancer péniblement dans la boue/la neige; **the ship ~ed through the waves** le bateau fendait les flots; **the lorry ~ed into the wall** le camion est allé se jeter contre le mur; **the car ~ed through the fence** la voi-

ture a défoncé la barrière; **to ~ through a book** lire laborieusement un livre; **he was ~ing through his maths** il bûchait* ses maths
[c] (*Brit*†* = *fail an exam*) [*candidate*] se faire recaler*, être recalé*
[4] COMP ▶ **plough horse** N cheval *m* de labour *or* de trait

▶ **plough back** [1] VT SEP [+ *profits*] réinvestir, reverser (**into** dans) [2] **~ing back** N → **ploughing**

▶ **plough in** VT SEP [a] (*also* ~ **under**) [+ *crops, grass*] recouvrir *or* enterrer en labourant [b] [+ *fertilizer*] enfouir en labourant

▶ **plough up** VT SEP [a] [+ *field, bushes, path, right of way*] labourer [b] (*fig* = *churn up*) **the tanks ~ed up the field** les tanks ont labouré *or* défoncé le champ

ploughing ['plaʊɪŋ] N (*NonC*) labour *m*; [*of field etc*] labourage *m*; (*fig*) **the ~ back of profits** le réinvestissement des bénéfices

ploughland ['plaʊlænd] N terre *f* de labour, terre *f* arable

ploughman ['plaʊmən] [1] N (*pl* -**men**) laboureur *m* [2] COMP ▶ **ploughman's lunch** N (*Brit Culin*) assiette de fromage et de pickles

ploughshare ['plaʊʃɛər] N soc *m* (de charrue) → **sword**

plover ['plʌvər] N pluvier *m*

plow [plaʊ] (*US*) → **plough**

ploy* [plɔɪ] N stratagème *m*, truc* *m* (**to do** pour faire)

PLP [ˌpiːelˈpiː] N (*Brit*) (ABBR = **Parliamentary Labour Party**) → **parliamentary**

PLR [ˌpiːelˈɑːr] (*Brit Admin*) (ABBR = **public lending right**) → **public**

pluck [plʌk] [1] VT [+ *fruit, flower*] cueillir; (*Mus*) [+ *strings*] pincer; [+ *guitar*] pincer les cordes de; (*Culin*) [+ *bird*] plumer; **to ~ one's eyebrows** s'épiler les sourcils; (*fig*) **it's an idea/example I ~ed out of the air** c'est une idée/un exemple qui m'est venu(e) comme ça [2] N [a] (*NonC:** = *courage*) courage *m*, cran* *m* [b] (*NonC: Culin*) fressure *f* [c] (= *tug*) petit coup *m*

▶ **pluck at** VT FUS **to ~ at sb's sleeve** tirer qn doucement par la manche

▶ **pluck off** VT SEP [+ *feathers*] arracher; [+ *fluff etc*] détacher, enlever

▶ **pluck out** VT SEP (*esp liter*) arracher

▶ **pluck up** VT SEP [a] [+ *weed*] arracher, extirper [b] (= *summon up*) **to ~ up courage** prendre son courage à deux mains; **he ~ed up (the) courage to tell her** il a enfin trouvé le courage de *or* il s'est (enfin) décidé à le lui dire

pluckily* ['plʌkɪlɪ] ADV courageusement, avec cran*

pluckiness* ['plʌkɪnɪs] N (*NonC*) courage *m*, cran* *m*

plucky* ['plʌkɪ] ADJ courageux, qui a du cran*

plug [plʌg] [1] N [a] (= *for draining*) [*of bath, basin*] bonde *f*, vidange *f*; [*of barrel*] bonde *f*; (*to stop a leak*) tampon *m*; (= *stopper*) bouchon *m*; (*for fixing*) cheville *f*; (*Geol: in volcano*) culot *m*; **a ~ of cotton wool** un tampon de coton; **to put in/pull out the ~** mettre/enlever *or* ôter la bonde; (*in lavatory*) **to pull the ~*** tirer la chasse d'eau; (*fig*) **to pull the ~ on‡** [+ *patient*] débrancher; [+ *accomplice, wrongdoer*] exposer; [+ *project etc*] laisser tomber* → **earplugs** [b] (*Elec*) (*on flex, apparatus*) prise *f* (de courant) (*mâle*); (* = *socket: also* **wall ~**) prise *f* (de courant) (*femelle*); [*of switchboard*] fiche *f* → **amp, fused, fuse** [c] (*Aut: also* **sparking ~**) bougie *f* [d] (*US: also* **fire ~**) bouche *f* d'incendie [e] (* = *publicity*) coup *m* de pouce (publicitaire), réclame *f or* publicité *f* (clandestine *or* indirecte); **to give sth/sb a ~** ◊ **to put in a ~ for sth/sb** donner un coup de pouce (publicitaire) à qch/qn, faire de la réclame *or* de la publicité indirecte pour qch/qn

[f] (*of tobacco*) (*for smoking*) carotte *f*; (*for chewing*) chique *f*
[2] VT [a] (*also* ~ **up**) [+ *hole, crack*] boucher, obturer; [+ *barrel, jar*] boucher; [+ *leak*] colmater; (*on boat*) aveugler; [+ *tooth*] obturer (**with** avec); (*fig*) **to ~ the gap in the tax laws** mettre fin aux échappatoires en matière de fiscalité; (*fig*) **to ~ the drain on gold reserves** arrêter l'hémorragie *or* la fuite des réserves d'or [b] **to ~ sth into a hole** enfoncer qch dans un trou; **~ the TV into the wall** branchez le téléviseur (sur le secteur) [c] (* = *publicize*) (*on one occasion*) faire de la réclame *or* de la publicité pour; (*repeatedly*) matraquer* [d]‡ (= *shoot*) flinguer‡, ficher* *or* flanquer* une balle dans la peau à; (= *punch*) ficher* *or* flanquer* un coup de poing à
[3] COMP ▶ **plug-and-play** ADJ (*Comput*) prêt à l'emploi ▶ **plug hat** N (*US*) (chapeau *m* en) tuyau *m* de poêle ▶ **plug-in** ADJ (*Elec*) qui se branche sur le secteur ▶ **plug-ugly**‡ N dur *m*, brute *f*

▶ **plug away*** VI bosser‡, travailler dur (**at doing** pour faire); **he was ~ging away at his maths** il bûchait* ses maths

▶ **plug in** [1] VT SEP [+ *lead, apparatus*] brancher [2] VI se brancher; **the TV ~s in over there** la télé se branche là-bas; **does your radio ~ in?** est-ce que votre radio peut se brancher sur le secteur? [3] **~-in** ADJ → **plug**

▶ **plug into*** VT FUS [+ *ideas etc*] se brancher à l'écoute de*

▶ **plug up** VT SEP → **plug 2a**

plughole ['plʌghəʊl] N trou *m* (d'écoulement *or* de vidange), bonde *f*, vidange *f*; **it went down the ~** (*lit*) c'est tombé dans le trou (du lavabo *or* de l'évier etc); (*fig*) [*idea, project*] c'est tombé à l'eau

plum [plʌm] [1] N (= *fruit*) prune *f*; (*also* ~ **tree**) prunier *m*; (*Brit hum*) **to speak with** *or* **have a ~ in one's mouth*** parler avec un accent snob [b] (* *fig*) (= *choice thing*) meilleur morceau *or* (*fig*), meilleure part *f* (*fig*); (= *good job*) boulot* *m* en or [2] ADJ [a] (*also* ~-**coloured**) prune *inv*, lie-de-vin *inv* [b] (* = *best, choice*) de choix, le plus chouette*; **he got the ~ job** c'est lui qui a décroché le meilleur travail *or* le travail le plus chouette*; **he has a ~ job** il a un boulot* en or [3] COMP ▶ **plum duff, plum pudding** N (plum-) pudding *m* ▶ **plum tomato** N (*Culin*) olivette *f*

plumage ['pluːmɪdʒ] N plumage *m*

plumb [plʌm] [1] N plomb *m*; **out of ~** hors d'aplomb
[2] ADJ vertical
[3] ADV [a] en plein, exactement; **~ in the middle of** en plein milieu de, au beau milieu de [b] (*esp US**) complètement, absolument, tout à fait
[4] VT [a] (= *descend to*) sonder; **to ~ the depths** (*lit*) sonder les profondeurs; (*fig*) toucher le fond; **to ~ the depths of desperation/loneliness** toucher le fond du désespoir/de la solitude; **to ~ the depths of stupidity/tastelessness/mediocrity** atteindre le comble de la stupidité/du mauvais goût/de la médiocrité; **the film ~s the depths of sexism and racism** ce film est d'un sexisme et d'un racisme inimaginables; **these terrorists have ~ed new depths** les terroristes sont allés encore plus loin; (*St Ex*) **the pound ~ed new depths yesterday** la livre a atteint son nouveau plus bas hier [b] (= *connect plumbing in*) [+ *sink, washing machine etc*] installer la plomberie de

▶ **plumb in** VT SEP [+ *sink, washing machine etc*] faire le raccordement de; [+ *gas fire*] brancher

plumbago [plʌmˈbeɪgəʊ] N (*pl* **plumbagos**)

a (= *graphite*) plombagine f b (*Bot*) plumbago m

plumber ['plʌmər] 1 N a plombier m b (*US‡*) agent m de surveillance gouvernementale, plombier* m 2 COMP ► **plumber's mate** N aide-plombier m ► **plumber's merchant** N grossiste m en plomberie

plumbic ['plʌmbɪk] ADJ plombifère

plumbing ['plʌmɪŋ] N (= *trade*) (travail m de) plomberie f; (= *system*) plomberie f, tuyauterie f

plumbline ['plʌmlaɪn] N (*Constr etc*) fil m à plomb; (*Naut*) sonde f

plumcake ['plʌmkeɪk] N (plum-)cake m

plume [plu:m] 1 N a (= *large feather*) (grande) plume f; (= *cluster of feathers*) (on bird) plumes fpl, aigrette f; (on hat, helmet) plumet m, aigrette f; (*larger*) panache m; **in borrowed ~s** portant des vêtements empruntés b (*fig*) [of smoke, dust] panache m; **a ~ of water** un jet d'eau 2 VT [bird] [+ wing, feather] lisser; **the bird was pluming itself** l'oiseau se lissait les plumes; (*fig*) **to ~ o.s. on sth** enorgueillir de qch

plumed [plu:md] ADJ [bird] à aigrette; [helmet] à plumet

plummet ['plʌmɪt] 1 VI [aircraft, bird] plonger, descendre or tomber à pic; [temperature] baisser or descendre brusquement; [prices, sales, popularity, amount] dégringoler; [spirits, morale] tomber à zéro 2 N plomb m

plummy* ['plʌmɪ] ADJ a (*Brit*) [accent, voice] snob b (= *colour*) prune inv, lie-de-vin inv

plump¹ [plʌmp] 1 ADJ [person] grassouillet, empâté; [baby, child, hand] potelé; [cheek, face] rebondi, plein; [lips] charnu; [arm, leg, chicken] dodu; [cushion] rebondi, bien rembourré 2 VT (*also* = **up**) [+ pillow] tapoter
► **plump out** VI devenir rondelet, grossir

plump² [plʌmp] 1 VT (= *drop*) laisser tomber lourdement, flanquer* 2 VI tomber lourdement 3 ADV a en plein, exactement; **~ in the middle of** au beau milieu de, au beau lieu de b (= *in plain words*) carrément, sans mâcher ses mots
► **plump down** 1 VI s'affaler 2 VT SEP laisser tomber lourdement; **to ~ o.s. down on the sofa** s'affaler sur le sofa
► **plump for*** VT FUS fixer son choix sur, se décider pour

plumpness ['plʌmpnɪs] N [of person] rondeur f, embonpoint m

plunder ['plʌndər] 1 N (= *act*) pillage m; (= *loot*) butin m 2 VT piller

plunderer ['plʌndərər] N pillard m

plundering ['plʌndərɪŋ] 1 N (NonC = *act*) pillage m 2 ADJ pillard

plunge [plʌndʒ] 1 N [of bird, diver] plongeon m; (= *steep fall*) chute f; (*fig* = *fall*) chute f, dégringolade* f; (*Fin* = *rash investment*) spéculation f hasardeuse (**on** sur); **to take a ~** (*diver etc*) plonger; [bather] faire un (petit) plongeon; [shares, prices etc] chuter, dégringoler; **his popularity has taken a ~** sa popularité a chuté; **prices started a downward ~** les prix ont commencé à chuter or dégringoler; **a ~ in the value of the pound** une chute de la valeur de la livre; (*fig*) **to take the ~** se jeter à l'eau, sauter le pas
2 VT [+ hand, knife, dagger] (gen) plonger, enfoncer (**into** dans); (*into water*) plonger (**into** dans); (*fig*) plonger; **they were ~d into war/darkness/despair** etc ils ont été plongés dans la guerre/l'obscurité/le désespoir etc
3 VI a (= *dive*) [diver, goalkeeper, penguin, submarine] plonger (**into** dans, **from** de); [ship] piquer de l'avant or du nez
b [road, cliff] plonger (**into** dans); **the stream/road ~d down the mountainside** le ruisseau/la route dévalait le flanc de la colline
c (= *fall*) [person] tomber, faire une chute

(from de); [vehicle] tomber (**from** de); [prices etc] chuter, dégringoler; **he ~d to his death** il a fait une chute mortelle; **he ~d over the cliff to his death** il s'est tué en tombant du haut de la falaise; **the plane ~d to the ground/into the sea** l'avion s'est écrasé au sol/est tombé dans la mer; **the car ~d over the cliff** la voiture est tombée de or a plongé par-dessus la falaise
d (= *rush, lurch*) **to ~ in/out/across** etc entrer/sortir/traverser etc précipitamment or à toute allure; **he ~d into the crowd** il s'est jeté dans la foule; **he ~d through the crowd** il s'est frayé un chemin à travers la foule; **he ~d through the hedge** il a piqué brusquement or s'est jeté au travers de la haie; **the truck ~d across the road** le camion a fait une embardée en travers de la route
e (*fig*) **to ~ into** [+ debt, recession, turmoil] sombrer dans; **he ~d into the argument** il s'est lancé dans la discussion
f (= *plummet*) [sales, prices, profits, currency] chuter, dégringoler; [temperature] tomber brusquement; **sales have ~d by 24%** les ventes ont chuté de 24 %
g * (= *gamble*) jouer gros jeu, flamber; (*St Ex* = *speculate rashly*) spéculer imprudemment
4 COMP ► **plunge pool** N (in sauna etc) bassin m
► **plunge in** 1 VI [diver etc] plonger; (*fig: into work etc*) s'y mettre de grand cœur 2 VT SEP (y) plonger

plunger ['plʌndʒər] N a (= *piston*) piston m; (*also* **sink ~**: for blocked pipe) (débouchoir m à) ventouse f b (= *gambler*) flambeur m; (*St Ex*) (spéculateur m) risque-tout m inv

plunging ['plʌndʒɪŋ] 1 N (NonC = *action*) plongement m; [of diver etc] plongées fpl; [of boat] tangage m 2 ADJ **~ neckline** décolleté m plongeant

plunk [plʌŋk] (*US*) = **plonk 1a, 2, 3**

pluperfect ['plu:'pɜ:fɪkt] N plus-que-parfait m

plural ['plʊərəl] 1 ADJ a (*Gram*) [form, number, ending, person] pluriel, du pluriel; [verb, noun] au pluriel b [vote] plural c [society] pluriel, diversifié 2 N (*Gram*) pluriel m; **in the ~** au pluriel

pluralism ['plʊərəlɪzəm] N (*Philos*) pluralisme m; (*Rel*) cumul m

pluralist ['plʊərəlɪst] ADJ, N pluraliste mf

pluralistic [plʊərə'lɪstɪk] ADJ pluraliste

plurality [plʊə'rælɪtɪ] N a (= *multitude, diversity*) pluralité f; [of benefices etc] cumul m b (*US Pol*) majorité f relative; **a ~ of 5,000 votes** une majorité de 5 000 voix

plus [plʌs] 1 PREP plus; **three ~ four** trois plus or et quatre; **... ~ what I've done already ...** plus ce que j'ai déjà fait; (*Bridge etc*) **we are ~ five** nous menons par cinq points
2 CONJ* en plus, d'ailleurs; **... ~ I don't like nightclubs** ... en plus or d'ailleurs, je n'aime pas les boîtes de nuit
3 ADJ a (*Elec, Math*) positif; (*lit*) **on the ~ side (of the account)** à l'actif du compte; (*fig*) **on the ~ side (of the account) we have his support** l'aspect positif, c'est que nous bénéficions de son soutien; (*fig*) **a ~ factor** un atout
b **ten-~ hours a week*** un minimum de dix heures or plus de dix heures par semaine; (*Scol*) **A/B** etc **~ A/B** etc plus; **we've sold 100 ~*** nous en avons vendu 100 et quelques or plus de 100
4 N a (*Math* = *sign*) (signe m) plus m
b (= *bonus, advantage*) avantage m additionnel, atout m; (of situation etc) **the ~es** les côtés mpl positifs
5 COMP ► **plus fours** NPL culotte f de golf ► **plus sign** N (*Math*) signe m plus

plush [plʌʃ] 1 N (*Tex*) peluche f 2 ADJ a (= *made of plush*) de or en peluche; (= *plush-like*)

pelucheux b (* = *sumptuous*) rupin‡, somptueux

plushly ['plʌʃlɪ] ADV somptueusement

plushy* ['plʌʃɪ] ADJ rupin*, somptueux

Plutarch ['plu:tɑ:k] N Plutarque m

Pluto ['plu:təʊ] N (*Astron*) Pluton f; (*Myth*) Pluton m

plutocracy [plu:'tɒkrəsɪ] N ploutocratie f

plutocrat ['plu:təʊkræt] N ploutocrate m

plutocratic [plu:təʊ'krætɪk] ADJ ploutocratique

plutonium [plu:'təʊnɪəm] N plutonium m

pluviometer [plu:vɪ'ɒmɪtər] N pluviomètre m

ply¹ [plaɪ] N a [of wood] feuille f, épaisseur f; [of wool] fil m, brin m; [of rope] toron m, brin m b (*compound ending*) **four-~ rope** corde f quatre fils; **four-~ wood** contreplaqué m quatre épaisseurs; **three-~ (wool)** laine f trois fils; **two-~ tissues/napkins** mouchoirs mpl/serviettes fpl (en papier) double épaisseur

ply² [plaɪ] 1 VT a [+ needle, tool] manier, jouer (habilement) de; [+ oar] manier; [ship] [+ river, sea] naviguer sur, voguer sur (*liter*); **they plied their oars with a will** ils faisaient force de rames; **to ~ one's trade (as)** exercer son métier (de) b [+ person] **to ~ sb with questions** presser qn de questions; **to ~ sb for information** demander continuellement des renseignements à qn; **he plied them with drink** il ne cessait de remplir leur verre 2 VI **to ~ between** [ship, coach etc] faire la navette entre; (*Jur*) **to ~ for hire** [taxi] faire un service de taxi

plywood ['plaɪwʊd] N contre-plaqué m

PM [pi:'em] N (*Brit*) (ABBR = **Prime Minister**) → prime

pm [pi:'em] N (ABBR = **post meridiem**) de l'après-midi; **3pm** 3 heures de l'après-midi, 15 heures; **10pm** 10 heures du soir, 22 heures

PMG [pi:em'dʒi:] N a (*Brit*) (ABBR = **Paymaster General**) → paymaster b (ABBR = **Postmaster General**) → postmaster

PMS [pi:em'es] N (ABBR = **premenstrual syndrome**) SPM m, syndrome m prémenstruel

PMT [pi:em'ti:] N (ABBR = **premenstrual tension**) SPM m, syndrome m prémenstruel

pneumatic [nju:'mætɪk] 1 ADJ pneumatique 2 COMP ► **pneumatic drill** N marteau-piqueur m ► **pneumatic tyre** N pneu m

pneumatically [nju:'mætɪkəlɪ] ADV [controlled, operated etc] pneumatiquement

pneumoconiosis [nju:məʊkəʊnɪ'əʊsɪs] N (*Med*) pneumoconiose f

pneumocystis carinii pneumonia [nju:məʊ'sɪstɪskə'raɪnɪaɪnju:'məʊnɪə] N pneumocystose f

pneumonia [nju:'məʊnɪə] N (NonC) pneumonie f

pneumonologist [nju:mə'nɒlədʒɪst] N pneumologue mf

pneumonology [nju:mə'nɒlədʒɪ] N pneumologie f

PO [pi:'əʊ] N a (ABBR = **post office**) PO Box 24 BP n° 24 b (ABBR = **Petty Officer**) → petty c (ABBR = **Pilot Officer**) → pilot

Po [pəʊ] N (= *river*) Pô m

po: [pəʊ] (*Brit*) 1 N († = *potty*) pot m (de chambre) 2 COMP ► **po-faced‡** ADJ à l'air pincé

p.o. [pi:'əʊ] (*Brit*) (ABBR = **postal order**) → postal

POA [pi:əʊ'eɪ] N (*Brit*) (ABBR = **Prison Officers' Association**) syndicat

poach¹ [pəʊtʃ] 1 VT (*Culin*) pocher 2 COMP ► **poached egg** N œuf m poché

poach² [pəʊtʃ] 1 VT [+ game] braconner, chasser illégalement; [+ fish] braconner, pêcher illégalement; (*fig*) [+ employee] débaucher 2 VI braconner; **to ~ for salmon** etc braconner du saumon etc; (*lit, fig*) **to ~ on sb's**

preserves or **territory** braconner sur les terres de qn ; (fig) **stop ~ing!*** (in tennis) arrête de me chiper la balle !* ; (in work) arrête de marcher sur mes plates-bandes !*

poacher¹ ['pəʊtʃəʳ] N (for eggs) pocheuse f

poacher² ['pəʊtʃəʳ] N (of game etc) braconnier m

poaching ['pəʊtʃɪŋ] N braconnage m

pock [pɒk] N (Med) pustule f de petite vérole

pocket ['pɒkɪt] ① N ⓐ (in garment, suitcase, file, wallet etc) poche f ; **with his hands in his ~s** les mains dans les poches ; **with (one's) ~s full of ...** les poches pleines de ... ; **in his trouser/ jacket ~** dans la poche de son pantalon/sa veste → **back**, **breast**, **hip¹** ; **to go through sb's ~s** faire les poches à qn ; (fig) **to be in sb's ~** être à la solde de qn ; **to have sb in one's ~** avoir qn dans sa manche or dans sa poche ; **to live in each other's** or **one another's ~s** vivre les uns sur les autres ; **he has the game in his ~** il a le jeu dans sa poche
ⓑ (fig = budget, finances) **it's a drain on his ~** ça grève son budget ; **the deal put £100 in his ~** l'affaire lui a rapporté 100 livres ; **that will hurt his ~** ça fera mal à son porte-monnaie ; **to line one's ~s** se remplir les poches ; **he is always putting his hand in his ~** il n'arrête pas de débourser ; **to pay for sth out of one's own ~** payer qch de sa poche ; **to be in ~** avoir une marge de bénéfice ; **to be out of ~** en être de sa poche ; **out-of-~** → **out** ; **I was £5 in/out of ~** j'avais fait un bénéfice/essuyé une perte de 5 livres ; **it left me £5 in/out of ~** ça m'a rapporté/coûté 5 livres ; (fig) **to have deep ~s** avoir de gros moyens ; **investors with deep ~s** les investisseurs mpl disposant de gros moyens
ⓒ (= small area) [of gas, fog] poche f ; [of land] parcelle f ; (Aviat: also **air ~**) trou m d'air ; (Billiards etc) blouse f ; **~ of infection** foyer m de contagion ; **~s of resistance** poches fpl de résistance ; **there are still some ~s of unemployment** il reste quelques petites zones de chômage
② VT ⓐ (lit, fig) [+ object, money, prize] empocher
ⓑ (* = steal) empocher, barboter*
③ COMP (flask, torch, dictionary, edition etc) de poche ► **pocket battleship** N cuirassé m de poche ► **pocket billiards** NPL (US) billard m américain ► **pocket calculator** N calculatrice f de poche, calculette f ► **pocket-handkerchief** N mouchoir m de poche ◆ ADJ (fig) grand comme un mouchoir de poche ► **pocket-money** N argent m de poche ► **pocket-size(d)** ADJ (lit) de poche ; (fig) [house, kingdom] tout petit ► **pocket veto** N (US Pol) veto implicite du Président qui ne signe pas un projet de loi dans les délais impartis

pocketbook ['pɒkɪtbʊk] N ⓐ (US) (= wallet) portefeuille m ; (= handbag) sac m à main ⓑ (= notebook) calepin m, carnet m

pocketful ['pɒkɪtfʊl] N (pl **pocketfuls**) poche f pleine ; **with ~s of ...** les poches pleines de ...

pocketknife ['pɒkɪtnaɪf] N (pl **-knives**) couteau m de poche, canif m

pockmark ['pɒkmɑːk] N cicatrice f de variole

pockmarked ['pɒkmɑːkt] ADJ [face] grêlé ; [surface] criblé de trous

pod [pɒd] N [of bean, pea etc] cosse f ; (Space) nacelle f ; (hum) **in ~:** (= pregnant) en cloque:

podgy* ['pɒdʒɪ] ADJ (esp Brit) grassouillet

podia ['pəʊdɪə] NPL of **podium**

podiatrist [pɒ'diːətrɪst] N (US) pédicure mf, podologue mf

podiatry [pɒ'diːətrɪ] N (US) (= science) podologie f ; (= treatment) soins mpl du pied, traitement m des maladies du pied

podium ['pəʊdɪəm] N (pl **podia**) podium m

Podunk ['pəʊdʌŋk] N (US) petit village m perdu, ≈ Trifouilly-les-Oies

POE (ABBR = **port of embarkation**) → **port**

poem ['pəʊɪm] N poème m ; **the ~s of Keats** les poèmes mpl de Keats

poet ['pəʊɪt] ① N poète m ② COMP ► **poet laureate** N (pl **poets laureate**) poète m lauréat

poetaster [,pəʊɪ'tæstəʳ] N mauvais poète m, rimailleur m

poetess ['pəʊɪtes] N poétesse f

poetic [pəʊ'etɪk] ADJ poétique ; **~ licence** licence f poétique ; **it's ~ justice** il y a une justice immanente

poetical [pəʊ'etɪkəl] ADJ poétique

poetically [pəʊ'etɪkəlɪ] ADV poétiquement

poeticize [pəʊ'etɪsaɪz] VT poétiser

poetics [pəʊ'etɪks] NPL poétique f

poetry ['pəʊɪtrɪ] ① N (NonC: lit, fig) poésie f ; **the ~ of Keats** la poésie de Keats ; **he writes ~** il écrit des poèmes, il est poète ② COMP ► **poetry reading** N lecture f de poèmes

pogo ['pəʊgəʊ] ① N pogo m ② VI (Brit = dance) pogoter, danser le pogo ③ COMP **pogo stick** N échasse f sauteuse

pogrom ['pɒgrəm] ① N pogrom m ② VT massacrer (au cours d'un pogrom)

poignancy ['pɔɪnjənsɪ] N **the ~ of the lyrics** le caractère poignant des paroles ; **it was a moment of extraordinary ~** c'était un moment très poignant

poignant ['pɔɪnjənt] ADJ [emotion, grief] poignant, intense, vif ; [look, entreaty] poignant

poignantly ['pɔɪnjəntlɪ] ADV [describe, express, evoke] d'une manière poignante ; [feel] vivement, intensément

poinsettia [pɔɪn'setɪə] N poinsettia m

▼**point** [pɔɪnt]

① NOUN		④ INTRANSITIVE VERB	
② PLURAL NOUN		⑤ COMPOUNDS	
③ TRANSITIVE VERB		⑥ PHRASAL VERBS	

① NOUN
ⓐ (= sharp end) [of pencil, needle, knife, jaw] pointe f ; **a knife with a sharp ~** un couteau très pointu ; **a star with ten ~s** une étoile à cinq branches ; **a stag with ten ~s** un cerf (de) dix cors ; (Ballet) **to be** or **dance on ~s** faire les pointes ; **at the ~ of a gun** sous la menace d'un revolver ; **not to put too fine a ~ on it** (= frankly) pour être franc
ⓑ (= dot) (Geom, Typ) point m ; (Math: also **decimal ~**) virgule f (décimale) ; **three ~ six (3.6)** trois virgule six (3,6) ; **eight-~ type** caractères mpl en corps huit ; (Geom) **~ A** le point A
ⓒ (on scale, in space, in time) point m ; **the highest ~ in the district** le point culminant de la région ; **at that ~ in the road** à cet endroit de la route ; **at the ~ where the road forks** là où la route bifurque ; **he had reached a ~ where he began to doubt whether ...** il en était arrivé à se demander si ... ; **to reach a low ~** [morale] être au plus bas ; [production, reputation] toucher le fond ; **this was the low ~ (of his career)** c'est à ce moment-là qu'il a touché le fond (dans sa carrière) ; **from that ~ onwards** à partir de ce moment ; **at this** or **that ~ (in space)** là, à cet endroit ; (in time) à ce moment-là ; **at this ~ in time** or **at this ~ in stade** ; **the train stops at Slough, and all ~s west** le train s'arrête à Slough et dans toutes les gares à l'ouest de Slough ; **the (thirty-two) ~s of the compass** les points mpl de la boussole ; **from all ~s (of the compass)** des quatre coins de l'horizon, de toutes parts, de tous côtés

◆ **point of** + noun: **there was no ~ of contact between them** ils n'avaient aucun point commun ; **he was strict to the ~ of cruelty** il était sévère au point d'être cruel ; **on** or **at the ~ of death** à l'article de la mort ; **~ of departure** point m de départ ; **~ of entry** (into a country) point m d'arrivée (dans un pays) ; **he had reached the ~ of no return** il avait atteint

le point de non-retour

◆ **the point of** + -ing: **to be on the ~ of doing sth** être sur le point de faire qch ; **when it came to the ~ of paying, ...** quand il s'est agi de payer, ... ; **he had reached the ~ of resigning** il en était arrivé au point de donner sa démission

◆ **up to a point** jusqu'à un certain point, dans une certaine mesure

ⓓ (= unit) (in score, on scale) point m ; (on thermometer) degré m ; (Boxing) **on ~s** aux points ; **the cost-of-living index went up two ~s** l'indice du coût de la vie a augmenté de deux points ; (St Ex) **to rise** or **gain three ~s** augmenter de or gagner trois points
ⓔ (= idea, question) point m ; **on this ~ we are agreed** sur ce point or là-dessus nous sommes d'accord ; **on all ~s** en tous points ; **12-~ plan** plan m en 12 points ; **the main ~s to remember** les principaux points à retenir ; **~ by ~** point par point → **5** ; **you have a ~ there!** c'est juste !, il y a du vrai dans ce que vous dites ! ; **to carry** or **gain** or **win one's ~** avoir or gain de cause ; **he made the ~ that ...** il fit remarquer que ... ; **he made a good ~ when he said that ...** il a mis le doigt dessus lorsqu'il a dit que ... ; **I'd like to make a ~ if I may** j'aurais une remarque à faire si vous le permettez ; **you've made your ~!** (= had your say) vous avez dit ce que vous aviez à dire ! ; (= convinced me) vous m'avez convaincu ! ; **I take your ~** je vois ce que vous voulez dire ; **~ taken!*** d'accord(, je te le concède) !
◆ **point of** + noun: **it's a ~ of detail** c'est un point de détail ; **it was a ~ of honour with him never to refuse** il se faisait un point d'honneur de ne jamais refuser, il mettait son point d'honneur à ne jamais refuser ; **~ of interest/of no importance** point m intéressant/sans importance ; **a ~ of law** un point de droit ; **on a ~ of principle** sur une question de principe → **order**
ⓕ (= important part, main idea) [of argument etc] objet m ; [of joke] astuce f ; **that's not the ~** il ne s'agit pas de ça, là n'est pas la question ; **that is hardly the ~** ◊ that is beside the **~** cela n'a rien à voir ; **the whole ~ was to do it today** tout l'intérêt était justement de le faire aujourd'hui ; **that's the (whole) ~** ◊ that's just the **~!** justement ! ; **the ~ is that you had promised it for today!** le fait est que vous l'aviez promis pour aujourd'hui ! ; **to come to the ~** [person] en venir au fait ; **when it comes to the ~, they don't value education** au fond, ils n'accordent pas beaucoup d'importance à l'éducation ; **we're getting off the ~** nous nous éloignons du sujet ; **get** or **come to the ~!** venez-en à l'essentiel !, cessez de tourner autour du pot !* ; **let's get back to the ~** revenons à nos moutons* ; **to keep** or **stick to the ~** ne pas s'éloigner du sujet
ⓖ (= meaning, purpose) **what was the ~ of his visit?** quel était le but or l'objet de sa visite ? ; **there's some** or **a ~ in it** ça a une utilité ; **a long story that seemed to have no ~ at all** une longue histoire sans rime ni raison ; **the ~ of this story is that ...** la morale de l'histoire, c'est que ... ; **(very much) to the ~** (très) pertinent ; **his remarks lack ~** ses remarques ne sont pas très pertinentes ; **the news gave ~ to his arguments** cette nouvelle a souligné la pertinence de ses arguments ; **to get** or **see the ~** comprendre ; **you get the ~?** vous saisissez ? * ; **to make a ~ of doing sth** ◊ to make it a **~ to do sth** ne pas manquer de faire qch
ⓗ (= use) **what's the ~?** à quoi bon ? ; **what's the ~ of** or **in waiting?** à quoi bon attendre ? ; **there's no ~ in waiting** ça ne sert à rien d'attendre ; **there's little ~ in saying ...** ça ne sert pas à grand-chose de dire ... ; **I don't see any ~ in doing that** je ne vois aucun intérêt à faire cela
ⓘ (= characteristic) caractéristique f ; **good ~s** qualités fpl ; **bad ~s** défauts mpl ; **it is not his strong ~** ce n'est pas son fort ; **he has his ~s** il a

ses bons côtés; **the ~s to look (out) for when buying a car** les choses *fpl* auxquelles il faut faire attention lorsqu'on achète une voiture

[j] Geog pointe *f*

[k] Aut vis *f* platinée

[l] Brit Elec: *also* power ~ prise *f* (de courant) (femelle)

[2] **points** NPL Brit Rail aiguillage *m*, aiguilles *fpl*

[3] TRANSITIVE VERB

[a] = aim, direct [+ telescope, hosepipe] pointer, diriger (at sur) [+ gun] braquer un revolver sur qn; **he ~ed his stick towards the house** il a indiqué la maison avec sa canne; **to ~ sb in the direction of** diriger qn vers; **she ~ed him in the right direction*** elle lui a montré le chemin; **he ~ed the boat towards the harbour** il a mis le cap sur le port; **he ~ed the car towards Paris** il a tourné en direction de Paris; **he ~ed his finger at me** il a pointé le doigt sur *or* vers moi

[b] = mark, show

♦ **to point the way**: **the signs ~ the way to London** les panneaux indiquent la direction de Londres; **it ~s the way to closer cooperation** cela montre la voie d'une plus grande coopération

[c] Constr [+ wall] jointoyer (with de)

[d] = punctuate ponctuer; [+ Hebrew, Arabic etc] mettre les points-voyelles à; [+ psalm] marquer de points

[e] + toes pointer

[4] INTRANSITIVE VERB

[a] person montrer *or* indiquer du doigt; **it's rude to ~** ce n'est pas poli de montrer du doigt; **to ~ at** *or* **towards sth/sb** indiquer *or* désigner qch/qn du doigt; **he ~ed at the house with his stick** il montra *or* indiqua la maison avec sa canne; **I want to ~ to one or two facts** je veux attirer votre attention sur un ou deux faits; **all the evidence ~s to him** *or* **to his guilt** tous les faits l'accusent; **everything ~s to a brilliant career for him** tout indique qu'il aura une brillante carrière; **it all ~s to the fact that ...** tout laisse à penser que ...; **everything ~s to murder/suicide** tout laisse à penser qu'il s'agit d'un meurtre/d'un suicide; **everything ~s that way** tout nous amène à cette conclusion

[b] signpost indiquer la direction (towards de); [gun] être braqué (at sur); [vehicle etc] être dirigé, être tourné (towards vers); **the needle is ~ing north** l'aiguille indique le nord; **the little hand is ~ing to four** la petite aiguille indique quatre heures; **the car isn't ~ing in the right direction** la voiture n'est pas tournée dans la bonne direction *or* dans le bon sens

[c] dancer faire des pointes

[d] dog tomber en arrêt

[5] COMPOUNDS

► **point-blank** ADJ → point-blank ► **point-by-point** ADJ méthodique ► **point duty** N (Brit Police etc) **to be on ~ duty** diriger la circulation ► **point of reference** N point *m* de référence ► **point of sale** N point *m* de vente ► **point-of-sale** ADJ **~-of-sale advertising** publicité *f* sur le lieu de vente, PLV *f*; **~-of-sale material** matériel *m* PLV; **~-of-sale terminal** terminal *m* point de vente ► **point of view** N point de vue; **from that/my ~ of view** de ce/mon point de vue; **from the social ~ of view** du point de vue social ► **points decision** N (Boxing) décision *f* aux points ► **points failure** N panne *f* d'aiguillage ► **points system** N (gen) système *m* par points; (Aut) permis *m* à points ► **points win** N victoire *f* aux points ► **point-to-point (race)** N (Racing) steeple-chase champêtre réservé à des cavaliers amateurs

[6] PHRASAL VERBS

► **point out** VT SEP [a] (= show) [+ person, object, place] montrer, indiquer, désigner

[b] (= mention) faire remarquer (**that** que); **to ~ sth out to sb** faire remarquer qch à qn, attirer l'attention de qn sur qch; **he ~ed out to me that I was wrong** il m'a fait remarquer que j'avais tort; **I should ~ out that ...** je dois vous dire *or* signaler que ...

► **point up** VT SEP mettre en évidence, souligner

point-blank ['pɔɪnt'blæŋk] [1] ADJ [shot] à bout portant; (fig) [refusal] net, catégorique; [request] de but en blanc, à brûle-pourpoint; **at** *or* **from ~ range** à bout portant [2] ADV [fire, shoot] à bout portant; (fig) [refuse] tout net, catégoriquement; [request, demand] de but en blanc, à brûle-pourpoint

pointed ['pɔɪntɪd] ADJ [a] [knife, stick, pencil, roof, chin, nose, shoes] pointu; [beard] en pointe, pointu; (Archit) [window, arch] en ogive; **the ~ end** le bout pointu [b] (fig) [remark, question, look] lourd de sous-entendus

pointedly ['pɔɪntɪdlɪ] ADV [say] d'un ton plein de sous-entendus; [behave, smile, ignore] ostensiblement; **she looked ~ at me** elle m'a lancé un regard qui en disait long

pointer ['pɔɪntər] N [a] (= stick) baguette *f*; (on scale) (= indicator) index *m*; (= needle) aiguille *f*; (on screen = arrow) flèche *f* lumineuse [b] (* = clue, indication) indice *m* (**to** de); (= piece of advice) conseil *m*, tuyau* *m*; **he gave me some ~s on what to do** il m'a donné quelques conseils (pratiques) *or* tuyaux* sur la marche à suivre; **here are a few ~s to help you make a choice** voici quelques indications pour vous aider à choisir; **there is at present no ~ to the outcome** rien ne permet de présumer *or* de conjecturer l'issue pour le moment; **they are looking for ~s on how the situation will develop** ils cherchent des indices permettant d'établir comment la situation va évoluer; **the elections should be a ~ to the public mood** les élections devraient permettre de prendre le pouls de l'opinion [c] (= dog) chien *m* d'arrêt

pointillism ['pwæntɪlɪzəm] N pointillisme *m*

pointing ['pɔɪntɪŋ] N (Constr) jointoiement *m*

pointless ['pɔɪntlɪs] ADJ [attempt, task, suffering] inutile, vain; [murder, violence] gratuit; [explanation, joke, story] sans rime ni raison, qui ne rime à rien; **it is ~ to complain** il ne sert à rien *or* il est inutile de se plaindre; **it is ~ for him to leave** ◊ **it is ~ him leaving** ça ne servirait à rien *or* il est inutile qu'il parte; **life seemed ~ to her** la vie lui paraissait dénuée de sens; **a ~ exercise*** une perte de temps

pointlessly ['pɔɪntlɪslɪ] ADV [try, work, suffer] inutilement, en vain; [say, protest] sans raison; [kill] gratuitement, sans raison; [die] pour rien; **the film is ~ violent/obscure** la violence/complexité de ce film n'est pas justifiée

pointlessness ['pɔɪntlɪsnɪs] N [of activity, organization, sb's death] absurdité *f*; [of existence] futilité *f*; **she stressed the ~ of protesting** elle a souligné à quel point il était inutile de protester

pointsman ['pɔɪntsmən] N (pl **-men**) (Rail) aiguilleur *m*

pointy* ['pɔɪntɪ] [1] ADJ [ears, hat, shoes] pointu; [beard] en pointe, pointu [2] COMP ► **pointy-headed*** ADJ (US fig pej) **a ~-headed intellectual** un intello* à lunettes; **that ~-headed professor** ce professeur Tournesol

poise [pɔɪz] [1] N (= balance) équilibre *m*; (= carriage) maintien *m*; [of head, body etc] port *m*; (fig) (= composure etc) calme *m*, sang-froid *m*; (= self-confidence) (calme) assurance *f*; (= grace) grâce *f*; **a woman of great ~** une femme pleine de grâce *or* empreinte d'une tranquille assurance; **he is young and lacks ~** il est jeune et manque d'assurance; (lit, fig) **to recover** *or*

regain one's ~ retrouver son calme *or* son sang-froid

[2] VT (= balance) mettre en équilibre; (= hold balanced) tenir en équilibre, maintenir en équilibre; **to be ~d** (= balanced) être en équilibre; (= held, hanging) être suspendu immobile; (= hovering) être immobile *or* suspendu (en l'air); **a waitress approached, pencil and pad ~d** une serveuse s'est approchée, armée de son bloc et de son crayon; **the swimmers stood** *or* **were ~d at the edge of the pool** les nageurs étaient en position sur les plots de départ; **the tiger was ~d (ready) to spring** le tigre se tenait prêt à bondir; **powerful military forces, ~d for invasion** des forces armées puissantes, prêtes pour l'invasion; (fig) **he was ~d to become champion** il était prêt à devenir champion; **~d on the brink of success/ruin** au bord de la réussite/la ruine; **to be ~d between life and death** être entre la vie et la mort; **the world was ~d between peace and war** le monde oscillait entre la paix et la guerre

poison ['pɔɪzn] [1] N (lit, fig) poison *m*; [of snake] venin *m*; **to take ~** s'empoisonner; **to die of ~** mourir empoisonné; **she's absolute ~**† c'est une vraie poison†; (hum: offering drink) **what's your ~?*** à quoi tu carbures? → **hate, rat**

[2] VT [person] [+ person, food, well, arrow] empoisonner; [chemicals] [+ air, water, land] contaminer; **to ~ o.s.** s'empoisonner; **a ~ed foot/finger** etc un pied/doigt etc infecté; **the drugs are ~ing his system** les drogues l'intoxiquent; **eggs ~ed with salmonella** des œufs contaminés par la salmonelle; (fig) **it is ~ing their friendship** cela empoisonne leur amitié; **an atmosphere ~ed by cruelty** une atmosphère empoisonnée par la cruauté; (esp Brit fig) **a ~ed chalice** un cadeau empoisonné; **to ~ sb's mind** (= corrupt) corrompre qn; (= instil doubts) faire douter qn; **he ~ed her mind against her husband** il l'a montée contre son mari

[3] COMP ► **poison fang** N crochet *m* venimeux (d'un serpent) ► **poison gas** N gaz *m* toxique *or* asphyxiant ► **poison gland** N glande *f* à venin ► **poison ivy** N (Bot) sumac *m* vénéneux ► **poison oak** N (NonC: Bot) sumac *m* vénéneux ► **poison-pen letter** N lettre *f* anonyme (de menace *or* d'insulte) ► **poison pill** N (Fin) pilule *f* empoisonnée (prix prohibitif visant à empêcher une société extérieure de lancer une OPA)

poisoner ['pɔɪznər] N empoisonneur *m*, -euse *f* (lit)

poisoning ['pɔɪznɪŋ] N (gen) empoisonnement *m*; (accidental) intoxication *f*; **the cause of his death was ~** il est mort empoisonné; **alcohol(ic) ~** empoisonnement *m* par l'alcool, éthylisme *m*; **arsenic(al) ~** empoisonnement *m* à l'arsenic; **mercury ~** intoxication *f* par le mercure, hydrargyrisme *m* → **blood, food, lead², salmonella, self**

poisonous ['pɔɪznəs] ADJ [snake] venimeux; [plant] vénéneux; [gas, fumes, substance, algae] toxique; (fig) [remark, allegation, comment, dispute] pernicieux

poke¹ [pəʊk] N (†† or dial) sac *m* → **pig**

poke² [pəʊk] [1] N [a] (= push) poussée *f*; (= jab) (petit) coup *m* (de canne, avec le doigt etc); (* = punch) coup *m* de poing; **she gave him a little ~** elle lui a donné un petit coup; **to give the fire a ~** tisonner le feu; **to give sb a ~ in the ribs** enfoncer son doigt dans les côtes de qn; **he gave the ground a ~ with his stick** il a tapoté le sol de sa canne; **it's better than a ~ in the eye (with a sharp stick)*** c'est mieux que rien; **to have a ~ around*** (= rummage) farfouiller*; **to take a ~ at sb*** (lit = punch) donner un coup de poing à qn; (fig) s'en prendre à qn; (fig) **a ~ at sth** une pique contre qch

b ** baise f** ; **he'd like to give her a good ~** il aimerait bien la baiser**

2 VT **a** (= *jab with finger, stick etc*) pousser, donner un coup (de canne *or* avec le doigt) à ; (* = *punch*) donner un coup de poing à ; (= *thrust*) [+ *stick, finger etc*] enfoncer (**into** dans, **through** à travers) ; [+ *rag etc*] fourrer (**into** dans) ; **to ~ the fire** tisonner le feu ; **he ~d me with his umbrella** il m'a donné un petit coup avec la pointe de son parapluie ; **he ~d his finger in her eye** il lui a mis le doigt dans l'œil ; **to ~ a finger into sth** enfoncer le doigt dans qch ; **he ~d the ground with his stick** il a tapoté le sol de sa canne ; **he ~d me in the ribs** il m'a enfoncé son doigt dans les côtes ; (*US*) **he ~d me one in the stomach*** il m'a envoyé son poing dans l'estomac ; **he ~d his finger up his nose** il s'est fourré le doigt dans le nez ; **to ~ one's head out of the window** passer la tête hors de *or* par la fenêtre ; **to ~ a hole in sth (with one's finger/stick etc)** faire un trou dans qch *or* percer qch (avec le doigt/sa canne *etc*) ; (*fig*) **to ~ holes in an argument** trouver des failles dans une argumentation → **fun**, **nose**

b (*Brit***) = *have sex with*) baiser**, tringler**

3 VI **a** (*also* ~ **out**) [*elbows, stomach, stick*] sortir, dépasser (**from, through** de)

b (*also* ~ **up**) dépasser

c (*also* ~ **through**) dépasser

d **he ~d at me with his finger** il m'a touché du bout du doigt ; **he ~d at the suitcase with his stick** il poussa la valise avec sa canne ; **she ~d at her food with a fork** elle jouait avec sa nourriture du bout de sa fourchette ; (*fig*) **to ~ into sth*** fourrer son nez dans qch

► **poke about***, **poke around*** VI farfouiller* ; **to ~ about in a drawer** farfouiller* *or* fourrager dans un tiroir ; **I spent the morning poking about in antique shops** j'ai passé la matinée à farfouiller* dans les magasins d'antiquités ; (*fig*) fouiner ; **I found him poking about among your cupboards** je l'ai pris à fouiner dans vos placards

► **poke in** VT SEP [+ *head*] passer (à l'intérieur) ; [+ *stick etc*] enfoncer ; [+ *rag*] fourrer ; (*fig*) **to ~ one's nose in*** fourrer son nez dans les affaires des autres, se mêler de ce qui ne vous regarde pas

► **poke out** **1** VI **a** = **poke²** 3a **b** (= *bulge*) [*stomach, chest, bottom*] être protubérant *or* proéminent **2** VT SEP **a** (= *stick out*) sortir ; **the tortoise ~d its head out** la tortue a sorti la tête **b** (= *remove, dislodge*) faire partir, déloger ; **he ~d the ants out with a stick** il a délogé les fourmis avec un bâton ; **to ~ sb's eyes out** crever les yeux à qn

poker¹ ['pəʊkə'] **1** N (*for fire etc*) tisonnier *m* → **stiff 2** COMP ► **poker work** N (*NonC*) (= *craft*) pyrogravure *f* ; (= *objects*) pyrogravures *fpl*

poker² ['pəʊkə'] **1** N (*Cards*) poker *m* **2** COMP ► **poker dice** N (*a* = *single dice*) dé *m* de poker d'as **b** (*NonC* = *game*) poker *m* d'as ► **poker face** N visage *m* impassible ► **poker-faced** ADJ au visage impassible

pokey ['pəʊkɪ] **1** N (*US** = *jail*) trou* *m*, taule* *f* **2** ADJ = **poky**

poky ['pəʊkɪ] ADJ (*pej*) [*house, room*] exigu (-guë *f*) et sombre

pol* [pɒl] N (*US*) ABBR = **politician**

Polack‡ ['pəʊlæk] N (*pej*) Polaque *mf* (*pej*), Polonais(e) *m(f)*

Poland ['pəʊlənd] N la Pologne

polar ['pəʊlə'] **1** ADJ (*Elec, Geog*) polaire ; **~ explorers** explorateurs *mpl* polaires ; **they are ~ opposites** ils sont aux antipodes l'un de l'autre **2** COMP ► **polar bear** N ours *m* blanc ► **Polar Circle** N cercle *m* polaire ► **polar front** N front *m* polaire ► **polar lights** NPL aurore *f* polaire *or* boréale

polarimeter [,pəʊlə'rɪmɪtə'] N polarimètre *m*

polariscope [pəʊ'lærɪskəʊp] N polariscope *m*

polarity [pəʊ'lærɪtɪ] N polarité *f*

polarization [,pəʊləraɪ'zeɪʃən] N (*lit, fig*) polarisation *f*

polarize ['pəʊləraɪz] VT (*lit, fig*) polariser

Polaroid® ['pəʊlərɔɪd] **1** ADJ Polaroïd® *inv* **2** N (*also* ~ **camera**) (appareil *m*) Polaroïd® *m* ; (*also* ~ **print**) photo *f* Polaroïd®, Polaroïd® *m* ; (*also* ~ **sunglasses**) **~s** lunettes *fpl* de soleil (en) Polaroïd®

Pole [pəʊl] N Polonais(e) *m(f)*

pole¹ [pəʊl] **1** N (= *rod*) perche *f* ; (*fixed*) poteau *m*, mât *m* ; (*also* **flagpole, tent ~**: *also in gymnastics, for climbing*) mât *m* ; (*also* **telegraph ~**) poteau *m* télégraphique ; (*also* **curtain ~**) tringle *f* ; (*also* **barber's ~**) enseigne *f* de coiffeur ; (*in fire station*) perche *f* ; (*for vaulting, punting*) perche *f* ; (*fig*) **to be up the ~*** (= *mistaken*) se gourer*, se planter* ; (= *mad*) dérailler* (*fig*) ; **to send** *or* **drive sb up the ~*** (= *mad*) rendre qn dingue* → **greasy, ski**

b (*Ski*) (= *ski stick*) bâton *m* ; (*marking run*) piquet *m*

c (= *archaic measure of length*) ≈ 5,029 mètres ; (= *measure of area*) ≈ 25,29 mètres carrés

2 VT [+ *punt etc*] faire avancer (à l'aide d'une perche)

3 COMP ► **pole jump** N (*Sport*) saut *m* à la perche ► **pole jumper** N sauteur *m*, -euse *f* à la perche, perchiste *mf* ► **pole jumping** N (*NonC*) saut *m* à la perche ► **pole position** N (*Motor Racing*) pole position *f* ; (*fig*) pole position *f*, meilleure place *f* ; **in ~ position** (*Motor Racing*) en pole position ; (*fig*) en pole position, à la meilleure place ► **pole vault** N = **pole jump** ► **pole-vault** VI sauter à la perche ► **pole-vaulter** N = **pole jumper** ► **pole-vaulting** N = **pole jumping**

pole² [pəʊl] **1** N (*Elec, Geog*) pôle *m* ; **North/South Pole** pôle *m* Nord/Sud ; **from ~ to ~** d'un pôle à l'autre ; **negative/positive ~** pôle *m* négatif/positif ; (*fig*) **they are ~s apart** ils sont aux antipodes l'un de l'autre ; (*fig*) **at opposite ~s of sth** aux deux pôles de qch **2** COMP ► **the Pole Star** N l'étoile *f* Polaire

poleaxe, poleax (*US*) ['pəʊlæks] **1** N (= *weapon*) hache *f* d'armes ; (*of butcher etc*) merlin *m* **2** VT [+ *cattle etc*] abattre, assommer ; (*fig*) [+ *person*] terrasser

polecat ['pəʊlkæt] N (*pl* **polecats** *or* **polecat**) putois *m* ; **lazy as a ~** fainéant

pol. econ. (ABBR = **political economy**) → **political**

polemic [pɒ'lemɪk] **1** ADJ polémique **2** N (= *argument*) **a ~ against sth** un réquisitoire contre qch ; **a ~ for sth** un plaidoyer pour qch

polemical [pɒ'lemɪkəl] ADJ polémique

polemicist [pɒ'lemɪsɪst] N polémiste *mf*

polemics [pɒ'lemɪks] N (*NonC*) arguments *mpl*

polenta [pəʊ'lentə] N polenta *f*

police [pə'liːs] **1** N (*NonC*) **a** (= *organization*) ≈ police *f*, gendarmerie *f* ; (*collective*) **the ~** la police, les gendarmes *mpl* ; **to join the ~** entrer dans la police, se faire policier *or* gendarme ; **he is in the ~** il est dans *or* de la police ; **one hundred ~** cent policiers *mpl or* gendarmes *mpl* ; **extra ~ were called in** on a fait venir des renforts de police ; **the ~ are looking for his car** la police recherche sa voiture ; **river/railway ~** police *f* fluviale/des chemins de fer → **mounted, transport**

b (*US Mil*) corvée *f* (militaire) de rangement et de nettoyage

2 VT **a** (*lit: with policemen*) [+ *place*] maintenir l'ordre dans ; **the demonstration was heavily ~d** d'importantes forces de police étaient présentes lors de la manifestation

b [*vigilantes, volunteers*] [+ *district, road*] faire la police dans ; (*Mil*) [+ *frontier, territory*] contrôler ; (*fig*) [+ *agreements, controls, ceasefires*] veiller à l'application de ; [+ *prices etc*] contrôler ; **the border is ~d by UN patrols** la frontière est sous la surveillance des patrouilles de l'ONU

c (*US* = *keep clean*) nettoyer

3 COMP (*gen*) de la police ; [*leave, vehicle, members*] de la police *or* de la gendarmerie ; [*campaign, control, inquiry*] policier, de la police *or* de la gendarmerie ; [*sergeant, inspector etc*] de police ; [*harassment*] par la police ► **police academy** N école *f* de police ► **police car** N voiture *f* de police ► **police chief** N préfet *m* (de police) ; (*US*) ≈ (commissaire *m*) divisionnaire *m* ► **Police Complaints Board** N ≈ Inspection *f* générale des services ► **police constable** N → **constable** ► **police court** N tribunal *m* de police ► **police custody** N → **custody** ► **police department** N (*US*) service *m* de police ► **police dog** N (*Police*) chien *m* policier ; (*US* = *Alsatian*) berger *m* allemand ► **police escort** N escorte *f* policière ► **the police force** N la police, les gendarmes *mpl*, les forces *fpl* de l'ordre ; **member of the ~ force** policier *m* ; **to join the ~ force** entrer dans la police ► **police headquarters** NPL quartier *m* général de la police, siège *m* central ► **police intervention** N intervention *f* de la police ► **police marksman** N tireur *m* d'élite (de la police) ► **police office** N gendarmerie *f* (bureaux) ► **police officer** N policier *m*, fonctionnaire *mf* de police ; **to become a ~ officer** entrer dans la police ► **police presence** N présence *f* policière ► **police protection** N protection *f* de la police ► **police record** N **to have a ~ record** avoir un casier judiciaire ; **he hasn't got a ~ record** il n'a pas de casier judiciaire, il a un casier judiciaire vierge ► **the police service** N la police ► **police state** N état *m* policier ► **police station** N poste *m or* commissariat *m* de police, gendarmerie *f* ► **police wagon** N (*US*) voiture *f or* fourgon *m* cellulaire ► **police work** N le métier de policier

policeman [pə'liːsmən] N (*pl* **-men**) (*in town*) agent *m* de police, gardien *m* de la paix ; (*in country*) gendarme *m* ; **to become a ~** entrer dans la police ; **I knew he was a ~** je savais qu'il était dans la police

policewoman [pə'liːs,wʊmən] N (*pl* **-women**) femme *f* policier, femme *f* agent (de police)

policing [pə'liːsɪŋ] N maintien *m* de l'ordre

policy¹ ['pɒlɪsɪ] **1** N **a** (= *aims, principles etc*) (*Pol*) politique *f* ; [*of newspaper, company, organization*] politique *f* (générale) ; (= *course of action*) politique *f* ; **complete frankness is the best ~** la franchise totale est la meilleure conduite à suivre *or* attitude à adopter ; **caution was the best ~** la prudence était la meilleure attitude à adopter → **honesty** ; **it's company ~** c'est la politique de l'entreprise *or* de la société ; (*Pol*) **economic/foreign/social ~** politique *f* étrangère/économique/sociale ; **to follow a ~ of doing sth** avoir pour règle de faire qch ; **it is good/bad ~ to ...** c'est une bonne/mauvaise politique que de ... ; **the government's policies** la politique du gouvernement ; **as a matter of ~** par principe ; **official ~** politique *f* officielle ; **it has always been our ~ to deliver goods free** nous avons toujours eu pour règle de livrer les marchandises franco de port ; **it is our ~ to use recycled paper** nous avons pour principe d'utiliser du papier recyclé ; **my ~ has always been to wait and see** j'ai toujours eu pour principe de voir venir

b (*NonC*:† = *prudence*) (bonne) politique *f* ; **it would not be ~ to refuse** il ne serait pas politique de refuser

2 COMP (*gen*) [*discussions etc*] de politique générale ► **policy committee** N comité *m* directeur ► **policy decision** N décision *f* de principe ► **policy document** N document *m* de politique générale ► **policy maker** N (*within organization, firm etc*) décisionnaire *mf*, décideur *m* ; (*for political party etc*) responsable *mf* politique ► **policy-making** N prise *f* de décisions ♦ ADJ [*process*] de décision ; [*body, role*] décisionnaire ► **policy matter** N question f de politique générale or de principe ► **policy paper** N = **policy document** ► **policy statement** N déclaration f de principe ; **to make a ~ statement** faire une déclaration de principe ► **policy unit** N (*Brit Pol*) conseillers *mpl* politiques ► **policy wonk***   N (*esp US: Pol*) conseiller *m*, -ère f politique

policy² ['pɒlɪsɪ] N (*Insurance*) police f (d'assurance) ; **to take out a ~** souscrire une (police d'assurance

policyholder ['pɒlɪsɪˌhəʊldəʳ] N assuré(e) *m(f)*

polio ['pəʊlɪəʊ] N (ABBR = **poliomyelitis**) polio f

poliomyelitis ['pəʊlɪəʊmaɪə'laɪtɪs] N poliomyélite f

Polish ['pəʊlɪʃ] ①   ADJ (*gen*) polonais ; [*ambassador, embassy*] de Pologne ; [*teacher, dictionary*] de polonais ② N (*Ling*) polonais *m*

polish ['pɒlɪʃ] ① N ⓐ (= *substance*) (for shoes) cirage *m*, crème f (pour chaussures) ; (for floor, furniture) encaustique f, cire f ; (for nails) vernis *m* (à ongles) ; **metal ~** produit *m* d'entretien pour les métaux ⓑ (= *act*) **to give sth a ~** faire briller qch ; **my shoes need a ~** mes chaussures ont besoin d'être cirées ⓒ (= *shine*) poli *m* ; **high ~** lustre *m* ; **to put a ~ on sth** faire briller qch ; **the candlesticks were losing their ~** les chandeliers perdaient de leur éclat ⓓ (*fig* = *refinement*) [*of person*] raffinement *m* ; [*of style, work, performance*] perfection f, élégance f ② VT (*also ~ up*) [+ *stones, glass*] polir ; [+ *shoes*] cirer ; [+ *floor, furniture*] cirer, astiquer ; [+ *car*] astiquer, briquer ; [+ *metal*] fourbir, astiquer ; [+ *leather*] lustrer ; (*fig*) [+ *person*] parfaire l'éducation de ; [+ *manners*] affiner ; [+ *style, language*] polir, châtier ; **to ~ (up) one's French** perfectionner or travailler son français ; **the style needs ~ing** le style aurait besoin d'être plus soigné → **polished**

► **polish off***   VT SEP [+ *food, drink*] finir ; [+ *work, correspondence*] expédier ; [+ *competitor, enemy*] régler son compte à, en finir avec ; **he ~ed off the meal** il a tout mangé jusqu'à la dernière miette ; **he ~ed off his scotch** il a avalé son whisky d'un trait ; **he ~ed off all the scotch** il a sifflé* tout le whisky ; **she ~ed off the cheese** elle a englouti* tout le fromage

► **polish up** VT SEP = **polish** 2

polished ['pɒlɪʃt] ADJ ⓐ (= *shiny*) [*surface*] poli, brillant ; [*floor, shoes*] ciré, brillant ; [*leather*] lustré ; [*silver, ornaments*] brillant, fourbi, astiqué ; [*stone, glass*] poli ⓑ (*fig* = *refined*) [*person*] qui a de l'éducation or du savoir-vivre ; [*manners*] raffiné ; [*style*] poli, châtié ; [*performer*] accompli ; [*performance*] impeccable

polisher ['pɒlɪʃəʳ] N (= *person*) polisseur *m*, -euse f ; (= *machine*) (*gen*) polissoir *m* ; (for floors) cireuse f ; (for pebbles etc) polisseuse f

Politburo ['pɒlɪtbjʊərəʊ] N Politburo *m*

polite [pə'laɪt] ADJ [*person, smile, request, refusal, applause*] poli ; **to be ~ to sb** être poli avec qn ; **when I said it was not his best work I was being ~** en disant que ce n'est pas sa meilleure œuvre j'ai été poli ; **be ~ about his car!** ne dis pas de mal de sa voiture ! ; **in ~ society** dans la bonne société ; **it is ~ to ask permission** il est poli de demander la permission ; **to make ~ conversation** échanger des politesses

politely [pə'laɪtlɪ] ADV poliment ; **what he ~ called an "inaccuracy"** ce qu'il a appelé poliment une « inexactitude »

politeness [pə'laɪtnɪs] N politesse f ; **to do sth out of ~** faire qch par politesse

politic ['pɒlɪtɪk] ADJ (*frm*) politique (*liter*) ; **he thought** or **deemed it ~ to refuse** il a jugé politique de refuser ; **it would be ~ to tell him**

before someone else does il serait diplomatique de le lui dire avant que quelqu'un d'autre ne le fasse → **body**

political [pə'lɪtɪkəl] ① ADJ ⓐ (*Pol*) politique ; **~ analyst** or **commentator** politologue *mf* → **party** ⓑ (*fig* = *politicized*) **he was always very ~** il a toujours été très politisé ; **he's a ~ animal** il a la politique dans le sang ⓒ (= *expedient, tactical*) **it was a ~ decision** c'était une décision tactique

② COMP ► **political action committee** N (*US*) comité *m* de soutien (*d'un candidat*) ► **political asylum** N **to ask for ~ asylum** demander le droit d'asile (politique) ► **political convention** N (*US*) convention f politique ► **political correctness** N (*esp pej*) **our society's obsession with ~ correctness** l'obsession de notre société pour ce qui est politiquement correct ; (*pej*) **in this age of ~ correctness** à l'heure de la pensée politiquement correcte, à l'heure du politiquement correct → POLITICALLY CORRECT ► **political economy** N économie f politique ► **political football***   N (*pej*) **the drug issue will continue to be a ~ football** la question de la drogue continuera à être une sorte de balle que tout le monde se renvoie dans le monde politique ; **he/this charter is being used as a ~ football** il/cette charte est le prétexte à des débats de politique politicienne ► **political geography** N géographie f politique ► **political prisoner** N prisonnier *m* politique ► **political science** N sciences *fpl* politiques ► **political scientist** N spécialiste *mf* des sciences politiques

politically [pə'lɪtɪkəlɪ] ① ADV d'un point de vue politique, politiquement ; **~ acceptable/expedient/sensitive** acceptable/opportun/délicat d'un point de vue politique, politiquement acceptable/opportun/délicat ; **~ stable** politiquement stable, stable d'un point de vue politique ; **~ motivated** ayant une motivation politique ; **~ aware** politisé ; **~ speaking** politiquement parlant ② COMP ► **politically correct** ADJ politiquement correct ► **politically incorrect** ADJ qui n'est pas politiquement correct ; **his jokes are ~ incorrect but very funny** ses plaisanteries ne sont pas politiquement correctes mais elles sont très drôles ► **politically-minded**, **politically-orientated** ADJ politisé

┌─────────────────────────┐
│ ▣ **POLITICALLY CORRECT** │
└─────────────────────────┘

Une personne politiquement correcte (politically correct, ou PC) évite d'employer certains termes, jugés dégradants ou insultants, pour désigner les membres de minorités ou de groupes défavorisés tels que les minorités ethniques, les femmes, les handicapés ou les homosexuels. Ainsi est-on passé successivement de « Negroes » (terme qu'utilisait Martin Luther King) à « coloured people », puis à « Black people » ; de même dira-t-on d'un aveugle qu'il est malvoyant (« he's visually impaired »). Les adeptes de ce mouvement d'origine américaine estiment ainsi remettre en question les présupposés idéologiques de la civilisation occidentale. Aujourd'hui, cependant, l'expression politically correct *est souvent utilisée de façon péjorative par les opposants à ces idées libérales.*

politician [ˌpɒlɪ'tɪʃən] N homme *m* politique, femme f politique

politicization [pəˌlɪtɪsaɪ'zeɪʃən] N politisation f

politicize [pə'lɪtɪsaɪz] VT politiser

politicking ['pɒlɪtɪkɪŋ] N (*pej*) politique f politicienne

politico*   [pə'lɪtɪkəʊ] N (*pl* **politicos**) (*pej*) (= *politician*) politicard *m* ; (= *political person*) **he's a real ~** il est très politisé

politico... [pə'lɪtɪkəʊ] PREF politico...

politics ['pɒlɪtɪks] ① N (*Pol*) politique f ; **to go into ~** se lancer dans la or entrer en politique ; **to be in ~** faire de la politique ; **to study ~** étudier les sciences politiques ; **to talk ~** parler politique ; **foreign ~** la politique étrangère ; (*pej*) **to play ~ (with education/the economy)** faire de la politique politicienne (*pej*) (en matière d'éducation/d'économie) ; **what they are doing is playing ~ with people's lives** ils jouent avec la vie des gens à des fins politiques → **office, party, sexual** ② NPL (= *political ideas*) opinions *fpl* politiques ; **what are your/his ~?** quelles sont vos/ses opinions politiques ? ; **the influence of socialist ideas on his ~** l'influence des idées socialistes sur ses opinions politiques

polity ['pɒlɪtɪ] N (= *system of government*) régime *m*, administration f politique ; (= *government organization*) constitution f politique ; (= *the State*) État *m*

polka ['pɒlkə] ① N (*pl* **polkas**) polka f ② COMP ► **polka dot** N pois *m* ► **polka-dot** ADJ **a ~-dot blouse** un chemisier à pois

poll [pəʊl] ① N ⓐ (= *vote in general: gen pl*) vote *m* ; (= *voting at election*) scrutin *m* ; (= *election*) élection(s) f(pl) ; (= *list of voters*) liste f électorale ; (= *voting place*) bureau *m* de vote ; (= *votes cast*) voix *fpl*, suffrages *mpl* ; **the result of the ~s** le résultat de l'élection or du scrutin ; **on the eve of the ~s** à la veille de l'élection or du scrutin ; **to go to the ~s** aller aux urnes, aller voter ; **a crushing defeat at the ~s** une écrasante défaite aux élections ; **there was a 64% turnout at the ~s** 64 % des inscrits ont voté, la participation électorale a été de (l'ordre de) 64 % ; **the conservatives' highest ~ for ten years** le meilleur score des conservateurs en dix ans ; **he got 20% of the ~** il a obtenu 20 % des suffrages exprimés ; **he achieved a ~ of 5,000 votes** il a obtenu 5 000 voix → **standing** ⓑ (= *opinion survey*) sondage *m* ; (**public**) **opinion ~** sondage *m* d'opinion ; **to take** or **conduct a ~** effectuer un sondage (**of** auprès de) ; **to take a ~ of 3,000 people** effectuer un sondage auprès de 3 000 personnes ; **a telephone ~** un sondage téléphonique ; **a ~ of ~s** une analyse de sondages → **Gallup** ⓒ († = *head*) chef† *m* ② VT ⓐ [+ *votes*] obtenir ; [+ *people*] sonder l'opinion de, interroger ; **they ~ed the students to find out whether ...** ils ont sondé l'opinion des étudiants pour savoir si ... ; **40% of those ~ed supported the government** 40 % des personnes interrogées étaient favorables au gouvernement ⓑ [+ *cattle*] décorner ; [+ *tree*] étêter, écimer ③ VI **the nationalists ~ed well** les nationalistes ont obtenu un bon score ④ COMP ► **poll taker** N (*US*) sondeur *m* ► **poll tax** N (*gen*) capitation f ; (*Brit: formerly*) ≈ impôts *mpl* locaux

pollack ['pɒlək] N (*pl* **pollacks** or **pollack**) lieu *m* jaune

pollard ['pɒləd] ① N (= *animal*) animal *m* sans cornes ; (= *tree*) têtard *m*, arbre *m* étêté or écimé ② VT [+ *animal*] décorner ; [+ *tree*] étêter, écimer

pollen ['pɒlən] ① N pollen *m* ② COMP ► **pollen count** N taux *m* de pollen

pollinate ['pɒlɪneɪt] VT féconder (avec du pollen)

pollination [ˌpɒlɪ'neɪʃən] N pollinisation f, fécondation f

pollinator ['pɒlɪneɪtəʳ] N (*Zool*) pollinisateur *m*, -trice f

polling ['pəʊlɪŋ] ① N élections *fpl* ; **~ is on Thursday** les élections ont lieu jeudi, on vote jeudi ; **the ~ was extremely low** le taux de participation était extrêmement faible ② COMP ► **polling booth** N isoloir *m* ► **polling day** N jour *m* des élections

► **polling place** N (US) = **polling station**
► **polling station** N (Brit) bureau m de vote

polliwog ['pɒlɪwɒg] N (US Zool) têtard m

pollock ['pɒlək] N = **pollack**

pollster ['pəʊlstə^r] N sondeur m, enquêteur m, -euse f

pollutant [pə'luːtənt] N polluant m

pollute [pə'luːt] VT polluer; (fig) contaminer; (= corrupt) corrompre; (= desecrate) profaner, polluer (liter); **the river was ~d with chemicals** la rivière était polluée par des produits chimiques

polluter [pə'luːtə^r] N pollueur m, -euse f; **the ~ pays** les pollueurs sont les payeurs

pollution [pə'luːʃən] N a [lit, Chem etc] pollution f; **air/atmospheric/marine ~** pollution f de l'air/atmosphérique/marine b (fig = impurity, corruption) souillure f (liter); **spiritual ~** souillure f (liter) de l'esprit → **light¹**, **noise**

Pollyanna [pɒlɪ'ænə] N optimiste m(f) béat(e)

pollywog ['pɒlɪwɒg] N = **polliwog**

polo ['pəʊləʊ] 1 N polo m → **water** 2 COMP
► **polo shirt** N polo m, chemise f polo
► **polo stick** N maillet m (de polo)

polonaise [pɒlə'neɪz] N (Mus, Dancing) polonaise f

polo-neck ['pəʊləʊnek] 1 N col m roulé 2 ADJ (also ~ed) à col roulé

polonium [pə'ləʊnɪəm] N polonium m

poltergeist ['pɔːltəgaɪst] N esprit m frappeur

poltroon† [pɒl'truːn] N poltron m

poly* ['pɒlɪ] N (in Brit) (ABBR = **polytechnic**) ≈ IUT m

poly... ['pɒlɪ] PREF poly...

polyandrous [pɒlɪ'ændrəs] ADJ polyandre

polyandry ['pɒlɪændrɪ] N polyandrie f

polyanthus [pɒlɪ'ænθəs] N primevère f (multiflore)

polyarchy ['pɒlɪˌɑːkɪ] N polyarchie f

polychlorinated biphenyl [ˌpɒlɪ'klɔːrɪneɪtɪdbaɪ'fenəl] N polychlorobiphényle m

polychromatic [ˌpɒlɪkrəʊ'mætɪk] ADJ polychrome

polychrome ['pɒlɪkrəʊm] 1 ADJ polychrome 2 N (= statue) statue f polychrome; (= picture) tableau m polychrome

polyclinic ['pɒlɪklɪnɪk] N polyclinique f

polycotton ['pɒlɪ'kɒtən] N polyester m et coton m

polyester [ˌpɒlɪ'estə^r] 1 N polyester m 2 COMP de or en polyester

polyethylene [ˌpɒlɪ'eθəliːn] N polyéthylène m, polythène m

polygamist [pɒ'lɪgəmɪst] N polygame mf

polygamous [pɒ'lɪgəməs] ADJ polygame

polygamy [pɒ'lɪgəmɪ] N polygamie f

polygenesis [ˌpɒlɪ'dʒenɪsɪs] N polygénisme m

polygenetic [ˌpɒlɪdʒɪ'netɪk] ADJ polygénétique

polyglot ['pɒlɪglɒt] ADJ, N polyglotte mf

polygon ['pɒlɪgən] N polygone m

polygonal [pɒ'lɪgənl] ADJ polygonal

polygraph ['pɒlɪgrɑːf] N détecteur m de mensonges

polyhedra [ˌpɒlɪ'hiːdrə] NPL of **polyhedron**

polyhedral [ˌpɒlɪ'hiːdrəl] ADJ polyédrique

polyhedron [ˌpɒlɪ'hiːdrən] N (pl **polyhedrons** or **polyhedra**) polyèdre m

polymath ['pɒlɪmæθ] N esprit m universel

polymer ['pɒlɪmə^r] N polymère m

polymerization ['pɒlɪmərəˈzeɪʃən] N polymérisation f

polymorphism [ˌpɒlɪ'mɔːfɪzəm] N polymorphisme m, polymorphie f

polymorphous [ˌpɒlɪ'mɔːfəs] ADJ polymorphe

Polynesia [ˌpɒlɪ'niːzɪə] N la Polynésie

Polynesian [ˌpɒlɪ'niːzɪən] 1 ADJ polynésien 2 N a (= person) Polynésien(ne) m(f) b (Ling) polynésien m

polynomial [ˌpɒlɪ'nəʊmɪəl] ADJ, N polynôme m

polyp ['pɒlɪp] N (Zool, Med) polype m

polyphase ['pɒlɪfeɪz] ADJ polyphasé

polyphonic [ˌpɒlɪ'fɒnɪk] ADJ polyphonique

polyphony [pə'lɪfənɪ] N polyphonie f

polypi ['pɒlɪpaɪ] NPL of **polypus**

polypropylene [ˌpɒlɪ'prəʊpiliːn] N polypropylène m

polypus ['pɒlɪpəs] N (pl **polypi**) (Med) polype m

polysemic [ˌpɒlɪ'siːmɪk] ADJ polysémique

polysemous [pɒ'lɪsəməs] ADJ polysémique

polysemy [pɒ'lɪsəmɪ] N polysémie f

polystyrene [ˌpɒlɪ'staɪriːn] 1 N (esp Brit) polystyrène m; **expanded ~** polystyrène m expansé 2 COMP ► **polystyrene cement** N colle f polystyrène ► **polystyrene chips** NPL billes fpl (de) polystyrène

polysyllabic [ˌpɒlɪsɪ'læbɪk] ADJ polysyllabe, polysyllabique

polysyllable [ˌpɒlɪ'sɪləbl] N polysyllabe m, mot m polysyllabique

polytechnic [ˌpɒlɪ'teknɪk] N (in Brit) ≈ IUT m, ≈ Institut m universitaire de technologie

polytheism ['pɒlɪθiːɪzəm] N polythéisme m

polytheistic [ˌpɒlɪθiː'ɪstɪk] ADJ polythéiste

polythene ['pɒlɪθiːn] (Brit) 1 N polyéthylène m, polythène m 2 COMP ► **polythene bag** N sachet m en plastique

polyunsaturate [ˌpɒlɪʌn'sætʃʊrɪt] N (acide m gras) polyinsaturé m

polyunsaturated [ˌpɒlɪʌn'sætʃʊˌreɪtɪd] ADJ polyinsaturé

polyurethane [ˌpɒlɪ'jʊərɪθeɪn] N polyuréthane m

polyvalent [pə'lɪvələnt] ADJ polyvalent

polyvinyl ['pɒlɪvaɪnl] N polyvinyle m

pom [pɒm] N = **pommy**

pomade [pə'mɑːd] 1 N pommade f 2 VT pommader

pomander [pəʊ'mændə^r] N (china) diffuseur m de parfum

pomegranate ['pɒməˌgrænɪt] N (= fruit) grenade f; (= tree) grenadier m

pomelo ['pɒmɪləʊ] N (pl **pomelos**) poméló m

Pomeranian [ˌpɒmə'reɪnɪən] N (= dog) loulou m (de Poméranie)

pommel ['pʌml] 1 N pommeau m 2 VT = **pummel** 3 COMP ► **pommel horse** N cheval m d'arçons

pommy ['pɒmɪ] (Austral pej) 1 N Anglais(e) m(f), rosbif m (pej) 2 ADJ anglais

pomp [pɒmp] N pompe f, faste m, apparat m; **~ and circumstance** grand apparat m, pompes fpl (liter); **with great ~** en grande pompe

Pompadour ['pɒmpəˌdʊə^r] N (US = hairstyle) banane f (coiffure)

Pompeii [pɒm'peɪiː] N Pompéi

Pompey ['pɒmpɪ] N Pompée m

pompom ['pɒmpɒm] N a (= bobble) pompon m b (Mil) canon-mitrailleuse m (de DCA)

pompon ['pɒmpɒn] 1 N (= bobble) pompon m 2 COMP ► **pompon dahlia** N (Bot) dahlia m pompon ► **pompon rose** N (Bot) rose f pompon

pomposity [pɒm'pɒsɪtɪ] N (pej) manières fpl pompeuses, air m or ton m pompeux, solennité f

pompous ['pɒmpəs] ADJ [person] pontifiant; [remark, speech, tone] pompeux, pontifiant; [style] pompeux, ampoulé

pompously ['pɒmpəslɪ] ADV [speak] sur un

ton pompeux; [write] dans un style pompeux; [behave] pompeusement

ponce* [pɒns] (Brit) 1 N a (= pimp) maquereau* m, souteneur m b (pej = homosexual) pédé* m 2 VI faire le maquereau, être souteneur

► **ponce about*, ponce around*** VI (pej) se pavaner

poncey* ['pɒnsɪ] ADJ (Brit pej) [person] affecté; [restaurant, school] snob; [clothes] de poseur

poncho ['pɒntʃəʊ] N (pl **ponchos**) poncho m

poncy* ['pɒnsɪ] ADJ → **poncey**

pond [pɒnd] N étang m; (stagnant) mare f; (artificial) bassin m → **big**, **millpond**

ponder ['pɒndə^r] VT considérer, peser, réfléchir à or sur 2 VI méditer (**over, on** sur), réfléchir (**over, on** à, sur)

ponderable ['pɒndərəbl] ADJ pondérable

ponderous ['pɒndərəs] ADJ [movement, object] lourd, pesant; [style, joke] lourd; [speech, tone, voice] pesant et solennel

ponderously ['pɒndərəslɪ] ADV [move] pesamment, lourdement; [write] avec lourdeur; [say, speak] d'un ton solennel et pesant

pondlife ['pɒndlaɪf] N (NonC) faune f et flore f des étangs

pondweed ['pɒndwiːd] N épi m d'eau, potamot m

pone [pəʊn] N (US) pain m de maïs

pong* [pɒŋ] (Brit) 1 N mauvaise odeur f; (stronger) puanteur f; **what a ~ in here!** ça (s)chlingue* ici! 2 VI (s)chlinguer*; **it ~s!*** pouah!, ça (s)chlingue!*

pons Varolii [pɒnzvə'rəʊlɪaɪ] N pont m de Varole, protubérance f annulaire

pontiff ['pɒntɪf] N (Rel) (= dignitary) pontife m; (= pope) souverain m pontife, pontife m romain

pontifical [pɒn'tɪfɪkəl] ADJ (Rel) pontifical; (fig) pontifiant

pontificate [pɒn'tɪfɪkɪt] 1 N (Rel) pontificat m 2 [pɒn'tɪfɪkeɪt] VI (fig) pontifier (**about** au sujet de, sur)

Pontius Pilate ['pɒnʃəs'paɪlət] N Ponce Pilate m

pontoon [pɒn'tuːn] 1 N a (gen) ponton m; (on aircraft) flotteur m b (Brit Cards) vingt-et-un m 2 COMP ► **pontoon bridge** N pont m flottant

pony ['pəʊnɪ] 1 N poney m; (Brit* = £25) 25 livres; (US Scol* = crib) traduc* f, corrigé m (utilisé illicitement) 2 COMP ► **pony express** N (US Hist) messageries fpl rapides par relais de cavaliers ► **pony trekking** N randonnée f équestre or à cheval

ponytail ['pəʊnɪteɪl] N queue f de cheval; **to have** or **wear one's hair in a ~** avoir une queue de cheval

poo* [puː] (Brit: baby talk) 1 N caca* m (baby talk); **to do a ~** faire caca* (baby talk) 2 VI faire caca* (baby talk)

pooch: [puːtʃ] N cabot* m, clebs: m

poodle ['puːdl] N caniche m; (fig = servile person) chien m

poof [pʊf] 1 N (Brit: pej) tante: f, tapette: f 2 EXCL hop!

poofter: ['pʊftə^r] N (Brit pej) = **poof**

poofy* ['pʊfɪ] ADJ (Brit pej) efféminé, du genre tapette*; **it's ~** ça fait fille

pooh [puː] 1 EXCL bah!, peuh! 2 N = **poo** 3 VI = **poo** 4 COMP ► **pooh-pooh** VT **to ~ ~ sth** faire fi de qch, dédaigner qch

pool¹ [puːl] 1 N a (= puddle) [of water, rain] flaque f (d'eau); [of spilt liquid] flaque f; (larger) mare f; (fig) [of light from lamp, spot, flood] rond m; [of sunlight] flaque f; [of shadow] zone f; **lying in a ~ of blood** étendu dans une mare de sang; **in a ~ of light** dans une flaque or un rond de lumière b (= pond) (natural) étang m; (artificial) bassin m, pièce f d'eau ; (*in river*) plan *m* d'eau ; (= *water hole*) point *m* d'eau ; (*also* **swimming ~**) piscine *f* → **paddle** [2] COMP ▶ **pool attendant** N surveillant(e) *m(f)* de baignade, maître *m* nageur

pool² [puːl] [1] N [a] (*Cards etc* = *stake*) poule *f*, cagnotte *f* ; (= *common fund*) cagnotte *f* [b] (*fig*) (*of things owned in common*) fonds *m* commun ; (= *reserve, source*) [*of ideas, experience, ability*] réservoir *m* ; [*of advisers, experts*] équipe *f* ; **a ~ of vehicles** un parc de voitures ; **typing ~** pool *m* de dactylos ; **~ of reporters** pool *m* de presse ; **a very good ~ of players/ talent** *etc* un très bon réservoir de joueurs/ talents *etc* ; **genetic ~** pool *m* génétique [c] (*Econ* = *consortium*) pool *m* ; (*US* = *monopoly trust*) trust *m* ; **the coal and steel ~** le pool charbon acier [d] (= *billiards*) billard *m* américain ; **to shoot** *or* **play ~** jouer au billard américain [2] **the pools*** NPL (*Brit*) = **the football pools** ; → **football** [3] VT [+ *money, resources, objects, knowledge, ideas*] mettre en commun ; [+ *efforts*] unir ; [+ *workers*] rassembler [4] COMP ▶ **pool table** N billard *m* (*table*)

poolroom ['puːlrʊm] N (*Billiards*) (salle *f* de) billard *m*

poop¹ [puːp] (*Naut*) [1] N poupe *f* [2] COMP ▶ **poop deck** N dunette *f*

poop²* [puːp] [1] N (*esp US* = *excrement*) crotte *f* [2] COMP ▶ **poop scoop** N ramasse-crottes *m inv*

poop³* [puːp] N (*US* = *information*) tuyau* *m*, bon renseignement *m*

pooped: [puːpt] ADJ (*esp US* = *exhausted*) pompé*, crevé*, à plat*

pooper-scooper* ['puːpəˈskuːpəʳ] N ramasse-crottes *m inv*

poor [pʊəʳ] [1] ADJ [a] (= *not rich*) [*person, family, nation*] pauvre ; **as ~ as a church-mouse** pauvre comme Job ; **how ~ is he really?** jusqu'à quel point est-il pauvre ? ; **to become ~er** s'appauvrir ; **he was a thousand pounds (the) ~er** il avait perdu mille livres ; **in ~ circumstances** dans le besoin, dans la gêne ; (*fig* = *lacking*) **soil that is ~ in zinc** un sol pauvre en zinc → **3** [b] (= *inferior*) [*amount, sales, harvest, output*] maigre, médiocre ; [*work, worker, soldier, film, result, performance, food, summer*] médiocre, piètre (*before n*) ; [*pay*] maigre, faible ; [*effort, ventilation*] insuffisant ; [*light*] faible ; [*sight*] faible, mauvais ; [*soil*] pauvre, peu productif ; [*quality*] médiocre ; [*housing*] insalubre ; [*hygiene, sanitation, visibility, conditions, management*] mauvais ; (*Scol etc: as mark*) **"~"** « faible », « médiocre » ; **to be ~ at (doing) sth** ne pas être doué pour (faire) qch ; **clients who have had ~ service** les clients qui ont eu à se plaindre de l'insuffisance du service ; **he had a very ~ attendance record** il avait souvent été absent ; **he has a ~ chance of survival** il a peu de chances de survivre ; **to be in ~ health** ne pas être en bonne santé, être en mauvaise santé ; **to have ~ hearing** être dur d'oreille ; **he has a ~ memory** il a mauvaise mémoire ; **people with ~ circulation** les gens qui ont une mauvaise circulation ; **she had a ~ grasp of German** son allemand n'était pas très bon ; **he showed a ~ grasp of the facts** il a manifesté un manque de compréhension des faits ; **to have a ~ opinion of o.s.** avoir une mauvaise opinion de soi-même ; **a ~ substitute (for sth)** un piètre substitut (de qch) ; **a ~ imitation of sth** une pâle imitation de qch ; **this sparkling wine is just a ~ relation of champagne** ce vin pétillant n'est qu'une pâle imitation de champagne ; **I'm a ~ sailor** je n'ai pas le pied marin ; **he is a ~ traveller** il supporte mal les voyages ; **he's a ~ loser** il est mauvais perdant → **second¹**, **show** [c] (= *pitiable*) pauvre ; **~ little thing!** pauvre

petit(e) ! ; **she's all alone, ~ woman** elle est toute seule, la pauvre ; **~ chap, he was killed in an air crash** le pauvre, il est mort dans un accident d'avion ; **~ things*, they look cold** les pauvres, ils ont l'air d'avoir froid ; **you ~ old thing!*** mon pauvre vieux !, ma pauvre vieille ! ; (*iro*) **~ little rich girl** pauvre petite fille *f* riche

[2] **the poor** NPL les pauvres *mpl*

[3] COMP ▶ **poor boy** N (*US Culin*) grand sandwich *m* mixte ▶ **poor law** N (*Hist*) **the ~ laws** les lois *fpl* sur l'assistance publique ▶ **poor-mouth*** VT (*US*) **to ~-mouth sb/sth** parler en termes désobligeants de qn/qch ▶ **poor-spirited** ADJ timoré, pusillanime ▶ **poor White** N (*esp pej*) petit Blanc *m*

poorbox ['pʊəbɒks] N (*Rel*) tronc *m* des pauvres

poorhouse ['pʊəhaʊs] N (*Hist*) hospice *m* (des pauvres)

poorly ['pʊəlɪ] [1] ADJ (*esp Brit:***) souffrant, malade ; **the hospital described his condition as ~** les médecins ont déclaré que son état était préoccupant [2] ADV [*live, dress*] pauvrement ; [*perform, eat, sell*] mal ; **~ lit/paid/ designed** *etc* mal éclairé/payé/conçu *etc* ; **to be ~ off** être pauvre

poorness ['pʊənɪs] N [a] (= *poverty*) pauvreté *f* [b] (= *poor quality*) mauvaise qualité *f*, médiocrité *f*

pop¹ [pɒp] [1] N [a] (= *sound*) [*of cork etc*] pan *m* ; [*of press stud etc*] bruit *m* sec ; **to go ~** [*cork*] sauter ; [*balloon*] éclater ; [*bulb, stud*] faire un (petit) bruit sec [b] (*NonC* = *drink*) boisson *f* gazeuse ; **orange ~** orangeade *f* [c] (= *try*) **to have** *or* **take a ~ at (doing) sth*** s'essayer à (faire) qch [d] (= *criticize*) **to have** *or* **take a ~ at sb/sth*** s'en prendre à qn/qch [e] (*US*) **the drinks go for $3.50 a ~*** les boissons sont à 3,50 chaque *or* chacune

[2] VT [a] [+ *balloon*] crever ; [+ *cork*] faire sauter ; [+ *corn*] faire éclater ; [+ *press stud*] fermer ; **to ~ one's cork** prendre son pied* ; (*Brit: hum*) **to ~ one's clogs** casser sa pipe* [b] (* = *put*) mettre ; **to ~ one's head round the door/out of the window** passer brusquement la tête par la porte/par la fenêtre ; **to ~ one's head in** passer la tête par la porte (*or* par la fenêtre *etc*) ; **to ~ sth into the oven** passer *or* mettre qch au four ; **he ~ped it into his mouth** il l'a fourré *or* l'a mis dans sa bouche ; **to ~ pills** se bourrer de médicaments ; **could you ~ this letter into the postbox?** tu peux mettre cette lettre à la boîte ? ; (*fig*) **to ~ the question** faire sa demande (en mariage) [c] († = *pawn*) mettre au clou*

[3] VI [a] [*balloon*] éclater ; [*cork, stud, buttons*] sauter ; **my ears ~ped** mes oreilles se sont débouchées ; **his eyes ~ped** il a écarquillé les yeux, il a ouvert des yeux ronds *or* de grands yeux ; **his eyes were ~ping out of his head** les yeux lui sortaient de la tête, il avait les yeux exorbités ; **her eyes were ~ping with amazement** elle écarquillait les yeux (sous l'effet de la surprise), elle ouvrait des yeux comme des soucoupes [b] (* = *go*) **I ~ped over** (*or* **round** *or* **across** *or* **out**) **to the grocer's** j'ai fait un saut à l'épicerie ; **he ~ped into a café** il est entré dans un café en vitesse ; **a letter ~ped through his letterbox** une lettre est tombée dans sa boîte aux lettres

[4] COMP ▶ **pop quiz** N (*US Scol*) interrogation *f* (écrite) surprise ▶ **pop socks** NPL (*Brit*) mi-bas *mpl* (fins) ▶ **pop-up book** N livre *m* animé ▶ **pop-up menu** N (*Comput*) menu *m* (qui s'affiche à l'écran sur commande) ▶ **pop-up toaster** N grille-pain *m inv* (à éjection automatique)

▶ **pop back*** VI revenir, retourner (en vitesse

or pour un instant)

▶ **pop in*** VI entrer en passant, ne faire que passer ; **I ~ped in to say hullo to them** je suis entré (en passant) leur dire bonjour ; **she kept ~ping in and out** elle n'a pas cessé d'entrer et de sortir

▶ **pop off** VI [a] (* = *leave*) partir ; **they ~ped off to Spain for a few days** ils sont partis passer quelques jours en Espagne [b] (* = *die*) mourir (subitement), claquer* [c] (*US:* = *shout*) donner de la gueule*

▶ **pop on*** VT SEP [a] (= *switch on*) allumer, mettre en marche ; **to ~ the kettle on** ≈ mettre de l'eau à chauffer [b] [+ *clothes, shirt etc*] enfiler

▶ **pop out** VI [*person*] sortir ; [*head*] émerger ; [*cork*] sauter

▶ **pop round*** VI passer, faire un saut ; **~ round anytime** passe n'importe quand → **pop 3b**

▶ **pop up** VI (*from water, above wall etc*) surgir ; **he ~ped up unexpectedly in Tangier*** il a réapparu inopinément à Tanger

pop² [pɒp] ABBR = **popular** [1] N (musique *f*) pop *m* ; **to be top of the ~s** ≈ être en tête du Top 50 [2] COMP [*music, song, singer, concert, group*] pop *inv* ▶ **pop art** N pop art *m* ▶ **pop psychology** N psychologie *f* bon marché (*pej*) *or* de quatre sous ▶ **pop star** N pop star *f*

pop³* [pɒp] N (*esp US*) papa *m* ; (*to old man*) **yes ~(s)** oui grand-père*, oui pépé*

popcorn ['pɒpkɔːn] N pop-corn *m inv*

pope [pəʊp] N pape *m* ; **Pope John Paul II** le pape Jean-Paul II ; (*Cards*) **~ Joan** le nain jaune

popemobile* ['pəʊpməbiːl] N *voiture blindée utilisée par le pape lors de bains de foule*

popery ['pəʊpərɪ] N (*pej*) papisme *m* (*pej*) ; **no ~!** à bas le pape !

popeyed [ˌpɒpˈaɪd] ADJ aux yeux exorbités

popgun ['pɒpgʌn] N pistolet *m* à bouchon

popinjay† ['pɒpɪndʒeɪ] N fat *m*, freluquet *m*

popish ['pəʊpɪʃ] ADJ (*pej*) papiste (*pej*)

poplar ['pɒpləʳ] N peuplier *m*

poplin ['pɒplɪn] [1] N popeline *f* [2] COMP de *or* en popeline

popover ['pɒpˌəʊvəʳ] N (*US Culin*) ≈ chausson *m*

poppa* ['pɒpə] N (*US*) papa *m*

poppadum ['pɒpədəm] N poppadum *m*

popper ['pɒpəʳ] N [a] (*Brit:** = *press stud*) pression *f*, bouton-pression *m* [b] (*Drugs**) popper *m*

poppet* ['pɒpɪt] N (*Brit*) **yes, (my) ~** oui, mon petit chou* ; **she's a (little) ~** elle est à croquer, c'est un amour

poppy ['pɒpɪ] [1] N [a] (= *flower*) pavot *m* ; (*growing wild*) coquelicot *m* [b] (*Brit: commemorative buttonhole*) coquelicot *m* en papier (*vendu le jour de l'Armistice*) [2] ADJ (= *colour*) ponceau *inv* [3] COMP ▶ **Poppy Day** (*Brit*) ≈ l'Armistice *m* ▶ **poppy seed** N graine *f* de pavot

---
POPPY DAY

Poppy Day, *littéralement « la journée du coquelicot », désigne familièrement « Remembrance Day », c'est-à-dire la commémoration des armistices des deux Guerres mondiales, fixée en Grande-Bretagne au deuxième dimanche de novembre. Dans les jours qui précèdent, des coquelicots de papier sont vendus dans la rue au profit des associations caritatives d'aide aux anciens combattants et à leurs familles.* → LEGION
---

poppycock†* ['pɒpɪkɒk] N (*NonC*) balivernes *fpl*

Popsicle® ['pɒpsɪkl] N (*US*) glace *f* à l'eau (*à deux bâtonnets*)

popsy†* ['pɒpsɪ] N (*Brit*) souris* *f*, fille *f*

populace ['pɒpjʊlɪs] N population f, populace f (pej)

popular ['pɒpjʊləʳ] **1** ADJ **a** (= well-liked) [person, decision, book, sport] populaire; (= fashionable) [style, model, place] prisé (**with** de), en vogue; [name] en vogue; [habit, practice] populaire, courant; **he's ~ with his colleagues** ses collègues l'aiment beaucoup, il jouit d'une grande popularité auprès de ses collègues; **he's ~ with the girls** il a du succès or il a la cote* auprès des filles; **I'm not very ~ with the boss just now*** je ne suis pas très bien vu du patron or je n'ai pas la cote* auprès du patron en ce moment; **computers are ~ among the young** les ordinateurs jouissent d'une grande popularité auprès des jeunes; (Comm) **this is a very ~ colour** cette couleur se vend beaucoup; **it is ~ to be patriotic** le patriotisme est à la mode or en vogue; **it is never ~ to raise taxes** les augmentations d'impôts ne sont jamais populaires **b** (= of, for, by the people) [music, concert, myth, newspaper, art, appeal] populaire; [lecture, journal] de vulgarisation; [government, discontent] populaire, du peuple; **at ~ prices** à la portée de toutes les bourses; **by ~ demand** or **request** à la demande générale; **contrary to ~ belief** or **opinion** contrairement aux idées reçues; (Pol) **~ opinion** opinion f publique; **~ support for the treaty** le soutien dont bénéficie le traité au sein de la population; (Pol) **~ vote** vote m populaire

2 COMP ► **popular etymology** N (Ling) étymologie f populaire ► **popular front** N (Pol) front m populaire

popularist ['pɒpjʊlərɪst] ADJ populaire, qui s'adresse au peuple

popularity [ˌpɒpjʊ'lærɪtɪ] N popularité f (**with** auprès de, **among** parmi); **to gain (in)** or **grow in ~** être de plus en plus populaire, acquérir une popularité de plus en plus grande; **to decline in ~** être de moins en moins populaire, perdre de sa popularité; **it enjoyed a certain ~** cela a joui d'une certaine popularité or faveur

popularization ['pɒpjʊləraɪ'zeɪʃən] N **a** (NonC) (= making prevalent) popularisation f; (= making accessible) vulgarisation f **b** (= popularized work) ouvrage m de vulgarisation

popularize ['pɒpjʊləraɪz] VT (= make prevalent) [+ sport, music, fashion, product] populariser, rendre populaire; (= make accessible) [+ science, ideas] vulgariser

popularizer ['pɒpjʊləraɪzəʳ] N **a** [of sport, fashion] promoteur m, -trice f; **Bruce Lee was a ~ of martial arts** Bruce Lee a popularisé les arts martiaux **b** [of science, ideas] vulgarisateur m, -trice f

popularly ['pɒpjʊləlɪ] ADV **~ known as ...** communément connu or connu de tous sous le nom de ...; **it is ~ supposed that ...** il est communément or généralement présumé que ..., on croit généralement que ...; **he is ~ believed to be rich** il passe communément or généralement pour être riche; **it's far more common than is ~ imagined** c'est bien plus fréquent qu'on ne l'imagine généralement; **~ elected** démocratiquement élu

populate ['pɒpjʊleɪt] VT peupler; **densely/sparsely ~d** très/peu peuplé, à forte/faible densité de population; **to be ~d with** être peuplé de

population [ˌpɒpjʊ'leɪʃən] **1** N population f; **a fall/rise in (the) ~** une diminution/un accroissement de la population; **the ~ of the town is 15,000** la population de la ville est de or la ville a une population de 15 000 habitants; **the working ~** la population active **2** COMP [increase] de la population, démographique ► **population explosion** N explosion f démographique ► **population figures** NPL (chiffres mpl de la) démographie f

► **population planning** N planification f démographique

populism ['pɒpjʊlɪzəm] N populisme m

populist ['pɒpjʊlɪst] ADJ, N populiste mf

populous ['pɒpjʊləs] ADJ populeux, très peuplé

porcelain ['pɔːsəlɪn] **1** N (NonC = substance, objects) porcelaine f; **a piece of ~** une porcelaine **2** COMP [dish] de or en porcelaine; [clay, glaze] à porcelaine ► **porcelain ware** N (NonC) vaisselle f en or de porcelaine

porch [pɔːtʃ] N [of house, church] porche m; [of hotel] marquise f; (US: also **sun ~**) véranda f

porcine ['pɔːsaɪn] ADJ (frm) porcin, de porc

porcupine ['pɔːkjʊpaɪn] **1** N porc-épic m → **prickly 2** COMP ► **porcupine fish** N (pl porcupine fish or fishes) poisson-globe m

pore¹ [pɔːʳ] N (in skin) pore m; (fig) **she oozes sexuality from every ~** la sensualité se dégage de toute sa personne

pore² [pɔːʳ] VI **to ~ over** [+ book] être absorbé dans; [+ letter, map] étudier de près; [+ problem] méditer longuement; **he was poring over the book** il était plongé dans or absorbé par le livre

pork [pɔːk] (Culin) **1** N porc m **2** COMP [chop etc] de porc ► **pork barrel*** (US Pol) N électoralisme m (travaux publics ou programme de recherche etc entrepris à des fins électorales) ♦ ADJ [project etc] électoraliste ► **pork butcher** N ≈ charcutier m, -ière f ► **pork pie** N **a** pâté m en croûte **b**‡ = **porky 2** ► **pork-pie hat** N (chapeau m en) feutre m rond ► **pork sausage** N saucisse f (de porc) ► **pork scratchings** NPL amuse-gueules de couennes de porc frites

porker ['pɔːkəʳ] N porc m à l'engrais, goret m

porky ['pɔːkɪ] **1** ADJ (*: pej) gras (grasse f) comme un porc, bouffi **2** N (‡ = lie: also ~ pie) bobard* m; **to tell porkies** raconter des bobards*

porn* [pɔːn] **1** N (NonC) (ABBR = **pornography**) porno* m **2** ADJ [magazine, video] porno*; [actor] de porno*; **~ shop** boutique f porno* → **hard, soft**

porno* ['pɔːnəʊ] ADJ [magazine, video] porno*; [actor] de porno*

pornographer [pɔː'nɒgrəfəʳ] N pornographe m

pornographic [ˌpɔːnə'græfɪk] ADJ pornographique

pornography [pɔː'nɒgrəfɪ] N pornographie f

porosity [pɔː'rɒsɪtɪ] N porosité f

porous ['pɔːrəs] ADJ poreux, perméable

porousness ['pɔːrəsnɪs] N porosité f

porphyry ['pɔːfɪrɪ] N porphyre m

porpoise ['pɔːpəs] N (pl **porpoise** or **porpoises**) marsouin m

porridge ['pɒrɪdʒ] N **a** porridge m, bouillie f de flocons d'avoine; **~ oats** flocons mpl d'avoine **b** (Brit‡) taule‡ f; **to do ~** faire de la taule‡

porringer† ['pɒrɪndʒəʳ] N bol m, écuelle f

port¹ [pɔːt] **1** N (= harbour, town) port m; (Naut) **~ of call** (port m d')escale f; (fig) **I've only one more ~ of call** il ne me reste plus qu'une course à faire; **~ of dispatch** or (US) **shipment** port m d'expédition; **~ of embarkation** port m d'embarquement; **~ of entry** port m de débarquement or d'arrivée; **naval/fishing ~** port m militaire/de pêche; **to come into ~** entrer dans le port; **they put into ~ at Dieppe** ils ont relâché dans le port de Dieppe; (Naut) **to make ~** arriver au port; **to run into ~** entrer au port; **to leave ~** appareiller, lever l'ancre; (fig) **a ~ in a storm** (= person offering help) une main secourable; (= refuge) un havre de paix; **the yen is the safest ~ in the current economic storm** le yen est la monnaie la plus sûre dans la crise actuelle; **any ~ in a storm**

nécessité n'a pas de loi (PROV) → **seaport, trading**

2 COMP [facilities, security] portuaire, du port ► **port authorities** NPL autorités fpl portuaires ► **port dues** NPL droits mpl de port

port² [pɔːt] N **a** = **porthole b** (Comput) port m, porte f (d'accès), point m d'accès

port³ [pɔːt] (Naut) **1** N (also **~ side**) bâbord m; **to ~** à bâbord; **land to ~!** terre par bâbord!; **to put the rudder to ~** mettre la barre à bâbord **2** ADJ [guns, lights] de bâbord **3** VT **to ~ the helm** mettre la barre à bâbord

port⁴ [pɔːt] N (= wine) porto m

portability [ˌpɔːtə'bɪlɪtɪ] N (esp Comput) portabilité f; [of software] transférabilité f

portable ['pɔːtəbl] **1** ADJ (gen) portatif; [computer, telephone, television, software] portable; (Comput) **a ~ language** un langage de programmation portable; **~ pension** pension f transférable **2** N (= computer) portable m; (= tape recorder) petit magnétophone m; (= television) téléviseur m portable

portage ['pɔːtɪdʒ] N (= action, route) portage m; (= cost) frais mpl de portage

Portakabin® ['pɔːtəkæbɪn] N (gen) bâtiment m préfabriqué; (= extension to office etc) petite annexe f préfabriquée; (= works office etc) baraque f de chantier

portal ['pɔːtl] **1** N portail m; (fig) porte f **2** COMP ► **portal vein** N veine f porte

Portaloo® ['pɔːtəluː] N (Brit) toilettes fpl publiques provisoires

portcullis [pɔːt'kʌlɪs] N herse f (de château fort)

portend [pɔː'tend] VT (liter) présager, annoncer

portent ['pɔːtent] N (liter) **a** (= omen) prodige m, présage m; **of evil ~** de mauvais présage **b** (= significance) grande importance f; **it's a day of ~** c'est un jour très important

portentous [pɔː'tentəs] ADJ (liter) (= ominous) de mauvais augure; (= marvellous) prodigieux; (= grave) solennel; (pej = pompous) pompeux, pontifiant

portentously [pɔː'tentəslɪ] ADV (liter) [say, announce] (pej = pompously) pompeusement; (pej = ominously) solennellement; **the sky was ~ dark** le ciel noir ne présageait rien de bon

porter ['pɔːtəʳ] **1** N **a** (for luggage: in station, hotel etc, on climb or expedition) porteur m **b** (US Rail = attendant) employé(e) m(f) des wagons-lits **c** (Brit = doorkeeper) [of private housing] concierge mf; [of public building] portier m, gardien(ne) m(f); (Univ) appariteur m **d** [of hospital] brancardier m, -ière f **e** (= beer) porter m, bière f brune **2** COMP ► **porter's lodge** N loge f du or de la concierge (or du portier etc)

porterage ['pɔːtərɪdʒ] N (= act) portage m; (= cost) frais mpl de portage

porterhouse ['pɔːtəhaʊs] N (also **~ steak**) chateaubriand m

portfolio [pɔːt'fəʊlɪəʊ] **1** N (pl **portfolios**) **a** (Pol = object, post) portefeuille m; **minister without ~** ministre m sans portefeuille **b** [of shares] portefeuille m **c** [of artist] portfolio m; [of model] book m **d** (Comm = range) gamme f **2** COMP ► **portfolio manager** N portefeuilliste mf

porthole ['pɔːthəʊl] N (Aviat, Naut) hublot m; (Naut: for guns, cargo) sabord m

portico ['pɔːtɪkəʊ] N (pl **porticoes** or **porticos**) portique m

portion ['pɔːʃən] **1** N (= part, percentage) portion f, partie f; [of train, ticket etc] partie f; (= share) portion f, (quote-)part f; [of estate, inheritance etc] portion f, part f; (of food = helping) portion f; (†: also **marriage ~**) dot f; (liter = fate) sort m, destin m **2** VT (also **~ out**) répartir (**among, between** entre)

portliness ['pɔːtlɪnɪs] N embonpoint *m*, corpulence *f*

portly ['pɔːtlɪ] ADJ corpulent

portmanteau [pɔːt'mæntəʊ] **1** N (*pl* **portmanteaus** *or* **portmanteaux** [pɔːt'mæntəʊz]) grosse valise *f* (*de cuir*) **2** COMP ▶ **portmanteau word** N (*Ling*) mot-valise *m*

portrait ['pɔːtrɪt] **1** N (*gen, Art*) portrait *m*; **to paint sb's ~** peindre (le portrait de) qn **2** COMP ▶ **portrait gallery** N galerie *f* de portraits ▶ **portrait lens** N (*Phot*) bonnette *f* ▶ **portrait mode** N (*Comput*) **to output sth in ~ mode** imprimer qch à la française or au format portrait ▶ **portrait painter** N portraitiste *mf* ▶ **portrait photographer** N photographe *mf* spécialisé(e) dans les portraits, portraitiste *mf* ▶ **portrait photography** N art *m* du portrait photographique; **to do ~ photography** faire des portraits photographiques

portraitist ['pɔːtrɪtɪst] N portraitiste *mf*

portraiture ['pɔːtrɪtʃə^r] N (*NonC*) (= *art*) art *m* du portrait; (= *portrait*) portrait *m*; (*NonC*; *collectively*) portraits *mpl*

portray [pɔː'treɪ] VT [*painter*] peindre, faire le portrait de; [*painting*] représenter; **he ~ed him as an embittered man** [*painter*] il l'a peint sous les traits d'un homme aigri; [*writer, speaker, actor*] il en a fait un homme aigri; **the film ~ed him as a saint** le film le présentait comme un saint

portrayal [pɔː'treɪəl] N (*in play, film, book*) évocation *f*; (*by actor*) [*of character*] interprétation *f*; **the novel is a hilarious ~ of Jewish life in the 1920s** ce roman dépeint or évoque d'une façon hilarante le monde juif des années 20

Portugal ['pɔːtjʊgəl] N le Portugal

Portuguese [ˌpɔːtjʊ'giːz] **1** ADJ (*gen*) portugais; [*ambassador, embassy*] du Portugal; [*teacher*] de portugais **2** N **a** (*pl inv*) Portugais(e) *m(f)* **b** (*Ling*) portugais *m* **3** **the Portuguese** NPL les Portugais *mpl* **4** COMP ▶ **Portuguese man-of-war** N (*pl* **Portuguese men-of-war**) (*Zool*) galère *f*

POS [ˌpiːəʊ'es] N (ABBR = **point of sale**) PLV *m*

pose [pəʊz] **1** N **a** (= *body position: gen, pej*) pose *f*, attitude *f*; (*Art*) pose *f*; (*fig*) pose *f*; **to strike a ~** (*lit*) poser (pour la galerie); (*fig*) se composer une attitude; **it's probably just a ~** ce n'est sans doute qu'une attitude **2** VI (*Art, Phot*) poser (**for** pour, **as** en); (*pej* = *attitudinize*) poser pour la galerie; **to ~ as a doctor** se faire passer pour un docteur; **to ~ nude** poser nu **3** VT **a** (= *present*) [+ *problem, question*] poser; [+ *difficulties*] poser, comporter; [+ *threat, challenge*] constituer, représenter; (*frm* = *state*) [+ *argument, claim, question*] formuler; [+ *solution*] présenter; **the danger ~d by nuclear weapons** le danger que constituent or représentent les armes nucléaires **b** [+ *artist's model*] faire prendre une pose à; [+ *person*] faire poser **4** COMP ▶ **posing pouch** N cache-sexe *m* (*pour homme*)

Poseidon [pɒ'saɪdən] N Poséidon *m*

poser ['pəʊzə^r] N **a** (*pej* = *person*) poseur *m*, -euse *f* (*pej*) **b** (= *problem, question*) question *f* difficile; **that's a bit of a ~!** c'est un véritable casse-tête or une sacrée colle!*; **how he did it remains a ~** nul ne sait comment il y est arrivé

poseur [pəʊ'zɜː^r] N (*pej*) poseur *m*, -euse *f* (*pej*)

posh [pɒʃ] **1** ADJ* **a** (= *distinguished*) [*house, neighbourhood, hotel, car, clothes*] chic; [*occasion*] select *inv* or sélect; **a ~ London restaurant** un restaurant londonien très chic; **he was looking very ~** il faisait très chic, il s'était mis sur son trente et un **b** (*pej*) [*person, accent*] snob (*f inv*); [*house, neighbourhood, school, car*] de riches; **~ people** les snob(s) *mpl*, les gens *mpl* de la haute*; **my ~ aunt** ma tante qui est très snob; **a ~ wedding** un mariage chic or en

grand tralala* **2** ADV (*pej*) **to talk ~**: parler comme les gens de la haute*

▶ **posh up**: VT SEP [+ *house, room*] redonner un coup de jeune à*; **to ~ o.s. up** se pomponner, se bichonner; **he was all ~ed up** il était sur son trente et un, il était bien pomponné

posidrive ['pɒzɪˌdraɪv] ADJ **~ screw/screwdriver** vis *f*/tournevis *m* cruciforme

posit ['pɒzɪt] VT postuler, poser comme postulat

▼ **position** [pə'zɪʃən] **1** N **a** (= *place, location*) [*of person, object*] position *f* (*also Geog, Math, Mil, Mus, Naut, Phys etc*), place *f*; [*of house, shop, town*] emplacement *m*, situation *f*; [*of gun*] emplacement *m*; **in(to) ~** en place, en position; **to change the ~ of sth** changer qch de place; **to take up (one's) ~** prendre position or place; **to get o.s. into ~** se placer; **to be in a good ~** être bien placé → **1d**; (*Mil etc*) **the enemy ~s** les positions *fpl* de l'ennemi; (*Sport*) **what ~ do you play (in)?** à quelle place jouez-vous?; (*lit, fig*) **to jockey** or **jostle** or **manoeuvre for ~** manœuvrer pour se placer avantageusement; (*in post office, bank*) **"~ closed"** « guichet fermé »

b (= *attitude, angle: gen, Art, Ballet*) position *f*; **in a horizontal ~** en position horizontale; **in an uncomfortable ~** dans une position incommode; **to change (one's) ~** changer de position; **in a sitting ~** en position assise

c (*in class, league*) position *f*, place *f*; (*socially*) position *f*, condition *f*; (= *job*) poste *m*, emploi *m*; **top management ~s** les postes *mpl* de cadre supérieur; **he finished in third ~** il est arrivé en troisième position or place; **his ~ in society** sa position dans la société; **a man in his ~ should not ...** un homme dans sa position or de sa condition ne devrait pas ... → **1d**; **his ~ in (the) government** son poste or sa fonction dans le gouvernement; **a high ~ in the Ministry** une haute fonction au ministère; **a ~ of trust** un poste de confiance; **he's in a ~ of power** il occupe un poste d'influence; **he is using his ~ of power for personal gain** il utilise son pouvoir à des fins personnelles

d (*fig* = *situation, circumstances*) situation *f*, place *f*; **what would you do in my ~?** que feriez-vous à ma place?; **our ~ is desperate** notre situation est désespérée; **the economic ~** la situation économique; **to be in a good/bad ~** être dans une bonne/mauvaise situation; **we were in an awkward ~** nous étions dans une situation délicate; **to be in a ~ to do sth** être en position or en mesure de faire qch; **he's in a good/bad ~ to judge** il est bien/mal placé pour juger; **he's in no ~ to decide** il n'est pas en position or en mesure de décider; **she's in no ~ to criticize** elle est mal placée pour critiquer; **put yourself in my ~** mettez-vous à ma place; **a man in his ~ cannot expect mercy** un homme dans sa situation ne peut s'attendre à la clémence → **1c**; **what's the ~ on deliveries/sales?** où en sont les livraisons/ventes?

e (*fig* = *point of view, opinion*) position *f*, opinion *f*; **you must make your ~ clear** vous devez dire franchement quelle est votre position; **the Church's ~ on homosexuality** la position de l'Église face à or sur l'homosexualité; **to take up a ~ on sth** prendre position sur qch; **he took up the ~ that ...** il a adopté le point de vue selon lequel ...

2 VT **a** (= *adjust angle of*) [+ *light, microscope, camera*] positionner **b** (= *put in place*) [+ *gun, chair, camera*] mettre en place, placer; [+ *house, school*] situer, placer; [+ *guards, policemen*] placer, poster; [+ *army, ship*] mettre en position; (*Marketing*) [+ *product*] positionner; **he ~ed each item with great care** il a très soigneusement disposé chaque article; **the company is well ~ed to sell a million cars this year** la société est bien placée pour vendre un million de voitures cette année

c (= *find position of*) déterminer la position de

positive ['pɒzɪtɪv] **1** ADJ **a** (= *not negative: gen, Elec, Gram, Math, Phot, Typ*) positif; [*test, result, reaction*] positif; (= *affirmative: Ling etc*) affirmatif; (= *constructive*) [*suggestion*] positif, concret (-ète *f*); [*attitude, criticism*] positif; [*response*] favorable, positif; **to take ~ action** prendre des mesures concrètes; **we need some ~ thinking** soyons positifs; **he's very ~ about it** il a une attitude très positive à ce sujet; **she is a very ~ person** c'est quelqu'un de très positif

b (= *definite, indisputable*) [*order, rule, instruction*] catégorique, formel; [*fact*] indéniable, irréfutable; [*change, increase, improvement*] réel, tangible; **~ proof** ◊ **proof ~** preuve *f* formelle; **there is ~ evidence that ...** il y a des preuves indéniables selon lesquelles ...; **to make a ~ identification** or **ID on a body** formellement identifier un corps; **progress has been made** un réel progrès or un progrès tangible a été fait; **he has made a ~ contribution to the scheme** il a apporté une contribution effective au projet, il a contribué de manière effective au projet; **it'll be a ~ pleasure to get rid of him!** ce sera un vrai or un véritable plaisir (que) de se débarrasser de lui!; **your room is a ~ disgrace** ta chambre est une véritable porcherie

c (= *sure, certain*) [*person*] sûr, certain (**about, on, of** de); **are you quite ~?** en êtes-vous bien sûr or certain?; **I'm absolutely ~ I put it back** je suis absolument sûr de l'avoir remis à sa place; **... he said in a ~ tone of voice** ... dit-il d'un ton très assuré; **I am ~ that I can mend it** je suis sûr de pouvoir le réparer

2 N (*Elec*) pôle *m* positif; (*Gram*) affirmatif *m*; (*Math*) nombre *m* positif, quantité *f* positive; (*Phot*) épreuve *f* positive, positif *m*; (*Ling*) **in the ~** à l'affirmatif; **he replied in the ~** il a répondu par l'affirmative; **the ~s far outweigh the negatives** les points positifs compensent largement les points négatifs

3 ADV (*Drugs, Sport*) **to test ~** subir un contrôle positif, être positif; **he tested ~ for HIV** son test du sida était positif; **to show ~** [*test*] se révéler positif; [*person*] être positif; **to think ~** être positif; **think ~!** soyez positif!

4 COMP ▶ **positive discrimination** N (*Brit*) discrimination *f* positive ▶ **positive feedback** N (*Elec*) réaction *f* positive; (= *praise*) réactions *fpl* positives; **to give sb/get ~ feedback (about sb/sth)** faire part à qn/recevoir des réactions positives (sur qn/qch) ▶ **positive vetting** N enquête *f* de sécurité (**of sb** sur qn); **a policy of ~ vetting** une politique d'enquêtes de sécurité

positively ['pɒzɪtɪvlɪ] ADV **a** (= *constructively, favourably*) [*act, contribute*] de façon positive, positivement; **to think ~** être positif; **to respond ~** (*in negotiations, to event etc*) réagir favorablement; **to respond ~ to treatment/medication** [*patient*] bien réagir à un traitement/un médicament; **to be ~ disposed to sb/sth** être bien disposé envers qn/qch

b (= *actively*) **I didn't object, in fact I ~ approved** je ne m'y suis pas opposé, j'étais même carrément d'accord; **she never refused his advances, but she never ~ invited them either** elle n'a jamais repoussé ses avances mais elle ne les a jamais encouragées non plus; **she doesn't mind being photographed, in fact she ~ loves it** cela ne la dérange pas qu'on la photographie, en fait, elle adore ça

c (= *absolutely, literally*) carrément; **she's ~ obsessed** c'est carrément une obsession chez elle; **this is ~ the worst thing that could happen** c'est vraiment la pire des choses qui pouvaient arriver; **he was ~ rude to me** il a été carrément grossier avec moi; **this is ~ the last time** cette fois, c'est vraiment la dernière; **I ~ forbid it!** je l'interdis formellement!; **she ~**

glowed with happiness elle rayonnait littéralement de bonheur
d (= definitely) [identify] formellement ; **cholesterol has been ~ associated with heart disease** le cholestérol a été formellement associé aux maladies cardiovasculaires
e he tested ~ for drugs/HIV ◊ he was ~ tested for drugs/HIV son test antidopage/du sida était positif
f (Elec, Phys) ~ **charged** chargé positivement, à charge positive

positivism ['pɒzɪtɪvɪzəm] N positivisme m

positivist ['pɒzɪtɪvɪst] ADJ, N positiviste mf

positron ['pɒzɪtrɒn] N positon m, positron m

poss* [pɒs] ADJ possible ; **as soon as ~** dès que possible

posse ['pɒsɪ] N (gen, fig hum) petite troupe f, détachement m

possess [pə'zes] VT **a** (= own, have) [+ property, qualities] posséder, avoir ; [+ documents, money, proof] posséder, être en possession de ; **all I ~** tout ce que je possède ; (illegally) **she was accused of ~ing a firearm/drugs** elle a été accusée de port d'armes prohibé/de détention illégale de stupéfiants ; **it ~es several advantages** cela présente plusieurs avantages ; **to ~ o.s. of sth** s'emparer de qch ; (frm) **to be ~ed of** posséder ; (liter) **to ~ one's soul in patience** s'armer de patience
b [demon, rage] (fig = obsess) posséder, obséder ; **he was ~ed by the devil** il était possédé du démon ; **~ed with** or **by jealousy** obsédé or dévoré par la jalousie, en proie à la jalousie ; **I was ~ed by an irrational fear** j'étais en proie à une peur irraisonnée ; **like one ~ed** comme un(e) possédé(e) ; **like a man/woman ~ed** comme un(e) possédé(e) ; **what can have ~ed him to say that?** qu'est-ce qui lui a pris de dire ça ?*

possession [pə'zeʃən] **1** N **a** (NonC = act, state) possession f ; (Jur = occupancy) jouissance f ; (illegal) [of drugs] détention f illégale ; **illegal ~ of a firearm** port m d'arme prohibé ; **in ~ of** en possession de ; **to have ~** (gen) posséder ; (Jur) avoir la jouissance de ; **to have sth in one's ~** avoir qch en sa possession ; **to get ~ of sth** obtenir qch ; (by force) s'emparer de qch ; (improperly) s'approprier qch ; (Rugby) **to get ~ of the ball** s'emparer du ballon ; **to come into ~ of** entrer en possession de ; **to come into sb's ~** tomber en la possession de qn ; **he was in full ~ of all his faculties** il était en pleine possession de ses facultés, il avait le plein usage de ses facultés ; **according to the information in my ~** selon les renseignements dont je dispose ; **to take ~ of sth** prendre possession de qch ; (improperly) s'approprier qch ; (= confiscate) confisquer qch ; (Jur) **to take ~** prendre possession de ; (Jur) **to be in ~** occuper les lieux ; (Jur etc) **a house with vacant ~** une maison avec jouissance immédiate ∎ (PROV) **~ is nine points** or **tenths of the law** ≈ (en fait de meubles) la possession vaut titre
b (= object) possession f, bien m ; (= territory) possession f ; **all his ~s** tous ses biens, tout ce qu'il possède ; **he had few ~s** il possédait très peu de choses

2 COMP ▶ **possession order** N (Brit Jur) injonction autorisant le propriétaire d'un logement à en reprendre possession en expulsant les occupants

possessive [pə'zesɪv] **1** ADJ **a** [person, nature, attitude, love] possessif ; **to be ~ about sth** ne pas vouloir partager qch ; **to be ~ towards** or **with sb** être possessif avec or à l'égard de qn ; **his mother is terribly ~** sa mère est très possessive, il a une mère abusive **b** (Gram) possessif **2** N (Gram) **the ~** le possessif ; **in the ~** au possessif **3** COMP ▶ **possessive adjective** N adjectif m possessif ▶ **possessive pronoun** N pronom m possessif

possessively [pə'zesɪvlɪ] ADV d'une façon possessive

possessiveness [pə'zesɪvnɪs] N (NonC) possessivité f

possessor [pə'zesər] N possesseur m ; (= owner) propriétaire mf ; **to be the ~ of** être possesseur de, posséder ; **he was the proud ~ of ...** il était l'heureux propriétaire de ...

▼ **possibility** [ˌpɒsə'bɪlɪtɪ] N **a** (NonC) possibilité f ; **within the bounds of ~** dans la limite du possible ; **not beyond the realms** or **bounds of ~** pas impossible ; **if by any ~ ...** si par impossible ..., si par hasard ... ; **there is some ~/not much ~ of success** il y a quelques chances/peu de chances que ça marche ; **there is no ~ of my leaving** il n'est pas possible que je parte
b (= possible event) possibilité f, éventualité f ; **to foresee all (the) possibilities** envisager toutes les possibilités or éventualités ; **there's a ~ that we might be wrong** il se peut or il est possible que nous nous trompions ; **it's a distinct ~** c'est bien possible ; **we must allow for the ~ that he may refuse** nous devons nous préparer à or nous devons envisager l'éventualité de son refus ; **he is a ~ for the job** c'est un candidat possible
c (= promise, potential) perspectives fpl, potentiel m ; **the firm saw good possibilities for expansion** la compagnie entrevoyait de bonnes perspectives d'expansion ; **the scheme/the job has real possibilities** c'est un projet/un emploi qui ouvre toutes sortes de perspectives ; **she agreed that the project had possibilities** elle a admis que le projet avait un certain potentiel

▼ **possible** ['pɒsəbl] **1** ADJ **a** possible ; [event, reaction, victory, loss] possible, éventuel ; **it's just ~** ce n'est pas impossible ; **it's not ~!** ce n'est pas possible !, pas possible !* ; **it is ~ that ...** il se peut que ... (+ subj), il est possible que ... (+ subj) ; **it's just ~ that ...** il n'est pas impossible que ... (+ subj), il y a une chance que ... (+ subj) ; **it's ~ to do so** il est possible de le faire, c'est faisable ; **it is ~ for us to measure his progress** il nous est possible de mesurer ses progrès ; **to make sth ~** rendre qch possible ; **he made it ~ for me to go to Spain** il a rendu possible mon voyage en Espagne ; **if (at all) ~** si possible ; **he visits her whenever ~** il va la voir aussi souvent que possible or chaque fois qu'il le peut ; **whenever** or **wherever ~, we try to find s** dans la mesure du possible, nous essayons de trouver ... ; **as far as ~** dans la mesure du possible ; **as much as ~** autant que possible ; **he did as much as ~** il a fait tout ce qu'il pouvait ; **as soon as ~** dès que possible, aussitôt que possible ; **as quickly as ~** le plus vite possible ; **at the worst ~ time** au pire moment ; **he chose the worst ~ job for a man with a heart condition** il a choisi le pire des emplois pour un cardiaque ; **the best ~ result** le meilleur résultat possible ; **one ~ result** un résultat possible or éventuel ; **what ~ interest can you have in it?** qu'est-ce qui peut bien vous intéresser là-dedans ? ; **what ~ motive could she have?** quels pouvaient bien être ses motifs ? ; **there is no ~ excuse for his behaviour** sa conduite n'a aucune excuse or est tout à fait inexcusable
b (= perhaps acceptable) [candidate, successor] possible, acceptable ; **a ~ solution** une solution possible or à envisager ; **it is a ~ solution to the problem** ce pourrait être une manière de résoudre le problème

2 N **a** **the art of the ~** l'art m du possible
b * **a list of ~s for the job** une liste de personnes susceptibles d'être retenues pour ce poste ; **he's a ~ for the match on Saturday** c'est un joueur éventuel pour le match de samedi ; (Sport) **the Possibles versus the Probables** la sélection B contre la sélection A

▼ **possibly** ['pɒsəblɪ] ADV **a** (with "can" etc) he did all he ~ could (to help them) il a fait tout

son possible (pour les aider) ; **I'll come if I ~ can** je ferai mon possible pour venir ; **I go as often as I ~ can** j'y vais aussi souvent que possible ; **I cannot ~ come** il m'est absolument impossible de venir ; **you can't ~ do that!** tu ne vas pas faire ça quand même ! ; **it can't ~ be true!** ce n'est pas possible ! **b** (= perhaps) peut-être ; **Belgian beer is ~ the finest in the world** la bière belge est peut-être la meilleure du monde ; ~ **they've left already** ils sont peut-être déjà partis, il se peut qu'ils soient déjà partis ; **was he lying? (very** or **quite)** ~ est-ce qu'il mentait ? c'est (tout à fait or très) possible ; ~ **not** peut-être pas, peut-être que non

possum* ['pɒsəm] N (US) (ABBR = **opossum**) opossum m ; (fig) **to play ~*** faire le mort

POST N (ABBR = **point-of-sale terminal**) → point

post¹ [pəust] **1** N (of wood, metal) poteau m ; (= stake) pieu m ; (for door etc: upright) montant m ; (also **goal ~**) poteau m (de but) ; (Sport) **starting/finishing** or **winning ~** poteau m de départ/d'arrivée ; (fig) **to be left at the ~** manquer le départ, rester sur la touche ; (Sport, fig) **to be beaten at the ~** être battu or coiffé sur le poteau → **deaf**, **gatepost**, **lamppost**, **pip³ 2** VT (also **~ up**) [+ notice, list] afficher **b** (= announce) [+ results] annoncer ; **to be ~ed (as) missing** être porté disparu **c** **to ~ a wall with advertisements** poser or coller des affiches publicitaires sur un mur

▼ **post²** [pəust] **1** N **a** (Mil, gen) poste m ; **at one's ~** à son poste → **forward**, **last¹ b** (esp Can, US: also **trading ~**) comptoir m **c** (= situation, job) poste m, situation f ; (in civil service, government etc) poste m ; **a ~ as a manager** un poste or une situation de directeur ; **his ~ as head of the ruling party** son poste de dirigeant du parti au pouvoir ; **to hold a ~** occuper un poste **2** VT **a** (Mil = position) [+ sentry, guard] poster ; **they ~ed a man by the stairs** ils ont posté un homme près de l'escalier **b** (esp Brit = send, assign) (Mil) poster (**to** à) ; (Admin, Comm) affecter, nommer (**to** à) ; **to ~ sb abroad/to Paris** envoyer qn à l'étranger/à Paris **c** (US Jur) **to ~ bail** déposer une caution ; **to ~ the collateral required** fournir les garanties **3** COMP ▶ **post exchange** N (US Mil) magasin m de l'armée

post³ [pəust] (esp Brit) **1** N **a** (NonC) poste f ; (= letters) courrier m ; **by ~** par la poste ; **by return (of)** ~ par retour du courrier ; **by first-/second-class** ~ ≈ tarif accéléré/normal ; **winners will be notified by ~** les gagnants seront avisés (personnellement) par courrier ; **your receipt is in the ~** votre reçu est déjà posté ; **I'll put it in the ~ today** je le posterai aujourd'hui ; **it went first ~ this morning** c'est parti ce matin par le premier courrier ; **to catch/miss the ~** avoir/manquer la levée ; **drop it in the ~ on your way** mettez-le à la boîte en route ; **the ~ was lifted** or **collected at 8 o'clock** la levée a eu lieu à 8 heures ; **has the ~ been** or **come yet?** le courrier est-il arrivé ?, le facteur est-il passé ? ; **the ~ is late** le courrier a du retard ; **is there any ~ for me?** est-ce que j'ai du courrier ?, y a-t-il une lettre pour moi ? ; **you'll get these through the ~** vous les recevrez par la poste ; (Brit) **Minister/Ministry of Posts and Telecommunications** ministre m/ ministère m des Postes et (des) Télécommunications → **registered**
b (Hist = riders etc) poste f → **general**

2 VT **a** (= send by post) envoyer or expédier par la poste ; (Brit = put in mailbox) poster, mettre à la poste
b (Accounts: also **~ up**) [+ transaction] inscrire ; **to ~ an entry to the ledger** passer une écriture dans le registre ; **to ~ (up) a ledger** tenir un registre à jour ; (fig) **to keep sb ~ed** tenir qn au courant

③ VI (*Hist* = *travel by stages*) voyager par la poste, prendre le courrier; (†† = *hasten*) courir le poste††, faire diligence†

④ COMP ► **post and packing** N (= *cost*) frais *mpl* de port et d'emballage ► **post chaise** N (*Hist*) chaise f de poste ► **post-free** ADJ (en) port payé ► **post horn** N (*Mus*) cornet *m* de poste *or* de postillon ► **post house** N (*Hist*) relais *m* de poste ► **Post-it®**, **Post-it note®** N Post-it® *m inv* ► **post office** N → **post office** ► **post-paid** ADJ port payé

► **post on** VT SEP [+ *letter, parcel*] faire suivre
► **post up** VT SEP = **post³ 2b**

post... [pəʊst] PREF post...; ~**glacial** postglaciaire; ~**-1950** (adj) postérieur (-eure f) à (l'année) 1950, d'après 1950 ♦ (adv) après 1950 → **postdate, postimpressionism**

postage ['pəʊstɪdʒ] ① N (*NonC*) tarifs *mpl* postaux *or* d'affranchissement; (*in account etc*) ~: **£2** frais *mpl* de port: 2 livres; ~ **due 20p** surtaxe 20 pence ② COMP ► **postage and packing** N (*Comm*) frais *mpl* de port et d'emballage ► **postage meter** N (*US*) machine f à affranchir (les lettres) ► **postage paid** ADJ port payé *inv* ► **postage rates** NPL tarifs *mpl* postaux ► **postage stamp** N timbre-poste *m*; **what she knows about children would fit on the back of a ~ stamp** les enfants, elle n'y connaît rien

postal ['pəʊstəl] ① ADJ [*code, zone*] postal; [*application*] par la poste; ~ **charges** ◊ ~ **rates** tarifs *mpl* postaux; ~ **dispute** conflit *m* (des employés) des postes; ~ **district** district *m* postal; **the** ~ **services** les services *mpl* postaux; **two-tier** ~ **service** courrier *m* à deux vitesses; ~ **strike** grève f des employés des postes; ~ **worker** employé(e) *m(f)* des postes, postier *m*, -ière f ② COMP ► **postal card** N (*US*) carte f postale ► **postal order** N (*Brit*) mandat *m* (postal); **a** ~ **order for 100 francs** un mandat de 100 F ► **postal vote** N (= *paper*) bulletin *m* de vote par correspondance; (= *system*) vote *m* par correspondance

postbag ['pəʊstbæg] N (*Brit*) sac *m* postal; **we've had a good ~* on this** nous avons reçu beaucoup de courrier à ce sujet

postbox ['pəʊstbɒks] N (*esp Brit*) boîte f à *or* aux lettres

postcard ['pəʊstkɑːd] N carte f postale

postcode ['pəʊstkəʊd] N (*Brit*) code *m* postal

postcoital [pəʊst'kɔɪtəl] ADJ (d')après l'amour

postdate [ˌpəʊst'deɪt] VT postdater

postdoctoral [pəʊst'dɒktərəl] ADJ (*Univ*) [*research, studies etc*] après le doctorat; ~ **fellow** chercheur *m* qui a son doctorat; ~ **fellowship** poste *m* de chercheur (qui a son doctorat)

poster ['pəʊstə'] ① N affiche f; (*decorative*) poster *m* ② COMP ► **poster paint** N gouache f

poste restante [ˌpəʊst'restɑ̃nt] N, ADV (*esp Brit*) poste f restante

posterior [pɒs'tɪərɪə'] ① ADJ (*frm*) postérieur (-eure f) (**to** à) ② N (* *hum*) derrière *m*, postérieur* *m*

posterity [pɒs'terɪtɪ] N postérité f; **to go down to** *or* **in** ~ **as sth/for sth** entrer dans la postérité en tant que qch/pour qch; **for** ~ pour la postérité

postern ['pɒstən] N poterne f

postfeminist [ˌpəʊst'femɪnɪst] ADJ, N postféministe *mf*

postgrad* ['pəʊst'græd] N, ADJ ABBR = **postgraduate**

postgraduate [pəʊst'grædjʊɪt] ① ADJ [*studies, course, grant, diploma*] ≈ de troisième cycle (universitaire) ② N (*also* ~ **student**) étudiant(e) *m(f)* de troisième cycle

posthaste [ˌpəʊst'heɪst] ADV à toute allure

posthumous ['pɒstjʊməs] ADJ posthume

posthumously ['pɒstjʊməslɪ] ADV à titre posthume

postiche [pɒs'tiːʃ] N, ADJ postiche *m*

postie* ['pəʊstɪ] N (*Austral, Brit dial*) facteur *m*, -trice f

postil(l)ion [pəs'tɪlɪən] N postillon *m*

postimpressionism ['pəʊstɪm'preʃənɪzəm] N postimpressionnisme *m*

postimpressionist ['pəʊstɪm'preʃənɪst] ADJ, N postimpressionniste *mf*

postindustrial [ˌpəʊstɪn'dʌstrɪəl] ADJ postindustriel

posting ['pəʊstɪŋ] ① N ⓐ (*NonC* = *sending by post*) expédition f *or* envoi *m* par la poste ⓑ (*Brit*) (= *assignment*) mutation f; (*Mil*) affectation f; **I've been given an overseas ~ to Japan** j'ai été muté *or* affecté au Japon ⓒ (*Accounts* = *entry*) passation f ② COMP ► **posting error** N (*Accounts*) erreur f d'écriture

postman ['pəʊstmən] ① N (*pl* **-men**) facteur *m*, préposé *m* (*Admin*) ② COMP ► **postman's knock** N (= *game*) ≈ le mariage chinois

postmark ['pəʊstmɑːk] ① N oblitération f, cachet *m* de la poste; **date as** ~ le cachet de la poste faisant foi; (*on letter*) pour la date, se référer au cachet de la poste; **letter with a French** ~ lettre f oblitérée en France; **it is ~ed Paris** ça porte le cachet de Paris ② VT tamponner, timbrer

postmaster ['pəʊst,mɑːstə'] ① N receveur *m* des postes ② COMP ► **Postmaster General** N (*pl* **Postmasters General**) (*Brit*) ministre *m* des Postes et Télécommunications

postmistress ['pəʊst,mɪstrɪs] N receveuse f des postes

postmodern [ˌpəʊst'mɒdən] ADJ postmoderne

postmodernism [ˌpəʊst'mɒdənɪzəm] N postmodernisme *m*

postmodernist [ˌpəʊst'mɒdənɪst] ADJ, N postmoderniste *mf*

post-mortem [pəʊst'mɔːtəm] ① ADJ ~ **examination** autopsie f ② N (*Med, also fig*) autopsie f; (*lit*) **to hold a** ~ faire une autopsie; **to hold** *or* **carry out a** ~ **on** (*lit*) faire l'autopsie de, autopsier; (*fig*) disséquer, faire l'autopsie de

postnatal ['pəʊst'neɪtl] ① ADJ postnatal ② COMP ► **postnatal depression** N dépression f post-partum, bébé blues* *m* ► **postnatal ward** N (service *m*) maternité f

post office ['pəʊst,ɒfɪs] N (= *place*) (bureau *m* de) poste f; (= *organization*) administration f des postes, service *m* des postes; **he works in the** ~ il travaille à la poste; **the main** ~ la grande poste; **Post Office Box No. 24** boîte postale *m* 24; (*US*) **Post Office Department** ministère *m* des Postes et Télécommunications; **he has £100 in** ~ **savings** *or* **in the Post Office Savings Bank** ≈ il a 100 livres sur son livret de caisse d'épargne (de la poste); ≈ il a 100 livres à la caisse d'épargne (de la poste); ~ **worker** employé(e) *m(f)* des postes, postier *m*, -ière f → **general**

postoperative [pəʊst'ɒprətɪv] ADJ postopératoire

postpartum [ˌpəʊst'pɑːtəm] (*frm*) ① ADJ postnatal ② COMP ► **postpartum depression** N dépression f post-partum

postpone [pəʊst'pəʊn] VT remettre à plus tard, reporter (**for** de, **until** à)

postponement [pəʊst'pəʊnmənt] N report *m*

postposition [ˌpəʊstpə'zɪʃən] N postposition f

postpositive [pəʊst'pɒzɪtɪv] ① ADJ postpositif ② N postposition f

postprandial [pəʊst'prændɪəl] ADJ (*liter or hum*) (d')après le repas

postproduction [ˌpəʊstprə'dʌkʃən] ① N travail *m* postérieur à la production ② COMP [*cost etc*] qui suit la production

postscript ['pəʊsskrɪpt] N (*to letter: abbr* PS) post-scriptum *m inv*; (*to book*) postface f; **to add sth as a** ~ ajouter qch en post-scriptum; (*fig*) **I'd like to add a ~ to what you have said** je voudrais ajouter un mot à ce que vous avez dit

poststructuralism [ˌpəʊst'strʌktʃərəlɪzəm] N poststructuralisme *m*

poststructuralist [ˌpəʊst'strʌktʃərəlɪst] ADJ, N poststructuraliste *mf*

postsynchronization [ˌpəʊst,sɪŋkrə-naɪ'zeɪʃən] N postsynchronisation f

postsynchronize [ˌpəʊst'sɪŋkrə,naɪz] VT postsynchroniser

post-Tertiary [ˌpəʊst'tɜːʃərɪ] ADJ (*Geol*) ~ **period** ère f posttertiaire

post-traumatic stress disorder [ˌpəʊst-trɔː'mætɪk'stresdɪs'ɔːdə'] N névrose f (post)traumatique

postulant ['pɒstjʊlənt] N (*Rel*) postulant(e) *m(f)*

postulate ['pɒstjʊlɪt] ① N postulat *m* ② ['pɒstjʊleɪt] VT poser comme principe; (*Philos*) postuler

postural ['pɒstjərəl] ADJ postural

posture ['pɒstʃə'] ① N posture f, position f; (*fig*) attitude f, position f; **his** ~ **is very poor** *or* **bad** ◊ **he has poor** ~ il se tient très mal; **in the** ~ **of** à la manière de ② VI (*pej*) poser, prendre des poses

posturing ['pɒstʃərɪŋ] N pose f, affectation f

postviral syndrome [ˌpəʊst,vaɪərəl-'sɪndrəʊm] N séquelles *fpl* d'une infection virale

postvocalic [pəʊstvəʊ'kælɪk] ADJ (*Phon*) postvocalique

postwar ['pəʊst'wɔː'] ADJ [*event*] de l'après-guerre; [*government, structure*] d'après-guerre; (*Brit Fin*) ~ **credits** crédits gouvernementaux résultant d'une réduction dans l'abattement fiscal pendant la seconde guerre mondiale; **the** ~ **period** ◊ **the** ~ **years** l'après-guerre *m*

postwoman ['pəʊst,wʊmən] N (*pl* **-women**) factrice f, préposée f (*Admin*)

posy ['pəʊzɪ] N petit bouquet *m* (de fleurs)

pot¹ [pɒt] ① N ⓐ (*for flowers, jam, dry goods etc*) pot *m*; (†: *for beer*) chope f; (= *piece of pottery*) poterie f; (*for cooking*) marmite f, pot† *m*; (= *saucepan*) casserole f; (*also* **teapot**) théière f; (*also* **coffeepot**) cafetière f; (= *potful*) (*of stew*) marmite f; (*of cream*) pot; (*also* **chamberpot**) pot *m* (de chambre), vase *m* de nuit; **jam** ~ pot *m* à confiture; ~ **of jam** pot *m* de confiture; ~**s and pans** casseroles *fpl*, batterie f de cuisine; (*making tea*) **... and one for the** ~ ... et une cuillerée pour la théière ■ (*PROV*) **it's the** ~ **calling the kettle black** c'est la paille et la poutre; (*fig*) **he can just keep the** ~ **boiling** il arrive tout juste à faire bouillir la marmite, il arrive à peine à joindre les deux bouts; (*in game etc*) **keep the** ~ **boiling!** allez-y!, à votre tour! → **flowerpot**
ⓑ (* *fig*) (= *prize*) coupe f; (= *large stomach*) brioche* f, bedaine* f; (*esp US* = *kitty*) cagnotte f; **to have** ~**s of money*** avoir un argent fou, rouler sur l'or; **to go/be to** ~* aller/être à vau-l'eau
ⓒ (*Billiards, Snooker*) **what a** ~! quel coup!; **if he sinks this** ~ **he's won** s'il met cette boule, il a gagné; (*fig*) **to take a** ~ **at sb*** (= *criticize*) chercher des crosses à qn*; (*Ftbl*) **to take a** ~ **at goal*** tirer au but

② VT ⓐ [+ *plant, jam etc*] mettre en pot → **potted**
ⓑ (*Billiards, Snooker*) mettre
ⓒ (* = *shoot*) [+ *duck, pheasant*] abattre, descendre*

③ VI ⓐ (= *make pottery*) faire de la poterie
ⓑ (= *shoot*) **to** ~ **at sth*** tirer qch, canarder qch

4 COMP ► **pot-bound** ADJ **this plant is ~ bound** cette plante est (trop) à l'étroit dans son pot ► **pot cheese** N (US) ≈ fromage m blanc (égoutté or maigre) ► **pot luck** N (fig) **to take ~ luck** (gen) s'en remettre au hasard ; (at meal) manger à la fortune du pot ► **pot plant** N (Brit) = **potted plant** ; → **potted** ► **pot roast** (Culin) N rôti m braisé, rôti m à la cocotte ► **pot-roast** VT faire braiser, faire cuire à la cocotte ► **pot scourer, pot scrubber** N tampon m à récurer ► **potting compost** N terreau m ► **potting shed** N abri m de jardin ► **pot-trained** ADJ [child] propre

pot²: [pɒt] N (= cannabis) marijuana f, herbe f ; (= hashish) hasch* m

potable ['pəʊtəbl] ADJ potable (lit)

potash ['pɒtæʃ] N (carbonate m de) potasse f

potassium [pə'tæsɪəm] **1** N potassium m **2** COMP de potassium

potation [pəʊ'teɪʃən] N (gen pl: frm) libation f

potato [pə'teɪtəʊ] (pl **potatoes**) **1** N pomme f de terre ; **is there any ~ left?** est-ce qu'il reste des pommes de terre ? ; (esp US fig) **it's small ~es*** c'est de la petite bière* → **fry³, hot, mash, sweet 2** COMP [field, salad, soup] de terre ► **potato beetle** N doryphore m ► **potato blight** N maladie f des pommes de terre ► **potato bug** N = **potato beetle** ► **potato cake** N croquette f de pommes de terre ► **potato chips** NPL (US) = **potato crisps** ► **potato crisps** NPL (Brit) chips fpl ► **potato-masher** N presse-purée m inv ► **potato omelette** N omelette f aux pommes de terre or Parmentier ► **potato-peeler** N économe m, épluche-légumes m inv ► **potato topping** N **with a ~ topping** recouvert de pommes de terre au gratin

potbellied [,pɒt'belɪd] ADJ (from overeating) ventru, bedonnant* ; (from malnutrition) au ventre ballonné ; [vase, stove] ventru, renflé

potbelly [,pɒt'belɪ] N (from overeating) gros ventre m, bedaine* f ; (from malnutrition) ventre m ballonné

potboiler ['pɒt,bɔɪlər] N (fig pej) œuvre f alimentaire

poteen [pɒ'tiːn, pə'tʃiːn] N whisky m (illicite)

potency ['pəʊtənsɪ] N (pl **potencies** or **potences** ['pəʊtənsɪz]) **a** [of remedy, drug, charm, argument] puissance f, force f ; [of drink] forte teneur f en alcool **b** [of male] virilité f

potent ['pəʊtənt] ADJ **a** [remedy, drug, charm] puissant ; [drink] fort ; [argument, reason] convaincant **b** [male] viril

potentate ['pəʊtənteɪt] N potentat m

potential [pəʊ'tenʃəl] **1** ADJ [buyer, investor, market, energy, resources] potentiel ; [sales, uses] possible, éventuel ; [earnings] éventuel ; [success, danger, enemy] potentiel, en puissance ; [meaning, value] virtuel ; (Gram) potentiel ; **he is a ~ prime minister** c'est un premier ministre en puissance

2 N (NonC) **a** (Elec, Gram, Math, Phys etc) potentiel m ; **military ~** potentiel m militaire ; **the destructive ~ of conventional weapons** le potentiel de destruction des armes conventionnelles

b (fig = promise, possibilities) possibilités fpl ; **to have ~** [person, company, business] être prometteur ; [scheme, plan, job] être prometteur, offrir toutes sortes de possibilités ; [building, land, area] offrir toutes sortes de possibilités ; **to have management ~** avoir les qualités requises pour devenir cadre supérieur ; **area with ~ as ...** zone f convertible or aménageable en ... ; **to have the ~ to do sth** être tout à fait capable de faire qch ; **he's got ~ as a footballer** il a de l'avenir en tant que footballeur, c'est un footballeur prometteur ; (Scol) **he's got ~ in maths** il a des aptitudes en maths ; **to have great ~** être très prometteur, promettre beaucoup ; **he hasn't yet realized his full ~** il

n'a pas encore donné toute sa mesure ; **to have no ~ for sth** ne pas avoir les capacités requises pour qch ; **our ~ for increasing production** les possibilités que nous avons d'augmenter la production

potentiality [pəʊ,tenʃɪ'ælɪtɪ] N potentialité f ; **potentialities = potential 2b**

potentially [pəʊ'tenʃəlɪ] ADV [dangerous, lethal, carcinogenic, serious] potentiellement ; **~ important/useful/lucrative** qui peut être or s'avérer important/utile/rentable ; **the sea level is rising, with ~ disastrous consequences** le niveau de la mer monte, ce qui pourrait avoir des conséquences désastreuses ; **it was a ~ violent confrontation** il s'agissait d'une confrontation qui pouvait prendre un tour violent or devenir violente ; **it's ~ a rich country** c'est un pays qui pourrait devenir riche ; **~, these problems are very serious** ces problèmes pourraient devenir très sérieux

potful ['pɒtfʊl] N [of rice, stew] casserole f ; [of jam] pot m

pothead†: ['pɒthed] N drogué(e) m(f) à la marijuana (or au hasch*)

pother* ['pɒðər] N (NonC) **a** (= fuss) agitation f ; (= noise) vacarme m, tapage m

potherbs ['pɒthɜːbz] NPL herbes fpl potagères

pothole ['pɒthəʊl] N **a** (in road) nid-de-poule m **b** (under ground) caverne f ; (larger) grotte f

potholed ['pɒthəʊld] ADJ plein de nids-de-poule

potholer ['pɒt,həʊlər] N (Brit) spéléologue mf

potholing ['pɒt,həʊlɪŋ] N (Brit) spéléologie f, spéléo* f ; **to go ~** faire de la spéléologie

pothook ['pɒthʊk] N (lit) crémaillère f ; (in handwriting) boucle f

pothunter* ['pɒt,hʌntər] N chasseur m acharné de trophées

potion ['pəʊʃən] N (= medicine) potion f ; (= magic drink) philtre m, breuvage m magique ; **love ~** philtre m (d'amour)

potlatch ['pɒtlætʃ] N (US) fête f où l'on échange des cadeaux

potpie ['pɒtpaɪ] N (US) tourte f à la viande

potpourri [pəʊ'pʊrɪ] N (pl **potpourris**) [of flowers] fleurs fpl séchées ; (fig, Literat, Mus) pot-pourri m

potsherd ['pɒtʃɜːd] N (Archeol) tesson m (de poterie)

potshot* ['pɒtʃɒt] N (with gun, missile) tir m au jugé ; (fig = criticism) attaque f, critique f ; **to take a ~ at sth** tirer sur qch au jugé

potted ['pɒtɪd] ADJ **a** (Culin) ~ **meat** rillettes de viande ; **~ shrimps** crevettes conservées dans du beurre fondu ; **~ plant** plante f verte, plante f d'appartement **b*** (fig) **a ~ version of "Ivanhoe"** un abrégé or une version abrégée d'« Ivanhoé » ; **he gave me a ~ lesson in car maintenance** il m'a donné un cours rapide sur l'entretien des voitures

potter¹ ['pɒtər] VI (esp Brit) mener sa petite vie tranquille, bricoler* ; **to ~ round the house** suivre son petit train-train* or faire des petits travaux dans la maison ; **to ~ round the shops** faire les magasins sans se presser

► **potter about** VI suivre son petit train-train*, bricoler*

► **potter along** VI aller son petit bonhomme de chemin, poursuivre sa route sans se presser ; **we ~ along** nous continuons notre train-train*

► **potter around** VI = **potter about**

potter² ['pɒtər] **1** N potier m, -ière f **2** COMP ► **potter's clay, potter's earth** N argile f or terre f de potier ► **potter's field** N (US = cemetery) cimetière m des pauvres ► **potter's wheel** N tour m de potier

pottery ['pɒtərɪ] **1** N **a** (NonC) (= craft, occupation) poterie f ; (= objects) poteries fpl ; (glazed) faïencerie f (NonC) ; (= ceramics) céra-

miques fpl ; **a piece of ~** une poterie ; **Etruscan ~** poterie(s) f(pl) étrusque(s) **b** (= place) poterie f ; (Brit Geog) **the Potteries** la région des Poteries (dans le Staffordshire) **2** COMP [jug, dish] de or en terre ; (ceramic) de or en céramique ; (glazed) de or en faïence

potty¹* ['pɒtɪ] **1** N pot m (de bébé) **2** COMP ► **potty-train** VT apprendre la propreté à ► **potty-trained** ADJ propre ► **potty-training** N apprentissage m de la propreté

potty²* ['pɒtɪ] ADJ (Brit) **a** [person] toqué*, dingue* ; [idea] farfelu ; **to be ~ about sb/sth** être toqué* de qn/qch ; **to go ~*** perdre la boule* **b** (slightly pej) **a ~ little house** une maison de rien du tout

pouch [paʊtʃ] N petit sac m ; (for money) bourse f ; (for ammunition) étui m ; (for cartridges) giberne f ; (for tobacco) blague f ; (US Diplomacy) valise f (diplomatique) ; [of kangaroo etc] poche f (ventrale) ; (under eye) poche f

pouf(fe) [puːf] N **a** (= stool) pouf m **b** (Brit:) = poof

poulterer ['pəʊltərər] N marchand(e) m(f) de volailles, volailler m, -ère f

poultice ['pəʊltɪs] **1** N cataplasme m **2** VT mettre un cataplasme à

poultry ['pəʊltrɪ] **1** N (NonC) volaille f (NonC), volailles fpl **2** COMP ► **poultry dealer** N volailler m ► **poultry farm** N élevage m de volaille(s) ► **poultry farmer** N volailleur m, -euse f, aviculteur m, -trice f ► **poultry farming** N (NonC) élevage m de volaille(s), aviculture f

pounce [paʊns] **1** N bond m, attaque f subite **2** VI bondir, sauter ; (also fig) **to ~ on** [+ prey etc] bondir sur, sauter sur ; [+ book, small object] se précipiter sur ; (fig) [+ idea, suggestion] sauter sur

pound¹ [paʊnd] **1** N **a** (= weight) livre f (= 453,6 grammes) ; **sold by the ~** vendu à la livre ; **$3 a ~** 3 dollars la livre ; (fig) **to demand one's ~ of flesh** exiger son dû impitoyablement → IMPERIAL SYSTEM **b** (= money) livre f ; **~ sterling** livre f sterling ; **ten ~s sterling** dix livres fpl sterling → **penny 2** COMP ► **pound cake** N quatre-quarts m inv ► **pound coin** N pièce f d'une livre ► **pound note** N billet m d'une livre

pound² [paʊnd] **1** VT [+ drugs, spices, nuts, rice etc] piler ; [+ meat] attendrir ; [+ dough] pétrir vigoureusement ; [+ rocks] concasser ; [+ earth, paving slabs] pilonner ; [guns, bombs, shells] pilonner ; **to ~ sth to a pulp** réduire or mettre qch en bouillie ; **to ~ sth to a powder** pulvériser qch, réduire or mettre qch en poudre ; **the ship was ~ed by huge waves** d'énormes vagues battaient contre le navire ; **to ~ sth with one's fists** marteler qch à coups de poing ; **he was ~ing the piano/typewriter** il tapait comme un sourd sur son piano/sa machine à écrire ; **to ~ the beat** [policeman] faire sa ronde ; (fig = be ordinary policeman) être simple agent

2 VI **a** [heart] battre fort ; (with fear, excitement) battre la chamade ; [sea, waves] battre **(on, against** contre) ; **he ~ed at** or **on the door** il martela à (à coups de poing), il frappa de grands coups à la porte ; **he ~ed on the table** il donna de grands coups sur la table, il frappa du poing sur la table ; **the drums were ~ing** les tambours battaient, on entendait battre le tambour

b (= move heavily) **to ~ in/out** etc (heavily) entrer/sortir etc à pas lourds ; (at a run) entrer/sortir etc en courant bruyamment ; **he was ~ing up and down his room** il arpentait sa chambre à pas lourds

► **pound away** VI **he was ~ing away at the piano/at** or **on the typewriter** il a tapé comme un sourd sur son piano/sa machine à écrire

► **pound down** VT SEP [+ drugs, spices, nuts] piler ; [+ rocks] concasser ; [+ earth, paving slabs] pilonner ; **to ~ sth down to a pulp** réduire or mettre qch en bouillie ; **to ~ sth down to a**

powder pulvériser qch, réduire or mettre qch en poudre
► **pound out** VT SEP **to ~ out a tune on the piano** marteler un air au piano; **to ~ out a letter on the typewriter** taper comme un sourd sur sa machine à écrire pour écrire une lettre
► **pound up** VT SEP [+ *drugs, spices, nuts*] piler; [+ *rocks*] concasser; [+ *earth, paving slabs*] pilonner

pound³ [paʊnd] N (*for dogs, cars*) fourrière *f*

poundage ['paʊndɪdʒ] N **a** (= *tax, commission*) impôt *m*/commission *f* de tant par livre (*sterling ou de poids*) **b** (= *weight*) poids *m* (en livres)

-pounder ['paʊndər] N (*in compounds*) **thirty-pounder** (= *gun*) pièce *f* or canon *m* de trente; **seven-pounder** (= *baby/fish*) bébé *m*/poisson *m* de 3,2 kg

pounding ['paʊndɪŋ] **1** ADJ [*heart*] (*gen*) battant à tout rompre; (*with fear, excitement*) battant la chamade; [*waves, surf*] d'une violence inouïe; **he could hear the sound of ~ hooves/feet/drums/artillery** il entendait le martèlement des sabots/des talons/des tambours/de l'artillerie; **with ~ heart** le cœur battant à tout rompre; **a ~ headache** un violent mal de tête
2 N **a** [*of heart, waves, surf*] battement *m*; [*of feet, hooves, drums*] martèlement *m*; [*of guns*] pilonnage *m*, martèlement *m*
b (*esp Brit*) **to take a ~** [*person*] en prendre pour son grade; **the city took a real ~ in the war/in the storm** la guerre/la tempête a fait des ravages dans cette ville; **the forwards often take a ~ in the scrum** les avants prennent souvent des coups dans la mêlée; **Manchester United took a real ~ from Liverpool** Manchester United s'est fait battre à plate couture par Liverpool or a pris une déculottée* contre Liverpool; **the Socialists took a terrible ~ in the last election** les socialistes se sont fait battre à plate couture lors des dernières élections; **the Conservatives have been taking a ~ from the press** les conservateurs se sont fait éreinter par la presse

pour [pɔːr] **1** VT [+ *liquid*] verser; **she ~ed him a cup of tea** elle lui a versé or servi une tasse de thé; **~ yourself some tea** prenez du thé, servez-vous or versez-vous du thé; **shall I ~ the tea?** je sers le thé?; **he ~ed me a drink** il m'a versé or servi à boire; **she ~ed the salt into the salt cellar** elle a versé le sel dans la salière; **she ~ed the water off the carrots** elle a vidé l'eau des carottes; **to ~ metal/wax into a mould** couler du métal/de la cire; (*fig*) **to ~ money into a scheme** investir énormément d'argent dans un projet; **to ~ scorn on sb/sth** dénigrer qn/qch; **she looked as if she had been ~ed into her dress** elle semblait moulée dans sa robe; (*US fig*) **to ~ it on*** y mettre le paquet*, foncer* → **oil**
2 VI **a** [*water, blood etc*] couler à flots (**from** de); **water came ~ing into the room** l'eau entra à flots dans la pièce; **water was ~ing down the walls** l'eau ruisselait le long des murs; **smoke was ~ing from the window** des nuages de fumée sortaient par la fenêtre; **sunshine ~ed into the room** le soleil entrait à flots dans la pièce; **the sweat ~ed off him** il ruisselait de sueur; **goods are ~ing out of the factories** les usines déversent des quantités de marchandises
b **it is ~ing (with rain)*** il pleut à verse; **it ~ed for four days** il n'a pas arrêté de pleuvoir à torrents pendant quatre jours → **rain**
c [*people, cars, animals*] affluer; **to ~ in/out** entrer/sortir en grand nombre or en masse; **refugees ~ed into the country** les réfugiés affluaient dans le pays; **cars ~ed off the ferry** un flot de voitures sortait du ferry; **complaints came ~ing in from all over the country** des plaintes affluaient de tout le pays
d [*jug, teapot*] verser; **this teapot doesn't ~**

very well cette théière ne verse pas très bien
e [*person*] servir; **shall I ~?** je vous sers?
f (*US = act as hostess*) jouer le rôle de maîtresse de maison
► **pour away** VT SEP [+ *dregs etc*] vider
► **pour down** VI **the rain** or **it was ~ing down** il pleuvait à verse or à flots or à torrents
► **pour forth** VT SEP = **pour out 2b**
► **pour in** **1** VI [*water, sunshine, rain*] entrer (à flots); [*people*] affluer; [*cars, animals*] arriver de toutes parts or en masse; **complaints/letters ~ed in** il y a eu un déluge or une avalanche de réclamations/de lettres **2** VT SEP [+ *liquid*] verser; (*fig*) **they ~ed in capital** ils y ont investi d'énormes capitaux
► **pour off** VT SEP [+ *liquid*] vider
► **pour out** **1** VI [*water*] sortir à flots; [*people, cars, animals*] sortir en masse; **the words came ~ing out** ce fut une cascade or un flot de paroles **2** VT SEP **a** [+ *tea, coffee, drinks*] verser, servir (**for sb** à qn); [+ *dregs, unwanted liquid*] vider; **the factory ~s out hundreds of cars a day** l'usine sort des centaines de voitures chaque jour **b** (*fig*) [+ *anger, emotion*] donner libre cours à; [+ *troubles*] épancher; [+ *complaint*] déverser; **to ~ out one's heart to sb** s'épancher avec or auprès de qn; **he ~ed out his story to me** il m'a raconté or sorti* toute son histoire

pouring ['pɔːrɪŋ] ADJ **a** (*also* **of ~ consistency**: *sauce etc*) liquide **b** (**in**) **the ~ rain** (sous) la pluie torrentielle or battante

pout [paʊt] **1** N moue *f*; **... she said with a ~** ... dit-elle en faisant la moue **2** VI faire la moue **3** VT **to ~ one's lips** faire la moue; **"no" she ~ed** « non » dit-elle en faisant la moue

poverty ['pɒvətɪ] N **a** (*lit*) pauvreté *f*; **to live in ~** vivre dans le besoin or dans la gêne; **to live in extreme ~** vivre dans une misère extrême **b** (*fig*) [*of ideas, information*] déficit *m*; **~ of resources** insuffisance *f* de ressources **2** COMP ► **poverty level, poverty line** N **at/below/above ~ level** or **the ~ line** au-dessous or au dessus du/au-dessus du seuil de pauvreté ► **poverty-stricken** ADJ (*lit*) [*person, family*] dans le dénuement; [*district*] miséreux; [*conditions*] misérable; (= *hard up*) **I'm ~-stricken** je suis fauché* (comme les blés), je suis sans le sou ► **the poverty trap** N (*Brit*) cercle vicieux auquel sont confrontés les bénéficiaires d'allocations de chômage ou d'insertion qui ne peuvent travailler, même de manière temporaire, sans perdre leurs droits

POW [ˌpiːəʊˈdʌbljuː] (*Mil*) (ABBR = **prisoner of war**) → **prisoner**

pow* [paʊ] EXCL bang*

powder ['paʊdər] **1** N **a** (= *particles*) poudre *f*; (*Culin*) **milk ~** lait *m* en poudre; **in the form of a ~** ◊ **in ~ form** en poudre; **to reduce sth to a ~** pulvériser qch, réduire qch en poudre; (*fig*) **to keep one's ~ dry** être paré; (*US*) **to take a ~** prendre la poudre d'escampette*, décamper* → **baking, face, talc**
b (= *fine snow*) poudreuse *f*
2 VT **a** [+ *chalk, rocks*] réduire en poudre, pulvériser; [+ *milk, eggs*] réduire en poudre; **~ed milk** lait *m* en poudre
b [+ *face, body*] poudrer; **to ~ one's nose** (*lit*) se mettre de la poudre; (* *euph*) (aller) se refaire une beauté (*euph*); **trees ~ed with snow** arbres *mpl* saupoudrés de neige
3 COMP ► **powder blue** N bleu *m* pastel *inv* ► **powder-blue** ADJ bleu pastel *inv*; **~-blue dress** robe *f* bleu pastel ► **powder burn** N brûlure *f* (superficielle) causée par la poudre ► **powder compact** N poudrier *m* ► **powdered sugar** N (*US*) sucre *m* glace ► **powder keg** N (*lit*) baril *m* de poudre; (*fig*) poudrière *f*; **the Prime Minister is sitting on a ~ keg** le Premier ministre est sur une poudrière ► **powder magazine** N poudrière *f* ► **powder puff** N houppette *f*; (*big, fluffy*)

houppe *f* ► **powder room** N (*euph*) toilettes *fpl* (pour dames)

powdering ['paʊdərɪŋ] N **a ~ of snow** une mince pellicule de neige; **a ~ of sugar** un saupoudrage de sucre

powdery ['paʊdərɪ] ADJ **a** (*in consistency*) [*substance, snow*] poudreux; [*stone*] friable **b** (= *covered with powder*) [*surface*] couvert de poudre

power ['paʊər] **1** N **a** (= *ability, capacity*) pouvoir *m*, capacité *f*; (= *faculty*) faculté *f*; **it is not (with)in my ~ to help you** il n'est pas en mon pouvoir de vous aider; **he did everything** or **all in his ~ to help us** il a fait tout son possible or tout ce qui était en son pouvoir pour nous aider; **it is quite beyond her ~ to save him** il n'est pas en son pouvoir de le sauver, elle est tout à fait impuissante à le sauver; **the ~ of hearing/movement** la faculté d'entendre/de se mouvoir; **he lost the ~ of speech** il a perdu (l'usage de) la parole; **mental ~s** facultés *fpl* mentales; **the body's recuperative ~** la puissance de récupération de l'organisme, la capacité régénératrice du corps; **his ~s of resistance** sa capacité de résistance; **his ~s of persuasion** son pouvoir or sa force de persuasion; **his ~s of imagination** sa faculté d'imagination; **earning ~** (niveau *m* de) rémunération *f*; **purchasing** or **spending ~** pouvoir *m* d'achat → **1c; height**
b (= *force*) [*of person, blow, sun, explosion*] puissance *f*, force *f*; (*Ling: of grammar*) puissance *f*; **the ~ of love/thought** la force de l'amour/de la pensée; **sea/air ~** puissance *f* navale/aérienne; **more ~ to your elbow!** tous mes vœux de réussite!
c (= *authority*) pouvoir *m* (*also Pol*), autorité *f*; **the ~ of the President/the police/the army** l'autorité *f* or le pouvoir du Président/de la police/de l'armée; **student/pupil etc ~** le pouvoir des étudiants/lycéens etc; **he has the ~ to act** il a le pouvoir d'agir; **they have no ~ in economic matters** ils n'ont aucune autorité en matière économique; **that does not fall within my ~(s)** ◊ **that is beyond** or **outside my ~(s)** ceci n'est pas or ne relève pas de ma compétence; **he exceeded his ~s** il a outrepassé or excédé ses pouvoirs; **at the height of his ~** à l'apogée de son pouvoir; **to have the ~ of life and death over sb** avoir droit de vie et de mort sur qn; **to have ~ over sb** avoir autorité sur qn; **to have sb in one's ~** avoir qn en son pouvoir; **to fall under sb's ~** tomber sous l'emprise de qn; (*Pol*) **in ~** au pouvoir; **Labour was in ~ at the time** le parti travailliste était alors au pouvoir; **to come to ~** accéder au pouvoir → **absolute, attorney, veto**
d (*fig*) **they are the real ~ in the government** ce sont eux qui détiennent le pouvoir réel dans le gouvernement; **he is a ~ in the university** il est très influent à l'université; **he is a ~ in the land** c'est un homme très puissant or très influent; **the ~ behind the throne** l'éminence *f* grise, celui (*or* celle) qui tire les ficelles; **the Church is no longer the ~ it was** l'Église n'est plus la puissance qu'elle était or n'a plus le pouvoir qu'elle avait; **the ~s that be** les autorités *fpl* constituées → **above, darkness, evil**
e (= *nation*) puissance *f*; **the nuclear/world ~s** les puissances *fpl* nucléaires/mondiales; **one of the great naval ~s** une des grandes puissances navales
f [*of engine, telescope etc*] puissance *f*; (*Elec, Phys, Tech etc*) puissance *f*, force *f*; (= *energy*) énergie *f*; (= *output*) rendement *m*; (= *electricity*) électricité *f*, courant *m*; **nuclear ~** l'énergie *f* nucléaire; (*Elec*) **they cut off the ~** ils ont coupé le courant; (*Elec*) **our consumption of ~ has risen** notre consommation d'électricité a augmenté; **a cheap source of ~** une source d'énergie bon marché; **a low-~ microscope** un microscope de faible puissance; **magnifying ~** grossissement *m*; **engines at half ~** mo-

teurs *mpl* à mi-régime ; **the ship returned to port under her own** ~ le navire est rentré au port par ses propres moyens ; **microwave on full** ~ **for a minute** faites chauffer au micro-ondes à puissance maximale pendant une minute → **horsepower, wind**[1]

[g] **a** ~ **of*** (= *a lot of*) un tas* de, énormément de ; **it did me a** ~ **of good** ça m'a fait un bien immense, ça m'a rudement* fait du bien ; **he made a** ~ **of money** il a gagné un argent fou

[h] (*Math*) puissance *f* ; **five to the** ~ **of three** cinq puissance trois ; **to the nth** ~ (à la) puissance n

[2] VT faire marcher, faire fonctionner ; ~**ed by nuclear energy** qui marche *or* fonctionne à l'énergie nucléaire ; ~**ed by jet engines** propulsé par des moteurs à réaction

[3] COMP [*saw, loom, lathe*] mécanique ; (*Aut*) [*brakes*] assisté ; (*Ind*) [*strike, dispute*] des travailleurs des centrales électriques ► **power-assisted** ADJ (*Aut*) assisté ► **power base** N (*Pol*) réseau *m* d'influence, support *m* politique ► **power broker** N (*Pol*) éminence *f* grise ► **power cable** N (*Elec*) câble *m* électrique ► **power cut** N (*Brit Elec*) coupure *f* de courant ► **power dive** N (*Aviat*) descente *f* en piqué ► **power dressing** N tenue élégante, sobre et sévère adoptée par certaines femmes cadres ► **power-driven** ADJ à moteur ; (*Elec*) électrique ► **power elite** N élite *f* au pouvoir ► **power failure** N (*Elec*) panne *f* de courant ► **power game** N (*Brit*) lutte *f* pour le pouvoir, jeu *m* de pouvoir ► **power lifting** N (*Sport*) power-lifting *m* ► **power line** N (*Elec*) ligne *f* à haute tension ► **power lunch** N déjeuner *m* d'affaires ► **power pack** N (*Elec*) bloc *m* d'alimentation ► **power plant** N (= *building*) centrale *f* (électrique) ; (*in vehicle etc*) groupe *m* moteur ► **power play** N (*Ice Hockey*) attaque *f* en force ; (*fig*) (= *attack*) attaque *f* en force ; (= *struggle*) épreuve *f* de force ► **power point** N (*Brit Elec*) prise *f* de courant ► **power politics** N politique *f* de coercition ► **power sharing** N (*Pol*) le partage du pouvoir ► **power station** N (*Elec*) centrale *f* (électrique) ► **power steering** N (*Aut*) direction *f* assistée ► **power structure** N (*Pol*) (= *way power is held*) répartition *f* des pouvoirs ; (= *those with power*) détenteurs *mpl* du pouvoir ► **power struggle** N lutte *f* pour le pouvoir ► **power supply** N (*Elec*) alimentation *f* électrique ► **power surge** N (*Elec*) surtension *f*, survoltage *m* ► **power tool** N outil *m* électrique ► **power workers** NPL (*Ind*) travailleurs *mpl* des centrales électriques

powerboat ['paʊəbəʊt] [1] N hors-bord *m inv*, (bateau *m*) offshore *m* [2] COMP ► **powerboat racing** N (*course*) offshore *m*

-powered ['paʊəd] ADJ (*in compounds*) **nuclear-powered** qui marche *or* fonctionne à l'énergie nucléaire → **high**

powerful ['paʊəfʊl] ADJ [*engine, machine, computer*] puissant ; [*kick, blow*] fort, violent ; [*person, build, smell*] fort ; [*influence, effect*] profond ; [*description, portrayal, performance*] (très) fort ; [*argument*] convaincant ; **I find his argument very** ~ je trouve son argument très convaincant ; **he gave a** ~ **performance as Hamlet** il a interprété le rôle de Hamlet avec force ; **a** ~ **earthquake** un violent tremblement de terre ; **a** ~ **lot of*** un tas de*, beaucoup de

powerfully ['paʊəfəlɪ] ADV [*hit, strike*] avec force ; [*affect*] fortement ; [*influence*] profondément ; [*erotic, evocative*] profondément ; **the room smelt** ~ **of cats** une forte odeur de chat régnait dans la pièce ; **to write** ~ écrire dans un style puissant *or* incisif ; **to argue** ~ **(for new legislation)** avancer des arguments percutants (en faveur d'une nouvelle législation) ; ~ **built** solidement charpenté, qui a une forte carrure ; ~ **addictive** à fort effet d'accoutumance

powerhouse ['paʊəhaʊs] N [a] (*lit*) centrale *f* électrique [b] (*fig*) personne *f* (*or* groupe *m*) très dynamique ; **a** ~ **of new ideas** une mine d'idées nouvelles

powerless ['paʊəlɪs] ADJ impuissant (**against** contre) ; **the government is** ~ **in the face of recession** le gouvernement est impuissant face à la récession ; **he is** ~ **to help you** il ne peut rien faire pour vous aider, il est impuissant à vous aider

powerlessly ['paʊəlɪslɪ] ADV **I looked on** ~ j'ai assisté au spectacle, impuissant *or* sans pouvoir rien faire

powerlessness ['paʊəlɪsnɪs] N impuissance *f*

powwow ['paʊwaʊ] [1] N assemblée *f* (*des Indiens d'Amérique*) ; (* *fig*) tête-à-tête *m inv* [2] VI (* *fig*) s'entretenir, palabrer (*pej*)

pox [pɒks] N (†: *gen*) variole *f*, petite vérole *f* ; (= *syphilis*) the ~* la vérole* ; **a** ~ **on** ...!† maudit soit ...! → **chickenpox, cowpox**

poxy: ['pɒksɪ] ADJ (*Brit*) merdique:

pp[1] [piː'piː] (ABBR = **per procurationem**) (= *by proxy*) [1] PREP p.p. [2] VT **to pp a letter (for sb)** signer une lettre pour qn

pp[2] [a] (ABBR = **parcel post**) → **parcel** [b] (ABBR = **post paid**) → **post**

PPE ['piː'piː'iː] (*Univ*) (ABBR = **philosophy, politics and economics**) philosophie, sciences politiques et économie *fpl*

ppm (ABBR = **parts per million**) → **part**

PPS ['piː'piː'es] [1] N [a] (*Brit Parl*) (ABBR = **Parliamentary Private Secretary**) ~ **parliamentary** [b] (ABBR = **post postscriptum**) PPS *m*

PQ (*Can Post*) ABBR = **Province of Quebec**

PR[1] [piː'ɑːr] N (ABBR = **public relations**) → **public**

PR[2] ABBR = **Puerto Rico**

PR[3] [piː'ɑːr] N (ABBR = **proportional representation**) RP *f*

Pr. ABBR = **Prince**

practicability [ˌpræktɪkə'bɪlɪtɪ] N [*of road, path*] praticabilité *f* ; [*of suggestion*] praticabilité *f*, possibilité *f* de réalisation ; **to question the** ~ **of a scheme** mettre en doute la possibilité de réaliser un projet

practicable ['præktɪkəbl] ADJ [*scheme, solution, suggestion*] praticable, réalisable ; [*road*] praticable

practical ['præktɪkəl] [1] ADJ [a] (= *concrete, not theoretical*) [*suggestion*] concret (-ète *f*) ; **a** ~ **way of ...** un moyen concret de ... ; **to be of no** ~ **use** n'avoir aucun intérêt pratique ; **for (all)** ~ **purposes** en pratique ; **to become** ~ [*scheme, idea etc*] devenir réalisable [b] (= *down-to-earth*) [*person*] pragmatique ; **to be** ~ avoir le sens pratique *or* le sens des réalités [c] (= *functional, appropriate*) [*clothes, shoes, gadget*] pratique [d] (= *near*) **it's a** ~ **certainty** c'est une quasi-certitude [2] (= *exam*) épreuve *f* pratique ; (= *lesson*) travaux *mpl* pratiques [3] COMP ► **practical joke** N farce *f* ► **practical joker** N farceur *m*, -euse *f* ► **practical nurse** N (*US*) infirmier *m*, -ière *f* auxiliaire, aide-soignant(e) *m(f)*

practicality [ˌpræktɪ'kælɪtɪ] [1] N (*NonC*) [*of person*] sens *m* *or* esprit *m* pratique ; [*of suggestion*] aspect *m* pratique ; **I doubt the** ~ **of this scheme** je doute de la faisabilité de ce projet, je doute que ce projet soit réalisable (d'un point de vue pratique) ; **they are worried about the** ~ **of building the system** ils craignent que ce système ne soit pas réalisable sur le plan pratique [2] **practicalities** NPL détails *mpl* pratiques

practically ['præktɪklɪ] ADV [a] (= *almost*) pratiquement [b] (= *from a practical point of view*) pratiquement, d'un point de vue pratique ; ~ **speaking** (= *in practice*) pour parler concrètement, en pratique [c] (= *in a practical way*) [*say, ask, suggest*] avec pragmatisme ; [*help*] sur le plan *or* d'un point de vue pratique ; **let's think** ~ soyons pratiques, faisons preuve de

sens pratique ; **he's very** ~ **minded** ◊ **he thinks very** ~ il a vraiment l'esprit *or* le sens pratique

practicalness ['præktɪkəlnɪs] N = **practicality 1**

practice ['præktɪs] [1] N [a] (= *habits, usage*) pratique *f*, usage *m* ; **to make a** ~ **of doing sth** ◊ **to make it a** ~ **to do sth** avoir l'habitude *or* se faire une habitude de faire qch ; **it is not my** ~ **to do so** il n'est pas dans mes habitudes de faire ainsi ; **it's common** ~ c'est courant ; **as is common** ~ ◊ **as is the** ~ comme il est d'usage → **restrictive, sharp** [b] (= *exercises*) exercices *mpl* ; (= *training*) entraînement *m* ; (= *experience*) expérience *f* ; (= *rehearsal*) répétition *f* ; **I need more** ~ je manque d'entraînement, je ne me suis pas assez exercé ; **he does six hours' piano** ~ **a day** il s'exerce au piano six heures par jour, il fait six heures de piano par jour ; **she's had lots of** ~ elle a de l'expérience ; **it takes years of** ~ il faut de longues années d'expérience ; **out of** ~ rouillé (*fig*) ; **with** ~ avec de l'entraînement ■ (*PROV*) ~ **makes perfect** c'est en forgeant qu'on devient forgeron (*PROV*) → **target** [c] (*NonC: as opposed to theory*) pratique *f* ; **in** ~ dans la pratique ; **to put sth into** ~ mettre qch en pratique [d] (= *profession: of law, medicine etc*) exercice *m* ; (= *business, clients*) clientèle *f*, cabinet *m* ; **to go into** ~ *or* **to set up in** ~ **as a doctor/lawyer** s'installer *or* s'établir docteur/avocat ; **he is in** ~ **in Valence** il exerce à Valence ; **he has a large** ~ il a une nombreuse clientèle, il a un cabinet important → **general** [2] VTI (*US*) = **practise** [3] COMP [*flight, run*] d'entraînement ► **practice exam** N examen *m* blanc ► **practice teacher** N (*US Scol*) professeur *m* stagiaire ; (*in primary school*) instituteur *m*, -trice *f* stagiaire ► **practice test** N = **practice exam**

practise, practice (*US*) ['præktɪs] [1] VT [a] (= *put into practice*) [+ *restraint, kindness, charity, technique, meditation, one's religion*] pratiquer ; [+ *method*] employer, appliquer ; **to** ~ **torture on sb** faire subir *or* infliger des tortures à qn ; **to** ~ **cruelty on sb** faire preuve de cruauté envers *or* à l'égard de qn ; **to** ~ **what one preaches** prêcher par l'exemple *or* d'exemple ; **to** ~ **medicine/law** exercer la médecine *or* la profession de médecin/la profession d'avocat [b] (= *exercise in*) [+ *sport*] s'entraîner à ; [+ *violin etc*] s'exercer à, travailler ; [+ *song, chorus, recitation*] travailler ; **she was practising her scales** elle faisait ses gammes ; **I need to** ~ **my backhand** j'ai besoin de travailler mon revers ; **to** ~ **doing sth** s'entraîner *or* s'exercer à faire qch ; **I'm going to** ~ **my German on him** je vais m'exercer à parler allemand avec lui → **practised**

[2] VI [a] (*Mus*) s'exercer ; (*Sport*) s'entraîner ; [*beginner*] faire des exercices ; **to** ~ **on the piano** s'exercer au piano, travailler le piano ; **he** ~**s for two hours every day** il fait deux heures d'entraînement *or* d'exercices par jour [b] (*doctor, lawyer*) exercer ; **to** ~ **as a doctor/lawyer** exercer la médecine *or* la profession de médecin/la profession d'avocat

practised, practiced (*US*) ['præktɪst] ADJ [*teacher, nurse, soldier*] expérimenté, chevronné ; [*eye, ear*] exercé ; [*movement*] expert ; [*performance*] accompli

practising, practicing (*US*) ['præktɪsɪŋ] ADJ [*doctor*] exerçant ; [*lawyer*] en exercice ; [*architect*] en activité ; [*Catholic, Buddhist*] pratiquant ; **a** ~ **Christian** un (chrétien) pratiquant ; **he's a** ~ **homosexual** c'est un homosexuel actif

practitioner [præk'tɪʃənər] N (*of an art*) praticien(ne) *m(f)* ; (*Med: also* **medical** ~) médecin *m* → **general**

praesidium [prɪ'sɪdɪəm] N présidium *m*

praetorian, **pretorian** (US) [prɪ'tɔːrɪən] [1] ADJ prétorien [2] COMP ► **praetorian guard** N (Hist, fig) garde f prétorienne

pragmatic [præg'mætɪk] ADJ (gen, Philos) pragmatique

pragmatical [præg'mætɪkl] ADJ pragmatique

pragmatically [præg'mætɪklɪ] ADV avec pragmatisme, d'une manière pragmatique

pragmatics [præg'mætɪks] N (NonC) pragmatique f

pragmatism [prægmətɪzəm] N pragmatisme m

pragmatist [prægmətɪst] ADJ, N pragmatiste mf

Prague [prɑːg] N Prague

prairie ['prɛərɪ] [1] N plaine f (herbeuse); (US) **the ~(s)** la Grande Prairie, les Prairies fpl [2] COMP ► **prairie chicken** N (US Zool) cupidon m (des prairies), tétras cupidon m ► **prairie cocktail** N (US) = **prairie oyster** ► **prairie dog** N chien m de prairie ► **prairie oyster** N (US) œuf m cru assaisonné et bu dans de l'alcool (remède contre la gueule de bois) ► **Prairie Provinces** NPL (Can) Provinces fpl des Prairies ► **prairie schooner** N (US) grand chariot m bâché (des pionniers américains) ► **the Prairie State** N (US) l'Illinois m ► **prairie wolf** N (US) coyote m

praise [preɪz] [1] N [a] éloge(s) m(pl), louange(s) f(pl); **in ~ of** à la louange de; **to speak** (or **write** etc) **in ~ of sb/sth** faire l'éloge de qn/qch; **it is beyond ~** c'est au-dessus de tout éloge; **to be full of ~ for sb/sth** ne pas tarir d'éloges sur qn/qch; **to give ~** être élogieux; **I have nothing but ~ for what he has done** je ne peux que le louer de ce qu'il a fait; **I have nothing but ~ for him** je n'ai qu'à me louer or me féliciter de lui; **all ~ to him for speaking out!** il a dit ce qu'il pensait et je lui tire mon chapeau!; **he was loud** or **warm in his ~(s) of ...** il n'a pas tari d'éloges sur ..., il a chanté les louanges de ... → **sing** [b] (Rel) **a hymn of ~** un cantique; **~ be to God!** Dieu soit loué!; **~ be!*** Dieu merci! [2] VT [a] (+ person, action, sb's courage etc) louer, faire l'éloge de; **to ~ sb for sth/for doing sth** louer qn de or pour qch/d'avoir fait qch; **to ~ sb to the skies** porter qn aux nues; **to ~ the virtues of sb/sth** vanter les mérites de qn/qch [b] (Rel) louer, glorifier; **~ God!** Dieu soit loué!

praiseworthily ['preɪz,wɜːðɪlɪ] ADV d'une manière louable or méritoire

praiseworthiness ['preɪz,wɜːðɪnɪs] N mérite m

praiseworthy ['preɪz,wɜːðɪ] ADJ [person] digne d'éloges; [cause, attempt] digne d'éloges, louable, méritoire

praline ['prɑːliːn] N (nutty) praline f; (= almond) dragée f

pram [præm] N (Brit) voiture f d'enfant, landau m; (Brit) **park** emplacement m réservé aux voitures d'enfants

prance [prɑːns] VI [horse, child] caracoler; [dancer] cabrioler; **the horse was prancing about** le cheval caracolait; **she was prancing* around** or **about with nothing on** elle se baladait* toute nue; **to ~ in/out** etc [horse] entrer/sortir en caracolant; [person] (gaily) entrer/sortir etc allégrement; (arrogantly) entrer/sortir etc en se pavanant

prang†‡ [præŋ] VT (Brit = crash) [+ plane, car] bousiller*; [+ bomb] pilonner

prank [præŋk] N (= joke) farce f, niche† f; **a childish ~** une gaminerie; **schoolboy ~** farce f d'écolier; **to play a ~ on sb** faire une farce or une niche† à qn

prankster† ['præŋkstər] N farceur m, -euse f

praseodymium [ˌpreɪzɪəʊ'dɪmɪəm] N praséodyme m

prat‡ [præt] N (Brit) con‡ m, conne‡ f

prate [preɪt] VI jaser, babiller (pej); **to ~ on about sth** parler à n'en plus finir de qch

pratfall‡ ['præt,fɔːl] N (US) chute f sur le derrière

prattle ['prætl] [1] VI [one person] jaser, babiller (pej); [several people] papoter, jacasser; [child] babiller, gazouiller; **to ~ on about sth** parler à n'en plus finir de qch; **he ~s on and on** c'est un vrai moulin à paroles [2] N [of one person] bavardage m, babillage m (pej); [of several people] jacasserie f, papotage m; [of child] babil m, babillage m

prawn [prɔːn] [1] N (esp Brit) crevette f rose, bouquet m → **Dublin** [2] COMP ► **prawn cocktail** N cocktail m de crevettes ► **prawn cracker** N beignet m de crevettes

pray [preɪ] [1] VI prier; **they ~ed to God to help them** ils prièrent Dieu de les secourir; **he ~ed to be released from his suffering** il pria le ciel de mettre fin à ses souffrances; **to ~ for sb/sb's soul** prier pour qn/l'âme de qn; **he ~ed for forgiveness** il pria Dieu de lui pardonner; **to ~ for rain** prier pour qu'il pleuve; **to ~ for guidance** demander conseil à Dieu; (fig) **we're ~ing for fine weather** nous prions pour qu'il fasse beau [2] VT [a] (†, liter = request) prier (**sb to do** qn de faire) [b] (Rel) prier (**that** pour que + subj); **they ~ed God to help him** ils prièrent Dieu de lui venir en aide [3] ADV†† **~ be seated** veuillez vous asseoir, asseyez-vous je vous prie; (iro) **what good is that, ~?** à quoi cela peut-il bien servir, je vous le demande?

prayer [prɛər] [1] N [a] (Rel) prière f (also NonC); **to be at ~** or **at one's ~s** être en prière; **he was kneeling in ~** il priait à genoux; **to say one's ~s** faire sa prière; **they said a ~ for him** ils ont fait or dit une prière pour lui, ils ont prié pour lui; (as service) **~s** office m; **he will lead us in ~** ◊ **he will lead our ~s** il va diriger nos prières; **he didn't have a ~*** il n'avait pas la moindre chance → **common, evening, lord** [b] (= desire, wish) vœu m, souhait m; **my one ~ is that I/he will be able to ...** mon seul vœu or souhait est de pouvoir/qu'il puisse ... [2] COMP ► **prayer beads** NPL chapelet m ► **prayer book** N livre m de prières; **the Prayer Book** le rituel de l'Église anglicane ► **prayer mat** N tapis m de prière ► **prayer meeting** N réunion f de prière ► **prayer rug** N tapis m de prière ► **prayer shawl** N (in Judaism) taleth m ► **prayer wheel** N moulin m à prières

praying ['preɪɪŋ] [1] N (NonC) prière(s) f(pl) [2] ADJ en prière [3] COMP ► **praying mantis** N (Zool) mante f religieuse

pre... [priː] PREF pré...; **~glacial** préglaciaire; **~-1950** (adj) antérieur (-eure f) à (l'année) 1950, d'avant 1950 ♦ (adv) avant 1950 → **predate, pre-record**

preach [priːtʃ] [1] VI (Rel) prêcher (also fig pej); évangéliser; (in church) prêcher; **to ~ to sb** prêcher qn; (fig pej) **to ~ to** or **at sb** prêcher or sermonner qn; **don't ~!** pas de morale, s'il te plaît!; (fig) **you're ~ing to the converted** vous prêchez un converti → **practise** [2] VT [+ religion, the Gospel, crusade, doctrine] prêcher; (fig) [+ patience] préconiser, prôner; [+ advantage] prôner; **to ~ a sermon** prêcher, faire un sermon; **to ~ that ...** proclamer que ...

preacher ['priːtʃər] N prédicateur m; (US = clergyman) pasteur m

preachify* ['priːtʃɪfaɪ] VI (pej) prêcher, faire la morale

preaching ['priːtʃɪŋ] N (NonC) prédication f, sermon m; (fig pej) prêchi-prêcha* m inv (pej)

preachy* ['priːtʃɪ] ADJ (pej) prêcheur, sermonneur

preamble [priː'æmbl] N préambule m; (in book) préface f

preamplifier [ˌpriː'æmplɪfaɪər] N préamplificateur m, préampli* m

prearrange ['priːə'reɪndʒ] VT arranger or organiser à l'avance

prebend ['prebənd] N prébende f

prebendary ['prebəndərɪ] N prébendier m

precancerous [ˌpriː'kænsərəs] ADJ précancéreux

precarious [prɪ'kɛərɪəs] ADJ (= uncertain) [situation, position] précaire; (= unsteady) [ladder etc] mal assuré, instable

precariously [prɪ'kɛərɪəslɪ] ADV [cling, hang, lean] d'une manière précaire or instable; **~ perched** or **balanced** en équilibre précaire; **to cling ~ to life** s'accrocher désespérément à la vie; **to live ~** (= in danger of poverty) vivre dans la précarité; (= live for the moment) vivre au jour le jour

precast ['priː'kɑːst] [1] ADJ (Theat, Cine) [play, film] dont les rôles sont distribués d'avance [2] COMP ► **precast concrete** N béton m précontraint

precaution [prɪ'kɔːʃən] N précaution f (**against** contre); **as a ~** par précaution; (also euph) **to take ~s** prendre ses précautions; **to take the ~ of doing** prendre la précaution de faire; **fire ~s** mesures fpl de sécurité contre les incendies; **safety** or **security ~s** mesures fpl de sécurité

precautionary [prɪ'kɔːʃənərɪ] ADJ de précaution, préventif; **as a ~ measure** par mesure de précaution; **to take ~ measures** prendre des mesures de précaution

precede [prɪ'siːd] VT (in space, time) précéder; (in rank) avoir la préséance sur; **the week preceding his death** la semaine qui a précédé sa mort, la semaine avant sa mort

precedence ['presɪdəns] N (in rank) préséance f; (in importance) priorité f; **to have** or **take ~ over sb** avoir la préséance or le pas sur qn; **this question must take ~ over all others** ce problème a la priorité sur tous les autres, ce problème passe en priorité or est prioritaire; **to give ~ to sth** donner or accorder la priorité à qch

precedent ['presɪdənt] N précédent m; **without ~** sans précédent; **to act as** or **form a ~** constituer un précédent; **to set** or **establish** or **create a ~** créer un précédent; **to break with ~** rompre avec la tradition

preceding [prɪ'siːdɪŋ] ADJ précédent; **the ~ day** le jour précédent, la veille

precentor [prɪ'sentər] N premier chantre m, maître m de chapelle

precept ['priːsept] N précepte m

preceptor [prɪ'septər] N précepteur m, -trice f

precession [prɪ'seʃən] [1] N précession f [2] COMP ► **precession of the equinoxes** N (Astron) précession f des équinoxes

pre-Christian [priː'krɪstʃən] ADJ préchrétien

precinct ['priːsɪŋkt] [1] N [a] (round cathedral) enceinte f; (= boundary) pourtour m; (fig) **within the ~s of ...** dans les limites de ...; **the ~s** (= neighbourhood) les alentours mpl, les environs mpl → **pedestrian, shopping** [b] (US Police) circonscription f administrative; (US Pol) circonscription f électorale, arrondissement m [2] COMP ► **precinct captain** N (US) (Pol) responsable mf politique de quartier; (Police) commissaire m (de police) de quartier ► **precinct cop*** N (US) flic* m de quartier ► **precinct police** N (US) police f de quartier ► **precinct station** N (US Police) poste m de police de quartier, commissariat m de quartier ► **precinct worker** N (US Pol) militant(e) politique à l'échelon du quartier

preciosity [ˌpresɪ'ɒsɪtɪ] N préciosité f

precious ['preʃəs] [1] ADJ [a] [person, moment] précieux; [object, book, possession] précieux, de valeur ; (* iro) chéri, cher ; **don't waste ~ time arguing** ne perds pas un temps précieux à discuter ; **this book is very ~ to me** ce livre a une très grande valeur pour moi, je tiens énormément à ce livre ; **the child is very ~ to him** il tient énormément à cet enfant ; (iro) **your ~ son*** ton fils chéri or adoré, ton cher fils ; (iro) **your ~ car** ta voiture chérie, ta chère voiture ; (iro) **your ~ career** ta chère carrière **b** [style, language] précieux, affecté **2** ADV* ~ **few** ◊ ~ **little** fort or bien peu **3** N (my) ~!† mon trésor ! **4** COMP ► **precious metal** N métal m précieux ► **precious stone** N pierre f précieuse

precipice ['presipis] N (gen) à-pic m inv ; **to fall over a ~** tomber dans un précipice

precipitance [prɪ'sɪpɪtəns], **precipitancy** [prɪ'sɪpɪtənsɪ] N précipitation f

precipitant [prɪ'sɪpɪtənt] **1** ADJ (frm) = **precipitate 4 2** N (Chem) précipitant m

precipitate [prɪ'sɪpɪteɪt] **1** VT **a** (frm) (= hasten) [+ event, crisis] hâter, précipiter ; (= hurl) [+ person] précipiter (**into** dans) **b** (Chem) précipiter ; (Met) condenser **2** VI (Chem) (se) précipiter ; (Met) se condenser **3** N (Chem) précipité m **4** [prɪ-'sɪpɪtɪt] ADJ (frm) irréfléchi, hâtif

precipitately [prɪ'sɪpɪtɪtlɪ] ADV (frm) précipitamment

precipitation [prɪˌsɪpɪ'teɪʃən] N précipitation f (also Chem, Met)

precipitous [prɪ'sɪpɪtəs] ADJ (frm) **a** escarpé, abrupt, à pic **b** = **precipitate 4**

precipitously [prɪ'sɪpɪtəslɪ] ADV (frm) à pic, abruptement

précis ['preɪsiː] **1** N (pl **précis** ['preɪsiːz]) résumé m, précis m **2** VT faire un résumé or précis de

precise [prɪ'saɪs] ADJ **a** [details, instructions, description] précis ; [measurement, meaning, account, nature, location] précis, exact ; **be (more) ~!** soyez (plus) précis ! ; **there were eight to be ~** il y en avait huit pour être exact or précis ; **the ~ amount of energy they need** la quantité exacte d'énergie dont ils ont besoin ; **at that ~ moment** à ce moment précis or même ; **I have to be up early, 4am to be ~** il faut que je me lève tôt, à 4 heures du matin pour être exact or précis **b** (= meticulous) [movement] précis ; [person, manner] méticuleux, minutieux ; (pej = over-precise) pointilleux, maniaque ; **in that ~ voice of hers** de sa façon de parler si nette

▼ **precisely** [prɪ'saɪslɪ] ADV [explain, describe] de façon précise ; [measure, define] avec précision, de façon précise ; [speak, enunciate] d'une voix très nette ; **10 o'clock ~** ◊ ~ **10 o'clock** 10 heures précises or sonnantes ; ~ **nine minutes** exactement or très précisément neuf minutes ; **hormones, or more ~, progesterone** des hormones, ou plus précisément or exactement de la progestérone ; ~ **what does that mean?** qu'est-ce que cela veut dire exactement or au juste ? ; **he said ~ nothing** il n'a absolument rien dit ; ~! précisément ! ; **I didn't feel the pain, ~ because I was so cold** justement, c'est parce que j'avais si froid que je ne sentais pas la douleur ; **that is ~ the problem** c'est bien là le problème

preciseness [prɪ'saɪsnɪs] N = **precision 1**

precision [prɪ'sɪʒən] **1** N précision f ; **with deadly/military/clinical ~** avec une précision implacable/militaire/chirurgicale **2** COMP [tool] de précision ► **precision bombing** N bombardement m de précision ► **precision engineering** N mécanique f de précision ► **precision instrument** N instrument m de précision ► **precision-made** ADJ de haute précision

preclude [prɪ'kluːd] VT [+ doubt] écarter, dissiper ; [+ misunderstanding] prévenir ; [+ possibility] exclure ; **to be ~d from doing** être empê-

ché de faire ; **to ~ sth happening** empêcher que qch n'arrive (subj) ; **that ~s his leaving** cela l'empêche de partir

precocious [prɪ'kəʊʃəs] ADJ (gen, pej) précoce ; (pej) **a ~ brat*** un petit prodige

precociously [prɪ'kəʊʃəslɪ] ADV ~ **mature** d'une maturité précoce ; **a ~ talented/brilliant player** un joueur au talent/génie précoce ; **"mummy, it's frankly horrifying", he said ~** « franchement maman, c'est l'horreur » dit-il avec une précocité étonnante

precociousness [prɪ'kəʊʃəsnɪs], **precocity** [prə'kɒsɪtɪ] N précocité f

precognition [ˌpriːkɒg'nɪʃən] N préconnaissance f

precombustion ['priːkəm'bʌstʃən] N précombustion f

preconceived ['priːkən'siːvd] ADJ ~ **notion** or **idea** idée f préconçue

preconception ['priːkən'sepʃən] N idée f préconçue, préconception f

preconcerted ['priːkən'sɜːtɪd] ADJ arrêté or concerté d'avance or au préalable

precondition ['priːkən'dɪʃən] **1** N condition f nécessaire or requise, condition f sine qua non **2** VT conditionner (**sb to do** qn à faire)

precook ['priː'kuːk] VT faire cuire à l'avance

precooked ['priː'kuːkt] ADJ précuit

precool ['priː'kuːl] VT refroidir d'avance

precursor [priː'kɜːsər] N (= person, thing) précurseur m ; (= event) annonce f, signe m avant-coureur

precursory [priː'kɜːsərɪ] ADJ [remark] préliminaire ; [taste, glimpse] annonciateur (-trice f)

predaceous, predacious [prɪ'deɪʃəs] ADJ = **predatory**

predate [priː'deɪt] VT **a** (= put earlier date on) [+ cheque, document] antidater **b** (= come before in time) [+ event] précéder, avoir lieu avant ; [+ document] être antérieur à, précéder

predator ['predətər] N prédateur m, rapace m

predatory ['predətərɪ] ADJ [animal, bird, insect] de proie, prédateur (-trice f), rapace ; [habits] de prédateur(s) ; [person] rapace ; [armies] pillard ; [look] vorace, avide ; (Comm) ~ **pricing** politique f de prix déloyale

predecease ['priːdɪ'siːs] VT prédécéder

predecessor ['priːdɪsesər] N prédécesseur m

predestination [priːˌdestɪ'neɪʃən] N prédestination f

predestine ['priː'destɪn] VT (also Rel) prédestiner (**to** à, **to do** à faire)

predetermination ['priːdɪˌtɜːmɪ'neɪʃən] N détermination f antérieure ; (Philos, Rel) prédétermination f

predetermine ['priːdɪ'tɜːmɪn] VT déterminer or arrêter au préalable or d'avance ; (Philos, Rel) prédéterminer

predeterminer [ˌpriːdɪ'tɜːmɪnər] N (Gram) prédéterminant m, préarticle m

predicable ['predɪkəbl] ADJ, N (Philos) prédicable m

predicament [prɪ'dɪkəmənt] N situation f difficile or fâcheuse ; **I'm in a real ~!** me voilà dans de beaux draps !

predicate ['predɪkeɪt] **1** VT **a** (= affirm: gen, Philos) affirmer (**that** que) **b** (= imply) [+ existence of sth etc] impliquer, supposer **c** (= base) [+ statement, belief, argument] baser, fonder (**on, upon** sur) ; **this is ~d on the fact that ...** ceci est fondé or basé sur le fait que ... **2** ['predɪkɪt] N (Gram) prédicat m ; (Philos) prédicat m, attribut m **3** ['predɪkɪt] ADJ (Gram) prédicatif ; (Philos) attributif

predicative [prɪ'dɪkətɪv] ADJ (Gram) prédicatif

predicatively [prɪ'dɪkətɪvlɪ] ADV (Gram) en tant que prédicat

predict [prɪ'dɪkt] VT prédire, prévoir (**that** que)

predictability [prɪdɪktə'bɪlɪtɪ] N prévisibilité f

predictable [prɪ'dɪktəbl] ADJ [behaviour] prévisible ; [person, book] sans surprise ; **his reaction was ~** sa réaction était prévisible

predictably [prɪ'dɪktəblɪ] ADV [behave, say, react] d'une manière prévisible ; **his father was ~ furious** ◊ ~, **his father was furious** comme on pouvait s'y attendre or comme on pouvait le prévoir, son père était furieux

prediction [prɪ'dɪkʃən] N prédiction f

predictive [prɪ'dɪktɪv] ADJ prophétique

predictor [prɪ'dɪktər] N indice m

predigested [ˌpriːdaɪ'dʒestɪd] ADJ prédigéré

predilection [ˌpriːdɪ'lekʃən] N prédilection f

predispose ['priːdɪs'pəʊz] VT prédisposer (**to** or **towards sth** à qch, **to do(ing)** à faire)

predisposition ['priːˌdɪspə'zɪʃən] N prédisposition f (**to** à)

predominance [prɪ'dɒmɪnəns] N prédominance f

predominant [prɪ'dɒmɪnənt] ADJ prédominant

predominantly [prɪ'dɒmɪnəntlɪ] ADV principalement, essentiellement ; **they are ~ French** ce sont principalement or essentiellement des Français ; **acne is ~ a teenage problem** l'acné est principalement or essentiellement un problème d'adolescent

predominate [prɪ'dɒmɪneɪt] VI prédominer (**over** sur), prévaloir

predominately [prɪ'dɒmɪneɪtlɪ] ADV = **predominantly**

preemie‡ ['priːmɪ] N (US Med) prématuré(e) m(f)

pre-eminence [priː'emɪnəns] N prééminence f

pre-eminent [priː'emɪnənt] ADJ prééminent

pre-eminently [priː'emɪnəntlɪ] ADV avant tout, essentiellement

pre-empt [priː'empt] VT **a** (= anticipate) [+ sb's decision, action] anticiper, devancer **b** (= prevent) prévenir ; **you can ~ pain by taking a painkiller** vous pouvez prévenir la douleur en prenant un calmant **c** [+ painting, land] acquérir par (droit de) préemption

pre-emption [priː'empʃən] N (droit m de) préemption f

pre-emptive [priː'emptɪv] ADJ [right] de préemption ; [attack, strike] préventif ; (Bridge) ~ **bid** (demande f de) barrage m

preen [priːn] **1** VT [+ feathers, tail] lisser ; **the bird was ~ing itself** l'oiseau se lissait les plumes ; **she was ~ing herself in front of the mirror** elle se pomponnait or s'arrangeait complaisamment devant la glace ; (liter) **to ~ o.s. on sth/on doing sth** s'enorgueillir de qch/de faire qch **2** VI [bird] se lisser les plumes ; [person] se pomponner

pre-establish ['priːɪs'tæblɪʃ] VT préétablir

pre-exist ['priːɪg'zɪst] **1** VI préexister **2** VT préexister à

pre-existence ['priːɪg'zɪstəns] N préexistence f

pre-existent ['priːɪg'zɪstənt], **pre-existing** ['priːɪg'zɪstɪŋ] ADJ préexistant

prefab* ['priːfæb] N (ABBR = **prefabricated building**) préfabriqué m

prefabricate [ˌpriː'fæbrɪkeɪt] VT préfabriquer

preface ['prefɪs] **1** N (to book) préface f, avant-propos m inv ; (to speech) introduction f, préambule m **2** VT [+ book] faire précéder (**by** de) ; **he ~d this by saying ...** en avant-propos il a dit ..., il a commencé par dire ... ; **he ~d his speech by saying ...** en guise d'introduction à son discours, il a dit ... ; **he had the irritating habit of prefacing his sentences with ...** il avait la manie agaçante de commencer toutes ses phrases par ...

prefaded [ˌpriː'feɪdɪd] ADJ [jeans etc] délavé

prefatory ['prefətərɪ] ADJ [remarks] préliminaire ; [page] liminaire

prefect ['pri:fekt] N (*French Admin*) préfet *m*; (*Brit Scol*) élève des grandes classes chargé(e) de la discipline

prefecture [,pri:fektjʊəʳ] N préfecture *f*

▼ **prefer** [prɪ'fɜːʳ] VT a préférer; **to ~ A to B** préférer A à B, aimer mieux A que B; **I ~ bridge to chess** je préfère le bridge aux échecs; **to ~ doing sth** *or* **to do sth** aimer mieux *or* préférer faire qch; **children ~ watching television to reading books** les enfants préfèrent la télévision à la lecture *or* aiment mieux regarder la télévision que lire; **would you ~ me to drive?** préférerais-tu que je prenne le volant?; **I'd ~ that you didn't come to New York with me** je préférerais que tu ne viennes pas à New York avec moi, j'aimerais mieux que tu ne viennes pas à New York avec moi; **I would ~ not to (do it)** je préférerais *or* j'aimerais mieux ne pas le faire; **she ~red not to give her name** elle a préféré ne pas donner son nom; **I much ~ Scotland** je préfère de beaucoup l'Écosse, j'aime beaucoup mieux l'Écosse; (*US Fin*) **~red stock** = **preference shares**; → **preference**

b (*Jur*) [+ *charge*] porter; [+ *action*] intenter; [+ *request*] formuler; [+ *petition*] adresser; [+ *argument*, *reason*] présenter; **to ~ a complaint against sb** déposer une plainte *or* porter plainte contre qn

c (*esp Rel = promote*) élever (**to** à)

▼ **preferable** ['prefərəbl] ADJ préférable (**to sth à** qch); **it is ~ to use vegetable oil for cooking** il est préférable de cuisiner à l'huile végétale; **any death is ~ to being drowned** il n'y a pas pire mort que la noyade

preferably ['prefərəblɪ] ADV de préférence

▼ **preference** ['prefərəns] 1 N (= *liking*) préférence *f* (**for** pour); (= *priority*: *also Econ*) priorité *f* (**over** sur), préférence *f*; **what is your ~?** que préférez-vous?; **in ~ to sth** de préférence à qch, plutôt que qch; **in ~ to doing sth** plutôt que de faire qch; **to give A ~ (over B)** accorder *or* donner la préférence à A (plutôt qu'à B); **I have no strong ~** je n'ai pas vraiment de préférence; **by ~** de préférence 2 COMP ▶ **preference shares** NPL (*Brit Fin*) actions *fpl* privilégiées *or* de priorité ▶ **preference stock** N = **preference shares**

preferential [,prefə'renʃəl] ADJ [*tariff*, *terms*] préférentiel; [*treatment*] de faveur; [*trade*, *ballot*, *voting*] préférentiel

preferentially [,prefə'renʃəlɪ] ADV (= *by preference*) de préférence; **no-one should be treated ~** personne ne devrait bénéficier d'un traitement préférentiel *or* de faveur

preferment [prɪ'fɜːmənt] N (*esp Rel*) avancement *m*, élévation *f* (**to** à)

prefiguration [,pri:fɪɡə'reɪʃən] N préfiguration *f*

prefigure [pri:'fɪɡəʳ] VT (= *foreshadow*) préfigurer; (= *imagine*) se figurer d'avance

prefix ['pri:fɪks] 1 N [*of word*] préfixe *m*; [*of phone number*] indicatif *m* 2 VT préfixer

preflight ['pri:'flaɪt] ADJ d'avant le décollage

preform ['pri:'fɔːm] VT préformer

preformation [,pri:fɔː'meɪʃən] N préformation *f*

prefrontal [,pri:'frʌntl] ADJ préfrontal

preggers‡ ['preɡəz] ADJ (*Brit* = *pregnant*) **to be ~** attendre un gosse*

pregnancy ['preɡnənsɪ] 1 N [*of woman*] grossesse *f*; [*of animal*] gestation *f* → **phantom**, **unwanted** 2 COMP ▶ **pregnancy test** N test *m* de grossesse

pregnant ['preɡnənt] ADJ [*woman*] enceinte; [*animal*] pleine; (*fig*) [*pause*, *silence*] lourd de sens; [*idea*] fécond; **three months ~** enceinte de trois mois; **to be ~ by sb** être enceinte de qn; **while she was ~ with Marie** alors qu'elle était enceinte de sa fille Marie; (*hum*) **you can't be half ~** il y a des choses que l'on ne peut pas faire à moitié; (*fig*) **~ with meaning** lourd de sens

preheat ['pri:'hi:t] VT préchauffer; **~ed oven** four *m* préchauffé; **~ the oven to ...** préchauffer le four à ...

prehensile [prɪ'hensaɪl] ADJ préhensile

prehistoric ['pri:hɪs'tɒrɪk] ADJ préhistorique

prehistory ['pri:'hɪstərɪ] N préhistoire *f*

pre-ignition ['pri:ɪɡ'nɪʃən] N autoallumage *m*

pre-industrial [pri:ɪn'dʌstrɪəl] ADJ préindustriel

prejudge ['pri:'dʒʌdʒ] VT [+ *question*] préjuger de; [+ *person*] juger d'avance

prejudice ['predʒʊdɪs] 1 N a préjugé *m*; (*NonC*) préjugés *mpl*; **racial ~** préjugés *mpl* raciaux; **to have a ~ against/in favour of sb/sth** avoir un préjugé contre/en faveur de qn/qch; **he is quite without ~ in this matter** il est sans parti pris dans cette affaire b (*esp Jur* = *detriment*) préjudice *m*; **to the ~ of** au préjudice de; **without ~ (to)** sans préjudice de 2 VT a [+ *person*] prévenir (**against** contre, **in favour of** en faveur de) → **prejudiced** b (*also Jur*) [+ *claim*, *chance*] porter préjudice à

prejudiced ['predʒʊdɪst] ADJ [*person*] plein de préjugés; [*idea*, *opinion*] préconçu, partial; **he was even more ~ than Harold** il avait encore plus de préjugés qu'Harold; **to be ~ against sb/sth** avoir un (*or* des) préjugé(s) contre qn/qch; **to be racially ~** avoir des préjugés raciaux

prejudicial [,predʒʊ'dɪʃəl] ADJ préjudiciable, nuisible (**to** à); **to be ~ to** nuire à

prelacy ['preləsɪ] N (= *office*) prélature *f*; (= *prelates collectively*) prélats *mpl*

prelate ['prelɪt] N prélat *m*

pre-law [,pri:'lɔː] N (*US Univ*: *also* **~ program**) enseignement *m* préparatoire aux études de droit

prelim* ['pri:lɪm] N (ABBR = **preliminary**) (*Univ*) examen *m* préliminaire; (*Sport*) (épreuve *f*) éliminatoire *f*

preliminary [prɪ'lɪmɪnərɪ] 1 ADJ [*exam*, *inquiry*, *report*, *remark*] préliminaire; [*stage*] premier, initial; (*Constr etc*) **~ estimate** devis *m* estimatif; (*Brit Jur*) **~ hearing** audience *f* préliminaire 2 N préliminaire *m*; **the preliminaries** les préliminaires *mpl*; **as a ~** en guise de préliminaire, au préalable 3 COMP ▶ **Preliminary Scholastic Aptitude Test** N (*US Scol*, *Univ*) test déterminant l'aptitude d'un candidat à présenter l'examen d'entrée à l'université

prelude ['prelju:d] 1 N (*gen*, *Mus*) prélude *m* (**to** de) 2 VT préluder à

premarital ['pri:'mærɪtl] ADJ avant le mariage; **~ contract** contrat *m* de mariage

premature ['prematʃʊəʳ] ADJ [*decision etc*] prématuré; [*birth*] prématuré, avant terme; [*senility*, *menopause*, *ejaculation*, *labour*] précoce; **~ baby** (enfant *mf*) prématuré(e) *m(f)*, enfant *mf* né(e) avant terme; (*fig*) **you are a little ~** vous anticipez un peu

prematurely ['prematʃʊəlɪ] ADV (*gen*) prématurément; [*be born*, *die*] avant terme; **his career was ~ ended by an arm injury** une blessure au bras a prématurément mis fin à sa carrière; **~ bald/menopausal** atteint(e) de calvitie/ménopause précoce; **~ old** *or* **aged** prématurément vieilli; **he's ~ middle-aged** il a vieilli avant l'âge

pre-med* ['pri:'med] 1 N a (*Brit*) ABBR = **pre-medication** b (*US*) = **pre-med program** 2 ADJ (*US*) (ABBR = **premedical**) **~ program** enseignement *m* préparatoire aux études de médecine; **~ student** étudiant(e) *m(f)* en année préparatoire de médecine

premedication [,pri:medɪ'keɪʃən] N prémédication *f*

premeditate [pri:'medɪteɪt] VT préméditer

premeditation [pri:,medɪ'teɪʃən] N préméditation *f*

premenstrual [pri:'menstrʊəl] 1 ADJ prémenstruel 2 COMP ▶ **premenstrual syndrome**, **premenstrual tension** N syndrome *m* prémenstruel

premier ['premɪəʳ] 1 ADJ premier, primordial 2 N (*Pol*) (= *Prime Minister*) Premier ministre *m*; (= *President*) chef *m* de l'État 3 COMP ▶ **Premier Division** N (*Ftbl*: *in Scot*) première division *f* d'Écosse ▶ **Premier League** N (*Ftbl*: *in England and Wales*) première division *f* d'Angleterre et du pays de Galles

première ['premɪəʳ] (*Cine*, *Theat*) 1 N première *f*; **the film has just received its London ~** la première londonienne du film vient d'avoir lieu 2 VT donner la première de; **the film was ~d in Paris** la première du film a eu lieu à Paris 3 VI **the movie ~d in May 1998** la première du film a eu lieu en mai 1998

premiership ['premɪəʃɪp] N (*Pol*) [*of Prime Minister*] fonction *f* de Premier ministre; [*of President*] fonction *f* de chef d'État; (*Ftbl*, *Rugby*) championnat *m* de première division; **during his ~** (*of Prime Minister*) sous son ministère, pendant qu'il était Premier ministre; (*of President*) pendant qu'il était chef de l'État; **he staked his claim for the ~** il revendiquait le poste de Premier ministre *or* de chef d'État

premise ['premɪs] 1 N (*gen*, *Philos* = *hypothesis*) prémisse *f*; **on the ~ that ...** en partant du principe que ..., si l'on pose en principe que ... 2 **premises** NPL (= *property*) locaux *mpl*, lieux *mpl*; **business ~s** locaux *mpl* commerciaux; **on the ~s** sur les lieux, sur place; **off the ~s** à l'extérieur, hors des lieux; **to escort sb off the ~s** escorter *or* accompagner qn dehors; **get off the ~s** videz *or* évacuez les lieux 3 VT (*frm*) **to be ~d on ...** être fondé *or* basé sur ...

premiss ['premɪs] N = **premise 1a**

premium ['pri:mɪəm] 1 N a (*gen*, *Comm*, *Fin*, *Insurance*) prime *f*; (*Jur*: *paid on lease*) reprise *f*; (*St Ex*) **to be sold at a ~** être vendu à prime; (*Comm*, *fig*) **to be at a ~** faire prime; **to set** *or* **put** *or* **place a (high) ~ on** [+ *person*] faire grand cas de; [+ *situation*, *event*] donner beaucoup d'importance à b (*US* = *gasoline*) super(carburant) *m* 2 ADJ [*goods*, *brand*] de qualité supérieure 3 COMP ▶ **premium bond** N (*Brit*) obligation *f* à prime, bon *m* à lots ▶ **premium fuel** (*Brit*) super(carburant) *m* ▶ **premium gasoline** N (*US*) → **premium fuel** ▶ **premium price** N prix *m* fort ▶ **premium-rate** ADJ (*Brit Telec*) facturé au tarif fort (*pour renseignements*, *téléphone rose*, *etc*)

premolar [pri:'məʊləʳ] N prémolaire *f*

premonition [,premə'nɪʃən] N prémonition *f*, pressentiment *m*; **to have a ~ that ...** avoir le pressentiment que ..., pressentir que ...

premonitory [prɪ'mɒnɪtərɪ] ADJ prémonitoire, précurseur

prenatal ['pri:'neɪtl] ADJ prénatal

prenuptial [,pri:'nʌpʃəl] ADJ prénuptial; **~ agreement** contrat *m* de mariage

preoccupation [pri:,ɒkjʊ'peɪʃən] N préoccupation *f*; **keeping warm was his main ~** sa grande préoccupation *or* son souci majeur était de se protéger du froid; **his ~ with money/with winning** son obsession *f* de l'argent/de gagner

preoccupy [pri:'ɒkjʊpaɪ] VT [+ *person*, *mind*] préoccuper; **to be preoccupied** être préoccupé (**by**, **with** de)

pre-op* ['pri:'ɒp] N prémédication *f*, médication *f* préopératoire

preordain [,pri:ɔː'deɪn] VT ordonner *or* régler d'avance; (*Philos*, *Rel*) préordonner

preordained [,pri:ɔː'deɪnd] ADJ prédestiné

prep* [prep] 1 N ABBR = **preparation** a (*Scol*) (= *work*) devoirs *mpl*, préparation *f*; (= *period*) étude *f* (surveillée) b (*US Med*) préparation *f*

(*d'un(e) malade*) [2] VI (*US*) [a] **to ~ for sth** se préparer pour qch [b] (*US Scol*) entrer en classe préparatoire (*pour l'université*) [3] VT (*US*) **to ~ o.s.** se préparer [4] COMP ► **prep school** N (*Brit*) = **preparatory school**; → **preparatory**

prepack ['priː'pæk], **prepackage** ['priː'pækɪdʒ] VT (*Comm*) préconditionner

prepaid ['priː'peɪd] [1] VB *pt, ptp* of **prepay** [2] ADJ (*gen*) payé (d'avance); (*Comm*) carriage ~ port payé; **reply ~** réponse payée; (*Fin etc*) ~ **expenses** compte *m* de régularisation de l'actif; (*in US*) ~ **health care** médecine *f* prépayée

preparation [,prepə'reɪʃən] N [a] (*NonC* = *act*) préparation *f*; (*Culin, Pharm etc* = *thing prepared*) préparation *f*; ~**s** préparatifs *mpl*; **the country's ~s for war** les préparatifs *mpl* de guerre du pays; **to make ~s for sth** prendre ses dispositions pour qch, faire les préparatifs de qch; **to be in ~** [*book, film etc*] être en préparation; **in ~ for** en vue de; **Latin is a good ~ for Greek** le latin prépare bien au grec, le latin est une bonne formation pour le grec [b] (*NonC: Scol*) (= *work*) devoirs *mpl*, préparation *f*; (= *period*) étude *f*

preparatory [prɪ'pærətərɪ] [1] ADJ [*work*] préparatoire; [*measure, step*] préliminaire, préalable; ~ **to** avant, préalablement à, en vue de; ~ **to sth/to doing sth** en vue de qch/de faire qch, avant qch/de faire qch [2] COMP ► **preparatory school** N (*Brit*) école *f* primaire privée; (*US*) école *f* secondaire privée

┌─────────────────────────┐
│ **PREPARATORY SCHOOL** │
└─────────────────────────┘

En Grande-Bretagne, une **preparatory school**, *ou* **prep school**, *est une école primaire, généralement non mixte, qui prépare les élèves à entrer dans un établissement secondaire privé. L'uniforme y est obligatoire et la discipline relativement stricte.*

Aux États-Unis, le terme désigne une école secondaire privée préparant les élèves aux études supérieures. Dans les deux cas, la clientèle de ces écoles est issue de milieux privilégiés. Le mot «preppy», utilisé comme substantif ou comme adjectif, désigne les élèves des **prep schools** *américaines, ou leur style vestimentaire BCBG.*

prepare [prɪ'pɛəʳ] [1] VT [+ *plan, speech, lesson, work, medicine, sauce*] préparer; [+ *meal, dish*] préparer, apprêter; [+ *surprise*] préparer, ménager (**for sb** à qn); [+ *room, equipment*] préparer (**for** pour); **to ~ sb for an exam/an operation** préparer qn à un examen/pour une opération; **to ~ sb for a shock/for bad news** préparer qn à un choc/à une mauvaise nouvelle; ~ **yourself for a shock!** prépare-toi à (recevoir) un choc!, tiens-toi bien!; **to ~ o.s. for** = **prepare for**; → **2**; **to ~ the way/ground for sth** préparer la voie/le terrain pour qch → **prepared**

[2] VI **to ~ for** (= *make arrangements*) [+ *journey, sb's arrival, event*] faire des préparatifs pour, prendre ses dispositions pour; (= *prepare o.s. for*) [+ *storm, flood, meeting, discussion*] se préparer pour; [+ *war*] se préparer à; [+ *examination*] préparer; **to ~ to do sth** s'apprêter or se préparer à faire qch

▼ **prepared** [prɪ'pɛəd] ADJ [*person, army, country*] prêt; [*statement, answer*] préparé à l'avance; (*Culin*) [*sauce, soup*] tout prêt; **be ~!** soyez sur le qui-vive!; **be ~ for bad news** préparez-vous à une mauvaise nouvelle; **I am ~ for anything** (= *can cope with anything*) j'ai tout prévu, je suis paré; (= *won't be surprised at anything*) je m'attends à tout; **to be ~ to do sth** être prêt or disposé à faire qch

preparedness [prɪ'pɛərɪdnɪs] N état *m* de préparation; (*Mil*) **state of ~** état *m* d'alerte préventive; **their ~ to help countries affected by the famine** leur disposition *f* à aider les pays touchés par la famine

prepay ['priː'peɪ] (*pret, ptp* **prepaid**) VT payer d'avance → **prepaid**

prepayment ['priː'peɪmənt] N paiement *m* d'avance

preponderance [prɪ'pɒndərəns] N (*in numbers*) supériorité *f* numérique; (*in influence*) prépondérance *f* (**over** sur)

preponderant [prɪ'pɒndərənt] ADJ (*in numbers*) numériquement supérieur; (*in influence*) prépondérant

preponderantly [prɪ'pɒndərəntlɪ] ADV principalement, essentiellement

preponderate [prɪ'pɒndəreɪt] VI (*in numbers*) être en supériorité numérique (**over** par rapport à); (*in influence*) l'emporter (**over** sur)

preposition [,prepə'zɪʃən] N préposition *f*

prepositional [,prepə'zɪʃənl] ADJ [*phrase*] prépositif, prépositionnel; [*use*] prépositionnel

prepositionally [,prepə'zɪʃənəlɪ] ADV prépositivement

prepossess [,priːpə'zes] VT (= *preoccupy*) préoccuper; (= *bias*) prévenir, influencer; (= *impress favourably*) impressionner favorablement

prepossessing [,priːpə'zesɪŋ] ADJ [*person, appearance*] avenant

preposterous [prɪ'pɒstərəs] ADJ ridicule, grotesque

preposterously [prɪ'pɒstərəslɪ] ADV ridiculement

preposterousness [prɪ'pɒstərəsnɪs] N (*NonC*) ridicule *m*, grotesque *m*

preppie*, **preppy*** ['prepɪ] (*US*) [1] ADJ bon chic bon genre*, BCBG* [2] N élève *mf* d'une boîte* privée → *PREPARATORY SCHOOL*

preprandial [,priː'prændɪəl] ADJ (*frm or hum*) [*drink*] avant le repas

preprepared [,priːprɪ'pɛəd] ADJ tout prêt

preproduction [,priːprə'dʌkʃən] [1] N travail *m* antérieur à la production [2] COMP ► **preproduction model** N prototype *m* ► **preproduction trial** N mise *f* à l'essai du prototype

preprogrammed [priː'prəʊgræmd] ADJ programmé à l'avance

prepubescent [,priːpjuː'besənt] ADJ prépubère

prepuce ['priːpjuːs] N prépuce *m*

prequel ['priːkwəl] N film ou roman ayant pour thème des événements antérieurs à ceux d'un film ou d'un roman déjà sorti, la jeunesse ou l'enfance d'un héros célèbre par exemple

Pre-Raphaelite [priː'ræfəlaɪt] ADJ, N préraphaélite *mf*

pre-record [,priːrɪ'kɔːd] VT [+ *song, programme*] enregistrer à l'avance; ~**ed broadcast** émission *f* en différé; ~**ed cassette** cassette *f* préenregistrée

prerelease showing [,priːrɪ'liːs'ʃəʊɪŋ] N (*Cine*) avant-première *f*

prerequisite ['priː'rekwɪzɪt] [1] N [a] (*gen*) condition *f* préalable [b] (*US Univ*) unité de valeur dont l'obtention est obligatoire pour pouvoir s'inscrire dans l'unité de valeur supérieure [2] ADJ nécessaire au préalable, préalablement nécessaire

prerogative [prɪ'rɒgətɪv] N prérogative *f*; (*Brit*) **to exercise the Royal Prerogative** faire acte de souverain

Pres. (ABBR = **president**) Pdt

presage ['presɪdʒ] (*frm*) [1] N (= *omen*) présage *m*; (= *foreboding*) pressentiment *m* [2] VT présager, annoncer

presbyopia [,prezbɪ'əʊpɪə] N presbytie *f*

Presbyterian [,prezbɪ'tɪərɪən] ADJ, N presbytérien(ne) *m(f)*

Presbyterianism [,prezbɪ'tɪərɪənɪzəm] N presbytérianisme *m*

presbytery ['prezbɪtərɪ] N (= *part of church*) chœur *m*; (= *residence*) presbytère *m*; (= *court*) consistoire *m*

pre-school [,priː'skuːl] ADJ [*years, age*] préscolaire; [*child*] d'âge préscolaire; ~ **education** enseignement *m* préscolaire; ~ **playgroup** ≈ garderie *f*

preschooler ['priːskuːləʳ] N (*US*) enfant *mf* d'âge préscolaire

prescience ['presɪəns] N prescience *f*

prescient ['presɪənt] ADJ prescient

prescribe [prɪs'kraɪb] VT (*gen, Admin, Jur, Med*) prescrire (**sth for sb** qch à qn); **the ~d dose/form/punishment** la dose/le formulaire/la punition prescrit(e); ~**d books** œuvres *fpl* (inscrites) au programme; **this diet is ~d in some cases** ce régime se prescrit dans certains cas; **he ~d complete rest** il a prescrit or ordonné le repos absolu; (*fig*) **what do you ~?** que me conseillez-vous?, que me recommandez-vous?

prescription [prɪs'krɪpʃən] [1] N [a] (*NonC: gen, Admin, Jur*) prescription *f* [b] (*Med*) ordonnance *f*; **to make out** or **write out a ~ for sb** une ordonnance pour qn; **to make up** or (*US*) **fill a ~** exécuter une ordonnance; **on ~** sur ordonnance; **he gets free ~s** les médicaments qu'on lui prescrit sont intégralement pris en charge [2] COMP [*medicine*] (= *made according to prescription*) prescrit; (= *available only on prescription*) vendu sur ordonnance seulement ► **prescription charge** N (*Brit*) montant forfaitaire payé sur les médicaments, ≈ ticket *m* modérateur ► **prescription glasses**, **prescription spectacles** NPL lunettes *fpl* de vue

┌─────────────────────────┐
│ **PRESCRIPTION CHARGE** │
└─────────────────────────┘

En Grande-Bretagne, les patients paient, à la façon du ticket modérateur en France, un montant forfaitaire sur tous les médicaments prescrits par un médecin: c'est la **prescription charge**, *dont sont néanmoins exemptées certaines catégories de personnes: enfants, femmes enceintes, personnes âgées ou bénéficiaires de prestations sociales.* → *NHS*

prescriptive [prɪs'krɪptɪv] ADJ (= *giving precepts*) (*gen, Gram*) normatif; (= *legalized by custom*) [*rights etc*] consacré par l'usage

prescriptivism [prɪs'krɪptɪˌvɪzəm] N (*Ling*) normativisme *m*

pre-select [,priːsɪ'lekt] VT présélectionner

presell [,priː'sel] VT vendre à l'avance

pre-seminal ['priː'semɪnəl] ADJ (*Med*) préséminal; ~ **fluid** liquide *m* préséminal

presence ['prezns] [1] N [a] présence *f*; **I felt comfortable in her ~** je me sentais à l'aise en sa présence; **in the ~ of** en présence de; (*Jur*) **your ~ is requested at ...** vous êtes prié d'assister à ...; (*liter, frm*) **they were admitted to the royal ~** ils furent admis en présence du roi (or de la reine); **he certainly made his ~ felt*** sa présence n'est vraiment pas passée inaperçue; **a ghostly ~** une présence surnaturelle; **this country will maintain a ~ in North Africa** ce pays maintiendra une présence en Afrique du Nord; **police ~** présence *f* policière; **there was a heavy police ~ at the match** il y avait une forte présence policière au match [b] (= *bearing etc*) présence *f*; **to lack ~** manquer de présence; **he has a good stage ~** il a de la présence (sur scène); (*liter*) **a man of noble ~** un homme de belle prestance or de belle allure [2] COMP ► **presence of mind** N présence *f* d'esprit

present ['preznt] [1] ADJ [a] (= *in attendance, in existence*) présent; ~ **at** présent à; **to be ~ at sth** être présent à qch, assister à qch; **my husband was ~ at the birth** mon mari a assisté à l'accouchement; **~ in** présent dans; **who was ~?** qui était là?; **is there a doctor ~?** y a-t-il un docteur ici *or* dans l'assistance?; **those ~** les personnes *fpl* présentes, l'assistance *f*; **~ company excepted** les personnes ici présentes exceptées, à l'exception des personnes ici présentes; **all ~ and correct!** tous présents à l'appel!

b (= *existing now*) [*state, epoch, year, circumstances, techniques, residence, job*] présent (*after n*), actuel; (= *in question*) présent (*before n*), en question; (*Gram*) présent (*after n*); **her ~ husband** son mari actuel; **the ~ writer believes that ...** l'auteur croit que ...; **the ~ government** le gouvernement actuel; **in the ~ day** aujourd'hui → **5**; **at the ~ moment** *or* **time** actuellement, à présent; (*more precisely*) en ce moment même; **the ~ month** le mois courant, ce mois-ci; **in the ~ case** dans le cas présent *or* qui nous intéresse *or* en question

2 N **a** (*also Gram*) présent *m*; **at ~** (= *right now*) actuellement, en ce moment; (= *for the time being*) pour le moment; **as things are at ~** dans l'état actuel des choses; **for the ~** pour le moment; (*Gram*) **in the ~** au présent; **to live in the ~** (= *not be hidebound*) vivre dans le présent; (= *live from day to day*) vivre au jour le jour; **(there's) no time like the ~!** il ne faut jamais remettre au lendemain ce que l'on peut faire le jour même!; **up to the ~** jusqu'à présent

b (= *gift*) cadeau *m*; **it's for a ~** c'est pour offrir; **she gave me the book as a ~** elle m'a offert le livre (en cadeau); (*lit, fig*) **to make sb a ~ of sth** faire cadeau *or* don de qch à qn → **birthday, Christmas**

c (*Jur*) **by these ~s** par les présentes

3 [prɪˈzent] VT **a** **to ~ sb with sth ◊ to ~ sth to sb** (= *give as gift*) offrir qch à qn, faire don *or* cadeau de qch à qn; (= *hand over*) [+ *prize, medal*] remettre qch à qn; **she ~ed him with a son** elle lui a donné un fils; **we were ~ed with a fait accompli** nous nous sommes trouvés devant un fait accompli; (*Mil*) **to ~ arms** présenter les armes; **~ arms!** présentez armes!

b [+ *tickets, documents, credentials, one's compliments, apologies*] présenter (**to** à); [+ *plan, account, proposal, report, petition, information*] présenter, soumettre (**to** à); [+ *complaint*] déposer; [+ *proof, evidence*] apporter, fournir; (*Parl*) [+ *bill*] introduire, présenter; (*Jur etc*) [+ *case*] exposer; **to ~ o.s. at the desk/for an interview** se présenter au bureau/à un entretien; **to ~ a cheque (for payment)** encaisser *or* présenter un chèque; **how is the data ~ed?** comment les données sont-elles présentées?; **his report ~s the matter in another light** son rapport présente la question sous un autre jour, son rapport jette une lumière différente sur la question; **to ~ o.s.** se présenter; **how you ~ yourself is very important** la manière dont vous vous présentez est très importante

c (= *constitute, offer*) [+ *problem*] présenter, poser; [+ *difficulties, features*] présenter; [+ *opportunity*] [+ *challenge*] constituer; **the bay ~s a magnificent sight** la baie présente un spectacle splendide; **the opportunity ~ed itself** l'occasion s'est présentée; **to ~ the appearance of sth** avoir *or* donner (toute) l'apparence de qch; **the patrol ~ed an easy target** la patrouille offrait *or* constituait une cible facile; **the Committee ~ed an easy target for criticism** le comité était une cible facile pour les critiques

d [+ *play, concert*] donner; [+ *film, play, programme*] donner, passer; (= *act as presenter of*) présenter; (*Theat*) **we are proud to ~ ...** nous sommes heureux de vous présenter ...; **"~ing Glenda Jackson as Lady Macbeth"** «avec Glenda Jackson dans le rôle de Lady Macbeth»

e (*frm* = *introduce*) présenter (**sb to sb** qn à qn); **may I ~ Miss Smith?** permettez-moi de

vous présenter Mademoiselle Smith; (*Brit*) **to be ~ed (at Court)** être présenté à la Cour

4 VI (*Med*) **he ~ed last month (here at the clinic)** [*patient*] il est venu nous consulter *or* il s'est présenté le mois passé (à la clinique); **she initially ~ed with headaches and insomnia** lorsqu'elle s'est présentée pour la première fois elle souffrait de maux de tête et d'insomnie; **the patient ~s with lesions to the abdomen** ce patient présente des lésions à l'abdomen; **he ~s as a chronic alcoholic** il présente tous les symptômes de l'alcoolisme chronique

5 COMP ► **present-day** ADJ d'aujourd'hui, contemporain ► **present perfect** N (*Gram*) passé *m* composé

presentable [prɪˈzentəbl] ADJ [*person, appearance, room*] présentable; [*clothes*] présentable, mettable; **go and make yourself (look) ~** va t'arranger un peu; **I'm not very ~** je ne suis guère présentable, je ne peux guère me montrer

presentably [prɪˈzentəbl] ADV de manière présentable

presentation [ˌprezənˈteɪʃən] **1** N **a** (*NonC* = *act or fact of presenting*) [*of plan, account, proposal, report, petition, evidence*] présentation *f*, soumission *f*; [*of complaint*] déposition *f*; [*of parliamentary bill*] présentation *f*, introduction *f*; [*of cheque*] encaissement *m*; [*of case*] exposition *f*; **on ~ of this ticket** sur présentation de ce billet

b (= *packaging, way of presenting*) présentation *f*; **the subject matter is good but the ~ is poor** le fond est bon mais la présentation laisse à désirer; **it's just a problem of ~** c'est une question de présentation; **his ~ of the play** (= *the way he did it*) sa mise en scène de la pièce; **a theatrical ~ of "Danton's Death"** une représentation théâtrale de «La mort de Danton»

c (= *introduction*) présentation *f* (**to** à)

d (= *ceremony*) remise *f* du cadeau (*or* de la médaille *etc*), ≈ vin *m* d'honneur; **who made the ~?** qui a remis le cadeau (*or* la médaille *etc*)?; **to make a ~ of sth to sb** remettre qch à qn

e (*Univ, Comm etc* = *lecture, talk*) exposé *m* oral; **a business ~** une présentation commerciale

2 COMP ► **presentation box, presentation case** N (*Comm*) coffret *m* de luxe ► **presentation copy** N [*of book*] (*for inspection, review*) spécimen *m* (gratuit), exemplaire *m* envoyé à titre gracieux; (*from author*) exemplaire *m* offert en hommage

presentational [ˌprezənˈteɪʃənl] ADJ **for ~ reasons** pour des raisons de présentation

presenter [prɪˈzentəʳ] N (*Brit Rad, TV*) présentateur *m*, -trice *f*, speaker(ine) *m(f)*

presentiment [prɪˈzentɪmənt] N pressentiment *m*

presently [ˈprezntlɪ] ADV **a** (*Brit*) (= *in a moment*) tout à l'heure; (= *some time later*) peu de temps après, un peu plus tard **b** (= *currently*) actuellement, à présent

presentment [prɪˈzentmənt] N [*of note, bill of exchange etc*] présentation *f*; (*Jur*) déclaration *f* émanant du jury

preservation [ˌprezəˈveɪʃən] **1** N (= *protection, safeguarding*) sauvegarde *f*, préservation *f*; (= *continuance, maintenance*) maintien *m*; **in a good state of ~** bien préservé, en bon état de conservation; **the ~ of the monument is our first priority** notre priorité est de sauvegarder le monument; **the ~ of peace in the Middle East** le maintien de la paix au Proche-Orient **2** COMP ► **preservation order** N (*Brit Admin*) **to put a ~ order on a building** classer un édifice (monument historique) ► **preservation society** N (*Archit*) association *f* pour la sauvegarde et la conservation des sites et monuments

preservationist [ˌprezəˈveɪʃnɪst] N (*esp US*) défenseur *m* de l'environnement

preservative [prɪˈzɜːvətɪv] N (*Culin*) agent *m* de conservation, conservateur *m*

preserve [prɪˈzɜːv] **1** VT **a** (= *keep, maintain*) [+ *building, traditions, manuscript, eyesight, position*] conserver; [+ *leather, wood*] entretenir; [+ *memory*] conserver, garder; [+ *dignity, sense of humour, reputation*] garder; [+ *peace*] maintenir; [+ *silence*] observer, garder; **well-/badly-~d** en bon/mauvais état de conservation; (*hum*) **she is very well-~d** elle est bien conservée; **to ~ one's looks** conserver sa beauté; **have you ~d the original?** avez-vous gardé *or* conservé l'original?

b (*from harm etc*) préserver, garantir (**from** de), protéger (**from** contre); **may God ~ you!†** Dieu vous garde!, que Dieu vous protège!; **(heaven** *or* **the saints) ~ me from that!†** le ciel m'en préserve!

c (*Culin*) [+ *fruit etc*] conserver, mettre en conserve; **~d** en conserve; **~d food** (*in bottles, cans*) conserves *fpl*; (*frozen*) produits *mpl* surgelés

2 N **a** (*Brit Culin*) (= *jam*) confiture *f*; (= *chutney*) condiment *m* à base de fruits

b (= *bottled fruit/vegetables*) fruits *mpl*/légumes *mpl* en conserve

c (*Hunting*) réserve *f*; **game ~** chasse *f* gardée *or* interdite

d (*fig* = *prerogative*) chasse *f* gardée; **that's his ~** c'est sa chasse gardée, c'est son domaine particulier

3 COMP ► **preserving pan** N bassine *f* à confiture

preserver [prɪˈzɜːvəʳ] N (= *person*) sauveur *m* → **life**

preset [ˈpriːˈset] VT (*pret, ptp* **preset**) programmer

preshrunk [ˈpriːˈʃrʌŋk] ADJ irrétrécissable

preside [prɪˈzaɪd] VI présider; **to ~ at** *or* **over a meeting** présider une réunion

presidency [ˈprezɪdənsɪ] N présidence *f*

president [ˈprezɪdənt] **1** N (*Pol etc*) président *m*; (*US Comm*) président-directeur *m* général, PDG *m*; (*US Univ*) président *m* (d'université) *m* **2** COMP ► **president-elect** N titre *que porte le président des États-Unis nouvellement élu* (en novembre) jusqu'à son investiture (en janvier de l'année suivante) ► **President of the Board of Trade** N (*Brit Parl*) ≈ ministre *m* du Commerce ► **Presidents' Day** N (*US*) jour férié le troisième lundi de février, en souvenir des présidents Lincoln et Washington

presidential [ˌprezɪˈdenʃəl] ADJ **a** (*gen*) [*decision, suite etc*] présidentiel, du président; **~ elections** élection *f* présidentielle; **his ~ hopes** l'espoir qu'il a de devenir président **b** (= *of one specific President*) [*staff, envoy, representative*] du Président; (*US Pol*) **~ adviser** conseiller *m* personnel du Président **c** (= *reminiscent of a president*) [*style, regime, politician*] présidentiel; **the new Prime Minister is more ~ (in style) than his predecessors** le nouveau Premier ministre a un style plus présidentiel que ses prédécesseurs; **a ~-style campaign** une campagne à l'américaine

presidentially [ˌprezɪˈdenʃəlɪ] ADV en tant que président

presidium [prɪˈsɪdɪəm] N = **praesidium**

pre-soak [ˈpriːˈsəʊk] VT faire tremper

press [pres] **1** N **a** (= *apparatus*) (for wine, olives, cheese etc) pressoir *m*; (for gluing, moulding etc) presse *f*; **cider ~** pressoir *m* à cidre; **hydraulic ~** presse *f* hydraulique; **racket ~** presse-raquette *m inv*; **trouser ~** presse *f* à pantalon

b (*Printing*) (= *machine: also* **printing ~**) presse *f* (typographique); (= *place, publishing firm*) imprimerie *f*; **rotary ~** presse *f* rotative; **to set the ~es rolling** mettre les presses en marche; (*Publishing*) **to pass sth for ~** donner le bon à tirer de qch; **to go to ~** [*book etc*] être mis sous presse; [*newspaper*] aller à l'impression; **correct at time of going to ~** correct au moment de mettre sous presse

c (= *reporting, journalists collectively*) presse *f*; **a free ~** une presse libre; **to get a good/bad ~** avoir bonne/mauvaise presse; **I saw it in the ~** je l'ai lu dans la presse *or* dans les journaux; **to advertise in the ~** (*Comm*) faire de la publicité dans la presse *or* dans les journaux; (*privately*) mettre une annonce dans les journaux; **a member of the ~** un(e) journaliste; **the national ~** la grande presse; **is (anyone from) the ~ present?** la presse est-elle représentée?; **the ~ reported that ...** la presse a relaté que ..., on a rapporté dans la presse que ...

d (= *pressure: with hand, instrument*) pression *f*; **he gave his trousers a ~** il a donné un coup de fer à son pantalon → **permanent**

e (*Weight Lifting*) développé *m*

f (*Ir, Scot* = *cupboard*) armoire *f*, placard *m*

g (= *pressure of people*) foule *f*, presse *f* (*liter*); **he lost his hat in the ~ to get out** il a perdu son chapeau dans la bousculade à la sortie

2 VT a (= *push*) [*+ button, switch, accelerator*] appuyer sur; (= *squeeze*) [*+ sb's hand etc*] serrer, presser; **he ~ed his fingertips together** il a pressé les extrémités de ses doigts les unes contre les autres; **he ~ed his nose against the window** il a collé son nez à la fenêtre; (*US*) **to ~ the flesh**[*] serrer une multitude de mains, prendre un bain de foule; **he ~ed her to him** il la serra *or* pressa contre lui; **as the crowd moved back he found himself ~ed (up) against a wall** au moment où la foule a reculé il s'est trouvé acculé *or* pressé contre un mur

b (= *crush*) [*+ grapes, olives, lemons, flowers*] presser

c (= *iron*) [*clothes etc*] repasser, donner un coup de fer à

d (= *make by pressing*) [*+ object, machine part*] mouler; [*+ record, disk*] presser

e (= *pressure*) (*in battle, game*) presser, attaquer constamment; [*pursuer*] talonner, serrer de près; [*creditor*] poursuivre, harceler; **to ~ sb to do sth** presser qn de *or* pousser qn à faire qch, insister pour que qn fasse qch; **I am really ~ed today** je suis débordé (de travail) aujourd'hui; **to ~ sb for payment/an answer** presser qn de payer/de répondre; **to be ~ed for time/money** être à court de temps/d'argent, manquer de temps/d'argent; **he didn't need much ~ing** il ne s'est guère fait prier; **to ~ a gift/money on sb** presser qn d'accepter *or* insister pour que qn accepte (*subj*) un cadeau/de l'argent, offrir avec insistance un cadeau/de l'argent à qn; († *or hum*) **to ~ one's suit** faire sa demande (en mariage) → **hard**

f (= *press-gang: lit, Hist*) enrôler de force; (*fig*) **to ~ sb into doing sth** forcer qn à faire qch; **we were all ~ed into service** nous avons tous été obligés d'offrir nos services *or* de mettre la main à la pâte*; **the church hall was ~ed into service as a school** la salle paroissiale a été réquisitionnée pour servir d'école; **buildings that were ~ed into service to house the victims** des bâtiments qui ont été réquisitionnés pour accueillir les victimes

g (= *pursue, press home*) [*+ attack, advantage*] pousser, poursuivre; [*+ claim, demand*] renouveler, insister sur; (*Jur*) **to ~ charges (against sb)** porter plainte (contre qn); **I shan't ~ the point** je n'insisterai pas

h (*Weight Lifting*) soulever

3 VI a (= *exert pressure: with hand etc*) appuyer (**on** sur); [*weight, burden*] faire pression, peser (**on** sur); [*debts, troubles*] peser (**on sb** à qn); **time ~es!** le temps presse!, l'heure tourne!; (*fig*) **to ~ for sth** faire pression pour obtenir qch, demander instamment qch; **they are ~ing to have the road diverted** ils font pression pour (obtenir)

que la route soit déviée

b **he ~ed through the crowd** il s'est frayé un chemin dans la foule; **he ~ed in/out** *etc* il est entré/sorti *etc* en jouant des coudes; **they ~ed in/out** *etc* ils sont entrés/sortis *etc* en masse; **crowds ~ed round him** une foule se pressait autour de lui

4 COMP [*campaign, card etc*] de presse ► **press agency** N agence *f* de presse ► **press agent** N agent *m* de publicité ► **the Press Association** N *agence de presse britannique* ► **press attaché** N attaché(e) *m(f)* de presse ► **press baron** N magnat *m* de la presse ► **press box** N tribune *f* de la presse ► **press button** N bouton(-poussoir) *m* ► **press clipping** N = **press cutting** ► **Press Complaints Commission** N (*in Brit*) *commission des plaintes contre la presse* ► **press conference** N conférence *f* de presse ► **press corps** N (*esp US*) la presse (*travaillant à un endroit donné*) ► **press cutting** N coupure *f* de presse *or* de journal; **~ cutting agency** argus *m* de la presse ► **press gallery** N (*esp Parl*) tribune *f* de la presse ► **press-gang** N (*Hist*) racoleurs *mpl* ♦ VT (*fig*) **to ~-gang sb into doing sth** faire pression sur qn *or* forcer la main à qn pour qu'il fasse qch ► **press hold** N (*Climbing*) appui *m* ► **press kit** N dossier *m* de presse ► **press lord** N = **press baron** ► **press office** N service *m* de presse ► **press officer** N attaché(e) *m(f)* de presse ► **press photographer** N photographe *mf* de (la) presse, reporter *m* photographe ► **press release** N communiqué *m* de presse ► **press report** N reportage *m* ► **press run** N (*US*) tirage *m* (d'une revue *etc*) ► **press secretary** N (*US*) **the White House** *etc* **~ secretary** le porte-parole de la Maison-Blanche *etc* ► **press stud** N (*Brit*) bouton-pression *m*, pression *f* ► **press-up** N (*Brit Gym*) traction *f*; **to do ~-ups** faire des tractions *or* des pompes* ► **press view** N (*Cine*) avant-première *f*

► **press ahead** VI = **press on**

► **press back** VT SEP [*+ crowd, enemy*] refouler

► **press down** 1 VI appuyer (**on** sur) 2 VT SEP [*+ knob, button, switch*] appuyer sur

► **press in** VT SEP [*+ panel etc*] enfoncer

► **press on** VI (*in work, journey etc*) continuer; **~ on!** *don't give up* persévérez!, n'abandonnez pas!; (**let's**) **~ on regardless!*** continuons quand même!; (*fig*) **to ~ on with sth** continuer résolument (à faire) qch; **they are ~ing on with the nuclear agreement** ils continuent à tout faire pour que l'accord nucléaire se réalise

► **press out** VT SEP [*+ juice, liquid*] exprimer

pressing ['presɪŋ] 1 ADJ (= *urgent*) [*business, problem*] urgent; [*danger, invitation*] pressant 2 N [*of clothes*] repassage *m*; **to send sth for ~** faire repasser qch

pressman ['presmən] N (*pl* **-men**) (*Brit*) journaliste *m*

pressmark ['presmɑːk] N (*Brit*) cote *f* (d'un livre de bibliothèque)

pressure ['preʃəʳ] 1 N a (*gen, Met, Phys, Tech*) pression *f*; **the boilers were running at full ~** la pression dans les chaudières était à son maximum; **at high ~** à haute pression; **to exert** *or* **put ~ on sth** faire pression *or* exercer une pression sur qch, presser *or* appuyer sur qch; **a ~ of 2kg to the square cm** une pression de 2 kg par cm²; **atmospheric ~** pression *f* atmosphérique; **oil ~** pression *f* d'huile; (*Aut: also* **tyre ~**) pression *f* (de gonflage); **water ~** pression *f* de l'eau → **blood pressure**

b (*fig* = *influence, compulsion*) pression *f*, contrainte *f*; **parental ~** la pression des parents; **to put ~ on sb (to do sth)** ◊ **to bring ~ to bear on sb (to do sth)** faire pression *or* exercer une pression sur qn (pour qu'il fasse qch); **they're putting the ~ on now** ils commencent à mettre la pression; **he was acting under ~ when he said ...** il agissait sous la contrainte *or* il n'agissait pas de son plein

gré quand il a dit ...; **under ~ from his staff** sous la pression de son personnel; **to come under ~** subir des pressions; **the Prime Minister came under ~ to resign** on a fait pression sur le Premier ministre pour qu'il démissionne → **1c**; **to use ~ to obtain a confession** user de contrainte pour obtenir une confession

c (*fig* = *stress, burden*) **the ~(s) of these events/of life today** la tension créée par ces événements/par la vie d'aujourd'hui; **~ of work prevented him from going** le travail l'a empêché d'y aller, il n'a pas pu y aller parce qu'il avait trop de travail; **the ~(s) of meeting deadlines** la contrainte des délais à respecter; **he has been under a lot of ~ recently** il a été sous pression* ces derniers temps; **I work badly under ~** je travaille mal quand je suis sous pression*; **I can't work well under such ~** je n'arrive pas à bien travailler quand je suis sous pression* à ce point

2 VT **don't ~ me!*** ne me bouscule pas!; **to ~ sb to do sth** faire pression sur qn pour qu'il fasse qch; **to ~ sb into doing sth** forcer qn à *or* contraindre qn à faire qch; **to feel ~d into sth** *or* **to do sth** se sentir forcé de faire qch; **do you feel ~d by your family to have a baby?** avez-vous le sentiment que votre famille fait pression sur vous pour que vous fassiez un enfant?; **don't feel ~d!*** ne te sens pas obligé!

3 COMP ► **pressure cabin** N (*Aviat*) cabine *f* pressurisée *or* sous pression ► **pressure-cook** VT cuire à la cocotte *or* à la cocotte-minute® *or* en autocuiseur ► **pressure cooker** N autocuiseur *m*, cocotte-minute® *f* ► **pressure-feed** N alimentation *f* par pression ► **pressure gauge** N manomètre *m*, jauge *f* de pression ► **pressure group** N (*Pol etc*) groupe *m* de pression ► **pressure point** N (*Anat*) point *m* de compression digitale d'une artère ► **pressure suit** N (*Space etc*) scaphandre *m* pressurisé

pressurization [ˌpreʃəraɪˈzeɪʃən] N pressurisation *f*, mise *f* en pression

pressurize ['preʃəraɪz] 1 VT a [*+ cabin, spacesuit*] pressuriser b (* *fig*) = **pressure 2** 2 COMP ► **pressurized cabin** N cabine *f* pressurisée *or* sous pression ► **pressurized water reactor** N réacteur *m* à eau sous pression

Prestel® ['pres,tel] N ≈ Télétel® *m*

prestidigitation ['presti,dɪdʒɪ'teɪʃən] N (*frm*) prestidigitation *f*

prestige [pres'tiːʒ] 1 N prestige *m* 2 ADJ [*car, production, politics etc*] de prestige

prestigious [pres'tɪdʒəs] ADJ prestigieux

presto ['prestəʊ] ADV (*Mus, gen*) presto; **hey ~!** le tour est joué!; **and hey ~! there he was** et abracadabra! il était là

prestressed ['priːˈstrest] ADJ précontraint; **~ concrete** (béton *m* armé) précontraint *m*

presumable [prɪˈzjuːməbl] ADJ présumable

presumably [prɪˈzjuːməblɪ] ADV sans doute

presume [prɪˈzjuːm] 1 VT a (= *suppose*) présumer (*also Jur*), supposer (**that** que); [*+ sb's death*] présumer; **to be ~d dead** être présumé mort; **every man is ~d (to be) innocent** tout homme est présumé (être) innocent; **he is ~d to be living in Spain** on présume *or* suppose qu'il vit en Espagne; **it may be ~d that ...** on peut présumer que ...; **I ~ so** je (le) présume, je (le) suppose; **I ~ not** je suppose que non; **you are presuming rather a lot** vous faites pas mal de suppositions, vous présumez pas mal de choses b (= *take liberty*) **to ~ to do sth** se permettre de faire qch 2 VI (*frm*) **you ~ too much!** vous êtes bien présomptueux!; **I hope I'm not presuming** je ne voudrais pas être impertinent; (*when asking a favour*) je ne voudrais pas abuser de votre gentillesse; **to ~ (up)on** abuser de

presumption [prɪ'zʌmpʃən] N [a] (= supposition) présomption f, supposition f; **the ~ is that ...** on présume que ..., on suppose que ...; **there is a strong ~ that ...** tout porte à croire que ... [b] (NonC: frm) présomption f; **if you'll excuse my ~** si vous me le permettez, si vous voulez bien pardonner mon audace

presumptive [prɪ'zʌmptɪv] ADJ [heir] présomptif; (Jur) [evidence] par présomption

presumptuous [prɪ'zʌmptjʊəs] ADJ [person, letter, question] présomptueux, impertinent

presumptuously [prɪ'zʌmptjʊəslɪ] ADV présomptueusement, avec présomption

presumptuousness [prɪ'zʌmptjʊəsnɪs] N (NonC) = **presumption b**

presuppose [ˌpriːsə'pəʊz] VT présupposer (**that** que)

presupposition [ˌpriːsʌpə'zɪʃən] N présupposition f

pre-tax [ˌpriː'tæks] ADJ, ADV avant impôts

pre-teen [ˌpriː'tiːn] [1] ADJ préadolescent [2] N **the ~s** les 10 à 12 ans

pretence, pretense (US) [prɪ'tens] N [a] (= pretext) prétexte m, excuse f; (= claim) prétention f; (NonC = affectation) prétention f; **he makes no ~ to learning** il n'a pas la prétention d'être savant; **under** or **on the ~ of (doing) sth** sous prétexte or sous couleur de (faire) qch → **false** [b] (= make-believe) **to make a ~ of doing sth** faire semblant or feindre de faire qch; **he made a ~ of friendship** il a feint l'amitié; **it's all (a) ~** tout cela est pure comédie or une feinte; **I'm tired of their ~ that all is well** je suis las de les voir faire comme si tout allait bien; **his ~ of sympathy did not impress me** sa feinte sympathie m'a laissé froid, ses démonstrations de feinte sympathie m'ont laissé froid

pretend [prɪ'tend] [1] VT [a] (= feign) [+ ignorance, concern, illness] feindre, simuler; **to ~ to do sth** faire semblant or faire mine de faire qch; **he ~ed to be ill** il a fait semblant or mine d'être malade; (as subterfuge) **they ~ed to be soldiers** ils se sont fait passer pour des soldats; (as game) **let's ~ we're soldiers** jouons aux soldats; **he ~ed he/she was out** il a essayé de faire croire qu'il/qu'elle était sorti(e) [b] (frm = claim) prétendre (**that** que); **I don't ~ to know everything about it** je ne prétends pas tout savoir là-dessus, je n'ai pas la prétention de tout savoir là-dessus [2] VI [a] (= feign) faire semblant; **the children were playing at "let's ~"** les enfants jouaient à faire semblant; **he's not really ill, he's just ~ing** il n'est pas malade, il fait semblant; (for fun) **I was only ~ing!** c'était pour rire!, je plaisantais!; **let's stop ~ing!** assez joué la comédie!; **let's not ~ to each other** ne nous jouons pas la comédie, soyons francs l'un avec l'autre [b] (frm = claim) **to ~ to learning/infallibility** avoir la prétention d'être or prétendre être érudit/infaillible [3] ADJ* [money, house etc] pour (de) rire*; **it's only ~** c'est pour rire!*

pretended [prɪ'tendɪd] ADJ (frm) prétendu, soi-disant inv

pretender [prɪ'tendəʳ] N prétendant(e) m(f); **a ~ to the throne (of ...)** un prétendant au trône (de ...); (Brit Hist) **the Young Pretender** le (Jeune) Prétendant (Charles Édouard Stuart)

pretense [prɪ'tens] N (US) = **pretence**

pretension [prɪ'tenʃən] N [a] (= claim: also pej) prétention f (**to sth** à qch); **this work has serious literary ~s** cette œuvre peut à juste titre prétendre à or cette œuvre a droit à la reconnaissance littéraire; (pej) **he has social ~s** il a des prétentions sociales [b] (NonC = pretentiousness) prétention f

pretentious [prɪ'tenʃəs] ADJ prétentieux

pretentiously [prɪ'tenʃəslɪ] ADV prétentieusement

pretentiousness [prɪ'tenʃəsnɪs] N (NonC) prétention f

preterite ['pretərɪt] N prétérit m, passé m simple

pre-term [ˌpriː'tɜːm] [1] ADJ [baby] prématuré [2] ADV prématurément, avant terme

preternatural [ˌpriːtə'nætʃrəl] ADJ surnaturel

preternaturally [ˌpriːtə'nætʃrəlɪ] ADV (frm) surnaturellement

pretext ['priːtekst] N prétexte m; **under** or **on the ~ of (doing) sth** sous prétexte de (faire) qch

pretorian [prɪ'tɔːrɪən] (US) = **praetorian**

pre-trial [ˌpriː'traɪəl] ADJ (Jur) avant procès

prettify ['prɪtɪfaɪ] VT [+ dress] enjoliver; [+ house, garden] essayer d'embellir

prettily ['prɪtɪlɪ] ADV [arrange, decorate] joliment; [smile, blush] de façon charmante

prettiness ['prɪtɪnɪs] N [of person, place] charme m

pretty ['prɪtɪ] [1] ADJ [a] (= attractive) [child, flower, music etc] joli (before n); **as ~ as a picture** [person] joli comme un cœur, joli à croquer; [garden etc] ravissant; **she's not just a ~ face*** elle n'a pas seulement un joli minois, elle a d'autres atouts que son joli visage; **it wasn't a ~ sight** ce n'était pas beau à voir; (to parrot) **~ Polly!** bonjour Jacquot! [b] (iro = fine) joli, beau (belle f); **that's a ~ state of affairs!** c'est du joli!; **you've made a ~ mess of it!** vous avez fait là de la jolie besogne! [c] (* = considerable) [sum, price] joli, coquet; **it will cost a ~ penny** cela coûtera une jolie somme or une somme coquette or une somme rondelette [2] ADV (* = fairly) assez; **it's ~ cold** il fait assez froid, il ne fait pas chaud; **how's it going? — ~ well!** ça va bien? — pas mal!; **we've ~ well finished** nous avons presque or pratiquement fini; **it's ~ much the same thing** c'est à peu près or pratiquement la même chose; **~ damn quick*** illico (presto)*; **you'd have to be ~ damn good* to get a job like that** il faut être drôlement* or sacrément* bon pour trouver un travail comme celui-là; **he's ~ nearly better** il est presque or pratiquement guéri; **to have a ~ good** or **fair idea of sth** avoir sa petite idée sur qch → **sit** [3] COMP ► **pretty-pretty*** ADJ un peu trop joli

► **pretty up*** VT SEP = **prettify**

pretzel ['pretsl] N bretzel m

prevail [prɪ'veɪl] VI [a] (= gain victory) prévaloir (**against** contre, **over** sur), l'emporter, avoir l'avantage (**against** contre, **over** sur); **let us hope that commonsense will ~** espérons que le bon sens prévaudra or s'imposera [b] [conditions, attitude, fashion] prédominer; [style] être en vogue; **the situation which now ~s** la situation actuelle [c] (frm) **to ~(up)on sb to do sth** décider qn à faire qch, persuader qn de faire qch; **can I ~ (up)on you to lend me some money?** accepteriez-vous de me prêter de l'argent?

prevailing [prɪ'veɪlɪŋ] ADJ [a] [wind] dominant [b] (= widespread) [belief, opinion, attitude] courant, répandu [c] (= current) [conditions, situation, customs] (today) actuel; (at that time) à l'époque; [style, taste, prices] (today) actuel, du jour; (at that time) de l'époque, du jour; (Econ) **~ market rate** cours m du marché [d] (Jur) **the ~ party** la partie gagnante

prevalence ['prevələns] N (= predominance, currency) [of illness] fréquence f; [of belief, opinion, attitude] prédominance f, fréquence f; [of conditions, situation, customs] caractère m généralisé; [of fashion, style] popularité f, vogue f; **I'm surprised by the ~ of that idea** je suis surpris que cette idée soit si répandue

prevalent ['prevələnt] ADJ [a] (= widespread) [belief, opinion, attitude] courant, répandu; [illness] répandu; **that sort of thing is very ~** ce genre de chose se voit (or se fait) partout, ce genre de chose est très courant [b] (= current) [conditions, customs] (today) actuel; (at that time) à l'époque; [style, taste] (today) actuel, du jour; (at that time) de l'époque, du jour

prevaricate [prɪ'værɪkeɪt] VI équivoquer, biaiser, tergiverser

prevarication [prɪˌværɪ'keɪʃən] N faux-fuyant(s) m(pl)

prevent [prɪ'vent] VT empêcher (**sb from doing, sb's doing** qn de faire); [+ event, action] empêcher; [+ illness] prévenir; [+ accident, fire, war] empêcher, éviter; **nothing could ~ him (from doing it)** rien ne pouvait l'en empêcher; **she couldn't ~ his death** elle n'a pu empêcher qu'il ne meure or l'empêcher de mourir; **I couldn't ~ the door from closing** je n'ai pas pu empêcher la porte de se fermer or éviter que la porte ne se ferme (subj)

preventable [prɪ'ventəbl] ADJ évitable

preventative [prɪ'ventətɪv] ADJ préventif

prevention [prɪ'venʃən] N (NonC) prévention f ■ (PROV) **~ is better than cure** mieux vaut prévenir que guérir; **Society for the Prevention of Cruelty to Animals** Société f protectrice des animaux → **accident, fire**

preventive [prɪ'ventɪv] [1] ADJ [medicine, measures] préventif; (Jur) **~ detention** (forte) peine f de prison [2] N (= measure) mesure f préventive (**against** contre); (= medicine) médicament m préventif (**against** contre)

preverbal [ˌpriː'vɜːbəl] ADJ préverbal

preview ['priːvjuː] N [of film, exhibition] avant-première f; (= art exhibition) vernissage m; (fig) **to give sb a ~ of sth** donner à qn un aperçu de qch; (Rad, TV) **for a ~ of today's main events over now to Jack Smith** et maintenant pour un tour d'horizon des principaux événements de la journée je passe l'antenne à Jack Smith

previous ['priːvɪəs] [1] ADJ [a] (gen) (= immediately before) précédent; (= sometime before) antérieur (-eure f); **have you made any ~ applications?** avez-vous déjà fait des demandes?; **the car has had two ~ owners** la voiture a déjà eu deux propriétaires, c'est une voiture de troisième main; **the ~ letter** la précédente lettre, la lettre précédente; **a ~ letter** une lettre précédente or antérieure; **the ~ week** la semaine précédente; **the ~ year** l'année f précédente; **the ~ day** la veille; **the ~ evening** la veille au soir; **in a ~ life** dans une vie antérieure; **on ~ occasions** précédemment, auparavant; **I have a ~ engagement** je suis déjà pris; (Jur) **to have no ~ convictions** avoir un casier judiciaire vierge; (Jur) **he has three ~ convictions** il a déjà eu trois condamnations; (Comm) **"no ~ experience necessary"** «débutants acceptés», «aucune expérience (préalable) exigée»; **~ to** antérieur à [b] (frm = hasty) prématuré; **this seems somewhat ~** ceci semble quelque peu prématuré; **you have been rather ~ in inviting him** votre invitation est quelque peu prématurée, vous avez été bien pressé de l'inviter [2] ADV [a] (= previously) **three months ~*** trois mois auparavant or plus tôt [b] (frm) **~ to: ~ to (his) leaving he ...** avant de partir or avant son départ il ...; **~ to his leaving we ...** avant son départ or avant qu'il ne parte nous ...

previously ['priːvɪəslɪ] ADV auparavant; **three months ~** trois mois auparavant or plus tôt; **~ unknown** jusque-là inconnu; **~ unreleased** or **unpublished** jusque-là inédit

prewar ['priː'wɔːʳ] [1] ADJ d'avant-guerre [2] ADV avant-guerre

prewash ['priːwɒʃ] N prélavage m

prex* [preks], **prexie***, **prexy*** ['preksɪ] N (US Univ) président m (d'université)

prey [preɪ] **1** N (*lit, fig*) proie *f*; **bird of ~** oiseau *m* de proie; **to be a ~ to** [+ *nightmares, illnesses*] être en proie à; **to fall (a) ~ to** devenir la proie de **2** VI **to ~ on** [*animal etc*] faire sa proie de; [*person*] faire sa victime de, s'attaquer (continuellement) à; [*fear, anxiety*] ronger, miner; **something is ~ing on her mind** il y a quelque chose qui la tourmente *or* la travaille*

prezzie: ['prezi] N (= *present*) cadeau *m*

Priam ['praɪəm] N Priam *m*

price [praɪs] **1** N **a** (*Comm etc*) (= *cost*) prix *m* (*also fig*); (= *estimate*) devis *m*; (*St Ex*) cours *m*; **he got a good ~ (for it)** il (en) a obtenu un bon prix; **he gave me a good ~ (on it)** il m'a fait un prix; **a special ~ of £50 per night** un tarif spécial de 50 livres la nuit; **book your tickets in advance at the special ~ of £4** achetez vos billets à l'avance au tarif préférentiel de 4 livres; **order any three videos for a special ~ of only £29.99** commandez trois cassettes vidéo au choix pour le prix promotionnel de 29,99 livres; **we pay top ~s for gold and silver** nous achetons l'or et l'argent au prix fort; **what is the ~ of this book?** combien coûte *or* vaut ce livre?, quel est le prix de ce livre?; **ask him for a ~ for putting in a new window** demandez-lui un devis *or* combien ça coûterait *or* quel est son prix pour poser une nouvelle fenêtre; **that's my ~, take it or leave it** c'est mon dernier prix, c'est à prendre ou à laisser; **he'll do it for a ~** il le fera si on y met le prix; **to put a ~ on sth** fixer le prix de qch → **1d**; **the ~ is right** (*fair price*) c'est un prix correct; (= *right for me*) le prix me convient; **to go up** *or* **rise in ~** augmenter; **to drop** *or* **fall in ~** baisser; **their products range in ~ from $12 to $48** le prix de leurs articles va de 12 à 48 dollars; **the ~ in dollars/sterling** ◊ **the dollar/sterling ~** le prix en dollars/livres sterling; (*St Ex*) **to make a ~** fixer un cours; (*St Ex*) **market ~** cours *m* du marché

b (*fig*) **every man has his ~** tout homme peut être acheté; **there's a ~ on his head** ◊ **he has got a ~ on his head** sa tête a été mise à prix; **to put a ~ on sb's head** mettre à prix la tête de qn; **he paid a high** *or* **big ~ for his success** il a payé cher *or* chèrement son succès; **it's a high** *or* **big ~ to pay for it** c'est le payer chèrement *or* cher, c'est consentir un grand sacrifice pour l'avoir; **it's a small ~ to pay for it** c'est consentir un bien petit sacrifice pour l'avoir → **cheap, closing, reduced**

c **at any ~: I wouldn't buy it at any ~** je ne l'achèterais à aucun prix; (*fig*) **I wouldn't help him at any ~!** je ne l'aiderais à aucun prix!; **they want peace at any ~** ils veulent la paix coûte que coûte *or* à tout prix; (*fig*) **will you do it? — not at any ~!** vous allez le faire? — pour rien au monde *or* pas question!; **you can get it but at a ~** vous pouvez l'avoir mais cela vous coûtera cher!; (*fig*) **he's famous now but at what a ~!** il est célèbre maintenant mais à quel prix!

d (= *value*) prix *m*, valeur *f*; **to put a ~ on a jewel/picture** évaluer un bijou/un tableau; (*fig*) **you can't put a ~ on friendship/honesty** l'honnêteté/l'amitié n'a pas de prix; **I cannot put a ~ on his friendship** son amitié n'a pas de prix (pour moi), je ne saurais dire combien j'apprécie son amitié; **he sets** *or* **puts a high ~ on loyalty** il attache beaucoup de valeur *or* un grand prix à la loyauté, il fait très grand cas de la loyauté; (*fig*) **what ~* all his promises now?** que valent toutes ses promesses maintenant?; (*liter*) **beyond ~** ◊ **without ~** qui n'a pas de prix, sans prix

e (*Betting* = *odds*) cote *f*; **what ~ are they giving on Black Beauty?** quelle est la cote de Black Beauty?; **what ~ he'll change his mind?*** vous pariez combien qu'il va changer d'avis?

2 VT **a** (= *fix price of*) fixer le prix de; (= *mark price on*) marquer le prix de; (= *ask price of*)

(*fig* = *estimate value of*) évaluer; **it is ~d at £10** ça coûte 10 livres, ça se vend 10 livres; **shares were ~d at 50p** les actions étaient cotées 50 pence; **tickets ~d (at) £20** billets *mpl* vendus 20 livres; (*St Ex*) **Japanese gas is ~d high** le gaz japonais est coté très cher

3 COMP [*control, index*] des prix; [*reduction, rise*] de(s) prix ► **price bracket** N = **price range** ► **Price Commission**† N (*Brit*) ≈ Direction *f* générale de la concurrence et de la consommation ► **price competitiveness** N compétitivité-prix *f* ► **price cut** N réduction *f*, rabais *m* ► **price cutting** N réduction(s) *f(pl)* de prix ► **price-earnings ratio** N (*St Ex*) rapport *m* cours-bénéfices, taux *m* *or* coefficient *m* de capitalisation (des résultats) ► **price escalation** N flambée *f* des prix; (*Jur*) **escalation clause** clause *f* de révision des prix ► **price-fixing** N (*by government*) contrôle *m* des prix; (*pej: by firms*) entente *f* (illicite) sur les prix ► **price freeze** N blocage *m* des prix ► **price inflation** N inflation *f* des coûts ► **price limit** N **to put a ~ limit on sth** fixer le prix maximum de qch; **my ~ limit is £400** je ne vais pas au-dessus de 400 livres ► **price list** N tarif *m*, prix *m* courant ► **price maintenance** N (*gen*) vente *f* à prix imposé; [*of manufacturer*] fixation *f* des prix ► **price range** N éventail *m* *or* gamme *f* de prix; **within my ~ range** dans mes prix; **in the medium ~ range** d'un prix modéré, dans les prix moyens ► **price-rigging** N (*pej: by firms*) entente *f* (illicite) sur les prix ► **price ring** N cartel *m* des prix ► **prices and incomes policy** N politique *f* des prix et des revenus ► **prices index** N (*Brit*) indice *m* des prix ► **price support** N (*US Econ*) (politique *f* de) soutien *m* des prix ► **price tag** N (*lit*) étiquette *f*; (*fig* = *cost*) prix *m*, coût *m*; (*fig*) **it's got a heavy ~ tag** son prix est très élevé, ça coûte cher; **what's the ~ tag on that house?** quel prix demandent-ils pour cette maison? ► **price ticket** N étiquette *f* ► **price variation clause** N (*Jur*) clause *f* de révision des prix ► **price war** N guerre *f* des prix

►**price down** VT SEP (*Comm*) (= *reduce price of*) réduire le prix de, solder; (= *mark lower price on*) inscrire un prix réduit sur

►**price out** VT SEP **to ~ one's goods out of the market** perdre un marché en voulant demander des prix trop élevés; **Japanese products have ~d ours out of the market** nos produits ne peuvent plus soutenir la concurrence des prix japonais; **the French have ~d us out of that market** les bas prix pratiqués par les Français nous ont chassés de ce marché; **the workers are in danger of pricing themselves out of the market** les ouvriers risquent de devenir trop chers sur le marché de l'emploi

►**price up** VT SEP (*Comm*) (= *raise price of*) augmenter; (= *mark higher price on*) inscrire un prix plus élevé sur

-priced [praɪst] ADJ (*in compounds*) **high-priced** coûteux, cher → **low**¹

priceless ['praɪslɪs] ADJ **a** [*picture, jewel*] qui n'a pas de prix, inestimable; [*friendship, contribution, gift*] inestimable, très précieux **b** (* = *amusing*) impayable*

pricey* ['praɪsɪ] ADJ cher, chérot* (*m only*)

pricing ['praɪsɪŋ] N (= *setting price*) détermination *f* *or* fixation *f* des prix; (*for service*) tarification *f*; [*of stock*] évaluation *f*; **~ policy** *or* **strategy** politique *f* des prix

prick [prɪk] **1** N **a** (= *act, sensation, mark*) piqûre *f*; **to give sth a ~** piquer qch; (*fig*) **the ~s of conscience** les aiguillons *mpl* de la conscience, le remords → **kick**

b (** = *penis*) bite** *or* bitte** *f*

c (** = *person*) con** *m*

2 VT **a** [*person, thorn, pin, hypodermic*] piquer; [+ *balloon, blister*] crever; [+ *name on list*

etc] piquer, pointer; **she ~ed her finger with a pin** elle s'est piqué le doigt avec une épingle; **to ~ a hole in sth** faire un trou d'épingle (*or* d'aiguille *etc*) dans qch; (*fig*) **his conscience was ~ing him** il avait mauvaise conscience, il n'avait pas la conscience tranquille

b **to ~ (up) one's ears** [*animal*] dresser les oreilles; [*person*] (*fig*) dresser *or* tendre *or* prêter l'oreille

3 VI **a** [*thorn etc*] piquer; (*fig*) **his conscience was ~ing** il avait mauvaise conscience

b (= *tingle*) **my eyes are ~ing** les yeux me cuisent; **my toe is ~ing** j'ai des fourmis dans l'orteil

4 COMP ► **prick-tease**** N (*pej* = *woman*) allumeuse* *f* ♦ VI [*woman*] faire l'allumeuse* ♦ VT allumer*

►**prick out** VT SEP **a** (= *plant*) [+ *seedlings*] repiquer **b** (*with pin etc*) [+ *outline, design*] piquer, tracer en piquant

►**prick up** **1** VI (*lit*) **the dog's ears ~ed up** le chien a dressé l'oreille; (*fig*) **his ears ~ed up** il a dressé l'oreille **2** VT SEP = **prick 2b**

pricking ['prɪkɪŋ] N picotement *m*, sensation *f* cuisante; (*fig*) **~s of conscience** remords *m(pl)*

prickle ['prɪkl] **1** N **a** (= *spine*) [*of plant*] épine *f*, piquant *m*; [*of hedgehog etc*] piquant *m* **b** (*pricking sensation: on skin etc*) picotement *m*, sensation *f* cuisante **2** VT piquer **3** VI [*skin, fingers etc*] fourmiller, picoter

prickly ['prɪklɪ] **1** ADJ **a** (= *spiky*) [*plant*] épineux, hérissé; [*animal*] hérissé, armé de piquants; **his beard was ~** sa barbe piquait; **my arm feels ~** j'ai des fourmis *or* des fourmillements dans le bras **b** (*fig* = *irritable*) [*person*] ombrageux, irritable; (= *delicate*) [*subject*] épineux, délicat; **he is as ~ as a porcupine** c'est un vrai hérisson **2** COMP ► **prickly heat** N fièvre *f* miliaire ► **prickly pear** N (= *fruit*) figue *f* de Barbarie; (= *tree*) figuier *m* de Barbarie

pride [praɪd] **1** N **a** (*NonC*) (= *self-respect*) fierté *f*, amour-propre *m*; (= *satisfaction*) fierté *f*; (*pej* = *arrogance*) orgueil *m*; **his ~ was hurt** il était blessé dans son orgueil *or* dans son amour-propre; **he has too much ~ to ask for help** il est trop fier pour demander de l'aide; **she has no ~** elle n'a pas d'amour-propre; **the sin of ~** le péché d'orgueil; **false ~** vanité *f* ■ (*PROV*) **~ comes** *or* **goes before a fall** l'orgueil précède la chute; **her son's success is a great source of ~** le succès s'enorgueillit et elle est très fière du succès de son fils; **her ~ in her family** la fierté qu'elle tire de sa famille; **he spoke of them with ~** il parla d'eux avec fierté; **to take** *or* **have (a) ~ in** [+ *children, achievements*] être très fier de; [+ *house, car etc*] prendre (grand) soin de; **she takes a ~ in her appearance** elle prend soin de sa personne; **to take (a) ~ in doing sth** mettre sa fierté à faire qch; **to take** *or* **have ~ of place** avoir la place d'honneur

b (= *object of pride*) fierté *f*; **she is her father's ~ and joy** elle est la fierté de son père

c (*Zool* = *group*) [*of lions*] troupe *f*

2 VT **to ~ o.s. (up)on (doing) sth** être fier *or* s'enorgueillir de (faire) qch

priest [priːst] **1** N (*Christian, pagan*) prêtre *m*; (= *parish priest*) curé *m* → **assistant, high** **2** COMP ► **priest-ridden** ADJ (*pej*) dominé par le clergé, sous la tutelle des curés (*pej*)

priestess ['priːstɪs] N prêtresse *f*

priesthood ['priːsthʊd] N (= *function*) prêtrise *f*, sacerdoce *m*; (= *priests collectively*) clergé *m*; **to enter the ~** se faire prêtre, entrer dans les ordres

priestly ['priːstlɪ] ADJ sacerdotal, de prêtre

prig [prɪg] N pharisien(ne) *m(f)*; **what a ~ she is!** ce qu'elle peut se prendre au sérieux!; **don't be such a ~!** ne fais pas le petit saint (*or* la petite sainte)!

priggish ['prɪgɪʃ] ADJ pharisaïque, suffisant, fat (*m only*)

priggishness ['prɪgɪʃnɪs] N (*NonC*) pharisaïsme *m*, suffisance *f*, fatuité *f*

prim [prɪm] ADJ [a] (*pej*) [*person*] (= *prudish: also* ~ **and proper**) collet monté *inv*, guindé; [*manner, smile, look, expression*] compassé, guindé, contraint; [*dress, hat*] très correct, très convenable; [*house, garden*] trop coquet *or* net *or* impeccable [b] (= *demure*) très convenable, comme il faut

prima ballerina ['priːmə,bælə'riːnə] N (*pl* **prima ballerina** *or* **prima ballerinas**) danseuse *f* étoile

primacy ['praɪməsɪ] N (= *supremacy*) primauté *f*; (*Rel*) primatie *f*

prima donna ['priːmə'dɒnə] N (*pl* **prima donna** *or* **prima donnas**) (*lit*) prima donna *f inv*; (*fig*) **she's a real** ~ elle est capricieuse, elle joue les divas

primaeval [praɪ'miːvəl] ADJ (*Brit*) = **primeval**

prima facie ['praɪmə'feɪʃɪ] (*frm*) [1] ADV à première vue, de prime abord [2] ADJ (*Jur*) recevable, bien fondé; (*gen*) légitime (à première vue); **to have a ~ case** (*Jur*) avoir une affaire recevable; (*gen*) avoir raison à première vue; (*Jur*) ~ **evidence** commencement *m* de preuve; **there are ~ reasons why ...** on peut a priori raisonnablement expliquer pourquoi ...

primal ['praɪməl] ADJ [a] (= *first in time, primeval*) primitif, des premiers âges; (*Psych*) ~ **scream** cri *m* primal [b] (= *first in importance, primordial*) principal, primordial

primarily ['praɪmərɪlɪ] ADV (= *chiefly*) essentiellement, surtout

primary ['praɪmərɪ] [1] ADJ [a] (= *first: Astron, Chem, Econ, Elec, Geol, Med etc*) primaire [b] (= *basic*) [*reason, cause*] principal; [*concern, aim*] principal, premier (*before n*); **of ~ importance** d'une importance primordiale, de la plus haute *or* de toute première importance; **the ~ meaning of a word** le sens premier d'un mot [2] N (= *school*) école *f* primaire; (= *colour*) couleur *f* fondamentale; (= *feather*) rémige *f*; (*Elec*) enroulement *m* primaire; (*US Pol*) primaire *f* [3] COMP ► **primary cause** N (*Philos*) cause *f* première ► **primary colour** N couleur *f* fondamentale ► **primary education** N enseignement *m* primaire ► **primary election** N (*US Pol*) élection *f* primaire ► **primary feather** N (*Zool*) rémige *f* ► **primary industries** NPL le secteur primaire ► **primary producer** N (*Econ*) producteur *m* du secteur primaire ► **primary producing country** N (*Econ*) pays *m* de production primaire ► **primary product** N (*Econ*) produit *m* primaire *or* de base ► **primary school** N (*esp Brit*) école *f* primaire ► **primary school-teacher** N (*esp Brit*) instituteur *m*, -trice *f* ► **primary stress** N (*Phon*) accent *m* principal ► **primary teacher** N = **primary school-teacher** ► **primary tense** N (*Gram*) temps *m* primitif ► **primary winding** N (*Elec*) enroulement *m* primaire

primate ['praɪmɪt] N [a] (*Rel*) primat *m* [b] ['praɪmeɪt] (*Zool*) primate *m*

prime [praɪm] [1] ADJ [a] (= *principal*) [*reason etc*] primordial, principal; [*concern, aim*] principal, premier (*before n*); **a ~ factor in ...** un facteur primordial *or* fondamental dans ... → **4**; **of ~ importance** d'une importance primordiale, de la plus haute *or* de toute première importance [b] (= *excellent, superior*) [*advantage*] de premier ordre; (= *best*) [*meat*] de premier choix; **in ~ condition** [*animal, athlete*] en parfaite condition; [*car*] en parfait état; (*Culin*) ~ **cut** morceau *m* de premier choix; **a ~ example of what to avoid** un excellent exemple de ce qu'il faut éviter; **of ~ quality** de première

qualité; ~ **ribs** côtes *fpl* premières; (*Rad, TV*) ~ **time** (*n*) prime time *m*, heure(s) *f(pl)* de grande écoute ♦ (*programme, audience etc*) aux heures de grande écoute [c] (*Math*) **7 is** ~ 7 est un nombre premier [2] N [a] (= *peak*) **when the Renaissance was in its** ~ quand la Renaissance était à son apogée, aux plus beaux jours de la Renaissance; **in the ~ of life ◊ in one's** ~ dans *or* à la fleur de l'âge; **he is past his** ~ il est sur le retour; (*hum*) **this grapefruit is past its** ~* ce pamplemousse n'est plus de la première fraîcheur, ce pamplemousse a vu de ses jours meilleurs (*hum*) [b] (*Math: also* ~ **number**) nombre *m* premier [c] (*Rel*) prime *f* [3] VT [a] [+ *gun, pump*] amorcer; (*fig*) **to ~ the pump** renflouer une entreprise *or* une affaire; **to ~ sb with drink** faire boire qn (tant et plus); **he was well ~d (with drink)** il avait bu plus que de raison [b] [+ *surface for painting*] apprêter [c] (*fig*) [+ *person*] mettre au fait, mettre au courant; **they ~d him about what he should say** ils lui ont bien fait répéter ce qu'il avait à dire; **he was ~d to say that** ils lui ont fait la leçon pour qu'il dise cela; **she came well ~d for the interview** elle est arrivée à l'entrevue tout à fait préparée [4] COMP ► **prime bill** N (*Econ, Fin*) effet *m* de premier ordre ► **prime cost** N (*Comm, Econ*) prix *m* de revient, prix *m* coûtant ► **prime factor** N (*Math*) facteur *m* premier, diviseur *m* premier ► **prime meridian** N (*Geog*) premier méridien *m* ► **prime minister** N Premier ministre *m* ► **prime ministerial** ADJ du Premier ministre ► **prime ministership**, **prime ministry** N ministère *m*, fonctions *fpl* de Premier ministre ► **prime mover** N (*Phys, Tech*) force *f* motrice; (*Philos*) premier moteur *m*, cause *f* première; (= *person*) instigateur *m*, -trice *f* ► **prime number** N nombre *m* premier ► **prime rate** N (*Econ, Fin*) taux *m* préférentiel *or* de base

primer ['praɪmər] N [a] (= *textbook*) premier livre *m*, livre *m* élémentaire [b] (= *reading book*) abécédaire *m* [c] (= *paint*) apprêt *m*

primeval, **primaeval** (*Brit*) [praɪ'miːvəl] ADJ primitif, primordial; ~ **forest** forêt *f* vierge

priming ['praɪmɪŋ] N [a] [*of pump*] amorçage *m*; [*of gun*] amorce *f* [b] (*Painting*) (= *substance*) couche *f* d'apprêt; (= *action*) apprêt *m*

primitive ['prɪmɪtɪv] ADJ, N (*all senses*) primitif *m*

primitivism ['prɪmɪtɪ,vɪzəm] N primitivisme *m*

primly ['prɪmlɪ] ADV (= *demurely*) bien sagement; **to be ~ dressed** être habillé très comme il faut, être tiré à quatre épingles [b] (*pej* = *priggishly*) [*say*] d'un ton guindé, d'un air bégueule; [*behave*] d'une manière guindée

primness ['prɪmnɪs] N [a] (= *demureness*) [*of person*] façons *fpl* très correctes *or* très convenables; [*of appearance, attire*] aspect *m* très comme il faut *or* très convenable [b] (= *prudishness*) [*of person*] façons *fpl* guindées *or* compassées, air *m* collet monté

primogeniture [,praɪməʊ'dʒenɪtʃər] N (*Jur etc*) primogéniture *f*

primordial [praɪ'mɔːdɪəl] ADJ primordial

primp [prɪmp] [1] VI se pomponner, se bichonner [2] VT pomponner, bichonner

primrose ['prɪmrəʊz] [1] N (*Bot*) primevère *f* (jaune); (*fig*) **the ~ path** le chemin *or* la voie de la facilité [2] ADJ (*also* ~ **yellow**) jaune pâle *inv*, jaune primevère *inv*

primula ['prɪmjʊlə] N (*Bot*) primevère *f* (*espèce*)

Primus® ['praɪməs] N (*esp Brit: also* ~ **stove**) réchaud *m* de camping (à pétrole), Primus® *m*

prince [prɪns] [1] N [a] prince *m* (*also fig*); **Prince Charles** le prince Charles; **the Prince of Wales** le prince de Galles; ~ **consort** prince *m* consort; ~ **regent** prince *m* régent; (*lit, fig*)

Prince Charming le prince charmant; **the Prince of Darkness** le prince des ténèbres *or* des démons; (*fig*) **the ~s of this world** les princes *mpl* de la terre, les grands *mpl* de ce monde [b] (*US fig* = *fine man*) chic type* *m* [2] COMP ► **Prince Edward Island** N l'île *f* du Prince-Édouard

princeling ['prɪnslɪŋ] N principicule *m*

princely ['prɪnslɪ] ADJ (*lit, fig*) princier; **the ~ sum of ...** la somme rondelette de ..., la coquette somme de ...

princess [prɪn'ses] N princesse *f*; **Princess Anne** la princesse Anne; **Princess Royal** Princesse Royale (*titre donné parfois à la fille aînée du monarque*)

principal ['prɪnsɪpəl] [1] ADJ principal; (*Brit Theat*) ~ **boy** jeune héros *m* (*rôle tenu par une actrice dans les spectacles de Noël*); (*Gram*) ~ **clause** (proposition *f*) principale *f*; (*Gram*) ~ **parts of a verb** temps *mpl* primitifs d'un verbe; (*Mus*) ~ **horn/violin** premier cor *m*/ violon *m*; (*Brit*) ~ **nursing officer** ≈ surveillant(e) *m(f)* général(e) (*dans un hôpital*) [2] N [a] (*Scol etc: gen*) chef *m* d'établissement; [*of lycée*] proviseur *m*; [*of college*] principal(e) *m(f)* [b] (*in orchestra*) chef *m* de pupitre; (*Theat*) vedette *f* [c] (*Fin, Jur* = *person employing agent, lawyer etc*) mandant *m*, commettant *m*; (*Jur* = *chief perpetrator of a crime*) auteur *m* (*d'un crime*), principal *m* responsable; (*Jur, Fin*) ~ **and agent** commettant *m* et agent *m* [d] (*Fin* = *capital sum*) principal *m*, capital *m*; ~ **and interest** principal *m* *or* capital *m* et intérêts *mpl*

principality [,prɪnsɪ'pælɪtɪ] N principauté *f*; **the Principality** (= *Wales*) le pays de Galles

principally ['prɪnsɪpəlɪ] ADV principalement

principle ['prɪnsɪpl] N (*all senses*) principe *m*; **to go back to first ~s** repartir sur de bonnes bases; **in** ~ en principe; **on** ~ ◊ **as a matter of** ~ par principe; **I make it a** ~ **never to lend money** ◊ **it's against my ~s to lend money** j'ai pour principe de ne jamais prêter d'argent; **that would be totally against my ~s** cela irait à l'encontre de tous mes principes; **for the ~ of the thing*** pour le principe; **he is a man of** ~(s) ◊ **he has high ~s** c'est un homme qui a des principes; **all these machines work on the same** ~ toutes ces machines marchent sur *or* selon le même principe

principled ['prɪnsɪpld] ADJ [*person*] qui a des principes; [*behaviour*] réglé par des principes

-principled ['prɪnsɪpld] ADJ (*in compounds*) → **high**, **low¹**

prink [prɪŋk] = **primp**

print [prɪnt] [1] N [a] (= *mark*) [*of hand, foot, tyre etc*] empreinte *f*; (= *finger print*) empreinte *f* (digitale); **a thumb/paw** *etc* ~ l'empreinte *f* d'un pouce/d'une patte *etc*; (*Police etc*) **to take sb's ~s** prendre les empreintes de qn → **fingerprint**, **footprint** [b] (*NonC: Typ*) (= *actual letters*) caractères *mpl*; (= *printed material*) texte *m* imprimé; **in small/large** ~ en petits/gros caractères; **read the small** *or* **fine** ~ **before you sign** lisez toutes les clauses avant de signer; **the ~ is poor** les caractères ne sont pas nets; **it was there in cold** ~! c'était là noir sur blanc!; **out of** ~ [*book*] épuisé; **in** ~ disponible (en librairie); **"books in ~"** «livres en librairie», «catalogue courant»; **he wants to see himself in** ~ il veut être publié; **to rush into** ~ se hâter *or* s'empresser de publier; **don't let that get into** ~ n'allez pas imprimer *or* publier cela [c] (*Art = etching, woodcut etc*) estampe *f*, gravure *f*; (*Art = reproduction*) tirage *m*; (*Phot*) tirage *m*, épreuve *f*; [*of cinema film*] copie *f*; (*Tex*) (= *material, design*) imprimé *m*; (= *printed dress*) robe *f* imprimée; (*Phot*) **to make a ~ from a negative** faire un tirage à partir d'un négatif, tirer une épreuve d'un cliché; **a cotton** ~ une cotonnade imprimée → **blueprint**

2 ADJ [*dress etc*] en (tissu) imprimé

3 VT **a** (*Typ, Comput*) imprimer ; (= *publish*) imprimer, publier ; **~ed in England** imprimé en Angleterre ; **the book is being ~ed just now** le livre est sous presse *or* à l'impression en ce moment ; **100 copies were ~ed** cela a été tiré *or* imprimé à 100 exemplaires, on en a tiré 100 exemplaires ; **they didn't dare ~ it** ils n'ont pas osé l'imprimer *or* le publier ; (*lit*) **to ~ money** imprimer des billets ; (*fig: Econ*) **it's a licence to ~ money** c'est une affaire extrêmement rentable *or* qui rapporte gros* → **printed**

b (*Tex*) imprimer ; (*Phot*) tirer

c (= *write in block letters*) écrire en capitales *or* en caractères d'imprimerie ; **~ it in block capitals** écrivez-le en lettres majuscules

d **the mark of horses' hooves ~ed in the sand** la marque de sabots de chevaux imprimée sur le sable, la trace *or* les empreintes *fpl* de sabots de chevaux sur le sable

4 VI **a** [*machine*] imprimer ; [*document*] être imprimé ; **the book is ~ing now** le livre est à l'impression *or* sous presse en ce moment ; (*Comput*) **"your document is ~ing"** « l'impression de votre document est en cours » ; **"~ing"** « impression en cours »

b (*on form*) **"please ~"** « écrivez en capitales »

5 COMP ► **print journalism** N journalisme *m* de presse écrite ► **print media** N presse *f* écrite ► **print reporter** N (*US*) journaliste *mf* de la presse écrite ► **print run** N (*Publishing*) tirage *m* ► **print shop** N (*Typ*) imprimerie *f* ; (= *art shop*) boutique *f* d'art (*spécialisée dans la vente de reproductions, affiches etc*) ► **print unions** NPL (*Ind*) syndicats *mpl* des typographes ► **print off** VT SEP (*Comput, Typ*) tirer, imprimer ; (*Phot*) tirer ► **print out** (*Comput*) **1** VT SEP imprimer **2** **~out** N → **printout**

printable ['prɪntəbl] ADJ (*lit*) imprimable ; (= *publishable*) publiable ; (*hum*) **what he said is just not ~*** ce qu'il a dit est franchement impubliable, il ne serait pas convenable de répéter ce qu'il a dit

printed ['prɪntɪd] ADJ imprimé ; **~ matter** ◊ **~ papers** imprimés *mpl* ; **the ~ word** tout ce qui est imprimé, la chose imprimée ; (*Elec*) **~ circuit (board)** circuit *m* imprimé

printer ['prɪntəʳ] **1** N **a** imprimeur *m* ; (= *typographer*) typographe *mf*, imprimeur *m* ; **the text has gone to the ~** le texte est chez l'imprimeur **b** (*Comput*) imprimante *f* **c** (*Phot*) tireuse *f* **2** COMP ► **printer's devil** N apprenti *m* imprimeur ► **printer's error** N faute *f* d'impression, coquille *f* ► **printer's ink** N encre *f* d'imprimerie ► **printer's mark** N marque *f* de l'imprimeur ► **printer's reader** N correcteur *m*, -trice *f* (d'épreuves)

printing ['prɪntɪŋ] **1** N (*Press, Tex, Typ*) impression *f* ; (*Phot*) tirage *m* ; (= *block writing*) écriture *f* en caractères d'imprimerie **2** COMP ► **printing frame** N (*Phot*) châssis-presse *m* ► **printing ink** N encre *f* d'imprimerie ► **printing office** N imprimerie *f* ► **printing press** N presse *f* typographique ► **printing works** N imprimerie *f* (*atelier*)

printmaker ['prɪnt,meɪkəʳ] N graveur *m*

printmaking ['prɪnt,meɪkɪŋ] N (*NonC*) gravure *f* (*de planches de reproduction*)

printout ['prɪntaʊt] N (*Comput*) listage *m*, listing *m*, sortie *f* sur imprimante *or* papier ; **to do a ~ of sth** imprimer qch

prion ['praɪɒn] N prion *m*

prior ['praɪəʳ] **1** ADJ précédent, antérieur (-eure *f*) ; [*consent*] préalable ; **~ to** antérieur à ; **without ~ notice** sans préavis, sans avertissement préalable ; **to have a ~ claim to sth** avoir droit à qch par priorité ; (*US Jur*) **restraint** interdiction *f* judiciaire **2** ADV **~ to** antérieurement à, préalablement à, avant ; **~ to (his) leaving he ...** avant de partir *or* avant son départ, il ...

son départ *or* avant qu'il ne parte, nous ...

3 N (*Rel*) prieur *m*

prioress ['praɪərɪs] N prieure *f*

prioritize [praɪ'ɒrɪtaɪz] **1** VT (= *give priority to*) donner la priorité à **2** VI (= *establish priorities*) établir la liste des priorités, identifier ses priorités

priority [praɪ'ɒrɪtɪ] **1** N priorité *f* ; **to have** *or* **take ~ (over)** avoir la priorité (sur) ; **housing must be given first** *or* **top ~** on doit donner la priorité absolue au logement ; **schools were low on the list of priorities** *or* **the ~ list** les écoles venaient loin sur la liste des priorités *or* étaient loin de venir en priorité ; **you must get your priorities right** vous devez décider de ce qui compte le plus pour vous ; **to give sb (a) high/low ~** donner/ne pas donner la priorité à qn ; **it is a high/low ~** c'est/ce n'est pas une priorité **2** COMP ► **priority case** N affaire *f* prioritaire ► **priority share** N (*St Ex*) action *f* prioritaire

priory ['praɪərɪ] N prieuré *m*

prise [praɪz] VT (*Brit*) **to ~ open a box** ouvrir une boîte en faisant levier, forcer une boîte ; **to ~ the lid off a box** forcer le couvercle d'une boîte ; (*fig*) **I ~d him out of his chair** je l'ai enfin fait décoller* de sa chaise ; (*fig*) **to ~ a secret out of sb** arracher un secret à qn ► **prise off** VT SEP enlever en faisant levier ► **prise up** VT SEP soulever en faisant levier

prism ['prɪzəm] N prisme *m* ; (*fig*) **through the ~ of time/memory** à travers le prisme du temps/ de la mémoire → **prune**[1]

prismatic [prɪz'mætɪk] ADJ [*surface, shape, colour*] prismatique (*also fig*) ; **~ compass** boussole *f* topographique à prismes

prison ['prɪzn] **1** N (= *place*) prison *f* ; (= *imprisonment*) prison *f*, réclusion *f* ; **he is in ~** il est en prison, il fait de la prison ; **to put sb in ~** mettre qn en prison, emprisonner qn ; **to send sb to ~** condamner qn à la prison ; **to send sb to ~ for five years** condamner qn à cinq ans de prison ; **he was in ~ for five years** il a fait cinq ans de prison **2** COMP [*food, life, conditions*] dans la (*or* les) prison(s), pénitentiaire ; [*system*] carcéral, pénitentiaire ; [*organization, colony*] pénitentiaire ► **prison authorities** NPL administration *f* pénitentiaire ► **prison camp** N camp *m* de prisonniers ► **prison farm** N ferme *f* dépendant d'une maison d'arrêt ► **prison governor** N directeur *m*, -trice *f* de prison ► **prison guard** N (*US*) gardien(ne) *m(f)* *or* surveillant(e) *m(f)* (de prison) ► **prison officer** N gardien(ne) *m(f)* *or* surveillant(e) *m(f)* (de prison) ► **prison population** N population *f* carcérale ► **prison riot** N mutinerie *f* (*dans une prison*) ► **prison van** N voiture *f* cellulaire ► **prison visitor** N visiteur *m*, -euse *f* de prison ► **prison yard** N cour *f* *or* préau *m* de prison

prisoner ['prɪznəʳ] N (*gen*) prisonnier *m*, -ière *f* ; (*in jail*) détenu(e) *m(f)*, prisonnier *m*, -ière *f* ; **~ of conscience** détenu(e) *m(f)* *or* prisonnier *m*, -ière *f* politique ; **~ of war** prisonnier *m*, -ière *f* de guerre ; (*Jur*) **~ at the bar** accusé(e) *m(f)*, inculpé(e) *m(f)* ; **he was taken ~ (by the enemy)** il a été fait prisonnier (par l'ennemi) ; **to hold sb ~** détenir qn, garder qn en captivité ; (*fig*) **to take no ~s** ne pas faire de quartier

prissy* ['prɪsɪ] ADJ (= *prudish*) bégueule ; (= *effeminate*) efféminé ; (= *fussy*) pointilleux

pristine ['prɪstaɪn] ADJ **a** (= *unspoiled*) parfait, virginal **b** (= *original*) original, d'origine

prithee ['prɪðiː] EXCL je vous prie

privacy ['prɪvəsɪ] **1** N intimité *f* ; **in ~** en toute intimité ; **in the ~ of your own home** dans l'intimité de votre foyer, tranquillement chez vous ; **his desire for ~** son désir d'être seul, son désir de solitude ; [*of public figure etc*] son désir de préserver sa vie privée ; **lack of ~** promiscuité *f*, impossibilité *f* de s'isoler ; **there is**

no ~ in these flats impossible de s'isoler *or* on ne peut avoir aucune vie privée dans ces appartements ; **everyone needs some ~** tout le monde a besoin de pouvoir s'isoler de temps en temps → **invasion** **2** COMP ► **Privacy Act** N (*Jur*) loi *f* sur la protection de la vie privée

private ['praɪvɪt] **1** ADJ **a** (= *not open to public*) [*conversation, meeting, interview, party, land, property, road*] privé ; [*gardens*] privatif ; [*letter*] personnel ; (*Jur*) **~ agreement** accord *m* à l'amiable ; **they have a ~ agreement to help each other** ils ont convenu (entre eux) de s'aider mutuellement, ils se sont entendus *or* se sont mis d'accord pour s'aider mutuellement ; **"~ fishing"** « pêche réservée *or* gardée » ; (*Theat etc*) **~ performance** représentation *f* à guichets *or* bureaux fermés ; (*in hotel etc*) **~ room** salon *m* réservé → **1b** ; **~ showing** [*of film*] séance *f* privée ; **a ~ wedding** un mariage célébré dans l'intimité ; **this matter is strictly ~** cette affaire est strictement confidentielle ; **I have ~ information that ...** je sais de source privée que ... ; **a ~ place** un coin retiré, un petit coin tranquille ; **it's not very ~ here** ce n'est pas très tranquille ici ; **let's go somewhere more ~** allons dans un endroit plus tranquille ; **he's a ~ person** (*gen*) c'est un homme très secret *or* qui ne se confie pas ; (*public figure etc*) il tient à préserver sa vie privée ; **"~"** (*on door etc*) « privé », « interdit au public » ; (*on envelope*) « personnel »

b (= *personal, domestic*) [*house, lesson, room*] particulier ; (= *personal*) [*car, bank account*] personnel ; [*plane, army*] privé ; **a ~ house** une maison particulière ; **a room with ~ bath(room)** une chambre avec salle de bain particulière ; **he has a ~ income** ◊ **he has ~ means** il a une fortune personnelle ; **a ~ citizen** un simple citoyen ; **in his ~ capacity** à titre personnel ; **for (his) ~ use** pour son usage personnel ; **in (his) ~ life** dans sa vie privée, dans le privé ; **the ~ life of Henry VIII** la vie privée d'Henri VIII ; **it's a ~ matter** *or* **affair** c'est une affaire privée ; **it is my ~ opinion that ...** pour ma part je pense que ... ; **for ~ reasons** pour des raisons personnelles ; **in his ~ thoughts** dans ses pensées secrètes *or* intimes ; **~ pupil** élève *mf* en leçons particulières ; **~ tutor** (*for full education*) précepteur *m*, -trice *f* ; (*for one subject*) répétiteur *m*, -trice *f* ; **he's got a ~ teacher** *or* **tutor for maths** il prend des leçons particulières en maths, il a un répétiteur en maths ; **~ tuition** leçons *fpl* particulières

c (= *outside public sector*) [*company, institution*] privé ; [*clinic, hospital, nursing home*] privé, non conventionné ; **~ pension (scheme)** (plan *m* de) retraite *f* complémentaire ; **~ health insurance** assurance *f* maladie privée ; (*Brit*) **~ patient** patient(e) *m(f)* consultant en clientèle privée ; (*Brit*) **his ~ patients** sa clientèle privée ; **~ treatment** ≈ traitement *m* non remboursé ; **to be in ~ practice** ≈ être médecin non conventionné

d (*Mil*) **~ soldier** simple soldat *m*, soldat *m* de deuxième classe

2 N **a** (*Mil*) (simple) soldat *m*, soldat *m* de deuxième classe ; **Private Martin** le soldat Martin ; **Private Martin!** soldat Martin ! ; (*US*) **~ first class** ≈ caporal *m*

b **in ~** = **privately** a *and* b

3 **privates*** NPL (*euph*) parties *fpl* intimes

4 COMP ► **private branch exchange** N (*Brit Telec*) commutateur *m* privé ► **private detective** N détective *m* privé ► **private dick*** N = **private eye** ► **private enterprise** N (*Econ*) entreprise *f* privée ► **private eye*** N privé* *m* ► **private hearing** N (*Admin, Jur*) audience *f* à huis clos ► **private hotel** N pension *f* de famille ► **private investigator** N = **private detective** ► **private joke** N plaisanterie *f* pour initiés ► **private member** N (*Parl*) simple député *m* ► **private member's bill** N (*Parl*) proposition *f* de loi (*émanant d'un simple député*) ► **private parts*** NPL (*euph*) parties *fpl* intimes ► **private property** N propriété *f* privée ► **private prosecution** N (*Jur*) poursuites pénales engagées *or* la partie civile ► **private school** N école *f* privée, ≈ école *f* libre ► **private secretary** N secrétaire *m* particulier, secrétaire *f* particulière ► **the private sector** N (*Econ, Ind*) le secteur privé ► **private study** N (*Brit Scol*) étude *f* ► **private view, private viewing** N (*Art etc*) vernissage *m*

privateer [ˌpraɪvəˈtɪəʳ] N (= *man, ship*) corsaire *m*

privately [ˈpraɪvɪtlɪ] ADV [a] (= *in private*) en privé; **may I speak to you ~?** puis-je vous parler en privé *or* vous dire un mot seul à seul?; **he told me ~ that ...** il m'a dit en privé que ...; **the committee sat ~** le comité s'est réuni en séance privée *or* à huis clos [b] (= *secretly, internally*) en *or* dans son (*or* mon *etc*) for intérieur, intérieurement; **~, he was against the scheme** dans son for intérieur *or* intérieurement, il était opposé au projet [c] (= *as private individual*) [*write, apply, object*] à titre personnel *or* privé; **I bought/sold my car ~,** not through a garage j'ai acheté/vendu ma voiture à un particulier, pas à un garage [d] (= *not through the state*) **~ owned** privé; **~ controlled** sous contrôle privé; **she is having the operation ~** (*private hospital*) elle se fait opérer dans un hôpital privé; (*private surgeon*) elle se fait opérer par un chirurgien non conventionné; **to be ~ educated** faire (*or* avoir fait) ses études dans une école privée (*or* des écoles privées)

privation [praɪˈveɪʃən] N privation *f*

privative [ˈprɪvətɪv] ADJ, N (*also Ling*) privatif *m*

privatization [ˌpraɪvətaɪˈzeɪʃən] N (*Econ*) privatisation *f*

privatize [ˈpraɪvətaɪz] VT (*Econ*) privatiser

privet [ˈprɪvɪt] [1] N troène *m* [2] COMP ► **privet hedge** N haie *f* de troènes

privilege [ˈprɪvɪlɪdʒ] [1] N privilège *m*; (*NonC: Parl etc*) prérogative *f*, immunité *f*; **to have the ~ of doing** avoir le privilège *or* jouir du privilège de faire; **I hate ~** je déteste les privilèges [2] VT [a] (= *favour*) privilégier [b] **to be ~d to do sth** avoir le privilège de faire qch; **I was ~d to meet him once** j'ai eu le privilège de le rencontrer une fois

privileged [ˈprɪvɪlɪdʒd] ADJ [*person, group, situation, position*] privilégié; **a ~ few** quelques privilégiés *mpl*; **the ~ few** les privilégiés *mpl*; **~ information** renseignements *mpl* confidentiels (*obtenus dans l'exercice de ses fonctions*) → **underprivileged**

privily†† [ˈprɪvɪlɪ] ADV en secret

privy [ˈprɪvɪ] [1] ADJ (†† *or Jur*) privé, secret (-ète *f*); **~ to** au courant de, dans le secret de [2] N† cabinets *mpl*, W.-C. *mpl* [3] COMP ► **Privy Council** N (*Brit*) conseil privé du souverain britannique ► **Privy Councillor** N (*Brit*) membre du conseil privé du souverain britannique ► **Privy Purse** N cassette *f* royale ► **Privy Seal** N Petit Sceau *m*

prize¹ [praɪz] [1] N [a] (*gen, Scol, fig*) prix *m*; (*in lottery*) lot *m*; **to win first ~** (*Scol etc*) remporter le premier prix (**in** de); (*in lottery*) gagner le gros lot; **there's a ~ for the best costume** il y a un prix pour le meilleur costume; **no ~s for guessing ...*** vous n'aurez aucun mal à deviner ...; **the Nobel Prize** le prix Nobel → **cash** [b] (*Naut*) prise *f* de navire (*or* de cargaison) [2] ADJ [a] (= *prize-winning*) primé, qui a remporté un prix; **a ~ sheep** un mouton primé; **he grows ~ onions** il cultive des oignons pour les concours agricoles [b] (*fig* = *outstanding*) **a ~ example of official stupidity** un parfait exemple de la bêtise des milieux officiels; **what a ~ fool he'd been*** il s'était conduit comme un parfait imbécile

[3] VT attacher beaucoup de prix à, apprécier, priser; **to ~ sth very highly** attacher énormément de prix à qch; **his most ~d possession was his car** la chose à laquelle il attachait le plus de prix *or* il tenait le plus était sa voiture; **gold is ~d for its beauty/its electrical conductivity** l'or est recherché *or* (très) apprécié pour sa beauté/sa conductivité; **lead soldiers are (greatly) ~d by collectors** les soldats de plomb sont très appréciés des collectionneurs *or* très prisés par les collectionneurs

[4] COMP ► **prize day** N (*Scol*) (jour *m* de la) distribution *f* des prix ► **prize draw** N tombola *f* ► **prize fight** N (*Boxing*) combat *m* professionnel ► **prize fighter** N boxeur *m* professionnel ► **prize fighting** N boxe *f* professionnelle ► **prize-giving** N (*Scol etc*) distribution *f* des prix ► **prize list** N palmarès *m*, liste *f* des lauréats *or* des gagnants ► **prize money** N (*NonC*) (*gen, Sport*) prix *m* (en argent); (*Naut*) part *f* de prise ► **prize ring** N (*Boxing*) ring *m* (*pour la boxe professionnelle*)

prize² [praɪz] = **prise**

prizewinner [ˈpraɪzˌwɪnəʳ] N (*Scol, gen*) lauréat(e) *m(f)*; (*in lottery*) gagnant(e) *m(f)*

prizewinning [ˈpraɪzˌwɪnɪŋ] ADJ [*essay, novel, entry etc*] primé, lauréat; [*ticket*] gagnant

PRO N (ABBR = **public relations officer**) → **public**

pro¹ [prəʊ] [1] PREP* pour; **are you ~ (or anti) the idea?** êtes-vous pour (ou contre) l'idée? [2] ADJ* pour; **he's very ~** il est tout à fait pour [3] N [a] (= *advantage*) **the ~s and the cons** le pour et le contre [b] (= *supporter*) **the ~s and the antis** les pour et les contre

pro²* [prəʊ] [1] N [a] (ABBR = **professional**) (*Sport etc*) pro *mf*; (*fig*) **you can see he's a ~** on voit bien qu'on a affaire à un professionnel, on dirait qu'il a fait ça toute sa vie [b] (= *prostitute*) professionnelle *f* [2] COMP ► **pro-am** ADJ (*Golf*) (ABBR = **professional-amateur**) pro-am; **~-am tournament** tournoi *m* pro-am ► **pro-celeb*** ADJ = **pro-celebrity** ► **pro-celebrity** ADJ **~-celebrity tournament** tournoi opposant des célébrités à des joueurs professionnels

pro- [prəʊ] PREF [a] (= *in favour of*) pro...; **~French/European** profrançais/proeuropéen; **~Europe** proeuropéen; **he was ~Hitler** il était hitlérien, il était partisan d'Hitler; **they were ~Moscow** ils étaient prosoviétiques [b] (= *acting for*) pro-, vice-→ **proconsul**

pro-abortion [ˌprəʊəˈbɔːʃən] ADJ en faveur de l'avortement

pro-abortionist [ˌprəʊəˈbɔːʃənɪst] N partisan(e) *m(f)* de l'avortement

proactive [ˌprəʊˈæktɪv] ADJ proactif

probabilistic [ˌprɒbəbəˈlɪstɪk] ADJ probabiliste

probability [ˌprɒbəˈbɪlɪtɪ] N probabilité *f*; **the ~ of sth** (*of an undesirable event*) les risques *mpl* de qch; (*of a desirable event*) les chances *fpl* de qch; **the ~ of sth happening** la probabilité que qch arrive; (*desirable event*) les chances *fpl* que qch arrive; **in all ~** selon toute probabilité; **the ~ is that ...** il est très probable que ... (+ *indic*), il y a de grandes chances pour que ... (+ *subj*); **there is little ~ that ...** il est peu probable que ... (+ *subj*)

probable [ˈprɒbəbl] [1] ADJ [a] (= *likely*) [*reason, success, event, election*] probable; **it is ~ that he will succeed** il est probable qu'il réussira; **it is not/hardly ~ that ...** il est improbable/peu probable que ... (+ *subj*) [b] (= *credible*) vraisemblable; **his explanation did not sound very ~** son explication ne m'a pas paru très vraisemblable [2] N **he is one of the ~s* for the match** il y a de fortes chances qu'il fasse partie des joueurs sélectionnés pour le match → **possible**

probably [ˈprɒbəblɪ] ADV probablement; **most ~** très probablement; **~ not** probablement pas

probate [ˈprəʊbɪt] (*Jur*) [1] N homologation *f* (*d'un testament*); **to value sth for ~** évaluer *or* expertiser qch pour l'homologation d'un testament; **to grant/take out ~ of a will** homologuer/faire homologuer un testament [2] VT (*US*) [+ *will*] homologuer [3] COMP ► **probate court** N tribunal *m* des successions

probation [prəʊˈbeɪʃən] [1] N [a] (*Jur*) ≈ mise *f* à l'épreuve; (*for minors*) mise *f* en liberté surveillée; **to be on ~** ≈ être en sursis avec mise à l'épreuve *or* en liberté surveillée; **to put sb on ~** ≈ mettre qn en sursis avec mise à l'épreuve *or* en liberté surveillée [b] (= *trial period*) **he is on ~** [*employee*] il a été engagé à l'essai; (*Rel*) il est novice; (*US Educ*) il a été pris (*or* repris) à l'essai; (*US Educ*) **a semester on ~** un semestre à l'essai, un semestre probatoire [2] COMP ► **probation officer** N (*Jur*) contrôleur *m* judiciaire

probationary [prəʊˈbeɪʃnərɪ] ADJ (*gen*) d'essai; (*Jur*) de sursis, avec mise à l'épreuve; (*Rel*) de probation, de noviciat; **~ year** année *f* probatoire; **for a ~ period** pendant une période d'essai; **a ~ period of three months** une période de probatoire de trois mois

probationer [prəʊˈbeɪʃnəʳ] N (*in business, factory etc*) employé(e) *m(f)* engagé(e) à l'essai; (*Brit Police*) stagiaire *mf*; (*Rel*) novice *mf*; (*Jur*) ≈ condamné(e) *m(f)* sursitaire avec mise à l'épreuve; (= *minor*) ≈ délinquant(e) *m(f)* en liberté surveillée

probe [prəʊb] [1] N [a] (*gen, Med, Dentistry, Space*) sonde *f*; (*Zool*) trompe *f*; (*Space*) **Venus ~** sonde *f* spatiale à destination de Vénus [b] (*fig* = *investigation*) enquête *f* (**into** sur), investigation *f* (**into** de) [2] VT [a] (*lit*) (= *explore*) [+ *hole, crack*] explorer, examiner; (*Med*) sonder; (*Space*) explorer; **he ~d the ground with his stick** il fouilla la terre de sa canne [b] (*fig* = *inquire into*) [+ *sb's subconscious*] sonder; [+ *past*] explorer; [+ *private life*] chercher à découvrir; [+ *causes, sb's death*] chercher à éclaircir; [+ *mystery*] approfondir; [+ *sb's activities*] enquêter sur [c] (= *inquire*) **"why did you say that?" ~d Dennis** «pourquoi avez-vous dit cela?» s'enquit Dennis [3] VI (*gen, Med etc*) faire un examen avec une sonde, faire un sondage; (*fig* = *inquire*) faire des recherches; **to ~ for sth** (*gen, Med*) chercher à localiser *or* à découvrir qch; (*fig: by investigation*) rechercher qch; **the police should have ~d more deeply** la police aurait dû pousser plus loin ses investigations; **to ~ into sth** = **to probe sth**; → **2b**

probing [ˈprəʊbɪŋ] [1] ADJ [a] [*instrument*] pour sonder [b] (*fig*) [*question, study*] pénétrant; [*interrogation*] serré; [*look*] inquisiteur (-trice *f*) [2] N (*NonC*) (*gen, Med*) sondage *m*; (*fig* = *investigations*) investigations *fpl* (**into** de)

probity [ˈprəʊbɪtɪ] N probité *f*

▼ **problem** [ˈprɒbləm] [1] N [a] (= *difficulty*) problème *m*; **the housing ~** le problème *or* la crise du logement; **he is a great ~ to his mother** il pose de gros problèmes à sa mère; **we've got ~s with the car** nous avons des ennuis avec la voiture; **he's got a drink ~** il boit, il est porté sur la boisson; **it's not my ~** ça ne me concerne pas; **that's YOUR ~!** ça c'est ton problème!; **that's no ~ (to him)** ça ne (lui) pose pas de problème; **no ~!*** pas de problème!*; **~ solved!*** (ça y est,) c'est réglé!; **what's the ~?** qu'est-ce qui ne va pas?, quel est le problème?; **hey, what's your ~?*** t'as un problème ou quoi?*; **I had no ~ in getting the money** ◊ **it was no ~ to get the money** je n'ai eu aucun mal à obtenir l'argent [b] (* = *objection*) **I have no ~ with that** j'y vois pas de problème*; **my ~ (with that) is that ...** ce qui me chiffonne *or* me gêne, c'est que ...; **do you have a ~ (with that)?** il y a quelque

chose qui te gêne?
c (Math etc = exercise) problème m
2 ADJ **a** (= causing problems) [situation] difficile; [family, group] qui pose des problèmes; [child] caractériel, difficile; (Sociol) ~ **cases** des cas mpl sociaux
b (Literat etc) [novel, play] à thèse
3 COMP ► **problem-free** ADJ sans problème ► **problem page** N (Press) courrier m du cœur ► **problem-solving** N résolution f de problèmes ♦ ADJ [technique, abilities] de résolution de problèmes

problematic(al) [ˌprɒblɪˈmætɪk(l)] ADJ problématique

proboscis [prəˈbɒsɪs], pl **proboscises** or **probocides** [prəˈbɒsɪˌdiːz] N (pl proboscises or probocides) (Zool) trompe f; (hum = nose) appendice m (hum)

procedural [prəˈsiːdjʊrəl] **1** ADJ (Admin, Insurance, Jur etc) de procédure **2** N (also **police** ~) (= novel) (roman m) policier m; (= film) film m policier

procedure [prəˈsiːdʒər] N procédure f; **what is the ~?** quelle est la procédure à suivre?, comment doit-on procéder?; **the correct** or **normal ~ is to apply to …** pour suivre la procédure normale il faut s'adresser à …; (Admin, Jur etc) **order of ~** règles fpl de procédure

proceed [prəˈsiːd] **1** VI **a** (frm, lit = move along) avancer; **he was ~ing along the road** il avançait sur la route; **"~ with caution"** (on foot) « avancer avec prudence »; (in vehicle) « rouler au pas »
b (frm = go on) continuer; **please ~!** veuillez continuer or poursuivre; **to ~ on one's way** poursuivre son chemin or sa route; **they then ~ed to London** ils se sont ensuite rendus à Londres; **let us ~ to the next item** passons à la question suivante; (lit, fig) **before we ~ any further** avant d'aller plus loin; ~ **with your work** continuez or poursuivez votre travail; **they ~ed with their plan** ils ont donné suite à leur projet; (Jur) **they did not ~ with the charges against him** ils ont abandonné les poursuites (engagées) contre lui; **to ~ to do sth** se mettre à faire qch, entreprendre de faire qch; **the police stopped the car and (then) ~ed to search it** les policiers arrêtèrent la voiture et entreprirent ensuite de la fouiller
c (fig = act, operate) procéder, agir; **you must ~ cautiously** il faut procéder or agir avec prudence; **I am not sure how to ~** je ne sais pas très bien comment procéder or m'y prendre; **it is all ~ing according to plan** tout se passe comme prévu; **the discussions are ~ing normally** les discussions se poursuivent normalement; **everything is ~ing well** les choses suivent leur cours de manière satisfaisante; **to ~ from the assumption** or **premise that …** [person, idea] partir du principe que …
d (= originate) **to ~ from** venir de, provenir de; (fig) relever de
e (Jur) **to ~ against sb** engager des poursuites contre qn
2 VT continuer; **"well"** she **~ed** « eh bien » continua-t-elle
3 N → **proceeds**

proceeding [prəˈsiːdɪŋ] **1** N (= course of action) façon f or manière f d'agir or de procéder
2 proceedings NPL **a** (= manoeuvres) opérations fpl; (= ceremony) cérémonie f; (= meeting) séance f, réunion f; (= discussions) débats mpl; **the ~s begin at 7 o'clock** la réunion or la séance commencera à 19 heures; **the secretary recorded the ~s** le secrétaire a enregistré les débats
b (esp Jur = measures) mesures fpl; **legal ~s** procès m; **to take ~s** prendre des mesures (**in order to do** pour faire, **against sb** contre qn); (Jur) **to take (legal) ~s against sb** engager des poursuites contre qn, intenter un procès à qn → **commence, divorce, institute**
c (= records) compte m rendu, rapport m; **it**

was **published in the Society's ~s** cela a été publié dans les actes de la Société; (as title) **Proceedings of the Historical Society** Actes mpl de la Société d'histoire

proceeds [ˈprəʊsiːdz] NPL montant m (des recettes); (Jur, Fin) ~ **of insurance** indemnité f versée par la compagnie

process¹ [ˈprəʊses] **1** N **a** (Chem, Bio, Ling, Sociol etc) processus m; (fig, Admin, Jur) procédure f; **the ~ of digestion/growing up** etc le processus de la digestion/de la croissance etc; **a natural/chemical ~** un processus naturel/chimique; **the thawing/preserving ~** le processus de décongélation/de conservation etc; **the legal/administrative ~ takes a year** la procédure juridique/administrative prend un an; **the ~es of the law** le processus de la justice; **it's a slow** or **long ~** (Chem etc) c'est un processus lent; (fig) ça prend du temps; **he supervised the whole ~** il a supervisé l'opération du début à la fin
b **to be in the ~ of modernization/negotiation/construction** être en cours de modernisation/négociation/construction; **to be in the ~ of moving/changing** être en train de déménager/changer; **in the ~ of cleaning the picture, they discovered …** au cours du nettoyage du tableau or pendant qu'ils nettoyaient le tableau ils ont découvert …; **she tried to help, and ruined everything in the ~** elle a essayé d'aider mais, ce faisant or du coup*, elle a tout gâché; **he saved the girl, but injured himself in the ~** il a sauvé la petite fille mais, ce faisant or du coup*, il s'est blessé; **in the ~ of time** avec le temps
c (= specific method) procédé m, méthode f; **the Bessemer ~** le procédé Bessemer; **he has devised a ~ for controlling weeds** il a mis au point un procédé or une méthode pour venir à bout des mauvaises herbes; **to work sth out by ~ of elimination** résoudre qch en procédant par élimination → **elimination**
d (Jur) (= action) procès m; (= summons) citation f à comparaître; **to bring a ~ against sb** intenter un procès à qn; **to serve a ~ on sb** signifier une citation à qn → **serve**
e (Anat, Bot, Zool) excroissance f, protubérance f

2 VT (Ind) [+ raw materials, food] traiter, transformer; [+ seeds, waste] traiter; (Phot) [+ film] développer; (Comput) [+ information, data] traiter; [+ tape] faire passer en machine; (Admin etc) [+ an application, papers, records] s'occuper de; **your application will take six weeks to ~** l'examen de votre candidature prendra six semaines; **they ~ 10,000 forms per day** 10 000 formulaires passent chaque jour entre leurs mains; (Comm) **in order to ~ your order** afin de donner suite à votre commande

3 COMP ► **process control** N (Ind) régulation f des processus industriels ► **processed cheese** N fromage m fondu ► **processed peas** NPL petits pois mpl en boîte ► **process printing** N quadrichromie f ► **process-server** N (Jur) huissier m de justice

process² [prəˈses] VI (Brit = go in procession) défiler, avancer en cortège; (Rel) aller en procession

processing [ˈprəʊsesɪŋ] **1** N (NonC) [of food, radioactive waste, application, papers, records] traitement m; [of raw materials] traitement m, transformation f; (Phot) [of film etc] développement m → **data, food, word 2** COMP ► **processing unit** N (Comput) unité f de traitement

procession [prəˈseʃən] N [of people, cars] cortège m, défilé m; (Rel) procession f; **to walk in (a) ~** défiler, aller en cortège or en procession → **funeral**

processional [prəˈseʃənl] (Rel) **1** ADJ processionnel **2** N hymne m processionnel

processor [ˈprəʊsesər] N **a** (Comput) processeur m → **data, word b** = **food processor**; → **food**

pro-choice [ˌprəʊˈtʃɔɪs] ADJ en faveur de l'avortement

pro-choicer* [ˌprəʊˈtʃɔɪsər] N partisan(e) m(f) de l'avortement

proclaim [prəˈkleɪm] VT **a** (= announce) proclamer, déclarer (**that** que); [+ holiday] instituer; [+ one's independence, innocence] proclamer; [+ war, one's love] déclarer; [+ edict] promulguer; **to ~ sb king** proclamer qn roi; **to ~ a state of emergency** décréter l'état d'urgence, proclamer l'état d'urgence; **to ~ peace** annoncer le rétablissement de la paix
b (= reveal, demonstrate) démontrer, révéler; **his tone ~ed his confidence** le ton de sa voix démontrait or révélait sa confiance; **their expressions ~ed their guilt** la culpabilité se lisait sur leurs visages

proclamation [ˌprɒkləˈmeɪʃən] N proclamation f

proclivity [prəˈklɪvɪtɪ] N (frm) propension f, inclination f (**to sth** à qch, **to do** à faire)

proconsul [ˈprəʊˈkɒnsəl] N proconsul m

procrastinate [prəʊˈkræstɪneɪt] VI atermoyer, tergiverser

procrastination [prəʊˌkræstɪˈneɪʃən] N (NonC) atermoiements mpl, tergiversations fpl

procrastinator [prəʊˈkræstɪˌneɪtər] N personne f qui remet tout au lendemain

procreate [ˈprəʊkrɪeɪt] **1** VI se reproduire **2** VT procréer, engendrer

procreation [ˌprəʊkrɪˈeɪʃən] N procréation f

Procrustean [prəʊˈkrʌstɪən] ADJ de Procuste

proctor [ˈprɒktər] N **a** (Jur etc) fondé m de pouvoir **b** (Univ) (Oxford, Cambridge) responsable mf de la discipline; (US = invigilator) surveillant(e) m(f) (à un examen)

procurable [prəˈkjʊərəbl] ADJ que l'on peut se procurer; **it is easily ~** on peut se le procurer facilement

procuration [ˌprɒkjʊˈreɪʃən] N **a** (= act of procuring) obtention f, acquisition f **b** (Jur = authority) procuration f **c** (= crime) proxénétisme m

procurator [ˈprɒkjʊreɪtər] **1** N (Jur) fondé m de pouvoir **2** COMP ► **Procurator Fiscal** N (Scot Jur) ≈ procureur m (de la République)

procure [prəˈkjʊər] **1** VT **a** (= obtain for o.s.) se procurer, obtenir; [+ sb's release etc] obtenir; **to ~ sth for sb ◊ to ~ sb sth** procurer qch à qn, faire obtenir qch à qn; **to ~ sb's death†** faire assassiner qn **b** (Jur) [+ prostitute etc] offrir les services de, procurer **2** VI (Jur) faire du proxénétisme

procurement [prəˈkjʊəmənt] **1** N (gen) obtention f; (Comm, Admin, Ind) approvisionnement m; (Mil) acquisition f de matériel militaire **2** COMP ► **procurement department** N (Comm, Ind) service m des achats or de l'approvisionnement

procurer [prəˈkjʊərər] N (Jur) entremetteur m, proxénète m

procuress [prəˈkjʊərɪs] N (Jur) entremetteuse f, proxénète f

procuring [prəˈkjʊərɪŋ] N **a** [of goods, objects] obtention f **b** (Jur) proxénétisme m

Prod: [prɒd], **Proddie** [ˈprɒdɪ]: N (Brit pej) protestant(e) m(f), parpaillot(e)* m(f)

prod [prɒd] **1** N (= push) poussée f; (= jab) (petit) coup m (de canne, avec le doigt etc); **to give sb a ~** pousser qn doucement (du doigt or du pied or avec la pointe d'un bâton etc); (fig) pousser qn; (fig) **he needs a ~ from time to time** il a besoin d'être poussé or qu'on le secoue* (subj) un peu de temps en temps **2** VT pousser doucement; **to ~ sb** pousser qn doucement (du doigt or du pied or avec la pointe d'un bâton etc); (fig) pousser qn; **she ~ded the jellyfish with a stick** elle a poussé la méduse avec la pointe d'un bâton ; **to ~ sb to do sth** or **into doing sth** pousser or inciter qn à faire qch ; **he needs ~ding** il a besoin d'être poussé or qu'on le secoue* (subj) **3** VI **to ~ at sb/sth** → **to prod sb/sth**; → **2**

prodigal ['prɒdɪgəl] ADJ prodigue (**of** de) ; **the ~ (son)** (Bible) le fils prodigue ; (fig) l'enfant m prodigue

prodigality [ˌprɒdɪ'gælɪtɪ] N prodigalité f

prodigally ['prɒdɪgəlɪ] ADV avec prodigalité

prodigious [prə'dɪdʒəs] ADJ (frm) prodigieux, extraordinaire

prodigiously [prə'dɪdʒəslɪ] ADV (frm) prodigieusement

prodigy ['prɒdɪdʒɪ] N prodige m, merveille f ; **child ~** ◊ **infant ~** enfant mf prodige ; **a ~ of learning** un puits de science

produce [prə'djuːs] **1** VT **a** (= make, yield, manufacture) [+ milk, oil, coal, ore, crops] produire ; [+ cars, radios] produire, fabriquer ; [writer, artist, musician etc] produire ; (Fin) [+ interest, profit] rapporter ; [+ offspring] [animal] produire, donner naissance à ; [woman] donner naissance à ; (Fin) **his shares ~ a yield of 7%** ses actions rapportent 7% ; **that investment ~s no return** cet investissement ne rapporte rien ; **Scotland ~s whisky** l'Écosse produit du whisky or est un pays producteur de whisky ; **coal ~s electricity** le charbon produit or donne de l'électricité ; **these magazines are ~d by the same firm** ces revues sont éditées par la même maison ; **he ~d a masterpiece** il a produit un chef-d'œuvre ; **well ~d** [+ book] bien présenté ; [+ goods] bien fait → **1d**; **he has ~d a new single** il a sorti un nouveau single **b** (= bring out, show) [+ gift, handkerchief, gun] sortir (**from** de) ; [+ ticket, documents etc] présenter ; [+ witness] produire ; [+ proof] fournir, apporter ; **he suddenly ~d a large parcel** il a soudain sorti un gros paquet ; **I can't ~ £100 just like that!** je ne peux pas trouver 100 livres comme ça! ; **he ~d a sudden burst of energy** il a eu un sursaut d'énergie **c** (= cause) [+ famine, deaths] causer, provoquer ; [+ dispute, bitterness] provoquer, causer ; [+ results] produire, donner ; [+ impression] faire, donner ; [+ pleasure, interest] susciter ; (Elec) [+ current] engendrer ; [+ spark] faire jaillir ; **it ~d a burning sensation in my finger** cela a provoqué une sensation de brûlure dans mon doigt **d** (Theat) mettre en scène ; (Cine) (Rad) [+ play] mettre en ondes ; [+ programme] réaliser ; (TV) [+ play, film] mettre en scène ; [+ programme] réaliser ; **well ~d** bien monté **e** (Geom) [+ line, plane] (= extend) prolonger, continuer

2 VI **a** [mine, oil well, factory] produire ; [land, trees, cows] produire, rendre **b** (Theat) assurer la mise en scène ; (Cine) assurer la production (d'un film) ; (Rad, TV) assurer la réalisation d'une émission

3 ['prɒdjuːs] N (NonC = food) produits mpl (d'alimentation) ; **agricultural/garden/foreign ~** produits mpl agricoles/maraîchers/étrangers ; **"~ of France"** « produit français », « produit de France » ; **"~ of more than one country"** « produit de différents pays » ; **we eat mostly our own ~** nous mangeons surtout nos propres produits or ce que nous produisons nous-mêmes

producer [prə'djuːsər] **1** N **a** (Agr, Ind etc) producteur m, -trice f **b** (Theat, Cine, Mus) producteur m, -trice f ; (Rad, TV) réalisateur m, -trice f, metteur m en ondes **2** COMP ► **producer gas** N gaz m fourni par gazogène ► **producer goods** NPL (Econ) biens mpl de production

-producing [prə'djuːsɪŋ] ADJ (in compounds) producteur (-trice f) de ... ; **oil-producing** producteur (-trice f) de pétrole ; **one of the coal-**

producing countries un des pays producteurs de charbon

product ['prɒdʌkt] **1** N **a** (Comm, Ind etc) produit m ; (fig) produit m, résultat m ; **food ~s** produits mpl alimentaires, denrées fpl (alimentaires) ; **it is the ~ of his imagination** c'est le fruit de son imagination ; **she is the ~ of a broken home** elle est le résultat d'un foyer désuni ; **a public-school ~** un (pur) produit des public schools → **finished, gross, waste b** (Math) produit m **2** COMP ► **product acceptance** N mesure f du succès d'un produit auprès des consommateurs ► **product liability** N responsabilité f du fabricant ► **product line** N gamme f or ligne f de produits ► **product manager** N (Comm) chef m de produit ► **product placement** N (Cine, Comm) placement m de produit(s)

production [prə'dʌkʃən] **1** N **a** (NonC: Ind, Bio etc = manufacturing) production f ; **to put sth into ~** entreprendre la production de qch ; **to take sth out of ~** retirer qch de la production ; **the factory is in full ~** l'usine tourne à plein rendement ; **car/oil** etc **~ has risen recently** la production automobile/pétrolière etc a récemment augmenté ; **industrial/agricultural ~ fell by 1.7% last month** la production industrielle/agricole a baissé de 1,7% le mois dernier ; **we hope to go into ~ soon** nous espérons commencer la production bientôt ; **the new model goes into ~ soon** on commencera bientôt la fabrication du nouveau modèle **b** (NonC = act of showing) présentation f ; **on ~ of this ticket** sur présentation de ce billet **c** (NonC = activity) (Theat) mise f en scène ; (Cine, Mus, Rad, TV) production f ; **film ~** la production cinématographique ; **TV ~** la production or création télévisuelle ; **he was writing plays for ~ at the Blackfriars Theatre** il écrivait des pièces pour les monter au « Blackfriars Theatre » **d** (= work produced) (Theat, Mus) représentation f, mise f en scène ; (Cine, Rad, TV) production f ; **a theatrical** or **stage ~** une pièce de théâtre ; **a new ~ of "Macbeth"** une nouvelle mise en scène de « Macbeth » ; **"Macbeth": a new ~ by ...** « Macbeth » : une nouvelle mise en scène de ... ; **the Theatre Royal's ~ of "Cats" ran for three years** « Cats » s'est joué pendant trois ans au « Theatre Royal »

2 COMP ► **production company** N (Cine, TV, Video) société f de production ► **production costs** NPL coûts mpl de production ► **production department** N (Publishing) service m fabrication ► **production line** N (Ind) chaîne f de fabrication ; **he works on the ~ line** il travaille à la chaîne ; **~ line work** travail m à la chaîne ► **production manager** N directeur m de (la) production ► **production number** N (Theat, Cine) numéro m de production ► **production run** N (Ind) série f ► **production values** NPL (Cine) **a film with high ~ values** un film à gros budget

productive [prə'dʌktɪv] ADJ [land, imagination] fertile, fécond ; [meeting, discussion, work] fructueux, productif ; (Econ) [employment, labour] productif ; (Ling) productif ; **to be ~ of sth** produire qch, engendrer qch, être générateur de qch ; **I've had a very ~ day** j'ai eu une journée très fructueuse, j'ai bien travaillé aujourd'hui ; (Fin) **~ life of an asset** vie f utile d'un bien

productively [prə'dʌktɪvlɪ] ADV de manière fructueuse or productive

productivity [ˌprɒdʌk'tɪvɪtɪ] **1** N (NonC: Econ, Ind) productivité f **2** COMP [fall, increase] de (la) productivité ► **productivity agreement** N (Brit) accord m de productivité ► **productivity bonus** N prime f à la productivité

prof. [prɒf] **1** N (Univ) (ABBR = **professor**) professeur m ; (on envelope) **Prof. C. Smith** Monsieur C. Smith **2** ADJ ABBR = **professional**

profanation [ˌprɒfə'neɪʃən] N profanation f

profane [prə'feɪn] **1** ADJ **a** (= secular, lay) [music etc] profane **b** (pej = blasphemous) [language etc] impie, sacrilège → **sacred 2** VT profaner

profanity [prə'fænɪtɪ] N **a** (= oath) juron m, blasphème m ; **he uttered a torrent of profanities** il a proféré un torrent d'injures **b** (NonC) [of language etc] caractère m profane

profess [prə'fes] VT **a** (= claim, declare) déclarer (**that** que) ; [+ faith, religion] professer ; (publicly) professer, faire profession de ; [+ an opinion, respect, hatred] professer ; **to ~ concern at sth** exprimer son inquiétude devant qch, se déclarer inquiet de qch ; **to ~ ignorance of sth** déclarer ne rien savoir sur qch ; **to ~ knowledge of sth** déclarer connaître qch ; **he ~ed himself satisfied** il s'est déclaré satisfait ; **he ~es to know all about it** il déclare tout savoir sur ce sujet ; **I don't ~ to be an expert** je ne prétends pas être expert en la matière **b** (frm = have as one's profession) **to ~ law/medicine** exercer la profession d'avocat/de médecin

professed [prə'fest] ADJ [atheist, communist etc] déclaré ; (Rel) [monk, nun] profès (-esse f)

professedly [prə'fesɪdlɪ] ADV de son (or leur etc) propre aveu, d'après lui (or eux etc) ; (= allegedly) soi-disant, prétendument

profession [prə'feʃən] N **a** (= calling) profession f ; (= body of people) (membres mpl d'une) profession f ; **by ~** de son (or une) métier or état ; **the medical ~** (= calling) la profession de médecin, la médecine ; (= doctors collectively) le corps médical, les médecins mpl ; **the ~s** les professions fpl libérales ; (euph) **the oldest ~** le plus vieux métier du monde → **learned b** (= declaration) profession f, déclaration f ; **~ of faith** profession f de foi ; **to make one's ~** [monk, nun] faire sa profession, prononcer ses vœux

professional [prə'feʃənl] **1** ADJ **a** [skill, organization, training, etiquette] professionnel ; **to be a ~ person** [doctor, lawyer etc] exercer une profession libérale ; [other white-collar worker] avoir une situation ; **the ~ classes** les (membres mpl des) professions fpl libérales ; **to take ~ advice** (medical/legal) consulter un médecin/un avocat ; (on practical problem) consulter un professionnel or un homme de métier ; **it is not ~ practice to do so** faire cela est contraire à l'usage professionnel **b** (= by profession) [writer, politician] professionnel, de profession ; [footballer, tennis player] professionnel ; [diplomat, soldier] de carrière ; (fig = of high standard) [play, piece of work] de haute qualité, excellent ; **~ football/tennis** etc football m/tennis m etc professionnel ; (Sport) **to turn** or **go ~** passer professionnel ; **to have a very ~ attitude to one's work** prendre son travail très au sérieux ; **it is well up to ~ standards** c'est d'un niveau de professionnel

2 N (all senses) professionnel(le) m(f) **3** COMP ► **professional army** N armée f de métier ► **professional foul** N (Ftbl) faute f délibérée ► **Professional Golfers' Association** N PGA f (association de golfeurs professionnels) ► **professional school** N (US) (Univ = faculty) faculté f de droit or de médecine ; (= business school) grande école f commerciale

professionalism [prə'feʃnəlɪzəm] N [of writer, actor etc] professionnalisme m ; (Sport) professionnalisme m ; [of play, piece of work] excellence f, haute qualité f

professionally [prə'feʃnəlɪ] ADV **a** (= vocationally) professionnellement ; **he sings/dances** etc **~** il est chanteur/danseur etc professionnel; **to be ~ qualified** avoir une qualification professionnelle; **I know him only ~** je n'ai que des rapports de travail avec lui; **she is known ~ as Julia Wills** dans la profession or le métier, elle est connue sous le nom de Julia Wills; **speaking ~, I have to tell you that ...** d'un point de vue professionnel, je dois vous dire que ...; **it was a difficult time both personally and ~** ce fut une période difficile sur le plan aussi bien personnel que professionnel; **the boat was ~ built** le bateau a été construit par des professionnels; **the play was ~ produced** la mise en scène (de la pièce) était l'œuvre d'un professionnel **b** (= *expertly*) de manière professionnelle **c** (= *according to professional standards*) en professionnel(le), de manière professionnelle; **he claims he acted ~ and responsibly throughout** il affirme qu'il s'est toujours comporté de manière professionnelle et responsable

professor [prə'fesər] N **a** (*Univ*) professeur m (titulaire d'une chaire); **~ of French** ◊ **French ~** professeur m (titulaire de la chaire) de français; **good morning, Professor Smith** bonjour Monsieur Smith, bonjour Monsieur (le professeur); (*in letters*) **Dear Professor Smith** monsieur, Cher Monsieur (*less frm*); (*if known to writer*) Cher Professeur; (*on envelope*) **Professor C. Smith** Monsieur C. Smith → **assistant b** (*US‡: iro*) maestro m, maître m

professorial [,prɒfə'sɔ:rɪəl] ADJ professoral

professorship [prə'fesəʃɪp] N chaire f (**of** de); **he has a ~** il est titulaire d'une chaire

proffer ['prɒfər] VT [+ *object, arm*] offrir, tendre; [+ *a remark, suggestion*] faire; [+ *one's thanks, apologies*] offrir, présenter; **to ~ one's hand to sb** tendre la main à qn

proficiency [prə'fɪʃənsɪ] N (grande) compétence f (**in** en); **Cambridge Certificate of Proficiency** diplôme d'anglais langue étrangère

proficient [prə'fɪʃənt] ADJ (très) compétent (**in** en)

profile ['prəʊfaɪl] **1** N **a** [*of head, building, hill etc*] profil m (*also Archit*); **in ~** de profil **b** (*fig* = *description*) [*of person*] profil m, portrait m; [*of situation etc*] profil m, esquisse f; **genetic ~** profil m génétique **c** (= *graph or table*) profil m **d** **to keep a low ~** essayer de ne pas (trop) se faire remarquer, adopter une attitude discrète → **low'**; **to keep a high ~** (*in media etc*) garder la vedette; (= *be seen on streets etc*) être très en vue or en évidence **2** VT **a** (= *show in profile*) profiler (*also Archit*) **b** (*gen*) (= *describe*) [+ *person*] établir le profil de, dresser le portrait de; [+ *situation*] établir le profil de, tracer une esquisse de; (*Police*) [+ *suspect*] établir le profil psychologique de

profit ['prɒfɪt] **1** N (*Comm*) profit m, bénéfice m; (*fig*) profit m, avantage m; **~ and loss** profits mpl et pertes fpl → **4**; **gross/net ~** bénéfice m brut/net; **to make** or **turn a ~** faire un bénéfice or des bénéfices; **to make a ~ of £100** faire un bénéfice de 100 livres (**on sth** sur qch); **to sell sth at a ~** vendre qch à profit; **to show** or **yield a ~** rapporter (un bénéfice); (*lit, fig*) **there's not much ~ in doing that** on ne gagne pas grand-chose à faire cela; (*Insurance*) **with ~s policy** police f (d'assurance) avec participation aux bénéfices; (*fig*) **with ~** avec profit, avec fruit; (*fig*) **to turn sth to ~** mettre à profit qch, tirer parti de qch

2 VI (*fig*) tirer un profit or un avantage; **to ~ by** or **from sth** tirer avantage or profit de qch, bien profiter de qch; **I can't see how he hopes to ~ (by it)** je ne vois pas ce qu'il espère en retirer or y gagner

3 VT (†† or *liter*) profiter à; **it will ~ him nothing** cela ne lui profitera en rien

4 COMP ▸ **profit and loss account** N (*Accounts*) compte m de profits et pertes, compte m de résultat ▸ **profit-making** ADJ rentable; **a ~-making/non-~-making organisa-**

tion une organisation à but lucratif/non lucratif ▸ **profit margin** N marge f bénéficiaire ▸ **profit motive** N recherche f du profit ▸ **profit-seeking** ADJ à but lucratif ▸ **profit sharing** N (*Ind*) participation f or intéressement m aux bénéfices ▸ **profit-sharing scheme** N système m de participation or d'intéressement aux bénéfices ▸ **profit squeeze** N compression f des bénéfices ▸ **profit taking** N (*St Ex*) prise f de bénéfices

profitability [,prɒfɪtə'bɪlɪtɪ] **1** N (*lit, fig*) rentabilité f **2** COMP ▸ **profitability study** N (*Comm*) étude f de rentabilité

profitable ['prɒfɪtəbl] ADJ (*Comm etc*) [*deal, sale, investment*] rentable, lucratif; [*company*] bénéficiaire, rentable; (*fig*) [*scheme, agreement, contract*] rentable; [*meeting, discussion, visit*] fructueux, payant (*fig*), profitable, fructueux; **we don't stock them any more as they were not ~** nous ne les stockons plus parce qu'ils n'étaient pas rentables; **it was a very ~ half-hour** cela a été une demi-heure très fructueuse or profitable; **you would find it ~ to read this** vous trouveriez la lecture de ceci utile or profitable

profitably ['prɒfɪtəblɪ] ADV **a** (*lit*) [*sell*] à profit; **the company is now trading ~** cette société enregistre à présent des bénéfices, cette société est à présent bénéficiaire **b** (*fig* = *usefully*) utilement, de manière utile; **the same technology could be ~ employed finding alternative sources of energy** on pourrait employer utilement cette même technologie pour trouver d'autres sources d'énergie; **there was little I could ~ do** je ne pouvais pas faire grand-chose d'utile

profiteer [,prɒfɪ'tɪər] **1** N profiteur m, mercanti m **2** VI faire des bénéfices excessifs

profiteering [,prɒfɪ'tɪərɪŋ] N (*pej*) réalisation f de bénéfices excessifs

profitless ['prɒfɪtlɪs] ADJ (*lit*) [*company, factory*] qui n'est pas rentable; [*shares*] qui ne rapporte rien; [*year*] improductif; (*fig*) infructueux

profitlessly ['prɒfɪtlɪslɪ] ADV (*lit*) sans dégager de bénéfices; (*fig*) d'une manière infructueuse

profligacy ['prɒflɪgəsɪ] N (*frm*) (= *debauchery*) débauche f, libertinage m; (= *extravagance*) extrême prodigalité f

profligate ['prɒflɪgɪt] (*frm*) **1** ADJ (= *debauched*) [*person, behaviour*] débauché, libertin, dissolu; [*life*] de débauche, de libertinage; (= *extravagant*) extrêmement prodigue **2** N débauché(e) m(f), libertin(e) m(f)

pro-form ['prəʊ,fɔ:m] N (*Ling*) proforme f

pro forma ['prəʊ'fɔ:mə] **1** ADJ pro forma *inv* **2** N (*also* = **invoice**) facture f pro forma; (*also* **~ letter**) (formule f de) lettre f toute faite **3** ADV selon les règles

profound [prə'faʊnd] ADJ (*all senses*) profond

profoundly [prə'faʊndlɪ] ADV [*different, moving, undemocratic etc*] profondément; [*deaf*] totalement, complètement

profundity [prə'fʌndɪtɪ] N **a** (*NonC*) profondeur f **b** (= *profound remark*) remarque f profonde

profuse [prə'fju:s] ADJ [*vegetation, bleeding*] abondant; [*thanks, praise, apologies*] profus, multiple; **~ in ...** prodigue de ...; **to be ~ in one's thanks/excuses** se confondre en remerciements/excuses

profusely [prə'fju:slɪ] ADV [*bleed, sweat*] abondamment; [*grow*] à profusion, en abondance; **to apologize ~** se confondre or se répandre en excuses; **to thank sb ~** remercier qn avec effusion

profusion [prə'fju:ʒən] N profusion f, abondance f (**of** de); **in ~** à profusion, à foison

prog.* [prɒg] N (*Brit TV etc*) (ABBR = **programme**) émission f, programme m

progenitor [prəʊ'dʒenɪtər] N (*lit*) ancêtre m; (*fig*) auteur m

progeny ['prɒdʒɪnɪ] N (= *offspring*) progéniture f; (= *descendants*) lignée f, descendants mpl

progesterone [prəʊ'dʒestə,rəʊn] N progestérone f

prognathous [prɒg'neɪθəs] ADJ prognathe

prognosis [prɒg'nəʊsɪs] N (*pl* **prognoses** [prɒg'nəʊsi:z]) pronostic m

prognostic [prɒg'nɒstɪk] N (*frm*) présage m, signe m avant-coureur

prognosticate [prɒg'nɒstɪkeɪt] **1** VT pronostiquer **2** VI faire des pronostics

prognostication [prɒg,nɒstɪ'keɪʃən] N pronostic m

program ['prəʊgræm] **1** N **a** (*Comput*) programme m **b** (*US*) = **programme 1a** **2** VI (*Comput*) établir un (or des) programme(s) **3** VT **a** (*Comput*) programmer; **to ~ sth to do** programmer qch de façon à faire **b** (*US*) = **programme 2a** **4** COMP (*Comput*) [*specification, costs*] du or d'un programme

programmable ['prəʊgræməbl] ADJ (*Comput*) programmable

programmatic [,prəʊgrə'mætɪk] ADJ programmatique

programme (*Brit*), **program** (*esp US*) ['prəʊgræm] **1** N **a** (*most senses*) programme m; (*Rad, TV* = *broadcast*) émission f (**on** sur, **about** au sujet de); [*of course*] emploi m du temps; (= *station*) (*Rad*) poste m; (*TV*) chaîne f; **what's the ~ for today?** (*during course etc*) quel est l'emploi du temps aujourd'hui?; (*fig*) qu'est-ce qu'on fait aujourd'hui?; **in the ~ for the day** au programme de la journée; **what's on the ~?** qu'est-ce qu'il y a au programme?; (*Rad, TV*) **details of the morning's ~s** le programme de la matinée → **detoxi(fi)cation, request b** (*Comput*) = **program**

2 VT **a** [+ *washing machine, video etc*] programmer (**to do** pour faire); (*fig*) [+ *person*] conditionner; **our bodies are ~d to fight disease** notre corps est programmé pour combattre la maladie; **we are genetically ~d for motherhood** nous sommes génétiquement programmées pour être mères; **~d learning** enseignement m programmé **b** (*Comput*) = **program**

3 COMP ▸ **programme editor** N (*Rad, TV*) éditorialiste mf ▸ **programme-maker** N (*TV, Rad*) réalisateur m, -trice f ▸ **programme music** N (*NonC*) musique f à programme ▸ **programme notes** NPL (*Mus, Theat*) commentaires mpl sur le programme ▸ **programme seller** N (*Theat*) vendeur m, -euse f de programmes

programmer ['prəʊgræmər] N (= *person: also* **computer ~**) programmeur m, -euse f; (= *device*) programmateur m

programming ['prəʊgræmɪŋ] **1** N **a** (*also* **computer ~**) programmation f **b** (*TV, Rad*) programmation f **2** COMP [*error, language etc*] de programmation

progress ['prəʊgres] **1** N **a** (*NonC: lit, fig*) progrès m(pl); **in the name of ~** au nom du progrès; **you can't stop ~** on n'arrête pas le progrès; **we made slow ~ through the mud** nous avons avancé lentement dans la boue; **~ was slow** les choses n'avançaient pas vite; **we are making good ~ in our search for a solution** nos travaux pour trouver une solution progressent de manière satisfaisante; **we have made little/no ~** nous n'avons guère fait de progrès/fait aucun progrès; **he is making ~** [*student etc*] il fait des progrès, il est en progrès; [*patient*] son état (de santé) s'améliore; **the ~ of events** le cours des événements; **the meeting is in ~** la réunion est en cours or a déjà commencé; **while the meeting was in ~** pendant la réunion; **the work in ~** les travaux en cours; **"silence: exam in ~"** « silence: examen » ; **to be in full ~** battre son plein

|b| (†† = *journey*) voyage *m* → **pilgrim**

|2| [prə'gres] VI (*lit*, *fig*) aller, avancer (**towards** vers); [*student etc*] faire des progrès, progresser; [*patient*] aller mieux; [*search, investigations, researches, studies etc*] progresser, avancer; **matters are ~ing slowly** les choses progressent lentement; **as the game ~ed** à mesure que la partie se déroulait; **while the discussions were ~ing** pendant que les discussions se déroulaient

|3| VT (= *advance*) faire progresser

|4| COMP ► **progress board** N tableau *m* de planning ► **progress chaser** N responsable *mf* du suivi (d'un projet) ► **progress chasing** N suivi *m* (d'un projet) ► **progress payment** N (*Fin*) acompte *m* (versé au prorata de l'avancement des travaux) ► **progress report** N (*gen*) compte *m* rendu (**on** de); (*Med*) bulletin *m* de santé; (*Scol*) bulletin *m* scolaire; (*Admin*) état *m* périodique, rapport *m* sur l'avancement des travaux; **to make a ~ report on** (*gen*) rendre compte de l'évolution de; (*Scol: on pupil*) rendre compte des progrès de; (*Med: on patient*) rendre compte de l'évolution de l'état de santé de; (*Admin*) dresser un état périodique de

progression [prə'greʃən] N (*gen, Math*) progression *f*; **by arithmetical/geometrical ~** selon une progression arithmétique/géométrique; **it's a logical ~** c'est une suite logique

progressive [prə'gresɪv] |1| ADJ |a| [*movement, taxation, disease, improvement*] progressif; [*idea, party, person, outlook*] progressiste (*also Pol*); [*age*] de ou du progrès; **in ~ stages** par degrés, par étapes |b| (*Gram, Phon*) progressif |2| |a| (*Pol etc*) progressiste *mf* |b| (*Gram*) temps *m* progressif |3| COMP ► **progressive education** N éducation *f* nouvelle

progressively [prə'gresɪvlɪ] ADV progressivement; **to get** or **grow** or **become ~ harder/easier** devenir de plus en plus difficile/facile; **the weather was getting ~ worse** le temps allait en empirant; **his health is getting ~ better** sa santé s'améliore de jour en jour

progressiveness [prə'gresɪvnɪs] N progressivité *f*

progressivity [ˌprəʊgre'sɪvɪtɪ] N progressivité *f*

prohibit [prə'hɪbɪt] |1| VT |a| (= *forbid*) interdire, défendre (**sb from doing** à qn de faire); (*Admin, Jur etc*) [+ *weapons, drugs, swearing*] prohiber; **smoking ~ed** défense de fumer; **feeding the animals is ~ed** il est interdit ou défendu de donner à manger aux animaux; **pedestrians are ~ed from using this bridge** il est interdit aux piétons d'utiliser ce pont; l'usage de ce pont est interdit aux piétons |b| (= *prevent*) empêcher (**sb from doing** qn de faire); **my health ~s me from swimming** mon état de santé m'interdit de nager, la natation m'est interdite pour des raisons de santé |2| COMP ► **prohibited substance** N substance *f* prohibée

prohibition [ˌprəʊɪ'bɪʃən] |1| N |a| [*of weapons, drugs, swearing etc*] interdiction *f*, prohibition *f*; **there was a strict ~ on speaking Welsh** il était strictement interdit de parler gallois |b| (*US Hist*) **Prohibition** la prohibition; **during Prohibition** pendant la prohibition |2| COMP (*US Hist: also* **Prohibition**) [*laws, party*] prohibitionniste

prohibitionism [ˌprəʊɪ'bɪʃənɪzəm] N prohibitionnisme *m*

prohibitionist [ˌprəʊɪ'bɪʃənɪst] ADJ, N prohibitionniste *mf*

prohibitive [prə'hɪbɪtɪv] ADJ [*price, tax, laws*] prohibitif

prohibitively [prə'hɪbɪtɪvlɪ] ADV **~ expensive** à un prix prohibitif; **internal flights are ~ ex-**

pensive le prix des vols intérieurs est prohibitif

prohibitory [prə'hɪbɪtərɪ] ADJ prohibitif

project ['prɒdʒekt] |1| N |a| (*gen*) projet *m*; (= *plan, scheme*) projet *m* (**to do, for doing** pour faire); (= *undertaking*) opération *f*, entreprise *f*; (*Constr*) grands travaux *mpl*; **they are studying the ~ for the new road** ils étudient le projet de construction de la nouvelle route; **the whole ~ will cost 20 million** l'opération ou le projet coûtera 20 millions en tout |b| (= *study*) étude *f* (**on** de); (*Scol*) dossier *m* (**on** sur); (*Univ*) mémoire *m* (**on** sur) |c| (*US: also* **housing ~**) cité *f*, lotissement *m*

|2| [prə'dʒekt] VT |a| (*gen, Psych, Math*) projeter; (*Psych*) **to ~ o.s.** se projeter; **she ~ed an image of innocence** elle projetait ou présentait l'image de l'innocence même; **in view of the ~ed contract** étant donné le projet de contrat; **to ~ quantities/costs** etc **from sth** prévoir la quantité/le coût etc à partir de qch |b| (= *propel*) [+ *object*] propulser; **to ~ one's voice** projeter sa voix |c| (= *cause to jut out*) [+ *part of building etc*] projeter en avant

|3| [prə'dʒekt] VI |a| (= *jut out*) faire saillie, saillir; **to ~ over sth** surplomber qch; **to ~ into sth** s'avancer (en saillie) dans qch |b| (= *show personality*) **how does he ~?** quelle image de lui-même présente-t-il ou projette-t-il? |c| [*actor, singer, speaker*] projeter sa (or leur etc) voix; **his voice ~s very well** sa voix porte vraiment bien

|4| COMP [*budget*] de l'opération; [*staff*] travaillant sur le projet ► **project leader, project manager** N (*gen*) chef *m* de projet; (*Constr*) maître *m* d'œuvre

projectile [prə'dʒektaɪl] N projectile *m*

projecting [prə'dʒektɪŋ] ADJ [*construction*] saillant, en saillie; [*tooth*] qui avance

projection [prə'dʒekʃən] |1| N |a| (*gen*) projection *f*; [*of rocket*] propulsion *f*; (*from opinion polls, sample votes etc*) prévisions *fpl* par extrapolation, projections *fpl* |b| (= *overhang*) saillie *f*, ressaut *m* |2| COMP ► **projection booth, projection room** N (*Cine*) cabine *f* de projection

projectionist [prə'dʒekʃənɪst] N projectionniste *mf*

projective [prə'dʒektɪv] ADJ projectif

projector [prə'dʒektəʳ] N (*Cine etc*) projecteur *m*

prolactin [prəʊ'læktɪn] N prolactine *f*

prolapse ['prəʊlæps] (*Med*) |1| N (*gen*) descente *f* d'organe, ptose *f*, prolapsus *m*; [*of womb*] descente *f* de matrice ou de l'utérus |2| VI descendre; **a ~d uterus** un utérus prolabé, un prolapsus de l'utérus)

prole [prəʊl] ADJ, N (*esp Brit: pej*) (ABBR = **proletarian**) prolo *m*

proletarian [ˌprəʊlə'tɛərɪən] |1| N prolétaire *mf* |2| ADJ [*class, party*] prolétarien; [*life, ways, mentality*] de prolétaire

proletarianize [ˌprəʊlə'tɛərɪənaɪz] VT prolétariser

proletariat [ˌprəʊlə'tɛərɪət] N prolétariat *m*

pro-life [ˌprəʊ'laɪf] ADJ contre l'avortement; **the ~ lobby** les adversaires *mpl* de l'avortement

pro-lifer [ˌprəʊ'laɪfəʳ] N adversaire *mf* de l'avortement

proliferate [prə'lɪfəreɪt] VI proliférer

proliferation [prəˌlɪfə'reɪʃən] N (*gen, Mil*) prolifération *f*

proliferous [prə'lɪfərəs] ADJ prolifère

prolific [prə'lɪfɪk] ADJ prolifique

prolix ['prəʊlɪks] ADJ (*frm*) prolixe

prolixity [prəʊ'lɪksɪtɪ] N (*frm*) prolixité *f*

prologue ['prəʊlɒg] N (*Literat etc*) prologue *m* (**to** de); (*fig*) prologue *m* (**to** à)

prolong [prə'lɒŋ] VT prolonger; (*fig*) **I won't ~ the agony** je vais abréger tes souffrances

prolongation [ˌprəʊlɒŋ'geɪʃən] N (*in space*) prolongement *m*; (*in time*) prolongation *f*

prolonged [prə'lɒŋd] ADJ prolongé; [*period*] long; **~ leave of absence** congé *m* prolongé ou de longue durée; **~ sick leave** congé *m* de longue maladie; **after a ~ absence** après une longue absence ou une absence prolongée

PROM N (*Comput*) (ABBR = **Programmable Read Only Memory**) PROM *f*, mémoire *f* morte programmable

prom* N (*Computer*) (ABBR = **promenade**) |a| (*Brit: by sea*) promenade *f*, front *m* de mer |b| (*Brit*) ~**s** série de concerts de musique classique |c| (*US*) bal *m* d'étudiants (or de lycéens)

PROM

*En Grande-Bretagne, les **proms** (pour «promenade concerts») sont des concerts de musique classique où une grande partie du public est debout. Les **proms** les plus célèbres sont les concerts organisés chaque été au Royal Albert Hall à Londres. Le dernier concert de la saison, appelé «Last Night of the **Proms**», est une grande manifestation mondaine, au cours de laquelle sont interprétés notamment des chants patriotiques.*

*Aux États-Unis, le **prom** est un grand bal organisé dans un lycée ou une université. Le «senior **prom**» des classes de terminale est une soirée particulièrement importante, à laquelle les élèves se rendent en tenue de soirée accompagnés de leur cavalier ou cavalière.*

---

promenade [ˌprɒmɪ'nɑːd] |1| N |a| (= *walk*) promenade *f* |b| (= *place*) (*by sea*) promenade *f*, front *m* de mer; (*in park etc*) avenue *f*; (*in theatre, hall etc*) promenoir *m* |c| (*US*) **prom** |c| |2| VI (*frm = walk*) se promener |3| VT (*frm*) [*person*] promener; [+ *avenue*] se promener le long de |4| COMP ► **Promenade Concerts** NPL → **prom** b ► **promenade deck** N (*Naut*) pont *m* promenade

promenader* [ˌprɒmɪ'nɑːdəʳ] N (*Brit Mus*) auditeur *m*, -trice *f* d'un «promenade concert» → **promenade**

Promethean [prə'miːθɪən] ADJ prométhéen

Prometheus [prə'miːθjuːs] N Prométhée *m*

promethium [prə'miːθɪəm] N prométhéum *m*

prominence ['prɒmɪnəns] N |a| (*lit*) [*of ridge, structure, nose, feature*] caractère *m* proéminent, proéminence *f* (*frm*); [*of cheekbones*] aspect *m* saillant; [*pattern, markings*] aspect *m* frappant; **the ~ of his teeth** ses dents en avant |b| (*fig*) importance *f*; **to give ~ to sth** accorder de l'importance à qch; **to come** or **rise (in)to ~** [*person*] venir occuper le devant de la scène; [*phenomenon*] prendre de l'importance; **Gough shot to ~ last year** Gough a été propulsé sur le devant de la scène l'année dernière; **to achieve national/international ~** venir occuper le devant de la scène nationale/internationale; **his sudden rise to ~** sa célébrité soudaine; **since the rise to ~ of the environmental movement** depuis que le mouvement écologique a pris de l'importance; **to bring sb (in)to ~** placer qn sur le devant de la scène; **to bring sth (in)to ~** attirer l'attention sur qch; **to be in a position of ~** (= *clearly visible*) être bien en évidence; (= *important*) occuper une place importante; **a position of ~** (= *important role*) un poste important |c| (*frm = protuberance*) proéminence *f*, relief *m*; (*Anat*) protubérance *f*

prominent ['prɒmɪnənt] ADJ [*ridge, structure, nose*] proéminent; [*cheekbones*] saillant; [*tooth*] qui avance; (*fig = striking*) [*pattern, markings*] frappant; [*feature*] marquant; (*fig =*

outstanding) [*person*] important, bien en vue; **he is a ~ member of ...** c'est un membre important de ...; **she is ~ in London literary circles** elle est très en vue dans les cercles littéraires londoniens; **he was very ~ in ...** ◊ **he played a ~ part in ...** il a joué un rôle important dans ...; **to put sth in a ~ position** mettre qch bien en vue *or* en valeur; (*fig*) **he occupies a ~ position in ...** il occupe une position importante *or* en vue dans ...

prominently ['prɒmɪnəntlɪ] ADV [*displayed, placed, set*] bien en évidence, bien en vue; **the murder was ~ reported in the press** ce meurtre a fait l'objet de nombreux articles dans la presse; **to figure** *or* **feature ~ (in sth)** occuper une place importante (dans qch); **his name figured** *or* **feature ~ in the case** on a beaucoup entendu parler de lui dans cette affaire, son nom revenait souvent dans cette affaire

promiscuity [ˌprɒmɪs'kjuːɪtɪ] N [a] (*pej: sexual*) promiscuité *f* sexuelle [b] (*gen*) promiscuité *f*

promiscuous [prə'mɪskjʊəs] ADJ [a] (*pej: in sexual matters*) [*person*] de mœurs faciles *or* légères; [*conduct*] immoral, très libre; **he/she is very ~** il/elle change sans arrêt de partenaire, il/elle couche avec n'importe qui [b] (= *disorderly, mixed*) [*collection, heap*] confus

promiscuously [prə'mɪskjʊəslɪ] ADV [a] (*pej*) [*behave*] immoralement [b] [*heap, collect*] confusément

promiscuousness [prə'mɪskjʊəsnɪs] N = **promiscuity**

promise ['prɒmɪs] [1] N [a] (= *undertaking*) promesse *f*; **~ of marriage** promesse *f* de mariage; **under (a** *or* **the) ~ of** sous promesse de; **to make sb a ~** faire une promesse à qn (**to do sth** de faire); **is that a ~?** c'est promis?; **to keep one's ~** tenir sa promesse; **to hold sb to his ~** faire tenir sa promesse à qn, obliger qn à tenir sa promesse; (*dismissively*) **~s, ~s!** oh, on dit ça, on dit ça! [b] (= *hope, prospect*) promesse(s) *f(pl)*, espérance(s) *f(pl)*; **a young man of great ~** un jeune homme très prometteur *or* qui donne de grandes espérances; **he shows great ~** il donne de grandes espérances; **it holds out a ~ of peace** cela promet *or* fait espérer la paix

[2] VT [a] promettre (**sth to sb** qch à qn, **sb to do** à qn de faire, **that** que); **I ~ you!** je vous le promets!; **"I will help you" she ~d** « je vous aiderai » promit-elle; **I can't ~ anything** je ne peux rien (vous) promettre; (*fig*) **to ~ sb the earth** *or* **the moon** promettre monts et merveilles à qn, promettre la lune à qn; **to ~ o.s. (to do) sth** se promettre (de faire) qch [b] (= *give outlook of*) promettre, annoncer; **they've ~d us rain for tomorrow** on nous a promis *or* annoncé de la pluie pour demain; **it ~d to be another scorching day** une nouvelle journée très chaude s'annonçait, la journée promettait encore d'être très chaude; **this ~s to be difficult** ça promet d'être *or* ça s'annonce difficile [c] (= *assure*) assurer; **he did say so, I ~ you** il l'a vraiment dit, je vous assure

[3] VI [a] (= *pledge*) promettre; **I ~!** je vous le promets!; **(will you) ~?** (c'est) promis?, juré?; **I can't ~ but I'll do my best** je ne (vous) promets rien mais je ferai de mon mieux [b] (*in outlook*) **to ~ well** [*situation, event*] être plein de promesses, être prometteur; [*crop, business*] s'annoncer bien; [*first book*] promettre, être prometteur; **this doesn't ~ well** ce n'est guère prometteur, ça ne s'annonce pas bien

promised ['prɒmɪst] ADJ promis; **the Promised Land** la Terre Promise

promising ['prɒmɪsɪŋ] ADJ [a] (= *encouraging*) [*situation, sign*] prometteur; (*Comm*) [*market*] porteur; **the future is ~** l'avenir s'annonce bien; **that's ~** c'est prometteur; (*iro*) ça promet! (*iro*); **it doesn't look very ~** ça ne semble guère prometteur, ça ne se présente *or*

s'annonce pas bien [b] (= *full of promise*) [*person*] prometteur; **we have two ~ candidates** nous avons deux candidats prometteurs; **he is a ~ pianist** c'est un pianiste d'avenir

promisingly ['prɒmɪsɪŋlɪ] ADV d'une façon prometteuse; **it began quite ~** s'annonçait bien, c'était bien parti; **it's going quite ~** c'est prometteur, ça marche bien

promissory note ['prɒmɪsərɪˌnəʊt] N billet *m* à ordre

promo* ['prəʊməʊ] N (*pl* **promos**) [a] (*Comm* = *promotional material*) matériel *m* promotionnel [b] (*US Comm*) (ABBR = **promotion**) promotion *f*

promontory ['prɒməntrɪ] N promontoire *m*

promote [prə'məʊt] VT [a] (+ *person*) promouvoir (**to** à); **to be ~d** être promu, monter en grade; **he was ~d (to) colonel** *or* **to the rank of colonel** il a été promu (au grade de) colonel; (*Ftbl etc*) **they've been ~d to the first division** ils sont montés en première division [b] (= *encourage, publicize*) [+ *plan, product, firm, campaign, cooperation*] promouvoir; [+ *trade*] promouvoir, encourager; [+ *cause, idea, language*] défendre; (*Parl*) [+ *bill*] présenter; **the government's efforts to ~ economic cooperation** les efforts du gouvernement pour promouvoir la coopération économique

promoter [prə'məʊtə'] N [*of sport*] organisateur *m*, -trice *f*; [*of concert*] [*of product*] promoteur *m* de vente; [*of business, company*] fondateur *m*, -trice *f*

promotion [prə'məʊʃən] [1] N [a] (*in job etc*) promotion *f*, avancement *m*; **to get ~** être promu, avoir une promotion [b] (*Sport: to higher division*) accession *f*, passage *m*; **the ~ of Westerhill Wanderers to the first division** l'accession *or* le passage de l'équipe des Westerhill Wanderers en première division [c] (*Comm*) promotion *f* [d] (*US Scol*) passage *m* de classe [e] (*NonC = encouragement, publicity*) [*of plan, product, firm, campaign*] promotion *f*; [*of cause, idea*] défense *f*; (*Parl*) [*of bill*] présentation *f*; **their priority is the ~ of healthy eating habits/economic cooperation** ils ont pour priorité d'encourager les gens à se nourrir sainement/de promouvoir la coopération économique; **she devoted her life to the ~ of the Breton language** elle a consacré sa vie à la défense de la langue bretonne

[2] COMP ► **promotion board** N comité *m* de promotion ► **promotion campaign** N campagne *f* publicitaire ► **promotion prospects** NPL possibilités *fpl* de promotion *or* d'avancement ► **promotions director** N directeur *m*, -trice *f* des promotions

promotional [prə'məʊʃənl] ADJ (*Comm*) promotionnel, publicitaire

prompt [prɒmpt] [1] ADJ [a] (= *speedy*) [*action*] rapide, prompt; [*delivery, reply, service*] rapide; **~ payment** paiement *m* rapide; (*Comm*) paiement *m* dans les délais; **they were ~ to offer their services** ils ont été prompts à offrir leurs services, ils ont offert leurs services sans tarder [b] (= *punctual*) ponctuel, à l'heure [2] ADV ponctuellement; **at 6 o'clock ~** à 6 heures pile *or* tapantes *or* sonnantes; **I want it on 6 May ~** je le veux le 6 mai sans faute *or* au plus tard [3] VT [a] (+ *person*) pousser, inciter (**to do** à faire); [+ *protest, reaction*] provoquer, susciter; **I felt ~ed to protest** cela m'a incité à protester, je me suis senti obligé de protester; **he was ~ed by a desire to see justice done** il était animé *or* poussé par un désir de voir la justice triompher; **it ~s the thought that ...** cela incite à penser que ..., cela vous fait penser que ...; **to ~ a great deal of interest** susciter beau-

coup d'intérêt; **a feeling of regret ~ed by the sight of ...** un sentiment de regret provoqué *or* suscité par la vue de ... [b] (*Theat*) souffler [4] N [a] (*Theat*) **to give sb a ~** souffler une réplique à qn [b] (*Comput*) (message *m* de) guidage *m*; **at the ~** à l'apparition du message de guidage [5] COMP ► **prompt box** N (*Theat*) trou *m* du souffleur ► **prompt side** N (*Theat*) (*Brit*) côté *m* cour; (*US*) côté *m* jardin; **off ~ side** (*Brit*) côté jardin; (*US*) côté cour

prompter ['prɒmptə'] N (*Theat*) souffleur *m*, -euse *f*

prompting ['prɒmptɪŋ] N incitation *f*; **he did it at my ~** il l'a fait à mon instigation; **he did it without (any) ~** il l'a fait de son propre chef

promptitude ['prɒmptɪtjuːd] N (*frm*) [a] (= *speed*) promptitude *f*, empressement *m* (**in doing** à faire) [b] (= *punctuality*) ponctualité *f*

promptly ['prɒmptlɪ] ADV [a] (= *without delay*) rapidement; **to pay ~** payer dans les délais [b] (= *punctually*) à l'heure; **he arrived ~ at three** il est arrivé à trois heures précises [c] (= *thereupon*) aussitôt, aussi sec*; **she sat down and ~ fell asleep** elle s'est assise et s'est aussitôt endormie

promptness ['prɒmptnɪs] N = **promptitude**

promulgate ['prɒməlgeɪt] VT (*frm*) [+ *law, decree, constitution*] promulguer; [+ *idea, doctrine, creed*] répandre, disséminer

promulgation [ˌprɒməl'geɪʃən] N (*frm*) [*of law, decree, constitution*] promulgation *f*; [*of idea, doctrine, creed*] diffusion *f*, dissémination *f*

prone [prəʊn] ADJ [a] (= *face down*) (couché) sur le ventre, étendu face contre terre [b] (= *liable*) enclin, sujet (**to sth** à qch, **to do** à faire)

proneness ['prəʊnnɪs] N tendance *f*, prédisposition *f* (**to sth** à qch, **to do** à faire)

prong [prɒŋ] N [a] [*of fork*] dent *f*; [*of antler*] pointe *f* [b] [*of policy, strategy*] front *m*

pronged [prɒŋd] ADJ à dents

-pronged [prɒŋd] ADJ (*in compounds*) **three-pronged** [*fork*] à trois dents; (*Mil etc*) [*attack, advance*] sur trois fronts, triple

pronominal [prəʊ'nɒmɪnl] ADJ pronominal

pronoun ['prəʊnaʊn] N pronom *m*

pronounce [prə'naʊns] [1] VT [a] [+ *letter, word*] prononcer; **how is it ~d?** comment ça se prononce?; **the "k" in "knee" is not ~d** on ne prononce pas le « k » dans « knee », le « k » dans « knee » est muet [b] déclarer, prononcer (**that** que); (*Jur*) **to ~ sentence** prononcer la sentence; **they ~d him unfit to drive** ils l'ont déclaré inapte à conduire; **he was ~d dead** ils l'ont déclaré mort; **he ~d himself in favour of the suggestion** il s'est prononcé *or* il s'est déclaré en faveur de la suggestion; **"I'm not going!" she ~d (to them)** « je n'y vais pas! » (leur) déclara-t-elle; **"I now ~ you man and wife"** « je vous déclare unis par les liens du mariage » [2] VI se prononcer (**on** sur, **for** en faveur de, **against** contre); (*Jur*) prononcer (**for** en faveur de, **against** contre), rendre un arrêt

pronounceable [prə'naʊnsəbl] ADJ prononçable

pronounced [prə'naʊnst] ADJ prononcé, marqué

pronouncement [prə'naʊnsmənt] N déclaration *f*

pronto* ['prɒntəʊ] ADV illico*

pronunciation [prəˌnʌnsɪ'eɪʃən] N prononciation *f*

proof [pruːf] [1] N [a] (= *evidence: gen, Jur, Math etc*) preuve *f*; **by way of ~** en guise de preuve, pour preuve; **as (a) ~ of** ◊ **in ~ of** pour preuve de; **I've got ~ that he did it** j'ai la preuve *or* je peux prouver qu'il l'a fait; **it is ~ that he is honest** c'est la preuve qu'il est honnête ; **he showed** or gave ~ **of great cour-age** il a fait preuve or il a témoigné de beau-coup de courage ; **to be living** ~ **of sth** être la preuve vivante de qch ; **to be living** ~ **that ...** être la preuve vivante que ... ; *(Jur)* **the burden of** ~ **lies with the prosecution** la charge de la preuve incombe au ministère public → **posi-tive**

b *(= test)* épreuve *f* ; **to put sth/sb to the** ~ mettre qch/qn à l'épreuve, éprouver qch/qn ■ *(PROV)* **the** ~ **of the pudding is in the eating** c'est à l'usage que l'on peut juger de la quali-té d'une chose

c *[of book, pamphlet, engraving, photograph]* épreuve *f* ; **to read** or **correct the ~s** corriger les épreuves ; **to pass the ~s** donner le bon à tirer → **galley, page¹**

d *(of alcohol)* teneur *f* en alcool ; **this whisky is 70°** ~ ≈ ce whisky titre 40° d'alcool ; **under/ over** ~ moins de/plus de la teneur normale or exigée en alcool

2 ADJ ~ **against** *[bullets, time, wear, erosion]* à l'épreuve de ; *[temptation, suggestion]* insensi-ble à

3 VT **a** *[+ fabric, anorak, tent]* imperméabili-ser

b *(Typ etc)* corriger les épreuves de

4 COMP ► **proof of identity** N *(NonC)* pa-piers *mpl* or pièce(s) *f(pl)* d'identité ► **proof of postage** N justificatif *m* d'expédition ► **proof of purchase** N justificatif *m* d'achat ► **proof sheets** NPL épreuves *fpl* ► **proof spirit** N *(Brit)* alcool *m* à 57° ; *(US)* alcool *m* à 60° ► **proof stage** N **at ~ stage** au stade des épreuves

...proof [pru:f] ADJ *(in compounds)* à l'épreuve de → **bulletproof, foolproof**

proofread ['pru:fri:d] VT corriger les épreuves de

proofreader ['pru:f,ri:dəʳ] N correcteur *m*, -trice *f* d'épreuves or d'imprimerie

proofreading ['pru:f,ri:dɪŋ] N correction *f* des épreuves

prop¹ [prɒp] **1** N **a** support *m* ; *(for wall, in mine, tunnel etc)* étai *m* ; *(for clothes-line)* perche *f* ; *(for vines, hops etc)* échalas *m* ; *(for beans, peas)* rame *f* ; *(for seedlings)* tuteur *m* ; *(fig)* sou-tien *m*, appui *m* *(to, for* de*)* ; *(fig)* **his presence was a great** ~ **to her morale** il lui trouvait beau-coup de réconfort dans sa présence, sa pré-sence lui était d'un grand réconfort (moral) ; **do you ever use alcohol as a ~?** vous arrive-t-il de boire (de l'alcool) pour vous donner du courage ?

b *(Rugby)* ~ **(forward)** pilier *m*

2 VT **a** *(also* ~ **up)** *(= lean)* *[+ ladder, cycle]* appuyer **(against** contre*)* ; *(= support, shore up)* *[+ tunnel, wall, building]* étayer ; *[+ clothes-line, lid]* caler ; *[+ vine, hops]* échalasser ; *[+ beans, peas]* mettre une rame à ; *[+ seedlings]* mettre un tuteur à ; *(fig)* *[+ régime]* maintenir ; *[+ busi-ness, company]* soutenir, renflouer ; *[+ organi-zation]* soutenir, patronner ; *(Fin)* *[+ the pound]* venir au secours de ; **to** ~ **o.s. (up) against** se caler contre, s'adosser à

b **he ~ped the door open with a book** il a maintenu la porte ouverte avec un livre

prop² [prɒp] N *(Theat)* *(ABBR =* **property)** accessoire *m*

prop³ ◆ [prɒp] **1** N *(Aviat)* = **propeller 2** COMP ► **prop shaft** ◆ N = **propeller shaft** ; → **pro-peller**

prop. *(Comm)* ABBR = **proprietor**

propaganda [,prɒpə'gændə] **1** N propa-gande *f* **2** COMP *[leaflet, campaign]* de propa-gande

propagandist [,prɒpə'gændɪst] ADJ, N propa-gandiste *mf*

propagandize [,prɒpə'gændaɪz] **1** VI faire de la propagande **2** VT *[+ doctrine]* faire de la propagande pour ; *[+ person]* soumettre à la propagande, faire de la propagande auprès de

propagate ['prɒpəgeɪt] *(lit, fig)* **1** VT propa-ger **2** VI se propager

propagation [,prɒpə'geɪʃən] N propagation *f*

propane ['prəupeɪn] N propane *m*

propel [prə'pel] **1** VT **a** *[+ vehicle, boat, ma-chine]* propulser, faire avancer **b** *(= push)* pousser ; **to** ~ **sth/sb along** faire avancer qch/ qn *(en le poussant)* ; **they** ~**led him into the room** ils l'ont poussé dans la pièce ; *(more vio-lently)* ils l'ont propulsé dans la pièce **2** COMP ► **propelling pencil** N *(Brit)* porte-mine *m*

propellant [prə'pelənt] N *[of rocket]* propergol *m*, combustible *m* *(pour fusée)* ; *[of aerosol]* propulseur *m*

propellent [prə'pelənt] **1** ADJ propulseur, propulsif **2** N = **propellant**

propeller [prə'peləʳ] **1** N *[of plane, ship]* héli-ce *f* **2** COMP ► **propeller shaft** N *(Aut)* arbre *m* de transmission ; *(Aviat, Naut)* arbre *m* d'hé-lice

propensity [prə'pensɪtɪ] N propension *f*, tendance *f* *(naturelle)* **(to, towards, for** à, **to do, for doing** à faire*)*

proper ['prɒpəʳ] **1** ADJ **a** *(= suitable)* conve-nable, adéquat ; *(= correct)* correct ; *(= appro-priate)* approprié ; **you'll have to put the lid on the** ~ **way** il faut que vous mettiez le couvercle comme il faut ; **you'll have to apply for it in the** ~ **way** il faudra faire votre de-mande dans les règles ; **the** ~ **dress for the oc-casion** la tenue de rigueur pour l'occasion ; **the** ~ **spelling** l'orthographe *f* correcte ; **in the** ~ **sense of the word** au sens propre du mot ; **if you had come at the** ~ **time** si vous étiez venu à la bonne heure or à l'heure dite ; **the staff were not given** ~ **training** le personnel n'a pas reçu une formation appropriée or adéquate ; **I regret not having had a** ~ **education** je regrette de ne pas avoir eu une véritable éducation or suivi de véritables études ; *(Admin etc)* **you must go through the** ~ **channels** vous devez passer par la filière officielle ; **the** ~ **reply would have been "no"** la réponse qui aurait convenu c'est « non » ; **to make a** ~ **job of sth** bien réussir qch *(also iro)* ; **to do the** ~ **thing by sb** bien agir or agir honorablement envers qn ; **do as you think** ~ faites ce qui vous sem-ble bon, faites comme bon vous semblera ; **if you think it** ~ **to do so** si vous jugez convena-ble d'agir ainsi ; **in a manner** ~ **to his position** ainsi que l'exigeait sa position ; **the qualities which are** ~ **to this substance** les qualités pro-pres à or typiques de cette substance → **right**

b *(= authentic)* véritable ; *(after n = strictly speaking)* proprement dit, même ; **he's not a** ~ **electrician** ce n'est pas un véritable électri-cien ; **I've never had a** ~ **job** je n'ai jamais eu un vrai or véritable travail ; **I'm not a** ~ **Lon-doner** or **a Londoner** ~ je ne suis pas à propre-ment parler londonien ; **outside Paris** ~ en dehors de Paris même or de Paris proprement dit

c *(= seemly)* *[person]* comme il faut*, conve-nable ; *[book, behaviour]* convenable, correct ; **it isn't** ~ **to do that** cela ne se fait pas ; **I don't think it would be** ~ **for me to comment** je ne pense pas qu'il serait convenable que je fasse des commentaires → **prim**

d *(* * *= real, total)* **he's a** ~ **fool** c'est un imbé-cile fini ; **I felt a** ~ **idiot** je me suis senti vrai-ment idiot ; **he's a** ~ **gentleman** c'est un monsieur très comme il faut*, c'est un vrai gentleman ; **he made a** ~ **mess of it** il (en) a fait un beau gâchis ; **it's a** ~ **mess in there!** c'est la pagaille complète* là-dedans !

2 ADV **a** ◆ *[behave, talk]* comme il faut

b *(dial)* vraiment, très ; **he did it** ~ **quick** il l'a fait vraiment très vite ; **it's** ~ **cruel!** qu'est-ce que c'est cruel ! * ; **he's** ~ **poorly** il n'est vrai-ment pas bien, il est vraiment malade

3 N *(Rel: also* **Proper)** propre *m*

4 COMP ► **proper fraction** N *(Math)* fraction *f* inférieure à l'unité ► **proper name**, **proper noun** N *(Gram)* nom *m* propre ► **proper psalm** N *(Rel)* psaume *m* du jour

▼ **properly** ['prɒpəlɪ] ADV **a** *(= correctly)* *[eat, be-have, dress]* correctement ; *(= in a seemly way)* convenablement, comme il faut ; **he didn't do it** ~ il ne l'a pas fait comme il le fallait ; ~ **speaking** à proprement parler ; **he very** ~ **re-fused** il a refusé à juste titre **b** *(* * *= complete-ly)* vraiment, drôlement* ; **to be** ~ **ashamed** avoir vraiment or drôlement* honte ; **we were** ~ **beaten** nous avons été battus à plate(s) cou-ture(s)

propertied ['prɒpətɪd] ADJ possédant

property ['prɒpətɪ] **1** N **a** *(NonC =possessions)* propriété *f*, biens *mpl* ; **is this your** ~? est-ce que cela vous appartient ?, est-ce à vous ? ; **it is the** ~ **of ...** cela appartient à ..., c'est la propriété de ... ; **personal** ~ **must not be left in the cloakroom** il ne faut pas laisser d'effets personnels dans le vestiaire ; *(Jur)* **per-sonal** ~ biens *mpl* personnels or mobiliers ; **government/company** ~ propriété *f* du gouvernement/de l'entreprise ; *(lit)* **it is com-mon** ~ c'est la propriété de tous, ce sont des biens communs ; *(fig)* **it is common** ~ **that ...** chacun sait que ..., il est de notoriété publi-que que ... ; **a man/woman of** ~ un homme/ une femme qui a du bien or des biens → **lost, real**

b *(NonC = estate)* propriété *f* ; *(= lands)* terres *fpl* ; *(= buildings)* biens *mpl* immobiliers ; **he has** or **owns** ~ **in Ireland** il a des terres or des biens immobiliers en Irlande, il est proprié-taire en Irlande ; **get off my** ~ décampez de ma propriété or de mes terres

c *(= house etc)* propriété *f* ; **a fine** ~ **with views over the lake** une belle propriété avec vue sur le lac

d *(Chem, Phys etc = quality)* propriété *f* ; **this plant has healing properties** cette plante a des propriétés or des vertus thérapeutiques

e *(Theat)* accessoire *m*

2 COMP ► **property centre** N *(Brit)* ≈ agence *f* immobilière ► **property develop-er** N promoteur *m* immobilier ► **property insurance** N assurance *f* sur le capital immo-bilier ► **property law** N droit *m* immobilier ► **property man** N *(pl* **property men)** *(Theat)* accessoiriste *m* ► **property market**, **prop-erty mart** N marché *m* immobilier ► **property mistress** N *(Theat)* accessoiriste *f* ► **property owner** N propriétaire *m* foncier ► **property settlement** N *(US Jur)* répartition *f* des biens (en cas de divorce) ► **property speculation** N spéculation *f* immobilière ► **property speculator** N spé-culateur *m* immobilier ► **property tax** N impôt *m* foncier

prophecy ['prɒfɪsɪ] N prophétie *f*

prophesy ['prɒfɪsaɪ] **1** VT prédire *(that* que*)* ; *[+ event]* prédire, prophétiser **2** VI prophéti-ser, faire des prophéties

prophet ['prɒfɪt] N prophète *m* ; **the Prophet Samuel** *etc* le prophète Samuel *etc* ; *(fig)* **a** ~ **of doom** un prophète de malheur

prophetess ['prɒfɪtɪs] N prophétesse *f*

prophetic(al) [prə'fetɪk(l)] ADJ prophétique

prophetically [prə'fetɪkəlɪ] ADV *[say, write]* prophétiquement ; **"sooner than you think",** **he commented** ~ « plus tôt que tu ne le penses », dit-il prophétiquement

prophylactic [,prɒfɪ'læktɪk] **1** ADJ prophy-lactique **2** N prophylactique *m* ; *(= contra-ceptive)* préservatif *m*

prophylaxis [,prɒfɪ'læksɪs] N prophylaxie *f*

propinquity [prə'pɪŋkwɪtɪ] N *(frm)* *(in time, space)* proximité *f* ; *(in relationship)* parenté *f* proche, consanguinité *f* ; *[of ideas etc]* ressem-blance *f*, affinité *f*

propitiate [prə'pɪʃɪeɪt] VT [+ *person, the gods*] se concilier

propitiation [prə,pɪʃɪ'eɪʃən] N propitiation *f*

propitiatory [prə'pɪʃɪətərɪ] ADJ propitiatoire

propitious [prə'pɪʃəs] ADJ propice, favorable (**to** à)

propitiously [prə'pɪʃəslɪ] ADV d'une manière propice, favorablement

proponent [prə'pəʊnənt] N partisan(e) *m(f)*, adepte *mf* (**of** de)

proportion [prə'pɔːʃən] **1** N **a** (= *ratio, relationship: also* Math) proportion *f*; **the ~ of men to women** la proportion *or* le pourcentage d'hommes par rapport aux femmes; (*lit, fig*) **he has no sense of ~** il n'a pas le sens des proportions **b** **in ~: in ~ as** à mesure que; **in ~ with** proportionnellement à; **add milk in ~ to the weight of flour** ajoutez du lait proportionnellement au poids de la farine; **her weight is not in ~ to her height** son poids n'est pas proportionné à sa taille; **contributions in ~ to one's earnings** contributions au prorata de *or* en proportion de ses revenus; **in ~ to what she earns, what she gives is enormous** en proportion de ce qu'elle gagne, ce qu'elle donne est énorme; **in due ~** selon une proportion équitable *or* une juste proportion; **to be in direct/inverse ~ to sth** être directement/inversement proportionnel à qch; (*fig*) **to see sth in ~** relativiser qch; **let's get things in ~** ne dramatisons pas **c** **out of (all) ~** hors de (toute) proportion; **out of ~ to** hors de proportion avec, disproportionné à *or* avec; **he's got it out of ~** (*lit*) [*artist etc*] il n'a pas respecté les proportions, c'est mal proportionné; (*fig*) il a exagéré, c'est hors de proportion **d** (= *part*) part *f*, partie *f*; **in equal ~s** à parts égales; **a certain ~ of the staff** une certaine partie *or* un certain pourcentage du personnel; **your ~ of the work** votre part du travail; **what ~ is rented?** quel est le pourcentage de ce qui est loué?; **a high ~ of women** une proportion élevée de femmes **2 proportions** NPL (= *size*) proportions *fpl*, dimensions *fpl* **3** VT proportionner (**to** à); **well-~ed** bien proportionné

proportional [prə'pɔːʃənl] **1** ADJ proportionnel, proportionnée (**to** à) **2** COMP ▶ **proportional representation** N (Pol) représentation *f* proportionnelle

proportionality [prə,pɔːʃə'nælɪtɪ] N (*frm*) proportionnalité *f*; **there is a need for ~ in sentencing** il faut que la peine soit proportionnée à la gravité du crime

proportionally [prə'pɔːʃnəlɪ] ADV proportionnellement; **men have ~ larger feet than women** proportionnellement, les hommes ont les pieds plus grands que les femmes

proportionate 1 [prə'pɔːʃənɪt] ADJ = **proportional 1 2** [prə'pɔːʃə,neɪt] VT = **proportion 3**

proportionately [prə'pɔːʃnɪtlɪ] ADV = **proportionally**

proposal [prə'pəʊzl] N **a** (= *offer*) proposition *f*, offre *f*; [*of marriage*] demande *f* en mariage, offre *f* de mariage **b** (= *plan*) projet *m*, plan *m* (**for sth** de *or* pour qch, **to do** pour faire); (= *suggestion*) proposition *f*, suggestion *f* (**to do** de faire); (Jur) **~s for the amendment of this treaty** projet *m* tendant à la révision du présent traité

propose [prə'pəʊz] **1** VT **a** (= *suggest*) proposer, suggérer (**sth to sb** qch à qn, **doing** de faire, **that** que + *subj*); [+ *measures, plan, motion, course, candidate*] proposer; [+ *toast*] porter; [+ *candidate*] proposer; **to ~ sb's health** porter un toast à la santé de qn; **to ~ marriage to sb** faire sa demande à qn, de-

mander qn en mariage; **he ~d Smith as** *or* **for chairman** il a proposé Smith pour la présidence **b** (= *have in mind*) **to ~ to do** *or* **doing** se proposer *or* avoir l'intention de faire, penser *or* compter faire **2** VI (= *offer marriage*) faire une demande en mariage (**to sb** à qn)

proposed [prə'pəʊzd] ADJ proposé; **your ~ solution** la solution que vous avez proposée; **a ~ nature reserve/housing scheme** un projet de réserve naturelle/de cité

proposer [prə'pəʊzər] N (*Admin, Parl etc*) auteur *m* de la proposition; (*for club membership etc*) parrain *m*, marraine *f*

proposition [,prɒpə'zɪʃən] **1** N **a** (*gen, Comm, Math, Philos etc* = *statement, offer*) proposition *f* **b** (= *affair, enterprise*) **that's quite another ~** *or* **a different ~** ça c'est une tout autre affaire; **the journey alone is quite a ~** *or* **is a big ~** le voyage n'est déjà pas une mince affaire *or* une partie de plaisir; **it's a tough ~** c'est ardu, ça présente de grandes difficultés; **he's a tough ~*** il est coriace, il n'est pas commode → **economic, paying c** (*pej: immoral*) proposition *f* malhonnête **2** VT faire des propositions (malhonnêtes) à

propound [prə'paʊnd] VT (= *put up*) [+ *theory, idea*] avancer, proposer; [+ *problem, question*] poser; (= *explain, develop*) [+ *programme*] exposer

proprietary [prə'praɪətərɪ] **1** ADJ **a** (Comm) [*article*] de marque déposée **b** [*duties etc*] de propriétaire **c** (= *possessive, protective*) [*behaviour, attitude*] possessif **2** COMP ▶ **proprietary brand** N (produit *m* de) marque *f* déposée ▶ **proprietary colony** N (*US Hist*) colonie accordée par la Couronne à une personne en pleine propriété ▶ **proprietary medicine** N spécialité *f* pharmaceutique ▶ **proprietary name** N marque *f* déposée ▶ **proprietary rights** NPL droit *m* de propriété

proprietor [prə'praɪətər] N propriétaire *m*

proprietorial [prə,praɪə'tɔːrɪəl] ADJ [*rights, duties*] de propriétaire; [*behaviour, attitude*] possessif

proprietorship [prə'praɪətəʃɪp] N (= *right*) droit *m* de propriété; **under his ~** quand il en était (*or* sera) le propriétaire, lui (étant) propriétaire

proprietress [prə'praɪətrɪs], **proprietrix** [prə'praɪətrɪks] N propriétaire *f*

propriety [prə'praɪətɪ] N **a** (= *decency*) propriétés *fpl*, bienséances *fpl*; **to observe the proprieties** respecter *or* observer les bienséances *or* les convenances **b** (NonC = *appropriateness, correctness etc*) [*of phrase, expression*] justesse *f*, correction *f*; **~ of behaviour** *or* **conduct** comportement *m* bienséant

propulsion [prə'pʌlʃən] N propulsion *f*

propulsive [prə'pʌlsɪv] ADJ [*energy*] propulsif; [*music, rhythm*] entraînant

pro rata [,prəʊ'rɑːtə] **1** ADV au prorata; **salary £20,000 ~** salaire au prorata du temps de travail (20000 livres pour un plein temps) **2** ADJ proportionnel

prorate ['prəʊreɪt] VT (*US*) distribuer au prorata

prorogation [,prəʊrə'geɪʃən] N prorogation *f*

prorogue [prə'rəʊg] VT (*esp Parl*) proroger

prosaic [prəʊ'zeɪk] ADJ (= *banal*) prosaïque (*liter*), commun

prosaically [prəʊ'zeɪkəlɪ] ADV prosaïquement (*liter*), communément; **more ~ known as ...** plus communément connu sous le nom de ...

proscenium [prəʊ'siːnɪəm] **1** N (*pl* **prosceniums** *or* **proscenia** [prəʊ'siːnɪə]) proscenium *m*, avant-scène *f* **2** COMP ▶ **proscenium arch** N (*Theat*) arc *m* de scène

proscribe [prəʊ'skraɪb] VT proscrire

proscription [prəʊ'skrɪpʃən] N proscription *f*

prose [prəʊz] **1** N **a** (*NonC: Literat*) prose *f*; **in ~** en prose **b** (*Scol, Univ: also ~ translation*) thème *m* **2** COMP [*poem, comedy*] en prose ▶ **prose writer** N prosateur *m*

prosecute ['prɒsɪkjuːt] **1** VT **a** (Jur) poursuivre (en justice), engager des poursuites (judiciaires) contre; **he was ~d for speeding** il a été poursuivi pour excès de vitesse → **trespasser b** (*frm* = *carry on*) [+ *enquiry, research, war*] poursuivre **2** VI (= *take legal action*) engager des poursuites judiciaires; **"we always ~"** « tout délit donnera lieu à des poursuites » **b** [*lawyer*] **Mr Paul Lambotte, prosecuting, pointed out that ...** Me Paul Lambotte, représentant la partie plaignante, a fait remarquer que ...; (*in higher court*) Me Paul Lambotte, représentant le ministère public *or* l'accusation, a fait remarquer que ... → **prosecuting**

prosecuting ['prɒsɪkjuːtɪŋ] **1** ADJ (Jur) **to appear as ~ counsel** représenter le ministère public **2** COMP ▶ **prosecuting attorney** N avocat *m* général

prosecution [,prɒsɪ'kjuːʃən] N **a** (Jur = *act of prosecuting*) poursuites *fpl* (judiciaires); **to bring a ~ against sb** engager des poursuites (judiciaires) contre qn; **to take out a private ~ (against sb)** engager des poursuites (contre qn) à titre privé; **there have been seven ~s in the last three years** il y a eu sept actions en justice au cours des trois dernières années →**crown, director b** (*Jur = side*) **the ~** (*in civil case*) la partie plaignante; (*in criminal case*) l'accusation *f*; **witness for the ~** témoin *m* à charge; **to give evidence for the ~** être témoin à charge; **to appear as counsel for the ~** (*in civil case*) représenter la partie plaignante; (*in criminal case*) représenter le ministère public *or* l'accusation; **Giles Harrison, for the ~, told the jury that ...** (*in civil case*) Giles Harrison, représentant la partie plaignante, a déclaré au jury que ...; (*in criminal case*) Giles Harrison, représentant le ministère public *or* l'accusation, a déclaré au jury que ... **c** (*frm* = *furtherance*) [*of enquiry, research, war*] poursuite *f*; **in the ~ of my duties** dans l'exercice de mes fonctions

prosecutor ['prɒsɪkjuːtər] N plaignant *m*; (*also* **public ~**) procureur *m* (de la République), ministère *m* public

proselyte ['prɒsɪlaɪt] **1** N prosélyte *mf* **2** VTI (*US*) = **proselytize**

proselytism ['prɒsɪlɪtɪzəm] N prosélytisme *m*

proselytize ['prɒsɪlɪtaɪz] **1** VI faire du prosélytisme **2** VT [+ *person*] convertir, faire un(e) prosélyte de

prosodic [prə'sɒdɪk] ADJ prosodique; (Phon) **~ feature** trait *m* prosodique

prosody ['prɒsədɪ] N prosodie *f*

prospect ['prɒspekt] **1** N **a** (= *view*) vue *f*, perspective *f* (**of, from** de); (*fig*) (= *outlook*) perspective *f*; (= *future*) (perspectives *fpl* d')avenir *m*; (= *hope*) espoir *m*; **this ~ cheered him up** cette perspective l'a réjoui; **what are his ~s?** quelles sont ses perspectives d'avenir?; **he has good ~s** il a de l'avenir; **he has no ~s** il n'a aucun avenir; **the job has no ~s** c'est un emploi sans avenir; **to improve one's career ~s** améliorer ses chances de promotion *or* d'avancement **b** **~ of: there is little ~ of his coming** il y a peu de chances *or* d'espoir (pour) qu'il vienne; **he has little ~ of succeeding** il a peu de chances de réussir, il y a peu de chances qu'il réussisse; **there is no ~ of that** rien ne laisse prévoir cela; **there is every ~ of success/of succeeding** tout laisse prévoir le succès/qu'on réussira; **to face the ~ of** faire face à la perspective de; **"good ~s of promotion"** « réelles perspectives d'évolution »; **the job offered the ~ of foreign travel** l'emploi offrait la possibilité de voyager à l'étranger **c** **~ for: the ~s for the harvest are good/poor**

la récolte s'annonce bien/mal; **future ~s for the steel industry** les perspectives d'avenir de la sidérurgie
d **in ~: to have sth in ~** avoir qch en perspective *or* en vue; **the events in ~** les événements *mpl* en perspective
e (= *likely person, thing: for marriage*) parti *m*; **he is a good ~ for the England team** c'est un bon espoir pour l'équipe anglaise; **he seems quite a good ~** il semble prometteur; **this product is an exciting ~ for the European market** ce produit ouvre des perspectives passionnantes en ce qui concerne le marché européen; **their offer/the deal seemed quite a good ~** leur proposition/l'affaire semblait prometteuse
2 [prə'spekt] VI prospecter; **to ~ for gold** *etc* prospecter pour trouver de l'or *etc*, chercher de l'or *etc*
3 [prə'spekt] VT [+ *land, district*] prospecter
prospecting [prə'spektɪŋ] N (*Min etc*) prospection *f*
prospective [prə'spektɪv] ADJ [*son-in-law, home, legislation*] futur (*before n*); [*journey*] en perspective; [*customer*] éventuel, potentiel
prospector [prə'spektəʳ] N prospecteur *m*, -trice *f*; **gold ~** chercheur *m* d'or
prospectus [prə'spektəs] N brochure *f*, prospectus *m*
prosper ['prɒspəʳ] **1** VI [*person*] prospérer; [*company, enterprise*] prospérer, réussir **2** VT (†, *liter*) favoriser, faire prospérer
prosperity [prɒs'perɪtɪ] N (*NonC*) prospérité *f*
prosperous ['prɒspərəs] ADJ [*person, city, business*] prospère, florissant; [*period, years*] prospère; [*undertaking*] prospère, qui réussit; [*look, appearance*] prospère, de prospérité; (*liter*) [*wind*] favorable
prosperously ['prɒspərəslɪ] ADV de manière prospère *or* florissante
prostaglandin [,prɒstə'glændɪn] N prostaglandine *f*
prostate ['prɒsteɪt] N (*also* **~ gland**) prostate *f*; **to have a ~ operation** se faire opérer de la prostate
prosthesis [prɒs'θiːsɪs] N (*pl* **prostheses** [prɒs'θiːsiːz]) prosthèse *or* prothèse *f*
prosthetic [prɒs'θetɪk] ADJ prosthétique *or* prothétique
prosthodontics [,prɒsθə'dɒntɪks] N prothèse *f* dentaire
prosthodontist ['prɒsθə'dɒntɪst] N prothésiste *mf* dentaire
prostitute ['prɒstɪtjuːt] **1** N prostituée *f*; **male ~** prostitué *m* **2** VT (*lit, fig*) prostituer; **to ~ o.s.** se prostituer
prostitution [,prɒstɪ'tjuːʃən] N (*NonC*) (*lit*) prostitution *f*; (*fig*) perversion *f*
prostrate ['prɒstreɪt] **1** ADJ (*lit*) à plat ventre; (*in respect, submission*) prosterné; (*in exhaustion*) prostré; (*fig: nervously, mentally*) prostré, accablé **2** [prɒs'treɪt] VT **a** **to ~ o.s.** se prosterner **b** (*fig*) accabler; **the news ~d him** la nouvelle l'a accablé *or* abattu; **~d with grief/by the heat** accablé de chagrin/par la chaleur
prostration [prɒs'treɪʃən] N (= *act*) prosternation *f*, prosternement *m*; (*Rel*) prostration *f*; (*fig* = *nervous exhaustion*) prostration *f*; **in a state of ~** prostré
prosy ['prəʊzɪ] ADJ ennuyeux, insipide
prot* [prɒt] N (*pej*) ABBR = **Protestant**
protactinium [,prəʊtæk'tɪnɪəm] N protactinium *m*
protagonist [prəʊ'tægənɪst] N protagoniste *mf*
Protagoras [prəʊ'tægəræs] N Protagoras *m*
protean ['prəʊtɪən] ADJ changeant, inconstant
protect [prə'tekt] **1** VT [+ *person, property, country, plants*] protéger (**from** de, **against**

contre); [+ *interests, rights*] sauvegarder; (*Econ*) [+ *industry*] protéger; **the tigress fought to ~ her cubs** la tigresse s'est battue pour défendre ses petits; **don't lie to ~ your brother** ne cherche pas à protéger ton frère en mentant **2** COMP ► **protected species** N espèce *f* protégée
protection [prə'tekʃən] **1** N **a** (*also Econ, Ind*) [*of person, property, country, plants*] protection *f* (**from** *or* **against sth** contre qch); [*of interests, rights*] sauvegarde *f*; **he wore a helmet for ~ against rock falls** il portait un casque pour se protéger des *or* contre les chutes de pierres; **the grease offers** *or* **affords some ~ against the cold** la graisse offre une certaine protection contre le froid
b (*Insurance*) garantie *f* (**against sth** contre qch), couverture *f* (**against sth** en cas de qch)
c (*gen pl* = *safeguard*) mesure *f* de protection; **benefits and ~s for employees** avantages *mpl* et garanties *fpl* *or* mesures *fpl* de protection pour les employés
d (*in protection racket*) protection *f*; **he pays 200 dollars a week (for** *or* **as) ~** il achète sa tranquillité 200 dollars par semaine → **police**
e (= *barrier contraception*) protection *f*; **they didn't use any ~** ils n'ont pas utilisé de protection
2 COMP ► **protection factor** N [*of sun cream*] indice *m* de protection ► **protection money** N **he pays 200 dollars a week ~ money** il achète sa tranquillité 200 dollars par semaine; **he pays ~ money to Big Joe** il verse de l'argent à Big Joe pour qu'on le laisse (*subj*) en paix ► **protection racket** N racket *m*; **he's running a ~ racket** il est à la tête d'un racket, il extorque de l'argent par intimidation
protectionism [prə'tekʃənɪzəm] N **a** (*Econ*) protectionnisme *m* **b** (*US*) [*of wildlife*] protection *f* de l'environnement
protectionist [prə'tekʃənɪst] **1** ADJ **a** (*Econ*) protectionniste **b** (*US: of wildlife*) [*measure etc*] pour la défense de l'environnement **2** N **a** (*Econ*) protectionniste *mf* **b** (*US: of wildlife*) défenseur *m* de l'environnement
protective [prə'tektɪv] ADJ [*layer, attitude, gesture*] protecteur (-trice *f*), de protection; [*clothing, covering*] de protection; (*Econ*) [*tariff, duty, system*] protecteur (-trice *f*); (*Zool*) ~ **colouring** *or* **coloration** mimétisme *m*, homochromie *f*; (*Jur*) ~ **custody** détention *f* provisoire (*comme mesure de protection*)
protectively [prə'tektɪvlɪ] ADV **he put his arm ~ around Julie's shoulders** il a passé un bras protecteur autour des épaules de Julie; **she stepped ~ in front of him** elle se mit devant lui pour le protéger; **he crossed his forearms ~ over his face** il croisa les avant-bras sur son visage pour se protéger
protectiveness [prə'tektɪvnɪs] N attitude *f* protectrice
protector [prə'tektəʳ] N (= *person*) protecteur *m*; (= *object, device*) dispositif *m* de protection; (*Brit Hist*) **the (Lord) Protector** le Protecteur
protectorate [prə'tektərɪt] N protectorat *m* (*also Brit Hist*)
protectress [prə'tektrɪs] N protectrice *f*
protégé ['prəʊtɪ,ʒeɪ, 'prɒtɪ,ʒeɪ] N protégé *m*
protégée ['prəʊtɪ,ʒeɪ, 'prɒtɪ,ʒeɪ] N protégée *f*
protein ['prəʊtiːn] **1** N protéine *f* **2** COMP [*intake, deficiency*] de protéines; [*foods, diet*] riche en protéines ► **protein content** N teneur *f* en protéines
pro tem ['prəʊ'tem], **pro tempore** † ['prəʊ'tempərɪ] **1** N temporairement; (*in jobs*) par intérim; **he's replacing the chairman ~** il remplace le président à titre temporaire **2** ADJ temporaire; **on a ~ basis** temporairement; **the ~ chairman** le président par intérim, le président intérimaire

▼**protest** ['prəʊtest] **1** N **a** (*gen*) protestation *f* (**against** contre, **about** à propos de); (= *demonstration*) manifestation *f*; **to do sth under ~** faire qch en protestant *or* contre son gré; **to make a ~** protester, élever une protestation (**against** contre); **in ~** en signe de protestation (**against** contre); **to stage a ~** organiser une manifestation **b** (*Fin, Jur: in case of dishonour of a bill*) protêt *m* **2** [prə'test] VT **a** (= *declare, affirm*) protester (**that** que); [+ *loyalty*] protester de; **"I didn't do it" he ~ed** « ce n'est pas moi » protesta-t-il ; ~ **innocence** **b** (*US*) protester contre **3** [prə'test] VI protester, élever une *or* des protestation(s) (**against** contre, **about** à propos de, **to sb** auprès de qn) **4** COMP (*Pol etc*) [*meeting*] de protestation ► **protest demonstration**, **protest march** N manifestation *f*
Protestant ['prɒtɪstənt] ADJ, N protestant(e) *m(f)*; ~ **ethic** morale *f* protestante
Protestantism ['prɒtɪstəntɪzəm] N protestantisme *m*
protestation [,prɒtes'teɪʃən] N protestation *f*
protester [prə'testəʳ] N protestataire *mf*; (*on march, in demonstration*) manifestant(e) *m(f)*
proto... ['prəʊtəʊ] PREF proto...
protocol ['prəʊtəkɒl] N (*also Comput*) protocole *m*
proton ['prəʊtɒn] N proton *m*
protoplasm ['prəʊtəʊplæzəm] N protoplasme *m*, protoplasma *m*
prototype ['prəʊtəʊtaɪp] N prototype *m*; **a ~ aircraft** le prototype d'un avion
prototypical [,prəʊtəʊ'tɪpɪkəl] ADJ par excellence; **he's a ~ socialist** c'est l'archétype du socialiste
protozoan, protozoon [,prəʊtə'zəʊən] N (*pl* **protozoa** [,prəʊtə'zəʊə]) (*Bio*) protozoaire *m*
protract [prə'trækt] VT prolonger, faire durer
protracted [prə'træktɪd] ADJ prolongé, très long (longue *f*)
protraction [prə'trækʃən] N prolongation *f*
protractor [prə'træktəʳ] N (*Geom*) rapporteur *m*
protrude [prə'truːd] **1** VI [*stick, gutter, rock, shelf*] dépasser, faire saillie; [*teeth*] avancer; [*eyes*] être globuleux **2** VT faire dépasser
protruding [prə'truːdɪŋ] ADJ [*teeth*] qui avance; [*eyes*] globuleux; [*chin*] saillant; [*shelf, rock*] en saillie
protrusion [prə'truːʒən] N saillie *f*, avancée *f*
protrusive [prə'truːsɪv] ADJ (*frm*) = **protruding**
protuberance [prə'tjuːbərəns] N (*frm*) protubérance *f*
protuberant [prə'tjuːbərənt] ADJ (*frm*) protubérant
proud [praʊd] ADJ **a** [*person*] fier (**of sb/sth** de qn/qch, **that** que + *subj*, **to do** de faire); (= *arrogant*) arrogant, orgueilleux; **the ~ father/owner** l'heureux père *m*/possesseur *m*; **that's nothing to be ~ of!** il n'y a pas de quoi être fier!; **I'm not very ~ of myself** je ne suis pas très fier de moi; **as ~ as a peacock** fier comme Artaban; (*pej*) fier comme un paon; **it was a ~ day for us when ...** nous avons été remplis de fierté *or* très fiers le jour où ... → **possessor**
b **my ~est possession** ce dont je suis le plus fier; **to do o.s. ~*** ne se priver de rien; **to do sb ~*** (= *entertain etc*) se mettre en frais pour qn, recevoir qn comme un roi (or une reine); (= *honour*) faire beaucoup d'honneur à qn **c** (*frm* = *splendid*) [*building, ship*] imposant, majestueux; [*stallion*] fier **d** (*Brit*) **to stand ~ of sth**† faire saillie sur qch
proudly ['praʊdlɪ] ADV fièrement
provable ['pruːvəbl] ADJ démontrable, prouvable

▼**prove** [pruːv] **1** VT **a** (= *give proof of*) prouver (*also Jur*); (= *show*) prouver, démontrer; **that ~s his innocence** *or* **him innocent** *or* **that he is innocent** cela prouve son innocence *or*

qu'il est innocent; **you can't ~ anything against me** vous n'avez aucune preuve contre moi; **that ~d that she did it** cela prouvait bien *or* c'était bien la preuve qu'elle l'avait fait; **he ~d that she did it** il a prouvé *or* démontré qu'elle l'avait (bien) fait; **he managed to ~ it against her** il a réussi à prouver qu'elle l'avait fait *or* qu'elle était coupable; **he couldn't ~ anything against her** il n'a rien pu prouver contre elle; **the theory remains to be ~d** il reste à prouver *or* démontrer cette théorie, cette théorie n'est pas encore prouvée; **whether he was right remains to be ~** à prouver *or* encore faut-il prouver qu'il avait raison; **he was ~d right** il s'est avéré qu'il avait raison, les faits lui ont donné raison; **it all goes to ~ that ...** tout cela montre bien *or* prouve que ...; **to ~ one's point** prouver ce que l'on avance (*or* a avancé *etc*); **to ~ a point** (= *show one is right*) montrer que l'on a raison; (= *show one is capable*) montrer qu'on en est capable; **can you ~ it?** pouvez-vous le prouver?; **that ~s it!** c'est la preuve!; **he ~d himself innocent** il a prouvé son innocence; **he ~d himself useful** il s'est révélé *or* montré utile → **proven**
[b] (= *test*) mettre à l'épreuve; [+ *will*] homologuer; **to ~ o.s.** faire ses preuves
[c] (*Culin*) [*dough*] laisser lever
[d] (*Jur, Fin*) **to ~ a debt** produire une dette (à la faillite)
[2] VI [a] [*person*] se révéler; [*fact, object*] s'avérer, se révéler; **he ~d (to be) incapable of helping us** il s'est montré *or* révélé incapable de nous aider; **the information ~d (to be) correct** les renseignements se sont avérés *or* révélés justes; **the money ~d to be in his pocket** l'argent s'est trouvé être dans sa poche; **it ~d very useful** cela s'est avéré *or* (*more frm*) s'est révélé très utile; **the car ~d (to be) a success** la voiture a été une réussite; **if it ~s otherwise** s'il en est autrement *or* différemment
[b] (*Culin*) [*dough*] lever
[3] COMP ► **proving ground** N terrain *m* d'essai, lieu *m* d'expérimentation

proven ['pru:vən, 'prəʊvən] [1] VB *ptp* of **prove** [2] ADJ [*formula, method*] qui a fait ses preuves; [*abilities*] indubitable; **a ~ track record** une expérience confirmée; (*Scot Jur*) **verdict of not ~** (ordonnance *f* de) non-lieu *m* (*en l'absence de charges suffisantes*); **the case was not ~** il n'y a eu d'ordonnance de non-lieu

provenance ['prɒvɪnəns] N provenance *f*

Provençal [,prɒvã:n'sɑ:l] [1] ADJ provençal [2] N [a] Provençal(e) *m(f)* [b] (*Ling*) provençal *m*

Provence [prɒ'vã:ns] N la Provence; **in ~** en Provence

provender† ['prɒvɪndər] N fourrage *m*, provende *f*

proverb ['prɒvɜ:b] N proverbe *m*; (*Bible*) **(the Book of) Proverbs** le livre des Proverbes

proverbial [prə'vɜ:bɪəl] ADJ proverbial; **it's like the ~ needle in a haystack** comme on dit, c'est chercher une aiguille dans une botte de foin

proverbially [prə'vɜ:bɪəlɪ] ADV [*say*] proverbialement; **prevention is ~ better than cure** comme le dit le proverbe, mieux vaut prévenir que guérir; **British food is ~ bad*** la mauvaise qualité de la nourriture en Grande-Bretagne est proverbiale *or* bien connue

provide [prə'vaɪd] [1] VT [a] (= *supply*) fournir (**sb with sth, sth for sb** qch à qn); (= *equip*) munir, pourvoir (**sb with sth** qn de qch), fournir (**sb with sth** qch à qn); **to ~ o.s. with sth** se procurer qch; **I will ~ food for everyone** c'est moi qui fournirai la nourriture pour tout le monde; **he ~d the school with a new library** il a pourvu l'école d'une nouvelle bibliothèque; **candidates must ~ their own pencils** les candidats doivent apporter leurs crayons; **can you ~ a substitute?** pouvez-vous

trouver un remplaçant?; **it ~s accommodation for five families** on peut loger cinq familles; **the field ~s plenty of space for a car park** le champ offre suffisamment d'espace pour le stationnement des voitures; **I am already ~d with all I need** je suis déjà bien pourvu, j'ai déjà tout ce qu'il me faut; **the car is ~d with a radio** la voiture est équipée d'une radio
[b] [*legislation, treaty etc*] stipuler, prévoir (**that** que); **unless otherwise ~d** sauf dispositions contraires
[2] VI [a] (*esp financially*) **to ~ for** (*gen*) pourvoir *or* subvenir aux besoins de; (*family*) entretenir; (*in the future*) assurer l'avenir de; **I'll see you well ~d for** je ferai le nécessaire pour que vous ne manquiez (*subj*) de rien; **the Lord will ~** Dieu y pourvoira
[b] (= *make arrangements*) **to ~ for sth** prévoir qch; [*treaty, legislation*] prévoir *or* stipuler qch; **they hadn't ~d for such a lot of spectators** le nombre de spectateurs les a pris au dépourvu; **he had ~d for any eventuality** il avait paré à toute éventualité; **to ~ against** se prémunir contre, prendre ses précautions contre

provided [prə'vaɪdɪd] CONJ **~ (that)** à condition que (+ *subj*), à condition de (+ *infin*); **you can go ~ it doesn't rain** tu peux y aller à condition qu'il ne pleuve pas; **you can go ~ you pass your exam** tu peux y aller à condition de réussir ton examen; **~ you always keep it closed** à condition de le garder toujours bien fermé; (*Admin, Jur*) **~ always that ...** sous réserve que ... (+ *subj*)

providence ['prɒvɪdəns] N [a] (*Rel etc*) providence *f*; **Providence** la Providence [b] († = *foresight*) prévoyance *f*, prudence *f*

provident ['prɒvɪdənt] ADJ [*person*] prévoyant, prudent; (*Brit*) [*fund, society*] de prévoyance

providential [,prɒvɪ'denʃəl] ADJ (*frm*) providentiel

providentially [,prɒvɪ'denʃəlɪ] ADV (*frm*) providentiellement; **~, he had brought a torch with him** par un heureux hasard, il avait apporté une lampe de poche

providently ['prɒvɪdəntlɪ] ADV (*frm*) avec prévoyance, prudemment

provider [prə'vaɪdər] N pourvoyeur *m*, -euse *f*; (*Comm*) fournisseur *m*, -euse *f*; (*Social Work*) **~s of care** dispensateurs *mpl* de soins; **she is the family's sole ~** elle est seule à subvenir aux besoins de la famille

providing [prə'vaɪdɪŋ] CONJ = **provided**

province ['prɒvɪns] [1] N [a] province *f* [b] (*fig*) domaine *m*, compétence *f* (*esp Admin*); **that is not my ~ ◊ it is not within my ~** cela n'est pas de mon ressort *or* ne relève pas de ma compétence; **his particular ~ is housing** le logement est son domaine *or* sa spécialité [c] (*Rel*) archevêché *m* [2] **the provinces** NPL la province; **in the ~s** en province

provincial [prə'vɪnʃəl] [1] ADJ (*gen, also pej*) provincial, de province; (*Comm*) **~ branch** branche *f or* agence *f* régionale [2] N provincial(e) *m(f)*

provincialism [prə'vɪnʃəlɪzəm] N (*pej*) provincialisme *m*

provirus ['prəʊ,vaɪrəs] N provirus *m*

provision [prə'vɪʒən] [1] N [a] (= *supply*) provision *f*; **to lay in** *or* **get in a ~ of coal** faire provision de charbon
[b] (*NonC* = *supplying*) [*of food*] fourniture *f*, approvisionnement *m*; [*of equipment*] fourniture *f*; [*of housing, education*] offre *f*; **~ of food to the soldiers** approvisionnement *m* des soldats en nourriture; (*Fin*) **~ of capital** apport *m or* fourniture *f* de capitaux; **~ of services** prestation *f* de services; **to make ~ for** [+ *one's family, dependents etc*] pourvoir aux besoins de, assurer l'avenir de; [+ *journey, siege, famine*] prendre des dispositions *or* des précautions pour

[c] (*Admin*) (= *funding*) financement *m* (**of, for** de); (= *funds*) fonds *mpl*
[d] (*Admin, Jur etc* = *stipulation*) disposition *f*, clause *f*; **according to the ~s of the treaty** selon les dispositions du traité; **it falls within the ~s of this law** cela tombe sous le coup de cette loi, c'est un cas prévu par cette loi; **~ to the contrary** clause *f* contraire; **there is no ~ for this in the rules ◊ the rules make no ~ for this** le règlement ne prévoit pas cela
[2] **provisions** NPL (= *food etc*) provisions *fpl*; **to get ~s in** faire des provisions
[3] VT approvisionner, ravitailler (**with** en)
[4] COMP ► **provision merchant** N marchand *m* de comestibles

provisional [prə'vɪʒənl] [1] ADJ [*government*] provisoire; [*arrangement, agreement, acceptance*] à titre conditionnel; (*Admin*) [*appointment*] à titre provisoire; (*Jur*) provisionnel [2] N (*Pol: in Ireland*) **the Provisionals** (les membres *mpl* de) l'IRA *f* provisoire [3] COMP ► **provisional driving licence** N (*Brit*) permis *m* de conduire provisoire (*obligatoire pour l'élève conducteur*) → DRIVING LICENCE ► **the Provisional IRA** N l'IRA *f* provisoire

provisionally [prə'vɪʒnəlɪ] ADV provisoirement

proviso [prə'vaɪzəʊ] N (*pl* **provisos** *or* **provisoes**) stipulation *f*, condition *f*; (*Jur*) clause *f* restrictive, condition *f* formelle; **with the ~ that ...** à condition que ... (+ *subj*)

provisory [prə'vaɪzərɪ] ADJ = **provisional 1**

Provo* ['prəʊvəʊ] N (*Pol: in Ireland*) **the ~s** (les membres *mpl* de) l'IRA *f* provisoire

provocation [,prɒvə'keɪʃən] N provocation *f*; (*Chem, Bio*) **under ~** en réponse à une provocation

provocative [prə'vɒkətɪv] ADJ [a] (= *aggressive*) [*gesture, remark*] provocant, provocateur (-trice *f*); **now you're trying to be ~** là vous essayez de me (*or* le *etc*) provoquer, là vous me (*or* lui *etc*) cherchez querelle [b] (= *thought-provoking*) [*book, title, talk*] qui force à réagir, qui ne laisse pas indifférent [c] (= *seductive*) [*woman, movement, smile*] provocant

provocatively [prə'vɒkətɪvlɪ] ADV (= *challengingly, suggestively*) [*say, ask, look, behave*] de manière provocante; **~ entitled ...** portant le titre provocateur de ...; **~ dressed** habillé de manière provocante

provoke [prə'vəʊk] VT [a] (= *rouse*) [+ *person*] provoquer; [+ *war, dispute, revolt*] provoquer, faire naître; [+ *reply*] provoquer, susciter; **to ~ sb to do sth** *or* **into doing sth** inciter qn à faire qch; **it ~d them to action** cela les a incités à agir [b] (= *anger*) **◊ to ~ sb's anger** provoquer qn

provoking [prə'vəʊkɪŋ] ADJ (= *annoying*) contrariant, agaçant; (= *thought-provoking*) provocateur (-trice *f*) → **thought**

provost ['prɒvəst] [1] N (*Brit Univ*) président *m*; (*US Univ*) ≈ doyen *m*; (*Scot*) maire *m*; (*Rel*) doyen *m* → **lord** [2] COMP ► **provost court** N (*Mil*) tribunal *m* prévôtal ► **provost guard** N prévôté *f* ► **provost marshal** N prévôt *m*

prow [praʊ] N proue *f*

prowess ['praʊɪs] N prouesse *f*

prowl [praʊl] [1] VI (*also* **~ about, ~ around**) rôder [2] N **to be on the ~** rôder [3] COMP ► **prowl car** N (*US Police*) voiture *f* de police

prowler ['praʊlər] N rôdeur *m*, -euse *f*

prowling ['praʊlɪŋ] ADJ rôdeur; [*taxi*] en maraude

proximity [prɒk'sɪmɪtɪ] [1] N proximité *f*; **in ~ to** ◊ **in the ~ of** à proximité de [2] COMP ► **proximity fuse** N fusée *f* de proximité

proximo ['prɒksɪməʊ] ADV (*Comm*) (du mois) prochain

proxy ['prɒksɪ] [1] N (= *power*) procuration *f*; (= *person*) fondé(e) *m(f)* de pouvoir, mandataire *mf*; **by ~** par procuration 2 COMP ► **proxy conflict** N (*Mil euph*) conflit *m* par personnes interposées ► **proxy vote** N vote *m* par procuration

Prozac® ['prəʊzæk] N Prozac® *m*

PRP [,pi:ɑː'pi:] N (ABBR = **performance-related pay**) → **performance**

PRS [pi:ɑː'es] N (ABBR = **Performing Rights Society**) ≈ SACEM *f*

prude [pru:d] N prude *f*, bégueule *f*; **he's a ~** il est pudibond

prudence ['pru:dəns] N prudence *f*, circonspection *f*

prudent ['pru:dənt] ADJ prudent, circonspect; **it is ~ to do** il est prudent de faire

prudential [pru(:)'denʃəl] ADJ prudent, de prudence

prudently ['pru:dəntlɪ] ADV prudemment, avec prudence

prudery ['pru:dərɪ] N pruderie *f*, pudibonderie *f*

prudish ['pru:dɪʃ] ADJ pudibond, bégueule*

prudishness ['pru:dɪʃnɪs] N = **prudery**

prune¹ [pru:n] N (= *fruit*) pruneau *m*; (‡ *pej* = *person*) repoussoir *m*; (*fig*) **~s and prisms** afféterie *f*, préciosité *f*

prune² [pru:n] VT (*to promote growth*) [+ *tree, bush*] tailler; (= *thin out*) élaguer, émonder; (*fig: also* **~ down**) [+ *article, essay*] élaguer, faire des coupures dans
► **prune away** VT SEP [+ *branches*] élaguer; (*fig*) [+ *paragraph, words*] élaguer

pruning ['pru:nɪŋ] 1 N a (*lit*) [*of tree, bush*] (*to promote growth*) taille *f*; (*to remove unwanted branches, dead wood etc*) élagage *m*, émondage *m* b (*fig*) [*of article, essay*] élagage *m* 2 COMP ► **pruning hook** N émondoir *m*, ébranchoir *m* ► **pruning knife** N (*pl* **pruning knives**) serpette *f* ► **pruning shears** NPL (= *secateurs*) cisailles *fpl*, coupe-branches *m*; (= *hedge shears*) taille-haies *m*, cisailles *fpl* à haies

prurience ['prʊərɪəns] N (*frm*) lascivité *f*, luxure *f*

prurient ['prʊərɪənt] ADJ (*frm*) lascif

Prussia ['prʌʃə] N la Prusse

Prussian ['prʌʃən] 1 ADJ prussien; **~ blue** bleu *m* de Prusse 2 N Prussien(ne) *m(f)*

prussic acid [,prʌsɪk'æsɪd] N acide *m* prussique

pry¹ [praɪ] VI mettre son nez dans les affaires des autres, s'occuper de ce qui ne vous regarde pas; **I don't want to ~ but ...** je ne veux pas être indiscret mais ...; **stop ~ing!** occupez-vous de ce qui vous regarde!; **to ~ into sb's secrets** chercher à découvrir les secrets de qn

pry² [praɪ] VT (*US*) = **prise**

prying ['praɪɪŋ] ADJ fureteur, indiscret (-ète *f*); **to keep sth safe from ~ eyes** mettre qch à l'abri des regards indiscrets

PS [pi:'es] N a (ABBR = **postscript**) P.-S. or PS *m* b (ABBR = **private secretary**) → **private**

psalm [sɑ:m] N psaume *m*; (*Bible*) **(the Book of) Psalms** le livre des Psaumes

psalmist ['sɑ:mɪst] N psalmiste *m*

psalmody ['sælmədɪ] N psalmodie *f*

psalter ['sɔːltər] N psautier *m*

PSAT [,pi:eseɪ'ti:] N (*US Scol, Univ*) (ABBR = **Preliminary Scholastic Aptitude Test**) → **preliminary**

PSBR [,pi:esbi:'ɑ:r] (*Econ*) (ABBR = **public sector borrowing requirement**) → **public**

psephologist [se'fɒlədʒɪst] N spécialiste *mf* des élections

psephology [sə'fɒlədʒɪ] N étude *f* des élections

pseud* [sju:d] (*Brit*) 1 N bêcheur* *m*, -euse* *f* 2 ADJ qui manque de sincérité, artificiel

pseudo* ['sju:dəʊ] ADJ insincère, faux (fausse *f*)

pseudo- ['sju:dəʊ] PREF pseudo-; **~antique** pseudoantique; **~autobiography** pseudoautobiographie *f*; **~apologetically** sous couleur de s'excuser

pseudonym ['sju:dənɪm] N pseudonyme *m*

pseudonymous [sju:'dɒnɪməs] ADJ pseudonyme

pshaw [pʃɔ:] EXCL peuh!

psi¹ [psi:es'aɪ] N (ABBR = **pounds per square inch**) ≈ kg/cm³

psi² [psi:es'aɪ] N (*NonC* = *psychic phenomena*) phénomènes *mpl* parapsychiques *or* paranormaux

psittacosis [,psɪtə'kəʊsɪs] N psittacose *f*

psoriasis [sɒ'raɪəsɪs] N psoriasis *m*

psst [pst] EXCL psitt, pst, hep

PST [,pi:es'ti:] (*US*) (ABBR = **Pacific Standard Time**) → **pacific**

PSV [,pi:es'vi:] (*Aut*) (ABBR = **public service vehicle**) → **public**

psych* [saɪk] VT ABBR = **psychoanalyse** a (= *guess, anticipate*) [+ *sb's reactions etc*] deviner, prévoir b (= *make uneasy: also* **~ out**) intimider, déconcerter (volontairement); **that doesn't ~ me (out)** ça ne me panique* pas c (= *prepare psychologically: also* **~ up**) préparer (mentalement) (**for sth** à *or* pour qch, **to do** pour faire); **to get o.s. ~ed up for sth** se préparer (mentalement) à qch; **he was all ~ed up to start, when ...** il était gonflé à bloc*, tout prêt à commencer, quand ...
► **psych out*** 1 VI (= *break down*) craquer* 2 VT SEP a (= *cause to break down*) faire craquer* b → **psych b** c (*US* = *analyse, work out*) piger*, comprendre (**that** que); (+ *situation etc*) analyser, comprendre; **to ~ sb out** voir clair dans le jeu de qn; **I ~ed it all out for myself** je m'y suis retrouvé tout seul
► **psych up*** VT SEP → **psych c**

psyche ['saɪkɪ] N psychisme *m*, psyché *f*

psychedelia [,saɪkə'deliə] N (*NonC*) (= *objects*) objets *mpl* psychédéliques; (= *atmosphere*) univers *m* psychédélique

psychedelic [,saɪkə'delɪk] ADJ psychédélique

psychiatric [,saɪkɪ'ætrɪk] ADJ [*hospital, treatment, medicine*] psychiatrique; [*disease*] mental

psychiatrist [saɪ'kaɪətrɪst] N psychiatre *mf*

psychiatry [saɪ'kaɪətrɪ] N psychiatrie *f*

psychic ['saɪkɪk] 1 ADJ a (= *supernatural*) [*phenomenon, powers etc*] parapsychologique; [*person*] télépathe; **~ research** recherches *fpl* parapsychologiques; **the ~ world** le monde du paranormal; **I'm not ~!** je ne suis pas devin! b (*Psych*) psychique 2 N médium *m*

psychical ['saɪkɪkəl] ADJ = **psychic 1**

psycho‡ ['saɪkəʊ] N ABBR = **psychopath, psychopathic, psychotic**

psycho... ['saɪkəʊ] PREF psych(o)...

psychoactive [,saɪkəʊ'æktɪv] ADJ (*Med*) psychotrope

psychoanalysis [,saɪkəʊə'nælɪsɪs] N psychanalyse *f*

psychoanalyst [,saɪkəʊ'ænəlɪst] N psychanalyste *mf*

psychoanalytic(al) [,saɪkəʊ,ænə'lɪtɪk(əl)] ADJ psychanalytique

psychoanalyze [,saɪkəʊ'ænəlaɪz] VT psychanalyser

psychobabble* ['saɪkəʊ,bæbəl] N (*NonC*) jargon *m* de psy*

psychodrama ['saɪkəʊdrɑ:mə] N psychodrame *m*

psychodynamic [,saɪkəʊdaɪ'næmɪk] 1 ADJ psychodynamique 2 N (*NonC*) **~s** psychodynamisme *m*

psychokinesis [,saɪkəʊkɪ'ni:sɪs] N psychokinèse *f*, psychokinésie *f*

psychokinetic [,saɪkəʊkɪ'netɪk] ADJ psychocinétique

psycholinguistic [,saɪkəʊlɪn'gwɪstɪk] 1 ADJ psycholinguistique 2 N (*NonC*) **~s** psycholinguistique *f*

psychological [,saɪkə'lɒdʒɪkəl] ADJ [*method, study, state, moment, warfare*] psychologique; **it's only ~** c'est psychologique

psychologically [,saɪkə'lɒdʒɪkəlɪ] ADV [*important, damaging, disturbed etc*] psychologiquement; **~, he's very strong** psychologiquement, il est très fort; **to be ~ prepared for sth** être psychologiquement prêt pour qch; **~ speaking** d'un point de vue psychologique

psychologist [saɪ'kɒlədʒɪst] N psychologue *mf* → **child, industrial**

psychology [saɪ'kɒlədʒɪ] N psychologie *f* → **child**

psychometric [,saɪkəʊ'metrɪk] ADJ psychométrique

psychometrics [,saɪkəʊ'metrɪks] N (*NonC*) psychométrie *f*

psychometry [saɪ'kɒmɪtrɪ] N psychométrie *f*

psychomotor ['saɪkəʊ'məʊtər] ADJ psychomoteur (-trice *f*)

psychoneurosis ['saɪkəʊnjʊə'rəʊsɪs] N (*pl* **psychoneuroses** ['saɪkəʊnjʊə'rəʊsi:z]) psychonévrose *f*

psychoneurotic ['saɪkəʊnjʊə'rɒtɪk] ADJ psychonévrotique

psychopath ['saɪkəʊpæθ] N psychopathe *mf*

psychopathic [,saɪkəʊ'pæθɪk] ADJ [*person*] psychopathe; [*condition*] psychopathique

psychopathology ['saɪkəʊpə'θɒlədʒɪ] N psychopathologie *f*

psychopharmacological ['saɪkəʊfɑ:məkə'lɒdʒɪkəl] ADJ psychopharmacologique

psychopharmacology ['saɪkəʊfɑ:mə'kɒlədʒɪ] N psychopharmacologie *f*

psychophysical [,saɪkəʊ'fɪzɪkəl] ADJ psychophysique

psychophysics [,saɪkəʊ'fɪzɪks] N (*NonC*) psychophysique *f*

psychophysiological ['saɪkəʊ,fɪzɪə'lɒdʒɪkəl] ADJ psychophysiologique

psychophysiology ['saɪkəʊfɪzɪ'ɒlədʒɪ] N psychophysiologie *f*

psychoses [saɪ'kəʊsi:z] NPL of **psychosis**

psychosexual [,saɪkəʊ'seksjʊəl] ADJ psychosexuel

psychosis [saɪ'kəʊsɪs] N (*pl* **psychoses**) psychose *f*

psychosocial ['saɪkəʊ'səʊʃəl] ADJ psychosocial

psychosomatic [,saɪkəʊsəʊ'mætɪk] ADJ psychosomatique

psychosurgery [,saɪkəʊ'sɜ:dʒərɪ] N psychochirurgie *f*

psychotherapist [,saɪkəʊ'θerəpɪst] N psychothérapeute *mf*

psychotherapy [,saɪkəʊ'θerəpɪ] N psychothérapie *f*

psychotic [saɪ'kɒtɪk] ADJ, N psychotique *mf*

psychotropic [,saɪkəʊ'trɒpɪk] ADJ [*drug*] psychotrope

PT† [pi:'ti:] N (*Scol*) (ABBR = **physical training**) → **physical**

pt ABBR = **part(s), pint(s), point(s)**

PTA [,pi:ti:'eɪ] N a (*Scol*) (ABBR = **Parent-Teacher Association**) → **parent** b (*Brit*) (ABBR = **Prevention of Terrorism Act**) *loi antiterroriste*

ptarmigan ['tɑ:mɪgən] N (*pl* **ptarmigans** or **ptarmigan**) lagopède *m* des Alpes

Pte (*Mil*) (ABBR = **Private**) (*on envelope*) **~ J. Smith** le soldat J. Smith

pterodactyl [,terə'dæktɪl] N ptérodactyle *m*

PTO [,pi:ti:'əʊ] (ABBR = **please turn over**) TSVP

Ptolemaic [,tɒlə'meɪɪk] ADJ ptolémaïque

Ptolemy ['tɒləmɪ] N Ptolémée *m*
ptomaine ['təʊmeɪn] N ptomaïne *f*; **~ poisoning** intoxication *f* alimentaire
ptosis ['təʊsɪs] N (*pl* **ptoses** ['təʊsiːz]) ptose *f*
PTSD [ˌpiːtiːesˈdiː] ABBR = **post-traumatic stress disorder**
ptyalin ['taɪəlɪn] N ptyaline *f*
pub [pʌb] (*Brit*) ABBR = **public house** ① N ≈ café *m*; (*in British or Irish context*) pub *m* ② COMP ► **pub-crawl*** N, VI **to go on a ~-crawl** ◊ **to go ~-crawling** faire la tournée des bars *or* des bistrots* *or* des pubs ► **pub food, pub grub*** N cuisine *f or* nourriture *f* de bistrot* ► **pub lunch** N repas *m* de bistrot*; **to go for a ~ lunch** aller manger au bistrot*

PUB

*Les pubs jouent un rôle essentiel dans la vie sociale britannique. Traditionnellement, l'accès au **pub** est interdit aux moins de 18 ans, mais certains établissements ont un espace réservé (ou une terrasse en jardin) pour les familles. En Angleterre et au pays de Galles, les **pubs** sont généralement ouverts de 11 heures à 23 heures alors qu'en Écosse et en Irlande, les horaires d'ouverture sont plus flexibles. Certains **pubs** appartiennent à des brasseries et ne vendent que leurs propres marques de bière; d'autres, les «free houses», appartiennent à des propriétaires privés et offrent, de ce fait, un plus grand choix de bières.*

pub. (ABBR = **published**) publié
pubertal ['pjuːbətəl] ADJ pubère
puberty ['pjuːbətɪ] N puberté *f*
pubes¹ ['pjuːbiːz] NPL *of* **pubis**
pubes² ['pjuːbiːz] NPL (= *pubic hair*) poils *mpl* du pubis, toison *f*
pubescence [pjuːˈbesəns] N pubescence *f*
pubescent [pjuːˈbesənt] ADJ pubescent
pubic ['pjuːbɪk] ① ADJ [*region etc*] pubien ② COMP ► **pubic hair** N poils *mpl* pubiens *or* du pubis ► **pubic lice** NPL morpions *mpl*
pubis ['pjuːbɪs] N (*pl* **pubes**) pubis *m*
public ['pʌblɪk] ① N ⓐ (*gen: Admin, Econ, Fin etc*) public (-ique *f*); (= *owned by the nation*) [*enterprise etc*] nationalisé, étatisé; (*copyright*) **in the ~ domain** dans le domaine public; (*Fin*) **to go ~** [*company*] s'introduire en Bourse → 3
ⓑ (= *of, for, by everyone*) [*meeting, park, indignation*] public (-ique *f*); "**this is a ~ announcement: would passengers ...**" «votre attention s'il vous plaît: les passagers sont priés de ...»; **to be in the ~ eye** être très en vue; **to disappear from the ~ eye** disparaître des feux de l'actualité; **he's a ~ figure** c'est quelqu'un qui est très en vue, c'est une personnalité très connue; **it is a matter of ~ interest** c'est une question d'intérêt public *or* général; **he has the ~ interest at heart** il a à cœur l'intérêt *or* le bien public; **a man in ~ life** un homme public; **to go into ~ life** se consacrer aux affaires publiques; **to be active in ~ life** prendre une part active aux affaires publiques; **he's really a ~ nuisance*** c'est une calamité publique*, il empoisonne le monde*; **there was a ~ protest against ...** il y a eu de nombreux mouvements de protestation contre ... → **1c**; (*Scot*) **the house has two ~ rooms and three bedrooms** la maison a cinq pièces dont trois chambres; **she is a good ~ speaker** elle parle bien en public; **~ speakers know that ...** les personnes amenées à parler fréquemment en public savent que ... → **image**
ⓒ (= *open to everyone, not secret*) public (-ique *f*); **to make sth ~** rendre qch public, publier qch, porter qch à la connaissance du public; **it was all quite ~** cela n'avait rien de secret, c'était tout à fait officiel; **he made a ~ protest** il a protesté publiquement; **his ~ support of**

the strikers son appui déclaré *or* ouvert aux grévistes; **let's go over there, it's too ~ here** allons là-bas, c'est trop public ici
② N public *m*; **the ~'s confidence in the government** la confiance des gens dans le gouvernement; **in ~** en public; **the reading/sporting ~** les amateurs *mpl* de lecture/de sport; **the French/English ~** les Français *mpl*/Anglais *mpl*; **the American voting ~** les électeurs *mpl* américains; (*hum*) **the great British ~** les sujets *mpl* de Sa (Gracieuse) Majesté; **the house is open to the ~** la maison est ouverte au public; (= *audience*) **he couldn't disappoint his ~** il ne pouvait pas décevoir son public → **general**
③ COMP ► **public access television** N (*US TV*) chaînes *fpl* câblées non commerciales ► **public-address system** N (système *m* de) sonorisation *f* ► **public affairs** NPL affaires *fpl* publiques ► **public analyst** N analyste *mf* d'État *or* officiel(le) ► **public assistance†** N (*NonC*) assistance *f* publique ► **public bar** N (*Brit*) bar *m* ► **public building** N édifice *m* public ► **public company** N société *f* anonyme par actions ► **public convenience** N (*Brit Admin*) toilettes *fpl* publiques ► **public corporation** N (*Brit*) entreprise *f* nationale ► **the public debt** N (*Econ*) la dette publique ► **public defender** N (*US Jur*) avocat *m* de l'assistance judiciaire ► **public enemy** N (*Admin*); (*fig*) **~ enemy number one*** ennemi *m* public numéro un ► **public examination** N (*Scol etc*) examen *m* national ► **public footpath** N (*Brit Admin*) passage *m* public ► **public gallery** N (*in parliament, courtroom*) tribune *f* réservée au public ► **public health** N santé *f or* hygiène *f* publique ► **Public Health Service** N (*US*) ≈ Direction *f* des affaires sanitaires et sociales ► **public holiday** N jour *m* férié, fête *f* légale ► **public house** N (*Brit*) pub *m* ► **public housing** N (*US*) logements *mpl* sociaux, ≈ HLM *fpl* ► **public housing project** N (*US*) cité *f* HLM ► **public lavatory** N toilettes *fpl* publiques ► **public law** N droit *m* public ► **public lending right** N (*Brit Admin*) droits dédommageant un auteur pour le prêt de ses ouvrages en bibliothèque ► **public library** N bibliothèque *f* municipale ► **public limited company** N (*Brit*) ≈ société *f* à responsabilité limitée ► **public medicine** N (*US*) = **public health** ► **public money** N (*Econ*) deniers *mpl* publics ► **public opinion** N opinion *f* publique ► **public opinion poll** N sondage *m* d'opinion publique ► **public ownership** N **under ~ ownership** nationalisé, étatisé; **to take sth into ~ ownership** nationaliser qch, étatiser qch ► **public property** N (*NonC* = *land etc*) biens *mpl* publics, propriété *f* publique; (*fig*) **to treat sb as ~ property** ne pas avoir d'égards pour la vie privée de qn ► **Public Prosecutor** N (*Jur*) procureur *m* (de la République), ≈ ministère *m* public ► **Public Prosecutor's Office** N (*Jur*) parquet *m* ► **the public purse** N (*Econ*) le trésor public ► **Public Record Office** N (*Brit*) ≈ Archives *fpl* nationales ► **public relations** NPL relations *fpl* publiques; **~ relations officer** responsable *mf* de relations publiques; **it's just a ~ relations exercise** il *etc* a fait ça uniquement dans le but de se faire bien voir ► **public school** N (*Brit* = *private school*) public school *m*, collège *m* secondaire privé; (*US* = *state school*) école *f* secondaire publique ► **public schoolboy, public schoolgirl** N (*Brit*) élève *mf* d'une public school ► **the public sector** N (*Econ*) le secteur public ► **public sector borrowing** N emprunts *mpl* d'État ► **public sector borrowing requirement** N besoins *mpl* de financement du secteur public ► **public servant** N fonctionnaire *mf* ► **public service** N service *m* public ► **public service**

corporation N (*US*) service *m* public non nationalisé ► **public service vehicle** N (*Brit Admin*) véhicule *m* de transport en commun ► **public speaking** N art *m* oratoire ► **public spending** N (*NonC*) dépenses *fpl* publiques ► **public spirit** N civisme *m*, sens *m* civique ► **public-spirited** ADJ **to be ~-spirited** faire preuve de civisme ► **public television** N (*US*) télévision *f* éducative (non commerciale) ► **public transport** N (*NonC*) transports *mpl* en commun, transports *mpl* publics ► **public utility** N service *m* public ► **public welfare** N assistance *f* publique ► **public works** NPL travaux *mpl* publics

PUBLIC ACCESS TELEVISION

*Aux États-Unis, **public access television** désigne les chaînes câblées non commerciales produites par des associations locales et autres institutions à but non lucratif. Le principe est de permettre aux communautés locales de s'exprimer et d'éviter que les chaînes câblées ne deviennent des monopoles. Selon la loi de 1984 sur la télévision câblée (Cable Act), une collectivité locale peut exiger du propriétaire d'une chaîne câblée qu'il lui réserve une **public access television** et mette à sa disposition le studio, le matériel d'enregistrement et le personnel technique nécessaires.*

publican ['pʌblɪkən] N ⓐ (*Brit* = *pub manager*) patron(ne) *m(f)* de bistrot ⓑ (*Bible* = *taxman*) publicain *m*
publication [ˌpʌblɪˈkeɪʃən] ① N ⓐ (*NonC* = *act of publishing*) [*of book etc*] publication *f*; (*Jur*) [*of banns*] publication *f*; [*of decree*] promulgation *f*, publication *f*; **after the ~ of the book** après la publication *or* la parution du livre; **this is not for ~** ceci doit rester entre nous ⓑ (= *published work*) publication *f* ② COMP ► **publication date** N date *f* de parution *or* de publication
publicist ['pʌblɪsɪst] N (*Jur*) spécialiste *mf* de droit public international; (*Press*) journaliste *mf*; (*Advertising*) (agent *m*) publicitaire *m*, agent *m* de publicité
publicity [pʌbˈlɪsɪtɪ] ① N (*NonC*) publicité *f* (**for** pour); **can you give us some ~ for the concert?** pouvez-vous nous faire de la publicité pour le concert?; **adverse ~** contre-publicité *f*; **I keep getting ~ about the society's meetings** je reçois tout le temps des circulaires concernant les réunions de la société; **I've seen some of their ~** j'ai vu des exemples de leur publicité ② COMP ► **publicity agency** N agence *f* publicitaire *or* de publicité ► **publicity agent** N (agent *m*) publicitaire *m*, agent *m* de publicité ► **publicity campaign** N campagne *f* d'information; (= *advertising*) campagne *f* de publicité ► **publicity stunt*** N coup *m* de pub*
publicize ['pʌblɪsaɪz] VT ⓐ (= *make public*) rendre public, publier; **I don't ~ the fact, but ...** je ne lie crie pas sur les toits, mais ...; **well-~d** dont on parle beaucoup (*or* dont on a beaucoup parlé *etc*) ► ⓑ (= *advertise*) faire de la publicité pour; **well-~d** annoncé à grand renfort de publicité
publicly ['pʌblɪklɪ] ① ADV ⓐ (= *in public*) publiquement, en public; **to be ~ accountable** devoir répondre de ses actes devant l'opinion ⓑ (*Econ*) **~-owned** d'État, du secteur public; **~ funded** financé par l'État ② COMP ► **publicly-quoted company** N société *f* anonyme cotée en Bourse
publish ['pʌblɪʃ] VT ⓐ [+ *news*] publier, faire connaître; (*Jur, Rel*) **to ~ the banns** publier les bans ⓑ [+ *book*] publier; [+ *periodical*] faire paraître; [+ *author*] éditer; **to be ~ed** [*book, author*] être publié; "**to be ~ed**" «à paraître»; "**just ~ed**" «vient de paraître»; "**~ed monthly**" «paraît tous les mois»
publisher ['pʌblɪʃə'] N éditeur *m*, -trice *f*

publishing ['pʌblɪʃɪŋ] [1] N [of book etc] publication f; **he's** or **he works in ~** il travaille dans l'édition [2] COMP ► **publishing house** N maison f d'édition

puce [pjuːs] ADJ puce inv

puck[1] [pʌk] N (= elf) lutin m, farfadet m

puck[2] [pʌk] N (Ice Hockey) palet m

pucker ['pʌkəʳ] [1] VI (also ~ **up**) [face, feature, forehead] se plisser; (Sewing) goder; **she ~ed up, waiting for his kiss** elle avança les lèvres, attendant son baiser [2] VT [a] (Sewing) froncer [b] (also ~ **up**) [+ lips] avancer; **to ~ (up) one's brow** or **forehead** plisser son front [3] N (Sewing) faux pli m

puckish ['pʌkɪʃ] ADJ (liter) de lutin, malicieux

pud: [pʊd] (Brit) ABBR = **pudding**

pudding ['pʊdɪŋ] [1] N [a] (= cooked dessert) **steamed ~** pudding m; **apple ~** dessert m aux pommes; **rice ~** riz m au lait → **milk**, **proof** [b] (Brit = dessert course in meal) dessert m; **what's for ~?** qu'y a-t-il comme dessert? [c] (= cooked meat etc dish) **steak-and-kidney ~** pain m de viande et de rognons à la vapeur [d] (= cooked sausage) **black/white ~** boudin m noir/blanc [e] (* pej = fat person) patapouf* mf [2] COMP ► **pudding basin** N (Brit) jatte f (dans laquelle on fait cuire le pudding) ► **pudding-face**: N (fig pej) (face f de) lune* f ► **pudding-head**: N (fig pej) empoté(e)* m(f), andouille* f ► **pudding rice** N (Culin) riz m à grains ronds

puddingstone ['pʊdɪŋstəʊn] N (Geol) poudingue m, conglomérat m

puddle ['pʌdl] [1] N flaque f [2] VI former une flaque

pudenda [puːˈdendə] NPL parties fpl génitales

pudgy ['pʌdʒɪ] ADJ = **podgy**

pueblo ['pwebləʊ] [1] N (pl **pueblos**) (in US) village indien du sud-ouest des États-Unis [2] COMP ► **the Pueblo Indians** NPL les (Indiens mpl) Pueblos mpl

puerile ['pjʊəraɪl] ADJ puéril (puérile f)

puerility [pjʊəˈrɪlɪtɪ] N puérilité f

puerperal [pjuː(ː)ˈɜːpərəl] ADJ puerpéral; **~ fever** fièvre f puerpérale

Puerto Rican ['pwɜːtəʊˈriːkən] [1] ADJ portoricain [2] N Portoricain(e) m(f)

Puerto Rico ['pwɜːtəʊˈriːkəʊ] N Porto Rico

puff [pʌf] [1] N [a] [of air] bouffée f, souffle m; (from mouth) souffle m; [of wind, smoke] bouffée f; (sound of engine) teuf-teuf m; **he blew out the candles with one ~** il a éteint les bougies d'un seul souffle; **our hopes vanished in a ~ of smoke** nos espoirs se sont évanouis or s'en sont allés en fumée; **to be out of ~**: être à bout de souffle, être essoufflé; **to get one's ~ back** reprendre son souffle, reprendre haleine; **he took a ~ at his pipe/cigarette** il a tiré une bouffée de sa pipe/cigarette; **just time for a quick ~!*** juste le temps de griller une clope* or d'en griller une*! [b] (also **powder ~**) houppe f; (small) houppette f; (in dress) bouillon m [c] (Press, Rad, TV* = advertisement) réclame f (NonC), boniment m (NonC); (= written article) papier m; **a ~ about his new book** un papier sur son nouveau livre [2] VI (= blow) souffler; (= pant) haleter; [wind] souffler; **smoke was ~ing from the ship's funnel** des bouffées de fumée sortaient de la cheminée du navire; **he was ~ing hard** or **~ing and panting** il soufflait comme un phoque or un bœuf; **to ~ (away) at** or **on one's pipe/cigarette** tirer des bouffées de sa pipe/cigarette; **the doctor came ~ing in** le docteur entra en haletant; **to ~ in/out** etc [train] entrer/sortir etc en envoyant des bouffées de fumée → **puffed** [3] VT [a] **to ~ (out) smoke** [person, chimney, engine, boat] envoyer des bouffées de fumée;

stop ~ing smoke into my face arrête de m'envoyer ta fumée dans la figure; **he ~ed his pipe** il tirait des bouffées de sa pipe [b] (also ~ **out**) [+ sails etc] gonfler; **to ~ (out) one's cheeks** gonfler ses joues; **to ~ out one's chest** gonfler or bomber sa poitrine; **the bird ~ed out** or **up its feathers** l'oiseau a hérissé ses plumes; **his eyes are ~ed (up)** il a les yeux gonflés or bouffis [c] (* = praise: also ~ **up**) faire mousser*, faire du battage autour de

[4] COMP ► **puff adder** N vipère f heurtante ► **puffed rice** N riz m soufflé ► **puffed sleeves** NPL = **puff sleeves**; → **puff** ► **puff paste** N (US) = **puff pastry** ► **puff pastry** N pâte f feuilletée ► **puff-puff*** N (baby talk = train) teuf-teuf* m (baby talk) ► **puff sleeves** NPL manches fpl bouffantes

►**puff along** VI [person] se déplacer en haletant; [steam train, bus] avancer en haletant

►**puff away** VI → **puff** 2

►**puff out** [1] VI [sails etc] se gonfler → **puff** 2 [2] VT SEP → **puff** 3a, 3b

►**puff up** [1] VI [sails etc] se gonfler; [eye, face] enfler [2] VT SEP (= inflate) gonfler; (fig) **to be ~ed up (with pride)** être bouffi d'orgueil → **puff** 3b, 3c

puffball ['pʌfbɔːl] N vesse-de-loup f

puffed* [pʌft] ADJ (= breathless: also ~ **out**) à bout de souffle

puffer ['pʌfəʳ] N [a] (also ~ **fish**) poisson-globe m [b] (* = train) train m à vapeur [c] (Med* = inhaler) inhalateur m [d] (* = smoker) fumeur m, -euse f

puffin ['pʌfɪn] N macareux m, perroquet m de mer

puffiness ['pʌfɪnɪs] N [of eye, face] gonflement m, bouffissure f

puffy ['pʌfɪ] ADJ [eye, face] gonflé, bouffi; [cloud] cotonneux

pug [pʌg] [1] N (= dog) carlin m [2] COMP ► **pug nose** N nez m retroussé ► **pug-nosed** ADJ au nez retroussé

pugilism ['pjuːdʒɪlɪzəm] N boxe f

pugilist† ['pjuːdʒɪlɪst] N pugiliste m, boxeur m

pugnacious [pʌgˈneɪʃəs] ADJ pugnace, querelleur

pugnaciously [pʌgˈneɪʃəslɪ] ADV avec pugnacité, d'un ton querelleur

pugnacity [pʌgˈnæsɪtɪ] N pugnacité f

puke: [pjuːk] [1] VI (also ~ **up**) dégueuler:, dégobiller:; (fig) **it makes you ~** c'est à faire vomir, c'est dégueulasse: [2] VT (also ~ **up**) dégueuler: [3] N [a] (= vomit) dégueulis: m [b] (US pej = person) salaud: m

►**puke up**: = **puke** 1, 2

pukka* ['pʌkə] ADJ (Brit) [a] (= genuine) vrai, véritable; (= excellent) de premier ordre [b] (= socially superior) snob inv

pulchritude ['pʌlkrɪtjuːd] N (liter or hum) vénusté f (liter)

pulchritudinous [ˌpʌlkrɪˈtjuːdɪnəs] ADJ (liter or hum) bien tourné, beau, belle f)

Pulitzer prize ['pʊlɪtsəˌpraɪz] N (US) prix m Pulitzer

┌─ **PULITZER PRIZE** ─┐

Aux États-Unis, les prix Pulitzer sont des récompenses prestigieuses décernées chaque année aux personnes jugées les plus méritantes dans les domaines du journalisme, de la littérature ou de la musique. Il existe treize catégories en journalisme (enquête, articles de fond, etc) et six en littérature. Ces prix ont été créés et financés par le journaliste et propriétaire de journaux Joseph Pulitzer (1847-1911).

---

pull [pʊl] [1] N [a] (= act, effect) traction f; [of moon] attraction f; (= attraction: magnetic, fig) (force f d')attraction f, magnétisme m; **one more ~ and we'll have it up** encore un coup et

on l'aura; **I felt a ~ at my sleeve** j'ai senti quelqu'un qui tirait ma manche; **to give sth a ~** ◊ **to give a ~ on** or **at sth** tirer (sur) qch; (fig) **he's got ~*** il a le bras long; **to ~ the current** la force du courant; (fig) **the ~ of family ties** la force des liens familiaux; (fig) **the ~ of the South/the sea** etc l'attraction f or l'appel m du Sud/de la mer etc; (fig) **to be on the ~:** draguer*; (fig) **to have a ~ over sb** (= have a hold over) avoir barre sur qn; (Rowing) **it was a long ~ to the shore** il a fallu ramer longtemps pour arriver jusqu'au rivage; **it was a long (hard) ~ up the hill** la montée était longue (et raide) pour aller jusqu'en haut de la colline; (fig) **to have (some) ~ with sb** avoir de l'influence auprès de qn → **leg** [b] (= swig, puff: at bottle, glass, drink) lampée f; **he took a ~ at the bottle** il but une lampée à même la bouteille; **he took a ~ at his beer** il but une lampée de bière; **he took a long ~ at his cigarette/pipe** il a tiré longuement sur sa cigarette/pipe [c] (= handle) poignée f; (= cord) cordon m → **bell**[1] [d] (Typ) épreuve f [e] (Golf) coup m hooké [2] VT [a] (= draw) [+ cart, carriage, coach, caravan, curtains] tirer; **she ~ed her jacket around her shoulders** elle ramena sa veste autour de ses épaules; **to ~ a door open** ouvrir une porte (en la tirant); **he ~ed the box over to the window** il a traîné la caisse jusqu'à la fenêtre; **to ~ a door shut** tirer une porte derrière soi; **~ your chair closer to the table** approchez votre chaise de la table; **he ~ed her towards him** il l'attira vers lui; **to ~ sb clear of** [+ wreckage, rubble] dégager qn de; [+ water, mud] retirer qn de [b] (= tug) [+ bell, rope, thread] tirer; [+ trigger] presser; [+ oars] manier; **to ~ to pieces** or **to bits** [+ toy, box etc] mettre en pièces or en morceaux, démolir; [+ daisy] effeuiller; (* fig) [+ argument, scheme, play, film] démolir*;* [+ person] éreinter; **to ~ sb's hair** tirer les cheveux à qn; **~ the other one (it's got bells on)!:** à d'autres!, mon œil!*; (Racing) **to ~ a horse** retenir un cheval; (Boxing, also fig) **to ~ one's punches** ménager son adversaire; **he didn't ~ any punches** il n'y est pas allé de main morte, il n'a pas pris de gants; (fig) **to ~ one's weight** faire sa part du travail, fournir sa part d'effort → **leg, string, wire** [c] (= draw out) [+ tooth] arracher, extraire; [+ cork, stopper] ôter, retirer; [+ gun, knife] sortir; [+ flowers] cueillir; [+ weeds] arracher, extirper; [+ beer] tirer; (Culin) [+ chicken] vider; **he ~ed a gun on me** il a sorti un revolver et l'a braqué sur moi; **he's ~ing pints* somewhere in London** il est barman quelque part à Londres; (Cards) **to ~ trumps*** faire tomber les atouts; (fig) **to ~ rank on sb** en imposer hiérarchiquement à qn [d] (= strain, tear) [+ muscle, tendon, ligament] se déchirer [e] (Typ) tirer [f] (Golf etc) [+ ball] hooker; **to ~ a shot** hooker [g] (* = cancel) [+ TV programme] annuler [h] (* = make, do) faire, commettre; **the gang ~ed several bank raids/several burglaries last month** le gang a fait or commis plusieurs hold-up de banques/plusieurs cambriolages le mois dernier; **to ~ a trick on sb** jouer un mauvais tour à qn → **face, fast**[1], **long**[1] [i] (* fig = attract) [+ public] attirer; [+ votes] ramasser [j] (Brit* = get off with) lever: [3] VI [a] (= tug) tirer (**at, on** sur); **stop ~ing!** arrête de tirer!; **he ~ed at her sleeve** il lui tira la manche, il la tira par la manche; **the car/the steering is ~ing to the left** la voiture/la direction porte à gauche; **the brakes ~ to the left** quand on freine la voiture porte à gauche *or est déportée sur la gauche* ; (*fig*) **to ~ for sb*** appuyer qn → **3b**

b (= *move*) **the train ~ed into/out of the station** le train est entré en gare/est sorti de la gare ; **he soon ~ed clear of the traffic** il eut vite fait de laisser le gros de la circulation derrière lui ; **he began to ~ ahead of his pursuers** il a commencé à prendre de l'avance sur or à distancer ses poursuivants ; **to ~ sharply to the left** [*car, driver*] virer brusquement à gauche → **3a; the car isn't ~ing very well** la voiture manque de reprises

c (= *swig, puff*) **he ~ed at his beer** il but une lampée de bière ; **to ~ at a cigarette/pipe** *etc* tirer sur une cigarette/pipe *etc*

d (= *row*) ramer (**for** vers)

4 COMP ► **pull-back** N (*Mil*) repli *m* ► **pull-down** ADJ [*bed*] rabattable, escamotable ; **~-down seat** strapontin *m* ► **pull-down menu** N (*Comput*) menu *m* déroulant ► **pull-in** N (*Brit*) (= *lay-by*) parking *m* ; (= *café*) café *m* de bord de route, routier *m* ► **pull-off** N (*US*) parking *m* ► **pull-out** N, ADJ → **pull-out** ► **pull-ring, pull-tab** N (*on can*) anneau *m*, bague *f* ► **pull-up** N (*Brit: by roadside*) = **pull-in** ; (*Gym*) traction *f* (*sur barre etc*)

► **pull about** VT SEP **a** [+ *wheeled object etc*] tirer derrière soi **b** (= *handle roughly*) [+ *object*] tirailler ; [+ *person*] malmener

► **pull ahead** VI (*in race, election etc*) prendre la tête

► **pull along** VT SEP [+ *wheeled object etc*] tirer derrière or après soi ; **to ~ o.s. along** se traîner

► **pull apart 1** VI **this box ~s apart** cette boîte est démontable or se démonte **2** VT SEP **a** (= *pull to pieces*) démonter ; (= *break*) mettre en pièces or en morceaux ; (*fig*) **the police ~ed the whole house apart looking for drugs*** la police a mis la maison sens dessus dessous en cherchant de la drogue ; (*fig*) **his parents' rows were ~ing him apart** les disputes de ses parents le déchiraient ; **nationalism was threatening to ~ the country apart** le nationalisme menaçait de déchirer le pays **b** (= *separate*) [+ *dogs, adversaries*] séparer ; [+ *sheets of paper etc*] détacher, séparer **c** (*fig* = *criticize play, performance*) éreinter ; [+ *argument, suggestion*] démolir

► **pull around** VT SEP = **pull about**

► **pull away 1** VI [*vehicle, ship*] démarrer ; [*train*] démarrer, s'ébranler ; **he ~ed away from the kerb** il s'est éloigné du trottoir ; **he began to ~ away from his pursuers** il a commencé à prendre de l'avance or à distancer ses poursuivants ; **she suddenly ~ed away from him** elle se dégagea soudain de son étreinte **2** VT SEP (= *withdraw*) (**from sb** à qn) ; (= *snatch*) ôter, arracher (**from sb** à qn, **des mains de** qn) ; **he ~ed the child away from the fire** il a éloigné or écarté l'enfant du feu

► **pull back 1** VI (*Mil, gen, fig* = *withdraw*) se retirer **2** VT SEP **a** (= *withdraw*) [+ *object*] retirer (**from** de) ; [+ *person*] tirer en arrière (**from** loin de) ; (*Mil*) retirer, ramener à or vers l'arrière ; **to ~ back the curtains** ouvrir les rideaux **b** [+ *lever*] tirer (sur)

► **pull down 1** VI (= *blind*) baisser, descendre ; **he ~ed his opponent down (to the ground)** il a mis à terre son adversaire ; **he ~ed his hat down over his eyes** il ramena or rabattit son chapeau sur ses yeux ; **~ your skirt down over your knees** ramène or tire ta jupe sur tes genoux ; **she slipped and ~ed everything down off the shelf with her** elle a glissé et entraîné dans sa chute tout ce qui était sur l'étagère **b** (= *demolish*) [+ *building*] démolir, abattre ; [+ *tree*] abattre ; **the whole street has been ~ed down** la rue a été complètement démolie ; (*fig*) **to ~ down the government** renverser le gouvernement **2** (= *weaken, reduce*) affaiblir, abattre ; **that bout of flu ~ed him down quite a lot** cette grippe l'a considé-

rablement affaibli ; **his geography marks ~ed him down** ses notes de géographie ont fait baisser sa moyenne

► **pull in 1** VI (*Aut etc*) (= *arrive*) arriver ; (= *enter*) entrer ; (= *stop*) s'arrêter ; **when the train ~ed in (at the station)** quand le train est entré en gare **2** VT SEP **a** [+ *rope, fishing line*] ramener ; **to ~ sb in** (*into room, car*) faire entrer qn, tirer qn à l'intérieur ; (*into pool etc*) faire piquer une tête dans l'eau à qn ; **~ your chair in (to the table)** rentre ta chaise (sous la table) ; **~ your stomach in!** rentre le ventre ! ; (*fig*) **the film is certainly ~ing people in** il est certain que ce film attire les foules → **belt, horn** **b** (* = *pick up*) **the police ~ed him in for questioning** la police l'a appréhendé pour l'interroger **c** (= *restrain*) [+ *horse*] retenir **d** (* = *earn*) [*person*] gagner ; [*business, shop etc*] rapporter **3** **~-in** N → **pull**

► **pull off 1** VT SEP **a** (= *remove*) [+ *handle, lid, cloth*] enlever, ôter ; [+ *gloves, shoes, coat, hat*] enlever, ôter **b** (*Aut*) **he ~ed the car off the road** or **onto the verge** il a arrêté la voiture sur le bord de la route **c** (*fig*) [+ *plan, aim*] réaliser ; [+ *deal*] mener à bien, conclure ; [+ *attack, hoax*] réussir ; **he didn't manage to ~ it off** il n'a pas réussi son coup **2** VI **a** (= *start*) [*car, bus etc*] démarrer, partir **b** **to ~ off the road** [*vehicle, driver*] quitter la route **3** **~-off** N → **pull**

► **pull on 1** VI **the cover ~s on** la housse s'enfile **2** VT SEP [+ *gloves, coat, cover*] mettre, enfiler ; [+ *shoes, hat*] mettre

► **pull out 1** VI **a** (= *leave*) [*train*] s'ébranler, démarrer ; [*car, bus, ship*] démarrer, partir **b** (= *withdraw*) (*lit, fig*) se retirer (**of** de) ; (*Aviat*) **to ~ out of a dive** se redresser ; **he ~ed out of the deal at the last minute** il a tiré son épingle du jeu or il s'est retiré à la dernière minute **c** (*Aut*) déboîter, sortir de la file ; **he ~ed out to overtake the truck** il a déboîté pour doubler le camion **d** **the drawers ~ out easily** les tiroirs coulissent bien ; **the table ~s out to seat eight** avec la rallonge huit personnes peuvent s'asseoir à la table ; **the centre pages ~ out** les pages du milieu sont détachables or se détachent **2** VT SEP **a** (= *extract, remove*) [+ *nail, hair, page*] arracher ; [+ *splinter*] enlever ; [+ *cork, stopper*] ôter, retirer ; [+ *tooth*] arracher, extraire ; [+ *weeds*] arracher, extirper ; [+ *gun, knife, cigarette lighter*] sortir ; **he ~ed a rabbit out of his hat** il a sorti or tiré un lapin de son chapeau ; **to ~ sb out of a room** faire sortir qn d'une pièce ; **they ~ed him out of the wreckage alive** ils l'ont tiré or sorti vivant des débris → **finger, stop** **b** (= *withdraw*) [+ *troops, police etc*] retirer (**of** de) ; **the union has ~ed all the workers out on strike** tous les ouvriers ont répondu à la consigne de grève donnée par le syndicat **c** (* *fig* = *produce*) [+ *reason, argument*] sortir* ; (*fig*) **he ~ed out one last trick** il a usé d'un dernier stratagème **3** **~-out** ADJ, N → **pull-out**

► **pull over 1** VI (*Aut*) **he ~ed over (to one side) to let the ambulance past** il s'est rangé or garé sur le côté pour laisser passer l'ambulance **2** VT SEP **a** **he ~ed the box over to the window** il a traîné la caisse jusqu'à la fenêtre ; **she ~ed the chair over and stood on it** elle a tiré la chaise à elle pour grimper dessus ; **they ~ed him over to the door** ils l'ont entraîné jusqu'à la porte **b** (* = *stop*) [+ *motorist, car*] contraindre à s'arrêter **c** **they climbed the wall and ~ed him over** ils ont grimpé sur le mur et l'ont hissé or fait passer de l'autre côté **d** (= *topple*) **the vandals ~ed the gatepost over** les vandales ont renversé or fait tomber le montant du portail ; **the bookcase on top of himself** il a entraîné la bibliothèque dans sa chute **3** **~-over** N → **pullover**

► **pull round 1** VI [*unconscious person*] revenir à soi, reprendre conscience ; [*sick person*] s'en sortir **2** VT SEP **a** [+ *chair etc*] faire pivoter, tourner ; **he ~ed me round to face him** il m'a fait me retourner pour me forcer à lui faire face **b** [+ *unconscious person*] ramener à la conscience

► **pull through 1** VI (*from illness*) s'en tirer, s'en sortir ; (*from difficulties*) s'en sortir, s'en tirer **2** VT SEP [+ *rope etc*] (*gen*) faire passer ; (*Climbing*) rappeler **3** VT FUS [+ *illness*] réchapper à ; [+ *difficulties, crisis*] se sortir de

► **pull together 1** VI (*on rope etc*) tirer ensemble or simultanément ; (*on oars*) ramer simultanément or à l'unisson **b** (*fig* = *co-operate*) (*s'entendre pour*) faire un effort **2** VT SEP **a** (= *join*) [+ *rope ends etc*] joindre ; **let me now ~ together the threads of my argument** je vais maintenant faire la synthèse de mes arguments ; **data exists but it needs ~ing together** les données existent mais il faut les rassembler **b** (* *fig*) **to ~ o.s. together** se prendre, se ressaisir ; **~ yourself together!** ressaisis-toi !, reprends-toi !

► **pull up 1** VI **a** (= *stop*) [*vehicle*] s'arrêter, stopper ; [*athlete, horse*] s'arrêter (net) **b** (= *draw level with*) **he ~ed up with the leaders** il a rattrapé or rejoint ceux qui menaient **2** VT SEP **a** (= *raise*) [+ *object*] remonter ; (= *haul up*) hisser ; [+ *stockings*] remonter, tirer ; [+ *chair*] approcher ; **when the bucket was full he ~ed it up** une fois le seau plein il l'a remonté ; **he leaned down from the wall and ~ed the child up** il s'est penché du haut du mur et a hissé l'enfant jusqu'à lui ; **he ~ed me out of the armchair** il m'a tiré or fait sortir du fauteuil ; (*fig*) **your geography mark has ~ed you up** votre note de géographie vous a remonté* → **sock¹** **b** (= *bring close*) **~ up a chair!** prends une chaise ! **c** [+ *tree etc*] arracher, déraciner ; [+ *weed*] arracher, extirper ; **to ~ up one's roots** se déraciner **d** (= *halt*) [+ *vehicle*] arrêter, stopper ; [+ *horse*] arrêter ; **the chairman ~ed the speaker up (short)** le président a coupé la parole à or a interrompu l'orateur ; **he ~ed himself up (short)** il s'arrêta net or pile ; **the police ~ed him up for speeding** la police l'a arrêté pour excès de vitesse ; (*fig*) **the headmaster ~ed him up for using bad language** il a été repris or réprimandé par le directeur pour avoir été grossier **3** **~-up** N → **pull**

pullet ['pʊlɪt] N jeune poule *f*, poulette *f*

pulley ['pʊlɪ] N **a** (= *block*) poulie *f* **b** (*Scot: for clothes-drying*) séchoir *m* à linge (suspendu)

Pullman® ['pʊlmən] N (*pl* **Pullmans**) (*Brit Rail: also* = **carriage**) pullman *m*, voiture-salon *f*, wagon-salon *m* ; (*US* = *sleeper: also* **~ car**) voiture-lit *f*, wagon-lit *m*

pull-out ['pʊlaʊt] **1** N **a** (*in magazine etc*) supplément *m* détachable **b** [*of troops*] retrait *m* **2** ADJ [*magazine section*] détachable ; [*table leaf, shelf*] rétractable ; **~ bed** meuble-lit *m*

pullover ['pʊl‚əʊvər] N (*esp Brit*) pull *m*, pullover *m*

pullulate ['pʌljʊleɪt] VI (*frm*) pulluler

pully* ['pʊlɪ] N (*Brit*) (ABBR = **pullover**) pull *m*

pulmonary ['pʌlmənərɪ] ADJ pulmonaire

pulp [pʌlp] **1** N **a** (= *paste*) pulpe *f* ; (= *part of fruit*) pulpe *f*, chair *f* ; (*for paper*) pâte *f* à papier, pulpe *f* (à papier) ; **to reduce** or **crush to a ~** [+ *wood*] réduire en pâte or en pulpe ; [+ *fruit*] réduire en pulpe or en purée or en marmelade ; (*fig*) **his arm was crushed to a ~** il a eu le bras complètement écrasé, il a eu le bras mis en bouillie or en marmelade* ; **to beat sb to a ~** passer qn à tabac*, tabasser* qn → **pound²** **b** (*pej* = *literature*) littérature *f* à sensation ; **~ fiction/novel** romans *mpl*/roman *m* à sensation ; **~ magazine** magazine *m* à sensation, torchon* *m* **2** VT [+ *wood, linen*] réduire en pâte *or* en pulpe; [+ *fruit*] réduire en pulpe *or* en purée *or* en marmelade; [+ *book*] mettre au pilon, pilonner; [+ *money, documents*] détruire (*par broyage*) ③ COMP ► **pulp cavity** N (*in tooth*) cavité *f* pulpaire

pulpit ['pʊlpɪt] N chaire *f* (*Rel*)

pulpy ['pʌlpɪ] ADJ [a] (= *soft*) [*fruit*] charnu, pulpeux; [*consistency*] pâteux; (*Bio*) [*tissue*] pulpeux [b] (* = *trashy*) [*novel, literature*] de gare (*pej*)

pulsar ['pʌlsɑːʳ] N pulsar *m*

pulsate [pʌl'seɪt] VI [*heart, vein*] palpiter; [*blood*] battre; [*music*] vibrer; **the pulsating rhythm of the drums** le battement rythmique des tambours

pulsating [pʌl'seɪtɪŋ] ADJ [*heart, vein*] palpitant; [*music*] vibrant; (*fig* = *exciting*) palpitant

pulsation [pʌl'seɪʃən] N [*of heart*] battement *m*, pulsation *f*; (*Elec, Phys*) pulsation *f*

pulse[1] [pʌls] ① N (*Med*) pouls *m*; (*Elec, Phys, Rad*) vibration *f*; [*of radar*] impulsion *f*; [*of drums etc*] battement *m* rythmique; [*of emotion*] frémissement *m*, palpitation *f*; (*also fig*) **to take sb's ~** prendre le pouls de qn; (*fig*) **to have** *or* **keep one's finger on the ~** se tenir au courant ② VI [*heart*] battre fort; [*blood*] battre; [*sound*] vibrer; **it sent the blood pulsing through his veins** cela lui fouetta le sang; **the life pulsing in a great city** la vie qui palpite au cœur d'une grande ville ③ COMP ► **pulse rate** N (*Med*) pouls *m*

pulse[2] [pʌls] N (*Bot*) légume *m* à gousse; (*Culin: dried*) légume *m* sec

pulsebeat ['pʌlsbiːt] N (*Med, Mus*) pulsation *f*

pulverization [ˌpʌlvəraɪˈzeɪʃən] N pulvérisation *f*

pulverize ['pʌlvəraɪz] VT (*lit, fig*) pulvériser

puma ['pjuːmə] N puma *m*

pumice ['pʌmɪs] N (*also* **~ stone**) pierre *f* ponce

pummel ['pʌml] VT (*in fight*) bourrer *or* rouer de coups; (*in massage*) pétrir

pummelling ['pʌməlɪŋ] N (*in fight*) volée *f* de coups; (*in massage*) pétrissage *m*; **to take a ~** (*lit*) se faire rouer de coups; (*Sport* = *be beaten*) se faire battre à plate(s) couture(s); (= *be criticized/attacked*) se faire violemment critiquer/attaquer

pump[1] [pʌmp] ① N (*all senses*) pompe *f* → **parish, petrol, door** ② VT [a] **to ~ water into sth** pomper de l'eau dans qch; **to ~ water out of sth** pomper l'eau de qch; **they ~ed the remaining oil out of the ship** ils ont pompé le pétrole qui restait dans le navire; **they ~ed the tank dry** ils ont vidé *or* asséché le réservoir (à la pompe), ils ont pompé toute l'eau (*or* l'essence *etc*) du réservoir; **to ~ air into sth** gonfler qch; **the water is ~ed up to the house** l'eau est amenée jusqu'à la maison au moyen d'une pompe; **the heart ~s the blood round the body** le cœur fait circuler le sang dans le corps; **to ~ oil through a pipe** faire passer *or* faire couler du pétrole dans un pipeline (à l'aide d'une pompe); (*Med*) **to ~ sb's stomach** faire un lavage d'estomac à qn; (*Sport*) **to ~ iron*** faire de l'haltérophilie; **to ~ sb full of drugs*** bourrer qn de calmants*; **to ~ bullets into sb*** cribler qn de balles → **lead**[2]; (*fig*) **they ~ed money into the project*** ils ont injecté de l'argent dans le projet; (*fig*) **he ~ed facts into their heads** il leur bourrait* la tête de faits précis [b] (* = *question*) **to ~ sb for sth** essayer de soutirer qch à qn; **they'll try to ~ you (for information)** ils essayeront de vous faire parler *or* de vous tirer les vers* du nez [c] [+ *handle etc*] lever et abaisser plusieurs fois *or* continuellement; [+ *accelerator, brake*] pomper sur ③ VI [*pump, machine, person*] pomper; [*heart*] battre fort; **blood ~ed from the artery** le sang

coulait à flots de l'artère; **the oil was ~ing along the pipeline** le pétrole coulait dans le pipeline; **the piston was ~ing up and down** le piston montait et descendait régulièrement

④ COMP ► **pump-action** ADJ [*shotgun*] à pompe ► **pump attendant** N (*Brit*) pompiste *mf* ► **pump house, pumping station** N station *f* d'épuisement *or* de pompage ► **pump prices** NPL **a rise in ~ prices** [*of petrol*] une hausse (des prix) à la pompe ► **pump priming** N (*Econ*) mesures *fpl* de relance de l'économie ► **pump room** N buvette *f* (*où l'on prend les eaux dans une station thermale*) ► **pump-water** N eau *f* de la pompe

► **pump away** VI [*heart*] battre la chamade; **he was ~ing away on the lever** il faisait fonctionner *or* actionnait le levier

► **pump in** VT SEP [+ *water, oil, gas etc*] refouler (à l'aide d'une pompe); **~ some more air in** donnez plus d'air

► **pump out** ① VI [*blood, oil*] couler à flots (**of** de) ② VT SEP [a] [+ *water, oil, gas etc*] pomper, aspirer (à l'aide d'une pompe) [b] (* = *produce*) pondre en masse*; (*TV, Rad*) **this station ~s out pop music 24 hours a day** cette station balance* de la musique pop 24 heures par jour

► **pump up** VT SEP [+ *tyre, airbed*] gonfler → **pump 3a**

pump[2] [pʌmp] N (*esp Brit* = *sports shoe*) (chaussure *f* de) tennis *m*; (= *slip-on shoe*) chaussure *f* sans lacet; (= *dancing shoe*) escarpin *m*

pumpernickel ['pʌmpənɪkl] N pumpernickel *m*, pain *m* de seigle noir

pumpkin ['pʌmpkɪn] N citrouille *f*; (*bigger*) potiron *m*; [*of Cinderella*] citrouille *f*; **~ pie** tarte *f* à la citrouille

pun [pʌn] ① N calembour *m*, jeu *m* de mots ② VI faire un *or* des calembour(s), faire un *or* des jeu(x) de mots; **"foot and mouth is a big problem, in fact it's a pig* of a problem" he ~ed** « la fièvre aphteuse est un problème très sérieux, c'est même vachement* sérieux » dit-il en voulant faire un jeu de mots

Punch [pʌntʃ] N Polichinelle *m*; **~ and Judy show** (*théâtre m de*) guignol *m* → **pleased**

punch[1] [pʌntʃ] ① N [a] (= *blow*) coup *m* de poing; **to give sb a ~ (on the nose)** donner un coup de poing (sur le nez) à qn; (*Boxing*) **he's got a good ~** il a du punch; (*esp US*) **to ride with the ~es** encaisser* → **pack, pull, rabbit** [b] (*NonC* = *punchiness*) punch* *m*; **a phrase with more ~** une expression plus frappante *or* plus incisive; **we need a presentation with some ~ to it** il nous faut une présentation énergique *or* vigoureuse; **a film with no ~ to it** un film qui manque de punch* [c] (= *tool*) (*for tickets*) poinçonneuse *f*; (*for holes in paper*) perforateur *m*; (*for metalworking*) poinçonneuse *f*, emporte-pièce *m inv*; (*for stamping design*) étampe *f*; (*smaller*) poinçon *m*; (*for driving in nails*) chasse-clou *m*

② VT [a] (*with fist*) [+ *person*] donner un coup de poing à; [+ *ball, door*] frapper d'un coup de poing; **to ~ sb's nose/face** ◊ **to ~ sb in the nose/face** donner un coup de poing sur le nez/dans la figure de qn; **to ~ sb in the stomach/in the kidneys/on the jaw** donner un coup de poing dans le ventre/les reins/la mâchoire à qn; **to ~ the air** lever le poing en signe de victoire; **he ~ed his fist through the glass** il a passé son poing à travers la vitre, il a brisé la vitre d'un coup de poing; **the goalkeeper ~ed the ball over the bar** d'un coup de poing le gardien de but a envoyé le ballon par-dessus la barre; **he ~ed his way through** il s'est ouvert un chemin à (force de) coups de poing *or* en frappant à droite et à gauche [b] (*US*) **to ~ cattle** conduire le bétail (à l'aiguillon) [c] (*with tool*) [+ *paper*] poinçonner, perforer

[+ *ticket*] (*by hand*) poinçonner; (*automatically*) composter; [+ *computer cards*] perforer; [+ *metal*] poinçonner, découper à l'emporte-pièce; [+ *design*] estamper; [+ *nails*] enfoncer profondément (au chasse-clou); **to ~ a hole in sth** faire un trou dans qch; (*Ind*) **to ~ the time clock** ◊ **to ~ one's card** pointer [d] (*with finger*) [+ *button*] taper

③ VI frapper (dur), cogner; (*Boxing*) **he ~es well** il sait frapper

④ COMP ► **punch bag** N (*Brit*) (*Sport*) sac *m* de sable; (*fig*) souffre-douleur *m inv*; (*fig*) **to use sb as a ~ bag** faire de qn son souffre-douleur, se servir de qn comme d'un punching-ball ► **punch card** N carte *f* perforée; **~ card system** système *m* à cartes perforées ► **punch-drunk** ADJ (*Boxing*) abruti par les coups, groggy, sonné*; (*fig*) abruti ► **punching bag** N (*US*) = **punch bag** ► **punching ball** N = **punchball** ► **punch line** N [*of joke etc*] chute *f*, conclusion *f* (*comique*); [*of speech etc*] mot *m* de la fin ► **punch operator** N (*Comput*) mécanographe *mf* ► **punch tape** N (*Comput*) bande *f* perforée ► **punch-up*** N bagarre *f*; (*Brit*) **to have a ~-up** se bagarrer*

► **punch in** ① VI (*Ind: on time clock*) pointer (en arrivant) ② VT SEP [a] [+ *door, lid etc*] ouvrir d'un coup de poing; **to ~ sb's face in** casser la gueule à qn* [b] (= *key in*) [+ *code number etc*] taper

► **punch out** ① VI (*Ind: on time clock*) pointer (en partant) ② VT SEP [+ *hole*] faire au poinçon *or* à la poinçonneuse; [+ *machine parts*] découper à l'emporte-pièce; [+ *design*] estamper

punch[2] [pʌntʃ] ① N (= *drink*) punch *m* ② COMP ► **punch bowl** N bol *m* à punch

punchball [pʌntʃbɔːl] N [a] (*Brit*) punching-ball *m* [b] (*US*) variante simplifiée du baseball, qui se joue sans batte

punchy* [pʌntʃɪ] ADJ [a] (= *forceful*) [*person*] qui a du punch*, dynamique; [*remark, reply*] incisif, mordant [b] = **punch-drunk**, →**punch**[1]

punctilio [pʌŋkˈtɪlɪəʊ] N (*pl* **punctilios**) (*NonC: frm*) (= *formality*) formalisme *m*; (= *point of etiquette*) point *m* *or* détail *m* d'étiquette

punctilious [pʌŋkˈtɪlɪəs] ADJ scrupuleux

punctiliously [pʌŋkˈtɪlɪəslɪ] ADV scrupuleusement

punctual ['pʌŋktjʊəl] ADJ [*person, train*] à l'heure; [*payment*] ponctuel; **he is always ~** il est très ponctuel, il est toujours à l'heure; **be ~** soyez *or* arrivez à l'heure

punctuality [ˌpʌŋktjʊˈælɪtɪ] N [*of person*] ponctualité *f*, exactitude *f*; [*of train*] exactitude *f*

punctually ['pʌŋktjʊəlɪ] ADV ponctuellement

punctuate ['pʌŋktjʊeɪt] VT (*lit, fig*) ponctuer (**with** de)

punctuation [ˌpʌŋktjʊˈeɪʃən] N ponctuation *f*; **~ mark** signe *m* de ponctuation

puncture ['pʌŋktʃəʳ] ① N (*in tyre*) crevaison *f*; (*in skin, paper, leather*) piqûre *f*; (*Med*) ponction *f*; (*Aut etc*) **I've got a ~** j'ai (un pneu) crevé; **they had a ~ outside Limoges** ils ont crevé près de Limoges ② VT [+ *tyre, balloon*] crever; [+ *skin, leather, paper*] piquer; (*Med*) [+ *abscess*] percer, ouvrir; **the bullet ~d his skull** la balle lui a transpercé le crâne; (*fig*) **his pride had been ~d** sa fierté en avait pris un coup ③ VI [*tyre etc*] crever ④ COMP ► **puncture repair kit** N trousse *f* à outils pour crevaisons ► **puncture wound** N perforation *f*

pundit ['pʌndɪt] N expert *m*, pontife *m*

pungency ['pʌndʒənsɪ] N [*of smell, taste*] âcreté *f*; [*of sauce*] goût *m* piquant *or* relevé; [*of remark, criticism*] mordant *m*, causticité *f*

pungent ['pʌndʒənt] ADJ [*fumes, smoke*] âcre; [*smell, taste*] âcre, piquant; [*sauce*] piquant, relevé ; [*remark, criticism, satire*] mordant, caustique

pungently ['pʌndʒəntlɪ] ADV [*remark*] d'un ton mordant *or* caustique ; [*criticize*] de façon mordante *or* caustique ; **~ flavoured** (au goût) relevé

Punic ['pjuːnɪk] ADJ punique

punish ['pʌnɪʃ] VT [a] [+ *person*] punir (**for sth** de qch, **for doing** pour avoir fait) ; [+ *theft, fault*] punir ; **he was ~ed by having to clean it all up** pour le punir on lui a fait tout nettoyer, pour sa punition il a dû tout nettoyer [b] (*fig*) [+ *opponent in fight, boxer, opposing team*] malmener ; [+ *engine*] fatiguer ; **the jockey really ~ed his horse** le jockey a vraiment forcé *or* fatigué son cheval

punishable ['pʌnɪʃəbl] ADJ [*offence*] punissable ; **~ by death/imprisonment** passible de la peine de mort/d'une peine de prison

punishing ['pʌnɪʃɪŋ] [1] N (= *act*) punition *f* ; (*fig*) **to take a ~** [*boxer, opponent, opposing team*] se faire malmener [2] ADJ [*speed, heat, game, work*] épuisant, exténuant

punishment ['pʌnɪʃmənt] N (*gen*) punition *f* ; (*solemn*) châtiment *m* ; (*formal: against employee, student etc*) sanctions *fpl* ; **as a ~ (for)** en punition (de) ; **he took his ~ bravely** *or* **like a man** il a subi sa punition sans se plaindre ; **to make the ~ fit the crime** adapter le châtiment au crime, proportionner la peine au délit ; (*fig*) **to take a lot of ~** [*boxer, opponent in fight*] encaisser* ; [*opposing team*] se faire malmener → **capital, corporal²**

punitive ['pjuːnɪtɪv] [1] ADJ [*expedition*] punitif ; [*measure*] de punition ; **a ~ bombing raid** un raid (aérien) de représailles [2] COMP ► **punitive damages** NPL (*Jur*) dommages-intérêts *mpl* dissuasifs (très élevés) ► **punitive taxation** N (*NonC*) fiscalité *f* dissuasive

Punjab [pʌn'dʒɑːb] N Pendjab *m*

Punjabi [pʌn'dʒɑːbɪ] [1] ADJ pendjabi [2] N [a] (= *person*) Pendjabi *mf* [b] (*Ling*) pendjabi *m*

punk [pʌŋk] [1] N [a] (= *music*) punk *m* [b] (*musician, fan*) punk *mf* [c] (*US** = *ruffian*) sale* petit voyou *m* [2] ADJ [a] [*band, music, style*] punk *inv* ; **~ rock** le punk rock [b] (*US** = *ill*) mal foutu*

punnet ['pʌnɪt] N (*Brit*) carton *m*, petit panier *m* (pour fraises etc)

punster ['pʌnstə'] N personne *f* qui fait des calembours

punt¹ [pʌnt] [1] N (= *boat*) bachot *m* *or* bateau *m* à fond plat [2] VT [+ *boat*] faire avancer à la perche ; [+ *goods*] transporter en bachot [3] VI **to go ~ing** faire un tour en rivière, aller se promener en bachot

punt² [pʌnt] (*Ftbl, Rugby*) [1] VT [+ *ball*] envoyer d'un coup de volée [2] N coup *m* de volée

punt³ [pʌnt] VI (*Brit* = *bet*) parier

punt⁴ [pʌnt] N livre *f* irlandaise

punter ['pʌntə'] N [a] (*Brit*) (*Racing*) turfiste *mf*, parieur *m* ; (*in casino*) joueur *m*, -euse *f* [b] (* = *customer*) client *m(f)* ; [*of prostitute*] micheton* *m* ; (*St Ex*) boursicoteur *m*, -euse *f* ; (*Brit* = *customer, member of public*) **the ~(s)** le public, la clientèle ; **your average ~** Monsieur Tout-le-monde

puny ['pjuːnɪ] ADJ [*person, animal*] chétif, malingre, frêle ; [*effort*] faible, piteux

pup [pʌp] [1] N [a] (= *dog*) chiot *m*, jeune chien(ne) *m(f)* ; (= *seal*) bébé *m* phoque, jeune phoque *m* ; **to sell sb a ~*** rouler* qn ; **to be sold a ~*** se faire rouler *or* avoir* [b] (↑* *pej*) (= *frivolous youth*) freluquet↑ *m* ; (= *inexperienced youth*) blanc-bec *m* [2] VI mettre bas [3] COMP ► **pup tent** N tente *f* à deux places

pupa ['pjuːpə] N (*pl* **pupae** ['pjuːpiː]) chrysalide *f*, pupe *f*

pupate ['pjuːpeɪt] VI devenir chrysalide *or* pupe

pupil¹ ['pjuːpl] [1] N (*Scol etc*) élève *mf* [2] COMP ► **pupil nurse** N (*Brit*) élève *mf* infirmier (-ière) (qui suit une formation courte) ► **pupil power** N pouvoir *m* des élèves ► **pupil teacher** N professeur *m* stagiaire

pupil² ['pjuːpl] N [*of eye*] pupille *f*

puppet ['pʌpɪt] [1] N [a] (*lit*) marionnette *f* ; (= *flat cutout*) pantin *m* [b] (*fig* = *pawn*) pantin *m* ; **he was like a ~ on a string** ce n'était qu'un pantin → **glove** [2] COMP [*theatre, play*] de marionnettes ; (*fig, esp Pol*) [*state, leader, cabinet*] fantoche ► **puppet show** N (spectacle *m* de) marionnettes *fpl*

puppeteer [pʌpɪ'tɪə'] N montreur *m*, -euse *f* de marionnettes, marionnettiste *mf*

puppetry ['pʌpɪtrɪ] N art *m* des marionnettes

puppy ['pʌpɪ] [1] N = **pup 1** [2] COMP ► **puppy farm** N centre *m* d'élevage de chiots de race ► **puppy fat*** N rondeurs *fpl* d'adolescent(e) ► **puppy love*** N premier amour *m* (d'adolescent)

purblind ['pɜːblaɪnd] ADJ (*liter*) [a] (= *blind*) aveugle ; (= *poorly sighted*) qui voit très mal, qui a une vue très faible [b] (*fig* = *stupid*) aveugle, borné, obtus

purchase ['pɜːtʃɪs] [1] N [a] (*Comm etc*) achat *m* ; **to make a ~** un achat [b] (= *grip, hold*) prise *f* ; **the wheels can't get enough ~ on this surface** les roues n'ont pas assez de prise sur cette surface ; **I can't get enough ~ on this rock** je n'arrive pas à trouver assez de prise sur ce rocher [2] VT acheter (**sth from sb** qch à qn, **sth for sb** qch pour *or* à qn) [3] COMP ► **purchase ledger** N grand livre *m* des achats ► **purchase money**, **purchase price** N prix *m* d'achat ► **purchase tax** N (*Brit*) taxe *f* à l'achat

purchaser ['pɜːtʃɪsə'] N acheteur *m*, -euse *f*

purchasing ['pɜːtʃɪsɪŋ] [1] N (*Ind, Comm etc*) achat *m* [2] COMP ► **purchasing department** N service *m* (des) achats ► **purchasing officer** N (*Ind, Comm etc*) responsable *mf* des achats ► **purchasing power** N pouvoir *m* d'achat

purdah ['pɜːdə] N (*Rel*) purdah *m* ; **to live in ~** vivre cloîtré ; (*fig*) **the President is in ~** le Président garde un profil bas

pure [pjʊə'] ADJ (*gen*) pur ; **as ~ as the driven snow** innocent comme l'enfant qui vient de naître ; (*Bible*) **~ in heart** au cœur pur ; **science** science *f* pure ; (*Genetics*) **~ line** hérédité *f* pure ; **~ alcohol** alcool *m* absolu ; **a ~ wool suit** un complet pure laine ; **~ and simple** pur et simple ; **it was ~ hypocrisy** c'était de la pure hypocrisie *or* de l'hypocrisie pure [2] COMP ► **pure-hearted** ADJ (au cœur) pur ► **pure-minded** ADJ pur (d'esprit) ► **pure new wool** N laine *f* vierge ► **pure vowel** N (*Phon*) voyelle *f* pure

purebred ['pjʊəbred] [1] ADJ de race [2] N animal *m* de race ; (= *horse*) pur-sang *m inv*

purée ['pjʊəreɪ] N purée *f* ; **tomato ~** purée *f* de tomates

purely ['pjʊəlɪ] ADV (*with adj*) purement ; **~ and simply** purement et simplement

pureness ['pjʊənɪs] N (*NonC*) pureté *f*

purgation [pɜː'geɪʃən] N (*Rel*) purgation *f*, purification *f* ; (*Pol*) purge *f*, épuration *f* ; (*Med*) purge *f*

purgative ['pɜːgətɪv] ADJ, N purgatif *m*

purgatory ['pɜːgətərɪ] N (*lit, fig*) purgatoire *m* ; (*fig*) **it was ~** c'était un vrai purgatoire *or* supplice ; **it was ~ for me** j'étais au supplice

purge [pɜːdʒ] [1] N (= *act*) (*gen, Med*) purge *f* ; (*Pol*) purge *f*, épuration *f* ; (= *medicament*) purge *f*, purgatif *m* ; **the (political) ~s which followed the revolution** les purges politiques qui ont *or* l'épuration politique qui a suivi la révolution ; **a ~ of the dissidents** une purge

des dissidents [2] VT [a] (*gen*) purger (**of** de) ; (*Med*) [+ *person, body*] purger ; (*Pol*) [+ *state, nation, party*] purger (**of** de) ; [+ *traitors, bad elements*] éliminer ; [+ *sins*] purger, expier [b] (*Jur*) [+ *person*] disculper (**of** de) ; [+ *accusation*] se disculper de ; **to ~ an offence** purger une peine ; (*US*) **to ~ one's contempt (of Congress)** purger sa contumace

purification [pjʊərɪfɪ'keɪʃən] N [a] [*of air, water, metal etc*] épuration *f* [b] (*Rel etc*) [*of person*] purification *f*

purifier ['pjʊərɪfaɪə'] N épurateur *m*, purificateur *m* ; **air ~** purificateur *m* d'air → **water**

purify ['pjʊərɪfaɪ] VT [+ *substance*] épurer, purifier ; [+ *person*] purifier

purism ['pjʊərɪzəm] N purisme *m*

purist ['pjʊərɪst] ADJ, N puriste *mf*

puritan ['pjʊərɪtən] ADJ, N puritain(e) *m(f)*

puritanical [ˌpjʊərɪ'tænɪkəl] ADJ puritain, de puritain

puritanism ['pjʊərɪtənɪzəm] N puritanisme *m*

purity ['pjʊərɪtɪ] N pureté *f*

purl [pɜːl] (*Knitting*) [1] N (*also* **~ stitch** = *one stitch*) maille *f* à l'envers ; **a row of ~** un rang à l'envers → **plain** [2] ADJ à l'envers [3] VT tricoter à l'envers → **knit**

purlieus ['pɜːljuːz] NPL (*frm*) alentours *mpl*, abords *mpl*, environs *mpl*

purloin [pɜː'lɔɪn] VT dérober

purple ['pɜːpl] [1] ADJ (*bluish*) violet ; (*reddish*) pourpre ; (*lighter*) mauve ; **to go ~ (in the face)** devenir cramoisi *or* pourpre ; (*Literat*) **~ passage** *or* **patch** morceau *m* de bravoure [2] N (= *colour*) (*bluish*) violet *m* ; (*reddish*) pourpre *m* ; (*Rel*) **the ~** la pourpre [3] COMP ► **Purple Heart** N (*US Mil*) décoration attribuée aux blessés de guerre ► **purple heart*** N (*Drugs*) pilule *f* du bonheur↑

purplish ['pɜːplɪʃ] ADJ violacé, qui tire sur le violet

purport ['pɜːpət] (*frm*) [1] N (= *meaning*) signification *f* [2] [pɜː'pɔːt] VT **to ~ to be sth/sb** [*person*] se présenter comme étant qch/qn, se faire passer pour qch/qn ; **to ~ to be objective** [*book, film, statement etc*] se vouloir objectif ; **he ~s to represent the views of the people** il prétend représenter l'opinion du (grand) public ; **a man ~ing to come from the Ministry** un homme qui se prétend (*or* prétendait) envoyé par le ministère ; **a document ~ing to come** *or* **be from the French embassy** un document censé émaner de l'ambassade de France ; **a book ~ing to be written for children** un livre censé s'adresser aux enfants

purportedly [pɜː'pɔːtədlɪ] ADV (*frm*) soi-disant ; **~ written by ...** censé avoir été écrit par ..., qui aurait été écrit par ...

▼ **purpose** ['pɜːpəs] [1] N [a] (= *aim, intention*) but *m*, objet *m* ; **what was the ~ of the meeting?** quel était le but *or* l'objet de cette réunion ? ; **what was the ~ of his visit?** quel était le but *or* l'objet de sa visite ?, dans quel but est-il venu ? ; **what is the ~ of this tool?** à quoi sert cet outil ? ; **a man with a ~ (in life)** un homme qui a un but *or* un objectif (dans la vie) ; **it's a film with a ~** c'est un film à thèse *or* qui contient un message ; **it is adequate for the ~** cela fait l'affaire ; **for the ~ of doing** dans le but *or* l'intention de faire, afin de faire ; **for this ~** dans ce but, à cet effet, à cette fin ; **for my ~s** pour ce que je veux faire ; **for our ~s we may disregard this** en ce qui nous concerne, nous n'avons pas besoin de tenir compte de cela ; **for the ~s of the meeting** pour (les besoins de) cette réunion ; (*Jur*) **for the ~s of this Act** aux fins de la présente loi ; **my ~ in doing this is ...** la raison pour laquelle je fais ceci est ... ; **with the ~ of ...** dans le but *or* l'intention de ... , afin de ... ; **to good ~** utilement, à profit ; **the money will be used to good ~** l'argent sera bien *or* utilement employé ; **to no ~** en vain, inutilement ; **to no ~**

at all en pure perte; **on ~** exprès, délibérément; **he did it on ~** il l'a fait exprès or délibérément; **he did it on ~ to annoy me** il l'a fait exprès pour me contrarier; **to the ~ à** propos; **not to the ~** hors de propos → **all, intent, practical, serve**

b (NonC = resolution) **(sense of) ~** résolution f; **he has no sense of ~** il manque de résolution; **his activities seem to lack ~** il semble agir sans but précis → **infirm, strength**

2 VT (frm) **to ~ to do sth** se proposer de faire qch

3 COMP ► **purpose-built** ADJ spécialement construit or conçu

purposeful ['pɜ:pəsfʊl] ADJ (= determined) [person] résolu, déterminé, qui sait ce qu'il veut; [gesture, look] résolu, décidé; (= intentional) [act] réfléchi, significatif

purposefully ['pɜ:pəsfəlɪ] ADV [move, act] dans un but précis, avec une intention bien arrêtée, délibérément

purposefulness ['pɜ:pəsfʊlnɪs] N résolution f, détermination f, ténacité f

purposeless ['pɜ:pəslɪs] ADJ [person] qui n'a pas de but, qui ne sait pas ce qu'il veut; [character] indécis, irrésolu; [act] sans but or objet (précis), inutile

purposely ['pɜ:pəslɪ] ADV exprès, à dessein, de propos délibéré; **he made a ~ vague statement** il a fait exprès de faire une déclaration peu précise; **the government's statement was ~ vague** la déclaration du gouvernement a été délibérément vague or a été vague à dessein

purposive ['pɜ:pəsɪv] ADJ (frm) calculé

purr [pɜ:r] **1** VI [cat] ronronner, faire ronron; [person, engine, car] ronronner **2** VT roucouler; **"sit down, darling", she ~ed** «assieds-toi, chéri», roucoula-t-elle **3** N [of cat] ronronnement m, ronron m; [of engine, car] ronronnement m

purring ['pɜ:rɪŋ] N = **purr 3**

purse [pɜ:s] **1** N **a** (Brit) (for coins) porte-monnaie m inv, bourse f; (= wallet) portefeuille m; (fig) **it's beyond my ~** c'est trop cher pour moi or pour ma bourse, c'est au-delà de mes moyens → **public b** (US = handbag) sac m à main **c** (= prize: esp Sport) prix m, récompense f **2** VT **to ~ (up) one's lips** faire la moue, pincer les lèvres **3** COMP ► **purse-proud** ADJ fier de sa fortune ► **purse-snatcher** N (US) voleur m, -euse f à la tire ► **purse strings** NPL (fig) **to hold/tighten the ~ strings** tenir/serrer les cordons de la bourse

purser ['pɜ:sər] N (Naut) commissaire m (du bord)

pursuance [pə'sju:əns] N (frm) exécution f; **in ~ of** dans l'exécution de

pursuant [pə'sju:ənt] ADJ (frm) **~ to** (= following on) suivant; (= in accordance with) conformément à

pursue [pə'sju:] VT **a** (= carry on) [+ studies, career, plan, theme, inquiry] poursuivre; [+ profession] exercer; [+ course of action] suivre; [+ policy] mener; **to ~ one's own interests** faire ce à quoi on s'intéresse; **to ~ one's interest in art** s'adonner à sa passion pour l'art **b** (= search for) [+ happiness] rechercher; [+ success, fame, objective] poursuivre **c** [+ matter] suivre, approfondir; **to ~ the matter** approfondir la question; (Jur) **to ~ a case** poursuivre une affaire **d** (= chase after) [+ person, animal] poursuivre, pourchasser; [+ vehicle] poursuivre; **his eyes ~d me round the room** il me suivait du regard à travers la pièce; (liter) **he is ~d by misfortune** la malchance le poursuit; (fig) **he won't stop pursuing her** il n'arrête pas de la poursuivre de ses assiduités

pursuer [pə'sju:ər] N poursuivant(e) m(f)

pursuit [pə'sju:t] **1** N **a** (= search) [of pleasure, happiness] recherche f, poursuite f; [of excellence, wealth] poursuite f; [of truth, peace, power] recherche f; **in ~ of** à la recherche de

b (= chase: also Cycling, Skating) poursuite f; **(to go) in ~ of sb/sth** (se mettre) à la poursuite de qn/qch; **he escaped with two policemen in hot ~** il s'est enfui avec deux agents à ses trousses **c** (= occupation) activité f; (= pastime) passe-temps m inv; **scientific ~s** travaux mpl or recherches fpl scientifiques **2** COMP ► **pursuit plane** N chasseur m, avion m de chasse

purulence ['pjʊərʊləns] N purulence f

purulent ['pjʊərʊlənt] ADJ purulent

purvey [pə'veɪ] VT (Comm etc) fournir (**sth to sb** qch à qn), approvisionner (**sth to sb** qn en qch)

purveyance [pə'veɪəns] N (Comm etc) approvisionnement m, fourniture f de provisions

purveyor [pə'veɪər] N (Comm etc) fournisseur m, -euse f, approvisionneur m, -euse f (**of sth** en qch, **to sb** de qn)

purview ['pɜ:vju:] N (frm) [of act, bill] articles mpl; [of the law] domaine m, limites fpl; [of inquiry] champ m, limites fpl; [of committee] capacité f, compétence f; [of book, film] limites fpl, portée f

pus [pʌs] N pus m

push [pʊʃ]

┌─────────────────────────────────┐
│ **1** NOUN   **4** COMPOUNDS   │
│ **2** TRANSITIVE VERB   **5** PHRASAL VERBS   │
│ **3** INTRANSITIVE VERB   │
└─────────────────────────────────┘

1 NOUN

a **= shove** poussée f; **to give sb/sth a ~** pousser qn/qch; **the car needs a ~** il faut pousser la voiture; **with one ~** en poussant une seule fois; **there was a great ~ as the crowd emerged** quand la foule est sortie, il y a eu une grande bousculade

b Brit* **= dismissal** **to give sb the ~** [employer] virer qn*; [boyfriend, girlfriend] plaquer qn*; **he got the ~** (from employer) il s'est fait virer*; (from girlfriend) il s'est fait plaquer*

c Mil, Pol **= advance** poussée f, avance f; **they made a ~ to the coast** ils ont fait une poussée or ils ont avancé jusqu'à la côte

d fig (= effort) gros effort m, coup m de collier; (= campaign) campagne f; **they made a ~ to get everything finished in time** ils ont fait un gros effort or ils ont donné un coup de collier pour tout terminer à temps; **they were having a ~ on sales** or **a sales ~** ils avaient organisé une campagne de promotion des ventes; **we're having a ~ for more teachers** nous menons une campagne pour une augmentation du nombre d'enseignants; **when it comes to the ~*** au moment critique or crucial; **when ~ comes to shove*** le moment venu

◆ **at a push*** à la rigueur

2 TRANSITIVE VERB

a lit [+ car, pram, barrow, door, person] pousser; [+ knob, button] appuyer sur; [+ stick, finger etc] enfoncer (**into** dans, **between** entre); [+ rag etc] fourrer (**into** dans); **don't ~ me!** ne (me) poussez pas!

◆ **to push** + preposition/adverb: **to ~ sb in/out/up** etc faire entrer/sortir/monter etc qn en le poussant; **to ~ sb against a wall** pousser qn contre un mur; **bulldozers ~ed the snow aside** des bulldozers déblayaient la neige; **he ~ed him down the stairs** il l'a poussé et l'a fait tomber dans l'escalier; **to ~ sb into a room** pousser qn dans une pièce; **he ~ed the book into my hand** il m'a fourré le livre dans la main; **they ~ed me off the pavement** ils m'ont poussé et m'ont forcé à descendre du trottoir; **he ~ed the cat off the table** il a poussé le chat et l'a forcé à descendre de la table; **she ~ed the books off the table** elle a poussé les livres et les a fait tomber de la table; **they ~ed the car off the cliff** ils ont poussé la voiture dans le précipice, ils ont poussé la voiture et l'ont fait tomber de la falaise; **they ~ed the car off the road** ils ont poussé la voi-

ture sur le bas-côté; **to ~ a door open** ouvrir une porte en la poussant, pousser une porte (pour l'ouvrir); **they ~ed him out of the car** ils l'ont poussé hors de la voiture; **to ~ sb/sth out of the way** écarter qn/qch en le poussant; **it ~ed the matter right out of his mind** cela m'a fait complètement oublier cette affaire; **to ~ a door shut** fermer une porte en la poussant, pousser une porte (pour la fermer); **he ~ed his head through the window** il a passé la tête par la fenêtre; **to ~ one's way through** a crowd se frayer or s'ouvrir un chemin dans la foule; **he ~ed the bill through Parliament** il a réussi à faire voter le projet de loi; **he ~ed the thought to the back of his mind** il a repoussé or écarté cette pensée; **he ~ed the box under the table** il a poussé la boîte sous la table

◆ **to be pushing** + age: **he must be ~ing* 60** il ne doit pas avoir loin de 60 ans, il doit friser la soixantaine

b fig **= press, advance** [+ one's views] mettre en avant; [+ claim] présenter avec insistance; [+ plan, method, solution] essayer d'imposer; [+ product] pousser la vente de; [+ candidate etc] essayer de placer; [+ business] développer en priorité

c fig **= go too far with** **that's ~ing it a bit!*** (indignantly) c'est un peu fort!; (not much time etc) c'est un peu juste!

d fig (= put pressure on) pousser; (= harass) importuner, harceler; **don't ~ him too hard** or **too far** n'insistez pas trop, ne le poussez pas à bout; **they ~ed him to the limits of his endurance** on l'a poussé jusqu'à la limite de ses forces; **to ~ sb to do sth** pousser qn à faire qch, insister pour que qn fasse qch; **to ~ sb for payment/for an answer** presser qn de payer/de répondre; **to ~ sb into doing forcer** or **obliger qn à faire; I was ~ed into it** on m'y a poussé or forcé; **he was ~ed into teaching** on l'a poussé à devenir professeur or à faire de l'enseignement; **to ~ o.s. hard** exiger beaucoup de soi-même; **he ~es himself too hard** il se surmène

◆ **to be pushed*** (= under pressure) **I'm really ~ed today** je suis vraiment bousculé or débordé aujourd'hui; **to be ~ed for time/money** être à court de temps/d'argent, manquer de temps/d'argent; **I'm rather ~ed for space** je suis à l'étroit

e US Golf **to ~ the ball** couper or faire dévier la balle

3 INTRANSITIVE VERB

a **= press** pousser; (on bell) appuyer (on sur); **you ~ and I'll pull** poussez et moi je vais tirer; **"~"** (on door) «poussez»; (on bell) «appuyez», «sonnez»; (fig) **to ~ for better conditions/higher wages** etc faire pression pour obtenir de meilleures conditions/une augmentation de salaire etc

b **= move** **they ~ed into/out of the room** ils sont entrés dans la pièce/sortis de la pièce en se frayant un passage; **he ~ed past me** il m'a dépassé en me bousculant; **she ~ed through the crowd** elle s'est frayé or ouvert un chemin dans la foule

c Mil (= advance) **to ~ into enemy territory** avancer en territoire ennemi

4 COMPOUNDS

► **push-bike*** N (Brit) vélo m ► **push-button** N, ADJ → push-button ► **push-pull circuit** N (Elec) push-pull m inv ► **push rod** N (Aut) tige f de culbuteur ► **push-start** N, VT **to give a car a ~-start** ◊ **to ~-start a car** faire démarrer une voiture en la poussant, pousser une voiture pour la faire démarrer ► **push-up** N (US Gym) traction f, pompe* f; **to do ~-ups** faire des tractions or des pompes*

5 PHRASAL VERBS

► **push about** VT SEP = push around

► **push ahead** VI (= make progress) avancer à grands pas; **to ~ ahead with** faire avancer à grands pas

▶ **push along** [1] VI [a] (* = *leave*) filer*, se sauver*

[b] (*Aut etc* = *move quickly*) rouler bon train

[2] VT SEP [+ *person, cart, chair*] pousser; (*fig* = *hasten*) [+ *work*] activer, accélérer

▶ **push around** VT SEP [a] [+ *cart, toy*] pousser de-ci de-là, pousser à droite et à gauche

[b] (*fig* = *bully*) marcher sur les pieds à*

▶ **push aside** VT SEP [+ *person, chair*] écarter (brusquement); (*fig*) [+ *objection, suggestion*] écarter, rejeter

▶ **push away** VT SEP [+ *person, chair, one's plate, sb's hand*] repousser; [+ *gift*] repousser, rejeter

▶ **push back** VT SEP [+ *cover, blankets, lock of hair*] rejeter or repousser (en arrière); [+ *curtains*] repousser; [+ *person, crowd, enemy*] repousser, faire reculer; (*fig*) [+ *desire, impulse*] réprimer

▶ **push down** [1] VI appuyer (**on** sur)

[2] VT SEP [a] [+ *switch, lever*] abaisser; [+ *knob, button*] appuyer sur; [+ *pin, stick*] enfoncer; [+ *fence, barrier, person*] renverser; he ~ed the tile down off the roof il a poussé la tuile et l'a fait tomber du toit, il a fait tomber la tuile du toit en la poussant; he ~ed his clothes down into the suitcase il a fourré ses vêtements dans la valise

[b] (*fig* = *reduce*) [+ *prices, inflation, value*] faire baisser

▶ **push forward** [1] VI avancer, se frayer or s'ouvrir un chemin

[2] VT SEP [+ *person, box etc*] pousser en avant, faire avancer; to ~ one's way forward se frayer or s'ouvrir un chemin; he ~ed himself forward il s'est frayé or ouvert un chemin; (*fig*) il s'est mis en avant, il s'est fait valoir

▶ **push in** [1] VI s'introduire de force; (*fig* = *interfere*) intervenir; he's always ~ing in where he's not wanted il se mêle toujours de or il intervient toujours dans ce qui ne le regarde pas

[2] VT SEP [a] [+ *stick, pin, finger*] enfoncer; [+ *rag*] fourrer dedans; [+ *person*] pousser dedans; [+ *knob, button*] appuyer sur; they opened the door and ~ed him in ils ouvrirent la porte et le poussèrent à l'intérieur; they took him to the pond and ~ed him in ils l'ont amené à l'étang et l'ont poussé dedans

[b] (= *break*) [+ *window, door, sides of box*] enfoncer

[c] to ~ one's way in s'introduire de force

▶ **push off** [1] VI [a] (*Naut*) pousser au large

[b] (* = *leave*) filer*, se sauver*; I must ~ off now il faut que je file* (*subj*) or que je me sauve* (*subj*); ~ off! fichez le camp!*, filez!*

[c] the top just ~es off il suffit de pousser le haut pour l'enlever

[2] VT SEP → push 2a

▶ **push on** [1] VI (*in journey*) pousser (**to** jusqu'à), continuer son chemin; (*in work*) continuer, persévérer; to ~ on with sth continuer (à faire) qch

[2] VT SEP [a] [+ *lid, cover*] placer or (re)mettre en place (en pressant or en appuyant)

[b] (*fig* = *incite*) pousser, inciter (**to do** à faire)

▶ **push out** [1] VI [*roots, branches*] pousser; [*shoots*] pointer, sortir

[2] VT SEP [a] [+ *person, object*] pousser dehors; [+ *stopper*] faire sortir (en poussant); (*fig*) [+ *employee, office holder*] évincer, se débarrasser de; to ~ the boat out (*lit*) pousser au large; (*fig*) faire la fête

[b] (*Bot*) [+ *roots, shoots*] produire

[c] (* = *produce*) [+ *information, products etc*] débiter

[d] to ~ one's way out se frayer or s'ouvrir un chemin (à travers la foule)

▶ **push over** VT SEP [a] (= *pass*) [+ *object*] pousser (**to sb** vers qn)

[b] (= *cause to fall off: over cliff, bridge etc*) pousser, faire tomber

[c] (= *cause to topple*) [+ *chair, vase, person*] renverser, faire tomber

[d] to ~ one's way over to sb se frayer or s'ouvrir un chemin vers qn

▶ **push through** [1] VI se frayer or s'ouvrir un chemin

[2] VT SEP [a] [+ *stick, hand etc*] enfoncer, (faire) passer

[b] (*fig*) [+ *deal, business*] conclure à la hâte; [+ *decision*] faire accepter à la hâte; (*Parl*) [+ *bill*] réussir à faire voter

[c] to ~ one's way through se frayer or s'ouvrir un chemin

▶ **push to** VT SEP [+ *door*] fermer (en poussant), pousser pour fermer

▶ **push up** VT SEP [a] [+ *stick, hand, lever, switch*] (re)lever; [+ *spectacles*] relever; (*hum*) he's ~ing up (the) daisies‡ (= *dead*) il mange les pissenlits par la racine*

[b] (*fig* = *increase*) [+ *numbers, taxes, sales, speed*] augmenter; [+ *prices, demand, sb's temperature, blood pressure*] faire monter; that ~es up the total to over 100 cela fait monter le total à plus de 100

push-button ['puʃ,bʌtn] [1] N bouton m, poussoir m [2] ADJ [*machine etc*] à commande automatique; [*telephone*] à touches; ~ **controls** commande f automatique; ~ **warfare** guerre f presse-bouton

pushcart ['puʃkɑːt] N charrette f à bras

pushchair ['puʃtʃɛəʳ] N (*Brit*) poussette f

pusher ['puʃəʳ] N [a] (*pej*) arriviste mf → **penpusher** [b] (*: also **drug-~**) revendeur m, -euse f (de drogue), dealer* m

pushfulness* ['puʃfʊlnɪs], **pushiness*** ['puʃɪnɪs] N (*pej*) arrivisme m, excès m d'ambition; [*of manner*] arrogance f

pushing ['puʃɪŋ] N [a] (*lit*) cohue f; ~ **and shoving** bousculade f [b] (*fig* = *persuasion*) persuasion f; he ~ed to do it, after a lot of ~ il a accepté (de le faire) après s'être fait beaucoup prier

Pushkin ['puʃkɪn] N Pouchkine m

pushover* ['puʃəʊvəʳ] N it was a ~ c'était la facilité même, c'était un jeu d'enfant; he's a ~ il se laisse facilement faire; he's a ~ **for blondes** il craque* dès qu'il voit une blonde

pushpin ['puʃpɪn] N épingle f (à tête de couleur)

pushy* ['puʃɪ] ADJ (*pej*) [*person*] arriviste, qui se fait valoir, qui se met trop en avant; [*manner*] arrogant

pusillanimity [,pjuːsɪlə'nɪmɪtɪ] N pusillanimité f

pusillanimous [,pjuːsɪ'lænɪməs] ADJ pusillanime

puss* [pʊs] N (= *cat*) minet(te) m(f), minou m; (*to cat*) ~, ~! minet, minet!, minou, minou!; **Puss in Boots** le Chat Botté

pussy ['pʊsɪ] [1] N [a] (* = *cat*) minet(te) m(f), minou m, chat(te) m(f) [b] (‡ = *female genitals*) chatte‡ f (*NonC:* ‡‡ = *intercourse*) baise‡‡ f [2] COMP ▶ **pussy willow** N (*Bot*) saule m (blanc)

pussycat* ['pʊsɪkæt] N (= *cat*) minet(te) m(f), minou m; (*US* = *sweetheart*) hi, ~! bonjour, mon chou* or mon ange!; he's a real ~ (= *harmless*) il ne ferait pas de mal à une mouche*

pussyfoot* ['pʊsɪfʊt] VI marcher à pas de loup; (*fig*) ne pas se mouiller*, ménager la chèvre et le chou

pussyfooting* ['pʊsɪˌfʊtɪŋ] [1] ADJ (*fig*) [*person*] qui a peur de se mouiller*; [*attitude*] timoré [2] N (*also ~ **about** or **around***) tergiversations fpl

pustule ['pʌstjuːl] N pustule f

▼**put** [pʊt]

vb: pret, ptp put	
[1] TRANSITIVE VERB	[4] COMPOUNDS
[2] INTRANSITIVE VERB	[5] PHRASAL VERBS
[3] NOUN	

[1] TRANSITIVE VERB

For set combinations consisting of put + *noun, eg* **put to use, put in danger/out of business/an end to**, *look up the noun. For* put + *preposition/adverb combinations, see also phrasal verbs.*

[a] = **place** mettre; ~ **it in the drawer** mettez-le dans le tiroir; to ~ sth in one's pocket mettre qch dans sa poche; he ~ her into a taxi il l'a mise dans un taxi; ~ yourself in my place mets-toi à ma place; I didn't know where to ~ myself!* je ne savais plus où me mettre!; to ~ an advertisement in the paper mettre or passer une annonce dans le journal; he ~ the shell to her ear il a mis le coquillage contre son oreille, il a porté le coquillage à son oreille; rather than ~ him in hospital he cared for him at home il a préféré s'occuper de lui à la maison plutôt que de le mettre à l'hôpital; *BUT* ~ the book in its proper place remets le livre à sa place; to ~ a bullet into sb tirer sur qn, coller une balle dans la peau de qn*; (= *give me your hand*) ~ it there!* tope là!, affaire conclue!

♦ **to put + on**: to ~ a button on a shirt mettre or coudre un bouton à une chemise; to ~ sb on a diet mettre qn au régime; he ~ some more coal on the fire il a remis or rajouté du charbon sur le feu; he ~ me on the train il m'a accompagné au train; to ~ one's signature on sth apposer sa signature sur qch, signer qch; to ~ sb on a committee nommer qn à un comité → put on

♦ **to put + over**: he ~ his hand over his mouth il a mis sa main devant la bouche; he ~ his hand over her mouth il a plaqué sa main sur sa bouche; he ~ his rucksack over the fence il a passé son sac à dos par-dessus la barrière; someone has been ~ over him at the office il a maintenant un chef au bureau → put over

♦ **to put one over on** or **across sb***(= *deceive*) pigeonner* qn, embobiner* qn; he tried to ~ one over on or across me il a essayé de me pigeonner* or de m'embobiner*; you'll never ~ one over on him on ne la lui fait pas*

♦ **to put + round**: to ~ one's arms round sb enlacer qn, prendre qn dans ses bras; he ~ his head round the door il a passé la tête par la porte → put round

♦ **to put + through**: he ~ his head through the window il a mis son nez à la fenêtre; to ~ one's fist through a window passer le poing à travers une vitre; to ~ one's pen through a word rayer or barrer un mot; she ~ a bullet through his head elle lui a tiré une balle dans la tête → put through

[b] = **set** [+ *clock, watch*] mettre; to ~ a watch to the right time mettre une montre à l'heure; I ~ him to work at once je l'ai aussitôt mis au travail; they had to ~ four men on to this job ils ont dû employer quatre hommes à ce travail or pour faire ce travail; she ~ my brother against me elle a monté mon frère contre moi

[c] = **rank** placer; I ~ Joyce above Lawrence je place Joyce au-dessus de Lawrence; I wouldn't ~ him among the greatest poets je ne le placerais or classerais pas parmi les plus grands poètes; *BUT* we should ~ happiness before or above money on devrait faire passer le bonheur avant l'argent; he ~s good health among his greatest blessings il estime que sa santé est l'un de ses meilleurs atouts

[d] = **express** dire; how shall I ~ it? comment dire?, comment dirais-je?; I don't quite know how to ~ it je ne sais pas trop comment le dire; try ~ting it another way essayez de le dire d'une autre façon; let me ~ it this way: she's not exactly diplomatic disons qu'elle n'a pas beaucoup de tact; how will you ~ it to him?

comment vas-tu lui présenter la chose?, comment vas-tu le lui dire?; **as Shakespeare ~s it** comme le dit Shakespeare; [BUT] **as the president memorably ~ it** selon la célèbre formule du président; **to ~ it bluntly** pour parler franc; **as he would ~ it** pour employer sa formule *or* son expression; **~ it so as not to offend her** présente la chose de façon à ne pas la blesser; **some expressions are impossible to ~ into French** certaines expressions sont impossibles à traduire en français; **to ~ into verse** mettre en vers

[e] **= suggest** **I ~ it to you that ...** n'est-il pas vrai *or* ...?; **it was ~ to me in no uncertain terms that I should resign** on m'a déclaré en termes très clairs que je devrais donner ma démission

[f] **= submit, expound** [+ *case, problem*] exposer, présenter; [+ *opinion, suggestion*] présenter; [+ *proposal*] soumettre; [+ *question*] poser; **he ~ the arguments for and against the project** il a présenté les arguments pour et contre le projet; **he ~ his views very clearly** il a présenté *or* exposé très clairement sa position

[g] **= cause to be** mettre; **to ~ sb in a good/ bad mood** mettre qn de bonne/mauvaise humeur

[h] **= invest**

♦ **to put + into**: **to ~ money into a company** placer *or* investir de l'argent dans une société; **he ~ all his savings into the project** il a placé *or* mis toutes ses économies dans ce projet; **he has ~ a lot into his marriage** il a fait beaucoup d'efforts pour que leur couple marche; **I've ~ a lot of time and trouble into it** j'y ai consacré beaucoup de temps et d'efforts

[i] **= estimate**

♦ **to put + at** estimer, évaluer; **they ~ the loss at £10,000** ils estiment *or* évaluent à 10 000 livres la perte subie; **the population was ~ at 50,000** on a évalué *or* estimé le nombre d'habitants à 50 000; **what would you ~ it at?** à combien l'estimez-vous *or* l'évaluez-vous?; [BUT] **I'd ~ her** *or* **her age at 50** je lui donnerais 50 ans

[j] **Sport** **to ~ the shot** *or* **the weight** lancer le poids

[k] **St Ex = offer to sell** [+ *stock, security*] se déclarer vendeur de

2 INTRANSITIVE VERB

Naut **to ~ into port** mouiller, jeter l'ancre; **the ship ~ into Southampton** le navire a mouillé *or* jeté l'ancre dans le port de Southampton; **to ~ to sea** appareiller

3 NOUN

St Ex = premium prime *f* pour livrer; **~ (option)** option *f* de vente, put *m*

4 COMPOUNDS

▶ **put-down*** N humiliation *f*, remarque *f* humiliante ▶ **put-in** N (*Rugby*) introduction *f* ▶ **put-on*** N (= *pretence*) comédie *f*; (= *hoax*) mystification *f*, farce *f* ♦ ADJ (= *feigned*) affecté, feint ▶ **put option** N → 3 ▶ **put-up job*** N coup *m* monté ▶ **put-upon*** ADJ **I feel ~-upon** je trouve qu'on profite de moi, je me sens exploité; **she is ~-upon** on abuse de sa gentillesse; **I won't be ~-upon any more!** je ne vais plus me laisser faire! *or* me laisser marcher sur les pieds!

5 PHRASAL VERBS

▶ **put about** **1** VI (*Naut*) virer de bord

2 VT SEP [a] (*esp Brit*) [+ *rumour*] faire courir, faire circuler; **he ~ it about that ...** il a fait courir *or* circuler le bruit que ...

[b] (*Naut*) **to ~ the ship about** virer de bord

[c] **to ~ o.s. about*** [*ambitious person*] se faire mousser*

▶ **put across** VT SEP (= *communicate*) [+ *ideas, intentions, desires*] faire comprendre, communiquer (**to sb** à qn); **to ~ sth across to sb** faire comprendre qch à qn; **the play ~s the message across very well** la pièce arrive très bien à faire

passer le message; **he knows his stuff but he can't ~ it across** il connaît son sujet à fond mais il n'arrive pas à le faire comprendre aux autres; **it all depends on how you ~ yourself across** tout dépend de la façon dont on se présente; **she ~ the song across beautifully** elle a donné une très belle interprétation de cette chanson

▶ **put around** VT SEP = put about 2a

▶ **put aside** VT SEP [a] [+ *object*] mettre de côté; (= *keep, save*) [+ *food, money*] mettre de côté, garder en réserve; **he ~ aside the document to read later** il a mis le document de côté pour le lire plus tard; **she ~ her book aside when I came in** elle a posé son livre quand je suis entré; (*Comm*) **I'll ~ one aside for you** je vous en mettrai un de côté [b] [+ *differences, disagreement, feeling*] mettre de côté

▶ **put away** VT SEP [a] = put aside a

[b] = put aside b

[c] (= *put in proper place*) [+ *clothes, toys, books*] ranger; **to ~ the car away** rentrer la voiture, mettre la voiture au garage; (*to person with weapon*) **~ that knife away!** pose *or* jette ce couteau!

[d] (*Sport*) [+ *ball*] mettre au fond des filets

[e] (* = *confine*) (*in prison*) enfermer, coffrer*; (*in mental hospital*) enfermer

[f] (* = *consume*) [+ *food*] avaler; [+ *drink*] siffler*

[g] (*US* = *beat*) battre

[h] = put down 2i

▶ **put back** **1** VI (*Naut*) **to ~ back to port** rentrer au port; **they ~ back to Dieppe** ils sont rentrés *or* retournés à Dieppe

2 VT SEP [a] (= *replace*) remettre (à sa place *or* en place); **~ it back!** remets-le à sa place!; **~ it back on the shelf** remettez-le sur l'étagère

[b] (= *retard*) [+ *development, progress*] retarder, freiner; [+ *clock*] retarder; **the disaster ~ the project back (by) ten years** ce désastre a retardé de dix ans la réalisation du projet; **this will ~ us back ten years** cela nous fera perdre dix ans → **clock**

[c] (= *postpone*) remettre (**to** à)

▶ **put by** VT SEP = put aside a

▶ **put down** **1** VI [*aircraft, pilot*] se poser, atterrir; (*on carrier*) apponter

2 VT SEP [a] [+ *parcel, book*] poser; [+ *child*] poser, mettre à terre (*or* sur un lit *etc*); [+ *passenger*] déposer, laisser; (*Cricket*) **he ~ down a simple catch** il a relâché une balle pourtant facile; **~ it down!** pose ça!; **she ~ her book down and stood up** elle posa son livre et se leva; **I simply couldn't ~ that book down** j'ai dévoré ce livre → **foot, root**

[b] [+ *aircraft*] poser

[c] [+ *umbrella*] fermer

[d] (= *pay*) [+ *deposit*] verser (**on** pour); **he ~ down £500 on the car** il a versé 500 livres d'arrhes pour la voiture

[e] [+ *wine*] mettre en cave

[f] (= *suppress*) [+ *revolt, movement*] réprimer, juguler

[g] * [+ *person*] (= *criticize*) critiquer; (= *denigrate*) dénigrer; **my boyfriend keeps ~ting me down** mon copain n'arrête pas de me critiquer; **it's a way of ~ting down minorities** c'est un moyen de dénigrer les minorités; **you must stop ~ting yourself down** arrête donc de te déprécier

[h] (= *record*) noter; **to ~ sth down in writing** *or* **on paper** mettre qch par écrit; (*Comm*) **~ it down on my account** mettez-le sur mon compte; **I've ~ you down as unemployed** j'ai mis que vous étiez chômeur; **~ me down for £10** je donnerai 10 livres; **I'll ~ you down for the next vacancy** je vais inscrire votre nom pour la prochaine place disponible → **name**

[i] (*Brit euph* = *have destroyed*) [+ *dog, cat*] faire piquer; [+ *horse*] faire abattre

▶ **put down as** VT SEP (= *consider, assess*) considérer comme; **he'll be ~ down as one of our best Prime Ministers** il passera à la postérité

comme l'un de nos meilleurs premiers ministres; **I had ~ him down as a complete fool** je l'avais catalogué comme un parfait imbécile, j'étais convaincu qu'il était complètement stupide; **I would ~ her down as about forty** je lui donnerais la quarantaine

▶ **put down to** VT SEP (= *attribute*) mettre sur le compte; **I ~ it down to his inexperience** je mets ça sur le compte de son manque d'expérience; **the accident must be ~ down to negligence** l'accident doit être imputé à la négligence

▶ **put forth** VT SEP (*liter*) [+ *leaves, roots, shoots*] produire; [+ *idea, suggestion, theory, proposal*] émettre; [+ *programme, plan*] proposer; [+ *effort*] fournir, déployer

▶ **put forward** VT SEP [a] (= *propose*) [+ *idea, suggestion, theory, proposal*] émettre; [+ *argument*] avancer, présenter; [+ *reason*] donner; [+ *opinion*] exprimer, émettre; [+ *plan*] proposer; **he ~ his name forward as a candidate** il s'est porté candidat; **he ~ himself forward for the job** il s'est porté candidat au poste, il a posé sa candidature au poste; **he ~ forward (the name of) Harry Green for the job** il a proposé Harry Green pour ce poste

[b] (= *advance*) [+ *meeting, starting time, clock, schedule, programme*] avancer (**by** de, **to, until** à)

▶ **put in** **1** VI (*Naut*) mouiller (**at** dans le port de)

2 VT SEP [a] (*into box, drawer, room*) mettre dans; [+ *seeds*] semer; [+ *plant*] planter; **he ~ his head in at the window** il a passé la tête par la fenêtre; **I've ~ the car in for repairs** j'ai donné la voiture à réparer; (= *pack*) **have you ~ in the camera?** est-ce que tu as pris l'appareil photo?

[b] (= *insert*) [+ *word, paragraph*] ajouter; [+ *remark*] ajouter, glisser; (= *include*) [+ *information*] inclure; **have you ~ in why you are not going?** est-ce que vous avez expliqué pourquoi vous n'y allez pas?; **"but it's cold" he ~ in** « mais il fait froid » fit-il remarquer

[c] (= *submit*) **to ~ in a request for sth** faire une demande de qch; **to ~ in a claim for damages** faire une demande d'indemnité; (*Jur*) **to ~ in a plea** plaider; **to ~ sb in for an exam** présenter qn à un examen; **to ~ sb in for a scholarship** recommander qn pour une bourse → **put in for**

[d] (= *install*) [+ *political party*] élire; [+ *person*] nommer; [+ *central heating, double glazing*] faire installer

[e] (= *spend*) [+ *time*] passer; **I've ~ in a lot of time on it** j'y ai passé *or* consacré beaucoup de temps; **she ~s in an hour a day at the piano** elle fait une heure de piano par jour

[f] (= *work*) travailler; **they ~ in at least 40 hours a week** ils travaillent plus de 40 heures par semaines; **can you ~ in a few hours at the weekend?** pourrais-tu travailler quelques heures ce week-end?

▶ **put in for** VT FUS [+ *job*] poser sa candidature à; [+ *promotion, transfer, divorce*] faire une demande de, demander; [+ *rise*] demander

▶ **put off** **1** VI (*Naut*) appareiller (**from** de)

2 VT SEP [a] (= *postpone*) [+ *departure, appointment, meeting*] retarder, repousser; [+ *decision*] remettre à plus tard, différer; [+ *visitor*] décommander; **to ~ sth off for ten days/ until January** remettre qch de dix jours/jusqu'à janvier; (*Brit*) **he is ~ting off the evil day** *or* **hour when he'll finally give up smoking** il repousse indéfiniment le moment où il devra s'arrêter de fumer; **I'm sorry to have to ~ you off** je suis désolé d'avoir à vous décommander; **he ~ off writing the letter** il a décidé d'écrire cette lettre plus tard

[b] (= *discourage*) dissuader; (= *repel*) dégoûter; **the failure may ~ them off trying again** il est possible que cet échec les dissuade d'essayer à nouveau; **his eccentricities ~ them off** ses petites manies les ont dégoûtés; **the divorce fig-**

ures don't seem to ~ **people off marriage** les statistiques de divorce ne semblent pas dégoûter les gens du mariage; **the country's reputation may ~ off tourists** la réputation du pays pourrait dissuader les touristes de s'y rendre; **it certainly ~ me off going to Greece** cela m'a certainement ôté l'envie d'aller en Grèce [c] (= *remove desire for*) **his remarks ~ me off my food** ses remarques m'ont coupé l'appétit [d] (= *distract*) **talking in the audience ~ him off** les bavardages de l'auditoire le déconcentraient; **it ~ her off revising for her exams** cela l'a distraite de son travail de révision pour ses examens → **scent, stroke** [e] (= *fob off*) **he ~ her off with vague promises** il la faisait patienter avec de vagues promesses; **you're not going to ~ me off with flattery** tu n'arriveras pas à m'amadouer en me flattant [f] [+ *passenger*] déposer, débarquer [g] (= *switch off*) [+ *light, gas, radio, TV, heater*] éteindre; **he ~ off the lights one by one** il a éteint les lumières une à une

► **put on** VT SEP [a] [+ *clothes, hat, glasses, lotion*] mettre; [+ *jumper, trousers, gloves, socks*] mettre, enfiler; **to ~ on one's make-up** se maquiller [b] (= *increase*) [+ *speed*] augmenter; **to ~ on weight** prendre du poids, grossir; **he ~ on 3 kilos** il a pris 3 kilos, il a grossi de 3 kilos; **they ~ on another goal in the second half** ils ont marqué un autre but en deuxième mi-temps; **the proposal could ~ 5p on a litre of petrol** cette proposition augmenterait le prix du litre d'essence de 5 pence [c] (= *assume*) [+ *air*] prendre, se donner; [+ *accent*] prendre; (= *pretend*) **to ~ on an act ◊ to ~ it on** faire semblant; **she ~ on a show of enthusiasm** elle faisait semblant d'être enthousiaste; **he's just ~ting it on** il fait semblant, c'est tout [d] (= *deceive*) [+ *person*] faire marcher*; **you're ~ting me on!*** tu me fais marcher!* [e] (= *organize*) [+ *concert, play, show*] organiser; [+ *film*] projeter; [+ *extra train, bus*] mettre en service; **the party ~ on a convincing display of unity** le parti a donné une image d'unité assez convaincante [f] (*Telec*) **~ me on to Mr Brown** passez-moi M. Brown; (*Telec*) **would you ~ on Mrs Smith?** pouvez-vous me passer Mme Smith? [g] (= *start functioning*) [+ *light, gas, radio, TV, heater*] allumer; [+ *tape, CD, music*] mettre; **to ~ the brakes on** freiner [h] (= *begin to cook, heat*) **~ the kettle on** mets de l'eau à chauffer; **I'll just ~ the potatoes on** je vais juste mettre les pommes de terre à cuire [i] (= *advance*) [+ *clock*] avancer (**by** de) [j] [+ *money, bet*] parier sur, miser sur; **he ~ £10 on Black Beauty** il a parié or misé 10 livres sur Black Beauty; **I wouldn't ~ money on it!** je n'en mettrais pas ma main au feu!

► **put onto, put on to** VT SEP **to ~ sb onto** or **on to sth** parler de qch à qn; **Alice ~ us onto him** Alice nous a parlé de lui; **a fellow journalist ~ me onto the story** c'est un collègue journaliste qui m'a mis sur l'affaire*; **they ~ the police onto him** ils l'ont signalé à la police; **can you ~ me onto a good dentist?** pourriez-vous m'indiquer un bon dentiste?; **Paul ~ us onto you** c'est Paul qui nous a dit de nous adresser à vous; **what ~ you onto it?** qu'est-ce qui vous en a donné l'idée?

► **put out** [1] VI (*Naut*) prendre le large; **to ~ out to sea** prendre le large, quitter le port; **to ~ out from Dieppe** quitter le port de Dieppe

[2] VT SEP [a] (= *put outside*) [+ *rubbish*] sortir, mettre dehors; (= *expel*) [+ *person*] expulser (**of** de); [+ *country, organization*] exclure (**of** de); **he ~ the rug out to dry** il a mis le tapis à sécher dehors; **he ~ the cat out for the night** il a fait sortir le chat or il a mis le chat dehors pour la nuit; **to ~ sb's eyes out** crever les yeux à qn; **to ~ sth out of one's head** or **mind** ne

plus penser à qch [b] (*Naut*) [+ *boat*] mettre à l'eau or à la mer [c] (= *stretch out, extend*) [+ *arm, leg*] allonger, étendre; [+ *foot*] avancer; [+ *tongue*] tirer (**at sb** à qn); [+ *leaves, shoots, roots*] produire; **to ~ out one's hand** tendre la main; [*traffic policeman*] tendre le bras; **to ~ one's head out of the window** passer la tête par la fenêtre; **the snail ~ out its horns** l'escargot a sorti ses cornes [d] (= *lay out in order*) [+ *cards, clothes*] étaler; [+ *chessmen*] disposer; [+ *best china*] sortir [e] (= *extinguish*) [+ *light, flames, gas, cigarette*] éteindre [f] (= *make unconscious*) endormir [g] (= *annoy*) contrarier (**about** par); **she looked very ~ out** elle avait l'air très contrariée; **he was very ~ out at finding her there** il était très contrarié de la trouver là [h] (= *disconcert*) déconcerter, dérouter (**by** par) [i] (= *inconvenience*) déranger, gêner; **I don't want to ~ you out** je ne voudrais pas vous déranger; **don't ~ yourself out** ne vous dérangez pas; (*iro*) surtout ne vous gênez pas!; **she really ~ herself out for us** elle s'est donné beaucoup de mal pour nous, elle s'est mise en quatre pour nous [j] (= *issue*) [+ *announcement, statement, report*] publier; [+ *news*] annoncer; [+ *appeal, warning*] lancer; [+ *propaganda*] faire; [+ *book, leaflet, edition*] sortir, publier; [+ *album*] sortir; **the government will ~ out a statement about it** le gouvernement va faire une déclaration or va publier un communiqué à ce sujet [k] (= *broadcast*) [+ *programme*] passer; (= *give out*) [+ *signal*] émettre [l] (= *spend*) dépenser [m] **to ~ out to tender** [+ *contract, service*] mettre en adjudication [n] (= *exert*) déployer, user de [o] (= *dislocate*) [+ *shoulder*] se déboîter; [+ *ankle, knee, back*] se démettre [p] (*Sport* = *eliminate*) [+ *team, contestant*] éliminer (**of** de); (*Baseball*) [+ *ball*] mettre hors jeu; **a knee injury ~ him out of the first two games** une blessure au genou l'a empêché de jouer les deux premiers matchs

► **put over** VT SEP = **put across**
► **put round** VT SEP [+ *rumour*] faire courir, faire circuler
► **put through** VT SEP [a] (= *make, complete*) [+ *reform, change*] instituer, instaurer; [+ *deal*] conclure; [+ *plan*] mener à bien; [+ *motion, amendment*] voter → **pace¹** [b] (*Telec* = *connect*) [+ *call*] passer; [+ *caller*] brancher, mettre en communication; **I'm ~ting you through now** vous êtes en ligne, je vous mets en communication; **~ me through to Mr Smith** passez-moi M. Smith [c] (*US*) **to ~ sb through college** payer les études de qn [d] (= *make suffer*) **to ~ sb through hell** mener la vie dure à qn; **they really ~ him through it*** ils lui en ont fait voir de dures*, ils lui ont fait passer un mauvais quart d'heure → **put 1a**
► **put together** VT SEP [a] (*lit*) mettre ensemble; **don't ~ two hamsters together** ne mettez pas deux hamsters ensemble; **don't ~ two hamsters together in one cage** ne mettez pas deux hamsters dans la même cage; **he's worth more than the rest of the family ~ together** à lui tout seul il vaut plus que toute la famille réunie; **it's more important than all the other factors ~ together** c'est plus important que tous les autres facteurs mis ensemble [b] (= *assemble*) [+ *table, bookcase*] assembler, monter; [+ *book, story, account*] composer; [+ *facts, what happened*] reconstituer; [+ *team*] monter, constituer; **she ~ together an excellent meal** elle a improvisé un délicieux repas [c] (= *design, draw up*) [+ *agreement, plan, package*] mettre au point
► **put up** [1] VI (= *stay*) descendre (**at** dans); **to ~ up for the night at a hotel** passer la nuit dans un hôtel

[b] (*Pol* = *offer o.s.*) se porter candidat(e) (**for** à), se présenter comme candidat(e) (**for** à); (*Parl*) **to ~ up for a constituency** chercher à avoir l'investiture de son parti dans une circonscription électorale
[2] VT SEP [a] (= *raise*) [+ *hand*] lever; [+ *flag, sail*] hisser; [+ *tent*] monter; [+ *collar, car window*] remonter; [+ *umbrella*] ouvrir; [+ *notice*] mettre, afficher (**on** sur); [+ *picture*] mettre, accrocher (**on** sur); [+ *building*] construire, ériger; [+ *fence, barrier*] ériger, dresser; **to ~ a ladder up against a wall** poser une échelle contre un mur → **back, foot** [b] (= *increase*) [+ *numbers, taxes, sales*] augmenter; [+ *prices*] faire monter; [+ *demand*] accroître; [+ *sb's temperature, blood pressure*] faire monter; **that ~s up the total to over 1,000** cela fait monter le total à plus de 1 000 [c] (= *offer*) [+ *proposal, case*] présenter, soumettre; [+ *prayer*] faire; [+ *resistance*] opposer; **to ~ sb up as a candidate for** proposer qn comme candidat à; **to ~ up a struggle** or **a fight** se battre; **he ~ up a real fight to keep you in your job** il s'est vraiment battu pour que tu conserves (*subj*) ton poste; **the matter was ~ up to the board for a decision** l'affaire a été soumise au conseil d'administration qui prendra une décision; **to ~ sth up for sale/auction** mettre qch en vente/aux enchères; **to ~ a child up for adoption** faire adopter un enfant; **he was ~ up by his local branch** il a été présenté comme candidat par sa section locale; **they ~ him up for the chairmanship** on l'a présenté or proposé comme candidat à la présidence; **I'll ~ you up for the club** je vous proposerai comme membre du club [d] (= *provide*) [+ *money, funds*] fournir (**for** pour); [+ *reward*] offrir; **to ~ up money for a project** financer un projet, fournir les fonds pour un projet; **how much can you ~ up?** combien pouvez-vous mettre? [e] (= *preserve*) [+ *fruit*] mettre en bocaux [f] (= *lodge*) loger, héberger

► **put up to** VT SEP [a] (= *incite*) **to ~ sb up to doing sth** pousser or inciter qn à faire qch; **someone must have ~ him up to it** quelqu'un a dû le pousser or l'inciter à le faire [b] (= *give information about*) **to ~ sb up to sth** renseigner qn sur qch; **he ~ her up to all the ways of avoiding tax** il l'a renseignée sur or lui a montré tous les moyens d'éviter de payer des impôts; **a friend of mine ~ me up to it** c'est un ami qui m'en a donné l'idée
► **put up with** VT FUS tolérer, supporter; **he has a lot to ~ up with** il n'a pas la vie facile; **it is difficult to ~ up with** c'est difficile à supporter, c'est difficilement supportable

putative ['pjuːtətɪv] ADJ (*frm*) putatif
putrefaction [ˌpjuːtrɪˈfækʃən] N putréfaction *f*
putrefy ['pjuːtrɪfaɪ] [1] VT putréfier [2] VI se putréfier
putrescence [pjuːˈtresns] N putrescence *f*
putrescent [pjuːˈtresnt] ADJ putrescent, en voie de putréfaction
putrid ['pjuːtrɪd] ADJ [a] (= *rotting*) putride, pourrissant [b] (‡ = *awful*) dégoûtant, dégueulasse‡
putsch [pʊtʃ] N putsch *m*, coup *m* d'État
putt [pʌt] (*Golf*) [1] N putt *m*, coup *m* roulé [2] VTI putter
puttee ['pʌtiː] N (*pl* **puttees** ['pʌtiːz]) bande *f* molletière
putter¹ ['pʌtər] N (*Golf*) putter *m*
putter² ['pʌtər] VI (*US*) = **potter¹**
putter³ ['pʌtər] VI [*engine, car, boat etc*] brouter
putting ['pʌtɪŋ] [1] N putting *m* [2] COMP
► **putting green** N (= *part of golf course*) green *m*

putty ['pʌtɪ] ① N mastic *m* (*ciment*); **she's (like) ~ in my hands** j'en fais ce que je veux ② VT mastiquer ③ COMP ► **putty knife** N (*pl* **putty knives**) couteau *m* de vitrier

put-you-up ['pʊt,juːʌp] N (*Brit*) canapé-lit *m*, divan *m*

putz [pʌts] N (*US*) ⓐ (* = *person*) couillon(ne)⁑ *m(f)* ⓑ (⁑ = *penis*) bitte⁑ *f*

puzzle ['pʌzl] ① N ⓐ (= *mystery*) énigme *f*, mystère *m*; **he's a real ~ to me** c'est une énigme vivante pour moi; **it's a ~ to me how** *or* **that he got the job** je trouve curieux qu'il ait pu obtenir ce poste ⓑ (= *game*) casse-tête *m inv*; (= *word game*) rébus *m*; (= *crossword*) mots *mpl* croisés; (= *jigsaw*) puzzle *m*; (= *riddle*) devinette *f* ② VT rendre *or* laisser perplexe; **that really ~d him** ça l'a vraiment rendu *or* laissé perplexe; **it ~s me that ...** je trouve curieux que ...; **to ~ one's head about sth** se creuser la tête au sujet de qch → **puzzled** ③ VI **to ~ over** *or* **about** essayer de comprendre; **I'm still puzzling over where he might have hidden it** j'en suis encore à me demander où il a bien pu le cacher ④ COMP ► **puzzle book** N livre *m* de jeux

► **puzzle out** VT SEP [+ *problem*] résoudre; [+ *mystery*] éclaircir, élucider; [+ *writing*] déchiffrer; [+ *answer, solution*] trouver, découvrir; [+ *sb's actions, attitude*] comprendre; **I'm trying to ~ out why he did it** j'essaie de comprendre *or* découvrir pourquoi il l'a fait

puzzled ['pʌzld] ADJ perplexe; **they were ~ to find/see ...** ils n'en revenaient pas de trouver/voir ...; **to be ~ that ...** ne pas arriver à comprendre pourquoi ...; **I am ~ (to know) why** je n'arrive pas à comprendre pourquoi; **he was ~ about what to say** il ne savait pas trop quoi dire → **puzzle**

puzzlement ['pʌzlmənt] N (*NonC*) perplexité *f*

puzzler ['pʌzlə] N (*gen*) énigme *f*; (= *problem*) question *f* difficile, casse-tête *m inv*

puzzling ['pʌzlɪŋ] ADJ curieux

PVC [,piːviːˈsiː] N (*Tex*) (ABBR = **polyvinyl chloride**) PVC *m*

PVS [,piːviːˈes] N ⓐ ABBR = **postviral syndrome** ⓑ (ABBR = **persistent vegetative state**) → **persistent**

Pvt. (*Mil*) ABBR = **Private 2a**

PW [piːˈdʌbljuː] N ⓐ (*US Mil*) (ABBR = **prisoner of war**) → **prisoner** ⓑ (*Brit*) ABBR = **policewoman**

p.w. (ABBR = **per week**) par semaine

PWR [piːˌdʌbljuˈɑːʳ] N (ABBR = **pressurized water reactor**) → **pressurize**

PX [piːˈeks] N (*US Mil*) (ABBR = **post exchange**) → **post**

pygmy ['pɪgmɪ] ① N Pygmée *mf*; (*fig*) pygmée *m* ② ADJ (*also fig*) pygmée (*f inv*)

pyjama [pɪˈdʒɑːmə] (*Brit*) ① **pyjamas** NPL pyjama *m*; **a pair of ~s** un pyjama; **in (one's) ~s** en pyjama ② COMP [*jacket, trousers*] de pyjama

pylon ['paɪlən] N pylône *m*

pylori [paɪˈlɔːraɪ] NPL of **pylorus**

pyloric [paɪˈlɔːrɪk] ADJ pylorique

pylorus [paɪˈlɔːrəs] N (*pl* **pylori**) pylore *m*

pyorrhea [paɪəˈrɪə] N pyorrhée *f* alvéolaire

pyramid ['pɪrəmɪd] ① N pyramide *f* ② VT (*US Fin*) **~ winnings** spéculer en réinvestissant les bénéfices réalisés ③ COMP ► **pyramid selling** N vente *f* pyramidale

pyramidal [pɪˈræmɪdl] ADJ pyramidal

Pyramus ['pɪrəməs] N **~ and Thisbe** Pyrame *m* et Thisbé *f*

pyre ['paɪəʳ] N bûcher *m* funéraire

Pyrenean [pɪrəˈniːən] ADJ pyrénéen, des Pyrénées

Pyrenees [pɪrəˈniːz] NPL Pyrénées *fpl*

pyrethrum [paɪˈriːθrəm] N pyrèthre *m*

pyretic [paɪˈretɪk] ADJ pyrétique

Pyrex® ['paɪreks] ① N pyrex® *m* ② COMP [*dish*] en pyrex®

pyrexia [paɪˈreksɪə] N pyrexie *f*

pyrexic [paɪˈreksɪk] ADJ pyrexique

pyrites [paɪˈraɪtiːz] N (*pl* **pyrites**) pyrite *f*; **iron ~** sulfure *m* de fer, fer *m* sulfuré

pyritic [paɪˈrɪtɪk] ADJ pyriteux

pyro... ['paɪərəʊ] PREF pyro...

pyromania [,paɪrəʊˈmeɪnɪə] N pyromanie *f*

pyromaniac [,paɪrəʊˈmeɪnɪæk] N pyromane *mf*, incendiaire *mf*

pyrotechnic [,paɪrəʊˈteknɪk] ① ADJ pyrotechnique; **~ display** feu(x) *m(pl)* d'artifice ② N (*NonC: Phys*) **~s** pyrotechnie *f*; (*pl: fig hum*) feux *mpl* d'artifice

Pyrrhic ['pɪrɪk] ADJ **~ victory** victoire *f* à la Pyrrhus

Pyrrhus ['pɪrəs] N Pyrrhus *m*

Pythagoras [paɪˈθægərəs] N Pythagore *m*

Pythagorean [paɪˈθægəˈrɪən] ADJ (*gen*) pythagoricien; [*number, letter*] pythagorique

python ['paɪθən] N python *m*

pyx [pɪks] N (*in church*) ciboire *m*; (*for sick communions*) pyxide *f*

pzazz⁎ [pəˈzæz] N (*US*) = **piz(z)azz**

Q

Q, q [kjuː] N (= *letter*) Q, q *m*; **Q for Queen** ≈ Q comme Québec → **P¹**

Qatar [kæ'tɑːʳ] **1** N **a** (= *country*) le Qatar **b** (= *inhabitant*) Qatari(e) *m(f)* **2** ADJ qatari

QC [,kjuː'siː] N (*Brit Jur*) (ABBR = **Queen's Counsel**) → **counsel**

QE2 [,kjuːiː'tuː] N (*Brit Naut*) (ABBR = **Queen Elizabeth II**) paquebot

QED [,kjuːiː'diː] (*Math*) (ABBR = **quod erat demonstrandum**) CQFD

qt N ABBR = **quart(s)**

q.t. [kjuː'tiː] N (ABBR = **quiet**) **on the ~*** en douce*, en cachette

Q-tip® ['kjuːtɪp] N coton-tige® *m*

qty N ABBR = **quantity**

qua [kweɪ] ADV **the actor ~ actor** l'acteur en tant que tel; **religion ~ religion** la religion en tant que telle

quack¹ [kwæk] **1** N coin-coin *m inv* (*cri du canard*) **2** VI faire coin-coin **3** COMP ► **quack-quack** N (*baby talk*) coin-coin *m inv*

quack²* [kwæk] N (= *imposter, bogus doctor*) charlatan *m*; (*hum = doctor*) toubib* *m*

quackery ['kwækərɪ] N (*NonC*) charlatanisme *m*

quad¹ [kwɒd] **1** N ABBR = **quadruplet, quadrangle** **2** COMP ► **quad bike** N moto *f* à quatre roues motrices

quad²* [kwɒd] N = **quod**

quadr... PREF = **quadri...**

Quadragesima [kwɒdrə'dʒesɪmə] N Quadragésime *f*

quadrangle ['kwɒdræŋgl] N **a** (*Math*) quadrilatère *m* **b** (= *courtyard*) cour *f*

quadrangular [kwɒ'dræŋgjʊləʳ] ADJ quadrangulaire

quadrant ['kwɒdrənt] N [*of circle*] quadrant *m*, quart *m* de cercle

quadraphonic [,kwɒdrə'fɒnɪk] ADJ quadriphonique, tétraphonique; **in ~ (sound)** en quadriphonie, en tétraphonie

quadraphonics [,kwɒdrə'fɒnɪks] N (*NonC*) quadriphonie *f*, tétraphonie *f*

quadraphony [kwɒd'rɒfənɪ] N = **quadraphonics**

quadraplegic [,kwɒdrə'pliːdʒɪk] N, ADJ tétraplégique *mf*

quadrasonic [,kwɒdrə'sɒnɪk] ADJ quadriphonique, tétraphonique

quadrasonics [,kwɒdrə'sɒnɪks] N (*NonC*) quadriphonie *f*, tétraphonie *f*

quadrat ['kwɒdrət] N quadrat *m*

quadratic [kwɒ'drætɪk] (*Math*) **1** ADJ quadratique **2** COMP ► **quadratic equation** N équation *f* quadratique *or* du second degré

quadrature ['kwɒdrətʃəʳ] N quadrature *f*

quadrennial [,kwɒ'drenɪəl] ADJ quadriennal

quadri... ['kwɒdrɪ] PREF quadri..., quadru...

quadriceps ['kwɒdrɪseps] N (*pl* **quadricepses** *or* **quadriceps**) quadriceps *m*

quadrilateral [,kwɒdrɪ'lætərəl] (*Math*) **1** ADJ quadrilatère, quadrilatéral **2** N quadrilatère *m*

quadrilingual [,kwɒdrɪ'lɪŋgwəl] ADJ quadrilingue

quadrille [kwə'drɪl] N (*Dancing*) quadrille *m*

quadrillion [kwɒ'drɪljən] N (*Brit*) quatrillion *m*; (*US*) ancien quatrillion *m* (10¹⁵)

quadripartite [,kwɒdrɪ'pɑːtaɪt] ADJ quadriparti (-tie *or* -tite *f*)

quadriplegia [,kwɒdrɪ'pliːdʒɪə] N tétraplégie *f*, quadriplégie *f*

quadriplegic [,kwɒdrɪ'pliːdʒɪk] ADJ, N tétraplégique *mf*, quadriplégique *mf*

quadroon [kwɒ'druːn] N quarteron(ne) *m(f)*

quadrophonic [,kwɒdrə'fɒnɪk] ADJ = **quadraphonic**

quadruped ['kwɒdrʊped] ADJ, N quadrupède *m*

quadruple ['kwɒdrʊpl] **1** ADJ, N quadruple *m* **2** [kwɒ'druːpl] VTI quadrupler

quadruplet [kwɒ'druːplɪt] N quadruplé(e) *m(f)*

quadruplicate [kwɒ'druːplɪkɪt] **1** ADJ quadruple **2** N **in ~** en quatre exemplaires

quaff [kwɒf] VT (†† *or hum*) [+ *glass*] vider à longs traits; [+ *wine*] lamper

quag [kwæg] N = **quagmire**

quagga ['kwægə] N (*pl* **quaggas** *or* **quagga**) couagga *m*

quagmire ['kwægmaɪəʳ] N (*lit, fig*) bourbier *m*

quahaug, quahog ['kwɑːhɒg] N (*US*) clam *m*

quail¹ [kweɪl] VI [*person*] perdre courage, reculer (**before** devant); **his heart** *or* **spirit ~ed** son courage l'a trahi

quail² [kweɪl] N (*pl* **quail** *or* **quails**) (= *bird*) caille *f*

quaint [kweɪnt] ADJ **a** (= *picturesque*) [*place*] pittoresque; [*person*] original; **a ~ little village** un petit village pittoresque *or* qui a du cachet **b** (= *old-fashioned*) [*custom, tradition, word, notion*] désuet (-ète *f*); (*pej*) vieillot; **how ~!** comme c'est curieux!

quaintly ['kweɪntlɪ] ADV (= *strangely*) curieusement; **~ old-fashioned** d'un charme désuet; **a pub ~ called** *or* **named "The Dew Drop"** un pub qui porte le nom désuet de «La Goutte de Rosée»

quaintness ['kweɪntnɪs] N **a** [*of place, object*] (= *picturesqueness*) pittoresque *m*; (= *old-fashionedness*) charme *m* désuet, charme *m* vieillot **b** (= *peculiarity*) [*of custom, word, idea, question*] côté *m* or aspect *m* curieux

quake [kweɪk] **1** VI [*earth, person*] trembler; **I was quaking (in my boots*)** je tremblais comme une feuille; **to ~ with fear** trembler de peur **2** N (ABBR = **earthquake**) tremblement *m* de terre, séisme *m*

Quaker ['kweɪkəʳ] **1** N quaker(esse) *m(f)* **2** COMP [*community, school*] de quakers; [*person, family*] quaker (*f inv*); [*beliefs*] des quakers ► **Quaker meeting** N réunion *f* de qua-

kers ► **Quaker meeting house** N église *f* de quakers

Quakerism ['kweɪkərɪzəm] N quakerisme *m*

qualification [,kwɒlɪfɪ'keɪʃən] N **a** (= *ability*) compétence *f* (**for** en, **to do** pour faire), aptitude *f* (**for** à), capacité *f* (**to do** pour faire); **I doubt his ~ to teach English** je doute qu'il ait les compétences requises *or* qu'il ait les capacités requises pour enseigner l'anglais; **we have never questioned his ~ for the job** nous n'avons jamais mis en doute son aptitude à remplir le poste **b** (= *degree, diploma etc*) diplôme *m*, titre *m* (**in** de); **his only ~ for the job was his experience in similar work** seule son expérience dans des domaines similaires le qualifiait pour ce travail; **what are your ~s?** (= *skill, degrees, experience etc*) quelle est votre formation?; (*also* **paper ~s**) qu'est-ce que vous avez comme diplômes *or* qualifications professionnelles?; **he has a lot of experience but no paper ~s** *or* **formal ~s** il a beaucoup d'expérience mais il n'a aucun diplôme *or* il n'a aucun titre *or* il n'a pas de qualifications professionnelles; **I have no teaching ~(s)** je n'ai pas le(s) diplôme(s) requis pour enseigner **c** (= *limitation*) réserve *f*, restriction *f*; **to accept a plan with ~(s)** accepter un projet avec des réserves *or* avec des restrictions; **without ~(s)** sans réserves *or* restrictions **d** (= *graduation*) **my first job after ~ (as a vet)** mon premier poste après que j'ai obtenu mon diplôme (de vétérinaire) **e** (*gen, Gram: qualifying*) qualification *f*

qualified ['kwɒlɪfaɪd] ADJ **a** (= *trained, suitable*) [*person, staff, craftsman, player, pilot*] qualifié; [*engineer, doctor, nurse, teacher, accountant*] diplômé; **suitably ~ candidates** les candidats ayant les qualifications requises; **~ for a job** qualifié pour un poste *or* un travail; **he was well ~ for the post of president** il avait les qualités requises pour être président; **~ to do sth** qualifié pour faire qch, habilité à faire qch (*frm*); **he is ~ to teach** il a les qualifications requises pour enseigner; **they are not ~ to vote** ils ne sont pas habilités à voter; **he is well ~ to captain the team** il est tout à fait qualifié pour être la capitaine de l'équipe; **I'm not ~ to speak for her** je ne suis pas habilité à parler en son nom; **I don't feel ~ to judge** je ne me sens pas en mesure d'en juger **b** (= *limited*) [*praise, support, approval*] mitigé; [*acceptance*] conditionnel; **a ~ success** une demi-réussite; **a ~ yes** un oui mitigé, un oui mais

qualifier ['kwɒlɪfaɪəʳ] N (*Gram*) qualificatif *m*, qualificateur *m*; (*Sport*) (= *team*) équipe *f* qualifiée; (= *person*) athlète *mf* qualifié(e)

▼ **qualify** ['kwɒlɪfaɪ] **1** VT **a** (= *make competent*) **to ~ sb to do/for sth** (*gen*) qualifier qn pour faire/pour qch; [*experience etc*] donner à qn les compétences *or* qualités requises pour faire/pour qch; [*degree, diploma*] donner à qn les diplômes *or* titres requis pour faire/pour qch; [*trade diploma, certificates*] donner à qn les qualifications professionnelles nécessaires

pour faire/pour qch; (*Jur*) **to ~ sb to do** habiliter qn à faire; **that doesn't ~ him to speak on it** cela ne lui donne pas qualité pour en parler
b (= *modify*) [+ *approval, support, praise*] mettre des réserves à; [+ *statement, opinion*] nuancer; **to ~ one's acceptance of sth** accepter qch sous réserve or sous condition; **I think you should ~ that remark** je pense que vous devriez nuancer cette remarque
c (= *describe*) qualifier (**as** de); (*Gram*) qualifier
2 VI obtenir son diplôme (or son brevet etc) (**in** en); **to ~ as a doctor/a nurse/an engineer** obtenir son diplôme de médecin/d'infirmière/d'ingénieur; **he has qualified as a teacher** il a obtenu son diplôme de professeur; **while he was ~ing as an architect** pendant qu'il faisait des études d'architecture; **to ~ for a job** avoir les compétences requises pour un poste; **he doesn't ~ for that post** il n'a pas les compétences requises (pour ce poste); **does he ~?** est-ce qu'il remplit les conditions requises?; (*Sport*) **to ~ for the final** se qualifier pour la finale; (*fig*) **he hardly qualifies as a poet** il ne mérite pas vraiment le nom de poète

qualifying ['kwɒlɪfaɪɪŋ] ADJ **a** [*mark*] de passage, qui permet de passer; [*examination*] d'entrée; [*score*] qui permet de se qualifier; **~ period** (*gen*) période f d'attente; (*Jur*) période f probatoire; (*Sport*) **~ heat** éliminatoire f; **~ round** série f éliminatoire; (*St Ex*) **~ shares** actions fpl de garantie **b** (*Gram*) qualificatif

qualitative ['kwɒlɪtətɪv] ADJ qualitatif
qualitatively ['kwɒlɪtətɪvlɪ] ADV qualitativement

quality ['kwɒlɪtɪ] **1** N **a** (= *nature, kind*) qualité f; **of the best ~** de première qualité, de premier ordre or choix; **of good** or **high ~** de bonne qualité, de qualité supérieure; **of poor** or **bad** or **low ~** de mauvaise qualité, de qualité inférieure; **the ~ of life** la qualité de la vie
b (*NonC* = *goodness*) qualité f; **guarantee of ~** garantie f de qualité; **it's ~ rather than quantity that counts** c'est la qualité qui compte plus que la quantité; **this wine has ~** ce vin a de la qualité or est de qualité; **he has real ~** il a de la classe
c (= *attribute*) qualité f; **natural qualities** qualités fpl naturelles; **one of his (good) qualities** une de ses qualités; **one of his bad qualities** un de ses défauts; **he has many artistic qualities** il a beaucoup de qualités or de dons mpl artistiques
d [*of voice, sound*] qualité f, timbre m
e († or *hum* = *high rank*) qualité† f
2 COMP [*car, film, product*] de qualité ► **quality control** N (*Ind*) contrôle m de qualité ► **quality controller** N (*Ind*) contrôleur m, -euse f de la qualité ► **quality papers** NPL (*Press*) presse f de qualité ► **quality time** N moments mpl de qualité

qualm [kwɑːm] N **a** (= *scruple*) doute m, scrupule m; (= *misgiving*) appréhension f, inquiétude f; **~s of conscience** scrupules mpl de conscience; **he did it without a ~** il l'a fait sans le moindre scrupule; **I would feel no ~s about doing that** je n'aurais pas le moindre scrupule à faire cela; **I had some ~s about his future** j'avais quelques inquiétudes sur or pour son avenir **b** (= *nausea*) nausée f

quandary ['kwɒndərɪ] N dilemme m; **to be in a ~** être pris dans un dilemme; **he was in a ~ about** or **as to** or **over what to do** il était bien embarrassé de savoir quoi faire; **that got him out of a ~** ça l'a sorti d'un dilemme

quango ['kwæŋɡəʊ] N (*Brit*) (ABBR = **quasi-autonomous nongovernmental organization**)

organisation f non gouvernementale quasi autonome

┌─ **QUANGO** ─┐

Cet acronyme de « *quasi-autonomous nongovernmental organization* » désigne des organismes mis en place par le gouvernement britannique dans les années 70 mais qui ne relèvent d'aucun ministère: c'est le cas par exemple de la Commission pour l'égalité des chances (*Equal Opportunities Commission*) ou de la Commission pour les relations interraciales (*Race Relations Board*). Certaines de ces organisations disposent d'un pouvoir de décision, d'autres ont un rôle purement consultatif. → EOC, EEOC

quanta ['kwɒntə] NPL of **quantum**
quantifiable [ˌkwɒntɪ'faɪəbl] ADJ quantifiable
quantifier ['kwɒntɪfaɪə'] N (*Ling, Philos, Math*) quantificateur m
quantify ['kwɒntɪfaɪ] VT (*gen, Philos*) quantifier
quantitative ['kwɒntɪtətɪv] ADJ (*gen*) quantitatif; (*Ling, Poetry*) de quantité
quantitatively ['kwɒntɪtətɪvlɪ] ADV quantitativement

quantity ['kwɒntɪtɪ] **1** N (*gen, Ling, Math, Poetry*) quantité f; **a small ~ of rice** une petite quantité de riz; **what ~ do you want?** quelle quantité (en) voulez-vous?; **in ~** en (grande) quantité; **in large quantities** en grandes quantités; **a ~ of** ◊ **any ~ of** ◊ **quantities of** une quantité de, (des) quantités de, un grand nombre de → **quality, unknown** COMP (*Comm*) [*production*] sur une grande échelle, en série ► **quantity mark** N (*Ling, Poetry*) signe m de quantité ► **quantity surveying** N (*NonC: Brit*) métrage m ► **quantity surveyor** N (*Brit*) métreur m (vérificateur)

quantum ['kwɒntəm] (*pl* **quanta**) **1** N quantum m **2** COMP ► **quantum leap** N (*fig*) bond m prodigieux; (*forwards*) bond m en avant; **to take** or **make a ~ leap** faire un bond (en avant) prodigieux ► **quantum mechanics** N (*NonC: Phys*) mécanique f quantique ► **quantum number** N nombre m quantique ► **quantum theory** N théorie f quantique or des quanta

quarantine ['kwɒrəntiːn] **1** N quarantaine f (*pour raisons sanitaires*); **in ~** en quarantaine **2** VT mettre en quarantaine **3** COMP [*regulations, period*] de quarantaine

quark [kwɑːk] N quark m

quarrel ['kwɒrəl] **1** N (= *dispute*) querelle f, dispute f; (*more intellectual*) différend m; (= *breach*) brouille f; **I had a ~ with him yesterday** je me suis disputé or querellé avec lui hier; **they've had a ~** (*argued*) ils se sont disputés or querellés; (= *fallen out*) ils se sont brouillés; **the ~ between the professor and his assistant** la querelle entre le professeur et son assistant; (*longer: more frm*) la querelle qui oppose (or opposait etc) le professeur à son assistant; **to start a ~** provoquer or susciter une querelle or dispute; **to pick a ~ with sb** ◊ **to try to start a ~ with sb** chercher querelle à qn; (*fig*) **I have no ~ with you** je n'ai rien contre vous; **he had no ~ with what we had done** il n'avait rien à redire à ce que nous avions fait
2 VI (= *have a dispute*) se quereller, se disputer (**with sb** avec qn, **about, over** à propos de); (= *break off friendship*) se brouiller (**with sb** avec qn); (*fig*) **I cannot ~ with that** je n'ai rien à redire à cela; **what he ~s with is ...** ce contre quoi il s'insurge c'est ...

quarrelling, quarreling (US) ['kwɒrəlɪŋ] **1** N (*NonC*) disputes fpl, querelles fpl; (*petty*) chamailleries* fpl **2** ADJ qui se disputent
quarrelsome ['kwɒrəlsəm] ADJ querelleur
quarrier ['kwɒrɪə'] N (ouvrier m) carrier m
quarry¹ ['kwɒrɪ] **1** N carrière f → **marble 2** VT **a** [+ *stone*] extraire **b** [+ *hillside*]

exploiter (*en carrière*) **3** VI exploiter une carrière; **they are ~ing for marble** ils exploitent une carrière de marbre **4** COMP ► **quarry tile** N carreau m ► **quarry-tiled floor** N sol m carrelé
► **quarry out** VT SEP [+ *block, stone*] extraire
quarry² ['kwɒrɪ] N [*of animal, bird etc*] proie f; (*Hunting* = *game*) gibier m; **the detectives lost their ~** les policiers ont perdu la trace de celui qu'il pourchassaient
quarryman ['kwɒrɪmən] N (*pl* **-men**) (ouvrier m) carrier m

quart [kwɔːt] N (= *measure*) ≈ litre m (*Brit* = 1,136 litre, *US* = 0,946 litre); (*fig*) **it's like trying to put a ~ into a pint pot** autant essayer de vider la mer avec une petite cuiller

quarter ['kwɔːtə'] **1** N **a** (= *fourth part*) quart m; **to divide sth into ~s** diviser qch en quatre (parties égales) or en (quatre) quartiers; **a ~ (of a pound) of tea** un quart (de livre) de thé; **a ~ full/empty** au quart plein/vide; **it's a ~ gone already** il y en a déjà un quart de parti; **a ~ as big as** quatre fois moins grand que; **I bought it for a ~ of the price** or **for ~ the price** je l'ai acheté au quart du prix or pour le quart de son prix
b (*in expressions of time*) quart m (d'heure); **a ~ of an hour** un quart d'heure; **a ~ to seven** ◊ **a ~ of seven** (*US*) sept heures moins le quart or moins un quart; **a ~ past six** ◊ **a ~ after six** (*US*) six heures un quart or et quart; (*on steering wheel*) **to drive with one's hands at a ~ to three** conduire avec les mains à neuf heures et quart; **it wasn't the ~ yet** il n'était pas encore le quart; **the clock strikes the ~s** l'horloge sonne les quarts
c (= *specific fourth parts*) [*of year*] trimestre m; (*US and Can money*) quart m de dollar, vingt-cinq cents mpl; (*Brit weight*) = 28 livres (= 12,7 kg); (*US weight*) = 25 livres (= 11,34 kg); (*Her*) quartier m; [*of beef, apple etc*] quartier m; [*of moon*] quartier m; **to pay by the ~** payer tous les trois mois or par trimestre; **a ~'s rent** un terme (de loyer) → **forequarters, hindquarters**
d (= *compass point*) point m cardinal; (*Naut*) **on the port/starboard ~** par la hanche de bâbord/tribord; **from all ~s** de toutes parts, de tous côtés; (*frm*) **you must report that to the proper ~** vous devez signaler cela à qui de droit; **in responsible ~s** dans les milieux autorisés
e (= *part of town*) quartier m; **the Latin ~** le quartier latin
f (*NonC: liter* = *mercy*) quartier m (liter), grâce f; **to give/cry ~** faire/demander quartier
2 quarters NPL (= *lodgings*) résidence f, domicile m; (*Mil*) quartiers mpl; (*temporary*) cantonnement m; **they are living in very cramped ~s** ils sont logés très à l'étroit → **married**
3 VT **a** (= *divide into four*) diviser en quatre (parts égales), diviser en (quatre) quartiers; [+ *traitor's body*] écarteler; (*Her*) écarteler → **hang b** (= *lodge*) (*Mil*) [+ *troops*] caserner; (*temporarily*) cantonner; (*gen*) loger (**on** chez)
c **to ~ the ground** [*dogs*] quêter; **to ~ a town in search of sb** [*police etc*] quadriller une ville à la recherche de qn
4 ADJ quart de; **the ~ part of** le quart de; **a ~ share in sth** (une part d')un quart de qch → **5**
5 COMP ► **quarter day** N (*Fin, Jur*) (jour m du) terme m ► **quarter-deck** N (*Naut*) plage f arrière; [*of sailing ship*] gaillard m d'arrière ► **quarter final** N (*Sport*) quart m de finale ► **quarter-finalist** N (*Sport*) quart de finaliste mf ► **quarter-hour** N (*period of time*) quart m d'heure; (*division of clock face*) **on the ~-hour** tous les quarts d'heure ► **quarter light** N (*Brit Aut*) déflecteur m ► **quarter mile** N (*Sport*) (course f d'un) quart m de mille ► **quarter note** N (*US Mus*) noire f ► **quarter pound** N quart m de livre ► **quarter-pound** ADJ d'un quart de livre

► **quarter-pounder** N (*Culin*) hamburger contenant un steak haché d'environ 100 grammes ► **quarter sessions** NPL (*Jur*) (= *sessions*) ≈ assises *fpl* trimestrielles (de tribunal de grande instance); (= *court*) ≈ tribunal *m* de grande instance (*jusqu'en 1972*) ► **quarter turn** N quart *m* de tour ► **quarter window** N (*US Aut*) déflecteur *m*

quarterback ['kwɔːtəbæk] (*US*) 1 N (*Ftbl*) stratège *m*, quarterback *m* 2 VT a (*Ftbl*) diriger la stratégie de b (*fig*) gérer 3 VI (*Ftbl*) servir de stratège

quartering ['kwɔːtərɪŋ] N (*NonC*) a (= *splitting into quarters*) division *f* en quatre; (*Her*) écartelure *f* b (*Mil* = *lodging*) cantonnement *m*

quarterly ['kwɔːtəlɪ] 1 ADJ trimestriel 2 N (= *periodical*) publication *f* trimestrielle 3 ADV tous les trois mois

quartermaster ['kwɔːtə,mɑːstə'] 1 a (*Mil*) intendant *m* militaire de troisième classe b (*Naut*) maître *m* de manœuvre 2 COMP ► **quartermaster general** (*Mil*) intendant *m* général d'armée de première classe ► **quartermaster sergeant** N (*Mil*) intendant *m* militaire adjoint

quartet(te) [kwɔː'tet] N (*of classical music players*) quatuor *m*; (*of jazz players*) quartette *m*; (*hum* = *four people*) quatuor* *m*

quarto ['kwɔːtəʊ] 1 N in-quarto *m* 2 ADJ (*paper*) in-quarto *inv*

quartz ['kwɔːts] 1 N quartz *m* 2 COMP de or en quartz ► **quartz clock** N pendule *f* à quartz ► **quartz crystal** N cristal *m* de quartz ► **quartz(-iodine) lamp** N lampe *f* à iode ► **quartz watch** N montre *f* à quartz

quartzite ['kwɔːtsaɪt] N quartzite *m*

quasar ['kweɪzɑː'] N quasar *m*

quash [kwɒʃ] VT (+ *decision, verdict, judgement*) casser, annuler; (+ *rebellion*) réprimer, étouffer; (+ *proposal, suggestion*) rejeter

quasi- ['kweɪzaɪ] PREF (+ *n*) quasi-; (+ *adj*) quasi, presque; **~marriage** quasi-mariage *m*; **~religious** quasi or presque religieux

quatercentenary [ˌkwætəsen'tiːnərɪ] N quatrième centenaire *m*

quaternary [kwə'tɜːnərɪ] 1 ADJ (*Chem, Geol, Math*) quaternaire 2 N (= *set of four*) ensemble *m* de quatre; (= *number four*) quatre *m*; (*Geol*) **the Quaternary** le quaternaire

quatrain ['kwɒtreɪn] N quatrain *m*

quaver ['kweɪvə'] 1 N a (*esp Brit Mus* = *note*) croche *f* b (= *voice tremor*) tremblement *m*, chevrotement *m* 2 VI (*voice*) chevroter, trembloter; (*person*) chevroter, parler d'une voix chevrotante or tremblotante 3 VT (*also* **~ out**) chevroter 4 COMP ► **quaver rest** N (*esp Brit Mus*) demi-soupir *m*

quavering ['kweɪvərɪŋ] 1 ADJ chevrotant, tremblotant 2 N tremblotement *m*

quaveringly ['kweɪvərɪŋlɪ] ADV d'une voix chevrotante or tremblotante, avec des tremblements dans la voix

quavery ['kweɪvərɪ] ADJ = **quavering 1**

quay [kiː] N (*Naut etc*) quai *m*; **on the ~** sur le quai; **along the ~** le long du quai

quayside ['kiːsaɪd] N quai *m*; (= *whole area*) quais *mpl*; **the ship drew up along the ~** le navire est arrivé à quai

queasiness ['kwiːzɪnɪs] N (*NonC*) nausée *f*, malaise *m*

queasy ['kwiːzɪ] ADJ a (= *nauseous*) **he was ~ ◊ he felt ~** il avait mal au cœur, il avait la nausée; **it makes me (feel) ~** ça me donne mal au cœur, ça me donne la nausée; **his stomach was ~** il avait l'estomac barbouillé b (= *uncomfortable*) mal à l'aise; **I had a ~ feeling about the whole thing** tout ça me mettait mal à l'aise; **to feel ~ (about sth)** se sentir mal à l'aise (à propos de qch)

Quebec [kwɪ'bek] 1 N a (= *city*) Québec b (= *province*) le Québec 2 ADJ québécois; (*Ling*) **~ French** québécois *m*

Quebec(k)er [kwɪ'bekə'] N Québécois(e) *m(f)*

Quebecois [kebe'kwɑː] N (*pl inv* = *person*) Québécois(e) *m(f)*

queen [kwiːn] 1 N a (*also fig*) reine *f*; **Queen Elizabeth** la reine Élisabeth; **she was ~ to George III** elle était l'épouse de Georges III; (*iro*) **Queen Anne's dead!*** ce n'est pas une nouvelle!, tu ne nous apprends rien! → **3**; **~ of the ball** reine *f* du bal → **beauty, Mary, May** b (= *ant, bee, wasp*) reine *f* c (*Chess*) dame *f*, reine *f* d (*Cards*) dame *f* e (* *pej* = *homosexual*) folle‡ *f*, tante‡ *f* 2 VT a* **to ~ it** faire la grande dame; **to ~ it over sb** prendre des airs d'impératrice avec qn b (*Chess*) (+ *pawn*) damer 3 COMP ► **Queen Anne** ADJ (*furniture etc*) de l'époque de la reine Anne (*début 18ᵉ*) ► **queen bee** N reine *f* des abeilles; (*fig*) **she's the ~ bee*** c'est elle qui commande ► **queen consort** N reine *f* (*épouse du roi*) ► **queen dowager** N reine *f* douairière ► **Queen Mother** N reine *f* mère ► **Queen's Bench** N (*Brit Jur*) cour *f* supérieure de justice ► **Queen's Counsel** N (*Jur*) avocat *m* de la Couronne ► **Queen's evidence** N (*Jur*) **to turn Queen's evidence** témoigner contre ses complices ► **the Queen's highway** la voie publique ► **queen-size bed** N grand lit double ► **Queen's Messenger** N courrier *m* diplomatique ► **Queen's speech** N (*Brit*) discours *m* de la reine

---
QUEEN'S SPEECH, KING'S SPEECH
---

*Chaque année, au moment de la rentrée parlementaire, le monarque britannique prononce une allocution devant les deux chambres du Parlement: c'est le discours de la reine (*Queen's speech*) ou du roi (*King's speech*), qui est diffusé à la télévision et à la radio. Ce discours est rédigé par le gouvernement, qui y expose son programme pour l'année à venir ainsi que les lois qu'il désire proposer. Conformément à la tradition, le souverain utilise l'expression « mon gouvernement ».*

queencake ['kwiːnkeɪk] N petit gâteau aux raisins secs

queenly ['kwiːnlɪ] ADJ (*woman*) au port de reine; (*behaviour*) de reine

Queensland ['kwiːnzlənd] N le Queensland; **in ~** dans le Queensland

queer [kwɪə'] 1 ADJ a (= *strange*) étrange, bizarre; (= *suspicious*) louche, suspect; **there's something ~ going on** il se passe quelque chose de louche; **there's something ~ about the way he always has money** c'est louche qu'il ait toujours de l'argent; **a ~ fellow** or **fish*** un curieux personnage or bonhomme; **a ~ customer*** un drôle d'individu or de type*; (*pej*) **~ in the head*** toqué*; (*Brit*) **to be in Queer Street*** être dans une mauvaise passe b (‡* = *homosexual*) (*gen pej*) (*man*) pédé‡ (*pej*); (*used by some homosexuals*) (*culture, politics, cinema*) gay *inv*; (*pej*) **he's/she's ~** c'est un pédé‡/une gouine‡ (*pej*) c (*Brit* † = *unwell*) **to feel ~** se sentir tout chose; **to come over ~** avoir un malaise d (*US*) **to be ~ for sth*** être dingue* de qch 2 N (†‡ *pej* = *homosexual*) (= *male*) pédé‡ *m*, pédale‡ *f*; (= *female*) gouine‡ *f* 3 VT gâter, abîmer; (*Brit fig*) **to ~ sb's pitch** couper l'herbe sous le pied à or de qn 4 COMP ► **queer-bashing*** N chasse *f* aux pédés‡, agressions *fpl* contre les homosexuels ► **queer-looking** ADJ **he was a ~-looking man** il avait une drôle d'allure ► **queer-**

sounding ADJ **it was a ~-sounding name** c'était un nom bizarre

queerly ['kwɪəlɪ] ADV bizarrement

queerness ['kwɪənɪs] N étrangeté *f*, bizarrerie *f*

quell [kwel] VT (+ *rebellion, rage, anxieties*) réprimer, étouffer; **she ~ed him with a glance** elle l'a fait rentrer sous terre d'un regard, elle l'a foudroyé du regard

quench [kwentʃ] VT (+ *flames, fire*) éteindre; (+ *steel etc*) tremper; (+ *hope, desire*) réprimer, étouffer; (+ *enthusiasm*) refroidir; **to ~ one's thirst** se désaltérer

quenchless ['kwentʃlɪs] ADJ (*liter*) inextinguible

quern [kwɜːn] N moulin *m* à bras (*pour le grain*)

querulous ['kwerʊləs] ADJ grincheux

querulously ['kwerʊləslɪ] ADV d'un ton grincheux

query ['kwɪərɪ] 1 N a (= *question*) question *f*; (= *doubt*) doute *m*; **readers' queries** questions *fpl* des lecteurs; **this raises a ~ about the viability of the scheme** cela met en question la viabilité de ce projet b (*Gram* = *question mark*) point *m* d'interrogation c (*Comput*) interrogation *f* 2 VT a (+ *statement, motive, evidence*) mettre en doute or en question; **I ~ that!** je me permets d'en douter!; **to ~ whether ...** demander si ..., chercher à savoir si ...; (+ *part of text*) marquer d'un point d'interrogation 3 COMP ► **query language** N (*Comput*) langage *m* d'interrogation

quest [kwest] (*liter*) 1 N quête *f* (*liter*) (**for** de); **in ~ of** en quête de 2 VI **to ~ for sth** être en quête de qch

questing ['kwestɪŋ] ADJ (*hand*) chercheur; (*look, voice*) interrogateur (-trice *f*)

▼ **question** ['kwestʃən] 1 N a question *f* (*also Parl*); **to ask sb a ~ ◊ to put a ~ to sb ◊ to put down a ~ for sb** (*Parl*) poser une question à qn; **what a ~ to ask!** quelle question!, belle question! (*iro*); (*prevaricating*) **(that's a) good ~!** (c'est une) bonne question!; (*Gram*) **indirect** or **oblique ~** interrogation *f* indirecte; **to put sth to the ~** soumettre qch au vote → **leading¹, pop¹, sixty** b (*NonC* = *doubt*) doute *m*; **there is no ~ about it** cela ne fait aucun doute; **there's no ~ that this is better** une chose est sûre, ceci est mieux; **to accept/obey without ~** accepter/obéir sans poser de questions; **her loyalty is beyond ~** sa loyauté ne fait pas l'ombre d'un doute; **she is without ~ one of the greatest writers of her generation** elle est sans conteste l'un des plus grands écrivains de sa génération → **bring** c (= *matter, subject*) question *f*; **that's the ~!** là est la question!, c'est là (toute) la question!; **that's not the ~** là n'est pas la question, il ne s'agit pas de cela; **that's another ~ altogether** ça c'est une tout autre affaire; **the person in ~** la personne en question or dont il s'agit; **to call sth into ~** remettre qch en question; **there's some/no ~ of closing the shop** il est/il n'est pas question de fermer or qu'on ferme (*subj*) le magasin; **there's no ~ of that ◊ that is out of the ~** il n'en est pas question, c'est hors de question; **the ~ is how many** la question c'est de savoir combien, il s'agit de savoir combien; (*in concluding*) reste à savoir combien; **the ~ is to decide ...** il s'agit de décider ...; (*in concluding*) reste à décider ...; **the German ~** la question allemande, le problème allemand; **it is a ~ of sincerity** c'est une question de sincérité; **it's (all) a ~ of what you want to do eventually** tout dépend de ce que tu veux faire en fin de compte; **it's an open ~** la question reste posée or ouverte; **it's an open ~ whether ...** il reste à savoir si ..., personne ne sait si ...; **success is merely a ~ of time** le succès n'est qu'une affaire or qu'une question de temps → **burning, time**

[2] VT [a] interroger, questionner (**on** sur, **about** au sujet de, à propos de); (Police) interroger; **we ~ed him closely to find out whether ...** nous l'avons soumis à un interrogatoire pour savoir si ...; **I will not be ~ed about it** je refuse d'être l'objet de questions à ce sujet [b] [+ motive, account, sb's honesty] mettre en doute or en question; [+ claim] contester; **to ~ whether ...** douter que ... (+ subj)

[3] COMP ► **question mark** N point *m* d'interrogation; (fig) **there is a ~ mark over whether he meant to do it** on ne sait pas au juste s'il avait l'intention de le faire; (fig) **a big ~ mark hangs over his future** l'incertitude plane sur son avenir ► **question tag** N fin *f* de phrase interrogative ► **question time** N (Brit Parl) questions *fpl* écrites ou orales (adressées par des parlementaires au gouvernement)

questionable ['kwestʃənəbl] ADJ [quality, taste] douteux; [value] douteux, discutable; [statement, figures] discutable; [motive, behaviour, practice, deal] suspect; **it is ~ whether ...** il est douteux que ... (+ subj)

questioner ['kwestʃənər] N personne *f* qui interroge; **she looked at her ~** elle regarda la personne qui l'interrogeait

questioning ['kwestʃənɪŋ] [1] N interrogation *f* [2] ADJ [a] (= curious) [nature] curieux; **to have a ~ mind** être curieux de nature [b] (= querying) [look, expression] interrogateur (-trice *f*)

questioningly ['kwestʃənɪŋlɪ] ADV d'un air interrogateur

questionmaster ['kwestʃən‚mɑːstər] N meneur *m*, -euse *f* de jeu; (Rad, TV) animateur *m*, -trice *f*

questionnaire [‚kwestʃə'neər] N questionnaire *m*

queue [kjuː] [1] N [a] (Brit) [of people] queue *f*, file *f* (d'attente); [of cars] file *f*; **to stand in a ~ ◊ to form a ~** faire la queue; **go to the end of the ~!** prenez la queue!; **he joined the theatre ~** il s'est joint aux personnes qui faisaient la queue au théâtre; **ticket ~** queue *f* devant les guichets → **jump** [b] (Comput) file *f* d'attente [2] VI (Brit: also ~ **up**) [people, cars] faire la queue (**for** pour); **we ~d (up) for an hour** nous avons fait une heure de queue; (Brit fig) **people are queuing up to ...** les gens se battent pour ... [3] COMP ► **queue-jump** VI (Brit) passer avant son tour, ne pas attendre son tour ► **queue-jumper** N (Brit) resquilleur *m*, -euse *f* (qui passe avant son tour) ► **queue-jumping** N (Brit) resquille *f* (pour passer avant son tour)

quibble ['kwɪbl] [1] N chicane *f*, argutie *f*; **that's just a ~** c'est couper les cheveux en quatre* [2] VI chicaner, ergoter (**over** sur)

quibbler ['kwɪblər] N chicaneur *m*, -euse *f*, chicanier *m*, -ière *f*, ergoteur *m*, -euse *f*

quibbling ['kwɪblɪŋ] [1] ADJ [person] ergoteur, chicaneur, chicanier; [argument] captieux, spécieux; [objection] spécieux [2] N (NonC) chicanerie *f*

quiche [kiːʃ] N quiche *f*

quick [kwɪk] [1] ADJ [a] (= rapid) [pulse, train, movement, route, decision, method] rapide; [recovery, answer] prompt; **be ~!** dépêche-toi!; **try to be ~er next time** essaie de faire plus vite la prochaine fois; **at a ~ pace** d'un pas vif or rapide, d'un bon pas; (Mil) **~ march!** en avant, marche!; **I had a ~ chat with her** or **a few ~ words with her** j'ai échangé quelques mots (rapides) avec elle; **going cheap for a ~ sale** sacrifié pour vente rapide; **we had a ~ meal** nous avons mangé en vitesse or sur le pouce*; **to have a ~ one** (* = drink) prendre un pot* en vitesse; (* = sex) tirer un coup en vitesse*; **it's ~er by train** c'est plus rapide or ça va plus vite par le train; **he's a ~ worker** il tra-

vaille vite; (* iro) il ne perd pas de temps (iro), il va vite en besogne (iro) → **double-quick**, **draw**

[b] (= lively) [mind] vif, rapide; [child] vif, éveillé; **he's too ~ for me** il est trop rapide pour moi, il va trop vite pour moi; **he has a ~ eye for mistakes** il repère vite les fautes; **to have a ~ ear** avoir l'oreille fine; **to have a ~ wit** avoir la repartie facile or de la repartie → **4**; **he was ~ to see that ...** il a tout de suite vu or remarqué que ...; **she was ~ to point out that ...** elle n'a pas manqué de faire remarquer que ...; **to be ~ to take offence** être prompt à s'offenser, s'offenser pour un rien; **to have a ~ temper** s'emporter facilement, être soupe au lait* → **4**; (liter) **to be ~ to anger** avoir la tête chaude, être prompt à s'emporter; **he is ~ at figures** il calcule vite

[2] N [a] (Anat) vif *m*; **to bite one's nails to the ~** se ronger les ongles jusqu'au sang; (fig) **to cut** or **sting sb to the ~** piquer or blesser qn au vif

[b] (††, liter) **the ~ and the dead** les vivants *mpl* et les morts *mpl*

[3] ADV (= quickly) **~, over here!** vite, par ici!; **as ~ as lightning** or **as a flash** avec la rapidité de l'éclair → **quickly**

[4] COMP ► **quick-acting** ADJ [drug etc] qui agit rapidement ► **quick-assembly furniture** N (NonC) meubles *mpl* en kit ► **quick assets** NPL (Fin) actif *m* disponible à court terme ► **quick-change artist** N (Theat) spécialiste *mf* des transformations rapides ► **quick-drying** ADJ [paint, concrete] qui sèche rapidement ► **quick-fire** ADJ **a series of ~-fire questions** un feu roulant de questions; **to shoot ~-fire questions at sb** mitrailler qn de questions ► **quick-firing** ADJ (Mil) à tir rapide ► **quick fix** N (pej) solution *f* de fortune; **there is no ~ fix to the country's economic problems** il n'y a pas de solution miracle aux problèmes économiques du pays ► **quick-freeze** VT surgeler ► **quick money** N (NonC: Fin) capital *m* investi réalisable sur demande ► **quick-setting** ADJ [cement] à prise rapide; [jelly] qui prend facilement ► **quick-tempered** ADJ **to be ~-tempered** s'emporter facilement, être soupe au lait* inv ► **quick time** N (US Mil) marche *f* normale (120 pas/minute) ► **quick-witted** ADJ à l'esprit vif or délié; (in answering) qui a la repartie facile or de la repartie

quicken ['kwɪkən] [1] VT [a] (lit) accélérer, presser; (Mus) **to ~ the tempo** presser l'allure or la cadence → **pace¹** [b] (fig) [+ feelings, imagination] exciter, stimuler; [+ appetite] stimuler, aiguiser [2] VI [a] [pace, movement] s'accélérer, devenir or se faire plus rapide [b] [hope] se ranimer [c] [foetus] remuer

quickie* ['kwɪkɪ] [1] N chose *f* faite en vitesse or à la hâte; (= drink) pot* *m* pris en vitesse; (= question) question *f* éclair inv; (* = sex) coup *m* rapide*; (Cine) court-métrage *m* vite fait [2] COMP ► **quickie divorce** N divorce *m* rapide

quicklime ['kwɪklaɪm] N chaux *f* vive

quickly ['kwɪklɪ] ADV [a] (= with great speed) [speak, work] vite; **~!** vite!, dépêchez-vous!; **as ~ as possible** aussi vite que possible, au plus vite; **as ~ as I can** aussi vite que je peux [b] (= in short time) [die, embrace etc] rapidement; (= without delay) [arrive, answer, react] sans tarder; **the police were ~ on the scene** la police est arrivée rapidement or sans tarder sur les lieux

quickness ['kwɪknɪs] N vitesse *f*, rapidité *f*; [of intelligence, sight, gesture] vivacité *f*; [of mind] promptitude *f*, vivacité *f*; [of pulse] rapidité *f*; [of hearing] finesse *f*; **~ of temper** promptitude *f* à s'emporter; **~ of wit** vivacité *f* d'esprit

quicksand(s) ['kwɪksænd(z)] N(PL) sables *mpl* mouvants; **to get stuck in ~** s'enliser

quickset hedge ['kwɪkset'hedʒ] N haie *f* vive; (= hawthorn) haie *f* d'aubépine

quicksilver ['kwɪk‚sɪlvər] [1] N vif-argent *m*, mercure *m* [2] ADJ [movements, changes] brusque, subit

quickstep ['kwɪkstep] N (Dancing) fox-trot *m*

quickthorn ['kwɪkθɔːn] N aubépine *f*

quid¹ [kwɪd] N (pl inv: Brit = pound) livre *f* (sterling); **to be ~s in** (= to have money) être en fonds

quid² [kwɪd] N [of tobacco] chique *f*

quiddity ['kwɪdɪtɪ] N (Philos) quiddité *f*

quid pro quo [‚kwɪdprəʊ'kwəʊ] N (pl quid pro quos) **it's a ~ (for)** c'est en contrepartie (de), c'est à titre de réciprocité (pour)

quiescence [kwaɪ'esns] N (frm) [of person] inactivité *f*; [of plant] dormance *f*; [of volcano] sommeil *m*

quiescent [kwaɪ'esnt] ADJ (frm) [person] (= passive) passif; (= quiet) tranquille; [symptoms, disease, problem] latent; [volcano] endormi; **in a ~ state** à l'état latent

quiet ['kwaɪət] [1] ADJ [a] (= not loud) [voice] bas (basse *f*); [music] doux (douce *f*); [sound] léger; **she spoke in ~ tones** elle parlait doucement; **... she said with a ~ laugh** ... dit-elle avec un petit rire → **1e**

[b] (= not noisy, not busy) [street, room, village, neighbour] tranquille; **isn't it ~!** quel calme!; **try to be a little ~er** essayez de ne pas faire autant de bruit; **this town is too ~ for me** cette ville est trop endormie pour moi; **business is ~** les affaires sont calmes; (St Ex) **the market was ~** la Bourse était calme

[c] (= silent) **to be ~** [person] être silencieux; **you're very ~ today** tu ne dis rien or pas grand-chose aujourd'hui; **be ~! ◊ keep ~!** taisez-vous!, silence!; **to keep** or **stay ~** garder le silence, ne pas piper mot; **that book should keep him ~ for a while** avec ce livre, il devrait se tenir tranquille un moment; **it was ~ as the grave** il y avait un silence de mort; **to be ~ as a mouse** ne faire aucun bruit

[d] (= placid) [person] calme; [child] calme, doux (douce *f*); [dog, horse] docile; **my daughter is a very ~ girl** ma fille est d'un tempérament très calme; **~ as a lamb** très calme

[e] (= discreet) [dinner] intime; [funeral, ceremony] dans l'intimité; [despair] silencieux; [irony] voilé, discret (-ète *f*); [optimism, diplomacy] discret (-ète *f*); **the wedding was very ~** le mariage a été célébré dans l'intimité; **they had a ~ laugh over it** ils en ont ri sous cape; **... he said with a ~ smile** ... dit-il avec un petit sourire; **with ~ humour** avec une pointe d'humour; **he had a ~ dig at his brother** il a lancé une petite pique à son frère; **to have a ~ word with sb** parler en particulier avec qn; **to keep ~ about sth ◊ to keep sth ~** ne pas ébruiter qch; **keep it ~** gardez-le pour vous

[f] (= untroubled) [night] paisible; [life] paisible, tranquille; **we had a ~ time on holiday** on a passé des vacances tranquilles or relax*; **he went to sleep with a ~ mind** il s'endormit l'esprit tranquille; (Mil or hum) **all ~** rien à signaler, RAS*; **all ~ on the western front** à l'ouest rien de nouveau

[g] (= muted) [colours, clothes] sobre, discret (-ète *f*); [decoration, style] sobre

[2] N (NonC) [a] (= silence) silence *m*, tranquillité *f*; **in the ~ of the night** dans le silence de la nuit; **let's have complete ~ for a few minutes** faisons silence complet pendant quelques minutes

[b] (= peace) calme *m*; **an hour of blessed ~** une heure de répit fort appréciée; **there was a period of ~ after the fighting** il y a eu une accalmie après les combats → **peace**

[c] **on the ~ en cachette, en douce*; **to do sth on the ~** faire qch en cachette or en dessous; **she had a drink on the ~** elle a pris un verre en douce* or en suisse; **he told me on the ~** il me l'a dit en confidence

3 VT (US) = **quieten**
► **quiet down** VI, VT SEP = **quieten down**

quieten ['kwaɪətn] VT (esp Brit) [+ person, crowd, horse, suspicion] calmer, apaiser; [+ fear] calmer, dissiper; [+ pain] calmer; [+ conscience] tranquilliser, apaiser
► **quieten down** **1** VI (= make less noise) se calmer; (fig: after unruly youth) se ranger; **their children have ~ed down a lot** leurs enfants se sont beaucoup assagis or calmés **2** VT SEP [+ person, dog, horse] calmer, apaiser

quietism ['kwaɪətɪzəm] N quiétisme m

quietist ['kwaɪətɪst] ADJ, N quiétiste mf

quietly ['kwaɪətlɪ] ADV **a** (= not loudly) [say, speak, sing] doucement **b** (= silently) sans bruit **c** (= discreetly) discrètement; **~ dressed** habillé simplement or discrètement; **I'm ~ confident about the future** je suis confiant en or dans l'avenir **d** (= without fuss) [get married, be buried] en toute simplicité; [read, sit] tranquillement; **she lives ~ in a cottage in Suffolk** elle mène une vie tranquille or paisible dans un cottage du Suffolk; **he was made to resign ~** on l'a forcé à démissionner sans faire de vagues **e** (Police = voluntarily) [go] de son plein gré; **are you going to come ~?** allez-vous nous suivre de votre plein gré?

quietness ['kwaɪətnɪs] N (= silence) silence m; (= stillness, peacefulness) calme m, tranquillité f; (= gentleness) douceur f

quietude ['kwaɪətjuːd] N quiétude f

quietus [kwaɪ'iːtəs] N (pl **quietuses**) (Jur) quittance f; (fig) (= release) coup m de grâce (lit, fig); (= death) mort f

quiff [kwɪf] N (Brit: also **~ of hair**) (on forehead) mèche f; (on top of head) épi m; (on baby's head) coque f

quill [kwɪl] N (= feather) penne f; (= part of feather) tuyau m de plume; (also **~-pen**) plume f d'oie; [of porcupine etc] piquant m

quilt [kwɪlt] **1** N (= bed cover) édredon m (piqué), courtepointe f; (= duvet: also **continental ~**) couette f **2** VT [+ eiderdown, cover] matelasser, ouater et piquer; [+ dressing gown] matelasser, ouatiner; [+ furniture, bedhead etc] capitonner

quilted ['kwɪltɪd] ADJ [jacket, dressing gown] matelassé, ouatiné; [bedspread] matelassé; [bedhead] capitonné

quilting ['kwɪltɪŋ] N (NonC) (= process) ouatage m, capitonnage m; (= material) ouate f, matelassé m, capitonnage m

quim [kwɪm] N (Brit) chatte f

quin [kwɪn] N (Brit) ABBR = **quintuplet**

quince [kwɪns] **1** N (= fruit) coing m; (= tree) cognassier m **2** COMP [jam] de coings

quincentenary [ˌkwɪnsen'tiːnərɪ] N cinquième centenaire m

quinine [kwɪ'niːn] N quinine f

Quinquagesima [ˌkwɪŋkwə'dʒesɪmə] N Quinquagésime f

quinquennia [kwɪŋ'kwenɪə] NPL of **quinquennium**

quinquennial [kwɪŋ'kwenɪəl] ADJ quinquennal

quinquennium [kwɪŋ'kwenɪəm] N (pl **quinquennia** [kwɪŋ'kwenɪə]) quinquennat m

quinsy ['kwɪnzɪ] N (Med††) amygdalite f purulente

quint [kwɪnt] N (US) ABBR = **quintuplet**

quintal ['kwɪntl] N **a** (= 100kg) quintal m **b** (= 100lb) 100 livres fpl (= 45,36 kg)

quintessence [kwɪn'tesns] N quintessence f

quintessential [ˌkwɪntɪ'senʃəl] ADJ par excellence; **he is the ~ English composer** c'est le compositeur anglais par excellence; **a ~ example of sth** un parfait exemple de qch

quintet(te) [kwɪn'tet] N quintette m

quintillion [kwɪn'tɪljən] N (pl **quintillions** or **quintillion**) (Brit) quintillion m; (US, Can) 10[18]

quintuple ['kwɪntjʊpl] **1** ADJ, N quintuple m **2** [kwɪn'tjuːpl] VTI quintupler

quintuplet [kwɪn'tjuːplɪt] N quintuplé(e) m(f)

quip [kwɪp] **1** N quolibet m **2** VI railler, lancer des pointes **3** VT **"never on a Sunday" she ~ped** « jamais le dimanche » dit-elle avec esprit

quire ['kwaɪər] N **a** (Bookbinding = part of book) cahier m (d'un livre) (quatre feuilles); **book in ~s** livre m en feuilles (détachées) or en cahiers **b** [of paper] = main f (de papier)

quirk [kwɜːk] N **a** bizarrerie f, excentricité f; **it's just one of his ~s** c'est encore une de ses excentricités; **by a ~ of fate** par un caprice du destin; **by some ~ of nature/of circumstance** par une bizarrerie de la nature/de(s) circonstance(s) **b** (= flourish) (Art, Mus) arabesque f; (in signature) paraphe or parafe m; (in handwriting) fioriture f

quirky ['kwɜːkɪ] ADJ [humour, behaviour, style] original, excentrique; [person] excentrique

quirt [kwɜːt] (US) **1** N cravache f tressée **2** VT cravacher

quisling ['kwɪzlɪŋ] N collaborateur m, -trice f (pej), collabo* mf

quit [kwɪt] (pret, ptp **quit** or **quitted**) **1** VT **a** (= leave) [+ place, premises] quitter, s'en aller de; [+ person] quitter, laisser; (esp US) **to ~ school** quitter l'école (or le collège etc); (esp US) **to ~ one's job** quitter sa place **b** (esp US = stop) cesser, arrêter (**doing** de faire); **to ~ hold** lâcher prise; **to ~ hold of sth** lâcher qch; **to ~ work** cesser le travail; **~ fooling!** arrête de faire l'idiot! **c** (Comput) [+ file window etc] sortir de, quitter **2** VI **a** (esp US) (= give up: in game etc) se rendre; (= accept defeat) abandonner la partie, renoncer; **I ~!** j'arrête!, j'abandonne!; **he ~s too easily** il se laisse décourager or il abandonne la partie trop facilement **b** (= leave) **to give a tenant notice to ~** donner congé à un locataire **c** (Comput) sortir, quitter **3** ADJ **~ of** débarrassé de

quite [kwaɪt] ADV **a** (= entirely) tout à fait; (also iro) **~ (so)!** exactement!; **I ~ agree with you** je suis entièrement or tout à fait de votre avis; **he ~ realizes that he must go** il se rend parfaitement compte qu'il doit partir; **I ~ understand** je comprends très bien; **I ~ believe it** je le crois volontiers or sans difficulté, je n'ai aucun mal à le croire; **I don't ~ know** je ne sais pas bien or trop; **I don't ~ see what he means** je ne vois pas tout à fait or pas trop ce qu'il veut dire; **that's ~ enough!** ça suffit comme ça!; **that's ~ enough for me** j'en ai vraiment assez; **it was ~ something** c'était épatant* or formidable*; **it wasn't ~ what I wanted** ce n'était pas exactement ce que je voulais; **not ~ as many as last week** pas tout à fait autant que la semaine dernière; **that's ~ another matter** c'est une tout autre affaire; **~ four days ago** il y a bien quatre jours; **he was ~ right** il avait bien raison or tout à fait raison; **my watch is ~ right** ma montre a l'heure exacte; **~ new** tout (à fait) neuf; **he was ~ alone** il était tout seul; **she was ~ a beauty** c'était une véritable beauté; **it is ~ splendid** c'est vraiment splendide! → **thing**
b (= to some degree, moderately) plutôt, assez; **it was ~ dark for 6 o'clock** il faisait plutôt sombre pour 6 heures; **~ a long time** assez longtemps; **~ a or some time** un bon moment, un bon bout de temps*; **~ a few people** un bon or assez grand nombre de gens; **your essay was ~ good** votre dissertation n'était pas mal inv or pas mauvaise du tout; **he is ~ a good singer** c'est un assez bon chanteur; **I ~ like this painting** j'aime assez ce tableau

quits [kwɪts] ADJ **to be ~ (with sb)** être quitte (envers qn); **to call it ~** s'en tenir là

quittance ['kwɪtəns] N (Fin etc) quittance f

quitter ['kwɪtər] N (pej) velléitaire mf; **he's no ~** il n'est pas du genre à baisser les bras

quiver[1] ['kwɪvər] **1** VI [person] frémir, frissonner (**with** de); [voice] trembler, trembloter; [leaves] frémir, frissonner; [flame] vaciller; [wings] battre, palpiter; [lips] trembler, frémir; [eyelids] battre, palpiter; [flesh, heart] frémir, palpiter; [violin] frémir **2** N [of lips, voice, hand] tremblement m; **a ~ of fear** un frisson de terreur

quiver[2] ['kwɪvər] N (for arrows) carquois m

qui vive [kiːˈviːv] N **on the ~** sur le qui-vive

Quixote ['kwɪksət] N **Don ~** don Quichotte m

quixotic [kwɪk'sɒtɪk] ADJ [person, mission, quest, venture] chimérique

quixotically [kwɪk'sɒtɪkəlɪ] ADV **to behave ~** jouer les don Quichotte; **he volunteered ~ to go himself** chevaleresque, il offrit d'y aller lui-même

quixotism ['kwɪksətɪzəm], **quixotry** ['kwɪksətrɪ] N donquichottisme m

quiz [kwɪz] **1** N (pl **quizzes**) **a** (Rad, TV) quiz m, jeu-concours m (radiophonique or télévisé); (in magazine etc) série f de questions; (= puzzle) devinette f **b** (US Scol) interrogation f rapide (orale ou écrite) **2** VT **a** (gen) interroger, presser de questions (**about** au sujet de) **b** (US Scol) interroger rapidement **3** COMP
► **quiz kid*** N (US) enfant mf prodige
► **quiz programme** N jeu m (radiophonique or télévisé), quiz m

quizmaster ['kwɪzmɑːstər] N meneur m, -euse f de jeu; (Rad, TV) animateur m, -trice f

quizzical ['kwɪzɪkəl] ADJ [smile, expression, look] interrogateur (-trice f), interrogatif; **she raised a ~ eyebrow** elle a levé un sourcil interrogateur

quizzically ['kwɪzɪkəlɪ] ADV [look at] d'un air interrogatif or interrogateur

quod [kwɒd] N (Brit) taule f; **to be in ~** être en taule

quoin [kwɔɪn] N (= angle) coin m or angle m d'un mur; (= stone) pierre f d'angle

quoit [kɔɪt] N palet m; **~s** (= game) jeu m du palet; **to play ~s** jouer au palet

quondam ['kwɒndæm] ADJ (liter) ancien (before n), d'autrefois

Quonset hut® ['kwɒnsɪt'hʌt] N (US) baraque f or hutte f préfabriquée (en tôle, cylindrique)

quorate ['kwɔːreɪt] ADJ (Brit Admin) qui a le quorum, où le quorum est atteint

Quorn® [kwɔːn] N substitut de viande à base de protéines végétales

quorum ['kwɔːrəm] N quorum m; **to make a ~** atteindre le quorum; **we have not got a ~** nous n'avons pas de quorum, le quorum n'est pas atteint

quota ['kwəʊtə] **1** N **a** (= share) quote-part f, part f **b** (= permitted amount) [of imports, immigrants] quota m, contingent m **2** COMP
► **quota system** N système m de quotas

quotable ['kwəʊtəbl] ADJ **a** (= which one may quote) que l'on peut (or puisse) citer; (= worth quoting) digne d'être cité, bon à citer **b** (St Ex) [securities] cotable

quotation [kwəʊ'teɪʃən] **1** N **a** (= passage cited) citation f (from de) **b** (St Ex) cours m, cote f; (Comm = estimate) devis m (estimatif) **2** COMP ► **quotation marks** NPL guillemets mpl; **in ~ marks** entre guillemets; **to open/close the ~ marks** ouvrir/fermer les guillemets

quote [kwəʊt] **1** VT **a** [+ author, poem, fact, text] citer; [+ words] rapporter, citer; [+ reference number etc] rappeler; **to ~ Shelley** citer Shelley; **to ~ sb as an example** citer or donner qn en exemple; **you can ~ me on that** vous pouvez rapporter mes paroles; **don't ~ me on that** ne me citez pas; **he was ~d as saying that ...** il aurait dit que ...; **she said the text was, and I ~, "full of mistakes"** ◊ **she said the text was, ~, unquote, "full of**

mistakes" elle m'a dit que le texte était, je cite, «plein de fautes»; **can you ~ (me) a recent instance of this?** pouvez-vous (m')en citer un exemple récent?; (*Comm*) **when ordering please ~ this number** pour toute commande prière de rappeler ce numéro

b (*Comm*) [+ *price*] indiquer; (*St Ex*) [+ *price*] coter (**at** à); **this was the best price he could ~ us** c'est le meilleur prix qu'il a pu nous faire or proposer; **she ~d me £500 for the job** elle

m'a fait un devis de 500 livres pour ces travaux; (*St Ex*) **~d company** société *f* cotée en Bourse

2 VI **a** (*Literat etc*) faire des citations; **to ~ from the Bible** citer la Bible

b (*Comm*) **to ~ for a job** établir or faire un devis pour un travail

3 N **a** (= *quotation*) citation *f* (**from** de)

b (= *short statement*: *to journalist etc*) déclaration *f*, commentaire *m*

c (*Comm*:* = *estimate*) devis *m*

4 **quotes*** NPL (*Gram*) guillemets *mpl*; **in ~s** entre guillemets

quoth [kwəʊθ] DEFECTIVE VB († *or hum*) ... ~ **he** ... fit-il, ... dit-il

quotidian [kwəʊˈtɪdɪən] ADJ (*frm*) quotidien

quotient [ˈkwəʊʃənt] N (*esp Math*) quotient *m* → **intelligence**

qv (ABBR = **quod vide**) q.v., voir ce mot

QWERTY, qwerty [ˈkwɜːtɪ] ADJ ~ **keyboard** clavier *m* QWERTY

R

R, r [ɑːʳ] N a (= letter) R, r m; **the three R's*** la lecture, l'écriture et l'arithmétique; **R for Robert** ◊ **R for Roger** (US) ≈ R comme Robert b (US Cine) (ABBR = **Restricted**) interdit aux moins de 17 ans c (ABBR = **right**) droite f d (Geog) ABBR = **river** e (ABBR = **Réaumur**) R f (Brit) (ABBR = **Rex, Regina**) George R le roi Georges; **Elizabeth R** la reine Élisabeth

® (ABBR = **registered trademark**) ®

RA [ɑːʳˈeɪ] N (Brit) (ABBR = **Royal Academy**) membre de l'Académie royale

RAAF [ˌɑːreɪəˈef] N ABBR = **Royal Australian Air Force**

Rabat [rəˈbɑːt] N Rabat

rabbet [ˈræbɪt] N feuillure f, rainure f

rabbi [ˈræbaɪ] N rabbin m; **Rabbi Schulman** le rabbin Schulman → **chief**

Rabbinic [rəˈbɪnɪk] N (Ling = medieval Hebrew) hébreu m rabbinique

rabbinic(al) [rəˈbɪnɪk(əl)] ADJ rabbinique

rabbit [ˈræbɪt] 1 N (pl **rabbit** or **rabbits**) lapin m; **doe ~** lapine f; **wild ~** lapin m de garenne; **~ food*** herbe f à lapins*; **like a ~ caught in the headlights** tétanisé; (fig) **to pull a ~ out of the** or **one's hat** sortir un lapin de son chapeau → **Welsh** 2 VI a (= shoot rabbits) **to go ~ing** chasser le lapin b (Brit*: also **~ on, go ~ing on**) ne pas cesser de parler; **to ~ on about sth** ne pas cesser de parler de qch, s'étendre à n'en plus finir sur qch 3 COMP ► **rabbit burrow, rabbit hole** N terrier m (de lapin) ► **rabbit hutch** N clapier m, cabane f or cage f à lapins ► **rabbit punch** N (Boxing etc) coup m du lapin ► **rabbit warren** N (lit) garenne f; (fig: streets, corridors) labyrinthe m

rabble [ˈræbl] 1 N (= disorderly crowd) cohue f; (pej = lower classes) **the ~** la populace (pej) 2 COMP ► **rabble-rouser** N (pej) fomentateur m, -trice f de troubles, agitateur m, -trice f ► **rabble-rousing** (pej) N incitation f à la révolte or à la violence ◆ ADJ qui incite à la révolte or à la violence, qui cherche à soulever les masses

Rabelaisian [ˌræbəˈleɪzɪən] ADJ (Literat) rabelaisien

rabid [ˈræbɪd] ADJ a (Med) [animal] qui a la rage, enragé; [person] atteint de la rage b (pej = fanatical) [nationalist, extremism, hysteria] fanatique; [hatred] farouche, féroce

rabidly [ˈræbɪdlɪ] ADV farouchement, fanatiquement

rabies [ˈreɪbiːz] 1 N rage f (Med) 2 COMP [virus] rabique, de la rage; [injection, precautions, laws] contre la rage, antirabique

RAC [ˌɑːreɪˈsiː] N (Brit) (ABBR = **Royal Automobile Club**) société de dépannage

raccoon [rəˈkuːn] 1 N (pl **raccoon** or **raccoons**) raton m laveur 2 COMP en (fourrure de) raton (laveur)

race¹ [reɪs] 1 N a (Sport, fig) course f; **the 100 metres ~** le 100 mètres, la course de 100 mètres; **horse ~** course f de chevaux; **cycle ~** course f cycliste; (Racing) **the ~s** les courses fpl

(de chevaux); **to ride a ~** [jockey] monter dans une course; (lit, fig) **~ against time** or **the clock** course f contre la montre; **the ~ for** or **to the White House** la course à la Maison-Blanche; **the ~ to find a cure for cancer** la course pour trouver un traitement contre le cancer → **arm², long¹, relay** b (= swift current) (in sea) raz m; (in stream) courant m fort → **mill** c (liter) [of sun, moon] cours m 2 VT a [+ person] faire la course avec; **I'll ~ you to school!** le premier à l'école a gagné!; **he ~d the train in his car** il faisait la course avec le train dans sa voiture b (= cause to speed) [+ car] lancer (à fond); (Aut) **to ~ the engine** emballer le moteur c (Sport) [+ horse, dog] faire courir; **to ~ pigeons** faire des courses de pigeon; **the champion ~s Ferrari** le champion court sur Ferrari 3 VI a (= compete) [racing driver, athlete, jockey etc] courir, faire la course; **to ~ against sb** faire la course avec qn; **we'll have to ~ against time** or **the clock** ça va être une course contre la montre; **he ~s at Cheltenham every week** [horse owner] il fait courir un cheval (or des chevaux) à Cheltenham toutes les semaines b (= rush) [person] aller or courir à toute allure or à toute vitesse; **to ~ in/out/across** etc entrer/sortir/traverser etc à toute allure; **to ~ after sb** courir après qn, essayer de rattraper qn; **to ~ for a taxi** courir pour avoir un taxi; **to ~ for the door** se précipiter vers la porte; **to ~ to the station** courir à la gare, foncer jusqu'à la gare; **to ~ to the telephone** se précipiter vers le téléphone; **to ~ along** filer (à toute allure); **he ~d down the street** il a descendu la rue à toute vitesse; **he ~d through his work** il a fait son travail à toute vitesse c [engine] s'emballer; [propeller] s'affoler; [pulse] être très rapide; **memories of the past ~d through her mind** les souvenirs du passé se sont mis à défiler dans son esprit; **thoughts ~d around in her head** les pensées se bousculaient dans sa tête; **my heart began to ~ with fear** mon cœur s'est mis à battre la chamade 4 COMP ► **race card** N programme m (des courses) ► **race meeting** N (Brit) courses fpl

race² [reɪs] 1 N (= species: lit, fig) race f; **the human ~** la race or l'espèce f humaine 2 COMP [hatred, prejudice] racial ► **race relations** NPL relations fpl interraciales; (Brit) **the Race Relations Board** commission pour les relations interraciales → **QUANGO** ► **race riot** N émeute(s) f(pl) raciale(s)

racecourse [ˈreɪskɔːs] N (esp Brit) champ m de courses, hippodrome m

racegoer [ˈreɪsɡəʊə] N (Brit) turfiste mf

racehorse [ˈreɪshɔːs] N cheval m de course

raceme [ræˈsiːm] N racème m (rare), grappe f

racer [ˈreɪsə] N a (= person) coureur m, -euse f; (= car, yacht) racer m; (= horse) cheval m de course; (= cycle) vélo m de course

racetrack [ˈreɪstræk] N (US) champ m de courses; (Brit) piste f

raceway [ˈreɪsweɪ] N (US: for horses, cars) piste f

Rachel [ˈreɪtʃəl] N Rachel f

rachitic [ræˈkɪtɪk] ADJ rachitique

rachitis [rəˈkaɪtɪs] N (Med) rachitisme m

Rachmanism [ˈrækməˌnɪzəm] N (Brit) intimidation de locataires par des propriétaires sans scrupule

racial [ˈreɪʃəl] ADJ [harmony, identity, purity] racial; [attack, prejudice, stereotype, violence] raciste; [inequality] entre les races; **~ discrimination** discrimination f raciale; **~ harassment** harcèlement m raciste; **~ minority** minorité f raciale; **~ segregation** ségrégation f raciale; **to vote along ~ lines** voter selon des critères raciaux

racialism† [ˈreɪʃəlɪzəm] N (esp Brit) racisme m

racialist† [ˈreɪʃəlɪst] ADJ, N (esp Brit) raciste mf

racially [ˈreɪʃəlɪ] ADV [sensitive, diverse, divided, pure, superior] d'un point de vue racial; **a ~ motivated attack** une agression raciste; **to be ~ prejudiced** avoir des préjugés raciaux; **to be ~ abused** être victime d'insultes racistes; **the schools are ~ segregated** les écoles pratiquent la ségrégation raciale; **the schools were ~ integrated** les écoles pratiquaient l'intégration raciale

racily [ˈreɪsɪlɪ] ADV [write] (= in risqué style) lestement; (= in lively style) avec verve

raciness [ˈreɪsɪnɪs] N [of story, style] caractère m leste; [of joke] grivoiserie f

racing [ˈreɪsɪŋ] 1 N courses fpl; (also **horse-~**) courses fpl de chevaux, hippisme m; **motor-~** course f automobile; **I'm not a ~ man** je ne suis pas amateur de courses; **the ~ world** le monde des courses 2 COMP [calendar, stables] de(s) courses ► **racing bicycle** N bicyclette f de course ► **racing bike** N vélo m de course ► **racing car** N voiture f de course ► **racing certainty** N (Brit fig) certitude f absolue ► **racing colours** NPL couleurs fpl d'une écurie (portées par le jockey) ► **racing cyclist** N coureur m, -euse f cycliste ► **racing driver** N coureur m, -euse f automobile, pilote m de courses ► **racing pigeon** N pigeon m voyageur de compétition ► **racing yacht** N racer m, yacht m de course

racism [ˈreɪsɪzəm] N racisme m

racist [ˈreɪsɪst] ADJ, N raciste mf

rack¹ [ræk] 1 N a (for bottles, documents) casier m; (for luggage) porte-bagages m inv; (for dishes) égouttoir m; (for hanging tools/ties etc) porte-outils/-cravates etc m; (for vegetables) bac(s) m(pl) à légumes; (for fodder, rifles, pipes) râtelier m; (US) **off the ~** en confection, en prêt-à-porter → **bicycle, hatrack, luggage, toast** b (Hist) (torture) chevalet m; **to put sb on the ~** (lit) infliger or faire subir à qn le supplice du chevalet; (fig) mettre qn au supplice 2 VT (Hist) (torture) faire subir le supplice du chevalet à; (fig) [pain] torturer, tourmenter; (fig) **~ed by remorse** tenaillé par le remords; **~ed by doubt** assailli de doutes; **to ~ one's brains** se creuser la tête or la cervelle*

3 COMP ► **rack and pinion** N (*Tech*) crémaillère *f* ► **rack (and pinion) railway** N chemin *m* de fer à crémaillère ► **rack rent** N loyer *m* exorbitant

rack² [ræk] N **to go to ~ and ruin** [*building*] tomber en ruine; [*business, economy*] aller à vau-l'eau; [*person, country*] aller à la ruine

racket¹ [ˈrækɪt] **1** N (*Sport*) raquette *f* **2** **rackets** NPL (= *game*) (jeu *m* de) paume *f* **3** COMP ► **racket press** N presse-raquette *m inv*, presse *f*

racket² [ˈrækɪt] **1** N **a** (= *noise*) [*of people*] tapage *m*, boucan* *m*; [*of machine*] vacarme *m*; **to make a ~** [*people*] faire du tapage *or* du boucan*; [*machine*] faire du vacarme **b** (= *organized crime*) trafic *m*; (= *dishonest scheme*) escroquerie *f*; **an extortion ~** un racket; **the drugs/stolen car ~** le trafic de drogue/des voitures volées; (*fig*) **he's in on the ~** il est dans le coup*; (*fig* = *job etc*) **what's your ~?** qu'est-ce que vous faites dans la vie?; **teaching isn't really my ~** l'enseignement n'est pas vraiment mon truc* **2** VI† (= *make a noise*) faire du tapage *or* du boucan*; (*also ~ about, ~ around* = *lead a hectic social life*) faire la bombe* *or* la bringue*

racketeer [ˌrækɪˈtɪə] N racketter *m*, racketteur *m*; **drugs ~** trafiquant *m* de drogue

racketeering [ˌrækɪˈtɪərɪŋ] N (*NonC*) racket *m*; **drugs ~** trafic *m* de drogue

racking [ˈrækɪŋ] ADJ [*pain, sobs*] déchirant; [*cough*] convulsif

raconteur [ˌrækɒnˈtɜːr] N conteur *m*, -euse *f*

racoon [rəˈkuːn] = **raccoon**

racquet [ˈrækɪt] = **racket¹**

racquetball [ˈrækɪtbɔːl] N (*NonC*) racket-ball *m*

racy [ˈreɪsɪ] ADJ **a** (= *risqué*) [*story, book, film, language*] leste **b** (= *lively*) [*style of writing, speaking*] plein de verve

RADA [ˈrɑːdə] N (*in Brit*) (ABBR = **Royal Academy of Dramatic Art**) ≈ Conservatoire *m* d'art dramatique

radar [ˈreɪdɑːr] **1** N radar *m*; **by ~** au radar **2** COMP [*antenna, echo, screen, station*] radar *inv* ► **radar astronomy** N radarastronomie *f* ► **radar beacon** N radiophare *m* pour radar ► **radar operator** N radariste *mf* ► **radar scanner** N (= *antenna*) antenne *f* radar *inv* ► **radar sensor** N détecteur *m* (radar *inv*) ► **radar trap** N (*Aut Police*) contrôle *m* radar *inv*; **to get caught in a ~ trap** se faire piéger par un radar

raddle [ˈrædl] **1** N ocre *f* rouge **2** VT [+ *sheep*] marquer (à l'ocre)

raddled [ˈrædld] ADJ [*face*] marqué, aux traits accusés, fripé; [*person*] au visage marqué, aux traits accusés

radial [ˈreɪdɪəl] **1** ADJ [*streets*] (*also Med*) radial; [*pattern*] en étoile **2** N (*also ~ tyre*) pneu *m* à carcasse radiale **3** COMP ► **radial engine** N moteur *m* en étoile ► **radial road** N radiale *f* ► **radial tyre** N pneu *m* à carcasse radiale

radially [ˈreɪdɪəlɪ] ADV [*arrange, extend*] en étoile

radiance [ˈreɪdɪəns], **radiancy** [ˈreɪdɪənsɪ] N [*of sun, lights etc*] éclat *m*; [*of face, personality, beauty*] éclat *m*, rayonnement *m*

radiant [ˈreɪdɪənt] **1** ADJ [*person, smile, beauty, sunshine*] radieux; [*optimism*] rayonnant; [*complexion, colour*] éclatant; **~ with joy/health** rayonnant de joie/de santé; **to look ~** être radieux **2** N (*Phys*) point *m* radiant; (*Math*) radian *m*; (*Astron*) (point *m*) radiant *m* **3** COMP ► **radiant energy** N (*Phys*) énergie *f* rayonnante ► **radiant heat** N (*Phys*) chaleur *f* radiante *or* rayonnante ► **radiant heater** N radiateur *m* à foyer rayonnant ► **radiant heating** N chauffage *m* par rayonnement

radiantly [ˈreɪdɪəntlɪ] ADV [*smile, say*] d'un air radieux; [*shine*] d'un vif éclat; **to be ~ happy** être rayonnant de bonheur; **~ beautiful** à la beauté radieuse

radiate [ˈreɪdɪeɪt] **1** VI (= *emit rays*) irradier, rayonner (*liter*); (= *emit heat*) rayonner; (*Phys*) irradier, (*fig*) [*lines, roads*] rayonner (**from** de), partir du même centre **2** VT [+ *heat*] (*Tech*) émettre; (*gen*) répandre; (*fig*) **to ~ happiness** être rayonnant *or* rayonner de bonheur; **he ~s enthusiasm** il respire l'enthousiasme

radiation [ˌreɪdɪˈeɪʃən] **1** N [*of light*] irradiation *f*; [*of heat*] rayonnement *m*; (= *radioactivity*) radiation *f* **2** COMP ► **radiation exposure** N irradiation *f* ► **radiation levels** NPL niveaux *mpl* de radiation ► **radiation sickness** N mal *m* des rayons ► **radiation treatment** N (*Med*) radiothérapie *f*

radiator [ˈreɪdɪeɪtər] **1** N (*also Aut*) radiateur *m* **2** COMP ► **radiator cap** N (*Aut*) bouchon *m* de radiateur ► **radiator grill(e)** N (*Aut*) calandre *f*

radical [ˈrædɪkəl] ADJ, N (*gen, Pol, Ling, Bot, Math*) radical *m*

radicalism [ˈrædɪkəlɪzəm] N radicalisme *m*

radicalize [ˈrædɪkəlaɪz] VT radicaliser

radically [ˈrædɪkəlɪ] ADV [*differ, change, affect, improve, reduce*] radicalement, de façon radicale; **~ different** radicalement différent; **there's something ~ wrong with this approach** il y a quelque chose qui ne va pas du tout avec cette méthode

radicchio [ræˈdiːkɪəʊ] N (*pl* **radicchios**) (*Culin*) trévise *f*

radices [ˈreɪdɪsiːz] NPL *of* **radix**

radicle [ˈrædɪkl] N (*Bot*) radicule *f*, radicelle *f*; (*Chem*) radical *m*

radii [ˈreɪdɪaɪ] NPL *of* **radius**

radio [ˈreɪdɪəʊ] **1** N **a** (*also ~ set*) radio *f*; **on the ~** à la radio; **he has got a ~** il a un poste de radio, il a la radio; **to put the ~ on/off** allumer/éteindre la radio *or* le poste → **transistor**
b (*NonC: Telec*) radio *m*; **to send a message by ~** envoyer un (message) radio; **they were communicating by ~** ils communiquaient par radio
2 VT [+ *person*] appeler *or* joindre par radio; [+ *information*] communiquer par radio; **to ~ a message** envoyer un (message) radio
3 VI **to ~ for help** appeler au secours par radio
4 COMP [*talk, programme*] de radio ► **radio alarm (clock)** N radio-réveil *m* ► **radio amateur** N radioamateur *m* ► **radio announcer** N speaker(ine) *m(f)* ► **radio astronomy** N radioastronomie *f* ► **radio beacon** N (*Aviat, Naut*) radiophare *m*, radiobalise *f* ► **radio beam** N faisceau *m* radio *inv* ► **radio broadcast** N émission *f* de radio *or* radiophonique ► **radio buoy** N radio sono-buoy ► **radio cab** N radio-taxi *m* ► **radio car** N voiture *f* radio *inv* ► **radio cassette (recorder)** N (*esp Brit*) radiocassette *m* ► **radio compass** N radiocompas *m* ► **radio contact** N radiocommunication *f* ► **radio control** N radiocommande *f* ► **radio-controlled** ADJ radiocommandé ► **radio direction finding** N radiogoniométrie *f* ► **radio engineer** N ingénieur *m* radio *inv* ► **radio frequency** N radiofréquence *f* ► **radio galaxy** N radiogalaxie *f* ► **radio ham** N radioamateur *m* ► **radio link** N liaison *f* radio ► **radio mast** N mât *m* d'antenne, pylône *m* ► **radio operator** N opérateur *m* (radio *inv*), radio *m* ► **radio play** N pièce *f* radiophonique, audiodrame *m* ► **radio programme** N émission *f* de radio *or* radiophonique ► **radio receiver** N récepteur *m* de radio ► **radio set** N poste *m* (de radio), radio *f* ► **radio silence** N silence *m* radio *inv*; **to maintain ~ silence** garder le silence radio ► **radio sono-buoy** N bouée *f* sonore ► **radio source, radio star** N radiosource *f* ► **radio station** N (= *broadcasting organization*) station *f* de radio; (= *installation*) poste *m* émetteur ► **radio taxi** N radio-taxi *m* ► **radio telescope** N radiotélescope *m* ► **radio valve** N valve *f*, tube *m* à vide ► **radio van** N (*Rad, TV*) studio *m* mobile (de radiodiffusion *or* d'enregistrement) ► **radio wave** N onde *f* hertzienne

radioactive [ˌreɪdɪəʊˈæktɪv] ADJ radioactif; **~ waste** déchets *mpl* radioactifs

radioactivity [ˌreɪdɪəʊækˈtɪvɪtɪ] N radioactivité *f*

radiobiology [ˌreɪdɪəʊbaɪˈɒlədʒɪ] N radiobiologie *f*

radiocarbon dating [ˌreɪdɪəʊˈkɑːbənˈdeɪtɪŋ] N datation *f* au carbone 14

radiochemistry [ˌreɪdɪəʊˈkemɪstrɪ] N radiochimie *f*

radiocommunication [ˌreɪdɪəʊkəˈmjuːnɪˈkeɪʃən] N contact(s) *m(pl)* radio *inv*

radioelement [ˌreɪdɪəʊˈelɪmənt] N radioélément *m*

radiogram [ˈreɪdɪəʊgræm] N **a** († = *message*) radiogramme *m*, radio *m* **b** (*Brit* = *apparatus*) combiné *m* (avec radio et pick-up)

radiograph [ˈreɪdɪəʊgrɑːf] N radio *f*, radiographie *f*

radiographer [ˌreɪdɪˈɒgrəfər] N radiologue *mf* (*technicien*)

radiography [ˌreɪdɪˈɒgrəfɪ] N radiographie *f*, radio *f*

radioisotope [ˌreɪdɪəʊˈaɪsətəʊp] N radio-isotope *m*

radiological [ˌreɪdɪəˈlɒdʒɪkəl] ADJ radiologique

radiologist [ˌreɪdɪˈɒlədʒɪst] N radiologue *mf* (*médecin*)

radiology [ˌreɪdɪˈɒlədʒɪ] N radiologie *f*

radiolysis [ˌreɪdɪˈɒlɪsɪs] N radiolyse *f*

radiometer [ˌreɪdɪˈɒmɪtər] N radiomètre *m*

radiopager [ˌreɪdɪəʊˈpeɪdʒər] N bip* *m*, pager *m*

radiopaging [ˌreɪdɪəʊˈpeɪdʒɪŋ] N (service *m* de) radiomessagerie *f*

radioscopy [ˌreɪdɪˈɒskəpɪ] N radioscopie *f*

radiotelegraph [ˌreɪdɪəʊˈtelɪgrɑːf] N radiotélégramme *m*, radiogramme *m*

radiotelegraphy [ˌreɪdɪəʊtɪˈlegrəfɪ] N radiotélégraphie *f*

radiotelephone [ˌreɪdɪəʊˈtelɪfəʊn] N radiotéléphone *m*

radiotelephony [ˌreɪdɪəʊtɪˈlefənɪ] N radiotéléphonie *f*

radiotherapist [ˌreɪdɪəʊˈθerəpɪst] N radiothérapeute *mf*

radiotherapy [ˌreɪdɪəʊˈθerəpɪ] N radiothérapie *f*; **to have ~ (treatment)** subir une radiothérapie

radish [ˈrædɪʃ] N radis *m*

radium [ˈreɪdɪəm] **1** N radium *m* **2** COMP ► **radium therapy, radium treatment** N (*Med*) radiumthérapie *f*, curiethérapie *f*

radius [ˈreɪdɪəs] N (*pl* **radiuses** *or* **radii**) (*Math, fig*) rayon *m*; (*Anat*) radius *m*; **within a 6km ~ of Paris** dans un rayon de 6 km autour de Paris

radix [ˈreɪdɪks] N (*pl* **radixes** *or* **radices**) (*Math*) base *f*; (*Ling*) radical *m*

radon [ˈreɪdɒn] N (*also ~ gas*) radon *m*

RAF [ˌɑːreɪˈef] N (*Brit*) (ABBR = **Royal Air Force**) RAF *f*

raffia [ˈræfɪə] **1** N raphia *m* **2** COMP en raphia

raffish [ˈræfɪʃ] ADJ [*charm, appearance, air, behaviour*] canaille; [*person*] à l'air canaille;

[*place*] louche ; **to cut a ~ figure** avoir l'air canaille

raffle ['ræfl] **1** N tombola f **2** VT mettre en tombola **3** COMP ► **raffle ticket** N billet m de tombola

raft [rɑːft] N **a** (*flat structure*) radeau m ; (*logs*) train m de flottage → **life b** (*fig*) **a ~ of ...** un tas de ...

rafter ['rɑːftəʳ] N (*Archit*) chevron m

rafting ['rɑːftɪŋ] N rafting m ; **to go ~** faire du rafting

rag¹ [ræg] **1** N **a** lambeau m, loque f ; (*for wiping etc*) chiffon m ; **to feel like a wet ~*** (*emotionally*) se sentir vidé or mou comme une chiffe ; (*physically*) se sentir ramollo* *inv* ; **~s** (*for paper-making*) chiffons *mpl*, peilles *fpl* ; (= *old clothes*) guenilles *fpl*, haillons *mpl* ; **his clothes were in ~s** ses vêtements étaient en lambeaux or tombaient en loques ; **to be (dressed) in ~s** être vêtu de guenilles or de haillons, être déguenillé ; **in ~s and tatters** tout en loques ; **to go from ~s to riches** passer de la misère à la richesse ; **to lose one's ~:** se mettre en rogne*, se foutre en rogne‡ → **glad, red**
b (* *pej* = *newspaper*) torchon* m, feuille f de chou*
c (‡ = *sanitary towel*) serviette f hygiénique ; **to be on the ~** avoir ses ragnagnas*
d (*Mus*) ragtime m
2 COMP ► **rag-and-bone man** N (*pl* **rag-and-bone men**) (*Brit*) chiffonnier m ► **rag doll** N poupée f de chiffon ► **rag rug** N carpette f faite de chutes de tissu ► **the rag trade*** N la confection

rag²* [ræg] (*Brit*) **1** N (= *joke*) farce f, blague* f ; **for a ~** par plaisanterie, pour s'amuser, pour blaguer* **2** VT† (= *tease*) taquiner, mettre en boîte* ; (= *play trick on*) faire une blague* à ; (*Scol*) [+ *teacher*] chahuter **3** COMP ► **rag week** N (*Univ*) semaine où les étudiants organisent des attractions au profit d'œuvres de bienfaisance

raga ['rɑːgə] N raga m *inv*

ragamuffin ['rægə,mʌfɪn] N (= *urchin*) galopin* m ; (= *ragged fellow*) va-nu-pieds *mf inv*

ragbag ['rægbæg] N **a** (*lit*) sac m à chiffons **b** (*Brit fig*) **a ~ of ...** un ramassis de ...

rage [reɪdʒ] **1** N rage f, fureur f ; [*of sea*] furie f ; **to be in a ~** être furieux or en fureur or en rage ; **to put sb into a ~** mettre qn en rage or en fureur ; **to fly into a ~** entrer en fureur, se mettre en rage, sortir de ses gonds ; **fit of ~** accès m or crise f de fureur or rage ; (*fig*) **to be (all) the ~** faire fureur **2** VI [*person*] être furieux, rager* (**against** contre) ; [*battle, fire*] faire rage ; [*sea*] être démonté, être en furie ; [*storm*] se déchaîner, faire rage ; [*wind*] être déchaîné ; (*fig*) **the fire ~d through the city** l'incendie s'est propagé dans la ville avec une violence inouïe

ragga ['rægə] N (*Mus*) raga(muffin) m

ragged ['rægɪd] **1** ADJ **a** (= *in tatters*) [*person*] déguenillé, en haillons ; [*clothes*] en lambeaux, en loques ; [*cuff*] effiloché **b** (= *uneven*) [*edge, rock*] déchiqueté ; [*hole*] aux bords déchiquetés or irréguliers ; [*line, beard*] irrégulier ; [*cloud*] effiloché ; (*US*) **on the ~ edge*** (= *anxious*) au bord de la crise de nerfs ; **to run sb ~*** éreinter or épuiser qn ; **to run o.s. ~*** s'épuiser **c** (= *disorganized*) [*performance*] inégal ; **the orchestra sounded rather ~ in places** l'orchestre a donné une prestation assez inégale **2** COMP ► **ragged robin** N (*Bot*) fleur f de coucou

raggedly ['rægɪdlɪ] ADV **a** (= *in rags*) **~ dressed** déguenillé, en haillons **b** (= *unevenly*) **they marched ~ up and down** ils ont défilé en désordre ; **the orchestra played ~** la prestation de l'orchestre a été assez inégale

raggle-taggle ['rægl'tægl] ADJ [*gipsy*] dépenaillé ; [*army, group*] disparate

raging ['reɪdʒɪŋ] **1** ADJ [*pain*] atroce ; [*storm, wind, torrent*] déchaîné ; [*sea*] déchaîné, démonté ; [*fire*] violent ; [*inflation*] galopant ; [*debate*] houleux ; [*feminist, nationalist, nationalism*] fanatique ; **a ~ inferno** un immense brasier ; **to be in a ~ temper ◊ to be ~ mad*** être dans une colère noire ; **~ temperature or fever** fièvre f de cheval ; **he had a ~ thirst** il mourait de soif ; **~ toothache** rage f de dents ; **a ~ success** un succès prodigieux **2** N [*of person*] rage f, fureur f ; [*of elements*] déchaînement m ; **the ~ of the sea** la mer en furie

raglan ['ræglən] ADJ, N raglan m *inv*

ragman ['rægmæn] N (*pl* **-men**) chiffonnier m

ragout ['ræguː] N ragoût m

ragtag ['ræg,tæg] N **~ and bobtail** racaille f, populace f

ragtime ['rægtaɪm] N ragtime m

ragtop* ['rægtɒp] N (*US Aut*) décapotable f

ragweed ['rægwiːd] N (*Bot*) ambroisie f

ragwort ['rægwɜːt] N (*Bot*) jacobée f

rah* [rɑː] (*US*) **1** EXCL hourra !, bravo ! **2** COMP ► **rah-rah*** ADJ enthousiaste, exubérant

raid [reɪd] **1** N (*Mil*) raid m, incursion f ; (*by police*) descente f (de police) ; (*with arrests*) rafle f ; (*by bandits*) razzia f ; (*Brit: by thieves*) hold-up m *inv* ; (*Fin*) raid m, tentative f de rachat ; **air ~** raid m (aérien), bombardement m aérien ; (*Brit*) **bank ~** hold-up m or braquage* m d'une banque **2** VT **a** (*Mil*) faire une incursion or un raid dans ; (*Aviat*) bombarder, faire un raid sur ; [*police*] faire une descente or une rafle dans ; [*bandits*] razzier ; (*Brit*) [*thieves*] faire un hold-up à, braquer* **b** (*fig*) [+ *orchard*] marauder dans ; (*hum*) [+ *cashbox, piggybank*] puiser dans ; (*hum*) [+ *larder, fridge*] dévaliser, faire une descente dans* ; (*Fin*) monter une OPA contre

raider ['reɪdəʳ] N (= *thief*) braqueur* m ; (= *ship*) navire m qui accomplit un raid, raider m ; (= *plane*) bombardier m ; (*Fin*) raider m

raiding ['reɪdɪŋ] **1** N (*Mil*) raids *mpl* ; [*of police*] raids *mpl*, descentes *fpl* **2** COMP ► **raiding party** N groupe m d'attaque

rail¹ [reɪl] **1** N **a** (= *bar*) [*of bridge, quay*] garde-fou m ; [*of boat*] bastingage m, rambarde f ; [*of balcony, terrace*] balustrade f ; (= *handrail: on wall*) main f courante ; (= *banister*) rampe f ; (*for carpet, curtains, spotlights etc*) tringle f ; (*Racing*) **the horse was close to the ~s** le cheval tenait la corde ; (= *fence*) **~s** grille f, barrière f → **altar, towel**
b (*for train, tram*) rail m ; **to travel by ~** voyager en train ; **to send by ~** envoyer par (le) train or par chemin de fer ; **to go off the ~s** (*lit*) [*train etc*] dérailler ; (*fig*) [*person*] (= *err*) s'écarter du droit chemin ; (= *be confused*) être déboussolé* ; (*fig*) **to keep sb on the ~s** maintenir qn sur le droit chemin → **live²**
2 COMP [*ticket*] de train, de chemin de fer ; [*journey*] en train, en chemin de fer ; [*dispute*] des employés des chemins de fer ► **rail strike** N grève f des employés des chemins de fer ► **rail traffic** N trafic m ferroviaire ► **rail transport** N transport m ferroviaire
► **rail in** VT SEP clôturer, entourer d'une clôture or d'une barrière
► **rail off** VT SEP fermer au moyen d'une clôture or d'une barrière

rail² [reɪl] VI (*frm*) **to ~ at** or **against sb** se répandre en injures contre qn

railcar ['reɪlkɑː] N autorail m

railcard ['reɪlkɑːd] N carte f de chemin de fer ; **family ~** carte f couple-famille ; **Senior Citizen ~** carte f vermeil ; **student ~** carte f de train tarif étudiant ; **young person's ~** carte f de train tarif jeune

railhead ['reɪlhed] N tête f de ligne

railing ['reɪlɪŋ] N **a** (= *rail*) [*of bridge, quay*] garde-fou m ; [*of balcony, terrace*] balustrade f ;

(*on stairs*) rampe f ; (*on wall*) main f courante **b** (= *part of fence*) barreau m ; (= *fence: also* **~s**) grille f

raillery ['reɪlərɪ] N taquinerie f, badinage m

railroad ['reɪlrəʊd] **1** N (*US*) = **railway 1a** **2** VT **a** (*US*) expédier par chemin de fer or par rail **b** (* = *force*) **to ~ a bill** faire voter un projet de loi (*après un débat sommaire*) ; **to ~ sb into doing sth** forcer qn à faire qch sans qu'il ait le temps de réfléchir or de faire ouf*

railway ['reɪlweɪ] **1** N **a** (= *system*) chemin m de fer ; (= *track*) voie f ferrée → **aerial, elevated, scenic, underground b** (*US: for trams etc*) rails *mpl* **2** COMP [*bridge, ticket*] de chemin de fer ► **railway carriage** N voiture f, wagon m ► **railway engine** N locomotive f ► **railway guide** N indicateur m des chemins de fer ► **railway journey** N voyage m en train or en chemin de fer ► **railway line** N ligne f de chemin de fer ; (= *track*) voie f ferrée ► **railway network** N réseau m ferroviaire ► **railway porter** N porteur m ► **railway station** N gare f ; (*small*) station f de chemin de fer ► **railway timetable** N horaire m des chemins de fer ► **railway workers** NPL employés *mpl* des chemins de fer, cheminots *mpl* ► **railway yard** N dépôt m (d'une gare)

railwayman ['reɪlweɪmən] N (*pl* **-men**) (*Brit*) cheminot m

railworkers ['reɪlwɜːkəz] NPL employés *mpl* des chemins de fer, cheminots *mpl*

raiment ['reɪmənt] N (*liter*) vêtements *mpl*

rain [reɪn] **1** N **a** (*Met*) pluie f ; **it looks like ~** le temps est à la pluie ; **in the ~** sous la pluie ; **heavy/light ~** pluie f battante/fine ; (*Scot*) **the ~'s on*** ça pleut* ; **(come) ~ (or hail) or shine** (*lit*) par tous les temps, qu'il pleuve ou qu'il vente ; (*fig*) quoi qu'il arrive ; **the ~s** la saison des pluies → **right**
b (*fig*) [*of arrows, blows, bullets*] pluie f **2** VT [+ *blows*] faire pleuvoir **3** VI pleuvoir ; **it is ~ing** il pleut ; **it is ~ing heavily** il pleut à verse ; **it's ~ing cats and dogs* ◊ it's ~ing buckets*** il pleut des cordes* ; **to ~ on sb's parade*** mettre des bâtons dans les roues de qn ■ (*PROV*) **it never ~s but it pours** un malheur n'arrive jamais seul **4** COMP ► **rain belt** N zone f des pluies ► **rain check*** N (*US*) billet m pour un autre match (*or pour un autre spectacle*) ; (*US fig*) **to give sb a ~ check** inviter qn une autre fois (*à la place*) ; (*esp US fig*) **I'll take a ~ check (on that)** ça sera pour une autre fois ► **rain cloud** N nuage m chargé de pluie ► **rain dance** N danse f de la pluie ► **rain gauge** N pluviomètre m ► **rain hood** N capuche f en plastique
► **rain down** VI [*bullets, stones etc*] pleuvoir
► **rain off, rain out** (*US*) VT SEP **the match was ~ed off** or **out** le match a été annulé (*or abandonné*) à cause de la pluie

rainbow ['reɪnbəʊ] **1** N arc-en-ciel m ; **of all colours of the ~** de toutes les couleurs de l'arc-en-ciel ; **to look for the pot** or **crock of gold at the end of the ~** poursuivre un rêve impossible **2** COMP ► **rainbow coalition** N (*Pol*) coalition f hétéroclite ► **rainbow trout** N truite f arc-en-ciel ► **rainbow wrasse** N girelle f

raincoat ['reɪnkəʊt] N imperméable m, imper* m

raindrop ['reɪndrɒp] N goutte f de pluie

rainfall ['reɪnfɔːl] N (= *shower*) chute f de pluie ; (= *amount*) pluviosité f, pluviométrie f

rainforest ['reɪnfɒrɪst] **1** N (*also* **tropical ~**) forêt f tropicale (humide) **2** COMP [*plant, species, conservation, destruction*] de la forêt tropicale (humide)

rainless ['reɪnlɪs] ADJ sec (sèche f), sans pluie

rainmaker ['reɪnmeɪkəʳ] N faiseur m, -euse f de pluie

rainmaking ['reɪnmeɪkɪŋ] ADJ [*ceremony etc*] destiné à faire venir la pluie

rainout ['reɪnaʊt] N (*US Sport*) *match annulé pour cause de pluie*

rainproof ['reɪnpruːf] [1] ADJ imperméable [2] VT imperméabiliser

rainstorm ['reɪnstɔːm] N pluie *f* torrentielle, trombes *fpl* d'eau

rainswept ['reɪnswept] ADJ [*place*] balayé par la pluie

rainwater ['reɪnwɔːtər] N eau *f* de pluie

rainwear ['reɪnwɛər] N (*NonC: Comm*) vêtements *mpl* de pluie

rainy ['reɪnɪ] ADJ [*place*] pluvieux; **the ~ season** la saison des pluies; **a ~ day** une journée pluvieuse *or* de pluie; (*fig*) **to put something away** *or* **save something for a ~ day** garder une poire pour la soif

▼ **raise** [reɪz] [1] VT [a] (= *lift, cause to rise*) [+ *arm, leg, eyes*] lever; [+ *object, weight*] lever, soulever; [+ *dust*] soulever; **to ~ a blind** (re)lever un store; (*Theat*) **to ~ the curtain** lever le rideau; (*lit*) **to ~ one's eyebrows** lever les sourcils; (*in surprise*) **they ~d their eyebrows when they heard ...** ils ont eu une expression perplexe *or* l'étonnement s'est lu sur leur visage quand ils ont entendu ...; (*fig*) **that will make him ~ his eyebrows** cela le fera tiquer; (*fig*) **he didn't ~ an eyebrow** il n'a pas sourcillé *or* tiqué; **she ~d a few eyebrows with her saucy jokes** elle a provoqué quelques froncements de sourcils avec ses plaisanteries grivoises; **to ~ one's hat to sb** donner un coup de chapeau à qn; (*fig*) tirer son chapeau à qn*; **to ~ one's glass to sb** lever son verre à qn, boire à la santé de qn; **to ~ one's hand to sb** lever la main sur qn; **to ~ one's fist to sb** menacer qn du poing; **to ~ sb from the dead** ressusciter qn (d'entre les morts); **to ~ one's voice** (= *speak louder*) hausser la voix; (= *get angry*) élever la voix, hausser le ton; **don't ~ your voice to me!** ne hausse pas le ton quand tu me parles!; **not a voice was ~d in protest** personne n'a élevé la voix pour protester; **to ~ sb's spirits** remonter le moral de qn; **to ~ sb's hopes** donner à espérer à qn; **he ~d the people to revolt** il souleva le peuple; (*fig*) **to ~ the roof*** faire un boucan monstre‡; (*in protest*) rouspéter ferme*; **to ~ the level of the ground** rehausser le niveau du sol; (*Naut*) **to ~ a sunken ship** renflouer un navire coulé → **tone**

[b] (= *increase*) [+ *salary*] augmenter, relever (*Admin*); [+ *price*] majorer, augmenter; [+ *standard, level*] élever; [+ *age limit*] reculer; [+ *temperature*] faire monter; **to ~ the school-leaving age** prolonger la scolarité obligatoire

[c] (= *build, erect*) [+ *monument*] élever, ériger; [+ *building*] édifier, bâtir

[d] (= *produce*) [+ *spirit*] évoquer; [+ *ghosts*] faire apparaître; [+ *problems, difficulties*] soulever, provoquer; **to ~ a blister** provoquer une ampoule; **to ~ a laugh** provoquer le rire, faire rire; **to ~ a cheer** (*oneself*) crier « hourra »; (*in others*) faire pousser des hourras; **to ~ a difficulties** soulever *or* faire des difficultés; **to ~ a smile** (*oneself*) ébaucher un sourire; (*in others*) faire sourire, donner à sourire; **to ~ suspicion in sb's mind** faire naître des soupçons dans l'esprit de qn; **to ~ Cain*** *or* **hell*** (= *make a noise*) faire un éclat *or* du boucan*; (= *make a fuss*) faire une scène de tous les diables*

[e] (= *bring to notice*) [+ *question, issue*] soulever; [+ *objection, protest*] élever

[f] (= *grow, breed*) [+ *animals, children, family*] élever; [+ *corn, wheat*] cultiver, faire pousser

[g] (= *get together*) [+ *army, taxes*] lever; [+ *money*] se procurer; **to ~ funds for sth** (*gen*) réunir *or* rassembler *or* se procurer les fonds pour qch; [*professional fundraiser*] collecter des fonds pour qch; (*Fin, Econ*) mobiliser des fonds pour qch; **to ~ a loan** [*government etc*] lancer *or* émettre un emprunt; [*person*] em-

prunter; **to ~ money on sth** emprunter de l'argent sur qch; **I can't ~ the £500 I need** je n'arrive pas à me procurer les 500 livres dont j'ai besoin → **mortgage**

[h] (= *end*) [+ *siege, embargo*] lever

[i] (*Cards*) faire une mise supérieure à; (*Bridge*) faire une annonce supérieure à; **I'll ~ you six/£10** je fais une relance *or* je relance de six/10 livres → **bid**

[j] (= *contact: on radio etc*) contacter

[2] N [a] (*US, also Brit***** = *pay rise*) augmentation *f* (de salaire)

[b] (*Cards*) relance *f*, mise *f* supérieure; (*Bridge*) annonce *f* supérieure, enchère *f*

▶ **raise up** VT SEP lever, soulever; **he ~d himself up on his elbow** il s'est soulevé sur son coude

raiser ['reɪzər] N [a] (*Agr*) éleveur *m*; **cattle-/sheep-~** éleveur *m* de bétail/de moutons

[b] (*in compounds*) → **fire, fund**

raisin ['reɪzən] [1] N raisin *m* sec [2] COMP ▶ **raisin bread** N pain *m* aux raisins secs

raising agent ['reɪzɪŋ,eɪdʒənt] N (*Culin*) poudre *f* à lever

raj [rɑːdʒ] N **the (British) Raj** l'empire *m* britannique des Indes

rajah ['rɑːdʒə] N raja(h) *or* radja(h) *m*

rake¹ [reɪk] [1] N (*for gardener, croupier*) râteau *m*; (*for grate*) râble *m*, ringard *m*

[2] VT [a] [+ *garden, leaves*] ratisser; [+ *hay*] râteler; **to ~ a fire** tisonner un feu; **to ~ the stones off the lawn** enlever les cailloux de la pelouse (à l'aide d'un râteau); **to ~ dead leaves into a pile** ratisser les feuilles mortes et en faire un tas; (*fig*) **to ~ through one's memory** fouiller dans sa mémoire *or* dans ses souvenirs

[b] (= *sweep*) **his glance ~d the crowd** il a parcouru la foule du regard; **enemy searchlights ~d the sea** les projecteurs ennemis balayaient la mer; **the car was ~d with bullets** la voiture a été criblée de balles

[3] VI (*fig* = *search*) **to ~ among** *or* **through** fouiller dans; **to ~ through dustbins** faire les poubelles

[4] COMP ▶ **rake-off*** N (*pej*) pourcentage *m*; **he gets a ~-off on each sale** il prélève son pourcentage sur chaque vente

▶ **rake in*** VT SEP [+ *money*] amasser; **he's just raking it in!** il remue le fric à la pelle!‡

▶ **rake out** VT SEP **to ~ out a fire** éteindre un feu en faisant tomber la braise

▶ **rake over** VT SEP [+ *flower bed*] ratisser; (*fig*) [+ *memories, past*] remuer; (*esp Brit fig*) **to ~ over the coals** *or* **ashes** remuer le passé

▶ **rake up** VT SEP [+ *leaves*] attiser; [+ *leaves*] ramasser avec un râteau, ratisser; (*fig*) [+ *grievance*] rappeler; **to ~ up the past** remuer le passé; **to ~ up sb's past** fouiller dans le passé de qn

rake²† [reɪk] N (= *person*) roué† *m*, débauché *m*, coureur *m*

rake³ [reɪk] [1] N (= *slope*) (*Naut*) [*of mast*] quête *f*; (*Theat*) [*of stage*] pente *f*; (*Aut*) [*of seat*] inclinaison *f* [2] VI (*Naut*) être incliné; (*Theat*) être en pente

raked [reɪkt] ADJ [*stage*] en pente

rakish¹ ['reɪkɪʃ] ADJ [a] († = *dissolute*) [*person, appearance, moustache*] canaille; **to look ~** avoir l'air canaille [b] (= *jaunty*) **worn at a ~ angle** porté de travers pour se donner un air désinvolte

rakish² ['reɪkɪʃ] ADJ (*Naut*) élancé, à la ligne élancée

rakishly ['reɪkɪʃlɪ] ADV [a] († = *dissolutely*) [*behave*] en débauché [b] (= *jauntily*) **a hat cocked ~ over one eye** un chapeau porté de travers pour se donner un air désinvolte; **he wore a ~-knotted cravat** sa façon de nouer son foulard lui donnait un air désinvolte

rally¹ ['rælɪ] [1] N [a] [*of troops*] rassemblement *m*, ralliement *m*; [*of people*] rassemblement *m*; (*Pol*) rassemblement *m*, meeting *m*; (*Aut*)

rallye *m*; (*Tennis*) échange *m*; **youth/peace ~** rassemblement *m* de la jeunesse/en faveur de la paix; **electoral ~** meeting *m* de campagne électorale

[b] (*in health*) amélioration *f*, mieux *m*; (*St Ex*) reprise *f*

[2] VT [+ *troops*] rassembler, rallier; [+ *supporters*] rallier; [+ *one's strength*] retrouver, reprendre; **hoping to ~ opinion within the party** en espérant rallier à sa cause des membres du parti

[3] VI [*troops, people*] se rallier; [*sick person*] aller mieux, reprendre des forces *or* le dessus; (*fig*) **to ~ to a movement/to the support of sb** se rallier à un mouvement/à la cause de qn; (*Aut*) **to go ~ing** faire un *or* des rallye(s); (*St Ex*) **the market rallied** les cours ont repris

[4] COMP ▶ **rally car** N voiture *f* de rallye ▶ **rally driver** N pilote *m* de rallye ▶ **rally driving** N rallye *m* ▶ **rallying call, rallying cry** N cri *m* de ralliement ▶ **rallying point** N point *m* de ralliement

▶ **rally round** [1] VI (*fig*) venir en aide [2] VT FUS **during her husband's illness everyone rallied round her** pendant la maladie de son mari tout le monde est venu lui apporter son soutien

rally² ['rælɪ] VT (= *tease*) taquiner, se moquer (gentiment) de

rallycross ['rælɪkrɒs] N (*NonC*) rallye-cross *m*

RAM [ræm] [1] N (*Comput*) (ABBR = **random access memory**) RAM *f inv* [2] COMP ▶ **RAM chip** N barrette *f* mémoire

ram [ræm] [1] N bélier *m* (*also Astron*); (*Tech*) hie *f*, dame *f*; [*of pile driver*] mouton *m*; (*for water*) bélier *m* hydraulique → **battering**

[2] VT [a] (= *push down*) enfoncer (*avec force*); (= *pack down*) tasser (**into** dans); **he ~med a newspaper into the pipe** il a enfoncé un journal dans le tuyau; **he ~med the clothes into the case** il a entassé les vêtements dans la valise; (*Mil, Min*) **to ~ a charge home** refouler une charge; (*fig*) **to ~ home an argument** donner beaucoup de poids à un argument, corroborer un argument; (*fig*) **to ~ sth down sb's throat** rebattre les oreilles à qn de qch; (*fig*) **to ~ sth into sb's head** enfoncer qch dans la tête *or* dans le crâne de qn

[b] (= *crash into*) (*Naut*) heurter (de l'avant *or* par l'étrave); (*in battle*) éperonner; (*Aut: deliberately or accidentally*) [+ *another vehicle*] emboutir; [+ *post, tree*] percuter (contre)

[3] COMP ▶ **ram raid** N casse-bélier* *m*, cambriolage éclair réalisé à l'aide d'une voiture lancée dans une vitrine ▶ **ram raider** N auteur *m* d'un casse-bélier* ▶ **ram raiding** N pillage de magasins avec une voiture-bélier

▶ **ram down** VT SEP [+ *earth*] tasser; (*Tech*) damer; [+ *piles*] enfoncer; **his hat ~med down over his ears** le chapeau enfoncé jusqu'aux oreilles

▶ **ram in** VT SEP enfoncer

Ramadan [,ræmə'dɑːn] N ramadan *m*; **in** *or* **at ~** pendant le ramadan; **to observe ~** faire le ramadan

ramble ['ræmbl] [1] N randonnée *f* (pédestre); **to go for a ~** faire une randonnée; **to go on a ~** partir en randonnée [2] VI [a] (= *wander about*) se promener au hasard; (*also* **go rambling** = *go on hike*) partir en randonnée *f* (pédestre) [b] (*pej: in speech: also ~ on*) parler pour ne rien dire; [*old person*] radoter; **he ~d on for half an hour** il a discouru *or* n'a cessé de discourir pendant une demi-heure

rambler ['ræmblər] N [a] (*Brit* = *hiker*) randonneur *m*, -euse *f*, promeneur *m*, -euse *f* [b] (*also* **~ rose**) rosier *m* grimpant

rambling ['ræmblɪŋ] [1] ADJ [a] (= *extensive*) [*building*] construit de manière anarchique; [*garden*] vaste et chaotique; [*plant*] qui pousse en tous sens [b] (*pej* = *confused*) [*conversation, story, speech, letter*] sans queue ni tête; [*person*] qui divague [2] N [a] (= *incoherent speech*) divagations *fpl*, radotages *mpl* [b] (= *walking in country*) randonnée *f* (pédestre) ; **to go ~** partir en randonnée [3] COMP ► **rambling club** N club *m* de randonnée ► **rambling rose** N (*Bot*) rosier *m* grimpant

Ramboesque* [ˌræmbəʊˈesk] ADJ digne de Rambo

rambunctious [ræmˈbʌŋkʃəs] ADJ (*US*) = **rumbustious**

RAMC [ˌɑːreɪemˈsiː] N (*Brit*) (ABBR = **Royal Army Medical Corps**) *service de santé de l'armée britannique*

ramekin [ˈræmɪkɪn] N ramequin *m*

ramification [ˌræmɪfɪˈkeɪʃən] N (= *complexities, consequences*) ramification *f*

ramify [ˈræmɪfaɪ] [1] VT ramifier [2] VI se ramifier

ramjet [ˈræmdʒet] N (*Aviat*) statoréacteur *m*

rammer [ˈræmər] N (*Tech*) dame *f*, hie *f* ; [*of cannon*] refouloir *m*

ramp [ræmp] N rampe *f* ; (*in road: for speed control*) ralentisseur *m* ; (*in garage etc*) pont *m* de graissage ; (*Aviat*) (**approach** or **boarding**-) passerelle *f* ; (*in garage*) **hydraulic ~** pont *m* élévateur ; (*sign on road*) **"~"** (= *speed bump*) « ralentisseur » ; (= *uneven road surface*) « chaussée déformée »

rampage [ræmˈpeɪdʒ] [1] N **to be** or **go on the ~** se déchaîner ; (= *looting etc*) se livrer au saccage [2] VI (*also* **~ about, ~ around**) se déchaîner

rampancy [ˈræmpənsɪ] N [*of plants*] exubérance *f* ; (*fig*) [*of evil etc*] déchaînement *m*

rampant [ˈræmpənt] ADJ [*vegetation*] luxuriant ; **to be** or **run ~** (*gen*) sévir ; [*person*] avoir la bride sur le cou ; (*Her*) **a lion ~** un lion rampant

rampart [ˈræmpɑːt] N (*lit, fig*) rempart *m*

rampike [ˈræmpaɪk] N (*US*) arbre *m* mort (debout)

ramrod [ˈræmrɒd] [1] N [*of gun*] baguette *f* ; [*of cannon*] refouloir *m* [2] COMP ► **ramrod straight** ADJ raide or droit comme un piquet

ramshackle [ˈræmˌʃækl] ADJ [*building*] délabré, branlant ; [*table*] branlant ; [*machine*] (tout) déglingué* ; [*system*] délabré ; [*alliance, coalition, collection*] fragile, précaire ; **a ~ old car** une vieille guimbarde

RAN [ˌɑːreɪˈen] N ABBR = **Royal Australian Navy**

ran [ræn] VB *pt of* **run**

ranch [rɑːntʃ] [1] N ranch *m* [2] COMP ► **ranch hand** N ouvrier *m* agricole ► **ranch house, ranch-type house** N maison *f* style ranch → HOUSE

rancher [ˈrɑːntʃər] N (*US*) (= *owner*) propriétaire *mf* de ranch ; (= *employee*) cow-boy *m*

ranching [ˈrɑːntʃɪŋ] N (*US*) élevage *m* en ranch

rancid [ˈrænsɪd] ADJ rance ; **to go ~** rancir, devenir rance

rancidity [rænˈsɪdɪtɪ], **rancidness** [ˈrænsɪdnɪs] N rance *m*

rancor [ˈræŋkər] N (*US*) = **rancour**

rancorous [ˈræŋkərəs] ADJ (*frm*) [*person*] rancunier ; [*argument*] plein de rancœur

rancour, rancor (*US*) [ˈræŋkər] N rancœur *f*, rancune *f*

rand [rænd] N (*pl inv* = *monetary unit*) rand *m*

R & B [ˌɑːrənˈbiː] N (ABBR = **rhythm and blues**) → **rhythm**

R & D [ˌɑːrənˈdiː] N (ABBR = **research and development**) R&D *f*

random [ˈrændəm] [1] N **at ~** au hasard, à l'aveuglette (*pej*) ; **chosen at ~** choisi au hasard ; **to walk about at ~** se promener à l'aventure ; **to hit out at ~** lancer des coups à l'aveuglette [2] ADJ [*selection, sampling*] aléatoire ; [*attack, killings*] aveugle ; **~ sample** échantillon *m* pris au hasard [3] COMP ► **random access** N (*Comput*) accès *m* sélectif or aléatoire ► **random ac-**

cess memory N (*Comput*) mémoire *f* vive ► **random number** N nombre *m* aléatoire

randomization [ˌrændəmaɪˈzeɪʃən] N (*Stat*) randomisation *f*, hasardisation *f*

randomize [ˈrændəmaɪz] VT (*Stat*) randomiser

randomly [ˈrændəmlɪ] ADV au hasard, à l'aveuglette (*pej*)

R & R [ˌɑːrəndˈɑːr] N (*US Mil*) (ABBR = **rest and recreation**) permission *f* ; **for a bit of ~*** pour se la couler douce*, pour se détendre

randy* [ˈrændɪ] ADJ (*Brit*) (= *aroused*) excité ; (*by nature*) porté sur la chose ; **to make sb ~** exciter qn ; **to feel ~** être tout excité ; **he's a ~ sod*** c'est un chaud lapin* ; **he's a ~ old devil** c'est un vieux cochon*

ranee [ˈrɑːniː] N = **rani**

rang [ræŋ] VB *pt of* **ring²**

range [reɪndʒ] [1] N [a] [*of mountains*] chaîne *f* ; (= *row*) rangée *f*, rang *m* [b] (= *scope, distance covered*) [*of telescope, gun, missile*] portée *f* ; [*of plane, ship, mooncraft*] rayon *m* d'action, autonomie *f* ; **at a ~ of ...** à une distance de ... ; **at long ~** à longue portée ; (*Mil*) **to find the ~** régler son tir ; (*lit, fig*) **to be out of ~** être hors de portée ; **within (firing) ~** à portée de tir ; (*fig*) **within my ~** à ma portée ; **~ of vision** champ *m* visuel → **free, long¹, shooting** [c] (= *extent between limits*) [*of temperature*] écarts *mpl*, variations *fpl* ; [*of prices, salaries*] échelle *f*, éventail *m* ; [*of musical instrument, voice*] étendue *f*, registre *m* [d] (= *selection*) [*of colours, feelings, speeds, goods, patterns*] gamme *f* ; **there will be a wide ~ of subjects** il y aura un grand choix de sujets ; (*Comm*) **a car/house at the lower end of the ~** une voiture/maison bas de gamme [e] [*of animal, plant*] habitat *m*, région *f* [f] (= *domain, sphere*) [*of activity*] champ *m*, rayon *m* ; [*of influence*] sphère *f* ; [*of knowledge*] étendue *f* ; **the ~ of his ideas is limited** le cercle de ses idées est restreint [g] (*US* = *grazing land*) prairie *f*, (grand) pâturage *m* [h] (*also* **shooting ~**) (*Mil*) champ *m* de tir ; (*at fair*) stand *m* (de tir) → **rifle²** [i] (*Surv*) direction *f*, alignement *m* ; **in ~ with** dans l'alignement or le prolongement de [j] (*also* **kitchen ~**) fourneau *m* de cuisine

[2] VT [a] (= *place in a row*) [+ *objects*] ranger ; [+ *troops*] aligner ; **books had been ~d on shelves on the walls** on avait rangé des livres sur des étagères, contre le mur ; (*fig*) **to ~ o.s. on the side of ...** se ranger du côté de ... ; **the prisoners were ~d along one wall of the cave** les prisonniers étaient alignés contre une paroi de la grotte ; **they ~d themselves along the pavement to see the procession** ils se sont postés le long du trottoir pour regarder le défilé ; **the boys ~d themselves in rows** les garçons se sont mis en rangs [b] (= *classify*) ranger, classer (**among** parmi) [c] (= *roam over*) parcourir ; **he ~d the whole country looking for ...** il a parcouru le pays à la recherche de ... ; **to ~ the seas** parcourir or sillonner les mers [d] (= *direct*) [+ *gun, telescope*] braquer (**on** sur)

[3] VI [a] (= *extend*) [*discussion, quest*] s'étendre (**from ... to** de ... à, **over** sur) ; [*results, opinions*] aller (**from ... to** de ... à), varier (**from ... to** entre ... et) ; **the search ~d over the whole country** les recherches se sont étendues sur tout le pays ; **the numbers ~ from 10 to 20** les numéros vont de 10 à 20 ; **the temperature ~s from 18° to 24°** or **between 18° and 24°** la température varie entre 18° et 24° ; (*fig*) **researches ranging over a wide field** recherches qui embrassent un large domaine [b] (= *roam*) errer, vagabonder ; **to ~ over the area** parcourir la région ; **animals ranging across the savannah** des animaux qui parcourent la savane

[c] **to ~ over** [*guns, missiles, shells*] avoir une portée de, porter à

rangefinder [ˈreɪndʒˌfaɪndər] N (*Mil, Naut, Phot*) télémètre *m*

rangeland [ˈreɪndʒlænd] N (*US*) prairie *f*

ranger [ˈreɪndʒər] N (*also* **forest ~**) garde *m* forestier → **park** [b] (*US* = *mounted patrolman*) gendarme *m* à cheval ; (*US*) **~s** gendarmerie *f* à cheval [c] **Ranger (Guide)** guide *f* aînée

Rangoon [ræŋˈguːn] N Rangoon

rangy [ˈreɪndʒɪ] ADJ grand et élancé, sans une once de graisse

rani [ˈrɑːniː] N rani *f*

rank¹ [ræŋk] [1] N [a] (= *row*) rang *m* ; (*Brit: also* **taxi ~**) station *f* de taxis ; **the taxi at the head of the ~** le taxi en tête de file ; **to break ~s** [*soldiers*] rompre les rangs ; (*fig*) [*splinter group*] faire bande à part ; **to serve in the ~s** servir dans les rangs ; (*Brit Mil*) **other ~s** les sous-officiers *mpl* et hommes *mpl* de troupe ; **the ~ and file** (*Mil*) les hommes de troupe ; (*fig*) la masse, le peuple ; (*Pol*) **the ~ and file of the party** la base du parti ; **the ~ and file workers** la base, les ouvriers *mpl* ; **to rise from the ~s** sortir du rang ; **to reduce to the ~s** casser ; (*fig*) **they were drawn from the ~s of the unemployed** on les avait tirés des rangs des chômeurs → **close²** [b] (*Mil* = *grade*) grade *m*, rang *m* ; **to reach the ~ of general** atteindre le grade de général → **pull** [c] (= *class, position*) rang *m* (social) ; **people of all ~s** gens *mpl* de toutes conditions ; **a person of ~** une personne de haut rang ; **a singer of the first ~** un chanteur de (tout) premier ordre ; **a second-~ painter** un peintre de seconde zone or de deuxième ordre [d] (*Gram*) rang *m* [e] [*of organ*] rang *m*

[2] VT [a] (= *place*) classer ; **I ~ it as one of the best red wines** je le classe parmi les meilleurs vins rouges ; **I ~ Beethoven among the great** je compte Beethoven parmi les grands ; (*US Scol*) **to be ~ed high/low in class** avoir un bon/mauvais classement [b] (*US Mil*) = **outrank**

[3] VI compter ; **he ~s among my friends** il compte parmi mes amis ; **to ~ above/below sb** être supérieur/inférieur à qn ; **to ~ high among ...** occuper un rang élevé parmi ... ; **the British team only ~ed tenth on the medals table** l'équipe britannique n'était que dixième au tableau des médaillés ; **the country ~s as one of the poorest in the world** ce pays compte parmi les plus pauvres du monde ; **it ~s with the best films of the decade** il se classe parmi les meilleurs films de la décennie → **ranking**

rank² [ræŋk] ADJ [a] (= *absolute*) [*outsider, amateur*] parfait (*before n*) ; [*prejudice, treachery*] pur (*before n*) ; [*beginner*] pur, parfait ; [*injustice*] criant, flagrant ; [*insolence*] caractérisé (*pej* = *pungent*) [*smell, breath, dustbin, drains*] fétide ; [*room*] nauséabond [c] (= *luxuriant*) [*vegetation, plants*] luxuriant ; [*weeds, grass*] touffu ; **the lawns were ~ with weeds** les pelouses étaient envahies par les mauvaises herbes

ranker [ˈræŋkər] N (*Mil*) (= *soldier*) simple soldat *m* ; (= *officer*) officier *m* sorti du rang

ranking [ˈræŋkɪŋ] [1] N classement *m* [2] **rankings** NPL (*Sport*) classement *m* officiel [3] ADJ [a] (*in hierarchy*) (*Mil, Admin*) **high-~** de haut rang or grade ; **low-~** de rang or grade inférieur ; **middle-~** de rang or grade intermédiaire ; (*Mil*) **the ~ officer** l'officier *m* responsable or le plus haut en grade [b] (*esp US* = *prominent*) renommé

rankle [ˈræŋkl] VI rester sur le cœur (**with** à) ; **it ~d with him** il l'avait sur le cœur, ça lui était resté sur le cœur

rankness [ˈræŋknɪs] N [a] (= *smell*) odeur *f* fétide; (= *taste*) goût *m* rance [b] [*of plants etc*] exubérance *f*, luxuriance *f*

rankshifted ['ræŋkʃɪftɪd] ADJ (*Gram*) déplacé d'une catégorie à une autre

ransack ['rænsæk] VT (= *pillage*) [+ *house, shop*] saccager, piller; [+ *town, region*] mettre à sac; (= *search*) [+ *room, luggage, drawer*] fouiller (à fond), mettre tout sens dessus dessous dans; [+ *files, one's memory*] fouiller dans (**for** pour trouver)

ransom ['rænsəm] [1] N (*lit, fig*) rançon *f*; **to hold sb to ~** mettre qn à rançon; (*fig*) **they are being held to ~** ils ont le couteau sur la gorge → **king** [2] VT racheter

rant [rænt] [1] VI [a] (*pej*) [*orator etc*] déclamer (de façon exagérée) [b] (*also* **~ on**) divaguer; **to ~ and rave** tempêter; **to ~ (and rave) at sb** tempêter *or* fulminer contre qn [2] N* (= *polemic*) diatribe *f*; **she went into a long ~ about her job** elle s'est lancée dans une longue diatribe sur son travail

ranting ['ræntɪŋ] [1] N tirade(s) *f(pl)* [2] ADJ [*person*] qui vocifère; [*style*] déclamatoire

ranunculus [rə'nʌŋkjʊləs] N (*pl* **ranunculuses** *or* **ranunculi** [rə'nʌŋkjʊˌlaɪ]) renoncule *f*

rap [ræp] [1] N [a] (= *noise*) petit coup *m* sec; (= *blow*) tape *f*; **there was a ~ at the door** on a frappé brusquement à la porte; **to give sb a ~ on the knuckles** donner un coup sur les doigts à qn; (*fig = rebuke*) taper sur les doigts de qn; **I don't care a ~*** je m'en fiche* éperdument
[b] (*esp US‡*) (= *criminal charge*) inculpation *f*; (= *prison sentence*) condamnation *f*; **to beat the ~** échapper à une condamnation; **to hang a murder ~ on sb** faire endosser un meurtre à qn; (*fig = blame*) **to take the ~*** devoir payer les pots cassés; (*US*) **to get the ~* for sth** trinquer* *or* écoper* pour qch
[c] (*Mus*) rap *m*
[d] (*US‡ = chat*) causette* *f*, conversation *f*
[2] VT [+ *door*] frapper bruyamment à; [+ *table*] frapper sur; **to ~ sb's knuckles ◊ to ~ sb over the knuckles** taper sur les doigts de qn; (*fig*) **to get one's knuckles ~ped ◊ to be ~ped over the knuckles** se faire taper sur les doigts
[3] VI [a] (= *knock*) frapper, donner un coup sec; (*fig = rebuke*) blâmer, réprouver
[b] (*esp US‡ = chat*) tailler une bavette*, bavarder
[c] (*Mus*) rapper
[4] COMP ► **rap artist** N rappeur *m*, -euse *f* ► **rap music** N musique *f* rap ► **rap session*** N (*US = chat*) discussion *f* à bâtons rompus ► **rap sheet** N (*US = police record*) casier *m* judiciaire

► **rap out** VT SEP [a] (= *say curtly*) dire brusquement; [+ *oath*] lâcher; [+ *order, retort*] lancer [b] (*Spiritualism*) [+ *message*] communiquer *or* annoncer au moyen de coups

rapacious [rə'peɪʃəs] ADJ rapace

rapaciously [rə'peɪʃəslɪ] ADV avec rapacité *or* avidité

rapacity [rə'pæsɪtɪ] N rapacité *f*, avidité *f*

rape¹ [reɪp] [1] N (*also Jur*) viol *m*; (†† = *abduction*) ravissement† *m*, rapt *m* [2] VT violer [3] COMP ► **rape crisis centre** N centre *m* d'aide aux victimes de viols

rape² [reɪp] [1] N (*Agr, Bot*) colza *m* [2] COMP ► **rape oil** N huile *f* de colza ► **rape seed** N graine *f* de colza

rape³ [reɪp] N (= *grape pulp*) marc *m* de raisin; (= *wine*) râpé *m*

Raphael ['ræfeɪəl] N Raphaël *m*

rapid ['ræpɪd] [1] ADJ rapide [2] **rapids** NPL (*in river*) rapides *mpl*; **they ran the ~s** ils ont franchi les rapides [3] COMP ► **rapid deployment force** N (*Mil*) = **rapid reaction force** ► **rapid eye movement** N mouvements *mpl* oculaires rapides (*pendant le sommeil paradoxal*) → **REM** ► **rapid eye movement**

sleep N sommeil *m* paradoxal ► **rapid fire** N (*Mil*) tir *m* rapide; **a hail of ~ fire** une pluie *or* une grêle de balles; (*fig*) **~ fire of questions** feu *m* roulant de questions ► **rapid reaction force** N (*Mil*) force *f* d'intervention rapide ► **rapid transit (system)** N (*US*) métro *m*

rapidity [rə'pɪdɪtɪ] N rapidité *f*

rapidly ['ræpɪdlɪ] ADV rapidement

rapier ['reɪpɪə'] [1] N rapière *f* [2] ADJ [*wit etc*] mordant [3] COMP ► **rapier thrust** N (*lit*) coup *m* de pointe; (*fig*) remarque *f* mordante

rapine ['ræpaɪn] N rapine *f*

rapist ['reɪpɪst] N (*Jur*) violeur *m*

rappel [ræ'pel] (*US*) [1] VI descendre en rappel [2] N (descente *f* en) rappel *m*

rapper ['ræpə'] N (*Mus*) rappeur *m*, -euse *f*

rapping ['ræpɪŋ] N (*NonC*) [a] (= *noise*) coups *mpl* secs et durs [b] (*Mus*) rap *m*

rapport [ræ'pɔːr] N rapport *m* (**with** avec, **between** entre); **in ~ with** en harmonie avec

rapprochement [ræ'prɒʃmɑ̃ː] N rapprochement *m* (*fig*)

rapscallion† [ræp'skæljən] N vaurien *m*, mauvais garnement *m*

rapt [ræpt] ADJ [*concentration, silence*] profond; [*interest*] profond, intense; [*person, expression*] captivé; **~ in contemplation/in thought** plongé dans la contemplation/dans ses pensées; **~ with wonder** émerveillé; **~ with attention** captivé; **she listened with ~ attention** elle écoutait, captivée

raptor ['ræptə'] N (*Orn*) rapace *m*

rapture ['ræptʃə'] N (= *delight*) ravissement *m*, enchantement *m*; **to be in ~s over** *or* **about** [+ *object*] être ravi *or* enchanté de; [+ *person*] être en extase devant; **to go into ~s over** *or* **about sth/sb** s'extasier sur qch/qn

rapturous ['ræptʃərəs] ADJ [*applause*] frénétique; [*reception, welcome*] enthousiaste; [*person*] enthousiaste, délirant; (*liter*) [*exclamation*] de ravissement, d'extase

rapturously ['ræptʃərəslɪ] ADV [*greet, listen*] avec ravissement; [*applaud*] avec frénésie

ra-ra skirt ['rɑːrɑːˌskɜːt] N jupe *f* à falbalas

rare [rɛə'] [1] ADJ [a] (= *uncommon, infrequent*) (*gen*) rare; [*opportunity*] unique; **on the ~ occasions when he spoke** les rares fois où il a parlé; **with ~ exceptions** à de rares exceptions près; **it is ~ for her to come** il est rare qu'elle vienne; **to grow ~(r)** [*animals, plants*] se raréfier; [*visits*] s'espacer; **a man who remembers birthdays is a ~ bird indeed** un homme qui se souvient des anniversaires est un oiseau rare; (*Brit*) **to have a ~ old time**†* s'amuser comme un fou *or* une folle* [b] (*Culin*) [*meat*] saignant; **a very ~ steak** un bifteck bleu → **medium** [c] (= *rarefied*) [*atmosphere*] raréfié; **to grow ~(r)** se raréfier [2] COMP ► **rare earth** N (*Chem*) terre *f* rare

rarebit ['rɛəbɪt] N → **Welsh**

rarefaction [ˌrɛərɪ'fækʃən] N raréfaction *f*

rarefied ['rɛərɪfaɪd] ADJ [*air, atmosphere*] raréfié; **to become ~** se raréfier; (*fig*) **the ~ world of particle physics** le monde à part de la physique des particules

rarefy ['rɛərɪfaɪ] [1] VT raréfier [2] VI se raréfier

rarely ['rɛəlɪ] ADV rarement

rareness ['rɛənɪs] N rareté *f*

raring* ['rɛərɪŋ] ADJ **to be ~ to go** être très impatient de commencer, ronger son frein; **to be ~ to do sth** être très impatient *or* brûler de faire qch

rarity ['rɛərɪtɪ] [1] N (= *scarcity*) rareté *f*; (= *rare thing*) chose *f* rare; **the ~ of such attacks** la rareté de telles attaques; **rain is a ~ here** la pluie est rare ici [2] COMP ► **rarity value** N **to have ~ value** avoir de la valeur de par sa rareté

rascal ['rɑːskəl] N [a] (= *scamp*) polisson(ne)

m(f), fripon(ne) *m(f)* [b] († = *scoundrel*) coquin *m*, vaurien *m*

rascally ['rɑːskəlɪ] ADJ **a ~ lawyer/merchant** un gredin d'avocat/de marchand; **a ~ trick** un tour pendable

rash¹ [ræʃ] N [a] (*Med: gen*) rougeur *f*, éruption *f*; (*from food etc*) (plaques *fpl* d')urticaire *f*; (*in measles etc*) éruption *f*, taches *fpl* rouges; **to come out** *or* **break out in a ~** avoir une éruption → **heat, nettlerash** [b] (*fig*) [*of strikes, attacks etc*] éruption *f*

rash² [ræʃ] ADJ [*person*] imprudent; [*action, behaviour, words, decision, promise*] imprudent, irréfléchi; **don't be ~!** sois prudent!; **don't do anything ~!** ne commets pas d'imprudences!; **in a ~ moment** dans un moment d'égarement; **it was ~ of him to do that** il s'est montré très imprudent en faisant cela

rasher ['ræʃə'] N (*Brit*) (mince) tranche *f* (de bacon)

rashly ['ræʃlɪ] ADV [*behave, act, offer, promise*] imprudemment, sans réfléchir

rashness ['ræʃnɪs] N imprudence *f*

rasp [rɑːsp] [1] N (= *tool*) râpe *f*; (= *noise*) grincement *m* [2] VT [a] (*Tech*) râper [b] (= *speak: also* **~ out**) dire *or* crier d'une voix râpeuse [3] VI grincer

raspberry ['rɑːzbərɪ] [1] N (= *fruit*) framboise *f*; **to blow a ~*** faire un bruit de dérision, faire pfft; (*fig*) **to blow a ~ at sth*** descendre qch en flammes*; (*fig*) **to get a ~ from*** se faire rabrouer *or* rembarrer par [2] COMP [*ice cream, tart*] (à la) framboise *inv*; [*jam*] de framboise ► **raspberry bush**, **raspberry cane** N framboisier *m*

rasping ['rɑːspɪŋ] [1] ADJ [*sound*] de râpe; [*voice*] râpeux; [*breath*] haletant [2] N (= *sound*) grincement *m*

Rasputin [ræ'spjuːtɪn] N Raspoutine *m*

raspy ['rɑːspɪ] ADJ = **rasping 1**

Rasta ['ræstə] N, ADJ (ABBR = **Rastafarian**) rasta *mf inv*

Rastafarian [ˌræstə'fɛərɪən] N, ADJ rastafari *mf inv*

Rastafarianism [ˌræstə'fɛərɪənɪzəm] N rastafarianisme *m*

rat [ræt] [1] N (*Zool*) rat *m*; (* *pej* = *person*) dégueulasse* *m*, salaud‡ *m*; (= *informer*) mouchard(e) *m(f)*; (* = *blackleg*) jaune *m*; (*: *abandoning friends*) lâcheur* *m*, -euse* *f*; **he's a dirty ~*** c'est un salaud‡ *or* une ordure‡; **you ~!*** espèce de dégueulasse!‡, espèce de salaud!‡; (*Brit*) (*expressing irritation*) **~s!*** zut alors!*; (*fig*) **the ~s are leaving the sinking ship** les rats quittent le navire → **smell** [2] VI [a] **to go ~ting** faire la chasse aux rats [b] **to ~ on sb*** (= *inform on*) donner qn, balancer qn*; (= *desert*) lâcher qn* [3] COMP ► **rat-arsed‡*** ADJ (*Brit*) bituré‡; **to get ~-arsed** se biturer‡ ► **rat-catcher** N chasseur *m* de rats ► **rat-catching** N chasse *f* aux rats; (= *extermination*) dératisation *f* ► **rat fink** N (*US*) salaud‡ *m*, vache‡ *f* ► **rat poison** N mort-aux-rats *f inv* ► **rat race** N foire *f* d'empoigne ► **rat run*** N (*Brit fig*) raccourci *m* ► **rats' tails*** NPL (*pej*) **her hair was in ~s' tails** des mèches de cheveux pendaient dans son cou ► **rat trap** N piège *m* à rats, ratière *f*

ratable ['reɪtəbl] = **rateable**

rat-a-tat ['rætə'tæt], **rat-a-tat-tat** ['rætəˌtæt'tæt] N (*at door*) toc toc *m*; (*of gunfire*) ta ta ta ta *m*; (*on drum*) rantanplan *m*

ratatouille [ˌrætə'twiː] N ratatouille *f*

ratbag‡ ['rætbæg] N peau *f* de vache*

ratchet ['rætʃɪt] [1] N (= *mechanism*) rochet *m* [2] COMP ► **ratchet wheel** N roue *f* à rochet

► **ratchet up** VI, VT SEP (*esp US*) augmenter

rate¹ [reɪt] [1] N (= *ratio, proportion*) taux *m*; (= *speed*) vitesse *f*, rythme *m*; **birth/death ~** taux *m* de natalité/mortalité; **the failure/success ~ for this exam is high** il y a un pourcentage élevé d'échecs/de réussites à cet examen; **~ of consumption** taux *m* de consommation; **~ of flow** [*of electricity, water*] débit *m* (moyen); **at the ~ of 100 litres an hour** à raison de 100 litres par heure; **to pay sb at the ~ of £10 per hour** payer qn à raison de 10 livres de l'heure; (= *speed*) **at a ~ of ...** à une vitesse de ...; (*Aviat*) **~ of climb** vitesse *f* ascensionnelle; **at a great ~ ◊ at a ~ of knots*** à fond de train*, à toute allure; **to go at a terrific ~** aller à un train d'enfer; **the population is growing at an alarming ~** la population augmente à un rythme inquiétant; **if you continue at this ~** si vous continuez à ce train-là *or* à ce rythme-là; **at his ~ of working**, he'll never finish au rythme auquel il travaille, il n'aura jamais terminé; (*fig*) **at the ~ you're going, you'll be dead before long** du train où vous allez, vous ne ferez pas de vieux os; **at this ~, I'll never find a job** si ça continue comme ça, je ne trouverai jamais de travail; **at any ~** en tout cas, de toute façon; **at that ~** à ce compte-là, dans ce cas → **first-rate, pulse¹**

b (*Comm, Fin, Econ, Med*) taux *m*; (*Fin*) cours *m*; (*Telec, Post, Transport*) tarif *m*; **~ of exchange** taux *m* de change, cours *m* du change; (*Econ*) **~ of growth ◊ growth ~** taux *m* de croissance; **~ of interest/pay/taxation** taux *m* d'intérêt/de rémunération/d'imposition; **postage/advertising ~s** tarifs *mpl* postaux/de publicité; **insurance ~s** primes *fpl* d'assurance; **there is a reduced ~ for children** les enfants bénéficient d'un tarif réduit *or* d'une réduction; **basic salary ~** traitement *m* de base → **basic**

2 rates NPL (*Brit Fin: formerly* = *municipal tax*) impôts *mpl* locaux; **~s and taxes** impôts *mpl* et contributions *fpl*; **a penny on/off the ~s** une augmentation/réduction d'un pour cent des impôts locaux → **water**

3 VT **a** (= *estimate worth of, appraise*) [+ *object*] évaluer (**at** à); (*fig* = *consider*) considérer (**as** comme); **to ~ sb/sth highly** faire grand cas de qn/qch; **how does he ~ that film?** que pense-t-il de ce film?; **I ~ him amongst my best pupils** je le considère comme un de mes meilleurs élèves, je le compte parmi mes meilleurs élèves; **I really ~ him*** je le trouve vraiment très bon; **I don't really ~ him*** je ne le trouve pas très bon; **I don't ~ any of his family*** je n'ai pas une très haute opinion des membres de sa famille; **how would you ~ your chances of getting a job?** quelles sont vos chances de trouver un emploi, à votre avis?

b (*Local Govt: formerly*) établir le montant des impôts locaux sur

c (= *deserve*) mériter; (*Scol*) **I think he ~s a pass (mark)** je pense qu'il mérite la moyenne

4 VI **he hardly ~s as a strong leader** on ne le considère pas vraiment comme un chef qui a de la poigne; **reading does not ~ highly among children as a hobby** la lecture n'est pas un passe-temps très prisé des enfants

5 COMP ► **rate-cap** VT (*Brit: formerly*) fixer un plafond aux impôts locaux de ► **rate-capping** N (*Brit: formerly*) plafonnement *m* des impôts locaux ► **rate collector** N (*Brit: formerly*) receveur *m* municipal ► **rate rebate** N (*Brit: formerly*) dégrèvement *m* (d'impôts locaux)

rate² [reɪt] VT (*liter*) = **berate**

rateable ['reɪtəbl] **1** ADJ [*property*] imposable **2** COMP ► **rateable value** N (*Brit: formerly*) loyer *m* matriciel (*Admin*), valeur *f* locative imposable

ratepayer ['reɪtpeɪəʳ] N (*Brit: formerly*) contribuable *mf* (*payant les impôts locaux*)

▼ rather ['rɑːðəʳ] ADV **a** (= *for preference*) plutôt; **~ than wait, he went away** plutôt que d'attendre, il est parti; **I would ~ have the blue dress** je préférerais *or* j'aimerais mieux avoir la robe bleue; **I would much ~ ...** je préférerais de beaucoup ...; **I would ~ be happy than rich**

j'aimerais mieux être heureux que riche; **I would ~ wait here than go** je préférerais attendre ici plutôt que de partir; **I would ~ you came yourself** je préférerais que vous veniez (*subj*) vous-même; **do you mind if I smoke? — I'd ~ you didn't** est-ce que je peux fumer? — j'aimerais mieux pas*, **I'd ~ not** je préfère pas*, j'aime mieux pas*; **I'd ~ not go** j'aimerais mieux ne pas y aller; **I'd ~ die!** plutôt mourir!; **~ you than me** je ne t'envie pas, je n'irai pas te disputer la place*

b (= *more accurately*) plus exactement, plutôt; **a car, or ~ an old banger** une voiture, ou plus exactement plutôt une vieille guimbarde; **he isn't on holiday, but ~ out of work** il n'est pas en vacances, mais bien plutôt au chômage

c (= *to a considerable degree*) plutôt; (= *to some extent*) un peu; (= *somewhat*) quelque peu; (= *fairly*) assez; (= *slightly*) légèrement; **he's a ~ clever person ◊ he's a ~ clever person** il est plutôt intelligent; **he felt ~ better** il se sentait un peu mieux; **he looked ~ silly** il a eu l'air plutôt stupide; **it's ~ more difficult than you think** c'est un peu plus difficile que vous ne croyez; **Latin is ~ too difficult for me** le latin est un peu trop difficile pour moi; **it's ~ a pity** c'est plutôt dommage; **his book is ~ good** son livre est plutôt bon; **that costs ~ a lot** cela coûte assez cher; **I ~ think he's wrong** je crois bien *or* j'ai l'impression qu'il a tort; (*esp Brit*) **~!†*** et comment!*

ratification [ˌrætɪfɪ'keɪʃən] N ratification *f*

ratify ['rætɪfaɪ] VT ratifier

rating¹ ['reɪtɪŋ] **1** N **a** (= *assessment*) estimation *f*, évaluation *f*; **the government's low ~ in the opinion polls** la mauvaise cote *or* la faiblesse du gouvernement dans les sondages **b** (*Brit Fin* = *tax on property*) montant *m* des impôts locaux **c** (= *placing*) classement *m* **d** (*Brit Naut*) (= *classification*) classe *f*; (= *sailor*) marin *m*, matelot *m*; **the ~s** les matelots et gradés *mpl* **2 ratings** NPL **the ~s** l'indice *m* d'écoute, l'audimat® *m*; **to get good ~s** [*programme*] avoir un bon indice d'écoute; [*person*] avoir la faveur du public; **high/low ~s** forts/faibles indices *mpl* d'écoute; **to boost ~s** faire grimper l'indice d'écoute *or* l'audimat®

rating² ['reɪtɪŋ] N réprimande *f*, semonce *f*

ratio ['reɪʃɪəʊ] N proportion *f*, rapport *m*; **in the ~ of 100 to 1** dans la proportion de 100 contre 1, dans le rapport de 100 contre *or* à 1; **inverse** *or* **indirect ~** raison *f* inverse; **in direct ~ to ...** en raison directe de ...

ratiocinate [ˌrætɪ'ɒsɪneɪt] VI (*frm*) raisonner, ratiociner (*pej*)

ratiocination [ˌrætɪɒsɪ'neɪʃən] N (*frm*) raisonnement *m*, ratiocination *f* (*pej*)

ration ['ræʃən] **1** N (= *allowance: of food, goods etc*) ration *f*; **it's off the ~*** ce n'est plus rationné; (= *food*) **~s** vivres *mpl*; **to put sb on short ~s** réduire les rations de qn → **iron 2** VT [+ *goods, food, people*] rationner; **he was ~ed to 1kg** sa ration était de 1 kg **3** COMP ► **ration book** N carnet *m* de rationnement ► **ration card** N carte *f* *or* ticket *m* de rationnement ► **ration out** VT SEP [+ *food etc*] rationner

rational ['ræʃənl] ADJ [*person, argument, behaviour*] raisonnable, sensé; [*creature, being*] doué de raison; [*action, thinking, explanation, decision*] (*also Math*) rationnel, logique; [*activity*] rationnel, conforme à la raison; (*Med* = *lucid*) lucide; **that wasn't very ~ of him** il n'a pas agi de façon très logique *or* rationnelle

rationale [ˌræʃə'nɑːl] N (= *reasoning*) raisonnement *m*; (= *statement*) exposé *m* raisonné

rationalism ['ræʃnəlɪzəm] N rationalisme *m*

rationalist ['ræʃnəlɪst] ADJ, N rationaliste *mf*

rationalistic [ˌræʃnə'lɪstɪk] ADJ rationaliste

rationality [ˌræʃə'nælɪtɪ] N rationalité *f*

rationalization [ˌræʃnəlaɪ'zeɪʃən] N rationalisation *f*

rationalize ['ræʃnəlaɪz] **1** VT **a** [+ *event, conduct etc*] (tenter de) trouver une explication logique à; (*Psych*) justifier *or* motiver après coup **b** (= *organize efficiently*) [+ *industry, production, problems*] rationaliser **c** (*Math*) rendre rationnel **2** VI (*Psych*) chercher une justification après coup

rationally ['ræʃnəlɪ] ADV [*think, behave, discuss, speak*] rationnellement, de façon rationnelle; **~, it should be possible** logiquement, ça devrait être possible

rationing ['ræʃnɪŋ] N rationnement *m*; **food ~** rationnement *m* de l'alimentation

ratline ['rætlaɪn] N (*Naut*) enfléchure *f*

ratpack ['rætpæk] N (*gen*) jeunes loups *mpl*; (= *journalists*) paparazzi *mpl*

rattan [ræ'tæn] **1** N rotin *m* **2** COMP de *or* en rotin

rat-tat-tat ['rætə'tæt] N = **rat-a-tat**

ratter ['rætəʳ] N (= *dog*) ratier *m*

rattiness* ['rætɪnɪs] N (= *bad temper*) (*in general*) caractère *m* grincheux; (*on one occasion*) mauvaise humeur *f*

rattle ['rætl] **1** N **a** (= *sound*) [*of vehicle*] bruit *m* (de ferraille), fracas *m*; [*of chains, bottles, typewriter*] cliquetis *m*; [*of door*] vibrations *fpl*; [*of hailstones, machine gun*] crépitement *m*; [*of rattlesnake*] sonnettes *fpl*; (*Med: also* **death ~**) râle *m* **b** (*baby's*) (*gen*) hochet *m*; (*strung on pram*) boulier *m* (de bébé); [*of sports fan*] crécelle *f* **2** VI [*box, container, object*] faire du bruit; [*articles in box*] s'entrechoquer; [*vehicle*] faire un bruit de ferraille; [*bullets, hailstones*] crépiter; [*machinery*] cliqueter; [*window*] trembler; **to ~ at the door** cogner à la porte; **there is something rattling** il y a quelque chose qui cogne; **to ~ along/away** etc [*vehicle*] rouler/partir etc dans un bruit de ferraille **3** VT **a** [+ *box*] agiter (avec bruit); [+ *bottles, cans*] faire s'entrechoquer; [+ *dice*] agiter, secouer; [+ *keys*] faire cliqueter; **to ~ sb's cage*** enquiquiner* qn **b** (* = *alarm*) [+ *person*] déconcerter, ébranler; **to get ~d** perdre son sang-froid, paniquer*; **don't get ~d!** pas de panique!*

► **rattle around** VI (*fig*) **I hate to think of her rattling around on her own in that big house** ça me fait mal au cœur de l'imaginer perdue dans cette grande maison

► **rattle away** VI = **rattle on**

► **rattle down** VI [*falling stones etc*] dégringoler *or* tomber avec fracas

► **rattle off** VT SEP [+ *poem, speech, apology*] débiter à toute allure

► **rattle on** VI parler sans arrêt (**about sth** de qch), jacasser

► **rattle through** VT FUS faire (*or* écrire *or* lire etc) à toute vitesse *or* au grand galop

rattler* ['rætləʳ] N (*esp US* = *rattlesnake*) serpent *m* à sonnette, crotale *m*

rattlesnake ['rætlsneɪk] N serpent *m* à sonnette, crotale *m*

rattletrap* ['rætltræp] N guimbarde *f*, tacot* *m*

rattling ['rætlɪŋ] **1** N = **rattle 1a 2** ADJ **a** (= *knocking*) bruyant; **I heard a ~ noise** [*of chains, bottles etc*] j'ai entendu un cliquetis; (= *knocking sound*) j'ai entendu quelque chose qui cognait **b** (= *fast*) **at a ~ pace** *or* **speed*** à toute *or* vive allure **3** ADV (*esp Brit*) **~ good†*** sacrément* bon

ratty* ['rætɪ] ADJ **a** (*Brit* = *bad-tempered*) grincheux; **don't get ~ with me!** ne passe pas tes nerfs sur moi!* **b** (*US* = *shabby*) [*person, coat*] miteux

raucous ['rɔːkəs] ADJ [*laughter*] gros (grosse *f*); [*song*] bruyant; [*party, evening*] bruyant, un peu trop animé; [*person, crowd*] braillard*, tapageur; [*bird cry*] rauque

raucously ['rɔːkəslɪ] ADV [laugh] bruyamment; **to shout ~** brailler*

raucousness ['rɔːkəsnɪs] N [of sound] son m rauque

raunch [rɔːntʃ] N (US) [of story, film] ambiance f torride; [of song] paroles fpl torrides

raunchy ['rɔːntʃɪ] ADJ [person, clothing] sexy inv; [story, film] torride; [song] paillard, grivois

ravage ['rævɪdʒ] [1] VT (= ruin) ravager, dévaster; (= plunder) ravager, piller; **body ~d by disease** corps m ravagé par la maladie [2] **ravages** NPL [of war etc] ravages mpl, dévastation f; **the ~s of time** les ravages mpl du temps, l'outrage m des ans

rave [reɪv] [1] VI (= be delirious) délirer, divaguer; (= talk wildly) divaguer, déraisonner; (= speak furiously) s'emporter, tempêter (**at, against** contre); (= speak enthusiastically) s'extasier (**about, over** sur), parler avec enthousiasme (**about, over** de) → rant [2] N (Brit = Acid House party) rave f [3] COMP ► **rave culture** N (NonC: Mus) culture f rave ► **rave notice***, **rave review*** N critique f dithyrambique ► **rave-up** (Brit = wild party) **to have a ~-up** faire la foire* or la fête*

► **rave up*** [1] VT SEP **to ~ it up** faire la foire* or la fête* [2] **~-up:** N

ravel ['rævl] [1] VT [a] (= entangle: lit, fig) emmêler, embrouiller, enchevêtrer [b] (= disentangle) = ravel out 2 [2] VI (= become tangled) s'embrouiller, s'enchevêtrer; (= fray) s'effilocher

► **ravel out** [1] VI s'effilocher [2] VT SEP [+ material] effilocher; [+ threads] démêler; [+ knitting] défaire; (fig) [+ difficulty] débrouiller; [+ plot] dénouer

raven ['reɪvn] [1] N corbeau m [2] COMP (in colour) noir comme (du) jais or comme l'ébène ► **raven-haired** ADJ aux cheveux de jais

ravening ['rævnɪŋ] ADJ vorace, rapace

Ravenna [rə'venə] N Ravenne

ravenous ['rævənəs] ADJ [animal] vorace; [appetite] vorace, féroce; [hunger] de loup; **I'm ~*** j'ai une faim de loup

ravenously ['rævənəslɪ] ADV [eat] voracement, avec voracité; [look at] d'un air vorace; **to be ~ hungry*** avoir une faim de loup

raver* ['reɪvə'] N (Brit) [a] (gen) noceur* m, -euse* f, fêtard(e)* m(f) [b] (= person attending a rave) raver* m

ravine [rə'viːn] N ravin m

raving ['reɪvɪŋ] [1] ADJ* ► **lunatic** fou m furieux, folle f furieuse; **she's a ~ beauty** elle est d'une beauté éblouissante → mad [2] N **~(s)** délire m, divagations fpl

ravioli ['rævɪ'əʊlɪ] N ravioli mpl

ravish ['rævɪʃ] VT [a] (liter = delight) ravir, transporter [b] († or liter) (= rape) violer; (= abduct) ravir

ravisher ['rævɪʃə'] N († or liter) ravisseur m

ravishing ['rævɪʃɪŋ] ADJ [woman] ravissant; [man] beau comme un dieu; [sight, beauty] enchanteur (-teresse f); [smile] ravageur; **to be ~ to look at** être un régal pour les yeux

ravishingly ['rævɪʃɪŋlɪ] ADV **she is ~ beautiful** elle est d'une beauté éblouissante; **the scenery is ~ beautiful** le paysage est magnifique; **the film is ~ photographed** les prises de vue du film sont superbes

ravishment ['rævɪʃmənt] N [a] (liter = delight) enchantement m, ravissement m [b] († or liter) (= rape) viol m; (= abduction) ravissement† m, rapt m

raw [rɔː] [1] ADJ [a] (= uncooked) [meat, fish, vegetables, egg] cru [b] (= unprocessed) [cotton, rubber, sugar, data, facts] brut; [cloth] écru; [alcohol, spirits] pur; [sewage] non traité; **~ colour** couleur f crue; (Sewing) ► **edge** bord m coupé [c] (= basic) [emotion, energy, ambition, talent] à l'état brut

[d] (= sore) [hands, back, skin] abîmé; [wound, nerves] à vif; [throat] très irrité; (fig) **his wife's words touched a ~ nerve** les paroles de sa femme ont touché la corde sensible

[e] (= inexperienced) [person] sans expérience, inexpérimenté; [troops] non aguerri; (Mil) **a ~ recruit** un bleu

[f] (= cold) [night, day, climate] glacial; [wind] âpre; [air] vif

[g] (= frank) [account] sans complaisance; [story] sans fard

[h] (= bawdy) [humour] cru, grossier

[i] (* = unfair) **he got a ~ deal** on ne lui a vraiment pas fait de cadeaux*; **he's had a ~ deal from life** il n'a pas été gâté par la vie*

[2] N **to get sb on the ~ nerve** toucher or piquer qn au vif; **life/nature in the ~** la vie/la nature telle qu'elle est; **in the ~*** (= naked) nu, à poil*

[3] COMP ► **raw material** N (Ind, fig) matière f première ► **raw score** N (US Scol) première approximation f de note ► **raw silk** N soie f grège

rawboned ['rɔːbəʊnd] ADJ [person] maigre, décharné; [horse] efflanqué

rawhide ['rɔːhaɪd] N (= whip) fouet m à lanières; (= material) cuir m brut or vert

Rawlbolt® ['rɔːlbəʊlt] N cheville d'ancrage en métal

Rawlplug® ['rɔːlplʌg] N cheville en plastique

rawness ['rɔːnɪs] N [a] (= lack of experience) inexpérience f [b] (= primitive nature) **the ~ of the music** le caractère primitif de la musique [c] (on skin) écorchure f [d] [of climate] froid m humide; **the ~ of the wind** l'âpreté f du vent

ray¹ [reɪ] [1] N [of light, heat, sun] rayon m; (fig) rayon m, lueur f; **a ~ of hope** une lueur d'espoir → cathode, death, X-ray [2] COMP ► **ray gun** N fusil m à rayons laser

ray² [reɪ] N (= fish) raie f → stingray

ray³ [reɪ] N (Mus) ré m

rayon ['reɪɒn] [1] N (Tex) rayonne f, soie f artificielle [2] ADJ en rayonne

raze [reɪz] VT raser; **to ~ to the ground** [+ town] raser; [+ building] raser, abattre à ras de terre

razor ['reɪzə'] [1] N rasoir m; **electric ~** rasoir m électrique; (fig) **on** or **at the ~'s edge** sur le fil du rasoir → safety [2] COMP ► **razor blade** N lame f de rasoir ► **razor burn** N feu m du rasoir ► **razor clam** N (US) couteau m ► **razor cut** N (Hairdressing) coupe f au rasoir ► **razor-edged** ADJ [knife etc] tranchant comme un rasoir; (fig) [wit] acéré ► **razor-sharp** ADJ [knife etc] tranchant comme un rasoir; (fig) [person, mind] délié, vif; [wit] acéré ► **razor shell** N (Brit) couteau m ► **razor-slashing** N taillades fpl à coup de rasoir ► **razor wire** N fil m de fer barbelé acéré

razorbill ['reɪzəbɪl] N petit pingouin m

razz [ræz] VT (US) mettre en boîte*

razzle* ['ræzl] N **to go (out) on the ~** (sortir) faire la bringue* or la nouba*

razzle-dazzle* ['ræzl'dæzl] N tape-à-l'œil m inv

razzmatazz* ['ræzmə'tæz] N [a] (= glitter) tape-à-l'œil m inv [b] (= double talk) propos mpl trompeurs

RC [ɑː'siː] (Rel) (ABBR = Roman Catholic) → Roman

RCAF [ɑːsiːeɪ'ef] N ABBR = **Royal Canadian Air Force**

RCMP [ɑːsiːem'piː] N (ABBR = **Royal Canadian Mounted Police**) → royal

RCN [ɑːsiː'en] N ABBR = **Royal Canadian Navy**

Rd (in addresses) (ABBR = **Road**) (in town) Rue f; (esp outside town) Rte (de)

RDA [ɑːdiː'eɪ] N (ABBR = **recommended daily allowance** or **amount**) AQR mpl

RDC [ɑːdiː'siː] N (Brit Local Govt) (ABBR = **Rural District Council**) → rural

RE [ɑːr'iː] N [a] (Brit Scol) (ABBR = **religious education**) → religious [b] (Brit Mil) (ABBR = **Royal Engineers**) → royal

re¹ [reɪ] N (Mus) ré m

re² [riː] PREP (Admin, Comm etc = referring to) concernant; (Jur: also **in re**) en l'affaire de

re... [riː] PREF (before consonant) re..., ré...; (before vowel) r..., ré...; **to redo** refaire; **to reheat** réchauffer; **to reopen** rouvrir; **to re-elect** réélire

reach [riːtʃ] [1] N [a] (= accessibility) portée f, atteinte f; **within ~** à portée; **out of ~** hors de portée or d'atteinte; **within sb's ~** à (la) portée de qn; **out of sb's ~** hors de (la) portée de qn; **within arm's ~** à portée de la main; **cars are within everyone's ~ nowadays** de nos jours les voitures sont à la portée de toutes les bourses or de tous; **out of the children's ~** hors de (la) portée des enfants; **I keep it within easy ~** or **within my ~** je le garde à portée de main or sous la main; **within easy ~ of the sea** à proximité de la mer, proche de la mer; **beyond the ~ of the law** à l'abri de la justice; **this subject is beyond his ~** ce sujet le dépasse [b] (esp Boxing) allonge f; **he has a long ~** (gen) il peut allonger le bras loin; (Boxing) il a une bonne allonge, il a de l'allonge [c] (= length) [of basin, river] étendue f; [of canal] bief m; **further to the north, there are great ~es of forest** plus au nord, il y a de grandes étendues de forêt; **the upper/lower ~es of the river** le cours supérieur/inférieur de la rivière

[2] VT [a] (= get as far as) [+ place, age, goal, limit, perfection] atteindre; [+ agreement, understanding] aboutir à, arriver à; [+ conclusion] arriver à; [+ compromise, decision] parvenir à; **when we ~ed him he was dead** quand nous sommes arrivés auprès de lui, il était mort; **to ~ the terrace you have to cross the garden** pour accéder à la terrasse, il faut traverser le jardin; **I hope this letter ~es him** j'espère que cette lettre lui parviendra; **the news ~ed us too late** nous avons appris or reçu la nouvelle trop tard; **to ~ page 50** arriver or en être à la page 50; **not a sound ~ed our ears** aucun bruit ne parvenait à nos oreilles; **he is tall enough to ~ the top shelf** il est assez grand pour atteindre l'étagère d'en haut; **he ~es her shoulder** il lui arrive à l'épaule; **her dress ~es the floor** sa robe descend jusqu'à terre; **the cancer has ~ed her liver** le cancer a atteint le foie; **you can ~ me at my hotel** vous pouvez me joindre à mon hôtel; **we hope to ~ a wider audience** nous espérons toucher un public plus large [b] (= get and give) passer; **~ me (over) that book** passez-moi ce livre; **~ (over) the salt for Richard** passez le sel à Richard [c] (US Jur = suborn) [+ witness] corrompre, suborner

[3] VI [a] [territory etc] s'étendre; [voice, sound] porter (**to** jusqu'à) → far- [b] (= stretch out hand: also **~ across**, **~ out**, **~ over**) tendre le bras; **to ~ for sth** essayer de prendre qch, tendre le bras pour prendre qch; **he ~ed into his pocket for his pencil** il mit la main dans sa poche pour prendre son crayon; **to ~ for the stars** viser haut; (US) **~ for the sky!:** haut les mains!

[4] COMP ► **reach-me-down** N **it is a ~-me-down from my sister** c'est un vêtement que ma sœur m'a passé

► **reach back** VI (fig) remonter (**to** à); **to ~ back to Victorian times** remonter à l'époque victorienne

► **reach down** [1] VI [clothes, curtains etc] descendre (**to** jusqu'à) [2] VT SEP (from hook) décrocher; (from shelf) descendre; **will you ~ down the book?** voulez-vous me descendre le livre?, voulez-vous me passer le livre qui est là-haut?

► **reach out** VT SEP tendre; **he ~ed out his hand**

for the cup il a étendu le bras pour prendre la tasse
► **reach up** VI [a] lever le bras; **he ~ed up to get the book from the shelf** il a levé le bras pour atteindre le livre sur le rayon [b] monter; **the flood water ~ed up to the windows** la crue (des eaux) est montée jusqu'aux fenêtres

reachable ['riːtʃəbl] ADJ [place, object] accessible; **he is ~* at ...** on peut le joindre à ...

react [riˈækt] VI [a] (gen) réagir (**against** contre, **on** sur, **to** à) [b] (Phys, Chem) réagir (**with** avec)

▼ **reaction** [riˈækʃən] [1] N (gen) réaction f; **what was his ~ to your suggestion?** comment a-t-il réagi or quelle a été sa réaction à votre proposition?; **this decision was a ~ against violence** cette décision a été une manière de riposter à la violence; (Pol) **forces of ~** forces fpl de la réaction, forces fpl réactionnaires → **chain** [2] COMP ► **reaction engine** N moteur m à réaction ► **reaction time** N temps m de réaction

reactionary [riˈækʃənrɪ] ADJ, N réactionnaire mf

reactivate [riˈæktɪveɪt] VT réactiver

reactivation [riːˌæktɪˈveɪʃən] N réactivation f

reactive [riˈæktɪv] ADJ (gen, Chem, Phys) réactif; (Psych) réactionnel

reactor [riˈæktər] N (Chem, Elec, Phys) réacteur m ► **nuclear**

read [riːd] (pret, ptp **read** [red]) [1] VT [a] [+ book, letter etc] lire; [+ music, bad handwriting] déchiffrer, lire; [+ hieroglyphs] déchiffrer; [+ proofs] corriger; **to ~ sb sth ◊ to ~ sth to sb** lire qch à qn; **I read him to sleep** je lui ai fait la lecture jusqu'à ce qu'il s'endorme; **I brought you something to ~** je vous ai apporté de la lecture; **to ~ sb's lips** lire sur les lèvres de qn; **~ my lips!** vous m'avez bien compris?; (Jur) **to ~ the Riot Act** ≈ faire les trois sommations; (fig) **he read them the riot act*** il leur a remonté les bretelles*; (fig) **to ~ sb a lesson*** faire la leçon à qn, sermonner qn; (fig) **to take sth as read** (= as self-evident) considérer qch comme allant de soi; (= as agreed) considérer qch comme convenu; (Admin) **they took the minutes as read** ils sont passés à l'ordre du jour (sans revenir sur le procès-verbal de la dernière séance); (in errata) **for "meet" ~ "met"** au lieu de «meet» prière de lire «met»; (Jur: on document) **read and approved** lu et approuvé → **well²**
[b] (= interpret) [+ dream] interpréter, expliquer; (= understand) comprendre; **to ~ sb's palm** lire les lignes de la main à qn; **to ~ the tea leaves** or **the teacups** ≈ lire dans le marc de café; (US fig) **to ~ the wind** flairer le vent; **these words can be read in several ways** ces mots peuvent s'interpréter de plusieurs façons; (fig) **to ~ between the lines** lire entre les lignes; **to ~ something into a text** faire dire à un texte quelque chose qu'il ne dit pas, solliciter un texte; (fig) **we mustn't ~ too much into this** nous ne devons pas y attacher trop d'importance; **to ~ sb's thoughts** lire (dans) la pensée de qn; **I can ~ him like a book** je sais or devine toujours ce qu'il pense; **I read disappointment in his eyes** j'ai lu la déception dans ses yeux
[c] (esp Brit Univ = study) étudier, faire; **to ~ medicine/law** faire (des études de) médecine/droit, faire sa médecine/son droit; **he is ~ing English/geography** etc il fait de l'anglais/de la géographie etc
[d] [+ thermometer, barometer etc] lire; **to ~ a meter** relever un compteur
[e] [instruments] marquer, indiquer; **the thermometer ~s 37°** le thermomètre indique (une température de) 37°
[f] (Telec) recevoir; **do you ~ me?** est-ce que vous me recevez?; (fig) vous me comprenez?

→ **loud**
[g] (Comput) lire
[2] VI [a] lire; **he can ~ and write** il sait lire et écrire; **she ~s well** elle lit bien, elle fait bien la lecture; [learner, beginner] elle sait bien lire; **he likes ~ing** il aime lire or bouquiner*, il aime la lecture; **to ~ aloud** lire à haute voix; **to ~ to oneself** lire; **do you like being read to?** aimez-vous qu'on vous fasse la lecture?; **I read about it in the paper** je l'ai lu or je l'ai vu dans le journal; **I've read about him** j'ai lu quelque chose à son sujet
[b] **the letter ~s thus ...** voici ce que dit la lettre ..., voici comment la lettre est rédigée ...; **the quotation ~s as follows ...** voici les termes exacts de la citation ...; **this book ~s well/badly** ce livre se lit bien/mal; **his article ~s like an official report** le style de son article fait penser à celui d'un rapport officiel, son article a l'allure d'un rapport officiel
[c] (esp Univ = study) étudier, faire des études; **to ~ for an examination** préparer un examen → **bar¹**
[3] N* lecture f; **she enjoys a good ~** elle aime bien la lecture, elle aime bouquiner*; **it's a good ~** ça se lit facilement, ça se laisse bien lire; **to have a quiet/a little ~** lire or bouquiner* tranquillement/un peu
[4] COMP ► **read head** N (Comput) tête f de lecture ► **read-only** ADJ (Comput) [file] à lecture seule ► **read-only memory** N mémoire f morte (Comput) ► **read-out** (Comput) N (on screen) affichage m; (on paper) sortie f papier or sur imprimante ► **read-write head** N (Comput) tête f de lecture-écriture ► **read-write memory** N (Comput) mémoire f lecture-écriture ► **read-write window** N (Comput) fenêtre f d'inscription-lecture
► **read back** VT SEP [+ one's notes etc] relire
► **read off** VT SEP [a] [+ text] (without pause) lire d'un trait; (at sight) lire à livre ouvert [b] [+ instrument readings] relever
► **read on** VI continuer à lire, poursuivre sa lecture; **"now ~ on"** «suite du feuilleton»
► **read out** [1] VT SEP [a] [+ text] lire à haute voix; [+ instrument readings] relever à haute voix [b] (Comput) extraire de la mémoire, sortir [2] **~-out** N → **read**
► **read over** VT SEP relire
► **read through** VT SEP (rapidly) parcourir; (thoroughly) lire en entier or d'un bout à l'autre
► **read up** VT SEP étudier (à fond), potasser*; **I must ~ up the Revolution** il faut que j'étudie (subj) or que je potasse* (subj) la Révolution
► **read up on** VT FUS → **read up**

readability [ˌriːdəˈbɪlɪtɪ] N lisibilité f

readable ['riːdəbl] ADJ [a] (= interesting) [book, account, style] agréable à lire; **it's very ~** ça se lit facilement [b] (= legible) [handwriting] lisible → **machine**

readdress [ˌriːəˈdres] VT [+ letter, parcel] réadresser; (= forward) faire suivre

reader ['riːdər] N [a] lecteur m, -trice f; **publisher's ~** lecteur m, -trice f dans une maison d'édition; **he's a great ~** il aime beaucoup lire, c'est un grand liseur → **lay⁴, proofreader** [b] (Brit Univ) ≈ chargé(e) m(f) d'enseignement; (US Univ) directeur m, -trice f de thèse or d'études [c] (= schoolbook) (to teach reading) livre m de lecture; (= anthology) recueil m de textes; **first French ~** recueil m de textes français pour première année [d] (**microfiche**) **~ lecteur m** de microfiche

readership ['riːdəʃɪp] N [a] [of newspaper, magazine] nombre m de lecteurs; **this paper has a big ~/a ~ of millions** ce journal a beaucoup de lecteurs/des millions de lecteurs [b] (Brit Univ) ≈ poste m (or fonctions fpl) de chargé(e) d'enseignement; (US Univ) fonctions fpl (or responsabilités fpl) de directeur m, -trice f de thèse or d'études

readily ['redɪlɪ] ADV [a] (= willingly) [accept, agree] volontiers, de bon cœur; [admit] volontiers [b] (= easily) [understand] facilement, aisément; **~ accessible** [place, data] facilement accessible; **to be ~ apparent** se voir (facilement); **exotic vegetables are ~ available these days** on trouve facilement des légumes exotiques de nos jours

readiness ['redɪnɪs] N [a] (= preparedness) **to be (kept) in ~** être (tenu) prêt (**for** à, pour) [b] (= willingness) empressement m, bonne volonté f; **his ~ to help us** son empressement à nous aider, l'empressement qu'il a montré à nous aider

reading ['riːdɪŋ] [1] N [a] (NonC) lecture f; [of proofs] correction f; **she likes ~** elle aime bien lire or la lecture; **this book is or makes very interesting ~** ce livre est très intéressant (à lire); **I'd prefer some light ~** je préférerais qch de distrayant or de facile à lire [b] (= recital) (séance f de) lecture f → **play, poetry** [c] (= interpretation) interprétation f, explication f; **my ~ of the sentence** mon explication or interprétation de cette phrase; (Cine, Theat) **his ~ of the part** son interprétation du rôle [d] (= variant) variante f, leçon f [e] (Elec, Med, Phys etc: from instrument) **to take a ~** lire un instrument, relever les indications d'un instrument; **the ~ is ...** l'instrument indique ... [f] (Parl) [of bill] discussion f, lecture f; **the House gave the bill its first ~** la Chambre a examiné le projet de loi en première lecture; **the third ~ of the bill was debated** le projet de loi a été discuté en troisième lecture [g] (NonC = knowledge) culture f, connaissances fpl; **of wide ~** instruit, cultivé [2] COMP ► **reading age** N (Scol) **he has a ~ age of eight** il a le niveau de lecture d'un enfant de huit ans; **she has a low/advanced ~ age** son niveau de lecture est bas/élevé pour son âge; **child of ~ age** enfant mf en âge de lire ► **reading book** N livre m de lecture ► **reading desk** N pupitre m; (Rel) lutrin m ► **reading glass** N loupe f ► **reading glasses** NPL lunettes fpl pour lire ► **reading knowledge** N **to have a ~ knowledge of Spanish** savoir lire l'espagnol ► **reading lamp, reading light** N (gen) lampe f de travail or de bureau; (in train, plane etc) liseuse f ► **reading list** N bibliographie f, (liste f d')ouvrages mpl recommandés ► **reading matter** N **I've got some ~ matter** j'ai des choses à lire or de quoi lire ► **reading room** N salle f de lecture or de travail ► **reading speed** N vitesse f de lecture

readjust [ˌriːəˈdʒʌst] [1] VT [+ position of sth, salary] rectifier; [+ clothes] rajuster; [+ strategy, approach] modifier; [+ one's life] réorganiser; [+ instrument] régler (de nouveau) [2] VI se réadapter (**to** à)

readjustment [ˌriːəˈdʒʌstmənt] N réadaptation f; [of salary] rajustement or réajustement m

ready ['redɪ] [1] ADJ [a] (= prepared) [person, thing] prêt; [answer, excuse] tout fait; **to be ~ to do sth** être prêt à or pour faire qch; (in restaurant) **are you ~ to order?** puis-je prendre votre commande?; **dinner is ~** le dîner est prêt; **dinner's ~!** à table!; **your glasses will be ~ (for you) in a fortnight** vos lunettes seront prêtes dans quinze jours; **the doctor's ~ for you now** le docteur est prêt à vous recevoir; **everything is ~ for his visit** tout est prêt pour sa visite; **~ for a challenge** préparé à un défi; **ready for an emergency** prêt à intervenir en cas d'urgence; **the troops were ~ for action** les troupes étaient prêtes à intervenir; **~ for anything** prêt à tout; **the contract will be ~ for signing tomorrow** le contrat sera prêt pour la signature demain; **"flight 211 is now ~ for boarding"** «vol 211, embarquement immédiat»; **the wine is ~ for drinking** ce vin est

bon à boire tout de suite ; **the crops are ~ for harvesting** c'est le moment de faire la récolte ; **~ for use** prêt à l'emploi ; **I'm ~ for him!** je l'attends de pied ferme ! ; **to get (o.s.) ~ (for sth)** se préparer (pour qch) ; **get ~ for it!** tenez-vous prêt ! ; *(before momentous news etc)* tenez-vous bien ! ; **to get sb/sth ~ (for sth/to do sth)** préparer qn/qch (pour qch/pour faire qch) ; **to get ~ to do sth** s'apprêter à faire qch, se préparer à faire qch ; **to be ~ (for sth/to do sth)** se préparer (pour qch/à faire qch) ; **to make sth ~** préparer qch ; *(Publishing)* **"now ~"** «vient de paraître» ; *(Brit Sport)* **steady, go!** à vos marques ! prêts ? partez ! ; **~ and waiting** fin prêt ; **~ when you are** quand tu veux ; **to be ~ with a joke/an excuse** avoir une plaisanterie/excuse toute prête *or* en réserve
b *(Comm)* **we have the goods you ordered ~ to hand** nous tenons à votre disposition les marchandises que vous avez commandées ; **money** ◊ **~ cash** (argent *m*) liquide *m* ; **to pay in ~ cash** payer en espèces ; **how much have you got in ~ money** *or* **~ cash?** combien avez-vous en liquide ?
c *(= willing)* **~ to do sth** prêt à faire qch ; **he is always ~ to help** il est toujours prêt à rendre service ; **I am quite ~ to see him** je suis tout à fait disposé à le voir ; **I'm ~, willing and able to do the job** je suis prêt à faire ce travail ; **to be only too ~ to do sth** n'être que trop disposé à faire qch
d *(= needing)* **I'm ~ for bed** j'irais me coucher ; **I'm ~ for a break** je ferais bien une pause ; **I'm ~ for a drink** je prendrais bien un verre
e *(= about to)* **he was ~ to hit her** il était sur le point de la frapper ; **he was ~ to cry** il était au bord des larmes
f *(= prompt)* *[wit]* vif ; *[reply]* prompt ; *[solution, explanation]* tout fait ; *[market]* tout trouvé ; *[availability]* immédiat ; **don't be so ~ to criticize** ne soyez pas si prompt à critiquer ; **to have a ~ smile** sourire facilement ; **to have a ~ tongue** avoir la langue déliée, avoir la parole facile ; **a ~ supply of sth** une réserve de qch facilement accessible *or* à portée de main ; **to have a ~ sale** *[goods]* se vendre facilement, être de vente courante
g *(Naut)* **~ about!** pare à virer !
2 N **a** *(Mil)* **to come to the ~** apprêter l'arme ; **at the ~** *(Mil)* prêt à faire feu ; *(Naut)* paré à faire feu ; *(fig)* fin prêt
b **the ~** *or* **readies** *(= money)* le fric⁑
3 COMP ► **ready-cooked** ADJ *[meal, dish]* cuisiné ► **ready-cut** ADJ *[shelves]* prédécoupé ► **ready-furnished** ADJ tout meublé ► **ready-made** ADJ *[curtains]* tout fait ; *[clothes]* de confection, prêt à porter ; *[solution, answer]* tout prêt ; **~-made ideas** des idées banales *or* toutes faites ► **ready meal** N *(Culin)* plat *m* cuisiné ► **ready-mix** N *(Culin)* **~-mix for cakes/pancakes** préparation *f* instantanée pour gâteaux/crêpes *etc* ♦ ADJ **she made a ~-mix cake** elle a fait un gâteau à partir d'une préparation *or* d'un sachet ► **ready-mixed** ADJ *[concrete]* prêt à l'emploi ► **ready-prepared** ADJ *[meal]* tout préparé ► **ready reckoner** N barème *m* ► **ready-to-eat, ready-to-serve** ADJ cuisiné ► **ready-to-wear** ADJ prêt à porter ♦ N prêt-à-porter *m*

reafforestation [ˈriːəˌfɒrɪsˈteɪʃən], **reforestation** *(US)* [ˌriːfɒrɪsˈteɪʃən] N reboisement *m*

reagent [riːˈeɪdʒənt] N *(Chem)* réactif *m*

real [rɪəl] **1** ADJ **a** *(gen)* vrai *(before n)* ; *(as opposed to apparent)* véritable, vrai *(before n)* ; *(Philos, Math)* réel ; **the danger was very ~** le danger était très réel ; **she wanted to see the ~ Africa** elle voulait voir l'Afrique, la vraie ; **he is the ~ boss** c'est lui le véritable *or* vrai patron ; **my ~ home is in Paris** c'est à Paris que je me sens chez moi ; **to show ~ interest** se montrer vraiment intéressé ; **in ~ life** dans la réali-

té ; **in the ~ world** dans la réalité ; *(Fin)* **in ~ terms** en termes réels ; **we have no ~ reason to suspect him** n'avons pas de véritable raison de le soupçonner ; **there was no ~ evidence that ...** il n'y avait pas de véritable preuve que ... ; **it came as no ~ surprise to him** ça n'a pas vraiment été une surprise pour lui ; **I'm in ~ trouble** j'ai de gros problèmes ; **I had ~ trouble getting them to leave** j'ai eu un mal fou à les faire partir ; **to make ~ money*** gagner des mille et des cents* ; **get ~!⁑** sois réaliste !, faut pas rêver !* ; **it's the ~ McCoy*** c'est du vrai de vrai*
b *(= not fake)* *[jewels]* vrai *(before n)*, véritable ; *[flowers]* vrai *(before n)*, naturel ; *[silk]* naturel ; *[leather, gold]* véritable
c **the ~ thing: it is a poor copy of the ~ thing** c'est une pâle copie de l'original ; **you're being recorded now — is this the ~ thing?** on vous enregistre — pour de bon ? ; **when you've tasted the ~ thing, this whisky ...** quand on a goûté du vrai whisky, celui-ci ... ; **climbing this hill isn't much when you've done the ~ thing** pour ceux qui ont fait de l'alpinisme, cette colline n'est rien du tout ; **this is love, the ~ thing** c'est l'amour avec un grand A ; **he's the ~ thing** *(= real film star, lion-tamer etc)* c'en est un vrai ; *(* = he's great)* il est super*
2 ADV *(esp US*)* **~ soon** sous peu
3 N **a** **for ~*** pour de vrai* ; **is this guy for ~?!⁑** il est incroyable, ce type* !
b *(Philos)* **the ~** le réel
4 COMP ► **real ale** N *(Brit)* bière *f* traditionnelle ► **real estate** N *(US Jur)* immobilier *m* ; **to work in ~ estate** *or* **the ~ estate business** travailler dans l'immobilier ► **real-estate agent** N *(US)* agent *m* immobilier ► **real-estate developer** N *(US)* promoteur *m* immobilier ► **real-estate office** N *(US)* agence *f* immobilière ► **real-estate register** N *(US)* cadastre *m* ► **Real Presence** N *(Rel)* présence *f* réelle ► **real property** N *(US Jur)* biens *mpl* immobiliers ► **real tennis** N jeu *m* de paume ► **real time** N *(Comput)* temps *m* réel ► **real-time computer** N ordinateur *m* exploité en temps réel ► **real-time processing** N *(Comput)* traitement *m* immédiat ► **real-time system** N *(Comput)* système *m* temps réel

realign [ˌriːəˈlaɪn] VT réaligner

realism [ˈrɪəlɪzəm] N réalisme *m*

realist [ˈrɪəlɪst] ADJ, N réaliste *mf*

realistic [rɪəˈlɪstɪk] ADJ réaliste ; **we had no ~ chance of winning** nous n'avions aucune chance réelle de gagner ; **it is not ~ to expect that ...** nous ne pouvons pas raisonnablement espérer que ...

realistically [rɪəˈlɪstɪkəlɪ] ADV *[expect, hope for]* d'une façon réaliste ; *[think, depict]* d'une façon réaliste, avec réalisme ; *[possible]* d'un point de vue réaliste ; **they are ~ priced** leur prix est réaliste ; **~, he had little chance of winning** soyons réalistes, il avait peu de chances de gagner

▼**reality** [rɪˈælɪtɪ] N **a** réalité *f* ; **to bring sb back to ~** ramener qn à la réalité ; **in ~** en réalité, en fait **b** *(= trueness to life)* réalisme *m*

realizable [ˈrɪəlaɪzəbl] ADJ réalisable

realization [ˌrɪəlaɪˈzeɪʃən] N **a** *(of assets, hope, plan)* réalisation *f* **b** *(= awareness)* prise *f* de conscience ; **he was hit by the sudden ~ that ...** il s'est subitement rendu compte que ...

realize [ˈrɪəlaɪz] VT **a** *(= become aware of)* se rendre compte de ; *(= understand)* comprendre ; **does he ~ the problems?** se rend-il compte des problèmes ? ; **the committee ~s the gravity of the situation** le comité se rend compte de la gravité de la situation ; **he had not fully ~d that his illness was so serious** il ne s'était pas vraiment rendu compte de la gravité de sa maladie ; **I ~d it was raining** je me suis rendu compte qu'il pleuvait ; **I made her ~ that I was right** je lui ai bien fait compren-

dre que j'avais raison ; **this made me ~ how lucky I'd been** c'est là que je me suis rendu compte de la chance que j'avais eue ; **I ~ that ...** je me rends compte du fait que ... ; **yes, I ~ that!** oui, je sais bien !, oui, je m'en rends bien compte ! ; **I ~d how he had done it** j'ai compris comment *or* je me suis rendu compte de la façon dont il l'avait fait ; **I ~d why ...** j'ai compris pourquoi ... ; **I ~ it's too late, but ...** je sais bien qu'il est trop tard, mais ...
b *[+ ambition, hope, plan]* réaliser ; **to ~ one's (full) potential** réaliser son plein potentiel ; **my worst fears were ~d** mes pires craintes se sont réalisées
c *(Fin)* *[+ assets]* réaliser ; *[+ price]* atteindre ; *[+ interest]* rapporter ; **how much did your Rembrandt ~?** ◊ **how much did you ~ on your Rembrandt?** combien votre Rembrandt vous a-t-il rapporté ?

reallocate [riːˈæləʊkeɪt] VT *[+ money, tasks]* réallouer, réaffecter ; *[+ time]* réallouer

reallocation [ˌriːæləˈkeɪʃən] N *[of resources, land, time]* réaffectation *f*

really [ˈrɪəlɪ] **1** ADV vraiment, réellement ; **I ~ don't know what to think** je ne sais vraiment pas quoi penser ; **he ~ is an idiot** c'est un véritable imbécile, il est vraiment idiot ; **it won't ~ last** ça ne durera guère ; **I don't REALLY like ...** je ne peux vraiment pas dire que j'aime ..., je n'aime guère ... ; **you ~ MUST visit Paris** il faut absolument que vous visitiez *(subj)* Paris **2** EXCL *(in doubt)* vraiment ?, sans blague ! ; *(in surprise)* c'est vrai ? ; *(in protest: also* **well ~!**)* vraiment !, ça alors ! ; **not ~!** pas vraiment ! ; *(in disbelief)* pas possible !

realm [relm] N *(liter = kingdom)* royaume *m* ; *(fig)* domaine *m* → **coin**

realpolitik [reɪˈɑːlpɒlɪtiːk] N realpolitik *f*

realtor [ˈrɪəltɔːr] N *(US)* agent *m* immobilier

realty [ˈrɪəltɪ] N *(Jur)* biens *mpl* immobiliers *or* immeubles

ream¹ [riːm] N *[of paper]* ≈ rame *f* (de papier) ; *(fig)* **he always writes ~s*** il écrit toujours des volumes *or* toute une tartine*

ream² [riːm] VT *(Tech)* fraiser

reamer [ˈriːmər] N *(Tech)* fraise *f*

reanimate [riːˈænɪmeɪt] VT ranimer, raviver

reanimation [ˈriːˌænɪˈmeɪʃən] N *(Med)* réanimation *f*

reap [riːp] **1** VT *(Agr)* moissonner, faucher ; *(fig)* *[+ profit]* récolter, tirer ; **to ~ the fruit of one's labours** recueillir le fruit de son labeur ; *(fig)* **to ~ what one has sown** récolter ce qu'on a semé ; *(fig, liter)* **they left him to ~ the bitter harvest of his corruption** ils l'ont laissé payer le prix de sa corruption → **sow²** **2** VI moissonner, faire la moisson

reaper [ˈriːpər] N *(= person)* moissonneur *m*, -euse *f* ; *(= machine)* moissonneuse *f* ; **~ and binder** moissonneuse-lieuse *f* ; *(fig, liter = death)* **the (Grim) Reaper** la Faucheuse

reaping [ˈriːpɪŋ] **1** N moisson *f* **2** COMP ► **reaping hook** N faucille *f* ► **reaping machine** N moissonneuse *f*

reappear [ˌriːəˈpɪər] VI réapparaître, reparaître

reappearance [ˌriːəˈpɪərəns] N réapparition *f*

reappoint [ˌriːəˈpɔɪnt] VT renommer *(to à)*

reappointment [ˌriːəˈpɔɪntmənt] N renouvellement *m* de nomination *(to à)*

reapportion [ˌriːəˈpɔːʃən] **1** VT réassigner, répartir à nouveau ; *(US Pol)* redécouper, procéder à une révision du découpage électoral de **2** VI *(US Pol)* subir un redécoupage électoral

reapportionment [ˌriːəˈpɔːʃənmənt] N *(US Pol)* redécoupage *m* électoral

reappraisal [ˌriːəˈpreɪzəl] N *[of situation, problem]* réévaluation *f*, réexamen *m* ; *[of author, film etc]* réévaluation *f*

reappraise [ˌriːəˈpreɪz] VT réévaluer

rear¹ [rɪəʳ] **1** N **a** (= back part) arrière m, derrière m; (* = buttocks) derrière* m; **in** or **at the ~** à l'arrière; **at the ~ of ...** derrière ..., à l'arrière de ...; **from the ~, he looks like Chaplin** (vu) de dos, il ressemble à Charlot; **from the ~ the car looks like ...** par l'arrière or vue de derrière la voiture ressemble à ... **b** (Mil) arrière-garde f, arrières mpl; [of squad] dernier rang m; [of column] queue f; **to attack an army in the ~** attaquer une armée à revers; (Mil, gen) **to bring up the ~** fermer la marche

2 ADJ de derrière, arrière inv

3 COMP ► **rear admiral** N vice-amiral m ► **rear bumper** N pare-chocs m arrière inv ► **rear door** N [of house] porte f de derrière; [of car] portière f arrière inv ► **rear-end** VT (US Aut) emboutir (l'arrière de) ► **rear-engined** ADJ [car] avec moteur m à l'arrière ► **rear gunner** N mitrailleur m arrière inv ► **rear-mounted** ADJ installé à l'arrière ► **rear projection** N (Cine) projection f par transparence ► **rear-view mirror** N [of car] rétroviseur m ► **rear wheel** N [of car] roue f arrière inv or de derrière ► **rear-wheel drive** N [of car] roues fpl arrière inv motrices; (= car) traction f arrière ► **rear window** N [of car] glace f arrière inv

rear² [rɪəʳ] **1** VT **a** [+ animal, family] élever; [+ plant] faire pousser, cultiver **b** **to ~ one's head** relever or dresser la tête; **the snake ~ed its head** le serpent s'est dressé; **violence ~s its ugly head again** la violence fait sa réapparition (dans toute son horreur), on voit poindre à nouveau l'horrible violence **c** (= set up) [+ monument] dresser, ériger **2** VI (also **~ up**) [animal, snake] se cabrer, se dresser

rearguard ['rɪəgɑːd] **1** N (Mil) arrière-garde f **2** COMP ► **rearguard action** N (lit, fig) combat m d'arrière-garde; (fig) **to fight a ~ action** mener un combat d'arrière-garde

rearm [ˌriːˈɑːm] VTI réarmer

rearmament [ˌriːˈɑːməmənt] N réarmement m

rearmost ['rɪəməust] ADJ [carriage] dernier, de queue; [rank] dernier

rearrange [ˌriːəˈreɪndʒ] VT réarranger

rearrangement [ˌriːəˈreɪndʒmənt] N réarrangement m, nouvel arrangement m

rearward ['rɪəwəd] **1** N arrière m **2** ADJ [part] arrière inv; [position] (situé) à l'arrière, de l'arrière; [movement] en arrière **3** ADV (also **~s**) vers l'arrière, par derrière

▼ **reason** ['riːzn] **1** N **a** (= cause, justification) (for behaviour) raison f, motif m; (for event) raison f, cause f; **~ for living** or **being** raison f d'être; **the ~s are ...** les raisons en sont ...; **the ~ for my lateness/the ~ why I am late is that ...** la raison de mon retard/pour laquelle je suis en retard, c'est que ...; **my ~ for leaving** ◊ **the ~ for my leaving** la raison de mon départ or pour laquelle je pars (or suis parti etc); **I want to know the ~ why** je veux savoir (le) pourquoi; **and that's the ~ why** et voilà pourquoi, et voilà la raison; **for no apparent ~** sans raison apparente; **I have (good** or **every) ~ to believe that ...** j'ai (tout) lieu or j'ai de bonnes raisons de croire que ...; **there is ~ to believe that he is dead** il y a lieu de croire qu'il est mort; **for the simple ~ that ...** pour la simple or bonne raison que ...; **for the very that ...** précisément parce que ...; **for that very ~** pour cette raison, pour cela même; **for no ~** sans raison, sans motif; **for some ~ (or another)** pour une raison ou pour une autre; **for ~s best known to himself** pour des raisons qu'il est seul à connaître, pour des raisons connues de lui seul; **all the more ~ for doing** or **to do** raison de plus pour faire; **with ~** avec (juste) raison, à juste titre; **by ~ of** en raison de, à cause de; **for personal/health ~s** pour des raisons personnelles/de santé etc **b** (NonC = mental faculty) raison f; **to lose one's ~** perdre la raison

c (NonC = common sense) raison f, bon sens m; **to see ~** entendre raison; **to make sb see ~** raisonner qn, faire entendre raison à qn; **he listened to ~** il s'est rendu à la raison; **he won't listen to ~** on ne peut pas lui faire entendre raison; **that stands to ~** cela va sans dire, cela va de soi; **it stands to ~ that ...** il va sans dire que ...; **I will do anything in** or **within ~** je ferai tout ce qu'il est raisonnablement possible de faire → **rhyme**

2 VI **a** (= think logically) raisonner **b** (= argue) **to ~ with sb** raisonner avec qn; **one can't ~ with her** il n'y a pas moyen de lui faire entendre raison

3 VT **a** (= work out) calculer (**that** que); (= argue) soutenir (**that** que) → **reasoned** **b** **to ~ sb into a sensible decision** amener qn à prendre une décision intelligente en le raisonnant

▶ **reason out** VT SEP [+ problem] résoudre (en raisonnant)

reasonable ['riːznəbl] ADJ **a** [person, behaviour, decision, explanation, request, price, rate, offer] raisonnable; **to be ~ about sth** être raisonnable à propos de qch; **within a ~ time** dans un délai raisonnable; **it is ~ to suppose that ...** on peut raisonnablement supposer que ... **b** [standard, results, essay] honnête; [distance] appréciable; **there is a ~ chance that ...** il y a des chances or de bonnes chances que ... (+ subj) **c** (Jur) doute m bien fondé; **to prove guilt beyond (a) ~ doubt** prouver la culpabilité de l'accusé avec quasi-certitude; (Jur) **to use ~ force** faire un usage modéré de la force; (esp Jur) **~ grounds for divorce** des motifs mpl valables de divorcer

reasonableness ['riːznəblnɪs] N caractère m or nature f raisonnable

reasonably ['riːznəbli] ADV **a** (= sensibly) [behave] d'une façon raisonnable; [say, expect] raisonnablement; **~ priced** à un prix raisonnable or acceptable; **one can ~ think that ...** il est raisonnable de penser que ... **b** (= fairly) [good, happy, easy, sure, safe] assez, relativement; **to be ~ successful** réussir assez or relativement bien

reasoned ['riːznd] ADJ sensé

reasoning ['riːznɪŋ] **1** N raisonnement m, dialectique f **2** ADJ [mind] doué de raison

reassemble [ˌriːəˈsembl] **1** VT [+ people, troops] rassembler; [+ tool, machine] remonter **2** VI se rassembler; **school ~s on 5 September** la rentrée des classes aura lieu le 5 septembre

reassembly [ˌriːəˈsembli] N [of machine] remontage m

reassert [ˌriːəˈsɜːt] VT réaffirmer; **to ~ o.s.** s'imposer à nouveau

reassess [ˌriːəˈses] VT [+ situation] réexaminer; (for taxation) [+ person] réviser la cote de; (Jur) [+ damages] réévaluer

reassessment [ˌriːəˈsesmənt] N [of situation] réexamen m; (for taxation) [of person] réévaluation f (fiscale); (Jur: damages) réévaluation f

reassurance [ˌriːəˈʃuərəns] N **a** (emotional) réconfort m **b** (factual) assurance f, garantie f; **to seek ~ that ...** chercher à obtenir l'assurance or la garantie que ...

reassure [ˌriːəˈʃuəʳ] VT rassurer

reassuring [ˌriːəˈʃuərɪŋ] ADJ rassurant; **it is ~ to know that ...** il est rassurant de savoir que ...

reassuringly [ˌriːəˈʃuərɪŋli] ADV [say] d'un ton rassurant; [smile, nod, look at] d'une manière rassurante; **~ familiar** familier et rassurant; **~ simple** d'une simplicité rassurante

reawaken [ˌriːəˈweɪkən] **1** VT [+ person] réveiller de nouveau; [+ interest] réveiller de nouveau, faire renaître **2** VI se réveiller de nouveau

reawakening [ˌriːəˈweɪknɪŋ] N réveil m; [of ideas, interest] renaissance f, réveil m

Reb*, reb* [reb] N (US) soldat m confédéré

rebarbative [rɪˈbɑːbətɪv] ADJ (frm) rébarbatif, rebutant

rebate ['riːbeɪt] N (= discount) rabais m, remise f; (= money back) remboursement m; (on tax, rates) dégrèvement m; (on rent) réduction f → **rate¹, rent¹, tax**

Rebecca [rɪˈbekə] N Rébecca f

rebel ['rebl] **1** N (also fig) rebelle mf **2** ADJ rebelle **3** [rɪˈbel] VI **a** (gen: lit, fig) se rebeller, se révolter (**against** contre) **b** (fig) **my feet ~led** mes pieds n'en pouvaient plus; **at the sight of all that food, his stomach ~led** à la vue de toute cette nourriture, il a eu un haut le cœur

rebellion [rɪˈbeljən] N rébellion f, révolte f; **to rise in ~** se rebeller, se révolter

rebellious [rɪˈbeljəs] ADJ (Mil, fig) rebelle

rebelliously [rɪˈbeljəsli] ADV [say] avec révolte; [act] de manière rebelle

rebelliousness [rɪˈbeljəsnɪs] N esprit m de rébellion

rebirth [ˌriːˈbɜːθ] N renaissance f

rebirthing [ˌriːˈbɜːθɪŋ] N rebirth m

reboot [ˌriːˈbuːt] VT (Comput) réinitialiser, réamorcer

rebore [ˌriːˈbɔːʳ] (Tech) **1** VT réaléser **2** ['riː.bɔːʳ] N réalésage m; **this engine needs a ~** ce moteur a besoin d'être réalésé

reborn [ˌriːˈbɔːn] ADJ **to be ~** [person] (= reincarnated) se réincarner (**as sth** en qch); (= redeemed, saved) renaître; [city] renaître; [hatred] se réveiller; [racism, fascism] renaître, resurgir

rebound [rɪˈbaʊnd] **1** VI **a** [ball] rebondir (**against** sur); (fig) **your violent methods will ~ (on** or **upon you)** vos méthodes violentes se retourneront contre vous **b** (after setback) reprendre du poil de la bête* **2** ['riːbaʊnd] N [of ball] rebond m; [of bullet] ricochet m; [of sales, economy] reprise f; (in prices) remontée f (**in** de); **to hit a ball on the ~** frapper une balle après le premier rebond; (fig) **to be on the ~ from a setback** etc (= feeling effects) être sous le coup d'un échec (or d'une déception etc); (= recovering) reprendre du poil de la bête* après un échec (or une déception etc); **she married him on the ~*** elle était encore sous le coup d'une déception (sentimentale) quand elle l'a épousé

rebroadcast [ˌriːˈbrɔːdkɑːst] **1** N retransmission f **2** VT retransmettre

rebuff [rɪˈbʌf] **1** N rebuffade f; **to meet with a ~** essuyer une rebuffade **2** VT [+ person] repousser, rabrouer; [+ offering, suggestion] repousser

rebuild [ˌriːˈbɪld] (pret, ptp **rebuilt**) VT rebâtir, reconstruire; (Med) [+ sb's face, nose] refaire

rebuilding [ˌriːˈbɪldɪŋ] N (NonC) reconstruction f

rebuilt [ˌriːˈbɪlt] VB pt, ptp of **rebuild**

rebuke [rɪˈbjuːk] **1** N reproche m, réprimande f **2** VT réprimander, faire des reproches à; **to ~ sb for sth** reprocher qch à qn; **to ~ sb for having done** reprocher à qn d'avoir fait

rebus ['riːbəs] N (pl **rebuses**) rébus m

rebut [rɪˈbʌt] VT réfuter

rebuttal [rɪˈbʌtl] N réfutation f

recalcitrance [rɪˈkælsɪtrəns] N caractère m or esprit m récalcitrant

recalcitrant [rɪˈkælsɪtrənt] ADJ récalcitrant

recalculate [riːˈkælkjʊleɪt] VT (gen) recalculer; [+ risk, probability] réévaluer

▼ **recall** [rɪˈkɔːl] **1** VT **a** (= summon back) [+ ambassador] rappeler; (Sport) [+ player] rappeler, sélectionner de nouveau; [+ library book] demander le retour de; (Comm) [+ faulty products] (*already sold*) rappeler; (*in shop*) retirer de la vente; (*Fin*) [+ *capital*] faire rentrer; (*fig*) **this music ~s the past** cette musique rappelle le passé; (*lit, fig*) **to ~ sb to life** rappeler qn à la vie; **to ~ Parliament** convoquer le Parlement (en session extraordinaire)

b (= *remember*) se rappeler (**that** que), se souvenir de; **I cannot ~ meeting him** or **whether I met him** je ne me rappelle pas l'avoir rencontré; **I ~ my mother telling me about it** je me souviens que or me rappelle que ma mère m'a parlé de ça; **can you ~ how you felt at the time?** vous rappelez-vous ce que or vous souvenez-vous de ce que vous ressentiez à l'époque?; **as I ~** si mes souvenirs sont bons, si je me souviens bien; **as far as I can ~** (pour) autant que je m'en souvienne, (pour) autant que je me rappelle (*subj*)

2 N rappel *m* (*also Mil*); **the company ordered the ~ of more than 900,000 cars for safety repairs** la société a demandé que 900 000 voitures soient renvoyées en usine pour des réparations concernant la sécurité; (*in library*) **this book is on ~** on a demandé le retour de ce livre; **they are demanding the ~ of parliament** ils demandent que le Parlement soit convoqué en session extraordinaire; (*fig*) **lost beyond ~** perdu à tout jamais

3 COMP ► **recall slip** N (*of library*) fiche *f* de rappel

recant [rɪˈkænt] **1** VT [+ *statement*] rétracter; [+ *religious belief*] abjurer; **to ~ one's opinion** se déjuger, changer d'avis **2** VI se rétracter; (*Rel*) abjurer

recantation [ˌriːkænˈteɪʃən] N rétractation *f*, reniement *m*; (*Rel*) abjuration *f*

recap[1]* [ˈriːkæp] **1** N ABBR = **recapitulation** **2** VTI [rɪˈkæp] (ABBR = **recapitulate**) well, to ~, ... eh bien, en résumé ...

recap[2] [ˈriːkæp] (*US*) **1** N (= *tyre*) pneu *m* rechapé **2** VT rechaper

recapitalization [ˌriːˌkæpɪtəlaɪˈzeɪʃən] N restructuration *f* financière or du capital

recapitalize [ˌriːˈkæpɪtəlaɪz] VT restructurer le capital de, changer la structure financière de

recapitulate [ˌriːkəˈpɪtjʊleɪt] **1** VT [+ *argument*] récapituler, faire le résumé de; [+ *facts*] reprendre **2** VI récapituler, faire un résumé

recapitulation [ˈriːkəˌpɪtjʊˈleɪʃən] N récapitulation *f*

recapture [riːˈkæptʃər] **1** VT [+ *animal, prisoner*] reprendre, capturer; (*esp Sport*) [+ *title*] reconquérir; [+ *emotion, enthusiasm*] retrouver; [*film, play, book*] [+ *atmosphere, period*] recréer **2** N [*of town, territory*] reprise *f*; [*of escapee*] arrestation *f*, capture *f*; [*of escaped animal*] capture *f*

recast [ˌriːˈkɑːst] **1** VT **a** (*Metal*) refondre **b** [+ *play, film*] changer la distribution (des rôles) de; [+ *actor*] donner un nouveau rôle à **c** (= *rewrite*) refondre, remanier **2** N (*Metal*) refonte *f*

recce* [ˈrekɪ] (*gen, Brit Mil*) ABBR = **reconnaissance, reconnoitre**

recd (*Comm*) (ABBR = **received**) reçu

recede [rɪˈsiːd] **1** VI **a** [*tide*] descendre; (*fig*) [*coast, person, threat, danger*] s'éloigner; [*memories, fear*] s'estomper; [*hopes of rescue*] s'amenuiser; [*lights*] s'évanouir (peu à peu); **the footsteps ~d** les pas se sont éloignés, le bruit des pas s'est estompé; **to ~ into the distance** s'éloigner, disparaître dans le lointain; **if untreated the gums ~** si les gencives ne sont pas traitées, les dents se déchaussent **b** [*chin, forehead*] être fuyant; [*gums*] se déchausser; **his hair(line) is receding** son front se dégarnit **c** [*price*] baisser **d** (*frm*) **to ~ from** [+ *opinion, promise*] revenir sur **2** COMP ► **receding chin** N menton *m* fuyant ► **receding forehead** N front *m* fuyant ► **receding hairline** N front *m* dégarni; **he has a receding hairline** son front se dégarnit

receipt [rɪˈsiːt] **1** N **a** (NonC: *esp Comm*) réception *f*; **to acknowledge ~ of** accuser réception de; **on ~ of** dès réception de; **I am in ~ of ...** j'ai reçu ...; **to pay on ~** payer à la réception **b** (= *paper*) (*for payment*) reçu *m*, récépissé *m* (**for** de); (*for parcel, letter*) accusé *m* de réception; (*for object purchased*) ticket *m* de caisse; (*for services*) reçu *m*; (*for taxi*) fiche *f*, reçu *m* **2** **receipts** NPL (*Comm, Fin* = *money taken*) recette(s) *f(pl)*; **tax ~s** recettes *fpl* fiscales, rentrées *fpl* de l'impôt **3** VT [+ *bill*] acquitter **4** COMP ► **receipt book** N livre *m* or carnet *m* de quittances, quittancier *m*

receivable [rɪˈsiːvəbl] **1** ADJ recevable **2** **receivables** NPL (*Fin*) créances *fpl* (recouvrables)

receive [rɪˈsiːv] **1** VT **a** (= *get*) [+ *letter, present, punch*] recevoir; [+ *money, salary*] recevoir, toucher; [+ *refusal, setback*] essuyer; (*Jur*) [+ *stolen goods*] receler; [+ *medical care*] recevoir; [+ *medical treatment*] subir; (*Jur*) **to ~ two years** or **two years' imprisonment** être condamné à deux ans de prison; **we ~d nothing but abuse** nous n'avons reçu que des insultes; (*Comm*) **we ~d your request yesterday** votre demande nous est parvenue hier; (*Comm*) **~d with thanks** pour acquit

b (= *welcome*) recevoir, accueillir; **to ~ sb with open arms** recevoir qn à bras ouverts; **his suggestion was well/not well ~d** sa suggestion a reçu un accueil favorable/défavorable; (*Rel*) **to be ~d into the Church** être reçu dans l'Église

c (*Rad, TV*) [+ *transmission*] capter, recevoir; **are you receiving me?** me recevez-vous? → **loud**

2 VI **a** (*frm*) recevoir; **the countess ~s on Mondays** Madame la comtesse reçoit le lundi **b** (*Jur*) être coupable de recel

received [rɪˈsiːvd] **1** ADJ [*opinion*] reçu; **the ~ wisdom** l'opinion *f* la plus répandue **2** COMP ► **Received Pronunciation** N (*Ling*) prononciation *f* standard (*de l'anglais*) → **ENGLISH**

receiver [rɪˈsiːvər] **1** N **a** receveur *m*, -euse *f*; [*of letter*] destinataire *mf*; [*of goods*] consignataire *m*, réceptionnaire *mf*; (*Jur*) [*of stolen property*] receleur *m*, -euse *f* **b** (*Fin, Jur*) ≈ administrateur *m* provisoire; (*in bankruptcy*) official = syndic *m* de faillite, administrateur *m* judiciaire; **to call in the (official) ~** placer la société en règlement judiciaire **c** [*of telephone*] récepteur *m*, combiné *m*; **to pick up** or **lift the ~** décrocher; **to put down** or **replace the ~** raccrocher **d** (= *radio set*) (poste *m*) récepteur *m* **2** COMP ► **receiver rest** N commutateur *m*

receivership [rɪˈsiːvəʃɪp] N (*Fin*) **the company has gone into ~** la société a été placée en règlement judiciaire

receiving [rɪˈsiːvɪŋ] **1** ADJ récepteur (-trice *f*), de réception; **he blew his top and I was on the ~ end*** il s'est mis dans une colère noire, et c'est moi qui ai écopé* or qui en ai fait les frais*; **he was on the ~ end* of their abuse/hatred/violence** il a fait les frais* de leurs insultes/leur haine/leur violence; (*Rad*) **~ set** poste *m* récepteur **2** N [*of stolen goods*] recel *m* **3** COMP ► **receiving line** N (*US*) rangée de personnes accueillant les invités à une réception

recension [rɪˈsenʃən] N **a** (NonC) révision *f* **b** (= *text*) texte *m* révisé

recent [ˈriːsnt] ADJ [*event, change, invention, survey, history, winner*] récent; [*acquaintance*] de fraîche date, nouveau (nouvelle *f*); **a ~ arrival** (= *person*) un nouveau venu, une nouvelle venue; **his ~ arrival** (= *action*) son arrivée récente; **in ~ years** ces dernières années; **in the ~ past** ces derniers temps; **his most ~ book** son tout dernier livre

recently [ˈriːsntlɪ] ADV (= *not long ago*) récemment; (= *lately*) dernièrement, récemment; **as ~ as ...** pas plus tard que ...; **un-**

til (quite) **~** jusqu'à ces derniers temps, il y a peu de temps encore

receptacle [rɪˈseptəkl] N récipient *m*; (*fig*) réceptacle *m*

reception [rɪˈsepʃən] **1** N **a** (NonC) réception *f* **b** (= *ceremony*) réception *f* **c** (= *welcome*) réception *f*, accueil *m*; **to get a favourable ~** être bien accueilli or reçu; **to give sb a warm/chilly ~** faire un accueil chaleureux/froid à qn **d** (*Rad, TV*) réception *f* **e** (*Brit: in hotel*) réception *f*; **at ~** à la réception **2** COMP ► **reception area** N (*gen*) accueil *m*; [*of hotel*] réception *f* ► **reception centre** N centre *m* d'accueil ► **reception class** N (*Brit Scol*) cours *m* préparatoire ► **reception clerk** N (*Brit*) réceptionniste *mf* ► **reception committee** N (*lit, fig*) comité *m* d'accueil ► **reception desk** N bureau *m* de réception ► **reception room** N (*in public building*) salle *f* de réception; (*in private house*) pièce *f* commune, salon *m*

receptionist [rɪˈsepʃənɪst] N réceptionniste *mf*

receptive [rɪˈseptɪv] ADJ [*person, mood*] réceptif (**to sth** à qch); **~ to new ideas** réceptif or ouvert aux nouvelles idées

receptiveness [rɪˈseptɪvnɪs], **receptivity** [ˌriːsepˈtɪvɪtɪ] N réceptivité *f*

receptor [rɪˈseptər] N (*Physiol, Rad*) récepteur *m*

recess [rɪˈses] **1** N **a** (= *holidays*) (*Jur*) vacances *fpl* (judiciaires); (*Parl*) vacances *fpl* (parlementaires); (*Parl*) **in ~** en vacances **b** (= *short break*) (*US Jur*) suspension *f* d'audience; (*esp US Scol*) récréation *f*; (*US Jur*) **the court is in ~** l'audience est suspendue **c** (= *alcove*) renfoncement *m*; [*of bed*] alcôve *f*; [*of door, window*] embrasure *f*; [*of statue*] niche *f* **d** (= *secret place*) recoin *m*; (*fig* = *depths*) recoin *m*, repli *m*; **in the ~es of his mind** dans les recoins de son esprit **2** VT (= *make an alcove in*) pratiquer un renfoncement dans; (= *put in alcove*) [+ *bed etc*] mettre dans un renfoncement **3** VI (*US Jur, Parl*) suspendre les séances, être en vacances **4** COMP ► **recess appointment** N (*US Pol*) nomination effectuée par le chef de l'exécutif pendant les vacances parlementaires

recessed [ˈrɪsest] ADJ [*doorway, cupboard, shelves*] en retrait; [*window*] en retrait, encastré; [*lighting*] encastré

recession [rɪˈseʃən] N **a** (NonC) recul *m*, régression *f* **b** (*Econ*) récession *f*

recessional [rɪˈseʃənl] (*Rel*) **1** N hymne *m* de sortie du clergé **2** ADJ de sortie

recessionary [rɪˈseʃənərɪ] ADJ de récession

recessive [rɪˈsesɪv] ADJ rétrograde; (*Genetics*) récessif

recharge [ˈriːˈtʃɑːdʒ] **1** VT [+ *battery, gun*] recharger; (*fig*) **to ~ one's batteries** recharger ses batteries* or ses accus* **2** VI [*battery*] se recharger

rechargeable [rɪˈtʃɑːdʒəbl] ADJ [*battery, torch*] rechargeable

recidivism [rɪˈsɪdɪvɪzəm] N récidive *f*

recidivist [rɪˈsɪdɪvɪst] ADJ, N récidiviste *mf*

recipe [ˈresɪpɪ] **1** N **a** (*Culin, Pharm*) recette *f* **b** (*fig*) **~ for happiness** secret *m* du bonheur; **what is your ~ for success?** quelle est votre recette pour réussir?; **lifting restrictions would be a ~ for disaster/anarchy/chaos** la levée des restrictions, c'est le meilleur moyen de s'attirer de gros ennuis/de tomber dans l'anarchie/de tomber dans le chaos **2** COMP ► **recipe book** N (*Culin*) livre *m* de cuisine or de recettes

recipient [rɪˈsɪpɪənt] N (*gen*) personne *f* qui reçoit (or a reçu etc); [*of letter*] destinataire *mf*; [*of cheque*] bénéficiaire *mf*; [*of award, decoration*] récipiendaire *m*; (*Jur*) donataire *mf*; (*Med*) [*of donated organ*] receveur *m*, -euse *f*

reciprocal [rɪ'sɪprəkəl] **1** ADJ (= *mutual*) [*agreement*] réciproque, mutuel; [*action, arrangement, feeling*] réciproque; (*Math*) réciproque, inverse; (*Gram*) réciproque; **~ visits** des échanges *mpl* de visites **2** N (*Math*) réciproque *f*

reciprocally [rɪ'sɪprəkəlɪ] ADV réciproquement, mutuellement; (*Math*) inversement

reciprocate [rɪ'sɪprəkeɪt] **1** VT **a** [+ *smiles, wishes*] rendre; [+ *help*] donner or offrir en retour; [+ *kindness*] retourner **b** (*Tech*) donner un mouvement alternatif à **2** VI **a** **he insulted me and I ~d** il m'a injurié, et je lui ai rendu la pareille; **he called me a fool and I ~d** il m'a traité d'imbécile et je lui ai retourné le compliment **b** (*Tech*) avoir un mouvement alternatif *or* de va-et-vient **3** COMP ► **reciprocating device** N dispositif *m* de va-et-vient ► **reciprocating engine** N moteur *m* alternatif

reciprocation [rɪ,sɪprə'keɪʃən] N **a** [*of help, kindness*] échange *m* **b** (*Tech*) alternance *f*, va-et-vient *m* inv

reciprocity [,resɪ'prɒsɪtɪ] N réciprocité *f*

recital [rɪ'saɪtl] **1** N **a** (= *account*) récit *m*; [*of details*] énumération *f* **b** [*of poetry*] récitation *f*, récital *m*; [*of music*] récital *m* **2** **recitals** NPL (*Jur: in contract*) préambule *m*

recitation [,resɪ'teɪʃən] N récitation *f*; **to give a poetry ~** dire des vers

recitative [,resɪtə'tiːv] N récitatif *m*

recite [rɪ'saɪt] **1** VT **a** [+ *poetry*] réciter, déclamer **b** [+ *facts*] exposer; [+ *details*] énumérer **2** VI réciter, déclamer

reckless ['reklɪs] **1** ADJ [*person, behaviour*] (= *heedless*) insouciant; (= *rash*) imprudent; [*disregard*] irresponsable; **with ~ abandon** avec une désinvolture imprudente; **~ of the consequences** insouciant des conséquences **2** COMP ► **reckless driver** N conducteur *m*, -trice *f* imprudent(e) ► **reckless driving** N conduite *f* imprudente ► **reckless endangerment** N (*US Jur*) mise en danger d'autrui par imprudence

recklessly ['reklɪslɪ] ADV imprudemment

recklessness ['reklɪsnɪs] N [*of person, behaviour*] (= *heedlessness*) insouciance *f*; (= *rashness*) imprudence *f*; [*of driving*] imprudence *f*

reckon ['rekən] **1** VT **a** (= *calculate*) [+ *time, numbers, points*] compter; [+ *cost, surface*] calculer **b** (= *judge*) considérer, estimer; **I ~ him among my friends** je le compte parmi *or* au nombre de mes amis; **she is ~ed (to be) a beautiful woman** elle est considérée comme une femme très belle; **the price is ~ed to be too high** on considère *or* estime le prix trop élevé; **her chances of survival cannot now be ~ed good** à l'heure actuelle on estime qu'elle a de faibles chances de survivre; **the number of victims was ~ed at around 300** on a estimé le nombre de victimes à environ 300 personnes **c** (* = *think*) penser; **what do you ~ one of these houses would cost?** d'après vous or à votre avis, combien coûte une maison comme celle-ci?; **I ~ we can start** je pense qu'on peut commencer; **I ~ he must be about forty** je lui donnerais la quarantaine; **about thirty, I ~** une trentaine, à mon avis **2** VI **a** calculer, compter; **~ing from tomorrow** en comptant à partir de demain, à compter de demain **b** (*fig*) **you can ~ on 30** tu peux compter sur 30; **I was ~ing on doing that tomorrow** j'avais prévu de faire *or* je pensais faire cela demain; **I wasn't ~ing on having to do that** je ne m'attendais pas à devoir faire cela; **they ~ to sell most of them abroad** ils comptent en vendre la majorité à l'étranger; **you'll have to ~ with six more** il faudra compter avec six de

plus; **she had not ~ed on** *or* **with an objection from them** elle ne s'attendait pas à une objection de leur part; **he's a person to be ~ed with** c'est une personne avec laquelle il faut compter; **if you insult him you'll have to ~ with the whole family** si vous l'insultez, vous aurez affaire à toute la famille; **he was ~ing without his secretary** il avait compté sans sa secrétaire; **he ~ed without the fact that ...** il n'avait pas prévu que ..., il n'avait pas tenu compte du fait que ...
► **reckon in** VT SEP prendre en compte
► **reckon up** VT SEP (*gen*) calculer; (= *add*) ajouter, additionner

reckoner ['rekənər] N → **ready**

reckoning ['rekənɪŋ] **1** N **a** (*Math etc*) (= *evaluation*) compte *m*; (= *calculation*) calcul *m*; **to be out in one's ~** s'être trompé dans ses calculs **b** (*Comm*) règlement *m* de compte(s) (*lit*); [*of hotel*] note *f*; [*of restaurant*] addition *f*; (*Rel*) **the day of ~** le jour du Jugement; (*fig*) **the day of ~ can't be far away** un de ces jours ça va lui (*or* nous *etc*) retomber dessus **c** (= *judgement*) estimation *f*; **to the best of my ~** (pour) autant que je puisse en juger; **in your ~** d'après vous, à votre avis **d** (*Naut*) estime *f* → **dead**

reclaim [rɪ'kleɪm] **1** VT **a** [+ *land*] (*gen*) reconquérir; (*from forest, bush*) défricher; (*from sea*) assécher, gagner sur la mer; (*with manure etc*) amender, bonifier; [+ *by-product*] récupérer; (= *demand back*) réclamer (**sth from sb** qch à qn); [+ *language, term*] récupérer; [+ *title*] reprendre; [+ *tax*] se faire rembourser; **the land has been ~ed from the sea** la terre a été gagnée sur la mer; **a campaign to ~ the night** *or* **streets** une campagne pour protester contre l'insécurité de la ville la nuit **2** N **past** *or* **beyond ~** perdu à tout jamais; **he is beyond ~** il ne se corrigera jamais

reclaimable [rɪ'kleɪməbl] ADJ [*land*] amendable; [*by-products*] récupérable

reclamation [,reklə'meɪʃən] N **a** (= *conversion*) [*of land*] (*gen*) mise *f* en valeur; (*from sea*) assèchement *m*; (*from marsh*) assèchement *m*, assainissement *m*; (*from forest, bush*) défrichement *m*; [*of marshland*] assèchement *m*, assainissement *m*; [*of desert*] reconquête *f*; [*of mine*] reconversion *f* **b** (= *recovery*) récupération *f*

reclassify [,riː'klæsɪfaɪ] VT reclasser, reclassifier

recline [rɪ'klaɪn] **1** VT [+ *head, arm*] reposer, appuyer **2** VI [*person*] être allongé, être étendu; **she was reclining in the armchair** elle était allongée *or* étendue sur le fauteuil; **reclining in his bath** étendu *or* allongé dans son bain; **the seat ~s** le siège est inclinable, le dossier (du siège) est réglable **3** COMP ► **reclining chair** N chaise *f* longue ► **reclining seat** N [*of coach, plane, car*] siège *m* inclinable *or* à dossier réglable

recluse [rɪ'kluːs] N reclus(e) *m(f)*, solitaire *mf*

reclusive [rɪ'kluːsɪv] ADJ reclus

recognition [,rekəg'nɪʃən] N **a** (*gen, Pol* = *acknowledgement*) reconnaissance *f*; **in ~ of ...** en reconnaissance de ... **b** (= *fame etc*) **he seeks ~** il veut être reconnu; **this brought him ~ at last** c'est ce qui lui a enfin permis d'être reconnu; **his exploits have gained world-wide ~** ses exploits ont été reconnus dans le monde entier; **to receive no ~** passer inaperçu **c** (= *identification*) reconnaissance *f*; (*Aviat*) identification *f*; **he has changed beyond** *or* **out of all ~** il est devenu méconnaissable; **he has changed it beyond** *or* **out of all ~** il l'a rendu méconnaissable; **to improve beyond** *or* **out of (all) ~** s'améliorer jusqu'à en être méconnaissable **d** (*Comput*) reconnaissance *f*; **speech ~** reconnaissance *f* de la parole

recognizable ['rekəgnaɪzəbl] ADJ reconnaissable; **she was easily ~ by her walk** elle était facilement reconnaissable à sa démarche; **it**

was instantly ~ to him il l'a reconnu immédiatement; **he was hardly ~ as the boy who ...** c'est à peine si l'on reconnaissait en lui le garçon qui ...

recognizably [,rekəg'naɪzəblɪ] ADV **it is ~ different/better** on voit que c'est différent/meilleur; **he was ~ a genius** on voyait bien que c'était un génie; **it was ~ a woman's face** on reconnaissait bien un visage de femme

recognizance [rɪ'kɒgnɪzəns] N (*esp US*) (*Jur*) engagement *m*; (= *sum of money*) caution *f* (personnelle); **to enter into ~s (for sb)** se porter caution (pour qn); **bail in his own ~ of £1,000** mise *f* en liberté sous caution personnelle de 1 000 livres

▼ **recognize** ['rekəgnaɪz] VT **a** (*gen*) reconnaître (**by** à, **as** comme étant, **that** que) **b** (*US*) [*chairman of meeting*] donner la parole à

recognized ['rekəgnaɪzd] ADJ (*gen*) reconnu; (*Comm*) attitré

recoil [rɪ'kɔɪl] **1** VI **a** [*person*] reculer, avoir un mouvement de recul (**from** devant); **to ~ in disgust** reculer de dégoût; **to ~ from doing** reculer devant l'idée de faire, se refuser à faire **b** [*gun*] reculer; [*spring*] se détendre; [*actions etc*] retomber (**on** sur) **2** N [*of gun*] recul *m*; [*of spring*] détente *f*; (*fig*) (*from disgusting sight*) dégoût *m* (**from** pour, de), horreur *f* (**from** de); (*from idea*) répugnance *f* (**from** pour)

recollect [,rekə'lekt] **1** VT se rappeler, se souvenir de; **to ~ o.s.** se recueillir **2** VI se souvenir; **as far as I (can) ~** autant que je m'en souvienne

recollection [,rekə'lekʃən] N souvenir *m*; **to the best of my ~** autant que je m'en souvienne; **his ~ of it is vague** il ne s'en souvient que vaguement; **I have some ~ of it** j'en ai un vague souvenir; **I have no ~ of it** je ne m'en souviens pas, je n'en ai aucun souvenir

recommence [,riːkə'mens] VTI recommencer (**doing** à faire)

▼ **recommend** [,rekə'mend] **1** VT **a** (= *speak good of*) recommander; **to ~ sth/sb to sb** recommander qch/qn à qn; **to ~ sb for a job** recommander qn pour un emploi; **to come highly ~ed** être vivement recommandé **b** (= *advise*) recommander, conseiller (**sb to do** à qn de faire); **to ~ doing sth** recommander *or* conseiller de faire qch; **what do you ~ for a sore throat?** que recommandez-vous pour guérir un mal de gorge?; **he was ~ed to accept** on lui a recommandé *or* conseillé d'accepter; **it is to be ~ed** c'est à conseiller; **it is not to be ~ed** c'est à déconseiller **c** (= *make acceptable*) **she has a lot to ~ her** elle a beaucoup de qualités en sa faveur, il y a beaucoup à dire en sa faveur; **she has little to ~ her** elle n'a pas grand-chose pour elle; **the apartment has little to ~ it** l'appartement est sans grand intérêt; **this biography has much to ~ it** cette biographie est vraiment à recommander **d** (*frm* = *commit*) [+ *child, one's soul*] recommander, confier (**to** à) **2** COMP ► **recommended daily allowance, recommended daily amount, recommended daily intake** N apport *m* quotidien *or* journalier recommandé ► **recommended reading** N (*NonC*) ouvrages *mpl* recommandés ► **recommended retail price** N (*Comm*) prix *m* conseillé

recommendable [,rekə'mendəbl] ADJ recommandable; **it is not ~** c'est à déconseiller

recommendation [,rekəmen'deɪʃən] N recommandation *f*; **on the ~ of ...** sur la recommandation de ...

recommendatory [,rekə'mendətərɪ] ADJ de recommandation

recommittal [,riːkə'mɪtl] N (*US Parl*) renvoi *m* en commission (*d'un projet de loi*)

recompense ['rekəmpens] **1** N **a** (= reward) récompense f; **in ~ for** en récompense de **b** (Jur: for damage) dédommagement m, compensation f **2** VT **a** (= reward) récompenser (**for** de) **b** (Jur etc = repay) [+ person] dédommager; [+ damage, loss] compenser, réparer

recompose [ˌriːkəm'pəʊz] VT **a** (= rewrite) recomposer **b** (= calm) **to ~ o.s.** se ressaisir, retrouver son calme or son sang-froid

reconcilable ['rekənsaɪləbl] ADJ [ideas, opinions] conciliable, compatible (**with** avec)

reconcile ['rekənsaɪl] VT [+ person] réconcilier (**to** avec); [+ two facts or ideas] concilier (**with** avec, **and** et); **to ~ a dispute** régler un litige; **they were ~d** ils se sont réconciliés; **to ~ o.s. to sth** se résigner à qch, se faire à qch; **to ~ sb to sth** faire accepter qch à qn

reconciliation [ˌrekənsɪlɪ'eɪʃən] N [of persons] réconciliation f; [of opinions, principles] conciliation f

recondite [rɪ'kɒndaɪt] ADJ (frm) abscons (frm)

recondition [ˌriːkən'dɪʃən] VT remettre à neuf or en état; (Aut) **~ed engine** moteur m refait à neuf or entièrement révisé; **~ed fridge/vacuum cleaner** réfrigérateur m/aspirateur m refait à neuf or remis en état

reconnaissance [rɪ'kɒnɪsəns] **1** N (Aviat, Mil) reconnaissance f **2** COMP ► **reconnaissance flight** N vol m de reconnaissance ► **reconnaissance patrol** N patrouille f de reconnaissance

reconnect ['riːkə'nekt] VT **a** [+ cable, machine, electricity, water supply] reconnecter, rebrancher; [+ pipe] raccorder **b** (Elec, Gas, Telec etc) [+ customer, household] reconnecter

reconnection fee [ˌriːkə'nekʃən ˌfiː] N (Elec, Telec etc) reprise f d'abonnement

reconnoiter, reconnoitre (US) [ˌrekə'nɔɪtər] (Aviat, Mil) **1** VT [+ region] reconnaître **2** VI faire une reconnaissance

reconnoitring [ˌrekə'nɔɪtərɪŋ] N (Aviat, Mil) reconnaissance f

reconquer [ˌriː'kɒŋkər] VT reconquérir

reconquest [ˌriː'kɒŋkwest] N reconquête f

reconsider [ˌriːkən'sɪdər] **1** VT [+ decision, opinion] reconsidérer, réexaminer; [+ judgement] réviser; **won't you ~ it?** est-ce que vous seriez prêt à reconsidérer la question? **2** VI (gen) reconsidérer or réexaminer la question; (= change one's mind) changer d'avis

reconsideration [ˈriːkənˌsɪdə'reɪʃən] N remise f en cause, nouvel examen m

reconstitute [ˌriː'kɒnstɪtjuːt] VT (gen) reconstituer; (Culin) réhydrater

reconstitution [ˈriːˌkɒnstɪ'tjuːʃən] N reconstitution f

reconstruct [ˌriːkən'strʌkt] VT [+ building] reconstruire, rebâtir; [+ crime] reconstituer; [+ policy, system] reconstruire

reconstruction [ˌriːkən'strʌkʃən] N [of building, policy, system] reconstruction f; [of crime] reconstitution f; (US Hist) **the Reconstruction** la Reconstruction de l'Union (après 1865)

reconstructive surgery [ˌriːkən'strʌktɪv 'sɜːdʒərɪ] N chirurgie f réparatrice

reconvene [ˌriːkən'viːn] **1** VT reconvoquer **2** VI [committee, jury etc] se réunir or s'assembler de nouveau; [meeting] reprendre; **we will ~ at 10 o'clock** la réunion (or l'audience etc) reprendra à 10 heures

▼ **record** [rɪ'kɔːd] **1** VT **a** (= register) [+ facts, story] enregistrer; [+ protest, disapproval] prendre acte de; [+ event etc] (in journal, log) noter, consigner; (= describe) décrire; **to ~ the proceedings of a meeting** tenir le procès-verbal d'une assemblée; (Parl) **to ~ one's vote** voter; **his speech was ~ed in the newspapers ...** son discours, tel que le rapportent les journaux ...; **history/the author ~s that ...** l'histoire/l'auteur rapporte que ...; **it's not ~ed anywhere** ce n'est pas attesté; **to ~ the population** recenser la population **b** [instrument, thermometer] enregistrer, marquer **c** [+ speech, music] enregistrer; **to ~ sth on tape** enregistrer qch sur bande; **to ~ sth on video** magnétoscoper qch; (Telec) **this is a ~ed message** ceci est or vous écoutez un message enregistré → **tape** **2** VI enregistrer; **he is ~ing at 5 o'clock** il enregistre à 5 heures; **his voice does not ~ well** sa voix ne se prête pas bien à l'enregistrement

3 ['rekɔːd] N **a** (= account, report) rapport m, récit m; (of attendance) registre m; (of act, decision) minute f; (of evidence, meeting) procès-verbal m; (= official report) rapport m officiel; (Jur) enregistrement m; (= historical report) document m; **the society's ~s** les actes mpl de la société; (public) **~s** archives fpl, annales fpl; **to make** or **keep a ~** noter, consigner; (fig) **this statue is a ~ of a past civilization** cette statue est un témoin d'une civilisation passée; (fig) **it is on ~ that ...** c'est un fait établi or il est établi que ...; **there is no similar example on ~** aucun exemple semblable n'est attesté; **to go/be on ~ as saying that ...** déclarer/avoir déclaré publiquement que ...; **to put on ~** consigner, mentionner (par écrit); **the highest temperatures on ~** les plus fortes températures enregistrées; **there is no ~ of his having said it** il n'est noté or consigné nulle part qu'il l'ait dit; **there is no ~ of it in history** l'histoire n'en fait pas mention; **to put** or **set the ~ straight** mettre les choses au clair, dissiper toute confusion possible; **just to put** or **set the ~ straight, let me point out that ...** pour qu'il n'y ait aucune confusion possible, disons bien que ...; (fig) **for the ~, they refuse ...** il faut noter or signaler qu'ils refusent ...; **this is strictly off the ~*** ceci est à titre (purement) confidentiel or officieux, ceci doit rester strictement entre nous; **the interview was off the ~*** l'interview n'était pas officielle; **off the ~*, he did come!** il est effectivement venu, mais que ceci reste entre nous or mais je ne vous ai rien dit; (Press etc) **on the ~, he admitted that ...** dans ses déclarations officielles, il a reconnu que ...

b (= case history) dossier m; (= card) fiche f; (Mil) **service ~** états mpl de service; (Jur) (police) **~** casier m judiciaire; **~ of previous convictions** dossier m du prévenu; (Jur, Police) **he's got a clean ~** ◊ **he hasn't got a ~*** il a un casier (judiciaire) vierge; **he's got a long ~** il a un casier judiciaire chargé; **France's splendid ~** les succès mpl glorieux de la France; **his past ~** sa conduite passée; **his war ~** son passé militaire; (Scol) **his attendance ~ is bad** il a été souvent absent; **to have a good ~ at school** avoir un bon dossier scolaire; **this airline has a good safety ~** cette compagnie aérienne a une bonne tradition de sécurité; **he left a splendid ~ of achievements** il avait à son compte de magnifiques réussites → **police, track**

c (Comput) article m

d (= recording) [of voice etc] enregistrement m

e (Audio) disque m; **to make** or **cut a ~** graver un disque

f (Sport, fig) record m; **to beat** or **break the ~** battre le record; **to hold the ~** détenir le record; **long-jump ~** record m du saut en longueur → **world**

g [of seismograph etc] courbe f enregistrée

4 COMP [amount, attendance, result] record inv ► **record breaker** N (= person) (gen) nouveau champion or nouvelle championne en titre; (Sport) nouveau recordman m, nouvelle recordwoman f; (= achievement) performance f qui établit un nouveau record ► **record-breaking** ADJ qui bat tous les records ► **record cabinet** N casier m à disques,

discothèque f (meuble) ► **record card** N fiche f ► **record company** N maison f de disques ► **record dealer** N disquaire mf ► **record deck** N platine f disques ► **record holder** N détenteur m, -trice f du record ► **record library** N discothèque f (collection) ► **record player** N tourne-disque m ► **record producer** N producteur m, -trice f de disques ► **record time** N **to do sth in ~ time** faire qch en un temps record ► **record token** N chèque-cadeau m (à échanger contre un disque), chèque-disque m

recorded [rɪ'kɔːdɪd] **1** ADJ **a** [music, message] enregistré; [programme] préenregistré, transmis en différé **b** (= noted) [fact, occurrence] attesté, noté; [crime] signalé; [history] écrit **2** COMP ► **recorded delivery** N (Brit Post) (= service) ≈ recommandé m (avec accusé de réception); [+ letter, parcel] envoi m en recommandé; **to send sth by ~ delivery** ≈ envoyer qch en recommandé

recorder [rɪ'kɔːdər] N **a** [of official facts] archiviste mf; (= registrar) greffier m **b** (Brit Jur) ≈ avocat m nommé à la fonction de juge; (US Jur) ≈ juge m suppléant **c** [of sounds] (= apparatus) appareil m enregistreur; (= tape recorder) magnétophone m; (= cassette recorder) magnétophone m à cassettes → **video** **d** (= person) artiste mf qui enregistre **e** (Mus) flûte f à bec; **descant/treble/tenor/bass ~** flûte f à bec soprano/alto/ténor/basse

recording [rɪ'kɔːdɪŋ] **1** N [of sound, facts] enregistrement m; (Rad) "**this programme is a ~**" « ce programme a été enregistré » **2** ADJ [artist] qui enregistre; [apparatus] enregistreur **3** COMP ► **the Recording Angel** N (Rel) l'ange qui tient le grand livre des bienfaits et des méfaits ► **recording equipment** N matériel m d'enregistrement ► **recording session** N séance f d'enregistrement ► **recording studio** N studio m d'enregistrement ► **recording tape** N bande f or ruban m magnétique ► **recording van** N (Rad, TV) car m de reportage

recount [rɪ'kaʊnt] VT (= relate) raconter, narrer

re-count ['riː'kaʊnt] **1** VT recompter, compter de nouveau **2** ['riː'kaʊnt] N [of votes] recomptage m or nouveau comptage m des voix

recoup [rɪ'kuːp] **1** VT **a** (= make good) [+ losses] récupérer; **to ~ costs** [person] rentrer dans ses fonds; [earnings] couvrir les frais; [course of action] permettre de couvrir les frais **b** (= reimburse) dédommager (**for** de); **to ~ o.s.** se dédommager, se rattraper **c** (Jur) déduire, défalquer **2** VI récupérer ses pertes

recourse [rɪ'kɔːs] N recours m (**to** à); **to have ~ to ...** avoir recours à ..., recourir à ...

recover [rɪ'kʌvər] **1** VT [+ sth lost, one's appetite, reason, balance] retrouver; [+ sth lent] reprendre (**from sb** à qn), récupérer; [+ lost territory] regagner, reconquérir; [+ sth floating] repêcher; [+ space capsule, wreck] récupérer; (Ind etc) [+ materials] récupérer; (Fin) [+ debt] recouvrer, récupérer; [+ goods, property] rentrer en possession de; **to ~ one's breath** reprendre haleine or sa respiration; **to ~ one's strength** reprendre des forces; **to ~ consciousness** revenir à soi, reprendre connaissance; **to ~ one's sight/health** retrouver or recouvrer la vue/la santé; **to ~ land from the sea** conquérir du terrain sur la mer; (fig) **to ~ lost ground** se rattraper; **to ~ o.s.** or **one's composure** se ressaisir, se reprendre; **to ~ expenses** rentrer dans ses frais, récupérer ses débours; **to ~ one's losses** réparer ses pertes; (Jur) **to ~ damages** obtenir des dommages-intérêts

2 VI **a** (after shock, accident) se remettre (**from** de); (from illness) guérir, se rétablir (**from** de); (= regain consciousness) revenir à soi, reprendre connaissance; (after error) se ressaisir; [economy, currency] se rétablir, se redresser; [stock market] reprendre; [shares] re-

monter ; **she has completely ~ed** elle est tout à fait rétablie
b (Jur) obtenir gain de cause ; **right to ~** droit m de reprise

re-cover [ˌriːˈkʌvə^r] VT recouvrir

recoverable [rɪˈkʌvərəbl] ADJ [goods, knowledge] récupérable ; [costs, debts] recouvrable ; [losses] réparable

recovered [rɪˈkʌvəd] **1** ADJ (after illness) guéri, remis **2** COMP ► **recovered memory** N (Psych) (= thing remembered) souvenir d'une expérience traumatisante rappelé par psychothérapie ; (NonC = ability to remember) rappel d'expériences traumatisantes par psychothérapie

▼ **recovery** [rɪˈkʌvərɪ] **1** N **a** (from illness) guérison f (**from sth** de qch) ; (from operation) rétablissement m ; **he is making a good ~** (gen) il se remet bien ; (from illness) il est en bonne voie de guérison ; (from operation) il est en bonne voie de rétablissement ; **to make a full ~** (from illness) guérir complètement ; (from operation) se remettre complètement ; **he made a good ~ from his stroke** il s'est bien remis de son attaque ; **best wishes for a speedy ~** meilleurs vœux de prompt rétablissement ; **to be (well) on the road** or **way to ~** être en (bonne) voie de guérison ; (from alcohol, drug addiction) **to be in ~** être en cure de désintoxication ; **to be past ~** [sick person] être dans un état désespéré ; [situation] être sans remède, être irrémédiable ; (Sport) **to make a ~** se ressaisir
b (Fin, Econ) [of economy, market] reprise f, redressement m ; [of shares] remontée f ; **a ~ in sales/in the housing market** une reprise des ventes/du marché de l'immobilier ; **to engineer the ~ of the economy** relancer l'économie ; **to be on the road to ~** être sur la voie de la reprise
c (= retrieval) (gen) récupération f ; [of body] (from water) repêchage m ; **a reward for the ~ of the Turner painting** une récompense à la personne qui permettra de retrouver or récupérer le tableau de Turner
d (= regaining) [of memory, sight, health] recouvrement m ; [of consciousness, breath, strength] reprise f ; [of territory] reconquête f ; **to bring about the ~ of sb's equanimity/reason/appetite** faire retrouver à qn sa sérénité/sa raison/son appétit
e (Fin) [of expenses] remboursement m ; [of debt] recouvrement m ; [of losses] réparation f ; (Jur) [of damages] obtention f
2 COMP ► **recovery operation** N opération f de récupération (d'un vaisseau spatial etc) ► **recovery position** N (Med) position f latérale de sécurité ; **to put sb in the ~ position** mettre qn en position latérale de sécurité ► **recovery room** N (Med) salle f de réveil ► **recovery ship** N (Space, Naut) navire m de récupération ► **recovery team** N (Aviat, Naut) équipe f de sauvetage ► **recovery vehicle** N (Aut) dépanneuse f ► **recovery vessel** N (Space, Naut) = **recovery ship**

recreant [ˈrekrɪənt] ADJ, N (liter) lâche mf, traître(sse) m(f)

recreate [ˌriːkrɪˈeɪt] VT recréer

recreation [ˌrekrɪˈeɪʃən] **1** N **a** (NonC) récréation f, détente f ; **for ~ I go fishing** je vais à la pêche pour me détendre **b** (Scol) récréation f, récré* f **2** COMP ► **recreation ground** N terrain m de jeux ► **recreation room** N [of school, hospital etc] salle f de récréation ; (US) [of home] salle f de jeux

recreational [ˌrekrɪˈeɪʃənl] **1** ADJ (gen) pour les loisirs ; **~ facilities** équipements mpl de loisirs **2** COMP ► **recreational drug** N drogue f euphorisante ► **recreational sex** N rapports mpl sexuels purement physiques ► **recreational therapist** N thérapeute qui soigne par le jeu ► **recreational therapy** N thérapie par le jeu ► **recreational vehicle** N (US) camping-car m, autocaravane f

recreative [ˈrekrɪˌeɪtɪv] ADJ récréatif, divertissant

recriminate [rɪˈkrɪmɪneɪt] VI récriminer (**against** contre)

recrimination [rɪˌkrɪmɪˈneɪʃən] N récrimination f

recriminatory [rɪˈkrɪmɪneɪtərɪ] ADJ [argument] récriminateur (-trice f), plein de récriminations ; [shout] de protestation ; **~ remark** récrimination f

rec room* [ˈrekrʊm] N (US) (ABBR = **recreation room**) salle f de jeux

recrudesce [ˌriːkruːˈdes] VI (liter) être en recrudescence

recrudescence [ˌriːkruːˈdesns] N (liter) recrudescence f

recrudescent [ˌriːkruːˈdesnt] ADJ (liter) recrudescent

recruit [rɪˈkruːt] **1** N (Mil, fig) recrue f ; **the party gained ~s from the middle classes** le parti faisait des recrues dans la bourgeoisie → **raw** **2** VT [+ member, soldier, staff] recruter ; **the party was ~ed from the middle classes** le parti se recrutait dans la bourgeoisie ; **he ~ed me to help** il m'a embauché* pour aider

recruiting [rɪˈkruːtɪŋ] **1** N recrutement m **2** COMP ► **recruiting office** N (Mil) bureau m de recrutement ► **recruiting officer** N (officier m) recruteur m

recruitment [rɪˈkruːtmənt] **1** N recrutement m **2** COMP ► **recruitment agency** N agence f de recrutement ► **recruitment consultant** N conseil m en recrutement

recta [ˈrektə] NPL of **rectum**

rectal [ˈrektəl] ADJ rectal

rectangle [ˈrekˌtæŋgl] N rectangle m

rectangular [rekˈtæŋgjʊlə^r] ADJ rectangulaire

rectifiable [ˈrektɪfaɪəbl] ADJ rectifiable

rectification [ˌrektɪfɪˈkeɪʃən] N (gen, Chem, Math) rectification f ; (Elec) redressement m

rectifier [ˈrektɪfaɪə^r] N (Elec) redresseur m

rectify [ˈrektɪfaɪ] VT **a** [+ error] rectifier, corriger ; **to ~ an omission** réparer une négligence or un oubli **b** (Chem, Math) rectifier **c** (Elec) redresser

rectilineal [ˌrektɪˈlɪnɪəl], **rectilinear** [ˌrektɪˈlɪnɪə^r] ADJ rectiligne

rectitude [ˈrektɪtjuːd] N rectitude f

rector [ˈrektə^r] N **a** (Rel) pasteur m (anglican) **b** (Scot Scol) proviseur m (de lycée) ; (Univ) ≈ recteur m

rectorship [ˈrektəʃɪp] N (Scot Scol) provisorat m ; (Univ) ≈ rectorat m

rectory [ˈrektərɪ] N presbytère m (anglican)

rectum [ˈrektəm] N (pl **rectums** or **recta**) rectum m

recumbent [rɪˈkʌmbənt] ADJ (liter) [person] allongé, étendu ; (Art) **~ figure** (gen) figure f couchée or allongée ; (on tomb) gisant m

recuperate [rɪˈkuːpəreɪt] **1** VI (Med) se rétablir, récupérer **2** VT [+ object] récupérer ; [+ losses] réparer

recuperation [rɪˌkuːpəˈreɪʃən] N (Med) rétablissement m ; [of materials etc] récupération f

recuperative [rɪˈkuːpərətɪv] ADJ [powers] de récupération ; [holiday, effect] réparateur (-trice f)

recur [rɪˈkɜː^r] VI **a** (= happen again) [error, event] se reproduire ; [idea, theme] se retrouver, revenir ; [illness, infection] réapparaître ; [opportunity, problem] se représenter **b** (= come to mind again) revenir à la mémoire (**to sb** de qn) **c** (Math) se reproduire périodiquement

recurrence [rɪˈkʌrəns] N [of problem, event, idea, theme] répétition f ; [of headache, symptom] réapparition f ; [of opportunity, problem] réapparition f, retour m ; **a ~ of the illness** un nouvel accès de la maladie, une rechute ;

let there be no ~ of this que ceci ne se reproduise plus

recurrent [rɪˈkʌrənt] **1** ADJ **a** (= recurring) récurrent ; **~ bouts of tonsillitis** de fréquentes angines fpl ; **~ bouts of malaria** des crises fpl de paludisme intermittentes ; **a ~ feature** un phénomène récurrent, une constante **b** (Anat) récurrent **2** COMP ► **recurrent expenses** NPL (gen) dépenses fpl courantes ; (Comm) frais mpl généraux

recurring [rɪˈkɜːrɪŋ] **1** ADJ **a** = **recurrent a** **b** (Math) **3.3333 ~** 3,3 à l'infini ; **0.2727 ~** 0,27 périodique **2** COMP ► **recurring decimal** N fraction f décimale récurrente or périodique

recursion [rɪˈkɜːʃən] N (Math, Gram) récurrence f

recursive [rɪˈkɜːsɪv] ADJ (Gram) récursif

recursively [rɪˈkɜːsɪvlɪ] ADV de façon récursive

recursiveness [rɪˈkɜːsɪvnɪs] N récursivité f

recusant [ˈrekjʊzənt] ADJ (Rel) réfractaire

recyclable [ˌriːˈsaɪkləbl] ADJ recyclable

recycle [ˌriːˈsaɪkl] **1** VT (gen) recycler ; [+ waste, water] retraiter ; (Ind) [+ revenue] réinvestir **2** COMP ► **recycled paper** N papier m recyclé

recycling [ˌriːˈsaɪklɪŋ] **1** N recyclage m **2** COMP ► **recycling plant** N (gen) usine f de recyclage ; (for large-scale or toxic waste) usine f de traitement des déchets ► **recycling scheme** N programme m de recyclage

red [red] **1** ADJ **a** (in colour) rouge ; [hair] roux (rousse f) ; **~ as a beetroot** (Brit) or **a beet** (US) rouge comme une tomate ; **to go as ~ as a beetroot** (Brit) or **a beet** (US) (gen, from effort, sun, alcohol, embarrassment) devenir rouge comme une tomate or une pivoine ; (from anger) devenir rouge de colère ; **he was rather ~ in the face** (naturally) il était rougeaud, il avait le teint rouge ; **her face was ~** (gen, from anger, effort, sun, heat, alcohol) elle avait le visage rouge ; (= ashamed, embarrassed) elle était rouge jusqu'aux oreilles ; **was I ~ in the face!*** ◊ **was my face ~!*** ◊ **did I have a ~ face!*** j'étais rouge jusqu'aux oreilles ! ; **he went ~ in the face** son visage est devenu tout rouge ; **~ with anger** rouge de colère ; **to go** or **turn ~ with embarrassment** rougir de confusion or d'embarras ; **nature ~ in tooth and claw** la nature impitoyable or sauvage ; (US) **to go into ~ ink*** [company] être dans le rouge ; [individual] se mettre à découvert ; **to bleed ~ ink*** [business, company] battre de l'aile ; (Brit) **it's like a ~ rag to a bull** c'est comme le rouge pour les taureaux ; (Brit) **that is like a ~ rag to him** il voit rouge quand on lui en parle (or quand on le lui montre etc) ; **to see ~** voir rouge ; (US) **it's not worth a ~ cent*** ça ne vaut pas un rond* ; (US) **I didn't get a ~ cent!** je n'ai pas touché un centime or un rond !* ■ (PROV) **~ sky at night, shepherd's delight, ~ sky in the morning, shepherd's warning** ciel rouge le soir, signe de beau temps, ciel rouge le matin, signe de mauvais temps → **3** ; → **blood, brick, man, paint**
b (Pol* pej) rouge ; **better ~ than dead** plutôt rouge que mort
2 N **a** (= colour, wine) rouge m
b (Pol = person) rouge mf, communiste mf ; **he sees ~s under the bed** il voit des communistes partout
c (Billiards) bille f rouge ; (Roulette) rouge m
d (fig) **to be in the ~*** [individual] être à découvert ; [company] être en déficit ; **to get out of the ~** ne plus être à découvert, combler le déficit ; **to be £100 in the ~** avoir un découvert or un déficit de 100 livres
e (US Hist) **the Reds** (= Indians) les Peaux-Rouges mpl
3 COMP ► **red admiral (butterfly)** N vulcain m ► **red alert** N alerte f maximale or rouge ; (Mil) **to be on ~ alert** être en état

► LANGUAGE IN USE: recovery 23.4

d'alerte maximale ► **the Red Army** N l'Armée f rouge ► **Red Army Faction** N Fraction f armée rouge ► **red-blooded** ADJ vigoureux ► **red-breasted merganser** N harle m huppé ► **red-brick** ADJ en briques rouges ♦ N (*Brit: also* ~-**brick university**) université f de fondation assez récente ► **red cabbage** N chou m rouge ► **red cap** N (*Brit Mil**) policier m militaire; (*US Rail*) porteur m ► **red card** N (*Ftbl*) carton m rouge ► **red carpet** N (*fig*) **to roll out the ~ carpet for sb** dérouler le tapis rouge pour recevoir qn, recevoir qn en grande pompe ► **red-carpet treatment** N accueil m en grande pompe ► **Red China** N la Chine communiste ► **Red Crescent** N Croissant-Rouge f ► **Red Cross (Society)** N Croix-Rouge f ► **red deer** N cerf m noble *or* élaphe ► **red duster***, **red ensign** N (*Naut*) pavillon m de la marine marchande (britannique) ► **red-eye** N (*Phot*) (effet m) yeux mpl rouges; (*US*) mauvais whisky m; (* = *night flight: also* ~-**eye flight**) avion m *or* vol m de nuit ► **red-eyed** ADJ aux yeux rouges ► **red-faced** ADJ (*lit*) rougeaud, rubicond; (*fig*) gêné, rouge de confusion ► **Red Flag** N drapeau m rouge; **"The Red Flag"** hymne du parti travailliste ► **red flag** N (= *danger signal*) avertissement m ► **red giant** N (*Astron*) géante f rouge ► **red grouse** N grouse f, lagopède m d'Écosse ► **the Red Guard** N (*in former USSR*) la garde rouge ► **the Red Guards** NPL (*in China*) les gardes mpl rouges ► **red-haired** ADJ roux (rousse f) ► **red-handed** ADJ **to be caught** ~-**handed** être pris en flagrant délit *or* la main dans le sac ► **red hat** N (*Rel*) chapeau m de cardinal ► **red-headed** ADJ = **red-haired** ► **red heat** N **to raise iron to ~ heat** chauffer le fer au rouge ► **red herring** N (*lit*) hareng m saur; (*fig*) **that's a ~ herring** c'est pour brouiller les pistes, c'est une diversion ► **red-hot** ADJ (*lit*) chauffé au rouge, brûlant; (*fig = enthusiastic*) ardent, enthousiaste; (*fig = up to the moment*) [*news, information*] de dernière minute; (*fig = very popular*) excellent ♦ N (*US Culin**) hot-dog m ► **Red Indian** N Peau-Rouge mf ► **red lead** N minium m ► **red-letter day** N jour m mémorable, jour m à marquer d'une pierre blanche ► **red light** N (*Aut*) feu m rouge; **to go through the ~ light** passer au rouge, griller* *or* brûler un feu rouge ► **red-light district** N quartier m chaud*, quartier m des prostituées ► **red man** N (*pl* **red men**) (*US*) Indien m (*aux USA*); (*Brit: at pedestrian crossing*) **it's the ~ man** c'est rouge (pour les piétons) ► **red meat** N viande f rouge ► **red mullet** N rouget m barbet ► **red pepper** N poivron m rouge ► **Red Riding Hood** N (*also* **Little Red Riding Hood**) le Petit Chaperon rouge ► **red salmon** N saumon m rouge ► **Red Sea** N (*Geog*) mer f Rouge ► **red sea bream** N daurade f (*or* dorade f) rose ► **red shank** N chevalier m gambette ► **red snapper** N vivaneau m (*Can*) ► **Red Square** N (*in Moscow*) la place Rouge ► **red squirrel** N écureuil m ► **red tape** N (*fig*) paperasserie f, bureaucratie f tatillonne ► **red wine** N vin m rouge

redact [rɪ'dækt] VT (*frm*) (= *draw up*) rédiger; (= *edit*) éditer

redaction [rɪ'dækʃən] N (*frm*) (= *version*) rédaction f; (= *editing*) édition f

redbreast ['redbrest] N rouge-gorge m

redcoat ['redkəʊt] N (*Hist*) soldat m anglais; (*Brit: in holiday camp*) animateur m, -trice f

redcurrant [red'kʌrənt] N groseille f (rouge)

redden ['redn] **1** VT rendre rouge, rougir **2** VI [*person*] rougir; [*foliage*] roussir, devenir roux

reddish ['redɪʃ] ADJ (*gen*) tirant sur le rouge, rougeâtre (*pej*); [*hair*] tirant sur le roux, roussâtre (*pej*); ~-**brown** (*gen*) d'un brun rou-

ge, brun-rougeâtre *inv* (*pej*); [*hair*] d'un brun roux, brun-roussâtre *inv* (*pej*)

redecorate [,ri:'dekəreɪt] **1** VT [+ *room, house*] (= *repaint*) repeindre; (= *redesign*) refaire la décoration de **2** VI (= *repaint*) refaire les peintures; (= *redesign*) refaire la décoration

redecoration [,ri:,dekə'reɪʃən] N remise f à neuf des peintures, remplacement m des papiers peints

redeem [rɪ'di:m] VT (= *buy back*) racheter; (*from pawn*) dégager; (*Fin*) [+ *debt*] amortir, rembourser; [+ *bill*] honorer; [+ *mortgage*] purger; [+ *insurance policy*] encaisser; (*Comm*) [+ *coupon, token*] échanger (**for** contre); (*US*) [+ *banknote*] convertir en espèces; [+ *promise*] tenir; [+ *obligation*] s'acquitter de, satisfaire à; (*Rel*) [+ *sinner*] racheter, rédimer (*frm*); (= *compensate for*) [+ *failing*] racheter, compenser; [+ *fault*] réparer; **to ~ o.s.** *or* **one's honour** se racheter; **to ~ sb/sth from sth** sauver qn/qch de qch

redeemable [rɪ'di:məbl] ADJ [*voucher*] échangeable (**against sth** contre qch); [*bond, bill*] remboursable; [*mortgage*] remboursable, amortissable; [*debt*] amortissable; [*insurance policy*] encaissable; (*from pawn*) qui peut être dégagé; **the vouchers are ~ on selected items** les bons sont à valoir sur l'achat de certains articles; **the catalogue costs £5, ~ against a first order** le catalogue coûte 5 livres, remboursées à la première commande

Redeemer [rɪ'di:mə] N (*Rel*) Rédempteur m

redeeming [rɪ'di:mɪŋ] ADJ **to have some ~ features** avoir des qualités qui rachètent *or* compensent les défauts; **I could not find a single ~ feature in this book** je n'ai pas trouvé la moindre qualité à ce livre; **a book with no ~ qualities** un livre qu'aucune qualité ne vient sauver, un livre sans la moindre qualité pour racheter ses défauts; **his one ~ quality is** ... la seule chose qui peut le racheter est ...

redefine [,ri:dɪ'faɪn] VT (*gen*) redéfinir; **to ~ the problem** modifier les données du problème

redemption [rɪ'dempʃən] **1** N **a** (= *salvation*) (*gen*) rédemption f, rachat m; (*Rel*) rédemption f; **beyond** *or* **past ~** [*person*] définitivement perdu (*fig*); [*object*] irréparable; [*situation*] irrémédiable **b** (*Fin*) [*of mortgage*] remboursement m, purge f (SPEC); [*of bond*] remboursement m; [*of debt*] remboursement m, amortissement m; (*from pawn*) dégagement m **2** COMP ► **redemption value** N valeur f de remboursement

redemptive [rɪ'demptɪv] ADJ rédempteur (-trice f)

redeploy [,ri:dɪ'plɔɪ] VT [+ *troops*] redéployer; [+ *workers, staff*] (*gen*) redéployer; (*to new location*) réaffecter; (*Econ*) [+ *sector etc*] redéployer

redeployment [,ri:dɪ'plɔɪmənt] N [*of troops, weapons, resources, funds*] redéploiement m (**(in)to sth** dans qch); [*of workers, staff*] (*gen*) redéploiement m (**to sth** dans qch); (*to new location*) réaffectation f

redesign [,ri:dɪ'zaɪn] VT reconcevoir

redevelop [,ri:dɪ'veləp] VT [+ *area*] rénover, réaménager

redevelopment [,ri:dɪ'veləpmənt] **1** N [*of area*] rénovation f, réaménagement m **2** COMP ► **redevelopment area** N zone f de rénovation *or* de réaménagement

redhead ['redhed] N roux m, rousse f, rouquin(e)* m(f)

redial [,ri:'daɪəl] (*Telec*) **1** VT recomposer **2** VI recomposer le numéro **3** ['ri:daɪəl] COMP ► **redial button** N touche f bis ► **redial facility** N rappel m du dernier numéro composé

redid [,ri:'dɪd] VB *pt of* **redo**

redirect [,ri:daɪ'rekt] VT [+ *letter, parcel*] faire suivre, réadresser; [+ *funds, resources*] réallouer; [+ *traffic*] dévier; **to ~ one's ener-**

gies réorienter *or* rediriger son énergie (**towards** vers)

rediscover [,ri:dɪs'kʌvə] VT redécouvrir

redistribute [,ri:dɪs'trɪbju:t] VT redistribuer

redistrict [,ri:'dɪstrɪkt] **1** VT (*US Pol, Admin*) soumettre à un redécoupage électoral (*or* administratif) **2** VI (*US Pol, Admin*) se soumettre à un redécoupage électoral (*or* administratif)

redistricting [,ri:'dɪstrɪktɪŋ] N (*US Pol, Admin*) redécoupage m électoral (*or* administratif)

redline ['redlaɪn] VT (*US Fin*) pratiquer une discrimination financière envers

redneck* ['rednek] N (*esp US*) rustre m, péquenaud(e)* m(f)

redness ['rednɪs] N rougeur f; [*of hair*] rousseur f

redo [,ri:'du:] (*pret* **redid**, *ptp* **redone**) VT refaire

redolence ['redəʊləns] N (*liter*) parfum m, odeur f agréable

redolent ['redəʊlənt] ADJ (*liter*) **a** (= *evocative*) ~ **of sth** évocateur (-trice f) de qch; **to be ~ of sth** évoquer qch **b** (= *smelling*) **to be ~ of sth** sentir qch; **the air was ~ with the smell of freshly-baked bread** l'air embaumait le pain frais

redone [,ri:'dʌn] VB *ptp of* **redo**

redouble [,ri:'dʌbl] **1** VT **a** redoubler; **to ~ one's efforts** redoubler ses efforts *or* d'efforts **b** (*Bridge*) surcontrer **2** VI redoubler **3** VI (*Bridge*) surcontre m

redoubt [rɪ'daʊt] N (*Mil*) redoute f

redoubtable [rɪ'daʊtəbl] ADJ redoutable, formidable

redound [rɪ'daʊnd] VI (*frm*) contribuer (**to** à); **to ~ upon** retomber sur; **to ~ to sb's credit** être (tout) à l'honneur de qn

redraft [,ri:'drɑ:ft] VT rédiger de nouveau

redress [rɪ'dres] **1** VT [+ *situation*] redresser; [+ *wrong, grievance*] réparer; **to ~ the balance (between)** rétablir l'équilibre (entre) **2** N réparation f (**for sth** pour qch); ~ **against sb** recours m contre qn; ~ **of grievances** réparation f; **to have no ~** n'avoir aucun recours; **to seek ~** exiger *or* demander réparation

redskin ['redskɪn] N Peau-Rouge mf

redstart ['redstɑ:t] N (*Orn*) rouge-queue m

reduce [rɪ'dju:s] **1** VT **a** (= *lessen*) réduire (**to** à, **by** de), diminuer; (= *shorten*) raccourcir; (= *weaken*) affaiblir; (= *lower*) abaisser; [+ *drawing, plan*] réduire; [+ *expenses*] réduire, restreindre; [+ *price*] baisser, diminuer; (*Med*) [+ *swelling*] résorber, résoudre; [+ *temperature*] faire descendre, abaisser; (*Culin*) [+ *sauce*] faire réduire; (*Ind*) [+ *output*] ralentir; (*Mil etc: in rank*) rétrograder, réduire à un grade inférieur; (*Aut*) **to ~ sb to the ranks** casser qn; **to ~ unemployment** réduire le chômage; (*gradually*) résorber le chômage; (*in car*) **to ~ speed** diminuer la vitesse, ralentir; **"~ speed now"** « ralentir »; **to ~ the age of retirement to 58** ramener l'âge de la retraite à 58 ans; (*Jur*) **to ~ a prisoner's sentence** réduire la peine d'un prisonnier
b (*Chem, Math, fig*) réduire (**to** en, à); **to ~ sth to powder/to pieces/to ashes** réduire qch en poudre/en morceaux/en cendres; **to ~ an argument to its simplest form** réduire un raisonnement à sa plus simple expression, simplifier un raisonnement au maximum; **it has been ~d to nothing** cela a été réduit à zéro; **he's ~d to a skeleton** il n'est plus qu'un squelette ambulant; **to ~ sb to silence/obedience/despair** réduire qn au silence/à l'obéissance/au désespoir; **to ~ sb to begging/to slavery** réduire qn à la mendicité/en esclavage; **to be ~d to begging** être réduit *or* contraint à mendier; **to ~ sb to submission** soumettre qn; **to ~ sb to tears** faire pleurer qn; (*Admin, Jur*) **to ~ sth to writing** consigner qch par écrit

2 VI (*esp US* = *slim*) maigrir; **to be reducing** être au régime

reduced [rɪ'djuːst] 1 ADJ (*gen*) réduit; **to buy at a ~ price** [+ *ticket*] acheter à prix réduit; [+ *goods*] acheter au rabais *or* en solde; (*Comm*) **to be ~** être soldé *or* en solde; (*on ticket*) "~" « prix réduit »; **on a ~ scale** [*reproduce*] à échelle réduite; [*act, plan*] sur une plus petite échelle; (*frm*) **in ~ circumstances** dans la gêne 2 COMP ► **reduced instruction set computer** N ordinateur *m* à jeu d'instructions réduit ► **reduced instruction set computing** N traitement *m* avec jeu d'instructions réduit

reducer [rɪ'djuːsər] N (= *slimming device*) appareil *m* d'amaigrissement; (*Phot*) réducteur *m*

reducible [rɪ'djuːsəbl] ADJ réductible

reductio ad absurdum [rɪ'dʌktɪəʊ,ædəb'seːdəm] N réduction *f* à l'absurde

reduction [rɪ'dʌkʃən] N (*gen, Chem, Math etc*) réduction *f*; (*in length*) raccourcissement *m*; (*in width*) diminution *f*; [*of expenses, staff*] réduction *f*, compression *f*; [*of prices, wages*] diminution *f*, baisse *f*; [*of temperature*] baisse *f*; (*Elec*) [*of voltage*] diminution *f*; (*Jur*) [*of sentence*] réduction *f*, modération *f*; (*Med*) [*of swelling*] résorption *f*, résolution *f*; (*Phot*) réduction *f*; (*Tech*) démultiplication *f*; **to make a ~ on an article** faire une remise sur un article; (*Comm*) **this is a ~** c'est un rabais; **to sell sth at a ~** vendre qch au rabais; **~ for cash** escompte *m* au comptant; **~ of taxes** dégrèvement *m* d'impôts; **~ of speed** ralentissement *m*; (*Mil etc*) **~ in strength** réduction *f or* diminution *f* des effectifs; **~ in rank** rétrogradation *f*

reductionism [rɪ'dʌkʃə,nɪzəm] N a (*pej*) approche *f* réductrice b (*Philos*) réductionnisme *m*

reductionist [rɪ'dʌkʃənɪst] 1 ADJ a (*pej*) réducteur b (*Philos*) réductionniste 2 N a (*pej*) personne *f* aux vues réductrices b (*Philos*) réductionniste *mf*

reductive [rɪ'dʌktɪv] ADJ (*pej* = *simplistic*) réducteur (-trice *f*), simplificateur (-trice *f*)

redundance [rɪ'dʌndəns] N = **redundancy 1b, 1c**

redundancy [rɪ'dʌndənsɪ] 1 N a (*Brit Ind*) licenciement *m* (économique), mise *f* au *or* en chômage (pour raisons économiques); **it caused a lot of redundancies** cela a causé de nombreux licenciements *or* la mise au chômage de nombreux employés; **he feared ~** il redoutait d'être licencié *or* mis au chômage; **he went in the last round of redundancies** il a perdu son emploi lors de la dernière série de licenciements, il fait partie de la dernière charrette*; **compulsory ~** licenciement *m* sec; **voluntary ~** départ *m* volontaire b (*gen*) excès *m* c (*Literat*) redondance *f* 2 COMP ► **redundancy money, redundancy payment** N (*Brit Ind*) indemnité *f* de licenciement

redundant [rɪ'dʌndənt] ADJ a (*Brit Ind*) licencié *or* au *or* en chômage (pour raisons économiques); **to make sb ~** licencier qn *or* mettre qn au chômage (pour raisons économiques) b (= *superfluous*) [*object, example, detail*] superflu; [*word, term, information*] redondant; (*Brit*) [*person*] en surnombre

reduplicate [rɪ'djuːplɪkeɪt] 1 VT redoubler; (*Ling*) rédupliquer 2 [rɪ'djuːplɪkɪt] ADJ redoublé, réduplicatif

reduplication [rɪ,djuːplɪ'keɪʃən] N redoublement *m*; (*Ling*) réduplication *f*

reduplicative [rɪ'djuːplɪkətɪv] ADJ (*Ling*) réduplicatif

redwing ['redwɪŋ] N (*Orn*) mauvis *m*

redwood ['redwʊd] N (*Bot*) séquoia *m*

re-echo [riː'ekəʊ] 1 VI retentir, résonner (de nouveau *or* plusieurs fois) 2 VT répéter, renvoyer en écho

---

reed [riːd] 1 N (*Bot*) roseau *m*; [*of wind instrument*] anche *f*; (*liter* = *pipe*) chalumeau *m*, pipeau *m*; (*Mus*) **the ~s** les instruments *mpl* à anche → **broken** 2 COMP [*basket etc*] de *or* en roseau(x) ► **reed bed** N roselière *f* ► **reed bunting** N (*Orn*) bruant *m* des roseaux ► **reed instrument** N (*Mus*) instrument *m* à anche ► **reed stop** N (*Mus*) jeu *m* d'anches *or* à anches

re-educate [riː'edjʊkeɪt] VT rééduquer

re-education ['riːedjʊ'keɪʃən] N rééducation *f*

reedy ['riːdɪ] ADJ a (*Bot*) [*bank*] couvert de roseaux; [*pond*] envahi par les roseaux b (*pej* = *high-pitched*) [*voice, sound, instrument*] aigu (-guë *f*)

reef¹ [riːf] N a récif *m*, écueil *m*; (*fig*) écueil *m*; **coral ~** récif *m* de corail b (*Min*) filon *m*

reef² [riːf] 1 N (*Naut*) ris *m* 2 VT (*Naut*) [+ *sail*] prendre un ris dans 3 COMP ► **reef knot** N nœud *m* plat

reefer [riːfər] N a (= *jacket*) caban *m* b* joint*; m c (*US* = *truck etc*) camion *m* (*or* wagon *m*) frigorifique

reek [riːk] 1 N puanteur *f*, relent *m* 2 VI a (= *smell*) puer, empester; **to ~ of sth** puer *or* empester qch b (*Scot*) [*chimney*] fumer

reel [riːl] 1 N a [*of thread, tape etc*] bobine *f*; (*Fishing*) moulinet *m*; [*of film*] (*Cine*) bande *f*; (*Phot*) bobine *f*, rouleau *m*; [*of cable, hose*] dévidoir *m*; (*Tech*) dévidoir *m*, touret *m*, bobine *f* → **inertia** b (= *dance*) reel *m*, quadrille *m* écossais 2 VT (*Tech*) [+ *thread*] bobiner 3 VI a (*gen*) chanceler; [*drunkenly*] tituber; **he lost his balance and ~ed back** il a perdu l'équilibre et il a reculé en chancelant *or* titubant; **he went ~ing down the street** il a descendu la rue en chancelant *or* titubant; **the blow made him ~** le coup l'a fait chanceler, il a chancelé sous le coup b (*fig*) **the street ~ed before her eyes** la rue a vacillé autour d'elle; **my head is ~ing** la tête me tourne; **the news made him** *or* **his mind ~** la nouvelle l'a ébranlé; **I ~ed at the very thought** cette pensée m'a donné le vertige; **I'm still ~ing from the shock of it** je ne me suis pas encore remis du choc; **to leave sb ~ing** ébranler qn; **the news left us ~ing with disbelief** la nouvelle nous a ébranlés et nous a laissés incrédules; **the news sent markets ~ing** la nouvelle a (profondément) perturbé les marchés 4 COMP ► **reel holder** N porte-bobines *m inv* ► **reel-to-reel** ADJ à bobines

►**reel in** VT SEP (*Fishing, Naut*) ramener, remonter

►**reel off** VT SEP [+ *verses, list*] débiter; [+ *thread*] dévider

►**reel up** VT SEP enrouler

re-elect [riːɪ'lekt] VT réélire

re-election [riːɪ'lekʃən] N (*Pol*) **to stand** (*Brit*) *or* **run for ~** se représenter (aux élections)

re-embark [riːɪm'baːk] VTI rembarquer

re-embarkation ['riːembaː'keɪʃən] N rembarquement *m*

re-emerge [riːɪ'mɜːdʒ] VI [*object, swimmer*] resurgir; [*facts*] ressortir

re-employ [riːɪm'plɔɪ] VT réembaucher

re-enact [riːɪ'nækt] VT a (*Jur*) remettre en vigueur b [+ *scene, crime*] reconstituer, reproduire

re-enactment [riːɪ'næktmənt] N (*Jur*) [*of law*] remise *f* en vigueur; [*of crime*] reconstitution *f*

re-engage [riːɪn'geɪdʒ] VT [+ *employee*] rengager, réembaucher; (*Aut*) **to ~ the clutch** rengréner, rengrener

re-engagement [riːɪn'geɪdʒmənt] N a [*of employee*] rengagement *m*, réengagement *m*, réemploi *m* b (*Aut*) [*of clutch*] rengrènement *m*

---

re-enlist [riːɪn'lɪst] 1 VI se rengager 2 VT rengager

re-enter [riː'entər] 1 VI a rentrer b **to ~ for an exam** se représenter à *or* se réinscrire pour un examen 2 VT rentrer dans; (*Space*) **to ~ the atmosphere** rentrer dans l'atmosphère

re-entry [riː'entrɪ] 1 N (*gen, Space*) rentrée *f*; **her ~ into politics** son retour à la politique 2 COMP ► **re-entry permit** N permis *m* de rentrée (*dans un pays où l'on voyage avec un visa*) ► **re-entry point** N (*Space*) point *m* de rentrée

re-erect [riːɪ'rekt] VT [+ *building, bridge*] reconstruire; [+ *scaffolding, toy*] remonter

▼**re-establish** [riːɪs'tæblɪʃ] VT [+ *relations, links, order, stability, monarchy, service*] rétablir; [+ *person*] réhabiliter; [+ *custom*] restaurer; **to ~ itself** [*species*] se réimplanter; **to ~ o.s. (as)** [*person*] (*after failure, setback*) retrouver sa place (de); **the Conservatives are trying to ~ themselves in Scotland** les conservateurs essaient de retrouver leur place *or* de regagner du terrain en Écosse

re-establishment [riːɪs'tæblɪʃmənt] N [*of relations, links, order, stability, monarchy, service*] rétablissement *m*; [*of species*] réintroduction *f*; [*of refugees*] réinstallation *f*

re-evaluate [riːɪ'væljueɪt] VT réévaluer

reeve¹ [riːv] N (*Hist*) premier magistrat *m*; (*Can*) président *m* du conseil municipal

reeve² [riːv] VT (*Naut*) [+ *rope*] passer dans un anneau *or* une poulie, capeler; [+ *shoal*] passer au travers de

re-examination ['riːɪgˌzæmɪ'neɪʃən] N nouvel examen *m*; (*Jur: of witness*) nouvel interrogatoire *m*

re-examine [riːɪg'zæmɪn] VT examiner de nouveau; (*Jur*) [+ *witness*] interroger de nouveau

re-export [riːik'spɔːt] 1 VT réexporter 2 [riː'ekspɔːt] N réexportation *f*

ref¹ (*Comm*) (ABBR = **with reference to**) → **reference**

ref²* [ref] N (*Sport*) (ABBR = **referee**) arbitre *m*

refection [rɪ'fekʃən] N (*frm*) (= *light meal*) collation *f*, repas *m* léger; (= *refreshment*) rafraîchissements *mpl*

refectory [rɪ'fektərɪ] 1 N réfectoire *m* 2 COMP ► **refectory table** N table *f* de réfectoire

refer [rɪ'fɜː] 1 VT a (= *pass*) [+ *matter, question, file*] soumettre (**to** à); **the problem was ~red to the UN** le problème a été soumis *or* renvoyé à l'ONU; **the dispute was ~red to arbitration** le litige a été soumis à l'arbitrage; **it was ~red to us for (a) decision** on nous a demandé de prendre une décision là-dessus; **I have to ~ it to my boss** je dois le soumettre à *or* en parler à mon patron; **I ~red him to the manager** je lui ai dit de s'adresser au gérant, je l'ai renvoyé au directeur; **the doctor ~red me to a specialist** le médecin m'a adressé à un spécialiste; **the patient was ~red for tests** on a envoyé le patient subir des examens; **to ~ sb to the article on …** renvoyer qn à l'article sur …, prier qn de se reporter *or* se référer à l'article sur …; **"the reader is ~red to page 10"** « prière de se reporter *or* se référer à la page 10 »; (*Banking*) **to ~ a cheque to drawer** refuser d'honorer un chèque b (*Jur*) [+ *accused*] déférer c (*Univ*) [+ *student*] refuser; **his thesis has been ~red** on lui a demandé de revoir *or* de reprendre sa thèse d (*liter, frm* = *attribute*) attribuer (**to** à) 2 VI a (= *allude*) (*directly*) parler (**to** de), faire référence (**to** à); (*indirectly*) faire allusion (**to** à); **I am not ~ring to you** je ne parle pas de vous; **we shall not ~ to it again** nous n'en reparlerons pas, nous n'en parlerons plus; **he never ~s to that evening** il ne parle jamais de ce soir-là ; **what can he be ~ring to?** de quoi parle-t-il ?, à quoi peut-il bien faire allusion ? ; **he ~red to her as his assistant** il l'a appelée son assistante ; *(Comm)* **~ring to your letter** (comme) suite *or* en réponse à votre lettre ; *(Banking)* **~ to drawer** voir le tireur **b** *(= apply)* s'appliquer **(to** à) ; **does that remark ~ to me?** est-ce que cette remarque s'applique à moi ?, **this ~s to you all** cela vous concerne tous **c** *(= consult)* se reporter, se référer **(to sth** à qch) ; **to ~ to one's notes** consulter ses notes, se reporter *or* se référer à ses notes ; **"please ~ to section 3"** « prière de se reporter *or* se référer à la section 3 » ; **you must ~ to the original** vous devez vous reporter *or* vous référer à l'original **3** COMP ► **referred pain** N *(Med)* douleur *f* irradiée

► **refer back** VT SEP *[+ decision]* remettre (à plus tard), ajourner ; **to ~ sth back to sb** consulter qn sur *or* au sujet de qch

referable [rɪˈfɜːrəbl] ADJ attribuable **(to** à)

referee [ˌrefəˈriː] **1** N **a** *(Ftbl etc, also fig)* arbitre *m* **b** *(Brit: giving a reference)* répondant(e) *m(f)* ; **to act as** *or* **be (a) ~ for sb** fournir des références *or* une attestation à qn ; **to give sb as a ~** donner qn en référence ; **may I give your name as a ~?** puis-je donner votre nom en référence ? **2** VT *(Sport, fig)* arbitrer **3** VI *(Sport, fig)* servir d'arbitre, être arbitre

▼ **reference** [ˈrefrəns] **1** N **a** *(NonC)* référence *f* **(to** à) ; *[of question for judgement]* renvoi *m* ; **outside the ~ of** hors de la compétence de ; **keep these details for ~** gardez ces renseignements pour information → **future, term** **b** *(= allusion) (direct)* mention *f* **(to** de) ; *(indirect)* allusion *f* **(to** à) ; **a ~ was made to his illness** on a fait allusion à *or* on a fait mention de sa maladie ; **in** *or* **with ~ to** quant à, en ce qui concerne ; *(Comm)* (comme) suite à ; **without ~ to** sans tenir compte de, sans égard pour **c** *(= testimonial)* **~(s)** références *fpl* ; **to give sb a good ~** *or* **good ~s** fournir de bonnes références à qn ; **a banker's ~** des références bancaires ; **I've been asked for a ~ for him** on m'a demandé de fournir des renseignements sur lui **d** **= referee 1b** **e** *(in book, article = note redirecting reader)* renvoi *m*, référence *f* ; *(on map)* coordonnées *fpl* ; *(Comm: on letter)* **please quote this ~** prière de rappeler cette référence → **cross** **f** *(= connection)* rapport *m* **(to** avec) ; **this has no ~ to ...** cela n'a aucun rapport avec ... **g** *(Ling)* référence *f* **2** VT **a** *[+ quotation]* référencer ; *[+ book]* fournir les références de **b** *(= refer to)* faire référence à **3** COMP ► **reference book** N ouvrage *m* de référence ► **reference library** N bibliothèque *f* d'ouvrages de référence ► **reference mark** N renvoi *m* ► **reference number** N *(Comm)* numéro *m* de référence ► **reference point** N point *m* de référence ► **reference strip** N *(Phot)* bande *f* étalon

referendum [ˌrefəˈrendəm] N *(pl* **referendums** *or* **referenda** [ˌrefəˈrendə]) référendum *m* ; **to hold a ~** organiser un référendum ; **a ~ will be held** un référendum aura lieu

referent [ˈrefərənt] N référent *m*

referential [ˌrefəˈrenʃəl] ADJ référentiel

referral [rɪˈfɜːrəl] N **a** *(Med, Psych)* (= *act)* orientation *f* d'un patient *(vers des services spécialisés)* ; *(= person)* patient(e) *m(f)* (orienté(e) vers des services spécialisés) ; **ask your doctor for a ~ to a dermatologist** demandez à votre médecin de vous envoyer chez un dermatologue ; **letter of ~** *lettre par laquelle un médecin adresse un patient à un spécialiste* **b** *(Jur)* **the ~**

of the case to the Appeal Courts le renvoi de l'affaire en appel ; **the ~ of the case to the Director of Public Prosecutions** la soumission de l'affaire au procureur général **c** *(NonC: to higher authority)* **he sanctioned the deal without ~** il a approuvé le marché sans en référer à une autorité supérieure

refill [ˌriːˈfɪl] **1** VT *[+ glass, bottle]* remplir à nouveau ; *[+ pen, lighter]* recharger **2** [ˈriːfɪl] N *(gen)* recharge *f* ; *(= cartridge)* cartouche *f* ; *(for propelling pencil)* mine *f* de rechange ; *(for notebook)* feuilles *fpl* de rechange ; *(for drink)* **would you like a ~?** encore un verre *(or* une tasse) ?

refinance [riːˈfaɪnæns] VT refinancer

refine [rɪˈfaɪn] **1** VT **a** *[+ ore]* affiner ; *[+ oil]* épurer ; *[+ crude oil, sugar]* raffiner **b** *(= improve)* *[+ language]* châtier ; *[+ manners]* réformer ; *[+ theory, technique, process, taste]* affiner ; *[+ model, engine]* perfectionner ; *[+ essay etc]* peaufiner* **2** VI **to ~ upon sth** raffiner sur qch

refined [rɪˈfaɪnd] ADJ **a** *(= processed)* *[food, ore]* traité ; *[sugar, oil]* raffiné ; *[flour]* bluté ; *[metal]* affiné ; *(St Ex, Econ)* **~ products** produits *mpl* raffinés **b** *(= genteel)* *[person, manners, taste]* raffiné **c** *(= sophisticated)* *[model, engine]* perfectionné

refinement [rɪˈfaɪnmənt] N **a** *(NonC = refining)* *[of crude oil, sugar]* raffinage *m* ; *[of ore]* affinage *m* ; *[of oil]* épuration *f* **b** *(NonC)* *[of person]* raffinement *m*, délicatesse *f* ; *[of language, style]* raffinement *m* **c** *(= improvement: in technique, machine etc)* perfectionnement *m* **(in** de) ; *(fig)* **that is a ~ of cruelty** c'est un raffinement de cruauté

refiner [rɪˈfaɪnər] N *[of crude oil, sugar]* raffineur *m* ; *[of metals]* affineur *m* ; *[of oil]* épureur *m*

refinery [rɪˈfaɪnərɪ] N *(for crude oil, sugar)* raffinerie *f* ; *(for metals)* affinerie *f*

refit [ˌriːˈfɪt] **1** VT *[+ ship etc]* *(also gen)* remettre en état ; *[+ factory]* équiper de nouveau, renouveler l'équipement de **2** VI *[ship]* être remis en état **3** [ˈriːfɪt] N *[of ship]* remise *f* en état ; *[of factory]* nouvel équipement *m* **4** COMP ► **refit yard** N chantier *m* de réarmement

refitting [ˌriːˈfɪtɪŋ], **refitment** [ˌriːˈfɪtmənt] N **= refit 3**

reflate [ˌriːˈfleɪt] VT *(Econ)* relancer

reflation [riːˈfleɪʃən] N *(Econ)* relance *f*

reflationary [riːˈfleɪʃənərɪ] ADJ *(Econ)* de relance

reflect [rɪˈflekt] **1** VT **a** *(= throw back)* *[+ heat, sound]* renvoyer ; *[+ light, image]* réfléchir ; *(fig)* *(gen)* refléter ; *[+ credit, discredit]* faire rejaillir, faire retomber **(on** sur) ; **the moon is ~ed in the lake** la lune se reflète dans le lac ; **I saw him ~ed in the mirror** j'ai vu son image dans le miroir *or* réfléchie par le miroir ; **he saw himself ~ed in the mirror** le miroir a réfléchi *or* lui a renvoyé son image ; **~ing prism** prisme *m* réflecteur ; *(fig)* **he basked** *or* **bathed in the ~ed glory of his friend's success** il tirait gloire *or* fierté de la réussite de son ami ; **the many difficulties are ~ed in his report** son rapport reflète les nombreuses difficultés ; **his music ~s his love for her** sa musique reflète son amour pour elle **b** *(= think)* se dire **(that** que) **2** VI **a** *(= meditate)* réfléchir **(on** à), méditer **(on** sur) **b** **to ~ off** être réfléchi par

► **reflect (up)on** VT FUS *(= affect)* *[+ person]* avoir des répercussions *or* des incidences sur la réputation de ; *[+ reputation]* avoir des répercussions *or* des incidences sur ; **to ~ well/ badly (up)on sb** faire honneur à/nuire à la réputation de qn

reflectingly [rɪˈflektɪŋlɪ] ADV **= reflectively**

reflection [rɪˈflekʃən] N **a** *(NonC = reflecting)* *[of light, heat, sound]* réflexion *f* **b** *(= image: in mirror etc)* reflet *m*, image *f* ; **to see one's ~ in a**

mirror voir son reflet dans un miroir ; *(fig)* **a pale ~ of former glory** un pâle reflet de la gloire passée **c** *(NonC = consideration)* réflexion *f* ; **on ~** *(toute)* réflexion faite, à la réflexion ; **on serious ~** après mûre réflexion ; **he did it without sufficient ~** il l'a fait sans avoir suffisamment réfléchi **d** *(= thoughts, comments)* **~s** réflexions *fpl* **(on, upon** sur) **e** *(= adverse criticism)* critique *f* **(on** de), réflexion *f* désobligeante **(on** sur) ; *(on sb's honour)* atteinte *f* **(on** à) ; **this is a ~ on your motives** cela fait douter de vos motifs ; **this is no ~ on ...** cela ne porte pas atteinte à ...

reflective [rɪˈflektɪv] ADJ **a** *(= pensive)* *[person, expression]* *(by nature)* réfléchi ; *(on one occasion)* pensif ; *[powers]* de réflexion ; **to be in a ~ mood** être d'humeur pensive ; **it was a ~ occasion** ce fut une occasion propice à la méditation **b** *(= typical)* **to be ~ of sth** refléter qch **c** *[surface, material, clothing]* réfléchissant ; *[light]* réfléchi **d** *(Gram)* **= reflexive a**

reflectively [rɪˈflektɪvlɪ] ADV *[look]* d'un air pensif ; *[say]* d'un ton pensif

reflectiveness [rɪˈflektɪvnɪs] N caractère *m* réfléchi *or* pensif

reflector [rɪˈflektər] N *(gen)* réflecteur *m* ; *[of car, bicycle]* réflecteur *m*, cataphote® *m*

reflex [ˈriːfleks] **1** ADJ *(Physiol, Psych, fig)* réflexe ; *(Math)* *[angle]* rentrant ; *(Phys)* réfléchi ; *(Phot)* **~ (camera)** (appareil *m*) reflex *m* **2** N réflexe *m* → **condition**

reflexion [rɪˈflekʃən] N **= reflection**

reflexive [rɪˈfleksɪv] **1** ADJ **a** *(Gram)* réfléchi **b** *(= reactive)* **a ~ movement** un réflexe **2** N *(Gram)* verbe *m* réfléchi **3** COMP ► **reflexive pronoun** N pronom *m* réfléchi ► **reflexive verb** N verbe *m* (pronominal) réfléchi

reflexively [rɪˈfleksɪvlɪ] ADV **a** *(Gram)* à la forme réfléchie **b** *(= instinctively)* *[move]* d'instinct

reflexology [ˌriːflekˈsɒlədʒɪ] N réflexologie *f*

refloat [ˌriːˈfləʊt] **1** VT *[+ ship, business etc]* renflouer, remettre à flot **2** VI être renfloué, être remis à flot

reflux [ˈriːflʌks] N reflux *m*

reforest [riːˈfɒrɪst] VT reboiser

reforestation [ˌriːfɒrɪsˈteɪʃən] *(US)* N **= reafforestation**

reform [rɪˈfɔːm] **1** N réforme *f* → **land** **2** VT *[+ law]* réformer ; *[+ institution, service]* réformer, faire des réformes dans ; *[+ conduct]* corriger ; *[+ person]* faire prendre de meilleures habitudes à ; **to ~ spelling** faire une réforme de *or* réformer l'orthographe **3** VI *[person]* s'amender, se réformer† **4** COMP *[measures etc]* de réforme ► **Reform Judaism** N judaïsme *m* non orthodoxe ► **the Reform Laws** NPL *(Brit Hist)* les lois *fpl* de réforme parlementaire ► **reform school** N *(US)* maison *f* de redressement

re-form [ˌriːˈfɔːm] **1** VT **a** *(= form again)* reformer, rendre sa première forme à ; *(Mil)* *[+ ranks]* reformer ; *[+ troops]* rallier, remettre en rangs **b** *(= give new form to)* donner une nouvelle forme à **2** VI se reformer ; *(Mil)* se reformer, reprendre sa formation

reformable [rɪˈfɔːməbl] ADJ réformable

reformat [ˌriːˈfɔːmæt] VT *(Comput)* reformater

reformation [ˌrefəˈmeɪʃən] N *(NonC)* *[of church, spelling, conduct]* réforme *f* ; *[of person]* assagissement *m*, retour *m* à une vie plus sage ; *(Hist)* **the Reformation** la Réforme, la Réformation

reformative [rɪˈfɔːmətɪv] ADJ de réforme, réformateur (-trice *f*)

reformatory [rɪˈfɔːmətərɪ] N *(Brit††)* maison *f* de correction *or* de redressement ; *(US Jur)* centre *m* d'éducation surveillée

reformed [rɪˈfɔːmd] ADJ **a** *[alcoholic]* ancien *(before n)* ; *[criminal]* repenti ; *[spelling]* réformé; **he's a ~ character** il s'est rangé or assagi [b] (Rel) [church] réformé; [Jew] non orthodoxe

reformer [rɪ'fɔ:mə'] N réformateur m, -trice f

reformist [rɪ'fɔ:mɪst] ADJ, N réformiste mf

reformulate [ri:'fɔ:mjʊ,leɪt] VT reformuler

refract [rɪ'frækt] VT réfracter

refracting [rɪ'fræktɪŋ] [1] ADJ (Phys) réfringent [2] COMP ► **refracting angle** N angle m de réfringence ► **refracting telescope** N lunette f d'approche

refraction [rɪ'frækʃən] N réfraction f

refractive [rɪ'fræktɪv] [1] ADJ réfractif, réfringent [2] COMP ► **refractive index** N indice m de réfraction

refractometer [,ri:fræk'tɒmɪtə'] N réfractomètre m

refractor [rɪ'fræktə'] N [a] (Phys) milieu m réfringent, dispositif m de réfraction [b] (= telescope) lunette f d'approche

refractory [rɪ'fræktərɪ] ADJ réfractaire

refrain¹ [rɪ'freɪn] VI se retenir, s'abstenir (**from doing** de faire); **he ~ed from comment** il s'est abstenu de tout commentaire; **they ~ed from measures leading to ...** ils se sont abstenus de toute mesure menant à ...; **please ~ from smoking** (on notice) prière de ne pas fumer; (spoken) ayez l'obligeance de ne pas fumer

refrain² [rɪ'freɪn] N (Mus, Poetry, fig) refrain m

refrangible [rɪ'frændʒɪbl] ADJ réfrangible

refresh [rɪ'freʃ] VT [drink, bath] rafraîchir; [food] revigorer, redonner des forces à; [sleep, rest etc] délasser, détendre; **to ~ o.s.** (with drink) se rafraîchir; (with food) se restaurer; (with sleep) se reposer, se délasser; **to ~ one's memory** se rafraîchir la mémoire; **to ~ one's memory about sth** se remettre qch en mémoire; **let me ~ your memory!** je vais vous rafraîchir la mémoire!*; **to feel ~ed** se sentir revigoré

refresher [rɪ'freʃə'] [1] N [a] (= drink etc) boisson f etc pour se rafraîchir [b] (Jur) honoraires mpl supplémentaires [2] COMP ► **refresher course** N stage m or cours m de recyclage

refreshing [rɪ'freʃɪŋ] ADJ [honesty, idea, approach, drink, fruit, taste, bath] rafraîchissant; [change, sight, news] agréable; [sleep] réparateur (-trice f); **it's ~ to see that ...** ça fait du bien de voir que ..., c'est agréable de voir que ...

refreshingly [rɪ'freʃɪŋlɪ] ADV [different] agréablement; **~ honest/frank/new** d'une honnêteté/franchise/originalité qui fait plaisir à voir; **~ cool** d'une fraîcheur vivifiante; **a ~ dry wine** un vin sec et agréable

refreshment [rɪ'freʃmənt] [1] N [a] [of mind, body] repos m, délassement m [b] (= food, drink) (light) **~s** rafraîchissements mpl; (= place) **~s** = **refreshment room** [2] COMP ► **refreshment bar** N buvette f ► **refreshment room** N (Rail) buffet m ► **refreshment stall** N = **refreshment bar**

refried beans [,ri:fraɪd'bi:nz] NPL préparation mexicaine à base de haricots

refrigerant [rɪ'frɪdʒərənt] ADJ, N réfrigérant m; (Med) fébrifuge m

refrigerate [rɪ'frɪdʒəreɪt] VT réfrigérer; (in cold room etc) frigorifier

refrigeration [rɪ,frɪdʒə'reɪʃən] N réfrigération f, frigorification f

refrigerator [rɪ'frɪdʒəreɪtə'] [1] N (= cabinet) réfrigérateur m, frigidaire® m, frigo* m; (= room) chambre f frigorifique; (= apparatus) condenseur m [2] COMP [truck etc] frigorifique

refrigeratory [rɪ'frɪdʒərətərɪ] ADJ, N (Chem) réfrigérant m

refringent [rɪ'frɪndʒənt] ADJ réfringent

refuel [,ri:'fjʊəl] [1] VI se ravitailler en carburant or en combustible [2] VT ravitailler

refuelling [,ri:'fjʊəlɪŋ] [1] N ravitaillement m (en carburant or en combustible) [2] COMP ► **refuelling stop** N (Aviat) escale f technique

refuge ['refju:dʒ] N (lit, fig) refuge m, abri m (**from** contre); (for climbers, pedestrians etc) refuge m; **place of ~** asile m; **a ~ for battered women** un foyer pour femmes battues; **to seek ~** chercher refuge or asile; **they sought ~ from the fighting in the city** ils ont cherché un refuge pour échapper aux combats dans la ville; **to seek ~ in silence** chercher refuge dans le silence; (lit, fig) **to take ~ in** se réfugier dans; **he took ~ in alcohol and drugs** il se réfugia dans l'alcool et la drogue; **she found ~ in a book** elle a trouvé refuge dans un livre; **God is my ~** Dieu est mon refuge

refugee [,refjʊ'dʒi:] [1] N réfugié(e) m(f) [2] COMP ► **refugee camp** N camp m de réfugiés ► **refugee status** N statut m de réfugié

refulgence [rɪ'fʌldʒəns] N (liter) splendeur f, éclat m

refulgent [rɪ'fʌldʒənt] ADJ (liter) resplendissant, éclatant

refund [rɪ'fʌnd] [1] VT [a] rembourser (**to sb** à qn); **to ~ sb's expenses** rembourser qn de ses frais or dépenses; **to ~ postage** rembourser les frais de port [b] (Fin) [+ excess payments] ristourner [2] ['ri:fʌnd] N remboursement m; (Fin) ristourne f; **tax ~** remboursement f de trop-perçu; **to get a ~** se faire rembourser

refundable [rɪ'fʌndəbl] ADJ remboursable

refurbish [,ri:'fɜ:bɪʃ] VT [+ building] réaménager, remettre à neuf; [+ furniture] remettre à neuf

refurbishment [,ri:'fɜ:bɪʃmənt] N réaménagement m, remise f à neuf

refurnish [,ri:'fɜ:nɪʃ] VT remeubler

refusal [rɪ'fju:zəl] N refus m (**to do** de faire); (Jur) **~ of justice** déni m de justice; **to get a ~ ◊ to meet with a ~** se heurter à or essuyer un refus; **to give a flat ~** refuser net; (Horse-riding) **three ~s** trois refus; **to give** or **offer sb first ~ of sth** accorder à qn l'option sur qch; **to have (the) first ~ of sth** recevoir la première offre de qch, avoir le droit de préemption sur qch

refuse¹ [rɪ'fju:z] [1] VT (gen) refuser (**sb sth** qch à qn, **to do** de faire), se refuser (**to do** à faire); [+ offer, invitation] refuser, décliner; [+ request] rejeter, repousser; **I absolutely ~ to do it** je me refuse catégoriquement à le faire; **to be ~d** essuyer un refus; **to be ~d sth** se voir refuser qch; **they were ~d permission to leave** on leur a refusé or ils se sont vu refuser la permission de partir; **she ~d him** elle l'a rejeté; **she ~d his proposal** elle a rejeté son offre; **to ~ a fence** [horse] refuser l'obstacle [2] VI refuser, opposer un refus; [horse] refuser l'obstacle

refuse² ['refju:s] [1] N détritus mpl, ordures fpl; (= industrial or food waste) déchets mpl; **household ~** ordures fpl ménagères; **garden ~** détritus mpl de jardin [2] COMP ► **refuse bin** N poubelle f, boîte f à ordures ► **refuse chute** N (at dump) dépotoir m; (in building) vide-ordures m inv ► **refuse collection** N ramassage m or collecte f des ordures ► **refuse collector** N éboueur m ► **refuse destructor** N incinérateur m (d'ordures) ► **refuse disposal** N traitement m des ordures ménagères ► **refuse disposal service** N service m de voirie ► **refuse disposal unit** N broyeur m d'ordures ► **refuse dump** N (public) décharge f (publique), dépotoir m; (in garden) monceau m de détritus ► **refuse lorry** N camion m des éboueurs

refus(e)nik [rɪ'fju:znɪk] N (Pol) refuznik mf

refutable [rɪ'fju:təbl] ADJ réfutable

refutation [,refjʊ'teɪʃən] N réfutation f

▼ **refute** [rɪ'fju:t] VT réfuter

reg. [redʒ] [1] N (Brit*) (ABBR = **registration number**) → **registration** [2] ADJ (ABBR = **registered**) ~ **no.** nᵒ

-reg² [redʒ] ADJ, N (Brit) (ABBR = **-registration**) **P-reg (car)** voiture dont l'immatriculation commence or finit par un P (la lettre indiquant l'année de mise en circulation)

regain [rɪ'geɪn] VT [+ one's composure, balance, self-confidence] retrouver; [+ sb's confidence] regagner, reconquérir; [+ one's health, sight etc] recouvrer; [+ title, initiative] reprendre; [+ independence, territory] reconquérir; (liter = arrive back at) [+ place] regagner; **to ~ one's strength** récupérer (ses forces), recouvrer ses forces; **to ~ consciousness** revenir à soi, reprendre connaissance; **to ~ lost time** regagner or rattraper le temps perdu; **to ~ one's footing** reprendre pied; **to ~ possession (of)** rentrer en possession (de)

regal ['ri:gəl] ADJ [suite, staircase, manner, bearing, gesture] royal; [splendour, dignity] majestueux; [disdain] souverain

regale [rɪ'geɪl] VT régaler (**sb with sth** qn de qch)

regalia [rɪ'geɪlɪə] N [of monarch] prérogatives fpl royales; (= insignia) insignes mpl royaux; [of Freemasons etc] insignes mpl; (hum) **she was in full ~** elle était dans ses plus beaux atours or en grand tralala*

regally ['ri:gəlɪ] ADV (lit, fig) royalement

▼ **regard** [rɪ'gɑ:d] [1] VT [a] (= look at) observer; (= consider) considérer (**as** comme); **to ~ with favour/horror** regarder d'un œil favorable/avec horreur; **we ~ it as worth doing** à notre avis ça vaut la peine de le faire; **we don't ~ it as necessary** nous ne le considérons pas comme nécessaire; **I ~ him highly** je le tiens en grande estime; **without ~ing his wishes** sans tenir compte de ses souhaits [b] (= concern) concerner, regarder; **as ~s ...** pour or en ce qui concerne ..., pour ce qui regarde ... [2] N [a] (= attention, concern) attention f, considération f; **to pay ~ to** or **to have ~ for sb/sth** tenir compte de qn/qch; **to have** or **show little ~ for sb/sth** faire peu de cas de qn/qch; **to have** or **show no ~ for sb/sth** ne faire aucun cas de qn/qch; **without ~ to** or **for sb/sth** sans égard pour qn/qch; **out of ~ for sb/sth** par égard pour qn/qch; **having ~ to sb/sth** si l'on tient compte de qn/qch; **in this** or **that ~** à cet égard, sous ce rapport; **with** or **in ~ to** pour or en ce qui concerne, quant à [b] (NonC = esteem) respect m, estime f; **to hold sb/sth in high ~** tenir qn/qch en haute estime; **to hold sb/sth in low ~** tenir qn/qch en piètre estime; **to have great ~ for sb** avoir beaucoup d'estime pour qn [c] (liter = look) regard m [3] **regards** NPL (in messages) **give him my ~s** transmettez-lui mon bon or meilleur souvenir; **Paul sends his kind ~s** Paul vous envoie son bon souvenir; (as letter-ending) (kindest) **~s** meilleurs souvenirs

regardful [rɪ'gɑ:dfʊl] ADJ **~ of** [feelings, duty] attentif à; [interests] soucieux de, soigneux de

regarding [rɪ'gɑ:dɪŋ] PREP (= with regard to) pour or en ce qui concerne, quant à; **information ~ sb/sth** des informations concernant qn/qch or relatives à qn/qch

regardless [rɪ'gɑ:dlɪs] [1] ADJ **~ of** [sb's feelings, fate] indifférent à; [future, danger] insouciant de; [sb's troubles] inattentif à; **~ of the consequences** sans se soucier des conséquences; **~ of expense** or **cost** même si cela revient cher; **~ of rank** sans distinction de rang; **~ of what the law says** indépendamment de ce que dit la loi [2] ADV [carry on] quand même

regatta [rɪ'gætə] N (one event) régate f; (regular event) régates fpl; **to take part in a ~** régater, prendre part à une régate

---

► LANGUAGE IN USE: **refuse** 8.3, 9.3, 12 **refute** 26.3 **regard** 21.2

Regency ['riːdʒənsɪ] ADJ [furniture, style] style Regency inv (anglaise)

regency ['riːdʒənsɪ] N régence f

regenerate [rɪ'dʒenəreɪt] **1** VT régénérer **2** VI se régénérer **3** [rɪ'dʒenərɪt] ADJ (frm) régénéré

regeneration [rɪˌdʒenə'reɪʃən] N régénération f

regenerative [rɪ'dʒenərətɪv] ADJ régénérateur (-trice f)

regent ['riːdʒənt] N régent(e) m(f); (US Univ) membre m du conseil d'université; **prince ~** prince régent

reggae ['regeɪ] N reggae m

regicide ['redʒɪsaɪd] N (= person) régicide mf; (= act) régicide m

régime [reɪ'ʒiːm] N régime m

regimen ['redʒɪmen] N (Med: frm) régime m

regiment ['redʒɪmənt] **1** N (Mil, fig) régiment m **2** ['redʒɪ pej] VT (fig peg) imposer une discipline trop stricte à, enrégimenter

regimental [ˌredʒɪ'mentl] **1** ADJ [duties, insignia, car, tie] régimentaire; [life, tradition, headquarters, commander] du régiment; [system] de régiments **2 regimentals** NPL (Mil) uniforme m; **in full ~s** en grand uniforme, en grande tenue **3** COMP ▶ **regimental band** N fanfare f du régiment ▶ **regimental sergeant major** N ≈ adjudant-chef m

regimentation [ˌredʒɪmen'teɪʃən] N (pej) discipline f excessive

regimented ['redʒɪmentɪd] ADJ (pej) [people, way of life, institution, society] enrégimenté; [appearance] trop strict

region ['riːdʒən] **1** N région f; (fig) **the lower ~s** les enfers mpl; **in the ~ of 5kg/10 francs** environ or dans les 5 kg/10 F, aux alentours de 5 kg/10 F **2 the regions** NPL (Brit) les provinces fpl

regional ['riːdʒənl] **1** ADJ (gen) régional; **on a ~ basis** sur le plan régional **2** COMP ▶ **regional council** N (Scot) ≈ conseil m général ▶ **regional development** N (Admin, Ind) aménagement m régional

regionalism ['riːdʒənəlɪzəm] N régionalisme m

regionalist ['riːdʒənəlɪst] ADJ, N régionaliste mf

register ['redʒɪstər] **1** N **a** (gen) registre m; (of members etc) liste f; (Scol: also **attendance ~**) registre m d'absences; **electoral ~** liste f électorale; **~ of births, marriages and deaths** registre m d'état civil **b** (Tech = gauge of speed, numbers etc) compteur m, enregistreur m **c** [of voice, organ etc] registre m **d** (Ling) registre m; **it's the wrong ~** ce n'est pas le bon registre **e** (Typ) registre m **f** (US = air vent) registre m **g** (US = cash register) caisse f (enregistreuse) **2** VT **a** (= record formally) [+ fact, figure] enregistrer; [+ birth, death, marriage] déclarer; [+ vehicle] (faire) immatriculer; **to ~ a trademark** déposer une marque de fabrique; **he ~ed his disapproval by refusing ...** il a manifesté sa désapprobation en refusant ...; **to ~ a protest** protester → **registered b** (= take note of) [+ fact] enregistrer;* (= realize) se rendre compte de, réaliser*; **I ~ed the fact that he had gone** je me suis rendu compte or j'ai réalisé* qu'il était parti **c** (= indicate) [machine] [+ speed, quantity] indiquer, marquer; [+ rainfall] enregistrer; [+ temperature] marquer; [face, expression] [+ happiness, sorrow] exprimer, refléter; **he ~ed or his face ~ed surprise** son visage or il a exprimé l'étonnement, il a paru étonné; **he ~ed or his face ~ed no emotion** il n'a pas exprimé d'émotion, il n'a pas paru ému

d (Post) [+ letter] recommander; (Rail) [+ luggage] (faire) enregistrer; **to ~ one's luggage through to London** (faire) enregistrer ses bagages jusqu'à Londres → **registered e** (Tech) [+ parts] faire coïncider; (Typ) mettre en registre **3** VI **a** (on electoral list etc) se faire inscrire, s'inscrire; (in hotel) s'inscrire sur or signer le registre; **to ~ with a doctor** se faire inscrire comme patient chez un médecin; **to ~ with the police** se déclarer à la police; **to ~ for military service** se faire recenser, se faire porter sur les tableaux de recensement; **to ~ for a course/for French literature** s'inscrire à un cours/en littérature française **b** (Tech) [two pages of machine] coïncider exactement; (Typ) être en registre **c** (* = be understood) être compris; **it hasn't ~ed (with him)** cela ne lui est pas entré dans la tête, il n'a pas saisi; **her death hadn't ~ed with him** il n'avait pas vraiment réalisé qu'elle était morte **4** COMP ▶ **register office** N (Brit) = **registry office**; → **registry** ▶ **register ton** N (Naut) tonneau m de jauge

registered ['redʒɪstəd] **1** ADJ **a** (= listed) [voter] inscrit (sur les listes électorales), [student] inscrit; [drug addict] inscrit (pour une cure de désintoxication); [nursing home] agréé; **a ~ childminder** une nourrice agréée; **~ to vote** inscrit sur les listes électorales; **to be ~ (as) blind/disabled** ≈ être titulaire d'une carte de cécité/d'invalidité; **a Greek-~ ship** un navire immatriculé en Grèce, un navire battant pavillon grec; **a British-~ car** une voiture immatriculée en Grande-Bretagne; **J-~ car** (Brit) voiture dont l'immatriculation commence ou finit par un J (la lettre indiquant l'année de mise en circulation) → **state b** (Post) [letter, mail] recommandé; (Rail) [luggage] enregistré **2** COMP ▶ **registered charity** N ≈ association f caritative reconnue d'utilité publique ▶ **registered company** N société f inscrite au registre du commerce ▶ **Registered General Nurse** N (Brit) ≈ infirmier m, -ière f diplômé(e) ▶ **registered name** N nom m déposé ▶ **registered nurse** N (US) ≈ infirmier m, -ière f diplômé(e) d'État ▶ **registered office** N siège m social ▶ **registered post** N **by ~ post** par envoi recommandé ▶ **registered share** N (St Ex) action f nominative ▶ **registered shareholder** N (St Ex) ≈ actionnaire mf inscrit(e) ▶ **registered stocks** NPL (St Ex) actions fpl or valeurs fpl nominatives, titres mpl nominatifs ▶ **registered trademark** N marque f déposée

registrar [ˌredʒɪ'strɑːr] **1** N **a** (Brit Admin) officier m de l'état civil; **to be married by the ~** se marier civilement or à la mairie **b** (Univ) (Brit) secrétaire mf (général(e)); (US) chef m du service des inscriptions **c** (Brit Med) chef m de clinique **d** (Jur) (in court) greffier m; (Fin) (companies') ~ conservateur m (du registre des sociétés) **2** COMP ▶ **registrar's office** N bureau m de l'état civil

registration [ˌredʒɪ'streɪʃən] **1** N **a** (= listing) [of voters] inscription f; [of dog] déclaration f; [of trademark] dépôt m; (Univ) inscription f; **~ for VAT** assujettissement m à la TVA (au-delà d'un certain chiffre d'affaires); **J-~ car** (Brit) voiture dont l'immatriculation commence ou finit par un J (la lettre indiquant l'année de mise en circulation) **b** (Post) [of letter] recommandation f; (Rail) [of luggage] enregistrement m **c** (Brit Scol: also **~ period**) appel m **2** COMP ▶ **registration document** N (Brit Aut) ≈ carte f grise ▶ **registration fee** N (Post) taxe f de recommandation; (Rail: for luggage) frais mpl d'enregistrement; (Univ) droits mpl d'inscription ▶ **registration**

number N (Brit Aut) numéro m minéralogique or d'immatriculation; **car (with) ~ number R971 VBW** voiture f immatriculée R971 VBW

registry ['redʒɪstrɪ] **1** N (= act) enregistrement m, inscription f; (= office) (gen) bureau m de l'enregistrement; (Brit Admin) bureau m de l'état civil; (Naut) certificat m d'immatriculation; (Naut) **port of ~** port m d'attache **2** COMP ▶ **registry office** N (Brit) bureau m d'état civil; **to get married in a ~ office** se marier civilement or à la mairie

regius professor ['riːdʒəsprə'fesər] N (Brit Univ) professeur m (titulaire d'une chaire de fondation royale)

regnal ['regnl] ADJ **~ year** année f du règne

regnant ['regnənt] ADJ régnant; **queen ~** reine f régnante

regorge [rɪ'gɔːdʒ] **1** VT vomir, régurgiter **2** VI refluer

regress [rɪ'gres] **1** VI **a** (Bio, Psych, fig) régresser (**to** au stade de), rétrograder **b** (= move backwards) retourner en arrière, reculer **2** ['riːgres] N = **regression**

regression [rɪ'greʃən] N (lit) retour m en arrière, recul m; (Bio, Psych, fig) régression f

regressive [rɪ'gresɪv] **1** ADJ régressif **2** COMP ▶ **regressive tax** N impôt m dégressif, taxe f dégressive

▼**regret** [rɪ'gret] **1** VT regretter (**doing, to do** de faire, **that** que + subj); [+ mistake, words, event] regretter, être désolé or navré de; [+ one's youth, lost opportunity] regretter; **I ~ to say that ...** j'ai le regret de dire que ...; **he is very ill, I ~ to say** il est très malade, hélas or je regrette de le dire; **we ~ to hear that ...** nous sommes désolés d'apprendre que ...; **we ~ that it was not possible to ...** (gen) nous sommes désolés de n'avoir pu ...; (Comm) nous sommes au regret de vous informer qu'il n'a pas été possible de ...; **it is to be ~ted that ...** il est regrettable que ... (+ subj); **you won't ~ it!** vous ne le regretterez pas!; **the President ~s he cannot see you today** le Président est au regret or exprime ses regrets de ne pouvoir vous recevoir aujourd'hui; **he is much ~ted** on le regrette beaucoup **2** N regret m (**for** de); **much to my ~** à mon grand regret; **I have no ~s** je ne regrette rien, je n'ai aucun regret; **to do with ~** faire qch à regret or à contrecœur; **to send (one's) ~s** envoyer ses excuses; **please give her my ~s that I cannot come** dites-lui, s'il vous plaît, combien je regrette de ne pouvoir venir

regretful [rɪ'gretfʊl] ADJ plein de regret; **to be ~ about sth** regretter qch

regretfully [rɪ'gretfʊlɪ] ADV **a** (= with regret) [say, decide, decline] à regret **b** (= unfortunately) **~, nationalism is flourishing again** malheureusement, le nationalisme est en pleine recrudescence

▼**regrettable** [rɪ'gretəbl] ADJ regrettable, fâcheux; **it is ~ that ...** il est regrettable que ... (+ subj)

regrettably [rɪ'gretəblɪ] ADV [poor, ignorant, true] malheureusement, tristement; **~ few people came** il est regrettable que si peu de gens soient venus; **~, he refused** malheureusement, il a refusé

regroup [ˌriː'gruːp] **1** VT regrouper **2** VI se regrouper; (fig) se ressaisir

regrouping [ˌriː'gruːpɪŋ] N regroupement m

regs: [regz] NPL (ABBR = **regulations**) règlement m

Regt. ABBR = **Regiment**

regular ['regjʊlər] **1** ADJ **a** (gen) [pulse, reminders, features, flight, order, meals] régulier; **on a ~ basis** régulièrement; **as ~ as clockwork** [person] réglé comme une horloge; [occurrence] très régulier; **to be in or have a ~**

contact with sb/sth avoir des contacts réguliers avec qn/qch; **to be in ~ employment** avoir un emploi fixe; **to take ~ exercise** faire régulièrement de l'exercice; **a ~ feature of sth** un aspect courant de qch; **to be a ~ feature on the menu** figurer régulièrement au menu; **to be ~ in one's habits** être régulier dans ses habitudes; **to keep ~ hours** mener une vie réglée, avoir des horaires très réguliers; **at ~ intervals** à intervalles réguliers; **~ meetings** se réunir régulièrement; **life took on a ~ pattern** la vie a commencé à prendre un cours normal; **to make ~ payments** effectuer des versements réguliers; **to have a ~ place on the team** avoir régulièrement sa place dans l'équipe; **to run regular advertisements in the press** faire paraître régulièrement des publicités dans la presse; **to make ~ trips to** se rendre régulièrement à; **to be in ~ use** être régulièrement utilisé
b (= even) [surface] uni
c (= habitual) [reader] assidu, fidèle (before n); [listener] fidèle (before n); **to be a ~ listener to sth** écouter régulièrement qch; **a ~ customer/visitor** un(e) habitué(e); **to be a ~ churchgoer** être pratiquant, aller régulièrement à l'église
d (esp US = customary) [event] habituel; [partner] régulier; **it's past his ~ bedtime** on a dépassé l'heure à laquelle il va habituellement se coucher; **the ~ staff** le personnel permanent; **our ~ cleaning woman** notre femme de ménage habituelle; **my ~ dentist** mon dentiste habituel; **my ~ doctor** mon médecin traitant
e (esp US) (= ordinary) ordinaire; (Comm) [size] normal; [price] normal, courant; (US) **I'm just a ~ guy*** je ne suis qu'un type* comme un autre; (US) **he's a ~ guy*** c'est un chic type*; **would you like ~, large, or extra-large?** normal, grand ou super*?; **~ fries** portion f de frites normale; **he's an acupuncturist, not a ~ doctor** ce n'est pas un médecin normal, c'est un acupuncteur; **it is quite ~ to apply in person** on fait tout à fait courant de faire sa demande en personne
f (Mil) (= not conscripted) [army, troops] régulier; [officer] de l'armée régulière; (Police) [officer] de carrière; **~ soldier** soldat m de métier; **the ~ police force** les forces fpl de police régulières (par rapport aux forces auxiliaires et spéciales)
g (* = real) véritable; **this is turning into a ~ epidemic** ça tourne à l'épidémie
h (Math, Gram, Rel) régulier
i * (in menstruation) **I'm quite ~** mes règles sont assez régulières; (= not constipated) **to be ~** aller régulièrement à la selle; **to keep sb ~** permettre à qn d'aller régulièrement à la selle; **~ bowel movements** selles fpl régulières
2 N **a** (Mil) soldat m de métier; (= police officer) policier m (de métier)
b (= habitual customer etc) habitué(e) m(f), bon(ne) client(e) m(f); (Rad, TV) **he's one of the ~s on that programme** il participe or prend part régulièrement à ce programme
c (Rel) régulier m, religieux m
d (US = gas) essence f (ordinaire), ordinaire m
3 COMP ► **regular gas(oline)** N = **regular 2d**

regularity [ˌregjʊˈlærɪtɪ] N régularité f

regularize [ˈregjʊləraɪz] VT régulariser

regularly [ˈregjʊləlɪ] ADV régulièrement

regulate [ˈregjʊleɪt] VT **a** (= control systematically) [+ amount, flow] régler; [+ expenditure] régler, calculer; **to ~ one's life by sth** se régler sur qch; **a well-~d life** une vie bien réglée
b [+ machine] régler, ajuster

regulation [ˌregjʊˈleɪʃən] **1** N (= rule) règlement m; (Admin) règlement m, arrêté m; **against (the) ~s** contraire au règlement → **fire, safety 2** COMP [style, size] réglementaire

► **regulation boots** NPL (Mil) brodequins mpl d'ordonnance ► **regulation dress** N (Mil) tenue f réglementaire

regulative [ˈregjʊlətɪv] ADJ régulateur (-trice f)

regulator [ˈregjʊleɪtər] N (= person) régulateur m, -trice f; (= instrument) régulateur m; **acidity ~** correcteur m d'acidité

regulatory [regjʊˈleɪtərɪ] ADJ [body, authority, system, role, changes] de réglementation; [control, framework] réglementaire; **~ reform** réforme f de la réglementation

Regulo® [ˈregjʊləʊ] N **~ (mark) 6** etc thermostat 6 etc

regurgitate [rɪˈgɜːdʒɪteɪt] **1** VT [animal, bird, person] régurgiter; [drainpipe etc] dégorger **2** VI refluer

regurgitation [rɪˌgɜːdʒɪˈteɪʃən] N régurgitation f

rehab: [ˈriːhæb] N (ABBR = **rehabilitation**) [of disabled, ill person] rééducation f; [of alcoholic, drug user] (= drying-out) désintoxication f; (to everyday life) réintégration f

rehabilitate [ˌriːəˈbɪlɪteɪt] VT [+ disabled, ill person] rééduquer; [+ refugees] réadapter; [+ demobilized troops] réintégrer (dans la vie civile); [+ ex-prisoner] réinsérer; [+ drug user, alcoholic] désintoxiquer; [+ disgraced person, sb's memory] réhabiliter

rehabilitation [ˈriːəˌbɪlɪˈteɪʃən] **1** N [of disabled, ill person] (to everyday life) rééducation f; (to work) réadaptation f; [of ex-prisoner] réinsertion f; [of refugee] réadaptation f; [of drug user, alcoholic] désintoxication f; [of demobilized troops] réintégration f (dans la vie civile); [of area, building, disgraced person] réhabilitation f **2** COMP ► **rehabilitation centre** N (for disabled, ill person) centre m de réadaptation; (for drug user, alcoholic) centre m de désintoxication; (for prisoner) centre m de réinsertion

rehash* [riːˈhæʃ] **1** VT [+ literary material etc] remanier, réarranger **2** [ˈriːhæʃ] N réchauffé m, resucée* f

rehearsal [rɪˈhɜːsəl] N **a** (Theat) répétition f; (fig = preparation) préparation f (**for sth** de qch); **this play is in ~** on répète cette pièce → **dress b** (NonC) [of facts etc] énumération f, récit m détaillé

rehearse [rɪˈhɜːs] VT (Theat) répéter; (gen) [+ facts, grievances] énumérer; **to ~ what one is going to say** préparer ce qu'on va dire; **well ~d** [+ play] répété avec soin; [+ actor] qui a soigneusement répété son texte; (fig) [+ intervention, protest] soigneusement étudié

reheat [ˌriːˈhiːt] VT réchauffer

rehouse [ˌriːˈhaʊz] VT reloger

reign [reɪn] **1** N (lit, fig) règne m; **in the ~ of** sous le règne de; (Hist) **the Reign of Terror** la Terreur; (fig) **~ of terror** régime m de terreur **2** VI (lit, fig) régner (**over** sur); **silence ~s** le silence règne; **to ~ supreme** [monarch] régner en or être le maître absolu; [champion] être sans rival; [justice, peace] régner en souverain(e)

reigning [ˈreɪnɪŋ] ADJ [monarch] régnant; [champion] en titre; (fig) [attitude] actuel, dominant

reimburse [ˌriːɪmˈbɜːs] VT rembourser (**sb for sth** qch à qn, qn de qch); **to ~ sb (for) his expenses** rembourser qn de ses dépenses

reimbursement [ˌriːɪmˈbɜːsmənt] N remboursement m

reimpose [ˌriːɪmˈpəʊz] VT réimposer

rein [reɪn] N (often pl: lit, fig) rêne f; [of horse in harness] guide f; **~s** [of child] rênes fpl; (lit, fig) **to hold the ~s** tenir les rênes; (lit, fig) **to keep a ~ on sb/sth** tenir qn/qch en bride; (fig) **to give (a) free ~ to** [+ anger, passions, one's imagination] donner libre cours à; **to give sb free ~ (to do sth)** donner carte blanche à qn (pour faire qch)

►**rein back** **1** VT SEP [+ horse] faire reculer **2** VI reculer

►**rein in** **1** VI (fig) ralentir **2** VT SEP [+ horse] serrer la bride à, ramener au pas; (fig) [+ passions] contenir, maîtriser

►**rein up** VI s'arrêter

reincarnate [ˌriːɪnˈkɑːneɪt] **1** VT réincarner **2** [ˌriːɪnˈkɑːnɪt] ADJ (frm) réincarné

reincarnation [ˌriːɪnkɑːˈneɪʃən] N réincarnation f

reindeer [ˈreɪndɪər] N (pl **reindeer** or **reindeers**) renne m

reinforce [ˌriːɪnˈfɔːs] VT (Mil) renforcer; (gen) [+ wall, bridge, heel] renforcer; [+ beam] armer, renforcer; [+ one's demands etc] appuyer; **~d concrete** béton m armé

reinforcement [ˌriːɪnˈfɔːsmənt] **1** N **a** (= action) renforcement m; (= thing) renfort m **b** (Mil = action) renforcement m; (also fig) **~s** renforts mpl **2** COMP [troops, supplies] de renfort

reinsert [ˌriːɪnˈsɜːt] VT réinsérer

reinstate [ˌriːɪnˈsteɪt] VT [+ employee] réintégrer, rétablir dans ses fonctions; [+ text] rétablir (**in** dans)

reinstatement [ˌriːɪnˈsteɪtmənt] N réintégration f, rétablissement m

reinstitute [ˌriːˈɪnstɪtjuːt] VT rétablir

reinstitution [ˌriːɪnstɪˈtjuːʃən] N rétablissement m

reinsurance [ˌriːɪnˈʃʊərəns] N réassurance f; [of underwriter etc] (against possible losses) contre-assurance f

reinsure [ˌriːɪnˈʃʊər] VT [+ policy, contract] réassurer, contracter une contre-assurance sur; [insurance company] réassurer; **to ~ o.s.** se réassurer, contracter une contre-assurance

reintegrate [ˌriːˈɪntɪgreɪt] VT réintégrer

reintegration [ˌriːɪntɪˈgreɪʃən] N réintégration f

reinvent [ˌriːɪnˈvent] VT **a to ~ the wheel** réinventer la roue **b to ~ o.s.** faire peau neuve; **to ~ o.s. as sth** se métamorphoser en qch

reinvest [ˌriːɪnˈvest] VT (Fin) réinvestir

reinvestment [ˌriːɪnˈvestmənt] N (Fin) nouveau placement m, nouvel investissement m

reinvigorate [ˌriːɪnˈvɪgəreɪt] VT revigorer

reissue [ˌriːˈɪʃjuː] **1** VT [+ book] donner une nouvelle édition de, rééditer; [+ film] ressortir, redistribuer **2** N (= act) [of book] réédition f; [of film] redistribution f; **it is a ~** [book] il a été réédité; [film] il est ressorti

reiterate [riːˈɪtəreɪt] VT réitérer, répéter

reiteration [riːˌɪtəˈreɪʃən] N réitération f, répétition f

reiterative [riːˈɪtərətɪv] ADJ réitératif

►**reject** [rɪˈdʒekt] **1** VT **a** (gen) rejeter, repousser; [+ damaged goods etc] [customer, shopkeeper] refuser; [maker, producer] mettre au rebut; [+ suitor] repousser, éconduire; [+ candidate, manuscript] refuser; [+ offer, proposal, application] rejeter; [+ plea, advances] repousser; [+ possibility] rejeter, repousser; [+ coins] [machine] refuser **b** (Med) [body] [+ medication, transplant] rejeter **c** (Comput) rejeter **2** [ˈriːdʒekt] N (Comm) pièce f or article m de rebut → **export b** (Comput) rejet m **3** [ˈriːdʒekt] COMP (Comm, Ind) [goods] de rebut ► **reject shop** N boutique f d'articles de second choix

rejection [rɪˈdʒekʃən] **1** N refus m, rejet m; (Med) rejet m **2** COMP ► **rejection slip** N (Publishing) lettre f de refus

rejig* [riːˈdʒɪg], **rejigger*** (US) [riːˈdʒɪgər] VT réorganiser, réarranger

rejoice [rɪˈdʒɔɪs] **1** VT réjouir; (frm, liter) **it ~d his heart to see ...** il s'est félicité du fond du cœur de voir ... **2** VI se réjouir (**at, over, in** de); **they ~d to see peace return to their country at last** ils se sont réjouis de voir enfin la paix revenir dans leur pays; *(hum, iro)* **he ~s in the name of Marmaduke** il a le privilège de s'appeler Marmaduke *(iro)*

rejoicing [rɪˈdʒɔɪsɪŋ] N [a] *(NonC)* réjouissance *f*, jubilation *f* [b] **~s** réjouissances *fpl*, fête *f*

rejoin[1] [ˌriːˈdʒɔɪn] [1] VT [+ *person, army*] rejoindre; *(Naut)* **to ~ ship** rallier le bord; **they ~ed the motorway at junction 15** ils ont rejoint l'autoroute à l'entrée n° 15 [2] VI se rejoindre

rejoin[2] [rɪˈdʒɔɪn] VI (= *reply*) répliquer, répondre

rejoinder [rɪˈdʒɔɪndəʳ] N réplique *f*, repartie *f*; *(Jur)* réplique *f*, réponse *f* à une réplique

rejuvenate [rɪˈdʒuːvɪneɪt] VTI rajeunir

rejuvenating [rɪˈdʒuːvɪneɪtɪŋ] ADJ rajeunissant

rejuvenation [rɪˌdʒuːvɪˈneɪʃən] N rajeunissement *m*

rekindle [ˌriːˈkɪndl] [1] VT [+ *fire*] rallumer, attiser; *(fig)* [+ *hope, enthusiasm, tensions, enmities*] ranimer, raviver [2] VI se rallumer, se ranimer

relapse [rɪˈlæps] [1] N *(Med, fig)* rechute *f*; **to have a ~** avoir *or* faire une rechute, rechuter [2] VI *(gen)* retomber (**into** dans); [*ill person*] rechuter

Relate [rɪˈleɪt] N *(Brit) centre de consultation conjugale*

relate [rɪˈleɪt] [1] VT [a] (= *recount*) [+ *story*] raconter, relater; [+ *details*] rapporter; **strange to ~ ...** chose curieuse (à dire) ...
[b] (= *associate*) établir un rapport entre, rapprocher; [+ *breeds*] apparenter; *(to a category)* rattacher, lier; **it is often difficult to ~ the cause to the effect** il est souvent difficile d'établir un rapport de cause à effet *or* d'établir un lien entre la cause et l'effet
[2] VI [a] (= *refer*) se rapporter, toucher (**to** à)
[b] *(Psych)* **to ~ to sb** (= *form relationship*) établir des rapports avec qn; (= *maintain relationship*) entretenir des rapports avec qn; **how do you ~ to your parents?** quels rapports entretenez-vous avec vos parents?; **he doesn't ~ to other people** il n'a pas le sens des contacts; **women ~ more to this than men** les femmes sentent mieux cela que les hommes; **I can ~ to that*** je comprends ça

related [rɪˈleɪtɪd] [1] ADJ [a] *(in family)* [*person*] parent; [*animal, species, language*] apparenté (**to sth** à qch); **she is ~ to us** elle est notre parente; **they are ~ to each other** ils sont parents; **he is ~ to the Royal family** c'est un parent de la famille royale; **he is ~ by marriage to our great aunt/the Royal family** c'est un parent *or* il est parent par alliance de notre grand-tante/de la famille royale; **they are closely/distantly ~** ce sont de proches parents/des parents éloignés; **two closely ~ species/languages** deux espèces/langues très proches
[b] (= *connected*) *(Chem)* apparenté; *(Philos)* connexe; *(Mus)* relatif; **to be ~ to sth** être lié à qch; **food allergies and ~ problems** les allergies alimentaires et les problèmes qui y sont liés; **cookware, cutlery, and ~ products** les ustensiles de cuisine, les couverts et les produits du même ordre; **geometry and other ~ subjects** la géométrie et les sujets connexes *or* qui s'y rattachent; **another ~ issue which this film deals with is ...** ce film aborde aussi un problème apparent, à savoir ...; **the two events are not ~** ces deux événements n'ont pas de rapport; **two closely ~ questions** deux questions fort proches l'une de l'autre *or* étroitement liées; **two distantly ~ questions** deux questions fort éloignées l'une de l'autre
[2] **-related** ADJ *(in compounds)* qui est lié à; **health-~ problems** problèmes *mpl* liés à la santé; **earnings-~ pensions** retraites *fpl* ramenées au salaire

relating [rɪˈleɪtɪŋ] ADJ **~ to** concernant, relatif à

relation [rɪˈleɪʃən] N [a] (*family = person*) parent(e) *m(f)*; (= *kinship*) parenté *f*; **I've got some ~s coming to dinner** j'ai de la famille à dîner; **is he any ~ to you?** est-il de vos parents?; **he is no ~ (of mine or to me)** il n'est pas de ma famille, il n'y a aucun lien de parenté entre nous; **what ~ is she to you?** quelle est sa parenté avec vous?
[b] (= *relationship*) rapport *m*, relation *f*; **to bear a ~ to** avoir rapport à; **to bear no ~ to** n'avoir aucun rapport avec, être sans rapport avec; **in** *or* **with ~ to** par rapport à, relativement à; **~s** relations *fpl*, rapports *mpl*; (= *personal ties*) rapports *mpl*; **to have business ~s with** être en rapports *mpl or* relations *fpl* d'affaires avec; **diplomatic/friendly/international ~s** relations *fpl* diplomatiques/d'amitié/internationales; **~s are rather strained** les relations *or* les rapports sont assez tendu(e)s; **sexual ~s** rapports *mpl* (sexuels) → **public**
[c] (= *telling*) [*of story*] récit *m*, relation *f*; [*of details*] rapport *m*

relational [rɪˈleɪʃənl] ADJ *(gen, Ling)* relationnel

relationship [rɪˈleɪʃənʃɪp] N [a] (= *family ties*) liens *mpl* de parenté; **what is your ~ to him?** quels sont les liens de parenté entre vous?, quels sont vos liens de parenté avec lui?
[b] (= *connection*) rapport *m*; (= *relations*) relations *fpl*, rapports *mpl*; (= *personal ties*) rapports *mpl*; **to see a ~ between two events** voir un rapport *or* un lien entre deux événements; **to have a ~ with sb** *(gen)* avoir des relations *or* être en relations avec qn; *(sexual)* avoir une liaison avec qn; **he has a good ~ with his clients** il est en bons rapports avec ses clients; **they have a good ~** ils s'entendent bien; **friendly/business ~** relations *fpl* d'amitié/d'affaires; **his ~ with his father was strained** ses rapports avec son père étaient tendus; **the ~ between mother and child** les rapports entre la mère et l'enfant

relative [ˈrelətɪv] [1] ADJ [a] (= *comparative*) [*safety, peace, comfort, luxury, weakness*] relatif; **with ~ ease** avec une relative facilité; **he is a newcomer** c'est plus ou moins un nouveau venu; **her ~ lack of experience** sa relative inexpérience; **in ~ terms** en termes relatifs; **petrol consumption is ~ to speed** la consommation d'essence est fonction de *or* relative à la vitesse; **there is a shortage of labour ~ to demand** il y a une pénurie de main d'œuvre par rapport à la demande; **all human values are ~** toutes les valeurs humaines sont relatives; **it's all ~** tout est relatif
[b] (= *respective*) [*importance, merits, strengths*] respectif
[c] (= *relevant*) **~ to sth** relatif à qch, qui se rapporte à qch; **the documents ~ to the problem** les documents relatifs au problème *or* qui se rapportent au problème
[d] *(Gram, Mus)* relatif
[2] N [a] (= *person*) parent(e) *m(f)*; **one of my ~s** un(e) parent(e) à moi, un membre de ma famille; **all my ~s came** toute ma famille est venue
[b] *(Gram)* relatif *m*
[3] COMP ► **relative clause** N *(Gram)* (proposition *f*) relative *f* ► **relative conjunction** N *(Gram)* conjonction *f* de subordination ► **relative major (key)** N *(Mus)* (ton *m*) majeur *m* relatif ► **relative minor (key)** N *(Mus)* (ton *m*) mineur *m* relatif ► **relative pronoun** N *(Gram)* pronom *m* relatif

relatively [ˈrelətɪvlɪ] ADV relativement; **~ speaking** comparativement

relativism [ˈrelətɪvɪzəm] N relativisme *m*

relativist [ˈrelətɪvɪst] ADJ, N relativiste *mf*

relativistic [ˌrelətɪˈvɪstɪk] ADJ relativiste

relativity [ˌreləˈtɪvɪtɪ] N *(gen, Ling, Philos, Phys)* relativité *f*; **theory of ~** théorie *f* de la relativité

relativization [ˌrelətɪvaɪˈzeɪʃən] N relativisation *f*

relativize [ˈrelətɪvaɪz] VT relativiser

relax [rɪˈlæks] [1] VT [+ *hold, grip*] relâcher, desserrer; *(Med)* [+ *bowels*] relâcher; [+ *muscles*] relâcher, décontracter; [+ *discipline, attention, effort*] relâcher; [+ *restrictions*] modérer; [+ *measures, tariffs*] assouplir; [+ *person, one's mind*] détendre, délasser → **relaxed** [2] VI [a] (= *rest*) se détendre, se relaxer; (* = *calm down*) **let's just ~!** restons calmes!, du calme! [b] [*hold, grip*] se relâcher, se desserrer; [*muscles*] se relâcher, se décontracter

relaxant [rɪˈlæksənt] N décontractant *m*; **muscle ~** décontractant *m* musculaire

relaxation [ˌriːlækˈseɪʃən] N [a] *(NonC)* [*of muscles, discipline, attention*] relâchement *m*; [*of mind*] détente *f*, relaxation *f*; [*of body*] décontraction *f*, relaxation *f*; [*of restrictions, measures, tariffs*] assouplissement *m*; *(Jur)* **measures of ~** mesures *fpl* d'assouplissement [b] (= *recreation*) détente *f*, délassement *m*; (= *rest*) repos *m*; **you need some ~ after work** on a besoin d'une détente après le travail; **books are her ~** pour se délasser *or* se détendre elle lit; **the ~s of the wealthy** les distractions *fpl* des riches

relaxed [rɪˈlækst] ADJ [*person, mood, discussion, attitude, approach, smile*] détendu, décontracté; [*discipline, muscle*] relâché; **to feel ~** se sentir détendu; *(fig)* **I feel fairly ~ about it*** je ne m'en fais pas pour ça*

relaxing [rɪˈlæksɪŋ] ADJ [*weekend, holiday, place*] reposant; [*atmosphere*] reposant, relaxant; [*music, massage*] relaxant; [*bath*] relaxant, délassant; **to have a ~ time** passer des moments reposants

relay [ˈriːleɪ] [1] N [a] [*of horses, men etc*] relais *m*; **to work in ~s** travailler par relais, se relayer [b] *(Rad, TV)* émission *f* relayée [c] *(Sport)* = **relay race** [d] *(Elec, Phys, Tech)* relais *m* [2] VT *(Elec, Rad, TV etc)* [+ *programme, information*] relayer, retransmettre; [+ *signal, message*] transmettre, retransmettre; **to ~ each other** se relayer [3] COMP ► **relay race** N course *f* de relais ► **relay station** N *(Rad, TV)* relais *m*

re-lay [ˌriːˈleɪ] VT *(pret, ptp* **re-laid***)* [+ *carpet*] reposer

release [rɪˈliːs] [1] N [a] *(NonC)* (*from captivity, prison, custody, obligation, responsibility*) libération *f*; (*from service*) dispense *f*, exemption *f*; (*Comm: from customs, bond*) congé *m*; **on his ~ from prison he ...** dès sa sortie de prison, il ...; **the ~ of the prisoners by the allied forces** la libération des prisonniers par les forces alliées; **death was a happy ~ for him** pour lui la mort a été une délivrance
[b] *(NonC: Comm)* [*of goods*] mise *f* en vente; [*of news*] autorisation *f* de publier; [*of film, record*] sortie *f*; [*of book*] parution *f*, sortie *f*; **this film is now on general ~** ce film n'est plus en exclusivité
[c] *(Comm* = *sth just brought out)* **new ~** (= *record, CD*) nouvel album *m*; (= *film*) nouveau film *m*; (= *book*) nouveauté *f*; (= *video*) nouvelle vidéo *f*; **their latest ~** leur dernier album *(or film etc)* → **press**
[d] *(NonC)* [*of bomb*] largage *m*; *(Phot etc)* déclenchement *m*; [*of steam*] échappement *m*
[e] *(also ~* **switch/button***)* touche *f* de déclenchement
[2] VT [a] (= *set free*) [+ *person*] *(from prison)* libérer, relâcher (**from** de), élargir *(Jur)*; *(from hospital)* autoriser à sortir (**from** de); *(from chains)* libérer (**from** de); *(from rubble, wreckage)* dégager (**from** de); *(from obligation, debt)* dégager, libérer (**from** de); *(from promise, vow)* relever (**from** de); [+ *captive animal*] relâcher; *(Jur)* **to ~ sb on bail** mettre qn en liberté pro-

visoire sous caution ; **death ~d him from pain** la mort mit fin à ses souffrances ; **his employer agreed to ~ him** son patron lui a permis de cesser son travail ; **can you ~ him for a few hours each week?** pouvez-vous le libérer quelques heures par semaine ?
b (= *let go*) [+ *object, sb's hand, pigeon*] lâcher ; [+ *bomb*] larguer, lâcher ; (*Chem*) [+ *gas*] dégager ; [+ *anger*] donner libre cours à ; **to ~ one's anger on sb** passer sa colère sur qn ; **to ~ one's hold** or **grip** lâcher prise ; **to ~ one's hold of** or **one's grip on sth** lâcher qch ; **humour is wonderful for releasing tension** l'humour est idéal pour relâcher les tensions ; **massage helps to ~ the tension in your shoulders and neck** les massages aident à décrisper les épaules et le cou
c (= *issue*) [+ *book, record*] sortir, faire paraître ; [+ *film*] (faire) sortir ; [+ *goods*] mettre en vente ; (= *publish, announce*) [+ *news*] autoriser la publication de ; [+ *details of sth*] publier ; **to ~ a statement** publier un communiqué (**about** au sujet de)
d (*Jur*) [+ *property*] céder
e [+ *spring, clasp, catch*] faire jouer ; (*Phot*) [+ *shutter*] déclencher ; [+ *handbrake*] desserrer ; (*Aut*) **to ~ the clutch** débrayer
3 COMP [*switch, knob, catch etc*] de déclenchement or de sortie etc ► **release date** N [*of film, record*] date f de sortie ; [*of book*] date f de parution ; [*of prisoner*] date f de libération, date f de sortie ► **release print** N (*Cine*) copie f d'exploitation ► **release valve** N soupape f de sûreté

relegate ['relɪgeɪt] VT **a** (= *demote*) [+ *person*] reléguer ; (*Sport*) [+ *team*] reléguer (**to** à, **en**), déclasser ; (*Brit Ftbl*) **to be ~d** descendre en seconde etc division ; **to ~ old furniture to the attic** reléguer de vieux meubles au grenier
b (= *hand over*) [+ *matter, question*] renvoyer (**to** à, se décharger de (**to** sur)

relegation [ˌrelɪ'geɪʃən] N relégation f (also *Sport*) ; [*of matter, question*] renvoi m (**to** à)

relent [rɪ'lent] VI s'adoucir, se laisser toucher, se laisser fléchir ; (= *reverse one's decision*) revenir sur une décision ; (*fig*) [*weather*] s'améliorer

relentless [rɪ'lentlɪs] ADJ [*search, pursuit, noise, demands, attacks, criticism*] incessant ; [*pressure, energy, determination, pace, growth*] implacable ; (*iro*) [*optimism, cheerfulness*] incorrigible ; [*person*] implacable, impitoyable ; **to be ~ in doing sth** or **in one's efforts to do sth** ne pas relâcher ses efforts pour faire qch ; **the ~ march of technology** l'avancée f inexorable de la technologie

relentlessly [rɪ'lentlɪslɪ] ADV **a** (= *tirelessly*) [*fight, pursue*] avec acharnement ; [*advance, march*] inexorablement ; **the sun beat down ~** le soleil était implacable **b** (= *unremittingly*) [*cheerful, happy, grim*] incurablement, incorrigiblement

relet [ˌriː'let] VT relouer

relevance ['reləvəns], **relevancy** ['reləvənsɪ] N [*of question, remark, argument*] pertinence f, intérêt m ; [*of fact, information*] importance f, intérêt m ; **I don't see the ~ of your question/that remark (to the issue)** je ne vois pas l'intérêt de votre question/cette remarque ; **to be of particular ~ (to sb)** être particulièrement pertinent (pour qn) ; **a curriculum which is of ~ to all pupils** un programme qui intéresse tous les élèves ; **to have no ~ to sth** n'avoir aucun rapport avec qch ; **outdated concepts which have no ~ to the present day** des concepts démodés qui sont sans rapport avec la réalité d'aujourd'hui

relevant ['reləvənt] ADJ **a** (= *pertinent*) [*information, fact, question, remark, argument*] pertinent ; [*law, regulation*] applicable (**to** à) ; **that is not ~** ce n'est pas pertinent ; **Molière's plays are still ~ today** les pièces de Molière sont toujours d'actualité ; **Ancient History may**

be fascinating but it's hardly ~ when it comes to finding a job l'histoire ancienne est peut-être fascinante mais ne sert pas à grand-chose quand il s'agit de trouver du travail ; (*gen*) **to be ~ to sth** être en rapport avec qch ; **to be ~ to sb/sth** [*law, regulation*] être applicable à qn/qch, concerner qn/qch ; (*Jur, Fin*) **the ~ year** l'année f de référence
b (= *in question, corresponding*) [*document, page, information, course*] approprié ; [*time, place, day etc*] en question ; [*law, regulation*] approprié, applicable ; [*official, authority*] compétent

reliability [rɪˌlaɪə'bɪlɪtɪ] N [*of person, character*] sérieux m ; [*of memory, description*] sûreté f, précision f ; [*of device, machine*] fiabilité f

reliable [rɪ'laɪəbl] ADJ [*person*] digne de confiance, sérieux ; [*account, report*] digne de foi, sérieux ; [*firm*] sérieux ; [*ally, source, information*] sûr ; [*machine, method, service, figures, guide, memory, description*] fiable ; [*evidence*] solide ; **he's very ~** on peut compter sur lui

reliably [rɪ'laɪəblɪ] ADV [*work, measure, date*] de manière fiable ; **I am ~ informed that …** j'ai appris de source sûre que …

reliance [rɪ'laɪəns] N (= *trust*) confiance f (**on** en) ; (= *dependence*) dépendance f (**on** de), besoin m (**on** de) ; **to place ~ on sb/in sth** avoir confiance en qn/en qch

reliant [rɪ'laɪənt] ADJ **to be ~ on sb (for sth)** être dépendant de qn (pour qch), dépendre de qn (pour qch) ; **to be ~ on sth** dépendre de qch → **self**

relic ['relɪk] N relique f (also *Rel*) ; **~s** (= *human remains*) dépouille f (mortelle) ; [*of past*] reliques fpl, vestiges mpl

relict†† ['relɪkt] N veuve f

relief [rɪ'liːf] **1** N **a** (*from pain, anxiety*) soulagement m ; **to bring ~ (to sb)** apporter or procurer du soulagement (à qn) ; **I felt great ~ when …** j'ai éprouvé un grand or vif soulagement quand … ; **to my ~** à mon grand soulagement ; **that's a ~!** ouf ! je respire !, j'aime mieux ça ! ; **(to me) it was a ~ to find it** j'ai été soulagé de le retrouver ; **it's a ~ to get out of the office once in a while** ça fait du bien de sortir du bureau de temps en temps → **comic**
b (= *assistance*) secours m, aide f ; **to go to the ~ of …** aller au secours de … ; **to come to the ~ of …** venir en aide à … ; **to send ~ to …** envoyer des secours à …
c (*US Admin*) aides fpl sociales ; **to be on** or **getting ~** bénéficier d'aides sociales
d (*Mil*) [*of town*] libération f ; [*of guard*] relève f
e (= *substitute or extra workers*) relève f
f (= *exemption*) (*Jur*) exonération f ; (*fiscal*) dégrèvement m
g (*Art, Geog*) relief m ; **high/low ~** haut-/bas-relief ; **to stand out in (bold** or **sharp** or **clear) ~ against …** se détacher sur … ; (*lit, fig*) **to bring** or **throw sth into ~** mettre qch en relief, faire ressortir qch

2 COMP [*train, coach*] supplémentaire ; [*typist, clerk*] suppléant ► **relief agency** N organisation f humanitaire ► **relief fund** N caisse f de secours ► **relief map** N carte f en relief ► **relief organization** N [*of refugees, earthquakes etc*] organisation f humanitaire ► **relief road** N (*Brit*) itinéraire m de délestage ► **relief supplies** NPL secours mpl ► **relief troops** NPL relève f, troupes fpl de secours ► **relief valve** N soupape f de sûreté ► **relief work** N travail m humanitaire ► **relief worker** N représentant m d'un organisme humanitaire

relieve [rɪ'liːv] VT **a** [+ *person*] soulager ; **to feel/look ~d** se sentir/avoir l'air soulagé ; **he was ~d to learn that …** il a été soulagé d'apprendre que … ; **to be ~d at sth** être soulagé par qch ; **to be ~d that …** être soulagé que … (+ *subj*) ; **to ~ sb of a burden** soulager qn d'un

fardeau ; **to ~ sb of a coat/suitcase** débarrasser qn d'un manteau/d'une valise ; **to ~ sb of a duty** décharger qn d'une obligation ; **to ~ sb of a post** ◊ **to ~ sb of a command** (*Mil*) relever qn de ses fonctions ; (*hum*) **a thief has ~d me of my purse** un voleur m'a soulagé de or délesté de mon porte-monnaie
b (= *mitigate*) [+ *anxiety, pain, stress, mental suffering*] soulager ; [+ *pressure*] diminuer ; [+ *fear, boredom*] dissiper ; [+ *poverty*] remédier à, pallier ; **to ~ sb's mind** tranquilliser (l'esprit de) qn ; **to ~ one's feelings** (*sorrow*) s'épancher ; (*anger*) décharger sa colère or sa bile ; **to ~ the symptoms of sth** soulager les symptômes de qch ; **to ~ a situation** remédier à une situation ; **the black of her dress was ~d by a white collar** un col blanc égayait sa robe noire ; **the new road ~s peak-hour congestion** la nouvelle route facilite la circulation aux heures de pointe ; **the new road ~s congestion in the town centre** la nouvelle route décongestionne le centre-ville ; (*Med*) **to ~ congestion** décongestionner ; (*euph*) **to ~ o.s.** se soulager, faire ses besoins*
c (= *help*) secourir, venir en aide à
d (= *take over from*) relayer ; **Paul will ~ you at six** Paul vous relayera à six heures ; (*Mil*) **to ~ the guard** relever la garde
e (*Mil*) [+ *town, fort, garrison*] libérer

relievo [rɪ'liːvəʊ] N (*Art*) relief m

religion [rɪ'lɪdʒən] N (= *belief*) religion f ; (= *form of worship*) culte m ; (*on form etc*) confession f ; **the Christian ~** la religion chrétienne ; **this new ~ already has many adherents** ce nouveau culte a déjà de nombreux adeptes ; **wars of ~** guerres fpl de religion ; (*fig*) **to make a ~ of doing sth** se faire une obligation (absolue) de faire qch ; (*lit*) **it's against my ~ (to do that)** c'est contraire à ma religion (de faire cela) ; (*hum*) **it's against my ~ to clean windows*** je ne fais jamais les vitres, c'est contraire à ma religion (*hum*) ; **to enter ~** entrer en religion ; **her name in ~** son nom de religion ; (*hum*) **to get ~*** découvrir Dieu

religiosity [rɪˌlɪdʒɪ'ɒsɪtɪ] N (*pej*) religiosité f

religious [rɪ'lɪdʒəs] **1** ADJ [*beliefs, practice, order, service, music, book, leader*] religieux ; [*freedom*] religieux, de religion ; [*person*] religieux, croyant ; [*war*] de religion ; **a ~ maniac** or **lunatic*** un fanatique religieux **2** N (*pl inv*) religieux m, -ieuse f **3** COMP ► **religious education** N (*Scol*) éducation f religieuse ► **religious instruction** N (*Scol*) instruction f religieuse

religiously [rɪ'lɪdʒəslɪ] ADV **a** (*Rel*) **a ~ diverse country** un pays qui présente une grande diversité religieuse ; **~ minded people** gens mpl très religieux ; **~ motivated** motivé par la religion **b** (= *conscientiously*) scrupuleusement, religieusement

religiousness [rɪ'lɪdʒəsnɪs] N piété f, dévotion f

reline [ˌriː'laɪn] VT [+ *coat, jacket*] mettre une nouvelle doublure à, redoubler ; (*Aut*) **to ~ the brakes** changer les garnitures de freins

relinquish [rɪ'lɪŋkwɪʃ] VT **a** (= *give up*) [+ *hope, power*] abandonner ; [+ *plan, right*] renoncer à (**to sb** en faveur de qn) ; [+ *habit*] renoncer à ; [+ *post*] quitter, abandonner ; [+ *goods, property etc*] se dessaisir de, abandonner **b** (= *let go*) [+ *object*] lâcher ; **to ~ one's hold on sth** lâcher qch

relinquishment [rɪ'lɪŋkwɪʃmənt] N abandon m (**of sth** de qch)

reliquary ['relɪkwərɪ] N reliquaire m

relish ['relɪʃ] **1** N **a** (= *enjoyment*) goût m (**for** pour) ; **to do sth with (great) ~** ◊ **to take ~ in doing sth** faire qch avec délectation ; **he ate with ~** il mangeait de bon appétit ; **he rubbed his hands with ~ at the prospect of …** il se frotta les mains de plaisir à la perspective de … **b** (*Culin*) (= *flavour*) goût m, saveur f ; (= *pickle: for hamburger etc*) achards mpl ; (= *seaso-*

ning) condiment *m*, assaisonnement *m*; (= *trace: of spices etc*) soupçon *m*; (*fig* = *charm*) attrait *m*, charme *m*; (*fig*) **it had lost all ~** cela avait perdu tout attrait **2** VT [+ *food, wine*] savourer; **to ~ doing sth** se délecter à faire qch, trouver du plaisir à faire qch; **I don't ~ the idea** *or* **prospect** *or* **thought of getting up at five** l'idée de me lever à cinq heures ne me sourit guère *or* ne me dit rien

relive [ˌriːˈlɪv] VT revivre

reload [ˌriːˈləʊd] VT, VI recharger

relocate [ˌriːləʊˈkeɪt] **1** VT (*gen*) installer ailleurs; [+ *company*] réimplanter; [+ *worker*] (*in a new place*) transférer, muter; (*in a new job*) reconvertir **2** VI (= *move house*) déménager, s'installer ailleurs; [*company*] se réimplanter; [*worker*] (*in a new place*) changer de lieu de travail; (*in a new job*) se reconvertir; **to ~ to ...** déménager à ..., s'installer à ...

relocation [ˌriːləʊˈkeɪʃən] **1** N (*gen*) déménagement *m*; [*of company*] réimplantation *f*, déménagement *m*; [*of worker*] (*in a new place*) transfert *m*, mutation *f*; (*in a new job*) reconversion *f*; [*of household*] déménagement *m* **2** COMP ► **relocation allowance** N prime *f* de relogement ► **relocation expenses** NPL (*paid to employee*) frais *mpl* de déménagement

reluctance [rɪˈlʌktəns] N **a** répugnance *f* (**to do** à faire); **to do sth with ~** faire qch à regret *or* à contrecœur; **to make a show of ~** se faire prier, se faire tirer l'oreille **b** (*Elec*) réluctance *f*

reluctant [rɪˈlʌktənt] ADJ [*person, animal*] réticent (**to do sth** à faire qch); [*acceptance*] peu enthousiaste; [*praise, consent, permission, response*] peu enthousiaste, donné à contrecœur; **the ~ soldier** le soldat malgré lui; **to give one's ~ approval to sth** donner son accord à qch avec réticence *or* à contrecœur; **to take the ~ decision to do sth** prendre avec réticence *or* à contrecœur la décision de faire qch

reluctantly [rɪˈlʌktəntlɪ] ADV à contrecœur

rely [rɪˈlaɪ] VI **to ~ (up)on sb/sth** compter sur qn/qch; **she relied on the trains being on time** elle comptait *or* tablait sur le fait que les trains seraient à l'heure; **I ~ on him for my income** je dépends de lui pour mes revenus; **you can ~ upon it** vous pouvez y compter; **you can ~ on me not to say anything about it** vous pouvez compter sur moi pour ne pas en parler, comptez sur ma discrétion; **she is not to be relied upon** on ne peut pas compter sur elle; **he relies increasingly on his assistants** il se repose de plus en plus sur ses assistants; **you mustn't ~ on other people for everything** il faut se prendre en charge; (*Jur*) **to ~ on sth** invoquer qch

REM [rem] N (ABBR = **rapid eye movement**) → **rapid**

remain [rɪˈmeɪn] VI **a** (= *be left*) rester; **much ~s to be done** il reste beaucoup à faire; **nothing ~s to be said** il ne reste plus rien à dire; **nothing ~s but to accept** il ne reste plus qu'à accepter; **it ~s to be seen whether ...** reste à savoir si ...; **that ~s to be seen** c'est ce que nous verrons, c'est ce qu'il reste à voir; **the fact ~s that he is wrong** il n'en est pas moins vrai *or* toujours vrai qu'il a tort; **take 2 from 4, 2 ~** 4 moins 2, il reste 2 **b** (= *stay*) rester, demeurer; **to ~ faithful** demeurer *or* rester fidèle; **~ seated** restez assis; **to ~ out/in** *etc* rester (en) dehors/(en) dedans *etc*; **to ~ up** rester levé; **let the matter ~ as it is** laissez l'affaire comme cela; **it ~s the same** ça ne change pas; **to ~ silent** garder le silence; **it ~s unsolved** ce n'est toujours pas résolu; **if the weather ~s fine** si le temps se maintient (au beau); (*in letters*) **I ~, Yours faithfully ...** je vous prie d'agréer *or* veuillez agréer l'expression de mes sentiments distingués ...

► **remain behind** VI rester

remainder [rɪˈmeɪndə^r] **1** N **a** (= *sth left over*) reste *m*; (= *remaining people*) autres *mfpl*; (*Math*) reste *m*; (*Jur*) usufruit *m* avec réversibilité; **for the ~ of the week** pendant le reste *or* le restant de la semaine **b** **~s** (*Comm*) (= *books etc*) invendus *mpl* soldés, soldes *mpl* d'éditeur; (= *clothes, articles*) fin(s) *f(pl)* de série **2** VT [+ *books etc*] solder

remaining [rɪˈmeɪnɪŋ] ADJ [*people, objects*] qui reste (*or* restait), restant; **use up the ~ olives in the sauce** utiliser le reste des olives dans la sauce; **she's one of his few ~ friends** elle fait partie des rares amis qui lui restent

remains [rɪˈmeɪnz] NPL [*of meal*] restes *mpl*; [*of fortune, army*] débris *mpl*; [*of building*] vestiges *mpl*, ruines *fpl*; **literary ~** œuvres *fpl* posthumes; **his (mortal) ~** ses restes *mpl*, sa dépouille mortelle; **human ~** restes *mpl* humains

remake [ˌriːˈmeɪk] **1** VT refaire; (*Cine*) [+ *film*] faire un remake de **2** [ˈriːmeɪk] N (*Cine*) remake *m*

remand [rɪˈmɑːnd] **1** VT (*gen, Jur*) [+ *case, accused person*] déférer, renvoyer (**to** à); (*Jur*) **to ~ sb to a higher court** renvoyer qn à une instance supérieure; **to ~ sb in custody** mettre qn en détention provisoire; **to ~ sb on bail** mettre qn en liberté sous caution; **case ~ed** la cause *f* renvoyée à huitaine → **further** **2** N renvoi *m* (à une autre audience); **to be on ~** (= *in custody*) être en détention provisoire; (= *on bail*) être en liberté provisoire **3** COMP ► **remand centre** N (*Brit*) centre *m* de détention provisoire ► **remand home†** N (*Brit*) ≈ maison *f* d'arrêt ► **remand prisoner** N personne *f* en détention provisoire ► **remand wing** N quartier *m* de détention provisoire

remark [rɪˈmɑːk] **1** N **a** (= *comment*) remarque *f*; **to make** *or* **pass the ~ that ...** faire remarquer *or* observer que ...; **I have a few ~s to make on that subject** j'ai quelques remarques à vous communiquer à ce sujet; **to make** *or* **pass unkind ~s about sb/sth** faire des remarques désagréables sur qn/qch; **~s were made about your absence** votre absence a fait l'objet de remarques **b** (*NonC*) **worthy of ~** digne d'attention, remarquable **2** VT **a** (= *say*) (faire) remarquer, (faire) observer; **"it's raining" he ~ed** « il pleut » observa-t-il **b** (= *notice*) remarquer, observer **3** VI (= *make remarks or observations*) (**on** sur); **he ~ed on it to me** il m'en a fait l'observation *or* la remarque

remarkable [rɪˈmɑːkəbl] ADJ remarquable (**for sth** par qch); **it is ~ that ...** il est remarquable que ... (+ *subj*); **there's nothing ~ about that** cela n'a rien de remarquable; **it is ~ how quickly children grow up** la vitesse à laquelle les enfants grandissent est incroyable, c'est incroyable ce que les enfants grandissent vite

remarkably [rɪˈmɑːkəblɪ] ADV remarquablement; **this has been a ~ difficult year for him** cette année a été extrêmement difficile pour lui; **~, the factory had escaped the bombing** fait étonnant *or* par miracle, l'usine avait échappé aux bombardements

remarriage [ˌriːˈmærɪdʒ] N remariage *m*

remarry [ˌriːˈmærɪ] **1** VI se remarier **2** VT remarier

remaster [ˌriːˈmɑːstə^r] VT [+ *recording*] remixer → **digitally**

rematch [ˈriːˌmætʃ] **1** N (*gen*) match *m* retour; (*Boxing*) deuxième combat *m* **2** [ˌriːˈmætʃ] VT opposer à nouveau

remediable [rɪˈmiːdɪəbl] ADJ remédiable

remedial [rɪˈmiːdɪəl] ADJ **a** (*Med*) [*treatment*] curatif; **~ exercises** gymnastique *f* corrective **b** (*Educ*) [*class*] de rattrapage; **~ education** soutien *m* scolaire; **~ teaching** cours *mpl* de rattrapage *or* de soutien; **~ help** soutien *m*; **~ (course in) English** cours *mpl* de rattrapage *or* de soutien en anglais **c** (= *corrective*) [*work*] de réparation; **~ action** *or* **measures** mesures *fpl* de redressement

remedy [ˈremədɪ] **1** N (*Med, fig*) remède *m* (**for** contre *or* pour); (*Jur*) recours *m*; **past** *or* **beyond ~** sans remède; **we must provide a ~ for injustice** nous devons trouver un remède à l'injustice; **the ~ for boredom is work** le travail est le remède de *or* contre l'ennui; **the ~ for despair** le remède contre le désespoir **2** VT (*Med*) remédier à; (*fig*) remédier à, porter remède à; **the situation cannot be remedied** la situation est sans remède

remember [rɪˈmembə^r] **1** VT **a** (= *recall*) [+ *person, date, occasion*] se souvenir de, se rappeler; **to ~ that ...** se rappeler que ...; **I ~ doing it** je me rappelle l'avoir fait, je me souviens de l'avoir fait; **I ~ed to do it** j'ai pensé à le faire, je n'ai pas oublié de le faire; **I ~ when an egg cost one penny** je me souviens de l'époque où un œuf coûtait un penny; **I cannot ~ your name** je ne me rappelle plus votre nom, je ne me souviens pas de votre nom; **don't you ~ me?** (*face to face*) vous ne me reconnaissez pas?; (*phone*) vous ne vous souvenez pas de moi?; **I ~ your face** je me souviens de votre visage, je vous reconnais; **I don't ~ a thing about it** je n'en ai pas le moindre souvenir, je ne me souviens de rien; **I can never ~ phone numbers** je n'ai aucune mémoire pour les *or* je ne me souviens jamais des numéros de téléphone; **let us ~ that ...** n'oublions pas que ...; **a night/occasion to ~** une soirée/un moment mémorable *or* inoubliable; **here's something to ~ him by** voici un souvenir de lui; **he is ~ed as a fine violinist** il a laissé le souvenir d'un violoniste talentueux; **she will be ~ed by millions (for her honesty/for supporting this cause)** des millions de gens se souviendront d'elle (pour son honnêteté/pour son soutien à cette cause); **I can't ~ the word at the moment** le mot m'échappe pour le moment; **we can't always ~ everything** on ne peut pas toujours songer à tout; **~ where you are!** ressaisissez-vous!; **to ~ o.s.** se reprendre; **to ~ sb in one's prayers** ne pas oublier qn dans ses prières; **that's worth ~ing** c'est bon à savoir **b** (= *commemorate*) [+ *the fallen, a battle*] commémorer **c** (= *give good wishes to*) rappeler (**to** au bon souvenir de); **~ me to your mother** rappelez-moi au bon souvenir de votre mère; **he asked to be ~ed to you** il vous envoie son meilleur souvenir **d** (= *give money or a present to*) ne pas oublier; **to ~ sb in one's will** ne pas oublier qn dans son testament

2 VI se souvenir; **I can't ~** je ne me souviens pas, je ne sais plus; **as far as I ~** autant que je m'en souvienne; **not as far as I ~** pas à ma connaissance, pas que je m'en souvienne; **if I ~ right(ly)** si j'ai bonne mémoire, si je m'en *or* me souviens bien; **the last time we had a party, if you ~, it took us days to clear up** la dernière fois que nous avons organisé une soirée, je te rappelle qu'il nous a fallu des jours pour tout ranger; **he was, you ~, a great man** il était, comme vous le savez, un grand homme

remembered [rɪˈmembəd] ADJ (*liter*) [*happiness etc*] inscrit dans la mémoire

remembrance [rɪˈmembrəns] N (= *memory, thing remembered*) souvenir *m*, mémoire *f*; (= *act of remembering, keepsake*) souvenir *m*; (*Brit*) **Remembrance Day** ≈ (le jour de) l'Armistice *m*, ≈ le 11 Novembre → POPPY DAY; **in ~ of** en souvenir de; **to the best of my ~** pour autant que je m'en souvienne; **within the ~ of man** de mémoire d'homme; **to have no ~ of sth** ne pas se souvenir de qch, n'avoir aucun souvenir de qch

▼ **remind** [rɪ'maɪnd] VT rappeler (**sb of sth** qch à qn, **sb that** à qn que); **you are ~ed that ...** nous vous rappelons que ...; **to ~ sb to do** faire penser à qn à faire; **must I ~ you (again)?** faut-il que je (vous) le redise or le rappelle (*subj*) encore une fois?; **she ~ed him of his mother** elle lui rappelait sa mère; **that ~s me!** à propos!, j'y pense!

reminder [rɪ'maɪndəʳ] [1] N (= *note, knot etc*) mémento *m*, pense-bête *m*; **as a ~ that ...** pour (vous or lui *etc*) rappeler que ...; **his presence was a ~ of ...** sa présence rappelait ...; **a gentle ~** un rappel discret; **give him a gentle ~** rappelez-le-lui discrètement; (*Comm*) **(letter of) ~** lettre *f* de rappel [2] COMP ► **reminder call** N (*Telec*) mémo appel *m*

reminisce [,remɪ'nɪs] VI évoquer or raconter ses souvenirs; **to ~ about sth** évoquer qch

reminiscence [,remɪ'nɪsəns] N réminiscence *f*

reminiscent [,remɪ'nɪsənt] ADJ [a] (= *similar*) **to be ~ of sth** rappeler qch, faire penser à qch [b] (= *nostalgic*) [*person, mood, smile*] nostalgique

reminiscently [,remɪ'nɪsəntlɪ] ADV **he smiled ~** il sourit à ce souvenir; **he talked ~ of the war** il évoquait des souvenirs de la guerre

remiss [rɪ'mɪs] ADJ (*frm*) négligent; **he has been ~ in not finishing his work** il s'est rendu coupable de négligence en ne terminant pas son travail; **that was very ~ of you** vous vous êtes montré très négligent; **it would be ~ of me to do that** ce serait négligent de ma part que de faire cela

remission [rɪ'mɪʃən] N (*gen, Med, Rel*) rémission *f*; (*Jur*) remise *f*; **the ~ of sins** la rémission des péchés; (*Brit Jur*) **he earned three years' ~ (for good conduct)** on lui a accordé trois ans de remise de peine (pour bonne conduite); (*Jur*) **~ from a debt** remise *f* d'une dette; **there can be no ~ of registration fees** il ne peut y avoir de dispense or d'exemption des droits d'inscription; (*Med*) **to be in ~** [*disease, person*] être en rémission; **to go into ~** [*disease, person*] entrer en rémission

remissness [rɪ'mɪsnɪs] N négligence *f*, manque *m* de zèle

▼ **remit**[1] [rɪ'mɪt] [1] VT [a] (*Rel*) [+ *sins*] pardonner, remettre; (*Jur etc*) [+ *fee, debt, penalty*] remettre; **to have part of one's sentence ~ted** bénéficier d'une remise de peine; **to ~ sb's sentence** faire bénéficier qn d'une remise de peine; **the prisoner's sentence was ~ted** on a remis la peine du détenu, le détenu a reçu une remise de peine [b] (*frm = send*) [+ *money*] envoyer, verser [c] (= *lessen*) relâcher, se relâcher de [d] (= *postpone*) différer [e] (*Jur*) renvoyer (*à une instance inférieure*) [2] VI (= *become less*) diminuer; [*storm*] se calmer; [*effort*] se relâcher

remit[2] ['ri:mɪt] N (*Brit*) attributions *fpl*

remittal [rɪ'mɪtl] N (*Jur*) renvoi *m* (à une instance inférieure)

remittance [rɪ'mɪtəns] [1] N [a] (*of money*) (*gen*) versement *m*; (*Banking, Econ, Fin*) remise *f* de fonds; (*Comm etc = payment*) paiement *m*, règlement *m*; **enclose your ~** joignez votre règlement [b] (*of documents*) remise *f* [2] COMP ► **remittance advice** N (*Comm*) avis *m* de versement ► **remittance man** N (*pl* **remittance men**) (*US*) résident étranger entretenu (*par ses parents etc*)

remittee [remɪ'ti:] N destinataire *mf* (*d'un envoi de fonds*)

remittent [rɪ'mɪtənt] ADJ (*Med*) rémittent; (*fig*) intermittent

remitter [rɪ'mɪtəʳ] N [a] remetteur *m*, -euse *f*; [*of money*] envoyeur *m*, -euse *f*; (*Comm*) remettant *m* [b] (*Jur*) renvoi *m* à une instance inférieure

remix ['ri:mɪks] [1] N (*Mus*) remix *m* [2] [,ri:-'mɪks] VT (*Mus*) remixer

remnant ['remnənt] [1] N (= *anything remaining*) reste *m*, restant *m*; (= *piece*) débris *m*, bout *m*; [*of custom, splendour*] vestige *m*; [*of food, fortune*] bribe *f*, débris *m*; [*of cloth*] coupon *m*; (*Comm*) **~s** soldes *mpl* (de fins de série); **the ~ of the army** ce qui restait (or reste) de l'armée [2] COMP ► **remnant day** N (*Comm*) jour *m* de soldes ► **remnant sale** N solde *m* (de coupons or d'invendus or de fins de série)

remodel [,ri:'mɒdl] VT (*also Art, Tech*) remodeler; (*fig*) [+ *society*] réorganiser; [+ *constitution*] remanier

remold [,ri:'məʊld] (*US*) = **remould**

remonstrance [rɪ'mɒnstrəns] N [a] (*NonC*) remontrance *f* [b] (= *protest*) protestation *f*; (= *reproof*) reproche *m*

remonstrant [rɪ'mɒnstrənt] [1] ADJ [*tone*] de remontrance, de protestation [2] N protestataire *mf*

remonstrate ['remənstreɪt] [1] VI protester (**against** contre); **to ~ with sb about sth** faire des remontrances à qn au sujet de qch [2] VT faire observer or remarquer (*avec l'idée de reproche ou de contradiction*) (**that** que)

remorse [rɪ'mɔ:s] N (*NonC*) remords *m* (**at** de, **for** pour); **a feeling of ~** un remords; **without ~** sans pitié

remorseful [rɪ'mɔ:sfʊl] ADJ plein de remords; **he was not ~ (about or for)** il n'avait aucun remords (pour)

remorsefully [rɪ'mɔ:sfəlɪ] ADV avec remords; **... he said ~** ... dit-il, plein de remords

remorsefulness [rɪ'mɔ:sfʊlnɪs] N (*NonC*) remords *m*

remorseless [rɪ'mɔ:slɪs] ADJ [a] (= *merciless*) [*person*] sans pitié, impitoyable [b] (= *relentless*) [*pressure*] implacable, impitoyable (**in sth** dans qch); [*ambition*] dévorant

remorselessly [rɪ'mɔ:slɪslɪ] ADV (= *mercilessly*) [*tease, pursue*] sans pitié, impitoyablement; (= *relentlessly*) implacablement, impitoyablement

remorselessness [rɪ'mɔ:slɪsnɪs] N absence *f* or manque *m* de pitié or de remords

remote [rɪ'məʊt] [1] ADJ [a] [*place*] (= *distant*) éloigné, lointain; (= *isolated*) isolé; [*relative, ancestor, descendant*] éloigné, lointain (**before n**); **in ~ country districts** dans les régions rurales isolées; **in a ~ spot** dans un lieu isolé; **in the ~ past/future** dans un passé/avenir lointain; **~ antiquity** la plus haute antiquité; **a village ~ from the world** un village à l'écart du monde; **a house ~ from a main road** une maison située loin or à l'écart des grands axes [b] (= *distanced*) éloigné (**from sth** de qch); **what he said was rather ~ from the subject in hand** ce qu'il a dit n'avait pas beaucoup de rapport avec le sujet; **subjects that seem ~ from our daily lives** des questions qui paraissent sans rapport avec notre vie quotidienne [c] (= *slight*) [*hope*] mince (*before n*); [*resemblance, chance, possibility*] vague; [*prospect*] lointain; [*risk*] ténu; **the odds of that happening are ~** il y a très peu de chances que cela se produise; **I haven't the ~st idea** je n'en ai pas la moindre idée [d] (= *aloof*) [*person*] distant [e] (= *remote-controlled*) à distance; **~ handset** télécommande *f* [2] N (*also* **~ control**) télécommande *f* [3] COMP ► **remote access** N (*Comput*) accès *m* à distance, téléconsultation *f* ► **remote control** N télécommande *f* ► **remote-controlled** ADJ télécommandé ► **remote job entry** N (*Comput*) télésoumission *f* de travaux ► **remote sensing** N télédétection *f*

remotely [rɪ'məʊtlɪ] ADV [a] (= *vaguely*) **it isn't ~ possible that ...** il est absolument impossible que ... (+ *subj*); **he failed to say anything ~ interesting** il n'a rien dit d'un tant soit peu intéressant; **I'm not ~ interested in art** l'art ne m'intéresse pas le moins du monde; **it doesn't ~ resemble ...** cela ne ressemble en rien à ...; **avoid saying anything ~ likely to upset him** évitez de dire quoi que ce soit qui puisse l'agacer; **I've never seen anything ~ like it** jamais de ma vie je n'ai vu une chose pareille; **the only person present even ~ connected with show business** la seule personne présente qui ait un rapport quelconque avec le monde du spectacle [b] (= *distantly*) **to be ~ situated** être situé loin de tout, être isolé; **we are ~ related** nous sommes (des) parents éloignés [c] (= *aloofly*) [*say*] d'un ton distant; [*behave*] d'un air distant [d] (= *from a distance*) [*control, detonate*] à distance

remoteness [rɪ'məʊtnɪs] N [a] (*in space*) éloignement *m*, isolement *m*; (*in time*) éloignement *m* [b] (= *aloofness*) attitude *f* distante or réservée (**from sb** envers qn)

remould, remold (*US*) [,ri:'məʊld] [1] VT (*Tech*) remouler; [+ *tyre*] rechaper; (*fig*) [+ *sb's character*] corriger [2] ['ri:məʊld] N (= *tyre*) pneu *m* rechapé

remount [,ri:'maʊnt] [1] VT [a] [+ *horse*] remonter sur; [+ *bicycle*] enfourcher de nouveau; [+ *ladder*] grimper de nouveau sur [b] [+ *picture*] rentoiler; [+ *photo*] faire un nouveau montage de [2] VI remonter à cheval (or à bicyclette)

removable [rɪ'mu:vəbl] ADJ amovible, détachable; **a sofa/cushion with a ~ cover** un canapé/coussin déhoussable

removal [rɪ'mu:vəl] [1] N [a] (= *taking away*) enlèvement *m*; (*esp Brit*) [*of furniture, household*] déménagement *m*; [*of abuse, evil*] suppression *f*; [*of pain*] soulagement *m*; (*from a job*) (= *demotion*) déplacement *m*; (= *sacking*) renvoi *m*, révocation *f*; (*Med*) ablation *f*; **stain ~** détachage *m* [b] (†: *from house*) déménagement *m*; **after our ~** après notre déménagement; **our ~ to this house** notre emménagement *m* dans cette maison; **our ~ from London** notre déménagement de Londres [2] COMP ► **removal expenses** NPL (*Brit*) frais *mpl* de déménagement ► **removal man** N (*pl* **removal men**) déménageur *m* ► **removal van** N (*Brit*) voiture *f* or camion *m* or fourgon *m* de déménagement

remove [rɪ'mu:v] [1] VT [+ *object*] enlever (**from** de); [+ *clothes*] enlever, ôter; [+ *furniture, lid*] enlever; [+ *stain, graffiti*] enlever, faire partir; [+ *paragraph, word, item on list, threat, tax*] supprimer; [+ *objection*] réfuter; [+ *difficulty, problem*] résoudre; (*lit, fig*) [+ *obstacle*] écarter; [+ *doubt*] chasser; [+ *suspicion, fear*] dissiper; [+ *employee*] destituer, révoquer; [+ *official*] déplacer; (*Med*) [+ *lung, kidney*] enlever; [+ *tumour*] extirper, enlever; [+ *splint, bandage*] enlever; **he was ~d to the cells** on l'a emmené en cellule; **to ~ sb to hospital** hospitaliser qn; **to ~ a child from school** retirer un enfant de l'école; (*Jur: in court*) **~ the prisoner!** faites sortir l'accusé!; **he ~d himself to another room** il s'est retiré dans une autre pièce; **to ~ sb's name** rayer qn, radier qn; **to ~ one's make-up** se démaquiller; **make-up removing cream** lait *m* démaquillant; **to ~ unwanted hair from one's legs** s'épiler les jambes; (*fig*) **to be far ~d from sth** être loin de qch; **cousin once/twice ~d** cousin(e) *m(f)* au deuxième/troisième degré [2] VI† déménager, changer de domicile; **to ~ to London** aller habiter à Londres, aller s'installer à Londres [3] N [a] (*in relationship*) degré *m* de parenté [b] (*frm: fig*) **to be only a few ~s from ...** être tout proche de ...; **this is but one ~ from disaster** nous frisons (or ils frisent *etc*) la catastrophe; **it's a far ~ from ...** c'est loin d'être ...

remover [rɪ'mu:vəʳ] N [a] (= *removal man*) déménageur *m* [b] (= *substance*) (for varnish) dissolvant m; (for stains) détachant m; **paint ~** décapant m (pour peintures) → **cuticle**, **hair**, **make-up**

remunerate [rɪ'mjuːnəreɪt] VT rémunérer

remuneration [rɪ,mjuːnə'reɪʃən] N rémunération f (**for** de)

remunerative [rɪ'mjuːnərətɪv] ADJ (frm) [scheme, investment] rémunérateur (-trice f), lucratif; [job, employment] rémunéré

Renaissance [rɪ'neɪsãːns] (Art, Hist) **1** N **the ~** la Renaissance **2** COMP [art, scholar] de la Renaissance; [style, palace] Renaissance inv ► **Renaissance man** N (pl **Renaissance men**) homme m aux talents multiples

renaissance [rɪ'neɪsãːns] N renaissance f

renal ['riːnl] **1** ADJ rénal **2** COMP ► **renal failure** N défaillance f or insuffisance f rénale

rename [,riː'neɪm] VT [+ person, street, town] rebaptiser (fig); (Comput) [+ file] renommer

renascence [rɪ'næsns] N = **renaissance**

renascent [rɪ'næsnt] ADJ renaissant

rend [rend] (pret, ptp **rent**) VT (liter) [+ cloth] déchirer; [+ armour] fendre; (fig) déchirer, fendre; (lit, fig) **to ~ sth from ...** arracher qch à or de ...; **a country rent by civil war** un pays déchiré par la guerre civile; **a cry rent the silence** un cri déchira le silence; **to ~ sb's heart** fendre le cœur à qn

render ['rendə'] VT **a** (frm = give) [+ service, homage, judgement] rendre; [+ help] donner; [+ explanation] donner, fournir; **~ unto Caesar the things which are Caesar's** il faut rendre à César ce qui est à César; **to ~ thanks to sb** remercier qn; **to ~ thanks to God** rendre grâce à Dieu; **to ~ assistance (to sb)** prêter assistance or secours (à qn); **to ~ an account of sth** rendre compte de qch; **for services ~ed** pour services rendus **b** (Comm) [+ account] remettre, présenter **c** [+ music] interpréter; [+ text] rendre, traduire (**into** en) **d** (= make) rendre; **his accident ~ed him helpless** son accident l'a rendu complètement infirme; **the blow ~ed him unconscious** or **insensible** le coup lui a fait perdre connaissance **e** (Culin) [+ fat] faire fondre **f** (Constr) enduire (**with** de)

► **render down** VT SEP [+ fat] faire fondre

► **render up** VT SEP (liter) [+ fortress] rendre; [+ prisoner, treasure] livrer

rendering ['rendərɪŋ] N **a** [of music, poem] interprétation f; [of text] traduction f (**into** en) **b** (Constr) enduit m

rendez-vous ['rɒndɪvuː] **1** N (pl **rendez-vous** ['rɒndɪvuːz]) rendez-vous m **2** VI (= meet) se retrouver; (= assemble) se réunir; **to ~ with sb** rejoindre qn; (Mil etc) **they ~ed with the patrol at dawn** ils ont rejoint la patrouille à l'aube

rendition [ren'dɪʃən] N = **rendering**

reneague [rɪ'niːg] VI = **renege**

renegade ['renɪɡeɪd] **1** N renégat(e) m(f) **2** ADJ [forces, faction, person] rebelle

renege [rɪ'neɪɡ] VI manquer à sa parole; (Cards) faire une renonce; **to ~ on a promise** manquer à sa promesse

▼ **renegotiate** [,riːnɪ'ɡəʊʃɪeɪt] VT renégocier

renegue [rɪ'neɪɡ] VI = **renege**

renew [rɪ'njuː] VT [+ appointment, attack, contract, passport, promise, one's strength] renouveler; [+ lease] renouveler, reconduire; [+ supplies] remplacer, renouveler; **to ~ negotiations/discussions** reprendre des négociations/discussions; **to ~ one's subscription** renouveler son abonnement, se réabonner; **to ~ one's acquaintance with sb** renouer connaissance avec qn → **renewed**

renewable [rɪ'njuːəbl] **1** ADJ [contract, resources, energy] renouvelable **2** **renewables** NPL énergies fpl renouvelables

renewal [rɪ'njuːəl] N **a** (= resumption) [of hostilities] reprise f; [of society] renouveau m;

[of attack] renouvellement m; [of interest, strength] regain m **b** (= improvement) [of city] rénovation f; [of district, area] réhabilitation f → **urban** **c** (= revalidating) [of licence, visa, passport, policy] renouvellement m; [of contract, lease] renouvellement m, reconduction f; **~ of subscription** réabonnement m **d** (Rel) renouveau m

renewed [rɪ'njuːd] ADJ **~ interest/hope/enthusiasm** un regain d'intérêt/d'espoir/d'enthousiasme; **with ~ vigour** avec une vitalité accrue; **~ fighting** une recrudescence des combats; **he has come under ~ pressure to resign** on fait de nouveau pression sur lui pour qu'il démissionne; **to make ~ efforts to do sth** renouveler ses efforts pour faire qch; **to feel a ~ sense of well-being** se sentir revivre

rennet ['renɪt] N (for junket) présure f

renounce [rɪ'naʊns] **1** VT [+ liberty, opinions, ideas, title] renoncer à; [+ religion] abjurer; [+ right] renoncer à, abandonner; [+ treaty] dénoncer; [+ friend] renier; [+ cause, party] renier, désavouer; [+ principles] répudier **2** VI (Bridge) défausser

renouncement [rɪ'naʊnsmənt] N = **renunciation**

renovate ['renəveɪt] VT [+ clothes, house] remettre à neuf, rénover; [+ building, painting, statue] restaurer

renovation [,renə'veɪʃən] N **a** (NonC = doing up) [of house, flat] rénovation f, remise f à neuf; (= restoration) [of historic building, painting, statue] restauration f; **to be in need of ~** être en mauvais état **b** (to building) **~s** travaux mpl

renown [rɪ'naʊn] N renommée f, renom m; **a wine of ~** un vin renommé; **a scholar of great or high ~** un érudit renommé or de renom

renowned [rɪ'naʊnd] ADJ [artist, scientist] renommé (**for sth** pour qch), célèbre (**for sth** pour qch); [expert, place] réputé (**for sth** pour qch), célèbre (**for sth** pour qch); **internationally ~ writers** des écrivains de renommée internationale; **garlic is ~ as an antiseptic** l'ail est réputé pour ses vertus antiseptiques

rent¹ [rent] **1** N [of house, room] loyer m; [of farm] fermage m; [of television etc] location f; (US) **for ~** à louer; **quarter's ~** terme m; **(one week) late** or **behind with one's ~** en retard (d'une semaine) sur son loyer; **to pay a high/low ~ for sth** payer un gros/petit loyer pour qch

2 VT **a** (= take for rent) louer; **we don't own it, we only ~ it** nous ne sommes pas propriétaires, mais locataires seulement; **~ed accommodation/flat** etc logement m/appartement m etc en location; **"~-a-bike"** « location de vélos » **b** (also **~ out**) louer, donner en location

3 COMP ► **rent-a-car** N (= firm) société f de location de voitures ► **rent-a-crowd*** ► **rent-a-mob** ► **rent allowance** N (Brit) indemnité f or allocation f (de) logement ► **rent-a-mob*** N (Brit) (gen) agitateurs mpl professionnels; (= supporters: at meeting etc) claque f ► **rent book** N (for accommodation) carnet m de quittances de loyer ► **rent boy*** N jeune prostitué m ► **rent collector** N personne f chargée d'encaisser les loyers ► **rent control** N encadrement m des loyers ► **rent-controlled** ADJ à loyer plafonné ► **rent-free** ADJ exempt de loyer, gratuit ♦ ADV sans payer de loyer ► **rent rebate** N réduction f de loyer ► **rent review** N (Brit Admin) réajustement m des loyers ► **rent strike** N grève f des loyers; **to go on ~ strike** ◊ **to stage a ~ strike** faire la grève des loyers

rent² [rent] **1** VB pt, ptp of **rend** **2** N (= tear) (in cloth) déchirure f, accroc m; (in rock) fissure f; (in clouds) déchirure f, trouée f; (fig: in party etc) rupture f, scission f

rental ['rentl] **1** N (esp Brit) **a** (= amount paid) [of house, land] (montant m du) loyer m; (esp for holiday accommodation) prix m de location; [of television etc] (prix m de) location f; [of telephone] abonnement m; (= income from rents) revenu m en loyers or fermages **b** (= activity) location f; **car/bike ~** location f de voitures/vélos **2** COMP ► **rental car** N voiture f de location ► **rental library** N (US) bibliothèque f de prêt (payante)

renumber [,riː'nʌmbə'] VT numéroter de nouveau, renuméroter

renunciation [rɪ,nʌnsɪ'eɪʃən] N (frm) [of violence, religion, citizenship, title, right, claim] renonciation f (**of sth** à qch); [of wife, husband, friend] reniement m (**of sb** de qn); [of cause, party] reniement m (**of sth** de qch), désaveu m (**of sth** de qch); [of treaty] dénonciation f (**of sth** de qch); [of principles] (also Jur) répudiation f (**of sth** de qch)

reoccupy [,riː'ɒkjʊpaɪ] VT réoccuper

reopen [,riː'əʊpən] **1** VT [+ box, door] rouvrir; [+ fight, battle, hostilities] reprendre; [+ debate, discussion] rouvrir; (Jur) **to ~ a case** rouvrir une affaire **2** VI [school] reprendre; [shop, theatre etc] rouvrir; [wound] se rouvrir

reopening [,riː'əʊpnɪŋ] N réouverture f

reorder [,riː'ɔːdə'] VT **a** [+ goods, supplies] commander de nouveau **b** (= reorganize) reclasser, réorganiser

reorganization ['riː,ɔːɡənaɪ'zeɪʃən] N réorganisation f

reorganize [,riː'ɔːɡənaɪz] **1** VT réorganiser **2** VI se réorganiser

rep¹* [rep] N ABBR = **repertory 1b**

rep² [rep] N (Tex) reps m

rep³* [rep] N ABBR = **representative a** (Comm) représentant(e) m(f) (de commerce) **b** (Admin, Pol = official) porte-parole m inv

Rep. (US Pol) **a** ABBR = **Representative b** ABBR = **Republican**

repackage [,riː'pækɪdʒ] VT [+ product] reconditionner; [+ parcel] remballer; (fig) [+ proposal, scheme] reformuler

repaid [rɪ'peɪd] VB pt, ptp of **repay**

repaint [,riː'peɪnt] VT repeindre

repair¹ [rɪ'peə'] **1** VT [+ tyre, shoes, chair] réparer; [+ clothes] réparer, raccommoder; [+ machine, watch] réparer, arranger; [+ roof, road] réparer, refaire; (Naut) [+ hull] radouber; (fig) [+ error, wrong] réparer, remédier à **2** N **a** (gen) réparation f; [of clothes] raccommodage m; [of shoes] ressemelage m; [of roof, road] réfection f; (Naut) [of hull] radoub m; **to be under ~** être en réparation; **to be beyond ~** être irréparable; **damaged** or **broken beyond ~** irréparable; **closed for ~s** fermé pour cause de travaux (NonC = condition) **to be in good/bad ~** être en bon/mauvais état; **to keep sth in (good) ~** entretenir qch **3** COMP ► **repair kit** N trousse f de réparation ► **repair man** N (pl **repair men**) réparateur m ► **repair outfit** N = **repair kit** ► **repair shop** N atelier m de réparations

repair² [rɪ'peə'] VI (liter = go) aller, se rendre

repairable [rɪ'peərəbl] ADJ réparable

repairer [rɪ'peərə'] N réparateur m, -trice f → **clock**, **shoe**

repaper [,riː'peɪpə'] VT retapisser, refaire les papiers peints de

reparable ['repərəbl] ADJ réparable

reparation [,repə'reɪʃən] N réparation f; (fig) **to make ~s for sth** réparer qch (une injure etc)

repartee [,repɑː'tiː] N (NonC) repartie or répartie f

repast [rɪ'pɑːst] N (liter) repas m, banquet m

repatriate (liter) [riː'pætrɪeɪt] **1** VT rapatrier **2** [riː'pætrɪət] N rapatrié(e) m(f)

repatriation [riː,pætrɪ'eɪʃən] N rapatriement m

repay [riː'peɪ] (*pret, ptp* **repaid**) VT [a] (= *pay back*) [+ *money*] rendre, rembourser; [+ *person*] rembourser; [+ *debt, obligation*] s'acquitter de; **if you lend me the money, I'll ~ you on Saturday** si tu me prêtes l'argent, je te le rendrai *or* je te rembourserai samedi; **to ~ sb's expenses** rembourser *or* indemniser qn de ses frais; (*fig*) **how can I ever ~ you?** comment pourrais-je jamais vous remercier?; (*fig*) **and this is how they ~ me!** c'est comme ça qu'ils me remercient!
[b] (= *give in return*) récompenser; **to ~ sb's kindness** payer de retour la gentillesse de qn, récompenser qn de sa gentillesse; (*iro*) **he repaid their kindness by stealing their camera** il les a remerciés de leur gentillesse en leur volant leur appareil photo, en guise de remerciement, il leur a volé leur appareil photo; **to be repaid for one's efforts** être récompensé de ses efforts; **it ~s obstinacy** la persévérance paie *or* est payante, cela vaut la peine de persévérer

repayable [riː'peɪəbl] ADJ remboursable; **the loan is ~ at any time** le créancier peut exiger le remboursement de cette dette à tout moment; **~ in ten monthly instalments** remboursable en dix mensualités; **~ over ten years** remboursable sur dix ans

repayment [riː'peɪmənt] [1] N [*of money*] remboursement *m*; [*of effort*] récompense *f*; **~s can be spread over three years** les remboursements peuvent s'échelonner sur trois ans [2] COMP ► **repayment mortgage** N (*Brit*) emprunt logement sans capital différé ► **repayment schedule** N (*Fin*) échéancier *m* de remboursement

repeal [riː'piːl] [1] VT [+ *law*] abroger, annuler; [+ *sentence*] annuler; [+ *decree*] révoquer [2] N abrogation *f*, annulation *f*, révocation *f*

▼**repeat** [riː'piːt] [1] VT (= *say again*) répéter; [+ *demand, promise*] réitérer; (*Mus*) reprendre; (= *recite*) [+ *poem etc*] réciter (par cœur); (= *do again*) [+ *action, attack*] répéter, renouveler; [+ *pattern, motif*] reproduire; (*Comm*) [+ *order*] renouveler; (*Comm*) **this offer will never be ~ed** (c'est une) offre unique *or* exceptionnelle; **you must not ~ what I tell you** il ne faut pas répéter ce que je vous dis; **to ~ o.s.** se répéter
[2] VI [a] **I ~, it is impossible** je le répète, c'est impossible [b] (*Math*) se reproduire périodiquement; **0.054 ~ing** 0,054 périodique [c] **radishes ~ on me*** les radis me donnent des renvois*
[3] N répétition *f*; (*Mus*) reprise *f*; (*esp Brit Rad, TV*) reprise *f*, rediffusion *f*
[4] ADJ [*business, customer*] **to get ~ business** réussir à fidéliser la clientèle; **we give reductions to ~ customers** nous accordons des réductions à nos fidèles clients
[5] COMP ► **repeat mark(s)** N(PL) (*Mus*) barre *f* de reprise, renvoi *m* ► **repeat offender** N (*Jur*) récidiviste *mf* ► **repeat order** N (*Brit Comm*) commande *f* renouvelée ► **repeat performance** N (*Theat*) deuxième représentation *f*; (*fig*) **he gave a ~ performance** il a fait exactement la même chose; (*pej*) il a fait la même comédie ► **repeat prescription** N (*Brit Med*) renouvellement d'une ordonnance ► **repeat sign** N (*Mus*) = **repeat mark(s)**

repeated [riː'piːtɪd] ADJ [*attacks, requests, warnings, criticism, efforts*] répété, renouvelé; **after ~ attempts** après plusieurs tentatives; **his plans have suffered ~ delays** ses projets ont subi une accumulation de retards

repeatedly [riː'piːtɪdlɪ] ADV à plusieurs reprises, sans cesse; **he had been ~ kicked in the head** il avait reçu plusieurs coups de pied à la tête

repeater [riː'piːtə'] [1] N [a] (= *gun/watch/ alarm clock*) fusil *m*/montre *f*/réveil *m* à répétition [b] (*Math*) fraction *f* périodique [c] (*US* *Scol*) redoublant(e) *m(f)*; (*US Jur*) récidiviste *mf*
[2] COMP ► **repeater loan** N (*Econ, Fin*) prêt-relais *m*

repeating [riː'piːtɪŋ] ADJ [*gun*] à répétition

repeg [riː'peg] VT (*Econ, Fin*) ne plus faire flotter, redonner une parité fixe à

repel [riː'pel] [1] VT [+ *enemy, sb's advances, magnetic pole*] repousser; (*fig = disgust*) dégoûter, inspirer de la répulsion à; (*fig*) **to be ~led by ...** être dégoûté par ..., éprouver de la répulsion pour ... [2] VI [*magnets, magnetic poles*] se repousser

repellant [riː'pelənt] N = **repellent 2**

repellent [riː'pelənt] [1] ADJ (*frm*) [*person, animal, character, sight, smell*] repoussant, répugnant; [*view, opinion*] abject; (*lit, fig*) **to be ~ to sb** dégoûter qn; **I find him ~** je le trouve répugnant, il me dégoûte → **water** [2] N → **insect**

repent [riː'pent] [1] VI se repentir (**of** de) [2] VT se repentir de, regretter

repentance [riː'pentəns] N repentir *m*

repentant [riː'pentənt] ADJ [*person, expression*] repentant; **to be ~** (= *repent*) se repentir

repercussion [ˌriːpə'kʌʃən] N [*of sounds*] répercussion *f*; [*of shock*] répercussion *f*, contrecoup *m*; (*fig*) **to have ~s on sth** se répercuter sur qch, avoir des répercussions sur qch; **the ~s of this defeat** le contrecoup *or* les répercussions de cet échec; **there will be no ~s** il n'y aura pas de répercussions; **the ~ on prices of the rise in costs** la répercussion sur les prix de la hausse du coût

repertoire ['repətwɑː'] N (*Theat, fig*) répertoire *m*

repertory ['repətərɪ] [1] N [a] (*Theat, fig*) = **repertoire** [b] (also ~ **theatre**) théâtre *m* de répertoire; **to act in ~** jouer à ◊ **to play ~** faire partie d'une troupe de répertoire; **he did three years in ~** il a joué pendant trois ans dans un théâtre de répertoire [2] COMP ► **repertory company** N compagnie *f* or troupe *f* (de théâtre) de répertoire

repetition [ˌrepɪ'tɪʃən] N [a] (= *recurrence*) répétition *f*; **I don't want a ~ of this!** que cela ne se reproduise pas!; **he didn't want a ~ of the scene with his mother** il ne voulait pas que cette scène avec sa mère se reproduise [b] (*NonC = duplication*) répétition *f*; **to learn by ~** apprendre en répétant

repetitious [ˌrepɪ'tɪʃəs] ADJ (*frm*) [*text, speech*] plein de répétitions *or* de redites; [*drumming, job*] répétitif

repetitive [riː'petɪtɪv] [1] ADJ [*writing*] plein de redites; [*work, movements, rhythms*] répétitif [2] COMP ► **repetitive strain injury** N (*Med*) troubles *mpl* musculosquelettiques (*dus à une activité répétée*), lésion *f* de surmenage

rephrase [ˌriː'freɪz] VT reformuler; **let me ~ that** ◊ **I'll ~ that** je vais m'exprimer autrement

repine [riː'paɪn] VI se plaindre, murmurer

replace [riː'pleɪs] VT [a] (= *put back*) remettre à sa place; (*Telec*) **to ~ the receiver** raccrocher [b] (= *take the place of*) remplacer, tenir la place de [c] (= *provide substitute for*) remplacer (**by, with** par)

replaceable [riː'pleɪsəbl] ADJ remplaçable

replacement [riː'pleɪsmənt] [1] N [a] (*NonC = putting back*) remise *f* en place, replacement *m* [b] (*NonC = substituting*) remplacement *m*, substitution *f* [c] (= *person*) remplaçant(e) *m(f)*; (= *product*) produit *m* de remplacement [2] COMP ► **replacement engine** N (*Aut*) moteur *m* de rechange; **to fit a ~ engine** faire l'échange standard du moteur ► **replacement part** N (*Tech*) pièce *f* de rechange

replant [ˌriː'plɑːnt] VT replanter

replay ['riːpleɪ] [1] N (*esp Brit: Sport*) **the ~ is on 15 October** le match sera rejoué le 15 octobre → **action, instant** [2] [ˌriː'pleɪ] VT [+ *match*] rejouer; [+ *cassette, video*] repasser

replenish [riː'plenɪʃ] VT remplir de nouveau (**with** de); **to ~ one's supplies of sth** se réapprovisionner en qch

replenishment [riː'plenɪʃmənt] N remplissage *m*; ~ **of supplies** réapprovisionnement *m*

replete [riː'pliːt] ADJ [a] (= *full up*) [*person*] rassasié, repu [b] (= *fully supplied*) ~ **with sth** rempli de qch, plein de qch

repletion [riː'pliːʃən] N satiété *f*

replica ['replɪkə] N (*gen*) copie *f* exacte; [*of painting*] réplique *f*; [*of document*] fac-similé *m*

replicate ['replɪkeɪt] [1] VT [a] (= *reproduce*) (*gen*) reproduire; (*Bio*) se reproduire par mitose ou méiose [b] (= *fold back*) replier [2] ['replɪkɪt] ADJ [*leaf etc*] replié

replication [ˌreplɪ'keɪʃən] N (*gen*) reproduction *f*; (*Bio*) reproduction *f* par mitose

▼**reply** [riː'plaɪ] [1] N réponse *f*; (*quick*) réplique *f*; (*Jur*) réplique *f*; **in ~ (to)** en réponse (à); (*liter*) **he made no ~** il n'a pas répondu [2] VTI répondre; (*quickly*) répliquer [3] COMP ► **reply coupon** N (*Post*) coupon-réponse *m* ► **reply-paid** ADJ préaffranchi

repoint [ˌriː'pɔɪnt] VT [+ *building etc*] rejointoyer

repointing [ˌriː'pɔɪntɪŋ] N rejointoiement *m*

repo man* ['riːpəʊˌmæn] (*pl* **repo men**) N (*US*) = **repossession man** → **repossession**

▼**report** [riː'pɔːt] [1] N [a] (= *account, statement*) rapport *m*; [*of speech*] compte rendu *m*; [*of debate, meeting*] compte rendu *m*, procès-verbal *m*; (*Press, Rad, TV*) reportage *m* (**on** sur); (*official*) rapport *m* (d'enquête); (*at regular intervals: on weather, sales, etc*) bulletin *m*; **monthly ~** bulletin *m* mensuel; (*Brit*) **school ~** bulletin *m* scolaire; **to make a ~ on** ... faire un rapport sur ...; (*Press, Rad, TV*) faire un reportage sur ...; (*Comm*) **annual ~** rapport *m* annuel (de gestion); **chairman's ~** rapport *m* présidentiel; (*Jur*) **law ~s** recueil *m* de jurisprudence *or* de droit; (*Jur*) **to make a ~ against** ... dresser un procès-verbal à ... → **progress, weather**
[b] (= *rumour*) rumeur *f*; **there is a ~ that** ... le bruit court que ..., on dit que ...; **as ~ has it** selon les bruits qui courent, selon la rumeur publique; **there are ~s of rioting** il y aurait (*or* il y aurait eu) des émeutes; **the ~s of rioting have been proved** les rumeurs selon lesquelles il y aurait eu des émeutes se sont révélées fondées; **I have heard a ~ that** ... j'ai entendu dire que ...
[c] († = *repute*) [*of person*] réputation *f*; [*of product*] renom *m*, renommée *f*; **of good ~** de bonne réputation, dont on dit du bien; **to know sth only by ~** ne savoir qch que par ouï-dire
[d] (= *explosion*) détonation *f*, explosion *f*; **with a loud ~** avec une forte détonation
[2] VT [a] (= *give account of*) rapporter, rendre compte de; (= *bring to notice esp of authorities*) signaler; (*Press, Rad, TV*) rapporter; **to ~ a speech** faire le compte rendu d'un discours; **to ~ one's findings** [*scientist etc*] rendre compte de l'état de ses recherches; [*commission*] présenter ses conclusions; **to ~ progress** rendre compte (des progrès); **only one paper ~ed his death** un seul journal a signalé *or* mentionné sa mort; **the papers ~ed the crime as solved** les journaux ont présenté le crime comme résolu; **our correspondent ~s from Rome that** ... notre correspondant à Rome nous apprend que ...; **he is ~ed as having said** ... il aurait dit ...; **it is ~ed that a prisoner has escaped** ◊ **a prisoner is ~ed to have escaped** un détenu se serait évadé; (*Parl*) **to ~ a bill** présenter un projet de loi; (*Parl*) **to move to ~ progress** demander la clôture des débats
[b] (= *announce*) déclarer, annoncer; **it is ~ed**

from the White House that ... on annonce à la Maison-Blanche que ...

[c] (= notify authorities of) [+ accident, crime, suspect] signaler; [+ criminal, culprit] dénoncer (often pej); **all accidents must be ~ed to the police** tous les accidents doivent être signalés à la police; **to ~ a theft to the police** signaler un vol à la police; **to ~ sb for bad behaviour** signaler qn pour mauvaise conduite; **to ~ sb's bad behaviour** signaler la mauvaise conduite de qn; **her colleague ~ed her to the boss out of jealousy** sa collègue l'a dénoncée au patron par jalousie

[d] (Mil, Naut) signaler; **to ~ sb sick** signaler que qn est malade; **~ed missing** porté manquant or disparu; **nothing to ~** rien à signaler; **to ~ one's position** signaler or donner sa position

[3] VI [a] (= announce o.s. ready) se présenter; **~ to the director on Monday** présentez-vous chez le directeur lundi; **to ~ for duty** se présenter au travail, prendre son service

[b] (Mil) (= join one's unit) rallier son unité; **to ~ sick** se faire porter malade

[c] (= give a report) rendre compte (**on** de), faire un rapport (**on** sur); (Press, Rad, TV) faire un reportage (**on** sur); **the committee is ready to ~** le comité est prêt à faire son rapport; (Rad, TV) **Michael Brown ~s from Rome** de Rome, (le reportage de) Michael Brown

[d] (Admin: in hierarchy) **he ~s to the sales manager** il est sous les ordres (directs) du directeur des ventes; **who do you ~ to?** qui est votre supérieur hiérarchique?

[4] COMP ▶ **report card** N (Scol) bulletin m scolaire ▶ **reported speech** N (Gram) style m or discours m indirect ▶ **report stage** N (Brit Parl) examen d'un projet de loi avant la troisième lecture; **the bill has reached the ~ stage** le projet de loi vient de passer en commission

▶ **report back** VI [a] (= return) (Mil etc) rentrer au quartier; (gen) **you must ~ back at 6 o'clock** il faut que vous soyez de retour à 6 heures [b] (= give report) donner or présenter son rapport (**to** à); **the committee was asked to investigate the complaint and ~ back to the assembly** le comité a été chargé d'examiner la plainte et de présenter son rapport à l'assemblée

reportage [ˌrepɔːˈtɑːʒ] N reportage m

reportedly [rɪˈpɔːtɪdlɪ] ADV **he had ~ seen her** il l'aurait vue; **~, several prisoners had escaped** plusieurs prisonniers se seraient échappés

reporter [rɪˈpɔːtəʳ] [1] N [a] (Press) journaliste mf; (on the spot) reporter m; (Rad, TV) reporter m; **special ~** envoyé(e) m(f) spécial(e) [b] (Parl) (= stenographer) sténographe mf; (Jur) greffier m [2] COMP ▶ **reporters' gallery** N (Jur, Parl) tribune f de la presse

reporting [rɪˈpɔːtɪŋ] [1] N (NonC: Press, Rad, TV) reportages mpl [2] COMP ▶ **reporting restrictions** NPL (Jur) restrictions fpl imposées aux médias (lors de la couverture d'un procès)

repose [rɪˈpəʊz] [1] N (= rest) repos m; (= sleep) sommeil m; (= peace) repos m, tranquillité f; **in ~** au repos [2] VT (frm) [+ confidence, trust] mettre, placer (**in** en); (= rest) **to ~ o.s.** se reposer [3] VI [a] (= rest) se reposer; [the dead] reposer [b] (= be based) reposer, être fondé (**on** sur)

repository [rɪˈpɒzɪtərɪ] N (gen, also Comm) (= warehouse) dépôt m, entrepôt m; (fig) [of knowledge, experience, facts etc] mine f; [of person) dépositaire mf (d'un secret etc)

repossess [ˌriːpəˈzes] VT reprendre possession de, rentrer en possession de

repossession [ˌriːpəˈzeʃən] [1] N reprise f de possession [2] COMP ▶ **repossession man*** N (US) récupérateur* m (huissier chargé de saisir un bien non payé) ▶ **repossession order** N (avis m de) saisie f

repot [ˌriːˈpɒt] VT rempoter

repp [rep] N = **rep²**

reprehend [ˌreprɪˈhend] VT [+ person] réprimander; [+ action, behaviour] blâmer, condamner

reprehensible [ˌreprɪˈhensɪbl] ADJ réprehensible

reprehensibly [ˌreprɪˈhensɪblɪ] ADV de manière répréhensible

represent [ˌreprɪˈzent] VT [a] (= stand for, symbolize) représenter; **a drawing ~ing prehistoric man** un dessin qui représente l'homme préhistorique; **phonetic symbols ~ sounds** les symboles phonétiques représentent des sons; (fig) **he ~s all that is best in his country's culture** il représente or personnifie le meilleur de la culture de son pays; **£200 doesn't ~ a good salary these days** 200 livres ne représentent or ne constituent plus un bon salaire de nos jours

[b] (= declare to be) [+ person, event] représenter; [+ grievance, risk etc] présenter (**as** comme étant); **he ~ed me to be a fool** or **as a fool** il m'a représenté or dépeint comme un imbécile; **I am not what you ~ me to be** je ne suis pas tel que vous me décrivez or dépeignez; **he ~s himself as a doctor** il se fait passer pour un médecin; **it is exactly as ~ed in the advertisement** cela est exactement conforme à la description de l'annonce (publicitaire)

[c] (= explain) exposer, représenter (liter); (= point out) faire remarquer, signaler; **can you ~ to him how much we need his help?** pouvez-vous lui faire comprendre à quel point nous avons besoin de son aide?

[d] (= act or speak for) représenter (also Parl); (Jur) représenter (en justice), postuler pour; **he ~s Warrington in Parliament** il représente Warrington au Parlement, c'est le député de Warrington; **the delegation ~ed the mining industry** la délégation représentait l'industrie minière; **he ~s their firm in London** il représente leur maison à Londres; (esp Sport) **to ~ one's country** représenter son pays; **many countries were ~ed at the ceremony** de nombreux pays étaient représentés à la cérémonie; **women artists were well/strongly ~ed at the exhibition** les femmes artistes étaient bien/fortement représentées à l'exposition; **I ~ Mr Thomas** je représente M. Thomas

[e] (Theat) [+ character] jouer (le rôle de); [+ part] jouer, interpréter

[f] (Jur: in contracts etc) déclarer

re-present [ˌriːprɪˈzent] VT présenter de nouveau

representation [ˌreprɪzenˈteɪʃən] [1] N [a] (Theat, gen) représentation f; [of coded system] interprétation f; (Parl) **proportional ~** représentation f proportionnelle [b] (= protest) **~s** protestation f officielle; **the ambassador made ~s to the government** l'ambassadeur a adressé une protestation officielle au gouvernement

representational [ˌreprɪzenˈteɪʃənl] ADJ (frm: Art) figuratif; [model, system] représentatif

representative [ˌreprɪˈzentətɪv] [1] ADJ (also Govt) représentatif (**of sth** de qch) [2] N représentant(e) m(f); (esp Brit Comm) représentant m (de commerce); (US Pol) député m; (= spokesperson) porte-parole m inv → **house**

repress [rɪˈpres] VT [+ revolt, sneeze, feelings, smile] réprimer; (Psych) refouler

repressed [rɪˈprest] ADJ [person, impulse] refoulé; [feeling] refoulé, réprimé

repression [rɪˈpreʃən] N [a] (political, social) répression f [b] (Psych) (voluntary) répression f; (involuntary) refoulement m

repressive [rɪˈpresɪv] ADJ [regime, law, policy, measures, action] répressif; [forces] de répression

reprieve [rɪˈpriːv] [1] N [a] (Jur) (lettres fpl de) grâce f, commutation f de la peine capitale;

(= delay) sursis m [b] (fig = respite) répit m, sursis m; **they won a ~ for the house** ils ont obtenu un sursis pour la maison [2] VT (Jur) accorder une commutation de la peine capitale à; (= delay) surseoir à l'exécution de; (fig) accorder un répit à; (fig) **the building has been ~d for a while** le bâtiment bénéficie d'un sursis

reprimand [ˈreprɪmɑːnd] [1] N (from parents, teachers) réprimande f; (from employer) blâme m [2] VT réprimander, blâmer

reprint [ˌriːˈprɪnt] [1] VT réimprimer; **this book is being ~ed** ce livre est en réimpression [2] VI [book] être en réimpression [3] [ˈriːprɪnt] N réimpression f; **cheap ~** réédition f bon marché

reprisal [rɪˈpraɪzl] N **~s** représailles fpl; **to take ~s** user de représailles; **as** a or **in ~ for ...** en représailles à ...; **by way of ~** par représailles

reprise [rɪˈpriːz] N (Mus) reprise f

repro* [ˈriːprəʊ] [1] N ABBR = **reprographics, reprography** [2] COMP (ABBR = reproduction) ~ **furniture** copie(s) f(pl) de meuble(s) ancien(s)

reproach [rɪˈprəʊtʃ] [1] N [a] (= rebuke) reproche m; **to heap ~es on sb** accabler qn de reproches; **term of ~** parole f de reproche [b] (NonC = discredit) honte f, opprobre m; (fig) **to be a ~ to ...** être la honte de ...; **to bring ~ on ...** jeter le discrédit sur ..., discréditer ...; **above** or **beyond ~** sans reproche(s), irréprochable [2] VT faire des reproches à; **to ~ sb for sth** reprocher qch à qn; **to ~ sb for having done sth** reprocher à qn d'avoir fait qch; **he has nothing to ~ himself with** il n'a rien à se reprocher

reproachful [rɪˈprəʊtʃfʊl] ADJ [look, tone] réprobateur (-trice f); [remark] lourd de reproches; [eyes] chargé de réprobation; **he was ~** il avait une attitude pleine de reproches

reproachfully [rɪˈprəʊtʃfəlɪ] ADV [say] sur un ton réprobateur or de reproche; [look at, shake one's head] d'un air réprobateur

reprobate [ˈreprəʊbeɪt] [1] ADJ, N (frm or hum) dépravé(e) m(f) [2] VT réprouver

reprobation [ˌreprəʊˈbeɪʃən] N réprobation f

reprocess [ˌriːˈprəʊses] VT retraiter

reprocessing [ˌriːˈprəʊsesɪŋ] N retraitement m → **nuclear**

reproduce [ˌriːprəˈdjuːs] [1] VT reproduire [2] VI se reproduire

reproducible [ˌriːprəˈdjuːsɪbl] ADJ reproductible

reproduction [ˌriːprəˈdʌkʃən] [1] N (gen, Art, Bio) reproduction f; **sound ~** reproduction f sonore; **this picture is a ~** ce tableau est une reproduction [2] COMP ▶ **reproduction furniture** N (NonC) copie(s) f(pl) de meuble(s) ancien(s)

reproductive [ˌriːprəˈdʌktɪv] ADJ reproducteur (-trice f)

reprographic [ˌriːprəˈgræfɪk] ADJ de reprographie

reprographics [ˌriːprəˈgræfɪks], **reprography** [rɪˈprɒgrəfɪ] N reprographie f

reproof [rɪˈpruːf] N reproche m, réprimande f; **a tone of ~** un ton de reproche; **in ~** en signe de désapprobation

re-proof [ˌriːˈpruːf] VT [+ garment] réimperméabiliser

reproval [rɪˈpruːvəl] N reproche m, blâme m

reprove [rɪˈpruːv] VT [+ person] blâmer (**for** de), réprimander; [+ action] réprouver, condamner

reproving [rɪˈpruːvɪŋ] ADJ [look, shake of one's head, tone] réprobateur (-trice f); [letter] de reproche(s)

reprovingly [rɪˈpruːvɪŋlɪ] ADV d'un air or ton de reproche

reptile [ˈreptaɪl] [1] N (lit, fig) reptile m [2] COMP ▶ **reptile house** N vivarium m

reptilian [rep'tɪlɪən] **1** ADJ (*Zool, fig, pej*) reptilien **2** N reptile *m* (*also fig*)

republic [rɪ'pʌblɪk] N république *f*; (*US*) **the Republic** les États-Unis d'Amérique

republican [rɪ'pʌblɪkən] **1** ADJ, N républicain(e) *m(f)* **2** COMP ► **Republican party** N (*Pol*) parti *m* républicain

republicanism [rɪ'pʌblɪkənɪzəm] N (*gen*) républicanisme *m*; (*US*) **Republicanism** politique *f* du parti républicain

republication [,ri:pʌblɪ'keɪʃən] N [*of book*] réédition *f*, republication *f*; [*of law, banns*] nouvelle publication *f*

republish [,ri:'pʌblɪʃ] VT [+ *book*] rééditer; [+ *banns*] publier de nouveau

repudiate [rɪ'pju:dɪeɪt] VT [+ *friend, ally*] renier, désavouer; [+ *accusation*] répudier, repousser; [*government etc*] [+ *debt, treaty, obligation*] refuser de respecter; **to ~ one's wife** répudier sa femme

repudiation [rɪ,pju:dɪ'eɪʃən] N [*of violence, doctrine, remarks*] condamnation *f*; [*of charge, evidence*] rejet *m*; **~ of a treaty/a debt** refus *m* de respecter un traité/d'honorer une dette

repugnance [rɪ'pʌgnəns] N répugnance *f*, aversion *f* (**to** pour); **he shows ~ to accepting charity** il répugne à accepter la charité

repugnant [rɪ'pʌgnənt] ADJ répugnant; **to be ~ to sb** répugner à qn

repulse [rɪ'pʌls] **1** VT (*Mil*) repousser, refouler; (*fig*) [+ *help, offer*] repousser, rejeter **2** N (*Mil*) échec *m*; (*fig*) refus *m*, rebuffade *f*; **to meet with** *or* **suffer a ~** essuyer un refus *or* une rebuffade

repulsion [rɪ'pʌlʃən] N (*also Phys*) répulsion *f*

repulsive [rɪ'pʌlsɪv] ADJ [*person, behaviour, sight, idea*] repoussant; (*Phys*) [*force*] répulsif; **I found it ~ to think that ...** il me répugnait de penser que ...

repulsively [rɪ'pʌlsɪvlɪ] ADV **~ ugly/large** *etc* d'une laideur/grosseur *etc* repoussante

repulsiveness [rɪ'pʌlsɪvnɪs] N aspect *m* or caractère *m* repoussant

repurchase [,ri:'pɜ:tʃɪs] **1** N rachat *m* **2** VT racheter

reputable ['repjʊtəbl] ADJ [*person, company*] de bonne réputation; [*brand, product*] réputé

reputably ['repjʊtəblɪ] ADV **to be ~ employed (as)** gagner honorablement sa vie (comme); **~ established in the business world** honorablement établi dans le monde des affaires

reputation [,repjʊ'teɪʃən] N réputation *f*; **to have a good/bad ~** avoir (une) bonne/(une) mauvaise réputation; **a good ~ as a singer** une bonne réputation de chanteur; **to have a ~ for honesty** avoir la réputation d'être honnête, être réputé pour son honnêteté; **to live up to one's ~** soutenir sa réputation; **she was by ~ a good organizer** elle avait la réputation d'être une bonne organisatrice

repute [rɪ'pju:t] N réputation *f*, renom *m*; **to know sb by ~** connaître qn de réputation; **to be of good ~** avoir (une) bonne réputation; **a restaurant of ~** un restaurant réputé *or* en renom; **place of ill ~** endroit *m* mal famé; (*euph*) **a house of ill ~** (= *brothel*) une maison close; **to hold sb in high ~** avoir une très haute opinion de qn

reputed [rɪ'pju:tɪd] ADJ **a** (= *supposed*) [*love affair, author*] soi-disant; **he bought the painting for a ~ $2,000,000** on dit qu'il a acheté le tableau 2 millions de dollars; **the buildings were ~ to be haunted** ces bâtiments étaient réputés hantés; **the story's ~ to be true** l'histoire est réputée authentique; **he is ~ to have worked miracles** à ce qu'on dit, il aurait fait des miracles **b** (= *esteemed*) [*person, organization*] réputé **c** (*Jur*) **~ father** père *m* putatif

reputedly [rɪ'pju:tɪdlɪ] ADV à ce que l'on dit (+ *cond*); **events that ~ took place thousands of**

years ago des événements qui, d'après ce qu'on dit, auraient eu lieu il y a des milliers d'années

▼ **request** [rɪ'kwest] **1** N **a** demande *f*, requête *f*; **at sb's ~** sur *or* à la demande de qn, à la requête de qn; **by general** *or* **popular ~** à la demande générale; **on** *or* **by ~** sur demande; **to make a ~ for sth** faire une demande de qch; **to make a ~ to sb for sth** demander qch à qn; **to grant a ~** accéder à une demande *or* à une requête

b (*Rad*) disque *m* des auditeurs *or* demandé par un auditeur; **to play a ~ for sb** passer un disque à l'intention de qn

2 VT demander; **to ~ sth from sb** demander qch à qn; **to ~ sb to do** demander à qn de faire, prier qn de faire; **"you are ~ed not to smoke"** « prière de ne pas fumer »; (*Comm etc*) **as ~ed in your letter of ...** comme vous (nous) l'avez demandé dans votre lettre du ...; (*Comm etc*) **herewith, as ~ed, my cheque for £50** ci-joint, comme vous l'avez demandé, un chèque de 50 livres; **it's all I ~ of you** c'est tout ce que je vous demande

3 COMP ► **request programme** N (*Rad*) programme *m* composé par les auditeurs ► **request stop** N (*Brit*) [*of bus*] arrêt *m* facultatif

requiem ['rekwɪem] **1** N requiem *m* **2** COMP ► **requiem mass** N messe *f* de requiem

▼ **require** [rɪ'kwaɪəʳ] VT **a** (= *need*) [*person*] avoir besoin de; [*thing, action*] demander, requérir; **I have all I ~** j'ai tout ce qu'il me faut *or* tout ce dont j'ai besoin; **the journey will ~ three hours** le voyage prendra *or* demandera trois heures; **it ~s great care** cela demande *or* requiert beaucoup de soin; **this plant ~s frequent watering** cette plante doit être arrosée souvent; **if ~d** quand il le faut; **when (it is) ~d** quand il le faut; **what qualifications are ~d?** quels sont les diplômes nécessaires *or* exigés? **b** (= *demand*) exiger; (= *order*) exiger, réclamer; **to ~ sb to do** exiger de qn qu'il fasse; **you are ~d to present yourself here tomorrow** vous êtes prié de vous présenter ici demain; **to ~ sth of sb** exiger qch de qn; **as ~d by law** comme la loi l'exige; **we ~ two references** nous exigeons deux références

required [rɪ'kwaɪəd] **1** ADJ [*conditions, amount*] requis; **by the ~ date** en temps voulu; **to meet the ~ standards** [*machine*] être conforme aux normes; [*student*] avoir le niveau requis; **in the ~ time** dans les délais prescrits **2** COMP ► **required course** N (*US Scol*) matière *f* obligatoire ► **required reading** N (*Scol, Univ*) ouvrage(s) *m(pl)* au programme; (*fig*) **his latest article is ~ reading for all those interested in the subject** tous ceux qui sont intéressés par ce sujet doivent absolument lire son dernier article

requirement [rɪ'kwaɪəmənt] N **a** (= *need*) exigence *f*, besoin *m*; **to meet sb's ~s** satisfaire aux exigences *or* aux besoins de qn; **there isn't enough to meet the ~** il n'y en a pas assez pour satisfaire la demande **b** (= *condition*) condition *f* requise; **to fit the ~s** remplir les conditions **c** (*US Univ*) cursus *m* obligatoire

requisite ['rekwɪzɪt] (*frm*) **1** N **a** (= *thing required*) chose *f* nécessaire *or* requise (**for** pour); **all the ~s** tout ce qui est nécessaire **b** **travel/toilet ~s** accessoires *mpl* de voyage/toilette **2** ADJ requis

requisition [,rekwɪ'zɪʃən] **1** N demande *f*; (*gen Mil*) réquisition *f*; **to put in a ~ for ...** faire une demande de ... **2** VT (*gen*) faire une demande de; (*Mil*) réquisitionner

requital [rɪ'kwaɪtl] N (= *repayment*) récompense *f*; (= *revenge*) revanche *f*

requite [rɪ'kwaɪt] VT **a** **~d love** amour *m* partagé **b** (*frm* = *repay*) [+ *person, action*] récompenser, payer (**for** de) **c** (*frm* = *avenge*) [+ *action*] venger; [+ *person*] se venger de

reran [,ri:'ræn] VB *pt of* **rerun**

reread [,ri:'ri:d] (*pret, ptp* **reread** ['ri:'red]) VT relire

reredos ['rɪədɒs] N retable *m*

reroof [,ri:'ru:f] VT refaire la toiture de

reroute [,ri:'ru:t] VT [+ *train, coach*] changer l'itinéraire de, dérouter; **our train was ~d through Leeds** on a fait faire à notre train un détour par Leeds, notre train a été dérouté sur Leeds

rerun ['ri:rʌn] (*vb: pret* **reran**, *ptp* **rerun**) **1** N [*of film, tape*] reprise *f*; [*of TV programme, series*] rediffusion *f*; **the opposition has demanded a ~ of the elections** l'opposition a demandé que l'on organise de nouvelles élections; **a ~ of the contest is almost certain** on va très certainement devoir recommencer l'épreuve; **the result could have been a ~ of 1931** le résultat aurait pu être la répétition de ce qui s'est passé en 1931 **2** [,ri:'rʌn] VT [+ *film, tape*] passer de nouveau; [+ *race*] courir de nouveau; **to ~ an election** organiser de nouvelles élections; (*Comput*) **to ~ a program** réexécuter un programme

resale [,ri:'seɪl] **1** N (*gen*) revente *f*; (*on package etc*) **"not for ~"** « échantillon gratuit » **2** COMP ► **resale price** N prix *m* à la revente ► **resale price maintenance** N prix *m* de vente imposé ► **resale value** N [*of car*] cote *f* or prix *m* à l'Argus; **what's the ~ value?** (*gen*) ça se revend combien?; [*car*] elle est cotée combien à l'Argus?

resat [,ri:'sæt] VB *pt, ptp of* **resit**

reschedule [,ri:'ʃedju:l, (*US*) ,ri:'skedju:l] VT [+ *meeting, visit*] changer l'heure (*or* la date) de; [+ *train service etc*] changer l'horaire de; [+ *repayments, debt*] rééchelonner; [+ *plans, course*] changer le programme de

rescind [rɪ'sɪnd] VT [+ *judgement*] rescinder, casser; [+ *law*] abroger; [+ *act*] révoquer; [+ *contract*] résilier, dissoudre; [+ *decision, agreement*] annuler

rescission [rɪ'sɪʒən] N [*of law*] abrogation *f*; [*of agreement*] annulation *f*; [*of contract*] résiliation *f*

rescript ['ri:skrɪpt] N (*Hist, Rel*) rescrit *m*

rescriptions [rɪ'skrɪpʃənz] NPL (*St Ex*) bons *mpl* du Trésor, emprunts *mpl* des collectivités publiques

rescue ['reskju:] **1** N (= *help*) secours *mpl*; (= *saving*) sauvetage *m*; (= *freeing*) délivrance *f*; **~ was difficult** le sauvetage a été difficile; **~ came too late** les secours sont arrivés trop tard; **to go to sb's ~** aller au secours *or* à la rescousse de qn; **to come to sb's ~** venir en aide à qn *or* à la rescousse de qn; **to the ~** à la rescousse → **air**

2 VT (= *save*) sauver, secourir; (= *free*) délivrer (**from** de); **you ~d me from a difficult situation** vous m'avez tiré d'une situation difficile; **the ~d were taken to hospital** les rescapés ont été emmenés à l'hôpital

3 COMP ► **rescue attempt** N tentative *f* or opération *f* de sauvetage ► **rescue operations** NPL opérations *fpl* de sauvetage ► **rescue party** N (*gen*) équipe *f* de secours; (*Ski, Climbing*) colonne *f* de secours ► **rescue services** NPL services *mpl* de secours ► **rescue worker** N sauveteur *m*, secouriste *mf*

rescuer ['reskjʊəʳ] N sauveteur *m*

resealable [,ri:'si:ləbl] ADJ [*container*] refermable

research [rɪ'sɜ:tʃ] **1** N recherche(s) *f(pl)*; **a piece of ~** un travail de recherche; **to do ~** faire des recherches *or* de la recherche; **to carry out ~ into the effects of ...** faire des recherches sur les effets de ... **2** VI faire des recherches (**into, on** sur) **3** VT [+ *article, book etc*] faire des recherches pour *or* en vue de; **well-~ed** bien documenté

► LANGUAGE IN USE: **request** 4, 10.1, 20.2, 25.1   **require** 10.1, 20.2

4 COMP ► **research and development** N (*Ind etc*) recherche *f* et développement *m*, recherche-développement *f* ► **research assistant, research associate** N (*Univ*) ≈ étudiant(e) *m(f)* en maîtrise (*ayant le statut de chercheur*) ► **research establishment** N centre *m* de recherches ► **research fellow** N (*Univ*) ≈ chercheur *m*, -euse *f* attaché(e) à l'université ► **research fellowship** N (*Univ*) poste *m* de chercheur (-euse *f*) attaché(e) à l'université ► **research laboratory** N laboratoire *m* de recherches ► **research scientist** N chercheur *m*, -euse *f* → **researcher** ► **research student** N (*Univ*) étudiant(e) *m(f)* qui fait de la recherche, étudiant(e) *m(f)* de doctorat (*ayant statut de chercheur*) ► **research work** N travail *m* de recherche, recherches *fpl* ► **research worker** N chercheur *m*, -euse *f* → **researcher**

researcher [rɪˈsɜːtʃəʳ] N chercheur *m*

reseat [ˌriːˈsiːt] VT a [+ *person*] faire changer de place à; **to ~ o.s.** se rasseoir b [+ *chair*] rempailler, refaire le siège de; [+ *trousers*] mettre un fond à

resection [riːˈsekʃən] N résection *f*

reselect [riːsɪˈlekt] VT (*Pol*) [*party*] accorder de nouveau son investiture à; **to be ~ed** [*candidate*] recevoir de nouveau l'investiture de son parti

reselection [riːsɪˈlekʃən] N (*Pol*) investiture *f* renouvelée

resell [ˌriːˈsel] (*pret, ptp* **resold**) VT revendre

resemblance [rɪˈzembləns] N ressemblance *f*; **to bear a strong/faint ~ (to)** avoir une grande/vague ressemblance (avec); **this bears no ~ to the facts** ceci n'a aucune ressemblance avec les faits; **there's not the slightest ~ between them** il n'y a pas la moindre ressemblance entre eux, ils ne se ressemblent pas du tout

▼ **resemble** [rɪˈzembl] VT [*person*] ressembler à; [*thing*] ressembler à, être semblable à; **they ~ each other** ils se ressemblent

resent [rɪˈzent] VT [+ *sb's reply, look, attitude*] être contrarié par; (*stronger*) être indigné de; **I ~ that!** je proteste!; **I ~ your tone** votre ton me déplaît fortement; **he ~ed my promotion** il n'a jamais pu accepter *or* admettre ma promotion; **he ~ed having lost his job/the fact that I married her** il n'acceptait pas la perte de son emploi/mon mariage avec elle, la perte de son emploi/mon mariage avec elle lui restait en travers de la gorge*; **he really ~ed this** ça lui est resté en travers de la gorge*; **he may ~ my being here** il n'appréciera peut-être pas ma présence

resentful [rɪˈzentfʊl] ADJ [*person, reply, look*] plein de ressentiment; **to be *or* feel ~ of *or* towards sb (for doing sth)** en vouloir à qn (d'avoir fait qch); **to be ~ of sb's success** mal accepter le succès de qn

resentfully [rɪˈzentfəlɪ] ADV avec ressentiment

resentment [rɪˈzentmənt] N ressentiment *m*

▼ **reservation** [ˌrezəˈveɪʃən] 1 N a (= *restriction*) réserve *f*; (*Jur*) réservation *f*; **mental ~** restriction *f* mentale; **without ~** sans réserve, sans arrière-pensée; **with ~s** avec certaines réserves, sous réserve; **to have ~s about** ... faire *or* émettre des réserves sur ... b (= *booking*) réservation *f*; **to make a ~ at the hotel/on the boat** réserver *or* retenir une chambre à l'hôtel/une place sur le bateau; **to have a ~** avoir une réservation c (= *area of land*) réserve *f*; (*US*) réserve *f* (*indienne*) d (*Brit: on roadway*) (**central**) **~** bande *f* médiane e (*Rel*) **Reservation (of the Sacrament)** les Saintes Réserves *fpl* 2 COMP ► **reservation desk** N (*in airport, hotels etc*) comptoir *m* des réservations

reserve [rɪˈzɜːv] 1 VT a (= *keep*) réserver, garder; **to ~ one's strength** ménager *or* garder ses forces; (*Sport*) se réserver; **to ~ o.s. for** ... se réserver pour ...; **to ~ the best wine for**

one's friends réserver *or* garder le meilleur vin pour ses amis; **to ~ judgement** réserver son jugement; **to ~ the right to do** se réserver le droit de faire; **to ~ a warm welcome for sb** ménager *or* réserver un accueil chaleureux à qn b (= *book in advance*) [+ *room, seat*] réserver, retenir

2 N a (= *sth stored*) réserve *f*, stock *m*; **to have great ~s of energy** avoir une grande réserve d'énergie; **cash ~** réserve *f* en devises; **gold ~s** réserves *fpl* d'or *or* en or; **world ~s of pyrites** réserves *fpl* mondiales de pyrite; **to keep *or* hold in ~** tenir en réserve b (= *restriction*) réserve *f*, restriction *f*; **without ~** sans réserve, sans restriction; **with all ~ *or* all proper ~s** sous toutes réserves c (*Brit: also* **~ price**) prix *m* minimum d (= *piece of land*) réserve *f* → **game¹, nature** e (*NonC* = *attitude*) réserve *f*, retenue *f*; **he treated me with some ~** il s'est tenu sur la réserve avec moi; **to break through sb's ~** amener qn à se départir de sa réserve *or* retenue f (*Mil*) **the Reserve** la réserve; (*Mil*) **the ~s** la réserve, les réservistes *mpl* g (*Sport*) **the ~s** l'équipe *f* B

3 COMP [*currency, fund*] de réserve ► **reserve bank** N (*US*) banque *f* de réserve ► **reserve list** N (*Mil*) cadre *m* de réserve ► **reserve player** N (*esp Brit Sport*) remplaçant(e) *m(f)* ► **reserve price** N (*Brit*) prix *m* minimum ► **reserve tank** N (*also* **~ petrol tank**) réservoir *m* (*d'essence*) de secours, nourrice *f* ► **reserve team** N (*Brit*) équipe *f* B

reserved [rɪˈzɜːvd] ADJ [*person, behaviour, room, table, seat*] réservé; **to be ~ about sth** se montrer réservé sur qch → **copyright, right**

reservedly [rɪˈzɜːvɪdlɪ] ADV avec réserve, avec retenue

reservist [rɪˈzɜːvɪst] N (*Mil*) réserviste *m*

reservoir [ˈrezəvwɑːʳ] N (*lit, fig*) réservoir *m*

reset [ˌriːˈset] (*pret, ptp* **reset**) 1 VT a [+ *precious stone*] remonter b [+ *clock, watch*] mettre à l'heure; **to ~ the alarm** remettre l'alarme c (*Comput*) redémarrer d (*Med*) [+ *limb*] remettre; **to ~ a broken bone** réduire une fracture e (*Typ*) recomposer 2 COMP ► **reset button, reset switch** N (*Comput*) bouton *m* de redémarrage

resettle [ˌriːˈsetl] 1 VT [+ *refugees*] établir (*ailleurs*), relocaliser; [+ *land*] repeupler 2 VI s'établir (*ailleurs*)

resettlement [ˌriːˈsetlmənt] 1 N [*of land*] repeuplement *m*; [*of people*] déplacement *m*, relocalisation *f* 2 COMP ► **resettlement programme** N programme visant à relocaliser une population dans une nouvelle région

reshape [ˌriːˈʃeɪp] VT [+ *dough, clay*] refaçonner, modeler de nouveau; [+ *text, policy, society, system*] réorganiser

reshuffle [ˌriːˈʃʌfl] 1 VT a [+ *cards*] battre de nouveau b (*fig*) [+ *cabinet, board of directors*] remanier 2 N a (*Cards*) **to have a ~** rebattre b (*in command etc*) remaniement *m*; (*Pol*) **Cabinet ~** remaniement *m* ministériel

reside [rɪˈzaɪd] VI (*lit, fig*) résider; **the power ~s in *or* with the President** le pouvoir est entre les mains du Président

residence [ˈrezɪdəns] 1 N a (*frm* = *house*) résidence *f*, demeure *f*; **the President's official ~** la résidence officielle du Président b (*US: also* **university ~, ~ hall**) résidence *f* (*universitaire*) c (*NonC* = *stay*) séjour *m*, résidence *f*; **to take up ~ in the country** élire domicile *or* s'installer à la campagne; **after five years' ~ in Britain** après avoir résidé en Grande-Bretagne pendant cinq ans; (*Admin*) **place/country of ~** lieu *m*/pays *m* de résidence; **to be in ~** [*monarch, governor etc*] être en résidence; **the students are now in ~** les étudiants sont maintenant rentrés; **there is always a doctor in ~** il y a toujours un médecin à demeure 2 COMP ► **residence hall** N (*US Univ*) résidence *f*

universitaire ► **residence permit** N (*Brit*) permis *m or* carte *f* de séjour

residency [ˈrezɪdənsɪ] N (*gen*) résidence *f* officielle; (*US Med*) internat *m* de deuxième et de troisième années; (*Mus* = *regular engagement*) **they've got a ~ at Steve's Bar** ils jouent régulièrement au Steve's Bar

resident [ˈrezɪdənt] 1 N a habitant(e) *m(f)*; (*in foreign country*) résident(e) *m(f)*; (*in street*) riverain(e) *m(f)*; (*in hostel*) pensionnaire *mf*; **"parking for ~s only"** « parking privé », **"~s only"** « interdit sauf aux riverains » b (*US Med*) interne *mf* de deuxième et de troisième années 2 ADJ a [*landlord*] occupant; [*chaplain, tutor, caretaker*] à demeure; [*doctor, dramatist, DJ*] attitré; **to be ~ abroad/in France** résider à l'étranger/en France; **the ~ population** la population fixe; (*hum*) **our ~ expert (on sth)** notre spécialiste (de qch) b (*Zool*) [*animal*] non migrateur (-trice *f*) 3 COMP ► **resident head** N (*US Univ*) directeur *m*, -trice *f* d'une résidence universitaire ► **resident physician** N (*Med*) interne *mf* ► **residents' association** N association *f* de riverains ► **resident student** N (*US Univ*) étudiant(e) *m(f)* d'une université d'État dont le domicile permanent est situé dans cet État

residential [ˌrezɪˈdenʃəl] 1 ADJ a (= *not industrial*) [*area*] d'habitation; **~ accommodation** logements *mpl* b (= *live-in*) [*post, job, course*] avec hébergement, résidentiel; [*staff*] logé sur place 2 COMP ► **residential care** N **to be in ~ care** être pris en charge en établissement spécialisé

residua [rɪˈzɪdjʊə] NPL *of* **residuum**

residual [rɪˈzɪdjʊəl] 1 ADJ restant; (*Chem*) résiduaire; [*radiation, fault*] résiduel; **the ~ powers of the British sovereign** les pouvoirs qui restent au souverain britannique 2 N (*Chem*) résidu *m*; (*Math*) reste *m* 3 **residuals** NPL (= *royalties*) droits versés aux acteurs et à l'auteur à l'occasion d'une rediffusion d'un programme télévisé ou d'un film 4 COMP ► **residual current** N courant *m* résiduel ► **residual current device** N disjoncteur *m* différentiel ► **residual heat** N chaleur *f* résiduelle ► **residual income** N revenu *m* net ► **residual unemployment** N chômage *m* résiduel

residuary [rɪˈzɪdjʊərɪ] ADJ restant; (*Chem*) résiduaire; (*Jur*) **~ estate** montant *m* net d'une succession; (*Jur*) **~ legatee** ≈ légataire *mf* universel(le)

residue [ˈrezɪdjuː] N reste(s) *m(pl)*; (*Chem*) résidu *m*; (*Math*) reste *m*; (*Jur*) reliquat *m*

residuum [rɪˈzɪdjʊəm] N (*pl* **residua**) résidu *m*, reste *m*

resign [rɪˈzaɪn] 1 VT a (= *give up*) se démettre de; [+ *one's job*] démissionner de; (= *hand over*) céder (**to** à); **he ~ed the leadership to his colleague** il a cédé la direction à son collègue; (*Mil etc*) **to ~ one's commission** (*se dit d'un officier*) (= *accept*) **to ~ o.s. to (doing) sth** se résigner à (faire) qch 2 VI démissionner, donner sa démission (**from** de)

resignation [ˌrezɪgˈneɪʃən] N a (*from job*) démission *f*; **to tender one's ~** donner sa démission b (*mental state*) résignation *f* c (*NonC*) [*of a right*] abandon *m* (**of** de), renonciation *f* (**of** à)

resigned [rɪˈzaɪnd] ADJ résigné; **to be ~ to (doing) sth** s'être résigné à (faire) qch; **to become ~ to (doing) sth** se résigner à (faire) qch

resignedly [rɪˈzaɪnɪdlɪ] ADV [*say*] avec résignation, d'un ton résigné; [*shrug, sigh*] avec résignation, d'un air résigné

resilience [rɪˈzɪliəns] N [*of person, character*] résistance *f*, faculté *f* de récupération; [*of rubber*] élasticité *f*

resilient [rɪ'zɪlɪənt] ADJ [*object, material, currency, market*] résistant; **he is very ~** (*physically*) il a beaucoup de résistance, il récupère bien; (*mentally*) il a du ressort, il ne se laisse pas abattre

resin ['rezɪn] N résine f

resinous ['rezɪnəs] ADJ résineux

resist [rɪ'zɪst] **1** VT [+ *attack, arrest, person*] résister à, s'opposer à; [+ *temptation*] résister à; [+ *order*] refuser d'obéir or d'obtempérer à; [+ *change*] s'opposer à; **I couldn't ~ (eating) another cake** je n'ai pas pu résister à l'envie de or je n'ai pas pu m'empêcher de manger encore un gâteau; **he ~s any advice** il s'oppose à or il est rebelle à tout conseil **2** VI résister, offrir de la résistance

resistance [rɪ'zɪstəns] **1** N (*gen, Elec, Med, Mil, Phys*) résistance f; (*Hist*) **the Resistance** la Résistance; **to meet with ~** se heurter à une résistance; **to offer ~ to sth** résister à qch; **to put up** or **offer stiff ~ to sth** opposer une vive résistance à qch; **he offered no ~** il n'opposa aucune résistance (**to** à); (*Med*) **his ~ was very low** il n'offrait presque plus de résistance; **that's the line of least ~** c'est la solution de facilité; **to take the line of least ~** choisir la solution de facilité → **passive 2** COMP ► **resistance fighter** N résistant(e) m(f) ► **resistance movement** N résistance f (mouvement)

resistant [rɪ'zɪstənt] ADJ [*person*] hostile (**to sth** à qch); [*virus, plant, material*] résistant (**to sth** à qch); **~ to penicillin** pénicillorésistant → **water**

-resistant [rɪ'zɪstənt] ADJ (*in compounds*) **disease-resistant** [*plant*] résistant aux maladies; **fire-resistant** [*paint, cloth*] ignifugé; **heat-resistant** résistant à la chaleur

resister [rɪ'zɪstə^r] N réfractaire m

resistor [rɪ'zɪstə^r] N (*Elec*) résistance f

resit [ˌriːˈsɪt] (*pret, ptp* **resat** (*Brit*)) **1** VT se représenter à, repasser **2** VI se présenter à la deuxième session **3** ['riːsɪt] N deuxième session f (*d'un examen*); **to have a ~ in law** devoir se représenter en droit; **to fail one's ~s/ one's ~ in chemistry** échouer une deuxième fois à ses examens/à son examen de chimie

resite [ˌriːˈsaɪt] VT [+ *factory*] réimplanter, transférer

resize [ˌriːˈsaɪz] VT (*Comput*) [+ *window*] redimensionner

resold [ˌriːˈsəʊld] VB *pt, ptp of* **resell**

resole [ˌriːˈsəʊl] VT ressemeler

resolute ['rezəluːt] ADJ [*person*] résolu, déterminé; [*opposition*] résolu; [*refusal*] ferme; [*faith*] solide; **to take ~ action** agir avec résolution or détermination; **to be ~ in doing sth** faire qch avec résolution or détermination; **to be ~ in one's opposition to sth** s'opposer résolument à qch; **to remain ~ in the fight against sb/sth** continuer résolument à se battre contre qn/qch

resolutely ['rezəluːtlɪ] ADV [*resist, oppose, stride, stare*] résolument; [*refuse*] fermement; **the Government remains ~ committed to the fight against unemployment** le gouvernement poursuit résolument son combat contre le chômage

resoluteness ['rezəluːtnɪs] N résolution f, détermination f

resolution [ˌrezə'luːʃən] N **a** (= *decision*) résolution f; **to make a ~ to do** prendre la résolution de faire; **good ~s** bonnes résolutions fpl → **New Year 2** (*Admin, Pol*) résolution f; **to make a ~** prendre une résolution; **to adopt/ reject a ~** adopter/rejeter une résolution **c** (*NonC = resoluteness*) fermeté f, résolution f; **to show ~** faire preuve de fermeté, faire preuve de décision **d** (*NonC = solving*) [*of problem, puzzle*] résolution f **e** (*NonC: Chem, Med, Mus, Phot*) résolution f (**into** en)

resolvable [rɪ'zɒlvəbl] ADJ résoluble

resolve [rɪ'zɒlv] **1** VT **a** [+ *problem, difficulty*] résoudre; [+ *doubt*] dissiper **b** (= *break up*) résoudre, réduire (**into** en); **to ~ sth into its elements** ramener or réduire qch à ses éléments; **water ~s itself into steam** l'eau se résout or se transforme en vapeur; **the meeting ~d itself into a committee** l'assemblée se constitua en commission **c** (*Med, Mus*) résoudre

2 VI **a** (= *decide*) résoudre, décider (**to do do** faire), se résoudre, se décider (**to do** à faire); **to ~ (up)on sth** se résoudre à qch; **to ~ that ...** décider que ...; **it has been ~d that ...** il a été décidé que ... **b** (= *break up*) se résoudre (**into** en); **the question ~s into four points** la question se divise en quatre points

3 N **a** (*NonC = resoluteness*) résolution f, fermeté f; **to do sth with ~** faire qch avec détermination **b** (= *decision*) résolution f, décision f; **to make a ~ to do** prendre la résolution de faire, résoudre de faire

resolved [rɪ'zɒlvd] ADJ résolu (**to do sth** à faire qch), décidé (**to do sth** à faire qch)

resonance ['rezənəns] N (*gen, Mus, Phon, Phys*) résonance f; [*of voice*] résonance f, sonorité f

resonant ['rezənənt] ADJ **a** (= *sonorous, echoing*) [*voice, room*] sonore; [*sound*] retentissant **b** (= *evocative*) **to be ~ of sth** rappeler qch; **it is a place ~ with memories for him** c'est un endroit qui éveille en lui une foule de souvenirs; **it was a place ~ with memories of him** c'est un endroit qui évoquait des souvenirs de lui

resonate ['rezəneɪt] VI **a** [*sound*] résonner **b** **the room ~d with the sound of laughter** la pièce résonnait de rires **c** (*fig*) **that ~s with me** je suis tout à fait d'accord là-dessus

resonator ['rezəneɪtə^r] N résonateur m

resorption [rɪ'zɔːpʃən] N résorption f

resort [rɪ'zɔːt] **1** N **a** (= *recourse*) recours m; **without ~ to violence** sans recourir or avoir recours à la violence; **as a last** or **final ~** ◊ **in the last** or **final ~** en dernier ressort; **it was/you were my last ~** c'était/tu étais mon dernier recours **b** (= *place*) lieu m de séjour or de vacances; **coastal ~** plage f; **seaside/summer ~** station f balnéaire/estivale; **winter sports ~** station f de sports d'hiver; (*fig liter*) **a ~ of thieves** un repaire de voleurs → **health, holiday 2** VI **to ~ to sth** avoir recours à qch, recourir à qch; **to ~ to sb** avoir recours à qn; **to ~ to doing sth** en venir à faire qch

resound [rɪ'zaʊnd] **1** VI retentir, résonner (**with** de); (*fig*) **his speech will ~ throughout France/history** son discours retentira dans toute la France/à travers l'histoire **2** VT faire retentir or résonner

resounding [rɪ'zaʊndɪŋ] ADJ **a** (= *loud*) [*thud, crack, crash, laugh*] sonore; [*voice*] sonore, tonitruant; **~ applause** un tonnerre d'applaudissements **b** (= *great*) [*triumph, victory, success*] retentissant; [*defeat*] écrasant; **a ~ silence** un silence pesant; **a ~ no** un non catégorique

resoundingly [rɪ'zaʊndɪŋlɪ] ADV **a** (= *loudly*) [*fall, crash*] bruyamment **b** (= *convincingly*) [*beat, defeat*] à plate(s) couture(s); **to be ~ successful** [*plan*] être couronné de succès; [*person*] remporter un succès retentissant

resource [rɪ'sɔːs] **1** N **a** (= *wealth, supplies etc*) ressource f; **financial/mineral/natural ~s** ressources fpl pécuniaires/en minerais/ naturelles; **~s of men and materials** ressources fpl en hommes et en matériel; (*Fin*) **the total ~s of a company** l'ensemble des ressources d'une société; (*fig*) **he has no ~s against boredom** il ne sait pas lutter or se défendre contre l'ennui; (*fig*) **left to his own ~s** livré à ses propres ressources or à lui-même **b** (*Comput*) ressources fpl **c** (= *resort*) ressource f; **you are**

my last ~ vous êtes ma dernière ressource or mon dernier espoir **2** COMP ► **resource centre** N (*Scol, Univ etc*) centre m de documentation

resourced [rɪ'sɔːst] ADJ (*Brit*) **well ~** qui dispose de bonnes ressources; **under-~** qui ne dispose pas des ressources nécessaires

resourceful [rɪ'sɔːsfʊl] ADJ [*person*] plein de ressources, ingénieux

resourcefully [rɪ'sɔːsfəlɪ] ADV d'une manière ingénieuse

resourcefulness [rɪ'sɔːsfʊlnɪs] N (*NonC*) ingéniosité f; **one's own inner ~** ses ressources fpl intérieures

resourcing [rɪ'sɔːsɪŋ] N (*NonC = resources*) ressources fpl

respect [rɪ'spekt] **1** N **a** (*NonC = esteem*) respect m; **to have ~ for** [+ *person*] avoir du respect pour, respecter; [+ *the law, sb's intelligence*] respecter; **I have the greatest ~ for him** j'ai infiniment de respect pour lui; **to treat with ~** traiter avec respect; **to be held in ~** être tenu en haute estime; **he can command ~** il impose le respect, il sait se faire respecter; **she has no ~ for other people's feelings** elle n'a aucune considération or aucun respect pour les sentiments d'autrui; **out of ~ for ...** par respect or égard pour ...; **with (due** or **the greatest) ~ I still think that ...** sans vouloir vous contredire or sauf votre respect je crois toujours que ...; (*frm*) **without ~ of persons** sans acception de personne; **without ~ to the consequences** sans penser or se soucier des conséquences, sans s'arrêter aux conséquences **b** (*NonC = reference, aspect*) **with ~ to ...** pour or en ce qui concerne ..., quant à ..., relativement à ...; **good in ~ of content** bon sous le rapport du contenu or quant au contenu; **in what ~?** sous quel rapport?, à quel égard?; **in some ~s** à certains égards, sous certains rapports; **in many ~s** à bien des égards; **in this ~** à cet égard, sous ce rapport; **in one ~** d'un certain côté; **in other ~s** à d'autres égards **c** **~s** (= *regards*) respects mpl; (*man to woman*) hommages mpl; **to pay one's ~s to sb** présenter ses respects à qn; **give my ~s to ...** présentez mes respects (or mes hommages) à ...

2 VT **a** [+ *person, customs, sb's wishes, opinions, grief, the law*] respecter; **to ~ o.s.** se respecter **b** (*frm*) **as ~s ...** quant à ..., en ce qui concerne ...

respectability [rɪˌspektə'bɪlɪtɪ] N respectabilité f

respectable [rɪ'spektəbl] ADJ [*person, behaviour, motives, size, amount, piece of work*] respectable; [*clothes*] convenable, comme il faut; **young people from ~ homes** des jeunes gens venant de foyers respectables; **he was outwardly ~ but ...** il avait l'apparence de la respectabilité mais ...; **in ~ society** entre gens respectables; **a ~ writer** un écrivain qui n'est pas sans talent; **to finish a ~ second/third** finir honorablement deuxième/troisième; **it is ~ to do sth** il est respectable de faire qch

respectably [rɪ'spektəblɪ] ADV **a** (= *decently*) [*dress, behave*] convenablement, comme il faut; **a ~ married man** un homme marié et respectable **b** (= *adequately*) **he finished ~ in fourth place** il a fini honorablement à la quatrième place

respecter [rɪ'spektə^r] N **death/the law is no ~ of persons** tout le monde est égal devant la mort/la loi; **death is no ~ of wealth** les riches et les pauvres sont égaux devant la mort; **he is no ~ of persons** il ne s'en laisse imposer par personne

respectful [rɪ'spektfʊl] ADJ respectueux (**of sth** de qch, **to(wards)** sb envers qn, à l'égard de qn)

respectfully [rɪˈspɛktfəlɪ] ADV [speak, bow, listen] respectueusement, avec respect; [stand, wait, ask, suggest] respectueusement; [treat] avec respect; **I would ~ disagree with Mr Brown** avec tout le respect que je lui dois, je suis en désaccord avec M. Brown; (in letters) **I remain ~ yours** or **yours ~** je vous prie d'agréer l'expression de mes sentiments respectueux; (man to woman) je vous prie d'agréer l'expression de mes très respectueux hommages

respectfulness [rɪˈspɛktfʊlnɪs] N [of person] attitude f respectueuse; [of tone, manner] caractère m respectueux

respecting [rɪˈspɛktɪŋ] PREP concernant, relatif à

respective [rɪˈspɛktɪv] ADJ respectif

respectively [rɪˈspɛktɪvlɪ] ADV respectivement

respiration [ˌrɛspɪˈreɪʃən] N (Bot, Med) respiration f

respirator [ˈrɛspəˌreɪtər] N (Med) respirateur m; (Mil) masque m à gaz

respiratory [ˈrɛspərətərɪ] **1** ADJ respiratoire **2** COMP ► **respiratory arrest** N arrêt m respiratoire ► **respiratory failure** N insuffisance f or défaillance f respiratoire ► **respiratory system** N système m or respiratoire ► **respiratory tract** N appareil m respiratoire

respire [rɪˈspaɪər] VTI respirer

respite [ˈrɛspaɪt] N répit m, relâche m or f; (Jur) sursis m; **without (a) ~** sans répit, sans relâche

resplendence [rɪˈsplɛndəns] N splendeur f

resplendent [rɪˈsplɛndənt] ADJ resplendissant; **to look ~** être resplendissant; **in a silk dress** resplendissant dans sa robe de soie; **to be ~ with sth** resplendir de qch, être resplendissant de qch

resplendently [rɪˈsplɛndəntlɪ] ADV splendidement

respond [rɪˈspɒnd] VI **a** (= reply) répondre (**to** à, **with** par); (Rel) chanter les répons; **~ to a toast** répondre à un toast **b** (= show reaction to) répondre (**to** à); **brakes that ~ well** freins mpl qui répondent bien; **car that ~s well to controls** voiture f qui a de bonnes réactions or qui répond bien aux commandes; **the patient ~ed to treatment** le malade a bien réagi au traitement; **the illness ~ed to treatment** le traitement a agi sur la maladie

respondent [rɪˈspɒndənt] **1** N **a** (Jur) défendeur m, -deresse f **b** (in opinion poll etc) personne f interrogée, sondé m **2** ADJ qui répond or réagit (**to** à)

response [rɪˈspɒns] **1** N **a** (lit, fig) réponse f; (to treatment) réaction f; **in ~ to** en réponse à; **in ~ to the radio appeal, the sum of £10,000 was raised** à la suite de or en réponse à l'appel radiodiffusé, on a recueilli la somme de 10 000 livres; **his only ~ was to nod** pour toute réponse, il a hoché la tête; **we had hoped for a bigger ~ from the public** nous n'avons pas reçu du public la réponse escomptée **b** (Rel) répons m **2** COMP ► **response time** N [of machine, person, police, ambulance etc] temps m de réponse

▼ **responsibility** [rɪˌspɒnsəˈbɪlɪtɪ] **1** N responsabilité f; **to lay** or **put** or **place the ~ for sth on sb** tenir qn pour responsable de qch, faire porter la responsabilité de qch à qn; **the report placed ~ for the accident on the company** le rapport a déclaré la société responsable de cet accident; **to take ~ for sth** prendre or assumer la responsabilité de qch; **"the company takes no ~ for objects left here"** ≈ «la compagnie décline toute responsabilité pour les objets en dépôt»; **to take on the ~** accepter or assumer la responsabilité; **the group which claimed ~ for the attack** le groupe qui a revendiqué l'attentat; **that's his ~** c'est à lui de s'en occuper; **it's not my ~ to do that** ce n'est pas à moi de faire ça; **on my own**

► **LANGUAGE IN USE:** **responsibility** 18.3

~ sous ma responsabilité; **he wants a position with more ~** il cherche un poste offrant plus de responsabilités; **he has too many responsibilities** il a trop de responsabilités; **it is a big ~ for him** c'est une lourde responsabilité pour lui

2 COMP ► **responsibility allowance, responsibility payment** N prime f de fonction

responsible [rɪˈspɒnsəbl] ADJ **a** (= trustworthy) [person, attitude, organization] responsable **b** (= in charge) responsable (**to sb** devant qn, **for sth** de qch); **~ for sth** responsable de qch, chargé de qch; **~ for doing sth** chargé de faire qch; **who is ~ here?** qui est le responsable ici? **c** (= the cause) **she is ~ for the success of the project** c'est à elle que l'on doit le succès du projet; **he was ~ for improving standards of service** c'est grâce à lui que le service s'est amélioré; **who is ~ for breaking the window?** qui a cassé la vitre?; **CFCs are ~ for destroying the ozone layer** les CFC sont responsables de la destruction de la couche d'ozone; **I demand to know who is ~ for this!** j'exige de savoir qui est responsable or de connaître le responsable!; **to hold sb ~ for sth** tenir qn responsable de qch **d** (= involving or demanding responsibility) **a ~ job** un travail à responsabilité(s)

responsibly [rɪˈspɒnsəblɪ] ADV avec sérieux, de façon responsable

responsive [rɪˈspɒnsɪv] ADJ **a** (= receptive) [audience, class, pupil] réceptif; **he wasn't very ~ when I spoke to him about it** quand je lui en ai parlé, il ne s'est pas montré très réceptif or il n'a pas beaucoup réagi **b** (= ready to react) [person] sensible, réceptif; **to be ~ to sb's needs** être sensible or réceptif aux besoins de qn; **to be ~ to criticism** être sensible à la critique **c** (Med) **to be ~ to antibiotics/treatment** réagir aux antibiotiques/au traitement **d** (= easily controlled) [machine, car, steering] sensible **e** (= answering) **to give a ~ smile/nod** faire un sourire/hocher la tête en guise de réponse

responsiveness [rɪˈspɒnsɪvnɪs] N (NonC = receptiveness) sensibilité f; **the government's ~ to social pressures** l'aptitude f du gouvernement à réagir aux pressions sociales

respray [riːˈspreɪ] **1** VT [+ car] refaire la peinture de **2** [ˈriːspreɪ] N **the car needs a ~** il faut refaire la peinture de la voiture

rest [rɛst] **1** N **a** (gen = relaxation etc) repos m; **a day of ~** un jour de repos; **to need ~** avoir besoin de repos; **to need a ~** avoir besoin de se reposer; **to have a ~** se reposer; **she took** or **had an hour's ~** elle s'est reposée pendant une heure; **we had a couple of ~s during the walk** pendant la promenade nous nous sommes arrêtés deux fois pour nous reposer; **no ~ for the wicked** pas de repos pour les braves; (US Mil) **~ and recuperation** (= leave) permission f; **take a ~!** reposez-vous!; **to have a good night's ~** passer une bonne nuit; (liter) **to retire to ~** se retirer; **at ~** au repos; **to be at ~** (= peaceful) être tranquille or calme; (= immobile) être au repos; (euph = dead) reposer en paix; (lit) **to lay to ~** porter en terre; (fig) **to lay** or **put to ~** [+ idea, notion] enterrer; **to set at ~** [+ fears, doubts] dissiper; **to put** or **set sb's mind** or **heart at ~** tranquilliser qn, rassurer qn; **you can set** or **put your mind at ~** tu peux être tranquille; **to come to ~** [ball, car etc] s'arrêter, s'immobiliser; [bird, insect] se poser; **give it a ~!** (= change the subject) change de disque!; (= stop working) laisse tomber!* **b** (= support for instrument, back, arm etc) support m, appui m → **armrest, receiver c** (= remainder) **the ~ of the money** le reste or ce qui reste de l'argent, l'argent qui reste; **the**

~ of the boys les garçons qui restent, les autres garçons; **I will take half of the money and you keep the ~** je prends la moitié de l'argent et tu gardes le reste or le restant; **I will take this book and you keep the ~** je prends ce livre et tu gardes le reste; **you go off and the ~ of us will wait here** pars, nous (autres) nous attendrons ici; **he was as drunk as the ~ of them** il était aussi ivre que les autres; **all the ~ of the money** tout ce qui reste de l'argent, tout l'argent qui reste; **all the ~ of the books** tous les autres livres; **and all the ~ (of it)** et tout ça*, et tout ce qui s'ensuit; **for the ~** quant au reste

d (Mus) pause f; (Poetry) césure f; (Mus) crotchet (Brit) or **quarter-note** (US) ~ soupir m

2 VI **a** (= repose) se reposer; [the dead] reposer; **she never ~s** elle ne se repose jamais; **you must ~ for an hour** il faut vous reposer pendant une heure; (fig) **he won't ~ till he finds out the truth** il n'aura de cesse qu'il ne découvre (subj) la vérité; (fig) **to ~ easy** dormir sur ses deux oreilles; **to ~ on one's oars** (lit) lever les avirons or les rames; (fig) prendre un repos bien mérité; (fig) **to ~ on one's laurels** se reposer or s'endormir sur ses lauriers; (euph) **to be ~ing** [actor] se trouver sans engagement; **may he ~ in peace** qu'il repose en paix; (Agr) **to let a field ~** laisser reposer un champ, laisser un champ en jachère; (Jur) **"the defence/prosecution ~s"** formule utilisée par les avocats pour conclure leur plaidoyer ou réquisitoire

b (= remain) rester, demeurer; **~ assured that ...** soyez certain or assuré que ...; **he refused to let the matter ~** il refusait d'en rester là; **they agreed to let the matter ~** ils ont convenu d'en rester là; **the matter must not ~ there** l'affaire ne doit pas en rester là; **and there the matter ~s for the moment** l'affaire en est là pour le moment; **the authority ~s with him** c'est lui qui détient l'autorité; **the decision ~s with him ◊ it ~s with him to decide** la décision lui appartient, il lui appartient de décider; **it doesn't ~ with me** cela ne dépend pas de moi **c** (= lean, be supported) [person] s'appuyer (**on** sur, **against** contre); [ladder] être appuyé (**on** sur, **against** contre); [roof etc] reposer (**on** sur); (fig) [argument, reputation, case] reposer (**on** sur); [eyes, gaze] se poser, s'arrêter (**on** sur); **her elbows were ~ing on the table** ses coudes reposaient sur la table; (fig) **a heavy responsibility ~s on him** il a une lourde responsabilité

3 VT **a** (= repose) faire or laisser reposer, donner du repos à; **to ~ o.s.** se reposer; **I am quite ~ed** je me sens tout à fait reposé; **to ~ the horses** laisser reposer les chevaux; **God ~ his soul!** que Dieu ait son âme!, paix à son âme! **b** (Jur) **to ~ one's case** conclure sa plaidoirie; (hum) **I ~ my case!** CQFD! **c** (= lean) poser, appuyer (**on** sur, **against** contre); (fig = base) [+ suspicions] fonder (**on** sur); **to ~ one's hand on sb's shoulder** poser la main sur l'épaule de qn; **to ~ one's elbows on the table** poser les coudes sur la table; **to ~ a ladder against a wall** appuyer une échelle contre un mur

4 COMP ► **rest camp** N (Mil) cantonnement m ► **rest centre** N centre m d'accueil ► **rest cure** N cure f de repos ► **rest day** N jour m de repos ► **rest home, rest house** N maison f de repos ► **resting place** N [of the dead] dernière demeure f ► **rest room** N (US) toilettes fpl ► **rest stop** N (US Aut) (= place) aire f de repos; (= break in journey) pause f (pendant un trajet en voiture ou en bus)

► **rest up*** VI se reposer

restart [riːˈstɑːt] **1** VT [+ work, activity, race] reprendre, recommencer; [+ engine] relancer, remettre en marche; [+ machine] remettre en marche **2** VI reprendre, recommencer; [engine, machine] se remettre en marche **3** N (of race, career) nouveau départ m

restate [ˌriːˈsteɪt] VT [+ argument, reasons] répéter; [+ problem] énoncer de nouveau; [+ theory, case, one's position] exposer de nouveau

restatement [ˌriːˈsteɪtmənt] N (gen) répétition f; [of plan, theory] nouvel énoncé m; (Jur) ~ of the law réexposé m du droit

restaurant [ˈrestərɔ̃ːŋ] **1** N restaurant m **2** COMP [food, prices] de restaurant ► **restaurant car** N (Brit Rail) wagon-restaurant m

restaurateur [ˌrestərəˈtɜːʳ] N restaurateur m, -trice f

restful [ˈrestfʊl] ADJ [sleep] (paisible et) réparateur (-trice f); [atmosphere, lighting, colour, holiday] reposant; [place] paisible, tranquille

restfully [ˈrestfəlɪ] ADV [sleep] paisiblement, tranquillement

restitution [ˌrestɪˈtjuːʃən] N **a** (NonC) restitution f; **to make ~ of sth** restituer qch; (Jur) **~ of conjugal rights** ordre m de réintégration du domicile conjugal **b** (= reparation) réparation f

restive [ˈrestɪv] ADJ **a** (= restless) [horse] rétif; [person] agité; **to grow ~** [horse] devenir rétif; [person] s'agiter **b** (= discontented) [group, crew] agité, indocile; **to grow ~** s'agiter, devenir difficile à contrôler

restiveness [ˈrestɪvnɪs] N agitation f; [of horse] rétivité f, nature f rétive

restless [ˈrestlɪs] **1** ADJ **a** (= unsettled, fidgety) [person, mind, attitude] agité; [child] agité, remuant; [curiosity] insatiable; **to grow ~** [person] s'agiter; **to be ~ (in one's sleep)** avoir un sommeil agité; **to have or spend a ~ night** avoir une nuit agitée **b** (= discontented) [group] agité, indocile; **to get or grow or become ~** s'agiter, devenir difficile à contrôler; [sea] agité; (hum) **the natives are ~** il y a de l'orage dans l'air, il y a de l'eau dans le gaz **c** (liter = moving) [wind] impétueux (liter); [sea] agité **2** COMP ► **restless spirit** N (lit, fig) âme f errante

restlessly [ˈrestlɪslɪ] ADV avec agitation, nerveusement; **to walk ~ up and down** faire nerveusement les cent pas, tourner comme un lion or un ours en cage

restlessness [ˈrestlɪsnɪs] N [of person] agitation f; [of manner] agitation f, nervosité f; [of crowd] impatience f

restock [ˌriːˈstɒk] VT [+ shop, freezer] réapprovisionner; [+ pond, river] repeupler, empoissonner

restoration [ˌrestəˈreɪʃən] **1** N **a** (NonC = return) rétablissement m; (Jur) [of property] restitution f; (Brit Hist) **the Restoration** la Restauration (de la monarchie en 1660) **b** [of text] rétablissement m; [of monument, work of art] restauration f **2** COMP ► **Restoration comedy** N (Brit Theat) théâtre m de la Restauration anglaise

restorative [rɪˈstɔːrətɪv] ADJ, N fortifiant m, reconstituant m

restore [rɪˈstɔːʳ] VT **a** (= give or bring back) [+ sth lost, borrowed, stolen] rendre, restituer (**to** à); [+ sb's sight etc] rendre; (Jur) [+ rights, law etc] rétablir; [+ confidence] redonner (**to sb** à qn, **in** dans); [+ order, calm] rétablir; **to ~ sb's health** rétablir la santé de qn, rendre la santé à qn; **~d to health** rétabli, guéri; **to ~ sb to life** ramener qn à la vie; **the brandy ~d my strength or me** le cognac m'a redonné des forces; **he was ~d to them safe and sound** il leur a été rendu sain et sauf; **to ~ a monarch to the throne** restaurer un monarque; **to ~ sb to power** ramener qn au pouvoir **b** (= repair) [+ building, painting, furniture etc] restaurer; [+ leather goods] rénover; [+ text] restituer, rétablir; **to ~ sth to its former condition** remettre qch en état

restorer [rɪˈstɔːrəʳ] N (Art etc) restaurateur m, -trice f → **hair**

restrain [rɪˈstreɪn] **1** VT **a** (= prevent: gen) retenir; **I was going to do it but he ~ed me** j'allais le faire mais il m'a retenu or m'en a empêché; **to ~ sb from doing sth** empêcher qn de faire qch **b** [+ dangerous person etc] (= overcome) maîtriser; (= control) contenir **c** (= control) [+ one's anger, feelings etc] réprimer, refréner; **please ~ yourself!** je vous en prie dominez-vous! **d** (= restrict) [+ trade etc] restreindre **2** COMP ► **restraining order** N (Jur) injonction f de ne pas faire, ordonnance f restrictive

restrained [rɪˈstreɪnd] ADJ [person] maître (maîtresse f) de soi; [tone, manner, response, reaction, performance, speech] mesuré; [emotion] contenu; [style, décor] sobre; **he was very ~ when he heard the news** quand il a appris la nouvelle, il est resté très maître de soi

restraint [rɪˈstreɪnt] **1** N **a** (= restriction) limitation f (**on sth** de qch), contrainte f; **without ~** sans contrainte **b** (NonC = limiting) frein m, contrôle m; **price ~** contrôle des prix; **fiscal ~** contrôle m de la fiscalité → **wage** **c** (NonC = moderation) [of person, behaviour] modération f, mesure f; [of style, speech] retenue f, mesure f; **his ~ was admirable** il se maîtrisait admirablement; **sexual ~** modération f sexuelle; **to exercise or show ~** faire preuve de modération or de retenue; **to show a lack of ~** manquer de retenue; **with/without ~** [say] avec/sans retenue; [act] avec/sans retenue or modération → **self** **d** (= restraining device: in prison, hospital) entrave f; **to be in ~s** être entravé or attaché; **to put sb in ~s** or (frm) **under ~** entraver qn, attacher qn **e** (= safety device: in car etc) dispositif de sécurité, p. ex. ceinture de sécurité, siège pour bébé; **head ~** appuie-tête m **2** COMP ► **restraint of trade** N (Jur, Fin) atteinte f or entraves fpl à la liberté du commerce

restrict [rɪˈstrɪkt] VT restreindre, limiter (**to** à); **visiting is ~ed to one hour per day** les visites sont limitées à une heure par jour; **to ~ sb's authority/freedom** restreindre or limiter l'autorité/la liberté de qn; **access ~ed to members of staff** accès réservé au personnel, accès interdit aux personnes étrangères à l'établissement

restricted [rɪˈstrɪktɪd] **1** ADJ **a** (= limited) [visibility] réduit; [number, choice, group, circulation] restreint, limité; [space, range, viewpoint, horizon] restreint; [access] (= partial) limité; (= forbidden to some people) réservé; **on a ~ diet** au régime **b** (= hindered) **to feel ~** [person] (physically) se sentir à l'étroit; (by clothes) sentir engoncé; (mentally) avoir l'impression d'étouffer **c** (= classified) [document, information] confidentiel **2** COMP ► **restricted area** N (Admin, Mil = prohibited) zone f interdite; (Brit Aut) zone f à vitesse limitée; (= delimited) **within a ~ area** dans une zone restreinte or limitée ► **restricted code** N (Ling) code m restreint

restriction [rɪˈstrɪkʃən] N restriction f, limitation f; **to place ~s on ...** imposer des restrictions à ...; (Aut) **speed ~** limitation f de vitesse; (Comm) **price ~** contrôle m de prix

restrictive [rɪˈstrɪktɪv] **1** ADJ **a** (= limiting) [measures] de restriction; [law, policy] restrictif; [environment] étouffant **b** (= tight) [clothing] qui gêne le mouvement **2** COMP ► **restrictive clause** N (Gram) proposition f déterminative ► **restrictive practices** NPL (Brit) (by trade unions) pratiques fpl syndicales restrictives; (by manufacturers) atteintes fpl à la libre concurrence ► **restrictive relative clause** N proposition f déterminative

re-string [ˌriːˈstrɪŋ] (pret, ptp **re-strung** [ˌriːˈstrʌŋ]) VT [+ pearls, necklace] renfiler; (Mus) [+ violin] remplacer les cordes de; (Sport) [+ racket] recorder; [+ bow] remplacer la corde de, remettre une corde à

restyle [ˌriːˈstaɪl] VT [+ product] donner un nouveau look* à; **to have one's hair ~d** changer de coiffure; **to ~ sb's hair** changer la coiffure de qn

▼**result** [rɪˈzʌlt] **1** N **a** résultat m, conséquence f; (Math) résultat m; **as a ~ he failed** en conséquence il a échoué, résultat — il a échoué; **to be the ~ of sth** être la conséquence de qch, être dû à qch, résulter de qch; **as a ~ of** (= directly because of: esp Admin) par suite de; **he died as a ~ of his injuries** il est décédé des suites de ses blessures; **without ~** sans résultat **b** [of election, exam, race] résultat m; **to demand ~s** exiger des résultats; **to get ~s*** [person] obtenir de bons résultats, arriver à quelque chose*; [action] donner de bons résultats, aboutir **2** VI résulter (**from** de); **it ~s that ...** il s'ensuit que ...
► **result in** VT FUS [+ higher/lower level, increased efficiency, changes, loss] entraîner, conduire à; [+ damage, injury, death] occasionner; [+ failure] se solder par

resultant [rɪˈzʌltənt] **1** ADJ **victims of the war and the ~ famine** les victimes de la guerre et de la famine qui en a résulté or qui s'est ensuivie **2** N (Math) résultante f

resume [rɪˈzjuːm] **1** VT **a** (= restart etc) [+ tale, account] reprendre; [+ activity, discussions] reprendre, recommencer; [+ relations] renouer; **to ~ work** reprendre le travail, se remettre au travail; **to ~ one's journey** reprendre la route, continuer son voyage; **"well" he ~d** « eh bien » reprit-il; (frm) **to ~ one's seat** se rasseoir; (frm) **to ~ possession of sth** reprendre possession de qch **b** (= sum up) résumer **2** VI [classes, work etc] reprendre, recommencer

résumé [ˈreɪzjuːmeɪ] N résumé m; (US) curriculum vitæ m inv

resumption [rɪˈzʌmpʃən] N reprise f; [of diplomatic relations] rétablissement m

resurface [ˌriːˈsɜːfɪs] **1** VT [+ road] refaire la surface de **2** VI [diver, submarine] remonter à la or en surface, faire surface; (fig = reappear) refaire surface; **she ~d* after a year of mourning** elle a recommencé à sortir après un an de deuil

resurgence [rɪˈsɜːdʒəns] N (gen) résurgence f; (Econ) reprise f

resurgent [rɪˈsɜːdʒənt] ADJ [nationalism, fundamentalism] renaissant, qui connaît un nouvel essor; (Econ) [spending] en nette augmentation

resurrect [ˌrezəˈrekt] VT (Rel) ressusciter; (fig) [+ fashion, ideas] ressortir du placard; [+ career, debate] reprendre; (* hum) [+ dress, chair etc] remettre en service

resurrection [ˌrezəˈrekʃən] N (Rel, fig) résurrection f

resuscitate [rɪˈsʌsɪteɪt] VT (gen) faire revivre; (Med) réanimer

resuscitation [rɪˌsʌsɪˈteɪʃən] N réanimation f

resuscitator [rɪˈsʌsɪteɪtəʳ] N (Med) réanimateur m

retail [ˈriːteɪl] **1** N (vente f au) détail m **2** VT vendre au détail; (fig) [+ gossip] colporter, répandre **3** VI [goods] se vendre (au détail) (**at** à) **4** ADV **to buy/sell ~** acheter/vendre au détail **5** COMP ► **retail banking** N (Fin) opérations bancaires portant sur les comptes personnels ► **retail business** N commerce m de détail ► **retail dealer** N détaillant(e) m(f) ► **retail outlet** N **they are looking for a ~ outlet for ...** ils cherchent un débouché pour ...; **50 ~ outlets** 50 points mpl de vente ► **retail park** N (Brit) centre m commercial ► **retail price** N prix m de détail; **~ price index** ≈ indice m des prix de l'INSEE ► **retail shop** (Brit), **retail store** (US) N magasin m de détail, détaillant m ► **the retail trade** N (=

► LANGUAGE IN USE: **result** 17, 26.3

traders) les détaillants *mpl* ; (= *selling*) la vente au détail

retailer [ˈriːteɪləʳ] N détaillant(e) *m(f)*

retain [rɪˈteɪn] VT **a** (= *keep*) conserver, garder ; (= *hold*) retenir, maintenir ; [+ *heat*] conserver ; **~ing wall** mur *m* de soutènement ; **to ~ control (of)** garder le contrôle (de) ; (*Fin*) **~ed earnings** bénéfices *mpl* non distribués **b** (= *remember*) garder en mémoire **c** (= *engage*) [+ *lawyer*] retenir, engager ; **~ing fee** = **retainer b**

retainer [rɪˈteɪnəʳ] N **a** (†, *liter* = *servant*) serviteur *m* **b** (= *fee*) acompte *m*, avance *f* sur honoraires ; (*to lawyer*) provision *f* ; (= *rent*) caution *f* (*versée à titre de loyer réduit par un locataire lors de son absence*) ; **to be on a ~** être sous contrat (*garantissant une disponibilité future*)

retake [ˈriːteɪk] (*vb: pret* **retook**, *ptp* **retaken**) **1** N **a** (*Cine*) nouvelle prise *f* (de vues) **b** (= *exam*) deuxième session *f* (*d'un examen*) ; **to fail one's (chemistry) ~s** échouer une deuxième fois à ses examens (de chimie) **2** [ˌriːˈteɪk] VT **a** reprendre ; [+ *prisoner*] reprendre, rattraper **b** (*Cine*) faire une nouvelle prise de **c** [+ *exam*] se représenter à, repasser

retaliate [rɪˈtælɪeɪt] VI se venger (**against sb/sth** de qn/qch), user de représailles (**against sb** envers qn) ; **he ~d by breaking a window** pour se venger il a brisé une fenêtre ; **he ~d by pointing out that ...** il a riposté *or* rétorqué que ..., pour sa part il a fait observer que ... ; **to ~ (up)on sb** rendre la pareille à qn, user de représailles envers qn

retaliation [rɪˌtælɪˈeɪʃən] N représailles *fpl* ; **in ~** par mesure de représailles ; **in ~ for ...** pour venger ..., pour se venger de ... ; **policy of ~** politique *f* de représailles

retaliatory [rɪˈtælɪətərɪ] ADJ (*frm*) de représailles ; **~ measures** (*gen, Mil*) (mesures *fpl* de) représailles *fpl* ; (*Econ*) mesures *fpl* de rétorsion

retard [rɪˈtɑːd] **1** VT retarder **2** N retard *m*

retarded [rɪˈtɑːdɪd] **1** ADJ (*also* **mentally ~**) arriéré **2 the retarded** NPL (*also* **the mentally ~**) les attardés *mpl* (mentaux) **3** COMP **► retarded acceleration** N (*Tech*) accélération *f* négative **► retarded ignition** N (*Aut*) retard *m* à l'allumage

retch [retʃ] **1** VI avoir des haut-le-cœur **2** N haut-le-cœur *m*

retching [ˈretʃɪŋ] N haut-le-cœur *m inv*

retd ABBR = **retired**

retell [ˌriːˈtel] (*pret, ptp* **retold**) VT raconter encore une fois

retention [rɪˈtenʃən] N (*NonC*) (= *keeping*) maintien *m* ; (*Med*) rétention *f* ; (= *memory*) mémoire *f*

retentive [rɪˈtentɪv] ADJ **a ~ memory** *or* **mind** une mémoire fidèle **b** **anal**, **anally**

retentiveness [rɪˈtentɪvnɪs] N faculté *f* de retenir, mémoire *f*

rethink [ˌriːˈθɪŋk] (*pret, ptp* **rethought** [ˌriːˈθɔːt]) **1** VT repenser **2** [ˈriːθɪŋk] N **we'll have to have a ~** nous allons devoir y réfléchir encore un coup*

reticence [ˈretɪsəns] N réticence *f*

reticent [ˈretɪsənt] ADJ réservé ; **~ about sth** réticent à parler de qch

reticently [ˈretɪsəntlɪ] ADV avec réticence, avec réserve

reticle [ˈretɪkl] N (*Opt*) réticule *m*

reticulate [rɪˈtɪkjʊlɪt], **reticulated** [rɪˈtɪkjʊleɪtɪd] ADJ réticulé

reticule [ˈretɪkjuːl] N **a** = **reticle b** (= *handbag*) réticule† *m*

retina [ˈretɪnə] N (*pl* **retinas** *or* **retinae** [ˈretɪniː]) rétine *f*

retinal [ˈretɪnl] ADJ rétinien

retinue [ˈretɪnjuː] N escorte *f*

retire [rɪˈtaɪəʳ] **1** VI **a** (= *withdraw*) se retirer, partir ; (*Mil*) reculer, se replier ; [*jury*] se retirer ; (*Sport*) abandonner ; **to ~ from the room** quitter la pièce ; **to ~ to the lounge** se retirer au salon, passer au salon ; (*Sport*) **to ~ hurt** abandonner à la suite d'une blessure ; **to ~ into o.s.** rentrer en *or* se replier sur soi-même ; **to ~ from the world/from public life** se retirer du monde/de la vie publique **b** († = *go to bed*) (aller) se coucher **c** (= *give up one's work*) prendre sa retraite **2** VT [+ *worker, employee*] mettre à la retraite ; (*Fin*) [+ *bond*] retirer de la circulation ; **to be compulsorily ~d** être mis à la retraite d'office

retired [rɪˈtaɪəd] **1** ADJ **a** (= *no longer working*) à la retraite ; **a ~ person** retraité(e) **b** (= *secluded*) [*life, spot*] retiré **2** COMP **► retired list** N (*Mil*) état *m* des mises à la retraite **► retired pay** N pension *f* de retraite

retiree [rɪtaɪˈriː] N (*US*) retraité(e) *m(f)*

retirement [rɪˈtaɪəmənt] **1** N **a** (= *stopping work*) retraite *f* ; **~ at 60** (mise *f* à la) retraite à 60 ans ; **to announce one's ~** annoncer que l'on prend sa retraite ; **to come out of ~** reprendre ses activités *or* une occupation *or* du service (*après avoir pris sa retraite*) ; **how will you spend your ~?** qu'est-ce que vous ferez quand vous aurez pris votre retraite ? → **compulsory, early**
b (= *seclusion*) isolement *m*, solitude *f* ; **to live in ~** vivre retiré du monde
c (*Mil*) retraite *f*, repli *m* ; (*Sport*) abandon *m* **2** COMP **► retirement age** N âge *m* de la retraite **► retirement benefit** N prime *f* *or* indemnité *f* de départ en retraite **► retirement community** N (*US*) communauté *f* de retraités **► retirement home** N (*personal*) maison *f* pour sa retraite ; (*communal*) maison *f* de retraite **► retirement pay** N retraite *f* **► retirement pension** N (pension *f* de) retraite *f* ; (*Mil*) solde *f* de retraite **► retirement relief** N (*Brit*) exonération, dont bénéficient les retraités, sur les plus-values en capital → **pension**

retiring [rɪˈtaɪərɪŋ] **1** ADJ **a** (= *shy*) [*person*] réservé **b** (= *outgoing*) [*chairman, president*] sortant **c** (= *taking retirement*) qui part en retraite **d ~ room** cabinet *m* particulier **2** COMP **► retiring age** N âge *m* de la retraite

retold [ˌriːˈtəʊld] VB *pt, ptp of* **retell**

retook [ˌriːˈtʊk] VB *pt of* **retake**

retool [ˌriːˈtuːl] **1** VT [+ *factory*] rééquiper ; [+ *machine*] renouveler **2** VI se rééquiper

retort [rɪˈtɔːt] **1** N **a** (= *answer*) réplique *f*, riposte *f* **b** (*Chem*) cornue *f* **2** VT répliquer (**that** que) ; **"not at all" he ~ed** « pas du tout » répliqua-t-il

retouch [ˌriːˈtʌtʃ] VT (*Art, Phot*) retoucher

retrace [rɪˈtreɪs] VT [+ *developments etc*] (= *research into*) reconstituer ; (= *give account of*) retracer ; **to ~ one's path** *or* **steps** revenir sur ses pas, rebrousser chemin

retract [rɪˈtrækt] **1** VT **a** (= *withdraw*) [+ *offer, evidence*] retirer ; [+ *statement*] retirer, revenir sur **b** (= *draw back*) [+ *undercarriage, aerial*] rentrer ; [+ *claws*] rentrer, rétracter ; [+ *tentacles, snail's horns*] rétracter **2** VI **a** (= *withdraw statement etc*) se rétracter **b** (= *draw back*) se rétracter ; [*undercarriage, blade, aerial*] rentrer

retractable [rɪˈtræktəbl] ADJ [*undercarriage, aerial, roof*] escamotable ; [*blade*] rentrant ; [*claws, tentacles etc*] rétractile ; [*ball-point pen*] à pointe rétractable ; **~ tape measure** mètre *m* ruban (à enrouleur)

retraction [rɪˈtrækʃən] N [*of statement, offer*] rétractation *f* ; [*of claws etc*] rétraction *f* ; [*of undercarriage*] escamotage *m*

retrain [ˌriːˈtreɪn] **1** VT recycler **2** VI se recycler

retraining [ˌriːˈtreɪnɪŋ] N recyclage *m*

retransmit [ˌriːtrænzˈmɪt] VT réexpédier ; (*Phys, Rad, TV*) retransmettre

retread [ˌriːˈtred] **1** VT [+ *tyre*] rechaper **2** [ˈriːtred] N (= *tyre*) pneu *m* rechapé

retreat [rɪˈtriːt] **1** N **a** (*also Mil*) retraite *f* ; **the army is in ~** l'armée bat en retraite ; **to sound the ~** battre la retraite ; **to make** *or* **beat a hasty ~** battre en retraite **b** (*St Ex: of currency*) repli *m* ; **the pound went into ~** la livre a cédé du terrain **c** (= *place: also Rel*) retraite *f* ; **to go on a ~** faire une retraite ; **a country ~** un endroit (*or* une maison *etc*) tranquille à la campagne **2** VI (*Mil*) battre en retraite ; (= *withdraw*) se retirer (**from** de) ; [*flood, glacier*] reculer ; [*chin, forehead*] être fuyant ; **~ing** [*army, troops*] en retraite ; (*fig*) **to ~ from** [+ *promise, belief etc*] abandonner, se défaire de **3** VT (*Chess*) ramener

retrench [rɪˈtrentʃ] **1** VI réduire ses dépenses **2** VT restreindre, réduire

retrenchment [rɪˈtrentʃmənt] N **a** (= *cutting back*) réduction *f* (des dépenses) **b** (*Mil*) retranchement *m*

retrial [ˌriːˈtraɪəl] N (*Jur*) révision *f* de procès

retribution [ˌretrɪˈbjuːʃən] N châtiment *m*

retributive [rɪˈtrɪbjʊtɪv] ADJ (*frm*) punitif

retrievable [rɪˈtriːvəbl] ADJ [*object, material*] récupérable ; [*money*] recouvrable ; [*error, loss*] réparable ; (*Comput*) accessible

retrieval [rɪˈtriːvəl] N **a** (*Comput*) extraction *f* ; **data ~** extraction *f* de données **b** (= *recovery*) [*of object*] récupération *f* ; [*of money*] recouvrement *m* ; [*of memories*] rappel *m*

retrieve [rɪˈtriːv] **1** VT (= *recover*) [+ *object*] récupérer (**from** de) ; [*dog*] rapporter ; (*Fin*) recouvrer ; (*Comput*) retrouver ; [+ *information*] rechercher et extraire ; [+ *fortune, honour, position*] rétablir ; (= *set to rights*) [+ *error*] réparer ; [+ *situation*] redresser, sauver ; (= *rescue*) sauver, tirer (**from** de) ; (*lit, fig*) **we shall ~ nothing from this disaster** nous ne sauverons *or* récupérerons rien de ce désastre **2** VI [*dog*] rapporter

retriever [rɪˈtriːvəʳ] N retriever *m*, chien *m* d'arrêt

retro [ˈretrəʊ] ADJ [*fashion, music*] rétro *inv*

retro- [ˈretrəʊ] PREF rétro...

retroactive [ˌretrəʊˈæktɪv] ADJ (*frm*) [*pay rise, legislation*] rétroactif ; **~ to 1 October** avec effet rétroactif au 1er octobre ; (*on salary*) **~ payment** rappel *m*

retroactively [ˌretrəʊˈæktɪvlɪ] ADV rétroactivement

retroengine [ˈretrəʊˌendʒɪn] N rétrofusée *f*

retrofit [ˈretrəʊfɪt] VT (*Tech*) [+ *machine, system*] modifier les équipements de

retroflex(ed) [ˈretrəʊfleks(t)] ADJ (*Ling*) apical, rétroflexe

retroflexion [ˌretrəʊˈflekʃən] N (*Med*) rétroflexion *f*

retrograde [ˈretrəʊgreɪd] **1** ADJ (*also Astron*) rétrograde **2** VI rétrograder

retrogress [ˌretrəʊˈgres] VI rétrograder

retrogression [ˌretrəʊˈgreʃən] N régression *f*

retrogressive [ˌretrəʊˈgresɪv] ADJ rétrograde ; (*Bio*) régressif

retropack [ˈretrəʊpæk] N système *m* de rétrofusées

retrorocket [ˈretrəʊˌrɒkɪt] N rétrofusée *f*

retrospect [ˈretrəʊspekt] N examen *m* *or* coup *m* d'œil rétrospectif ; **in ~** rétrospectivement

retrospection [ˌretrəʊˈspekʃən] N examen *m* rétrospectif

retrospective [ˌretrəʊˈspektɪv] **1** ADJ [*survey, emotion*] rétrospectif ; [*pay rise, effect, legislation*] rétroactif ; (*Art*) **~ exhibition** rétrospective *f* **2** N (*Art*) rétrospective *f*

retrospectively [ˌretrəʊˈspektɪvlɪ] ADV (gen) rétrospectivement; (Admin, Jur) rétroactivement

retrovirus [ˈretrəʊˌvaɪərəs] N rétrovirus m

retry [ˌriːˈtraɪ] VT (Jur) juger de nouveau

retune [ˌriːˈtjuːn] **1** VI (Rad) (= adjust tuning) rajuster le réglage; (= change station/frequency) changer de station/fréquence; **to ~ to FM** passer sur FM **2** VT [+ musical instrument] réaccorder; [+ engine] modifier le réglage de; (Rad) [+ set] régler **3** [ˈriːtjuːn] N [of engine] révision f

return [rɪˈtɜːn] **1** VI [person, vehicle etc] (= come back) revenir; (= go back) retourner; [property] retourner, revenir (**to** à); [symptoms, doubts, fears] réapparaître; **to ~ home** rentrer; **have they ~ed?** sont-ils revenus ou rentrés?; **his good spirits ~ed** sa bonne humeur est revenue; **to ~ to one's work** se remettre à ou reprendre son travail; **to ~ to school** rentrer (en classe); **to ~ to a subject/an idea** revenir à un sujet/une idée; **to ~ to what we were talking about, he ...** pour en revenir à la question, il ...; **to ~ to one's bad habits** reprendre ses mauvaises habitudes

2 VT **a** (= give back) (gen) rendre; [+ sth borrowed, stolen, lost] rendre, restituer; (= bring back) rapporter; [+ goods to shop] rendre, rapporter; (= put back) remettre; (= send back) renvoyer, retourner; [+ ball, sound, light] renvoyer; [+ compliment, salute, blow, visit] rendre; [+ sb's love] répondre à; **to ~ money to sb** rembourser qn; **he ~ed the £5 to him** il lui a remboursé les 5 livres, il l'a remboursé des 5 livres; **to ~ a book to the library** rapporter ou rendre un livre à la bibliothèque; **to ~ a book to the shelf** remettre un livre sur le rayon; **he ~ed it to his pocket** il l'a remis dans sa poche; (on letter) "**~ to sender**" «retour à l'envoyeur»; (liter) **to ~ thanks** rendre grâce, remercier; **to ~ the favour** renvoyer l'ascenseur* (fig); **to ~ sb's favour** rendre service à qn (en retour); **I hope to ~ your kindness** j'espère pouvoir vous rendre service en retour; **his love was not ~ed** elle n'a pas répondu à son amour; **to ~ good for evil** rendre le bien pour le mal; **to ~ like for like** rendre la pareille; (Bridge) **to ~ hearts** rejouer du cœur, renvoyer cœur; (Tennis etc) **to ~ the ball** renvoyer la balle; **backhand well ~ed by ...** revers bien repris par ... → **fire**

b (= reply) répondre, répliquer

c (= declare) [+ income, details] déclarer; (Jur) **to ~ a verdict** rendre ou prononcer un verdict; (Jur) **to ~ a verdict of guilty on sb** déclarer qn coupable; **to ~ a verdict of murder** conclure au meurtre

d (Fin) [+ profit, income] rapporter, donner

e (Parl) [+ candidate] élire; **he was ~ed by an overwhelming majority** il a été élu à ou avec une très forte majorité

3 N **a** (= coming, going back) [of person, illness, seasons] retour m; **on my ~** à mon retour; **my ~ home** mon retour; **after their ~ to school** après la rentrée (des classes); **by ~ of post** par retour du courrier; **a ~ to one's old habits** un retour à ses vieilles habitudes; **many happy ~s (of the day)!** bon anniversaire! → **point**

b (= giving back) retour m; (= sending back) renvoi m; (= putting back) remise f en place; [of sth lost, stolen, borrowed] restitution f; [of money] remboursement m → **sale**

c (Brit: also **~ ticket**) aller et retour m, aller-retour m; **two ~s to London** deux allers et retours pour Londres, deux allers-retours pour Londres

d (= recompense) récompense f (**for** de); (from land, business, mine) rendement m, rapport m; (from investments, shares) rapport m; **~s** (= profits) bénéfice m, profit m; (= receipts) rentrées fpl, recettes fpl; **small profits and quick ~s** de bas prix et un gros chiffre d'affaires; (Fin) **~ on capital** rapport m de capital; **~ on**

investments rentabilité f des investissements; **to get a poor ~ for one's kindness** être mal récompensé ou mal payé de sa gentillesse; **in ~** en revanche; **in ~ for** en récompense de, en échange de

e (= act of declaring) [of verdict] déclaration f; [of election results] proclamation f; (= report) rapport m, relevé m; (= statistics) statistique f; **official ~s** statistiques fpl officielles; **the population ~s show that ...** le recensement montre que ...; **the election ~s** les résultats mpl de l'élection; **tax ~** (feuille f de) déclaration f de revenus ou d'impôts

f (Parl) [of candidate] élection f

g (Sport) riposte f; (Tennis) retour m; **~ of service** retour m de service

h (Comput etc) **~ (key)** (touche f) «retour»

4 COMP ► **return fare** N (Brit) (prix m) aller-retour m, aller et retour m ► **return flight** N (Brit) (= journey back) vol m (de) retour; (= two-way journey) vol m aller-retour ► **return half** N [of ticket] coupon m de retour ► **returning officer** N (Pol) président m du bureau de vote ► **return item** N (Fin) impayé m ► **return journey** N (Brit) (voyage m ou trajet m de) retour m ► **return match** N (Brit) revanche f, match m retour ► **return stroke** N (Tech) mouvement m de retour ► **return ticket** N (Brit) (billet m d')aller (et) retour m ► **return visit** N → **return visit**

returnable [rɪˈtɜːnəbl] ADJ [bottle, container] consigné; **~ deposit** caution f

returnee [rɪˌtɜːˈniː] N (Pol) personne qui retourne dans son pays après une longue absence

returner [rɪˈtɜːnə⟩] N (Ind) femme qui reprend le travail après avoir élevé ses enfants

return visit [rɪˈtɜːnˈvɪzɪt] N **a** (= repeat visit) deuxième ou nouvelle visite f; (for check-up) visite f de contrôle; **to make** ou **pay a ~** (= go back) retourner; (= come back) revenir; **in 1979, the Pope made his first ~ to Poland** en 1979, le pape est retourné (ou revenu) pour la première fois en Pologne; **towards the end of his career he made a nostalgic ~ to Germany** vers la fin de sa carrière, il est retourné (or revenu) en Allemagne par nostalgie **b** (= returning sb's visit: to person who has visited you) **it is hoped that a ~ by our German friends can be arranged** on espère que nos amis allemands pourront nous rendre visite à leur tour; **the exchange went well and Moscow was invited to send an economist on a ~** l'échange s'est bien passé et on a invité Moscou à envoyer à son tour un économiste

retype [ˌriːˈtaɪp] VT retaper (à la machine)

reunification [ˌriːjuːnɪfɪˈkeɪʃən] N réunification f; **since German ~** depuis la réunification allemande

reunify [ˌriːˈjuːnɪfaɪ] VT réunifier

reunion [rɪˈjuːnjən] N réunion f

Réunion [riːˈjuːnjən] N **~ (Island)** (l'île f de) la Réunion

reunite [ˌriːjuːˈnaɪt] **1** VT réunir; **they were ~d at last** ils se sont enfin retrouvés **2** VI se réunir

re-up‡ [ˌriːˈʌp] VI (US Mil) rempiler*, se réengager

re-usable [ˌriːˈjuːzəbl] ADJ réutilisable

re-use [ˌriːˈjuːz] VT réutiliser

rev [rev] **1** N (Aut) (ABBR = **revolution**) tour m; **~ counter** compte-tours m inv; **4,000 ~s per minute** 4 000 tours minute **2** VT = **rev up 2a** **3** VI = **rev up 1a**

► **rev up**‡ **1** VI **a** [engine] s'emballer; [driver] emballer le moteur **b** (= prepare) se préparer (**for** pour) **2** VT SEP **a** [+ engine] emballer **b** (fig) [+ production] accélérer; **to be ~ved up for sth** (= eager) être fin prêt pour qch

Rev. ABBR = **Reverend**

revaluation [ˌriːvæljʊˈeɪʃən] N (Fin) réévaluation f

revalue [ˌriːˈvælju:] VT (Fin) réévaluer

revamp* [ˌriːˈvæmp] VT [+ company, department] réorganiser; [+ house, room, object] retaper*

revanchism [rɪˈvæntʃɪzəm] N revanchisme m

revanchist [rɪˈvæntʃɪst] N, ADJ revanchiste mf

Revd ABBR = **Reverend**

reveal [rɪˈviːl] VT (gen) révéler; (= make visible) [+ hidden object etc] découvrir, laisser voir; (= make known) révéler (**that** que); [+ truth, facts] révéler, faire connaître; [+ corruption] révéler, mettre à jour; **I cannot ~ to you what he said** je ne peux pas vous révéler ce qu'il a dit; **to ~ one's identity** se faire connaître, révéler son identité; **he ~ed himself as being ...** il s'est révélé comme étant ...; **his condition ~ed itself as (being) psychological in origin** ses problèmes se sont avérés avoir une cause psychologique; **~ed religion** religion f révélée

revealing [rɪˈviːlɪŋ] ADJ **a** (= telling) [insight, glimpse, book, comment] révélateur (-trice f) **b** [dress, blouse etc] (gen) suggestif; (= see-through) transparent; (= low-cut) très décolleté

revealingly [rɪˈviːlɪŋlɪ] ADV **~, most of his clients are women** il est révélateur que la plupart de ses clients soient des femmes; **he ~ remarked that he'd never read the book in question** il a eu une remarque révélatrice lorsqu'il a dit qu'il n'avait jamais lu le livre en question

reveille [rɪˈvælɪ] N (Mil) réveil m → **sound**¹

revel [ˈrevl] **1** VI **a** (= make merry) s'amuser, se divertir; (= carouse) faire la fête **b** (= delight) se délecter (**in sth** de qch); **to ~ in doing sth** se délecter à faire qch, prendre grand plaisir à faire qch **2** **revels** NPL (= entertainment) divertissements mpl; (= carousing) festivités fpl

revelation [ˌrevəˈleɪʃən] N révélation f; (Rel) **(the Book of) Revelation** l'Apocalypse f

revelatory [ˌrevəˈleɪtərɪ] ADJ révélateur (-trice f) → **self**

reveller, reveler (US) [ˈrevlə⟩] N fêtard m, joyeux convive m; **the ~s** les gens mpl de la fête, les fêtards mpl

revelry [ˈrevlrɪ] N (NonC) festivités fpl

revenge [rɪˈvendʒ] **1** N (lit) vengeance f; (fig, Sport etc) revanche f; **to take ~ on sb for sth** se venger de qch sur qn; **to get one's ~** se venger; **to do sth out of** ou **in ~** faire qch par vengeance; **in ~ he killed him** pour se venger il l'a tué **2** VT [+ insult, murder] venger; **to ~ o.s. ◊ to be ~d** (gen) se venger (**on sb** de qn, **on sb for sth** de qch sur qn); (in sport competition etc) prendre sa revanche (**on sb** sur qn, **for sth** de qch)

revengeful [rɪˈvendʒfʊl] ADJ [person] vindicatif; [act] vengeur (-geresse f)

revengefully [rɪˈvendʒfəlɪ] ADV vindicativement

revenger [rɪˈvendʒə⟩] N vengeur m, -geresse f

revenue [ˈrevənju:] **1** N [of state] recettes fpl; [of individual] revenu m → **inland** **2** COMP ► **revenue man**† N (pl **revenue men**) douanier m ► **revenue officer** N agent m ou employé(e) m(f) des douanes ► **revenue sharing** N (US Econ) redistribution d'une partie des impôts fédéraux aux autorités locales ► **revenue stamp** N timbre m fiscal

reverb* [rɪˈvɜːb] N (NonC = effect) écho m

reverberate [rɪˈvɜːbəreɪt] **1** VI [sound] retentir, résonner, se répercuter; [room] résonner (**with** de); (fig) [protests etc] se propager **2** VT [+ sound] renvoyer, répercuter; [+ light] réverbérer, réfléchir; [+ heat] réverbérer

reverberation [rɪˌvɜːbəˈreɪʃən] N [of sound] répercussion f; [of room] résonance f; (fig = effect) retentissements mpl; (fig) **to send ~s around the world** avoir des répercussions dans le monde entier

reverberator [rɪˈvɜːbəreɪtə⟩] N réflecteur m

revere [rɪˈvɪə⟩] VT révérer, vénérer

revered [rɪˈvɪəd] ADJ vénéré

reverence ['revərəns] **1** N **a** (= *respect*) vénération *f*; **to have** or **for sb ◊ to hold sb in** ~ révérer qn; **to show** or **pay** ~ **to** rendre hommage à **b** **your Reverence** ≈ mon (révérend) père **2** VT révérer

reverend ['revərənd] **1** ADJ **a** (*Rel*) (*Anglican*) **the** ~ **gentleman** le révérend; (*in titles*) **the Reverend (Robert) Martin** (*Anglican*) le révérend (Robert) Martin; (*Nonconformist*) le pasteur (Robert) Martin; (*Anglican, Nonconformist*) **yes, Reverend*** oui, mon révérend; **the Most Reverend** le Révérendissime; (*Anglican*) **the Very** or **Right Reverend Robert Martin** le très révérend Robert Martin; **Reverend Mother** révérende mère *f* **b** († = *venerable*) vénérable **2** N (*: Protestant*) pasteur *m*

reverent ['revərənt] ADJ (*frm*) déférent

reverential [,revə'renʃəl] ADJ (*frm*) [*tone, attitude, respect*] révérencieux

reverently ['revərəntlɪ] ADV (*frm*) [*say*] révérencieusement, avec déférence; [*speak, look at*] avec déférence

reverie ['revərɪ] N rêverie *f*

revers [rɪ'vɪə'] N (*pl* **revers** [rɪ'vɪəz]) revers *m* (*d'un vêtement*)

reversal [rɪ'vɜːsəl] N **a** (= *turning upside down*) (*also fig*) [*of policy, roles, trend*] renversement *m*; (= *switching over of two objects*) interversion *f*; [*of opinion, view etc*] revirement *m*; (*Jur*) [*of judgement*] arrêt *m* d'annulation, réforme *f* **b** (= *failure*) revers *m*

▼ **reverse** [rɪ'vɜːs] **1** ADJ [*process, situation, motion*] inverse; [*effect*] inverse, contraire; **in the** ~ **direction** en sens inverse; **in** ~ **order** dans l'ordre inverse; ~ **side** [*of coin, medal*] revers *m*; [*of sheet of paper*] verso *m*; [*of cloth*] envers *m*; [*of painting*] dos *m*

2 N **a** (= *opposite*) contraire *m*; **quite the** ~! au contraire!; **it is quite the** ~ c'est tout le contraire; **he is the** ~ **of polite** il est tout sauf poli; (*fig*) **in** ~ dans l'ordre inverse → **2d** **b** (= *back*) [*of coin, medal*] revers *m*; [*of sheet of paper*] verso *m*; [*of cloth*] envers *m*; [*of painting*] dos *m* **c** (= *setback, loss*) revers *m*, échec *m*; (= *defeat*) revers *m*, défaite *f* **d** (*Aut*) **in** ~ en marche arrière; (*fig*) **to go into** ~ [*process, one's fortunes etc*] renverser la vapeur

3 VT **a** (= *turn the other way round*) renverser, retourner; [*garment*] retourner; [+ *situation*] renverser, changer complètement; [+ *photo, result*] inverser; **to** ~ **the order of things** inverser l'ordre des choses; **to** ~ **one's policy** faire volte-face (*fig*); **to** ~ **a procedure** procéder par ordre inverse; **to** ~ **a trend** renverser une tendance; (*Brit Telec*) **to** ~ **the charges** téléphoner en PCV; **to** ~ **the position(s) of two objects** intervertir or inverser deux objets **b** (= *cause to move backwards*) [+ *moving belt*] renverser la direction or la marche de; [+ *typewriter ribbon*] changer de sens; (*Tech*) **to** ~ **the engine** faire machine arrière; **to** ~ **one's car into the garage/down the hill** rentrer dans le garage/descendre la côte en marche arrière; **he** ~**d the car into a tree** il a heurté un arbre en faisant une marche arrière; **to** ~ **one's car across the road** faire une marche arrière en travers de la route **c** (*Jur* = *annul*) [+ *decision, verdict*] réformer, annuler; [+ *judgement*] réformer, déjuger; [+ *sentence*] révoquer, casser **4** VI (*Brit*) (= *move backwards*) [*car*] faire marche arrière; [*dancer*] renverser; (*Aut*) **to** ~ **into the garage/out of the driveway/down the hill** rentrer dans le garage/sortir de l'allée/descendre la côte en marche arrière; **to** ~ **into a tree** heurter un arbre en faisant une marche arrière; **to** ~ **across the road** faire une marche arrière en travers de la route **5** COMP ► **reverse-charge call** N (*Brit Telec*) (appel *m* or communication *f* en) PCV *m*

► **reverse discrimination** N (*US*) discrimination *f* en faveur des minorités ► **reverse gear** N (*Aut*) marche *f* arrière ► **reverse racism** N (*US*) racisme *m* à l'envers ► **reverse turn** N (*Aut*) virage *m* en marche arrière; (*Dancing*) renversement *m* ► **reversing light** N (*Brit Aut*) feu *m* de marche arrière, feu *m* de recul

► **reverse out** VT FUS (*Typ*) passer du noir au blanc

reversibility [rɪ,vɜːsɪ'bɪlɪtɪ] N réversibilité *f*

reversible [rɪ'vɜːsəbl] ADJ [*process, effect, operation, coat, jacket*] réversible; [*decision*] révocable

reversion [rɪ'vɜːʃən] N **a** (= *return to former state*) retour *m* (**to** à); (*Bio*) réversion *f*; **b** (*Jur*) **to** ~ **type** réversion *f* au type primitif **b** (*Jur*) réversion *f*, droit *m* de retour **c** (*Phot*) inversion *f*

reversionary [rɪ'vɜːʃnərɪ] ADJ **a** (*Jur*) de réversion, réversible **b** (*Bio*) atavique, régressif

revert [rɪ'vɜːt] VI **a** (= *return*) revenir (**to** à); (*Jur*) revenir, retourner (**to** à); [*property*] faire retour (**to** à); **to** ~ **to the question** pour en revenir à la question; (*Bio*) **to** ~ **to type** retourner or revenir au type primitif; (*fig*) **he has** ~**ed to type** le naturel a repris le dessus **b** (= *become again*) **fields** ~**ing to woodland** des champs qui retournent à l'état de forêt

review [rɪ'vjuː] **1** N **a** [*of situation, events, the past*] examen *m*, bilan *m*; [*of wages, prices, contracts*] révision *f*; (= *printed etc report*) rapport *m* d'enquête; **under** ~ [*salaries, policy*] en cours de révision; **the agreement comes up for** ~ or **comes under** ~ **next year** l'accord doit être révisé l'année prochaine; **I shall keep your case under** ~ je suivrai votre cas de très près; **he gave a** ~ **of recent developments in photography** il a passé en revue les progrès récents de la photographie **b** (*Mil, Naut* = *inspection*) revue *f*; **to hold a** ~ passer une revue **c** (*US Scol etc* = *revision*) révision *f* **d** (= *critical article*) [*of book, film, play etc*] critique *f*, compte rendu *m*; ~ **copy** [*of book*] exemplaire *m* de service de presse **e** (= *magazine*) revue *f*, périodique *m* **2** VT **a** (= *consider again*) [+ *one's life, the past*] passer en revue; **we shall** ~ **the situation next year** nous réexaminerons la situation l'année prochaine **b** [+ *troops*] passer en revue **c** (*US Scol etc*) revoir, réviser **d** [+ *book, play, film*] faire la critique de, donner or faire un compte rendu de **3** COMP ► **review body** N commission *f* de révision ► **reviewing stand** N tribune *f* des officiels ► **review panel** N comité *m* de révision

reviewer [rɪ'vjuːə'] N critique *mf*; **book/film** etc ~ critique *mf* littéraire/de cinéma etc

revile [rɪ'vaɪl] **1** VT honnir (*liter*), vilipender **2** VI proférer des injures (**at, against** contre)

revise [rɪ'vaɪz] **1** VT **a** (= *change*) [+ *opinion, estimate*] réviser, modifier; **to** ~ **sth upward(s)** réviser en hausse qch **b** (= *update*) [+ *text, dictionary etc*] réviser; (= *correct*) [+ *proof*] corriger, revoir; ~**d edition** édition *f* revue et corrigée; **Revised Standard Version** [*of Bible*] traduction anglaise de la bible de 1953; (*Brit*) **Revised Version** [*of Bible*] traduction anglaise de la Bible de 1884 **c** (*Brit Scol*) revoir, réviser **2** VI (*Brit Scol*) réviser; **to** ~ **for exams** réviser or faire des révisions pour les examens; **to start revising** commencer à réviser or (à faire) ses révisions **3** N (*Typ*) (épreuve *f* de) mise *f* en pages, seconde épreuve *f*

reviser [rɪ'vaɪzə'] N [*of text*] réviseur *m*; [*of proof*] correcteur *m*, -trice *f*

revision [rɪ'vɪʒən] N révision *f*

revisionism [rɪ'vɪʒənɪzəm] N révisionnisme *m*

revisionist [rɪ'vɪʒənɪst] ADJ, N révisionniste *mf*

revisit [,riː'vɪzɪt] VT **a** (= *study, discuss again*) [+ *issue*] réexaminer; [+ *author, one's past*] visiter; [+ *book*] relire; [+ *film*] revoir **b** [+ *place*] revisiter; [+ *person*] retourner voir

revitalize [,riː'vaɪtəlaɪz] VT (*gen*) redonner de la vitalité à, revivifier; **to** ~ **the economy** relancer l'économie

revival [rɪ'vaɪvəl] N **a** (= *bringing back*) [*of custom, ceremony*] reprise *f*; (*Jur*) remise *f* en vigueur; (*Hist*) **the Revival of Learning** la Renaissance **b** (*Theat*) [*of play*] reprise *f*; (*Rel*) [*of faith*] renouveau *m*, réveil *m*; ~ **meeting** réunion *f* pour le renouveau de la foi

revivalism [rɪ'vaɪvəlɪzəm] N (*Rel*) revivalisme *m*

revivalist [rɪ'vaɪvəlɪst] ADJ, N revivaliste *mf*

revive [rɪ'vaɪv] **1** VT **a** [+ *person*] (*from fainting*) ranimer; (*from near death, esp Med*) réanimer; **a glass of brandy will** ~ **you** un verre de cognac vous remontera or vous requinquera **b** [+ *fire, feeling, pain, memory*] ranimer, raviver; [+ *conversation*] ranimer; [+ *hope, interest*] faire renaître, raviver; [+ *trade, business*] relancer, réactiver; [+ *fashion*] remettre en vogue; [+ *law*] remettre en vigueur; [+ *custom, usage*] rétablir; [+ *play*] reprendre; **to** ~ **sb's courage** redonner du courage à qn; **to** ~ **sb's spirits** remonter le moral à qn **2** VI [*person*] reprendre connaissance; [*hope, feelings*] renaître; [*business, trade*] reprendre

reviver [rɪ'vaɪvə'] N (= *drink*) remontant *m*

revivify [,riː'vɪvɪfaɪ] VT revivifier (*liter*)

revocation [,revə'keɪʃən] N [*of order, promise, edict*] révocation *f*; [*of law, edict*] abrogation *f*; [*of licence*] retrait *m*; [*of decision*] annulation *f*

revoke [rɪ'vəʊk] **1** VT [+ *law*] rapporter, abroger; [+ *order, edict*] révoquer; [+ *promise*] revenir sur, révoquer; [+ *decision*] revenir sur, annuler; [+ *licence*] retirer **2** VI (*Cards*) faire une (fausse) renonce **3** N (*Cards*) (fausse) renonce *f*

revolt [rɪ'vəʊlt] **1** N révolte *f*; **to break out in** ~ ◊ **to rise in** ~ se révolter, se soulever; **to be in** ~ (**against**) se révolter or être révolté (contre) → **stir¹** **2** VI **a** (= *rebel*) se révolter, se soulever (**against** contre) **b** (= *be disgusted*) se révolter (**at** contre), être dégoûté (**at** par) **3** VT révolter, dégoûter; **to be** ~**ed by sth/sb** être révolté or dégoûté par qch/qn

revolting [rɪ'vəʊltɪŋ] ADJ **a** (= *repulsive, disgusting*) dégoûtant, répugnant **b** (* = *unpleasant*) [*weather, colour*] épouvantable; [*dress*] affreux

revoltingly [rɪ'vəʊltɪŋlɪ] ADV **dirty** d'une saleté révoltante or repoussante; ~ **ugly** d'une laideur repoussante

revolution [,revə'luːʃən] N **a** (= *turn*) [*of planet*] révolution *f*; [*of wheel*] révolution *f*, tour *m* **b** (*Pol etc* = *uprising*) révolution *f*, coup *m* d'État; (*fig*) révolution *f*; (*Hist*) **the French Revolution** la Révolution française; **a** ~ **in farming methods** une révolution dans les méthodes d'exploitation agricole; (*Hist*) **Industrial/Agricultural Revolution** Révolution *f* industrielle/agricole

revolutionary [,revə'luːʃnərɪ] ADJ, N (*lit, fig*) révolutionnaire *mf*

revolutionize [,revə'luːʃənaɪz] VT révolutionner, transformer radicalement

revolve [rɪ'vɒlv] **1** VT (*lit*) faire tourner; (*fig*) **to** ~ **a problem in one's mind** tourner et retourner un problème dans son esprit **2** VI tourner; **to** ~ **on an axis/around the sun** tourner sur un axe/autour du soleil; (*fig*) **the discussion** ~**d around two topics** la discussion tournait autour de deux sujets; (*fig*) **everything** ~**s around him** tout dépend de lui

revolver [rɪ'vɒlvə'] N revolver *m*

revolving [rɪ'vɒlvɪŋ] **1** ADJ [*chair, bookcase, stand*] pivotant; [*stage*] tournant; (*Astron*) en rotation, qui tourne; (*Tech*) rotatif, à rotation; ~ **light** (*gen*) feu *m* tournant, feu *m* à

► LANGUAGE IN USE: **reverse** 27.6

éclats; (on police car etc) gyrophare m [2] COMP ► **revolving credit** N (US) crédit m documentaire renouvelable ► **revolving door** N tambour m; (fig) **the ~ door of senior executives** la valse* des cadres supérieurs; (fig) **the ~ door between government and the private sector** les chassés-croisés mpl de personnel entre le service public et le secteur privé; (fig) **the ~ door of the justice system** le cercle vicieux du système judiciaire ► **revolving presidency** N présidence f tournante

revue [rɪ'vjuː] N (Theat) (satirical) revue f; (spectacular) revue f, spectacle m de music-hall; **~ artist** artiste mf de music-hall

revulsion [rɪ'vʌlʃən] N [a] (= disgust) écœurement m, répugnance f (**at** devant) [b] (= sudden change) revirement m; (= reaction) réaction f (**against** contre)

reward [rɪ'wɔːd] [1] N récompense f; **as a ~ for your honesty** en récompense de votre honnêteté; **as (a) ~ for helping me** pour vous (or le etc) récompenser de m'avoir aidé; **1,000 francs' ~** 1 000 F de récompense; **to offer a ~** offrir une récompense [2] VT récompenser (**for** de); (with money) récompenser, rémunérer (**for** de); **"finder will be ~ed"** « récompense à qui rapportera l'objet »; **to ~ sb with a smile** remercier qn d'un sourire; (fig) **to ~ attention/investigation** mériter de l'attention/des recherches

rewarding [rɪ'wɔːdɪŋ] ADJ (financially) rémunérateur (-trice f); (mentally, morally) qui en vaut la peine; **this is a very ~ book** ce livre vaut la peine d'être lu; **a ~ film** un film qui vaut la peine d'être vu; **bringing up a child is exhausting but ~** élever un enfant est une occupation exténuante mais qui a sa récompense

rewind [ˌriː'waɪnd] (pret, ptp **rewound**) VT (Tex) rebobiner, rembobiner; [+ film, ribbon, tape] rembobiner; [+ watch] remonter

rewinding [ˌriː'waɪndɪŋ] N [of film, tape, video, thread] rembobinage m; [of clock, watch] remontage m

rewire [ˌriː'waɪə'] VT **to ~ a house** refaire l'installation électrique d'une maison; **the house needs rewiring** l'installation électrique de la maison doit être refaite

reword [ˌriː'wɜːd] VT [+ paragraph, question] reformuler; [+ idea] exprimer en d'autres termes

rework [ˌriː'wɜːk] VT retravailler

rewound [ˌriː'waʊnd] VB pt, ptp of **rewind**

rewrite [ˌriː'raɪt] (pret **rewrote**, ptp **rewritten**) [1] VT (gen) récrire; (= rework) remanier; (= copy) recopier [2] N* remaniement m [3] COMP ► **rewrite rule, rewriting rule** N (Gram) règle f de réécriture

rewriter [ˌriː'raɪtə'] N (US Press) rewriter m, rédacteur-réviseur m

rewritten [ˌriː'rɪtn] VB ptp of **rewrite**

rewrote [ˌriː'rəʊt] VB pt of **rewrite**

Reykjavik ['reɪkjəvɪk] N Reykjavik

RGN [ˌɑːdʒiː'en] N (ABBR = **Registered General Nurse**) → **registered**

Rh [1] N (ABBR = **rhesus**) Rh [2] COMP ► **Rh factor** N facteur m Rhésus

rhapsodic [ræp'sɒdɪk] ADJ (Mus) [passage, style] r(h)apsodique; (fig = lyrical) [account, description, verse] dithyrambique

rhapsodize ['ræpsədaɪz] VI s'extasier (**over, about** sur)

rhapsody ['ræpsədɪ] N (Mus) r(h)apsodie f; (fig) éloge m dithyrambique

rhea ['riːə] N nandou m

rheme [riːm] N rhème m

Rhenish ['renɪʃ] ADJ [wine] du Rhin

rhenium ['riːnɪəm] N rhénium m

rheostat ['riːəʊstæt] N rhéostat m

---

rhesus ['riːsəs] [1] N rhésus m [2] COMP ► **rhesus baby** N enfant mf rhésus ► **rhesus factor** N facteur m Rhésus ► **rhesus monkey** N (singe m) rhésus m ► **rhesus negative** ADJ rhésus négatif ► **rhesus positive** ADJ rhésus positif

rhetic ['riːtɪk] ADJ (Ling) rhétique

rhetoric ['retərɪk] N (also pej) rhétorique f; (= art) art m oratoire

rhetorical [rɪ'tɒrɪkəl] ADJ (de) rhétorique; [style] ampoulé (pej); **~ question** question f pour la forme or l'effet

rhetorically [rɪ'tɒrɪkəlɪ] ADV [ask] pour la forme; [speak, declaim] en orateur

rhetorician [ˌretə'rɪʃən] N rhétoricien m, -ienne f, rhéteur m (also pej)

rheumatic [ruː'mætɪk] [1] N (= person) rhumatisant(e) m(f) [2] ADJ [pain] rhumatismal; [person] rhumatisant, qui souffre de rhumatismes; [hands, fingers] plein de rhumatismes [3] COMP ► **rheumatic fever** N rhumatisme m articulaire aigu

rheumaticky* [ruː'mætɪkɪ] ADJ [person] rhumatisant; [hands, fingers] plein de rhumatismes; [pain] rhumatismal

rheumatics* [ruː'mætɪks] NPL rhumatismes mpl

rheumatism ['ruːmətɪzəm] N rhumatisme m

rheumatoid ['ruːmətɔɪd] ADJ **~ arthritis** polyarthrite f chronique évolutive, rhumatisme m chronique polyarticulaire

rheumatologist [ˌruːmə'tɒlədʒɪst] N rhumatologue mf

rheumatology [ˌruːmə'tɒlədʒɪ] N rhumatologie f

rheumy ['ruːmɪ] ADJ (liter) [eyes] chassieux (frm)

Rhine [raɪn] N Rhin m

Rhineland ['raɪnlænd] N **the ~** la Rhénanie

rhinestone ['raɪnstəʊn] N diamant m fantaisie

rhinitis [raɪ'naɪtɪs] N (Med) rhinite f

rhino* ['raɪnəʊ] N (pl **rhino** or **rhinoes**) ABBR = **rhinoceros**

rhinoceros [raɪ'nɒsərəs] N (pl **rhinoceros** or **rhinoceroses**) rhinocéros m

rhizome ['raɪzəʊm] N rhizome m

Rhode Island ['rəʊd'aɪlənd] N le Rhode Island

Rhodes [rəʊdz] N (Geog) Rhodes f; **in ~** à Rhodes

Rhodesia [rəʊ'diːʒə] N la Rhodésie

Rhodesian [rəʊ'diːʒən] [1] ADJ rhodésien [2] N Rhodésien m, -ienne f

rhodium ['rəʊdɪəm] N rhodium m

rhododendron [ˌrəʊdə'dendrən] N rhododendron m

rhomb [rɒm] N = **rhombus**

rhombi ['rɒmbaɪ] NPL of **rhombus**

rhombic ['rɒmbɪk] ADJ rhombique

rhomboid ['rɒmbɔɪd] [1] N rhomboïde m [2] ADJ rhomboïdal

rhombus ['rɒmbəs] N (pl **rhombuses** or **rhombi**) losange m, rhombe m

Rhône [rəʊn] N Rhône m

rhubarb ['ruːbɑːb] [1] N [a] (Bot, Culin) rhubarbe f [b] (Theat) "~, ~, ~" ≈ brouhaha m (mot employé pour reconstituer un murmure de fond) [c] (US* = quarrel) prise f de bec, éclats mpl de voix [2] COMP [jam] de rhubarbe; [tart] à la rhubarbe

rhyme [raɪm] [1] N [a] (= identical sound) rime f; **for (the sake of) the ~** pour la rime; (fig) **without ~ or reason** sans rime ni raison; (fig) **there seems to be neither ~ nor reason to it** cela ne rime à rien, cela n'a ni rime ni raison [b] (= poetry) vers mpl; (= a poem) poème m; **in ~** en vers (rimés); **to put sth into ~** mettre qch en vers → **nursery** [2] VT faire rimer (**with** avec) [3] VI [a] [word] rimer (**with** avec) [b] (pej

---

(= write verse) faire de mauvais vers, rimailler (pej) [4] COMP ► **rhyme scheme** N agencement m des rimes

rhymed ['raɪmd] ADJ rimé

rhymer ['raɪmə'], **rhymester** ['raɪmstə'] N (pej) rimailleur m, -euse f (pej)

rhyming ['raɪmɪŋ] [1] ADJ qui rime [2] COMP ► **rhyming dictionary** N dictionnaire m des rimes ► **rhyming game** N jeu m de rimes ► **rhyming slang** N argot des Cockneys

---

▭ RHYMING SLANG

L'« argot rimé » est une forme d'argot utilisée par les Cockneys; il consiste à remplacer un mot par une expression qui rime avec ce mot: par exemple, on dira « apples and pears » pour « stairs ». Cette forme de langage est parfois difficile à comprendre, surtout lorsque la rime est supprimée; ainsi, à la place de « butcher's hook » (pour « look »), les Cockneys vont simplement dire « butcher's », par exemple dans « let's take a butcher's » (jetons un coup d'œil). Certaines expressions de ce **rhyming slang** sont passées dans la langue courante et sont comprises par tous les Britanniques; pour « use your head » (réfléchis un peu), on entendra ainsi « use your loaf », « loaf » étant une réduction de « loaf of bread » (pour « head »).

---

rhythm ['rɪðəm] [1] N rythme m; (Mus) **~ and blues** rhythm and blues m [2] COMP ► **rhythm guitar** N guitare f rythmique ► **rhythm method** N [of contraception] méthode f Ogino or des températures ► **rhythm section** N (Mus) section f rythmique

rhythmic(al) ['rɪðmɪk(əl)] ADJ [movement, beat] rythmique; [music] rythmé, cadencé

rhythmically ['rɪðmɪkəlɪ] ADV de façon rythmique, en rythme

RI [ɑː'raɪ] [a] (ABBR = **religious instruction**) → **religious** [b] ABBR = **Rhode Island**

rib [rɪb] [1] N [a] (Anat, Culin) côte f; **true/false ~** vraie/fausse côte f → **dig, floating, poke²**, **stick** [b] [of leaf, ceiling] nervure f; [of ship] membre m, membrure f; [of shell] strie f; [of umbrella] baleine f; [of knitting] côte f [2] VT (* = tease) taquiner, mettre en boîte* [3] COMP ► **rib cage** N cage f thoracique ► **rib roast** N (Culin) côte f de bœuf ► **rib-tickler*** N blague* f ► **rib-tickling** ADJ tordant*

ribald ['rɪbəld] ADJ [comment, joke] grivois, égrillard; [laughter] égrillard

ribaldry ['rɪbəldrɪ] N (NonC) grivoiserie f; (= comments) grivoiseries fpl

riband† ['rɪbənd] N = **ribbon**; → **blue**

ribbed [rɪbd] ADJ [cotton, sweater, socks] à côtes; [shell] strié; [ceiling] à nervures

ribbing ['rɪbɪŋ] N [a] (NonC: Knitting) côtes fpl [b] (* = teasing) **to give sb a ~** taquiner qn; **to get a ~** se faire taquiner

ribbon ['rɪbən] [1] N [a] [of dress, hair, typewriter, decoration] ruban m; **velvet ~** ruban m de velours → **bunch** [b] **in ~s** (= in tatters) en lambeaux; **to tear sth to ~s** (lit) mettre qch en lambeaux; (fig) [+ play etc] éreinter qch [2] COMP ► **ribbon development** N (NonC) croissance f urbaine linéaire (le long des grands axes routiers)

riboflavin [ˌraɪbəʊ'fleɪvɪn] N riboflavine f

ribonucleic [ˌraɪbəʊnjuː'kliːɪk] ADJ **~ acid** acide m ribonucléique

rice [raɪs] [1] N riz m [2] COMP ► **rice bowl** N (= bowl) bol m à riz; (= region) région f rizicole ► **rice growing** N riziculture f ► **rice-growing** ADJ rizicole, producteur (-trice f) de riz ► **rice paper** N papier m de riz ► **rice pudding** N riz m au lait ► **rice wine** N saké m

ricefield ['raɪsfiːld] N rizière f

ricer ['raɪsə'] N (US Culin) presse-purée m inv

rich [rɪtʃ] **1** ADJ **a** (gen) [person, country, variety, life, soil, food, sound, colour] riche; [smell] riche, puissant; [tapestries] riche, somptueux; [gift, clothes, banquet] somptueux; [voice] chaud, aux tonalités riches; [profit] gros (grosse f); [wine] généreux; **~ people** les riches mpl; **~ and famous** riche et célèbre; **to grow** or **get ~(er)** s'enrichir; **to make sb ~** enrichir qn; (gen pej) **to get ~ quick*** s'enrichir rapidement → **get**; **to be (all) the ~er for sth** gagner beaucoup à faire qch; **~ in minerals/vitamins/detail/history** etc riche en mineraux/vitamines/détails/histoire etc; (in marriage service) **for ~er, for poorer** ≈ pour le meilleur et pour le pire → **Croesus, picking**
b (= unreasonable) **that's ~!** c'est un peu fort!, elle est bonne, celle-là!
c († = funny) [humour, tale] savoureux
2 ~es richesse(s) f(pl)
3 the rich NPL les riches mpl
4 COMP ► **rich tea biscuit** N ≈ petit-beurre m

-rich [rɪtʃ] ADJ (in compounds) **calcium-/protein-rich** riche en calcium/protéines; **oil-rich** [nation, region] riche en pétrole

Richard ['rɪtʃəd] N Richard m; **~ (the) Lionheart** Richard m Cœur de Lion

richly ['rɪtʃlɪ] ADV [decorated, flavoured, scented, coloured] richement; [dressed] richement, somptueusement; [illustrated] abondamment; [deserved] largement; [rewarded] généreusement; [satisfying] profondément; **to be ~ endowed with courage/talent** avoir du courage/talent à revendre; **~ patterned** à riches motifs; **a ~ rewarding experience** une expérience extrêmement enrichissante

richness ['rɪtʃnɪs] N [of person, life, culture, soil, voice, food, colour] richesse f; [of tapestries] richesse f, somptuosité f; [of gift, clothes, banquet] somptuosité f; **~ in oil/vitamins** richesse f en pétrole/vitamines

Richter ['rɪxtə'] N **the ~ scale** l'échelle f de Richter

rick¹ [rɪk] N (Agr) meule f (de foin etc)

rick² [rɪk] = **wrick**

rickets ['rɪkɪts] N (NonC) rachitisme m; **to have ~** être rachitique

rickety ['rɪkɪtɪ] ADJ (Med) rachitique; (fig) [building, fence, stairs] branlant; [furniture] bancal; [vehicle] bringuebalant

rickey ['rɪkɪ] N (US) cocktail au citron vert

rickrack ['rɪkræk] N (NonC: US) ganse f en zigzag

rickshaw ['rɪkʃɔ:] N (pulled by man) pousse(-pousse) m inv; (pulled by bicycle etc) rickshaw m

ricky-tick* ['rɪkɪtɪk] ADJ (US) démodé, vieillot

ricochet ['rɪkəʃeɪ] **1** N ricochet m **2** VI ricocher

ricotta [rɪ'kɒtə] N ricotte f

rictus ['rɪktəs] N (pl rictus or rictuses) rictus m

rid [rɪd] (pret, ptp **rid** or **ridded**) VT (of pests, disease) débarrasser; (of bandits etc) délivrer (**of** de); **to get ~ of** [+ spots, cold, cough, fleas, possessions, rubbish] se débarrasser de; [+ habit, illusion, desire, tendency] perdre, se défaire de; [+ fears, doubts] perdre; [+ unwanted goods] se débarrasser de, se défaire de; [+ boyfriend, girlfriend] laisser tomber*, se débarrasser de; (frm) **to ~ o.s. of** = to get rid of; **to be ~ of sb/sth** être débarrassé de qn/qch; **to get ~ of one's debts** liquider or régler ses dettes; **the body gets ~ of waste** l'organisme élimine les déchets

riddance ['rɪdəns] N débarras m; **good ~ (to bad rubbish)!** bon débarras!*

ridden ['rɪdn] **1** VB ptp of **ride 2** ADJ **~ by** tourmenté or hanté par; **~ by fears** hanté par la peur; **~ by remorse** tourmenté par le remords

-ridden [,rɪdn] ADJ (in compounds) **disease-/guilt-/remorse-ridden** accablé par la maladie/la culpabilité/le remords; **angst-/fear-ridden** tourmenté par l'angoisse/la peur → **debt, hag**

riddle¹ ['rɪdl] **1** N crible m, claie f **2** VT **a** [+ coal, soil etc] cribler, passer au crible; [+ stove] agiter la grille de **b** [+ person, target] cribler; **~d with holes/bullets** criblé de trous/balles; **the council is ~d with corruption** la corruption règne au conseil; **the committee is ~d with troublemakers** le comité grouille de provocateurs

riddle² ['rɪdl] N (= puzzle) énigme f, devinette f; (= mystery) énigme f, mystère m; **to speak** or **talk in ~s** parler par énigmes; **to ask sb a ~** poser une devinette à qn

ride [raɪd] (vb: pret **rode**, ptp **ridden**) **1** N **a** (= outing) promenade f, tour m; (= distance covered) trajet m; **he gave the child a ~ on his back** il a promené l'enfant sur son dos; **to go for a ~ in a car** faire une promenade en voiture; **he gave me a ~ into town in his car** il m'a emmené en ville dans sa voiture; **it's my first ~ in a Rolls** c'est la première fois que je me promène or que je roule en Rolls; **we went for a ~ in a train** nous avons fait un voyage en train; **can I have a ~ on your bike?** est-ce que je peux emprunter ton vélo?; **to have a ~ in a helicopter** faire un tour en hélicoptère; **we got a ~ in a taxi** nous avons pris un taxi; **it was the taxi ~ they liked best** c'est le tour en taxi qu'ils ont préféré; **bike ~** tour m or promenade f à vélo; **car ~** tour m en voiture; **coach ~** tour m or excursion f en car; **it's a short taxi ~ to the airport** ce n'est pas loin en taxi jusqu'à l'aéroport; **he has a long (car/bus) ~ to work** il a un long trajet (en voiture or en autobus) jusqu'à son lieu de travail; **it's only a short ~ by bus/coach/train/car/taxi** il n'y en a pas pour longtemps or c'est un court trajet en bus/en car/en train/en voiture/en taxi; **it's a 60p ~ from the station** le trajet depuis la gare coûte 60 pence; **three ~s on the merry-go-round** trois tours de manège; **to steal a ~** voyager sans billet or sans payer; (fig) **I just came along for the ~** je suis venu pour voir; **to take sb for a ~** (in car etc) emmener qn faire un tour; (fig) (= make fool of) faire marcher qn*, mener qn en bateau*; (= swindle) rouler qn*, posséder qn*; (US* euph = kill) emmener qn faire un tour → **joyride, Valkyrie**
b (on horseback) promenade f or tour m à cheval; (= long journey) chevauchée f; **after a hard ~ across country** après une chevauchée pénible à travers la campagne
c (at fairground) tour m; **a ~ on the roller-coaster** un tour de montagnes russes
d (* fig) **motherhood was no easy ~** la maternité n'était pas facile à assumer; **he faces a rough ~ from the media** il risque de se faire malmener par les médias; **he was given a rough ~ over his remarks about the homeless** on lui a fait payer ses remarques sur les SDF; **the company has not had a smooth** or **an easy ~ lately** tout n'a pas été rose pour l'entreprise ces derniers temps, l'entreprise a eu sa part d'ennuis ces derniers temps
e (= path for horses) allée f cavalière
f (Horse-riding = mount) **Castilian Queen is a difficult ~** Castilian Queen est difficile à monter
2 VI **a** (= ride a horse) monter à cheval, faire du cheval; **can you ~?** savez-vous monter à cheval?; **she ~s a lot** elle fait beaucoup d'équitation; **he has ridden since childhood** il monte à cheval or il fait de l'équitation depuis son enfance; **she learnt to ~ on Oscar** elle a appris à monter (à cheval) sur Oscar; **to go riding** faire de l'équitation; **to ~ astride/sidesaddle** monter à califourchon/en amazone; **he ~s well** il est bon cavalier; **the jockey was riding just under 65 kilos** (en tenue) le jockey pesait un peu moins de 65 kilos → **hound**

b (= go on horseback/by bicycle/by motorcycle) aller à cheval/à bicyclette/à or en moto; **to ~ down/away** etc descendre/s'éloigner etc à cheval (or à bicyclette or à or en moto etc); **he stopped then rode on** il s'est arrêté puis a repris sa route; **they had ridden all day** ils avaient passé toute la journée à cheval or en selle; **he rode to London** il est allé à Londres à cheval (or à bicyclette etc); **he was riding on a bicycle/a camel** il était à bicyclette/à dos de chameau; **the child was riding on his father's back** le père portait l'enfant sur son dos; **he was riding on his mother's shoulders** sa mère le portait sur ses épaules; **the witch was riding on a broomstick** la sorcière était à cheval or à califourchon sur un balai; **they were riding on a bus/in a car/in a train** ils étaient en autobus/en voiture/en train; **they rode in a bus to ...** ils sont allés en bus à ...; **she ~s to work on a bike** elle va au travail à bicyclette; (fig liter) **the seagull ~s on the wind** la mouette est portée par le vent; (fig) **the moon was riding high in the sky** la lune voguait haut dans le ciel; (fig) **he's riding high** il a le vent en poupe; **he was riding high in public opinion** il avait la cote (auprès du public); **he was riding high on his latest success** tout baignait* pour lui après son dernier succès; (fig) **we'll just have to let the matter** or **to let things ~ for a while** nous allons devoir laisser l'affaire suivre son cours or laisser courir* pendant un certain temps; (fig) **she had to let things ~** elle a dû laisser courir* → **anchor, fall, roughshod, punch¹, shank**
c **to ~ well** [horse] être une bonne monture
d (Tech etc) (= overlap) chevaucher; (= work out of place) travailler
3 VT **a** **to ~ a horse** monter à cheval; **have you ever ridden a horse?** êtes-vous déjà monté à cheval?; **I have never ridden Flash** je n'ai jamais monté Flash; **he rode Cass at Newmarket** il montait Cass à Newmarket; **he rode Buster into town** il a pris Buster pour aller en ville, il est allé en ville sur Buster; **Jason will be ridden by J. Bean** Jason sera monté par J. Bean; **who is riding Omar?** qui monte Omar?; **he rode his horse straight at me** il a dirigé son cheval droit sur moi; **he rode his horse up the stairs** il a fait monter l'escalier à son cheval; **he rode his horse away/back** etc il est parti/revenu etc à cheval; (Brit fig) **to ~ two horses at the same time** courir deux lièvres à la fois; **he ~s his pony to school** il va à l'école à dos de poney; **have you ever ridden a donkey/camel?** êtes-vous déjà monté à dos de chameau?; **he was riding a donkey** il était à dos d'âne; **he was riding a motorbike** il était à or en moto; **he rode his motorbike to the station** il est allé à la gare à or en moto; **I have never ridden a bike/a motorbike** je ne suis jamais monté à vélo/à moto; **can I ~ your bike?** est-ce que je peux emprunter ton vélo?; **he was riding a bicycle** il était à bicyclette; **he rode his cycle into town** il est allé en ville à bicyclette; **he always ~s a bicycle** il va partout à or il se déplace toujours à bicyclette; **witches ~ broomsticks** les sorcières chevauchent des balais; **she was riding a broomstick** elle était à cheval or à califourchon sur un balai; **they had ridden 10km** ils avaient fait 10 km à cheval (or à bicyclette or à or en moto etc); **they had ridden all the way** ils avaient fait tout le trajet à cheval (or à bicyclette etc); **he rode the country looking for ...** il a parcouru le pays à la recherche de ...; (US) **to ~ sb on a rail** expulser qn de la ville (en l'emmenant à califourchon sur un poteau); (fig) **the birds rode the wind** les oiseaux se laissaient porter par le vent; (liter) **the ship rode the waves** le bateau voguait sur les vagues; (fig) **he's riding (on) a wave of personal popularity** il jouit d'une excellente cote de popularité → **ride on**; → **herd, race¹**

b (esp US* = nag etc) être toujours sur le dos de*, ne pas ficher la paix à* (**about** au sujet de); **don't ~ him too hard** ne soyez pas trop dur avec lui

▶**ride about**, **ride around** VI se déplacer or faire un tour (à cheval or à bicyclette or en voiture etc)

▶**ride behind** VI (on same horse) monter en croupe; (on motorcycle) monter derrière or en croupe; (in car) être assis à l'arrière; (different horse, motorcycle, car) être derrière

▶**ride down** VT SEP **a** (= trample) renverser, piétiner **b** (catch up with) rattraper

▶**ride on** VT FUS dépendre de; **billions of dollars are riding on the outcome of the election** de l'issue des élections dépendent des milliards de dollars; **his reputation's riding on the outcome of the trial** sa réputation dépend de l'issue du procès, c'est sa réputation qui est en jeu dans ce procès

▶**ride out** **1** VI sortir (à cheval or à bicyclette etc) **2** VT SEP (fig) surmonter; **to ~ out the storm** (Naut) étaler la tempête; (fig) surmonter la crise; **to ~ out a difficult time** se tirer d'une or surmonter une mauvaise passe; **the company managed to ~ out the depression** la société a réussi à survivre à la dépression

▶**ride up** VI **a** [horseman, cyclist etc] arriver **b** [skirt, trousers] remonter; **her underskirt had ridden up (a)round her hips** son jupon lui était remonté sur les hanches

rider ['raɪdər] N **a** (= person) [of horse] cavalier m, -ière f; [of racehorse] jockey m; [of circus horse] écuyer m, -ère f; [of bicycle] cycliste mf; [of motorcycle] motocycliste mf; **a good ~** un bon cavalier, une bonne cavalière → **dispatch, outrider b** (= addition: to document) annexe f; (to bill) clause f additionnelle; (to insurance policy, jury's verdict) avenant m; **the committee added a ~ condemning ...** la commission ajouta une clause condamnant ...

ridge [rɪdʒ] **1** N **a** (= top of a line of hills or mountains) arête f, crête f; (= extended top of a hill) faîte m; (= ledge on hillside) corniche f; (= chain of hills, mountains) chaîne f; (in sea = reef) récif m **b** (of roof, on nose) arête f; (on sand) ride f; (in ploughed land) billon m; (on cliff, rock face) strie f; (Met) **a ~ of high pressure** une ligne de hautes pressions; (Agr) **~ and furrow (formation)** crêtes fpl de labours → **alveolar 2** VT **a** [+ earth] billonner; [+ rock face] strier; [+ sand] rider **3** COMP ▶ **ridge piece**, **ridge pole** N poutre f de faîte m, faîtage m ▶ **ridge tent** N tente f (à toit en arête) ▶ **ridge tile** N (tuile f) faîtière f, enfaîteau m ▶ **ridge way** N chemin m or route f de crête

ridicule ['rɪdɪkjuːl] **1** N raillerie f, ridicule m; **to hold sb/sth up to ~** tourner qn/qch en ridicule or en dérision; **to lay o.s. open to ~** s'exposer aux railleries; **she's an object of ~** elle est un objet de risée **2** VT ridiculiser, tourner en ridicule or en dérision

ridiculous [rɪ'dɪkjʊləs] ADJ ridicule; **she was made to look ~** elle a été ridiculisée; **to make o.s. (look) ~** se rendre ridicule, se ridiculiser; **to take things to ~ extremes** pousser les choses trop loin; **to go to ~ lengths** trop en faire; **to go to ~ lengths to do sth** se ridiculiser à force de faire qch → **sublime**

ridiculously [rɪ'dɪkjʊləslɪ] ADV ridiculement; **~, he blamed himself for the accident** il se sentait responsable de l'accident, ce qui est ridicule

ridiculousness [rɪ'dɪkjʊləsnɪs] N ridicule m

riding ['raɪdɪŋ] **1** N (also **horse-~**) équitation f; (= horsemanship) monte f **2** COMP ▶ **riding boots** NPL bottes fpl de cheval ▶ **riding breeches** NPL culotte f de cheval ▶ **riding crop** N = **riding whip** ▶ **riding habit** N habit m or tenue f d'amazone

▶ **riding jacket** N veste f de cheval or d'équitation ▶ **riding master** N professeur m d'équitation ▶ **riding school** N manège m, école f d'équitation ▶ **riding stable(s)** N(PL) centre m d'équitation, manège m ▶ **riding whip** N cravache f

rife [raɪf] ADJ **a** to be ~ [disease, racism, crime, corruption, unemployment] sévir; **rumours are/speculation is ~ (that)** les rumeurs/les spéculations vont bon train (comme quoi) **b** (= full of) **a city ~ with violence** une ville en proie à la violence, une ville où sévit la violence; **the whole company is ~ with corruption/jealousy** la corruption/jalousie sévit dans toute l'entreprise; **the media is ~ with rumours/speculation** les rumeurs/spéculations vont bon train dans les médias

riff [rɪf] N (Mus) riff m

riffle ['rɪfl] VT (also **~ through**) [+ pages, papers] feuilleter rapidement, parcourir

riffraff ['rɪf,ræf] N racaille f

rifle¹ ['raɪfl] VT [+ town] piller; [+ tomb] violer; [+ drawer, till] vider; [+ house] dévaliser, vider; **to ~ sb's pockets** faire les poches à qn; **she ~d through the papers** elle feuilletait rapidement les documents

rifle² ['raɪfl] **1** N (= gun) fusil m (rayé); (for hunting) carabine f de chasse; (Mil) **the Rifles** ≈ les chasseurs mpl à pied, ≈ (le régiment de) l'infanterie f légère **2** COMP ▶ **rifle butt** N crosse f de fusil ▶ **rifle range** N (outdoor) champ m de tir; (indoor) stand m de tir; **within ~ range** à portée de fusil ▶ **rifle shot** N coup m de fusil; (= marksman) tireur m; **within ~ shot** à portée de fusil

rifleman ['raɪflmən] N (pl **-men**) fusilier m

rift [rɪft] **1** N **a** (lit) fissure f; (deeper) crevasse f; (in clouds) trouée f **b** (fig = disagreement) désaccord m; (Pol) (in party) division f; (in cabinet, group) division f, désaccord m; **this caused a ~ in their friendship** ceci a causé une faille dans leur amitié; **the ~ between them was widening** ils s'éloignaient de plus en plus l'un de l'autre **2** COMP ▶ **rift valley** N (Geol) graben m

rig [rɪg] **1** N **a** (Naut) gréement m **b** (also **oil ~**) (on land) derrick m; (at sea: also **floating ~**) plateforme f (pétrolière) flottante **c** (* = outfit: also **~ out**) tenue f, accoutrement m (pej) **d** (US = tractor-trailer) semi-remorque m **2** VT **a** (Naut) gréer **b** (= fix dishonestly) [+ election, competition, game] truquer; [+ prices] fixer illégalement; **it was ~ged** c'était un coup monté; (St Ex) **to ~ the market** manipuler le marché, provoquer une hausse (or une baisse) factice dans les cours **3** VI (Naut) être gréé

▶ **rig out** VT SEP (= clothe) habiller (**with** de, **as** en)

▶ **rig up** VT (+ boat) gréer; (with mast) mâter; (+ equipment) monter, installer; (fig) (= make hastily) faire avec des moyens de fortune or avec les moyens du bord; (= arrange) arranger

rigger ['rɪgər] N **a** (Naut) gréeur m; (Aviat) monteur-régleur m **b** (St Ex) agioteur m, manipulateur m

rigging ['rɪgɪŋ] N **a** (Naut) (= ropes etc) gréement m; (= action) gréage m **b** (US = clothes) vêtements mpl, fringues* fpl **c** (* = dishonest interference) [of election, competition] truquage m; [of prices] fixation f illégale; (St Ex) agiotage m manipulation f

▼**right** [raɪt]

1 ADJECTIVE	**4** PLURAL NOUN
2 ADVERB	**5** TRANSITIVE VERB
3 NOUN	**6** COMPOUNDS

1 ADJECTIVE

a = morally good bien inv; **it isn't ~ to lie** ◊ lying isn't ~ ce n'est pas bien de mentir; **it's not ~, leaving her like this** ce n'est pas bien de la laisser comme ça; **I have always tried to**

do what was ~ j'ai toujours essayé de bien agir; **to do what is ~ by sb** agir pour le bien de qn; **you were ~ to refuse** vous avez bien fait de or vous avez eu raison de refuser; **he thought it ~ to warn me** il a cru or jugé bon de m'avertir; **would it be ~ to tell him?** est-ce que ce serait une bonne chose de le lui dire?; **to do the ~ thing by sb** bien agir or agir honorablement envers qn

♦ **only right**: **it seemed only ~ to give him the money** il ne semblait que juste de lui donner l'argent; **it is only ~ for her to go** or **that she should go** il n'est que juste qu'elle y aille; **it is only ~ to point out that ...** il faut néanmoins signaler que ...; **that's only ~ and proper!** ce n'est que justice!, c'est bien le moins!; **it's only ~ and proper that ...** il n'est que juste que ... (+ subj)

b = accurate juste, exact; **that's ~** c'est juste, c'est exact; **that can't be ~!** ce n'est pas possible!; **is that ~?** (checking) c'est bien ça?; (expressing surprise) vraiment?; (by the clock) **the ~ time** l'heure exacte or juste → **1c**; **is the clock ~?** est-ce que la pendule est à l'heure?; **my guess was ~** j'avais deviné juste

♦ **to be right** [person] avoir raison; **you're quite ~** vous avez parfaitement raison; **how ~ you are!*** je suis entièrement d'accord avec vous!, et comment!*

♦ **to get sth right**: **I got all the answers ~** j'ai répondu juste à toutes les questions; **to get one's sums ~** ne pas se tromper dans ses calculs; **to get one's facts ~** ne pas se tromper; **let's get it ~ this time!** cette fois-ci, il s'agit de ne pas nous tromper!

♦ **to put** or **set right** [+ error] corriger, rectifier; [+ situation] redresser; [+ clock] remettre à l'heure; [+ sth broken] réparer, remettre en état; **that can easily be put ~** on peut (facilement) arranger ça; **I tried to put things ~ after their quarrel** j'ai essayé d'arranger les choses après leur dispute; **the plumber came and put things ~** le plombier est venu et a fait les réparations nécessaires

♦ **to put** or **set sb right** (= correct) corriger qn; (= disabuse) détromper qn; (= cure) guérir qn; **the medicine soon put** or **set him ~** ce médicament l'a vite guéri; **put me ~ if I'm wrong** corrigez-moi si je me trompe

c = correct bon (before n); **the ~ answer** la bonne réponse; **it is just the ~ size** c'est la bonne taille; (lit) **on the ~ road** sur le bon chemin; **is this the ~ road for Lyons?** est-ce que c'est bien la route de Lyon or la bonne route pour Lyon?; (fig) **on the ~ road** ◊ **on the ~ track** sur la bonne voie; **to come at the ~ time** arriver au bon moment, bien tomber; **to do sth at the ~ time** faire qch au bon moment; **the ~ word** le mot juste; **she is on the ~ side of forty** elle n'a pas encore quarante ans; **to get on the ~ side of sb*** s'attirer les bonnes grâces de qn; **to know the ~ people** avoir des relations; **your assumption was ~** tu avais vu juste

d = best meilleur (-eure f); **what's the ~ thing to do?** quelle est la meilleure chose à faire?; **I don't know what's the ~ thing to do** je ne sais pas ce qu'il faut faire or ce qu'il convient de faire; **we will do what is ~ for the country** nous ferons ce qui est dans l'intérêt du pays; **the ~ man for the job** l'homme de la situation, l'homme qu'il nous (or leur etc) faut

e = necessary **I haven't got the ~ papers with me** je n'ai pas les documents nécessaires sur moi; **I didn't have the ~ books for the course** je n'avais pas les livres qu'il fallait pour ce cours

f = proper **to do sth the ~ way** faire qch comme il faut; **that is the ~ way of looking at it** c'est bien ainsi qu'il faut aborder la question; **she wasn't wearing the ~ clothes** (socially inappropriate) elle n'avait pas la tenue requise, elle n'était pas habillée comme il fallait; **if you go hiking you must wear the ~ shoes** lorsque l'on fait de la randonnée, il faut porter des chaussures adaptées

➤ **LANGUAGE IN USE**: **right** 11, 13, 26.3

g = in proper state [*person*] guéri, rétabli ; [*part of body*] guéri ; **David's ankle is still not ~** la cheville de David n'est pas encore guérie ; **I don't feel quite ~ today** je ne me sens pas très bien *or* pas dans mon assiette aujourd'hui ; **the brakes aren't ~** les freins ne fonctionnent pas bien, il y a quelque chose qui cloche dans les freins ; **to be in one's ~ mind** avoir toute sa raison ; **he's not ~ in the head*** il déraille* ; (*Brit*) **to be as ~ as rain*** (*after illness*) se porter comme un charme → **all right**

h = real: esp Brit* **it's a ~ mess in there** c'est la pagaille* complète là-dedans ; **I felt a ~ fool** je me suis senti complètement idiot ; **she gave them a ~ telling off** elle les a enguirlandés* quelque chose de bien

i agreeing, confirming etc **~!** ◊ **~ you are!*** d'accord !, entendu ! ; (*approvingly*) **~ on!*‡** c'est ça ! ; **~, who's next?** bon, c'est à qui le tour ? ; **(oh) ~!*** (= *I see*) ah, d'accord ! ; **she was the last to leave, ~?** elle est partie la dernière, c'est bien ça ? ; **too ~!** et comment !

◆ **right enough**: **it was him ~ enough!** c'était bien lui, aucun doute là-dessus !

j = opposite of left droit ; **~ hand** main *f* droite ; **on my ~ hand you see the bridge** sur ma droite vous voyez le pont ; **it's a case of the ~ hand not knowing what the left hand's doing** il y a un manque total de communication et de coordination → **6**; **I'd give my ~ arm to know the truth** je donnerais n'importe quoi pour connaître la vérité

2 ADVERB

a = straight, directly droit ; **~ ahead of you** droit devant vous ; **~ in front of you** sous vos yeux ; **the blow hit me ~ in the face** j'ai reçu le coup en pleine figure ; (*gen*) **~ behind you** juste derrière vous ; **you'll have the wind ~ behind you** vous aurez le vent dans le dos ; **public opinion would be ~ behind them** ils auraient l'opinion publique pour eux ; **go ~ on** continuez tout droit ; **I'll be ~ back** je reviens tout de suite

◆ **right away** (= *immediately*) tout de suite, sur-le-champ ; (= *at the first attempt*) du premier coup

◆ **right off*** du premier coup

b = exactly **~ then** sur-le-champ ; **I had to decide ~ then** j'ai dû décider sur-le-champ ; **~ now** (= *at the moment*) en ce moment ; (= *at once*) tout de suite ; **~ here** ici même ; **~ in the middle** au beau milieu, en plein milieu ; **~ at the start** au tout début ; **~ from the start** dès le début

c = completely, all the way tout ; **~ round the house** tout autour de la maison ; **to fall ~ to the bottom** tomber tout au fond ; **~ (up) against the wall** tout contre le mur ; **~ at the top of the mountain** tout en haut de la montagne ; **~ at the back** ◊ **~ at the bottom** tout au fond ; **pierced ~ through** transpercé *or* percé de part en part ; **to turn ~ round** se retourner, faire volte-face ; **push it ~ in** enfoncez-le complètement ; (*in race*) **he's ~ up there** il est en tête

d = correctly, well bien ; **you haven't put the lid on ~** tu n'as pas bien mis le couvercle ; **if I remember ~** si je me souviens bien ; **to guess ~** deviner juste ; **to answer ~** répondre correctement, bien répondre ; **you did ~ to refuse** vous avez bien fait *or* eu raison de refuser ; **if everything goes ~** si tout va bien ; **nothing goes ~ for them** rien ne leur réussit ; **if I get you ~*** si je vous comprends bien

e †, dial (= *very*) très ; **she's doing ~ well** elle va très bien

f = opposite of left à droite ; **to look ~** regarder à droite ; **the party has now moved ~ of centre** le parti se situe maintenant à la droite du centre, c'est devenu un parti de centre droit ; (*Mil*) **eyes ~!** tête droite ! ; (*Mil*) **~ about turn!** demi-tour *m* (à) droite !

◆ **right and left** (= *on every side*) **to be cheated ~ and left** se faire avoir* par tout le monde ; **to owe money ~ and left** devoir de l'argent à tout le monde

◆ **right, left and centre*** (= *everywhere*) partout, de tous côtés

3 NOUN

a = moral bien *m* ; **he doesn't know ~ from wrong** il ne sait pas discerner le bien du mal ; **to be in the ~** avoir raison, être dans le vrai ; **to know the ~s and wrongs of a question** connaître les tenants et les aboutissants d'une question

b = entitlement droit *m* ; **by ~** de droit ; **to have a ~ to sth** avoir droit à qch ; **to have a** *or* **the ~ to do sth** avoir le droit de faire qch ; **he has no ~ to sit here** il n'a pas le droit de s'asseoir ici ; **what ~ have you to say that?** de quel droit dites-vous cela ? ; **by what ~?** de quel droit ? ; **he has no ~ to the money** il n'a pas droit à cet argent ; **he is within his ~s** il est dans son droit ; **I know my ~s** je connais mes droits ; **to stand on** *or* **assert one's ~s** faire valoir ses droits ; **I won't stand on my ~ to do so** je ne ferai pas valoir mon droit à le faire ; **women's ~s** les droits *mpl* de la femme *or* des femmes ; **women's ~s movement** mouvement *m* pour les droits de la femme ; (*Jur*) **~ of appeal** droit *m* d'appel → **4**

◆ **by rights** en toute justice

◆ **in one's own right**: **Taiwan wants membership in its own ~** Taïwan veut adhérer indépendamment ; **she's a poet in her own ~** elle est elle-même poète

c = opposite of left droite *f* ; **to drive on the ~** conduire à droite ; **to keep to the ~** tenir la *or* sa droite, serrer à droite ; **on my ~** à ma droite ; **on** *or* **to the ~ of the church** à droite de l'église ; (*Mil*) **by the ~, march!** à droite, droite ! ; (*US*) **to take a ~** tourner à droite ; (*Pol*) **the Right** la droite

d Boxing droite *f*

4 **rights** PLURAL NOUN

a Comm droits *mpl* ; **manufacturing/publication ~s** droits *mpl* de fabrication/publication ; **TV/film ~s** droits *mpl* d'adaptation pour la télévision/le cinéma ; **"all ~s reserved"** « tous droits réservés » ; **to have the (sole) ~s of** *or* **to sth** avoir les droits (exclusifs) de qch

b = proper state **to put** *or* **set sth to ~s** mettre qch en ordre ; **to put the world** *or* **things to ~s** refaire le monde

c **to have sb bang** *or* **dead to ~s*** (= *have evidence against sb*) avoir coincé* qn ; (= *understand sb well*) avoir bien cerné qn

5 TRANSITIVE VERB

a = return to normal [+ *car, ship*] redresser ; **the car ~ed itself** la voiture s'est redressée (toute seule) ; **the problem should ~ itself** le problème devrait s'arranger tout seul *or* se résoudre de lui-même

b = make amends for [+ *wrong*] redresser ; [+ *injustice*] réparer

6 COMPOUNDS

► **right angle** N angle *m* droit ; **to be at ~ angles (to)** être perpendiculaire à ► **right-angled** ADJ à angle droit ► **right-angled triangle** N triangle *m* rectangle ► **right-hand** ADJ **~-hand drive car** voiture *f* avec (la) conduite à droite ; (*fig*) **his ~-hand man** son bras droit (*fig*) ; **the ~-hand side** le côté droit ► **right-handed** ADJ [*person*] droitier ; [*punch, throw*] du droit ; [*screw*] fileté à droite ; [*scissors, tin-opener etc*] pour droitiers ► **right-hander** N (*Motor Racing*) virage *m* à droite ; (*Boxing*) droite *f* ; (= *person*) droitier *m*, -ière *f* ► **right-ho*** EXCL = righto ► **Right Honourable** ADJ (*Brit*) le Très Honorable ► **right-minded** ADJ = right-thinking ► **right-of-centre** ADJ (*Pol*) (de) centre droit ► **right of way** N (*across property*) droit *m* de passage ; (*Aut*) (= *priority*) priorité *f* ; (*Aut*) **it's his ~ of way** c'est lui qui a (la) priorité ; **he has (the) ~ of way** il a (la) priorité ► **right-oh** EXCL = righto ► **right-on*** ADJ vertueux ► **rights issue** N (*St Ex*) émission *f* de droits de souscription ► **right-thinking** ADJ sensé ► **right-to-life** ADJ [*movement, group*] (*gen*) pour le droit à la vie ; (*anti-abortion*) antiavortement *inv* ► **right-to-lifer** N (*US*) adversaire *mf* de l'avortement ► **right triangle** N (*US*) = right-angled triangle ► **right whale** N (*Zool*) baleine *f* franche ► **right wing** N (*Sport*) ailier *m* droit ; (*Pol*) droite *f* ; **the ~ wing of the party** l'aile droite du parti ► **right-wing** ADJ (*Pol*) de droite ; **to be ~-wing** être de droite ► **right-winger** N (*Pol*) homme *m or* femme *f* de droite ; (*Sport*) ailier *m* droit

righteous ['raɪtʃəs] 1 ADJ a (*frm* = *virtuous*) [*person, behaviour*] droit, vertueux b (= *self-righteous*: *esp pej*) [*person, manner, tone, article*] moralisateur (-trice *f*) ; [*indignation, anger*] justifié ; **stop being so ~!** cesse de faire la morale ! → **self** 2 **the righteous** NPL (*Bible*) les justes *mpl*

righteously ['raɪtʃəslɪ] ADV vertueusement

righteousness ['raɪtʃəsnɪs] N droiture *f*, vertu *f*

rightful ['raɪtfʊl] ADJ [*owner, heir, inheritance, position, claim*] légitime ; **one day all minorities will take their ~ place in society** un jour, toutes les minorités obtiendront la place qui leur revient dans la société ; **~ claimant** ayant droit *m*

rightfully ['raɪtfəlɪ] ADV légitimement ; **we demand only what is ~ ours** nous n'exigeons que ce qui nous appartient légitimement

rightism ['raɪtɪzəm] N droitisme *m*, opinions *fpl* de droite

rightist ['raɪtɪst] (*Pol*) 1 N homme *m or* femme *f* de droite 2 ADJ de droite

▼ **rightly** ['raɪtlɪ] ADV a (= *correctly*) bien, avec raison ; **he ~ assumed that ...** il supposait avec raison que ... ; **she hoped she'd chosen ~** elle espérait qu'elle avait bien choisi *or* qu'elle avait fait le bon choix ; **I don't ~ know*** je ne sais pas très bien ; **it shouldn't ~ do that** cela ne devrait vraiment pas faire ça b (= *justifiably*) à juste titre ; **~ or wrongly** à tort ou à raison ; **~ so** à juste titre

righto* [,raɪt'əʊ] EXCL (*Brit*) d'accord, OK

rightward(s) ['raɪtwəd(z)] ADJ, ADV à droite, vers la droite

righty ho* [,raɪtɪ'həʊ] EXCL (*Brit*) = **righto**

rigid ['rɪdʒɪd] ADJ a (*lit*) [*material, structure*] rigide ; [*muscle*] raide ; **~ with fear** paralysé par la peur ; **~ with rage** *or* **anger** blême de colère ; **to be bored ~*** s'ennuyer à mourir ; **this kind of music bores me ~*** ce genre de musique m'ennuie à mourir b (*fig* = *strict, inflexible*) [*specifications, interpretation, principles, rule, discipline*] strict ; [*system, hierarchy, adherence, person, approach, attitude*] rigide ; [*control, censorship*] rigoureux

rigidity [rɪ'dʒɪdɪtɪ] N a (*lit*) [*of material, structure*] rigidité *f* ; [*of muscle*] raideur *f* b (*fig* = *strictness, inflexibility*) [*of control, censorship, principles, rule, discipline*] rigueur *f* ; [*of specifications, interpretation, system, person, attitude*] rigidité *f*

rigidly ['rɪdʒɪdlɪ] ADV a (= *stiffly*) [*stand, move, gesture*] avec raideur ; **~ constructed** construit de manière rigide ; **to stand ~ to attention** être figé dans un garde-à-vous impeccable ; **to sit ~ erect** *or* **upright** être assis droit comme un i b (*fig*) [*enforce, control, disciplined, organized etc*] rigoureusement ; **to stick ~ to sth** s'en tenir rigoureusement à qch ; **~ authoritarian/conformist/dogmatic** d'un autoritarisme/conformisme/dogmatisme rigide ; **nursing is still a ~ hierarchical profession** la profession d'infirmière reste très hiérarchisée

rigmarole ['rɪgmərəʊl] N comédie *f*, cinéma

➤ LANGUAGE IN USE: **rightly** 13, 26.3

m; **to go through the whole** *or* **same ~ again** recommencer le même cinéma*

rigor ['rɪgəʳ] N (*US*) = **rigour**

rigor mortis ['rɪgəʳ'mɔːtɪs] N rigidité *f* cadavérique

rigorous ['rɪgərəs] ADJ [*examination, test, control, person*] rigoureux; **he is ~ about quality** il est très strict sur la qualité; **to be ~ in doing sth** faire qch rigoureusement

rigorously ['rɪgərəslɪ] ADV [*enforce, control, observe, define, test*] rigoureusement

rigour, rigor (*US*) ['rɪgəʳ] N rigueur *f*

rile* [raɪl] VT agacer, mettre en boule*

Riley ['raɪlɪ] N (*Brit*) **to live the life of ~*** avoir *or* mener la belle vie

rill [rɪl] N (*liter*) ruisselet *m*

rim [rɪm] **1** N (*gen*) bord *m*; [*of wheel*] jante *f*; [*of spectacles*] monture *f*; **a ~ of dirt** *or* **a dirty ~ around the bath** une trace sale sur le bord de la baignoire **2** VT border; [+ *wheel*] janter, cercler

rimaye [rɪ'meɪ] N (*Climbing*) rimaye *f*

rime[1]† [raɪm] = **rhyme**

rime[2] [raɪm] N (*liter*) givre *m*

rimless ['rɪmlɪs] ADJ [*spectacles*] sans monture

rind [raɪnd] N [*of orange, lemon*] peau *f*, pelure *f*; (= *grated zest*) zeste *m*; (= *peel*) écorce *f*; (= *peelings*) pelure *f*; [*of cheese*] croûte *f*; [*of bacon*] couenne *f*; **melon ~** écorce *f* de melon

▼ **ring**[1] [rɪŋ] **1** N **a** (*gen*) anneau *m*; (*on finger*) anneau *m*; (*with stone*) bague *f*; [*of bishop*] anneau *m*; (*on bird's foot*) bague *f*; (*for napkin*) rond *m*; (*for swimmer*) bouée *f* de natation; (*for invalid to sit on*) rond *m* (*pour malade*); [*of piston*] segment *m*; [*of turbine*] couronne *f*; **diamond ~** bague *f* de diamant(s); **wedding ~** alliance *f*, anneau *m* de mariage; (*for cooking*) **electric ~** plaque *f* électrique; **gas ~** brûleur *m* (de cuisinière à gaz) → **earring, key, signet** **b** (= *circle*) cercle *m*, rond *m*; [*of people*] cercle *m*; [*of smoke*] rond *m*; (*in water*) rond *m*; (*in tree trunk*) cercle *m*; **the ~s of Saturn** les anneaux *mpl* de Saturne; **to have ~s round the eyes** avoir les yeux cernés *or* battus; **to stand in a ~** se tenir en cercle *or* en rond, former un cercle; (*fig*) **to run ~s round sb*** dominer qn de la tête et des épaules **c** (= *group*) coterie *f*, clique *f* (*pej*); [*of dealers*] groupe *m*, cartel *m*; [*of gangsters*] bande *f*, gang *m*; [*of spies*] réseau *m*; (*at auction*) **there is a ~ operating** il y a un système d'enchères privées **d** (= *enclosure*) (*at circus*) piste *f*; (*at exhibition*) arène *f*, piste *f*; (*Racing*) enceinte *f* des bookmakers; (*Boxing*) ring *m*; (*Boxing*) **the ~** la boxe, le ring **2** VT (= *surround*) entourer; (*with quoit, hoop*) jeter un anneau sur; (= *circle*) [+ *item on list etc*] entourer d'un cercle; [+ *bird, tree*] baguer; [+ *bull*] mettre un anneau au nez de **3** COMP ▸ **ring-a-ring-a-roses** N *ronde enfantine* ▸ **ring binder** N classeur *m* à anneaux ▸ **ring exercise** N (*Gym*) exercice *m* aux anneaux ▸ **ring-fence** VT [+ *money*] allouer; **to ~-fence a local authority** obliger une municipalité à utiliser l'argent destiné à un usage particulier ▸ **ring finger** N annulaire *m* ▸ **ring ouzel** N merle *m* à plastron ▸ **ring-pull** N (*Brit*: *on can*) anneau *m* (d'ouverture), bague *f*; **~-pull can** boîte *f* avec anneau (d'ouverture) ▸ **ring road** N (*Brit*) rocade *f*; (*motorway-type*) périphérique *m* ▸ **ring spanner** N clef *f* polygonale ▸ **ring-tailed** ADJ à queue zébrée

ring[2] [rɪŋ] (*vb*: *pret* **rang**, *ptp* **rung**) **1** N **a** (= *sound*) son *m*; [*of bell*] sonnerie *f*; (*lighter*) tintement *m*; [*of electric bell*] retentissement *m*; [*of coins*] tintement *m*; **there was a ~ at the door** on a sonné à la porte; **to hear a ~ at the door** entendre sonner à la porte; **give two ~s for the maid** sonne deux coups *or* deux fois

pour (appeler) la bonne; **his voice had an angry ~ (to it)** il y avait un accent *or* une note de colère dans sa voix; **that has the ~ of truth (to it)** ça sonne juste **b** (*esp Brit** = *phone call*) coup *m* de téléphone *or* de fil*; **to give sb a ~** donner *or* passer un coup de téléphone *or* de fil* à qn **c** **~ of bells** jeu *m* de cloches **2** VI **a** [*bell*] sonner, retentir; (*lightly*) tinter; [*alarm clock, telephone*] sonner; **the bell rang** la cloche a sonné *or* tinté, la sonnette a retenti; **the bell rang for dinner** la cloche a sonné le dîner; **to ~ for sb** sonner qn; **to ~ for sth** sonner pour demander qch; **please ~ for attention** prière de sonner; **to ~ for the lift** appeler l'ascenseur; **to ~ at the door** sonner à la porte; **you rang, sir?** Monsieur a sonné? **b** (= *telephone*) téléphoner **c** (= *sound*) [*words*] retentir, résonner; [*voice*] vibrer; [*coin*] sonner, tinter; (= *resound*) résonner, retentir; [*ears*] tinter, bourdonner; **to ~ false/true** [*coin*] sonner faux/clair; (*fig*) **that ~s true** ça sonne juste; **that doesn't ~ true** ça sonne faux; **the room rang with their shouts** la pièce résonnait de leurs cris; **the town rang with his praises** la ville entière chantait ses louanges; **the news set the town ~ing** toute la ville parlait de la nouvelle, dans toute la ville il n'était bruit que de la nouvelle†; **his voice rang with emotion** sa voix vibrait d'émotion; **his words still ~ in my ears** ses mots retentissent encore à mes oreilles **3** VT **a** (= *sound: gen*) sonner; [+ *coin*] faire sonner, faire tinter; **to ~ the doorbell** sonner (à la porte); **to ~ the bell** (*lit*) sonner, donner un coup de sonnette; (*handbell*) agiter la sonnette; (** fig = succeed*) décrocher la timbale*, réussir magnifiquement; **they rang the church bells** (*gen*) ils ont fait sonner les cloches; [*bell ringers*] ils ont sonné les cloches; (*fig*) **his name ~s a bell*** son nom me dit quelque chose *or* me rappelle quelque chose; (*US*) **he/it ~s my bell*** il/ça me botte*; **to ~ the knell (of)** sonner le glas (de); **to ~ the hours** sonner les heures; **to ~ the changes** [*bells*] carillonner (*en variant l'ordre des cloches*); (*fig*) **to do sth to ~ the changes** faire qch pour changer; **to ~ the changes on an outfit/the menu** *etc* varier un ensemble/le menu *etc* **b** (*Telec*: *also* ~ **up**) téléphoner à, donner *or* passer un coup de téléphone *or* de fil* à qn

▸ **ring around** = **ring round**

▸ **ring back** VI, VT SEP (*Brit Telec*) rappeler

▸ **ring down** VT SEP (*Theat*) **to ~ down the curtain** (*faire*) baisser le rideau; (*fig*) **to ~ down the curtain on sth** marquer la fin de qch

▸ **ring in 1** VI (*Brit* = *report by telephone*) téléphoner un reportage **2** VT SEP **to ~ in the New Year** carillonner le Nouvel An

▸ **ring off** VI (*Brit Telec*) raccrocher

▸ **ring out** VI [*bell*] sonner; [*electric bell*] retentir; [*voice*] résonner; [*shot*] éclater, retentir

▸ **ring round** (*Brit*) **1** VI (*Telec*) donner des coups de téléphone **2** VT FUS **I'll ~ round my friends** je vais appeler (tous) mes amis

▸ **ring up** VT SEP **a** (*Brit Telec*) donner un coup de téléphone *or* de fil* à **b** (*Theat*) **to ~ up the curtain** frapper les trois coups, (*sonner pour faire*) lever le rideau; (*fig*) **to ~ up the curtain on a new career** *etc* marquer le début d'une nouvelle carrière *etc* **c** (*on cash register*) [+ *amount*] enregistrer; (*fig*) [+ *profits, sales*] réaliser

ringbolt ['rɪŋbəʊlt] N (*Tech*) piton *m*; (*Naut*) anneau *m* (d'amarrage)

ringdove ['rɪŋdʌv] N ramier *m*

ringer ['rɪŋəʳ] N **a** (*also* **bell ~**) sonneur *m*, carillonneur *m* **b** (= *lookalike*) sosie *m*; **he is a dead ~* for the President** c'est le sosie du président

ringing ['rɪŋɪŋ] **1** ADJ [*bell*] qui sonne *or* tinte; [*voice, tone*] sonore; [*endorsement*] vibrant; [*declaration*] retentissant; **in ~ tones** avec des accents vibrants **2** N [*of bell*] sonne-

rie *f*, son *m*; (*lighter*) tintement *m*; [*of electric bell*] retentissement *m*; [*of telephone*] sonnerie *f*; (= *ears*) tintement *m*, bourdonnement *m* **3** COMP ▸ **ringing tone** N (*Brit Telec*) tonalité *f* d'appel

ringleader ['rɪŋliːdəʳ] N chef *m*, meneur *m*

ringlet ['rɪŋlɪt] N frisette *f*; (*long*) anglaise *f*

ringmaster ['rɪŋmɑːstəʳ] N **the ~** ≈ Monsieur Loyal

ringside ['rɪŋsaɪd] N **at the ~** au premier rang; (*fig*) **to have a ~ seat** être aux premières loges

ringway ['rɪŋweɪ] N = **ring road**; → **ring**[1]

ringworm ['rɪŋwɜːm] N teigne *f*

rink [rɪŋk] N (*for ice-hockey, ice-skating*) patinoire *f*; (*for roller-skating*) skating *m*

rinky-dink* ['rɪŋkɪdɪŋk] ADJ (*US*) (*old-fashioned; also small-time*) ringard*; (= *poor quality*) de camelote*; (= *broken down*) déglingué*, démoli

rinse [rɪns] **1** N **a** (= *act*) rinçage *m*; **give the cup a ~** rincez la tasse, passez la tasse sous le robinet **b** (*for hair*) rinçage *m* **2** VT **a** [+ *clothes etc*] rincer; **to ~ one's hands** se passer les mains à l'eau; **to ~ the soap off one's hands** se rincer les mains **b** (= *colour with a rinse*) **to ~ one's hair** se faire un *or* des rinçage(s); **she ~d her hair black** elle s'est fait un rinçage noir

▸ **rinse out** VT SEP **a** [+ *hair tint, colour, dirt*] faire partir à l'eau **b** [+ *cup*] rincer; **to ~ out one's mouth** se rincer la bouche

Rio ['riːəʊ] N **~ (de Janeiro)** Rio (de Janeiro); **~ Grande** Rio Grande

riot ['raɪət] **1** N **a** (= *uprising*) émeute *f*; (*Jur*) actes *mpl* séditieux; **the ~s against the régime** les émeutes *fpl* contre le régime **b** (*fig*) **a ~ of colour(s)** une débauche de couleurs; **a ~ of reds and blues** une profusion de rouges et de bleus; **a ~ of flowers** une profusion de fleurs; **he's a ~*** c'est un (type) rigolo*; **she's a ~*** elle est rigolote*; **the film is a ~*** (= *funny*) le film est tordant*; **to run ~** [*people, imagination*] être déchaîné; [*vegetation*] pousser dans tous les sens **2** VI faire une émeute; (*Jur*) se livrer à des actes séditieux **3** COMP ▸ **Riot Act** N (*Hist*) loi *f* contre les attroupements séditieux → **read** ▸ **riot control** N (*NonC*) répression *f* des émeutes ▸ **riot-control** ADJ antiémeute ▸ **riot gear** N (*NonC*) tenue *f* antiémeute ▸ **the riot police** N les unités *fpl* antiémeute ▸ **riot shield** N bouclier *m* antiémeute ▸ **the Riot Squad** N = **the riot police**

rioter ['raɪətəʳ] N émeutier *m*, -ière *f*; (*vandalizing*) casseur *m*

rioting ['raɪətɪŋ] **1** N (*NonC*) émeutes *fpl* **2** ADJ [*mob, youths etc*] en émeute

riotous ['raɪətəs] ADJ **a** (= *uproarious*) [*party, evening*] très animé; [*performance, comedy, welcome*] délirant*; **they had a ~ time*** ils se sont amusés comme des fous; **she burst into ~ laughter** elle s'est mise à hurler de rire **b** (= *disorderly*) [*behaviour*] séditieux; [*crowd*] déchaîné; **to engage in ~ living** mener une vie dissipée *or* de débauche; (*Jur*) **~ assembly** attroupements *mpl* séditieux

riotously ['raɪətəslɪ] ADV **a** [*behave, act*] (= *noisily*) de façon tapageuse; (*Jur*) de façon séditieuse **b** **it was ~ funny*** c'était tordant*

RIP [ˌɑːraɪ'piː] (ABBR = **rest in peace**) R.I.P.

rip [rɪp] **1** N déchirure *f* **2** VT déchirer, fendre; **to ~ open a letter** ouvrir une lettre en hâte, fendre une enveloppe; **to ~ the buttons from a shirt** arracher les boutons d'une chemise **3** VI [*cloth*] se déchirer, se fendre **b*** **the fire/explosion ~ped through the house** l'incendie a fait rage à travers la maison/l'explosion a soufflé la maison de part en part; **the jet ~ped through the sky** le jet a fendu le ciel; **the car ~s along** la voiture roule à toute vitesse *or* roule à toute biture*; **let her** *or* **it ~!*** [*boat, car*] appuie!, fonce!*; **to let ~** (*gen*) laisser courir*; (*in anger*) éclater, exploser (*de colère etc*); **he let ~ a string of oaths** il a lâché un chapelet de jurons; **he let ~ at me** il m'a passé un bon savon*; **to ~ into sb** (= *criticize, tell off*) descendre qn en flammes* [4] COMP ► **rip-off:** N → **rip-off** ► **rip-roaring*** ADJ (*gen*) d'une gaieté bruyante, exubérant; [*success*] monstre*

► **rip off** [1] VT SEP [a] (*lit*) arracher (**from** de) [b] (:= *steal*) [+ *object, goods*] voler; (= *defraud etc*) [+ *customer*] arnaquer*, filouter*; [+ *employee*] exploiter; **they're ~ping you off!** c'est du vol manifeste *or* de l'arnaque*! [2] **~-off:** → **rip-off**

► **rip out** VT SEP arracher

► **rip up** VT SEP déchirer

riparian [raɪˈpɛərɪən] ADJ, N riverain(e) *m(f)*

ripcord [ˈrɪpkɔːd] N poignée *f* d'ouverture

ripe [raɪp] ADJ [a] (*lit*) [*fruit*] mûr; [*cheese*] fait [b] (*fig* = *mature*) [*age, judgement*] mûr; **to live to a ~ old age** vivre vieux *or* jusqu'à un âge avancé; **to live to the ~ old age of 88** atteindre l'âge respectable de 88 ans; **wait until the time is ~** attendez le moment opportun; **the market is ~ for the picking** ce marché vous tend les bras*; **the time is ~ to begin afresh** il est temps de tout reprendre à zéro; **the time is ~ for revolution** le temps est venu de faire la révolution; **conditions were ~ for an outbreak of cholera/a military uprising** toutes les conditions étaient réunies pour une épidémie de choléra/une insurrection armée [c] (* = *fetid*) [*smell*] fétide; **he smelled rather ~** il ne sentait pas la rose [d] (* = *crude*) [*language, humour*] égrillard → **overripe**

ripen [ˈraɪpən] [1] VT (faire) mûrir [2] VI mûrir; [*cheese*] se faire

ripeness [ˈraɪpnɪs] N maturité *f*

rip-off: [ˈrɪpɒf] [1] N [a] (= *swindle*) escroquerie *f*; **it's a ~!** c'est du vol *or* de l'arnaque*! [b] (= *copy*) imitation *f* [2] COMP ► **rip-off artist:** N escroc *m*

riposte [rɪˈpɒst] [1] N (*Fencing: also fig*) riposte *f* [2] VI riposter

ripper [ˈrɪpəʳ] N (= *murderer*) éventreur *m*; **Jack the Ripper** Jack l'éventreur

ripping†‡ [ˈrɪpɪŋ] ADJ (*Brit*) épatant*, sensationnel*

ripple [ˈrɪpl] [1] N [a] (= *movement*) [*of water*] ride *f*, ondulation *f*; [*of crops*] ondulation *f* [b] (= *noise*) [*of waves*] clapotis *m*; [*of voices*] murmure(s) *m(pl)*, gazouillement *m*; [*of laughter*] cascade *f* [c] (= *ice-cream*) **chocolate/ raspberry ~** glace à la vanille marbrée de glace au chocolat/à la framboise [2] VI [*water*] se rider; [*crops, hair*] onduler; [*waves*] clapoter [3] VT [+ *water*] rider; [+ *crops*] faire onduler [4] COMP ► **ripple effect** N effet *m* de vague

ripsaw [ˈrɪpsɔː] N scie *f* à refendre

riptide [ˈrɪptaɪd] N contre-courant *m*, turbulence *f*

RISC [ˌɑːraɪesˈsiː] N (*Comput*) [a] (ABBR = **reduced instruction set computer**) → **reduced** [b] (ABBR = **reduced instruction set computing**) → **reduced**

rise [raɪz] (*vb: pret* **rose**, *ptp* **risen**) [1] N [a] [*of theatre curtain, sun*] lever *m*; (*Mus*) hausse *f*; (= *increase*) élévation *f*, hausse *f*; (*in pressure*) hausse *f*; [*of tide*] flux *m*, flot *m*; [*of river*] crue *f*; (*Brit: in wages*) augmentation *f*, relèvement *m* (*Admin*); (*in prices*) hausse *f*, augmentation *f*; (*in bank rate*) relèvement *m*; **prices are on the ~** les prix sont en hausse; (*Brit*) **to ask for a ~** [*employee*] demander une augmentation (de salaire); **there has been a ~ in the number of people looking for work** le nombre des demandeurs d'emploi a augmenté; (*fig*) **his meteoric ~** son ascension *f* fulgurante; **her ~ to power** son ascension *f* au pouvoir; **his ~ to fame took 20 years** il a mis 20 ans à parvenir à la gloire *or* à devenir célèbre; **the ~ of Bristol/the steel industry** l'essor *m* de Bristol/de l'industrie de l'acier; **the ~ of**

the working classes l'ascension du prolétariat; **the ~ and fall of an empire** l'essor et la chute d'un empire, la grandeur et la décadence d'un empire; (*fig*) **to get a ~ out of sb*** ◊ **to take the ~ out of sb*** se payer la tête de qn*

[b] (= *small hill*) éminence *f*, hauteur *f*; (= *slope*) côte *f*, pente *f*

[c] (= *origin*) [*of river*] source *f*; **the river has** *or* **takes its ~ (in)** la rivière prend sa source *or* a son origine (dans); (*fig*) **to give ~ to** [+ *trouble*] causer, provoquer; [+ *speculation, rumour*] donner lieu à, engendrer; [+ *bitterness*] occasionner, causer; [+ *fear, suspicions*] donner naissance à, susciter; [+ *pleasure, interest*] susciter; [+ *impression*] faire, donner

[2] VI [a] (= *get up*) (*from sitting, lying*) se lever, se mettre debout; (*from bed*) se lever; (*after falling*) se relever; **he ~s early/late** il se lève tôt/tard; **~ and shine!** allez, lève-toi!, debout, là-dedans!*; **he rose to go** il s'est levé pour partir; **to ~ to one's feet** se mettre debout, se lever; **to ~ on tiptoe** se mettre sur la pointe des pieds; **to ~ from (the) table** se lever de table; **he rose from his chair** il s'est levé de sa chaise; **he rose from his sickbed to go and see her** il a quitté son lit pour aller la voir; **to ~ from the dead** ressusciter (des morts); **the horse rose on its hind legs** le cheval s'est dressé (sur ses jambes de derrière) *or* s'est cabré

[b] (= *go up, ascend*) [*smoke, mist*] s'élever, monter; [*balloon*] s'élever; [*aircraft, lift*] monter; [*theatre curtain, sun, moon, wind, bread*] se lever; [*dough*] lever; [*hair*] se dresser; [*ground*] monter (en pente); [*voice*] monter, devenir plus aigu; [*sea*] devenir houleux; [*water, river, tide, blood pressure, temperature, exchange rate*] monter; [*barometer*] remonter, être en hausse; [*hopes, anger*] croître, grandir; [*prices*] monter, augmenter; [*cost of living*] augmenter, être en hausse; [*stocks, shares*] monter, être en hausse; **to ~ to the surface** [*swimmer, object, fish*] remonter à la *or* en surface; **the fish are rising well** les poissons mordent bien; **the mountain ~s to 3,000 metres** la montagne a une altitude de 3 000 mètres; **the mountains rising before him** les montagnes qui se dressaient *or* s'élevaient devant lui; **he won't ~ to any of your taunts** il ne réagira à aucune de vos piques; **his eyebrows rose at the sight of her** quand il l'a vue il a levé les sourcils (d'étonnement); **the idea/ image rose in his mind** l'idée/l'image s'est présentée à son esprit; **great cheers rose from the audience** de nombreux hourras s'élevèrent de la foule; **to ~ to the occasion** se montrer à la hauteur de la situation *or* des circonstances; **I can't ~ to £50** je ne peux pas aller jusqu'à 50 livres; **to ~ in price** augmenter (de prix); **to ~ above a certain temperature/a certain level** dépasser une température donnée/un niveau donné; **her spirits rose** son moral a remonté; **the colour rose to her cheeks** ses joues se sont empourprées, le rouge lui est monté aux joues → **bait, challenge, gorge**

[c] (*fig: in society, rank*) s'élever; **to ~ in the world** réussir, faire son chemin dans le monde; **to ~ from nothing** partir de rien; (*Mil*) **to ~ from the ranks** sortir du rang; **he rose to be President/a captain** il s'est élevé jusqu'à devenir Président/jusqu'au grade de capitaine; **to ~ to fame** connaître la célébrité

[d] (= *adjourn*) [*assembly*] clore la session; [*meeting*] lever la séance; (*Parl*) **the House rose at 2am** l'Assemblée a levé la séance à 2 heures du matin; **Parliament will ~ on Thursday next** les vacances parlementaires commenceront jeudi prochain

[e] (= *originate*) [*river*] prendre sa source *or* sa naissance (**in** dans)

[f] (= *rebel: also* **~ up**) se soulever, se révolter (**against** contre); **to ~ (up) in revolt** se révolter (**against** contre); **they rose (up) in anger and**

assassinated the tyrant emportés par la colère ils se sont soulevés et ont assassiné le tyran; **a feeling of inadequacy rose (up) within him** un sentiment de médiocrité montait en lui

risen [ˈrɪzn] [1] VB *ptp of* **rise** [2] ADJ (*Rel*) **the ~ Christ** *or* **Lord** le Christ ressuscité

riser [ˈraɪzəʳ] N [a] (= *person*) **to be an early ~** être lève-tôt *inv* *or* matinal; **to be a late ~** être lève-tard *inv* [b] [*of stair*] contremarche *f*

risibility [ˌrɪzɪˈbɪlɪtɪ] N (*frm*) caractère *m* drôle

risible [ˈrɪzɪbl] ADJ (*frm*) risible

rising [ˈraɪzɪŋ] [1] N [a] (= *rebellion*) soulèvement *m*, insurrection *f*

[b] (*NonC*) [*of sun, star*] lever *m*; [*of barometer*] hausse *f*; [*of prices*] augmentation *f*, hausse *f*; [*of river*] crue *f*; [*of person from dead*] résurrection *f*; [*Theat*] [*of curtain*] lever *m*; [*of ground*] élévation *f*; **the ~ and falling of the waves** le mouvement des vagues; **the ~ and falling of the boat on the water** le mouvement du bateau qui danse sur les flots

[c] [*of Parliament, court*] ajournement *m*, clôture *f* de séance

[2] ADJ [a] [*sun*] levant; [*barometer, prices, temperature*] en hausse; [*tide*] montant; [*wind*] qui se lève; [*tone*] qui monte; [*anger, fury*] croissant; [*ground*] qui monte en pente; **the ~ sap** la sève ascendante *or* brute

[b] (*fig*) nouveau (nouvelle *f*); **a ~ young doctor** un jeune médecin d'avenir; **the ~ generation** la nouvelle génération, les jeunes *mpl* → **4**

[3] ADV* **she's ~ six** elle va sur ses six ans; (*Brit Scol*) **the ~ fives** les enfants qui auront cinq ans dans l'année

[4] COMP ► **rising damp** N humidité *f* (par capillarité) ► **rising star** N (*lit, fig*) étoile *f* montante

▼ **risk** [rɪsk] [1] N [a] (= *possible danger*) risque *m*; **to take** *or* **run ~s** courir des risques; **to take** *or* **run the ~ of doing** courir le risque de faire; **you're running the ~ of being arrested** *or* **of arrest** vous risquez de vous faire arrêter; **that's a ~ you'll have to take** c'est un risque à courir; **there's too much ~ involved** c'est trop risqué; **it's not worth the ~** ça ne vaut pas la peine de courir un tel risque; **there is no ~ of his coming** il n'y a pas de risque qu'il vienne, il ne risque pas de venir; **you do it at your own ~** vous le faites à vos risques et périls; (*Comm*) **goods sent at sender's ~** envois *mpl* faits aux risques de l'expéditeur; **at the ~ of seeming stupid** au risque de *or* quitte à paraître stupide; **at the ~ of his life** au péril de sa vie; **at ~** [*person*] en danger; [*plan, custom*] menacé; **children at ~** l'enfance *f* en danger; **some jobs are at ~** des emplois risquent d'être supprimés *or* sont menacés → **occupational, owner**

[b] (*Insurance*) risque *m*; **fire ~** risque *m* d'incendie; **he is a bad accident ~** il présente des risques élevés d'accident; **he is a bad ~** on court trop de risques avec lui → **security**

[2] VT [a] [+ *life, career, future, reputation, savings*] risquer; **you ~ falling** vous risquez de tomber; **he ~ed life and limb to rescue the drowning child** il a risqué sa vie pour sauver l'enfant qui se noyait → **neck**

[b] [+ *battle, defeat, quarrel*] s'exposer aux risques de; [+ *accident*] risquer d'avoir, courir le risque de; (= *venture*) [+ *criticism, remark*] risquer, hasarder; **she won't ~ coming today** elle ne se risquera pas à venir aujourd'hui; **I'll ~ it** je vais risquer *or* tenter le coup*; **I can't ~ it** je ne peux pas prendre un tel risque

[3] COMP ► **risk capital** N capitaux *mpl* à risques ► **risk factor** N facteur *m* de risque ► **risk management** N gestion *f* des risques ► **risk-taking** N he does not like **~-taking** il n'aime pas prendre de risques, il n'a pas le goût du risque

riskily [ˈrɪskɪlɪ] ADV de manière risquée; **~, he's**

► LANGUAGE IN USE: **risk** 2.3

decided to resign il a décidé de démissionner, ce qui est risqué

riskiness ['rɪskɪnɪs] N (NonC) risques mpl, aléas mpl

risky ['rɪskɪ] ADJ [enterprise, deed] risqué; [joke, story] risqué, osé; **it's ~** ◊ **it's a ~ business** c'est risqué

risotto [rɪ'zɒtəʊ] N risotto m

risqué ['riːskeɪ] ADJ [story, joke] risqué, osé

rissole ['rɪsəʊl] N (Brit) rissole f

rite [raɪt] **1** N rite m; **funeral ~s** rites mpl funèbres; (Mus) **the Rite of Spring** le Sacre du printemps → **last**[1] **2** COMP ► **rite of passage** N rite m de passage; **a ~(s)-of-passage novel** un roman d'initiation

ritual ['rɪtjʊəl] **1** ADJ rituel **2** N rituel m; (fig) **he went through the ~(s)** il a fait les gestes rituels, il s'est conformé aux rites; **he went through the ~ of apologizing** il a fait les excuses rituelles, il s'est excusé comme de coutume

ritualism ['rɪtjʊəlɪzəm] N ritualisme m

ritualist ['rɪtjʊəlɪst] ADJ, N ritualiste mf

ritualistic [‚rɪtjʊə'lɪstɪk] ADJ ritualiste

ritualize ['rɪtjʊəlaɪz] VT ritualiser

ritually ['rɪtjʊəlɪ] ADV rituellement

ritzy* ['rɪtsɪ] ADJ luxueux

rival ['raɪvəl] **1** N rival(e) m(f) **2** ADJ [firm, enterprise] rival, concurrent; [attraction] rival; **two ~ firms** deux entreprises rivales, deux concurrents **3** VT (gen) rivaliser avec (**in** de); (Comm) être en concurrence avec; (= equal) égaler (**in** en); **he can't ~ her in intelligence** pour ce qui est de l'intelligence, elle le domine de la tête et des épaules; **his achievements ~ even yours** ses réussites sont presque égales aux vôtres

rivalry ['raɪvəlrɪ] N rivalité f (**with** avec, **between** entre)

rive [raɪv] (pret **rived**, ptp **riven** ['rɪvən]) (liter) **1** VT fendre **2** VI se fendre; **riven by** fendu par; (fig) déchiré par

river ['rɪvəʳ] **1** N rivière f; (major) fleuve m (also fig); (Admin, Econ, Geog etc) cours m d'eau; **down ~** en aval; **up ~** en amont; the Seine (Brit) ◊ **the Seine ~** (US) la Seine; (fig) **~s of blood** des fleuves mpl de sang → **sell 2** COMP [police, port, system] fluvial ► **river basin** N bassin m fluvial ► **river blindness** N (Med) cécité f des rivières, onchocercose f ► **river fish** N poisson m d'eau douce or de rivière ► **river fishing** N (NonC) pêche f fluviale or en eau douce ► **river head** N source f (de rivière or de fleuve) ► **river horse*** N hippopotame m ► **river lamprey** N lamproie f de rivière ► **river-mouth** N bouche f d'une rivière (or d'un fleuve), embouchure f ► **river traffic** N (NonC) trafic m fluvial, navigation f fluviale

riverbank ['rɪvəbæŋk] N rive f, berge f

riverbed ['rɪvəbed] N lit m de rivière or de fleuve

riverboat ['rɪvəbəʊt] N embarcation f fluviale; **a Mississippi ~** un bateau du Mississippi; **by ~** en bateau

riverine ['rɪvəraɪn] ADJ fluvial; [person] riverain

riverside ['rɪvəsaɪd] **1** N bord m de l'eau (or de la rivière or du fleuve), rive f; **by the ~** au bord de l'eau (or de la rivière etc); **along the ~** le long de la rivière (or du fleuve) **2** ADJ (situé) au bord de la rivière etc

rivet ['rɪvɪt] **1** N rivet m **2** VT (Tech) riveter, river; (fig) **it ~ed our attention** ça nous a fascinés; **~ed with fear** rivé or cloué sur place par la peur **3** COMP ► **rivet joint** N rivetage m

riveter ['rɪvɪtəʳ] N (= person) riveur m; (= machine) riveuse f

rivet(t)ing ['rɪvɪtɪŋ] **1** N rivetage m **2** ADJ (= fascinating) fascinant

Riviera [‚rɪvɪ'eərə] N **the (French) ~** la Côte d'Azur; **the Italian ~** la Riviera (italienne)

rivulet ['rɪvjʊlɪt] N (petit) ruisseau m

Riyadh [rɪ'jɑːd] N Riyad

riyal [rɪ'jɑːl] N riyal m

RL N (ABBR = **Rugby League**) → **rugby**

RM [ɑːr'em] N (Brit Mil) (ABBR = **Royal Marines**) → **royal**

RMT [‚ɑːrem'tiː] N (Brit) (ABBR = **National Union of Rail, Maritime and Transport Workers**) syndicat

RN [a] (Brit Mil) (ABBR = **Royal Navy**) → **royal** [b] (US) ABBR = **registered nurse**

RNA [‚ɑːren'eɪ] N (Med) (ABBR = **ribonucleic acid**) ARN m

RNAS (Brit) (ABBR = **Royal Naval Air Services**) aéronavale britannique

RNLI [‚ɑːrenel'laɪ] N (Brit) (ABBR = **Royal National Lifeboat Institution**) ≈ Société f nationale de sauvetage en mer

RNR (Brit Mil) (ABBR = **Royal Naval Reserve**) → **royal**

RNZAF ABBR = **Royal New Zealand Air Force**

RNZN ABBR = **Royal New Zealand Navy**

roach[1] [rəʊtʃ] N (pl **roach** or **roaches**) (= fish) gardon m

roach[2] [rəʊtʃ] **1** N [a] (esp US*) (ABBR = **cockroach**) cafard m, blatte f [b] (for joint, cigarette) filtre m **2** COMP ► **roach clip** N (US: for joint) pince métallique servant à tenir un joint

road [rəʊd] **1** N [a] (gen) route f; (minor) chemin m; (in town) rue f; (fig) chemin m, voie f; **trunk ~** (route f) nationale f, grande route f; **country ~** route f de campagne, (route f) départementale f; **"~ up"** "attention travaux"; **she lives across the ~ (from us)** elle habite en face de chez nous; **just across the ~ is a bakery** il y a une boulangerie juste en face; **my car is off the ~ just now** ma voiture est au garage; **I hope to put it back on the ~ soon** j'espère qu'elle sera bientôt en état (de rouler); **my car is (back) on the ~ again** ma voiture est à nouveau en état de marche; **this vehicle shouldn't be on the ~** on ne devrait pas laisser circuler un véhicule dans cet état; **a spot of petrol will get us on the ~ again** un peu d'essence va nous dépanner; **he is a danger on the ~** (au volant) c'est un danger public; **to take (to) the ~** prendre la route, se mettre en route; **to be on the ~** [salesman, theatre company] être en tournée; **we were on the ~ at 6 in the morning** nous étions sur la route à 6 heures du matin; **we've been on the ~ since this morning** nous voyageons depuis ce matin; **we were on the ~ to Paris** nous étions en route pour Paris; **is this the ~ to London** or **the London ~?** c'est (bien) la route de Londres?; (in towns) **London Road** rue f de Londres; **you're on the right ~** vous êtes sur la bonne route; (fig) vous êtes sur la bonne voie; **on the ~ to ruin/success** sur le chemin de la ruine/du succès ■ (PROV) **the ~ to hell is paved with good intentions** l'enfer est pavé de bonnes intentions (PROV); **somewhere along the ~ he changed his mind** à un moment donné or en cours de route* il a changé d'avis; **you're in my ~*** vous me barrez le passage; **(get) out of the ~!*** dégagez!*, ôtez-vous de là!; (dial) **any ~*** de toute façon; **to have one for the ~*** prendre un dernier verre avant de partir, boire le coup de l'étrier; (US fig) **to take the high/low ~** se comporter de façon irréprochable/malhonnête; (Naut) **~s** rade f; (Brit: car sales) **on-the-~ price** prix m clés en mains → **arterial, end, hit, main, Rome** [b] (US) ABBR = **railroad**

2 COMP ► **road accident** N accident m de la route or de la circulation ► **road atlas** N recueil m de cartes routières ► **road bike** N vélo m de route ► **road book** N guide m routier ► **road bridge** N pont m routier ► **road construction** N construction f routière or de routes ► **road fund licence** N (Brit) vignette f (automobile) ► **road gang** N (US) équipe f de forçats (employés à construire des routes) ► **road haulage** N transports mpl routiers ► **road haulier** N entrepreneur m de transports routiers ► **road hog** N chauffard* m ► **road hump** N ralentisseur m ► **road manager** N (Mus) organisateur m, -trice f de tournées ► **road map** N carte f routière ► **road metal** N empierrement m ► **road movie** N road movie m ► **road pricing** N (Brit) système de péage ► **road race** N course f sur route ► **road racer** N (Cycling) routier m, -ière f ► **road racing** N compétition f sur route ► **road rage** N agressivité f au volant ► **road rider** N (Cycling) = **road racer** ► **road runner** N (US = bird) coucou m terrestre (du Sud-Ouest) ► **road safety** N sécurité f routière ► **road sense** N **he has no ~ sense** [driver] il n'a aucun sens de la conduite; [pedestrian] il ne fait jamais attention à la circulation; **to teach a child ~ sense** apprendre à un enfant à faire attention à la circulation ► **road show** N (Theat) spectacle m en tournée; (Rad, TV) émission f itinérante ► **road sign** N panneau m indicateur or de signalisation; **international ~ signs** signalisation f routière internationale ► **road stability** N (Aut) tenue f de route ► **road surveyor** N agent m des Ponts et Chaussées, agent m voyer ► **road sweeper** N (= person) balayeur m, -euse f; (= vehicle) balayeuse f ► **road tax** N (Brit) taxe f sur les véhicules à moteur; (Brit) **~ tax disc** vignette f (automobile) ► **road test** N essai m sur route ► **road-test** VT **they are ~-testing the car tomorrow** ils vont faire les essais sur route demain ► **road traffic** N (NonC) circulation f routière ► **road traffic accident** N accident m de la route ► **road transport** N transports mpl routiers ► **road-trials** NPL (= road test) essais mpl sur route; (= rally) épreuves fpl sur route ► **road-user** N (gen) usager m de la route; **~-user charges** taxation f des usagers de la route

---

ROADS

Les Britanniques et les Américains n'utilisent pas les mêmes termes pour désigner les différents types de routes. En Grande-Bretagne, les routes nationales sont des « A-roads » ou « trunk roads », les routes secondaires des « B-roads ». Dans la première catégorie, certaines sont des quatre voies séparées par un terre-plein central: elles portent alors le nom de « dual carriageways » (le terme américain équivalent est « divided highways »). Les autoroutes (« motorways ») sont gratuites.

Aux États-Unis, le terme générique pour une autoroute est « superhighway », mais l'on distingue les « interstate highways », qui vont d'un État à l'autre - certaines étant gratuites (« freeways »), les autres payantes (« toll roads » ou « turnpikes ») - et les « expressways », qui sont les autoroutes urbaines ou périurbaines.

---

roadbed ['rəʊdbed] N (US) [of railroad] ballast m; [of road] empierrement m

roadblock ['rəʊdblɒk] N barrage m routier

roadholding ['rəʊdhəʊldɪŋ] N tenue f de route

roadhouse ['rəʊdhaʊs] N (US) relais m routier

roadie* ['rəʊdɪ] N (Mus) roadie* m

roadmaking ['rəʊdmeɪkɪŋ] N (NonC) construction f routière or des routes

roadman ['rəʊdmən] N (pl **-men**) cantonnier m

roadmender ['rəʊdmendəʳ] N = **roadman**

roadroller ['rəʊdrəʊləʳ] N rouleau m compresseur

roadside ['rəʊdsaɪd] **1** N (gen) bord m de la route; (= verge) bas-côté m, accotement m; **along** or **by the ~** au bord de la route **2** COMP [inn] (situé) au bord de la route ► **roadside**

repairs NPL (*professional*) dépannage *m* ; (*done alone*) réparations *fpl* de fortune

roadstead ['rəʊdsted] N (*Naut*) rade *f*

roadster ['rəʊdstər] N (= *car*) roadster *m* ; (= *cycle*) bicyclette *f* routière

roadway ['rəʊdweɪ] N chaussée *f* ; (*on bridge*) tablier *m*

roadwork ['rəʊdwɜːk] ① N (*NonC* : *Sport*) jogging *m* sur route ② **roadworks** NPL travaux *mpl* (d'entretien des routes)

roadworthy ['rəʊdwɜːðɪ] ADJ **a ~ car** une voiture conforme aux normes de sécurité

roam [rəʊm] ① VT [+ *streets, countryside*] parcourir, errer dans or par ; **to ~ the (seven) seas** courir or écumer les mers, bourlinguer sur toutes les mers ; **to ~ the streets** traîner dans les rues ② VI errer ; [*thoughts*] vagabonder ; **to ~ about the house** errer dans la maison ; **to ~ about the world** parcourir le monde ; **to ~ about the streets** traîner dans les rues
► **roam about, roam around** VI (= *wander*) errer, vagabonder ; (= *travel*) bourlinguer*, rouler sa bosse*

roamer ['rəʊmər] N vagabond *m*

roaming ['rəʊmɪŋ] ① ADJ [*person*] errant, vagabond ; [*dog*] errant ; [*thoughts*] vagabond ② N vagabondage *m*

roan[1] [rəʊn] ADJ, N (= *horse*) rouan *m* → **strawberry**

roan[2] [rəʊn] N (= *leather*) basane *f*

roar [rɔːr] ① VI [*person, crowd*] hurler, pousser de grands cris ; (*with anger*) rugir ; [*lion, wind, sea*] rugir ; [*bull*] mugir, beugler ; [*thunder, guns, waterfall, storm, forest fire*] gronder ; [*engine, vehicle*] vrombir, ronfler ; [*fire in hearth*] ronfler ; **to ~ with pain** hurler de douleur ; **to ~ with laughter** rire à gorge déployée, hurler de rire ; **this will make you ~!*** tu vas hurler de rire !, tu vas rigoler !* ; **the trucks ~ed past us** les camions nous ont dépassé dans un ronflement or hurlement de moteur ; **the car ~ed up the street** la voiture remonta la rue dans un ronflement or hurlement de moteur ; **he ~ed away on his motorbike** il est parti en faisant vrombir sa moto
② VT **a** (*also* ~ **out**) [+ *order, one's disapproval*] hurler ; [+ *song*] chanter à tue-tête **b** (*Aut*) **to ~ the engine*** faire ronfler or faire vrombir le moteur
③ N **a** [*of crowd*] clameur *f*, hurlement *m* ; [*of lion*] rugissement *m* ; [*of bull*] mugissement *m* ; [*of river, waterfall, traffic*] grondement *m* ; [*of engine*] vrombissement *m* ; [*of furnace*] ronflement *m* ; **~s of laughter** une explosion de rires ; **the ~s of the crowd** les clameurs *fpl* de la foule

roaring ['rɔːrɪŋ] ① ADJ **a** [*lion, engine*] rugissant ; [*wind, sea*] mugissant ; [*traffic*] assourdissant ; [*crowd*] hurlant ; [*guns, waterfall, storm*] grondant ; [*forest fire*] ronflant ; **a ~ fire** (*in hearth*) une belle flambée ; (*Brit* : *fig*) **a ~ success** un succès fou* ; **to be doing a ~ trade (in sth)** faire des affaires d'or en vendant qch) ② ADV (*Brit*) **~ drunk*** soûl comme une bourrique ③ N [*of crowd*] hurlements *mpl*, clameur *f* ; [*of lion*] rugissement *m* ; [*of bull*] mugissement *m* ; [*of river, waterfall, traffic*] grondement *m* ④ COMP ► **the Roaring Forties** NPL (*Geog*) les quarantièmes *mpl* rugissants ► **the Roaring Twenties** NPL (= *1920s*) les années *fpl* folles

roast [rəʊst] ① N **a** rôti *m* ; **~ of veal/pork** *etc* rôti *m* de veau/porc *etc* ; **~ of beef** rôti *m* de bœuf, rosbif *m* ; **a slice off the ~** une tranche de or du rôti **b** (*US* = *barbecue*) barbecue *m* ② ADJ [*pork, veal, chicken*] rôti ; **~ beef** rôti *m* de bœuf, rosbif *m* ; **~ potatoes** pommes *fpl* de terre rôties ③ VT **a** [+ *meat*] (faire) rôtir ; [+ *chestnuts*] griller, rôtir ; [+ *coffee beans*] griller, torréfier ; [+ *minerals*] calciner, griller ; **to ~ o.s. by the fire** se rôtir au coin du feu **b** (*US*

= *criticize*) éreinter **④** VI [*meat*] rôtir → **roasting**

roaster ['rəʊstər] N (= *device*) rôtissoire *f* ; (= *bird*) volaille *f* à rôtir

roasting ['rəʊstɪŋ] ① N (*lit*) rôtissage *m* ; (*fig*) **to give sb a ~ :** sonner les cloches à qn* ② ADJ (* = *hot*) [*day, weather*] torride ; **it's ~ in here*** on crève* (de chaleur) ici, on rôtit* ici ; **I'm ~!*** je crève* de chaleur ! **b** (*Culin*) [*chicken etc*] à rôtir ③ COMP ► **roasting jack, roasting spit** N tournebroche *m*

rob [rɒb] VT **a** (= *steal from*) [+ *person*] voler, dévaliser ; [+ *shop*] dévaliser ; [+ *orchard*] piller ; **to ~ sb of sth** (*purse etc*) voler qch à qn ; (*rights, privileges*) dépouiller or priver qn de qch ; **to ~ an orchard** piller un verger ; **to ~ the till** voler de l'argent dans la caisse ; **to ~ Peter to pay Paul** déshabiller Pierre pour habiller Paul ; **I've been ~bed of my watch** on m'a volé ma montre ; **I've been ~bed** j'ai été volé ; **the bank was ~bed** la banque a été dévalisée, il y a eu un vol à la banque ; (*Sport*) **we were ~bed*** on nous a volé la victoire ; (*fig*) **he has been ~bed of the pleasure of seeing her** il a été privé du plaisir de la voir ; **the shock ~bed him of speech** (*briefly*) le choc lui a fait perdre la parole ; (*long-term*) le choc lui a ôté l'usage de la parole **b** (* = *steal*) piquer*

robber ['rɒbər] ① N bandit *m*, voleur *m* ② COMP ► **robber baron** N (*US Ind*) requin *m* de l'industrie or de la finance

robbery ['rɒbərɪ] N vol *m* ; (*Jur*) **~ with violence** vol *m* avec voies de fait or coups et blessures ; **at that price it's sheer ~!*** à ce prix-là c'est du vol manifeste or de l'escroquerie ! → **armed, daylight, highway**

robe [rəʊb] ① N **a** (= *ceremonial garment*) robe *f* de cérémonie ; (= *dressing gown*) peignoir *m* ; **he was wearing his ~ of office** il portait la robe or la toge de sa charge ; **ceremonial ~s** vêtements *mpl* de cérémonie ; **christening ~** robe *f* de baptême → **coronation b** (*US* = *rug*) couverture *f* ② VT revêtir (d'une robe) ; (*fig, liter*) parer, revêtir (**in** de) ③ VI [*judge etc*] revêtir sa robe

Robert ['rɒbət] N Robert *m*

robin ['rɒbɪn] N **a** (*in Europe* : *also* ~ **redbreast**) rouge-gorge *m* **b** (*in US*) merle *m* américain → **round**

robot ['rəʊbɒt] ① N robot *m* ; (*fig*) robot *m*, automate *m* ② COMP [*worker, guidance, pilot*] automatique, -robot ► **robot bomb** N bombe *f* volante ► **robot plane** N avion-robot *m*

robotic [rəʊˈbɒtɪk] ADJ [*manner, movements*] d'automate, de robot

robotics [rəʊˈbɒtɪks] N (*NonC*) robotique *f*

robotization [ˌrəʊbɒtaɪˈzeɪʃən] N robotisation *f*

robotize ['rəʊbɒtaɪz] VT robotiser

robust [rəʊˈbʌst] ADJ **a** (= *strong*) [*person, appetite, economy*] robuste ; [*plant*] robuste, résistant ; [*material*] résistant ; [*object, structure, design*] solide ; [*economic growth*] soutenu ; **to have a ~ constitution** avoir une constitution robuste ; **to be in ~ health** avoir une santé robuste **b** (= *vigorous*) [*activity, attitude, speech*] énergique ; [*humour*] jovial ; **to put up a ~ defence of sb/sth** défendre vigoureusement or énergiquement qn/qch **c** (= *intense*) [*flavour, wine*] corsé, robuste

robustly [rəʊˈbʌstlɪ] ADV (= *strongly*) **~ built** [*person*] de robuste constitution ; [*object*] solide **b** (= *vigorously*) [*oppose, attack, defend*] vigoureusement, énergiquement ; [*reply*] avec vigueur ; **to campaign ~ (for/against sth)** mener une campagne vigoureuse or énergique (en faveur de/contre qch)

robustness [rəʊˈbʌstnɪs] N robustesse *f*, vigueur *f*

roc [rɒk] N roc(k) *m*

rock[1] [rɒk] ① VT **a** (= *swing to and fro*) [+ *child*] bercer ; [+ *cradle*] balancer ; **to ~ a child to sleep** endormir un enfant en le berçant ; **a boat ~ed by the waves** un bateau bercé par les vagues → **1b** ; **to ~ o.s. in a rocking chair** se balancer dans un rocking-chair **b** (= *shake*) ébranler, secouer ; [+ *ship*] [*waves*] ballotter ; [*explosion*] ébranler ; (* *fig* = *startle*) ébranler, secouer ; **town ~ed by an earthquake** ville *f* ébranlée par un tremblement de terre ; (*fig*) **country ~ed by rioting** *etc* pays *m* ébranlé par des émeutes *etc* ; (*fig*) **to ~ the boat*** jouer les trouble-fête, semer le trouble or la perturbation ; (*fig*) **don't ~ the boat*** ne compromets pas les choses, ne fais pas l'empêcheur de danser en rond* ; **that bit of news will ~ her!*** cette nouvelle va la bouleverser or lui faire un choc ! ② VI **a** (= *sway gently*) [*cradle, hammock*] (se) balancer ; [*person, ship*] se balancer ; **he was ~ing back and forth** il se balançait d'avant en arrière **b** (= *sway violently*) [*person*] chanceler ; [*building*] être ébranlé or secoué ; **the mast was ~ing in the wind** le mât oscillait dans le vent ; **the ground ~ed beneath our feet** le sol a tremblé sous nos pieds ; **they ~ed with laughter*** ils étaient écroulés or pliés de rire* ③ N (*also* ~ **music**) rock *m* → **5, glam, punk** ④ ADJ (*Mus*) [*ballet, musical etc*] rock *inv* ; **~ musician** rocker *m* ⑤ COMP ► **rock 'n' roll, rock-and-roll** N rock (and roll) *m* ; **to do the ~-and-roll** danser le rock (and roll) ♦ ADJ rock *inv* ► **rock star** N (*Mus*) rock star *f*

rock[2] [rɒk] ① N **a** (*NonC* = *substance*) (*any kind*) roche *f* ; (*hard*) roc *m* ; (*also* = *face*) rocher *m*, paroi *f* rocheuse ; **caves hewn out of the ~** des cavernes *fpl* creusées dans la roche or le roc ; **hewn out of solid ~** creusé à même le roc, creusé dans le roc ; (*lit, fig*) **built on ~** bâti sur le roc ; **they were drilling into ~ and not clay** ils foraient la roche or le roc et non l'argile ; **plants that grow in ~** plantes *fpl* qui poussent sur la roche ; **porous/volcanic** *etc* **~** roche *f* poreuse/volcanique *etc* ; **the study of ~s** l'étude *f* des roches **b** (= *large mass, huge boulder*) rocher *m*, roc *m* (*liter*) ; (*smaller*) roche *f* ; **a huge ~ blocked their way** un énorme rocher leur bouchait le passage ; **fallen ~s** éboulis *mpl* ; (*Geog*) **the Rock (of Gibraltar)** le rocher de Gibraltar ; (*fig*) **as solid as a ~** solide comme un roc ; **the ship went on the ~s** le bateau s'est échoué sur les rochers or contre les écueils ; **on the ~s** [*drink*] avec des glaçons ; (*fig*) **he's on the ~s*** il n'a plus le sou, il est à sec* or dans la dèche* ; **that firm went on the ~s last year*** cette firme a fait faillite l'an dernier ; (*fig*) **their marriage is on the ~s*** leur mariage est en train de craquer* ; **to be between a ~ and a hard place** être pris dans un dilemme **c** (*US* = *small stone*) galet *m* **d** (* = *diamond*) diam* *m* ; **~s** (= *jewels*) quincaillerie* *f* **e** (*Brit* = *sweet*) ≈ sucre *m* d'orge ; **Blackpool ~** bâton de sucre d'orge marqué au nom de Blackpool **f** **to get one's ~s off** prendre son pied* ② COMP ► **rock bass** N perche *f*, achigan *m* ► **rock bottom** N (*Geol*) fond *m* rocheux ; (*fig*) **this is ~ bottom*** c'est la fin de tout, c'est la catastrophe ; **her spirits reached ~ bottom*** elle avait le moral à zéro* ; **prices were at ~ bottom** les prix étaient au plus bas ► **rock-bottom** ADJ (*Comm*) **"~-bottom prices"** « prix sacrifiés », « prix défiant toute concurrence » ► **rock bun, rock cake** N (*Brit*) rocher *m* (*Culin*) ► **rock candy** N (*US*) ≈ sucre *m* d'orge ► **rock carving** N sculpture *f* sur roc ► **rock-climber** N varappeur *m*, -euse *f*, rochassier *m*, -ière *f* ► **rock-climbing** N varappe *f*, escalade *f* ► **rock crystal** N cristal *m* de roche ► **rock face** N paroi *f* rocheuse

► **rock fall** N chute *f* de pierres *or* de rochers
► **rock garden** N (jardin *m* de) rocaille *f*
► **rock-hard** ADJ (*lit*) dur comme la pierre; (*fig* = *tough*) **she's ~-hard*** c'est une coriace
► **rock painting** N (*Art*) peinture *f* rupestre *or* pariétale ► **rock plant** N plante *f* alpestre *or* de rocaille ► **rock pool** N flaque *f or* flache *f* laissée par la marée (*en bord de mer*)
► **rock-ribbed** ADJ (*US fig*) inébranlable, à toute épreuve ► **rock rose** N hélianthème *m*
► **rock salmon** N (*Brit*) roussette *f* ► **rock salt** N sel *m* gemme ► **rock-solid** ADJ (*lit, fig*) solide comme un roc ► **rock-steady** ADJ [*hand, voice*] parfaitement ferme; [*camera, gun, moving car*] parfaitement stable

rockabilly ['rɒkəbɪlɪ] N (*Mus*) rockabilly *m*

rocker ['rɒkər] N **a** [*of cradle etc*] bascule *f*; (*esp US* = *rocking chair*) rocking-chair *m*, berceuse *f*; **to be off one's ~*** être cinglé*, avoir une case en moins*; **to go off one's ~*** perdre la boule* **b** (= *person*) rockeur *m*, -euse *f*

rockery ['rɒkərɪ] N (jardin *m* de) rocaille *f*

rocket ['rɒkɪt] **1** N (*Mil*) fusée *f*, roquette *f*; (*Aviat, also firework*) fusée *f*; **to fire** *or* **send up a ~** lancer une fusée; **distress ~** fusée *f* de détresse; **space ~** fusée *f* interplanétaire; (*Brit fig*) **he's just had a ~* from the boss** le patron vient de lui passer un savon* *or* de l'enguirlander*
2 VI [*prices*] monter en flèche; **he went ~ing past my door** il est passé en trombe devant ma porte; **to ~ to fame** devenir célèbre du jour au lendemain
3 COMP ► **rocket attack** N attaque *f* à la roquette ► **rocket base** N = rocket range ► **rocket fuel** N (*NonC*) propergol *m* ► **rocket gun** N fusil *m* lance-roquettes *inv or* lance-fusées *inv* ► **rocket launcher** N lance-roquettes *m inv*, lance-fusées *m inv* ► **rocket plane** N avion-fusée *m* ► **rocket-propelled** ADJ autopropulsé ► **rocket propulsion** N propulsion *f* par fusée, autopropulsion *f* ► **rocket range** N base *f* de lancement de missiles; **within ~ range** à portée de missiles ► **rocket research** N recherches *fpl* aérospatiales ► **rocket science** N technologie *f* des fusées ► **rocket scientist** N (*esp US*) spécialiste *mf* des fusées; **it doesn't take a ~ scientist to ...** pas besoin de sortir de Saint-Cyr pour ..., pas besoin d'être un génie pour ... ► **rocket ship** N vaisseau *m* spatial ► **rocket technology** N technologie *f* des fusées

rocketry ['rɒkɪtrɪ] N (= *science*) technologie *f* des fusées; (= *rockets collectively*) (panoplie *f* de) fusées *fpl*

rockfish ['rɒkfɪʃ] N (*pl* **rockfish** *or* **rockfishes**) rascasse *f*

rocking ['rɒkɪŋ] **1** N balancement *m*, ballottement *m* **2** COMP ► **rocking chair** N rocking-chair *m*, berceuse *f* ► **rocking horse** N cheval *m* à bascule

rockling ['rɒklɪŋ] N (*pl* **rockling** *or* **rocklings**) loche *f* de mer

rocky¹ ['rɒkɪ] ADJ **a** (* = *precarious*) [*marriage*] fragile, instable; [*health*] précaire, chancelant; **his finances are ~** sa situation financière est précaire; **to be going through a ~ patch** traverser une période difficile **b** (= *unsteady*) [*table, chair*] branlant

rocky² ['rɒkɪ] **1** ADJ **a** (*lit*) [*shore, mountain*] rocheux; [*road, path*] rocailleux; (*fig* = *difficult*) **I knew it would be a ~ road to recovery** je savais que mon rétablissement n'était pas du tout cuit* *or* que mon rétablissement serait long et difficile; **on the ~ road to fame** sur le dur chemin de la gloire **2** COMP ► **the Rocky Mountains** NPL (*also* **the Rockies**: *Geog*) les (montagnes *fpl*) Rocheuses *fpl*

rococo [rəʊ'kəʊkəʊ] **1** N rococo *m* **2** ADJ rococo *inv*

---

rod [rɒd] **1** N **a** (*wooden*) baguette *f*; (*metallic*) tringle *f*; [*of machinery*] tige *f*; (*for punishment*) baguette *f*, canne *f*; (*symbol of authority*) verge *f*; **curtain/stair ~** tringle *f* à rideaux/d'escalier; (*fig*) **to make a ~ for one's own back** donner des verges pour se faire battre *or* fouetter; **to rule with a ~ of iron** [+ *country*] gouverner d'une main de fer; [+ *person, family*] mener à la baguette *or* à la trique* → **black, connecting, piston, spare** **b** (*also* **fishing ~**) canne *f* (à pêche); **to fish with ~ and line** pêcher à la ligne **c** (= *measure*) perche *f* (= 5,03 m) **d** [*of eye*] bâtonnet *m* **e** (*US** = *gun*) flingue* *m* **f** (*Aut** = *hotrod*) hotrod *m*, voiture *f* gonflée **g** (** = *penis*) bite** *f* **2** COMP ► **rod bearing** N (*Tech*) manchon *m* de bielle

rode [rəʊd] VB *pt of* **ride**

rodent ['rəʊdənt] **1** N rongeur *m* **2** ADJ rongeur; (*Med*) **~ cancer** ◊ **~ ulcer** cancer *m* de la peau

rodeo ['rəʊdɪəʊ] N rodéo *m*

rodomontade [,rɒdəmɒn'teɪd] N rodomontade *f*

roe¹ [rəʊ] **1** N (*pl* **roe** *or* **roes**) (*species: also* **~ deer**) chevreuil *m* **2** COMP ► **roe buck** N chevreuil *m* mâle ► **roe deer** N (*female*) chevreuil *m* femelle, chevrette *f*

roe² [rəʊ] N [*of fish*] **hard ~** œufs *mpl* de poisson; **soft ~** laitance *f*; **herring ~** œufs *mpl* *or* laitance *f* de hareng

roentgen ['rɒntjən] N Roentgen *or* Röntgen *m*

rogation [rəʊ'geɪʃən] (*Rel*) **1** N (*gen pl*) rogations *fpl* **2** COMP ► **Rogation Days** NPL les trois jours qui précèdent l'Ascension ► **Rogation Sunday** N dimanche *m* des Rogations

rogatory ['rɒgətərɪ] ADJ (*Jur*) rogatoire → **letter**

Roger ['rɒdʒər] N Roger *m*; (*Telec*) **"roger!"** « compris ! » → **jolly**

roger** ['rɒdʒər] VT tringler**

rogue [rəʊg] **1** N **a** (= *scoundrel*) coquin *m*, gredin *m*; (= *scamp*) coquin(e) *m(f)*, fripon(ne) *m(f)*; **you little ~!** petit coquin ! **b** (*Zool*) solitaire *m* **2** ADJ (*Zool*) [*elephant, lion, male*] solitaire; (*Bio, Med*) [*gene*] aberrant; **~ cop*** (= *criminal*) ripou* *m*; (= *vigilante*) flic* *m* qui agit en justicier solitaire **3** COMP ► **rogues' gallery** N (*Police*) photographies *fpl* de l'identité judiciaire *or* des sommiers*; (*fig*) **they look like a ~s' gallery** ils ont des têtes de repris de justice

roguery ['rəʊgərɪ] N (= *wickedness*) coquinerie *f*, malhonnêteté *f*; (= *mischief*) espièglerie *f*

roguish ['rəʊgɪʃ] ADJ (= *mischievous*) [*person, smile, charm, humour*] malicieux; (= *rascally*) [*person*] coquin

roguishly ['rəʊgɪʃlɪ] ADV [*smile, say*] malicieusement; **he winked at me ~** il m'a fait un clin d'œil malicieux

roil ['rɔɪl] (*esp US*) **1** VI [*water*] bouillonner **2** VT (*fig*) perturber; **to ~ the waters** semer la trouble

roily ['rɔɪlɪ] ADJ (*esp US*) [*water, sea*] troublé, agité; (*fig*) [*person*] exaspéré

roister ['rɔɪstər] VI s'amuser bruyamment

roisterer ['rɔɪstərər] N fêtard(e)* *m(f)*

Roland ['rəʊlənd] N Roland *m*; **a ~ for an Oliver** un prêté pour un rendu

role, rôle [rəʊl] **1** N (*Theat, fig*) rôle *m* → **leading¹** **2** COMP ► **role model** N modèle *m* ► **role-play(ing)** N (*Psych*) psychodrame *m*; (*Scol*) jeu *m* de rôle ► **role reversal** N inversion *f* des rôles

roll [rəʊl] **1** N **a** [*of cloth, paper, netting, wire, hair etc*] rouleau *m*; [*of banknotes*] liasse *f*; [*of tobacco*] carotte *f*; [*of butter*] coquille *f*; [*of flesh, fat*] bourrelet *m*; (*Phot*) **~ of film** (rouleau *m* de) pellicule *f*
b (*also* **bread ~**) petit pain *m* → **sausage, Swiss**
c (= *movement*) [*of ship*] roulis *m*; [*of sea*]

---

houle *f*; [*of plane*] tonneau *m*; **to walk with a ~** se balancer en marchant, avoir une démarche chaloupée; **the ship gave a sudden ~** le bateau roula brusquement; **the horse was having a ~ on the grass** le cheval se roulait dans l'herbe; **to have a ~ in the hay with sb*** batifoler* dans l'herbe avec qn → **rock¹**
d (= *sound*) [*of thunder, drums*] roulement *m*; [*of organ*] ronflement *m*
e (= *list, register*) liste *f*, tableau *m*; (*for court, ship's crew etc*) rôle *m*; (*Scol*) **class ~** liste *f* (nominative) des élèves; **we have 60 pupils on our ~(s)** nous avons 60 élèves inscrits; (*Scol*) **falling ~s** diminutions *fpl* des effectifs; **to call the ~** faire l'appel; (*Brit*) **~ of honour** (*Mil*) noms *mpl* des combattants morts pour la patrie *or* tombés au champ d'honneur; (*Scol*) tableau *m* d'honneur; (*Jur*) **to strike sb's name off the ~s** radier qn des listes *or* du tableau → **electoral**
f **to be on a ~*** (= *prospering*) avoir le vent en poupe

2 VI **a** (= *turn over*) rouler; **to ~ over and over** [*object*] rouler sur soi-même; [*person*] se rouler; **the coin ~ed under the table** la pièce a roulé sous la table; **stones ~ed down the hill** des pierres ont roulé *or* déboulé jusqu'au pied de la colline; **the car ~ed down the hill** (*brakes off*) la voiture a descendu la pente toute seule; (*over and over*) la voiture a dévalé la pente en faisant une série de tonneaux; **the lorries ~ed through the streets** les camions roulaient dans les rues; **his car ~ed to a stop** sa voiture s'arrêta doucement; **to ~ headlong down a slope** dégringoler une pente; **the children were ~ing down the slope** les enfants dévalaient la pente en roulant sur eux-mêmes; **tears were ~ing down her cheeks** les larmes coulaient sur ses joues; **the waves were ~ing on to the beach** les vagues déferlaient sur la plage; **the newspapers were ~ing off the presses** les journaux tombaient des rotatives; **the wheels kept ~ing** les roues continuaient à tourner; (*fig*) **heads will ~** il y aura des limogeages*, des têtes tomberont; (*in car*) **we were ~ing along at 100km/h** nous roulions à 100 (km) à l'heure; **the horse ~ed in the mud** le cheval s'est roulé dans la boue; (*fig*) **he's ~ing in money*** *or* **in it*** il roule sur l'or; (*fig*) **they were ~ing in the aisles*** ils se tordaient de rire, ils se tenaient les côtes*; **she is trainer and manager ~ed into one** elle est entraîneur et manager tout à la fois *or* en même temps; **to ~ with the punches** encaisser les coups
b [*ship*] rouler; **he ~ed from side to side as he walked** il se balançait en marchant; **his eyes were ~ing** ses yeux roulaient, il roulait les yeux
c [*thunder*] gronder, rouler; [*drums, words*] rouler; [*voice*] retentir; [*organ*] rendre un son grave et prolongé; [*noises*] se répercuter
d (= *function, operate*) [*machine*] marcher, fonctionner; [*film cameras*] tourner; **cameras ~!** on tourne !; (*Theat*) **to keep the show ~ing*** s'arranger pour que le spectacle continue (*subj*); (*fig*) **you must keep the ball** *or* **things ~ing while I'm away*** arrangez-vous pour que ça tourne (*subj*) rond *or* pour que tout marche (*subj*) pendant mon absence

3 VT **a** [+ *barrel, hoop, ball*] faire rouler; [+ *umbrella, cigarette*] rouler; [+ *pastry, dough*] étendre *or* abaisser au rouleau; [+ *metal*] laminer; [+ *lawn*] rouler; [+ *road*] cylindrer; **to ~ one's eyes** rouler des yeux; **to ~ one's r's** rouler les r; **to ~ sth between one's fingers** rouler qch avec *or* entre ses doigts; **to ~ string into a ball** enrouler de la ficelle en pelote; **the hedgehog ~ed itself up into a ball** le hérisson s'est roulé en boule; **he ~ed himself in a blanket** il s'est enroulé dans une couverture; **they ~ed the car to the side of the road** ils ont poussé la voiture sur le bas-côté → **rolled**
b (*US** = *rob*) dévaliser

[4] COMP ► **roll bar** N (Aut) arceau m de sécurité ► **roll call** N (gen, Mil, Scol) appel m; (fig) **a ~ call of sporting giants** brochette de sommités du sport ► **roll-collar** N (Brit) = roll-neck ► **roll film** N rouleau m or bobine f de pellicule photo(graphique) ► **roll-neck** [of sweater] col m roulé ♦ ADJ ~neck(ed) à col roulé ► **roll-on** → roll-on ► **roll-top desk** N bureau m à cylindre ► **roll-up**, **roll-your-own*** N (Brit) cigarette f roulée

► **roll about** VI [coins, marbles] rouler çà et là; [ship] rouler; [person, dog] se rouler par terre

► **roll along** [1] VI [a] [ball, vehicle] rouler [b] (* = arrive) s'amener*, se pointer* [2] VT SEP [+ ball] faire rouler; [+ car] pousser

► **roll around** VI = roll about

► **roll away** [1] VI [clouds, mist, vehicle] s'éloigner; [ball] rouler au loin; **the ball ~ed away from me** le ballon a roulé loin de moi [2] VT SEP [+ trolley, table] pousser

► **roll back** [1] VI [object] rouler en arrière; [eyes] chavirer [2] VT SEP [a] [+ object] rouler en arrière; [+ carpet] rouler; [+ sheet] enlever (en roulant) [b] (fig = bring back) ramener; **if only we could ~ back the years** si seulement nous pouvions ramener le temps passé [c] (US fig = reduce) réduire [3] ~**back*** N → rollback

► **roll by** VI [vehicle, procession] passer; [clouds] traverser le ciel, dériver dans le ciel; [time, years] s'écouler, passer

► **roll down** [1] VI [ball, person] rouler de haut en bas; [tears] couler [2] VT SEP [a] [+ cart] descendre (en roulant) [b] (= wind down) [+ car window] descendre, baisser [c] [+ socks, sleeves] baisser; [+ stockings] rouler

► **roll in** [1] VI [waves] déferler;* [letters, contributions, suggestions] affluer;* s'amener*, se pointer*; **he ~ed in*** **half an hour late** il s'est amené* or pointé* avec une demi-heure de retard; **the money keeps ~ing in*** l'argent continue à affluer [2] VT SEP [+ barrel, trolley] faire entrer (en roulant)

► **roll off** VI [vehicle, procession] s'ébranler, se mettre en marche [b] (= fall off) dégringoler

► **roll on** [1] VI [vehicle etc] continuer de rouler; [time] s'écouler; [dim] **~ on the holidays!*** vivement les vacances!; (Brit) **~ on Tuesday!*** vivement mardi! [2] VT SEP [+ stockings] enfiler [3] ~**on** N → roll-on [4] ~**on-~off** (Brit) → roll-on

► **roll out** VT SEP [a] [+ barrel, trolley] rouler or pousser dehors [b] [+ sentence, verse] débiter [c] [+ pastry] étendre or abaisser au rouleau; [+ metal] laminer [d] (= introduce) [+ system, offer] introduire

► **roll over** [1] VI [person, animal] (once) se retourner (sur soi-même); (several times: also = **over and over**) se rouler [2] VT SEP [+ person, animal, object] retourner

► **roll past** VI = roll by

► **roll up** [1] VI [a] [animal] se rouler (**into** en) [b] (* = arrive) arriver, s'amener*; (at fairground) **~ up and see the show!** approchez, venez voir le spectacle! [2] VT SEP [+ cloth, paper, map] rouler; **to ~ up one's sleeves** retrousser ses manches [3] ~**up*** N → roll

rollaway bed ['rəʊlə,weɪ'bed] N (US) lit m pliant (sur roulettes)

rollback ['rəʊlbæk] N (US) (gen) réduction f; (Econ) baisse f forcée des prix (sur ordre du gouvernement)

rolled [rəʊld] [1] ADJ [a] (also ~ up) [carpet, newspaper, blanket, garment] roulé, enroulé; [trousers, sleeves] retroussé; [umbrella] plié [b] (Phon) roulé [2] COMP ► **rolled gold** plaqué m or ► **rolled-gold** ADJ [bracelet] (en) plaqué or ► **rolled oats** NPL flocons mpl d'avoine ► **rolled-steel joist** N poutrelle f ► **rolled tobacco** N tabac m en carotte

roller ['rəʊlə'] [1] N [a] (gen) rouleau m; (for pastry) rouleau m à pâtisserie; (for roads) rouleau m compresseur; (for lawn) rouleau m de

jardin; (for metal) laminoir m, cylindre m lamineur; (in papermaking: also Tex) calandre f [b] (for painting and decorating) rouleau m (à peinture); (for inking) rouleau m (encreur) [c] (for winding sth round) rouleau m; [of blind] enrouleur m; (for hair) bigoudi m, rouleau m à mise en plis; **to put one's hair in ~s** se mettre des bigoudis [d] (for moving things) rouleau m; (= wheel) roulette f, galet m; **table on ~s** table f à roulettes [e] (part of harness) surfaix m [f] (= wave) lame f de houle [2] COMP ► **roller bandage** N bande f (roulée) ► **roller blade** N (Sport) patin m en ligne ► **roller blind** N store m ► **roller coaster** N montagnes fpl russes ► **roller skate** N patin m à roulettes ► **roller-skate** VI faire du patin à roulettes ► **roller-skating** N patinage m à roulettes ► **roller towel** N rouleau m essuie-main(s)

rollerball ['rəʊlə,bɔ:l] N stylo m à bille

rollerdrome ['rəʊlə,drəʊm] N (US) piste f de patin à roulettes

rollick* ['rɒlɪk] VI (also ~ **about**) s'amuser bruyamment

rollicking* ['rɒlɪkɪŋ] [1] ADJ [person] d'une gaieté exubérante, joyeux; [play, farce] bouffon; [occasion] (bruyant et) joyeux; **to lead a ~ life** mener joyeuse vie or une vie de patachon*; **to have a ~ time** s'amuser follement or comme des fous; **it was a ~ party** nous nous sommes amusés comme des petits fous à la soirée [2] N (= telling off) savon* m; **to give sb a (real) ~** passer un (sacré or bon) savon à qn*; **to get a (real) ~** recevoir un (sacré or bon) savon*

rolling ['rəʊlɪŋ] [1] ADJ [a] (= undulating) [countryside, landscape] vallonné; [hills, lawns] onduleux [b] (= pitching) [ship] qui roule; [sea] houleux; **~ waves** (vagues fpl) déferlantes fpl [c] (= swaying) [gait, walk] chaloupé [d] (= ongoing) [contract] révisable; [programme] constamment remis à jour; **~ news service** service m d'informations permanentes [2] ADV **to be ~ drunk*** être rond comme une queue de pelle* [3] COMP ► **rolling mill** N (= factory) laminerie f, usine f de laminage; (= machine) laminoir m ► **rolling pin** N rouleau m à pâtisserie ► **rolling plan** N (Fin) plan m pluriannuel (révisable chaque année) ► **rolling stock** N (Rail) matériel m roulant ► **rolling stone** N ■ (PROV) **a ~ stone gathers no moss** pierre qui roule n'amasse pas mousse (PROV); **he's a ~ stone** il mène une vie nomade ► **rolling targets** NPL (US Econ) objectifs mpl économiques révisables

rollmop ['rəʊlmɒp] N (Brit: also ~ **herring**) rollmops m

roll-on ['rəʊlɒn] [1] N (= corset) gaine f [2] ADJ [deodorant etc] à bille [3] COMP ► **roll-on-roll-off** N (manutention f par) roulage m ► **roll-on-roll-off ferry** N ferry m roulier or roll-on roll-off ► **roll-on-roll-off ship** N roulier m

rollover ['rəʊləʊvə'] [1] N [a] (NonC: Fin) [of loan, debt] refinancement m [b] (Brit: in lottery) remise f en jeu du prix [2] ADJ (Brit: in lottery) **it's a ~ week** le gros lot de la semaine précédente a été remis en jeu

Rolodex® ['rəʊlədeks] N fichier m Rolodex®

roly-poly ['rəʊlɪ'pəʊlɪ] [1] ADJ* [person, figure] rondelet; [child] potelé [2] N [a] (Brit: also ~ **pudding**) (gâteau m) roulé m à la confiture [b] (* = plump child) poupard m

ROM [rɒm] N (Comput) (ABBR = **Read-Only-Memory**) → read

Romagna ['rɒmaɲa] N la Romagne

romaine [rəʊ'meɪn] N (US: also ~ **lettuce**) (laitue f) romaine f

Roman ['rəʊmən] [1] N [a] (= person) Romain(e) m(f); (Bible) **the Epistle to the ~s** l'épître f aux Romains [b] (Typ) romain m [2] ADJ (Archit, Geog, Hist, Rel, Typ) romain → holy [3] COMP ► **the Roman alphabet** N l'alphabet m romain ► **Roman arch** N voûte f (en) plein cintre, arc m plein cintre ► **the Roman calendar** N le calendrier romain ► **Roman candle** N chandelle f romaine ► **Roman Catholic** ADJ, N catholique mf (romain) ► **the Roman Catholic Church** N l'Église f catholique (romaine) ► **Roman Catholicism** N catholicisme m ► **the Roman Empire** N l'Empire m romain ► **Roman law** N droit m romain ► **Roman letters** NPL (Typ) caractères mpl romains ► **Roman nose** N nez m aquilin ► **Roman numeral** N chiffre m romain ► **the Roman Rite** N (Rel) le rite romain

romance [rəʊ'mæns] [1] N [a] (= tale of chivalry) roman m; (= love story/film) roman m/ film m sentimental; (Mus) romance f; (= love affair) idylle f; (= love) amour m; (NonC = charm, attraction) charme m; **it's quite a ~** c'est un vrai roman; (fig = lies) **it's pure ~** c'est de la pure invention, c'est tout du roman; **their ~ lasted six months** leur idylle a duré six mois; **he was her first ~** il était son premier amoureux or amour; **they had a beautiful ~** ils ont vécu un beau roman (d'amour); **the ~ of the sea/of foreign lands** la poésie de la mer/des pays étrangers [b] (Ling) **Romance** romance m [2] ADJ (Ling) **Romance** roman [3] VI enjoliver, broder (fig) [4] VT (= woo) faire la cour à, courtiser

romancer [rəʊ'mænsə'] N conteur m, -euse f; (fig) **he's a ~** il enjolive toujours tout

Romanesque [,rəʊmə'nesk] ADJ [architecture] roman

Romania [rəʊ'meɪnɪə] N la Roumanie

Romanian [rəʊ'meɪnɪən] [1] ADJ (gen) roumain; [ambassador, embassy] de Roumanie [2] N [a] Roumain(e) m(f) [b] (Ling) roumain m

Romanic [rəʊ'mænɪk] ADJ [language] roman

Romanize ['rəʊmənaɪz] VT (Hist) romaniser; (Rel) convertir au catholicisme

Romans(c)h [rəʊ'mænʃ] N romanche m

romantic [rəʊ'mæntɪk] [1] ADJ [a] (= amorous) [relationship, interlude, assignation] amoureux; [novel, film] sentimental; [novelist, holiday, dinner] romantique [b] (= picturesque, glamorous) [appearance, landscape, castle] romantique; **a ~ figure like Lawrence of Arabia** un personnage romantique comme Lawrence d'Arabie [c] (= unrealistic) [person] romantique, sentimental; [idea, view, image] romantique [d] (Art, Literat, Mus) **Romantic** romantique [2] N romantique mf, sentimental(e) m(f); (Art, Literat, Mus) romantique mf [3] COMP ► **romantic comedy** N (Cine, Theat) comédie f sentimentale ► **romantic fiction** N (NonC) les romans mpl roses ► **romantic lead** N (Cine, Theat) jeune premier m, -ière f ► **romantic love** N amour m romantique ► **the Romantic Movement** N (Art, Literat, Mus) le Mouvement romantique, le romantisme

romantically [rəʊ'mæntɪkəlɪ] ADV [a] (= picturesquely, glamorously) **the castle is ~ sited on a cliff top** le château occupe une situation très romantique au sommet d'une falaise; **~ named ...** au nom romantique de ... [b] (= amorously) [behave, kiss] amoureusement; **~ inclined** or **minded** romantique; **to be ~ involved with sb** avoir une liaison avec qn; **she has been ~ linked with the prince** on a parlé d'une idylle entre le prince et elle; **~, things are looking up** sur le plan sentimental, les choses s'annoncent bien [c] (= unrealistically) [talk, describe] sentimentalement

romanticism [rəʊˈmæntɪsɪzəm] N (Art, Literat, Mus) romantisme m

romanticist [rəʊˈmæntɪsɪst] N (Art, Literat, Mus) romantique mf

romanticize [rəʊˈmæntɪsaɪz] VTI romancer

romanticized [rəʊˈmæntɪsaɪzd] ADJ [idea, view, depiction] très romantique

Romany ['rɒmənɪ] **1** N **a** Rom mf inv, tzigane or tsigane mf **b** (Ling) romani m **2** ADJ [person, society, culture, language] rom inv, tzigane or tsigane ; **a ~ caravan** une roulotte de tziganes or tsiganes

Rome [rəʊm] N ■ (PROV) **when in ~ (do as the Romans do)** à Rome il faut vivre comme les Romains ■ (PROV) **~ wasn't built in a day** Paris or Rome ne s'est pas fait en un jour ■ (PROV) **all roads lead to ~** tous les chemins mènent à Rome ; **the Church of ~** l'Église f (catholique) romaine ; (Rel) **to go over to ~** se convertir au catholicisme

Romeo ['rəʊmɪəʊ] N Roméo m

Romish ['rəʊmɪʃ] ADJ (pej) catholique

romp [rɒmp] **1** N **a** (hum = sex) ébats mpl amoureux **b** (= energetic play) jeux mpl bruyants, ébats mpl ; **the play was just a ~** la pièce n'était (guère) qu'une farce **2** VI [children, puppies] jouer bruyamment, s'ébattre ; **the horse ~ed home** le cheval est arrivé dans un fauteuil* ; (fig) **to ~ through an exam** bien se débrouiller à un examen

rompers ['rɒmpəz] NPL, **romper suit** ['rɒmpəsuːt] N barboteuse f

Romulus ['rɒmjʊləs] N **~ and Remus** Romulus m et Remus m

Roncesvalles ['rɒnsəvælz] N Roncevaux

rondeau ['rɒndəʊ] (pl rondeaux ['rɒndəʊz]), **rondel** ['rɒndl] N (Mus, Poetry) rondeau m

rondo ['rɒndəʊ] N (Mus) rondeau m

Roneo® ['rəʊnɪəʊ] VT polycopier, ronéoter

rood [ruːd] **1** N **a** (Rel Archit) crucifix m **b** (Brit = measure) quart m d'arpent **2** COMP ► **rood screen** N jubé m

roof [ruːf] N **1** N [of building, car] toit m (also Climbing) ; [of cave, tunnel] plafond m ; (fig: of sky, branches) voûte f ; (Anat) **the ~ of the mouth** la voûte du palais ; **without a ~ over one's head** sans abri or toit ; **a room in the ~** une chambre sous les combles or sous les toits ; **I couldn't live under her ~** je ne pourrais pas vivre chez elle ; **to live under the same ~ as sb** vivre sous le même toit avec or que qn ; **under one ~** (gen) sous le même toit ; (in shopping arcade, hypermarket etc) réuni(s) au même endroit ; (fig) **to go through** or **to hit the ~*** [person] exploser, piquer une crise* ; [price, claim] crever le plafond **2** VT [+ house] couvrir (d'un toit) ; **red-~ed** à toit rouge **3** COMP ► **roof garden** N jardin m sur le toit ► **roof light** N plafonnier m ► **roof rack** N (esp Brit) galerie f
► **roof in** VT SEP couvrir d'un toit
► **roof over** VT SEP recouvrir d'un toit

roofer ['ruːfə'] N couvreur m

roofing ['ruːfɪŋ] **1** N **a** (on house) toiture f, couverture f **b** (= act) pose f de la toiture or de la couverture **2** COMP ► **roofing felt** N couverture f bitumée or goudronnée

roofless ['ruːflɪs] ADJ sans toit

rooftop ['ruːftɒp] N toit m ; (fig) **to shout** or **proclaim sth from the ~s** crier qch sur tous les toits (fig)

rook[1] [rʊk] **1** N (Orn) (corbeau m) freux m **2** VT (‡ = swindle) rouler (dans la farine)*, escroquer

rook[2] [rʊk] N (Chess) tour f

rookery ['rʊkərɪ] N colonie f de freux ; [of seals, penguins] colonie f ; (fig pej = overcrowded slum) taudis m surpeuplé

rookie‡ ['rʊkɪ] N (US: esp Mil) bleu* m

room [rʊm] **1** N **a** (in house) pièce f ; (large) salle f ; (= bedroom) chambre f ; (= office, study) bureau m ; (in hotel) chambre f ; **~s to let** chambres fpl à louer ; **~ and board** pension f ; **his ~s** son appartement ; **come to my ~s for coffee** venez prendre le café chez moi ; **they live in ~s** ils habitent un meublé or un garni (pej) → **double, lecture, roof**
b (NonC = space) place f ; **is there ~?** y a-t-il de la place? ; **there is ~ for two people** il y a de la place pour deux personnes ; **there's no ~** il n'y a pas de place ; (fig) **there's not enough** or **no ~ to swing a cat*** c'est grand comme un mouchoir de poche ; **to take up ~/too much ~** prendre de la place/trop de place ; **to make ~ for sb** faire de la place pour qn ; **to make ~ for sth** faire de la place pour qch ; (fig) **there is still ~ for hope** il y a encore lieu d'espérer ; **there is little ~ for hope** il ne reste pas beaucoup d'espoir ; **there is no ~ for doubt** il n'y a pas de doute possible ; **there is ~ for improvement in your work** votre travail laisse à désirer

2 VI (US) partager une chambre (**with** avec) ; **to ~ with a landlady** louer une chambre meublée

3 COMP ► **room clerk** N (US) réceptionniste mf ► **room divider** N meuble m de séparation ► **rooming house** N (US) immeuble m (avec chambres à louer) ; **he lives in a ~ing house** il habite un meublé ► **rooming-in** N (in maternity wards) possibilité pour les accouchées de garder leur nouveau-né dans leur chambre ► **room service** N service m des chambres (d'hôtel), room-service m ; **ring for ~ service** appelez le garçon d'étage ► **room temperature** N température f ambiante ; **to bring a wine to ~ temperature** chambrer un vin ; **wine at ~ temperature** vin m chambré

-roomed [rʊmd] ADJ (in compounds) **a six-roomed house** une maison de six pièces ; **a two-roomed flat** un deux-pièces

roomer ['rʊmə'] N (US) locataire mf

roomette [ruːˈmet] N (US Rail) compartiment m individuel de wagons-lits

roomful ['rʊmfʊl] N pleine salle f

roominess ['rʊmɪnɪs] N dimensions fpl spacieuses

roommate ['rʊmmeɪt] N camarade mf de chambre ; (US: sharing lodgings) personne f avec laquelle on partage un appartement

roomy ['rʊmɪ] ADJ [flat, car] spacieux ; [bag] grand ; [garment] ample

roost [ruːst] **1** N perchoir m, juchoir m → **rule 2** VI (= settle) se percher, se jucher ; (= sleep) jucher ; (fig) **all her little schemes are coming home to ~** toutes ses petites combines vont lui retomber dessus or se retourner contre elle

rooster ['ruːstə'] N (esp US) coq m

root [ruːt] **1** N **a** (gen, Bot, Math etc) racine f ; (fig) [of trouble etc] origine f, cause f ; **to pull up** or **out by the ~s** déraciner, extirper ; (lit, fig) **to take ~** prendre racine ; (fig) **to pull up one's ~s** se déraciner ; **her ~s are in France** elle est restée française de cœur or d'esprit ; **she has no ~s** elle n'a pas de racines, c'est une déracinée ; **to put down ~s in a country** s'enraciner dans un pays ; (fig) **~ and branch** entièrement, radicalement ; **the ~ of the matter** la vraie raison ; **to get to the ~ of the problem** trouver la cause or aller au fond du problème ; **that is at the ~ of ...** cela est à l'origine de ... ; **what lies at the ~ of his attitude?** quelle est la raison fondamentale de son attitude ? → **cube, grass, square**
b (Ling) (gen) racine f ; (Gram) [of verb] radical m ; [of non-verb] base f
c [of tooth] racine f ; [of tongue] base f
d (Mus) fondamentale f

2 VT (Bot) enraciner ; (fig) **a deeply ~ed belief** une croyance bien enracinée ; (fig) **to be** or **stand ~ed to the spot** être cloué sur place

3 VI **a** [plants etc] s'enraciner, prendre racine
b [pigs] fouiller (avec le groin)

4 COMP ► **root beer** N (US) boisson gazeuse à base d'extraits végétaux ► **root canal** N [of tooth] canal m dentaire ► **root-canal therapy, root-canal work** N (Dentistry) dévitalisation f, pulpectomie f ► **root cause** N cause f première ► **root crops** NPL racines fpl comestibles ► **root ginger** N gingembre m frais ► **root sign** N (Math) radical m ► **roots music** N (= world music) world music f ; (= reggae) reggae m (des origines) ► **root vegetable** N racine f (comestible) ► **root word** N (Ling) mot m souche inv
► **root about** VI fouiller (**among** dans, **for sth** pour trouver qch)
► **root among** VI fouiller dans
► **root around** VI = root about
► **root for*** VT FUS [+ team] encourager, applaudir
► **root out** VT SEP (fig) (= find) dénicher ; (= remove) extirper
► **root through** VI = root among
► **root up** VT SEP [+ plant] déraciner ; [pigs] déterrer ; (fig) extirper

rootless ['ruːtlɪs] ADJ (lit, fig) sans racine(s)

rootstock ['ruːtstɒk] N (Bot) rhizome m

rope [rəʊp] **1** N **a** (gen) corde f ; (Naut) cordage m ; [of bell] cordon m ; (fig) **to give sb more ~** lâcher la bride à qn ; **give him enough ~ and he'll hang himself** si on le laisse faire il se passera lui-même la corde au cou or il creusera sa propre tombe ; (Boxing etc) **the ~s** les cordes fpl ; **on the ~s** (Boxing) dans les cordes ; (* fig) [person] sur le flanc* ; [business] qui bat de l'aile* ; (fig) **to know the ~s*** connaître toutes les ficelles* ; **to show sb the ~s*** mettre qn au courant ; **to learn the ~s*** se mettre au courant ; (US) **to be at the end of one's ~** (= annoyed, impatient) être à bout de nerfs ; (= desperate) être sur le point de craquer ; **a ~ of pearls** un collier de perles ; **a ~ of onions** un chapelet d'oignons ; **a ~ of hair** une torsade de cheveux → **clothes, skipping, tightrope**
b (Climbing) corde f ; (people on rope) cordée f ; **a ~ of climbers** une cordée d'alpinistes ; **to put on the ~** s'encorder ; **there were three of them on the ~** ils formaient une cordée de trois

2 VT **a** [+ box, case] corder ; **to ~ sb to a tree** lier qn à un arbre ; **to ~ climbers (together)** encorder des alpinistes ; (Climbing) **~d party** cordée f
b (US = catch) [+ cattle] prendre au lasso

3 COMP ► **rope burn** N brûlure f (provoquée par une corde) ► **rope ladder** N échelle f de corde ► **rope-length** N (Climbing) longueur f de corde ► **rope maker** N cordier m ► **rope trick** N Indian ~ trick tour de prestidigitation réalisé avec une corde ► **roping-off** N (Climbing) rappel m
► **rope in** VT SEP [+ area] entourer de cordes, délimiter par une corde ; (fig) **to ~ sb in*** enrôler qn, embringuer qn* ; **he got himself ~d in* to help at the fête** il s'est laissé embringuer* pour aider à la fête ; **I don't want to get ~d in* for anything** je ne veux pas me laisser embringuer*
► **rope off** VT SEP (= section off) réserver par une corde ; (= block off) interdire l'accès de
► **rope up** (Climbing) **1** VI s'encorder **2** VT SEP encorder ; **to be ~d up** être encordé

ropedancer ['rəʊpdɑːnsə'], **ropewalker** ['rəʊpwɔːkə'] N funambule mf, danseur m, -euse f de corde

rop(e)y ['rəʊpɪ] ADJ **a** (Brit* = mediocre) pas terrible* **b** (Brit = ill) **to feel a bit ~*** être or se sentir patraque* **c** (= rope-like) [muscles, arm, neck] noueux

RORO (ABBR = roll-on-roll-off) → roll-on

rosary ['rəʊzərɪ] N **a** (Rel) chapelet m ; (=

fifteen decades) rosaire *m* [b] (*in garden*) rose-raie *f*

rose¹ [rəʊz] VB *pt of* **rise**

rose² [rəʊz] [1] N [a] (= *flower*) rose *f*; (*also* ~**bush**, ~ **tree**) rosier *m*; **wild** ~ églantine *f*; (*fig*) **life isn't all** ~**s** la vie n'est pas rose tous les jours; (*fig*) **it isn't all** ~**s** tout n'est pas rose ■ (*PROV*) **there is no** ~ **without a thorn** il n'y a pas de roses sans épines; (*fig*) **she's an English** ~ elle est belle comme une fleur *or* fraîche comme une rose; (*fig*) **that will put** ~**s back in your cheeks** cela va te rendre tes belles couleurs; (*fig liter*) **under the** ~ en confidence; (*Brit Hist*) **the Wars of the Roses** la guerre des Deux-Roses; (*fig*) **everything is coming up** ~**s*** tout marche comme sur des roulettes*; **to come up smelling of** ~**s*** s'en sortir très bien → **bed, Christmas, rock²**

[b] [*of hose, watering can*] pomme *f*; (*on hat, shoe*) rosette *f*; [*of pump*] crépine *f*; (*on ceiling*) rosace *f* (de plafond) → **compass**

[c] (= *colour*) rose *m*

[2] ADJ rose

[3] COMP [*leaf, petal*] de rose ► **rose-coloured** ADJ rose, couleur de rose *inv*; (*fig*) **to see everything/life through** ~**-coloured spectacles** voir tout/la vie en rose ► **rose diamond** N (diamant *m* en) rose *f* ► **rose garden** N roseraie *f* ► **rose grower** N rosiériste *mf* ► **rose pink** ADJ rose, rosé ► **rose-red** ADJ vermeil ► **rose-tinted** ADJ = rose-coloured ► **rose water** N eau *f* de rose (*lit*) ► **rose window** N rosace *f*, rose *f*

rosé [rəʊzeɪ] N rosé *m* (*vin*)

roseate [rəʊzɪɪt] ADJ (*liter*) [a] (= *pink*) rose [b] (*pej* = rose-tinted) [*picture, vision*] idyllique

rosebay [rəʊzbeɪ] N laurier-rose *m*

rosebed [rəʊzbed] N parterre *m or* massif *m* de roses

rosebowl [rəʊzbəʊl] N coupe *f* à fleurs

rosebud [rəʊzbʌd] [1] N bouton *m* de rose [2] COMP ► **rosebud mouth** N bouche *f* en cerise

rosebush [rəʊzbʊʃ] N rosier *m*

rosehip [rəʊzhɪp] [1] N cynorhodon *m*, gratte-cul *m* [2] COMP ► **rosehip syrup** N sirop *m* d'églantine

roselike [rəʊzlaɪk] ADJ rosacé

rosemary [rəʊzmərɪ] N romarin *m*

roseola [rəʊziːələ] N roséole *f*

rosette [rəʊzet] N (= *ribbons etc*) rosette *f*; (*Sport: as prize*) cocarde *f*; (*Archit*) rosace *f*

rosewood [rəʊzwʊd] [1] N bois *m* de rose [2] COMP en bois de rose

Rosh Hashanah [ˌrɒʃhəˈʃɑːnə] N Rosh ha-Shana, Roch ha-Shana

Rosicrucian [ˌrəʊzɪˈkruːʃən] ADJ, N rosicrucien(ne) *m(f)*

rosin [rɒzɪn] N colophane *f*

RoSPA [rɒspə] N (*Brit*) (ABBR = **Royal Society for the Prevention of Accidents**) *société pour la prévention des accidents*

roster [rɒstə^r] N liste *f*, tableau *m* (de service) → **duty**

rostrum [rɒstrəm] N (*pl* **rostrums** *or* **rostra** [rɒstrə]) tribune *f*; (*Roman Hist*) rostres *mpl*

rosy [rəʊzɪ] ADJ [a] (= *pink*) [*colour*] rosé; [*face, cheeks, complexion, light*] rose [b] (= *optimistic*) [*view*] optimiste; **the situation looks** ~ (**for her**) la situation se présente bien (pour elle); **things don't look very rosy for her** la situation n'est pas rose pour elle; **his future looks** ~ l'avenir se présente bien pour lui; **the party seemed to have a** ~ **future ahead of it** l'avenir du parti était prometteur; **to paint a** ~ **picture of sth** faire *or* brosser un tableau idyllique de qch

rot [rɒt] [1] N (*NonC*) [a] pourriture *f*; (*Bot, Med*) carie *f*; (*fig*) **he worked well at the beginning then the** ~ **set in*** au début il travaillait bien mais par la suite il a flanché* *or* les pro-

blèmes ont commencé; (*fig*) **to stop the** ~ redresser la situation → **dry** [b] (*esp Brit*†* = *nonsense*) balivernes *fpl*; **to talk** ~ dire *or* débiter des balivernes; **that's utter** ~ ◊ **that's a lot of** ~ ce ne sont que des balivernes [2] VI pourrir; (*fig*) [*person*] croupir; **to** ~ **in jail** croupir en prison; **let him** ~!* qu'il aille se faire pendre !* [3] VT (faire) pourrir

► **rot away** VI tomber en pourriture

rota [rəʊtə] [1] N [a] (*esp Brit*) liste *f*, tableau *m* (de service) [b] (*Rel*) **Rota** rote *f*

Rotarian [rəʊˈtɛərɪən] ADJ, N rotarien *m*

rotary [rəʊtərɪ] [1] ADJ [a] [*tin-opener, dial, control, movement*] rotatif [b] **Rotary (Club)** Rotary Club *m* [2] COMP ► **rotary clothes dryer** N séchoir *m* rotatif ► **rotary cultivator** N motoculteur *m* ► **rotary engine** N moteur *m* rotatif ► **rotary kiln** N four *m* rotatif ► **rotary (lawn)mower** N tondeuse *f* à lame rotative ► **rotary press** N rotative *f* ► **rotary printer** N tireuse *m* rotative ► **rotary printing press** N = rotary press ► **rotary shutter** N (*Phot*) obturateur *m* rotatif ► **rotary-wing aircraft** N aéronef *m* à voilure tournante

rotate [rəʊˈteɪt] [1] VT (= *revolve*) faire tourner; (*on axis*) faire pivoter; (= *change round*) [+ *crops*] alterner; [*two people*] [+ *work, jobs*] faire à tour de rôle [2] VI tourner; (*on pivot*) pivoter; [*crops*] être alterné

rotating [rəʊˈteɪtɪŋ] ADJ (*gen*) tournant; (= *pivoting*) pivotant

rotation [rəʊˈteɪʃən] N (= *turning*) rotation *f*; (= *turn*) rotation *f*, tour *m*; **in** *or* **by** ~ à tour de rôle; ~ **of crops** assolement *m*, rotation *f* (des cultures)

rotatory [rəʊˈteɪtərɪ] ADJ rotatoire

Rotavator® [rəʊtəveɪtə^r] N (*Brit*) = **Rotovator**

rote [rəʊt] [1] N **by** ~ [*learn*] machinalement, sans essayer de comprendre; [*recite*] comme un perroquet [2] COMP ► **rote learning** N apprentissage *m* par cœur

rotgut: [rɒtgʌt] N (*pej*) tord-boyaux* *m inv*

rotisserie [rəʊˈtɪsərɪ] N (= *grill or oven*) rôtissoire *f*; (= *fitment*) tournebroche *m*; (= *restaurant*) rôtisserie *f*

rotogravure [ˌrəʊtəʊɡrəˈvjʊə^r] N rotogravure *f*

rotor [rəʊtə^r] [1] N (*Aviat, Elec*) rotor *m* [2] COMP ► **rotor arm** N (*Aut*) rotor *m* ► **rotor blade** N pale *f* de rotor

rotorcraft [rəʊtəkrɑːft] N giravion *m*, hélicoptère *m*

rototill [rəʊtəʊtɪl] VT (*US*) labourer avec un motoculteur

Rototiller® [rəʊtəʊtɪlə^r] N (*US*) motoculteur *m*

rotovate [rəʊtəveɪt] VT (*Brit*) labourer avec un motoculteur

Rotovator® [rəʊtəveɪtə^r] N (*Brit*) motoculteur *m*

rotproof [rɒtpruːf] ADJ imputrescible

rotten [rɒtn] [1] ADJ [a] (= *decayed*) [*wood, vegetation, vegetable, egg*] pourri; [*meat*] pourri, avarié; [*fruit, tooth*] pourri, gâté [b] (= *corrupt*) véreux, corrompu; ~ **to the core** pourri jusqu'à la moelle → **3** [c] (* = *useless*) nul (**at sth** en qch, **at doing sth** pour faire qch) [d] (* = *unpleasant*) [*weather*] **what** ~ **weather!** quel temps pourri !*; **what** ~ **luck!** quelle guigne !*, quelle poisse !*; **we had a** ~ **time** on ne s'est pas marrés*; **what a** ~ **trick!** quel sale tour !*; **that's a** ~ **thing to say/do!** c'est moche* de dire/faire ça !; **it's a** ~ **business** c'est une sale affaire; **isn't it** ~ **about poor Anne?** pauvre Anne! quel sale coup !*; (= *ill*) **to feel/look** ~* se sentir/avoir l'air mal fichu*; (= *guilty*) **to feel** ~* (**about doing sth**) se sentir minable* (de faire qch) [e] (*: expressing annoyance*) fichu*, sale* (*before n*) **you can keep your** ~ **bike** tu peux te le garder, ton sale vélo*

[2] ADV* **to spoil sb** ~ pourrir qn; (*Brit*) **to fancy sb** ~ être entiché de qn

[3] COMP ► **rotten apple** N (*fig*) brebis *f* galeuse ■ (*PROV*) **one** ~ **apple spoils the (whole) barrel** il ne faut qu'une brebis galeuse pour infecter le troupeau

rottenness [rɒtnɪs] N (état *m* de) pourriture *f*

rotter†* [rɒtə^r] N (*Brit*) sale type* *m*

rotting [rɒtɪŋ] ADJ en pourriture, qui pourrit

Rottweiler [rɒt,vaɪlə^r] N Rottweiler *m*

rotund [rəʊˈtʌnd] ADJ [a] (= *round*) [*person, body*] replet (-ète *f*), rondelet; [*object, building*] arrondi; **his** ~ **stomach** son ventre rebondi [b] (= *sonorous*) [*voice, tone*] sonore

rotunda [rəʊˈtʌndə] N rotonde *f*

rotundity [rəʊˈtʌndɪtɪ] N [*of person*] embonpoint *m*; (*fig*) [*of style*] grandiloquence *f*; [*of voice*] sonorité *f*

rouble, ruble (*US*) [ruːbl] N rouble *m*

roué [ruːeɪ] N roué *m*, débauché *m*

rouge [ruːʒ] [1] N rouge *m* (à joues) [2] VT **to** ~ **one's cheeks** se farder les joues, se mettre du rouge aux joues

rough [rʌf] [1] ADJ [a] (= *not smooth*) [*skin, hands, cloth*] rêche; (*harder*) rugueux; [*bark*] rugueux; [*ground, road, track*] raboteux; ~ **edges** aspérités *fpl*; (*fig*) **the proposal still has some** ~ **edges** le projet n'est pas encore tout à fait au point; (*fig*) **he'll be a good salesman once we knock off the** ~ **edges** il fera un bon vendeur lorsque nous l'aurons un peu dégrossi; (*Brit*) **to give sb the** ~ **side of one's tongue** passer un savon* à qn

[b] (= *harsh*) [*sound*] rude, âpre; [*voice*] rude; [*taste*] âpre; [*wine*] grossier; **to taste** ~ avoir un goût âpre

[c] (= *unrefined*) [*person, speech, manners*] rude; [*tone, voice*] brusque

[d] (* = *difficult*) [*life*] dur; **to have a** ~ **time (of it)** en voir de rudes *or* de dures*; **to give sb a** ~ **time** en faire voir de toutes les couleurs à qn*; **it's** ~ **on him** c'est dur pour lui; **don't be too** ~ **on him** ne sois pas trop dur avec lui → **ride**

[e] (*Brit*** = *ill*) **to feel** ~ ne pas se sentir bien, être mal fichu*; **you sound** ~! tu as l'air mal fichu !

[f] (= *violent*) [*person, game, treatment*] rude; [*sex*] brutal; **to be** ~ **with sb** (*physically*) malmener qn; (*verbally*) être dur avec qn; **a** ~ **customer** un dur*; (*fig*) **he'll be a good salesman** ~ **handling** rudoiement *m*; **a** ~ **neighbourhood** un mauvais quartier; (*Sport*) ~ **play** jeu *m* brutal; ~ **stuff*** brutalités *fpl*; **no** ~ **stuff!** mollo !*

[g] (= *stormy*) [*weather*] gros (grosse *f*); [*sea*] agité, mauvais; [*crossing*] agité; **it was very** ~ la mer était très agitée *or* mauvaise

[h] (= *rudimentary*) [*shelter*] rudimentaire; [*clothes*] grossier; (= *approximate*) [*calculation, translation, estimate, description*] approximatif; [*plan*] vague, approximatif; **a** ~ **guess** une approximation; **at a** ~ **estimate** *or* **guess** à vue de nez; **can you give me a** ~ **idea (of) how long it will take?** à votre avis, ça prendra combien de temps environ ?; **I've got a** ~ **idea (of) what it looks like** je vois à peu près à quoi ça ressemble; **as a** ~ **guide** à titre indicatif; **he gave a** ~ **outline of the proposals** il a donné les grandes lignes des propositions; ~ **draft** brouillon *m*; ~ **sketch** croquis *m*, ébauche *f*

[i] (= *uncultivated*) ~ **pasture** prés *mpl* incultes; **a piece of** ~ **ground** un terrain vague

[2] ADV **to sleep** ~ coucher sur la dure; **to live** ~ vivre à la dure; **to play** ~ [*child, sportsperson*] jouer de manière brutale; [*gangster*] avoir des méthodes brutales; **we can either keep it friendly, or we can play** ~ soit on continue à l'amiable, soit on devient méchants; (*Brit*) **to cut up** ~* (*angry*) se mettre en rogne*; (*violent*) devenir violent

3 N **a** (= *ground*) terrain *m* accidenté *or* rocailleux ; (*Golf*) rough *m* ; (*fig*) **to take the ~ with the smooth** prendre les choses comme elles viennent
b (= *draft*) brouillon *m*, premier jet *m* ; **to write sth out in ~** rédiger qch au brouillon ; (*US*) **a diamond in the ~ = a rough diamond**
c (* = *person*) voyou *m*
4 VT **to ~ it*** vivre à la dure
5 COMP ► **rough-and-ready** ADJ [*method*] fruste, rudimentaire ; [*work*] grossier, fait à la hâte ; [*installation, equipment*] rudimentaire, de fortune ; [*person*] fruste ► **rough-and-tumble** ADJ désordonné, confus ♦ N mêlée *f*, bagarre *f* ; **after the ~-and-tumble of his life in the navy** après sa vie mouvementée de marin ► **rough diamond** N (*lit*) diamant *m* brut ; (*fig: Brit*) **he's a ~ diamond** sous ses dehors frustes, il a un cœur d'or ► **rough-dry** VT sécher sans repasser ► **rough-hewn** ADJ dégrossi, ébauché ► **rough justice** N justice *f* sommaire ► **rough paper** N (*NonC: Brit*) papier *m* de brouillon ► **rough puff pastry** N pâte *f* feuilletée (simplifiée) ► **rough-spoken** ADJ au langage grossier ► **rough trade‡** N partenaire homosexuel des bas-fonds ► **rough work** N (*NonC*) brouillon *m*
► **rough out** VT SEP [*+ plan, drawing*] ébaucher
► **rough up** VT SEP [*+ hair*] ébouriffer ; (*fig*) **to ~ sb up*** malmener qn ; (*stronger*) tabasser‡ qn

roughage ['rʌfɪdʒ] N (*NonC*) fibres *fpl*

roughcast ['rʌfkɑːst] **1** ADJ, N crépi *m* **2** VT crépir

roughen ['rʌfn] **1** VT rendre rude *or* rugueux **2** VI devenir rude *or* rugueux

roughhouse* ['rʌfhaʊs] N bagarre *f*

roughly ['rʌflɪ] ADV **a** (= *violently*) [*pull, push, play*] brutalement ; **to treat sb/sth ~** malmener qn/qch
b (= *brusquely*) [*speak, answer, order*] durement
c (= *crudely*) [*make, sew, chop, slice*] grossièrement
d (= *approximately*) à peu près ; **~ comparable/equal** à peu près comparable/égal ; **it costs ~ 100 francs** ça coûte environ 100 F ; **~ half of the population** environ la moitié de la population ; **he was ~ the same age as me** il avait environ *or* à peu près le même âge que moi ; **tell me ~ what it's all about** dites-moi grosso modo *or* en gros de quoi il s'agit ; **he ~ outlined the proposals** il a donné les grandes lignes des propositions ; **to sketch sth ~** faire un croquis de qch ; **to fall ~ into two categories** se répartir approximativement en deux catégories ; **~ translated, the name means ...** traduit approximativement, ce nom veut dire ... ; **~ speaking** en gros, grosso modo

roughneck* ['rʌfnek] N (*esp US*) voyou *m*, dur *m* à cuire*

roughness ['rʌfnɪs] N (*NonC*) **a** [*of skin, hands, cloth*] rudesse *f* ; [*of ground, road, track*] inégalité *f* ; [*of edges*] rugosité *f* **b** (= *harshness*) [*of sound, voice, taste, wine*] rudesse *f* **c** (= *lack of refinement*) [*of person, manners, speech*] rudesse *f* ; [*of tone, voice*] brusquerie *f* **d** (= *violence*) [*of person, game, treatment*] brutalité *f* ; [*of neighbourhood*] caractère *m* dangereux **e** (= *storminess*) [*of sea*] agitation *f* ; **the ~ of the weather** les mauvais temps **f** (= *rudimentary nature*) [*of shelter*] caractère *m* rudimentaire ; [*of clothes*] grossièreté *f* **g** (= *approximate nature*) [*of calculation, translation, estimate, description*] caractère *m* approximatif ; [*of plan*] manque *m* de détails

roughrider [ˌrʌfˈraɪdə'] N dresseur *m*, -euse *f or* dompteur *m*, -euse *f* de chevaux

roughshod ['rʌfʃɒd] ADV (*fig*) **to ride ~ over** [*+ objection, person*] faire peu de cas de

roulette [ruːˈlet] **1** N roulette *f* → **Russian 2** COMP ► **roulette table** N table *f* de roulette ► **roulette wheel** N roulette *f*

Roumania [ruːˈmeɪnɪə] N = **Rumania**
Roumanian [ruːˈmeɪnɪən] = **Rumanian**

round [raʊnd]

> When *round* is an element in a phrasal verb, eg *ask round, call round, rally round*, look up the verb.

1 ADV **a** (= *around*) autour ; **there was a wall right ~** *or* **all ~** il y avait un mur tout autour ; **he went ~ by the bridge** il a fait le détour *or* il est passé par le pont ; **you can't get through here, you'll have to go ~** vous ne pouvez pas passer par ici, il faut faire le tour ; **the long way ~** le chemin le plus long ; **it's a long way ~** ça fait un grand détour *or* un grand crochet ; **spring will soon be ~ again** le printemps reviendra bientôt → **gather round, look round**
b **~ and ~** en rond ; (*looking for sth*) **to go** (*or* **drive** *or* **ride**) **~ and ~** tourner en rond ; **the idea was going ~ and ~ in his head** il tournait et retournait l'idée dans sa tête
c **all ~:** **all (the) year ~** pendant toute l'année ; **drinks all ~!*** je paie une tournée !*, c'est ma tournée !* ; (*esp Brit fig*) **taking things all ~ ◊ taken all ~** tout compte fait ; **this ought to make life much easier all ~** (= *for everybody*) cela devrait simplifier la vie de tout le monde
d (*to sb's place*) **she ran ~ to her mother's** elle a couru chez sa mère ; **come ~ and see me** venez me voir ; **I asked him ~ for a drink** je l'ai invité à (passer) prendre un verre chez moi ; **I'll be ~ at 8 o'clock** je serai là à 8 heures
e **~ about →** 2b
2 PREP **a** (*of place etc*) autour de ; **sitting ~ the table** assis autour de la table ; **sitting ~ the fire** assis au coin du feu *or* auprès du feu ; **all ~ the house** tout autour de la maison ; **the villages ~ Brighton** les villages *mpl* des environs *or* des alentours de Brighton ; **she knows everybody ~ about** elle connaît tout le monde dans le coin ; **the house is just ~ the corner** la maison est au coin de la rue *or* juste après le coin de la rue ; **come and see me if you're ~ this way** viens me voir si tu passes par ici *or* si tu es dans le coin* ; **to go ~ a corner** tourner un coin ; (*Aut*) prendre un virage ; **to go ~ an obstacle** contourner un obstacle ; **to look ~ a house** visiter une maison ; **to show sb ~ a town** faire visiter une ville à qn ; **they went ~ the castle** ils ont visité le château ; **they went ~ the cafés looking for ...** ils ont fait le tour des cafés à la recherche de ... ; **she's 75cm ~ the waist** elle fait 75 cm de tour de taille ; **put a blanket ~ him** enveloppez-le dans une couverture → **clock, world**
b (*esp Brit = approximately: also ~ about*) autour de, environ ; **~ (about) 7 o'clock** autour de 7 heures, vers les 7 heures ; **~ (about) £800** 800 livres environ, dans les 800 livres
3 ADJ **a** (= *circular*) rond, circulaire ; (= *rounded*) rond, arrondi ; **to have ~ shoulders** avoir le dos rond *or* voûté ; **~ handwriting** écriture *f* ronde
b (= *complete*) **a ~ dozen** une douzaine tout rond ; **~ figure ◊ number** chiffre *m* rond ; **in ~ figures that will cost 20 million** cela coûtera 20 millions en chiffres ronds *or* pour donner un chiffre rond
c (*fig uses*) **in rich ~ tones** d'une voix riche et sonore ; **at a ~ pace** à vive allure ; **a (good) ~ sum** une somme rondelette *or* coquette* ; **he told me in ~ terms why ...** il m'a expliqué tout net pourquoi ... → **6**
4 N **a** (= *circle etc*) rond *m*, cercle *m* ; (*Brit = slice*) [*of bread, meat*] tranche *f* ; **a ~ of toast** un toast, une tranche de pain grillé
b (*esp Brit: also* **delivery ~**) tournée *f* ; **to do** *or* **make one's ~(s)** [*watchman, policeman*] faire sa ronde *or* sa tournée ; [*postman, milkman*] faire sa tournée ; [*doctor*] faire ses visites ; **to do** *or* **make the ~s of ...** faire le tour de ... ; **to go** *or* **do the ~s** [*infection, a cold etc*] faire des ravages ; [*news, joke etc*] courir, circuler ; **the story**

is going the ~s that ... le bruit court que ..., on raconte *or* on dit que ... ; **the story went the ~s of the club** l'histoire a fait le tour du club ; **this coat has gone the ~s of the family*** ce manteau a fait le tour de la famille ; (*fig*) **the daily ~** la routine quotidienne, le train-train quotidien ; **your life is just one long ~ of pleasures** tu ne penses qu'à t'amuser
c [*of cards, golf, competition, tournament*] partie *f* ; (*Boxing*) round *m*, reprise *f* ; (*Horse-riding*) tour *m* de piste, parcours *m* ; [*of election*] manche *f* ; [*of talks, discussions*] série *f* ; (*Horse-riding*) **to have a clear ~** faire un tour de piste *or* un parcours sans fautes ; **a new ~ of negotiations** une nouvelle série de négociations → **ammunition, applause, shot**
d [*of drinks*] tournée* *f* ; **to pay for a ~ (of drinks)** payer une tournée* ; **it's my ~** c'est ma tournée*
e (*Mus*) canon *m* ; (*Dancing*) ronde *f*
f **in the ~** (*Sculp*) en ronde-bosse ; (*Theat*) en rond ; (*fig = taken as a whole*) globalement
5 VT **a** (= *make round*) arrondir
b (*Comput, Math*) [*+ figure*] arrondir
c (= *go round*) [*+ corner*] tourner ; [*+ bend*] prendre ; (*Naut*) [*+ cape*] doubler ; [*+ obstacle*] contourner
6 COMP ► **round arch** N (*Archit*) (arc *m* en) plein cintre *m*, arc *m* roman ► **round-cheeked** ADJ aux joues rondes, joufflu ► **round dance** N ronde *f* ► **round-eyed** ADJ (*lit*) aux yeux ronds ; (*with surprise*) avec des yeux ronds ► **round-faced** ADJ au visage rond ► **rounding error** N erreur *f* d'arrondi ► **round-necked pullover** N pull(-over) *m* ras du cou ► **round robin** N (= *petition*) pétition *f* (où les signatures sont disposées en rond) ; (*esp US Sport*) tournoi où tous les joueurs se rencontrent ► **round-shouldered** ADJ voûté ► **Round Table** N (*Myth*) Table *f* ronde ► **round-table discussion** N table *f* ronde ► **round-the-clock** ADJ 24 heures sur 24 → **clock** ► **round trip** N aller *m* et retour ; **Concorde does three ~ trips a week** le Concorde effectue trois voyages *fpl* par semaine ► **round trip ticket** N billet *m* aller-retour
► **round down** VT SEP [*+ prices etc*] arrondir (au chiffre inférieur)
► **round off** VT SEP [*+ speech, list, series*] terminer ; [*+ sentence*] parachever ; [*+ debate, meeting*] mettre fin à, clore ; [*+ meal*] terminer, finir (*with par*) ; **and now, to ~ off, I must say ...** et maintenant, pour conclure *or* en dernier lieu, je dois dire ...
► **round on** VT FUS = **round upon**
► **round up** **1** VT SEP **a** (= *bring together*) [*+ people*] rassembler, réunir ; [*+ cattle*] rassembler ; [*+ criminals*] ramasser* **b** [*+ prices etc*] arrondir (au chiffre supérieur) **2** **~up** N **roundup**
► **round upon** VT FUS (*in words*) s'en prendre à ; (*in actions*) sauter sur, attaquer

roundabout ['raʊndəbaʊt] **1** ADJ [*route*] détourné, indirect ; **we came (by) a ~ way** nous avons fait un détour ; **by ~ means** par des moyens détournés ; **~ phrase** circonlocution *f* ; **what a ~ way of doing things!** quelle façon contournée *or* compliquée de faire les choses ! **2** N (*Brit = merry-go-round*) manège *m* ; (*esp Brit = playground apparatus*) tourniquet *m* ; (*at road junction*) rond-point *m* (à sens giratoire) ; (*on traffic sign*) sens *m* giratoire → **swing**

rounded ['raʊndɪd] ADJ **a** (= *curved*) [*shape, edge, hill*] arrondi ; [*face, breasts, hips, handwriting*] rond ; [*shoulders*] voûté ; [*spine*] courbé **b** (= *complete*) [*education*] complet (-ète *f*) et équilibré ; [*film, book*] étoffé ; [*wine, tone*] rond ; [*flavour*] plein ; [*person, character*] équilibré ; [*character in book*] étoffé ; **a ~ picture of the situation** une description complète et impartiale de la situation **c** (*Culin*) [*tablespoon*] gros (grosse *f*) **d** (*Phon*) [*vowel*] arrondi

roundel ['raʊndl] N (= *decoration*) rond *m*; (= *symbol, logo*) insigne *m* rond; (*on warplane*) cocarde *f*

roundelay†† ['raʊndɪleɪ] N (*Mus*) rondeau *m*

rounder ['raʊndə'] N (*US*) fêtard* *m*, noceur* *m*

rounders ['raʊndəz] N (*Brit*) sorte de baseball

Roundhead ['raʊndhed] N (*Brit Hist*) Tête *f* ronde

roundhouse ['raʊndhaʊs] N (*US Rail*) rotonde *f*

roundly ['raʊndlɪ] ADV [*condemn, criticize*] sans ambages; [*reject*] catégoriquement; [*defeat*] à plate(s) couture(s)

roundness ['raʊndnɪs] N rondeur *f*

roundsman ['raʊndzmən] N (*pl* **-men**) (*Brit*) livreur *m*; **milk ~** laitier *m*

roundup ['raʊndʌp] N [*of cattle, people*] rassemblement *m*; [*of criminals, suspects*] rafle *f*; (= *meeting*) tour *m* d'horizon; (= *news summary*) résumé *m* de l'actualité

roundworm ['raʊndwɜːm] N ascaride *m*

rouse [raʊz] **1** VT (= *awaken*) réveiller, éveiller; (= *stimulate*) activer, éveiller; [+ *feeling*] exciter, stimuler; [+ *admiration, interest*] susciter; [+ *indignation*] provoquer, soulever; [+ *suspicions*] éveiller; **~ yourself!** secouez-vous!*; **to ~ the masses** soulever les masses; **to ~ sb to action** inciter or pousser qn à agir; **to ~ sb (to anger)** mettre qn en colère; **he's a terrible man when he's ~d** il est redoutable quand il est en colère **2** VI (= *waken*) se réveiller; (= *become active*) sortir de sa torpeur

rousing ['raʊzɪŋ] ADJ [*cheers, applause, speech, chorus, reception*] enthousiaste; [*music*] entraînant

roust [raʊst], **roust out** VT (*US*) (= *evict*) chasser; (= *call out*) faire venir; **to ~ sb out of bed/his home** arracher qn de son lit/de sa maison

roustabout ['raʊstəbaʊt] N (*US*) débardeur *m*; (*Austral*) manœuvre *m*

rout¹ [raʊt] **1** N **a** (*Mil* = *defeat*) déroute *f*, débâcle *f*; **to put to ~** mettre en déroute **b** (†† = *revels*) raout† *m*, fête *f* mondaine **c** (*Jur* = *mob*) attroupement *m* illégal **2** VT (= *defeat*) mettre en déroute

rout² [raʊt] VI (= *search: also* **~ about**) fouiller ► **rout out** VT (= *find*) dénicher; (= *force out*) déloger; **to ~ sb out of bed** tirer qn de son lit

route [ruːt] **1** N **a** (*gen, also of train, plane, ship etc*) itinéraire *m*; (*Climbing*) itinéraire *m*, voie *f*; **shipping/air ~s** routes *fpl* maritimes/aériennes; (*Aut*) **all ~s** toutes directions; **what ~ does the 39 bus take?** par où passe le 39?, quel est l'itinéraire du 39?; **we're on a bus ~** nous sommes sur une ligne d'autobus; **the ~ to the coast goes through ...** pour aller à la côte on passe par ...; **I know a good ~ to London** je connais un bon itinéraire pour aller à Londres; **en ~ (for)** en route (pour) → **sea, trade** **b** [*often* raʊt] (*Mil*) ordres *mpl* de marche, route *f* à suivre **c** (*US*) [*often* raʊt] (= *delivery round*) tournée *f*; **he has a paper ~** il distribue des journaux **d** (*US*) [*often* raʊt] (*in highway names*) **Route 39** ≈ la nationale 39 **2** VT (= *plan route of*) [+ *train, coach, bus*] fixer le parcours or l'itinéraire de; [+ *phone call*] acheminer; **to ~ a train through Leeds** faire passer un train par Leeds; **my luggage was ~d through Amsterdam** mes bagages ont été expédiés via Amsterdam; **they've ~d the train by Leeds** le train passe maintenant par Leeds **3** COMP ► **route map** N (= *road map*) carte *f* routière; (*for ramblers*) topo* *m*; (*for trains etc*) carte *f* du réseau ► **route march** N (*Mil*) marche *f* d'entraînement ► **route planner** N (= *map*) carte *f* routière; (= *road atlas*) recueil *m* de cartes routières

routine [ruː'tiːn] **1** N **a** routine *f*; **daily ~** (*gen*) occupations *fpl* journalières, routine *f* quotidienne; (*pej*) train-train *m inv* de la vie quotidienne; (*Mil, Naut*) emploi *m* du temps; **business** or **office ~** travail *m* courant du bureau; **as a matter of ~** automatiquement, systématiquement; **dance ~** numéro *m* de danse; (*Theat*) numéro *m*; (*fig*) **he gave me the old ~* about his wife not understanding him** il m'a ressorti la vieille rengaine du mari incompris, il m'a mis le disque* du mari incompris **2** ADJ **a** (= *normal*) [*work, matter, check, maintenance, flight*] de routine; [*procedure, questions*] de routine, d'usage; **it was quite ~** c'était de la simple routine; **on a ~ basis** de façon routinière; **~ duties** obligations *fpl* courantes; **to make ~ inquiries** mener une enquête de routine **b** (= *predictable*) [*report, problem, banter*] banal

routinely [ruː'tiːnlɪ] ADV couramment; **to be ~ tested** [*person*] passer un examen de routine; [*blood*] être systématiquement examiné

rove [rəʊv] **1** VI errer, vagabonder; [*eyes*] errer **2** VT [+ *countryside*] parcourir, errer dans or sur; [+ *streets*] errer dans, aller au hasard dans

rover ['rəʊvə'] N vagabond(e) *m(f)*

roving ['rəʊvɪŋ] **1** ADJ [*reporter*] volant; [*ambassador, musician*] itinérant; [*gang*] errant; **to have a ~ commission to do sth** avoir carte blanche or toute latitude pour faire qch; **to have a ~ eye** être toujours à l'affût d'une aventure (amoureuse) **2** N vagabondage *m*

row¹ [rəʊ] **1** N [*of objects, people*] (*beside one another*) rang *m*, rangée *f*; (*behind one another*) file *f*, ligne *f*; [*of seeds, plants*] rayon *m*, rang *m*; [*of houses, trees, figures*] rangée *f*; [*of cars*] file *f*; (*Knitting*) rang *m*; **in the front ~** au premier rang; (*Rugby*) **the front/second/back ~ (of the scrum)** la première/deuxième/troisième ligne (de mêlée); **they were sitting in a ~** ils étaient assis en rang; (*fig*) **four failures in a ~** quatre échecs d'affilée or de suite; (*fig*) **a hard** or **long** or **tough ~ to hoe** une rude besogne **2** COMP ► **row house** N (*US*) maison qui fait partie d'une rangée de maisons identiques et contiguës → [HOUSE]

row² [rəʊ] **1** VT [+ *boat*] faire aller à la rame or à l'aviron; [+ *person, object*] transporter en canot (**to** à); **to ~ sb across** faire traverser qn en canot; **to ~ a race** faire une course d'aviron → **stroke 2** (*gen*) ramer; (*Sport*) faire de l'aviron; **to ~ away/back** s'éloigner/revenir à la rame; **he ~ed across the Atlantic** il a traversé l'Atlantique à la rame or à l'aviron; **to go ~ing** (*for pleasure*) canoter, faire du canotage; (*Sport*) faire de l'aviron **3** N promenade *f* en canot; **to go for a ~** canoter, faire un tour en canot; **it will be a hard ~ upstream** ce sera dur de remonter la rivière à la rame or à l'aviron

row³* [raʊ] (*esp Brit*) **1** N (= *noise*) vacarme *m*, boucan* *m*; (= *quarrel*) dispute *f*; **to make a ~** faire du vacarme or du boucan*; **what a ~!** quel vacarme or boucan*!; **to have a ~ with sb** se disputer avec qn, s'engueuler* avec qn; **to give sb a ~** passer un savon à qn*, sonner les cloches à qn*; **to get (into) a ~** se faire passer un savon* or sonner les cloches* **2** VI se disputer, s'engueuler* (**with** avec)

rowan ['raʊən] N (= *tree*) sorbier *m* des oiseleurs; (= *berry*) sorbe *f*

rowboat ['rəʊbəʊt] N (*US*) canot *m* (à rames)

rowdiness ['raʊdɪnɪs] N tapage *m*, chahut *m*

rowdy ['raʊdɪ] **1** ADJ [*person, behaviour*] chahuteur; [*party*] un peu trop animé; [*demonstration*] bruyant; **~ scenes in Parliament** scènes *fpl* de chahut au parlement; **to be ~** [*person*] chahuter **2** N* bagarreur* *m*, voyou *m*; **football rowdies** hooligans *mpl* (des matchs de football)

rowdyism ['raʊdɪɪzəm] N tapage *m*, chahut *m*

rower ['rəʊə'] N rameur *m*, -euse *f*; (*in navy*) nageur *m*, -euse *f*

rowing ['rəʊɪŋ] **1** N (*for pleasure*) canotage *m*; (*Sport*) aviron *m*; (*in navy*) nage *f* **2** COMP ► **rowing boat** N (*Brit*) canot *m* (à rames) ► **rowing club** N club *m* d'aviron ► **rowing machine** N rameur *m*

rowlock ['rɒlək] N (*esp Brit*) dame *f* de nage, tolet *m*

royal ['rɔɪəl] **1** ADJ **a** (*lit, fig*) royal; **the ~ household** la maison royale; **~ occasion** événement honoré de la présence d'un membre de la famille royale; **the "~ we"** le pluriel de majesté; (*fig*) **the ~ road to freedom/success** la voie royale de la liberté/du succès; (*fig*) **to give sb a (right) ~ welcome** réserver à qn un accueil royal; **he's a ~ pain in the backside*** c'est le roi des enquiquineurs* → **prerogative, princess b** [*paper*] de format grand raisin; **~ octavo** in-huit raisin **2** N* membre *m* de la famille royale; **the ~s** la famille royale **3** COMP ► **the Royal Academy (of Arts)** N (*Brit*) l'Académie *f* royale des Beaux-Arts ► **the Royal Air Force** N (*Brit*) la Royal Air Force ► **royal assent** N (*Brit*) sanction *f* royale (*d'un projet de loi*); **to receive** or **be given ~ assent** être approuvé par le souverain ► **royal blue** N bleu roi *m inv* ► **royal-blue** ADJ bleu roi *inv* ► **the Royal Canadian Mounted Police** N la Gendarmerie royale canadienne ► **Royal Commission** N (*Brit*) commission *f* d'enquête parlementaire ► **royal correspondent** N correspondant(e) chargé(e) des affaires royales ► **the Royal Engineers** NPL (*Brit Mil*) le génie (militaire britannique) ► **royal family** N famille *f* royale ► **royal flush** N (*Cards*) flush *m* royal ► **Royal Highness** N Your/His Royal Highness Votre/Son Altesse Royale ► **royal jelly** N gelée *f* royale ► **the Royal Mail** N (*Brit*) le service postal britannique ► **the Royal Marines** NPL (*Brit Mil*) l'infanterie *f* de marine; **a Royal Marine** un soldat de l'infanterie de marine ► **the Royal Mint** N (*Brit*) l'hôtel *m* des Monnaies ► **the Royal Naval Reserve** N (*Brit Mil*) le corps de réservistes de la marine ► **the Royal Navy** N (*Brit Mil*) la marine nationale ► **royal pardon** N grâce *f* royale ► **the Royal Shakespeare Company** N (*Brit*) troupe de théâtre spécialisée dans le répertoire shakespearien ► **the Royal Society** N (*Brit*) ≈ l'Académie *f* des sciences ► **the Royal Society for the Prevention of Cruelty to Animals** N (*Brit*) → RSPCA ► **the Royal Ulster Constabulary** N (*Brit Police*) la police de l'Irlande du Nord ► **royal warrant** N (*Brit*) autorisation que reçoit un commerçant de fournir la famille royale

┌─────────────────────────────────┐
│ **ROYAL SHAKESPEARE COMPANY** │
└─────────────────────────────────┘

La Royal Shakespeare Company, ou RSC, est une troupe de théâtre fondée en 1960 à Stratford-on-Avon, lieu de naissance de Shakespeare. Basée à Stratford et au Barbican à Londres, elle présente naturellement des pièces de Shakespeare mais aussi d'autres auteurs classiques ou contemporains. La RSC fait chaque année des tournées de six mois dans toute la Grande-Bretagne et elle a acquis une solide réputation internationale.

royalism ['rɔɪəlɪzəm] N royalisme *m*

royalist ['rɔɪəlɪst] ADJ, N royaliste *mf*

royally ['rɔɪəlɪ] ADV **a** (= *lavishly*) [*entertain, treat*] royalement **b** (* = *completely*) **to get ~ drunk** se soûler à mort*; **to be ~ pissed off (with sb)*** en avoir sa claque* (de qn); **to have ~ screwed up*** avoir merdé en beauté**

royalty ['rɔɪəltɪ] N **a** (= *position, dignity, rank*) royauté *f* **b** (= *royal person*) membre *m* de la famille royale; (= *royal persons*) (membres *mpl* de) la famille royale; **when speaking to ~** quand on s'adresse à un membre de la famille royale [c] (*also* **royalties**) (*from book*) royalties *fpl*, droits *mpl* d'auteur; (*from oil well, patent*) royalties *fpl*

rozzer ['rɒzəʳ] N (*Brit*) flic* *m*, poulet* *m*

RP [ɑː'piː] N (*Ling*) (ABBR = **Received Pronunciation**) → **received**; → ENGLISH

RPI [ˌɑːpiː'aɪ] N (*Brit*) (ABBR = **retail price index**) → **retail**

rpm [ˌɑːpiː'em] N [a] (ABBR = **revolutions per minute**) tr/min [b] (*Comm*) (ABBR = **resale price maintenance**) → **resale**

RR (*US*) ABBR = **railroad**

RRP [ˌɑːrɑː'piː] N (*Comm*) (ABBR = **recommended retail price**) → **recommend**

RSA [ˌɑːres'eɪ] N [a] (ABBR = **Royal Society of Arts**) *organisme habilité à conférer des diplômes* [b] (ABBR = **Royal Scottish Academy**) Académie *f* royale d'Écosse

RSC [ˌɑːres'siː] N (*Brit*) (ABBR = **Royal Shakespeare Company**) → **royal**

RSI [ˌɑːres'aɪ] N (ABBR = **repetitive strain injury**) TMS *mpl*

RSM [ˌɑːres'em] N (*Mil*) (ABBR = **Regimental Sergeant Major**) → **regimental**

RSPB [ˌɑːrespiː'biː] N (*Brit*) (ABBR = **Royal Society for the Protection of Birds**) *société britannique de protection des oiseaux*

RSPCA [ˌɑːrespiːsiː'eɪ] N (*Brit*) (ABBR = **Royal Society for the Prevention of Cruelty to Animals**) ≈ SPA *f*

RSV N (ABBR = **Revised Standard Version**) → **revise**

RSVP [ˌɑːresviː'piː] (ABBR = **please reply**) RSVP

RTA [ˌɑːtiː'eɪ] N (ABBR = **road traffic accident**) → **road**

Rt Hon. (*Brit Pol*) (ABBR = **Right Honourable**) → **right**

Rt Rev. (ABBR = **Right Reverend**) → **reverend**

RU N (ABBR = **Rugby Union**) → **rugby**

rub [rʌb] [1] N [a] (*on thing*) frottement *m*; (*on person*) friction *f*; (*with duster etc*) coup *m* de chiffon *or* de torchon; **to give sth a ~** [+ *furniture, shoes, silver*] donner un coup de chiffon *or* de torchon à qch [+ *sore place, one's arms*] frotter qch; **to give sb a ~** frictionner qn [b] (= *obstacle*) **there's the ~!** c'est là la difficulté!, voilà le hic!*; **the ~ is that ...** l'ennui *or* le hic*, c'est que ...; (*esp Brit*) **we didn't have the ~ of the green** nous n'avons pas été vernis* *or* pas eu de chance [c] (= *massage cream*) crème *f* de massage; (= *massage oil*) huile *f* de massage

[2] VT frotter; (= *polish*) astiquer, frotter; (*Art*) [+ *brass, inscription*] prendre un frottis de; **~ yourself and you'll soon be dry** frictionne-toi *or* frotte-toi, tu seras bientôt sec; **to ~ one's nose** se frotter le nez; (*fig*) **to ~ sb's nose in sth** ne jamais laisser oublier qch à qn; **to ~ one's hands (together)** se frotter les mains; (*esp Brit*) **to ~ one's hands with glee** se frotter les mains; **to ~ sth dry** sécher qch en le frottant; **to ~ a hole in sth** faire un trou dans qch à force de frotter; **to ~ sth through a sieve** passer qch au tamis; **to ~ lotion into the skin** faire pénétrer de la lotion dans la peau; (*fig*) **to ~ shoulders** (*Brit*) *or* **elbows** (*US*) **with all sorts of people** côtoyer toutes sortes de gens; (*US*) **to ~ sb the wrong way** prendre qn à rebrousse-poil → **salt**

[3] VI [*thing*] frotter (**against** contre); [*person, cat*] se frotter (**against** contre)

[4] COMP ► **rub-down** N **to give a horse a ~-down** bouchonner un cheval; **to give sb a ~-down** faire une friction à qn, frictionner qn ► **rub-up** N **to give sth a ~-up** frotter *or* astiquer qch

► **rub along*** VI (*Brit*) faire *or* poursuivre son petit bonhomme de chemin; **to ~ along (to-**

gether) [*two people*] vivre *or* s'accorder tant bien que mal; (*fig*) **he can ~ along in French** ◊ **he knows enough French to ~ along with** il sait assez de français pour se tirer d'affaire tant bien que mal *or* pour se débrouiller

► **rub away** VT SEP [+ *mark*] faire disparaître (en frottant), effacer; **she ~bed her tears away** elle a essuyé ses larmes

► **rub down** [1] VT SEP [+ *horse*] bouchonner; [+ *person*] frictionner (**with** avec); [+ *wall, paintwork*] (= *clean*) frotter, nettoyer du haut en bas; (= *sandpaper*) poncer, polir [2] **~-down** N → **rub**

► **rub in** VT SEP [+ *oil, liniment*] faire pénétrer en frottant; (*fig*) [+ *idea*] insister sur; [+ *lesson*] faire entrer (**to** à); (*fig*) **don't ~ it in!*** pas besoin de me le rappeler!; **he's always ~bing in how rich he is** il ne vous laisse jamais oublier à quel point il est riche

► **rub off** [1] VI [*mark*] partir, s'en aller; [*writing*] s'effacer, disparaître, s'en aller; **the blue will ~ off on to your hands** tu vas avoir les mains toutes bleues; (*fig*) **I hope some of his politeness will ~ off on to his brother*** j'espère qu'il passera un peu de sa politesse à son frère, j'espère que sa politesse déteindra un peu sur son frère [2] VT SEP [+ *writing on blackboard*] effacer; [+ *dirt*] enlever en frottant

► **rub on** VT SEP [+ *cream, polish etc*] passer

► **rub out** [1] VI [*mark, writing*] s'effacer, s'en aller; **that ink won't ~ out** cette encre ne s'effacera pas [2] VT SEP (= *erase*) effacer; (* = *kill*) descendre*, liquider*

► **rub up** [1] VI **to ~ up against all sorts of people** côtoyer toutes sortes de gens; [2] VT SEP [+ *vase, table*] frotter, astiquer; (*fig*) **to ~ sb up the right way** savoir s'y prendre avec qn; (*Brit fig*) **to ~ sb up the wrong way** prendre qn à rebrousse-poil; (* = *revise*) **to ~ up one's French** dérouiller* son français [3] **~-up** N → **rub**

rubato [ruː'bɑːtəʊ] N, ADV rubato *m*

rubber[1] ['rʌbəʳ] [1] N [a] (= *material: no pl*) caoutchouc *m*; **synthetic ~** caoutchouc *m* synthétique; **to burn ~*** (= *start*) démarrer sur les chapeaux de roue; (= *pass*) passer en trombe → **foam** [b] (*Brit* = *eraser*) gomme *f* [c] (*esp US* = *condom*) préservatif *m*, capote *f* anglaise [2] **rubbers** NPL (= *shoes*) caoutchoucs *mpl* [3] ADJ *de* or *en caoutchouc* → **4** [4] COMP ► **rubber band** N élastique *m* ► **rubber boots** NPL (*US*) bottes *fpl* de *or* en caoutchouc ► **rubber bullet** N balle *f* de *or* en caoutchouc ► **rubber cement** N dissolution *f* de caoutchouc ► **rubber cheque*** N chèque *m* en bois* *or* sans provision ► **rubber gloves** NPL gants *mpl* de *or* en caoutchouc ► **rubber plant** N caoutchouc *m* (*plante verte*) ► **rubber plantation** N plantation *f* d'hévéas ► **rubber ring** N (*for swimming*) bouée *f* (de natation); (*for sitting on*) rond *m* (pour malade) ► **rubber solution** N dissolution *f* ► **rubber stamp** N tampon *m* en caoutchouc ► **rubber-stamp*** VT (*lit*) tamponner; (*fig*) approuver sans discussion ► **rubber tree** N arbre *m* à gomme, hévéa *m* ► **rubber-tyred** ADJ sur pneus

rubber[2] ['rʌbəʳ] N (*Cards*) rob *m*, robre *m*; **to play a ~** faire un robre *or* une partie; (*Bridge*) **that's game and ~** c'est la partie

rubberized ['rʌbəraɪzd] ADJ caoutchouté

rubberneck*[?] ['rʌbənek] (*US*) [1] N (= *tourist*) touriste *mf*; (= *onlooker*) badaud(e) *m(f)* [2] VI faire le badaud

rubbery ['rʌbəri] ADJ [*object, substance, skin, food*] caoutchouteux; [*lips*] lippu; [*legs*] en coton

rubbing ['rʌbɪŋ] [1] N (= *action*) frottement *m*, friction *f*; (*Art*) frottis *m*, reproduction *f* par

frottage → **brass** [2] COMP ► **rubbing alcohol** N (*US*) alcool *m* à 90°

rubbish ['rʌbɪʃ] [1] N [a] (= *waste material*) détritus *mpl*; (*Brit* = *household rubbish*) ordures *fpl*, immondices *fpl*; [*of factory*] déchets *mpl*; [*of building site*] décombres *mpl*; (*pej* = *worthless things*) camelote* *f*; **household ~** ordures *fpl* ménagères; **garden ~** détritus *mpl* de jardin; **this shop sells a lot of ~** ce magasin ne vend que de la camelote*; **it's just ~** ça ne vaut rien → **1b** [b] (*fig* = *nonsense*) bêtises *fpl*; **to talk ~** dire des bêtises *or* des inepties; **(what a lot of) ~!*** n'importe quoi!*; **this book is ~** ce livre ne vaut strictement rien; **that's just ~** ça ne veut rien dire, ça n'a aucun sens; **it is ~ to say that ...** c'est idiot de dire que ... [2] ADJ (* = *useless*) nul; **I'm ~ at golf** je suis nul en golf [3] VT (* *fig* = *denigrate*) débiner* [4] COMP ► **rubbish bin** N (*Brit*) poubelle *f*, boîte *f* à ordures ► **rubbish chute** N (*at dump*) dépotoir *m*; (*in building*) vide-ordures *m inv* ► **rubbish collection** N ramassage *m* *or* collecte *f* des ordures ► **rubbish dump**, **rubbish heap** N (*public*) décharge *f* publique, dépotoir *m*; (*in garden*) monceau *m* de détritus

rubbishy* ['rʌbɪʃi] ADJ (*esp Brit*) [*film, book, magazine*] nul, débile*; [*goods*] de mauvaise qualité, qui ne vaut rien; **this is ~ stuff** ça ne vaut rien

rubble ['rʌbl] N [*of ruined house, bomb site, demolition site*] décombres *mpl*; (*smaller pieces*) gravats *mpl*; (*in road-building*) blocaille *f*, blocage *m*; **the building was reduced to a heap of ~** il ne restait du bâtiment qu'un tas de décombres

rube*[?] [ruːb] N (*US*) péquenaud* *m*

Rube Goldberg ['ruːb'ɡəʊldbɜːɡ] N (*US*) **a ~ machine** un engin bricolé avec les moyens du bord

rubella [ruː'belə] N rubéole *f*

Rubicon ['ruːbɪkən] N Rubicon *m*; **to cross the ~** passer *or* franchir le Rubicon

rubicund ['ruːbɪkənd] ADJ (*liter*) rubicond

rubidium [ruː'bɪdɪəm] N rubidium *m*

ruble ['ruːbl] N (*US*) = **rouble**

rubric ['ruːbrɪk] N rubrique *f*

ruby ['ruːbɪ] [1] N rubis *m*; (= *colour*) couleur *f* rubis [2] COMP (= *colour*) [*wine*] (de couleur) rubis *inv*; [*lips*] vermeil; (= *made of rubies*) [*necklace, ring*] de rubis ► **ruby wedding** N noces *fpl* de rubis

RUC [ˌɑːjuː'siː] N (*Brit Police*) (ABBR = **Royal Ulster Constabulary**) → **royal**

ruche [ruːʃ] N ruche *f*

ruched [ruːʃt] ADJ ruché

ruck[1] [rʌk] N (*Racing*) peloton *m*; (*Rugby*) mêlée *f* ouverte *or* spontanée; (*Brit* = *fight*) bagarre *f*; (*fig*) **the (common) ~** les masses *fpl*, la foule, le peuple; (*fig*) **to get out of the ~** se distinguer du commun des mortels

ruck[2] [rʌk] N (= *crease*) faux pli *m*, godet *m*

► **ruck up** VI [*skirt, blouse*] remonter en faisant des plis

ruckle ['rʌkl] N = **ruck**[2]

rucksack ['rʌksæk] N (*esp Brit*) sac *m* à dos

ruckus* ['rʌkəs] N (*pl* **ruckuses**) (*US*) grabuge* *m*

ruction* ['rʌkʃən] N (*gen pl*) (= *rows*) disputes *fpl*, grabuge* *m*; (= *riots*) troubles *mpl*, bagarres *fpl*; **there'll be ~s if you break that glass** si tu casses ce verre tu vas te faire sonner les cloches* *or* il va y avoir du grabuge*

rudder ['rʌdəʳ] N (*Aviat, Naut, fig*) gouvernail *m*; (*Aviat*) **vertical/horizontal ~** gouvernail *m* de direction/de profondeur

rudderless ['rʌdəlɪs] ADJ [*boat*] sans gouvernail; [*government, country*] à la dérive

ruddiness ['rʌdɪnɪs] N **the ~ of her complexion** son teint rose ; (pej) son teint rougeaud

ruddy ['rʌdɪ] **1** ADJ **a** [face] rose ; (pej) rougeaud ; [complexion] rose ; (pej) rougeaud, coloré ; [sky, glow] rougeoyant ; **her face had a ~ glow** elle avait les joues roses **b** (Brit† euph = bloody) sacré ; **he's a ~ fool** c'est un imbécile fini ; **you're a ~ nuisance** tu me casses vraiment les pieds* ; **what the ~ hell are you doing?** mais qu'est-ce que tu fiches ?* **2** ADV (Brit†* euph = bloody) bougrement† ; **how could you be so ~ stupid?** comment as-tu pu être aussi bougrement†* idiot ?

rude [ru:d] **1** ADJ **a** (= impolite) [person, behaviour, reply] impoli (**to sb** avec qn, **about sth** à propos de qch) ; [remark] impoli ; **he's always ~** c'est un grossier personnage, **it's ~ to stare/to speak with your mouth full** c'est mal élevé de dévisager les gens/de parler la bouche pleine **b** (= obscene) [noise] incongru ; [joke] grossier ; [story] scabreux ; [song] grivois ; [gesture] obscène **c** (= unexpected) [shock] brutal ; (fig) **to have** or **get a ~ awakening** être brutalement rappelé à la réalité **d** (liter = primitive) [shelter, table, implement] rudimentaire **e** (= vigorous) [health] de fer ; **to be in ~ health** avoir une santé de fer **2** COMP ► **rude word** N gros mot *m*

rudely ['ru:dlɪ] ADV **a** (= impolitely) [say] impoliment ; [push, interrupt] impoliment, brutalement ; **before I was so ~ interrupted** avant qu'on ne m'interrompe aussi impoliment **b** (= unexpectedly) [awaken] en sursaut, brusquement **c** (liter = primitively) [carved, shaped] grossièrement

rudeness ['ru:dnɪs] N **a** (= impoliteness) [of person, behaviour, reply] impolitesse *f* ; [of remark] impolitesse *f*, grossièreté *f* **b** (= obscenity) [of joke] grossièreté *f* ; [of story] côté *m* scabreux ; [of song] grivoiserie *f* ; [of gesture] obscénité *f* **c** (= unexpectedness) [of shock] brutalité *f*

rudiment ['ru:dɪmənt] N (Anat) rudiment *m* ; (fig) **~s** rudiments *mpl*, éléments *mpl*, notions *fpl* élémentaires

rudimentary [,ru:dɪ'mentərɪ] ADJ rudimentaire ; **I've only got ~ French** je n'ai que quelques rudiments de français, mon français est rudimentaire

rue¹ [ru:] VT (liter) se repentir de, regretter amèrement ; **to ~ the day (when)** maudire le jour (où)

rue² [ru:] N (Bot) rue *f*

rueful ['ru:fʊl] ADJ contrit

ruefully ['ru:fəlɪ] ADV [say, admit] avec regret ; [smile] d'un air contrit

ruff [rʌf] N **a** (Dress) collerette *f* ; (Hist) fraise *f* ; [of bird, animal] collier *m*, collerette *f* **b** (Orn) (= sandpiper) combattant *m* ; (= pigeon) pigeon *m* capucin

ruff² [rʌf] (Cards) **1** N action *f* de couper (avec un atout) **2** VTI couper (avec un atout)

ruffian ['rʌfɪən] N voyou *m*, brute *f* ; **you little ~!** petit polisson !

ruffianly ['rʌfɪənlɪ] ADJ [person] brutal ; [behaviour] de voyou, de brute ; [looks, appearance] de brigand, de voyou

ruffle ['rʌfl] **1** N (on wrist) manchette *f* (en dentelle etc) ; (on chest) jabot *m* ; (round neck) fraise *f* ; (= ripple: on water) ride *f*, ondulation *f* **2** VT **a** (= disturb) [+ hair, feathers] ébouriffer ; [+ surface, water] agiter, rider ; [+ one's clothes] déranger, froisser ; **the bird ~d (up) its feathers** l'oiseau a hérissé ses plumes **b** (fig) (= upset) froisser ; (= annoy) contrarier, irriter ; **she wasn't at all ~d** elle était restée parfaitement calme ; **to ~ sb's feathers** froisser qn

Rufflette® ['rʌf'let] N (also ~ **tape**) galon *m* fronceur, ruflette® *f*

rug [rʌg] N **a** (for floor) petit tapis *m* ; (bedside) descente *f* de lit, carpette *f* ; (fireside) carpette *f* ; (fig) **to pull the ~ out from under sb's**

feet◊ **to pull the ~ from under sb** couper l'herbe sous le pied de qn **b** (esp Brit = blanket) couverture *f* ; (in tartan) plaid *m* → **travelling c** (⋮ = wig) moumoute* *f*, postiche *m*

rugby ['rʌgbɪ] **1** N (also ~ **football**) rugby *m* **2** COMP ► **rugby league** N (le) rugby à treize ► **rugby player** N rugbyman *m*, joueur *m* de rugby ► **rugby tackle** N plaquage *m* ♦ VT plaquer ► **rugby union** N (le) rugby à quinze

rugged ['rʌgɪd] ADJ **a** (= rough) [terrain] accidenté ; [coastline, cliffs] déchiqueté ; [mountains] aux contours déchiquetés ; [landscape, beauty] sauvage **b** (= masculine) [man] rude ; [features] rude, taillé à coups de serpe **c** (= tough) [person, personality, character, manners] rude ; [individualism, independence, determination] farouche ; [resistance] acharné ; **hill farmers are a ~ breed** les éleveurs des montagnes sont de solides gaillards **d** (= durable) [machine, construction, clothing] solide

ruggedness ['rʌgɪdnɪs] N [of landscape] aspect *m* sauvage ; [of character, features] rudesse *f*

rugger* ['rʌgə*] N (Brit) rugby *m*

Ruhr [rʊə*] N Ruhr *f*

ruin ['ru:ɪn] **1** N **a** (= destruction, cause of destruction) ruine *f* ; **the palace was going to ~** or **falling into ~** le palais tombait en ruine or menaçait ruine ; **he was on the brink of ~** ◊ **stared him in the face** il était au bord de la ruine ; **the ~ of my hopes** la ruine or la faillite de mes espérances ; **drink was his ~** l'alcool a été sa perte ; **it will be the ~ of him** ça sera sa ruine ; **you will be the ~ of me** tu seras ma perte or ma ruine → **rack² b** (gen pl = remains) ruine(s) *f(pl)* ; (lit, fig) **in ~s** en ruine ; **the castle is now a ~** le château est maintenant une ruine **2** VT [+ building, reputation, hopes, health, person] ruiner ; [+ clothes] abîmer ; [+ event, enjoyment] gâter

ruination [,ru:ɪ'neɪʃən] N ruine *f*, perte *f* ; **to be the ~ of** être la ruine de

ruined ['ru:ɪnd] ADJ [building, city] en ruine ; [economy] délabré, en ruine ; [person] (morally) perdu ; (financially) ruiné ; [career] ruiné

ruinous ['ru:ɪnəs] ADJ **a** (= expensive) [cost] exorbitant ; [expense] exorbitant, ruineux **b** (= disastrous) [effects, consequences] dévastateur (-trice *f*) ; [war, policy] désastreux ; **to be ~ for sb/sth** entraîner la ruine de qn/qch, ruiner qn/qch **c** (liter = dilapidated) [building] délabré ; **to be in a ~ state** être délabré

ruinously ['ru:ɪnəslɪ] ADV **~ expensive** ruineux ; **~ high interest rates** des taux *mpl* d'intérêt ruineux or exorbitants

rule [ru:l] **1** N **a** (= guiding principle) règle *f* ; (= regulation) règlement *m* ; (Gram) règle *f* ; **the ~s of the game** la règle du jeu ; **school ~s** règlement *m* intérieur de l'école (or du lycée etc) ; **it's against the ~s** c'est contraire à la règle or au règlement ; **running is against the ~s** ◊ **it's against the ~s to run** il est interdit or il n'est pas permis de courir ; (lit, fig) **to play by the ~s** jouer suivant or selon les règles, respecter les règles ; (fig) **to bend** or **stretch the ~s** faire une entorse au règlement ; **~s and regulations** statuts *mpl* ; **standing ~** règlement *m* ; **it's a ~ that ...** il est de règle que ... (+ *subj*) ; **~ of the road** (Aut) règle *f* générale de la circulation ; (Naut) règles *fpl* générales du trafic maritime ; **to do sth by ~** faire qch selon les règles ; (Math) **the ~ of three** la règle de trois ; **a rough ~ of thumb is that it is best to ...** en règle générale il vaut mieux ... ; **by ~ of thumb** à vue de nez ; **golden ~** règle *f* d'or → **exception**, **work b** (= custom) coutume *f*, habitude *f* ; **ties are the ~ in this hotel** les cravates sont de règle dans cet hôtel ; **bad weather is the ~ in winter** le mauvais temps est habituel or normal en hiver ; **he makes it a ~ to get up early** il a pour

règle de se lever tôt ; **to make tidiness a ~** faire de l'ordre une règle ; **as a (general) ~** en règle générale, normalement, en principe **c** (NonC = authority) autorité *f*, empire *m* ; **under British ~** sous l'autorité britannique ; **under a tyrant's ~** sous l'empire or la domination d'un tyran ; (Pol etc) **majority ~** ◊ **the ~ of the majority** le gouvernement par la majorité ; **the ~ of law** l'autorité *f* de la loi → **home d** (for measuring) règle *f* (graduée) ; **a foot ~** une règle d'un pied ; **folding ~** mètre *m* pliant → **slide e** (Rel) règle *f* **2** VT **a** [+ country] gouverner ; (fig) [+ passions, emotion] maîtriser ; [+ person] dominer, mener ; (fig) **to ~ the roost** faire la loi ; **he ~d the company for 30 years** il a dirigé la compagnie or il a été à la tête de la compagnie pendant 30 ans ; **to be ~d by jealousy** être mené or dominé par la jalousie ; **to ~ one's passions** maîtriser ses passions ; **he is ~d by his wife** il est mené par sa femme ; **if you would only be ~d by what I say ...** si seulement tu voulais consentir à écouter mes conseils ... ; **I won't be ~d by what he wants** je ne veux pas me plier à ses volontés **b** [judge, umpire etc] décider, déclarer (**that** que) ; (Jur) **the judge ~d the defence out of order** le juge a déclaré non recevables les paroles de l'avocat pour la défense ; **the judge ~d that the child should go to school** le juge a décidé que l'enfant irait à l'école **c** (= draw lines on) [+ paper] régler, rayer ; [+ line] tirer à la règle ; **~d paper** papier *m* réglé or rayé **3** VI **a** (= reign) régner (**over** sur) ; (in graffiti) **United ~ OK** United vaincra **b** **the prices ruling in Paris** les cours pratiqués à Paris **c** (Jur) statuer (**against** contre, **in favour of** en faveur de, **on** sur) **4** COMP ► **the rule book** N le règlement ; (fig) **to do sth by the ~ book** faire qch dans les règles ; (fig) **to throw the ~ book at sb*** remettre qn à sa place, rembarrer qn*

► **rule off** VT (Comm) [+ account] clore, arrêter ; **to ~ off a column of figures** tirer une ligne sous une colonne de chiffres

► **rule out** VT SEP [+ word, sentence] barrer, rayer ; (fig) [+ possibility, suggestion, date, person] exclure, écarter ; **the age limit ~s him out** il est exclu du fait de la limite d'âge ; **murder can't be ~d out** il est impossible d'écarter or d'exclure l'hypothèse d'un meurtre

ruler ['ru:lə*] N **a** (= sovereign) souverain(e) *m(f)* ; (= political leader) chef *m* (d'État) ; **the country's ~s** les dirigeants *mpl* du pays **b** (for measuring) règle *f*

ruling ['ru:lɪŋ] **1** ADJ [class, body] dirigeant ; [elite] dirigeant, au pouvoir ; [party] au pouvoir ; [principle] souverain ; [passion] dominant ; [price] en vigueur **2** N (Admin, Jur) décision *f*, jugement *m* ; [of judge] décision *f* ; **to give a ~** rendre un jugement

rum¹ [rʌm] **1** N rhum *m* **2** COMP ► **rum-running** N contrebande *f* d'alcool ► **rum toddy** N grog *m*

rum²†* [rʌm] ADJ (Brit) [person, situation] loufoque* ; [idea] loufoque*, biscornu*

Rumania [ru:'meɪnɪə] N la Roumanie

Rumanian [ru:'meɪnɪən] **1** ADJ roumain **2** N **a** (= person) Roumain(e) *m(f)* **b** (Ling) roumain *m*

rumba ['rʌmbə] N rumba *f*

rumble ['rʌmbl] **1** N **a** (= noise) [of thunder, cannon] grondement *m* ; [of train, lorry] roulement *m*, grondement *m* ; [of pipe, stomach] gargouillement *m*, borborygme *m* **b** (⋮ = fight) bagarre *f*, baston* *m* or *f* **2** VI [thunder, cannon] gronder ; [stomach, pipes] gargouiller ; **to ~ past** [vehicle] passer avec fracas **3** VT **a** (Brit⋮ = see through) [+ swindle] flairer, subodorer* ; [+ trick] piger* ; [+ person] voir venir ;

(= *find out*) piger* (**what/why** *etc* ce que/pourquoi *etc*); **I soon ~d him** *or* **his game** *or* **what he was up to!** j'ai tout de suite pigé sa combine!* **b** (*also* **~ out**) [+ *comments, remarks*] dire en grondant, grommeler **4** COMP ► **rumble seat** N strapontin *m* ► **rumble strip** N (*on road*) bande *f* rugueuse

►**rumble on** VI (*Brit*) [*argument, controversy*] traîner en longueur

rumbling ['rʌmblɪŋ] N [*of thunder*] grondement *m*; [*of vehicle*] roulement *m*, grondement *m*; [*of stomach, pipe*] gargouillement *m*; (*fig*) **~s of discontent** murmures *mpl* de mécontentement; **tummy ~s*** gargouillis *mpl*, borborygmes *mpl*

rumbustious [rʌm'bʌstʃəs] ADJ (*Brit*) exubérant

ruminant ['ruːmɪnənt] ADJ, N ruminant *m*

ruminate ['ruːmɪneɪt] **1** VI (*lit, fig*) ruminer; (*fig*) **to ~ over** *or* **about** *or* **on sth** ruminer qch, retourner qch dans sa tête **2** VT ruminer

rumination [ˌruːmɪ'neɪʃən] N (*lit, fig*) rumination *f*

ruminative ['ruːmɪnətɪv] ADJ [*person*] pensif; [*mood*] méditatif, pensif

ruminatively ['ruːmɪnətɪvlɪ] ADV d'un air pensif, pensivement

rummage ['rʌmɪdʒ] **1** N **a** (= *action*) **to have a good ~ round** fouiller partout **b** (*US* = *jumble*) bric-à-brac *m* **2** VI (*also* **~ about, ~ around**) farfouiller*, fouiller (**among, in** dans, **for** pour trouver) **3** COMP ► **rummage sale** N (*US*) vente *f* de charité (*de bric-à-brac*)

rummy¹* ['rʌmɪ] **1** ADJ (= *rum²*) **2** N (*US** = *drunk*) poivrot* *m*

rummy² ['rʌmɪ] N (*Cards*) rami *m*

rumour, rumor (*US*) ['ruːməʳ] **1** N rumeur *f* (**that** selon laquelle); **there is a disturbing ~ (to the effect) that ...** il court un bruit inquiétant selon lequel ...; **all these nasty ~s** toutes ces rumeurs pernicieuses; **~ has it that ...** on dit que ..., le bruit court que ...; **there is a ~ of war** le bruit court *or* on dit qu'il va y avoir la guerre **2** VT **it is ~ed that ...** on dit que ..., le bruit court que ...; **he is ~ed to be in London** il serait à Londres, le bruit court qu'il est à Londres; **he is ~ed to be rich** on le dit riche **3** COMP ► **rumour-monger** N colporteur *m*, -euse *f* de rumeurs ► **rumour-mongering** N (*NonC*) commérages *mpl*, colportage *m* de rumeurs

rump [rʌmp] **1** N **a** [*of animal*] croupe *f*; [*of fowl*] croupion *m*; (*Culin*) culotte *f* (de bœuf);* [*of person*] derrière *m*, postérieur* *m* **b** (*esp Brit pej*) [*of group, organization*] derniers vestiges *mpl* **2** ADJ (*Pol*) **a ~ party/opposition** *etc* un parti/une opposition *etc* croupion; **~ Yugoslavia** ce qui reste de la Yougoslavie; (*Brit Hist*) **the Rump Parliament** le Parlement croupion

rumple ['rʌmpl] VT [+ *clothes, paper*] froisser; [+ *hair*] ébouriffer

rumpsteak ['rʌmpsteɪk] N rumsteck *m*

rumpus* ['rʌmpəs] **1** N (*pl* **rumpuses**) chahut *m*; (= *noise*) tapage *m*, boucan* *m*; (= *quarrel*) prise *f* de bec*; **to make** *or* **kick up a ~** faire du chahut *or* du boucan*; **to have a ~ with sb** se chamailler* avec qn, avoir une prise de bec* avec qn **2** COMP ► **rumpus room** N (*esp US*) salle *f* de jeux

rumpy-pumpy* ['rʌmpɪ'pʌmpɪ] N (*NonC*) partie *f* de jambes en l'air*

rumrunner ['rʌmrʌnəʳ] N (*Hist*) (= *person*) contrebandier *m* (*d'alcool*); (= *ship*) bateau *m* servant à la contrebande d'alcool

run [rʌn]

vb: pret **ran**, ptp **run**	
1 NOUN	**4** TRANSITIVE VERB
2 PLURAL NOUN	**5** COMPOUNDS
3 INTRANSITIVE VERB	**6** PHRASAL VERBS

1 NOUN

a = *act of running* action *f* de courir, course

f; **to go for a ~** aller courir; **to go for a 2-km ~** faire 2 km de course à pied; **at a ~** en courant; **to break into a ~** se mettre à courir; **to make a ~ for it** se sauver, filer*; (*fig*) **I'll give them a (good) ~ for their money!** ils vont voir à qui ils ont affaire!; (*on sb's death*) **he's had a good ~** il a bien profité de l'existence

b = *outing* tour *m*; **to go for a ~ in the car** re un tour en voiture; **they went for a ~ in the country** ils ont fait un tour à la campagne; **we had a pleasant ~ down** le voyage a été agréable

c = *distance travelled* trajet *m*; (= *route*) ligne *f*; **it's a 30-minute ~** il y a une demi-heure de trajet; **it's a 30-minute bus ~** il y a une demi-heure de bus; **it's a short car ~** le trajet n'est pas long en voiture; **the boat no longer does that ~** le bateau ne fait plus cette traversée, ce service n'existe plus; **the ferries on the Dover-Calais ~** les ferrys sur la ligne Douvres-Calais; **the ships on the China ~** les paquebots qui font la Chine

d = *series* série *f*; (*Cards*) séquence *f*; **a ~ of misfortunes** une série de malheurs, une série noire; **a ~ of bad luck** une période de malchance; **she's having a ~ of luck** la chance lui sourit; (*Roulette*) **a ~ on the red** une série à la rouge; **the ~ of the cards** le hasard du jeu

e Theat, TV = *period of performance* **when the London ~ was over** une fois la saison à Londres *or* la série de représentations à Londres terminée; **the play had a long ~** la pièce a tenu longtemps l'affiche; **her new series begins a ~ on BBC1** sa nouvelle série d'émissions va bientôt passer sur BBC1

f = *great demand* (*Econ*) ruée *f*; **there was a ~ on the pound** il y a eu une ruée sur la livre; (*St Ex*) **a ~ on shares** une ruée sur les actions; **there was a ~ on the banks** les guichets (des banques) ont été assiégés; **there has been a ~ on sugar** les gens se sont précipités (dans les magasins) pour acheter du sucre, il y a une ruée sur le sucre

g = *use* **they have the ~ of the garden** ils ont la jouissance du jardin; **they gave us the ~ of the garden** ils nous ont donné la jouissance du jardin

h *of tide* flux *m*

i = *trend* [*of market*] tendance *f*; [*of events*] tournure *f*; **the decisive goal arrived, against the ~ of play** le but décisif a été marqué contre le cours du jeu; **against the ~ of the polls, he was re-elected** contrairement à la tendance indiquée par les sondages, il a été réélu

j = *type* **he was outside the common ~ of lawyers** ce n'était pas un avocat ordinaire; **she didn't fit the usual ~ of petty criminals** elle n'avait pas le profil du petit malfaiteur ordinaire; **the usual ~ of problems** les problèmes *mpl* habituels

k = *track for sledging, skiing* piste *f*; **ski ~** piste *f* de ski

l = *animal enclosure* enclos *m*

m *in tights* échelle *f*

n Mus roulade *f*

o *Printing* tirage *m*; **a ~ of 5,000 copies** un tirage de 5 000 exemplaires

p *Cricket* course *f*; **to make a ~** marquer une course

q *Mil* = *raid, mission* raid *m* (aérien); **a bombing ~** un bombardement

r *US Pol* = *bid for leadership* candidature *f* (**for** à)

s *SET STRUCTURES*

♦ **in the long run** à long terme; **it will be more economical in the long ~** ce sera plus économique à long terme; **things will sort themselves out in the long ~** les choses s'arrangeront avec le temps

♦ **in the short run** à court terme; **the most effective policy in the short ~** les mesures les plus efficaces à court terme; **no improvement is likely in the short ~** il y a peu de chances que la si-

tuation s'améliore à court terme *or* dans l'immédiat

♦ **on the run**: **a criminal on the ~ (from the police)** un criminel recherché par la police; **he is still on the ~** il court toujours, il est toujours en cavale*; **he was on the ~ for several months** il n'a été repris qu'au bout de plusieurs mois; **to have the enemy on the ~** mettre l'ennemi en fuite; **to keep the enemy on the ~** harceler l'ennemi; **I knew I had him on the ~** je savais que j'avais réussi à le mettre en mauvaise posture; **she has so much to do she's always on the ~*** elle a tant à faire qu'elle est toujours en train de courir

2 **runs** NPL **to have the ~s** avoir la courante* *or* la chiasse*

3 INTRANSITIVE VERB

a gen courir; (= *hurry*) courir, se précipiter; **don't ~ across the road** ne traverse pas la rue en courant; (*Brit*) **he's trying to ~ before he can walk** il essaie de brûler les étapes; (*fig*) **to ~ behind sb** avoir du retard par rapport à qn; **to ~ down/off** descendre/partir en courant; **to ~ down a slope** dévaler une pente *or* descendre une pente en courant; **to ~ for the bus** courir pour attraper le bus; **he used to ~ for his school** il représentait son lycée dans les épreuves de course à pied; **it ~s in the family** [*disease*] c'est héréditaire; [*characteristic*] c'est de famille; **my thoughts ran on Jenny** je pensais à Jenny; **she came ~ning out** elle est sortie en courant; **she ran over to her neighbour's** elle a couru *or* s'est précipitée chez son voisin; **three men ran past him** trois hommes l'ont dépassé en courant; **laughter ran round the room** le rire gagnait toute la salle; **a rumour ran through the school** un bruit courait à l'école; **this theme ~s through the whole Romantic movement** c'est un thème récurrent chez les romantiques; **all sorts of thoughts were ~ning through my head** toutes sortes d'idées me venaient à l'esprit; **that tune is ~ning through my head** cet air me trotte dans la tête; **the rope ran through his fingers** la corde lui a filé entre les doigts; **money simply ~s through his fingers** c'est un panier percé, l'argent lui file entre les doigts; **she ran to meet him** elle a couru *or* s'est précipitée à sa rencontre; **she ran to help him** elle a couru l'aider, elle a volé à son secours → 6

b = *flee* fuir, prendre la fuite; **~ for it!** sauvez-vous!

c *drawer, curtains* coulisser; **the drawer ~s smoothly** le tiroir coulisse facilement

d = *flow, leak* [*river, tears, tap, cheese*] couler; [*sore, abscess*] suppurer; [*colour*] déteindre; [*dye, ink*] baver; **to ~ into the sea** [*river*] se jeter dans la mer; **the river ~s between wooded banks** la rivière coule entre des berges boisées; **your bath is ~ning now** votre bain est en train de couler; **to leave a tap ~ning** laisser un robinet ouvert; **tears ran down her cheeks** les larmes coulaient sur ses joues; **his eyes are ~ning** il a les yeux qui coulent *or* pleurent; **his nose was ~ning** il avait le nez qui coulait; **the milk ran all over the floor** le lait s'est répandu sur le sol; **a heavy sea was ~ning** la mer était grosse; **where the tide is ~ning strongly** là où les marées sont fortes

♦ **to run high** [*river*] être haut; [*sea*] être gros; **feelings were ~ning high** les passions étaient exacerbées; **tension was ~ning high** l'atmosphère était très tendue

♦ **to run with** (= *be saturated*) **the floor was ~ning with water** le plancher était inondé; **the walls were ~ning with moisture** les murs ruisselaient (d'humidité); **his face was ~ning with sweat** son visage ruisselait de sueur

e *words, text* **how does the last sentence ~?** quelle est la dernière phrase?; **so the story ~s** c'est ce que l'on raconte

f *Pol etc* = *stand* être candidat, se présenter; **he isn't ~ning this time** il n'est pas candidat *or* il ne se présente pas cette fois-ci ; **he won't ~ again** il ne se représentera plus ; **to ~ for President** *or* **the Presidency** être candidat à la présidence

[g] = be I'm ~ning a bit late j'ai un peu de retard, je suis un peu en retard ; **to ~ wild** [*person*] être déchaîné ; [*animal*] courir en liberté ; [*plants, garden*] retourner à l'état sauvage

♦ **to run at** [*amount*] **inflation is ~ning at 3%** le taux d'inflation est de 3% ; **the deficit is now ~ning at 300 million dollars a year** le déficit est maintenant de 300 millions de dollars par an

[h] = extend, continue [*play*] être à l'affiche, se jouer ; [*film*] passer ; [*contract*] valoir, être valide ; **the play has been ~ning for a year** la pièce est à l'affiche *or* se joue depuis un an ; **this contract has ten months to ~** ce contrat expire dans dix mois *or* vaut (encore) pour dix mois ; (*Jur*) **the two sentences to ~ concurrently/consecutively** avec/sans confusion des deux peines ; (*Rad, TV*) **the programme ran for an extra ten minutes** l'émission a duré dix minutes de plus que prévu ; (*TV, Rad*) **the programme is ~ning to time** l'émission passera à l'heure prévue ; **the book has ~ into five editions** ce livre en est à sa cinquième édition

[i] bus, train, coach, ferry assurer le service ; **this train ~s between London and Manchester** ce train assure le service Londres-Manchester *or* entre Londres et Manchester ; **the buses ~ once an hour** les bus passent toutes les heures ; **the buses are ~ning early/late/to** *or* **on time** les bus sont en avance/en retard/à l'heure ; **there are no trains ~ning today** il n'y a pas de trains aujourd'hui ; **that train doesn't ~ on Sundays** ce train n'assure le service *or* n'est pas en service le dimanche

[j] = function [*machine*] marcher ; [*factory*] fonctionner, marcher ; [*wheel*] tourner ; **the car is ~ning smoothly** la voiture marche bien ; **you mustn't leave the engine ~ning** il ne faut pas laisser tourner le moteur ; **this car ~s on diesel** cette voiture marche au gazole ; **the radio ~s off the mains/off batteries** cette radio marche sur secteur/sur piles ; **things are ~ning smoothly** tout se passe bien

[k] = pass [*road, river etc*] passer (**through** à travers) ; [*mountain range*] s'étendre ; **the road ~s past our house** la route passe devant notre maison ; **the road ~s right into town** la route va jusqu'au centre-ville ; **the main road ~s north and south** la route principale va du nord au sud ; **he has a scar ~ning across his chest** il a une cicatrice en travers de la poitrine ; **a wall ~s round the garden** un mur entoure le jardin ; **the river ~s through the valley** la rivière coule dans la vallée ; **the roots ~ under the house** les racines passent sous la maison

[l] = unravel [*knitting*] se démailler ; [*tights*] filer

4 TRANSITIVE VERB

[a] gen courir ; **he ran 2km non-stop** il a couru (pendant) 2 km sans s'arrêter ; **he ~s 15km every day** il fait 15 km de course à pied tous les jours ; **he ran the distance in under half an hour** il a couvert la distance en moins d'une demi-heure ; **to ~ the 100 metres** courir le 100 mètres ; **to ~ a race** participer à une (épreuve de) course ; **you ran a good race** vous avez fait une excellente course ; **the first race will be ~ at 2 o'clock** la première épreuve se courra à 2 heures ; **but if it really happened he'd ~ a mile*** mais si ça se produisait, il aurait vite fait de se débiner* ; **to ~ the streets** [*child, dog*] traîner dans les rues ; (*US*) **to ~ a red** *or* **a stoplight** brûler *or* griller un feu rouge ; **they beat Wales and ran Scotland very close** ils ont battu le pays de Galles et ont bien failli battre l'Écosse ; **you're ~ning things a bit close*** *or* **fine*!** ça va être juste !, tu calcules un peu juste !

[b] = chase, hunt [+ *fox, deer*] chasser ; (= make run) [+ *person*] chasser ; [+ *animal*] poursuivre, pourchasser ; (*Sport*) [+ *horse*] faire courir ; **to ~**

a horse in the Derby engager *or* faire courir un cheval dans le Derby ; **the sheriff ran him out of town** le shérif l'a chassé de la ville ; **they ran him out of the house** ils l'ont chassé de la maison ; **to ~ sb into debt** endetter qn

[c] Pol [+ *candidate*] présenter ; **the party is ~ning 100 candidates this year** le parti présente 100 candidats (aux élections) cette année

[d] = transport [+ *person*] conduire ; [+ *goods*] transporter ; **to ~ sb into town** conduire qn en ville ; **he ran her home** il l'a ramenée chez elle ; **I'll ~ your luggage to the station** j'apporterai vos bagages à la gare

[e] = smuggle [+ *guns, whisky*] passer en contrebande ; **he was ~ning guns to the island** il faisait passer *or* il passait des fusils dans l'île en contrebande

[f] = operate: esp Brit [+ *machine*] faire marcher ; (*Comput*) [+ *program*] exécuter ; **to ~ a radio off the mains** faire marcher une radio sur secteur ; **it would be cheaper to ~ the heating system on gas** ce serait plus économique si le chauffage fonctionnait en gaz ; **I can't afford to ~ a car** je ne peux pas me permettre d'avoir une voiture ; **he ~s a Rolls** il a une Rolls ; **this car is very cheap to ~** cette voiture est très économique

[g] = organize, manage [+ *business, company, organization, school*] diriger, gérer ; [+ *mine*] gérer, administrer ; [+ *shop, hotel, club*] tenir ; [+ *newspaper*] être directeur de ; [+ *competition*] organiser ; [+ *public transport*] gérer ; **the company ~s extra buses at rush hours** la société met en service des bus supplémentaires aux heures de pointe ; **the school is ~ning courses for foreign students** le collège organise des cours pour les étudiants étrangers ; **to ~ a house** tenir une maison ; **I want to ~ my own life** je veux mener ma vie comme je l'entends ; **she's the one who really ~s everything** en réalité c'est elle qui dirige tout

[h] = put, move **he ran a line of stitches along the hem** il a fait une série de points le long de l'ourlet ; **to ~ a boat ashore** pousser un bateau sur le rivage ; **to ~ the car into/out of the garage** rentrer la voiture au/sortir la voiture du garage ; **he ran the car into a tree** sa voiture est rentrée dans un arbre, il a percuté un arbre (avec sa voiture) ; **to ~ a pipe into a room** faire passer un tuyau dans une pièce ; **to ~ wires under the floorboards** faire passer des fils électriques sous le plancher ; **to ~ one's eye over a page** jeter un coup d'œil sur une page ; **he ran the vacuum cleaner over the carpet** il a passé l'aspirateur sur le tapis ; **to ~ one's hand over sth** passer la main sur qch ; **to ~ one's fingers over the piano keys** promener ses doigts sur le clavier ; **to ~ one's fingers through one's hair** se passer la main dans les cheveux

[i] = publish publier ; **the paper ran a series of articles on genetic engineering** le journal a publié une série d'articles sur les manipulations génétiques ; **the papers ran the story on the front page** les journaux ont publié l'article en première page, cette histoire a fait la une des journaux

[j] = present [+ *film*] présenter, donner ; (*Comm*) vendre ; **the supermarket is ~ning a new line in fresh pasta** le supermarché vend une nouvelle gamme de pâtes fraîches

[k] = cause to flow faire couler ; **to ~ water into a bath** faire couler de l'eau dans une baignoire ; **I'll ~ you a bath** je vais te faire couler un bain ; **he ~s his words together** il mange ses mots

5 COMPOUNDS

► **run-around*** N **he gave me the ~-around** il s'est défilé* ► **run-down** ADJ [*person*] à plat*, mal fichu* ; [*building, area*] délabré ; **I feel a little ~-down** je me sens à plat* ► **run-in** N (* = quarrel) engueulade* f, prise f de bec (**over** à propos de) ; (= rehearsal) répétition f ; (= ap-

proach) approche f ► **run-off** N (*Sport*) finale f (d'une course) ; (*Agr*) infiltrations fpl ► **run-of-the-mill** ADJ banal, ordinaire ► **run-on** ADJ (*Typ*) [*text*] composé sans alinéa ; **~-on line** enjambement m ► **run-resist** ADJ runproof ► **run-through** N (before test) essai m ; (*Theat*) répétition f ► **run time** N (*Comput*) durée f d'exploitation ► **run-up** N (*Sport*) course f d'élan ; (= preparation) période f préparatoire (**to** à) ; (*US* = increase) augmentation f (**in** de) ; **the ~-up to the elections** la période qui précède les élections ; **the ~-up in prices** la flambée des prix

6 PHRASAL VERBS

► **run about** VI (*gen*) courir çà et là ; (*looking for sth, working etc*) courir dans tous les sens ; **the children were ~ning about all over the house** les enfants couraient partout dans la maison ; (*fig*) **she has been ~ning about* with him for several months** elle sort avec lui depuis plusieurs mois

► **run across** **1** VI traverser en courant

2 VT FUS (= meet) [+ *person*] rencontrer par hasard, tomber sur ; (= find) [+ *object, quotation, reference*] trouver par hasard, tomber sur

► **run after** VT FUS courir après ; (*fig*) **he doesn't ~ after women** ce n'est pas un coureur ; (*fig*) **I'm not going to spend my days ~ning after you!** je ne suis pas à ton bonne !

► **run against** VT FUS **the game was ~ning against them** ils étaient en train de perdre la partie ; (*Pol*) **to ~ against sb** se présenter contre qn

► **run along** VI courir ; (= go away) s'en aller ; **~ along!** sauvez-vous !, filez !*

► **run around** VI = run about

► **run at** VT FUS (= attack) se jeter *or* se précipiter sur

► **run away** **1** VI [a] partir en courant ; (= flee) [*person*] se sauver, s'enfuir ; [*horse*] s'emballer ; **to ~ away from home** faire une fugue ; **don't ~ away, I need your advice** ne te sauve pas, j'ai besoin d'un conseil ; (= elope) **she ran away with another man** elle est partie avec un autre homme ; (= steal) **he ran away with the funds** il est parti avec la caisse

[b] [*water*] s'écouler ; **he let the bath water ~ away** il a laissé la baignoire se vider

2 VT SEP [+ *water*] vider

► **run away with** VT FUS [a] (= win easily) [+ *race, match*] gagner haut la main ; [+ *prize*] remporter haut la main

[b] (= use up) [+ *funds, money, resources*] épuiser

[c] **you're letting your imagination ~ away with you** tu te laisses emporter par ton imagination ; **don't let your emotions ~ away with you** ne te laisse pas dominer par tes émotions ; **don't ~ away with the idea that ...** n'allez pas vous mettre dans la tête que ... → run away 1a

► **run back** **1** VI revenir *or* retourner en courant

2 VT SEP [a] [+ *person*] ramener (en voiture)

[b] (= rewind) [+ *tape, film*] rembobiner

► **run by** = run past

► **run down** **1** VI [a] [*person*] descendre en courant

[b] [*watch etc*] s'arrêter (faute d'être remonté) ; [*battery*] se décharger

2 VT SEP [a] (= knock over) renverser ; (= run over) écraser

[b] (*Naut*) [+ *ship*] heurter *or* aborder par l'avant *or* par l'étrave ; (in battle) éperonner

[c] (esp Brit = limit, reduce) [+ *production*] diminuer ; [+ *factory*] diminuer la production de ; **they are ~ning down their DIY stores** ils vont réduire le nombre (or la taille) de leurs magasins de bricolage

[d] (* = disparage) critiquer, dire du mal de

[e] (= pursue and capture) [+ *criminal*] découvrir la cachette de ; [+ *stag etc*] mettre aux abois

[f] [+ *list, page*] parcourir

► **run in** **1** VI entrer en courant ; (* = call) passer ; **I'll ~ in and see you tomorrow*** je passerai vous voir demain

2 VT SEP **a** (*Brit*) [+ *car*] roder; **"~ning in, please pass"** « en rodage »

b (* = *arrest*) emmener au poste

▶ **run into** VT FUS **a** (= *meet*) rencontrer par hasard, tomber sur; **to ~ into difficulties** *or* **trouble** se heurter à des difficultés; **to ~ into danger** se trouver dans une situation dangereuse; **to ~ into debt** s'endetter; **we've ~ into a problem** il y a un problème

b (= *collide with*) rentrer dans; **the car ran into a tree** la voiture est rentrée dans un arbre

c (= *merge*) **the colours are ~ning into each other** les couleurs déteignent les unes sur les autres; **I was so tired, my words began to ~ into one another** j'étais si fatigué que je commençais à bredouiller

d (= *amount to*) s'élever à; **the cost will ~ into thousands of pounds** le coût va s'élever *or* se chiffrer à des milliers de livres

▶ **run off 1** VI = **run away 1**

2 VT SEP **a** = **run away 2**

b (*Typ*) tirer; **to ~ off 600 copies** tirer 600 exemplaires

c (*Sport*) **to ~ off the heats** [*runner*] disputer les éliminatoires

▶ **run on 1** VI **a** continuer de courir; (* *fig: in talking*) parler sans arrêt; **but here am I ~ning on, and you're in a hurry** mais je parle, je parle, alors que vous êtes pressé; **it ran on for four hours** ça a duré quatre heures

b [*letters, words*] ne pas être séparés, être liés; [*line of writing*] suivre sans alinéa; [*verse*] enjamber; [*time*] passer, s'écouler

2 VT SEP [+ *letters, words, sentences*] faire suivre sur la même ligne

▶ **run out 1** VI **a** [*person*] sortir en courant; [*rope, chain*] se dérouler; [*liquid*] couler; **the pier ~s out into the sea** la jetée s'avance dans la mer

b (= *come to an end*) [*lease, contract*] expirer; [*supplies*] être épuisé, venir à manquer; [*period of time*] être écoulé, tirer à sa fin; **my patience is ~ning out** ma patience est à bout, je suis à bout de patience; **when the money ~s out** quand il n'y aura plus d'argent, quand l'argent sera épuisé; **their luck ran out** la chance les a lâchés

2 VT SEP [+ *rope, chain*] laisser filer

▶ **run out of** VT FUS [+ *supplies, money*] venir à manquer de, se trouver à court de; [+ *patience*] être à bout de; **we're ~ning out of time** il ne nous reste plus beaucoup de temps; (*TV, Rad*) **we've ~ out of time** il est temps de rendre l'antenne, le temps qui nous était imparti est écoulé; **to ~ out of petrol** (*Brit*) *or* **gas** (*US*) tomber en panne d'essence; (*US fig*) **to ~ out of gas*** s'essouffler

▶ **run out on*** VT FUS [+ *person*] laisser tomber*

▶ **run over 1** VI **a** (= *overflow*) [*liquid, container*] déborder; (*Rad, TV etc*) **the play ran over by ten minutes** la pièce a duré dix minutes de plus que prévu; (*Rad, TV etc*) **we're ~ning over** nous avons pris du retard

b (= *go briefly*) passer; **I'll ~ over tomorrow** je passerai demain; **she ran over to her neighbours'** elle a fait un saut chez ses voisins

2 VT FUS **a** (= *recapitulate*) [+ *story, part in play*] revoir, reprendre; **I'll ~ over your part with you** je vous ferai répéter votre rôle; **let's just ~ over it again** reprenons cela encore une fois

b (= *reread*) [+ *notes*] parcourir

3 VT SEP (*in car etc*) [+ *person, animal*] écraser

▶ **run past 1** VI passer en courant

2 VT SEP* [+ *idea*] expliquer; **could you ~ that past me again?** est-ce que tu pourrais m'expliquer ça encore une fois ?

▶ **run through 1** VI passer *or* traverser en courant

2 VT FUS **a** (= *use up*) [+ *fortune*] gaspiller

b (= *read quickly*) [+ *notes, text*] parcourir, jeter un coup d'œil sur

c (= *rehearse*) [+ *play*] répéter; [+ *verse, movement*] reprendre; (= *recapitulate*) récapituler,

reprendre; **let's ~ through the chorus again** reprenons le refrain encore une fois; **if I may just ~ through the principal points once more?** pourrais-je reprendre *or* récapituler les points principaux ?

3 VT SEP **a** **to ~ sb through (with a sword)** passer qn au fil de l'épée, transpercer qn d'un coup d'épée

b (*Comput*) [+ *data*] passer (en revue)

▶ **run to** VT FUS **a** (= *seek help from*) faire appel à; (= *take refuge with*) se réfugier dans les bras de; **as usual she ran to her parents** comme d'habitude elle a fait appel à papa et maman *or* elle est allée se réfugier dans les bras de *or* chez ses parents; **I wouldn't go ~ning to the police** je ne me précipiterais pas au commissariat de police; **go on then, ~ to mummy!** c'est ça, va te réfugier dans les jupes de ta mère !

b (= *afford*) **I can't ~ to a new car** je ne peux pas me payer une nouvelle voiture; **the funds won't ~ to a meal in a restaurant** il n'y a pas assez d'argent pour un repas au restaurant

c (= *develop*) **to ~ to fat** grossir

d (= *amount to*) **the article ~s to several hundred pages** l'article fait plusieurs centaines de pages

▶ **run up 1** VI (= *climb quickly*) monter en courant; (= *approach quickly*) s'approcher en courant; **a man ran up and fired several shots** un homme est arrivé en courant et a tiré plusieurs coups de feu

2 VT SEP **a** **to ~ up a hill** monter une colline en courant

b [+ *flag*] hisser

c [+ *bills*] accumuler; **to ~ up a debt** s'endetter (**of** de); **she's ~ up a huge bill at the garage** ça va lui coûter cher chez le garagiste

d (* = *make quickly*) [+ *garment*] faire *or* coudre rapidement; **she can ~ up a dress in no time** elle peut faire *or* coudre une robe en un rien de temps

▶ **run up against** VT FUS [+ *problem, difficulty*] se heurter à

---

runabout ['rʌnəbaʊt] **1** N (= *car*) petite voiture *f*; (= *boat*) runabout *m* **2** COMP
▶ **runabout ticket** N (*Rail etc*) billet *m* circulaire

runaway ['rʌnəweɪ] **1** N (*gen*) fuyard *m*, fugitif *m*, -ive *f*; (= *teenager, pupil etc*) fugueur *m*, -euse *f* **2** ADJ [*slave, person*] fugitif; [*horse*] emballé; [*car, railway truck*] fou (folle *f*); ~ **wedding** mariage *m* clandestin; **the ~ couple** le couple clandestin, les amants *mpl*; (*Fin*) ~ **inflation** inflation *f* galopante; (*fig*) ~ **success** succès *m* à tout casser*, succès *m* monstre*; **he had a ~ victory** il a remporté une victoire haut la main

rundown ['rʌndaʊn] N **a** (= *reduction: gen*) réduction *f*, diminution *f*; [*of industry, business*] réductions *fpl* délibérées; **there will be a ~ of staff** il y aura une réduction de personnel

b (= *summary*) **to give sb a ~ on sth*** mettre qn au courant *or* au parfum‡ de qch

rune [ruːn] N rune *f*; (*Brit fig*) **to read the ~s** interpréter la situation; (*Brit fig*) **they read the ~s correctly** ils ont vu juste

rung¹ [rʌŋ] VB ptp of **ring²**

rung² [rʌŋ] N [*of ladder*] barreau *m*, échelon *m*; [*of chair*] bâton *m*, barreau *m*

runic ['ruːnɪk] ADJ runique

runnel ['rʌnl] N (= *brook*) ruisseau *m*; (= *gutter*) rigole *f*

runner ['rʌnəʳ] **1** N **a** (= *athlete*) coureur *m*; (= *horse*) partant *m*; (= *messenger*) messager *m*, courrier *m*; (= *smuggler*) contrebandier *m*; **to do a ~*** déguerpir*, mettre les bouts‡; (*Brit Hist*) **Bow Street Runner** sergent *m* (de ville) → **blockade, gunrunner** **b** (= *sliding part*) [*of car seat, door etc*] glissière *f*; [*of curtain*] suspendur *m*; [*of sledge*] patin *m*; [*of skate*] lame *f*; [*of turbine*] couronne *f* mobile; [*of drawer*] coulisseau *m* **c** (= *hall carpet*) chemin *m*

de couloir; (= *stair carpet*) chemin *m* d'escalier; (*also* **table-~**) chemin *m* de table **d** (*Bot* = *plant*) coulant *m*, stolon *m*

2 COMP ▶ **runner bean** N (*Brit*) haricot *m* grimpant *or* à rames ▶ **runner-up** N (*pl* **runners-up**) (*Scol, Sport etc*) (*coming second*) second(e) *m(f)*; (*after first, second, third place*) ~**s-up will each receive ...** les autres gagnants recevront chacun ...

running ['rʌnɪŋ] **1** N **a** (= *action: in race etc*) course *f*; (*Brit*) **to make the ~** (*Sport*) faire le lièvre; (*fig*) (*in work*) mener la course; (*in relationship*) prendre l'initiative; **to be in the ~** avoir des chances de réussir; **to be out of the ~*** ne plus être dans la course; **to be in the ~ for promotion/for the job** être sur les rangs pour obtenir de l'avancement/pour avoir le poste

b (*NonC* = *functioning*) [*of machine*] marche *f*, fonctionnement *m*; [*of train*] marche *f*

c (*NonC: gen*) gestion *f*; [*of competition*] organisation *f*

d (*NonC* = *smuggling*) contrebande *f* → **gunrunning**

2 ADJ **a** (= *flowing*) [*tap*] ouvert; ~ **water** ◊ a ~ **stream** un petit cours d'eau, un ruisseau; (*from tap*) ~ **water** eau *f* courante; ~ **water in every room** eau *f* courante dans toutes les chambres; **hot and cold ~ water** eau *f* courante chaude et froide; **to wash sth under hot/cold ~ water** laver qch sous le robinet d'eau chaude/froide; **to have a ~ nose** avoir le nez qui coule; (*Med*) ~ **cold** rhume *m* de cerveau

b (= *continuous*) **to become a ~ joke between ...** devenir un inépuisable *or* perpétuel sujet de plaisanterie entre ...; a ~ **argument** une vieille querelle; ~ **battle** (*lit*) combat où l'un des adversaires bat en retraite; (*fig*) lutte *f* continuelle; **to keep up a ~ battle (with sb)** mener un combat de harcèlement (contre qn); ~ **sore** (*Med*) plaie *f* suppurante; (*fig*) véritable plaie *f* → **long¹**

3 ADV **four days/times** ~ quatre jours/fois de suite; **(for) three years** ~ pendant trois ans; **for the third year** ~ pour la troisième année consécutive

4 COMP ▶ **running account** N (*Fin*) compte *m* courant (*entre banques etc*); **to have** *or* **keep a ~ account with sb** être en compte avec qn ▶ **running board** N [*of car, train*] marchepied *m* ▶ **running bowline** N (*Naut*) laguis *m* ▶ **running commentary** N (*Rad, TV*) commentaire *m* suivi (**on sth** de qch); (*fig*) **she gave us a ~ commentary on what was happening** elle nous a fait un commentaire détaillé de ce qui se passait ▶ **running costs** NPL (*esp Brit*) [*of business*] frais *mpl* de fonctionnement *or* d'exploitation, dépenses *fpl* courantes; [*of machine*] frais *mpl* d'entretien; **the ~ costs of the car/the central heating are high** la voiture/le chauffage central revient cher ▶ **running fire** N (*Mil*) feu *m* roulant ▶ **running hand** N écriture *f* cursive ▶ **running head** N (*Typ*) = **running title** ▶ **running jump** N saut *m* avec élan; (**go and) take a ~ jump!*** va te faire cuire un œuf ! ▶ **running kick** N coup *m* de pied donné en courant ▶ **running knot** N nœud *m* coulant ▶ **running mate** N (*US Pol*) candidat(e) *m(f)* à la vice-présidence ▶ **running order** N **in ~ order** en état de marche ▶ **running repairs** NPL réparations *fpl* courantes ▶ **running shoe** N chaussure *f* de course ▶ **running stitch** N (*Sewing*) point *m* de devant ▶ **running tally** N = **running total** ▶ **running time** N [*of film*] durée *f* ▶ **running title** N (*Typ*) titre *m* courant ▶ **running total** N cumul *m*, total *m* cumulé; **to keep a ~ total (of sth)** tenir un compte régulier (de qch) ▶ **running track** N (*Sport*) piste *f*

runny* ['rʌnɪ] ADJ [*sauce, honey, consistency*] liquide; [*omelette*] baveux; [*eyes*] qui pleure; **a**

~ egg (*boiled*) un œuf à la coque; (*fried, poached*) un œuf dont le jaune est crémeux; **to have a ~ nose** avoir le nez qui coule

runproof ['rʌnpruːf] ADJ [*tights*] indémaillable; [*mascara*] waterproof

runt [rʌnt] N (= *animal*) avorton *m*; (*pej* = *person*) nabot(e) *m(f)*, avorton *m*; **a little ~ of a man** un bonhomme tout riquiqui*

runway ['rʌnweɪ] N (*Aviat*) piste *f*; (*Tech*) chemin *m* or piste *f* de roulement

rupee [ruːˈpiː] N roupie *f*

rupture ['rʌptʃər] 1 N (*lit, fig*) rupture *f*; (*Med* = *hernia*) hernie *f* 2 VT rompre; (*Med*) **~d appendix** appendice *m* rompu; **to ~ o.s.** se donner une hernie 3 VI se rompre

rural ['rʊərəl] 1 ADJ [*area, village, school, life, economy, poverty*] rural; [*setting, landscape*] rural, champêtre (*liter*); [*household*] paysan; [*policeman, services, crime*] en milieu rural; [*postmaster, housing*] en zone rurale; [*accent*] campagnard; **~ England** l'Angleterre *f* rurale; (*Brit Rel*) **~ dean** doyen *m* rural; **~ depopulation** exode *m* rural 2 COMP ► **rural development** N développement *m* rural ► **rural district council** N (*Brit*) conseil *m* municipal rural ► **rural planning** N aménagement *m* rural

ruse [ruːz] N ruse *f*, stratagème *m*

rush¹ [rʌʃ] 1 N **a** (= *rapid movement*) course *f* précipitée, ruée *f*; [*of crowd*] ruée *f*; (*with jostling*) bousculade *f*; (*Mil* = *attack*) bond *m*, assaut *m*; **he was caught in the ~ for the door** il a été pris dans la ruée vers la porte; **it got lost in the ~** ça s'est perdu dans la bousculade; **to make a ~ at** se précipiter sur; **there was a ~ for the empty seats** il y a eu une ruée vers les places libres, on s'est rué vers or sur les places libres; **gold ~** ruée *f* vers l'or; (*Comm*) **there's a ~ on matches** on se rue sur les allumettes; **we have a ~ on in the office just now** c'est le coup de feu en ce moment au bureau; (*in shops*) **the Christmas ~** la bousculade dans les magasins avant Noël; **we've had a ~ of orders** on nous a submergés de commandes; **a ~ of warm air** une bouffée d'air tiède; **there was a ~ of water** l'eau a jailli; **he had a ~ of blood to the head** il a eu un coup de sang **b** (= *hurry*) hâte *f*; **the ~ of city life** le rythme effréné de la vie urbaine; **to be in a ~** être extrêmement pressé; **I had a ~ to get here in time** j'ai dû me dépêcher pour arriver à l'heure; **I did it in a ~** je l'ai fait à toute vitesse or en quatrième vitesse*; **what's all the ~?** pourquoi est-ce que c'est si pressé?; **is there any ~ for this?** est-ce que c'est pressé? or urgent?; **it all happened in a ~** tout est arrivé or tout s'est passé très vite **c** (*Cine*) (projection *f* d')essai *m* **d** (*Drugs*) flash* *m* **e** (*US Univ: of fraternity etc*) campagne *f* de recrutement

2 VI [*person*] se précipiter; [*car*] foncer; **the train went ~ing into the tunnel** le train est entré à toute vitesse dans le tunnel; **they ~ed to help her** ils se sont précipités pour l'aider; **I ~ed to her side** je me suis précipité à ses côtés; **I'm ~ing to finish it** je me presse or je me dépêche pour le finir; **to ~ through** [+ *book*] lire à la hâte or en diagonale; [+ *meal*] prendre sur le pouce*; [+ *museum*] visiter au pas de course; [+ *town*] traverser à toute vitesse; [+ *work*] expédier; **to ~ in/out/back** *etc* entrer/sortir/rentrer *etc* précipitamment or à toute vitesse → **rush in, rush out**; **to ~ to the attack** se jeter or se ruer à l'attaque; **to ~ to conclusions** tirer des conclusions hâtives; **the blood ~ed to his face** le sang lui est monté au visage; **memories ~ed into his mind** des souvenirs lui affluèrent à l'esprit; (*fig*) **he ~ed into marriage** il s'est marié hâtivement or à la hâte; **the wind ~ed through the stable** le vent s'engouffrait dans l'écurie; **a torrent of water**

~ed down the slope un véritable torrent a dévalé la pente → **headlong**

3 VT **a** (= *cause to move quickly*) entraîner or pousser vivement; **to ~ sb to hospital** transporter qn d'urgence à l'hôpital; **they ~ed more troops to the front** ils ont envoyé or expédié d'urgence des troupes fraîches sur le front; **they ~ed him out of the room** ils l'ont fait sortir précipitamment or en toute hâte de la pièce; **I don't want to ~ you** je ne voudrais pas vous bousculer; **don't ~ me!** laissez-moi le temps de souffler!; **to ~ sb off his feet** ne pas laisser à qn le temps de souffler; **to ~ sb into a decision** forcer or obliger qn à prendre une décision à la hâte; **to ~ sb into doing sth** forcer or obliger qn à faire qch à la hâte; **they ~ed the bill through Parliament** ils ont fait voter la loi à la hâte → **rushed** **b** (= *take by storm*: *Mil*) [+ *town, position*] prendre d'assaut; [+ *fence, barrier*] franchir (sur son élan); **her admirers ~ed the stage** ses admirateurs ont envahi la scène; **the mob ~ed the line of policemen** la foule s'est élancée contre le cordon de police **c** (= *do hurriedly*) [+ *job, task*] dépêcher; [+ *order*] exécuter d'urgence; (*Comm*) **"please ~ me three tickets"** «envoyez-moi de toute urgence trois billets» **d** ‡ (= *charge*) faire payer; (= *swindle*) faire payer un prix exorbitant à, estamper*; **how much were you ~ed for it?** combien on te l'a fait payer?; **you really were ~ed for that!** tu t'es vraiment fait estamper* pour ça! **e** (*US Univ: of fraternity etc*) recruter

4 COMP ► **rush hour** N heures *fpl* de pointe or d'affluence ► **rush-hour traffic** N circulation *f* aux heures de pointe ► **rush job** N (*gen*) travail *m* urgent; **that was a ~ job** = urgent) c'était urgent; (*pej* = *too rushed*) c'était fait à la va-vite* ► **rush order** N (*Comm*) commande *f* pressée or urgente

► **rush about, rush around** VI courir çà et là

► **rush at** VT FUS se jeter sur, se ruer sur; [+ *enemy*] se ruer sur, fondre sur; **don't ~ at the job, take it slowly** ne fais pas ça trop vite, prends ton temps

► **rush down** VI [*person*] descendre précipitamment; [*stream*] dévaler

► **rush in** VI (*lit*) entrer précipitamment or à toute vitesse; (*fig*) se précipiter (**to** pour) → **rush¹ 2**

► **rush out** 1 VI sortir précipitamment or à toute vitesse 2 VT SEP (= *produce quickly*) [+ *goods*] sortir rapidement; (= *deliver*) **we'll ~ it out to you right away** nous vous le livrerons directement dans les plus brefs délais

► **rush through** VT SEP (*Comm*) [+ *order*] exécuter d'urgence; [+ *goods, supplies*] envoyer or faire parvenir de toute urgence; **they ~ed medical supplies through to him** on lui a fait parvenir des médicaments de toute urgence → **rush¹ 2**

► **rush up** 1 VI (= *arrive*) accourir 2 VT SEP [+ *help, reinforcements*] faire parvenir or (faire) envoyer d'urgence (**to** à)

rush² [rʌʃ] 1 N (*Bot*) jonc *m*; (*for chair*) jonc *m*, paille *f* 2 COMP ► **rush light** N chandelle *f* à mèche de jonc ► **rush mat** N natte *f* de jonc ► **rush matting** N (*NonC*) natte *f* de jonc

rushed [rʌʃt] ADJ **a** (= *hurried*) [*meal*] expédié; [*decision*] hâtif, précipité; [*work*] fait à la va-vite* **b** (= *busy*) [*person*] débordé; **to be ~ off one's feet** être (complètement) débordé; **she was ~ off her feet trying to get everything ready** elle était complètement débordée avec tous les préparatifs

rusk [rʌsk] N (*esp Brit*) biscotte *f*

russet ['rʌsɪt] 1 N **a** (= *colour*) couleur *f* feuille-morte *inv*, brun roux *inv* **b** (= *apple*) reinette *f* grise 2 ADJ brun roux *inv*

Russia ['rʌʃə] N la Russie

Russian ['rʌʃən] 1 ADJ (*gen*) russe; [*ambassador, embassy*] de Russie; [*teacher*] de russe

2 N **a** Russe *mf* **b** (*Ling*) russe *m* 3 COMP ► **Russian doll** N poupée *f* russe or gigogne ► **Russian dressing** N (*Culin*) sauce *f* rouge relevée (*pour la salade*) ► **the Russian Federation** N la Fédération de Russie ► **Russian Orthodox** ADJ (*Rel*) orthodoxe russe ► **Russian Orthodox Church** N Église *f* orthodoxe russe ► **Russian roulette** N roulette *f* russe ► **Russian salad** N salade *f* russe

Russkie*, **Russky*** [rʌskɪ] (*esp US†, pej* or *hum*) 1 N Rus(s)kof* *m*, Popov* *mf inv* 2 ADJ russe

Russo- ['rʌsəʊ] PREF russo-; **~Japanese** russo-japonais

rust [rʌst] 1 N (*on metal, also Bot*) rouille *f*; (= *colour*) couleur *f* rouille, roux *m* 2 VT (*lit, fig*) rouiller 3 VI (*lit, fig*) se rouiller 4 COMP ► **the Rust Belt** N (*US*) la région industrielle des États-Unis; **the Rust Belt states** les États *mpl* industriels américains ► **rust bucket*** N (= *car, boat*) tas *m* de rouille* ► **rust-coloured** ADJ (couleur) rouille *inv* ► **rust-resistant** ADJ = **rustproof 1**

► **rust in** VI [*screw*] se rouiller dans son trou

► **rust up** VI se rouiller

rusted ['rʌstɪd] (*esp US*) ADJ rouillé

rustic ['rʌstɪk] 1 N campagnard(e) *m(f)*, paysan(ne) *m(f)* 2 ADJ **a** (= *rural*) [*scene, charm, simplicity, appearance*] rustique, champêtre (*liter*); [*restaurant*] rustique; [*novel*] pastoral **b** (= *roughly-made*) [*furniture*] rustique; [*wall*] grossier **c** (*pej* = *crude*) frustre (*pej*), grossier (*pej*)

rusticate ['rʌstɪkeɪt] 1 VI habiter la campagne 2 VT (*Brit Univ*) exclure (temporairement)

rusticity [rʌsˈtɪsɪtɪ] N rusticité *f*

rustiness ['rʌstɪnɪs] N rouillure *f*, rouille *f*

rustle ['rʌsl] 1 N [*of leaves*] bruissement *m*; [*of silk, skirt*] bruissement *m*, froufrou *m*; [*of paper*] froissement *m* 2 VI [*leaves, wind*] bruire; [*paper*] produire un froissement or un bruissement; [*clothes, skirt*] faire froufrou; **she ~d into the room** elle est entrée en froufroutant dans la pièce; **something ~d in the cupboard** il y a eu un froissement or un bruissement dans le placard 3 VT **a** [+ *leaves*] faire bruire; [+ *paper*] froisser; [+ *programme*] agiter avec un bruissement; [+ *petticoat, skirt*] faire froufrouter **b** (*esp US* = *steal*) [+ *cattle*] voler

► **rustle up*** VT SEP se débrouiller* pour trouver (or faire), préparer (à la hâte); **can you ~ me up a cup of coffee?** tu pourrais me donner un café en vitesse?

rustler ['rʌslər] N **a** (*esp US* = *cattle thief*) voleur *m* de bétail **b** (*US* = *energetic person*) type* *m* énergique or expéditif

rustling ['rʌslɪŋ] N **a** (= *cattle theft*) vol *m* de bétail **b** = **rustle 1**

rustproof ['rʌstpruːf] 1 ADJ [*metal, alloy*] inoxydable, qui ne rouille pas; [*paint, treatment*] antirouille *inv*, anticorrosion *inv*; [*bodywork*] traité contre la rouille or la corrosion 2 VT traiter contre la rouille or la corrosion

rustproofing ['rʌstpruːfɪŋ] N traitement *m* antirouille or anticorrosion

rusty ['rʌstɪ] ADJ **a** (*lit, fig*) rouillé; **to go** or **get ~** (*lit, fig*) se rouiller; **my English is pretty ~** mon anglais est un peu rouillé; **his ~ typing skills** ses notions de dactylographie, qui ne datent pas d'hier; **your skills are a little ~** vous avez un peu perdu la main; **I'm very ~ on criminal law** il y a longtemps que je n'ai plus pratiqué le droit pénal **b** (*in colour: also* **~ brown**) brun roux *inv*

rut¹ [rʌt] (*Zool*) 1 N rut *m* 2 VI être en rut 3 COMP ► **rutting season** N saison *f* du rut

rut² [rʌt] ① N (*in track, path*) ornière *f*; (*fig*) routine *f*, ornière *f*; (*fig*) **to be (stuck) in** *or* **to get into a ~** [*person*] s'encroûter; [*mind*] devenir routinier; (*fig*) **to get out of the ~** sortir de l'ornière ② VT sillonner; **~ted** [*road, path*] défoncé

rutabaga [ˌruːtəˈbeɪɡə] N (*US*) rutabaga *m*

Ruth [ruːθ] N Ruth *f*

ruthenium [ruːˈθiːnɪəm] N ruthénium *m*

ruthless [ˈruːθlɪs] ADJ [*person*] impitoyable, sans pitié (**in sth** dans qch); [*treatment, determina-tion, investigation, deed*] impitoyable; **to be ~ in doing sth** faire qch impitoyablement

ruthlessly [ˈruːθlɪslɪ] ADV [*suppress, crush*] impitoyablement, sans pitié; **~ efficient** d'une efficacité redoutable; **she was a ~ ambi-tious woman** c'était une femme dont l'ambi-tion n'épargnait rien ni personne

ruthlessness [ˈruːθlɪsnɪs] N caractère *m or* na-ture *f* impitoyable

RV [ɑːˈviː] N ⓐ (*Bible*) (ABBR = **Revised Version**) → **revise** ⓑ (*US*) (ABBR = **recreational vehicle**) camping-car *m*; **RV park** terrain *m* pour camping-cars

Rwanda [rʊˈændə] N le Rwanda

Rwandan [rʊˈændən] ① ADJ rwandais ② N Rwandais(e) *m(f)*

rye [raɪ] ① N ⓐ (= *grain*) seigle *m* ⓑ (*US*) = **rye whisky, rye bread** ② COMP ► **rye bread** N pain *m* de seigle ► **rye whisky** N whisky *m* (de seigle)

ryegrass [ˈraɪɡrɑːs] N ray-grass *m inv*

S

S, s [es] N [a] (= *letter*) S, s *m*; **S for sugar** ≈ S comme Suzanne [b] (ABBR = **south**) S [c] **S** (*Rel*) (ABBR = **Saint**) St(e) [d] **S** (ABBR = **small**) (taille *f*) S *m*

SA [es'eɪ] N (ABBR = **South Africa, South America, South Australia**) → **south**

Saar [zɑːʳ] N (= *river, region*) **the ~** la Sarre

sab* [sæb] N (*Brit*) *activiste cherchant à saboter les chasses à courre*

sabbatarian [ˌsæbəˈtɛərɪən] [1] N (= *Christian*) partisan(e) *m(f)* de l'observance stricte du dimanche; (= *Jew*) personne *f* qui observe le sabbat [2] ADJ (= *Jewish Rel*) de l'observance du sabbat

Sabbath [ˈsæbəθ] N (*Jewish*) sabbat *m*; (*Christian*) repos *m* dominical; († = *Sunday*) dimanche *m*; **to keep** *or* **observe/break the ~** observer/ne pas observer le sabbat *or* le repos dominical; **(witches') sabbath** sabbat *m*

sabbatical [səˈbætɪkəl] [1] N congé *m* sabbatique; **to be on ~** être en congé sabbatique; **to take a ~** prendre un congé sabbatique [2] COMP ► **sabbatical leave** N congé *m* sabbatique ► **sabbatical term** N trois mois *mpl* de congé sabbatique ► **sabbatical year** N (*Univ*) année *f* sabbatique

sabbing* [ˈsæbɪŋ] N (*NonC: Brit: also* **hunt-~**) sabotage *m* des chasses à courre

saber [ˈseɪbəʳ] (*US*) = **sabre**

sable [ˈseɪbl] [1] N [a] (*Zool*) zibeline *f*, martre *f* [b] (*Her*) sable *m* [2] COMP [a] [*fur*] de zibeline, de martre; [*brush*] en poil de martre [b] (*liter* = *black*) noir

sabot [ˈsæbəʊ] N (*all wood*) sabot *m*; (*leather etc upper*) socque *m*

sabotage [ˈsæbətɑːʒ] [1] N (*NonC*) sabotage *m*; **an act of ~** un sabotage [2] VT (*lit, fig*) saboter

saboteur [ˌsæbəˈtɜːʳ] N saboteur *m*, -euse *f*

sabre, saber (*US*) [ˈseɪbəʳ] [1] N sabre *m* [2] COMP ► **sabre rattling** N (*esp Pol*) bruits *mpl* de sabre†, tentatives *fpl* d'intimidation ► **sabre-toothed tiger** N tigre *m* à dents de sabre

sac [sæk] N (*Anat, Bio*) sac *m*

saccharin [ˈsækərɪn] N (*US*) = **saccharine 2**

saccharine [ˈsækəriːn] [1] ADJ [a] (*Culin*) [*product*] à la saccharine; [*pill, flavour*] de saccharine [b] (= *sentimental*) [*story, ending*] mièvre; [*ballad, melody*] sirupeux; [*sweetness, smile*] mielleux; **~ sentimentality** sensiblerie *f*, mièvrerie *f* [2] N saccharine *f*

sacerdotal [ˌsæsəˈdəʊtl] ADJ sacerdotal

sachet [ˈsæʃeɪ] N sachet *m*; [*of shampoo*] berlingot *m*

sack¹ [sæk] [1] N [a] (= *bag*) sac *m*; **coal ~** sac *m* à charbon; **~ of coal** sac *m* de charbon; **a ~(ful) of potatoes** un (plein) sac de pommes de terre; **that dress makes her look like a ~ of potatoes** dans cette robe elle ressemble à un sac de pommes de terre; **she flopped down on to the sofa like a ~ of potatoes** elle s'est affalée sur le canapé [b] (* = *dismissal*) renvoi

m; **to give sb the ~** renvoyer qn, virer* qn; **to get the ~** être renvoyé, se faire virer*; **he got the ~ for stealing** il s'est fait virer* parce qu'il avait volé [c] (*esp US*✱ = *bed*) pieu✱ *m*, plumard✱ *m*; **to hit the ~** aller se pieuter✱ [2] VT (* = *dismiss*) [+ *employee*] renvoyer, virer*; **to ~ sb for doing sth** virer* qn pour avoir fait qch [3] COMP ► **sack dress** N robe *f* sac ► **sack race** N course *f* en sac

► **sack out*, sack up*** VI (*US = go to bed*) aller se pieuter✱

sack² [sæk] (*liter*) [1] N (= *plundering*) sac *m*, pillage *m* [2] VT [+ *town*] mettre à sac, saccager, piller

sack³ [sæk] N (= *wine*) vin *m* blanc sec

sackbut [ˈsækbʌt] N (*Mus*) saquebute *f*

sackcloth [ˈsækklɒθ] N grosse toile *f* d'emballage, toile *f* à sac; (*Rel*) **~ and ashes** le sac et la cendre; (*fig*) **to be in ~ and ashes** être contrit

sacking¹ [ˈsækɪŋ] N [a] (*NonC: Tex*) grosse toile *f* d'emballage, toile *f* à sac [b] (= *dismissal: gen*) renvoi *m*; **large scale ~s** renvois *mpl* massifs, largage *m*

sacking² [ˈsækɪŋ] N (= *plundering*) sac *m*, pillage *m*

sacra [ˈsækrə] NPL *of* **sacrum**

sacral [ˈseɪkrəl] ADJ (*Anat*) sacré

sacrament [ˈsækrəmənt] N sacrement *m*; **to receive the ~s** communier → **blessed**

sacramental [ˌsækrəˈmentl] [1] ADJ sacramentel [2] N sacramental *m*

sacred [ˈseɪkrɪd] [1] ADJ [a] (= *holy*) [*place, object, animal, symbol*] sacré (**to** pour) [b] (= *religious*) [*art, music, rite*] sacré, religieux; **~ writings** livres *mpl* sacrés; **~ and profane love** l'amour *m* sacré et l'amour *m* profane [c] (= *sacrosanct*) [*principle, duty, promise*] sacré (**to** pour); **~ to the memory of sb** consacré à la mémoire de qn; **is nothing ~?** les gens ne respectent plus rien!; **to her nothing was ~** elle ne respectait rien (ni personne) [2] COMP ► **sacred cow** N (*lit, fig*) vache *f* sacrée ► **the Sacred Heart** N le Sacré-Cœur ► **Sacred History** N l'Histoire *f* sainte

sacredness [ˈseɪkrɪdnɪs] N caractère *m* sacré

sacrifice [ˈsækrɪfaɪs] [1] N (*all senses*) sacrifice *m*; (*Rel*) **the ~ of the mass** le saint sacrifice (de la messe); (*fig*) **to make great ~s** faire *or* consentir de grands sacrifices (**for sb** pour qn, **to do sth** pour faire qch) → **self** [2] VT (*all senses*) sacrifier (**to** à); **to ~ o.s. for sb** se sacrifier pour qn; (*in small ads etc*) **"cost £25: ~ for £5"*** « prix 25 livres: sacrifié à 5 livres »

sacrificial [ˌsækrɪˈfɪʃəl] [1] ADJ [*rite*] sacrificiel; [*animal*] du sacrifice [2] COMP ► **sacrificial lamb** N (*Bible*) agneau *m* pascal; (*fig*) bouc *m* émissaire ► **sacrificial victim** N (*lit*) victime *f* du sacrifice; (*fig*) victime *f* expiatoire

sacrilege [ˈsækrɪlɪdʒ] N (*lit, fig*) sacrilège *m*

sacrilegious [ˌsækrɪˈlɪdʒəs] ADJ sacrilège; **it would be ~ to do such a thing** ce serait (un) sacrilège de faire une chose pareille

sacrist(an) [ˈsækrɪst(ən)] N sacristain(e) *m(f)*, sacristine *f*

sacristy [ˈsækrɪstɪ] N sacristie *f*

sacroiliac [ˌseɪkrəʊˈɪlɪæk] [1] ADJ sacro-iliaque [2] N articulation *f* sacro-iliaque

sacrosanct [ˈsækrəʊsæŋkt] ADJ sacro-saint

sacrum [ˈseɪkrəm] N (*pl* **sacra**) sacrum *m*

SAD [sæd] N (ABBR = **seasonal affective disorder**) → **seasonal**

▼ **sad** [sæd] [1] ADJ [a] (= *unhappy*) [*person, expression, eyes*] triste; [*feeling*] de tristesse; **to become ~** devenir triste, s'attrister; **the more he thought about it, the ~der he became** plus il y pensait, plus ça le rendait triste; **to make sb ~** attrister qn, rendre qn triste; **it makes me ~ to think that ...** ça me rend triste *or* ça m'attriste de penser que ...; **he eventually departed a ~der and (a) wiser man** il partit, mûri par la dure leçon de l'expérience; **I'm ~ that I/you won't be able to come** je suis désolé de ne pouvoir venir/que vous ne puissiez pas venir; **I shall be ~ to leave** je serai désolé de partir; **he was ~ to see her go** il était triste de la voir partir; **(I'm) ~ to say he died five years ago** malheureusement, il est mort il y a cinq ans

[b] (= *saddening*) [*story, news, situation, duty, occasion*] triste; [*loss*] douloureux; **it's a ~ business** c'est une triste affaire; **it's a ~ state of affairs** c'est un triste état de choses; **the ~ fact** *or* **truth is that ...** la triste vérité est que ...; **it's ~ that they can't agree** c'est désolant qu'ils n'arrivent pas à se mettre d'accord; **it's ~ to see such expertise wasted** c'est désolant de voir ce talent gâché; **~ to say, he died soon after** c'est triste à dire *or* malheureusement, il est mort peu après

[c] (* *pej* = *pathetic*) [*person*] minable*, pitoyable; **that ~ little man** ce pauvre type

[2] COMP ► **sad bastard**✱✱ N pauvre con✱✱ *m* ► **sad case*** N **he's a real ~ case** c'est vraiment un cas navrant ► **sad-eyed** ADJ aux yeux tristes ► **sad-faced** ADJ au visage triste ► **sad sack*** N (*US*) (*gen*) nullité *f*; (= *soldier*) troufion *m* nullard*

sadden [ˈsædn] VT attrister, rendre triste, affliger

saddening [ˈsædnɪŋ] ADJ attristant, triste; **it is ~ to think that ...** c'est triste de penser que ...

saddle [ˈsædl] [1] N [a] [*of horse, cycle*] selle *f*; (*lit*) **in the ~** en selle; **he leapt into the ~** il sauta en selle; (*fig*) **when he was in the ~** quand c'était lui qui tenait les rênes → **sidesaddle** [b] [*of hill*] col *m* [c] (*Culin*) **~ of lamb** selle *f* d'agneau [2] VT [a] (*also* **~ up**) [+ *horse*] seller [b] (* *fig*) **to ~ sb with sth** [*person*] [+ *job, debts, responsibility*] refiler* qch à qn; **I've been ~d with organizing the meeting** je me retrouve avec l'organisation de la réunion sur les bras; **the war ~d the country with a huge debt** à cause de la guerre le pays s'est retrouvé lourdement endetté; **we're ~d with it** nous voilà avec ça sur les bras; **to ~ o.s. with sth** s'encombrer de qch

3 COMP ► **saddle-backed** ADJ [*horse*] ensellé ► **saddle horse** N cheval *m* de selle ► **saddle joint** N (*Culin: of mutton or lamb*) selle *f* ► **saddle shoes** NPL (*US*) chaussures *fpl* basses bicolores ► **saddle-sore** ADJ meurtri à force d'être en selle ► **saddle-stitched** ADJ cousu à longs points

saddlebag ['sædlbæg] N [*of horse*] sacoche *f* (de selle); [*of cycle*] sacoche *f* (de bicyclette)

saddlebow ['sædlbəʊ] N pommeau *m* de selle

saddlecloth ['sædlklɒθ] N tapis *m* de selle

saddler ['sædlər] N sellier *m*

saddlery ['sædlərɪ] N (= *articles, business*) sellerie *f*

Sadducee N Sad(d)ucéen(ne) *m(f)*

sadism ['seɪdɪzəm] N sadisme *m*

sadist ['seɪdɪst] ADJ, N sadique *mf*

sadistic [sə'dɪstɪk] ADJ sadique

sadistically [sə'dɪstɪkəlɪ] ADV sadiquement, avec sadisme

sadly ['sædlɪ] ADV **a** (= *sorrowfully*) [*say, smile, look at, shake one's head*] tristement, avec tristesse **b** (= *woefully*) [*familiar, evident, neglected*] tristement; [*disappointed*] profondément; **to be ~ lacking in sth** manquer cruellement de qch; **to be ~ in need of sth** avoir bien besoin de qch; **to be ~ mistaken** se tromper lourdement; **he will be ~ missed** il sera regretté de tous **c** (= *unfortunately*) malheureusement; **~ for sb/sth** malheureusement pour qn/qch; **Jim, who ~ died in January ...** Jim, qui, à notre grande tristesse, est mort en janvier ...

sadness ['sædnɪs] N (*NonC*) tristesse *f*, mélancolie *f*

sadomasochism [ˌseɪdəʊ'mæsəkɪzəm] N sadomasochisme *m*

sadomasochist [ˌseɪdəʊ'mæsəkɪst] N sadomasochiste *mf*

sadomasochistic [ˌseɪdəʊmæsə'kɪstɪk] ADJ sadomasochiste

s.a.e. [ˌeseɪ'iː] N (*Brit*) **a** (ABBR = **stamped addressed envelope**) → **stamp** **b** (ABBR = **self-addressed envelope**) → **self**

safari [sə'fɑːrɪ] **1** N safari *m*; **to be/go on (a) ~** faire/aller faire un safari **2** COMP ► **safari hat** N chapeau *m* de brousse ► **safari jacket** N saharienne *f* ► **safari park** N (*Brit*) réserve *f* d'animaux ► **safari shirt** N saharienne *f* ► **safari suit** N ensemble *m* saharien

safe [seɪf] **1** ADJ **a** (= *not risky*) [*substance, toy*] sans danger; [*nuclear reactor*] sûr, sans danger; [*place, vehicle*] sûr; [*ladder, structure*] solide; **the water is ~ to drink** on peut boire cette eau sans danger, l'eau est potable; **government assurances that beef is perfectly ~ to eat** les affirmations du gouvernement selon lesquelles la consommation de viande de bœuf ne présente aucun danger; **to make a place ~ for sb/sth** éliminer tous les dangers qu'un endroit pourrait présenter pour qn/qch; **to make a bomb ~** désamorcer une bombe; **to make a building ~** assurer la sécurité d'un bâtiment; **in a ~ place** en lieu sûr; **a ~ anchorage** un bon mouillage; **the ice isn't ~ la glace** n'est pas solide; **he's a ~ pair of hands** c'est quelqu'un de sûr; **to be in ~ hands** être en de bonnes mains; **is that dog ~?** ce chien n'est pas méchant?; **that dog isn't ~ with** or **around children** ce chien peut présenter un danger pour les enfants; **he's ~ in jail*** for the moment pour le moment on est tranquille, il est en prison **b** (*impersonal uses*) **it is ~ to say/assume that ...** on peut affirmer/supposer sans trop s'avancer que ...; **is it ~ to come out?** est-ce qu'on peut sortir sans danger?; **is it ~ to use rat poison with children around?** n'est-ce pas dangereux d'utiliser de la mort-aux-rats là où

il y a des enfants?; **they assured him that it was ~ to return** ils lui ont assuré qu'il pouvait revenir en toute sécurité; **it might be ~r to wait** il serait peut-être plus prudent d'attendre; **the ~st thing (to do) would be to wait here** le plus sûr serait d'attendre ici; **it's not ~ to go out after dark** il est dangereux de sortir la nuit **c** [*choice, job*] sûr; [*method*] sans risque; [*limit, level*] raisonnable; **keep your alcohol consumption (to) within ~ limits** buvez avec modération; **a ~ margin** une marge de sécurité; **to keep a ~ distance from sb/sth** or **between o.s. and sb/sth** (*gen*) se tenir à bonne distance de qn/qch; (*Aut*) maintenir la distance de sécurité par rapport à qn/qch; **to follow sb at a ~ distance** suivre qn à une distance respectueuse; **(just) to be on the ~ side*** par précaution, pour plus de sûreté **d** (= *successful, problem-free*) **to wish sb a ~ journey** souhaiter bon voyage à qn; **(have a) ~ journey!** bon voyage!; **a ~ landing** un atterrissage réussi; **he wrote to acknowledge the ~ arrival of the photographs** il a écrit pour dire que les photos étaient bien arrivées; **to ensure the ~ delivery of supplies** veiller à ce que les vivres arrivent (*subj*) à bon port; **let us pray for the ~ return of the troops** prions pour que nos troupes reviennent saines et sauves; **to ensure the ~ return of the hostages** faire en sorte que les otages soient libérés sains et saufs; **a reward for the ~ return of the stolen equipment** une récompense à qui rapportera en bon état l'équipement volé **e** (= *likely to be right*) **it is a ~ assumption that ...** on peut dire sans trop s'avancer que ...; **a ~ bet (for sb)** un bon choix (pour qn); **the house wine is always a ~ bet** choisir la cuvée du patron, c'est sans risque; **it is a ~ bet that ...** il y a toutes les chances pour que ... (+ *subj*); **it's a ~ bet he'll win** il gagnera à coup sûr; **this was a pretty ~ guess** on ne s'avançait pas trop en supposant cela **f** (= *not in danger*) [*person*] en sécurité; (= *no longer in danger*) hors de danger; [*object*] en sécurité; **I don't feel very ~ on this ladder** je ne me sens pas très en sécurité sur cette échelle; **I won't feel ~ until he is behind bars** je ne serai pas tranquille tant qu'il ne sera pas derrière les barreaux; **I feel so ~ here with you** je me sens tellement en sécurité ici auprès de toi; **he's ~ for re-election** il sera réélu à coup sûr; **to be ~ from sth** être à l'abri de qch; **I'm ~ from him now** il ne peut plus me nuire or me faire de mal maintenant; **to be ~ from being sued** ne pas risquer de procès; **~ in the knowledge that ...** avec la certitude que ...; **~ and sound** sain et sauf; (*Sport*) **a ~ winner** un gagnant certain or assuré; **to be ~ with sb** être en sécurité avec qn; **I'll keep it ~ for you** je vais vous le garder en lieu sûr; **your reputation is ~** votre réputation ne craint rien; **your secret is ~ (with me)** je ne le répéterai pas, (avec moi) votre secret ne risque rien; (*fig*) **no girl is ~ with him** c'est un séducteur impénitent ■ (*PROV*) **better ~ than sorry** deux précautions valent mieux qu'une (*PROV*)

2 N (*for money, valuables*) coffre-fort *m* → **meat**

3 COMP ► **safe area** N (*Pol*) zone *f* de sécurité ► **safe-blower** N perceur *m* de coffre-fort (*qui utilise des explosifs*) ► **safe-breaker** N perceur *m* de coffre-fort ► **safe-conduct** N (*Mil etc*) sauf-conduit *m* ► **safe-cracker** N = **safe-breaker** ► **safe deposit** N (= *vault*) chambre *f* forte, salle *f* des coffres; (*also* ~ **deposit box**) coffre(-fort) *m* (*à la banque*) ► **safe haven** N **a** (*Mil, Pol*) zone *f* de refuge **b** (= *refuge*) (*gen*) abri *m* sûr; (*for terrorists, criminals*) repaire *m*; (*for people in danger*) refuge *m*; **to provide ~ haven for sb** ◊ **to offer ~ haven to sb** offrir un abri sûr or un repaire or un refuge à qn **c** (*fig = escape*) refuge *m* (**from** contre);

the idea of the family as a ~ haven from the brutal outside world la famille perçue comme un refuge contre la brutalité du monde extérieur; **the district was once a ~ haven from Manhattan's hustle and bustle** le quartier était autrefois à l'abri du tourbillon d'activité de Manhattan ► **safe house** N lieu *m* sûr ► **safe passage** N **to guarantee sb/sth (a) ~ passage to/from a country** assurer la protection de qn/qch à son entrée dans un pays/à sa sortie d'un pays ► **the safe period*** N (*Med*) la période sans danger ► **safe seat** N siège *m* sûr; (*Brit Pol*) **it was a ~ Conservative seat** c'était un siège acquis au parti conservateur → MARGINAL SEAT ► **safe sex** N rapports *mpl* sexuels sans risque; (*specifically with condom*) rapports *mpl* sexuels protégés

safeguard ['seɪfgɑːd] **1** VT sauvegarder, protéger (**against** contre) **2** N sauvegarde *f*, garantie *f* (**against** contre); **as a ~ against** comme sauvegarde contre, pour éviter **3** COMP ► **safeguard clause** N (*Jur*) clause *f* de sauvegarde

safekeeping [ˌseɪf'kiːpɪŋ] N bonne garde *f*; **in ~** sous bonne garde, en sécurité; **I gave it to him for ~** ◊ **I put it in his ~** je le lui ai donné à garder; **the key is in his ~** on lui a confié la clé

safely ['seɪflɪ] ADV **a** (= *without risk*) sans risque or danger, en toute sécurité; **you can walk about quite ~ in the town centre** vous pouvez vous promener sans risque or sans danger dans le centre-ville; **most food can ~ be frozen for months** on peut congeler la plupart des aliments sans risque or sans danger pendant plusieurs mois; **drive ~!** sois prudent!; **he was ~ tucked up in bed** il était en sécurité or bien au chaud dans son lit **b** (= *without mishap*) [*return, land*] sans encombre; [*arrive*] bien, à bon port; **give me a ring to let me know you've got home ~** passe-moi un coup de fil pour que je sache que tu es bien rentré; (*Comm*) **the consignment reached us ~** nous avons bien reçu les marchandises **c** (= *securely*) [*shut, locked, stowed*] bien; **to put sth away ~** ranger qch en lieu sûr **d** (= *well and truly*) **now that the election is ~ out of the way, the government can ...** maintenant que le gouvernement n'a plus à se soucier des élections, il peut ...; **he's ~ through to the semi-final** il est arrivé sans encombre en demi-finale **e** (*confidently*) **I think I can ~ say that ...** je pense pouvoir dire sans trop m'avancer que ...

safeness ['seɪfnɪs] N (= *freedom from danger*) sécurité *f*; (*of construction, equipment*) solidité *f*

safety ['seɪftɪ] **1** N **a** (= *freedom from danger*) sécurité *f*; **~ first!** la sécurité d'abord!; **his ~ must be our first consideration** sa sécurité doit être notre premier souci; **for his (own) ~** pour sa (propre) sécurité; **for ~'s sake** pour plus de sûreté, par mesure de précaution; **to ensure sb's ~** veiller sur or assurer la sécurité de qn; **the government must ensure the ~ of nuclear power plants** le gouvernement doit garantir la sécurité des centrales nucléaires; **he sought ~ in flight** il chercha le salut dans la fuite; **there is ~ in numbers** plus on est nombreux, moins il y a de danger; **in a place of ~** en lieu sûr; **he reached ~ at last** il fut enfin en sûreté or en sécurité; **to play for ~** ne pas prendre de risques, jouer au plus sûr → **2, road** **b** [*of construction, equipment*] solidité *f*

2 COMP ► **safety belt** N ceinture *f* de sécurité ► **safety blade** N lame *f* de sûreté ► **safety bolt** N verrou *m* de sûreté ► **safety catch** N cran *m* de sûreté ► **safety chain** N chaîne *f* de sûreté ► **safety curtain** N (*Theat*) rideau *m* de sûreté ► **safety-deposit box** N (*US*) coffre(-fort) *m* (*à la banque*) ► **safety device** N dispositif *m* de sécurité ► **safety factor** N coefficient *m* de sécurité

► **safety glass** N verre m securit® or de sécurité ► **safety island** N (US Aut) refuge m ► **safety lamp** N lampe f de mineur ► **safety lock** N serrure f de sécurité ► **safety margin** N marge f de sécurité ► **safety match** N allumette f de sûreté or suédoise ► **safety measure** N mesure f de sécurité ; **as a ~ measure** pour plus de sûreté, par mesure de sécurité ► **safety mechanism** N dispositif m de sécurité ► **safety net** N (lit) filet m (de protection) ; (fig) filet m de sécurité ► **safety pin** N (gen) épingle f de sûreté or de nourrice ; [of hand grenade] goupille f ► **safety precaution** N mesure f de sécurité ► **safety razor** N rasoir m mécanique or de sûreté ► **safety regulations** NPL règles fpl de sécurité ► **safety screen** N écran m de sécurité ► **safety valve** N (lit, fig) soupape f de sûreté ► **safety zone** N (US Aut) refuge m (pour piétons)

saffron ['sæfrən] [1] N safran m [2] ADJ [colour, robe] safran inv ; [flavour] safrané, de safran [3] COMP ► **saffron-coloured** ADJ safran inv ► **saffron powder** N safran m ► **saffron rice** N riz m safrané or au safran ► **saffron strands, saffron threads** NPL pistils mpl de safran, stigmates mpl de safran ► **saffron yellow** ADJ jaune inv safran inv

sag [sæg] [1] VI [roof, chair] s'affaisser ; [beam, floorboard] s'arquer, fléchir ; [cheeks, breasts, hemline] pendre ; [rope] pendre au milieu, être détendu ; [gate] être affaissé ; [prices] fléchir, baisser [2] N [of prices, sales, credibility] baisse f ; [of roof] affaissement m ; **the ~ in the market** la contraction du marché

saga ['sɑːgə] N (Literat) saga f ; (= film, story) aventure f épique ; (= novel) roman-fleuve m ; (fig) **he told me the whole ~ of what had happened** il m'a raconté tout ce qui était arrivé or toutes les péripéties en long et en large

sagacious [sə'geɪʃəs] ADJ (frm) [person, remark] sagace ; [choice] judicieux

sagaciously [sə'geɪʃəslɪ] ADV (frm) avec sagacité

sagaciousness [sə'geɪʃəsnɪs], **sagacity** [sə'gæsɪtɪ] N sagacité f

sage¹ [seɪdʒ] [1] N (Bot, Culin) sauge f ; **~ and onion stuffing** farce f à l'oignon et à la sauge [2] COMP ► **sage green** N, ADJ vert m cendré inv

sage² [seɪdʒ] (liter) [1] ADJ [person, advice] sage ; **~ words of warning** une sage mise en garde [2] N sage m

sagebrush ['seɪdʒbrʌʃ] N (US) armoise f ; **the Sagebrush State** le Nevada

sagely ['seɪdʒlɪ] ADV (= wisely) [say] avec sagesse ; (iro = importantly) avec componction ; **to nod ~** opiner de la tête avec componction

sagging ['sægɪŋ] ADJ [a] (= drooping) [armchair, ceiling] affaissé ; [beam] arqué, fléchi ; [rope] détendu ; [stomach] qui s'affaisse ; [breasts] qui tombent, flasque ; [cheeks, hemline] pendant ; [skin] distendu [b] (= flagging) [morale, spirits] défaillant ; [stock market, dollar] mou (molle f) ; **to bolster one's ~ popularity** soutenir sa popularité en baisse ; **the president's ~ ratings** la cote de popularité en baisse du président

saggy* ['sægɪ] ADJ [mattress, sofa] défoncé ; [garment] avachi ; [bottom, breasts] flasque

Sagittarian [,sædʒɪ'teərɪən] [1] N **to be (a) ~** être (du) Sagittaire [2] ADJ [person] du Sagittaire ; [character trait] propre au Sagittaire

Sagittarius [,sædʒɪ'teərɪəs] N (Astron) le Sagittaire ; (Astrol) **I'm (a) ~** je suis (du) Sagittaire

sago ['seɪgəʊ] [1] N sagou m [2] COMP ► **sago palm** N sagoutier m ► **sago pudding** N sagou m au lait

Sahara [sə'hɑːrə] N **the ~ (Desert)** le (désert du) Sahara

sahib ['sɑːhɪb] N (in India) sahib m ; **yes, ~** oui, sahib ; **Smith Sahib** Monsieur Smith

said [sed] VB pt, ptp of **say**

Saigon [saɪ'gɒn] N Saigon

sail [seɪl] [1] N [a] [of boat] voile f ; **under ~** à la voile ; **to set ~** [boat] prendre la mer ; [person] partir en bateau ; **to set ~ for** [boat] partir à destination de ; **he has set ~ for America** il est parti pour l'Amérique (en bateau) ; **he set ~ from Dover** il est parti de Douvres (en bateau) → **hoist, wind**¹ [b] (= trip) **to go for a ~** faire un tour en bateau or en mer ; **Spain is two days' ~ from here** l'Espagne est à deux jours de mer [c] [of windmill] aile f [2] VI [a] [boat] **the steamer ~s at 6 o'clock** le vapeur prend la mer or part à 6 heures ; **the boat ~ed up/down the river** le bateau remonta/descendit la rivière ; **the ship ~ed into Cadiz** le bateau entra dans le port de Cadix ; **to ~ into harbour** entrer au port ; **the ship ~ed out of Southampton/round the cape** le bateau a quitté le port de Southampton/a doublé le cap ; **to ~ at 10 knots** filer 10 nœuds [b] **he ~s** or **goes sailing every weekend** [person] il fait du bateau or de la voile tous les week-ends ; **to ~ away/back** etc partir/revenir etc en bateau ; **we ~ at 6 o'clock** nous partons à 6 heures, le bateau part à 6 heures ; **we ~ed into Southampton** nous sommes entrés dans le port de Southampton ; **we ~ed for Australia** nous sommes partis pour l'Australie (en bateau) ; **to ~ round the world** faire le tour du monde en bateau ; **to ~ into the wind** avancer contre le vent ; **to ~ close to the wind** (Naut) naviguer au plus près ; (fig) **to ~ close or near to the wind** (= take a risk) jouer un jeu dangereux ; (= nearly break law) friser l'illégalité ; (in jokes etc) friser la vulgarité ; (fig) **to ~ under false colours** agir sous de faux prétextes [c] (fig) [swan etc] glisser ; **clouds were ~ing across the sky** des nuages glissaient or couraient dans le ciel ; **she ~ed into the room*** elle est entrée dans la pièce d'un pas nonchalant ; **the plate ~ed past my head and hit the door** l'assiette est passée à côté de ma tête et a heurté la porte [3] VT [a] (liter) **to ~ the seas** parcourir les mers ; **he ~ed the Atlantic last year** l'année dernière il a fait la traversée de or il a traversé l'Atlantique (en bateau) [b] [+ boat] (= manoeuvre) manœuvrer ; **she ~ed her boat into the harbour** elle a manœuvré (son bateau) pour entrer dans le port ; **he ~ed his boat round the cape** il a doublé le cap ; **he ~s his own yacht** (= owns it) il a son propre yacht ; (= captains it) il barre or pilote son yacht lui-même [4] COMP ► **sail maker** N voilier m (personne)

► **sail into*** VT FUS [a] (= scold) voler dans les plumes à* [b] **he ~ed into the work** il a attaqué le travail avec entrain

► **sail through*** [1] VI réussir haut la main [2] VT FUS **to ~ through one's degree/one's driving test** avoir sa licence/son permis de conduire haut la main

sailboard ['seɪlbɔːd] N planche f à voile

sailboarder ['seɪlbɔːdər] N véliplanchiste mf

sailboarding ['seɪlbɔːdɪŋ] N planche f à voile ; **to go ~** faire de la planche à voile

sailboat ['seɪlbəʊt] N (US) bateau m à voiles, voilier m

sailcloth ['seɪlklɒθ] N toile f à voile

sailing ['seɪlɪŋ] [1] N [a] (NonC = activity, hobby) (dinghies etc) navigation f à voile ; (yachts) navigation f de plaisance ; **a day's ~** une journée de voile or en mer ; **his hobby is ~** son passe-temps favori est la voile → **plain** [b] (= departure) départ m [2] COMP ► **sailing boat** N (Brit) bateau m à voiles, voilier m ► **sailing date** N date f de départ (d'un bateau) ► **sailing dinghy** N canot m à voiles, dériveur m ► **sailing orders** NPL instructions fpl de navigation ► **sailing ship** N grand voilier m, navire m à voiles

sailor ['seɪlər] [1] N (gen) marin m ; (before the mast) matelot m ; **to be a good/bad ~** avoir/ne pas avoir le pied marin [2] COMP ► **sailor hat** N chapeau m de marin ► **sailor suit** N costume m marin

sailplane ['seɪlpleɪn] N planeur m

sainfoin ['sænfɔɪn] N sainfoin m

saint [seɪnt] [1] N saint(e) m(f) ; **~'s day** fête f (de saint) ; **All Saints' (Day)** la Toussaint ; **he's no ~*** ce n'est pas un petit saint [2] COMP ► **Saint Bernard** N (= dog) saint-bernard m ► **Saint Helena** N (Geog) Sainte-Hélène f ; **on Saint Helena** à Sainte-Hélène ► **Saint John** N saint m Jean ► **Saint John's wort** N mille-pertuis m or millepertuis m inv ► **the Saint Lawrence** N le Saint-Laurent ; **the Saint Lawrence Seaway** la voie maritime du Saint-Laurent ► **saint-like** ADJ = **saintly** ► **Saint Lucia** N (Geog) Sainte-Lucie f ; **in Saint Lucia** à Sainte-Lucie ► **Saint Lucian** ADJ saint-lucien ♦ N Saint-Lucien(ne) m(f) ► **Saint Patrick's Day** N la Saint-Patrick ► **Saint Peter's Church** N (l'église f) Saint-Pierre ► **Saint Pierre and Miquelon** N (Geog) Saint-Pierre-et-Miquelon ► **Saint Vincent and the Grenadines** N (Geog) Saint-Vincent-et-Grenadines ► **Saint Vitus' dance** N (Med) danse f de Saint-Guy

sainted ['seɪntɪd] ADJ († or hum) **your ~ father** votre saint homme de père ; (esp Brit) **my ~ aunt!*** sacrebleu !*

sainthood ['seɪnthʊd] N sainteté f

saintliness ['seɪntlɪnɪs] N sainteté f

saintly ['seɪntlɪ] ADJ [man, woman] saint (before n) ; [quality, behaviour, generosity etc] digne d'un saint ; [smile] angélique, de sainte nitouche ; **to be ~** [person] être un(e) saint(e)

saithe [seɪθ] (Brit) N lieu noir m, colin m

sake¹ [seɪk] N **for the ~ of sb** pour l'amour de qn, par égard pour qn ; **for the ~ of your career/my health** pour ta carrière/ma santé ; **for God's ~** pour l'amour de Dieu ; **for my ~** pour moi, par égard pour moi ; **for your own ~** pour ton bien ; **for their ~(s)** pour eux ; **do it for both our ~s** fais-le (par égard) pour nous deux ; **to eat for the ~ of eating** manger pour (le plaisir de) manger ; **for old times' ~** en souvenir du passé ; **for argument's ~** à titre d'exemple ; **art for art's ~** l'art pour l'art ; **for the ~ of peace** pour avoir la paix → **goodness, heaven, pity, safety**

sake², **saké, saki** ['sɑːkɪ] N saké m

Sakhalin (Island) ['sækəlɪn(,aɪlənd)] N (l'île f de) Sakhaline f

sal [sæl] [1] N sel m [2] COMP ► **sal ammoniac** N sel m ammoniac ► **sal volatile** N sel m volatil

salaam [sə'lɑːm] [1] N salutation f (à l'orientale) [2] VI saluer (à l'orientale) [3] EXCL salam

salability [,seɪlə'bɪlɪtɪ] N (US) = **saleability**

salable ['seɪləbl] ADJ (US) = **saleable**

salacious [sə'leɪʃəs] ADJ (frm) salace, lubrique

salaciousness [sə'leɪʃəsnɪs] N salacité f

salad ['sæləd] [1] N salade f ; **ham ~** jambon m accompagné de salade ; **tomato ~** salade f de tomates → **fruit, potato** [2] COMP ► **salad bowl** N buffet m de crudités ► **salad bowl** N saladier m ► **salad cream** N (Brit) (sorte f de) mayonnaise f (en bouteille etc) ► **salad days** NPL (fig) années fpl de jeunesse et d'inexpérience ► **salad dish** N = **salad bowl** ► **salad dressing** N (oil and vinegar) vinaigrette f ; (made with egg) mayonnaise f ► **salad oil** N huile f de table ► **salad servers** NPL couverts mpl à salade ► **salad shaker** N panier m à salade ► **salad spinner** N essoreuse f à salade

salamander ['sælə,mændər] N (Myth, Zool) salamandre f

salami [sə'lɑːmɪ] N salami m

salaried ['sælərɪd] ADJ [employment, post] salarié ; **a ~ employee** un(e) salarié(e)

▼ **salary** ['sælərɪ] **1** N (*monthly, professional etc*) traitement *m*, appointements *mpl*; (= *pay in general*) salaire *m*; **he couldn't do that on his ~** il ne pourrait pas faire ça avec ce qu'il gagne *or* avec son salaire **2** COMP ▶ **salary bracket** N fourchette *f* des traitements ▶ **salary earner** N personne *f* qui touche un traitement ▶ **salary range** N éventail *m* des salaires ▶ **salary scale** N échelle *f* des salaires

sale [seɪl] **1** N **a** (= *act*) vente *f*; **"for ~"** «à vendre»; **"not for ~"** «cet article n'est pas à vendre»; **to put sth up for ~** mettre qch en vente; **our house is up for ~** notre maison est à vendre *or* en vente; (*Brit*) **on ~** en vente; (*Brit*) **on ~ at all good chemists** en vente dans toutes les bonnes pharmacies; **we made a quick ~** la vente a été vite conclue; **he finds a ready ~ for his vegetables** il n'a aucun mal à vendre ses légumes; **his vegetables find a ready ~** ses légumes se vendent sans aucun mal; **on ~ or return** ◊ **on a ~-or-return basis** avec possibilité de reprise des invendus, avec faculté de retour; **~s are up/down** les ventes ont augmenté/baissé; **she is in ~s** elle est *or* travaille dans la vente; **~ by auction** vente *f* publique, vente *f* aux enchères → **cash, quick** **b** (= *event: gen*) vente *f*; (*also* **auction ~**) vente *f* (aux enchères); (*Comm: also* **~s**) soldes *mpl*; **the ~s are on** c'est la saison des soldes; **the ~ begins** *or* **the ~s begin next week** les soldes commencent la semaine prochaine; **this shop is having a ~ just now** il y a des soldes dans ce magasin en ce moment; **to put sth in the ~** solder qch; **in a ~** en solde; **they are having a ~ in aid of the blind** on organise une vente (de charité) en faveur des aveugles → **bring, clearance, jumble**

2 COMP ▶ **sale of produce** N vente *f* de produits ▶ **sale of work** N vente *f* de charité ▶ **sale price** N prix *m* soldé ▶ **sales assistant** N (*Brit*) vendeur *m*, -euse *f* ▶ **sales clerk** N (*US*) = **sales assistant** ▶ **sales conference** N réunion *f* de la force de vente ▶ **sales department** N service *m* des ventes ▶ **sales director** N directeur *m*, -trice *f* *or* chef *m* des ventes ▶ **sales drive** N campagne *f* de promotion des ventes ▶ **sales force** N force *f* de vente ▶ **sales leaflet** N argumentaire *m* ▶ **sales manager** N directeur *m*, -trice *f* commercial(e) ▶ **sales office** N bureau *m* de vente ▶ **sales pitch** N baratin* *m* publicitaire, boniment *m* ▶ **sales promotion** N promotion *f* des ventes ▶ **sales rep***, **sales representative** N représentant(e) *m(f)* (de commerce), VRP *m* ▶ **sales resistance** N réaction *f* défavorable (à la publicité), résistance *f* de l'acheteur ▶ **sales slip** N (*in shops*) ticket *m* (de caisse) ▶ **sales talk*** N baratin* *m* publicitaire, boniment *m* ▶ **sales tax** N taxe *f* à l'achat ▶ **sale value** N valeur *f* marchande

saleability [,seɪlə'bɪlɪtɪ] N **establish the ~ of the property before you buy it** avant d'acheter la propriété, vérifiez si elle est facile à vendre

saleable, salable (*US*) ['seɪləbl] ADJ [*object*] vendable; [*skill*] monnayable; [*artist*] dont les œuvres sont vendables; **a highly ~ commodity** un produit qui se vend très bien; **small cars are more ~ than big ones at the moment** les petites voitures se vendent mieux que les grosses en ce moment

Salerno [sə'lɜːnəʊ] N Salerne

saleroom ['seɪlrʊm] N (*Brit*) salle *f* des ventes

salesgirl ['seɪlzgɜːl] N = **sales assistant**

salesman ['seɪlzmən] N (*pl* **-men**) (*in shop*) vendeur *m*; (= *representative*) représentant *m*; (de commerce), VRP *m*; **he's a good ~** il sait vendre → **door**

salesmanship ['seɪlzmənʃɪp] N art *m* de la vente

salesperson ['seɪlzpɜːsn] N vendeur *m*, -euse *f*

salesroom ['seɪlzrʊm] N (*US*) = **saleroom**

saleswoman ['seɪlzwʊmən] N (*pl* **-women**) (*in shop*) vendeuse *f*; (= *representative*) représentante *f* (de commerce), VRP *m*

salient ['seɪlɪənt] ADJ, N saillant *m*

salina [sə'liːnə] N **a** (= *marsh etc*) (marais *m*) salant *m*, salin *m*, saline *f*; (= *saltworks*) saline(s) *f(pl)*, raffinerie *f* de sel **b** (= *mine*) mine *f* de sel

saline ['seɪlaɪn] **1** ADJ salin **2** N **a** = **salina a b** (*Chem, Med* = *solution*) solution *f* saline **3** COMP ▶ **saline drip** N perfusion *f* de sérum physiologique *or* isotonique ▶ **saline solution** N (*Med, Chem: for contact lenses*) solution *f* saline

salinity [sə'lɪnɪtɪ] N salinité *f*

saliva [sə'laɪvə] N salive *f*

salivary ['sælɪvərɪ] ADJ salivaire

salivate ['sælɪveɪt] VI saliver; **to ~ over sth** se lécher les babines *or* saliver en pensant à qch

salivation [,sælɪ'veɪʃən] N salivation *f*

sallow[1] ['sæləʊ] ADJ [*complexion, face, skin*] cireux; [*person*] au teint cireux

sallow[2] ['sæləʊ] N (*Bot*) saule *m*

sallowness ['sæləʊnɪs] N teint *m* jaunâtre

sally ['sælɪ] N **a** (*Mil*) sortie *f* **b** (= *flash of wit*) saillie *f*, boutade *f*; **to make a ~** dire une boutade

▶ **sally forth**, **sally out** VI sortir gaiement

Sally Army* [,sælɪ'ɑːmɪ] N (*Brit*) (ABBR = **Salvation Army**) → **salvation**

salmon ['sæmən] **1** N (*pl* **salmons** *or* **salmon**) saumon *m* → **rock**[2], **smoke 2** COMP ▶ **salmon farm** N élevage *m* de saumons ▶ **salmon fishing** N pêche *f* au saumon ▶ **salmon pink** N, ADJ (rose *m*) saumon *m inv* ▶ **salmon steak** N darne *f* de saumon ▶ **salmon trout** N truite *f* saumonée

salmonella [,sælmə'nelə] **1** N (*pl* **salmonellae** [,sælmə'nelɪ]) salmonelle *f* **2** COMP ▶ **salmonella poisoning** N salmonellose *f*

salmonellosis [,sælmənə'ləʊsɪs] N salmonellose *f*

Salome [sə'ləʊmɪ] N Salomé *f*

salon ['sælɒn] N (*all senses*) salon *m* → **beauty, hair**

saloon [sə'luːn] **1** N **a** (= *large room*) salle *f*, salon *m*; (*on ship*) salon *m* **b** (*Brit: also* **~ bar**) bar *m*; (*US* = *bar*) bar *m*, saloon *m* **c** (*Brit* = *car*) berline *f* **2** COMP ▶ **saloon bar** N (*Brit*) bar *m* ▶ **saloon car** N (*Brit Aut*) berline *f*; (*US Rail*) voiture-salon *f*

salsa ['sɑːlsə] N **a** (*Culin*) sauce aux oignons, tomates et poivrons, spécialité portoricaine **b** (*Mus*) salsa *f*

salsify ['sælsɪfɪ] N salsifis *m*

SALT [sɔːlt] **1** ABBR = **Strategic Arms Limitation Talks 2** COMP ▶ **SALT negotiations** N négociations *fpl* SALT

salt [sɔːlt] **1** N (*NonC: Chem, Culin*) sel *m*; **kitchen/table ~** sel *m* de cuisine/de table; **there's too much ~ in the potatoes** les pommes de terre sont trop salées; **I don't like ~ in my food** je n'aime pas manger salé; (*fig*) **to rub ~ in(to) the wound** retourner le couteau dans la plaie; (*fig*) **he's not worth his ~** il ne vaut pas grand-chose; (*fig*) **to take sth with a pinch** *or* **grain of ~** ne pas prendre qch au pied de la lettre; (*fig*) **the ~ of the earth** le sel de la terre; **below the ~**† socialement inférieur; **an old (sea) ~** un vieux loup de mer → **bath, smell**

2 ADJ **a** (= *salty*) [*taste*] salé; [*air*] marin; (*liter*) **to shed ~ tears** verser des larmes amères **b** (= *salted*) [*fish, meat, porridge*] salé

3 VT [+ *meat, one's food*] saler

4 COMP ▶ **salt beef** N bœuf *m* salé ▶ **salt box** N (*US* = *house*) maison à deux étages et à toit dissymétrique ▶ **salt flat** N salant *m*

▶ **salt-free** ADJ sans sel ▶ **salt lake** N lac *m* salé ▶ **salt lick** N (= *block of salt*) pierre *f* à lécher; (= *place*) salant *m* ▶ **salt marsh** N marais *m* salant ▶ **salt mine** N mine *f* de sel; (*fig hum*) **back to the ~ mines!*** allez, il faut reprendre le collier!* ▶ **salt pan** N puits *m* salant ▶ **salt pork** N porc *m* salé ▶ **salt shaker** N salière *f* ▶ **salt spoon** N cuiller *f or* cuillère *f* à sel ▶ **salt tax** N (*Hist*) gabelle *f* ▶ **salt water** N eau *f* salée

▶ **salt away** VT SEP [+ *meat*] saler; (*fig*) [+ *money*] mettre à gauche*

▶ **salt down** VT FUS saler, conserver dans le sel

saltcellar ['sɔːlt,selər] N salière *f*

saltine [sɔːl'tiːn] N (*US* = *cracker*) petit biscuit *m* salé

saltiness ['sɔːltɪnɪs] N [*of water*] salinité *f*; [*of food*] goût *m* salé

salting ['sɔːltɪŋ] N **a** (= *act of putting salt on*) salaison *f* **b** (= *place: esp Brit*) (marais *m*) salant *m*

saltpetre, saltpeter (*US*) ['sɔːlt,piːtər] N salpêtre *m*

saltwater ['sɔːltwɔːtər] ADJ [*fish*] de mer

saltworks ['sɔːltwɜːks] N (*NonC*) saline(s) *f(pl)*

salty ['sɔːltɪ] ADJ **a** (= *containing salt*) [*food, water, taste*] salé; [*soil*] salin; [*deposit*] de sel **b** († = *risqué*) [*language, story*] salé

salubrious [sə'luːbrɪəs] ADJ (*frm*) (= *healthy*) [*place*] salubre; [*climate*] sain; (*fig* = *desirable, pleasant*) **not a very ~ district** un quartier peu recommandable

salubrity [sə'luːbrɪtɪ] N salubrité *f*

saluki [sə'luːkɪ] N sloughi *m*

salutary ['sæljʊtərɪ] ADJ salutaire

salutation [,sæljʊ'teɪʃən] N salut *m*; (*exaggerated*) salutation *f*; **in ~** pour saluer

salutatorian [sə,luːtə'tɔːrɪən] N (*US Scol*) deuxième *mf* de la promotion (*qui prononce un discours de fin d'année*)

salute [sə'luːt] **1** N (*with hand*) salut *m*; (*with guns*) salve *f*; [*military*] ~ salut *m* militaire; **to give (sb) a ~** faire un salut (à qn); **to take the ~** passer les troupes en revue; **to raise one's hand in ~** saluer de la main → **fire, gun 2** VT (*Mil etc*) saluer (*de la main*); (*fig* = *acclaim*) saluer (**as** comme); **to ~ the flag** saluer le drapeau; **he ~d the historic achievement of the government** il a salué ce succès historique du gouvernement **3** VI (*Mil etc*) faire un salut

Salvador(i)an [,sælvə'dɔː(r)ɪən] **1** ADJ salvadorien **2** N Salvadorien(ne) *m(f)*

salvage ['sælvɪdʒ] **1** N (*NonC*) **a** (= *saving*) [*of ship, cargo*] sauvetage *m*; (*for re-use*) récupération *f* **b** (= *things saved from fire, wreck*) objets *mpl or* biens *mpl* sauvés *or* récupérés; (= *things for re-use*) objets *mpl* récupérables; **to collect old newspapers for ~** récupérer les vieux journaux **c** (= *payment*) prime *f or* indemnité *f* de sauvetage

2 VT **a** (= *save*) sauver; [+ *pride, reputation*] préserver; **to ~ one's marriage** sauver son mariage; **we'll have to ~ what we can from the situation** il nous faudra sauver ce que nous pourrons de la situation; **she was lucky to (be able to) ~ her career** c'est tout juste si elle a pu sauver sa carrière **b** [+ *ship*] sauver, effectuer le sauvetage de; [+ *material, cargo*] sauver (**from** de) **c** [+ *objects for re-use*] récupérer **3** COMP [*operation, work, company, vessel*] de sauvetage

salvation [sæl'veɪʃən] **1** N (*Rel etc*) salut *m*; (*economic*) relèvement *m*; (*fig*) **work has been his ~** c'est le travail qui l'a sauvé, il a trouvé son salut dans le travail **2** COMP ▶ **Salvation Army** N Armée *f* du Salut; **Salvation Army band** fanfare *f* de l'Armée du Salut

salvationist [sæl'veɪʃənɪst] N salutiste *mf*

salve¹ [sælv] **1** N (*lit, fig*) baume *m* **2** VT [+ *pain*] soulager, apaiser; **to ~ his conscience he ...** pour soulager sa conscience, il ...

salve² [sælv] VT (= *salvage*) sauver

salver ['sælvəʳ] N plateau *m* (*de métal*)

salvia ['sælvɪə] N sauge *f* à fleurs rouges, salvia *f*

salvo¹ ['sælvəʊ] N (*pl* **salvos** *or* **salvoes**) (*Mil*) salve *f* → **fire**

salvo² ['sælvəʊ] N (*pl* **salvos**) (*Jur*) réserve *f*, réservation *f*

salvor ['sælvəʳ] N sauveteur *m* (*en mer*)

Salzburg ['sæltsbɜːg] N Salzbourg

SAM [sæm] N (*Mil*) (ABBR = **surface-to-air missile**) SAM *m*

Sam [sæm] **1** N *dim of* **Samuel**; → **uncle** **2** COMP ▶ **Sam Browne (belt)** N (*Mil*) ceinturon *m* et baudrier *m*; (*for cyclist*) bande *f* fluorescente

Samaria [sə'mɛərɪə] N la Samarie

Samaritan [sə'mærɪtən] **1** N Samaritain(e) *m(f)*; (*Rel*) **the Good ~** le bon Samaritain; **he was a good ~** il faisait le bon Samaritain; (*US*) **Good ~ Laws** *lois mettant un sauveteur à l'abri des poursuites judiciaires qui pourraient être engagées par le blessé*; (= *organization*) **the ~s** ≈ SOS-Amitié **2** ADJ samaritain

samarium [sə'mɛərɪəm] N samarium *m*

samba ['sæmbə] N samba *f*

sambo ['sæmbəʊ] N (*pej*) noiraud(e)‡ *m(f)*, moricaud(e)‡ *m(f)* (*pej*)

▼ **same** [seɪm] **1** ADJ même (**as que**); **to be the ~ age/shape** avoir le même âge/la même forme; **the carpet was the ~ colour as the wall** la moquette était de la même couleur que le mur; **we come from the ~ place** nous venons du même endroit; **the ~ books as** *or* **that ...** les mêmes livres que ...; **is that the ~ man (that) I saw yesterday?** est-ce bien l'homme que j'ai vu hier?; **the ~ woman that spoke to me** la femme qui m'a parlé; **the ~ girl as I saw yesterday** la fille que j'ai vue hier; **but in the ~ breath he said ...** mais il a ajouté ...; **the ~ day** le même jour; **the very ~ day** le jour même, exactement le même jour; **the ~ day as last year** le même jour que l'année dernière; **that ~ day** ce même jour; **~ difference!*** c'est du pareil au même!*, c'est kif-kif!*; **it's the ~ old rubbish on TV tonight** il y a les bêtises habituelles à la télé ce soir; **they turned out to be one and the ~ person** en fin de compte il s'agissait d'une seule et même personne; **I'm still the ~ person I was before** je n'ai pas changé; **for the ~ reason** pour la même raison; **it comes to the ~ thing** cela revient au même → **one**; **they both arrived at the ~ time** ils sont arrivés en même temps; **don't all talk at the ~ time** ne parlez pas tous en même temps *or* à la fois; **at the ~ time we must remember that ...** il ne faut cependant pas oublier que ...; **at the very ~ time as ...** au moment même *or* précis où ...; **we sat at the ~ table as usual** nous avons pris notre table habituelle; **how are you? — ~ as usual!*** comment vas-tu? — comme d'habitude!; **in the ~ way** de même; **in the ~ way as** *or* **that ...** de la même façon que ... → **story, token, way** **2** PRON **ⓐ** **the ~** (*gen*) la même chose; (*specific reference*) le *or* la même; (*Jur* = *aforementioned*) le susdit, la susdite; **it's the ~ as ...** c'est la même chose que ...; **the film is the ~ as before** le film est le même qu'avant; **the price is the ~ as last year** c'est le même prix que l'année dernière; (*in health*) **she's much** *or* **about the ~** son état est inchangé; **we must all write the ~** il faut que nous écrivions tous la même chose; **do the ~ as your brother** fais comme ton frère; **he left and I did the ~** il est parti et j'ai fait de même *or* j'en ai fait autant; **I'll do the ~ for you** je te le revaudrai; **I would do the ~ again** (si c'était à refaire), je

recommencerais; **don't do the ~ again!** ne recommence pas!; (*in bar etc*) **(the) ~ again please*** la même chose, s'il vous plaît, remettez-moi (*or* remettez-nous) ça*; **I don't feel the ~ about it as I did** maintenant je vois la chose différemment; **I still feel the ~ about you** mes sentiments à ton égard n'ont pas changé; **it's all** *or* **just the ~ to me** cela m'est égal; **thanks all** *or* **just the ~** merci tout de même *or* quand même*; **all** *or* **just the ~, he refused** il a refusé quand même *or* tout de même, n'empêche qu'il a refusé; **things go on just the ~** (= *monotonously*) rien ne change; (= *in spite of everything*) rien n'a changé, la vie continue (quand même); **it's not the ~ at all** ce n'est pas du tout la même chose, ce n'est pas du tout pareil; **it's not the ~ as before** ce n'est plus pareil, ce n'est plus comme avant; **it's the ~ everywhere** c'est partout pareil; **and the ~ to you!** (*good wishes*) à vous aussi!, vous de même!; (*as retort*) je te souhaite la pareille!; **you idiot! — ~ to you!*** toi-même!; **~ here!*** moi aussi!; **it's the ~ with us** (et) nous aussi! **ⓑ** (*Comm: frm*) le *or* la même; **"to repairing ~, £20"** « réparation du même (*or* de la même), 20 livres » **3** COMP ▶ **same-day** ADJ (*Comm*) [*delivery, service etc*] (garanti) le jour même *or* dans la journée ▶ **same-sex** ADJ [*relationship, marriage*] homosexuel

sameness ['seɪmnɪs] N identité *f*, similitude *f*; (= *monotony*) monotonie *f*, uniformité *f*

samey* ['seɪmɪ] ADJ (*Brit*) répétitif; **her songs are very ~** ses chansons se ressemblent toutes

samizdat [,sæmɪz'dæt] N samizdat *m*; **~ publication** samizdat *m*

Samoa [sə'məʊə] N le Samoa

Samoan [sə'məʊən] **1** ADJ samoan **2** N Samoan(e) *m(f)*

samosa [sə'məʊsə] N (*pl* **samosas** *or* **samosa**) samosa *m*

samovar [,sæməʊ'vɑːʳ] N samovar *m*

sampan ['sæmpæn] N sampan(g) *m*

sample ['sɑːmpl] **1** N (*gen*) échantillon *m*; (*Med*) [*of urine*] échantillon *m*; [*of blood, tissue*] prélèvement *m*; **as a ~** à titre d'échantillon; **to take a ~** prélever un échantillon, faire un prélèvement (*also Geol*); **to take a blood ~** faire une prise *or* un prélèvement de sang (**from** à); **to choose from ~s** choisir sur échantillons; (*Comm*) **all the goods are up to ~** toutes les marchandises sont d'aussi bonne qualité que les échantillons; (*Comm*) **free ~** échantillon *m* gratuit; **a ~ of his poetry** un exemple de sa poésie → **random** **2** VT **ⓐ** [+ *food, wine*] goûter, (*fig*) [+ *lifestyle*] goûter à **ⓑ** (*Mus*) sampler **ⓒ** [+ *opinion*] sonder; **the newspaper has ~d public opinion on ...** le journal a fait un sondage sur ... **3** COMP [*bottle, cigarette, selection etc*] échantillon *m*; [*line, sentence etc*] exemple *m* ▶ **sample book** N (*Comm*) catalogue *m* d'échantillons ▶ **sample section** N a ~ **section of the population** un échantillon représentatif de la population ▶ **sample survey** N enquête *f* par sondage

sampler ['sɑːmpləʳ] N (*Sewing*) échantillon *m* de broderie; (*Mus*) sampler *m*, échantillonneur *m*

sampling ['sɑːmplɪŋ] N (*gen*) échantillonnage *m*; (*Mus*) sampling *m*; (*Comm etc*) **~ technique** technique *f* d'échantillonnage

Samson ['sæmsn] N Samson *m*

Samuel ['sæmjʊəl] N Samuel *m*

samurai ['sæmʊˌraɪ] **1** N (*pl inv*) samouraï *or* samurai *m* **2** COMP ▶ **samurai bond** N (*Fin*) obligation *f* libellée en yens émise par des emprunteurs étrangers ▶ **samurai sword** N épée *f* de samouraï ▶ **samurai tradition** N

tradition *f* samouraï ▶ **samurai warrior** N (guerrier *m*) samouraï *m*

San Andreas [,sænæn'dreɪəs] N **the ~ Fault** la faille de San Andreas

sanatorium [,sænə'tɔːrɪəm] N (*pl* **sanatoriums** *or* **sanatoria** [,sænə'tɔːrɪə]) (*Brit*) sanatorium *m*; (*Scol*) infirmerie *f*

Sancho Panza [,sæntʃəʊ'pænzə] N Sancho Pança *m*

sancta ['sæŋktə] NPL *of* **sanctum**

sanctification [,sæŋktɪfɪ'keɪʃən] N sanctification *f*

sanctify ['sæŋktɪfaɪ] VT sanctifier

sanctimonious [,sæŋktɪ'məʊnɪəs] ADJ [*person, comment, speech etc*] moralisateur (-trice *f*)

sanctimoniously [,sæŋktɪ'məʊnɪəslɪ] ADV d'une manière moralisatrice; [*speak*] d'un ton moralisateur *or* prêcheur

sanctimoniousness [,sæŋktɪ'məʊnɪəsnɪs] N [*of comment, speech etc*] ton *m* moralisateur; [*of person*] attitude *f* moralisatrice

sanction ['sæŋkʃən] **1** N **ⓐ** (*NonC* = *authorization*) sanction *f*, approbation *f*; **he gave it his ~** il a donné son approbation; **with the ~ of sb** avec le consentement de qn **ⓑ** (= *enforcing measure*) sanction *f*; **to impose economic ~s against** *or* **on ...** prendre des sanctions économiques contre ...; **to lift the ~s on ...** lever les sanctions contre ... **2** VT **ⓐ** [+ *law, conduct*] sanctionner, approuver; **I will not ~ such a thing** je ne peux approuver *or* sanctionner une chose pareille; **this expression has been ~ed by usage** cette expression est consacrée par l'usage **ⓑ** (= *impose sanctions on*) prendre des sanctions contre **3** COMP ▶ **sanctions-busting** N violation *f* de sanctions

sanctity ['sæŋktɪtɪ] N [*of person, behaviour*] sainteté *f*; [*of oath, place*] caractère *m* sacré; [*of property, marriage*] inviolabilité *f*; **odour of ~** odeur *f* de sainteté

sanctuary ['sæŋktjʊərɪ] N (= *holy place*) sanctuaire *m*; (= *refuge*) asile *m*; (*for wildlife*) réserve *f*; **right of ~** droit *m* d'asile; **to seek ~** chercher asile → **bird**

sanctum ['sæŋktəm] N (*pl* **sanctums** *or* **sancta**) **ⓐ** (= *holy place*) sanctuaire *m* **ⓑ** (* = *sb's study etc*) retraite *f*, tanière *f*; (*hum*) **the (inner) ~** le saint des saints (*hum*)

sand [sænd] **1** N **ⓐ** sable *m*; **a grain of ~** un grain de sable; **this resort has miles and miles of golden ~(s)** cette station balnéaire a des kilomètres de plages de sable doré; (*fig*) **to be built on ~** [*plan, agreement*] être un château de cartes, être voué à l'échec; (*fig*) **the ~s are running out** nos instants sont comptés; **~s** [*of beach*] plage *f* (de sable); [*of desert*] désert *m* (de sable) **ⓑ** (*US* * = *courage*) cran* *m* **2** VT **ⓐ** [+ *path*] sabler, couvrir de sable; (*against ice*) sabler **ⓑ** (also **~ down**) poncer **3** COMP ▶ **sand bar** N barre *f* (de rivière) ▶ **sand blind** ADJ (*US*) qui a mauvaise vue ▶ **sand castle** N château *m* de sable ▶ **sand desert** N désert *m* de sable ▶ **sand dollar** N (*US Zool*) oursin *m* plat ▶ **sand dune** N dune *f* (de sable) ▶ **sand eel** N anguille *f* de sable, lançon *m*, équille *f* ▶ **sand flea** N (= *beach flea*) puce *f* de mer; (*tropical*) chique *f* ▶ **sand martin** N hirondelle *f* de rivage ▶ **sand trap** N (*US Golf*) bunker *m* ▶ **sand yacht** N char *m* à voile ▶ **sand-yachting** N **to go ~-yachting** faire du char à voile

sandal ['sændl] N sandale *f*

sandal(wood) ['sændl(wʊd)] **1** N santal *m* **2** COMP [*box, perfume*] de santal

sandbag ['sændbæg] **1** N sac *m* de sable *or* de terre **2** VT **ⓐ** (* = *stun*) assommer **ⓑ** [+ *wall, door, dam*] renforcer avec des sacs de sable *or* de terre

sandbank ['sændbæŋk] N banc *m* de sable

sandblast ['sændblɑːst] [1] N jet *m* de sable [2] VT décaper à la sableuse

sandblaster ['sænd,blɑːstəʳ] N sableuse *f*

sandblasting ['sænd,blɑːstɪŋ] N décapage *m* à la sableuse; ~ **machine** = **sandblaster**

sandbox ['sændbɒks] N bac *m* à sable; (*Rail*) sablière *f*

sandboy ['sændbɔɪ] N **happy as a ~** heureux comme un poisson dans l'eau *or* comme un roi

sander ['sændəʳ] N (= *tool*) ponceuse *f*

sandfly ['sændflaɪ] N phlébotome *m*; (= *biting midge*) simulie *f*

sandglass ['sændglɑːs] N sablier *m*

Sandhurst ['sændhɜːst] N (*Brit*) école militaire, ≈ Saint-Cyr

sanding ['sændɪŋ] N [*of road*] sablage *m*; (= *sandpapering*) ponçage *m* au papier de verre

S & L [,esənd'el] N (*US Fin*) (ABBR = **savings and loan association**) → **saving**

sandlot ['sændlɒt] (*US*) [1] N terrain *m* vague [2] N ► **sandlot baseball** N baseball *m* pratiqué dans les terrains vagues

S & M [,esənd'em] [1] N ABBR = **sadomasochism** [2] ADJ (ABBR = **sadomasochistic**) sadomaso*, SM*

sandman ['sændmæn] N (*pl* **-men**) (*fig*) marchand *m* de sable

sandpaper ['sænd,peɪpəʳ] [1] N papier *m* de verre [2] VT (*also* ~ **down**) poncer

sandpapering ['sænd,peɪpərɪŋ] N ponçage *m*

sandpile ['sændpaɪl] N (*US*) tas *m* de sable

sandpiper ['sænd,paɪpəʳ] N (*Orn*) bécasseau *m*, chevalier *m*

sandpit ['sændpɪt] N (*esp Brit*) sablonnière *f*, carrière *f* de sable; (*for children*) bac à sable

sandshoes ['sændʃuːz] NPL (*rubber-soled*) tennis *mpl* or *fpl*; (*rope-soled*) espadrilles *fpl*

sandstone ['sændstəʊn] [1] N grès *m* [2] COMP ► **sandstone quarry** N carrière *f* de grès, grésière *f*

sandstorm ['sændstɔːm] N tempête *f* de sable

sandwich ['sænwɪdʒ] [1] N sandwich *m*; **cheese ~** sandwich *m* au fromage; **open ~** canapé *m*; (*Brit*) **he's the meat *or* filling in the ~*** il est pris entre deux feux [2] VT (*also* ~ **in**) [+ *person, appointment*] intercaler; **to be ~ed (between)** être pris en sandwich (entre)*; **three pieces of wood, ~ed together** trois couches de bois superposées [3] COMP ► **sandwich bar** N sandwicherie *f* ► **sandwich board** N panneau *m* publicitaire (*porté par un homme-sandwich*) ► **sandwich cake** N (*Brit Culin*) gâteau *m* fourré ► **sandwich course** N (*Ind*) stage *m* de formation (professionnelle) en alternance ► **sandwich loaf** N pain *m* de mie ► **sandwich man** N (*pl* **sandwich men**) homme-sandwich *m*

sandworm ['sændwɜːm] N arénicole *f*

sandy ['sændɪ] ADJ [a] (= *covered with, containing sand*) [*soil, ground*] sablonneux; [*beach*] de sable; [*water, deposit*] sableux [b] (= *light-brown*) couleur (de) sable *inv*; [*hair, moustache*] blond roux *inv*

sane [seɪn] ADJ [a] (*Psych*) [*person*] sain d'esprit; [*behaviour*] sain [b] (= *sensible*) [*system, policy, advice*] sensé; [*person*] sensé, raisonnable

sanely ['seɪnlɪ] ADV sainement, raisonnablement

Sanforized® ['sænfəraɪzd] ADJ irrétrécissable, qui ne rétrécit pas au lavage

San Francisco [,sænfræn'sɪskəʊ] N San Francisco

sang [sæŋ] VB *pt of* **sing**

sangfroid ['sɑ̃ːŋ'frwɑː] N sang-froid *m inv*

sangria [sæŋ'griːə] N sangria *f*

sanguinary ['sæŋgwɪnərɪ] ADJ (*frm*) [a] (= *bloody*) [*battle, struggle*] sanglant; [*violence*] sanguinaire [b] (= *bloodthirsty*) [*person*] sanguinaire

sanguine ['sæŋgwɪn] ADJ [a] (*frm* = *optimistic*) [*person, view, temperament*] optimiste (**about** quant à); **of (a) ~ disposition** d'un naturel optimiste, porté à l'optimisme [b] (*liter*) [*complexion*] sanguin [c] (*Med Hist*) [*person, temperament*] sanguin

sanguinely ['sæŋgwɪnlɪ] ADV avec optimisme

sanguineous [sæŋ'gwɪnɪəs] ADJ sanguinolent

sanitarium [,sænɪ'tɛərɪəm] N (*pl* **sanitariums** or **sanitaria** [,sænɪ'tɛərɪə]) (*esp US*) = **sanatorium**

sanitary ['sænɪtərɪ] ADJ [a] (= *hygienic*) [*place*] hygiénique [b] (= *to do with hygiene*) [*conditions, system, services*] sanitaire; ~ **facilities** (installations *fpl*) sanitaires *mpl*; ~ **arrangements** dispositions *fpl* sanitaires [2] COMP ► **sanitary engineer** N ingénieur *m* des services sanitaires ► **sanitary inspector** N inspecteur *m*, -trice *f* de la santé publique ► **sanitary napkin** N (*US*) = **sanitary towel** ► **sanitary protection** N (*NonC*) protections *fpl* périodiques ► **sanitary towel** N (*Brit*) serviette *f* hygiénique

sanitation [,sænɪ'teɪʃən] [1] N (*in house*) installations *fpl* sanitaires, sanitaires *mpl*; (*in town*) système *m* sanitaire; (= *science*) hygiène *f* publique [2] COMP ► **sanitation man** N (*pl* **sanitation men**) (*US*) éboueur *m* (municipal)

sanitize ['sænɪtaɪz] VT (*lit*) assainir, désinfecter; (*fig*) assainir, expurger

sanitized ['sænɪtaɪzd] ADJ (*fig*) [*account, view of events*] édulcoré, expurgé

sanity ['sænɪtɪ] N [*of person*] santé *f* mentale; [*of judgement, reasoning*] rectitude *f*; **he was restored to ~** il retrouva sa santé mentale *or* sa raison; ~ **demands that ...** le bon sens exige que ... (+ *subj*); **fortunately ~ prevailed** heureusement le bon sens l'emporta

sank [sæŋk] VB *pt of* **sink¹**

San Marinese [,sæn,mærɪ'niːz] [1] ADJ san-marinais [2] N San-Marinais(e) *m(f)*

San Marino [,sænmə'riːnəʊ] N Saint-Marin *n*; **in ~** à Saint-Marin

San Salvador [sæn'sælvədɔːʳ] N San Salvador

sansevieria [,sænsɪ'vɪərɪə] N sansevière *f*

Sanskrit ['sænskrɪt] ADJ, N sanscrit *m*

Santa* ['sæntə] N = **Santa Claus**

Santa Claus [,sæntə'klɔːz] N le père Noël

Santiago [,sæntɪ'ɑːgəʊ] N (*also* ~ **de Chile**) Santiago (du Chili); (*also* ~ **de Compostela**) Saint-Jacques-de-Compostelle

Saone [sɔːn] N Saône *f*

sap¹ [sæp] N (*Bot*) sève *f*

sap² [sæp] [1] N (*Mil* = *trench*) sape *f* [2] VT [+ *strength, confidence*] saper, miner

sap³* [sæp] N (= *fool*) cruche* *f*, andouille* *f*

saphead ['sæphed] N (*US*) cruche* *f*, andouille* *f*

sapless ['sæplɪs] ADJ [*plant*] sans sève, desséché

sapling ['sæplɪŋ] N jeune arbre *m*; (*fig liter*) jeune homme *m*; ~**s** boisage *m*

sapper ['sæpəʳ] N (*Brit Mil*) soldat *m* du génie; **the Sappers*** le génie

sapphic ['sæfɪk] ADJ saphique

sapphire ['sæfaɪəʳ] [1] N (= *jewel, gramophone needle*) saphir *m* [2] COMP [*ring*] de saphir(s); [*sky*] (*also* ~ **blue**) de saphir

sappiness ['sæpɪnɪs] N abondance *f* de sève

sappy¹ ['sæpɪ] ADJ [*leaves*] plein de sève; [*wood*] vert

sappy²* ['sæpɪ] ADJ (= *foolish*) cruche*

saraband ['særəbænd] N sarabande *f*

Saracen ['særəsn] [1] ADJ sarrasin [2] N Sarrasin(e) *m(f)*

Saragossa [,særə'gɒsə] N Saragosse

Sarah ['sɛərə] N Sara(h) *f*

Saranwrap® [sə'rænræp] N (*US*) film *m* alimentaire (transparent), Scellofrais® *m*

Saratoga [,særə'təʊgə] [1] N Saratoga [2] COMP ► **Saratoga trunk** N (*US*) grosse malle *f* à couvercle bombé

sarcasm ['sɑːkæzəm] N (*NonC*) sarcasme *m*, raillerie *f*

sarcastic [sɑː'kæstɪk] ADJ sarcastique

sarcastically [sɑː'kæstɪkəlɪ] ADV [*say*] d'un ton sarcastique

sarcoma [sɑː'kəʊmə] N (*pl* **sarcomas** or **sarcomata** [sɑː'kəʊmətə]) (*Med*) sarcome *m*

sarcomatosis [sɑː,kəʊmə'təʊsɪs] N sarcomatose *f*

sarcophagus [sɑː'kɒfəgəs] N (*pl* **sarcophaguses** or **sarcophagi** [sɑː'kɒfəgaɪ]) sarcophage *m*

sardine [sɑː'diːn] N (*pl* **sardine** or **sardines**) sardine *f*; **tinned** or (*US*) **canned ~s** sardines *fpl* en boîte *or* en conserve; (*fig*) **packed like ~s** serrés comme des sardines

Sardinia [sɑː'dɪnɪə] N la Sardaigne; **in ~** en Sardaigne

Sardinian [sɑː'dɪnɪən] [1] ADJ sarde [2] N [a] (= *person*) Sarde *mf* [b] (*Ling*) sarde *m*

sardonic [sɑː'dɒnɪk] ADJ sardonique

sardonically [sɑː'dɒnɪkəlɪ] ADV [*smile*] d'un air sardonique, sardoniquement; [*say*] d'un ton sardonique, sardoniquement; **to laugh ~** avoir un rire sardonique

Sargasso Sea [sɑː'gæsəʊ,siː] N mer *f* des Sargasses

sarge* [sɑːdʒ] N (ABBR = **sergeant**) sergent *m*

sari ['sɑːrɪ] N sari *m*

Sark [sɑːk] N (île *f* de) Sercq

sarky* ['sɑːkɪ] ADJ sarcastique

sarnie* ['sɑːnɪ] N (*Brit*) sandwich *m*

sarong [sə'rɒŋ] N sarong *m*

sarsaparilla [,sɑːsəpə'rɪlə] N (= *plant*) salsepareille *f*; (= *drink*) boisson *f* à la salsepareille

sartorial [sɑː'tɔːrɪəl] ADJ (*frm*) [*elegance, habits, matters*] vestimentaire; ~ **art** art *m* du tailleur

sartorius [sɑː'tɔːrɪəs] N (*pl* **sartorii** [sɑː'tɔːrɪaɪ]) (*Anat*) muscle *m* couturier

SAS [,eseɪ'es] N (*Brit Mil*) (ABBR = **Special Air Service**) ≈ GIGN *m*

SASE [,eseɪes'iː] N (*US*) (ABBR = **self-addressed stamped envelope**) → **self**

sash¹ [sæʃ] N (*on uniform*) écharpe *f*; (*on dress etc*) large ceinture *f* à nœud

sash² [sæʃ] [1] N (*of window*) châssis *m* à guillotine [2] COMP ► **sash cord** N corde *f* (*d'une fenêtre à guillotine*) ► **sash window** N fenêtre *f* à guillotine

sashay* ['sæʃeɪ] VI (= *walk stylishly*) évoluer d'un pas léger, glisser

sashimi ['sæʃɪmɪ] N sashimi *m*

Sask. ABBR = **Saskatchewan**

Saskatchewan ['sæs'kætʃɪ,wən] N (= *province*) le Saskatchewan

sasquatch ['sæskwætʃ] N animal hypothétique des forêts du nord-ouest des États-Unis et du Canada

sass* [sæs] (*US*) [1] N toupet* *m*, culot* *m* [2] VT être insolent avec

Sassenach ['sæsənæx] N (*Scot: gen pej*) nom donné aux Anglais par les Écossais, ≈ Anglicho* *mf*

sassy* ['sæsɪ] ADJ (*US*) insolent, impertinent; **don't be ~ with me** je n'aime pas qu'on (me) réponde

SAT [,eseɪ'tiː] N (*US Educ*) (ABBR = **Scholastic Aptitude test**) examen *m* d'entrée à l'université

SAT

Aux États-Unis, les **SAT** (*Scholastic Aptitude Tests*) *sont un examen national de fin d'enseignement secondaire, composé surtout de tests de logique permettant d'évaluer le*

*raisonnement verbal et mathématique des élèves. La note maximale est de 1 600 points et la moyenne tourne généralement autour des 900. Les résultats obtenus à cet examen (**SAT** scores) sont adressés aux universités dans lesquelles le lycéen a fait une demande d'inscription, et celles-ci font leur sélection sur la base à la fois de ces notes et du dossier scolaire de l'élève. Il est possible de se présenter aux **SAT** autant de fois qu'on le désire.*

sat [sæt] VB *pt, ptp of* **sit**

Sat. ABBR = **Saturday**

Satan ['seɪtn] N Satan *m* → **limb**

satanic [sə'tænɪk] ① ADJ ⓐ (*Rel, Occultism*) [*ritual, cult, forces*] satanique ⓑ (= *evil*) [*reputation*] démoniaque ② COMP ▶ **satanic abuse** N (*NonC*) sévices *mpl* sexuels associés à des rites sataniques

satanically [sə'tænɪkəlɪ] ADV d'une manière satanique

Satanism ['seɪtənɪzəm] N satanisme *m*

Satanist ['seɪtənɪst] ① N sataniste *mf* ② ADJ = **satanic**

satay ['sæteɪ] ① N **chicken/pork** ~ petite brochette de poulet/porc accompagnée d'une sauce aux cacahuètes ② COMP ▶ **satay sauce** N sauce *f* aux cacahuètes, sauce *f* satay

satchel ['sætʃəl] N cartable *m*

Satcom ['sæt,kɒm] N centre *m* de communications par satellite

sate [seɪt] VT = **satiate**

sated ['seɪtɪd] ADJ = **satiated**

sateen [sæ'tiːn] ① N satinette *f* ② COMP en satinette

satellite ['sætəlaɪt] ① N ⓐ (*Astron, Space, Telec*) satellite *m*; **artificial** ~ satellite *m* artificiel; **communications** ~ satellite *m* de télécommunications, satellite-relais *m* ⓑ (*Pol*) satellite *m* ⓒ (*US = dormitory town*) ville *f* satellite ② VT (= *transmit via satellite*) transmettre par satellite ③ COMP [*town, country etc*] satellite ▶ **satellite broadcasting** N diffusion *f* par satellite ▶ **satellite dish** N antenne *f* parabolique ▶ **satellite link(-up)** N liaison *f* satellite ▶ **satellite nation** N (*Pol*) nation *f* satellite ▶ **satellite photograph** N photo *f* satellite ▶ **satellite telephone** N téléphone *m* (par) satellite ▶ **satellite television** N télévision *f* par satellite

satiate ['seɪʃɪeɪt] VT (*lit*) assouvir, rassasier (**with** de); (*fig*) blaser (**with** par)

satiated ['seɪʃɪeɪtɪd] ADJ (*with food*) repu, rassasié; (*with pleasures*) comblé, blasé (*pej*)

satiation [seɪʃɪ'eɪʃən] N (*lit, fig*) assouvissement *m*; **to** ~ (**point**) (jusqu'à) satiété

satiety [sə'taɪətɪ] N (*frm*) satiété *f*

satin ['sætɪn] ① N satin *m* → **silk** ② COMP [*dress, slipper*] en or de satin; [*paper, finish*] satiné ▶ **satin-smooth** ADJ satin ▶ **satin stitch** N plumetis *m*

satinette [sætɪ'net] ① N satinette *f* ② COMP en satinette

satinwood ['sætɪnwʊd] N bois *m* de citronnier

satire ['sætaɪə'] N satire *f* (**on** contre)

satiric(al) [sə'tɪrɪk(əl)] ADJ satirique

satirically [sə'tɪrɪkəlɪ] ADV d'une manière satirique

satirist ['sætərɪst] N (= *writer*) écrivain *m* satirique; (= *cartoonist*) caricaturiste *mf*; (*in cabaret etc*) ≈ chansonnier *m*; **he's TV's greatest** ~ il n'a pas son pareil à la télévision pour la satire

satirize ['sætəraɪz] VT faire la satire de

satisfaction [sætɪs'fækʃən] N ⓐ (*NonC = pleasure*) satisfaction *f*; **to feel ~/great ~** éprouver de la satisfaction/une satisfaction profonde; **his ~ at having completed his book** la satisfaction qu'il éprouvait d'avoir terminé son livre; **he expressed his ~ at the results of the vote** il a exprimé sa satisfaction devant

les résultats de l'élection; **sexual** ~ satisfaction *f* sexuelle; **it gave us great ~ to hear that ...** nous avons appris avec beaucoup de satisfaction que ...; **to my (great)** ~ **he ...** à ma grande satisfaction il ...; **to everybody's** ~ à la satisfaction de tous; **has the repair been done to your** ~? est-ce que vous êtes satisfait de la réparation?; **his innocence has not been proved to my** ~ on n'a pas réussi à me convaincre de son innocence; **she would not give him the** ~ **of seeing how annoyed she was** elle ne voulait pas lui faire le plaisir de lui montrer à quel point elle était contrariée → **job**

ⓑ (*NonC*) [*of demand, need*] satisfaction *f*; [*of wrong*] réparation *f*, dédommagement *m*; [*of appetite*] assouvissement *m*; [*of debt*] règlement *m*, acquittement *m*; **to give/obtain** ~ donner/obtenir satisfaction; **I demand** ~† je demande réparation

ⓒ (= *satisfying experience etc*) satisfaction *f*; **one of her greatest ~s comes from her work with children** son travail avec les enfants lui apporte l'une de ses plus grandes satisfactions

satisfactorily [sætɪs'fæktərɪlɪ] ADV de manière satisfaisante

satisfactory [sætɪs'fæktərɪ] ADJ satisfaisant; **to bring sth to a** ~ **conclusion** mener qch à bon terme, conclure qch de manière satisfaisante; (*Med*) **he's in a** ~ **condition** son état est satisfaisant; (*Med*) **to make a** ~ **recovery** se rétablir or se remettre de manière satisfaisante; (*in commercial letters etc*) **we are sorry it was not** ~ nous regrettons que vous n'en soyez pas satisfait or que cela ne vous ait pas donné (entière) satisfaction

satisfied ['sætɪsfaɪd] ADJ ⓐ (= *content*) [*person*] satisfait (**with** de, **to do sth** de faire qch); **in a** ~ **voice** d'un ton satisfait; **some people are never** ~! il y en a qui ne sont jamais contents!; (*angrily*) **I'll stay then: (are you)** ~? alors je reste: tu es content?; **you've made her cry: (are you)** ~? tu l'as fait pleurer: tu es content de toi or satisfait? ⓑ (= *convinced*) [*person*] satisfait (**with** de), convaincu (**with** par); **I'm** ~ **that her death was accidental** je suis convaincu que sa mort a été accidentelle; **I'm** ~ **that I'm right** je suis convaincu d'avoir raison → **satisfy**

satisfy ['sætɪsfaɪ] ① VT ⓐ (+ *person*) satisfaire, contenter; (*Scol, Univ: frm*) **to** ~ **the examiners (in History)** être reçu (en histoire or à l'examen d'histoire) → **satisfied** ⓑ (+ *hunger, need, want, creditor*) satisfaire; (+ *condition*) satisfaire, remplir; (+ *objection*) répondre à; (+ *debt, obligation*) s'acquitter de; (*Comm*) (+ *demand*) satisfaire à ⓒ (= *convince*) convaincre, assurer (**sb that** qn que, **of** de); **to** ~ **o.s. of sth** s'assurer de qch; **I am satisfied that you have done your best** je suis convaincu or persuadé que vous avez fait de votre mieux ② VI donner satisfaction

satisfying ['sætɪsfaɪɪŋ] ADJ [*life, relationship, work, career*] satisfaisant; [*task, experience*] gratifiant; [*food, meal*] substantiel

satrap ['sætrəp] N satrape *m*

satsuma [sæt'suːmə] N satsuma *f*

saturate ['sætʃəreɪt] ① VT saturer (**with** de); (*Comm*) **to** ~ **the market** saturer le marché; **my shoes are ~d** mes chaussures sont trempées ② COMP ▶ **saturated fat** N graisse *f* saturée

saturation [sætʃə'reɪʃən] ① N saturation *f* ② COMP ▶ **saturation bombing** N bombardement *m* intensif ▶ **saturation point** N point *m* de saturation; **to reach** ~ **point** arriver à saturation

Saturday ['sætədɪ] N samedi *m*; **on** ~ samedi; **on ~s** le samedi; **next ~** ◊ ~ **next** samedi prochain or qui vient; **last ~** samedi dernier; **the first/last** ~ **of the month** le premier/dernier samedi du mois; **every** ~ tous les samedis, chaque samedi; **every other** ~ ◊ **every second** ~

un samedi sur deux; **it is** ~ **today** nous sommes samedi aujourd'hui, on est samedi; **~ 18 December** samedi 18 décembre; **on ~ 23 January** le samedi 23 janvier; **the** ~ **after next** samedi en huit; **a week on** ~ ◊ ~ **week** samedi en huit; **a fortnight on** ~ ◊ ~ **fortnight** samedi en quinze; **a week/fortnight past on** ~ il y a huit/quinze jours samedi dernier; **the following** ~ le samedi suivant; **the** ~ **before last** l'autre samedi; ~ **morning** samedi matin; ~ **afternoon** samedi après-midi; ~ **evening** samedi soir; ~ **night** samedi soir; (*overnight*) la nuit de samedi; (*Comm*) ~ **closing** fermeture *f* le samedi; (*Press*) **the** ~ **edition** l'édition *f* de or du samedi; (*US* = *gun*) ~ **night special*** revolver *m* bon marché → **holy**

Saturn ['sætən] N (*Myth*) Saturne *m*; (*Astron*) Saturne *f*

Saturnalia [sætə'neɪlɪə] N (*pl* **Saturnalia** or **Saturnalias**) saturnale(s) *f(pl)*

saturnine ['sætənaɪn] ADJ (*liter*) [*man, face*] ténébreux; [*features*] sombre

satyr ['sætə'] N satyre *m*

sauce [sɔːs] ① N ⓐ (*Culin*) sauce *f* ■ (*PROV*) **what's ~ for the goose is ~ for the gander** ce qui est bon pour l'un l'est pour l'autre → **apple, mint, tomato, white** ⓑ (†* = *impudence*) toupet* *m*; **none of your ~!** (*to child*) petit(e) impertinent(e)!; (*to adult*) assez d'impertinence! ⓒ (*US:* = *drink*) **the** ~ l'alcool *m*; **to hit the** ~ ◊ **to be on the** ~ picoler* ② COMP ▶ **sauce boat** N saucière *f*

saucepan ['sɔːspən] N casserole *f* → **double**

saucer ['sɔːsə'] N soucoupe *f*, sous-tasse *f*; ~-**eyed** ◊ **with eyes like ~s** avec des yeux comme des soucoupes → **flying**

saucily* ['sɔːsɪlɪ] ADV [*behave, speak*] avec impertinence, impertinemment; [*dress*] avec coquetterie; [*look*] d'un air coquin

sauciness* ['sɔːsɪnɪs] N (= *cheekiness*) toupet* *m*, impertinence *f*; (= *smartness*) coquetterie *f*

saucy* ['sɔːsɪ] ADJ ⓐ (= *cheeky*) [*person*] impertinent (**with** avec); [*look*] coquin ⓑ (*esp Brit* = *suggestive*) [*joke, humour*] grivois; [*postcard, photo*] osé; [*clothes*] suggestif

Saudi ['saʊdɪ] ① ADJ (*gen*) saoudien; [*ambassador, embassy*] d'Arabie Saoudite; [*capital*] de l'Arabie Saoudite ② N Saoudien(ne) *m(f)* ③ COMP ▶ **Saudi Arabia** N l'Arabie *f* Saoudite ▶ **Saudi Arabian** ADJ saoudien ♦ N Saoudien(ne) *m(f)*

sauerkraut ['saʊəkraʊt] N (*NonC*) choucroute *f*

Saul [sɔːl] N Saül *m*

sauna ['sɔːnə] N (*also* ~ **bath**) sauna *m*; **at the** ~ au sauna; **in the** ~ dans le sauna

saunter ['sɔːntə'] ① VI flâner; **to** ~ **in/out/away** *etc* entrer/sortir/s'éloigner *etc* d'un pas nonchalant ② N **to go for a** ~* faire une petite promenade or une balade*

saurian ['sɔːrɪən] ADJ, N saurien *m*

sausage ['sɒsɪdʒ] ① N saucisse *f*; (*pre-cooked*) saucisson *m*; **beef/pork** ~ saucisse *f* de bœuf/ de porc; (*Brit*) **not a** ~* rien, des clous* → **cocktail, garlic, liver'** ② COMP ▶ **sausage dog*** N teckel *m*, saucisson *m* à pattes* (*hum*) ▶ **sausage machine** N machine *f* à faire les saucisses ▶ **sausage meat** N chair *f* à saucisse ▶ **sausage roll** N (*esp Brit*) ≈ friand *m*

sauté ['səʊteɪ] ① VT (+ *potatoes, meat*) faire sauter ② ADJ ~ **potatoes** pommes *fpl* (de terre) sautées

savage ['sævɪdʒ] ① ADJ ⓐ (= *violent, harsh*) [*person*] féroce, brutal; [*animal, attack, criticism, look*] féroce; [*blow*] brutal; [*temper*] sauvage ⓑ (= *drastic*) **a** ~ **pay cut** une très forte réduction de salaire; ~ **cuts in the education budget** des coupes *fpl* claires dans le budget de l'éducation ⓒ († = *primitive*) [*tribe*] sauvage ② N sauvage *mf* ③ VT† [*dog etc*] attaquer férocement; (fig) [critics etc] éreinter, attaquer violemment

savagely ['sævɪdʒlɪ] ADV a (= violently, harshly) [beat] sauvagement; [criticize] violemment, férocement; [say] brutalement; [funny] férocement; ~ **beautiful** d'une beauté sauvage; **to attack sb/sth** ~ (lit) attaquer qn/qch sauvagement; (fig) attaquer qn/qch violemment b (= drastically) **the film has been ~ cut** or **edited** ce film a été monstrueusement coupé; **to cut staff/a budget** ~ faire des coupes claires dans un budget/parmi le personnel

savageness ['sævɪdʒnɪs], **savagery** ['sævɪdʒrɪ] N (= cruelty) sauvagerie f, brutalité f, férocité f; (= primitiveness) barbarie f

savanna(h) [sə'vænə] N savane f

savant ['sævənt] N érudit(e) m(f), homme m de science, lettré(e) m(f)

save¹ [seɪv] 1 VT a (= rescue) [+ person, animal, jewels, building, marriage] sauver (**from** de); **surgeons could not ~ his leg** les chirurgiens n'ont pas pu sauver sa jambe; **a campaign to ~ the hospital** une campagne pour le maintien or la survie de l'hôpital; **we must ~ the planet for future generations** il faut préserver or sauvegarder la planète pour les générations à venir; **to ~ the situation** sauver la situation; **to ~ sb from death/drowning** etc sauver qn de la mort/de la noyade etc; **to ~ sb from falling** empêcher qn de tomber; **to ~ sb from himself** protéger qn de or contre lui-même; **to ~ sth from the shipwreck/the fire** etc sauver qch du naufrage/de l'incendie etc → **wreckage**; **to ~ a building from demolition** sauver un bâtiment de la démolition, empêcher la démolition d'un bâtiment; **to ~ sb's life** sauver la vie à or de qn; (fig) **thanks, you ~d my life!** merci, tu m'as sauvé la vie!; **I couldn't do it to ~ my life** or **my soul** je ne pourrais pas le faire, même si ma vie en dépendait; **to ~ one's (own) skin*** or **neck*** or **hide*** sauver sa peau*; (esp Brit fig) **to ~ one's (own) bacon*** se tirer du pétrin; **to ~ sb's bacon** or **neck** tirer qn d'affaire; (US) **to ~ sb's ass**•• or **butt**•• sortir qn de la merde••; **to be ~d by the bell** être sauvé par le gong; **to ~ the day** sauver la mise; **to ~ face** sauver la face; **God ~ the Queen!** vive la reine!
b (Rel) [+ sinner] sauver, délivrer; **to ~ one's soul** sauver son âme
c (= store away: also ~ **up**) [+ money] mettre de côté; [+ food] mettre de côté, garder; **he has money ~d** il a de l'argent de côté; **I've ~d you a piece of cake** je t'ai gardé un morceau de gâteau; **to ~ o.s. (up) for sth** se réserver pour qch; **he ~d the last sweet for himself** il s'est gardé le dernier bonbon; **I was saving the wine for later** je gardais le vin pour plus tard; **to ~ sth till (the) last** garder qch pour la bonne bouche; **to ~ the best for last** garder le meilleur pour la fin; **to ~ (up) old newspapers for charity** garder les vieux journaux pour les bonnes œuvres; (= collect) **to ~ stamps/ matchboxes** etc collectionner les timbres/les boîtes d'allumettes etc; **will you ~ me a place at your table?** me garderez-vous une place à votre table?
d (= not spend, not use) [+ money, labour] économiser; [+ time] (faire) gagner; (= avoid) [+ difficulty etc] éviter (**sb sth** qch à qn); **you have ~d me a lot of trouble** vous m'avez évité bien des ennuis; **to ~ time let's assume that ...** pour aller plus vite or pour gagner du temps admettons que ... (+ subj); **this route will ~ you 10 miles** cet itinéraire vous fera gagner 16 kilomètres; **going by plane will ~ you four hours (on the train journey)** vous gagnerez quatre heures en prenant l'avion (au lieu du train); **that will ~ my going** or **me from going** cela m'évitera d'y aller; **think of all the money you'll ~** pensez à tout l'argent que vous économiserez or à toutes les économies que vous ferez; (Comm) **"~ 10p on this packet"** « 10 pence d'économie sur ce paquet »; **you ~ £1 if**

you buy three packets en achetant trois paquets vous économisez une livre; **to ~ petrol** faire des économies d'essence, économiser l'essence; **industry must be encouraged to ~ energy** il faut encourager l'industrie à faire des économies d'énergie; **he's saving his strength** or **himself for tomorrow's race** il se ménage pour la course de demain; (euph, hum) **to ~ o.s. for sb** se réserver pour qn; (Brit) **~ as you earn** plan d'épargne par prélèvements mensuels, aux intérêts exonérés d'impôts → **penny, stitch**
e (Sport) **to ~ a goal/penalty** arrêter un but/ penalty
f (Comput) sauvegarder
2 VI a (also ~ **up**) mettre (de l'argent) de côté, faire des économies; **to ~ for the holidays/ for a new bike** mettre de l'argent de côté pour les vacances/pour (acheter) un nouveau vélo
b **to ~ on sth** économiser sur qch, faire des économies sur qch
c (Sport) faire une parade
3 N a (Sport) parade f
b (Comput) sauvegarde f
► **save up** 1 VI = **save¹ 2a** 2 VT SEP = **save¹ 1c**

save² [seɪv] PREP (liter) sauf, à l'exception de; ~ **that ...** sauf que ..., à ceci près que ...

saveloy ['sævəlɔɪ] N cervelas m

saver ['seɪvə'] N épargnant(e) m(f)

Savile Row ['sævɪl'rəʊ] 1 N (Brit) rue de Londres où se trouvent les plus grands tailleurs 2 COMP ► **a Savile Row suit** N un costume de Savile Row

saving ['seɪvɪŋ] 1 N a (= rescue) sauvetage m → **face, life**
b (Rel) [of sinner] salut m
c [of time, money] économie f; (Banking) épargne f; **we must make ~s** il faut économiser or faire des économies; **this means a great ~ of time/petrol** etc cela représente une grande économie de temps/d'essence etc; **a ~ of £12** une économie de 12 livres; **a considerable ~ in time and money** une économie considérable de temps et d'argent; **the government is trying to encourage ~** le gouvernement cherche à encourager l'épargne
d (Comput) sauvegarde f
2 **savings** NPL économies fpl; **small ~s** la petite épargne; **to live on one's ~s** vivre de ses économies → **national, post office**
3 PREP† sauf; ~ **your presence** sauf votre respect
4 COMP ► **saving clause** N (Jur) clause f de sauvegarde ► **saving grace** N **the film's/ John's only ~ grace is ...** la seule chose qui rachète or sauve le film/John est ... ► **savings account** N (Brit) compte m d'épargne; (US) compte m de dépôt ► **savings and loan association** N (US) ≈ société f de crédit immobilier ► **savings bank** N caisse f d'épargne ► **savings stamp** N timbre-épargne m

saviour, **savior** (US) ['seɪvjə'] N sauveur m; (Rel) **the Saviour** le Sauveur

savoir-faire ['sævwɑː'feə'] N savoir-vivre m inv

savor etc ['seɪvə'] (US) = **savour**

savory ['seɪvərɪ] 1 N a (= herb) sarriette f
b (US) = **savoury 2** 2 ADJ (US) = **savoury 1**

savour, **savor** (US) ['seɪvə'] 1 N (= flavour: lit, fig) saveur f 2 VT [+ food, drink] savourer, déguster; [+ triumph] savourer; **to ~ every moment** savourer chaque instant or chaque moment; **to ~ the delights of ...** goûter aux plaisirs de ...; **he was ~ing the excitement of the competition** il était pris par la fièvre de la compétition 3 VI a (lit, liter) **to ~ of sth** sentir qch; (fig) **to ~ of fascism/heresy** sentir le fascisme/l'hérésie, avoir des relents de fascisme/d'hérésie; **she hated anything that ~ed of the supernatural** elle détestait tout ce qui avait trait au surnaturel

savouriness, **savoriness** (US) ['seɪvərɪnɪs] N saveur f, succulence f

savourless, **savorless** (US) ['seɪvəlɪs] ADJ sans saveur, sans goût, insipide, fade

savoury, **savory** (US) ['seɪvərɪ] 1 ADJ a (Brit = not sweet) [food, dish] salé (par opposition à sucré); **a ~ pie** une tourte b (= appetizing) [smell] appétissant; [taste] savoureux c (= respectable) **not a very ~ subject** un sujet peu appétissant or peu ragoûtant; **some not very ~ episodes in her past** des épisodes pas très reluisants de son passé; **the main square is none too ~ at night** la place principale est assez mal fréquentée la nuit; **one of the book's less ~ characters** l'un des personnages les moins recommandables du roman 2 N (Culin) mets m non sucré; (on toast) canapé m chaud

Savoy [sə'vɔɪ] 1 N la Savoie 2 ADJ savoyard; (Brit) ~ **cabbage** chou m frisé de Milan

Savoyard [sə'vɔɪɑːd] 1 N Savoyard(e) m(f) 2 ADJ savoyard

savvy ['sævɪ] 1 N* jugeote* f, bon sens m 2 VI a (= know) **no ~**‡ sais pas, moi* b (‡ = understand) piger‡, comprendre; **I can take care of myself, ~?** je me débrouille tout seul, tu piges?‡ 3 ADJ‡ calé*, futé

saw¹ [sɔː] (vb: pret **sawed**, ptp **sawed** or **sawn**) 1 N scie f; ~ **circular** 2 VT scier, débiter à la scie; (US fig) **to ~ wood**‡ (= sleep) roupiller*; (= snore) ronfler → **sawn** 3 VI **to ~ through a plank/the bars of a cell** scier une planche/les barreaux d'une cellule 4 COMP ► **saw edge** N lame f dentée ► **saw-edged knife** N (pl **saw-edged knives**) couteau-scie m
► **saw away*** VI (pej) **to ~ away at the violin** racler du violon
► **saw off** 1 VT SEP enlever à la scie 2 ~**ed-off** ADJ ► **sawed** 3 ~**n-off** ADJ → **sawn**
► **saw up** VT SEP débiter à la scie

saw² [sɔː] N (= saying) dicton m

saw³ [sɔː] VB pt of **see¹**

sawbones†* ['sɔːbəʊnz] N (pej) chirurgien m, charcutier‡ m (pej)

sawbuck ['sɔːbʌk] N (US) (= sawhorse) chevalet m de scieur de bois; ‡ (= ten-dollar bill) billet m de dix dollars

sawdust ['sɔːdʌst] N (NonC) sciure f (de bois)

sawed [sɔːd] 1 VB pt, ptp of **saw¹** 2 COMP ► **sawed-off*** ADJ (US pej = short) court sur pattes*, petit; ~**-off shotgun** carabine f à canon scié

sawfish ['sɔːfɪʃ] N (pl **sawfish** or **sawfishes**) poisson-scie m

sawhorse ['sɔːhɔːs] N chevalet m de scieur de bois

sawmill ['sɔːmɪl] N scierie f

sawn [sɔːn] 1 VB ptp of **saw¹** 2 ADJ scié; ~ **timber** bois m de sciage 3 COMP ► **sawn-off shotgun** N (Brit) carabine f à canon scié

sawyer ['sɔːjə'] N scieur m

sax* [sæks] N (ABBR = **saxophone**) saxo* m

saxhorn ['sækshɔːn] N saxhorn m

saxifrage ['sæksɪfrɪdʒ] N saxifrage f

Saxon ['sæksn] 1 ADJ saxon 2 N a (= person) Saxon(ne) m(f) b (Ling) saxon m

Saxony ['sæksənɪ] N la Saxe

saxophone ['sæksəfəʊn] N saxophone m

saxophonist [ˌsæk'sɒfənɪst] N saxophoniste mf, saxo* m

▼ **say** [seɪ] (pret, ptp **said**) 1 VT a (= speak, utter, pronounce) dire (**sth to sb** qch à qn; **about** au sujet de, à propos de); [+ lesson, poem] réciter; [+ prayer] faire, dire; (Rel) **to ~ mass** dire la messe; **I should like to ask Mr Buchanan to ~ a few words** je demande maintenant à M. Buchanan de dire quelques mots, je passe la parole à M. Buchanan qui va nous dire quelques mots; **as I said yesterday** comme je l'ai dit hier; **as I said in my letter/on the phone** comme je vous l'ai (or le lui ai etc) dit dans ma lettre/au téléphone; **well said!** bien dit!; **to ~ yes/no to an invitation** accepter/ refuser une invitation; **your father said no** ton père a dit (que) non; **I invited him but he said no** je l'ai invité (à venir) mais il a refusé; **something was said about it** on en a parlé, il en a été question; **all of that can be said in two sentences** tout cela tient en deux phrases; **~ after me ...** répétez après moi ...; **could you ~ that again?** pourriez-vous répéter (ce que vous venez de dire)?; **so ~ing, he sat down** sur ces mots or sur ce, il s'assit; **she hasn't much to ~ for herself** elle n'a jamais grand-chose à dire; **he always has a lot to ~ for himself** il parle toujours beaucoup, il a toujours quelque chose à dire; **what have you (got) to ~ for yourself?** qu'est-ce que tu as comme excuse?; **to ~ one's piece** dire ce qu'on a à dire; **just ~ the word and I'll go** vous n'avez qu'un mot à dire pour que je parte; **it's easier or sooner said than done!** c'est plus facile à dire qu'à faire!, facile à dire!; **when all is said and done** tout compte fait, au bout du compte; **interesting, not to ~ encouraging** intéressant, pour ne pas dire encourageant; **to ~ nothing of ...** sans parler de ...; (hum) **though ~ it myself** ◊ **though I ~ it as shouldn't ...** ce n'est pas à moi de dire ça mais ... → least, less

[b] (direct speech) **"yes" she said** « oui » dit-elle; **"10 o'clock" he said to himself** « 10 heures » se dit-il

[c] (= state) dire; **it ~s in the rules (that)** ◊ **the rules ~ (that)** il est dit dans le règlement (que); **it ~s on the radio there's going to be snow** la radio annonce de la neige; **it is said that ...** on dit que ...; **he is said to be seriously ill** on dit qu'il est gravement malade

[d] (= claim) dire, prétendre; **he got home at 6 so he ~s** il est rentré à 6 heures à ce qu'il dit or prétend; (expressing doubt) **that's what you ~!** ◊ **so you ~!** c'est ce que vous dites!, c'est vous qui le dites!

[e] (giving instructions) dire; **he said to wait here** il a dit d'attendre ici; **he said I was to give you this** il m'a dit de vous donner ceci

[f] (expressing opinions, estimating) dire; **what will people ~?** qu'est-ce que les gens vont dire?; **he doesn't care what people ~** il se moque du qu'en-dira-t-on; **you might as well ~ the earth is flat!** autant dire que la terre est plate!; **I ~ he should do it** je suis d'avis qu'il le fasse; **I can't ~ I'm fond of anchovies** je ne peux pas dire que j'aime (subj) les anchois; **to see him you would ~ he was drunk** à le voir on dirait qu'il est ivre; **what would you ~ is the population of Paris?** à votre avis or d'après vous, combien y a-t-il d'habitants à Paris?; **I would ~ she's intelligent** je dirais qu'elle est intelligente; **I would ~ she was 50** je dirais qu'elle a 50 ans, je lui donnerais 50 ans; **would you really ~ so?** (le pensez-vous) vraiment?; **he hadn't a good word to ~ for or about her** il n'a rien trouvé à dire en sa faveur; **I'll ~ this or I'll ~ one thing for him, he's clever** je dirai ceci en sa faveur, il est intelligent; **~ what you like or will (about him), he's not a bad guy*** tu peux dire ce que tu veux (de lui), ce n'est pas un mauvais bougre*; **that's ~ing a lot*** ce n'est pas peu dire; **he's cleverer than his brother but that isn't ~ing much or a lot*** il est plus intelligent que son frère, mais ça ne veut rien dire; **there's something to be said for it** cela a du bon or des avantages; **there's something to be said for being obstinate** cela peut avoir du bon or des avantages d'être têtu; **he stuck to what he believes in and there's something to be said for that** il est resté fidèle à ses convictions et on ne peut pas lui en vouloir; **there's something to be said for waiting** il y aurait peut-être intérêt à attendre, on ferait peut-être mieux d'attendre

[g] (= be telling, indicative) **that doesn't ~ much for him** ce n'est pas à son honneur; **that doesn't ~ much for his intelligence** cela en dit long (iro) sur son intelligence; **it ~s much or a lot for his courage that he stayed** le fait qu'il

soit resté en dit long sur son courage; **his clothes ~ a lot about him** ses vêtements en disent long sur lui or sa personnalité

[h] (= imagine) imaginer; **~ someone left you a fortune, what would you do with it?** imaginons que vous héritiez d'une fortune, qu'en feriez-vous?; (let us) **~ for argument's sake that ...** mettons à titre d'exemple que ... → 1f; **there's no ~ing what he'll do next** (il est) impossible de dire or on ne peut pas savoir ce qu'il va faire ensuite

[i] (= admit) dire, reconnaître; **I must ~ (that) she's very pretty** je dois dire or reconnaître qu'elle est très jolie

[j] (proposals) **shall we ~ £5/Tuesday?** disons or mettons 5 livres/mardi?; **what do you ~ to a cup of tea? — I wouldn't or won't ~ no*** que diriez-vous d'une tasse de thé? — j'en boirais bien une or ce ne serait pas de refus* or je ne dirais pas non; **what would you ~ to a round of golf?** si on faisait une partie de golf?

[k] (= register) [dial, gauge etc] marquer, indiquer; **my watch ~s 10 o'clock** ma montre marque or indique 10 heures; **the thermometer ~s 30°** le thermomètre marque or indique 30°

[l] (emphatic) **you('ve) said it!*** tu l'as dit!*; **you can ~ that again!*** c'est le cas de le dire!; **don't ~ it's broken!*** ne me dis pas que c'est cassé!; **enough said!*** ◊ **'nuff said!*** (ça) suffit!, assez parlé!; **~ no more** (= I understand) ça va, j'ai compris; **let's ~ no more about it!** n'en parlons plus!; **it goes without ~ing that ...** il va sans dire que ..., il va de soi que ...; **is he right? — I should ~ he is** or **I should ~ so** (expressing certainty) est-ce qu'il a raison? — et comment or pour avoir raison il a raison!; (expressing doubt) est-ce qu'il a raison? — il me semble or je pense que oui; **didn't I ~ so?** je l'avais bien dit, n'est-ce pas?; **and so ~ all of us!*** nous sommes tous d'accord là-dessus; **I should ~ he is right!** il a bien raison, c'est moi qui vous le dis! → goodbye, nothing, thank

2 VI dire; **so to ~** pour ainsi dire; **that is to ~** c'est-à-dire; **it is (as) one** or **you might ~ a new method** c'est comme qui dirait* une nouvelle méthode; (I) **~!** dites donc!; (iro) **you don't ~!*** sans blague!* (iro), pas possible! (iro); (US) **~*, what time is it?** dites, quelle heure est-il?; **if there were, ~, 500 people** s'il y avait, mettons or disons, 500 personnes; (iro) **~s you!*** que tu dis!*; **~s who?*** ah oui? (iro); **as they ~** comme on dit, comme dirait l'autre*; **it seems rather rude, I must ~** cela ne me paraît guère poli, je dois dire; (expressing indignation) **well, I must ~!** ça alors!*; **it's not for me to ~** (= not my responsibility) ce n'est pas à moi de décider or de juger; (= not my place) ce n'est pas à moi de le dire

3 N **to have a** or one's **~** (= say one's piece) dire ce qu'on a à dire; **to have a ~/no ~ in the matter** avoir/ne pas avoir voix au chapitre, avoir/ne pas avoir son mot à dire; **let him have his ~!** laissez-le s'exprimer!; **I will have my ~!** je dirai ce que j'ai à dire!; **to have a ~ in selecting ...** avoir son mot à dire dans la sélection de ...; **to have the final ~** être celui qui décide or qui prend les décisions; **to have a strong ~ in sth** jouer un rôle déterminant dans qch

4 COMP ► **say-so*** N **on your ~-so** parce que vous le dites (or l'aviez dit etc); **on his ~-so** parce qu'il le dit (or l'a dit etc), sur ses dires; **it's his ~-so** c'est lui qui décide, c'est à lui de dire

SAYE [,eseɪwaɪ'i:] (Brit) (ABBR = **Save As You Earn**) → save

saying ['seɪɪŋ] N dicton m; **as the ~ goes** comme dit le proverbe, comme on dit; **~s of the week** les mots mpl or les citations fpl de la semaine

SBU [,esbi:'ju:] N (ABBR = **strategic business unit**) → strategic

---

SC ABBR = **South Carolina**

s/c (ABBR = **self-contained**) → self

scab [skæb] 1 N [a] [of wound] croûte f, escarre f [b] (* pej = strikebreaker) jaune m (pej), briseur m de grève 2 VI [a] (also ~ **over**) se cicatriser, former une croûte [b] (* pej = strikebreaker) refuser de faire grève, faire le jaune

scabbard ['skæbəd] N [of dagger] gaine f; [of sword] fourreau m

scabby ['skæbɪ] ADJ [a] (= covered with scabs) [knees, hands, skin] couvert de croûtes [b] (= having scabies) [person, animal] galeux, scabieux (Med) [c] (Brit* = despicable) [person] minable*; [behaviour] dégueulasse*

scabies ['skeɪbi:z] N (NonC: Med) gale f

scabious[1] ['skeɪbɪəs] ADJ (Med) scabieux

scabious[2] ['skeɪbɪəs] N (Bot) scabieuse f

scabrous ['skeɪbrəs] ADJ [a] [question, topic] scabreux, risqué [b] (Bot, Zool) rugueux

scads* [skædz] NPL ~ **of** beaucoup de, plein* de

scaffold ['skæfəld] N [a] (= gallows) échafaud m [b] (Constr) échafaudage m

scaffolding ['skæfəldɪŋ] N (NonC) [a] (= structure) échafaudage m; (= material) matériel m pour échafaudages

scag* [skæg] N (Drugs) héro* f

scalawag* ['skæləwæg] N (US) = scallywag

scald [skɔ:ld] 1 VT [+ jar, teapot, tomatoes] échauder, ébouillanter; (= sterilize) stériliser; **to ~ one's hand** s'ébouillanter la main; **to ~ o.s.** s'ébouillanter; (Culin) **to ~ the milk** chauffer le lait sans le faire bouillir; (Brit) **to run off** or **set off like a ~ed cat** filer comme un zèbre, prendre ses jambes à son cou 2 N brûlure f (causée par un liquide bouillant)

scalding ['skɔ:ldɪŋ] 1 ADJ [a] (= hot) [water, steam, coffee, sun, tears] brûlant; [heat] torride; **a bath of ~ water** un bain brûlant; **I have a ~ pain when urinating** j'ai une sensation de brûlure quand j'urine [b] (= severe) [criticism] virulent 2 ADV ~ **hot** [water, coffee, sun] brûlant; [weather] terriblement chaud; **it's ~ hot today** il fait terriblement chaud aujourd'hui, il fait une chaleur torride aujourd'hui

scale[1] [skeɪl] 1 N [a] [of thermometer, ruler] graduation f, échelle f (graduée); [of numbers] série f; [of wages] barème m, échelle f; ~ **of charges** liste f des tarifs; **social** ~ échelle f sociale → **centigrade, Fahrenheit, sliding**
[b] [of map, drawing] échelle f; (**drawn** or **true**) **to** ~ à l'échelle; **drawn to a** ~ **of ...** rapporté à l'échelle de ...; **on a** ~ **of 1cm to 5km** à une échelle de 1 cm pour 5 km; **this map is not to** ~ les distances ne sont pas respectées sur cette carte
[c] (fig) (= scope) échelle f; (= size etc) importance f; **on a large** ~ sur une grande échelle, en grand; **on a small** ~ sur une petite échelle, en petit; **on a national** ~ à l'échelle nationale, à l'échelon national; **a disaster of** or **on this** ~ une catastrophe de cette importance; **the ~ and intensity of the fighting** l'ampleur f et l'intensité f des combats; **grand in** ~ [plans, programme] à grande échelle, de grande envergure
[d] (Mus) gamme f; **the ~ of C** la gamme de do; **to practise one's ~s** faire ses gammes

2 VT [a] (= climb) [+ wall, mountain] escalader [b] [+ map] dessiner à l'échelle

3 COMP ► **scale drawing** N dessin m à l'échelle ► **scale model** N modèle m réduit → **full-scale**

► **scale back** VT SEP (US) = scale down

► **scale down** VT SEP (gen) réduire; [+ salary] (Scol) [+ marks] réduire proportionnellement; [+ drawing] réduire l'échelle de; [+ production] réduire, baisser

► **scale up** VT SEP augmenter proportionnellement

scale² [skeɪl] [1] N → **scales** [2] VTI peser
[3] COMP ► **scale maker** N fabricant *m* de
balances ► **scale pan** N plateau *m* de balance

scale³ [skeɪl] [1] N [a] [*of fish, reptile, rust*]
écaille *f*; [*of skin*] squame *f*; **metal ~** écaille *f*
métallique; (*fig*) **the ~s fell from his eyes** les
écailles lui sont tombées des yeux [b] (*NonC*)
(*of water pipes, kettle*) tartre *m*, dépôt *m* calcaire; (*of teeth*) tartre *m* [2] VT [a] [+ *fish*] écailler
[b] [+ *teeth, kettle*] détartrer
► **scale off** VI s'en aller en écailles, s'écailler

scales [skeɪlz] NPL (*for weighing*) (*gen: in kitchen,
shop*) balance *f*; (*in bathroom*) pèse-personne
m inv, balance *f*; (*for babies*) pèse-bébé *m inv*;
(*for luggage, heavy goods*) bascule *f*; (*for letters*)
pèse-lettre *m inv*; (*manual, with weight on a
rod*) balance *f* romaine; **kitchen or household
~** balance *f* de ménage; **pair of ~** balance *f* (à
plateaux); (*Astrol, Astron*) **the Scales** la Balance; **to turn the ~ at 80 kilos** peser 80 kilos;
(*fig*) **to tip the ~ (in sb's favour/against sb)** faire
pencher la balance (en faveur/défaveur de
qn) → **platform**

scallion [skælɪən] N (*gen*) oignon *m*; (*US =
shallot*) échalote *f*; (*US = leek*) poireau *m*

scallop [skɒləp] [1] N [a] coquille *f* Saint-
Jacques, pétoncle *m* [b] (*Sewing*) **~s** festons
mpl [2] VT [a] **~ed fish/lobster** coquille *f* de
poisson/de homard [b] [+ *hem etc*] festonner;
(*Sewing*) **~ed edge** bordure *f* festonnée or à
festons; (*Culin*) **to ~ (the edges of) a pie**
canneler le bord d'une tourte [3] COMP
► **scallop shell** N coquille *f*

scallywag [skælɪwæg] N [a] (= *rascal*) petit(e)
polisson(ne) *m(f)* [b] (*US Hist pej*) Sudiste républicain favorable à l'émancipation des Noirs et
considéré comme traître par les autres Sudistes

scalp [skælp] [1] N [a] cuir *m* chevelu; (= *trophy*)
scalp *m* [2] VT [a] [+ *person*] scalper [b] (*US**) [+
tickets] revendre (*au marché noir*) [3] VI (*St Ex**)
boursicoter

scalpel [skælpəl] N (*Med*) scalpel *m*; (*for paper
etc*) cutter *m*

scalper* [skælpər] N [a] (*St Ex*) spéculateur *m*
sur la journée [b] (= *ticket tout*) vendeur *m*,
-euse *f* de billets à la sauvette

scaly [skeɪlɪ] ADJ [a] (= *covered in scales*) [*creature, body*] écailleux, couvert d'écailles
[b] (= *peeling*) [*skin*] qui pèle, qui se desquame
(*Med*), squameux (*Med*); [*paint*] écaillé, qui
s'écaille [c] (= *having limescale deposits*) [*kettle,
pipe*] entartré

scam* [skæm] [1] N arnaque* *f*, escroquerie *f*
[2] VI faire de la gratte* *or* des bénefs*

scamp¹* [skæmp] N (= *child*) polisson(ne) *m(f)*,
galopin* *m*; (= *adult*) coquin(e) *m(f)*

scamp² [skæmp] VT [+ *one's work etc*] bâcler*

scamper [skæmpər] [1] N galopade *f*; [*of mice*]
trottinement *m* [2] VI [*children*] galoper; [*mice*]
trottiner; **to ~ in/out** etc [*children*] entrer/sortir
etc en gambadant
► **scamper about** VI [*children*] gambader;
[*mice*] trottiner çà et là
► **scamper away, scamper off** VI [*children,
mice*] s'enfuir, détaler*

scampi [skæmpɪ] NPL langoustines *fpl* (frites),
scampi *mpl*

scan [skæn] [1] VT [a] (= *examine closely*) [+ *horizon, sb's face*] scruter; [+ *crowd*] fouiller du regard; [+ *newspaper*] lire attentivement (**for sth**
pour y trouver qch) [b] (= *glance quickly over*)
[+ *horizon*] promener son regard sur; [+
crowd] parcourir des yeux; [+ *newspaper*]
parcourir rapidement, feuilleter [c] (*Comput*)
scruter [d] (*TV, Radar*) balayer; (*Med*) [*machine*] balayer; [*person*] faire une scanographie
de [e] (*Poetry*) scander [2] VI se scander; **this
line does not ~** ce vers est faux [3] N [a] (*Rad,
TV*) balayage *m* [b] (*Med*) (= *scanning*) scanographie *f*, tomodensitométrie *f*; (= *picture*)
scanographie *f*, scanner* *m*; (*Med*) (**ultra-**

sound) **~** échographie *f*; **to have a ~** passer un
scanner*, passer une échographie

scandal [skændl] [1] N [a] (= *disgrace*) scandale *m*; (*Jur*) diffamation *f*; **we can't afford another ~** nous ne pouvons pas nous permettre
d'être impliqués dans un nouveau scandale;
to cause a ~ causer un scandale; **the Webb ~**
le scandale Webb; **a financial ~** un scandale
financier; **it's a (real) ~** c'est scandaleux, c'est
une honte; **it's a ~ that ...** c'est un scandale *or*
une honte que ... ; (= *gossip*) **~** cancans *mpl*, ragots* *mpl*; **there's a lot of ~
going around about him** il y a beaucoup de ragots* qui circulent sur son compte [2] COMP
► **scandal sheet*** N (*pej*) journal *m* à
scandale

scandalize [skændəlaɪz] VT scandaliser, indigner; **to be ~d by sth** se scandaliser de qch,
s'indigner de qch; **she was quite ~d** elle était
vraiment scandalisée *or* indignée

scandalmonger [skændl,mʌŋgər] N mauvaise langue *f*, colporteur *m*, -euse *f* de ragots*;
(*US Press*) torchon* *m*

scandalous [skændələs] ADJ scandaleux; **it's
~ that ...** c'est un scandale *or* une honte que
... (+ *subj*), c'est scandaleux que ... (+ *subj*); **I
think it's a ~ price to charge (for)** je trouve
scandaleux qu'on demande ce prix-là (pour)

scandalously [skændələslɪ] ADV [*behave*] de
façon scandaleuse; [*expensive, rich, poor*]
scandaleusement

Scandinavia [ˌskændɪneɪvɪə] N la Scandinavie

Scandinavian [ˌskændɪneɪvɪən] [1] ADJ
scandinave [2] N Scandinave *mf*

scandium [skændɪəm] N scandium *m*

scanner [skænər] N [a] (*Med*) (also **CAT ~**)
scanner *m*, tomodensitomètre *m*; (*also* **ultrasound ~**) échographe *m* [b] (*Rad, Telec*)
scanner *m* [c] (*Radar*) antenne *f* [d] (*Comput*:
also **optical ~**) scanner *or* scanneur *m*

scanning [skænɪŋ] [1] N (*electronic*) balayage
m; (*Med: by ultrasound*) échographie *f*
[2] COMP ► **scanning device** N (*Telec*) organe *m* explorateur; (*Med*) dispositif *m* de scanographie ► **scanning electron microscope** N microscope *m* électronique à balayage

scansion [skænʃən] N scansion *f*

scant [skænt] ADJ (= *insufficient*) [*reward*]
(bien) maigre; [*information*] (bien *or* très)
insuffisant; **to pay ~ attention to sth** ne guère
prêter attention à qch; **there is ~ evidence of
the success they talk about** il n'y a guère de
preuves du succès dont ils parlent; **to receive
~ praise (from sb) (for sth)** recevoir des éloges
parcimonieux (de qn) (pour qch); **to have ~
regard for sth** peu se soucier de qch; **to show
~ respect for sth** ne pas manifester beaucoup
de respect pour qch [b] (= *bare*) **it measures a
~ 2cm** ça fait à peine 2 cm; **a ~ two months
later** à peine deux mois plus tard

scantily [skæntɪlɪ] ADV [*furnished*] chichement; **~ clad** *or* **dressed** en tenue légère; **~
clad in a light cotton blouse** légèrement vêtu
d'un fin chemisier de coton; **a ~ cut blouse**
un chemisier très échancré

scantiness [skæntɪnɪs] N (= *insufficiency*)
insuffisance *f*

scanty [skæntɪ] ADJ [*information*] maigre,
sommaire; [*evidence*] maigre; [*news*] sommaire; [*knowledge*] limité, sommaire; [*swimsuit*]
minuscule; [*blouse*] échancré; **a ~ income** de
maigres revenus

scapegoat [skeɪpgəʊt] [1] N bouc *m* émissaire [2] VT **to ~ sb** faire de qn un bouc émissaire

scapegrace [skeɪpgreɪs] N coquin(e) *m(f)*,
vaurien(ne) *m(f)*

scapula [skæpjʊlə] N (*pl* **scapulas** *or* **scapulae**
[skæpjʊliː]) omoplate *f*

scapular [skæpjʊlər] ADJ, N scapulaire *m*

scar¹ [skɑːr] [1] N (= *mark: lit, fig*) cicatrice *f*;
(*from knife wound, esp on face*) balafre *f*; **the
quarrying left a ~ on the hillside** l'exploitation
de la carrière a laissé une cicatrice sur *or* a
mutilé le flanc de la colline; **emotional ~s** cicatrices *fpl* psychologiques; **the ~s of war** les
cicatrices *fpl* de la guerre; **it left a deep ~ on
his mind** il en est resté profondément marqué
[2] VT marquer d'une cicatrice; (*with knife*) balafrer; **he was ~red with many wounds** il
portait les cicatrices de nombreuses blessures; **face ~red by smallpox** visage grêlé par la
petite vérole; **war-~red town** ville qui porte
des cicatrices de la guerre; **walls ~red by bullets** des murs portant des traces de balles;
(*fig*) **this is something that's going to ~ him
forever** c'est quelque chose qui va le marquer
profondément; **she was ~red by the death of
her parents** elle avait été profondément
marquée par la mort de ses parents
[3] COMP ► **scar tissue** N (*Med*) tissus *mpl* cicatrisés

scar² [skɑːr] N (= *crag*) rocher *m* escarpé

scarab [skærəb] N (= *beetle, gem*) scarabée *m*

scarce [skeəs] [1] ADJ [*food, water, money*] peu
abondant, rare; [*people, jobs*] rare, peu nombreux; [*goods*] rare; [*resources*] limité; **to become** *or* **get ~** commencer à manquer, se faire
rare; **to make o.s. ~*** (= *leave*) s'éclipser*
[2] ADV† = **scarcely**

scarcely [skeəslɪ] ADV [a] (= *barely*) à peine,
guère; **they could ~ have imagined that ...** ils
auraient à peine pu imaginer que ..., ils n'auraient guère pu imaginer que ...; **the landscape has ~ altered** le paysage n'a guère
changé *or* n'a presque pas changé; **I could ~
believe it** je pouvais à peine le croire; **I ~
know what to say** je ne sais trop que dire;
they were ~ ever apart ils étaient presque toujours ensemble; **he was ~ more than a boy** il
sortait à peine *or* tout juste de l'enfance; **it is
~ surprising that ...** il n'est guère surprenant
que ...; **with ~ a sound** pratiquement *or*
presque sans faire de bruit; **there was ~ a ripple on the sea** il n'y avait pratiquement
aucune ride sur la mer; **there was ~ a building left undamaged** il ne restait pratiquement
aucun bâtiment intact; **it could ~ have been
a less promising start** ça aurait difficilement
pu commencer plus mal; **the press is ~ an advertisement for self-restraint** on ne peut guère
dire que la presse soit un modèle de retenue
[b] (*no sooner*) à peine, tout juste; **~ had the
car stopped when the police surrounded it** à
peine la voiture s'était-elle arrêtée que les policiers l'encerclèrent

scarceness [skeəsnɪs] N = **scarcity**

scarcity [skeəsɪtɪ] [1] N [*of product, foodstuff
etc*] rareté *f*, pénurie *f*; [*of money*] manque *m*;
there is a ~ of good artists today il n'y a plus
guère de bons artistes [2] COMP ► **scarcity
value** N valeur *f* de rareté

scare [skeər] [1] N [a] (* = *fright*) **to give sb a ~**
effrayer qn, faire peur à qn, donner la frousse
à qn*; **what a ~ he gave me!** il m'a fait une de
ces peurs *or* frousses!* [b] (*rumour etc*) bruit
m alarmant *or* alarmiste; **to raise a ~** semer la
panique, faire courir des bruits alarmants;
the invasion les bruits *mpl* alarmistes d'invasion; **bomb/gas/typhoid** etc ~ alerte *f* à la
bombe/au gaz/à la typhoïde etc; **because of
the war ~** à cause des rumeurs de guerre;
there have been several war ~s this year à plusieurs reprises cette année les gens ont craint
la guerre [2] VT effrayer, faire peur à; **to ~ sb
stiff** *or* **out of their wits*** faire une peur bleue
à qn, ficher la frousse* *or* la trouille* à qn; **to
~ the life** *or* **wits out of sb*** faire une peur
bleue à qn, ficher la frousse* *or* la trouille* à
qn → **scared**; → **hell, shit** [3] COMP [*headlines,
tactics*] alarmiste ► **scare story** N rumeur *f*
alarmiste
► **scare away, scare off** VT SEP **the dog ~d him**

away la peur du chien l'a fait fuir, il a fui par peur du chien ; *(fig)* **the price ~d him away** le prix lui a fait peur
► **scare up*** VT SEP *(US)* [+ *food, money*] arriver à trouver

scarecrow ['skɛəkrəʊ] N *(lit, fig)* épouvantail *m*

scared [skɛəd] ADJ effrayé ; **he was terribly ~** il était terrifié or épouvanté ; **to be running ~*** avoir la frousse* ; **to be ~ (of sb/sth)** avoir peur (de qn/qch) ; **to be ~ of doing sth** or **to do sth** avoir peur de faire qch ; **too ~ to move** trop effrayé pour bouger ; **to be ~ that ...** avoir peur que ... (+ *subj*) ; **I'm ~ that he'll try to find me** j'ai peur qu'il n'essaie *(subj)* de me trouver ; **to be ~ stiff*** avoir une peur bleue, avoir une de ces frousses* or trouilles* ; **to be ~ to death*** être mort de frousse* or trouille* ; **he's ~ to death of women*** il a une peur bleue des femmes ; **to be ~ out of one's wits*** avoir une peur bleue ; **to be ~ shitless*‡** chier dans son froc*‡ ; **I'm ~ shitless of flying*‡** ça me fout la pétoche de prendre l'avion‡

scaredy* ['skɛədɪ] N *(baby talk)* **~ (cat)** trouillard(e)* *m(f)*, poule *f* mouillée*

scarehead* ['skɛəhed] N *(US Press)* manchette *f* à sensation

scaremonger ['skɛə,mʌŋgəʳ] N alarmiste *mf*, oiseau *m* de malheur

scaremongering ['skɛə,mʌŋgərɪŋ] N alarmisme *m*

scarf¹ [skɑːf] **1** N *(pl* **scarfs** or **scarves)** écharpe *f* ; *(square)* foulard *m* **2** COMP ► **scarf-ring** N coulant *m* or anneau *m* pour foulard → **headscarf**

scarf²‡ [skɑːf] VT *(US: also* **~ down)** engloutir, s'enfiler‡

Scarface ['skɑːfeɪs] N le Balafré

scarify ['skɛərɪfaɪ] VT *(Agr, Med)* scarifier ; *(fig)* éreinter

scarlatina [,skɑːlə'tiːnə] N scarlatine *f*

scarlet ['skɑːlɪt] **1** ADJ écarlate ; **to go** or **blush ~ (with shame/embarrassment)** devenir écarlate or cramoisi (de honte/de gêne) **2** N écarlate *f* **3** COMP ► **scarlet fever** N scarlatine *f* ► **scarlet pimpernel** N mouron *m* ► **scarlet runner (bean)** N haricot *m* grimpant ► **scarlet woman†** N *(pl* **scarlet women)** *(pej)* femme *f* de mauvaise vie

scarp [skɑːp] N escarpement *m*

scarper‡ ['skɑːpəʳ] VI *(Brit)* ficher le camp*

scarves [skɑːvz] NPL of **scarf**

scary* ['skɛərɪ] ADJ [*person, monster*] effrayant ; [*moment, feeling*] effrayant, angoissant ; [*experience*] effrayant, angoissant, qui fiche la frousse* ; [*movie*] qui donne le frisson or la chair de poule ; **that's a ~ thought** c'est une idée qui fait peur

scat¹‡ [skæt] EXCL allez ouste !*

scat² [skæt] N *(Jazz)* scat *m* *(style d'improvisation vocale)*

scathing ['skeɪðɪŋ] ADJ [*person, remark, criticism*] cinglant **(about** au sujet de) ; **to give sb a ~ look** jeter un regard plein de mépris à qn

scathingly ['skeɪðɪŋlɪ] ADV [*say*] sur un ton cinglant ; [*write*] sur un ton cinglant, en termes cinglants ; **to look ~ at sb** jeter un regard plein de mépris à qn

scatological [,skætə'lɒdʒɪkəl] ADJ scatologique

scatter ['skætəʳ] **1** VT **a** *(also* **~ about, ~ around)** [+ *crumbs, papers, seeds*] éparpiller ; [+ *sand, salt, sawdust, nails*] répandre ; *(fig)* **to ~ sth to the four winds** semer qch aux quatre vents ; **to ~ cushions on a divan** jeter des coussins çà et là sur un divan **b** [+ *clouds, crowd*] disperser ; [+ *enemy*] mettre en déroute ; [+ *light*] diffuser ; **my relatives are ~ed all over the country** ma famille est dispersée aux quatre coins du pays **2** VI [*clouds, crowd*] se disperser ; **the robbers ~ed at the approach of the police** les voleurs

se sont dispersés or enfuis dans toutes les directions à l'arrivée de la police
3 N *(Math, Tech)* dispersion *f* ; **a ~ of houses** des maisons dispersées or éparses ; **a ~ of raindrops** quelques gouttes de pluie éparses
4 COMP ► **scatter cushions** NPL petits coussins *mpl* ► **scatter-gun** N fusil *m* de chasse ♦ ADJ *(fig)* [*approach*] tous azimuts* ► **scatter rugs** NPL carpettes *fpl*

scatterbrain ['skætəbreɪn] N écervelé(e) *m(f)*, hurluberlu* *m*

scatterbrained ['skætəbreɪnd] ADJ écervelé, hurluberlu*

scattered ['skætəd] **1** ADJ **a** *(= dispersed)* [*books*] éparpillé ; [*buildings*] dispersé, éparpillé, épars ; [*trees*] dispersé, éparpillé ; [*population*] dispersé, disséminé ; [*light*] diffus ; [*riots*] sporadique, intermittent ; **~ fighting** combats *mpl* sporadiques or intermittents ; **the village is very ~** les maisons du village sont très dispersées **b** **~ with sth** *(= strewn with: gen)* parsemé de qch ; [+ *nails, flowers, corpses*] jonché de qch **2** COMP ► **scattered showers** NPL *(Met)* averses *fpl* intermittentes or éparses

scattering ['skætərɪŋ] N [*of clouds, crowd*] dispersion *f* ; [*of light*] diffusion *f* ; **there was a ~ of people in the hall** il y avait quelques personnes dispersées or çà et là dans la salle

scattershot ['skætəʃɒt] ADJ **the money has been spent in (a) ~ fashion** l'argent a été dépensé à tort et à travers ; **he fielded the committee's ~ questions** il a répondu aux questions du comité, qui partaient dans tous les sens

scattiness* ['skætɪnɪs] N *(NonC: Brit)* [*of person*] étourderie *f*

scatty* ['skætɪ] ADJ *(Brit)* **a** *(= scatterbrained)* [*person*] étourdi ; **she's so ~!** quelle tête de linotte ! **b** *(= distracted)* **to drive sb ~** rendre qn zinzin* *inv*

scavenge ['skævɪndʒ] **1** VT [+ *streets*] enlever les ordures de ; [+ *object*] récupérer **2** VI **to ~ in the dustbins (for sth)** faire les poubelles (pour trouver qch)

scavenger ['skævɪndʒəʳ] **1** N **a** *(Zool)* charognard *m* **b** *(= street cleaner)* éboueur *m* **c** *(= person: on rubbish dumps, in bins etc)* pilleur *m* de poubelles **2** COMP ► **scavenger hunt** N chasse *f* au trésor, rallye *m*

SCE [,essiː'iː] N *(ABBR = **Scottish Certificate of Education**)* examen de fin d'études secondaires en Écosse

scenario [sɪ'nɑːrɪəʊ] N **a** *(Cine)* scénario *m* **b** *(fig)* *(= sequence of events)* scénario *m* ; *(= plan of action)* plan *m* d'action, stratégie *f* **(for** pour) ; *(Mil, Pol etc)* **best-/worst-case ~** meilleure/pire hypothèse *f* ; **in the worst-case ~** dans le pire des cas or la pire des hypothèses

scenarist ['siːnərɪst] N scénariste *mf*

scene [siːn] **1** N **a** *(Theat etc)* *(= part of play)* scène *f* ; *(= setting)* scène *f*, décor *m* ; **a bedroom ~** une scène de lit *(dans un film)* ; **the garden ~ in "Richard II"** la scène du jardin dans « Richard II » ; **the balcony ~ from "Romeo and Juliet"** la scène du balcon de « Roméo et Juliette » ; *(Cine, TV)* **outdoor** or **outside ~** extérieur *m* ; **~ from a film** scène *f* or séquence *f* (tirée) d'un film ; **the big ~ in the film** la grande scène du film ; **it was his big ~** c'était sa grande scène ; **the ~ is set in Paris** la scène se passe à Paris, l'action se déroule à Paris ; *(fig)* **the ~ was set for their romance** toutes les conditions étaient réunies pour leur idylle ; **this set the ~ for the discussion** ceci a préparé le terrain pour les discussions ; **now let our reporter set the ~ for you** notre reporter va maintenant vous mettre au courant de la situation ; *(Theat, fig)* **behind the ~s** dans les coulisses ; *(fig)* **to work behind the ~s** tra-

vailler dans l'ombre or dans les coulisses → **change**
b *(= sight)* spectacle *m*, tableau *m* ; *(= view)* vue *f* ; *(fig)* scène *f* ; *(= happening)* incident *m* ; **the hills make a lovely ~** les collines offrent un très joli spectacle or tableau ; **the ~ spread out before you** la vue or le panorama qui s'offre à vous ; **picture the ~ ...** imaginez la scène ... ; **~s of violence** scènes *fpl* de violence ; **there were angry ~s at the meeting** des incidents violents ont eu lieu au cours de la réunion ; **it was a ~ of utter destruction/chaos/horror** c'était une scène de destruction totale/de chaos total/d'horreur totale ; *(fig)* **it's a bad ~‡** c'est pas brillant*, la situation n'est pas brillante
c *(= place)* lieu(x) *m(pl)*, endroit *m* ; **the ~ of the crime/accident** le lieu du crime/de l'accident ; **the town had once been the ~ of a great battle** la ville avait été jadis le théâtre d'une grande bataille ; *(Mil)* **~ of operations** théâtre *m* des opérations ; **he needs a change of ~** il a besoin de changer d'air or de décor ; **they were soon on the ~** ils furent vite sur les lieux ; **to appear** or **come on the ~** faire son apparition ; **when I came on the ~** quand je suis arrivé
d *(* = fuss)* scène *f* ; **try not to make a ~ about it** tâche de ne pas en faire toute une histoire ; **to have a ~ with sb** avoir une scène avec qn → **1f** ; **I hate ~s** je déteste les scènes
e *(= sphere of activity)* scène *f*, monde *m* ; **the political ~** la scène politique ; **the (gay) ~** le monde gay or des homosexuels ; **the jazz/pop/rave ~** le monde du jazz/de la pop/des raves ; **the drug(s) ~ in our big cities** le milieu de la drogue dans nos grandes villes ; **it's not my ~‡** ce n'est pas mon truc*
f *(sexually)* **to have a ~* with sb** avoir une liaison avec qn → **1d**
2 COMP ► **scene change** N *(Theat)* changement *m* de décor(s) ► **scene painter** N peintre *m* de décors ► **scene shift** N changement *m* de décor(s) ► **scene shifter** N machiniste *mf*

scenery ['siːnərɪ] N **a** paysage *m*, vue *f* ; **the ~ is very beautiful** le paysage est très beau, la vue est très belle ; **mountain ~** paysage *m* de montagnes ; *(fig)* **a change of ~ will do you good** un changement d'air or de décor* vous fera du bien **b** *(Theat)* décor(s) *m(pl)*

scenic ['siːnɪk] **1** ADJ pittoresque ; **to take the ~ route** *(lit)* prendre l'itinéraire touristique ; *(fig hum)* prendre le chemin des écoliers* **2** COMP ► **scenic car** N *(esp US Rail)* voiture *f* panoramique ► **scenic design** N *(Theat)* *(= sets)* décors *mpl* ; *(= profession)* conception *f* de décors ► **scenic designer** N *(Theat)* décorateur *m*, -trice *f* de théâtre ► **scenic railway** N *(= miniature railway)* petit train *m* (d'agrément) ; *(Brit = roller coaster)* montagnes *fpl* russes, scenic railway *m*

scenography [siː'nɒgrəfɪ] N scénographie *f*

scent [sent] **1** N **a** *(= odour)* parfum *m*, senteur *f* *(liter)*
b *(esp Brit = perfume)* parfum *m* ; **to use ~** se parfumer
c *(= animal's track)* fumet *m* ; *(fig)* piste *f*, voie *f* ; *(Hunting, fig)* **to lose the ~** perdre la piste ; **to throw** or **put sb off the ~** dépister or déjouer qn ; **to put** or **throw dogs off the ~** dépister les chiens, brouiller or faire perdre la piste aux chiens ; **to be on the (right) ~** être sur la bonne piste or voie ; **he got the ~ of something suspicious** il a flairé quelque chose de louche
d *(= sense of smell)* [*of person*] odorat *m* ; [*of animal*] flair *m*
2 VT **a** *(= put scent on)* [+ *handkerchief, air*] parfumer **(with** de) ; *(fig)* **the ~ed air** l'air *m* parfumé or odorant
b *(= smell)* [+ *game*] flairer ; *(fig)* [+ *danger, trouble*] flairer, pressentir ; *(fig)* **to ~ blood** deviner une faille chez son adversaire

3 COMP ► **scent bottle** N (*esp Brit*) flacon *m* à parfum ► **scent spray** N (*esp Brit*) vaporisateur *m* (à parfum) ; (= *aerosol*) atomiseur *m* (à parfum)

scentless ['sentlɪs] ADJ inodore, sans odeur

scepter ['septər] N (*US*) = **sceptre**

sceptic, skeptic (*US*) ['skeptɪk] ADJ, N sceptique *mf*

sceptical, skeptical (*US*) ['skeptɪkəl] ADJ [*person, attitude*] sceptique (**about, of** sur) ; **to cast a ~ eye on** *or* **over sth** porter un regard sceptique sur qch ; **I'm ~ about it** cela me laisse sceptique ; **to be ~ about doing sth** douter qu'il soit bon de faire qch ; **to be ~ that** *or* **about whether ...** douter que ... (+ *subj*) ; **they are ~ about how genuine his commitment is** ils ont des doutes sur la sincérité de son engagement

sceptically, skeptically (*US*) ['skeptɪkəlɪ] ADV [*ask*] d'un ton sceptique, avec scepticisme ; [*look at*] d'un air sceptique, avec scepticisme ; **he raised his eyebrows ~** il haussa les sourcils d'un air sceptique

scepticism, skepticism (*US*) ['skeptɪsɪzəm] N scepticisme *m*

sceptre, scepter (*US*) ['septər] N sceptre *m*

schedule ['ʃedjuːl, (*US*) 'skedjuːl] **1** N **a** (= *timetable*) [*of work, duties*] programme *m*, planning *m* ; [*of trains etc*] horaire *m* ; [*of events*] calendrier *m* ; **production/building** *etc* ~ calendrier *m* *or* planning *m* pour la production/la construction *etc* ; **to make out a ~** établir un programme *or* un plan *or* un horaire ; **our ~ does not include the Louvre** notre programme ne comprend pas le Louvre **b** (= *forecasted timings*) **to be ahead of ~** (*in work*) avoir de l'avance sur son programme ; [*train*] avoir de l'avance ; **the train is behind ~** le train a du retard ; **the preparations are behind ~** il y a du retard dans les préparatifs ; **our work has fallen behind ~** nous sommes en retard dans notre travail ; **the train is on ~** le train est à l'heure ; **the preparations are on ~** il n'y a pas de retard dans les préparatifs ; **the work is on ~** les travaux avancent conformément aux prévisions *ou* au calendrier ; **the ceremony will take place on ~** la cérémonie aura lieu à l'heure prévue (*or* à la date prévue *etc*) ; **the ceremony went off according to ~** la cérémonie s'est déroulée comme prévu ; (*fig*) **it all went (off) according to ~** tout s'est passé comme prévu ; **to work to a very tight ~** avoir un programme très serré **c** (= *list*) [*of goods, contents*] liste *f*, inventaire *m* ; [*of prices*] barème *m*, tarif *m* ; **~ of charges** liste *f* *or* barème *m* des prix **d** (*Jur. to contract*) annexe *f* (**to** à)

2 VT **a** (*gen pass*) [+ *activity*] établir le programme *or* l'horaire de ; **his ~d speech** le discours qu'il doit (*or* devait *etc*) prononcer ; **his ~d departure** son départ prévu ; **at the ~d time/date** *etc* à l'heure/à la date *etc* prévue *or* indiquée ; **~d price** prix *m* tarif ; **as ~d** comme prévu ; **~d service** [*train, bus*] service *m* régulier ; **~d flight** vol *m* régulier ; **this stop is not ~d** cet arrêt n'est pas prévu ; **he is ~d to leave at midday** son départ est fixé pour midi ; **you are ~d to speak after him** d'après le programme vous parlez après lui ; **the talks are ~d for this weekend** les pourparlers sont prévus *or* programmés pour ce week-end ; **the train is ~d for 11 o'clock** *or* **to arrive at 11 o'clock** (selon l'horaire) le train doit arriver à 11 heures, le train arrive normalement à 11 heures ; **the government has ~d elections for 5th January** le gouvernement a prévu des élections pour le 5 janvier, le gouvernement a fixé les élections au 5 janvier ; **~d territories** zone *f* sterling

b [+ *object*] inscrire sur une liste ; (*Brit Admin, Archit*) **~d building** bâtiment *m* classé (*comme monument historique*)

schema ['skiːmə] N (*pl* **schemata** [skiː'mɑːtə]) schéma *m*

schematic [skɪ'mætɪk] ADJ schématique

schematically [skɪ'mætɪkəlɪ] ADV schématiquement

scheme [skiːm] **1** N **a** (= *plan*) plan *m* (**to do** pour faire) ; (= *project*) projet *m* ; (= *method*) procédé *m* (**for doing** pour faire) ; **he's got a ~ for re-using plastic bottles** il a un plan *or* un projet *or* un procédé pour réutiliser les bouteilles en plastique ; **a ~ of work** un plan de travail ; **profit-sharing ~** système *m* de participation (aux bénéfices) ; **pension ~** régime *m* de retraite ; **a ~ for greater productivity** un plan destiné à augmenter la productivité ; **man's place in the ~ of things** le rôle de l'homme dans l'ordre des choses ; **where does he stand in the ~ of things?** où se situe-t-il dans tout cela ? ; (*iro*) **where does he stand in the great** *or* **grand ~ of things?** quelle place occupe-t-il dans le grand ordre de l'univers ? ; **in my/your** *etc* **~ of things** dans ma/votre *etc* vision des choses ; **the ~ for the new bridge** le projet pour le nouveau pont ; **it's some crazy ~ of his** c'est une de ses idées invraisemblables ; **it's not a bad ~** ça n'est pas une mauvaise idée → **supplementary**

b (= *plot*) complot *m*, machination(s) *f(pl)* ; (= *dishonest plan*) procédé *m* malhonnête, combine* *f* ; **it's a ~ to get him out of the way** c'est un complot pour l'éliminer **c** (= *arrangement*) arrangement *m*, combinaison *f* → **colour, rhyme**

2 VT combiner, machiner

3 VI [*group*] comploter, conspirer ; [*individual*] intriguer (**to do** pour faire)

schemer ['skiːmər] N (*pej*) intrigant(e) *m(f)*

scheming ['skiːmɪŋ] **1** ADJ (*pej*) [*person*] intrigant **2** N machinations *fpl*, intrigues *fpl*

scherzo ['skɜːtsəʊ] N (*pl* **scherzos** *or* **scherzi** ['skɜːtsiː]) scherzo *m*

schilling ['ʃɪlɪŋ] N schilling *m*

schism ['sɪzəm] N schisme *m*

schismatic [sɪz'mætɪk] ADJ, N schismatique *mf*

schist [ʃɪst] N schiste *m* cristallin

schizo ['skɪtsəʊ] ADJ, N (ABBR = **schizophrenic**) schizo* *mf*

schizoid ['skɪtsɔɪd] ADJ, N schizoïde *mf*

schizophrenia [ˌskɪtsəʊ'friːnɪə] N schizophrénie *f*

schizophrenic [ˌskɪtsəʊ'frenɪk] ADJ, N schizophrène *mf*

schlemiel:, schlemihl: [ʃlə'miːl] N (*US*) pauvre bougre* *m*, minable* *f*

schlep(p): [ʃlep] (*US*) **1** VI se traîner, crapahuter* **2** VT trimballer*, (se) coltiner*

schlock: [ʃlɒk] **1** N pacotille *f* **2** ADJ de pacotille

schlong: [ʃlɒŋ] N (*US*) bite: *f*

schmaltz* [ʃmɔːlts] N (*NonC*) sentimentalisme *m* excessif

schmaltzy* ['ʃmɔːltsɪ] ADJ à la guimauve, à l'eau de rose

schmear: [ʃmɪər] N (*US*) **the whole ~** tout le bataclan*

schmo [ʃməʊ] N (*pl* **schmoes**) (*US*) ballot* *m*, andouille* *f*

schmooze* [ʃmuːz] VI (*US*) (= *gossip*) jaser* ; (= *bootlick*) faire de la lèche:

schmuck: [ʃmʌk] N (*US*) con: *m*, connard: *m*, connasse: *f*

schnapps [ʃnæps] N schnaps *m*

schnook: [ʃnʊk] N (*US*) ballot* *m*, pauvre type* *m*

schnorkel ['ʃnɔːkl] N = **snorkel**

schnorrer: ['ʃnɔːrər] N (*US*) mendigot *m*, tapeur* *m*

schnozzle: ['ʃnɒzl] N (*US*) gros pif* *m*, tarin* *m*

scholar ['skɒlər] N **a** lettré(e) *m(f)*, érudit(e) *m(f)* ; **a ~ and a gentleman** un homme cultivé et raffiné ; **a Dickens ~** un(e) spécialiste de Dickens ; **I'm not much of a ~** je ne suis pas bien savant *or* instruit **b** (= *scholarship holder*) boursier *m*, -ière *f* ; († = *pupil*) écolier *m*, -ière *f*

scholarly ['skɒləlɪ] ADJ [*person, publication, account*] érudit, savant ; [*approach*] érudit ; [*debate*] d'érudits ; **to have a ~ interest in a subject** s'intéresser à un sujet en tant que spécialiste

scholarship ['skɒləʃɪp] **1** N **a** érudition *f*, savoir *m* **b** (= *award*) bourse *f* (d'études) ; (*US Univ*) bourse *f* (*pour étudiant de licence*) ; **to win a ~ to Cambridge** obtenir une bourse pour Cambridge (*par concours*) **2** COMP ► **scholarship holder** N boursier *m*, -ière *f*

scholastic [skə'læstɪk] **1** ADJ **a** (= *educational*) [*work, level*] scolaire ; **~ achievement** réussite *f* scolaire **b** (*among scholars*) [*debate, controversy*] parmi les érudits **2** N (*Philos*) scolastique *mf* **3** COMP ► **scholastic aptitude test** N (*US Educ*) examen *m* d'entrée à l'université → [SAT] ► **scholastic philosophy** N philosophie *f* scolastique ► **the scholastic profession** N (*gen*) l'enseignement *m* ; (= *teachers collectively*) les enseignants *mpl*

scholasticism [skə'læstɪsɪzəm] N scolastique *f*

school¹ [skuːl] **1** N **a** (*gen*) école *f*, établissement *m* ; (= *primary school*) école *f* ; (= *secondary school*) (*gen*) lycée *m* ; (*up to 16 only*) collège *m* ; [*of dancing*] école *f*, académie *f* ; [*of music*] école *f*, conservatoire *m* ; (*US* = *university*) fac* *f* ; **~ of motoring** auto-école *f* ; **to go to ~** aller à l'école (*or* au collège *or* au lycée *etc*) ; **to leave ~** quitter l'école *etc* ; **to send a child to ~** (*gen*) envoyer un enfant à l'école ; (*Admin*) [*local authority etc*] scolariser un enfant ; **at ~** *or* **in ~** à l'école *etc* ; **we were at ~ together** nous étions à la même école *etc* ; **he wasn't at ~ yesterday** il n'était pas à l'école *etc* or en classe hier ; (= *pupils collectively*) **she gave a talk to the ~** elle a fait un exposé à l'école (*or* au collège *or* au lycée *etc*) ; **to go camping/sailing with the ~** aller faire du camping/de la voile avec l'école *etc* ; **to go skiing with the ~** ≈ partir en classe de neige ; **television for ~s** télévision *f* scolaire ; **programmes** *or* **broadcasts for ~s** émissions *fpl* éducatives → **boarding, high, old, summer** **b** (= *lessons*) classe(s) *f(pl)* ; (*gen secondary*) cours *mpl* ; **~ reopens in September** la rentrée scolaire *or* la rentrée des classes est en septembre ; **there's no ~ this morning** il n'y a pas classe ce matin, il n'y a pas (de) cours ce matin ; **we met every day after ~** nous nous retrouvions tous les jours après l'école **c** (*Univ*) faculté *f* ; (*at Oxford and Cambridge*) **Schools** (= *building*) salle d'examen ; (= *finals*) ≈ examens *mpl* de licence ; **he's at law/medical ~** il fait son droit/sa médecine, il est en droit/médecine ; **I went to art/business ~** je suis allé dans une école d'art/de commerce **d** (= *institute*) institut *m* ; (= *department*) département *m* ; **School of Linguistics/African Studies** *etc* Institut *m* *or* Département *m* de Linguistique/d'Études africaines *etc* ; (*US*) **~ of education** école *f* normale (*primaire*) **e** (*fig*) école *f* ; **the hard ~ of poverty** la dure école de la pauvreté ; **the ~ of life** l'école *f* de la vie ; **he graduated from the ~ of hard knocks** il a été à rude école **f** (*Hist* = *scholastic*) **the ~s** l'École *f*, la scolastique **g** [*of painting, philosophy etc*] école *f* ; (*Art*) **the Dutch ~** l'école *f* hollandaise ; **the Freudian ~** l'école *f* freudienne ; **a ~ of thought** une école de pensée ; **an aristocrat/doctor** *etc* **of the old ~** un aristocrate/un médecin *etc* de la vieille école ; **he's one of the old ~** il est de la vieille école

2 VT [+ *animal*] dresser ; [+ *feelings, reactions*]

contrôler ; [+ *voice etc*] discipliner ; **to ~ o.s. to do sth** s'astreindre à faire qch

3 COMP [*equipment, edition, television, doctor*] scolaire ► **school-age child** N (*pl* **school-age children**) enfant *mf* d'âge scolaire ► **school attendance** N scolarisation *f*, scolarité *f* ► **school board** N (*US Scol*) commission *f* scolaire ► **school bus** N car *m* de ramassage scolaire ; **~ bus service** service *m* de ramassage scolaire ► **school certificate** N (*formerly*) ≈ BEPC *m* ► **school council** N (*Brit Scol*) (*secondary*) comité *m* des délégués de classe ► **school counsellor** N (*US*) conseiller *m*, -ère *f* général(e) d'éducation ► **school crossing patrol** N → **crossing** ► **school dinner** N = **school lunch** ► **school district** N (*US*) secteur *m* scolaire ► **school fees** NPL frais *mpl* de scolarité ► **school fund** N fonds *collectés grâce à diverses opérations organisées par les élèves d'une école* ► **school holidays** NPL vacances *fpl* scolaires ► **school hours** NPL **during ~ hours** pendant les heures de cours *or* de classe ; **out of ~ hours** en dehors des heures de cours *or* de classe ► **school inspector** N (*Brit Scol*) (*secondary*) ≈ inspecteur *m*, -trice *f* d'académie ; (*primary*) ≈ inspecteur *m*, -trice *f* primaire ► **school leaver** N (*Brit*) jeune *mf* qui a terminé ses études secondaires ► **school-leaving age** N âge *m* de fin de scolarité ; **to raise the ~-leaving age** prolonger la scolarité (*to jusqu'à*) ► **school librarian** N (*books only*) bibliothécaire *mf* scolaire ; (*books and other resources*) documentaliste *mf* scolaire ► **school life** N vie *f* scolaire ► **school lunch, school meal** N déjeuner *m* à la cantine (scolaire) ; **he hates ~ lunches** *or* **meals** il déteste manger à la cantine ► **school medical officer** N (*Brit*) médecin *m* scolaire ► **school outing** N (*Brit*) sortie *f* (éducative) scolaire ► **school phobia** N phobie *f* de l'école ► **school record** N dossier *m* scolaire ► **school report** N bulletin *m* (scolaire) ► **school run** N **to do the ~ run** emmener les enfants à l'école ► **schools inspector** N = **school inspector** ► **schools medical officer** N = **school medical officer** ► **school superintendent** N (*US*) inspecteur *m*, -trice *f* (*responsable du bon fonctionnement des établissements scolaires*) ► **school tie** N cravate *f* de l'école → **old** ► **school time** N **in ~ time** pendant les heures de cours *or* de classe ► **school trip** N = **school outing** ► **school uniform** N uniforme *m* scolaire ► **school year** N année *f* scolaire

school² [skuːl] N [*of fish*] banc *m*

schoolbag ['skuːlbæg] N cartable *m*

schoolbook ['skuːlbʊk] N livre *m* scolaire *or* de classe

schoolboy ['skuːlbɔɪ] **1** N (*gen*) élève *m* ; (*at primary school*) écolier *m* ; (*at secondary school*) lycéen *m* ; (*up to age 16 only*) collégien *m* → **public** **2** COMP ► **schoolboy crush*** N béguin* *m* (**on** pour) ► **schoolboy slang** N argot *m* des écoles *or* des lycées

schoolchild ['skuːltʃaɪld] N (*pl* **-children**) (*gen*) élève *mf* ; (*at primary school*) écolier *m*, -ière *f* ; (*at secondary school*) lycéen(ne) *m(f)* ; (*up to age 16 only*) collégien(ne) *m(f)*

schooldays ['skuːldeɪz] NPL années *fpl* de scolarité *or* d'école ; **during my ~** du temps où j'allais en classe

schooled [skuːld] ADJ **to be ~ in sth** avoir l'expérience de qch ; **to be well ~ in sth** être rompu à qch

schoolfellow ['skuːlfeləʊ], **schoolfriend** ['skuːlfrend] N camarade *mf* de classe

schoolgirl ['skuːlgɜːl] **1** N (*gen*) élève *f* ; (*at primary school*) écolière *f* ; (*at secondary school*) lycéenne *f* ; (*up to age 16 only*) collégienne *f* **2** COMP ► **schoolgirl complexion** N teint *m* de jeune fille ► **schoolgirl crush*** N béguin* *m* (**on** pour)

schoolhouse ['skuːlhaʊs] N (*US*) (= *school building*) école *f* ; (*for head teacher*) maison *f* du directeur

schooling ['skuːlɪŋ] N **a** (*Scol*) instruction *f*, études *fpl* ; **~ is free** les études sont gratuites ; **compulsory ~** scolarité *f* obligatoire ; **~ is compulsory up to age 16** la scolarité est obligatoire jusqu'à 16 ans ; **he had very little formal ~** il n'a pas fait une scolarité complète ; **he lost a year's ~** il a perdu une année (d'école) **b** [*of horse*] dressage *m*

schoolkid* ['skuːlkɪd] N écolier *m*, -ière *f*

schoolmarm ['skuːlmɑːm] N (*pej*) institutrice *f*, maîtresse *f* d'école

schoolmarmish ['skuːlˌmɑːmɪʃ] ADJ (*pej*) **she is very ~** elle fait *or* est très maîtresse d'école

schoolmaster ['skuːlˌmɑːstər] N (*primary*) instituteur *m* ; (*secondary*) professeur *m*

schoolmate ['skuːlmeɪt] N = **schoolfellow**

Schoolmen ['skuːlmən] NPL (*Philos*) scolastiques *mpl*

schoolmistress ['skuːlˌmɪstrɪs] N (*primary*) institutrice *f* ; (*secondary*) professeur *m*

schoolroom ['skuːlrʊm] N salle *f* de classe ; **in the ~** dans la (salle de) classe, en classe

schoolteacher ['skuːlˌtiːtʃər] N (*primary*) instituteur *m*, -trice *f* ; (*secondary*) professeur *m*

schoolteaching ['skuːlˌtiːtʃɪŋ] N enseignement *m*

schoolwork ['skuːlwɜːk] N travail *m* scolaire

schoolyard ['skuːljɑːd] N (*esp US*) cour *f* d'école

schooner ['skuːnər] N **a** (*Naut*) schooner *m*, goélette *f* **b** (*Brit* = *sherry glass*) grand verre *m* (à Xérès) ; (*US* = *beer glass*) demi *m* (de bière)

schtick [ʃtɪk] N (*US*) numéro *m* (*de comédien*)

schuss [ʃʊs] N (*Ski*) schuss *m*

schwa [ʃwɑː] N (*Phon*) schwa *m*

sciatic [saɪˈætɪk] ADJ sciatique

sciatica [saɪˈætɪkə] N sciatique *f*

science ['saɪəns] **1** N **a** science(s) *f(pl)* ; **we study ~ at school** nous étudions les sciences au lycée ; **gardening for him is quite a ~** pour lui le jardinage est une véritable science ; (*Univ*) **the Faculty of Science** ◊ **the Science Faculty** la faculté des Sciences ; (*Brit*) **Secretary (of State) for Science** ◊ **Minister of Science** ministre *m* de la Recherche scientifique ; **Department** *or* **Ministry of Science** ministère *m* de la Recherche scientifique → **applied, natural, social** **b** († = *knowledge*) science† *f* ; **to blind sb with ~** éblouir qn de sa science **2** COMP [*equipment, subject*] scientifique ; [*exam*] de sciences ► **science fiction** N science-fiction *f* ♦ ADJ de science-fiction ► **science park** N parc *m* scientifique ► **science teacher** N professeur *m* de sciences

scientific [ˌsaɪənˈtɪfɪk] **1** ADJ **a** scientifique ; **on a ~ basis** sur des bases scientifiques, sur une base scientifique ; **the ~ community** la communauté scientifique ; **she received her ~ training in the US** elle a fait ses études de sciences aux États-Unis **b** (= *methodical*) méthodique ; **to be ~ about sth** être méthodique par rapport à qch **2** COMP ► **the scientific method** N la méthode scientifique ► **scientific officer** N (*Brit Police*) expert *m* (de la police)

scientifically [ˌsaɪənˈtɪfɪkəlɪ] ADV **a** [*prove, explain*] scientifiquement ; **to be ~ based** reposer sur des bases scientifiques ; **to be ~ trained** avoir une formation scientifique ; **~ speaking** d'un point de vue scientifique **b** (= *methodically*) [*search*] de manière méthodique ; [*plan*] de manière systématique

scientist ['saɪəntɪst] N (*as career*) scientifique *mf* ; (= *scientific scholar*) savant *m* ; **my daughter is a ~** ma fille est une scientifique ; **one of our leading ~s** l'un de nos plus grands savants → **Christian, social**

scientologist [ˌsaɪənˈtɒlədʒɪst] ADJ, N scientologue *mf*

scientology ['saɪənˈtɒlədʒɪ] N scientologie *f*

sci-fi* ['saɪfaɪ] ABBR = **science-fiction 1** N science-fiction *f*, SF *f* **2** ADJ de science-fiction, de SF

Scillies ['sɪlɪz] NPL **the ~** = **the Scilly Isles** les Sorlingues *fpl*, les îles *fpl* Scilly

scimitar ['sɪmɪtər] N cimeterre *m*

scintilla [sɪnˈtɪlə] N **not a ~ of evidence** pas l'ombre d'une preuve, pas la moindre preuve ; **not a ~ of (a) doubt** pas l'ombre d'un doute, pas la moindre doute

scintillate ['sɪntɪleɪt] VI [*star, jewel*] scintiller ; (*fig*) [*person*] briller, pétiller d'esprit

scintillating ['sɪntɪleɪtɪŋ] ADJ [*person, performance, wit*] brillant ; [*conversation*] brillant, spirituel ; **in ~ form** dans une forme éblouissante

scion ['saɪən] N (= *person*) descendant(e) *m(f)* ; (*Bot*) scion *m*

Scipio ['sɪpɪəʊ] N Scipion *m*

scissor ['sɪzər] **1** **scissors** NPL ciseaux *mpl* ; **a pair of ~s** une paire de ciseaux → **kitchen, nail 2** VT* couper avec des ciseaux **3** COMP ► **scissor bill** N bec *m* en ciseaux ► **scissor jump** N (*Sport*) saut *m* en ciseaux ► **scissor kick** N ciseaux *mpl* → **multiple** ► **scissors-and-paste job** N (*lit*) montage *m* ; (* *fig*) compilation *f*

sclera ['sklɪərə] N (*Anat*) sclérotique *f*

sclerosis [sklɪˈrəʊsɪs] N (*pl* **scleroses** [sklɪˈrəʊsiːz]) sclérose *f* → **multiple**

sclerotic [sklɪˈrɒtɪk] ADJ (*Anat*) sclérotique

SCM [ˌesiːˈem] N (*Brit*) (ABBR = **State-Certified Midwife**) → **state**

scoff¹ [skɒf] VI se moquer ; **to ~ at sb/sth** se moquer de qn/qch, mépriser qn/qch ; **he was ~ed at by the whole town** il a été l'objet de risée de toute la ville

scoff²* [skɒf] VTI (*esp Brit*) bouffer‡

scoffer ['skɒfər] N moqueur *m*, -euse *f*, railleur *m*, -euse *f*

scoffing ['skɒfɪŋ] **1** ADJ [*remark, laugh*] moqueur, railleur **2** N moqueries *fpl*, railleries *fpl*

scofflaw ['skɒflɔː] N (*US*) personne *f* qui se moque des lois et des règlements

scold [skəʊld] **1** VT réprimander (**for doing** pour avoir fait) ; [+ *child*] gronder (**for doing** pour avoir fait) ; **he got ~ed** il s'est fait réprimander ; [*child*] il s'est fait attraper *or* gronder **2** VI grogner, rouspéter* **3** N (= *woman*) mégère *f*, chipie *f*

scolding ['skəʊldɪŋ] N gronderie *f*, réprimande *f* ; **to get a ~ from sb** se faire gronder *or* attraper par qn ; **to give sb a ~** réprimander *or* gronder qn

scoliosis [ˌskɒlɪˈəʊsɪs] N scoliose *f*

scollop ['skɒləp] = **scallop**

sconce [skɒns] N (*on wall*) applique *f* ; (*for carrying candle*) bougeoir *m*

scone [skɒn] N scone *m* (*petit pain au lait*)

scoop [skuːp] **1** N **a** (*for flour, sugar*) pelle *f* (à main) ; (*for water*) écope *f* ; (*for ice cream*) cuiller *f* à glace ; (*for mashed potatoes*) cuiller *f* à purée ; [*of bulldozer*] lame *f* ; [*of dredger*] benne *f* preneuse ; (*also* **~ful**) pelletée *f* **b** (*Press*) scoop *m*, exclusivité *f* ; (*Comm*) bénéfice *m* important ; **to make a ~** (*Comm*) faire un gros bénéfice ; (*Press*) publier une exclusivité, faire un scoop ; (*Press*) **it was a ~ for the "Globe"** le « Globe » l'a publié en exclusivité, cela a été un scoop pour le « Globe » **2** VT (*Comm*) [+ *market*] s'emparer de ; [+ *competitor*] devancer ; [+ *profit*] ramasser ; [+ *prize, award*] décrocher* ; (*Press*) [+ *story*] publier en exclusivité ; (*fig*) **to ~ the pool** tout rafler

► **scoop out** VT SEP **to ~ water out of a boat** écoper un bateau ; **he ~ed the sand out (of the bucket)** il a vidé le sable (du seau) ; **he**

~ed out a hollow in the soft earth il a creusé un trou dans la terre molle
► **scoop up** VT SEP [+ *earth, sweets*] ramasser; (*with instrument*) ramasser à la pelle; **the eagle ~ed up the rabbit** l'aigle a saisi le lapin dans ses serres; **he ~ed up the child and ran for his life** il a ramassé l'enfant en vitesse et s'est enfui à toutes jambes

scoot* [sku:t] VI se sauver*, filer*; **~!** fichez le camp!*, filez!*; **to ~ in/out** *etc* entrer/sortir *etc* rapidement *or* en coup de vent
► **scoot away***, **scoot off*** VI se sauver*, filer*

scooter ['sku:tə'] N (*also* **motor ~**) scooter *m*; (*child's*) trottinette *f*

scope [skəʊp] N **a** (= *range*) [*of law, regulation*] étendue *f*, portée *f*; [*of undertaking*] envergure *f*; [*of powers, disaster*] étendue *f*; [*of changes*] ampleur *f*; **reforms of considerable ~** des réformes d'une portée considérable; **a programme of considerable ~** un programme d'une envergure considérable; **to extend the ~ of one's activities** élargir le champ de ses activités, étendre son rayon d'action; **limited in ~** d'une portée limitée; **this project is more limited in ~** ce projet est de moins grand envergure *or* est moins ambitieux; **to be broad in ~** [*project*] être de grande envergure; [*research*] être d'une portée considérable; [*book*] être ambitieux; **his evaluation of the situation is very broad in ~** son évaluation de la situation porte sur de nombreux aspects; **the service is comprehensive in ~** ce service est très complet
b (= *possibility, potential*) (*for activity, action etc*) possibilité *f*, occasion *f*; **he wants a job with more ~** (*more varied*) il voudrait un travail plus varié; (*with more prospects*) il voudrait un travail offrant davantage de perspectives d'évolution; **his job gave him plenty of ~ to show his ability** son travail lui a amplement permis de faire la preuve de ses compétences; **there's not much ~ for originality/creativity** ça ne laisse pas beaucoup de place à l'originalité/la créativité; **there is ~ for improvement** ça pourrait être mieux; **there is ~ for increasing our share of the market** il nous est possible d'augmenter notre part du marché; **there is little ~ for reducing our costs** il ne nous est pas vraiment possible de réduire nos coûts, nous n'avons pas beaucoup de marge de manœuvre pour réduire nos coûts; **it gave him full ~ to decide for himself** cela le laissait entièrement libre de *or* cela lui donnait carte blanche pour prendre les décisions lui-même; **the subject is within/beyond the ~ of this book** ce sujet entre dans le cadre/dépasse le cadre de ce livre; **that is within the ~ of the new regulations** ceci est prévu par le nouveau règlement
c (= *competences, capabilities*) compétences *fpl*; **this work is within/beyond his ~** ce travail entre dans ses compétences/dépasse ses compétences

scorbutic [skɔ:'bju:tɪk] ADJ scorbutique

scorch [skɔ:tʃ] **1** N (*also* **~ mark**) brûlure *f* (légère); **there was a ~ on her dress** sa robe avait été roussie **2** VT [+ *linen*] roussir, brûler (légèrement); [+ *grass*] [*fire etc*] brûler; [*sun*] dessécher, roussir **3** VI **a** [*linen*] brûler (légèrement) **b** (*Brit** = *drive fast: also* **~ along**) [*driver*] conduire à un train d'enfer; [*car*] rouler à toute vitesse; [*cyclist*] pédaler à fond de train *or* comme un fou* (*or* une fou*) **4** COMP ► **scorched earth policy** N tactique *f* de la terre brûlée

scorcher* ['skɔ:tʃə'] N journée *f* de canicule; **today's going to be a ~** aujourd'hui ça va être la canicule; **it was a (real) ~ (of a day)** il faisait une chaleur caniculaire *or* une de ces chaleurs*

scorching* ['skɔ:tʃɪŋ] **1** ADJ **a** (= *hot*) [*day*] de canicule; [*heat*] caniculaire; [*sand*] brûlant; [*sun*] de plomb; **~ weather** canicule *f*

b (= *fast*) **at a ~ pace** à une vitesse folle **2** ADV **~ hot** [*food*] brûlant; [*liquid*] bouillant; **~ hot weather** canicule *f*; **it was a ~ hot day** il faisait une chaleur caniculaire *or* une de ces chaleurs*; **the sun is ~ hot** il fait un soleil de plomb

score [skɔ:'] **1** N **a** (= *amount won etc*) (*Sport*) score *m*; (*Cards*) marque *f*; (*US Scol* = *mark*) note *f*; **to keep (the) ~** (*gen*) compter *or* marquer les points; (*Cards*) tenir la marque; (*Tennis*) tenir le score; (*Ftbl*) **there's no ~ yet** on n'a pas encore marqué (de but); **there was no ~ in the match between Leeds and York** Leeds et York ont fait match nul; **what's the ~?** (*Sport*) où en est le match?, on en est à combien?; (* *fig*) où en sont les choses?; (*fig*) **to know the ~*** savoir de quoi il retourne → **half**
b (= *debt*) compte *m*, dette *f*; (*fig*) **to settle a ~ with sb** régler ses comptes avec qn; **I've got a ~** *or* **an old ~ to settle with him** j'ai un compte à régler avec lui
c (= *subject, account*) **on the ~ of ...** pour cause de ..., en raison de ...; **on more ~s than one** à plus d'un titre; **on that ~** à cet égard, à ce sujet; **on what ~?** à quel titre?; **on several ~s** à plusieurs titres
d (= *mark, cut*) (*on metal, wood*) rayure *f*; (*deeper*) entaille *f*; (*on rock*) strie *f*; (*on skin, leather*) (*accidental*) éraflure *f*; (*deliberate*) incision *f*
e [*of film*] musique *f*; **who wrote the ~?** qui est l'auteur de la musique *or* de la bande originale?
f (*Mus = sheets of music*) partition *f*; **piano ~** partition *f* de piano; **to follow the ~** suivre la partition → **vocal**
g (= *twenty*) **a ~** vingt; **a ~ of people** une vingtaine de personnes; **three ~ and ten**†† soixante-dix; (*fig*) **~s of times** trente-six fois*; **there were ~s of mistakes** il y avait un grand nombre de *or* des tas* de fautes
2 VT **a** [+ *goal, point*] marquer; (*Scol etc*) **to ~ 70% (in an exam)** avoir 70 sur 100 (à un examen); (*Tennis*) **he went five games without scoring a point** il n'a pas marqué un seul point pendant cinq jeux; **they had 14 goals ~d against them** leurs adversaires ont marqué 14 buts; **to ~ a hit** (*Fencing*) toucher; (*Shooting*) viser juste; (*Drugs*‡) se procurer de la dope*; **to ~ a hit of crack/speed/smack**‡ se procurer sa dose de crack/de speed*/d'héro*; (*fig*) **to ~ a great success** *or* **a hit** remporter *or* se tailler un grand succès; **he certainly ~d a hit with her*** il lui a vraiment fait bonne impression; (*fig*) **to ~ points** marquer des points; (*fig*) **to ~ a point over** *or* **off sb** marquer un point aux dépens de qn, damer le pion à qn
b (= *cut*) [+ *stick*] entailler; [+ *rock*] strier; [+ *ground*] entamer; [+ *wood, metal*] rayer; [+ *leather, skin*] (*deliberately*) inciser; (*accidentally*) érafler; (*Culin*) inciser; **lines had been ~d on the wall** des lignes avaient été tracées sur le mur
c (*Mus*) (= *arrange*) adapter (**for** pour); (= *orchestrate*) orchestrer (**for** pour); (= *compose*) composer; **the film was ~d by Michael Nyman** la musique *or* la bande originale du film a été composée par Michael Nyman; **it is ~d for piano and cello** c'est écrit pour piano et violoncelle
3 VI **a** (*Sport*) (= *win points*) marquer un *or* des point(s); (= *score goal*) marquer un but; (= *keep the score*) marquer les points; **to ~ well in a test** avoir *or* obtenir un bon résultat à un test; (*Ftbl*) **they failed to ~** ils n'ont pas réussi à marquer (un but); (*Ftbl*) **Barnes ~d from a distance of twenty feet** Barnes a marqué à sept mètres; (*fig*) **that is where he ~s** c'est là qu'il a le dessus *or* l'avantage; **to ~ over** *or* **off sb** marquer un point aux dépens de qn, damer le pion à qn
b (‡ = *succeed*) (*gen*) avoir du succès; (= *get*

off with) lever*; (*with woman*) lever* une nana‡; (*with man*) lever* un mec‡; (*in buying drugs*) se procurer de la dope*
4 COMP ► **score draw** N (*Brit Ftbl*) match *m* nul (*avec un minimum de un but*)
► **score out**, **score through** VT SEP rayer, barrer
► **score up** VT SEP [+ *points*] marquer, faire; [+ *debt*] porter en compte, inscrire; (*fig*) **that remark will be ~d up against you** on ne vous pardonnera pas cette réflexion

scoreboard ['skɔ:bɔ:d] N (*gen*) tableau *m* d'affichage (*des scores*); (*Billiards*) boulier *m*

scorecard ['skɔ:kɑ:d] N [*of game*] carte *f or* fiche *f* de score; (*Shooting*) carton *m*; (*Golf*) carte *f* de parcours; (*Cards*) feuille *f* de marque

scorekeeper ['skɔ:,ki:pə'] N (= *person*) marqueur *m*, -euse *f*

scoreless ['skɔ:lɪs] ADJ (*Sport*) **the game was ~** *or* **it was a ~ game** aucun point n'a été marqué pendant le jeu; **a ~ draw** un match nul zéro à zéro

scoreline ['skɔ:laɪn] N (*Sport*) score *m*

scorer ['skɔ:rə'] N **a** (*keeping score*) marqueur *m* **b** (*also* **goal ~**) marqueur *m* (de but); **to be the top ~** être le meilleur marqueur

scoresheet ['skɔ:ʃi:t] N (*in games*) feuille *f* de match; (*Ftbl*) **they're ahead on the ~** ils mènent à la marque

scoring ['skɔ:rɪŋ] N (*NonC*) **a** (*Sport*) buts *mpl*; (*Cards*) points *mpl*; **all the ~ was in the second half** tous les buts ont été marqués pendant la deuxième mi-temps; **to open the ~** ouvrir le score; **"rules for ~"** « comment marquer les points » **b** (= *cut*) incision *f*, striage *m*; (*Culin*) incision *f* **c** (*Mus*) arrangement *m*

scorn ['skɔ:n] **1** N (*NonC*) mépris *m*, dédain *m*; **to be filled with ~ (for)** n'avoir que du mépris *or* du dédain (pour); **to heap** *or* **pour ~ on sb/sth** traiter qn/qch avec mépris; **my suggestion was greeted with ~** ma proposition a été accueillie avec mépris *or* dédain → **laugh** **2** VT [+ *person*] mépriser; [+ *action*] dédaigner, mépriser; [+ *advice*] faire fi de; [+ *suggestion*] rejeter, passer outre à; [+ *idea*] dédaigner; **he was ~ed as ineffectual/naive** on le méprisait parce qu'on le considérait comme incompétent/naïf; **he was ~ed as an amateur/a mercenary** on le méprisait parce qu'on le considérait comme un simple amateur/un mercenaire; (*liter*) **he ~s telling lies** *or* **to tell a lie** il ne s'abaisserait pas à mentir

scornful ['skɔ:nful] ADJ méprisant, dédaigneux; **to be ~ of sb/sth** mépriser qn/qch; **to be ~ about sth** manifester son mépris *or* son dédain pour qch

scornfully ['skɔ:nfəlɪ] ADV avec mépris, avec dédain

Scorpio ['skɔ:pɪəʊ] N (*Astron*) le Scorpion; (*Astrol*) **I'm (a) ~** je suis (du) Scorpion

scorpion ['skɔ:pɪən] **1** N scorpion *m*; (*Astrol, Astron*) **the Scorpion** le Scorpion **2** COMP ► **scorpion fish** N rascasse *f*

Scorpionic [,skɔ:pɪ'ɒnɪk] N **to be a ~** être (du) Scorpion

Scot [skɒt] N Écossais(e) *m(f)*; **the ~s** les Écossais *mpl* → **Scots**

Scotch [skɒtʃ] **1** N (*also* **~ whisky**) whisky *m*, scotch *m* **2** **the Scotch*** NPL les Écossais *mpl* **3** ADJ écossais **4** COMP ► **Scotch broth** N *potage écossais à base de mouton, de légumes et d'orge* ► **Scotch egg** N (*esp Brit*) œuf dur enrobé de chair à saucisse et pané ► **Scotch-Irish** ADJ (*US*) irlando-écossais ► **Scotch mist** N bruine *f*, crachin *m* ► **Scotch pine** N pin *m* sylvestre ► **Scotch tape**® N (*US*) scotch® *m*, ruban *m* adhésif ► **Scotch terrier** N scotch-terrier *m* ► **Scotch woodcock** N (*Culin*) toast *m* aux œufs brouillés et aux anchois

scotch [skɒtʃ] VT [+ *rumour*] étouffer ; [+ *plan, attempt*] faire échouer ; [+ *revolt, uprising*] réprimer ; [+ *claim*] démentir

scot-free ['skɒt'fri:] ADV **to get off ~** s'en tirer à bon compte

Scotland ['skɒtlənd] N l'Écosse *f* ; **Secretary of State for ~** ministre *m* des Affaires écossaises → **yard²**

Scots [skɒts] **1** N (*Ling*) écossais *m* **2** ADJ écossais **3** COMP ► **the Scots Guards** NPL (*Mil*) la Garde écossaise ► **Scots law** N droit *m* écossais ► **Scots pine** N pin *m* sylvestre

Scotsman ['skɒtsmən] N (*pl* **-men**) Écossais *m*

Scotswoman ['skɒts,wʊmən] N (*pl* **-women**) Écossaise *f*

Scotticism ['skɒtɪsɪzəm] N expression *f* écossaise

Scottie ['skɒtɪ] N (ABBR = **Scotch terrier**) → **Scotch**

Scottish ['skɒtɪʃ] **1** ADJ écossais **2** COMP ► **Scottish country dancing** N danses *fpl* folkloriques écossaises ► **Scottish Nationalism** N nationalisme *m* écossais ► **Scottish Nationalist** N nationaliste *mf* écossais(e) ◆ ADJ de or des nationaliste(s) écossais(es) ► **the Scottish National Party** N (*Brit Pol*) le Parti national écossais ► **the Scottish Office** N (*Brit Pol*) le ministère des Affaires écossaises ► **Scottish Secretary** N (*Brit Pol*) ministre *m* des Affaires écossaises ► **Scottish terrier** N scotch-terrier *m*

scoundrel ['skaʊndrəl] N fripouille *f*, vaurien *m* ; (*stronger*) crapule *f* ; (= *child*) coquin(e) *m(f)*, (petit) chenapan *m* ; **you little ~!** (espèce de) petit coquin or chenapan !

scoundrelly† ['skaʊndrəlɪ] ADJ de gredin, de vaurien

scour ['skaʊər] **1** VT **a** [+ *pan, sink*] récurer ; [+ *metal*] décaper ; [+ *table, floor*] frotter **b** [+ *channel*] creuser, éroder **c** (= *search*) fouiller ; **I ~ed the newspaper for the article** j'ai cherché partout dans le journal pour trouver l'article ; **they ~ed the neighbourhood in search of the murderer** ils ont fouillé le quartier pour trouver l'assassin ; **to ~ the area/the woods/the countryside** battre le secteur/les bois/la campagne ; **I've ~ed the house and I can't see my keys anywhere** j'ai fouillé la maison de fond en comble et je n'arrive pas à trouver mes clés **2** COMP ► **scouring pad** N tampon *m* à récurer ► **scouring powder** N poudre *f* à récurer

► **scour off** VT SEP enlever en frottant

► **scour out** VT SEP récurer

scourer ['skaʊərər] N (= *powder*) poudre *f* à récurer ; (= *pad*) tampon *m* à récurer

scourge [skɜ:dʒ] **1** N (*fig*) fléau *m* ; (= *whip*) discipline *f*, fouet *m* **2** VT (*fig*) châtier, être un fléau pour ; (= *whip*) fouetter ; **to ~ o.s.** se flageller

scouse* [skaʊs] (*Brit*) **1** N **a** (= *person*) originaire *mf* de Liverpool **b** (= *dialect*) dialecte *m* de Liverpool **2** ADJ de Liverpool

Scouser* ['skaʊsər] N (*Brit*) originaire *mf* de Liverpool ; **Janet's dad is a ~** le père de Janet est (originaire) de Liverpool

scout [skaʊt] **1** N **a** (*Mil*) éclaireur *m* ; **he's a good ~†*** c'est un chic type* → **talent b** (*gen Catholic*) scout *m* ; (*gen non-Catholic*) éclaireur *m* → **cub c** **to have a ~ round** reconnaître le terrain ; **have a ~ round to see if he's there** allez jeter un coup d'œil pour voir s'il est là **d** (*also* **talent ~**) (*Sport*) découvreur *m*, -euse *f* or dénicheur *m*, -euse *f* de futurs grands joueurs ; (*Cine, Theat*) découvreur *m*, -euse *f* or dénicheur *m*, -euse *f* de talents **e** (*Brit Univ*) domestique *mf* **2** VI (*Mil*) aller en reconnaissance **3** VT explorer ; **to ~ an area for sth** explorer un endroit pour trouver qch **4** COMP ► **scout camp** N camp *m* scout ► **scout car** N (*Mil*) voiture *f* de reconnaissance ► **scout movement** N mouve-ment *m* scout ► **scout uniform** N uniforme *m* de scout

► **scout about, scout around** VI (*Mil*) aller en reconnaissance ; (*fig*) **to ~ about for sth** chercher qch, aller or être à la recherche de qch

scouting ['skaʊtɪŋ] N (*NonC*) **a** (= *youth movement*) scoutisme *m* **b** (*Mil*) reconnaissance *f*

scoutmaster ['skaʊt,mɑ:stər] N chef *m* scout

scow [skaʊ] N chaland *m*

scowl [skaʊl] **1** N air *m* de mauvaise humeur, mine *f* renfrognée ; **... he said with a ~** ... dit-il en se renfrognant or d'un air renfrogné **2** VI se renfrogner ; **to ~ at sb/sth** jeter un regard mauvais à qn/qch **3** VT **"shut up!" he ~ed** « tais-toi ! » dit-il en se renfrognant or l'œil mauvais

scowling ['skaʊlɪŋ] ADJ [*face, look*] renfrogné, maussade

SCR N (*Brit Univ*) (ABBR = **senior common room**) → **senior**

scrabble ['skræbl] **1** VI **a** (*also* **~ about, ~ around**) **to ~ in the ground for sth** gratter la terre pour trouver qch ; **she ~d (about or around) in the sand for the keys she had dropped** elle cherchait à tâtons dans le sable les clés qu'elle avait laissé tomber ; **he ~d (about or around) for a pen in the drawer** il a tâtonné dans le tiroir à la recherche d'un stylo **b** (= *scramble*) **to ~ to do sth** chercher à faire qch au plus vite ; **his mind ~d for alternatives** il se creusait la tête pour trouver au plus vite d'autres solutions **2** N (= *game*) Scrabble® Scrabble® *m*

scrag [skræg] **1** N (*Brit Culin: also* **~ end**) collet *m* (de mouton) **2** VT‡ [+ *person*] tordre le cou à*

scragginess ['skrægɪnɪs] N (= *scrawniness*) maigreur *f*

scraggly* ['skrægli] ADJ (*US*) [*beard, hair*] en bataille ; [*plant*] difforme

scraggy ['skrægi] ADJ **a** (= *scrawny*) maigre **b** (= *unkempt, scanty*) [*hair, beard, fur*] peu fourni et hérissé

scram* [skræm] VI ficher le camp* ; **~!** fiche(-moi) le camp !* ; **I'd better ~** je dois filer*

scramble ['skræmbl] **1** VI **a** (= *clamber*) **to ~ up/down** *etc* grimper/descendre *etc* tant bien que mal ; **he ~d along the cliff** il a avancé avec difficulté le long de la falaise ; **they ~d over the rocks/up the cliff** en s'aidant des pieds et des mains ils ont avancé sur les rochers/escaladé la falaise ; **he ~d into/out of the car** il est monté dans/est descendu de la voiture à toute vitesse, il s'est précipité dans/hors de la voiture ; **he ~d down off the wall** il a dégringolé du mur ; **he ~d through the hedge** il s'est frayé tant bien que mal un passage à travers la haie ; **to ~ for** [+ *coins, seats*] se bousculer pour (avoir), se disputer ; [+ *jobs etc*] faire des pieds et des mains pour (avoir) **b** (*Brit Sport*) **to go scrambling** faire du trial **c** (*Aviat*) décoller sur alerte **2** VT (*Culin, Telec*) brouiller ; (*TV*) coder, crypter **3** N **a** ruée *f* ; **the ~ for seats** la ruée pour les places ; **there was a ~ for seats** (*lit*) on s'est rué sur les places ; (*fig*) on s'est arraché les places **b** (*also* **motorcycle ~**) (réunion *f* de) trial *m* **4** COMP ► **scrambled eggs** NPL œufs *mpl* brouillés

scrambler ['skræmblər] N **a** (*Telec* = *device*) brouilleur *m* ; (*TV*) brouilleur *m*, codeur *m* **b** (*Brit* = *motorcyclist*) trialiste *mf*

scrambling ['skræmblɪŋ] N (*Brit Sport*) trial *m*

scrap¹ [skræp] **1** N **a** (= *small piece*) [*of paper, cloth, bread, string*] (petit) bout *m* ; [*of verse, writing*] quelques lignes *fpl* ; [*of conversation*] bribe *f* ; [*of news*] fragment *m* ; **~s** (= *broken pieces*) débris *mpl* ; (= *food remnants*) restes *mpl* ; (*fig*) **there isn't a ~ of evidence** il n'y a pas la moindre preuve ; **it wasn't a ~ of use** cela n'a servi absolument à rien ; **there wasn't a ~ of truth in it** il n'y avait pas un brin de vérité là-dedans ; **not a ~** pas du tout **b** (*NonC* = *scrap iron*) ferraille *f* ; **to collect ~** récupérer de la ferraille ; **I put it out for ~** je l'ai envoyé à la ferraille ; **to sell a car/ship for ~** vendre une voiture/un bateau comme épave or à la casse ; **what is it worth as ~?** qu'est-ce que cela vaudrait (vendu) comme épave or à la casse ? **2** VT jeter, bazarder* ; [+ *car, ship*] envoyer à la ferraille or à la casse ; [+ *equipment*] mettre au rebut ; [+ *project*] abandonner, mettre au rancart* ; **let's ~ the idea** laissons tomber cette idée **3** COMP ► **scrap car** N voiture *f* mise en épave or à la casse ► **scrap dealer** N marchand *m* de ferraille, ferrailleur *m* ► **scrap iron** N ferraille *f* ► **scrap merchant** N = **scrap dealer** ► **scrap metal** N = **scrap iron** ► **scrap paper** N (*for scribbling on*) (papier *m* de) brouillon *m* ; (= *old newspapers etc*) vieux papiers *mpl* ► **scrap value** N **its ~ value is £10** (vendu) à la casse cela vaut 10 livres

scrap²* [skræp] **1** N (= *fight*) bagarre *f* ; **to get into or have a ~** se bagarrer* (**with** avec) **2** VI se bagarrer*

scrapbook ['skræpbʊk] N album *m* (*de coupures de journaux etc*)

scrape [skreɪp] **1** N **a** (= *action*) coup *m* de grattoir or de racloir ; (= *sound*) grattement *m*, raclement *m* ; (= *mark*) éraflure *f*, égratignure *f* ; **to give sth a ~** gratter or racler qch ; **to give one's knee a ~** s'érafler or s'égratigner le genou **b** [*of butter etc*] fine couche *f*, lichette* *f* **c** (* = *trouble*) **to get (o.s.) into a ~** s'attirer des ennuis, se mettre dans un mauvais pas ; **he's always getting into ~s** il lui arrive toujours des histoires* ; **to get (o.s.) out of a ~** se tirer d'affaire or d'embarras ; **to get sb into a ~** attirer des ennuis à qn, mettre qn dans un mauvais pas ; **to get sb out of a ~** tirer qn d'affaire or d'embarras **2** VT (= *graze*) érafler, égratigner ; (= *just touch*) frôler, effleurer ; (= *clean: gen*) gratter, racler ; [+ *vegetables*] gratter ; **to ~ (the skin off) one's knees** s'érafler les genoux ; **to ~ one's plate clean** tout manger, nettoyer or racler* son assiette ; (*Aut*) **I ~d his bumper** je lui ai frôlé or éraflé le pare-chocs ; **to ~ a living** vivoter ; **to ~ a violin*** racler du violon ; (*Naut*) **to ~ the bottom** talonner (le fond) ; **to ~ (the bottom of) the barrel** en être réduit aux raclures (*fig*) → **scrape up 3** VI (= *make scraping sound*) racler, gratter ; (= *rub*) frotter (**against** contre) ; **to ~ along the wall** frôler le mur ; **the car ~d past the lamp-post** la voiture a frôlé le réverbère ; **to ~ through the doorway** réussir de justesse à passer par la porte ; (*fig*) **he just ~d clear of a prison sentence** il a frisé la peine de prison, il a tout juste évité une peine de prison ; **to ~ through an exam** réussir un examen de justesse ; **to ~ and save** économiser sur tout → **bow²**

► **scrape along** VI = **scrape by**

► **scrape away 1** VI **to ~ away* at the violin** racler du violon **2** VT SEP enlever en grattant or en raclant

► **scrape by** VI (*financially*) vivoter ; **she ~d by on £30 per week** elle vivotait avec 30 livres par semaine ; **I can just ~ by in Spanish** j'arrive tout juste à me faire comprendre en espagnol

► **scrape off** VT SEP = **scrape away 2**

► **scrape out** VT SEP [+ *contents*] enlever en grattant or en raclant ; [+ *pan*] nettoyer en raclant, récurer

► **scrape through** VI passer de justesse ; (*fig* =

succeed) réussir de justesse

▶ **scrape together** VT SEP [a] **to ~ two bits of metal together** frotter deux morceaux de métal l'un contre l'autre [b] (*fig*) [+ *objects*] rassembler, ramasser; [+ *money*] réunir or rassembler à grand-peine or en raclant les fonds de tiroirs*

▶ **scrape up** VT SEP [+ *earth, pebbles*] ramasser, mettre en tas; (*fig*) [+ *money*] réunir or rassembler à grand-peine or en raclant les fonds de tiroirs*

scraper ['skreɪpəʳ] N racloir *m*, grattoir *m*; (*at doorstep*) décrottoir *m*, gratte-pieds *m inv*

scraperboard ['skreɪpəbɔːd] N carte *f* à gratter

scrapheap ['skræphiːp] N tas *m* de ferraille; (*fig*) **to throw** or **toss sth on the ~** mettre qch au rebut, bazarder qch*; **to throw** or **toss sb on the ~*** mettre qn au rancart*; **only fit for the ~*** bon à mettre au rancart*; (*fig*) **to end up on the ~** être mis au rebut

scrapie ['skreɪpɪ] N (*Vet*) tremblante *f*

scraping ['skreɪpɪŋ] [1] ADJ [*noise*] de grattement, de raclement [2] N [a] [*of butter*] fine couche *f*, lichette* *f*; **~s** [*of food*] restes *mpl*; [*of dirt, paint*] raclures *fpl* [b] (= *action*) grattement *m*, raclement *m* → **bow²**

scrappy ['skræpɪ] ADJ [a] (= *disjointed*) [*conversation, essay, film*] décousu; [*education*] incomplet (-ète *f*); [*football match*] confus; **a ~ goal** un but marqué à la suite d'un cafouillage [b] [*piece of paper*] en piteux état

scrapyard ['skræpjɑːd] N (*esp Brit*) dépôt *m* de ferraille; (*for cars*) cimetière *m* de voitures, casse* *f*

scratch [skrætʃ] [1] N [a] (= *mark*) (*on skin*) égratignure *f*, éraflure *f*; (*on paint*) éraflure *f*; (*on glass, record*) rayure *f*; **they came out of it without a ~** ils s'en sont sortis indemnes or sans une égratignure; **it's only a ~** ce n'est qu'une égratignure [b] (= *action*) grattement *m*; (*by claw*) coup *m* de griffe; (*by fingernail*) coup *m* d'ongle; **the cat gave her a ~** le chat l'a griffée; **to have a good ~*** se gratter un bon coup* [c] (= *noise*) grattement *m*, grincement *m* [d] (*Sport*) **to be on** or **start from ~** être scratch *inv*; (*fig*) **to start from ~** partir de zéro*; **we'll have to start from ~ again** il nous faudra repartir de zéro*; **he didn't come up to ~** il ne s'est pas montré à la hauteur; **his work doesn't come up to ~** son travail n'est pas à la hauteur or au niveau; **to bring up to ~** amener au niveau voulu; **to keep sb up to ~** maintenir qn au niveau voulu

[2] VT [a] (*with nail, claw*) griffer; [+ *varnish*] érafler; [+ *record, glass*] rayer; **to ~ a hole in sth** creuser un trou en grattant qch; **he ~ed his hand on a nail** il s'est éraflé or écorché la main sur un clou; **he ~ed his name on the wood** il a gravé son nom dans le bois; (*fig*) **it only ~ed the surface** (*gen*) c'était très superficiel; [*report, lecture*] ça n'a fait qu'effleurer la question, c'était très superficiel; **we've only managed to ~ the surface of the problem** nous n'avons fait qu'effleurer or aborder le problème; (*fig* = *write*) **to ~ a few lines** griffonner quelques mots

[b] (= *to relieve itch*) gratter; **to ~ o.s.** se gratter; (*lit, fig*) **to ~ one's head** se gratter la tête; (*fig*) **you ~ my back and I'll ~ yours** un petit service en vaut un autre [c] (= *cancel*) [+ *meeting*] annuler; (*Comput*) effacer; (*Sport etc*) [+ *competitor, horse*] scratcher; [+ *match, game*] annuler; [+ *candidate*] rayer de la liste; (*US Pol*) **to ~ a ballot** modifier un bulletin de vote (*en rayant un nom etc*)

[3] VI [a] (*with nail, claw*) griffer; (= *to relieve itch*) se gratter; [*hen*] gratter le sol; [*pen*] gratter, grincer; **the dog was ~ing at the door** le chien grattait à la porte

[b] (*Sport etc*) [*competitor*] se faire scratcher; [*candidate*] se désister

[4] COMP [*crew, team*] de fortune, improvisé; [*vote*] par surprise; [*golfer*] scratch *inv*, de handicap zéro ▶ **scratch and sniff** ADJ *que l'on gratte pour sentir un parfum* ▶ **scratch file** N (*Comput*) fichier *m* de travail or de manœuvre ▶ **scratch 'n' sniff** N = **scratch and sniff** ▶ **scratch pad** N (*gen*) bloc-notes *m*; (*Comput*) mémoire *f* bloc-notes ▶ **scratch paper** N (*US*) = **scrap paper** → **scrap** ▶ **scratch race** N course *f* scratch ▶ **scratch score** N (*Golf*) scratch score *m*, score *m* ramené à zéro ▶ **scratch sheet*** N (*US Racing*) journal *m* des courses (*hippiques*) ▶ **scratch tape** N (*Comput*) bande *f* de travail or de manœuvre ▶ **scratch test** N (*Med*) cuti(-réaction) *f*, test *m* cutané

▶ **scratch out** VT SEP [a] (*from list*) rayer, effacer [b] [+ *hole*] creuser en grattant; **to ~ sb's eyes out** arracher les yeux à qn

▶ **scratch together** VT SEP (*fig*) [+ *money*] réussir à amasser (en raclant les fonds de tiroirs*)

▶ **scratch up** VT SEP [+ *bone*] déterrer; (*fig*) [+ *money*] = **scratch together**

scratchcard ['skrætʃkɑːd] N (*Brit*) carte *f* à gratter

scratchy ['skrætʃɪ] ADJ [*surface, material*] rêche, qui accroche; [*pen*] qui grince, qui gratte; [*handwriting*] en pattes de mouche; [*record*] rayé, éraillé

scrawl [skrɔːl] [1] N [a] (*gen*) gribouillage *m*, griffonnage *m*; **I can't read her ~** je ne peux pas déchiffrer son gribouillage; **the word finished in a ~** le mot se terminait par un gribouillage; **her letter was just a ~** sa lettre était griffonnée à la hâte [b] (= *brief letter, note*) mot *m* griffonné [2] VT gribouiller, griffonner; **to ~ a note to sb** griffonner un mot à qn; **there were rude words ~ed all over the wall** il y avait des mots grossiers gribouillés sur tout le mur [3] VI gribouiller

scrawny ['skrɔːnɪ] ADJ maigre

scream [skriːm] [1] N [a] [*of pain, fear*] cri *m* aigu or perçant, hurlement *m*; [*of laughter*] éclat *m*; **to give a ~** pousser un cri [b]* **it was a ~** c'était à se tordre*, c'était vraiment marrant*; **he's a ~** il est désopilant or impayable* [2] VI (*also* **~ out**) [*person*] crier; (*stronger*) hurler; [*baby*] crier, brailler; [*siren, brakes, wind*] hurler; **to ~ with laughter** rire aux éclats or aux larmes; **to ~ with pain/with rage** hurler de douleur/de rage; **to ~ for help** crier à l'aide or au secours; **to ~ at sb** crier après qn [3] VT (*also* **~ out**) [a] [*abuse etc*] hurler (**at** à); **"shut up" he ~ed** "taisez-vous" hurla-t-il; **to ~ o.s. hoarse** s'enrouer à force de crier, s'égosiller [b] [*headlines, posters*] annoncer en toutes lettres

▶ **scream down** VT SEP **to ~ the place down** crier comme un damné or sourd

▶ **scream out** [1] VI = **scream 2** [2] VT SEP = **scream 3**

screamer* ['skriːməʳ] N (*US*) [a] (= *headline*) énorme manchette *f* [b] (= *joke*) histoire *f* désopilante; **he's a ~** il est désopilant or impayable*

screamingly* ['skriːmɪŋlɪ] ADV **~ funny** à mourir de rire, tordant*; **~ boring** à mourir d'ennui

scree ['skriː] N éboulis *m* (*en montagne*)

screech [skriːtʃ] [1] N (*gen*) cri *m* strident; (*from pain, fright, rage*) hurlement *m*; [*of brakes*] grincement *m*; [*of tyres*] crissement *m*; [*of owl*] cri *m* (rauque et perçant); [*of siren*] hurlement *m*; **she gave a ~ of laughter** elle est partie d'un rire perçant [2] VI [*person*] pousser des cris stridents, hurler; [*brakes*] grincer; [*tyres*] crisser; [*singer, owl*] crier; [*siren*] hurler [3] VT crier à tue-tête [4] COMP ▶ **screech owl** N chouette *f* effraie, chat-huant *m*

screed [skriːd] N [a] (= *discourse*) laïus* *m*, topo* *m* (**about** sur); (*letter*) longue missive *f* (**about** sur); (*fig* = *a lot*) **to write ~s*** écrire des volumes or toute une tartine* [b] (*Constr*) (= *depth guide strip*) guide *m*; (= *levelling device*) règle *f* à araser le béton; (*NonC* = *surfacing material*) matériau *m* de ragréage

screen [skriːn] [1] N [a] (*in room*) paravent *m*; (*for fire*) écran *m* de cheminée; (*fig: of troops, trees*) rideau *m*; (= *pretence*) masque *m* → **safety, silk, smoke** [b] (*Cine, TV, Comput etc*) écran *m*; **to show sth on a ~** projeter qch; (*TV*) **a 50-cm ~** un écran de 50 cm; (*Cine*) **the ~** l'écran *m*, le cinéma; (*Cine*) **the big** or **large ~** le grand écran; (*TV*) **the small ~** le petit écran; **to write for the ~** écrire des scénarios; **stars of the ~** les vedettes *fpl* de l'écran; **the violence children see on ~** la violence que les enfants voient à l'écran; **they are married off ~ as well as on** ils sont mari et femme à la scène or à l'écran comme à la ville; (*Comput*) **information can be accessed on ~** on peut afficher les renseignements à l'écran; (*Comput*) **to work on ~** travailler sur écran → **panoramic, television, wide** [c] (= *sieve*) crible *m*, claie *f*

[2] VT [a] (= *hide*) masquer, cacher; (= *protect*) faire écran à, protéger; **the trees ~ed the house** les arbres masquaient or cachaient la maison; **to ~ sth from sight** or **view** dérober or masquer qch aux regards; **he ~ed the book with his hand** il a caché le livre de sa main; **to ~ sth from the wind/sun** protéger qch du vent/du soleil; **to ~ one's eyes** se protéger les yeux avec la main, faire écran de sa main pour se protéger les yeux; **in order to ~ our movements from the enemy** pour cacher or masquer nos mouvements à l'ennemi [b] (*Cine, TV*) [+ *film*] projeter [c] (= *sieve*) [+ *coal*] cribler [d] (= *check*) [+ *candidates*] présélectionner; **to ~ sb (for a job)** passer au crible la candidature de qn; **the candidates were carefully ~ed** les candidats ont été passés au crible; (*Med*) **to ~ sb for cancer** faire subir à qn un test de dépistage du cancer

[3] COMP ▶ **screen actor** N acteur *m* de cinéma, vedette *f* de l'écran ▶ **screen door** N porte *f* grillagée ▶ **screen memory** N (*Psych*) souvenir-écran *m* ▶ **screen rights** NPL droits *mpl* d'adaptation cinématographique ▶ **screen test** N bout *m* d'essai; **to do a ~ test** tourner un bout d'essai ▶ **screen wash** N (*Brit Aut*) liquide *m* lave-glace ▶ **screen washer** N (*Brit Aut*) lave-glace *m* ▶ **screen writer** N scénariste *mf*

▶ **screen off** VT SEP **the kitchen was ~ed off from the rest of the room** la cuisine était séparée du reste de la pièce or était cachée (par un rideau or un paravent); **the nurses ~ed off his bed** les infirmiers ont mis un paravent autour de son lit; **the trees ~ed off the house from the road** les arbres cachaient la maison de la route, les arbres faisaient écran entre la maison et la route; **a cordon of police ~ed off the accident from the onlookers** les agents de police ont formé un cordon pour cacher l'accident aux badauds

screening ['skriːnɪŋ] [1] N [a] [*of film*] projection *f* [b] [*of coal*] criblage *m*; (*fig*) [*of person*] tri *m*, procédure *f* de sélection sur dossier; (*Med*) [*of person*] examen *m* de dépistage (**of sb** pratiquer sur qn); **the ~ of women for breast cancer** le dépistage du cancer du sein chez les femmes [2] COMP ▶ **screening room** N (*Cine*) salle *f* de projection

screenplay ['skriːnpleɪ] N scénario *m*

screenwriting ['skriːnraɪtɪŋ] N écriture *f* de scénarios

screw [skruː] [1] N [a] vis *f*; (= *action*) tour *m* de vis; (*Brit*) **a ~ of tea/sweets/tobacco** *etc*†

un cornet de thé/de bonbons/de tabac *etc*; (*fig*) **he's got a ~ loose*** il lui manque une case*; (*fig*) **to put** *or* **tighten the ~(s) on sb*** ◊ **to turn the ~ on sb*** augmenter la pression sur qn → **thumbscrew**
  [b] (*Aviat, Naut*) hélice *f* → **airscrew, twin**
  [c] (‡ = *sex*) **it was a good ~** on a bien baisé‡; **she's a good ~** c'est un bon coup‡
  [d] (‡ = *prison warder*) maton(ne)‡ *m(f)*
  [e] (*Brit* †‡ = *income*) salaire *m*; **he gets a good ~** son boulot paie bien*

2 VT [a] visser (**on** sur, to à), fixer avec une vis; **to ~ sth tight** visser qch à bloc
  [b] (= *twist*) **to ~ one's face into a smile** grimacer un sourire
  [c] (= *extort*) [+ *money*] extorquer, soutirer (**out of** à); [+ *information*] arracher (**out of** à); (‡ = *defraud*) [+ *person*] arnaquer*, pigeonner*
  [d] (‡‡ = *have sex with*) baiser‡‡
  [e] (‡: *in exclamations*) **~ you!** va te faire voir‡‡ *or* foutre‡‡!; **~ the cost/the neighbours!** on se fout du prix/des voisins!‡

3 VI se visser

4 COMP ► **screw bolt** N boulon *m* à vis ► **screw joint** N joint *m* à vis ► **screw propeller** N hélice *f* ► **screw thread** N filet *m* *or* filetage *m* de vis ► **screw top** N couvercle *m* à pas de vis ► **screw-top(ped)** ADJ avec couvercle à pas de vis ► **screw-up‡** N (*fig* = *muddle*) pagaille* f complète

► **screw around** VI [a] (‡ = *waste time*) glander‡, glandouiller‡ [b] (‡‡: *sexually*) baiser‡‡ avec tout le monde, coucher à droite à gauche*

► **screw down** [1] VI se visser [2] VT SEP visser (à fond)

► **screw off** [1] VI se dévisser [2] VT SEP dévisser

► **screw on** [1] VI se visser [2] VT SEP visser, fixer avec des vis; [+ *lid*] visser; (*fig*) **he's got his head ~ed on all right*** *or* **the right way*** il a la tête sur les épaules

► **screw round** VT SEP tourner, visser; (*fig*) **to ~ one's head round** se dévisser la tête *or* le cou

► **screw together** VT SEP [+ *two parts*] fixer avec une vis; **to ~ sth together** assembler qch avec des vis

► **screw up** [1] VT SEP [a] visser (à fond), resserrer (à fond) [b] [+ *paper*] chiffonner, froisser; [+ *handkerchief*] rouler, tortiller; **to ~ up one's eyes** plisser les yeux; **to ~ up one's face** faire la grimace; (*fig*) **to ~ up (one's) courage** prendre son courage à deux mains* (**to do** pour faire) [c] (‡ = *spoil*) foutre en l'air‡‡, bousiller* [d]‡ **to ~ sb up** détraquer‡ *or* perturber qn; **he is ~ed up** il est paumé‡ [2]‡ VI merder‡‡ [3] **~-up‡** N → **screw**

screwball‡ ['skruːbɔːl] ADJ, N cinglé(e)* *m(f)*, tordu(e)‡ *m(f)*

screwdriver ['skruːˌdraɪvəʳ] N (= *tool*) tournevis *m*; (= *drink*) vodka-orange *f*

screwed‡ ['skruːd] ADJ (*Brit* = *drunk*) paf* *inv*, bourré‡ → **screw up**

screwy‡ ['skruːɪ] ADJ [*person*] cinglé*; [*idea, situation*] tordu*

scribble ['skrɪbl] [1] VI gribouiller; **he was scribbling in a notebook** il gribouillait sur un carnet; **we were scribbling away furiously, trying to finish the exam** nous écrivions frénétiquement pour essayer de terminer l'épreuve; **someone has ~d all over the wall** quelqu'un a gribouillé sur le mur [2] VT griffonner, gribouiller; **to ~ a note to sb** griffonner *or* gribouiller un mot à qn; **there were comments ~d all over the page** il y avait des commentaires griffonnés *or* gribouillés sur toute la page [3] N gribouillage *m*; **I can't read her ~** je ne peux pas déchiffrer son gribouillage; **the word ended in a ~** le mot se terminait par un gribouillage; **her letter was just a ~** sa lettre était griffonnée

► **scribble down** VT SEP [+ *notes*] griffonner

► **scribble out** VT SEP [a] (= *erase*) rayer, ratu-

rer [b] [+ *essay, draft*] jeter sur le papier, ébaucher

scribbler ['skrɪbləʳ] N (*lit*) gribouilleur *m*, -euse *f*; (*fig* = *bad author*) plumitif *m*

scribbling ['skrɪblɪŋ] N gribouillage *m*, gribouillis *m* [2] COMP ► **scribbling pad** N (*Brit*) bloc-notes *m*

scribe [skraɪb] N scribe *m*

scrimmage ['skrɪmɪdʒ] N (*gen, Sport*) mêlée *f*

scrimp [skrɪmp] VI lésiner (**on** sur), être chiche (**on** de); **to ~ and save** *or* **scrape** économiser sur tout

scrimshank* ['skrɪmʃæŋk] (*Brit Mil*) [1] N = **scrimshanker** [2] VI tirer au flanc*

scrimshanker* ['skrɪmˌʃæŋkəʳ] N (*Brit Mil*) tire-au-flanc* *mf inv*

scrip [skrɪp] N (*Fin*) titre *m* provisoire (d'action)

scripholder ['skrɪphəʊldəʳ] N (*Fin*) détenteur *m*, -trice *f* de titres (provisoires)

script [skrɪpt] [1] N [a] (*Cine*) scénario *m*; (*Rad, Theat, TV*) texte *m*; (*in exam*) copie *f*; (*Jur*) document *m* original [c] (*NonC* = *handwriting*) script *m*, écriture *f* script; (*Typ*) scriptes *fpl* → **italic** [2] VT [+ *film*] écrire le scénario de; (*Rad, TV*) **~ed talk/discussion** *etc* conversation *f*/discussion *f etc* préparée d'avance

scriptural ['skrɪptʃərəl] ADJ biblique

Scripture ['skrɪptʃəʳ] N (*also* **Holy ~(s)**) Écriture *f* sainte, Saintes Écritures *fpl*; (*Scol*) **~ (lesson)** (cours *m* d')instruction *f* religieuse

scripture ['skrɪptʃəʳ] N texte *m* sacré

scriptwriter ['skrɪptˌraɪtəʳ] N (*Cine, TV*) scénariste *mf*

scrivener †† ['skrɪvnəʳ] N (= *scribe*) scribe *m*; (= *notary*) notaire *m*

scrod [skrɒd] N (*US*) jeune morue *f or* cabillaud *m* (spécialité du Massachusetts)

scrofula ['skrɒfjʊlə] N scrofule *f*

scrofulous ['skrɒfjʊləs] ADJ scrofuleux

scroll [skrəʊl] [1] N [a] [*of parchment*] rouleau *m*; (= *ancient book*) manuscrit *m* → **dead** [b] (*Archit*) volute *f*, spirale *f*; (*in writing*) enjolivement *m*; [*of violin*] volute *f* [2] VI (*Comput*) défiler [3] VT (*Comput*) **to ~ sth up/down** dérouler *or* faire défiler qch vers le haut/le bas

Scrooge [skruːdʒ] N harpagon *m*

scrotum ['skrəʊtəm] N (*pl* **scrotums** *or* **scrota** ['skrəʊtə]) scrotum *m*

scrounge* [skraʊndʒ] [1] VT [+ *meal, clothes etc*] réussir à se faire offrir (**from** *or* **off sb** par qn); **to ~ money from sb** taper qn*; **he ~d £5 off him** il l'a tapé de 5 livres*; **can I ~ your pen?** je peux te piquer* ton stylo? [2] VI (= *cadge*) **to ~ on sb** vivre aux crochets de qn; **he's always scrounging** c'est un parasite; (*for meals*) c'est un pique-assiette [3] N **to be on the ~ for sth** essayer d'emprunter qch; **he's always on the ~** c'est un parasite

scrounger* ['skraʊndʒəʳ] N parasite *m*, profiteur *m*, -euse *f*; (*for meals*) pique-assiette *mf inv*

scroungy‡ ['skraʊndʒɪ] ADJ (*US* = *scruffy*) dépenaillé*, débraillé

scrub¹ [skrʌb] [1] N nettoyage *m* à la brosse, bon nettoyage *m*; **to give sth a good ~** bien nettoyer qch (à la brosse *or* avec une brosse); **give your face a ~!** lave-toi bien la figure!; **it needs a ~** cela a besoin d'être bien nettoyé [2] VT [a] [+ *floor*] nettoyer *or* laver à la brosse; [+ *washing*] frotter; [+ *pan*] récurer; **to ~ one's hands** se brosser les mains, bien se nettoyer les mains; **she ~bed the walls clean** elle a nettoyé les murs à fond; **he ~bed the walls with bleach** il a nettoyé les murs à fond avec de l'eau de Javel; **to ~ o.s. (all over)** se frotter vigoureusement (tout le corps)
  [b] (* = *cancel*) [+ *match etc*] annuler; **let's ~ that** laissons tomber

3 VI frotter; **she's been on her knees ~bing all day** elle a passé sa journée à genoux à frotter les planchers; **to ~ at sth** récurer qch; **he was ~bing away at the oven** il récurait le four; (*fig*) **let's ~ round it:** laissons tomber*, n'en parlons plus

4 COMP ► **scrubbing brush** N (*Brit*) brosse *f* à récurer

► **scrub away** VT SEP [+ *dirt*] enlever en frottant; [+ *stain*] faire partir (en frottant)

► **scrub down** VT SEP [+ *room, walls*] nettoyer à fond; **to ~ o.s. down** faire une toilette en règle

► **scrub off** VT SEP → **scrub away**

► **scrub out** VT SEP [+ *name*] effacer; [+ *stain*] faire partir; [+ *pan*] récurer

► **scrub up** VI [*surgeon etc*] se brosser les mains avant d'opérer

scrub² [skrʌb] N (*NonC* = *brushwood*) broussailles *fpl*

scrubber¹ ['skrʌbəʳ] N (*also* **pan-~**) tampon *m* à récurer

scrubber²‡ ['skrʌbəʳ] N pute‡ *f*

scrubby ['skrʌbɪ] ADJ [*land*] broussailleux; [*trees, grass*] rabougri

scrubland ['skrʌblænd] N (*gen*) brousse *f*; (*in Austral*) scrub *m*

scrubwoman ['skrʌbˌwʊmən] N (*pl* **-women**) (*US*) femme *f* de ménage

scruff [skrʌf] N [a] **by the ~ of the neck** par la peau du cou [b] (* = *untidy person*) individu *m* débraillé *or* peu soigné

scruffily ['skrʌfɪlɪ] ADV **~ dressed** débraillé, dépenaillé*

scruffiness ['skrʌfɪnɪs] N [*of person*] tenue *f* débraillée *or* dépenaillée*; [*of clothes, building*] miteux *m*

scruffy ['skrʌfɪ] ADJ [*person, appearance, clothes*] débraillé, dépenaillé*; [*building*] miteux; [*hair*] en désordre

scrum [skrʌm] [1] N [a] (*Rugby*) mêlée *f*; **to put the ball into the ~** introduire le ballon dans la *or* en mêlée [b] (* *fig* = *pushing*) bousculade *f*, mêlée *f*; **the ~ of reporters** la bousculade *or* la mêlée des journalistes; **she pushed through the ~ of photographers** elle s'est frayé un chemin à travers la mêlée des photographes [2] COMP ► **scrum half** N demi *m* de mêlée

scrummage ['skrʌmɪdʒ] [1] N = **scrum** [2] VI (*Rugby*) jouer en mêlée; (*fig*) se bousculer

scrump* [skrʌmp] VT (*Brit*) [+ *apples etc*] chaparder

scrumptious* ['skrʌmpʃəs] ADJ délicieux; **it smells ~** ça sent délicieusement bon

scrumpy ['skrʌmpɪ] N (*Brit*) cidre *m* fermier

scrunch [skrʌntʃ] [1] VI **her feet ~ed on the gravel** ses pas crissaient sur le gravier [2] VT (*also* **~ up** = *crush*) écraser; **to ~ sth into a ball** faire une boule de qch

scrunchie ['skrʌntʃɪ] N (*for hair*) chouchou *m*

scruple ['skruːpl] [1] N scrupule *m*; **moral/religious ~s** scrupules *mpl* moraux/religieux; **to have ~s about sth** avoir des scrupules au sujet de qch; **he has no ~s** il est sans scrupules, il est dénué de scrupules; **to have no ~s about sth** n'avoir aucun scrupule au sujet de qch; **to have no ~s about doing sth** n'avoir aucun scrupule à faire qch, ne pas avoir scrupule à faire qch [2] VI (*frm*) **I did not ~ to accept his offer** je n'ai pas hésité à accepter *or* je n'ai pas eu scrupule (*liter*) à accepter son offre

scrupulous ['skruːpjʊləs] ADJ [a] (= *honest*) [*person, organization, honesty*] scrupuleux; **it is not ~ to do that** ce n'est pas honnête de faire cela [b] (= *meticulous*) [*person, research, care*] scrupuleux, méticuleux; [*attention*] scrupuleux; **he was ~ about paying his debts** il payait scrupuleusement ses dettes; **he is ~ about hygiene** il fait très attention aux questions d'hygiène; **he spoke with the most**

~ **politeness** il s'exprimait avec une extrême politesse

scrupulously ['skruːpjʊləslɪ] ADV [a] (= honestly) [behave] d'une manière scrupuleuse; ~ **honest/fair** d'une honnêteté/équité scrupuleuse [b] (= meticulously) [avoid] soigneusement; ~ **clean** d'une propreté irréprochable; **to be ~ careful** faire preuve d'un soin méticuleux

scrupulousness ['skruːpjʊləsnɪs] N (NonC) (= honesty) scrupules mpl, esprit m scrupuleux; (= exactitude) minutie f

scrutineer [ˌskruːtɪˈnɪər] N (Brit) scrutateur m, -trice f

scrutinize ['skruːtɪnaɪz] VT [+ writing, document] scruter, examiner minutieusement; [+ votes] pointer

scrutiny ['skruːtɪnɪ] N [a] (= act of scrutinizing) [of document, conduct] examen m minutieux or rigoureux; [of votes] pointage m [b] (= watchful gaze) regard m insistant or scrutateur (frm); **to keep sb under close ~** surveiller qn de près; **under his ~, she felt nervous** son regard insistant or scrutateur la mettait mal à l'aise

SCSI ['skʌzɪ] N (Comput) (ABBR = **small computer systems interface**) SCSI f

scuba ['skuːbə] [1] N (ABBR = **self-contained underwater breathing apparatus**) scaphandre m autonome [2] COMP ► **scuba dive** VI faire de la plongée sous-marine ► **scuba diver** N plongeur m, -euse f ► **scuba diving** N plongée f sous-marine (autonome)

scud [skʌd] VI (also ~ **along**) [clouds, waves] courir (à toute allure); [boat] filer (vent arrière); **the clouds were ~ding across the sky** les nuages couraient (à toute allure) dans le ciel

scuff [skʌf] [1] VT [+ shoes, furniture] érafler; **~ed shoes** chaussures fpl éraflées; **to ~ one's feet** traîner les pieds [2] VI traîner les pieds [3] COMP ► **scuff marks** NPL (on shoes) éraflures fpl, marques fpl d'usure

scuffle ['skʌfl] [1] N bagarre f, échauffourée f, rixe f [2] VI se bagarrer* (**with** avec) [b] (= shuffle) traîner les pieds

scull [skʌl] [1] N [a] (= one of a pair of oars) aviron m; (= single oar for stern) godille f [b] (= boat) outrigger m [2] VI (with two oars) ramer (en couple); (with single oar) godiller; **to go ~ing** faire de l'aviron [3] VT (with two oars) faire avancer à l'aviron; (with single oar) faire avancer à la godille

scullery ['skʌlərɪ] [1] N (esp Brit) arrière-cuisine f [2] COMP ► **scullery maid** N fille f de cuisine

sculpt [skʌlp(t)] [1] VT sculpter (**out of** dans) [2] VI sculpter, faire de la sculpture

sculptor ['skʌlptər] N sculpteur m

sculptress ['skʌlptrɪs] N femme f sculpteur, sculpteur m; **I met a ~** j'ai rencontré une femme sculpteur; **she is a ~** elle est sculpteur

sculptural ['skʌlptʃərəl] ADJ sculptural

sculpture ['skʌlptʃər] [1] N sculpture f; **a (piece of) ~** une sculpture [2] VTI sculpter

scum [skʌm] N [a] (gen) écume f; (foamy) écume f, mousse f; (dirty) couche f de saleté; (on bath) crasse f; **to remove the ~ (from)** (= foam) écumer; (= dirt) décrasser, nettoyer [b] (pej = people) rebut m, lie f; **the ~ of the earth** le rebut du genre humain [c] (‡ pej = person: also ~**bag**) salaud‡ m, ordure‡ f

scummy ['skʌmɪ] ADJ (lit) écumeux, couvert d'écume, mousseux; (‡ pej) de salaud‡

scunner‡ ['skʌnər] (Scot) [1] N **what a ~!** quelle barbe !*; **to take a ~ to sb/sth** prendre qn/qch en grippe [2] VI **to be ~ed** en avoir marre‡

scupper ['skʌpər] [1] N (Naut) dalot or daleau m [2] VT (Brit*) [+ plan, negotiations] faire capoter*; [+ effort] saboter; **we're ~ed** nous sommes fichus*

scurf [skɜːf] N (on scalp) pellicules fpl (du cuir chevelu); (on skin) peau f morte

scurfy ['skɜːfɪ] ADJ [scalp] pelliculeux; [skin] dartreux

scurrility [skʌˈrɪlɪtɪ] N [a] (= slander) caractère m calomnieux [b] (= obscenity) obscénité f

scurrilous ['skʌrɪləs] ADJ [a] (= defamatory) [rumour, article] calomnieux [b] (= obscene) obscène

scurrilously ['skʌrɪləslɪ] ADV [a] (= slanderously) [suggest, abuse] calomnieusement [b] (= obscenely) ~ **funny jokes** des plaisanteries fpl obscènes

scurry ['skʌrɪ] [1] N débandade f, sauve-qui-peut m inv; **a ~ of footsteps** des pas précipités [2] VI se précipiter, filer* (à toute allure)
► **scurry away, scurry off** VI [person] détaler, se sauver (à toutes jambes); [animal] détaler

scurvy ['skɜːvɪ] [1] N scorbut m [2] ADJ (†† or liter) bas (basse f), mesquin, vil (vile f)

scut [skʌt] N [of rabbit, deer] queue f

scutcheon ['skʌtʃən] N = **escutcheon**

scuttle[1] ['skʌtl] N (for coal) seau m (à charbon)

scuttle[2] ['skʌtl] VI courir précipitamment; **to ~ in/out/through** etc entrer/sortir/traverser etc précipitamment
► **scuttle away, scuttle off** VI déguerpir, filer*

scuttle[3] ['skʌtl] [1] N [a] (Naut) écoutille f [b] (US: in ceiling etc) trappe f [2] VT [a] (Naut) saborder; **to ~ one's own ship** se saborder [b] (fig) [+ hopes, plans] faire échouer

scuttlebutt ['skʌtlbʌt] N [a] (Naut = water cask) baril m d'eau douce [b] (US fig = gossip) ragots mpl, commérages mpl

scuzzy‡ ['skʌzɪ] ADJ (= dirty) dégueulasse‡; (= seedy) louche

Scylla ['sɪlə] N Scylla f; (fig) **to be between ~ and Charybdis** tomber de Charybde en Scylla

scythe [saɪð] [1] N faux f [2] VT faucher
► **scythe down** VT SEP (fig) [+ opponents, critics] descendre en flammes*
► **scythe through** VT FUS (fig) [+ troops, army] décimer; [+ building] pulvériser

SD ABBR = **South Dakota**

SDI [ˌesdiːˈaɪ] N (US Mil, Space) (ABBR = **Strategic Defense Initiative**) → **strategic**

SDLP [ˌesdiːelˈpiː] N (Ir Pol) (ABBR = **Social Democratic and Labour Party**) → **social**

SDP [ˌesdiːˈpiː] N (Brit Pol: formerly) (ABBR = **Social Democratic Party**) → **social**

SE (ABBR = **south-east**) S.-E.

sea [siː] [1] N (not land) mer f; **to swim in the ~** nager or se baigner dans la mer; **on the ~** [boat] en mer; [town] au bord de la mer; **by** or **beside the ~** au bord de la mer; **by ~** par mer, en bateau; **to be swept** or **carried out to ~** être emporté par la mer; **to go to ~** [boat] prendre la mer; [person] devenir or se faire marin; **to put to ~** prendre la mer; **look out to ~** regardez au or vers le large; **over** or (liter) **beyond the ~(s)** outre-mer; **from over** or (liter) **beyond the ~(s)** d'outre-mer; (lit) **(out) at ~** en mer; (fig) **I'm all at ~*** (= unable to understand, follow etc) je nage complètement*; (= unable to get used to new situation) je suis complètement désorienté or déboussolé*; **I'm all at ~ over how to answer this question** je ne sais absolument pas comment répondre à cette question; **he was all at ~ in the discussion** il était complètement perdu dans la discussion; **it left him all at ~** cela l'a complètement désorienté → **burial, call, follow, half, high**
[b] (= particular area) mer f; **the Sea of Galilee** la mer de Galilée
[c] (NonC = state of the sea) (état m de la) mer f; **what's the ~ like?** (for sailing) comment est la mer?; (for swimming) est-ce que l'eau est bonne?; **a rough** or **heavy ~** une mer houleuse; **a calm ~** une mer calme; (Naut) **to ship a ~** embarquer un paquet de mer
[d] (fig) [of flowers, corn etc] mer f; [of blood,

mare f, mer f; [of difficulties, troubles, doubts, confusion] océan m; **a ~ of faces** une multitude de visages
[2] COMP ► **sea air** N air m marin or de la mer ► **sea anchor** N ancre f flottante ► **sea anemone** N anémone f de mer ► **sea bathing** N bains mpl de mer ► **sea battle** N bataille f navale ► **sea bed** N fond m de la mer ► **sea bird** N oiseau m de mer, oiseau m marin ► **sea biscuit** N biscuit m de mer ► **sea boot** N botte f de caoutchouc ► **sea bream** N dorade or daurade f ► **sea breeze** N brise f de mer or du large ► **sea calf** N veau m marin, phoque m ► **sea captain** N capitaine m (de la marine marchande) ► **sea change** N (fig) profond changement m ► **sea chest** N malle-cabine f ► **sea coast** N côte f ► **sea cow** N vache f marine ► **sea crossing** N traversée f (par mer) ► **sea defences** NPL ouvrages mpl de défense (contre la mer) ► **sea dog** N (= fish) roussette f, chien m de mer; (= seal) phoque m commun; (= sailor) (**old**) ~ **dog** (vieux) loup m de mer ► **sea eagle** N aigle m de mer ► **sea eel** N anguille f de mer ► **sea elephant** N éléphant m de mer ► **sea fight** N combat m naval ► **sea fish** N poisson m de mer; ~ **fish farming** aquaculture f marine ► **sea floor** N fond m de la mer ► **sea front** N bord m de (la) mer, front m de mer ► **sea god** N dieu m marin ► **sea-green** N vert m glauque inv ◊ ADJ glauque ► **sea horse** N hippocampe m ► **sea kale** N chou m marin, crambe m ► **sea lamprey** N lamproie f de mer ► **sea lane** N couloir m or voie f de navigation maritime ► **sea lavender** N statice m ► **sea legs** NPL **to find** or **get one's ~ legs** s'amariner, s'habituer à la mer; **he's got his ~ legs** il a retrouvé le pied marin ► **sea level** N niveau m de la mer; **100 metres above/below ~ level** 100 mètres au-dessus/au-dessous du niveau de la mer ► **sea lift** N (Mil etc) évacuation f par mer ► **sea lion** N otarie f ► **sea loch** N (Scot) bras m de mer ► **Sea Lord** N (Brit) ≈ amiral m; **First Sea Lord** ≈ amiral m chef d'état-major de la Marine ► **sea mile** N mille m marin ► **sea otter** N loutre f de mer ► **sea perch** N perche f de mer ► **sea power** N puissance f navale ► **sea route** N route f maritime ► **sea rover** N (= ship) bateau m pirate; (= person) pirate m ► **sea salt** N sel m de mer ► **Sea Scout** N scout m marin ► **sea serpent** N serpent m de mer ► **sea shanty** N chanson f de marins ► **sea shell** N coquillage m ► **sea transport** N transports mpl maritimes ► **sea trout** N truite f de mer ► **sea urchin** N oursin m ► **sea view** N (esp Brit) vue f sur la mer ► **sea wall** N digue f ► **sea water** N eau f de mer

Seabee ['siːbiː] N (US Mil) militaire m du Génie maritime

seaboard ['siːbɔːd] N littoral m, côte f

seaborne ['siːbɔːn] ADJ [goods] transporté par mer; [trade] maritime

seafarer ['siːˌfɛərər] N marin m

seafaring ['siːˌfɛərɪŋ] N (also ~ **life**) vie f de marin; ~ **man** = **seafarer**

seafood ['siːfuːd] N fruits mpl de mer

seagirt ['siːgɜːt] ADJ (liter) ceint par la mer

seagoing ['siːgəʊɪŋ] ADJ (Naut) long-courrier; [theme, experience] maritime; ~ **man** marin m; ~ **ship** (navire m) long-courrier m, navire m de mer

seagull ['siːgʌl] N mouette f

seal[1] [siːl] [1] N phoque m [2] VI **to go ~ing** chasser le phoque [3] COMP ► **seal cull, seal culling** N massacre m des bébés phoques

seal[2] [siːl] [1] N [a] (= stamping device) sceau m, cachet m; (on document) sceau m, cachet m; (on envelope) cachet m; (on package) plomb m; (Jur: on door etc) scellé m; (frm) **to be under ~** [document] être sous scellés; (fig) **under ~ of secrecy** sous le sceau du secret; **under the ~**

of confession dans le secret de la confession; (*Comm*) **~ of quality** label *m* de qualité; (*Jur*) **given under my hand and ~** signé et scellé par moi; **to put** *or* **set one's ~ to sth** apposer son sceau à qch; (*fig*) **to set** *or* **give one's ~ of approval to sth** donner son approbation à qch; (*fig*) **this set the ~ on their alliance** ceci a scellé leur alliance → **privy, self**

b (= *ornamental stamp*) **Christmas ~** timbre *m* ornemental de Noël

c (= *device for sealing*: *also Aut*) joint *m* (d'étanchéité); **the ~ is not very good** ce n'est pas très étanche

2 VT **a** (= *put seal on*) [+ *document*] sceller, apposer un sceau sur; (= *stick down*) [+ *envelope, packet*] coller, fermer; (= *close with seal*) [+ *envelope*] cacheter; [+ *package*] plomber; [+ *jar*] sceller, fermer hermétiquement; [+ *tin*] souder; **~ed orders** instructions *fpl* secrètes; (*hum*) **my lips are ~ed** mes lèvres sont scellées; (*Culin*) **to ~ a steak** saisir un bifteck → **hermetically**

b (= *close off*) [+ *area*] boucler; [+ *border*] fermer

c (= *decide*) [+ *fate*] régler, décider (de); [+ *bargain*] conclure; **this ~ed his fate** cela a décidé (de) *or* a réglé son sort

3 COMP ► **seal ring** N chevalière *f*

► **seal in** VT SEP enfermer (hermétiquement); **our special process ~s the flavour in** notre procédé spécial garde *or* conserve toute la saveur

► **seal off** VT SEP (= *close up*) [+ *door, room*] condamner; (= *forbid entry to*) [+ *passage, road, room*] interdire l'accès de; (*with troops, police etc*) [+ *area*] boucler

► **seal up** VT SEP [+ *window, door, jar*] fermer hermétiquement, sceller; [+ *tin*] souder

sealant ['siːlənt] N (= *device*) joint *m*; (= *substance*) enduit *m* étanche

sealer ['siːlər] N (= *person*) chasseur *m* de phoques; (= *ship*) navire *m* équipé pour la chasse au(x) phoque(s)

sealing[1] ['siːlɪŋ] N chasse *f* aux phoques

sealing[2] ['siːlɪŋ] **1** N [of *document*] scellage *m*; [of *letter*] cachetage *m*; [of *package*] plombage *m* **2** COMP ► **sealing wax** N cire *f* à cacheter

sealskin ['siːlskɪn] **1** N peau *f* de phoque **2** ADJ en peau de phoque

seam [siːm] **1** N **a** (*in cloth, canvas*) couture *f*; (*in plastic, rubber*) couture *f*, joint *m*; (*in planks, metal*) joint *m*; (*in welding*) soudure *f*; **to fall** *or* **come apart at the ~s** [*garment*] se découdre; [*relationship*] battre de l'aile; [*system, country*] s'écrouler; **to be bursting at the ~s*** [*suitcase, room*] être plein à craquer **b** (*Min*) filon *m*, veine *f*; (*Geol*) couche *f* **c** (*on face*) (= *wrinkle*) ride *f*; (= *scar*) balafre *f*, couture *f* **2** VT faire une couture *or* un joint à

seaman ['siːmən] **1** N (*pl* **-men**) (*gen*) marin *m*; (*US Navy*) quartier-maître *m* de 2ᵉ classe → **able, ordinary 2** COMP ► **seaman apprentice** N (*US Navy*) matelot *m* breveté ► **seaman recruit** N (*US Navy*) matelot *m*

seamanlike ['siːmənlaɪk] ADJ de bon marin

seamanship ['siːmənʃɪp] N habileté *f* dans la manœuvre, qualités *fpl* de marin

seamed [siːmd] ADJ **a** [*stockings, tights*] à couture **b** [*face*] sillonné de rides; **a face ~ with wrinkles** un visage sillonné de rides; **the cave was ~ with crevices** la paroi de la caverne était entaillée de fissures; **grey rock ~ with white** de la roche grise veinée de blanc

seamen ['siːmən] NPL *of* **seaman**

seamless ['siːmlɪs] ADJ **a** [*stockings, bra, garment*] sans couture **b** (= *smooth*) [*transition*] sans heurts, en douceur; [*blend*] homogène; **a ~ whole** un ensemble homogène

seamstress ['sɛmstrɪs] N couturière *f*

seamy ['siːmɪ] ADJ [*event, details*] sordide; [*dis-*

---

trict] mal famé, louche; **the ~ side of life** le côté sordide de la vie

séance ['seɪɑːns] N [of *spiritualists*] séance *f* de spiritisme; [of *committee etc*] séance *f*, réunion *f*

seaplane ['siːpleɪn] **1** N hydravion *m* **2** COMP ► **seaplane base** N hydrobase *f*

seaport ['siːpɔːt] N port *m* de mer

sear [sɪər] **1** ADJ desséché, flétri **2** VT (= *wither*) [+ *flower, grain, leaves*] [*heat*] dessécher, flétrir; [*frost*] flétrir; (= *burn*) brûler; (*Med* = *cauterize*) cautériser; [= *brand*] marquer au fer rouge; (*fig* = *make callous*) [+ *person, conscience, feelings*] endurcir

► **sear through** VT FUS [+ *walls, metal*] traverser, percer

search [sɜːtʃ] **1** N **a** (*for sth lost*) recherche(s) *f(pl)*; **in ~ of** à la recherche de; **a ~ was made for the child** on a entrepris des recherches pour retrouver l'enfant; **the ~ for the missing man** les recherches entreprises pour retrouver l'homme; **to begin a ~ for** [+ *person*] partir à la recherche de; [+ *thing*] se mettre à la recherche de; **in my ~ I found an interesting book** au cours de mes recherches j'ai découvert un livre intéressant → **house**

b [of *drawer, box, pocket, district*] fouille *f*; (*Admin*) [of *luggage etc*] visite *f*; (*Jur*) [of *building etc*] perquisition *f*; **the ~ did not reveal anything** la fouille n'a rien donné; **his ~ of the drawer revealed nothing** il a fouillé le tiroir sans rien trouver *or* pour ne rien trouver; **the thieves' ~ of the house** la fouille de la maison par les voleurs; (*Police*) **house ~** perquisition *f* à domicile, visite *f* domiciliaire; (*Jur*) **right of ~** droit *m* de visite; **passengers must submit to a ~** les passagers doivent se soumettre à une fouille

c (*Comput*) recherche *f*; **~ and replace** recherche *f* et remplacement *m*

2 VT **a** (= *hunt through*) [+ *house, park, woods, district*] fouiller; (*Jur*) [+ *house etc*] perquisitionner; **they ~ed the woods for the child** ils ont fouillé les bois *or* ils ont passé les bois au peigne fin à la recherche de l'enfant; **we have ~ed the library for it** nous l'avons cherché partout dans la bibliothèque **b** (= *examine*) [+ *pocket, drawer, suitcase*] fouiller (dans) (**for** pour essayer de retrouver); [+ *luggage*] (*gen*) fouiller; (*Customs, Police etc*) visiter; [+ *suspect*] fouiller; **they ~ed him for a weapon** ils l'ont fouillé pour s'assurer qu'il n'avait pas d'arme; **~ me!*** je n'en sais rien!, je n'en ai pas la moindre idée! **c** (= *scan*) [+ *documents, records, photograph*] examiner (en détail) (**for** pour trouver); (*fig*) **he ~ed her face for some sign of affection** il a cherché sur son visage un signe d'affection; **to ~ one's conscience** sonder sa conscience; **to ~ one's memory** chercher dans *or* fouiller dans ses souvenirs

d (*Comput*) [+ *file*] consulter; **to ~ a file for sth** rechercher qch dans un fichier

3 VI **a** (*gen*) chercher; **to ~ after** *or* **for sth** chercher *or* rechercher qch; **to ~ through sth** fouiller qch, chercher dans qch; **they ~ed through his belongings** ils ont fouillé ses affaires

b (*Comput*) **to ~ for** rechercher

4 COMP ► **search-and-destroy** ADJ (*Mil*) [*mission, operation*] de recherche et destruction ► **search engine** N (*Comput*) moteur *m* de recherche ► **search party** N équipe *f* *or* caravane *f* *or* expédition *f* de secours ► **search warrant** N (*Jur*) mandat *m* de perquisition

► **search about**, **search around** VI **to ~ about for sth** chercher qch un peu partout, fouiller un peu partout pour trouver qch

► **search out** VT SEP chercher partout; (*and find*) trouver

searcher ['sɜːtʃər] N chercheur *m*, -euse *f* (**for, after** en quête de)

---

searching ['sɜːtʃɪŋ] ADJ [*look, glance, eyes*] scrutateur (-trice *f*), inquisiteur (-trice *f*); [*mind*] pénétrant; [*question*] perspicace; [*examination*] rigoureux; **it was a ~ test of his ability** cela a mis ses compétences à rude épreuve → **heart**

searchingly ['sɜːtʃɪŋlɪ] ADV [*look*] d'un air inquisiteur

searchlight ['sɜːtʃlaɪt] N projecteur *m*

searing ['sɪərɪŋ] ADJ **a** (= *intense*) [*heat*] torride; [*sun*] brûlant, de plomb; [*light*] aveuglant; [*pain*] fulgurant **b** (= *forceful*) [*indictment, criticism, article*] virulent

seascape ['siːskeɪp] N (= *view*) paysage *m* marin; (*Art*) marine *f*

seashore ['siːʃɔːr] N rivage *m*, bord *m* de (la) mer; **by** *or* **on the ~** au bord de la mer; **children playing on the ~** des enfants qui jouent sur la plage

seasick ['siːsɪk] ADJ **to be ~** avoir le mal de mer; **to feel ~** avoir le mal de mer

seasickness ['siːsɪknɪs] N mal *m* de mer

seaside ['siːsaɪd] **1** N (*NonC*) bord *m* de la mer; **at** *or* **beside** *or* **by the ~** au bord de la mer, à la mer; **we're going to the ~** nous allons à la mer *or* au bord de la mer **2** COMP [*town*] au bord de la mer; [*holiday*] à la mer; [*hotel*] en bord de mer, au bord de la mer ► **seaside resort** N station *f* balnéaire

▼**season** ['siːzn] **1** N **a** (*spring, summer etc*) saison *f*; **the dry ~** la saison sèche → **monsoon, rainy**

b (*Sport, Comm, Zool, Agr, Hunting etc*) saison *f*; (= *period of activity, availability etc*) époque *f*, saison *f*; (*also* **social ~**) saison *f* des réunions mondaines; **it isn't the ~ for lily of the valley** ce n'est pas la saison du muguet; (*Sport*) **when does the new ~ begin?** quand commence la nouvelle saison?; (*Sport*) **his first ~ in the Celtic team** sa première saison dans l'équipe du Celtic; **the start of the ~** (*for tourism, hotels etc*) le début de (la) saison; (*Shooting*) l'ouverture de la chasse; (*social*) le commencement de la saison (mondaine); **early in the ~** (*gen*) en début de saison; (*very beginning*) au début de la saison; **late in the ~** dans l'arrière-saison, tard dans la saison; **the busy ~** (*for shops etc*) la période de grande activité; (*for hotels etc*) la pleine saison; (*Brit*) **the peak/high/low ~** la pleine/haute/basse saison; **the hunting/fishing** *etc* **~** la saison de la chasse/de la pêche *etc*; **the strawberry/sweetcorn ~** la saison des fraises/du maïs; **the football ~** la saison de football; **the tourist ~** la saison touristique; **the holiday ~** la période *or* la saison des vacances; **the Christmas ~** la période de Noël *or* des fêtes; **"Season's greetings"** « Joyeux Noël et bonne année »; **to be out of/in ~** [*food*] ne pas être/être de saison; (*for hunting*) être fermé/ouvert → **1f**; **are pheasants in ~ now?** les faisans sont-ils en saison?; **to go somewhere out of/in ~** aller quelque part hors saison *or* en basse saison/en haute saison; **strawberries out of/in ~** fraises hors de/de saison → **breeding, festive, silly**

c (*fig*) moment *m* opportun; **a word in ~** un mot dit à propos *or* au moment opportun; **in (~) and out of ~** à tout bout de champ; **in due ~** en temps utile, au moment opportun

d (*Theat*) saison *f* (théâtrale); **he did a ~ at the Old Vic** il a joué à l'Old Vic pendant une saison; **the film is here for a short ~** le film sera projeté quelques semaines; (*on notice*) **for a ~, Laurence Olivier in "Macbeth"** pour quelques semaines, Laurence Olivier dans « Macbeth »; (*TV*) **a Dustin Hoffman ~** ◊ **a ~ of Dustin Hoffman films** un cycle Dustin Hoffman

e = **season ticket**

f (*Vet*) [*animals*] (*for mating*) **to be out of/in ~** [*males*] ne pas être/être en (période de) rut; [*females*] ne pas être/être en chaleur

---

$\boxed{2}$ VT $\boxed{a}$ [+ *wood*] faire sécher, dessécher ; [+ *cask*] abreuver → **seasoned**
$\boxed{b}$ (*Culin*) (*with condiments*) assaisonner ; (*with spice*) épicer, relever ; **a highly ~ed dish** un plat relevé ; (*fig*) **a speech ~ed with humour** un discours assaisonné *or* pimenté d'humour

$\boxed{3}$ COMP ▸ **season ticket** N (*Rail, Theat etc*) carte *f* d'abonnement ; **to take out a ~ ticket** prendre un abonnement, s'abonner **(for à)** ▸ **season ticket holder** N abonné(e) *m(f)*

seasonable ['si:znəbl] ADJ $\boxed{a}$ [*weather*] de saison $\boxed{b}$ (*frm* = *timely*) [*advice, arrival*] opportun

seasonal ['si:zənl] $\boxed{1}$ ADJ [*work, migration*] saisonnier ; [*changes, fruit, vegetable*] de saison ; **the holiday business is ~** le tourisme est une industrie saisonnière $\boxed{2}$ COMP ▸ **seasonal adjustment** N (*Econ, Pol*) correction *f* des variations saisonnières, **after ~ adjustments** en données corrigées des variations saisonnières, après correction des variations saisonnières ▸ **seasonal affective disorder** N dépression *f* saisonnière ▸ **seasonal worker** N (ouvrier *m*, -ière *f*) saisonnier *m*, -ière *f*

seasonally ['si:zənəlɪ] ADV [*migrate*] de manière saisonnière ; **~ available fruit and vegetables** les fruits *mpl* et légumes *mpl* de saison ; **~ adjusted figures** données *fpl* corrigées des variations saisonnières ; **according to the ~ adjusted figures** en données corrigées des variations saisonnières, après correction des variations saisonnières

seasoned ['si:znd] ADJ $\boxed{a}$ (= *experienced*) [*professional, performer*] chevronné, expérimenté ; [*observer, traveller*] expérimenté ; [*troops*] aguerri ; (*fig*) **campaigner** vieux routier *m* ; **a ~ campaigner for civil rights** un vétéran des campagnes pour les droits civils $\boxed{b}$ [*wood, timber*] séché → **season**

seasoning ['si:znɪŋ] N assaisonnement *m* ; **to check the ~** vérifier l'assaisonnement ; **add ~** assaisonnez ; **there wasn't enough ~ in the soup** la soupe n'était pas assez assaisonnée *or* était fade ; (*fig*) **with a ~ of humour** avec un grain *or* une pointe d'humour

seat [si:t] $\boxed{1}$ N $\boxed{a}$ (= *chair etc*) (*gen*) siège *m* ; (*in theatre, cinema*) fauteuil *m* ; (*in bus, train*) banquette *f* ; (*Aut*) (*individual*) siège *m* ; (*for several people*) banquette *f* ; [*of cycle*] selle *f* → **back, driver, hot**
$\boxed{b}$ (= *place or right to sit*) place *f* ; **to take a ~** s'asseoir ; **to take one's ~** prendre place → **1d** ; **to keep one's ~** rester assis ; **to lose one's ~** perdre sa place → **1d** ; (*Cine, Theat*) **I'd like two ~s for ...** je voudrais deux places pour ... ; **keep a ~ for me** gardez-moi une place ; **there are ~s for 70 people** il y a 70 places assises → **book**
$\boxed{c}$ (= *part of chair*) siège *m* ; [*of trousers*] fond *m* ; (* = *buttocks*) derrière *m*, postérieur* *m* ; (*fig*) **he was flying by the ~ of his pants** il a dû faire appel à toute la présence d'esprit dont il était capable
$\boxed{d}$ (*Parl*) siège *m* ; **to keep/lose one's ~** être/ne pas être réélu ; (*Brit*) **to take one's ~ in the Commons/in the Lords** prendre son siège aux Communes/à la Chambre des lords, ≈ être validé comme député à l'Assemblée nationale/comme sénateur ; **the socialists won/lost ten ~s** les socialistes ont gagné/perdu dix sièges ; **they won the ~ from the Conservatives** ils ont pris le siège aux conservateurs ; **a majority of 50 ~s** une majorité de 50 (députés *etc*) → **safe**
$\boxed{e}$ (*on company board, committee*) siège *m*
$\boxed{f}$ (= *location, centre*) [*of government*] siège *m* ; [*of commerce*] centre *m* ; (*Med*) [*of infection*] foyer *m* ; **~ of learning** siège *m or* haut lieu *m* du savoir ; **he has a (country) ~ in the north** il a un manoir *or* un château dans le nord
$\boxed{g}$ (*Horse-riding*) **to have a good ~** avoir une bonne assiette, bien se tenir en selle ; **to keep one's ~** rester en selle ; **to lose one's ~** être désarçonné, vider les étriers

$\boxed{2}$ VT $\boxed{a}$ [+ *child*] (faire) asseoir ; (*at table*) [+ *guest*] placer ; **to ~ o.s.** s'asseoir ; **please be ~ed** veuillez vous asseoir, asseyez-vous je vous prie ; **to remain ~ed** rester assis ; **the waiter ~ed him at my table** le garçon l'a placé à ma table → **deep**
$\boxed{b}$ (= *have or find room for*) **we cannot ~ them all** nous n'avons pas assez de sièges pour tout le monde ; **how many does the hall ~?** combien y a-t-il de places assises *or* à combien peut-on s'asseoir dans la salle ? ; **this car ~s six in comfort** on tient confortablement à six dans cette voiture ; **this table ~s eight** on peut tenir à huit à cette table, c'est une table pour huit personnes *or* couverts
$\boxed{c}$ (*also* **reseat**) [+ *chair*] refaire le siège de ; [+ *trousers*] (re)mettre un fond à
$\boxed{3}$ VI (*frm*) **this skirt won't ~** cette jupe ne va pas se déformer à l'arrière
$\boxed{4}$ COMP ▸ **seat back** N dossier *m* (de chaise *etc*) ▸ **seat belt** N (*Aut, Aviat*) ceinture *f* de sécurité ▸ **seat cover** N housse *f* (*de siège*)

-seater ['si:tə'] ADJ, N (*in compounds*: Aut) **a two-seater** une deux places ; **two-seater car/plane** voiture *f*/avion *m* biplace *or* à deux places ; **a 50-seater coach** un car de 50 places

seating ['si:tɪŋ] $\boxed{1}$ N (*NonC*) $\boxed{a}$ (= *act*) répartition *f or* allocation *f* des places ; **is the ~ (of the guests) all right?** est-ce qu'on a bien placé les invités ? $\boxed{b}$ (= *seats*) sièges *mpl* ; (*as opposed to standing room*) places *fpl* assises ; **~ for 600** 600 places assises $\boxed{2}$ COMP ▸ **seating accommodation** N nombre *m* de places assises ▸ **seating arrangements** NPL **we must think about the ~ arrangements** nous devons réfléchir à la manière dont nous allons placer les gens ; **what are the ~ arrangements?** comment va-t-on placer les gens ? ▸ **seating capacity** N = seating accommodation ▸ **seating plan** N (*at dinner*) plan *m* de table

seatmates ['si:tmeɪts] NPL (*US*) **we were ~** nous étions assis l'un(e) à côté de l'autre

SEATO ['si:təʊ] N (ABBR = **South East Asia Treaty Organisation**) OTASE *f*

seatwork ['si:tw3:k] N (*US Scol*) travail *m* fait en classe

seaward ['si:wəd] $\boxed{1}$ ADJ $\boxed{a}$ (= *towards the sea*) [*side, face, end*] qui fait face à la mer, côté mer ; [*journey*] vers la mer $\boxed{b}$ (= *from the sea*) [*wind*] (venant) du large $\boxed{2}$ ADV (*also* **~s**) (= *towards sea*) vers la mer ; (= *out to sea*) vers le large

seaway ['si:weɪ] N route *f* maritime

seaweed ['si:wi:d] N algue(s) *f(pl)*

seaworthiness ['si:,w3:ðɪnɪs] N navigabilité *f* → **certificate**

seaworthy ['si:,w3:ðɪ] ADJ en état de naviguer

sebaceous [sɪ'beɪʃəs] ADJ sébacé

Sebastian [sɪ'bæstjən] N Sébastien *m*

seborrhoea [,sebə'rɪə] N séborrhée *f*

sebum ['si:bəm] N sébum *m*

SEC [,esi:'si:] N (*US*) (ABBR = **Securities and Exchange Commission**) ≈ COB *f*

sec* [sek] N ABBR = **second**

SECAM ['si:,kæm] (*TV*) (ABBR = **séquentiel à mémoire**) SECAM *m*

secant ['si:kənt] $\boxed{1}$ N sécante *f* $\boxed{2}$ ADJ sécant

secateurs [,sekə'tз:z] NPL (*esp Brit: also* **pair of ~**) sécateur *m*

secede [sɪ'si:d] VI faire sécession, se séparer (**from** de)

secession [sɪ'seʃən] N sécession *f*, séparation *f*

secessionist [sɪ'seʃnɪst] ADJ, N sécessionniste *mf*

seclude [sɪ'klu:d] VT éloigner *or* isoler (du monde)

secluded [sɪ'klu:dɪd] ADJ [*place, beach, house*] retiré, à l'écart ; [*valley, garden*] retiré ; [*life*] retiré (du monde) ; [*village*] isolé

seclusion [sɪ'klu:ʒən] N solitude *f* ; **to live in ~** vivre en solitaire, vivre retiré du monde

second¹ ['sekənd] $\boxed{1}$ ADJ $\boxed{a}$ (*one of many*) deuxième ; (*one of two*) second ; **a ~ chance** une seconde *or* autre chance ; **you may not get a ~ chance** l'occasion ne se représentera peut-être pas ; **Britain's ~ city** la deuxième ville de Grande-Bretagne ; **the ~ day I was there** le lendemain de mon arrivée ; **every ~ day** tous les deux jours, un jour sur deux ; **every ~ Thursday** un jeudi sur deux ; **on the ~ floor** (*Brit*) au deuxième (étage) ; (*US*) au premier (étage) ; **to hear** *or* **learn sth at ~ hand** (= *indirectly*) apprendre qch de seconde main → **secondhand** ; **to be ~ in the queue** être le (*or* la) deuxième dans la queue ; (*Scol*) **he was ~ in French** il était deuxième en français ; **this is her ~ marriage** c'est la deuxième fois qu'elle se marie, c'est son second mariage ; **in the ~ place** deuxièmement, en second lieu ; **in the first place ... in the ~ place ...** d'abord ... ensuite ... ; **to be** *or* **lie in ~ place** être en deuxième position, occuper la deuxième place ; **to finish in ~ place** terminer deuxième ; **that's the ~ time you've asked me that** c'est la deuxième fois que vous me posez la question ; **a ~ time** une deuxième fois ; **for the** *or* **a ~ time** pour la deuxième fois ; **for the ~ and last time** pour la seconde et dernière fois ; **~ time around** la deuxième fois ; **to be ~ to none** être sans pareil, être sans égal ; **San Francisco is ~ only to New York as the tourist capital of the States** seul New York surpasse San Francisco comme capitale touristique des États-Unis → **2** ; → **helping, look, row** ; *for other phrases see* **sixth**
$\boxed{b}$ (= *additional*) [*car*] deuxième ; **to have a ~ home** avoir une résidence secondaire
$\boxed{c}$ (*in comparisons*) second ; **there are fears of a ~ Chernobyl** on craint un second Tchernobyl ; **England is like a ~ home to him** l'Angleterre est une seconde patrie pour lui ; **she's like a ~ mother to me** elle est (comme) une deuxième mère pour moi ; **~ self** autre soi-même *m* ; **my ~ self** un(e) autre moi-même
$\boxed{d}$ (*Mus*) **~ violin** second violon *m* ; **to play ~ violin** être second violon ; **she's singing ~ soprano in the concert** elle est seconde soprano pour ce concert
$\boxed{e}$ (*in titles*) **Queen Elizabeth the Second** la reine Élisabeth II ; **Pope John Paul the Second** le pape Jean-Paul II ; *for other phrases see* **sixth**
$\boxed{2}$ ADV $\boxed{a}$ (*one of many*) deuxième ; (*one of two*) second ; (*in poll, league table*) **to come ~** arriver deuxième *or* second, arriver en deuxième *or* seconde position ; (*in race, competition, election*) **to come** *or* **finish ~** arriver *or* terminer deuxième *or* second ; **he was placed ~** il s'est classé deuxième *or* second ; (*at meeting, party etc*) **he arrived ~** il a été le deuxième à arriver
$\boxed{b}$ (= *secondly*) deuxièmement
$\boxed{c}$ (+ *superl adj*) **the ~ tallest building in the world** le deuxième immeuble du monde par sa hauteur ; **the ~ largest shareholder** le deuxième actionnaire par ordre d'importance ; **the ~ most common question** la deuxième parmi les questions les plus souvent posées → **second-best**
$\boxed{3}$ N $\boxed{a}$ deuxième *mf*, second(e) *m(f)* ; **he came a good** *or* **close ~** il a été battu de justesse ; **he came a poor ~** il est arrivé deuxième, loin derrière le vainqueur
$\boxed{b}$ (*Boxing*) soigneur *m* ; (*in duel*) second *m*, témoin *m* ; (*Boxing*) **~s out (of the ring)!** soigneurs hors du ring !
$\boxed{c}$ (*Brit Univ*) licence *f* avec mention (assez) bien ; **he got an upper/a lower ~** ≈ il a eu sa licence avec mention bien/assez bien ; **many students get a ~** ≈ de nombreux étudiants sont reçus avec la mention assez bien
$\boxed{d}$ (*also* **~ gear**) seconde *f* ; **in ~** en seconde
$\boxed{e}$ (*Mus* = *interval*) seconde *f*

4 **seconds** NPL [a] (*Comm* = *imperfect goods*) articles *mpl* de second choix, articles *mpl* comportant un défaut

[b] (* = *second helping*) rab❉ *m*, rabiot* *m*; **any-one for ~s?*** qui en reveut?, qui veut du rab?❉

5 VT [a] [+ *motion*] appuyer; [+ *speaker*] appuyer la motion de; **I'll ~ that** (*at meeting*) j'appuie cette proposition or cette demande; (*gen*) je suis d'accord or pour*

[b] [sɪˈkɒnd] (*Brit Admin, Mil*) affecter provisoirement (**to** à), détacher (**to** à)

6 COMP ► **second-best** → **second-best** ► **second chamber** N (*Parl*) (*gen*) deuxième chambre *f*; (*Brit*) **the ~ chamber** la Chambre haute, la Chambre des lords ► **second childhood** N **to be in one's ~ childhood** être retombé en enfance ► **second-class** → **second-class** ► **the second coming** N (*Rel*) le second avènement (du Christ) ► **second cousin** N petit(e) cousin(e) *m(f)* (*issu(e) de germains*) ► **second fiddle** N (*fig*) **to play ~ fiddle** jouer les seconds rôles (**to sb** à côté de qn) ► **second gear** N seconde *f* ► **second-guess*** VT (*esp US*) [+ *person, sb's reaction*] (essayer d')anticiper ► **the second house** N (*Theat*) la deuxième or seconde représentation (de la journée) ► **second-in-command** N (*Mil*) commandant *m* en second; (*Naut*) second *m*; (*gen*) second *m*, adjoint *m*; **to be ~ in command** être deuxième dans la hiérarchie ► **second language** N (*in education system*) première langue *f* (étrangère); (*of individual*) deuxième langue *f* ► **second lieutenant** N (*Mil etc*) sous-lieutenant *m* ► **second mate** N (*Merchant Navy*) commandant *m* en second ► **second mortgage** N hypothèque *f* de second rang ► **second name** N nom *m* de famille ► **second nature** N **it's ~ nature (to him)** c'est une seconde nature (chez lui); **it was ~ nature for him to help his friends** aider ses amis était chez lui une seconde nature ► **second officer** N = **second mate** ► **second opinion** N (*gen*) un autre avis, l'avis *m* de quelqu'un d'autre; (*from doctor, lawyer, etc*) un deuxième avis; **I'd like a ~ opinion** j'aimerais avoir un autre avis or l'avis de quelqu'un d'autre ► **the second person** N (*Gram*) la deuxième personne; **in the ~ person** à la deuxième personne; **the ~ person singular/ plural** la deuxième personne du singulier/du pluriel ► **second-rate** ADJ [*goods*] de qualité inférieure; [*work*] médiocre; [*writer*] de seconde zone ► **second-rater*** N médiocre *mf*, médiocrité *f* ► **second sight** N **to have ~ sight** avoir le don de double vue ► **second string** N (*esp US Sport*) (= *player*) remplaçant(e) *m(f)*; (= *team*) équipe *f* de réserve; **he has a ~ string to his bow** il a plus d'une corde à son arc ► **second teeth** NPL seconde dentition *f* ► **second thought** N **without** or **with hardly a ~ thought** sans hésiter; **not to give sb/sth a ~ thought** ne plus penser à qn/ qch; **he didn't give it a ~ thought** il l'a fait sans hésiter; **on ~ thoughts** (*Brit*) or **thought** (*US*) réflexion faite, à la réflexion; **to have ~ thoughts (about sth)** (= *be doubtful*) avoir des doutes (sur qch); **to have ~ thoughts about doing sth** (= *be doubtful*) se demander si l'on doit faire qch; (= *change mind*) changer d'avis et décider de ne pas faire qch ► **second wind** N **to get one's ~ wind** trouver un or son second souffle

second² [ˈsekənd] **1** N (*in time*) seconde *f*; **it won't take a ~** il y en a pour une seconde; **at that very ~** à cet instant précis; **just a ~!** ◊ **half a ~!*** un instant!, une seconde!; **I'm coming in half a ~** j'arrive tout de suite or dans une seconde; **I'll be with you in (just) a ~** je suis à vous dans une seconde → **split** **2** COMP ► **second hand** N trotteuse *f*

secondary [ˈsekəndərɪ] **1** ADJ [a] (= *less important*) [*character, role, effect, source*] se-

condaire; **of ~ importance** (d'une importance) secondaire; **the cost is a ~ consideration** la question du coût est secondaire; **my desire to have children was always ~ to my career** ma carrière a toujours primé sur mon désir d'avoir des enfants

[b] (*Educ*) [*education*] secondaire, du second degré; [*schooling*] secondaire; [*student, teacher*] du secondaire; **after five years of ~ education** après cinq années d'enseignement secondaire, après cinq années dans le secondaire; **subjects taught at ~ level** les matières *fpl* enseignées dans le secondaire

2 N [a] (*Univ etc* = *minor subject*) matière *f* secondaire, sous-dominante *f*

[b] (*also* **~ school**) (*gen*) établissement *m* d'enseignement secondaire; (*age 11 to 15*) collège *m* (d'enseignement secondaire); (*from age 15 to 18*) lycée *m*

[c] (*Med*: *also* **~ tumour**) tumeur *f* secondaire, métastase *f*

3 COMP ► **secondary action** N (*Pol*) mouvement *m* de solidarité ► **secondary cancer** N (*Med*) métastase *f* du cancer ► **secondary cause** N (*Philos*) cause *f* seconde ► **secondary era** N (*Geol*) (ère *f*) secondaire *m* ► **secondary infection** N (*Med*) surinfection *f* ► **secondary modern (school)** N (*Brit*: *formerly*) établissement secondaire d'enseignement général et technique ► **secondary picketing** N (*Pol*) mise en place de piquets de grève autour d'établissements traitant avec une entreprise en grève ► **secondary product** N (*Chem, Ind*) sous-produit *m* ► **secondary road** N ≈ route *f* départementale, route *f* secondaire ► **secondary school** N = **2b** ► **secondary sex(ual) characteristics** NPL caractères *mpl* sexuels secondaires ► **secondary stress** N (*Phon*) accent *m* secondaire ► **secondary tumour** N = **2c**

second-best [ˈsekəndˈbest] **1** N **it is the ~** (*gen*) c'est ce qu'il y a de mieux après; (= *poor substitute*) c'est un pis-aller; **as a ~** faute de mieux, au pis-aller **2** ADJ [*jacket etc*] de tous les jours; **his ~ novel** de tous ses romans celui qui vient en second du point de vue de la qualité **3** ADV **to come off ~** perdre, se faire battre

second-class [ˈsekəndˈklɑːs] **1** ADJ (*lit*) de deuxième classe; (*Rail*) [*ticket, compartment*] de seconde (classe); [*hotel*] de seconde catégorie, (*pej*) [*food, goods etc*] de qualité inférieure; **~ citizen** citoyen(ne) *m(f)* de deuxième ordre; (*Univ*) **~ degree** = **second**[1] **3c**; **~ mail** (*Brit*) courrier *m* à tarif réduit; (*Brit*) **~ stamp** timbre *m* à tarif réduit; (*Rail*) **a ~ return to London** un aller et retour en seconde (classe) pour Londres; (*Rail*) **~ seat** seconde *f* **2** ADV (*Rail etc*) **to travel ~** voyager en seconde; **to send sth ~** envoyer qch en courrier ordinaire

seconder [ˈsekəndə^r] N [*of motion*] personne *f* qui appuie une motion; [*of candidate*] deuxième parrain *m*

secondhand [ˈsekəndˈhænd] **1** ADJ [*clothes, car*] d'occasion, de seconde main; (*fig*) [*information, account*] de seconde main **2** ADV [*buy*] d'occasion; **to hear sth ~** entendre dire qch, entendre qch de quelqu'un d'autre **3** COMP ► **secondhand bookseller** N bouquiniste *mf* ► **secondhand bookshop** N bouquiniste *m*, magasin *m* de livres d'occasion ► **secondhand dealer** N marchand(e) *m(f)* d'occasion ► **secondhand smoke*** N la fumée des cigarettes (*des autres*)

▼ **secondly** [ˈsekəndlɪ] ADV deuxièmement; **firstly ... ~ ...** premièrement ... deuxièmement ...; (*Admin, Comm, Jur*) primo ... secundo ...

secondment [sɪˈkɒndmənt] N (*Brit*) affectation *f* provisoire, détachement *m*; **on ~** (*at*

home) en détachement, détaché (**to** à); (*abroad*) en mission (**to** à)

secrecy [ˈsiːkrəsɪ] N (*NonC*) secret *m*; **in ~** en secret, secrètement; **in strict ~** en grand secret, dans le plus grand secret; **under pledge of ~** sous le sceau du secret; **a veil of ~** un voile de mystère; **there's no ~ about it** on n'en fait pas (un) mystère; **there was an air of ~ about her** elle avait un petit air mystérieux; **I rely on your ~** je compte sur votre discrétion; **a country where ~ reigns** un pays qui a la manie du secret → **swear**

secret [ˈsiːkrɪt] **1** N [a] secret *m*; **to keep a ~** garder un secret; **to keep sth a ~** garder or tenir qch secret; **to keep sth a ~ from sb** cacher qch à qn; **I told you it was a ~** je vous l'ai dit en confidence; **to let sb into the ~** mettre qn dans le secret; **to let sb into a ~** révéler or confier un secret à qn; **to be in (on) the ~** être au courant; **there's no ~ about it** cela n'a rien de secret; **to have no ~s from sb** ne pas avoir de secrets pour qn; **to make no ~ of sth** ne pas cacher qch; **he makes no ~ of the fact that ...** il ne cache pas que ...; **lovers' ~** confidence *f* d'amoureux; **the ~ of success** le secret du succès; **the ~ of being a good teacher is listening** or **is to listen to one's pupils** le secret, pour être un bon professeur, c'est de savoir écouter ses élèves; **the ~s of nature** les secrets *mpl* or les mystères *mpl* de la nature → **open, state**

[b] (*NonC* = *secrecy*) **in ~** en secret

2 ADJ [a] (= *clandestine*) [*talks, plan, life, ingredient*] secret (-ète *f*); **it's all highly ~** tout cela est top secret; **~ funds** caisse *f* noire; **to be sent on a ~ mission** être envoyé en mission secrète; **to keep sth ~** tenir or garder qch secret; **to keep sth ~ from sb** cacher qch à qn → **top¹**

[b] (= *concealed*) [*drawer, passage*] secret (-ète *f*); [*entrance*] secret (-ète *f*), dérobé

[c] (*Pol*) [*ballot, vote, voting, election*] à bulletin secret

[d] (= *private*) **you've got a ~ admirer!** vous avez un admirateur!; **I'm a ~ admirer of her novels** j'avoue que j'apprécie ses romans; **to be a ~ drinker/drug user** boire/se droguer en cachette

3 COMP ► **secret agent** N agent *m* secret ► **secret police** N police *f* secrète ► **the Secret Service** N (*Brit*) les services *mpl* secrets; (*US*) les services *mpl* chargés de la protection du président ► **secret society** N société *f* secrète ► **secret weapon** N (*lit, fig*) arme *f* secrète

secretaire [ˌsekrɪˈtɛə^r] N secrétaire *m*

secretarial [ˌsekrəˈtɛərɪəl] **1** ADJ [*course, work*] de secrétariat; [*job*] de secrétaire; [*skills*] en secrétariat; **his duties are mostly ~** il fait essentiellement un travail de secrétaire, ses tâches sont avant tout administratives **2** COMP ► **secretarial agency** N agence *f* de placement de secrétaires ► **secretarial college, secretarial school** N école *f* de secrétariat

secretariat [ˌsekrəˈtɛərɪət] N secrétariat *m*

secretary [ˈsekrətrɪ] **1** N [a] (*in office, of club etc*) secrétaire *mf*; (*also* **company ~**) secrétaire *mf* général(e) (d'une société) → **foreign, parliamentary, under** [b] (= *writing desk*) secrétaire *m* **2** COMP ► **secretary-general** N (*pl* **secretaries-general**) secrétaire *mf* général(e) ► **Secretary of State** N (*Pol*) (*Brit*) ministre *m* (**of, for** de); (*US*) secrétaire *m* d'État, ≈ ministre *m* des Affaires étrangères ► **Secretary of State for Scotland** N (*Brit Pol*) ministre *m* des Affaires écossaises ► **secretary to the board** N secrétaire *mf* (auprès) du comité de gestion

secrete [sɪˈkriːt] VT [a] (*Anat, Bio, Med*) sécréter [b] (= *hide*) cacher

secretion [sɪˈkriːʃən] N [a] (= *process, fluid*) sécrétion *f* [b] (*NonC* = *hiding*) action *f* de cacher

secretive ['siːkrətɪv] ADJ [person, behaviour, air] secret (-ète f), cachottier; [organization] impénétrable; **to be ~ about sth** faire mystère de qch

secretively ['siːkrətɪvlɪ] ADV [smile] d'une manière impénétrable; **she's been behaving very ~ lately** elle est très renfermée ces derniers temps, on dirait qu'elle nous cache quelque chose ces derniers temps

secretiveness ['siːkrətɪvnɪs] N (NonC) réserve f, cachotteries fpl

secretly ['siːkrətlɪ] ADV [meet, marry, plan] en secret; [film] en cachette, secrètement; [hope, want] secrètement; **she was ~ relieved** en son for intérieur, elle était soulagée; **he was ~ pleased** il était content, mais ne le montrait pas, en son for intérieur, il n'était pas mécontent

sect [sekt] N secte f

sectarian [sek'tɛərɪən] **1** ADJ [violence, killings] motivé par le sectarisme; [motive, divisions, organization] sectaire; **~ school** école f confessionnelle **2** N sectaire mf

sectarianism [sek'tɛərɪənɪzəm] N sectarisme m

section ['sekʃən] **1** N **a** [of book, document, law, population, text] section f, partie f; [of country] partie f; [of road, pipeline] section f, tronçon m; [of town] quartier m; [of machine, furniture] élément m; (Mil) groupe m (de combat); **the brass/string ~** [of orchestra] les cuivres mpl/les cordes fpl; (Press) **the financial ~** la ou les page(s) financière(s); (Admin, Jur) **~ two of the municipal by-laws** l'article deux des arrêtés municipaux; **this bookcase comes in ~s** cette bibliothèque se vend par éléments; **there is a ~ of public opinion which maintains ...** il y a une partie ou une section de l'opinion publique qui maintient ... **b** (Admin, Ind) section f; (Comm) rayon m ▸ **consular** **c** (Rail) (= part of network) canton m (de voie ferrée); (US) (= extra train) train m supplémentaire, train-bis m; (in sleeping car) compartiment-lits m **d** (= cut) coupe f, section f; (for microscope) coupe f, lamelle f; **longitudinal/vertical ~** coupe f longitudinale/verticale → **cross** **e** (= act of cutting) section f, sectionnement m

2 VT **a** (= divide) diviser **b** [+ mentally ill person] interner

3 COMP ▸ **section hand** N (US Rail) cantonnier m (des chemins de fer), agent m de la voie ▸ **section mark** N paragraphe m (signe typographique)

▸ **section off** VT SEP séparer

sectional ['sekʃənl] ADJ **a** (= factional) [interests] d'un groupe, particulier; [conflict] interne **b** (= made of several parts) [bookcase, furniture] modulaire **c** (Archit) [drawing] en coupe

sectionalism ['sekʃənəlɪzəm] N défense f des intérêts d'un groupe

sector ['sektər] **1** N **a** secteur m; (Mil) secteur m, zone f; (Comput) secteur m; (fig) secteur m, domaine m; **private/public ~** secteur m privé/public **b** (Geom) secteur m; (= instrument) compas m (de proportions) **2** VT sectoriser

sectoral ['sektərəl] ADJ (Econ) sectoriel(le)

sectorial [sek'tɔːrɪəl] ADJ sectoriel

secular ['sekjʊlər] ADJ [society, education, school] laïque; [life, priest, clergy] séculier; [matter, music, writer] profane

secularism ['sekjʊlərɪzəm] N (= policy) laïcité f; (= doctrine) laïcisme m

secularization [ˌsekjʊləraɪ'zeɪʃən] N (NonC) [of society, education, art] sécularisation f, laïcisation f

secularize ['sekjʊləraɪz] VT [+ society, schools, education] séculariser

secure [sɪ'kjʊər] **1** ADJ **a** (= stable) [job, position] sûr; [career, future] assuré; [relationship] solide; [environment] sécurisant **b** (= unworried) [person] tranquille, sans inquiétude; **to feel ~** se sentir en sécurité or sécurisé; **to feel ~ about sth** ne pas avoir d'inquiétudes quant à qch; **to make sb feel ~** sécuriser qn; **a child must be (emotionally) ~** un enfant a besoin de sécurité affective, un enfant a besoin d'être sécurisé; **to be financially ~** être à l'abri des soucis financiers; **~ in the knowledge that ...** avec la certitude que ... **c** (= impregnable) [building, car, computer system] protégé, à l'abri des effractions; [code] inviolable; **I want to make my home ~ against burglars** je veux protéger ma maison des cambrioleurs or contre les cambrioleurs **d** [door, window, base, knot, lock, rope] solide; [structure, ladder] stable; **to get a ~ foothold in a market** prendre solidement pied sur un marché; (fig) **to be on ~ ground** être en terrain connu

2 VT **a** (= get) [+ object] se procurer, obtenir; [+ staff, performer] engager; [+ agreement, deal, ceasefire, sb's freedom, support] obtenir; **to ~ sth for sb** ◊ **to ~ sb sth** obtenir qch pour qn; **I did everything possible to ~ him the job** j'ai fait tout ce que j'ai pu pour lui obtenir ce travail; **a win that ~d them a place in the final** une victoire qui leur a valu une place en finale; **to ~ victory** remporter la victoire **b** (= fix) [+ rope] fixer, attacher; [+ door, window] bien fermer; [+ tile] fixer; (= tie up) [+ person, animal] attacher; **to ~ X to Y** fixer X à Y **c** (= make safe: from danger) protéger (against, from contre); [+ debt, loan] garantir; [+ future] assurer **d** (Mil = capture) prendre (le contrôle de); **their troops have ~d the bridge/the airport** leurs troupes ont pris le contrôle du pont/de l'aéroport or ont pris le pont/l'aéroport

3 COMP ▸ **secure accommodation** N (Brit Jur) ≈ centre m d'éducation surveillée ▸ **secure unit** N (Brit) (for young offenders) ≈ centre m d'éducation surveillée; (for mental patients) pavillon m d'hôpital psychiatrique réservé aux malades dangereux

securely [sɪ'kjʊəlɪ] ADV **a** (= firmly) [fasten, fix] solidement, bien; [lock] bien **b** (= safely) **he remains ~ in power** il est solidement installé au pouvoir; **the strike was ~ under the union's control** le syndicat avait la grève bien en main; **~ established** solidement établi

Securicor® [sɪ'kjʊərɪkɔːr] **1** N société de surveillance et de convoi de fonds **2** COMP ▸ **Securicor guard** N employé m du service de surveillance, convoyeur m de fonds

securitization [sɪˌkjʊərɪtaɪ'zeɪʃən] N (Fin) titrisation f

securitize [sɪ'kjʊərɪtaɪz] VT [+ loan] titriser

security [sɪ'kjʊərɪtɪ] **1** N **a** (= safety, confidence) sécurité f; **in ~** en sécurité; (Admin, Ind) **job ~** sécurité f de l'emploi; **~ of tenure** (in one's job) sécurité f totale de l'emploi; (Jur: of tenant) bail m assuré; (Psych) **a child needs ~** un enfant a besoin de sécurité sur le plan affectif, un enfant a besoin d'être sécurisé **b** (Ind, Pol etc: against spying, escape etc) sécurité f; **~ was very lax** les mesures de sécurité étaient très relâchées; **maximum** or **top** or **high ~ wing** [of jail] quartier m de haute surveillance → **maximum** **c** (Fin: for loan) caution f, garantie f; **loans without ~** crédit m à découvert; **up to £10,000 without ~** jusqu'à 10000 livres sans caution or sans garantie; **to go** or **stand ~ for sb** se porter garant pour or de qn

2 securities NPL (St Ex) valeurs fpl, titres mpl; **government securities** fonds mpl d'État

3 COMP ▸ **securities market** N (Fin) marché m des valeurs ▸ **security agreement** N accord m de sécurité ▸ **security blanket** N [of child] doudou* f; (Psych) objet m transitionnel; [of police] dispositif m de sécurité; (fig) **he's my ~ blanket** c'est quelqu'un sur qui je peux compter ▸ **security camera** N caméra f de surveillance ▸ **security clearance** N autorisation officielle accordée par les services de sécurité ▸ **Security Council** N Conseil m de sécurité ▸ **security firm** N société f de surveillance ▸ **security forces** NPL forces fpl de sécurité ▸ **security guard** N (gen) garde m chargé de la sécurité; (transporting money) convoyeur m de fonds ▸ **security leak** N fuite f (de documents, de secrets etc) ▸ **security officer** N (Mil, Naut) officier m chargé de la sécurité; (Comm, Ind) inspecteur m (chargé) de la sécurité ▸ **security police** N services mpl de la sûreté ▸ **security risk** N personne susceptible de compromettre la sûreté de l'État, la sécurité d'une organisation etc; **that man is a ~ risk** cet homme constitue un risque or n'est pas sûr ▸ **security vetting** N enquête f de sécurité (of sb sur qn); **a policy of ~ vetting** une politique d'enquêtes de sécurité

sedan [sɪ'dæn] N **a** (also ~ **chair**) chaise f à porteurs **b** (US = car) conduite f intérieure, berline f

sedate [sɪ'deɪt] **1** ADJ **a** [person] posé, calme; [behaviour] calme, pondéré; [place, event] tranquille, paisible; **the ~ world of antique dealing** le monde tranquille du commerce des antiquités; **at a ~ pace** or **speed** posément, sans se presser; **in a ~ manner** posément **b** (= conservative) [dress, furnishings] conventionnel **2** VT (Med) donner des sédatifs à, mettre sous sédation

sedately [sɪ'deɪtlɪ] ADV **a** (= slowly) [walk, drive] posément, sans se presser **b** (= conservatively) [dressed, furnished] de manière conventionnelle

sedateness [sɪ'deɪtnɪs] N [of person] calme m; [of place, dancing] calme m, tranquillité f; [of pace] lenteur f

sedation [sɪ'deɪʃən] N sédation f; **under ~** sous calmants

sedative ['sedətɪv] ADJ, N calmant m, sédatif m

sedentary ['sedntrɪ] ADJ sédentaire

sedge [sedʒ] **1** N laîche f, carex m **2** COMP ▸ **sedge warbler** N phragmite m des joncs, rousserolle f

sediment ['sedɪmənt] N (Geol, Med) sédiment m; (in boiler, liquids) dépôt m; (in wine) dépôt m, lie f

sedimentary [ˌsedɪ'mentərɪ] ADJ sédimentaire

sedimentation [ˌsedɪmen'teɪʃən] N sédimentation f

sedition [sə'dɪʃən] N sédition f

seditious [sə'dɪʃəs] ADJ séditieux

seduce [sɪ'djuːs] VT (gen, sexually) séduire; **to ~ sb from sth** détourner qn de qch; **to ~ sb into doing sth** entraîner qn à faire qch

seducer [sɪ'djuːsər] N séducteur m, -trice f

seduction [sɪ'dʌkʃən] N séduction f

seductive [sɪ'dʌktɪv] ADJ [person, voice, notion, argument, smile] séduisant; [offer] séduisant, alléchant; [message] attrayant; [garment] sexy*; **the ~ charms of sth** les séductions fpl or les charmes mpl irrésistibles de qch

seductively [sɪ'dʌktɪvlɪ] ADV **a** (= alluringly) [smile, look at, dress] de manière séduisante **b** (= temptingly) **~ simple** d'une simplicité exquise; **a ~ domestic atmosphere** une ambiance cosy*; **a ~ illustrated book** un livre avec de ravissantes illustrations

seductiveness [sɪ'dʌktɪvnɪs] N caractère m séduisant, séduction f

seductress [sɪ'dʌktrɪs] N séductrice f

sedulous ['sedjʊləs] ADJ assidu, persévérant, attentif

sedulously ['sedjʊləslɪ] ADV assidûment, avec persévérance

▼ **see¹** [si:] (*pret* **saw**, *ptp* **seen**) ⊡ VT ⓐ (*gen*) voir ; **I can ~ him** je le vois ; **I saw him read/reading the letter** je l'ai vu/qui lisait la lettre ; **he was ~n to read the letter** on l'a vu lire la lettre ; **she saw him knocked down** elle l'a vu se faire renverser ; **there was not a house to be ~n** il n'y avait pas une seule maison en vue ; **there was no one at all** or **not a soul to be ~n** il n'y avait pas âme qui vive, il n'y avait pas un chat* ; **to ~ sth with one's own eyes** voir qch de ses propres yeux ; **~ page 10** voir (à la) page 10 ; **can you ~ your way without a torch?** est-ce que vous pouvez trouver votre chemin or est-ce que vous y voyez assez sans lampe de poche? ; (*fig*) **I could ~ it** or **that one coming*** je le sentais venir, je m'y attendais

ⓑ (= *understand, conceive*) voir ; **I fail to ~** or **I can't ~ how you're going to do it** je ne vois pas du tout or je ne vois vraiment pas comment vous allez le faire ; **the French ~ it differently** les Français voient la chose différemment ; **the way I ~ it** ◊ **as I ~ it** à mon avis, selon moi ; **this is how** or **the way I ~ it** voici comment je vois la chose ; **do you ~ what I mean?** vous voyez ce que je veux dire? ; **I ~ what you're getting at** je vois où vous voulez en venir ; **I don't ~ why** je ne vois pas pourquoi ; **I don't ~ why not** (*granting permission*) je n'y vois aucune objection ; (*not understanding sb's refusal*) je ne vois pas pourquoi ; **to ~ the joke** comprendre or saisir la plaisanterie

ⓒ (= *notice, learn, discover*) voir ; **I saw in the paper that he had died** j'ai vu or lu dans le journal qu'il était décédé ; **I ~ they've bought a new car** je vois qu'ils ont acheté une nouvelle voiture ; **~ who's at the door** voir qui est à la porte ; **not until I ~ how many there are** pas avant de savoir or de voir combien il y en a ; **I'll ~ what I can do** je verrai or je vais voir ce que je peux faire ; **let's ~ what you're capable of** voyons (un peu) ce que vous savez faire

ⓓ (= *have an opinion*) trouver ; **I ~ nothing wrong in it** je n'y trouve rien à redire ; **I don't know what she ~s in him** (*what good qualities*) je ne sais pas ce qu'elle lui trouve (de bien) ; (*what attracts her*) je ne sais pas ce qui l'attire en lui

ⓔ (= *meet, speak to*) voir ; [+ *doctor, lawyer*] voir, consulter ; **to go and** or **to ~ sb** aller voir qn ; **I'm ~ing the doctor tomorrow** je vais chez le docteur or je vois le docteur demain ; **the manager wants to ~ you** le directeur veut vous voir, le directeur vous demande ; **I can't ~ you today** je ne peux pas vous voir aujourd'hui ; **I want to ~ you about my son** je voudrais vous voir or vous parler au sujet de mon fils ; (*greeting*) **how nice to ~ you!** ça me fait plaisir de vous voir! ; **I'll ~ you in hell first!*** jamais de la vie!, il faudra que vous me passiez sur le corps d'abord!

ⓕ (= *visit*) [+ *country, town*] visiter ; **to ~ the sights** [*of town*] visiter la ville ; [*of country*] visiter le pays ; **to ~ the sights of Paris** visiter ce qu'il y a à voir à Paris ; **I want to ~ the world** je veux voyager

ⓖ (= *have relationship with*) (*social*) voir, fréquenter ; (*romantic*) sortir avec, fréquenter ; **they ~ a lot of him** ils le voient souvent ; **we've ~n less of him lately** on l'a moins vu ces derniers temps ; **she's ~ing John just now** elle sort avec John en ce moment

ⓗ (*saying goodbye*) **(it was) nice to ~ you!** ça m'a fait plaisir de vous voir! ; **~ you!*** à bientôt!* ; **~ you later!*** à tout à l'heure! ; **~ you some time!*** à un de ces jours! ; **~ you soon!** à bientôt! ; **~ you (on) Sunday** à dimanche ; **~ you next week** à la semaine prochaine

ⓘ (= *experience, know*) voir ; **1963 saw the assassination of John F. Kennedy** (l'année) 1963 a vu l'assassinat de John F. Kennedy ; **I've ~n some things in my time but ...** j'en ai vu (des choses) dans ma vie mais ... ; (*Mil*) **he saw service in Libya** il a servi en Libye, il a fait la campagne de Libye ; **since she's started going round with that crowd she has certainly ~n life** depuis qu'elle fait partie de cette bande elle en a vu des choses ; **I'm going to Australia because I want to ~ life** je pars en Australie parce que je veux voir or découvrir le monde ; **since becoming a social worker she's certainly ~n life** depuis qu'elle est assistante sociale elle a pu se rendre compte de ce que c'est que la vie

ⓙ (= *find*) **can you ~ your way to helping us?** est-ce que vous trouveriez le moyen de nous aider? ; **I can't ~ my way to doing that** je ne vois pas comment je pourrais le faire

ⓚ (= *accompany, escort*) (re)conduire, (r)accompagner ; **to ~ sb to the station** accompagner or conduire qn à la gare ; **to ~ sb home/to the door** reconduire or raccompagner qn jusque chez lui/jusqu'à la porte ; **to ~ the children to bed** coucher les enfants ; **he was so drunk we had to ~ him to bed** il était tellement ivre que nous avons dû l'aider à se coucher → **see off, see out**

ⓛ (= *allow to be*) **I couldn't ~ her left alone** je ne pouvais pas supporter or permettre qu'on la laisse (*subj*) toute seule

ⓜ (= *ensure*) s'assurer ; **~ that he has all he needs** veillez à ce qu'il ne manque de rien ; **that you have it ready for Monday** faites en sorte que ce soit prêt pour lundi ; **I'll ~ he gets the letter** je ferai le nécessaire pour que la lettre lui parvienne, je me charge de lui faire parvenir la lettre ; **I'll ~ you (all) right*** je veillerai à ce que vous n'y perdiez (*subj*) pas, vous n'en serez pas de votre poche* → **see to**

ⓝ (= *imagine*) voir, (s')imaginer ; **I can't ~ him as Prime Minister** je ne le vois or ne l'imagine pas du tout en Premier ministre ; **I can't ~ myself doing that** je me vois mal or je m'imagine mal faire cela ; **I can't ~ myself being elected** je ne vois pas très bien comment je pourrais être élu ; **can you ~ him as a father?** est-ce que vous l'imaginez père de famille? ; **I can't ~ myself as a father** je ne m'imagine dans le rôle de père ; **I can just ~ her!** je l'imagine tout à fait! ; **I must be ~ing things*** je dois avoir des visions* or des hallucinations

ⓞ (*Poker etc*) **(I'll) ~ you** je demande à vous voir, je vous vois

⊡ VI ⓐ voir ; **to ~ in/out/through** *etc* voir à l'intérieur/à l'extérieur/à travers *etc* ; **let me ~** (= *show me*) montre-moi, fais voir ; (*at window etc*) laisse-moi regarder → **2d** ; **~ for yourself** voyez vous-même ; **he couldn't ~ to read** il n'y voyait pas assez clair pour lire ; **I can hardly ~ without my glasses** je n'y vois pas grand-chose sans mes lunettes ; **cats can ~ in the dark** les chats voient clair la nuit ; **you can ~ for miles** on y voit à des kilomètres → **eye**

ⓑ (= *find out*) voir ; **I'll go and ~** je vais (aller) voir ; **I'll go and ~ if dinner's ready** je vais (aller) voir si le dîner est prêt

ⓒ (= *understand*) voir, comprendre ; **as far as I can ~** à ce que je vois ; **I ~!** je vois!, ah bon! ; **as you can ~** comme vous pouvez (le) constater ; **so I ~** c'est bien ce que je vois ; (*in anger*) **now ~ here!** non, mais dites donc!* ; (*in explanations etc*) **... you ~** ... voyez-vous, ... vous voyez ; **it's all over now, ~?** c'est fini, compris?* ; **she was bound to win, don't you ~?** tu ne comprends pas qu'elle allait forcément gagner?

ⓓ (= *think, deliberate*) voir ; **let me ~** ◊ **let's ~** voyons (un peu) ; **let me ~ what have I got to do?** voyons, qu'est-ce que j'ai à faire? ; **I'll have to ~ (if)** je vais voir (si) ; **we'll soon ~** nous le saurons bientôt ; **we'll soon ~ if ...** nous saurons bientôt si ... ; **can I go out? — we'll ~** est-ce que je peux sortir? — on verra

⊡ COMP ▶ **see-through** ADJ [*garment*] transparent

▶ **see about** VT FUS ⓐ (= *deal with*) s'occuper de ; **he came to ~ about buying the house** il est venu voir s'il pouvait acheter la maison ; **he came to ~ about the washing machine** il est venu au sujet de la machine à laver ⓑ (= *consider*) **to ~ about sth** voir si qch est possible ; **can I go? — we'll ~ about it** est-ce que je peux y aller? — on va voir or on verra (ça) ; **he said he wouldn't do it — we'll ~ about that!** il a dit qu'il ne le ferait pas — c'est ce qu'on va voir! ; **we must ~ about (getting) a new television** il va falloir songer à s'acheter une nouvelle télévision

▶ **see after** VT FUS s'occuper de

▶ **see in** VT SEP [+ *person*] faire entrer ; **to ~ the New Year in** fêter la nouvelle année, faire le réveillon du nouvel an

▶ **see into** VT FUS (= *study, examine*) s'enquérir de, examiner ; **we shall have to ~ into this** il va falloir examiner la question or se renseigner là-dessus

▶ **see off** VT SEP ⓐ (= *accompany*) **I saw him off at the station/airport** *etc* je l'ai accompagné au train or à la gare/à l'aéroport *etc* ; **we'll come and ~ you off** on viendra vous dire au revoir ⓑ (* *fig* = *defeat*) damer le pion à

▶ **see out** VT SEP ⓐ [+ *person*] reconduire or raccompagner à la porte ; **I'll ~ myself out** pas la peine de me raccompagner!* ; **he saw himself out** il est sorti sans qu'on le raccompagne (*subj*) ⓑ **this coat will have to ~ the winter out** il faut que ce manteau lui (or me *etc*) fasse l'hiver ; **he was so ill we wondered whether he'd ~ the week out** il était si malade que nous nous demandions s'il passerait la semaine ; **I saw the third act out then left** je suis resté jusqu'à la fin du troisième acte puis je suis parti

▶ **see over** VT FUS [+ *house, factory, gardens*] visiter

▶ **see through** ⊡ VT FUS [+ *person*] voir clair dans, deviner les intentions de ; [+ *behaviour, promises*] ne pas se laisser tromper or duper par ; **I saw through him at once** j'ai tout de suite vu clair dans son jeu or deviné ses intentions ; **she saw through his scheming** elle ne s'est pas laissé tromper or duper par ses machinations ⊡ VT SEP (*never fus*) [+ *project, deal*] mener à bonne fin ; **£50 should ~ you through** 50 livres devraient vous suffire ; **don't worry, I'll ~ you through** ne vous inquiétez pas, vous pouvez compter sur moi ; **she saw me through all the hard times** elle m'a aidé dans tous les moments difficiles ⊡ **~-through** ADJ → **see¹**

▶ **see to** VT FUS (= *mend*) réparer ; (= *deal with*) s'occuper de ; **to ~ to it that ...** veiller à ce que ... (+ *subj*) ; **I'll ~ to the car** je m'occuperai de la voiture ; **please ~ to it that ...** veillez s'il vous plaît à ce que ... (+ *subj*) ; **~ to it that they are paid on time** veillez à ce qu'ils soient payés à temps ; **I'll ~ to it** j'y veillerai ; **the sweets didn't last long, the children saw to that!** les bonbons n'ont pas fait long feu, les enfants se sont chargés de les faire disparaître!

see² [si:] N [*of bishop*] siège *m* épiscopal, évêché *m* ; [*of archbishop*] archevêché *m* → **holy**

seed [si:d] ⊡ N ⓐ (*Agr, Bot etc*) graine *f* ; (*collective n: for sowing*) graines *fpl*, semence *f* ; (*in apple, grape etc*) pépin *m* ; **to run** or **go to ~** [*plant*] monter en graine ; [*person*] (= *grow slovenly*) se négliger, se laisser aller ; (= *lose vigour*) se décatir

ⓑ (*fig* = *source, origin*) germe *m*, semence *f* ; **the ~s of discontent** les germes *mpl* du mécontentement ; **to sow ~s of doubt in sb's mind** semer le doute dans l'esprit de qn

ⓒ (*liter*) (= *sperm*) semence *f*, sperme *m* ; (= *offspring*) progéniture *f*

ⓓ (*Tennis etc: also* **~ed player**) tête *f* de série ; **first** or **number one ~** tête *f* de série numéro un ; **the top ~s** les premières têtes *fpl* de série

[2] VT [a] [+ *lawn*] ensemencer ; [+ *raisin, grape*] épépiner ; **to ~ clouds** ensemencer les nuages [b] (*Tennis*) **he was ~ed third** il était (classé) troisième tête de série → **1d**

[3] VI monter en graine

[4] COMP ► **seed box** N germoir *m* ► **seed corn** N blé *m* de semence ; (*fig*) **they are eating their ~ corn** ils mangent leur blé en herbe ► **seeding machine** N semoir *m* ► **seed merchant** N grainetier *m* ► **seed money** N (*Econ, Fin*) capital *m* initial, mise *f* de fonds initiale ► **seed pearls** NPL semence *f* de perles, très petites perles *fpl* ► **seed pod** N tégument *m* ► **seed potato** N pomme *f* de terre de semence ► **seed tray** N = **seed box**

seedbed ['si:dbed] N semis *m*, couche *f*

seedcake ['si:dkeɪk] N gâteau *m* au carvi

seedily ['si:dɪlɪ] ADV [*dress*] minablement, de façon minable

seediness ['si:dɪnɪs] N (= *shabbiness*) aspect *m* minable *or* miteux

seedless ['si:dlɪs] ADJ sans pépins

seedling ['si:dlɪŋ] N semis *m*, (jeune) plant *m*

seedsman ['si:dzmən] N (*pl* **-men**) = **seed merchant**

seedy ['si:dɪ] ADJ [a] (= *shabby*) [*clothes*] râpé, miteux ; [*person, hotel*] minable, miteux [b] (* = *ill*) **I'm feeling ~** je suis *or* je me sens mal fichu*, je me sens patraque* ; **he looks rather ~** il a l'air mal fichu*

▼ **seeing** ['si:ɪŋ] [1] N vue *f*, vision *f* ▪ (*PROV*) **~ is believing** voir c'est croire [2] CONJ **~ that** *or* **as*** vu que, étant donné que [3] COMP ► **Seeing Eye dog** N (*US*) chien *m* d'aveugle

seek [si:k] (*pret, ptp* **sought**) [1] VT [a] (= *look for*) [+ *object, person, solution, death*] chercher ; [+ *fame, honours*] rechercher ; [+ *happiness, peace*] chercher, rechercher ; **to ~ one's fortune in Canada** chercher *or* tenter fortune au Canada ; **to ~ work** chercher du travail ; **they sought shelter from the storm** ils ont cherché un abri *or* un refuge contre la tempête ; **we sought shelter in the embassy/under a big tree** nous nous sommes réfugiés à l'ambassade/sous un grand arbre ; **the reason is not far to ~** la raison n'est pas difficile à trouver, on n'a pas à chercher loin pour trouver la raison ; (*in advertisements*) **candidates are urgently sought for the post of chef** on recherche de toute urgence un chef de cuisine ; **American male, ~s attractive, intelligent female** Américain désire faire connaissance belle femme intelligente [b] (= *ask*) demander (**from sb** à qn) ; **to ~ advice/help from sb** demander conseil/de l'aide à qn ; **to ~ (political) asylum** demander l'asile politique ; **to ~ compensation for sth** demander à être indemnisé de qch ; **the prosecutors are ~ing the death penalty** l'accusation réclame la peine de mort [c] (*frm* = *attempt*) chercher (**to do** à faire) ; **they sought to kill him** ils ont cherché à le tuer [2] VI **to ~ for** *or* **after sth/sb** rechercher qch/qn ; **much sought after** très recherché, très demandé

► **seek out** VT SEP [+ *person*] aller voir, (aller) s'adresser à ; [+ *trouble etc*] (re)chercher

seeker ['si:kər] N [a] (= *person*) chercheur *m*, -euse *f* ; **to be a ~ after** [+ *truth, knowledge etc*] être en quête de → **asylum, job, self** [b] (*Mil* = *device*) autodirecteur *m*

▼ **seem** [si:m] VI [a] sembler, avoir l'air ; **he ~s honest** il semble (être) honnête, il a l'air honnête ; **he ~ed nice enough** il semblait *or* avait l'air plutôt gentil ; **further strikes ~ unlikely** il semble peu probable qu'il y ait de nouvelles grèves ; **she makes it ~ so simple!** avec elle tout paraît si simple! ; **she ~s to know you** elle semble vous connaître, elle a l'air de vous connaître ; **she ~s not to want to leave** elle semble ne pas vouloir partir, elle

n'a pas l'air de vouloir partir ; **we ~ to have met before** il me semble *or* j'ai l'impression que nous nous sommes déjà rencontrés ; **I ~ to have heard that before** il me semble avoir déjà entendu cela ; **I can't ~ to do it** je n'arrive pas à le faire ; **I ~ed to be floating** j'avais l'impression de planer ; **how did she ~ to you?** comment l'as-tu trouvée? ; **how does it ~ to you?** qu'en penses-tu? ; **it all ~s like a dream** on croit rêver

[b] (*impers vb*) sembler, paraître ; **it ~s that the** *or* **as if the government is going to fall** (= *looks as if*) il semble bien que le gouvernement va tomber ; **it ~s that the government is going to fall** (= *people say*) il paraît que le gouvernement va tomber ; **I've checked and it ~s she's right** j'ai vérifié et il semble qu'elle a raison *or* on dirait qu'elle a raison *or* elle semble avoir raison ; **it ~s she's right for everybody says so** il semble bien qu'elle a raison puisque tout le monde est d'accord là-dessus ; **I've checked and it doesn't ~ right** *or* **it ~s she's not right** j'ai vérifié et il ne semble pas qu'elle ait raison ; **from what people say it doesn't ~ she's right** d'après ce qu'on dit il ne semble pas qu'elle ait raison ; **does it ~ that she is right?** est-ce qu'elle semble avoir raison? ; **the heat was so terrible it ~ed that the whole earth was ablaze** il faisait une chaleur si terrible qu'il semblait que la terre entière fût *or* était en feu ; **it ~s to me that he refused** il me semble qu'il a refusé ; **it ~s to me that we should leave at once** il me semble que nous devrions partir tout de suite ; **it does not ~ to me that we can accept** il ne me semble pas que nous puissions accepter ; **does it ~ to you as though it's going to rain?** est-ce qu'il te semble qu'il va pleuvoir?, est-ce que tu crois qu'il va pleuvoir? ; **they're getting married next week, so it ~s** ils se marient la semaine prochaine à ce qu'il paraît or semble-t-il ; **it ~s not** il paraît que non ; **it ~s that he died yesterday** il paraît qu'il est mort hier ; **he died yesterday it ~s** il est mort hier paraît-il ; **I did what ~ed best** j'ai fait ce que j'ai jugé bon ; **it ~s ages since we last met** j'ai l'impression que ça fait des siècles* que nous ne nous sommes pas vus ; **there ~s to be a mistake in this translation** il semble y avoir une erreur dans cette traduction ; **there ~s to be a mistake, I'm the one who booked this room** il semble y avoir erreur, c'est moi qui ai retenu cette chambre

seeming ['si:mɪŋ] ADJ apparent, soi-disant *inv*

seemingly ['si:mɪŋlɪ] ADV apparemment ; **there has ~ been a rise in inflation** à ce qu'il paraît il y a eu une hausse de l'inflation ; **he's left then? — ~** il est donc parti? — (à ce qu'il) paraît or d'après ce qu'on dit

seemliness ['si:mlɪnɪs] N [*of behaviour*] bienséance *f* ; [*of dress*] décence *f*

seemly ['si:mlɪ] ADJ [*behaviour*] convenable, bienséant ; [*dress*] décent, correct

seen [si:n] VB *ptp of* **see¹**

seep [si:p] VI suinter, filtrer ; **water was ~ing through the walls** l'eau suintait des murs *or* filtrait à travers les murs, les murs suintaient

► **seep away** VI s'écouler peu à peu *or* goutte à goutte

► **seep in** VI s'infiltrer

► **seep out** VI [a] [*fluid*] suinter [b] [*information, news*] filtrer

seepage ['si:pɪdʒ] N [*of water, blood*] suintement *m* ; [*from tank*] fuite *f*, déperdition *f*

seer [sɪər] N (*liter*) voyant(e) *m(f)*, prophète *m*, prophétesse *f*

seersucker ['sɪə,sʌkər] N crépon *m* de coton

seesaw ['si:sɔ:] [1] N (jeu *m* de) bascule *f* [2] ADJ (*fig*) en yoyo® [3] VI (*lit*) jouer à la bascule ; (*fig*) osciller [4] COMP ► **seesaw motion** N mouvement *m* de bascule, va-et-vient *m*

seethe [si:ð] VI [a] [*boiling liquid, sea*] bouillonner [b] (*fig*) **to ~ with anger/rage**

bouillir de colère/rage ; **he was (positively) seething*** il était fumasse* *or* furibard* ; **a country seething with discontent** un pays où le mécontentement couve *or* fermente ; **resentment ~d in him** il était rongé par le ressentiment ; **the crowd ~d round the film star** la foule se pressait autour de la vedette ; **the streets were seething with people** les rues grouillaient de monde ; **a seething mass of people** une masse grouillante de gens, une foule grouillante

segment ['segmənt] [1] N (*gen, Anat, Geom, Ling, Zool*) segment *m* ; [*of orange etc*] quartier *m*, morceau *m* [2] [seg'ment] VT segmenter, couper en segments [3] [seg'ment] VI se segmenter

segmental [seg'mentl] ADJ (*gen*) segmentaire ; (*Ling*) segmental

segmentation [,segmən'teɪʃən] N segmentation *f*

segregate ['segrɪgeɪt] VT séparer, isoler (**from** de) ; (*Pol*) séparer ; **to ~ the sexes** séparer les sexes ; **they decided to ~ the contagious patients** ils ont décidé d'isoler les (malades) contagieux ; **the political prisoners were ~d from the others** les prisonniers politiques ont été séparés *or* isolés des autres

segregated ['segrɪgeɪtɪd] ADJ (*Pol*) [*school, club, bus*] où la ségrégation est appliquée ; **a ~ school system** un système d'enseignement où la ségrégation est appliquée

segregation [,segrɪ'geɪʃən] N (*Pol*) ségrégation *f* ; [*of group, person, object*] séparation *f*, isolement *m* (**from** de)

segregationist [,segrɪ'geɪʃnɪst] [1] N ségrégationniste *mf* [2] ADJ [*riot, demonstration*] ségrégationniste ; [*policy*] de ségrégation, ségrégationniste

segue ['segweɪ] [1] VI **the band ~d from "These Foolish Things" into "Blue Moon"** après « These Foolish Things » l'orchestre a enchaîné « Blue Moon » ; **the film attempts to ~ (from tragedy) into comedy** le film essaie de passer subtilement (de la tragédie) à la comédie [2] N (*Mus*) enchaînement *m* (**from** de, **into** à)

Seine [seɪn] N Seine *f*

seine [seɪn] N seine *f*

seismic ['saɪzmɪk] ADJ (*lit*) sismique ; (*fig*) [*events, changes, effects, efforts*] cataclysmique

seismograph ['saɪzməgrɑːf] N sismographe *m*

seismography [saɪz'mɒgrəfɪ] N sismographie *f*

seismologist [saɪz'mɒlədʒɪst] N sismologue *mf*

seismology [saɪz'mɒlədʒɪ] N sismologie *f*

seize [si:z] [1] VT [a] (= *clutch, grab*) saisir, attraper ; **she ~d (hold of) his hand** ◊ **she ~d him by the hand** elle lui a saisi la main ; **he ~d her by the hair** il l'a empoignée par les cheveux ; **to ~ sb bodily** attraper qn à bras-le-corps ; **to ~ the opportunity to do sth** saisir l'occasion *or* sauter sur l'occasion de faire qch ; **to ~ the day** vivre dans l'instant ; **to be ~d with rage** avoir un accès de rage ; **to be ~d with fear** être saisi de peur ; **she was ~d with the desire to see him** un désir soudain de le voir s'est emparé d'elle *or* l'a saisie ; **he was ~d with a bout of coughing** il a été pris d'un accès de toux, il a eu un accès de toux → **bull¹** [b] (= *get possession of by force*) s'emparer de, se saisir de ; (*Mil*) [+ *territory*] s'emparer de ; [+ *person, gun, ship*] capturer, s'emparer de ; **to ~ power** s'emparer du pouvoir [c] (*Jur*) [+ *person*] arrêter, détenir ; [+ *property*] saisir ; [+ *contraband*] confisquer, saisir

[2] VI (*Tech*) se gripper

► **seize on** VT FUS = **seize upon**

► **seize up** VI (*Tech*) se gripper ; (*Med*) s'ankyloser ; (*fig*) [*traffic*] se paralyser, s'immobiliser

► **seize upon** VT FUS [+ *opportunity, chance*] saisir ; [+ *idea*] se saisir de ; **his opponents ~d**

upon these revelations ses opposants se sont saisis de ces révélations

seizure ['siːʒəʳ] N **a** (NonC) [of goods, gun, property] saisie f; [of city, ship] capture f; [of power, territory] prise f; [of criminal] capture f, arrestation f; (Jur) appréhension f (au corps); [of contraband] saisie f, confiscation f **b** (Med) crise f, attaque f; **to have a ~** avoir une crise or une attaque

seldom ['seldəm] ADV rarement, peu souvent; **he ~ worked** il travaillait rarement, il ne travaillait pas souvent; **~ if ever** rarement pour ne pas dire jamais

select [sɪ'lekt] **1** VT [+ team, candidate] sélectionner (**from, among** parmi); [+ gift, book, colour] choisir (**from, among** parmi); **to ~ a sample of** [+ rock] prélever un échantillon de; [+ colours, materials] choisir un échantillon de; **~ed poems** poèmes mpl choisis; **~ed works** œuvres fpl choisies; (Comm) **~ed fruit** fruits mpl sélectionnés or de premier choix **2** ADJ [audience] choisi, d'élite; [club] fermé; [restaurant] chic inv, sélect; **a ~ few** quelques privilégiés; **a ~ group of friends** quelques amis choisis; **they formed a small ~ group** ils formaient un petit groupe fermé **3** COMP **► select committee** N (Brit Parl) commission f parlementaire (d'enquête)

selectee [sɪlek'tiː] N (US Mil) appelé m

selection [sɪ'lekʃən] **1** N sélection f, choix m; **to make a ~** faire une sélection or un choix; (Literat, Mus) **~s from ...** morceaux mpl choisis de ... → **natural 2** COMP **► selection committee** N comité m de sélection

selective [sɪ'lektɪv] ADJ [recruitment, classification, memory] sélectif; **one must be ~** il faut savoir faire un choix; **~ breeding** élevage m à base de sélection; (Scol) **~ entry** (Brit) ◊ **~ admissions** (US) sélection f; (Brit) **~ school** école f (or lycée m or collège m) à recrutement sélectif; (US Mil) **~ service** service m militaire obligatoire, conscription f; (Ind) **~ strike** grève f ponctuelle or limitée

selectively [sɪ'lektɪvlɪ] ADV [terrorists etc] **to strike** ~ se livrer à des actions ponctuelles

selectivity [sɪlek'tɪvɪtɪ] N **a** [of procedure, system] sélectivité f; (Scol) sélection f **b** (Elec, Rad) sélectivité f

selectman [sɪ'lektmən] N (pl **-men**) (US) conseiller m municipal (en Nouvelle-Angleterre)

selector [sɪ'lektəʳ] N (= person) sélectionneur m, -euse f; (Tech) sélecteur m

selenium [sɪ'liːnɪəm] N sélénium m

self [self] **1** N (pl **selves**) **a** (gen, Philos, Psych) **the** ~ le moi inv; **the cult of** ~ le culte du moi; **the conscious** ~ le moi conscient; **his better** ~ le meilleur de lui-même; **her real** ~ son vrai moi; **my former** ~ le moi or la personne que j'étais auparavant; **she's her old** ~ **again** elle est redevenue complètement elle-même; **he'll soon be his usual** ~ **again** il retrouvera bientôt sa santé (or sa gaieté etc); **she had no thought of** ~ elle ne pensait pas à elle-même or à son intérêt personnel ■ (PROV) **to thine own** ~ **be true** demeure fidèle à toi-même → **second**[1], **shadow**
b (Comm etc) moi-même etc; **your good** ~ vous-même; **your good selves** vous-mêmes; (on cheque) **pay** ~ payez à l'ordre de moi-même

2 COMP **► self-abasement** N abaissement m de soi, avilissement m **► self-absorbed** ADJ égocentrique **► self-absorption** N égocentrisme m **► self-abuse**† N masturbation f **► self-accusation** N autoaccusation f **► self-acting** ADJ automatique **► self-addressed envelope** N enveloppe f à son nom et adresse **► self-addressed stamped envelope** N enveloppe f affranchie à son nom et adresse **► self-adhesive** ADJ autoadhésif **► self-adjusting** ADJ à réglage

automatique **► self-advertisement** N to indulge in **~-advertisement** faire sa propre réclame **► self-aggrandizement** N autoglorification f **► self-analysis** N autoanalyse f **► self-apparent** ADJ évident, qui va de soi **► self-appointed** ADJ **he was a ~-appointed critic of ...** il a pris sur lui de critiquer ... **► self-appraisal** N autoévaluation f **► self-assembly** ADJ en kit **► self-assertion** N affirmation f de soi **► self-assertive** ADJ très sûr de soi **► self-assessment** N autoévaluation f; (Brit Fin) **~-assessment system** le système de déclaration des revenus (avec autoévaluation des impôts à payer) **► self-assurance** N assurance f, confiance f en soi **► self-assured** ADJ sûr de soi, plein d'assurance **► self-aware** ADJ **to be ~-aware** avoir pris conscience de soi **► self-awareness** N (prise f de) conscience f de soi **► self-belay**, **self-belaying system** N (Climbing) autoassurance f **► self-belief** N (NonC) confiance f en soi **► self-betterment** N amélioration f de soi-même or de sa condition **► self-catering** N appartement m etc indépendant (avec cuisine) ◆ ADJ indépendant (avec cuisine) **► self-censorship** N (NonC) autocensure f **► self-centred** ADJ égocentrique **► self-centredness** N égocentrisme m **► self-certification** N (NonC: Brit Admin) justification par l'employé d'un arrêt de travail de sept jours maximum pour cause de maladie **► self-cleaning** ADJ autonettoyant **► self-closing** ADJ à fermeture automatique **► self-coloured** ADJ uni **► self-composed** ADJ posé, calme **► self-composure** N calme m, sang-froid m **► self-conceit** N vanité f, suffisance f **► self-conceited** ADJ vaniteux, suffisant **► self-confessed** ADJ **he is a ~-confessed thief** il avoue être voleur, il reconnaît être voleur **► self-confidence** N confiance f en soi **► self-confident** ADJ sûr de soi, plein d'assurance **► self-congratulation** N autosatisfaction f **► self-congratulatory** ADJ satisfait de soi **► self-conscious** ADJ (= shy) [person, manner] emprunté, embarrassé, gauche; (= aware of oneself or itself) [art, person, political movement] conscient (de son image); **to be ~-conscious about sth** être gêné or embarrassé par qch **► self-consciously** ADV (= shyly) de façon empruntée, timidement; (= deliberately) volontairement **► self-consciousness** N (= shyness) gêne f, timidité f; (= awareness) conscience f (de son image) **► self-contained** ADJ [person] indépendant; (Brit) [flat] indépendant, avec entrée particulière **► self-contempt** N mépris m de soi **► self-contradiction** N contradiction f avec soi-même **► self-contradictory** ADJ [text] contradictoire (en soi); [person] qui se contredit **► self-control** N maîtrise f de soi, sang-froid m **► self-controlled** ADJ maître (maîtresse f) de soi **► self-correcting** ADJ autocorrecteur (-trice f) **► self-critical** ADJ qui se critique; (Pol, Rel) qui fait son autocritique **► self-criticism** N critique f de soi; (Pol, Rel) autocritique f **► self-deception** N aveuglement m **► self-defeating** ADJ [action, plan] qui va à l'encontre du but recherché **► self-defence** N (= skill, art) autodéfense f; (Jur) **in ~-defence** pour se défendre, en légitime défense; (Jur) **in ~-defence** pour se défendre, en légitime défense; (Jur) **self-delusion** N aveuglement m **► self-denial** N abnégation f, sacrifice m de soi **► self-denying** ADJ [person] qui fait preuve d'abnégation, qui se sacrifie; [decision etc] qui impose le sacrifice de ses intérêts **► self-deprecating** ADJ **to be ~-deprecating** [person] se dénigrer soi-même **► self-deprecatory** ADJ [thoughts] qui s'autodénigre **► self-destruct** VI s'autodétruire, se désintégrer ◆ ADJ [device, program] autodestructeur (-trice f) **► self-destruction** N autodestruction f **► self-destructive** ADJ [person, behaviour] autodestructeur (-trice f); **she has a tendency**

to be **~-destructive** elle a tendance à s'autodétruire **► self-determination** N autodétermination f **► self-determined** ADJ autodéterminé **► self-determining** ADJ qui s'autodétermine **► self-discipline** N autodiscipline f **► self-disciplined** ADJ qui fait preuve d'autodiscipline **► self-discovery** N (Psych) découverte f de soi **► self-doubt** N fait m de douter de soi-même **► self-doubting** ADJ qui doute de soi-même **► self-drive** ADJ (Brit) [car] sans chauffeur **► self-educated** ADJ autodidacte **► self-effacement** N modestie f, effacement m **► self-effacing** ADJ effacé, modeste **► self-elected** ADJ (Pol) qui s'est élu lui-même; **he was a ~-elected critic of ...** il avait pris sur lui de critiquer ... **► self-employed** ADJ indépendant, qui travaille à son compte **► the self-employed** NPL les travailleurs mpl indépendants **► self-employment** N **in ~-employment** = self-employed **► self-esteem** N respect m de soi, amour-propre m; **to have low/high ~-esteem** avoir une mauvaise/bonne opinion de soi-même **► self-evaluation** N auto-évaluation f **► self-evident** ADJ évident, qui va de soi **► self-evidently** ADV fort or bien évidemment **► self-examination** N examen m de conscience; (Med) [of breasts, testicles] autopalpation f **► self-explanatory** ADJ qui se passe d'explication, évident **► self-expression** N expression f (libre) **► self-fertilization** N autofécondation f **► self-fertilizing** ADJ autofertile **► self-filling** ADJ à remplissage automatique **► self-financing** N autofinancement m ◆ ADJ qui s'autofinance **► self-flattery** N louanges fpl que l'on s'adresse à soi-même **► self-forgetful** ADJ désintéressé **► self-forgetfulness** N désintéressement m **► self-fulfilling prophecy** N prédiction f qui se réalise **► self-fulfilment** N (NonC) accomplissement m de soi **► self-glorification** N autoglorification f **► self-governing** ADJ autonome **► self-government** N autonomie f **► self-hate** N haine f de soi **► self-hating** ADJ qui se déteste **► self-hatred** N = **self-hate ► self-help** N (gen) efforts mpl personnels, débrouillardise* f; (Econ) autoassistance f **► self-help group** N groupe m d'entraide **► self-hypnosis** N autohypnose f **► self-ignite** VI s'enflammer spontanément **► self-ignition** N (gen) combustion f spontanée; (Aut) autoallumage m **► self-image** N image f de soi-même **► self-importance** N suffisance f **► self-important** ADJ suffisant, m'as-tu-vu* inv **► self-imposed** ADJ auto-imposé, que l'on s'impose à soi-même **► self-improvement** N progrès mpl personnels **► self-induced** ADJ [illness, misery, problems] que l'on a provoqué soi-même **► self-indulgence** N (gen) amour m de son propre confort; (= self-pity) apitoiement m sur soi-même **► self-indulgent** ADJ (gen) qui ne se refuse rien; (= self-pitying) qui s'apitoie sur son (propre) sort **► self-inflicted** ADJ que l'on s'inflige à soi-même, volontaire **► self-interest** N intérêt m (personnel) **► self-interested** ADJ intéressé, qui recherche son avantage personnel **► self-justification** N autojustification f **► self-justifying** ADJ justificatif **► self-knowledge** N connaissance f de soi **► self-levelling foot** N (pl **self-levelling feet**) (on furniture) pied m de nivellement, pied m auto-réglable **► self-loader** N arme f automatique **► self-loading** ADJ [gun] automatique **► self-loathing** N dégoût m de soi-même ◆ ADJ qui a horreur de soi-même **► self-locking** ADJ à fermeture automatique **► self-love** N narcissisme m, amour m de soi-même **► self-lubricating** ADJ autolubrifiant **► self-lubrication** N autolubrification f **► self-made** ADJ qui a réussi par ses propres moyens **► self-made man** N self-made man *m*, fils *m* de ses œuvres (*frm*) ► **self-maintenance** N entretien *m* automatique ► **self-mastery** N maîtrise *f* de soi ► **self-mockery** N autodérision *f* ► **self-mocking** ADJ [*person*] qui se moque de soi-même ; [*humour*] empreint d'autodérision ► **self-mockingly** ADV par autodérision ► **self-motivated** ADJ très motivé (de par soi-même) ► **self-murder** N suicide *m* ► **self-mutilation** N (*NonC*) automutilation *f* ► **self-neglect** N négligence *f* de soi ► **self-obsessed** ADJ égocentrique ► **self-obsession** N égocentrisme *m* ► **self-opinionated** ADJ entêté, opiniâtre ► **self-ordained** ADJ he was a ~-ordained critic of ... il avait pris sur lui de critiquer ... ► **self-parody** N autoparodie *f* ► **self-perpetuating** ADJ it's ~-perpetuating ça se perpétue ► **self-pity** N apitoiement *m* sur soi-même ► **self-pitying** ADJ qui s'apitoie sur son (propre) sort ► **self-poisoning** N empoisonnement *m* ; **paracetamol ~-poisoning** suicide *m* par surdose de paracétamol ► **self-portrait** N autoportrait *m* ► **self-possessed** ADJ qui garde son sang-froid, maître (maîtresse *f*) de soi ► **self-possession** N sang-froid *m*, maîtrise *f* de soi ► **self-praise** N éloge *m* de soi-même, auto-louange *f* ► **self-preoccupied** ADJ égocentrique ► **self-preservation** N instinct *m* de conservation ► **self-pride** N orgueil *m* personnel, fierté *f* ► **self-proclaimed** ADJ he was a ~-proclaimed critic of ... il avait pris sur lui de critiquer ... ► **self-propelled** ADJ autopropulsé ► **self-protection** N from ~ protection pour sa propre protection ► **self-publicist** N spécialiste *mf* de la publicité personnelle ► **self-punishment** N autopunition *f* ► **self-raising flour** N (*Brit*) farine *f* pour gâteaux (*avec levure incorporée*) ► **self-regard** N ► **self-esteem** ► **self-regulating** ADJ autorégulateur (-trice *f*) ► **self-regulation** N autorégulation *f* ► **self-regulatory** ADJ = **self-regulating** ► **self-reliance** N autonomie *f* ► **self-reliant** ADJ autonome ; **to be ~-reliant** être autonome, ne pas avoir besoin des autres ► **self-renewal** N renouvellement *m* automatique ► **self-renewing** ADJ qui se renouvelle automatiquement ► **self-replicating** ADJ [*computer, machine etc*] autoreproducteur (-trice *f*) ► **self-reproach** N repentir *m*, remords *m* ► **self-reproachful** ADJ plein de reproches à l'égard de soi-même ► **self-respect** N respect *m* de soi ► **self-respecting** ADJ qui se respecte ; **no ~-respecting teacher would agree that ...** aucun professeur qui se respecte (*subj*) ne conviendrait que ... ► **self-restraint** N retenue *f* ► **self-revelation** N révélation *f* de soi-même ► **self-revelatory** ADJ d'inspiration autobiographique ► **self-ridicule** N autodérision *f* ► **self-righteous** ADJ pharisaïque, satisfait de soi ► **self-righteousness** N pharisaïsme *m*, autosatisfaction *f* ► **self-righting** ADJ inchavirable ► **self-rising flour** N (*US*) = **self-raising flour** ► **self-rule** N (*Pol*) autonomie *f* ► **self-ruling** ADJ (*Pol*) autonome ► **self-sacrifice** N abnégation *f*, dévouement *m* ► **self-sacrificing** ADJ qui se sacrifie, qui a l'esprit de sacrifice ► **self-satisfaction** N contentement *m* de soi, fatuité *f* ► **self-satisfied** ADJ [*person*] content de soi, suffisant ; [*smile*] suffisant, de satisfaction ► **self-sealing** ADJ [*envelope*] autocollant, autoadhésif ; [*container*] à obturation automatique ► **self-seeker** N égoïste *mf* ► **self-seeking** ADJ égoïste ► **self-service** N, ADJ libre-service *m inv* ; **~-service shop/restaurant** (magasin *m*/restaurant *m*) libre-service *m inv* or self-service *m inv* ; **~-service garage** station *f* (d'essence) libre-service ► **self-serving** ADJ égoïste, intéressé ► **self-starter** N (*Aut*) démarreur *m* (automatique or électrique) ; (*fig* = hard-working person) personne *f* motivée et pleine d'initiative ► **self-steering** ADJ à pi-

lotage automatique ► **self-styled** ADJ soi-disant *inv*, prétendu ► **self-sufficiency** N (*economic*) autarcie *f* ; (= self-confidence) auto-suffisance *f* ► **self-sufficient** ADJ (*economically*) autarcique ; (= self-confident) auto-suffisant ► **self-supporting** ADJ [*person*] qui subvient à ses (propres) besoins ; [*firm*] financièrement indépendant ► **self-sustaining growth** N (*Econ*) croissance *f* autonome ► **self-tapping** ADJ [*screw*] autotaraudeur ► **self-taught** ADJ autodidacte ; **"French ~-taught"** «apprenez le français par vous-même» ► **self-timer** N (*Phot*) retardateur *m* ► **self-torture** N torture *f* délibérée de soi-même ► **self-treatment** N (*Med*) automédication *f* ► **self-will** N volonté *f* inébranlable ► **self-willed** ADJ entêté, volontaire ► **self-winding** ADJ (à remontage) automatique ► **self-worship** N adulation *f* de soi-même

selfhood ['selfhʊd] N (*Psych*) individualité *f*

selfish ['selfɪʃ] ADJ [*person, behaviour*] égoïste ; [*motive*] intéressé

selfishly ['selfɪʃlɪ] ADV égoïstement, en égoïste

selfishness ['selfɪʃnɪs] N égoïsme *m*

selfless ['selflɪs] ADJ désintéressé, altruiste

selflessly ['selflɪslɪ] ADV sans penser à soi, d'une façon désintéressée, par altruisme

selflessness ['selflɪsnɪs] N désintéressement *m*, altruisme *m*

selfsame ['selfseɪm] ADJ même ; **this is the ~ book** c'est bien le même livre ; **I reached Paris the ~ day** je suis arrivé à Paris le même jour or le jour même

sell [sel] (*pret, ptp* **sold**) **1** VT **a** [+ *goods, item*] vendre ; [+ *stock*] écouler ; **"to be sold"** «à vendre» ; **to ~ sth for $25** vendre qch 25 dollars ; **he sold it (to) me for £10** il me l'a vendu 10 livres ; **he sold the books at $10 each** il a vendu les livres 10 dollars pièce or chaque ; **he was ~ing them at or for £10 a dozen** il les vendait 10 livres la douzaine ; **do you ~ stamps?** est-ce que vous vendez des timbres ? ; **are stamps sold here?** est-ce qu'on vend des timbres ici ? ; **I was sold this in Grenoble** on m'a vendu cela à Grenoble ; **he's a commercial traveller who ~s shirts** c'est un voyageur de commerce qui vend des chemises ; **it's not the price but the quality that ~s this item** ce n'est pas le prix mais la qualité qui fait vendre cet article ; (*sexually*) **to ~ o.s.** se vendre → 1b ; **to ~ one's body** vendre son corps ; **to ~ sb into slavery** vendre qn comme esclave ; **to ~ one's life dearly** vendre chèrement sa vie ; (*fig*) **to ~ the pass** abandonner or trahir la cause ; **to ~ a secret** vendre or trahir un secret ; **to ~ sb short** (= cheat) avoir qn*, posséder qn* ; (= belittle) ne pas faire or rendre justice à qn ; **to ~ o.s. short** ne pas savoir se vendre ; **he sold his soul for political power** il a vendu son âme contre le pouvoir (politique) ; **I'd ~ my soul for a coat/body like that!*** je donnerais n'importe quoi or je vendrais mon âme pour avoir un manteau/un corps comme ça ! → **bill, pup**
b (* = put across) **to ~ sb an idea** faire accepter une idée à qn ; **if we can ~ coexistence to Ruritania** si nous arrivons à faire accepter le principe de la coexistence à la Ruritanie ; **he doesn't ~ himself very well** il n'arrive pas à se faire valoir or à se mettre en valeur ; **if you can ~ yourself to the voters** si vous arrivez à convaincre les électeurs ; **to be sold on* an idea** etc être emballé* or enthousiasmé par une idée etc ; **to be sold on sb*** être complètement emballé* par qn
c (* = betray) **I've been sold!** on m'a vendu !* ; **to ~ sb down the river** trahir qn
2 VI se vendre ; **these books ~ at or for $10 each** ces livres se vendent 10 dollars pièce or chaque ; **they ~ at £10 a dozen** ils se vendent 10 livres la douzaine ; **your car should ~ for £8,000** votre voiture devrait se vendre 8 000

livres ; **it ~s well** cela se vend bien ; **that line doesn't ~** cet article se vend mal ; (*St Ex*) **to ~ short** vendre à découvert ; **the idea didn't ~** l'idée n'a pas été acceptée → **cake**
3 N **a**: (= disappointment) déception *f* ; (= fraud) attrape-nigaud *m* ; **what a ~!** ce que je me suis (or tu t'es etc) fait avoir !* **b** (*Comm*) → **hard, soft**
4 COMP ► **sell-by date** N (*Comm*) date *f* limite de vente ; **to be past one's ~-by date*** avoir fait son temps ► **sell-through** ADJ [*video*] réservé à la vente
► **sell back** VT SEP revendre (à la même personne etc)
► **sell off** VT SEP [+ *stock*] liquider ; [+ *goods*] solder ; [+ *shares*] vendre, liquider
► **sell on** [sel] VT SEP revendre
► **sell out** **1** VI **a** (*US Comm* = sell up) (*business*) vendre son fonds or son affaire ; (*stock*) liquider son stock
b (= be used up) [*product, tickets*] se vendre tous
c [*shopkeeper etc*] **to ~ out of sth** (*temporarily*) être à court de qch ; (= use up supply of) épuiser son stock de qch
d (*fig*) renier ses principes ; **to ~ out to the enemy** passer à l'ennemi ; **to ~ out on sb** trahir qn
2 VT SEP **a** (*St Ex*) vendre
b (*Comm*) vendre tout son stock de ; **this item is sold out** cet article est épuisé ; **we are sold out of everything** nous avons tout vendu ; **we are sold out of milk** nous n'avons plus de lait, nous sommes à court de lait ; (*Theat*) **the house was sold out** toutes les places étaient louées ; **tickets for the ballet were sold out** il n'y avait plus de billets pour le ballet, tous les billets pour le ballet avaient été vendus ; **the concert is sold out** il n'y a plus de billets pour le concert, le concert se jouera à guichets fermés
3 **~out** N → **sellout**
► **sell up** (*esp Brit*) **1** VI **a** (*gen*) se défaire de or vendre toutes ses possessions **b** (*Comm*) = **sell out 1a 2** VT SEP **a** (*Jur*) [+ *goods*] opérer la vente forcée de, saisir ; [+ *debtor*] vendre les biens de **b** (*Comm*) [+ *business*] vendre, liquider

seller ['selər] N **a** (*in compounds*) vendeur *m*, -euse *f*, marchand(e) *m(f)* ; **newspaper-~** vendeur *m*, -euse *f* de journaux ; **onion-~** marchand(e) *m(f)* d'oignons → **bookseller b** (*as opposed to buyer*) vendeur *m* ; **~'s market** marché *m* favorable au vendeur **c** **this book is a (good) ~** ce livre se vend bien or comme des petits pains* → **bestseller**

selling ['selɪŋ] **1** N vente(s) *f(pl)* **2** COMP ► **selling point** N (*Comm*) avantage *m* pour le client ; (*fig*) atout *m* ► **selling price** N prix *m* de vente ► **selling rate** N (*Fin*) cours *m* vendeur

selloff ['selɒf] N (*Econ*) vente *f*

Sellotape® ['seləʊteɪp] (*Brit*) **1** N scotch® *m*, ruban *m* adhésif **2** VT **sellotape** scotcher, coller avec du ruban adhésif

sellout ['selaʊt] N **a** (*Cine, Theat etc*) **the play was a ~** tous les billets (pour la pièce) ont été vendus, on a joué à guichets fermés or à bureaux fermés **b** (= betrayal) trahison *f*, capitulation *f* ; **a ~ of minority opinion** une trahison de l'opinion de la minorité ; (*Pol*) **a ~ to the left** une capitulation devant la gauche

seltzer ['seltsər] N (*US: also ~ water*) eau *f* de Seltz

selvage, selvedge ['selvɪdʒ] N lisière *f* (*d'un tissu*)

selves [selvz] NPL of **self**

semantic [sɪˈmæntɪk] ADJ sémantique

semantically [sɪˈmæntɪkəlɪ] ADV sémantiquement, d'un point de vue sémantique

semanticist [sɪˈmæntɪsɪst] N sémanticien(ne) *m(f)*

semantics [sɪˈmæntɪks] N (NonC) sémantique f

semaphore [ˈseməfɔːʳ] 1 N a signaux mpl à bras ; **in ~** par signaux à bras b (Rail) sémaphore m 2 VT transmettre par signaux à bras

semblance [ˈsembləns] N semblant m, apparence f ; **without a ~ of respect** sans le moindre semblant de respect ; **to put on a ~ of sorrow** faire semblant d'avoir de la peine

seme [siːm] N (Ling) sème m

semen [ˈsiːmən] N sperme m, semence f

semester [sɪˈmestəʳ] N (esp US) semestre m

semi [ˈsemɪ] 1 PREF a → 3 b (= not completely: + adj) plus ou moins ; **it's ~ tidy** c'est plus ou moins bien rangé 2 N a (Brit*) ABBR = **semi-detached** b* ABBR = **semifinal** c (US) ABBR = **semitrailer** 3 COMP ► **semi-monthly** ADJ, N (US Press) bimensuel m ► **semi-skimmed** ADJ demi-écrémé

semiautomatic [ˌsemɪɔːtəˈmætɪk] ADJ semi-automatique

semibasement [ˈsemɪˌbeɪsmənt] N ≈ rez-de-jardin m

semibreve [ˈsemɪbriːv] (esp Brit Mus) 1 N ronde f 2 COMP ► **semibreve rest** N pause f

semicircle [ˈsemɪsɜːkl] N demi-cercle m

semicircular [ˌsemɪˈsɜːkjʊləʳ] ADJ demi-circulaire, semi-circulaire, en demi-cercle

semicolon [ˌsemɪˈkəʊlən] N point-virgule m

semicommercial [ˌsemɪkəˈmɜːʃəl] ADJ semi-commercial

semiconductor [ˌsemɪkənˈdʌktəʳ] N semi-conducteur m

semiconscious [ˌsemɪˈkɒnʃəs] ADJ à demi conscient

semiconsonant [ˌsemɪˈkɒnsənənt] N semi-consonne f, semi-voyelle f

semidarkness [ˌsemɪˈdɑːknɪs] N pénombre f, demi-jour m

semidesert [ˌsemɪˈdezət] ADJ semi-désertique

semi-detached [ˌsemɪdɪˈtætʃt] (Brit) 1 N (also ~ **house**) maison f jumelle 2 ADJ ~ **houses** maisons fpl mitoyennes

semifinal [ˌsemɪˈfaɪnl] N demi-finale f ; **to go out in the ~s** être éliminé en demi-finale

semifinalist [ˌsemɪˈfaɪnəlɪst] N demi-finaliste mf ; (= team) équipe f demi-finaliste

semiliquid [ˌsemɪˈlɪkwɪd] ADJ semi-liquide

semiliterate [ˌsemɪˈlɪtərɪt] ADJ quasiment illettré

seminal [ˈsemɪnl] ADJ (Physiol) séminal ; (fig) qui fait école, riche et original

seminar [ˈsemɪnɑːʳ] N séminaire m, colloque m ; (Univ) séminaire m, séance f de travaux pratiques or de TP

seminarian [ˌsemɪˈnɛərɪən], **seminarist** [ˈsemɪnərɪst] N séminariste m

seminary [ˈsemɪnərɪ] N (= priests' college) séminaire m ; (= school) petit séminaire m

semiofficial [ˌsemɪəˈfɪʃəl] ADJ semi-officiel, officieux

semiologist [ˌsemɪˈɒlədʒɪst] N sémiologue mf

semiology [ˌsemɪˈɒlədʒɪ] N sémiologie f

semiotic [ˌsemɪˈɒtɪk] ADJ sémiotique

semiotics [ˌsemɪˈɒtɪks] N (NonC) sémiotique f

semipolitical [ˌsemɪpəˈlɪtɪkəl] ADJ semi-politique

semiprecious [ˌsemɪˈpreʃəs] ADJ semi-précieux ; **~ stone** pierre f semi-précieuse

semiprivate room [ˌsemɪpraɪvɪtˈrʊm] N (US Med) chambre f d'hôpital à plusieurs lits

semiprofessional [ˌsemɪprəˈfeʃənl] ADJ semi-professionnel

semiquaver [ˈsemɪkweɪvəʳ] N (esp Brit Mus) double croche f

semiskilled [ˌsemɪˈskɪld] ADJ [work] d'ouvrier

spécialisé ; **~ worker** ouvrier m, -ière f spécialisé(e), OS mf

semisolid [ˌsemɪˈsɒlɪd] ADJ semi-solide

Semite [ˈsiːmaɪt] N Sémite or sémite mf

Semitic [sɪˈmɪtɪk] ADJ [language] sémitique ; [people] sémite

semitone [ˈsemɪtəʊn] N demi-ton m

semitrailer [ˌsemɪˈtreɪləʳ] N (Aut) semi-remorque f

semitropical [ˌsemɪˈtrɒpɪkəl] ADJ semi-tropical

semivowel [ˈsemɪvaʊəl] N semi-voyelle f, semi-consonne f

semiweekly [ˌsemɪˈwiːklɪ] ADJ, N (US Press) bi-hebdomadaire m

semolina [ˌseməˈliːnə] N semoule f ; (also ~ **pudding**) semoule f au lait

sempiternal [ˌsempɪˈtɜːnl] ADJ (liter) éternel, perpétuel

sempstress [ˈsempstrɪs] N = **seamstress**

SEN [ˌesiˈen] N (Brit) (ABBR = **State-Enrolled Nurse**) → **state**

Sen. (US) ABBR = **Senator**

sen. ABBR = **senior**

senate [ˈsenɪt] N a (Pol) sénat m ; (in US, Can, Austral) **the Senate** le Sénat b (Univ) conseil m d'université

senator [ˈsenɪtəʳ] N sénateur m

senatorial [ˌsenəˈtɔːrɪəl] ADJ sénatorial

send [send] (pret, ptp **sent**) 1 VT a (= dispatch) [+ thing] envoyer (**to sb** à qn) ; **I sent him a letter to say that ...** je lui ai envoyé une lettre pour lui dire que ... ; **I sent the letter to him yesterday** je lui ai envoyé la lettre hier ; **I wrote the letter but didn't ~ it (off)** j'ai écrit la lettre mais je ne l'ai pas envoyée ; **to ~ good wishes** adresser or envoyer ses bons vœux ; **Paul ~s his best wishes** Paul vous (or nous etc) envoie ses bons vœux ; **~ her my regards** faites-lui or transmettez-lui mes amitiés ; (fig) **this decision ~s the wrong signal** or **message** cette décision risque d'être mal interprété ; **to ~ help** envoyer des secours ; **to ~ word that ...** faire savoir que ..., faire dire que ... ; **I'll ~ a car (for you)** j'enverrai une voiture (vous chercher) ; **to ~ washing to the laundry** donner or envoyer du linge au blanchissage ; **God sent a plague to punish the Egyptians** Dieu envoya or infligea un fléau aux Égyptiens pour les punir ; **the rain has been sent to save our crops** cette pluie nous a été envoyée or donnée pour sauver nos récoltes ; (hum) **these things are sent to try us!** c'est le ciel qui nous envoie ces épreuves !

b (= cause to go) [+ person] envoyer ; **to ~ sb for sth** envoyer qn chercher qch ; **to ~ sb to do sth** envoyer qn faire qch ; **I sent him (along) to see her** je l'ai envoyé la voir ; **~ him (along) to see me**, **send him to venir me voir**, envoie-le-moi ; **to ~ sb to bed** envoyer qn se coucher ; **to ~ sb home** renvoyer qn chez lui ; (to a different country) rapatrier qn ; (Ind) **to ~ workers home** mettre des employés en chômage technique ; **they sent him to school in London** ils l'ont mis en pension à Londres ; **I won't ~ you to school today** je ne t'envoie pas à l'école aujourd'hui ; **children are sent to school at the age of five** les enfants doivent aller à l'école à partir de cinq ans ; **some children are sent to school without breakfast** il y a des enfants qui vont à l'école sans avoir pris de petit déjeuner ; **he was sent to prison** on l'a envoyé en prison ; **the rain sent us indoors** la pluie nous a fait rentrer ; **they sent the dogs after the escaped prisoner** ils ont envoyé les chiens à la poursuite or à la recherche du prisonnier évadé ; (lit, fig) **to ~ sb to sleep** endormir qn ; **to ~ sb into fits of laughter** faire rire qn de rire ; **to ~ sb packing** or **about his business** envoyer promener qn*, envoyer paître qn* ; **to ~ prices/**

shares etc **soaring** faire monter les prix/les actions etc en flèche ; → **Coventry**

c (= propel, cause to move) [+ ball] envoyer, lancer ; [+ stone, arrow] lancer ; **to ~ an astronaut/a rocket into space** lancer or envoyer un astronaute/une fusée dans l'espace ; **he sent the ball over the trees** il a envoyé or lancé le ballon par-dessus les arbres ; **he screwed up the paper and sent it straight into the basket** il a froissé le papier et l'a envoyé or l'a lancé tout droit dans la corbeille ; **the explosion sent a cloud of smoke into the air** l'explosion a projeté un nuage de fumée (en l'air) ; **the news sent a thrill through her** la nouvelle l'a électrisée ; **the sight of the dog sent her running to her mother** en voyant le chien elle s'est précipitée vers sa mère ; **the blow sent him sprawling** le coup l'a envoyé par terre ; **he sent the plate flying** il a envoyé voler* l'assiette ; **to ~ sb flying** envoyer qn rouler à terre

d (= cause to become) rendre ; **the noise is ~ing me mad** le bruit me rend fou

e (†* = make ecstatic) emballer* ; **this music ~s me** cette musique m'emballe*, **he ~s me** je le trouve sensationnel

2 VI (frm, liter) **they sent to ask if ...** ils envoyèrent demander si ...

3 COMP ► **send-off** N **they were given a warm ~-off** on leur a fait des adieux chaleureux ; **they gave him a big ~-off** ils sont venus nombreux lui souhaiter bon voyage ► **send-up*** N (Brit) parodie f

► **send away** 1 VI **to ~ away for sth** (= order by post) commander qch par correspondance ; (= order and receive) se faire envoyer qch 2 VT SEP a envoyer ; (= expel: from country, town) expulser ; **to ~ one's children away to school** mettre ses enfants en pension ; **to ~ a radio/car away to be fixed** donner une radio/une voiture à réparer b (= dismiss) [+ person] congédier c [+ parcel, letter, goods] envoyer ; (= post) envoyer (par la poste)

► **send back** VT SEP [+ person, thing] renvoyer

► **send down** VT SEP a (lit) [+ person] faire descendre, envoyer en bas b [+ prices, sb's temperature, blood pressure] faire baisser c (Brit Univ) renvoyer (de l'université) d (* = jail) coffrer*, envoyer en prison

► **send for** VT FUS a [+ doctor, police etc] faire venir, appeler ; (= send sb to get) faire appeler, envoyer chercher ; **to ~ for help** chercher de l'aide, se faire envoyer des secours b (= order by post) commander par correspondance ; (= order and receive) se faire envoyer

► **send forth** VT SEP (liter) [+ light] diffuser ; [+ leaf] produire ; [+ smell] répandre, exhaler ; [+ army] envoyer

► **send in** VT SEP a [+ person] faire entrer ; [+ troops] envoyer b [+ resignation] envoyer, donner ; [+ report, entry form] envoyer, soumettre ; **to ~ in an application** faire une demande ; (for job) poser sa candidature ; **to ~ in a request** envoyer or faire une demande ; **~ in your name and address if you wish to receive ...** envoyez vos nom et adresse si vous désirez recevoir ...

► **send off** 1 VI = **send away** 1 2 VT SEP a [+ person] envoyer ; **I sent him off to think it over/get cleaned up** etc je l'ai envoyé méditer là-dessus/se débarbouiller etc ; **she sent the child off to the grocer's** elle a envoyé l'enfant chez l'épicier b (= say goodbye to) dire au revoir à ; **there was a large crowd to ~ him off** une foule de gens était venue or étaient venus lui dire au revoir or lui souhaiter bon voyage c [+ letter, parcel, goods] envoyer, expédier ; (= post) mettre à la poste d (Ftbl etc) [+ player] expulser 3 **~-off** N → **send**

► **send on** VT SEP (Brit) [+ letter] faire suivre ; [+ luggage] (in advance) expédier à l'avance ; (afterwards) faire suivre ; [+ object left behind] renvoyer

►**send out** [1] VI **to ~ out for sth** (= order by phone) [+ pizza etc] commander qch par téléphone; (= send sb to fetch) envoyer chercher qch [2] VT SEP [a] [+ person] faire sortir; **she sent the children out to play** elle a envoyé les enfants jouer dehors; **I sent her out for a breath of air** je l'ai envoyée prendre l'air; **they were sent out for talking too loudly** on les a mis à la porte parce qu'ils parlaient trop fort [b] (= post) [+ correspondence, leaflets] envoyer (par la poste) [c] [+ scouts, messengers, emissary] envoyer [d] (= emit) [+ smell] répandre, exhaler; [+ heat] diffuser, répandre; [+ light] diffuser, émettre; [+ smoke] répandre; [+ signal] (gen) émettre; (Rad) diffuser [e] (= put out) [+ shoots, roots] produire, donner

►**send round** VT SEP [a] (= circulate) [+ document, bottle etc] faire circuler [b] faire parvenir; **I'll ~ it round to you as soon as it's ready** je vous le ferai parvenir or porter dès que cela sera prêt [c] [+ person] envoyer; **I sent him round to the grocer's** je l'ai envoyé chez l'épicier

►**send up** [1] VT SEP [a] [+ person, luggage] faire monter; [+ aeroplane] envoyer; [+ spacecraft, flare] lancer; [+ smoke] envoyer; [+ prices] faire monter en flèche [b] (Brit* = make fun of) [+ person] mettre en boîte*; (= imitate) [+ person, book] parodier [c] [+ entry form] envoyer [d] (= blow up) faire sauter*, faire exploser [e] (* = jail) coffrer*, envoyer en prison [2] **~-up*** N (Brit) → **send**

sender ['sendər] N expéditeur m, -trice f, envoyeur m, -euse f → **return**

sending-off [ˌsendɪŋ'ɒf] N (Ftbl etc) expulsion f

Seneca ['senɪkə] N Sénèque m

Senegal [ˌsenɪ'gɔːl] N le Sénégal

Senegalese [ˌsenɪgə'liːz] [1] ADJ sénégalais [2] N (pl inv) Sénégalais(e) m(f)

senile ['siːnaɪl] [1] ADJ sénile; **~ decay** dégénérescence f sénile [2] COMP ► **senile dementia** N démence f sénile

senility [sɪ'nɪlɪtɪ] N sénilité f

senior ['siːnɪər] [1] ADJ [a] (= older) aîné, plus âgé; **he is three years ~ to me** ◊ **he is ~ to me by three years** il est mon aîné de trois ans, il est plus âgé que moi de trois ans; **(Mr) Smith Senior** (M.) Smith père; **Mrs Smith Senior** Mme Smith mère [b] (= of higher rank) [employee] de grade supérieur; [officer] supérieur (-eure f); [position, rank] supérieur (-eure f), plus élevé; (Sport) **at ~ level** en senior; **he is ~ to me in the firm** (in rank) il est au-dessus de moi dans l'entreprise, son poste dans l'entreprise est plus élevé que le mien; (in service) il a plus d'ancienneté que moi dans la maison; (Mil) **~ officer** officier m supérieur; **a ~ official** (Admin) un haut fonctionnaire; (in private firm) un cadre supérieur or haut placé; (Brit) **~ CID officer** officier m de police judiciaire haut placé; **~ police officer** officier m de police haut placé [2] N [a] (= older) aîné(e) m(f); **he is my ~ by three years** ◊ **he is three years my ~** (in age) il est mon aîné de trois ans, il est plus âgé que moi de trois ans; (in service) il a trois ans d'ancienneté de plus que moi [b] (US Univ) étudiant(e) m(f) de licence; (US Scol) élève mf de terminale; (Brit Scol) **the ~s** les grand(e)s m(f)(pl) [3] COMP ► **senior aircraftman** N (pl senior aircraftmen) (Brit Air Force) ≈ soldat m ► **senior aircraftwoman** N (pl senior aircraftwomen) (Brit Air Force) ≈ soldat m ► **senior airman** N (pl senior airmen) (US Air Force) caporal-chef m ► **senior chief petty officer** N (US Navy) premier maître m ► **senior citizen** N personne f du troisième âge; **~ citizens' club** club m du troisième âge ► **senior clerk** N premier commis m, commis m principal ► **senior common room** N (Brit Univ) salle f des professeurs ► **senior editor** N rédacteur m, -trice f en chef ► **senior executive** N cadre m supérieur ► **senior high school** N (US) ≈ lycée m ► **senior master** N (Brit Scol) professeur m principal ► **senior master sergeant** N (US Air Force) adjudant m ► **senior partner** N associé m principal ► **senior prom** N (US) bal m des classes de terminale ► **senior school** N (= oldest classes) grandes classes fpl; (= secondary school) collège m d'enseignement secondaire ► **Senior Service** N (Brit) marine f (de guerre) ► **senior year** N (US Scol) (classe f) terminale f, dernière année f d'études (scolaires)

seniority [ˌsiːnɪ'ɒrɪtɪ] N (in age) priorité f d'âge; (in rank) séniorité f; (in years of service) ancienneté f; **promotion by ~** avancement m à l'ancienneté

senna ['senə] [1] N séné m [2] COMP ► **senna pod** N gousse f de séné

sensation [sen'seɪʃən] N [a] (= feeling) sensation f; **to lose all ~ in one's arm** perdre toute sensation dans le bras; **to have a dizzy ~** avoir une sensation de vertige [b] (= impression) sensation f; **to have the ~ of doing sth** avoir la sensation de faire qch; **I felt a ~ of being watched** j'avais l'impression or le sentiment que l'on m'observait [c] (= excitement, success) sensation f; [press] sensation f; **to create or cause a ~** faire sensation; **it was a ~ in Paris** cela a fait sensation à Paris; **it's a ~!** c'est sensationnel!; **the film that turned her into an overnight ~** le film qui a fait d'elle une star du jour au lendemain

sensational [sen'seɪʃənl] ADJ [a] [event] qui fait sensation, sensationnel; [fashion] qui fait sensation; **~ murder** meurtre m qui fait sensation [b] [film, novel, newspaper] à sensation; **he gave a ~ account of the accident** il a fait un récit dramatique de l'accident [c] (* = marvellous) sensationnel*, formidable*

sensationalism [sen'seɪʃnəlɪzəm] N (NonC) [a] (Press etc) recherche f or exploitation f du sensationnel [b] (Philos) sensualisme m

sensationalist [sen'seɪʃnəlɪst] [1] N colporteur m, -euse f de nouvelles à sensation; (= writer) auteur m à sensation [2] ADJ à sensation; **they described it in ~ terms** ils l'ont décrit en recherchant le sensationnel

sensationalize [sen'seɪʃnəlaɪz] VT dramatiser

sensationally [sen'seɪʃnəlɪ] ADV **it was ~ successful/popular** etc cela a connu un succès/une popularité etc inouï(e) or fantastique

sense [sens] [1] N [a] (= faculty) sens m; **~ of hearing** ouïe f; **~ of smell** odorat m; **~ of sight** vue f; **~ of taste** goût m; **~ of touch** toucher m; **to come to one's ~s** (= regain consciousness) reprendre connaissance, revenir à soi → **1d**; → **sixth** [b] (= awareness) sens m, sentiment m; **~ of colour** sens m de la couleur; **~ of direction** sens m de l'orientation; **~ of duty** sentiment m du devoir; **~ of humour** sens m de l'humour; **he has no ~ of humour** il n'a pas le sens de l'humour; **to lose all ~ of time** perdre toute notion de l'heure; **the ~ of my own inadequacy** le sentiment de mon impuissance; **to have no ~ of shame** ne pas savoir ce que c'est que la honte; **he has no ~ of occasion** il n'a aucun sens de ce qui est opportun; **well-chosen flowers can add to the ~ of occasion at a wedding** pour un mariage, une judicieuse sélection de fleurs peut ajouter au caractère exceptionnel de l'occasion → **business, road, strong** [c] (= sensation, impression) (physical) sensation f; (mental) sentiment m; **a ~ of warmth** une sensation de chaleur; **a ~ of guilt** un sentiment de culpabilité [d] (= sanity) ~s raison f; **to take leave of one's ~s** perdre la tête or la raison; **to come to one's ~s** (= become reasonable) revenir à la raison; **to bring sb to his ~s** ramener qn à la raison; **anyone in his ~s would know ...** tout homme sensé or tout homme jouissant de sa raison saurait ...; **no one in his ~s would do that** il faudrait être fou pour faire ça [e] (= wisdom, sound judgement: also **commonsense**) bon sens m, intelligence f; **haven't you enough ~** or **the (good) ~ to refuse?** n'avez-vous pas assez de bon sens pour refuser?; **there is some ~ in what he says** il y a du bon sens dans ce qu'il dit; **to have more ~ than to do** avoir trop de bon sens pour faire, être trop sensé pour faire; **you should have had more ~ than to do it** vous auriez dû avoir assez de bon sens pour ne pas le faire [f] (= reasonable quality) sens m; **there's no ~ in (doing) that** cela n'a pas de sens, cela ne rime à rien; **what's the ~ of** or **in (doing) that?** à quoi bon (faire) cela?; **to see ~** entendre raison; **he won't see ~** il ne veut pas entendre raison; **try to make him see ~** essaie de lui faire entendre raison → **sound², talk** [g] (= meaning) [of word, phrase, writing, text etc] sens m (also Ling), signification f; **in the literal/figurative ~** au sens propre/figuré; **in every ~ of the word** dans toute l'acception du terme; **alcoholism is not a disease in the usual ~ of the word** l'alcoolisme n'est pas une maladie au sens habituel du terme; **she is in no ~ suitable for the job** elle n'est pas du tout la personne qu'il faut pour le poste; **in a ~** dans un (certain) sens, dans une certaine mesure; **in a very real ~** de fait; **to get the ~ of what sb says** saisir l'essentiel de ce que dit qn [h] (= rational meaning) [of words, writing, action, event] sens m; **to make ~** [words, speech etc] avoir du sens; **not to make ~** [words, speech etc] ne pas avoir de sens, être dénué de sens; **what she did makes ~** ce qu'elle a fait est logique or se tient; **what she did just doesn't make ~** ce qu'elle a fait n'est pas logique or ne tient pas debout*; **why did she do it? — I don't know, it doesn't make ~** pourquoi est-ce qu'elle a fait ça? — je n'en sais rien, ça n'a aucun sens or ça ne tient pas debout*; **to make ~ of sth** arriver à comprendre qch, saisir la signification de qch [i] (= opinion) **the general ~ of the meeting** l'opinion générale or le sentiment de ceux présents; (US Pol) **the ~ of the Senate** la recommandation du Sénat [2] VT [a] (= become aware of, feel) [+ sb's uneasiness, grief, happiness etc] sentir (intuitivement); [+ trouble] pressentir; **to ~ danger** pressentir le danger; **they ~ victory** ils ont le sentiment qu'ils vont gagner; **to ~ somebody's presence** sentir une présence, se rendre compte d'une présence; **I could ~ his eyes on me** je sentais qu'il me regardait; **I ~d his interest in what I was saying** j'ai senti que ce que je disais l'intéressait; **to ~ that one is unwelcome** sentir or deviner qu'on n'est pas le bienvenu; **she can ~ when her children are unhappy** elle le sent or devine quand ses enfants sont malheureux [b] [machine, sensor device] [+ movement, heat, change] détecter; **the camera ~s when a film has reached the end** la caméra le détecte quand un film est arrivé au bout [3] COMP ► **sense organ** N organe m des sens or sensoriel

senseless ['senslɪs] ADJ [a] (= stupid) [person] insensé; [action, idea] stupide, qui ne tient pas debout; (stronger) absurde, insensé; **a ~ waste of energy resources** un gâchis insensé des ressources d'énergie; **it was a ~ waste of human life** il (or elle etc) est mort(e) pour rien; **what a ~ thing to do!** (or **to say!** etc) c'est d'une stupidité sans nom!, ça n'a pas le sens commun! [b] (= unconscious) sans connaissance; **to fall ~ (to the floor)** tomber sans connaissance → **knock**

senselessly ['senslıslı] ADV stupidement, d'une façon insensée

senselessness ['senslısnıs] N [of person] manque m de bon sens; [of action, idea] absurdité f; **the absolute ~ of war** l'absurdité f totale de la guerre

sensibility [ˌsensı'bılıtı] N [a] (NonC) sensibilité f [b] **sensibilities** susceptibilité f

sensible ['sensəbl] ADJ [a] (= wise, of sound judgement) [person] sensé, raisonnable; **she's a ~ person** or **type** elle est très raisonnable or sensée; **try to be ~ about it** sois raisonnable; **that was ~ of you** tu as très bien fait, c'était la chose à faire [b] (= reasonable, practicable) [act, decision, choice] sage, raisonnable; [clothes] pratique, commode; [shoes] pratique; **the most ~ thing (to do) would be to see her** le plus sage or raisonnable serait de la voir [c] (frm = perceptible) [change, difference, rise in temperature] appréciable [d] (frm = aware) **I am ~† of the honour you do me** je suis sensible à or conscient de l'honneur que vous me faites

sensibleness ['sensəblnıs] N bon sens m, jugement m

sensibly ['sensəblı] ADV [a] (= reasonably) [act, decide] raisonnablement, sagement, judicieusement; **to be ~ dressed** porter des vêtements pratiques [b] (= perceptibly) sensiblement

sensitive ['sensıtıv] [1] ADJ [a] [person] (= emotionally aware, responsive) sensible; (= easily hurt) sensible (**to** à); (= easily offended) facilement blessé (**to** par), susceptible; (= easily influenced) impressionnable, influençable; **she is ~ about her nose** elle fait une fixation sur son nez; **she's a ~ soul** c'est quelqu'un de très sensible or émotif [b] (= delicate) [eyes, matter, skin, subject, topic] délicat, sensible; [situation] névralgique, délicat; (Phot) [film] sensible (**to** à); (Phot) [paper] sensibilisé; **public opinion is very ~ to hints of corruption** l'opinion publique réagit vivement à tout soupçon de corruption; **this is politically very ~** sur le plan politique ceci est très délicat; **that is a very ~ area** (= place) c'est un point chaud; (fig = subject matter) c'est un domaine très délicat or sensible [c] (= sore) [tooth, skin, sore place] sensible [d] (affecting national security) [document etc] sensible [e] (St Ex, Comm) [market] nerveux [2] ADJ (in compounds) **heat-/light-~** sensible à la chaleur/la lumière

sensitively ['sensıtıvlı] ADV avec sensibilité, d'une manière sensible

sensitiveness ['sensıtıvnıs] N (= responsiveness) (physical, emotional) sensibilité f; (to criticism) susceptibilité f

sensitivity [ˌsensı'tıvıtı] N [a] [of person, instrument, gauge, machine] sensibilité f; **their ~ to this problem** leur sensibilisation à ce problème; **~ to pain** sensibilité à la douleur; (= soreness) **if you experience any ~, discontinue use** en cas de réaction (allergique), cesser l'utilisation [b] (= delicacy) [of subject] caractère m délicat; [of information] caractère m sensible; **an issue of great ~** un sujet très délicat

sensitize ['sensıtaız] VT (gen, Phot) sensibiliser

sensor ['sensər] N (Tech) détecteur m; **heat ~** palpeur m

sensory ['sensərı] ADJ des sens; (Physiol) [organ, nerve] sensoriel

sensual ['sensjʊəl] ADJ sensuel

sensualism ['sensjʊəlızəm] N sensualité f; (Philos) sensualisme m

sensualist ['sensjʊəlıst] N personne f sensuelle, voluptueux m, -euse f; (Philos) sensualiste mf

sensuality [ˌsensjʊ'ælıtı] N sensualité f

sensually ['sensjʊəlı] ADV sensuellement

sensuous ['sensjʊəs] ADJ [person, temperament, poetry, music] voluptueux, sensuel

sensuously ['sensjʊəslı] ADV avec volupté, voluptueusement

sensuousness ['sensjʊəsnıs] N [of poetry, music] qualité f voluptueuse or sensuelle; [of person, temperament] sensualité f

sent [sent] VB pt, ptp of **send**

sentence ['sentəns] [1] N [a] (Gram) phrase f [b] (Jur) (= judgement) condamnation f, sentence f; (= punishment) peine f; (lit, fig) **to pass ~ on sb** prononcer une condamnation or une sentence contre qn; **~ of death** arrêt m de mort, condamnation f à mort; **under ~ of death** condamné à mort; **he got a five-year ~** il a été condamné à cinq ans de prison; **a long ~** une longue peine → **commute, life, serve** [2] VT prononcer une condamnation or une sentence contre; **to ~ sb to death/to five years** condamner qn à mort/à cinq ans de prison [3] COMP ▸ **sentence structure** N (Gram) structure f de la phrase

sententious [sen'tenʃəs] ADJ sentencieux, pompeux

sententiously [sen'tenʃəslı] ADV sentencieusement

sententiousness [sen'tenʃəsnıs] N [of speech] ton m sentencieux; [of person] caractère m sentencieux

sentient ['senʃənt] ADJ sensible, doué de sensation

sentiment ['sentımənt] N [a] (NonC = feeling) sentiment m; **public ~** le sentiment général; **there is growing nationalist ~ in the country** on observe dans le pays une montée du sentiment nationaliste; **his actions were motivated by religious ~** ses actes ont été motivés par un sentiment religieux; **anti-government ~ was strong** il y avait un fort sentiment anti-gouvernemental [b] (= opinion, thought) sentiment m; **what are your ~s on this?** quels sont vos sentiments à ce sujet?; **what a marvellous ~!** quelle idée charmante!; **my ~s exactly!** c'est exactement ce que je pense! [c] (= emotion) sentiment m; **my ~s towards your daughter** les sentiments que j'éprouve pour votre fille or que m'inspire votre fille [d] (NonC = sentimentality) sentimentalité f, sensiblerie f (pej)

sentimental [ˌsentı'mentl] ADJ [person, novel] sentimental (also pej); **it's of ~ value only** sa valeur est purement sentimentale; (Literat) **~ comedy** comédie f larmoyante

sentimentalism [ˌsentı'mentəlızəm] N sentimentalisme m, sensiblerie f (pej)

sentimentalist [ˌsentı'mentəlıst] N sentimental(e) m(f)

sentimentality [ˌsentımen'tælıtı] N sentimentalité f, sensiblerie f (pej)

sentimentalize [ˌsentı'mentəlaız] [1] VT rendre sentimental [2] VI faire du sentiment*

sentimentally [ˌsentı'mentəlı] ADV sentimentalement, d'une manière (or d'une voix etc) sentimentale

sentinel ['sentınl] N sentinelle f, factionnaire m

sentry ['sentrı] [1] N (Mil) sentinelle f, factionnaire m; (fig) sentinelle f [2] COMP ▸ **sentry box** N guérite f ▸ **sentry duty** N **to be on ~ duty** être en or de faction

Seoul [səʊl] N Séoul

Sep. ABBR = **September**

sepal ['sepəl] N sépale m

separable ['sepərəbl] ADJ séparable

separate ['seprət] [1] ADJ [section, piece] séparé, distinct; [treaty, peace] séparé; [career, existence] indépendant; [organization, unit] distinct, indépendant; [entrance] particulier; [occasion, day] différent; [question, issue] différent, autre; **the children have ~ rooms** les enfants ont chacun leur (propre) chambre; **Paul and his wife sleep in ~ beds/rooms** Paul et sa femme font lit/chambre à part; **they live completely ~ lives** ils mènent des vies complètement séparées; (in restaurant etc) **we want ~ bills** nous voudrions des additions séparées, nous voudrions chacun notre addition; **the two houses though semi-detached are quite ~** les deux maisons bien que jumelées sont tout à fait indépendantes (l'une de l'autre); **I wrote it on a ~ sheet** je l'ai écrit sur une feuille séparée or sur une feuille à part; **take a ~ sheet for each answer** prenez une nouvelle feuille pour chaque réponse; **there will be ~ discussions on this question** cette question sera discutée à part or séparément; **there is a ~ department for footwear** il y a un rayon séparé or spécial pour les chaussures; **"with ~ toilet"** «avec WC séparé»; **keep the novels ~ from the textbooks** ne mélangez pas les romans et les livres de classe [2] **separates** NPL (= clothes) vêtements mpl coordonnés [3] ['sepəreıt] VT séparer (**from** de); (= sort out) séparer, trier; (= divide up) diviser; [+ strands] dédoubler; [+ milk] écrémer; **to ~ truth from error** distinguer le vrai du faux; **only three points now ~ the two teams** trois points seulement séparent maintenant les deux équipes → **separated, sheep, wheat** [4] ['sepəreıt] VI [a] [liquids] se séparer (**from** de); [metals etc] se séparer, se détacher (**from** de) [b] [people] se séparer, se quitter; [fighters] rompre; [married couple] se séparer; [non-married couple] rompre [5] COMP ▸ **separate opinion** N (US Jur) avis m divergeant de la minorité des juges ▸ **separate school** N (Can) école f or collège m privé(e)

▸ **separate out** VT SEP séparer, trier

separated ['sepəreıtıd] ADJ [couple, person] séparé

separately ['seprətlı] ADV [a] (= apart) séparément, à part [b] (= one by one) séparément, un par un, un à la fois; **these articles are sold ~** ces articles se vendent séparément

separateness ['seprətnıs] N séparation f (**from** de); **feeling of ~** sentiment m de séparation or d'être à part

separation [ˌsepə'reıʃən] [1] N séparation f; [of ore] triage m; (Pol, Rel) scission f, séparation f; (after marriage) séparation f (**from** d'avec); **judicial ~** séparation f de corps [2] COMP ▸ **separation allowance** N (Mil) allocation f militaire; (Jur = alimony) pension f alimentaire

separatism ['sepərətızəm] N séparatisme m

separatist ['sepərətıst] ADJ, N séparatiste mf

separator ['sepəreıtər] N (all senses) séparateur m

Sephardi [se'fɑːdı] N (pl **Sephardim** [se'fɑːdım]) séfarade mf

Sephardic [se'fɑːdık] ADJ séfarade

sepia ['siːpjə] [1] N [a] (= colour) sépia f [b] (= fish) seiche f [2] COMP ▸ **sepia drawing** N sépia f

sepoy ['siːpɔı] N cipaye m

sepsis ['sepsıs] N (Med) septicité f, état m septique

Sept. ABBR = **September**

septa ['septə] NPL of **septum**

September [sep'tembər] [1] N septembre m, mois m de septembre; **the first of ~** le premier septembre; **the tenth of ~** le dix septembre; **on the tenth of ~** le dix septembre; **in ~** en septembre; **in the month of ~** au mois de septembre; **each** or **every ~** tous les ans or chaque année en septembre; **at the beginning of ~** au début (du mois) de septembre, début septembre; **in the middle of ~** ◊ **in mid ~** au milieu (du mois) de septembre, à la mi-

septembre; **at the end of ~** à la fin (du mois) de septembre, fin septembre; **during ~** pendant le mois de septembre; **there are 30 days in ~** il y a 30 jours au mois de septembre, septembre a 30 jours; **~ was cold** septembre a été froid, il a fait froid en septembre; **early in ~** ◊ **in early ~** au début de septembre; **late in ~** ◊ **in late ~** vers la fin de septembre; **last/next ~** septembre dernier/prochain

2 COMP ► **September holidays** NPL congés *mpl* (du mois) de septembre ► **September Massacre** N (*Hist*) massacres *mpl* de septembre ► **September rains** NPL pluies *fpl* (du mois) de septembre ► **September weather** N **it's ~ weather** il fait un temps de septembre

Septembrist [sep'tembrɪst] N septembriseur *m*

septet [sep'tet] N septuor *m*

septic ['septɪk] 1 ADJ septique; [*wound*] infecté; **to go** or **become ~** s'infecter 2 COMP ► **septic poisoning** N septicémie *f* ► **septic tank** N fosse *f* septique

septicaemia, **septicemia** (*US*) [ˌseptɪ'siːmɪə] N septicémie *f*

septuagenarian [ˌseptjʊədʒɪ'nɛərɪən] ADJ, N septuagénaire *mf*

Septuagesima [ˌseptjʊə'dʒesɪmə] N Septuagésime *f*

Septuagint ['septjʊədʒɪnt] N version *f* des Septante

septum ['septəm] N (*pl* **septa**) (*Anat, Bot*) cloison *f*, septum *m*

septuplet [sep'tʌplɪt] N septuplé(e) *m(f)*

sepulcher ['seplkə'] N (*US*) = **sepulchre**

sepulchral [sɪ'pʌlkrəl] ADJ sépulcral; (*fig* = *gloomy*) funèbre, sépulcral

sepulchre, **sepulcher** (*US*) ['seplkə'] N sépulcre *m*, tombeau *m*; (*Rel*) sépulcre *m* → **holy**, **white**

sequel ['siːkwəl] N a (= *consequence*) suite *f*, conséquence *f*; (*to illness etc*) séquelles *fpl*; **it had a tragic ~** cela a eu des suites or des conséquences tragiques b [*of book, film etc*] suite *f*

sequence ['siːkwəns] 1 N a (= *order*) ordre *m*, suite *f*; **in ~** par ordre, les uns à la suite des autres; **in historical ~** par ordre chronologique; **logical ~** ordre *m* or enchaînement *m* logique b (= *series*) suite *f*, succession *f*; (*Cards*) séquence *f* c [*film*] séquence *f* d (*Mus*) séquence *f*; **~ of tenses** concordance *f* des temps 2 VT [+ *genes, DNA*] séquencer

sequencer ['siːkwənsə'] N (*Mus*) séquenceur *m*

sequential [sɪ'kwenʃəl] ADJ a (= *in regular sequence*) séquentiel b (= *following*) qui suit; **~ upon** or **from ...** qui résulte de ... c (*Comput*) séquentiel; **~ access/processing** accès *m*/traitement *m* séquentiel

sequester [sɪ'kwestə'] VT a (= *isolate*) isoler; (= *shut up*) enfermer, séquestrer b (*Jur*) [+ *property*] séquestrer

sequestered [sɪ'kwestəd] ADJ a [*life*] isolé, retiré; [*spot*] retiré, peu fréquenté b (*Jur*) [*property*] mis or placé sous séquestre

sequestrate [sɪ'kwestreɪt] VT (*Jur*) a = **sequester b** b (= *confiscate*) confisquer, saisir

sequestration [ˌsiːkwes'treɪʃən] N (*Jur*) a [*of property*] séquestration *f*, mise *f* sous séquestre b (= *confiscation*) confiscation *f*, saisie *f* conservatoire

sequin ['siːkwɪn] N paillette *f*

sequinned, **sequined** (*US*) ['siːkwɪnd] ADJ pailleté, cousu de paillettes

sequoia [sɪ'kwɔɪə] N séquoia *m*

sera ['sɪərə] NPL of **serum**

seraglio [se'rɑːlɪəʊ] N sérail *m*

---

serape [sə'rɑːpɪ] N (*US*) poncho *m*, couverture *f* mexicaine

seraph ['serəf] N (*pl* **seraphs** or **seraphim**) (*Rel, liter etc*) séraphin *m*

seraphic [sə'ræfɪk] ADJ (*lit, fig*) séraphique

seraphim ['serəfɪm] NPL of **seraph**

Serb [sɜːb] 1 ADJ serbe 2 N a Serbe *mf* b (*Ling*) serbe *m*

Serbia ['sɜːbɪə] N la Serbie

Serbian ['sɜːbɪən] N = **Serb**

Serbo-Croat ['sɜːbəʊ'krəʊæt], **Serbo-Croatian** ['sɜːbəʊkrəʊ'eɪʃən] 1 ADJ serbo-croate 2 N a Serbo-Croate *mf* b (*Ling*) serbo-croate *m*

sere [sɪə'] ADJ = **sear 1**

serenade [ˌserə'neɪd] 1 N sérénade *f* 2 VT donner une sérénade à

serendipitous [ˌserən'dɪpɪtəs] ADJ [*discovery etc*] heureux; **his timing was ~** il ne pouvait pas mieux tomber

serendipity [ˌserən'dɪpɪtɪ] N (*NonC: hum*) hasard *m* heureux

serene [sə'riːn] ADJ [*person, smile, place, atmosphere*] serein, paisible; [*face*] serein; [*sky*] serein, clair; [*sea, river*] calme; **to become** or **grow ~** [*person*] devenir serein, se rasséréner; [*sky*] redevenir serein; [*sea, river*] redevenir calme; **His Serene Highness** Son Altesse *f* Sérénissime

serenely [sə'riːnlɪ] ADV [*smile*] avec sérénité, sereinement; [*say*] d'un ton serein; **~ indifferent to the noise** suprêmement indifférent au bruit

serenity [sɪ'renɪtɪ] N [*of person, place, smile, lifestyle*] sérénité *f*

serf [sɜːf] N serf *m*, serve *f*

serfdom ['sɜːfdəm] N servage *m*

serge [sɜːdʒ] 1 N serge *f* 2 COMP de serge ► **serge suit** N complet *m* en serge; **blue ~ suit** complet *m* en serge bleue

sergeant ['sɑːdʒənt] 1 N a (*Brit Mil, Air Force*) sergent *m*; **yes, ~** oui, chef → **2, colour, drill²**, **flight²** b (*US Air Force*) caporal-chef *m* c (*Police*) ≈ détective 2 COMP ► **sergeant at arms** N huissier *m* d'armes ► **sergeant first class** N (*US Mil*) sergent-chef *m* ► **sergeant-major** N (*Mil*) (*Brit*) sergent-major *m*; (*US*) adjudant-chef *m* → **company, regimental**

serial ['sɪərɪəl] 1 N a (*Rad, TV*) feuilleton *m*; (*in magazine etc: also* **~ story**) roman-feuilleton *m*, feuilleton *m*; **television/radio ~** feuilleton *m* à la télévision/à la radio, feuilleton *m* télévisé/radiophonique; **13-part ~** feuilleton *m* en 13 épisodes b [*of publication, journal*] publication *f* périodique, périodique *m* 2 ADJ a (*Comput*) [*disk, transmission, processing, programming etc*] série *inv*; [*access*] séquetiel b [*music*] sériel 3 COMP ► **serial killer** N meurtrier *m* tuant en série, tueur *m* en série ► **serial killings** NPL meurtres *mpl* en série ► **serial monogamy** N série de liaisons monogamiques ► **serial number** N [*of goods, car engine*] numéro *m* de série; [*of soldier*] (numéro *m*) matricule *m*; [*of cheque, banknote*] numéro *m* ► **serial port** N (*Comput*) port *m* série ► **serial rights** NPL droits *mpl* de reproduction en feuilleton ► **serial writer** N feuilletoniste *mf*

serialism ['sɪərɪəˌlɪzəm] N (*Mus*) sérialisme *m*

serialization [ˌsɪərɪəlaɪ'zeɪʃən] N (*Press*) publication *f* en feuilleton; (*Rad, TV*) adaptation *f* en feuilleton

serialize ['sɪərɪəlaɪz] VT (*Press*) publier en feuilleton; (*Rad, TV*) adapter en feuilleton; **it was ~d in six parts** cela a été publié or adapté en six épisodes; **it has been ~d in the papers** cela a paru or été publié en feuilleton dans les journaux

---

serially ['sɪərɪəlɪ] ADV a [*number*] en série b **to appear/be published ~** [*story*] paraître/être publié en feuilleton; [*magazine, journal*] paraître/être publié en livraisons périodiques

seriatim [ˌsɪərɪ'eɪtɪm] ADV (*frm*) successivement, point par point

sericulture [ˌserɪ'kʌltʃə'] N sériciculture *f*

series ['sɪəriːz] 1 N (*pl inv*) a (*gen, Chem, Comm, Elec, Ling, Mus*) série *f*; (*Math*) série *f*, suite *f*; (*Elec*) **in ~** en série; **~ of stamps/coins** série *f* de timbres/de monnaies; **~ of colours** gamme *f* or échelle *f* de couleurs; **a ~ of volumes on this subject** une série de volumes sur ce sujet; **there has been a ~ of incidents** il y a eu une série or une succession d'incidents, il y a eu plusieurs incidents successifs; **it will be one of a ~ of measures intended to ...** cette mesure entrera dans le cadre d'une série de mesures destinées à ... b (*Rad, TV*) série *f* (d'émissions); (= *set of books*) collection *f*; (= *set of stamps*) série *f*; (*Rad, TV*) **this is the last in the present ~** voilà la dernière émission de notre série; (*Publishing*) **a new paperback ~** une nouvelle collection de poche → **world** 2 COMP ► **series connection** N (*Elec*) montage *m* en série

serio-comic [ˌsɪərɪəʊ'kɒmɪk] ADJ mi-sérieux mi-comique

serious ['sɪərɪəs] 1 ADJ a (= *in earnest, not frivolous*) [*person, offer, suggestion, interest*] sérieux, sincère; [*publication, conversation, discussion, occasion*] sérieux, important; [*report, information, account*] sérieux, sûr; [*literature, music*] respectable; [*attitude, voice, smile, look*] plein de sérieux, grave; [*tone*] sérieux, grave; (= *unsmiling*) [*person*] sérieux, grave; [*look*] grave, sévère; (= *thoughtful*) [*pupil*] sérieux, appliqué; **are you ~?** (parlez-vous) sérieusement ?; **I'm quite ~** je suis sérieux, je parle sérieusement, je ne plaisante pas; **to give ~ thought to sth** (= *ponder*) bien réfléchir à qch; (= *intend*) songer sérieusement à qch; **to be ~ about one's work** être sérieux dans son travail; **the ~ student of jazz will maintain that ...** quelqu'un qui s'intéresse sérieusement au jazz affirmera que ...; **marriage is a ~ business** le mariage est une affaire sérieuse; **she earns ~ money*** elle gagne un bon paquet*; **~ wine*** vin *m* décent b (= *causing concern*) [*illness, injury, mistake, situation*] grave, sérieux; [*damage*] important, considérable; [*threat*] sérieux; [*loss*] grave, lourd; **I have ~ doubts about ...** je doute sérieusement de ..., j'ai de graves doutes sur ...; **the patient's condition is ~** le patient est dans un état grave 2 COMP ► **Serious Fraud Office** N (*Brit*) service de la répression des fraudes majeures

seriously ['sɪərɪəslɪ] ADV a (= *in earnest*) sérieusement, avec sérieux; (= *not jokingly*) sérieusement, sans plaisanter; **he said it all quite ~** il l'a dit tout à fait sérieusement; **yes, but ~ ...** oui, mais sérieusement ...; **~ now ...** sérieusement ..., toute plaisanterie (mise) à part ...; **to take sth/sb ~** prendre qch/qn au sérieux; **to think ~ about sth** (= *ponder*) bien réfléchir à qch; (= *intend*) songer sérieusement à qch b (= *dangerously*) gravement, sérieusement; [*ill*] gravement; [*wounded*] grièvement; [*worried*] sérieusement c (= *very*) **to be ~ rich*** avoir beaucoup de fric*

seriousness ['sɪərɪəsnɪs] N a [*of intention, offer, suggestion, interest*] sérieux *m*, sincérité *f*; [*of publication, discussion, conversation, occasion*] sérieux *m*, importance *f*; [*of report, information, account*] caractère *m* sérieux or sûr; [*of attitude, character, voice, smile, tone, look*] sérieux *m*; **in all ~** sérieusement, en toute sincérité b [*of situation, illness, mistake, threat, loss, injury*] gravité *f*; [*of damage*] importance *f*, ampleur *f*

serjeant ['sɑːdʒənt] = **sergeant**

sermon [ˈsɜːmən] N (Rel) sermon m; (fig pej) sermon m, laïus* m; **the Sermon on the Mount** le Sermon sur la Montagne; (fig pej) **to give sb a** ~ faire un sermon à qn

sermonize [ˈsɜːmənaɪz] (fig pej) 1 VT sermonner 2 VI prêcher, faire des sermons

sermonizing [ˈsɜːmənaɪzɪŋ] (fig pej) N propos mpl moralisateurs

seropositive [ˌsɪərəʊˈpɒzɪtɪv] ADJ séropositif

serous [ˈsɪərəs] ADJ séreux

serpent [ˈsɜːpənt] N (lit, fig) serpent m → **sea**

serpentine [ˈsɜːpəntaɪn] 1 ADJ (liter) [river, road] sinueux, tortueux, qui serpente; (= treacherous) perfide; (Zool) de serpent 2 N (Miner) serpentine f, ophite m

SERPS [sɜːps] N (Brit) (ABBR = **state earnings-related pension scheme**) assurance-vieillesse de la Sécurité sociale

serrate [seˈreɪt] VT denteler, découper en dents de scie

serrated [seˈreɪtɪd] ADJ [edge, blade] en dents de scie; ~ **knife** couteau-scie m

serration [seˈreɪʃən] N dentelure f

serried [ˈserɪd] ADJ serré; **in** ~ **ranks** en rangs serrés

serum [ˈsɪərəm] N (pl **serums** or **sera**) sérum m; **tetanus** ~ sérum m antitétanique

servant [ˈsɜːvənt] 1 N (in household) domestique mf; (= maid) bonne f; (fig) serviteur m, servante f; **to keep a** ~ avoir un(e) domestique; **a large staff of** ~**s** une nombreuse domesticité; **the** ~**s' hall** l'office m or f; **I'm not your** ~ je ne suis pas votre domestique; **the government is the** ~ **of the people** le gouvernement est le serviteur or est au service du peuple; (in letters) **your obedient** ~† ≈ veuillez agréer, Monsieur (or Madame etc), l'assurance de ma considération distinguée → **civil, humble, manservant, public** 2 COMP ► **servant girl** N servante f, bonne f

serve [sɜːv] 1 VT a (= work for) [+ master, employer, family] servir, être au service de; [+ God, one's country] servir; **he** ~**d his country well** il a bien servi son pays, il a bien mérité de la patrie (frm); **he has** ~**d the firm well** il a bien servi la compagnie, il a rendu de grands services à la compagnie; **he has** ~**d our cause well** il a bien servi notre cause; (fig) **to** ~ **two masters** servir deux maîtres à la fois; **if my memory** ~**s me (right)** si j'ai bonne mémoire, si je me souviens bien; **his knowledge of history** ~**d him well** ses connaissances en histoire or d'histoire lui ont été très utiles or se sont avérées très utiles or lui ont bien servi; **that excuse won't** ~ **you when ...** cette excuse ne vous servira à rien quand ... b (Rel) **to** ~ **mass** servir la messe c (= be used as) [object etc] servir (**as** de); (= be useful to) rendre service à, être utile à; **it** ~**s her as a table** ça lui sert de table; **it's not very good but it will** ~ **me** ça n'est pas parfait mais ça fera l'affaire; **it will** ~ **my** (or your etc) **purpose** or **needs** cela fera l'affaire; **it** ~**s its purpose** or **turn** cela fait l'affaire, cela suffit bien; **it** ~**s a variety of purposes** cela sert à divers usages; **it** ~**s no useful purpose** cela ne sert à rien (de spécial) d (phrases) ~**s him right** c'est bien fait pour lui, il ne l'a pas volé; (it) ~**s you right for being so stupid** cela t'apprendra à être si stupide; **it would have** ~**d them right if they hadn't got any** ça aurait été bien fait pour eux s'ils n'en avaient pas reçu e (in shop, restaurant) servir; **to** ~ **sb (with) sth** servir qch à qn; **are you being** ~**d?** est-ce qu'on s'occupe de vous? f [+ food, meal] servir (**to sb** à qn); **dinner is** ~**d** le dîner est servi; (as formal announcement) Madame est servie (or Monsieur est servi); **this fish should be** ~**d with mustard sauce** ce poisson se sert or se mange avec une sauce à la moutarde; (in recipe etc) **"**~**s five"** « pour cinq personnes » → **first, serving** g (with transport, church services) desservir; (with gas, electricity) alimenter; **the bus** ~**s six villages** le car dessert six villages; **the power station** ~**s a large district** la centrale alimente une zone étendue h (= work out) **to** ~ **one's apprenticeship** or **time (as)** faire son apprentissage (de); **to** ~ **one's time** (Mil) faire son temps de service; (Prison) faire son temps de prison; (Prison) **to** ~ **time** faire de la prison; **to** ~ **(out) a prison sentence** purger une peine (de prison); (Prison) **he has** ~**d over 25 years altogether** en tout il a fait plus de 25 ans de prison i (Jur) **to** ~ **legal process** signifier or notifier un acte judiciaire; **to** ~ **notice on sb (to the effect) that ...** notifier or signifier à qn que ...; **to** ~ **a summons on sb** ◊ **to** ~ **sb with a summons** remettre une assignation à qn; **to** ~ **a warrant on sb** ◊ **to** ~ **sb with a warrant** délivrer à qn un mandat; **to** ~ **a writ on sb** ◊ **to** ~ **sb with a writ** assigner qn j (Tennis etc) servir k [bull, stallion etc] servir

2 VI a [servant, waiter] servir; **to** ~ **at table** servir à table; **is there anyone serving at this table?** est-ce que quelqu'un fait le service or s'occupe du service à cette table? b (= work, do duty) **to** ~ **on a committee/jury** être membre d'un comité/d'un jury; **he has** ~**d for two years as chairman of this society** cela fait deux ans qu'il exerce la fonction de président de cette société → **serving** c (Mil) servir; **to** ~ **in the army** servir dans l'armée; **he** ~**d in Germany** il a servi en Allemagne; **he** ~**d as a Sapper in the Engineers** il a servi comme simple soldat dans le génie; **to** ~ **under sb** servir sous (les ordres de) qn; **he** ~**d with my brother** mon frère et lui ont été soldats ensemble d (= be useful) servir (**for, as** de), être utile; **that table is not exactly what I want but it will** ~ cette table n'est pas exactement ce que je veux mais elle fera l'affaire; **it** ~**s to show/explain ...** cela sert à montrer/expliquer ... e (Rel) servir f (Tennis) servir, être au service

3 N (Tennis etc) service m; **he has a strong** ~ il a un service puissant; **it's your** ~ c'est à vous de servir

► **serve out** VT SEP a [+ meal, soup] servir; [+ rations, provisions] distribuer b [+ term of office, contract] finir; [+ prison sentence] purger → **serve 1h**

► **serve up** VT SEP servir, mettre sur la table

server [ˈsɜːvəʳ] N a (Comput) serveur m b (= person) (Rel) servant m; (Tennis etc) serveur m, -euse f c (= tray) plateau m; (= utensil) couvert m à servir → **salad**

servery [ˈsɜːvərɪ] N (Brit) office f

service [ˈsɜːvɪs] 1 N a (NonC = act of serving: gen, domestic, Mil etc) service m; ~ **at sea** service m dans la marine; (Mil) **to see** ~ **(as)** avoir du service or servir (comme); **this coat has seen** or **given good** ~ ce manteau a fait de l'usage; **ten years'** ~ dix ans de service; **on Her Majesty's** ~ au service de Sa Majesté; **to be in** ~ [domestic servant] être domestique or en service; **to be in sb's** ~ être au service de qn; **at your** ~ à votre service or disposition; **our company is always at your** ~ notre compagnie est toujours à votre service; **to be of** ~ **to sb** être utile à qn, rendre service à qn; **can I be of** ~? est-ce que je peux vous aider?; (in shop) **qu'y a-t-il pour votre service?**; **to bring/come into** ~ mettre/entrer en service; **this machine is out of** ~ cette machine est hors service; **how long has this machine been in** ~? depuis quand cette machine fonctionne-t-elle?; (in shop, hotel etc) **the** ~ **is very poor** le service est très mauvais; (Brit: on bill) **15%** ~ **included** service 15% compris → **active, military** b (= department; system) service m; **medical/**public/social etc ~**s** services mpl médicaux/publics/sociaux etc; **customs** ~ service m des douanes; (Mil) **when I was in the Services** quand j'étais dans l'armée (or la marine or l'aviation etc); (Mil) **the Services were represented** il y avait des représentants des forces armées; **the train** ~ **to London is excellent** il y a d'excellentes liaisons ferroviaires avec Londres, Londres est très bien desservi par le train; **do you know what the train** ~ **is (to London)?** connaissez-vous l'horaire des trains (pour Londres)?; **the number 4 bus** ~ la ligne (de bus numéro) 4 → **civil, health, postal** c (= help etc rendered) service m; **to do sb a** ~ rendre service à qn; **for** ~**s rendered (to)** pour services rendus (à); **they dispensed with his** ~**s** ils se sont passés or privés de ses services; **do you need the** ~**s of a lawyer?** avez-vous besoin (des services) d'un avocat? d (Rel) (gen) service m; (Catholic) service m, office m; (Protestant) service m, culte m → **evening, funeral** e (= maintenance work) [of car etc] révision f; [of household machine] service m après-vente; (Aut) **30,000-km** ~ révision des 30 000 km; **to put one's car in for** ~ donner sa voiture à réviser → **after** f (= set of crockery) service m; **coffee** ~ service m à café → **dinner, tea** g (Tennis etc) service m h (Jur) ~ **of documents** signification f or notification f d'actes; (Jur) ~ **of process** signification f d'un acte judiciaire or d'une citation

2 **services** NPL (on motorway) = **service station**

3 VT [+ car, washing machine etc] réviser; (Fin) [+ debt] servir les intérêts de; [+ organization, group etc] pourvoir aux besoins de, offrir ses services à; **I put my car in to be** ~**d** j'ai donné ma voiture à réviser

4 COMP ► **service academy** N (US Mil) école f militaire ► **service agreement** N (Brit) contrat m de service après-vente ► **service area** N [of motorway] aire f de services ► **service break** N (Tennis) break m ► **service bus** N autobus m régulier ► **service charge** N service m ► **service department** N (= office etc) service m des réparations or d'entretien; (= repair shop) atelier m de réparations ► **service dress** N (Brit Mil) tenue f de gala ► **service elevator** N (US) = **service lift** ► **service families** NPL (Mil) familles fpl de militaires ► **service flat** N (Brit) appartement m avec service (assuré par le personnel de l'immeuble) ► **service game** N (Tennis) jeu m de service ► **service hatch** N passe-plat m ► **service industries** NPL (Econ) services mpl, industries fpl de service ► **service lift** N (Brit) (for goods) monte-charge m inv; (for personnel) ascenseur m de service ► **service line** N (Tennis) ligne f de service ► **service module** N (Space) module m de service ► **service provider** N prestataire m de services ► **service rifle** N (Mil) fusil m de guerre ► **service road** N (Brit) (= access road) voie f or chemin m d'accès; (for works traffic) voie f de service ► **service sector** N (Econ) secteur m tertiaire ► **service station** N (Aut) station-service f ► **service tunnel** N tunnel m de service

serviceable [ˈsɜːvɪsəbl] ADJ a (= practical) fonctionnel; **the furniture was plain but** ~ les meubles étaient simples mais fonctionnels b (= usable, operative) utilisable; **an old but still** ~ **washing machine** une vieille machine à laver encore utilisable or qui marche encore

serviceman [ˈsɜːvɪsmən] N (pl **-men**) (Mil) militaire m

servicewoman [ˈsɜːvɪsˌwʊmən] N (pl **-women**) (Mil) femme f soldat

servicing [ˈsɜːvɪsɪŋ] N [of car] révision f; [of washing machine etc] entretien m

serviette [ˌsɜːvɪˈet] (esp Brit) **1** N serviette f (de table) **2** COMP ► **serviette ring** N rond m de serviette

servile [ˈsɜːvaɪl] ADJ [person, behaviour] servile, obséquieux, rampant; [flattery etc] servile

servility [sɜːˈvɪlɪtɪ] N servilité f

serving [ˈsɜːvɪŋ] **1** N **a** (= action) service m **b** (= portion) portion f, part f **2** ADJ (in office) **the ~ chairman** le président etc en exercice **3** COMP ► **serving dish** N plat m ► **serving hatch** N passe-plat m ► **serving spoon** N grande cuillère or cuiller f (pour servir)

servitude [ˈsɜːvɪtjuːd] N servitude f, asservissement m; (= slavery) esclavage m → **penal**

servo [ˈsɜːvəʊ] N (ABBR = **servo-mechanism, servo-motor**) → **servo-**

servo- [ˈsɜːvəʊ] PREF servo...; **~assisted** assisté; **~control** servocommande f; **~mechanism** servomécanisme m; **~motor** servomoteur m

sesame [ˈsesəmɪ] **1** N sésame m; **open Sesame!** Sésame ouvre-toi! **2** COMP ► **sesame oil** N huile f de sésame ► **sesame seeds** NPL graines fpl de sésame

sesquipedalian [ˌseskwɪpɪˈdeɪlɪən] ADJ polysyllabe

session [ˈseʃən] **1** N **a** (= sitting: gen, Admin, Jur, Parl etc) séance f; (= lesson) cours m; **a yoga ~** ◊ **a ~ of yoga** un cours or une séance de yoga; **two afternoon ~s a week** deux séances (or cours) par semaine l'après-midi; (Brit Scol) **the morning/afternoon ~** les cours mpl du matin/de l'après-midi; **a photo ~** une séance de photos; **I had a ~ with him yesterday** (working) nous avons travaillé ensemble hier; (in discussion) nous avons eu une (longue) discussion hier; **we're in for a long ~** nous n'aurons pas fini de sitôt → **jam²**, **recording**
b (NonC: Admin, Jur, Parl etc) séance f, session f; **to be in ~** siéger; **this court is now in ~** le tribunal est en session or en séance, l'audience est ouverte; **to go into secret ~** siéger en séance secrète or à huis clos → **quarter**
c (Scol, Univ) (= year) année f (universitaire or scolaire); (US = term) trimestre m (universitaire)
2 COMP ► **session musician** N (Mus) musicien(ne) m(f) de studio

set [set] (vb: pret, ptp **set**) **1** N **a** [of objects] jeu m, série f, assortiment m; (= kit) trousse f; [of sails, oars, keys, golf clubs, knives, spanners] jeu m; [of ties, pens] jeu m, assortiment m; [of chairs, saucepans, weights, numbers, stamps] série f; [of books, ornaments, toy cars] collection f; [of bracelets, magazines] collection f, série f; [of dishes, plates, mugs] service m; [of tyres] train m; [of jewels] parure f; [of theories] corps m, ensemble m; **I need two more to make up the ~** il m'en manque deux pour avoir le jeu complet or toute la série; **in ~s of three** par séries or jeux de trois; **in ~s** en jeux complets, en séries complètes; **it makes a ~ with those over there** cela forme un ensemble avec les autres là-bas; **a ~ of rooms** un appartement; **a ~ of kitchen utensils** une batterie de cuisine; **I bought her a ~ of hairclasps** je lui ai acheté des barrettes assorties; **~ of teeth** (natural) dentition f, denture f; (false) dentier m; **top/bottom ~** [of false teeth] appareil m pour la mâchoire supérieure/inférieure; **a ~ of dining-room furniture** un mobilier or un ensemble de salle à manger; **he had a whole ~ of telephones on his desk** il avait toute une collection or batterie de téléphones sur son bureau; **sewing ~** trousse f de couture; **painting ~** boîte f de peinture; **chess/draughts ~** jeu m d'échecs/de dames → **tea**
b (Tennis) set m; (Tennis) **~ to Henman** set Henman
c (Math, Philos) ensemble m
d (Elec) appareil m; (Rad, TV) poste m → **headset, transistor, wireless**

e (= group of people) groupe m, bande f (also pej); (larger) cercle m, monde m, milieu m; **the golfing ~** le monde du golf; **the literary ~** le monde des lettres, les milieux mpl littéraires; **I'm not in their ~** ◊ **we're not in the same ~** nous ne sommes pas du même monde or milieu, je n'appartiens pas à leur cercle; **a ~ of thieves/gangsters etc** une bande de voleurs/ gangsters etc; **they're just a ~ of fools!** ce n'est qu'une bande d'imbéciles! → **jet¹**
f (Brit Scol) groupe m de niveau
g (= stage) (Cine) plateau m; (Theat) scène f; (= scenery) décor m; **on (the) ~** (Cine) sur le plateau; (Theat) en scène
h (Mus = part of concert) set m, partie f
i (Hairdressing) mise f en plis; **to have a ~** se faire faire une mise en plis → **shampoo**
j (NonC = position, posture, direction etc) [of body] position f, attitude f; [of head] port m; [of shoulders] position f; [of tide, wind] direction f; [of opinion, sb's mind etc] tendance f
k (liter) **at ~ of sun** au coucher du soleil
l (Hunting) arrêt m → **dead**
m (Hort) plante f à repiquer; **onion ~s** oignons mpl à repiquer

2 ADJ **a** (= unchanging) [rule, price, time] fixe; [smile etc] figé; [purpose, dogma] fixe, (bien) déterminé; [opinion, idea] (bien) arrêté; [lunch] à prix fixe; **~ in one's ways** conservateur (-trice f), routinier, qui tient à ses habitudes; **~ in one's opinions** immuable dans ses convictions; (in restaurant) **the ~ meal** ◊ **the ~ menu** le menu; **~ expression** ◊ **~ phrase** expression f consacrée or toute faite, locution f figée (frm) → **stone**
b (Hort) **the fruit is ~** les fruits ont (bien) noué → **fair**
c (= prearranged) [time, date] fixé, décidé d'avance; (Scol etc) [book, subject] au programme; [speech, talk] étudié, préparé d'avance; [prayer] liturgique
d (= determined) résolu, déterminé; **to be ~ (up)on sth** vouloir qch à tout prix, avoir jeté son dévolu sur qch; **since you are so ~ on it** puisque vous y tenez tant; **to be ~ on doing sth** être résolu à faire qch, vouloir à tout prix faire qch; **to be (dead) ~ against sth** s'opposer (absolument or formellement) à qch
e (= ready) prêt; **they're all ~!** ils sont fin prêts!; **to be all ~ to do sth** être prêt à or pour faire qch; (fig) **the scene is ~ for ...** tout est prêt pour ...; (Sport) **on your marks, get ~, go!** à vos marques, prêts, partez!
f (Rugby) **~ scrum** mêlée f ordonnée

3 VT **a** (= place, put) [+ object] mettre, poser, placer; [+ signature etc] apposer; [+ sentry, guard] poster; **~ it on the table/beside the window/over there** mettez-le or posez-le or placez-le sur la table/près de la fenêtre/là-bas; **the house is ~ on a hill** la maison est située sur une colline; **his stories, ~ in the Paris of 1890, ...** ses histoires, situées or qui se passent or qui se déroulent dans le Paris de 1890, ...; **he ~ the scheme before the committee** il a présenté le projet au comité; **I ~ him above Wordsworth** je le place or mets au-dessus de Wordsworth, je le considère supérieur à Wordsworth; **what value do you ~ on this?** (lit) quelle valeur or à quel prix estimez-vous cela?; (fig) quelle valeur accordez-vous à cela?; **we must ~ the advantages against the disadvantages** il faut peser le pour et le contre, il faut mettre en balance les avantages et les inconvénients → **fire, foot, heart, store**
b (= arrange, adjust) [+ clock, mechanism] régler; [+ alarm] mettre; (on display) [+ specimen, butterfly etc] monter; [+ hen] faire couver; [+ plant] repiquer; (Typ) [+ type, page] composer; (Med) [+ arm, leg] (in plaster) plâtrer; (with splint) mettre une attelle à; [+ fracture] réduire; **he ~s his watch by the radio** il règle sa montre sur la radio; **~ your watch to the right time/to 2pm** mettez votre montre à l'heure/à

14 heures; **have you ~ the alarm clock?** est-ce que tu as mis le réveil?; **I've ~ the alarm for six** or **to wake me at six** j'ai mis le réveil à or pour six heures; (Aviat) **he ~ the controls to automatic** il a mis les commandes sur automatique; **to ~ sb's hair** faire une mise en plis à qn; **to have one's hair ~** se faire faire une mise en plis → **sail, table**
c (= fix, establish) [+ date, deadline, limit] fixer; **let's ~ a time for the meeting** fixons l'heure de la réunion; **I've ~ myself a time limit** je me suis fixé une limite (de temps) or un délai; **he ~ a new record for the 100 metres** il a établi un nouveau record pour le 100 mètres; **they ~ the pass mark at ten** on a fixé la moyenne à dix → **agenda, course, fashion, pace**
d (= give, assign) [+ task, subject] donner; [+ exam, test] composer or choisir les questions de; [+ texts, books] mettre au programme; **I ~ them a difficult translation** je leur ai donné une traduction difficile (à faire); **to ~ sb a problem** poser un problème à qn; **Molière is not ~ this year** Molière n'est pas au programme cette année; **I ~ him the task of clearing up** je l'ai chargé de ranger or du rangement → **example**
e (Brit Scol) **to ~ pupils for** or **in maths** répartir les élèves en groupes de niveau en maths
f (= cause to be, do, begin etc) **to ~ a dog on sb** lâcher or lancer un chien contre qn → **set upon**; **they ~ the police on to him** ils l'ont signalé à la police; **she ~ my brother against me** elle a monté mon frère contre moi; **to ~ sth going** mettre qch en marche; **the news ~ me thinking** la nouvelle m'a fait réfléchir or m'a donné à réfléchir; **that ~ him wondering whether ...** cela l'a porté or poussé à se demander si ...; **this ~ everyone laughing** cela a fait rire tout le monde, à cela tout le monde s'est mis à rire; **to ~ sb to do sth** faire faire qch à qn, donner à qn la tâche de faire qch; **I ~ him to work at once** je l'ai mis au travail aussitôt; **they ~ him to work mending the fence** ils lui ont fait réparer la barrière; **to ~ o.s. to do sth** entreprendre de faire qch
g [+ gem] sertir (in dans), monter (in sur); **to ~ sth with jewels** orner or incruster qch de pierres précieuses
h [+ jelly, jam] faire prendre; [+ concrete] faire prendre, faire durcir; [+ dye, colour] fixer

4 VI **a** [sun, moon] se coucher; **the ~ting sun** le soleil couchant
b [broken bone, limb] se ressouder; [jelly, jam] prendre; [glue] durcir; [concrete] prendre, durcir; [fruit] nouer; (fig) [character] se former, s'affermir; **quick-~ting cement** ciment m prompt or à prise rapide; **his face ~ in a hostile expression** son visage s'est figé dans une expression hostile
c (= begin) se mettre, commencer (**to doing** à faire); **to ~ to work** se mettre au travail, s'y mettre*; **to ~ to work mending** or **to mend the lawnmower** entreprendre de or se mettre à réparer la tondeuse à gazon

5 COMP ► **set designer** N (Theat) décorateur m, -trice f de théâtre ► **set-in sleeve** N manche f rapportée ► **set piece** N (= fireworks) pièce f (de feu) d'artifice; (Art, Literat, Mus) morceau m traditionnel; (in music competition etc) morceau m de concours; (Sport) combinaison f calculée or prévue ► **set point** N (Tennis) balle f de set ► **set square** N équerre f (à dessin) ► **set theory** N (Math) théorie f des ensembles ► **set-to** N (= fight) bagarre f; (= quarrel) prise f de bec*; **to have a ~-to with sb** se bagarrer avec qn*, avoir une prise de bec avec qn*

► **set about** **1** VT FUS **a** (= begin) [+ task, essay] se mettre à; **to ~ about doing sth** se mettre à faire qch, entreprendre de faire qch; **I don't know how to ~ about it** je ne sais pas comment m'y prendre **b** (= attack) attaquer; **they ~ about each other** (blows) ils en sont venus aux coups or aux mains; (words) ils ont commencé à s'injurier **2** VT SEP [+ *rumour etc*] faire courir; **he ~ it about that ...** il a fait courir le bruit que ...

►**set apart** VT SEP [+ *object etc*] mettre de côté or à part; **his eyes are ~ wide apart** il a les yeux très écartés; (fig) **that ~s him apart from the others** cela le distingue des autres

►**set aside** VT SEP **a** (= *keep, save*) mettre de côté, garder en réserve **b** **she ~ her book aside when I came in** elle a posé son livre quand je suis entré **c** (= *reject, annul*) [+ *request, objection, proposal, petition*] rejeter; [+ *decree, will*] annuler; (Jur) [+ *judgement, verdict*] casser

►**set back** **1** VT SEP **a** (= *replace*) remettre; **~ it back on the shelf** remets-le sur l'étagère **b** **the house was ~ back from the road** la maison était (construite) en retrait de la route **c** (= *retard*) [+ *development, progress*] retarder; [+ *clock*] retarder (**by** de); **the disaster ~ back the project by ten years** le désastre a retardé de dix ans la réalisation du projet **d** (* = *cost*) coûter; **that car must have ~ him back a packet** * or **a good deal** cette voiture a dû lui coûter les yeux de la tête; **how much did all that ~ you back?** combien tu as casqué* pour tout ça? **2** **~back** N → **setback**

►**set by** VT SEP = **set aside a**

►**set down** VT SEP **a** (= *put down*) [+ *object*] poser, déposer; [+ *passenger*] laisser, déposer **b** (Aviat) [+ *plane*] poser **c** (= *record*) noter, inscrire; [+ *rules, guidelines*] établir, définir; **the 1990 convention ~ down rules for the treatment of asylum seekers** la convention de 1990 a établi or défini des règles relatives au traitement des demandeurs d'asile; **to ~ sth down in writing** or **on paper** coucher or mettre qch par écrit; (Comm) **~ it down on** or **to my account** mettez-le or portez-le sur mon compte **d** (= *attribute*) attribuer (**sth to sth** qch à qch); **the accident must be ~ down to negligence** l'accident doit être imputé à la négligence; **we ~ it all down to the fact that he was tired** nous avons expliqué tout cela par sa fatigue, nous avons attribué tout cela à sa fatigue **e** (= *assess, estimate*) **I had already ~ him down as a liar** je le tenais déjà pour menteur

►**set forth** **1** VI = **set off 1** **2** VT SEP [+ *idea, plan, opinion*] faire connaître, exposer; [+ *conditions, rules*] inclure

►**set in** **1** VI (= *begin*) [*complications, difficulties*] survenir, surgir; [*disease*] se déclarer; **a reaction ~ in after the war** une réaction s'est amorcée après la guerre; **the rain will soon ~ in** il va bientôt commencer à pleuvoir; **the rain has ~ in for the night** il va pleuvoir toute la nuit; **the rain has really ~ in now!** la pluie a l'air bien installée! **2** VT SEP (Sewing) [+ *sleeve*] rapporter **3** **~in** ADJ → **set**

►**set off** **1** VI (= *leave*) se mettre en route, partir; **to ~ off on a journey/an expedition** partir en voyage/en expédition; (fig) **he ~ off on a long explanation** il s'est lancé dans une longue explication **2** VT SEP **a** [+ *bomb*] faire exploser; [+ *firework*] faire partir; [+ *mechanism, alarm, rise in inflation*] déclencher; **to ~ sb off (laughing/ crying etc)** faire rire/pleurer etc qn; **her remark ~ him off and she couldn't get a word in edgeways** après sa remarque il s'est lancé et elle n'a pas pu placer un mot **b** (= *enhance*) [+ *hair, eyes, picture, furnishings*] mettre en valeur, faire valoir; [+ *complexion, colour*] rehausser, mettre en valeur **c** (= *balance etc*) **to ~ off profits against losses** balancer les pertes et les profits, opposer les pertes aux profits; **we must ~ off the expenses against the profits** il faut déduire les dépenses des bénéfices; **the profit on hats will ~ off the loss on ties** le bénéfice sur les chapeaux compensera le déficit sur les cravates

►**set on** VT FUS = **set upon**

►**set out** **1** VI **a** (= *leave, depart*) se mettre en route (**for** pour), partir (**for** pour, **from** de, **in search of** à la recherche de) **b** (= *intend, propose*) **he ~ out to explain why it had happened** il a cherché à or s'est proposé d'expliquer pourquoi cela s'était produit; **I didn't ~ out to prove you were wrong** il n'était pas dans mon intention de prouver or montrer mais n'était pas de prouver que vous aviez tort; **I ~ out to convince him he should change his mind** j'ai entrepris de le persuader de changer d'avis; **the book ~s out to show that ...** ce livre a pour objet or but de montrer que ... **2** VT SEP [+ *books, goods*] exposer; [+ *chessmen etc on board*] disposer; (fig) [+ *reasons, ideas*] présenter, exposer; **the conditions are ~ out in paragraph three** les modalités sont indiquées or prévues au paragraphe trois; **it's very clearly ~ out here** c'est expliqué or exposé ici de façon très claire; **the information is well ~ out on the page** l'information est bien présentée sur la page

►**set to** **1** VI (= *start*) commencer, se mettre (**to do** à faire); (= *start work*) s'y mettre*; **they ~ to with their fists** ils en sont venus aux coups (de poing) **2** **~-to*** N → **set**

►**set up** **1** VI (= *establish o.s.*) **to ~ up in business as a grocer** s'établir épicier; **he ~ up in business in London** il a monté une affaire or une entreprise à Londres **2** VT SEP **a** (= *place in position*) [+ *chairs, table, stall*] placer, installer; [+ *tent*] dresser; [+ *monument, statue*] ériger, dresser; (Typ) **to ~ up type** assembler les caractères, composer; **to ~ up camp** établir un camp **b** (= *start, establish*) [+ *school, institution*] fonder; [+ *business, company, fund*] créer, lancer; [+ *tribunal, government, committee*] constituer; [+ *fashion*] lancer; [+ *record*] établir; [+ *theory*] avancer; **to ~ up an inquiry** ouvrir une enquête; **to ~ up house** or **home** s'installer; **they've ~ up home in Toulon/Spain** ils se sont installés à Toulon/en Espagne; **they ~ up house** or **home together** ils se sont mis en ménage; **to ~ up shop** (Comm) ouvrir un commerce or un magasin, s'établir; (fig) s'établir, s'installer; **he ~ up shop as a grocer** il s'est établi épicier, il a ouvert une épicerie; (fig) **he ~ up shop as a doctor*** il s'est installé comme médecin; **to ~ sb up in business** établir or lancer qn dans les affaires; **he's all ~ up now** il est bien établi or lancé maintenant; **I've ~ it all up for you** je vous ai tout installé or préparé **c** (= *pose*) **I've never ~ myself up as a scholar** je n'ai jamais prétendu être savant **d** (after illness) rétablir, remettre sur pied **e** (= *equip*) munir, approvisionner (**with** de) **f** (* = *falsely incriminate*) monter un coup contre; **I've been ~ up** je suis victime d'un coup monté **g** (* = *lure into a trap*) piéger **3** **~up*** N → **setup** **4** **~-ting-up** N → **setting**

►**set upon** VT FUS (= *attack*) (physically) attaquer, se jeter sur; (verbally) attaquer

setback ['setbæk] N (= *hitch*) contretemps *m*; (*more serious*) revers *m*, échec *m*; (*in health*) rechute *f*

sett [set] N **a** (in roadway etc) pavé *m* **b** [of badger] terrier *m*

settee [se'ti:] **1** N canapé *m* **2** COMP ►**settee bed** N canapé-lit *m*

setter ['setər] N **a** (= *dog*) setter *m*, chien *m* d'arrêt **b** (= *person*) [of gems] sertisseur *m* → **typesetter**

setting ['setɪŋ] **1** N **a** (= *surroundings, background*) cadre *m* **b** [of jewel] monture *f* **c** (Mus) [poem etc] mise *f* en musique; **~ for piano** arrangement *m* pour piano **d** (NonC) [of sun, moon] coucher *m*; (= *act of*

placing) mise *f*; [of machine etc] réglage *m*; (Typ) composition *f*; [of cement] (Med) [of fracture] réduction *f*; [of limb, bone] pose *f* d'un plâtre or d'une attelle (**of** à) **e** (= *hardening*) [of jam] épaississement *m*; [of cement] solidification *f*, durcissement *m* **f** (Brit Scol) répartition *f* par groupes de niveaux **2** COMP ►**setting lotion** N lotion *f* or fixateur *m* pour mise en plis ►**setting ring** N (Phot) bague *f* de réglage ►**setting-up** N [of institution, company etc] création *f*, lancement *m*; (Typ) composition *f* ►**setting-up exercises** NPL exercices *mpl* d'assouplissement

settle¹ ['setl] N banc *m* à haut dossier

settle² ['setl] **1** VT **a** (= *install, make comfortable*) [+ *child, patient*] installer; **to ~ a child for the night** installer un enfant pour la nuit; **he ~d his daughter in a flat** il a installé sa fille dans un appartement; **she ~d her head back against the head-rest** elle a reposé sa tête sur l'appui-tête; **he ~d himself into the chair** il s'est installé (confortablement) dans le fauteuil; **he ~d himself in the saddle** il s'est installé sur la selle; **he is a difficult horse to ~** c'est un cheval nerveux; **he ~d his gaze** or **his eyes on my face** son regard se posa or s'arrêta sur mon visage → **settled** **b** (= *sort out, resolve*) [+ *question, matter, argument, legal dispute, case*] régler; [+ *problem*] résoudre; [+ *one's affairs*] régler, mettre en ordre; (= *fix, agree on*) [+ *conditions, terms, details, date*] fixer; **to ~ one's difficulties** résoudre ses problèmes; **they have ~d their differences** ils ont réglé leurs différends; **several points remain to be ~d** il reste encore plusieurs points à régler; (Ftbl etc) **the result was ~d in the first half** la première mi-temps a décidé du résultat; **that ~s it** (= *no more problem*) comme ça le problème est réglé; (= *that's made my mind up*) ça me décide; **~ it among yourselves** réglez or arrangez ça entre vous; **that's ~d then?** alors c'est entendu?; **nothing is ~d** on n'a encore rien décidé; **I'll ~ him!** * je vais lui régler son compte!* → **settled** → **score** **c** (= *pay*) [+ *debt*] rembourser, s'acquitter de; [+ *bill, account*] régler → **account** **d** (= *calm, stabilize*) [+ *nerves*] calmer; [+ *doubts*] apaiser, dissiper; **he sprinkled water on the floor to ~ the dust** il a aspergé le sol d'eau pour empêcher la poussière de voler; **to ~ one's stomach** or **digestion** calmer or soulager les douleurs d'estomac **e** (Jur = *bequeath*) **to ~ sth on sb** faire don de qch à qn; (in will) léguer qch à qn **f** [+ *land*] (= *colonize*) coloniser; (= *inhabit*) peupler → **settled**

2 VI **a** (= *land, alight*) [bird, insect] se poser (**on** sur) **b** (= *sink*) [sediment, coffee grounds, tea leaves] se déposer; [wall] se tasser; [building] s'affaisser; (Comm) **contents of the packet may ~ during transit** le contenu du paquet peut se tasser pendant le transport **c** (= *become permanent*) [snow] tenir; [dust etc] retomber → **2e**; **to ~ on sth** [dust, snow] couvrir qch; **the wind ~d in the east** le vent a définitivement tourné à l'est; **the weather has ~d** le temps s'est mis au beau fixe; **the cold has ~d on his chest** son rhume s'est transformé en bronchite; **a feeling of calm/ gloom ~d on him** un sentiment de calme descendit sur lui/de tristesse s'abattit sur lui; **an expression of sorrow ~d on his face** une expression de tristesse apparut sur son visage; **her eyes** or **gaze ~d on him** son regard s'arrêta or se posa sur lui → **settled** **d** (= *get comfortable*) **to ~ into an armchair** s'installer (confortablement) dans un fauteuil; **to ~ into one's new job** s'habituer or se faire à son nouvel emploi; **to ~ into a routine** adopter une routine; **to ~ into a habit** prendre une habitude or un pli; **to ~ to sth** se mettre (sérieusement) à qch, s'appliquer à qch; **I can't ~ to anything** je suis incapable de

me concentrer; **let your meal ~ before you go swimming** attends d'avoir digéré avant de te baigner; **things are settling into shape** cela commence à prendre tournure
[e] (= *calm down*) [*emotions*] s'apaiser; [*conditions*] redevenir normal; [*situation*] redevenir normal, s'arranger; (*fig*) **when the dust has ~d** quand les choses se seront tassées*
[f] (= *go to live*) s'installer, se fixer; (*as colonist*) s'établir; **he ~d in London/in France** il s'est installé *or* fixé à Londres/en France; **the Dutch ~d in South Africa** les Hollandais se sont établis en Afrique du Sud
[g] (= *sort out, accept*) **to ~ with sb for the cost of the meal** régler qn pour le prix du repas, régler le prix du repas à qn; **I'll ~ for all of us** je vais régler la note (pour tout le monde); (*Jur*) **to ~ out of court** arriver à un règlement à l'amiable; **he ~d for £200** il s'est contenté de 200 livres, il a accepté 200 livres; **they ~d on £200** ils se sont mis d'accord sur 200 livres; **will you ~ for a draw?** accepteriez-vous un match nul?
[h] (= *choose, decide on*) **to ~ on sth** fixer son choix sur qch, opter *or* se décider pour qch
► **settle down** [1] VI [*person*] (*in armchair etc*) s'installer (**in** dans); (= *take up one's residence etc*) s'installer, se fixer; (= *become calmer*) se calmer; (*after wild youth etc*) se ranger, s'assagir; [*excitement, emotions*] s'apaiser; [*situation, conditions*] s'arranger, redevenir normal, se tasser*; **he ~d down to read the document** il s'est installé pour lire tranquillement le document; **to ~ down to work** se mettre (sérieusement) au travail; **he has ~d down in his new job** il s'est bien adapté *or* s'est fait à son nouvel emploi; **to ~ down at school** s'habituer *or* s'adapter à l'école; **it's time he got married and ~d down** il est temps qu'il se marie (*subj*) et qu'il mène (*subj*) une vie stable; **he can't ~ down anywhere** il n'arrive à se fixer nulle part; **he took some time to ~ down in Australia/to civilian life** il a mis du temps à s'habituer *or* à s'adapter à la vie en Australie/ à la vie civile; **when things have ~d down again** quand les choses se seront calmées *or* se seront tassées*
[2] VT SEP installer; **to ~ o.s. down in an armchair** s'installer confortablement dans un fauteuil; **he ~d the child down on the settee** il a installé l'enfant sur le canapé
► **settle in** VI (= *get things straight*) s'installer; (= *get used to things*) s'adapter; **the house is finished and they're quite ~d in** la maison est terminée et ils sont tout à fait installés; **we took some time to ~ in** nous avons mis du temps à nous adapter
► **settle up** [1] VI régler (la note); **to ~ up with sb** (*financially*) régler qn; (*fig*) régler son compte à qn*; **let's ~ up** faisons nos comptes [2] VT SEP [+ *bill*] régler

settled ['setld] [1] VB *pret ptp of* **settle**² [2] ADJ [a] [*weather*] stable; **the weather is ~** le temps est stable [b] [*land, area*] (= *colonized*) colonisé; (= *inhabited*) habité, peuplé [c] (= *unchanging*) [*social order, life, team*] établi; **a man of ~ habits** un homme aux habitudes régulières [d] (= *at ease: in new job, home etc*) **I feel ~** j'ai fait mon trou*, je me suis bien habitué; **to get ~** s'installer [e] [*question, matter*] réglé

settlement ['setlmənt] N [a] (*NonC*) [*of question, argument, bill, debt*] règlement *m*; [*of conditions, terms, details, date*] décision *f* (**of** concernant); [*of problem*] solution *f*; **in ~ of an account** pour *or* en règlement d'un compte [b] (= *agreement*) accord *m*; **to reach a ~** arriver à *or* conclure un accord; **the chances of a ~** les chances d'un accord → **negotiate, wage** [c] (*Jur*) donation *f* (**on sb** en faveur de qn); (= *act of settling*) constitution *f*; (= *income*) rente *f*; (= *dowry*) dot *f* → **marriage** [d] (= *colonization*) colonisation *f*; (= *colony*) colonie *f*; (= *village*) village *m*, hameau *m*; (= *homestead*) ferme *f* or habitation *f* (isolée) →

penal [e] (*for social work: also* ~ **house**) centre *m* d'œuvres sociales [f] (*Constr: of building etc*) tassement *m*
settler ['setlər] N colon *m*, colonisateur *m*, -trice *f*
settlor ['setlər] N (*Fin, Jur*) constituant *m*
setup ['setʌp] [1] N [a] (= *way sth is organised*) **what's the ~?** comment est-ce que c'est organisé *or* que ça marche?; **it's an odd ~** c'est une drôle de situation; **I don't like that ~ at all** je n'aime pas l'allure de tout ça*; **when did he join the ~?** quand est-ce qu'il est entré là-dedans? [b]* (= *trick*) coup *m* monté, machination *f*; (= *trap*) piège *m* [2] COMP ► **setup file** N (*Comput*) fichier *m* de configuration
seven ['sevn] [1] ADJ sept *inv* [2] N sept *m inv*; *for phrases see* **six** [3] PRON sept; **there are ~** il y en a sept [4] COMP ► **the seven deadly sins** NPL (*liter*) les sept péchés *mpl* capitaux ► **seven-league boots** NPL bottes *fpl* de sept lieues ► **the seven seas** NPL (*liter*) toutes les mers *fpl* (du globe); **to sail the ~ seas** parcourir les mers ► **the Seven Sisters** NPL (*Astron, Myth*) les Pléiades *fpl*; (*US Univ*) groupe *m* de sept universités pour jeunes filles dans le nord-est des États-Unis ► **the seven wonders of the world** NPL les sept merveilles *fpl* du monde ► **the seven-year itch*** NN sentiment d'insatisfaction après sept ans de mariage
sevenfold ['sevnˌfəʊld] [1] ADJ septuple [2] ADV au septuple
seventeen [ˌsevn'tiːn] [1] ADJ dix-sept *inv* [2] N dix-sept *m inv*; *for phrases see* **six** [3] PRON dix-sept; **there are ~** il y en a dix-sept
seventeenth [ˌsevn'tiːnθ] [1] ADJ dix-septième [2] N dix-septième *mf*; (= *fraction*) dix-septième *m*; *for phrases see* **sixth**
seventh ['sevnθ] [1] ADJ septième [2] N [a] septième *mf*; (= *fraction*) septième *m*; *for phrases see* **sixth** [b] (*Mus*) septième *f* [3] COMP ► **Seventh Day Adventist** N adventiste *mf* du septième jour → **heaven**
seventieth ['sevntɪθ] [1] ADJ soixante-dixième, septantième (*Belg, Helv*) [2] N soixante-dixième *mf*; (= *fraction*) soixante-dixième *m*; *for phrases see* **sixth**
seventy ['sevntɪ] [1] ADJ soixante-dix *inv*, septante *inv* (*Belg, Helv*) [2] N soixante-dix *m inv*; **he's in his seventies** il est septuagénaire, il a plus de soixante-dix ans; *for phrases see* **sixty** [3] PRON soixante-dix; **there are ~** il y en a soixante-dix
sever ['sevər] [1] VT [+ *rope etc*] couper, trancher; (*fig*) [+ *relations*] rompre, cesser; [+ *communications*] interrompre; **to ~ one's connections with sb** cesser toutes relations avec qn; (*Comm*) se dissocier de qn [2] VI [*rope etc*] se rompre
severability [ˌsevərə'bɪlɪtɪ] N (*Jur*) autonomie *f* des dispositions d'un contrat
several ['sevrəl] [1] ADJ [a] (*in number*) plusieurs; **~ times** plusieurs fois; **~ hundred people** plusieurs centaines de personnes [b] (*frm* = *separate*) **they went their ~ ways** (*lit*) ils sont partis chacun de leur côté; (*fig*) la vie les a séparés; **their ~ occupations** leurs diverses *or* différentes occupations *fpl* → **joint** [2] PRON plusieurs *mfpl*; **~ of them** plusieurs d'entre eux (*or* elles); **~ of us saw the accident** plusieurs d'entre nous ont vu l'accident, nous sommes plusieurs à avoir vu l'accident; **~ of us passed the exam** nous sommes plusieurs à avoir été reçus à l'examen
severally ['sevrəlɪ] ADV séparément, individuellement
severance ['sevərəns] [1] N séparation *f* (**from** de); [*of relations*] rupture *f*; [*of communications*] interruption *f* [2] COMP ► **severance motion** N (*US Jur*) demande *f* de procès séparés (*par des coaccusés*) ► **severance pay** N (*Ind*) indemnité *f* de licenciement

severe [sɪ'vɪər] ADJ [a] (= *serious, intense*) [*problem, consequences, damage, shortage, injury, illness, disability*] grave; [*blow, defeat*] sévère; [*loss*] sévère, lourd; [*hardship, setback*] sérieux; [*competition*] serré, acharné; [*pain*] vif (*before n*); [*migraine, pressure*] fort; [*storm*] violent; [*frost*] fort; [*climate, winter*] rigoureux; [*cold*] intense; **a ~ cold** un gros rhume [b] (= *strict*) [*person, expression, penalty, measure*] sévère; **it was a ~ test of her patience** cela a mis sa patience à rude épreuve [c] (= *austere*) [*clothes*] sévère; **her style of dress was somewhat ~** elle s'habillait de façon un peu austère
severely [sɪ'vɪəlɪ] ADV [a] [*damage, disrupt, injure, affect*] gravement; [*strain, limit, hamper*] sérieusement; **~ ill/depressed/disabled** gravement malade/déprimé/handicapé; **he's ~ subnormal** c'est un débile profond [b] [*punish, reprimand, criticize, look*] sévèrement [c] [*dress*] sévèrement
severity [sɪ'verɪtɪ] N (*NonC*) [*of problem, crisis, recession, illness, injury*] gravité *f*; [*of punishment, criticism, building, clothes, tone*] sévérité *f*; [*of pain, storm*] violence *f*; [*of winter*] rigueur *f*
Seville [sə'vɪl] [1] N Séville [2] COMP ► **Seville orange** N (*Brit*) orange *f* amère, bigarade *f* ► **Seville orange tree** N (*Brit*) bigaradier *m*
sew [səʊ] (*pret* **sewed**, *ptp* **sewn, sewed**) [1] VT **to ~ a button on sth** coudre un bouton à qch; (*if button missing*) recoudre un bouton à qch [2] VI coudre, faire de la couture
► **sew on** VT SEP [+ *button etc*] (*gen*) coudre; (*also* ~ **back on**) recoudre
► **sew up** VT SEP [+ *tear*] recoudre; [+ *seam*] faire; [+ *sack*] fermer par une couture; [+ *wound*] (re)coudre, suturer; **to ~ sth up in a sack** coudre qch dans un sac; **we've got the contract all ~n up*** le contrat est dans le sac* *or* dans la poche*; **the French market is pretty well ~n up*** le marché français est pratiquement verrouillé; **they've got the match all ~n up*** ils ont le match dans leur poche*; **it's all ~n up now*** l'affaire est dans le sac*
sewage ['sjuːɪdʒ] [1] N (*NonC*) eaux *fpl* d'égout *or* usées [2] COMP ► **sewage disposal** N évacuation *f* des eaux usées ► **sewage farm** N champ *m* d'épandage ► **sewage pipe** N égout *m* ► **sewage works** N = **sewage farm**
sewer ['sjuːər] [1] N égout *m* → **main** [2] COMP ► **sewer gas** N gaz *m* méphitique (d'égouts) ► **sewer rat** N rat *m* d'égout
sewerage ['sjuːərɪdʒ] N [a] (= *disposal*) évacuation *f* des vidanges; (= *system*) (système *m* d'égouts *mpl*; (= *cost of service*) frais *mpl* de vidange [b] = **sewage**
sewing ['səʊɪŋ] [1] N (*NonC*) (= *activity, skill*) couture *f*; (= *piece of work*) ouvrage *m*; **I like ~** j'aime coudre *or* la couture; **she put her ~ down** elle a posé son ouvrage [2] COMP ► **sewing basket** N boîte *f* à couture ► **sewing bee** N (*US*) they have a ~ **bee on Thursdays** elles se réunissent pour coudre le jeudi ► **sewing cotton** N fil *m* de coton, fil *m* à coudre ► **sewing machine** N machine *f* à coudre ► **sewing silk** N fil *m* de soie
sewn [səʊn] VB *ptp of* **sew**
sex [seks] [1] N [a] sexe *m*; († *or hum*) **the gentle** *or* **weaker ~** le sexe faible [b] (*NonC* = *sexual act*) rapports *mpl* sexuels, relations *fpl* sexuelles; **to have ~ (with sb)** faire l'amour (avec qn), avoir des rapports (sexuels) avec qn; **all he ever thinks about is ~*** ◊ **he's got ~ on the brain*** il ne pense qu'au sexe *or* qu'à ça*; **~ outside marriage** relations *fpl* sexuelles hors mariage [2] VT [+ *chick etc*] déterminer le sexe de [3] COMP [*education, instinct*] sexuel ► **sex act** N acte *m* sexuel ► **sex aid** N gadget *m* érotique ► **sex-and-shopping** ADJ (*Brit*) **~-and-shopping novel** roman *m* de gare, érotique et su-

perficiel ► **sex appeal** N sex-appeal *m* ► **sex change (operation)** N (opération *f* de) changement *m* de sexe ; **to have** *or* **undergo a ~ change (operation)** se faire opérer pour changer de sexe ► **sex clinic** N clinique *f* de sexologie ► **sex-crazy** ADJ **he is ~-crazy** c'est un obsédé (sexuel) ► **sex discrimination** N discrimination *f* sexuelle ► **sex drive** N pulsion *f* sexuelle ► **sex fiend** N satyre* *m* ► **sex goddess** N bombe *f* sexuelle ► **sex hormone** N hormone *f* sexuelle ► **sex hygiene** N (*US*) hygiène *f* sexuelle ► **the sex industry** N l'industrie *f* du sexe ► **sex kitten*** N minette *f* très sexy ► **sex life** N vie *f* sexuelle ► **sex-linked** ADJ (*Bio*) lié au sexe ► **sex-mad*** ADJ ► **sex-crazy** ► **sex maniac** N obsédé(e) sexuel(le) *m(f)* ► **sex manual** N ouvrage *m* sur le sexe ► **sex object** N objet *m* sexuel ► **sex offender** N délinquant(e) sexuel(le) *m(f)* ► **sex organ** N organe *m* sexuel ► **sex partner** N partenaire *mf* sexuel(le) ► **sex pot*** N fille *f or* femme *f* très sexy* ► **sex-ridden** ADJ [*person*] qui ramène tout au sexe ; [*book*] farci de sexe ► **sex scene** N (*Cine, Theat*) scène *f* érotique ► **sex shop** N sex-shop *m*, boutique *f* porno *inv* ► **sex show** N spectacle *m* érotique ► **sex-starved*** ADJ (sexuellement) frustré* ► **sex symbol** N sex-symbol *m* ► **sex therapist** N sexologue *mf* ► **sex therapy** N sexologie *f* ► **sex tourism** N tourisme *m* sexuel ► **sex urge** N ► **sex drive**

sexagenarian [ˌseksədʒɪˈnɛərɪən] ADJ, N sexagénaire *mf*

Sexagesima [seksəˈdʒesɪmə] N Sexagésime *f*

sexed [sekst] ADJ **[a]** (*Bio, Zool*) sexué **[b] to be highly ~** avoir une forte libido

sexiness [ˈseksɪnɪs] N (*NonC*) [*of person, voice, eyes*] sex-appeal *m* ; (* *fig*) [*of subject, issue*] côté *m* excitant

sexism [ˈseksɪzəm] N sexisme *m*

sexist [ˈseksɪst] ADJ sexiste

sexless [ˈsekslɪs] ADJ [*person*] (*also Bio*) asexué ; **a ~ marriage** une vie conjugale sans rapports sexuels

sexologist [sekˈsɒlədʒɪst] N sexologue *mf*

sexology [sekˈsɒlədʒɪ] N sexologie *f*

sexploitation* [ˌseksplɔɪˈteɪʃən] N *utilisation de l'image de la femme-objet dans la publicité etc*

sextant [ˈsekstənt] N sextant *m*

sextet [seksˈtet] N (= *players, composition*) sextuor *m*

sexton [ˈsekstən] N sacristain *m*, bedeau *m*

sextuplet [ˈsekstjuːplɪt] N sextuplé(e) *m(f)*

sexual [ˈseksjʊəl] **1** ADJ sexuel **2** COMP ► **sexual abuse** N sévices *mpl* sexuels, abus *m* sexuel ► **sexual equality** N égalité *f* des sexes ► **sexual harassment** N harcèlement *m* sexuel ► **sexual intercourse** N rapports *mpl* sexuels ► **sexual orientation** N orientation *f* sexuelle ► **sexual politics** N *conventions définissant la place des individus dans la société en fonction de leur sexe ou de leurs préférences sexuelles* ► **sexual services** NPL commerce *m* sexuel tarifé ► **sexual stereotyping** N catégorisation *f* en stéréotypes sexuels

sexuality [ˌseksjʊˈælɪtɪ] N sexualité *f*

sexually [ˈseksjʊəlɪ] **1** ADV **[a]** [*attractive, exciting, explicit, available, inadequate*] sexuellement ; [*threatening*] du point de vue sexuel ; **to be ~ abused** subir des sévices sexuels ; **to be ~ active** avoir une activité sexuelle ; **to be ~ aroused** excité sexuellement ; **to be ~ attracted to sb** avoir une attirance sexuelle pour qn ; **~ harassed** soumis à un harcèlement sexuel **[b]** (= *by sex*) [*segregated*] par le sexe **2** COMP ► **sexually transmitted disease** N maladie *f* sexuellement transmissible

sexy [ˈseksɪ] ADJ **[a]** (= *sexually exciting*) [*person, clothes*] sexy* *inv* ; [*voice*] séduisant ; [*image*] de

séducteur (-trice *f*) ; **to look ~** avoir l'air sexy* *or* séduisant **[b]** (= *interested in sex*) **to be** *or* **feel ~** avoir des envies ; **to make sb feel ~** donner des envies à qn, exciter qn **[c]** (* = *exciting*) [*subject, issue*] excitant

Seychelles [seɪˈʃel(z)] NPL **the ~** les Seychelles *fpl*

Seychellois [ˌseɪʃelˈwɑː] **1** ADJ seychellois **2** N Seychellois(e) *m(f)*

sez* [sez] = **says** ; → **say** ; (*iro*) ► **you!** que tu dis !* ; ~ **who?*** ah oui ? (*iro*)

SF [esˈef] N (ABBR = **science fiction**) SF *f*

SFA [ˌesefˈeɪ] (ABBR = **Scottish Football Association**) fédération *f* écossaise de football

SFO N (*Brit*) (ABBR = **Serious Fraud Office**) → **serious**

sgd (ABBR = **signed**) → **sign 2a**

Sgt (ABBR = **Sergeant**) (*on envelopes*) ~ **J. Smith** le Sergent J. Smith

shabbily [ˈʃæbɪlɪ] ADV **[a]** (= *tattily*) [*dressed*] pauvrement **[b]** (= *unfairly*) [*behave*] mesquinement ; [*treat*] avec mesquinerie

shabbiness [ˈʃæbɪnɪs] N [*of dress*] aspect *m* élimé *or* râpé ; [*of person*] mise *f* pauvre ; [*of behaviour, treatment*] mesquinerie *f*, petitesse *f*

shabby [ˈʃæbɪ] **1** ADJ **[a]** (= *tatty*) [*person, clothes, district, house, furnishings*] miteux **[b]** (= *unfair*) [*treatment, behaviour, compromise*] mesquin ; **a ~ trick** un vilain tour, une mesquinerie **2** COMP ► **shabby-genteel** ADJ pauvre mais digne ► **shabby-looking** ADJ de pauvre apparence

shack [ʃæk] N cabane *f*, hutte *f*

► **shack up*** VI (= *live*) se mettre en ménage (**with sb** avec qn) ; **to ~ up together** vivre ensemble

shackle [ˈʃækl] **1 shackles** NPL chaînes *fpl*, fers *mpl* ; (*fig*) chaînes *fpl*, entraves *fpl* **2** VT mettre aux fers, enchaîner ; (*fig*) entraver

shad [ʃæd] N (*pl* **shad** *or* **shads**) alose *f*

shade [ʃeɪd] **1** N **[a]** (*NonC*) ombre *f* ; **in the ~ of a tree** à l'ombre *or* sous l'ombrage d'un arbre ; **40° in the ~** 40° à l'ombre ; (*fig*) **to put sb/sth in the ~** éclipser qn/qch **[b]** [*of colour*] nuance *f*, ton *m* ; [*of opinion*] nuance *f* ; **several ~s darker than that** plus sombre de plusieurs tons (que cela) ; **several ~s of red** plusieurs nuances *or* tons de rouge ; **a new ~ of lipstick** un nouveau ton *or* une nouvelle couleur de rouge à lèvres ; **a ~ of meaning** une nuance **[c]** (= *hint, small amount*) **a ~ of vulgarity** un soupçon de vulgarité ; **there's not a ~ of difference between them** il n'y a pas la moindre différence entre eux ; **a ~ bigger** un tout petit peu *or* légèrement *or* un tantinet* plus grand ; **~s of Sartre!** voilà qui fait penser à Sartre !, ça rappelle Sartre ! **[d]** (= *lampshade*) abat-jour *m inv* ; (= *eyeshade*) visière *f* ; (*US* = *blind*) store *m* **[e]** (*liter* = *ghost*) ombre *f*, fantôme *m* **2 shades*** NPL (= *sunglasses*) lunettes *fpl* de soleil **3** VT **[a]** [*trees, parasol*] donner de l'ombre à ; [*person*] [+ *one's work etc*] abriter du soleil *or* de la lumière ; **~d place** endroit *m* ombragé *or* à l'ombre ; **he ~d his eyes with his hands** il s'abrita les yeux de la main ; **to ~ a light** voiler une lampe **[b]** (*also ~ in*) [+ *painting etc*] ombrer, nuancer ; (*by hatching*) [+ *outline, drawing etc*] hachurer ; (= *colour in*) colorer (**in** en) **[c]** [+ *price*] baisser *or* diminuer progressivement ; **prices ~d for quantities** tarif *m* dégressif pour commandes en gros ; **~d charges** tariff *m* dégressif **[d]** (= *narrowly win*) gagner de justesse **4** VI (*also ~ off*) **[a]** se dégrader (**into** jusqu'à), se fondre (**into** en) ; **the red ~s (off) into pink** le rouge se fond en rose **[b]** [*prices*] baisser

► **shade off** **1** VI = **shade 4** **2** VT SEP [+ *colours etc*] estomper

shadiness [ˈʃeɪdɪnɪs] N **[a]** (= *shade*) ombre *f* **[b]** (*fig*) caractère *m* suspect *or* louche

shading [ˈʃeɪdɪŋ] N **[a]** (*NonC*) (*in painting etc*) ombres *fpl*, noirs *mpl* ; (= *hatching*) hachure(s) *f(pl)* ; (*fig*) nuance *f* **[b]** (*for plants*) **to provide ~** faire de l'ombre

shadow [ˈʃædəʊ] **1** N **[a]** (= *shade*) ombre *f* ; **in the ~ of the tree** à l'ombre de l'arbre ; **in the ~ of the porch** dans l'ombre du porche ; **he was standing in (the) ~** il se tenait dans l'ombre ; **I could see his ~ on the wall** je voyais son ombre (projetée) sur le mur ; **he's afraid** *or* **frightened** *or* **scared of his own ~** il a peur de son ombre ; **to live in sb's ~** vivre dans l'ombre de qn ; **to cast a ~ over sth** (*lit*) projeter une ombre sur qch ; (*fig*) assombrir qch ; **he's only a ~ of his former self** il n'est plus que l'ombre de lui-même ; **to have (dark) ~s under one's eyes** avoir les yeux cernés, avoir des cernes *mpl* sous les yeux **[b]** (= *darkness*) **the ~s** l'obscurité *f*, les ténèbres *fpl* **[c]** (= *hint*) **without a ~ of doubt** sans l'ombre d'un doute ; **not a ~ of truth** pas le moindre atome de vérité **[d]** (*fig* = *detective etc*) personne *f* (*or* policier *m* *or* détective *m* etc) qui file quelqu'un ; **to put a ~ on sb** faire filer qn, faire prendre qn en filature **[e]** (= *inseparable companion*) ombre *f* **2** VT (= *follow*) filer, prendre en filature **3** COMP ► **shadow-box** VI boxer dans le vide ► **shadow-boxing** N (*Sport*) boxe *f* dans le vide ; (*fig*) attaque *f* de pure forme, attaque *f* purement rituelle ► **shadow cabinet** N (*Brit Parl*) cabinet *m* fantôme ► **shadow Foreign Secretary** N (*Brit Parl*) **he is (the) ~ Foreign Secretary** il est le porte-parole de l'opposition pour les Affaires étrangères ► **shadow minister** N (*Brit Pol*) ministre *m* fantôme ► **shadow play** N spectacle *m* d'ombres chinoises

---

SHADOW CABINET

*Dans le système parlementaire britannique, le « cabinet fantôme » (**Shadow Cabinet**) se compose des députés du principal parti d'opposition qui deviendraient ministres si leur parti était élu. Chaque ministre en fonction a donc un homologue dans l'opposition : au ministre de l'Intérieur (**Home Secretary**) ou des Finances (**Chancellor**) correspond donc un « **Shadow Home Secretary** » et un « **Shadow Chancellor** ». Leur rôle est d'interroger le gouvernement sur sa politique dans leurs domaines de spécialité et d'être les porte-parole des opinions de leur parti.*

---

shadowy [ˈʃædəʊɪ] ADJ **[a]** (= *shady*) [*place*] ombragé ; [*woods*] sombre, ombreux **[b]** (= *indistinct*) [*figure, shape, outline, form*] confus, vague, indistinct ; [*idea, plan*] vague, indistinct **[c]** (= *mysterious*) [*figure, group*] indéfini ; **the ~ world of espionage** le monde mystérieux de l'espionnage

shady [ˈʃeɪdɪ] ADJ **[a]** (= *shadowy*) [*place*] ombragé ; **under a ~ tree** à l'ombre d'un arbre **[b]** (= *dishonest*) [*person, behaviour*] louche ; [*lawyer, deal*] véreux ; **to have a ~ past** avoir un passé louche

shaft [ʃɑːft] **1** N **[a]** (= *stem, handle*) [*of arrow, spear*] hampe *f* ; [*of tool, golf club*] manche *m* ; [*of feather*] tuyau *m* ; [*of column*] fût *m* ; [*of bone*] diaphyse *f* ; (*on cart, carriage, plough etc*) brancard *m* ; (*Aut, Tech*) arbre *m* → **camshaft** **[b]** (*liter* = *arrow*) flèche *f* ; **Cupid's ~s** les flèches *fpl* de Cupidon ; **~ of light** rayon *m* *or* trait *m* de lumière ; **~ of lightning** éclair *m* ; **~ of sarcasm/wit** trait *m* de raillerie/d'esprit **[c]** [*of mine*] puits *m* ; [*of lift, elevator*] cage *f* ; (*for ventilation*) puits *m*, cheminée *f* **2** ADJ (** = *have sex with*) baiser**, baiser** ; (*fig* = *defeat,* *ruin)* **we'll be ~ed if that happens** si ça arrive, on sera baisés‡ *or* niqués‡‡

shag¹ [ʃæg] N (= *tobacco*) tabac *m* très fort

shag² [ʃæg] N (*Orn*) cormoran *m* huppé

shag³ [ʃæg] **1** N (*Brit*) **to have a ~**‡‡ baiser‡‡ **2** VT (*Brit*‡‡ = *have sex with*) baiser‡‡ **3** VI **a** (*Brit*‡‡ = *have sex*) baiser‡‡ **b** (*US*) **to ~ off**‡ se tirer‡, foutre le camp‡

shag⁴‡ [ʃæg] VT (*US* = *retrieve*) [+ *ball*] récupérer

shag⁵ [ʃæg] **1** N (= *napped fabric*) laine *f* à longues mèches **2** COMP ► **shag (pile) carpet** N moquette *f* à longues mèches ► **shag (pile) rug** N tapis *m* à longues mèches

shagged‡‡ [ʃægd] ADJ **to be ~ (out)** être claqué* *or* crevé‡

shaggy [ˈʃægɪ] **1** ADJ [*hair, beard*] hirsute; [*eyebrows, mane*] broussailleux; [*animal, fur*] à longs poils hirsutes; [*carpet, rug*] à longs poils **2** COMP ► **shaggy dog story** N histoire *f* sans queue ni tête

shagreen [ʃæˈgriːn] N chagrin *m* (*cuir*)

Shah [ʃɑː] N schah *or* chah *m*

shake [ʃeɪk] (*vb: pret* **shook**, *ptp* **shaken**) **1** N **a** (= *movement*) secousse *f*, ébranlement *m*; (= *quiver*) tremblement *m*; **to give sth a ~** secouer qch; **with a ~ of his head** en refusant d'un hochement de tête, en hochant la tête en signe de refus; **with a ~ in his voice** la voix tremblante, d'une voix tremblante; **to be all of a ~** être tout tremblant; **to have the ~s** (*from nerves*) avoir la tremblote*; (*from drink*) trembler, être agité de tremblements; **I'll be there in a ~** j'arrive dans un instant *or* une seconde; **in a brace** *or* **couple of ~s** ◊ **in two ~s (of a lamb's tail)*** en un clin d'œil, en moins de deux*; **he's no great ~s at swimming** *or* **as a swimmer** il n'est pas fameux *or* il ne casse rien* comme nageur **b** (= *drink*) milk-shake *m* → **handshake, milk 2** VT **a** [+ *duster, rug, person*] secouer; [+ *dice, bottle, medicine, cocktail*] agiter; [+ *house, windows etc*] ébranler, faire trembler; (= *brandish*) [+ *stick etc*] brandir; **"~ the bottle"** « agiter avant emploi »; **to ~ one's head** (*in refusal*) dire *or* faire non de la tête, hocher la tête en signe de refus; (*at bad news*) secouer la tête; **he shook his finger at me** (*playfully, warningly*) il m'a fait signe du doigt; (*threateningly*) il m'a menacé du doigt; **to ~ one's fist/stick at sb** menacer qn du poing/de sa canne; **to ~ hands with sb** ◊ **to ~ sb's hand** serrer la main à qn; **they shook hands** ils se sont serré la main; **they shook hands on it** ils se sont serré la main en signe d'accord; (*fig*) **~ a leg!** remue-toi!, bouge-toi!*; **to ~ o.s. (***or* **itself)** [*person, animal*] se secouer; (*to remove sand, water etc*) s'ébrouer; **a man with more medals than you can ~ a stick at*** un homme qui avait des tonnes* de médailles **b to ~ apples from a tree** secouer un arbre pour en faire tomber les pommes; **he shook the sand out of his shoes** il a secoué ses chaussures pour en vider le sable; **he shook two aspirins into his hand** il a fait tomber deux comprimés d'aspirine dans sa main; **he shook pepper on to his steak** il a saupoudré son bifteck de poivre; **he shook himself free** il s'est libéré d'une secousse; (*liter*) **he shook (off) the dust of that country from his feet** il a décidé de ne plus remettre les pieds dans le pays **c** (*fig* = *weaken, impair*) [+ *confidence, belief, resolve*] ébranler; [+ *opinion*] affecter; [+ *health*] ébranler, compromettre; [+ *reputation*] nuire à, compromettre; **even torture could not ~ him** même la torture ne l'a pas fait céder **d** (*fig*) (= *amaze*) stupéfier; (= *disturb*) secouer, bouleverser; **this will ~ you!** tu vas en être soufflé!*, ça va t'en boucher un coin!‡; **four days which shook the world** quatre jours qui ébranlèrent le monde; **he needs to be ~n out of his smugness** il faudrait qu'il lui arrive

(subj) quelque chose qui lui fasse perdre de sa suffisance → **shaken**
 e (*US**) **= shake off b**

 3 VI **a** [*person, hand, table*] trembler; [*building, windows, walls*] trembler, être ébranlé; [*leaves, grasses*] trembler, être agité; [*voice*] trembler, trembloter; **he was shaking with laughter** ◊ **his sides were shaking** il se tordait (de rire); **to ~ with cold** trembler de froid, grelotter; **to ~ with fear** trembler de peur; (*fig*) **the walls shook at the sound** le bruit a fait trembler les murs → **boot, shoe b** (= *shake hands*) **they shook on the deal** ils ont scellé leur accord d'une poignée de main; **(let's) ~ on it!** tope là!, topez là!

 4 COMP ► **shake-out** N (*US Econ*) tassement *m* ► **shake-up** N grande réorganisation *f*, grand remaniement *m*

► **shake down 1** VI **a** (* = *settle for sleep*) se coucher, se pieuter‡; **I can ~ down anywhere** je peux pioncer‡ *or* me pieuter‡ n'importe où **b** (= *learn to work etc together*) **they'll be a good team once they've ~n down** ils formeront une bonne équipe quand ils se seront habitués *or* faits les uns aux autres **2** VT SEP **a to ~ down apples from a tree** faire tomber des pommes en secouant l'arbre, secouer l'arbre pour en faire tomber les pommes; **to ~ down the contents of a packet** secouer un paquet pour en tasser le contenu **b** (*US*) **to ~ sb down for £50**‡ soutirer *or* faire cracher‡ 50 livres à qn **c** (*US*‡ = *frisk, search*) [+ *person*] fouiller **3** **~down** N → **shakedown**

► **shake off** VT SEP **a to ~ off dust/sand/water from sth** secouer la poussière/le sable/l'eau de qch **b** (*fig = get rid of*) [+ *cold, cough*] se débarrasser de; [+ *yoke etc*] se libérer de, s'affranchir de; [+ *habit*] se défaire de, perdre; [+ *pursuer*] se débarrasser de, semer*

► **shake out 1** VT SEP **a** [+ *flag, sail*] déployer; [+ *blanket*] bien secouer; [+ *bag*] vider en secouant; **she picked up the bag and shook out its contents** elle a pris le sac et l'a vidé en le secouant; **she shook 50p out of her bag** elle a secoué son sac et en a fait tomber 50 pence **b** (*Ind*) dégraisser **2** **~-out** N → **shake**

► **shake up 1** VT SEP **a** [+ *pillow, cushion*] secouer, taper; [+ *bottle, medicine*] agiter **b** (*fig = disturb*) bouleverser, secouer; **he was considerably ~n up by the news** il a été très secoué *or* il a été bouleversé par la nouvelle, la nouvelle lui a fait un coup* ► **shook c** (*fig = rouse, stir*) [+ *person*] secouer, secouer les puces à*; [+ *firm, organization*] réorganiser de fond en comble **2** **~-up** N → **shake**

shakedown [ˈʃeɪkdaʊn] N (= *bed*) lit *m* de fortune; (*US*‡) (= *search*) fouille *f*; (= *extortion*) extorsion *f*, chantage *m*

shaken [ˈʃeɪkn] ADJ (*by being in accident*) secoué; (*by seeing accident*) bouleversé; (*by news*) ébranlé; **~ but not stirred** [*martini*] préparé en secouant plutôt qu'en mélangeant; (*hum*) [*person*] secoué mais pas franchement ému

shaker [ˈʃeɪkər] N (*for cocktails*) shaker *m*; (*for dice*) cornet *m*; (*for salad*) panier *m* à salade → **flour**

Shakespearean, Shakespearian [ʃeɪksˈpɪərɪən] ADJ shakespearien

shakily [ˈʃeɪkɪlɪ] ADV [*stand up*] en chancelant; [*walk*] d'un pas mal assuré; [*speak*] d'une voix mal assurée; [*write*] d'une main tremblante

shakiness [ˈʃeɪkɪnɪs] N (*NonC*) [*of hand*] tremblement *m*; [*of table, chair etc*] manque *m* de stabilité *or* solidité; [*of building*] manque *m* de solidité; [*of voice*] chevrotement *m*; (*fig*) [*of position*] instabilité *f*; [*of health*] faiblesse *f*; [*of knowledge*] insuffisance *f*, faiblesse *f*

shako [ˈʃækəʊ] N (*pl* **shakos** *or* **shakoes**) s(c)hako *m*

shaky [ˈʃeɪkɪ] ADJ **a** (= *weak*) [*person*] (*from illness*) chancelant; (*from nerves*) mal à l'aise **b** (= *trembling*) [*person, legs*] (*from fear, illness*) flageolant, tremblant; (*from age*) tremblant; [*voice*] (*from fear, illness*) tremblant; (*from age*) chevrotant; (*from nerves*) mal assuré; [*hand*] tremblant; [*handwriting*] tremblé; **her legs were ~** elle flageolait sur ses jambes **c** (= *wobbly*) [*table, building*] branlant, peu solide **d** (= *uncertain*) [*start*] incertain; [*business, firm, deal*] à l'avenir incertain; [*argument*] boiteux; [*knowledge*] hésitant; [*health*] chancelant; [*prospects*] précaire; **~ finances** une situation financière incertaine; **my Spanish is very ~** mon espagnol est très hésitant; **to get off to a ~ start** partir sur un mauvais pied

shale [ʃeɪl] **1** N argile *f* schisteuse, schiste *m* argileux **2** COMP ► **shale oil** N huile *f* de schiste

shall [ʃæl] MODAL AUX VB (*2nd person sg* **shalt**, *neg* **shall not** *often abbr to* **shan't**) → **should 1** (*in 1st pers fut tense*) **I ~** *or* **I'll arrive on Monday** j'arriverai lundi; **we ~ not** *or* **we shan't be there before 6 o'clock** nous n'y serons pas avant 6 heures; **I'll come in a minute** je vais venir *or* je viens dans un instant **b** (*in 1st pers questions*) **~ I open the door?** dois-je ouvrir la porte?, voulez-vous que j'ouvre (*subj*) la porte?, j'ouvre la porte?*; **I'll buy three, ~ I?** je vais en acheter trois, n'est-ce pas or d'accord*?; **let's go in, ~ we?** entrons, voulez-vous?; **~ we ask him to come with us?** si on lui demandait de venir avec nous? **c** (*indicating command, guarantee etc*) **it ~ be done this way and no other** cela sera fait *or* doit être fait de cette façon et d'aucune autre; (*Bible*) **thou shalt not kill** tu ne tueras point; **you ~ obey me** vous m'obéirez, vous devez m'obéir; **you shan't have that job!** tu n'auras pas ce poste!

shallot [ʃəˈlɒt] N échalote *f*

shallow [ˈʃæləʊ] **1** ADJ **a** (= *not deep*) [*water, lake, grave, depression, container*] peu profond; [*soil*] mince; [*breathing*] superficiel; **the ~ end of the bathing pool** le petit bain *or* bassin de la piscine **b** (*pej = superficial*) [*person, mind, character, argument, novel, film*] superficiel; [*conversation*] futile; **to be ~-minded** manquer de profondeur d'esprit **2** **shallows** NPL basfond *m*, haut-fond *m*

shallowly [ˈʃæləʊlɪ] ADV [*breathe*] superficiellement

shallowness [ˈʃæləʊnɪs] N **a** (*lit*) manque *m* de profondeur **b** (*pej*) [*of person*] esprit *m* superficiel; [*of character*] manque *m* de profondeur; [*of conversation*] futilité *f*; [*of knowledge*] caractère *m* superficiel

shalt†† [ʃælt] VB *2nd person sg* of **shall**

sham [ʃæm] **1** N (= *pretence*) comédie *f*, imposture *f*; (= *person*) imposteur *m*; (= *jewellery, furniture*) imitation *f*; **this diamond is a ~** ce diamant est faux *or* du toc*; **the election was a ~** l'élection n'était qu'une comédie; **his promises were a ~** ses promesses n'étaient que du vent; **the whole organization was a ~** l'organisation tout entière n'était qu'une imposture

 2 ADJ [*jewellery, doctor, priest, title*] faux (fausse *f*); [*deal*] fictif; [*piety*] feint; [*illness*] feint, simulé; [*fight*] simulé; **a ~ marriage** un simulacre de mariage; **a ~-Tudor house** une maison pseudo-Tudor; **~ olde-worlde decor** décor *m* en faux ancien; **~ Louis XVI** de l'imitation *or* du faux Louis XVI

 3 VT feindre, simuler; **to ~ ill** *or* **illness** feindre *or* simuler une maladie, faire semblant d'être malade; **she ~med dead** elle a fait la morte, elle a fait semblant d'être morte

 4 VI faire semblant, jouer la comédie; **he's only ~ming** il fait seulement semblant

shaman [ˈʃæmən] N chaman *m*

shamanism [ˈʃæməˌnɪzəm] N chamanisme *m*

shamateur* ['ʃæmətər] N (Sport) sportif m, -ive f prétendu(e) amateur (qui se fait rémunérer)

shamble ['ʃæmbl] VI marcher en traînant les pieds; **to ~ in/out/away** etc entrer/sortir/ s'éloigner etc en traînant les pieds

shambles ['ʃæmblz] N (NonC) (gen = muddle) confusion f, désordre m; (stronger: after battle, disaster) scène f or spectacle m de dévastation; **what a ~!** quelle (belle) pagaille!*; **his room was (in) a ~** sa chambre était sens dessus dessous or tout en l'air; **the match degenerated into a ~** le match s'est terminé dans la pagaille*; **your essay is a ~*** votre dissertation est un fouillis sans nom*; **it's a bloody ~**: c'est complètement bordélique:

shambolic* ['ʃæmˈbɒlɪk] ADJ (Brit) bordélique:

shame [ʃeɪm] 1 N a (NonC) (= feeling) honte f, confusion f; (= humiliation) honte f; **to my eternal** or **lasting ~** à ma très grande honte; **he hung his head in ~** il a baissé la tête de honte or de confusion; **to bring ~ (up)on sb** être or faire la honte de qn, déshonorer qn; **to put sb/sth to ~** faire honte à qn/qch; **~ on you!** quelle honte!, c'est honteux de votre part!; **the ~ of it!** quelle honte!, c'est honteux!; **the ~ of that defeat** la honte de cette défaite, cette défaite déshonorante; **she has no sense of ~** elle ne sait pas ce que c'est que la honte, elle n'a aucune pudeur; **he has lost all sense of ~** il a perdu toute honte, il a toute honte bue (liter) → **cry, crying**
b (NonC = pity) dommage m; **it is a ~** c'est dommage (that que + subj, to do de faire); **it's a dreadful ~!** c'est tellement dommage!; **it would be a ~ if he were to refuse** or **if he refused** il serait dommage qu'il refuse (subj); **what a ~!** (quel) dommage!; **what a ~ he isn't here** (quel) dommage qu'il ne soit pas ici; **nice legs, ~ about the face!** jolies jambes, on ne peut pas en dire autant de son visage!
2 VT (= bring disgrace on) couvrir de honte, faire la honte de; (= make ashamed) faire honte à; **to ~ sb into doing sth** obliger qn à faire qch en lui faisant honte, piquer l'amour-propre de qn pour qu'il fasse qch; **to be ~d into doing sth** faire qch par amour-propre or pour conserver son amour-propre

shamefaced ['ʃeɪmfeɪst] ADJ (= ashamed) honteux, penaud; (= confused) confus, timide; **he was rather ~ about it** il en était tout honteux or penaud

shamefacedly ['ʃeɪmfeɪsɪdlɪ] ADV d'un air penaud or honteux

shamefacedness ['ʃeɪmfeɪstnɪs] N (NonC) air m penaud or honteux

shameful ['ʃeɪmfʊl] ADJ [behaviour, attitude, event, experience, secret] honteux; [record] déplorable; **there is nothing ~ about it** il n'y a pas de honte à cela; **it is ~ that ...** c'est une honte que ... (+ subj); **it's ~ to do that** c'est une honte de faire cela

shamefully ['ʃeɪmfəlɪ] ADV [act, behave, treat] de façon honteuse; [bad, late] scandaleusement; **~ lazy/ignorant** si paresseux/ignorant que c'en est une honte; **the government have ~ neglected this sector** le gouvernement a négligé ce secteur d'une façon scandaleuse

shameless ['ʃeɪmlɪs] ADJ a (= brazen) [person, liar, behaviour, attempt] éhonté; [lie] éhonté, sans vergogne; († or hum) **hussy** petite effrontée f; **to be quite ~ about (doing) sth** ne pas avoir du tout honte de (faire) qch b (= immodest) [person] sans vergogne, impudique; [act] impudique

shamelessly ['ʃeɪmlɪslɪ] ADV a (= brazenly) [declare, lie, cheat, flirt] sans vergogne, effrontément, sans la moindre gêne; [steal] sans vergogne; **~ sentimental/theatrical** d'une sentimentalité/théâtralité éhontée b (= immodestly) [act, behave] sans pudeur, de façon impudique

shamelessness N (NonC) [of person, behaviour] (= brazenness) effronterie f, impudence f; (= immodesty) impudeur f

shaming ['ʃeɪmɪŋ] ADJ mortifiant, humiliant; **it's too ~!** quelle humiliation!

shammy* ['ʃæmɪ] N (also ~ leather) peau f de chamois

shampoo [ʃæmˈpuː] 1 N (= product, process) shampooing or shampoing m; **~ and set** shampooing m (et) mise f en plis; **to give o.s. a ~** se faire un shampooing, se laver la tête → **dry** 2 VT [+ person] faire un shampooing à; [+ hair, carpet] shampouiner; **to have one's hair ~ed and set** se faire faire un shampooing (et) mise en plis

shamrock ['ʃæmrɒk] N trèfle m (emblème national de l'Irlande)

shamus: ['ʃeɪməs] N (US) (= policeman) flic* m; (= detective) détective m privé

shandy ['ʃændɪ] N (Brit) panaché m

Shanghai ['ʃæŋˈhaɪ] N Shanghai

shanghai [ʃæŋˈhaɪ] VT (Naut††) embarquer de force comme membre d'équipage; (fig) **to ~ sb into doing*** contraindre qn à faire

Shangri-la ['ʃæŋrɪˈlaː] N paradis m terrestre

shank [ʃæŋk] 1 N a (Anat) jambe f; [of horse] canon m; (Culin) jarret m; (= handle) manche m 2 COMP ► **Shanks's pony** N **to go** or **ride on Shanks's pony** aller à pied, prendre le train onze:

shan't [ʃaːnt] = shall not; → **shall**

shantung [ʃænˈtʌŋ] N shant(o)ung m

shanty[1] ['ʃæntɪ] N (= hut) baraque f, cabane f

shanty[2] ['ʃæntɪ] N (Brit: also **sea ~**) chanson f de marins

shantytown ['ʃæntɪˌtaʊn] N bidonville m

SHAPE [ʃeɪp] N (ABBR = **Supreme Headquarters Allied Powers Europe**) SHAPE m (quartier général des forces alliées de l'OTAN en Europe)

shape [ʃeɪp] 1 N a (= form, outline) forme f; **what ~ is the room?** ◊ **what is the ~ of the room?** quelle est la forme de la pièce?, de quelle forme est la pièce?; **stamps of all ~s** des timbres de toutes formes; **of all ~s and sizes** de toutes les formes et de toutes les tailles; **children of all ~s and sizes** des enfants d'allures diverses; **they come in all ~s and sizes** (lit) il y en a de toutes sortes et de toutes les tailles; (fig) il y en a une variété infinie; **his nose is a funny ~** son nez a une drôle de forme; **this hat has lost its ~** ce chapeau s'est déformé; **it's like a mushroom in ~** cela a la forme d'un champignon, cela ressemble à un champignon; **it's triangular in ~** c'est en forme de triangle, c'est triangulaire; **in the ~ of a cross** en forme de croix; **a prince in the ~ of a swan** un prince sous la forme d'un cygne; **a monster in human ~** un monstre à figure humaine; **I can't stand racism in any ~ or form** je ne peux pas tolérer le racisme sous quelque forme que ce soit; (lit, fig) **to take the ~ of sth** prendre la forme de qch; **the news reached him in the ~ of a telegram from his brother** c'est par un télégramme de son frère qu'il a appris la nouvelle; (fig) **perks in the ~ of luncheon vouchers** des avantages sous la forme de chèques-restaurant; **that's the ~ of things to come** cela donne une idée de ce qui nous attend; **who knows what ~ the future will take?** qui sait comment se présentera l'avenir?; **to take** [dress, vase, project] prendre forme or tournure; **to be in good ~** [person] être en (bonne) forme; [business etc] marcher bien; **in poor ~** [person, business] mal en point; **she's in really bad ~** elle ne va vraiment pas bien; **he carved the wood into ~** il a façonné le bois; **he beat the silver into ~** il a façonné l'argent; (= misshapen) **out of ~** être déformé; (= unfit) ne pas être en forme, être en mauvaise forme; (fig) **to knock** or **lick*** **into ~** [+ assistant] former, dresser*; [+ soldier] entraîner, dresser*; **to knock** or **lick*** **sth into** **~** arranger qch, rendre qch présentable; **he managed to knock** or **lick*** **the team into ~** il a réussi à mettre l'équipe au point; **to get (o.s.) into** or **to** (re)trouver la forme; **to keep o.s. in good ~** rester or se maintenir en forme; **to get one's ideas into ~** formuler or préciser ses idées
b (= human figure) forme f, figure f; (= silhouette) forme f, silhouette f; (= thing dimly seen) forme f vague or imprécise; (= ghost etc) fantôme m, apparition f; **a ~ loomed up out of the darkness** une forme imprécise surgit de l'obscurité
c (for jellies etc) moule m; (in hat-making) forme f
d (Culin) **rice ~** gâteau m de riz; **meat ~** pain m de viande
2 VT [+ clay] façonner, modeler; [+ stone, wood] façonner, tailler; (fig) [+ statement, explanation] formuler; **he ~d the clay into a tree** ◊ **he ~d a tree out of the clay** il a façonné un arbre dans l'argile; **oddly ~d** d'une forme bizarre; **a nicely ~d stone** une pierre d'une jolie forme; (Phot) **~d canvas** détourage m; **~d like a ball/a pole** etc en forme de boule/de piquet etc; **to ~ sb's ideas/character** modeler or former les idées/le caractère de qn; **to ~ sb's life** déterminer le destin de qn; **to ~ the course of events** influencer la marche des événements
3 VI (fig) prendre forme or tournure → **shape up**

► **shape up** VI a (= get on) progresser; (= progress) [project] prendre forme or tournure; **our plans are shaping up well** nos projets prennent tournure or s'annoncent bien or sont en bonne voie; **things are shaping up well** tout marche bien, on avance; **how is he shaping up?** comment s'en sort-il?*, est-ce qu'il se fait?; **he is shaping up nicely as a goalkeeper** il est en train de devenir un bon gardien de but; **~ up!*** secoue-toi un peu!*; **~ up or ship out!*** rentre dans le rang ou fiche le camp!* b (esp US = slim etc) retrouver la forme

-shaped [ʃeɪpt] ADJ (in compounds) en forme de; **heart-shaped** en forme de cœur → **egg**

shapeless ['ʃeɪplɪs] ADJ [dress, hat, cardigan] informe, sans forme; [mass, lump, bundle] informe; [person] aux formes lourdes; [book, plan, monologue] sans aucune structure; **to become ~** [clothes] se déformer, s'avachir

shapelessness ['ʃeɪplɪsnɪs] N absence f de forme

shapeliness ['ʃeɪplɪnɪs] N belles proportions fpl, beauté f (de forme), galbe m

shapely ['ʃeɪplɪ] ADJ [woman] bien proportionné; [legs] bien galbé; [body] harmonieux; **her ~ figure** sa silhouette harmonieuse or bien proportionnée

shard [ʃaːd] N tesson m (de poterie)

▼ **share** [ʃɛər] 1 N a part f; **here's your ~** voici votre part, voici ce qui vous est dû; **my ~ is £5** (receiving) ma (quote-)part s'élève à or j'ai droit à or je dois recevoir 5 livres; (paying) ma (quote-)part s'élève à or je dois (payer) 5 livres; **his ~ of the inheritance** sa part or sa portion de l'héritage; **his ~ of** or **in the profits** sa part des bénéfices; **he will get a ~ of** or **in the profits** il aura part aux bénéfices; **he has a ~ in the business** il est l'un des associés dans cette affaire; **he has a half-~ in the firm** il possède la moitié de l'entreprise; **to have a ~ in doing sth** contribuer à faire qch; **he had some ~ in it** il y était pour quelque chose; **I had no ~ in that** je n'y étais pour rien; **to take a ~ in sth** participer à qch; **to pay one's ~** payer sa (quote-)part; **to bear one's ~ of the cost** participer aux frais; **he wants more than his ~** il veut plus qu'il ne lui est dû, il tire la couverture à lui (fig); **he isn't doing his ~** il ne fournit pas sa part d'efforts; **he's had more than his (fair) ~ of misfortune** il a eu plus que

➤ **LANGUAGE IN USE:** **share** 11.1, 12.1, 26.3

sa part de malheurs; **to take one's ~ of the blame** accepter sa part de responsabilité; **he does his full ~ of work** il fournit toute sa (quote-)part de travail; **they went ~s in the cost of the holiday** ils ont payé les vacances à deux (*or* à trois *etc*), ils ont partagé le coût des vacances entre eux → **fair¹, lion**

b (*St Ex*) action *f*; **he has 500 ~s in an oil company** il a 500 actions d'une compagnie de pétrole → **ordinary, preference, qualifying**

c (*Agr = ploughshare*) soc *m* (*de charrue*)

2 VT **a** (*gen*) partager; [+ *room, prize*] partager (**with sb** avec qn); [+ *expenses, work*] partager (**with sb** avec qn), participer à; [+ *profits*] avoir part à; [+ *sorrow, joy*] partager, prendre part à; [+ *responsibility, blame, credit*] partager; **they ~d the money (between them)** ils se sont partagé l'argent; (*in school etc*) **you can ~ Anne's book** tu peux suivre avec Anne; (*Comput*) **~d facility** installation *f* commune; (*Telec*) **~d line** ligne *f* partagée; **they ~ certain characteristics** ils ont certaines caractéristiques en commun; **I do not ~ that view** je ne partage pas cette opinion; **I ~ your hope that ...** j'espère avec *or* comme vous que ...

b (*also* **~ out**) partager, répartir (**among, between** entre)

3 VI partager; **~ and ~ alike** à chacun sa part; **to ~ in** [+ *sorrow, joy*] partager, prendre part à; [+ *responsibility*] partager; [+ *profits*] avoir part à; [+ *expenses, work*] participer à, partager

4 COMP ► **share capital** N (*Fin*) capital *m* actions ► **share certificate** N (*Fin etc*) titre *m or* certificat *m* d'actions ► **share index** N (*St Ex*) indice *m* de la Bourse ► **share option** N (*St Ex*) possibilité de prise de participation des employés dans leur entreprise ► **share-out** N partage *m*, distribution *f* ► **share premium** N (*St Ex*) prime *f* d'émission ► **share price** N (*St Ex*) cours *m* d'une action

► **share out** **1** VT SEP = **share 2b** **2** **~-out** N → **share**

sharecropper ['ʃɛəˌkrɒpəʳ] N (*esp US Agr*) métayer *m*, -ère *f*

sharecropping ['ʃɛəˌkrɒpɪŋ] N (*esp US*) métayage *m*

shareholder ['ʃɛəˌhəʊldəʳ] N (*Fin etc*) actionnaire *mf*

shareholding ['ʃɛəˌhəʊldɪŋ] N (*Fin*) actionnariat *m*

shareware ['ʃɛəwɛəʳ] N (*NonC: Comput*) shareware *m*

shark [ʃɑːk] N (= *fish: gen*) requin *m*; (*generic name*) squale *m*; (*fig pej = sharp businessman*) requin *m*; (= *swindler*) escroc *m*, aigrefin *m*

sharkskin ['ʃɑːkskɪn] N (*Tex*) peau *f* d'ange

sharon ['ʃærən] N (*also* **~ fruit**) charon *m or* sharon *m*

sharp [ʃɑːp] **1** ADJ **a** (= *good for cutting*) [*knife, razor, blade*] (bien) aiguisé *or* affûté; [*piece of glass, tin, edge*] coupant; **the ~ edge of knife** le (côté) tranchant

b (= *pointed*) [*pencil*] bien taillé; [*needle, pin*] très pointu; [*teeth, fingernails, beak, nose, chin*] pointu; [*fang*] acéré; [*point*] acéré, aigu (-guë *f*); [*corner*] aigu (-guë *f*); [*features*] anguleux; (*fig*) **to be at the ~ end of sth** être en première ligne de *or* pour qch

c (= *well-defined*) [*contrast*] vif, net; [*image, TV picture*] net; [*distinction, difference*] net, marqué; [*outline*] net, distinct; [*division*] fort; **to be in ~ contrast to sth** contraster vivement *or* nettement avec qch; **to bring into ~ focus** (*Phot*) bien mettre au point; [+ *problem, issue*] faire ressortir nettement → **relief**

d (= *acute*) [*person*] dégourdi, malin (-igne *f*); [*intelligence*] vif, pénétrant; [*wit*] vif; [*mind*] pénétrant; [*awareness*] aigu (-guë *f*); [*eyesight*] perçant; [*hearing*] fin; **to have ~ ears** avoir l'oreille *or* l'ouïe fine; **to have ~ eyes** ne pas avoir les yeux dans sa poche; **he has a ~ eye for a bargain** il sait repérer *or* flairer une

bonne affaire; **to keep a ~ look-out for sb/sth** guetter qn/qch avec vigilance *or* d'un œil attentif; **he's (as) ~ as a needle** (= *clever*) il a l'esprit très vif; (= *missing nothing*) rien ne lui échappe; **his mind is (as) ~ as a razor** il a l'esprit très vif

e (= *abrupt*) [*rise, fall, decline, reduction, cut*] fort; [*increase, drop*] brusque, soudain; [*bend, corner*] serré; [*angle*] aigu; [*change*] brutal; **the motorcycle made a ~ right turn** la moto a pris un virage serré à droite; **he gave the handle a ~ turn** il a tourné la poignée brusquement

f (= *intense*) [*pain*] cuisant, vif; [*sensation*] vif; [*wind, cold*] vif, pénétrant; [*frost*] fort; [*blow*] sec (sèche *f*); [*cry*] perçant, aigu (-guë *f*)

g (= *severe*) [*criticism, attack*] mordant, incisif; [*retort, words*] mordant, cinglant; [*rebuke*] vif; [*order, tone, voice*] cassant; **to be a ~ reminder of sth** rappeler qch de façon brutale; (*fig*) **to have a ~ tongue** avoir la langue acérée, être caustique

h (*pej* = *unscrupulous*) [*business practices*] déloyal → **4**

i (* = *stylish*) [*person*] classe* *inv*; [*suit*] chic *inv*; **to be a ~ dresser** s'habiller très classe* *inv*

j (= *acrid*) [*smell, perfume*] piquant, âcre (*pej*); [*taste, sauce*] piquant, âpre (*pej*); [*cheese*] au goût prononcé

k (= *brisk*) [*pace*] vif; (*esp Brit*) **look** *or* **be ~ (about it)!*** grouille-toi!*

l (*Mus*) [*note*] trop haut; **C ~** do dièse; **you were a little ~** vous avez chanté (*or* joué) un peu trop haut

2 ADV **a** (= *abruptly*) [*stop*] brusquement, net; **to turn ~ left/right** prendre un virage serré à gauche/à droite

b (*Mus*) [*sing, play*] trop haut

c (= *precisely*) **at 8 (o'clock) ~** à 8 heures précises *or* sonnantes *or* pile

3 N **a** (*Mus*) dièse *m*

b (*Med* = *hypodermic*) aiguille *f*

4 COMP ► **sharp-eared** ADJ (*fig*) qui a l'oreille *or* l'ouïe fine ► **sharp-eyed** ADJ qui a un œil de lynx, à qui rien n'échappe ► **sharp-faced, sharp-featured** ADJ aux traits anguleux ► **sharp practice** N pratique *f* déloyale ► **sharp-sighted** ADJ = **sharp-eyed** ► **sharp-tempered** ADJ coléreux, soupe au lait* *inv* ► **sharp-tongued** ADJ caustique ► **sharp-witted** ADJ à l'esprit vif *or* prompt

sharpen ['ʃɑːpən] **1** VT (*also* **~ up**) **a** [+ *blade, knife, razor, tool*] affûter, aiguiser; [+ *scissors*] aiguiser; [+ *pencil*] tailler; **the cat was ~ing its claws on the chair leg** le chat aiguisait ses griffes *or* se faisait les griffes sur le pied de la chaise **b** (*fig*) [+ *outline, picture, focus*] rendre plus net; [+ *difference, contrast*] rendre plus marqué; [+ *appetite*] aiguiser; [+ *de-sire*] exciter; [+ *pain*] aggraver, aviver; [+ *feel-ing*] aviver; [+ *intelligence*] affiner, rendre plus fin; **to ~ one's wits** se dégourdir **c** (*esp Brit: Mus*) diéser **2** VI [*voice*] devenir plus perçant; [*desire, pain*] devenir plus vif, s'aviver

sharpener ['ʃɑːpnəʳ] N (= *knife sharpener*) (*on wall, on metal etc*) aiguisoir *m* à couteaux, affiloir *m*; (*long, gen with handle*) fusil *m* à repasser les couteaux; (= *pencil sharpener*) taille-crayons *m inv*

sharpening ['ʃɑːpnɪŋ] N aiguisage *m*, affilage *m*, affûtage *m*

sharper ['ʃɑːpəʳ] N escroc *m*, filou *m*, aigrefin *m*; (= *card sharper*) tricheur *m*, -euse *f* (*professionnel(le)*)

sharpie ['ʃɑːpɪ] N (*US*) (= *alert person*) petit(e) futé(e) *m(f)*; (= *crook*) filou *m*, escroc *m*

sharpish ['ʃɑːpɪʃ] **1** ADJ **a** (= *good for cutting*) [*knife, razor, blade*] assez aiguisé *or* affûté; [*edge*] assez coupant **b** (= *pointed*) [*pencil*] assez bien taillé; [*teeth, fingernails, beak, nose, chin*] assez pointu; [*point*] assez aigu; [*features*] assez anguleux → **sharp 2** ADV (*Brit* = *quickly*) en vitesse*

sharply ['ʃɑːplɪ] ADV **a** (= *abruptly*) [*fall, drop, increase, decline, change*] brusquement; [*stop*] brusquement, net; [*reduce*] nettement; **prices have risen ~** les prix ont monté en flèche; **to turn ~ to the left** tourner tout de suite à gauche; **to corner ~** (*in country*) prendre un virage à la corde; (*in town*) prendre un tournant serré

b (= *clearly*) [*show up, stand out, differ, divide*] nettement; **~ defined** [*image*] qui se détache nettement; (*Phot, fig*) **~ in focus** parfaitement net; **a ~ focused strategy** une stratégie bien ciblée; **to bring ~ into focus** (*Phot*) bien mettre au point; [+ *issue, differences*] faire ressortir nettement; **to contrast ~ with sth** contraster vivement avec qch

c (= *severely*) [*criticise, react*] vivement; [*say, ask, comment, reply*] avec brusquerie; [*look at*] sévèrement; **a ~ worded attack** une attaque mordante *or* incisive; **to speak ~ to sb about sth** parler à qn de qch en termes sévères

d (= *acutely, alertly*) [*say, ask*] vivement, avec intérêt; **he looked at me ~** il m'a regardé soudain avec intérêt

e (= *distinctly*) [*click, tap*] sèchement

f **~ pointed** [*knife, scissors*] effilé, (très) pointu; [*nose*] pointu

g (= *quickly*) rapidement

sharpness ['ʃɑːpnɪs] N **a** [*of razor, knife*] tranchant *m*; [*of pencil, needle, nail*] pointe *f* aiguë **b** (*fig*) [*of turn, bend*] angle *m* brusque; [*of outline etc*] netteté *f*; [*of pain*] violence *f*, acuité *f*; [*of criticism, reproach, rebuke*] sévérité *f*, tranchant *m*; [*of tone, voice*] brusquerie *f*, aigreur *f*; [*of taste, smell*] piquant *m*, âcreté *f* (*pej*); [*of wind, cold*] âpreté *f*; **there's a ~ in the air** il fait frais

sharpshooter ['ʃɑːpˌʃuːtəʳ] N (*esp US*) tireur *m* d'élite

shat [ʃæt] VB *pt, ptp* of **shit**

shatter ['ʃætəʳ] **1** VT [+ *window, door*] fracasser (**against** contre); [+ *health*] ruiner, briser; [+ *self-confidence*] briser; [+ *faith*] détruire; (*fig*) [+ *hopes, chances*] ruiner, détruire; [+ *career*] briser; **the sound ~ed the glasses** le bruit a brisé les verres; **to ~ sb's nerves** démolir les nerfs de qn; (*fig*) **she was ~ed by his death** sa mort l'a anéantie → **shattered** **2** VI [*glass, windscreen, cup*] voler en éclats; [*box etc*] se fracasser

shattered ['ʃætəd] ADJ **a** (= *grief-stricken*) anéanti, consterné; (= *aghast, overwhelmed*) bouleversé, complètement retourné **b** (* = *exhausted*) éreinté*, claqué*

shattering ['ʃætərɪŋ] ADJ **a** (= *devastating*) [*ex-perience, news*] bouleversant; [*blow, effect*] dé-vastateur (-trice *f*); [*defeat*] écrasant (*Brit* = *exhausting*) [*day, journey*] claquant*, tuant*

shatterproof glass [ˌʃætəpruːfˈglɑːs] N verre *m* securit® *inv*

shave [ʃeɪv] (*vb: pret* **shaved**, *ptp* **shaved, shaven**) **1** N **to give sb a ~** raser qn; **to have** *or* **give o.s. a ~** se raser, se faire la barbe; (*fig*) **to have a close** *or* **narrow ~** l'échapper belle, y échapper de justesse; **that was a close** *or* **nar-row ~!** il était moins une!*, on l'a échappé belle! → **aftershave** **2** VT [+ *person, face, legs etc*] raser; [+ *wood*] raboter, planer; (*fig* = *brush against*) raser, frôler; (*fig*) **to ~ the price of sth** faire un rabais sur le prix de qch **3** VI se raser

► **shave off** VT SEP **a** **to ~ off one's beard** se raser la barbe **b** **the joiner ~d some of the wood off** le menuisier a enlevé un peu du bois au rabot; (*fig*) **to ~ off a few pounds** faire un rabais de quelques livres

shaven [ʃeɪvn] **1** VB †† *ptp* of **shave 2** ADJ ra-sé → **clean**

shaver ['ʃeɪvəʳ] **1** N **a** rasoir *m* électrique **b** (**young**) **~** †* gosse* *m*, gamin *m* **2** COMP ► **shaver outlet** N (*US*) = **shaver point** ► **shaver point** N prise *f* pour rasoir électri-que

Shavian ['ʃeɪvɪn] ADJ à la or de George Bernard Shaw

shaving ['ʃeɪvɪn] **1** N **a** (= piece of wood, metal etc) copeau m **b** (NonC: with razor etc) rasage m; **~ is a nuisance** c'est embêtant* de se raser **2** COMP ► **shaving brush** N blaireau m ► **shaving cream** N crème f à raser ► **shaving foam** N mousse f à raser ► **shaving gel** N gel m à raser ► **shaving soap** N savon m à barbe ► **shaving stick** N bâton m de savon à barbe

shawl [ʃɔːl] N châle m

she [ʃiː] **1** PERS PRON **a** (stressed, unstressed) elle; **~ has come** elle est venue; **here ~ is** la voici; **~ is a doctor** elle est médecin, c'est un médecin; **~ is a small woman** elle est petite; **it is ~** c'est elle; (frm) **if I were ~** si j'étais elle, si j'étais à sa place; **SHE didn't do it** ce n'est pas elle qui l'a fait; **younger than ~** plus jeune qu'elle; **~'s a fine boat/car** faire un beau bateau/une belle voiture **b** (+ rel pron) celle; **~ who** or **that can ...** celle qui peut ... **2** N* femelle f; (= animal) c'est une femelle; [baby] c'est une fille **3** COMP (gen: with names of animals) femelle (after n) ► **she-bear** N ourse f ► **she-cat** N (fig) mégère f, furie f ► **she-devil** N (fig) démon m, furie f ► **she-goat** N chèvre f → **wolf**

s/he (ABBR = he or she) il ou elle

shea [ʃiː] N karité m

sheaf [ʃiːf] N (pl **sheaves**) [of corn] gerbe f; [of papers] liasse f; [of arrows] faisceau m

shear [ʃɪəʳ] (vb: pret **sheared**, ptp **sheared** or **shorn**) **1** N **shears** NPL cisaille(s) f(pl); (Hort) cisaille(s) f(pl); (Sewing, gen) grands ciseaux mpl; **a pair of ~s** une paire de cisailles → **pruning 2** VT [+ sheep] tondre; (fig) **shorn of** dépouillé de
► **shear off 1** VI [branch etc] partir, se détacher **2** VT SEP [+ wool] tondre; [+ projecting part, nail] faire partir, arracher; [+ branch] couper, élaguer; **the ship had its bow shorn off in the collision** dans la collision l'avant du navire a été emporté
► **shear through** VT FUS [+ paper, cloth] trancher; [+ wood, metal] fendre; (fig) [+ the waves, the crowd] fendre

shearer ['ʃɪərəʳ] N (= person) tondeur m, -euse f; (= machine) tondeuse f

shearing ['ʃɪərɪn] N (= process) tonte f; (= wool etc) ~s tonte

sheath [ʃiːθ] **1** N (pl **sheaths** [ʃiːðz]) **a** [of dagger] gaine f; [of sword] fourreau m; [of scissors etc] étui m; [of electric cable, flex] gaine f; (Bio) gaine f, enveloppe f; (Bot) enveloppe f; (Brit = contraceptive) préservatif m **b** (also ~ **dress**) fourreau m (robe) **2** COMP ► **sheath knife** N (pl **sheath knives**) couteau m à gaine

sheathe [ʃiːð] VT **a** [+ sword, dagger] rengainer; [+ cable] gainer; [cat etc] [+ claws] rentrer **b** (= cover) recouvrir, revêtir (with de)

sheaves [ʃiːvz] NPL of **sheaf**

Sheba ['ʃiːbə] N Saba; **the Queen of ~** la reine de Saba

shebang* [ʃə'bæŋ] N **the whole ~** toute l'affaire, tout le tremblement*

shebeen [ʃɪ'biːn] N (Ir) débit m de boissons clandestin

shed¹ [ʃed] N **a** (gen) abri m; (smallish) abri m, cabane f; (larger) remise f, resserre f; (large open-sided: Rail, Agr etc) hangar m; (lean-to) appentis m; **bicycle ~** abri m à vélos, remise f pour les vélos; **garden ~** abri m de jardin, cabane f → **cowshed, toolshed b** (= part of factory) atelier m

shed² [ʃed] (pret, ptp **shed**) VT **a** (= lose, get rid of) [+ petals, leaves, fur, horns] perdre; [+ shell] dépouiller; [truck] [+ load] déverser, perdre; (Space) [+ rocket, section of craft] larguer, éjecter; [+ tears] verser, répandre; [+ coat etc] enlever, se dépouiller de (frm); [+ unwanted thing] se débarrasser de, se défaire de; [+ assistant, employee] se défaire de, se séparer

de; **to ~ hairs** [dog, cat] perdre ses poils; **the snake ~s its skin** le serpent mue; **to ~ blood** (one's own) verser son sang; (other people's) faire couler le sang, verser or répandre le sang; **I'm trying to ~ 5 kilos** j'essaie de perdre 5 kilos; **to ~ water** ne pas laisser pénétrer l'eau
b (= send out) [+ light] répandre, diffuser; [+ warmth, happiness] répandre; **to ~ light on** (lit) éclairer; (fig) [+ sb's motives etc] jeter de la lumière sur; [+ problem] éclaircir; [+ little-known subject] éclairer

she'd [ʃiːd] = **she had**, **she would**; → **have, would**

sheen [ʃiːn] N (on silk) lustre m, luisant m; (on hair) brillant m, éclat m; **to take the ~ off sth** (lit) délustrer qch; (fig) diminuer l'éclat de qch

sheep [ʃiːp] **1** N (pl inv) mouton m (animal); (= ewe) brebis f; **they followed him like a lot of ~** ils l'ont suivi comme des moutons, ils l'ont suivi comme les moutons de Panurge; **to make ~'s eyes at sb** faire les yeux doux à qn; (fig) **we must divide** or **separate the ~ from the goats** il ne faut pas mélanger les torchons et les serviettes* **2** COMP ► **black, lost 2** COMP ► **sheep-dip** N bain m parasiticide (pour moutons) ► **sheep farm** N ferme f d'élevage de moutons ► **sheep farmer** N éleveur m de moutons ► **sheep farming** N élevage m de moutons ► **sheep track** N piste f à moutons ► **sheep-worrying** N harcèlement m des moutons (par des chiens)

sheepdog ['ʃiːpdɒg] N chien m de berger → **trial**

sheepfold ['ʃiːpfəʊld] N parc m à moutons, bergerie f

sheepherder ['ʃiːp,hɜːdəʳ] N (US) berger m, gardien m de moutons

sheepish ['ʃiːpɪʃ] ADJ penaud (about sth de qch)

sheepishly ['ʃiːpɪʃlɪ] ADV d'un air penaud

sheepishness ['ʃiːpɪʃnɪs] N timidité f, air m penaud

sheepshank ['ʃiːpʃæŋk] N (Naut) jambe f de chien

sheepshearer ['ʃiːp,ʃɪərəʳ] N (= person) tondeur m, -euse f (de moutons); (= machine) tondeuse f (à moutons)

sheepshearing ['ʃiːp,ʃɪərɪn] N (NonC) tonte f (des moutons)

sheepskin ['ʃiːpskɪn] **1** N **a** peau f de mouton **b** (US Univ* fig) peau f d'âne, diplôme m **2** COMP [waistcoat etc] en peau de mouton ► **sheepskin jacket** N canadienne f

sheer¹ [ʃɪəʳ] **1** ADJ **a** (= utter) [beauty, terror, boredom, stupidity, joy, delight] (à l'état) pur; [waste, carelessness, survival] pur et simple; [variety] même (after n); [impossibility, necessity] absolu; **by ~ accident** tout à fait par hasard; **by ~ coincidence** par pure coïncidence; **in ~ desperation** en désespoir de cause; **by ~ force of will** par la seule force de la volonté; **to succeed through ~ hard work** réussir grâce à or par son seul travail; **by ~ luck** tout à fait par hasard; **it was ~ luck I was there** c'était tout à fait par hasard que j'étais là; **it's ~ madness** c'est de la folie pure; **a sigh of ~ pleasure** un soupir de pur plaisir; **the ~ pleasure of reading a good story** le simple plaisir de lire une bonne histoire; **the ~ scale of the disaster/size of the job** l'importance même du désastre/du travail; **the ~ strength of the animal** la force même de l'animal; **delays are occurring because of the ~ volume of traffic** il y a des ralentissements dus uniquement à la densité de la circulation
b (= fine) [tights, stockings, fabric etc] très fin
c (= smooth) [make-up] satiné
d (= vertical) [cliff, rock] à pic, abrupt; **a ~ drop** un à-pic, un abrupt
2 ADV à pic, abruptement

sheer² [ʃɪəʳ] (Naut = swerve) **1** N embardée f **2** VI faire une embardée
► **sheer off** VI [ship] faire une embardée; (gen) changer de direction

sheet [ʃiːt] **1** N **a** (on bed) drap m; (= shroud) linceul m; (= dust sheet) housse f; (= tarpaulin) bâche f → **white**
b (= piece) [of plastic, rubber] morceau m; [of paper, notepaper] feuille f; [of iron, steel] tôle f; [of glass, metal etc] feuille f, plaque f; **an odd** or **loose ~** une feuille volante; (Comm) **order ~** bulletin m de commande; **baking ~** plaque f à gâteaux or de four → **balance**
c (= expanse) [of water, snow etc] étendue f; **a ~ of ice** (large) une plaque or nappe de glace; (thin film) une couche de glace; (on road) une plaque de verglas; **a ~ of flame** un rideau de flammes; **~s of rain** des trombes fpl d'eau; **the rain came down in ~s** il pleuvait à seaux
d (= periodical) périodique m; (= newspaper) journal m
e (Naut) écoute f; (fig) **he's three ~s to** or **in the wind†*** il est gris → **main**
2 COMP ► **sheet anchor** N (Naut) ancre f de veille; (fig) ancre f de salut ► **sheet ice** N verglas m ► **sheet lightning** N (NonC) éclair m en nappe(s) ► **sheet metal** N (NonC: gen) tôle f; **~ metal (work)shop** tôlerie f ► **sheet music** N (NonC) partitions fpl
► **sheet down** VI [rain] tomber à seaux; [snow] tomber à gros flocons; **it's ~ing down** (rain) il pleut à seaux; (snow) il neige à gros flocons

sheeting ['ʃiːtɪn] N (NonC) feuilles fpl

Sheherazade [ʃə,herə'zɑːdə] N Schéhérazade f

sheik(h) [ʃeɪk] N **a** cheik m → **oil b** (US fig) séducteur m, Roméo m

sheik(h)dom ['ʃeɪkdəm] N tribu or territoire sous l'autorité d'un cheik

sheila* ['ʃiːlə] N (Austral) nana* f

shekel ['ʃekl] N (modern) shekel m; (Hist: Bible etc) sicle m; (US* fig = coin) pièce f de monnaie; (fig) **~s* fric* m, sous* mpl; (US fig) **to be in the ~s*** être en fonds, avoir du fric*

sheldrake ['ʃel,dreɪk], **shelduck** ['ʃel,dʌk] N tadorne m de Bellon

shelf [ʃelf] **1** N (pl **shelves**) **a** étagère f; (in shop) rayon m; (in oven) plaque f; **a ~ of books** un rayon de livres; **a set of shelves** une étagère, un rayonnage; (Comm) **there are more luxury goods on the shelves nowadays** il y a plus d'articles de luxe sur les rayons or dans les magasins aujourd'hui; **to buy sth off the ~** acheter qch tout fait → **off;** (fig) **to leave sth on the ~** (= postpone) laisser qch de côté or au placard*; (fig) **to be (left) on the ~** [woman] monter en graine (fig), être laissée pour compte **b** (= edge) (in rock) rebord m, saillie f; (underwater) écueil m → **continental 2** COMP ► **shelf life** N (Comm) durée f de conservation en stock; (fig hum) **most pop stars have a short ~ life** la plupart des stars de la pop ne durent pas longtemps ► **shelf mark** N (in library) cote f

shell [ʃel] **1** N **a** [of egg, nut, oyster, snail etc] coquille f; [of tortoise, lobster, crab] carapace f; (on beach, in collection etc) coquillage m; [of peas] cosse f; (lit, fig) **to come out of/go back into one's ~** sortir de/rentrer dans sa coquille; (US) **"clam on the ~"** ≈ « dégustation de clams » → **cockle**
b [of building] carcasse f; [of ship] coque f; (Culin) **pastry ~** fond m de tarte
c (Mil) obus m; (US = cartridge) cartouche f
d (= racing boat) outrigger m
2 VT **a** [+ peas] écosser; [+ nut] décortiquer, écaler; [+ oyster] écailler, retirer de sa coquille; [+ crab, prawn, shrimp, lobster] décortiquer → **shelled**
b (Mil) bombarder (d'obus)

3 COMP [*necklace, ornament etc*] de or en coquillages ► **shell game** N (*US*) (= *trick*) tour m de passe-passe (pratiqué avec des coques de noix); (*fig* = *fraud*) escroquerie f ► **shell shock** N (*Med*) psychose f traumatique (*du soldat*), commotion f (*due aux combats*) ► **shell-shocked** ADJ (*Med*) commotionné; (*fig*) abasourdi ► **shell suit** N survêtement m

►**shell out*** **1** VI casquer‡, payer; **to ~ out for sth** payer qch, casquer‡ pour qch **2** VT SEP cracher‡, aligner*

she'll [ʃiːl] = **she will**; → **will**

shellac [ʃəˈlæk] **1** N (*NonC*) (gomme f) laque f **2** VT **a** (*lit*) laquer **b** (*US** = *beat*) battre à plates coutures

shellacking* [ʃəˈlækɪŋ] N (*US*) **a** (*Sport* = *defeat*) raclée f, déculottée f **b** (= *telling-off*) **to get** or **take a ~ (from)** se faire enguirlander (par)

shelled [ʃeld] ADJ [*nut, prawn*] décortiqué; [*pea*] écossé

shellfire [ˈʃelfaɪər] N (*Mil*) tirs mpl d'obus, pilonnage m à l'artillerie

shellfish [ˈʃelfɪʃ] **1** N (*pl* **shellfish** or **shellfishes**) (= *lobster, crab*) crustacé m; (= *mollusc*) coquillage m **2** NPL (*Culin*) fruits mpl de mer

shelling [ˈʃelɪŋ] N (*NonC: Mil*) bombardement m (par obus), pilonnage m d'artillerie

shellproof [ˈʃelpruːf] ADJ (*Mil*) blindé

shelter [ˈʃeltər] **1** N **a** (*NonC*) abri m, couvert m; **under the ~ of ...** à l'abri sous ...; **to take ~** ◊ **to get under ~** se mettre à l'abri or à couvert; **to take ~ from/under** s'abriter de/sous; **to seek/offer ~** chercher/offrir un abri (**from** contre); **she gave him ~ for the night** elle lui a donné (un) asile pour la nuit; **we must find ~ for the night** nous devons trouver un abri pour cette nuit; (*Brit*) **Shelter** organisation bénévole d'aide aux SDF **b** (= *hut etc*) (*on mountain*) abri m, refuge m; (*for sentry*) guérite f; (= *bus shelter*) Abribus® m; (= *air-raid shelter*) abri m **c** (*for homeless*) asile m, refuge m **2** VT **a** (= *protect*) (*from wind, rain, sun, shells etc*) abriter (**from** de), protéger (**from** de, **contre**); (*from blame etc*) protéger (**from** de); [+ *criminal etc*] protéger; (= *hide*) cacher; **~ed from the wind** à l'abri du vent → **sheltered b** (= *give lodging to*) recueillir, donner un asile or le couvert à; [+ *fugitive etc*] donner asile à, recueillir **3** VI s'abriter (**from** de, **under** sous), se mettre à l'abri or à couvert

sheltered [ˈʃeltəd] **1** ADJ **a** (= *protected from weather*) [*place, garden, harbour, waters*] abrité **b** (= *protected*) [*life, upbringing, environment etc*] protégé **c** (*Brit* = *supervised*) [*work, employment*] en milieu protégé **d** (*Econ*) [*industry*] protégé (*contre la concurrence étrangère*) **2** COMP ► **sheltered accommodation**, **sheltered housing** N (*NonC*) (*Brit*) (*for elderly*) logement-foyer m; (*for disabled*) foyer m d'hébergement pour handicapés ► **sheltered workshop** N (*Brit*) atelier m protégé

shelve [ʃelv] **1** VT **a** (*fig* = *postpone*) [+ *plan, project, problem*] mettre en sommeil or en suspens **b** (*lit*) (= *put on shelf*) [+ *book*] mettre (or remettre) en place; (= *fit with shelves*) [+ *cupboard, wall*] garnir de rayons or d'étagères **2** VI (= *slope: also ~* **down**) descendre en pente douce

shelves [ʃelvz] NPL of **shelf**

shelving [ˈʃelvɪŋ] N (*NonC*) rayonnage(s) m(pl), étagères fpl; [*of project etc*] mise f en sommeil or en suspens

shemozzle* [ʃəˈmɒzl] N (*Brit*) bagarre* f, chamaillerie* f; **there was quite a ~!** ça a bardé‡!

shenanigan(s)* [ʃəˈnænɪɡən(z)] N (*NonC*) (= *trickery*) manigances fpl, entourloupettes* fpl; (= *rowdy fun*) chahut m

shepherd [ˈʃepəd] **1** N **a** berger m; (*Rel*) pasteur m; (*Rel*) **the Good Shepherd** le bon Pasteur or Berger **b** (*also ~* **dog**) chien m de berger **2** VT [+ *sheep*] garder, soigner; **the dog ~ed the flock into the field** le chien a fait entrer le troupeau dans le pré; (*fig*) **to ~ sb in** faire entrer qn; **to ~ sb out** escorter qn jusqu'à la porte; **he ~ed us round Paris** il nous a escortés or nous a guidés or nous a servi de guide dans Paris **3** COMP ► **shepherd boy** N jeune pâtre m (*liter*), jeune berger m ► **shepherd's check** N = **shepherd's plaid** ► **shepherd's crook** N houlette f ► **shepherd's pie** N (*esp Brit Culin*) ≈ hachis m Parmentier ► **shepherd's plaid** N plaid m noir et blanc ► **shepherd's purse** N (*Bot*) bourse-à-pasteur f

shepherdess [ˈʃepədɪs] N bergère f

sherbet [ˈʃɜːbət] N **a** (*Brit*) (= *fruit juice*) jus m de fruit glacé; (*fizzy*) boisson f gazeuse; (= *powder*) poudre f acidulée or de sorbet **b** (*US* = *water ice*) sorbet m

sheriff [ˈʃerɪf] **1** N **a** (*Brit Jur*) shérif m **b** (*US*) shérif m, ≈ capitaine m de gendarmerie **2** COMP ► **Sheriff Court** N (*Scot*) ≈ tribunal m de grande instance; (*US*) ≈ tribunal m de police

Sherpa [ˈʃɜːpə] N (*pl* **Sherpas** or **Sherpa**) sherpa m

sherry [ˈʃerɪ] N xérès m, sherry m

she's [ʃiːz] = **she is, she has**; → **be, have**

Shetland [ˈʃetlənd] **1** N **the ~s** les îles fpl Shetland **2** ADJ (*gen*) [*people, customs, village*] des îles Shetland; [*sweater*] en shetland **3** COMP ► **the Shetland Islands, the Shetland Isles** NPL = **the Shetlands** ► **Shetland pony** N poney m des Shetland ► **Shetland pullover** N pull-over m en shetland ► **Shetland wool** N shetland m

Shetlander [ˈʃetləndər] N Shetlandais(e) m(f)

shew†† [ʃəʊ] VTI = **show**

shhh [ʃː] EXCL chut!

Shiah [ˈʃiːə] **1** N **a** (= *doctrine*) chiisme m **b** (= *follower: also ~* **Muslim**) chiite mf **2** ADJ chiite

shiatsu [ˌʃiːˈætsuː] N shiatsu m

shibboleth [ˈʃɪbəleθ] N (*Bible*) schibboleth m; (*fig*) (= *doctrine*) doctrine f or principe m arbitraire; (= *password*) mot m de passe; (= *characteristic*) caractéristique f, signe m distinctif

shield [ʃiːld] **1** N (*gen*) bouclier m; (*not round*) (*Her*) écu m; (*on gun*) blason m; (*on gun*) bouclier m; (*on or around machine*) écran m de protection, tôle f protectrice; (*against radiation*) écran m; (*fig*) (= *safeguard*) sauvegarde f, bouclier m (*liter*) (**against** contre); (= *person*) protecteur m, -trice f; (*Space*) **thermal ~** bouclier m thermique → **dress, windshield 2** VT protéger (**from** de, contre); [+ *fugitive, criminal*] protéger, couvrir; (*Tech*) [+ *machine operator*] protéger; [+ *gun, machine*] fixer un écran de protection à; **to ~ one's eyes from the sun** se protéger les yeux du soleil; **to ~ sb with one's body** faire à qn un bouclier or un rempart de son corps

shift [ʃɪft] **1** N **a** (= *change*) changement m (**in** de), modification f (**in** de); (*Ling*) mutation f; (= *movement*) [*of cargo, load etc*] déplacement m (**in** de); **there has been a ~ in policy/attitude** la politique/l'attitude a changé; **a sudden ~ in policy/attitude** un retournement or un bouleversement de la politique/de l'attitude; **~ of emphasis** changement m d'éclairage; **a sudden ~ in the wind** une saute de vent → **scene, vowel b** (*Ind etc*) (= *period of work*) poste m, période f de travail d'une équipe; (= *people*) poste m, équipe f (*de relais*); **he works ~s** ◊ **he's on ~s** il travaille par équipes, il fait un travail posté; **they used to work a ten-hour ~ in that factory** ils avaient des postes de dix heures dans cette usine; **I work an eight-hour ~** je fais les trois-huit, je fais un poste de huit heures; **this factory operates on three ~s per 24-hour period** dans cette usine ils font les trois-huit, dans cette usine trois équipes se relaient sur 24 heures; **to be on day/night ~** être (au poste) de jour/de nuit; **which ~ do you prefer?** quel poste préférez-vous?; **the next ~ were late in coming on** le poste suivant or l'équipe suivante était en retard pour prendre le relais or la relève; **they worked in ~s to release the injured man** ils se sont relayés pour (essayer de) libérer le blessé → **day, night c to make ~ with sth/sb** se contenter de or s'accommoder de or se débrouiller avec qch/qn; **to make ~ without sth/sb** se passer de qch/qn, se débrouiller* sans qch/qn; **to make ~ to do sth** se débrouiller* pour faire qch; **as a last desperate ~ he ...** en désespoir de cause il ... **d** (*Aut* = *gearshift*) changement m de vitesse **e** (= *straight dress*) robe f droite; († = *woman's slip*) chemise f **f** (*Comput*) décalage m **2** VT **a** (= *move*) [+ *object, furniture*] déplacer, changer de place; [+ *one's head, arm etc*] bouger, remuer; [+ *chair, car etc*] déplacer, changer de place; (*Theat*) [+ *scenery*] changer; [+ *screw*] débloquer, faire bouger; [+ *lid, top, cap*] faire bouger; [+ *stain*] enlever, faire disparaître; [+ *employee*] (*to another town*) muter (**to** à); (*on another job, department*) affecter (**to** à); (*fig*) [+ *blame, responsibility*] rejeter (**on, on to** sur); **he ~ed his chair nearer the fire** il a approché sa chaise du feu; **to ~ sth in/out/away etc** rentrer/sortir/écarter etc qch; **we couldn't ~ him (from his opinion)** nous n'avons pas réussi à le faire changer d'avis or à l'ébranler; **I can't ~ this cold*** je n'arrive pas à me débarrasser de ce rhume **b** (= *change, exchange*) changer de; (*lit, fig*) **to ~ position** changer de position; (*Aut*) **to ~ gears** changer de vitesse, passer les vitesses → **ground**† **3** VI **a** (= *go*) aller; (= *move house*) déménager; (= *change position, stir*) [*person, animal, planet etc*] changer de place or de position, bouger; [*limb*] remuer, bouger; [*wind*] tourner; [*ballast, cargo, load*] se déplacer; [*opinions, ideas*] changer, se modifier; [*stain*] s'en aller, disparaître; (*over*) **a minute to let me past*** pousse-toi or bouge-toi* une minute pour me laisser passer; **~ off the rug*** dégage* du tapis; (*on seat etc*) **can you ~ down** or **up along a little?** pourriez-vous vous pousser un peu?; **he has ~ed into another class** il a été transféré or il est passé dans une autre classe; (*Theat etc*) **the scene ~s to Paris** la scène est maintenant à Paris; (*Aut*) **to ~ into second (gear)** passer la deuxième; **he won't ~** il ne bougera pas; **the government has not ~ed from its original position** le gouvernement n'a pas modifié sa première position; (= *go fast*) **he/that car certainly ~s*** il/cette voiture fonce!; (= *hurry*) **come on, ~!*** allez, remue-toi* or grouille-toi‡! **b** (= *for o.s.*) se débrouiller* tout seul **4** COMP ► **shift key** N [*of typewriter*] touche f de majuscule ► **shift lock** N (*Typ*) touche f de verrouillage des majuscules ► **shift register** N (*Comput*) registre m à décalage ► **shift work** N (*Brit Ind etc*) travail m posté or par relais or par roulement; **to do ~ work** ◊ **to be on ~ work** travailler par équipes, faire un travail posté ► **shift worker** N travailleur m, -euse f posté(e)

►**shift about, shift around 1** VI **a** (= *change job*) changer souvent d'emploi; (*within same firm*) être muté plusieurs fois **b** (= *fidget*) bouger, remuer **2** VT SEP [+ *furniture etc*] déplacer, changer de place

►**shift back 1** VI (= *withdraw*) (se) reculer **2** VT SEP [+ *chair etc*] reculer

►**shift over** VI s'écarter, se pousser; **~ over!*** pousse-toi!

shiftily ['ʃɪftɪlɪ] ADV [say] d'un ton faux; [tell] sournoisement; [look] d'un air sournois

shiftiness ['ʃɪftɪnɪs] N [of person, behaviour] sournoiserie f; [of look, eyes] aspect m fuyant; [of answer] caractère m évasif

shifting ['ʃɪftɪŋ] ① ADJ [winds, currents] variable; [attitudes, pattern, colours] changeant; [alliances, population, balance of power] instable ② COMP ► **shifting cultivation** N culture f itinérante ► **shifting sands** NPL (lit) sables mpl mouvants; (fig) terrain m mouvant

shiftless ['ʃɪftlɪs] ADJ (frm) apathique, indolent

shiftlessness ['ʃɪftlɪsnɪs] N manque m de ressources

shifty* ['ʃɪftɪ] ① ADJ [person, behaviour] sournois; [look, eyes] fuyant; [answer] évasif ② COMP ► **shifty-eyed*** ADJ aux yeux fuyants ► **shifty-looking*** ADJ à l'aspect fuyant

shiitake mushroom [ˌʃiːtækɪ'mʌʃrʊm] N champignon m shiitaké

Shiite, Shi'ite ['ʃiːaɪt] (also ~ **Muslim**) N, ADJ chiite mf

shiksa, shikse(h) ['ʃɪksə] N (esp US: gen pej) jeune fille f goy

shill [ʃɪl] N (US: at fairground etc) compère m

shillelagh [ʃə'leɪlə] N gourdin m irlandais

shilling ['ʃɪlɪŋ] N (Brit) shilling m

shilly-shally ['ʃɪlɪˌʃælɪ] ① VI hésiter; (deliberately) tergiverser, atermoyer; **stop ~ing!** décide-toi enfin! ② VT = **shilly-shallying**

shilly-shallying ['ʃɪlɪˌʃælɪŋ] N (NonC) hésitations fpl, valse-hésitation f; (deliberate) tergiversations fpl, atermoiements mpl

shimmer ['ʃɪmər] ① VI [satin, jewels] chatoyer; [water, lake, heat haze, road surface] miroiter; **the moonlight ~ed on the lake** le clair de lune faisait miroiter le lac ② N [of satin, jewels] chatoiement m; [of water, lake] miroitement m

shimmering ['ʃɪmərɪŋ], **shimmery** ['ʃɪmərɪ] ADJ [material, jewel] chatoyant; [water, lake] miroitant; **the ~ moonlight on the lake** le clair de lune qui faisait miroiter le lac

shimmy ['ʃɪmɪ] ① N ⓐ (US Aut) shimmy m ⓑ (= dance) shimmy m ② VI (US Aut) avoir du shimmy

shin [ʃɪn] ① N ⓐ tibia m ⓑ (Brit Culin) ► **of beef** jarret m de bœuf ② VI **to ~ up a tree** grimper à un arbre; **to ~ down a tree** descendre d'un arbre; **to ~ over a wall** escalader un mur ③ COMP ► **shin guard, shin pad** N protège-tibia m

shinbone ['ʃɪnbəʊn] N tibia m

shindig* ['ʃɪndɪg] N (= dance, party etc) fiesta f, soirée f joyeuse

shindy* ['ʃɪndɪ] N ⓐ (= brawl) bagarre f; (= row, commotion) tapage m, boucan* m; **to kick up** or **make a ~** faire du boucan* ⓑ = **shindig**

shine [ʃaɪn] (vb: pret, ptp **shone**) ① N [of sun] éclat m; [of metal] éclat m, brillant m; [of shoes] brillant m; **to give sth a ~** faire briller qch, faire reluire qch; **to take the ~ off** [+ brass, shoes] rendre mat or terne (pej); (fig) [+ success, news] diminuer l'attrait de, faire tomber à plat; [+ sb else's achievement] éclipser; **the ~ on his trousers** son pantalon lustré; **to take a ~ to sb*** se toquer de qn* → **moonshine, rain**
② VI [sun, stars, lamp] briller; [metal, shoes] briller, reluire; (fig = excel) briller; **the sun is shining** il fait (du) soleil, il y a du soleil, le soleil brille; **the moon is shining** il y a clair de lune; **to ~ on sth** éclairer or illuminer qch; **the light was shining in my eyes** j'avais la lumière dans les yeux; **her face shone with happiness** son visage rayonnait de bonheur; **her eyes shone with pleasure/envy** ses yeux brillaient de plaisir/luisaient d'envie; (fig) **to ~ at football/Spanish** briller or faire des étincelles* au football/en espagnol

③ VT ⓐ **~ your torch** or **the light over here** éclairez par ici; **he shone his torch on the car** il a braqué sa lampe de poche sur la voiture, il a éclairé la voiture ⓑ (pret, ptp **shone** or **shined**) [+ furniture, brass, shoes] astiquer, faire briller
► **shine down** VI [sun, moon, stars] briller
► **shine through** VI [light etc] passer, filtrer; (fig) [courage etc] transparaître
► **shine up** VI (US fig) **to ~ up to sb*** (to girl) faire du plat* à qn; (to boss) faire de la lèche* à qn

shiner ['ʃaɪnər] N (* = black eye) œil m au beurre noir*

shingle ['ʃɪŋgl] ① N (NonC: on beach etc) galets mpl; (on roof) bardeau m; (coated in tar) shingle m; (US* = signboard) petite enseigne f (de docteur, de notaire etc); († = hairstyle) coupe f à la garçonne ② VT† [+ hair] couper à la garçonne ③ COMP ► **shingle beach** N plage f de galets

shingles ['ʃɪŋglz] N (NonC) zona m; **to have ~** avoir un zona

shingly ['ʃɪŋglɪ] ADJ [beach] (couvert) de galets

shininess ['ʃaɪnɪnɪs] N éclat m, brillant m

shining ['ʃaɪnɪŋ] ADJ ⓐ (= gleaming) [eyes, hair] brillant; [face] rayonnant; [furniture, floor, metal] luisant ⓑ (= outstanding) [success, moment] remarquable; **she was a ~ example to everyone** c'était un modèle pour tout le monde; **~ light (in sth)** (fig) (person) lumière f (en qch); (thing) phare f (de qch) → **improve**

shinny ['ʃɪnɪ] VI = **shin 2**

Shinto ['ʃɪntəʊ] N shinto m

Shintoism ['ʃɪntəʊɪzəm] N shintoïsme m

Shintoist ['ʃɪntəʊɪst] ADJ, N shintoïste mf

shinty ['ʃɪntɪ] N sorte de hockey sur gazon

shiny ['ʃaɪnɪ] ADJ [surface, hair, shoes, coin] brillant; [car] rutilant; [furniture, metal, fabric] luisant; [nose] qui brille (or brillait); **the company's ~ new offices** les nouveaux bureaux rutilants de la société

ship [ʃɪp] ① N (gen) bateau m; (large) navire m; (= vessel) vaisseau m, bâtiment m; **His (or Her) Majesty's Ship Maria/Falcon** la Maria/le Falcon († liter) **the good ~ Caradoc** la nef† Caradoc, le Caradoc, (fig) **when my ~ comes in** quand j'aurai fait fortune; (fig) **he runs** or **keeps a tight ~** il ne plaisante pas sur l'organisation (or la discipline); (fig) **it was a case of "~s that pass in the night"** ce fut une rencontre sans lendemain; (fig) **the ~ of the desert** le vaisseau du désert, le chameau → **board, jump, warship**
② VT ⓐ (= transport) transporter; (= send by ship) expédier (par bateau); (= send by any means) expédier; (Comm) **the goods were ~ped on SS Wallisdown** la marchandise a été expédiée à bord du Wallisdown
ⓑ (= put or take on board) [+ cargo] embarquer, charger; [+ water] embarquer; **~ the oars** rentrer les avirons
③ COMP ► **ship canal** N canal m maritime or de navigation ► **ship chandler** N **ship's chandler** ► **ship of the line** N (Hist) bâtiment m de ligne ► **ship's biscuit** N (NonC) biscuit m (de mer) ► **ship's boat** N chaloupe f ► **ship's boy** N mousse m ► **ship's chandler** N fournisseur m d'équipement pour bateaux, shipchandler m ► **ship's company** N équipage m, hommes mpl du bord ► **ship's papers** N papiers mpl de bord or d'un navire ► **ship-to-shore radio** N liaison f radio avec la côte
► **ship off, ship out** ① VI s'embarquer (**to** pour) ② VT SEP ⓐ (= send by ship) [+ goods, troops etc] envoyer (par bateau or par mer) ⓑ (* = send) [+ goods, person] expédier*

shipboard ['ʃɪpbɔːd] ① ADJ [task] à bord; [personnel] de bord; **a ~ romance** une histoire d'amour le temps d'une croisière ② N **on ~** à bord

shipbuilder ['ʃɪpˌbɪldər] N constructeur m naval

shipbuilding ['ʃɪpˌbɪldɪŋ] N construction f navale

shipload ['ʃɪpləʊd] N (lit) charge f; (fig) grande quantité f, masse* f; **tourists were arriving by the ~** les touristes arrivaient par bateaux entiers

shipmate ['ʃɪpmeɪt] N camarade m de bord

shipment ['ʃɪpmənt] N (= load) cargaison f; (= act of shipping) expédition f (par bateau); (Comm) **ready for ~** prêt à l'expédition

shipowner ['ʃɪpˌəʊnər] N armateur m

shipper ['ʃɪpər] N expéditeur m, affréteur m

shipping ['ʃɪpɪŋ] ① N (NonC) ⓐ (= ships collectively) navires mpl; (= traffic) navigation f; (Rad) **attention all ~!** avis à la navigation!; **it was a danger to ~** cela constituait un danger pour la navigation; **the canal is closed to British ~** le canal est fermé aux navires britanniques ⓑ (= act of loading) chargement m, embarquement m ⓒ (= charges for transporting cargo) frais mpl de transport ② COMP ► **shipping agent** N agent m maritime ► **shipping clerk** N expéditionnaire m ► **shipping company** N compagnie f de navigation ► **shipping lane** N voie f de navigation ► **shipping line** N = **shipping company** ► **shipping losses** NPL **losses during 1944** les pertes en navires au cours de l'année 1944

shipshape ['ʃɪpʃeɪp] ADJ bien rangé, en ordre; **all ~ and Bristol fashion** arrangé d'une façon impeccable

shipwreck ['ʃɪprek] ① N (= event) naufrage m; (= wrecked ship) épave f ② VT (lit) faire sombrer; (fig) ruiner, anéantir; **to be ~ed** faire naufrage; **~ed on a desert island** [vessel] échoué sur une île déserte; [person] naufragé sur une île déserte; **a ~ person** un(e) naufragé(e); **a ~ed sailor/vessel** un marin/vaisseau naufragé

shipwright ['ʃɪprart] N (= builder) constructeur m de navires; (= carpenter) charpentier m (de chantier naval)

shipyard ['ʃɪpjɑːd] N chantier m naval

shire ['ʃaɪər] N (Brit) comté m; **~ horse** shire m, cheval m de gros trait

shirk [ʃɜːk] ① VT [+ task, work] éviter de faire, s'arranger pour ne pas faire; [+ obligation, duty] esquiver, se dérober à; [+ difficulty, problem, issue] éluder, esquiver; **to ~ doing sth** éviter de faire qch, s'arranger pour ne pas faire qch ② VI tirer au flanc*

shirker ['ʃɜːkər] N tire-au-flanc* mf inv

shirr [ʃɜːr] VT ⓐ (Sewing) froncer ⓑ (US Culin) **~ed eggs** œufs mpl en cocotte or au four

shirring ['ʃɜːrɪŋ] ① N fronces fpl ② COMP ► **shirring elastic** N (fil m) élastique m à froncer, ≈ Lastex® m

shirt [ʃɜːt] ① N (man's) chemise f; (woman's) chemisier m; (footballer's etc) maillot m; (fig) **keep your ~ on!** ne vous mettez pas en rogne* or en pétard*!; (Betting etc) **to put one's ~ on sth** jouer (toute) sa fortune or tout ce qu'on a sur qch; (Betting etc) **to lose one's ~** perdre (toute) sa fortune or tout ce qu'on a, y laisser sa chemise → **boil, nightshirt, stuff** ② COMP ► **shirt front** N plastron m ► **shirt-lifter*** N (pej) pédé* m, pédale* f ► **shirt sleeves** NPL **in (one's) ~ sleeves** en bras or manches de chemise ► **shirt-tail** N pan m de chemise; **in (one's) ~-tails** en chemise ► **shirt-tail cousin*** N (US) cousin(e) m(f) éloigné(e), cousin(e) m(f) à la mode de Bretagne

shirtdress ['ʃɜːtdres] N robe f chemisier

shirting ['ʃɜːtɪŋ] N (NonC) shirting m

shirtwaist ['ʃɜːtweɪst] ① N (US) (= blouse) chemisier m; (= dress) robe f chemisier ② COMP ► **shirtwaist(ed) dress** N = **shirtwaister**

shirtwaister [ˈʃɜːtˌweɪstə] N robe f chemisier

shirty* [ˈʃɜːti] ADJ (*Brit*) [*person, reply*] vache*; **to get ~** (**with sb**) (**about sth**) se mettre en rogne* (contre qn) (à propos de qch)

shish kebab [ˈʃiːʃkəˈbæb] N chiche-kebab *m*

shit** [ʃit] (*vb: pret, ptp* **shat**) **1** N **a** (*lit, fig*) (= *excrement, rubbish*) merde** f; **~!** merde!*; **no ~?** sans blague?*; (*fig*) **to be in the ~** être dans la merde** jusqu'au cou; **in deep ~** dans la merde** jusqu'au cou; **don't give me that ~!** arrête de déconner!*; **to have** or **take a ~** chier** un coup; **I don't give a ~!** j'en ai rien à branler!**, je m'en contrefous** (**about** de); **he's a ~** c'est un salaud*; **to scare the ~ out of sb** flanquer une de ces trouilles* à qn; **to beat** or **kick** or **knock the ~ out of sb** passer qn à tabac*, dérouiller qn*; (*fig*) **then the ~ really hit the fan** alors ça a bardé* or chié** **b** (= *bastard*) salaud* *m* **c** (*Drugs* = *resin*) shit *m* **2** VI chier**; (*US*) **it's time to ~ or get off the pot** il est temps de s'y mettre ou bien de passer la main **3** VT (*lit, fig*) **to ~ o.s.** chier** dans son froc; **to ~ a brick** or **bricks** chier** or faire dans son froc (*fig*) **4** ADJ merdique*, nul à chier** **5** COMP ▶ **shit-hole**** N endroit *m* de merde** ▶ **shit-hot*** ADJ vachement bon* ▶ **shit-scared**** ADJ **to be ~-scared** avoir une trouille bleue* ▶ **shit-stirrer*** N fouteur *m*, -euse f de merde**

shite** [ʃaɪt] N (*Brit*) merde** f

shitface* [ˈʃitfeɪs] N = **shithead**

shitfaced** [ˈʃitfeɪst] ADJ pété*, cassé*

shithead** [ˈʃithed] N connard* *m*, connasse* f

shithouse** [ˈʃithaʊs] N (= *lavatory*) chiottes* fpl; (*fig*) **this ~ of a country** ce pays de merde** → **built**

shitless** [ˈʃitlɪs] ADJ **to scare sb ~** flanquer une de ces trouilles* à qn; **to be scared ~** avoir une trouille bleue*; **to bore sb ~** casser les couilles à qn**; **to be bored ~** se faire chier**

shitlist* [ˈʃitlɪst] N liste f noire

shitty* [ˈʃiti] ADJ [*person, mood, food*] dégueulasse*; [*place, job*] merdique*; **what a ~ thing to do/say!** c'est dégueulasse* de faire/dire ça!

shitwork** [ˈʃitwɜːk] N (*NonC; US*) boulot *m* merdique*

shiv* [ʃiv] N (= *knife*) surin* *m*, couteau *m*

shiver¹ [ˈʃɪvə] **1** VI (*with cold, fear*) frissonner, trembler (**with** de); (*with pleasure*) frissonner, tressaillir (**with** de) → **boot, shoe 2** N (*from cold*) frisson *m*; (*from fear, emotion*) frisson *m*, tressaillement *m*; **it sent ~s down his spine** cela lui a donné froid dans le dos; **he gave a ~** il a frissonné, il a eu un frisson; **to give sb the ~s** donner le frisson à qn

shiver² [ˈʃɪvə] **1** N (= *fragment*) éclat *m*, fragment *m* **2** VI (= *shatter*) voler en éclats, se fracasser **3** VT fracasser; **~ my timbers!** mille sabords!

shivery [ˈʃɪvəri] ADJ (*from cold*) frissonnant, grelottant; (*from emotion, fever*) frissonnant, tremblant

shoal¹ [ʃəʊl] N [*of fish*] banc *m* (*de poissons*); (*fig*) **they came in (their) ~s** ils sont venus en foule; **~s of applications** une avalanche de demandes

shoal² [ʃəʊl] N (= *shallows*) haut-fond *m*, bas-fond *m*; (= *sandbank*) banc *m* de sable, écueil *m*

shock¹ [ʃɒk] **1** N **a** (= *impact*) [*of collision etc*] choc *m*, heurt *m*; [*of earthquake, explosion*] secousse f **b** (*Elec*) décharge f (électrique); **to get a ~** recevoir une décharge (électrique), prendre le jus*; **she got a ~ from the refrigerator** ◊ **the refrigerator gave her a ~** elle a reçu une décharge en touchant le réfrigérateur **c** (*to sensibilities etc*) choc *m*, coup *m*; (= *feel-*

ing, emotion) horreur f; **he got such a ~ when he heard that ...** cela lui a donné un tel choc or coup d'apprendre que ...; **he hasn't yet got over the ~ of her death** il ne s'est pas encore remis du choc que lui a causé sa mort; **the ~ killed him** le choc l'a tué; **the ~ of the election results** les résultats *mpl* stupéfiants des élections; **their refusal came as a ~ to me** leur refus m'a stupéfié or ébahi; **it comes as a ~ to hear that ...** il est stupéfiant d'apprendre que ...; **you gave me a ~!** vous m'avez fait peur!; **I got such a ~!** j'en étais tout retourné!*; (*hum*) **~ horror!*** quelle horreur! → **4**; **pale with ~** pâle de saisissement; **my feeling is one of ~ at the idea that ...** j'éprouve un sentiment d'horreur à l'idée que ..., je suis bouleversé à l'idée que ...

d (*Med*) commotion f, choc *m*; **anaphylactic ~** choc *m* anaphylactique; **to be suffering from ~** être en état de choc, être commotionné; **in a state of ~** en état de choc, commotionné → **shell**

e (*US Aut*) **~s*** amortisseurs *mpl*

2 ADJ [*defeat, victory, news, resignation, decision*] surprise

3 VT (= *take aback*) secouer, retourner*; (*stronger*) bouleverser; (= *disgust*) dégoûter; (= *scandalize*) choquer, scandaliser; **to ~ sb out of his complacency** déstabiliser qn; **he's easily ~ed** il se choque facilement or pour un rien

4 COMP [*tactics*] de choc ▶ **shock absorber** N (*Aut*) amortisseur *m* ▶ **shock-horror*** ADJ [*story, film*] d'épouvante; [*headline*] sensationnel, à sensation ▶ **shock jock*** N (*esp US*) présentateur de radio qui cherche à provoquer de vives controverses en exprimant des opinions extrémistes ▶ **shock resistant** ADJ résistant aux chocs ▶ **shock therapy, shock treatment** N (*Med*) (traitement *m* par) électrochoc *m* ▶ **shock troops** NPL troupes *fpl* de choc ▶ **shock wave** N (*Phys*) onde f de choc

shock² [ʃɒk] N **a ~ of hair** une tignasse*

shocked [ʃɒkt] ADJ **a** (= *unpleasantly surprised*) [*person, voice, expression, face*] abasourdi (**at sth** par qch); [*reaction*] choqué; **a ~ silence** un silence consterné; **to listen in ~ silence** écouter muet de stupéfaction; **~ to see/hear/learn sth** abasourdi de voir/d'entendre/d'apprendre qch **b** (= *scandalized*) choqué **c** (*Med*) commotionné

shocker* [ˈʃɒkə] N **a** **he's a ~** il est impossible or imbuvable*; **his essay's a ~** sa dissertation est une catastrophe*; **what a ~ of a day!** quel temps épouvantable or de cochon*! **b** (= *cheap book*) livre *m* à sensation

shocking [ˈʃɒkɪŋ] **1** ADJ **a** (= *scandalous*) [*act, behaviour, book*] choquant, scandaleux; [*sight*] choquant, atroce; [*decision, waste of money*] scandaleux; [*price*] scandaleux, exorbitant; [*murder, cruelty*] odieux, atroce; [*crime*] odieux, atroce, affreux; [*news*] atroce, bouleversant; **the film wasn't really ~** le film n'avait rien de vraiment choquant; **it may be ~ to the older generation** cela pourrait choquer les générations plus âgées; **it is ~ to think that ...** il est scandaleux de penser que ... (+ *subj*); **it is ~ that ...** il est scandaleux que ... (+ *subj*); **the ~ truth** la terrible vérité **b** (*Brit** = *dreadful*) [*weather, results, cold, cough*] affreux, épouvantable; [*quality, handwriting*] épouvantable; **in a ~ state** dans un état épouvantable **2** COMP ▶ **shocking pink** N rose *m* criard *inv*

shockingly [ˈʃɒkɪŋli] ADV **a** (= *disturbingly*) [*effective, frank*] terriblement; **~, children are more likely to be killed in an accident in the home** chose terrible, un enfant a plus de chances d'être tué dans un accident domestique **b** (* = *badly*) [*play, act*] de façon lamentable; [*behave*] affreusement mal; (= *scandalously*) scandaleusement, de façon choquante; (*Brit** = *extremely*) [*bad, unfair,*

expensive, difficult] terriblement, affreusement

shockproof [ˈʃɒkpruːf] ADJ (*Tech*) antichoc *inv*; (* *fig*) [*person*] difficile à choquer

shod [ʃɒd] VB *pt, ptp of* **shoe**

shoddily [ˈʃɒdɪli] (*pej*) ADV [*made, built*] mal; [*behave, treat*] très mal

shoddiness [ˈʃɒdɪnɪs] N [*of work, goods*] mauvaise qualité f; [*of behaviour*] bassesse f, mesquinerie f

shoddy [ˈʃɒdi] **1** ADJ (*pej*) [*workmanship, goods*] de mauvaise qualité; [*service*] de mauvaise qualité, mauvais; [*treatment*] indigne; [*behaviour, attempt*] mesquin; [*building*] miteux **2** N (= *cloth*) lirette f

shoe [ʃuː] (*vb: pret, ptp* **shod**) **1** N chaussure f, soulier *m*; (= *horseshoe*) fer *m* (à cheval); (= *brake shoe*) sabot *m* (de frein); **to have one's ~s on/off** être chaussé/déchaussé; **to put on one's ~s** mettre ses chaussures, se chausser; **to take off one's ~s** enlever ses chaussures, se déchausser; (*fig*) **to quake** or **shake** or **tremble** or **shiver in one's ~s** avoir une peur bleue; (*fig*) **I wouldn't like to be in his ~s** je n'aimerais pas être à sa place; (*fig*) **to step into** or **fill sb's ~s** succéder à qn; **he's waiting for dead men's ~s** il attend que quelqu'un meure pour prendre sa place; (*fig*) **you'll know where the ~ pinches when ...** vous vous trouverez serré or à court quand ...; (*fig*) **that's another pair of ~s** c'est une autre paire de manches; (*fig*) **that's where the ~ pinches** c'est là que le bât blesse; (*US fig*) **to drop the other ~** finir ce que l'on a commencé; (*US*) **if the ~ fits, wear it** qui se sent morveux (qu'il) se mouche, il n'y a que la vérité qui blesse → **court**

2 VT [+ *horse*] ferrer; **to be well/badly shod** [*person*] être bien/mal chaussé ◊ (*PROV*) **the cobbler's children are always the worst shod** ce sont les cordonniers qui sont les plus mal chaussés (*PROV*)

3 COMP ▶ **shoe cream** N crème f pour chaussures ▶ **shoe leather** N cuir *m* pour chaussures; (*fig*) **I wore out a lot of ~ leather** ◊ **it cost me a lot in ~ leather** ça m'est revenu cher en chaussures, j'ai dû faire des kilomètres à pied ▶ **shoe polish** N cirage *m* ▶ **shoe repairer** N cordonnier *m*; **~ repairer's (shop)** cordonnerie f ▶ **shoe repairing** N (*NonC*) cordonnerie f ▶ **shoe repairs** NPL cordonnerie f ▶ **shoe size** N pointure f; **what ~ size are you?** quelle est votre pointure?, quelle pointure faites-vous?

shoeblack† [ˈʃuːblæk] N cireur *m*, -euse f de chaussures

shoebrush [ˈʃuːbrʌʃ] N brosse f à chaussures

shoehorn [ˈʃuːhɔːn] **1** N chausse-pied *m* **2** VT **the cars are ~ed into tiny spaces** les voitures sont casées dans des emplacements minuscules; **I was ~ing myself into a skin-tight ball gown** j'enfilais non sans mal une robe de bal moulante

shoelace [ˈʃuːleɪs] N lacet *m* (de chaussure); (*fig*) **you are not fit** or **worthy to tie his ~s** vous n'êtes pas digne de délier le cordon de ses souliers

shoemaker [ˈʃuːmeɪkə] N (= *cobbler*) cordonnier *m*; (= *manufacturer*) fabricant *m* de chaussures; (= *shoeshop owner*) chausseur *m*; **~'s shop** cordonnerie f

shoeshine boy [ˌʃuːʃaɪnˈbɔɪ] N cireur *m* de chaussures

shoeshop [ˈʃuːʃɒp] N magasin *m* de chaussures

shoestring [ˈʃuːstrɪŋ] N (*US*) (*lit*) = **shoelace**; (*fig*) **to do sth on a ~** faire qch à peu de frais or avec peu d'argent; **they're living on a ~** ils sont gênés, ils doivent se serrer la ceinture*; **~ budget** budget *m* minime or infime

shoetree [ˈʃuːtriː] N embauchoir *m*

shone [ʃɒn] VB *pt, ptp of* **shine**

shoo [ʃuː] **1** EXCL (*to animals*) pschtt!; (*to person*) ouste!* **2** VT (*also* ~ **away**, ~ **off**) chasser **3** COMP ► **shoo-in** N (*US*) **it's a ~-in** c'est du tout cuit*, c'est du gâteau*; **the president looks a ~-in for a second term** le président sera réélu à coup sûr

shook [ʃʊk] **1** VB *pt of* **shake 2** COMP ► **shook-up** ADJ **to be ~-up about sth** être secoué par qch; **a ~-up generation** une génération de paumés*

shoot [ʃuːt] (*vb: pret, ptp* **shot**) **1** N **a** (*on branch etc*) pousse f, rejeton m (*Bio*); (= *seedling*) pousse f
b (= *chute*) glissière f, déversoir m
c (= *shooting party*) partie f de chasse; (= *land*) (terrain m de) chasse f; (*fig*) **the whole (bang) ~** tout le tremblement*, tout le bataclan*
d (= *photo assignment*) séance f (de photos); (= *filming session*) séance f (de tournage)
e ~!* zut!*, mercredi!*
2 VT **a** [+ *animal*] (= *hunt*) chasser; (= *kill*) abattre, tirer; [+ *injured horse etc*] abattre; [+ *person*] (= *hit*) atteindre d'un coup de feu; (= *wound*) blesser par balle(s); (= *kill*) tuer par balle(s), abattre; (= *execute*) fusiller; **~ him!** tire!, descends-le!*; **to be shot in the head** être atteint or blessé or tué d'une balle dans la tête; **to be shot in the arm** recevoir une balle dans le bras, être atteint d'une balle au bras; **he had been shot through the heart** il avait reçu une balle en plein cœur; **to ~ sb dead** abattre qn; **he was shot as a spy** il a été fusillé pour espionnage; (*hum*) **people have been shot for less!** on en a tué pour moins que ça!; (*hum*) **you'll get shot for that!** tu vas te faire incendier pour ça!*; **to ~ from the hip** (*lit*) tirer l'arme à la hanche; (*fig*) (*challenging sb*) attaquer impulsivement; (*answering sb*) riposter impulsivement; (*Aut*) **to ~ the lights** griller or brûler le feu rouge; (*fig*) **to ~ o.s. in the foot** scier la branche sur laquelle on est assis; **it's a case of ~ the messenger** c'est se tromper de cible; **it's like ~ing fish in a barrel** c'est un combat gagné d'avance
b (= *fire*) [+ *gun*] tirer un coup de (**at** sur); [+ *arrow*] décocher, tirer (**at** sur); [+ *bullet*] tirer (**at** sur); [+ *rocket, missile*] lancer (**at** sur); (*fig*) **the volcano shot lava high into the air** le volcan projetait de la lave dans les airs; **they shot the coal into the cellar** ils ont déversé le charbon dans la cave; **to ~ a goal** ◊ **to ~ the ball into the net** marquer un but; **he shot the bolt** (*fastened*) il a mis or poussé le verrou; (*opened*) il a tiré le verrou; (*fig*) **he has shot his bolt** il a joué sa dernière carte, il a brûlé ses dernières cartouches; (*US fig*) **to ~ the breeze** bavarder; (*US fig*) **to ~ the bull** raconter des conneries*; (*fig*) **to ~ a line** faire de l'épate*, en mettre plein la vue*; (*Brit fig*) **to ~ a line about sth** raconter des histoires or des bobards* à propos de qch; (*US fig*) **to ~ the works* on sth** (= *spend all*) claquer* tout son argent pour acheter qch; **to ~ dice** jeter les dés; (*fig*) **to ~ (for) the moon** viser (très) haut → **pool²**
c (= *direct*) [+ *look, glance*] décocher, lancer (**at** à); [*sun*] [+ *ray of light*] darder; **he shot a smile at her** il lui a lancé or décoché un sourire; **to ~ questions at sb** bombarder or mitrailler qn de questions
d (*Cine etc*) [+ *film, scene*] tourner; [+ *subject of snapshot etc*] prendre (en photo)
e [+ *rapids*] franchir, descendre; [+ *bridge*] passer rapidement sous
f * (= *send*) envoyer, expédier; (= *give*) donner; (= *throw*) jeter, flanquer*
g (*Drugs*) [+ *heroin*] se shooter* à l'héroïne
3 VI **a** (*with gun, bow*) tirer (**at** sur); (*Sport: at target*) tirer (à la cible); (*Brit* = *hunt*) **to go ~ing** aller à la chasse, tirer le gibier; **to ~ to kill** tirer pour abattre; **to ~ on sight** tirer à vue; **he can't ~ straight** il tire mal or

comme un pied*; (*fig*) **they're both ~ing for** or **at the same target** ils travaillent de concert
b (= *move quickly*) **to ~ in/out/past** *etc* [*person, car, ball etc*] entrer/sortir/passer *etc* en flèche; **to ~ along** filer; **he shot to the door** il s'est précipité vers la porte; **to ~ to fame/stardom** devenir très vite célèbre/une star; **the car shot out of a side street** la voiture a débouché à toute vitesse d'une rue transversale; **he shot across the road** il a traversé la rue comme une flèche; **the bullet shot past his ears** la balle lui a sifflé aux oreilles; **the cat shot up the tree** le chat a grimpé à l'arbre à toute vitesse; **the pain went ~ing up his arm** la douleur au bras le lancinait, son bras l'élançait; (*in class etc*) **he has shot ahead in the last few weeks** il a fait des progrès énormes depuis quelques semaines
c (*Ftbl etc*) shooter, tirer; **to ~ at goal** shooter, faire un shoot; (*fig: in conversation*) ~!* vas-y!, dis ce que tu as à dire!, dis!*
d (*Bot*) bourgeonner, pousser
4 COMP ► **shoot-'em-up** N (*Cine*) film m de violence; (= *video game*) jeu m vidéo violent ► **shoot-out** N (= *fight*) fusillade f; (*Ftbl*) épreuve f des tirs au but ► **shoot-the-chute** N (*US*) toboggan m (*appareil de manutention*)

► **shoot away 1** VI **a** (*Mil etc* = *fire*) continuer à tirer, tirer sans arrêt **b** (= *move*) partir comme une flèche, s'enfuir à toutes jambes **2** VT SEP = **shoot off 2b**

► **shoot back** VI **a** (*Mil etc*) retourner le (or son *etc*) feu (**at** à) **b** (= *move*) retourner or rentrer or revenir en flèche

► **shoot down** VT SEP **a** [+ *plane*] abattre, descendre; (*Aviat*) **he was shot down in flames** son avion s'est abattu en flammes; (*fig*) **to ~ down in flames** [+ *project*] démolir; (*fig*) [+ *person*] descendre en flammes* **b** (= *kill*) [+ *person*] abattre, descendre*

► **shoot off 1** VI = **shoot away 1b 2** VT SEP **a** [+ *gun*] décharger, faire partir; (*fig*) **he's always ~ing his mouth off** il faut toujours qu'il l'ouvre (*subj*) le bec* or sa grande gueule*; **to ~ one's mouth off about sth** raconter des histoires or des bobards* au sujet de qch **b** **he had a leg shot off** il a eu une jambe emportée par un éclat d'obus, un éclat d'obus lui a emporté la jambe

► **shoot out 1** VI [*person, car etc*] sortir comme une flèche; [*flame, water*] jaillir **2** VT SEP **a** **to ~ out one's tongue** [*person*] tirer la langue; [*snake*] darder sa langue; **he shot out his arm and grabbed my stick** il a avancé brusquement le bras et a attrapé ma canne; **he was shot out of the car** il a été éjecté de la voiture **b** **to ~ it out** avoir un règlement de compte (à coups de revolvers or de fusils), s'expliquer à coups de revolvers or de fusils **3** **~-out** N → **shoot**

► **shoot up 1** VI **a** [*flame, water*] jaillir; [*rocket, price etc*] monter en flèche **b** (= *grow quickly*) [*tree, plant*] pousser vite; [*child*] bien pousser* **c** (*Drugs*) se shooter* **2** VT SEP (*: with gun*) flinguer*, tirer sur **3 shot up!** ADJ → **shot 3**

shooter [ˈʃuːtəʳ] N **a** (* = *gun*) flingue* m
b (*also* **target** ~) personne qui pratique le tir → **peashooter, sharpshooter, six, troubleshooter**

shooting [ˈʃuːtɪŋ] **1** N **a** (*NonC* = *shots*) coups mpl de feu; (*continuous*) fusillade f; **I heard some ~ over there** j'ai entendu des coups de feu par là-bas; **the ~ caused ten deaths** la fusillade a fait dix morts
b (= *act*) (*murder*) meurtre m or assassinat m (avec une arme à feu); (*execution*) fusillade f, exécution f; **the ~ of a policeman in the main street** le meurtre d'un agent de police abattu dans la grand-rue
c (*esp Brit* = *hunting*) chasse f; **rabbit ~** la chasse au lapin; **there's good ~ there** il y a une bonne chasse là-bas
d (*Cine*) [*of film, scene*] tournage m

2 ADJ [*pain*] lancinant
3 COMP ► **shooting brake†** N (*Brit Aut*) break m ► **shooting-down** N **the ~-down of the diplomat** l'attentat m à l'arme à feu contre le diplomate; **the ~-down of the plane (by the enemy)** la perte or la destruction de l'avion (abattu par l'ennemi) ► **shooting gallery** N tir m, stand m (de tir) ► **shooting incident** N **there were a few ~ incidents last night** la nuit dernière il y a eu quelques échanges de coups de feu ► **shooting iron†** N (*US*) flingue* m ► **shooting match** N (*Brit fig*) **the whole ~ match** tout le bataclan*, tout le tremblement* ► **shooting party** N partie f de chasse ► **shooting range** N tir m, stand m (de tir); **within ~ range** à portée (de tir) ► **shooting script** N (*Cine*) découpage m ► **shooting spree** N **to go on a ~ spree** être pris d'un accès or d'une crise de folie meurtrière ► **shooting star** N étoile f filante ► **shooting stick** N canne-siège f ► **shooting war** N lutte f armée

shop [ʃɒp] **1** N **a** (*esp Brit Comm*) magasin m; (*small*) boutique f; **wine ~** marchand m de vins; **at the butcher's ~** à la boucherie, chez le boucher; **"The Toy Shop"** « la Maison du Jouet »; **mobile** or **travelling ~** épicerie f *etc* roulante; **he's just gone (round) to the ~s** il est juste sorti faire des courses; **to set up ~** (*Comm*) ouvrir un commerce or un magasin, s'établir, s'installer; (*fig*) s'établir, s'installer; (*lit, fig*) **to shut up ~** fermer boutique; (*fig*) **you've come to the wrong ~*** tu te trompes d'adresse* (*fig*); (*fig*) **to talk ~** parler boutique or affaires or métier; (*fig*) **all over the ~*** (= *everywhere*) partout; (= *in confusion*) en désordre, bordélique* → **back, corner, grocer**
b (*Brit* = *shopping*) **to do one's weekly ~** faire ses courses de la semaine
c (= *workshop*) atelier m
d (= *part of factory*) atelier m; **assembly ~** atelier m de montage → **closed, machine**
2 VI **to ~ at Harrods** faire ses courses or ses achats chez Harrods; (*sign*) **"~ at Brown's"** « achetez chez Brown »; **to go ~ping** (*specific errands*) faire les courses; (*leisurely browsing*) faire les magasins, faire du shopping*; **I was ~ping for a winter coat** je cherchais un manteau d'hiver; **she's ~ping for a husband/a new sales director** elle cherche un mari/un nouveau directeur des ventes
3 VT (*esp Brit*: = *betray*) vendre, donner*
4 COMP (= *bought in shop*) [*cakes etc*] acheté dans le commerce ► **shop assistant** N (*Brit*) vendeur m, -euse f, employé(e) m(f) (de magasin) ► **the shop floor** N (*Brit Ind, lit*) l'atelier m; (*fig* = *workers*) les ouvriers mpl; **he works on the ~ floor** c'est un ouvrier ► **shop front** N (*Brit*) devanture f ► **shop steward** N (*Brit Ind*) délégué(e) m(f) syndical(e) ► **shop talk** N (= *jargon*) jargon m (de métier); **I'm getting tired of ~ talk** je commence à en avoir assez de parler affaires or boulot* ► **shop window** N vitrine f

► **shop around** VI (= *go around shops*) faire les magasins; (= *compare prices*) comparer les prix; **to ~ around for sth** faire les magasins or comparer les prix avant d'acheter qch; (*fig*) **it's worth ~ping around before you decide on a university** ça vaut la peine de comparer or se renseigner avant de choisir une université

shopaholic* [ʃɒpəˈhɒlɪk] N accro mf du shopping*

shopfitter [ˈʃɒpˌfɪtəʳ] N (*esp Brit*) décorateur m de magasin

shopgirl [ˈʃɒpgɜːl] N (*Brit*) vendeuse f

shopkeeper [ˈʃɒpˌkiːpəʳ] N commerçant(e) m(f), marchand(e) m(f); **small ~** petit commerçant m

shoplift [ˈʃɒplɪft] VTI voler à l'étalage

shoplifter [ˈʃɒpˌlɪftəʳ] N voleur m, -euse f à l'étalage

shoplifting [ˈʃɒpˌlɪftɪŋ] N (NonC) vol m à l'étalage

shopper [ˈʃɒpəʳ] N **ⓐ** (= person) personne f qui fait ses courses ; (= customer) client(e) m(f) **ⓑ** (= bag) sac m (à provisions), cabas m ; (on wheels) caddie® m

shopping [ˈʃɒpɪŋ] **1** N (NonC) **ⓐ** courses fpl ; **to do the/some ~** faire les/des courses ; **~ is very tiring** faire les courses est très fatigant ; **"open Thursdays for late evening ~"** « ouvert le jeudi en nocturne », « nocturne le jeudi » → **mall, window, shop ⓑ** (= goods) achats mpl **2** COMP [street, district] commerçant ► **shopping bag** N sac m (à provisions), cabas m ► **shopping basket** N panier m (à provisions) ► **shopping cart** N (US) = **shopping trolley** ► **shopping centre, shopping complex** N centre m commercial ► **shopping list** N liste f de(s) courses ; (fig) **a ~ list of requests/demands** une liste de requêtes/revendications ► **shopping mall** N centre m commercial ► **shopping precinct** N (Brit) zone f commerciale (piétonnière) ► **shopping spree** N **to go on a ~ spree** aller faire du shopping ► **shopping trip** N **to go on a ~ trip** partir faire les magasins or les boutiques ► **shopping trolley** N (Brit) caddie® m

shopsoiled [ˈʃɒpsɔɪld] ADJ (Brit) qui a fait l'étalage or la vitrine, défraîchi

shopwalker† [ˈʃɒpˌwɔːkəʳ] N (Brit) chef m de rayon

shopworn [ˈʃɒpwɔːn] ADJ (US) = **shopsoiled**

shore¹ [ʃɔːʳ] **1** N [of sea] rivage m, bord m ; [of lake] rive f, bord m ; (= coast) côte f, littoral m ; (= beach) plage f ; (fig liter) **these ~s** ces rives ; (esp Naut) **on ~** à terre ; (Naut) **to go on ~** débarquer **2** COMP ► **shore leave** N (Naut) permission f à terre ► **shore patrol** N (US Navy) détachement m de police militaire (de la Marine)

shore² [ʃɔːʳ] **1** N (for wall, tunnel) étai m, étançon m ; (for tree) étai m ; (for ship) accore m, étançon m **2** VT étayer, étançonner, accorer ► **shore up** VT SEP **ⓐ** = **shore² 2 ⓑ** (fig) consolider

shoreline [ˈʃɔːlaɪn] N littoral m

shoreward(s) [ˈʃɔːwəd(z)] ADJ, ADV (from sea) vers le rivage or la côte ; (from river, lake) vers la rive

shorn [ʃɔːn] VB ptp of **shear**

▼ **short** [ʃɔːt] **1** ADJ **ⓐ** (gen) court ; [person] (= not tall) petit, de petite taille ; [step, walk] petit ; [visit, message, conversation] court, bref ; [programme] court ; **the ~est route** le chemin le plus court ; **the ~est distance between two points** le plus court chemin d'un point à un autre ; **a ~ distance away** ◊ **a ~ way off** à peu de distance, à une faible distance ; **he's got rather ~ legs** [person] il a les jambes plutôt courtes ; [dog etc] il est plutôt court sur pattes ; **these trousers are ~ in the leg** ce pantalon est court de jambes ; (Ski) ~ **ski** ski m court → **7** ; **make the skirt ~er** raccourcis la jupe ; (fig) **the ~ answer is that he ...** tout simplement il ... ; **I'd like a ~ word** or **a few ~ words with you** j'aimerais vous dire un mot ; ~ **and to the point** bref et précis ; (hum) **that was ~ and sweet** ça n'a pas traîné (hum), ça a été du vite fait* ; (fig) **to have sb by the ~ hairs⁑** or ~ **and curlies⁑** tenir qn à la gorge or par les couilles⁑ ; (fig) **he got the ~ end of the stick** c'est lui qui en a pâti ; **to win by a ~ head** (Racing) gagner d'une courte tête ; (fig) gagner de justesse ; (fig) **to make ~ work of sth** ne pas mettre beaucoup de temps à faire qch ; (fig) **to make ~ work of sb*** envoyer promener qn* → **7** ; → **shrift, story, term ⓑ** [period, time] **a ~ time** or **while, ago** il y a peu de temps ; **in a ~ time** or **while** dans peu de temps, bientôt ; **time is getting ~** il ne reste

plus beaucoup de temps ; **the days are getting ~er** les jours raccourcissent ; **one ~ year of happiness** une petite or brève année de bonheur ; **to take a ~ holiday** prendre quelques jours de vacances ; (Ind) ~**er hours and better pay** une réduction du temps de travail et une augmentation de salaire ; **they want a ~er working week** ils veulent réduire la durée du travail hebdomadaire ; **at ~ notice** à bref délai ; (Ind) **to be on ~ time** ◊ **to work ~ time** être au chômage partiel → **7** ; **to put sb on ~ time** mettre qn au chômage partiel **ⓒ** (Ling) [vowel, syllable] bref **ⓓ** (= abbreviated) **"TV" is ~ for "television"** « TV » est l'abréviation de « television » ; **Fred is ~ for Frederick** Fred est le diminutif de Frederick ; **he's called Fred for ~** son diminutif est Fred **ⓔ** (= lacking) **they never went ~** ils n'ont jamais manqué du nécessaire ; **to be ~ of sugar** être à court de sucre, manquer de sucre ; **I'm a bit ~ this month*** je suis un peu fauché* or à court ce mois-ci ; **we're ~ of three** il nous en manque trois ; **we're not ~ of volunteers** nous ne manquons pas de volontaires ; **he's long on muscle but a bit ~ on brains*** il a beaucoup de muscle mais pas tellement de cervelle ; (hum) **he's one sandwich ~ of a picnic** or **several cards ~ of a full deck** il lui manque une case*, il a une case vide* ; **petrol is ~** or **in ~ supply at the moment** on manque d'essence en ce moment ; **to give sb ~ change** ne pas rendre la monnaie juste à qn, ne pas rendre assez à qn ; (deliberately) tricher en rendant la monnaie à qn ; **to give ~ weight** or **measure** ne pas donner le poids juste ; (deliberately) tricher sur le poids → **breath, commons ⓕ** (= curt) [reply, manner] brusque, sec (sèche f) ; **he was rather ~ with me** il m'a répondu (or parlé etc) assez sèchement or brusquement, il s'est montré assez sec or brusque à mon égard **ⓖ** (Fin) [bill] à courte échéance ; [loan] à court terme ; ~ **sale** vente f à découvert

2 ADV **ⓐ** **to cut ~** [+ speech, TV programme etc] couper court à, abréger ; [+ class, visit, holiday] écourter ; [+ person] couper la parole à ; **to take sb up ~** couper la parole à qn ; **to be taken** or **caught ~*** être pris d'un besoin pressant ; **the ball fell ~** le ballon n'est pas tombé assez loin → **fall** ; **to go ~ of sth** (= lack sth) manquer de qch ; (= deprive o.s. of sth) se priver de qch ; **we never went ~** nous n'avons jamais manqué du nécessaire ; **to run ~ of sth** se trouver à court de qch, venir à manquer de qch ; **supplies are running ~** les provisions s'épuisent or commencent à manquer ; **the car stopped ~ of the house** la voiture s'est arrêtée avant (d'arriver au niveau de) la maison ; (fig) **I'd stop ~ of murder** je n'irais pas jusqu'au meurtre **ⓑ** ~ **of** (= less than) moins de, en dessous de ; (= except) sauf ; (= before) avant ; **£10 ~ of what they needed** 10 livres de moins que ce dont ils avaient besoin ; **it's well ~ of the truth** c'est bien en deçà de la vérité ; **a week ~ of their arrival/his birthday** etc une semaine avant leur arrivée/son anniversaire etc ; **we're three ~** il nous en manque trois ; **I'm £2 ~** il me manque 2 livres ; **not far ~ of £100** pas loin de 100 livres, presque 100 livres ; **we are £2,000 ~ of our target** il nous manque encore 2 000 livres pour atteindre notre objectif ; **he fell down 10 metres ~ of the winning post** il est tombé à 10 mètres du poteau d'arrivée ; **it's little ~ of suicide** c'est presque un suicide, peu s'en faut que ce ne soit un suicide ; **it's little ~ of folly** cela frise la folie ; **it's nothing ~ of robbery** c'est du vol ni plus ni moins ; **nothing ~ of a revolution will satisfy them** seule une révolution saura les satisfaire, il ne leur faudra rien moins qu'une révolution pour les satisfaire ; **I don't see what you can do ~ of asking him yourself** je ne vois pas ce que vous pouvez faire à moins de or si ce

n'est lui demander vous-même ; **he did everything ~ of asking her to marry him** il a tout fait sauf or hormis lui demander de l'épouser → **stop, bring up, sell ⓒ** (St Ex) **to sell ~** vendre à découvert **3** N **ⓐ** **in ~** (enfin) bref **ⓑ** * (Cine) court métrage m ; (Elec) court-circuit m → **long¹ ⓒ** (Brit = drink) alcool m fort **4** **shorts** NPL (= garment: also **pair of ~s**) (gen) short m ; [of football etc] culotte f ; (US = men's underwear) caleçon m **5** VT (Elec) court-circuiter **6** VI (Elec) se mettre en court-circuit **7** COMP ► **short-acting** ADJ [drug] à effet rapide ► **short-arse**⁑ N (Brit) demi-portion* f (pej) ; **to be a ~arse** être bas du cul⁑ ► **short back-and-sides** N coupe très courte derrière et sur les côtés ► **short-change** VT **to ~-change sb** (lit: in shop etc) ne pas rendre assez à qn ; (fig) rouler* qn ► **short-circuit** N (Elec) court-circuit m ♦ VT (Elec, fig = bypass) court-circuiter ; (fig = cause to fail) faire capoter ♦ VI se mettre en court-circuit ► **short covering** N (St Ex) rachat m pour couvrir un découvert ► **short cut** N (lit, fig) raccourci m ; **I took a ~ cut through the fields** j'ai pris un raccourci or j'ai coupé à travers champs ; **you'll have to do it all with no ~ cuts** il faudra que tu fasses tout sans rien omettre ► **short-dated** ADJ (Fin) à courte échéance ► **short division** N (Math) division f simple ► **short-haired** ADJ [person] aux cheveux courts ; [animal] à poil ras ► **short-handed** ADJ à court de personnel or de main-d'œuvre ► **short-haul** N [of truck] camionnage m à or sur courte distance ; [of plane] vol m à or sur courte distance ♦ ADJ à courte distance ► **short-life** ADJ (Brit Comm) [food] à durée de conservation limitée ; [garment] qui n'est pas fait pour durer ► **short-list** (Brit) N liste f de(s) candidats sélectionnés ♦ VT mettre sur la liste de(s) candidats sélectionnés, présélectionner ; **he was ~-listed for the post of ...** il était parmi les candidats sélectionnés pour le poste de ... ► **short-lived** ADJ [animal] à la vie éphémère ; [happiness] de courte durée ► **short-order** ADJ (US) ~-**order cook** cuisinier m, -ière f préparant des plats rapides ; ~-**order service** service m de plats rapides ► **short pastry** N = **shortcrust pastry** ► **short-range** ADJ [shot, gun] de or à courte portée ; [aircraft] à court rayon d'action ; (fig) [plan, weather forecast] à court terme ► **short seller** N (St Ex) vendeur m à découvert ► **short sharp shock** N (Brit = punishment) sanction f sévère (mais de courte durée) ; (fig) électrochoc m ► **short sharp shock treatment** N (Brit) traitement m brutal (visant à dissuader les jeunes délinquants de récidiver) ► **short sight** N myopie f ► **short-sighted** ADJ (lit) myope ; (fig) [person] myope, qui manque de perspicacité ; [policy, measure] qui manque de vision ► **short-sightedness** N (lit) myopie f ; (fig) [of person] myopie f intellectuelle, manque m de perspicacité ; [of policy, measure] manque m de vision ► **short ski method** N ski m évolutif ► **short-sleeved** ADJ à manches courtes ► **short-staffed** ADJ **to be ~-staffed** manquer de personnel, souffrir d'une pénurie de personnel ► **short-stay** ADJ [parking, visa] de courte durée ; [hospital ward] pour séjours de courte durée ► **short-stay car park** N parc m de stationnement de courte durée ► **short story** N nouvelle f ; ~-**story writer** nouvelliste mf ► **short-tempered** ADJ **to be ~-tempered** (in general) être coléreux, s'emporter facilement ; (= in a bad temper) être de mauvaise humeur ► **short-term** ADJ [parking etc] de courte durée ; [loan, planning, solution] à court terme ; ~-**term car park** = **short-stay car park** ► **short-termism** N (pej) vision f à court terme ► **short-time working** N (Ind) chômage m partiel ► **short trou-**

sers NPL culottes *fpl* courtes (*de petit garçon*)
► **short-winded** ADJ qui manque de souffle, au souffle court

shortage ['ʃɔːtɪdʒ] N [*of corn, coal, energy, cash*] manque *m*, pénurie *f*; [*of resources*] manque *m*, insuffisance *f*; **in times of ~** en période de pénurie; **there was no ~ of water** on ne manquait pas d'eau; **owing to the ~ of staff** à cause du manque de personnel; **the food ~** la pénurie de vivres, la disette; **the housing ~** la crise du logement

shortbread ['ʃɔːtbred] N (*Culin*) sablé *m*

shortcake ['ʃɔːtkeɪk] N (*US*) **strawberry** *etc* **~** tarte *f* sablée aux fraises *etc*

shortcoming ['ʃɔːt,kʌmɪŋ] N défaut *m*

shortcrust pastry [,ʃɔːtkrʌst'peɪstrɪ] N (*Culin*) pâte *f* brisée

shorten ['ʃɔːtn] **1** VT [+ *skirt, rope*] raccourcir; [+ *visit, holiday, journey*] écourter; [+ *life*] abréger; [+ *book, programme, letter*] raccourcir, abréger; [+ *syllabus*] alléger; [+ *distance, time*] réduire **2** VI [*days etc*] raccourcir; **the odds are ~ing** (*lit*) la cote baisse; (*fig*) les chances augmentent

shortening ['ʃɔːtnɪŋ] N (*NonC*) **a** (= *action*) [*of skirt, rope, days*] raccourcissement *m*; [*of book, programme, letter*] raccourcissement *m*, abrègement *m*; [*of life, visit, holiday, journey*] abrègement *m*; [*of syllabus*] allègement *m*; [*of distance, time*] réduction *f* **b** (*esp US Culin*) matière *f* grasse

shortfall ['ʃɔːtfɔːl] N (*in payments, profits, savings*) montant *m* insuffisant (**in** de); (*in numbers*) nombre *m* insuffisant (**in** de); **in earnings** manque *m* à gagner; **there is a ~ of £5,000** il manque 5000 livres; **the ~ of £5,000** les 5000 livres qui manquent; **there is a ~ of 200 in the registrations for this course** il manque 200 inscriptions à ce cours

shorthand ['ʃɔːthænd] **1** N **a** (*lit*) sténographie *f*; **to take sth down in ~** prendre qch en sténo, sténographier qch **b** (*fig*) (= *abbreviation*) abréviation *f*; (= *code of behaviour, coded message*) code *m*; **"motivation essential": that's ~ for "you'll be working 24 hours a day"** «motivation indispensable»: c'est une façon de dire que tu vas travailler 24 heures sur 24 **2** ADJ (*fig* = *abbreviated*) [*term, version, formula*] abrégé **3** COMP ► **shorthand notebook** N carnet *m* de sténo ► **shorthand notes** NPL notes *fpl* en *or* de sténo ► **shorthand typing** N sténodactylo *f* ► **shorthand typist** N sténodactylo *mf* ► **shorthand writer** N sténo(graphe) *mf*

shorthorn ['ʃɔːthɔːn] N (*Zool*) race *f* shorthorn (*race bovine*)

shortie ['ʃɔːtɪ] N = **shorty**

shortish ['ʃɔːtɪʃ] ADJ [*person*] assez petit; [*hair, skirt*] plutôt court; [*period*] assez bref

shortly ['ʃɔːtlɪ] ADV **a** (= *soon*) [*go, visit*] bientôt; (= *in a few days*) prochainement; **details will be released ~** des précisions seront communiquées prochainement; **more of that ~** nous reviendrons sur ce sujet d'ici peu; **~ before/after sth** peu avant/après qch; **~ after seven** peu après sept heures; **~ before half past two** peu avant deux heures et demie; **~ afterwards** peu (de temps) après **b** (= *curtly*) [*say, speak*] sèchement, brusquement **c** (= *concisely*) [*explain*] brièvement

shortness ['ʃɔːtnɪs] N **a** [*of stick, skirt, hair, grass, arms*] peu *m or* manque *m* de longueur; [*of person*] petite taille *f*, petitesse *f*; [*of visit, message, conversation, programme*] brièveté *f*, courte durée *f*; [*of vowel, syllable*] brièvété *f*; **because of its ~** parce que c'est (*or* c'était) si court **b** (= *curtness*) brusquerie *f*, sécheresse *f*

shortsheet ['ʃɔːtʃiːt] VT (*US*) [+ *bed*] mettre en portefeuille

shortstop ['ʃɔːtstɒp] N (*Baseball*) bloqueur *m*

shortwave ['ʃɔːtweɪv] (*Rad*) **1** N ondes *fpl*

courtes **2** ADJ [*radio*] à ondes courtes; [*transmission*] sur ondes courtes

shorty* ['ʃɔːtɪ] N courtaud(e) *m(f)*; **hey ~!** hé toi le *or* la petit(e)!

Shostakovich [,ʃɒstə'kəʊvɪtʃ] N Chostakovitch *m*

shot [ʃɒt] **1** N **a** (*from gun*) coup *m* (de feu); (= *bullet*) balle *f*; (*NonC: also* **lead ~**) plomb *m*; **not a single ~ was fired** pas un seul coup de feu n'a été tiré; **to take** *or* **have** *or* **fire a ~ at sb/sth** tirer sur qn/qch; **good ~!** (c'était) bien visé! → **1c**; (*lit, fig*) **a ~ across the bows** un coup de semonce; **at the first ~** du premier coup; **the first ~ killed him** la première balle l'a tué; **I've got four ~s left** il me reste quatre coups *or* balles; **a round of five ~s** une salve de cinq coups; **he is a good/bad ~** il est bon/ mauvais tireur; (*fig*) **to make a ~ in the dark** tenter le coup, deviner à tout hasard; (*fig*) **that was just a ~ in the dark** c'était dit à tout hasard; **he was off like a ~** il est parti comme une flèche; **he agreed like a ~*** il y a consenti sans hésiter *or* avec empressement; **would you go? — like a ~!*** est-ce que tu irais? — sans hésiter *or* et comment!*; **he's only got one ~ (left) in his locker** c'est sa dernière chance *or* cartouche* → **crack**, **long¹**, **Parthian**, **parting**
b (*Space*) lancement *m* → **moon**, **space**
c (*Sport*) (*Ftbl, Hockey*) tir *m*; (*Golf, Tennis etc*) coup *m*; (= *throw*) lancer *m*; **good ~!** bien joué!; **a ~ at goal** un shoot, un tir au but; (*Sport*) **to put the ~** lancer le poids; **the biggest by a long ~** de loin le plus grand; (*fig*) **to call the ~s*** mener la barque
d (= *attempt*) essai *m*; (= *guess*) hypothèse *f*; (= *turn to play*) tour *m*; **to have a ~ at (doing) sth** essayer de faire qch; **to give something one's best ~*** mettre le paquet*, faire de son mieux; **have a ~ at it!** (= *try it*) tentez le coup!; (= *guess*) devinez!, dites voir!*
e (*Phot*) photo(graphie) *f*; (*Cine*) prise *f* de vue(s), plan *m*
f (= *injection*) piqûre *f* (**against** contre); (*fig*) **a ~ in the arm** un coup de fouet, un stimulant
g [*of whisky etc*] coup *m*; **put a ~ of gin in it** ajoute donc un peu *or* une goutte de gin

2 ADJ **a** (= *iridescent*) [*silk*] changeant
b (= *suffused*) **black hair ~ (through) with silver** des cheveux noirs striés d'argent; **his work is ~ through with humour** son œuvre est imprégnée d'humour
c (* = *rid*) **~ of sb/sth** débarrassé de qn/qch; **to get ~ of sb/sth** se débarrasser de qn/qch
d (* = *destroyed: also* **~ to pieces**) [*object, machine*] bousillé*; **my nerves are totally ~** j'ai les nerfs en capilotade; **her confidence was ~ to pieces** sa confiance était totalement anéantie; **to get/be ~ of ...** se débarrasser/être débarrassé de ...; **to be (all) ~ up‡** (= *exhausted*) être exténué *or* sur les rotules‡

3 COMP ► **shot angle** N (*Cine, Phot*) angle *m* de prise de vue(s) ► **shot put** N (*Sport*) lancer *m* du poids ► **shot putter** N lanceur *m*, -euse *f* de poids

shotgun ['ʃɒtgʌn] **1** N fusil *m* de chasse; (*US*) **to ride ~** voyager comme passager, accompagner **2** COMP ► **shotgun marriage**, **shotgun wedding** N (*fig*) régularisation *f* (précipitée), mariage *m* forcé

should [ʃʊd] MODAL AUX VB *cond of* **shall** (*neg* **should not**, *abbr* **shouldn't**) **a** (*indicating obligation, advisability, desirability*) **I ~ go and see her** je devrais aller la voir, il faudrait que j'aille la voir; **~ I go too? — yes you ~** devrais-je y aller aussi? — oui vous devriez *or* ça vaudrait mieux; **he thought he ~ tell you** il a pensé qu'il ferait bien de vous le dire *or* qu'il devrait vous le dire; (*frm*) **you ~ know that we have spoken to him** il faut que vous sachiez que nous lui avons parlé; **you ~ have been a teacher** vous auriez dû être professeur; **~n't you go and see her?** est-ce que

vous ne devriez pas aller la voir?, est-ce que vous ne feriez pas bien d'aller la voir?; **everything is as it ~ be** tout est comme il se doit, tout est en ordre; **... which is as it ~ be ...** comme il se doit; **how ~ I know?** comment voulez-vous que je (le) sache?
b (*indicating probability*) **he ~ win the race** il devrait gagner la course, il va probablement gagner la course; **he ~ have got there by now I expect** je pense qu'il est arrivé, il a dû arriver à l'heure qu'il est; **that ~ be Marie at the door now** ça doit être Marie (qui frappe *or* qui sonne); **this ~ do the trick*** ça devrait faire l'affaire; **why ~ he suspect me?** pourquoi me soupçonnerait-il?
c (*often used to form cond tense in 1st pers*) **I ~** *or* **I'd go if he invited me** s'il m'invitait, j'irais; **we ~ have come if we had known** si nous avions su, nous serions venus; **will you come? — I ~ like to** est-ce que vous viendrez? — j'aimerais bien; **I ~n't be surprised if he comes** *or* **came** *or* **were to come** ça ne m'étonnerait pas qu'il vienne; **I ~ think there were about 40** (je pense qu')il devait y en avoir environ 40; **was it a good film? — I ~ think it was!** est-ce que c'était un bon film? — je pense bien *or* et comment!*; **he's coming to apologize — I ~ think so too!** il vient présenter ses excuses — j'espère bien!; **I ~ hope not!** il ne manquerait plus que ça!*; **I ~ say so!** et comment!*
d (*subj uses*) (*frm*) **it is necessary that he ~ be told** il faut qu'on le lui dise; (*frm*) **lest he ~ change his mind** de crainte qu'il ne change (*subj*) d'avis; **it is surprising that he ~ be so young** c'est étonnant qu'il soit si jeune; **who ~ come in but Paul!** et devinez qui est entré? Paul!

shoulder ['ʃəʊldə*] **1** N **a** (*Anat, Culin, Dress etc*) épaule *f*; **to have broad ~s** (*lit*) être large d'épaules *or* de carrure; (*fig*) avoir les reins solides (*fig*); **the ~s are too wide ◊ it's too wide across the ~s** c'est trop large d'épaules *or* de carrure; **put my jacket round your ~s** mets *or* jette ma veste sur tes épaules *or* sur ton dos; (*lit, fig*) **to cry** *or* **weep on sb's ~** pleurer sur l'épaule de qn; **she had her bag on** *or* **over one ~** elle portait son sac à l'épaule; **they stood ~ to ~** (*lit*) ils étaient coude à coude *or* côte à côte; ils se serraient les coudes; (*fig*) **all the responsibilities had fallen on his ~s** toutes les responsabilités étaient retombées sur lui *or* sur ses épaules; (*fig*) **to put** *or* **set one's ~ to the wheel** s'atteler à la tâche → **cold, head, look, rub, straighten**
b [*of road*] accotement *m*, bas-côté *m*; [*of hill*] contrefort *m*, épaulement *m*; (*Climbing*) épaule *f* → **hard**

2 VT **a** [+ *load, case*] charger sur son épaule; [+ *child etc*] hisser sur ses épaules; (*fig*) [+ *responsibility*] endosser; [+ *task*] se charger de; (*Mil*) **to ~ arms** porter l'arme; **~ arms!** portez arme!
b **to ~ sb aside** *or* **out of the way** écarter qn d'un coup d'épaule; **to ~ one's way through the crowd** se frayer un chemin à travers *or* dans la foule à coups d'épaules

3 COMP ► **shoulder bag** N sac *m* à bandoulière ► **shoulder blade** N omoplate *f*; **it hit him between the ~ blades** cela l'a atteint entre les épaules ► **shoulder-high** ADJ [*grass, hedge, wall*] à hauteur d'épaule; **to carry sb ~-high** porter qn en triomphe ► **shoulder holster** N étui *m* de revolver (*porté à l'épaule*) ► **shoulder joint** N (*Anat*) articulation *f* de l'épaule ► **shoulder-length hair** N (*NonC*) cheveux *mpl* mi-longs *or* jusqu'aux épaules ► **shoulder pad** N épaulette *f* (*rembourrage d'épaules de vêtement*) ► **shoulder strap** N [*of garment*] bretelle *f*; [*of bag*] bandoulière *f*; (*Mil*) patte *f* d'épaule

shouldn't ['ʃʊdnt] = **should not**; → **should**
should've ['ʃʊdv] = **should have**; → **should**

shout [ʃaʊt] **1** N cri *m*; **a ~ of joy** un cri de joie; **there were ~s of applause/protest/laughter** des acclamations/des protestations bruyantes/des éclats de rire ont retenti; **he gave a ~ of laughter** il a éclaté de rire; **to give sb a ~** appeler qn; **~s of "long live the queen" could be heard** on entendait crier « vive la reine »; (*Brit* = round of drinks) **it's my ~** c'est ma tournée*

2 VT [+ *order, slogan*] crier; **"no" he ~ed** « non » cria-t-il; **to ~ o.s. hoarse** s'enrouer à force de crier → **head**

3 VI **a** crier, pousser des cris; **stop ~ing, I'm not deaf!** ne crie pas comme ça, je ne suis pas sourd!; **to ~ for joy** crier de joie, pousser des cris de joie; **to ~ with laughter** éclater de rire; **to ~ for help** crier or appeler au secours; **she ~ed for Jane to come** elle a appelé Jane en criant or à grands cris; **she ~ed for someone to come and help her** elle a appelé pour qu'on vienne l'aider; **he ~ed to or at me to throw him the rope** il m'a crié de lui lancer la corde; (*fig*) **it's nothing to ~ about** ça n'a rien d'extraordinaire, il n'y a pas de quoi en faire un plat*

b (= *scold etc*) **to ~ at sb** engueuler* qn, crier après* qn

▶ **shout after** VT FUS [+ *person*] crier à

▶ **shout down** VT SEP **a** (= boo, express disagreement) [+ *speaker*] huer; **they ~ed down the proposal** ils ont rejeté la proposition avec de hauts cris **b** (= shout loudly) **to ~ the place** or **house down** crier comme un damné or un sourd; **I thought she was going to ~ the place down** elle criait tellement que j'ai crû que tout allait s'écrouler

▶ **shout out** **1** VI (*gen*) pousser un cri; **to ~ out to sb** interpeller qn **2** VT SEP [+ *order*] crier; [+ *slogan*] crier, lancer

shouting [ˈʃaʊtɪŋ] **1** N (*NonC*) cris *mpl*, clameur *f*; (= noise of quarrelling) éclats *mpl* de voix; (*fig*) **it's all over bar the ~** l'important est fait (il ne reste plus que les détails) **2** COMP ▶ **shouting match*** N engueulade* *f*

shove [ʃʌv] **1** N poussée *f*; **to give sb/sth a ~** pousser qn/qch; **give it a good ~** poussez-le un bon coup

2 VT **a** (= push) pousser; (with effort) pousser avec peine or effort; (= thrust) [+ *stick, finger etc*] enfoncer (**into** dans, **between** entre); [+ *rag*] fourrer (**into** dans); (= jostle) bousculer; **to ~ sth in/out/down** etc faire entrer/sortir/descendre etc qch en le poussant; **to ~ sth/sb aside** pousser qn/qch de côté, écarter qch/qn (d'un geste); **to ~ sth into a drawer/one's pocket** fourrer qch dans un tiroir/sa poche; **stop shoving me!** arrêtez de me pousser or bousculer!; **to ~ sb into a room** pousser qn dans une pièce; **to ~ sb against a wall** pousser or presser qn contre un mur; **to ~ sb off the pavement** pousser qn du trottoir; (by jostling) obliger qn à descendre du trottoir (en le bousculant); **to ~ sb/sth out of the way** écarter qn/qch en le poussant, pousser qn/qch pour l'écarter; **he ~d the box under the table** (= moved) il a poussé or fourré la boîte sous la table; (= hid) il a vite caché la boîte sous la table; **they ~d the car off the road** ils ont poussé la voiture sur le bas-côté; **she ~d the books off the table** elle a poussé or balayé les livres de dessus la table; **he ~d his finger into my eye** il m'a mis le doigt dans l'œil; **he ~d his head through the window** il a mis or passé la tête par la fenêtre; **he ~d the book into my hand** il m'a fourré le livre dans la main; **to ~ a door open** ouvrir une porte en la poussant or d'une poussée, pousser une porte (pour l'ouvrir); **to ~ one's way through the crowd** se frayer un chemin dans or à travers la foule, s'ouvrir un passage dans la foule en poussant

b (* = put) fourrer*, mettre

3 VI pousser; **stop shoving!** arrêtez de pousser!, ne bousculez pas!; **he ~d (his way) past me** il m'a dépassé en me bousculant; **two men ~d (their way) past** deux hommes sont passés en jouant des coudes or en bousculant les gens; **he ~d (his way) through the crowd** il s'est frayé un chemin dans or à travers la foule

4 COMP ▶ **shove-ha'penny** N (*Brit*) jeu *m* de palet de table

▶ **shove about, shove around** VT SEP (lit) [+ *object*] pousser çà et là or dans tous les sens; [+ *person*] bousculer; (*fig* = treat high-handedly) en prendre à son aise avec

▶ **shove away** VT SEP [+ *person, object*] repousser

▶ **shove back** VT SEP (= push back) [+ *person, chair*] repousser; (= replace) remettre (à sa place); (into pocket etc) fourrer de nouveau, remettre

▶ **shove down*** VT SEP [+ *object*] poser; **he ~d down a few notes before he forgot** il a griffonné or gribouillé quelques notes pour ne pas oublier

▶ **shove off** **1** VI (*Naut*) pousser au large; (* = leave) filer* le camp*, filer* **2** VT SEP [+ *boat*] pousser au large, déborder

▶ **shove on*** VT SEP **a** [+ *one's coat etc*] enfiler; [+ *hat*] enfoncer **b** **~ on another record** mets donc un autre disque

▶ **shove out** VT SEP [+ *boat*] pousser au large, déborder; [+ *person*] mettre à la porte

▶ **shove over** **1** VI (* = move over) se pousser **2** VT SEP **a** (= knock over) [+ *chair etc*] renverser; [+ *person*] faire tomber (par terre) **b** (over cliff etc) pousser **c** **it over to me*** passe-le-moi

▶ **shove up** VI = shove over 1

shovel [ˈʃʌvl] **1** N pelle *f*; (mechanical) pelleteuse *f*, pelle *f* mécanique **2** VT [+ *coal, grain*] pelleter; (also **~ out**) [+ *snow, mud*] enlever à la pelle; **to ~ earth into a pile** pelleter la terre pour en faire un tas; **he ~led the food into his mouth*** il fourrait* or enfournait* la nourriture dans sa bouche

▶ **shovel up** VT SEP [+ *sth spilt etc*] ramasser avec une pelle or à la pelle; [+ *snow*] enlever à la pelle

shoveler [ˈʃʌvələr] N (canard *m*) souchet *m*

shovelful [ˈʃʌvlfʊl] N pelletée *f*

show [ʃəʊ] (vb: pret **showed**, ptp **shown** or **showed**) **1** N **a** [of hatred etc] manifestation *f*, démonstration *f*; [of affection etc] démonstration *f*, témoignage *m*; (= semblance) apparence *f*, semblant *m*; (= ostentation) parade *f*; **there were some fine pieces on ~** quelques beaux objets étaient exposés; **an impressive ~ of strength** un impressionnant étalage de force, une impressionnante démonstration de force; **the dahlias make** or **are a splendid ~** les dahlias sont splendides (à voir) or offrent un spectacle splendide; **they make a great ~ of their wealth** ils font parade or étalage de leur richesse; **with a ~ of emotion** en affectant l'émotion, en affectant d'être ému; **they made a ~ of resistance** ils ont fait semblant de résister, ils ont offert un simulacre de résistance; **to make a ~ of doing** faire semblant or mine de (faire); **just for ~** pour l'effet

b (= exhibition) (Agr, Art, Tech etc) exposition *f*; (Comm) foire *f*; (= contest: Agr) concours *m*; **flower ~** floralies *fpl*; (smaller) exposition *f* de fleurs; **dress ~** défilé *m* de couture; **he's holding his first London ~** [artist, sculptor etc] il expose à Londres pour la première fois; **the Boat Show** le Salon de la Navigation → **dogshow, fashion, motor**

c (*Theat* etc) spectacle *m*; (= variety show) show *m*; **there are several good ~s on in London** on donne plusieurs bons spectacles à Londres en ce moment; **I often go to a ~** je vais souvent au spectacle; **the last ~ starts at 9** (*Theat*) la dernière représentation commence à 21 heures; (*Cine*) la dernière séance commence à 21 heures; **there is no ~ on Sundays** (*Theat*) il n'y a pas de représentation le dimanche; (*Cine*) il n'y a pas de séance le dimanche; **on with the ~!** que la représentation commence (subj) or continue (subj)!; (*Theat, fig*) **the ~ must go on** il faut continuer malgré tout; (*fig*) **let's get this ~ on the road*** il faut faire démarrer* tout ça, passons à l'action; **this is Paul's ~*** c'est Paul qui commande ici; **to run the ~*** tenir les rênes; (*fig*) **he runs the whole ~*** c'est lui qui commande or a tout en main; **to give the ~ away*** vendre la mèche*; (*fig*) **to put up a good ~** faire bonne figure, bien se défendre*; **to make a poor ~** faire triste or piètre figure; **it's a poor ~*** c'est lamentable, il n'y a pas de quoi être fier; **it's a poor ~* that ...** il est malheureux que ... (+ subj); (esp *Brit*) **good ~!*** bravo! → **steal**

2 VT **a** (= display, make visible) montrer, faire voir; [+ *ticket, passport*] montrer, présenter; (= exhibit) [+ *goods for sale, picture, dog*] exposer; **~ it me!** faites voir!, montrez-le-moi!; **we're going to ~ (you) some slides** nous allons (vous) passer or projeter quelques diapositives; **they ~ a film during the flight** on passe un film or il y a une projection de cinéma pendant le vol; **what is ~ing at that cinema/at the Odeon** qu'est-ce qu'on donne or qu'est-ce qui passe dans ce cinéma/à l'Odéon?; **the film was first ~n in 1974** ce film est sorti en 1974; **it has been ~n on television** c'est passé à la télévision; (in shop) **what can I ~ you?** que puis-je vous montrer?, que désirez-vous voir?; **as ~n by the graph** comme le montre or l'indique le graphique; **as ~n in the illustration on page 4** voir l'illustration page 4; (*fig*) **there's nothing to ~ for it** on ne le dirait pas, ça ne se voit or ne se remarque pas; **he has nothing to ~ for it** il n'en a rien tiré, ça ne lui a rien donné or apporté; **he has nothing to ~ for all the effort he has put into it** les efforts qu'il y a consacrés n'ont rien donné; **I ought to ~ myself** or **my face at Paul's party** il faudrait que je fasse acte de présence à la soirée de Paul; **he daren't ~ himself** or **his face there again** il n'ose plus s'y montrer or montrer son nez là-bas*; (*fig*) **to ~ one's hand** or **cards** dévoiler ses intentions, abattre son jeu or ses cartes; (*fig*) **to ~ a clean pair of heels** se sauver à toutes jambes; (*Brit fig*) **~ a leg!*** lève-toi!, debout!; (lit, *fig*) **to ~ one's teeth** montrer les dents; (*fig*) **to ~ sb the door** mettre qn à la porte; (*fig*) **to ~ the flag** être là pour le principe, faire acte de présence

b (= indicate) [dial, clock etc] indiquer, marquer; (*gen*) montrer, indiquer; **what time does your watch ~?** quelle heure est-il à votre montre?; (*Comm, Fin*) **to ~ a loss/profit** indiquer une perte/un bénéfice; **the figures ~ a rise over last year's sales** les chiffres montrent or indiquent que les ventes ont augmenté par rapport à l'année dernière; **the roads are ~n in red** les routes sont marquées en rouge

c (= demonstrate) montrer, faire voir; (= reveal) montrer, laisser voir; (= explain) montrer, expliquer; (= prove) prouver; [+ *one's intelligence, kindness, courage, tact*] montrer, faire preuve de; [+ *one's interest, enthusiasm, surprise, agreement*] montrer, manifester; [+ *one's approval*] montrer, indiquer; [+ *one's gratitude, respect*] témoigner; **to ~ loyalty** se montrer loyal (**to sb** envers qn); **that dress ~s her bra** cette robe laisse voir son soutien-gorge; **this skirt ~s the dirt** cette jupe est salissante; **it's ~ing signs of wear** cela porte des signes d'usure; **he was ~ing signs of tiredness** il montrait des signes de fatigue; **it ~ed signs of having been used** il était visible qu'on s'en était servi, manifestement on s'en était servi; **to ~ fight** se montrer combatif; **her choice of clothes ~s good taste** sa façon de s'habiller témoigne de son bon goût; **he ~ed that he was angry** il a manifesté or laissé voir sa colère; **he's beginning to ~ his age** il commence à faire son âge; **this ~s great intelligence** cela révèle or dénote beaucoup d'intelligence; **he ~ed himself (to be) a coward** il s'est montré or révélé lâche; **to ~ sth to be true** démontrer la vérité de qch, montrer que qch est vrai; **it all goes to ~ that ...** tout cela montre or prouve bien que ...; **it only** or **just goes to ~!*** tu m'en diras tant!*, c'est bien ça la vie!; **I ~ed him that it was impossible** je lui ai prouvé or démontré que c'était impossible; **he ~ed me how it works** il m'a montré or il m'a fait voir comment cela fonctionne; (fig) **I'll ~ him!*** je lui apprendrai!; **to ~ sb the way** montrer or indiquer le chemin à qn; **I'll ~ you the way** suivez-moi (je vais vous montrer le chemin) → willing

[d] (= guide, conduct) **to ~ sb into the room** faire entrer qn dans la pièce; **to ~ sb to his seat** placer qn; **to ~ sb to the door** reconduire qn jusqu'à la porte; **to ~ sb over** or **round a house** faire visiter une maison à qn

[3] VI [a] [emotion] être visible; [stain, scar] se voir; [underskirt etc] dépasser; **it doesn't ~** cela ne se voit pas, on ne dirait pas; **don't worry, it won't ~** ne t'inquiète pas, ça ne se verra pas; **his fear ~ed on his face** la peur se lisait sur son visage

[b] (esp US = arrive) = **show up 1b**

[4] COMP ► **show bill** N (Theat) affiche f de spectacle ► **show biz*** N le monde du spectacle, le showbiz* ► **show business** N le monde du spectacle, le show business ► **show flat** N (Brit) appartement m témoin ► **show girl** N girl f ► **show home, show house** N (Brit) maison f témoin ► **show jumping** N (NonC) concours m hippique, jumping m ► **show-me attitude*** N (US) scepticisme m ► **the Show-Me State** N (US) le Missouri ► **show-off** N frimeur m, -euse f, m'as-tu-vu(e)* m(f) pl inv ► **show of hands** N vote m à main levée; **to vote by ~ of hands** voter à main levée ► **show-stopper** N **it was a ~-stopper*** c'était le clou* du spectacle ► **show-stopping*** ADJ sensationnel* ► **show trial** N (Jur) procès pour l'exemple ► **show window** N (lit, fig) vitrine f

►**show about, show around** VT SEP faire visiter les lieux mpl (or la ville or la maison etc) à

►**show in** VT SEP [+ visitor etc] faire entrer

►**show off** [1] VI (gen) frimer*, poser (pour la galerie); [child] chercher à se rendre intéressant, faire l'intéressant; **she's always ~ing off** c'est une frimeuse* or une poseuse; **stop ~ing off** (gen) arrête de frimer*; (showing off knowledge) arrête d'étaler ta science* [2] VT SEP [a] [+ sb's beauty, complexion etc] faire valoir, mettre en valeur [b] (pej) [+ one's wealth, knowledge etc] faire étalage de, étaler; **he wanted to ~ off his new car** il voulait faire admirer sa nouvelle voiture [3] **~-off** N → **show** [4] **~ing-off** N → **showing**

►**show out** VT SEP [+ visitor etc] accompagner or reconduire (jusqu'à la porte)

►**show round** VT SEP = **show about, show around**

►**show through** VI (= be visible) se voir au travers

►**show up** [1] VI [a] (= stand out) [feature] ressortir; [mistake] être visible or manifeste; [stain] se voir (nettement); **the tower ~ed up clearly against the sky** la tour se détachait nettement sur le ciel [b] (* = arrive, appear) se pointer*, s'amener* [2] VT SEP [a] [+ visitor etc] faire monter [+ fraud, impostor] démasquer, dénoncer; [+ flaw, defect] faire ressortir [c] (= embarrass) faire honte à (en public)

showboat ['ʃəʊbəʊt] [1] N (US) (lit) bateau-théâtre m; (‡ fig = person) m'as-tu-vu(e)* m(f) pl inv [2] VI crâner*, en mettre plein la vue

showcase ['ʃəʊkeɪs] [1] N (lit, fig) vitrine f [2] COMP ► **showcase project** N opération f de prestige

showdown ['ʃəʊdaʊn] N épreuve f de force

---

shower ['ʃaʊə^r] [1] N [a] [of rain] averse f; (fig) [of blows] volée f, grêle f; [of sparks, stones, arrows] pluie f; [of blessings] déluge m; [of insults] torrent m, flot m

[b] douche f; **to have** or **take a ~** prendre une douche; (US) **to send sb to the ~s*** (Sport) expulser qn; (fig) mettre qn sur la touche (fig)

[c] (Brit: pej = people) bande f de crétins*

[d] (before wedding etc) **to give a ~ for sb** organiser une soirée pour donner ses cadeaux à qn

[2] VT (fig) **to ~ sb with gifts/praise ◊ to ~ gifts/praise on sb** combler qn de cadeaux/de louanges; **to ~ blows on sb** faire pleuvoir des coups sur qn; **to ~ abuse** or **insults on sb** accabler or couvrir qn d'injures; **invitations were/advice was ~ed (up)on him** les invitations/les conseils pleuvaient (sur lui)

[3] VI [a] (= wash) se doucher, prendre une douche

[b] (= fall) **small stones/hailstones ~ed (down) on to the car** des petites pierres/grêlons pleuvaient sur la voiture; **advice ~ed upon him** les conseils pleuvaient sur lui

[4] COMP ► **shower attachment** N douchette f à main, douchette f de lavabo ► **shower cap** N bonnet m de douche ► **shower cubicle** N cabine f de douche ► **shower curtain** N rideau m de douche ► **shower stall** N = **shower cubicle** ► **shower unit** N bloc-douche m

showerproof ['ʃaʊəpruːf] ADJ imperméable

showery ['ʃaʊərɪ] ADJ [weather, day] pluvieux; **~ rain** averses fpl; **it will be ~** il y aura des averses

showground ['ʃəʊgraʊnd] N champ m de foire

showing ['ʃəʊɪŋ] [1] N [a] [of pictures etc] exposition f; [of film] projection f; (Cine) **the first ~ is at 8pm** la première séance est à 20 heures; (Cine, TV) **another ~ of this film** une nouvelle projection de ce film [b] (= performance) performance f, prestation* f; **on this ~ he doesn't stand much chance** si c'est tout ce dont il est capable or à en juger d'après cette prestation, il n'a pas de grandes chances; **he made a good ~** il s'en est bien tiré; **he made a poor ~** il ne s'est vraiment pas distingué [c] **on his own ~** de son propre aveu [2] COMP ► **showing-off** N (NonC) frime f, pose f

showjumper ['ʃəʊˌdʒʌmpə^r] N (= rider) cavalier m, -ière f de concours hippique; (= horse) cheval m (de saut) d'obstacles

showman ['ʃəʊmən] N (pl **-men**) (in fair, circus etc) forain m; (fig) **he's a real ~** il a vraiment le sens de la mise en scène (fig)

showmanship ['ʃəʊmənʃɪp] N art m or sens m de la mise en scène

shown [ʃəʊn] VB ptp of **show**

showpiece ['ʃəʊpiːs] N [a] [of exhibition etc] trésor m, joyau m; **this vase is a real ~** ce vase est une pièce remarquable [b] (fig) **the new school is a ~** la nouvelle école est un modèle du genre

showplace ['ʃəʊpleɪs] [1] N [a] (= tourist attraction) lieu m de grand intérêt touristique [b] (fig) = **showpiece b** [2] COMP ► **showplace home** N (US) maison f de rêve

showroom ['ʃəʊrʊm] N magasin m or salle f d'exposition; (Aut) **in ~ condition** à l'état m neuf

showtime ['ʃəʊtaɪm] N **it's ~!** le spectacle commence!; **ten minutes till ~!** le spectacle commence dans dix minutes!

showy* ['ʃəʊɪ] ADJ (pej) [clothes, jewellery, décor] voyant, tape-à-l'œil inv; [colour] voyant, criard; [person, manner] plein d'ostentation

shrank [ʃræŋk] VB pt of **shrink**

shrapnel ['ʃræpnl] N (Mil) [a] obus m à balles, shrapnel m [b] (NonC) éclats mpl d'obus

---

shred [ʃred] [1] N [of cloth, paper, skin, plastic sheeting] lambeau m; (fig) [of truth] parcelle f, grain m; [of common sense] grain m, once f; **not a ~ of evidence** pas la moindre or plus petite preuve; **her dress hung in ~s** sa robe était en lambeaux; **without a ~ of clothing on** nu comme un ver, complètement nu [2] VT [a] [+ paper] (gen) mettre en lambeaux, déchiqueter; (in shredder) détruire (par lacération), déchiqueter [b] [+ carrots] râper; [+ cabbage, lettuce] couper en lanières

shredder ['ʃredə^r] N [a] [of food processor] (disque m) râpe m [b] (also **paper** or **document ~**) destructeur m (de documents), déchiqueteuse f; **to put sth through the ~** détruire qch, passer qch à la déchiqueteuse

shrew [ʃruː] N [a] (Zool) musaraigne f [b] (= woman) mégère f → **taming**

shrewd [ʃruːd] ADJ [person] (= clear-sighted) perspicace; (= cunning) astucieux; [plan] astucieux; [businessman, politician] habile; [assessment, reasoning, investment, move] judicieux; **a ~ judge of character** un fin psychologue; **I can make a ~ guess at what he wanted** je crois que je devine ce qu'il voulait; **to have a ~ suspicion that ...** être assez perspicace pour soupçonner que ...

shrewdly ['ʃruːdlɪ] ADV [look at] d'un air perspicace; [say, ask, assess, suspect] avec perspicacité; [realize, recognize, perceive, comment] judicieusement; [reason] habilement; [guess] astucieusement

shrewdness ['ʃruːdnɪs] N [of person] perspicacité f, habileté f, sagacité f; [of assessment] perspicacité f; [of plan] astuce f

shrewish ['ʃruːɪʃ] ADJ (pej) [woman] acariâtre; [behaviour] de mégère; **a ~ woman** une mégère

shriek [ʃriːk] [1] N hurlement m, cri m perçant or aigu; **to let out** or **give a ~** pousser un hurlement or un cri; **~s of laughter** de grands éclats mpl de rire; **~s of laughter** en riant à gorge déployée [2] VI hurler, crier (with de); **to ~ with laughter** rire à gorge déployée, se tordre de rire; (fig) **the colour simply ~s at you** cette couleur hurle or est vraiment criarde [3] VT hurler, crier; **to ~ abuse at sb** hurler des injures à qn; **"no" he ~ed** « non » hurla-t-il

shrift [ʃrɪft] N **to give sb short ~** expédier qn sans ménagement, envoyer promener qn*; **I got short ~ from him** il m'a traité sans ménagement, il m'a envoyé promener*

shrike [ʃraɪk] N pie-grièche f

shrill [ʃrɪl] [1] ADJ (pej) [a] (= piercing) [voice, cry] strident, perçant; [laughter, music] strident; [whistle] strident, aigu (-guë f) [b] (= vehement) [demand] outrancier; [protest] violent [2] VI [whistle, telephone] retentir [3] VT **"stop!" she ~ed** « arrête! » cria-t-elle d'une voix perçante or stridente

shrillness ['ʃrɪlnɪs] N (NonC) ton m aigu or perçant

shrilly ['ʃrɪlɪ] ADV (pej) [a] (= piercingly) [say, sing] d'une voix stridente or perçante; **her voice sounded ~ from the corridor** on entendait sa voix perçante dans le couloir; **to whistle ~** émettre un sifflement strident or aigu [b] (= vehemently) [demand] de façon outrancière; [protest, condemn] violemment

shrimp [ʃrɪmp] [1] N crevette f; (fig) **he's just a little ~** il n'est pas plus haut que trois pommes [2] VI **to go ~ing** aller pêcher la crevette [3] COMP ► **shrimp cocktail** N (Culin) cocktail m de crevettes ► **shrimp sauce** N sauce f crevette

shrine [ʃraɪn] N (= place of worship) lieu m saint, lieu m de pèlerinage; (= reliquary) châsse f; (= tomb) tombeau m; (fig) haut lieu m

shrink [ʃrɪŋk] (pret **shrank**, ptp **shrunk**) [1] VI [a] (= get smaller) [clothes] rétrécir; [area] se réduire; [boundaries] se resserrer; [piece of meat] réduire; [body, person] se ratatiner, rapetisser;

[*wood*] se contracter ; [*quantity, amount*] diminuer ; (*on label*) **"will not ~"** « irrétrécissable » **b** (*also* **~ away, ~ back**) reculer, se dérober (**from sth** devant qch, **from doing** devant l'idée de faire) ; **she shrank (away** *or* **back) from him** elle a eu un mouvement de recul ; **he did not ~ from saying that …** il n'a pas craint de dire que … **2** VT (**+** *wool*) (faire) rétrécir ; (**+** *metal*) contracter **3** N (**:** = *psychiatrist*) psychiatre *mf*, psy* *mf* **4** COMP ► **shrink-wrap** VT emballer sous film plastique ► **shrink-wrapped** ADJ emballé sous film plastique

shrinkage ['ʃrɪŋkɪdʒ] N (*NonC*) [*of clothes*] rétrécissement *m* ; [*of wood, market*] contraction *f* ; [*of industry*] recul *m* ; [*of quantity, amount*] diminution *f* ; [*of metal*] retrait *m* ; (*in material*) **to allow for ~** prévoir un rétrécissement

shrinking ['ʃrɪŋkɪŋ] **1** ADJ craintif **2** COMP ► **shrinking violet** N sensitive *f*, personne *f* sensible et timide

shrive†† [ʃraɪv] (*pret* **shrived** *or* **shrove**, *ptp* **shrived** *or* **shriven**) VT confesser et absoudre

shrivel ['ʃrɪvl] (*also* **~ up**) **1** VI [*apple, body*] se ratatiner ; [*skin*] se rider, se flétrir ; [*leaf*] se flétrir, se racornir ; [*steak*] se racornir, se ratatiner ; (*fig*) **her answer made him ~ (up)** sa réponse lui a donné envie de rentrer sous terre **2** VT dessécher, flétrir

shriven ['ʃrɪvn] VB *ptp of* **shrive**

shroud [ʃraʊd] **1** N **a** linceul *m*, suaire *m* (*liter*) ; [*of mist*] voile *m*, linceul *m* (*liter*) ; [*of snow*] linceul *m* (*liter*) ; [*of mystery*] voile *m* ; [*of mast*] hauban *m* ; [*of parachute*] suspentes *fpl* **c** (*Space: of rocket*) coiffe *f* **2** VT (**+** *corpse*) envelopper dans un linceul, ensevelir ; (*fig*) **~ed in mist/snow** enseveli sous la brume/la neige, sous un linceul de brume/de neige (*liter*) ; **~ed in mystery/secrecy** enveloppé de mystère/d'une atmosphère de secret

shrove [ʃrəʊv] **1** VB *pt of* **shrive** **2** COMP ► **Shrove Tuesday** N (le) Mardi gras

Shrovetide ['ʃrəʊvtaɪd] N les jours *mpl* gras (*les trois jours précédant le Carême*)

shrub [ʃrʌb] N arbrisseau *m* ; (*small*) arbuste *m* → **flowering**

shrubbery ['ʃrʌbərɪ] N (massif *m* d')arbustes *mpl*

shrubby ['ʃrʌbɪ] ADJ arbustif ; **a ~ tree** un arbuste

shrug [ʃrʌg] **1** N haussement *m* d'épaules ; **to give a ~ of contempt** hausser les épaules (en signe) de mépris ; **… he said with a ~** dit-il en haussant les épaules *or* avec un haussement d'épaules **2** VTI **to ~ (one's shoulders)** hausser les épaules ► **shrug off** VT SEP (**+** *suggestion, warning*) dédaigner, faire fi de ; (**+** *remark*) ignorer, ne pas relever ; (**+** *infection, a cold*) se débarrasser de

shrunk [ʃrʌŋk] VB *ptp of* **shrink**

shrunken ['ʃrʌŋkən] ADJ [*person, body*] ratatiné, rabougri ; **~ head** tête *f* réduite

shtick [ʃtɪk] N = **schtick**

shtoom: [ʃtʊm] ADJ **to keep ~ (about sth)** garder bouche cousue* (à propos de qch)

shuck [ʃʌk] (*US*) **1** N (= *pod*) cosse *f* ; [*of nut*] écale *f* ; [*of chestnut*] bogue *f* ; [*of corn*] spathe *f* **2** EXCL **~s!*** mince alors !*, zut alors !* **3** VT (**+** *bean*) écosser ; (**+** *nut*) écaler ; (**+** *chestnut*) éplucher ; (**+** *corn*) égrener ; **to ~ one's clothes** se déshaper* ► **shuck off*** VT SEP (*US*) (**+** *garment*) enlever ; **to ~ off one's clothes** se déshaper* ; **to ~ off one's jacket** tomber la veste*

shudder ['ʃʌdər] **1** N (*from cold*) frisson *m* ; (*from horror*) frisson *m*, frémissement *m* ; [*of vehicle, ship, engine*] vibration *f*, trépidation *f* ; **to give a ~** [*person*] frissonner, frémir ; [*vehicle, ship*] avoir une forte secousse, être ébranlé ; **it gives me the ~s*** ça me donne des frissons ; **he realized with a ~ that …** il a frissonné *or* frémi, comprenant que … **2** VI (*from cold*) frissonner ; (*from horror*) frémir, frissonner ;

[*engine, motor*] vibrer, trépider ; [*vehicle, ship*] vibrer, trépider ; (*on striking sth*) avoir une forte secousse, être ébranlé ; (*for mechanical reasons*) vibrer, trépider ; **I ~ to think what might have happened** je frémis rien qu'à la pensée de ce qui aurait pu se produire ; **what will he do next? — I ~ to think!** qu'est-ce qu'il va encore faire ? — j'en frémis d'avance !

shuffle ['ʃʌfl] **1** N **a** **the ~ of footsteps** le bruit d'une démarche traînante **b** (*Cards*) battage *m* ; (*fig*) réorganisation *f* ; **give the cards a good ~** bats bien les cartes ; (*Parl*) **a cabinet (re)shuffle** un remaniement ministériel ; (*US*) **to get lost in the ~** [*person*] passer inaperçu ; [*fact, issue etc*] être mis aux oubliettes *or* au placard **2** VT **a** **to ~ one's feet** traîner les pieds **b** (**+** *cards*) battre ; (**+** *dominoes*) mêler, brouiller ; (**+** *papers*) remuer, déranger **3** VI **a** traîner les pieds, **to ~ in/ out/along** *etc* entrer/sortir/avancer *etc* d'un pas traînant *or* en traînant les pieds **b** (*Cards*) battre les cartes ► **shuffle off 1** VI s'en aller *or* s'éloigner d'un pas traînant *or* en traînant les pieds **2** VT SEP (**+** *garment*) enlever maladroitement ; (*fig*) (**+** *responsibility*) rejeter (**on to sb** sur qn), se dérober à ► **shuffle out of** VT FUS (*fig*) (**+** *duty, responsibility*) se dérober à

shuffleboard ['ʃʌflbɔːd] N jeu *m* de palets

shufti, shufty ['ʃʌftɪ, 'ʃʊftɪ] N (*Brit*) **to have** *or* **take a ~ (at sth)** jeter un œil *or* un coup d'œil (à qch)*

shun [ʃʌn] VT (**+** *place, temptation*) fuir ; (**+** *person, publicity*) fuir, éviter ; (**+** *work, obligation*) éviter, esquiver ; **I ~ned his company** j'ai fui sa présence ; **to ~ doing** éviter de faire

shunt [ʃʌnt] **1** VT **a** (*Rail*) (= *direct*) aiguiller ; (= *divert*) dériver, détourner ; (= *move about*) manœuvrer ; (= *position*) garer **b** (*fig*) (**+** *conversation, discussion*) aiguiller, détourner (**on to** sur) ; (**+** *person*) expédier* (**to** à) ; (*fig*) **they ~ed the visitors to and fro between the factory and the offices*** ils ont fait faire la navette aux visiteurs entre l'usine et les bureaux ; **~ that book over to me!:** passe-moi *or* file-moi ce bouquin !* **c** (*Elec*) shunter, dériver **2** VI (*fig*) **to ~ (to and fro)*** [*person, object, document*] faire la navette (**between** entre) **3** N (*Rail*) aiguillage *m* ; (* *fig*) collision *f*

shunter ['ʃʌntər] N (*Brit Rail*) (= *person*) aiguilleur *m* (de train) ; (= *engine*) locomotive *f* de manœuvre

shunting ['ʃʌntɪŋ] (*Rail*) **1** N manœuvres *fpl* d'aiguillage **2** COMP ► **shunting operation** N (*Brit*) opération *f* de triage ► **shunting yard** N voies *fpl* de garage et de triage

shush [ʃʊʃ] **1** EXCL chut ! **2** VT* faire chut à ; (= *silence: also* **~ up**) faire taire

shut [ʃʌt] (*pret, ptp* **shut**) **1** VT (**+** *eyes, door, factory, shop*) fermer ; (**+** *drawer*) (re)fermer, repousser ; **the shop is ~ now** le magasin est fermé maintenant ; **the shop is ~ on Sundays** le magasin ferme *or* est fermé le dimanche ; **we're ~ting the office for two weeks in July** nous fermons le bureau pour deux semaines au mois de juillet ; **to ~ one's finger in a drawer** se pincer *or* se prendre le doigt dans un tiroir ; **to ~ sb in a room** enfermer qn dans une pièce ; **~ your mouth!:** ferme-la !:, boucle-la !: ; **~ your face!:** ta gueule !:, la ferme !: → **door, ear!, open, stable²** **2** VI [*door, box, lid, drawer*] se fermer, fermer ; [*museum, theatre, shop*] fermer ; **the door ~** la porte s'est (re)fermée ; **the door ~s badly** la porte ferme mal ; **the shop ~s on Sundays/at 6 o'clock** le magasin ferme le dimanche/à 18 heures **3** COMP ► **shut-eye:** N **to get a bit of ~-eye** *or* **some ~-eye** piquer un roupillon:, dormir un peu ► **shut-in** ADJ (*esp US*) enfermé, confiné ► **shut-out** N (*Ind*) lock-out *m inv* ; (*US Sport*) victoire *f* (*remportée du fait que l'équi-*

pe adverse n'a marqué aucun point) ► **shut-out bid** N (*Bridge*) (annonce *f* de) barrage *m* ► **shut away** VT SEP (**+** *person, animal*) enfermer ; (**+** *valuables*) mettre sous clé ; **he ~s himself away** il s'enferme chez lui, il vit en reclus ► **shut down 1** VI [*business, shop, theatre*] fermer (définitivement), fermer ses portes **2** VT SEP (**+** *lid*) fermer, rabattre ; (**+** *business, shop, theatre*) fermer (définitivement) ; (**+** *machine*) arrêter **3** **~down** N → **shutdown** ► **shut in 1** VT SEP (**+** *person, animal*) enfermer ; (= *surround*) entourer (**with** de) ; **to feel ~ in** se sentir enfermé *or* emprisonné (*fig*) **2** **~-in** ADJ → **shut** ► **shut off 1** VT SEP **a** (= *stop, cut*) (**+** *electricity, gas*) couper, fermer ; (**+** *engine*) couper ; (**+** *supplies*) arrêter, couper **b** (= *isolate*) (**+** *person*) isoler, séparer (**from** de) ; **we're very ~ off here** nous sommes coupés de tout ici *or* très isolés ici **2** **~off** N → **shutoff** ► **shut out 1** VT SEP **a** **he found that they had ~ him out** ◊ **he found himself ~ out** il a trouvé qu'il était à la porte *or* qu'il ne pouvait pas entrer ; **don't ~ me out, I haven't got a key** ne ferme pas la porte, je n'ai pas de clé ; **I ~ the cat out at night** je laisse *or* mets le chat dehors pour la nuit ; **close the door and ~ out the noise** ferme la porte pour qu'on n'entende pas le bruit ; **he ~ them out of his will** il les a exclus de son testament ; **you can't ~ him out of your life** tu ne peux pas l'exclure *or* le bannir de ta vie **b** (= *block*) (**+** *view*) boucher ; (**+** *memory*) chasser de son esprit **c** (*US Sport*) (**+** *opponent*) bloquer **2** **~-out** N, ADJ → **shut** ► **shut to 1** VI [*door*] se (re)fermer **2** VT SEP (re)fermer ► **shut up 1** VI (* = *be quiet*) se taire ; **~ up!** tais-toi !, la ferme !: ; **better just ~ up and get on with it** mieux vaut se taire *or* la boucler* et continuer **2** VT SEP **a** (**+** *factory, business, theatre, house*) fermer → **shop b** (**+** *person, animal*) enfermer ; (**+** *valuables*) mettre sous clé ; **to ~ sb up in prison** emprisonner qn, mettre qn en prison **c** (* = *silence*) faire taire, clouer le bec à*

shutdown ['ʃʌtdaʊn] N fermeture *f*

shutoff ['ʃʌtɒf] N (*also* **~ device**) interrupteur *m* automatique, dispositif *m* d'arrêt automatique

shutter ['ʃʌtər] **1** N volet *m* ; (*Phot*) obturateur *m* ; **to put up the ~s** mettre les volets ; (*Comm*) fermer (le magasin) ; (*fig: permanently*) fermer boutique, fermer définitivement **2** COMP ► **shutter release** N (*Phot*) déclencheur *m* d'obturateur ► **shutter speed** N vitesse *f* d'obturation

shuttered ['ʃʌtəd] ADJ [*house, window*] (= *fitted with shutters*) muni de volets ; (= *with shutters closed*) aux volets clos ; **the windows were ~** les fenêtres étaient munies de volets *or* avaient leurs volets fermés

shuttle ['ʃʌtl] **1** N **a** [*of loom, sewing machine*] navette *f* **b** (= *plane, train etc*) navette *f* ; **air ~** navette *f* aérienne ; **space ~** navette *f* spatiale **c** (*: in badminton* = *shuttlecock*) volant *m* **2** VI [*person, vehicle, boat, documents*] faire la navette (**between** entre) **3** VT **to ~ sb to and fro** envoyer qn à droite et à gauche ; **he was ~d (back and forth) between the factory and the office** on l'a renvoyé de l'usine au bureau et vice versa, il a dû faire la navette entre l'usine et le bureau ; **the papers were ~d (backwards and forwards) from one department to another** les documents ont été renvoyés d'un service à l'autre **4** COMP ► **shuttle bus** N navette *f* ► **shuttle diplomacy** N navettes *fpl* diplomatiques ► **shuttle movement** N (*Tech*) mouvement *m* alternatif ► **shuttle service** N (Aviat, Rail etc) (service *m* de) navettes *fpl*

shuttlecock ['ʃʌtlkɒk] N (in badminton) volant *m*

shy[1] [ʃaɪ] [1] ADJ [a] (= nervous) [person, smile, look] timide; **he's a ~ person** ◊ **he's ~ of people** c'est un timide; **to be ~ with people** être timide avec les gens; **don't be ~** ne sois pas timide, ne fais pas le (or la) timide; **to make sb (feel) ~** intimider qn; **she went all ~* when asked to give her opinion** elle a été tout intimidée quand on lui a demandé de donner son avis
[b] (= wary) **to be ~ of sb/sth** avoir peur de qn/qch; **he was so ~ about his private life** il craignait tellement de parler de sa vie privée; **to be ~ of doing sth** avoir peur de faire qch → **bite, camera, fight, workshy**
[c] (Zool) [animal, bird] craintif → **gun**
[d] (esp US = short) **he is two days ~ of his 95th birthday** il va avoir 95 ans dans deux jours; **I'm $5 ~** il me manque 5 dollars; **they are $65,000 ~ of the $1 million that's needed** il leur manque 65 000 dollars pour avoir le million nécessaire
[2] VI [horse] broncher (**at** devant)
► **shy away** VI (fig) **to ~ away from doing** répugner à faire, s'effaroucher à l'idée de faire

shy[2] [ʃaɪ] (Brit) [1] VT (= throw) lancer, jeter
[2] N (lit) **to take** or **have a ~ at sth** lancer un projectile (or une pierre etc) vers qch; **"20p a ~"** « 20 pence le coup »; (fig = try) **to have a ~ at doing** tenter de faire → **coconut**

shyly ['ʃaɪlɪ] ADV timidement

shyness ['ʃaɪnɪs] N (NonC) [of person] timidité *f*; [of animal, bird] caractère *m* craintif

shyster* ['ʃaɪstər] N (US) (gen) escroc *m*; (= lawyer) avocat *m* véreux or marron

SI [es'aɪ] N (ABBR = **Système international (d'unités)**) SI *m*

si [si:] N (Mus) si *m*

Siam [saɪ'æm] N le Siam

Siamese [,saɪə'mi:z] [1] ADJ (gen) siamois
[2] N [a] (pl inv) Siamois(e) *m(f)* [b] (Ling) siamois *m* [3] COMP ► **Siamese cat** N chat *m* siamois ► **Siamese twins** NPL (frères *mpl*) siamois *mpl*, (sœurs *fpl*) siamoises *fpl*

SIB [,esaɪ'bi:] N (Brit) (ABBR = **Securities and Investments Board**) ≈ COB *f*

Siberia [saɪ'bɪərɪə] N la Sibérie

Siberian [saɪ'bɪərɪən] [1] ADJ sibérien, de Sibérie [2] N Sibérien(ne) *m(f)*

sibilant ['sɪbɪlənt] [1] ADJ (frm, also Phon) sifflant [2] N (Phon) sifflante *f*

sibling ['sɪblɪŋ] [1] N **~s** enfants *mfpl* de mêmes parents, fratrie *f*; **one of his ~s** l'un de ses frères et sœurs; **Paul and Julie are ~s** Paul et Julie sont frère et sœur; **she's my ~** c'est ma sœur [2] COMP ► **sibling rivalry** N rivalité *f* fraternelle

sibyl ['sɪbɪl] N sibylle *f*

sibylline ['sɪbɪlaɪn] ADJ sibyllin

sic [sɪk] ADV sic

Sicilian [sɪ'sɪlɪən] [1] ADJ (gen) sicilien; [2] N [a] Sicilien(ne) *m(f)* [b] (Ling) sicilien *m*

Sicily ['sɪsɪlɪ] N la Sicile; **in ~** en Sicile

sick [sɪk] [1] ADJ [a] (= ill) [person] malade; **he's a ~ man** il est (très) malade; **to fall** or **take†** **ill** tomber malade; **to be off ~** (= off work) être en congé maladie; (= off school) être absent pour maladie; **she's off ~ with 'flu** elle n'est pas là or elle est absente, elle a la grippe; **to go ~** se faire porter malade; **to call in** or **phone in ~** téléphoner pour dire que l'on est malade; **to be ~ of a fever†** avoir la fièvre → **homesick**
[b] **to be ~** (= vomit) vomir; **to be as ~ as a dog*** être malade comme un chien; **to make sb ~** faire vomir qn; **to make o.s. ~** se faire vomir; (= nauseous) **to feel ~** avoir mal au cœur, avoir envie de vomir; **I get ~ in planes**

j'ai mal au cœur or je suis malade en avion, j'ai le mal de l'air; **a ~ feeling** (lit) un haut-le-cœur; (fig) une (sensation d')angoisse; **worried ~** ◊ **with worry** fou or malade d'inquiétude → **airsick, car, seasick, travel**
[c] (= disgusted) **to make sb ~** rendre qn malade, écœurer qn; **you make me ~!** tu m'écœures!, tu me dégoûtes!; **it's enough to make you ~** il y a de quoi vous écœurer or dégoûter; **it makes me ~ to my stomach** ça m'écœure, ça me fait gerber*; **he felt ~ about the whole business** toute l'affaire le rendait malade; **it makes me ~ to think that ...** ça me rend malade de penser que ...; **he was really ~ at failing the exam*** ça l'a vraiment rendu malade d'avoir échoué à l'examen; **to be as ~ as a parrot** en être malade*; (liter) **to be ~ at heart** (= unhappy) avoir la mort dans l'âme
[d] (= fed up) **to be ~ of sb/sth/doing sth** en avoir assez or marre* de qn/qch/faire qch; **to be ~ of the sight of sb** en avoir assez or marre* de voir qn; **to be/get ~ and tired*** or **~ to death*** or **~ to the (back) teeth* of ...** en avoir/finir par en avoir par-dessus la tête* or ras le bol* or plein le dos* de ...
[e] (pej = offensive) [person, mind, joke, humour, suggestion] malsain; **~ comedian** comique *m* porté sur l'humour malsain
[f] (US = inferior) **they made our team look ~** à côté d'eux, notre équipe avait l'air nulle or minable
[2] N (Brit* = vomit) vomi* *m*, vomissure *f*
[3] **the sick** NPL les malades *mfpl*
[4] COMP ► **sick bag** N sac *m* vomitoire ► **sick bay** N infirmerie *f* ► **sick building syndrome** N syndrome *m* du bâtiment malsain ► **sick headache** N migraine *f* ► **sick leave** N **on ~ leave** en congé *m* (de) maladie ► **sick list** N **to be on the ~ list** (Admin) être porté malade; (* = ill) être malade ► **sick-making*** ADJ dégoûtant, gerbant* ► **sick note*** N (for work) certificat *m* médical; (for school) billet *m* d'excuse ► **sick-out** N (US Ind) mouvement de protestation où tous les travailleurs se font porter malade ► **sick pay** N indemnité *f* de maladie (versée par l'employeur)
► **sick up*** VT SEP (Brit) dégueuler*, vomir

sickbed ['sɪkbed] N lit *m* de malade

sicken ['sɪkn] [1] VT rendre malade, donner mal au cœur à; (fig) dégoûter, écœurer [2] VI tomber malade; **to ~ for sth** [person] couver qch; (fig) **to ~ of ...** se lasser de ..., en avoir assez de ...

sickening ['sɪknɪŋ] ADJ (= disgusting) [sight, smell] écœurant, qui soulève le cœur; [cruelty] révoltant; [waste] révoltant, dégoûtant; [crime] ignoble, révoltant; **a ~ feeling of failure** un écœurant sentiment d'échec; **a ~ feeling of panic** une affreuse sensation de panique; **a ~ feeling of foreboding** un horrible sentiment d'appréhension [b] (* = annoying) [person, behaviour, situation] agaçant, énervant [c] (= unpleasant) [blow] mauvais; [crunch] sinistre; **with a ~ thud** avec un bruit sourd et sinistre

sickeningly ['sɪknɪŋlɪ] ADV [familiar] tristement; **~ violent/polite** d'une violence/d'une politesse écœurante; **it is ~ sweet** c'est si sucré que c'est écœurant; **he made it all look ~ easy** avec lui, tout paraissait d'une facilité écœurante; **he seems ~ happy** il semble si heureux que c'en est écœurant; **he stood at the top of a ~ steep gully** il se tenait au sommet d'une ravine vertigineuse; **the ship was rolling ~** le roulis du bateau soulevait le cœur

sickle ['sɪkl] [1] N faucille *f* [2] COMP ► **sickle-cell anaemia** N (Med) anémie *f* à hématies falciformes, drépanocytose *f*

sickliness ['sɪklɪnɪs] N [of person] état *m* maladif; [of cake] goût *m* écœurant

sickly ['sɪklɪ] [1] ADJ [a] (= unhealthy) [person, face, complexion, pallor] maladif; [business,

company] mal en point; [climate] malsain; [plant] étiolé; **she gave a ~ smile** elle eut un pâle sourire [b] (Brit = nauseating) [smell, colour, cake] écœurant; [smile] mielleux [2] ADV **~ green** d'un vert nauséeux; **~ yellow** cireux; **~ sweet** [smell, taste] douceâtre; [book] mièvre; [person, expression] mielleux

sickness ['sɪknɪs] [1] N (NonC) (= illness) maladie *f*; **there's a lot of ~ in the village** il y a beaucoup de malades dans le village; **there's ~ on board** il y a des malades à bord; (= vomiting) **bouts of ~** vomissements *mpl*; **mountain ~** mal *m* des montagnes; (in marriage service) **in ~ and in health** ≈ pour le meilleur et pour le pire → **travel** [2] COMP ► **sickness benefit** N (Brit) (prestations *fpl* de l')assurance-maladie *f* ► **sickness insurance** N assurance-maladie *f*

sicko* ['sɪkəʊ] (esp US pej) [1] N taré(e)* *m(f)* [2] ADJ [person] taré; [group] de tarés*

sickroom ['sɪkrum] N (in school etc) infirmerie *f*; (at home) chambre *f* de malade

side [saɪd] [1] N [a] [of person] côté *m*; **wounded in the ~** blessé au côté; **to sleep on one's ~** dormir sur le côté; **to hold one's ~s with laughter** se tenir les côtes; **he had the telephone by his ~** il avait le téléphone à côté de lui or à portée de la main; **his assistant was at** or **by his ~** son assistant était à ses côtés; (fig) **she remained by his ~ through thick and thin** elle est restée à ses côtés or elle l'a soutenu à travers toutes leurs épreuves; **~ by ~** (lit) côte à côte; (fig: in agreement) en parfait accord (**with** avec) → **split**
[b] [of animal] flanc *m*; (Culin) **a ~ of bacon** une flèche de lard; **a ~ of beef/mutton** un quartier de bœuf/mouton
[c] (as opposed to top, bottom) [of box, house, car, triangle] côté *m*; [of ship] flanc *m*, côté *m*; [of mountain] (gen) versant *m*; (= flank) flanc *m*; (inside) [of cave, ditch, box] paroi *f*; [of mountain] **the north ~** le versant nord; **vines growing on the ~ of the hill** des vignes qui poussent sur le flanc de la colline; **by the ~ of the church** à côté de or tout près de l'église; **set the box on its ~** pose la caisse sur le côté; **go round the ~ of the house** contournez la maison; **you'll find him round the ~ of the house** tournez le coin de la maison et vous le verrez; **she's (built) like the ~ of a house*** c'est un monument*, elle est colossale → **near, off**
[d] [of cube, record, coin] côté *m*, face *f*; [of garment, cloth, slice of bread, sheet of paper, shape] côté *m*; (fig) [of matter, problem etc] aspect *m*; [of sb's character] facette *f*; **the right ~** (of garment, cloth) l'endroit *m*; **the wrong ~** (of garment, cloth) l'envers *m*; **right/wrong out** (of cloth) à l'endroit/l'envers; **right/wrong ~ up** dans le bon/mauvais sens; (on box etc) **"this ~ up"** « haut »; **write on both ~s of the paper** écrivez des deux côtés de la feuille, écrivez recto verso; **I've written six ~s** j'ai écrit six pages; (fig) **the other ~ of the coin** or **picture** le revers de la médaille; (fig) **they are two ~s of the same coin** [issues] ce sont deux facettes d'un même problème; [people] ils représentent deux facettes d'une même tendance; **there are two ~s to every quarrel** dans toute querelle il y a deux points de vue; (fig) **look at it from his ~ (of it)** considère cela de son point de vue; **now listen to my ~ of the story** maintenant écoute ma version des faits; **he's got a nasty ~* to him** or **to his nature** il a un côté méchant → **bright, flip, right**
[e] (= edge) [of road, lake, river] bord *m*; [of wood, forest] lisière *f*; [of field, estate] bord *m*, côté *m*; **by the ~ of the road/lake** etc au bord de la route/du lac etc
[f] (= part away from centre) côté *m*; **on the other ~ of the street/room** de l'autre côté de la rue/la pièce; **he crossed to the other ~ of the room** il a traversé la pièce; **he was on the wrong ~ of the road** il était du mauvais côté de la route; **the east ~ of the town** la partie

est *or* les quartiers est de la ville ; **he got out of the train on the wrong ~** il est descendu du train à contre-voie ; **he is paralysed down one ~ of his face** il a un côté du visage paralysé ; **from all ~s ◊ from every ~** de tous côtés, de toutes parts ; **from ~ to ~** d'un côté à l'autre ; **he moved to one ~** il s'est écarté ; **to take sb on** *or* **to one ~** prendre qn à part ; **to put sth to** *or* **on one ~** mettre qch de côté ; **leaving that question to one ~ for the moment ...** laissant la question de côté pour le moment ... ; **it's on this ~ of London** c'est de notre côté de Londres ; (*between here and London*) c'est avant Londres, c'est entre ici et Londres ; (*fig*) **the science ~ of the college** la section sciences du collège ; (*Brit Parl*) **members on the other ~ of the House** (= *the government*) les députés *mpl* de la majorité ; (= *the opposition*) les députés *mpl* de l'opposition ; (*fig*) **he got out of bed on the wrong ~** il s'est levé du pied gauche ; (*fig*) **he's on the wrong ~ of 50** il a passé la cinquantaine ; **he's on the right ~ of 50** il n'a pas encore 50 ans ; **this ~ of Christmas** avant Noël ; **he makes a bit (of money) on the ~ by doing ...**; il se fait un peu d'argent en plus *or* il arrondit ses fins de mois en faisant ... ; **a cousin on his mother's ~** un cousin du côté de sa mère ; **my grandfather on my mother's ~** mon grand-père maternel ; (*TV*) **on the other ~** sur l'autre chaîne ; **it's on the heavy/big ~** c'est plutôt lourd/grand ; **it's on the hot/chilly ~** [*weather*] il fait plutôt chaud/froid → **safe, sunny**

g (= *group, team, party*) (*gen*) camp *m* ; (*Sport*) équipe *f* ; (*Pol etc*) parti *m* ; **he's on our ~** il est dans notre camp *or* avec nous ; **God was on their ~** Dieu était avec eux ; **to be on the ~ of the angels** avoir raison d'un point de vue moral ; **we have time on our ~** nous avons le temps pour nous, le temps joue en notre faveur ; **whose ~ are you on?** dans quel camp êtes-vous?, qui soutenez-vous? ; (*fig*) **to get on the wrong ~ of sb** se faire mal voir de qn ; **there are faults on both ~s** les deux camps ont des torts *or* sont fautifs ; **with a few concessions on the government ~** avec quelques concessions de la part du gouvernement ; **to take ~s (with sb)** prendre parti (pour qn) ; **to pick** *or* **choose ~s** (= *decide one's viewpoint*) choisir son camp ; (*for game etc*) faire *or* tirer les équipes ; (*Sport*) **they've picked** *or* **chosen the England ~** on a sélectionné l'équipe d'Angleterre → **change**

h (*Brit* = *conceit*) **he's got no ~ ◊ there's no ~ to him** c'est un homme très simple, ce n'est pas un crâneur* ; **to put on ~** prendre des airs supérieurs, crâner*

2 COMP [*chapel, panel, elevation, seat*] latéral ► **side arms** NPL armes *fpl* de poing ► **side dish** N plat *m* d'accompagnement ► **side door** N entrée *f* latérale, petite porte *f* ► **side drum** N tambour *m* plat, caisse *f* claire ► **side effect** N effet *m* secondaire ► **side entrance** N entrée *f* latérale ► **side face** ADJ, ADV (*Phot*) de profil ► **side glance** N regard *m* oblique *or* de côté ► **side-impact bars** NPL = **side-impact protection** ► **side-impact protection** N (*NonC: Aut*) protections *fpl* latérales, renforts *mpl* latéraux ► **side issue** N question *f* secondaire, à-côté *m* ► **side judge** N (*US Jur*) juge *m* adjoint ► **side-on** ADJ [*collision, crash*] latéral ; [*view*] latéral, de côté ► **side order** N (*Culin*) garniture *f* ► **side plate** N petite assiette *f* (*que l'on place à la gauche de chaque convive*) ► **side road** N (*Brit*) petite route *f*, route *f* transversale ; (*in town*) petite rue *f*, rue *f* transversale ► **side salad** N salade *f* (*pour accompagner un plat*) ► **side show** N (*at fair*) attraction *f* ; (*fig* = *minor point*) détail *m* ► **side-slipping** (*Ski*) dérapage *m* ► **side-splitting*** ADJ tordant*, gondolant* ► **side street** N petite rue *f*, rue *f* transversale ► **side stroke** N

(*Swimming*) nage *f* indienne ► **side trim** N (*Aut*) moulure *f* latérale ► **side view** N vue *f* latérale ► **side-wheeler** N (*US*) bateau *m* à aubes ► **side whiskers** NPL favoris *mpl*

► **side against** VT FUS **to ~ against sb** prendre parti contre qn

► **side with** VT FUS **to ~ with sb** se ranger du côté de qn, prendre parti pour qn

sideboard ['saɪdbɔːd] N buffet *m*

sideboards (*Brit*) ['saɪdbɔːdz], **sideburns** ['saɪdbɜːnz] NPL pattes *fpl*, favoris *mpl*

sidecar ['saɪdkɑːʳ] N side-car *m*

-sided ['saɪdɪd] ADJ (*in compounds*) **three-sided** à trois côtés, trilatéral ; **many-sided** multilatéral → **one**

sidekick* ['saɪdkɪk] N (= *assistant*) acolyte *m* ; (= *friend*) copain* *m*, copine* *f*

sidelight ['saɪdlaɪt] N (*Brit Aut*) feu *m* de position, veilleuse *f* ; (*fig*) **it gives us a ~ on ...** cela projette un éclairage particulier sur ..., cela révèle un côté *or* aspect inattendu de ...

sideline ['saɪdlaɪn] **1** N **a** (*Sport*) (ligne *f* de) touche *f* ; **on the ~s** (*Sport*) sur la touche ; (*fig*) dans les coulisses ; (*fig*) **he stayed** *or* **stood on the ~s** il n'a pas pris position, il n'est pas intervenu ; **to be relegated to the ~s** être mis sur la touche **b** activité *f* (*or* travail *m* etc) secondaire ; **he sells wood as a ~** il a aussi un petit commerce de bois ; (*Comm*) **it's not a ~** ce n'est pas notre spécialité **2** VT (*Sport, fig*) mettre sur la touche

sidelong ['saɪdlɒŋ] **1** ADJ oblique, de côté **2** ADV de côté, en oblique

sidereal [saɪˈdɪərɪəl] ADJ sidéral

sidesaddle ['saɪdsædl] ADV **to ride ~** monter en amazone

sideslip ['saɪdslɪp] (*Aviat*) **1** N glissade *f* *or* glissement *m* sur l'aile **2** VI glisser sur l'aile

sidesman ['saɪdzmæn] N (*pl* **-men**) (*Brit Rel*) ≈ bedeau *m*

sidestep ['saɪdstep] **1** VT [+ *blow*] éviter, esquiver ; [+ *question*] éviter, éluder ; [+ *rules etc*] ne pas tenir compte de **2** VI (*lit*) faire un pas de côté ; (*Ski*) monter en escalier ; (*fig*) rester évasif ; (*Boxing*) esquiver

sidestepping ['saɪdstepɪŋ] N (*Ski*) montée *f* en escalier ; (*Boxing*) esquives *fpl*

sideswipe ['saɪdswaɪp] N (= *blow*) coup *m* oblique ; (*fig*) allusion *f* désobligeante

sidetable ['saɪdteɪbl] N desserte *f*

sidetrack ['saɪdtræk] VT [+ *train*] dériver, dérouter ; (*fig*) [+ *person*] faire s'écarter de son sujet ; (*fig*) **to get ~ed** s'écarter de son sujet

sidewalk ['saɪdwɔːk] **1** N (*US*) trottoir *m* **2** COMP ► **sidewalk artist** N (*US*) = **pavement artist** → **pavement** ► **sidewalk café** N (*US*) = **pavement café** → **pavement**

sideways ['saɪdweɪz] **1** ADV **a** (= *to one side, side-on*) [*glance, look*] de biais, de côté ; [*move*] latéralement ; [*walk*] en crabe ; [*stand*] de profil ; [*sit*] de côté ; [*fall*] sur le côté ; **to slide ~** déraper ; **to turn ~** se tourner ; **it goes in ~** ça rentre de côté ; **a car parked ~ on to the kerb** une voiture garée le long du trottoir → **knock b** (*in career*) **to move ~** changer de poste au même niveau hiérarchique **2** ADJ **a** (= *to one side*) [*glance, look, movement*] de biais, de côté **b** (*in career*) **~ move** *or* **step** changement *m* de poste au même niveau hiérarchique ; **the Justice Minister's recent ~ move to Defence** la récente mutation du ministre de la Justice au ministère de la Défense

siding ['saɪdɪŋ] N **a** (*Rail*) voie *f* de garage *or* d'évitement → **goods b** (*US* = *wall covering*) revêtement *m* extérieur

sidle ['saɪdl] VI **to ~ along** marcher de côté, avancer de biais ; **to ~ in/out** etc entrer/sortir etc furtivement ; **he ~d into the room** il s'est faufilé dans la pièce ; **he ~d up to me** il s'est glissé jusqu'à moi

Sidon ['saɪdən] N Sidon

SIDS N (*Med*) (ABBR = **sudden infant death syndrome**) MSN *f*

siege [siːdʒ] **1** N (*Mil, fig*) siège *m* ; **in a state of ~** en état de siège ; **to lay ~ to** assiéger une ville ; **to be under ~** [*town*] être assiégé ; (*fig: by questioning etc*) être sur la sellette, être en butte à de nombreuses critiques ; **to raise** *or* **lift the ~** lever le siège (*lit*) **2** COMP ► **siege economy** N économie *f* de siège ► **siege mentality** N **to have a ~ mentality** être toujours sur la défensive ► **siege warfare** N guerre *f* de siège

Siena, Sienna [sɪˈenə] N Sienne

Sienese [sɪəˈniːz] ADJ siennois

sienna [sɪˈenə] N (= *earth*) terre *f* de Sienne *or* d'ombre ; (= *colour*) ocre *m* brun → **burnt**

sierra [sɪˈerə] N sierra *f*

Sierra Leone [sɪˈerəlɪˈəʊn] N la Sierra Leone

Sierra Leonean [sɪˈerəlɪˈəʊnɪən] **1** ADJ sierra-léonais **2** N Sierra-Léonais(e) *m(f)*

siesta [sɪˈestə] N sieste *f* ; **to have** *or* **take a ~** faire une *or* la sieste

sieve [sɪv] **1** N (*for coal, stones*) crible *m* ; (*for sugar, flour, sand, soil*) tamis *m* ; (*for wheat*) van *m* ; (*for liquids*) passoire *f* ; (*Culin*) **to rub** *or* **put through a ~** passer au tamis ; **he's got a head** *or* **memory** *or* **brain like a ~*** sa mémoire est une (vraie) passoire* **2** VT [+ *fruit, vegetables*] passer ; [+ *sugar, flour, sand, soil*] tamiser ; [+ *coal, stones*] passer au crible, cribler

sift [sɪft] **1** VT **a** [+ *flour, sugar, sand*] tamiser, passer au tamis ; [+ *coal, stones*] cribler, passer au crible ; [+ *wheat*] vanner ; (*fig*) [+ *evidence*] passer au crible ; **to ~ flour on to sth** saupoudrer qch de farine (au moyen d'un tamis) **b** (*also* ~ **out**) (*lit*) séparer (à l'aide d'un crible) ; (*fig*) [+ *facts, truth*] dégager (**from** de) **2** VI (*fig*) **to ~ through sth** passer qch en revue, examiner qch

sifter ['sɪftəʳ] N (*for flour, sugar, sand*) tamis *m* ; (*for soil*) cribleuse *f*, crible *m*

sigh [saɪ] **1** N soupir *m* ; **to heave** *or* **give a ~** soupirer, pousser un soupir **2** VT **"if only he had come" she ~ed** « si seulement il était venu » dit-elle dans un soupir *or* soupira-t-elle **3** VI soupirer, pousser un soupir ; [*wind*] gémir ; **he ~ed with relief** il a poussé un soupir de soulagement ; **to ~ for sth** soupirer après *or* pour qch ; (*for sth lost*) regretter qch ; **to ~ over sth** se lamenter sur qch, regretter qch

sighing ['saɪɪŋ] N [*of person*] soupirs *mpl* ; [*of wind*] gémissements *mpl*

sight [saɪt] **1** N **a** (= *faculty, act of seeing, range of vision*) vue *f* ; **to have good/poor ~** avoir une bonne/mauvaise vue ; **to lose one's ~** perdre la vue ; **to get back** *or* **regain one's ~** recouvrer la vue ; **to know sb by ~** connaître qn de vue ; **to shoot on** *or* **at ~** tirer à vue ; **he translated it at ~** il l'a traduit à livre ouvert ; **he played the music at ~** il a déchiffré le morceau de musique ; **at the ~ of ...** à la vue de ..., au spectacle de ... ; **the train was still in ~** on voyait encore le train, le train était encore visible ; **the end is (with)in ~** la fin est en vue, on entrevoit la fin ; **we are within ~ of a solution** nous entrevoyons une solution ; **we live within ~ of the sea** de chez nous on voit *or* aperçoit la mer ; **to come into ~** apparaître ; **keep the luggage in ~ ◊ keep ~ of the luggage** surveillez les bagages ; **out of ~** hors de vue ; **don't let the luggage out of your ~** ne perdez pas les bagages de vue ; **to keep out of ~** (*vi*) se cacher, ne pas se montrer (*vt*) cacher, ne pas montrer ; **it is out of ~** on ne le voit pas, ce n'est pas visible, ce n'est pas à portée de vue ; **he never lets it out of his ~** il le garde toujours sous les yeux ; (*liter*) **out of my ~!** hors de ma vue ! ; **keep out of his ~!** qu'il ne te voie pas ! ; ■(*PROV*) **out of ~ out of mind** loin des yeux loin du cœur (*PROV*) ; **to catch ~ of sb/sth** apercevoir qn/qch ; (*lit, fig*) **to lose ~ of**

sb/sth perdre qn/qch de vue; **at first ~ it seems to be ...** à première vue or au premier abord cela semble être ...; **love at first ~** le coup de foudre; **it was my first ~ of Paris** c'était la première fois que je voyais Paris; **I got my first ~ of that document yesterday** j'ai vu ce document hier pour la première fois; **their first ~ of land came after 30 days at sea** la terre leur est apparue pour la première fois au bout de 30 jours en mer; **the ~ of the cathedral** la vue de la cathédrale; **I can't bear or stand the ~ of blood** je ne peux pas supporter la vue du sang; **I can't bear or stand the ~ of him** ◊ **I hate the ~ of him** je ne peux pas le voir (en peinture*) or le sentir*; (Comm) **to buy/accept sth ~ unseen** acheter/accepter qch sans l'avoir examiné; (fig liter) **to find favour in sb's ~** trouver grâce aux yeux de qn; **all men are equal in the ~ of God** tous les hommes sont égaux devant Dieu; **in the ~ of the law** aux yeux de la loi, devant la loi → **heave, second**[1], **short**

[b] (= spectacle) spectacle m (also pej); **the tulips are a wonderful ~** les tulipes sont magnifiques; **it is a ~ to see** or **a ~ to be seen** cela vaut la peine d'être vu, il faut le voir; **the Grand Canyon is one of the ~s of the world** le Grand Canyon est l'un des plus beaux spectacles or paysages au monde; **it's one of the ~s of Paris** c'est l'une des attractions touristiques de Paris, c'est l'une des choses à voir à Paris; **it's a sad ~** c'est triste (à voir), ça fait pitié; **it's not a pretty ~** ça n'est pas beau à voir; **it was a ~ for sore eyes** (welcome) cela réchauffait le cœur; (* pej) c'était à pleurer; **his face was a ~!** (amazed etc) il faisait une de ces têtes!*; (after injury etc) il avait une tête à faire peur!*; **I must look a ~!** je dois avoir une de ces allures or j'ai l'air de Dieu sait quoi!*; **doesn't she look a ~ in that hat!** elle a l'air d'un épouvantail avec ce chapeau! → **see**[1]

[c] (on gun) mire f; **to take ~** viser; **to have sth in one's ~s** avoir qch dans sa ligne de mire; (fig) **to have sb in one's ~s** avoir qn dans le collimateur or dans sa ligne de mire; (fig) **to set one's ~s too high** viser trop haut (fig); **to set one's ~s on sth** avoir des vues sur qch

[d] (phrases) **not by a long ~** loin de là, loin s'en faut; **it's a (far** or **long) ~ better than the other*** c'est infiniment mieux que l'autre; **he's a ~ too clever*** il est par or bien trop malin

[2] VT **[a]** (= see) [+ land, person] apercevoir **[b]** (= aim) prendre sa mire, viser; (= adjust) régler le viseur d'un canon

[3] COMP ► **sight draft** N (Comm, Fin) effet m à vue ► **sight-read** VT (Mus) déchiffrer ► **sight-reading** N déchiffrage m

sighted ['saɪtɪd] **[1]** ADJ qui voit; **partially ~** malvoyant **[2] the sighted** NPL les voyants mpl (lit), ceux mpl qui voient

-sighted ['saɪtɪd] ADJ (in compounds) **weak-sighted** à la vue faible → **clear**, **short**

sighting ['saɪtɪŋ] N **numerous ~s of the monster have been reported** le monstre aurait été aperçu à plusieurs reprises

sightless ['saɪtlɪs] ADJ [person] aveugle; (liter) [eyes] privé de la vue (liter)

sightline ['saɪtlaɪn] N champ m de vision

sightly ['saɪtlɪ] ADJ **it's not very ~** ce n'est pas beau à voir

sightseeing ['saɪtsiːɪŋ] N tourisme m; **to go ~** ◊ **to do some ~** (gen) faire du tourisme; (in town) visiter la ville

sightseer ['saɪtsiːə'] N touriste mf

sign [saɪn] **[1]** N **[a]** (with hand etc) signe m, geste m; **he made a ~ of recognition** il m'a (or lui a etc) fait signe qu'il me (or le etc) reconnaissait; **they communicated by ~s** ils communiquaient par signes; **to make a ~ to sb** faire signe à qn (**to do** de faire); **to make the ~ of the Cross** faire le signe de la croix

(over sb/sth sur qn/qch); (= cross o.s.) se signer; **he made a rude ~** il a fait un geste grossier

[b] (= symbol: Astron, Ling, Math, Mus etc) signe m; **this ~ means "do not machine-wash"** ce symbole signifie : « ne pas laver en machine »; **the ~s of the zodiac** les signes mpl du zodiaque; (Astrol) **born under the ~ of Leo** né sous le signe du Lion; (Astrol) **air/earth/fire/water ~** signe m d'air/de terre/de feu/d'eau → **minus**

[c] (= indication) signe m, indication f; (Med) signe m; (= trace) trace f, trace f; **in ~ of ...** en signe de ...; **it's a good/bad ~** c'est bon/mauvais signe; **all the ~s are that ...** tout laisse à penser or indique que ...; **those clouds are a ~ of rain** ces nuages annoncent la pluie or sont signe de pluie; **violence is a ~ of fear** la violence est signe de peur, la violence dénote or indique la peur; **it's a ~ of the times** c'est un signe des temps; **it's a sure ~** c'est un signe infaillible; **at the slightest ~ of disagreement** au moindre signe de désaccord; **there is no ~ of his agreeing** rien ne laisse à penser or rien n'indique qu'il va accepter; **he gave no ~ of wishing to come with us** il ne donnait aucun signe de or il n'avait pas du tout l'air de vouloir venir avec nous; **he gave no ~ of having heard us** rien n'indiquait qu'il nous avait entendus; **there was no ~ of life** il n'y avait aucun signe de vie; (lit, fig) **he gave no ~ of life** il n'a pas donné signe de vie; **there's no ~ of him anywhere** on ne le trouve nulle part, il n'y a aucune trace de lui; **there's no ~ of it anywhere** c'est introuvable, je (or il etc) n'arrive pas à le (re)trouver → **show**

[d] (= notice) panneau m; (on inn, shop) enseigne f; (Aut = traffic warnings etc) panneau m (de signalisation); (Aut = directions on motorways etc) panneau m (indicateur); (= writing on signpost) direction f, indication f; (on road) **I can't read the ~** je n'arrive pas à lire le panneau

[2] VT **[a]** [+ letter, document, register, visitors' book] signer; **to ~ one's name** signer (son nom); **he ~s himself John Smith** il signe « John Smith »; (in letters) **~ed John Smith** signé John Smith; **~ed and sealed** [agreement] conclu en bonne et due forme; [new law] voté en bonne et due forme; (fig) **it was ~ed, sealed and delivered by twelve noon** à midi, l'affaire était entièrement réglée → **pledge**

[b] (Ftbl etc) **to ~ a player** engager un joueur **[c]** [+ spoken language] traduire en langue des signes

[3] VI **[a]** signer; **you have to ~ for the key** vous devez signer pour obtenir la clé; **he ~ed for the parcel** il a signé le reçu pour le colis; (Ftbl) **Smith has ~ed for Celtic** Smith a signé un contrat avec le Celtic → **dotted**

[b] **to ~ to sb to do sth** faire signe à qn de faire qch

[c] (= use sign language) s'exprimer dans le langage des signes, signer

[4] COMP ► **sign language** N langage m des signes; **to talk in ~ language** parler or communiquer par signes ► **sign writer** N peintre mf d'enseignes

► **sign away** VT SEP **to ~ sth away** signer sa renonciation à qch, signer l'abandon de son droit sur qch; (fig) **to ~ one's life away** hypothéquer son avenir

► **sign in [1]** VI (in factory) pointer (en arrivant); (in hotel, club etc) signer le registre (en arrivant) **[2]** VT SEP (at club) **to ~ sb in** faire entrer qn en tant qu'invité (en signant le registre)

► **sign off** VI **[a]** (Rad, TV) terminer l'émission; **this is Jacques Dupont ~ing off** ici Jacques Dupont qui vous dit au revoir **[b]** (on leaving work) pointer en partant; (Brit: DSS) informer la sécurité sociale que l'on a retrouvé du travail **[c]** (at end of letter) terminer sa lettre

► **sign on [1]** VI **[a]** (= enrol) (for course etc) s'inscrire; (Ind etc: for job) se faire embaucher

(as comme, en tant que); (Mil) s'engager (as comme, en tant que); (Brit: at employment office) pointer au chômage, pointer à la sécurité sociale; **I've ~ed on for German conversation** je me suis inscrit au cours de conversation allemande **[b]** (on arrival at work) pointer en arrivant **[2]** VT SEP [+ employee] embaucher; (Mil) engager

► **sign out [1]** VT SEP [+ library book, sports equipment etc] signer pour emprunter **[2]** VI (in hotel, club etc) signer le registre (en partant); (in office) pointer (en partant)

► **sign over** VT SEP céder par écrit (**to** à)

► **sign up [1]** VI = **sign on 1a [2]** VT SEP = **sign on 2**

signal ['sɪgnl] **[1]** N **[a]** (gen, Ling, Naut, Psych, Rail) signal m; **at a prearranged ~** à un signal convenu; **the ~ for departure** le signal du départ; (Naut) **flag ~s** signaux mpl par pavillons; **(traffic) ~s** feux mpl de circulation; (Rail) **the ~ is at red** le signal est au rouge; (Aut) **I didn't see his ~** je n'ai pas vu son clignotant → **distress, hand**

[b] (= electronic impulse, message: Rad, Telec, TV) signal m; **I'm getting the engaged ~** ça sonne occupé or pas libre; **send a ~ to HQ to the effect that ...** envoyez un signal or message au QG pour dire que ...; (Rad, Telec, TV) **the ~ is very weak** le signal est très faible; (Rad, TV) **station ~** indicatif m de l'émetteur; (Mil) **the Signals** les Transmissions fpl

[2] ADJ [success, triumph] éclatant, insigne (liter); [failure] notoire, insigne (liter); [contribution] remarquable, insigne (liter); [importance] capital

[3] VT [+ message] communiquer par signaux; **to ~ sb on/through** etc faire signe à qn d'avancer/de passer etc; (Aut) **to ~ a turn** indiquer or signaler un changement de direction

[4] VI (gen) faire des signaux; (Aut) mettre son clignotant; **to ~ to sb** faire signe à qn (**to do** de faire)

[5] COMP ► **signal book** N (Naut) code m international de signaux, livre m des signaux ► **signal box** N (Rail) cabine f d'aiguillage, poste m d'aiguillage or de signalisation ► **signal flag** N (Naut) pavillon m de signalisation

signalize ['sɪgnəlaɪz] VT (= mark, make notable) marquer; (= point out) distinguer, signaler

signally ['sɪgnəlɪ] ADV manifestement; **a task they have ~ failed to accomplish** une tâche qu'ils n'ont manifestement pas su accomplir; **the present law has ~ failed** la loi actuelle a manifestement échoué

signalman ['sɪgnəlmæn] N (pl **-men**) (Rail) aiguilleur m; (Naut) signaleur m, sémaphoriste m

signatory ['sɪgnətərɪ] **[1]** ADJ signataire **[2]** N signataire mf (**to** de)

signature ['sɪgnətfə'] **[1]** N **[a]** signature f; **to set** or **put one's ~ to sth** apposer sa signature à qch **[b]** (Mus = key signature) armature f **[2]** COMP ► **signature tune** N (esp Brit) indicatif m (musical)

signboard ['saɪnbɔːd] N (for advertisements) panneau m publicitaire

signer ['saɪnə'] N signataire mf

signet ['sɪgnɪt] **[1]** N sceau m, cachet m **[2]** COMP ► **signet ring** N chevalière f → **writer**

significance [sɪg'nɪfɪkəns] N (= meaning) signification f; (= importance) [of event, speech] importance f, portée f; **a look of deep ~** un regard lourd de sens; **what he thinks is of no ~** peu importe ce qu'il pense

▼ **significant** [sɪg'nɪfɪkənt] **[1]** ADJ **[a]** (= appreciable) [number, amount, difference, factor, role, implications] significatif; [event] significatif, d'une grande portée; **a ~ number of people** un nombre significatif de personnes, un grand nombre de gens **[b]** (= meaningful: gen)

significatif; [*look, sigh, tone*] lourd de sens; **it is ~ that ...** il est significatif que ... (+ *subj*); **statistically/politically/historically** ~ statistiquement/politiquement/historiquement significatif [2] COMP ▶ **significant figure** N (*Math*) chiffre *m* significatif ▶ **significant other** N partenaire *mf*

significantly [sɪɡˈnɪfɪkəntlɪ] ADV [a] (= *appreciably*) [*higher, lower, different, better, reduced*] considérablement; [*contribute*] fortement; **to change/improve/increase ~** changer/s'améliorer/augmenter considérablement [b] (= *notably*) **he was ~ absent** son absence a été remarquée; **~, most applicants are men** il est significatif que la plupart des candidats soient des hommes; **~, he refused** il est significatif qu'il ait refusé [c] (= *meaningfully*) **to look at sb** ~ jeter à qn un regard lourd de sens; **to smile ~** avoir un sourire lourd de sens

signification [ˌsɪɡnɪfɪˈkeɪʃən] N signification *f*, sens *m*

signify [ˈsɪɡnɪfaɪ] [1] VT [a] (= *mean*) signifier, vouloir dire (**that** que); (= *indicate*) indiquer, dénoter; **it signifies intelligence** cela indique or dénote de l'intelligence [b] (= *make known*) signifier, indiquer (**that** que); [+ *one's approval*] signifier; [+ *one's opinion*] faire connaître [2] VI avoir de l'importance; **it does not ~** cela n'a aucune importance, cela importe peu

signing [ˈsaɪnɪŋ] N [a] [*of letter, contract, treaty etc*] signature *f* [b] (*Sport*) **Clarke, their recent ~ from Liverpool** Clarke, leur récent transfert or transfuge de Liverpool [c] (= *sign language*) langage *m* des signes

signpost [ˈsaɪnpəʊst] [1] N poteau *m* indicateur [2] VT [+ *direction, place*] indiquer; **Lewes is ~ed at the crossroads** Lewes est indiqué au carrefour; **the road is badly ~ed** (= *not indicated*) la route est mal indiquée; (= *no signposts on it*) la route est mal signalisée

signposting [ˈsaɪnpəʊstɪŋ] N signalisation *f* (verticale)

Sikh [siːk] [1] N Sikh *mf* [2] ADJ sikh

Sikhism [ˈsiːkɪzəm] N sikhisme *m*

silage [ˈsaɪlɪdʒ] N (= *fodder*) fourrage *m* ensilé or vert; (= *method*) ensilage *m*

silence [ˈsaɪləns] [1] N silence *m*; **he called for ~** il a demandé or réclamé le silence; **when he finished speaking, there was ~** quand il a eu fini de parler, le silence s'est installé; **the ~ was broken by a cry** un cri a rompu or déchiré le silence; **they listened in ~** ils ont écouté en silence; **a two minutes' ~** deux minutes de silence; **your ~ on this matter ...** le mutisme dont vous faites preuve à ce sujet ...; (*fig*) **there is ~ in official circles** dans les milieux autorisés on garde le silence; **to pass sth over in ~** passer qch sous silence ■ (*PROV*) **~ gives or means consent** qui ne dit mot consent (*PROV*) ■ (*PROV*) **~ is golden** le silence est d'or (*PROV*) → **dead, radio, reduce**

[2] VT [a] [+ *person, critic, guns*] (*gen*) faire taire; (*by force etc*) réduire au silence; [+ *noise*] étouffer; [+ *conscience*] faire taire; **to ~ criticism** faire taire les critiques; **to ~ the opposition** faire taire l'opposition, réduire l'opposition au silence [b] (= *kill*) **to ~ sb** faire taire qn définitivement

silencer [ˈsaɪlənsəʳ] N (*on gun, Brit: on car*) silencieux *m*

silent [ˈsaɪlənt] [1] ADJ [a] (= *making no noise*) [*person, machine, place, prayer, demonstration, tribute*] silencieux; **to be** or **keep ~** garder le silence, rester silencieux; **to fall** or **become ~** se taire; **be ~!** taisez-vous!, silence!; **~ tears rolled down his cheeks** des larmes coulaient en silence sur ses joues; **to look at sb in ~ contempt** dévisager qn en silence et avec mépris; **she looked at me in ~ admiration** elle me regarda, muette d'admiration; **to watch in ~ despair** observer avec un désespoir muet; **to sit in ~ contemplation of sth** rester assis à contempler qch en silence; **his mouth was open in a ~ scream** il avait la bouche ouverte pour crier mais aucun son n'en sortait; **to make a ~ protest** protester en silence; **it was (as) ~ as the grave** or **the tomb** il régnait un silence de mort → **1b**

[b] (= *saying nothing*) **to be ~ (on** or **about sth)** [*person, organization*] garder le silence (sur qch), rester muet (sur qch); **the law is ~ on this point** la loi ne dit rien à ce sujet; **to keep** or **remain** or **stay ~ (on** or **about sth)** garder le silence (sur qch); **he was (as) ~ as the grave** or **tomb** il était muet comme une tombe → **1a**; (*Police*) **you have the right to remain ~** vous avez le droit de garder le silence; **to give sb the ~ treatment** ne plus parler à qn

[c] (= *taciturn*) [*person*] taciturne; **he's the strong, ~ type** il est du genre géant taciturne [d] (*Cine*) [*film, movie*] muet; **the ~ era** l'époque *f* du (cinéma) muet [e] (*Ling* = *not pronounced*) [*letter*] muet; **~ "h"** « h » muet

[2] N (*Cine: gen pl*) **the ~s** les films *mpl* muets, le (cinéma) muet

[3] COMP ▶ **silent killer** N *maladie mortelle aux symptômes indécelables* ▶ **the silent majority** N la majorité silencieuse ▶ **silent partner** N (*US Comm*) (associé *m*) commanditaire *m* ▶ **silent revolution** N révolution *f* silencieuse ▶ **the silent screen** (*Cine*) le (cinéma) muet ▶ **silent witness** N témoin *m* muet

silently [ˈsaɪləntlɪ] ADV (= *without speaking*) en silence; (= *without making any noise*) silencieusement

Silesia [saɪˈliːʃə] N la Silésie

silex [ˈsaɪleks] N silex *m*

silhouette [ˌsɪluːˈet] [1] N (*gen, Art*) silhouette *f*; **to see sth in ~** voir la silhouette de qch, voir qch en silhouette [2] VT **to be ~d against** se découper contre, se profiler sur, se silhouetter sur; **~d against** se découpant contre, se profilant sur, silhouetté sur

silica [ˈsɪlɪkə] [1] N silice *f* [2] COMP ▶ **silica gel** N gel *m* de silice

silicate [ˈsɪlɪkɪt] N silicate *m*

siliceous [sɪˈlɪʃəs] ADJ siliceux

silicon [ˈsɪlɪkən] [1] N silicium *m* [2] COMP ▶ **silicon carbide** N carbure *m* de silicium ▶ **silicon chip** N puce *f* électronique, pastille *f* de silicium, microplaquette *f*

silicone [ˈsɪlɪkəʊn] N silicone *f*

silicosis [ˌsɪlɪˈkəʊsɪs] N silicose *f*

silk [sɪlk] [1] N [a] (= *material*) soie *f*; (= *thread*) (fil *m* de) soie *f*; **they were all in their ~s and satins** elles étaient toutes en grande toilette; **the shelves were full of ~s and satins** les rayonnages regorgeaient de soieries et de satins → **artificial, raw, sewing**

[b] (*Brit Jur* = *barrister*) avocat *m* de la couronne; **to take ~** être nommé avocat de la couronne

[2] ADJ de or en soie ■ (*PROV*) **you can't make a ~ purse out of a sow's ear** on ne peut pas arriver à un excellent résultat sans de bonnes bases

[3] COMP ▶ **silk factory** N fabrique *f* de soie ▶ **silk finish** N **with a ~ finish** [*cloth*] similisé, mercerisé; [*paintwork*] satiné ▶ **silk hat** N haut-de-forme *m* ▶ **silk industry** N soierie *f* ▶ **silk manufacturer** N fabricant *m* en soierie; (*in Lyons*) soyeux *m* ▶ **silk-screen printing** N (*NonC*) sérigraphie *f* ▶ **silk stocking** N bas *m* de soie ▶ **silk thread** N fil *m* de soie, soie *f* à coudre

silken [ˈsɪlkən] [1] ADJ [a] (= *made of silk*) [*ribbon, fabric*] de soie, en soie [b] (= *like silk*) [*hair, eyelashes, skin*] soyeux; [*voice*] suave; **a ~ sheen** un lustre soyeux [2] COMP ▶ **the Silken Ladder** N (*Mus*) l'Échelle *f* de soie

silkiness [ˈsɪlkɪnɪs] N qualité *f* or douceur *f* soyeuse, soyeux *m*

silkworm [ˈsɪlkwɜːm] N ver *m* à soie; **~ breeding** sériciculture *f* (*Tech*), élevage *m* des vers à soie

silky [ˈsɪlkɪ] ADJ [*hair, skin, fabric*] soyeux; [*voice*] suave; **a ~ sheen** un lustre soyeux; **~ smooth** or **soft** d'une douceur soyeuse

sill [sɪl] N [*of window*] rebord *m*, appui *m*; [*of door*] seuil *m*; (*Aut*) bas *m* de marche

silliness [ˈsɪlɪnɪs] N sottise *f*, stupidité *f*, niaiserie *f*

silly [ˈsɪlɪ] [1] ADJ [a] (= *foolish*) [*person*] bête, sot; [*behaviour, mistake*] bête; [*remark, idea, game*] ridicule; **I hope he won't do anything ~** j'espère qu'il ne va pas faire de bêtises; **don't be ~!** ne fais pas l'idiot(e)!; **to drink o.s. ~*** boire à en devenir idiot; **you ~ fool!** espèce d'idiot(e)!; **the ~ idiot!** quel(le) imbécile!; **you're a ~ little boy** tu es un gros bêta*; **shut up, you ~ old fool!** tais-toi, vieux fou!; **(if you) ask a ~ question, (you) get a ~ answer** à question idiote, réponse idiote; **I'm sorry, it was a ~ thing to say** excusez-moi, j'ai dit une bêtise; **that was a ~ thing to do** c'était bête de faire ça; **it's the silliest thing I ever heard** c'est la plus grosse bêtise que j'aie jamais entendue; **I used to worry about the silliest little things** je m'inquiétais des moindres vétilles; **he was ~ to resign** il a été bête de démissionner

[b] (= *ridiculous*) [*name, hat, price*] ridicule; **I feel ~ in this hat** je me sens ridicule avec ce chapeau; **to make sb look ~** rendre qn ridicule

[2] N* idiot(e) *m(f)*; **you big ~!** espèce d'imbécile!

[3] COMP ▶ **silly billy*** N gros bêta*, grosse bêtasse* ▶ **silly money*** N sommes *fpl* ridiculement élevées ▶ **the silly season** N (*Brit Press*) la période creuse (*pour la presse*)

silo [ˈsaɪləʊ] N (*gen, Mil*) silo *m*

silt [sɪlt] N (*gen*) limon *m*; (= *mud*) vase *f* ▶**silt up** [1] VI (*with mud*) s'envaser; (*with sand*) s'ensabler [2] VT SEP engorger

silting [ˈsɪltɪŋ] N envasement *m*, ensablement *m*

Silurian [saɪˈlʊərɪən] ADJ, N (*Geol*) silurien *m*

silver [ˈsɪlvəʳ] [1] N (*NonC*) [a] (= *metal*) argent *m*; (= *silverware, cutlery etc*) argenterie *f* [b] (= *money*) argent *m* (monnayé), monnaie *f* (*en pièces d'argent ou de nickel*); **have you got any ~? — sorry, only notes and coppers** est-ce que vous avez de la monnaie? — désolé, je n'ai que des billets ou alors de la petite monnaie or des pièces jaunes; **£2 in ~** 2 livres en pièces d'argent

[2] ADJ [a] (= *made of silver*) en argent; (*fig*) **to be born with a ~ spoon in one's mouth** naître avec une cuiller d'argent dans la bouche [b] (*in colour*) argenté; [*car*] gris métallisé *inv* → **cloud**

[3] VT [+ *mirror, fork*] argenter

[4] COMP ▶ **silver age** N âge *m* d'argent ▶ **silver birch** N bouleau *m* argenté ▶ **silver collection** N (*at meeting etc*) quête *f*; **"there will be a ~ collection"** « vous êtes priés de contribuer généreusement à la quête » ▶ **silver disc** N (*Brit Mus*) disque *m* d'argent ▶ **silver fir** N sapin *m* argenté ▶ **silver foil** N = **silver paper** ▶ **silver fox** N renard *m* argenté ▶ **silver gilt** N plaqué *m* argent ▶ **silver-grey** ADJ gris argenté *inv* ▶ **silver-haired** ADJ aux cheveux argentés ▶ **silver jubilee** N (fête *f* du) vingt-cinquième anniversaire *m* (*d'un événement*) ▶ **silver lining** N (fig) **to have a ~ lining** avoir de bons côtés; **to look for the ~ lining** attendre une éclaircie; **to look for the ~ lining in sth** chercher le bon côté de qch → **cloud** ▶ **silver medal** N mé-

daille f d'argent ► **silver medallist** N médaillé(e) m(f) d'argent ► **silver paper** N papier m d'argent ► **silver plate** N (NonC) (= solid silver articles) argenterie f; (= electroplate) plaqué m argent ► **silver-plated** ADJ argenté, plaqué argent inv ► **silver plating** N argenture f ► **the silver screen** N (Cine) le grand écran ► **the Silver State** N (US) le Nevada ► **silver tongue** N (fig) **to have a ~ tongue** être beau parleur; **his ~ tongue** ses belles paroles ► **silver-tongued** ADJ à la langue déliée, éloquent ► **silver wedding** N noces fpl d'argent

silverfish ['sɪlvəfɪʃ] N (pl silverfish) poisson m d'argent, lépisme m

silverside ['sɪlvəsaɪd] N (Brit Culin) ≈ gîte m à la noix

silversmith ['sɪlvəsmɪθ] N orfèvre mf

silverware ['sɪlvəweəʳ] N (NonC) argenterie f

silvery ['sɪlvərɪ] ADJ (colour, light, hair] argenté; [sound, voice, laugh] argentin; **~ grey/white** gris/blanc argenté inv

silviculture ['sɪlvɪˌkʌltʃəʳ] N sylviculture f

simian ['sɪmɪən] ADJ, N simien(ne) m(f)

similar ['sɪmɪləʳ] **1** ADJ semblable (**to sb/sth** à qn/qch); (= roughly similar) similaire (**to sb/sth** à qn/qch); **we have a ~ house** notre maison est presque la même or presque pareille; **your case is ~** votre cas est semblable or similaire; **the two houses are so ~ that ...** les deux maisons sont si semblables que or se ressemblent à tel point que ...; **on a ~ occasion** dans des circonstances semblables or similaires, en semblable occasion; **in a ~ situation** dans une situation semblable or similaire; **in a ~ way** à peu près de la même façon; **everyone is of a ~ age** tout le monde a à peu près le même âge; **they all taste somewhat ~** ils ont tous à peu près le même goût; **paint removers and ~ products** les décapants et les produits similaires; **he asked for 38 ~ offences to be considered** il a demandé à ce que 38 délits similaires soient pris en considération; **~ in appearance** d'aspect semblable; **to be ~ in design** être d'une conception similaire; **the two houses are ~ in size** les deux maisons sont de dimensions similaires or comparables; **he is ~ in character to his father** il a un tempérament qui se rapproche de celui de son père; **it is ~ in colour** c'est à peu près de la même couleur; **it is ~ in colour to ruby** c'est d'une couleur semblable à celle du rubis; **vehicles ~ to the bicycle** véhicules mpl voisins de or apparentés à la bicyclette; **the feeling is ~ to being drunk** la sensation est semblable à celle de l'ivresse

2 COMP ► **similar triangles** NPL (Geom) triangles mpl semblables

▼ **similarity** [ˌsɪmɪ'lærɪtɪ] N ressemblance f (**to** avec, **between** entre), similitude f (**between** entre), similarité f (**between** entre)

similarly ['sɪmɪləlɪ] ADV [treat, behave etc] de la même façon, de façon similaire; [pleasant, unpleasant, angry etc] tout aussi; **they were ~ dressed** ils étaient habillés de façon similaire, leurs vêtements se ressemblaient; **~, we don't agree with ...** de même, nous ne sommes pas d'accord avec ...

simile ['sɪmɪlɪ] N (Literat) comparaison f; **style rich in ~** style m riche en comparaisons

similitude [sɪ'mɪlɪtjuːd] N similitude f, ressemblance f; (Literat etc) comparaison f

SIMM (chip) ['sɪm(tʃɪp)] ABBR = **single in-line memory module** N barrette f SIMM

simmer ['sɪməʳ] **1** N (= slight boil) faible ébullition f; **the stew was just on the ~** le ragoût cuisait à feu doux or mijotait **2** VI [water] frémir; [vegetables] cuire à feu doux; [soup, stew] mijoter, cuire à feu doux; (fig) (with excitement) être en ébullition; (with anticipation) être tout excité d'avance; (with discontent) bouillir de mécontentement; [revolt] couver; [anger] couver, monter; **he was**

~ing (with rage) il bouillait (de rage) **3** VT [+ water, dye] faire cuire à petits bouillons; [+ soup, stew] faire mijoter or cuire à feu doux; [+ vegetables] faire cuire à feu doux

► **simmer down*** VI (fig) s'apaiser, se calmer; **~ down!** calme-toi!, un peu de calme!

simnel cake ['sɪmnlkeɪk] N (Brit) gâteau m aux raisins recouvert de pâte d'amandes (généralement servi à Pâques)

Simon ['saɪmən] N Simon m; (= game) **~ says ...** Jacques a dit ...

simonize ['saɪmənaɪz] VT lustrer, polir

simony ['saɪmənɪ] N simonie f

simper ['sɪmpəʳ] **1** N sourire m affecté; **~s** minauderie(s) f(pl) **2** VTI minauder; **"yes" she ~ed** « oui » dit-elle en minaudant

simpering ['sɪmpərɪŋ] **1** N minauderies fpl, mignardises fpl **2** ADJ [person] minaudier; [smile] affecté; **to give sb a ~ smile** sourire à qn en minaudant

simperingly ['sɪmpərɪŋlɪ] ADV d'une manière affectée, avec affectation

simple ['sɪmpl] **1** ADJ **a** (= uncomplicated) [question, task, machine, food, person, substance, life form] simple (after n); **it's as ~ as ABC** c'est simple comme bonjour; **a dangerously ~ way of ...** une façon dangereusement simpliste de ...; **a ~ black dress** une robe noire toute simple; **in ~ English** ◊ **in ~ language** en termes simples, en langage clair; **the ~ life** la vie simple; **she likes the ~ life** elle aime vivre simplement or avec simplicité; **the ~ things in or of life** les choses simples de la vie; **they're ~ people** ce sont des gens simples; **I'm a ~ soul** je suis tout simple; **in ~ terms** en termes simples; **to make simple(r)** simplifier; **it's a ~ matter to have the clock repaired** c'est très simple de faire réparer la pendule → **1b**; **nothing could be simpler!** c'est tout ce qu'il y a de plus simple!; **it is ~ to fix** c'est facile à réparer; **the camcorder is ~ to use** ce caméscope est simple à utiliser; **the ~ truth** la vérité pure → **pure**

b (= mere) simple (before n); **the ~ fact that ...** le simple fait que ...; **the ~ fact is I haven't the time** je n'ai tout simplement pas le temps; **the ~ fact is he's a liar** c'est simplement un menteur; **he's a ~ labourer** c'est un simple manœuvre; **it's a ~ matter of money/practice** c'est une simple question d'argent/de pratique; **it's a ~ matter of buying another key** il s'agit tout simplement d'acheter une autre clef → **1a**; **a ~ phone call could win you a week's holiday in Florida** un simple appel et vous pourriez gagner une semaine de vacances en Floride; **for the ~ reason that ...** pour la simple raison que ...

c (*: mentally) [person] simplet

2 COMP ► **simple division** N (Math) division f simple ► **simple equation** N (Math) équation f du premier degré ► **simple fracture** N (Med) fracture f simple ► **simple-hearted** ADJ candide, franc (franche f), ouvert ► **simple interest** N (Fin) intérêts mpl simples ► **simple majority** N majorité f simple ► **simple-minded** ADJ simplet, simple d'esprit, naïf (naïve f) ► **simple-mindedness** N simplicité f d'esprit, naïveté f ► **simple sentence** N phrase f simple ► **Simple Simon** N nigaud m, naïf m ► **simple tense** N temps m simple ► **simple time** N (Mus) mesure f simple

simpleton ['sɪmpltən] N nigaud(e) m(f), niais(e) m(f)

simplicity [sɪm'plɪsɪtɪ] N simplicité f; **it's ~ itself** c'est la simplicité même, c'est tout ce qu'il y a de plus simple

simplifiable ['sɪmplɪfaɪəbl] ADJ simplifiable

simplification [ˌsɪmplɪfɪ'keɪʃən] N simplification f

simplify ['sɪmplɪfaɪ] VT simplifier

simplistic [sɪm'plɪstɪk] ADJ (pej) simpliste; **it is ~ to say that ...** il est simpliste de dire que ...

Simplon Pass ['sɪmplɒnˌpɑːs] N col m du Simplon

simply ['sɪmplɪ] ADV **a** (= merely) simplement; **I ~ said that ...** j'ai simplement dit que ...; **she could ~ refuse** elle pourrait refuser purement et simplement; **he was known ~ as Jay** on l'appelait simplement Jay; **it ~ isn't possible** ◊ **it's ~ impossible** c'est absolument or tout simplement impossible; **that's ~ the way it is** c'est comme ça; **it's ~ a question of money** c'est simplement une question d'argent; **they sacked her ~ because she's pregnant** ils l'ont renvoyée simplement parce qu'elle était enceinte

b (= absolutely) **you ~ must come!** il faut absolument que vous veniez (subj)!; **I ~ can't believe it** je n'arrive vraiment pas à y croire; **that is ~ not true** c'est tout simplement faux; **that is ~ not good enough!** c'est lamentable!; **he is quite ~ the best** il est tout simplement le meilleur, il est le meilleur, cela ne fait aucun doute; **it was quite ~ the worst moment of my life** ce fut sans aucun doute le pire moment de ma vie

c (= straightforwardly) [speak] simplement; **very ~, he was short of money** il était tout simplement à court d'argent; **to put it ~, we've got a problem** en deux mots, nous avons un problème

d (= modestly) [live, dress, furnish] simplement, avec simplicité

simulacrum [ˌsɪmjʊ'leɪkrəm] N (pl simulacra [sɪmjʊ'leɪkrə]) simulacre m

simulate ['sɪmjʊleɪt] **1** VT **a** (Aviat, Comput, Space, Tech etc) simuler **b** [+ passion, enthusiasm, grief, illness] simuler, feindre **2** COMP ► **simulated leather** N imitation f cuir

simulation [ˌsɪmjʊ'leɪʃən] N (gen, Comput) simulation f

simulator ['sɪmjʊleɪtəʳ] N (Aut, Space) simulateur m; (Aviat: also **flight ~**) simulateur m de vol

simulcast ['sɪmlkɑːst] **1** VT diffuser simultanément à la radio et à la télévision **2** N émission f radiotélévisée

simultaneity [ˌsɪmltə'niːɪtɪ] N simultanéité f

simultaneous [ˌsɪml'teɪnɪəs] **1** ADJ simultané **2** COMP ► **simultaneous broadcast** N émission f simultanée ► **simultaneous equations** NPL (Math) système m d'équations ► **simultaneous translation** N traduction f simultanée

simultaneously [ˌsɪml'teɪnɪəslɪ] ADV simultanément; **~ with sb/sth** en même temps que qn/qch

sin [sɪn] **1** N péché m; **~s of omission/commission** péchés mpl par omission/par action; **a ~ against (the law of) God** un manquement à la loi de Dieu; **it's a ~ to do that** (Rel) c'est un péché de faire cela; (hum) c'est une honte or un crime de faire cela; **to live in ~†** (unmarried) vivre dans le péché (**with sb** avec qn) → **seven, ugly 2** VI pécher (**against** contre); **he was more ~ned against than ~ning** il était plus victime que coupable **3** COMP ► **sin bin** N (US Ice Hockey etc) prison f ► **sin tax*** N (US) taxe f sur le tabac et les alcools

Sinai ['saɪneɪaɪ] N (the) **~** le Sinaï; **the ~ Desert** le désert du Sinaï; **Mount ~** le mont Sinaï

Sinbad ['sɪnbæd] N ► **the Sailor** Sinbad le Marin

▼ **since** [sɪns] **1** CONJ **a** (in time) depuis que; **~ I have been here** depuis que je suis ici; **ever ~ I met him** depuis que or depuis le jour où je l'ai rencontré; **it's a week ~ I saw him** cela fait une semaine que je ne l'ai (pas) vu, je ne l'ai pas vu depuis une semaine; **it is a long time ~ I last saw you** il y a longtemps que je ne vous ai vu; **it's ages ~ I saw you** cela fait des siècles qu'on ne s'est pas vus*

b (= *because*) puisque; **why don't you buy it, ~ you are so rich!** achète-le donc, puisque tu es si riche!

2 ADV depuis; **he has not been here ~** il n'est pas venu depuis; **he has been my friend ever ~** il est resté mon ami depuis (ce moment-là); **a short time ~** ◊ **not long ~** il y a peu de temps; **it's many years ~** il y a bien des années de cela, cela fait bien des années

3 PREP depuis; **~ arriving** or **his arrival** depuis son arrivée, depuis qu'il est arrivé; **I have been waiting ~ 10 o'clock** j'attends depuis 10 heures; **~ then** depuis (lors); **~ when has he had a car?** depuis quand a-t-il une voiture?; (*iro*) **~ when?* ~** when? depuis quand?; **he left in June, ~ when we have not heard from him** il est parti en juin et nous sommes sans nouvelles depuis or et depuis lors nous sommes sans nouvelles; **ever ~ 1900 France has attempted to ...** depuis 1900 la France tente de or a sans cesse tenté de ...; **ever ~ then** or **that time she's never gone out alone** depuis ce temps-là elle ne sort plus jamais seule; **how long is it ~ the accident** il s'est passé combien de temps depuis l'accident?, l'accident remonte à quand?

▼ **sincere** [sɪnˈsɪəʳ] ADJ sincère (**about sth** à propos de qch); **my ~ good wishes** mes vœux les plus sincères; **it is my ~ belief that ...** je crois sincèrement que ...; **to be ~ in one's desire to do sth** or **in wanting to do sth** désirer or vouloir sincèrement faire qch

sincerely [sɪnˈsɪəlɪ] ADV **a** (= *genuinely*) [*hope, believe, regret, say*] sincèrement; **his ~ held religious beliefs** les croyances religieuses auxquelles il est sincèrement attaché **b** (*in letters*) **Yours ~** (*Brit*) ◊ **Sincerely yours** (*US*) Veuillez agréer, Monsieur (or Madame *etc*), l'expression de mes salutations distinguées

sincerity [sɪnˈserɪtɪ] N [*of person, emotion*] sincérité *f*; **in all ~** en toute sincérité

sine [saɪn] N (*Math*) sinus *m*

sinecure [ˈsaɪnɪkjʊəʳ] N sinécure *f*

sine qua non [ˈsaɪnɪˈkweɪˈnɒn] N condition *f* sine qua non

sinew [ˈsɪnjuː] N (*Anat*) tendon *m*; **~s** (= *muscles*) muscles *mpl*; (= *strength*) force(s) *f(pl)*; (= *energy*) vigueur *f*, nerf *m*; **money is the ~s of war** l'argent est le nerf de la guerre; **a man of great moral ~** un homme d'une grande force morale

sinewy [ˈsɪnjʊɪ] ADJ (= *muscular*) [*person*] musclé; [*body, arms*] nerveux; [*muscles*] bien dessiné; (*Culin*) [*meat*] tendineux; (= *vigorous*) [*music, performance*] vigoureux; [*writing, style*] nerveux

sinfonietta [ˌsɪnfənˈjetə] N (= *short symphony*) sinfonietta *f*; (= *small symphony orchestra*) sinfonietta *m*

sinful [ˈsɪnfʊl] ADJ [*behaviour*] honteux, immoral; [*city, world*] plein de péchés, de perdition; [*act, waste, system*] honteux; [*thought, pleasure, desire*] coupable; **a ~ act** un péché; **he was taught that sex was ~** on lui a appris que les rapports sexuels étaient un péché; **her ~ past** son passé dissolu or de pécheresse (*hum*); **a fridge filled with ~ goodies** un réfrigérateur rempli de bonnes choses qui invitent au péché; **it was ~ to ...** on considérait cela comme un péché de ...

sinfully [ˈsɪnfəlɪ] ADV [*behave, think*] d'une façon coupable; [*waste*] scandaleusement

sinfulness [ˈsɪnfʊlnɪs] N (*NonC*) [*of person*] péchés *mpl*; [*of deed*] caractère *m* coupable or scandaleux

sing [sɪŋ] (*pret* **sang**, *ptp* **sung**) **1** VT [*person, bird*] chanter; (*fig*) [+ *sb's beauty etc*] chanter, célébrer; **she sang the child to sleep** elle a chanté jusqu'à ce que l'enfant s'endorme; **she was ~ing the child to sleep** elle chantait pour que l'enfant s'endorme; **to ~ mass**

chanter la messe; **sung mass** messe *f* chantée, grand-messe *f*; (*fig*) **to ~ another tune** déchanter, changer de ton; (*fig*) **to ~ sb's/sth's praises** chanter les louanges de qn/qch; **to ~ one's own praises** vanter ses propres mérites

2 VI [*person, bird, violin*] chanter; [*ears*] bourdonner, tinter; [*wind, kettle*] siffler; **to ~ like a lark** chanter comme un rossignol; **to ~ soprano** chanter soprano; **to ~ small*** se faire tout petit, filer doux*; (*Brit fig*) **they are ~ing from the same hymn sheet** or **song sheet** ils ont le même discours

b (*US**) moucharder*, se mettre à table*

3 COMP ► **sing-along** N **to have a ~-along** chanter tous en chœur

► **sing along** VI **he invited the audience to ~-along** il a invité la salle à chanter en chœur avec lui; **I like records that get people ~ing along** j'aime les disques qui incitent les gens à chanter en chœur; **to ~ along with** or **to a record/a song/the radio** accompagner un disque/une chanson/la radio de la voix; **the audience was ~ing along to his latest hit** la salle chantait son dernier tube en chœur avec lui

► **sing out** VI chanter fort; (* *fig*) crier; **if you want anything just ~ out*** si vous voulez quoi que ce soit vous n'avez qu'à appeler (bien fort); **to ~ out for sth*** réclamer qch à grands cris

► **sing up** VI chanter plus fort; **~ up!** plus fort!

sing. (ABBR = *singular*) sing.

Singapore [ˌsɪŋəˈpɔːʳ] N Singapour; **in ~** à Singapour

Singaporean [ˌsɪŋəˈpɔːrɪən] **1** ADJ (*gen*) singapourien; [*ambassador, embassy*] de Singapour **2** N Singapourien(ne) *m(f)*

singe [sɪndʒ] **1** VT brûler légèrement; [+ *cloth, clothes*] roussir; [+ *poultry*] flamber; (*fig*) **to ~ one's wings** se brûler les ailes or les doigts **2** N (*also* **~ mark**) légère brûlure *f*; (= *scorch mark on cloth*) tache *f* de roussi, roussissure *f*

singer [ˈsɪŋəʳ] **1** N chanteur *m*, -euse *f* → **opera 2** COMP ► **singer-songwriter** N auteur-compositeur *m* (de chansons)

Singhalese [ˌsɪŋəˈliːz] **1** ADJ cing(h)alais **2 a** (*pl* **Singhaleses** or **Singhalese**) Cing(h)alais(e) *m(f)* **b** (*Ling*) cing(h)alais *m*

singing [ˈsɪŋɪŋ] **1** N (*NonC*) [*of person, bird, violin*] chant *m*; [*of kettle, wind*] sifflement *m*; (*in ears*) bourdonnement *m*, tintement *m* **2** COMP ► **singing lesson** N **to have ~ lessons** prendre des cours de chant, apprendre le chant ► **singing teacher** N professeur *m* de chant ► **singing telegram** N service qui consiste à envoyer des filles chanter des compliments à des gens dont c'est l'anniversaire ► **singing voice** N **to have a good ~ voice** avoir de la voix, avoir une belle voix

single [ˈsɪŋgl] **1** ADJ **a** (= *just one*) [*rose, shot*] seul; [*survivor*] seul, unique; [*market*] unique; **in a ~ day** en un seul jour; **a ~ diamond** un diamant monté seul; (*as ring*) un solitaire; **every ~ day** tous les jours sans exception; **to drink sth in a ~ gulp** boire qch d'un seul coup or en une seule gorgée; **I did not, for a ~ moment, doubt her sincerity** je n'ai pas douté un seul instant de sa sincérité; **there isn't a ~ moment to lose** il n'y a pas une minute à perdre; **not a ~ person had come** absolument personne n'était venu, pas une seule personne n'était venue; **she didn't mention it to a ~ one of her friends** elle ne l'a mentionné à aucun des ses amis; **if there is a ~ or one ~ objection to this proposal** s'il y a une seule or la moindre objection à cette proposition; **I didn't see a ~ soul** je n'ai vu absolument personne, je n'ai pas vu âme qui vive; **I couldn't think of a ~ thing to say** je ne savais absolument pas quoi dire

b (*esp Econ* = *unique, not several*) [*market*] unique; **a ~ or one ~ department should deal with all of these matters** un service unique or un

même service devrait traiter toutes ces affaires

c (*intensifying* = *individual*) **the biggest ~ issue in the election campaign** le sujet principal de la campagne électorale; **the ~ biggest producer of coal** le plus grand producteur de charbon; **the ~ greatest problem** le plus grand problème; **the ~ most important invention since the wheel** la plus grande invention depuis la roue

d (= *not double or multiple*) [*knot, flower, thickness, wardrobe*] simple; [*garage*] pour une voiture; **a ~ sheet** un drap pour un lit d'une personne; **a ~ whisky/gin** un whisky/gin simple, une mesure normale de whisky/gin; **to be in ~ figures** [*number, score*] être inférieur à dix; [*rate*] être inférieur à 10%; **in ~ file** en file indienne → **spacing**

e (= *unmarried*) [*person*] célibataire; [*life*] de célibataire; **she's a ~ woman** elle est célibataire, c'est une célibataire; **~ people** célibataires *mpl*; **the ~ homeless** les gens *mpl* seuls et sans abri; **"marital status?" — "~"** «situation familiale?» — «célibataire»

f (*Brit Rail etc*) **~ ticket** aller *m* simple; **how much is the ~ fare to London?** combien coûte l'aller simple pour Londres?

2 N **a** (*Cricket* = *one run*) **a ~** une seule course, un seul point; **three ~s** trois fois une course or un point

b (*Brit Rail etc* = *ticket*) aller *m* (simple)

c (*in cinema, theatre*) **there are only ~s left** il ne reste que des places séparées or isolées

d (= *record*) **a ~** un 45 tours; **his latest ~** son dernier 45 tours

e (*Brit* = *pound coin or note*) billet *m* or pièce *f* d'une livre; (*US* = *dollar note*) billet *m* d'un dollar

f (*also* **~ room**) chambre *f* simple or d'une personne

g (*drink* = *one measure*) **make mine a ~** donnez-moi un simple; **double or ~?** double ou simple?

3 **singles** NPL **a** (*Tennis etc*) simple *m*; **ladies' ~s** simple *m* dames

b (* = *unmarried people*) célibataires *mpl*; **~s bar/club** bar *m*/club *m* de rencontres pour célibataires

4 COMP ► **single-barrelled** ADJ à un canon ► **single bed** N lit *m* d'une personne ► **single-breasted** ADJ [*jacket, coat*] droit ► **single-celled** ADJ unicellulaire ► **single combat** N **in ~ combat** en combat singulier ► **single cream** N (*Brit*) crème *f* fraîche liquide ► **single-crop farming** N monoculture *f* ► **single currency** N monnaie *f* unique ► **single-decker** (*Brit*) ADJ sans impériale ◆ N autobus *m* (or tramway *m* etc) sans impériale ► **single-density** ADJ → **density** ► **single-engined** ADJ monomoteur (-trice *f*) ► **single-entry book-keeping** N comptabilité *f* en partie simple ► **single European currency** N monnaie *f* unique européenne ► **the Single European Market** N (*Pol*) le marché unique européen ► **single-handed** ADV tout seul, sans aucune aide ◆ ADJ [*achievement*] fait sans aucune aide; (*Naut*) [*sailing, voyage, race*] en solitaire; **to be ~-handed** [*person*] n'avoir aucune aide, être tout seul ► **single-handedly** ADV tout(e) seul(e), à lui *etc* tout seul ► **single honours** N (*Brit Univ: also* **~ honours degree**) ≈ licence *f* préparée dans une seule matière ► **single lens reflex** N (*also* **~ lens reflex camera**) reflex *m* (à un objectif) ► **single malt** N (*also* **~ malt whisky**) (whisky *m*) single malt *m* ► **single-masted** ADJ à un mât ► **single-minded** ADJ [*person*] résolu, ferme; [*attempt*] énergique, résolu; [*determination*] tenace; **to be ~-minded about sth** concentrer tous ses efforts sur qch; **to be ~-minded in one's efforts to do sth** tout faire en vue de faire qch ► **single-mindedly** ADV résolument ► **single-mindedness** N détermination *f*, ténacité *f* ► **single mother** N mère *f* célibataire ► **single parent** N père *m* or mère *f* célibataire ► **single-parent family** N famille *f* monoparentale ► **single-party** ADJ (*Pol*) [*state, government*] à parti unique ► **single room** N chambre *f* simple *or* individuelle ► **single-seater** N (*also* **~-seater aeroplane**) (avion *m*) monoplace *m* ► **single-sex** ADJ (*Brit*) [*school, education, class*] non mixte ► **single-sided disk** N (*Comput*) disque *m* simple face ► **single-storey** ADJ de plain-pied ► **single track** N (*Rail*) voie *f* unique ► **single-track** ADJ (*Rail*) à voie unique ; (*fig*) **to have a ~-track mind** (= *one thing at a time*) ne pouvoir se concentrer que sur une seule chose à la fois ; (= *obsessive idea*) n'avoir qu'une idée en tête ► **Single Transferable Vote** N (*Pol*) ≈ scrutin *m* de liste à représentation proportionnelle

► **single out** VT SEP (= *distinguish*) distinguer ; (= *pick out*) choisir ; **I don't want to ~ anyone out** je ne veux pas faire de distinctions ; **he's ~d out for all the nasty jobs** on le choisit pour toutes les corvées ; **to ~ o.s. out** se singulariser

singleness ['sɪŋlnɪs] N **~ of purpose** persévérance *f*, ténacité *f*

singlet ['sɪŋlɪt] N (*Brit*) maillot *m* or tricot *m* de corps, débardeur *m*

singleton ['sɪŋltən] N (*Cards*) singleton *m*

singly ['sɪŋlɪ] ADV séparément

singsong ['sɪŋsɒŋ] 1 N (*Brit*) **to have a ~** chanter en chœur 2 ADJ **~ voice** voix *f* qui psalmodie ; **to repeat sth in a ~ voice** répéter qch d'une voix chantante

singular ['sɪŋɡjʊləʳ] 1 ADJ a (*Gram*) [*noun, verb, form, ending*] au singulier b (= *exceptional, unusual*) [*lack of success*] singulier ; **a woman of ~ beauty** une femme d'une singulière beauté ; **his ~ manner of dress** sa manière singulière de s'habiller 2 N (*Gram*) singulier *m* ; **in the ~** au singulier ; **in the masculine ~** au masculin singulier

singularity [,sɪŋɡjʊ'lærɪtɪ] N singularité *f*

singularize ['sɪŋɡjʊləraɪz] VT singulariser

singularly ['sɪŋɡjʊləlɪ] ADV singulièrement

Sinhalese [,sɪnə'liːz] = **Singhalese**

sinister ['sɪnɪstəʳ] ADJ a (= *ominous*) sinistre b (*Her*) sénestre, senestre

sinisterly ['sɪnɪstəlɪ] ADV sinistrement

sink¹ [sɪŋk] (*pret* **sank**, *ptp* **sunk**) 1 VI a (= *go under*) [*ship*] couler, sombrer ; [*person, object*] couler ; **to ~ to the bottom** couler *or* aller au fond ; **to ~ like a stone** couler à pic ; (*fig*) **they left him to ~ or swim** ils l'ont laissé se sortir* *or* s'en tirer* tout seul ; **it was ~ or swim** il fallait bien s'en sortir* *or* s'en tirer* tout seul ; **~ or swim he'll have to manage by himself** il n'a qu'à se débrouiller comme il peut b [*ground*] s'affaisser ; [*foundation, building*] s'affaisser, se tasser ; [*level, river, fire*] baisser ; **the land ~s towards the sea** le terrain descend en pente vers la mer ; **the sun was ~ing** le soleil se couchait ; **the sun sank below the horizon** le soleil a disparu au-dessous de l'horizon ; **to ~ out of sight** disparaître ; **to ~ to one's knees** tomber à genoux ; **to ~ to the ground** s'affaisser, s'écrouler ; **he sank into a chair** il s'est laissé tomber *or* s'est affaissé *or* s'est effondré dans un fauteuil ; **he sank into the mud up to his knees** il s'est enfoncé dans la boue jusqu'aux genoux ; **she let her head ~ into the pillow** elle a laissé retomber sa tête sur l'oreiller ; **the water slowly sank into the ground** l'eau a pénétré *or* s'est infiltrée lentement dans le sol ; **he is ~ing fast** (= *dying*) il décline *or* il baisse rapidement c (*fig*) **to sink into a deep sleep** tomber *or* sombrer dans un profond sommeil ; **to ~ into despondency** tomber dans le découragement, se laisser aller au découragement ; **to ~ into insignificance/poverty/despair** sombrer dans l'insignifiance/la misère/le désespoir ; **he has**

sunk in my estimation il a baissé dans mon estime ; **his voice sank** sa voix s'est faite plus basse ; **his voice sank to a whisper** il s'est mis à chuchoter, sa voix n'était plus qu'un murmure ; **his heart** *or* **his spirits sank** le découragement *or* l'abattement s'est emparé de lui, il en a eu un coup de cafard* ; **his heart sank at the thought** son cœur s'est serré à cette pensée ; **it's enough to make your heart ~** c'est à vous démoraliser *or* à vous donner le cafard*

d [*prices, value, temperature, sales, numbers*] chuter ; (*St Ex*) **the shares have sunk to three dollars** les actions ont chuté jusqu'à trois dollars ; (*Fin*) **the pound has sunk to a new low** la livre est tombée plus bas que jamais *or* a atteint sa cote la plus basse

2 VT a [+ *ship*] couler, faire sombrer ; [+ *object*] immerger ; (*fig*) [+ *theory*] démolir ; [+ *business, project*] ruiner, couler ; [+ *play, book*] couler, démolir* ; [+ *person*] couler, ruiner la réputation de ; (*fig*) **they sank their differences** ils ont enterré *or* oublié *or* mis de côté leurs querelles ; **to be sunk in thought/depression/despair** être plongé dans ses pensées/la dépression/le désespoir ; **I'm sunk*** je suis fichu* *or* perdu b [+ *mine, well*] creuser, forer ; [+ *foundations*] creuser ; [+ *pipe*] noyer ; **to ~ a post 2 metres in the ground** enfoncer un pieu 2 mètres dans le sol ; **the dog sank his fangs into my leg** le chien a enfoncé *or* planté ses crocs dans ma jambe ; **he sank his teeth into the sandwich** il a mordu (à belles dents) dans le sandwich ; (*Brit*) **he can ~ a glass of beer in five seconds*** il peut avaler *or* descendre* une bière en cinq secondes ; (*Golf*) **to ~ the ball** faire entrer la balle dans le trou ; **to ~ a lot of money in a project** (= *invest*) investir *or* placer beaucoup d'argent dans une entreprise ; (= *lose*) perdre *or* engloutir beaucoup d'argent dans une entreprise

► **sink back** VI [*person*] (se laisser) retomber ; **it sank back into the water** c'est retombé dans l'eau ; **he managed to sit up but soon sank back exhausted** il a réussi à s'asseoir mais s'est bientôt laissé retomber épuisé ; **he sank back into his chair** il s'est enfoncé dans son fauteuil

► **sink down** VI [*building*] s'enfoncer, s'affaisser ; [*post*] s'enfoncer ; **to ~ down into a chair** s'enfoncer dans un fauteuil ; **to ~ down on one's knees** tomber à genoux ; **he sank down (out of sight) behind the bush** il a disparu derrière le buisson

► **sink in** VI a [*person, post etc*] s'enfoncer ; [*water, ointment etc*] pénétrer b (*fig*) [*explanation*] rentrer* ; [*remark*] faire son effet ; **when the facts sank in, he ...** quand il a eu pleinement compris les faits, il ... ; **as it hadn't really sunk in yet he ...** comme il ne réalisait pas encore, il ... ; **my explanation took a long time to ~ in** mon explication a eu du mal à rentrer*, il a (*or* ils ont *etc*) mis longtemps à comprendre mon explication

sink² [sɪŋk] 1 N (*in kitchen*) évier *m* ; (*US: in bathroom*) lavabo *m* ; **double ~** évier *m* à deux bacs ; (*fig*) **a ~ of iniquity** un lieu de perdition *or* de débauche → **kitchen** 2 COMP ► **sink unit** N bloc-évier *m*

sinker ['sɪŋkəʳ] N a (= *lead*) plomb *m* → **hook** b (*US**) (= *doughnut*) beignet *m*

sinking ['sɪŋkɪŋ] 1 ADJ a (= *foundering*) **a ~ ship** (*lit*) un bateau qui sombre ; (*fig*) [*organization, cause*] un navire en perdition (*fig*) → **rat** b **to have a ~ feeling that ...** (= *dread*) avoir le sentiment angoissant que ... ; **that ~ feeling** ce sentiment d'angoisse ; **with a ~ heart** la mort dans l'âme ; (*Fin*) **a ~ pound/dollar** une livre/un dollar en (forte) baisse 2 N **the ~ of a ship** (*accidental*) le naufrage d'un navire ; (*in battle*) la destruction d'un navire 3 COMP ► **sinking fund** N (*Fin*) fonds *mpl* d'amortissement

sinless ['sɪnlɪs] ADJ sans péché, pur, innocent

sinner ['sɪnəʳ] N pécheur *m*, -eresse *f*

Sinn Féin [,ʃɪn'feɪn] N Sinn Fein *m*

Sino- ['saɪnəʊ] PREF sino- ; **~Soviet** sino-soviétique

Sinologist [,saɪ'nɒlədʒɪst] N sinologue *mf*

Sinology [,saɪ'nɒlədʒɪ] N sinologie *f*

Sinophobia [,saɪnəʊ'fəʊbɪə] N sinophobie *f*

sinuosity [,sɪnjʊ'ɒsɪtɪ] N sinuosité *f*

sinuous ['sɪnjʊəs] ADJ [*shape, curve, road, roots*] sinueux ; [*snake, dance, music, style*] ondulant ; [*movement*] onduleux ; **with ~ grace** avec une grâce ondoyante

sinus ['saɪnəs] N (*pl* **sinuses**) sinus *m inv* ; **to have ~ trouble** avoir de la sinusite

sinusitis [,saɪnə'saɪtɪs] N (*NonC*) sinusite *f* ; **to have ~** avoir de la sinusite

Sioux [suː] 1 ADJ sioux *inv* ; (*US*) **the ~ State** le Dakota du Nord 2 N a (*pl inv*) Sioux *mf* b (*Ling*) sioux *m*

sip [sɪp] 1 N petite gorgée *f* ; **do you want a ~ of rum?** voulez-vous une goutte de rhum ? ; **he took a ~** il a bu une petite gorgée 2 VT (= *drink a little at a time*) boire à petites gorgées *or* à petits coups ; (= *take a sip*) boire une petite gorgée de ; (*with enjoyment*) siroter* 3 VI **he ~ped at his whisky** (= *drank a little at a time*) il a bu du whisky à petites gorgées ; (= *took a sip*) il a bu une petite gorgée de son whisky

siphon ['saɪfən] 1 N siphon *m* → **soda** 2 VT siphonner

► **siphon off** VT SEP (*lit*) siphonner ; (*fig*) [+ *people*] mettre à part ; [+ *profits, funds*] canaliser ; (*illegally*) détourner

sir [sɜːʳ] N monsieur *m* ; **yes ~** oui, Monsieur ; (*to officer in Army, Navy, Air Force*) oui, mon commandant (*or* mon lieutenant *etc*) ; (*to surgeon*) oui docteur ; (*emphatic*) **yes/no ~!*** ça oui/non ! ; (*in letter*) **Dear Sir** (Cher) Monsieur ; (*to newspaper editor*) **Sir** Monsieur (le Directeur) ; (*iro*) **my dear/good ~** mon cher/bon Monsieur ; **Sir John Smith** sir John Smith

sire ['saɪəʳ] 1 N (*Zool*) père *m* ; († = *father*) père *m* ; (†† = *ancestor*) aïeul *m* ; (*to king*) **yes ~** oui sire 2 VT engendrer

siree* [sɪ'riː] N (*US: emphatic*) **yes/no ~!** ça oui/non !

siren ['saɪərən] 1 N a (= *device*) sirène *f* b (*Myth*) **the Sirens** les sirènes *fpl* 2 ADJ (*liter*) [*charms*] séducteur (-trice *f*) ; [*song*] de sirène, enchanteur (-teresse *f*)

sirloin ['sɜːlɔɪn] 1 N aloyau *m* 2 COMP ► **sirloin steak** N bifteck *m* dans l'aloyau *or* d'aloyau

sirocco [sɪ'rɒkəʊ] N sirocco *m*

sis* [sɪs] N (ABBR = **sister**) sœurette *f*, frangine* *f*

sisal ['saɪsəl] 1 N sisal *m* 2 COMP en *or* de sisal

sissy* ['sɪsɪ] (*pej*) 1 N (= *coward*) poule *f* mouillée ; **he's a bit of a ~** (= *effeminate*) il est un peu efféminé 2 ADJ [*boy*] efféminé ; [*voice, clothes, sport*] de fille ; **a ~ man** une chochotte* ; **Mummy's little ~ boy** le petit chéri à sa maman ; **poetry is ~ stuff** la poésie est un truc de filles ; **it's ~ doing** *or* **to do that** c'est un truc* de fille

sister ['sɪstəʳ] 1 N a sœur *f* ; **her younger ~** sa (sœur) cadette, sa petite sœur → **half, step-sister** b (*Rel*) religieuse *f*, (bonne) sœur *f* ; **yes ~** oui, ma sœur ; **Sister Mary Margaret** sœur Marie Marguerite ; **the Sisters of Charity** les sœurs de la Charité c (*Brit Med: also* **nursing ~**) infirmière *f* chef ; **yes ~** oui Madame (*or* Mademoiselle) d (*US*) **listen ~!*** écoute ma vieille !* 2 ADJ [*company, party*] frère (sœur *f*) ; [*publication, hotel, radio station*] jumeau (-elle *f*) ; **~ organization** organisation *f* sœur ; **~ country** pays *m* frère ; **~ ship** sistership *m* 3 COMP ► **sister-in-law** N (*pl* **sisters-in-law**) belle-sœur *f* ► **sister school** N (*US Univ*) uni-

versité pour femmes jumelée avec une université pour hommes

sisterhood ['sɪstəhʊd] N (= *solidarity*) solidarité *f* féminine; (*Rel*) communauté *f* (religieuse); (= *group of women*) **the ~** la communauté (des femmes)

sisterly ['sɪstəlɪ] ADJ fraternel, de sœur

Sistine ['sɪstiːn] ADJ **the ~ Chapel** la chapelle Sixtine

Sisyphus ['sɪsɪfəs] N Sisyphe *m*

sit [sɪt] (*pret, ptp* **sat**) [1] VI [a] (*also* **~ down**) s'asseoir; **to be ~ting** être assis; (*to dog*) **~!** assis!; **~ by me** assieds-toi près de moi; **he was ~ting at his desk/at table** il était (assis) à son bureau/à table; **they spent the evening ~ting at home** ils ont passé la soirée (tranquillement) à la maison; **he just ~s at home all day** il reste chez lui toute la journée à ne rien faire; **he was ~ting over his books all evening** il a passé toute la soirée dans ses livres; **to ~ through a lecture/play** assister à une conférence/à une pièce jusqu'au bout; **don't just ~ there, do something!** ne reste pas là à ne rien faire!; **to ~ still** rester *or* se tenir tranquille, ne pas bouger; **to ~ straight** *or* **upright** se tenir droit; (*Art, Phot*) **to ~ for one's portrait** poser pour son portrait; **she sat for Picasso** elle a posé pour Picasso; **to ~ on a committee/jury** être membre *or* faire partie d'un comité/jury; **to ~ for an exam** passer un examen, se présenter à un examen; **he sat for Sandhurst** il s'est présenté au concours d'entrée de Sandhurst; (*Brit Parl*) **he ~s for Brighton** il est (le) député de Brighton; **to be ~ting pretty*** avoir le bon filon*, tenir le bon bout*; (*fig: hum or liter*) **to ~ at sb's feet** suivre l'enseignement de qn → **tight** [b] [*bird, insect*] se poser, se percher; **to be ~ting** être perché; (*on eggs*) couver; **the hen is ~ting on three eggs** la poule couve trois œufs [c] [*committee, assembly etc*] être en séance, siéger; **the committee is ~ting now** le comité est en séance; **the House ~s from November to June** la Chambre siège de novembre à juin; **the House sat for 16 hours** la Chambre a été en séance pendant 16 heures [d] [*dress, coat etc*] tomber (**on sb** sur qn); **the jacket ~s badly across the shoulders** la veste tombe mal aux épaules; (*fig*) **this policy would ~ well with their allies** cette politique serait bien vue de leurs alliés; (*liter*) **it sat heavy on his conscience** cela lui pesait sur la conscience; (*liter*) **how ~s the wind?** d'où vient *or* souffle le vent?

[2] VT [a] (*also* **~ down**) asseoir, installer; (*invite to sit*) faire asseoir; **he sat the child (down) on his knee** il a assis *or* installé l'enfant sur ses genoux; **they sat him (down) in a chair** (= *placed him in it*) ils l'ont assis *or* installé dans un fauteuil; (= *invited him to sit*) ils l'ont fait asseoir dans un fauteuil [b] **~ a horse well/badly** monter bien/mal, avoir une bonne/mauvaise assiette [c] (*esp Brit*) [+ *exam*] passer, se présenter à

[3] COMP ► **sit-down*** N **he had a ten-minute ~-down** il s'est assis dix minutes (pour se reposer) ♦ ADJ **we had a ~-down lunch** nous avons déjeuné à table; **~-down strike** grève *f* sur le tas ► **sit-in** N → **sit-in** ► **sit-up** N (*Gym*) redressement *m* assis

► **sit about**, **sit around** VI rester assis (à ne rien faire), traîner

► **sit back** VI **to ~ back in an armchair** s'enfoncer *or* se carrer *or* se caler dans un fauteuil; **to ~ back on one's heels** s'asseoir sur les talons; **just ~ back and listen to this** installe-toi bien et écoute un peu (ceci); (*fig*) **he sat back and did nothing about it** il s'est abstenu de faire quoi que ce soit, il n'a pas levé le petit doigt; **I can't just ~ back and do nothing!** je ne peux quand même pas rester là à ne rien faire *or* à me croiser les bras!; **the Government sat back and did nothing to help**

them le gouvernement n'a pas fait le moindre geste pour les aider

► **sit by** VI rester sans rien faire; (*fig*) **to ~ (idly) by (while ...)** rester sans rien faire (pendant que ...)

► **sit down** [1] VI s'asseoir; **to be ~ting down** être assis; **he sat down to a huge dinner** il s'est attablé devant un repas gigantesque; (*fig*) **to take sth ~ting down*** rester les bras croisés devant qch [2] VT SEP = **sit 2a** [3] **~-down*** N, ADJ → **sit**

► **sit in** [1] VI [a] **she sat in all day waiting for him to come** elle est restée à la maison toute la journée à l'attendre, elle a passé la journée chez elle à l'attendre; **to ~ in on a discussion** assister à une discussion (sans y prendre part); (*fig = replace*) **to ~ in for sb** remplacer qn [b] (*as protest*) **the demonstrators sat in in the director's office** les manifestants ont occupé le bureau du directeur [2] **~-in** N → **sit-in**

► **sit on*** VT FUS (*fig*) [a] (= *keep to oneself*) [+ *news, facts, report*] garder secret, garder le silence sur; (= *not pass on*) [+ *file, document*] garder (pour soi), accaparer; **the committee sat on the proposals for weeks, then decided to ...** pendant des semaines, le comité ne s'est pas occupé des propositions, puis a décidé de ... [b] (= *silence*) [+ *person*] faire taire, fermer *or* clouer le bec à*; **he won't be sat on** il ne se laisse pas marcher sur les pieds [c] (= *reject*) [+ *idea, proposal*] rejeter, repousser

► **sit out** [1] VI (= *sit outside*) (aller) s'asseoir dehors, se mettre *or* s'installer dehors [2] VT SEP [a] **to ~ a lecture/play out** rester jusqu'à la fin d'une conférence/d'une pièce, assister à une conférence/à une pièce jusqu'au bout [b] **she sat out the waltz** elle n'a pas dansé la valse

► **sit up** [1] VI [a] (= *sit upright*) se redresser, s'asseoir bien droit; **to be ~ting up** être assis bien droit, se tenir droit; **he was ~ting up in bed** il était assis dans son lit; **you can ~ up now** vous pouvez vous asseoir maintenant; (*fig*) **to make sb ~ up** secouer *or* étonner qn; (*fig*) **to ~ up (and take notice)** (*gen*) se secouer, se réveiller; (*after illness*) **he began to ~ up and take notice** il a commencé à reprendre intérêt à la vie *or* à refaire surface [b] (= *stay up*) rester debout, ne pas se coucher; **to ~ up late** se coucher tard, veiller tard; **to ~ up all night** ne pas se coucher de la nuit; **don't ~ up for me** couchez-vous sans m'attendre; **the nurse sat up with him** l'infirmière est restée à son chevet *or* l'a veillé [2] VT SEP [+ *doll, child*] asseoir, redresser [3] **~-up** N → **sit**

► **sit upon*** VT FUS = **sit on**

sitar [sɪˈtɑːr] N sitar *m*

sitcom* ['sɪtkɒm] N (*Rad, TV*) (ABBR = **situation comedy**) sitcom *f*, comédie *f* de situation

site [saɪt] [1] N [*of town, building*] emplacement *m*; (*Archeol*) site *m*; (*Constr*) chantier *m* (de construction *or* de démolition *etc*); (*Camping*) (terrain *m* de) camping *m*; **the ~ of the battle** le champ de bataille → **building, launching** [2] VT [+ *town, building, gun*] placer; **they want to ~ the steelworks in that valley** on veut placer *or* construire l'aciérie dans cette vallée; **the factory is very badly ~d** l'usine est très mal située *or* placée [3] COMP ► **site measuring** N (*Civil Engineering*) métré *m* ► **Site of Special Scientific Interest** N (*Brit*) site *m* d'intérêt scientifique, ≈ réserve *f* naturelle

sit-in ['sɪtɪn] N [*of demonstrators*] sit-in *m*, manifestation *f* avec occupation de locaux; [*of workers*] grève *f* sur le tas; **the workers held a ~** les ouvriers ont organisé une grève sur le tas; **the students held a ~ in the university offices** les étudiants ont occupé les bureaux de l'université; **the ~ at the offices** l'occupation *f* des bureaux

siting ['saɪtɪŋ] N **the ~ of the new town there was a mistake** c'était une erreur de bâtir *or* placer la ville nouvelle à cet endroit; **the ~ of the new factories has given rise to many ob-**

jections le choix de l'emplacement pour les nouvelles usines a soulevé de nombreuses critiques

sitter ['sɪtər] N (*Art*) modèle *m*; (= *baby-sitter*) baby-sitter *mf*; (= *hen*) couveuse *f*; (*Sport*) **he missed a ~** il a raté un coup enfantin; **it's a ~!** tu ne peux pas (*or* il ne peut pas *etc*) le rater!

sitting ['sɪtɪŋ] [1] N [*of committee, assembly etc*] séance *f*; (*for portrait*) séance *f* de pose; (*in canteen etc*) service *m*; **they served 200 people in one ~/in two ~s** ils ont servi 200 personnes à la fois/en deux services; **second ~ for lunch** deuxième service pour le déjeuner; **at one** *or* **a single ~** (= *in one go*) d'une seule traite [2] ADJ [*committee*] en séance; [*official*] en exercice; [*game bird*] posé, au repos; (*Jur*) **~ judge** juge *m* en exercice; (*Brit Parl*) **~ member** député *m* en exercice; (*Brit*) **~ tenant** locataire *mf* en possession des lieux *or* en place [3] COMP ► **sitting and standing room** N places *fpl* debout et assises ► **sitting duck*** N (*fig*) cible *f* facile ► **sitting room** N salon *m* ► **sitting target** N (*lit, fig*) cible *f* facile

situate ['sɪtjʊeɪt] VT (= *locate*) [+ *building, town*] placer; (= *put into perspective*) [+ *problem, event*] situer; **the house is ~d in the country** la maison se trouve *or* est située à la campagne; **the shop is well ~d** le magasin est bien situé *or* bien placé; **we are rather badly ~d as there is no bus service** nous sommes assez mal situés car il n'y a pas d'autobus; (*fig*) **he is rather badly ~d at the moment** il est dans une situation assez défavorable *or* en assez mauvaise posture en ce moment; (*financially*) il est assez gêné *or* il a des ennuis d'argent en ce moment; **I am well ~d to appreciate the risks** je suis bien placé pour apprécier les risques; **how are you ~d for money?** ça va du point de vue argent?, où en es-tu question argent?

situation [ˌsɪtjʊˈeɪʃən] [1] N [a] (= *location*) [*of town, building etc*] situation *f*, emplacement *m*; **the house has a fine ~** la maison est bien située [b] (= *circumstances*) situation *f* (*also Literat*); **he was in a very difficult ~** il se trouvait dans une situation très difficile; **they managed to save the ~** ils ont réussi à sauver *or* redresser la situation; **the international ~** la situation internationale, la conjoncture internationale; **they're in a waiting/discussion etc ~** ils sont en situation d'attente/de dialogue *etc*; **in an exam ~, you must ...** à un examen, il faut ... [c] (= *job*) situation *f*; **"~s vacant/wanted"** « offres/demandes d'emploi » [2] COMP ► **situation comedy** N comédie *f* de situation

situational [ˌsɪtjʊˈeɪʃənl] ADJ situationnel

Situationism [ˌsɪtjʊˈeɪʃəˌnɪzəm] N (*Philos*) situationnisme *m*

Situationist [ˌsɪtjʊˈeɪʃəˌnɪst] ADJ, N (*Philos*) situationniste *mf*

six [sɪks] [1] ADJ six *inv*; **he is ~ (years old)** il a six ans → **4**; **he'll be ~ on Saturday** il aura six ans samedi; **he lives in number ~** il habite au (numéro) six; **~ times ~** six fois six [2] N [a] six *m inv*; **it is ~ o'clock** il est six heures; **come at ~** venez à six heures; **it struck ~** six heures ont sonné; **they are sold in ~es** c'est vendu *or* cela se vend par (lots *or* paquets de) six; **the children arrived in ~es** les enfants sont arrivés par groupes de six; **he lives at ~ Churchill Street** il habite (au) six Churchill Street; (*Cards*) **the ~ of diamonds** le six de carreaux; **two ~es are twelve** deux fois six douze [b] (*fig phrases*) (*Brit*) **~ of the best*** six grands coups; **to be (all) at ~es and sevens** [*books, house etc*] être en désordre *or* en pagaille*, être sens dessus dessous; [*person*] être tout retourné*; (*hum*) **to be ~ foot under*** manger les pissenlits par la racine*; **it's ~ of one and half a dozen of the other*** ◊ **it's ~ and half a dozen*** c'est blanc bonnet et bonnet blanc, c'est du pareil au même*

[c] (*Cricket*) **to hit a** ~ marquer six courses *fpl or* points *mpl* (*d'un seul coup*); **he hit three ~es** il a marqué trois fois six courses *or* points → **knock**

[3] PRON six; **there were about** ~ il y en avait six environ *or* à peu près; **~ of the girls came** six des filles sont venues; **there are** ~ **of us** nous sommes *or* on est* six; **all** ~ **(of us) left** nous sommes partis tous les six; **all** ~ **(of them) left** tous les six sont partis, ils sont partis tous les six

[4] COMP ► **the Six Counties** NPL (*Brit*) les six comtés *mpl* de l'Irlande du Nord ► **six-cylinder** (*Aut*) ADJ à six cylindres ♦ N (voiture *f* à) six cylindres *f* ► **six-eight time** N (*Mus*) mesure *f* à six-huit ► **six-footer*** N personne *f* qui mesure plus d'un mètre quatre-vingts ► **six-gun*** N = **six-shooter** ► **six-pack** N pack *m* de six ► **six-seater** ADJ à six places ♦ N (= *car etc*) (voiture *f etc* à) six places *f*; (= *plane etc*) (avion *m etc* à) six places *m* ► **six-shooter** N six-coups *m inv* ► **six-sided** ADJ hexagonal ► **six-speed gearbox** N (*Aut*) boîte *f* (à) six vitesses ► **six-storey** N à six étages ► **six-yard box** N (*Ftbl*) surface *f* de but ► **six-year-old** ADJ [*child, horse*] de six ans; [*house, car*] vieux (vieille *f*) de six ans ♦ N (= *child*) enfant *mf* (âgé(e)) de six ans; (= *horse*) cheval *m* de six ans

sixfold ['sıksfəʊld] [1] ADJ sextuple [2] ADV au sextuple

sixish ['sıksıʃ] ADJ **he is** ~ il a dans les six ans, il a six ans environ; **he came at** ~ il est venu vers (les) six heures

sixpence ['sıkspəns] N (*Brit*) (= *coin*) (ancienne) pièce *f* de six pence; (= *value*) six pence *mpl*

sixpenny ['sıkspənı] ADJ à six pence

sixteen ['sıks'tiːn] [1] ADJ seize *inv*; **she was sweet** ~ c'était une fraîche jeune fille (de seize ans) [2] N seize *m inv*; *for phrases see* **six** [3] PRON seize; **there are** ~ il y en a seize

sixteenth ['sıks'tiːnθ] [1] ADJ seizième [2] N seizième *mf*; (= *fraction*) seizième *m*; *for phrases see* **sixth**

sixth [sıksθ] [1] ADJ sixième; **to be** ~ **in an exam/in German** être sixième à un concours/en allemand; **she was the** ~ **to arrive** elle est arrivée la sixième; **Charles the Sixth** Charles six; **the** ~ **of November** ◊ **November the** ~ le six novembre

[2] N sixième *mf*; (= *fraction*) sixième *m*; (*Mus*) sixte *f*; **he wrote the letter on the** ~ il a écrit la lettre le six, sa lettre est du six; **your letter of the** ~ votre lettre du six (courant); (*Brit Scol*) **the** ~ = **the sixth form**

[3] ADV [a] (*in race, exam, competition*) en sixième position *or* place; **he came** *or* **was placed** ~ il s'est classé sixième

[b] = **sixthly**

[4] COMP ► **sixth form** N (*Brit Scol*) ≈ classes *fpl* de première et terminale; **to be in the** ~ **form** ≈ être en première *or* en terminale ► **sixth-form college** N lycée *n'ayant que des classes de première et de terminale* ► **sixth-former, sixth-form pupil** N ≈ élève *mf* de première *or* de terminale ► **the sixth grade** N (*US Scol*) ≈ le CM2 ► **sixth sense** N sixième sens *m*

sixthly ['sıksθlı] ADV sixièmement, en sixième lieu

sixtieth ['sıkstıθ] [1] ADJ soixantième [2] N soixantième *mf*; (= *fraction*) soixantième *m*; *for phrases see* **sixth**

sixty ['sıkstı] [1] ADJ soixante *inv*; **he is about** ~ il a une soixantaine d'années, il a dans les soixante ans; **about** ~ **books** une soixantaine de livres

[2] N soixante *m inv*; **about** ~ une soixantaine, environ soixante; **to be in one's sixties** avoir entre soixante et soixante-dix ans, être

sexagénaire; **he is in his early sixties** il a un peu plus de soixante ans; **he is in his late sixties** il approche de soixante-dix ans; **she's getting on** *or* **going on for** ~ elle approche de la soixantaine, elle va sur ses soixante ans; **in the sixties** (= *1960s*) dans les années soixante; **in the early/late sixties** au début/vers la fin des années soixante; **the temperature was in the sixties** ≈ il faisait entre quinze et vingt degrés; **the numbers were in the sixties** le nombre s'élevait à plus de soixante; (*in car*) **to do** ~* faire du soixante milles (à l'heure), ≈ faire du cent (à l'heure); *for other phrases see* **six**

[3] PRON soixante; **there are** ~ il y en a soixante

[4] COMP ► **sixty-first** ADJ soixante et unième ♦ N soixante et unième *mf*; (= *fraction*) soixante et unième *m* ♦ PRON soixante et unième ► **sixty-four (thousand) dollar question*** N that's the ~-four (thousand) dollar question c'est la question à mille francs ► **sixty-odd*** PRON there were ~-odd il y en avait soixante et quelques*, il y en avait une soixantaine; ~-odd books un peu plus de soixante livres, soixante et quelques livres ► **sixty-one** ADJ soixante et un(e) ♦ PRON soixante et un ► **sixty-second** ADJ soixante-deuxième ♦ N soixante-deuxième *mf*; (= *fraction*) soixante-deuxième *m* ► **sixty-two** ADJ soixante-deux *inv* ♦ N soixante-deux *m inv* ♦ PRON soixante-deux; **there are** ~-**two** il y a soixante-deux

sizable ['saızəbl] ADJ = **sizeable**

sizably ['saızəblı] ADV = **sizeably**

size¹ [saız] [1] N (*for plaster, paper*) colle *f*; (*for cloth*) apprêt *m* [2] VT encoller, apprêter

size² [saız] [1] N [a] [*of person, animal, sb's head, hands*] taille *f*; [*of room, building*] grandeur *f*, dimensions *fpl*; [*of car, chair*] dimensions *fpl*; [*of egg, fruit, jewel*] grosseur *f*; [*of parcel*] grosseur *f*, dimensions *fpl*; [*of book, photograph, sheet of paper, envelope*] taille *f*, dimensions *fpl*; [*of format*] format *m*; [*of sum*] montant *m*; [*of estate, park, country*] étendue *f*, superficie *f*; [*of problem, difficulty, obstacle*] ampleur *f*, étendue *f*; [*of operation, campaign*] ampleur *f*, envergure *f*; **the small/large** ~ [*of packet, tube etc*] le petit/grand modèle; **the** ~ **of the town** l'importance *f* de la ville; **a building of vast** ~ un bâtiment de belles dimensions; **the** ~ **of the farm** (*building*) les dimensions *fpl* de la ferme; (*land*) l'étendue *f* de la ferme; **the** ~ **of the fish you caught** la taille du poisson que tu as attrapé; **the** ~ **of the sum involved was so large that ...** la somme en question était d'une telle importance que ...; **sort them according to** ~ triez-les selon la grosseur (*or* le format *etc*); **to alter/cut/make sth to** ~ transformer/couper/faire qch sur mesure; **it's the** ~ **of a brick** c'est de la taille d'une brique; **it's the** ~ **of a walnut** c'est de la grosseur d'une noix; **it's the** ~ **of a house/elephant** c'est grand comme une maison/un éléphant; **a child of that** ~ shouldn't be allowed to do that un enfant de cette taille ne devrait pas avoir le droit de faire ça; **he's about your** ~ il est à peu près de la même taille que vous; (*fig*) **that's about the** ~ **of it!** c'est à peu près ça!, quelque chose dans ce genre-là!; **he cut the wood to** ~ il a coupé le bois à la dimension voulue; **they are all of a** ~* ils sont tous de la même grosseur (*or* de la même taille *etc*) → **cut down, shape**

[b] [*of coat, skirt, dress, trousers etc*] taille *f*; [*of shoes, gloves*] pointure *f*; [*of shirt*] encolure *f*; **what** ~ **are you?** ◊ **what** ~ **do you take?** (*in dress etc*) quelle taille faites-vous?; (*in shoes, gloves*) quelle pointure faites-vous?; (*in shirts*) vous faites combien d'encolure *or* de tour de cou?; (*in hats*) quel est votre tour de tête?; **what** ~ **of collar** *or* **shirt?** quelle encolure?; **I take** ~ **12** je prends du 12 *or* la taille 12; **what** ~ **(of) shoes do you take?** quelle pointure faites-

vous?, vous chaussez du combien?; **I take** ~ **5 (shoes)** ≈ je chausse *or* je fais du 38; **what** ~ **of waist are you?** quel est votre tour de taille?; **we are out of** ~ **5** ≈ nous n'avons plus de 38; **we haven't got your** ~ nous n'avons pas votre taille (*or* pointure *etc*) → **try**; **"one** ~**"** « taille unique »; **I need a** ~ **smaller** il me faut la taille (*or* la pointure *etc*) en-dessous; **it's two** ~**s too big for me** c'est deux tailles (*or* pointures *etc*) au-dessus de ce qu'il me faut; **hip** ~ tour *m* de hanches

[2] VT classer *or* trier selon la grosseur (*or* la dimension *or* la taille *etc*)

► **size up** VT SEP [+ *person*] juger, jauger; [+ *situation*] mesurer; **to** ~ **up the problem** mesurer l'étendue du problème; **I can't quite** ~ **him up** (*don't know what he is worth*) je n'arrive pas vraiment à le juger *or* à décider ce qu'il vaut; (= *don't know what he wants*) je ne vois pas vraiment où il veut en venir

-size [saız] ADJ (*in compounds*) = **-sized**

sizeable ['saızəbl] ADJ [*amount, number, problem, operation, proportion*] assez important, assez considérable; [*object, building, estate*] assez grand; [*majority*] assez large, assez confortable

sizeably ['saızəblı] ADV considérablement, de beaucoup

-sized [saızd] ADJ (*in compounds*) → **size²**; **medium-sized** de taille (*or* grandeur *or* grosseur *etc*) moyenne → **life**

sizzle ['sızl] [1] VI grésiller [2] N grésillement *m*

sizzler* ['sızləʳ] N journée *f* torride *or* caniculaire

sizzling ['sızlıŋ] [1] ADJ [*fat, bacon*] grésillant; **a** ~ **noise** un grésillement [2] ADV ~ **hot** brûlant; **it was a** ~ **hot day*** il faisait une chaleur torride *or* caniculaire ce jour-là

ska [skɑː] N (*Mus*) ska *m*

skate¹ [skeɪt] N (*pl* skate *or* skates) (= *fish*) raie *f*

skate² [skeɪt] [1] N patin *m*; (*fig*) **put** *or* **get your** ~**s on!*** grouille-toi!*, magne-toi!* → **iceskate, rollerskate** [2] VI patiner; **to go skating** (*ice*) faire du patin *or* du patinage; (*roller*) faire du patin à roulettes *or* du skating; **he ~d across the pond** il a traversé l'étang (en patinant *or* à patins); (*fig*) **it went skating across the room** cela a glissé à travers la pièce → **ice, roller**

► **skate around, skate over, skate round** VT FUS [+ *problem, difficulty, objection*] esquiver autant que possible

skateboard ['skeɪtbɔːd] [1] N skateboard *m*, planche *f* à roulettes [2] VI faire de la planche à roulettes

skateboarder ['skeɪtbɔːdəʳ] N skateur *m*, -euse *f*

skateboarding ['skeɪtbɔːdɪŋ] N skateboard *m*, planche *f* à roulettes

skater ['skeɪtəʳ] N (*ice*) patineur *m*, -euse *f*; (*roller*) personne *f* qui fait du skating *or* du patinage à roulettes

skating ['skeɪtɪŋ] [1] N (*ice*) patinage *m*; (*roller*) skating *m*, patinage *m* à roulettes [2] COMP [*champion, championship, display*] (*ice*) de patinage; (*roller*) de skating, de patinage à roulettes ► **skating rink** N (*ice*) patinoire *f*; (*roller*) skating *m* ► **skating turn** N (*Ski*) pas *m* du patineur

skean dhu ['skiːənˈduː] N (*Scot*) poignard *m* (*porté dans la chaussette*)

skedaddle* ['skıˈdædl] VI (= *run away*) décamper*, déguerpir*; (= *flee in panic*) fuir en catastrophe

skeet shooting ['skiːtˈʃuːtɪŋ] N skeet *m*, tir *m* au pigeon d'argile, ball-trap *m*

skein [skeɪn] N [*of wool etc*] écheveau *m*

skeletal ['skelɪtl] ADJ [a] (*Anat*) [*structure, development*] du squelette; [*remains*] de squelette;

~ structure or **system** squelette *m* [b] (= *emaciated*) [*person, body*] squelettique; [*face*] émacié [c] (= *schematic*) [*timetable*] schématique

skeleton ['skelitn] [1] N (*Anat*) squelette *m*; [*of building, ship, model etc*] squelette *m*, charpente *f*; [*of plan, scheme, suggestion, novel etc*] schéma *m*, grandes lignes *fpl*; **he was a mere** or **a walking** or **a living ~** c'était un véritable cadavre ambulant; **he was reduced to a ~** il n'était plus qu'un squelette, il était devenu (d'une maigreur) squelettique; **the staff was reduced to a ~** le personnel était réduit au strict minimum; (*fig*) **a ~ in the cupboard** (*Brit*) or **closet** (*US*) un cadavre dans le placard*; **the family ~** le secret de famille → **feast** [2] COMP [*army, crew, staff*] squelettique, réduit au strict minimum ► **skeleton key** N passe *m*, passe-partout *m inv* ► **skeleton law** N (*Ind*) loi-cadre *f* ► **skeleton map** N carte *f* schématique ► **skeleton outline** N [*of drawing, map, plan*] schéma *m* simplifié; [*of proposals, report*] résumé *m*, grandes lignes *fpl*

skep [skep] N [a] (= *beehive*) ruche *f* [b] (= *basket*) panier *m*

skeptic etc ['skeptik] (*US*) = **sceptic**

sketch [sketʃ] [1] N [a] (= *drawing*) (*rough*) croquis *m*; (*preliminary*) esquisse *f*; (*fig*) [*of ideas, proposals etc*] aperçu *m*, ébauche *f*; (= *drawing*) **a rough ~** une ébauche; (*fig*) **he gave me a (rough) ~ of what he planned to do** il m'a donné un aperçu de or il m'a dit en gros ce qu'il comptait faire [b] (*Theat*) sketch *m*, saynète *f* [2] VI (*roughly*) faire des croquis; (= *make preliminary drawing*) faire des esquisses; **to go ~ing** aller or partir faire des croquis [3] VT [+ *view, castle, figure*] (*roughly*) faire un croquis de, croquer; (= *make preliminary drawing*) faire une esquisse de, esquisser; [+ *map*] faire à main levée; (*fig*) [+ *ideas, proposals, novel, plan*] ébaucher, esquisser [4] COMP ► **sketch(ing) book** N carnet *m* à croquis or à dessins ► **sketching pad** N bloc *m* à dessins ► **sketch map** N carte *f* faite à main levée ► **sketch pad** N = **sketching pad**
► **sketch in** VT SEP [+ *detail in drawing*] ajouter, dessiner; (*fig*) [+ *details*] ajouter; [+ *facts*] indiquer
► **sketch out** VT SEP [+ *plans, proposals, ideas*] ébaucher, esquisser; (*lit, fig*) **to ~ out a picture of sth** ébaucher qch, dessiner les grandes lignes de qch

sketchily ['sketʃɪlɪ] ADV sommairement; **the ideas are ~ developed** les idées sont (sommairement) esquissées

sketchy ['sketʃɪ] ADJ [*details*] incomplet (-ète *f*), lacunaire; [*account, report*] peu détaillé, sommaire; [*piece of work*] peu détaillé; [*knowledge*] rudimentaire, sommaire

skew [skju:] [1] N **to be on the ~** être de travers or en biais or mal posé [2] ADJ de travers [3] ADV [*hang*] de travers [4] VI [a] (*also* = *round*) obliquer; (*fig*) **negotiations ~ed off course** les négociations ont dévié de leur but initial [b] (= *squint*) loucher [5] COMP ► **skew-eyed*** ADJ qui louche, qui a un œil qui dit merde à l'autre*; ► **skew-whiff*** ADJ (*Brit*) (**on the**) **~-whiff** de travers, de guingois*, de traviole*

skewbald ['skju:bɔ:ld] [1] ADJ pie *inv* [2] N cheval *m* pie *inv*

skewed [skju:d] ADJ [a] (= *slanting*) de travers [b] (= *distorted*) [*conception, view, graph*] déformé; [*statistics*] faussé

skewer ['skju:ə'] [1] N (*for roast etc*) broche *f*; (*for kebabs*) brochette *f* [2] VT [+ *chicken*] embrocher; [+ *pieces of meat*] mettre en brochette; (*fig*) transpercer, embrocher*

ski [ski:] [1] N (*pl* **skis** or **ski**) ski *m*, planche* *f*; (*Aviat*) patin *m* → **water** [2] VI faire du ski, skier; **to go ~ing** (*as holiday*) partir aux sports d'hiver; (= *go out skiing*)

(*aller*) faire du ski; **I like ~ing** j'aime le ski or faire du ski or skier; **to ~ down a slope** descendre une pente à *or* en skis [3] COMP [*school, clothes*] de ski ► **ski binding** N fixation *f* ► **ski boot** N chaussure *f* de ski ► **ski bunny*** N (*US* = *girl*) minette *f* de station de ski ► **ski instructor** N moniteur *m*, -trice *f* de ski ► **ski jump** N (= *action*) saut *m* à skis; (= *place*) tremplin *m* (de ski) ► **ski-jumping** N saut *m* à skis ► **ski lift** N télésiège *m*, remonte-pente *m inv* ► **ski-mountaineering** N ski *m* de haute montagne ► **ski pants** NPL fuseau *m* (de ski) ► **ski-pass** N forfait *m* skieur(s) ► **ski pole** N = **ski stick** ► **ski-rack** N [*of car*] porte-skis *m* ► **ski resort** N station *f* de ski or de sports d'hiver ► **ski run** N piste *f* de ski ► **ski slope** N pente *f* or piste *f* de ski ► **ski stick** N bâton *m* de ski ► **ski-suit** N combinaison *f* (de ski) ► **ski-touring** N ski *m* de randonnée, randonnée *f* à ski ► **ski tow** N téléski *m*, remonte-pente *m inv* ► **ski trousers** NPL fuseau *m* (de ski) ► **ski wax** N fart *m* ► **ski-wear** N vêtements *mpl* de ski

skibob ['ski:bɒb] N ski-bob *m*, véloski *m*

skid [skɪd] [1] N [a] [*of car etc*] dérapage *m*; **to get** or **go into a ~** déraper, faire un dérapage; **to get out of a ~** ◊ **to correct a ~** redresser or contrôler un dérapage [b] (*on wheel*) cale *f* [c] (*under heavy object*) (*rollers, logs etc*) traîneau *m*; **to put the ~s* on** or **under** (= *cause to fail*) [+ *person*] faire un croc-en-jambe à (*fig*); [+ *plan etc*] faire tomber à l'eau*; **her marriage/career is on the ~s*** son mariage/sa carrière bat de l'aile; (*US*) **to hit the ~s*** devenir clochard(e) [2] VI (*in car etc*) déraper; [*person*] déraper, glisser; **the car ~ded to a halt** or **stop** la voiture a dérapé et s'est immobilisée; **I ~ded into a tree** j'ai dérapé et percuté un arbre; **he went ~ding into the bookcase** il a glissé or dérapé et est allé se cogner contre la bibliothèque; **the toy ~ded across the room** le jouet a glissé jusqu'à l'autre bout de la pièce; (*US*) **prices ~ded*** les prix ont dérapé [3] COMP ► **skid row** N (*esp US*) quartier *m* de clochards, cour *f* des miracles; (*fig*) **he's heading for ~ row** il finira clochard*

skidlid* ['skɪdlɪd] N casque *m* (de moto)

skidmark ['skɪdmɑːk] N trace *f* de pneu, trace *f* de dérapage

skidoo [skɪ'du:] N skidoo *m*, motoneige *f*, scooter *m* des neiges

skidpad ['skɪdpæd], **skidpan** ['skɪdpæn] N piste *f* d'entraînement au dérapage (*pour apprendre à contrôler un véhicule*)

skidproof ['skɪdpru:f] ADJ antidérapant

skier ['ski:ə'] N skieur *m*, -euse *f*

skiff [skɪf] N skiff *m*, yole *f*

skiing ['ski:ɪŋ] [1] N (*NonC*) ski *m* → **water** [2] COMP [*clothes, school*] de ski ► **skiing holiday** N vacances *fpl* aux sports d'hiver, vacances *fpl* de neige; **to go on a ~ holiday** partir aux sports d'hiver ► **skiing instructor** N moniteur *m*, -trice *f* de ski ► **skiing pants** NPL fuseau *m* (de ski) ► **skiing resort** N station *f* de ski or de sports d'hiver ► **skiing trousers** NPL = **skiing pants**

skilful, skillful (*US*) ['skɪlfʊl] ADJ [*person, player*] habile (**at doing sth** à faire qch), adroit; [*use, choice, management*] intelligent; **~ at hunting** habile à la chasse; **to be ~ in doing sth** faire preuve d'habileté or d'adresse pour faire qch; **to be ~ with sth** savoir se servir de qch

skilfully, skillfully (*US*) ['skɪlfəlɪ] ADV [*organize, carry out, use*] habilement, intelligemment; [*avoid*] adroitement; [*write*] avec habileté

skilfulness, skillfulness (*US*) ['skɪlfʊlnɪs] N (*NonC*) habileté *f*, adresse *f*

skill [skɪl] N [a] (*NonC* = *competence, ability*) habileté *f*, adresse *f*; (*gen manual*) dextérité *f*; (= *talent*) savoir-faire *m*, talent *m*; **the ~ of the dancers** l'adresse *f* or l'habileté *f* or le talent des danseurs; **the ~ of the juggler** l'adresse *f* or la dextérité or le talent du jongleur; **his ~ at billiards** son habileté or son adresse au billard; **his ~ in negotiation** son savoir-faire or son talent or son habileté en matière de négociations; **her ~ in persuading them** l'habileté dont elle a fait preuve pour les persuader; **lack of ~** maladresse *f* [b] (*in craft etc*) technique *f*; **~s** (*gen*) capacités *fpl*, compétences *fpl*; (*Scol: innate*) aptitudes *fpl*; (*Scol: learnt*) savoir *m*; **it's a ~ that has to be acquired** c'est une technique qui s'apprend; **we could make good use of his ~s** ses capacités or ses compétences nous seraient bien utiles; **what ~s do you have?** quelles sont vos compétences?; **learning a language is a question of learning new ~s** apprendre une langue consiste à acquérir de nouvelles compétences

Skillcentre ['skɪlsentə'] N (*Brit*) centre de formation professionnelle pour demandeurs d'emploi

skilled [skɪld] ADJ [a] (= *skilful*) [*person, driver*] habile, adroit; **to be ~ in the use of sth** savoir bien se servir de qch, faire un usage habile de qch; **to be ~ in diplomacy** être un habile diplomate; **~ in the art of negotiating** versé or maître dans l'art de la négociation; **~ in** or **at doing sth** habile à faire qch; **to be ~ in reading and writing** savoir bien lire et écrire [b] (*Ind*) [*job, labour, worker*] qualifié; **a low-~ clerical job** un emploi or un travail peu qualifié dans un bureau; (*US*) **~ nursing care** soins dispensés par un personnel médical qualifié; (*US*) **~ nursing facility** centre de soins dispensés par un personnel médical qualifié → **semiskilled**

skillet ['skɪlɪt] N poêlon *m*

skillful ['skɪlfʊl] ADJ (*US*) = **skilful**

skillfully ['skɪlfəlɪ] ADV (*US*) = **skilfully**

skillfulness ['skɪlfʊlnɪs] N (*US*) = **skilfulness**

skim [skɪm] [1] VT [a] [+ *milk*] écrémer; [+ *soup*] écumer; **to ~ the cream/scum/grease from sth** écrémer/écumer/dégraisser qch [b] **to ~ the ground/water** [*bird etc*] raser or effleurer or frôler le sol/la surface de l'eau; **to ~ a stone across the pond** faire ricocher une pierre sur l'étang [c] (*US* fig*) [+ *one's income*] ne pas déclarer en totalité au fisc [2] VI [a] **to ~ across the water/along the ground** raser l'eau/le sol; **the stone ~med across the pond** la pierre a ricoché d'un bout à l'autre de l'étang; (*fig*) **to ~ through a book** parcourir or feuilleter un livre; **he ~med over the difficult passages** il s'est contenté de parcourir rapidement les passages difficiles [b] (*US* fig* = *cheat on taxes*) frauder (le fisc) [3] COMP ► **skim(med) milk** N lait *m* écrémé
► **skim off** VT SEP [+ *cream, grease*] enlever; (*fig*) **they ~med off the brightest pupils** ils ont mis à part les élèves les plus brillants

skimmer ['skɪmə'] N (*Orn*) rhyncops *m*, bec-en-ciseaux *m*

skimming ['skɪmɪŋ] N (*US* = tax fraud*) ≈ fraude *f* fiscale

skimp [skɪmp] VI lésiner, économiser; **to ~ on** [+ *butter, cloth, paint etc*] lésiner sur; [+ *money*] économiser; [+ *praise, thanks*] être chiche de; [+ *piece of work*] faire à la va-vite, bâcler*

skimpily ['skɪmpɪlɪ] ADV [*serve, provide*] avec parcimonie; [*live*] chichement

skimpiness ['skɪmpɪnɪs] N [*of meal, helping, allowance*] insuffisance *f*; [*of dress etc*] ampleur *f* insuffisante; [*of person*] avarice *f*

skimpy ['skɪmpɪ] ADJ [*meal*] frugal, maigre (*before n*); [*pay*] maigre (*before n*); [*dress*] très réduit; [*bikini, underwear*] minuscule

skin [skɪn] **1** N **a** [of person, animal] peau f; **she has (a) good/bad ~** elle a une jolie/vilaine peau; **to wear wool next to the ~** porter de la laine sur la peau or à même la peau; **wet** or **soaked to the ~** trempé jusqu'aux os; **the snake casts** or **sheds its ~** le serpent mue; **rabbit ~** peau f de lapin
b (phrases) **to be (all** or **only) ~ and bone** n'avoir que la peau sur les os; **with a whole ~** indemne, sain et sauf, sans une écorchure; **to escape by the ~ of one's teeth** l'échapper belle; **we caught the last train by the ~ of our teeth** nous avons attrapé le dernier train de justesse; **to have a thick ~** avoir une peau d'éléphant, être insensible; **to have a thin ~** être susceptible, avoir l'épiderme sensible; **to get under sb's ~*** (= annoy) porter or taper* sur les nerfs à qn; (= understand) se mettre à la place or dans la peau de qn; **I've got you under my ~*** je t'ai dans la peau, je suis amoureux fou de toi; **it's no ~ off my nose!*** (= does not hurt me) pour ce que ça me coûte!; (= does not concern me) ce n'est pas mon problème!
→ **pigskin, save¹**
c [of fruit, vegetable, milk pudding, sausage, drum] (unpeeled) peau f; (peeled) pelure f; [of boat, aircraft] revêtement m; (for duplicating) stencil m; (for wine) outre f; **to cook potatoes in their ~(s)** faire cuire des pommes de terre en robe des champs or en robe de chambre; **a banana ~** une peau de banane
d (Ski) ~s peaux fpl (de phoque), peluches fpl
e (‡ = cigarette paper) papier m à cigarette
2 VT **a** [+ animal] dépouiller, écorcher; [+ fruit, vegetable] éplucher; **I'll ~ him alive!*** je vais l'écorcher tout vif!; **to ~ one's knee** s'érafler or s'écorcher le genou; **there are more ways than one** or **there is more than one way to ~ a cat** il y a plusieurs façons de plumer un canard → **eye**
b (‡ = steal from) estamper*, plumer*
3 COMP [colour, texture] de (la) peau ▶ **skin cancer** N cancer m de la peau ▶ **skin-deep** ADJ superficiel; **it's only ~-deep** ça ne va pas (chercher) bien loin ▶ **beauty ~ skin disease** N maladie f de (la) peau ▶ **skin diver** N plongeur m, -euse f sous-marin(e) ▶ **skin diving** N plongée f sous-marine ▶ **skin flick‡** N (Cine) (film m) porno* m inv ▶ **skin game*** N (US) escroquerie f ▶ **skin graft** N greffe f de la peau ▶ **skin grafting** N greffe f de la peau ▶ **skin mag(azine)*** N (US) revue f porno* ▶ **skin patch** N (Med) patch m, timbre m transdermique ▶ **skin test** N (Med) cuti-(réaction) f
▶ **skin up** VI‡ rouler un joint*

skinflint ['skɪnflɪnt] N grippe-sou m, radin(e)* m(f)

skinful‡ ['skɪnfʊl] N **to have (had) a ~** être bourré‡, être noir‡; **he's got a ~ of whisky** il s'est soûlé* or il a pris une biture‡ au whisky

skinhead ['skɪnhed] N (Brit = thug) skinhead m

skinless ['skɪnlɪs] ADJ [meat, sausage, fish] sans (la) peau

-skinned [skɪnd] ADJ (in compounds) **fair-skinned** à (la) peau claire → **thick, thin**

skinner ['skɪnə*] N peaussier m

skinny ['skɪnɪ] **1** ADJ **a** (= thin) [person, legs, arms] maigre; (Fashion) **the ~ look** la mode ultra-mince **b** (= close-fitting) [sweater] moulant **2** COMP ▶ **skinny-dip*** N baignade f à poil* ♦ VI se baigner à poil* ▶ **skinny-dipping*** N (NonC) baignade f à poil*; **to go ~-dipping** se baigner à poil* ▶ **skinny-rib (sweater** or **jumper)*** N pull-chaussette m

skint‡ [skɪnt] ADJ (Brit) fauché*

skintight [skɪn'taɪt] ADJ collant, ajusté

skip¹ [skɪp] **1** N petit bond m, petit saut m; **to give a ~** faire un petit bond or saut
2 VI **a** gambader, sautiller; (with rope) sauter à la corde; **to ~ with joy** sauter or bondir de joie; **the child ~ped in/out** etc l'enfant est entré/sorti etc en gambadant or en sautillant; **she ~ped lightly over the stones** elle sautait légèrement par-dessus les pierres; **he ~ped out of the way of the cycle** il a bondi pour éviter le vélo, il a évité le vélo d'un bond; (fig) **he ~ped over that point** il est passé sur ce point, il a sauté par-dessus or a glissé sur ce point; **to ~ from one subject to another** sauter d'un sujet à un autre; **the author** or **book ~s about a lot** l'auteur papillonne beaucoup dans ce livre
b (fig) **I ~ped up to London yesterday** j'ai fait un saut à Londres hier; **he ~ped off without paying** il a décampé or filé* sans payer; **I ~ped round to see her** j'ai fait un saut chez elle, je suis passé la voir en vitesse
3 VT (= omit) [+ chapter, page, paragraph] sauter, passer; [+ class, meal] sauter; **I'll ~ lunch** je vais sauter le déjeuner, je vais me passer de déjeuner; **~ it!*** laisse tomber!*; **~ the details!** laisse tomber les détails!*, épargne-nous les détails!; **to ~ school** sécher les cours
4 COMP ▶ **skip rope** N (US) corde f à sauter

skip² [skɪp] N (Brit = container) benne f

skipper ['skɪpə*] **1** N (Naut) capitaine m, patron m; (Sport*) capitaine m, chef m d'équipe; (in race) skipper m **2** VT* [+ boat] commander; [+ team] être le chef de, mener

skipping ['skɪpɪŋ] **1** N saut m à la corde **2** COMP ▶ **skipping rope** N (Brit) corde f à sauter

skirl [skɜːl] N son m aigu (de la cornemuse)

skirmish ['skɜːmɪʃ] **1** N (gen) échauffourée f; (Mil) escarmouche f; (fig) escarmouche f, accrochage* m **2** VI (Mil) s'engager dans une escarmouche; (fig) **to ~ with sb** avoir un accrochage* avec qn

skirt [skɜːt] **1** N **a** (= garment) jupe f; [of frock coat] basque f **b** (= girl) **a bit of ~‡** une nana‡ **c** (Tech: on machine, vehicle) jupe f **d** (Culin = steak) flanchet m **2** VT (also ~ round) (= go round) contourner, longer; (= miss, avoid) [+ town, obstacle] contourner, éviter; [+ problem, difficulty] esquiver, éluder; **the road ~s (round) the forest** la route longe or contourne la forêt; **we ~ed (round) Paris to the north** nous sommes passés au nord de Paris, nous avons contourné Paris par le nord; **to ~ (round) the issue (of whether)** esquiver or éluder la question (de savoir si) **3** VI **to ~ round → 2 4** COMP ▶ **skirt length** N hauteur f de jupe

skirting ['skɜːtɪŋ] N (Brit: also ~ board) plinthe f

skit [skɪt] N parodie f (on de); (Theat) sketch m satirique

skitter ['skɪtə*] VI **to ~ across the water/along the ground** [bird] voler en frôlant l'eau/le sol; [stone] ricocher sur l'eau/le sol

skittish ['skɪtɪʃ] ADJ (= frivolous) capricieux; (= nervous) nerveux; (= coquettish) coquet; (= excitable) [horse] ombrageux

skittishly ['skɪtɪʃlɪ] ADV (= coquettishly) en faisant la coquette

skittle ['skɪtl] **1** N quille f; (esp Brit) **~s** (jeu m de) quilles fpl → **beer 2** COMP ▶ **skittle alley** N (piste f de) jeu m de quilles, bowling m

skive* [skaɪv] (Brit) **1** VI tirer au flanc* **2** N **to be on the ~** tirer au flanc*
▶ **skive off*** VI (Brit) se défiler*

skiver* ['skaɪvə*] N (Brit) tire-au-flanc* m inv

skivvy* ['skɪvɪ] **1** N **a** (Brit pej = servant) boniche f (pej), bonne f à tout faire **b** (US = underwear) **skivvies** sous-vêtements mpl (d'homme) **2** VI (Brit) faire la boniche

Skopje ['skɒpje] N Skopje

skua ['skjuːə] N stercoraire m, labbe m

skulduggery* [skʌl'dʌɡərɪ] N (NonC) maquignonnage m, trafic m; **a piece of ~** un maquignonnage

skulk [skʌlk] VI (also ~ about) rôder en se cachant, rôder furtivement; **to ~ in/away** etc entrer/s'éloigner etc furtivement

skull [skʌl] N crâne m; **~ and crossbones** (= emblem) tête f de mort; (= flag) pavillon m à tête de mort; **I can't get it into his (thick) ~* that ...** pas moyen de lui faire comprendre que ..., je n'arrive pas à lui faire entrer dans le crâne* que ...

skullcap ['skʌlkæp] N calotte f

skunk [skʌŋk] N (pl skunk or skunks) (= animal) mouffette f; (= fur) sconse m; (* pej = person) mufle* m, canaille f, salaud‡ m

sky [skaɪ] **1** N ciel m; **the skies** le(s) ciel(s); (fig) les cieux mpl; **there was a clear blue ~** le ciel était clair et bleu; **in the ~** dans le ciel; **under the open ~** à la belle étoile; **under a blue ~ ◊ under blue skies** sous un ciel bleu; **the skies over** or **of England** les ciels mpl d'Angleterre; **the skies of Van Gogh** les ciels mpl de Van Gogh; **under warmer skies** sous des cieux plus cléments; **to praise sb to the skies** porter qn aux nues; (fig) **it came out of a clear (blue) ~** c'est arrivé de façon tout à fait inattendue, on ne s'y attendait vraiment pas; **the ~'s the limit*** tout est possible
2 VT [+ ball] envoyer très haut or en chandelle
3 COMP ▶ **sky ad** N publicité f or annonce f aérienne ▶ **sky blue** N bleu m ciel ▶ **sky-blue** ADJ bleu ciel inv ▶ **sky-high** ADJ très haut (dans le ciel); (fig) extrêmement haut; **he hit the ball ~-high** il a envoyé le ballon très haut (dans le ciel); **the bridge was blown ~-high** le pont a sauté, le pont a volé en morceaux; **to blow a theory ~-high** démolir une théorie; **prices are ~-high** les prix sont exorbitants; **the crisis sent sugar prices ~-high** la crise a fait monter en flèche le prix du sucre ▶ **sky pilot†‡** N (fig) aumônier m, curé m ▶ **sky train** N (Aviat) avion qui remorque un ou plusieurs planeurs

skycap ['skaɪkæp] N (US) porteur m (dans un aéroport)

skydive ['skaɪdaɪv] **1** N saut m (en parachute) en chute libre **2** VI faire du parachutisme en chute libre

skydiver ['skaɪdaɪvə*] N parachutiste mf (faisant de la chute libre)

skydiving ['skaɪdaɪvɪŋ] N parachutisme m (en chute libre)

Skye [skaɪ] N (l'île f de) Skye f

skyjack* ['skaɪdʒæk] VT [+ plane] détourner, pirater

skyjacker* ['skaɪdʒækə*] N pirate m de l'air

skyjacking* ['skaɪdʒækɪŋ] N détournement m d'avion, piraterie f aérienne

Skylab ['skaɪlæb] N (Space) laboratoire m spatial, Skylab m

skylark ['skaɪlɑːk] **1** N (= bird) alouette f (des champs) **2** VI* chahuter, faire le fou

skylarking* ['skaɪlɑːkɪŋ] N rigolade* f, chahut m

skylight ['skaɪlaɪt] N lucarne f

skyline ['skaɪlaɪn] N ligne f d'horizon; [of city] ligne f des toits; [of buildings] profil m, silhouette f

skyrocket ['skaɪrɒkɪt] **1** N fusée f **2** VI [prices] monter en flèche

skyscraper ['skaɪskreɪpə*] N gratte-ciel m inv

skyward ['skaɪwəd] ADJ, ADV vers le ciel

skywards ['skaɪwədz] ADV [soar, point] vers le ciel; [gaze] en l'air

skyway ['skaɪweɪ] N (Aviat*) route f or voie f aérienne; (US Aut) route f surélevée

skywriting ['skaɪraɪtɪŋ] N publicité f aérienne (tracée dans le ciel par un avion)

slab [slæb] **1** N **a** (large piece) [of stone, wood, slate] bloc m; (flat) plaque f; [of meat] pièce f; (smaller) carré m, pavé m; [of cake] pavé m;

(*smaller*) grosse tranche *f*; [*of chocolate*] plaque *f*; (*smaller*) tablette *f* **b** (= *paving slab*) dalle *f*; (= *table, surface*) [*in butcher's slab*] étal *m*; (*in mortuary*) table *f* de dissection *or* d'autopsie **2** COMP ▶ **slab cake** N grand cake *m* rectangulaire

slack [slæk] **1** ADJ **a** (= *loose*) [*skin, sail*] flasque, mou (molle *f*); [*rope*] lâche, mal tendu; [*joint, knot*] desserré; [*hold, grip*] faible; [*muscle*] relâché; **to be ~** [*screw*] avoir du jeu; [*rope*] avoir du mou; **keep it ~!** [*rope*] laissez du mou!; **to have a ~ mouth/jaw** avoir la lèvre inférieure/la mâchoire pendante **b** (= *not busy*) [*time, season, month*] creux; [*demand*] faible; [*market, trade*] faible, stagnant; **during ~ periods** (*weeks, months etc*) pendant les jours *or* mois creux, pendant les périodes creuses; (*in the day*) aux heures creuses; **business is ~ this week** les affaires marchent au ralenti *or* ne vont pas fort* cette semaine **c** (= *lax*) [*discipline, security*] relâché; [*student*] inappliqué; [*worker*] peu sérieux, peu consciencieux; **to be ~ in** *or* **about one's work** se relâcher dans son travail

2 N **a** (*in rope: Climbing*) mou *m*; (*in cable*) ballant *m*; (*in joint etc*) jeu *m*; **to take up the ~ in a rope** raidir un cordage; (*fig*) **to take up the ~ in the economy** relancer les secteurs affaiblis de l'économie; (*fig*) **to cut sb some ~** faciliter les choses à qn **b** (= *coal*) poussier *m*

3 slacks NPL (= *trousers*) pantalon *m*

4 VI* ne pas travailler comme il le faudrait

5 COMP ▶ **slack water** N étale *mf*

▶ **slack off** **1** VI **a** (* = *stop working/trying etc*) se relâcher (dans son travail/dans ses efforts etc) **b** [*business, trade, demand*] ralentir **2** VT SEP [+ *rope, cable*] détendre, donner du mou à

▶ **slack up*** VI ralentir (ses efforts *or* son travail)

slacken ['slækn] **1** VT (*also* **~ off**) [+ *rope*] relâcher, donner du mou à; [+ *cable*] donner du ballant à; [+ *reins*] relâcher; [+ *screw*] desserrer; [+ *pressure etc*] diminuer, réduire; **to ~ one's pace** ralentir l'allure; (*in car*) **to ~ speed** diminuer de vitesse, ralentir **2** VI (*also* **~ off**) [*rope*] se relâcher, prendre du mou; [*cable*] prendre du ballant; [*screw*] se desserrer; [*gale*] diminuer de force; [*speed*] diminuer; [*activity, business, trade*] ralentir, diminuer; [*effort, enthusiasm, pressure*] diminuer, se relâcher

▶ **slacken off** (*esp Brit*) **1** VI **a** = **slacken 2 b** [*person*] se relâcher, se laisser aller **2** VT SEP = **slacken 1**

▶ **slacken up** VI = **slacken off 1b**

slackening ['slæknɪŋ] N (*NonC*) [*of effort, grip, rope, muscles*] relâchement *m*; [*of output, pace*] ralentissement *m*; **a ~ of demand** une diminution *or* baisse de la demande; **a ~ in sb's determination** un fléchissement de la détermination de qn

slacker* ['slækər] N flemmard(e)* *m(f)*, fainéant(e) *m(f)*

slackly ['slæklɪ] ADV **a** (= *loosely*) [*hang*] lâchement, mollement **b** (= *laxly*) [*work, play*] négligemment; [*supervise*] sans fermeté

slackness ['slæknɪs] N [*of rope etc*] manque *m* de tension;* [*of person*] négligence *f*, laisser-aller *m inv*; **the ~ of trade** le ralentissement *or* la stagnation des affaires

slag [slæg] **1** N **a** (*Metal*) scories *fpl*, crasses *fpl* **b** (*Min*) stériles *mpl* **c** (*Brit:* = *slut*) salope: *f* **2** VT (*Brit*) → **slag off 3** COMP ▶ **slag heap** N (*Metal*) crassier *m*; (*Min*) terril *m*

▶ **slag off:** VT SEP (*esp Brit*) **to ~ sb off** (= *scold, insult*) engueuler: qn; (= *speak badly of*) débiner* qn

slain [sleɪn] (*liter*) **1** VB ptp of **slay 2 the slain** NPL (*Mil*) les morts *mpl*, les soldats *mpl* tombés au champ d'honneur

---

slake [sleɪk] VT [+ *lime*] éteindre; [+ *one's thirst*] étancher; (*fig*) [+ *desire for revenge etc*] assouvir, satisfaire

slalom ['slɑːləm] **1** N slalom *m* **2** VI slalomer **3** COMP ▶ **slalom descent** N descente *f* en slalom ▶ **slalom racer, slalom specialist** N slalomeur *m*, -euse *f*

slam [slæm] **1** N **a** [*of door*] claquement *m* **b** (*Bridge*) chelem *m*; **to make a grand/little ~** faire un grand/petit chelem

2 VT **a** [+ *door*] (faire) claquer, fermer violemment; [+ *lid*] (faire) claquer, rabattre violemment; **to ~ the door shut** claquer la porte; **she ~med the books on the table** elle a jeté brutalement *or* a flanqué* les livres sur la table; **he ~med the ball into the grandstand** d'un coup violent il a envoyé le ballon dans la tribune; (*fig*) **our team ~med yours*** notre équipe a écrasé la vôtre **b** (** = *criticize*) éreinter*, descendre en flammes*

3 VI **a** [*door, lid*] claquer; **the door ~med shut** la porte s'est refermée en claquant **b** **to ~ into** (*or* **against**) **sth** s'écraser contre qch

4 COMP ▶ **slam dancing** N (*NonC*) slam *m* (*danse punk qui consiste à se jeter contre les autres spectateurs*) ▶ **slam-dunk** (*US Basketball*) N slam-dunk *m*, smash *m* ♦ VT, VI smasher

▶ **slam down** VT SEP (*gen*) poser *or* jeter brutalement, flanquer*; [+ *lid*] rabattre brutalement; **to ~ the phone down** raccrocher brutalement; **he ~med the phone down on me** il m'a raccroché au nez

▶ **slam on** VT SEP **to ~ on the brakes** freiner à mort; (*fig*) **to ~ the brakes on sth*** (= *put a stop to*) mettre le holà à qch

▶ **slam to** **1** VI se refermer en claquant **2** VT SEP refermer en claquant

slammer ['slæmər] N (= *prison*) **the ~**: la taule:, la prison

slander ['slɑːndər] **1** N calomnie *f*; (*Jur*) diffamation *f*; **it's a ~ to suggest that ...** c'est de la calomnie que de suggérer que ... **2** VT calomnier, dire du mal de; (*Jur*) diffamer

slanderer ['slɑːndərər] N calomniateur *m*, -trice *f*; (*Jur*) diffamateur *m*, -trice *f*

slanderous ['slɑːndərəs] ADJ calomnieux; (*Jur*) diffamatoire

slanderously ['slɑːndərəslɪ] ADV calomnieusement; (*Jur*) de façon diffamatoire

slang [slæŋ] **1** N (*NonC*) argot *m*; **in ~** en argot; **in army/school ~** en argot militaire/d'écolier, dans l'argot des armées/des écoles; **that word is ~** c'est un mot d'argot *or* argotique, c'est un argotisme; **to talk ~** parler argot; **he uses a lot of ~** il emploie beaucoup d'argot, il s'exprime dans une langue très verte → **rhyming 2** ADJ [*phrase, word*] d'argot, argotique; **a ~ expression** un argotisme **3** VT* traiter de tous les noms **4** COMP ▶ **slanging match*** N (*Brit*) prise *f* de bec*

slangily* ['slæŋɪlɪ] ADV **to talk ~** parler argot, employer beaucoup d'argot

slangy* ['slæŋɪ] ADJ [*style, language, expression*] argotique; [*person*] qui emploie beaucoup d'argot

slant [slɑːnt] **1** N **a** inclinaison *f*, aspect *m* penché; (*fig* = *point of view*) point *m* de vue (**on** sur), angle *m*, perspective *f*; **what's his ~ on it?** quel est son point de vue sur la question?; (*fig*) **his mind has a curious ~** il a une curieuse tournure *or* forme d'esprit; **to give/get a new ~* on sth** présenter/voir qch sous un angle *or* jour nouveau **b** (*Typ: also* **~ mark**) (barre *f*) oblique *f* **2** VI [*line, handwriting*] pencher, être incliné; [*light, sunbeam*] passer obliquement **3** VT [+ *line, handwriting*] faire pencher, incliner; (*fig*) [+ *account, news*] présenter avec parti pris; **~ed eyes** yeux *mpl* bridés; **a ~ed report** un rapport orienté *or*

---

tendancieux **4** COMP ▶ **slant-eyed** ADJ aux yeux bridés

slanting ['slɑːntɪŋ] ADJ [*line, rays, light, rain*] oblique; [*roof, surface*] en pente, incliné; [*handwriting*] penché, couché; [*eyes*] bridé

slantwise ['slɑːntwaɪz] ADV, ADJ obliquement, de biais

slanty* ['slɑːntɪ] ADJ **~-eyed** aux yeux bridés; **~ eyes** yeux *mpl* bridés

slap [slæp] **1** N claque *f*; (*on face*) gifle *f*; (*on back*) grande tape *f*; (*stronger*) grande claque *f*; **a ~ on the bottom** une fessée; (*lit, fig*) **a ~ in the face** une gifle; **a ~ on the back** une grande tape *or* claque dans le dos; **to give sb a ~** donner une gifle à qn; (*fig*) **to give sb a ~ on the wrist** réprimander qn; (*fig*) **to get a ~ on the wrist** se faire taper sur les doigts

2 ADV* en plein, tout droit; **he ran ~ into the wall** il est rentré en plein dans *or* tout droit dans le mur; **~ in the middle** en plein *or* au beau milieu

3 VT **a** (= *hit*) [+ *person*] donner une tape à; (*stronger*) donner une claque à; **to ~ sb on the back** donner une tape *or* une claque dans le dos à qn; **to ~ a child's bottom** donner une fessée à un enfant; **to ~ sb's face** *or* **sb in the face** gifler qn; (*in amusement etc*) **to ~ one's knees** *or* **thighs** se taper les cuisses **b** (= *put*) mettre brusquement, flanquer*; (= *apply*) appliquer *or* mettre à la va-vite *or* sans soin; **he ~ped the book on the table** il a flanqué* le livre sur la table; **he ~ped a coat of paint on the wall** il a flanqué* une couche de peinture sur le mur, il a donné un coup de pinceau au mur; **he ~ped £5 on to the price*** il a collé* 5 livres de plus sur le prix, il a gonflé son prix de 5 livres; **she ~ped some foundation on her face*** elle s'est collé* un peu de fond de teint sur le visage, elle s'est mis du fond de teint sur le visage à la va-vite

4 COMP ▶ **slap and tickle*** N (*Brit*) **they were having a bit of the old ~ and tickle** ils étaient en train de se peloter* ▶ **slap-bang*** ADV (*Brit*) **~-bang into the wall** en plein *or* tout droit dans le mur; **he ran ~-bang(-wallop) into his mother** il s'est cogné en plein contre sa mère; (*fig* = *met*) il est tombé tout d'un coup sur sa mère, il s'est retrouvé tout d'un coup nez à nez avec sa mère ▶ **slap-happy*** ADJ (= *carelessly cheerful*) insouciant, décontracté*, relaxe*; (*US* = *punch-drunk*) groggy, abruti par les coups ▶ **slap-up meal*** N (*Brit*) repas *m* fameux *or* extra*

▶ **slap around** VT SEP donner des claques à; **he ~s his wife around** il bat sa femme

▶ **slap down** VT SEP [+ *object*] poser brusquement *or* violemment; (*fig*) **to ~ sb down*** rembarrer* qn, envoyer qn sur les roses*

▶ **slap on** VT SEP [+ *paint etc*] appliquer à la va-vite *or* n'importe comment; (*fig*) [+ *tax*] flanquer*, imposer brusquement; **to ~ on make-up** se maquiller à la va-vite

slapdash ['slæpdæʃ] **1** ADJ [*person*] négligent; [*work*] bâclé* **2** ADV à la va-vite, n'importe comment

slaphead: ['slæphed] N (*pej or hum* = *bald person*) **he's a ~** c'est un crâne d'œuf*, il est chauve comme un œuf*

slapper: ['slæpər] N garce: *f*

slapstick ['slæpstɪk] N (*also* **~ comedy**) grosse farce *f*, comédie *f* bouffonne

slash [slæʃ] **1** N **a** (= *cut: gen*) entaille *f*, taillade *f*; (*on face*) entaille *f*, balafre *f*; (*Sewing: in sleeve*) crevé *m* **b** (*Typ: also* **~ mark**) (barre *f*) oblique *f* **c** **to go for a ~**: (= *urinate*) aller pisser une jatte: *or* un coup: **2** VT **a** (*with knife, sickle etc*) taillader; (*several cuts*) taillader; [+ *rope*] couper net, trancher; [+ *face*] balafrer; (*with whip, stick*) cingler; (*Sewing*) [+ *sleeve*] faire des crevés dans; **~ed sleeves** manches *fpl* à crevés; **to ~ sb**

taillarder qn ; **his attacker ~ed his face/his jacket** son assaillant lui a balafré le visage/a tailladé sa veste ; **to ~ one's wrists** s'ouvrir les veines

b (fig) [+ prices] casser*, écraser* ; [+ costs, expenses] réduire radicalement ; [+ speech, text] couper or raccourcir radicalement ; **"prices ~ed"** « prix cassés », « prix sacrifiés »

c (* = condemn) [+ book, play] éreinter*, démolir*

3 VI **he ~ed at me with his stick** il m'a flanqué* un or des coup(s) de bâton ; **he ~ed at the grass with his stick** il cinglait l'herbe de sa canne

4 COMP ► **slash-and-burn** ADJ (Agr) **~-and-burn agriculture** or **farming** culture f sur brûlis

slasher film* ['slæʃəfilm], **slasher movie*** ['slæʃəmuːvi] N film m d'horreur (particulièrement violent)

slashing ['slæʃɪŋ] ADJ (fig) [criticism, attack] cinglant, mordant

slat [slæt] N lame f ; (wooden) latte f ; [of blind] lamelle f

slate [sleɪt] **1** N (= substance, object: Constr, Scol etc) ardoise f ; (fig: Pol) liste f provisoire de candidats ; (Pol) **they've got a full ~ there** ils ont des candidats dans toutes les circonscriptions ; (Brit Comm) **put it on the ~*** mettez-le sur mon compte, ajoutez ça à mon ardoise* ; (fig) **to start with a clean ~** repartir sur une bonne base → **wipe 2** VT **a** [+ roof] ardoiser **b** (US Pol) [+ candidate] proposer **c** (Brit*) (= criticize) éreinter*, démolir* ; (= cold) attraper*, engueuler* **d** (US) **to be ~d* for sth** (= destined) être désigné pour qch **3** COMP [deposits] d'ardoise, ardoisier ; [industry] ardoisier, de l'ardoise ; [roof] en ardoise, d'ardoise ► **slate-blue** ADJ, N bleu ardoise m inv ► **slate-coloured** ADJ ardoise inv ► **slate-grey** ADJ, N gris ardoise m inv ► **slate quarry** N ardoisière f, carrière f d'ardoise

slater ['sleɪtər] N (in quarry) ardoisier m ; [of roof] couvreur m

slatted ['slætɪd] ADJ à lames ; (wooden) à lattes ; [blind] à lamelles

slattern ['slætən] N souillon f

slatternly ['slætənlɪ] ADJ [woman, appearance] négligé ; [behaviour, habits] de souillon

slaty ['sleɪtɪ] ADJ (in texture) ardoisier, semblable à l'ardoise ; (in colour) (couleur) ardoise inv

slaughter ['slɔːtər] **1** N [of animals] abattage m ; [of people] massacre m ; **the ~ on the roads** les hécatombes fpl sur la route ; **there was great ~** cela a été un carnage or un massacre **2** VT [+ animal] abattre ; [+ person] tuer sauvagement ; [+ people] massacrer ; (= beat) **our team really ~ed them*** notre équipe les a écrasés or massacrés*

slaughterer ['slɔːtərər] N [of animals] tueur m, assommeur m ; [of person] meurtrier m ; [of people] massacreur m

slaughterhouse ['slɔːtəhaʊs] N abattoir m

Slav [slɑːv] N, ADJ slave mf

slave [sleɪv] **1** N (lit, fig) esclave mf ; (fig) **to be a ~ to** être (l')esclave de → **white 2** VI (also **~ away**) travailler comme un nègre, trimer ; **to ~ (away) at sth/at doing** s'escrimer sur qch/à faire **3** COMP ► **slave driver** N (lit) surveillant m d'esclaves ; (fig) négrier m, -ière f ► **slave labour** N (NonC) (= exploitation) exploitation f des esclaves ; (= work) travail m fait par les esclaves ; (* fig) travail m de forçat or de galérien ; **~ labour camp** camp m de travaux forcés ► **slave ship** N (vaisseau m) négrier m ► **slave trade** N commerce m des esclaves, traite f des Noirs ► **slave trader** N marchand m d'esclaves, négrier m ► **slave traffic** N trafic m d'esclaves

slaver¹ ['sleɪvər] N (= person) marchand m d'esclaves, négrier m ; (= ship) (vaisseau m) négrier m

slaver² ['slævər] (= dribble) **1** N bave f **2** VI baver ; (fig) **to ~ over sth** baver* devant qch

slavery ['sleɪvərɪ] N (lit, fig) esclavage m ; **housework is nothing but ~** le ménage est un véritable esclavage or une perpétuelle corvée → **sell**

slavey* ['sleɪvɪ] N boniche* f

Slavic ['slɑːvɪk] ADJ, N slave m

slavish ['sleɪvɪʃ] ADJ [imitation] servile ; [devotion] béat ; [remake] sans aucune originalité ; **to be a ~ follower of sb/sth** suivre qn/qch aveuglément

slavishly ['sleɪvɪʃlɪ] ADV [follow] servilement, aveuglément ; [copy] bêtement ; **their ~ pro-American attitude** leur attitude aveuglément pro-américaine ; **the film is ~ faithful to the novel** le film est trop proche du roman

Slavonic [slə'vɒnɪk] ADJ, N slave m

slavophile ['slævəʊˌfaɪl] N, ADJ slavophile mf

slaw [slɔː] N (esp US) = **coleslaw**

slay [sleɪ] (pret **slew**, ptp **slain**) VT (liter) tuer ; (fig) **he ~s me!** il me fait mourir or crever* de rire ! → **slain**

slayer ['sleɪər] N (liter) tueur m, -euse f

SLD [esel'diː] N (Brit Pol) (ABBR = Social and Liberal Democrats) → **social**

sleaze* [sliːz] N **a** (Pol = corruption) corruption f **b** (= filth) sordidité f ; **that film is pure ~** ce film est complètement sordide

sleazebag* ['sliːzbæg], **sleazeball*** ['sliːzbɔːl] N ordure* f

sleaziness* ['sliːzɪnɪs] N aspect m sordide ; [of person] air m louche

sleazy* ['sliːzɪ] ADJ [place, atmosphere, behaviour] sordide ; [person] louche ; [magazine] cochon

sled [sled] N (US) = **sledge 1**

sledding ['sledɪŋ] N (US) **hard** or **tough ~*** période f (or tâche f) difficile

sledge [sledʒ] **1** N traîneau m ; (child's) luge f **2** VI **to go sledging** faire de la luge, se promener en traîneau ; **to ~ down/across** etc descendre/traverser etc en luge or en traîneau

sledgehammer ['sledʒˌhæmər] N marteau m de forgeron ; (fig) **to strike sb/sth a ~ blow** assener un coup violent or magistral à qn/qch

sleek [sliːk] ADJ [hair, fur] lustré, lisse et brillant ; [cat] au poil lustré ; [person] soigné ; [car, boat, aircraft, furniture] aux lignes pures

► **sleek down** VT SEP **to ~ one's hair down** se lisser les cheveux

sleekly ['sliːklɪ] ADV [smile, reply] doucereusement, avec onction

sleekness ['sliːknɪs] N [of person] allure f soignée ; [of car, plane] lignes fpl profilées ; [of structure, building] finesse f or pureté f (de lignes)

sleep [sliːp] (vb: pret, ptp **slept**) **1** N **a** sommeil m ; **to be in a deep** or **sound ~** dormir profondément ; **to be in a very heavy ~** dormir d'un sommeil de plomb ; **to talk in one's ~** parler en dormant or dans son sommeil ; **to walk in one's ~** marcher en dormant ; **to sleep the ~ of the just** dormir du sommeil du juste ; **overcome by ~** ayant succombé au sommeil ; **to have a ◊** or **get some ~** dormir ; (for a short while) faire un somme ; **to get** or **go to ~** s'endormir ; **my leg has gone to ~** j'ai la jambe engourdie ; **I didn't get a wink of ~** or **any ~ all night** je n'ai pas fermé l'œil de la nuit ; **she sang the child to ~** elle a chanté jusqu'à ce que l'enfant s'endorme ; **to put** or **send sb to ~** endormir qn ; (euph) **to put a cat to ~** (= put down) faire piquer un chat ; **I need eight hours' ~ a night** il me faut (mes) huit heures de sommeil chaque nuit ; **a three-hour ~** trois heures de sommeil ; **I haven't had enough ~ lately** je manque de sommeil ces temps-ci ; **I had a good ~ last night** j'ai bien dormi la nuit

dernière ; **to have a good night's ~** passer une bonne nuit ; **a ~ will do you good** cela vous fera du bien de dormir ; **let him have his ~ out** laisse-le dormir tant qu'il voudra → **beauty**, **lose**

b (* = matter in eyes) chassie f

2 VI **a** dormir ; **to ~ tight** or **like a log** or **like a top** dormir à poings fermés or comme une souche or comme un loir ; **~ tight!** dors bien ! ; **to ~ heavily** dormir d'un sommeil de plomb ; **he was ~ing deeply** or **soundly** il dormait profondément, il était profondément endormi ; **to ~ soundly** (= without fear) dormir sur ses deux oreilles ; **to ~ lightly** (regularly) avoir le sommeil léger ; (on one occasion) dormir d'un sommeil léger ; **I didn't ~ a wink all night** je n'ai pas fermé l'œil de la nuit ; **to ~ the clock round** faire le tour du cadran ; (fig) **he was ~ing on his feet** il dormait debout

b (= spend night) coucher ; **he slept in the car** il a passé la nuit or dormi dans la voiture ; **he slept at his aunt's** il a couché chez sa tante ; **he ~s on a hard mattress** il couche or dort sur un matelas dur

c (= have sex) **to ~ with sb** coucher* avec qn

3 VT **the house ~s eight (people)** on peut loger or coucher huit personnes dans cette maison ; **this room will ~ four (people)** on peut coucher quatre personnes or coucher à quatre dans cette chambre ; **the hotel ~s 500** l'hôtel peut loger or contenir 500 personnes ; **can you ~ us all?** pouvez-vous nous coucher tous ?

4 COMP ► **sleep-learning** N hypnopédie f

► **sleep around*** VI coucher* avec n'importe qui, coucher* à droite et à gauche

► **sleep away** VT SEP **to ~ the morning away** passer la matinée à dormir, ne pas se réveiller de la matinée

► **sleep in** VI **a** (= lie late) faire la grasse matinée, dormir tard ; (= oversleep) ne pas se réveiller à temps, dormir trop tard **b** [nurse, servant etc] être logé sur place

► **sleep off** VT SEP **to ~ sth off** dormir pour faire passer qch, se remettre de qch en dormant ; **go to bed and ~ it off** va te coucher et cela te passera en dormant ; **to ~ off a hangover ◊ to ~ it off*** dormir pour faire passer sa gueule de bois* ; cuver son vin*

► **sleep on** **1** VI **he slept on till ten** il a dormi jusqu'à dix heures, il ne s'est pas réveillé avant dix heures ; **let him ~ on for another hour** laisse-le dormir encore une heure **2** VT FUS **to ~ on a problem/a letter/a decision** attendre le lendemain pour résoudre un problème/répondre à une lettre/prendre une décision ; **let's ~ on it** nous verrons demain, la nuit porte conseil ; **I'll have to ~ on it** il faut que j'attende demain pour décider

► **sleep out** VI **a** (in open air) coucher à la belle étoile ; (in tent) coucher sous la tente **b** [nurse, servant etc] ne pas être logé (sur place)

► **sleep over** VI passer la nuit, coucher

► **sleep through** **1** VI **I slept through till the afternoon** j'ai dormi comme une souche or sans me réveiller jusqu'à l'après-midi **2** VT FUS **he slept through the storm** l'orage ne l'a pas réveillé ; **he slept through the alarm clock** il n'a pas entendu son réveil (sonner)

► **sleep together** VI (= have sex) coucher ensemble

sleeper ['sliːpər] N **a** (= person) dormeur m, -euse f ; (fig = spy) espion(ne) m(f) en sommeil ; **to be a light/heavy ~** avoir le sommeil léger/lourd ; **that child is a good ~** cet enfant dort très bien or fait sa nuit sans se réveiller **b** (Brit Rail) (on track) traverse f ; (= berth) couchette f ; (= rail car) voiture-lit f ; (= train) train-couchettes m ; **I took a ~ to Marseilles** j'ai pris un train-couchettes pour aller à Marseille, je suis allé à Marseille en train-couchettes **c** (esp Brit = earring) clou m (bou-

cle d'oreille) **d** *(fig = sudden success)* révélation *f*

sleepily ['sli:pɪlɪ] ADV *[smile, blink etc]* d'un air endormi; *[say, ask]* d'un ton endormi

sleepiness ['sli:pɪnɪs] N *[of person]* envie *f* de dormir, torpeur *f*; *[of town]* somnolence *f*, torpeur *f*

sleeping ['sli:pɪŋ] **1** ADJ *[person, village]* endormi ■ *(PROV)* **let ~ dogs lie** il ne faut pas réveiller le chat qui dort *(PROV)*; **to let ~ dogs lie** ne pas réveiller le chat qui dort; **(the) Sleeping Beauty** la Belle au bois dormant **2** COMP ► **sleeping accommodation** N *(in house)* place *f* pour dormir, lits *mpl*; *(on train)* couchettes *fpl* ► **sleeping area** N *(in house)* chambres *fpl* à coucher; *(in studio flat)* coin *m* à dormir ► **sleeping bag** N sac *m* de couchage ► **sleeping berth** N couchette *f* ► **sleeping car** N *(Rail)* wagon-lit *m*, voiture-lit *f* ► **sleeping draught** N soporifique *m* ► **sleeping partner** N *(Brit Comm)* (associé *m*) commanditaire *m* ► **sleeping pill** N somnifère *m* ► **sleeping policeman** N *(pl* **sleeping policemen**) *(Brit: in road)* ralentisseur *m*, gendarme *m* couché ► **sleeping porch** N *(US)* chambre-véranda *f* ► **sleeping position** N position *f* pour dormir ► **sleeping problems** NPL troubles *mpl* du sommeil; **I have terrible ~ problems** je dors très mal ► **sleeping quarters** NPL chambres *fpl* (à coucher); *(in barracks)* chambrées *fpl*; *(= dormitory)* dortoir *m* ► **sleeping sickness** N maladie *f* du sommeil ► **sleeping suit** N grenouillère *f* ► **sleeping tablet** N = **sleeping pill**

sleepless ['sli:plɪs] ADJ *[person]* qui ne dort pas, insomniaque; **a ~ baby can be very tiring** ça peut être très fatigant d'avoir un bébé qui ne dort pas; **(to have) a ~ night** (passer) une nuit blanche; **he arrived exhausted after a ~ journey** il est arrivé épuisé, n'ayant pas dormi de tout le trajet; **he spent many ~ hours worrying** il a passé de longues heures sans sommeil à se faire du souci

sleeplessly ['sli:plɪslɪ] ADV sans pouvoir dormir

sleeplessness ['sli:plɪsnɪs] N insomnie *f*

sleepwalk ['sli:pwɔ:k] VI être somnambule

sleepwalker ['sli:pwɔ:kəʳ] N somnambule *mf*

sleepwalking ['sli:pwɔ:kɪŋ] N *(NonC)* somnambulisme *m*

sleepwear ['sli:pwɛəʳ] N *(NonC: Comm etc)* vêtements *mpl or* lingerie *f* de nuit

sleepy ['sli:pɪ] ADJ **a** *(= drowsy)* *[person]* qui a sommeil; *[voice, look]* endormi; **to be or feel ~** avoir sommeil **b** *(= quiet)* *[village, town]* somnolent

sleepyhead* ['sli:pɪhed] N endormi(e) *m(f)*

sleepyheaded* ['sli:pɪ'hedɪd] ADJ (à moitié) endormi

sleet [sli:t] **1** N neige *f* fondue **2** VI **it is ~ing** il tombe de la neige fondue

sleeve [sli:v] **1** N *[of garment]* manche *f*; *[of record]* pochette *f*; *[of cylinder etc]* chemise *f*; *(fig)* **he's always got something up his ~** il a plus d'un tour dans son sac; **he's bound to have something up his ~** il a certainement quelque chose en réserve, il garde certainement un atout caché; **I don't know what he's got up his ~** je ne sais pas ce qu'il nous réserve (comme surprise); **I've got an idea up my ~** j'ai une petite idée en réserve *or* dans la tête; **to have or wear one's heart on one's ~** laisser voir ses sentiments, être transparent → **laugh**, **shirt 2** COMP ► **sleeve board** N jeannette *f* ► **sleeve note** N *(Brit: on record sleeve)* texte *m (sur pochette de disque)*

-sleeved [sli:vd] ADJ *(in compounds)* **long-sleeved** à manches longues

sleeveless ['sli:vlɪs] ADJ sans manches; **~ T-shirt** tee-shirt *m* sans manches

sleigh [sleɪ] **1** N traîneau *m* **2** VI aller en traîneau **3** COMP ► **sleigh bell** N grelot *m or* clochette *f* (de traîneau) ► **sleigh ride** N **to go for a ~ ride** faire une promenade en traîneau

sleight [slaɪt] N **~ of hand** *(= skill)* habileté *f*, dextérité *f*; *(= trick)* tour *m* de passe-passe; **by (a) ~ of hand** par un tour de passe-passe

slender ['slendəʳ] ADJ **a** *(lit)* *[person, figure]* svelte, mince; *[legs, arms, fingers, waist]* fin; *[neck]* fin, gracieux; *[column]* élancé **b** *(fig)* *[hope, chance, margin]* faible; *[income, means, resources]* maigre

slenderize ['slendəraɪz] VT *(US)* amincir

slenderly ['slendəlɪ] ADV **~ built** svelte, mince

slenderness ['slendənɪs] N **a** *(lit)* *[of figure, person]* sveltesse *f*, minceur *f*; *[of legs, arms, fingers, waist, neck]* finesse *f* **b** *(fig)* *[of income, means, resources]* maigreur *f*; **the ~ of the Conservative majority** la faible majorité des conservateurs; **the ~ of his chances of winning** le peu de chances qu'il a de gagner

slept [slept] VB *pt, ptp of* **sleep**

sleuth [slu:θ] **1** N *(= dog: also* **~ hound**) limier *m*; *(* = *detective)* limier *m*, détective *m* **2** VI *(*:* also* **~ around**) fureter, fouiner*

slew¹ [slu:] VB *pt of* **slay**

slew² [slu:] *(also* **~ round**) **1** VI virer, pivoter; *(Naut)* virer; *[car]* déraper par l'arrière; *(right round)* faire un tête-à-queue; **the car ~ed (round) to a stop** la voiture s'est arrêtée après un tête-à-queue **2** VT faire pivoter, faire virer; **he ~ed the car (round)** il a fait déraper la voiture par l'arrière; *(= right round)* il a fait un tête-à-queue

slew³ [slu:] N *(esp US)* **a ~ of ...** un tas* de ..., un grand nombre de ...

slewed†‡ [slu:d] ADJ *(Brit = drunk)* paf‡ *inv*, soûl*

slice [slaɪs] **1** N **a** *[of cake, bread, meat]* tranche *f*; *[of lemon, cucumber, sausage]* rondelle *f*, tranche *f*; **~ of bread and butter** tranche *f* de pain beurré, tartine *f* beurrée **b** *(fig)* *(= part)* partie *f*; *(= share)* part *f*; **it took quite a ~ of our profits** cela nous a pris une bonne partie de nos bénéfices; **a large ~ of the credit** une grande part du mérite; **~ of life** tranche *f* de vie; **~ of luck** coup *m* de chance **c** *(= kitchen utensil)* spatule *f*, truelle *f* **d** *(Sport)* balle *f* coupée, slice *m* **2** VT **a** *[+ bread, cake, meat]* couper (en tranches); *[+ lemon, sausage, cucumber]* couper (en rondelles); *[+ rope etc]* couper net, trancher; **to ~ sth thin** couper qch en tranches *or* rondelles fines; **~d bread** le pain en tranches; **a ~d loaf** un pain en tranches; **it's the best thing since ~d bread*** on n'a pas vu mieux depuis l'invention du fil à couper le beurre **b** *(Sport)* *[+ ball]* couper, slicer **3** VI **this knife won't ~** ce couteau coupe très mal; **this bread won't ~** ce pain se coupe très mal *or* est très difficile à couper

► **slice off** VT SEP *[+ piece of rope, finger etc]* couper net; **to ~ off a piece of sausage** couper une rondelle de saucisson; **to ~ off a steak** couper *or* tailler un bifteck

► **slice through** VT FUS *[+ rope]* couper net, trancher; *(fig)* *[+ restrictions etc]* (réussir à) passer au travers de, court-circuiter*; *(fig)* **to ~ through the air/the waves** fendre l'air/les flots

► **slice up** VT SEP couper *or* débiter en tranches *or* en rondelles

slicer ['slaɪsəʳ] N *(= knife)* couteau *m* électrique; *(= machine)* trancheuse *f*

slick [slɪk] **1** ADJ **a** *(= efficient, skilful)* **the robbery was an extremely ~ operation** le braquage a été rondement mené **b** *(pej = superficial, glib)* *[person]* qui a du bagout*; *[explanation]* trop prompt; *[excuse]* facile; *[style]* superficiel; *[manner]* doucereux, mielleux; **he**

always has a ~ answer il a toujours réponse à tout **c** *(= shiny, slippery)* *[hair]* lissé; *[road, surface]* glissant; **~ tyres** pneus *mpl* lisses **2** N *(also* **oil ~**) nappe *f* de pétrole; *(on beach)* marée *f* noire **3** VT **to ~ (down) one's hair** *(with comb etc)* se lisser les cheveux; *(with hair cream)* mettre de la brillantine; **~ed-back hair** cheveux *mpl* lissés en arrière

slicker ['slɪkəʳ] N *(US)* combinard(e)* *m(f)* → **city**

slickly ['slɪklɪ] ADV élégamment, habilement

slickness ['slɪknɪs] N **a** *(= efficiency, skill)* habileté *f* **b** *(pej = superficiality, glibness)* caractère *m* superficiel **c** *(= shininess, slipperiness)* *[of hair]* brillant *m*; *[of road]* surface *f* glissante

slide [slaɪd] *(vb: pret, ptp* **slid**) **1** N **a** *(= action)* glissade *f*; *(also* **landslide**) glissement *m* (de terrain); *(fig: in prices, temperature etc)* baisse *f*, chute *f* **(in** de) **b** *(in playground, pool etc)* toboggan *m*; *(= polished ice etc)* glissoire *f*; *(for logs etc)* glissoir *m* **c** *(Phot)* diapositive *f*, diapo* *f*; *[of microscope]* porte-objet *m*; **illustrated with ~s** accompagné de diapositives; **a film for ~s** une pellicule à diapositives → **colour**, **lantern d** *(Tech = runner)* coulisse *f*; *(on trombone etc)* coulisse *f*; *(Mus: between notes)* coulé *m*; *(= hair slide)* barrette *f*

2 VI **a** *[person, object]* glisser; *(on ice etc)* *[person]* faire des glissades, glisser; **to ~ down the bannisters** descendre en glissant sur la rampe; **to ~ down a slope** descendre une pente en glissant, glisser le long d'une pente; **the drawer ~s in and out easily** le tiroir glisse bien, le tiroir s'ouvre et se ferme facilement; **the top ought to ~ gently into place** on devrait pouvoir mettre le haut en place en le faisant glisser doucement; **the book slid off my knee** le livre a glissé de mes genoux; **to let things ~** laisser les choses aller à la dérive; **he let his studies ~** il a négligé ses études **b** *(= move silently)* se glisser; **he slid into the room** il s'est glissé dans la pièce; *(fig)* **to ~ into bad habits** prendre insensiblement de mauvaises habitudes

3 VT faire glisser, glisser; **he slid the chair across the room** il a fait glisser la chaise à travers la pièce; **he slid the packing case into a corner** il a glissé la caisse dans un coin; **he slid the photo into his pocket** il a glissé la photo dans sa poche; **to ~ the top (back) onto a box** remettre le couvercle sur une boîte en le faisant glisser; **~ the drawer into place** remets le tiroir en place; **he slid the gun out of the holster** il a sorti le revolver de l'étui

4 COMP ► **slide box** N *(Phot)* classeur *m* pour diapositives, boîte *f* à diapositives ► **slide changer** N *(Phot)* passe-vue *m* ► **slide fastener** N *(Dress etc)* fermeture *f* éclair®, fermeture *f* à glissière ► **slide guitar** N slide guitar *f* ► **slide magazine** N *(Phot)* panier *m* ► **slide projector** N *(Phot)* projecteur *m* de diapositives ► **slide rule** N règle *f* à calcul ► **slide show** N projection *f* de diapositives

► **slide down** VI *[person, animal, vehicle]* descendre en glissant; *[object]* glisser

► **slide off** VI **a** *[top, lid etc]* s'enlever facilement *or* en glissant **b** *(fig = leave quietly)* *[guest]* s'en aller discrètement, s'éclipser*; *[thief]* s'éloigner furtivement

sliding ['slaɪdɪŋ] **1** ADJ *[movement]* glissant; *[part]* qui glisse, mobile; *[panel, door, seat]* coulissant; *(Aut)* **~ roof** toit *m* ouvrant; *(Admin, Comm, Ind etc)* **~ scale** échelle *f* mobile; *(US)* **~ time** horaire *m* flexible **2** N glissement *m*

slight [slaɪt] **1** ADJ **a** *(= minor)* *(gen)* petit, léger *(before n)*; *[error]* petit; **to be at a ~ angle** être légèrement incliné; **it doesn't make the ~est bit of difference** *(= is unimportant)* cela n'a aucune importance; *(= is useless)* ça ne sert à rien; **without the ~est hint of**

embarrassment/disappointment sans manifester la moindre gêne/la moindre déception ; **I haven't the ~est idea** je n'en ai pas la moindre idée ; **I haven't the ~est idea (of) where he's gone/what to do** je n'ai pas la moindre idée de l'endroit où il est allé/de ce qu'il faut faire ; **nobody showed the ~est interest** personne n'a manifesté le moindre intérêt ; **not in the ~est** pas le moins du monde ; **he takes offence at the ~est thing** il se vexe pour un rien ; **just the ~est bit short** un tout petit peu trop court
[b] (= *slim*) [*person, figure*] mince, menu ; **to be of ~ build** être menu, avoir les attaches fines [c] (= *inconsiderable*) insignifiant ; **a book of very ~ scholarship** un livre vraiment peu érudit ; **it is no ~ accomplishment** c'est un exploit, et non des moindres
[2] VT (= *ignore*) ignorer, manquer d'égards envers ; (= *offend*) blesser, offenser ; **he felt (himself) ~ed** il s'est senti blessé or offensé
[3] N (= *insult*) affront m ; **this is a ~ on all of us** c'est un affront qui nous touche tous

slighting ['slaɪtɪŋ] ADJ offensant

slightingly ['slaɪtɪŋlɪ] ADV d'une manière blessante

slightly ['slaɪtlɪ] ADV [a] [*different, deaf, injured, damaged*] légèrement ; [*expensive, more, less, better etc*] un peu ; [*change, rise, fall, improve etc*] légèrement ; **~ unfair** un peu injuste, pas très juste ; **~ uneasy** pas très à l'aise ; **I know her ~** je la connais un peu ; **ever so ~** un tout petit peu [b] **~ built** [*person*] menu, aux attaches fines

slightness ['slaɪtnɪs] N (= *slimness*) minceur f ; (= *frailty*) fragilité f ; [*of difference, increase etc*] caractère m insignifiant or négligeable

slim [slɪm] [1] ADJ [a] [*person*] = *thin*] mince, svelte [b] (fig) [*majority*] faible ; [*chance, hope*] faible, mince ; **(the) chances are ~ of England winning** or **that England will win** il y a peu de chances que l'Angleterre gagne (*subj*) ; **his chances of winning are ~ ◊ he has only a ~ chance of winning** il a peu de chances de gagner, ses chances de gagner sont minces [2] VI maigrir, (= *diet*) suivre un régime amaigrissant ; **she's ~ming** elle suit un régime (amaigrissant) [3] VT (*also ~ down*) [*diet etc*] faire maigrir ; [*dress etc*] amincir [4] N (*East African name for AIDS*) **Slim*** sida m
► **slim down** [1] VI [*person*] maigrir, perdre du poids [b] [*business, company*] réduire ses effectifs, dégraisser* [2] VT SEP [a] = **slim** 3 [b] (fig) **~med down** [*business, company*] allégé, dégraissé*

slime [slaɪm] N (= *mud*) vase f ; (*on riverbeds*) limon m ; (= *sticky substance*) dépôt m visqueux or gluant ; (*from snail*) bave f

slimeball: ['slaɪmbɔːl] N (*esp US*) ordure⁂ f

sliminess ['slaɪmɪnɪs] N [a] (*lit*) [*of substance, creature, surface*] viscosité f [b] (fig) [*of person*] obséquiosité f

slimline ['slɪmlaɪn] ADJ [*drink*] light, hypocalorique ; [*body, person*] mince, svelte ; [*dishwasher, freezer etc*] mini *inv*

slimmer ['slɪmə'] N personne f au régime ; **if you are a ~** si vous suivez un régime

slimming ['slɪmɪŋ] [1] N fait m de suivre un régime amaigrissant, amaigrissement m ; **~ can be very tiring** un régime amaigrissant peut être très fatigant, ça peut être très fatigant d'être au régime [2] ADJ [*garment*] qui amincit ; [*food*] amincissant [3] COMP ► **slimming aid** N (= *food*) (produit m) amincissant

slimness ['slɪmnɪs] N [a] (*lit* = *thinness*) minceur f [b] (fig) **the ~ of their majority** leur faible majorité ; **the ~ of his chances** le peu de chances or les faibles chances qu'il a

slimy ['slaɪmɪ] ADJ [a] (*lit*) [*substance, creature, surface*] visqueux [b] (*Brit* fig) [*person*]

mielleux, obséquieux ; **he's a ~ toad** c'est un lécheur or un lèche-bottes*

sling [slɪŋ] (*vb: pret, ptp* **slung**) [1] N [a] (= *weapon*) fronde f ; (*child's*) lance-pierre(s) m *inv* ; **they were quite unable to cope with the ~s and arrows of outrageous fortune** ils n'étaient pas à même de faire face à l'adversité
[b] (= *hoist*) cordages mpl, courroies fpl ; (*for oil drums etc*) courroie f ; (*Naut*) (*for loads, casks, boats*) élingue f ; (*for mast*) cravate f ; (*for rifle*) bretelle f ; (*Med*) écharpe f ; **to have one's arm in a ~** avoir le bras en écharpe
[c] (*Climbing*) anneau m (de corde) ; (*also* **gear ~**) baudrier m
[2] VT [a] (= *throw*) [+ *objects, stones*] lancer, jeter (**at** or **to sb** à qn, **at sth** sur qch) ; [+ *insults, accusations*] lancer (**at sb** à qn) ; (*Brit*) **~ your hook!*** fiche le camp !*
[b] (= *hang*) [+ *hammock etc*] suspendre ; [+ *load etc*] hisser ; (*Naut*) élinguer ; **to ~ across one's shoulder** [+ *rifle*] mettre en bandoulière or à la bretelle ; [+ *satchel*] mettre en bandoulière ; [+ *load, coat*] jeter par derrière l'épaule ; **with his rifle slung across his shoulder** avec son fusil en bandoulière or à la bretelle
► **sling away*** VT SEP (= *get rid of*) bazarder*
► **sling out*** VT SEP (= *put out*) [+ *person*] flanquer* à la porte or dehors ; [+ *object*] bazarder*
► **sling over*** VT SEP (= *pass*) balancer*, envoyer
► **sling up** VT SEP suspendre

slingbacks ['slɪŋbæks] NPL escarpins mpl à bride (arrière)

slingshot ['slɪŋʃɒt] N (*US*) lance-pierre(s) m *inv*

slink [slɪŋk] (*pret, ptp* **slunk**) VI **to ~ away/out** etc s'en aller/sortir etc furtivement or sournoisement or honteusement

slinkily* ['slɪŋkɪlɪ] ADV [*walk*] d'une démarche ondoyante or ondulante, avec un mouvement onduleux

slinking ['slɪŋkɪŋ] ADJ furtif

slinky* ['slɪŋkɪ] ADJ [*dress, skirt*] moulant, sinueux ; [*figure*] ondoyant ; [*walk*] ondoyant, ondulant

slip [slɪp] [1] N [a] (= *slide*) dérapage m ; (= *trip*) faux pas m ; (*of earth*) éboulement m ; (fig = *mistake*) bévue f, erreur f ; (= *oversight*) étourderie f, oubli m ; (*moral*) écart m, faute f légère ▪ (*PROV*) **there's many a ~ 'twixt cup and lip** il y a loin de la coupe aux lèvres (*PROV*) ; **~ of the tongue** ◊ **~ of the pen** lapsus m ; **it was a ~ of the tongue** c'était un lapsus, la langue lui a (or m'a etc) fourché ; **he made several ~s** il a fait or commis plusieurs lapsus ; **to give sb the ~** fausser compagnie à qn
[b] (*also* **pillowslip**) taie f (d'oreiller) ; (= *underskirt*) combinaison f → **gym**
[c] **the ~s** (*Naut*) la cale ; (*Theat*) les coulisses fpl ; (*Cricket*) partie du terrain se trouvant diagonalement derrière le batteur ; **in the ~s** (*Naut*) sur cale ; (*Theat*) dans les coulisses
[d] (= *plant-cutting*) bouture f ; (= *paper: in filing system*) fiche f ; **a ~ of paper** (= *small sheet*) un bout or un morceau de papier ; (= *strip*) une bande de papier ; (fig) **a (mere) ~ of a boy/girl** un gamin/une gamine, un jeune homme/une jeune fille gracile
[e] (*NonC: Pottery*) engobe m
[f] (*Aviat: also* **sideslip**) glissade f or glissement m sur l'aile
[2] VI [a] (= *slide*) [*person, foot, hand, object*] glisser ; **he ~ped on the ice** il a glissé or dérapé sur la glace ; **my foot/hand ~ped** mon pied/ma main a glissé ; (*Aut*) **the clutch ~ped** l'embrayage a patiné ; **the knot has ~ped** le nœud a glissé or coulissé ; **the fish ~ped off the hook** le poisson s'est détaché de l'hameçon ; **the drawer ~s in and out easily** le tiroir glisse bien, le tiroir s'ouvre et se ferme facilement ; **the top ought to ~ gently into place** on devrait pouvoir mettre le haut en place en le faisant glisser doucement ; **the saw ~ped and cut my**

hand la scie a glissé or dérapé et m'a entaillé la main ; **the book ~ped out of his hand/off the table** le livre lui a glissé des doigts/a glissé de la table ; **the beads ~ped through my fingers** les perles m'ont glissé entre les doigts ; (fig) **money ~s through her fingers** l'argent lui file entre les doigts ; **to let sth ~ through one's fingers** laisser qch filer entre ses doigts ; **the thief ~ped through their fingers** le voleur leur a filé entre les doigts ; **several errors had ~ped into the report** plusieurs erreurs s'étaient glissées dans le rapport ; **to let an opportunity ~ ◊ to let ~ an opportunity** laisser passer or laisser échapper une occasion ; **he let ~ an oath** il a laissé échapper un juron ; **he let (it) ~ that ...** il a laissé échapper que ... ; **he's ~ping*** (= *getting old, less efficient*) il baisse, il n'est plus ce qu'il était ; (= *making more mistakes*) il ne fait plus assez attention, il ne se concentre plus assez → **net¹**
[b] (= *move quickly*) [*person*] se glisser, passer ; [*vehicle*] se faufiler, passer ; **he ~ped into/out of the room** il s'est glissé or coulé dans/hors de la pièce ; **he ~ped through the corridors** il s'est faufilé dans les couloirs ; **I'll just ~ through the garden** je vais passer par le jardin ; **the motorbike ~ped through the traffic** la motocyclette s'est faufilée à travers la circulation ; **he ~ped over** or **across the border** il se faufila de l'autre côté de la frontière ; **to ~ into bed** se glisser or se couler dans son lit ; **to ~ into a dress** etc se glisser dans or enfiler (rapidement) une robe etc ; **to ~ out of a dress** etc enlever (rapidement) une robe etc ; (fig) **he ~ped easily into his new role** il s'est adapté or il s'est fait facilement à son nouveau rôle ; **to ~ into bad habits** prendre insensiblement de mauvaises habitudes
[3] VT [a] (= *slide*) glisser ; **to ~ a coin to sb/ into sb's hand** glisser une pièce à qn/dans la main de qn ; **he ~ped the book back on the shelf** il a glissé or remis le livre à sa place sur l'étagère ; **he ~ped the ring on her finger** il lui a glissé or passé la bague au doigt ; **he ~ped the photo into his pocket** il a glissé la photo dans sa poche ; **to ~ the top (back) onto a box** remettre le couvercle sur une boîte en le faisant glisser ; **~ the drawer (back) into place** remets le tiroir en place ; **he ~ped the gun out of its holster** il a retiré or sorti le revolver de son étui ; (*Aut*) **to ~ the clutch** faire patiner l'embrayage ; **a question on Proust was ~ped into the exam** l'épreuve a comporté une question inattendue sur Proust ; (*Med*) **a ~ped disc** une hernie discale ; (*Knitting*) **to ~ a stitch** glisser une maille
[b] (= *escape from*) échapper à ; (*Naut*) [+ *anchor, cable, moorings*] filer ; **the dog ~ped its collar** le chien s'est dégagé de son collier ; **he ~ped the dog's leash** il a lâché le chien ; **that ~ped his attention** or **his notice** cela lui a échappé ; **it ~ped his notice that ...** il ne s'est pas aperçu que ..., il n'a pas remarqué que ..., il lui a échappé que ... ; **it ~ped my memory** or **my mind** j'avais complètement oublié cela, cela m'était complètement sorti de la tête
[4] COMP ► **slip-on** ADJ facile à mettre or à enfiler* ► **slip-ons, slip-on shoes** NPL chaussures fpl sans lacets ► **slip road** N (*Brit*) (*to motorway*) bretelle f d'accès ; (= *bypass road*) voie f de déviation ► **slip stitch** N (*Knitting*) maille f glissée ► **slip-up*** N bévue f, cafouillage* m ; **there has been a ~-up somewhere** quelqu'un a dû faire une gaffe*, quelque chose a cafouillé* ; **a ~-up in communication(s)** une défaillance or un cafouillage* dans les communications
► **slip along** VI faire un saut, passer ; **he has just ~ped along to the shops** il a fait un saut jusqu'aux magasins ; **~ along to Mary's and ask her ...** fais un saut or passe chez Marie et demande-lui ...
► **slip away** VI [*car, boat*] s'éloigner doucement ; [*guest*] partir discrètement, s'esquiver ;

[*thief*] filer*, s'esquiver ; **I ~ped away for a few minutes** je me suis esquivé *or* éclipsé* pour quelques minutes ; **her life was ~ping away (from her)** la vie la quittait
▶ **slip back** 1 VI [*car, boat*] revenir *or* retourner doucement ; [*guest*] revenir *or* retourner discrètement ; [*thief, spy*] revenir *or* retourner furtivement *or* subrepticement ; **I'll just ~ back and get it** je retourne le chercher 2 VT SEP → **slip 3a**
▶ **slip by** VI = **slip past**
▶ **slip down** VI a [*object, car*] glisser ; [*person*] glisser *et* tomber ; **I'll just ~ down and get it** je descends le chercher b [*food, drink*] descendre* tout seul
▶ **slip in** 1 VI [*car, boat*] entrer doucement ; [*person*] entrer discrètement *or* sans se faire remarquer ; [*thief*] entrer furtivement *or* subrepticement ; [*cat etc*] entrer inaperçu ; **several errors have ~ped in** plusieurs erreurs s'y sont glissées ; **I'll just ~ in and tell him** je vais juste entrer le lui dire ; **I've only ~ped in for a minute** je ne fais que passer, je ne fais qu'entrer *et* sortir 2 VT SEP [*+ object*] glisser, placer ; [*+ part, drawer*] glisser à sa place ; [*+ remark, comment*] glisser, placer ; (*Aut*) **to ~ in the clutch** embrayer
▶ **slip off** 1 VI a = **slip away** b [*coat, lid, cover*] glisser 2 VT SEP [*+ cover, ring, bracelet, glove, shoe*] enlever ; [*+ garment*] enlever, ôter
▶ **slip on** 1 VT SEP [*+ garment*] passer, enfiler* ; [*+ ring, bracelet, glove*] mettre, enfiler ; [*+ shoe*] mettre ; [*+ lid, cover*] (re)mettre, placer 2 **~-on** ADJ → **slip**
▶ **slip out** 1 VI [*guest*] sortir discrètement, s'esquiver ; [*thief*] sortir furtivement, filer* ; **I must just ~ out for some cigarettes** il faut que je sorte un instant chercher des cigarettes ; **she ~ped out to the shops** elle a fait un saut jusqu'aux magasins ; **the secret ~ped out** le secret a été révélé par mégarde ; **the words ~ped out before he realized it** les mots lui ont échappé avant même qu'il ne s'en rende compte 2 VT SEP sortir doucement (*or* discrètement *etc*)
▶ **slip over** 1 VI a = **slip along** b (= *fall*) glisser *et* tomber 2 VT SEP **to ~ one over on sb*** rouler qn* 3 **~over*** N = **slipover**
▶ **slip past** VI [*person, vehicle*] passer, se faufiler ; **the years ~ped past** les années passèrent
▶ **slip round** VI = **slip along**
▶ **slip through** VI [*person, error*] passer, s'introduire
▶ **slip up** 1 VI (= *make mistake*) se ficher dedans* 2 **~-up** N → **slip**

slipcase ['slɪpkeɪs] N [*of book*] coffret *m*

slipcover ['slɪpkʌvəʳ] N (*esp US*) (*on book*) jaquette *f* ; (*on furniture*) housse *f*

slipknot ['slɪpnɒt] N nœud *m* coulant

slipover* ['slɪpəʊvəʳ] N pull-over *m* sans manches

slippage ['slɪpɪdʒ] N (*Ind*) [*of output*] dérapage *m* (**in** de) ; (*in schedule*) retard *m*

slipper ['slɪpəʳ] N pantoufle *f* ; (*warmer*) chausson *m* ; (= *mule*) mule *f* → **glass**

slippery ['slɪpərɪ] ADJ a (*lit*) [*surface, road, soap, mud, shoes*] glissant ; **his fingers were ~ with blood/sweat** le sang/la sueur rendait ses doigts glissants ; **the roads were ~ with ice** les routes étaient verglacées ; (*fig*) **to be on the ~ slope** être sur la pente savonneuse b (*fig pej*) [*person*] fuyant, insaisissable ; (= *unreliable*) sur qui on ne peut pas compter ; **he's a ~ customer** il est retors

slippy* ['slɪpɪ] ADJ glissant ; (*Brit*) **look ~ (about it)!‡** grouille-toi !*

slipshod ['slɪpʃɒd] ADJ [*person*] (*in dress etc*) débraillé, négligé ; (*in work*) négligent ; [*work, style*] négligé, peu soigné

slipslop* ['slɪpslɒp] N (= *liquor*) lavasse* *f*, bibine* *f* ; (= *talk, writing*) bêtises *fpl*

slipstream ['slɪpstriːm] N (*Aviat*) sillage *m*

slipway ['slɪpweɪ] N (*Naut*) (*for building, repairing*) cale *f* (de construction) ; (*for launching*) cale *f* de lancement

slit [slɪt] (*vb: pret, ptp* **slit**) 1 N a (= *opening*) fente *f* ; (= *cut*) incision *f* ; (= *tear*) déchirure *f* ; **to make a ~ in sth** fendre *or* inciser *or* déchirer qch ; **the skirt has a ~ up the side** la jupe a une fente *or* est fendue sur le côté b (*‡* = *vagina*) fente‡ *f* 2 ADJ **to have ~ eyes** (= *slanting*) avoir les yeux bridés ; **he looked at me through ~ eyes** (*concentrating*) il m'a regardé en plissant les yeux 3 VT (= *make an opening in*) fendre ; (= *cut*) inciser, faire une fente dans ; (= *tear*) déchirer ; **to ~ sb's throat** trancher la gorge à qn, égorger qn ; **to ~ one's wrists** s'ouvrir les veines ; **to ~ a letter open** ouvrir une lettre ; **to ~ a sack open** éventrer *or* fendre un sac ; **a ~ skirt** une jupe fendue 4 COMP ▶ **slit-eyed** ADJ (= *with eyes nearly closed*) aux yeux plissés ; (= *with slanting eyes*) aux yeux bridés

slither ['slɪðəʳ] VI [*person, animal*] glisser ; [*snake*] onduler ; **he ~ed about on the ice** il dérapait sur la glace, il essayait de se tenir en équilibre sur la glace ; **the car ~ed (about) all over the place** la voiture dérapait dans tous les sens ; **he ~ed down the slope/down the rope** il a dégringolé* la pente/le long de la corde ; **the snake ~ed across the path** le serpent a traversé le sentier en ondulant

slithery ['slɪðərɪ] ADJ glissant

sliver ['slɪvəʳ] N [*of glass, wood*] éclat *m* ; [*of cheese, ham etc*] lamelle *f*

slivovitz ['slɪvəʊvɪts] N (*NonC*) slivowitz *m*

Sloane Ranger* [ˌsləʊn'reɪndʒəʳ] N (*Brit*) ≈ personne *f* BCBG

slob* [slɒb] N rustaud(e) *m(f)*, plouc‡ *mf*
▶ **slob out*** VI glander*

slobber ['slɒbəʳ] 1 VI [*person, dog etc*] baver ; **to ~ over sth** (*lit*) baver sur qch ; (*fig pej*) s'attendrir *or* s'extasier exagérément sur qch ; **to ~ over sb** [*dog*] couvrir qn de grands coups de langue ; (*pej = kiss*) [*person*] faire des mamours* à qn, donner une fricassée de museau à qn‡ 2 N (*NonC*) bave *f*, salive *f* ; (*fig pej*) sensiblerie *f*, attendrissement *m* exagéré

slobbery ['slɒbərɪ] ADJ (*pej*) baveux

sloe [sləʊ] 1 N prunelle *f* ; (= *bush*) prunellier *m* 2 COMP ▶ **sloe-eyed** ADJ aux yeux de biche ▶ **sloe gin** N gin *m* à la prunelle

slog [slɒg] 1 N (= *work*) long travail *m* pénible, travail *m* de Romain* *or* de nègre* ; (= *effort*) gros effort *m* ; **the programme was one long ~** le programme exigeait un grand effort *or* représentait un travail de Romain* ; **it was a (hard) ~ to pass the exam** il a fallu fournir un gros effort *or* travailler comme un nègre* pour réussir à l'examen ; **after a long ~ he reached the top of the hill** après un gros effort il a atteint le sommet de la colline ; **he found it nothing but a ~** c'était une vraie corvée pour lui
2 VT [*+ ball*] donner un grand coup à ; [*+ opponent*] donner un grand coup à, donner un gnon‡ ; **we ~ged it to ~ it out** nous nous sommes laissé s'expliquer à coups de poing
3 VI a (= *work etc*) travailler très dur *or* comme un nègre* ; **he ~ged (his way) through the book** il s'est forcé à lire le livre, il a poursuivi péniblement la lecture du livre b (= *walk etc*) marcher d'un pas lourd, avancer avec obstination ; **he ~ged up the hill** il a gravi la colline avec effort
▶ **slog along** VI marcher d'un pas lourd, avancer avec obstination ; **we ~ged along for 10km** nous nous sommes traînés sur 10 km
▶ **slog away** VI travailler dur *or* comme un nègre* ; **to ~ away at sth** trimer* sur qch
▶ **slog on** VI = **slog along**

slogan ['sləʊgən] N slogan *m*

sloganeering [ˌsləʊgə'nɪərɪŋ] N (*NonC: pej*) **politics should be about ideas, rather than ~** en politique, il faut des idées, pas des slogans

slogger* ['slɒgəʳ] N (= *hard worker*) bourreau *m* de travail ; (*Boxing*) cogneur *m*

slo-mo* [ˌsləʊ'məʊ] N (ABBR = **slow-motion**) ralenti *m* ; **in ~** au ralenti

sloop [sluːp] N sloop *m*

slop [slɒp] 1 VT [*+ liquid*] (= *spill*) renverser, répandre ; (= *tip carelessly*) répandre (**on to** sur, **into** dans) ; **you've ~ped paint all over the floor** tu· as éclaboussé tout le plancher de peinture 2 VI (*also* **~ over**) [*water, tea etc*] déborder, se renverser (**into** dans, **on to** sur) ; [*bowl, bucket*] déborder 3 SLOPS NPL (= *dirty water*) eaux *fpl* sales ; (*in teacup etc*) fond *m* de tasse ; (= *liquid food*) (*for invalids etc*) bouillon *m*, aliment *m* liquide ; (*for pigs*) pâtée *f*, soupe *f* 4 COMP ▶ **slop basin** N vide-tasses *m inv* ▶ **slop bucket**, **slop pail** N (*in kitchen etc*) poubelle *f* ; (*in bedroom*) seau *m* de toilette ; (*on farm*) seau *m* à pâtée ▶ **slopping out** N (*NonC: Brit Prison*) corvée *f* de tinettes
▶ **slop about**, **slop around** 1 VI a **the water was ~ping about in the bucket** l'eau clapotait dans le seau ; **they were ~ping about in the mud** ils pataugeaient dans la boue b (*fig*) **she ~s about in a dressing gown all day*** elle traîne *or* traînasse* toute la journée en robe de chambre 2 VT SEP renverser *or* mettre un peu partout
▶ **slop out** VI (*Brit Prison*) faire la corvée de tinettes, vider les seaux hygiéniques
▶ **slop over** 1 VI = **slop 2** 2 VT SEP renverser

slope [sləʊp] 1 N [*of roof, floor, ground, surface*] inclinaison *f*, pente *f* ; [*of handwriting etc*] inclinaison *f* ; **roof with a slight/steep ~** toit *m* (qui descend) en pente douce/raide ; **road with a ~ of 1 in 8** route *f* avec une pente de 12,5 % ; (*Mil*) **rifle at the ~** fusil *m* sur l'épaule b (= *rising ground, gentle hill*) côte *f*, pente *f* ; (= *mountainside*) versant *m*, flanc *m* ; **~ up** montée *f* ; **~ down** descente *f* ; **the car got stuck on a ~** la voiture est restée en panne dans une côte ; **halfway up** *or* **down the ~** à mi-côte, à mi-pente ; **on the ~s of Mount Etna** sur les flancs de l'Etna ; **the southern ~s of the Himalayas** le versant sud de l'Himalaya ; **on the (ski) ~s** sur les pistes (de ski)
2 VI [*ground, roof, ground*] être en pente, être incliné ; [*handwriting*] pencher ; **the garden ~s towards the river** le jardin descend en pente vers la rivière
3 VT incliner, pencher ; (*Mil*) **to ~ arms** mettre l'arme sur l'épaule ; **"~ arms!"** « portez arme ! »
▶ **slope away**, **slope down** VI [*ground*] descendre en pente (**to** jusqu'à, **towards** vers)
▶ **slope off*** VI se tirer‡, se barrer‡
▶ **slope up** VI [*road, ground*] monter

sloping ['sləʊpɪŋ] ADJ [*ground, roof*] en pente, incliné ; [*handwriting*] penché ; [*shoulders*] tombant

sloppily ['slɒpɪlɪ] ADV (= *carelessly*) [*dress, work*] sans soin, n'importe comment ; [*eat, drink*] salement ; [*speak*] mal ; **~ acted/written** écrit/joué n'importe comment

sloppiness ['slɒpɪnɪs] N a (= *carelessness*) (*gen*) négligence *f*, manque *m* de soin ; (*in thinking, logic*) manque *m* de rigueur ; **the ~ of his work** son travail peu soigné ; **the ~ of their English** leur anglais très relâché b (= *sentimentality*) sensiblerie *f* c (= *sloppy consistency*) [*of cement, paste, food etc*] consistance *f* trop liquide

sloppy ['slɒpɪ] 1 ADJ a (= *careless*) [*work, handwriting, spelling*] négligé, peu soigné ; [*language*] relâché ; [*thinking, logic*] qui manque de rigueur ; [*appearance*] négligé, débraillé ; **his ~ attitude** son je-m'en-foutisme* ; **their ~ English** leur anglais *m* très relâché ; **to get ~** [*person*] se relâcher ; **to be a ~ worker**

travailler n'importe comment; **to be a ~ eater** manger salement **b** (= *sentimental*) [*film, book, story*] à l'eau de rose; **a big ~ kiss** un gros baiser mouillé **c** (*gen pej*) [*cement, paste, food*] trop liquide **d** [*garment*] lâche, ample **2** COMP ► **sloppy Joe** N (= *sweater*) grand pull *m*; (*US* = *sandwich*) hamburger *m*

slosh [slɒʃ] **1** VT **a** (*Brit* = *hit*) flanquer* un coup *or* un gnon* à **b*** (= *spill*) renverser, répandre; (= *apply lavishly*) répandre (**on to, over** sur, **into** dans); **to ~ paint on a wall** barbouiller un mur de peinture, flanquer* de la peinture sur un mur; **he ~ed water over the floor** (*deliberately*) il a répandu de l'eau par terre; (*accidentally*) il a renversé *or* fichu* de l'eau par terre **2** VI **water was ~ing everywhere** l'eau se répandait partout; **to ~ through mud/water** patauger dans la boue/l'eau

► **slosh about***, **slosh around*** **1** VI = **slop about 1a** **2** VT SEP = **slop about 2**

sloshed: [slɒʃt] ADJ (*esp Brit* = *drunk*) beurré:, rond:; **to get ~** prendre une biture:

slot [slɒt] **1** N **a** (= *slit*) fente *f*; (= *groove*) rainure *f*; (*in door, for mail*) fente *f*; **to put a coin in the ~** mettre *or* introduire une pièce dans la fente **b** (*fig* = *space in schedule etc*) (*gen, also Rad, TV*) créneau *m*, tranche *f* horaire; (*Scol etc: in timetable*) heure *f*, plage *f* horaire; (*Rad, TV etc*) they are looking for something to fill the early-evening comedy* on cherche quelque chose pour la tranche comédie du début de soirée; (= *job etc*) **who will fit this ~?** qui fera l'affaire pour ce créneau? **2** VT **to ~ a part into another part** emboîter *or* encastrer une pièce dans une autre pièce; (*fig*) **to ~ sth into a programme/timetable** insérer *or* faire rentrer qch dans une grille de programmes/d'horaires **3** VI **this part ~s into that part** cette pièce-ci s'emboîte *or* s'encastre dans celle-là; (*fig*) **the song will ~ into the programme here** on peut insérer *or* faire figurer la chanson à ce moment-là du programme **4** COMP ► **slot car** N (*US*) petite voiture *f* (*de circuit électrique*) ► **slot machine** N (*for tickets, cigarettes etc*) distributeur *m* (automatique); (*in fair etc*) appareil *m* *or* machine *f* à sous ► **slot meter** N compteur *m* (de gaz etc) (à pièces) ► **slotted spoon** N écumoire *f*

► **slot in** **1** VI [*piece, part*] s'emboîter; (*fig*) [*item on programme etc*] s'insérer, figurer **2** VT SEP [+ *piece, part*] emboîter, encastrer; (*fig*) [+ *item on programme*] insérer, faire figurer

► **slot together** **1** VI [*pieces, parts*] s'emboîter *or* s'encastrer les un(e)s dans les autres **2** VT SEP [+ *pieces, parts*] emboîter *or* encastrer les un(e)s dans les autres

sloth [sləʊθ] N **a** (*NonC*) paresse *f* **b** (*Zool*) paresseux *m*

slothful [ˈsləʊθfʊl] ADJ (*liter*) paresseux

slothfully [ˈsləʊθfəlɪ] ADV paresseusement

slouch [slaʊtʃ] **1** N **a** **to walk with a ~** mal se tenir en marchant **b** **he's no ~*** il n'est pas empoté* **2** VI **he was ~ing in a chair** il était affalé dans un fauteuil; **she always ~es** elle ne se tient jamais droite, elle est toujours avachie; **stop ~ing!** redresse-toi!, tiens-toi droit!; **he ~ed in/out** *etc* il entra/sortit *etc* en traînant les pieds, le dos voûté **3** COMP ► **slouch hat** N chapeau *m* (mou) à larges bords

► **slouch about**, **slouch around** VI traîner à ne rien faire

slough[1] [slaʊ] N (= *swamp*) bourbier *m*, marécage *m*; (*fig*) **the Slough of Despond** l'abîme *m* du désespoir

slough[2] [slʌf] **1** N [*of snake*] dépouille *f*, mue *f* **2** VT (*also ~ off*) **the snake ~ed (off) its skin** le serpent a mué

► **slough off** VT SEP **a** = **slough**[2] **2** **b** (*fig*) [+ *habit etc*] perdre, se débarrasser de

Slovak [ˈsləʊvæk] **1** ADJ slovaque **2** N **a** Slovaque *mf* **b** (*Ling*) slovaque *m* **3** COMP ► **the Slovak Republic** N la République slovaque

Slovakia [sləʊˈvækɪə] N la Slovaquie

Slovakian [sləʊˈvækɪən] = **Slovak**

sloven [ˈslʌvn] N souillon *f*

Slovene [ˈsləʊviːn] **1** ADJ slovène **2** N **a** Slovène *mf* **b** (*Ling*) slovène *m*

Slovenia [sləʊˈviːnɪə] N la Slovénie

Slovenian [sləʊˈviːnɪən] = **Slovene**

slovenliness [ˈslʌvnlɪnɪs] N (= *untidiness*) aspect *m* négligé *or* débraillé; (= *carelessness*) je-m'en-foutisme* *m*

slovenly [ˈslʌvnlɪ] ADJ [*person, appearance, work*] négligé; **his ~ attitude** son je-m'en-foutisme*

slow [sləʊ] **1** ADJ **a** (*gen*) lent; **the ~ movement of the symphony** le mouvement lent de la symphonie; **after a ~ start** après un départ laborieux; **the pace of life there is ~** là-bas on vit au ralenti; **it's ~ but sure** on (*or* ça) avance lentement mais sûrement; (*Brit*) **a ~ train** = *stopping-train* un (train) omnibus; **at a ~ speed** à petite vitesse; (*lit, fig*) **it's ~ going** cela n'avance pas vite; **it's ~ work** c'est un travail qui avance lentement; **he's a ~ learner** il n'apprend pas vite; (*frm*) **to be ~ of speech** parler lentement; **to be ~ to do sth** *or* **in doing sth** mettre du temps à faire qch; **she was not ~ to notice** *or* **in noticing** ... il ne lui a pas fallu longtemps pour remarquer ... → **mark**[2], **progress, uptake** **b** [*pitch, track, surface*] lourd **c** (*euph* = *stupid*) [*person*] à l'esprit lent; **he's a bit ~** il a l'esprit un peu lent **d** (= *boring*) [*party, evening, play, film etc*] ennuyeux **e** (*pej* = *slack, sluggish*) [*market, trading, demand*] stagnant; [*growth*] lent; **business is ~** les affaires stagnent **f** (*watch, clock*) **my watch is ~** ma montre retarde; **my watch is ten minutes ~** ma montre retarde de dix minutes **g** (*Culin*) **in a ~ oven** à feu doux; **over a ~ heat** à feu doux **h** (*Phot*) [*film*] lent **2** ADV (= *slowly*) lentement; **to go ~er** ralentir; (*Ind*) **to go ~** faire la grève perlée → **astern, dead** **3** VT (*also ~ down, ~ up*) [+ *person*] (*in walk*) faire ralentir; (*in activity*) ralentir, retarder; [+ *vehicle, machine*] ralentir (la marche de); [+ *traffic*] ralentir; [+ *horse*] ralentir l'allure *or* le pas de; [+ *progress, production, negotiations*] ralentir, retarder; [*reaction*] rendre moins rapide; **his injury ~ed him down** *or* **up** sa blessure l'a ralenti; **all these interruptions have ~ed us down** *or* **up** toutes ces interruptions nous ont retardés **4** VI (*also ~ down, ~ off, ~ up*) [*driver, worker, walker, vehicle, machine, production, progress*] ralentir; [*reactions*] devenir plus lent *or* moins rapide; (*Aut*) **"~"** « ralentir »; (*Aut*) **a "~" signal** un panneau « attention, ralentir »; (*fig*) **you must ~ down or you will make yourself ill** il faut que vous travailliez moins, sinon vous allez tomber malade; **since his retirement his life has ~ed down** depuis qu'il a pris sa retraite il vit au ralenti **5** COMP ► **slow-acting** ADJ à action lente; **it is ~-acting** cela agit lentement ► **slow burn:** N (*US*) **he did a ~ burn** il a fini par péter les plombs: ► **slow-burning** ADJ à combustion lente; **it is ~-burning** cela brûle lentement ► **slow cooker** N (*Culin*) cocotte *f* électrique ► **slow handclap** N (*Brit: by audience*) applaudissements *mpl* rythmés (*pour exprimer le mécontentement*) ► **slow lane*** N (*Aut*) (*in France*) voie *f* de droite; (*in Brit, Austral etc*) voie *f* de gauche → **life** ► **slow match** N mèche *f* à combustion lente ► **slow motion** N (*Cine etc*) **in ~ motion** au ralenti ◆ ADJ **~-motion film/shot** *etc* (film *m*/prise *f* de vues *etc* au ralenti *m* ► **slow-moving** ADJ [*person, animal*] lent, aux mouvements lents; [*vehicle*] lent; [*play*] lent, dont l'action est lente ► **slow puncture** N (*Brit*) pneu qui se dégonfle lentement ► **slow-speaking, slow-spoken** ADJ qui parle lentement ► **slow virus** N virus *m* lent ► **slow-witted** ADJ lourdaud, qui a l'esprit lent *or* lourd ► **slow worm** N (*Zool*) orvet *m*

► **slow down** **1** VT SEP = **slow 3** **2** VI = **slow 4** **3** **~down** N → **slowdown**

► **slow off** VI = **slow 4**

► **slow up** **1** VT SEP = **slow 3** **2** VI = **slow 4**

slowcoach [ˈsləʊkəʊtʃ] N (*Brit* = *dawdler*) lambin(e)* *m(f)*

slowdown [ˈsləʊdaʊn] N ralentissement *m*; (*US Ind*) grève *f* perlée

slowly [ˈsləʊlɪ] ADV (*gen*) lentement; [*realize, start, increase*] peu à peu; **~ but surely** lentement mais sûrement

slowness [ˈsləʊnɪs] N [*of person, vehicle, movement etc*] lenteur *f*; [*of pitch, track*] lourdeur *f*; [*of party, evening*] manque *m* d'entrain *or* d'intérêt; [*of novel, plot, play*] lenteur *f*, manque *m* de mouvement *or* d'action; (= *lack of energy etc*) allure *f* posée; (= (*of mind*)) lenteur *f* *or* lourdeur *f* d'esprit; **his ~ to act** *or* **in acting** la lenteur avec laquelle *or* le retard avec lequel il a agi

slowpoke* [ˈsləʊpəʊk] N (*US*) = **slowcoach**

SLR [ˌeselˈɑːr] N (*Phot*) (ABBR = **single lens reflex (camera)**) → **single**

sludge [slʌdʒ] N (*NonC*) (= *mud*) boue *f*, vase *f*; (= *sediment*) boue *f*, dépôt *m*; (= *sewage*) vidanges *fpl*; (= *melting snow*) neige *f* fondue

slug [slʌɡ] **1** N (*Zool*) limace *f*; (= *bullet*) balle *f*; (= *blow*) coup *m*; (*Min, Typ*) lingot *m*; (*esp US* = *metal token*) jeton *m*; (*US*: = *false coin*) fausse pièce *f*; (*US*) **a ~ of whisky:** un peu *or* un coup* de whisky sec **2** VT (* = *hit*) frapper (comme une brute)

► **slug out*** VT SEP **to ~ it out** se taper dessus* (*pour régler une question*)

slugfest: [ˈslʌɡfest] N bagarre *f*, rixe *f*

sluggard [ˈslʌɡəd] N paresseux *m*, -euse *f*, fainéant(e) *m(f)*

slugger [ˈslʌɡər] N (*Baseball*) joueur *m* qui frappe fort

sluggish [ˈslʌɡɪʃ] ADJ [*person, temperament*] mou (molle *f*), léthargique; (= *slow-moving*) lent; (= *lazy*) paresseux; [*growth, reaction, movement, circulation, digestion*] lent; [*liver*] paresseux; [*market, business*] stagnant; (*Aut*) **the engine is ~** le moteur manque de reprise *or* de nervosité; (*Comm*) **sales are ~** les ventes ne vont pas fort

sluggishly [ˈslʌɡɪʃlɪ] ADV [*move*] lentement; [*react, respond, flow*] mollement; (*Econ, Fin*) [*trade, perform*] faiblement

sluggishness [ˈslʌɡɪʃnɪs] N [*of person*] mollesse *f*, lenteur *f*; [*of engine*] manque *m* de nervosité

sluice [sluːs] **1** N **a** (*whole structure*) écluse *f*; (= *gate: also ~ gate, ~ valve*) vanne *f* *or* porte *f* d'écluse; (= *channel: also ~way*) canal *m* (à vannes); (= *water*) écluse *f* **b** **to give sth/o.s. a ~ (down)** laver qch/se laver à grande eau **2** VT (*also ~ down*) laver à grande eau **3** COMP ► **sluice gate, sluice valve** N vanne *f* *or* porte *f* d'écluse

sluiceway [ˈsluːsweɪ] N → **sluice 1a**

slum [slʌm] **1** N (= *house*) taudis *m*; **the ~s** les quartiers *mpl* pauvres; (*in suburb*) la zone; (= *shanty towns*) les bidonvilles *mpl* **2** VI (* = *live cheaply: also ~ it: esp Brit*) vivre à la dure, manger de la vache enragée*; (*iro*) **we don't see you often round here — I'm ~ming (it) today!** on ne te voit pas souvent ici —

aujourd'hui je m'encanaille ! **3** VT **to ~ it*** → **2** **4** COMP ► **slum area** N quartier *m* pauvre ► **slum clearance** N aménagement *m* des quartiers insalubres ; **~ clearance area** zone *f* de quartiers insalubres en voie d'aménagement ; **~ clearance campaign** campagne *f* pour la démolition des taudis ► **slum-dweller** N habitant(e) *m(f)* de taudis ► **slum dwelling** N taudis *m*

slumber ['slʌmbəʳ] **1** N (*liter: also* **~s**) sommeil *m* (paisible) **2** VI dormir paisiblement **3** COMP ► **slumber party** N (*US*) soirée entre adolescentes qui restent dormir chez l'une d'entre elles ► **slumber wear** N (*NonC: Comm*) vêtements *mpl* de nuit

slumb(e)rous ['slʌmb(ə)rəs] ADJ (*liter*) (= *drowsy*) somnolent ; (= *soporific*) assoupissant (*liter*)

slumgullion [slʌm'gʌljən] N (*US*) ragoût *m*

slumlord* ['slʌmlɔːd] N (*US pej*) marchand* *m* de sommeil

slummy* ['slʌmɪ] ADJ sordide

slump [slʌmp] **1** N (*in numbers, popularity, morale etc*) forte baisse *f*, baisse *f* soudaine (**in** de) ; (*Econ*) dépression *f* (**in** de) ; (*Comm: in sales etc*) baisse *f* soudaine (**in** de) ; (*in prices*) effondrement *m* (**in** de) ; **the 1929 ~** la crise (économique) de 1929 **2** VI (*popularity, morale, production, trade*) baisser brutalement ; (*prices, rates*) s'effondrer ; **business has ~ed** les affaires sont en baisse, c'est le marasme (économique) **b** (*also ~ down*) s'effondrer, s'écrouler (**into** dans, **onto** sur) ; **he lay ~ed on the floor** il gisait effondré or écroulé par terre ; **he was ~ed over the wheel** il était affaissé sur le volant **c** (= *stoop*) avoir le dos rond or voûté
► **slump back** VI [*person*] retomber en arrière
► **slump down** VI = **slump 2b**
► **slump forward** VI [*person*] tomber en avant

slung [slʌŋ] VB *pt, ptp of* **sling**

slunk [slʌŋk] VB *pt, ptp of* **slink**

slur [slɜːʳ] **1** N **a** (= *stigma*) tache *f* (**on** sur), atteinte *f* (**on** à), insinuation *f* (**on** contre) ; (= *insult*) insulte *f*, affront *m* ; **to be a ~ on sb's reputation** porter atteinte à or être une tache sur la réputation de qn ; **that is a ~ on him** cela porte atteinte à son intégrité ; **to cast a ~ on sb** porter atteinte à la réputation de qn ; **it's no ~ on him to say ...** ce n'est pas le calomnier que de dire ... **b** (*Mus*) liaison *f* **2** VT (= *join*) [+ *several sounds, words*] lier à tort ; (*Mus*) lier ; (= *enunciate indistinctly*) [+ *word etc*] mal articuler, ne pas articuler ; **his speech ~red** ◊ **he ~red his words** il n'arrivait pas à articuler, il n'articulait pas **3** VI [*sounds etc*] être or devenir indistinct
► **slur over** VT FUS [+ *incident, mistake, differences, discrepancies*] passer sous silence, glisser sur

slurp [slɜːp] **1** VTI boire à grand bruit **2** N slurp *m*

slurry ['slʌrɪ] N boue *f*, pâte *f*

slush [slʌʃ] **1** N (*NonC*) (= *snow*) neige *f* fondue ; (= *mud*) gadoue *f* ; (*fig = sentiment*) sensiblerie *f* **2** COMP ► **slush fund** N fonds *mpl* secrets, caisse *f* noire ► **the slush pile*** N (*Publishing*) les manuscrits *mpl* refusés

slushy ['slʌʃɪ] ADJ **a** [*snow*] fondu ; [*road, street*] couvert de neige fondue **b** (* = *sentimental*) [*film, book, story*] à l'eau de rose ; [*song*] sentimental

slut [slʌt] N (*pej*) (*dirty*) souillon *f* ; (*immoral*) salope* *f*, pute* *f*

sluttish ['slʌtɪʃ] ADJ [*appearance*] sale, de souillon ; [*morals, behaviour*] de salope* ; **a ~ woman** une souillon

sly [slaɪ] **1** ADJ **a** (= *crafty, roguish*) [*person, animal*] rusé ; [*plan*] astucieux ; [*smile, look*] entendu, narquois ; [*remark, reference, suggestion*] narquois ; **he's a ~ dog** or **a ~ (old) fox*** c'est une fine mouche ; **(as) ~ as a fox** ru-

sé comme un renard **b** (*pej = underhand, cunning*) [*person, trick*] sournois (*pej*) **c** (* = *secretive*) **she gave me a ~ kick under the table** elle m'a donné un coup de pied en douce* sous la table ; **they were having a ~ cigarette in the toilets** ils fumaient en douce* dans les toilettes **2** N **on the ~** en cachette, en douce*

slyboots* ['slaɪbuːts] N malin *m*, -igne *f*

slyly ['slaɪlɪ] ADV **a** (= *craftily, roguishly*) [*say, smile, look, suggest*] d'un air entendu, d'un air narquois **b** (*pej = cunningly*) sournoisement (*pej*)

slyness ['slaɪnɪs] N **a** (= *craftiness, roguishness*) [*of person, look*] ruse *f* ; **the ~ of her smile/comment** son sourire/commentaire narquois **b** (*pej = underhandedness, cunning*) sournoiserie *f* (*pej*)

smack¹ [smæk] **1** VI (*lit, fig*) **to ~ of sth** sentir qch **2** N **a** (= *small taste*) léger or petit goût *m* ; (*fig*) soupçon *m* **b** (* = *heroin*) héroïne *f*, (poudre *f*) blanche* *f*

smack² [smæk] **1** N (= *slap*) tape *f* ; (*stronger*) claque *f* ; (*on face*) gifle *f* ; (= *sound*) bruit *m* sec, claquement *m* ; (* *fig* = *kiss*) gros baiser *m* (qui claque) ; **he gave the ball a good ~** il a donné un grand coup dans le ballon ; (*esp Brit fig*) **it was a ~ in the eye for them*** (= *snub*) c'était une belle gifle pour eux ; (= *setback*) c'était un revers pour eux
2 VT [+ *person*] donner une tape à ; (*stronger*) donner une claque à ; (*on face*) gifler ; **to ~ sb's face** gifler qn, donner une paire de gifles à qn ; **I'll ~ your bottom!** je vais te donner la fessée !, tu vas avoir la fessée ! ; **he ~ed the table (with his hand)** il a frappé sur la table (de la main) ; **to ~ one's lips** se lécher les babines
3 ADV* en plein ; **~ in the middle** en plein milieu ; **he kissed her ~ on the lips** il l'a embrassée en plein sur la bouche ; **he ran ~ into the tree** il est rentré en plein or tout droit dans l'arbre

smack³ [smæk] N (*also* **fishing ~**) smack *m*, sémaque *m*

smacker* ['smækəʳ] N **a** (= *kiss*) gros baiser *m*, grosse bise* *f* ; (= *blow*) grand coup *m* (retentissant) ; (*Brit* = *pound*) livre *f* ; (*US* = *dollar*) dollar *m*

smacking ['smækɪŋ] **1** N fessée *f* ; **to give sb a ~** donner une or la fessée à qn **2** ADJ **a ~ kiss** un baiser sonore, un gros baiser

small [smɔːl] **1** ADJ **a** (*gen*) petit ; [*family, audience, population*] peu nombreux ; [*waist*] mince ; [*meal*] léger ; **the ~est possible number of books** le moins de livres possible ; **a ~ proportion of the business is international** une faible proportion des transactions commerciales sont internationales ; **"I'm sorry" he said in a ~ voice** « je suis désolé » dit-il d'une petite voix ; **he is a ~ eater** il mange très peu, il a un petit appétit ; **in ~ letters** en minuscules *fpl* ; **with a ~ "e"** avec un « e » minuscule ; (*euph hum*) **the ~est room**† le petit coin* ; **~ shopkeeper/farmer/businessman** petit commerçant *m*/agriculteur *m*/entrepreneur *m* ; (*fig*) **to feel ~** être dans ses petits souliers, se sentir honteux ; **to make sb feel ~** humilier qn ; **to make sb look ~** rabaisser qn devant tout le monde ; **it's a ~ world!** le monde est petit ! ; **to get** or **grow ~er** (= *shrink*) [*income, difficulties, population, amount, supply*] diminuer ; [*object*] rapetisser ; **mobile phones are getting ~er** les téléphones portables sont de plus en plus petits or compacts ; **to make sth ~er** [+ *income, amount, supply*] diminuer qch ; [+ *organization*] réduire qch ; [+ *garment*] reprendre qch → **4** ; → **hour, print, way** **b** (= *young*) [*child*] petit, jeune ; **I was very ~ at the time** j'étais tout petit or jeune à l'époque **c** (*frm* = *slight, scant*) **a matter of ~ importance** une affaire de peu d'importance ; **it's ~ comfort to them to know that ...** cela ne les consolera guère de savoir que ... ; **to have ~**

cause or **reason to do sth** n'avoir guère de raison de faire qch ; **a matter of no ~ consequence** une affaire d'une grande importance ; **they paid ~ attention to his suggestion** ils ont prêté peu d'attention à sa suggestion ; **this is of ~ concern to them** cela ne les préoccupe guère → **wonder**
2 ADV **to cut sth up ~** [+ *paper*] couper qch en petits morceaux ; [+ *meat*] hacher qch menu
3 N **a** **the ~ of the back** le creux des reins **b** (*Brit: npl*) **~s†*** (= *underwear*) dessous *mpl*, sous-vêtements *mpl*
4 COMP ► **small ads** NPL (*Brit Press*) petites annonces *fpl* ► **small-arms** NPL (*Mil*) armes *fpl* portatives, armes *fpl* légères ► **small barbel** N (*Zool*) barbillon *m*, colinot or colineau *m* ► **small beer** N (*Brit fig*) **it's ~ beer** c'est de la petite bière* ; **he's ~ beer** il ne compte pas beaucoup ► **small-bore** ADJ de petit calibre ► **small business** N (*Econ*) petite entreprise *f* ► **small change** N (*NonC*) petite or menue monnaie *f* ► **small claims court** N (*Jur*) tribunal *m* d'instance (*s'occupant d'affaires mineures*) ► **small end** N (*Aut*) pied *m* de bielle ► **small fry** N menu fretin *m* ; (= *children*) les gosses* *mfpl* ; **they're just ~ fry** c'est du menu fretin ► **small intestine** N (*Anat*) intestin *m* grêle ► **small-minded** ADJ mesquin ► **small-mindedness** N petitesse *f* d'esprit, mesquinerie *f* ► **small-mouth bass** N (*Zool*) achigan *m* à petite bouche ► **small potatoes** NPL (*esp US*) = **small beer** ► **small-scale** ADJ peu important ; [*undertaking*] de peu d'importance, de peu d'envergure ; [*map*] à petite échelle ► **the small screen** N (*TV*) le petit écran ► **small-size(d)** ADJ petit ► **small talk** N (*NonC*) papotage *m*, menus propos *mpl* ; **he's got plenty of ~ talk** il a la conversation facile ► **small-time** ADJ peu important, de troisième ordre ; **a ~-time crook** un escroc à la petite semaine ► **small-timer*** N moins *m* que rien, individu *m* insignifiant ► **small town** N (*US*) petite ville *f* ► **small-town** ADJ (*esp US pej*) provincial → **print**

smallholder ['smɔːlhəʊldəʳ] N (*Brit Agr*) ≈ petit agriculteur *m*

smallholding ['smɔːlhəʊldɪŋ] N (*Brit Agr*) ≈ petite ferme *f*

smallish ['smɔːlɪʃ] ADJ (*in size*) plutôt or assez petit ; (*in importance*) peu important ; **a ~ number of ...** un nombre restreint de ...

smallness ['smɔːlnɪs] N [*of object*] petitesse *f* ; [*of sum of money*] petitesse *f*, modicité *f* ; [*of population*] caractère *m* limité or peu nombreux

smallpox ['smɔːlpɒks] N variole *f*, petite vérole *f*

smarm* [smɑːm] VI (*Brit*) flatter, flagorner ; **to ~ over sb** lécher les bottes* à qn, passer de la pommade* à qn

smarmy* ['smɑːmɪ] ADJ (*Brit*) [*person*] lèche-bottes* *inv*, obséquieux* ; [*manner*] de lèche-bottes*

smart [smɑːt] **1** ADJ **a** (= *not shabby*) [*hotel, restaurant, club, neighbourhood, party, dinner*] chic *inv* ; [*person, clothes, appearance*] élégant ; [*house, car*] beau (belle *f*) ; [*garden, lawn*] soigné ; **you're looking very ~** tu es très élégant

b (= *fashionable*) à la mode, dernier cri *inv*; **the ~ set** le beau monde; **the Paris/London ~ set** le tout Paris/le tout Londres

c (*esp US** = *clever*) [*person*] intelligent; [*idea*] astucieux, malin (-igne *f*); [*deed, act*] intelligent, astucieux; **that wasn't very ~ (of you)** ce n'était pas très malin (de ta part); **he's too ~ for me** il est trop malin pour moi; **(that was) ~ work!** (= *clever*) beau travail!; (= *swift*) ça n'a pas traîné!*

d (* *pej* = *cheeky*) culotté*; **don't get ~ with me!** ne la ramène pas!*; **she's got a ~ answer to everything** elle a toujours réponse à tout

e (= *brisk*) [*pace*] vif; **give the nail a ~ tap** tapez un bon coup sur le clou; **look ~ (about it)!*** grouille-toi!*, remue-toi!

2 VI **a** [*cut, graze*] brûler; [*iodine etc*] piquer; **my eyes were ~ing** j'avais les yeux qui me piquaient; **the smoke made his throat ~** la fumée lui irritait la gorge

b (*fig*) être piqué au vif; **he was ~ing under the insult** l'insulte l'avait piqué au vif; **you'll ~ for this!** il vous en cuira!, vous me le payerez!

3 NPL (*US*) **~s** (= *brains*) jugeote* *f*

4 COMP ▶ **smart alec(k)***, **smart ass*** (*US*) N (*pej*) (Monsieur *or* Madame *or* Mademoiselle) je-sais-tout* *mf inv* ▶ **smart bomb** N bombe *f* intelligente ▶ **smart card** N carte *f* à mémoire *or* à puce ▶ **smart drug** N smart drug *f*, médicament *m* psychoénergétique ▶ **smart money** N réserve *f* d'argent (*destinée à faire des investissements au moment opportun*); **the ~ money is on him winning** dans les milieux bien informés, on le donne gagnant

smartarse* ['smɑːtɑːs], **smartass*** (*US*) ['smɑːtæs] N bêcheur* *m*, -euse* *f*

smarten ['smɑːtn] VT = **smarten up 2**
▶ **smarten up 1** VI **a** (= *make o.s. tidy etc*) [*person*] devenir plus élégant *or* soigné; [*town*] devenir plus élégant *or* pimpant; **you'd better ~ up for dinner** il faut que tu t'arranges (*subj*) (un peu) *or* que tu te fasses beau (belle *f*) pour le dîner **b** (= *speed up*) [*production, pace*] s'accélérer **2** VT SEP **a** (= *tidy up*) [*person*] rendre plus élégant *or* plus soigné; [+ *child*] pomponner, bichonner; [+ *house, room, town*] (bien) arranger, rendre élégant *or* pimpant; **to ~ o.s. up** se faire beau (belle *f*) *or* élégant **b** (= *speed up*) accélérer

smartly ['smɑːtlɪ] ADV **a** (= *elegantly*) [*dress*] élégamment, avec beaucoup d'élégance; **~ dressed** *or* **turned out** élégamment vêtu; **she wore a ~ tailored suit** elle portait un tailleur bien coupé **b** (= *briskly*) [*move*] rapidement; (*person*) vivement; [*reply*] du tac au tac; **to tap sth ~** taper sur qch un bon coup

smartness ['smɑːtnɪs] N (*NonC*) [*of person, clothes*] chic *m*, élégance *f*; (= *cleverness*) intelligence *f*; (= *skilfulness*) habileté *f*; (= *quickness*) rapidité *f*

smarty* ['smɑːtɪ] N (*also* **~-pants**) bêcheur* *m*, -euse* *f*, (Monsieur *or* Madame *or* Mademoiselle) je-sais-tout* *mf inv*

smash [smæʃ] **1** N **a** (= *sound*) fracas *m*; (= *blow*) coup *m* violent; (*Tennis etc*) smash *m*; **the ~ as the car hit the lamppost** le choc quand la voiture a percuté le réverbère; **the cup fell with a ~** la tasse s'est fracassée (en tombant) par terre; **he fell and hit his head a nasty ~ on the kerb** en tombant il s'est violemment cogné la tête contre le trottoir **b** (*also* **~-up***) (= *accident*) accident *m*; (*Aut, Rail* = *collision*) collision *f*, tamponnement *m*; (*very violent*) télescopage *m*; **car/rail ~** accident *m* de voiture/de chemin de fer **c** (*Econ, Fin* = *collapse*) effondrement *m* (financier), débâcle *f* (financière); (*St Ex*) krach *m*; (= *bankruptcy*) faillite *f*; (= *ruin*) ruine *f*, débâcle *f* complète **d** = **smash hit** **e** **whisky/brandy ~** whisky *m*/cognac *m* glacé à la menthe

2 ADV* **to run ~ into a wall** heurter un mur de front *or* de plein fouet, rentrer en plein dans un mur; **the cup fell ~ to the ground** la tasse s'est fracassée par terre; (*Fin*) **to go ~** faire faillite

3 VT **a** (= *break*) casser, briser; (= *shatter*) fracasser; **I've ~ed my watch** j'ai cassé ma montre; **the waves ~ed the boat on the rocks** les vagues ont fracassé le bateau contre les rochers; **to ~ sth to pieces** *or* **to bits** briser qch en mille morceaux, mettre qch en miettes; **when they ~ed the atom*** quand on a désintégré *or* fissionné l'atome; **to ~ a door open** enfoncer une porte; **he ~ed the glass with the hammer ◊ he ~ed the hammer through the glass** il a fracassé la vitre avec le marteau; **he ~ed his fist into Paul's face** il a envoyé *or* balancé* son poing dans la figure de Paul; (*Tennis*) **to ~ the ball** faire un smash, smasher; (*Tennis*) **he ~ed the ball into the net** il a envoyé son smash dans le filet **b** (*fig*) [+ *spy ring etc*] briser, détruire; [+ *hopes*] ruiner; [+ *enemy*] écraser; [+ *opponent*] battre à plate(s) couture(s), pulvériser*; (*Sport etc*) **he ~ed* the record in the high jump** il a pulvérisé* le record du saut en hauteur

4 VI **a** se briser (en mille morceaux), se fracasser; **the cup ~ed against the wall** la tasse s'est fracassée contre le mur; **the car ~ed into the tree** la voiture s'est écrasée contre l'arbre; **his fist ~ed into my face** il a envoyé *or* balancé* son poing sur ma figure, il m'a asséné son poing sur la figure **b** (*Fin*) [*person, firm*] faire faillite

5 COMP ▶ **smash-and-grab** N (*also* **~-and-grab raid**) cambriolage *m* (commis en brisant une devanture); **there was a ~-and-grab (raid) at the jeweller's** des bandits ont brisé la vitrine du bijoutier et raflé les bijoux ▶ **smash hit*** N **it was a ~ hit** cela a fait un malheur*, cela a eu un succès foudroyant; **it was the ~ hit of the year** c'était le succès de l'année ▶ **smash-up*** N → **1b**
▶ **smash down** VT SEP [+ *door, fence*] fracasser
▶ **smash in** VT SEP [+ *door*] enfoncer; **to ~ sb's face** *or* **head in*** casser la gueule à qn*
▶ **smash up 1** VT SEP [+ *room, house, shop*] tout casser dans, tout démolir dans; [+ *car*] accidenter, bousiller*; **he was ~ed up* in a car accident** il a été grièvement blessé *or* sérieusement amoché dans un accident de voiture **2** **~-up*** N → **smash 1b**

smashed [smæʃt] ADJ **a** (* = *drunk*) pété*, bourré*; **to get ~** se soûler* **b** (*: *on drugs*) défoncé*; **to get ~** se défoncer* **c** (= *broken*) [*vehicle*] bousillé*; [*skull, limb, bone*] fracassé

smasher*†‡ ['smæʃə'] N (*Brit*) (*in appearance*) **he's a ~** il est vachement‡ beau; **she's a ~** elle est vachement‡ jolie *or* bien roulée*; (*in character etc*) **to be a ~** être épatant* *or* vachement chouette‡; **it's a ~** c'est épatant* *or* sensationnel*

smashing* ['smæʃɪŋ] ADJ (*Brit*) sensationnel, sensass†; **we had a ~ time** on s'est amusé comme des fous*

smattering ['smætərɪŋ] N connaissances *fpl* vagues *or* superficielles; **a ~ of** un petit nombre de; **he has a ~ of German** il sait un peu l'allemand, il sait quelques mots d'allemand; **I've got a ~ of maths** j'ai quelques connaissances vagues *or* quelques notions en maths

smear [smɪə'] **1** N **a** (= *mark*) trace *f*; (*longer*) traînée *f*; (= *stain*) (légère) tache *f*, salissure *f*; **a long ~ of ink** une traînée d'encre; **there is a ~ on this page** il y a une légère tache *or* une salissure sur cette page, cette page est tachée *or* salie **b** (= *defamation*) diffamation *f* (**on, against** de); **this ~ on his honour/reputation** cette atteinte à son honneur/sa réputation **c** (*Med*) frottis *m*, prélèvement *m* → **cervical**

2 VT **a** (= *wipe*) **to ~ cream on one's hands** ◊ **to ~ one's hands with cream** s'enduire les mains de crème; **he ~ed his face with mud** ◊ **he ~ed mud on his face** il s'est barbouillé le visage de boue; **his hands were ~ed with ink** il avait les mains barbouillées *or* tachées d'encre, il avait des traînées d'encre sur les mains; **you've ~ed it all over the place** tu en a mis partout; **he ~ed butter on the slice of bread** il a étalé du beurre sur la tranche de pain **b** [+ *page of print*] maculer; [+ *wet paint*] faire une trace *or* une marque sur; [+ *lettering*] étaler (*accidentellement*) **c** (*fig*) [+ *reputation, integrity*] salir, entacher; **to ~ sb** [*story, report*] salir *or* entacher la réputation de qn; [*person*] calomnier qn **d** (*US** = *defeat*) battre à plates coutures

3 VI [*ink, paint*] se salir

4 COMP ▶ **smear campaign** N campagne *f* de diffamation ▶ **smear tactics** NPL procédés *mpl* diffamatoires ▶ **smear test** N (*Med*) = **1c** ▶ **smear word** N **it is a ~ word** c'est de la diffamation

smeary ['smɪərɪ] ADJ [*face*] barbouillé; [*window*] couvert de taches *or* de traînées; [*ink, paint*] sali

smell [smel] (*vb: pret, ptp* **smelled** *or* **smelt**) **1** N **a** (= *sense of smell*) odorat *m*; [*of animal*] odorat *m*, flair *m*; (= *odour*) odeur *f*; (= *bad smell*) mauvaise odeur *f*; **he has a keen sense of ~** il a l'odorat très développé, il a le nez très fin; **he has no sense of ~** il n'a pas d'odorat; **the mixture has no ~** le mélange est inodore *or* n'a pas d'odeur *or* ne sent rien; **a gas with no ~** un gaz inodore *or* sans odeur; **it has a nice/nasty ~** cela sent bon/mauvais; **what a ~ in here!** ce que ça sent mauvais ici!; **there was a ~ of burning in the room** il y avait une odeur de brûlé dans la pièce, la pièce sentait le brûlé; **to have a ~ at sth** [*person*] sentir qch; (*more carefully*) renifler qch; [*dog etc*] flairer *or* renifler qch

2 VT sentir; (= *sniff at*) sentir, renifler; **he could ~ or he smelt something burning** il sentait que quelque chose brûlait; **he smelt the meat to see if it was bad** il a senti *or* reniflé la viande pour voir si elle était encore bonne; **the dog could ~ or the dog smelt the bone** le chien a flairé *or* éventé l'os; **the dog smelt the bone suspiciously** le chien a flairé *or* reniflé l'os d'un air soupçonneux; (*fig*) **I ~ a rat!** il y a anguille sous roche!, il y quelque chose de louche là-dedans *or* là-dessous!; **he ~ed danger** il a flairé *or* deviné le danger; **I (can) ~ danger!** je pressens un danger!

3 VI **a** **since the accident he cannot ~** depuis l'accident il n'a plus d'odorat; **to ~ at sth** [*person*] sentir *or* renifler qch; [*dog etc*] renifler *or* flairer qch **b** **that mixture doesn't ~ (at all)** ce mélange ne sent rien *or* n'a pas (du tout) d'odeur; **this gas doesn't ~** ce gaz est inodore; **these socks ~!** ces chaussettes sentent mauvais!; **this room ~s!** cette pièce sent mauvais *or* pue!; **his breath ~s** il a mauvaise haleine; **that ~s like chocolate** ça sent le chocolat, on dirait du chocolat; **to ~ of onions/burning** *etc* sentir l'oignon/le brûlé *etc*; **to ~ good** *or* **sweet** sentir bon; **to ~ bad** sentir mauvais; **to ~ foul** empester; **it ~s delicious!** quelle odeur délicieuse!; **it ~s dreadful!** ça pue!; **the deal ~s a bit*** cette affaire semble plutôt louche *or* ne semble pas très catholique*; (*fig*) **that idea ~s!*** cette idée ne vaut rien!, c'est une idée catastrophique!*; (*fig*) **I think he ~s!*** je trouve que c'est un sale type!*

4 COMP ▶ **smelling salts** NPL sels *mpl*
▶ **smell out** VT SEP **a** (= *discover*) [*dog etc*] découvrir en flairant *or* en reniflant; [*person*] [+ *criminal, traitor*] découvrir, dépister; [+ *treachery, plot*] découvrir **b** **it's ~ing the room out** ça empeste la pièce

smelliness ['smelinis] N (NonC) mauvaise odeur f

smelly ['smeli] ADJ [person, feet, armpits] qui sent mauvais; [breath] mauvais; [cheese] qui sent fort; **it's rather ~ in here** ça sent mauvais ici

smelt[1] [smelt] VB pt, ptp of **smell**

smelt[2] [smelt] N (pl smelt or smelts) (= fish) éperlan m

smelt[3] [smelt] VT [+ ore] fondre; [+ metal] extraire par fusion

smelter ['smeltə'] N haut fourneau m

smelting ['smeltiŋ] [1] N (= process) extraction f par fusion [2] COMP ► **smelting furnace** N haut-fourneau m ► **smelting works** N (pl inv) fonderie f

smidgen*, **smidgin*** ['smidʒən] N **a ~ of** (gen) un tout petit peu de; [+ truth] un grain de, un brin de

smile [smaıl] [1] N sourire m; **with a ~ on his lips** le sourire aux lèvres; **... he said with a ~** ... dit-il en souriant; **... he said with a nasty ~** ... dit-il en souriant méchamment or avec un mauvais sourire; **he had a happy ~ on his face** il avait un sourire heureux, il souriait d'un air heureux; **to give sb a ~** faire or adresser un sourire à qn, sourire à qn; **she gave a little ~** elle a eu un petit sourire; **to be all ~s** être tout souriant or tout sourire; **take that ~ off your face!** arrête donc de sourire comme ça!; **I'll wipe** or **knock the ~ off his face!** il verra s'il a encore envie de sourire!, je vais lui faire passer l'envie de sourire! → **raise**, **wear**, **wreathe**

[2] VI sourire (**at** or **to sb** à qn); **to ~ to oneself** sourire intérieurement; **to ~ sadly** avoir un sourire triste, sourire tristement or d'un air triste; **to keep smiling** garder le sourire; **he ~d at my efforts** il a souri de mes efforts; (fig) **fortune ~d (up)on him** la fortune lui sourit

[3] VT **to ~ a bitter smile** avoir un sourire amer, sourire amèrement or avec amertume; **to ~ one's thanks** remercier d'un sourire

smiley ['smaılı] [1] ADJ (* = smiling, friendly) [person, face] souriant; [eyes] rieur [2] N (Comput) emoticon m, smiley m; (as badge) badge m de tête souriante

smiling ['smaılıŋ] ADJ [person, face, eyes, mouth] souriant

smilingly ['smaılıŋlı] ADV en souriant, avec un sourire

smirch [smɜːtʃ] [1] VT (lit) salir, souiller; (fig liter) ternir, entacher [2] N (lit, fig) tache f

smirk [smɜːk] [1] N (= self-satisfied smile) petit sourire m satisfait or suffisant; (knowing) petit sourire m narquois; (affected) petit sourire m affecté [2] VI sourire d'un air satisfait (or suffisant or narquois or affecté)

smite [smaıt] (pret **smote**, ptp **smitten**) [1] VT (†† or liter) (= strike) frapper (d'un grand coup); (= punish) châtier (liter); (fig) [pain] déchirer; [one's conscience] tourmenter; [light] frapper → **smitten** [2] N coup m violent

smith [smıθ] N (shoes horses) maréchal-ferrant m; (forges iron) forgeron m → **goldsmith**, **silversmith**

smithereens [ˌsmıðə'riːnz] NPL **to smash sth to ~** briser qch en mille morceaux, faire voler qch en éclats; **it lay in ~** cela s'était brisé en mille morceaux, cela avait volé en éclats

Smithsonian Institution [smıθ'səʊnıən,ınstı'tjuːʃən] N (US) **the ~** la Smithsonian Institution

---

SMITHSONIAN INSTITUTION

La Smithsonian Institution, située dans la ville de Washington, est le plus grand musée du monde. Créé par le Congrès en 1846 grâce au don d'un scientifique anglais, James Smithson, ce complexe aujourd'hui financé par le Congrès réunit quatorze musées consacrés notamment à l'aviation et à l'espace, à l'histoire de l'Amérique, aux Indiens d'Amérique, aux beaux-arts. Riche de 100 millions de pièces, il est surnommé le grenier de la nation (the nation's attic). Il comporte également un zoo et un institut de recherche scientifique.

---

smithy ['smıðı] N forge f

smitten ['smıtn] [1] VB ptp of **smite** [2] ADJ (= in love) amoureux; **he was really ~ with her** il en était vraiment amoureux, il était fou d'elle; **to be ~ with** or **by** [+ remorse, desire, urge] être pris de; [+ terror, deafness] être frappé de;* [+ sb's beauty] être enchanté par;* [+ idea] s'enthousiasmer pour

smock [smɒk] [1] N (= dress, peasant's garment etc) blouse f; (= protective overall) blouse f, sarrau m; (= maternity top) blouse f de grossesse; (= maternity dress) robe f de grossesse [2] VT faire des smocks à

smocking ['smɒkıŋ] N (NonC) smocks mpl

smog [smɒg] N smog m; **~ mask** masque m antibrouillard

smoggy ['smɒgı] ADJ [city, air] pollué par le smog; [sky] obscurci par le smog

smoke [sməʊk] [1] N (NonC) fumée f; **to go up in ~** [house etc] brûler; [plans, hopes etc] partir en fumée, tomber à l'eau; (fig) **the ~ is beginning to clear** on commence à y voir plus clair; (US) **it's all ~ and mirrors** on n'y voit que du feu ■ (PROV) **there's no ~ without fire** il n'y a pas de fumée sans feu (PROV); (Brit) **the (Big) Smoke** Londres → **cloud, holy, puff**

[b] **to have a ~** fumer; **have a ~!** prends une cigarette!; **I've no ~s** je n'ai plus de sèches!

[c] (Drugs* = marijuana) marijuana f

[2] VI [a] [chimney, lamp etc] fumer

[b] [person] fumer; **he ~s like a chimney*** il fume comme un sapeur

[3] VT [a] [+ cigarette etc] fumer; **he ~s cigarettes/a pipe** il fume la cigarette/la pipe

[b] [+ meat, fish, glass] fumer; **~d salmon/trout** etc saumon m/truite f etc fumé(e); **~d glass** verre m fumé; **~d-glass** [window, windscreen etc] en verre fumé → **haddock**

[4] COMP ► **smoke alarm** N détecteur m de fumée ► **smoke bomb** N bombe f fumigène ► **smoke detector** N détecteur m de fumée ► **smoke-dry** VT fumer ► **smoke-filled** ADJ (during fire) rempli de fumée; (from smoking etc) enfumé; (fig) **~-filled room** salle f de réunion très animée, PC m de crise ► **smoke pollution** N (Ind) pollution f par les fumées; (tobacco) pollution f par la fumée de tabac ► **smoke ring** N rond m de fumée; **to blow ~ rings** faire des ronds de fumée ► **smoke screen** N (Mil) rideau m or écran m de fumée; (fig) paravent m ► **smoke shop** N (US) tabac m ► **smoke signal** N signal m de fumée; (fig) **~ signals** (vagues) indications fpl

► **smoke out** VT SEP [+ insects, snake etc] enfumer; (fig) [+ traitor, culprit etc] dénicher, débusquer; **it was smoking the room out** c'était en train d'enfumer la pièce

smokeless ['sməʊklıs] ADJ **~ fuel** combustible m non fumigène; **~ zone** zone où l'on n'a le droit d'utiliser que des combustibles non fumigènes; **the ~ cigarette** la cigarette sans fumée

smoker ['sməʊkə'] N [a] (= person) fumeur m, -euse f; **he has a ~'s cough** il a une toux de fumeur → **heavy** [b] (Rail) wagon m fumeurs

smokestack ['sməʊkstæk] [1] N cheminée f (extérieure) [2] ADJ **~ America** l'Amérique f industrielle; (Econ) **~ industries** industries fpl traditionnelles

smokey ['sməʊkı] = **smoky**

smoking ['sməʊkıŋ] [1] N tabagisme m; **I hate ~** (other people) je déteste qu'on fume, je déteste le tabagisme; (myself) je déteste fumer; **"no ~"** « défense de fumer »; **campaign against ~** campagne f contre le tabac or le tabagisme; **"~ can seriously damage your health"** « le tabac nuit gravement à la santé »; **to give up ~** arrêter de fumer [2] ADJ [fireplace] qui fume; [gun] dont le canon fume (encore) → 3 [3] COMP ► **smoking car** N (US) wagon m fumeurs ► **smoking compartment** N (Rail) wagon m fumeurs ► **smoking gun*** N (esp US fig = proof) preuve f tangible; **we don't have a ~ gun** nous n'avons pas de preuve tangible ► **smoking-jacket** N veste f d'intérieur ► **smoking room** N fumoir m

smoky ['sməʊkı] [1] ADJ [atmosphere, room] enfumé; [fire] qui fume; [flame] fumeux; [surface] (= smoke-covered) sali or noirci par la fumée; [glass] (= smoked) fumé; [taste] fumé; **~ grey** gris cendré inv; **~ blue** bleu ardoise inv [2] N (US*) motard m (de la police routière)

smolder ['sməʊldə'] VI (US) = **smoulder**

smoldering ['sməʊldərıŋ] ADJ (US) = **smouldering**

smooch* [smuːtʃ] [1] VI (= kiss) se bécoter*; (pet) se peloter*; (= dance) se frotter l'un contre l'autre [2] N **to have a ~** = 1

smoochy* ['smuːtʃı] ADJ [record, song] langoureux

smooth [smuːð] [1] ADJ [a] (= not rough) (gen) [sea, surface, texture, road, stone, tyre, hair] lisse; [lake] d'huile; [fabric] lisse, soyeux; [skin] lisse, doux (douce f); (= unwrinkled) [cheek, brow] lisse, sans rides; (= hairless) [face, chin] glabre, lisse; **the flagstones had been worn ~ by centuries of use** les dalles étaient patinées par les années; **as ~ as silk** or **satin** [skin, fabric, hair] doux comme de la soie; **the sea was as ~ as glass** la mer était d'huile

[b] (= not lumpy) [paste, sauce, mixture, consistency] onctueux, homogène

[c] (= not harsh) [flavour, wine, whisky etc] moelleux; [voice, sound] doux (douce f)

[d] (= even, not jerky) [flow, stride, breathing] régulier; [takeoff, landing, transition] en douceur; [sea crossing] calme, par mer calme; [flight] sans heurts; [engine] qui tourne parfaitement; **~ running** [of machinery] bon fonctionnement m; [of organization, business, economy] bonne marche f; **the takeoff/landing was ~** le décollage/l'atterrissage s'est fait en douceur; **the bill had a ~ passage through Parliament** le Parlement n'a pas fait obstacle au projet de loi

[e] (slightly pej = suave) [person, manners] doucereux (pej), suave; [talk] mielleux (pej); **he's a ~ talker** c'est un beau parleur; **he's a ~ operator** il sait s'y prendre → **satin, silky**

[2] VT [a] [+ sheets, cloth, piece of paper, skirt] lisser, défroisser; [+ pillow, hair, feathers] lisser; [+ wood] rendre lisse, planer; [+ marble] rendre lisse, polir; **to ~ cream into one's skin** faire pénétrer la crème dans la peau (en massant doucement); (fig) **that ~ed her ruffled** or **rumpled feathers** cela lui a rendu le sourire

[b] (fig) **to ~ sb's way** or **path to the top** faciliter le chemin de qn vers le sommet; **to ~ the way** or **path of an application/request** faciliter l'acceptation d'une candidature/demande

[3] COMP ► **smooth-faced** ADJ au visage glabre or lisse; (fig: slightly pej) trop poli, doucereux ► **smooth-running** ADJ [engine, machinery] qui fonctionne sans à-coups; [car] qui ne secoue pas, qui ne donne pas d'à-coups; [business, organization, scheme] qui marche bien or sans heurts ► **smooth-shaven** ADJ rasé de près ► **smooth-spoken, smooth-talking, smooth-tongued** ADJ enjôleur, doucereux

► **smooth back** VT SEP [+ one's hair] ramener doucement en arrière; [+ sheet] rabattre en lissant or en défroissant

► **smooth down** VT SEP [+ hair, feathers] lisser; [+ sheet, cover] lisser, défroisser; (fig) [+ person] calmer, apaiser

► **smooth out** VT SEP [+ material, dress] défroisser; [+ wrinkles, creases] faire disparaître; (fig) [+ anxieties] chasser, faire disparaître; [+ difficulties] aplanir, faire disparaître

► **smooth over** VT SEP [+ soil] aplanir, égaliser;

[+ *sand*] égaliser, rendre lisse ; [+ *wood*] rendre lisse, planer ; (*fig*) **to ~ things over** arranger les choses

smoothie: ['smuːðɪ] N (*pej*) beau parleur *m*

smoothly ['smuːðlɪ] ADV a (= *evenly, not jerkily*) [*move*] en douceur, sans à-coups ; **to run ~** [*engine*] (bien) tourner b (= *efficiently, suavely*) [*act*] habilement, (*pej*) [*speak*] d'un ton douceureux (*pej*) ; **to run** or **go ~** [*event, operation*] bien se passer ; **the move to the new house went off** or **passed off ~** le déménagement s'est bien passé

smoothness ['smuːðnɪs] N (*NonC*) a [*of surface, texture, road, stone, tyre, hair, sea, skin*] aspect *m* lisse ; [*of fabric*] aspect *m* lisse or soyeux ; [*of paste, sauce, mixture*] onctuosité *f* ; [*of flavour, wine, whisky etc*] rondeur *f*, moelleux *m* ; [*of voice, sound*] douceur *f* b (= *evenness*) [*of flow, stride, breathing*] régularité *f* ; [*of sea crossing*] calme *m* ; **the ~ of the landing** l'atterrissage *m* en douceur ; **listen to the ~ of the engine!** écoutez comme le moteur tourne bien ! c (*pej* = *suaveness*) [*of person, manners*] caractère *m* douceureux or mielleux

smoothy: ['smuːðɪ] N = **smoothie**

smorgasbord ['smɔːɡəsˌbɔːd] N (*Culin*) smorgasbord *m*, buffet *m* scandinave

smote [sməʊt] VB *pt of* **smite**

smother ['smʌðəʳ] 1 VT a (= *stifle*) [+ *person, flames*] étouffer ; [+ *noise*] étouffer, amortir ; (*fig*) [+ *scandal, feelings*] étouffer ; [+ *criticism, doubt, yawn*] étouffer, réprimer ; [+ *one's anger*] contenir, réprimer b (= *cover*) (re)couvrir (**with** de) ; **she ~ed the child with kisses** elle a couvert or dévoré l'enfant de baisers ; **books ~ed in dust** des livres enfouis sous la poussière or tout (re)couverts de poussière ; **a child ~ed in dirt** un enfant tout sale or tout couvert de crasse ; **a face ~ed in make-up** une figure toute emplâtrée de maquillage ; **he was ~ed in blankets** il était tout emmailloté de couvertures, il était tout emmitouflé dans ses couvertures 2 VI [*person*] être étouffé, mourir étouffé 3 COMP ► **smother-love** N (*iro*) amour *m* maternel possessif or dévorant

smoulder, smolder (*US*) ['sməʊldəʳ] VI [*fire, emotion*] couver ; [*woman*] être très sexy* ; **to ~ with rage** être blême de rage

smouldering, smoldering (*US*) ['sməʊldərɪŋ] ADJ a (*lit*) [*fire*] qui couve ; [*ashes, rubble*] qui fume b (*fig*) [*expression, look*] provocant, aguichant ; [*emotion*] qui couve ; **his ~ hatred** la haine qui couve en lui

SMP [ˌesemˈpiː] N (*Brit*) (ABBR = **Statutory Maternity Pay**) → **statutory**

smudge [smʌdʒ] 1 N (*on paper, cloth*) (légère) tache *f*, traînée *f* ; (*in text, print etc*) bavure *f*, tache *f* 2 VT [+ *face*] salir ; [+ *print*] maculer ; [+ *paint*] faire une trace or une marque sur ; [+ *lettering, writing*] étaler accidentellement 3 VI s'étaler

smudgy ['smʌdʒɪ] ADJ [*photo*] indistinct ; [*page*] sali, taché ; [*writing*] à moitié effacé ; **~ newsprint** papier *m* journal salissant

smug [smʌɡ] ADJ [*person, voice, attitude, smile*] suffisant ; [*optimism, satisfaction*] béat ; [*remark, speech*] plein de suffisance

smuggle ['smʌɡl] 1 VT [+ *tobacco, drugs*] faire la contrebande de, passer en contrebande or en fraude ; **to ~ in/out** etc [+ *contraband*] faire entrer/sortir etc ; [+ *goods*] faire entrer/sortir etc en contrebande ; (*fig*) [+ *letters etc*] faire entrer/sortir etc clandestinement or en fraude ; [+ *person, animal*] faire entrer/sortir etc clandestinement ; **to ~ sth past** or **through the customs** passer qch en contrebande, passer qch sans le déclarer à la douane ; **~d goods** contrebande *f* ; **~d whisky** whisky *m* de contrebande 2 VI faire de la contrebande

smuggler ['smʌɡləʳ] N contrebandier *m*, -ière *f*

smuggling ['smʌɡlɪŋ] 1 N (*NonC*) [*of goods*] contrebande *f* (*action*) 2 COMP ► **smuggling ring** N réseau *m* de contrebandiers

smugly ['smʌɡlɪ] ADV [*say*] d'un ton suffisant ; [*behave, smile*] d'un air suffisant

smugness ['smʌɡnɪs] N [*of person*] suffisance *f* ; [*of voice, reply*] ton *m* suffisant

smut [smʌt] N a (= *dirt*) petite saleté *f* ; (= *soot*) flocon *m* de suie ; (*in eye*) escarbille *f* ; (= *dirty mark*) tache *f* de suie ; (*Bot*) charbon *m* du blé ; b (*NonC* = *obscenity*) obscénité(s) *f(pl)*, cochonneries* *fpl* ; (*TV*) **programme full of ~** émission *f* cochonne*

smuttiness ['smʌtɪnɪs] N (*NonC: fig*) obscénité *f*, grossièreté *f*

smutty ['smʌtɪ] ADJ a (* = *rude*) [*joke, film, book*] cochon* ; [*person*] grossier b (= *smudged with dirt*) [*face, object*] sali

snack [snæk] 1 N a (*gen*) casse-croûte *m inv* ; **to have a ~** casser la croûte, manger (un petit) quelque chose b (= *party snack*) amuse-gueule *m inv* 2 VI **to have a snack** → **1a** 3 COMP ► **snack bar** N snack-bar *m*, snack *m*

snaffle ['snæfl] 1 N (*also* **~ bit**) mors *m* brisé 2 VT (*Brit* * = *steal*) chiper*, faucher*

snafu: [snæˈfuː] (*US*) 1 ADJ en pagaille* 2 VT mettre la pagaille* dans ~

snag [snæɡ] 1 N a (= *drawback*) inconvénient *m* ; (= *hidden obstacle*) obstacle *m* caché ; (= *stump of tree, tooth etc*) chicot *m* ; (= *tear*) (*in cloth*) accroc *m* ; (*in stocking*) fil *m* tiré ; **there's a ~ in it somewhere** il y a sûrement un os* ; **to run into** or **hit a ~** tomber sur un os* ; **that's the ~!** voilà le hic !* ; **the ~ is that you must ...** l'embêtant* c'est que vous devez ... 2 VT [+ *cloth*] faire un accroc à ; [+ *stockings, tights*] accrocher (**on sth** qch), tirer un fil à 3 VI [*rope etc*] s'accrocher (à quelque chose) ; [*stockings, tights etc*] s'accrocher

snail [sneɪl] 1 N escargot *m* ; **at a ~'s pace** [*walk*] comme un escargot, à un pas de tortue ; (*fig*) [*progress, continue*] à un pas de tortue → **pace¹** 2 COMP ► **snail mail*** N (*NonC: hum*) **to send sth by ~ mail** envoyer qch par la poste ► **snail shell** N coquille *f* d'escargot

snake [sneɪk] 1 N a serpent *m* ; (*fig pej* = *person*) traître(sse) *m(f)*, faux frère *m* ; (*fig*) **~ in the grass** (= *person*) ami(e) *m(f)* perfide, traître(sse) *m(f)* ; (= *danger*) serpent *m* caché sous les fleurs ; (*Pol Econ*) **the Snake** le serpent (monétaire) → **grass, water** 2 VI [*road, river*] serpenter (**through** à travers) ; **the road ~d down the mountain** la route descendait en lacets or en serpentant au flanc de la montagne ; **the whip ~d through the air** la lanière du fouet a fendu l'air en ondulant 3 COMP ► **snake charmer** N charmeur *m* de serpent ► **snake eyes:** NPL (*US: at dice*) double un *m*, deux *m* (aux dés) ► **snake fence** N (*US*) barrière *f* en zigzag, barrière *f* pliante ► **snake oil** N (*US*) (= *quack remedy*) remède *m* de charlatan ; (= *nonsense*) inepties *fpl*, foutaises* *fpl* ► **snake pit** N fosse *f* aux serpents ► **snakes and ladders** N sorte de jeu de l'oie

► **snake along** VI [*road, river*] serpenter ; [*rope, lasso etc*] fendre l'air en ondulant

snakebite ['sneɪkbaɪt] N morsure *f* de serpent

snakeskin ['sneɪkskɪn] 1 N peau *f* de serpent 2 COMP [*handbag etc*] en (peau de) serpent

snaky: ['sneɪkɪ] ADJ a (= *winding*) [*road, river*] sinueux b (= *treacherous*) [*person, behaviour, remark*] sournois

snap [snæp] 1 N a (= *noise*) [*of fingers, whip, elastic*] claquement *m* ; [*of sth breaking*] bruit *m* sec, craquement *m* ; [*of sth shutting*] bruit *m* sec, claquement *m* ; (= *action*) [*of whip*] claquement *m* ; [*of breaking twig etc*] rupture *f* or cassure *f* soudaine ; **he closed the lid with a ~** il a refermé le couvercle avec un bruit sec or

d'un coup sec ; **with a ~ of his fingers he ...** faisant claquer ses doigts il ... ; **the dog made a ~ at my leg** le chien a essayé de me mordre la jambe ; (*fig*) **put some ~ into it!** allons, un peu de nerf or d'énergie ! ; **he has plenty of ~** il a du nerf*, il est très dynamique → **brandy, ginger** b (*Met*) **a cold ~** une brève vague de froid, un coup de froid c (*also* **~shot**) photo *f* (d'amateur) ; (*not posed*) instantané *m* ; **here are our holiday ~s** voici nos photos de vacances ; **it's only a ~** ce n'est qu'une photo d'amateur d (*US: also* **~ fastener**) pression *f*, bouton-pression *m* e (*Brit Cards*) (sorte *f* de jeu de) bataille *f* f (*US* = *easy*) **it's a ~*** c'est du gâteau*, c'est facile comme tout, c'est un jeu d'enfant 2 ADJ a (= *sudden*) [*vote, strike*] subit, décidé à l'improviste ; [*judgement, answer, remark*] fait sans réflexion, irréfléchi ; **to make a ~ decision** (se) décider tout d'un coup or subitement b (*US** = *easy*) facile comme tout, facile comme pas deux* 3 ADV **to go ~** se casser net or avec un bruit sec 4 EXCL (*gen*) tiens ! on est or fait pareil ! ; (*Cards*) ≈ bataille ! 5 VI a (= *break*) se casser net or avec un bruit sec b [*whip, elastic, rubber band*] claquer ; **to ~ shut/open** se fermer/s'ouvrir avec un bruit sec or avec un claquement ; **the rubber band ~ped back into place** l'élastique est revenu à sa place avec un claquement c **to ~ at sb** [*dog*] essayer de mordre qn ; [*person*] parler à qn d'un ton brusque, rembarrer* qn ; **the dog ~ped at the bone** le chien a essayé de happer l'os 6 VT a (= *break*) casser net or avec un bruit sec b [+ *whip, rubber band etc*] faire claquer ; **to ~ one's fingers** faire claquer ses doigts ; **to ~ one's fingers at** [+ *person*] faire la nique à ; (*fig*) [+ *suggestion, danger*] se moquer de ; **to ~ sth open/shut** ouvrir/fermer qch d'un coup sec or avec un bruit sec c (*Phot*) prendre en photo d **"shut up!" he ~ped** « silence ! » fit-il d'un ton brusque 7 COMP ► **snap fastener** N (*US*) (*on clothes*) pression *f*, bouton-pression *m* ; (*on handbag, bracelet etc*) fermoir *m* ► **snap-in, snap-on** ADJ [*hood, lining*] amovible (à pressions)

► **snap back** VI a [*elastic, rope etc*] revenir en place brusquement or avec un claquement b (*fig: after illness, accident*) se remettre très vite c (*in answering*) répondre d'un ton brusque

► **snap off** 1 VI se casser or se briser net 2 VT SEP casser net ; (*fig*) **to ~ sb's head off** rabrouer qn, rembarrer* qn

► **snap out** 1 VI **to ~ out of** [+ *gloom, lethargy, self-pity*] se sortir de, se tirer de ; [+ *bad temper*] contrôler, dominer ; **~ out of it!** [+ *gloom etc*] secoue-toi !*, réagis ! ; [+ *bad temper*] contrôle-toi or domine-toi un peu ! 2 VT SEP [+ *question/order*] poser/lancer d'un ton brusque or cassant

► **snap up** VT SEP [*dog etc*] happer, attraper ; (*fig*) **to ~ up a bargain** sauter sur or se jeter sur une occasion ; **they are ~ped up as soon as they come on the market** on se les arrache or on saute dessus dès qu'ils sont mis en vente

snapdragon ['snæpdræɡən] N (*Bot*) gueule-de-loup *f*

snapper ['snæpəʳ] N (*pl* **snapper** or **snappers**) (*Zool, Culin*) lutjanidé *m*

snappish ['snæpɪʃ] ADJ a (= *irritable*) [*person, reply, tone*] cassant ; [*dog*] hargneux

snappishness ['snæpɪʃnɪs] N [*of person*] caractère *m* cassant ; (*temporary*) brusquerie *f* ; [*of voice, reply*] ton *m* brusque *or* cassant

snappy ['snæpɪ] ADJ [a] (= *punchy*) [*title, phrase, slogan*] qui a du punch* ; [*dialogue*] nerveux ; [*reply*] bien envoyé [b] (= *snazzy*) [*clothes*] chic *inv* ; **he's a ~ dresser** il est toujours bien sapé* [c]* **make it ~!** ◊ **look ~ (about it)!** grouille-toi !*, remue-toi ! [d] = **snappish**

snapshot ['snæpʃɒt] N → **snap 1c**

snare [snɛəʳ] [1] N piège *m* ; (*fig*) piège *m*, traquenard *m* ; (*fig*) **these promises are a ~ and a delusion** ces promesses ne servent qu'à allécher *or* appâter [2] VT (*lit, fig*) attraper, prendre au piège [3] COMP ► **snare drum** N tambour *m* à timbre

snarky* ['snɑːkɪ] ADJ râleur*

snarl[1] [snɑːl] [1] N [*of dog*] grondement *m* féroce ; **to give a ~ of fury** [*dog*] gronder férocement ; [*person*] pousser un rugissement de fureur ; **... he said with a ~** ... dit-il d'une voix rageuse *or* avec hargne [2] VI [*dog*] gronder en montrant les dents *or* férocement ; [*person*] lancer un grondement (**at sb** à qn), gronder ; **when I went in the dog ~ed at me** quand je suis entré le chien a grondé en montrant les dents [3] VT [+ *order*] lancer d'un ton hargneux *or* d'une voix rageuse ; **to ~ a reply** répondre d'un ton hargneux *or* d'une voix rageuse ; **"no" he ~ed** « non » dit-il avec hargne *or* d'une voix rageuse

snarl[2] [snɑːl] [1] N (*in wool, rope, hair etc*) nœud *m*, enchevêtrement *m* ; (*fig*) **a traffic ~** un embouteillage → **snarl-up** [2] VI (*also* **~ up, get ~ed up**) [*wool, rope, hair*] s'emmêler, s'enchevêtrer ; [*traffic*] se bloquer ;* [*plans, programme*] cafouiller* [3] VT (*also* **~ up**) [+ *wool, rope, hair*] emmêler, enchevêtrer [4] COMP ► **snarl-up** N **a traffic ~-up** ◊ **a ~-up (in the traffic)** un embouteillage ; (*fig: in plans etc*) **there's been a ~-up** il y a eu du cafouillage* *or* quelques anicroches

► **snarl up** [1] VI = **snarl**[2] **2** [2] VT SEP [a] = **snarl**[2] **3** [b] [+ *traffic*] bloquer ;* [+ *plans, programme*] mettre la pagaille* dans **→ ~-up** N → **snarl**[2]

snatch [snætʃ] [1] N [a] (= *action*) geste *m* vif (*pour saisir quelque chose*) ; (*fig*) [*of jewellery, wages etc*] vol *m* (à l'arraché) ; [*of child etc*] enlèvement *m* ; **there was a jewellery/wages ~ yesterday** hier des voleurs se sont emparés de bijoux/de salaires [b] (= *small piece*) fragment *m* ; **a ~ of music/poetry** quelques mesures *fpl*/vers *mpl* ; **a ~ of conversation** des bribes *fpl* *or* un fragment de conversation ; **a few ~es of Mozart** quelques mesures *or* un fragment de Mozart ; **to work in ~es** travailler de façon intermittente *or* par accès *or* par à-coups [c] (*Weight Lifting*) arraché *m* [d] ("** = *vagina*) chatte** *f* [2] VT (= *grab*) [+ *object*] saisir, s'emparer (brusquement) de ; [+ *a few minutes' peace, a holiday*] réussir à avoir ; [+ *opportunity*] saisir, sauter sur ; [+ *kiss*] voler, dérober (**from sb** à qn) ; [+ *sandwich, drink*] avaler à la hâte ; (= *steal*) voler, chiper* (**from sb** à qn), saisir ; (= *kidnap*) enlever ; **she ~ed the book from him** elle lui a arraché le livre ; **he ~ed the child from the railway line just in time** il a saisi *or* attrapé *or* empoigné l'enfant et l'a tiré hors de la voie juste à temps ; **Cantona ~ed victory from the jaws of defeat with two last-minute goals** Cantona a arraché la victoire in extremis en marquant deux buts à la dernière minute ; **to ~ some sleep/rest** (réussir à) dormir/se reposer un peu ; **to ~ a meal** déjeuner (*or* dîner) à la hâte [3] VI **to ~ at** [+ *object, end of rope etc*] essayer de saisir, faire un geste vif pour saisir ; [+ *opportunity, chance*] saisir, sauter sur [4] COMP ► **snatch squad** N (*Brit*) forces de l'ordre chargées d'appréhender les meneurs de manifestations

►**snatch away, snatch off** VT SEP enlever

d'un geste vif *or* brusque

►**snatch up** VT SEP [+ *object, child*] saisir

-snatcher ['snætʃəʳ] N (*in compounds*) → **cradle**

snazzy* ['snæzɪ] ADJ qui en jette*, chouette* ; **she's a ~ dresser** elle est toujours bien sapée*

sneak [sniːk] (*vb: pret, ptp* **sneaked** *or* (*US* *) **snuck**) [1] N (* = *underhand person*) faux jeton* *m* ; (*Brit Scol* = *telltale*) mouchard(e)* *m(f)*, rapporteur* *m*, -euse *f*

[2] ADJ [*attack, visit*] furtif, subreptice ; **~ preview** (*Cine*) avant-première *f* ; (*gen*) avant-goût *m* ; **~ thief** chapardeur* *m*, -euse* *f*

[3] VI [a] **to ~ in/out** etc entrer/sortir etc furtivement ; **he ~ed into the house** il s'est faufilé *or* s'est glissé dans la maison ; **he ~ed up behind** *or* **on me** il s'est approché de moi sans faire de bruit ; **success can ~ up on you** le succès peut arriver sans crier gare [b] (*Brit Scol*) moucharder*, cafarder* (**on sb** qn)

[4] VT [a] **I ~ed the letter onto his desk** j'ai glissé la lettre discrètement *or* furtivement *or* en douce* sur son bureau ; **he ~ed the envelope from the table** il a enlevé furtivement *or* subrepticement l'enveloppe de la table ; **to ~ a look at sth** lancer un coup d'œil furtif à qch, regarder qch à la dérobée ; **he was ~ing* a cigarette** il était en train de fumer en cachette [b] (* = *pilfer*) faucher*, piquer*

►**sneak away, sneak off** VI s'esquiver, s'éclipser*

sneaker ['sniːkəʳ] N (*esp US*) tennis *m*, basket *f*

sneaking ['sniːkɪŋ] ADJ (= *grudging*) [*dislike, preference etc*] inavoué ; **I had a ~ feeling that ...** je ne pouvais m'empêcher de penser que ... ; **to have a ~ suspicion that ...** soupçonner que ... ; **I have a ~ admiration/respect for him** je ne peux pas m'empêcher de l'admirer/de le respecter

sneaky* ['sniːkɪ] ADJ [*person, character, action*] sournois

sneer [snɪəʳ] [1] VI ricaner, sourire d'un air méprisant *or* sarcastique ; **to ~ at sb** se moquer de qn d'un air méprisant ; **to ~ at sth** tourner qch en ridicule [2] N (= *act*) ricanement *m* ; (= *remark*) sarcasme *m*, raillerie *f* ; **... he said with a ~** ... dit-il d'un air méprisant

sneerer ['snɪərəʳ] N ricaneur *m*, -euse *f*

sneering ['snɪərɪŋ] [1] ADJ [*person, contempt, remark*] sarcastique ; [*tone*] railleur [2] N (*NonC*) raillerie(s) *f(pl)*

sneeringly ['snɪərɪŋlɪ] ADV sarcastiquement

sneeze [sniːz] [1] N éternuement *m* [2] VI éternuer ; (*fig*) **it's not to be ~d at** ce n'est pas à dédaigner, il ne faut pas cracher dessus* ; (*Brit*) **when America ~s, Britain catches cold** quand l'Amérique éternue, la Grande-Bretagne s'enrhume

snick [snɪk] [1] N petite entaille *f*, encoche *f* [2] VT [+ *stick etc*] faire une petite entaille *or* une encoche dans ; (*Sport*) [+ *ball*] juste toucher

snicker ['snɪkəʳ] [1] N [a] [*of horse*] petit hennissement *m* [b] = **snigger 1** [2] VI [a] [*horse*] hennir doucement [b] = **snigger 2**

snide [snaɪd] ADJ narquois

sniff [snɪf] [1] N [a] (*from cold, crying etc*) reniflement *m* ; **to give a ~** renifler (une fois) ; (*disdainfully*) faire la grimace *or* la moue ; **... he said with a ~** ... dit-il en reniflant ; (*disdainfully*) ... dit-il en faisant la grimace *or* la moue ; **I got a ~ of gas** j'ai senti l'odeur du gaz ; **to have** *or* **take a ~ at sth** [*person*] renifler qch ; (*suspiciously*) flairer qch ; [*dog*] renifler *or* flairer qch ; **one ~ of that is enough to kill you** il suffit de respirer cela une fois pour en mourir ; (*fig*) **I didn't get a ~* of the whisky** je n'ai pas eu droit à une goutte de whisky [b] (* = *hint*) **to get a ~ of sth** flairer qch ; **at the first ~ of danger** au moindre danger

[2] VI (*from cold, crying*) renifler ; (*disdainfully*) faire la grimace *or* la moue ; [*dog*] renifler ; **to ~ at sth** renifler qch ; (*fig*) faire la grimace *or* la moue à qch ; **it's not to be ~ed at** ce n'est pas à dédaigner, il ne faut pas cracher dessus*

[3] VT [*dog etc*] renifler, flairer ; [*person*] renifler, sentir l'odeur de ; (*suspiciously*) flairer ; [+ *air, perfume, aroma*] humer ; [+ *drug*] aspirer ; [+ *smelling salts*] respirer ; (*Pharm*) [+ *inhalant etc*] aspirer ; **to ~ glue** respirer de la colle, sniffer**

►**sniff out** VT (= *discover*) flairer

sniffer dog N chien *m* renifleur

sniffle ['snɪfl] [1] N (= *sniff*) reniflement *m* ; (= *slight cold*) petit rhume *m* de cerveau ; **... he said with a ~** ... dit-il en reniflant ; **to have a ~** *or* **the ~s** avoir un petit rhume, être légèrement enrhumé [2] VI [*person, dog*] renifler ; (*from catarrh etc*) avoir le nez bouché, renifler

sniffy* ['snɪfɪ] ADJ (= *disdainful*) dédaigneux, méprisant ; **to be ~ about sth** se montrer désagréable à propos de qch

snifter ['snɪftəʳ] N [a] (*Brit* = *drink*) petit (verre *m* d')alcool *m* ; **to have a ~** prendre un petit verre, boire la goutte* [b] (*US* = *glass*) verre *m* ballon

snigger ['snɪgəʳ] [1] N rire *m* en dessous ; (*cynical*) ricanement *m* [2] VI pouffer de rire ; (*cynically*) ricaner ; **to ~ at** [+ *remark, question*] pouffer de rire *or* ricaner en entendant ; [+ *sb's appearance etc*] se moquer de ; **stop ~ing!** arrête de rire *or* de ricaner comme ça !

sniggering ['snɪgərɪŋ] [1] N ricanements *mpl* [2] ADJ qui n'arrête pas de pouffer de rire *or* de ricaner

snip [snɪp] [1] N [a] (= *cut*) petit coup *m* (de ciseaux etc), petite entaille *f* ; (= *small piece*) petit bout *m* (d'étoffe etc), échantillon *m* ; (*Brit* = *bargain*) bonne affaire *f*, (bonne) occasion *f* ; (*Racing*) gagnant *m* sûr [2] VT couper (à petits coups de ciseaux etc) [3] VI **to ~ at sth** donner des petits coups dans qch

►**snip off** VT SEP couper *or* enlever *or* détacher (à coups de ciseaux etc)

snipe [snaɪp] [1] N (*pl* **snipe** *or* **snipes**) (*Orn*) bécassine *f* [2] VI (= *shoot*) tirer (en restant caché), canarder* ; **to ~ at sb/sth** canarder* qn/qch ; (*fig: verbally*) critiquer qn/qch par en dessous *or* sournoisement

sniper ['snaɪpəʳ] N tireur *m* isolé, sniper *m*

snippet ['snɪpɪt] N [*of cloth, paper*] petit bout *m* ; [*of conversation, news, information*] fragment *m*, bribes *fpl*

snippy* ['snɪpɪ] ADJ (*US*) [*person, tone*] hargneux ; **to be in a ~ mood** être de mauvais poil*

snitch* [snɪtʃ] [1] VI moucharder* (**on sb** qn) [2] VT chiper*, piquer* [3] N (= *nose*) pif** *m* ; (= *telltale*) mouchard(e)* *m(f)*, rapporteur* *m*, -euse* *f*

snivel ['snɪvl] VI (= *whine*) pleurnicher, larmoyer ; (= *sniff*) renifler ; (= *have a runny nose*) avoir le nez qui coule, avoir la morve au nez (*pej*)

sniveler ['snɪvləʳ] N (*US*) = **sniveller**

sniveling ['snɪvlɪŋ] ADJ (*US*) = **snivelling**

sniveller ['snɪvləʳ] N pleurnicheur *m*, -euse *f*

snivelling ['snɪvlɪŋ] [1] ADJ pleurnicheur, larmoyant [2] N pleurnicherie(s) *f(pl)*, reniflement(s) *m(pl)*

snob [snɒb] N snob *mf* ; **he's a terrible ~** il est terriblement snob ; **she's a musical/wine ~** c'est une snob en matière de musique/vin

snobbery ['snɒbərɪ] N snobisme *m*

snobbish ['snɒbɪʃ] ADJ snob *inv* ; **to be ~ about sb/sth** faire preuve de snobisme à l'égard de qn/en matière de qch

snobbishness ['snɒbɪʃnɪs] N snobisme *m*

snobby* ['snɒbɪ] ADJ snob *inv*

snog: [snɒg] (Brit) [1] VI se bécoter* [2] N **to have a ~** se bécoter*

snood [snu:d] N résille f

snook[1] [snu:k] N (pl **snook** or **snooks**) (= fish) brochet m de mer

snook[2] [snu:k] N → **cock 2b**

snooker ['snu:kər] [1] N (= game) snooker m, ≈ jeu m de billard; (= shot) snooker m [2] VT (lit) faire un snooker à; (US = hoodwink) tromper, avoir*; (Brit) **to be ~ed**: (= be in difficulty) être coincé*, être dans le pétrin*

snoop [snu:p] [1] N **to have a ~ around** jeter un coup d'œil discret; **I had a ~ around the kitchen** j'ai fureté discrètement or sans être vu dans la cuisine [b] = **snooper** [2] VI se mêler des affaires des autres; **to ~ (around)** rôder or fureter or fouiller en essayant de passer inaperçu; **he's been ~ing (around) here again** il est revenu fourrer son nez* par ici; **to ~ on sb** surveiller qn, espionner qn; **he was ~ing into her private life** il fourrait son nez* dans or il se mêlait de sa vie privée

snooper ['snu:pər] N (pej) fouineur* m, -euse f; **all the ~s from the Ministry** tous les espions du ministère, tous les enquêteurs du ministère qui fourrent leur nez* partout; **he's a terrible ~** il met son nez partout, c'est un terrible fouineur*

snoot: [snu:t] N pif*: m, nez m

snooty: ['snu:tɪ] ADJ snob inv

snooze: [snu:z] [1] N petit somme m, roupillon* m; **afternoon ~** sieste f; **to have a ~ =** **to snooze;** → **2** [2] VI piquer un roupillon* [3] COMP ► **snooze button** N bouton m d'arrêt momentané (d'un radio-réveil)

snore [snɔ:ʳ] [1] N ronflement m (d'un dormeur) [2] VI ronfler

snorer ['snɔ:rəʳ] N ronfleur m, -euse f

snoring ['snɔ:rɪŋ] N (NonC) ronflement(s) m(pl)

snorkel ['snɔ:kl] [1] N [of submarine] schnorkel or schnorchel m; [of swimmer] tuba m [2] VI nager avec un masque et un tuba

snorkelling ['snɔ:kəlɪŋ] N plongée f (avec un masque et un tuba)

snort [snɔ:t] [1] N [a] [of person] grognement m; [of horse etc] ébrouement m [b]: = **snorter b** [c] (Drugs:) sniff: m, prise f [2] VI [a] [horse etc] s'ébrouer; [person] (angrily, contemptuously) grogner, ronchonner; (laughing) s'étrangler de rire [b] (Drugs*) sniffer: de la drogue [3] VT [a] (= say) (angrily etc) grogner, dire en grognant; (laughing) dire en s'étranglant de rire [b] (Drugs*) sniffer:

snorter: ['snɔ:təʳ] N [a] **a (real) ~ of a question/problem** une question/un problème vache:; **a ~ of a game** un match formidable* [b] (= drink) petit (verre m d')alcool m; **to have a ~** prendre un petit verre, boire la goutte*

snot: [snɒt] N [a] (NonC: in nose) morve f [b] (* = snooty person) morveux:* m, -euse*f

snotty: ['snɒtɪ] [1] ADJ [a] (= covered in snot) [nose] qui coule; [face, child] morveux; [handkerchief] plein de morve [b] (= snooty) snob inv [2] N (= midshipman) midship m, ≈ aspirant m [3] COMP ► **snotty-faced**: ADJ morveux, qui a le nez qui coule ► **snotty-nosed**: ADJ (lit, fig) snob inv

snout [snaʊt] N [a] (gen) museau m; [of pig] museau m, groin m; (* pej) [of person] pif: m [b] (NonC: Police:) tabac m, perlot: m

snow [snəʊ] [1] N [a] neige f; **hard/soft ~** neige f dure/molle; **the eternal ~s** les neiges fpl éternelles → **fall, white** [b] (fig: on TV screen) neige f [c] (Culin) apple etc ~ purée f de pommes etc (aux blancs d'œufs battus en neige) [d] (Drugs*: = cocaine) neige* f [2] VI neiger; **it is ~ing** il neige, il tombe de la neige

[3] VT (US: = charm glibly) avoir qn au charme*; **she ~ed: him into believing that he would win** elle a réussi à lui faire croire qu'il allait gagner

[4] COMP ► **snow bank** N talus m de neige, congère f ► **snow-blind** ADJ **to be ~-blind** souffrir de or être atteint de cécité des neiges ► **snow blindness** N cécité f des neiges ► **snow blower** N chasse-neige m inv à souffleuse, souffleuse f (Can) ► **snow-boot** N (Ski) après-ski m ► **snow buggy** N skidoo m, autoneige f ► **snow bunny**: N (US = girl) minette f de station de ski ► **snow cap** N couronne f or couverture f de neige ► **snow-capped** ADJ couronné de neige ► **snow-clad, snow-covered** ADJ (liter) enneigé, enfoui sous la neige ► **snow goose** N (pl snow geese) oie f des neiges ► **snow job**: N (US) **it's a ~ job** c'est du baratin*; **to give sb a ~ job** baratiner* qn ► **snow leopard** N léopard m des neiges, once f ► **snow line** N limite f des neiges éternelles ► **the Snow Queen** N (Myth) la Reine des neiges ► **snow report** N (Met) bulletin m d'enneigement ► **snow tyre** N pneu-neige m, pneu m clouté ► **snow-white** ADJ blanc (blanche f) comme neige, d'une blancheur de neige ► **Snow White (and the Seven Dwarfs)** N Blanche-Neige f (et les sept nains)

► **snow in** VT (pass only) **to be ~ed in** être bloqué par la neige

► **snow under** VT (fig: pass only) **he was ~ed under with work** il était complètement submergé or débordé de travail, il avait tellement de travail qu'il ne savait pas où donner de la tête; **to be ~ed under with letters/offers** être submergé de lettres/d'offres, recevoir une avalanche de lettres/d'offres

► **snow up** VT (Brit) **to be ~ed up** [road, village, farm, person] être bloqué par la neige

snowball ['snəʊbɔ:l] [1] N boule f de neige; **it hasn't got a ~'s chance in hell**: ça n'a pas l'ombre d'une chance; **~(ing) effect** effet m boule de neige; **~ fight** bataille f de boules de neige [2] VT lancer des boules de neige à, bombarder de boules de neige [3] VI (lit) se lancer des or se bombarder de boules de neige; (fig) [project etc] faire boule de neige; (fig) **~ing costs** coûts mpl qui montent en flèche

snowbelt ['snəʊbelt] N (US) régions fpl neigeuses

snowboard ['snəʊbɔ:d] [1] N surf m des neiges [2] VI faire du surf sur neige

snowboarding ['snəʊbɔ:dɪŋ] N surf m des neiges

snowbound ['snəʊbaʊnd] ADJ [road, country] complètement enneigé; [village, house, person] bloqué par la neige

snowcat ['snəʊkæt] N (Aut) autoneige f

Snowdon ['snəʊdən] N (Brit) le (mont) Snowdon

Snowdonia [snəʊ'dəʊnɪə] N le massif or le parc national du Snowdon

snowdrift ['snəʊdrɪft] N congère f, amoncellement m de neige

snowdrop ['snəʊdrɒp] N (Bot) perce-neige m inv

snowfall ['snəʊfɔ:l] N chute f de neige

snowfield ['snəʊfi:ld] N champ m de neige

snowflake ['snəʊfleɪk] N flocon m de neige

snowman ['snəʊmæn] N (pl -men) bonhomme m de neige → **abominable**

snowmobile ['snəʊmə,bi:l] N (US Aut) autoneige f, motoneige f

snowplough, snowplow (US) ['snəʊplaʊ] N (also Ski) chasse-neige m inv; (Ski) **~ (turn)** stem m

snowshoe ['snəʊʃu:] N raquette f

snowslide ['snəʊslaɪd] N (US) avalanche f

snowstorm ['snəʊstɔ:m] N tempête f de neige

snowsuit ['snəʊsu:t] N combinaison f de ski

snowy ['snəʊɪ] [1] ADJ [a] [weather, climate, winter] neigeux; [valley, region, landscape, mountain, street] enneigé; [roof] couvert de neige; **a ~ day/morning** une journée/matinée de neige; **it was very ~ yesterday** il a beaucoup neigé hier [b] (in colour: also ~ **white**) [linen, shirt] blanc (blanche f) comme neige; [hair, beard] de neige [2] COMP ► **snowy owl** N harfang m

SNP [esen'pi:] N (Brit Pol) (ABBR = **Scottish National Party**) → **Scottish**

Snr (esp US) ABBR = **senior**

snub[1] [snʌb] [1] N rebuffade f [2] VT [+ person] snober; [+ offer] repousser, rejeter; **to be ~bed** essuyer une rebuffade

snub[2] [snʌb] ADJ [nose] retroussé, camus (pej); **~-nosed** au nez retroussé or camus (pej)

snuck [snʌk] (US) VB pt, ptp of **sneak**

snuff[1] [snʌf] [1] N tabac m à priser; **pinch of ~** prise f; **to take ~** priser; (Brit) **he/his work isn't up to ~**:† il/son travail n'est pas à la hauteur; (Brit) **his lectures didn't come up to ~**:† ses cours ne valaient pas grand-chose [2] VTI = **sniff 2, 3**

snuff[2] [snʌf] [1] VT [+ candle] moucher; (Brit euph) **to ~ it**: (= die) claquer*, casser sa pipe* [2] COMP ► **snuff film, snuff movie** N film m porno sadique (dont la scène principale est un meurtre filmé en direct)

► **snuff out** [1] VI (: = die) mourir, casser sa pipe* [2] VT SEP [a] [+ candle] moucher [b] [+ interest, hopes, enthusiasm, sb's life] mettre fin à [c] (: = kill) zigouiller:

snuffbox ['snʌfbɒks] N tabatière f

snuffer ['snʌfəʳ] N (also **candle-~**) éteignoir m; **~s** mouchettes fpl

snuffle ['snʌfl] [1] N [a] = **sniffle 1** [b] **to speak in a ~** parler du nez or d'une voix nasillarde, nasiller [2] VI [a] = **sniffle 2** [b] (sing or chanter) d'une voix nasillarde, nasiller [3] VT dire or prononcer d'une voix nasillarde

snug [snʌg] [1] ADJ [a] (= cosy) [house, bed, garment] douillet; **it's nice and ~ here** on est bien ici; **he was ~ in bed** il était bien au chaud dans son lit; **to be as ~ as a bug in a rug**: être bien au chaud, être douillettement installé [b] (= close-fitting) bien ajusté; **it's a ~ fit** [garment] ça va, mais juste; [object] cela rentre juste bien [2] N (Brit: in pub) petite arrière-salle f

snuggery ['snʌgərɪ] N (Brit) = **snug 2**

snuggle ['snʌgl] [1] VI se blottir, se pelotonner (into sth dans qch, beside sb contre qn) [2] VT [+ child etc] serrer or attirer contre soi

► **snuggle down** VI se blottir, se pelotonner (beside sb contre qn), se rouler en boule; **~ down and go to sleep** installe-toi bien confortablement et dors

► **snuggle together** VI se serrer or se blottir l'un contre l'autre

► **snuggle up** VI se serrer, se blottir (to sb contre qn)

snugly ['snʌglɪ] ADV [a] (= cosily) douillettement; **~ tucked in** bien au chaud sous ses couvertures [b] (= tightly) **these trousers fit ~** ce pantalon va juste bien; **the washing machine fitted ~ into the space** la machine à laver s'encastrait parfaitement

▼ **so** [səʊ]

[1] ADVERB	[3] COMPOUNDS
[2] CONJUNCTION	

[1] ADVERB

[a] **degree = to such an extent** si, tellement, aussi; **so easy/quickly** tellement facile/rapidement; **is it really so tiring?** est-ce vraiment si or tellement fatigant?, est-ce vraiment aussi fatigant (que cela)?; **do you really need so long?** vous faut-il vraiment si longtemps or tellement de temps or aussi longtemps (que cela)?; **so early** si tôt, telle-

ment tôt, d'aussi bonne heure

◆ **so ... (that)** si *or* tellement ... que; **he was so clumsy (that) he broke the cup** il était si *or* tellement maladroit qu'il a cassé la tasse; **the body was so decomposed that it was unidentifiable** le cadavre était tellement décomposé qu'il était impossible de l'identifier

◆ **so ... as to do sth** assez ... pour faire qch; **he was so stupid as to tell her what he'd done** il a eu la stupidité de *or* il a été assez stupide pour lui raconter ce qu'il avait fait; *(frm)* **would you be so kind as to open the door?** auriez-vous l'amabilité *or* la gentillesse *or* l'obligeance d'ouvrir la porte?

◆ **not so ... as** pas aussi ... que; **he is not so clever as his brother** il n'est pas aussi *or* si intelligent que son frère; **it's not so big as all that!** ce n'est pas si grand que ça!; **it's not so big as I thought it would be** ce n'est pas aussi grand que je le pensais *or* que je l'imaginais; **it's not nearly so difficult as you think** c'est loin d'être aussi difficile que vous le croyez; **it's not so early as you think** il n'est pas aussi tôt que vous le croyez; **he's not so good a teacher as his father** il n'est pas aussi bon professeur que son père *or* il ne vaut pas son père comme professeur; **he's not so stupid as he looks** il n'est pas aussi *or* si stupide qu'il en a l'air; **he was not so stupid as to say that to her** il n'a pas été bête au point de lui dire cela, il a eu l'intelligence de ne pas lui dire cela

[b] = **very, to a great extent** si, tellement; **I'm so tired!** je suis si *or* tellement fatigué!; **I'm very tired!** je suis vraiment si *or* tellement fatigué!; **there's so much to do** il y a tellement *or* tant (de choses) à faire; **thanks so much** *◊* **thanks ever so:** merci beaucoup *or* mille fois; **it's not so very difficult!** cela n'est pas si difficile que ça!; **Elizabeth, who so loved France ...** Elizabeth, qui aimait tant la France ...

[c] **unspecified amount** **how tall is he?** — oh, **about so tall** *(accompanied by gesture)* quelle taille fait-il? — oh, à peu près (grand) comme ça; **so much per head** tant par tête; **their skulls were crushed like so many eggshells** leurs crânes furent écrasés comme autant de coquilles d'œufs; **his speech was so much nonsense** son discours était complètement stupide; **how long will it take?** — **a week or so** combien de temps cela va-t-il prendre? — une semaine environ *or* à peu près; **twenty or so** à peu près vingt, une vingtaine

[d] **manner = thus, in this way** ainsi, comme ceci *or* cela, de cette façon; **you should stand (just** *or* **like) so** vous devriez vous tenir comme ceci, voici comment vous devriez vous tenir; **as A is to B so C is to D** C est à D ce que A est à B; **as he failed once so he will fail again** il échouera comme il a déjà échoué; **you don't believe me but it is so** vous ne me croyez pas mais il en est bien ainsi; **it was that ...** c'est ainsi que ...; *(frm)* **so be it** soit; **it so happened that ...** il s'est trouvé que ...

◆ **so (that)** *(intention)* pour (+ *infin*), afin de (+ *infin*), pour que (+ *subj*), afin que (+ *subj*); *(result)* si bien que (+ *indic*), de (telle) sorte que (+ *indic*); **I'm going early so (that) I'll get a ticket** j'y vais tôt pour obtenir *or* afin d'obtenir un billet; **I brought it so (that) you could read it** je l'ai apporté pour que *or* afin que vous puissiez le lire; **he arranged the timetable so (that) the afternoons were free** il a organisé l'emploi du temps de façon à laisser les après-midi libres *or* de (telle) sorte que les après-midi soient libres; **he refused to move, so (that) the police had to carry him away** il a refusé de bouger, si bien que *or* de sorte que les agents ont dû l'emporter de force

◆ **so as to do** afin de faire, pour faire; **he stood up so as to see better** il s'est levé pour mieux voir

◆ **so as not to do:** **she put it down gently so as not to break it** elle l'a posé doucement pour

ne pas le casser; **he hurried so as not to be late** il s'est dépêché pour ne pas être *or* afin de ne pas être en retard

[e] **used as substitute for phrase, word etc** **so saying ...** ce disant ..., sur ces mots ...; **so I believe** c'est ce que je crois, c'est ce qu'il me semble; **is that so?** pas possible!, tiens!; **that is so** c'est bien ça, c'est exact; **if that is so ...** s'il en est ainsi ...; **just so!** *◊* **quite so!** exactement!, tout à fait!; **I told you so yesterday** je vous l'ai dit hier; **so it seems!** à ce qu'il paraît!; **he certainly said so** c'est ce qu'il a dit, il a bien dit ça; **please do so** faites-le, faites ainsi; **I think so** je (le) crois, je (le) pense; **I hope so** *(answering sb)* j'espère que oui; *(agreeing with sb)* je l'espère, j'espère bien; **how so?** comment (ça se fait)?; **why so?** pourquoi (donc)?; **he said they would be there and so they were** il a dit qu'ils seraient là, et en effet ils y étaient; **so do I!** *◊* **so have I!** *◊* **so am I!** *etc* moi aussi!; **he's going to bed and so am I** il va se coucher et moi aussi *or* et je vais en faire autant; **if you do that so will I si** tu fais ça, j'en ferai autant; **I'm tired — so am I!** je suis fatigué — moi aussi!; **he said he was French — so he did!** il a dit qu'il était français — c'est vrai *or* en effet!; **it's raining — so it is!** il pleut — en effet *or* c'est vrai!; **I want to see that film — so you shall!** je veux voir ce film — eh bien, tu le verras!; **I didn't say that! — you did so!** je n'ai pas dit ça! — mais si, tu l'as dit!*; **so to speak** *◊* **so to say** pour ainsi dire; **and so forth** *◊* **and so on (and so forth)** et ainsi de suite; **so long!** *tchao!*, salut!*; **I'm not going, so there!** je n'y vais pas, voilà!

[2] CONJUNCTION

[a] = **therefore** donc, par conséquent; **he was late, so he missed the train** il est arrivé en retard, donc *or* par conséquent il a manqué le train; **the roads are busy so be careful** il y a beaucoup de circulation, alors fais bien attention

[b] **exclamatory** **so there he is!** le voilà donc!; **so you're selling it?** alors vous le vendez?; **he's come at last!** il est donc enfin arrivé!; **and so you see ...** alors comme vous voyez ...; **I'm going home — so?*** je rentre — et alors?; **so (what)?*** et alors?, et après?

[3] COMPOUNDS

► **so-and-so*** N *(pl* **so-and-sos)** **Mr/Mrs So-and-so** Monsieur/Madame Untel; **then if so-and-so says ...** alors si quelqu'un *or* Machin Chouette* dit ...; **he's an old so-and-so** c'est un vieux schnock:; **if you ask him to do so-and-so** si vous lui demandez de faire quoi que ce soit ► **so-called** ADJ soi-disant *inv*, prétendu ► **so-so*** ADJ comme ci comme ça, couci-couça*; **his work is only so-so** son travail n'est pas fameux*

---

s/o *(Banking)* (ABBR = **standing order**) → **standing**

soak [səʊk] [1] N [a] **to give sth a (good) ~** (bien) faire tremper qch, (bien) laisser tremper qch; **the sheets are in ~** les draps sont en train de tremper [b] (: = *drunkard*) soûlard* m, poivrot* m [2] VT [a] faire *or* laisser tremper (**in** dans); **to be/get ~ed to the skin** être trempé/se faire tremper jusqu'aux os *or* comme une soupe*; **to ~ o.s. in the bath** faire trempette dans la baignoire; **bread ~ed in milk** pain m imbibé de lait *or* qui a trempé dans du lait; *(fig)* **he ~ed himself in the atmosphere of Paris** il s'est plongé dans l'atmosphère de Paris [b] (: = *take money from*) *(by overcharging)* estamper*; *(by taxation)* faire payer de lourds impôts à; **the government's policy is to ~ the rich** la politique du gouvernement est de faire casquer* les riches [3] VI [a] tremper; **to put sth in to ~** faire tremper qch, mettre qch à tremper [b] (: = *drink*) boire comme une éponge, avoir la dalle en pente* [4] COMP ► **soak test** N *(Comput)* rodage m

► **soak in** VI [*liquid*] pénétrer, être absorbé

► **soak out** [1] VI [*stain etc*] partir *(au trempage)* [2] VT SEP [+ *stains*] faire partir en trempant

► **soak through** [1] VI [*liquid*] traverser, filtrer au travers [2] VT SEP **to be ~ed through** [*person*] être trempé (jusqu'aux os); [*object, garment*] être trempé

► **soak up** VT SEP *(lit, fig)* absorber

soaking ['səʊkɪŋ] [1] N trempage m; **to get a ~** se faire tremper (jusqu'aux os); **to give sth a ~** faire *or* laisser tremper qch [2] ADJ (*also* **~ wet**) [*person*] trempé (jusqu'aux os); [*object, garment*] trempé

soap [səʊp] [1] N [a] savon m; (* *fig: also* **soft ~**) flatterie(s) f(pl), flagornerie f *(pej)*; *(US fig)* **no ~!:** rien à faire!, des clous!: → **shaving, toilet** [b] **soap opera** [2] VT SEP savonner [3] COMP ► **soap bubble** N bulle f de savon ► **soap opera** N *(fig: Rad, TV)* soap-opéra m, soap* m, feuilleton m mélo* *or* à l'eau de rose ► **soap powder** N lessive f (en poudre), poudre f à laver

► **soap down** VT SEP savonner

soapbox ['səʊpbɒks] [1] N [a] *(lit)* caisse f à savon; *(fig: for speaker)* tribune f improvisée [b] (= *go-cart*) auto f sans moteur (pour enfants), caisse f à savon* [2] COMP ► **soapbox derby** N course f en descente d'autos sans moteur (pour enfants) ► **soapbox orator** N orateur m de carrefour, harangueur m, -euse f de foules ► **soapbox oratory** N harangue(s) f(pl) de démagogue

soapdish ['səʊpdɪʃ] N porte-savon m

soapflakes ['səʊpfleɪks] NPL savon m en paillettes, paillettes fpl de savon

soapstone ['səʊpstəʊn] N stéatite f

soapsuds ['səʊpsʌdz] NPL (= *lather*) mousse f de savon, (= *soapy water*) eau f savonneuse

soapy ['səʊpɪ] ADJ [a] *(lit)* [*water, taste, smell*] savonneux; [*floor, object*] recouvert de savon; [*cloth, hands, face*] plein de savon [b] *(Brit* * = *sentimental*) mièvre

soar [sɔːʳ] VI (*also* **~ up**) [*bird, aircraft*] monter (en flèche); [*ball etc*] voler (**over** par-dessus); *(fig)* [*tower, cathedral*] s'élancer (vers le ciel); [*voice, music*] s'élever (**above** au-dessus de); [*prices, costs, profits*] monter en flèche; [*ambitions, hopes*] grandir démesurément; [*spirits, morale*] remonter en flèche → **send**

► **soar up** VI → **soar**

soaraway* ['sɔːrəweɪ] ADJ [*success, career etc*] fulgurant

soaring ['sɔːrɪŋ] [1] N [*of bird*] essor m; [*of plane*] envol m [2] ADJ [a] (= *increasing*) [*prices, costs, profits, unemployment*] qui monte en flèche; [*inflation*] galopant; **Britain's ~ crime rate** la forte hausse de la criminalité en Grande-Bretagne [b] (= *tall*) [*spire, skyscraper*] qui s'élance vers le ciel

sob [sɒb] [1] N sanglot m; **... he said with a ~ ...** dit-il en un sanglot [2] VI sangloter [3] VT **"no" she ~bed** «non» dit-elle en sanglotant; **to ~ o.s. to sleep** s'endormir à force de sangloter *or* en sanglotant [4] COMP ► **sob sister*** N *(US)* journaliste f qui se spécialise dans les histoires larmoyantes ► **sob story*** N histoire f mélodramatique *or* larmoyante; *(Press etc)* **the main item was a ~ story about a puppy** l'article principal était une histoire à vous fendre le cœur concernant un chiot; **he told us a ~ story about his sister's illness** il a cherché à nous apitoyer *or* à nous avoir au sentiment* en nous parlant de la maladie de sa sœur ► **sob stuff*** N **there's too much ~ stuff in that film** il y a trop de sensiblerie *or* de mélo* dans ce film; **he gave us a lot of ~ stuff** il nous a fait tout un baratin* larmoyant

► **sob out** VT SEP [+ *story*] raconter en sanglotant; *(fig)* **to ~ one's heart out** pleurer à chaudes larmes *or* à gros sanglots

s.o.b.: [ˌesəʊˈbiː] N *(US)* (ABBR = **son of a bitch**) salaud: m, fils m de garce:

sobbing [ˈsɒbɪŋ] ① N sanglots *mpl* ② ADJ sanglotant

sober [ˈsəʊbəʳ] ① ADJ ⓐ (= *not drunk*) pas ivre or soûl ; (= *sobered-up*) dessoûlé* ; **I'm perfectly ~** je ne suis pas du tout soûl ; **he's stone cold ~ ◊ he's (as) ~ as a judge*** il n'est pas du tout soûl ; **are you ~ yet?** tu as dessoûlé ? ⓑ (= *abstinent*) sobre ; **she has been ~ now for three years** cela fait maintenant trois ans qu'elle ne boit plus or qu'elle est sobre ⓒ (= *serious*) [*person, attitude*] pondéré ; [*expression*] grave ; [*assessment, statement, judgement*] mesuré ; [*fact, reality*] sans fard ; **upon ~ reflection** après mûre réflexion ⓓ (= *plain*) [*suit, tie, colour, style*] sobre

② VT ⓐ (*fig: also ~ up*) (= *calm*) calmer ; (= *deflate*) dégriser ⓑ (*also ~ up = stop being drunk*) dessoûler*, désenivrer

③ COMP ► **sober-headed** ADJ [*person*] sérieux, posé ; [*decision*] réfléchi, posé ► **sober-minded** ADJ sérieux, sensé ► **sober-sided** ADJ sérieux, grave, qui ne rit pas souvent

► **sober up** ① VI dessoûler*, désenivrer ② VT SEP = **sober 2**

sobering [ˈsəʊbərɪŋ] ADJ (*fig*) [*experience*] qui fait réfléchir ; **a ~ reminder of sth** un brusque rappel à la réalité de qch ; **it is a ~ thought** cela fait réfléchir ; **it had a ~ effect on him** cela l'a fait réfléchir

soberly [ˈsəʊbəlɪ] ADV ⓐ (= *seriously*) [*speak, behave*] avec pondération ⓑ (= *plainly*) [*dress*] sobrement, avec sobriété

soberness [ˈsəʊbənɪs] N ⓐ (= *seriousness*) pondération *f*, sérieux *m* ⓑ (= *plainness*) [*of style, design*] sobriété *f*

sobersides* [ˈsəʊbəsaɪdz] N bonnet *m* de nuit (*fig*)

sobriety [səˈbraɪətɪ] N ⓐ = **soberness** ⓑ (= *abstinence*) **the struggle for ~** la lutte constante pour rester sobre ; **she maintained her ~ for seven years** elle a réussi à rester sobre pendant sept ans ; (*frm or hum*) **his ~ was in question** on le soupçonnait d'avoir bu

sobriquet [ˈsəʊbrɪkeɪ] N sobriquet *m*

soc. [sɒk] N ABBR = **society**

soccer [ˈsɒkəʳ] ① N football *m*, foot* *m* ② COMP [*match, pitch, team*] de football, de foot* ► **soccer player** N footballeur or footballer *m* ► **soccer season** N saison *f* de football or de foot*

sociability [ˌsəʊʃəˈbɪlɪtɪ] N sociabilité *f*

sociable [ˈsəʊʃəbl] ADJ [*person, mood*] sociable ; **I'll have a drink just to be ~** je vais prendre un verre juste pour vous (or lui *etc*) faire plaisir ; **I'm not feeling very ~ this evening** je n'ai pas envie de voir des gens ce soir

sociably [ˈsəʊʃəblɪ] ADV [*behave*] de façon sociable, aimablement ; [*invite, say*] amicalement

social [ˈsəʊʃəl] ① ADJ ⓐ (*Sociol etc*) [*class, status, problem, customs*] social ; **she's a ~ acquaintance** c'est une relation (personnelle) ; **~ event** or **activity** activité* *f* socioculturelle ; **we work together but we don't have a ~ relationship** nous travaillons ensemble mais nous ne nous voyons pas en dehors du travail ; **he has little ~ contact with his business colleagues** il a peu de contacts avec ses collègues en dehors du travail ; **this isn't a ~ visit** or **call** il ne s'agit pas d'une visite de courtoisie ; **she didn't regard him as her ~ equal** pour elle, il n'appartenait pas au même milieu social ; **~ mobility** mobilité *f* sociale ; **upward ~ mobility** ascension *f* sociale ; **~ research** recherches *fpl* en sciences sociales ; **~ scale** échelle *f* sociale → **3**

ⓑ (*Zool, Anthropology*) [*insect, animal*] social ; **man is a ~ animal** l'homme est un animal social or sociable → **3**

② N (petite) fête *f*

③ COMP ► **social administration** N gestion *f* sociale ► **Social and Liberal Democrats**

N (*Brit Pol*) parti *m* social et libéral-démocrate ► **social anthropologist** N spécialiste *mf* de l'anthropologie sociale ► **social anthropology** N anthropologie *f* sociale ► **social benefits** NPL prestations *fpl* sociales ► **the Social Chapter** N (*Pol*) le chapitre social ► **social circle** N sphère *f* de la société ► **social climber** N (*still climbing*) arriviste *mf* ; (*arrived*) parvenu(e) *m(f)* ► **social climbing** N arrivisme *m* ► **social-climbing** ADJ [*wife*] arriviste ► **social club** N club *m* (de rencontres) ► **social column** N (*Press*) carnet *m* mondain, mondanités *fpl* ► **social conscience** N conscience *f* sociale ► **social contract** N contrat *m* social ► **Social Democracy** N social-démocratie *f* ► **Social Democrat** N social-démocrate *mf* ► **Social Democratic** ADJ social-démocrate ► **Social Democratic and Labour Party** N (*Ir Pol*) parti *m* social-démocrate et travailliste ► **Social Democratic Party** N (*Brit Pol: formerly*) parti *m* social-démocrate ► **social disease** N (*gen*) maladie *f* due à des facteurs socioéconomiques ; (*venereal*) maladie *f* honteuse ► **social drinker** N **to be a ~ drinker** boire seulement en compagnie ► **social drinking** N fait *m* de boire seulement en compagnie ► **social engineering** N manipulation *f* des structures sociales ► **social evening** N soirée *f* (*entre amis*) ► **social fund** N (*Brit*) ≈ fonds *m* de solidarité ► **social gathering** N réunion *f* entre amis ► **social history** N histoire *f* sociale ► **social housing** N (*NonC: Brit*) logements *mpl* sociaux ► **social insurance** N (*US*) sécurité *f* sociale ► **social life** N **to have an active ~ life** (= *go out frequently*) sortir beaucoup ; (= *see people frequently*) voir du monde ; (*in high society*) avoir une vie mondaine active ► **social misfit** N inadapté(e) *m(f)* social(e) ► **social order** N ordre *m* social ► **social realism** N (*Art, Literat*) réalisme *m* social ⓑ = **socialist realism** → **socialist** ► **the social register** N (*US*) ≈ le bottin® mondain ► **social science** N sciences *fpl* humaines ; (*Univ*) **Faculty of Social Science** faculté *f* des sciences humaines ► **social scientist** N spécialiste *mf* des sciences humaines ► **social secretary** N [*of organization*] responsable *mf* des programmes de loisirs ; [*of person*] secrétaire *mf* particulier (-ière) ► **social security** N (*gen*) aide *f* sociale ; (*also ~ security benefits*) prestations *fpl* sociales ; **to be on ~ security** recevoir l'aide sociale ; **Department of Social Security** (*Brit*) ≈ Sécurité *f* sociale ► **Social Security Administration** N (*US*) service des pensions ► **social security card** N (*US*) ≈ carte *f* d'assuré social ► **social security number** N (*US*) numéro *m* de Sécurité sociale ► **social service** N = **social work** ► **social services** NPL services *mpl* sociaux ; **Secretary of State for/Department of Social Services** ministre *m*/ministère *m* des Affaires sociales ► **social skills** NPL savoir-vivre *m inv* ; **to have no ~ skills** ne pas savoir se comporter en société ; **poor ~ skills** manque *m* de savoir-vivre ; **to develop one's ~ skills** améliorer son comportement en société ► **social spending** N dépenses *fpl* d'aide sociale ► **social studies** NPL sciences *fpl* sociales ► **social welfare** N sécurité *f* sociale ► **social work** N assistance *f* sociale ► **social worker** N assistant(e) *m(f)* social(e), travailleur *m*, -euse *f* sociale(e)

┌─────────────────────────┐
│ **SOCIAL SECURITY NUMBER** │
└─────────────────────────┘

Aux États-Unis, le numéro de Sécurité sociale, formé de neuf chiffres, est indispensable pour bénéficier des prestations sociales, mais il est également utilisé de plus en plus comme numéro d'identité à l'échelle nationale : il figure sur les carnets de chèques ; certains États l'utilisent comme numéro de permis de conduire et certaines universités comme numéro d'inscription

des étudiants. Depuis 1987, tous les enfants se voient attribuer un **social security number.**

socialism [ˈsəʊʃəlɪzəm] N socialisme *m*

socialist [ˈsəʊʃəlɪst] ① ADJ socialiste ; **the Socialist Republic of ...** la République socialiste de ... ② N socialiste *mf* ③ COMP ► **socialist realism** N (*Art, Literat*) réalisme *m* socialiste ► **Socialist Workers' Party** N (*in Brit*) parti *m* d'extrême gauche

socialistic [ˌsəʊʃəˈlɪstɪk] ADJ socialisant

socialite [ˈsəʊʃəlaɪt] N mondain(e) *m(f)* ; **a Paris ~** un membre du Tout-Paris

sociality [ˌsəʊʃɪˈælɪtɪ] N socialité *f*, sociabilité *f*

socialization [ˌsəʊʃəlaɪˈzeɪʃən] N socialisation *f* (*Pol*)

socialize [ˈsəʊʃəlaɪz] ① VT (*Pol, Psych*) socialiser ② VI (= *be with people*) fréquenter des gens ; (= *make friends*) se faire des amis ; (= *chat*) s'entretenir, bavarder (**with sb** avec qn)

socializing [ˈsəʊʃəlaɪzɪŋ] **he doesn't like ~** il n'aime pas fréquenter les gens ; **there isn't much ~ on campus** on ne se fréquente pas beaucoup sur le campus

socially [ˈsəʊʃəlɪ] ADV ⓐ (= *not professionally etc*) [*meet, interact*] en société ; **I don't really mix with him ~** je ne fréquente guère (en dehors du travail) ; **to know sb ~** fréquenter qn en dehors du travail ⓑ [*disadvantaged, acceptable, conservative*] socialement ; **~ prominent** en vue dans la société ; **~ superior/inferior** d'un rang social supérieur/inférieur ; **to be ~ aware** or **conscious** avoir conscience des problèmes sociaux ; **~ adept** qui sait se comporter en société ; **to be ~ inadequate** être un(e) inadapté(e) social(e) ; **to be ~ conditioned to do sth** être conditionné par son milieu social à faire qch

societal [səˈsaɪətl] ADJ sociétal

society [səˈsaɪətɪ] ① N ⓐ (= *social community*) société *f* ; **to live in ~** vivre en société ; **for the good of ~** dans l'intérêt social or de la société or de la communauté ; **it is a danger to ~** cela constitue un danger social, cela met la société en danger ; **modern industrial societies** les sociétés *fpl* industrielles modernes ⓑ (*NonC = high society*) (haute) société *f*, grand monde *m* ; **polite ~** la bonne société ; **the years she spent in ~** ses années de vie mondaine ⓒ (*NonC = company, companionship*) société *f*, compagnie *f* ; **in the ~ of ...** dans la société de ..., en compagnie de ... ; **I enjoy his ~** je me plais en sa compagnie, j'apprécie sa compagnie ⓓ (= *organized group*) société *f*, association *f* ; (= *charitable society*) œuvre *f* de charité, association *f* de bienfaisance ; (*Scol, Univ etc*) club *m*, association *f* ; **dramatic ~** club *m* théâtral, association *f* théâtrale ; **learned ~** société *f* savante ; (*Rel*) **the Society of Friends** la Société des Amis, les Quakers *mpl* ; (*Rel*) **the Society of Jesus** la Société de Jésus → **royal**

② COMP [*correspondent, news, photographer, wedding*] mondain, de la haute société ► **society column** N (*Press*) chronique *f* mondaine, carnet *m* mondain

socio... [ˈsəʊsɪəʊ] PREF socio... ; **~cultural** socioculturel ; **~economic** socioéconomique ; **~political** sociopolitique → **sociological**

sociobiology [ˌsəʊsɪəʊbaɪˈɒlədʒɪ] N sociobiologie *f*

sociolect [ˈsəʊsɪəʊˌlekt] N (*Ling*) sociolecte *m*

sociolinguistic [ˌsəʊsɪəʊlɪŋˈɡwɪstɪk] ADJ sociolinguistique

sociolinguistics [ˌsəʊsɪəʊlɪŋˈɡwɪstɪks] N (*NonC*) sociolinguistique *f*

sociological [ˌsəʊsɪəˈlɒdʒɪkəl] ADJ sociologique

sociologically [ˌsəʊsɪəˈlɒdʒɪkəlɪ] ADV [important, significant] sociologiquement

sociologist [ˌsəʊsɪˈɒlədʒɪst] N sociologue mf

sociology [ˌsəʊsɪˈɒlədʒɪ] N sociologie f

sociometry [ˌsəʊsɪˈɒmɪtrɪ] N sociométrie f

sociopath [ˈsəʊsɪəʊpæθ] N inadapté(e) m(f) social(e)

sociopathic [ˌsəʊsɪəʊˈpæθɪk] ADJ socialement inadapté, sociopathe

sock¹ [sɒk] N [a] (pl **socks**) (= short stocking) chaussette f; (shorter) socquette f; (= inner sole) semelle f; (of tooth) alvéole f; (Elec: for light bulb) douille f; (Brit fig) **to pull one's ~s up** se secouer*, faire un effort; (fig) **put a ~ in it!** la ferme!*, ta gueule!*; **this will knock** or **blow your ~s off!*** ça va t'en mettre plein la vue!*; **it knocks the ~s off most science fiction films*** ça dame le pion à la plupart des films de science-fiction; **to work one's ~s off*** s'éreinter (au travail); **to dance/act one's ~s off*** se défoncer* en dansant/jouant, danser/ jouer en se donnant à fond [b] (= windsock) manche f à air

sock²* [sɒk] [1] N (= slap) beigne* f; (= punch) gnon* m; **to give sb a ~ on the jaw** flanquer un coup* or son poing sur la gueule* à qn [2] VT (= strike) flanquer une beigne* or un gnon* à; **~ him one!** cogne dessus!*, fous-lui une beigne!*; **~ it to me!** vas-y envoie!*; **~ it to them!** montre-leur un peu!

sockdolager* [sɒkˈdɒlədʒəʳ] N (US) [a] (= decisive event) coup m décisif [b] (= great person/ thing) personne f/chose f fantastique

socket [ˈsɒkɪt] [1] N (gen) cavité f, trou m (où qch s'emboîte); (of hipbone) cavité f articulaire; (of eye) orbite f; (of tooth) alvéole f; (Elec: for light bulb) douille f; (Elec: also **wall ~**) prise f de courant, prise f femelle; (Carpentry) mortaise f; (in candlestick etc) trou m; **to pull sb's arm out of its ~** désarticuler or démettre l'épaule à qn [2] COMP ▶ **socket joint** N (Tech) joint m à rotule; (Anat) énarthrose f ▶ **socket wrench** N (Tech) clé f à pipe or à douille

socko* [ˈsɒkəʊ] (US) ADJ fantastique, du tonnerre

Socrates [ˈsɒkrətiːz] N Socrate m

Socratic [sɒˈkrætɪk] ADJ socratique

sod¹ [sɒd] N (NonC: = turf) gazon m; (= piece of turf) motte f (de gazon)

sod²** [sɒd] (Brit) [1] N con** m, couillon** m; (pej) salaud* m, salopard* m; **the poor ~s who tried** les pauvres cons** or couillons** or bougres* qui l'ont essayé; **poor little ~!** pauvre petit bonhomme!; **he's a real ~** c'est un salaud* or un salopard*; **~ all** que dalle* [2] VT ~ **it!** merde (alors)!*; ~ **him!** il m'emmerde!**, qu'il aille se faire foutre!** [3] COMP ▶ **Sod's Law** N (Brit) loi f de l'emmerdement* maximum; **that's Sod's Law** un emmerdement* n'arrive jamais seul

▶ **sod off** VI fous le camp!*; ~ **off!** fous le camp!*, va te faire foutre!**

soda [ˈsəʊdə] [1] N [a] (Chem) soude f; (also **washing ~**, ~ **crystals**) soude f du commerce, cristaux mpl (de soude) → **baking**, **caustic** [b] (also ~ **water**) eau f de Seltz; **whisky and ~** whisky m soda or à l'eau de Seltz → **club**, **ice** [c] (US: also ~ **pop**) boisson f gazeuse (sucrée) [2] COMP ▶ **soda ash** N (Chem) soude f du commerce ▶ **soda biscuit** N (US) biscuit m sec à la levure chimique ▶ **soda bread** N pain m irlandais (au bicarbonate) ▶ **soda cracker** N (US) → **soda biscuit** ▶ **soda crystals** NPL → **1a** ▶ **soda fountain** N (US) (= siphon) siphon m d'eau de Seltz; (= place) buvette f ▶ **soda jerk(er)** N (US) serveur m, -euse f (dans une buvette) ▶ **soda pop** N (US) soda m ▶ **soda siphon** N siphon m (d'eau de Seltz) ▶ **soda water** N → **1b**

sodality [səʊˈdælɪtɪ] N camaraderie f; (= association, also Rel) confrérie f

sodden [ˈsɒdn] ADJ [ground] détrempé; [clothes, paper] trempé (**with** de); (fig) ~ **with drink** ◊ **drink-~** abruti par l'alcool

sodding** [ˈsɒdɪŋ] (Brit) [1] ADJ **her ~ dog** son foutu chien*, son putain de chien**; **shut the ~ door!** ferme cette putain de porte!**; **what a ~ disgrace!** c'est une honte, nom de Dieu!*; ~ **hell!** bordel de merde!** [2] ADV **it's ~ difficult** c'est foutrement* difficile; **he's ~ crazy!** il déconne** complètement!

sodium [ˈsəʊdɪəm] [1] N sodium m [2] COMP ▶ **sodium bicarbonate** N bicarbonate m de soude ▶ **sodium carbonate** N carbonate m de sodium ▶ **sodium chloride** N chlorure m de sodium ▶ **sodium light** N lampe f (à vapeur) de sodium ▶ **sodium nitrate** N nitrate m de soude ▶ **sodium sulphate** N sulfate m de soude ▶ **sodium-vapor lamp** N (US) = **sodium light**

Sodom [ˈsɒdəm] N Sodome f

sodomite [ˈsɒdəmaɪt] N sodomite m

sodomize [ˈsɒdəmaɪz] VT sodomiser

sodomy [ˈsɒdəmɪ] N sodomie f

sofa [ˈsəʊfə] [1] N sofa m, canapé m [2] COMP ▶ **sofa bed** N canapé-lit m

Sofia [ˈsəʊfɪə] N Sofia

soft [sɒft] [1] ADJ [a] (= not hard) [ground, snow, butter, penis] mou (molle f); [fabric, skin, hand, breasts, body] doux (douce f); [food, bread, fruit, pencil, wood] tendre; [bed, carpet, texture] moelleux; [fur, hair, beard] soyeux; [brush, toothbrush] doux (douce f), souple; [leather] souple; **as ~ as silk** or **velvet** doux comme (de) la soie; **to get** or **become ~(er)** [ground, pitch] devenir mou; [butter] se ramollir; [leather] s'assouplir; [skin] s'adoucir; **to make ~(er)** [+ leather] assouplir; [+ skin] adoucir; **to go ~** [onions, biscuits] ramollir → **4**; → **roe²**, **soap**, **solder** [b] (= gentle, not intense) [breeze, wind, kiss, light, colour] doux (douce f); [rain, touch, tap] léger; [accent] mélodieux; [lighting] doux (douce f), tamisé [c] (= quiet) [sound, voice, laugh, music] doux (douce f); **the music is too ~** la musique n'est pas assez forte, on n'entend pas assez la musique [d] (in shape) [outline, lines] doux (douce f); [pleat, fold] souple [e] (pej = unfit) [person, body, muscles] mou (molle f); **this sort of life makes you ~** ce genre de vie vous ramollit; **to get** or **go ~** [body] s'avachir; [muscles] se ramollir [f] (= kind) [person] doux (douce f); **she had another, ~er side to her** il y avait une autre facette, plus douce, de sa personnalité; **to have a ~ heart** avoir le cœur tendre [g] (pej = lenient) [person] indulgent; [sentence] léger; **to get ~** [person] devenir trop indulgent or trop bon; **to be (too) ~ on sb** être trop indulgent envers qn; **to be (too) ~ on sth** [+ crime, drugs] être trop laxiste en matière de qch; **to go ~ (on sth)** devenir plus laxiste (en matière de qch); **to have a ~ spot for sb/sth** avoir un faible pour qn/qch; **to be a ~ touch*** être une (bonne) poire* [h] (= moderate) [approach] modéré; **to take a ~ line (on sth)** adopter une ligne modérée (en matière de qch); (Pol) **the ~ left** la gauche modérée [i] (* = easy) [life, job] pépère, peinard*; **to take the ~ option** choisir la solution de facilité [j] (* = stupid) **to be ~ in the head** (= stupid) avoir le cerveau ramolli*; (= mad) avoir perdu la boule*; (= senile) être gâteux [k] **to be ~ on sb†*** (= attracted to) avoir le béguin† * pour qn [l] [water] non calcaire, doux [m] (Ling) [consonant] doux (douce f) [n] (Econ, Fin, St Ex) [prices, stocks, market] mou (molle f), qui tend à la baisse; [economy] amorphe; [currency] faible; **sales are ~** les

ventes ne marchent pas très fort; ~ **loan** prêt m à taux bonifié [2] ADV [a] (liter = quietly) doucement [b] (= stupidly) **don't talk ~!** tu dis n'importe quoi! [3] EXCL †† (= wait) un instant!; (= be quiet) silence! [4] COMP ▶ **soft-boiled egg** N œuf m à la coque ▶ **soft-bound book** N livre m broché; (= paperback) livre m de poche ▶ **soft brown sugar** N sucre m roux ▶ **soft centre** N (Brit) chocolat m fourré ▶ **soft-centred** ADJ (Brit) [a] [chocolate, boiled sweet] fourré [b] (fig pej) à l'eau de rose ▶ **soft cheese** N fromage m à pâte molle ▶ **soft coal** N houille f grasse ▶ **soft contact lens** N lentille f (de contact) souple ▶ **soft copy** N (Comput) visualisation f sur écran ▶ **soft-core** ADJ [pornography] soft* inv ▶ **soft-cover** ADJ → **softback** ▶ **soft currency** N (Fin) devise f faible ▶ **soft drinks** NPL boissons fpl non alcoolisées ▶ **soft drugs** NPL drogues fpl douces ▶ **soft focus** N (Phot) flou m artistique ▶ **soft-focus** ADJ (Phot) [image, picture] (artistiquement) flou; (Phot) ~**-focus filter** filtre m pour flou artistique; (Phot) ~**-focus lens** objectif m pour flou artistique ▶ **soft-footed** ADJ à la démarche légère, qui marche à pas feutrés or sans faire de bruit ▶ **soft fruit** N (Brit) baies fpl comestibles, ≈ fruits mpl rouges ▶ **soft furnishings** NPL (Brit Comm) tissus mpl d'ameublement (rideaux, tentures, housses etc) ▶ **soft goods** NPL (Brit Comm) textiles mpl, tissus mpl ▶ **soft hat** N chapeau m mou ▶ **soft-headed*** ADJ faible d'esprit, cinglé* ▶ **soft-hearted** ADJ au cœur tendre, compatissant ▶ **soft ice-cream** N glace f à l'italienne ▶ **soft iron** N fer m doux ▶ **soft landing** N (Aviat, Space) atterrissage m en douceur ▶ **soft margarine** N margarine f ultra-légère ▶ **soft palate** N (Anat) voile m du palais ▶ **soft pedal** N (Mus) pédale f douce ▶ **soft-pedal** VI (Mus) mettre la pédale douce ◆ VT (esp US fig) ne pas trop insister sur ▶ **soft pencil** N crayon m à mine grasse ▶ **soft porn** N soft porn m ▶ **soft sell** N (Comm) technique f (de vente) non agressive; (fig) **he's a master of the ~ sell** il est maître dans l'art de persuader les clients en douceur ▶ **soft-shelled** ADJ [egg, mollusc] à coquille molle; [crustacean, turtle] à carapace molle ▶ **soft shoulder** N [road] accotement m non stabilisé ▶ **soft soap** N (lit) savon m vert; (* fig pej = flattery) flatterie f ▶ **soft-soap*** VT (fig pej) caresser dans le sens du poil*, passer de la pommade à ▶ **soft-spoken** ADJ à la voix douce ▶ **soft steel** N acier m doux ▶ **soft target** N cible f facile ▶ **soft toilet paper** N papier m hygiénique doux ▶ **soft top** N (Aut) décapotable f ▶ **soft toy** N (jouet m en) peluche f ▶ **soft verge** N (Aut) accotement m non stabilisé ▶ **soft X-rays** NPL rayons mpl X diffus

softback [ˈsɒftbæk] N livre m broché; (= paperback) livre m de poche

softball [ˈsɒftbɔːl] N (US) sorte de base-ball, softball m

soften [ˈsɒfn] [1] VT [+ butter, clay, ground, pitch] (r)amollir; [+ colour, leather] assouplir; [+ skin, colour, outline] adoucir; [+ sound] adoucir, atténuer; [+ lights, lighting] adoucir, tamiser; [+ pain, anxiety] atténuer; [+ sb's anger, reaction, effect, impression] adoucir, atténuer; [+ resistance] amoindrir, réduire; (fig) **to ~ the blow** adoucir or amortir le choc [2] VI [butter, clay, ground, pitch] devenir mou (molle f), se ramollir; [collar, leather] s'assouplir; [skin] s'adoucir; [colour] s'adoucir, s'atténuer; [sb's anger] s'atténuer; **his heart ~ed at the sight of her** il s'attendrit en la voyant; **his eyes ~ed as he looked at her** son regard s'est adouci à sa vue

▶ **soften up** [1] VI [butter, clay, ground, pitch] devenir mou, se ramollir; [collar, leather]

s'assouplir; [skin] s'adoucir; (= grow less stern) s'adoucir; **we must not ~ up towards** or **on these offenders** nous ne devons pas faire preuve d'indulgence envers ces délinquants [2] VT SEP [a] [+ butter, clay, pitch, ground] (r)amollir; [+ collar, leather] assouplir; [+ skin] adoucir [b] [+ person] attendrir; (*: by cajoling) [+ customer etc] bonimenter*, baratiner*; (*: by bullying) intimider, malmener; [+ resistance, opposition] réduire; (Mil: by bombing etc) affaiblir par bombardement intensif

softener ['sɒfnər] N (also **water ~**) adoucisseur m; (also **fabric ~**) produit m assouplissant

softening ['sɒfnɪŋ] N [a] [of leather] assouplissement m; [of skin] adoucissement m [b] (Med) **~ of the brain** ramollissement m cérébral [c] (= moderating) [of attitude, position, policy] assouplissement m [d] (Ling) [of consonant] adoucissement m

softie* ['sɒftɪ] N (too tender-hearted) tendre mf; (no stamina etc) mauviette f, mollasson(ne) m(f); (= coward) poule f mouillée, dégonflé(e)* m(f); **you silly ~, stop crying!** ne pleure plus, grand(e) nigaud(e)!

softly ['sɒftlɪ] [1] ADV [a] (= quietly) [say, call, sing, whistle] doucement; [swear] à voix basse; [walk] à pas feutrés; **a ~ spoken man** un homme à la voix douce [b] (= gently) [touch, tap] légèrement; [kiss] tendrement [c] (= not brightly) [shine, gleam, gleam] faiblement; **~ lit** à la lumière tamisée [2] COMP ► **softly-softly** ADJ précautionneux; **he adopted a ~-~ approach** il a pris beaucoup de précautions

softness ['sɒftnɪs] N [a] [of ground, snow, butter] mollesse f; [of fabric, skin, hand, breasts, body] douceur f; [of bread, wood, fruit] tendreté f; [of bed, carpet] moelleux m; [of fur, hair, beard] soyeux m; [of brush, toothbrush, leather] souplesse f; **the ~ of its consistency** sa consistance moelleuse [b] (= gentleness) [of breeze, wind, kiss] douceur f; [of rain, touch, tap] légèreté f [c] (= lack of brightness) [of light, lighting, colour] douceur f [d] (= quietness) [of sound, accent, laugh, music] douceur f [e] (in shape) [of outline, lines] douceur f; [of pleat, fold] souplesse f [f] (pej = unfitness) [of person, body, muscles] mollesse f [g] (= leniency) [of person] indulgence f; [of sentence] légèreté f [h] (= moderation) [of approach, line] modération f [i] (* = easiness) [of life, job] tranquillité f [j] (* = stupidity) débilité f; **~ in the head** (= stupidity, madness) débilité f; (= senility) gâtisme m [k] [of water] douceur f

software ['sɒft,wɛər] (Comput) [1] N (NonC) software* m, logiciel m [2] COMP ► **software engineer** N ingénieur-conseil m en informatique, ingénieur m (en) logiciel ► **software engineering** N génie m logiciel ► **software house** N société f de services et de conseils en informatique, SSCI f ► **software library** N logithèque f ► **software package** N progiciel m

softwood ['sɒftwʊd] N bois m tendre

softy* ['sɒftɪ] N = **softie**

soggy ['sɒgɪ] ADJ [clothes] trempé; [ground] détrempé; [vegetables, pasta] trop cuit, ramolli; [bread] pâteux, ramolli

soh [səʊ] N (Mus) sol m

soil¹ [sɔɪl] N sol m, terre f; **rich/chalky ~** sol m or terre f riche/calcaire; **cover it over with ~** recouvre-le de terre; (liter) **a man of the ~** un terrien, un homme de la terre; (fig) **my native ~** ma terre natale, mon pays natal; **on French ~** sur le sol français, en territoire français

soil² [sɔɪl] [1] VT (lit) salir; (fig) [+ reputation, honour] souiller (frm); **this dress is easily ~ed** cette robe se salit vite or est salissante; **~ed**

linen linge m sale; (Comm) **~ed copy/item** exemplaire m/article m défraîchi → **shop-soiled** [2] VI [material, garment] se salir, être salissant [3] N (= excrement) excréments mpl, ordures fpl; (= sewage) vidange f [4] COMP ► **soil pipe** N tuyau m d'écoulement; (vertical) tuyau m de descente

soirée ['swɑːreɪ] N soirée f

sojourn ['sɒdʒɜːn] (liter) [1] N séjour m [2] VI séjourner, faire un séjour

solace ['sɒlɪs] (liter) [1] N consolation f, réconfort m; **to be a ~ to sb** être un réconfort pour qn [2] VT [+ person] consoler; [+ pain] soulager, adoucir

solanum [səʊ'leɪnəm] N solanacée f

solar ['səʊlər] [1] ADJ solaire [2] COMP ► **solar battery** N batterie f solaire, photopile f ► **solar calendar** N calendrier m solaire ► **solar cell** N pile f solaire, photopile f ► **solar collector** N capteur m solaire ► **solar eclipse** N éclipse f de soleil ► **solar flare** N facule f solaire ► **solar furnace** N four m solaire ► **solar heating** N chauffage m (à l'énergie) solaire ► **solar panel** N panneau m solaire ► **solar plexus** (Anat) plexus m solaire ► **solar power** N énergie f solaire ► **solar system** N système m solaire ► **solar wind** N vent m solaire ► **solar year** N année f solaire

solarium [səʊ'lɛərɪəm] N (pl **solariums** or **solaria** [səʊ'lɛərɪə]) solarium m

sold [səʊld] VB pt, ptp of **sell**

solder ['səʊldər] [1] N soudure f; **hard ~** brasure f; **soft ~** claire soudure f [2] VT souder [3] COMP ► **soldering iron** N fer m à souder

soldier ['səʊldʒər] [1] N [a] soldat m (also fig), militaire m; **woman ~** femme f soldat; **~s and civilians** les militaires mpl et (les) civils mpl; **Montgomery was a great ~** Montgomery était un grand homme de guerre or un grand soldat; **he wants to be a ~** il veut se faire soldat or être militaire de carrière or entrer dans l'armée; **to play (at) ~s** (pej) jouer à la guerre; [children] jouer aux soldats; **~ of fortune** soldat m de fortune, mercenaire m; **old ~** vétéran m → **foot, private** [b] (Brit* = finger of bread or toast) mouillette f [2] VI servir dans l'armée, être soldat; **he ~ed for ten years in the East** il a servi (dans l'armée) pendant dix ans en Orient; **after six years' ~ing** après six ans de service dans l'armée; **to be tired of ~ing** en avoir assez d'être soldat or d'être dans l'armée [3] COMP ► **soldier ant** N (fourmi f) soldat m

► **soldier on** VI (Brit fig) persévérer (malgré tout)

soldierly ['səʊldʒəlɪ] ADJ [values, bravery, discipline] de soldat; [person] à l'allure militaire

soldiery ['səʊldʒərɪ] N (collective) soldats mpl, militaires mpl

sole¹ [səʊl] N (pl **sole** or **soles**) (= fish) sole f → **Dover, lemon**

sole² [səʊl] [1] N [of shoe, sock, stocking] semelle f; [of foot] plante f → **inner** [2] VT ressemeler; **to have one's shoes ~d** faire ressemeler ses chaussures; **crepe-/rubber-/leather-~d** avec semelles de crêpe/caoutchouc/cuir

sole³ [səʊl] [1] ADJ [a] (= only, single) unique, seul; **for the ~ purpose of** ... dans l'unique or le seul but de ...; **the ~ reason** la seule or l'unique raison; **their ~ surviving daughter** la seule de leurs filles qui soit encore en vie [b] (= exclusive) [right, possession] exclusif; [responsibility] entier; [heir] universel; [owner] unique; **for the ~ use of** ... à l'usage exclusif de ...; **to have ~ ownership of sth** être l'unique propriétaire de qch; (Comm) **~ supplier** fournisseur m exclusif [2] COMP ► **sole agent** N (Comm) concessionnaire mf exclusif(-ive), dépositaire mf exclusif(-ive); **~ agent for Australia/for Col-**

lins dictionaries distributeur m exclusif en Australie/des dictionnaires Collins ► **sole beneficiary** N (Jur) légataire m universel ► **sole legatee** N (Jur) légataire mf universel(le) ► **sole stockholder** N unique actionnaire mf ► **sole trader** N (Comm) gérant m or propriétaire m unique

solecism ['sɒlɪsɪzəm] N (Ling) solécisme m; (= social offence) manque m de savoir-vivre, faute f de goût

solei ['sɒlɪaɪ] NPL of **soleus**

solely ['səʊllɪ] ADV uniquement; **to be ~ responsible for sth** être seul(e) responsable de qch; **I am ~ to blame** je suis seul coupable, c'est entièrement de ma faute

solemn ['sɒləm] ADJ [mood, occasion, promise, music, warning] solennel; [silence] plein de solennité or de gravité; [face, expression] grave; [person] grave, solennel; **it is my ~ duty to inform you that** ... il est de mon devoir de vous informer que ... (frm)

solemnity [sə'lemnɪtɪ] N [a] (NonC = solemnness) [of person, tone, occasion, music] solennité f [b] (= occasion) solennité f; **the solemnities** les solennités fpl

solemnization ['sɒləmnar'zeɪʃən] N [of marriage] célébration f

solemnize ['sɒləmnaɪz] VT [+ marriage] célébrer; [+ occasion, event] solenniser

solemnly ['sɒləmlɪ] ADV [swear, promise, utter] solennellement; [say] gravement, d'un ton solennel; [smile, nod, look at] gravement

solenoid ['səʊlənɔɪd] N (Elec) solénoïde m

soleus ['sɒlɪəs] N (pl **solei**) muscle m soléaire

sol-fa ['sɒl'fɑː] N (also **tonic ~**) solfège m

soli ['səʊlɪ] NPL of **solo**

solicit [sə'lɪsɪt] [1] VT solliciter (**sb for sth, sth from sb** qch de qn); [+ vote] solliciter, briguer; [+ alms] quémander [2] VI [prostitute] racoler

solicitation [sə,lɪsɪ'teɪʃən] N sollicitation f

soliciting [sə'lɪsɪtɪŋ] N racolage m

solicitor [sə'lɪsɪtər] [1] N [a] (Jur) (Brit) (for sales, wills etc) ≈ notaire m; (in divorce, police, court cases) ≈ avocat m; (US) ≈ juriste m conseil or avocat m conseil attaché à une municipalité etc [b] (US) (for contribution) solliciteur m, -euse f; (for trade) courtier m, placier m [2] COMP ► **Solicitor General** N (pl **Solicitors General**) (Brit) adjoint m du procureur général; (US) adjoint m du ministre de la Justice

solicitous [sə'lɪsɪtəs] ADJ (frm) plein de sollicitude (**of sb** envers qn); **to be ~ of sb's interests/wishes** se soucier des intérêts/désirs de qn

solicitously [sə'lɪsɪtəslɪ] ADV (frm) avec sollicitude

solicitude [sə'lɪsɪtjuːd] N (frm) sollicitude f

solid ['sɒlɪd] [1] ADJ [a] (= not liquid or gas) solide; **~ food** aliments mpl solides; **to freeze ~** (gen) geler; [water, lake, pond, pipes] geler; [oil] se congeler; **frozen ~** complètement gelé; **to go** or **become ~** se solidifier → **2** [b] (= not hollow or plated) [tyre, ball, block] plein; [layer, mass] compact; [rock, oak, mahogany, gold, silver etc] massif; **the chain is made of ~ gold** la chaîne est en or massif; **the door is made of ~ steel** la porte est tout en acier; **cut in** or **out of (the) ~ rock** taillé à même le roc or dans la masse; **the garden was a ~ mass of colour** le jardin resplendissait d'une profusion de couleurs; **the square was ~ with cars*** la place était complètement embouteillée; **the room was ~ with people*** la pièce était noire de monde → **4** [c] (= continuous) [row, line] continu, ininterrompu; [rain] ininterrompu; **he was six foot six of ~ muscle** c'était un homme de deux mètres tout en muscles; **I waited a ~ hour** j'ai attendu une heure entière; **he slept**

18 ~ hours il a dormi 18 heures d'affilée; **they worked for two ~ days** ils ont travaillé deux jours sans s'arrêter or sans relâche; **it will take a ~ day's work** cela exigera une journée entière de travail; **a rug like this would take three ~ weeks to make** un tapis comme celui-ci demande bien trois semaines de travail [d] (= *substantial, reliable*) [*building, bridge, structure, grip, basis, relationship, majority, evidence, reasons*] solide; [*meal*] consistant; [*scholarship, piece of work, character, advice*] sérieux; [*support*] indéfectible, ferme; [*gains*] substantiel; [*information*] sûr; **a ~ grounding in mathematics** des connaissances or des bases solides en mathématiques; **a man of ~ build** un homme solidement or bien bâti; **a ~ citizen** un bon citoyen; **~ middle-class values** les bonnes valeurs *fpl* bourgeoises; (*US Pol, Hist*) **the Solid South** *États du Sud des États-Unis qui, depuis la guerre de Sécession, votaient traditionnellement pour le parti démocrate*; **(as) ~ as a rock** (*lit*) [*structure, substance*] dur comme la pierre; (*fig*) [*person*] solide comme un roc; [*relationship*] indestructible → **rock²**; → **ground¹** [e] (*US*⸸ = *excellent*) super*

[2] ADV **jammed ~** complètement bloqué or coincé; **rusted ~** bloqué par la rouille, complètement rouillé; **he was stuck ~ in the mud** il était complètement enlisé dans la boue; **packed ~ (with people)** noir de monde; **to be booked ~ (for three weeks)** [*hotel, venue, performer etc*] être complet (pendant trois semaines); **he slept for 18 hours ~** il a dormi 18 heures d'affilée; **they worked for two days ~** ils ont travaillé deux jours de suite sans s'arrêter or sans relâche

[3] N (*gen, Chem, Math, Phys*) solide *m*; (= *food*) **~s** aliments *mpl* solides

[4] COMP ► **solid angle** N (*Math*) angle *m* solide ► **solid compound** N (*Ling*) mot *m* composé ► **solid figure** N (*Math*) solide *m* ► **solid fuel** N (= *coal etc*) combustible *m* solide; (*for rockets etc: also* ► **propellant**) propergol *m* solide ► **solid-fuel heating** N chauffage *m* central au charbon or à combustibles solides ► **solid geometry** N (*Math*) géométrie *f* dans l'espace ► **solid propellant** N → **solid fuel** ► **solid-state** ADJ [*physics*] des solides; [*electronic device*] à circuits intégrés ► **solid word** N (*Ling*) mot *m* simple

solidarity [ˌsɒlɪ'dærɪtɪ] N (*NonC*) solidarité *f*; (*Ind*) **~ strike** grève *f* de solidarité

solidi ['sɒlɪˌdaɪ] NPL *of* **solidus**

solidification [səˌlɪdɪfɪ'keɪʃən] N [*of liquid, gas*] solidification *f*; [*of oil*] congélation *f*

solidify [sə'lɪdɪfaɪ] [1] VT [+ *liquid, gas*] solidifier; [+ *oil*] congeler [2] VI se solidifier, se congeler

solidity [sə'lɪdɪtɪ] N solidité *f*

solidly ['sɒlɪdlɪ] ADV [a] (= *firmly*) [*made, constructed*] solidement; **~ built** [*structure*] solidement construit; [*person*] solidement or bien bâti; **Russia was ~ under communist rule** le communisme exerçait fermement son emprise sur la Russie; **the idea was ~ based on the best psychological theory** cette idée était solidement fondée sur la meilleure théorie psychologique [b] (= *continuously*) sans arrêt [c] [*vote*] massivement, en masse; **to be ~ behind sb/sth** soutenir qn/qch sans réserve; **a ~ middle-class area** un quartier tout ce qu'il y a de bourgeois; **the district of Morningside is ~ Conservative** le quartier de Morningside est un bastion conservateur

solidus ['sɒlɪdəs] N (*pl* **solidi**) (*Typ*) barre *f* oblique

soliloquize [sə'lɪləkwaɪz] VI soliloquer, monologuer; **"perhaps" he ~d** « peut-être » dit-il, se parlant à lui-même

soliloquy [sə'lɪləkwɪ] N soliloque *m*, monologue *m*

solipsism ['sɒlɪpsɪzəm] N solipsisme *m*

solitaire [ˌsɒlɪ'tɛəʳ] N [a] (= *stone, board game*) solitaire *m* [b] (*US Cards*) réussite *f*, patience *f*

solitariness [ˈsɒlɪtərɪnɪs] N [*of life, task*] solitude *f*

solitary ['sɒlɪtərɪ] [1] ADJ [a] (= *lone, lonely*) [*person, life, activity, childhood*] solitaire; [*place*] solitaire, retiré; **a ~ hour** une heure de solitude; **a ~ journey** un voyage en solitaire; **she ate a ~ dinner** elle a pris son dîner seule or en solitaire; **in ~ splendour** dans un splendide isolement [b] (= *sole*) seul, unique; **one ~ tourist** un seul or unique touriste; **with the ~ exception of ...** à la seule or l'unique exception de ...; **not a ~ one*** pas un seul [2] N* = **solitary confinement** [3] COMP ► **solitary confinement** N **(in) ~ confinement** (*Jur*) (en) isolement *m* cellulaire

solitude ['sɒlɪtjuːd] N solitude *f*

solo ['səʊləʊ] (*pl* **solos** or **soli**) [1] N [a] (*Mus*) solo *m*; **piano ~** solo *m* de piano [b] (*Cards: also ~ whist*) whist-solo *m* [2] ADV [*play, sing*] en solo; [*fly*] en solo, en solitaire; **he left the band to go ~** il a quitté le groupe pour entamer une carrière (en solo) [3] ADJ [*instrument, album, artist*] solo *inv*; [*performance*] en solo; [*voice*] seul; [*flight, crossing, journey*] en solitaire; **a ~ piece** or **passage** un solo; **his ~ career** sa carrière (en) solo

soloist ['səʊləʊɪst] N soliste *mf*

Solomon ['sɒləmən] [1] N Salomon *m*; **the judgement of ~** le jugement de Salomon → **song** [2] COMP ► **the Solomon Islands** NPL les îles *fpl* Salomon

solon ['səʊlən] N (*US*) législateur *m*

solstice ['sɒlstɪs] N solstice *m*; **summer/winter ~** solstice *m* d'été/d'hiver

solubility [ˌsɒljʊ'bɪlɪtɪ] N solubilité *f*

soluble ['sɒljʊbl] ADJ [*substance*] soluble; [*problem*] résoluble, soluble → **water**

solus ['səʊləs] ADJ (*Advertising*) [*advertisement, site, position*] isolé [2] N annonce *f* isolée

▼ **solution** [sə'luːʃən] N [a] (*to problem etc*) solution *f* (**to** de) [b] (*Chem*) (= *act*) solution *f*, dissolution *f*; (= *liquid*) solution *f*; (*Pharm*) solution *f*, soluté *m*; **in ~** en solution → **rubber¹**

solvable ['sɒlvəbl] ADJ soluble, résoluble

solve [sɒlv] VT [+ *equation, difficulty, problem*] résoudre; [+ *crossword puzzle*] réussir; [+ *murder*] élucider, trouver l'auteur de; [+ *mystery*] élucider; **to ~ a riddle** trouver la solution d'une énigme or d'une devinette, trouver la clef d'une énigme; **that question remains to be ~d** cette question est encore en suspens

solvency ['sɒlvənsɪ] N solvabilité *f*

solvent ['sɒlvənt] [1] ADJ [a] (*Fin*) [*company, client*] solvable [b]* [*person*] qui a une bonne situation [c] (*Chem*) dissolvant [2] N (*Chem*) solvant *m*, dissolvant *m* [3] COMP ► **solvent abuse** N usage *m* de solvants

Solzhenitsyn [ˌsɒlʒə'nɪtsɪn] N Soljenitsyne *m*

Som. ABBR = **Somerset**

soma ['səʊmə] N (*pl* **somas** or **somata**) (*Physiol*) soma *m*

Somali [səʊ'mɑːlɪ] [1] ADJ (*gen*) somalien, somali; [*ambassador, embassy*] de Somalie [2] N [a] Somali(e) *m(f)*, Somalien(ne) *m(f)* [b] (*Ling*) somali *m*

Somalia [səʊ'mɑːlɪə] N la Somalie

Somaliland [səʊ'mɑːlɪlænd] N le Somaliland

somata ['səʊmətə] NPL *of* **soma**

somatic [səʊ'mætɪk] ADJ somatique

sombre, somber (*US*) ['sɒmbəʳ] ADJ [*colour, clothes, mood, outlook, prediction, prospect*] sombre; [*person, thoughts, expression, voice*] sombre, morne; [*message, speech, news*] pessimiste; [*day, weather*] morne, maussade; [*atmosphere*] lugubre; **on a ~ note** sur un ton pessimiste; **to be in a ~ mood** être d'humeur sombre; **her face grew ~** son visage s'assombrit

sombrely, somberly (*US*) ['sɒmbəlɪ] ADV [*say*] d'un ton morne; [*look, nod*] d'un air sombre; **~ dressed** habillé de sombre

sombreness, somberness (*US*) ['sɒmbənɪs] N caractère *m* or aspect *m* sombre; (= *colour*) couleur *f* sombre; (= *darkness*) obscurité *f*

sombrero [sɒm'brɛərəʊ] N sombrero *m*

---

some [sʌm]

[1] ADJECTIVE		[3] ADVERB
[2] PRONOUN		

[1] ADJECTIVE

[a] = **a certain amount of, a little**   du, de la, de l'; **~ tea/ice cream/water** du thé/de la glace/de l'eau; **have you got ~ money?** est-ce que tu as de l'argent?; **will you have ~ more meat?** voulez-vous encore de la viande or encore un peu de viande?

[b] = **a certain number of**   des; **~ cakes** des gâteaux; **there are ~ children outside** il y a des enfants dehors; **I haven't seen him for ~ years** cela fait des années que je ne l'ai pas vu

Before an adjective **de** *is often used without the article:*

~ wonderful memories de merveilleux souvenirs; **I found ~ small mistakes** j'ai trouvé de petites erreurs

[c] **indefinite** un, une; **~ woman was asking for her** il y avait une dame qui la demandait; **give it to ~ child** donnez-le à un enfant; **there must be ~ solution** il doit bien y avoir une solution; **~ other day** un autre jour; **at ~ restaurant in London** dans un restaurant de Londres; **~ time last week** (un jour) la semaine dernière; **in ~ way or (an)other** d'une façon ou d'une autre; **~ other time maybe!** une autre fois peut-être!; **~ day** un de ces jours, un jour (ou l'autre); *BUT* **~ more talented person** quelqu'un de plus doué; **I read it in ~ book (or other)** je l'ai lu quelque part dans un livre

[d] = **a certain** if you are worried about **~ aspect** of your health ... si un aspect quelconque de votre santé vous préoccupe ...

[e] **as opposed to others** **~ children like school** certains enfants aiment l'école; **~ coffee is bitter** certains cafés sont amers; **in ~ ways, he's right** dans un sens, il a raison; **~ people like spinach, others don't** certains aiment les épinards, d'autres pas, il y a des gens qui aiment les épinards et d'autres non; **~ people just don't care** il y a des gens qui ne s'en font pas; **~ people say that ...** il y a des gens qui disent que ..., on dit que ...; (*in exasperation*) **~ people!** il y en a qui exagèrent!, il y a des gens, je vous jure!

[f] = **a considerable amount of** **it took ~ courage to do that!** il a fallu du courage pour faire ça!; **he spoke at ~ length** il a parlé assez longuement; **it's a matter of ~ importance** c'est une question assez importante; **~ distance away, a shepherd was shouting to his dog** au loin, un berger criait après son chien

[g] = **a limited** **this will give you ~ idea of ...** cela vous donnera une petite idée de ...; **that's ~ consolation!** c'est quand même une consolation!; **surely there's ~ hope she will recover?** il doit quand même y avoir une chance qu'elle guérisse?; **the book was ~ help, but not much** le livre m'a aidé un peu mais pas beaucoup

[h] *: **in exclamations** (*admiring*) **that's ~ fish!** ça c'est ce qu'on appelle un poisson!; **she's ~ girl!** c'est une fille formidable!*; **that was ~ party!** ça a été une super fête!*; (*iro*) **you're ~ help!** tu parles d'une aide!*; (*iro*) **I'm trying to help! — ~ help!** j'essaie de t'aider! — tu parles!*; (*iro*) **he says he's my friend — ~ friend!** il dit être mon ami — drôle d'ami!*

[2] PRONOUN

[a] = **as opposed to others** certain(e)s *m(f)pl*; **~ cheered, others shouted questions** certains

applaudissaient, d'autres posaient des questions en criant à tue-tête ; **~ of my friends** certains de mes amis

Note the use of **d'entre** *with personal pronouns:* **~ of them were late** certains d'entre eux étaient en retard ; **~ of us knew him** certains d'entre nous le connaissaient

[b] **as opposed to all of them** quelques-un(e)s *m(f)pl* ; **I don't want them all, but I'd like ~** je les veux pas tous mais j'en voudrais quelques-uns

Even if not expressed, **of them** *must be translated in French, by* **en:** **I've still got ~** (of them) j'en ai encore quelques-uns ; **~ (of them) have been sold** on en a vendu quelques-uns *or* un certain nombre

[c] **= a certain amount or number: when object of the verb** en ; **I've got ~** j'en ai ; **have ~!** prenez-en ! ; **have ~ more** reprenez-en ; **give me ~!** donnez-m'en ! ; **if you find ~ tell me** si vous en trouvez dites-le-moi ; **do you want stamps? — it's okay, I've got ~** est-ce que tu as besoin de timbres ? — non, ça va, j'en ai

[d] **= a part** une partie ; **~ (of it) has been eaten** on en a mangé une partie ; **put ~ of the sauce into a bowl** versez une partie de la sauce dans un bol ; [BUT] **have ~ of this cake** prenez un peu de gâteau ; **~ of this essay is interesting** cette dissertation est intéressante par endroits, il y a des choses intéressantes dans cette dissertation ; **I agree with ~ of what you said** je suis d'accord avec certaines des choses que vous avez dites ; **~ of what you say is true** il y a du vrai dans ce que vous dites

♦ **... and then some*** : it would cost twice that much and then ~ ça coûterait deux fois plus et même davantage ; **they accomplished all their objectives, and then ~** ils ont atteint tous leurs objectifs et les ont même dépassés

[3] **ADVERB**

[a] **= about** environ ; **there were ~ twenty houses** il y avait environ vingt maisons, il y avait une vingtaine de maisons

[b] **esp US* = a bit** **you'll feel better when you've slept ~** tu te sentiras mieux une fois que tu auras dormi un peu ; **I'll kill time by looking round ~** en attendant, je vais faire un petit tour

[c] * : **emphatic** that's going ~! c'est quelque chose ! ; **Edinburgh-London in five hours, that's going ~!** Édimbourg-Londres en cinq heures, c'est quelque chose !

...some [səm] N (*in compounds*) groupe *m* de ... ; **threesome** groupe de trois personnes ; **we went in a threesome** nous y sommes allés à trois → **foursome**

somebody ['sʌmbədɪ] PRON [a] (= *some unspecified person*) quelqu'un ; **there is ~ at the door** il y a quelqu'un à la porte ; **there is ~ knocking at the door** on frappe à la porte ; **~ else** quelqu'un d'autre ; **he was talking to ~ tall and dark** il parlait à quelqu'un de grand aux cheveux sombres ; **we need ~ really strong to do that** il nous faut quelqu'un de vraiment fort *or* quelqu'un qui soit vraiment fort pour faire cela ; **ask ~ French** demande à un Français (quelconque) ; **they've got French staying with them** ils ont un Français *or* quelqu'un de français chez eux en ce moment ; **~ from the audience** quelqu'un dans l'auditoire *or* l'assemblée ; **~ or other** quelqu'un, je ne sais qui ; (*hum*) **~ up here loves me*/hates me*** c'est/ce n'est pas mon jour de veine* ; **Mr Somebody-or-other** Monsieur Chose *or* Machin* ; **you must have seen ~!** tu as bien dû voir quelqu'un !

[b] (= *important person*) personnage *m* important ; **she thinks she's ~** elle se prend pour quelqu'un, elle se croit quelqu'un ; **they think they are ~** *or* **somebodies** ils se

prennent pour *or* ils se croient des personnages importants

somehow ['sʌmhaʊ] ADV **~ or other** (= *in some way*) d'une manière ou d'une autre ; (= *for some reason*) pour une raison ou pour une autre ; **it must be done ~** il faut que ce soit fait d'une manière ou d'une autre ; **I managed it ~** j'y suis arrivé je ne sais comment ; **we'll manage ~** on se débrouillera* ; **~ we must find £100** d'une manière ou d'une autre nous devons nous procurer 100 livres, nous devons nous débrouiller* pour trouver 100 livres ; **Taiwan is ~ different from the rest of China** d'une certaine manière, Taïwan est différente du reste de la Chine ; **I ~ doubt it** je ne sais pas pourquoi, mais j'en doute ; **it seems odd ~** je ne sais pas pourquoi mais ça semble bizarre ; **~ he's never succeeded** pour une raison ou pour une autre *or* je ne sais pas pourquoi, il n'a jamais réussi

someone ['sʌmwʌn] PRON = **somebody**

someplace ['sʌmpleɪs] ADV (*US*) = **somewhere**

somersault ['sʌməsɔːlt] [1] N [a] (*on ground, also accidental*) culbute *f* ; (*by child*) galipette *f* ; (*in air*) saut *m* périlleux ; (*by car*) tonneau *m* ; **to turn a ~** faire la culbute *or* un saut périlleux *or* un tonneau [b] (*fig* = *change of policy*) volte-face *f inv* ; (*fig*) **to do a ~** faire volte-face [2] VI (*person*) faire la culbute, faire un *or* des saut(s) périlleux ; (*car*) faire un *or* plusieurs tonneau(x)

something ['sʌmθɪŋ] [1] PRON [a] quelque chose *m* ; **~ moved over there** il y a quelque chose qui a bougé là-bas ; **~ must have happened to him** il a dû lui arriver quelque chose ; **~ unusual** quelque chose d'inhabituel ; **there must be ~ wrong** il doit y avoir quelque chose qui ne va pas ; **did you say ~?** pardon ?, comment ?, vous dites ? ; **I want ~ to read** je veux quelque chose à lire ; **I need ~ to eat** j'ai besoin de manger quelque chose ; **would you like ~ to drink?** voulez-vous boire quelque chose ? ; **give him ~ to drink** donnez-lui (quelque chose) à boire ; **he has ~ to live for at last** il a enfin une raison de vivre ; **you can't get ~ for nothing** on n'a rien pour rien ; **I have ~ else to do** j'ai quelque chose d'autre à faire, j'ai autre chose à faire ; **it's ~ else!*** (= *incredible*) c'est (vraiment) autre chose !, c'est une autre paire de manches !* ; **I'll have to tell him ~ or other** il faudra que je lui dise quelque chose *or* que je trouve (*subj*) quelque chose à lui dire ; **he whispered ~ or other in her ear** il lui a chuchoté quelque chose *or* on ne sait quoi à l'oreille ; **~ of the kind** quelque chose dans ce genre-là ; **there's ~ about her** *or* **she's got ~ about her I don't like** il y a chez elle *or* en elle quelque chose que je n'aime pas ; **there's ~ in what you say** il y a du vrai dans ce que vous dites ; **~ tells me that ...** j'ai l'impression que ... ; **here's ~ for your trouble** voici pour votre peine ; **give him ~ for himself** donnez-lui la pièce* *or* un petit quelque chose ; **you've got ~ there!** là tu n'as pas tort !, c'est vrai ce que tu dis là ! ; (*challengingly*) **do you want to make ~ (out) of it?** tu cherches la bagarre ?* ; **that's (really) ~!*** ◊ **that really is ~!*** c'est pas rien !*, ça se pose là !* ; **she has a certain ~*** elle a un petit quelque chose, elle a un certain je ne sais quoi ; **that certain ~* which makes all the difference** ce petit je ne sais quoi qui fait toute la différence ; **the 4-~* train** le train de 4 heures et quelques ; **it's sixty-~** c'est soixante et quelques ; **he's called Paul ~** il s'appelle Paul Chose *or* Paul quelque chose ; **that has ~ to do with accountancy** ça a quelque chose à voir avec la comptabilité ; **he's got ~ to do with it** (= *is involved*) il a quelque chose à voir là-dedans (*or* avec ça) ; (= *is responsible*) il y est pour quelque chose ; **he is ~ to do with Brown and Co** il a quelque chose à voir avec Brown et Cie ; **he is ~ (or other) in aviation** il est quelque chose dans l'aéronautique ; **I hope to**

see ~ of you j'espère vous voir un peu ; **it is really ~ to find good coffee nowadays** ça n'est pas rien* de trouver du bon café aujourd'hui ; **he scored 300 points, and that's ~!** il a marqué 300 points et ça c'est quelque chose* *or* et ça n'est pas rien ! ; **that's always ~** c'est toujours quelque chose, c'est mieux que rien ; **he thinks he's ~*** il se croit quelque chose, il se prend pour quelqu'un

[b] **or ~** ou quelque chose dans ce genre-là, ou quelque chose comme ça ; **he's got flu or ~** il a la grippe ou quelque chose comme ça *or* dans ce genre-là ; **do you think you're my boss or ~?** tu te prends pour mon patron ou quoi ?* ; **he fell off a wall or ~** il est tombé d'un mur ou quelque chose dans ce genre-là*, je crois qu'il est tombé d'un mur

[c] **he is ~ of a miser** il est quelque peu *or* plutôt avare ; **he is ~ of a pianist** il est assez bon pianiste, il joue assez bien du piano, il est assez doué pour le piano ; **it was ~ of a failure** c'était plutôt un échec

[2] ADV [a] **he left ~ over £5,000** il a laissé plus de 5 000 livres, il a laissé dans les 5 000 livres et plus ; **~ under £10** un peu moins de 10 livres ; **he won ~ like 10,000 francs** il a gagné quelque chose comme 10 000 F, il a gagné dans les 10 000 F ; **it's ~ like 10 o'clock** il est 10 heures environ, il est quelque chose comme 10 heures ; **it weighs ~ around 5 kilos** ça pèse 5 kilos environ, ça pèse dans les 5 kilos, ça fait quelque chose comme 5 kilos ; **there were ~ like 80 people there** 80 personnes environ étaient présentes, il y avait quelque chose comme 80 personnes ; **he talks ~ like his father** il parle un peu comme son père ; **now that's ~ like a claret!** voilà ce que j'appelle un bordeaux !, ça au moins c'est du bordeaux ! ; **now that's ~ like it!*** ça au moins c'est bien *or* c'est vraiment pas mal !

[b] (* : *emphatic*) **it was ~ dreadful!** c'était vraiment épouvantable ! ; **the weather was ~ shocking!** comme mauvais temps ça se posait là !* ; **the dog was howling ~ awful** le chien hurlait que c'en était abominable*, le chien hurlait fallait voir comme*

-something ['sʌmθɪŋ] [1] ADJ (*in compounds*) **he's thirty-something** il a une trentaine d'années ; **thirty-something couples** les couples *mpl* d'une trentaine d'années [2] N (*in compounds*) **most American twenty-somethings do not vote** la plupart des Américains d'une vingtaine d'années ne votent pas

sometime ['sʌmtaɪm] [1] ADV [a] (*in past*) **~ last month** le mois dernier, au cours du mois dernier ; **~ last May** au (cours du) mois de mai dernier ; **it was ~ last winter** c'était durant *or* pendant *or* au cours de l'hiver dernier (je ne sais pas *or* plus exactement quand) ; **it was ~ before 1950** c'était avant 1950 (je ne sais pas *or* plus exactement quand) [b] (*in future*) un de ces jours, un jour ou l'autre ; **~ soon** bientôt, avant peu ; **~ before January** d'ici janvier ; **~ next year** (dans le courant de) l'année prochaine ; **~ after my birthday** après mon anniversaire ; **~ or (an)other** it will have to be done il faudra (bien) le faire à un moment donné *or* tôt ou tard *or* un jour ou l'autre [2] ADJ [a] (= *former*) ancien (*before n*) ; (*US*) **it's a ~ thing*** cela appartient au passé [b] (*US* = *occasional*) intermittent

sometimes ['sʌmtaɪmz] ADV quelquefois, parfois ; **Burma, ~ known as Myanmar** la Birmanie, parfois appelée Myanmar ; **it is ~ difficult to ...** il est parfois difficile de ..., il peut être difficile de ... ; **he ~ forgets his glasses** il lui arrive d'oublier ses lunettes ; **you can be a real pain ~!*** qu'est-ce que tu peux être embêtant des fois !* ; **~ he agrees, ~ not** tantôt il est d'accord et tantôt non

somewhat ['sʌmwɒt] ADV (*frm*) quelque peu ; (*with comparatives*) un peu ; **~ surprising**

quelque peu *or* relativement surprenant ; **~ easier** un peu plus facile ; **it amused him ~** cela l'a quelque peu amusé ; **he greeted me ~ brusquely** il m'a salué avec une certaine brusquerie ; **it was ~ of a failure** c'était plutôt un échec, c'était plus ou moins un échec ; **more than ~** vraiment ; *(hum)* **I was more than ~ annoyed** j'étais plus qu'irrité

somewhere [ˈsʌmweə] ADV quelque part ; **~ or other** quelque part, je ne sais où ; **~ in France** quelque part en France ; **~ near Paris** (quelque part) près de *or* dans les environs de Paris ; **~ about** *or* **around here** quelque part par ici, pas loin d'ici ; **~ around 10 million people** environ *or* à peu près 10 millions de personnes ; **~ else** ailleurs ; *(restaurant etc)* **let's go ~ nice/cheap** allons dans un endroit agréable/bon marché ; **he's in the garden or ~** il est dans le jardin je crois ; **have you got ~ to stay?** avez-vous un endroit où loger ? ; **now we're getting ~!** enfin nous faisons des progrès !

Somme [sɒm] N (= *river*) Somme *f* ; **the Battle of the ~** la bataille de la Somme

somnambulism [sɒmˈnæmbjʊlɪzəm] N somnambulisme *m*

somnambulist [sɒmˈnæmbjʊlɪst] N somnambule *mf*

somniferous [sɒmˈnɪfərəs] ADJ somnifère, soporifique

somnolence [ˈsɒmnələns] N somnolence *f*

somnolent [ˈsɒmnələnt] ADJ somnolent

son [sʌn] **1** N fils *m* ; **I've got three ~s** j'ai trois fils *or* trois garçons ; *(Rel)* **Son of God/Man** Fils de Dieu/de l'Homme ; **his ~ and heir** son héritier ; *(liter)* **the ~ of men** les hommes *mpl* ; **he is his father's ~** *(in looks)* c'est tout le portrait de son père ; *(in character)* c'est bien le fils de son père ; **every mother's ~ of them** tous tant qu'ils sont *(or* étaient *etc)* ; **come here ~!** viens ici mon garçon *or* mon gars* *or* fiston !* → **father 2** COMP ▶ **son-in-law** N *(pl* **sons-in-law)** gendre *m*, beau-fils *m* ▶ **son-of-a-bitch** N *(pl* **sons-of-bitches)** salaud* *m*, fils *m* de pute* ▶ **son-of-a-gun** N *(pl* **sons-of-guns)** (espèce *f* de) vieille fripouille *f* *or* vieux coquin *m*

sonar [ˈsəʊnɑː] N sonar *m*

sonata [səˈnɑːtə] **1** N sonate *f* **2** COMP ▶ **sonata form** N forme *f* sonate

sonatina [ˌsɒnəˈtiːnə] N sonatine *f*

sonde [sɒnd] N *(Met, Space)* sonde *f*

sone [səʊn] N sone *f*

song [sɒŋ] **1** N *(gen)* chanson *f* ; *(more formal)* chant *m* ; *(of birds)* chant *m*, ramage *m* ; **festival of French ~** festival *m* de chant français *or* de la chanson française ; **to break** *or* **burst into ~** se mettre à chanter (une chanson *or* un air), entonner une chanson *or* un air ; **give us a ~** chante-nous quelque chose ; *(fig)* **it was going for a ~** c'était à vendre pour presque rien *or* pour une bouchée de pain ; **what a ~ and dance* there was!** ça a fait une de ces histoires !* ; **there's no need to make a ~ and dance* about it** il n'y a pas de quoi en faire toute une histoire* *or* tout un plat* ; *(US)* **to give sb the same old ~ and dance*** (= *excuse)* débiter les excuses habituelles à qn ; *(Brit fig)* **to be on ~** être en pleine forme → **marching, singsong**

2 COMP ▶ **song cycle** N cycle *m* de chansons ▶ **song hit** N chanson *f* à succès, tube* *m* ▶ **the Song of Solomon, the Song of Songs** N le cantique des cantiques ▶ **song sheet** N feuillet *m* de chanson ▶ **song thrush** N grive *f* musicienne ▶ **song without words** N romance *f* sans paroles ▶ **song writer** N *(words)* parolier *m*, -ière *f*, auteur *m* de chansons ; *(music)* compositeur *m*, -trice *f* de chansons ; *(both)* auteur-compositeur *m*

songbird [ˈsɒŋbɜːd] N oiseau *m* chanteur

songbook [ˈsɒŋbʊk] N recueil *m* de chansons

songfest [ˈsɒŋfest] N *(US)* festival *m* de chansons

songsmith [ˈsɒŋsmɪθ] N parolier *m*, -ière *f*

songster [ˈsɒŋstə] N (= *singer)* chanteur *m* ; (= *bird)* oiseau *m* chanteur

songstress [ˈsɒŋstrɪs] N chanteuse *f*

sonic [ˈsɒnɪk] **1** ADJ *[speed]* sonique ; *[wave]* sonore **2** N *(NonC)* **~s** l'acoustique *f* *(dans le domaine transsonique)* **3** COMP ▶ **sonic barrier** N mur *m* du son ▶ **sonic boom** N bang *m inv* (supersonique) ▶ **sonic depth-finder** N sonde *f* à ultra-sons ▶ **sonic mine** N mine *f* acoustique

sonnet [ˈsɒnɪt] N sonnet *m*

sonny* [ˈsʌnɪ] N mon (petit) gars*, fiston* *m* ; **~ boy** ◊ **~ Jim** mon gars*, fiston*

sonority [səˈnɒrɪtɪ] N sonorité *f*

sonorous [ˈsɒnərəs] ADJ *[voice]* sonore ; *[sound]* éclatant, retentissant ; *[language, rhetoric]* grandiloquent

sonorously [ˈsɒnərəslɪ] ADV *[say]* d'une voix sonore

sonorousness [ˈsɒnərəsnɪs] N sonorité *f*

soon [suːn] ADV **a** (= *before long)* bientôt ; (= *quickly)* vite ; **we shall ~ be in Paris** nous serons bientôt à Paris, nous serons à Paris dans peu de temps *or* sous peu ; **you would ~ get lost** vous seriez vite perdu ; **he ~ changed his mind** il a vite changé d'avis, il n'a pas mis longtemps *or* il n'a pas tardé à changer d'avis ; **I'll ~ finish that!** j'aurai bientôt terminé !, j'aurai vite *or* tôt fait ; **(I'll) see you ~!** à bientôt ! ; **very ~** très vite, très bientôt ; **quite ~** dans assez peu de temps, assez vite ; **~ afterwards** peu après ; **quite ~ afterwards** assez peu de temps après ; **all too ~ it was over** ce ne fut que trop vite fini ; **all too ~ it was time to go** malheureusement il a bientôt fallu partir ; **the holidays can't come ~ enough!** vivement les vacances !

b (= *early)* tôt ; **why have you come so ~?** pourquoi êtes-vous venu si tôt ? ; **I expected you much ~er than this** je vous attendais bien plus tôt (que cela) *or* bien avant ; **I couldn't get here any ~er** je n'ai pas pu arriver plus tôt ; **how ~ can you get here?** dans combien de temps au plus tôt peux-tu être ici ?, quel jour *(or* à quelle heure *etc)* peux-tu venir au plus tôt ? ; **how ~ will it be ready?** dans combien de temps *or* quand est-ce que ce sera prêt ? ; **Friday is too ~** vendredi c'est trop tôt ; **we were none too ~** il était temps que nous arrivions *(subj)*, nous sommes arrivés juste à temps *or* tout juste ; **and none too ~ at that!** et ce n'est pas trop tôt ! ; **must you leave so ~?** faut-il que vous partiez *(subj)* déjà *or* si tôt ?, quel dommage que vous deviez *(subj)* partir déjà *or* si tôt ! ; **so ~?** déjà ? ; **on Friday at the ~est** vendredi au plus tôt, pas avant vendredi ; **in five years or at his death, whichever is the ~er** dans cinq ans ou à sa mort, s'il meurt avant cinq ans *or* si cela survient avant

c *(in phrases)* **as ~ as possible** dès que possible, aussitôt que possible ; **I'll do it as ~ as I can** je le ferai dès que je pourrai *or* aussitôt que je le pourrai *or* aussitôt que possible ; **let me know as ~ as you've finished** prévenez-moi dès que *or* aussitôt que vous aurez fini ; **as ~ as he spoke to her he knew ...** aussitôt qu'il lui a parlé il a su ... ; **as ~ as 7 o'clock** dès 7 heures ; **the ~er we get started the ~er we'll be done** plus tôt nous commencerons plus tôt nous aurons fini, plus tôt commencé plus tôt fini ; **the ~er the better!** le plus tôt sera le mieux ! ; *(iro)* **it would be ~er** il serait grand temps !, ça ne serait pas trop tôt ! ; **~er or later** tôt ou tard ; **no ~er had he finished than his brother arrived** à peine avait-il fini que son frère est arrivé ; **no ~er said than done!** aussitôt dit aussitôt fait ! ; **he could (just) as ~ fly to the moon as pass that exam** il a autant de chances de réussir cet examen que d'aller sur la lune

d *(expressing preference)* **I'd ~er you didn't tell him** je préférerais que vous ne le lui disiez *(subj)* pas ; **I'd as ~ you ...** j'aimerais autant que vous ... (+ *subj)* ; **I would ~er stay here than go** je préférerais rester ici (plutôt) que d'y aller ; **I would just as ~ stay here with you** j'aimerais tout autant rester ici avec vous, cela me ferait tout autant plaisir de rester ici avec vous ; **he would as ~ die as betray his friends** il préférerait mourir plutôt que de trahir ses amis ; **will you go? — I'd ~er not** est-ce que tu iras ? — je n'y tiens pas *or* je préférerais pas !* ; **I'd ~er die!** plutôt mourir ! ; **what would you ~er do?** qu'est-ce que vous aimeriez mieux (faire) *or* vous préféreriez (faire) ? ; **~er than have to speak to her, he left** plutôt que d'avoir à lui parler il est parti ; **she'd marry him as ~ as not** elle l'épouserait volontiers, elle aimerait bien l'épouser ; **~er you than me!*** je n'aimerais pas être à ta place, je te souhaite bien du plaisir !* *(iro)*

sooner [ˈsuːnə] **1** ADV *compar of* **soon 2** N *(US)* pionnier *m* de la première heure *(dans l'Ouest des États-Unis)* **3** COMP ▶ **the Sooner State** N *(US)* l'Oklahoma *m*

soot [sʊt] N *(NonC)* suie *f*

▶ **soot up 1** VI s'encrasser **2** VT SEP encrasser

sooth†† [suːθ] N **in ~** en vérité

soothe [suːð] VT *[+ person]* calmer, apaiser ; *[+ nerves, mind, pain]* calmer ; *[+ anger, anxieties]* apaiser ; *[+ sb's vanity]* flatter ; **to ~ sb's fears** apaiser les craintes de qn, tranquilliser qn

soothing [ˈsuːðɪŋ] ADJ *[bath, massage]* relaxant ; *[voice, words, music, manner]* apaisant ; *[drink]* calmant ; *[lotion, ointment]* adoucissant ; *[presence]* rassurant, réconfortant ; **the ~ effect of lavender oil/a glass of sherry** l'effet apaisant de l'huile de lavande/d'un verre de sherry

soothingly [ˈsuːðɪŋlɪ] ADV *[say, whisper]* d'un ton apaisant ; **~ familiar** familier et réconfortant ; **~ cool** frais et apaisant

soothsayer [ˈsuːθseɪə] N devin *m*, devineresse *f*

soothsaying [ˈsuːθseɪɪŋ] N divination *f*

sooty [ˈsʊtɪ] ADJ *[object, surface]* couvert *or* noir de suie ; *[fumes, exhaust]* chargé de suie ; *[chimney, flue]* plein de suie ; *[flame]* fuligineux ; *[powder]* qui a l'aspect de la suie ; **~ particles** particules *fpl* de suie ; **a ~ black colour** un noir charbonneux *or* fuligineux

SOP [ˌesəʊˈpiː] N *(ABBR = standard operating procedure)* → **standard**

sop [sɒp] N **a** *(Culin)* pain *m* trempé *(dans du lait, du jus de viande etc)*, mouillette *f* ; **he can eat only ~s** il ne peut rien manger de trop solide, il doit se nourrir d'aliments semi-liquides ; *(fig)* **it's just a ~ to Cerberus** c'est simplement pour le *(or* les *etc)* ramener à de meilleures dispositions *or* pour l'amadouer *(or* les *etc* amadouer) ; **he gave the guard £10 as a ~** il a donné 10 livres au gardien pour s'acheter ses bons services *or* pour lui graisser la patte* ; **it's a ~ to my conscience** c'est pour faire taire ma conscience ; **as a ~ to his pride, I agreed** j'ai accepté pour flatter son amour-propre ; **he only said that as a ~ to the unions** il a dit cela uniquement pour amadouer les syndicats **b** (* = *sissy)* *(man)* poule *f* mouillée, lavette* *f* ; *(woman)* femme *f* très fleur bleue

▶ **sop up** VT SEP *[+ spilt liquid]* *[sponge, rag]* absorber ; *[person]* éponger (**with** avec) ; **he ~ped up the gravy with some bread** il a saucé son assiette avec un morceau de pain

Sophia [səˈfaɪə] N Sophie *f*

sophism [ˈsɒfɪzəm] N = **sophistry**

sophist [ˈsɒfɪst] N sophiste *mf* ; *(Hist Philos)* **Sophists** sophistes *mpl*

sophistical [səˈfɪstɪkəl] ADJ sophistique, captieux

sophisticate [səˈfɪstɪkeɪt] N raffiné(e) m(f), élégant(e) m(f)

sophisticated [səˈfɪstɪkeɪtɪd] ADJ a (= complex, advanced) [equipment, system, technique] sophistiqué, (très) élaboré b (= refined) [person, tastes, lifestyle] raffiné c (= intelligent, subtle) [person] averti; [approach, analysis, understanding] subtil; [play, film, book] subtil, complexe

sophistication [səˌfɪstɪˈkeɪʃən] N a (= complexity) [of equipment, system, technique] sophistication f b (= refinement) [of person, tastes, lifestyle] raffinement m c (= intelligence, subtlety) raffinement m; [of approach, analysis, understanding] subtilité f; [of film, novel] subtilité f, complexité f; the job demands a high level of political ~ cet emploi exige une grande subtilité politique or un grand sens politique

sophistry [ˈsɒfɪstrɪ] N (NonC) sophistique f; (piece of) ~ sophisme m; (Hist Philos) **Sophistry** sophistique f

Sophocles [ˈsɒfəkliːz] N Sophocle m

sophomore [ˈsɒfəmɔːʳ] N (US) étudiant(e) m(f) de seconde année

sophomoric [ˌsɒfəˈmɔːrɪk] ADJ (US pej) aussi prétentieux qu'ignorant

soporific [ˌsɒpəˈrɪfɪk] 1 ADJ a (= sedative) soporifique; **too much wine can be ~** trop de vin peut avoir un effet soporifique b (* = boring) soporifique* 2 N somnifère m

sopping* [ˈsɒpɪŋ] ADJ (also **~ wet**) [person] trempé (jusqu'aux os); [clothes] à tordre

soppy* [ˈsɒpɪ] ADJ (Brit) a (= sentimental) [person] fleur bleue inv, sentimental; [film, book, story] à l'eau de rose, sentimental; **people who are ~ about cats** les gens qui sont gagas* avec les chats b (= silly) [person] bébête*; [action] bête; **don't be so ~!** ne sois pas si bête! c († = feeble, weedy) mollasson*; **he's a ~ git** c'est une mauviette or un mollasson*

soprano [səˈprɑːnəʊ] 1 N (pl **sopranos** or **soprani** [səˈprɑːniː]) (= singer) soprano mf, soprano mf; (= voice, part) soprano m → **boy** 2 ADJ [part, voice, repertoire] de soprano; [aria] pour soprano; [instrument] soprano inv; **the ~ saxophone** le saxophone soprano; **the ~ clef** la clef d'ut dernière ligne

sorb [sɔːb] N (= tree) sorbier m; (= fruit) sorbe f

sorbet [ˈsɔːbeɪ, ˈsɔːbɪt] N a (= water ice) sorbet m; **lemon ~** sorbet m au citron b (US) = **sherbet a**

sorbic [ˈsɔːbɪk] ADJ **~ acid** acide m sorbique

sorbitol [ˈsɔːbɪtɒl] N sorbitol m

sorcerer [ˈsɔːsərəʳ] N sorcier m; (Mus etc) **the Sorcerer's Apprentice** l'Apprenti sorcier m

sorceress [ˈsɔːsərɛs] N sorcière f

sorcery [ˈsɔːsərɪ] N sorcellerie f

sordid [ˈsɔːdɪd] ADJ [conditions, surroundings, affair, episode, detail] sordide; [motive, action] sordide, honteux; [behaviour] abject, honteux

sordidly [ˈsɔːdɪdlɪ] ADV sordidement

sordidness [ˈsɔːdɪdnɪs] N [of conditions, surroundings] aspect m sordide; (fig) [of behaviour, motive, method] bassesse f; [of agreement, deal] caractère m honteux; [of crime, greed, gains] caractère m sordide; [of film, book] saleté f

sore [sɔːʳ] 1 ADJ a (= inflamed) irrité b (= painful) douloureux; **to have a ~ throat** avoir mal à la gorge; **I'm ~ all over** j'ai mal partout; **to have a ~ head** (= headache) avoir mal à la tête; **to stick out** or **stand out like a ~ thumb*** (= be obvious) crever les yeux; (= stand out visually) faire tache, détonner; **a ~ spot** (lit) une zone sensible; (fig) un sujet délicat; (fig) **it's a ~ point (with him)** c'est un sujet qu'il vaut mieux éviter (avec lui) → **bear²**, **sight** c (esp US* = offended, resentful) vexé; **I really feel ~ about it** ça m'a vraiment vexé; **to get ~**

se vexer; **don't get ~!** ne te vexe pas!; **to be** or **feel ~ at** or **with sb** en vouloir à qn; **to get ~ at** or **with sb** s'emporter contre qn d (†† or liter) **to be in ~ need of sth** avoir grandement besoin de qch; **to be ~ at heart** être affligé or désolé 2 ADV **to be ~ afraid**†† avoir grand-peur 3 N (Med) plaie f; (fig) **to open up old ~s** rouvrir or raviver d'anciennes blessures (fig) → **running**

sorehead* [ˈsɔːhed] N (US) râleur* m, -euse* f, rouspéteur* m, -euse* f

sorely [ˈsɔːlɪ] ADV (frm) [wounded] gravement, grièvement; [disappointed] cruellement; **~ tempted** fortement tenté; **modern equipment is ~ lacking** on manque cruellement de matériel moderne, le matériel moderne fait cruellement défaut; **reform is ~ needed** on a grand besoin de réformes; **to be ~ tested** or **tried** [person, patience] être mis à rude épreuve; **she will be ~ missed** sa présence nous manquera énormément

soreness [ˈsɔːnɪs] N a (Med etc = painfulness) endolorissement m b (* fig) (= annoyance) contrariété f, irritation f; (= bitterness) amertume f; (= anger) colère f, rogne* f

sorghum [ˈsɔːgəm] N sorgho m

soroptimist [səˈrɒptɪmɪst] N membre d'une association internationale pour les femmes dans les professions libérales

sorority [səˈrɒrɪtɪ] N (US Univ) association f d'étudiantes

SORORITY, FRATERNITY

Beaucoup d'universités américaines possèdent des associations d'étudiants très sélectives, appelées **sororities** pour les femmes et **fraternities** pour les hommes, qui organisent des soirées, récoltent des fonds pour des œuvres de bienfaisance et cherchent à se nuisser (pas) entre elles du même type. Le nom de ces associations est souvent formé à partir de deux ou trois lettres de l'alphabet grec: par exemple, « Kappa Kappa Gamma **sorority** » ou « Sigma Chi **fraternity** ».

---

sorrel [ˈsɒrəl] 1 N a (Bot) oseille f b (= horse) alezan m clair; (= colour) roux m, brun rouge m 2 ADJ [horse] alezan inv

▼ **sorrow** [ˈsɒrəʊ] 1 N peine f, chagrin m; (stronger) douleur f; **his ~ at the loss of his son** la peine or le chagrin or la douleur qu'il a éprouvé(e) à la mort de son fils; **to my (great) ~** à mon grand chagrin, à ma grande douleur; **this was a great ~ to me** j'en ai eu beaucoup de peine or de chagrin; **he was a great ~ to her** il lui a causé beaucoup de peine or de chagrin; **more in ~ than in anger** avec plus de peine que de colère; (Rel) **the Man of Sorrows** l'Homme m de douleur → **drown** 2 VI **to ~ over** [+ sb's death, loss] pleurer; [+ news] déplorer, se lamenter de; **she sat ~ing by the fire** elle était assise au coin du feu toute à son chagrin

sorrowful [ˈsɒrəʊfʊl] ADJ triste

sorrowfully [ˈsɒrəʊflɪ] ADV [look, shake head] tristement, d'un air triste; [say] d'un ton triste

sorrowing [ˈsɒrəʊɪŋ] ADJ affligé

▼ **sorry** [ˈsɒrɪ] ADJ a (= regretful) désolé; **I was ~ to hear of your accident** j'étais désolé or très peiné or navré d'apprendre que vous avez eu un accident; **I am ~ I cannot come** je regrette or je suis désolé de ne (pas) pouvoir venir; **I am ~ she cannot come** je regrette or je suis désolé qu'elle ne puisse (pas) venir; **I have to have to tell you that ...** je regrette d'avoir à vous dire que ...; (frm) **we are ~ to inform you ...** nous avons le regret de vous informer ...; **he didn't pass, I'm ~ to say** il a échoué hélas or malheureusement; **(I'm) ~ I am late** ◊ **I'm ~ to be late** excusez-moi or je suis désolé d'être en retard; **say you're ~!** dis or demande pardon!;

~! ◊ ~ about that!* pardon!, excusez-moi!, je suis désolé!; **I'm very** or **terribly ~** je suis vraiment désolé or navré; **awfully ~! ◊ so ~!** oh pardon!, excusez-moi!, je suis vraiment désolé!; **will you go? — I'm ~ I can't** est-ce que tu vas y aller? — impossible hélas or (je suis) désolé mais je ne peux pas; **can you do it? — no, ~** est-ce que tu peux le faire? — non, désolé or désolé, je ne peux pas or malheureusement pas; **I am ~ to disturb you** je suis désolé de vous déranger, excusez-moi de vous déranger; **I am** or **feel ~ about all the noise yesterday** je regrette beaucoup qu'il y ait eu tellement de bruit hier; **~ about that vase!** excusez-moi pour ce vase!; **you'll be ~ for this!** vous le regretterez!, vous vous en repentirez!

b (= pitying) **to be** or **feel ~ for sb** plaindre qn; **I feel so ~ for her since her husband died** elle me fait pitié depuis la mort de son mari; **I'm ~ for you but you should have known better** je suis désolé pour vous or je vous plains mais vous auriez dû être plus raisonnable; (iro) **if he can't do better than that then I'm ~ for him** s'il ne peut pas faire mieux, je regrette pour lui or je le plains; **there's no need to feel** or **be ~ for him** il est inutile de le plaindre, il n'est pas à plaindre; **to be** or **feel ~ for o.s.** se plaindre (de son sort), s'apitoyer sur soi-même or sur son propre sort; **he looked very ~ for himself** il faisait piteuse mine

c (= woeful) [condition] triste; [excuse] piètre; **to be in a ~ plight** être dans une triste situation, être en fâcheuse situation; **to be in a ~ state** être dans un triste état, être en piteux état; **he was a ~ figure** il faisait triste or piteuse figure; **a ~ sight** un triste spectacle, un spectacle désolant or affligeant; **it was a ~ tale of mismanagement and inefficiency** c'était une lamentable or déplorable histoire de mauvaise gestion et d'inefficacité

sort [sɔːt] 1 N a (= class, variety, kind, type) (gen) sorte f, genre m; [of animal, plant] sorte f, espèce f; (= make) [of car, machine, coffee etc] marque f; **this ~ of book** cette sorte or ce genre de livre; **books of all ~s** des livres de toutes sortes or de tous genres; **... and all ~s of things ...** et toutes sortes de choses encore, ... et j'en passe, ... et que sais-je; **this ~ of thing(s)** ce genre de chose(s); **what ~ of flour do you want? — the ~ you gave me last time** quelle sorte or quel genre de farine voulez-vous? — la même que vous m'avez donnée (or le même que vous m'avez donné) la dernière fois; **what ~ do you want?** vous en (or le or la etc) voulez de quelle sorte?; **what ~ of car is it?** quelle marque de voiture est-ce?; **what ~ of man is he?** quel genre or type d'homme est-ce?; **what ~ of dog is he?** qu'est-ce que c'est comme (race de) chien?; **he is not the ~ of man to refuse** ce n'est pas le genre d'homme à refuser, il n'est pas homme à refuser; **he's not that ~ of person** ce n'est pas son genre; **I'm not that ~ of girl!** ce n'est pas mon genre!, mais pour qui me prenez-vous?; **that's the ~ of person I am** c'est comme ça que je suis (fait); **what ~ of people does he think we are?** (mais enfin) pour qui nous prend-il?; **what ~ of a fool does he take me for?** (non mais*) il me prend pour un imbécile!; **what ~ of behaviour is this?** qu'est-ce que c'est que cette façon de se conduire?; **what ~ of an answer do you call that?** vous appelez ça une réponse?; **classical music is the ~ she likes most** c'est la musique classique qu'elle préfère; **and all that ~ of thing** et autres choses du même genre, et tout ça*; **you know the ~ of thing I mean** vous voyez (à peu près) ce que je veux dire; **I don't like that ~ of talk/behaviour** je n'aime pas ce genre de conversation/de conduite; **he's the ~ that will cheat** il est du genre à tricher; **I know his ~!** je connais les gens de son genre or espèce!; **your ~* never did any good** les

gens de votre genre *or* espèce ne font rien de bien ; **they're not our ~*** ce ne sont pas des gens comme nous ; **it's my ~* of film** c'est le genre de film que j'aime *or* qui me plaît **b** (*in phrases*) **something of the ~** quelque chose de ce genre(-là) *or* d'approchant ; **this is wrong — nothing of the ~!** c'est faux — pas le moins du monde ! ; **I shall do nothing of the ~!** je n'en ferai rien !, certainement pas ! ; **I will have nothing of the ~!** je ne tolérerai pas cela ! ; (*pej*) **it was beef of a ~** c'était quelque chose qui pouvait passer pour du bœuf ; **he is a painter of ~s** c'est un peintre si l'on peut dire ; **after a ~ ◊ in some** = dans une certaine mesure, en quelque sorte ; **to be out of ~s** ne pas être dans son assiette ■ (*PROV*) **it takes all ~s (to make a world)** il faut de tout pour faire un monde (*PROV*) ; (*fig*) **a good ~*** un brave garçon, un brave type*, une brave fille ; **he's the right ~*** c'est un type bien*
c **a ~ of** une sorte *or* espèce de, un genre de ; **there was a ~ of box in the middle of the room** il y avait une sorte *or* une espèce *or* un genre de boîte au milieu de la pièce, il y avait quelque chose qui ressemblait à une boîte au milieu de la pièce ; **there was a ~ of tinkling sound** il y avait une sorte *or* une espèce de bruit de grelot, on entendait quelque chose qui ressemblait à un bruit de grelot ; **in a ~ of way*** I'm sorry d'une certaine façon je le regrette ; **I had a ~ of fear that ... ◊ I was ~ of* frightened that ...** j'avais comme peur que ... + ne (+ *subj*) ; **I ~ of* thought that he would come** j'avais un peu l'idée qu'il viendrait ; **he was ~ of* worried-looking** il avait un peu l'air inquiet, il avait l'air comme qui dirait* inquiet ; **it's ~ of* blue** c'est plutôt bleu ; **aren't you pleased? — ~ of!*** tu n'es pas content ? — ben si !*

2 VT **a** (*also* **~ out**) (= *classify*) [+ *documents, stamps*] classer ; (= *select those to keep*) [+ *documents, clothes, apples*] trier, faire le tri de ; (= *separate*) séparer (**from** de) ; **he spent the morning ~ing (out) his stamp collection** il a passé la matinée à classer *or* trier les timbres de sa collection ; **to ~ things (out) into sizes** *or* **according to size** trier des objets selon leur taille ; (*Cards*) **to ~ out one's cards** *or* **one's hand** arranger ses cartes, mettre de l'ordre dans ses cartes ; **to ~ (out) the clothes into clean and dirty** séparer les vêtements sales des propres, mettre les vêtements sales à part ; **can you ~ out the green ones and leave them aside?** pourriez-vous les trier et mettre les verts à part ?
b (*Post*) [+ *letters etc*] (*Comput*) [+ *data, file*] trier
c **to get sth ~ed*** [+ *problem, situation*] régler qch
d (*Scot* = *mend*) arranger ; **I've ~ed your bike** j'ai arrangé *or* réparé ton vélo

3 COMP ▸ **sort code** N (*Banking*) code *m* guichet ▸ **sort-out*** N **to have a ~-out** faire du rangement ; **I've had a ~-out of all these old newspapers** j'ai trié tous ces vieux journaux
▸ **sort out 1** VT SEP **a** = **sort 2a**
b (*fig*) (= *tidy*) [+ *papers, toys, clothes*] ranger, mettre de l'ordre dans ; [+ *ideas*] mettre de l'ordre dans ; (= *solve*) [+ *problem*] régler, résoudre ; [+ *difficulties*] venir à bout de ; (= *fix, arrange*) arranger ; **I just can't ~ the twins out* (one from the other)** je ne peux pas distinguer les jumeaux (l'un de l'autre) ; **can you ~ this out for me?** est-ce que vous pourriez débrouiller ça pour moi ? ; **we've got it all ~ed out now** nous avons réglé *or* résolu la question ; **we'll soon ~ it out** nous aurons vite fait d'arranger ça *or* de régler ça ; **things will ~ themselves out** les choses vont s'arranger d'elles-mêmes ; **he was so excited I couldn't ~ out what had happened** il était tellement excité que je n'ai pas pu débrouiller *or* comprendre ce qui s'était passé ; **did you ~**

out with him when you had to be there? est-ce que tu as décidé *or* fixé avec lui l'heure à laquelle tu dois y être ? ; **to ~ o.s. out** se reprendre, résoudre ses problèmes ; (*Brit*) **to ~ sb out*** (*by punishing, threatening etc*) régler son compte à qn* ; (= *get out of difficulty etc*) tirer qn d'affaire ; (*after depression, illness etc*) aider qn à reprendre pied (*fig*)
c (= *explain*) **to ~ sth out for sb** expliquer qch à qn
2 **~-out** N → **sort**

sorter [ˈsɔːtər] N **a** (= *person*) trieur *m*, -euse *f* **b** (= *machine*) (*for letters*) trieur *m* ; (*for punched cards*) trieuse *f* ; (*for grain*) trieur *m* ; (*for wool, coke*) trieur *m*, trieuse *f*

sortie [ˈsɔːtɪ] N (*Aviat, Mil*) sortie *f* ; **they made** *or* **flew 400 ~s** ils ont fait 400 sorties

sorting [ˈsɔːtɪŋ] **1** N (*Comput, Post*) tri *m* **2** COMP ▸ **sorting office** N (*Post*) bureau *m* *or* centre *m* de tri

SOS [ˌesəʊˈes] N (= *signal*) SOS *m* ; (*fig*) SOS *m*, appel *m* au secours (**for sth** pour demander qch)

sot [sɒt] N ivrogne *m* invétéré

sottish [ˈsɒtɪʃ] ADJ abruti par l'alcool

sotto voce [ˌsɒtəʊˈvəʊtʃɪ] ADV tout bas, à mi-voix ; (*Mus*) sotto voce

sou' [saʊ] ADJ (*in compounds: Naut*) = **south**

soubriquet [ˈsuːbrɪkeɪ] N → **sobriquet**

Soudan [suˈdɑːn] N = **Sudan**

Soudanese [ˌsuːdəˈniːz] = **Sudanese**

soufflé [ˈsuːfleɪ] **1** N soufflé *m* ; **cheese/fish ~** soufflé *m* au fromage/au poisson **2** COMP ▸ **soufflé dish** N moule *m* à soufflé ▸ **soufflé omelette** N omelette *f* soufflée

sough [saʊ] (*liter*) **1** N murmure *m* (du vent) **2** VI [*wind*] murmurer

sought [sɔːt] VB *pt, ptp of* **seek**

souk [suːk] N souk *m*

soul [səʊl] **1** N **a** âme *f* ; **with all one's ~** de toute son âme, de tout son cœur ; **All Souls' Day** le jour des Morts ; **upon my ~!** †* grand Dieu ! ; **he cannot call his ~ his own** il ne s'appartient pas, il est complètement dominé ; (*fig*) **he was the ~ of the movement** c'était lui l'âme *or* l'animateur du mouvement ; **he is the ~ of discretion** c'est la discrétion même *or* personnifiée ; **he has no ~** il est trop terre à terre, il a trop les pieds sur terre ; **it lacks ~** cela manque de sentiment → **bare, body, heart, sell**
b (= *person*) âme *f*, personne *f* ; **a village of 300 ~s** un village de 300 âmes ; **the ship sank with 200 ~s** le bateau a sombré avec 200 personnes à bord ; **the ship sank with all ~s** le bateau a péri corps et biens ; **I didn't see a (single** *or* **living) ~** je n'ai pas vu âme qui vive ; **don't tell a ~** surtout n'en soufflez mot à personne ; **(you) poor ~!** mon (*or* ma) pauvre ! ; **the poor ~!** le (*or* la) pauvre ! ; **he's a good ~** il est bien brave* ; **she's a kind** *or* **kindly ~** elle est la gentillesse même ; **lend me your pen, there's a good ~*** sois gentil *or* sois un ange, prête-moi ton stylo → **simple**
c (*US: esp of black Americans*) soul *m* (façon de ressentir des Noirs)
d (*US**) ABBR = **soul brother, soul food, soul music**
2 ADJ (*US*: of black Americans*) **~ brother/sister** frère *m*/sœur *f* de race (*terme employé par les Noirs entre eux*) ; **Soul City** Harlem ; **~ food** nourriture *f* soul (*nourriture traditionnelle des Noirs du sud des États-Unis*) ; **~ band** groupe *m* de (musique) soul ; **~ music** musique *f* soul
3 COMP ▸ **soul-destroying** ADJ (= *boring*) abrutissant ; (= *depressing*) démoralisant ▸ **soul mate** N âme *f* sœur ▸ **soul-searching** N introspection *f* ; **after a lot of ~-searching** après un long examen de conscience ▸ **soul-stirring** ADJ très émouvant

soulful [ˈsəʊlfʊl] ADJ [*eyes, look*] expressif ; [*expression*] attendrissant ; [*person, music*] sentimental

soulfully [ˈsəʊlfəlɪ] ADV [*sing, write*] de façon sentimentale *or* attendrissante ; [*look*] d'un air expressif *or* éloquent

soulless [ˈsəʊllɪs] ADJ [*place, building, music*] sans âme ; [*work*] abrutissant ; [*system*] inhumain ; [*eyes, look*] insensible, inexpressif ; [*existence*] vide

sound¹ [saʊnd] **1** N (*gen*) son *m* ; [*of sea, storm, breaking glass, car brakes etc*] bruit *m* ; [*of voice, bell, violins etc*] son *m* ; **the speed of ~** la vitesse du son ; **to the ~(s) of the national anthem** au(x) son(s) de l'hymne national ; **there was not a ~ to be heard** on n'entendait pas le moindre bruit ; **without (making) a ~** sans bruit, sans faire le moindre bruit ; **we heard the ~ of voices** nous avons entendu un bruit de voix ; **he lives within the ~ of the cathedral bells** depuis chez lui, on entend les cloches de la cathédrale ; **the Glenn Miller ~** la musique de Glenn Miller ; (*fig*) **I don't like the ~ of it** (= *it doesn't attract me*) ça ne me dit rien, ça ne me plaît pas ; (= *it's worrying*) ça m'inquiète ; **I don't like the ~ of his plans** ses projets ne me disent rien qui vaille ; **the news has a depressing ~** les nouvelles semblent déprimantes
2 VI **a** [*bell, trumpet, voice*] sonner, retentir ; [*car horn, siren, signal, order*] retentir ; **footsteps/a gun ~ed a long way off** on a entendu un bruit de pas/un coup de canon dans le lointain ; (*fig*) **a note of warning ~s through his writing** un avertissement retentit dans ses écrits ; **it ~s better if you read it slowly** c'est mieux *or* ça sonne mieux si vous le lisez lentement
b (= *suggest by sound*) **that instrument ~s like a flute** le son de cet instrument ressemble à celui de la flûte, on dirait le son de la flûte ; **it ~s empty** (au son) on dirait que c'est vide ; **a language which ~ed (to me) like Dutch** une langue qui aurait pu être *or* qui (me) semblait être du hollandais ; **he ~s (like an) Australian** à l'entendre parler on dirait un Australien ; **the train ~ed a long way off ◊ it ~ed as if** *or* **as though the train were a long way off** le train semblait être encore bien loin ; **it ~ed as if someone were coming in** on aurait dit que quelqu'un entrait ; **that ~s like Paul arriving** ça doit être Paul qui arrive ; **she ~s tired** elle semble fatiguée ; **you ~ like your mother when you say things like that** quand tu parles comme ça, tu me rappelles ta mère *or* on croirait entendre ta mère ; (*to sick person*) **you ~ terrible** (à t'entendre) tu sembles en triste état
c (*fig* = *seem, appear*) sembler (être) ; **that ~s like an excuse** cela a l'air d'une excuse, cela ressemble à une excuse ; **how does it ~ to you?** qu'en penses-tu ? ; **it ~s like a good idea** ça a l'air d'(être) une bonne idée, ça a l'air d'être une bonne idée ; **it doesn't ~ too good** cela n'annonce rien de bon, ce n'est pas très prometteur ; **it ~s as if she isn't coming** j'ai l'impression qu'elle ne viendra pas ; **you don't ~ like the kind of person we need** (à en juger par ce que vous dites) vous ne semblez pas être le genre de personne qu'il nous faut
3 VT **a** [+ *bell, alarm*] sonner ; [+ *trumpet, bugle*] sonner de ; (*Mil*) [+ *reveille, retreat*] sonner ; (*Mil*) **to ~ the last post** envoyer la sonnerie aux morts ; **to ~ the** *or* **one's horn** [*of car*] klaxonner ; (*fig*) **to ~ a (note of) warning** lancer un avertissement ; **to ~ sb's praises** faire l'éloge de qn, chanter les louanges de qn
b (*Ling*) **to ~ one's "t"s** faire sonner ses « t » ; **the "n" in "hymn" is not ~ed** le « n » de « hymn » ne se prononce pas
c (= *examine*) [+ *rails, train wheels*] vérifier au marteau ; (*Med*) **to ~ sb's chest** ausculter qn
4 COMP [*film, recording*] sonore ▸ **sound archives** NPL phonothèque *f* ▸ **sound barrier**

N mur *m* du son ; (*Aviat*) **to break the ~ barrier** franchir le mur du son ► **sound bite** N petite phrase *f* (*prononcée par un homme politique pour être citée dans les médias*) ; **to talk in ~ bites** parler à coups de petites phrases ► **sound board** N = **sounding board**; →**sounding¹** ► **sound box** N (*Mus*) caisse *f* de résonance ► **sound card** N (*Comput*) carte *f* son ► **sound change** N (*Phon*) changement *m* phonétique ► **sound check** N (*Mus*) sound check ► **sound effects** NPL (*Rad etc*) bruitage *m* ► **sound effects man** N (*pl* **sound effects men**) (*Cine, TV, Rad*) bruiteur *m* ► **sound engineer** N (*Cine, Rad etc*) ingénieur *m* du son ► **sound hole** N (*Mus*) ouïe *f* ► **sound law** N (*Phon*) loi *f* phonétique ► **sound library** N phonothèque *f* ► **sound pollution** N nuisance *f* due au bruit ► **sound-producing** ADJ (*Phon*) phonatoire ► **sound shift** N (*Phon*) mutation *f* phonétique ► **sound stage** N (*Recording*) salle *f* de tournage ► **sound system** N (*Ling*) système *m* de sons ; (= *hi-fi*) chaîne *f* hi-fi ; (*for disco, concert*) sonorisation *f*, sono* *f* ► **sound truck** N (*US*) camionnette *f* équipée d'un haut-parleur ► **sound wave** N (*Phys*) onde *f* sonore

► **sound off** VI [a]⁑ (= *proclaim one's opinions*) faire de grands laïus* (**about** sur) ; (= *boast*) se vanter (**about** de) ; (= *grumble*) rouspéter*, râler* (**about** à propos de) ; **to ~ off at sb** engueuler⁑ qn [b] (*US Mil = number off*) se numéroter

sound² [saʊnd] [1] ADJ [a] (= *healthy, robust*) [*person*] en bonne santé, bien portant ; [*heart*] solide ; [*constitution, teeth, lungs, fruit, tree*] sain ; [*timber*] sain, solide ; [*structure, floor, bridge*] solide, en bon état ; (*fig*) [*firm, business, financial position*] sain, solide ; [*bank, organization*] solide ; [*investment*] sûr ; **the bullet struck his ~ leg** la balle a atteint sa jambe valide ; **of ~ mind** sain d'esprit ; **in body and mind** sain de corps et d'esprit ; **to be ~ in wind and limb** avoir bon pied bon œil ; **to be as ~ as a bell** être en parfait état → **safe** [b] (= *competent, judicious, sensible*) [*judgement*] sain ; [*doctrine*] orthodoxe, solide ; [*argument, reasoning*] solide, valable ; [*decision, advice, opinion*] sensé ; [*case, training*] solide ; [*rule, policy, behaviour, tactics*] sensé, valable ; [*claim, title*] valable, sérieux ; [*statesman, player etc*] compétent ; **he is a ~ worker** il sait travailler, il est compétent dans son travail ; **he is a ~ socialist** c'est un bon socialiste, c'est un socialiste bon teint ; **he is ~ enough on theory ...** il connaît très bien la théorie ... ; **he's a ~ guy*** (= *sensible*) il est très sérieux or sensé ; (= *we can trust him*) c'est un type fiable* ; **~ sense** bon sens *m*, sens *m* pratique ; **that was a ~ move** c'était une action judicieuse or sensée [c] (= *thorough*) [*defeat*] complet (-ète *f*), total ; [*sleep*] profond ; **a ~ thrashing** une bonne or belle correction ; **he is a ~ sleeper** il a un bon sommeil, il dort bien

[2] ADV **to be ~ asleep** être profondément endormi, dormir à poings fermés ; **to sleep ~** bien dormir

sound³ [saʊnd] [1] N (*Med* = *probe*) sonde *f* [2] VT (*gen, Med, Naut etc*) sonder ; (fig: also ~ **out**) [+ *person*] sonder (**on, about** sur) ; **to ~ sb's opinions/feelings on sth** sonder qn sur ses opinions/ses sentiments à propos de qch [3] VI sonder [4] COMP ► **sound line** N = **sounding line** ; →**sounding²**

sound⁴ [saʊnd] N (*Geog*) détroit *m*, bras *m* de mer

sounding¹ [ˈsaʊndɪŋ] [1] N [a] [*of trumpet, bell etc*] son *m* ; **the ~ of the retreat/the alarm** le signal de la retraite/de l'alerte [b] (*Med*) auscultation *f* [2] COMP ► **sounding board** N (*Mus*) table *f* d'harmonie ; (*behind rostrum etc*) abat-voix *m inv* ; (*fig*) **he used the committee as a ~ board for his new idea** il a d'abord

essayé sa nouvelle idée sur les membres du comité

sounding² [ˈsaʊndɪŋ] [1] N (*Aviat, Naut, Space etc*) (= *act*) sondage *m* ; (= *measurement, data*) ~**s** sondages *mpl* ; (*lit, fig*) **to take ~s** faire des sondages [2] COMP ► **sounding line** N ligne *f* de sonde

-sounding [ˈsaʊndɪŋ] ADJ (*in compounds*) qui sonne ; **foreign-sounding name** nom *m* à consonance étrangère ; **strange-/respectable-sounding** qui sonne étrange/respectable or bien

soundless [ˈsaʊndlɪs] ADJ silencieux

soundlessly [ˈsaʊndlɪslɪ] ADV [*move*] sans bruit, en silence ; [*laugh, cry*] en silence ; [*say*] sans émettre un son

soundly [ˈsaʊndlɪ] ADV [a] (= *thoroughly*) [*defeat*] à plate(s) couture(s) ; [*condemn*] sévèrement ; **to whip sb ~** donner de bons coups de fouet à qn ; **he was ~ beaten** or **thrashed** (= *defeated*) il a été battu à plate(s) couture(s) ; (= *punished*) il a reçu une bonne or belle correction [b] (= *deeply*) [*asleep*] profondément ; **to sleep ~** (*lit*) dormir profondément or à poings fermés ; (*fig*) dormir sur ses deux oreilles [c] (= *firmly*) ~ **based** [*business, financial position*] sain, solide ; [*decision*] qui repose sur des bases solides [d] (= *strongly*) [*constructed*] solidement [e] (= *safely*) [*invest*] bien, judicieusement [f] (= *competently*) [*organize, manage*] bien, de façon saine or sûre ; [*play*] correctement, bien, comme il faut [g] (= *sensibly, logically*) [*advise, reason, argue*] judicieusement

soundness [ˈsaʊndnɪs] N (*NonC*) [a] (= *health*) [*of body, horse*] santé *f* ; [*of mind*] équilibre *m* [b] (= *stability*) [*of company, economy*] bonne santé *f* [c] (= *strength*) [*of structure*] solidité *f* [d] (= *sensibleness, logicality*) [*of judgement*] justesse *f* ; [*of advice, proposal, argument, philosophy, policy*] bon sens *m* [e] (= *deepness*) [*of sleep*] profondeur *f*

soundpost [ˈsaʊndpəʊst] N (*Mus*) âme *f*

soundproof [ˈsaʊndpruːf] [1] VT insonoriser [2] ADJ insonorisé

soundproofing [ˈsaʊndpruːfɪŋ] N insonorisation *f*

soundtrack [ˈsaʊndtræk] N (*Cine*) bande *f* sonore

soup [suːp] [1] N [a] soupe *f* ; (*thinner or sieved*) potage *m* ; (*very smooth*) velouté *m* ; **clear ~** potage *m* clair ; **mushroom/tomato ~** velouté *m* de champignons/de tomate ; **onion ~** soupe *f* à l'oignon ; **vegetable ~** soupe *f* or potage *m* aux légumes ; (*fig*) **to be in the ~*** être dans le pétrin *m* or dans de beaux draps → **pea** [b] (*US*⁑ = *nitroglycerine*) nitroglycérine *f* [2] COMP ► **soup cube** N potage *m* en cube ; (= *stock cube*) bouillon *m* Kub® or en cube ► **soup kitchen** N soupe *f* populaire ► **soup plate** N assiette *f* creuse or à soupe ► **soup spoon** N cuiller *f* à soupe ► **soup tureen** N soupière *f*

► **soup up*** VT SEP (*Aut*) [+ *engine*] gonfler* ; **he was driving a ~ed-up Mini®** il conduisait une Mini® au moteur gonflé* or poussé

soupçon [ˈsuːpsɒn] N [*of garlic etc, malice*] soupçon *m*, pointe *f*

soupy [ˈsuːpɪ] ADJ [*liquid*] (= *thick*) épais (-aisse *f*) ; (= *unclear*) trouble ; [*fog, atmosphere*] épais (-aisse *f*), dense ; (* fig = *sentimental*) [*film, story, voice*] sirupeux

sour [ˈsaʊəʳ] [1] ADJ [a] (*in taste, smell*) [*fruit, wine, beer, cream, smell, taste*] aigre ; [*milk*] tourné, aigre ; **to go** or **turn ~** [*milk*] tourner ; [*cream*] devenir aigre ; **this milk tastes ~** ce lait a tourné [b] (*Agr*) [*soil*] trop acide [c] (= *embittered*) [*person, voice*] aigre ; [*face, expression, mood*] revêche ; [*comment*] acerbe ; **to give sb a ~ look** lancer un regard mauvais à

qn ; **to turn** or **go ~** [*situation, relationship*] mal tourner, tourner à l'aigre [2] VT (*lit, fig*) aigrir ; [+ *milk*] faire tourner [3] VI [a] (*lit*) s'aigrir ; [*milk*] tourner [b] (*fig*) [*person, character*] s'aigrir ; [*relations*] se dégrader ; [*situation*] mal tourner, se dégrader [4] N **whisky** *etc* ~ cocktail *m* de whisky *etc* au citron [5] COMP ► **sour(ed) cream** N (*for cooking*) crème *f* fermentée ► **sour-faced** ADJ à la mine revêche or rébarbative ► **sour grapes** NPL (*fig*) dépit *m* ; **it was clearly ~ grapes on his part** c'était évidemment du dépit de sa part ; **it sounds like ~ grapes** ça ressemble à du dépit ► **sour milk** N (*for cooking*) lait *m* fermenté

source [sɔːs] [1] N [*of river*] source *f* ; (*fig*) source *f*, origine *f* ; [*Literat etc*] ~**s** sources *fpl* ; **a ~ of heat** une source de chaleur ; (*Med*) **a ~ of infection** un foyer d'infection ; **we have other ~s of supply** nous avons d'autres sources d'approvisionnement, nous pouvons nous approvisionner ailleurs ; **what is the ~ of this information?** quelle est l'origine or la provenance de cette nouvelle ? ; **I have it from a reliable ~ that ...** je tiens de bonne source or de source sûre que ... ; **at ~** à la source [2] VT (*Comm* = *find supplier for*) rechercher des fournisseurs de ; **to be ~d from** provenir de [3] COMP ► **source language** N (*Ling*) langue *f* de départ, langue *f* source ; (*Comput*) langage *m* source ► **source materials** NPL (*Literat etc*) sources *fpl* ► **source program** N (*Comput*) programme *m* source

sourcing [ˈsɔːsɪŋ] N (*Comm*) approvisionnement *m*

sourdine [sʊəˈdiːn] N sourdine *f*

sourdough [ˈsaʊədəʊ] N (*US*) levain *m*

sourish [ˈsaʊərɪʃ] ADJ (*lit, fig*) aigrelet

sourly [ˈsaʊəlɪ] ADV (= *disagreeably*) [*say, complain, think*] avec aigreur, aigrement ; [*look*] d'un air revêche [b] **to smell ~ of sth** avoir une odeur aigre de qch

sourness [ˈsaʊənɪs] N (*NonC*) [*of fruit, flavour, milk, cream, wine, beer, person, comment*] aigreur *f* ; **the ~ of her expression/mood/tone** son expression *f*/humeur *f*/ton *m* revêche

sourpuss* [ˈsaʊəpʊs] N grincheux *m*, -euse *f*

sousaphone [ˈsuːzəfəʊn] N sousaphone *m*

souse [saʊs] [1] VT [a] (= *immerse*) tremper (**in** dans) ; (= *soak*) faire or laisser tremper (**in** dans) ; **to ~ sth with water** inonder qch d'eau ; (*fig*) ~**d**⁑ (= *drunk*) rond*, noir⁑ [b] (*Culin*) mariner ; ~**d herrings** harengs *mpl* marinés ; (*rolled up*) rollmops *mpl* [2] N (*Culin*) marinade *f* (*à base de vinaigre*) [b] (⁑ = *drunkard*) poivrot* *m*, ivrogne *mf*

south [saʊθ] [1] N sud *m* ; **to the ~ of** au sud de ; **in the ~ of Scotland** dans le sud de l'Écosse ; **house facing the ~** maison *f* exposée au sud or au midi ; **to veer to the ~** or **to go into the ~** [*wind*] tourner au sud ; **the wind is in the ~** le vent est au sud ; **the wind is (coming** or **blowing) from the ~** le vent vient or souffle du sud ; **to live in the ~** habiter dans le Sud ; (*in France*) habiter dans le Midi ; **the South of France** le Sud de la France, le Midi ; (*US Hist*) **the South** le Sud, les États *mpl* du Sud → **deep**

[2] ADJ sud *inv*, du or au sud ; **~ wind** vent *m* du sud ; **~ coast** côte *f* sud or méridionale ; **on the ~ side** du côté sud ; **room with a ~ aspect** pièce *f* exposée au sud or au midi ; (*Archit*) **~ transept/door** transept *m*/portail *m* sud or méridional ; **in ~ Devon** dans le sud du Devon ; **in the South Atlantic** dans l'Atlantique Sud → **4**

[3] ADV [*go*] vers le sud, en direction du sud ; [*be, lie*] au sud, dans le sud ; **~ of the island** [*go, sail*] au sud de l'île ; [*be, lie*] dans le sud de l'île ; **the town lies ~ of the border** la ville est située au sud de la frontière ; **further ~** plus au sud ; **we drove ~ for 100km** nous avons roulé

pendant 100 km en direction du sud *or* du midi ; **go ~ till you get to Crewe** allez en direction du sud jusqu'à Crewe ; **to sail due ~** aller droit vers le sud ; (*Naut*) avoir le cap au sud ; **by ~-west** sud quart sud-ouest

4 COMP ▶ **South Africa** N l'Afrique *f* du Sud ▶ **South African** ADJ sud-africain, d'Afrique du Sud ♦ N Sud-Africain(e) *m(f)* ▶ **South America** N l'Amérique *f* du Sud ▶ **South American** ADJ sud-américain, d'Amérique du Sud ♦ N Sud-Américain(e) *m(f)* ▶ **South Australia** N l'Australie-Méridionale *f* ▶ **South Carolina** N la Caroline du Sud ; **in South Carolina** en Caroline du Sud ▶ **South Dakota** N le Dakota du Sud ; **in South Dakota** dans le Dakota du Sud ▶ **south-east** N sud-est *m* ♦ ADJ du sud-est *inv* ♦ ADV vers le sud-est ▶ **South-East Asia** N le Sud-Est asiatique, l'Asie *f* du sud-est ▶ **south-easter** N vent *m* du sud-est ▶ **south-easterly** ADJ [*wind, direction*] du sud-est ; [*situation*] au sud-est ♦ ADV vers le sud-est ▶ **south-eastern** ADJ (du *or* au) sud-est ▶ **south-eastward(s)** ADV vers le sud-est ▶ **south-facing** ADJ exposé au sud *or* au midi ▶ **South Georgia** N la Géorgie du Sud ▶ **South Moluccan** N les Moluquois(e) *m(f)* du Sud ▶ **the South Pacific** N le Pacifique Sud ▶ **South Pole** N pôle *m* Sud ▶ **the South Sea Islands** NPL l'Océanie *f* ▶ **the South Seas** NPL les mers *fpl* du Sud ▶ **south-south-east** N sud-sud-est *m* ♦ ADJ (du *or* au) sud-sud-est *inv* ♦ ADV vers le sud-sud-est ▶ **south-south-west** N sud-sud-ouest *m* ♦ ADJ (du *or* au) sud-sud-ouest *inv* ♦ ADV vers le sud-sud-ouest ▶ **south-west** N sud-ouest *m* ♦ ADJ (du *or* au) sud-ouest *inv* ♦ ADV vers le sud-ouest ▶ **South West Africa** N l'Afrique *f* du sud-ouest ▶ **south-wester** N vent *m* du sud-ouest, suroît *m* ▶ **south-westerly** ADJ [*wind, direction*] du sud-ouest ; [*situation*] au sud-ouest ♦ ADV vers le sud-ouest ▶ **south-western** ADJ (du *or* au) sud-ouest *inv* ▶ **south-westward(s)** ADV vers le sud-ouest → **Korea, Vietnam**

southbound ['saʊθbaʊnd] ADJ [*traffic, vehicles*] (se déplaçant) en direction du sud ; [*carriageway*] sud *inv* ; **to be ~ on the M1** être sur la M1 en direction du sud

southerly ['sʌðəlɪ] **1** ADJ [*wind*] du sud ; [*situation*] au sud, au midi ; **in a ~ direction** en direction du sud *or* du midi, vers le sud *or* le midi ; **~ latitudes** latitudes *fpl* australes ; **~ aspect** exposition *f* au sud *or* au midi **2** ADV vers le sud

southern ['sʌðən] **1** ADJ sud *inv*, du sud ; **the ~ coast** la côte sud *or* méridionale ; **house with a ~ outlook** maison *f* exposée au sud *or* au midi ; **~ wall** mur *m* exposé au sud *or* au midi ; **~ hemisphere** hémisphère *m* sud *inv or* austral ; **Southern Africa** Afrique *f* australe ; **~ France** le Sud de la France, le Midi ; **in ~ Spain** dans le Sud de l'Espagne, en Espagne méridionale **2** COMP ▶ **the Southern Cross** N la Croix-du-Sud

southerner ['sʌðənəʳ] N **a** homme *m or* femme *f* du Sud, habitant(e) *m(f)* du Sud ; (*in France*) Méridional(e) *m(f)* ; **he is a ~** il vient du Sud ; **the ~s** les gens *mpl* du Sud **b** (*US Hist*) sudiste *mf*

southernmost ['sʌðənməʊst] ADJ le plus au sud, à l'extrême sud

southpaw ['saʊθpɔː] N (*Sport*) gaucher *m*

southward ['saʊθwəd] **1** ADJ au sud **2** ADV (*also* ~s) vers le sud

souvenir [ˌsuːvəˈnɪəʳ] N souvenir *m* (*objet*)

sou'wester [saʊˈwɛstəʳ] N (= *hat*) suroît *m* ; (= *wind*) = **south-wester** → **south**

sovereign ['sɒvrɪn] **1** N souverain(e) *m(f)* ; (*Brit* = *coin*) souverain *m* (*ancienne pièce d'or qui valait 20 shillings*) **2** ADJ [*state, independence, body, law, powers*] souverain (*after n*) ; [*contempt, indifference*] souverain (*before n*) ; **a ~**

remedy for *or* **against sth**† un remède souverain contre qch

sovereignty ['sɒvrɪntɪ] N souveraineté *f*

soviet ['saʊvɪət] **1** N soviet *m* ; **the Supreme Soviet** le Soviet suprême ; (= *people*) **the Soviets** les Soviétiques *mpl* **2** ADJ soviétique **3** COMP ▶ **Soviet Russia** N la Russie soviétique ▶ **the Soviet Union** N l'Union *f* soviétique

sovietize ['saʊvɪətaɪz] VT soviétiser

Sovietologist [ˌsaʊvɪəˈtɒlədʒɪst] N soviétologue *mf*

sow[1] [saʊ] N (= *pig*) truie *f*

sow[2] [saʊ] (*pret* **sowed**, *ptp* **sown** *or* **sowed**) **1** VT [+ *seed, grass*] semer ; [+ *field*] ensemencer (**with** en) ; (*fig*) [+ *mines, pebbles, doubt, discord*] semer ■ (*PROV*) **~ the wind and reap the whirlwind** qui sème le vent récolte la tempête (*PROV*) → **seed, wild** **2** VI semer

sowbelly ['saʊbɛlɪ] N (*US*) petit salé *m*

sower ['saʊəʳ] N (= *person*) semeur *m*, -euse *f* ; (= *machine*) semoir *m*

sowing ['saʊɪŋ] **1** N **a** (= *work*) semailles *fpl* ; (= *period, seeds*) semailles *fpl* ; (= *young plants*) semis *mpl* **b** (*NonC* = *act*) [*of field*] ensemencement *m* ; **the ~ of seeds** les semailles **2** COMP ▶ **sowing machine** N semoir *m*

sown [saʊn] VB *ptp of* **sow**[2]

soy [sɔɪ] N **a** (*also* ~ **sauce**) sauce *f* de soja **b** (*US*) = **soya**

soya ['sɔɪə] **1** N (*esp Brit: also* ~ **bean**) (= *plant*) soja *or* soya *m* ; (= *bean*) graine *f* de soja **2** COMP ▶ **soya flour** N farine *f* de soja

soybean ['sɔɪbiːn] N (*US*) = **soya bean** → **soya**

sozzled†* ['sɒzld] ADJ (*Brit*) paf* *inv*, noir*

SP [ɛsˈpiː] N (*Brit*) ABBR = **starting price** **a** (*Racing*) cote *f* de départ **b** (* = *information*) **what's the SP on him?** qu'est-ce qu'il se dit sur lui ? ; **to give sb the SP on sb/sth** donner des infos* à qn sur qn/qch

spa [spɑː] N **a** (= *town*) station *f* thermale, ville *f* d'eau ; (= *spring*) source *f* minérale **b** (*US: also* **health ~**) établissement *m* de cure de rajeunissement

space [speɪs] **1** N **a** (*NonC*: gen, Astron, Phys) espace *m* ; **the rocket vanished into ~** la fusée a disparu dans l'espace ; **he was staring into ~** il regardait dans l'espace *or* dans le vide → **outer** **b** (*NonC* = *room*) espace *m*, place *f* ; **to clear (a** *or* **some) ~** *or* **make ~ for sb/sth** faire de la place pour qn/qch ; **to take up a lot of ~** [*car, books, piece of furniture*] prendre une grande place *or* beaucoup de place, être encombrant ; [*building*] occuper un grand espace ; **the ~ occupied by a car/a building** l'encombrement *m* d'une voiture/d'un bâtiment ; **there isn't enough ~ for it** il n'y a pas assez de place pour ça ; **I haven't enough ~ to turn the car** je n'ai pas assez de place pour *or* je n'ai pas la place de tourner la voiture ; **to buy ~ in a newspaper (for an advertisement)** acheter de l'espace (publicitaire) dans un journal **c** (*fig* = *freedom*) **she needed a bit of ~** elle avait besoin qu'on la laisse un peu tranquille ; **we give each other ~** nous nous accordons *or* nous nous laissons à chacun une certaine liberté **d** (= *gap, empty area*) espace *m*, place *f* (*NonC*) ; (*Mus*) interligne *m* ; (*Typ*: between two words etc) espace *m*, blanc *m* ; (*Typ* = *blank type*) espace *m* ; **in the ~s between the trees** (dans les espaces) entre les arbres ; **a ~ of 10 metres between the buildings** un espace *or* un écart *or* une distance de 10 mètres entre les bâtiments ; **leave a ~ for the name** laisse de la place *or* un espace *or* un blanc pour le nom ; **in the ~ provided** dans le ~ réservé à cet effet ; **in an enclosed ~** dans un espace clos *or* fermé ; **I'm looking for a ~ to park the car in** *or* **a parking ~** je cherche une place (pour me garer) → **blank, open**

e (= *interval, period*) espace *m* (de temps), intervalle *m* ; **after a ~ of ten minutes** après un intervalle de dix minutes ; **for the ~ of a month** pendant une durée *or* une période d'un mois ; **a ~ of five years** une période de cinq ans ; **in the ~ of three generations/one hour** en l'espace de trois générations/d'une heure ; **a short ~ of time** un court laps de temps *or* espace de temps ; **for a ~** pendant un certain temps

2 VT **a** (*also* ~ **out**) [+ *chairs, words, visits, letters*] espacer ; [+ *payments*] échelonner (**over** sur) ; **~ the posts (out) evenly** espacez les poteaux régulièrement, plantez les poteaux à intervalles réguliers ; **you'll have to ~ them further out** *or* **further apart** ◊ **you'll have to ~ them out more** il faudra laisser plus d'espace entre eux *or* les espacer davantage ; **to be single-/double-~d** [*text*] avoir des interlignes *mpl* simples/doubles ; **to ~ type out to fill a line** espacer *or* répartir les caractères sur toute une ligne ; **the houses were well ~d (out)** les maisons étaient bien *or* largement espacées **b** **to be ~d (out)**‡ être défoncé‡

3 COMP [*journey, programme, research, rocket*] spatial ▶ **the Space Age** N l'ère *f* spatiale ▶ **space-age** ADJ de l'ère spatiale, futuriste ▶ **space bar** N [*of typewriter, keyboard*] barre *f* d'espacement ▶ **space cadet**‡ N (*esp US*) allumé(e)* *m(f)* ▶ **space capsule** N capsule *f* spatiale ▶ **space fiction** N science-fiction *f* (*sur le thème des voyages dans l'espace*) ▶ **space-filler** N (*Press*) article *m* bouche-trou *inv* ▶ **space flight** N (= *journey*) voyage *m* spatial *or* dans l'espace ; (*NonC*) voyages *mpl or* vols *mpl* spatiaux ▶ **space heater** N radiateur *m* ▶ **space helmet** N casque *m* d'astronaute *or* de cosmonaute ▶ **Space Invaders**® N Space Invaders *mpl* (*jeu vidéo mettant en scène des envahisseurs extraterrestres*) ; **Space Invaders machine** Space Invaders *m* ▶ **space lab** N laboratoire *m* spatial ▶ **space opera** N space opera *m* (*film ou série de science-fiction sur le thème des voyages dans l'espace*) ▶ **space plane** N = space shuttle ▶ **space platform** N = space station ▶ **space probe** N sonde *f* spatiale ▶ **the space race** N la course à l'espace ▶ **space-saving** ADJ qui économise *or* gagne de la place ▶ **space science** N spatiologie *f* ▶ **space scientist** N spécialiste *mf* en spatiologie, spatiologue *mf* ▶ **space shot** N (= *launching*) lancement *m* d'un engin spatial ; (= *flight*) vol *m* spatial ▶ **space shuttle** N navette *f* spatiale ▶ **space sickness** N mal *m* de l'espace ▶ **space station** N station *f* orbitale *or* spatiale ▶ **space-time** N espace-temps *m* ▶ **space-time continuum** N continuum *m* espace-temps ▶ **space travel** N voyages *mpl* spatiaux *or* interplanétaires *or* dans l'espace ▶ **space writer** N (*Press*) journaliste *mf* payé(e) à la ligne

spacecraft ['speɪskrɑːft] N engin *m or* vaisseau *m* spatial

spaceman ['speɪsmæn] N (*pl* **-men**) (*gen*) spationaute *m* ; (*American*) astronaute *m* ; (*Russian*) cosmonaute *m*

spaceport ['speɪspɔːt] N base *f* de lancement (*d'engins spatiaux*)

spaceship ['speɪsʃɪp] N = **spacecraft**

spacesuit ['speɪssuːt] N combinaison *f* spatiale

spacewalk ['speɪswɔːk] **1** N marche *f* dans l'espace **2** VI marcher dans l'espace

spacewalker ['speɪswɔːkəʳ] N marcheur *m*, -euse *f* de l'espace

spacewoman ['speɪswʊmən] N (*pl* **-women**) (*gen*) spationaute *f* ; (*American*) astronaute *f* ; (*Russian*) cosmonaute *f*

spacey* ['speɪsɪ] ADJ [*music*] planant* ; [*person*] qui plane*

spacing ['speɪsɪŋ] N (*esp Typ*) espacement *m* ; (*between two objects*) espacement *m*, écartement *m*; (*also* ~ **out**: *of payments, sentries*) échelonnement *m*; (*Typ*) **to type sth in single/double** ~ taper qch à simple/double interligne *or* avec un interligne simple/double

spacious ['speɪʃəs] ADJ [*room, house, car*] spacieux; [*garden*] grand; [*garment*] ample; ~ **accommodation** logement *m* spacieux

spaciousness ['speɪʃəsnɪs] N grandes dimensions *fpl*, grandeur *f*

spade [speɪd] N **[a]** bêche *f*, pelle *f*; (*child's*) pelle *f*; (*fig*) **to call a ~ a** ~ appeler un chat un chat, ne pas avoir peur des mots **[b]** (*Cards*) pique *m*; **the six of ~s** le six de pique; (*fig*) **in ~s*** par excellence; *for other phrases see* **club [c]** (✿ *pej*) nègre *m*, négresse *f*

spadeful ['speɪdfʊl] N pelletée *f*; (*fig*) **by the ~** en grandes quantités

spadework ['speɪdwɜːk] N (*NonC*: *fig*) travail *m* préliminaire

spag bol [ˌspæɡ'bɒl] N (*Brit*) spaghettis *mpl* bolognaise

spaghetti [spə'ɡetɪ] **[1]** N spaghettis *mpl* **[2]** COMP ► **spaghetti bolognese** N spaghettis *mpl* bolognaise ► **spaghetti junction** N échangeur à niveaux multiples ► **spaghetti western*** N western-spaghetti* *m*, western *m* italien

Spain [speɪn] N l'Espagne *f*

spake †† [speɪk] VB *pt of* **speak**

Spam® [spæm] N ≈ mortadelle *f*

span¹ [spæn] **[1]** N **[a]** [*of hands, arms*] envergure *f*; [*of girder*] portée *f*; [*of bridge*] travée *f*; [*of arch*] portée *f*, ouverture *f*; [*of roof*] portée *f*, travée *f*; [*of plane, bird*] (*also* **wingspan**) envergure *f*; **a bridge with three ~s** un pont à trois travées; **single-~ bridge** pont à travée unique; **the bridge has a ~ of 120 metres** le pont a une travée *or* une portée de 120 mètres **[b]** (*in time*) espace *m* (de temps), durée *f*; **the average ~ of life** la durée moyenne de vie; (*liter*) **man's ~ is short** la vie humaine est brève; **for a brief** *or* **short ~ (of time)** pendant un bref moment, pendant un court espace de temps → **life [c]** († = *measure*) empan *m* **[d]** (= *yoke*) [*of oxen etc*] paire *f* **[2]** VT **[a]** [*bridge, rope, plank etc*] [+ *stream, ditch*] enjamber; [+ *bridge-builder*] jeter *or* construire un pont sur; (*fig*) **Christianity ~s almost 2,000 years** le christianisme embrasse presque 2 000 ans; **his life ~s almost the whole of the 18th century** sa vie s'étend sur *or* couvre presque tout le 18ᵉ siècle; **his compositions ~ all types of music** ses compositions couvrent *or* embrassent tous les types de musique **[b]** (= *measure*) mesurer à l'empan

span² †† [spæn] VB *pt of* **spin**

spandex ['spændeks] N (*Tex*) fibre *f* (synthétique) élastique

spangle ['spæŋɡl] **[1]** N paillette *f*; **dress with ~s on it** robe *f* pailletée *or* à paillettes **[2]** VT orner de paillettes; (*fig*) **~d with** pailleté de → **star**

spangly* ['spæŋɡlɪ] ADJ à paillettes, pailleté

Spaniard ['spænjəd] N Espagnol(e) *m(f)*

spaniel ['spænjəl] N épagneul *m*

Spanish ['spænɪʃ] **[1]** ADJ (*gen*) espagnol; [*ambassador, embassy, monarch*] d'Espagne; [*teacher*] d'espagnol; **the ~ way of life** la vie espagnole, la façon de vivre des Espagnols; **the ~ people** les Espagnols *mpl* **[2]** N (*Ling*) espagnol *m* **[3]** **the Spanish** NPL les Espagnols *mpl* **[4]** COMP ► **Spanish America** N l'Amérique *f* hispanophone ► **Spanish-American** ADJ hispano-américain ► **the Spanish Armada** N (*Hist*) l'Invincible Armada *f* ► **Spanish chestnut** N châtaigne *f*, marron *m* ► **the**

Spanish Civil War N la guerre civile espagnole, la guerre d'Espagne ► **Spanish fly** N (*NonC*) (poudre *f* de) cantharide *f* ► **Spanish guitar** N guitare *f* classique ► **the Spanish Main** N la mer des Antilles *or* des Caraïbes ► **Spanish moss** N (*US*) mousse *f* espagnole ► **Spanish omelette** N omelette *f* aux pommes de terre et aux légumes ► **Spanish onion** N oignon *m* d'Espagne ► **Spanish rice** N riz *m* à l'espagnole

spank [spæŋk] **[1]** **to give sb a ~** donner un coup *or* une claque à qn sur les fesses **[2]** VT (*gen, for sexual pleasure*) donner une fessée à **[3]** VI **to be** *or* **go ~ing along** [*horse, vehicle, ship*] aller *or* filer à bonne allure

spanking ['spæŋkɪŋ] **[1]** N fessée *f*; **to give sb a ~** donner une fessée à qn **[2]** ADJ* **[a]** (= *excellent*) super*; **in ~ condition** en excellent état **[b]** (= *fast*) [*pace*] fulgurant; **to move at a ~ pace** [*film, events*] se dérouler à un rythme échevelé; **to speed along at a ~ pace** [*car*] passer à toute berzingue* **[c]** (= *fresh*) [*breeze*] fort, bon **[3]** ADV†* ► **new** flambant neuf*; ~ **white/clean** d'une blancheur/d'une propreté éclatante

spanner ['spænər] **[1]** N (*Brit*) clé *f* (à écrous); (*fig*) **to put a ~ in the works** mettre des bâtons dans les roues **[2]** COMP ► **spanner wrench** N clé *f* à ergots

spar¹ [spɑːr] N (*Geol*) spath *m*

spar² [spɑːr] N (*Naut*) espar *m*

spar³ [spɑːr] **[1]** VI (*Boxing*) s'entraîner (à la boxe) (**with sb** avec qn); (*rough and tumble*) se bagarrer* amicalement (**with sb** avec qn); [*two people*] échanger des coups de poing pour rire; (*fig* = *argue*) se disputer (**with sb** avec qn); [*two people*] se défier en paroles **[2]** COMP ► **sparring match** N (*Boxing*) combat *m* d'entraînement; (*fig*) échange *m* verbal ► **sparring partner** N (*Boxing*) sparring-partner *m*, partenaire *mf* d'entraînement; (*fig*) adversaire *mf*

spare [speər] **[1]** ADJ **[a]** (= *reserve*) de réserve; (= *replacement*) de rechange; (= *surplus*) de *or* en trop; **take a ~ pen in case that one runs out** prends un stylo de rechange *or* de réserve au cas où celui-ci n'aurait plus d'encre; **I've a ~ pen if you want it** j'ai un autre stylo *or* un stylo de *or* en trop, si tu veux; **have you any ~ cups?** (*in case you need more*) est-ce que tu as des tasses de réserve?; (*which you're not using*) est-ce que tu as des tasses de *or* en trop?; **take some ~ clothes** prends des vêtements de rechange; **there were no ~ chairs** *or* **no chairs** ~ il n'y avait pas de chaise libre; **a ~ bed** (*gen*) un lit de libre; (*for houseguests*) un lit d'amis; ~ **cash** (*small amount*) argent *m* de reste; (*larger*) argent *m* disponible; **I'll lend you my ~ key** je vais te prêter mon double (de clé); **I've got a ~ ticket for the play** j'ai une place en plus pour la pièce de théâtre; **there are two going ~*** il en reste deux; **thousands of tickets are going ~*** il reste des milliers de billets; (*hum*) **I felt like a ~ prick**✿ **at a wedding** je me demandais ce que je foutais là✿ **[b]** (= *lean*) [*person, body*] sec (sèche *f*) **[c]** (= *austere*) [*prose, style, design, room*] dépouillé; [*music*] sobre; [*diet, meal*] frugal **[d]** (*Brit*✿ = *crazy*) **to go** ~ devenir dingue*; **to drive sb** ~ rendre qn dingue* **[2]** N (= *part*) pièce *f* de rechange, pièce *f* détachée; (= *tyre*) pneu *m* de rechange; (= *wheel*) roue *f* de secours **[3]** VT **[a]** (= *do without*) se passer de; **we can't ~ him just now** nous ne pouvons pas nous passer de lui en ce moment; **can you ~ it?** vous n'en avez pas besoin?; **can you ~ £10?** est-ce que tu aurais 10 livres?; **can you ~ me £5?** est-ce que tu peux me passer 5 livres?; **I can only ~ a few minutes** ◊ **I've only a few minutes to** ~ je ne dispose que de quelques minutes, je n'ai que quelques minutes de libres *or* devant moi; **I can't ~ the time (to do it)** je

n'ai pas le temps (de le faire), je n'ai pas une minute (à y consacrer); **he had time to ~ so** he went to the pictures il n'était pas pressé *or* il avait du temps devant lui, alors il est allé au cinéma; **did you have a rush to get here?** — **no, I had time (and) to ~** est-ce que tu as dû te dépêcher pour arriver? — non, j'ai eu plus de temps qu'il ne m'en fallait; **I can only ~ an hour for my piano practice** je peux seulement consacrer une heure à *or* je ne dispose que d'une heure pour mes exercices de piano; **I can ~ you five minutes** je peux vous accorder *or* consacrer cinq minutes; **to ~ a thought for** penser à, dédier une pensée à; **there are three to ~** il en reste trois; **I've got none** *or* **nothing to ~** j'ai juste ce qu'il me faut, je n'en ai pas trop; **I've enough and to ~** j'en ai plus qu'il ne m'en faut; **she had a metre to ~** elle en avait un mètre de trop *or* de plus que nécessaire; **with two minutes to** ~ avec deux minutes d'avance; **we did it with £5 to** ~ nous l'avons fait et il nous reste encore 5 livres **[b]** (= *show mercy to*) [+ *person, sb's life, tree etc*] épargner; (*lit, fig*) **he ~d no one** il n'a épargné personne, il n'a fait grâce à personne; **the plague ~d no one** la peste n'a épargné personne; **if I'm ~d†** si Dieu me prête vie; **to ~ sb's feelings** ménager (les sentiments de) qn; ~ **my blushes!** épargnez ma modestie!, ne me faites pas rougir! **[c]** [+ *suffering, grief etc*] éviter, épargner (**to sb** à qn); **to ~ sb embarrassment** épargner *or* éviter de l'embarras à qn; **I wanted to ~ him trouble** je voulais lui éviter de se déranger; **you could have ~d yourself the trouble** vous auriez pu vous épargner tout ce mal; **I'll ~ you the details** je vous fais grâce des détails **[d]** (= *refrain from using etc*) [+ *one's strength, efforts*] ménager; **we have ~d no expense to make her stay a pleasant one** nous n'avons pas reculé devant la dépense pour que son séjour soit agréable; **he ~d no expense to modernize the house** il a dépensé sans compter pour moderniser la maison; **no expense** ~**d** peu importe le prix; **he didn't ~ himself** ◊ he ~**d no pains** il s'est donné beaucoup de mal, il n'a pas épargné sa peine; **he could have ~d his pains** ◊ he could have ~**d himself the trouble** il s'est donné du mal pour rien; ~ **your pains, it's too late now** pas la peine de te donner du mal, c'est trop tard maintenant ■ (*PROV*) ~ **the rod and spoil the child** qui aime bien châtie bien (*PROV*)

[4] COMP ► **spare bedroom** N = spare room ► **spare part** N (*Aut, Tech*) pièce *f* de rechange, pièce *f* détachée ► **spare-part surgery*** N chirurgie *f* de transplantation ► **spare room** N chambre *f* d'amis ► **spare time** N temps *m* libre; **to do sth in one's ~ time** faire qch pendant son temps libre *or* ses moments de libre ► **spare-time** ADJ (fait) à temps perdu *or* pendant les moments de loisir; ~**-time activities** (activités *fpl* de) loisirs *mpl* ► **spare tyre** N [*of car*] roue *f* de secours; (* *fig* = *fat*) bourrelet *m* (de graisse) (à la taille); **to get a ~ tyre*** prendre de l'embonpoint; **to get rid of one's ~ tyre*** se débarrasser de son bourrelet (de graisse) ► **spare wheel** N [*of car*] roue *f* de secours

sparerib ['speərɪb] N (*Culin*) travers *m* (de porc)

sparing ['speərɪŋ] ADJ [*person*] économe; [*amount*] limité, modéré; **she was ~ with heat and light** elle faisait des économies de chauffage et d'électricité; **I've not been ~ with the garlic** je n'ai pas lésiné sur l'ail; **he was ~ with** *or* (*frm*) **of the wine** il a lésiné sur le vin; (*frm*) ~ **of words** avare *or* chiche de paroles; (*frm*) **you must be more ~ of your strength** vous devez ménager vos forces; ~ **in one's praise (for sb)** avare de ses louanges (à l'égard de qn); **to be ~ in one's use of sth** utiliser qch avec modération

sparingly ['speərɪŋlɪ] ADV [*use, apply*] avec modération ; [*eat*] frugalement ; [*drink*] peu ; [*spend, praise*] avec parcimonie

spark [spɑːk] 1 (*Elec*) étincelle *f* ; (*fig*) [*of intelligence, wit, life*] étincelle *f* ; [*of commonsense, interest*] lueur *f* ; (*fig*) **to make the ~s fly** (= *start a row*) mettre le feu aux poudres (*fig*) ; (= *fight*) se bagarrer un bon coup* ; **they'll strike ~s off each other** ils se stimuleront (l'un l'autre) → **bright** 2 **sparks** NPL (*Brit = electrician*) électricien *m* ; (= *radio operator*) radio *m* (de bord) 3 VI jeter des étincelles 4 VT (*also* ~ **off**) [+ *rebellion, complaints, quarrel*] provoquer, déclencher ; [+ *interest, enthusiasm*] susciter, éveiller (**in sb** chez qn) ; **to ~ a fire** provoquer un incendie 5 COMP ► **spark gap** N (*Elec*) écartement *m* des électrodes ► **spark(ing) plug** N (*Aut*) bougie *f*

sparkle ['spɑːkl] 1 N (*NonC*) [*of stars, dew, tinsel*] scintillement *m*, étincellement *m* ; [*of diamond*] éclat *m*, feux *mpl* ; (*in eye*) étincelle *f*, éclair *m* ; (*fig*) vie *f*, éclat *m* 2 VI [*glass, drops of water, snow etc*] étinceler, briller ; [*surface of water, lake etc*] scintiller, miroiter ; [*diamond*] étinceler, jeter des feux, scintiller ; [*fabric*] chatoyer ; [*wine*] pétiller ; [*eyes*] étinceler, pétiller (**with** de) ; [*person*] briller ; [*conversation, play, book*] étinceler, pétiller (**with** de), être brillant *or* étincelant

sparkler ['spɑːklər] N a (= *firework*) cierge *m* magique b (* = *sparkling wine*) vin *m* pétillant c (‡ = *diamond*) diam◦ *m*

sparkling ['spɑːklɪŋ] 1 ADJ a (= *bright*) [*glass, diamond, snow, sand, sea, eyes*] étincelant (**with sth** de qch) ; [*day, sky*] radieux ; [*surface of water, lake*] scintillant, miroitant b (= *scintillating*) [*person, conversation, script, performance, results*] brillant ; **he was in ~ form** il était dans une forme éblouissante c (= *fizzy*) [*wine*] mousseux ; [*water*] (*naturally*) gazeux naturel ; (*artificially*) gazéifié ; ~ **cider** cidre *m* 2 ADV ~ **clean** d'une propreté éclatante

sparkly* ['spɑːklɪ] ADJ brillant

sparrow ['spærəʊ] N moineau *m* → **hedgesparrow**

sparrowgrass ['spærəʊgrɑːs] N (*dial*) asperge(s) *f(pl)*

sparrowhawk ['spærəʊhɔːk] N épervier *m*

sparse [spɑːs] ADJ [*population, hair, vegetation*] clairsemé ; [*traffic*] léger ; [*furniture*] rare ; [*dialogue*] entrecoupé de longs silences

sparsely ['spɑːslɪ] ADV [*wooded, furnished*] peu ; ~ **populated** peu peuplé

Sparta ['spɑːtə] N Sparte

Spartacus ['spɑːtəkəs] N Spartacus *m*

Spartan ['spɑːtən] 1 N Spartiate *mf* 2 ADJ a (= *from Sparta*) spartiate b (= *austere: also* **spartan**) [*lifestyle, accommodation, conditions, diet*] spartiate

spasm ['spæzəm] N (*Med*) spasme *m* ; (*fig*) accès *m* (**of** de) ; **a ~ of coughing** un accès *or* une quinte de toux ; **to work in ~s** travailler par à-coups *or* par accès

spasmodic [spæz'mɒdɪk] ADJ a (= *intermittent*) [*work, movements, attempts, service*] intermittent, irrégulier ; **the team had only ~ success** l'équipe n'a connu que des succès intermittents ; **to mount ~ raids** lancer des raids répétés b (*Med*) spasmodique

spasmodically [spæz'mɒdɪkəlɪ] ADV a (= *intermittently*) [*continue, campaign*] de façon intermittente ; [*work, try*] par à-coups, de façon intermittente *or* irrégulière b (*Med*) **to jerk ~** [*person, body, chest*] être agité de spasmes irréguliers

spastic ['spæstɪk] 1 ADJ a († = *handicapped*) [*person*] handicapé moteur (handicapée motrice *f*) b (*Med*) [*movement, paralysis*] spasmodique c (*pej = clumsy*) [*movement*] convulsif 2 N (*Med†*) handicapé(e) *m(f)* moteur (*f inv*)

3 COMP ► **spastic colon** N colopathie *f* spasmodique

spasticity [spæs'tɪsɪtɪ] N (*Med*) paralysie *f* spasmodique

spat¹ [spæt] VB *pt, ptp of* **spit¹**

spat² [spæt] N (= *gaiter*) demi-guêtre *f*

spat³ [spæt] N (= *oyster*) naissain *m*

spat⁴* [spæt] (*US = quarrel*) 1 N prise *f* de bec* 2 VI avoir une prise de bec*

spate [speɪt] N (*Brit*) a [*of river*] crue *f* b (*fig*) [*of letters, orders etc*] avalanche *f* ; [*of words, abuse*] torrent *m* ; [*of bombings etc*] série *f* ; **in ~** en crue ; **to be in full ~** (= *talking at length*) être parti (dans son sujet) ; **to have a ~ of work** être débordé *or* submergé de travail ; **a fresh ~ of sabotage/attacks** une recrudescence d'actes de sabotage/d'attaques

spatial ['speɪʃəl] (*frm*) 1 ADJ a (= *physical*) [*relationship, variation*] spatial ; [*constraints*] d'espace ; ~ **distribution of employment** répartition *f or* distribution *f* géographique de l'emploi b (*Psych*) ~ **awareness/ability/skills** perception *f* spatiale 2 COMP ► **spatial frequency** N (*Elec*) fréquence *f* spatiale

spatiotemporal ['speɪʃɪəʊ'tempərəl] ADJ spatiotemporel

spatter ['spætər] 1 VT (*accidentally*) éclabousser (**with** de) ; (*deliberately*) asperger (**with** de) ; **to ~ mud on** *or* **over a dress** éclabousser de boue une robe 2 VI (= *splash*) gicler (**on** sur) ; (= *sound*) crépiter (**on** sur) 3 N (= *mark*) éclaboussure(s) *f(pl)* ; (= *sound*) crépitement *m*

-spattered ['spætəd] ADJ (*in compounds*) **the butcher's blood-spattered apron** le tablier éclaboussé de sang du boucher ; **mud-spattered car** voiture *f* éclaboussée de boue

spatula ['spætjʊlə] N (*Culin*) spatule *f* ; (*Med*) abaisse-langue *m inv*

spavin ['spævɪn] N éparvin *m*

spawn [spɔːn] 1 N [*of fish, frog*] frai *m*, œufs *mpl* ; [*of mushroom*] mycélium *m* ; (*pej = person*) progéniture *f* (*iro*) 2 VT pondre ; (*fig pej*) engendrer, faire naître 3 VI frayer ; (*fig pej*) se reproduire, se multiplier

spawning ['spɔːnɪŋ] 1 N (*NonC*) frai *m* 2 COMP ► **spawning ground** N frayère *f*

spay [speɪ] VT [+ *animal*] enlever les ovaires de

SPCA [,espiːsiː'eɪ] N (*US*) (ABBR = **Society for the Prevention of Cruelty to Animals**) ≈ SPA *f*

SPCC [,espiːsiː'siː] N (*US*) (ABBR = **Society for the Prevention of Cruelty to Children**) association pour la protection de l'enfance

speak [spiːk] (*pret* **spoke, spake**, *ptp* **spoken**) 1 VI a (= *talk*) parler (**to** à, **of, about** de) ; (= *converse*) parler, s'entretenir (**with** avec) ; (= *be on speaking terms*) parler, adresser la parole (**to** à) ; (*fig*) [*gun, trumpet etc*] retentir, se faire entendre ; **to ~ in a whisper** chuchoter ; ~ **normally, don't shout!** parle normalement, ne crie pas ! ; **to ~ to o.s.** parler tout seul ; **I'll ~ to him about it** je vais lui en parler, je vais lui en toucher un mot *or* deux mots ; **I don't know him to ~ to** je ne le connais pas assez bien pour lui parler *or* pour lui adresser la parole ; **I'll never ~ to him again** je ne lui adresserai plus jamais la parole ; **did you ~?** pardon ?, tu m'as parlé ?, tu dis ?* ; **you have only to ~** tu n'as qu'un mot à dire ; **so to ~** pour ainsi dire ; **biologically/philosophically ~ing ...** biologiquement/philosophiquement parlant ... ; ~**ing personally ...** pour ma part ..., personnellement ... ; ~**ing as a member of the society I ...** en tant que membre de la société je ...

b (*Telec*) **who's (that) ~ing?** qui est à l'appareil ? ; (*passing on call*) c'est de la part de qui ? ; (*Telec*) (**this is**) **Paul ~ing** ici Paul, (c'est) Paul à l'appareil ; (*Telec*) ~**ing!** lui-même (*or* ellemême) !, c'est moi-même ! → **action, badly, roughly**

c (= *make a speech*) parler (**on** *or* **about sth** de qch) ; (= *begin to speak*) prendre la parole ; **to**

~ **in public** parler en public ; **he rose to ~** il s'est levé pour prendre la parole *or* pour parler ; **Mr Latimer will ~ next** ensuite c'est M. Latimer qui prendra la parole ; **the chairman asked him to ~** le président lui a donné la parole ; **Mr King will now ~ on "The Incas"** M. King va maintenant (nous) parler des Incas ; **to ~ in a debate** (*proposer, seconder*) faire un discours *or* prendre la parole au cours d'un débat ; (*from floor of house*) participer à un débat, intervenir dans un débat

d (*phrases*) **to ~ for sb** (= *be spokesman for*) parler pour qn *or* au nom de qn ; (= *give evidence for*) parler *or* témoigner en faveur de qn ; ~**ing for myself ...** personnellement ..., pour ma part ..., en ce qui me concerne ... ; ~ **for yourself!*** parle pour toi !* ; **let him ~ for himself** laisse-le s'exprimer, laisse-le dire luimême ce qu'il a à dire ; **it ~s for itself** c'est évident, c'est tout ce qu'il y a de plus clair ; **the facts ~ for themselves** les faits parlent d'eux-mêmes *or* se passent de commentaires ; **I can ~ for** *or* **to his honesty** je peux témoigner de *or* répondre de son honnêteté ; **it ~s to the chaos that was inside me** cela dit *or* montre bien la confusion qui régnait en moi ; **that ~s well for his generosity** ceci montre bien *or* prouve bien qu'il est généreux ; **that is already spoken for** c'est déjà réservé *or* retenu ; **she is already spoken for** elle est déjà prise ; **to ~ of sth as sth** appeler qch qch ; **he always ~s well of her** il dit toujours du bien d'elle ; **he is very well spoken of** on dit beaucoup de bien de lui ; ~**ing of holidays ...** à propos de vacances ..., puisqu'on parle de vacances ... ; **he has no friends/money to ~ of** il n'a pour ainsi dire pas d'amis/d'argent ; **nobody to ~ of** pour ainsi dire personne ; **it's nothing to ~ of** ce n'est pas grand-chose, cela ne vaut pas la peine qu'on en parle (*subj*), c'est trois fois rien* ; **everything spoke of wealth** tout indiquait *or* révélait *or* dénotait la richesse ; **everything spoke of fear/hatred** tout révélait *or* trahissait la peur/la haine ; (*Parl etc*) **to ~ to a motion** soutenir une motion

2 VT a [+ *language*] parler ; **"English spoken"** « ici on parle anglais » ; **French is spoken all over the world** le français se parle dans le monde entier

b (*liter*) [+ *a poem, one's lines, the truth*] dire ; **I didn't ~ a word** je n'ai rien dit ; **to ~ one's mind** dire ce que l'on pense

3 N (*in compounds*) langage *m* de ..., jargon *m* de ... ; **computerspeak** langage *m or* jargon *m* de l'informatique, langage *m or* jargon *m* des informaticiens

► **speak out** VI = **speak up** b

► **speak up** VI a (= *talk loudly*) parler fort *or* haut ; (= *raise one's voice*) parler plus fort *or* plus haut ; ~ **up!** (*parle*) plus fort *or* plus haut ! ; (= *don't mumble*) parle plus clairement ! b (*fig*) parler franchement, ne pas mâcher ses mots ; **he's not afraid to ~ up** il n'a pas peur de dire ce qu'il pense *or* de parler franchement, il ne mâche pas ses mots ; **I think you ought to ~ up** je crois que vous devriez dire franchement ce que vous pensez ; **to ~ up for sb** parler en faveur de qn, défendre qn ; **to ~ up against sth** s'élever contre qch

speakeasy* ['spiːkiːzɪ] N (*US Hist*) bar *m* clandestin (*pendant la prohibition*)

speaker ['spiːkər] N a (*gen*) celui *m* (*or* celle *f*) qui parle ; (*in dialogue, discussion*) interlocuteur *m*, -trice *f* ; (*in public*) orateur *m*, -trice *f* ; (= *lecturer*) conférencier *m*, -ière *f* ; **he's a good/poor ~** il parle bien/mal, c'est un bon/ mauvais orateur *or* conférencier ; **the previous ~** la personne qui a parlé la dernière, l'orateur *or* le conférencier précédent b **Speaker (of the House)** (*Brit*) président(e) *m(f)* de la Chambre des communes ; (*US*) président(e) *m(f)* de la Chambre des représentants c **French ~** personne *f* qui parle français ; (*as* native or official language) francophone mf; **he is not a Welsh ~** il ne parle pas gallois → **native** d (also **loudspeaker**: for PA system, musical instruments) haut-parleur m, enceinte f; [of hi-fi] baffle m, enceinte f.

SPEAKER (OF THE HOUSE)

En Grande-Bretagne, le **Speaker** est le président de la Chambre des communes, qui veille au respect du règlement et au bon déroulement des séances. Élu au début de chaque législature, il n'appartient pas nécessairement au parti au pouvoir, mais il perd son droit de vote et se doit de rester impartial. Au début de chacune de leurs interventions, les députés s'adressent au président de l'assemblée par ces mots: « Mister/Madam Speaker ».

Aux États-Unis le président de la Chambre des représentants est le **Speaker of the House**: il est le leader du parti majoritaire et joue le rôle de porte-parole de son parti. Politiquement, il vient en seconde position, après le vice-président des États-Unis, pour remplacer le président en cas de besoin.

speaking ['spi:kɪŋ] 1 ADJ (= talking) [doll, machine] parlant 2 N (= skill) art m de parler → **public** 3 COMP ► **the speaking clock** N (Brit) l'horloge f parlante ► **speaking part**, **speaking role** N (Cine, Theat) rôle m (autre que de figuration) ► **speaking terms** NPL **they're on ~ terms again** ils se parlent à nouveau, ils s'adressent à nouveau la parole; **they're not on ~ terms** ils ne s'adressent plus la parole, ils ne se parlent plus; **she's on ~ terms with him again** elle lui parle à nouveau, elle lui adresse à nouveau la parole ► **speaking tube** N tuyau m acoustique ► **speaking voice** N **his ~ voice** le timbre de sa voix quand il parle; **he has a pleasant ~ voice** il a une voix agréable (à entendre).

-speaking ['spi:kɪŋ] ADJ (in compounds) **English-speaking** [country] anglophone, de langue anglaise; [person] anglophone, parlant anglais; **slow-speaking** au débit lent, à la parole lente.

spear [spɪəʳ] 1 N a [of warrior, hunter] lance f b [of broccoli, asparagus] pointe f 2 VT transpercer d'un coup de lance; **he ~ed a potato with his fork** il a piqué une pomme de terre avec sa fourchette 3 COMP ► **spear grass** N (Brit) chiendent m ► **spear gun** N fusil m sous-marin or à harpon.

spearcarrier ['spɪəkæərɪəʳ] N (Theat) (lit) soldat m; (fig) **he started as a ~** il a débuté en jouant les hallebardiers, il a commencé par être figurant.

spearfish ['spɪəfɪʃ] VI (US: also **go ~ing**) pratiquer la pêche sous-marine.

spearhead ['spɪəhed] 1 N (Mil, fig) fer m de lance 2 VT [+ attack, offensive] être le fer de lance de; [+ campaign] mener.

spearmint ['spɪəmɪnt] 1 N (Bot) menthe f verte; (= chewing gum) chewing-gum m (à la menthe) 2 COMP [sweet] à la menthe; [flavour] de menthe.

spec* [spek] 1 N (ABBR = **speculation**) **to buy sth on ~** risquer or tenter le coup* en achetant qch; **I went along on ~** j'y suis allé à tout hasard 2 **specs** NPL (ABBR = **specifications**) spécifications fpl, caractéristiques fpl (techniques).

special ['speʃəl] 1 ADJ a (= particular, exceptional) [occasion, assignment, permission, arrangements, adviser, price, study, skill] spécial; [purpose, use, equipment] spécial, particulier; [day] grand, exceptionnel; [event, situation, goods] exceptionnel; [circumstances] exceptionnel, extraordinaire; [powers, meeting] extraordinaire; [case] particulier, à part; [status, interest] particulier; [effort, pleasure, attention] (tout) particulier; [treatment] de faveur; **what is so ~ about it?** qu'est-ce que cela

a de si exceptionnel or extraordinaire?; **is there anything ~ you would like?** as-tu envie de quelque chose de particulier or de spécial?; **to take ~ care** faire (tout) particulièrement attention; **take ~ care of it** fais-y (tout) particulièrement attention, prends-en un soin tout particulier; **by ~ command of ...** sur ordre spécial or exprès de ...; **are you thinking of any ~ date?** est-ce que tu penses à une date particulière or en particulier?; **this is rather a ~ day for me** c'est une journée particulièrement importante pour moi; **can I ask a ~ favour?** peux-tu me rendre un grand service?; **it's a ~ feature of the village** c'est une caractéristique or une particularité du village; **in this one ~ instance** dans ce cas bien particulier; **my ~ chair** mon fauteuil préféré, le fauteuil que je me réserve; **what are you doing this weekend? — nothing ~** que fais-tu ce week-end? — rien de spécial or de particulier; **there is nothing ~ about being a journalist** le fait d'être journaliste n'a rien d'extraordinaire; **I've no ~ person in mind** je ne pense à personne en particulier; **to have a ~ place in sb's heart** occuper une place à part dans le cœur de qn; **he has a ~ place in our affections** nous sommes tout particulièrement attachés à lui; **Britain had its own ~ problems** la Grande-Bretagne avait ses propres problèmes; **he had no ~ reason for suspecting him** je n'avais aucune raison particulière de le soupçonner; **why do you say that? — oh, no ~ reason** pourquoi est-ce dit ça? — oh, j'ai dit ça sans raison particulière; (Pol) **with ~ responsibility for sth** chargé du dossier de qch; **I've cooked something ~ for dinner** j'ai préparé quelque chose de spécial pour le dîner; **she is something ~** elle n'est pas comme tout le monde; **~ to that country** particulier or propre à ce pays; **as a ~ treat my grandfather would take me to the zoo** quand il voulait me gâter, mon grand-père m'emmenait au zoo; **we had roast beef as a ~ treat** nous nous sommes offert un extra et avons mangé du rosbif; **he has his own ~ way with the children** il a une façon toute particulière or bien à lui de s'y prendre avec les enfants b (= dear) [person] **is there anyone ~ in your life?** y a-t-il quelqu'un dans votre vie?; **"professional woman seeks someone ~ to share her life with"** « femme exerçant profession libérale cherche âme sœur »; **tender moments with a ~ person** moments de tendresse avec une personne qu'on aime; **her ~ friend** son meilleur ami, un ami intime; **you're extra ~!** tu es vraiment tout pour moi!; **she's very ~ to us** elle nous est très chère.

2 N (= train) train m supplémentaire; (= newspaper) édition f spéciale; (= policeman) auxiliaire m de police; (Rad, TV* = programme) émission f spéciale; **the chef's ~** la spécialité du chef or de la maison; (on menu) **today's ~** le plat du jour; (on item in shop) **this week's ~** l'affaire f de la semaine → **football**.

3 COMP ► **special agent** N (= spy) agent m secret ► **Special Air Service** N (Brit Mil) ≈ Groupement m d'intervention de la gendarmerie nationale ► **Special Branch** N (Brit Police) les renseignements mpl généraux ► **special constable** N (Brit) auxiliaire m de police ► **special correspondent** N (Press, Rad, TV) envoyé(e) m(f) spécial(e) ► **special delivery** N (Post) **by ~ delivery** en exprès ► **special-delivery letter** N (Post) lettre f exprès ► **special edition** N [of book] édition f spéciale; [of programme] diffusion f spéciale; [of car] modèle m spécial ► **special education** N (Brit) = **special schooling** ► **special effects** NPL (Cine etc) effets mpl spéciaux ► **special feature** N (Press) article m spécial ► **special handling** N (US Post) acheminement m rapide ► **special interest group** N (Pol etc) groupe m de pression ► **special jury** N (Jur) jury m spécial ► **special licence** N

(Jur) (gen) dispense f spéciale; (for marriage) dispense f de bans ► **special messenger** N **by ~ messenger** par messager spécial ► **special needs** NPL (Educ, Admin) problèmes mpl de scolarité; **children with ~ needs** ◊ **~ needs children** enfants mpl ayant des problèmes de scolarité; **~ needs teacher** enseignant(e) m(f) spécialisé(e) pour enfants ayant des problèmes de scolarité ► **special offer** N (Comm) promotion f, réclame f ► **Special Patrol Group** N (Brit Police) ≈ brigade f antiémeute ► **special relationship** N (Pol) lien m privilégié (with avec) ► **special school** N (Brit) établissement m scolaire spécialisé ► **special schooling** N (Brit) enseignement m spécialisé (pour handicapés mentaux) ► **special school teacher** N (Brit) instituteur m, -trice f spécialisé(e) ► **special slalom** N (Ski) slalom m spécial ► **special student** N (US Univ) auditeur m, -trice f libre (ne préparant pas de diplôme) ► **special subject** N (Scol, Univ) option f; (advanced) sujet m spécial.

specialism ['speʃəlɪzəm] N a (= subject, skill) spécialité f b (= specialization) spécialisation f.

specialist ['speʃəlɪst] 1 N (gen, Med) spécialiste mf; (in de); (Med) **an eye/heart ~** un(e) ophtalmologue/cardiologue; (gen) **you need a ~ to tell you that** seul un spécialiste or un expert peut vous dire cela 2 COMP [knowledge, dictionary] spécialisé, spécial ► **specialist teacher** N (primary) instituteur m, -trice f spécialisé(e) dans une matière); (secondary) professeur m spécialisé(e) dans une matière) ► **specialist work** N **it's ~ work** cela requiert un spécialiste or un professionnel, un amateur ne peut pas le faire.

speciality [,speʃɪ'ælɪtɪ] N spécialité f; **to make a ~ of sth** se spécialiser dans qch; **his ~ is Medieval English** c'est un spécialiste de l'anglais médiéval; **it is a ~ of the village** c'est une spécialité du village; **armchairs are this firm's ~** cette firme se spécialise dans les fauteuils; **the chef's ~** la spécialité du chef or de la maison.

specialization [,speʃəlaɪ'zeɪʃən] N spécialisation f (**in** dans).

specialize ['speʃəlaɪz] VI [student, firm, chef etc] se spécialiser (**in** dans); (hum) **he ~s in making a fool of himself** il se fait un point de passer pour un imbécile.

specialized ['speʃəlaɪzd] 1 ADJ [knowledge, equipment] spécial; [vocabulary, department, training] spécialisé; [tools] à usage spécial 2 COMP ► **specialized subject** N (Scol, Univ) option f; (advanced) sujet m spécialisé.

specially ['speʃəlɪ] ADV a (= expressly) [designed, made, built, adapted] spécialement; [commissioned, prepared, selected, formulated] (tout) spécialement; **to be ~ trained** avoir reçu une formation spéciale; **~ written for children** écrit spécialement pour les enfants; **I asked for it** je l'ai demandé exprès or tout spécialement b (* = exceptionally) [good, difficult] particulièrement; [important] spécialement, particulièrement c (= in particular) [think] surtout, tout particulièrement; **he is ~ interested in Proust** il s'intéresse spécialement or tout particulièrement à Proust; **we would ~ like to see the orchard** nous aimerions particulièrement or surtout voir le verger.

specialty ['speʃəltɪ] N (US) = **speciality**.

specie ['spi:ʃɪ] N (Fin) espèces fpl (monnayées).

species ['spi:ʃi:z] N (pl inv: all senses) espèce f.

specific [spə'sɪfɪk] 1 ADJ [person, description, instructions, meaning, reason, plan] précis; [issue, charge, case] précis, particulier; [area, conditions, group, need] spécifique, particulier; **he refused to be more ~** il a refusé d'être plus précis; **he was very ~ on that point** il s'est montré très explicite sur ce point; **nothing very ~** rien de bien précis; **~ to sb/sth** propre à qn/qch ② N **a** (Med) (remède m) spécifique m (**for** de, contre); (fig) remède m spécifique m **b** (pl = details etc) **let's get down to ~s** entrons dans les détails, prenons des exemples précis ③ COMP ► **specific gravity** N (Phys) densité f ► **specific heat** N (Phys) chaleur f massique or spécifique ► **specific name** N (Bio) nom m d'espèce

-specific [spə'sɪfɪk] ADJ (in compounds) **most predators are species-specific** la plupart des prédateurs sont spécifiques à certaines espèces; **most societies impose gender-specific clothing** la plupart des sociétés imposent des habitudes vestimentaires propres à chaque sexe

specifically [spə'sɪfɪkəlɪ] ADV **a** (= especially) [design] tout spécialement, expressément; [aim at, relate to] tout spécialement; [intend, plan] expressément, particulièrement **b** (= in particular) en particulier; **more ~** plus particulièrement **c** (= explicitly) [mention, refer to, authorize, warn, recommend] expressément; **to state sth ~** préciser qch; **I told you quite ~** je vous l'avais bien précisé or spécifié; **he ~ asked us not to mention the fact** il nous a bien spécifié de ne pas mentionner ce fait, il nous a expressément demandé de ne pas mentionner ce fait **d** (= uniquely) **~ medical/socialist/political** spécifiquement médical/socialiste/politique

specification [ˌspesɪfɪ'keɪʃən] N **a** (NonC: act of specifying) spécification f, précision f **b** (= item in contract etc) stipulation f, prescription f; **this ~ was not complied with** cette stipulation or cette prescription n'a pas été respectée; **~s** (for building, machine etc) spécifications fpl, caractéristiques fpl (techniques); (in contract etc) cahier m des charges → **outline**

specify ['spesɪfaɪ] VT spécifier, préciser; **unless otherwise specified** sauf indication contraire; **not elsewhere specified** non dénommé ailleurs; **at a specified time** à un moment précis, à une heure précise

specimen ['spesɪmən] ① N [of rock, species, style] spécimen m; [of blood, tissue] prélèvement m; [of urine] échantillon m; (fig = example) spécimen m, exemple m (of de); **that trout is a fine ~** cette truite est un magnifique spécimen or est magnifique; (fig) **an odd ~*** (man or woman) un drôle d'échantillon d'humanité*; (man) un drôle de type*; (woman) une drôle de bonne femme*; **you're a pretty poor ~*** tu es un (or une) pas grand-chose* ② COMP ► **specimen copy** N spécimen m ► **specimen page** N page f spécimen ► **specimen signature** N spécimen m de signature

specious ['spiːʃəs] ADJ (frm) [logic, argument, theory, rhetoric] spécieux

speciousness ['spiːʃəsnɪs] N (NonC: frm) [of logic, argument, theory, rhetoric] caractère m spécieux

speck [spek] ① N [of dust, soot] grain m; [of dirt, mud, ink] toute petite tache f; (on fruit, leaves, skin) tache f, tavelure f; (= tiny amount) [of sugar, butter] tout petit peu m; [of truth etc] grain m, atome m; **it has got black ~s all over it** c'est entièrement couvert de toutes petites taches noires; **I've got a ~ in my eye** j'ai une poussière or une escarbille dans l'œil; **just a ~ on the horizon/in the sky** rien qu'un point noir à l'horizon/dans le ciel; **cream?** — **just a ~*, thanks** de la crème? — rien qu'un tout petit peu, merci ② VT tacheter, moucheter; [+ fruit] tacheter, taveler

speckle ['spekl] ① N tacheture f, moucheture f ② VT tacheter, moucheter

speckled ['spekld] ADJ [egg] tacheté, moucheté (**with sth** de qch); **~ with (patches of) brown and white** tacheté or moucheté de brun et de blanc; **the sky was ~ with stars** le ciel était

constellé d'étoiles; **the beach was ~ with people** il y avait des gens éparpillés sur la plage

specs* [speks] NPL **a** ABBR = **spectacles** **b** → **spec**

spectacle ['spektəkl] ① N (= sight) (gen, pej) spectacle m; (Cine/Theat etc) superproduction f, film m/revue f etc à grand spectacle; **the coronation was a great ~** le couronnement a été un spectacle somptueux; (pej) **to make a ~ of o.s.** se donner en spectacle ② COMP ► **spectacle case** N (Brit) étui m à lunettes

spectacled ['spektəkld] ADJ (also Zool) à lunettes

spectacles ['spektəklz] NPL (Brit) (**pair of**) ~ lunettes fpl

spectacular [spek'tækjʊləʳ] ① ADJ (gen) spectaculaire; [sight] impressionnant; [failure, collapse] retentissant ② N (Cine/Theat) superproduction f, film m/revue f à grand spectacle

spectacularly [spek'tækjʊləlɪ] ADV [good, bad, beautiful, handsome] extraordinairement; [crash, increase, grow, fail] de manière spectaculaire; **to prove ~ successful** connaître un succès spectaculaire; **her ~ successful career** sa spectaculaire réussite professionnelle; **everything went ~ wrong** tout s'est extraordinairement mal passé; **in ~ bad taste** d'un extraordinaire mauvais goût; **they beat us ~ easily** ils nous ont battus avec une facilité spectaculaire

spectate [spek'teɪt] VI être présent en tant que spectateur (or spectatrice)

spectator [spek'teɪtəʳ] ① N spectateur m, -trice f; **the ~s** les spectateurs mpl, le public, l'assistance f ② COMP ► **spectator sport** N **I don't like ~ sports** je n'aime pas le sport en tant que spectacle; **rugby, the most exciting of ~ sports** le rugby, sport qui passionne le plus le public; **this tends to be rather a ~ sport** c'est un sport qui attire plus de spectateurs que de joueurs

specter ['spektəʳ] N (US) = **spectre**

spectra ['spektrə] NPL of **spectrum**

spectral ['spektrəl] ADJ **a** (liter = ghostly) spectral (liter) **b** (Phys) spectral

spectre, specter (US) ['spektəʳ] N spectre m, fantôme m

spectrogram ['spektrəʊɡræm] N spectrogramme m

spectrograph ['spektrəʊɡrɑːf] N spectrographe m

spectroscope ['spektrəʊskəʊp] N spectroscope m

spectroscopic [ˌspektrəskɒpɪk] ADJ spectroscopique

spectroscopy [spek'trɒskəpɪ] N spectroscopie f

spectrum ['spektrəm] ① N (pl **spectra**) (Phys) spectre m; (fig) [of ideas, opinions] gamme f (fig); **the political ~** l'éventail m politique ② COMP [analysis, colours] spectral

specula ['spekjʊlə] NPL of **speculum**

speculate ['spekjʊleɪt] VI **a** (Philos) spéculer (**about, on** sur); (gen = ponder) s'interroger (**about, on** sur, **whether** pour savoir si); **he was speculating about going** il se demandait s'il devait y aller ou non **b** (Fin) spéculer (St Ex) spéculer or jouer à la Bourse

speculation [ˌspekjʊ'leɪʃən] N **a** (NonC) (Philos) spéculation f; (gen = guessing) conjecture(s) f(pl), supposition(s) f(pl) (**about** sur); **it is the subject of much ~** cela donne lieu à bien des conjectures; **it is pure ~** ce n'est qu'une supposition; **after all the ~ about ...** après toutes ces conjectures or suppositions sur ... **b** (gen, Fin, St Ex) spéculation f (**in, on** sur); **he bought it as a ~** il a spéculé en achetant cela; **it proved a good ~** ce fut une spéculation réussie or une bonne affaire; **that picture he bought was a good ~** il a fait une

bonne affaire en achetant ce tableau, il a eu du nez en achetant ce tableau

speculative ['spekjʊlətɪv] ADJ **a** (= hypothetical: also Fin, Comm) [theory, idea, venture, activity, investment] spéculatif; [story] basé sur des suppositions; [builder, developer] qui spécule; **~ investors** spéculateurs mpl **b** (= inquiring) [look] scrutateur (-trice f) (liter), inquisiteur (-trice f)

speculatively ['spekjʊlətɪvlɪ] ADV **a** (= hypothetically) [suggested, mentioned] de façon spéculative **b** (= inquiringly) [look at, say] avec curiosité **c** (Fin) dans un but spéculatif

speculator ['spekjʊleɪtəʳ] N spéculateur m, -trice f

speculum ['spekjʊləm] N (pl **speculums** or **specula**) [of telescope] miroir m; (Med) spéculum m

sped [sped] VB pt, ptp of **speed**

speech [spiːtʃ] ① N **a** (NonC = faculty) parole f; (= enunciation) articulation f, élocution f; (= manner of speaking) façon f de parler, langage m; (as opposed to writing) parole f; (= language) [of district, group] parler m, langage m; **to lose the power of ~** perdre (l'usage de) la parole; **his ~ was very indistinct** il parlait or articulait très indistinctement; **he expresses himself better in ~ than in writing** il s'exprime mieux oralement que par écrit; **the ~ of the playground is different from that of the classroom** le langage or le parler des enfants qui jouent diffère de celui des enfants en classe; **his ~ betrays his origins** son langage or sa façon de s'exprimer trahit ses origines ■ (PROV) **~ is silver but silence is golden** la parole est d'argent mais le silence est d'or (PROV); **free ~ ◊ freedom of ~** liberté f de parole or d'expression → **figure, part** **b** (= formal address) discours m (**on** sur); (short, less formal) speech* m, allocution f; **to make a ~** faire un discours; **~, ~!** un discours! → **king, maiden, queen** **c** (Ling) (= utterances) parole f; (= spoken language) langage m parlé; (Gram) **direct/indirect ~** discours m direct/indirect ② COMP ► **speech act** N (Ling) acte m de parole ► **speech bubble** N (in comic, cartoon) bulle f ► **speech clinic** N centre m d'orthophonie ► **speech community** N (Ling) communauté f linguistique ► **speech day** N (Brit Scol) distribution f des prix ► **speech defect** N troubles mpl du langage ► **speech difficulty** N défaut m d'élocution ► **speech disorder** N = **speech defect** ► **speech from the throne** N (Britain and Commonwealth) discours m du Trône (discours du monarque pour l'ouverture de la saison parlementaire) ► **speech impediment** N = **speech difficulty** ► **speech maker** N orateur m, -trice f ► **speech making** N (NonC: slightly pej) discours mpl, beaux discours mpl (pej) ► **speech organ** N (Anat) organe m de la parole ► **speech recognition** N (Comput) reconnaissance f de la parole ► **speech sound** N (Ling) phonème m ► **speech synthesis** N (Comput) synthèse f vocale ► **speech synthesizer** N (Comput) synthétiseur m de parole ► **speech therapist** N orthophoniste mf, phoniatre mf ► **speech therapy** N orthophonie f, phoniatrie f ► **speech training** N leçons fpl d'élocution ► **speech writer** N **her ~ writer** la personne qui écrit ses discours

speechify ['spiːtʃɪfaɪ] VI (pej) faire des laïus, laïusser

speechifying ['spiːtʃɪfaɪɪŋ] N (pej) laïus* mpl, beaux discours mpl

speechless ['spiːtʃlɪs] ADJ [person] muet; **I'm ~!** je suis sans voix!; **I was so happy I was ~** j'étais si heureux que j'en suis resté muet or sans voix; **to leave sb ~** laisser qn sans voix; **she was left ~** elle en est restée sans voix; **she stared at him in ~ disbelief/horror** elle le fixa, muette d'incrédulité/d'horreur; **~ with astonishment/fear/rage/shock** muet d'étonnement/de peur/de rage/de stupeur

speed [spiːd] (*vb: pret, ptp* **sped** *or* **speeded**) **1** N **a** (= *rate of movement*) vitesse *f*; (= *rapidity*) rapidité *f*; (= *promptness*) promptitude *f*; **the ~ of light/sound** la vitesse de la lumière/du son; **his reading ~ is low** il lit lentement; **shorthand/typing ~s** nombre *m* de mots-minute en sténo/en dactylo; **a secretary with good ~s** une secrétaire qui a une bonne vitesse (de frappe et de sténo); (*in car etc*) **what ~ were you going at** *or* **doing?** quelle vitesse faisiez-vous?, à quelle vitesse rouliez-vous?; **at a ~ of 80km/h** à une vitesse de 80 km/h; **at a great ~** à toute vitesse; **at top ~** [*go, run, move, drive*] à toute vitesse *or* allure; [*do sth*] très vite, en quatrième vitesse*; **with all possible ~** le plus vite possible; **with such ~** si vite; **to pick up** *or* **gather ~** prendre de la vitesse; **to be up to ~** (= *functioning properly*) être opérationnel; **to bring up to ~** [+ *student*] mettre au niveau **b** (*Aut, Tech* = *gear*) vitesse *f*; **four forward ~s** quatre vitesses avant; **a three-~ gear** une boîte à trois vitesses **c** (*NonC: Phot*) [*of film*] rapidité *f*; (= *width of aperture*) degré *m* d'obturation; (= *length of exposure*) durée *f* d'exposition **d** (* = *drug*) amphétamines *fpl* **e** **good ~!**†† Dieu vous garde!† **2** VT (*pret, ptp* **sped** *or* **speeded**) (*liter*) [+ *arrow etc*] lancer, décocher; **to ~ sb on his way** souhaiter bon voyage à qn; **to ~ the parting guest** précipiter *or* brusquer le départ de l'invité; **God ~ you!**†† Dieu vous garde!† **3** VI **a** (*pret, ptp* **sped**) (= *move fast*) [*person, vehicle, horse, boat, plane etc*] **to ~ along** aller à toute vitesse *or* à toute allure, filer comme un éclair; (*liter*) **the arrow sped from his bow** la flèche jaillit de son arc **b** (*pret, ptp* **speeded**) (*in car etc* = *go too fast*) conduire trop vite, excéder la limitation de vitesse; **you're ~ing!** tu vas trop vite!, tu fais un *or* des excès de vitesse! **4** COMP ▶ **speed bump** N ralentisseur *m* ▶ **speed camera** N (*Brit Police*) cinémomètre *m* ▶ **speed chess** N blitz *m* ▶ **speed cop*** N (*Brit*) motard* *m* (*policier*) ▶ **speed limit** N **there's no ~** il n'y a pas de limitation de vitesse; **the ~ limit is 80km/h** la vitesse est limitée à 80 km/h; **to keep within the ~ limit** respecter la limitation de vitesse; **to go over the ~ limit** dépasser la limitation de vitesse ▶ **speed merchant*** N mordu(e)* *m(f)* de vitesse ▶ **speed reading** N lecture *f* rapide ▶ **speed restriction** N limitation de vitesse ▶ **speed skating** N (*Sport*) patinage *m* de vitesse ▶ **speed trap** N (*on road*) contrôle *m* de vitesse ▶ **speed-up** N accélération *f*; (*Ind: of production*) amélioration *f* de rendement ▶ **speed zone** N (*US*) zone *f* à vitesse limitée

▶**speed along** **1** VI (*pret, ptp* **sped along**) [*person, vehicle*] aller à toute allure *or* à toute vitesse, filer comme l'éclair **2** VT SEP (*pret, ptp* **speeded along**) [+ *work, production*] activer

▶**speed up** (*pret, ptp* **speeded up**) **1** VI (*gen*) aller plus vite; [*walker/worker/singer/pianist/train etc*] marcher/travailler/chanter/jouer/rouler *etc* plus vite; [*car*] accélérer; [*engine, machine etc*] tourner plus vite; **do ~ up!** plus vite!, active!* **2** VT SEP [+ *machine*] faire tourner plus vite; [+ *service, work, delivery*] activer, accélérer; [+ *production*] accélérer, augmenter; [+ *person*] faire aller *or* faire travailler plus vite, presser; [+ *film*] accélérer; **to ~ things up** activer les choses **3** **~-up** N → **speed**

speedball [spiːdbɔːl] N **a** (= *game*) speedball *m* **b** (‡ = *drug*) mélange *m* de cocaïne et d'héroïne

speedboat [spiːdbəʊt] N vedette *f*; (*with outboard motor*) hors-bord *m inv*

speeder [spiːdər] N (= *fast driver*) fou *m*, folle *f* de la vitesse; (*convicted*) automobiliste *mf* coupable d'excès de vitesse

speedily [spiːdɪlɪ] ADV [*react, move, deal with, finish, work*] rapidement; [*reply, return*] rapidement, promptement; **as ~ as possible** aussi rapidement *or* vite que possible

speediness [spiːdɪnɪs] N [*of service, decision, reply, recovery*] rapidité *f*, promptitude *f*

speeding [spiːdɪŋ] **1** N (*in car etc*) excès *m* de vitesse **2** COMP ▶ **speeding conviction** N condamnation *f* pour excès de vitesse ▶ **speeding fine** N amende *f* pour excès de vitesse ▶ **speeding ticket** N P.-V. *m* pour excès de vitesse

speedo* [spiːdəʊ] N (*Brit*) compteur *m* (de vitesse)

speedometer [spɪˈdɒmɪtər] N [*of car etc*] compteur *m* (de vitesse), indicateur *m* de vitesse

speedster* [spiːdstər] N fou *m*, folle *f* de la route (*pej*), mordu(e)* *m(f)* de la vitesse

speedwalk [spiːdwɔːk] N (*US*) tapis *m* roulant

speedway [spiːdweɪ] N (*Sport* = *racetrack*) piste *f* de vitesse pour motos; (*US* = *road*) voie *f* express; (*NonC: Sport: also* **~ racing**) course(s) *f(pl)* de motos

speedwell [spiːdwel] N (*Bot*) véronique *f*

▼**speedy** [spiːdɪ] ADJ [*action, movement, process, solution, decision, service, car*] rapide; [*response, reply*] rapide, prompt; **to bring sth to a ~ conclusion** mener rapidement qch à terme; **there is little prospect of a ~ end to the recession** il est peu probable que la récession touche à sa fin; **we wish her a ~ recovery** nous lui souhaitons un prompt rétablissement

speleologist [ˌspiːlɪˈɒlədʒɪst] N spéléologue *mf*

speleology [ˌspiːlɪˈɒlədʒɪ] N spéléologie *f*

spell¹ [spel] N (= *magic power*) charme *m* (*also fig*), sortilège *m*; (= *magic words*) formule *f* magique, incantation *f*; **an evil ~** un maléfice; **to put** *or* **cast** *or* **lay a ~ on** *or* **over sb** ◊ **to put sb under a ~** jeter un sort à qn, ensorceler qn, envoûter qn; (*fig*) ensorceler qn, envoûter qn; **under a ~** ensorcelé, envoûté, sous le charme; (*fig*) **under the ~ of sb/sth** ◊ **under sb's/sth's ~** ensorcelé *or* envoûté par qn/qch; (*lit, fig*) **to break the ~** rompre le charme; (*fig*) **the ~ of the East** le charme *or* les sortilèges *mpl* de l'Orient

spell² [spel] **1** N **a** (= *period of work, turn*) tour *m*; **we each took a ~ at the wheel** nous nous sommes relayés au volant, nous avons conduit chacun à notre tour; **~ of duty** tour *m* de service **b** (= *brief period*) (courte) période *f*; (*Met*) **cold/sunny ~s** périodes *fpl* de froid/ensoleillées; **for/after a ~** pendant/après un certain temps; **for a short ~** pendant un petit moment; **he has done a ~ in prison** il a été en prison pendant un certain temps, il a fait de la prison; **he's going through a bad ~** il traverse une mauvaise période, il est dans une mauvaise passe; **to have a dizzy** *or* **giddy ~** avoir un vertige **c** (*Scot, Austral* = *short rest*) petite sieste *f* **2** VT relayer; **to ~ sb at the wheel/at the oars** relayer qn au volant/aux avirons

spell³ [spel] (*pret, ptp* **spelt** *or* **spelled**) **1** VT **a** (*in writing*) écrire, orthographier; (*aloud*) épeler; **how do you ~ it?** comment est-ce que cela s'écrit?, comment écrit-on cela?; **can you ~ it for me?** pouvez-vous me l'épeler?; **he spelt "address" with one "d"** il a écrit « address » avec un seul « d » **b** [*letters*] former, donner; (*fig* = *mean*) signifier, représenter; (= *entail*) mener à; **d-o-g ~s "dog"** d-o-g forment *or* donnent *or* font (le mot) « dog »; (*fig*) **that would ~ ruin for him** cela signifierait *or* représenterait *or* serait la ruine pour lui; **effort ~s success** l'effort mène au succès

2 VI épeler; **to learn to ~** apprendre à épeler, apprendre l'orthographe; **he can't ~** ◊ **he ~s badly** il fait des fautes d'orthographe, il ne sait pas l'orthographe, il a une mauvaise orthographe

3 COMP ▶ **spell-check** (*Comput*) N vérificateur *m* *or* correcteur *m* orthographique ♦ VT effectuer la vérification orthographique de ▶ **spell-checker** N (*Comput*) vérificateur *m* *or* correcteur *m* orthographique

▶**spell out** VT SEP **a** (= *read letter by letter*) épeler; (= *decipher*) déchiffrer **b** (*fig*) [+ *consequences, alternatives*] expliquer bien clairement (**for sb** à qn); **let me ~ it out for you** laissez-moi vous expliquer bien clairement, laissez-moi mettre les points sur les i; **do I have to ~ it out for you?** faut-il que je mette les points sur les i?

spellbinder [spelbaɪndər] N (= *speaker*) orateur *m*, -trice *f* fascinant(e), ensorceleur *m*, -euse *f*; **that film was a ~** ce film était ensorcelant *or* était envoûtant *or* vous tenait en haleine

spellbinding [spelbaɪndɪŋ] ADJ ensorcelant, envoûtant

spellbound [spelbaʊnd] ADJ (*lit, fig*) ensorcelé, envoûté; (*fig*) **to hold sb ~** (*with a story*) tenir qn sous le charme; (*with one's charm*) subjuguer qn, fasciner qn

speller [spelər] N **a** **to be a good/bad ~** [*person*] savoir/ne pas savoir l'orthographe **b** (= *book*) livre *m* d'orthographe

spelling [spelɪŋ] **1** N orthographe *f*; **reformed ~** nouvelle orthographe *f* **2** COMP [*test, practice*] d'orthographe ▶ **spelling bee** N concours *m* d'orthographe ▶ **spelling book** N livre *m* d'orthographe ▶ **spelling checker** N (*Comput*) vérificateur *m* d'orthographe ▶ **spelling error, spelling mistake** N faute *f* d'orthographe ▶ **spelling pronunciation** N prononciation *f* orthographique

spelt¹ [spelt] VB (*esp Brit*) pt, ptp of **spell³**

spelt² [spelt] N (*Bot*) épeautre *m*

spelunker [spɪˈlʌŋkər] N (*US*) spéléologue *mf*

spelunking [spɪˈlʌŋkɪŋ] N (*US*) spéléologie *f*

spend [spend] (*pret, ptp* **spent**) **1** VT **a** [+ *money*] dépenser; **he ~s a lot (of money) on food/bus fares/clothes** *etc* il dépense beaucoup en nourriture/tickets d'autobus/vêtements *etc*; **he ~s a lot (of money) on his house/car/girlfriend** il dépense beaucoup *or* il fait de grosses dépenses pour sa maison/sa voiture/sa petite amie; **he spent a fortune on having the roof repaired** il a dépensé une somme folle *or* une fortune pour faire réparer le toit; **without ~ing a penny** *or* **a ha'penny** sans dépenser un sou, sans bourse délier; (*Brit fig euph*) **to ~ a penny*** aller au petit coin* → **money** **b** (= *pass*) [+ *holiday, evening, one's life*] passer; (= *devote*) [+ *labour, care*] consacrer (**on sth** à qch, **doing, in doing** à faire); [+ *time, afternoon*] passer; **to ~ time on sth** passer du temps sur qch, consacrer du temps à qch; **to ~ time (in) doing** passer *or* consacrer *or* employer du temps à faire; **he ~s his time reading** il passe son temps à lire, il consacre son temps à la lecture; **I spent two hours on that letter** j'ai passé deux heures sur cette lettre, cette lettre m'a pris deux heures; **he spent a lot of effort (in) getting it just right** il a fait beaucoup d'efforts pour que ce soit juste comme il faut **c** (= *consume, exhaust*) [+ *ammunition, provisions*] épuiser; **to be spent** [*hatred, enthusiasm*] être tombé; **her fury was now spent** sa fureur était maintenant apaisée; (*liter*) **the storm had spent its fury** la tempête s'était calmée → **spent**

2 VI dépenser

spender [spendər] N **to be a big ~** dépenser beaucoup

---

spending ['spendɪŋ] **1** N (NonC) dépenses fpl; **government ~** dépenses fpl publiques **2** COMP ► **spending money** N (NonC) argent m de poche ► **spending power** N pouvoir m d'achat ► **spending spree** N **to go on a ~ spree** faire des folies

spendthrift ['spendθrɪft] **1** N dépensier m, -ière f, panier m percé‡ **2** ADJ [habits, attitude etc] de prodigalité; **he's a ~** il est très dépensier, il jette l'argent par les fenêtres

spent [spent] **1** VB pt, ptp of **spend 2** ADJ **a** (= burnt out) [cartridge, match] utilisé; [fuel, fuel rod, uranium] épuisé; (fig) **to be a ~ force** ne plus avoir d'influence, ne plus avoir l'influence que l'on avait **b** (liter = exhausted) [person] recru (liter); **they collapsed, their energy ~** ils se sont effondrés, à bout de forces

sperm [spɜːm] **1** N (pl inv) (single) spermatozoïde m; (= semen) sperme m **2** COMP ► **sperm bank** N banque f de sperme ► **sperm count** N nombre m de spermatozoïdes ► **sperm oil** N huile f de baleine ► **sperm whale** N cachalot m

spermaceti [,spɜːmə'setɪ] N spermaceti m, blanc m de baleine

spermatic [spɜː'mætɪk] ADJ (Anat) spermatique

spermatozoon [,spɜːmətəʊ'zəʊɒn] N (pl **spermatozoa** [,spɜːmətəʊ'zəʊə]) spermatozoïde m

spermicidal [,spɜːmɪ'saɪdl] ADJ spermicide

spermicide ['spɜːmɪsaɪd] N spermicide m

spew [spjuː] VT **a** (‡: also ~ **up**) dégueuler‡, vomir; **it makes me ~** ça (me) donne envie de dégueuler‡ or vomir, c'est dégueulasse‡ **b** (fig: also ~ **forth**, ~ **out**) [+ fire, lava, curses] vomir

SPG [espiː'dʒiː] N (Brit Police) (ABBR = **Special Patrol Group**) → **special**

sphagnum ['sfægnəm] N (also ~ **moss**) sphaigne f

sphere [sfɪər] N (gen, Astron, Math etc) sphère f; (fig) sphère f, domaine m; **the music of the ~s** la musique des sphères célestes; **~ of interest/influence** sphère f d'intérêt/d'influence; **the ~ of poetry** le domaine de la poésie; **in the social ~** dans le domaine social; **distinguished in many ~s** renommé dans de nombreux domaines; **that is outside my ~** cela n'entre pas dans mes compétences; **within a limited ~** dans un cadre or domaine restreint

spherical ['sferɪkəl] ADJ sphérique

spheroid ['sfɪərɔɪd] **1** N sphéroïde m **2** ADJ sphéroïdal

sphincter ['sfɪŋktər] N sphincter m

sphinx [sfɪŋks] N (pl **sphinxes**) sphinx m; **the Sphinx** le Sphinx

spic⁑ [spɪk] N (US pej) = **spick**

spice [spaɪs] **1** N **a** (Culin) épice f; **mixed ~(s)** épices fpl mélangées; **there's too much ~ in it** c'est trop épicé **b** (fig) piquant m, sel m; **the papers like a story with a bit of ~ to it** les journaux aiment les nouvelles qui ont du piquant or qui ne manquent pas de sel; **a ~ of irony/humour** une pointe d'ironie/d'humour; **the ~ of adventure** le piment de l'aventure **2** VT (Culin) épicer, relever (**with** de); (fig) relever, pimenter (**with** de) **3** COMP ► **spice rack** N casier m or étagère f à épices

spiciness ['spaɪsɪnɪs] N (NonC) [of food] goût m épicé or relevé; [of story] piquant m

spick⁑ [spɪk] N (US pej) Latino mf

spick-and-span ['spɪkən'spæn] ADJ [room, object] impeccable, reluisant de propreté, nickel*; [person] qui a l'air de sortir d'une boîte

spicy ['spaɪsɪ] ADJ **a** (Culin) [food, flavour, smell] épicé **b** (= racy) [story] croustillant, épicé; [detail] croustillant; [language] salé

spider ['spaɪdər] **1** N **a** (Zool) araignée f **b** (for luggage) pieuvre f (à bagages) **c** (US = fry-pan) poêle f à trépied **2** COMP ► **spider crab** N araignée f de mer ► **spider plant** N chlorophytum m, parachute m ► **spider's web** N toile f d'araignée

spiderman ['spaɪdəmæn] N (pl -**men**) (Constr) ouvrier travaillant en hauteur, sur un échafaudage, un toit etc

spiderweb ['spaɪdəweb] N (US) = **spider's web**; → **spider**

spidery ['spaɪdərɪ] ADJ [writing] en pattes de mouche; [shape] en forme d'araignée

spiel* [spiːl] N laïus* m inv, baratin* m; (Advertising etc) boniment(s)* m(pl), baratin* m ► **spiel off*** VT SEP (US) débiter, réciter à toute allure

spiffing†* ['spɪfɪŋ] ADJ (Brit) épatant*

spigot ['spɪgət] N **a** (= plug for barrel) fausset m **b** (Brit = part of tap) clé f (d'un robinet); (US = faucet) robinet m

spik⁑⁑ [spɪk] N (US pej) = **spick**

spike [spaɪk] **1** N **a** (= sharp point) (wooden, metal) pointe f; (on railing) pointe f de fer, (fer m de) lance f; (on shoe) pointe f; (for letters, bills etc) pique-notes m inv; (= nail) gros clou m à large tête; (= tool) pointe f; [of antler] dague f; [of bulb] épi m; (on graph) pointe f, haut m **b** (Sport) ~**s*** (shoes) chaussures fpl à pointes **c** (Climbing) **rocky ~** becquet m **d** (Volleyball) smash m **2** VT **a** (= pierce) transpercer; (= put spikes on) garnir de pointes or de clous; (fig = frustrate) [+ plan, hopes] contrarier; (Sport) **~d shoes** chaussures fpl à pointes; (fig) **to ~ sb's guns** mettre des bâtons dans les roues à qn **b** * [+ drink] corser (**with** de); **~d coffee** café m arrosé d'alcool **c** (Press = suppress) [+ article, story, quote] supprimer **d** **~d hair** cheveux mpl en brosse **3** VI (Volleyball) smasher **4** COMP ► **spike heels** NPL (US) talons mpl aiguilles ► **spike lavender** N (Bot) (lavande f) aspic m

spikenard ['spaɪknɑːd] N (NonC) nard m (indien)

spiky ['spaɪkɪ] ADJ **a** (= pointed) [shape, flower, leaf] pointu; [hair] hérissé **b** (= covered with spikes) [cactus, leaf] couvert d'épines **c** (Brit* = irritable) [person] irascible, irritable

spill¹ [spɪl] (vb: pret, ptp **spilt** or **spilled**) **1** N **a** (= act of spilling) fait m de renverser, renversement m → **oil b** (from horse, cycle) chute f, culbute f; (Aut) accident m; **to have a ~** faire une chute or une culbute, avoir un accident **2** VT [+ water, sand, salt] renverser, répandre; [+ rider, passenger] jeter à terre; **she spilt the salt** elle a renversé le sel; **she spilt wine all over the table** elle a renversé or répandu du vin sur toute la table; **you're ~ing water from that jug** tu laisses tomber de l'eau de cette cruche; **to ~ blood** verser or faire couler le sang; (fig) **to ~ the beans*** (gen) vendre la mèche (**about** à propos de); (under interrogation) se mettre à table‡, parler; (fig) **to ~ one's guts‡** (= talk) (gen) raconter sa vie; (under interrogation) se mettre à table‡, parler; (Naut) **to ~** (**wind from**) **a sail** étouffer une voile **3** VI [liquid, salt etc] se répandre; **the light was ~ing under the door** un filet de lumière passait sous la porte ► **spill out 1** VI se répandre; (fig) [people etc] sortir en masse; **the crowd ~ed out into the streets** la foule s'est déversée dans la rue **2** VT SEP [+ contents, sand, liquid] répandre; (fig) [+ story, truth, details] révéler, raconter (précipitamment) ► **spill over 1** VI [liquids] déborder, se répandre; (fig) [population] déborder, se déverser (**into** dans); **these problems ~ed over into his private life** ces problèmes ont gagné sa vie privée **2** ~**over** N → **spillover**, **overspill**

spill² [spɪl] N (for lighting with) longue allumette f (de papier etc)

spillage ['spɪlɪdʒ] N [of oil, toxic waste, chemicals] déversement m accidentel; **he swerved to avoid an oil ~** il a donné un coup de volant pour éviter une flaque d'huile

spillikins ['spɪlɪkɪnz] N (Brit) (jeu m de) jonchets mpl, mikado m

spillover ['spɪləʊvər] N (= quantity spilt) quantité f renversée; (fig) (= excess part) excédent m; (Econ = effect) retombées fpl, effet m d'entraînement

spillway ['spɪlweɪ] N (US) déversoir m

spilt [spɪlt] VB (esp Brit) pt, ptp of **spill¹**

spin [spɪn] (vb: pret **spun** or **span**, ptp **spun**) **1** N **a** (= turning motion) tournoiement m; (Aviat) (chute f en) vrille f; **to give a wheel a ~** faire tourner une roue; (on washing machine) **long/short ~** essorage m complet/léger; (Sport) **to put (a) ~ on a ball** donner de l'effet à une balle; (Aviat) **to go into a ~** tomber en vrille or en vrillant; (Aviat) **to pull** or **get out of a ~** se sortir d'une (chute or) vrille; (fig) **to get into a ~** [person] s'affoler, perdre la tête, paniquer*; **everything was in such a ~** c'était la pagaille* complète; (fig) **to give sth a ~‡** (= try out) essayer qch → **flat¹ b** (* = ride) petit tour m, balade* f; **to go for a ~** faire un petit tour or une balade* (en voiture or à bicyclette etc) **c** **to put a new/different ~ on sth*** présenter qch sous un nouvel angle/un angle différent **2** VT **a** [+ wool, yarn, fibres, glass] filer (**into** en, pour en faire); [+ thread etc] fabriquer, produire; [spider, silkworm] filer, tisser; (fig) **to ~ a yarn** or **story** inventer or raconter une histoire; **spun glass** verre m filé; **hair like spun gold** des cheveux ressemblant à de l'or filé; **spun silk** schappe m or f; (Naut) **spun yarn** bitord m → **fine²** **b** [+ wheel, nut, revolving stand etc] faire tourner; [+ top] lancer, fouetter; (Sport) [+ ball] donner de l'effet à; **to ~ a coin** jouer à pile ou face; (US) **he's just ~ning his wheels*** il loupe* tout ce qu'il tente **c** (Brit) = **spin-dry 3** VI **a** [spinner etc] filer; [spider] filer or tisser sa toile **b** (also ~ **round**) [suspended object, top, dancer] tourner, tournoyer; [planet, spacecraft] tourner (sur soi-même); [machinery wheel] tourner; [car wheel] patiner; [aircraft] vriller, tomber en vrillant; (Sport) [ball] tournoyer; **to ~ round and round** continuer à tourner (or tournoyer etc); **to send sth/sb ~ning** envoyer rouler qch/qn; **the disc went ~ning away over the trees** le disque s'envola en tournoyant par-dessus les arbres; **he spun round as he heard me come in** il s'est retourné vivement or sur ses talons en m'entendant entrer; (fig) **my head is ~ning (round)** j'ai la tête qui tourne; (fig) **the room was ~ning (round)** la chambre tournait (autour de moi or lui etc) **c** (= move quickly) **to ~** or **go ~ning along** [vehicle] rouler à toute vitesse, filer (à toute allure) **d** (Fishing) **to ~ for trout** etc pêcher la truite etc à la cuiller **4** COMP ► **spin doctor*** N (Pol) spécialiste en communication chargé de l'image d'un parti politique ► **spin-dry** VT essorer (à la machine) ► **spin-dryer** N (Brit) essoreuse f ► **spin-drying** N (NonC) essorage m à la machine ► **spin-off** N → **spin-off** ► **spin off 1** VI **to ~ off from** (= arise as result of) résulter de **2** ~**-off** N → **spin-off** ► **spin out** VT SEP [+ story, explanation] faire durer, délayer; [+ visit, money, food] faire durer ► **spin round 1** VI → **spin 3b 2** VT SEP [+ wheel, nut, revolving stand] faire tourner; [+ person] faire pivoter; [+ dancing partner] faire tourner or tournoyer

spina bifida ['spaɪnə'bɪfɪdə] N spina-bifida m

spinach ['spinidʒ] N (= *plant*) épinard *m*; (*Culin*) épinards *mpl*

spinal ['spainl] [1] ADJ (*Anat*) [*injury*] à la colonne vertébrale; [*surgery, disorder, deformity, tumour, problem*] de la colonne vertébrale; [*nerve, muscle*] spinal; [*ligament, disc*] vertébral; **a very painful ~ condition** une affection de la colonne vertébrale très douloureuse [2] COMP ► **spinal anaesthesia** N rachianesthésie *f* ► **spinal anaesthetic** N **to give sb a ~ anaesthetic** faire une rachianesthésie à qn ► **spinal column** N colonne *f* vertébrale ► **spinal cord** N moelle *f* épinière ► **spinal fluid** N liquide *m* rachidien ► **spinal meningitis** N méningite *f* cérébrospinale

spindle ['spindl] [1] N [a] (*Spinning*) fuseau *m*; (*on machine*) broche *f* [b] (*Tech*) [*of pump*] axe *m*; [*of lathe*] arbre *m*; [*of valve*] tige *f* [2] COMP ► **spindle-legged***, **spindle-shanked*** ADJ qui a de longues échasses* (*fig*) ► **spindleshanks*** N = **spindlelegs**

spindlelegs* ['spindllegz] N (= *person*) grand échalas* *m*

spindly ['spindli] ADJ grêle

spindrift ['spindrift] N (= *spray from sea*) embrun(s) *m(pl)*, poudrin *m*

spine [spain] [1] N [a] (*Anat*) (= *backbone*) colonne *f* vertébrale, épine *f* dorsale; [*of fish*] épine *f*; (= *spike*) [*of hedgehog*] piquant *m*, épine *f*; [*of plant*] (*Bot*) épine *f*, piquant *m*; [*of book*] dos *m*; [*of hill etc*] crête *f* [b] (*US fig* = *courage*) courage *m*, résolution *f* [2] COMP ► **spine-chiller** N roman *m* or film *m etc* à vous glacer le sang ► **spine-chilling** ADJ à vous glacer le sang ► **spine-tingling** ADJ (= *frightening*) à vous glacer le sang; (= *moving*) prenant

spineless ['spainlis] ADJ [a] (= *cowardly*) [*person*] sans caractère, mou (molle *f*); [*attitude*] mou (molle *f*); **he's ~** il manque de caractère [b] (*Zool*) invertébré

spinelessly ['spainlisli] ADV (*fig*) lâchement, mollement

spinet [spi'net] N (*Mus*) épinette *f*

spinnaker ['spinəkə'] N spinnaker *m*, spi *m*

spinner ['spinə'] N (= *person*) fileur *m*, -euse *f*; (*Fishing*) cuiller *f*; (= *spin-dryer*) essoreuse *f*; (= *revolving display stand*) tourniquet *m*; (*Baseball, Cricket*) **he sent down a ~*** il a donné de l'effet à la balle → **money**

spinneret [,spinə'ret] N (*Tex, Zool*) filière *f*

spinney ['spini] N (*Brit*) bosquet *m*, petit bois *m*

spinning ['spiniŋ] [1] N (*by hand*) filage *m*; (*by machine*) filature *f*; (*Fishing*) pêche *f* à la cuiller [2] COMP ► **spinning jenny** N jenny *f* ► **spinning machine** N machine *f* or métier *m* à filer ► **spinning mill** N filature *f* ► **spinning top** N toupie *f* ► **spinning wheel** N rouet *m*

spin-off ['spinɔf] N (*gen*) profit *m* or avantage *m* inattendu; (*Ind, Tech etc*) sous-produit *m*, application *f* secondaire; (*Fin*) **~ effect** retombées *fpl*; **this TV series is a ~ from the famous film** ce feuilleton télévisé est tiré or issu du célèbre film

Spinoza [spi'nəʊzə] N Spinoza *m*

spinster ['spinstə'] N (*gen, Admin*) célibataire *f*; (*pej*) vieille fille *f*; **she is a ~** elle est célibataire, elle n'est pas mariée

spinsterhood† ['spinstəhʊd] N célibat *m* (*pour une femme*); **a last attempt to avoid ~** une dernière tentative pour éviter de rester vieille fille (*pej*) or pour éviter le célibat; **a life of ~** une vie de vieille fille (*pej*)

spiny ['spaini] [1] ADJ épineux [2] COMP ► **spiny anteater** N échidné *m* ► **spiny lobster** N langouste *f*

spiracle ['spaiərəkl] N (= *air hole*) orifice *m* d'aération; [*of whale etc*] évent *m*; [*of insect etc*] stigmate *m*; (*Geol*) cassure *f*

spiral ['spaiərəl] [1] ADJ [*pattern, movement, dive*] en spirale; [*spring*] en spirale, à boudin; [*curve, shell*] en spirale, spiroïdal; [*nebula*] spiral; (*Aviat*) en vrille [2] N spirale *f*; **in a ~** en spirale; (*fig*) **the wage-price ~** la montée inexorable des salaires et des prix; **the inflationary ~** la spirale inflationniste [3] VI [*staircase, smoke*] monter en spirale; [*ball, missile etc*] tourner en spirale; [*plane*] vriller; (*fig*) [*prices*] monter en flèche; [*prices and wages*] former une spirale [4] COMP ► **spiral galaxy** N galaxie *f* spirale ► **spiral notebook** N carnet *m* à spirale ► **spiral staircase**, **spiral stairway** N escalier *m* en colimaçon

► **spiral down** VI [*plane*] descendre en vrille

► **spiral up** VI [*plane*] monter en vrille; [*staircase, smoke, missile*] monter en spirale; [*prices*] monter en flèche

spirally ['spaiərəli] ADV en spirale, en hélice

spire ['spaiə'] N (*Archit*) flèche *f*, aiguille *f*; [*of tree, mountain*] cime *f*; [*of grass, plant*] brin *m*, pousse *f*

spirit ['spirit] [1] N [a] (= *soul*) esprit *m*, âme *f*; **the life of the ~** la vie de l'esprit, la vie spirituelle; **he was there in ~** il était présent en esprit or de cœur; **the ~ is willing but the flesh is weak** l'esprit est prompt mais la chair est faible; **God is pure ~** Dieu est un pur esprit → **holy, move** [b] (= *supernatural being*) esprit *m*; (*Spiritualism*) esprit *m*; **evil ~** esprit malin or du mal [c] (= *person*) esprit *m*, âme *f*; **one of the greatest ~s of his day** un des plus grands esprits de son temps; **the courageous ~ who ...** l'esprit courageux or l'âme courageuse qui ...; **a few restless ~s** quelques mécontents; **the leading ~ in the party** l'âme *m* du parti → **kindred, moving** [d] (= *attitude etc*) esprit *m*, disposition *f*; [*of proposal, regulations etc*] esprit *m*; **he's got the right ~** il a la disposition or l'attitude qu'il faut; **in a ~ of forgiveness** dans un esprit or une intention de pardon; **he has great fighting ~** il ne se laisse jamais abattre; **you must take it in the ~ in which it was meant** prenez-le dans l'esprit où c'était dit or voulu; **to take sth in the right/wrong ~** prendre qch en bonne/mauvaise part or du bon/mauvais côté; **you must enter into the ~ of the thing** il faut y participer de bon cœur; **in a ~ of revenge** par esprit de vengeance; **in a ~ of mischief etc** par espièglerie etc; **the ~, not the letter of the law** l'esprit et non la lettre de la loi; **the film is certainly in the ~ of the book** le film est certainement conforme à l'esprit du livre; **the ~ of the age** or **the times** l'esprit *m* des temps or de l'époque; **that's the ~!** c'est ça!, voilà comment il faut réagir!, voilà l'attitude à prendre! → **community, public, team** [e] (= *courage*) courage *m*, cran* *m*; (= *energy*) énergie *f*; (= *vitality*) entrain *m*; **man of ~** homme *m* énergique or de caractère; **he replied with ~** il a répondu courageusement or énergiquement or avec fougue; **he sang/played with ~** il a chanté/joué avec fougue or brio [f] (*Chem*) alcool *m*; **preserved in ~(s)** conservé dans de l'alcool; **~(s) of ammonia** sel *m* ammoniaque; **~(s) of salt** esprit-de-sel *m*; **~(s) of turpentine** (essence *f* de) térébenthine *f*; (= *drink*) **~s** spiritueux *mpl*, alcool *m*; **raw ~s** alcool *m* pu → **methylated spirit(s), surgical**

[2] **spirits** NPL (= *frame of mind*) humeur *f*, état *m* d'esprit; (= *morale*) moral *m*; **in good ~s** de bonne humeur; **in high ~s** enjoué; **in poor** or **low ~s** ◊ **out of ~s** déprimé, qui n'a pas le moral; **depression can alternate with high ~s** des périodes de dépression peuvent alterner avec des moments d'exaltation; **to keep one's ~s up** ne pas se laisser abattre, garder le moral; **my ~s rose** j'ai repris courage; **to raise sb's ~s** remonter le moral à qn

[3] VT **he was ~ed out of the castle** on l'a fait sortir du château comme par enchantement or magie; **the documents were mysteriously ~ed off his desk** les documents ont été mystérieusement escamotés or subtilisés de son bureau

[4] COMP [*lamp, stove, varnish*] à alcool; (*Spiritualism*) [*help, world*] des esprits ► **spirit gum** N colle *f* gomme ► **spirit level** N niveau *m* à bulle

► **spirit away**, **spirit off** VT SEP [+ *person*] faire disparaître comme par enchantement; [+ *object, document etc*] escamoter, subtiliser

spirited ['spiritid] ADJ [*person*] plein d'entrain; [*horse*] fougueux; [*reply, speech*] plein de verve, fougueux; [*defence*] plein de verve; [*attempt, attack*] courageux; [*conversation*] animé; [*music*] plein d'allant; **to put up** or **make a ~ defence of sth** défendre qch avec vigueur; (*Mus, Theat, Cine, Sport*) **he gave a ~ performance** il a joué avec brio → **free, high, low¹, mean³, public**

spiritless ['spiritlis] ADJ [*person*] sans entrain, sans énergie, sans vie; [*acceptance, agreement*] veule, lâche

spiritual ['spiritjʊəl] [1] ADJ (*gen*) spirituel; [*person*] d'une grande spiritualité; **his ~ home** sa patrie d'adoption (*fig*) or spirituelle; (*Brit*) **the lords ~** les lords *mpl* spirituels (*évêques siégeant à la Chambre des lords*) [2] N chant *m* religieux; (*also* **Negro ~**) (negro-)spiritual *m* [3] COMP ► **spiritual adviser** N (*Rel*) conseiller *m*, -ère *f* spirituel(le), directeur *m*, -trice *f* de conscience

spiritualism ['spiritjʊəlizəm] N (*Rel*) spiritisme *m*; (*Philos*) spiritualisme *m*

spiritualist ['spiritjʊəlist] ADJ, N (*Rel*) spirite *mf*; (*Philos*) spiritualiste *mf*

spirituality [,spiritjʊ'æliti] N [a] (*NonC*) spiritualité *f*, qualité *f* spirituelle [b] (*Rel*) spiritualities biens *mpl* et bénéfices *mpl* ecclésiastiques

spiritually ['spiritjʊəli] ADV spirituellement

spirituous ['spiritjʊəs] ADJ spiritueux, alcoolique; **~ liquor** spiritueux *mpl*

spirt [spɜːt] = **spurt**

spit¹ [spit] (*vb: pret, ptp spat*) [1] N (= *spittle*) crachat *m*; (= *saliva*) [*of person*] salive *f*; [*of animal*] bave *f*; (*Bot*) écume *f* printanière, crachat *m* de coucou; (= *action*) crachement *m*; (*esp Mil*) **~ and polish** briquage *m*, astiquage *m*; **there was just a ~ of rain** il tombait quelques gouttes de pluie; (*Brit*) **a ~ and sawdust pub*** un pub miteux; (*fig*) **he's the dead** or **very ~* of his uncle** c'est le portrait craché* de son oncle, son oncle et lui se ressemblent comme deux gouttes d'eau [2] VT [+ *blood, curses, flames etc*] cracher; (*Austral fig*) **to ~ (out) the dummy*** bouder comme un gamin* [3] VI [*person, cat etc*] cracher (**at sb** sur qn); [*fire, fat*] crépiter; **she spat in his face** elle lui a craché à la figure; (*Brit*) **it was ~ting (with rain)** il tombait quelques gouttes de pluie; (*fig*) **to ~ in the wind*** pisser dans un violon*; (*fig*) **to ~ in sb's eye** faire face à qn

► **spit out** VT SEP [+ *pip, pill*] (re)cracher; [+ *tooth, curses, information*] cracher; **~ it out!*** (= *say it*) allons, accouche* or vide ton sac!*

► **spit up** VT SEP [+ *blood etc*] cracher

spit² [spit] [1] N (*Culin*) broche *f*; (*Geog*) pointe *f* or langue *f* (de terre) [2] VT embrocher

spit³ [spit] N (*Hort*) **to dig sth two ~s deep** creuser qch à une profondeur de deux fers de bêche

spite [spait] [1] N (*NonC*) [a] (= *ill feeling*) rancune *f*, dépit *m*; **out of pure ~** par pure rancune or malveillance; **to have a ~ against sb*** avoir une dent contre qn, en vouloir à qn [b] **in ~ of** malgré, en dépit de; **in ~ of it** malgré cela, en dépit de cela; **in ~ of the fact that he has seen me** bien qu'il m'ait vu, malgré qu'il m'ait vu; **in ~ of everyone** envers et contre tous [2] VT vexer, contrarier

spiteful ['spaɪtfʊl] ADJ [person] méchant, malveillant; [behaviour, story] malveillant; [tongue] venimeux; **a ~ remark** or **comment** une méchanceté, une remarque malveillante

spitefully ['spaɪtfəlɪ] ADV méchamment

spitefulness ['spaɪtfʊlnɪs] N méchanceté f, malveillance f

spitfire ['spɪtfaɪəʳ] N **to be a ~** [person] s'emporter pour un rien, être soupe au lait

spitroast ['spɪtrəʊst] VT faire rôtir à la broche

spitroasted ['spɪtrəʊstɪd] ADJ (rôti) à la broche

spitting ['spɪtɪŋ] N **"~ prohibited"** «défense de cracher»; (fig) **within ~ distance*** à deux pas (of de) → **image**

spittle ['spɪtl] N (ejected) crachat m; (dribbled) [of person] salive f; [of animal] bave f

spittoon [spɪ'tu:n] N crachoir m

spitz [spɪts] N loulou m (chien)

spiv* [spɪv] N (Brit) chevalier m d'industrie

splash [splæʃ] 1 N a (= act) éclaboussement m; (= sound) floc m, plouf m; (= series of sounds) clapotement m; (= mark) éclaboussure f, tache f; (fig) [of colour] tache f; **he dived in with a ~** il a plongé dans un grand éclaboussement or en faisant une grande gerbe; **it made a great ~ as it hit the water** c'est tombé dans l'eau avec un gros plouf or en faisant une grande gerbe; (fig) **to make a ~*** faire sensation, faire du bruit; (fig) **a great ~ of publicity** un grand étalage de or une débauche de publicité
b (in drinks etc = small amount) **a ~ of** (gen) un petit peu de; [+ soda water] une giclée de
2 ADV **it went ~ into the stream** c'est tombé dans l'eau (en faisant floc or plouf)
3 VT a (gen) éclabousser (**sth over sb/sth** qch sur qn/qch, **sb/sth with sth** qn/qch de qch); **to ~ milk on the floor** renverser du lait par terre; **he ~ed paint on the floor** il a fait des éclaboussures de peinture par terre; (in swimming etc) **don't ~ me!** ne m'éclabousse pas!; **to ~ one's way through a stream** traverser un ruisseau en éclaboussant or en pataugeant; **~ed with red/colour/light** avec des taches de rouge/de couleur/de lumière
b (= apply hastily) **to ~ o.s. with water** ◊ **to ~ water on o.s.** s'asperger d'eau; **he ~ed paint on the wall** il a barbouillé le mur de peinture
c (fig) [+ headlines] mettre en manchette; (Press) **the news was ~ed across the front page** la nouvelle a été mise en manchette, la nouvelle a fait cinq colonnes à la une
4 VI a [liquid, mud etc] faire des éclaboussures; **the milk ~ed on** or **over the tablecloth** le lait a éclaboussé la nappe; **tears ~ed on to her book** les larmes s'écrasaient sur son livre
b [person, animal] barboter, patauger; **to ~ across a stream** traverser un ruisseau en éclaboussant or en pataugeant; **the dog ~ed through the mud** le chien pataugeait dans la boue; **to ~ into the water** [person] plonger dans l'eau dans un grand éclaboussement or en faisant une grande gerbe; [stone etc] tomber dans l'eau avec un gros floc or plouf
5 COMP ► **splash guard** N [of car etc] garde-boue m inv

► **splash about** 1 VI [person, animal] barboter, patauger (**in** dans) 2 VT SEP [+ ink, mud] faire des éclaboussures de; (fig) [+ money] faire étalage de

► **splash down** 1 VI [spacecraft] amerrir 2 **~down** N → **splashdown**

► **splash out*** (Brit) 1 VI (= spend money) faire une folie 2 VT SEP [+ money] claquer*, dépenser

► **splash up** 1 VI gicler (**on sb** sur qn) 2 VT SEP faire gicler

splashback ['splæʃbæk] N revêtement m (au dessus d'un évier etc)

splashboard ['splæʃbɔːd] N [of car etc] garde-boue m inv

splashdown ['splæʃdaʊn] N (Space) amerrissage m

splashy* ['splæʃɪ] ADJ (US) tape-à-l'œil inv

splat [splæt] 1 N **with a ~** avec un flac or floc 2 EXCL flac!, floc!

splatter ['splætəʳ] = **spatter**

splay [spleɪ] 1 VT [+ window frame] ébraser; [+ end of pipe etc] évaser; [+ feet, legs] tourner en dehors 2 VI (also **~ out**) [window frame] s'ébraser; [end of pipe etc] se tourner en dehors

splayfeet ['spleɪfiːt] NPL pieds mpl tournés en dehors

splayfooted [ˌspleɪ'fʊtɪd] ADJ [person] aux pieds plats; [horse] panard

spleen [spliːn] N (Anat) rate f; (fig = bad temper) mauvaise humeur f, humeur f noire; (†† = melancholy) spleen m; **to vent one's ~ on ...** décharger sa bile sur ...

splendid ['splendɪd] ADJ [view, collection, building, painting, performance] magnifique, splendide; [idea] magnifique; [book] (in content) merveilleux; (in appearance) splendide; [meal] merveilleux; [example] superbe; [person] (= excellent) excellent; (= imposing) magnifique; [player, teacher] excellent; **~!** formidable!; **to do a ~ job** faire un travail formidable; **~ isolation** splendide isolement m

splendidly ['splendɪdlɪ] ADV [play, sing] magnifiquement, à merveille; [dressed, carved, restored, appointed] magnifiquement, superbement; [get along, come along] à merveille, merveilleusement; **~ named** merveilleusement nommé; **~ arrogant/vulgar/ugly** merveilleusement arrogant/vulgaire/laid; **you did ~** tu as été magnifique; **everything is going ~** tout se passe à merveille

splendiferous†* [splen'dɪfərəs] ADJ (Brit hum) mirobolant*, mirifique† (also hum)

splendour, splendor (US) ['splendəʳ] N splendeur f, magnificence f, éclat m

splenetic [splɪ'netɪk] ADJ a (frm = bad-tempered) hargneux, atrabilaire† b (†† = melancholy) porté au spleen

splice [splaɪs] 1 VT [+ rope, cable] épisser; [+ film, tape] coller; [+ timbers] enter, abouter; **to ~ the mainbrace** (Naut) distribuer une ration de rhum; (* fig = have a drink) boire un coup*; (fig) **to get ~d*** convoler 2 N (in rope) épissure f; (in film) collure f; (in wood) enture f

splicer ['splaɪsəʳ] N (for film) colleuse f (à bandes adhésives)

spliff* [splɪf] N (Drugs) pétard* m, joint* m

splint [splɪnt] N (Med) éclisse f, attelle f; **to put sb's arm in ~s** éclisser le bras de qn; **she had her leg in ~s** elle avait la jambe éclissée

splinter ['splɪntəʳ] 1 N [of glass, shell, wood] éclat m; [of bone] esquille f; (in one's finger etc) écharde f 2 VT [+ wood] fendre en éclats; [+ glass, bone] briser en éclats; (fig) [+ party] scinder, fragmenter 3 VI [wood] se fendre en éclats; [glass, bone] se briser en éclats; (fig) [party] se scinder, se fragmenter 4 COMP ► **splinter group** N groupe m dissident or scissionniste, faction f dissidente

splinterproof glass ['splɪntəpruː'glɑːs] N verre m securit® inv

split [splɪt] (vb: pret, ptp **split**) 1 N a (in garment, fabric, canvas) (at seam) fente f; (= tear) déchirure f; (in wood, rock) crevasse f, fente f; (in earth's surface) fissure f; (in skin) fissure f, déchirure f; (from cold) gerçure f, crevasse f; (= quarrel) rupture f; (Pol) scission f, schisme m; **there was a three-way ~ in the committee** le comité s'est trouvé divisé en trois clans
b (= share) **I want my ~*** je veux ma part (du gâteau*); **they did a four-way ~ of the profits** ils ont partagé les bénéfices en quatre
c (= small bottle) **soda/lemonade ~** petite bouteille f d'eau gazeuse/de limonade; (=

cake) **jam/cream ~** gâteau m fourré à la confiture/à la crème; (= ice cream etc) **banana ~** banana split m inv
2 **splits** NPL **to do the ~s** faire le grand écart
3 VT a (= cleave) [+ wood, pole] fendre; [+ slate, diamond] cliver; [+ stones] fendre, casser; [+ fabric, garment] déchirer; [+ seam] fendre; [lightning, frost, explosion, blow] fendre; (fig) [+ party] diviser, créer une scission or un schisme dans; **to ~ the atom** fissionner l'atome; **to ~ sth open** ouvrir qch en le coupant en deux or en fendant; **he ~ his head open as he fell** il s'est fendu le crâne en tombant; **the sea had ~ the ship in two** la mer avait brisé le bateau en deux; **he ~ it in two** il l'a fendu (en deux); **he ~ it into three** il l'a coupé en trois; **~ the loaf lengthwise** fendez le pain dans le sens de la longueur; (fig) **to ~ hairs** couper les cheveux en quatre, chercher la petite bête, chinoiser; (Gram) **to ~ an infinitive** intercaler un adverbe entre « to » et le verbe; (fig) **to ~ one's sides** (laughing or with laughter) se tordre de rire; **this decision ~ the radical movement** cette décision a divisé le mouvement radical, cette décision a provoqué une scission or un schisme dans le mouvement radical; **it ~ the party down the middle** cela a littéralement divisé le parti en deux; **the voters were ~ down the middle** l'électorat était divisé or coupé en deux
b (= divide, share) [+ work, profits, booty, bill] (se) partager, (se) répartir; **let's ~ a bottle of wine** si on prenait une bouteille de vin à deux (or trois etc)?; **they ~ the money three ways** ils ont divisé l'argent en trois; **to ~ the difference** (lit) partager la différence; (fig) couper la poire en deux; **they ~ the work/the inheritance** ils se sont partagé le travail/l'héritage
4 VI a [wood, pole, seam] se fendre; [stones] se fendre, se casser; [fabric, garment] se déchirer; (fig) [party, Church, government] se diviser, se désunir; **to ~ open** se fendre; (fig) **my head is ~ting** j'ai atrocement mal à la tête; **the party ~ over nationalization** le parti s'est divisé sur la question des nationalisations, il y a eu une scission or un schisme dans le parti à propos de la question des nationalisations
b (= divide: also **~ up**) [cells] se diviser; [people, party etc] se diviser, se séparer; **the crowd ~ into smaller groups** la foule s'est divisée or séparée en petits groupes; **Latin ~ into the Romance languages** le latin s'est divisé or ramifié en langues romanes
c (Brit* = tell tales, inform) vendre la mèche*; **to ~ on sb** donner qn, vendre qn, cafarder qn*
d (* = depart) filer*, mettre les bouts*
5 COMP ► **split cane** N osier m ♦ ADJ en osier ► **split decision** N (Boxing etc) décision f majoritaire ► **split ends** NPL (in hair) fourches fpl ► **split infinitive** N (Gram) infinitif où un adverbe est intercalé entre « to » et le verbe ► **split-level cooker** N cuisinière f à éléments de cuisson séparés ► **split-level house** N maison f à deux niveaux ► **split-new** ADJ tout neuf (tout neuve f) ► **split-off** N séparation f, scission f (**from** de) ► **split peas** NPL pois mpl cassés ► **split-pea soup** N soupe f de pois cassés ► **split personality** N double personnalité f ► **split pin** N (Brit) goupille f fendue ► **split ring** N bague f fendue ► **split screen** N (Cine, TV, Comput) écran m divisé ► **split-screen facility** N (Comput) écran m divisible en fenêtres, fonction f écran divisé ► **split second** N fraction f de seconde; **in a ~ second** en un rien de temps ► **split-second timing** N [of military operation etc] précision f à la seconde près; [of actor, comedian] sens m du moment ► **split-site** ADJ [school etc] dont les locaux ne sont pas regroupés ► **split ticket** N (US Pol) **to vote a ~ ticket** voter pour une liste avec panachage ► **split-up** N [of engaged couple, friends] rupture f; [of married couple] sé-

paration f; [of political party] scission f
► **split off** ⓵ VI [piece of wood, branch etc] se détacher (en se fendant) (**from** de); (fig) [group, department, company etc] se séparer (**from** de); **a small group of children ~ off and wandered away** un petit groupe d'enfants s'est séparé des autres et est parti de son côté ⓶ VT SEP [+ branch, splinter, piece] enlever (en fendant or en cassant) (**from** de); (fig) [+ company, group, department] séparer (**from** de) ⓷ **~-off** N → **split**
► **split up** ⓵ VI [ship] se briser; [boulder, block of wood etc] se fendre; (fig) [meeting, crowd] se disperser; [party, movement] se diviser, se scinder; [friends] rompre, se brouiller; [married couple] se séparer; [engaged couple] rompre ⓶ VT SEP [+ wood, stones] fendre (**into** en); [+ money, work] partager, répartir (**among** entre), diviser (**into** en); [+ compound] diviser (**into** en); [+ party, group, organization] diviser, scinder (**into** en); [+ meeting] mettre fin à; [+ crowd] disperser; [+ friends] séparer; **to ~ up a book into six chapters** diviser un livre en six chapitres; **we must ~ the work up amongst us** nous devons nous partager or nous répartir le travail; **you'll have to ~ up those two boys if you want them to do any work** il faut que vous sépariez (subj) ces deux garçons si vous voulez qu'ils travaillent (subj) ⓷ **~-up** N → **split**

splitting ['splɪtɪŋ] ⓵ N [of nation, organization] division f; [of roles] partage m; (Gram) **the ~ of an infinitive** l'insertion d'un adverbe entre « to » et le verbe; **the ~ of the atom** la fission de l'atome → **hair** ⓶ ADJ **to have a ~ headache** avoir un mal de tête atroce → **ear**[1], **side**

splodge [splɒdʒ], **splotch** [splɒtʃ] ⓵ N [of ink, paint, colour, dirt, mud] éclaboussure f, tache f; **strawberries with a great ~ of cream** des fraises avec un monceau de crème ⓶ VT [+ windows, dress etc] éclabousser, barbouiller (**with** de); [+ mud, ink etc] faire des taches or des éclaboussures de (**on** sur) ⓷ VI [mud etc] gicler (**on** sur)

splurge* [splɜːdʒ] ⓵ N (= ostentation) tralala* m; (= spending spree) folles dépenses fpl, folie f; **the wedding reception was** or **made a great ~** la réception de mariage était à grand tralala*; **she went on a ~ or had a ~ and bought a Rolls** elle a fait une vraie folie et s'est payé* une Rolls ⓶ VI (also **~ out**) faire une or des folie(s) (**on** en achetant) ⓷ VT dépenser (en un seul coup) (**on sth** pour qch), engloutir (**on sth** dans qch)

splutter ['splʌtə[r]] ⓵ N [of person] (= spitting) crachotement m; (= stuttering) bredouillement m, bafouillage* m; [of engine] bafouillage* m; [of fire, frying pan, fat, candle] crépitement m ⓶ VI [person] (= spit) crachoter, postillonner; (= stutter) bredouiller, bafouiller*; [pen] cracher; [engine] bafouiller*, tousser; [fire, frying pan, fat, candle] crépiter; **he ~ed indignantly** il a bredouillé or bafouillé d'indignation ⓷ VT (also **~ out**) [+ words, excuse] bredouiller, bafouiller*

spoil [spɔɪl] (vb: pret, ptp **spoiled** or **spoilt**) ⓵ N ⒜ (gen pl) **~(s)** (= booty) butin m; (fig: after business deal etc) bénéfices mpl, profits mpl; (US Pol) poste m or avantage m reçu en récompense de services politiques rendus; **the ~s of war** le butin or les dépouilles fpl de la guerre; (fig) **he wants his share of the ~s** il veut sa part du gâteau ⒝ (NonC: from excavations etc) déblais mpl ⓶ VT ⒜ (= damage) abîmer; **to ~ one's eyes** s'abîmer la vue; **fruit ~ed by insects** des fruits abîmés par les insectes; **the drought has really ~t the garden** la sécheresse a vraiment fait de dégâts dans le jardin; **to ~ a ballot paper** rendre un bulletin de vote nul ⒝ (= detract from) [+ view, style, effect] gâter; [+ holiday, occasion, pleasure] gâter, gâcher;

these weeds quite ~ the garden ces mauvaises herbes enlaidissent or défigurent le jardin; **his peace of mind was ~t by money worries** sa tranquillité était empoisonnée par des soucis d'argent; **to ~ one's appetite** s'enlever or se couper l'appétit; **if you eat that now you'll ~ your lunch** si tu manges ça maintenant tu n'auras plus d'appétit pour le déjeuner; **don't ~ your life by doing that** ne gâche pas ta vie en faisant cela; **if you tell me the ending you'll ~ the film for me** si vous me racontez la fin vous me gâcherez tout l'intérêt du film; **she ~t the meal by overcooking the meat** elle a gâté le repas en faisant trop cuire la viande; **she ~t the meal by telling him the bad news** elle a gâché le repas en lui racontant la triste nouvelle; **the weather ~ed our holiday** le temps nous a gâté or gâché nos vacances ▪ (PROV) **to ~ the ship for a ha'p'orth of tar** tout gâcher en faisant des économies de bout de chandelle → **fun** ⒞ (= pamper) [+ child, one's spouse, dog etc] gâter; **to ~ o.s.** se gâter soi-même, se faire plaisir; **to ~ sb rotten**‡ pourrir qn → **spare** ⓷ VI ⒜ [food] s'abîmer; (in ship's hold, warehouse, shop) s'avarier ⒝ **to be ~ing for a fight** brûler de se battre, chercher la bagarre* ⓸ COMP ► **spoils system** N (US Pol) système m des dépouilles (consistant à distribuer des postes administratifs à des partisans après une victoire électorale)

spoilage ['spɔɪlɪdʒ] N (NonC) (= process) détérioration f; (= thing, amount spoilt) déchet(s) m(pl)

spoiled [spɔɪld] = **spoilt**

spoiler ['spɔɪlə[r]] N (Aut) becquet m; (Aviat) aérofrein m; (= person) empêcheur m de danser en rond; (Press) **a rival publisher brought out a ~** un éditeur concurrent leur a coupé l'herbe sous le pied

spoilsport ['spɔɪlspɔːt] N trouble-fête mf inv, rabat-joie m inv; **don't be such a ~!** ne joue pas les trouble-fête or les rabat-joie!

spoilt [spɔɪlt] ⓵ VB pt, ptp of **spoil** ⓶ ADJ ⒜ (= indulged) [child] gâté; **to be ~ for choice** avoir l'embarras du choix ⒝ (= invalid) [ballot paper] nul ⒞ (= rotten) [food] abîmé

spoke[1] [spəʊk] N [of wheel] rayon m; [of ladder] barreau m, échelon m; (Brit fig) **to put a ~ in sb's wheel** mettre des bâtons dans les roues à qn

spoke[2] [spəʊk] VB pt of **speak**

spoken ['spəʊkən] ⓵ VB ptp of **speak** ⓶ ADJ [dialogue, recitative] parlé; **a robot capable of understanding ~ commands** un robot capable de comprendre la commande vocale; **the ~ language** la langue parlée; **the ~ word** l'oral m, la langue parlée; **~ English** l'anglais m parlé → **well**[2]

spokeshave ['spəʊkʃeɪv] N (Tech) vastringue f

spokesman ['spəʊksmən] N (pl **-men**) porte-parole m inv (**of, for** de)

spokesperson ['spəʊks,pɜːsən] N porte-parole m inv

spokeswoman ['spəʊks,wʊmən] N (pl **-women**) porte-parole m inv (femme)

Spoleto [spəʊ'letəʊ] N Spolète

spoliation [,spəʊlɪ'eɪʃən] N (esp Naut) pillage m, spoliation f

spondaic [spɒn'deɪɪk] ADJ spondaïque

spondee ['spɒndiː] N spondée m

spondulicks‡, **spondulix**‡ [spɒn'duːlɪks] NPL († or hum) pépètes†‡ fpl

sponge [spʌndʒ] ⓵ N ⒜ (Zool, gen) éponge f; **to give sth a ~** donner un coup d'éponge à or sur qch; (fig) **to throw in** or **up the ~*** s'avouer vaincu, abandonner la partie ⒝ (Culin: also **~ cake**) gâteau m or biscuit m de Savoie

⓶ VT ⒜ [+ face, person, carpet] éponger, essuyer or nettoyer à l'éponge; [+ wound] éponger; [+ liquid] éponger, étancher ⒝ (* = cadge) [+ meal] se faire payer* (**from** or **off sb** par qn); **to ~ money from sb** taper* qn; **he ~d £10 off his father** il a tapé* son père de 10 livres ⓷ VI (* = cadge) **to ~ on sb** vivre aux crochets de qn; **he's always sponging** c'est un parasite; (for meals) c'est un pique-assiette ⓸ COMP ► **sponge bag** N (Brit) trousse f de toilette ► **sponge bath** N toilette f à l'éponge ► **sponge cake** N (Culin) → **1b** ► **sponge-down** N [of person] toilette f à l'éponge; [of walls] coup m d'éponge ► **sponge finger** N (Culin) boudoir m ► **sponge mop** N balai m à laver ► **sponge pudding** N (Culin) ≈ pudding m (sorte de gâteau de Savoie) ► **sponge rubber** N caoutchouc m mousse®

► **sponge down** ⓵ VT SEP [+ person] laver à l'éponge; [+ horse] éponger; [+ walls etc] nettoyer or laver or essuyer à l'éponge; **to ~ o.s. down** se laver à l'éponge, s'éponger ⓶ **~-down** N → **sponge**

► **sponge out** VT SEP [+ wound] éponger; [+ stain, writing] effacer à l'éponge

► **sponge up** VT SEP [+ liquid] éponger, étancher

sponger* ['spʌndʒə[r]] N (pej) parasite m; (for meals) pique-assiette mf inv

sponginess ['spʌndʒɪnɪs] N spongiosité f

spongy ['spʌndʒɪ] ADJ spongieux

sponsor ['spɒnsə[r]] ⓵ N (gen) [of appeal, proposal, announcement etc] personne f qui accorde son patronage, membre m d'un comité de patronage; (Fin: for loan etc) répondant(e) m(f), caution f; (for commercial enterprise) promoteur m, parrain m; (Rel = godparent) parrain m, marraine f; (for club membership) parrain m, marraine f; (Rad, TV = advertiser) personne f or organisme m qui assure le patronage; [of concert, event] personne f or organisme m qui accorde son parrainage; [of sports event] sponsor m; (individual: for fund-raising event) donateur m, -trice f (à l'occasion d'une « sponsored walk » etc); (US) [of club] animateur m, -trice f; **to be sb's ~ ◊ to stand ~ to sb ◊ to act as ~ for sb** être le (or la) répondant(e) de qn, se porter caution pour qn ⓶ VT [+ appeal, proposal, announcement] patronner, présenter; (Fin) [+ borrower] se porter caution pour; [+ commercial enterprise] être le promoteur de, parrainer; (Rel) être le parrain (or la marraine) de; [+ club member, concert, event] parrainer; (Rad, TV) [+ programme] patronner; [+ sporting event] sponsoriser, être le(s) sponsor(s) de; [+ fund-raising walker, swimmer etc] s'engager à rémunérer (en fonction de sa performance); (in fund-raising) **~ed walk** marche entreprise pour récolter des dons en faveur d'une œuvre de bienfaisance

┌─────────────────┐
│ **SPONSORED** │
└─────────────────┘

Les « **sponsored** events » sont un moyen souvent employé pour récolter des dons en faveur d'une œuvre de bienfaisance. Ils consistent à prendre part à un événement sportif (course à pied, course cycliste, saut en parachute) après avoir demandé à sa famille, ses amis ou ses collègues de s'engager à faire un don si on finit la course. Pour une « **sponsored** walk », on promet généralement de donner une certaine somme par kilomètre parcouru.

-sponsored ['spɒnsəd] ADJ (in compounds) **government-sponsored** à l'initiative du gouvernement

sponsorship ['spɒnsəʃɪp] N (Rad, TV) commande f publicitaire; [of appeal, announcement] patronage m; (Sport) sponsoring m; (Comm) mécénat m d'entreprise; [of *loan*] cautionnement *m* ; [*of child, member*] parrainage *m*

spontaneity [ˌspɒntə'neɪɪtɪ] N spontanéité *f*

spontaneous [spɒn'teɪnɪəs] **1** ADJ spontané **2** COMP ► **spontaneous abortion** N avortement *m* spontané ► **spontaneous combustion** N combustion *f* spontanée ► **spontaneous generation** N génération *f* spontanée ► **spontaneous miscarriage** N avortement *m* spontané ► **spontaneous remission** N rémission *f* spontanée

spontaneously [spɒn'teɪnɪəslɪ] ADV [*behave, abort, combust*] spontanément ; [*arise*] spontanément, soudainement ; **to miscarry ~** avoir un avortement spontané ; **to be ~ warm/ friendly** se montrer spontanément chaleureux/amical

spoof* [spuːf] **1** N (= *hoax*) blague* *f*, canular *m* ; (= *parody*) parodie *f*, satire *f* (**on** de) **2** ADJ **a ~ horror film/documentary** une parodie de film d'épouvante/de documentaire ; **a ~ announcement** une déclaration bidon* **3** VT [+ *reader, listener etc*] faire marcher ; (= *parody*) [+ *book etc*] parodier

spook [spuːk] **1** N **a** (* *hum* = *ghost*) apparition *f*, revenant *m* **b** (*US** = *secret agent*) barbouze* *f* **2** VT (*US*) **a** (= *haunt*) [+ *person, house*] hanter **b** (= *frighten*) effrayer, faire peur à

spooky* [ˈspuːkɪ] ADJ [*person, place, atmosphere, music*] sinistre ; [*film*] qui fait froid dans le dos, qui donne la chair de poule ; [*feeling*] à vous faire froid dans le dos, à vous donner la chair de poule ; **to bear a ~ resemblance to sb/sth** ressembler d'une manière étrange à qn/qch

spool [spuːl] N [*of camera, film, tape, thread, typewriter ribbon*] bobine *f* ; [*of fishing reel*] tambour *m* ; [*of sewing machine, weaving machine*] canette *f* ; [*of wire*] rouleau *m*

spoon [spuːn] **1** N cuillère *or* cuiller *f* ; (= *spoonful*) cuillerée *f*, cuiller *f* ; (*Golf*) spoon *m*, bois *m* trois → **dessertspoon, silver 2** VT **to ~ sth into a plate/out of a bowl** *etc* verser qch dans une assiette/enlever qch d'un bol *etc* avec une cuiller **3** VI (†* *fig*) flirter **4** COMP ► **spoon-feed** VT (*lit*) **to ~-feed sb** nourrir qn à la cuiller ; (*fig*) **he needs to be ~-fed all the time** il faut toujours qu'on lui mâche (*subj*) le travail

► **spoon off** VT SEP [+ *fat, cream etc*] enlever avec une cuiller

► **spoon out** VT SEP (= *take out*) verser avec une cuiller ; (= *serve out*) servir avec une cuiller

► **spoon up** VT SEP [+ *food, soup*] manger avec une cuiller ; [+ *spillage*] ramasser avec une cuiller

spoonbill [ˈspuːnbɪl] N spatule *f*

spoonerism [ˈspuːnərɪzəm] N contrepèterie *f*

spoonful [ˈspuːnfʊl] N cuillerée *f*, cuiller *f*

spoor [spʊəʳ] N (*NonC*) [*of animal*] foulées *fpl*, trace *f*, piste *f*

sporadic [spə'rædɪk] ADJ sporadique ; **~ fighting** combats *mpl* sporadiques, échauffourées *fpl*

sporadically [spə'rædɪkəlɪ] ADV sporadiquement

spore [spɔːʳ] N spore *f*

sporran [ˈspɒrən] N (*Scot*) escarcelle *f* en peau (*portée avec le kilt*)

sport [spɔːt] **1** N **a** sport *m* ; **he is good at ~** il est doué pour le sport, il est très sportif ; **he is good at several ~s** il est doué pour plusieurs sports ; **outdoor/indoor ~s** sports *mpl* de plein air/d'intérieur ; (*meeting*) **~s** réunion *f* sportive ; **school ~s** réunion *f* or compétition *f* sportive scolaire → **field b** † (*NonC* = *fun, amusement*) divertissement *m*, amusement *m* ; (*fig liter* = *plaything*) jouet *m* ; **it was great ~** c'était très divertissant *or* amusant ; **in ~** pour rire, pour s'amuser ; **we had (some) good ~** (*gen*) nous nous sommes

bien divertis *or* amusés ; (*Hunting/Fishing*) nous avons fait bonne chasse/bonne pêche ; (*liter*) **to make ~ of sb** se moquer de qn, tourner qn en ridicule → **spoilsport**

c (* = *person*) (**good**) ~ chic* *or* brave type* *m*, chic* *or* brave fille *f* ; **be a ~!** sois chic !* ; (*Austral*) **come on, ~!** allez, mon vieux* *or* mon pote‡ !

d (*Bio, Zool*) variété *f* anormale

2 VI (*liter*) folâtrer, batifoler

3 VT [+ *tie, hat, beard, buttonhole*] arborer, exhiber ; [+ *black eye*] exhiber

4 COMP ► **sport coat, sport jacket** N (*US*) = sports jacket → **sports**

sportiness [ˈspɔːtɪnɪs] N (*lit, fig*) caractère *m* sportif

sporting [ˈspɔːtɪŋ] **1** ADJ **a** (*Sport*) [*event, activity, organization, career, prowess*] sportif ; **a ~ injury** une blessure *or* un traumatisme du sport ; **the ~ world** le monde du sport ; **~ goods** articles *mpl* de sport **b** (= *fair*) [*gesture*] généreux ; [*person*] chic* *inv* ; **that's very ~ of you** c'est très chic* de votre part ; **to have a ~ chance (of winning)** avoir de bonnes chances (de gagner) ; **to give sb a ~ chance (of winning)** donner à qn une chance (de gagner) **2** COMP ► **sporting gun** N fusil *m* de chasse ► **sporting house**† N (*US euph*) maison *f* de passe

sportingly [ˈspɔːtɪŋlɪ] ADV très sportivement

sportive [ˈspɔːtɪv] ADJ folâtre, badin

sports [spɔːts] **1** ADJ [*programme, reporting, newspaper etc*] de sport, sportif ; [*commentator, reporter, news, editor, club*] sportif ; [*clothes*] sport *inv* **2** COMP ► **sports bra** N soutien-gorge *m* de sport ► **sports car** N voiture *f* de sport ► **sports coat** = **sports jacket** ► **sports day** N (*Brit Scol*) réunion *f* or compétition *f* sportive scolaire ► **sports desk** N (*Press*) rédaction *f* sportive ► **sports enthusiast** = **sports fan** ► **sports equipment** N (*NonC*) équipement *m* sportif, matériel *m* de sport ► **sports fan*** N fanatique *mf* de sport ► **sports ground** N terrain *m* de sport, stade *m* ► **sports injuries clinic** N clinique *f* du sport ► **sports injury** N blessure *f* sportive, traumatisme *m* du sport ► **sports jacket** N veste *f* sport *inv* ► **sports medicine** N médecine *f* sportive ► **sports page** N (*Press*) page *f* sportive *or* des sports ► **sports shop** N magasin *m* de sports

sportscast [ˈspɔːtskɑːst] N (*US Rad, TV*) émission *f* sportive

sportscaster [ˈspɔːtskɑːstəʳ] N (*US Rad, TV*) reporter *m* sportif

sportsman [ˈspɔːtsmən] N (*pl* -**men**) sportif *m* ; (*fig*) **he's a real ~** il est beau joueur, il est très sport *inv*

sportsmanlike [ˈspɔːtsmənlaɪk] ADJ (*lit, fig*) sportif, chic* *inv*

sportsmanship [ˈspɔːtsmənʃɪp] N (*lit, fig*) sportivité *f*, esprit *m* sportif

sportsperson [ˈspɔːtspɜːsən] N sportif *m*, -ive *f*

sportswear [ˈspɔːtsweəʳ] N (*NonC*) vêtements *mpl* de sport

sportswoman [ˈspɔːtswʊmən] N (*pl* -**women**) sportive *f*

sportswriter [ˈspɔːtsraɪtəʳ] N rédacteur *m* sportif

sporty* [ˈspɔːtɪ] ADJ **a** (= *fast*) [*car*] de sport **b** (*Sport*) [*person*] sportif **c** (*Fashion*) [*clothes*] sport *inv*

spot [spɒt] **1** N **a** [*of blood, ink, paint*] (= *mark, dot etc*) tache *f* ; (= *splash*) éclaboussure *f* ; (*on fruit*) tache *f*, tavelure *f* ; (= *polka dot*) pois *m* ; (*on dice, domino*) point *m* ; [*of leopard etc*] tache *f*, moucheture *f* ; (*fig: on reputation etc*) tache *f*, souillure *f* (**on** sur) ; **a ~ of dirt** une tache, une salissure ; **a ~ of red** une tache

or un point rouge ; **a dress with red ~s** une robe à pois rouges ; (*Brit*) **~s of rain** quelques gouttes *fpl* de pluie ; **to have ~s before one's eyes** *or* **the eyes** voir des mouches volantes devant les yeux ; (*Cards*) **the ten ~ of spades** le dix de pique ; (*US*) **a five/ten ~‡** (= *money*) un billet de cinq/dix dollars ; (*fig liter*) **without a ~ or stain** sans la moindre tache *or* souillure → **beauty, knock, sunspot**

b (= *pimple*) bouton *m* ; (*freckle-type*) tache *f* (de son) ; **he came out in ~s** il a eu une éruption de boutons ; **these ~s are measles** ce sont des taches de rougeole

c (*esp Brit* = *small amount*) **a ~ of** un peu de ; [+ *whisky, coffee etc*] une goutte de ; [+ *irony, jealousy*] une pointe de ; [+ *truth, commonsense*] un grain de ; **he did a ~ of work** il a travaillé un peu ; **brandy? — just a ~** du cognac ? — juste une goutte *or* un soupçon ; **there's been a ~ of trouble** il y a eu un petit incident *or* un petit problème ; **how about a ~ of lunch?*** et si on déjeunait ?, et si on mangeait un morceau ? ; **we had a ~ of lunch** nous avons mangé un morceau → **bother**

d (= *place*) endroit *m* ; **show me the ~ on the map** montrez-moi l'endroit sur la carte ; **a good ~ for a picnic** un bon endroit *or* coin pour un pique-nique ; **it's a lovely ~** c'est un endroit *or* un coin ravissant ! ; **there's a tender ~ on my arm** j'ai un point sensible au bras ; **the ~ in the story where ...** l'endroit *or* le moment dans l'histoire où ... → **high, hit, soft**

e (*phrases*) **the police were on the ~ in two minutes** la police est arrivée sur les lieux en deux minutes ; **it's easy if you're on the ~** c'est facile si vous êtes sur place *or* si vous êtes là ; **leave it to the man on the ~ to decide** laissez décider la personne qui est sur place ; (*Press*) **our man on the ~** notre envoyé spécial ; **an on-the-~ broadcast/report** une émission/un reportage sur place ; **an on-the-~ enquiry** une enquête sur le terrain ; **an on-the-~ fine** une amende payable sur-le-champ *or* avec paiement immédiat ; **he was fined on the ~** on lui a infligé une amende sur-le-champ ; **he decided on the ~** il s'est décidé sur le coup *or* sur-le-champ *or* tout de suite ; **he was killed on the ~** il a été tué sur le coup ; **to put sb on the ~** mettre qn en difficulté *or* dans l'embarras ; **to be in a (bad *or* tight) ~*** être dans le pétrin*, être dans de beaux draps

f (*Rad, Theat, TV:* in show*) numéro *m* ; (*Rad, TV: also* ~ **ad** *or* **advertisement**) spot *m*, message *m* publicitaire ; **a solo ~ in cabaret** un numéro individuel dans une revue ; **he got a ~ in the Late Show** il a fait un numéro dans le Late Show ; **Glo-kleen had a ~ (ad*) before the news** Glo-kleen a fait passer un spot *or* un message publicitaire avant les informations ; **there was a ~ (announcement) about the referendum** il y a eu une brève annonce au sujet du référendum

g (*: *also* **nightspot**) boîte *f* de nuit

h = **spotlight 1**

i (*Billiards, Snooker*) mouche *f*

2 VT **a** (= *speckle, stain*) tacher (**with** de) ; **a tie ~ted with fruit stains** une cravate portant des taches de fruit → **spotted**

b (= *recognize, notice*) [+ *person, object, vehicle*] apercevoir, repérer* ; [+ *mistake*] trouver, repérer ; [+ *bargain, winner, sb's ability*] déceler, découvrir ; **can you ~ any bad apples in this tray?** est-ce que tu vois *or* tu trouves des pommes gâtées sur cette claie ?

3 VI **a** [*material, garment etc*] se tacher, se salir

b **it is ~ting (with rain)** il commence à pleuvoir, il tombe quelques gouttes de pluie

c (*Mil etc* = *act as spotter*) observer

4 COMP [*transaction, goods, price*] payé comptant ; [*count, test*] intermittent, fait à l'improviste ► **spot ad***, **spot advertisement, spot announcement** N → **1f** ► **spot cash** N (*NonC*) argent *m* comptant *or* liquide

► **spot check** N contrôle *m* inopiné *or* impromptu ► **spot-check** VT contrôler *or* vérifier de façon impromptue ► **spot fine** N amende *f* à régler immédiatement ► **spot market** N marché *m* au comptant ► **spot-on*** ADJ (*Brit*) (= *right*) **what he said was ~-on** ce qu'il a dit était en plein dans le mille* ; **he guessed ~-on** il a mis en plein dans le mille* ; (= *very good*) **your new jacket is ~-on** ta nouvelle veste est super* ► **spot rate** N (*Fin*) cours *m* du disponible ► **spot remover** N détachant *m* ► **spot survey** N sondage *m* ► **spot-weld** VT souder par points

spotless ['spɒtlɪs] ①ADJ ⓐ (= *clean*) [*room, street, beach, clothes*] impeccable ; **she keeps the house ~** elle entretient impeccablement la maison ⓑ (= *flawless*) [*reputation, image*] sans tache ②ADV* = **spotlessly**

spotlessly ['spɒtlɪslɪ] ADV **~ clean** impeccable, reluisant de propreté

spotlessness ['spɒtlɪsnɪs] N propreté *f* (impeccable *or* immaculée)

spotlight ['spɒtlaɪt] ① N (*Theat* = *beam*) rayon *m or* feu *m* de projecteur ; (*Theat* = *lamp*) projecteur *m*, spot *m* ; (*in home*) spot *m* ; (*Aut*) phare *m* auxiliaire ; **in the ~** (*Theat*) sous le feu du *or* des projecteur(s) ; (*fig*) en vedette, sous le feu des projecteurs ; (*fig*) **the ~ was on him** il était en vedette ; (*in the public eye*) les feux de l'actualité étaient braqués sur lui ; (*Theat, fig*) **to turn the ~ on sb/sth = to spotlight sb/sth** ; → **2** ②VT (*Theat*) diriger les projecteurs sur ; (*fig*) [+ *sb's success, achievements*] mettre en vedette ; [+ *changes, differences, a fact*] mettre en lumière

spotlit ['spɒtlɪt] ADJ illuminé

spotted ['spɒtɪd] ①ADJ ⓐ (= *patterned*) [*handkerchief, tie, dress, crockery*] à pois ; [*animal*] tacheté ; **blue eggs ~ with brown** œufs *mpl* bleus tachetés de marron ; **a yellow tie ~ with grey** une cravate jaune à pois gris ⓑ (= *blemished*) **~ with paint** taché de peinture ; **~ with stains** couvert de taches ; **~ with nasty green mould** couvert d'horribles taches de moisissure verte ②COMP ► **spotted dick** N (*Brit Culin*) *pudding aux raisins de Corinthe* ► **spotted fever** N fièvre *f* éruptive ► **spotted flycatcher** N (*Orn*) gobe-mouches *m* gris

spotter ['spɒtə'] ① N ⓐ (*Brit: as hobby*) **train/plane ~** passionné(e) *m(f)* de trains/d'avions ⓑ (*Mil etc*) (*for enemy aircraft*) guetteur *m* ; (*during fighting*) observateur *m* ; (*US Comm**) surveillant(e) *m(f)* du personnel ②COMP ► **spotter plane** N avion *m* d'observation

spotting ['spɒtɪŋ] N ⓐ repérage *m* ; (*Brit*) **train/plane ~** *passe-temps consistant à identifier le plus grand nombre possible de trains/d'avions* ⓑ (*Med*) traces *fpl* (de sang)

spotty ['spɒtɪ] ADJ ⓐ [*person, face, skin*] boutonneux ⓑ (*esp US = patchy*) [*support*] irrégulier, inégal ; [*bus service*] irrégulier ; [*knowledge*] inégal (* = *patterned*) [*handkerchief, shirt, crockery*] à pois ⓓ (= *dirty*) [*garment*] taché

spousal ['spaʊzl] ADJ (*esp US*) [*duties, violence*] conjugal ; [*consent*] du conjoint

spouse [spaʊz] N (*frm or hum*) époux *m*, épouse *f* ; (*Jur*) conjoint(e) *m(f)*

spout [spaʊt] ① N [*of teapot, jug, can*] bec *m* ; (*for tap*) brise-jet *m inv* ; [*of gutter, pump etc*] dégorgeoir *m* ; [*of pipe*] orifice *m* ; [*of fountain*] jet *m*, ajutage *m* ; (= *stream of liquid*) jet *m*, colonne *f* ; (*Brit fig*) **to be up the ~*** [*plans, timetable etc*] être fichu* *or* foutu* ; [*person*] (= *in trouble*) être dans un mauvais cas, être dans de beaux draps ; (= *pregnant*) être en cloque* ; **that's another £50 (gone) up the ~*** voilà encore 50 livres de foutues en l'air* *or* de parties en fumée → **waterspout** ② VI ⓐ [*liquid*] jaillir, sortir en jet (**from, out of** de) ; [*whale*] lancer un jet d'eau, souffler (* *fig pej = harangue*) pérorer, laïusser* (**about** sur) ③ VT (*also ~ out*) ⓐ [+ *liquid*] faire jaillir,

laisser échapper un jet de ; [+ *smoke, lava*] lancer *or* émettre un jet de, vomir ⓑ (* *fig* = *recite*) débiter, déclamer ; **he can ~ columns of statistics** il peut débiter *or* dévider des colonnes entières de statistiques

sprain [spreɪn] ① N entorse *f* ; (*less serious*) foulure *f* ② VT [+ *muscle, ligament*] fouler, étirer ; **to ~ one's ankle** se faire *or* se donner une entorse à la cheville ; (*less serious*) se fouler la cheville ; **to have a ~ed ankle** s'être fait une entorse à la cheville ; (*less serious*) s'être foulé la cheville

sprang [spræŋ] VB *pt of* **spring**

sprat [spræt] N sprat *m* ; (*fig*) **it was a ~ to catch a mackerel** c'était un appât

sprawl [sprɔ:l] ① VI (*also ~ out*) (= *fall*) tomber, s'étaler* ; (= *lie*) être affalé *or* vautré ; [*handwriting*] s'étaler (*dans tous les sens*) ; [*plant*] ramper, s'étendre (**over** sur) ; [*town*] s'étaler (**over** dans) ; **he was ~ing** *or* **lay ~ed in an armchair** il était affalé *or* vautré dans un fauteuil ; **to send sb ~ing** faire tomber qn de tout son long *or* les quatre fers en l'air, envoyer qn rouler par terre ② N (*position*) attitude *f* affalée ; [*of building, town*] étendue *f* ; **an ugly ~ of buildings down the valley** d'affreux bâtiments qui s'étalent dans la vallée ; **London's suburban ~** l'étalement *m or* l'extension *f* de la banlieue londonienne ; **the seemingly endless ~ of suburbs** l'étendue *f* apparemment infinie des banlieues, les banlieues *fpl* tentaculaires

sprawling ['sprɔ:lɪŋ] ADJ [*person, position, body*] affalé ; [*house*] grand et informe ; [*city*] tentaculaire ; [*novel, handwriting*] qui part (*or* partait) dans tous les sens

spray¹ [spreɪ] ① N ⓐ (*gen*) (nuage *m* de) gouttelettes *fpl* ; (*from sea*) embruns *mpl* ; (*from hosepipe*) pluie *f* ; (*from atomizer*) spray *m* ; (*from aerosol*) pulvérisation *f* ; **wet with the ~ from the fountain** aspergé par le jet de la fontaine ⓑ (= *container*) (= *aerosol*) bombe *f*, aérosol *m* ; (*for scent etc*) atomiseur *m*, spray *m* ; (*refillable*) vaporisateur *m* ; (*for lotion*) brumisateur *m* ; (*larger: for garden etc*) pulvérisateur *m* ; **insecticide ~** (= *aerosol*) bombe *f* (d')insecticide ; (*contents*) insecticide *m* (*en bombe*) → **hair** ⓒ (*also ~ attachment, ~ nozzle*) pomme *f*, ajutage *m* ② VT ⓐ [+ *roses, garden, crops*] faire des pulvérisations sur ; [+ *room*] faire des pulvérisations dans ; [+ *hair*] vaporiser (**with** de) ; (= *spray-paint*) peindre à la bombe ; **to ~ the lawn with weedkiller** pulvériser du désherbant sur la pelouse ; **they ~ed the oil slick with detergent** ils ont répandu du détergent sur la nappe de pétrole ; (*fig*) **to ~ sth/sb with bullets** arroser qch/qn de balles, envoyer une grêle de balles sur qch/qn ⓑ [+ *water*] vaporiser, pulvériser (**on** sur) ; [+ *scent*] vaporiser ; [+ *insecticide, paint*] pulvériser ; **they ~ed foam on the flames** ils ont projeté de la neige carbonique sur les flammes ③ VI ⓐ **it ~ed everywhere** ça a tout arrosé ; **it ~ed all over the carpet** ça a arrosé tout le tapis ⓑ (= *spray insecticide*) pulvériser des insecticides ④ COMP [*deodorant, insecticide etc*] (présenté) en bombe ► **spray can** N bombe *f* ► **spray gun** N pistolet *m* (*à peinture etc*) ► **spraying machine** N (*Agr*) pulvérisateur *m* ► **spray-on** ADJ (*lit*) en aérosol, en bombe ; (* *hum*) [*jeans, dress etc*] hypermoulant* ► **spray-paint** N peinture *f* en bombe ♦ VT peindre à la bombe ► **spray out** VI [*liquid*] jaillir (**on to, over** sur) ; **water ~ed out all over them** ils ont été complètement aspergés *or* arrosés d'eau

spray² [spreɪ] N [*of flowers*] gerbe *f* ; [*of greenery*] branche *f* ; (= *brooch*) aigrette *f*

sprayer ['spreɪə'] N ⓐ = **spray¹ 1b** ⓑ (= *aircraft: also* **crop-~**) avion-pulvérisateur *m*

spread [spred] (*vb: pret, ptp* **spread**) ① N ⓐ (*NonC*) [*of fire, disease, infection*] propagation *f*, progression *f* ; [*of nuclear weapons*] prolifération *f* ; [*of idea, knowledge*] diffusion *f*, propagation *f* ; **to stop the ~ of a disease** empêcher une maladie de s'étendre, arrêter la propagation d'une maladie ; [*of education*] **the ~ of education** le progrès de l'éducation ; (*Insurance*) **the ~ of risk** la division des risques ⓑ (= *extent, expanse*) [*of wings*] envergure *f* ; [*of arch*] ouverture *f*, portée *f* ; [*of bridge*] travée *f* ; [*of marks, prices, ages*] gamme *f*, échelle *f* ; [*of wealth*] répartition *f*, distribution *f* ; (*Naut*) **a ~ of canvas** *or* **of sail** un grand déploiement de voiles ; **he's got middle-age(d) ~** il a pris de l'embonpoint avec l'âge ⓒ (= *cover*) (*for table*) dessus *m or* tapis *m* de table ; (*for meals*) nappe *f* ; (= *bedspread*) dessus-de-lit *m inv*, couvre-lit *m* ⓓ (*Culin*) pâte *f* (*à tartiner*) ; **cheese ~** fromage *m* à tartiner ⓔ (* *fig* = *meal*) festin *m* ; **what a lovely ~!** c'est un vrai festin !, comme c'est appétissant ! ⓕ (*Cards*) séquence *f* ⓖ (*Press, Typ*) (= *two pages*) double page *f* ; (*across columns*) deux (*or* trois *etc*) colonnes *fpl* ② ADJ (*Ling*) [*vowel*] non arrondi ; [*lips*] étiré ③ VT ⓐ (*also ~ out*) [+ *cloth, sheet, map*] étendre, étaler (**on sth** sur qch) ; [+ *carpet, rug*] étendre, dérouler ; [+ *wings, bird's tail, banner, sails*] déployer ; [+ *net*] étendre, déployer ; [+ *fingers, toes, arms, legs*] écarter ; [+ *fan*] ouvrir ; **the peacock ~ its tail** le paon a fait la roue ; (*fig*) **to ~ one's wings** élargir ses horizons ; **to ~ o.s.** (*lit: also ~* **o.s. out**) s'étaler, prendre plus de place ; (= *speak at length*) s'étendre, s'attarder (**on** sur) ; (= *extend one's activities*) s'étendre ⓑ [+ *bread*] tartiner (**with** de) ; [+ *butter, jam, glue*] étaler (**on** sur) ; [+ *face cream*] étendre (**on** sur) ; **~ both surfaces with glue ◊ ~ glue on both surfaces** étalez de la colle sur les deux surfaces, enduisez de colle les deux surfaces ; **to ~ butter on a slice of bread ◊ to ~ a slice of bread with butter** tartiner de beurre une tranche de pain, beurrer une tartine ⓒ (= *distribute*) [+ *sand etc*] répandre (**on, over** sur) ; [+ *fertilizer*] répandre, étendre (**over, on** sur) ; (*also ~ out*) [+ *objects, cards, goods*] étaler (**on** sur) ; [+ *soldiers, sentries*] disposer, échelonner (**along** le long de) ; **he ~ sawdust on the floor** il a répandu de la sciure sur le sol, il a couvert le sol de sciure ; **he ~ his books (out) on the table** il a étalé ses livres sur la table ; **there were policemen ~ (out) all over the hillside** il y avait des agents de police éparpillés *or* dispersés sur toute la colline ; **the wind ~ the flames** le vent a propagé les flammes ⓓ (= *diffuse*) [+ *disease, infection*] propager ; [+ *germs*] disséminer ; [+ *wealth*] distribuer ; [+ *rumours*] faire courir ; [+ *news*] faire circuler, communiquer ; [+ *knowledge*] répandre, diffuser ; [+ *panic, fear, indignation*] répandre, semer ; (*in time: also ~ out*) [+ *payment, studies*] échelonner, étaler (**over** sur) ; **his visits were ~ (out) over three years** ses visites se sont échelonnées *or* étalées sur une période de trois ans ; **he ~ his degree (out) over five years** il a échelonné ses études de licence sur cinq ans ; **his research was ~ over many aspects of the subject** ses recherches embrassaient *or* recouvraient de nombreux aspects du sujet ; **our resources are ~ very thinly** nous n'avons plus aucune marge dans l'emploi de nos ressources ; **the new regulations ~ the tax burden more evenly** les nouveaux règlements répartissent la charge fiscale plus uniformément ; (*fig*) **to ~ o.s. too thin** trop disperser ses efforts ; (*fig*) **to ~ the word** (= *propagate ideas*) prêcher la bonne parole ; (= *announce*) **to ~ the word about sth** annoncer qch

4 VI **a** (= *widen, extend further*) [*river, stain*] s'élargir, s'étaler ; [*flood, oil slick, weeds, fire, infection, disease*] gagner du terrain, s'étendre ; [*water*] se répandre ; [*pain*] s'étendre ; [*panic, indignation*] se propager ; [*news, rumour, knowledge*] se propager, se répandre ; **to ~ into** or **over sth** [*river, flood, water, oil slick*] se répandre dans or sur qch ; [*fire, pain*] se communiquer à qch, atteindre qch ; [*weeds, panic*] envahir qch ; [*disease*] atteindre qch, contaminer qch ; [*news, education*] atteindre qch, se répandre dans or sur qch ; **under the ~ing chestnut tree** sous les branches étendues du marronnier
b (= *stretch, reach: also* ~ **out**) [*lake, plain, oil slick, fire*] s'étendre (**over** sur) ; **the desert ~s over 500 square miles** le désert s'étend sur or recouvre 500 miles carrés ; **his studies ~ (out) over four years** ses études se sont étendues sur quatre ans
c [*butter, paste etc*] s'étaler
5 COMP ▶ **spread eagle** N (*Her*) aigle f éployée ▶ **spread-eagle** ADJ (*US*) chauvin (*employé à propos d'un Américain*) ◆ VT **to ~ eagle sb** envoyer qn rouler par terre ; **to be** or **lie ~eagled** être étendu bras et jambes écartés, être vautré
▶ **spread out 1** VI **a** [*people, animals*] se disperser, s'éparpiller ; ~ **out!** dispersez-vous ! **b** (= *open out*) [*map*] s'ouvrir ; [*wings*] se déployer ; [*valley*] s'élargir **c** = **spread 4b 2** VT SEP **the valley lay ~ out before him** la vallée s'étendait à ses pieds ; **he was ~ out on the floor** il était étendu de tout son long par terre → **spread 3a, 3c, 3d**

spreader ['spredə^r] N (*for butter*) couteau m à tartiner ; (*for glue*) couteau m à palette ; (*Agr: for fertilizer*) épandeur m, épandeuse f

spreadsheet ['spredʃiːt] N (*Comput*) (= *chart*) tableau m ; (= *software*) tableur m

spree [spriː] N fête f ; **to go on** or **have a ~** faire la fête or la noce* → **buying, crime, drinking, spending, shooting, shopping**

sprig [sprɪg] N brin m

sprightliness ['spraɪtlɪnɪs] N (*NonC*) (*physical*) vivacité f, vitalité f ; (*mental*) vivacité f

sprightly ['spraɪtlɪ] ADJ (= *physically*) alerte ; (= *mentally*) alerte, vif

spring [sprɪŋ] (*vb: pret* **sprang**, *ptp* **sprung**) **1** N **a** (= *leap*) bond m, saut m ; **in** or **with** or **at one ~** d'un bond, d'un saut ; **to give a ~** bondir, sauter
b (*for chair, mattress, watch: also Tech*) ressort m ; **the ~s** [*of car*] la suspension → **hairspring, mainspring**
c (*NonC = resilience*) [*of mattress*] élasticité f ; [*of bow, elastic band*] détente f ; **he had a ~ in his step** il marchait d'un pas élastique or souple
d [*of water*] source f ; **hot ~** source f chaude
e (*fig*) ~**s** (= *cause, motive*) mobile m, motif m, cause f ; (= *origin*) source f, origine f
f (= *season*) printemps m ; **in (the) ~** au printemps ; **~ is in the air** on sent venir le printemps
2 VI **a** (= *leap*) bondir, sauter ; **to ~ in/out/across** etc entrer/sortir/traverser etc d'un bond ; **to ~ at sth/sb** bondir or sauter or se jeter sur qch/qn ; **to ~ to one's feet** se lever d'un bond
b (*fig*) **to ~ to attention** bondir au garde-à-vous ; **to ~ to sb's help** bondir or se précipiter à l'aide de qn ; **to ~ to the rescue** se précipiter pour porter secours ; **he sprang into action** il est passé à l'action ; **they sprang into the public eye** ils ont tout à coup attiré l'attention du public ; **to ~ into existence** apparaître du jour au lendemain ; **to ~ into view** apparaître soudain, surgir ; **to ~ to mind** venir or se présenter à l'esprit ; **tears sprang to her eyes** les larmes lui sont venues aux yeux, les larmes

lui sont montées aux yeux ; **a denial sprang to his lips** une dénégation lui est venue or montée aux lèvres ; **his hand sprang to his gun** il a saisi or attrapé son pistolet ; **the door sprang open** la porte s'est brusquement ouverte ; **where did you ~ from?** d'où est-ce que tu sors ? ; **hope ~s eternal** l'espoir fait vivre
c (= *originate from*) provenir, découler (**from** de) ; **the oak sprang from a tiny acorn** le chêne est sorti d'un tout petit gland ; **all his actions ~ from the desire to ...** toutes ses actions proviennent or découlent de son désir de ... ; **it sprang from his inability to cope with the situation** c'est venu or né de son incapacité à faire face à la situation
d [*timbers etc*] (= *warp*) jouer, se gondoler ; (= *split*) se fendre
3 VT **a** [+ *trap, lock*] faire jouer ; [+ *mine*] faire sauter ; (*fig*) **to ~ a surprise on sb** surprendre qn ; **to ~ a question on sb** poser une question à qn à brûle-pourpoint or de but en blanc ; **to ~ a piece of news on sb** annoncer une nouvelle à qn de but en blanc ; **he sprang the suggestion on me suddenly** il me l'a suggéré de but en blanc or à l'improviste ; **he sprang it on me** il m'a pris de court or au dépourvu
b (= *put springs in*) [+ *mattress*] pourvoir de ressorts ; [+ *car*] suspendre ; **well-sprung** [*car*] bien suspendu
c (*Hunting*) [+ *game*] lever ; (: *fig*) [+ *prisoner*] aider à se tirer de la belle: ; **he was sprung: from Dartmoor** on l'a aidé à se cavaler: de Dartmoor
d (= *leap over*) [+ *ditch, fence etc*] sauter, franchir d'un bond
e [+ *timbers, mast*] (= *warp*) gondoler, faire jouer ; (= *split*) fendre → **leak**
4 COMP [*weather, day, flowers*] printanier, de printemps ; [*mattress*] à ressorts ▶ **spring balance** N balance f à ressort ▶ **spring binder** N (= *file*) classeur m à ressort ▶ **spring binding** N [*of file*] reliure f à ressort ▶ **spring chicken** N (*Culin*) poussin m ; (*fig*) **he/she is no ~ chicken** il/elle n'est pas de toute première jeunesse ▶ **spring-clean** N (*NonC: also* **~-cleaning**) grand nettoyage m (de printemps) ◆ VT nettoyer de fond en comble ▶ **spring fever** N fièvre f printanière ▶ **spring greens** NPL (*Brit*) choux mpl précoces ▶ **spring-like** ADJ printanier, de printemps ▶ **spring-loaded** ADJ tendu par un ressort ▶ **spring lock** N serrure f à fermeture automatique ▶ **spring onion** N (*Brit*) ciboule f ▶ **spring roll** N (*Culin*) rouleau m de printemps ▶ **spring snow** N (*Ski*) neige f de printemps ▶ **spring tide** N (*gen*) grande marée f ; (*at equinox*) marée f d'équinoxe (de printemps) ▶ **spring water** N eau f de source
▶ **spring up** VI [*person*] se lever d'un bond or précipitamment ; [*flowers, weeds*] surgir de terre ; [*corn*] lever brusquement ; [*new buildings, settlements*] pousser comme des champignons ; [*wind, storm*] se lever brusquement ; [*rumour*] naître, s'élever ; [*doubt, fear*] naître, jaillir ; [*friendship, alliance*] naître, s'établir ; [*problem, obstacle, difficulty*] se présenter, surgir

springboard ['sprɪŋbɔːd] N (*lit, fig*) tremplin m

springbok ['sprɪŋbɒk] N (*pl* **springbok** or **springboks**) springbok m

springe [sprɪndʒ] N collet m

springiness ['sprɪŋɪnɪs] N [*of rubber, mattress*] élasticité f ; [*of ground, turf, step, hair*] souplesse f ; [*of plank*] flexibilité f ; [*of carpet*] moelleux m

springtide ['sprɪŋtaɪd] N (*liter*) = **springtime**

springtime ['sprɪŋtaɪm] N printemps m

springy ['sprɪŋɪ] ADJ [*rubber, mattress, texture*] élastique, souple ; [*carpet*] moelleux ; [*plank*] flexible, qui fait ressort ; [*ground, turf, step*] souple ; [*step*] alerte, souple ; [*hair*] frisé

sprinkle ['sprɪŋkl] VT **to ~ sth with water** ◊ **to ~ water on sth** asperger qch d'eau ; **to ~ water**

on the garden arroser légèrement le jardin ; **a rose ~d with dew** une rose couverte de rosée ; **to ~ sand on** or **over sth** ◊ **to ~ sth with sand** répandre une légère couche de sable sur qch, couvrir qch d'une légère couche de sable ; **to ~ sand/grit on the roadway** sabler/cendrer la route ; (*Culin*) **to ~ sugar over a cake** ◊ **to ~ a cake with sugar** saupoudrer un gâteau de sucre ; **lawn ~d with daisies** pelouse parsemée or émaillée (*liter*) de pâquerettes ; (*fig*) **they are ~d about here and there** ils sont éparpillés or disséminés ici et là

sprinkler ['sprɪŋklə^r] **1** N (*for lawn*) arroseur m ; (*for sugar etc*) saupoudreuse f ; (*larger*) saupoudroir m ; (*in ceiling: for fire-fighting*) diffuseur m (*d'extincteur automatique d'incendie*), sprinkler m **2** COMP ▶ **sprinkler system** N (*for lawn*) combiné m d'arrosage ; (*for fire-fighting*) installation f d'extinction automatique d'incendie

sprinkling ['sprɪŋklɪŋ] N **a** (= *act*) (*with water*) (*gen, Rel*) aspersion f ; (*on garden, road, street*) arrosage m ; (*with sugar*) saupoudrage m ; **to give sth a ~ (of water)** (*gen*) asperger qch (d'eau) ; [+ *garden, road, street*] arroser qch ; **to give sth a ~ (of sugar)** saupoudrer qch (de sucre) **b** (= *quantity*) [*of sand, snow*] mince couche f ; **top off with a ~ of icing sugar/grated Parmesan** terminer en saupoudrant de sucre glace/parmesan râpé ; **a ~ of water** quelques gouttes fpl d'eau ; **a ~ of freckles** quelques taches fpl de rousseur ; **a ~ of sightseers** quelques rares touristes mpl ; **a ~ of women ministers** un petit nombre de femmes ministres ; **a ~ of literary allusions in the text** des allusions littéraires émaillant le texte

sprint [sprɪnt] **1** N (*Sport*) sprint m ; **to make a ~ for the bus** piquer* un sprint or foncer pour attraper l'autobus **2** VI (*Sport*) sprinter ; (*gen*) foncer, piquer* un sprint ; **to ~ down the street** descendre la rue à toutes jambes

sprinter ['sprɪntə^r] N (*Sport*) sprinter m, sprinteur m, -euse f

sprit [sprɪt] N (*Naut*) livarde f, balestron m

sprite [spraɪt] N lutin m, farfadet m ; (*Comput = icon in game*) joueur m, lutin m

sprocket ['sprɒkɪt] **1** N pignon m **2** COMP ▶ **sprocket wheel** N pignon m (d'engrenage)

sprog: [sprɒg] N (*Brit*) **a** (= *child*) morpion* m, -ionne* f (*pej*) **b** (*Mil*) bleu m

sprout [spraʊt] **1** N (*Bot*) (*on plant, branch etc*) pousse f ; (*from bulbs, seeds*) germe m ; (**Brussels**) choux m de Bruxelles **2** VI **a** [*bulbs, onions etc*] germer, pousser **b** (*also* ~ **up** = *grow quickly*) [*plants, crops, weeds*] bien pousser ; [*child*] grandir or pousser vite **c** (*also* ~ **up** = *appear*) [*mushrooms etc*] pousser ; [*weeds*] surgir de terre ; [*new buildings*] surgir de terre, pousser comme des champignons **3** VT **to ~ new leaves** pousser or produire de nouvelles feuilles ; **to ~ shoots** [*potatoes, bulbs*] germer ; **the wet weather has ~ed the barley** le temps humide a fait germer l'orge ; **the deer has ~ed horns** les cornes du cerf ont poussé, le cerf a mis ses bois ; **Paul has ~ed* a moustache** Paul s'est laissé pousser la moustache

spruce¹ [spruːs] N (*also* ~ **tree**) épicéa m spruce ; (*Can*) **white/black ~** épinette f blanche/noire

spruce² [spruːs] ADJ [*person*] pimpant, soigné ; [*garment*] net, impeccable ; [*house*] coquet, pimpant
▶ **spruce up** VT SEP [+ *child*] faire beau ; [+ *house*] bien astiquer ; **all ~d up** [*person*] tiré à quatre épingles, sur son trente et un ; [*house*] bien astiqué, reluisant de propreté ; **to ~ o.s. up** se faire tout beau (toute belle f)

sprucely ['spruːslɪ] ADV **~ dressed** tiré à quatre épingles, sur son trente et un

spruceness ['spru:snɪs] N [of person] mise f soignée ; [of house] aspect m coquet

sprung [sprʌŋ] **1** VB ptp of **spring 2** ADJ [seat, mattress] à ressorts

spry [spraɪ] ADJ alerte, plein d'entrain

SPUC [ˌespiˈjuːˈsiː] N (Brit) (ABBR = **Society for the Protection of the Unborn Child**) association antiavortement

spud [spʌd] **1** N (= tool) sarcloir m ; (* = potato) patate* f **2** COMP ► **spud-bashing:** N (Mil) corvée f de patates*

spume [spju:m] N (liter) écume f

spun [spʌn] VB pt, ptp of **spin**

spunk [spʌŋk] N **a** (NonC* = courage) cran* m, courage m **b** (Brit** = semen) foutre** m

spunky: ['spʌŋkɪ] ADJ plein de cran*

spur [spɜːʳ] **1** N **a** [of horse, fighting cock, mountain, masonry] éperon m ; [of bone] saillie f ; (fig) aiguillon m ; **to dig in one's ~s** enfoncer ses éperons, éperonner son cheval ; (Brit) **to win** or **gain** or **earn one's ~s** (Hist) gagner ses éperons ; (fig) faire ses preuves ; **on the ~ of the moment** sous l'impulsion du moment, sur un coup de tête ; **the ~ of hunger** l'aiguillon m de la faim ; **it will be a ~ to further efforts** cela nous (or les etc) poussera à inciter à faire des efforts supplémentaires **b** (Rail: also **~ track**) (= siding) voie f latérale, voie f de garage ; (= branch) voie f de desserte, embranchement m **c** (on motorway etc) embranchement m

2 VT (also **~ on**) [+ horse] éperonner, aiguillonner ; **he ~red his horse on** (= applied spurs once) il a éperonné son cheval, il a donné de l'éperon à son cheval ; (= sped on) il a piqué des deux ; **~red on by ambition** éperonné or aiguillonné par l'ambition ; **to ~ sb (on) to do sth** pousser or encourager or inciter qn à faire qch ; **this ~red him (on) to greater efforts** ceci l'a encouragé à redoubler d'efforts

3 COMP ► **spur gear** N = **spur wheel** ► **spur-of-the-moment** ADJ fait sur l'impulsion du moment ► **spur wheel** N roue f à dents droites

spurge [spɜːdʒ] **1** N euphorbe f **2** COMP ► **spurge laurel** N daphné m

spurious ['spjʊərɪəs] ADJ (gen) faux (fausse f) ; [document, writings] faux (fausse f), apocryphe ; [claim] fallacieux ; [interest, affection, desire] simulé, feint

spuriously ['spjʊərɪəslɪ] ADV faussement

spurn [spɜːn] VT [+ help, offer] repousser, rejeter ; [+ lover] éconduire

spurt [spɜːt] **1** N [of water, flame] jaillissement m, jet m ; [of anger, enthusiasm, energy] sursaut m, regain m ; (= burst of speed) accélération f ; (fig: at work etc) effort m soudain, coup m de collier ; (Racing) **final ~** emballage m, rush m ; **to put on a ~** (Sport) démarrer, sprinter ; (in running for bus) piquer* un sprint, foncer ; (fig: in work) donner un coup de collier, faire un soudain effort ; **in ~s** (= sporadically) par à-coups **2** VI (also **~ out, ~ up**) [water, blood] jaillir, gicler (**from** de) ; [flame] jaillir (**from** de) **b** [runner] piquer* un sprint, foncer ; (Sport) démarrer, sprinter **3** VT (also **~ out**) [+ flame, lava] lancer, vomir ; [+ water] laisser jaillir, projeter

sputa ['spju:tə] NPL of **sputum**

sputnik ['spʊtnɪk] N spoutnik m

sputter ['spʌtəʳ] VI (= progress unevenly) piétiner ; **the economy is already ~ing** l'économie piétine déjà ; **the battle ~ed to a halt** la bataille s'est enlisée et a pris fin → **splutter 2, 3**

sputum ['spju:təm] N (pl sputa) crachat m, expectorations fpl

spy [spaɪ] **1** N (gen, Ind, Pol) espion(ne) m(f) ; **police ~** indicateur m, -trice f de police **2** VI (gen) espionner, épier ; (Ind, Pol) faire de l'espionnage ; **to ~ for a country** faire de l'espionnage au service or pour le compte d'un pays ; **to ~ on sb** espionner qn ; **to ~ on sth** épier qch, **stop ~ing on me!** arrête de m'espionner or de me surveiller! ; **to ~ into sth** chercher à découvrir qch subrepticement **3** VT (= catch sight of) apercevoir, **I spied him coming** je l'ai vu qui arrivait or s'approchait ; **I ~, with my little eye, something beginning with A** je vois quelque chose qui commence par A, essaie de deviner (jeu d'enfant) **4** COMP [film, story etc] d'espionnage ► **spy-in-the-sky*** N satellite-espion m ► **spy plane** N avion-espion m ► **spy ring** N réseau m d'espionnage ► **spy satellite** N satellite-espion m

► **spy out** VT SEP reconnaître, (lit, fig) **to ~ out the land** reconnaître le terrain

spycatcher ['spaɪkætʃəʳ] N (Brit) chasseur m d'espions

spyglass ['spaɪglɑːs] N lunette f d'approche

spyhole ['spaɪhəʊl] N judas m

spying ['spaɪɪŋ] N (NonC) espionnage m

spymaster ['spaɪmɑːstəʳ] N chef m des services secrets

Sq ABBR = **Square**

sq. (ABBR = **square**) carré ; **4sq. m** 4 m²

squab [skwɒb] N (pl squabs or squab) **a** (Orn) pigeonneau m **b** (Brit Aut) assise f

squabble ['skwɒbl] **1** N chamaillerie* f, prise f de bec* **2** VI se chamailler*, se disputer (over sth à propos de qch)

squabbler* ['skwɒblə'] N chamailleur* m, -euse f

squabbling ['skwɒblɪŋ] N (NonC) chamaillerie(s)* f(pl)

squad [skwɒd] **1** N [of soldiers, policemen, workmen, prisoners] escouade f, groupe m ; (Sport) équipe f ; (Sport) **the England ~** l'équipe f d'Angleterre → **firing, flying 2** COMP ► **squad car** N (esp US Police) voiture f de police

squaddie, squaddy* ['skwɒdɪ] N (Brit = private soldier) deuxième classe m inv

squadron ['skwɒdrən] **1** N (Mil) escadron m ; (Aviat, Naut) escadrille f **2** COMP ► **squadron leader** N (Brit Aviat) commandant m

squalid ['skwɒlɪd] ADJ [place, conditions, love affair, experience] sordide ; [motive] bas (basse f), ignoble ; **it was a ~ business** c'était une affaire sordide

squall [skwɔːl] **1** N **a** (Met) rafale f or bourrasque f (de pluie) ; (at sea) grain m ; (fig) **there are ~s ahead** il y a de l'orage dans l'air, il va y avoir du grabuge* **b** (= cry) hurlement m, braillement m **2** VI [baby] hurler, brailler

squalling ['skwɔːlɪŋ] ADJ criard, braillard*

squally ['skwɔːlɪ] ADJ [wind] qui souffle en rafales ; [weather] à bourrasques, à rafales ; [day] entrecoupé de bourrasques

squalor ['skwɒləʳ] N (NonC) conditions fpl sordides, misère f noire ; **to live in ~** vivre dans des conditions sordides or dans la misère noire ; (pej) vivre comme un cochon (or des cochons)*

squander ['skwɒndəʳ] VT [+ time, money, talents] gaspiller ; [+ fortune, inheritance] dissiper, dilapider ; [+ opportunity, chances] laisser filer, laisser passer

square [skwɛəʳ] **1** N **a** (= shape: gen, Geom, Mil) carré m ; [of chessboard, crossword, graph paper] case f ; (= square piece) [of fabric, chocolate, toffee] carré m ; [of cake] part f (carrée) ; (= window pane) carreau m ; **to fold paper into a ~** plier une feuille de papier en carré ; **divide the page into ~s** divisez la page en carrés, quadrillez la page ; **linoleum with black and white ~s on it** du linoléum en damier noir et blanc or à carreaux noirs et blancs ; **the troops were drawn up in a ~** les troupes avaient formé le carré ; **form (yourselves into) a ~** placez-vous en carré, formez un carré ; (fig) **to start again from ~ one*** repartir à zéro*, repartir de la case départ ; **now we're back to ~ one*** nous nous retrouvons à la case départ*, nous repartons à zéro* **b** (in town) place f ; (with gardens) square m ; (esp US = block of houses) pâté m de maisons ; (Mil: also **barrack ~**) cour f (de caserne) ; **the town ~** la (grand-)place **c** (= drawing instrument) équerre f ; **out of ~** qui n'est pas d'équerre ; **to cut sth on the ~** équarrir qch ; (fig) **to be on the ~*** (offer, deal) être honnête or régulier* ; [person] jouer franc jeu, jouer cartes sur table → **set, T d** (Math) carré m ; **four is the ~ of two** quatre est le carré de deux **e** (* pej = conventional person) **he's a real ~** il est vraiment ringard* ; **don't be such a ~!** ne sois pas si ringard*!

2 ADJ **a** (in shape) [object, shape, hole, face, jaw, shoulders] carré ; **a ~ corner** un coin à angle droit ; **of ~ build** trapu, ramassé ; **to be a ~ peg in a round hole*** ne pas être dans son élément **b** **~ with** or **to sth** (= parallel) parallèle à qch ; (= at right angles) à angle droit avec qch, perpendiculaire à qch **c** (Math) **6 ~ metres** 6 mètres carrés ; **6 metres ~** (de) 6 mètres sur 6 ; **a 25-cm ~ baking dish** un moule de 25 centimètres sur 25 **d** (Fin) [accounts, books, figures] en ordre ; **to get one's accounts ~** mettre ses comptes en ordre, balancer ses comptes ; **to get ~ with sb** (financially) régler ses comptes avec qn ; (fig = get even with) rendre la pareille à qn **e** (= not indebted) **to be (all) ~ (with sb)*** être quitte (envers qn) **f** (Sport) **to be all ~** être à égalité **g** (= honest) [dealings] honnête ; **a ~ deal** un arrangement équitable or honnête ; **to get a ~ deal** être traité équitablement ; **to give sb a ~ deal** agir honnêtement avec qn ; **to be ~ with sb** être honnête avec qn → **fair¹ h** (* pej = conventional) [person, habit, attitude] ringard* ; (hum) **be there or be ~!** tous les gens branchés* y seront **i** (= unequivocal) [refusal, denial] net, catégorique **j** (Cricket) à angle droit ; **to be ~ of the wicket** être placé perpendiculairement au guichet

3 ADV **a** (= squarely) **to hit** or **catch sb ~ on the forehead/on the jaw** atteindre qn en plein front/en pleine mâchoire ; **to hit sb ~ in the chest** frapper qn en pleine poitrine ; **a huge wave hit the ship ~ on** une énorme lame a frappé le bateau de plein fouet ; **to kiss sb ~ on the mouth** embrasser qn à pleine bouche ; **~ in the middle** en plein milieu ; (fig) **to be ~ in the middle of sth** être au beau milieu de qch ; **to look sb ~ in the face** regarder qn bien en face ; **to stand ~** être bien campé sur ses jambes ; **the bomb landed ~ on target** la bombe est tombée en plein sur l'objectif → **fair¹ b** (= parallel) **~ to** or **with sth** parallèlement à qch ; **he turned to face me ~ on** il s'est tourné pour être juste en face de moi ; **to stand ~ on to the camera** se tenir bien en face de la caméra **c** (= at right angles) **to cut sth ~** équarrir qch, couper qch au carré or à angle droit ; **~ to** or **with sth** à angle droit avec qch, d'équerre avec qch ; **the ship ran ~ across our bows** le navire nous a complètement coupé la route

4 VT **a** (= make square) [+ figure, shape] rendre carré, carrer ; [+ stone, timber] équarrir, carrer ; [+ corner] couper au carré or à angle droit ; **to ~ one's shoulders** redresser les épaules ; (fig) **to try to ~ the circle** chercher à faire la quadrature du cercle **b** (= settle, sort out) [+ books, accounts] mettre en ordre, balancer ; [+ debts] acquitter, régler ; [+ creditors] régler, payer ; (= reconcile) concilier, faire cadrer (**with** avec) ; **to ~ one's ac-**

count with sb régler ses comptes avec qn ; **to ~ o.s. with sb** régler ses comptes avec qn ; **I can't ~ that with what he told me yesterday** ça ne cadre pas avec ce qu'il m'a dit hier ; **he managed to ~ it with his conscience** il s'est arrangé avec sa conscience ; **can you ~* it with the boss?** est-ce que vous pouvez arranger ça avec le patron ? ; **I can ~* him** (= *get him to agree*) je m'occupe de lui, je me charge de lui [c] (*Math*) [+ *number*] élever au carré ; **four ~d is sixteen** quatre au carré fait seize

[5] VI cadrer, correspondre ; **that doesn't ~ with the facts** cela ne cadre pas avec les faits, cela ne correspond pas aux faits ; **that ~s!** ça cadre !, ça colle !*

[6] COMP ► **square-bashing*** N (*Brit Mil*) exercice *m* ► **square bracket** N (*Typ*) crochet *m* ► **square-built** ADJ trapu ► **square-cut** ADJ coupé à angle droit, équarri ► **square dance** N ≈ quadrille *m* ► **square-dancing** N (*NonC*) quadrille *m* ► **square-faced** ADJ au visage carré ► **square-jawed** ADJ à la mâchoire carrée ► **square knot** N (*US*) nœud *m* plat ► **square leg** N (*Cricket*) position du joueur de champ lorsqu'il est placé à angle droit avec le batteur ► **square meal** N repas *m* substantiel ► **square number** N (*Math*) carré *m* ► **square-rigged** ADJ gréé (en) carré ► **square rigger** N (*Naut*) navire *m* gréé en carré ► **square root** N racine *f* carrée ► **square-shouldered** ADJ aux épaules carrées, carré d'épaules ► **square-toed** ADJ [*shoes*] à bout carré

► **square off** [1] VI (*in quarrel*) se faire face ; (*in fist fight*) se mettre en garde (**to sb** devant qn) [2] VT SEP [+ *paper, plan*] diviser en carrés, quadriller ; [+ *wood, edges*] équarrir

► **square up** [1] VI [a] [*boxers, fighters*] se mettre en garde (**to sb** devant qn) ; (*fig*) **to ~ up to a problem** faire face à un problème [b] (= *pay debts*) régler ses comptes (**with sb** avec qn) [2] VT SEP [a] (= *make square*) [+ *paper*] couper au carré *or* à angle droit ; [+ *wood*] équarrir [b] [+ *account, debts*] régler, payer ; **I'll ~ things up*** **for you** je ne vous en fais pas, je vais arranger ça

squarely ['skweəlɪ] ADV [a] (= *completely*) complètement ; **responsibility rests ~ with the President** la responsabilité incombe complètement au président ; **to lay** *or* **place the blame for sth ~ on sb** faire rejeter complètement la responsabilité de qch sur qn [b] (= *directly*) **to look at sb ~** regarder qn droit dans les yeux ; **to look sb ~ in the eye** regarder qn dans le blanc des yeux ; **a film that looks ~ at social problems** un film qui traite sans détour des problèmes sociaux ; **to face one's guilt ~** assumer sa culpabilité sans détour ; **she faced her mother ~** elle s'est campée devant sa mère d'un air résolu ; **a film aimed ~ at family audiences** un film visant un public familial ; **to hit sb ~ in the stomach** frapper qn en plein dans le ventre ; **set ~ in the middle of the wall** placé en plein milieu du mur [c] (= *honestly*) [*deal with*] honnêtement → **fairly**

squash¹ [skwɒʃ] [1] N [a] (*Brit*) **lemon/orange ~** citronnade *f*/orangeade *f* (concentrée) [b] (*Sport*) squash *m* [c] (= *crowd*) cohue *f*, foule *f* ; (= *crush*) cohue *f*, bousculade *f* ; **we all got in, but it was a ~** on est tous entrés mais on était serrés ; **a great ~ of people** une cohue, une foule ; **I lost him in the ~ at the exit** je l'ai perdu dans la cohue *or* dans la bousculade à la sortie [2] VT [+ *fruit, beetle, hat, box*] écraser ; (*fig*) [+ *argument*] réfuter ; (= *snub*) [+ *person*] rabrouer ; **to ~ flat** [+ *fruit, beetle*] écraser, écrabouiller* ; [+ *hat, box*] aplatir ; **he ~ed his nose against the window** il a écrasé son nez contre la vitre ; **you're ~ing me!** tu m'écrases ! ; **she ~ed the shoes into the suitcase** elle a réussi à

caser* les chaussures dans la valise ; **can you ~ two more people in the car?** est-ce que tu peux faire tenir *or* caser* deux personnes de plus dans la voiture ?

[3] VI [a] [*people*] **they ~ed into the elevator** ils se sont serrés *or* entassés dans l'ascenseur ; **they ~ed through the gate** ils ont franchi le portail en se bousculant [b] [*fruit, parcel etc*] s'écraser ; **will it ~?** est-ce que cela risque de s'écraser ?

[4] COMP ► **squash court** N (*Sport*) court *m* de squash ► **squash player** N joueur *m*, -euse *f* de squash ► **squash racket** N raquette *f* de squash

► **squash in** [1] VI [*people*] s'empiler, s'entasser ; **when the car arrived they all ~ed in** quand la voiture est arrivée ils se sont tous empilés *or* entassés dedans ; **can I ~ in?** est-ce que je peux me trouver une petite place ? [2] VT SEP (*into box, suitcase etc*) réussir à faire rentrer

► **squash together** [1] VI [*people*] se serrer (les uns contre les autres) [2] VT SEP [+ *objects*] serrer, tasser ; **we were all ~ed together** nous étions très serrés *or* entassés

► **squash up** [1] VI [*people*] se serrer, se pousser ; **can't you ~ up a bit?** pourriez-vous vous serrer *or* vous pousser un peu ? [2] VT SEP [+ *object*] écraser ; [+ *paper*] chiffonner en boule

squash² [skwɒʃ] N (*pl* **squashes** *or* **squash**) (= *gourd*) gourde *f* ; (*US* = *marrow*) courge *f*

squashy* ['skwɒʃɪ] ADJ [*fruit, sofa*] mou (molle *f*)

squat¹ [skwɒt] [1] ADJ [*person*] trapu, courtaud ; [*building*] ramassé, trapu ; [*armchair, jug, teapot*] trapu ; [*glass*] court [2] VI [a] (*also* **~ down**) [*person*] s'accroupir, s'asseoir sur ses talons ; [*animal*] se tapir, se ramasser ; **to be ~ting (down)** [*person*] être accroupi, être assis sur ses talons ; [*animal*] être tapi *or* ramassé [b] [*squatters*] squatter ; **to ~ in a house** squatter *or* squattériser une maison [3] N (= *act of squatting, place*) squat *m* [4] COMP ► **squat thrust** N (*Gym*) saut *m* de main

squat²* [skwɒt] N (*US*: *also* **diddly-~**) **you don't know ~ (about that)** t'y connais que dalle* ; **that doesn't mean ~ (to me)** (pour moi,) ça veut dire que dalle*

squatter ['skwɒtər] N squatter *m* ; **~'s rights** droit *m* de propriété par occupation du terrain

squatting ['skwɒtɪŋ] N squat *m*, squattage *m*

squaw [skwɔː] N squaw *f*, femme *f* peau-rouge

squawk [skwɔːk] [1] VI [*hen, parrot*] pousser un *or* des gloussement(s) ; [*baby*] brailler ; [*person*] pousser un *or* des cri(s) rauque(s) ; (* *fig* = *complain*) râler*, gueuler* [2] N gloussement *m*, braillement *m*, cri *m* rauque [3] COMP ► **squawk box*** N (*US* = *loudspeaker*) haut-parleur *m*

squeak [skwiːk] [1] N [*of hinge, wheel, pen, chalk*] grincement *m* ; [*of shoes*] craquement *m* ; [*of mouse, doll*] petit cri *m* aigu, vagissement *m* ; [*of person*] petit cri *m* aigu, glapissement *m* ; **to let out** *or* **give a ~ of fright/surprise** etc pousser un petit cri *or* glapir de peur/de surprise etc ; **not a ~*, mind!** (= *be quiet*) pas de bruit, hein ! ; (= *keep it secret*) pas un mot !, motus et bouche cousue !* ; **I don't want another ~ out of you** je ne veux plus t'entendre → **narrow** [2] VI [a] (= *make sound*) [*hinge, wheel, chair, gate, pen, chalk*] grincer ; [*shoe*] craquer ; [*mouse, doll*] vagir, pousser un *or* des petit(s) cri(s) ; [*person*] glapir [b] (*in exam, election*) **to ~ through** être accepté de justesse [3] VT **"no"** she ~ed « non » glapit-elle

squeaker ['skwiːkər] N (*in toy etc*) sifflet *m*

squeaky ['skwiːkɪ] [1] ADJ [*hinge, gate, wheel, chair*] grinçant ; [*pen*] qui crisse ; [*toy*] qui grince ; [*shoes*] qui craque ; [*voice*] aigu (-guë *f*) [2] COMP ► **squeaky-clean*** ADJ (*lit*) (= *very*

clean) [*hair*] tout propre ; [*office, home*] ultra-propre ; (= *above reproach*) [*person*] blanc comme neige ; [*reputation, image*] irréprochable ; [*company*] à la réputation irréprochable

squeal [skwiːl] [1] N [*of person, animal*] cri *m* aigu *or* perçant ; [*of brakes*] grincement *m*, hurlement *m* ; [*of tyres*] crissement *m* ; **to let out** *or* **give a ~ of pain** pousser un cri de douleur ; **... he said with a ~ of laughter** ... dit-il avec un rire aigu [2] VI [a] [*person, animal*] pousser un *or* des cri(s) (aigu(s) *or* perçant(s)) ; [*brakes*] grincer, hurler ; [*tyres*] crisser ; **he ~ed like a (stuck) pig** il criait comme un cochon qu'on égorge ; **she tickled the child and he ~ed** elle a chatouillé l'enfant et il a poussé un petit cri [b] (* = *inform*) vendre la mèche* ; **to ~ on sb** balancer* *or* donner* qn ; **somebody ~ed to the police** quelqu'un les (*or* nous etc) a balancés* *or* donnés* à la police [3] VT **"help"** he ~ed « au secours » cria-t-il (d'une voix perçante)

squeamish ['skwiːmɪʃ] ADJ facilement dégoûté (**about sth** par qch) ; **I'm not ~ about blood** je ne suis pas facilement dégoûté par la vue du sang ; **don't be so ~!** ne fais pas le délicat !

squeamishness ['skwiːmɪʃnɪs] N (*NonC*) délicatesse *f* exagérée

squeegee [ˌskwiːˈdʒiː] [1] N (*for windows*) raclette *f* (à bord de caoutchouc) ; (= *mop*) balai-éponge *m* [2] COMP ► **squeegee merchant*** N (*Brit*) laveur *m* de pare-brise

squeeze [skwiːz] [1] N [a] (= *act, pressure*) pression *f*, compression *f* ; (*NonC*: *in crowd*) cohue *f*, bousculade *f* ; **to give sth a ~** → **2a** ; **he gave her a big ~** il l'a serrée très fort dans ses bras ; **a ~ of lemon** quelques gouttes *fpl* de citron ; **a ~ of toothpaste** un peu de dentifrice ; **it was a real ~ in the bus** on était serrés comme des sardines* *or* on était affreusement tassés dans l'autobus ; **it was a (tight) ~ to get through** il y avait à peine la place de passer ; (*fig*) **to put the ~ on sb** presser qn, harceler qn [b] (*Econ*: *also* **credit ~**) restrictions *fpl* de crédit [c] (*Bridge*) squeeze *m* (**in** à) [d] (* = *romantic partner*) (petit) copain *m*, (petite) copine *f*

[2] VT [a] (= *press*) [+ *handle, tube, plastic bottle, lemon, sponge*] presser ; [+ *cloth*] tordre ; [+ *doll, teddy bear*] appuyer sur ; [+ *sb's hand, arm*] serrer ; **he ~d his finger in the door** il s'est pris *or* pincé le doigt dans la porte ; **she ~d another sweater into the case** elle a réussi à caser* un autre chandail dans la valise ; **to ~ one's eyes shut** fermer les yeux en serrant fort ; (*fig*) **he ~d his victim dry*** il a saigné sa victime à blanc [b] (= *extract*: *also* **~ out**) [+ *water, juice, toothpaste*] exprimer (**from, out of** de) [c] (* *fig*) [+ *information*] soutirer, arracher ; [+ *names, contribution*] arracher ; [+ *money*] soutirer, extorquer (**out of** à) ; **you won't ~ a penny out of me** tu ne me feras pas lâcher* un sou ; **the government hopes to ~ more money out of the taxpayers** le gouvernement espère pressurer encore les contribuables [d] (*Fin*) [+ *wages, prices*] bloquer, geler

[3] VI **he ~d past me** il s'est glissé devant moi en me poussant un peu ; **he managed to ~ into the bus** il a réussi à se glisser *or* à s'introduire dans l'autobus en poussant ; **they all ~d into the car** ils se sont entassés *or* empilés dans la voiture ; **can you ~ underneath the fence?** est-ce que tu peux te glisser sous la barrière ? ; **he ~d through the crowd** il a réussi à se faufiler à travers la foule ; **she ~d through the window** elle s'est glissée par la fenêtre ; **the car ~d into the empty space** il y avait juste assez de place pour se garer

[4] COMP ► **squeeze bottle** N (*US*) flacon *m* en plastique déformable ► **squeeze-box*** N (= *accordion*) accordéon *m* ; (= *concertina*)

concertina *m*

►**squeeze in** [1] VI [*person*] trouver une petite place ; [*car etc*] rentrer tout juste, avoir juste la place ; **can I ~ in?** est-ce qu'il y a une petite place pour moi ? [2] VT SEP [+ *object into box*] (* *fig*) [+ *item on programme etc*] réussir à faire rentrer, trouver une petite place pour ; **can you ~ two more people in?** est-ce que vous avez de la place pour deux autres personnes ?, est-ce que vous pouvez prendre deux autres personnes ? ; **I can ~ you in*** to-morrow at nine je peux vous prendre (en vitesse) *or* vous caser* demain à neuf heures

►**squeeze past** VI [*person*] passer en se faufilant *or* en poussant ; [*car*] se faufiler, se glisser

►**squeeze through** VI [*person*] se faufiler, frayer un chemin ; [*car*] se faufiler, se glisser (**between** entre)

►**squeeze up*** VI [*person*] se serrer, se pousser

squeezer ['skwiːzə*r*] N presse-fruits *m inv* ; **lemon ~** presse-citron *m inv*

squelch [skweltʃ] [1] N [a] bruit *m* de succion *or* de pataugeage ; **I heard the ~ of his footsteps in the mud** je l'ai entendu patauger dans la boue ; **the tomato fell with a ~** la tomate s'est écrasée par terre avec un bruit mat [b] (: *fig = crushing retort*) réplique *f* qui coupe le sifflet* [2] VI [*mud etc*] faire un bruit de succion ; **to ~ in/out** *etc* [*person*] entrer/sortir *etc* en pataugeant ; **to ~ (one's way) through the mud** avancer en pataugeant dans la boue ; **the water ~ed in his boots** l'eau faisait flic flac* dans ses bottes [3] VT (= *crush underfoot*) piétiner, écraser

squib [skwɪb] N pétard *m* → **damp**

squid [skwɪd] N (*pl* **squid** *or* **squids**) calmar *m*, encornet *m*

squidgy* ['skwɪdʒɪ] ADJ (*Brit*) visqueux

squiffy †* ['skwɪfɪ] ADJ (*Brit*) éméché* ; **to get ~** se noircir†*

squiggle ['skwɪgl] [1] N (= *scrawl*) gribouillis *m* ; (= *wriggle*) tortillement *m* [2] VI (*in writing etc*) gribouiller, faire des gribouillis ; [*worm etc*] se tortiller

squiggly ['skwɪglɪ] ADJ ondulé

squillion* ['skwɪlɪən] N (*Brit*) myriade *f* ; **~s of pounds** des millions et des millions de livres ; **a ~ reasons** une myriade de raisons

squinch [skwɪntʃ] (*US*) [1] VT [+ *eyes*] plisser ; **he ~ed his eyes at the sunlight** il a plissé les yeux à cause du soleil, le soleil lui a fait plisser les yeux [2] VI plisser les yeux

squint [skwɪnt] [1] N [a] (*Med*) strabisme *m* ; **to have a ~** loucher, être atteint de strabisme [b] (= *sidelong look*) regard *m* de côté ; (* = *quick glance*) coup *m* d'œil ; **to have** *or* **take a ~ at sth*** (*obliquely*) regarder qch du coin de l'œil, lorgner qch ; (*quickly*) jeter un coup d'œil à qch ; **let's have a ~!*** donne voir !, montre voir !* ; **have a ~* at this** jette un coup d'œil là-dessus, zieute: ça [2] VI (*Med*) loucher [b] (= *screw up eyes*) **he ~ed in the sunlight** il a plissé les yeux à cause du soleil, le soleil lui a fait plisser les yeux [c] (= *take a look*) jeter un coup d'œil ; **he ~ed down the tube** il a jeté un coup d'œil dans le tube ; **to ~ at sth** (*obliquely*) regarder qch du coin de l'œil, lorgner qch ; (*quickly*) jeter un coup d'œil à qch ; **he ~ed at me quizzically** il m'a interrogé du regard [3] COMP ► **squint-eyed** ADJ qui louche

squirarchy ['skwaɪərɑːkɪ] N = **squirearchy**

squire ['skwaɪə*r*] [1] N (= *landowner*) propriétaire *m* terrien, ≈ châtelain *m* ; (*Hist* = *knight's attendant*) écuyer *m* ; **the ~ told us ...** le châtelain nous a dit ... ; **the ~ of Barcombe** le seigneur† *or* le châtelain de Barcombe ; (*Brit*) **yes ~!**: oui chef *or* patron !* [2] VT [+ *lady*] escorter, servir de cavalier à ; **she was ~d by ...** elle était escortée par ...

squirearchy ['skwaɪərɑːkɪ] N (*NonC*) hobereaux *mpl*, propriétaires *mpl* terriens

squirm [skwɜːm] VI [a] [*worm etc*] se tortiller ; **to ~ through a window** [*person*] passer par une fenêtre en faisant des contorsions [b] (*fig*) [*person*] (*from embarrassment*) ne pas savoir où se mettre, être au supplice ; (*from distaste*) avoir un haut-le-corps ; **spiders make me ~** j'ai un haut-le-corps quand je vois une araignée ; **her poetry makes me ~** ses poèmes me mettent mal à l'aise

squirrel ['skwɪrəl] [1] N (*pl* **squirrels** *or* **squirrel**) écureuil *m* ; **red ~** écureuil *m* ; **grey ~** écureuil *m* gris [2] COMP [*coat etc*] en petit-gris

►**squirrel away** VT SEP [+ *nuts etc*] amasser

squirt [skwɜːt] [1] N [a] [*of water*] jet *m* ; [*of detergent*] giclée *f* ; [*of scent*] quelques gouttes *fpl* [b] (* *pej* = *person*) petit morveux* *m*, petite morveuse* *f* [2] VT [+ *water*] faire jaillir, faire gicler (**at, on, onto** sur, **into** dans) ; [+ *detergent*] verser une giclée de ; [+ *oil*] injecter ; [+ *scent*] faire tomber quelques gouttes de ; **he ~ed the insecticide onto the roses** il a pulvérisé de l'insecticide sur les roses ; **to ~ sb with water** asperger *or* arroser qn d'eau ; **to ~ scent on sb ◊ to ~ sb with scent** asperger qn de parfum [3] VI [*liquid*] jaillir, gicler ; **the water ~ed into my eye** j'ai reçu une giclée d'eau dans l'œil ; **water ~ed out of the broken pipe** l'eau jaillissait du tuyau cassé [4] COMP ► **squirt gun** N (*US*) pistolet *m* à eau

squirter ['skwɜːtə*r*] N poire *f* (en caoutchouc)

squishy* ['skwɪʃɪ] ADJ [*fruit*] mollasson ; [*ground, texture*] spongieux

Sr (ABBR = **Senior**) Sr

SRC [ˌesɑːˈsiː] N (*Brit*) (ABBR = **Science Research Council**) ≈ CNRS *m*

Sri Lanka [ˌsriːˈlæŋkə] N le Sri Lanka

Sri Lankan [ˌsriːˈlæŋkən] [1] ADJ (*gen*) sri-lankais ; [*ambassador, embassy*] du Sri Lanka [2] N Sri-Lankais(e) *m(f)*

SRN [ˌesɑːˈren] N (*Brit*) (ABBR = **State-Registered Nurse**) → **state**

SS [esˈes] N [a] (ABBR = **steamship**) *navire de la marine marchande britannique* ; **SS Charminster** le Charminster [b] (ABBR = **Saints**) St(e)s *m(f)pl* [c] (= *Nazi*) SS *m inv*

SSA [ˌesesˈeɪ] N (*US*) (ABBR = **Social Security Administration**) → **social**

SSSI [ˌeseseˈsaɪ] N (*Brit*) (ABBR = **Site of Special Scientific Interest**) → **site**

St [1] N [a] (ABBR = **Street**) rue *f* ; **Churchill St** rue Churchill [b] (= **Saint**) St(e) ; **St Peter** saint Pierre ; **St Anne** sainte Anne [2] COMP ► **St John Ambulance** N (*Brit*) *association bénévole de secouristes* ► **St Lawrence** N (*Geog* = *river*) Saint-Laurent *m* ► **St Lawrence Seaway** N (*Geog*) voie *f* maritime du Saint-Laurent

st ABBR = **stone(s)**

stab [stæb] [1] N [a] (*with dagger/knife etc*) coup *m* (de poignard/de couteau etc) ; (*fig*) **a ~ in the back** un coup bas *or* déloyal ; **a ~ of pain** un élancement ; **a ~ of remorse/grief** un remords/une douleur lancinant(e) [b] (* = *attempt*) **to have** *or* **make a ~ at (doing) sth** s'essayer à (faire) qch ; **I'll have a ~ at it** je vais tenter le coup [2] VT (*with knife etc*) (= *kill*) tuer d'un coup de *or* à coups de couteau etc ; (= *wound*) blesser d'un coup de *or* à coups de couteau etc ; (= *kill or wound with dagger*) poignarder ; **to ~ sb with a knife** frapper qn d'un coup de couteau, donner un coup de couteau à qn ; **to ~ sb to death** tuer qn d'un coup de *or* à coups de couteau etc ; **he was ~bed through the heart** il a reçu un coup de couteau etc dans le cœur ; (*lit, fig*) **to ~ sb in the back** poignarder qn dans le dos ; **he ~bed his penknife into the desk** il a planté son canif dans le bureau ; **he ~bed the pencil through the map** il a transpercé la carte d'un coup de crayon [3] VI **he ~bed at the book with his finger** il a frappé le livre du doigt [4] COMP ► **stab-wound** N coup *m* de poignard (*or* couteau etc) ; (= *mark*) trace *f* de coup de poignard (*or* couteau etc) ; **to die of ~-wounds** mourir poignardé

stabbing ['stæbɪŋ] [1] N agression *f* (à coups de couteau etc) ; **there was another ~ last night** la nuit dernière une autre personne a été attaquée à coups de couteau etc [2] ADJ [*gesture*] comme pour frapper ; [*sensation*] lancinant ; **~ pain** douleur *f* lancinante, élancement *m*

stabile ['steɪbaɪl] N (*Art*) stabile *m*

stability [stəˈbɪlɪtɪ] N (*NonC: gen*) stabilité *f* ; [*of marriage*] solidité *f*

stabilization [ˌsteɪbəlaɪˈzeɪʃən] N stabilisation *f*

stabilize ['steɪbəlaɪz] VT stabiliser

stabilizer ['steɪbəlaɪzə*r*] [1] N (*Aut, Naut, Aviat*) stabilisateur *m* ; (*in food*) stabilisant *m* [2] **stabilizers** NPL (*Brit*) [*of bicycle*] stabilisateurs *mpl* [3] COMP ► **stabilizer bar** N (*US Aut*) barre *f* antiroulis, stabilisateur *m*

stable¹ ['steɪbl] ADJ (*gen*) stable ; [*marriage*] solide ; (*Med*) stationnaire, stable ; **to be in a ~ relationship** avoir une relation stable ; **he is not a very ~ character** il est plutôt instable ; (*Med*) **to be in a serious but ~ condition** être dans un état grave mais stationnaire *or* stable ; **sterling has remained ~ against the franc** la livre sterling est restée stable par rapport au franc

stable² ['steɪbl] [1] N (= *building*) écurie *f* ; (*also* **racing ~**) écurie *f* (de courses) ; (*riding*) **~(s)** centre *m* d'équitation, manège *m* ; (*fig*) **another bestseller from the HarperCollins ~** un nouveau best-seller qui sort de chez HarperCollins [2] VT [+ *horse*] mettre dans une *or* à l'écurie [3] COMP ► **stable-boy** N garçon *m* or valet *m* d'écurie ► **stable companion** N = **stablemate** ► **stable door** N ■ (*PROV*) **to shut** *or* **close the ~ door after the horse has bolted** *or* **has gone** prendre des précautions après coup ► **stable girl** N valet *m* d'écurie ► **stable lad** N (*Brit*) lad *m*

stablemate ['steɪblmeɪt] N (= *horse*) compagnon *m* de stalle ; (*fig* = *person*) camarade *mf* d'études *or* de travail etc

staccato [stəˈkɑːtəʊ] [1] ADV (*Mus*) staccato [2] ADJ (*Mus*) [*notes*] piqué ; [*passage*] joué en staccato ; [*gunfire, voice, style*] saccadé

stack [stæk] [1] N [a] (*Agr*) meule *f* ; [*of rifles*] faisceau *m* ; [*of wood, books, papers*] tas *m*, pile *f* ; (*US*) [*of tickets*] carnet *m* ; **~s* of** un tas* de, plein* de ; **I've got ~s*** *or* **a ~* of things to do** j'ai des tas* de choses *or* plein* de choses à faire ; **to have ~s* of money** rouler sur l'or, être bourré de fric: ; **we've got ~s* of time** on a tout le temps → **haystack** [b] (= *group of chimneys*) souche *f* de cheminée ; (*on factory, boat etc*) (tuyau *m* de) cheminée *f* [c] (*in library, bookshop*) **~s** rayons *mpl*, rayonnages *mpl* [d] (*Comput*) pile *f* [2] VT [a] (*Agr*) mettre en meule ; (*also* **~ up**) [+ *books, wood*] empiler, entasser ; [+ *dishes*] empiler ; **the table was ~ed with books** la table était couverte de piles de livres ; (*hum*) **she's well-~ed:** il y a du monde au balcon* [b] [+ *supermarket shelves*] remplir ; (*gen*) **she ~ed the shelf with books** elle a entassé des livres sur le rayon [c] (= *hold waiting*) [+ *incoming calls, applications etc*] mettre en attente ; (*Aviat*) [+ *aircraft*] mettre en attente (à différentes altitudes) [d] * (*pej*) **to ~ a jury** composer un jury favorable ; **he had ~ed the committee with his own supporters** il avait noyauté le comité en y plaçant ses partisans ; **to ~ the cards** *or* (*US*) **the deck** tricher (en battant les cartes) ; (*fig*)

the cards or odds are ~ed against me tout joue contre moi
► **stack up** 1 VI (US = measure, compare) se comparer (**with, against** à) 2 VT SEP (gen) empiler, entasser; [+ wheat, barrels] gerber → **stack 2a**

stadium ['steɪdɪəm] N (pl **stadiums** or **stadia** ['steɪdɪə]) stade m (sportif)

staff[1] [stɑːf] N (pl **staffs**) (= work force) (Comm, Ind) personnel m; (Scol, Univ) personnel m enseignant, professeurs mpl; (= servants) domestiques mfpl; (Mil) état-major m; **a large** ~ un personnel etc nombreux; **to be on the** ~ faire partie du personnel; **we have 30 typists on the** ~ notre personnel comprend 30 dactylos; **15** ~ (gen) 15 employés; (teachers) 15 professeurs or enseignants; **he's left our** ~ il nous a quittés, il est parti, il ne fait plus partie de notre personnel; **he joined our** ~ **in 1984** il est entré chez nous en 1984, il a commencé à travailler chez nous en 1984; **he's** ~ il fait partie du personnel → **chief, editorial**
2 VT [+ school, hospital etc] pourvoir en personnel; **it is** ~ed **mainly by immigrants** le personnel se compose surtout d'immigrants; **the hotel is well-**~ed l'hôtel est pourvu d'un personnel nombreux → **overstaffed, short, understaffed**
3 COMP ► **staff association** N association f du personnel, ≈ comité m d'entreprise ► **staff canteen** N (in firm etc) restaurant m d'entreprise, cantine f (des employés) ► **staff college** N (Mil) école f supérieure de guerre ► **staff corporal** N (Brit) ≈ adjudant m ► **staff discount** N remise f pour le personnel ► **staff meeting** N (Scol, Univ) conseil m des professeurs ► **staff nurse** N (Med) infirmier m, -ière f ► **staff officer** N (Mil) officier m d'état-major ► **staff sergeant** N (Brit, US Army) ≈ sergent-chef m; (US Air Force) sergent m ► **staff-student ratio** N = **staffing ratio**; → **staffing** ► **staff training** N formation f du personnel

staff[2] [stɑːf] N (pl **staves** or **staffs**) (liter = rod, pole) bâton m; (longer) perche f; (= walking stick) bâton m; (shepherd's) houlette f; (= weapon) bâton m, gourdin m; (= symbol of authority) bâton m de commandement; (Rel) crosse f, bâton m pastoral; (also **flagstaff**) mât m; †† (of spear, lance etc) hampe f; (fig = support) soutien m; (fig) **a** ~ **for my old age** mon bâton de vieillesse; (fig) **bread is the** ~ **of life** le pain est l'aliment vital or le soutien de la vie

staff[3] [stɑːf] N (pl **staves**) (Mus) portée f

staffed [stɑːft] ADJ (permanently) où il y a du personnel en permanence

staffer ['stɑːfər] N (esp US) (in journalism) membre m de la rédaction; (in organization) membre m du personnel

staffing ['stɑːfɪŋ] 1 N dotation f en personnel 2 COMP [problems etc] de personnel ► **staffing officer** N (Can) agent m de dotation ► **staffing ratio** N (Scol etc) taux m d'encadrement; **the** ~ **ratio is good/bad** le taux d'encadrement est élevé/faible

staffroom ['stɑːfrʊm] N (Scol, Univ) salle f des professeurs

Staffs ABBR = **Staffordshire**

stag [stæg] 1 N a (= deer) cerf m; (= other animal) mâle m b (Brit St Ex) loup m 2 ADJ a (= men only) [event, evening] entre hommes; ~ **night** or **party** (gen = men-only party) soirée f entre hommes; (before wedding) enterrement m de la vie de garçon; **he's having a** ~ **night** or **party** il enterre sa vie de garçon; (US) **the** ~ **line** le coin des hommes seuls (dans une soirée) b (US* = pornographic) [film] porno* inv; ~ **show** spectacle m porno 3 COMP ► **stag beetle** N cerf-volant m (Zool), lucane m ► **stag hunt(ing)** N chasse f au cerf

stage [steɪdʒ] 1 N a (Theat = place) scène f; (= profession) **the** ~ le théâtre; **on (the)** ~ sur scène; **to come on** ~ entrer en scène; **to go on the** ~ monter sur la scène; (as career) monter sur les planches, commencer à faire du théâtre; **on the** ~ **as in real life** à la scène comme à la ville; **she has appeared on the** ~ elle a joué au théâtre; **to write for the** ~ écrire des pièces de théâtre; **the book was adapted for the** ~ le livre a été adapté pour le théâtre or porté à la scène; **his play never reached the** ~ sa pièce n'a jamais été jouée; (fig) **to set the** ~ **for sth** préparer le terrain pour qch; **the** ~ **is set for a memorable match** tout annonce un match mémorable; **to hold the** ~ être le point de mire; **it was the** ~ **of a violent confrontation** cela a été le cadre or le théâtre de violents affrontements → **downstage**
b (= platform: in hall etc) estrade f; (Constr = scaffolding) échafaudage m; (also **landing** ~) débarcadère m; (of microscope) platine f
c (= point, section) [of journey] étape f; [of road, pipeline] section f; [of rocket] étage m; [of operation] étape f, phase f; [of process, disease] stade m, phase f; **a four-**~ **rocket** une fusée à quatre étages; **the second** ~ **fell away** le deuxième étage s'est détaché; **a critical** ~ une phase or un stade critique; **the first** ~ **of his career** le premier échelon de sa carrière; **in** ~s par étapes, par degrés; **by** ~s [travel] par étapes; **in** or **by easy** ~s [travel] par petites étapes; [study] par degrés; ~ **by** ~ étape par étape; **the reform was carried out in** ~s la réforme a été appliquée en plusieurs étapes or temps; **in the early** ~s au début; **at an early** ~ **in its history** vers le début de son histoire; **at this** ~ **in the negotiations** à ce point or à ce stade des négociations; **what** ~ **is your project at?** à quel stade or où en est votre projet?; **it has reached the** ~ **of being translated** c'en est au stade de la traduction; **we have reached a** ~ **where ...** nous (en) sommes arrivés à un point or à un stade où ...; **the child has reached the talking** ~ l'enfant en est au stade où il commence à parler; **he's going through a difficult** ~ il passe par une période difficile; **it's just a** ~ **in his development** ce n'est qu'une phase or un stade dans son développement → **fare**
d (also ~**coach**) diligence f
2 VT (Theat) monter, mettre en scène; (fig) **they** ~d **an accident/a reconciliation** (= organize) ils ont organisé un accident/une réconciliation; (feign) ils ont monté un accident/fait semblant de se réconcilier; **they** ~d **a demonstration** (= organize) ils ont organisé une manifestation; (= carry out) ils ont manifesté; **to** ~ **a strike** (= organize) organiser une grève; (= go on strike) faire la grève; **that was no accident, it was** ~d ce n'était pas un accident, c'était un coup monté
3 COMP ► **stage designer** N décorateur m, -trice f de théâtre ► **stage direction** N (= instruction) indication f scénique; (NonC = art, activity) (art m de la) mise f en scène ► **stage director** N metteur m en scène ► **stage door** N entrée f des artistes ► **stage effect** N effet m scénique (fig) N trac* m ► **stage fright** N trac* m ► **stage left** N côté m cour ► **stage-manage** VT [+ play, production] s'occuper de la régie de; (fig) [+ event, confrontation etc] mettre en scène, orchestrer ► **stage manager** N (Theat) régisseur m ► **stage name** N nom m de scène ► **stage play** N (Theat) pièce f de théâtre ► **stage production** N production f théâtrale ► **stage race** N (Sport) course f par étapes ► **stage right** N côté m jardin ► **stage set** N (Theat) décor m ► **stage show** N = **stage production** ► **stage-struck** ADJ **to be** ~**-struck** brûler d'envie de faire du théâtre ► **stage whisper** N (fig) aparté m; **in a** ~ **whisper** en aparté

stagecraft ['steɪdʒkrɑːft] N (NonC: Theat) technique f de la scène

stagehand ['steɪdʒhænd] N machiniste m

stager ['steɪdʒər] N old ► vétéran m, vieux routier m

stagey ['steɪdʒɪ] ADJ = **stagy**

stagflation [stæg'fleɪʃən] N (Econ) stagflation f

stagger ['stægər] 1 VI chanceler, tituber; **he** ~**d to the door** il est allé à la porte d'un pas chancelant or titubant; **to** ~ **along/in/out** etc avancer/entrer/sortir etc en chancelant or titubant; **he was** ~**ing about** il se déplaçait en chancelant or titubant, il vacillait sur ses jambes
2 VT a (= amaze) stupéfier, renverser; (= horrify) atterrer; **this will** ~ **you** tu vas trouver cela stupéfiant or renversant; **I was** ~**ed to learn that ...** (= amazed) j'ai été absolument stupéfait d'apprendre que ...; (= horrified) j'ai été atterré d'apprendre que ... b [+ spokes, objects] espacer; [+ visits, payments] échelonner; [+ holidays] étaler; **they work** ~**ed hours** leurs heures de travail sont étalées or échelonnées; (Sport) ~**ed start** départ m décalé
3 N allure f chancelante or titubante
4 **staggers** NPL (Vet) vertigo m

staggering ['stægərɪŋ] 1 ADJ a (= astounding) [number, amount, losses, success, news] stupéfiant, ahurissant; [increase] stupéfiant b (= powerful) (lit) ~ **blow** coup m de massue; (fig) **to be a** ~ **blow (to sb/sth)** être un coup de massue (pour qn/qch) 2 N a (= action) démarche f chancelante or titubante b [of hours, visits etc] échelonnement m; [of holidays] étalement m

staggeringly ['stægərɪŋlɪ] ADJ [difficult] extraordinairement; ~ **beautiful** d'une beauté stupéfiante; **the team's** ~ **bad performance** la prestation extrêmement décevante de l'équipe; ~ **high prices** des prix exorbitants

staghound ['stæghaʊnd] N espèce de foxhound

staging ['steɪdʒɪŋ] 1 N a (= scaffolding) (plateforme f d')échafaudage m b (Theat: of play) mise f en scène c (Space) largage m (d'un étage de fusée) 2 COMP ► **staging post** N (Mil, also gen) relais m, point m de ravitaillement

stagnancy ['stægnənsɪ] N stagnation f

stagnant ['stægnənt] ADJ [water] stagnant; [pond] à l'eau stagnante; [air] confiné; [mind] inactif; [economy, market, business, output, society] stagnant; ~ **growth** stagnation f

stagnate [stæg'neɪt] VI [water] être stagnant, croupir; (fig) [business] stagner, être dans le marasme; [person] stagner, croupir; [mind] être inactif

stagnation [stæg'neɪʃən] N stagnation f

stagy ['steɪdʒɪ] ADJ (pej) [appearance, diction, mannerisms] théâtral; [person] cabotin

staid [steɪd] ADJ (pej) [person, appearance] collet monté inv; [behaviour, place, community] sclérosé; [image] guindé; [car, suit] très ordinaire

staidness ['steɪdnɪs] N (pej) [of person, appearance] aspect m collet monté; [of institution, community] sclérose f; [of place, behaviour] caractère m sclérosé; [of image] caractère m guindé; [of car, suit] caractère m très ordinaire

stain [steɪn] 1 N a (lit, fig = mark) tache f (**on** sur); **blood/grease** ~ tache f de sang/graisse; **without a** ~ **on his character** sans une tache à sa réputation b (= colouring) colorant m; **wood** ~ couleur f pour bois 2 VT a (= mark, soil) tacher; (fig) [+ reputation] ternir, entacher; [+ career] porter atteinte à, nuire à; ~**ed with blood** taché de sang b (= colour) [+ wood] teinter, teindre; [+ glass] colorer 3 VI **this material will** ~ ce tissu se tache facilement or est très salissant 4 COMP ► **stained glass** N (= substance) verre m coloré; (windows collectively) vitraux mpl ► **stained-glass window** N vitrail m, verrière f ► **stain remover**

N détachant m ► **stain resistant** ADJ antitaches

-stained ['steɪnd] ADJ (in compounds) **grease-stained** taché de graisse; **nicotine-stained** taché par la nicotine or le tabac; **oil-stained** taché d'huile → **bloodstained, tear²**

stainless ['steɪnlɪs] 1 ADJ sans tache, pur 2 COMP ► **stainless steel** N acier m inoxydable, inox m

stair [stɛəʳ] 1 N (= step) marche f; (also **~s, flight of ~s**) escalier m; **to pass sb on the ~(s)** rencontrer qn dans l'escalier; **below ~s** à l'office 2 COMP [carpet] d'escalier ► **stair rod** N tringle f d'escalier

staircase ['stɛəkeɪs] N escalier m → **moving, spiral**

stairway ['stɛəweɪ] N escalier m

stairwell ['stɛəwel] N cage f d'escalier

stake [steɪk] 1 N a (for fence, tree) pieu m, poteau m; (as boundary mark) piquet m, jalon m; (for plant) tuteur m; (Hist) bûcher m; **to die** or **be burnt at the ~** mourir sur le bûcher; (Brit) **I would go to the ~ to defend their rights** je serais prêt à mourir pour défendre leurs droits; (US) **to pull up ~s*** déménager b (Betting) enjeu m; (fig = share) intérêt m; (= horse-race) **~s** course f de chevaux; (Racing) **the Newmarket ~s** le Prix de Newmarket; (lit, fig) **to play for high ~s** jouer gros jeu; (fig) **to raise the ~s** faire monter les enchères; **to have a ~ in sth** avoir des intérêts dans qch; **he has got a ~ in the success of the firm** il est intéressé matériellement or financièrement au succès de l'entreprise; **Britain has a big ~ in North Sea oil** la Grande-Bretagne a de gros investissements or a engagé de gros capitaux dans le pétrole de la mer du Nord

c **at ~: the issue at ~** ce dont il s'agit, ce qui est en jeu, ce qui se joue ici; **our future is at ~** notre avenir est en jeu, il s'agit de or il y va de notre avenir; **there is a lot at ~** l'enjeu est considérable, il y a gros à perdre; **there is a lot at ~ for him** il a gros à perdre; **he has got a lot at ~** il joue gros jeu, il risque gros, il a misé gros

2 VT a [+ territory, area] marquer or délimiter (avec des piquets etc); [+ path, line] marquer, jalonner; [+ claim] établir; **to ~ one's claim to sth** revendiquer qch, établir son droit à qch b (also **~ up**) [+ fence] soutenir à l'aide de poteaux or de pieux; [+ plants] mettre un tuteur à, soutenir à l'aide d'un tuteur c (= bet) [+ money, jewels etc] jouer, miser (**on** sur); [+ one's reputation, life] risquer, jouer (**on** sur); **he ~d everything** or **his all on the committee's decision** il a joué le tout pour le tout or il a joué son va-tout sur la décision du comité; **I'd ~ my life on it** j'en mettrais ma tête à couper d (= back financially) [+ show, project, person] financer, soutenir financièrement

► **stake out** 1 VT SEP a [+ piece of land] marquer or délimiter (avec des piquets etc); [+ path, line] marquer, jalonner; (fig) [+ section of work, responsibilities etc] s'approprier, se réserver; **to ~ out a position as ...** se tailler une position de ... b (Police) [+ person, house] mettre or garder sous surveillance, surveiller 2 **~out** N → **stakeout**

stakeholder ['steɪkhəʊldəʳ] N (Betting) dépositaire mf d'enjeux

stakeout ['steɪkaʊt] N (Police) surveillance f; **to be on a ~** effectuer une surveillance

stalactite ['stæləktaɪt] N stalactite f

stalagmite ['stæləgmaɪt] N stalagmite f

stale [steɪl] 1 ADJ a (= not fresh) [food] qui n'est plus frais (fraîche f); [bread, cake] rassis (rassie f); [biscuit] vieux (vieille f); [cheese] desséché; [beer, perfume] éventé; [air] confiné; [breath, sweat, urine] fétide; **to smell of ~ cigarette smoke** sentir le tabac froid; **to**

go ~ [bread, cake] rassir; [biscuit] s'abîmer; [beer] s'éventer; [room] sentir le renfermé b [person] qui a perdu tout enthousiasme, las (lasse f); [idea, joke] éculé; [news] dépassé; **to become ~** [person] perdre tout enthousiasme; [relationship] s'étioler; [situation] stagner c (Fin) **~ cheque** chèque m prescrit 2 VI (liter) [pleasures etc] perdre de sa (or leur) fraîcheur or nouveauté

stalemate ['steɪlmeɪt] 1 N (Chess) pat m; (fig) impasse f; **the discussions have reached ~** les discussions sont dans l'impasse; **the ~ is complete** c'est l'impasse totale; **to break the ~** sortir de l'impasse 2 VT (Chess) faire pat inv; (fig) [+ project] contrecarrer; [+ adversary] paralyser, neutraliser

stalemated ['steɪlmeɪtɪd] ADJ [discussions] au point mort (**on** sth en ce qui concerne qch), dans l'impasse (**on** sth en ce qui concerne qch); [project] au point mort

staleness ['steɪlnɪs] N (NonC) a (= lack of freshness) [of food] manque m de fraîcheur; [of air] mauvaise qualité f; [of breath, sweat, urine] mauvaise odeur f b [of person] manque m d'enthousiasme; [of news, situation] manque m de fraîcheur; [of relationship] étiolement m

Stalin ['stɑːlɪn] N Staline m

Stalinism ['stɑːlɪnɪzəm] N stalinisme m

Stalinist ['stɑːlɪnɪst] 1 N stalinien(ne) m(f) 2 ADJ stalinien

stalk¹ [stɔːk] 1 N [of plant] tige f; [of fruit] queue f; [of cabbage] trognon m; (Zool) pédoncule m; **his eyes were out on ~s*** il ouvrait des yeux ronds, il écarquillait les yeux 2 COMP ► **stalk-eyed** ADJ (Zool) aux yeux pédonculés

stalk² [stɔːk] 1 VT a [+ game, prey] traquer; [+ victim] suivre partout; [+ suspect] filer b **to ~ the streets/town** etc [fear, disease, death] régner dans les rues/la ville etc 2 VI **to ~ in/out/off** etc entrer/sortir/partir etc d'un air digne or avec raideur; **he ~ed in haughtily/angrily/indignantly** il est entré d'un air arrogant/furieux/indigné 3 COMP ► **stalking-horse** N (fig) prétexte m; (Pol) **I've no intention of standing as a ~ing-horse candidate** je n'ai aucunement l'intention de me présenter comme candidat bidon*

stalker ['stɔːkəʳ] N **she complained of being followed by a ~** elle s'est plainte d'un désaxé qui la suit partout

stalking ['stɔːkɪŋ] N (Jur) traque f (forme de harcèlement sexuel pathologique consistant suivre partout sa victime)

stall [stɔːl] 1 N a (in stable, cowshed) stalle f; (Racing) (starting) **~s** stalles fpl de départ b (in market, street, at fair) éventaire m, boutique f (en plein air); (in exhibition) stand m; **newspaper/flower~** kiosque m à journaux/de fleuriste; **bookstall** petite librairie f; **coffee ~** buvette f; (fig) **to set out one's ~** définir ses objectifs; **to set out one's ~ to achieve sth** faire en sorte d'arriver à qch c (Brit Theat) (fauteuil m d')orchestre m; **the ~s** l'orchestre m d (in showers etc) cabine f; (in church) stalle f → **choir** e (US: in car park) place f, emplacement m f (= finger stall) doigtier m g (Aut) fait m de caler; (US fig) **in a ~** au point mort

2 VI a [car, engine, driver] caler; [aircraft] être en perte de vitesse, décrocher b (fig) **to ~ (for time)** essayer de gagner du temps, atermoyer; **he managed to ~ until ...** il a réussi à trouver des faux-fuyants jusqu'à ce que ...; **stop ~ing!** cesse de te dérober!

3 VT a (Aut) [+ engine, car] caler; (Aviat) causer une perte de vitesse or un décrochage à; **to be ~ed** [car] avoir calé; (fig) [project etc] être au point mort b [+ person] tenir à distance; **I managed to ~**

him until ... j'ai réussi à le tenir à distance or à esquiver ses questions jusqu'à ce que ...; **try to ~ him for a while** essaie de gagner du temps

4 COMP ► **stall-fed** ADJ (Agr) engraissé à l'étable

stallholder ['stɔːlhəʊldəʳ] N marchand(e) m(f) (à l'étal); (at fair) forain(e) m(f); (at exhibition) exposant(e) m(f)

stallion ['stæljən] N étalon m (cheval)

stalwart ['stɔːlwət] 1 ADJ a (= dependable) [person] loyal, [supporter, ally] inconditionnel; [work] exemplaire b (= sturdy) [person] vigoureux, robuste 2 N brave homme m (or femme f); [of party etc] fidèle mf, pilier m

stamen ['steɪmen] N (pl **stamens** or **stamina** ['stæmɪnə]) (Bot) étamine f

stamina ['stæmɪnə] N (NonC) (physical) résistance f, endurance f; (intellectual) vigueur f; (moral) résistance f, endurance f; **he's got ~** il est résistant, il a de l'endurance → **stamen**

stammer ['stæməʳ] 1 N bégaiement m, balbutiement m; (Med) bégaiement m; **to have a ~** bégayer, être bègue 2 VI bégayer, balbutier; (Med) bégayer, être bègue 3 VT (also **~ out**) [+ name, facts] bégayer, balbutier; **to ~ (out) a reply** bégayer or balbutier une réponse, répondre en bégayant or balbutiant; **"n-not t-too m-much"** he **~ed** « p-pas t-trop » bégaya-t-il

stammerer ['stæmərəʳ] N bègue mf

stammering ['stæmərɪŋ] 1 N (NonC) bégaiement m, balbutiement m; (Med) bégaiement m 2 ADJ [person] (from fear, excitement) bégayant, balbutiant; (Med) bègue; [answer] bégayant, hésitant

stammeringly ['stæmərɪŋlɪ] ADV en bégayant, en balbutiant

stamp [stæmp] 1 N a (= postage stamp) timbre(-poste) m; (= fiscal stamp, revenue stamp) timbre m (fiscal); (= savings stamp) timbre(-épargne) m; (= trading stamp) timbre(-prime) m; **(National) Insurance ~** cotisation f à la Sécurité sociale; **to put** or **stick a ~ on a letter** coller un timbre sur une lettre, timbrer une lettre; **used/unused ~** timbre m oblitéré/non oblitéré b (= implement) (for metal) étampe f, poinçon m; (= rubber stamp) timbre m, tampon m; (= date stamp) timbre dateur m c (= mark, impression) (on document) cachet m; (on metal) empreinte f, poinçon m; (Comm = trademark) estampille f; **look at the date ~** regardez la date sur le cachet; **here's his address ~** voici le cachet indiquant son adresse; **it's got a receipt ~ on it** il y a un cachet accusant paiement; (fig) **he gave the project his ~ of approval** il a approuvé le projet; **the ~ of genius/truth** la marque or le sceau du génie/de la vérité; **men of his ~** des hommes de sa trempe or de son envergure or de son acabit (pej) d [of foot] (from cold) battement m de pied; (from rage) trépignement m; **with a ~ (of his foot)** en tapant du pied

2 VT a **to ~ one's foot** taper du pied; **to ~ one's feet** (in rage) trépigner; (in dance) frapper du pied; (to keep warm) battre la semelle; **he ~ed the peg into the ground** il a tapé du pied sur le piquet pour l'enfoncer en terre b (= stick a stamp on) [+ letter, parcel] timbrer, affranchir; [+ savings book, insurance card] timbrer, apposer un or des timbre(s) sur; (= put fiscal stamp on) timbrer; **this letter isn't sufficiently ~ed** cette lettre n'est pas suffisamment affranchie c (= mark with stamp) tamponner, timbrer; [+ passport, document] viser; [+ metal] estamper, poinçonner; **to ~ a visa on a passport** apposer un visa sur un passeport; **to ~ the date on a form** ◊ **to ~ a form with the date** apposer la date sur un formulaire (avec un timbre dateur); **he ~ed a design on the metal** il

a estampillé le métal d'un motif; (fig) **to ~ sth on one's memory** graver qch dans sa mémoire; **his accent ~s him as a (a) Belgian** son accent montre bien or indique bien qu'il est belge; **to ~ o.s. on sth** laisser sa marque or son empreinte sur qch → **die²**

3 VI a taper du pied; (angrily) taper du pied, trépigner; [horse] piaffer; **he ~ed on my foot** il a fait exprès de me marcher sur le pied; **he ~ed on the burning wood** il a piétiné les tisons, il a éteint les tisons du pied; (fig) **to ~ on a suggestion** rejeter une suggestion b (angrily) **to ~ in/out etc** entrer/sortir etc en tapant du pied; (to keep warm) taper du pied, battre la semelle 4 COMP ► **Stamp Act** N (Hist) loi f sur le timbre ► **stamp album** N album m de timbres(-poste) ► **stamp-book** N carnet m de timbres(-poste) ► **stamp collecting** N (NonC) philatélie f ► **stamp collection** N collection f de timbres(-poste) ► **stamp collector** N collectionneur m, -euse f de timbres(-poste), philatéliste mf ► **stamp dealer** N marchand(e) m(f) de timbres(-poste) ► **stamp duty** N droit m de timbre ► **stamped addressed envelope** N (Brit) enveloppe f affranchie à son nom et adresse; **I enclose a ~ed addressed envelope (for your reply)** veuillez trouver ci-joint une enveloppe affranchie pour la réponse ► **stamping ground⁰** N (fig) lieu m favori, royaume m ► **stamp machine** N distributeur m (automatique) de timbres(-poste)

► **stamp down** VT SEP [+ peg etc] enfoncer du pied; (fig) [+ rebellion] écraser, étouffer; [+ protests] refouler

► **stamp out** VT SEP a [+ fire] piétiner, éteindre en piétinant; [+ cigarette] écraser sous le pied; (fig) [+ rebellion] enrayer, juguler; [+ custom, belief, tendency] déraciner, détruire b [+ coin etc] frapper; [+ design] découper à l'emporte-pièce c [+ rhythm] marquer en frappant du pied

stampede [stæm'pi:d] 1 N (aimless) [of animals] débandade f, fuite f précipitée; [of people] sauve-qui-peut m inv; [of retreating troops] débâcle f, déroute f; (fig: with purpose = rush) ruée f; **there was a ~ for the door** on s'est précipité or rué vers la porte; **he got knocked down in the ~ for seats** il a été renversé dans la ruée vers les sièges 2 VI [animals, people] s'enfuir en désordre or à la débandade (**from** de), fuir en désordre or à la débandade (**towards** vers); (fig = rush) se ruer (**for sth** pour obtenir qch); **to ~ for the door** se ruer vers la porte 3 VT [+ animals, people] jeter la panique parmi; (fig) **they ~d him into agreeing** il a accepté parce qu'ils ne lui ont pas laissé le temps de la réflexion; **we mustn't let ourselves be ~d** il faut que nous prenions (subj) le temps de réfléchir

stance [stæns] N (lit, fig) position f; (Climbing) relais m; (bus) **~** quai m; **to take up a ~** (lit) prendre place or position; (fig) prendre position (**on** sur, **against** contre)

stanch [stɑːntʃ] VT = **staunch¹**

stanchion ['stɑːnʃən] N (as support) étançon m, étai m; (for cattle) montant m

▼**stand** [stænd]

vb: pret, ptp **stood**
1 NOUN	4 COMPOUNDS
2 TRANSITIVE VERB	5 PHRASAL VERBS
3 INTRANSITIVE VERB	

1 NOUN a = position: lit, fig] position f; **to take (up) one's ~** (lit) prendre place or position; (fig) prendre position (**on** sur, **against** contre); **he took (up) his ~ beside me** il s'est placé or mis à côté de moi, il a pris position à côté de moi; **I admired the firm ~ he took on that point** j'ai admiré sa fermeté sur cette question; **I make**

my **~ upon these principles** je me base sur ces principes; (fig = fight) **to make** or **take a ~ against sth** lutter contre qch; **we must take a ~ against racism** nous devons lutter contre le racisme; (Mil) **they turned and made a ~** ils ont fait volte-face et se sont défendus; (Mil) **the ~ of the Australians at Tobruk** la résistance des Australiens à Tobrouk; **Custer's last ~** le dernier combat de Custer

b also taxi **~** station f (de taxis)

c Comm: for displaying goods étal m, étalage m; (also newspaper **~**) kiosque m à journaux; (= market stall) étal m (étals pl), éventaire m; (at exhibition, funfair, trade fair) stand m

d = seating area tribune f; **I've got a ticket for the ~(s)** j'ai une tribune, j'ai un billet de tribune(s)

e = witness stand barre f; **to take the ~** venir à la barre

f = holder, support (for plant, bust etc) guéridon m; (for lamp) pied m (de lampe); (= hat stand) porte-chapeaux m inv; (= coat stand) portemanteau m; (= music stand) pupitre m à musique

g of trees bouquet m, bosquet m; **a ~ of grass** une étendue d'herbe

h Cricket **the ~ between Gooch and Hussein** le nombre de points que Gooch et Hussein ont marqué

i = standstill

2 TRANSITIVE VERB a = place [+ object] mettre; **~ the plant in a sunny spot** mettez cette plante dans un endroit ensoleillé; **he stood the child on the chair** il a mis l'enfant debout sur la chaise; **to ~ sth (up) against a wall** mettre qch debout contre le mur; **to ~ sth on its end** mettre qch debout

b = tolerate [+ heat, pain, criticism, insolence, attitude] supporter; **I can't ~ it any longer** (pain etc) je ne peux plus le supporter; (boredom etc) j'en ai assez, j'en ai par-dessus la tête*; **I can't ~ (the sight of) her** je ne peux pas la supporter or la sentir* or la voir*; **she can't ~ being laughed at** elle ne supporte pas qu'on se moque (subj) d'elle; **I can't ~ gin/Wagner/wet weather** je déteste le gin/Wagner/la pluie

c = withstand [+ pressure, heat] supporter, résister à; **she stood the journey quite well** elle a bien supporté le voyage; **these shoes won't ~ much wear** ces chaussures ne vont pas faire beaucoup d'usage; **it won't ~ close examination** cela ne résistera pas à un examen approfondi; **that doll won't ~ much more of that treatment** cette poupée ne va pas faire long feu à ce rythme-là

d * = pay for payer, offrir; **to ~ sb a drink** offrir un verre à qn, payer un pot à qn*; **he stood the next round of drinks** il a payé la tournée suivante; **to ~ sb a meal** inviter qn au restaurant; **to ~ the cost of sth** payer qch; **they agreed to ~ the cost of my course** ils ont accepté de payer mon stage

3 INTRANSITIVE VERB a = be upright: also ~ up [person, animal] être or se tenir debout; **he is too weak to ~** il est trop faible pour se tenir debout or tenir sur ses jambes; **my niece has just learnt to ~** ça ne fait pas longtemps que ma nièce sait se tenir debout; **we had to ~ as far as Calais** nous avons dû rester debout or voyager debout jusqu'à Calais; **you must ~ (up)** or **stay ~ing (up) till the music stops** vous devez rester debout jusqu'à ce que la musique s'arrête (subj); **~ (up) straight!** tiens-toi droit!; **we couldn't get the tent to ~ (up)** nous n'arrivions pas à monter la tente or à faire tenir la tente debout; **the post must ~ upright** le poteau doit être bien droit; **the house is still ~ing** la maison est encore debout or est toujours là; **not much still ~s of the walls** il ne reste plus grand-chose des murs; **not a stone was left ~ing in the old town** la vieille ville a été complètement détruite

♦ **to stand or fall**: **the project will ~ or fall by ...** le succès du projet repose sur ...; **I ~ or fall by this** il en va de ma réputation

b = rise: also ~ up se lever; **all ~!** levez-vous s'il vous plaît!; (fig) **to ~ (up) and be counted** déclarer ouvertement sa position

c = stay, stand still rester (debout); **we stood talking for an hour** nous sommes restés debout à bavarder pendant une heure; **don't just ~ there, do something!** ne reste pas là à ne rien faire or les bras ballants!; **~ over there till I'm ready** mets-toi or reste là-bas jusqu'à ce que je sois prêt; **I left him ~ing on the bridge** je l'ai laissé sur le pont; **they stood patiently in the rain** ils attendaient patiemment sous la pluie; (fig) **he left the others ~ing** il dépassait les autres de la tête et des épaules (fig); **~ and deliver!** la bourse ou la vie!

d = be positioned, be [person] être, se tenir; [object, vehicle, tree] être, se trouver; [town, building] se trouver; **he stood there ready to shoot** il était or se tenait là, prêt à tirer; **the man ~ing over there** cet homme là-bas; (fig) **I like to know where I ~** j'aime savoir où j'en suis; **where do you ~ with him?** où en êtes-vous avec lui?; **as things ~ at the moment** dans l'état actuel des choses; **how do things ~ between them?** comment ça va entre eux?; **how do things** or **matters ~?** où en sont les choses?

♦ **to stand** + preposition: **three chairs stood against the wall** il y avait trois chaises contre le mur; **nothing ~s between you and success** rien ne s'oppose à votre réussite; **this is all that ~s between him and ruin** sans cela il aurait déjà fait faillite; **he stood in the doorway** il était debout dans l'embrasure de la porte; **they stood in a circle around the grave** ils se tenaient en cercle autour de la tombe; **tears stood in her eyes** elle avait les larmes aux yeux; **the village ~s in the valley** le village se trouve or est (situé) dans la vallée; **the house ~s in its own grounds** la maison est entourée d'un parc; **a lamp stood in the middle of the table** il y avait une lampe au milieu de la table; **where do you ~ on this question?** quel est votre position sur cette question?; **beads of perspiration stood on his brow** des gouttes de sueur perlaient sur son front; **he was ~ing over the stove, stirring a sauce** il était penché au-dessus du fourneau, occupé à remuer une sauce; **she looked up to see Faith ~ing over her** elle leva les yeux et vit que Faith se tenait près d'elle → **5**

♦ **to stand in the way**: **to ~ in sb's way** bloquer or barrer le passage à qn; (fig) se mettre en travers du chemin de qn; **I won't ~ in your way** je ne me mettrai pas en travers de votre chemin, je ne vous ferai pas obstacle; **nothing now ~s in our way** maintenant la voie est libre; **his age ~s in his way** son âge est un handicap; **to ~ in the way of sth** faire obstacle à qch; **to ~ in the way of progress** faire obstacle au progrès

♦ **to stand to do sth**: **to ~ to lose** risquer de perdre; **the managers ~ to gain millions if the company is sold** les directeurs devraient gagner des millions si l'entreprise est vendue; **he ~s to make a fortune on it** ça va sans doute lui rapporter une fortune

♦ **to stand** + past participle/adjective/adverb: **the car stood abandoned by the roadside** la voiture était abandonnée au bord de la route; **to ~ accused of murder** être accusé de meurtre; **he ~s alone in this matter** personne ne partage son avis sur cette question; **this ~s alone** c'est unique en son genre; **to ~ clear** s'écarter, se tenir à distance; **~ clear of the doors!** ≈ attention, fermeture des portes!; **to ~ convicted of manslaughter** être condamné pour homicide; **I ~ corrected** je reconnais mon erreur; **to ~ opposed to sth** être opposé à qch, s'opposer à qch; **they were ~ing ready to leave** ils se tenaient prêts à partir; **the rec-**

ord ~s **unbeaten** le record n'a pas encore été battu; **to ~ well with sb** être bien vu de qn

e = *tread* marcher; **you're ~ing on my foot** tu me marches sur le pied; **he stood on the beetle** il a marché sur *or* écrasé le scarabée; **to ~ on the brakes** piler*

f = *measure* [*person*] faire, mesurer; [*building, tree*] faire; **he ~s over six feet in his socks** il mesure *or* fait plus de 1 mètre 80 sans chaussures; **the tree ~s 30 metres high** l'arbre fait 30 mètres de haut

g = *be mounted, based* [*statue etc*] reposer (on sur); [*argument, case*] être basé (on sur); **the lamp ~s on an alabaster base** la lampe a un pied d'albâtre

h = *be at the moment, have reached* **to ~ at** [*thermometer, clock*] indiquer; [*price, value*] s'élever à; [*score*] être de; **you must accept the offer as it ~s** cette offre n'est pas négociable; **the record stood at four minutes for several years** pendant plusieurs années le record a été de quatre minutes; **sales ~ at 5% up on last year** les ventes sont en hausse de 5% par rapport à l'année dernière; (*Banking*) **to have £500 ~ing to one's account** avoir 500 livres sur son compte; **the amount ~ing to your account** le solde de votre compte, la somme que vous avez sur votre compte

i = *remain undisturbed, unchanged* [*liquid, mixture, dough*] reposer; [*tea, coffee*] infuser; **the offer/agreement still ~s** l'offre/l'accord tient toujours; **the objection still ~s** l'objection demeure; **they agreed to let the regulation ~** ils ont décidé de ne rien changer au règlement

j Brit Parl = *be candidate* se présenter, être candidat; **he stood for Neath** il s'est présenté *or* il était candidat à Neath; **to ~ against sb in an election** se présenter contre qn à des élections; **to ~ for election** se présenter *or* être candidat aux élections; **to ~ for re-election** se représenter; **he stood for the council but wasn't elected** il était candidat au poste de conseiller municipal mais n'a pas été élu

k Naut **to ~ (out) to sea** (= *move*) mettre le cap sur le large; (= *stay*) être *or* rester au large

4 COMPOUNDS
▶ **stand-alone** ADJ [*system*] autonome, indépendant ▶ **stand-by** N → stand-by ▶ **stand-in** N remplaçant(e) *m(f)*; (*Cine*) doublure *f* ▶ **stand-offish** ADJ → stand-offish ▶ **stand-to** N (*Mil*) alerte *f* ▶ **stand-up** ADJ → stand-up

5 PHRASAL VERBS
▶**stand about, stand around** VI rester là; **don't ~ about doing nothing!** ne reste pas là à ne rien faire!; **they were ~ing about wondering what to do** ils restaient là à se demander ce qu'ils pourraient bien faire; **they kept us ~ing about for hours** ils nous ont fait attendre debout pendant des heures

▶**stand aside** VI s'écarter, se pousser; **he stood aside to let me pass** il s'est écarté pour me laisser passer; **~ aside!** écartez-vous!; **to ~ aside in favour of sb** laisser la voie libre à qn, ne pas faire obstacle à qn; (*fig*) **to ~ aside from something** rester en dehors de qch, ne pas se mêler de qch

▶**stand back** VI (= *move back*) reculer, s'écarter; (*fig*) prendre du recul; **you must ~ back and get the problem into perspective** il faut que vous preniez (*subj*) du recul pour voir le problème dans son ensemble; **the farm ~s back from the road** la ferme est en retrait de la route

▶**stand by** **1** VI **a** (*pej* = *be onlooker*) rester là (à ne rien faire); **how could you ~ (idly) by while they attacked him?** comment avez-vous pu rester sans rien faire alors qu'ils l'attaquaient?; **we will not ~ (idly) by and let democracy be undermined** nous n'allons pas laisser attaquer la démocratie sans rien faire

b (= *be ready for action*) [*troops*] être en état d'alerte; [*person, ship, vehicle*] être *or* se tenir

prêt; (= *be at hand*) attendre *or* être sur place; (*Aviat*) **~ by for takeoff** paré pour le décollage; **~ by for further revelations** apprêtez-vous à entendre d'autres révélations

2 VT FUS **a** (= *support*) [+ *friend*] ne pas abandonner; [+ *colleague, spouse*] soutenir, épauler; **she stood by her husband** elle a soutenu son mari

b (= *keep to*) [+ *promise*] tenir; [+ *sb else's decision*] respecter, se conformer à; [+ *one's own decision*] s'en tenir à; **I ~ by what I have said** je m'en tiens à ce que j'ai dit

▶**stand down** **1** VI (= *resign*) [*official, chairman*] se démettre de ses fonctions, démissionner; (= *withdraw*) [*candidate*] se désister; (*Jur*) [*witness*] quitter la barre; **he stood down as chairman last January** il a démissionné de ses fonctions *or* de son poste de président en janvier dernier; **he stood down in favour of his brother** il s'est désisté en faveur de son frère

2 VT FUS (= *withdraw*) [+ *troops*] donner l'ordre de se retirer; **to be made to ~ down** être contraint de démissionner

▶**stand for** VT FUS **a** (= *represent*) représenter; **what does UNO ~ for?** qu'est-ce que l'abréviation UNO veut dire *or* signifie?; **I dislike all he ~s for** je déteste tout ce qu'il représente *or* incarne

b (= *support*) promouvoir; **our party ~s for equality of opportunity** notre parti milite pour l'égalité des chances → stand 3j

c (= *tolerate*) supporter, tolérer; **I won't ~ for it!** je ne le tolérerai pas!

▶**stand in** VI **to ~ in for sb** remplacer qn; **I offered to ~ in when he was called away** j'ai proposé de le remplacer quand il a dû s'absenter

▶**stand off** **1** VI **a** (= *move away*) s'écarter; (= *keep one's distance*) se tenir à l'écart (**from** de), garder ses distances (**from** par rapport à); (= *remain uninvolved*) ne pas intervenir

b (= *reach stalemate*) aboutir à une impasse

2 VT SEP (*Brit*) [+ *workers*] mettre temporairement au chômage

▶**stand out** VI **a** (= *project*) [*ledge, buttress*] avancer (**from** sur), faire saillie; [*vein*] saillir (**on** sur)

b (= *be conspicuous, clear*) ressortir, se détacher; **to ~ out against the sky** ressortir *or* se détacher sur le ciel; **the yellow ~s out against the dark background** le jaune ressort sur le fond sombre; **his red hair stood out in the crowd** ses cheveux roux le faisaient remarquer dans la foule; **that ~s out a mile!*** cela saute aux yeux!, cela crève les yeux!

c (= *be outstanding*) se distinguer; **he ~s out from all the other students** il se distingue de tous les autres étudiants; **he ~s out above all the rest** il surpasse tout le monde

d (= *remain firm*) tenir bon, tenir ferme; **how long can you ~ out?** combien de temps peux-tu tenir?; **to ~ out for sth** revendiquer qch; **to ~ out against** [+ *attack, domination, attacker*] résister à; [+ *demand, change, proposal*] s'élever contre

▶**stand over** **1** VI [*items for discussion*] **these questions can ~ over until ...** ces questions peuvent attendre jusqu'à ce que ...

2 VT FUS [+ *person*] surveiller, être derrière le dos de; **I hate people ~ing over me while I work** je déteste avoir toujours quelqu'un derrière *or* sur le dos quand je travaille; **he would never have done it if I hadn't stood over him** il ne l'aurait jamais fait si je n'avais pas été constamment derrière lui; **stop ~ing over him!** laisse-le donc un peu tranquille!

▶**stand to** (*Mil*) VI être en état d'alerte

▶**stand up** **1** VI **a** (= *rise*) se lever, se mettre debout; (= *be standing*) [*person*] être debout; [*tent, structure*] tenir debout; **she had nothing but the clothes she was ~ing up in** elle ne possédait que les vêtements qu'elle avait sur le dos; (*fig*) **to ~ up and be counted** déclarer ouvertement sa position

b (= *resist challenge*) tenir debout; **they made accusations that did not ~ up** les accusations qu'ils avaient faites ne tenaient pas debout; **that argument won't ~ up in court** cet argument va être rapidement réfuté par la partie adverse

2 VT SEP **a** (= *place upright*) mettre; **to ~ sth up against a wall** mettre *or* appuyer qch contre un mur; **the soup was so thick you could ~ a spoon up in it** la soupe était si épaisse qu'on pouvait y faire tenir une cuiller debout

b (* = *fail to meet*) [+ *friend*] faire faux bond à; [+ *boyfriend, girlfriend*] poser un lapin à*

▶**stand up for** VT FUS [+ *person, principle, belief*] défendre; **you must ~ up for what you think is right** vous devez défendre ce qui vous semble juste; **~ up for me if he asks you what you think** prenez ma défense *or* soutenez-moi s'il vous demande votre avis; **to ~ up for o.s.** savoir se défendre

▶**stand up to** VT FUS [+ *opponent, bully, superior*] affronter; [+ *person in argument*] tenir tête à; [+ *use, conditions*] résister à; **it won't ~ up to that sort of treatment** cela ne résistera pas à ce genre de traitement; **the report won't ~ up to close examination** ce rapport ne résiste pas à l'analyse

standard ['stændəd] **1** N **a** (= *flag*) étendard *m*; (*Naut*) pavillon *m*

b (= *norm*) norme *f*; (= *criterion*) critère *m*; (*for weights and measures*) étalon *m*; (*for silver*) titre *m*; (*fig: intellectual etc*) niveau *m* (voulu); **monetary ~** titre *m* de monnaie; **the metre is the ~ of length** le mètre est l'unité de longueur; (*fig*) **to be** *or* **come up to ~** [*person*] être à la hauteur; [*thing*] être de la qualité voulue, être conforme à la norme; **I'll never come up to his ~** je n'arriverai jamais à l'égaler; **judging by that ~** selon ce critère; **you are applying a double ~** vous avez deux poids, deux mesures; **his ~s are high** il recherche l'excellence, il ne se contente pas de l'à-peu-près; (*morally, artistically*) **he has set us a high ~** il a établi un modèle difficile à surpasser; **the exam sets a high ~** cet examen exige un niveau élevé; **the ~ of the exam was low** le niveau de l'examen était bas; **to have high moral ~s** avoir un sens moral très développé; **high/low ~ of living** niveau *m* de vie élevé/bas; **to be first-year university ~** être du niveau de première année d'université; **their ~ of culture** leur niveau de culture; **I couldn't accept their ~s** je ne pouvais pas accepter leur échelle de valeurs → gold

c (= *support*) support *m*; (*for lamp, street light*) pied *m*; (= *actual streetlight*) réverbère *m*; (= *water/gas pipe*) tuyau *m* vertical d'eau/de gaz; (= *tree, shrub*) arbre *m* de haute tige → lamp

d (*Mus*) (= *jazz tune*) standard *m*; (= *pop tune*) classique *m*

2 ADJ **a** (= *regular*) [*size, height*] normal, standard *inv*; [*amount, charge, procedure*] normal; [*measure, weight*] étalon *inv*; [*model, design, feature*] standard *inv*; [*product*] ordinaire; **a ~ car** une voiture de série; **it's ~ equipment on all their cars** c'est monté en série sur toutes leurs voitures; **he's below ~ height for the police** il n'a pas la taille requise pour être agent de police; **~ operating procedure** procédure *f* à suivre; **~ practice** pratique *f* courante; **the ~ rate of income tax** le taux d'imposition ordinaire pour l'impôt sur le revenu

b (*Ling* = *orthodox*) [*spelling, pronunciation, grammar, usage*] correct

c (= *recommended*) [*text, book*] de base, classique

d [*shrub*] de haute tige

3 COMP ▶ **standard bearer** N (*lit*) porte-étendard *m*, porte-drapeau *m*; (*fig*) porte-drapeau *m* ▶ **standard class** N (*Rail*) seconde classe *f* ▶ **standard clause** N (*Jur*) clause-type *f* ▶ **standard deviation** N (*Stat*) écart *m* type ► **Standard English** N anglais *m* correct → ENGLISH ► **standard error** N (*Stat*) erreur *f* type ► **standard gauge** N (*Rail*) écartement *m* normal ► **standard-gauge** ADJ à écartement *m* normal ► **Standard Grade** N (*Scot Scol*) ≈ épreuve *f* du brevet des collèges ► **standard issue** N **to be ~ issue** (*Mil*) être standard *inv*; (*gen*) être la norme ► **standard-issue** ADJ (*Mil*) réglementaire; (*gen*) standard *inv* ► **standard lamp** N (*Brit*) lampadaire *m* ► **standard rose** N rosier *m* à haute tige ► **standard time** N heure *f* légale

standardization [ˌstændədaɪˈzeɪʃən] N (*NonC: gen*) standardisation *f*; [*of product, terminology*] normalisation *f*

standardize [ˈstændədaɪz] VT (*gen*) standardiser; [+ *product, terminology*] normaliser; (*US Scol*) **~d test** test de connaissances commun à tous les établissements

stand-by [ˈstændbaɪ] **1** N (= *person*) remplaçant(e) *m(f)*; (*US Theat* = *understudy*) doublure *f*; (= *car/battery/boots*) voiture *f*/pile *f*/bottes *fpl* de réserve *or* de secours; **if you are called away you must have a ~** si vous vous absentez, vous devez avoir un remplaçant *or* quelqu'un qui puisse vous remplacer en cas de besoin; **aspirin is a useful ~** l'aspirine est toujours bonne à avoir *or* peut toujours être utile; **lemon is a useful ~ if you have no vinegar** le citron peut être utilisé à la place du vinaigre le cas échéant; **to be on ~** [*troops*] être sur pied d'intervention; [*plane*] se tenir prêt à décoller; [*doctor*] être de garde; (*Mil*) **to be on 24-hour ~** être prêt à intervenir 24 heures sur 24; (*Mil*) **to put on ~** mettre sur pied d'intervention

2 ADJ [*car, battery etc*] de réserve; [*generator, plan*] de secours; (*Aviat*) **~ ticket** billet *m* sans garantie; **~ passenger** (passager *m*, -ère *f* en) stand-by *mf inv*; (*Jur, Fin*) **~ credit** crédit *m* d'appoint *or* stand-by; **~ loan** prêt *m* conditionnel *or* stand-by

standee* [stænˈdiː] N (*US*) (*at match etc*) spectateur *m*, -trice *f* debout; (*on bus etc*) voyageur *m*, -euse *f* debout

standing [ˈstændɪŋ] **1** ADJ **a** (= *upright*) [*passenger*] debout *inv*; [*statue*] en pied; [*corn, crop*] sur pied **b** (= *permanent*) [*invitation*] permanent; [*rule*] fixe; [*grievance, reproach*] constant, de longue date; **it's a ~ joke** c'est un sujet de plaisanterie continuel; **it's a ~ joke that he wears a wig** on dit qu'il porte une perruque, c'est un sujet de plaisanterie continuel

2 N **a** (= *position, importance etc*) [*of person*] rang *m*; (= *social status*) standing *m*; (= *reputation*) réputation *f*; [*of restaurant, business*] réputation *f*, standing *m*; [*of newspaper*] réputation *f*; **social ~** rang *m or* position *f* social(e), standing *m*; **professional ~** réputation *f* professionnelle; **what's his financial ~?** quelle est sa situation financière?; **his ~ in public opinion polls** sa cote de popularité; **what's his ~?** quelle est sa réputation?, que pense-t-on de lui?; **firms of that ~** des compagnies aussi réputées; **a man of (high *or* some *or* good) ~** un homme considéré *or* estimé; **he has no ~ in this matter** il n'a aucune autorité *or* son opinion ne compte pas *or* il n'a pas voix au chapitre dans cette affaire **b** (= *duration*) durée *f*; **of ten years' ~** [*friendship*] qui dure depuis dix ans; [*agreement, contract*] qui existe depuis dix ans; [*doctor, teacher*] qui a dix ans de métier; **of long ~** de longue date; **friends of long ~** des amis de longue date; **he has 30 years' ~ in the firm** il a 30 ans d'ancienneté dans l'entreprise, il travaille dans l'entreprise depuis 30 ans → **long** **c** (*US Sport*) **the ~** le classement **d** (*US Aut*) **"no ~"** « stationnement interdit »

3 COMP ► **standing army** N armée *f* de métier ► **standing charge** N (frais *mpl* d')abonnement *m* ► **standing committee** N comité *m* permanent ► **standing expenses** NPL frais *mpl* généraux ► **standing jump** N (*Sport*) saut *m* à pieds joints ► **standing order** N (*Banking*) virement *m* automatique; (*Comm*) commande *f* permanente; (*Admin, Parl*) règlement *m* intérieur; (*Comm*) **~ orders** règlement *m*; **to place a ~ order for a newspaper** passer une commande permanente pour un journal; (*Mil*) **~ orders** règlement *m* ► **standing ovation** N ovation *f*; **to get a ~ ovation** se faire ovationner; **to give sb a ~ ovation** se lever pour ovationner qn ► **standing room** N (*NonC*) (*in bus, theatre*) places *fpl* debout; **"~ room only"** (= *seats all taken*) « il n'y a plus de places assises »; (= *no seats provided*) « places debout seulement » ► **standing start** N (*Sport*) départ *m* debout; (*Aut*) départ *m* arrêté ► **standing stone** N pierre *f* levée

stand-off [ˈstændɒf] **1** N **a** (= *pause: in negotiations etc*) temps *m* d'arrêt **b** (= *stalemate*) impasse *f* **c** (= *counterbalancing situation*) contrepartie *f* **2** COMP ► **stand-off half** N (*Rugby*) demi *m* d'ouverture

stand-offish [ˌstændˈɒfɪʃ] ADJ (*pej*) distant

stand-offishly [ˌstændˈɒfɪʃlɪ] ADV (*pej*) d'une manière distante

stand-offishness [ˌstændˈɒfɪʃnɪs] N (*pej*) froideur *f*, réserve *f*

standpat* [ˈstændpæt] ADJ (*US: esp Pol*) immobiliste

standpipe [ˈstændpaɪp] N colonne *f* d'alimentation

standpoint [ˈstændpɔɪnt] N (*lit, fig*) point *m* de vue

standstill [ˈstændstɪl] N arrêt *m*; **to come to a ~** [*person, car*] s'immobiliser; [*production*] s'arrêter; [*discussions*] aboutir à une impasse; **to bring to a ~** [+ *car*] immobiliser; [+ *discussion*] paralyser; [+ *discussion*] aboutir à; **to be at a ~** [*person, car*] être immobile; [*production*] être interrompu; [*discussion*] être au point mort; **trade is at a ~** les affaires sont au point mort

stand-up [ˈstændʌp] **1** ADJ [*collar*] droit; [*meal etc*] (pris) debout; **~ comedian** *or* **comic** comique *m* (qui se produit en solo); **a ~ fight** (*physical*) une bagarre violente; (= *argument*) une discussion violente **2** N* (= *comedian*) comique *mf* (qui se produit seul sur scène); (*NonC*) (= *stand-up comedy*) one man show(s) *m(pl)* comique(s)

stank [stæŋk] VB *pt of* **stink**

Stanley® [ˈstænlɪ] N **~ knife** cutter *m*

stannic [ˈstænɪk] ADJ stannique

stanza [ˈstænzə] N (*Poetry*) strophe *f*; (*in song*) couplet *m*

stapes [ˈsteɪpiːz] N (*pl* **stapes** *or* **stapedes** [stæˈpiːdiːz]) étrier *m*

staphylococcus [ˌstæfɪləˈkɒkəs] N (*pl* **staphylococci** [ˌstæfɪləˈkɒkaɪ]) staphylocoque *m*

staple¹ [ˈsteɪpl] **1** ADJ [*product, food, industry*] de base; [*crop*] principal; **~ commodity** article *m* de première nécessité; **~ diet** nourriture *f* de base; **their ~ meals of fish and rice** leurs repas à base de poisson et de riz **2** N **a** (*Econ*) (= *chief commodity*) produit *m* *or* article *m* de base; (= *raw material*) matière *f* première **b** (= *chief item*) (*Comm: held in stock*) produit *m* *or* article *m* de base; (*gen: of conversation etc*) élément *m* *or* sujet *m* principal; (*in diet etc*) aliment *m* *or* denrée *f* de base **c** (*Tex* = *fibre*) fibre *f*

staple² [ˈsteɪpl] **1** N (*for papers*) agrafe *f*; (*Tech*) crampon *m*, cavalier *m* **2** VT (*also* **~ together**) [+ *papers*] agrafer; [+ *wood, stones*] cramponner; **to ~ sth on to sth** agrafer qch à qch **3** COMP ► **staple gun** N agrafeuse *f* d'artisan *or* d'atelier

stapler [ˈsteɪplə*] N agrafeuse *f*

star [stɑː*] **1** N **a** (*Astron*) étoile *f*, astre *m*; (*Typ etc* = *asterisk*) astérisque *m*; (*Scol: for merit*) bon point *m*; **morning/evening ~** étoile *f* du matin/du soir; (*US*) **the Stars and Stripes** la Bannière étoilée; (*US Hist*) **the Stars and Bars** le drapeau des États confédérés; **Star of David** étoile *f* de David; **the ~ of Bethlehem** l'étoile *f* de Bethléem → **4**; (*fig*) **to have ~s in one's eyes** être naïvement plein d'espoir; (*fig*) **to see ~s** voir trente-six chandelles; **he was born under a lucky/an unlucky ~** il est né sous une bonne/une mauvaise étoile; **you can thank your (lucky) ~s* that ...** tu peux remercier le ciel de ce que ...; (= *horoscope*) **the ~s** l'horoscope *m*; **it was written in his ~s that he would do it** il était écrit qu'il le ferait; **three-/five-~ hotel** hôtel *m* trois/cinq étoiles → **five**, **four**, **guiding**, **pole²**, **shooting**, **two** **b** (*Cine, Sport etc* = *person*) vedette *f*; (= *actress*) vedette *f*, star *f*; **the film made him into a ~** le film en a fait une vedette *or* l'a rendu célèbre → **all**, **film**

2 VT **a** (= *decorate with stars*) étoiler; **lawn ~red with daisies** pelouse *f* parsemée *or* émaillée (*liter*) de pâquerettes **b** (= *put asterisk against*) marquer d'un astérisque **c** (*Cine, Theat*) avoir pour vedette; **the film ~s John Wayne** John Wayne est la vedette du film; **~ring Mel Gibson as ...** avec Mel Gibson dans le rôle de ...

3 VI (*Cine, Theat*) être la vedette; (*fig*) briller; **to ~ in a film** être la vedette d'un film; **he ~red as Hamlet** c'est lui qui a joué le rôle de Hamlet

4 COMP ► **star anise** N anis *m* étoilé ► **star-chamber** ADJ (*fig*) arbitraire ► **star-crossed** ADJ maudit par le sort ► **star fruit** N carambole *f* ► **star grass** N herbe *f* étoilée ► **star-of-Bethlehem** N (*Bot*) ornithogale *m*, dame-d'onze-heures *f* ► **star part** N (*Cine, Theat*) premier rôle *m* ► **starring role, star role** N (*Cine, Theat*) premier rôle *m* ► **star route** N (*US Post*) liaison *f* postale ► **star shell** N (*Mil*) fusée *f* éclairante ► **star sign** N signe *m* zodiacal *or* du zodiaque ► **star-spangled** ADJ parsemé d'étoiles, étoilé; (*US flag, anthem*) **the Star-Spangled Banner** la Bannière étoilée ► **star-studded** ADJ [*sky*] parsemé d'étoiles; [*cast*] prestigieux; [*play*] à la distribution prestigieuse ► **star system** N **a** (*Astron*) système *m* stellaire **b** (*Cine*) **the ~ system** le star-système *or* star-system ► **the star turn** N (*Theat: fig*) la vedette ► **Star Wars** N (*gen, Cine, US Mil**) la guerre des étoiles; (*US Mil*) **the "Star Wars"* plan** *or* **program** le projet *or* le programme « Star Wars » *or* « Guerre des étoiles »

starboard [ˈstɑːbəd] (*Naut*) **1** N tribord *m*; **to ~** à tribord; **land to ~!** terre par tribord! **2** ADJ [*wing, engine, guns, lights*] de tribord; **on the ~ beam** par le travers tribord; **~ bow** tribord *m* avant; **on the ~ bow** par tribord avant; **~ side** tribord *m*; **on the ~ side** à tribord → **watch²** **3** VT **to ~ the helm** mettre la barre à tribord

starburst [ˈstɑːbɜːst] N (*liter*) étoile *f*

starch [stɑːtʃ] **1** N **a** (*in food*) amidon *m*, fécule *f*; (*for stiffening*) amidon *m*; **he was told to cut out all ~(es)** on lui a dit de supprimer tous les féculents; (*US fig*) **it took the ~ out of him*** cela l'a mis à plat, cela lui a ôté toute son énergie **b** (*pej: formal manner*) raideur *f*, manières *fpl* apprêtées *or* empesées **2** VT [+ *collar*] amidonner, empeser **3** COMP ► **starch-reduced** ADJ [*bread*] de régime; [*diet*] pauvre en féculents

starchy [ˈstɑːtʃɪ] ADJ **a** [*food*] féculent; **~ foods** féculents *mpl* **b** (*pej: formal*) [*person, attitude*] guindé

stardom [ˈstɑːdəm] N (*NonC: Cine, Sport, Theat etc*) vedettariat *m*, célébrité *f*; **to rise to ~** ◊ **to achieve ~** devenir une vedette *or* une star

stardust ['stɑːdʌst] N (fig) la vie en rose

stare [steəʳ] **1** N regard m (fixe); **cold/curious/vacant ~** (long) regard m froid/curieux/vague

2 VI **to ~ at sb** dévisager qn, fixer qn du regard, regarder qn fixement; **to ~ at sth** regarder qch fixement, fixer qch du regard; **to ~ at sb/sth in surprise** regarder qn/qch avec surprise or d'un air surpris, écarquiller les yeux devant qn/qch; **they all ~d in astonishment** ils ont tous regardé d'un air ébahi or en écarquillant les yeux; **he ~d at me stonily** il m'a regardé d'un air dur; **what are you staring at?** qu'est-ce que tu regardes comme ça?; **it's rude to ~** il est mal élevé de regarder les gens fixement; **to ~ into space** regarder dans le vide or dans l'espace, avoir le regard perdu dans le vague

3 VT **~ sb in the face** dévisager qn, fixer qn du regard, regarder qn dans le blanc des yeux; **where are my gloves? — here, they're staring you in the face!** où sont mes gants? — ils sont sous ton nez or tu as le nez dessus!; **they're certainly in love, that ~s you in the face** ils sont vraiment amoureux, cela crève les yeux; **ruin ~d him in the face** il était au bord de la ruine; **the truth ~d him in the face** la vérité lui crevait les yeux or lui sautait aux yeux

▶ **stare out** VT SEP faire baisser les yeux à

starfish ['stɑːfɪʃ] N (pl inv) étoile f de mer

stargazer ['stɑːgeɪzəʳ] N **a** (= astronomer) astronome mf; (= astrologer) astrologue mf **b** (= fish) uranoscope m

stargazing ['stɑːgeɪzɪŋ] N contemplation f des étoiles, (= predictions) prédictions fpl astrologiques; (fig = dreaming) rêverie f, rêvasserie f (pej)

staring ['steərɪŋ] ADJ [crowd] curieux; **his ~ eyes** son regard fixe; (in surprise) son regard étonné or ébahi; (in fear) son regard effrayé

stark [stɑːk] **1** ADJ **a** (= austere) [landscape, beauty, building, décor, colour] austère; [cliff] désolé, morne **b** (= harsh) [choice] difficile; [warning, reminder] sévère; [reality] dur; **those are the ~ facts of the matter** voilà les faits bruts or tels qu'ils sont; **the ~ fact is that ...** le fait est que ... **c** (= absolute) [terror] pur; **in ~ contrast** tout à l'opposé; **to be in ~ contrast to sb/sth** contraster vivement avec qn/qch **2** ADV **~ naked** tout nu

starkers ['stɑːkəz] ADJ (Brit) à poil*

starkly ['stɑːklɪ] ADV **a** (= austerely) [furnished] de façon austère; **~ beautiful** d'une beauté sauvage **b** (= clearly) [illustrate, outline] crûment; [stand out] âprement; [different] carrément; [apparent] nettement; **to contrast ~ with sth** contraster de façon frappante avec qch; **to be ~ exposed** être exposé sans ambages

starkness ['stɑːknɪs] N (NonC) **a** (= austerity) [of landscape, beauty, building, décor, colour] austérité f **b** (= harshness) [of choice] difficulté f; [of warning, reminder] sévérité f; [of facts] caractère m brut; [of reality] dureté f **c** (= absoluteness) **the ~ of the contrast between ...** le contraste absolu entre ...

starless ['stɑːlɪs] ADJ sans étoiles

starlet ['stɑːlɪt] N (Cine) starlette f

starlight ['stɑːlaɪt] N **by ~** à la lumière des étoiles

starling ['stɑːlɪŋ] N étourneau m, sansonnet m

starlit ['stɑːlɪt] ADJ [night, sky] étoilé; [countryside, scene] illuminé par les étoiles

starry ['stɑːrɪ] **1** ADJ [sky, night] étoilé **2** COMP ▶ **starry-eyed** ADJ [person] (= idealistic) idéaliste; (= innocent) innocent, ingénu; (from wonder) éberlué; (from love) éperdument amoureux; **in ~-eyed wonder** le regard plein d'émerveillement, complètement ébloui

starstruck ['stɑːstrʌk] ADJ ébloui (devant une célébrité)

▼ **start** [stɑːt]

1 NOUN	**4** COMPOUNDS
2 TRANSITIVE VERB	**5** PHRASAL VERBS
3 INTRANSITIVE VERB	

1 NOUN

a = **beginning** [of speech, book, film, career etc] commencement m, début m; [of negotiations] ouverture f, amorce f; (Sport) [of race etc] départ m; (= starting line) (point m de) départ m; **the ~ of the academic year** la rentrée universitaire et scolaire; **that was the ~ of all the trouble** c'est là que tous les ennuis ont commencé; **at the ~** au commencement, au début; **from the ~** dès le début, dès le commencement; **for a ~** d'abord, pour commencer; **from ~ to finish** du début à la fin; **to get off to a good or brisk or fast ~** bien commencer, bien démarrer; **to get a good ~ in life** bien débuter dans la vie; **they gave their son a good ~ in life** ils ont fait ce qu'il fallait pour que leur fils débute (subj) bien dans la vie; **that was a good ~ to his career** cela a été un bon début or un début prometteur pour sa carrière; (lit, fig) **to get off to a bad or slow ~** mal démarrer, mal commencer; **it's off to a good/bad ~** c'est un bon/mauvais début; **to make a ~** commencer; **to make a ~ on sth** commencer qch, se mettre à qch; **to make an early ~** commencer de bonne heure; (in journey) partir de bonne heure; (Sport) **to be lined up for the ~** être sur la ligne de départ; (Sport) **the whistle blew for the ~ of the race** le coup de sifflet a annoncé le départ de la course; (Sport) **wait for the ~** attendez le signal du départ

b = **advantage** (Sport) avance f; (fig) avantage m; **will you give me a ~?** est-ce que vous voulez bien me donner une avance?; **to give sb 10 metres' or a 10-metre ~** donner 10 mètres d'avance à qn; (fig) **that gave him a ~ over the others in the class** cela lui a donné un avantage sur les autres élèves de sa classe, cela l'a avantagé par rapport aux autres élèves de sa classe

c = **sudden movement** sursaut m, tressaillement m; **to wake with a ~** se réveiller en sursaut; **to give a ~** sursauter, tressaillir; **to give sb a ~** faire sursauter or tressaillir qn; **you gave me such a ~!** ce que vous m'avez fait peur!

2 TRANSITIVE VERB

a = **begin** commencer (**to do, doing** à faire, de faire), se mettre (**to do, doing** à faire); [+ work] commencer, se mettre à; [+ task] entreprendre; [+ song] commencer (à chanter), entonner; [+ attack] déclencher; [+ bottle] entamer, déboucher; **to ~ a cheque book/a new page** commencer or prendre un nouveau carnet de chèques/une nouvelle page; **to ~ a journey** partir en voyage; **he ~ed the day with a glass of milk** il a bu un verre de lait pour bien commencer la journée; **to ~ the day right** bien commencer la journée, se lever du pied droit; **to ~ life as ...** débuter dans la vie comme ...; **that doesn't (even) ~ to compare with ...** cela est loin d'être comparable à ..., cela n'a rien de comparable avec ...; **it soon ~ed to rain** il n'a pas tardé à pleuvoir; **I'd ~ed to think you weren't coming** je commençais à croire que tu ne viendrais pas; **to ~ again or afresh** recommencer (**to do** à faire), recommencer à zéro*; **don't ~ that again!** tu ne vas pas recommencer!; **"it's late" he ~ed** « il est tard » commença-t-il

◆ **to get started** commencer, démarrer; **to get ~ed on (doing) sth** commencer (à faire) qch; **let's get ~ed!** allons-y!, on s'y met!*; **once I get ~ed I work very quickly** une fois

lancé je travaille très vite; **just to get ~ed, they ...** rien que pour mettre l'affaire en route or rien que pour démarrer, ils ...

b = **originate, initiate**: also **~ off, ~ up** [+ discussion] commencer, ouvrir; [+ conversation] amorcer, engager; [+ quarrel, argument, dispute] déclencher, faire naître; [+ reform, movement, series of events] déclencher; [+ fashion] lancer; [+ phenomenon, institution] donner naissance à; [+ custom, policy] inaugurer; [+ war] causer; [+ rumour] donner naissance à, faire naître; **to ~ (up) a fire** (in grate etc) allumer un feu, faire du feu; (accidentally) mettre le feu, provoquer un incendie; **you'll ~ a fire if you go on doing that!** tu vas mettre le feu à la maison or tu vas provoquer un incendie si tu fais ça!; **she has ~ed a baby*** elle est enceinte

c = **cause to start** (also **~ up**) [+ engine, vehicle] mettre en marche, démarrer; [+ clock] mettre en marche; (also **~ off**) [+ race] donner le signal du départ de; (fig) **he ~ed the ball rolling by saying ...** pour commencer, il a dit ...; **he blew the whistle to ~ the runners (off)** il a sifflé pour donner le signal du départ; **he ~ed the new clerk (off) in the sales department** il a d'abord mis or affecté le nouvel employé au service des ventes; **they ~ed her (off) as a typist** d'abord or pour commencer ils l'ont employée comme dactylo; **to ~ sb (off or out) on a career** lancer or établir qn dans une carrière; **if you ~ him (off) on that subject ...** si tu le lances sur ce sujet ...; **that ~ed him (off) sneezing/remembering** etc alors il s'est mis à éternuer/à se souvenir etc; (lit, fig) **to ~ a hare** lever un lièvre

◆ **to get sth started** [+ engine, vehicle] mettre qch en marche, faire démarrer qch; [+ clock] mettre qch en marche; [+ project] faire démarrer qch

◆ **to get sb started** (gen) mettre qn en selle; [+ film star, pop star etc] lancer qn; **to get sb ~ed on (doing) sth** faire commencer qch à qn

3 INTRANSITIVE VERB

a = **begin**: also **~ off, ~ out, ~ up** [person] commencer, s'y mettre; [speech, programme, meeting, ceremony] commencer; **let's ~!** commençons!, allons-y!, on s'y met!*; **we must ~ at once** il faut commencer or nous y mettre immédiatement; **well, to ~ at the beginning** eh bien, pour commencer par le commencement; **it's ~ing (off)** rather well/badly cela s'annonce plutôt bien/mal; **to ~ (off) well in life** bien débuter dans la vie; **to ~ (out or up) in business** se lancer dans les affaires; **to ~ again or afresh** recommencer (à zéro*); **classes ~ on Monday** les cours commencent or reprennent lundi; **the classes ~ (up) again soon** les cours reprennent bientôt, c'est bientôt la rentrée; **~ing from Monday** à partir de lundi; **to ~ (off) by doing** commencer par faire; **~ by putting everything away** commence par tout ranger; **~ on a new page** prenez une nouvelle page; **he ~ed (off) in the sales department/as a secretary** il a débuté dans le service des ventes/comme secrétaire; **he ~ed (off or out) as a Marxist** il a commencé par être marxiste, au début or au départ il a été marxiste

◆ **to start with** commencer par; **to ~ with sth** commencer or débuter par qch; **~ with me!** commencez par moi!; **to ~ with, there were only three of them, but later ...** (tout) d'abord ils n'étaient que trois, mais plus tard ...; **to ~ with, this is untrue** pour commencer or d'abord, c'est faux; **we only had 100 francs to ~ with** nous n'avions que 100 F pour commencer or au début; **he ~ed (off) with the intention of writing a thesis** au début son intention était d'écrire or il avait l'intention d'écrire une thèse

b = **broach to ~ on a book** commencer un livre; **to ~ on a course of study** commencer or entreprendre un programme d'études; **they had ~ed on a new bottle** ils avaient débouché or entamé une nouvelle bouteille; **I ~ed on the job last week** (*employment*) j'ai commencé à travailler la semaine dernière; (*task*) je m'y suis mis la semaine dernière → **start on**

c = originate, initiate: *also* ~ **up** [*music, noise, guns*] commencer, retentir; [*fire*] commencer, prendre; [*river*] prendre sa source; [*road*] partir (**at** de); [*political party, movement, custom*] commencer, naître; **that's when the trouble ~s** c'est alors *or* là que les ennuis commencent; **it all ~ed when he refused to pay** toute cette histoire a commencé *or* tout a commencé quand il a refusé de payer

d = leave: *also* ~ **off**, ~ **out** [*person*] partir, se mettre en route; [*ship*] partir; [*train*] démarrer, se mettre en marche; **to ~ (off or out) from London/for Paris/on a journey** partir de Londres/pour Paris/en voyage; (*Sport*) **ten horses ~ed and only three finished** dix chevaux ont pris le départ mais trois seulement ont fini la course; **he ~ed (off) along the corridor** il s'est engagé dans le couloir; **he ~ed (off) down the street** il a commencé à descendre la rue

e = get going: *also* ~ **up** [*car, engine, machine*] démarrer, se mettre en route; [*clock*] se mettre à marcher; **my car won't ~** ma voiture ne veut pas démarrer*

f = jump nervously [*person*] sursauter, tressaillir; [*animal*] tressaillir, avoir un soubresaut; **to ~ to one's feet** sauter sur ses pieds, se lever brusquement; **he ~ed forward** il a fait un mouvement brusque en avant; (*fig*) **his eyes were ~ing out of his head** les yeux lui sortaient de la tête; **tears ~ed to her eyes** les larmes lui sont montées aux yeux

g timbers jouer

4 COMPOUNDS
► **starting block** N (*Athletics*) starting-block *m*, bloc *m* de départ; (*fig*) **to be fast/slow off the ~ing blocks** être rapide/lent à démarrer ► **starting gate** N (*Racing*) starting-gate *m* ► **starting grid** N (*Motor Racing*) grille *f* de départ ► **starting handle** N (*Brit Aut*) manivelle *f* ► **starting line** N (*Sport*) ligne *f* de départ ► **starting pistol** N pistolet *m* de starter ► **starting point** N point *m* de départ ► **starting post** N (*Sport*) ligne *f* de départ ► **starting price** N (*St Ex*) prix *m* initial; (*Racing*) cote *f* de départ ► **starting salary** N salaire *m* d'embauche ► **starting stalls** NPL (*Racing*) stalles *fpl* de départ ► **start-up** N [*of machine*] démarrage *m*, mise *f* en route; [*of business*] lancement *m*, mise *f* en route; (*Comm etc*) **~-up costs** frais *mpl* de lancement *or* de démarrage; **~-up money** capital *m* initial ► **Start-Up scheme** N (*Brit*) programme d'aide aux chômeurs pour la création d'entreprises

5 PHRASAL VERBS
► **start back** VI **a** (= return) prendre le chemin du retour, repartir
b (= recoil) [*person, horse etc*] reculer soudainement, faire un bond en arrière
► **start in** VI s'y mettre, s'y coller*; **~ in!** allez-y!
► **start off 1** VI → start 3a, 3d
2 VT SEP → start 2b, 2c
► **start on*** VT FUS (= pick on) s'en prendre à → start 3b
► **start out** VI → start 3a, 3d
► **start over 1** VI (*esp US*) repartir à zéro
2 VT recommencer
► **start up 1** VI → start 3a, 3c, 3e
2 VT SEP → start 2b, 3c

starter ['stɑːtə*r*] **1** N **a** (*Sport*) (= *official*) starter *m*; (= *horse*) partant *m*; **to be under ~'s orders** [*runner*] être à ses marques; [*horse*] être sous les ordres (du starter); (*fig*) être sur *or* dans les starting-blocks; **to be a slow ~** être lent au départ *or* à démarrer; (*Scol etc*) **the child was a late ~** cet enfant a mis du temps à se développer → **nonstarter b** (*Aut*)

---

démarreur *m*; (*on machine etc*) bouton *m* de démarrage; (*also* ~ **motor**) démarreur *m*
c (*Brit: in meal*) hors-d'œuvre *m inv*; **for ~s*** (= food) comme hors-d'œuvre; (*fig* = *for a start*) pour commencer, d'abord **2** COMP
► **starter flat** N (*Brit*) appartement idéal pour une personne souhaitant accéder à la propriété
► **starter home** N (*Brit*) logement idéal pour une personne souhaitant accéder à la propriété
► **starter pack** N (*Comm*) kit *m* de base

startle ['stɑːtl] VT [*sound, sb's arrival*] faire sursauter *or* tressaillir; [*news, telegram*] alarmer; **it ~d him out of his sleep** cela l'a réveillé en sursaut; **to ~ sb out of his wits** donner un (drôle* de) choc à qn; **you ~d me!** tu m'as fait sursauter!, tu m'as fait peur!

startled ['stɑːtld] ADJ [*animal*] effarouché; [*person*] très surpris; [*expression*] de saisissement; **in a ~ voice** d'une voix qui montrait sa surprise; **he gave her a ~ look** il lui lança un regard interloqué; **she was ~ to see him** elle fut très surprise de le voir

startling ['stɑːtlɪŋ] ADJ [*success, conclusion, results, evidence, news*] surprenant; [*contrast*] saisissant

startlingly ['stɑːtlɪŋlɪ] ADV [*different, similar*] étonnamment; **~ original** d'une originalité surprenante; **~ beautiful/modern** d'une beauté/modernité saisissante; **his ~ blue eyes** ses yeux d'un bleu saisissant

starvation [stɑːˈveɪʃən] **1** N (*NonC*) inanition *f*; **they are threatened with ~** ils risquent de mourir d'inanition *or* de faim, la famine les menace **2** COMP [*rations, wages*] de famine
► **starvation diet** N **to be on a ~ diet** (*lit*) être sérieusement *or* dangereusement sous-alimenté; (*fig*) suivre un régime draconien
► **starvation level** N **to be living at ~ level** = **to be on a starvation diet**

starve [stɑːv] **1** VT **a** affamer; **to ~ sb to death** laisser qn mourir de faim; **to ~ o.s. to death** se laisser mourir de faim; **she ~d herself to feed her children** elle s'est privée de nourriture pour donner à manger à ses enfants; **you don't have to ~ yourself in order to slim** tu peux maigrir sans te laisser mourir de faim; **to ~ sb into submission** soumettre qn par la faim; (*Mil*) **to ~ a town into surrender** amener une ville à se rendre par la famine **b** (= deprive) priver (**sb of sth** qn de qch); **~d of affection** privé d'affection; **engine ~d of petrol** moteur *m* à sec **2** VI manquer de nourriture, être affamé; **to ~ (to death)** mourir de faim; (*deliberately*) se laisser mourir de faim → **starving**
► **starve out** VT SEP [+ *person, animal*] obliger à sortir en affamant

starveling ['stɑːvlɪŋ] N (= person) affamé(e) *m(f)*

starving ['stɑːvɪŋ] ADJ (*lit*) affamé, famélique; (*fig*) **I'm ~*** je meurs de faim, j'ai une faim de loup

stash* [stæʃ] **1** VT (*also* ~ **away**) (= hide) cacher, planquer*; (= save up, store away) mettre à gauche*, mettre de côté; **he had £500 ~ed away** (= saved up) il avait mis 500 livres de côté; (= in safe place) il avait 500 livres en lieu sûr **2** N (= place) planque* *f*, cachette *f*; **a ~ of jewellery/drugs** des bijoux cachés/des drogues cachées; **a ~ of money** un magot, un bas de laine

stasis ['steɪsɪs] N (*Med, Literat*) stase *f*

state [steɪt] **1** N **a** (= condition) état *m*; **~ of alert/emergency/siege/war** état *m* d'alerte/d'urgence/de siège/de guerre; **the ~ of the art** l'état *m* actuel de la technique *or* des connaissances → **3**; **in your ~ of health/mind** dans votre état de santé/d'esprit; **he was in an odd ~ of mind** il était d'une humeur étrange; **you're in no ~ to reply** vous n'êtes pas en état de répondre; (*in bank*) **I'd like to know the ~ of my account** j'aimerais connaître la position de mon compte; (*fig*) **what's the ~ of play?** où

---

en est-on?; **in a good/bad ~ of repair** bien/mal entretenu; **to be in a good/bad ~** [*chair, car, house*] être en bon/mauvais état; [*person, relationship, marriage*] aller bien/mal; **you should have seen the ~ the car was in** vous auriez dû voir l'état de la voiture; **it wasn't in a (fit) ~ to be used** c'était hors d'état de servir, c'était inutilisable; **he's not in a (fit) ~ to drive** il est hors d'état *or* il n'est pas en état de conduire; **what a ~ you're in!** vous êtes dans un bel état!; **he got into a terrible ~ about it*** ça l'a mis dans tous ses états; **he's not in a (fit) ~ to drive**; **don't get into such a ~!*** ne vous affolez pas! → **affair, declare**

b (*Pol*) État *m*; **the State** l'État *m*; **the States*** les États-Unis *mpl*; **the State of Virginia** l'État *m* de Virginie; **the affairs of ~** les affaires *fpl* de l'État; **a ~ within a ~** un État dans l'État → **evidence, minister, police, secretary**

c (*US* = State Department) **State** le Département d'État

d (= rank) rang *m*; **every ~ of life** tous les rangs sociaux

e (*NonC* = pomp) pompe *f*, apparat *m*; **the robes of ~** les costumes *mpl* d'apparat; **in ~** en grande pompe, en grand apparat; **to live in ~** mener grand train → **lie**[1]

2 VT déclarer, affirmer (**that** que); [+ *one's views, the facts*] exposer; [+ *time, place*] fixer, spécifier; [+ *conditions*] poser, formuler; [+ *theory, restrictions*] formuler; [+ *problem*] énoncer, poser; **I also wish to ~ that ...** je voudrais ajouter que ...; **it is ~d in the records that ...** il est écrit *or* mentionné dans les archives que ...; **I have seen it ~d that ...** j'ai lu quelque part que ...; **as ~d above** ainsi qu'il est dit plus haut; **~ your name and address** déclinez vos nom, prénoms et adresse; (*written*) inscrivez vos nom, prénoms et adresse; **cheques must ~ the sum clearly** les chèques doivent indiquer la somme clairement; **he was asked to ~ his case** on lui a demandé de présenter ses arguments; (*Jur*) **to ~ the case for the prosecution** présenter le dossier de l'accusation

3 COMP [*business, documents, secret*] d'État; [*security, intervention*] de l'État; [*medicine*] étatisé; (*US: also* **State**) [*law, policy, prison, university*] de l'État ► **state apartments** NPL appartements *mpl* officiels ► **state banquet** N banquet *m* de gala ► **State Capitol** N (*US*) Capitole *m* ► **state-certified midwife** N (*Brit Med*) sage-femme *f* diplômée d'État ► **state coach** N (*Brit*) carrosse *m* d'apparat (*de cérémonie officielle*) ► **state control** N contrôle *m* de l'État; **under ~ control** = **state-controlled** ► **state-controlled** ADJ étatisé ► **State Department** N (*US*) Département *m* d'État, ≈ ministère *m* des Affaires étrangères ► **state education** N (*Brit*) enseignement *m* public ► **state-enrolled nurse** N (*Brit*) infirmier *m*, -ière *f* auxiliaire, aide-soignant(e) *mf* ► **state funeral** N funérailles *fpl* nationales ► **State legislature** N (*US Jur*) législature *f* de l'État ► **State line** N (*US*) frontière *f* entre les États ► **state-maintained** ADJ (*Brit Scol*) public ► **state militia** N (*US*) milice *f* (formée de volontaires d'un État) ► **state-of-the-art** ADJ (*fig* = up-to-date) [*computer, video*] dernier cri; (*fig*) **it's ~-of-the-art** c'est ce qui se fait de mieux, c'est le dernier cri ► **State of the Union Address** N (*US Pol*) discours *m* sur l'état de l'Union ► **state-owned** ADJ étatisé ► **State police** N (*NonC: US*) police *f* de l'État; **Michigan State police** la police de l'État du Michigan ► **state-registered nurse** N (*Brit: formerly*) infirmier *m*, -ière *f* diplômé(e) d'État ► **State Representative** N (*US Pol*) membre *m* de la Chambre des représentants d'un État ► **State rights** NPL (*US*) = **State's rights** ► **state-run** ADJ d'état ► **State's attorney** N (*US*) procureur *m* ► **state school** N (*Brit*) école f publique ► **state sector** N (Econ etc) secteur m public ► **State Senator** N (US Pol) membre m du Sénat d'un État ► **state socialism** N (NonC: Pol Econ) socialisme m d'État ► **State's rights** NPL (US) droits mpl des États ► **state-subsidised** ADJ subventionné par l'État ► **state-trading countries** NPL (Econ) pays mpl à commerce d'État ► **state trooper** N (US) ≈ gendarme m ► **State university** N (US) université f d'État ► **state visit** N **to go on** or **make a ~ visit to a country** se rendre en visite officielle or faire un voyage officiel dans un pays ► **state-wide** ADJ, ADV (US) d'un bout à l'autre de l'État

---
STATE OF THE UNION ADDRESS

Le discours sur l'état de l'Union est l'allocution que prononce le président des États-Unis devant le Congrès le 3 janvier de chaque année, au début de la session parlementaire. Dans cette intervention, diffusée à la radio et à la télévision, le président dresse un bilan de son action, expose ses projets et donne au Congrès des «informations sur l'état de l'Union», comme le demande la Constitution.

STATE'S RIGHTS

Le dixième amendement de la Constitution américaine accorde aux États un certain nombre de droits (State's rights) sur toutes les questions qui ne relèvent pas des prérogatives du gouvernement fédéral: enseignement, fiscalité, lois et réglementations diverses. Cependant, l'interprétation de ce texte a provoqué de nombreuses controverses: les États du Sud l'ont utilisé pour justifier la sécession avant la guerre civile, puis pour s'opposer à l'intégration raciale dans les années 50. La question du degré d'autonomie dont disposent les États par rapport au pouvoir fédéral reste un sujet politiquement sensible.

---

statecraft ['steɪtkrɑːft] N (NonC) habileté f politique

stated ['steɪtɪd] ADJ [date, sum] fixé; [interval] fixe; [limit] prescrit; **on ~ days** à jours fixes; **at the ~ time** ◊ **at the time ~** à l'heure dite

statehood ['steɪthʊd] N (NonC) **to achieve ~** devenir un État

statehouse ['steɪthaʊs] N (US) siège m de la législature d'un État

stateless ['steɪtlɪs] ADJ apatride; **~ person** apatride mf

statelet ['steɪtlɪt] N (Pol) mini-État m

stateliness ['steɪtlɪnɪs] N majesté f, caractère m imposant

stately ['steɪtlɪ] 1 ADJ [person] plein de dignité; [building, pace] majestueux; **to make ~ progress** progresser majestueusement 2 COMP ► **stately home** N (Brit) manoir m ancestral (ouvert au public)

statement ['steɪtmənt] N a (NonC) [of one's views, the facts] exposition f, formulation f; [of time, place] spécification f; [of theory, restrictions, conditions] formulation f; [of problem] énonciation f b (written, verbal) déclaration f; (Jur) déposition f ► **official ~** communiqué m officiel; **to make a ~** (gen, Press) faire une déclaration; (Jur) faire une déposition, déposer; (Jur) **~ of grounds** exposé m des motifs c (Fin) [of accounts etc] (= bill) relevé m; (Comm = bill) facture f; (also **bank ~**) relevé m de compte d (Ling) assertion f

stateroom ['steɪtrʊm] N (Brit) [of palace] grande salle f de réception; [of ship, train] cabine f de luxe

stateside* ['steɪtsaɪd] ADJ (US) aux États-Unis, ≈ chez nous

statesman ['steɪtsmən] N (pl **-men**) homme m d'État; (fig) **he is a real ~** il est extrêmement diplomate → **elder¹**

statesmanlike ['steɪtsmənlaɪk] ADJ diplomatique

statesmanship ['steɪtsmənʃɪp] N (NonC) habileté f politique, diplomatie f

statesmen ['steɪtsmən] NPL of **statesman**

static ['stætɪk] 1 ADJ a (= stationary) statique; **a series of ~ images** une série d'images fixes or statiques b (= unchanging) immuable; **the ~ quality of their lives** leur vie immuable c (= fixed) [population, output] stationnaire 2 N (NonC) a **~s** statique f b (Elec, Rad, TV etc) parasites mpl; (US) **he gave me a lot of ~ about ...** il m'a passé un savon* à propos de ... 3 COMP ► **static electricity** N électricité f statique

station ['steɪʃən] 1 N a (= place) poste m, station f; (= fire station) caserne f de pompiers; (= lifeboat station) centre m or poste m (de secours en mer); (Mil) poste m (militaire); (Police) poste m or commissariat m (de police), gendarmerie f; (Elec = power station) centrale f (électrique); (Rad) station f de radio, poste m émetteur; (in Australia = sheep/cattle ranch) élevage m (de moutons/de bétail), ranch m; **naval ~** station f navale; (Rad) **foreign ~s** stations fpl étrangères; (Telec) **calling all ~s** appel m à tous les émetteurs; (Rel) **the Stations of the Cross** les stations fpl de la Croix, le chemin de (la) Croix → **frontier, petrol, pump¹, signal** b (Rail) gare f; [of underground] station f; **bus** or **coach ~** gare f routière; **the train came into the ~** le train est entré en gare; (in underground) la rame est entrée dans la station → **change** c (= position) poste m (also Mil), position f; **to take up one's ~** prendre position, se placer; **from my ~ by the window** de la fenêtre où je m'étais posté or où je me trouvais d (= rank) condition f, rang m; **one's ~ in life** son rang or sa situation social(e), sa place dans la société; **to get ideas above one's ~** avoir des idées de grandeur; **to marry beneath one's ~†** faire une mésalliance, se mésallier; **to marry above one's ~** se marier au-dessus de sa condition e (US Telec) poste m; **give me ~ 101** je voudrais le poste 101 2 VT [+ people] placer; [+ guards, observers, look-out, troops, ship] poster; [+ tanks, guns] placer, installer; **to ~ o.s.** se placer, se poster; **to be ~ed at** [troops, regiment] être en or tenir garnison à; [ships, sailors] être en station à 3 COMP (Rail) [staff, bookstall etc] de (la) gare ► **station break** N (US Rad, TV) page f de publicité ► **station house** N (US) (for police) commissariat m; (for firefighters) caserne f de pompiers ► **station master** N (Rail) chef m de gare ► **station officer** N (Brit Police) responsable mf d'un poste de police ► **station wag(g)on** N (US Aut) break m

stationary ['steɪʃənərɪ] 1 ADJ a (= motionless) [vehicle] à l'arrêt; [person, ship] stationnaire, immobile; [target] immobile b (= fixed) [crane] fixe 2 COMP ► **stationary bicycle** N bicyclette f fixe

stationer ['steɪʃənəʳ] N papetier m, -ière f; **~'s (shop)** papeterie f

stationery ['steɪʃənərɪ] 1 N (NonC) papeterie f, papier m et petits articles mpl de bureau; (= writing paper) papier m à lettres 2 COMP ► **Stationery Office** N (Brit) **His (or Her) Majesty's Stationery Office** ≈ l'Imprimerie f nationale (fournit aussi de la papeterie à l'administration et publie une gamme étendue d'ouvrages et de brochures didactiques)

statist ['steɪtɪst] ADJ (Pol) étatiste mf

statistic [stə'tɪstɪk] 1 N statistique f, chiffre m; **a set of ~s** une statistique; **these ~s are not reliable** on ne peut pas se fier à ces chiffres or à ces statistiques; **~s suggest that ...** la statistique or les statistiques suggère(nt) que

...; (hum: woman's) **(vital) ~s** mensurations fpl → **statistics** 2 ADJ = **statistical**

statistical [stə'tɪstɪkəl] ADJ [analysis, evidence, data, probability, table, significance] statistique; [error] de statistiques; [expert] en statistique(s)

statistically [stə'tɪstɪkəlɪ] ADV statistiquement

statistician [ˌstætɪs'tɪʃən] N statisticien(ne) m(f)

statistics [stə'tɪstɪks] N (NonC) statistique f

stative ['steɪtɪv] ADJ (Ling) **~ verb** verbe m d'état

stator ['steɪtəʳ] N stator m

stats [stæts] NPL (ABBR = **statistics**) stats* fpl

statuary ['stætjʊərɪ] 1 ADJ statuaire 2 N (= art) statuaire f; (= statues collectively) statues fpl

statue ['stætjuː] N statue f; **the Statue of Liberty** la statue de la Liberté

statuesque [ˌstætjʊ'esk] ADJ sculptural

statuette [ˌstætjʊ'et] N statuette f

stature ['stætʃəʳ] N stature f, taille f; (fig) [of person] envergure f, stature f; (fig) [of institution] envergure f; **to be of small ~** ◊ **to be small in** or **of ~** être petit or fluet; **of short ~** court de stature or de taille; **he is a writer of some ~** c'est un écrivain d'une certaine envergure or d'une certaine stature; **his ~ as a painter increased when ...** il a pris de l'envergure en tant que peintre quand ...; **moral/intellectual ~** envergure f sur le plan moral/intellectuel

status ['steɪtəs] 1 N (pl **statuses**) a (= economic etc position) situation f, position f; (Admin, Jur) statut m; **social ~** standing m; **civil ~** état m civil; **what is his (official) ~?** quel est son titre officiel?, quelle est sa position officielle?; **the economic ~ of the country** la situation or position économique du pays; **the financial ~ of the company** l'état financier de la compagnie; **the ~ of the black population** la condition sociale or (Admin) le statut de la population noire; **his ~ as an assistant director** son standing de directeur adjoint b (= prestige) [of person] prestige m, standing m; [of job, post] prestige m; **it is the ~ more than the salary that appeals to him** c'est le prestige plus que le salaire qui a de l'attrait pour lui; **he hasn't got enough ~ for the job** il ne fait pas le poids* pour le poste 2 COMP ► **status report** N (gen, Mil etc) **to make a ~ report on ...** faire le point sur ... ► **status symbol** N (gen) signe m extérieur de (la) réussite; (marking financial success) signe m extérieur de richesse

status quo ['steɪtəs'kwəʊ] N statu quo m inv

statute ['stætjuːt] 1 N (Jur etc) loi f; **by ~** selon la loi; (US Jur) **the ~ of limitations is seven years** au bout de sept ans il y a prescription 2 COMP ► **statute book** N (esp Brit) ≈ code m; **to be on the ~ book** figurer dans les textes de loi, ≈ être dans le code ► **statute law** N droit m écrit

statutorily ['stætjʊtərəlɪ] ADV légalement

statutory ['stætjʊtərɪ] 1 ADJ a (= legal) [duty, powers, provision, right, control] légal; [offence] prévu or défini par la loi; **to have ~ effect** faire force de loi b (pej = token) [woman etc] de service (pej); **I was the ~ pensioner on the committee** j'étais la retraitée-alibi or le retraité de service au comité 2 COMP ► **statutory body** N organisme m de droit public ► **statutory change** N (US Jur) modification f législative ► **statutory corporation** N société f d'État ► **statutory holiday** N jour m férié; **Monday is a ~ holiday** lundi est (un jour) férié ► **statutory maternity pay** N (Brit) allocation f minimum de maternité ► **statutory rape** N (Jur) détournement m de mineur

staunch¹ [stɔːntʃ] VT [+ flow] contenir, arrêter; [+ blood] étancher; [+ wound] étancher le sang de

staunch² [stɔːntʃ] ADJ [*supporter, defender, Republican, Protestant*] ardent; [*friend*] loyal; [*ally*] sûr; [*support*] fidèle

staunchly ['stɔːntʃlɪ] ADV [*oppose*] fermement; [*defend, support*] vigoureusement; [*conservative, Protestant*] résolument

staunchness ['stɔːntʃnɪs] N dévouement *m*, loyauté *f*

stave [steɪv] (*vb: pret, ptp* **stove** *or* **staved**) N [*of barrel etc*] douve *f*; (*Mus*) portée *f*; (*Poetry*) stance *f*, strophe *f*
► **stave in** VT SEP défoncer, enfoncer
► **stave off** VT SEP [+ *danger*] écarter, conjurer; [+ *threat*] dissiper, conjurer; [+ *ruin, disaster, defeat*] éviter, conjurer; [+ *hunger*] tromper; [+ *attack*] parer; **in an attempt to ~ off the time when ...** en essayant de retarder le moment où ...

staves [steɪvz] NPL *of* **staff²**, **staff³**

stay¹ [steɪ] ① N ⓐ séjour *m*; **he is in Rome for a short ~** il est à Rome pour une courte visite *or* un bref séjour; **a ~ in hospital** un séjour à l'hôpital; **will it be a long ~?** est-ce qu'il restera (*or* vous resterez *etc*) longtemps? ⓑ (*Jur*) suspension *f*; **~ of execution** sursis *m* à l'exécution (d'un jugement); **to put a ~ on proceedings** surseoir aux poursuites
② VT ⓐ (= *check*) arrêter; [+ *disease, epidemic*] enrayer; [+ *hunger*] tromper; (= *delay*) retarder; (*Jur*) [+ *judgement*] surseoir à, différer; [+ *proceedings*] suspendre; [+ *decision*] ajourner, remettre; **to ~ one's hand** se retenir ⓑ (= *last out*) [+ *race*] terminer, aller jusqu'au bout de; [+ *distance*] tenir; **to ~ the course** (*Sport*) aller jusqu'au bout; (*fig*) tenir bon, tenir le coup*
③ VI ⓐ (= *remain*) rester, demeurer; **~ there!** restez là! **here I am and here I** ~ j'y suis j'y reste; **to ~ still** ◊ **to ~ put*** ne pas bouger; **to ~ for** *or* **to dinner** rester (à) dîner; **to ~ faithful** rester *or* demeurer fidèle; (*Rad*) **~ tuned!** restez à l'écoute!, ne quittez pas l'écoute!; **to ~ ahead of the others** garder son avance sur les autres; **it is here to ~** c'est bien établi; **he is here to ~** il est là pour de bon; **things can't be allowed to ~ that way** on ne peut pas laisser les choses comme ça; **if the weather ~s fine** si le temps se maintient (au beau); **he ~ed (for) the whole week** il est resté toute la semaine; **he ~ed a year in Paris** il est resté un an à Paris, il a séjourné un an à Paris; **to ~ with a company** [*customers, employees*] rester fidèle à une entreprise; **to ~ off school/work** ne pas aller à l'école/au travail; **to ~ off drugs/alcohol** ne plus prendre de drogue(s)/d'alcool ⓑ (*on visit*) **has she come to ~?** est-ce qu'elle est venue avec l'intention de rester?; **she came to ~ (for) a few weeks** elle est venue passer quelques semaines; **I'm ~ing with my aunt** je loge chez ma tante; **to ~ in a hotel** être à l'hôtel; **where do you ~ when you go to London?** où logez-vous quand vous allez à Londres?; **he was ~ing in Paris when he fell ill** il séjournait à Paris quand il est tombé malade ⓒ (*Scot* = *live permanently*) habiter ⓓ (= *persevere*) tenir; **to ~ to the finish** tenir jusqu'à la ligne d'arrivée; **to ~ with a scheme*** ne pas abandonner un projet; **~ with it!*** tenez bon! ⓔ (*liter* = *pause*) s'arrêter
④ COMP ► **stay-at-home** N, ADJ casanier *m*, -ière *f*, pantouflard(e)* *m(f)* ► **staying power** N résistance *f*, endurance *f*; **he hasn't a lot of ~ing power** il se décourage facilement
► **stay away** VI **he ~ed away for three years** il n'est pas rentré avant trois ans; **he ~ed away from the meeting** il n'est pas allé (*or* venu) à la réunion, il s'est abstenu d'aller à la réunion; **to ~ away from school** ne pas aller à l'école, manquer l'école
► **stay behind** VI rester en arrière; **you'll be-**
hind after school! tu resteras en classe!
► **stay down** VI ⓐ rester en bas; (*bending*) rester baissé; (*lying down*) rester couché; (*under water*) rester sous l'eau; (*fig Scol*) redoubler ⓑ (*food etc*) **nothing he eats will ~ down** il n'assimile rien *or* il ne garde rien de ce qu'il mange
► **stay in** VI ⓐ [*person*] (*at home*) rester à la maison, ne pas sortir; (*Scol*) être en retenue ⓑ [*nail, screw, tooth filling*] tenir
► **stay out** VI ⓐ [*person*] (*away from home*) ne pas rentrer; (= *outside*) rester dehors; **get out and ~ out!** sortez et ne revenez pas!; **he always ~s out late on Fridays** il rentre toujours tard le vendredi; **he ~ed out all night** il n'est pas rentré de la nuit; **don't ~ out after 9 o'clock** rentrez avant 9 heures ⓑ (*Ind: on strike*) rester en grève ⓒ (*fig*) **to ~ out of** [+ *argument*] ne pas se mêler de; [+ *prison*] éviter; **to ~ out of trouble** se tenir tranquille; **you ~ out of this!** mêlez-vous de vos (propres) affaires!
► **stay over** VI s'arrêter (un *or* plusieurs jour(s)), faire une halte; **can you ~ over till Thursday?** est-ce que vous pouvez rester jusqu'à jeudi?
► **stay up** VI ⓐ [*person*] rester debout, ne pas se coucher; **don't ~ up for me** ne m'attendez pas pour aller vous coucher; **you can ~ up to watch the programme** vous pouvez voir l'émission avant de vous coucher; **we always ~ up late on Saturdays** nous veillons *or* nous nous couchons toujours tard le samedi ⓑ (= *not fall*) [*trousers, fence etc*] tenir; **this zip won't ~ up** cette fermeture éclair® ne veut pas rester fermée

stay² [steɪ] ① N (*for pole, flagstaff etc: Naut*) étai *m*, hauban *m*; (*for wall*) étai *m*, étançon *m*; (*fig*) soutien *m*, support *m* ② **stays** † NPL (= *corsets*) corset *m* ③ VT (*also* ~ **up**: *Naut*) haubaner, étayer

stayer ['steɪəʳ] N (= *horse*) stayer *m*, cheval *m* qui a du fond; (= *runner*) coureur *m*, -euse *f* qui a du fond *or* de la résistance physique; **he's a ~** (*Sport*) il a du fond, il est capable d'un effort prolongé; (*fig*) il n'abandonne pas facilement, il va jusqu'au bout de ce qu'il entreprend

STD [ˌestiːˈdiː] ⓐ (*Brit Telec*) (ABBR = **subscriber trunk dialling**) automatique *m*; **to phone ~** téléphoner par l'automatique; **~ code** indicatif *m* de zone ⓑ (ABBR = **sexually transmitted disease**) MST *f*; **~ clinic** ≈ service *m* de (dermato-)vénérologie

stead [sted] N **in my/his** *etc* **~** à ma/sa *etc* place; **to stand sb in good ~** rendre grand service à qn, être très utile à qn

steadfast ['stedfəst] (*liter*) ADJ ⓐ (= *unshakable*) [*person, refusal, belief*] inébranlable; [*loyalty, support*] inébranlable, indéfectible; [*intention, desire*] ferme; [*gaze*] ferme, résolu; **~ in adversity/danger** inébranlable au milieu des infortunes/du danger; **to be ~ in one's belief that ...** rester fermement persuadé que ...; **to be ~ in one's praise of sb/sth** ne pas tarir d'éloges sur qn/qch; **to be ~ in one's opposition to sth** rester fermement opposé à qch ⓑ (= *loyal*) [*person*] constant, loyal; **~ in love** constant en amour

steadfastly ['stedfəstlɪ] ADV [*refuse, reject, deny, maintain*] inébranlablement; **~ loyal** d'une loyauté inébranlable; **to remain ~ at one's post** rester ferme à son poste

steadfastness ['stedfəstnɪs] N fermeté *f*, résolution *f* (*liter*); **~ of purpose** ténacité *f*

Steadicam® ['stedɪkæm] N (*TV*) Steadycam® *m*

steadily ['stedɪlɪ] ADV ⓐ (= *continuously*) [*increase, worsen, improve, work*] régulièrement; [*breathe, beat*] avec régularité; [*advance, rain, sob*] sans interruption; **a ~ increasing number of people** un nombre toujours croissant de personnes; **the poor are ~ getting poorer** les
pauvres deviennent de plus en plus pauvres *or* toujours plus pauvres; **the engine ran ~** le moteur tournait sans à-coups ⓑ [*look at*] (= *without flinching*) sans détourner les yeux; (= *intimidatingly*) droit dans les yeux, avec insistance; [*reply*] (= *calmly*) fermement, avec fermeté ⓒ [*firmly*] [*walk*] d'un pas ferme; [*hold, grasp*] d'une main ferme

steadiness ['stedɪnɪs] N (*NonC*) ⓐ (= *regularity*) [*of progress, supply, pace, breath, beat, demand*] régularité *f*; [*of prices, sales, market, economy*] stabilité *f* ⓑ (= *composure*) [*of voice*] fermeté *f*; **the ~ of her look** *or* **gaze** (= *unflinching*) son regard qui ne cillait pas; (= *intimidating*) l'insistance de son regard; **the ~ of his game** la régularité de son jeu; **~ of nerve** sang-froid *m*; **~ of purpose** détermination *f* inébranlable ⓒ (= *firm*) [*of chair, table, ladder, boat*] stabilité *f*; [*of hand*] (*in drawing*) sûreté *f*; (*in holding*) fermeté *f*; [*gait*] fermeté *f* ⓓ (= *dependability*) [*of person*] sérieux *m*

steady ['stedɪ] ① ADJ ⓐ (= *regular*) [*supply, rain, breathing, beat, demand, income*] régulier; [*prices, sales, market*] stable; [*temperature, wind*] constant; **to make ~ progress** progresser régulièrement, faire des progrès constants; **there was a ~ downpour for three hours** il n'a pas cessé de pleuvoir pendant trois heures; **at a ~ pace** à une allure régulière; **a ~ stream** *or* **flow of sth** un flux régulier de qch; **we were doing a ~ 60km/h** nous roulions à une vitesse régulière *or* constante de 60 km/h; **to hold** *or* **keep sth** ~ [+ *prices, demand*] stabiliser qch → **1c**; **a ~ job** un emploi stable; **~ boyfriend** petit ami *m* attitré; **~ girlfriend** petite amie *f* attitrée; **to have a ~ relationship with sb** avoir une relation stable avec qn ⓑ (= *composed*) [*voice*] ferme; [*nerves*] solide; [*look, gaze*] (= *unflinching*) calme; (= *intimidating*) soutenu, insistant; **to look at sb with a ~ gaze** ◊ **to give sb a ~ look** (= *unflinching*) regarder qn sans détourner les yeux; (= *intimidating*) regarder qn droit dans les yeux *or* avec insistance; **he plays a very ~ game** il a un jeu très régulier ⓒ (= *firm*) [*chair, table*] stable, solide; [*boat*] stable; [*hand*] (*in drawing*) sûr; (*in holding*) ferme; **to hold** *or* **keep sth ~** maintenir fermement qch → **1a**; **to hold ~** (*on one's feet*) être solide sur ses jambes; **the car is not very ~ on corners** la voiture ne tient pas très bien la route dans les tournants ⓓ (= *dependable*) [*person*] sérieux
② EXCL ⓐ (*Brit: also* ~ **on!**) (= *be careful*) doucement!; (= *calm down*) du calme! → **ready** ⓑ (*Naut*) **~ as she goes!** ◊ **keep her ~!** comme ça droit!
③ ADV †* **they've been going ~ for six months** ils sortent ensemble depuis six mois; **to go ~ with sb** sortir avec qn
④ N* (*male*) copain* *m*; (*female*) copine* *f*
⑤ VT [+ *wobbling object*] assujettir; [+ *chair, table*] (*with hand*) maintenir; (= *wedge*) caler; [+ *nervous person, horse*] calmer; **to ~ o.s.** se remettre d'aplomb; **to ~ one's nerves** se calmer (les nerfs); **to have a ~ing effect on sb** (= *make less nervous*) calmer qn; (= *make less wild*) assagir qn, mettre du plomb dans la cervelle de qn*
⑥ VI (*also* ~ **up**) (= *regain balance*) se remettre d'aplomb; (= *grow less nervous*) se calmer; (= *grow less wild*) se ranger, s'assagir; [*prices, market*] se stabiliser
⑦ COMP ► **steady-state theory** N (*Phys*) théorie *f* de la création continue

steak [steɪk] ① N (= *beef*) bifteck *m*, steak *m*; (*of other meat*) tranche *f*; (*of fish*) tranche *f*, darne *f* → **fillet, frying, rumpsteak, stew 3**
② COMP ► **steak and kidney pie** N tourte *f* à la viande de bœuf et aux rognons ► **steak and kidney pudding** N pudding

m à la viande de bœuf et aux rognons ► **steak knife** N (*pl* **steak knives**) couteau *m* à viande *or* à steak

steakhouse ['steɪkhaʊs] N ≈ grill-room *m*

steal [stiːl] (*pret* **stole**, *ptp* **stolen**) **1** VT [+ *object, property*] voler, dérober (*liter*) (**from sb** à qn); (*fig*) [+ *kiss*] voler (**from sb** à qn); **he stole a book from the library** il a volé un livre à la bibliothèque; **he stole money from the till/drawer** *etc* il a volé de l'argent dans la caisse/dans le tiroir *etc*; **to ~ the credit for sth** s'attribuer tout le mérite de qch; **to ~ a glance at ...** jeter un coup d'œil furtif à ...; **to ~ a march on sb*** gagner *or* prendre qn de vitesse; (*Theat, also fig*) **to ~ the show from sb** ravir la vedette à qn; (*fig*) **he stole the show** il n'y en a eu que pour lui, on n'a eu d'yeux que pour lui; **to ~ sb's thunder** éclipser qn en lui coupant l'herbe sous le pied; (*Brit*) **Labour have stolen the Tories' clothes** les travaillistes se sont appropriés les idées des conservateurs

2 **a** VI voler; (*Bible*) **thou shalt not ~** tu ne voleras point **b** (= *move silently*) **to ~ up/down/out** *etc* monter/descendre/sortir *etc* à pas furtifs *or* feutrés *or* de loup; **he stole into the room** il s'est glissé *or* faufilé dans la pièce; (*fig*) **a smile stole across her lips** un sourire erra sur ses lèvres; **a tear stole down her cheek** une larme furtive glissa sur sa joue; **the light was ~ing through the shutters** la lumière filtrait à travers les volets

3 N (*US* = *theft*) vol *m*; (*fig* = *bargain*) **it's a ~*** c'est une bonne affaire

► **steal away** VI s'esquiver **2** VT SEP [+ *child etc*] prendre, enlever (**from sb** à qn); [+ *sb's husband*] voler, prendre (**from sb** à qn); [+ *sb's affections*] détourner

stealing ['stiːlɪŋ] N (*NonC*) vol *m*; **~ is wrong** c'est mal de voler

stealth [stelθ] **1** N **by ~** furtivement, à la dérobée **2** COMP ► **Stealth bomber** N (*Aviat*) bombardier *m* furtif

stealthily ['stelθɪlɪ] ADV [*move, remove, exchange*] furtivement, à la dérobée; [*creep, enter, leave*] furtivement, à pas furtifs

stealthiness ['stelθɪnɪs] N caractère *m* furtif, manière *f* furtive

stealthy ['stelθɪ] ADJ furtif

steam [stiːm] **1** N (*NonC*) vapeur *f*; (= *condensation: on window etc*) buée *f*; **it works by ~** ça marche *or* fonctionne à la vapeur; (*Naut*) **full ~ ahead!** en avant toute!; (*fig*) **the building project is going full ~ ahead** le projet de construction va de l'avant à plein régime; **to get up** *or* **pick up ~** [*train, ship*] prendre de la vitesse; [*driver etc*] faire monter la pression; (*fig*) [*worker, programme, project*] démarrer vraiment* (*fig*); (*fig*) **when she gets up** *or* **picks up ~ she can** ... quand elle s'y met *or* quand elle est lancée elle peut ...; (*fig*) **to run out of ~** [*speaker, worker*] s'essouffler (*fig*); [*programme, project*] tourner court, s'essouffler; **the strike is running out of ~** le mouvement de grève commence à s'essouffler; (*fig*) **under one's own ~** par ses propres moyens; (*fig*) **to let off** *or* **blow off ~*** (= *energy*) se défouler*; (= *anger*) épancher sa bile

2 VT (*for cleaning, disinfecting purposes*) passer à la vapeur; (*Culin*) cuire à la vapeur; **to ~ open an envelope** décacheter une enveloppe à la vapeur; **to ~ off a stamp** décoller un timbre à la vapeur

3 VI **a** [*kettle, liquid, horse, wet clothes*] fumer **b to ~ along/away** *etc* [*steamship, train*] avancer/partir *etc*; (* *fig*) [*person, car*] avancer/partir* à toute allure*; **they were ~ing along at 12 knots** ils filaient 12 nœuds; **the ship ~ed up the river** le vapeur remontait la rivière; **the train ~ed out of the station** le train est sorti de la gare dans un nuage de fumée; **to ~ ahead** [*steamship*] avancer;* [*person*]

avancer à toute vapeur*; (* *fig* = *make great progress*) faire des progrès à pas de géant

4 COMP [*boiler, iron, turbine*] à vapeur; [*bath*] de vapeur ► **steam-driven** ADJ à vapeur ► **steamed pudding** N pudding *m* cuit à la vapeur ► **steamed up*** ADJ (*fig*) **to get ~ed up** se mettre dans tous ses états (**about sth** à propos de qch); **don't get so ~ed up about it!** ne te mets pas dans tous tes états pour ça! ► **steam engine** N (*Rail*) locomotive *f* à vapeur ► **steam heat** N chaleur *f* fournie par la vapeur ► **steam organ** N orgue *m* à vapeur ► **steam room** N sauna *m* ► **steam shovel** N (*US*) excavateur *m*

► **steam up** **1** VI [*window, mirror*] se couvrir de buée; [*bathroom*] se remplir de buée **2** VT SEP embuer **3** **~ed up*** ADJ → **steam**

steamboat ['stiːmbəʊt] N (bateau *m* à) vapeur *m*

steamer ['stiːmə*r*] N **a** (*Naut*) (bateau *m* à) vapeur *m*; (= *liner*) paquebot *m* **b** (= *saucepan*) couscoussier *m*

steaming ['stiːmɪŋ] ADJ **a** (*also* **~ hot**) fumant **b** (* = *angry*) [*person*] fumasse*; [*letter*] furibond* **c** (*Scot** = *drunk*) bourré*

steamroller ['stiːmrəʊlə*r*] **1** N rouleau *m* compresseur **2** VT (*fig*) [+ *opposition etc*] écraser, briser; [+ *obstacles*] aplanir; **to ~ a bill through Parliament** faire approuver un projet de loi au Parlement sans tenir compte de l'opposition **3** COMP ► **steamroller tactics** NPL technique *f* du rouleau compresseur

steamship ['stiːmʃɪp] N paquebot *m*; **~ company** ligne *f* de paquebots

steamy ['stiːmɪ] ADJ **a** (= *humid*) [*room, city, air*] plein de vapeur; [*window*] embué **b** (* = *erotic*) [*affair, film, novel*] torride

steed [stiːd] N (*liter*) coursier *m* (*liter*)

steel [stiːl] **1** N (*NonC*) acier *m*; (*fig*) **to be made of ~** avoir une volonté de fer; **nerves of ~** nerfs *mpl* d'acier → **stainless** **b** (= *sharpener*) aiguisoir *m*, fusil *m*; (*for striking sparks*) briquet† *m*, fusil† *m*; (*liter* = *sword, dagger*) fer *m* → **cold**

2 VT (*fig*) **to ~ o.s.** *or* **one's heart to do** s'armer de courage pour faire; **to ~ o.s. against** se cuirasser contre

3 COMP (= *made of steel*) [*knife, tool*] en acier; (*Ind*) [*manufacture*] de l'acier; (*gen, also of steel production*) sidérurgique; [*dispute, strike*] des sidérurgistes, des (ouvriers) métallurgistes; (*St Ex*) [*shares, prices*] de l'acier ► **steel band** N steel band *m* ► **steel-clad** ADJ bardé de fer ► **steel engraving** N gravure *f* sur acier ► **steel grey** ADJ gris acier *inv*, gris métallisé *inv* ► **steel guitar** N steel-guitar *f*, guitare *f* à cordes métalliques ► **steel helmet** N casque *m* ► **steel industry** N sidérurgie *f*, industrie *f* sidérurgique ► **steel maker**, **steel manufacturer** N métallurgiste *m*, aciériste *m* ► **steel mill** N = **steelworks** ► **steel-plated** ADJ revêtu d'acier ► **steel tape** N (*Carpentry etc*) mètre *m* à ruban métallique ► **steel wool** N (*NonC*) (*for floors*) paille *f* de fer; (*for saucepans*) tampon *m* métallique

steelworker ['stiːlwɜːkə*r*] N (ouvrier *m*, -ière *f*) sidérurgiste *mf*, (ouvrier *m*, -ière *f*) métallurgiste *mf*

steelworks ['stiːlwɜːks] N aciérie *f*

steely ['stiːlɪ] **1** ADJ **a** [*sky*] (= *blue*) bleu acier *inv*; (= *grey*) gris acier *inv*; [*colour*] acier *inv*; **b** (= *grim*) [*person, smile*] dur et menaçant; [*look, stare*] d'acier; [*determination*] inébranlable; [*refusal, attitude*] inébranlable, inflexible; **his look of ~ concentration** son regard d'intense concentration **c** (= *like steel*) [*material, substance*] dur comme l'acier; [*appearance*] de l'acier **2** COMP ► **steely blue** ADJ bleu acier *inv* ► **steely-eyed** ADJ au regard d'acier ► **steely grey** ADJ gris acier *inv*, gris métallisé *inv* ► **steely-hearted** ADJ au cœur de pierre

steelyard ['stiːljɑːd] N balance *f* romaine

steep¹ [stiːp] ADJ **a** [*slope, incline, road, street, stairs*] raide; [*hill, bank*] escarpé; [*cliff*] abrupt; [*roof*] en pente; [*descent*] rapide; [*ascent, climb*] rude; [*dive*] à la verticale; **a ~ path** un raidillon, un sentier raide **b** (= *great*) [*rise, fall*] fort **c** (* = *expensive*) [*price, fees*] élevé, raide*; [*bill*] salé* **d** (*Brit** = *unreasonable*) **that's** *or* **it's a bit ~** or **a bit too raide*** *or* **fort***; **it's a bit ~ to expect us to do that!** c'est un peu raide* *or* fort* de s'attendre à ce qu'on fasse ça!

steep² [stiːp] **1** VT (*in water, dye etc*) tremper (**in** dans); [+ *washing*] faire tremper, mettre à tremper; (*Culin*) macérer, mariner (**in** dans); (*fig*) **~ed in ignorance/vice** croupissant dans l'ignorance/le vice; **~ed in prejudice** imbu de préjugés; **a town ~ed in history** une ville imprégnée d'histoire; **a scholar ~ed in the classics** un érudit imprégné des auteurs classiques **2** VI [*clothes etc*] tremper; (*Culin*) macérer, mariner

steepen ['stiːpən] VI (*lit*) [*slope, ground*] devenir plus raide; (*fig*) [*slump, decline*] s'accentuer

steeple ['stiːpl] N clocher *m*, flèche *f*

steeplechase ['stiːpltʃeɪs] N steeple (-chase) *m*

steeplechaser ['stiːpltʃeɪsə*r*] N (= *horse*) coureur *m*, -euse *f* de steeple

steeplechasing ['stiːpltʃeɪsɪŋ] N steeple (-chase) *m*

steeplejack ['stiːpldʒæk] N réparateur *m* de hautes cheminées et de clochers

steeply ['stiːplɪ] ADV **a** (= *precipitously*) [*rise, climb, fall, drop*] en pente raide; **to bank ~** faire un virage serré sur l'aile; **the lawn slopes ~ down to the river** la pelouse descend en pente raide vers la rivière; **~ sloping roof/land** toit *m*/terrain *m* en pente raide; **~ terraced vineyards** des vignobles en terrasses escarpées **b** (= *greatly*) [*to rise/fall* ~] [*prices, costs, profits*] monter en flèche/baisser fortement

steepness ['stiːpnɪs] N [*of road etc*] pente *f* (raide); [*of slope*] abrupt *m*

steer¹ [stɪə*r*] N (= *ox*) bœuf *m*; (*esp US: castrated*) bouvillon *m*

steer² [stɪə*r*] **1** VT **a** (= *handle controls of*) [+ *ship*] gouverner; [+ *boat*] barrer **b** (= *move, direct*) [+ *ship, car*] diriger (**towards** vers); (*fig*) [+ *person*] guider; [+ *conversation*] diriger; (*Naut*) **to ~ a** *or* **one's course to** faire route vers *or* sur; **to ~ one's way through a crowd** se frayer un passage à travers une foule; **he ~ed her over to the bar** il l'a guidée vers le bar; (*fig*) **he ~ed me into a good job** c'est lui qui m'a permis de trouver un bon boulot*

2 VI (*Naut*) tenir le gouvernail *or* la barre, gouverner; **to ~ by the stars** se guider sur les étoiles; **he ~ed for the lighthouse** il a fait route vers *or* il a mis le cap sur le phare; **~ due north!** cap au nord!; **this car/boat doesn't ~ well** cette voiture n'a pas une bonne direction/ce bateau gouverne mal; **to ~ clear of sth** (*Naut*) passer au large de qch; (*Aut*) passer à l'écart de qch; (*fig*) **to ~ clear of sb/sth** éviter qn/qch

3 N (*US** = *tip*) tuyau* *m*, conseil *m*; **a bum ~** un tuyau qui ne vaut rien

steerage ['stɪərɪdʒ] (*Naut*) **1** N entrepont *m* **2** ADV dans l'entrepont, en troisième classe

steerageway ['stɪərɪdʒweɪ] N erre *f*

steering ['stɪərɪŋ] **1** N (*NonC*) (*Aut*) (= *action*) conduite *f*; (= *mechanism*) direction *f*; (*Naut*) conduite *f*, pilotage *m* **2** COMP ► **steering arm** N (*Aut*) bras *m* de direction ► **steering column** N (*Aut*) colonne *f* de direction ► **steering committee** N (*Admin etc*) comité *m* de pilotage ► **steering gear** N (*Aut*) boîte *f* de direction; (*Naut*) servomoteur *m* de barre *or* de gouvernail; (*Aviat*) direction *f* ► **steering lock** N (*Aut*) (*when driving*) rayon *m* de braquage ; (= *anti-theft device*) antivol *m* de direction ► **steering system** N (*Aut*) direction *f* ► **steering wheel** N (*Aut*) volant *m* ; (*Naut*) barre *f* à roue

steersman ['stɪəzmən] N (*pl* **-men**) (*Naut*) timonier *m*, homme *m* de barre

stellar ['stelər] ADJ a (*Astron*) stellaire b (*Cine, Theat etc*) [*person, cast*] brillant ; [*talent, quality, reputation*] sublime c (= *superb*) [*profits, education*] excellent

stem¹ [stem] 1 VT a (= *stop*) [+ *flow*] contenir, endiguer ; [+ *flood, river*] contenir, endiguer ; [+ *course of disease*] enrayer, juguler ; [+ *attack*] juguler, stopper ; (*fig*) **to ~ the course of events** endiguer la marche des événements ; (*fig*) **to ~ the tide** *or* **flow of** ... endiguer (le flot de) ... b [+ *ski*] ramener or écarter en chasse-neige 2 COMP ► **stem parallel** N (*Ski*) stem(m) *m* parallèle ► **stem turn** N (*Ski*) virage *m* en stem(m) *m*

▼ **stem²** [stem] 1 N a [*of flower, plant*] tige *f* ; [*of tree*] tronc *m* ; [*of fruit, leaf*] queue *f* ; [*of glass*] pied *m* ; [*of tobacco pipe*] tuyau *m* ; [*of feather*] tige *f*, tuyau *m* ; (*in handwriting, Printing: of letter*) hampe *f* ; (*Mus: of note*) queue *f* ; (*Ling: of word*) radical *m* b (*Naut*) (= *timber*) étrave *f* ; (= *part of ship*) avant *m*, proue *f* ; **from ~ to stern** de bout en bout 2 VI **to ~ from** ... provenir de ..., découler de ..., dériver de ... 3 COMP ► **stem ginger** N gingembre *m* confit ► **stem-winder** N montre *f* à remontoir

-stemmed [stemd] ADJ (*in compounds*) **short-/thick-stemmed** [*pipe*] à tuyau court/épais ; **thin-/green-stemmed** [*plant*] à tige fine/verte ; **slim-/thick-stemmed** [*glass*] au pied fin/épais

stench [stentʃ] N puanteur *f*, odeur *f* nauséabonde *or* fétide

stencil ['stensl] 1 N (*of metal, cardboard*) pochoir *m* ; (*of paper*) poncif *m* ; (*in typing etc*) stencil *m* ; (= *decoration*) peinture *f* or décoration *f* au pochoir ; (= *Typing*) **to cut a ~** préparer un stencil 2 VT [+ *lettering, name*] peindre or marquer au pochoir ; (*in typing etc*) [+ *document*] polycopier, tirer au stencil

Sten gun ['stengʌn] N (*Brit Hist*) mitraillette *f* légère

steno* ['stenəʊ] N (*US*) = **stenographer, stenography**

stenographer [ste'nɒgrəfər] N sténographe *mf*

stenography [ste'nɒgrəfi] N (*US*) sténographie *f*

stentorian [sten'tɔːrɪən] ADJ (*liter*) [*voice, tones*] de stentor ; [*shout*] puissant

step [step] 1 N a (= *movement, sound, track*) pas *m* ; **to take a ~ back/forward** faire un pas en arrière/en avant ; **with slow ~s** à pas lents ; (*lit, fig*) **at every ~** à chaque pas ; **~ by ~** (*lit*) pas à pas ; (*fig*) petit à petit → **4** ; **he didn't move a ~** il n'a pas bougé d'un pas ; **we heard ~s in the lounge** nous avons entendu des pas or un bruit de pas dans le salon ; **we followed his ~s in the snow** nous avons suivi (la trace de) ses pas dans la neige ; (*fig*) **to follow in sb's ~s** marcher sur les pas *or* suivre les brisées de qn ; (*fig = distance*) **it's a good ~*** *or* **quite a ~* to the village** il y a un bon bout de chemin or ça fait une bonne trotte* d'ici au village ; (*fig*) **every ~ of the way** [*complain etc*] continuellement, constamment ; [*argue, object*] point par point ; **I'll fight this decision every ~ of the way** je combattrai cette décision jusqu'au bout ; **to be** *or* **stay one ~ ahead of sb** avoir une longueur d'avance sur qn → **retrace, watch²** b (*fig*) pas *m* (**towards** vers) ; (= *measure*) disposition *f*, mesure *f* ; **it is a great ~ for the nation to take** c'est pour la nation un grand pas à faire or à franchir ; **the first ~s in one's career** les premiers pas or les débuts *mpl* de sa carrière ; **it's a ~ up in his career** c'est une promotion pour lui ; **to take ~s (to do)** prendre

des dispositions *or* des mesures (pour faire) ; **to take legal ~s** avoir recours à la justice, engager des poursuites (**to do** pour faire) ; **what's the next ~?** qu'est-ce qu'il faut faire maintenant *or* ensuite ? ; **the first ~ is to decide ...** la première chose à faire est de décider ... → **false** c (*NonC: in marching, dancing*) pas *m* ; **a waltz ~** un pas de valse ; **to keep (in) ~** (*in marching*) marcher au pas ; (*in dance*) danser en mesure ; (*lit, fig*) **to keep ~ with sb** ne pas se laisser distancer par qn ; (*in dance*) danser en mesure ; **to fall into ~** se mettre au pas ; **to get out of ~** rompre le pas ; (*fig*) **to be in ~ with** [+ *person*] agir conformément à, être au diapason de ; [+ *regulations*] être conforme à ; **to be/march etc out of ~** ne pas être/marcher *etc* au pas ; (*Mil*) **to break ~** rompre le pas ; (*fig*) **to be out of ~ with** [+ *person*] être déphasé par rapport à ; [+ *regulations*] ne pas être conforme à ; **the unions and their leaders are out of ~** il y a déphasage entre les syndicats et leurs dirigeants d (= *stair*) marche *f* (*also Climbing*) ; (= *doorstep*) pas *m* de la porte, seuil *m* ; (*on bus etc*) marchepied *m* ; (**flight of**) **~s** (*indoors*) escalier *m* ; (*outdoors*) perron *m*, escalier *m* ; (*Brit*) (**pair of**) **~s** escabeau *m* ; **mind the ~** attention à la marche e (*also* ~ **aerobics**) step *m* 2 VT a (= *place at intervals*) échelonner b (*Naut*) [+ *mast*] arborer, mettre dans son emplanture 3 VI **~ this way** venez par ici ; **to ~ off sth** descendre de qch, quitter qch ; **he ~ped into the car/onto the pavement** il est monté dans la voiture/sur le trottoir ; **he ~ped into his slippers/trousers** il a mis ses pantoufles/son pantalon ; (*Brit fig*) **to ~ into sb's boots** succéder à qn ; **to ~ on sth** marcher sur qch ; **to ~ on the brakes** donner un coup de frein ; (*US Aut*) **to ~ on the gas*** appuyer sur le champignon* ; (*fig*) **~ on it!*** dépêche-toi !, grouille-toi !* ; **to ~ out of line** (*gen*) sortir des rangs ; (*morally*) s'écarter du droit chemin ; **to ~ over sth** enjamber qch → **shoe** 4 COMP ► **step aerobics** N (*NonC: Sport*) step *m* ► **step-by-step** ADJ [*instructions*] point par point ► **step-parent** N beau-père *m*/belle-mère *f* ; **~-parents** beaux-parents *mpl* ► **stepped-up** ADJ [*campaign, efforts*] intensifié ; [*production, sales*] augmenté, accru ► **stepping stone** N (*lit*) pierre *f* de gué ; (*fig*) marchepied *m*

► **step aside** VI (*lit*) faire un pas de côté ; (= *give up position*) s'effacer

► **step back** VI (*lit*) faire un pas en arrière, reculer ; (*fig*) **we ~ped back into Shakespeare's time** nous nous sommes retrouvés à l'époque de Shakespeare

► **step down** VI (*lit*) descendre (**from** de) ; (*fig*) se retirer, se désister (**in favour of sb** en faveur de qn)

► **step forward** VI faire un pas en avant ; (= *show o.s., make o.s. known*) s'avancer, se faire connaître ; (= *volunteer*) se présenter

► **step in** VI entrer ; (*fig*) intervenir, s'interposer

► **step inside** VI entrer

► **step out** VI (= *go outside*) sortir ; (= *hurry*) allonger le pas ; (*US* *fig*) faire la bombe* 2 VT SEP (= *measure*) [+ *distance*] mesurer en comptant les pas

► **step up** 1 VI **to ~ up to sb/sth** s'approcher de qn/qch 2 VT SEP [+ *production, sales*] augmenter, accroître ; [+ *campaign*] intensifier ; [+ *attempts, efforts*] intensifier, multiplier ; (*Elec*) [+ *current*] augmenter 3 **~ped-up** ADJ → **step**

stepbrother ['step,brʌðər] N demi-frère *m*

stepchild ['steptʃaɪld] N beau-fils *m*, belle-fille *f*

stepchildren ['step,tʃɪldrən] NPL beaux-enfants *mpl*

stepdaughter ['step,dɔːtər] N belle-fille *f*

stepfather ['step,fɑːðər] N beau-père *m*

Stephen ['stiːvn] N Étienne *m*, Stéphane *m*

stepladder ['step,lædər] N escabeau *m*

stepmother ['step,mʌðər] N belle-mère *f*

steppe [step] N steppe *f*

Step Reebok® [,step'riːbɒk] N step *m*

stepsister ['step,sɪstər] N demi-sœur *f*

stepson ['stepsʌn] N beau-fils *m*

stereo ['stɪərɪəʊ] 1 N a (ABBR = **stereophonic**) (= *system*) stéréo *f*, stéréophonie *f* ; (= *record player/radio etc*) chaîne *f*/radio *f* etc stéréophonique or stéréo *inv* ; (= *record/tape etc*) disque *m*/bande *f* magnétique etc stéréophonique or stéréo ; **recorded in ~** enregistré en stéréo(phonie) 2 ABBR = **stereoscope, stereotype** etc 2 COMP [*record player, cassette recorder, tape etc*] stéréophonique, stéréo *inv* ; [*broadcast, recording*] en stéréophonie ► **stereo effect** N effet *m* stéréo(phonique) ► **stereo sound** N son *m* stéréo

stereo... ['stɪərɪəʊ] PREF stéréo...

stereochemistry [,stɪərɪə'kemɪstrɪ] N stéréochimie *f*

stereogram ['stɪərɪəgræm], **stereograph** ['stɪərɪəgrɑːf] N stéréogramme *m*

stereophonic [,stɪərɪə'fɒnɪk] ADJ stéréophonique

stereoscope ['stɪərɪəskəʊp] N stéréoscope *m*

stereoscopic [,stɪərɪəs'kɒpɪk] ADJ stéréoscopique

stereoscopy [,stɪərɪ'ɒskəpɪ] N stéréoscopie *f*

stereotype ['stɪərɪətaɪp] 1 N a (*fig*) stéréotype *m* b (*Typ*) cliché *m* ; (= *process*) clichage *m* 2 VT a (*fig*) stéréotyper b (*Printing*) clicher

stereotypical [,stɪərɪə'tɪpɪkl] ADJ stéréotypé

stereovision [,stɪərɪə'vɪʒən] N vision *f* stéréoscopique

sterile ['steraɪl] ADJ (*all senses*) stérile

sterility [ste'rɪlɪtɪ] N stérilité *f*

sterilization [,sterɪlaɪ'zeɪʃən] N stérilisation *f*

sterilize ['sterɪlaɪz] VT stériliser

sterling ['stɜːlɪŋ] 1 N (*NonC*) a (*Econ*) livres *fpl* sterling *inv* b (*also* ~ **silver**) argent *m* fin or de bon aloi 2 ADJ a (*Metal*) [*gold, silver*] fin, de bon aloi b (*also* ~ **silver**) [*bracelet*] d'argent fin *or* de bon aloi c (*esp Brit* = *excellent*) [*qualities, work, service, efforts*] remarquable ; [*advice*] excellent ; **a man of ~ worth** un homme de très grande valeur d (*Fin*) **pound ~** livre *f* sterling *inv* 3 COMP ► **the sterling area, the sterling bloc** N la zone sterling

stern¹ [stɜːn] N (*Naut*) arrière *m*, poupe *f* ;* [*of horse etc*] croupe *f* ;* [*of person*] derrière *m*, postérieur* *m* ; (*Naut*) ~ **foremost** par l'arrière, en marche arrière → **stem²**

stern² [stɜːn] ADJ [*person, look, measure, rebuke, test*] sévère ; [*task*] rude ; [*opposition, resistance*] farouche ; [*warning*] sévère, sérieux ; **to be made of ~er stuff** être d'une autre trempe

sterna ['stɜːnə] NPL of **sternum**

sternly ['stɜːnlɪ] ADV a (= *severely*) [*say, rebuke*] sévèrement ; [*look at*] d'un air sévère ; [*warn*] sur un ton comminatoire ; **to deal ~ with sb/sth** se montrer sévère à l'égard de qn/qch ; **a ~ worded statement** une déclaration au ton comminatoire ; **a ~ factual account** un récit rigoureux basé sur les faits b (= *firmly*) [*forbid*] strictement ; [*oppose*] farouchement ; [*resist*] avec opiniâtreté

sternness ['stɜːnnɪs] N [*of person, look, speech, measure, reprimand, test*] sévérité *f* ; [*of task*] difficulté *f* ; [*of opposition, resistance*] fermeté *f*

Sterno® ['stɜːnəʊ] (*US*) 1 N ≈ méta® *m* 2 COMP ► **Sterno can** N récipient pour tablette de méta

sternum ['stɜːnəm] N (*pl* **sternums** *or* **sterna**) sternum *m*

► LANGUAGE IN USE: **stem** 17.1

steroid ['stɪərɔɪd] N stéroïde m

stertorous ['stɜːtərəs] ADJ (frm) [breathing] stertoreux

stet [stet] [1] IMPERS VB (Typ) bon, à maintenir [2] VT maintenir

stethoscope ['steθəskəʊp] N stéthoscope m

Stetson® ['stetsən] N Stetson® m

stevedore ['stiːvɪdɔːʳ] N arrimeur m, débardeur m, docker m

Steven ['stiːvn] N Étienne m

stew [stjuː] [1] N (meat) ragoût m; (rabbit, hare) civet m; **to be/get in a ~*** (= trouble) être/se mettre dans le pétrin*; (= worry) être/se mettre dans tous ses états → **Irish** [2] VT [+ meat] (faire) cuire en ragoût, faire en daube; [+ rabbit, hare] cuire en civet; [+ fruit] faire cuire; **~ed fruit** (gen) fruits mpl cuits; (mushy) **~ed apples/rhubarb** etc compote f de pommes/de rhubarbe etc; (fig = drunk) **to be ~ed*** être pinté* [3] VI [meat] cuire en ragoût or à l'étouffée; [fruit] cuire; [tea] devenir trop infusé; (fig) **to let sb ~ in his own juice** laisser qn cuire or mijoter dans son jus [4] COMP ▶ **stewing steak** N bœuf m à braiser

steward ['stjuːəd] N (on ship, plane) steward m; (on estate etc) intendant m, régisseur m; (in club, college) intendant m, économe m; (at meeting) membre m du service d'ordre; (at dance) organisateur m; (at meeting etc) **the ~s** le service d'ordre → **shop**

stewardess ['stjuːədes] N hôtesse f

stewardship ['stjuːədʃɪp] N (= duties) intendance f; **under his ~** (in club, college) quand il était intendant or économe; (on estate) quand il était intendant or régisseur

stewpan ['stjuːpæn], **stewpot** ['stjuːpɒt] N cocotte f

stg (Fin) ABBR = **sterling**

stick [stɪk]

vb: pret, ptp **stuck**	
[1] NOUN	[4] INTRANSITIVE VERB
[2] PLURAL NOUN	[5] COMPOUNDS
[3] TRANSITIVE VERB	[6] PHRASAL VERBS

[1] NOUN

[a] = **length of wood** bâton m; (= twig) petite branche f, brindille f; (= walking stick) canne f; (= stake: for peas, flowers etc) bâton m, tuteur m; (taller) rame f; (for lollipop etc) bâton m; (Mil, Mus) baguette f; (Aviat = joystick) manche m à balai; (Hockey, Lacrosse) crosse f; (Ice Hockey) stick m; **a few ~s of furniture** quelques pauvres meubles; **every ~ of furniture** chaque meuble; (fig) **to carry a big ~** user du bras long; (fig) **to use** or **wield the big ~** manier la trique; (Pol) faire de l'autoritarisme; **the policy of the big ~** la politique du bâton; (fig) **to find a ~ to beat sb with** profiter de l'occasion pour s'en prendre à qn; (fig) **to get (hold of) the wrong end of the ~** mal comprendre; (US fig) **to get on the ~*** s'y coller*, s'y mettre

[b] of chalk, charcoal, sealing wax, candy bâton m, morceau m; [of dynamite] bâton m; [of chewing gum] tablette f, palette f (Can); [of celery] branche f; [of rhubarb] tige f; **a ~ of bombs** un chapelet de bombes; **a ~ of parachutists** un groupe de saut

[c] esp Brit* fig = criticism critiques fpl désobligeantes; **to give sb a lot of ~** éreinter qn (for, over à propos de); **to take** or **get a lot of ~** se faire éreinter (for, over à propos de)

[d] Brit* = person **he is a dull** or **dry old ~** il est rasoir*; **he's a funny old ~** c'est un numéro*

[e] Drugs* stick m

[2] **sticks** PLURAL NOUN

[a] = **firewood** petit bois m

[b] Sport = **hurdles** haies fpl

[c] pej = **backwoods** (out) **in the ~s*** en pleine cambrousse*

[d] **one summer they upped ~s and left for Canada*** un été, ils ont tout plaqué* et sont partis au Canada

[3] TRANSITIVE VERB

[a] = **thrust, stab** [+ pin, needle, fork] piquer, planter (into dans); [+ knife, dagger, bayonet] plonger, planter (into dans); [+ spade, rod] planter, enfoncer (into dans); **to ~ a pin through sth** transpercer qch avec une épingle; **I stuck the needle into my finger** je me suis piqué le doigt avec l'aiguille; **we found this place by ~ing a pin in the map** nous avons trouvé ce coin en plantant une épingle au hasard sur la carte; **a board stuck with drawing pins/nails** un panneau couvert de punaises/hérissé de clous; **to ~ a pig** égorger un cochon; **to squeal like a stuck pig** brailler comme un cochon qu'on égorge

[b] * = **put** mettre; (inside sth) mettre, fourrer*; **he stuck it on the shelf/under the table** il l'a mis sur l'étagère/sous la table; **to ~ sth into a drawer** mettre or fourrer* qch dans un tiroir; **to ~ one's hands in one's pockets** mettre or fourrer* ses mains dans ses poches; **he stuck his finger into the hole** il a mis or fourré* son doigt dans le trou; **he stuck the lid on the box** il a mis le couvercle sur la boîte; **he stuck his head through the window/round the door** il a passé la tête par la fenêtre/dans l'embrasure de la porte; **I'll have to ~ a button on that shirt** il faudra que je mette un bouton à cette chemise; **he had stuck £30 on the price** il avait majoré le prix de 30 livres; **to ~ an advertisement in the paper** mettre or passer une annonce dans le journal; **they stuck him on the committee** ils l'ont mis or collé* au comité; (fig) **you know where you can ~ that!** ◊ ~ **it up your ass!** tu sais où tu peux te le mettre?*; **she told him to ~ his job** elle lui a dit d'aller se faire voir* avec son boulot*

[c] with glue etc coller; **to ~ a poster on the wall/a door** coller une affiche au mur/sur une porte; **to ~ a stamp on a letter** coller un timbre sur une lettre; "~ **no bills**" « défense d'afficher »; **it was stuck fast** c'était bien collé or indécollable; (fig) **he tried to ~ the murder on his brother*** il a essayé de mettre le meurtre sur le dos de son frère; (fig) **you can't ~ that on me!** vous ne pouvez pas me mettre ça sur le dos!; (fig) **he stuck me with the bill** il m'a laissé régler la note; (fig) **he stuck* me (for) £10 for that old book** il m'a fait payer or il m'a pris 10 livres pour ce vieux bouquin*

◆ **to be stuck** [key, lock, door, drawer, gears, valve, lid] être coincé, être bloqué; [vehicle, wheels] être coincé, être bloqué; (in mud) être embourbé; (in sand) être enlisé; [machine, lift] être bloqué, être en panne; **to be stuck in the lift** être coincé or bloqué dans l'ascenseur; **the train was stuck at the station** le train était bloqué or immobilisé en gare; **the car was stuck between two trucks** la voiture était bloquée or coincée entre deux camions; **I was stuck in a corner and had to listen to him all evening** j'étais bloqué dans un coin et j'ai dû l'écouter toute la soirée; **he was stuck in town all summer** il a été obligé de rester en ville tout l'été; **I'm stuck at home all day** je suis cloué à la maison toute la journée; **we're stuck here for the night** nous allons être obligés de passer la nuit ici; (fig) **he's really stuck* on her** il est vraiment entiché d'elle; **to be stuck for an answer** ne pas savoir que répondre; (in crossword puzzle, guessing game, essay etc) **I'm stuck*** je sèche*; **I'll help you if you're stuck*** je t'aiderai si tu n'y arrives pas; **I'm stuck for £10*** il me manque 10 livres; **he's not stuck for money*** ce n'est pas l'argent qui lui manque; **I was stuck* with the job of organizing it all** je me suis retrouvé avec toute l'organisation sur les bras* or à devoir tout organiser; **I was stuck*** c'est moi qui ai dû casquer*; **I was stuck* with him all evening** je l'ai eu sur le dos or sur les bras toute la soirée

◆ **to get stuck**: **to get stuck in the mud** s'embourber, s'enliser dans la boue; **to get stuck in the sand** s'enliser dans le sable; **a bone got stuck in my throat** une arête s'est mise en travers de ma gorge

[d] esp Brit = **tolerate** [+ sb's presence, mannerisms etc] supporter; **I can't ~ it any longer** j'en ai marre, j'en ai ras le bol*; **I wonder how he ~s it at all** je me demande comment il peut tenir le coup; **I can't ~ her*** je ne peux pas la blairer*

[4] INTRANSITIVE VERB

[a] = **embed itself** etc [needle, spear] se planter, s'enfoncer (into dans); **he had a knife ~ing in(to) his back** il avait un couteau planté dans le dos

[b] = **adhere** [glue, paste] tenir; [stamp, label] être collé, tenir (to à); (fig) [habit, name etc] rester; **the paper stuck to the table** le papier est resté collé à la table; **the eggs have stuck to the pan** les œufs ont attaché (à la casserole); **it ~s to your ribs*** [food] ça tient au corps or à l'estomac; **the nickname stuck (to him)** le surnom lui est resté; **to make a charge ~** prouver la culpabilité de quelqu'un

[c] = **remain, stay** rester; **to ~ close to sb** rester aux côtés de qn, ne pas quitter qn

◆ **to stick to sb/sth**: **she stuck to him all through the holiday** elle ne l'a pas lâché d'une semelle pendant toutes les vacances; **to ~ to sb like a limpet** or **a leech** se cramponner à qn; **they stuck to the fox's trail** ils sont restés sur les traces du renard; **to ~ to one's word** or **promise** tenir parole; **to ~ to one's principles** rester fidèle à ses principes; **to ~ to one's post** rester à son poste; **to ~ to one's guns*** camper sur ses positions; **he stuck to his story** il a maintenu ce qu'il avait dit; **decide what you're going to say then ~ to it** décidez ce que vous allez dire et tenez-vous-y; **to ~ to the facts** s'en tenir aux faits; **~ to the point!** ne vous éloignez pas or ne sortez pas du sujet!; (fig) **to ~ to one's knitting** se cantonner dans ce que l'on sait faire

◆ **to stick to/by sb**: **to ~ to** or **by sb through thick and thin** rester fidèle à qn envers et contre tout; **will you ~ by me?** est-ce que vous me soutiendrez?

◆ **to stick to/at/in sth**: **to ~ to** or at a job rester dans un emploi; **I'll ~ in the job for a bit longer** pour le moment je garde ce boulot* or je vais rester où je suis; **~ at it!** persévère!, tiens bon!

◆ **to stick with sb/sth** [+ person] (= stay beside) rester avec, ne pas quitter; [+ person, brand] (= stay loyal) rester fidèle à; [+ activity, sport] s'en tenir à; **~ with him!*** ne le perdez pas de vue!

[d] = **get jammed** etc [wheels, vehicle] se coincer, se bloquer; (= get stuck in mud) s'embourber; (= get stuck in sand) s'enliser; [key, lock, door, drawer, gears, valve, lid] se coincer, se bloquer; [machine, lift] se bloquer, tomber en panne; **the car stuck in the mud** la voiture s'est embourbée; **a bone stuck in my throat** une arête s'est mise en travers de ma gorge; (fig) **that ~s in my throat** or **gizzard*** je n'arrive pas à le digérer*; **the word "please" seems to ~ in her throat** on dirait qu'elle n'arrive pas à dire « s'il te plaît »; **the bidding stuck at £100** les enchères se sont arrêtées à 100 livres; **I got halfway through and stuck there** je suis resté coincé à mi-chemin; **he stuck halfway through the second verse** il s'est arrêté or il a eu un trou au milieu de la deuxième strophe; **it may ~ for a few weeks, but it'll sell in the end** (house for sale) ça risque de traîner quelques semaines, mais ça finira par se vendre — **fast**!

[e] = **balk** reculer, regimber (at, on devant); **he will ~ at nothing to get what he wants** il ne recule devant rien pour obtenir ce qu'il veut; **they may ~ on** or **at that clause** il se peut qu'ils regimbent (subj) devant cette clause

bras toute la soirée

f = extend, protrude the nail was ~ing through the plank le clou dépassait or sortait de la planche; the rod was ~ing into the next garden la barre dépassait dans le jardin d'à côté; a narrow finger of land ~ing into enemy territory une étroite bande de terre s'enfonçant en territoire ennemi

g Cards (I) ~! ◊ I'm ~ing (je suis) servi

5 COMPOUNDS

► **stick figure** N bonhomme m ► **sticking plaster** N sparadrap m ► **sticking point** N (fig) point m de friction ► **stick insect** N phasme m; she's like a ~ insect elle est maigre comme un clou ► **stick-in-the-mud*** ADJ, N sclérosé(e) m(f), encroûté(e) m(f) ► **stick-on** ADJ adhésif ► **stick shift** N (US Aut) levier m de vitesses ► **stick-to-itiveness*** N (US) ténacité f, persévérance f ► **stick-up*** N braquage* m, hold-up m

6 PHRASAL VERBS

► **stick around*** VI rester dans les parages; (= be kept waiting) attendre, poireauter*; ~ around for a few minutes restez dans les parages un moment; I was tired of ~ing around doing nothing j'en avais assez de poireauter* sans rien faire

► **stick away** VT SEP cacher, planquer*; he stuck it away behind the bookcase il l'a caché or planqué* derrière la bibliothèque

► **stick back** VT SEP **a** (= replace) remettre (into dans, on to sur)

b (with glue etc) recoller

► **stick down** **1** VI [envelope etc] (se) coller

2 VT SEP **a** [+ envelope etc] coller

b (* = put down) poser, mettre; he stuck it down on the table il l'a posé or mis sur la table

c * [+ notes, details] noter en vitesse; he stuck down a few dates before he forgot avant d'oublier il a rapidement noté quelques dates

► **stick in** **1** VI* (= make an effort) s'y mettre sérieusement; (= persevere) persévérer; you'll have to ~ in if you want to succeed vous devrez vous y mettre sérieusement si vous voulez réussir; he stuck in at his maths il a fait un gros effort en maths

2 VT SEP **a** (= put in) [+ needle, pin, fork] piquer; (forcefully) planter; [+ dagger, knife, bayonet, spade] planter, enfoncer; [+ photo in album etc] coller; he stuck in a few quotations* il a collé* quelques citations par-ci par-là; try to ~ in a word about our book essaie de glisser un mot sur notre livre

b (fig) to get stuck in* s'y mettre sérieusement

► **stick on** **1** VI [label, stamp etc] rester collé

2 VT SEP **a** [+ label] coller; [+ stamp] mettre, coller

b (* = put on) [+ hat, coat, lid] mettre; ~ on another CD mets un autre CD; (fig) to ~ it on* (= put the price up) augmenter le prix

► **stick out** **1** VI **a** (= protrude) [shirttails] dépasser, sortir; [rod etc] dépasser; [balcony etc] faire saillie; his ears ~ out il a les oreilles décollées; his teeth ~ out il a les dents en avant; I could see his legs ~ing out from under the car je voyais ses jambes qui sortaient de sous la voiture; to ~ out beyond sth dépasser qch; (fig) it ~s out a mile* ça crève les yeux (that que)

b (= persevere etc) tenir (bon); can you ~ out a little longer? est-ce que vous pouvez tenir un peu plus longtemps?; to ~ out for more money tenir bon dans ses revendications pour une augmentation de salaire

2 VT SEP **a** [+ rod etc] faire dépasser; [+ one's arm, head] sortir (of de); to ~ one's chest out bomber la poitrine; to ~ one's tongue out tirer la langue

b (* = tolerate) supporter; to ~ it out tenir le coup

► **stick through** **1** VI (= protrude) dépasser

2 VT SEP [+ pen, rod, one's finger etc] passer à travers

► **stick together** **1** VI **a** [labels, pages, objects] être collés ensemble; the pieces won't ~ together les morceaux ne veulent pas rester collés or se coller ensemble

b (= stay together) rester ensemble; (fig) se serrer les coudes; ~ together till you get through the park restez ensemble jusqu'à la sortie or ne vous séparez pas avant la sortie du parc; (fig) we must all ~ together! nous devons nous serrer les coudes!

2 VT SEP coller (ensemble)

► **stick up** **1** VI **a** there was a rock ~ing up out of the water il y avait un rocher qui sortait or émergeait de l'eau; his head was ~ing up above the crowd sa tête était visible au-dessus de la foule; your hair is ~ing up vos cheveux rebiquent*

b * to ~ up for sb prendre la défense or le parti de qn; to ~ up for o.s. défendre ses intérêts, ne pas se laisser faire; to ~ up for one's rights défendre ses droits, ne pas se laisser faire

2 VT SEP **a** [+ notice etc] afficher

b to ~ up one's hand lever la main; ~ 'em up!* haut les mains!; to ~ sb up* dévaliser qn (sous la menace d'un revolver); they stuck up the bank* ils ont braqué* la banque

► **stick with** VT FUS → stick 4c

stickball ['stɪkbɔːl] N (US) sorte de base-ball

sticker ['stɪkər] **1** N **a** (= label) autocollant m; a ban the bomb ~ un autocollant antinucléaire → **billsticker** **b** (fig) he's a ~ il n'abandonne pas facilement, il n'est pas du genre à baisser les bras* **2** COMP ► **sticker price** N (US: in car sales) prix m clés en mains

stickiness ['stɪkɪnɪs] N (NonC) **a** (Brit = gumminess) the label has lost its ~ l'étiquette ne colle plus **b** [of substance, toffee, dough, clay] consistance f collante; [of object, paste] consistance f collante or poisseuse; [of paint, syrup] consistance f poisseuse; [of road, surface] caractère m gluant; [of ground] lourdeur f **d** (= sweatiness, mugginess) [of hands, heat] moiteur f; [of weather, climate, day] chaleur f humide, moiteur f **e** (* = difficulty) [of situation, problem, moment, conversation] difficulté f

stickleback ['stɪklbæk] N épinoche f

stickler ['stɪklər] N to be a ~ for [+ discipline, obedience, correct clothing, good manners] insister sur, tenir rigoureusement à; [+ etiquette] être à cheval sur, être pointilleux sur; [+ grammar, spelling] être rigoriste en matière de; [+ figures, facts] être pointilleux sur le chapitre de, insister sur; to be a ~ for detail être tatillon

stickpin ['stɪkpɪn] N (US) épingle f de cravate

stickweed ['stɪkwiːd] N (US) jacobée f

stickwork ['stɪkwɜːk] N (NonC) his ~ is very good [of hockey player etc] il manie bien la crosse or le stick; [of drummer] il manie bien les baguettes

sticky ['stɪkɪ] **1** ADJ **a** (Brit = gummed) [label] adhésif; to be ~ on both sides avoir deux faces adhésives

b (= clinging) [substance, toffee, dough, clay] collant; [object, fingers] collant, poisseux; [paste] collant, gluant; [syrup] poisseux; [road, surface] gluant; [blood, paint, oil] visqueux; a ~ mark une tache collante; to have ~ eyes avoir des yeux chassieux; (euph) to have ~ fingers* être clepto(mane)*

c (Sport) [ground] lourd; (Racing) to find the going ~ trouver le terrain lourd

d (= sweaty, muggy) [person, palms, heat] moite; [weather, climate, day] chaud et humide; his shirt was wet and ~ at the back sa chemise pleine de sueur lui collait au dos; to feel hot and ~ [person] transpirer; it was hot and ~ l'atmosphère était moite

e (* = difficult) [situation, problem, moment] délicat, difficile; [conversation] pénible; to go

through a ~ patch ◊ to be or to bat on a ~ wicket (Brit) être dans le pétrin*; to have a ~ time passer un mauvais quart d'heure

f (Brit = violent) to come to or meet a ~ end* mal finir

g (Brit = unhelpful) to be ~ about doing sth* faire des histoires* pour faire qch

2 COMP ► **sticky-fingered***, **sticky-handed*** ADJ (fig = dishonest) clepto(mane)* ► **sticky tape** N (Brit) ruban m adhésif, scotch® m

stiff [stɪf] **1** ADJ **a** (= rigid, hard to move) [card, paper] rigide; [material] raide; [collar, brush, door, drawer, lock] dur

b (Culin) [mixture, paste] ferme; **whisk the egg whites until ~** battre les blancs en neige ferme

c (Physiol) [person] (gen) raide; (from exercise) courbaturé; [limb, muscle] raide; [corpse] raide, rigide; [joint] ankylosé; [finger] engourdi; [movement] difficile; to have a ~ neck avoir un torticolis → 3; to have a ~ back avoir des courbatures dans le dos; you'll be or feel ~ tomorrow vous aurez des courbatures demain; my back felt very ~ j'avais très mal au dos, j'avais des courbatures dans le dos; ~ with cold frigorifié*; to go ~ with terror être paralysé par la peur; her face was ~ with tension elle avait les traits crispés; (as) ~ as a board or as a poker raide comme un piquet; to keep a ~ upper lip rester impassible, garder son flegme

d (* = to be bored) s'ennuyer à mourir; to bore sb ~ raser* qn; to be frozen ~ être frigorifié*; to be scared ~ être mort de trouille*; to scare sb ~ ficher la trouille* à qn; worried ~ mort d'inquiétude

e (= severe) [penalty, sentence, fine, warning] sévère; [competition] rude; [challenge] sérieux; [opposition, resistance] tenace; [test, exam] difficile; [climb] raide, pénible

f (= formal) [person] guindé; [smile] contraint; [bow] raide; to give a ~ bow s'incliner avec raideur; ~ and formal [person, manner, letter, atmosphere] guindé

g (= high) [price] élevé; [price rise] fort; [bill] salé*

h (= strong) [whisky] bien tassé; I could use a ~ drink j'ai besoin d'un (petit) remontant

i (Met) [breeze, wind] fort

2 N **a** (* = corpse) macchabée* m

b (= fool) big ~* gros balourd m or bêta m

c (US*) (= tramp) vagabond m; (= laborer: also working ~) ouvrier m

3 COMP ► **stiff arm** N (US) to give sb the ~ arm écarter qn (d'un geste) du bras ► **stiff-arm** VT (US) to ~ sb écarter qn (d'un geste) du bras ► **stiff-necked** ADJ (fig) opiniâtre, entêté

stiffen ['stɪfn] (also ~ up) **1** VT **a** [+ card, fabric] raidir, renforcer; (= starch) empeser

b [+ dough, paste] donner de la consistance à **c** [+ limb] raidir; [+ joint] ankyloser **d** (fig) [+ morale, resistance etc] affermir **2** VI **a** [card, fabric] devenir raide or rigide **b** [dough, paste] prendre de la consistance, devenir ferme **c** [limb] se raidir; [joint] s'ankyloser; [door, lock] devenir dur; he ~ed when he heard the noise il s'est raidi quand il a entendu le bruit **d** [breeze] augmenter d'intensité, fraîchir **e** (fig) [resistance] devenir opiniâtre; [morale] s'affermir

stiffener ['stɪfənər] N **a** (= starch etc) amidon m **b** (= plastic strip: in collar etc) baleine f

stiffening ['stɪfnɪŋ] N (= cloth) toile f (pour raidir les revers etc)

stiffly ['stɪflɪ] ADV [move, say, smile, greet] avec raideur; to stand ~ se tenir raide; ~ starched très amidonné; ~ sprung bien suspendu; ~ beaten or whipped [egg white] battu en neige ferme; [cream] fouetté en chantilly ferme

stiffness ['stɪfnɪs] N (NonC) **a** (= lack of suppleness) [of person, knees, back etc] raideur f; [of joints] raideur f, ankylose f; ~ in or of the neck torticolis *m*; **the ~ you feel after exercise** les courbatures *fpl* dues au sport **b** (= *formality*) [*of manner*] raideur *f* **c** (= *rigidity*) [*of card, paper*] rigidité *f*; [*of material*] raideur *f*; [*of collar, brush*] dureté *f* **d** (= *difficulty of operating*) [*of door, drawer, lock*] résistance *f* **e** (= *severity*) [*of penalty, sentence, fine, warning*] sévérité *f*; [*of competition*] âpreté *f*; [*of challenge*] sérieux *m*; [*of opposition, resistance*] ténacité *f*; [*of climb*] caractère *m* ardu, difficulté *f*; [*of test, exam*] difficulté *f* **f** (*Culin*) [*of mixture, paste*] fermeté *f* **g** [*of breeze, wind*] âpreté *f*

stifle ['staɪfl] **1** VT **a** (+ *person*) étouffer, suffoquer; (+ *fire*) étouffer; (+ *sobs*) réprimer, étouffer; (+ *anger, smile, desire*) réprimer; **to ~ a yawn/sneeze** réprimer une envie de bâiller/d'éternuer **2** VI étouffer, suffoquer **3** N (*Anat*) [*of horse etc*] grasset *m*

stifling ['staɪflɪŋ] ADJ [*heat, atmosphere*] étouffant, suffocant; [*situation, place*] étouffant, suffocant; [*smoke, fumes*] suffocant; **it's ~ today/in here** on étouffe aujourd'hui/ici

stigma ['stɪɡmə] N (*pl* **stigmas** *or* **stigmata** [stɪɡ'mɑːtə]) stigmate *m*; (*Rel*) **the ~ta** les stigmates *mpl*

stigmatic [stɪɡ'mætɪk] ADJ, N (*Rel*) stigmatisé(e) *m(f)*

stigmatize ['stɪɡmətaɪz] VT (*all senses*) stigmatiser

stile [staɪl] N **a** (= *steps over fence, wall*) échalier *m*; (= *turnstile*) tourniquet *m* (*porte*) **b** (*Constr etc* = *upright*) montant *m*

stiletto [stɪ'letəʊ] N (*pl* **stilettos** *or* **stilettoes**) (= *weapon*) stylet *m*; (*also* **~ heel**) talon *m* aiguille

still[1] [stɪl] ADV **a** (= *up to this time*) encore, toujours; **he was ~ wearing his coat** il n'avait pas encore *or* toujours pas enlevé son manteau; **she ~ lives in London** elle vit toujours à Londres; **he's ~ as stubborn as ever** il est toujours aussi entêté; **I can ~ remember it** je m'en souviens encore; **he ~ hasn't arrived** il n'est toujours pas arrivé; **I ~ don't understand** je ne comprends toujours pas; **you could ~ change your mind** vous pouvez encore changer d'avis, il est encore temps de changer d'avis **b** (*stating what remains*) encore; **I've ~ got three left** il m'en reste encore trois; **there's ~ time** il y a *or* on a encore le temps; **the details have ~ to be worked out** il reste encore à régler les détails; **there are further redundancies ~ to come** il y aura encore d'autres licenciements; **there are many things ~ to do** il y a encore beaucoup de choses à faire; **there are many questions ~ to be answered** il reste encore beaucoup de questions sans réponse; **there are ten weeks ~ to go** il reste encore dix semaines; **~ to come, the financial news ...** dans quelques instants, les informations financières ... **c** (= *nonetheless*) quand même, tout de même; **he's ~ your brother** c'est quand même *or* tout de même ton frère; **I didn't win; ~, it's been good experience** je n'ai pas gagné, mais ça a quand même *or* tout de même été une bonne expérience; **~ and all*** tout compte fait **d** (= *however*) **I've got to find the money from somewhere; ~, that's my problem** il faut que je trouve l'argent quelque part, mais ça, c'est mon problème; **I missed the bus; ~, that's life** j'ai raté le bus, mais c'est la vie! **e** (*in comparisons = even*) encore; **he was ~ more determined after the debate** il était encore plus résolu après le débat; **living standards have fallen ~ further** les niveaux de vie sont tombés encore plus bas; **more serious ~** *or* **more serious is the problem of ethnic unrest** il y a le problème autrement plus sérieux des troubles ethniques **f** (= *yet*) encore; **there is ~ another reason** il y a encore une autre raison

still[2] [stɪl] **1** ADJ **a** (= *motionless*) [*person, hands, air, water*] immobile **b** (= *calm*) [*place, night, day*] calme; **all was ~** tout était calme; **the ~ waters of the lake** les eaux calmes du lac ■ (*PROV*) **~ waters run deep** il n'est pire eau que l'eau qui dort (*PROV*); **a ~, small voice** une petite voix insistante **c** (*Brit = not fizzy*) [*drink, orange*] non gazeux; [*water*] plat **d** (= *silent*) **be ~!** †† paix! ††

2 ADV **hold ~!** (*gen*) ne bouge pas!; (= *don't fidget*) reste tranquille!; **to keep** *or* **stay** *or* **stand ~** [*person*] (*gen*) ne pas bouger; (= *not fidget*) rester tranquille; **to sit ~** [*person*] (*gen*) rester assis sans bouger; (= *not fidget*) rester tranquillement assis; **time stood ~** le temps s'est arrêté; **her heart stood ~** son cœur a cessé de battre

3 N **a** (*liter*) silence *m*, calme *m*; **in the ~ of the night** dans le silence de la nuit **b** (*Cine*) = **still photograph**

4 VT (+ *anger, fear*) calmer; (+ *person*) apaiser, tranquilliser; (= *silence*) faire taire

5 COMP ▸ **still life** N (*pl* **still lifes**) (*Art*) nature *f* morte ▸ **still photograph** N (*Cine*) photo *f* de film

still[3] [stɪl] N **a** (= *apparatus*) alambic *m*; (= *place*) distillerie *f* **2** VT distiller

stillbirth ['stɪlbɜːθ] N (= *birth*) mort *f* à la naissance; (= *child*) enfant *m(f)* mort-né(e)

stillborn ['stɪlbɔːn] ADJ mort-né (*mort-née f*)

stillness ['stɪlnɪs] N [*of person, hands, air, water*] immobilité *f*; (= *calm*) [*of place, night, day*] calme *m*; **an eerie ~** un calme inquiétant

stilt [stɪlt] N échasse *f*; (*Archit*) pilotis *m*

stilted ['stɪltɪd] ADJ [*person, conversation, language, manner*] guindé; **the actors' ~ performances** le manque de naturel des acteurs

stimulant ['stɪmjʊlənt] **1** ADJ stimulant **2** N (*lit, fig*) stimulant *m*; (*fig*) **to be a ~ to ...** stimuler ...

stimulate ['stɪmjʊleɪt] VT (*gen, Physiol*) stimuler; **to ~ sb to sth/to do** inciter *or* pousser qn à qch/à faire

stimulating ['stɪmjʊleɪtɪŋ] ADJ (*gen*) stimulant; (*sexually*) excitant

stimulation [ˌstɪmjʊ'leɪʃən] N (= *stimulus*) stimulant *m*; (= *state*) stimulation *f*

stimulative ['stɪmjʊlətɪv] ADJ stimulant

stimulus ['stɪmjʊləs] N (*pl* **stimuli** ['stɪmjʊlaɪ]) (*Physiol*) stimulus *m*; (*fig*) stimulant *m*; (*fig*) **to be a ~ to** *or* **for** (+ *exports, efforts, imagination*) stimuler; **it gave trade a new ~** cela a donné une nouvelle impulsion *or* un coup de fouet au commerce; **under the ~ of ...** stimulé par ...

stimy ['staɪmɪ] = **stymie**

sting [stɪŋ] (*vb: pret, ptp* **stung**) **1** N **a** [*of insect*] dard *m*, aiguillon *m*; (*fig*) **but there's a ~ in the tail** mais il y a une mauvaise surprise à la fin; (*fig: of plan, draft, legislation etc*) **it's had its ~ removed** on l'a rendu inopérant; (*fig*) **to take the ~ out of** (+ *words*) adoucir; (+ *situation*) désamorcer

b (= *pain, wound, mark*) [*of insect, nettle etc*] piqûre *f*; [*of iodine etc*] brûlure *f*; [*of whip*] douleur *f* cuisante; (*fig*) [*of attack*] mordant *m*, vigueur *f*; [*of criticism, remark*] causticité *f*, mordant *m*; **I felt the ~ of the rain on my face** la pluie me cinglait le visage; **the ~ of salt water in the cut** la brûlure de l'eau salée dans la plaie

c (*esp US**) (= *confidence trick*) arnaque* *f*, coup *m* monté

2 VT **a** [*insect, nettle*] piquer; [*iodine, ointment*] brûler; [*rain, hail, whip*] cingler, fouetter; (*fig*) [*remark, criticism*] piquer au vif, blesser; **stung by remorse** bourrelé de remords; **my remark stung him into action** ma remarque (l'a piqué au vif et) l'a poussé à agir; **he was stung into replying brusquely** pi-

qué *or* blessé, il répondit brusquement → **quick**

b ■ avoir*, estamper*; **he stung me for £10 for that meal** il m'a eu* *or* estampé* en me faisant payer ce repas 10 livres, il a eu le toupet* de me faire payer ce repas 10 livres; **I've been stung!** je me suis fait avoir *or* estamper!*

3 VI **a** [*insect, nettle*] piquer; [*iodine, ointment*] brûler; [*blow, slap, whip*] provoquer une sensation cuisante; [*remark, criticism*] être cuisant; **that ~s!** ça pique!, ça brûle!

b [*eyes*] cuire, piquer; [*cut, skin*] cuire, brûler; **the smoke made his eyes ~** la fumée lui picotait les yeux

stinger ['stɪŋər] N **a** (= *cocktail*) cocktail à base de crème de menthe **b** (*US*) [*of insect*] piqûre *f* **c** (*US**= *remark*) pique *f*, pointe *f*

stingily ['stɪndʒɪlɪ] ADV [*praise*] chichement; [*spend*] avec avarice; [*serve*] en lésinant

stinginess ['stɪndʒɪnɪs] N [*of person*] ladrerie *f*, avarice *f*; [*of portion*] insuffisance *f*

stinging ['stɪŋɪŋ] **1** ADJ [*blow, slap, pain*] cuisant; [*sensation*] cuisant, de piqûre; [*rain, wind, comment, attack, criticism*] cinglant **2** (= *sensation*) sensation *f* cuisante **3** COMP ▸ **stinging nettle** N ortie *f*

stingray ['stɪŋreɪ] N pastenague *f*

stingy ['stɪndʒɪ] ADJ [*person*] radin*; [*portion, amount*] misérable, mesquin; **to be ~ with** (+ *food, wine*) lésiner sur; (+ *praise*) être chiche de; **~ with money** avare (*de ses sous*)

stink [stɪŋk] (*vb: pret* **stank**, *ptp* **stunk**) **1** N **a** puanteur *f*, odeur *f* infecte; **what a ~!** ce que ça pue!; (*fig*) **there's a ~ of corruption** cela pue la corruption, cela sent la corruption à plein nez

b (* *fig* = *row, trouble*) esclandre *m*, grabuge* *m*; **there was a dreadful ~ about the broken windows** il y a eu du grabuge* à propos des carreaux cassés; **to kick up** *or* **cause** *or* **make a ~** faire toute une scène, râler*; **to kick up a ~ about sth** causer un esclandre à propos de qch, faire du grabuge* à cause de qch

2 VI **a** puer, empester; **it ~s of fish** cela pue or empeste le poisson; **it ~s in here!** cela pue or empeste ici!; (*lit*) **it ~s to high heaven*** cela empeste, ça fouette*; (*fig*) **it ~s of corruption** cela pue la corruption, cela sent la corruption à plein nez; (*fig*) **the whole business ~s** c'est une sale affaire; **they're ~ing with money*** ils sont bourrés de fric*

b (* = *be very bad*) [*person, thing*] être dégueulasse*

3 VT (+ *room etc*) empester

4 COMP ▸ **stink-bomb** N boule *f* puante ▸ **stink-horn** N satyre *m* puant

▸ **stink out** VT SEP (+ *fox etc*) enfumer; (+ *room*) empester

stinker* ['stɪŋkər] N (*pej*) (= *person*) salaud* *m*, salope* *f*; (= *angry letter*) lettre *f* d'engueulade*; **to be a ~** [*person*] être salaud *or* salope*)*; [*problem, question*] être un casse-tête

stinking ['stɪŋkɪŋ] **1** ADJ **a** (= *smelly*) [*person, lavatory, rubbish*] puant **b** (* = *horrible*) sale* (*before n*); **take your ~ hands off me!** retire tes sales pattes!*, bas les pattes!*; **this ~ little town** cette sale* petite ville; **what a ~ thing to do!** quelle vacherie!*; **a ~ letter** une lettre de réclamation virulente **c** (*Brit = bad*) **a ~ cold** un sale rhume, un rhume carabiné*; **a ~ hangover** une gueule de bois carabinée* **2** ADV **~ rich*** bourré de fric*, plein aux as*

stinkpot* ['stɪŋkpɒt] N salaud* *m*, salope* *f*

stinkweed ['stɪŋkwiːd] N diplotaxis *m*

stinky* ['stɪŋkɪ] ADJ puant

stint [stɪnt] **1** N **a** ration *f* de travail, besogne *f* assignée; **to do one's ~** (= *daily work*) faire son travail quotidien; (= *do one's share*) faire sa part de travail; **he does a ~ in the gym/at the typewriter every day** il passe un certain temps chaque jour au gymnase/à la machine; **I've done my ~ at the wheel** j'ai pris mon tour au volant; **I've finished my ~ for today** j'ai fini ce que j'avais à faire aujourd'hui **b** **without ~** [*spend*] sans compter; [*give, lend*] généreusement, avec largesse **2** VT [+ *food*] lésiner sur; [+ *compliments*] être chiche de; **to ~ sb of sth** mesurer qch à qn; **he ~ed himself in order to feed the children** il s'est privé afin de nourrir les enfants; **he didn't ~ himself** il ne s'est privé de rien **3** VI **to ~ on** [+ *food*] lésiner sur; [+ *compliments*] être chiche sur; **to ~ on money** être avare or ladre

stipend ['staɪpend] N (*esp Rel*) traitement *m*

stipendiary [staɪ'pendɪərɪ] **1** ADJ [*services, official*] rémunéré; [*priest*] qui reçoit un traitement **2** N *personne qui reçoit une rémunération or un traitement fixe*; (*Brit Jur: also* **~ magistrate**) juge *m* au tribunal de police

stipple ['stɪpl] VT pointiller

stipulate ['stɪpjʊleɪt] **1** VT stipuler (**that** que); [+ *price*] stipuler, convenir expressément de; [+ *quantity*] stipuler, prescrire **2** VI **to ~ for sth** stipuler qch, spécifier qch, convenir expressément de qch

stipulation [ˌstɪpjʊ'leɪʃən] N stipulation *f*; **on the ~ that ...** à la condition expresse que ... (+ *fut or subj*)

stir¹ [stɜːʳ] **1** N **a** **to give sth a ~** remuer or tourner qch **b** (*fig*) agitation *f*, sensation *f*; **there was a great ~ in Parliament about ...** il y a eu beaucoup d'agitation au Parlement à propos de ...; **it caused** or **made quite a ~** cela a fait une certaine sensation, cela a eu un grand retentissement, cela a fait du bruit **2** VT **a** [+ *tea, soup*] remuer, tourner; [+ *mixture*] tourner; [+ *fire*] tisonner; **he ~red sugar into his tea** il a remué or tourné son thé après y avoir mis du sucre; **she ~red milk into the mixture** elle a ajouté du lait au mélange **b** (= *move*) remuer; (*quickly*) agiter; **the wind ~red the leaves** le vent a agité or remué or fait trembler les feuilles; **nothing could ~ him from his chair** rien ne pouvait le tirer de son fauteuil; **to ~ o.s.*** se secouer, se bouger⁕; **to ~ one's stumps*** se grouiller⁕ **c** (*fig*) [+ *curiosity, passions*] exciter; [+ *emotions*] éveiller; [+ *imagination*] stimuler, exciter; [+ *person*] émouvoir, exalter; **to ~ sb to do sth** inciter qn à faire qch; **to ~ a people to revolt** soulever un peuple à la révolte; **to ~ sb to pity** émouvoir la compassion de qn; **it ~red his heart** cela lui a remué le cœur; **to ~ sb's blood** réveiller l'enthousiasme de qn; **it was a song to ~ the blood** c'était une chanson enthousiasmante **3** VI **a** [*person*] remuer, bouger; [*leaves, curtains etc*] remuer, trembler; [*feelings*] être excité; **I will not ~ from here** je ne bougerai pas d'ici; **he hasn't ~red from the spot** il n'a pas quitté l'endroit; **he wouldn't ~ an inch** (*lit*) il ne voulait pas bouger d'un centimètre; (*fig*) il ne voulait pas faire la moindre concession; **to ~ in one's sleep** bouger en dormant or dans son sommeil; **nobody is ~ring yet** personne n'est encore levé, tout le monde dort encore; **nothing was ~ring in the forest** rien ne bougeait dans la forêt; **the curtains ~red in the breeze** la brise a agité les rideaux; **anger ~red within her** la colère est montée en elle **b** (* *fig* = *try to cause trouble*) essayer de mettre la pagaille* or de causer des problèmes **4** COMP ► **stir-fry** VT faire sauter (en remuant) ♦ ADJ [*vegetables*] sauté
► **stir in** VT SEP [+ *milk etc*] ajouter en tournant
► **stir round** VT SEP (*Culin etc*) tourner
► **stir up** VT SEP [+ *soup etc*] tourner, remuer; [+ *fire*] tisonner; (*fig*) [+ *curiosity, attention, anger*] exciter; [+ *imagination*] exciter, stimuler; [+ *memories, the past*] réveiller; [+ *revolt*] susciter; [+ *hatred*] attiser; [+ *mob*] ameuter; [+ *opposition, discord*] fomenter; [+ *trouble*] provoquer;

[+ *person*] secouer; **to ~ sb up to sth/to do sth** pousser or inciter qn à qch/à faire qch

stir²⁕ [stɜːʳ] (*esp US*) **1** N (= *prison*) taule⁕ or tôle⁕ *f*; **in ~** en taule⁕, au bloc⁕ **2** COMP ► **stir-crazy⁕** ADJ rendu dingue⁕ par la réclusion

stirrer⁕ [stɜːrəʳ] N (= *troublemaker*) fauteur *m* de troubles, fouteur *m*, -euse *f* de merde⁕

stirring ['stɜːrɪŋ] **1** ADJ [*speech*] vibrant; [*tale*] passionnant; [*music*] entraînant; [*performance*] enthousiasmant; [*victory*] grisant **2** N (= *first sign*) [*of discontent, revolt*] frémissement *m*; [*of love*] frisson *m*; **a ~ of interest** un début d'intérêt

stirrup ['stɪrəp] **1** N **a** [*of rider*] étrier *m*; **to put one's feet in the ~s** chausser les étriers **b** (*US Climbing*) escarpolette *f*, étrier *m* **c** (*Med*) **~s** étriers *mpl* **2** COMP ► **stirrup cup** N coup *m* de l'étrier ► **stirrup leather** N étrivière *f* ► **stirrup pump** N pompe *f* à main portative ► **stirrup strap** N = **stirrup leather**

stitch [stɪtʃ] **1** N (*Sewing*) point *m*; (*Knitting*) maille *f*; (*Surg*) point *m* de suture; (= *sharp pain*) point *m* de côté; **she put a few ~es in the tear** elle a fait un point à la déchirure; (*Knitting*) **to drop a ~** sauter or laisser échapper une maille; **to put ~es in a wound** suturer or recoudre une plaie; **he had ten ~es** on lui a fait dix points de suture; **to get one's ~es out** se faire retirer ses fils (de suture) ■ (*PROV*) **a ~ in time saves nine** un point à temps en vaut cent; **he hadn't a ~ (of clothing) on*** il était nu comme un ver; **he hadn't a dry ~ on him** il n'avait pas un fil de sec sur le dos; **to be in ~es*** se tenir les côtes, se tordre de rire; **her stories had us in ~es*** ses anecdotes nous ont fait rire aux larmes → **cable** **2** VT [+ *seam, hem, garment*] (*gen*) coudre; (*on machine*) piquer; [+ *book*] brocher; (*Med*) suturer → **hand**, **machine** **3** VI coudre **4** COMP ► **stitch-up⁕** N (*Brit*) coup *m* monté
► **stitch down** VT SEP rabattre
► **stitch on** VT SEP [+ *pocket, button*] coudre; (= *mend*) recoudre
► **stitch up** VT SEP **a** (*Sewing*) coudre; (= *mend*) recoudre; (*Med*) suturer **b** (* = *arrange, finalize*) [+ *agreement*] (réussir à) conclure **c** (⁕ *fig* = *frame*) monter un coup contre; **I was ~ed up** j'ai été victime d'un coup monté

stitching ['stɪtʃɪŋ] N couture *f*, points *mpl*

stoat [stəʊt] N hermine *f*

stock [stɒk] **1** N **a** (= *supply*) [*of cotton, sugar, books, goods*] réserve *f*, provision *f*, stock *m* (*Comm*); [*of money*] provision *f*; (*Comm*) **in ~** en stock, en magasin; **out of ~** épuisé; **the shop has a large ~** le magasin est bien approvisionné; **coal ~s are low** les réserves or les stocks de charbon sont réduit(e)s; (*Theat*) **~ of plays** répertoire *m*; **I've got a ~ of cigarettes** j'ai une provision or un stock⁕ de cigarettes; **to get in** or **lay in a ~ of** s'approvisionner en, faire provision de; **it adds to our ~ of facts** cela complète les données en notre possession; **a great ~ of learning** un grand fonds d'érudition; (*Ling*) **the linguistic** or **word ~** le fonds lexical; **to take ~** (*Comm*) faire l'inventaire; (*fig*) faire le point; **to take ~ of** [+ *situation, prospects etc*] faire le point de; [+ *person*] jauger → **dead**, **surplus** **b** (*Agr* = *animals and equipment*) cheptel *m* (*vif et mort*); (*Agr: also* **livestock**) cheptel *m* vif, bétail *m*; (*Rail*) matériel *m* roulant; (*Ind* = *raw material*) matière *f* première; (*for papermaking*) pâte *f* à papier → **fatstock**, **livestock**, **rolling** **c** (*Fin*) valeurs *fpl*, titres *mpl*; (= *company shares*) actions *fpl*; **~s and shares** valeurs *fpl* (*mobilières*), titres *mpl*; **railway ~(s)** actions *fpl* des chemins de fer; (*fig*) **to put ~ in sth** faire cas de qch; (*fig*) **his ~ has risen** sa cote a remonté → **preference**, **registered**

d (= *tree trunk*) tronc *m*; (= *tree stump*) souche *f*; (*Hort: for grafting*) porte-greffe *m*, ente *f* → **laughing** **e** (= *base, stem*) [*of anvil*] billot *m*; [*of plough*] fût *m*; [*of rifle*] fût *m* et crosse *f*; [*of plane*] fût *m*, bois *m*; [*of whip*] manche *m*; [*of fishing rod*] gaule *f*; [*of anchor*] jas *m* → **lock¹** **f** (= *descent, lineage*) origine *f*, souche *f*; **of good Scottish ~** de bonne souche écossaise; **he comes of farming ~** il vient d'une famille d'agriculteurs, il est d'origine or de souche paysanne **g** (*Cards*) talon *m* **h** (*Culin*) bouillon *m*; **chicken ~** bouillon *m* de poulet **i** (= *flower*) giroflée *f*, matthiole *f* **j** (*Hist*) **the ~s** le pilori **k** **to be on the ~s** [*ship*] être sur cale; (*fig*) [*book, piece of work, scheme*] être en chantier **l** (= *tie*) cravate *f* foulard **2** ADJ **a** (*Comm*) [*goods, model*] courant, de série; **~ line** article *m* suivi; **~ size** taille *f* courante or normalisée; **she is not ~ size** elle n'est pas une taille courante **b** (*Theat*) [*play*] du répertoire; **~ character** personnage *m* type **c** (= *standard, hackneyed*) [*argument, joke, excuse, comment, response*] classique; **~ phrase** cliché *m*, expression *f* toute faite **d** (*for breeding*) destiné à la reproduction; **~ mare** jument *f* poulinière **3** VT **a** (= *supply*) [+ *shop, larder, cupboard*] approvisionner (**with** en); [+ *library/farm*] monter en livres/en bétail; [+ *river, lake*] peupler (**with** de), empoissonner; **well-~ed** [*shop etc*] bien approvisionné; [*library, farm*] bien fourni or pourvu **b** (*Comm* = *hold in stock*) [+ *milk, hats, tools etc*] avoir, vendre **4** COMP ► **stock book** N livre *m* d'inventaire(s) ► **stock car** N (*Rail*) wagon *m* à bestiaux; (*Aut Sport*) stock-car *m*; (*Aut Sport*) **~ car racing** course *f* de stock-cars ► **stock certificate** N (*Fin*) titre *m* ► **stock company** N (*Fin*) société *f* par actions, société *f* anonyme → **joint**; (*US Theat*) compagnie *f* or troupe *f* de répertoire ► **stock control** N (*Comm*) = **stock management** ► **stock cube** N (*Culin*) bouillon *m* Kub® ► **stock dividend** N dividende *m* sous forme d'actions ► **stock exchange** N Bourse *f* (des valeurs); **on the ~ exchange** à la Bourse ► **stock-in-trade** N (= *goods*) marchandises *fpl* en magasin or en stock; (= *tools, materials, also fig: of comedian, writer etc*) outils *mpl* du métier ► **stock level** N (*Comm*) niveau *m* des stocks ► **stock list** N (*Fin*) cours *m* de la Bourse; (*Comm*) liste *f* des marchandises en stock, inventaire *m* commercial ► **stock management** N gestion *f* des stocks ► **stock market** N Bourse *f*, marché *m* financier; **~ market closing report** compte rendu des cours de clôture ► **stock option** N (*US Fin*) droit *m* (préférentiel) de souscription ► **stock-still** ADJ **to stand** or **be ~-still** rester planté comme un piquet; (*in fear, amazement*) rester cloué sur place
► **stock up** **1** VI s'approvisionner (**with, on** en, de, **for** pour), faire ses provisions (**with, on** de, **for** pour) **2** VT SEP [+ *shop, larder, cupboard, freezer*] garnir; [+ *library*] accroître le stock de livres de; [+ *farm*] accroître le cheptel de; [+ *river, lake*] aleviner, empoissonner

stockade [stɒ'keɪd] **1** N **a** (= *fencing, enclosure*) palissade *f* **b** (*US: for military prisoners*) salle *f* de police (*d'une caserne*), bloc⁕ *m* **2** VT palanquer

stockbreeder ['stɒkˌbriːdəʳ] N éleveur *m*, -euse *f*

stockbreeding ['stɒkˌbriːdɪŋ] N élevage *m*

stockbroker ['stɒkˌbrəʊkəʳ] **1** N agent *m* de change **2** COMP ► **the stockbroker belt** N

(Brit) la banlieue résidentielle ► **stock-broker Tudor** N (Brit) style Tudor des banlieues résidentielles

stockbroking ['stɒkbrəʊkɪŋ] N commerce m des valeurs en Bourse, transactions fpl boursières

stockfish ['stɒkfɪʃ] N stockfisch m inv

stockholder ['stɒkhəʊldər] N (US) actionnaire mf

stockholding ['stɒkhəʊldɪŋ] N [a] (Comm) stockage m [b] (Fin) actions fpl

Stockholm ['stɒkhəʊm] N Stockholm

stockily ['stɒkɪlɪ] ADV ~ **built** trapu, râblé

stockiness ['stɒkɪnɪs] N aspect m trapu or râblé

stockinet(te) [,stɒkɪ'net] N (= fabric) jersey m; (= knitting stitch) (point m de) jersey m

stocking ['stɒkɪŋ] [1] N bas m → **Christmas, nylon** [2] COMP ► **stocking feet** NPL **in one's ~ feet** sans chaussures ► **stocking-filler** N tout petit cadeau m de Noël ► **stocking mask** N bas m (d'un bandit masqué) ► **stocking stitch** N (Knitting) (point m de) jersey m

stockist ['stɒkɪst] N (Brit) revendeur m

stockjobber ['stɒkdʒɒbər] N (Brit) intermédiaire qui traite directement avec l'agent de change; (US: often pej) agent m de change, agioteur m

stockman ['stɒkmən] N (pl **-men**) gardien m de bestiaux

stockpile ['stɒkpaɪl] [1] VT [+ food etc] stocker, faire or constituer des stocks de; [+ weapons] amasser, accumuler [2] VI faire des stocks [3] N stock m, réserve f

stockpiling ['stɒkpaɪlɪŋ] N (NonC) stockage m, constitution f de stocks

stockpot ['stɒkpɒt] N (Culin) marmite f de bouillon

stockroom ['stɒkrʊm] N magasin m, réserve f, resserre f

stocktaking ['stɒkteɪkɪŋ] N (Brit Comm) (= action) inventaire m; **to do ~** (Comm) faire l'inventaire; (fig) faire le point

stocky ['stɒkɪ] ADJ [a] (= thickset) [man] trapu, râblé; **his ~ build** sa forte carrure [b] (Hort) [plant, growth] dense

stockyard ['stɒkjɑːd] N parc m à bestiaux

stodge* [stɒdʒ] N (NonC: Brit) [a] (= food) aliment m bourratif, étouffe-chrétien* m inv [b] (in book etc) littérature f indigeste

stodgy ['stɒdʒɪ] ADJ (pej) [a] (Culin) [food, meal, pudding] bourratif; [cake] pâteux, lourd [b] (* = dull) [person] rasant*, barbant*; [writing, book] indigeste

stogie, stogy ['stəʊgɪ] N (US) cigare m

stoic ['stəʊɪk] [1] N stoïque mf; (Philos) **Stoic** stoïcien m [2] ADJ [a] (= uncomplaining) [person, acceptance] stoïque; **to be ~ about sth** accepter qch stoïquement [b] (Philos) **Stoic** stoïcien

stoical ['stəʊɪkəl] ADJ stoïque

stoically ['stəʊɪkli] ADV stoïquement

stoicism ['stəʊɪsɪzəm] N stoïcisme m

stoke [stəʊk] VT (also ~ **up**) [+ fire] garnir, entretenir; [+ furnace] alimenter; [+ engine, boiler] chauffer

► **stoke up** [1] VI (furnace) alimenter la chaudière; (open fire) entretenir le feu; (* fig = eat) se garnir or se remplir la panse* [2] VT SEP = **stoke**

stokehole ['stəʊkhəʊl] N (Naut) chaufferie f; [of boiler, furnace] porte f de chauffe

stoker ['stəʊkər] N (Naut, Rail etc) chauffeur m

STOL [stɒl] (Aviat) (ABBR = **short take-off and landing**) ADAC m

stole¹ [stəʊl] N (Dress) étole f, écharpe f; (Rel) étole f

stole² [stəʊl] VB pt of **steal**

stolen ['stəʊlən] VB ptp of **steal**

stolid ['stɒlɪd] ADJ [person, manner, expression, face] impassible

stolidity [stɒ'lɪdɪtɪ] N flegme m, impassibilité f

stolidly ['stɒlɪdlɪ] ADV [say, stare, ignore, stand, sit] impassiblement; **to be ~ British (in one's attitudes)** être d'un flegme tout britannique (dans ses attitudes)

stolidness ['stɒlɪdnɪs] N = **stolidity**

stomach ['stʌmək] [1] N (Anat) estomac m; (= belly) ventre m; **he was lying on his ~** il était couché or allongé sur le ventre, il était à plat ventre; **to have a pain in one's ~** avoir mal à l'estomac or au ventre; (fig) **I have no ~ for this journey** je n'ai aucune envie de faire ce voyage; **an army marches on its ~** une armée ne se bat pas le ventre creux → **empty, full** [2] VT [+ food] digérer; (fig) [+ behaviour, sb's jokes] supporter, encaisser*; (fig) **he couldn't ~ this** il n'a pas pu l'encaisser* [3] COMP [disease] de l'estomac; [ulcer] à l'estomac ► **stomach ache** N mal m de ventre; **I have (a) ~ ache** j'ai mal au ventre ► **stomach pump** N pompe f stomacale ► **stomach trouble** N (NonC) ennuis mpl gastriques

stomatologist [,stəʊmə'tɒlədʒɪst] N stomatologiste mf, stomatologue mf

stomatology [,stəʊmə'tɒlədʒɪ] N stomatologie f

stomp [stɒmp] [1] VI **to ~ in/out** etc entrer/sortir etc d'un pas lourd et bruyant; **we could hear him ~ing about** on entendait le bruit lourd de ses pas [2] VT (esp US) **to ~ one's feet** (in rage) trépigner; (in dance) frapper du pied [3] N [a] [of feet] martèlement m [b] (= dance) swing m

stone [stəʊn] [1] N [a] (= substance, gem: single piece) pierre f; (= pebble) caillou m; (on beach etc) galet m; (commemorative) stèle f (commémorative); (= gravestone) pierre f tombale, stèle f; **(made) of ~** de pierre; (fig) **within a ~'s throw (of)** à deux pas (de); (fig) **to leave no ~ unturned** remuer ciel et terre (**to do** pour faire); **to turn to ~** ◊ **to change into ~** (vt) pétrifier, changer en pierre ♦ (vi) se pétrifier; **it isn't set** or **cast** or **carved in ~** cela n'a rien d'immuable → **paving, precious, rolling, stand, tombstone** [b] (esp Brit: in fruit) noyau m [c] (Med) calcul m; **to have a ~ in the kidney** avoir un calcul rénal; **to have a ~ removed from one's kidney** se faire enlever un calcul rénal → **gallstone** [d] (pl gen inv: Brit = weight) = 14 livres, = 6,348 kg — gen inv: Brit IMPERIAL SYSTEM [2] VT [a] [+ person, object] lancer or jeter des pierres sur, bombarder de pierres; **to ~ sb to death** lapider qn, tuer qn à coups de pierre; (Brit) **~ the crows!*** vingt dieux! [b] [+ date, olive] dénoyauter [3] COMP [building, wall] en pierre ► **Stone Age** N l'âge m de pierre ► **stone-blind** ADJ complètement aveugle ► **stone-broke*** ADJ (US) = **stony-broke**; → **stony** ► **stone circle** N (Brit) cromlech m ► **stone-cold** ADJ complètement froid; **~-cold sober*** pas du tout ivre ► **stone-dead** ADJ raide mort ► **stone-deaf** ADJ sourd comme un pot ► **stone fruit** N fruit m à noyau ► **stoneground** ADJ [flour, wheat] meulé à la pierre

stonebreaker ['stəʊn,breɪkər] N (= person) casseur m de pierres; (= machine) casse-pierre(s) m, concasseur m

stonechat ['stəʊntʃæt] N (Orn) traquet m (pâtre)

stonecrop ['stəʊnkrɒp] N (Bot) orpin m

stonecutter ['stəʊnkʌtər] N (= person) tailleur m de pierre(s) précieuse(s), lapidaire m; (= machine) sciotte f, scie f (de carrier)

stoned* ['stəʊnd] ADJ (on drugs) défoncé* (on sth à qch); (= drunk) complètement beurré* or

bourré*; **to get ~** (on drugs) se défoncer*; (on alcohol) se beurrer*, se bourrer*

stonemason ['stəʊnmeɪsn] N tailleur m de pierre

stonewall ['stəʊnwɔːl] VI (Cricket) jouer très prudemment; (fig) donner des réponses évasives

stoneware ['stəʊnwɛər] N (NonC) pots mpl de grès

stonewashed ['stəʊnwɒʃt] ADJ [jeans] délavé

stonework ['stəʊnwɜːk] N (NonC) maçonnerie f

stonily ['stəʊnɪlɪ] ADV avec froideur, froidement; [stare, look] d'un œil froid

stonking* ['stɒŋkɪŋ] ADJ (= fantastic) génial*

stony ['stəʊnɪ] [1] ADJ [a] (= containing stones, stone-like) [soil, path, floor, tiles] pierreux; [beach] de galets → **fall** [b] (= made of stone) [outcrop, cliff] rocheux [c] (= unsympathetic) [person] dur, insensible; [look, stare, expression] dur; [face] de marbre; [silence] glacial [2] COMP ► **stony-broke*** ADJ (Brit) fauché comme les blés* ► **stony-faced** ADJ au visage impassible

stood [stʊd] VB pt, ptp of **stand**

stooge [stuːdʒ] N (Theat) comparse mf, faire-valoir m; (gen: pej) laquais m
► **stooge about*, stooge around*** VI rôder, errer

stook [stuːk] [1] N moyette f [2] VI moyetter

stool [stuːl] [1] N [a] tabouret m; (folding) pliant m; (= footstool) tabouret m, marche-pied†; (fig) **to fall between two ~s** se retrouver le bec dans l'eau* ► **music, piano** [b] [of window] rebord m; (Med) selle f; (Bot) pied m (de plante), plante f mère [2] COMP ► **stool pigeon*** N indicateur m, -trice f, mouchard(e) m(f); (in prison) mouton m

stoolie*, stooly* ['stuːlɪ] N (US) = **stool pigeon** → **stool**

stoop¹ [stuːp] [1] N [a] **to have** or **walk with a ~** avoir le dos voûté or rond [b] [of bird of prey] attaque f plongeante [2] VI [a] (= have a stoop) avoir le dos voûté or rond, être voûté [b] (also **~ down**) se pencher, se baisser; (fig) s'abaisser (**to sth** jusqu'à qch, **to do, to doing** jusqu'à faire); (fig) **he would ~ to anything** il est prêt à toutes les bassesses [c] [bird of prey] plonger

stoop² [stuːp] N (US) véranda f

stooping ['stuːpɪŋ] ADJ [person, back] voûté; [shoulders] tombant; [position, posture] courbé

stop [stɒp] [1] N [a] (= halt) arrêt m (also Ski); (= short stay) halte f; **we had a ~ of a few days in Arles** nous avons fait une halte de quelques jours à Arles; **we had a ~ for coffee** nous avons fait une pause-café; **they worked for six hours without a ~** ils ont travaillé six heures d'affilée or sans s'arrêter; **a five-minute ~ ◊ five minutes' ~** cinq minutes d'arrêt; **to be at a ~** [vehicle] être à l'arrêt; [traffic] être bloqué; [work, progress, production] s'être arrêté, avoir cessé; **to come to a ~** [traffic, vehicle] s'arrêter; [work, progress, production] cesser; **to bring to a ~** [+ traffic, vehicle] arrêter; [+ work, progress, production] arrêter, faire cesser; **to make a ~** [bus, train] s'arrêter; [plane, ship] faire escale; **to put a ~ to sth** mettre fin à qch, mettre un terme à qch; **I'll put a ~ to that!** je vais mettre un terme or le holà à tout ça! [b] (= stopping place) [of bus, train] arrêt m; [of plane, ship] escale f → **bus, request** [c] [of organ] jeu m; (fig) **to pull out all the ~s** faire un suprême effort, remuer ciel et terre (**to do** pour faire) [d] (Punctuation) point m; (in telegrams) stop m → **full** [e] (= device) (on drawer, window) taquet m; (on door stop) butoir m de porte; (on typewriter: also **margin ~**) margeur m; (Tech) mentonnet m [f] (Phon) (consonne f) occlusive f [g] (Phot) diaphragme m

2 VT a (= *block*) [+ *hole, pipe*] boucher, obturer; (*accidentally*) boucher, bloquer; [+ *leak*] boucher, colmater; [+ *jar, bottle*] boucher; [+ *tooth*] plomber; **to ~ one's ears** se boucher les oreilles; (*fig*) **to ~ one's ears to sth** rester sourd à qch; **to ~ a gap** (*lit*) boucher un trou; (*fig*) combler une lacune → **stopgap**; **to ~ the way** barrer le chemin

b (= *halt*) [+ *person, vehicle, ball, machine, process*] arrêter; [+ *traffic*] arrêter, interrompre; [+ *progress*] interrompre; [+ *light*] empêcher de passer; [+ *pain, worry, enjoyment*] mettre fin à; (*fig, Sport etc = beat*) battre; **he ~ped the show with his marvellous medley of old hits** il a fait un tabac* avec son merveilleux pot-pourri de vieilles chansons à succès; **to ~ sb short** (*lit*) arrêter qn net *or* brusquement; (= *interrupt*) interrompre qn; **to ~ sb (dead) in his tracks** (*lit*) arrêter qn net *or* brusquement; (*fig*) couper qn dans son élan; (*fig*) **to ~ sth (dead) in its tracks** interrompre qch; **he ~ped a bullet*** il a reçu une balle; **the walls ~ some of the noise** les murs étouffent *or* absorbent une partie du bruit

c (= *cease*) arrêter, cesser (**doing** de faire); **~ it!** assez!, ça suffit!; **~ that noise!** assez de bruit!; **to ~ work** arrêter *or* cesser de travailler, cesser le travail

d (= *interrupt*) [+ *activity, building, production*] interrompre, arrêter; (= *suspend*) suspendre; (*Boxing*) [+ *fight*] suspendre; [+ *allowance, leave, privileges*] supprimer; [+ *wages*] retenir; [+ *gas, electricity, water supply*] couper; **rain ~ped play** la pluie a interrompu *or* arrêté la partie; **they ~ped £15 out of his wages** ils ont retenu 15 livres sur son salaire; **to ~ one's subscription** résilier son abonnement; **to ~ (payment on) a cheque** faire opposition au paiement d'un chèque; **to ~ payment** [*bank*] suspendre ses paiements; **he ~ped the milk for a week** il a fait interrompre *or* il a annulé la livraison du lait pendant une semaine

e (= *prevent*) empêcher (**sb's doing, sb from doing** qn de faire, **sth happening, sth from happening** que qch n'arrive (*subj*)); **there's nothing to ~ you** rien ne vous en empêche; **he ~ped the house (from) being sold** il a empêché que la maison (ne) soit vendue *or* la vente de la maison

f (*Mus*) [+ *string*] presser; [+ *hole of trumpet etc*] boucher, mettre le doigt sur

3 VI a [*person, vehicle, machine, clock, sb's heart*] s'arrêter; (= *to do sth*) s'arrêter pour faire qch; **~ thief!** au voleur!; (*in work etc*) **you can ~ now** vous pouvez (vous) arrêter maintenant; (*in lesson etc*) **we'll ~ here for today** nous nous arrêterons *or* nous nous en tiendrons là pour aujourd'hui; **he ~ped (dead) in his tracks** il s'est arrêté net *or* pile*; **he ~ped in mid sentence** il s'est arrêté au beau milieu d'une phrase; **~ and think** réfléchissez bien; **~ and consider if** *or* **whether ...** réfléchissez si ...; **he never knows where to ~** il ne sait pas s'arrêter; **he will ~ at nothing** il est prêt à tout, il ne recule devant rien (**to do** pour faire) → **dead, shortstop**

b [*supplies, production, process, music*] s'arrêter, cesser; [*attack, pain, worry, enjoyment, custom*] cesser; [*allowance, privileges*] être supprimé; [*play, programme, concert*] finir, se terminer; [*conversation, discussion, struggle*] cesser, se terminer

c * (= *remain*) rester; (= *live temporarily*) loger; **~ where you are!** restez là où vous êtes!; **I'm ~ping with my aunt** je loge chez ma tante

4 COMP [*button, lever, signal*] d'arrêt; (*Phot*) [*bath, solution*] d'arrêt ► **stop-and-go** N (*US*) → **stop-go** ► **stop consonant** N (*Phon*) (consonne *f*) occlusive *f* ► **stop-go** N → **stop-go** ► **stop-off** N arrêt *m*, courte halte *f* ► **stop order** N (*St Ex*) ordre *m* stop ► **stop-press** N (*Brit Press*) (= *news*) nouvelles *fpl* de dernière heure; (*as heading*) « dernière heure » ► **stop sign** N (*Aut*) (panneau *m*)

stop *m*

► **stop away*** VI **he ~ped away for three years** il est resté trois ans sans revenir *or* trois ans absent; **he ~ped away from the meeting** il n'est pas allé à la réunion

► **stop behind*** VI rester en arrière *or* à la fin

► **stop by*** VI s'arrêter en passant

► **stop down*** VI (*bending*) rester baissé; (*lying down*) rester couché; (*under water*) rester sous l'eau

► **stop in*** VI a (*at home*) rester à la maison *or* chez soi, ne pas sortir b = **stop by**

► **stop off** 1 VI s'arrêter; (*on journey*) s'arrêter, faire une halte; **let's ~ off and get a pizza** arrêtons-nous pour acheter une pizza 2 **~-off** N → **stop**

► **stop out*** VI rester dehors, ne pas rentrer; **he always ~s out late on Fridays** il rentre toujours tard le vendredi

► **stop over** 1 VI s'arrêter (un *or* plusieurs jour(s)), faire une halte 2 **~over** N → **stopover**

► **stop up** 1 VI (*Brit**) ne pas se coucher, rester debout; **don't ~ up for me** ne m'attendez pas pour aller vous coucher 2 VT SEP [+ *hole, pipe, jar, bottle*] boucher; **my nose is ~ped up** j'ai le nez bouché

stopcock ['stɒpkɒk] N robinet *m* d'arrêt

stopgap ['stɒpgæp] 1 N bouche-trou *m* 2 ADJ [*measure, solution*] provisoire

stop-go ['stɒpgəʊ] 1 N (*gen, Econ*) **a period of ~** une période d'activité intense suivie de relâchement, une période de « stop and go » 2 COMP ► **stop-go policy** N politique *f* en dents de scie

stoplight ['stɒplaɪt] N (*US*) (= *traffic light*) feu *m* rouge; (= *brake light*) feu *m* de stop

stopover ['stɒpəʊvə'] N halte *f*

stoppage ['stɒpɪdʒ] 1 N a (*in traffic, work*) arrêt *m*, interruption *f*; (*Sport*) arrêt *m* de jeu; (= *strike*) arrêt *m* de travail, grève *f*; [*of leave, wages, payment*] suspension *f*; (= *amount deducted*) retenue *f* b (= *blockage*) obstruction *f*, engorgement *m*; (*Med*) occlusion *f* 2 COMP ► **stoppage time** N (*Sport*) arrêts *mpl* de jeu; **to play ~ time** jouer les arrêts de jeu

stopper ['stɒpə'] 1 N a [*of bottle, jar*] bouchon *m*; [*of bath, basin*] bonde *f*; **to take the ~ out of a bottle** déboucher une bouteille; **to put the ~ into a bottle** boucher une bouteille; (*fig*) **to put a ~ on sth*** mettre un terme *or* le holà à qch → **conversation** 2 VT boucher

stopping ['stɒpɪŋ] 1 N a (*NonC = halting*) [*of activity, progress, vehicle, process*] arrêt *m*; [*of cheque*] opposition *f* au paiement; [*of match, game, payment*] suspension *f*; [*of allowance, leave, privileges*] suppression *f*; [*of wages*] retenue *f* (**of** sur) b (*NonC = blocking*) [*of hole, pipe*] obturation *f*, bouchage *m*; [*of leak*] colmatage *m*, bouchage *m*; (*Mus*) → **double** c [*of tooth*] plombage *m* 2 COMP ► **stopping place** N (= *lay-by etc*) endroit *m* où s'arrêter; **we were looking for a ~ place** nous cherchions un endroit où nous arrêter ► **stopping train** N (train *m*) omnibus *m*

stopwatch ['stɒpwɒtʃ] N chronomètre *m*

storage ['stɔːrɪdʒ] 1 N a (*NonC*) [*of goods, fuel*] entreposage *m*, emmagasinage *m*; [*of furniture*] entreposage *m*; [*of food, wine*] rangement *m*, conservation *f*; [*of radioactive waste*] stockage *m*; [*of heat, electricity*] accumulation *f*; [*of documents*] conservation *f*; **to put in(to) ~** entreposer, emmagasiner; [+ *furniture*] mettre au garde-meuble → **cold** b (*Comput*) (= *state*) mémoire *f*; (= *action*) mise *f* en mémoire 2 COMP [*problems*] d'entreposage, d'emmagasinage; [*charges*] de magasinage ► **storage battery** N accumulateur *m*, accu* *m* ► **storage capacity** N (*gen, Comput*) capacité *f* de stockage ► **storage heater** (*also* elec-

tric ~ **heater**) N radiateur *m* électrique à accumulation, accumulateur *m* de chaleur ► **storage space** N (*in house*) espace *m* de rangement; (*in firm etc*) espace *m* de stockage ► **storage tank** N (*for oil etc*) réservoir *m* de stockage; (*for rainwater*) citerne *f* ► **storage unit** N (= *furniture*) meuble *m* de rangement

store [stɔː'] 1 N a (= *supply, stock, accumulation*) provision *f*, réserve *f*, stock *m* (*Comm*); [*of learning, information*] fonds *m*; **to get in** *or* **lay in a ~ of sth** faire provision de qch; **to keep a ~ of sth** avoir une provision de qch; (*fig*) **to set great ~/little ~ by sth** faire grand cas/peu de cas de qch, attacher du prix/peu de prix à qch b **~s** (= *supplies*) provisions *fpl*; **to take on** *or* **lay in ~s** s'approvisionner, faire des provisions c (*Brit = depot, warehouse*) entrepôt *m*; (= *furniture store*) garde-meuble *m*; (*in office, factory etc: also* **~s**) réserve *f*; (*larger*) service *m* des approvisionnements; **ammunition ~** dépôt *m* de munitions; **to put in(to) ~** [+ *goods*] entreposer; [+ *furniture*] mettre au garde-meuble; **I am keeping this in ~ for winter** je garde cela en réserve pour l'hiver; (*fig*) **I've got a surprise in ~ for you** j'ai une surprise en réserve pour vous, je vous réserve une surprise; **what does the future hold** *or* **have in ~ for him?** ◊ **what is** *or* **lies in ~ for him?** que lui réserve l'avenir? d (*esp US = shop*) magasin *m*, commerce *m*; (*large*) grand magasin *m*; (*small*) boutique *f*; **book ~** magasin *m* de livres, librairie *f* → **chain, department, general**

2 VT a (= *keep in reserve, collect: also* **~ up**) [+ *food, fuel, goods*] mettre en réserve; [+ *documents*] conserver; [+ *electricity, heat*] accumuler, emmagasiner; (*fig: in one's mind*) [+ *facts, information*] noter *or* enregistrer dans sa mémoire; **this cellar can ~ enough coal for the winter** cette cave peut contenir assez de charbon pour passer l'hiver b (= *place in store: also* **~ away**) [+ *food, fuel, goods*] emmagasiner, entreposer; [+ *furniture*] mettre au garde-meuble; [+ *crops*] mettre en grange, engranger; (*Comput*) mettre en réserve; **he ~d the information (away)** (*in filing system etc*) il a rangé les renseignements; (*in his mind*) il a noté les renseignements; **I've got the camping things ~d (away) till we need them** j'ai rangé *or* mis de côté les affaires de camping en attendant que nous en ayons besoin; **where do you ~ your wine?** où est-ce que vous entreposez *or* conservez votre vin? c (*Comput*) mémoriser

3 VI **these apples ~ well/badly** ces pommes se conservent bien/mal

4 COMP (*gen: esp US*) [*item, line*] de série; (*US: also* **~-bought**) [*clothes*] de confection *or* de série; [*cake*] du commerce ► **store card** N (*Comm*) carte *f* privative ► **store detective** N vigile *m* en civil (*dans un grand magasin*)

► **store away** VT SEP → **store 2b**

► **store up** VT SEP → **store 2a**

storefront ['stɔːfrʌnt] N (*US*) devanture *f*

storehouse ['stɔːhaʊs] N entrepôt *m*; (*fig: of information etc*) mine *f*

storekeeper ['stɔːˌkiːpə'] N magasinier *m*; (*esp US = shopkeeper*) commerçant(e) *m(f)*

storeroom ['stɔːrʊm] N réserve *f*, magasin *m*

storey, story (*US*) ['stɔːrɪ] N étage *m*; **on the 3rd** *or* (*US*) **4th ~** au troisième (étage); **a four-~(ed)** *or* (*US*) **four-storied building** un bâtiment de quatre étages

-storeyed, -storied (*US*) ['stɔːrɪd] ADJ (*in compounds*) → **storey**

stork [stɔːk] N cigogne *f*

storm [stɔːm] 1 N a tempête *f*; (= *thunderstorm*) orage *m*; (*on Beaufort scale*) tempête *f*; **~ of rain/snow** tempête *f* de pluie/de neige; **magnetic ~** orage *m* magnétique; (*Brit fig*) **it was a ~ in a teacup** c'était une

tempête dans un verre d'eau → **dust, hailstorm, sandstorm**
b (fig) [of arrows, missiles] pluie f, grêle f; [of insults, abuse] torrent m; [of cheers, protests, applause, indignation] tempête f; **there was a political ~** les passions politiques se sont déchaînées; **his speech caused or raised quite a ~** son discours a provoqué une véritable tempête or un ouragan; **to bring a ~ about one's ears** soulever un tollé (général); **a period of ~ and stress** une période très orageuse or très tourmentée
c (Mil) **to take by ~** prendre or emporter d'assaut; (fig) **the play took London by ~** la pièce a obtenu un succès foudroyant or fulgurant à Londres; **he took her by ~** il a eu un succès foudroyant or fulgurant auprès d'elle, elle a eu le coup de foudre pour lui
2 VT (Mil) prendre or emporter d'assaut; (fig) **angry ratepayers ~ed the town hall** les contribuables en colère ont pris d'assaut or ont envahi la mairie
3 VI [wind] souffler en tempête, faire rage; [rain] tomber à torrents, faire rage; (fig) [person] fulminer; **to ~ at sb** tempêter or fulminer contre qn; **to ~ (one's way) in/out etc** entrer/sortir etc comme un ouragan
4 COMP [signal, warning] de tempête ► **storm belt** N zone f des tempêtes ► **storm cellar** N (US) abri m contre les tempêtes or cyclones ► **storm centre** N centre m de dépression, œil m du cyclone; (fig) centre m de l'agitation ► **storm cloud** N nuage m orageux; (fig) nuage m noir or menaçant; (fig) **the ~ clouds are gathering** l'avenir est sombre ► **storm cone** N cône m de tempête ► **storm damage** N dégâts mpl occasionnés par la tempête ► **storm door** N double porte f (à l'extérieur) ► **storm drain** N collecteur m d'eaux pluviales ► **storm force** N ~ **force** [wind] atteindre force 10 ► **storm-force** ADJ [wind] de force 10 ► **storm lantern** N lampe-tempête f, lanterne-tempête f ► **storm-lashed** ADJ battu par l'orage or la tempête ► **storm petrel** N (Orn, fig) = **stormy petrel**; → **stormy** ► **storm sewer** N collecteur m d'eaux pluviales ► **storm-tossed** ADJ ballotté or battu par la tempête ► **storm trooper** N (Mil) (gen) membre m d'une troupe d'assaut; (= Nazi) membre m des sections d'assaut nazies ► **storm troops** NPL troupes fpl d'assaut ► **storm water** N eau(x) f(pl) pluviale(s) ► **storm window** N double fenêtre f (à l'extérieur)

stormbound ['stɔːmbaʊnd] ADJ bloqué par la tempête

storming ['stɔːmɪŋ] **1** N (= attack, invasion) assaut m; **the ~ of the Bastille** la prise de la Bastille **2** ADJ (* = impressive) spectaculaire, impressionnant

stormproof ['stɔːmpruːf] ADJ à l'épreuve de la tempête

stormy ['stɔːmɪ] **1** ADJ **a** [weather, night, skies] orageux; [seas, waters] démonté; **on a ~ night** par une nuit d'orage **b** (fig = turbulent) [meeting, scene, relationship] orageux, houleux; [period] tumultueux; [career] mouvementé; [temperament, person] violent, emporté; **~ waters** période f tumultueuse; **the bill had a ~ passage through Parliament** l'adoption du projet de loi au Parlement a donné lieu à des débats houleux **2** COMP ► **stormy petrel** N (Orn) pétrel m; (fig) enfant mf terrible

story[1] ['stɔːrɪ] **1** N **a** (= account) histoire f; **it's a long ~** c'est toute une histoire, c'est une longue histoire; **that's only part of the ~** mais ce n'est pas tout; **you're not telling me the whole or full ~** ◊ **you're only telling me part of the ~** tu ne me dis pas tout, tu me caches quelque chose; **according to your ~** d'après ce que vous dites, selon vous; **I've heard his ~** j'ai entendu sa version des faits; (fig) **a differ-**
ent ~ une autre histoire; **it's quite another ~ or a very different ~** c'est une tout autre histoire; **it's the same old ~** c'est toujours la même histoire or la même chanson*; **these scars tell their own ~** ces cicatrices parlent d'elles-mêmes or en disent long; (hum) **that's the ~ of my life!** ça m'arrive tout le temps!
b (= tale) histoire f, conte m; (= legend) histoire f, légende f; (Literat) histoire f, récit m; (short) nouvelle f; (= anecdote, joke) histoire f, anecdote f; **there's an interesting ~ attached to that** on raconte une histoire intéressante à ce sujet; **or so the ~ goes** ou du moins c'est ce que l'on raconte, d'après les on-dit; **he writes stories** il écrit des histoires or des nouvelles; **she told the children a ~** elle a raconté une histoire aux enfants; **do you know the ~ about ...?** connaissez-vous l'histoire de ...?; **what a ~ this house could tell!** que de choses cette maison pourrait nous (or vous etc) raconter! → **bedtime, fairy, short**
c (= plot) [of film] scénario m; [of book] intrigue f; [of play] intrigue f, action f; **the ~ of the film is taken from his book** le scénario du film est tiré de son roman; **he did the ~ for the film** il a écrit le scénario du film
d (Press, Rad, TV) (= event etc) affaire f; (= article) article m; **they devoted two pages to the ~ of ...** ils ont consacré deux pages à l'affaire de ...; **did you read the ~ on ...?** avez-vous lu l'article sur ...?; **I don't know if there's a ~ in it** je ne sais pas s'il y a matière à un article; **he was sent to cover the ~ of the refugees** on l'a envoyé faire un reportage sur les réfugiés
e (* fig) histoire f; **to tell stories** raconter des histoires
2 COMP ► **story line** N [of film] scénario m; [of book] intrigue f; [of play] intrigue f, action f ► **story-writer** N nouvelliste mf

story[2] ['stɔːrɪ] N (US) = **storey**

storyboard ['stɔːrɪbɔːd] N (Cine, TV) story-board m

storybook ['stɔːrɪbʊk] **1** N livre m de contes or d'histoires **2** ADJ (fig) [situation, love affair] romanesque; **a meeting with a ~ ending** une rencontre qui se termine comme dans les romans

storyteller ['stɔːrɪtelə*] N conteur m, -euse f; (* = fibber) menteur m, -euse f

storytelling ['stɔːrɪtelɪŋ] N (NonC) **they pass on their tradition through ~** leurs traditions se transmettent à travers les contes

stoup [stuːp] N (Rel) bénitier m; (†† = tankard) pichet m

stout [staʊt] **1** ADJ **a** (= fat) [person] corpulent, gros (grosse f); **to get or grow ~** prendre de l'embonpoint **b** (= sturdy) [legs] solide, robuste; [stick, door, rope, shoes] solide; [horse] vigoureux; [branch] gros (grosse f) **c** (= resolute) [soldier, defence, resistance, opposition, heart] vaillant; [support] résolu; **he is a ~ fellow**† c'est un brave type* **2** N (= beer) stout m or f, bière f brune **3** COMP ► **stout-hearted** ADJ vaillant, intrépide

stoutly ['staʊtlɪ] ADV **a** (= resolutely) [fight, defend, resist] vaillamment; [deny] vigoureusement; [believe, maintain] dur comme fer **b** **~ built** [hut] solidement bâti

stoutness ['staʊtnɪs] N (NonC) **a** (= fatness) [of person] corpulence f, embonpoint m **b** (= sturdiness) [of horse, branch] vigueur f; [of stick, door, rope, shoes] solidité f **c** (= resoluteness) [of defence, resistance, opposition] vaillance f; [of support] détermination f; **the ~ of his resolve** sa résolution inébranlable; **~ of heart** vaillance f

stove[1] [staʊv] N **a** (= heater) poêle m → **wood b** (= cooker) (solid fuel) fourneau m; (gas, electric) cuisinière f; (small) réchaud m **c** (Ind, Tech) four m, étuve f

stove[2] [staʊv] VB pt, ptp of **stave**
stovepipe ['staʊvpaɪp] N (lit, also fig = hat) tuyau m de poêle

stow [staʊ] VT ranger, mettre; (out of sight: also **~ away**) faire disparaître, cacher; (Naut) [+ cargo] arrimer; (also **~ away**) [+ ropes, tarpaulins etc] ranger; **where can I ~ this?** où puis-je déposer ceci?; **~ it!**‡ la ferme!‡, ferme-la!‡
► **stow away** **1** VI s'embarquer clandestinement; **he ~ed away to Australia** il s'est embarqué clandestinement pour l'Australie **2** VT SEP (= put away) ranger; (= put in its place) ranger, placer; (= put out of sight) faire disparaître, cacher; (‡ fig) [+ meal, food] enfourner* → **stow 3** **~away** N → **stowaway**

stowage ['staʊɪdʒ] N (Naut) (= action) arrimage m; (= space) espace m utile; (= costs) frais mpl d'arrimage

stowaway ['staʊəweɪ] N passager m clandestin, passagère f clandestine

strabismus [strə'bɪzməs] N strabisme m

strabotomy [strə'bɒtəmɪ] N strabotomie f

straddle ['strædl] **1** VT [+ horse, cycle] enfourcher; [+ chair] se mettre à califourchon or à cheval sur; [+ fence, ditch] enjamber; **to be straddling sth** être à califourchon or à cheval sur qch; **the village ~s the border** le village est à cheval sur la frontière; **the enemy positions ~d the river** l'ennemi avait pris position des deux côtés de la rivière; (Mil: gunnery) **to ~ a target** encadrer un objectif; (US fig) **to ~ an issue** nager entre deux eaux, ménager la chèvre et le chou **2** VI être à califourchon; (US* fig) nager entre deux eaux, ménager la chèvre et le chou; **straddling legs** jambes fpl écartées

strafe [strɑːf] VT (Mil etc) (with machine guns) mitrailler au sol; (with shellfire, bombs) bombarder, marmiter

strafing ['strɑːfɪŋ] N (Mil, Aviat) mitraillage m au sol

straggle ['strægl] VI **a** [vines, plants] pousser tout en longueur, pousser au hasard; [hair] être or retomber en désordre; [houses, trees] être épars or disséminés; [village] s'étendre en longueur; **the branches ~d along the wall** les branches tortueuses grimpaient le long du mur; **the village ~s for miles along the road** les maisons du village s'égrènent or le village s'étend sur des kilomètres le long de la route; **her hair was straggling over her face** ses cheveux rebelles or des mèches folles retombaient en désordre sur son visage **b** **to ~ in/out etc** [people, cars, planes] entrer/sortir etc petit à petit
► **straggle away**, **straggle off** VI se débander or se disperser petit à petit

straggler ['stræglə*] N (= person) traînard(e) m(f); (= also Mil) (= plane etc) avion m etc isolé (qui traîne derrière les autres); (Bot) branche f gourmande, gourmand m

straggling ['stræglɪŋ], **straggly** ['stræglɪ] ADJ qui traîne en longueur; [plant] (qui pousse) tout en longueur; [village] tout en longueur; **~ hair** cheveux mpl fins rebelles or en désordre or décoiffés; **a ~ row of houses** un rang de maisons disséminées; **a long ~ line** une longue ligne irrégulière

straight [streɪt] **1** ADJ **a** (= not curved) [road, edge, stick, nose, skirt, trousers] droit; [posture] bien droit; [course, route] en ligne droite; [chair] à dossier droit; [hair] raide; **a ~ line** (gen) une ligne droite; (Math) une droite; **to walk in a ~ line** marcher en ligne droite; **on a ~ course** en ligne droite; **to have a ~ back** avoir le dos droit; **to keep one's back ~** se tenir droit; **to play (with) a ~ bat** (Cricket) jouer avec la batte verticale; (Brit fig = prevaricate) être sur la défensive; († = act decently) jouer franc jeu
b (= not askew) [picture, rug, tablecloth tie, hat, hem] droit; **the picture isn't ~** le tableau n'est pas droit or est de travers; **to put or set ~** [+ picture, hat, tie] redresser, remettre droit;

[+ *rug, tablecloth*] remettre droit

[c] (= *frank*) [*person, answer, question*] franc (franche *f*) (**with sb** avec qn); [*dealing*] loyal, régulier; [*denial, refusal*] net, catégorique; **to be ~ about sth** exprimer franchement qch; **let's be ~ about this** soyons francs, ne nous leurrons pas; **~ talk(ing)** ◊ **~ speaking** franc-parler *m*; **it's time for some ~ talking** soyons francs; **to play a ~ game** jouer franc jeu; (*Racing, St Ex etc*) **~ tip** tuyau* *m* sûr

[d] (= *unambiguous*) clair; **say nothing, is that ~?** tu ne dis rien, c'est clair?; **have you got that ~?** est-ce bien clair?; **let's get this ~** entendons-nous bien sur ce point; **let's get that ~ right now** mettons cela au clair tout de suite; **to get things ~ in one's mind** mettre les choses au clair dans son esprit; **to put sth ~** mettre qch au clair; **to put** or **set sb ~ (about sth)** éclairer qn (sur qch); **to keep sb ~ (about sth)** empêcher qn de se tromper (sur qch); **to put** or **set o.s. ~ with sb** faire en sorte de ne pas être en reste avec qn → **record**

[e] (= *tidy*) [*house, room, books, affairs, accounts*] en ordre; **to put** or **set** or **get sth ~** [+ *house, room, books*] mettre qch en ordre, mettre de l'ordre dans qch; [+ *affairs, accounts*] mettre de l'ordre dans qch

[f] (= *pure, simple*) **it was a ~ choice between A and B** il n'y avait que deux solutions, A ou B; **the election was a ~ fight between the Tories and Labour** l'élection a mis aux prises conservateurs et travaillistes; **her latest novel is ~ autobiography** son dernier roman est de l'autobiographie pure; (*US*) **to get ~ As** obtenir les notes les plus élevées; (*US*) **a ~ A student** un étudiant qui obtient les notes les plus élevées partout

[g] (= *consecutive*) [*victories, defeats, games, months*] consécutif; **to win ten ~ victories** remporter dix victoires d'affilée or consécutives; **for five ~ days** pendant cinq jours d'affilée or consécutifs; (*Tennis*) **in ~ sets** en deux/trois sets (*pour les matchs en trois/cinq sets*); (*Tennis*) **to win/lose in ~ sets** gagner/perdre trois sets

[h] (* = *not owed or owing money*) quitte; **if I give you £5, then we'll be ~** si je te donne cinq livres, nous serons quittes

[i] (= *unmixed*) [*whisky, vodka*] sec (sèche *f*), sans eau

[j] (*Theat*) (= *mainstream*) [*theatre*] traditionnel; (= *non-comic*) [*play, role, actor*] sérieux

[k] (= *unsmiling*) **to keep a ~ face** garder son sérieux; **to say sth with a ~ face** dire qch sans sourire or avec un grand sérieux → **4**

[l] (*Geom*) [*angle*] plat

[m] (* = *conventional*) [*person*] conventionnel, conformiste

[n] (* = *heterosexual*) hétéro*

[o] * (= *not criminal*) [*person*] honnête, régulier; (*not on drugs*) **I've been ~ for three years** ça fait trois ans que je n'ai pas pris de drogue

2 N [a] **the ~** [*of racecourse, railway line, river etc*] la ligne droite; (*fig*) **now we're in the ~** nous sommes maintenant dans la dernière ligne droite

[b] **to cut sth on the ~** couper qch (de) droit fil; **out of the ~** de travers, en biais

[c] (*fig*) **to follow** or **keep to the ~ and narrow** rester dans le droit chemin; (*fig*) **to keep sb~ on the ~ and narrow** faire suivre le droit chemin à qn

3 ADV [a] (= *in a straight line*) [*walk*] droit; [*grow*] (bien) droit; [*fly*] en ligne droite; [*shoot*] juste; **~ above us** juste au-dessus de nous; **~ across from the house** juste en face de la maison; **to go ~ ahead** aller tout droit; **he looked ~ ahead** il a regardé droit devant lui; **he came ~ at me** il s'est dirigé droit sur moi; **to look ~ at sb** regarder qn droit dans les yeux; **to hold o.s. ~** se tenir droit; **to look sb ~ in the face/the eye** regarder qn bien en face/droit dans les yeux; **to go ~ on** aller tout droit; **to sit ~** s'asseoir bien droit; **to sit up ~**

se redresser; **to stand ~** se tenir droit; **to stand up ~** se redresser; **the bullet went ~ through his chest** la balle lui a traversé la poitrine de part en part; **to go ~ towards sb/sth** se diriger droit vers qn/qch; **the cork shot ~ up in the air** le bouchon est parti droit en l'air

[b] (= *level*) **to hang ~** [*picture*] être bien droit

[c] (= *directly*) **~ after this** tout de suite après; **~ away** tout de suite, sur-le-champ; **to come ~ back** (= *without detour*) revenir directement; (= *immediately*) revenir tout de suite; (*fig*) **~ from the horse's mouth** de source sûre; **to go ~ home** (= *without detour*) rentrer directement chez soi; (= *immediately*) rentrer chez soi tout de suite; **~ off** (= *immediately*) tout de suite, sur-le-champ; (= *without hesitation*) sans hésiter; (= *without beating about the bush*) sans ambages, sans mâcher ses mots; **~ out** (= *without hesitation*) sans hésiter; (= *without beating about the bush*) sans ambages, sans mâcher ses mots; **he went ~ to London** (= *without detour*) il est allé directement or tout droit à Londres; (= *immediately*) il s'est immédiatement rendu à Londres; **to go ~ to bed** aller tout de suite se coucher; **I may as well come ~ to the point** autant que j'en vienne droit au fait

[d] (* = *frankly*) **give it to me** or **tell me ~** dis-le-moi carrément; **to tell sb sth ~** out dire franchement qch à qn; (*fig*) **I let him have it ~ from the shoulder** je le lui ai dit carrément; (*Brit*) **~ up, I got fifty quid for it*** sans blaguer*, j'en ai tiré cinquante livres; (*Brit*) **I got fifty quid for it — ~ up?*** j'en ai tiré cinquante livres — sans blague?*

[e] (= *neat*) **to drink one's whisky ~** boire son whisky sec or sans eau

[f] (= *clearly*) **he couldn't think ~** il avait le cerveau brouillé, il n'avait plus les idées claires; **I couldn't see ~** je n'y voyais plus clair

[g] **to go ~*** (= *reform*) revenir dans le droit chemin

[h] (= *consecutively*) **for five days ~** pendant cinq jours d'affilée or consécutifs

[i] (*Theat*) **he played the role ~** il a joué le rôle avec mesure

4 COMP ► **straight-cut tobacco** N tabac *m* coupé dans la longueur de la feuille ► **straight-faced** ADV en gardant son sérieux, d'un air impassible ♦ ADJ qui garde son sérieux, impassible ► **straight flush** N (*Cards*) quinte *f* flush ► **straight-laced** ADJ = **strait-laced**; → **strait** ► **straight-line** ADJ [*depreciation*] constant ► **straight man** N (*pl* **straight men**) (*Theat*) comparse *m*, faire-valoir *m* ► **straight-out*** ADJ [*answer, denial, refusal*] net, catégorique; [*supporter, enthusiast, communist*] pur jus*; [*liar, thief*] fieffé (*before n*) ► **straight razor** N (*US*) rasoir *m* à main or de coiffeur ► **straight ticket** N (*US Pol*) **to vote a ~ ticket** choisir une liste sans panachage

straightedge ['streɪtedʒ] N règle *f* large et plate, limande *f* (*Carpentry*)

straighten ['streɪtn] **1** VT [+ *wire, nail*] redresser, défausser; [+ *hair*] décrêper; [+ *road*] refaire en éliminant les tournants; [+ *tie, hat*] ajuster; [+ *picture*] redresser, remettre d'aplomb; [+ *room*] mettre de l'ordre dans, mettre en ordre; [+ *papers*] ranger; **to ~ one's back** or **shoulders** se redresser, se tenir droit; **to ~ the hem of a skirt** arrondir une jupe **2** VI (*also ~ out*) [*road etc*] devenir droit; (*also ~ out, ~ up*) [*growing plant etc*] pousser droit; (*also ~ up*) [*person*] se redresser

► **straighten out** **1** VI → **straighten 2** **2** VT SEP [+ *wire, nail*] redresser, défausser; [+ *road*] refaire en éliminant les tournants; (*fig*) [+ *situation*] débrouiller; [+ *problem*] résoudre; [+ *one's ideas*] mettre de l'ordre dans, débrouiller; **he managed to ~ things out*** il a réussi à arranger les choses; **I'm trying to ~ out how much I owe him*** j'essaie de trouver combien je lui dois; **to ~ sb out:** remettre qn

dans la bonne voie; **I'll soon ~ him out!:** je vais aller le remettre à sa place!, je vais lui apprendre!

► **straighten up** **1** VI [a] → **straighten 2** [b] (= *tidy up*) mettre de l'ordre, ranger **2** VT SEP [+ *room, books, papers*] ranger, mettre de l'ordre dans

straightforward [ˌstreɪt'fɔːwəd] ADJ (= *frank*) honnête, franc (franche *f*); (= *plain-spoken*) franc (franche *f*), direct; (= *simple*) simple; **it's very ~** c'est tout ce qu'il y a de plus simple; **it was ~ racism** c'était du racisme pur et simple or du racisme à l'état pur

straightforwardly [ˌstreɪt'fɔːwədlɪ] ADV [*answer*] franchement, sans détour; [*behave*] avec droiture, honnêtement; **everything went quite ~** il n'y a pas eu de problèmes, tout s'est bien passé

straightforwardness [ˌstreɪt'fɔːwədnɪs] N (= *frankness*) honnêteté *f*, franchise *f*; (= *plain-spokenness*) franchise *f*; (= *simplicity*) simplicité *f*

straightjacket ['streɪtdʒækɪt] N = **straitjacket**

straightness ['streɪtnɪs] N [a] (= *frankness*) franchise *f*; (= *honesty*) rectitude *f* [b] (* = *heterosexual attitudes*) attitudes *fpl* hétéro*

straightway †† ['streɪtweɪ] ADV incontinent, sur-le-champ

strain[1] [streɪn] **1** N [a] (*Tech etc*) tension *f*, pression *f*; **the ~ on the rope** la tension de la corde, la force exercée sur la corde; **it broke under the ~** cela s'est rompu sous la tension; **that puts a great ~ on the beam** cela exerce une forte pression sur la poutre; **to take the ~ off sth** diminuer la pression sur qch; (*fig*) **it put a great ~ on their friendship** cela a mis leur amitié à rude épreuve; **it was a ~ on the economy/their resources/his purse** cela grevait l'économie/leurs ressources/son budget; **to stand the ~** [*rope, beam*] supporter la tension (*or* le poids *etc*); [*person*] tenir le coup* → **breaking**

[b] (*physical*) effort *m* (physique); (= *overwork*) surmenage *m*; (= *tiredness*) fatigue *f*; **the ~(s) of city life** la tension de la vie urbaine; **the ~ of six hours at the wheel** la fatigue nerveuse que représentent six heures passées au volant; **listening for three hours is a ~** écouter pendant trois heures demande un grand effort; **all the ~ and struggle of bringing up the family** toutes les tensions et les soucis qui sont le lot d'un parent qui élève ses enfants; **the ~ of climbing the stairs** l'effort requis pour monter l'escalier; **he has been under a great deal of ~** ses nerfs ont été mis à rude épreuve; **the situation put a great ~ on him** or **put him under a great ~** la situation l'a épuisé or l'a beaucoup fatigué nerveusement → **stress**

[c] (*Med* = *sprain*) entorse *f*, foulure *f* → **eye-strain**

[d] **~s** (*Mus*) accords *mpl*, accents *mpl*; (*Poetry*) accents *mpl*, chant *m*; **to the ~s of the "London March"** aux accents de la « Marche londonienne »

2 VT [a] [+ *rope, beam*] tendre fortement or excessivement; (*Med*) [+ *muscle*] froisser; [+ *arm, ankle*] fouler; (*fig*) [+ *friendship, relationship, marriage*] mettre à rude épreuve; [+ *resources, savings, budget, the economy*] grever; [+ *meaning*] forcer; [+ *word*] forcer le sens de; [+ *sb's patience*] mettre à l'épreuve; [+ *one's authority*] outrepasser, excéder; (*Med*) **to ~ one's back** se donner un tour de reins; **to ~ one's heart** se fatiguer le cœur; **to ~ one's shoulder** se froisser un muscle dans l'épaule; **to ~ one's voice** (*action*) forcer sa voix; (*result*) se casser la voix; **to ~ one's eyes** s'abîmer or se fatiguer les yeux; **he ~ed his eyes to make out what it was** il a plissé les yeux pour mieux distinguer ce que c'était; **to ~ one's ears to hear sth** tendre l'oreille pour entendre qch; **to ~ every nerve to do** fournir un effort intense pour faire; **to ~ o.s.** (= *damage muscle* etc) se froisser un muscle; (= *overtire o.s.*) se surmener; (*iro*) **don't ~ yourself!** surtout ne te fatigue pas!

b († or *liter*) **to ~ sb to o.s.** or **to one's heart** serrer qn contre son cœur, étreindre qn **c** (= *filter*) [+ *liquid*] passer, filtrer; [+ *soup, gravy*] passer; [+ *vegetables*] (faire) égoutter

3 VI **to ~ to do** (*physically*) peiner pour faire, fournir un gros effort pour faire; (*mentally*) s'efforcer de faire; **to ~ at sth** (*pushing/pulling*) pousser/tirer qch de toutes ses forces; (*fig = jib at*) renâcler à qch; **to ~ at the leash** [*dog*] tirer fort sur sa laisse ■ (*PROV*) **to ~ at a gnat (and swallow a camel)** faire une histoire pour une vétille et passer sur une énormité; (*fig*) **to ~ after sth** faire un grand effort pour obtenir qch; **to ~ under a weight** ployer sous un poids

► **strain off** VT SEP [+ *liquid*] vider

strain² [streɪn] N (= *breed, lineage*) race *f*, lignée *f*; [*of animal etc*] race *f*; [*of virus*] souche *f*; (= *tendency, streak*) tendance *f*; **there is a ~ of madness in the family** il y a dans la famille des tendances à or une prédisposition à la folie; (*fig*) **there was a lot more in the same ~** il y en avait encore beaucoup du même genre; **he continued in this ~** il a continué sur ce ton or dans ce sens

strained [streɪnd] ADJ **a** (= *tense*) [*person, voice, relations, atmosphere, silence*] tendu **b** (= *unnatural*) [*smile*] contraint; [*laugh, jollity, politeness*] forcé; [*manner*] emprunté; [*style*] affecté **c** (*Physiol*) (= *damaged*) [*muscle*] froissé; [*arm, ankle*] foulé; [*eyes*] fatigué; [*voice*] (= *overtaxed*) forcé; (= *injured*) cassé; **he has a ~ shoulder/back** il s'est froissé un muscle dans l'épaule/le dos **d** (*Culin*) [*baby food*] en purée; [*vegetables*] égoutté; [*liquid, soup, gravy*] passé

strainer ['streɪnə'] N (*Culin*) passoire *f*; (*Tech*) épurateur *m*

strait [streɪt] **1** N **a** (*Geog: also* **~s**) détroit *m*; **the Strait of Gibraltar** le détroit de Gibraltar; **the Straits of Dover** le Pas de Calais; **the Strait of Hormuz** le détroit d'Hormuz or d'Ormuz **b** (*fig*) **~s** situation *f* difficile; **to be in financial ~s** avoir des ennuis d'argent → **dire 2** ADJ († *esp Biblical*) étroit **3** COMP ► **strait-laced** ADJ collet monté *inv*

straitened ['streɪtnd] ADJ (*frm*) [*times*] de gêne; **in ~ circumstances** dans la gêne; **the more ~ economic circumstances of the 1990s** la situation économique plus difficile des années 1990

straitjacket ['streɪtdʒækɪt] N camisole *f* de force

strand¹ [strænd] **1** N (*liter* = *shore*) grève *f* **2** VT [+ *ship*] échouer; (*also* **to leave ~ed**) [+ *person*] laisser en rade* or en plan*; **they were (left) ~ed without passports or money** ils se sont retrouvés en rade* or coincés sans passeport ni argent; **he took the car and left me ~ed** il a pris la voiture et m'a laissé en plan* or en rade*

strand² [strænd] N [*of thread, wire*] brin *m*; [*of rope*] toron *m*; [*of fibrous substance*] fibre *f*; [*of pearls*] rang *m*; (*fig: in narrative etc*) fil *m*, enchaînement *m*; **a ~ of hair** une mèche; (*fig*) **the ~s of one's life** le fil de sa vie

strange [streɪndʒ] ADJ **a** (= *peculiar*) [*person, behaviour, feeling, fact, event, place, situation*] étrange; **there's something ~ about him** il a quelque chose de bizarre; **the ~ thing is that ...** ce qu'il y a d'étrange, c'est que ...; **it feels ~ (to do sth)** ça fait bizarre (de faire qch), ça paraît étrange (de faire qch); **it is ~ that ...** c'est étrange que ... (+ *subj*); **it is ~ to do sth** c'est étrange de faire qch; **to seem ~ to sb** paraître étrange à qn; **~ as it may seem ...** aussi étrange que cela puisse paraître ...; **~ to say I have never met her** chose étrange, je ne l'ai jamais rencontrée, ce qu'il y a d'étrange, c'est que je ne l'ai jamais rencontrée → **bedfellow, truth**

b (= *unfamiliar*) [*country, city, house, language*] inconnu (**to sb** à qn); **a ~ man** un inconnu; **there were several ~ people there** il y avait plusieurs personnes qu'il ne connaissais pas (or qu'il ne connaissait pas *etc*); **don't talk to any ~ men** n'adresse pas la parole à des inconnus; **never get in a ~ car** ne monte jamais dans la voiture d'un inconnu; **a ~ car was parked in front of my house** une voiture inconnue était garée devant chez moi; **I awoke in a ~ bed** je me suis réveillé dans un lit qui n'était pas le mien

c (= *unaccustomed*) [*work, activity*] inhabituel; **you'll feel rather ~ at first** vous vous sentirez un peu dépaysé pour commencer **d** (= *unwell*) **to feel ~** [*person*] se sentir mal, ne pas se sentir bien

strangely ['streɪndʒlɪ] ADV [*act, behave*] de façon étrange, bizarrement; [*familiar, quiet*] étrangement; **~ named** au nom étrange; **to be ~ reminiscent of sb/sth** rappeler étrangement qn/qch; **~ (enough), I have never met her** chose étrange, je ne l'ai jamais rencontrée

strangeness ['streɪndʒnɪs] N étrangeté *f*, bizarrerie *f*

stranger ['streɪndʒə'] **1** N (*unknown*) inconnu(e) *m(f)*; (*from another place*) étranger *m*, -ère *f*; **he is a perfect ~ (to me)** il m'est totalement inconnu; **I'm a ~ here** je ne suis pas d'ici; **I am a ~ to Paris** je ne connais pas Paris; **a ~ to politics** un novice en matière de politique; (*liter*) **he was no ~ to misfortune** il connaissait bien le malheur, il avait l'habitude du malheur; **you're quite a ~!** vous vous faites or vous devenez rare!, on ne vous voit plus! **2** COMP ► **Strangers' Gallery** N (*Brit Parl*) tribune *f* réservée au public

strangle ['stræŋgl] VT étrangler; (*fig*) [+ *free speech*] étrangler, museler; [+ *protests*] étouffer; **~d** [*person, voice, cry, laugh*] étranglé; [*sneeze, sob*] étouffé

stranglehold ['stræŋglhəʊld] N (*lit, fig*) **to have a ~ on sb** tenir qn à la gorge; (*Econ, Comm etc*) **a ~ on the market** une domination or un quasi-monopole du marché

strangler ['stræŋglə'] N étrangleur *m*, -euse *f*

strangling ['stræŋglɪŋ] N (*lit*) strangulation *f*, étranglement *m*; (*fig*) étranglement *m*; **there have been several ~s in Boston** plusieurs personnes ont été étranglées à Boston

strangulate ['stræŋgjʊleɪt] VT (*Med*) étrangler

strangulation [ˌstræŋgjʊ'leɪʃən] N (*NonC*) strangulation *f*

strap [stræp] **1** N (*of leather*) (*thin*) lanière *f*; (*broader*) sangle *f*; (*of cloth*) bande *f*; (*on shoe, also Climbing*) lanière *f*; (*on harness etc*) sangle *f*, courroie *f*; (*on suitcase, around book*) sangle *f*, lanière *f*; (*on garment*) bretelle *f*; (*on shoulder bag, camera etc*) bandoulière *f*; (= *watch strap*) bracelet *m*; (*for razor*) cuir *m*; (*in bus, tube*) poignée *f* de cuir; (*Scol Hist*) lanière *f* de cuir; (*Tech*) lien *m*; (*Scol Hist*) **to give sb the ~** administrer une correction à qn (avec une lanière de cuir)

2 VT **a** (= *tie*) attacher (**sth to sth** qch à qch) **b** (*also* **~ up**) [+ *sb's ribs etc*] bander or maintenir avec une sangle; [+ *suitcase, books*] attacher avec une sangle or une courroie **c** [+ *child etc*] administrer une correction à **3** COMP ► **strap-hang** VI voyager debout (*dans les transports en commun*) ► **strap-hanger** N (*standing*) voyageur *m*, -euse *f* debout *inv* (*dans les transports en commun*); (*US: public transport user*) usager *m* des transports en commun

► **strap down** VT SEP attacher avec une sangle or une courroie

► **strap in** VT SEP [+ *object*] attacher avec une sangle or une courroie; [+ *child in car, pram etc*] attacher avec une ceinture de sécurité or un harnais; **he isn't properly ~ped in** il est

mal attaché, sa ceinture de sécurité or son harnais est mal mis(e)

► **strap on** VT SEP [+ *object*] attacher; [+ *watch*] mettre, attacher

► **strap up** VT SEP = **strap 2b**

strapless ['stræplɪs] ADJ [*dress, bra*] sans bretelles

strapline ['stræplaɪn] N (*Press = headline*) gros titre *m*

strapped* [stræpt] ADJ **to be financially ~ ◊ to be ~ for funds** or **for cash** être à court (d'argent)

strapper* ['stræpə'] N gaillard(e) *m(f)*

strapping ['stræpɪŋ] **1** ADJ bien bâti, costaud*; **a ~ fellow** un solide gaillard **2** N (*NonC*) **a** (*for cargo*) courroies *fpl*, sangles *fpl* **b** (*Med*) bandages *mpl*

Strasbourg ['stræzbɜːg] N Strasbourg

strata ['strɑːtə] NPL *of* **stratum**

stratagem ['strætɪdʒəm] N stratagème *m*

strategic [strə'tiːdʒɪk] **1** ADJ stratégique; (*Mil*) **to put sth in a ~ position** mettre qch à un endroit stratégique **2** COMP ► **Strategic Air Command** N (*US Aviat*) l'aviation *f* militaire stratégique (américaine) ► **strategic business unit** N domaine *m* d'activité stratégique ► **Strategic Defense Initiative** N (*US Mil, Space*) Initiative *f* de défense stratégique

strategical [strə'tiːdʒɪkəl] ADJ stratégique

strategically [strə'tiːdʒɪkəlɪ] ADV **a** **~ placed** [*town, room*] stratégiquement situé; [*object*] stratégiquement placé **b** (*esp Mil*) [*important, sensitive*] du point de vue stratégique; **~, speed is vital in a desert campaign** la vitesse est un élément stratégique fondamental lors d'une campagne dans le désert; **~, a merger would make sense** du point de vue stratégique, une fusion serait souhaitable

strategist ['strætɪdʒɪst] N stratège *m*

strategy ['strætɪdʒɪ] N stratégie *f*

stratification [ˌstrætɪfɪ'keɪʃən] N stratification *f*

stratificational [ˌstrætɪfɪ'keɪʃənl] ADJ (*Ling*) stratificationnel

stratify ['strætɪfaɪ] VTI stratifier

stratocruiser ['strætəʊˌkruːzə'] N avion *m* stratosphérique

stratosphere ['strætəʊsfɪə'] N stratosphère *f*; **this would send oil prices into the ~** cela ferait exploser le prix du pétrole

stratospheric [ˌstrætəʊs'ferɪk] ADJ stratosphérique

stratum ['strɑːtəm] N (*pl* **stratums** or **strata**) (*Geol*) strate *f*, couche *f*; (*fig*) couche *f*

straw [strɔː] **1** N paille *f*; **to drink sth through a ~** boire qch avec une paille; **to draw ~s** tirer à la courte paille; **to draw the short ~** (*lit*) tirer la paille la plus courte; (*fig*) tirer le mauvais numéro; (*fig*) **man of ~** homme *m* de paille; (*fig*) **to clutch** or **catch** or **grasp at ~s** se raccrocher désespérément à un semblant d'espoir; **it's a ~ in the wind** c'est une indication des choses à venir; **when he refused, it was the last ~** quand il a refusé, ça a été la goutte d'eau qui fait déborder le vase; **that's the last ~** or **the ~ that breaks the camel's back!** ça c'est le comble!; **I don't care a ~*** je m'en fiche*, j'en ai rien à cirer*

2 COMP (= *made of straw: gen*) de or en paille; [*roof*] de paille, de chaume ► **straw boss** N (*US*) sous-chef *m* ► **straw-coloured** ADJ paille *inv* ► **straw hat** N chapeau *m* de paille ► **straw man** N (*pl* **straw men**) (*fig*) homme *m* de paille ► **straw mat** N paillasson *m* ► **straw mattress** N paillasse *f* ► **straw poll** N sondage *m* d'opinion ► **straw-poll elections** NPL (*US Pol*) élection-pilote *f*, élection-témoin *f* ► **straw vote** N (*esp US*) = **straw poll**

strawberry ['strɔːbərɪ] **1** N (= *fruit*) fraise *f*; (= *plant*) fraisier *m*; **wild ~** fraise *f* des bois, fraise *f* sauvage **2** COMP [*jam*] de fraises; [*ice cream*] à la fraise; [tart] aux fraises ► **strawberry bed** N fraiseraie f, fraisière f ► **strawberry blonde** ADJ blond vénitien inv ♦ N femme f or fille f etc aux cheveux blond vénitien ► **strawberry mark** N (Anat) tache f de vin, envie f ► **strawberry roan** N cheval m rouan, jument f rouanne

stray [streɪ] **1** N **a** (= dog, cat, etc) animal m errant or perdu; (= sheep, cow etc) animal m égaré; (= child) enfant mf perdu(e) or abandonné(e); **this dog is a ~** c'est un chien perdu or errant → **waif**
b (Rad) **~s** parasites mpl, friture f
2 ADJ **a** (= lost) [dog, cat] errant; [cow, sheep] égaré; [child] perdu, abandonné
b (= random) [bullet] perdu; [shot, fact, plane, taxi] isolé; [thought] vagabond; [hairs, bits of food] épars; **he picked a ~ hair off her shoulder** il a enlevé un cheveu de son épaule; **~ strands of hair fell across her forehead** des mèches folles lui tombaient sur le front; **a few ~ houses** quelques maisons éparses; **a few ~ cars** quelques rares voitures; **a ~ red sock had got into the white wash** une chaussette rouge s'était égarée dans le linge blanc
3 VI (also **~ away**) [person, animal] s'égarer; [thoughts] vagabonder, errer; (lit, fig) **to ~ (away) from** [+ place, plan, subject] s'écarter de; [+ course, route] dévier de; **they ~ed into enemy territory** ils se sont égarés or ont fait fausse route et se sont retrouvés en territoire ennemi; **his thoughts ~ed to the coming holidays** il se prit à penser aux vacances prochaines

streak [striːk] **1** N **a** (= line, band) raie f, bande f; [of ore, mineral] veine f; [of light] rai m, filet m; [of blood, paint] filet m; **his hair had ~s of grey in it** ses cheveux commençaient à grisonner; **he had (blond) ~s put in his hair** il s'est fait faire des mèches (blondes); **a ~ of cloud across the sky** une traînée nuageuse dans le ciel; **a ~ of lightning** un éclair; **he went past like a ~ (of lightning)** il est passé comme un éclair
b (fig = tendency) tendance(s) f(pl), propension f; **he has a jealous ~ or a ~ of jealousy** il a des tendances or une propension à la jalousie; **she has a ~ of Irish blood** elle a du sang irlandais dans les veines; **a lucky ~ ◊ a ~ of luck** une période de chance; **an unlucky ~ ◊ a ~ of bad luck** une période de malchance; **a winning ~** (Sport) une suite or une série de victoires; (Gambling) une bonne passe; **to be on a winning ~** (Sport) accumuler les victoires; (Gambling) être dans une bonne passe
2 VT zébrer, strier (**with** de); **a mirror ~ed with dirt** un miroir zébré de longues traînées sales; **sky ~ed with red** ciel m strié or zébré de bandes rouges; **cheeks ~ed with tear-marks** joues fpl sillonnées de larmes; **clothes ~ed with mud/paint** vêtements mpl maculés de longues traînées de boue/de peinture; **his hair was ~ed with grey** ses cheveux commençaient à grisonner; **she's got ~ed hair ◊ she's had her hair ~ed** elle s'est fait faire des mèches; **rock ~ed with quartz** roche f veinée de quartz; **meat ~ed with fat** viande f persillée
3 VI **a** (= rush) **to ~ in/out/past** etc entrer/sortir/passer etc comme un éclair
b (*= dash naked) courir tout nu en public

streaker* [striːkəʳ] N streaker m, -euse f

streaky [striːkɪ] **1** ADJ [glass, window, mirror] plein de traînées; [pattern, sky] strié, zébré; **the first coat of paint looked rather ~** la première couche de peinture avait l'air plutôt irrégulière; **he had ~ fair hair** il avait les cheveux blonds avec des mèches **2** COMP ► **streaky bacon** N (Brit) bacon m entrelardé

stream [striːm] **1** N **a** (= brook) ruisseau m
b (= current) courant m; (lit, fig) **to go with the ~** suivre le courant; (lit, fig) **to go against the ~** aller contre le courant or à contre-

courant → **downstream**, **upstream**
c (= flow) [of water] flot m, jet m; [of lava] flot m, torrent m; [of blood, light, oaths, excuses, cars, trucks] flot m; [of tears] torrent m, ruisseau m; [of curses] flot m, torrent m; [of cold air etc] courant m; **a thin ~ of water** un mince filet d'eau; **the water flowed out in a steady ~** l'eau s'écoulait régulièrement; **to be on ~** [oil] être en service; **to come on ~** être mis en service; **to bring the oil on ~** mettre le pipeline en service; **~s of people were coming out** des flots de gens sortaient, les gens sortaient à flots; (Literat, Psych) **the ~ of consciousness** la vie mouvante et insaisissable de la conscience, le « stream of consciousness »
d (Brit Scol) groupe m de niveau; (Brit Scol) **divided into five ~s** réparti en cinq groupes de niveau; **the top/middle/bottom ~** la section forte/moyenne/faible
2 VI **a** [water, tears, oil, milk] ruisseler; [blood] ruisseler, dégouliner; **to ~ with blood/tears** etc ruisseler de sang/de larmes etc; **the fumes made his eyes ~** les émanations l'ont fait pleurer à chaudes larmes; **cold air/ sunlight ~ed through the window** l'air froid/le soleil entra à flots par la fenêtre
b (in wind etc: also **~ out**) flotter au vent
c **to ~ in/out/past** etc [people, cars etc] entrer/sortir/passer etc à flots
3 VT **to ~ blood/water** etc ruisseler de sang/d'eau etc
b (Scol) [+ pupils] répartir par niveau; **to ~ French** or **the French classes** répartir les élèves par niveaux en français

streamer [striːməʳ] N (of paper) serpentin m; (= banner) banderole f; (Astron) flèche f lumineuse; (Press) manchette f

streaming [striːmɪŋ] **1** N (Scol) répartition f des élèves par niveaux **2** ADJ (Brit) **to have a ~ cold** avoir un gros rhume; **to have a ~ nose** avoir le nez qui n'arrête pas de couler; **to have ~ eyes** avoir les yeux qui pleurent

streamline [striːmlaɪn] VT **a** (Aut, Aviat) donner un profil aérodynamique à **b** (fig) [+ organization, system, process] rationaliser

streamlined [striːmlaɪnd] ADJ **a** (Aviat) [aeroplane, shape, body] aérodynamique; (Aut) [car, shape, body] caréné, profilé; (Zool) [shape, body] (in air) aérodynamique; (in water) hydrodynamique **b** (= reduced) [organization, system, process] rationalisé **c** (= uncluttered) [room, appearance] dépouillé; **a ~ new kitchen** une nouvelle cuisine aux lignes dépouillées **d** (= slim) [silhouette] svelte

streamlining [striːmlaɪnɪŋ] N (fig) [of organization, system, process] rationalisation f, dégraissage m

street [striːt] **1** N **a** rue f; **I saw him in the ~** je l'ai vu dans la rue; **to take to the ~s** [demonstrators, protesters] descendre dans la rue; **to turn** or **put sb (out) into the ~** mettre qn à la rue; **to be out on the ~(s)** (= homeless) être à la rue, être SDF; **a woman of the ~s†** une prostituée; **she is on the ~s* ◊ she works the ~s*** elle fait le trottoir
b (fig) (Brit) **that's right up my ~*** c'est tout à fait dans mes cordes; (Brit) **he is not in the same ~ as you*** il ne vous arrive pas à la cheville; (Brit) **to be ~s ahead of sb*** dépasser qn de loin; **they're ~s apart*** un monde or tout les sépare; **~s better*** beaucoup mieux → **back**, **high**, **man**, **queer**, **walk**
2 COMP [noises etc] de la rue; [singer etc] des rues ► **street accident** N accident m de la circulation ► **street arab†** N gamin(e) m(f) des rues ► **street cleaner** N (= person) balayeur m; (= machine) balayeuse f ► **street cred*, street credibility** N **to have ~ cred** or **credibility** être branché; **this will do wonders for your ~ cred** or **credibility** c'est excellent pour ton image de marque ► **street directory** N = **street guide** ► **street door** N porte f donnant sur la rue, porte f d'entrée

► **street fighting** N (NonC; Mil) combats mpl de rue ► **street furniture** N mobilier m urbain ► **street guide** N plan m de la ville, répertoire m des rues ► **street hawker** N colporteur m ► **street level** N **at ~ level** au rez-de-chaussée ► **street lighting** N (NonC) éclairage m des rues or de la voie publique ► **street map** N plan m de la ville, répertoire m des rues ► **street market** N marché m en plein air or à ciel ouvert ► **street musician** N musicien m, -ienne f des rues ► **street photographer** N photostoppeur m, -euse f ► **street plan** N plan m de la ville ► **street price** N (US St Ex) cours m après Bourse or hors Bourse ► **street seller** N marchand m ambulant ► **street smart*** ADJ (US = shrewd) futé, dégourdi ► **street sweeper** N (= person) balayeur m; (= machine) balayeuse f ► **street theatre** N (NonC) théâtre m de rue ► **street trading** N (NonC) vente f ambulante ► **street urchin** N gamin(e) m(f) des rues ► **street value** N [of drugs] valeur f à la revente ► **street vendor** N marchand m ambulant

streetcar [striːtkɑːʳ] N (US) tramway m

streetlamp [striːtlæmp], **streetlight** [striːtlaɪt] N réverbère m

streetwalker [striːtwɔːkəʳ] N prostituée f

streetwise [striːtwaɪz] ADJ (lit) [child] conscient des dangers de la rue; (fig) [worker, policeman] futé, dégourdi

strength [streŋθ] N (NonC) **a** [of person, animal, hand, voice, magnet, lens] force f, puissance f; (= health) forces fpl, robustesse f; [of enemy, team, nation, one's position] force f; [of building, wall, wood] solidité f; [of shoes, material] solidité f, robustesse f; [of wind] force f; [of current] intensité f; [of character, accent, emotion, influence, attraction] force f; [of belief, opinion] force f, fermeté f; [of arguments, reasons] force f, solidité f; [of protests] force f, vigueur f; [of claim, case] solidité f; [of tea, coffee, cigarette] force f; [of sauce] goût m relevé; [of drink] teneur f en alcool; [of solution] titre m; **he hadn't the ~ to lift it** il n'avait pas la force de le soulever; **his ~ failed him** ses forces l'ont abandonné; **give me ~!*** Dieu qu'il faut être patient!; **to get one's ~ back** reprendre des forces, recouvrer ses forces; **to go from ~ to ~** devenir de plus en plus fort; **~ of character** force de caractère; **~ of purpose** résolution f, détermination f; **he has great ~ of purpose** il est très résolu or déterminé; **~ of will** volonté f, fermeté f; (Fin) **the ~ of the pound** la solidité de la livre; **the pound has gained in ~** la livre s'est consolidée; **to be bargaining from ~** être en position de force pour négocier; (fig) **on the ~ of ...** en vertu de ... → **show**, **tensile**
b (Mil, Naut) effectif(s) m(pl); **fighting ~** effectif(s) m(pl) mobilisable(s); **they are below** or **under ~** leur effectif n'est pas au complet; **to bring up to ~** compléter l'effectif de; **his friends were there in ~** ses amis étaient là en grand nombre; **to be on the ~** (Mil) figurer sur les contrôles; (gen) faire partie du personnel

strengthen [streŋθən] **1** VT [+ muscle, limb] fortifier, rendre fort; [+ eyesight] améliorer; [+ person] fortifier, remonter, tonifier; (morally) fortifier, tonifier, enhardir; [+ enemy, nation, team, one's position, protest, case] renforcer; (Fin) [+ the pound, stock market] consolider; [+ building, table] consolider, renforcer; [+ wall] étayer; [+ fabric, material] renforcer; [+ affection, emotion, effect] augmenter, renforcer; [+ opinion, belief] confirmer, renforcer **2** VI [muscle, limb] devenir fort or vigoureux, se fortifier; [wind] augmenter, redoubler; [desire, influence, characteristic] augmenter; [prices] se raffermir

strengthening [streŋθənɪŋ] **1** N [of nation, team, one's position, case, building, material] renforcement *m*; [*of currency, stock market*] consolidation *f*; [*of affection*] augmentation *f* ☐2 ADJ ~ **exercises** exercices *mpl* de raffermissement; **a ~ economy** une économie en croissance; **to have a ~ effect on sth** consolider qch

strenuous ['strenjʊəs] ADJ [*exercise, life, holiday, game, march, campaign*] épuisant; [*activity, work, job*] ardu; [*efforts, attempts, opposition, resistance, attack*] acharné; [*objection, protest, denial*] vigoureux; **it was all too ~ for me** tout cela était trop ardu pour moi; **I'd like to do something less ~** j'aimerais faire quelque chose de moins pénible; (*Med*) **he mustn't do anything ~** il ne faut pas qu'il se fatigue (*subj*)

strenuously ['strenjʊəslɪ] ADV [*exercise, deny, oppose, object, protest*] vigoureusement; [*resist, try*] avec acharnement

strenuousness ['strenjʊəsnɪs] N (degré *m* d')effort *m* requis (**of** par)

strep throat• [ˌstrep'θrəʊt] N (*NonC: Med*) angine *f* (streptococcique)

streptococcal [ˌstreptəʊ'kɒkl], **strepto-coccic** [ˌstreptəʊ'kɒksɪk] ADJ streptococcique

streptococcus [ˌstreptəʊ'kɒkəs] N (*pl* **strep-tococci** [ˌstreptəʊ'kɒkaɪ]) streptocoque *m*

streptomycin [ˌstreptəʊ'maɪsɪn] N streptomycine *f*

▼ **stress** [stres] ☐1 N ☐a (= *pressure etc*) pression *f*, stress *m*; (*Med*) stress *m*; (*also* **mental ~, nervous ~**) tension *f* (nerveuse); **in times of ~** à des moments *or* à une période de grande tension; **the ~es and strains of modern life** toutes les pressions et les tensions de la vie moderne, les agressions de la vie moderne; **to be under ~** [*person*] être stressé; [*relationship*] être tendu; **this put him under great ~** ceci l'a considérablement stressé; **he reacts well under ~** il réagit bien dans des conditions difficiles ☐b (= *emphasis*) insistance *f*; **to lay ~ on** insister sur ☐c (*Ling, Poetry*) (*NonC: gen*) accentuation *f*; (= *accent: on syllable*) accent *m*; (= *accented syllable*) syllabe *f* accentuée; (*Mus*) accent *m*; (*Ling*) **the ~ is on the first syllable** l'accent tombe sur la première syllabe → **primary, secondary** ☐d (*Tech, Mechanics, Constr*) effort *m*, contrainte *f*; (*on rope, cable*) charge *f*; **the ~ acting on a metal** l'effort qui agit sur un métal; **the ~ produced in the metal** le travail du métal; **to be in ~** [*beam, metal*] travailler; **the ~ to which a beam is subjected** la charge qu'on fait subir à une poutre; **a ~ of 500 kilos per square millimetre** une charge de 500 kilos par millimètre carré → **tensile** ☐2 VT ☐a (= *emphasize*) [+ *good manners, one's innocence etc*] insister sur; [+ *fact, detail*] faire ressortir, souligner ☐b (*Ling, Mus, Poetry*) accentuer ☐c (*Tech: natural process*) fatiguer, faire travailler; (*Tech: industrial process*) [+ *metal*] mettre sous tension ☐3 COMP ► **stress fracture** N (*Med*) fracture *f* de marche ► **stress mark** N (*Ling*) accent *m* ► **stress quotient** N **this job has a high ~ quotient** ce travail provoque une grande tension nerveuse ► **stress-related** ADJ [*illness*] causé par le stress

stressed [strest] ADJ ☐a (= *tense*) [*person*] stressé; **what are you getting so ~ out• about?** pourquoi es-tu si stressé?•, il n'y a pas de quoi stresser• ☐b (*Ling, Poetry*) accentué ☐c (*Phys*) soumis à une contrainte

stressful ['stresfʊl] ADJ [*situation, environment, life, day, job*] stressant; [*event*] stressant, éprouvant

stretch [stretʃ] ☐1 N ☐a (= *act, gesture*) étirement *m*; (= *distance, span: of wing etc*) envergure *f*; **with a ~ of his arm** en étendant le bras; **to give a rope a ~** étirer une corde; **to give shoes a ~** élargir des chaussures; **there's not much ~ left in this elastic** cet élastique a beaucoup perdu de son élasticité; **there's a lot of ~ in this material** ce tissu donne *or* prête à l'usage; **to be at full ~** [*arms, rope etc*] être complètement tendu; (*fig*) [*engine etc*] tourner à plein régime *or* rendement; [*factory*] tourner à plein régime; [*person*] donner son plein; **by a ~ of the imagination** en faisant un effort d'imagination; **by no** *or* **not by any ~ of the imagination can one say that ...** même en faisant un gros effort d'imagination, on ne peut pas dire que ...; **not by a long ~!** loin de là! ☐b (= *period of time*) période *f*; **for a long ~ of time** (pendant) longtemps; **for hours at a ~** des heures durant; **he read it all in one ~** il l'a lu d'une (seule) traite; **to do a ~•** faire de la prison *or* de la taule•; **he's done a ten-year ~•** il a fait dix ans de taule•, il a tiré• dix ans ☐c (= *area*) étendue *f*; (= *part*) partie *f*, bout *m*; **vast ~es of sand/snow** de vastes étendues de sable/de neige; **there's a straight ~ (of road) after you pass the lake** la route est toute droite une fois que vous avez dépassé le lac; **a magnificent ~ of country** une campagne magnifique; **in that ~ of the river** dans cette partie de la rivière; **for a long ~ the road runs between steep hills** sur des kilomètres la route serpente entre des collines escarpées; (*Racing, Running, also fig*) **to go into the final ~** entrer dans la dernière ligne droite → **home** ☐d (*Naut*) bordée *f* (courue sous les mêmes amures) ☐2 ADJ [*garment, fabric, cushion-cover*] extensible ☐3 VT ☐a (= *make longer, wider etc*) [+ *rope, spring*] tendre; [+ *elastic*] étirer; [+ *shoe, glove, hat*] élargir; (*Med*) [+ *muscle, tendon*] distendre; (*fig*) [+ *law, rules*] tourner; [+ *meaning*] forcer; [+ *one's principles*] adapter; [+ *one's authority*] outrepasser, excéder; (*fig*) (**if you were**) **to ~ a point you could say that ...** on pourrait peut-être aller jusqu'à dire que ...; **you could ~ a point and allow him to ...** vous pourriez faire une petite concession et lui permettre de ...; **to ~ the truth** forcer la vérité, exagérer; **to ~ one's imagination** faire un effort d'imagination ☐b (= *extend: also* ~ **out**) [+ *wing*] déployer; [+ *rope, net, canopy*] tendre (**between** entre, **above** au-dessus de); [+ *rug*] étendre, étaler; [+ *linen*] étendre; (*after sleep etc*) **to ~ o.s.** s'étirer → **3d**; **he had to ~ his neck to see** il a dû tendre le cou pour voir; **he ~ed (out) his arm to grasp the handle** il tendit *or* allongea le bras pour saisir la poignée; **he ~ed his arms and yawned** il s'étira et bâilla; **he ~ed his leg to ease the cramp** il a étendu *or* allongé la jambe pour atténuer la crampe; (*fig*) **I'm just going to ~ my legs•** (= *go for a walk*) je vais juste me dégourdir les jambes; **the blow ~ed him (out) cold** le coup l'a mis K.-O.•; **to be fully ~ed** [*rope etc*] être complètement tendu → **3c, 3d** ☐c (*fig*) [+ *resources, supplies, funds, income*] (= *make them last*) faire durer, tirer le maximum de; (= *put demands on them*) mettre à rude épreuve; **to be fully ~ed** [*engine*] tourner à plein régime; [*factory*] tourner à plein régime *or* rendement; **our supplies/resources etc are fully ~ed** nos provisions/ressources *etc* sont utilisées au maximum, nos provisions/ressources *etc* ne sont pas élastiques; **we're very ~ed at the moment** on tourne à plein en ce moment → **3b, 3d** ☐d (*fig*) [+ *athlete, student etc*] pousser, exiger le maximum de; **the work he is doing does not ~ him enough** le travail qu'il fait n'exige pas assez de lui; **to be fully ~ed** travailler à la limite de ses possibilités; **to ~ sb to the limits** pousser qn au maximum; **to ~ o.s. too far** vouloir en faire trop → **3b, 3c**

☐4 VI ☐a [*person, animal*] s'étirer; **he ~ed lazily** il s'est étiré paresseusement; **he ~ed across me to get the book** il a tendu le bras devant moi pour prendre le livre ☐b (= *lengthen*) s'allonger; (= *widen*) s'élargir; [*elastic*] s'étirer, se tendre; [*fabric, jersey, gloves, shoes*] prêter, donner ☐c (= *extend, reach, spread out: also often* ~ **out**) [*rope etc*] s'étendre, aller; [*forest, plain, procession, sb's authority, influence*] s'étendre; **the rope won't ~ to that post** la corde ne va pas jusqu'à ce poteau; **how far will it ~?** jusqu'où va-t-il?; (*fig*) **my money won't ~ to a new car** je n'ai pas les moyens de m'acheter une nouvelle voiture; **the festivities ~ed (out) into January** les festivités se sont prolongées pendant une partie du mois de janvier; **a life of misery ~ed (out) before her** une vie de misère s'étendait *or* s'étalait devant elle

☐5 COMP ► **stretch limo•** N limousine *f* extralongue ► **stretch mark** N vergeture *f*
► **stretch across** VI **he ~ed across and touched her cheek** il a tendu la main et touché sa joue
► **stretch down** VI **she ~ed down and picked up the book** elle a tendu la main et ramassé le livre, elle a allongé le bras pour ramasser le livre
► **stretch out** ☐1 VI [*person, arm etc*] s'étendre, s'allonger; [*countryside etc*] s'étendre; **he ~ed (himself) out on the bed** il s'est étendu *or* allongé sur le lit → **stretch 4c** ☐2 VT SEP ☐a (= *reach*) [+ *arm, hand, foot*] tendre, allonger; (= *extend*) [+ *leg etc*] allonger, étendre; [+ *wing*] déployer; [+ *net, canopy, rope*] tendre; [+ *rug*] étendre, étaler; [+ *linen*] étendre; (= *lengthen*) [+ *meeting, discussion*] prolonger; [+ *story, explanation*] allonger ☐b = **stretch 3b**
► **stretch over** VI = **stretch across**
► **stretch up** VI **he ~ed up to reach the shelf** il s'est étiré pour atteindre l'étagère

stretcher ['stretʃər] ☐1 N ☐a (*Med*) brancard *m*, civière *f* ☐b (= *device*) (*for gloves*) ouvre-gants *m inv*; (*for shoes*) forme *f*; (*for fabric*) cadre *m*; (*for artist's canvas*) cadre *m*, châssis *m*; (*on umbrella*) baleine *f* ☐c (*Constr* = *brick*) panneresse *f*, carreau *m*; (= *crosspiece in framework*) traverse *f*; (= *crossbar in chair, bed etc*) barreau *m*, bâton *m*; (= *cross-plank in canoe etc*) barre *f* de pieds ☐2 VT porter sur un brancard *or* une civière; **the goalkeeper was ~ed off** le gardien de but a été emmené sur un brancard *or* une civière ☐3 COMP ► **stretcher-bearer** N (*Med*) brancardier *m* ► **stretcher case** N malade *mf or* blessé(e) *m(f)* qui ne peut pas marcher ► **stretcher party** N équipe *f* de brancardiers

stretchy ['stretʃɪ] ADJ extensible

strew [stru:] (*pret* **strewed**, *ptp* **strewed** *or* **strewn**) VT [+ *straw, sand, sawdust*] répandre, éparpiller (**on, over** sur); [+ *flowers, objects*] éparpiller, semer (**on, over** sur); [+ *wreckage etc*] éparpiller, disséminer (**over** sur); [+ *ground, floor*] joncher, parsemer (**with** de); [+ *room, table*] joncher (*also fig*)

strewth• [stru:θ] EXCL ça alors!•, bon sang!•

striate ['straɪeɪt] VT strier

stricken ['strɪkən] ☐1 VB (*rare*) *ptp of* **strike** ☐2 ADJ ☐a [*area, city, vehicle*] (*by famine, drought, earthquake, eruption etc*) sinistré; (*by war, famine*) dévasté; [*ship*] en détresse; [*industry, firm*] gravement touché; [*economy*] dévasté; **to be ~ by famine/drought** être frappé par la famine/la sécheresse ☐b (= *wounded*) [*person, animal*] gravement blessé; **~ with grief** accablé de douleur; **~ with** *or* **by panic** saisi de panique; **to be ~ with** *or* **by polio/cancer** être atteint de polio/d'un cancer; **I was ~ with** *or* **by guilt** j'ai été pris d'un sentiment de culpabilité ☐c (= *afflicted*) [*person, look, expression*] affligé → **strike**

-stricken ['strɪkən] ADJ (*in compounds*) frappé

de, atteint de, accablé de; **plague-stricken** touché par de la peste → **grief**

strict [strɪkt] **1** ADJ **a** (= severe, inflexible: gen) strict; [person] strict, sévère; [curfew, control, hygiene] rigoureux; [order] formel; [secrecy] absolu; **security was ~ for the President's visit** de strictes mesures de sécurité avaient été mises en place pour la visite du Président; **to be under ~ orders (not) to do sth** avoir reçu l'ordre formel de (ne pas) faire qch; **to reveal/treat sth in ~ confidence** révéler/traiter qch de façon strictement confidentielle; **"write in ~ confidence to Paul Jackson"** « écrire à Paul Jackson: discrétion assurée »; **this is in the ~est confidence** c'est strictement confidentiel **b** (= precise, absolute) [meaning, truth] strict; **in the ~ sense (of the word)** au sens strict (du mot), stricto sensu; **in ~ order of precedence** suivant strictement l'ordre de préséance; **a ~ time limit** un délai impératif **2** COMP ► **strict liability** N (Jur) responsabilité f inconditionnelle

▼**strictly** ['strɪktlɪ] ADV **a** (= sternly, severely) [treat, bring up] d'une manière stricte **b** [controlled, enforced, observed, adhered to] rigoureusement; **~ confidential/personal/limited** strictement confidentiel/privé/limité; (gen) **~ prohibited or forbidden** formellement interdit; **"smoking ~ prohibited"** « défense absolue de fumer »; **~ between us or ourselves or you and me** strictement entre nous; **this is ~ business** c'est strictement professionnel; **our relationship is ~ professional** notre relation est strictement professionnelle; **that's not ~ true** ce n'est pas tout à fait vrai; **it's not ~ necessary** ce n'est pas absolument nécessaire; **you should avoid medication unless ~ necessary** évitez de prendre des médicaments si ce n'est pas indispensable; **fox-hunting is ~ for the rich** la chasse au renard est réservée aux riches; **this car park is ~ for the use of residents** ce parking est exclusivement or strictement réservé aux résidents; **~ speaking** à proprement parler; **that's ~ for the birds!*** ça c'est bon pour les imbéciles!*

strictness ['strɪktnɪs] N sévérité f

stricture ['strɪktʃə'] N (= criticism) critique f (hostile) (**on** de); (= restriction) restriction f (**on** de); (Med) sténose f, rétrécissement m

stridden ['strɪdn] VB ptp of **stride**

stride [straɪd] (vb: pret **strode**, ptp **stridden**) **1** N grand pas m, enjambée f; [of runner] foulée f; **with giant ~s** à pas de géant; **in or with a few ~s he had caught up with the others** il avait rattrapé les autres en quelques enjambées or foulées; (fig) **to make great ~s (in French/in one's studies)** faire de grands progrès (en français/dans ses études); **to get into one's ~** ◊ **to hit one's ~** trouver son rythme (de croisière); **to take sth in one's ~** (Brit) ◊ **to take sth in ~** (US) accepter qch sans sourciller or sans se laisser démonter; (gen) **he took it in his ~** (Brit) ◊ **he took it in ~** (US) il a continué sans se décontenancer, il ne s'est pas laissé démonter; **to put sb off their ~** faire perdre sa concentration à qn, déboussoler* qn; (US fig) **to be caught off ~** être pris au dépourvu **2** VI marcher à grands pas or à grandes enjambées; **to ~ along/in/away** etc avancer/entrer/s'éloigner à grands pas or à grandes enjambées; **he was striding up and down the room** il arpentait la pièce **3** VT **a** [+ deck, yard, streets] arpenter **b** † = **bestride**

stridency ['straɪdənsɪ] N **a** [of tone, rhetoric etc] véhémence f **b** [of sound, voice] stridence f

strident ['straɪdənt] ADJ **a** (gen pej = vociferous) [critic, criticism] acharné, véhément; [tone, rhetoric, feminist] véhément; **there were ~ calls for his resignation/for him to resign** on a demandé à grands cris sa démission/qu'il

démissionne **b** [sound, voice] strident (also Phon)

stridently ['straɪdntlɪ] ADV **a** (= noisily) [hoot, sound, whistle] d'une façon stridente **b** (= vociferously) [demand, declare] à grands cris; **~ anti-American** farouchement antiaméricain

strife [straɪf] **1** N (NonC) conflit m, dissensions fpl; (less serious) querelles fpl; (Pol) **a party crippled by internal ~** un parti paralysé par des dissensions or des querelles intestines; **industrial ~** conflits mpl sociaux; **domestic ~** querelles fpl de ménage, dissensions fpl domestiques; (liter) **to cease from ~** déposer les armes **2** COMP ► **strife-ridden, strife-torn** ADJ [country] déchiré par les conflits; [party] déchiré par les dissensions

▼**strike** [straɪk] (vb: pret **struck**, ptp **struck**, (rare) **stricken**) **1** N **a** (= act) coup m (frappé); (Aviat, Mil) raid m (aérien); (Mil) **first ~ weapon** arme f de première frappe **b** (Ind) grève f (**of, by** de); **the coal ~** la grève des mineurs; **the electricity/gas ~** la grève (des employés) de l'électricité/du gaz; **the transport/hospital ~** la grève des transports/des hôpitaux; **the Ford ~** la grève chez Ford; **to be (out) on ~** être en grève, faire grève (**for** pour obtenir, **against** pour protester contre); **to call a ~** lancer un ordre de grève; **to go on ~** ◊ **to come out on ~** se mettre en grève, faire grève → **general, hunger, rail[1], steel, sympathy** **c** (Min, Miner etc = discovery) découverte f; **to make a ~** découvrir un gisement; (fig) **a lucky ~** un coup de chance **d** (Fishing: by angler) ferrage m; (Fishing: by fish) touche f, mordage m; (Baseball, Bowling) strike m; (US fig) **you have two ~s against you** tu es mal parti*, ça se présente mal pour toi; (US fig) **the building/government has three ~s against it** les jours du bâtiment/du gouvernement sont comptés; (US Jur) **three ~s and you're out** principe selon lequel une troisième récidive entraîne une condamnation à perpétuité **e** [of clock] sonnerie f des heures **2** VT **a** (= hit) [+ person] frapper, donner un or des coup(s) à; [+ ball] toucher, frapper; [+ nail, table] frapper sur, taper sur; (Mus) [+ string] toucher, pincer; [snake] mordre, piquer; **to ~ sth with one's fist** ◊ **to ~ one's fist on sth** frapper du poing or donner un coup de poing sur qch; **to ~ sth with a hammer** frapper or taper or cogner sur qch avec un marteau; **he struck me (a blow) on the chin** il m'a frappé au menton, il m'a donné un coup de poing au menton; **to ~ the first blow** donner le premier coup, frapper le premier (or la première); (fig) **to ~ a blow for freedom** rompre une lance pour la liberté; (fig) **he struck his rival a shrewd blow by buying the land** il a porté à son rival un coup subtil en achetant la terre; **he struck the knife from his assailant's hand** d'un coup de poing il a fait tomber le couteau de la main de son assaillant; **the pain struck him as he bent down** la douleur l'a saisi quand il s'est baissé; **disease struck the city** la maladie a frappé la ville or s'est abattue sur la ville; **to be stricken by or with remorse** être pris de remords; **the city was struck or stricken by fear** la ville a été prise de peur, la peur s'est emparée de la ville; **to ~ fear into sb or sb's heart** remplir (le cœur de) qn d'effroi; **it struck terror and dismay into the whole population** cela a terrorisé la population tout entière → **heap** **b** (= knock against) [person, one's shoulder etc, spade] cogner contre, heurter; [car etc] heurter, rentrer dans*; [+ rocks, the bottom] toucher, heurter; (fig) [lightning, light] frapper; **he struck his head on or against the table as he fell** il s'est heurté la tête quand il est tombé, il s'est cogné la tête à or contre la table en tombant; **the stone struck him on the head** la pierre l'a frappé or l'a heurté à la tête; **he was struck by two bullets** il a reçu

deux balles; **to be struck by lightning** être frappé par la foudre, être foudroyé; **a piercing cry struck his ear** un cri perçant lui a frappé l'oreille or les oreilles; **the horrible sight that struck his eyes** le spectacle horrible qui lui a frappé les yeux or le regard or la vue **c** (= find, discover) [+ gold] découvrir, trouver; (fig) [+ hotel, road] tomber sur, trouver; (fig) [+ difficulty, obstacle] rencontrer; (fig) **to ~ gold** trouver le filon*; **to ~ oil** (Miner) trouver du pétrole; (fig) trouver le filon*; (fig) **to ~ it rich** faire fortune → **patch** **d** (= make, produce etc) [+ coin, medal] frapper; [+ sparks, fire] faire jaillir (**from** de); [+ match] frotter, gratter; (fig) [+ agreement, truce] arriver à, conclure; **to ~ a light** allumer une allumette (or un briquet etc); (Bot) **to ~ roots** prendre racine; (Hort) **to ~ cuttings** faire prendre racine à des boutures; **to ~ an average** établir une moyenne; **to ~ a balance** trouver un équilibre, trouver le juste milieu; **to ~ a bargain** conclure un marché; **to ~ an attitude** poser → **pose** **e** [+ chord, note] sonner, faire entendre; [clock] sonner; (fig) **to ~ a false note** sonner faux; **to ~ a note of warning** donner or sonner l'alarme; **the clock struck three** la pendule a sonné trois heures; **it has just struck six** six heures viennent juste de sonner; (Naut) **to ~ four bells** piquer quatre **f** (= take down) [+ tent] démonter, plier; [+ sail] amener; [+ camp] lever; [+ flag] baisser, amener; (Theat) **to ~ the set** démonter le décor **g** (= delete) [+ name] rayer (**from** de); [+ person] (from list) rayer; (from professional register) radier (**from** de); **the judge ordered the remark to be struck or stricken from the record** le juge a ordonné que la remarque soit rayée du procès-verbal **h** (= cause to be or become) rendre (subitement); (lit, fig) **to ~ sb dumb** rendre qn muet; **to be struck dumb** (lit) être frappé de mutisme; (fig) rester muet, être sidéré*; **to ~ sb dead** porter un coup mortel à qn; (fig) **~ me pink!‡** j'en suis soufflé!* **i** (= make impression on) sembler, paraître (**sb** à qn); **I was struck by his intelligence** j'ai été frappé par son intelligence; **I wasn't very struck* with him** il ne m'a pas fait très bonne impression; **to be struck on sb‡** (= impressed by) être très impressionné par qn; (= in love with) être toqué* de qn; **the funny side of it struck me later** le côté drôle de la chose m'est apparu or m'a frappé plus tard; **that ~s me as a good idea** cela me semble or paraît une bonne idée; **an idea suddenly struck him** soudain il a eu une idée, une idée lui est venue soudain à l'esprit; **it ~s me that or ~s me* he is lying** j'ai l'impression qu'il ment, à mon avis il ment; **how did he ~ you?** quelle impression or quel effet vous a-t-il fait?; **how did the film ~ you?** qu'avez-vous pensé du film? **j** (Fishing) [angler] ferrer; **the fish struck the bait** le poisson a mordu à l'appât **3** VI **a** (= hit) frapper; (= attack) (Mil) attaquer; [snake] mordre, piquer; [tiger] sauter sur sa proie; (fig) [disease etc] frapper; [panic] s'emparer des esprits; (lit, fig) **to ~ home** frapper or toucher juste, faire mouche; (esp Brit fig) **to ~ lucky** avoir de la chance; **he struck at his attacker** il porta un coup à son assaillant; **we must ~ at the root of this evil** nous devons attaquer or couper ce mal dans sa racine; **it ~s at the root of our parliamentary system** cela porte atteinte aux fondements mêmes de notre système parlementaire; **his speech ~s at the heart of the problem** son discours porte sur le fond même du problème; **his foot struck against or on a rock** son pied a buté contre or heurté un rocher; **when the ship struck** quand le bateau a touché; **the sun was striking through the mist** le soleil perçait la brume ; **the chill struck through to his very bones** le froid a pénétré jusqu'à la moelle de ses os → **iron** .

b [*match*] s'allumer

c [*clock*] sonner ; **has 6 o'clock struck?** est-ce que 6 heures ont sonné ?

d (*Ind* = *go on strike*) faire grève (**for** pour obtenir, **against** pour protester contre)

e (= *turn, move, go*) aller, prendre ; **~ left on leaving the forest** prenez à gauche en sortant de la forêt ; **to ~ uphill** se mettre à grimper la côte

f (*Hort* = *take root*) prendre racine ; (*Fishing* = *seize bait*) mordre

4 COMP (*Ind*) [*committee, fund*] de grève ► **strike force** N (*gen: of police etc*) brigade *f* d'intervention ; (*Mil*) force *f* de frappe ► **strike fund** N (*Ind*) caisse *f* syndicale de grève ► **strike leader** N (*Ind*) leader *m* de la grève ► **strike pay** N (*Ind*) salaire *m* de gréviste

► **strike back** VI (*Mil, gen*) rendre les coups (**at sb** à qn), se venger (**at sb** de qn), user de représailles (**at sb** à l'égard de qn)

► **strike down** VT SEP **a** abattre ; (*fig*) [*esp disease*] terrasser **b** (*US* = *abolish*) [+ *law*] abolir

► **strike in** VI (*fig* = *interrupt*) interrompre

► **strike off** **1** VI (= *change direction*) prendre, aller ; **he struck off across the fields** il a pris *or* il s'en est allé à travers champs **2** VT SEP **a** [+ *sb's head*] trancher, couper ; [+ *branch*] couper **b** (= *score out, delete: from list*) rayer ; **to be struck off** [*doctor etc*] être radié **c** (*Typ*) tirer

► **strike on** VT FUS [+ *idea*] avoir ; [+ *solution*] tomber sur, trouver

► **strike out** **1** VI **a** (= *hit out*) se débattre ; **he struck out wildly** il s'est débattu furieusement ; **he struck out at his attackers** il lança une volée de coups dans la direction de ses attaquants **b** (= *set off*) **to ~ out for the shore** [*swimmer*] se mettre à nager vers le rivage ; [*rower*] se mettre à ramer vers le rivage ; (*fig*) **he left the firm and struck out on his own** il a quitté l'entreprise et s'est mis à son compte **2** VT SEP (= *delete*) [+ *word, question*] rayer

► **strike through** VT SEP = **strike out 2**

► **strike up** **1** VI [*band etc*] commencer à jouer ; [*music*] commencer **2** VT SEP (*Mus*) [*band*] se mettre à jouer ; [*singers*] se mettre à chanter ; **~ up the band!** faites jouer l'orchestre ! ; **to ~ up an acquaintance** faire *or* lier connaissance (**with sb** avec qn) ; **to ~ up a friendship** lier amitié (**with sb** avec qn)

► **strike upon** VT FUS = **strike on**

strikebound ['straɪkbaʊnd] ADJ bloqué par une (*or* la) grève

strikebreaker ['straɪk,breɪkəʳ] N (*Ind*) briseur *m* de grève

strikebreaking ['straɪk,breɪkɪŋ] N **he was accused of ~** on l'a accusé d'être un briseur de grève

striker ['straɪkəʳ] N **a** (*Ind*) gréviste *mf* **b** (= *clapper*) frappeur *m* ; (*on clock*) marteau *m* ; (*on gun*) percuteur *m* **c** (*Ftbl*) buteur *m*

striking ['straɪkɪŋ] **1** ADJ **a** (= *impressive, outstanding*) [*feature, contrast, similarity, difference*] frappant, saisissant ; **to be in ~ contrast to sth** offrir un contraste frappant *or* saisissant avec qch ; **to bear a ~ resemblance to sb** ressembler à qn de manière frappante, présenter une ressemblance frappante avec qn ; **his/her ~ good looks** sa beauté saisissante, sa grande beauté ; **she was a ~ redhead** c'était une superbe rousse

b **to be within ~ distance (of sth)** être à proximité (de qch) ; **he had come within ~ distance of a medal/the presidency** une médaille/la présidence était maintenant à sa portée ; **to be within ~ distance of doing sth** être bien placé pour faire qch

c [*clock*] **a ~ clock** une horloge qui sonne les heures, une horloge à carillon ; **the ~ mechanism** le carillon

d (*Mil*) [*force, power*] de frappe

e (= *on strike*) [*workers*] en grève, gréviste

2 N **a** [*of coins*] frappe *f*

b [*of clock*] carillon *m*

strikingly ['straɪkɪŋlɪ] ADV **a** de façon frappante, de façon saisissante ; **~ different (from sth)** différent à tous points de vue (de qch) ; **~ beautiful** d'une beauté saisissante, d'une grande beauté ; **~ modern/bold** d'une modernité/audace saisissante, extrêmement moderne/audacieux ; **to be ~ similar to sb/sth** ressembler à qn/qch de façon frappante *or* saisissante ; **to be ~ evident** sauter aux yeux, crever les yeux **b** [*contrast*] **~ with sth** offrir un contraste frappant *or* saisissant avec qch ; **to differ ~ (from sth)** différer à tous points de vue (de qch) ; **~, inflation is now higher than ever** ce qui est frappant, c'est que l'inflation n'a jamais été aussi forte

Strimmer® ['strɪməʳ] N (*small*) coupe-bordure *m* ; (*heavy-duty*) débroussailleuse *f*

string [strɪŋ] (*vb: pret, ptp* **strung**) **1** N **a** (= *cord*) ficelle *f* ; [*of violin, piano, bow, racket etc*] corde *f* ; [*of puppet*] ficelle *f*, fil *m* ; [*of apron, bonnet, anorak*] cordon *m* ; (*Bot: on bean etc*) fil(s) *m(pl)* ; **a piece of ~** un bout de ficelle ; **he has got her on a ~** il la tient, il la mène par le bout du nez ; **to have more than one ~ to one's bow** avoir plus d'une corde à son arc ; **his first ~** sa première ressource ; **his second ~** sa deuxième ressource, la solution de rechange ; (*Mus*) **the ~s** les cordes *fpl*, les instruments *mpl* à cordes ; (*fig*) **he had to pull ~s to get the job** il a dû user de son influence *or* se faire pistonner *or* faire jouer le piston pour obtenir le poste ; **to pull ~s for sb** exercer son influence pour aider qn, pistonner qn ; **he's the one who pulls the ~s** (= *has control*) c'est lui qui tire les ficelles ; (*fig*) **there are no ~s attached** cela ne vous (*or* nous *etc*) engage à rien ; **with no ~s attached** sans condition(s) ; **with ~s (attached)** assorti de conditions → **apron, heartstrings**

b [*of beads, pearls*] rang *m* ; [*of onions*] chapelet *m* ; [*of garlic*] chaîne *f* ; (*fig*) [*of people, vehicles*] file *f* ; [*of racehorses*] écurie *f* ; [*of curses, lies, insults, excuses*] kyrielle *f*, chapelet *m*

c (*Ling*) séquence *f*

d (*Comput*) chaîne *f* ; **a numeric/character ~** une chaîne numérique/de caractères

e (*Sport*) équipe *f* (provisoire)

2 VT **a** [+ *violin etc*] monter ; [+ *bow*] garnir d'une corde ; [+ *racket*] corder → **highly**

b [+ *beads, pearls*] enfiler ; [+ *rope*] tendre (**across** en travers de, **between** entre) ; **they strung lights in the trees** ils ont suspendu *or* attaché des (guirlandes de) lampions dans les arbres

c [+ *beans*] enlever les fils de

3 COMP (*Mus*) [*orchestra, quartet*] à cordes ; [*serenade, piece*] pour cordes ► **string bag** N filet *m* à provisions ► **string bean** N (= *vegetable*) haricot *m* vert ; (*US* = *tall thin person*) asperge* *f*, grande perche *f* ► **string correspondent** N (*US Press*) correspondant(e) *m(f)* local(e) à temps partiel ► **string(ed) instrument** N (*Mus*) instrument *m* à cordes ► **string player** N (*Mus*) musicien(ne) *m(f)* qui joue d'un instrument à cordes ► **string-puller** N **he's a ~-puller** il n'hésite pas à se faire pistonner *or* à faire jouer ses relations ► **string-pulling** N piston *m* ► **string tie** N cravate-lacet *f* ► **string vest** N tricot *m* de corps à grosses mailles

► **string along*** **1** VI suivre ; **to ~ along with sb** (= *accompany*) accompagner qn ; (*fig* = *agree with*) se ranger à l'avis de qn **2** VT SEP (*pej*) faire marcher, bercer de fausses espérances

► **string out** **1** VI [*people, things*] se déployer (**along** le long de) ; **~ out a bit more!** espacez-vous un peu plus ! **2** VT SEP **a** [+ *lanterns, washing etc*] suspendre ; [+ *guards, posts*] échelonner ; [*people, things*] **to be strung out along**

the road être déployé le long de la route **b** (*fig*) **to be strung out**: (*gen*) (= *debilitated*) être à plat ; (= *disturbed*) être perturbé ; (*Drugs = addicted*) être accro• ; (*Drugs = under influence*) être défoncé• ; (*Drugs: with withdrawal symptoms*) être en manque

► **string together** VT SEP [+ *words, sentences*] enchaîner ; **he can barely ~ a sentence** *or* **two words together** il a du mal à aligner deux phrases

► **string up** VT SEP **a** [+ *lantern, onions, nets*] suspendre (au moyen d'une corde) **b** (*fig*) **he had strung himself up to do it** il avait aiguisé toutes ses facultés en vue de le faire ; **to be strung up (about sth)** être très tendu *or* nerveux (à la pensée de qch) **c** (* = *hang, lynch*) pendre

stringed [strɪŋd] ADJ → **string 3**

-stringed [strɪŋd] ADJ (*in compounds*) **four-stringed** à quatre cordes

stringency ['strɪndʒənsɪ] N (= *strictness*) [*of control, regulations, test*] rigueur *f* ; [*of reforms*] caractère *m* draconien ; **thanks to the ~ of the security** grâce aux strictes mesures de sécurité ; **financial** *or* **economic ~** austérité *f*

stringent ['strɪndʒənt] ADJ **a** (= *strict*) [*control, regulations, standards, test*] rigoureux ; [*reforms*] draconien ; **the meeting took place amid ~ security** de strictes mesures de sécurité ont été mises en place pour cette réunion **b** (= *compelling*) [*reasons, arguments*] solide ; [*necessity*] impérieux

stringently ['strɪndʒəntlɪ] ADV rigoureusement

stringer ['strɪŋəʳ] N (= *journalist*) correspondant(e) *m(f)* local(e) à temps partiel

stringy ['strɪŋɪ] ADJ [*beans, celery, meat*] filandreux ; [*molasses, cooked cheese*] filant, qui file ; [*plant, seaweed*] tout en longueur ; (*fig*) [*person*] filiforme

strip [strɪp] **1** N **a** [*of metal, wood, paper, grass*] bande *f* ; [*of fabric*] bandelette *f* ; [*of ground*] bande *f*, langue *f* ; [*of water, sea*] bras *m* ; **a ~ of garden** un petit jardin tout en longueur ; **to tear sb off a ~**: ◊ **to tear a ~ off sb**: sonner les cloches à qn*

b (*Aviat: also* **landing ~**) piste *f* d'atterrissage

c (*also* **comic ~**) = **strip cartoon**

d (*Brit Ftbl etc* = *clothes*) tenue *f* ; **the England ~** la tenue de l'équipe (de football) d'Angleterre

e * = **striptease**

2 VT **a** (= *remove everything from*) [+ *person*] déshabiller, dévêtir ; (*also* **~ down**) [+ *room, house*] démeubler, vider ; [*thieves*] dévaliser, vider ; [+ *car, engine, gun*] démonter complètement ; (*Tech*) [+ *nut, screw, gears*] arracher le filet de ; [*wind, people, birds*] [+ *branches, bushes*] dépouiller, dégarnir ; [= *take paint etc off*] [+ *furniture, door*] décaper ; **to ~ sb naked** *or* **to the skin** déshabiller *or* dévêtir qn complètement ; **to ~ a bed (down)** défaire un lit complètement ; **to ~ (down) the walls** enlever *or* arracher le papier peint ; **~ped pine** pin *m* décapé ; **~ped pine furniture** vieux meubles *mpl* en pin décapé

b (= *remove*) [+ *old covers, wallpaper, decorations, ornaments*] enlever ; [+ *old paint*] décaper, enlever ; **to ~ the bark from the tree** dépouiller un arbre de son écorce

c (= *deprive etc*) [+ *person, object*] dépouiller (**of** de) ; **to ~ a tree of its bark** dépouiller un arbre de son écorce ; **to ~ a room of all its pictures** enlever tous les tableaux dans une pièce ; **to ~ sb of his titles/honours** dépouiller qn de ses titres/honneurs ; (*Fin*) **to ~ a company of its assets** cannibaliser* une compagnie → **asset**

3 VI se déshabiller, se dévêtir ; [*striptease artist*] faire du strip-tease ; **to ~ naked** *or* **to the skin** se mettre nu ; **to ~ to the waist** se déshabiller *or* se dévêtir jusqu'à la ceinture, se mettre torse nu ; **to be ~ped to the waist** être nu jusqu'à la ceinture, être torse nu

4 COMP ► **strip cartoon** N (*Brit*) bande *f* dessinée ► **strip club** N boîte *f* de striptease ► **strip cropping** N (*Agr*) cultures alternées selon les courbes de niveaux ► **strip joint** N (*US*) = **strip club** ► **strip light** N (tube *m* au) néon *m* ► **strip lighting** N (*Brit*) éclairage *m* au néon *or* fluorescent ► **strip mine** N (*US*) mine *f* à ciel ouvert ► **strip mining** N (*US*) extraction *f* à ciel ouvert ► **strip poker** N strip-poker *m* ► **strip-search** N fouille *f* corporelle ♦ VT he was ~-searched at the airport on l'a fait se déshabiller et soumis à une fouille corporelle à l'aéroport ► **strip show** N strip-tease *m* ► **strip-wash** N (grande) toilette *f* ♦ VT faire la (grande) toilette de

►**strip away** VT SEP [+ *paint, varnish*] décaper ; [+ *layer of dirt, turf, bark*] retirer ; (*fig*) [+ *pretence, hypocrisy, artifice*] exposer ; **chemicals that ~ away the skin's protective outer layer** des produits qui attaquent la couche protectrice de l'épiderme ; **to ~ away sb's dignity** priver qn de sa dignité

►**strip down** 1 VI = **strip off 1** 2 VT SEP (*Tech etc*) [+ *machine, engine, gun*] démonter complètement → **strip 2a**

►**strip off** 1 VI se déshabiller *or* se dévêtir complètement, se mettre nu 2 VT SEP [+ *buttons, ornaments*] enlever, ôter (**from** de) ; [+ *paper*] enlever, arracher (**from** de) ; [+ *leaves*] faire tomber (**from** de) ; [+ *berries*] prendre (**from** de)

stripe [straɪp] N a (*of one colour: also Zool*) raie *f*, rayure *f* ; (*pattern*) **~s** rayures *fpl* ; **yellow with a white ~** jaune rayé de blanc → **pinstripe, star** b (*Mil*) galon *m* ; **to get one's ~s** gagner ses galons ; **to lose one's ~s** être dégradé c †(= *lash*) coup *m* de fouet ; (= *weal*) marque *f* (d'un coup de fouet)

striped [straɪpt] ADJ [*garment, wallpaper, fabric*] rayé, à rayures ; [*animal, insect*] rayé ; **a pair of ~ trousers** (*broad stripes*) un pantalon rayé ; (*pinstripes*) un pantalon à fines rayures ; **~ with red** rayé de rouge

stripey* ['straɪpɪ] ADJ = **stripy**

stripling ['strɪplɪŋ] N adolescent *m*, tout jeune homme *m*, gringalet *m* (*pej*)

strippagram ['strɪpəɡræm] N *message envoyé à l'occasion d'une célébration par l'intermédiaire d'une personne qui fait un strip-tease ; cette personne*

stripper ['strɪpə^r] N a (*also* **paint-~**) décapant *m* b (= *striptease artist*) strip-teaseuse *f* ; **male ~** strip-teaseur *m*

striptease ['strɪptiːz] N strip-tease *m*, effeuillage *m* ; **~ artist** strip-teaseuse *f*, effeuilleuse* *f*

stripteaser ['strɪptiːzə^r] N strip-teaseuse *f*, effeuilleuse* *f*

stripy* ['straɪpɪ] ADJ [*garment, wallpaper, fabric*] rayé, à rayures ; [*animal, insect*] rayé

strive [straɪv] (*pret* **strove**, *ptp* **striven** ['strɪvn]) VI a (= *try hard*) s'efforcer (**to do** de faire), faire son possible (**to do** pour faire), s'évertuer (**to do** à faire) ; **to ~ after** *or* **for sth** s'efforcer de *or* faire son possible pour *or* s'évertuer à obtenir qch b (*liter* = *struggle, fight*) lutter, se battre (**against, with** contre)

striving ['straɪvɪŋ] N efforts *mpl* (**for** pour obtenir)

strobe [strəʊb] 1 ADJ [*lights*] stroboscopique 2 N a (*also* **~ light, ~ lighting**) lumière *f* stroboscopique b = **stroboscope**

stroboscope ['strəʊbəskəʊp] N stroboscope *m*

strode [strəʊd] VB *pt of* **stride**

stroke [strəʊk] 1 N a (= *movement, blow: gen*, Billiards, Cricket, Golf, Tennis *etc*) coup *m* ; (*Swimming* = *movement*) mouvement *m* des bras (*pour nager*) ; (*Rowing, Swimming* = *style*) nage *f* ; (*Rowing* = *movement*) coup *m* de rame

or d'aviron ; **he gave the cat a ~** il a fait une caresse au chat ; **with a ~ of his axe** d'un coup de hache ; **with a ~ of the pen** d'un trait de plume ; **~ of lightning** coup *m* de foudre ; (*Golf, Tennis etc*) **good ~!** bien joué ! ; **to row at 38 ~s to the minute** ramer *or* nager à une cadence de 38 coups d'aviron minute ; (*Rowing, fig*) **to set the ~** donner la cadence ; **to put sb off his ~** (*Sport*) faire perdre le rythme à qn ; (*fig*) faire perdre tous ses moyens à qn ; **he swam the pool with powerful ~s** il a traversé le bassin d'une manière puissante → **backstroke, breast**

b (*fig*) **at a (single) ~** ◊ **at one ~** d'un (seul) coup ; **it was a tremendous ~ to get the committee's agreement** cela a été un coup de maître que d'obtenir l'accord du comité ; **he hasn't done a ~ (of work)** il n'a rien fait du tout, il n'en a pas fichu une rame* ; **~ of diplomacy** chef-d'œuvre *m* de diplomatie ; **~ of genius** trait *m* de génie ; **~ of luck** coup *m* de chance *or* de veine → **master**

c (= *mark*) [*of pen, pencil*] trait *m* ; [*of brush*] touche *f* ; (*Typ* = *oblique*) barre *f* ; **thick ~s of the brush** des touches *fpl* épaisses ; (*Typ*) **5 ~ 6** 5 barre 6 → **brush**

d [*of bell, clock*] coup *m* ; **on the ~ of ten** sur le coup de dix heures, à dix heures sonnantes ; **in the ~ of time** juste à temps

e (*Med*) attaque *f* (d'apoplexie) ; **to have a ~** avoir une attaque (d'apoplexie) → **heatstroke, sunstroke**

f (*Tech: of piston*) course *f* ; **a two-/four-~ engine** un moteur à deux/quatre temps → **two**

g (*Rowing* = *person*) chef *m* de nage ; **to row ~** être chef de nage, donner la nage

2 VT a [+ *cat, sb's hand, one's chin*] caresser ; [+ *sb's hair*] caresser, passer la main dans ; (*fig*) **to ~ sb (up) the wrong way** prendre qn à rebrousse-poil *or* à contre-poil

b (*Rowing*) **to ~ a boat** être chef de nage, donner la nage

c (= *draw line through: also* **~ out**) biffer

d (*Sport*) [+ *ball*] frapper

3 VI (*Rowing*) être chef de nage, donner la nage

4 COMP ► **stroke play** N (*NonC: Golf*) comptage des points au coup par coup ► **stroke-play tournament** N (*Golf*) stroke-play *m*

►**stroke down** VT SEP [+ *cat's fur*] caresser ; [+ *hair*] lisser ; (*fig*) **to ~ sb down** apaiser *or* amadouer qn

►**stroke out** VT SEP = **stroke 2c**

►**stroke up** VT SEP → **stroke 2a**

stroll [strəʊl] 1 N petite promenade *f* ; **to have** *or* **take a ~** *or* **go for a ~** aller faire un tour 2 VI se promener nonchalamment, flâner ; **to ~ in/out/away** *etc* entrer/sortir/s'éloigner *etc* sans se presser *or* nonchalamment ; **to ~ up and down the street** descendre et remonter la rue en flânant *or* sans se presser *or* nonchalamment ; **to ~ around** flâner

stroller ['strəʊlə^r] N a (= *person*) promeneur *m*, -euse *f*, flâneur *m*, -euse *f* b (*esp US* = *push chair*) poussette *f* ; (*folding*) poussette-canne *f*

strolling ['strəʊlɪŋ] ADJ [*player, minstrel*] ambulant

stroma ['strəʊmə] N (*pl* **stromata** ['strəʊmətə]) stroma *m*

strong [strɒŋ] 1 ADJ a (= *powerful*) fort (*also* Mil, Pol, Sport *etc*) ; (= *healthy*) robuste ; [*heart*] robuste, solide ; [*nerves*] solide ; [*eyesight*] très bon ; [*leg*] vigoureux ; [*arm, limb*] fort, vigoureux ; [*voice, accent*] fort ; [*magnet*] puissant ; [*wind*] fort ; (*Elec*) [*current*] intense ; [*lens, spectacles*] fort, puissant ; (= *solid, robust*) [*building, wall*] solide ; [*table, shoes, bolt, nail*] solide, robuste ; [*glue*] fort ; [*fabric, material*] solide, résistant ; **to be (as) ~ as an ox** *or* **a horse** *or* **a bull** (= *powerful*) être fort comme un bœuf *or* comme un Turc ; (= *healthy*) avoir

une santé de fer ; **do you feel ~?** est-ce que vous avez des forces ?, est-ce que vous vous sentez en forme ? ; (*in health*) **when you are ~ again** quand vous aurez repris des forces, quand vous aurez retrouvé vos forces ; **she has never been very ~** elle a toujours eu une petite santé ; (*fig*) **you need a ~ stomach for that job** il faut avoir l'estomac solide *or* bien accroché* pour faire ce travail → **constitution**

b (*fig: morally*) fort, courageux ; [*character, personality*] fort, puissant ; [*characteristic*] marqué, frappant ; [*accent*] fort, marqué ; [*emotion, desire, interest*] vif ; [*reasons, argument, evidence*] solide, sérieux ; (*St Ex*) [*market*] ferme ; (*Econ*) [*the pound, dollar*] solide ; [*candidate, contender*] sérieux, qui a des chances de gagner ; [*letter*] bien senti ; [*protest*] vigoureux, vif ; [*measures, steps*] énergique ; [*influence, attraction*] fort, profond ; (*Mus*) [*beat*] fort ; (*in courage etc*) **you must be ~** soyez courageux, vous devez faire preuve de courage ; (*mentally etc*) **he's a very ~ person** c'est un homme bien trempé *or* un homme qui a du ressort ; **we are in a ~ position to make them obey** nous sommes bien placés pour les faire obéir ; **his ~ suit** (*Cards*) sa couleur forte ; (*fig: also* **his ~ point**) son fort ; **to be ~ in maths** être fort en maths ; **to be ~ on*** (= *good at*) être bon en ... ; (*emphasizing*) mettre l'accent sur ... ; **in ~ terms** en termes non équivoques ; **there are ~ indications that ...** tout semble indiquer que ... ; **a ~ effect** beaucoup d'effet ; **I had a ~ sense of ...** je ressentais vivement ... ; **I've a ~ feeling that ...** j'ai bien l'impression que ... ; **he's got ~ feelings on this matter** cette affaire lui tient à cœur ; **it is my ~ opinion** *or* **belief that ...** je suis fermement convaincu *or* persuadé que ... ; **a ~ socialist** un socialiste fervent ; **~ supporters of ...** d'ardents partisans de ..., des fervents de ... ; **I am a ~ believer in ...** je crois fermement à *or* profondément à ... → **case**[1]

c (= *intense, pungent*) [*coffee, cheese, wine, cigarette*] fort ; (*pej*) [*butter*] rance ; [*sauce, taste*] fort, relevé ; [*solution*] concentré ; [*light*] fort, vif ; **it has a ~ smell** ça sent fort

d (*in numbers*) **an army 500 ~** une armée (forte) de 500 hommes ; **they were 100 ~** ils étaient au nombre de 100

e (*Ling*) [*verb, form*] fort

2 ADV **to be going ~** [*person*] être toujours solide ; [*car etc*] marcher toujours bien ; [*relationship etc*] aller bien ; [*firm, business*] aller bien, être florissant ; **that's pitching it** *or* **coming it** *or* **going it a bit ~*** il pousse (*or* vous poussez *etc*) un peu*, il y va (*or* vous y allez *etc*) un peu fort ; **to come on ~*** (*gen* = *be overbearing*) insister lourdement ; (*sexually*) faire du rentre-dedans* ; (*US* = *make progress*) progresser fortement

3 COMP ► **strong-arm** ADJ → **strong-arm** ► **strong breeze** N (*on Beaufort scale*) vent *m* frais ► **strong drink** N (*NonC*) alcool *m*, boisson *f* alcoolisée ► **strong gale** N (*on Beaufort scale*) fort coup *m* de vent ► **strong-minded** ADJ → **strong-minded** ► **strong-willed** ADJ résolu ; **to be ~-willed** avoir de la volonté

strong-arm* ['strɒŋɑːm] 1 ADJ [*method, treatment*] brutal ; **~ man** gros bras *m* (*fig*) ; **~ tactics** la manière forte 2 VT faire violence à ; **to ~ sb into doing sth** forcer la main à qn pour qu'il fasse qch

strongbox ['strɒŋbɒks] N coffre-fort *m*

stronghold ['strɒŋhəʊld] N (*Mil*) forteresse *f*, fort *m* ; (*fig*) bastion *m*

strongly ['strɒŋlɪ] ADV a [*influence, hint, accentuate, remind, indicate, imply*] fortement ; [*attract, recommend, advise, interest, desire*] fortement, vivement ; [*criticize, protest*] vivement ; [*deny, condemn, protest, defend*] vigoureusement ; [*fight, attack*] énergiquement ; [*support, oppose*] fermement ; [*feel, sense, believe*] profondément ; **to argue ~ for** *or* **in fa-**

vour of sth plaider vigoureusement *or* avec force pour qch; **to argue ~ against sth** s'élever avec véhémence contre qch; **to argue ~ that** ... soutenir fermement que ...; **to taste ~ of sth** avoir un goût prononcé de qch; **to smell ~ of sth** avoir une forte odeur de qch; **the kitchen smelled ~ of smoke** il y avait une forte odeur de fumée dans la cuisine; **fish features ~ in the Japanese diet** le poisson occupe une place importante dans l'alimentation des Japonais; **if you feel ~ about this problem, write to us** si ce problème vous tient à cœur, écrivez-nous; **I feel very ~ that** ... je suis convaincu que ...
b ~ **recommended** vivement recommandé; **you are ~ recommended** *or* **advised to leave the country** nous vous recommandons vivement de quitter le pays; ~ **held views** *or* **opinions** opinions *fpl* très arrêtées; **to be ~ critical of sb/sth** critiquer vivement qn/qch; **to be ~ in favour of sth** être très favorable à qch; **to be ~ against** *or* **opposed to sth** s'opposer fermement à qch; ~ **anti-American/nationalist** farouchement antiaméricain/nationaliste; **a ~ worded letter** une lettre virulente; **his accent was ~ northern** il avait un très net *or* fort accent du nord; ~ **built** [*person*] costaud*; ~ **constructed** *or* **made** *or* **built** solide.

strongman ['strɒŋmæn] N (*pl* **-men**) (*in circus etc*) hercule *m*; (*fig, Comm, Pol etc*) homme *m* fort

strong-minded [,strɒŋ'maɪndɪd] ADJ résolu, qui a beaucoup de volonté, qui sait ce qu'il veut

strong-mindedly [,strɒŋ'maɪndɪdlɪ] ADV avec une persévérance tenace, avec ténacité

strong-mindedness [,strɒŋ'maɪndɪdnɪs] N volonté *f*, force *f* de caractère

strongroom ['strɒŋrʊm] N (*gen*) chambre *f* forte; (*in bank*) chambre *f* forte, salle *f* des coffres

strontium ['strɒntɪəm] N strontium *m*; ~ **90** strontium *m* 90, strontium *m* radioactif

strop [strɒp] **1** N cuir *m* (à rasoir) **2** VT [+ *razor*] repasser sur le cuir

strophe ['strəʊfɪ] N strophe *f*

stroppy: ['strɒpɪ] ADJ (*Brit*) buté et râleur*; **to get ~** se mettre à râler*; **to get ~ with sb** se mettre en rogne contre qn*

strove [strəʊv] VB *pt of* **strive**

struck [strʌk] VB *pt, ptp of* **strike**

structural ['strʌktʃərəl] **1** ADJ **a** (*also Econ = relating to structure*) [*change, problem, reform etc*] structurel; ~ **complexity** complexité *f* de structure; ~ **unemployment** chômage *m* structurel **b** (*Ling, Psych = relating to structuralism*) structural; ~ **psychology/linguistics** psychologie *f*/linguistique *f* structurale **c** (*Archit, Constr, Aviat, Naut*) (*= load-bearing*) [*repair, alteration, failure, integrity, weakness, alteration, damage, fault*] au niveau de la structure; (*in building*) ~ **defect** vice *f* de construction; **the house was in good ~ condition** la structure de la maison était saine **2** COMP ► **structural engineer** N ingénieur *m* en génie civil ► **structural engineering** N génie *m* civil ► **structural inspection** N ► **structural survey** ► **structural steel** N acier *m* (de construction) ► **structural survey** N (*Archit, Constr*) expertise *f* détaillée

structuralism ['strʌktʃərəlɪzəm] N structuralisme *m*

structuralist ['strʌktʃərəlɪst] ADJ, N structuraliste *mf*

structurally ['strʌktʃərəlɪ] ADV **the building is ~ sound/unsound** la structure du bâtiment est saine/peu saine; ~**, the film is quite complex** structurellement, c'est un film assez complexe

structure ['strʌktʃəʳ] **1** N **a** (*Anat, Bot, Chem, Geol, Ling, Math, Philos, Phys, Psych etc*) structu-

re *f*; (*Literat, Poetry*) structure *f*, composition *f*; **social/administrative ~** structure *f* sociale/administrative **b** (*Constr*) [*of building etc*] structure *f*; (*the building, bridge etc itself*) construction *f*, édifice *m* **2** VT structurer

structured ['strʌktʃəd] ADJ structuré; (*Educ*) ~ **activity** activité *f* structurée

struggle ['strʌgl] **1** N (*lit, fig*) lutte *f* (**for** pour, **against** contre, **with** avec, **to do** pour faire); (*= fight*) bagarre *f*; **to put up a ~** résister (*also fig*), se débattre; **he lost his glasses in the ~** il a perdu ses lunettes dans la bagarre; (*Mil*) **they surrendered without a ~** ils n'ont opposé aucune résistance; **you won't succeed without a ~** vous ne réussirez pas sans vous battre, il faudra vous battre si vous voulez réussir; **her ~ to feed her children** sa lutte quotidienne pour nourrir ses enfants; **the ~ to find somewhere to live** les difficultés qu'on a à trouver *or* le mal qu'il faut se donner pour trouver un logement; **I had a ~ to persuade him** j'ai eu beaucoup de mal à le persuader, je ne l'ai persuadé qu'au prix de grands efforts; **it was a ~ but we made it** cela nous a demandé beaucoup d'efforts mais nous y sommes arrivés
2 VI **a** (*gen*) lutter (**against** contre, **for** pour); (*= fight*) se battre; (*= thrash around*) se débattre, se démener; (*fig = try hard*) se démener, se décarcasser* (**to do** pour faire), s'efforcer (**to do** de faire); **he was struggling with the thief** il était aux prises *or* se battait avec le voleur; **he ~d fiercely as they put on the handcuffs** il a résisté avec acharnement quand on lui a passé les menottes; **he ~d to get free from the ropes** il s'est débattu *or* démené pour se dégager des cordes; **they were struggling for power** ils se disputaient le pouvoir; (*fig*) **he was struggling to make ends meet** il avait beaucoup de mal à joindre les deux bouts, il tirait le diable par la queue; **he is struggling to finish it before tomorrow** il se démène *or* il se décarcasse* pour le terminer avant demain
b (*= move with difficulty*) **to ~ in/out etc** entrer/sortir *etc* avec peine *or* à grand-peine; **he ~d up the cliff** il s'est hissé péniblement *or* à grand-peine jusqu'au sommet de la falaise; **he ~d through the tiny window** il s'est contorsionné pour passer par la minuscule fenêtre; **to ~ through the crowd** se frayer péniblement *or* tant bien que mal un chemin à travers la foule; **he ~d to his feet** il s'est levé péniblement *or* à grand-peine; **he ~d into a jersey** il a enfilé tant bien que mal un pullover
► **struggle along** VI (*lit*) avancer avec peine *or* à grand-peine; (*fig: financially*) subsister *or* se débrouiller tant bien que mal
► **struggle back** VI (*= return*) revenir (*or* retourner) avec peine *or* à grand-peine; (*fig*) **to ~ back to solvency** s'efforcer de redevenir solvable
► **struggle on** VI **a** = **struggle along** **b** (*= continue the struggle*) continuer de lutter, poursuivre la lutte (**against** contre)
► **struggle through** VI (*fig*) venir à bout de ses peines, s'en sortir

struggling ['strʌglɪŋ] ADJ [*artist etc*] qui tire le diable par la queue

strum [strʌm] **1** VT **a** [+ *piano*] tapoter de; [+ *guitar, banjo etc*] gratter de, racler (de) **b** (*also ~ out*) [+ *tune*] (*on piano*) tapoter; (*on guitar etc*) racler **2** VI **~ on** = **1a 3** N (*also ~ming*) [*of guitar etc*] raclement *m*

strumpet†† ['strʌmpɪt] N catin *f*

strung [strʌŋ] VB *pt, ptp of* **string**; → **highly, string up**

strut[1] [strʌt] VI (*also ~ about, ~ around*) se pavaner; **to ~ in/out/along** *etc* entrer/sortir/avancer *etc* en se pavanant *or* en se rengorgeant *or* d'un air important; **to ~ one's stuff** frimer*

strut[2] [strʌt] N (= *support*) étai *m*, support *m*; (*for wall, trench, mine*) étrésillon *m*; (*more solid*) étançon *m*; (*Carpentry*) contrefiche *f*; (*between uprights*) lierne *f*, traverse *f*, entretoise *f*; (*Constr: in roof*) jambe *f* de force

strychnine ['strɪkniːn] N strychnine *f*

stub [stʌb] **1** N [*of tree, plant*] souche *f*, chicot *m*; [*of pencil, broken stick*] bout *m*, morceau *m*; [*of cigarette, cigar*] bout *m*, mégot* *m*; [*of tail*] moignon *m*; [*of cheque, ticket*] talon *m* **2** VT **to ~ one's toe/one's foot** se cogner le doigt de pied/le pied (**against** contre) **3** COMP ► **stub end** N [*of pencil etc*] bout *m* (de crayon *etc*)
► **stub out** VT SEP [+ *cigar, cigarette*] écraser

stubble ['stʌbl] N (*NonC*) (*Agr*) chaume *m*, éteule *f*; (*on chin*) barbe *f* de plusieurs jours; **field of ~** champ *m* de chaume, éteule *f*

stubbly ['stʌblɪ] ADJ [*field*] couvert de chaume; [*chin, face*] mal rasé; [*beard*] de plusieurs jours; [*hair*] court et raide, en brosse

stubborn ['stʌbən] ADJ **a** [*person*] têtu, entêté; [*animal*] rétif; [*opposition, campaign, resistance*] opiniâtre, acharné; [*denial, refusal, defiance, insistence, determination*] opiniâtre; **his attitude** son entêtement; **she has a ~ streak** elle a un côté têtu *or* entêté → **mule**[1] **b** [*stain*] rebelle, récalcitrant; [*cold, fever etc*] rebelle, persistant; [*problem*] persistant, tenace

stubbornly ['stʌbənlɪ] ADV obstinément; **he ~ refused** il a refusé obstinément; **he was ~ determined** sa détermination était inébranlable; **interest rates have remained ~ high** les taux d'intérêt ont persisté à rester élevés

stubbornness ['stʌbənnɪs] N [*of person*] entêtement *m*; [*of animal*] caractère *m* rétif; [*of opposition, campaign, resistance*] opiniâtreté *f*, acharnement *m*; [*of denial, refusal, defiance, insistence*] obstination *f*, opiniâtreté *f*

stubby ['stʌbɪ] ADJ [*person*] courtaud; [*finger*] boudiné; [*pencil, crayon*] gros et court; **a dog with ~ legs** un chien court sur pattes

stucco ['stʌkəʊ] **1** N (*pl* **stuccoes** *or* **stuccos**) stuc *m* **2** VT stuquer **3** COMP de *or* en stuc, stuqué

stuccowork ['stʌkəʊwɜːk] N stuc *m*

stuck [stʌk] **1** VB *pt, ptp of* **stick** **2** COMP ► **stuck-up*** ADJ bêcheur*

stud[1] [stʌd] **1** N (= *knob, nail*) clou *m* à grosse tête; (*on door, shield etc*) clou *m* décoratif; (*on boots*) clou *m* à souliers, caboche *f*; (*on football boots*) crampon *m*; (*on tyre, roadway*) clou *m*; (*Aut = cat's-eye*) clou *m* à catadioptre; (*also collar ~*) bouton *m* de col; (*in chain*) étai *m*; (*Constr*) montant *m*; (*Tech = double-headed screw*) goujon *m*; (= *pivot screw*) tourillon *m* **2** VT [+ *boots, shield, door*] clouter; (*Aut*) **~ded tyre** pneu *m* clouté *or* à clous; (*fig*) **~ded with** parsemé de, émaillé de; **sky ~ded with stars** ciel *m* constellé, ciel *m* parsemé *or* semé *or* piqueté *or* criblé d'étoiles

stud[2] [stʌd] **1** N **a** (*also racing ~*) écurie *f* (de courses); (*also ~ farm*) haras *m*; **to be at ~** ◊ **to have been put (out) to ~** être au haras **b** (* = *young man*) jeune mec* *m*; (*promiscuous*) tombeur* *m* **2** COMP ► **stud farm** N haras *m* ► **stud fee** N prix *m* de la saillie ► **stud mare** N (jument *f*) poulinière *f* ► **stud poker** N (*Cards*) variété de poker

studbook ['stʌdbʊk] N stud-book *m*

student ['stjuːdənt] **1** N (*Univ*) étudiant(e) *m(f)*; (*esp US Scol*) élève *mf*, lycéen(ne) *m(f)*; (*Univ*) **medical ~** étudiant(e) *m(f)* en médecine; **~'s book** livre *m* de l'élève; **he is a ~ of bird life** il étudie la vie des oiseaux; **he is a keen ~** il est très studieux
2 COMP (*Univ*) [*life*] étudiant, estudiantin; (*Univ*) [*residence, restaurant*] universitaire; (*Univ*) [*power, unrest*] étudiant; [*attitudes, opinions*] (*Univ*) des étudiants; (*Scol*) des élèves, des lycéens ► **the student community** N les étudiants *mpl* ► **student council** N (*Scol*)

comité *m* des délégués de classe ► **student councillor** N (*Scol, Univ*) délégué(e) *m(f)* de classe ► **student driver** N (*US*) jeune conducteur *m*, -trice *f* ► **student file** N (*US Scol*) dossier *m* scolaire ► **student grant** N bourse *f* ► **student ID card** N (*US*) carte *f* d'étudiant ► **student lamp** N (*US*) lampe *f* de bureau (*orientable*) ► **student loan** N prêt *m* étudiant (*accordé par l'État*) ► **student nurse** N (*Med*) élève *mf* infirmier(-ière) ► **student participation** N (*Univ*) participation *f* des étudiants; (*Scol*) participation *f* (en classe) ► **Students' Union** N = **Student Union** ► **student teacher** N professeur *m* stagiaire; (*in primary school*) instituteur *m*, -trice *f* stagiaire ► **student teaching** N stage *m* pédagogique ► **Student Union** N (*Univ*) (= *association*) association *f* d'étudiants; (= *building*) locaux *d'une association d'étudiants*)

studentship ['stju:dəntʃɪp] N bourse *f* (d'études)

studhorse ['stʌdhɔ:s] N étalon *m*

studied ['stʌdɪd] ADJ **a** [*indifference, casualness, politeness, calm*] affecté, étudié; [*elegance*] recherché; [*insult*] délibéré, voulu; **to maintain a ~ silence** garder délibérément le silence; **to maintain a ~ neutrality** rester délibérément neutre **b** (*pej = affected*) [*pose, style*] affecté

studio ['stju:dɪəʊ] **1** N [*of artist, photographer, musician etc*] studio *m*, atelier *m*; (*Cine, Rad, Recording, TV etc*) studio *m* → **mobile, recording 2** COMP ► **studio apartment** N (*US*) studio *m* (*logement*) ► **studio audience** N (*Rad, TV*) public *m* (*invité à une émission*) ► **studio couch** N divan *m* ► **studio flat** N (*Brit*) studio *m* (*logement*) ► **studio portrait** N (*Phot*) portrait *m* photographique

studious ['stju:dɪəs] ADJ **a** [*person*] studieux, appliqué **b** (= *deliberate, careful*) [*insult, avoidance*] délibéré, voulu; [*politeness, calm*] affecté, étudié

studiously ['stju:dɪəslɪ] ADV (= *deliberately, carefully*) [*avoid, ignore*] soigneusement; **~ polite/ambiguous** d'une politesse/ambiguïté affectée or étudiée

studiousness ['stju:dɪəsnɪs] N application *f* (à l'étude), amour *m* de l'étude

▼ study ['stʌdɪ] **1** N **a** (*gen, Art, Mus, Phot, Sociol etc*) étude *f*; **to make a ~ of sth** faire une étude de qch, étudier qch; **it is a ~ of women in industry** c'est une étude sur les femmes dans l'industrie; **his studies showed that ...** ses recherches ont montré que ...; (*fig = model, ideal*) **it is a ~ in social justice** c'est un modèle de justice sociale; (*fig hum*) **his face was a ~** il fallait voir son visage, son visage était un poème → **brown**
b (*NonC*) étude *f*; (*Scol*) études *fpl*; **he spends all his time in ~** il consacre tout son temps à l'étude or à ses études, il passe tout son temps à étudier
c (= *room*) bureau *m*, cabinet *m* de travail
2 VT [+ *nature, an author, text*] étudier; (*Scol, Univ*) [+ *maths etc*] faire des études de, étudier; [+ *project, proposal, map, ground*] étudier, examiner soigneusement; [+ *person, sb's face, reactions*] étudier, observer attentivement; [+ *stars*] observer → **studied**
3 VI (*gen*) étudier; (*Scol, Univ etc*) étudier, faire ses études; **to ~ hard** travailler dur; **to ~ under sb** travailler sous la direction de qn; [*painter, composer*] être l'élève de qn; **to ~ for an exam** préparer un examen; **he is ~ing to be a doctor/a pharmacist** il fait des études de médecine/de pharmacie; **he is ~ing to be a teacher** il fait des études pour entrer dans l'enseignement or pour devenir professeur
4 COMP [*visit, hour*] d'étude; [*group*] de travail ► **study hall** N (*US Scol*) (*gen*) permanence *f*; (*in boarding school*) (salle *f* d')étude *f*; (*US Scol*) **~ hall teacher** surveillant(e) *m(f)* d'étude ► **study period** N (*Brit*) (heure *f* de)

permanence *f*, (heure *f* d')étude *f* surveillée ► **study room** N (*Scol*) permanence *f*; (*in boarding school*) (salle *f* d')étude *f* ► **study tour** N voyage *m* d'études

stuff [stʌf] **1** N (*NonC*) **a** (*: gen*) chose *f*, truc* *m*; **look at that ~** regarde ça, regarde ce truc*; **it's dangerous ~** c'est dangereux; **radioactive waste is dangerous ~** les déchets radioactifs sont (des trucs) vraiment dangereux; **what's this ~ in this jar?** qu'est-ce que c'est que ça or que ce truc* dans ce pot?; **his new book is good ~** son nouveau livre est bien; **there's some good ~ in what he writes** il y a de bonnes choses dans ce qu'il écrit; **his painting is poor ~** sa peinture ne vaut pas grand-chose; **Joyce? I can't read his ~ at all** Joyce? je ne supporte pas du tout (ses livres); **I can't listen to his ~ at all** je ne supporte pas sa musique; (*pej*) **all that ~ about how he wants to help us** toutes ces promesses en l'air comme quoi il veut nous aider; **that's the ~ (to give them** or **to give the troops)!** bravo!, c'est ça!; **~ and nonsense!** balivernes!; **he knows his ~** il connaît son sujet or son métier; **do your ~!** vas-y!, c'est à toi!; **he did his ~ very well** il s'en est bien sorti; **she's a nice bit of ~** elle est canon* or bien roulée*; → **greenstuff, hot, stern²**
b * (= *miscellaneous objects*) trucs *mpl*; (*jumbled up*) fatras *m*; (= *possessions*) affaires *fpl*, fourbi* *m*; (= *tools etc*) [*of workman*] attirail* *m*; **he brought back a lot of ~ from China** il a rapporté des tas de choses de Chine; **put your ~ away** range tes affaires
c (= *fabric, cloth*) étoffe *f*; (*fig*) **it is the (very) ~ of life/politics** *etc* c'est l'essence même de la vie/la politique *etc*; (*liter*) **he is the ~ that heroes are made from** ◊ **he is the ~ of heroes** il a l'étoffe d'un héros
d (*Drugs**: gen*) came* *f*
2 VT **a** (= *fill, pack*) [+ *cushion, quilt, chair, toy, mattress*] rembourrer (**with** avec); (*Taxidermy*) [+ *animal*] empailler; [+ *sack, box, pockets*] bourrer, remplir (**with** de); (*Culin*) [+ *chicken, tomato*] farcir (**with** avec); (= *stop up*) [+ *hole*] boucher (**with** avec); (= *cram, thrust*) [+ *objects, clothes, books*] fourrer (**in, into** dans); **to ~ one's ears** se boucher les oreilles; **to ~ one's fingers into one's ears** fourrer ses doigts dans ses oreilles; **he ~ed the papers down the drain** il a fourré or enfoncé les papiers dans le tuyau; **he ~ed some money into my hand** il m'a fourré de l'argent dans la main; (*fig*) **he is a ~ed shirt*** c'est un grand ponte* suffisant; **~ed toy** jouet *m* de peluche; **to ~ o.s. with food** ◊ **to ~ food into one's mouth** se gaver or se bourrer de nourriture; **he was ~ing himself*** il s'empiffrait*; **they ~ed him with morphine** ils l'ont bourré de morphine; **to ~ one's head with useless facts** se farcir or se bourrer la tête or la mémoire de connaissances inutiles; **he's ~ing your head with silly ideas*** il te bourre le crâne or il te farcit la cervelle d'idées niaises; **the museum is ~ed with interesting things*** le musée est bourré de choses intéressantes; (*US Pol*) **to ~ a ballot box** mettre des bulletins de vote truqués dans une urne; (*Brit*) **get ~ed!*** va te faire cuire un œuf!*, va te faire foutre**!*; **~ him!*** qu'il aille se faire voir* or foutre**!*; **the council tax/decency!*** j'en ai rien à foutre** des impôts locaux/des convenances!*
b (* = *put*) mettre; **~ your books on the table** mets or fous* tes livres sur la table; (*fig*) **(you know where) you can ~ that!*** tu sais où tu peux te le mettre!*
c (*: = *defeat, ruin*) baiser**, niquer**; **we'll be ~ed if that happens** si ça arrive, on sera baisés** or niqués**
d (** = *have sex with*) baiser**
3 VI (* = *guzzle*) se gaver, se gorger
4 COMP† [*dress etc*] en laine, en lainage

► stuff away VT SEP [+ *food*] enfourner*, engloutir

► stuff up VT SEP [+ *hole*] boucher; **my nose is ~ed up** ◊ **I'm ~ed up** j'ai le nez bouché

stuffily* ['stʌfɪlɪ] ADV [*say etc*] d'un ton désapprobateur

stuffiness ['stʌfɪnɪs] N (*in room*) manque *m* d'air; [*of person*] pruderie *f*, esprit *m* étriqué or vieux jeu *inv*

stuffing ['stʌfɪŋ] N (*NonC*) (= *padding material*) [*of quilt, cushion, mattress*] bourre *f*, rembourrage *m*; [*of toy, chair*] rembourrage *m*; (*Taxidermy*) paille *f*; (*Culin*) farce *f*; (*fig*) **he's got no ~** c'est une chiffe molle; **to knock the ~ out of sb*** (= *demoralize*) démoraliser qn; (= *take down a peg*) remettre qn à sa place

stuffy ['stʌfɪ] ADJ **a** (= *airless*) [*room*] mal aéré; [*atmosphere*] étouffant; **it's ~ in here** on manque d'air ici; **the room was ~ after the meeting** on manquait d'air dans la salle après la réunion **b** (= *stick-in-the-mud*) vieux jeu *inv*; (= *snobby*) guindé; **golf has a rather ~ image in England** le golf a une image assez vieux jeu et guindée en Angleterre; **Delphine's father is a nice man, but rather ~** le père de Delphine est un homme gentil, mais il est un peu collet monté **c** (= *congested*) [*nose, sinuses*] bouché, pris

stultify ['stʌltɪfaɪ] VT [+ *person*] abrutir, déshumaniser; [+ *sb's efforts, action*] rendre vain; [+ *argument, reasoning, claim*] enlever toute valeur à

stultifying ['stʌltɪfaɪɪŋ] ADJ [*work, system, regime*] abrutissant; [*atmosphere, effect*] débilitant

stumble ['stʌmbl] **1** N **a** (*in walking*) faux pas *m*, trébuchement *m*; [*of horse*] faux pas *m* **b** **he recited it without a ~** il l'a récité sans trébucher or se reprendre une seule fois **2** VI **a** trébucher (**over** sur, contre), faire un faux pas; [*horse*] broncher; **he ~d against the table** il a trébuché or fait un faux pas et a heurté la table; **to ~ in/out/along** *etc* entrer/sortir/avancer *etc* en trébuchant **b** (*in speech*) trébucher (**at, over** sur); **he ~d through the speech** il a prononcé le discours d'une voix hésitante or trébuchante **3** COMP ► **stumbling block** N pierre *f* d'achoppement

► stumble across, stumble (up)on VT FUS (*fig*) tomber sur

stumblebum* ['stʌmbl,bʌm] N (*US*) empoté(e)* *m(f)*, abruti(e)* *m(f)*

stump [stʌmp] **1** N **a** [*of tree*] souche *f*, chicot *m*; [*of limb, tail*] moignon *m*; [*of tooth*] chicot *m*; [*of cigar*] bout *m*, mégot* *m*; [*of pencil, chalk, sealing wax, crayon etc*] bout *m* (*qui reste de qch*); (*US*) **to find o.s. up a ~*** ne savoir que répondre, être perplexe
b (*Cricket*) piquet *m*
c (*US Pol*) estrade *f* (*d'un orateur politique*); **to be** or **go on the ~** faire campagne, faire une tournée de discours
d **~s*** (= *legs*) guiboles* *fpl* → **stir¹**
2 VT **a** (* = *puzzle, nonplus*) coller*, faire sécher*; **to be ~ed by a problem** buter sur un problème; **to be ~ed by a question** sécher* sur une question; (*during quiz, crossword etc*) **that's got me ~ed** ◊ **I'm ~ed** je sèche*
b (*Cricket*) éliminer
c (*US Pol*) **to ~ a state** faire une tournée électorale dans un état
3 VI **a** **to ~ in/out/along** *etc* (*heavily*) entrer/sortir/avancer *etc* à pas lourds; (*limping*) entrer/sortir/avancer *etc* clopin-clopant*
b (*US Pol*) faire une tournée électorale

► stump up* (*Brit*) **1** VI casquer*, cracher* **2** VT SEP cracher*, y aller de

stumpy ['stʌmpɪ] ADJ [*person, leg, tail*] courtaud; [*object, plant*] court et épais (-aisse *f*)

stun [stʌn] **1** VT étourdir, assommer; (*fig = amaze*) abasourdir, stupéfier **2** COMP ► **stun grenade** N grenade *f* incapacitante or paralysante ► **stun gun** N pistolet *m* hypodermique

stung [stʌŋ] VB *pt, ptp of* **sting**

stunk [stʌŋk] VB *ptp of* **stink**

stunned [stʌnd] ADJ **a** (*lit*) assommé **b** (*fig = flabbergasted*) abasourdi, stupéfait (**by sth** de qch); **in ~ silence** muet de stupeur; **there was a ~ silence** tout le monde s'est tu, abasourdi *or* stupéfait; **the news was received in ~ disbelief** la nouvelle a été accueillie par un sentiment de stupéfaction incrédule

stunner: [ˈstʌnəʳ] N (= *girl/dress/car etc*) fille *f*/ robe *f*/voiture *f etc* fantastique* *or* sensationnelle*

stunning [ˈstʌnɪŋ] ADJ **a** (* = *fantastic, impressive*) (*gen*) remarquable, (*très*) étonnant; [*woman*] superbe; **a ~ blonde** une superbe blonde; **a ~ success** un formidable succès; **you look ~** tu es superbe **b** **he gave me a ~ blow on the jaw** il m'a envoyé un coup à la mâchoire qui m'a assommé **c** (= *amazing, overwhelming*) [*success, news, defeat*] stupéfiant; **news of his death came as a ~ blow** la nouvelle de sa mort a été un coup terrible; **it was a ~ blow to the government's credibility** ça a porté un coup terrible à la crédibilité du gouvernement

stunningly [ˈstʌnɪŋlɪ] ADV [*simple, original etc*] remarquablement; ~ **beautiful** d'une beauté extraordinaire *or* incroyable

stunt¹ [stʌnt] **1** N (= *feat*) tour *m* de force, exploit *m* (*destiné à attirer l'attention du public*); [*of stuntman*] cascade *f*; (*Aviat*) acrobatie *f*; [*of students*] canular* *m*; (*also* **publicity ~**) truc* *m* publicitaire; **don't ever pull a ~ like that again**! ne recommence plus jamais un truc* pareil; **it's a ~ to get your money** c'est un truc* *or* c'est un coup monté pour avoir votre argent; **that was a good ~** c'était un truc* ingénieux *or* une combine* ingénieuse **2** VI [*pilot etc*] faire des acrobaties; (*Cine*) faire le cascadeur **3** COMP ► **stunt double** N cascadeur *m*, -euse *f*, doublure *f* ► **stunt flier** N (*Aviat*) aviateur *m* qui fait de l'acrobatie, aviateur *m* de haute voltige ► **stunt flying** N acrobatie *f* aérienne, haute voltige *f* ► **stunt kite** N cerf-volant *m* pilotable

stunt² [stʌnt] VT [+ *growth*] retarder, arrêter; [+ *person, plant*] retarder la croissance *or* le développement de

stunted [ˈstʌntɪd] ADJ [*person*] rachitique, chétif; [*plant*] rabougri; [*growth, development*] retardé

stuntman [ˈstʌntmæn] N (*pl* **-men**) (*Cine, TV*) cascadeur *m*

stuntwoman [ˈstʌntˌwʊmən] N (*pl* **-women**) (*Cine, TV*) cascadeuse *f*

stupefaction [ˌstjuːpɪˈfækʃən] N stupéfaction *f*, stupeur *f*

stupefy [ˈstjuːpɪfaɪ] VT [*blow*] étourdir; [*drink, drugs, lack of sleep*] abrutir; (*fig = astound*) stupéfier, abasourdir

stupefying [ˈstjuːpɪfaɪɪŋ] ADJ **a** (*frm = stultifying*) abrutissant **b** (* = *boring*) mortel* **c** (* = *stupendous*) stupéfiant

stupendous [stjuːˈpɛndəs] ADJ **a** (= *amazing, impressive*: *gen*) extraordinaire, remarquable; [*sum, quantity*] prodigieux; (*vulgarity, ignorance*) incroyable **b** (* *fig = wonderful*) sensationnel*, formidable

stupendously [stjuːˈpɛndəslɪ] ADV [*good*] extraordinairement; [*rich*] prodigieusement; ~ **vulgar/thick*** *etc* incroyablement *or* prodigieusement vulgaire/stupide *etc*, d'une vulgarité/ stupidité *etc* incroyable *or* prodigieuse

stupid [ˈstjuːpɪd] ADJ **a** (= *unintelligent*) [*person, question, idea, mistake*] stupide, idiot, bête; **to make sb look ~** ridiculiser qn; **it was ~ of me to refuse** ◊ **I refused, which was ~ of me** j'ai eu la bêtise de refuser, j'ai été assez bête pour refuser; **how ~ of me!** que je suis bête!; **to do something ~** faire une bêtise; **what**

a ~ thing to do! c'était vraiment idiot *or* bête (de faire ça)!; **that hat looks really ~ (on you)** tu as l'air vraiment idiot avec ce chapeau; **don't be ~**! ne sois pas bête!; **to act ~** faire l'imbécile → **bore²**
b (*: expressing annoyance*) **I hate this ~ machine**! je déteste cette maudite *or* fichue* machine!; **it was just a ~ quarrel/ misunderstanding** ce n'était qu'une querelle/ un malentendu stupide; **you can keep your ~ presents, I don't want them!** tu peux garder tes cadeaux débiles*, je n'en veux pas!; **even just ~ things like missing a bus get me depressed** un rien me déprime, même des bêtises comme manquer le bus; **you ~ idiot!** espèce d'idiot(e)!*; **you ~ moron*/bastard**!* espèce d'idiot/de con!; **that ~ bitch!**‡ cette espèce de conne!‡
c († = *insensible, dazed*) (*from blow, drink etc*) abruti, hébété; **to knock sb ~** assommer qn; **to knock o.s. ~** s'assommer; **to laugh o.s. ~** rire comme un bossu *or* comme une baleine*; **to drink o.s. ~** s'abrutir d'alcool

stupidity [stjuːˈpɪdɪtɪ] N stupidité *f*, sottise *f*, bêtise *f*

stupidly [ˈstjuːpɪdlɪ] ADV **a** (= *foolishly*) [*behave*] stupidement, bêtement; ~, **I told him your name** ◊ **I ~ told him your name** j'ai eu la bêtise de *or* j'ai été assez bête pour lui dire votre nom; ~ **generous/zealous** d'une générosité/d'un zèle stupide **b** (= *absently, as if stunned*) [*smile, say*] d'un air hébété *or* stupide†; **"but ... she's dead!" he said ~** «mais ... elle est morte!» dit-il d'un air hébété *or* stupide†

stupidness [ˈstjuːpɪdnɪs] N = **stupidity**

stupor [ˈstjuːpəʳ] N stupeur *f*

sturdily [ˈstɜːdɪlɪ] ADV **a** ~ **built** [*person*] de constitution robuste; [*furniture, structure, vehicle, equipment*] solide, robuste; [*building*] (de construction) solide **b** (= *stoically*) [*say*] d'un air résolu *or* déterminé; ~ **independent** résolument indépendant

sturdiness [ˈstɜːdɪnɪs] N **a** [*of furniture, structure, vehicle, equipment*] solidité *f*; [*of building*] construction *f* solide; [*of plant, person*] robustesse *f*, vigueur *f* **b** [*of resistance, defence, refusal*] caractère *m* énergique

sturdy [ˈstɜːdɪ] ADJ **a** [*person, plant*] robuste, vigoureux; [*object, structure, body*] solide **b** (*fig*) [*resistance, defence, refusal*] énergique, vigoureux; ~ **common sense** solide bon sens *m*

sturgeon [ˈstɜːdʒən] N (*pl inv*) esturgeon *m*

stutter [ˈstʌtəʳ] **1** N bégaiement *m*; **to have a ~** bégayer **2** VI bégayer; (*fig*) **to ~ on/along** progresser difficilement **3** VT (*also* ~ **out**) bégayer, dire en bégayant

stutterer [ˈstʌtərəʳ] N bègue *mf*

stuttering [ˈstʌtərɪŋ] **1** N (*NonC*) bégaiement *m* **2** ADJ **a** (= *stammering*) [*voice*] bégayant, qui bégaie **b** (*fig = jerky*) hésitant; **a ~ start** un début hésitant

Stuttgart [ˈstʊtgɑːt] N Stuttgart

STV [ˌestiːˈviː] N (*Pol*) (ABBR = **Single Transferable Vote**) → **single**

sty¹ [staɪ] N [*of pigs*] porcherie *f*

sty², **stye** [staɪ] N (*Med*) orgelet *m*, compère-loriot *m*

Stygian [ˈstɪdʒɪən] ADJ (*fig*) sombre *or* noir comme le Styx, ténébreux; ~ **darkness** ténèbres *fpl* impénétrables, nuit *f* noire

style [staɪl] **1** N **a** (*gen, Art, Literat, Mus, Sport, Typ etc*) style *m*; **in the ~ of Mozart** dans le style *or* à la manière de Mozart; **building in the Renaissance ~** édifice *m* (de) style Renaissance; ~ **of life** *or* **living** style *m* de vie; **he won in fine ~** il l'a emporté haut la main; **I like his ~ of writing** j'aime sa manière d'écrire *or* son style; (*fig*) **I don't like his ~** je n'aime pas son genre; **that house is not my ~** ce n'est pas mon genre de maison; **that's the ~!** bravo! → **cramp¹**

b (*Dress etc*) (*gen*) mode *f*; (*specific*) modèle *m*; (*Hairdressing*) coiffure *f*; **in the latest ~** (*adv*) à la dernière mode ◊ (*adj*) du dernier cri; **these coats are made in two ~s** ces manteaux sont disponibles en deux modèles; **the four ~s are all the same price** les quatre modèles sont tous au même prix; **I want something in that ~** je voudrais quelque chose dans ce genre-là *or* dans ce goût-là
c (*NonC* = *distinction, elegance*) [*of person*] allure *f*, chic *m*; [*of building, car, film, book*] style *m*, cachet *m*; **that writer lacks ~** cet écrivain manque de style *or* d'élégance, le style de cet écrivain manque de tenue; **to live in ~** mener grand train, vivre sur un grand pied; **he does things in ~** il fait bien les choses; **they got married in ~** ils se sont mariés en grande pompe; **he certainly travels in ~** quand il voyage il fait bien les choses, il voyage dans les règles de l'art
d (= *sort, type*) genre *m*; **just the ~ of book/ car I like** justement le genre de livre/de voiture qui j'aime
e (= *form of address*) titre *m*
2 VT **a** (= *call, designate*) appeler; **he ~s himself "Doctor"** il se fait appeler « Docteur »; **the headmaster is ~d "rector"** le directeur a le titre de « recteur » → **self**
b (= *design etc*) [+ *dress, car, boat*] créer, dessiner; **to ~ sb's hair** créer une nouvelle coiffure pour qn; **it is ~d for comfort not elegance** c'est un modèle conçu en fonction du confort et non de l'élégance
c (*Typ*) [+ *manuscript*] préparer (*selon le style de l'éditeur*)
3 COMP ► **style book** N (*Typ*) manuel *m* des règles typographiques ► **style sheet** N (*Comput*) feuille *f* de style

-style [staɪl] ADJ (*in compounds*) **western-style democracy** démocratie *f* de style occidental; **to dress 1920s-style** s'habiller dans le style des années 20

styli [ˈstaɪlaɪ] NPL *of* **stylus**

styling [ˈstaɪlɪŋ] **1** N (*NonC*) [*of dress*] forme *f*, ligne *f*, façon *f*; [*of car*] ligne *f*; (*Hairdressing*) coupe *f* **2** COMP [*mousse, gel, lotion*] coiffant, structurant ► **styling brush** N brosse *f* ronde

stylish [ˈstaɪlɪʃ] ADJ [*person, car, clothes*] élégant, chic *inv*; [*district, resort, bar, hotel etc*] chic *inv*; [*film, book*] qui a du style; [*performer, performance*] de grande classe

stylishly [ˈstaɪlɪʃlɪ] ADV [*dress*] élégamment; [*write*] avec style; [*designed, decorated*] avec élégance; ~ **dressed** élégamment vêtu, habillé avec élégance; **she wore a ~-cut black suit** elle portait un tailleur noir d'une coupe élégante

stylishness [ˈstaɪlɪʃnɪs] N [*of person, car, clothes*] élégance *f*, chic *m*

stylist [ˈstaɪlɪst] N (*Literat*) styliste *mf*; (*Dress etc*) modéliste *mf*; (*Hairdressing*) coiffeur *m*, -euse *f*, artiste *mf* (capillaire)

stylistic [staɪˈlɪstɪk] ADJ (*Ling, Literat, Mus, Art, Cine etc*) stylistique; **a ~ device** un procédé stylistique *or* de style

stylistically [staɪˈlɪstɪkəlɪ] ADV d'un point de vue stylistique; ~, **he owes much to Hemingway** d'un point de vue stylistique, il doit beaucoup à Hemingway

stylistics [staɪˈlɪstɪks] N (*NonC*) stylistique *f*

stylize [ˈstaɪlaɪz] VT styliser

stylus [ˈstaɪləs] N (*pl* **styluses** *or* **styli**) (= *tool*) style *m*; [*of record player*] pointe *f* de lecture

stymie [ˈstaɪmɪ] **1** N (*Golf*) trou *m* barré **2** VT (*Golf*) barrer le trou à; (* *fig*) coincer*; **I'm ~d*** je suis coincé*, je suis dans une impasse

styptic [ˈstɪptɪk] **1** ADJ styptique; ~ **pencil** crayon *m* hémostatique **2** N styptique *m*

Styrofoam® [ˈstaɪrəˌfəʊm] **1** N (*US*) polystyrène *m* expansé **2** COMP [*cup*] en polystyrène

Styx [stɪks] N Styx *m*

suasion ['sweɪʒən] N (*also* **moral ~**) pression *f* morale

suave [swɑːv] ADJ (*esp pej*) [*person*] mielleux, doucereux; [*manner*] doucereux, onctueux; [*voice, smile*] mielleux

suavely ['swɑːvlɪ] ADV [*say*] d'un ton mielleux *or* doucereux; **to smile ~** avoir un sourire mielleux

suavity ['swɑːvɪtɪ] N (*NonC*) manières *fpl* doucereuses *or* onctueuses (*pej*)

sub* [sʌb] ABBR = **subaltern, subedit, subeditor, sub-lieutenant, submarine, subscription, substitute**

sub... [sʌb] PREF sub..., sous- → **subculture**

subagent [sʌb'eɪdʒənt] N sous-agent *m*

subalpine ['sʌb'ælpaɪn] ADJ subalpin

subaltern ['sʌbltən] 1 N (*Brit Mil*) officier d'un rang inférieur à celui de capitaine 2 ADJ subalterne

subaqua [sʌb'ækwə] ADJ **~ club** club *m* de plongée

subaqueous ['sʌb'eɪkwɪəs] ADJ subaquatique, aquatique

subarctic ['sʌb'ɑːktɪk] ADJ subarctique; (*fig*) presque arctique

subassembly [sʌbə'semblɪ] N sous-assemblée *f*

subatomic ['sʌbə'tɒmɪk] ADJ subatomique

sub-basement ['sʌb'beɪsmənt] N second sous-sol *m*

sub-branch ['sʌb'brɑːntʃ] N sous-embranchement *m*

subclass ['sʌb'klɑːs] N sous-classe *f*

subcommittee ['sʌbkə,mɪtɪ] N sous-comité *m*; (*larger*) sous-commission *f*; **the Housing Subcommittee** la sous-commission du logement

subcompact [sʌb'kɒmpækt] N (*US Aut*) petite voiture *f*

subconscious [sʌb'kɒnʃəs] ADJ, N subconscient *m*

subconsciously [sʌb'kɒnʃəslɪ] ADV a (= *without realizing*) inconsciemment b (*Psych*) au niveau du subconscient, de manière subconsciente

subcontinent [sʌb'kɒntɪnənt] N sous-continent *m*; **the (Indian) Subcontinent** le sous-continent indien

subcontract [sʌb'kɒntrækt] 1 N sous-traité *m* 2 [sʌbkən'trækt] VT sous-traiter

subcontracting [sʌbkən'træktɪŋ] 1 N sous-traitance *f* 2 ADJ [*firm*] qui sous-traite

subcontractor [sʌbkən'træktə*] N sous-entrepreneur *m*, sous-traitant *m*

subculture ['sʌb,kʌltʃə*] N (*Sociol*) subculture *f*; (*Bacteriology*) culture *f* repiquée

subcutaneous [sʌbkjʊ'teɪnɪəs] ADJ sous-cutané

subcutaneously [sʌbkjʊ'teɪnəslɪ] ADV en sous-cutané

subdeacon [sʌb'diːkən] N sous-diacre *m*

subdeb* [sʌbdeb], **subdebutante** ['sʌb,debjuːtɑːnt] N (*US*) jeune fille *f* qui n'a pas encore fait son entrée dans le monde

subdistrict ['sʌb,dɪstrɪkt] N subdivision *f* d'un quartier

subdivide ['sʌbdɪ'vaɪd] 1 VT subdiviser (**into** en) 2 VI se subdiviser

subdivision ['sʌbdɪ,vɪʒən] N subdivision *f*

subdominant [sʌb'dɒmɪnənt] N (*Ecol*) (espèce *f*) sous-dominante *f*; (*Mus*) sous-dominante *f*

subdue [səb'djuː] VT [+ *people, country*] subjuguer, assujettir, soumettre; [+ *feelings, passions, desire*] contenir, refréner, maîtriser; [+ *light, colour*] adoucir, atténuer; [+ *voice*] baisser; [+ *pain*] atténuer, amortir

subdued [səb'djuːd] ADJ a (= *morose*) [*person, mood, atmosphere*] sombre; [*voice*] qui

---

manque d'entrain; **she was very ~** elle avait perdu son entrain b (= *restrained, unobtrusive*) [*reaction, response*] prudent c (= *quiet, dim*) [*colour*] doux (douce *f*); [*light, lighting*] tamisé, voilé; [*voice*] bas (basse *f*); [*conversation, discussion*] à voix basse

subedit [sʌb'edɪt] VT (*Brit Press, Typ*) corriger, mettre au point, préparer pour l'impression

subeditor [sʌb'edɪtə*] N (*Brit Press, Typ*) secrétaire *mf* de (la) rédaction

sub-entry [sʌb,entrɪ] N (*Accounts*) sous-entrée *f*

subfamily ['sʌb,fæmɪlɪ] N sous-famille *f*

subfield ['sʌbfiːld] N (*Math*) subdivision *f*

sub-frame ['sʌbfreɪm] N (*Aut*) faux-châssis *m*

subfusc ['sʌbfʌsk] N toge *f* et mortier noirs

subgroup ['sʌbgruːp] N sous-groupe *m*

subhead(ing) ['sʌb,hed(ɪŋ)] N sous-titre *m*

subhuman [sʌb'hjuːmən] 1 ADJ [*conditions*] inhumain; **to treat/portray foreigners as ~** traiter/dépeindre les étrangers comme des sous-hommes 2 N sous-homme *m*

subject ['sʌbdʒɪkt] 1 N a (*esp Brit* = *citizen etc*) sujet(te) *m(f)*; **the king and his ~s** le roi et ses sujets; **British ~** sujet *m* britannique; **he is a French ~** (*in France*) il est de nationalité française; (*elsewhere*) c'est un ressortissant français
b (*Med, Phot, Psych etc* = *person*) sujet *m*; **he's a good ~ for treatment by hypnosis** c'est un sujet qui répond bien au traitement par l'hypnose; **he's a good ~ for research into hypnosis** c'est un bon sujet pour une étude sur l'hypnose
c (= *matter, topic: gen, Art, Literat, Mus etc*) sujet *m* (**of, for** de); (*Scol, Univ*) matière *f*, discipline *f*; **to get off the ~** sortir du sujet; **that's off the ~** c'est hors du sujet *or* à côté du sujet; **let's get back to the ~** revenons à nos moutons; **on the ~ of ...** au sujet de ..., sur le sujet de ...; **while we're on the ~ of ...** pendant que nous parlons de ..., à propos de ...; **let's change the ~** changeons de sujet; (*Scol, Univ*) **his best ~** sa matière *or* sa discipline forte → **drop**
d (= *reason, occasion*) sujet *m*, motif *m* (**of, for** de); **it is not a ~ for rejoicing** il n'y a pas lieu de se réjouir
e (*Gram, Logic, Philos*) sujet *m*
2 ADJ a (*frm* = *subservient*) [*people, tribes, state*] asservi, soumis; **the police are ~ to the law, like the rest of us** la police doit obéir à la loi, comme nous tous
b **~ to** (= *prone to*) sujet à; **the area is ~ to drought** la région est sujette à la sécheresse; **he is ~ to back pain** il est sujet au mal de dos *or* à des maux de dos; **to French rule** sous (la) domination française; **your gift will be ~ to VAT** votre cadeau sera soumis à la TVA
c (= *depending on*) **~ to the approval of the committee** sous réserve de l'accord du comité; **you may leave the country ~ to producing the necessary documents** vous pouvez quitter le territoire à condition de fournir les documents nécessaires; **the building is being sold ~ to certain conditions** le bâtiment est à vendre sous certaines conditions; **my offer is ~ to the following conditions** mon offre est soumise aux conditions suivantes; **the decision is ~ to approval/confirmation (by the minister)** cette décision doit être approuvée/confirmée (par le ministre); **they have authority to decide, ~ to the minister's approval** ils ont le pouvoir de décision, sous réserve de l'approbation du ministre; **"~ to availability"** [*holiday, concert, flight*] « dans la limite des places disponibles »; [*free gift*] « dans la limite des stocks disponibles »; **"prices are ~ to alteration"** « ces prix sont sujets à modifications »; **~ to prior sale** sous réserve de vente (antérieure)
3 [səb'dʒekt] VT (= *subdue*) [+ *country*] soumettre, assujettir (*liter*); **to ~ sb to sth** sou-

---

mettre qn à qch, faire subir qch à qn; **to ~ sth to heat/cold** exposer qch à la chaleur/au froid; **he was ~ed to much criticism** il a été en butte à de nombreuses critiques, il a fait l'objet de nombreuses critiques, il a été très critiqué; **to ~ o.s. to criticism** s'exposer à la critique
4 COMP ► **subject heading** N rubrique *f* ► **subject index** N (*in book*) index *m* thématique; (*in library*) fichier *m* par matières ► **subject matter** N (= *theme*) sujet *m*; (= *content*) contenu *m* ► **subject pronoun** N (*Gram*) pronom *m* sujet

subjection [səb'dʒekʃən] N sujétion *f*, soumission *f*; **to hold** *or* **keep in ~** maintenir dans la sujétion *or* sous son joug; **to bring into ~** soumettre, assujettir (*liter*); **they were living in a state of complete ~** ils vivaient dans la sujétion *or* dans la soumission *or* dans les chaînes

subjective [səb'dʒektɪv] 1 ADJ a subjectif b (*Gram*) [*case, pronoun*] sujet 2 N (*Gram*) nominatif *m*

subjectively [səb'dʒektɪvlɪ] ADV subjectivement

subjectivism [səb'dʒektɪvɪzəm] N subjectivisme *m*

subjectivity [sʌbdʒek'tɪvɪtɪ] N subjectivité *f*

subjoin [sʌb'dʒɔɪn] VT adjoindre, ajouter

sub judice [sʌb'dʒuːdɪsɪ] ADJ (*Jur*) **the matter is ~** l'affaire est en instance *or* devant les tribunaux

subjugate ['sʌbdʒʊgeɪt] VT [+ *people, country*] subjuguer, soumettre, assujettir; [+ *animal, feelings*] dompter

subjugation [sʌbdʒʊ'geɪʃən] N subjugation *f*, assujettissement *m*

subjunctive [səb'dʒʌŋktɪv] ADJ, N subjonctif *m*; **in the ~ (mood)** au (mode) subjonctif

subkingdom ['sʌb,kɪŋdəm] N (*Bot, Zool etc*) embranchement *m*

sublease ['sʌbliːs] 1 N sous-location *f* 2 VTI sous-louer (**to** à, **from** à)

sublet [sʌb'let] (*vb: pret, ptp* **sublet**) 1 N sous-location *f* 2 VTI sous-louer (**to** à)

sub-librarian [sʌblaɪ'brɛərɪən] N bibliothécaire *mf* adjoint(e)

sub-lieutenant [sʌblef'tenənt] N (*Brit Naut*) enseigne *m* de vaisseau (de première classe)

sublimate ['sʌblɪmeɪt] 1 VT (*all senses*) sublimer 2 ['sʌblɪmɪt] ADJ, N (*Chem*) sublimé *m*

sublimation [sʌblɪ'meɪʃən] N sublimation *f*

sublime [sə'blaɪm] 1 ADJ a [*being, beauty, painting, scenery, music*] sublime; [*moment*] divin b (* = *delightful*) [*dinner, hat, person*] divin, sensationnel* c [*indifference, disregard*] suprême (*before n*), souverain (*before n*); [*innocence*] suprême (*before n*); [*incompetence*] prodigieux 2 N sublime *m*; **from the ~ to the ridiculous** du sublime au grotesque

sublimely [sə'blaɪmlɪ] ADV a **~ beautiful** d'une beauté sublime b (* = *delightfully*) [*dance, sing etc*] divinement c [*indifferent, ignorant*] souverainement, au plus haut point; **the government seems ~ unaware of the danger** le gouvernement semble totalement inconscient du danger

subliminal [sʌb'lɪmɪnl] 1 ADJ subliminal 2 COMP ► **subliminal advertising** N publicité *f* subliminale ► **subliminal image** N image *f* subliminale ► **subliminal message** N message *m* subliminal

subliminally [sʌb'lɪmɪnəlɪ] ADV [*evoke, influence etc*] de manière subliminale

sublimity [sə'blɪmɪtɪ] N sublimité *f*

sublingual [sʌb'lɪŋgwəl] ADJ sublingual

submachine gun [sʌbmə'ʃiːngʌn] N mitraillette *f*

submarine [sʌbmə'riːn] 1 N a (*Naut*) sous-marin *m* b (*US**: *also* **~ sandwich, sub**

sandwich) gros sandwich *m* mixte [2] ADJ sous-marin [3] COMP ► **submarine chaser** N chasseur *m* de sous-marins ► **submarine pen** N abri *m* pour sous-marins

submariner [ˌsʌbˈmɑːrɪnəʳ] N sous-marinier *m*

submaxillary [ˌsʌbˈmæksɪləri] ADJ sous-maxillaire

submediant [ˌsʌbˈmiːdɪənt] N (*Mus*) sus-dominante *f*

sub-menu [ˈsʌbmenjuː] N (*Comput*) sous-menu *m*

submerge [səbˈmɜːdʒ] [1] VT [*flood, tide, sea*] submerger ; [+ *field*] inonder, submerger ; **to ~ sth in sth** immerger qch dans qch ; (*fig*) **to ~ o.s. in sth** se plonger totalement dans qch [2] VI [*submarine, diver etc*] s'immerger

submerged [səbˈmɜːdʒd] ADJ submergé ; (*fig*) **~ in work** submergé *or* débordé de travail

submergence [səbˈmɜːdʒəns] N submersion *f*

submersible [səbˈmɜːsəbl] ADJ, N submersible *m*

submersion [səbˈmɜːʃən] N [a] (*in liquid*) submersion *f* [b] **total ~ in an interesting hobby can be very relaxing** se plonger totalement dans un hobby intéressant peut apporter une grande détente

submission [səbˈmɪʃən] N [a] (= *submissiveness*) soumission *f* (**to** à) ; **she nodded her head in ~** elle a incliné la tête d'un air soumis ; **to starve/beat sb into ~** soumettre qn en le privant de nourriture/en le battant [b] (*Wrestling*) abandon *m* [c] (*NonC = handing in*) [*of documents, sample, application, report*] dépôt *m* ; [*of thesis*] remise *f* (au rapporteur) [d] (= *proposal*) proposition *f* [e] (*Jur*) **~s** conclusions *fpl* (d'une partie) ; (*Jur*) **to file ~s with a court** déposer des conclusions auprès d'un tribunal [f] (*frm* = *assertion*) **it is my ~ that ...** ma thèse est que ... ; **in my/our ~** selon ma/notre thèse

submissive [səbˈmɪsɪv] ADJ [*person, behaviour, attitude*] soumis, docile ; **children were expected to be ~ to their elders** on attendait des enfants qu'ils se soumettent à leurs aînés

submissively [səbˈmɪsɪvlɪ] ADV docilement

submissiveness [səbˈmɪsɪvnɪs] N soumission *f*, docilité *f*

submit [səbˈmɪt] [1] VT [a] **to ~ o.s. to sb/sth** se soumettre à qn/qch [b] (= *put forward*) [+ *documents, sample, proposal, report, evidence*] soumettre (**to** à) ; **to ~ that ...** suggérer que ... ; **I ~ that ...** ma thèse est que ... [2] VI (*Mil*) se soumettre (**to** à) ; (*fig*) se soumettre, se plier (**to** à)

subnormal [ˌsʌbˈnɔːməl] [1] ADJ [a] (*also* **mentally ~**) [*person*] attardé, arriéré [b] [*weight, height, temperature etc*] inférieur (-eure *f*) à la normale [2] N **the subnormal** NPL **the mentally/educationally ~** les attardés *mpl or* retardés *mpl* (sur le plan intellectuel/éducatif)

suborbital [ˌsʌbˈɔːbɪtəl] ADJ (*Space*) sous-orbital

sub-order [ˈsʌbɔːdəʳ] N sous-ordre *m*

subordinate [səˈbɔːdnɪt] [1] ADJ [a] (*officer, role, position*) subalterne (**to** à) [b] (*Gram*) subordonné [2] N subordonné(e) *m(f)*, subalterne *mf* [3] [səˈbɔːdɪneɪt] VT subordonner (**to** à) ; (*Gram*) **subordinating conjunction** subordonnant *m*, conjonction *f* de subordination

subordination [səˌbɔːdɪˈneɪʃən] N subordination *f*

suborn [səˈbɔːn] VT suborner

subparagraph [ˈsʌbˌpærəɡrɑːf] N sous-paragraphe *m*

subplot [ˈsʌbplɒt] N (*Literat*) intrigue *f* secondaire

subpoena [səˈpiːnə] (*Jur*) [1] N citation *f*, assignation *f* (*pour le témoin*) [2] VT citer *or* assigner (à comparaître)

subpopulation [ˈsʌbˌpɒpjʊˈleɪʃən] N subpopulation *f*

sub-postmaster [ˌsʌbˈpəʊstmɑːstəʳ] N (*Brit*) receveur *m* des postes

sub-postmistress [ˌsʌbˈpəʊstmɪstrɪs] N (*Brit*) receveuse *f* des postes

sub-post office [ˌsʌbˈpəʊstɒfɪs] N agence *f* postale

subregion [ˈsʌbˌriːdʒən] N sous-région *f*

subrogate [ˈsʌbrəɡɪt] ADJ subrogé ; (*Ling*) **~ language** langage *m* subrogé

sub rosa [ˌsʌbˈrəʊzə] ADV en confidence, sous le sceau du secret

subroutine [ˈsʌbruːˌtiːn] N (*Comput*) sous-programme *m*

▼**subscribe** [səbˈskraɪb] [1] VT [a] [+ *money*] donner, verser (**to** à) [b] [+ *one's signature, name*] apposer (**to** au bas de) ; [+ *document*] signer ; **he ~s himself John Smith** il signe John Smith [2] VI **to ~ to** [+ *book, new publication, fund*] souscrire à ; [+ *newspaper*] (= *become a subscriber*) s'abonner à ; (= *be a subscriber*) être abonné à ; [+ *charity*] verser une somme d'argent à, apporter une contribution à ; (*fig*) [+ *opinion, project, proposal*] souscrire à ; **I don't ~ to the idea that money should be given to ...** je ne suis pas partisan de donner de l'argent à ... ; **to ~ for shares** souscrire à des actions

subscriber [səbˈskraɪbəʳ] [1] N (*to fund, new publication etc*) souscripteur *m*, -trice *f* (**to** de) ; (*to newspaper, also Telec*) abonné(e) *m(f)* (**to** de) ; (*to opinion, idea*) adepte *mf*, partisan *m* (**to** de) [2] COMP ► **subscriber trunk dialling** N (*Brit Telec*) automatique *m*

subscript [ˈsʌbskrɪpt] (*Typ*) [1] ADJ inférieur (-eure *f*) [2] N indice *m*

subscription [səbˈskrɪpʃən] [1] N (*to fund, charity*) souscription *f* ; (*to club*) cotisation *f* ; (*to newspaper*) abonnement *m* ; **to pay one's ~** (*to club*) payer *or* verser sa cotisation ; (*to newspaper*) payer *or* régler son abonnement ; (*Press*) **to take out a ~ to ...** s'abonner à ... [2] COMP ► **subscription rate** N (*Press*) tarif *m* d'abonnement

subsection [ˈsʌbˌsekʃən] N (*Jur etc*) subdivision *f*, article *m*

subsequent [ˈsʌbsɪkwənt] [1] ADJ (= *later in past*) postérieur (-eure *f*), ultérieur (-eure *f*) ; (= *in future*) à venir [2] ADV (*frm*) **~ to this** par la suite ; **~ to his arrival** à la suite de son arrivée ; **events that occurred ~ to March 1995** les événements postérieurs à mars 1995

subsequently [ˈsʌbsɪkwəntlɪ] ADV par la suite, ultérieurement

subserve [səbˈsɜːv] VT (*frm*) favoriser

subservience [səbˈsɜːvɪəns] N [a] (= *submission*) [*of person, nation*] asservissement *m* (**to sb/sth** à qn/qch) [b] (*pej* = *servility*) [*of person, manner, behaviour*] servilité *f* (*pej*) (**to sb** envers qn) [c] (*frm* = *secondary role*) rôle *m* accessoire *or* secondaire (**to sb/sth** par rapport à qn/qch)

subservient [səbˈsɜːvɪənt] ADJ [a] (= *submissive*) [*person, nation*] asservi, soumis ; **~ to** soumis à [b] (*pej* = *servile*) [*person, manner, behaviour*] servile (*pej*) [c] (*frm* = *secondary*) accessoire, secondaire (**to sb/sth** par rapport à qn/qch)

subset [ˈsʌbset] N sous-ensemble *m*

subside [səbˈsaɪd] VI [*land, pavement, foundations, building*] s'affaisser, se tasser ; [*flood, river*] baisser, décroître ; [*wind, anger, excitement*] tomber, se calmer ; [*threat*] s'éloigner ; [*person*] (*into armchair etc*) s'affaisser, s'écrouler (**into** dans, **on to** sur)

subsidence [ˈsʌbsɪdns, səbˈsaɪdəns] N [*of land, pavement, foundations, building*] affaissement *m* ; **"road liable to ~"** « chaussée instable » ; **the crack in the wall is caused by ~** la faille dans le mur est due à l'affaissement du terrain

subsidiarity [ˌsʌbsɪdɪˈærɪtɪ] N subsidiarité *f*

subsidiary [səbˈsɪdɪərɪ] [1] ADJ [a] [*role*] secondaire, accessoire ; [*motive, reason, aim*] subsidiaire (**to** par rapport à) ; (*Theat, Literat*) [*character*] secondaire ; [*advantage, income*] accessoire [b] (*Univ*) [*subject, course*] optionnel ; **to do ~ Latin** étudier le latin en option [c] (*Fin, Comm*) **~ company/bank** filiale *f* (d'une société/d'une banque) [2] N (*Fin*) filiale *f*

subsidize [ˈsʌbsɪdaɪz] VT subventionner ; **heavily ~d** [*agriculture, housing*] fortement subventionné

subsidy [ˈsʌbsɪdɪ] N subvention *f* ; **government** *or* **state ~** subvention *f* de l'État ; **there is a ~ on butter** l'État subventionne les producteurs *or* la production de beurre

subsist [səbˈsɪst] VI subsister ; **to ~ on bread/£60 a week** vivre de pain/avec 60 livres par semaine

subsistence [səbˈsɪstəns] [1] N [a] existence *f*, subsistance *f* ; **means of ~** moyens *mpl* d'existence *or* de subsistance [b] (*also* **~ allowance, ~ benefit**) frais *mpl or* indemnité *f* de subsistance [2] COMP ► **subsistence crops** NPL cultures *fpl* vivrières de base ► **subsistence economy** N économie *f* de subsistance ► **subsistence farmer** N agriculteur *m* qui produit le minimum vital ► **subsistence farming** N agriculture *f* vital de subsistance ► **subsistence level** N minimum *m* vital ; **to live at ~ level** avoir tout juste de quoi vivre ► **subsistence wage** N salaire *m* tout juste suffisant pour vivre, salaire *m* de subsistance

subsoil [ˈsʌbsɔɪl] N (*Agr, Geol*) sous-sol *m*

subsonic [ˌsʌbˈsɒnɪk] ADJ [*plane, speed etc*] subsonique

subspecies [ˈsʌbˌspiːʃiːz] N (*pl inv*) sous-espèce *f*

substance [ˈsʌbstəns] [1] N (= *matter, material, essential meaning, gist*) substance *f* (*also Chem, Philos, Phys, Rel etc*) ; (= *solid quality*) solidité *f* ; (= *consistency*) consistance *f* ; (= *wealth etc*) biens *mpl*, fortune *f* ; **that is the ~ of his speech** voilà la substance *or* l'essentiel de son discours ; **I agree with the ~ of his proposals** je suis d'accord sur l'essentiel de ses propositions ; **the meal had not much ~ (to it)** le repas n'était pas très substantiel ; **to lack ~** [*film, book, essay*] manquer d'étoffe ; [*argument*] être plutôt mince ; [*accusation, claim, allegation*] être sans grand fondement ; **in ~** en substance ; **a man of ~†** (= *rich*) un homme riche *or* cossu ; (*Jur*) **the ~ of the case** le fond de l'affaire → **sum** [2] COMP ► **substance abuse** N abus *m* de substances toxiques

substandard [ˌsʌbˈstændəd] ADJ [a] (= *low-quality*) [*goods, service, materials*] de qualité inférieure ; [*work*] médiocre [b] (= *below a certain standard*) [*housing, conditions, abattoir etc*] non conforme aux normes [c] (*Ling*) incorrect

substantial [səbˈstænʃəl] ADJ [a] (= *considerable, sizeable*) important, considérable ; [*business*] gros (grosse *f*) ; [*house*] grand ; **to be in ~ agreement** être d'accord sur l'essentiel *or* dans l'ensemble [b] (= *durable*) [*object, structure*] solide [c] (= *sustaining*) [*meal*] substantiel [d] (= *convincing*) [*proof*] convaincant, solide ; [*objection*] fondé ; [*argument*] de poids [e] (*frm* = *real, tangible*) substantiel

substantially [səbˈstænʃəlɪ] ADV [a] (= *considerably*) considérablement ; **~ bigger/higher** *etc* beaucoup plus grand/plus haut *etc* ; **~ more refugees** beaucoup plus de réfugiés ; **~ different** fondamentalement différent [b] (= *to a large extent*) [*correct, true, the same*] en grande partie ; **this is ~ true** c'est en grande partie vrai ; **to remain ~ unchanged** rester inchangé dans l'ensemble ; **it is ~ the same book** c'est en grande partie le même livre [c] **~ constructed** solidement construit

substantiate [səbˈstænʃɪeɪt] VT fournir des

preuves à l'appui de, justifier; **he could not ~ it** il n'a pas pu fournir de preuves

substantiation [səb,stænʃɪ'eɪʃən] N preuve f, justification f

substantival [,sʌbstən'taɪvəl] ADJ (Gram) substantif, à valeur de substantif

substantive ['sʌbstəntɪv] **1** N (Gram) substantif m **2** ADJ **a** (frm = substantial) important **b** (Gram) substantif

substation ['sʌb,steɪʃən] N sous-station f

substitute ['sʌbstɪtjuːt] **1** N (= person: gen, Sport) remplaçant(e) m(f), suppléant(e) m(f) (**for** de); (= thing) produit m de substitution or de remplacement (**for** de); (Gram) terme m suppléant; **you must find a ~** (**for yourself**) vous devez vous trouver un remplaçant, il faut vous faire remplacer; **~s for rubber** ◊ **rubber ~s** succédanés mpl or ersatz m inv de caoutchouc; (Comm) **"beware of ~s"** « se méfier des contrefaçons »; **there is no ~ for wool** rien ne peut remplacer la laine; **a correspondence course is no/a poor ~ for personal tuition** les cours par correspondance ne remplacent pas/remplacent mal les cours particuliers → **turpentine**

2 ADJ (Sport) (à titre de) remplaçant; **~ coffee** ersatz m inv or succédané m de café; (Educ) **~ teacher** suppléant(e) m(f), remplaçant(e) m(f)

3 VT substituer (**A for B** A à B), remplacer (**A for B** B par A)

4 VI **to ~ for sb** remplacer or suppléer qn

substitution [,sʌbstɪ'tjuːʃən] N substitution f (also Chem, Ling, Math etc), remplacement m; **~ of x for y** substitution de x à y, remplacement de y par x; (Sport) **to make a ~** remplacer un joueur

substrata ['sʌb,strɑːtə] NPL of **substratum**

substrate ['sʌbstreɪt] N (Chem) substrat m

substratum ['sʌb,strɑːtəm] N (pl **substrata** ['sʌb,strɑːtə]) gen (Geol, Ling, Sociol etc) substrat m; (Agr) sous-sol m; (fig) fond m

substructure ['sʌb,strʌktʃəʳ] N infrastructure f

subsume [səb'sjuːm] VT subsumer

subsystem ['sʌb,sɪstəm] N sous-système m

subteen [,sʌb'tiːn] N (esp US) préadolescent(e) m(f)

subtemperate [,sʌb'tempərɪt] ADJ subtempéré

subtenancy [,sʌb'tenənsɪ] N sous-location f

subtenant [,sʌb'tenənt] N sous-locataire mf

subtend [səb'tend] VT sous-tendre

subterfuge ['sʌbtəfjuːdʒ] N subterfuge m

subterranean [,sʌbtə'reɪnɪən] ADJ (lit, fig) souterrain

subtext ['sʌbtekst] N sujet m sous-jacent

subtilize ['sʌtɪlaɪz] VTI subtiliser

subtitle ['sʌb,taɪtl] (Cine) **1** N sous-titre m **2** VT sous-titrer

subtitling ['sʌb,taɪtlɪŋ] N sous-titrage m

subtle ['sʌtl] ADJ (gen) subtil (subtile f); [mind, humour, irony, joke] subtil (subtile f), fin; [perfume, flavour] subtil (subtile f), délicat; [pressure, implication, suggestion, reminder, rebuke] discret (-ète f); [plan] ingénieux; [flaw] léger; **a ~ form of racism** une forme insidieuse de racisme; **the ~ message of the film is that ...** le message implicite or en filigrane de ce film est que ...

subtleness ['sʌtlnɪs] N = **subtlety a**

subtlety ['sʌtltɪ] N **a** (NonC: gen) subtilité f; [of mind, humour, irony, joke] subtilité f, finesse f; [of perfume, flavour] subtilité f, délicatesse f; [of pressure, implication, suggestion, reminder, rebuke] discrétion f; [of plan] ingéniosité f **b** (= detail) subtilité f

subtly ['sʌtlɪ] ADV [imply, suggest, remind, rebuke] discrètement; [change, enhance] de façon subtile; **~ flavoured** au goût subtil or délicat;

~ coloured aux couleurs subtiles; **~ spicy** délicatement épicé; **~ erotic** d'un érotisme subtil

subtonic [,sʌb'tɒnɪk] N sous-tonique f

subtopic [,sʌb'tɒpɪk] N sous-thème m, subdivision f d'un thème

subtotal ['sʌb,təʊtl] N total m partiel

subtract [səb'trækt] VT soustraire, retrancher, déduire (**from** de)

subtraction [səb'trækʃən] N soustraction f

subtropical ['sʌb'trɒpɪkəl] ADJ subtropical

subtropics ['sʌb'trɒpɪks] NPL régions fpl subtropicales

suburb ['sʌbɜːb] N faubourg m; **the ~s** la banlieue; **in the ~s** en banlieue; **the outer ~s** la grande banlieue; **it is now a ~ of London** c'est maintenant un faubourg de Londres, ça fait désormais partie de la banlieue de Londres

suburban [sə'bɜːbən] ADJ **a** [house, street, community, train] de banlieue; **a ~ area** une banlieue, une zone suburbaine (frm); **~ development** or **growth** développement m suburbain; (NonC: pej) **~ sprawl** (= phenomenon) développement anarchique des banlieues; (= particular suburb) banlieue f tentaculaire **b** (pej) [attitude, values, accent] banlieusard (pej); **his ~ lifestyle** sa vie étriquée (pej) de banlieusard

suburbanite [sə'bɜːbənaɪt] N habitant(e) m(f) de la banlieue, banlieusard(e) m(f) (pej)

suburbanize [sə'bɜːbənaɪz] VT donner le caractère or les caractéristiques de la banlieue à, transformer en banlieue

suburbia [sə'bɜːbɪə] N (NonC) la banlieue

subvention [səb'venʃən] N subvention f

subversion [səb'vɜːʃən] N (Pol) subversion f

subversive [səb'vɜːsɪv] **1** ADJ (lit, fig) subversif **2** N élément m subversif

subvert [səb'vɜːt] VT [+ the law, tradition] bouleverser, renverser; (= corrupt) [+ person] corrompre

subway ['sʌbweɪ] N (= underpass: esp Brit) passage m souterrain; (= railway: esp US) métro m

sub-zero [,sʌb'zɪərəʊ] ADJ [temperature] au-dessous de zéro

succeed [sək'siːd] **1** VI **a** (= be successful) réussir (**in sth** dans qch); (= prosper) réussir, avoir du succès; [plan, attempt] réussir; **to ~ in doing** réussir or parvenir or arriver à faire; **he ~s in all he does** tout lui réussit, il réussit tout ce qu'il entreprend; (PROV) **nothing ~s like success** un succès en entraîne un autre; **to ~ in business/as a politician** réussir or avoir du succès en affaires/en tant qu'homme politique; **to ~ in life/one's career** réussir dans la vie/sa carrière

b (= follow) succéder (**to** à); **he ~ed (to the throne) in 1911** il a succédé (à la couronne) en 1911; **there ~ed a period of peace** il y eut ensuite une période de paix

2 VT [person] succéder à, prendre la suite de; [event, storm, season etc] succéder à, suivre; **he ~ed his father as leader of the party** il a succédé à or pris la suite de son père à la direction du parti; **he was ~ed by his son** son fils lui a succédé; **as year ~ed year** comme les années passaient, comme les années se succédaient

succeeding [sək'siːdɪŋ] ADJ (in past) suivant; (in future) à venir; **each ~ year brought ...** cha-que année qui passait apportait ...; **many Armenians left their homeland in ~ years** beau-coup d'Arméniens ont quitté leur patrie pendant les années qui ont suivi; **each ~ year will bring ...** chacune des années à venir apportera ...; **this issue will need serious consideration in ~ weeks** il faudra sérieusement réfléchir à ce problème pendant les semaines à venir; **my sight gets worse with each ~ year** ma vue baisse d'année en année; **she returns

to this idea in the ~ chapters** elle reprend cette idée dans les chapitres suivants

▼ **success** [sək'ses] **1** N [of plan, venture, attempt, person] succès m, réussite f; **~ in an exam** le succès or la réussite à un examen; **his ~ in doing sth** le fait qu'il ait réussi à faire qch; **his ~ in his attempts** la réussite qui a couronné ses efforts; **without ~** sans succès, en vain; **to meet with ~** avoir or obtenir or remporter du succès; **to have great ~** faire fu-reur, avoir un succès fou; **to make a ~ of sth** (project, enterprise) faire réussir qch, mener qch à bien; (job, meal, dish) réussir qch; **we wish you every ~** nous vous souhaitons très bonne chance; **congratulations on your ~** je vous félicite de votre succès, (toutes mes) féli-citations pour votre succès; **congratulations on your ~ in obtaining ...** je vous félicite d'avoir réussi à obtenir ...; **he was a ~ at last** il avait enfin réussi, il était enfin arrivé, il avait enfin du succès; **he was a great ~ at the dinner/as Hamlet/as a writer/in business** il a eu beaucoup de succès au dîner/dans le rôle de Hamlet/en tant qu'écrivain/en affaires; **it was a ~** [holiday, meal, evening, attack] c'était une réussite, c'était réussi; [play, book, record] ça a été couronné de succès; **the hotel was a great ~** on a été très content de l'hôtel → **rate¹**, **succeed**

2 COMP ► **success story** N (histoire f d'une) réussite f

successful [sək'sesfʊl] ADJ **a** [plan, attempt, venture, treatment, policy] couronné de succès; [campaign, deal, effort, mission, meeting] fructueux, couronné de succès; [candidate in exam] reçu, admis; [election candidate] victo-rieux; [application] retenu; [marriage] heu-reux; **there have been only three ~ prosecu-tions so far** jusqu'ici, seules trois actions en justice ont abouti; **to be ~** (= succeed) réussir, être couronné de succès; **the tests were ~** les tests ont produit de bons résultats; **the strike proved very ~** la grève a été couronnée de succès; **(up)on** or **after ~ completion of** [+ course] après avoir été reçu à l'issue de; [+ deal] après avoir conclu; **her application was ~** sa candidature a été retenue; **to be (very) ~ in** or **at doing sth** (très bien) réussir à faire qch; **to be ~ in one's efforts** voir ses efforts aboutir; **to be ~ in sth** (attempt, mission, exam) réussir qch; **unfortunately your application has not been ~** nous avons le re-gret de vous faire savoir que votre candidatu-re n'a pas été retenue; **let us hope that the government will be ~ in its efforts to obtain ratification** espérons que les efforts du gou-vernement pour obtenir la ratification abouti-ront or seront fructueux; **to reach a ~ con-clusion** or **outcome** aboutir; **this option offers the best chance of a ~ outcome** ce choix offre la meilleure chance de réussite; **the show had a ~ run on Broadway** ce spectacle a eu une bonne saison or a eu beaucoup de succès à Broadway

b (= prosperous, popular etc) [businessman, business, company] prospère; [doctor, surgeon, lawyer, barrister, academic] réputé; [writer, painter, book, film] à succès; [career] brillant; **she has a ~ career as a novelist/journalist** elle mène une brillante carrière de romancière/ journaliste → **bidder**

successfully [sək'sesfəlɪ] ADV avec succès; **a certificate showing you ~ completed the course** un certificat indiquant que vous avez été reçu à l'issue ce stage

succession [sək'seʃən] N **a** [of victories, dis-asters, delays, kings] succession f, série f; **in ~** (= one after the other) successivement, l'un(e) après l'autre; (= by turns) successivement, tour à tour, alternativement; (= on each occa-sion) successivement, progressivement; **four times in ~** quatre fois de suite; **for ten years in ~** pendant dix années consécutives or dix ans de suite; **in close** or **rapid ~** [walk] à la file;

► LANGUAGE IN USE: **success** 23.5, 23.6

[happen] coup sur coup; **the ~ of days and nights** la succession or l'alternance f des jours et des nuits [b] (NonC) (= act of succeeding: to title, throne, office, post) succession f (**to** à); **he is second in ~ (to the throne)** il occupe la deuxième place dans l'ordre de succession (à la couronne); **in ~ to his father** à la suite de son père

successive [sək'sesɪv] ADJ successif; **on three ~ occasions** trois fois de suite; **on four ~ days** pendant quatre jours consécutifs or de suite; **for the third ~ year/time** pour la troisième année/fois consécutive; **with each ~ failure** à chaque nouvel échec

successively [sək'sesɪvlɪ] ADV successivement; **~ higher levels of unemployment** des taux de chômage de plus en plus élevés

successor [sək'sesə'] N (= person, thing) successeur m (**to, of** de); **the ~ to the throne** l'héritier m, -ière f de la couronne; (Jur) **~ in title** ayant droit m, ayant cause m

succinct [sək'sɪŋkt] ADJ [account, instructions etc] concis, succinct; [person] concis

succinctly [sək'sɪŋktlɪ] ADV succinctement

succinctness [sək'sɪŋktnɪs] N concision f

succor ['sʌkə'] (US) = **succour**

succotash ['sʌkətæʃ] N (US Culin) plat de maïs en grain et de fèves de Lima

succour, succor (US) ['sʌkə'] (liter) [1] (NonC) secours m, aide f [2] VT secourir, soulager, venir à l'aide de

succubus ['sʌkjʊbəs] N (pl succubi ['sʌkjʊ,baɪ]) succube m

succulence ['sʌkjʊləns] N succulence f

succulent ['sʌkjʊlənt] [1] ADJ (also Bot) succulent [2] N (Bot) plante f grasse; **~s** plantes fpl grasses, cactées fpl

succumb [sə'kʌm] VI (to temptation etc) succomber (**to** à); (= die) mourir (**to** de), succomber

such [sʌtʃ] [1] ADJ [a] (= of that sort) tel, pareil; **~ a book** un tel livre, un livre pareil, un pareil livre, un livre de cette sorte; **~ books** de tels livres, des livres pareils, de pareils livres, des livres de cette sorte; **~ people** de telles gens, des gens pareils, de pareilles gens; **we had ~ a case last year** nous avons eu un cas semblable l'année dernière; **in ~ cases** en pareil cas; **did you ever hear of ~ a thing?** avez-vous jamais entendu une chose pareille?; **there's no ~ thing!** ça n'existe pas! → **1b**; **there is no ~ thing in France** il n'y a rien de tel en France; **I said no ~ thing!** je n'ai jamais dit cela!, je n'ai rien dit de la sorte!; **no ~ thing!** pas du tout!; **... or some ~ (thing)** ... ou une chose de ce genre; **no ~ book exists** un tel livre n'existe pas; **Robert was ~ a one** Robert était comme ça; **~ was my reply** telle a été ma réponse, c'est ce que j'ai répondu; **~ is not the case** ce n'est pas le cas ici; **it was ~ weather!** quel temps il a fait!, il a fait un de ces temps! [b] (gen) **~ as** tel que, comme; **a friend ~ as Paul** ◊ **a friend as Paul** un ami tel que or comme Paul; **only ~ a fool as Martin would do that** il fallait un idiot comme Martin or quelqu'un d'aussi bête que Martin pour faire cela; **~ a book as this** ◊ **a book ~ as this** un livre tel que or comme celui-ci; **animals ~ as cats** ◊ **~ animals as cats** les animaux tels que or comme les chats; **~ writers as** or **writers ~ as Molière and Corneille** des écrivains tels (que) or comme Molière et Corneille; **until ~ time** jusqu'à ce moment-là; **until ~ time as ...** jusqu'à ce que ... (+ subj), en attendant que ... (+ subj); **he's not ~ a fool as you think** il n'est pas aussi or si bête que vous croyez; **I'm not ~ a fool as to believe that!** je ne suis pas assez bête pour croire ça!; **there are no ~ things as unicorns** les licornes n'existent pas; **have you ~ a thing as a penknife?** auriez-vous un canif par hasard?; **~ as?** quoi, par exemple?; **it is**

not ~ as to cause concern cela ne doit pas être une raison d'inquiétude; **his health was ~ as to alarm his wife** son état de santé était de nature à alarmer sa femme; **it caused ~ scenes of grief as are rarely seen** cela a provoqué des scènes de douleur telles qu'on or comme on en voit peu; **~ people as knew him** les gens qui le connaissaient; **~ books as I have** le peu de livres or les quelques livres que je possède; **you can take my car, ~ as it is** vous pouvez prendre ma voiture pour ce qu'elle vaut [c] (= so much) tellement, tant; **embarrassed by ~ praise** embarrassé par tant or tellement de compliments; **he was in ~ pain** il souffrait tellement; **don't be in ~ a rush** ne soyez pas si pressé; **we had ~ a surprise!** quelle surprise nous avons eue!, nous avons eu une de ces surprises!, nous avons été drôlement surpris!*; **there was ~ a noise that ...** il y avait tellement or tant de bruit que ...; **his rage was ~ that ...** ◊ **~ was his rage that ...** il était tellement or tant furieux que ...

[2] ADV [a] (= so very) si, tellement; **he gave us ~ good coffee** il nous a offert un si bon café; **~ big boxes** de si grandes boîtes; **~ a lovely present** un si joli cadeau; **it was ~ a long time ago!** il y a si or tellement longtemps de ça!; **he bought ~ an expensive car that ...** il a acheté une voiture si or tellement chère que ... [b] (in comparisons) aussi; **I haven't had ~ good coffee for years** ça fait des années que je n'ai pas bu un aussi bon café; **~ lovely children as his** des enfants aussi gentils que les siens

[3] PRON ceux mpl, celles fpl; **~ as wish to go** ceux qui veulent partir; **all ~** tous ceux; **I'll give you ~ as I have** je vous donnerai ceux que j'ai or le peu que j'ai; **I know of no ~** je n'en connais point; **as ~** (= in that capacity) à ce titre, comme tel(le), en tant que tel(le); (= in itself) en soi; **the soldier, as ~, deserves respect** tout soldat, comme tel, mérite le respect; **the work as ~ is boring, but the pay is good** le travail en soi est ennuyeux, mais le salaire est bon; **and as ~ he was promoted** et en tant que tel il a obtenu de l'avancement; **he was a genius but not recognized as ~** c'était un génie mais il n'était pas reconnu pour tel or considéré comme tel; **there are no houses as ~** il n'y a pas de maisons à proprement parler; **teachers and doctors and ~(like)*** les professeurs et les docteurs et autres (gens de la sorte); **rabbits and hares and ~(like)*** les lapins, les lièvres et autres animaux de ce genre or de la sorte; **shoes and gloves and ~(like)*** les souliers, les gants et autres choses de ce genre or de la sorte

[4] COMP ► **such-and-such** ADJ tel (et or ou tel); **Mr Such-and-~*** Monsieur Untel; **in ~-and-~ a street** dans telle (or telle) rue

suchlike* ['sʌtʃlaɪk] [1] ADJ de la sorte, de ce genre [2] PRON → **such 3**

suck [sʌk] [1] VT [+ fruit, pencil] sucer; [+ juice, poison] sucer (**from** de); (through straw) [+ drink] aspirer (**through** avec); [+ sweet] sucer, suçoter; [baby breast, bottle] téter; [leech] sucer; [pump, machine] aspirer (**from** de); **to ~ one's thumb** sucer son pouce; **child ~ing its mother's breast** enfant qui tète sa mère; **to ~ dry** [+ orange etc] sucer tout le jus de; (fig) [+ person] sucer jusqu'au dernier sou; (of money) sucer jusqu'à la moelle; (fig) **to be ~ed into a situation** être entraîné dans une situation; **~ it and see*** il faut se lancer* (pour savoir si ça marchera) → **teach**

[2] VI [a] [baby] téter [b] **to ~ at** [+ fruit, pencil, pipe] sucer [c] (esp US‡ = be very bad) **it ~s!** c'est un tas de conneries‡!

[3] N [a] **to have a ~ at sth** to give sth a ~ sucer qch [b] (at breast) tétée f; (liter) **to give ~ to ...** allaiter ..., donner le sein à ...

► **suck down** VT SEP [sea, mud, sands] engloutir

► **suck in** [1] VI (fig) **to ~ in with sb** faire de la lèche à qn‡, lécher les bottes de qn [2] VT SEP [sea, mud, sands] engloutir; [porous surface] absorber; [pump, machine] aspirer; (fig) [+ knowledge, facts] absorber, assimiler

► **suck off‡** VT SEP tailler une pipe à‡

► **suck out** VT SEP [person] sucer, faire sortir en suçant (**of, from** de); [machine] refouler à l'extérieur (**of, from** de)

► **suck up** [1] VI (fig) **to ~ up to sb** faire de la lèche à qn‡, lécher les bottes* de qn [2] VT SEP [person] aspirer, sucer; [pump, machine] aspirer; [porous surface] absorber

sucker ['sʌkə'] [1] N [a] (on machine) ventouse f; (= plunger) piston m; (Bot) surgeon m, drageon m; [of leech, octopus] ventouse f; [of insect] suçoir m [b] (‡ = person) poire* f, gogo* m; **to be a ~ for sth** ne pouvoir résister à qch; (US) **never give a ~ an even break*** ne donne jamais une chance à un imbécile; **to play sb for a ~** mener qn en bateau*, rouler* qn [2] VT (US‡ = swindle) embobiner*; **to get ~ed out of 500 dollars** se faire refaire de 500 dollars [3] COMP ► **sucker punch*** N (fig) coup m bas

sucking-pig ['sʌkɪŋpɪg] N cochon m de lait

suckle ['sʌkl] [1] VT [+ child] allaiter, donner le sein à; [+ young animal] allaiter [2] VI téter

suckling ['sʌklɪŋ] [1] N (= act) allaitement m; (= child) nourrisson m, enfant mf à la mamelle [2] COMP ► **suckling pig** N = **sucking-pig**

sucrase ['sjuː'kreɪz] N sucrase f, invertase f

sucrose ['suː'krəʊz] N saccharose m

suction ['sʌkʃən] [1] N succion f; **it works by ~** cela marche par succion; **to adhere by ~ (on)** faire ventouse (sur) [2] VT [+ liquid] aspirer [3] COMP [apparatus, device] de succion ► **suction disc** N ventouse f ► **suction pad** N ventouse f ► **suction pump** N pompe f aspirante ► **suction valve** N clapet m d'aspiration

Sudan [suː'dɑːn] N (the) ~ le Soudan

Sudanese [,suːdə'niːz] [1] ADJ soudanais [2] N (pl inv = person) Soudanais(e) m(f)

sudden ['sʌdn] [1] ADJ (gen) soudain; [death] subit, soudain; [attack, marriage] inattendu; [inspiration] subit; **it's all so ~!** on s'y attendait tellement peu!, c'est arrivé tellement vite!; **all of a ~** soudain, tout à coup [2] COMP ► **sudden-death** N (Brit Ftbl, Golf: also ~-death play-off) mort f subite; (US Sport: also ~-death overtime) prolongation où les ex aequo sont départagés dès le premier point marqué ► **sudden infant death syndrome** N (Med) mort f subite du nourrisson

suddenly ['sʌdnlɪ] ADV soudain, tout à coup; **to die ~** mourir subitement; **~, the door opened** soudain or tout à coup, la porte s'est ouverte

suddenness ['sʌdnnɪs] N (gen) caractère m soudain, soudaineté f; [of death, inspiration] caractère m subit; [of attack, marriage] caractère m imprévu or inattendu

suds [sʌdz] NPL [a] (also soapsuds) (= lather) mousse f de savon; (= soapy water) eau f savonneuse [b] (US‡ = beer) bière f

sudsy ['sʌdzɪ] ADJ savonneux

sue [suː] [1] VT (Jur) poursuivre en justice, intenter un procès à (**for sth** pour obtenir qch, **over, about** au sujet de); **to ~ sb for damages** poursuivre qn en dommages-intérêts; **to ~ sb for libel** intenter un procès en diffamation à qn; **to be ~d for damages/libel** être poursuivi en dommages-intérêts/en diffamation; **to ~ sb for divorce** entamer une procédure de divorce contre qn [2] VI (Jur) intenter un procès, engager des poursuites; **to ~ for divorce** entamer une procédure de divorce [b] (liter) **to ~ for peace/pardon** solliciter la paix/le pardon

suede [sweɪd] [1] N daim *m*, cuir *m* suédé ; **imitation ~** suédine *f* [2] COMP [*shoes, handbag, coat, skirt*] de daim ; [*gloves*] de suède ; [*leather*] suédé

suet [sʊɪt] N (*Culin*) graisse *f* de rognon ; **~ pudding** gâteau sucré ou salé à base de farine et de graisse de bœuf

Suetonius [swiːˈtəʊnɪəs] N Suétone *m*

Suez [ˈsuːɪz] N **~ Canal** canal *m* de Suez ; **Gulf of ~** golfe *m* de Suez ; (*Brit Hist*) **before/after ~** avant/après l'affaire de Suez

suffer [ˈsʌfəʳ] [1] VT [a] (= *undergo*) (*gen*) subir ; [+ *hardship, bereavement, martyrdom, torture*] souffrir, subir ; [+ *punishment, change in circumstances, loss*] subir ; [+ *damage, setback*] essuyer, subir ; [+ *pain, headaches, hunger*] souffrir de ; **he ~ed a lot of pain** il a beaucoup souffert ; (*liter*) **to ~ death** mourir ; **her popularity ~ed a decline** sa popularité a souffert or a décliné [b] (= *allow*) [+ *opposition, sb's rudeness, refusal etc*] tolérer, permettre ; **I can't ~ it a moment longer** je ne peux plus le souffrir or le tolérer, c'est intolérable, c'est insupportable ; **he doesn't ~ fools gladly** il n'a aucune patience pour les imbéciles ; (*liter*) **to ~ sb to do** souffrir que qn fasse
[2] VI [a] [*person*] souffrir ; **to ~ in silence** souffrir en silence ; **to ~ for one's sins** expier ses péchés ; **he ~ed for it later** il en a souffert les conséquences or il en a pâti plus tard ; **you'll ~ for this** il vous en cuira, vous me le paierez ; **I'll make him ~ for it!** il me le paiera ! [b] (= *be afflicted by*) **to ~ from** [+ *rheumatism, heart trouble, the cold, hunger*] souffrir de ; [+ *deafness*] être atteint de ; [+ *a cold, influenza, frostbite, pimples, bad memory*] avoir ; **he ~s from a limp/stammer** etc il boite/bégaie etc ; **he was ~ing from shock** il était commotionné ; **to ~ from the effects of** [+ *fall, illness*] se ressentir de, souffrir des suites de ; [+ *alcohol, drug*] subir le contrecoup de ; **to be ~ing from having done** souffrir or se ressentir d'avoir fait ; **the child was ~ing from its environment** l'enfant subissait les conséquences fâcheuses de son milieu or était la victime de son milieu ; **she ~s from lack of friends** son problème c'est qu'elle n'a pas d'amis ; **the house is ~ing from neglect** la maison se ressent d'avoir été négligée or du manque d'entretien ; **his style ~s from overelaboration** son style souffre or a le défaut d'être trop élaboré → **delusion** [c] (= *be injured, impaired*) [*limb*] souffrir, être blessé ; [*eyesight, hearing, speech*] souffrir, se détériorer ; [*health, reputation, plans, sales, wages*] souffrir, pâtir ; [*car, town, house*] souffrir, être endommagé ; [*business*] souffrir, péricliter ; **your health will ~** votre santé en souffrira or en pâtira ; **the regiment ~ed badly** le régiment a essuyé de grosses pertes

sufferance [ˈsʌfərəns] N tolérance *f*, souffrance *f* (*Jur*) ; **on ~** par tolérance

sufferer [ˈsʌfərəʳ] N (*from illness*) malade *mf* ; (*from misfortune*) victime *f* ; (*from accident*) accidenté(e) *m(f)*, victime *f* ; **~ from diabetes/AIDS/asthma** etc ◊ diabetes/AIDS/asthma etc ~ diabétique *mf*/sidéen(ne) *m(f)*/asthmatique *mf* etc ; (*hum*) **my fellow ~s at the concert** mes compagnons *mpl* d'infortune au concert

suffering [ˈsʌfərɪŋ] [1] N souffrance(s) *f(pl)* ; **"after much ~ patiently borne"** « après de longues souffrances patiemment endurées » ; **her ~ was great** elle a beaucoup souffert [2] ADJ souffrant, qui souffre

suffice [səˈfaɪs] (*frm*) [1] VI suffire, être suffisant ; **~ it to say ...** qu'il (me) suffise de dire ..., je me contenterai de dire ... [2] VT suffire à, satisfaire

sufficiency [səˈfɪʃənsɪ] N (*pl* **sufficiencies**) (*frm*) quantité *f* suffisante ; **a ~ of coal** une quantité suffisante de charbon, suffisamment de charbon, du charbon en quantité suffisante or en suffisance → **self**

sufficient [səˈfɪʃənt] ADJ [*number, quantity, cause, condition*] suffisant ; **~ time/money/evidence** suffisamment de temps/d'argent/de preuves ; **to be ~ (for)** être suffisant (pour), suffire (for à) ; **I've got ~** j'en ai suffisamment ; **to have ~ to eat** avoir suffisamment à manger ; **he earns ~ to live on** il gagne de quoi vivre ; **one song was ~ to show he couldn't sing** une chanson a suffi à or pour démontrer qu'il ne savait pas chanter ■ (*PROV*) **~ unto the day (is the evil thereof)** à chaque jour suffit sa peine (*PROV*) → **self**

sufficiently [səˈfɪʃəntlɪ] ADV suffisamment ; **a ~ large number/quantity** un nombre/une quantité suffisant(e) ; **he is ~ clever to do that** il est suffisamment intelligent pour faire ça

suffix [ˈsʌfɪks] [1] N [*of word*] suffixe *m* ; **these ships were all numbered with the ~ LBK** ces bateaux avaient tous un numéro suivi des trois lettres LBK [2] VT suffixer (**to** à)

suffocate [ˈsʌfəkeɪt] [1] VI suffoquer, étouffer ; (*fig: with anger, indignation, surprise*) suffoquer (**with** de) [2] VT suffoquer, étouffer ; (*fig*) [*anger, indignation, surprise*] suffoquer ; **he felt ~d in that small town atmosphere** il étouffait dans cette atmosphère de petite ville

suffocating [ˈsʌfəkeɪtɪŋ] ADJ [a] [*heat, atmosphere*] étouffant, suffocant ; [*fumes*] asphyxiant, suffocant ; [*smell*] suffocant ; **it's ~ in here** on étouffe ici ; **the room was ~** l'atmosphère de la pièce était étouffante or suffocante [b] (*fig*) [*atmosphere, regime, relationship, life*] étouffant ; [*respectability*] oppressant

suffocation [ˌsʌfəˈkeɪʃən] N suffocation *f*, étouffement *m* ; (*Med*) asphyxie *f* ; **to die from ~** mourir asphyxié

suffragan [ˈsʌfrəgən] [1] ADJ suffragant [2] N **~ (bishop)** (évêque *m*) suffragant *m*

suffrage [ˈsʌfrɪdʒ] N [a] (= *franchise*) droit *m* de suffrage or de vote ; **universal ~** suffrage *m* universel ; **elected by universal ~** élu au suffrage universel [b] (*frm* = *vote*) suffrage *m*, vote *m*

suffragette [ˌsʌfrəˈdʒet] N suffragette *f* ; (*Hist*) **the Suffragette Movement** le Mouvement des Suffragettes

suffragist [ˈsʌfrədʒɪst] N partisan(e) *m(f)* du droit de vote pour les femmes

suffuse [səˈfjuːz] VT [*light*] baigner, se répandre sur ; [*emotion*] envahir ; **the room was ~d with light** la pièce baignait dans une lumière douce ; **~d with red** rougi, empourpré

sugar [ˈʃʊgəʳ] [1] (*NonC*) sucre *m* ; **come here ~!** viens ici chéri(e) or mon petit lapin en sucre ! ; (*euph*) **~!*** mercredi !* → **icing**
[2] VT [+ *food, drink*] sucrer → **pill**
[3] COMP ► **sugar almond** N = **sugared almond** ► **sugar basin** N (*Brit*) sucrier *m* ► **sugar beet** N betterave *f* sucrière or à sucre ► **sugar bowl** N = **sugar basin** ► **sugar cane** N canne *f* à sucre ► **sugar-coated** ADJ (*lit*) dragéifié ; (*fig = falsely pleasant*) doucereux, mielleux ► **sugar cube** N morceau de sucre ► **sugar daddy*** N vieux protecteur *m* ► **sugar diabetes**†* N diabète *m* sucré ► **sugared almond** N dragée *f* ► **sugar-free** ADJ sans sucre ► **sugar loaf** N pain *m* de sucre ► **sugar lump** N = **sugar cube** ► **sugar maple** N (*Can, US*) érable *m* à sucre ► **sugar pea** N (pois *m*) mange-tout *m inv* ► **sugar plantation** N plantation *f* de canne à sucre ► **sugar refinery** N raffinerie *f* de sucre ► **sugar shaker** N saupoudreuse *f*, sucrier *m* verseur ► **sugar tongs** NPL pince *f* à sucre

sugarless [ˈʃʊgəlɪs] ADJ sans sucre

sugarplum [ˈʃʊgəplʌm] N bonbon *m*, dragée *f*

sugary [ˈʃʊgərɪ] ADJ [a] [*food, drink, taste*] sucré [b] (*fig pej*) [*film, music, lyrics*] sirupeux ; [*person, voice, smile*] doucereux, mielleux

▼ **suggest** [səˈdʒest] VT [a] (= *propose*) suggérer, proposer (**sth to sb** qch à qn) ; (*pej = hint*) insinuer (**sth to sb** qch à qn) ; **I ~ that we go to the museum** je suggère or je propose qu'on aille au musée ; **I ~ed that they (should) go to London** il leur a suggéré or proposé d'aller à Londres ; **an idea ~ed itself (to me)** une idée m'est venue à l'esprit ; **what are you trying to ~?** que voulez-vous dire par là ?, qu'insinuez-vous ? (*pej*) ; (*esp Jur*) **I ~ to you that ...** mon opinion est que ... [b] (= *imply*) [*facts, data, sb's actions*] suggérer (**that** que) ; (= *evoke*) suggérer, faire penser à ; **what does that smell ~ to you?** à quoi cette odeur vous fait-elle penser ?, qu'est-ce que cette odeur vous suggère ? ; **the coins ~ a Roman settlement** les monnaies suggèrent l'existence d'un camp romain ; **it doesn't exactly ~ a careful man** on ne peut pas dire que cela dénote un homme soigneux

suggestibility [səˌdʒestɪˈbɪlɪtɪ] N suggestibilité *f*

suggestible [səˈdʒestɪbl] ADJ influençable ; (*Psych*) suggestible

▼ **suggestion** [səˈdʒestʃən] [1] N [a] (*gen*) suggestion *f* ; (= *proposal*) suggestion *f*, proposition *f* ; (= *insinuation*) allusion *f*, insinuation *f* ; **to make** or **offer a ~** faire une suggestion or une proposition ; **if I may make a ~** si je peux me permettre de faire une suggestion ; **have you any ~s?** avez-vous quelque chose à suggérer ? ; **my ~ is that ...** je suggère or je propose que ... ; **there is no ~ of corruption** il ne saurait être question de corruption, rien n'autorise à penser qu'il y ait eu corruption [b] (*NonC: Psych etc*) suggestion *f* ; **the power of ~** la force de suggestion [c] (= *trace*) soupçon *m*, pointe *f* [2] COMP ► **suggestions box** N boîte *f* à idées

suggestive [səˈdʒestɪv] ADJ [a] (*sexually*) [*remark, look, pose, clothing*] suggestif [b] (= *reminiscent*) **to be ~ of sth** suggérer qch

suggestively [səˈdʒestɪvlɪ] ADV [*move, dance*] de façon suggestive ; [*say*] d'un ton suggestif ; **to wink ~** faire un clin d'œil suggestif

suggestiveness [səˈdʒestɪvnɪs] N (*pej*) caractère *m* suggestif, suggestivité *f*

suicidal [ˌsʊɪˈsaɪdl] ADJ [a] [*person, feelings, tendencies*] suicidaire ; **he was not the ~ type** il n'était pas du genre suicidaire or à se suicider ; **I feel absolutely ~** j'ai vraiment envie de me tuer [b] (*fig = ruinous*) [*act, decision, carelessness*] suicidaire ; **it would be absolutely ~ (to do that)** ce serait complètement suicidaire or un véritable suicide (de faire ça) !

suicide [ˈsʊɪsaɪd] [1] N (= *act: lit, fig*) suicide *m* ; (= *person*) suicidé(e) *m(f)* ; **there were two attempted ~s** il y a eu deux tentatives *fpl* de suicide, deux personnes ont tenté de se suicider ; **such an act was political ~** un tel acte représentait un véritable suicide politique, il (or elle etc) se suicidait politiquement en faisant cela ; **it would be ~ to do so** le faire équivaudrait à un suicide, ce serait se suicider que de le faire → **attempt, commit** [2] COMP [*attack etc*] suicide *inv* ► **suicide attempt, suicide bid** N tentative *f* de suicide ► **suicide bomber** N auteur *m* d'un (or de l')attentat-suicide, tueur-kamikaze *m* ► **suicide note** N lettre *f* or note *f* de suicide ► **suicide pact** N pacte *m* suicidaire

▼ **suit** [suːt] [1] N [a] (*tailored garment*) (*for man*) costume *m*, complet *m* ; (*for woman*) tailleur *m* ; (*non-tailored, also for children*) ensemble *m* ; [*of racing driver, astronaut*] combinaison *f* ; **~ of clothes** tenue *f* ; **~ of armour** armure *f* complète ; (*Naut*) **a ~ of sails** un jeu de voiles ; (*Brit*) **the men in (grey) ~s** les décideurs *mpl* → **lounge, trouser** [b] (*frm = request*) requête *f*, pétition *f* ; (*liter: for marriage*) demande *f* en mariage → **press** [c] (*Jur*) poursuite *f*, procès *m*, action *f* en justice (*Jur*) ; **to bring a ~** intenter un procès (**against sb** à qn), engager des poursuites (**against sb** contre qn) ; **criminal ~** action *f* cri-

---

► LANGUAGE IN USE: **suggest** 1, 2.2   **suggestion** 1.1   **suit** 4, 7.4, 11.3, 19.2

minelle → **file²**, **lawsuit**, **party**

d (Cards) couleur f; **long** or **strong ~** couleur f longue; (fig) fort m; **short ~** couleur f courte → **follow**

e (* = business executive) cadre sup* m

2 VT **a** (= be convenient, satisfactory for) [arrangements, date, price, climate, food, occupation] convenir à; **it doesn't ~ me to leave now** cela ne m'arrange pas de partir maintenant; **I'll do it when it ~s me** je le ferai quand ça m'arrangera; **such a step ~ed him perfectly** or **just ~ed his book*** une telle mesure lui convenait parfaitement or l'arrangeait parfaitement; **~ yourself!*** c'est comme vous voudrez!, faites comme vous voudrez or voulez!; **~s me!*** ça me va!, ça me botte!*; **it ~s me here** je suis bien ici; **that ~s me down to the ground*** ça me va tout à fait

b (= be appropriate to) convenir à, aller à; **the job doesn't ~ him** l'emploi ne lui convient pas, ce n'est pas un travail fait pour lui; **such behaviour hardly ~s you** une telle conduite ne vous va guère or n'est guère digne de vous; (Theat) **the part ~ed him perfectly** le rôle lui allait comme un gant or était fait pour lui; **he is not ~ed to teaching** il n'est pas fait pour l'enseignement; **the hall was not ~ed to such a meeting** la salle n'était pas faite pour or ne se prêtait guère à une telle réunion; **it ~s their needs** cela leur convient; **they are well ~ed (to one another)** ils sont faits l'un pour l'autre, ils sont très bien assortis

c [garment, colour, hairstyle] aller à; **it ~s her beautifully** cela lui va à merveille

d (= adapt) adapter, approprier (**sth to sth** qch à qch); **to ~ the action to the word** joindre le geste à la parole

3 VI faire l'affaire, convenir; **will tomorrow ~?** est-ce que demain vous conviendrait or ferait l'affaire?

suitability [ˌsuːtəˈbɪlɪtɪ] N [of action, remark, example, choice] à-propos m, pertinence f; [of time, accommodation, clothes] caractère m approprié; **I have doubts about his ~ (as captain of England)** je doute qu'il possède (subj) les qualités requises (pour être capitaine de l'équipe d'Angleterre); **his ~ (for the position) is not in doubt** le fait qu'il possède les qualités requises (pour ce poste) n'est pas mis en doute

suitable [ˈsuːtəbl] ADJ [place, time, action, clothes] approprié (**for** à); [remark, reply, example, choice] approprié (**for** à), pertinent; [behaviour] convenable (**for** pour); [climate, job] qui convient (**for** à); [food, colour] qui convient (**for** à), approprié (**for** à); [size] qui va (**for** à); [donor, epitaph] approprié (**for** à); (gen) **it's not ~** ça ne convient pas; **an especially ~ form of exercise** une forme d'exercice particulièrement indiquée or appropriée; **he is not at all a ~ person** ce n'est pas du tout quelqu'un comme lui qu'il faut; **I can't find anything ~** je ne trouve or je ne vois rien qui convienne or qui fasse l'affaire; **a ~ caption for the illustration** une légende qui aille avec or qui convienne à l'illustration; **the most ~ man for the job** l'homme le plus apte à occuper ce poste, l'homme le plus indiqué pour ce poste; **these products are ~ for all skin types** ces produits conviennent à tous les types de peau; **these flats are not ~ for families** ces appartements ne conviennent pas aux familles or ne sont pas vraiment appropriés pour les familles; **the 25th is the most ~ for me** c'est le 25 qui m'arrange or me convient le mieux; **the film isn't ~ for children** ce n'est pas un film pour les enfants

suitably [ˈsuːtəblɪ] ADV [reply, thank, apologize] comme il convient, comme il se doit; [behave] convenablement, comme il faut; [equipped] comme il faut; **I'm not ~ dressed for gardening** je ne suis pas habillé comme il faut pour jardiner; **to be ~ qualified** posséder les compétences requises or qu'il faut; **he was**

~ impressed when I told him that ... il a été assez impressionné quand je lui ai dit que ...

suitcase [ˈsuːtkeɪs] N valise f; (fig) **to live out of a ~** vivre sans jamais vraiment défaire ses bagages

suite [swiːt] N **a** (= furniture) mobilier m; (= rooms: in hotel etc) appartement m, suite f; **a dining-room ~** un mobilier or un ensemble de salle à manger, une salle à manger → **bedroom**, **bridal** **b** (Mus) suite f **c** (= retainers) suite f, escorte f

suiting [ˈsuːtɪŋ] N (NonC: Tex) tissu m pour complet

suitor [ˈsuːtər] N soupirant m, prétendant m; (Jur) plaideur m, -euse f; (Comm) acquéreur m potentiel, repreneur m potentiel

Sulawesi [ˌsuːləˈweɪsɪ] N Sulawesi, les Célèbes fpl

sulcus [ˈsʌlkəs] N (pl sulci [ˈsʌlsaɪ]) scissure f

Suleiman [ˌsuːlɪˈmɑːn] N **~ the Magnificent** Soliman or Suleyman le Magnifique

sulfa [ˈsʌlfə] N (US) = **sulpha**

sulfate [ˈsʌlfeɪt] N (US) = **sulphate**

sulfide [ˈsʌlfaɪd] N (US) = **sulphide**

sulfonamide [sʌlˈfɒnəmaɪd] N (US) = **sulphonamide**

sulfur [ˈsʌlfər] N (US) = **sulphur**

sulfureous [sʌlˈfjʊərɪəs] ADJ (US) = **sulphureous**

sulfuric [sʌlˈfjʊərɪk] ADJ (US) = **sulphuric**

sulfurous [ˈsʌlfərəs] ADJ (US) = **sulphurous**

sulk [sʌlk] **1** N bouderie f, maussaderie f; **to be in a ~** ◊ **to have (a fit of) the ~s** bouder, faire la tête **2** VI bouder, faire la tête

sulkily [ˈsʌlkɪlɪ] ADV [behave, look, say] d'un air boudeur

sulkiness [ˈsʌlkɪnɪs] N (= state) bouderie f; (= temperament) caractère m boudeur or maussade

sulky [ˈsʌlkɪ] ADJ [person, voice, expression, silence] boudeur; **to be** or **look ~ (about sth)** faire la tête (à propos de qch)

sullen [ˈsʌlən] ADJ [person, look, comment, silence, sky] maussade; [clouds] menaçant

sullenly [ˈsʌlənlɪ] ADV [say, reply] d'un ton maussade; [look, stare] d'un air maussade or renfrogné; [promise, agree] de mauvaise grâce; **the ~ resentful expression on her face** son air or son visage maussade et irrité; **to be ~ silent** être enfermé dans un silence maussade

sullenness [ˈsʌlənnɪs] N [of person] humeur f maussade, maussaderie f; [of attitude, voice, silence] maussaderie f; **the ~ of the sky/clouds** l'aspect menaçant du ciel/des nuages

sully [ˈsʌlɪ] VT (liter) souiller; **to ~ one's hands with sth/by doing sth** se salir les mains en faisant qch

sulpha [ˈsʌlfə] N **~ drug** sulfamide m

sulphate [ˈsʌlfeɪt] N sulfate m; **copper ~** sulfate m de cuivre

sulphide [ˈsʌlfaɪd] N sulfure m

sulphonamide [sʌlˈfɒnəmaɪd] N sulfamide m

sulphur [ˈsʌlfər] **1** N soufre m **2** ADJ (colour: also **~ yellow**) jaune soufre inv **3** COMP ► **sulphur bath** N bain m sulfureux ► **sulphur dioxide** N anhydride m sulfureux ► **sulphur spring** N source f sulfureuse

sulphureous [sʌlˈfjʊərəs] ADJ sulfureux; (in colour) couleur m de soufre, soufré

sulphuric [sʌlˈfjʊərɪk] ADJ sulfurique

sulphurous [ˈsʌlfərəs] ADJ sulfureux

sultan [ˈsʌltən] N sultan m

sultana [sʌlˈtɑːnə] **1** N **a** (esp Brit = fruit) raisin m de Smyrne **b** (= woman) sultane f **2** COMP ► **sultana cake** N (esp Brit) cake m (aux raisins de Smyrne)

sultanate [ˈsʌltənət] N sultanat m

sultriness [ˈsʌltrɪnɪs] N (= heat) chaleur f étouffante; [of weather] lourdeur f

---

sultry [ˈsʌltrɪ] ADJ **a** (= hot) [day] étouffant; [weather, air] lourd; [heat] lourd, suffocant; [atmosphere] étouffant, pesant; **it was hot and ~** il faisait chaud et lourd **b** (fig = sensual) [person, voice, look, smile] sensuel

▼ **sum** [sʌm] **1** N (= total after addition) somme f, total m (**of** de); (= amount of money) somme f (d'argent); (Math = problem) calcul m, opération f; (specifically adding) addition f; (Scol) **~s** (= arithmetic) le calcul; **to do a ~ in one's head** faire un calcul mental or de tête; **he is good at ~s** il est bon en calcul; **the ~ of its parts** la somme de ses composants or parties; **the ~ of our experience** la somme de notre expérience; **the ~ and substance of what he said** les grandes lignes de ce qu'il a dit; **in ~** en somme, somme f toute → **lump¹**, round **2** COMP ► **summing-up** N récapitulation f, résumé m (also Jur) ► **sum total** N (= amount) somme f totale; (= money) montant m (global); (fig) **the ~ total of all this was that he ...** le résultat de tout cela a été qu'il ...

► **sum up** **1** VI récapituler, faire un or le résumé; (Jur) résumer; **to ~ up, let me say that ...** en résumé or pour récapituler je voudrais dire que ... **2** VT SEP **a** (= summarize) [+ speech, facts, arguments] résumer, récapituler; [+ book etc] résumer; **that ~s up all I felt** cela résume tout ce que je ressentais **b** (= assess) [+ person] jauger, se faire une idée de; [+ situation] apprécier d'un coup d'œil **3** ~**ming-up** N → **sum**

sumac(h) [ˈsuːmæk] N sumac m

Sumatra [suːˈmɑːtrə] N Sumatra

Sumatran [suːˈmɑːtrən] **1** ADJ de Sumatra **2** N habitant(e) m(f) or natif m, -ive f de Sumatra

summa cum laude [ˌsʌmɑːkʊmˈlaʊdeɪ] ADV (US Univ) **to graduate ~** ≈ obtenir son diplôme avec mention très honorable

summarily [ˈsʌmərɪlɪ] ADV sommairement

summarize [ˈsʌməraɪz] **1** VT [+ book, text, speech] résumer; [+ facts, arguments] résumer, récapituler **2** VI faire un résumé

summary [ˈsʌmərɪ] **1** N **a** (NonC) résumé m, récapitulation f; **in ~** en résumé **b** (= printed matter, list etc) sommaire m, résumé m; (Fin) [of accounts] relevé m; (Rad, TV) **here is a ~ of the news** voici les nouvelles fpl en bref **2** ADJ sommaire

summat: [ˈsʌmət] N (dial) = **something**

summation [sʌˈmeɪʃən] N (= addition) addition f; (= summing-up) récapitulation f, résumé m (also Jur)

summer [ˈsʌmər] **1** N été m; **in (the) ~** en été; **in the ~ of 1997** pendant l'été (de) 1997; (liter) **a girl of 17 ~s** une jeune fille de 17 printemps → **high**, **Indian** **2** VI passer l'été **3** COMP [weather, heat, season, activities] d'été, estival; [day, residence] d'été ► **summer camp** N (US Scol) colonie f de vacances ► **summer clothes** NPL vêtements mpl d'été, tenue f estivale or d'été ► **summer holidays** NPL grandes vacances fpl ► **summer house** N maison f de vacances; (in country) maison f de campagne → **summerhouse** ► **summer lightning** N éclair m de chaleur ► **summer resort** N station f estivale ► **summer school** N université f d'été ► **summer squash** N (US) courgette f ► **summer time** N (Brit: by clock) heure f d'été ► **summer visitor** N estivant(e) m(f)

summerhouse [ˈsʌməhaʊs] N pavillon m d'été

summertime [ˈsʌmətaɪm] N (= season) été m

summery [ˈsʌmərɪ] ADJ [clothes] d'été, estival; [colours, food] d'été; **the ~ weather** le temps estival

summit [ˈsʌmɪt] **1** N **a** [of mountain] sommet m, cime f **b** (fig) [of power, honours, glory] sommet m; [of ambition] summum m **c** (Pol) sommet m; **at ~ level** au plus haut niveau

[2] COMP (*Pol*) [*talks*] au sommet ► **summit conference** N (conférence *f* au) sommet *m* ► **summit meeting** N rencontre *f* au sommet

summitry* [ˈsʌmɪtrɪ] N (*esp US Pol*) tactique *f* de la rencontre au sommet

summon [ˈsʌmən] VT [+ *servant, police*] appeler, faire venir; (*to meeting*) convoquer (**to** à); [*monarch, president, prime minister*] mander (**to** à); (*Jur*) citer, assigner (**as** comme); [+ *help, reinforcements*] requérir; **the Queen ~ed Parliament** la reine a convoqué le Parlement; **to ~ sb to do sth** sommer qn de faire qch; (*Jur*) **~ sb to appear** citer qn à comparaître, assigner qn; (*Mil*) **they ~ed the town to surrender** ils ont sommé la ville de *or* ils ont mis la ville en demeure de se rendre; **I was ~ed to his presence** j'ai été requis de paraître devant lui, il m'a mandé auprès de lui; (*Admin etc*) **to ~ sb in/down** *etc* sommer qn d'entrer/de descendre *etc*

► **summon up** VT SEP [+ *one's energy, strength*] rassembler, faire appel à; [+ *interest, enthusiasm*] faire appel à; **to ~ up (one's) courage** faire appel à *or* rassembler tout son courage, s'armer de courage, prendre son courage à deux mains (**to do** pour faire); **he ~ed up the courage to fight back** il a trouvé le courage de riposter

summons [ˈsʌmənz] [1] N (*pl* **summonses**) sommation *f* (*also Mil*), injonction *f*; (*Jur*) citation *f*, assignation *f*; (*Jur*) **to take out a ~ against sb** faire assigner qn; **he got a ~ for drunken driving** il a reçu une citation à comparaître *or* une assignation pour conduite en état d'ivresse; (*Mil*) **they sent him a ~ to surrender** ils lui ont fait parvenir une sommation de se rendre → **issue, serve** [2] VT (*Jur*) citer, assigner (**à comparaître**) (**for sth** pour qch)

sumo [ˈsuːməʊ] N sumo *m*

sump [sʌmp] [1] N (*Tech*) puisard *m* (*pour eaux-vannes etc*); (*Brit Aut*) carter *m*; (= *deep cave*) fosse *f* [2] COMP ► **sump oil** N (*Aut*) huile *f* de carter

sumptuary [ˈsʌmptjʊərɪ] ADJ (*frm*) somptuaire; (*Hist*) ~ **law** loi *f* somptuaire

sumptuous [ˈsʌmptjʊəs] ADJ somptueux

sumptuously [ˈsʌmptjʊəslɪ] ADV somptueusement

sumptuousness [ˈsʌmptjʊəsnɪs] N somptuosité *f*

sun [sʌn] [1] N soleil *m*; **the ~ is shining** il fait (du) soleil, le soleil brille; **in the ~** au soleil; **right in the ~** en plein soleil; **a place in the ~** (*lit*) un endroit ensoleillé *or* au soleil; (*fig*) une place au soleil; **this room certainly catches the ~** cette pièce reçoit beaucoup de soleil; **to catch the ~** (= *get a tan*) prendre des bonnes couleurs; (= *get sunburned*) prendre un coup de soleil; **in the July ~** au soleil de juillet; **come out of the ~** ne restez pas au soleil; **the ~ is in my eyes** j'ai le soleil dans les yeux; **he rose with the ~** il se levait avec le soleil; **everything under the ~** tout ce qu'il est possible d'imaginer; **nothing under the ~** rien au monde; **there's no prettier place under the ~** il n'est pas de plus joli coin au monde *or* sur la terre; **no reason under the ~** pas la moindre raison; **there is nothing new under the ~** il n'y a rien de nouveau sous le soleil → **midnight** [2] VT **to ~ o.s.** [*lizard, cat*] se chauffer au soleil; [*person*] prendre un bain de soleil, lézarder au soleil [3] COMP ► **sun bonnet** N capeline *f* ► **sun dance** N danse *f* du soleil (*rituel du solstice chez les Indiens d'Amérique*) ► **sun deck** N [*of house, hotel etc*] véranda *f*; (*Naut*) pont *m* supérieur ► **sun-drenched** ADJ inondé de soleil ► **sun dress** N robe *f* bain de soleil ► **sun-filled** ADJ ensoleillé, rempli de soleil ► **sun-god** N dieu *m* soleil *or* Soleil ► **sun helmet** N casque *m* colonial ► **the Sun King** N (*Hist*) le Roi-Soleil ► **sun-kissed** ADJ

baigné de soleil ► **sun lamp** N lampe *f* à bronzer *or* à ultraviolets ► **sun lotion** N = **suntan lotion**; → **suntan** ► **sun lounge** N véranda *f*; (*in health institution etc*) solarium *m* ► **sun-lounger** N chaise *f* longue (*pour bronzer*) ► **sun oil** N = **suntan oil**; → **suntan** ► **sun porch** N petite véranda *f* ► **sunshield** N (*Aut*) pare-soleil *m inv* ► **sun umbrella** N parasol *m* ► **sun visor** N (*for eyes, on cap*) visière *f*; (*Aut*) pare-soleil *m inv* ► **sunworship** N (*Rel*) culte *m* du soleil ► **sunworshipper** N (*Rel*) adorateur *m*, -trice *f* du soleil; (*gen*) adepte *mf or* fanatique *mf* du bronzage

Sun. ABBR = **Sunday**

sunbaked [ˈsʌnbeɪkt] ADJ brûlé par le soleil

sunbath [ˈsʌnbɑːθ] N bain *m* de soleil

sunbathe [ˈsʌnbeɪð] VI prendre un bain *or* des bains de soleil, se (faire) bronzer

sunbather [ˈsʌnbeɪðəʳ] N personne *f* qui prend un bain de soleil

sunbathing [ˈsʌnbeɪðɪŋ] N bains *mpl* de soleil

sunbeam [ˈsʌnbiːm] N rayon *m* de soleil

sunbed [ˈsʌnbed] N (*with sunray lamp*) lit *m* solaire; (*for outdoors*) lit *m* pliant

Sunbelt [ˈsʌnbelt] N (*US*) **the ~** les États du sud des États-Unis

---

┌─ **SUNBELT** ─┐

La « région du soleil » désigne les États du sud des États-Unis (de la Caroline du Nord à la Californie), caractérisés par un climat chaud et ensoleillé et qui connaissent, depuis quelque temps, un fort développement économique dû notamment aux mouvements migratoires en provenance du nord du pays. Les États du nord, par opposition, sont parfois appelés « Frostbelt » (région du gel) ou « Rustbelt » (région de la rouille) à cause de leurs vieilles infrastructures industrielles.

---

sunblind [ˈsʌnblaɪnd] N store *m*

sunblock [ˈsʌnblɒk] N écran *m* (solaire) total

sunburn [ˈsʌnbɜːn] N coup *m* de soleil

sunburned [ˈsʌnbɜːnd], **sunburnt** [ˈsʌnbɜːnt] ADJ (= *tanned*) bronzé, hâlé; (*painfully*) brûlé par le soleil; **to get ~** (= *tan*) (se faire) bronzer; (*painfully*) prendre un coup de soleil

sunburst [ˈsʌnbɜːst] [1] N rayon *m* de soleil (*entre les nuages*) [2] COMP ► **sunburst clock** N horloge *f* en forme de soleil

sundae [ˈsʌndeɪ] N sundae *m*, coupe *f* glacée Chantilly

Sunday [ˈsʌndɪ] [1] N [a] dimanche *m* → **Easter, month, palm²**; *for phrases see* **Saturday** [b] **the ~s*** (= *Sunday papers*) les journaux *mpl* du dimanche [2] COMP [*clothes, paper*] du dimanche; [*walk, rest, peace*] dominical ► **Sunday best** N **in one's ~ best** tout endimanché, en habits du dimanche ► **Sunday driver** N (*pej*) chauffeur *m* du dimanche ► **Sunday-go-to-meeting*** ADJ (*US*) [*clothes*] du dimanche ► **Sunday motorist** N (*pej*) = **Sunday driver** ► **Sunday observance** N observance *f* du repos dominical ► **Sunday opening** N (*Comm*) ouverture *f* des magasins le dimanche, commerce *m* dominical ► **Sunday papers** NPL journaux *mpl* du dimanche ► **Sunday school** N école *f* du dimanche, ≈ catéchisme *m*; **~ school teacher** catéchiste *mf* (*qui s'occupe de l'école du dimanche*) ► **Sunday trading** N (*Comm*) = **Sunday opening**; **~ trading laws** réglementation *f* du commerce dominical

---

┌─ **SUNDAY PAPERS** ─┐

Les journaux du dimanche occupent une place essentielle parmi les activités dominicales des Britanniques, qui en achètent souvent plusieurs. Il s'agit soit de journaux paraissant uniquement le dimanche (« Observer » et « News of the World »,

---

par exemple), soit d'éditions du dimanche de quotidiens (« Sunday Times », « Sunday Telegraph », « Independent on Sunday », « Sunday Express », etc.). Un **Sunday paper** *contient généralement des rubriques très variées sur les arts, les sports, les voyages ou les affaires, et s'accompagne d'un supplément magazine en couleurs.*

Aux États-Unis, le plus grand journal du dimanche est l'édition dominicale du « New York Times », mais les Américains préfèrent généralement la presse locale à la presse nationale.

---

sunder [ˈsʌndəʳ] (*liter*) [1] VT fractionner, scinder [2] N **in ~** (= *apart*) écartés; (= *in pieces*) en morceaux

sundial [ˈsʌndaɪəl] N cadran *m* solaire

sundown [ˈsʌndaʊn] N (*US*) = **sunset**

sundowner* [ˈsʌndaʊnəʳ] N (*Austral* = *tramp*) chemineau *m*, clochard *m*; (*Brit* = *drink*) boisson alcoolisée prise en début de soirée

sundried [ˌsʌnˈdraɪd] ADJ séché au soleil

sundry [ˈsʌndrɪ] [1] ADJ divers (*after n*); **all and ~** tout le monde [2] **sundries** NPL articles *mpl* divers

sunfish [ˈsʌnfɪʃ] N (*pl inv: Zool*) poisson *m* lune

sunflower [ˈsʌnˌflaʊəʳ] [1] N (*Bot*) tournesol *m*, soleil *m*; **the Sunflower State** (*US*) le Kansas [2] COMP ► **sunflower oil** N (*Culin*) huile *f* de tournesol ► **sunflower seeds** NPL (*Culin*) graines *fpl* de tournesol

sung [sʌŋ] VB *ptp of* **sing**

sunglasses [ˈsʌnˌɡlɑːsɪz] NPL lunettes *fpl* de soleil

sunhat [ˈsʌnhæt] N chapeau *m* de soleil *or* de plage

sunk [sʌŋk] [1] VB *ptp of* **sink¹** [2] COMP ► **sunk costs** NPL (*Ind*) frais *mpl or* coûts *mpl* fixes

sunken [ˈsʌŋkən] ADJ [*ship, treasure*] englouti; [*rock*] submergé; [*garden, road*] en contrebas; [*bath*] encastré; [*eyes*] enfoncé; [*cheeks*] creux

sunless [ˈsʌnlɪs] ADJ sans soleil

sunlight [ˈsʌnlaɪt] N (lumière *f* du) soleil *m*; **in the ~** au soleil, à la lumière du soleil

sunlit [ˈsʌnlɪt] ADJ ensoleillé

Sunni [ˈsʌnɪ] [1] N (= *religion*) sunnisme *m*; (= *person*) sunnite *mf* [2] ADJ sunnite

sunny [ˈsʌnɪ] [1] ADJ [a] (= *bright*) [*climate, room, morning*] ensoleillé; [*side*] (*of street, building etc*) exposé au soleil, ensoleillé; **it's ~ today** il y a du soleil aujourd'hui; **the outlook is ~** on prévoit du soleil, on peut s'attendre à un temps ensoleillé; (*Brit Met*) **~ intervals** ◊ ~ **periods** éclaircies *fpl* [b] (= *cheerful*) [*smile*] rayonnant, radieux; [*person*] épanoui; [*personality*] enjoué; **to have a ~ disposition** avoir un naturel enjoué; **to be in a ~ mood** être d'humeur enjouée; **the ~ side of life** les bons côtés de la vie [2] COMP ► **sunny side up** ADJ (*US Culin*) **eggs ~ side up** œufs *mpl* sur le plat (*frits sans avoir été retournés*)

sunray lamp [ˈsʌnreɪˌlæmp] N (*Med*) = **sun lamp** → **sun**

sunray treatment [ˈsʌnreɪˌtriːtmənt] N héliothérapie *f*

sunrise [ˈsʌnraɪz] [1] N lever *m* de soleil [2] COMP ► **sunrise industry** N industrie *f* en pleine expansion

sunroof [ˈsʌnruːf] N (*Aut*) toit *m* ouvrant

sunscreen [ˈsʌnskriːn] N écran *m* solaire

sunseeker [ˈsʌnsiːkəʳ] N amateur *m* de soleil

sunset [ˈsʌnset] [1] N coucher *m* de soleil [2] COMP ► **sunset clause** N (*US Jur*) clause *f* de révision ► **sunset industry** N industrie *f* en déclin ► **sunset law** N (*US*) loi stipulant que le vote approuvant la création d'un organisme gouvernemental doit être périodiquement reconduit pour que l'organisme continue d'exister

sunshade [ˈsʌnʃeɪd] N (for eyes) visière f; (for table, on pram) parasol m; (in car) pare-soleil m inv; (= parasol) ombrelle f

sunshine [ˈsʌnʃaɪn] **1** N (NonC) (lumière f du) soleil m; **in the ~** au soleil; (Met) **five hours of ~** cinq heures d'ensoleillement; (fig) **a ray of ~** (= person, event) un rayon de soleil; (iro) **he's a real ray of ~ today** il est gracieux comme une porte de prison aujourd'hui; **hallo ~!*** bonjour mon rayon de soleil! **2** COMP ▶ **sunshine law** N (US) loi imposant la publicité des débats pour les décisions administratives ▶ **sunshine roof** N (Aut) toit m ouvrant ▶ **the Sunshine State** N (US) la Floride

sunspecs* [ˈsʌnspeks] NPL = **sunglasses**

sunspot [ˈsʌnspɒt] N tache f solaire

sunstroke [ˈsʌnstrəʊk] N (NonC) (Med) insolation f

sunsuit [ˈsʌnsuːt] N bain m de soleil

suntan [ˈsʌntæn] **1** N bronzage m; **to get a ~** se (faire) bronzer **2** COMP ▶ **suntan lotion** N lotion f or lait m solaire ▶ **suntan oil** N huile f solaire

suntanned [ˈsʌntænd] ADJ bronzé

suntrap [ˈsʌntræp] N coin m très ensoleillé

sunup [ˈsʌnʌp] N (US) = **sunrise**

sup [sʌp] **1** VI souper (**on, off** de) **2** VT (also **~ up**) boire or avaler à petites gorgées **3** N petite gorgée f

super [ˈsuːpəʳ] **1** ADJ (esp Brit*) merveilleux, sensationnel* **2** N **a** (Police:*) ABBR = **superintendent b** (Cine:*) ABBR = **supernumerary c** (US = gasoline) super(carburant) m **3** COMP ▶ **Super Bowl** N (US Ftbl) Super Bowl m (championnat de football américain) ▶ **super-duper***: ADJ formid* inv, sensass* inv ▶ **Super Tuesday** N (US Pol) super-mardi m (second mardi du mois de mars, date-clé des élections primaires)

super... [ˈsuːpəʳ] PREF super...; **~-salesman** super-vendeur m → **superannuate**

superable [ˈsuːpərəbl] ADJ surmontable

superabundance [ˌsuːpərəˈbʌndəns] N surabondance f

superabundant [ˌsuːpərəˈbʌndənt] ADJ surabondant

superannuate [ˌsuːpəˈrænjʊeɪt] VT mettre à la retraite; **~d** retraité, à la or en retraite; (fig) suranné, démodé

superannuation [ˌsuːpəˌrænjʊˈeɪʃən] **1** N (= act) (mise f à la) retraite f; (Brit = pension) pension f de retraite; (Brit: also **~ contribution**) versements mpl or cotisations fpl pour la pension **2** COMP ▶ **superannuation fund** N (Brit) caisse f de retraite

superb [suːˈpɜːb] ADJ (view, weather, day) superbe; (quality, opportunity) merveilleux, exceptionnel; **in ~ condition** en excellent état

superblock [ˈsuːpəblɒk] N (US) zone urbaine aménagée en quartier piétonnier

superbly [suːˈpɜːbli] ADV superbement; **they have done ~ well** ils ont superbement bien réussi; **he is ~ fit** il est dans une forme (physique) éblouissante

supercargo [ˈsuːpəˌkɑːgəʊ] N (Naut) subrécargue m

supercharged [ˈsuːpətʃɑːdʒd] ADJ surcomprimé

supercharger [ˈsuːpəˌtʃɑːdʒəʳ] N compresseur m

supercilious [ˌsuːpəˈsɪlɪəs] ADJ (person) hautain, dédaigneux; (smile) dédaigneux

superciliously [ˌsuːpəˈsɪlɪəslɪ] ADV (look at) dédaigneusement, d'un air hautain; (say) dédaigneusement, d'un ton hautain

superciliousness [ˌsuːpəˈsɪlɪəsnɪs] N hauteur f, arrogance f

super-class [ˈsuːpəˌklɑːs] N superclasse f

supercomputer [ˌsuːpəkəmˈpjuːtəʳ] N supercalculateur m, superordinateur m

superconductive [ˌsuːpəkənˈdʌktɪv] ADJ supraconducteur

superconductivity [ˈsuːpəˌkɒndʌkˈtɪvɪtɪ] N supraconductivité f

superconductor [ˈsuːpəkənˈdʌktəʳ] N supraconducteur m

supercool [ˌsuːpəˈkuːl] VT (Chem) sous-refroidir

supercover [ˈsuːpəˌkʌvəʳ] N (Insurance) garantie f totale, couverture f complète

superego [ˌsuːpərˈiːgəʊ] N surmoi m

supererogation [ˈsuːpərˌerəˈgeɪʃən] N surérogation f

superficial [ˌsuːpəˈfɪʃəl] ADJ superficiel

superficiality [ˌsuːpəˌfɪʃɪˈælɪtɪ] N caractère m superficiel, manque m de profondeur

superficially [ˌsuːpəˈfɪʃəlɪ] ADV (discuss, examine) superficiellement; (attractive) en apparence

superficies [ˌsuːpəˈfɪʃɪːz] N (pl inv) superficie f

superfine [ˈsuːpəfaɪn] ADJ (goods, quality) extrafin, superfin, surfin; (pej) (distinction) trop ténu, bien mince

superfluity [ˌsuːpəˈfluːɪtɪ] N **a** surabondance f (**of** de) **b** = **superfluousness**

superfluous [suːˈpɜːfluəs] ADJ (goods, explanation) superflu; **it is ~ to say that ...** inutile de dire que ...; **he felt rather ~*** il se sentait de trop

superfluously [suːˈpɜːfluəslɪ] ADV d'une manière superflue

superfluousness [suːˈpɜːfluəsnɪs] N caractère m superflu

supergiant [ˌsuːpəˈdʒaɪənt] N (Astron) supergéante f

superglue [ˈsuːpəgluː] N supercolle f

supergrass* [ˈsuːpəgrɑːs] N (Brit) super-indicateur m de police

supergroup [ˈsuːpəgruːp] N (Mus) supergroupe m

superheat [ˌsuːpəˈhiːt] VT surchauffer

superhero [ˈsuːpəˌhɪərəʊ] N super-héros m

superhighway [ˈsuːpəˌhaɪweɪ] N (US) voie f express (à plusieurs files) → ROADS information

superhuman [ˌsuːpəˈhjuːmən] **1** ADJ surhumain **2** N surhomme m

superimpose [ˌsuːpərɪmˈpəʊz] VT superposer (**on** à); (Cine, Phot, Typ) **~d** en surimpression

superintend [ˌsuːpərɪnˈtend] VT (+ work, shop, department) diriger; (+ exam) surveiller; (+ production) contrôler; (+ vote-counting) présider à

superintendence [ˌsuːpərɪnˈtendəns] N (NonC) (of activity) contrôle m; (of child, prisoner) surveillance f; **under the ~ of sb** sous la surveillance de qn

superintendent [ˌsuːpərɪnˈtendənt] N **a** (of institution, orphanage) chef m, -trice f; (of department) chef m **b** (Brit: also **police ~, ~ of police**) ≈ commissaire m (de police)

Superior [suˈpɪərɪəʳ] ADJ Lake **~** le lac Supérieur

▼**superior** [suˈpɪərɪəʳ] **1** ADJ **a** (= better) supérieur (-eure f) (**to** à); **~ in number to ...** supérieur en nombre à ..., numériquement supérieur à ...; **in ~ numbers** en plus grand nombre, plus nombreux; **the vastly ~ numbers of the enemy** les effectifs largement supérieurs de l'ennemi **b** (= high-quality) (product, goods) de qualité supérieure; **a very ~ model** un modèle très supérieur **c** (pej = supercilious) (person) hautain, dédaigneux; (air, smile) supérieur (-eure f), de supériorité; **to feel ~** se sentir supérieur **d** (in hierarchy) supérieur (**to** à); **his ~ officer** l'officier qui lui était supérieur → **mother e** (Anat) (limb) supérieur (-eure f) **f** (Typ) (letter, number) en exposant,

superior (-eure f) **2** N supérieur(e) m(f) **3** COMP ▶ **superior court** N (US Jur) juridiction intermédiaire

superiority [suˌpɪərɪˈɒrɪtɪ] **1** N supériorité f (**to, over** par rapport à) **2** COMP ▶ **superiority complex** N complexe m de supériorité

superjacent [ˌsuːpəˈdʒeɪsənt] ADJ sus-jacent

superlative [suˈpɜːlətɪv] **1** ADJ **a** (= excellent) (artist, quality, achievement) exceptionnel, extraordinaire **b** (Gram) superlatif **2** N (Gram) superlatif m; **in the ~** au superlatif; (fig) **he tends to talk in ~s** il a tendance à exagérer

superlatively [suˈpɜːlətɪvlɪ] ADV (play, perform) de façon extraordinaire; (rich, well) extraordinairement

superman [ˈsuːpəmæn] N (pl -men) surhomme m; (on TV etc) **Superman** Superman m

supermarket [ˈsuːpəˌmɑːkɪt] N supermarché m

supermen [ˈsuːpəmen] NPL of **superman**

supermodel [ˈsuːpəmɒdl] N top model m

supernal [suːˈpɜːnəl] ADJ (liter) céleste, divin

supernatural [ˌsuːpəˈnætʃərəl] **1** ADJ surnaturel **2** N surnaturel m

supernormal [ˌsuːpəˈnɔːməl] ADJ au-dessus de la normale

supernova [ˌsuːpəˈnəʊvə] N (pl **supernovae** [ˌsuːpəˈnəʊviː]) (Astron) supernova f

supernumerary [ˌsuːpəˈnjuːmərərɪ] **1** ADJ (Admin, Bio etc) surnuméraire; (= superfluous) superflu **2** N (Admin etc) surnuméraire mf; (Cine) figurant(e) m(f)

superorder [ˈsuːpərɔːdəʳ] N superordre m

superordinate [ˌsuːpərˈɔːdɪnɪt] **1** ADJ dominant, supérieur **2** N (Ling) terme m générique

superphosphate [ˌsuːpəˈfɒsfeɪt] N superphosphate m

superpose [ˌsuːpəˈpəʊz] VT (also Geom) superposer (**on** à)

superposition [ˌsuːpəpəˈzɪʃən] N superposition f

superpower [ˈsuːpəpaʊəʳ] N (Pol) superpuissance f, supergrand m

superscript [ˈsuːpəˌskrɪpt] (Typ) **1** ADJ supérieur (-eure f) **2** N (= number) chiffre m supérieur; (= letter) lettre f supérieure

superscription [ˌsuːpəˈskrɪpʃən] N suscription f

supersede [ˌsuːpəˈsiːd] VT (+ belief, object, order) remplacer; (+ person) supplanter, prendre la place de; **this edition ~s previous ones** cette édition remplace et annule les précédentes; **~d idea/method** idée f/méthode f périmée

supersensitive [ˌsuːpəˈsensɪtɪv] ADJ hypersensible

supersonic [ˌsuːpəˈsɒnɪk] ADJ (aircraft, vehicle, speed) supersonique; (flight, travel) en avion supersonique

supersonically [ˌsuːpəˈsɒnɪkəlɪ] ADV en supersonique

superstar [ˈsuːpəstɑːʳ] N (Cine, Theat) superstar f; (Sport) superchampion(ne) m(f)

superstate [ˈsuːpəsteɪt] N (pej) super-État m

superstition [ˌsuːpəˈstɪʃən] N superstition f

superstitious [ˌsuːpəˈstɪʃəs] ADJ superstitieux

superstitiously [ˌsuːpəˈstɪʃəslɪ] ADV superstitieusement

superstore [ˈsuːpəstɔːʳ] N (esp Brit) hypermarché m

superstratum [ˌsuːpəˈstrɑːtəm] N (pl **superstratums** or **superstrata** [ˌsuːpəˈstrɑːtə]) (Ling) superstrat m

superstructure [ˈsuːpəˌstrʌktʃəʳ] N superstructure f

supertanker [ˈsuːpəˌtæŋkəʳ] N pétrolier m géant, supertanker m

---

▶ **LANGUAGE IN USE:** **superior** 5.2

supertax ['su:pətæks] N tranche *f* supérieure de l'impôt sur le revenu

supervene [,su:pə'vi:n] VI survenir

supervention [,su:pə'venʃən] N apparition *f*, manifestation *f*

supervise ['su:pəvaɪz] [1] VT [+ *person, worker*] surveiller, avoir l'œil sur ; [+ *organization, department*] diriger ; [+ *work*] surveiller, diriger, superviser ; [+ *exam*] surveiller ; (*Univ*) [+ *research*] diriger [2] VI exercer la surveillance, surveiller

supervision [,su:pə'vɪʒən] [1] N (= *watch*) surveillance *f* ; (= *monitoring*) contrôle *m* ; (= *management*) direction *f* (*esp Comm*) ; **under the ~ of ...** sous la surveillance or direction de ... ; **to keep sth under strict ~** exercer une surveillance or un contrôle sévère sur qch [2] COMP ► **supervision order** N (*Brit Jur*) ordonnance *f* de surveillance

supervisor ['su:pəvaɪzər] N (*gen*) surveillant(e) *m(f)* ; (*Comm*) chef *m* de rayon ; (*at exam*) surveillant(e) *m(f)* ; (*Univ*) directeur *m*, -trice *f* or patron *m* de thèse

supervisory ['su:pəvaɪzərɪ] ADJ [*post, role, powers, body*] de surveillance ; **~ staff** personnel *m* chargé de la surveillance ; **in a ~ capacity** à titre de surveillant(e)

superwoman ['su:pə,wʊmən] N (*pl* **-women**) superwoman *f*

supine ['su:paɪn] ADJ (*liter*) [a] (*lit* = *prostrate*: *also* **lying ~**: *also* **in a ~ position**) allongé sur le dos [b] (*pej* = *passive*) [*person, attitude*] mollasse (*pej*)

supper ['sʌpər] [1] N (= *main evening meal*) dîner *m* ; (*after theatre etc*) souper *m* ; (= *snack*) collation *f* ; **to have ~** dîner (or souper *etc*) ; (*fig*) **we made him sing for his ~** nous l'avons aidé *etc*, mais c'était donnant donnant → **lord** [2] COMP ► **supper club** N (*US*) petit restaurant nocturne, avec danse et éventuellement spectacle

suppertime ['sʌpətaɪm] N l'heure *f* du dîner (*or du souper etc*) ; **at ~** au dîner (*or souper etc*)

supplant [sə'plɑ:nt] VT [+ *person*] supplanter, évincer ; [+ *object*] supplanter, remplacer

supple ['sʌpl] ADJ (*lit, fig*) souple ; **to become ~r** s'assouplir

supplement ['sʌplɪmənt] [1] N (*also Press*) supplément *m* (**to** à) → **colour** [2] ['sʌplɪ,ment] VT [+ *income*] augmenter, arrondir (**by doing** en faisant) ; [+ *book, information, one's knowledge*] ajouter à, compléter

supplemental [,sʌplɪ'mentəl] ADJ (*esp US*) supplémentaire

supplementary [,sʌplɪ'mentərɪ] [1] ADJ (*gen, Geom, Mus*) supplémentaire ; [*food, vitamins*] complémentaire ; **you may need ~ iron** vous pourriez avoir besoin d'un complément de fer ; **~ to** en plus de [2] COMP ► **supplementary benefit** N (*NonC: Brit Admin: formerly*) allocation *f* supplémentaire ► **supplementary question** N (*Brit Parl*) question *f* orale ► **supplementary scheme** N (*Jur*) régime *m* complémentaire

suppleness ['sʌplnɪs] N souplesse *f*

suppletion [sə'pli:ʃən] N (*Ling*) suppléance *f*

suppletive [sə'pli:tɪv] ADJ (*Ling*) supplétif

suppliant ['sʌplɪənt], **supplicant** ['sʌplɪkənt] ADJ, N suppliant(e) *m(f)*

supplicate ['sʌplɪkeɪt] [1] VT supplier, implorer (**sb to do** qn de faire) ; [+ *mercy etc*] implorer (**from sb** de qn) [2] VI **to ~ for sth** implorer qch

supplication [,sʌplɪ'keɪʃən] N supplication *f* ; (*written*) supplique *f*

supplier [sə'plaɪər] N (*Comm*) fournisseur *m*

supply[1] [sə'plaɪ] [1] N [a] (= *amount, stock*) provision *f*, réserve *f* ; **a good ~ of coal** une bonne provision or réserve de charbon ; **to get** or **lay in a ~ of ...** faire des provisions de

..., s'approvisionner de ... ; **to get in a fresh ~ of sth** renouveler sa provision or sa réserve de qch ; **supplies** (*gen*) provisions *fpl*, réserves *fpl* ; (= *food*) vivres *mpl* ; (*Mil*) substances *fpl*, approvisionnements *mpl* ; **electrical supplies** matériel *m* électrique ; **office supplies** fournitures *fpl* or matériel de bureau
[b] (*NonC*) (= *act of supplying*) [*of fuel etc*] alimentation *f* ; [*of equipment, books etc*] fourniture *f* ; **the ~ of fuel to the engine** l'alimentation du moteur en combustible ; **the electricity/gas ~** l'alimentation en électricité/gaz ; (*Econ*) **~ and demand** l'offre *f* et la demande ; (*Brit*) **Ministry of Supply** ≈ services *mpl* de l'Intendance → **short, water**
[c] (*person* = *temporary substitute*) remplaçant(e) *m(f)*, suppléant(e) *m(f)* ; **to teach** or **be on ~** faire des suppléances or des remplacements
[d] (*Parl*) **supplies** crédits *mpl*
[2] VT [a] (= *provide, furnish*) [+ *tools, books, goods*] fournir, procurer (**to sb** à qn) ; (*Comm*) fournir, approvisionner ; (= *equip*) [+ *person, city*] fournir, approvisionner (**with sth** en or de qch) ; (*Mil: with provisions*) ravitailler, approvisionner ; (*Comm*) **we ~ most of the local schools** nous fournissons or nous approvisionnons la plupart des écoles locales ; (*Comm*) **to ~ from stock** livrer sur stock ; **sheep ~ wool** les moutons donnent de la laine ; **we ~ the tools for the job** nous fournissons or nous procurons les outils nécessaires pour faire le travail ; **to ~ electricity/gas/water to the town** alimenter la ville en électricité/gaz/eau ; **to ~ sb with food** nourrir or alimenter qn ; **they kept us supplied with milk** grâce à eux nous n'avons jamais manqué de lait ; **the car was supplied with a radio** la voiture était munie or pourvue d'une radio ; **a battery is not supplied with the torch** une pile n'est pas livrée avec la torche ; **to ~ sb with information/details** fournir des renseignements/des détails à qn
[b] (= *make good*) [+ *need, deficiency*] suppléer à, remédier à ; [+ *sb's needs*] subvenir à ; [+ *loss*] réparer, compenser
[3] COMP [*train, wagon, truck, convoy*] de ravitaillement, ravitailleur ; [*pharmacist etc*] intérimaire ► **supply line** N voie *f* de ravitaillement ► **supply management** N (*Econ*) régulation *f* de l'offre ► **supply ship** N navire *m* ravitailleur ► **supply-side economics** NPL (*Econ*) théorie *f* de l'offre ► **supply teacher** N (*Brit*) suppléant(e) *m(f)*

supply[2] ['sʌplɪ] ADV [*move, bend*] avec souplesse, souplement

▼ **support** [sə'pɔ:t] [1] N [a] (*NonC: lit, fig*) appui *m*, soutien *m* ; (*financial*) aide *f* (financière) ; **he couldn't stand without ~** il ne pouvait pas se soutenir (sur ses jambes) ; **he leaned on me for ~** il s'est appuyé sur moi ; **to give ~ to sb/ sth** soutenir qn/qch ; **this bra gives good ~** ce soutien-gorge maintient bien la poitrine ; **he depends on his father for (financial) ~** il dépend financièrement de son père ; (*financial*) **he has no visible means of ~** il n'a pas de moyens d'existence connus ; **what means of ~ has he got?** quelles sont ses ressources ? ; (*fig*) **he looked to his friends for ~** il a cherché un soutien or un appui auprès de ses amis ; **he needs all the ~ he can get** il a bien besoin de tout l'appui qu'on pourra lui donner ; **he got a lot of ~ from his friends** ses amis l'ont vraiment soutenu or appuyé ; **the proposal got no ~** personne n'a parlé en faveur de la proposition ; **he spoke in ~ of the motion** il a parlé en faveur de la motion ; **in ~ of his theory/claim** à l'appui de sa théorie/revendication ; **have I your ~ in this?** est-ce que je peux compter sur votre appui or soutien dans cette affaire ? ; **to give** or **lend one's ~ to ...** prêter son appui à ... ; **that lends ~ to his theory** ceci corrobore or vient corroborer sa théorie ; **they demonstrated in ~ of the prisoners** ils ont manifesté en

faveur des prisonniers, ils ont fait une manifestation de soutien aux prisonniers ; **a collection in ~ of the accident victims** une quête au profit des victimes de l'accident ; **they stopped work in ~** ils ont cessé le travail par solidarité → **moral**
[b] (= *object*) (*gen*) appui *m* ; (*Constr, Tech*) support *m*, soutien *m* ; (*fig: moral, financial etc*) soutien *m* ; (*US Econ* = *subsidy*) subvention *f* ; **use the stool as a ~ for your foot** prenez le tabouret comme appui pour votre pied ; **he is the sole (financial) ~ of his family** il est le seul soutien (financier) de sa famille ; **he has been a great ~ to me** il a été pour moi un soutien précieux
[2] VT [a] (= *hold up*) [*pillar, beam*] supporter, soutenir ; [*bridge*] porter ; [*person, neck*] soutenir ; **the elements necessary to ~ life** les éléments nécessaires à l'entretien de la vie, les éléments vitaux
[b] (= *uphold*) [+ *motion, theory, cause, party, candidate*] (*passively*) être pour ; (*actively*) soutenir ; [+ *sb's application, action, protest*] soutenir, appuyer ; [+ *team*] être supporter de, supporter* ; **with only his courage to ~ him** avec son seul courage comme soutien, n'ayant de soutien que son courage ; **his friends ~ed him in his refusal to obey** ses amis l'ont soutenu or l'ont appuyé or ont pris son parti lorsqu'il a refusé d'obéir ; **the socialists will ~ it** les socialistes seront or voteront pour ; **I cannot ~ what you are doing** je ne peux pas approuver ce que vous faites ; (*Cine, Theat*) **~ed by a cast of thousands** avec le concours de milliers d'acteurs et figurants ; **the proofs that ~ my case** les preuves à l'appui de ma cause ; (*Econ*) **a subsidy to ~ the price of beef** une subvention pour maintenir le prix du bœuf ; (*Ftbl*) **he ~s Celtic** c'est un supporter du Celtic, il supporte* le Celtic
[c] (*financially*) subvenir aux besoins de ; **she has a husband and three children to ~** elle doit subvenir aux besoins de son mari et de ses trois enfants ; **to ~ o.s.** (*gen*) subvenir à ses propres besoins ; (= *earn one's living*) gagner sa vie ; **the school is ~ed by money from ...** l'école reçoit une aide financière de ...
[d] (= *endure*) supporter, tolérer
[3] COMP (*Mil etc*) [*troops, convoy, vessel*] de soutien ► **support act** N (*Mus*) groupe *m* (or chanteur *m*, -euse *f*) de première partie (*d'un concert*) ► **support band** N (*Mus*) groupe *m* de première partie (*d'un concert*) ► **support hose** N (*pl inv*) bas *mpl* (or collants *mpl*) de contention or antifatigue ► **support price** N (*Econ*) prix *m* de soutien ► **support stockings** NPL bas *mpl* de contention or antifatigue

supportable [sə'pɔ:təbl] ADJ supportable, tolérable

supporter [sə'pɔ:tər] N [a] (*Constr, Tech*) soutien *m*, support *m* ; (*Her*) tenant *m* [b] (= *person*) [*of party*] sympathisant(e) *m(f)* ; [*of theory, cause, opinion*] partisan *m* ; **she's a ~ of ...** elle soutient ..., elle est pour ... ; (*Sport*) supporter *m* ; **football ~s** supporters *mpl* de football

supporting [sə'pɔ:tɪŋ] [1] ADJ [a] (= *corroborating*) [*document*] de confirmation ; **~ evidence** preuves *fpl* à l'appui [b] (*Cine, Theat*) [*role, part*] second (*before n*) ; **~ actor** acteur *m* qui a un second rôle *m* ; **she won an Oscar for Best Supporting Actress** elle a reçu l'Oscar du meilleur second rôle féminin ; **the ~ cast** les seconds rôles *mpl* ; **to be in the ~ cast** avoir un second rôle [c] (*Constr*) [*wall*] de soutènement → **self** [2] COMP ► **supporting film** N (*Cine*) film *m* qui passe en première partie

supportive [sə'pɔ:tɪv] ADJ [*role*] de soutien ; [*relationship*] d'un grand soutien or secours ; **she has a very ~ family** sa famille lui est d'un grand soutien ; **to provide a ~ environment for sb** créer autour de qn un environnement favorable ; **my father was very ~ of the idea** mon père soutenait tout à fait cette idée

> ► LANGUAGE IN USE: **support** 11.2, 13, 26.2

supportively [sə'pɔːtɪvlɪ] ADV [*act, behave*] de façon très positive

supportiveness [sə'pɔːtɪvnɪs] N soutien *m*, aide *f*

▼ **suppose** [sə'pəʊz] **1** VT **a** (= *imagine*) supposer (**that** que + *subj*); (= *assume, postulate*) supposer (**that** que + *indic*); **~ he doesn't come? — he will — yes but just ~!** et s'il ne vient pas? — il viendra — oui, mais à supposer qu'il ne vienne pas *or* oui, mais au cas où il ne viendrait pas?; **if we ~ that the two are identical** si nous supposons que les deux sont identiques; (*Math*) **~ A equals B** soit A égale B; **~ ABC a triangle** soit un triangle ABC **b** (= *believe*) croire; (= *think*) penser (**that** que); **what do you ~ he wants?** à votre avis que peut-il bien vouloir?; **I went in, and who do you ~ was there?** je suis entré et devine qui se trouvait là?; **he is (generally) ~d to be rich ◊ it is (generally) ~d that he is rich** il passe pour être riche, on dit qu'il est riche; **I never ~d him to be a hero** je n'ai jamais pensé *or* imaginé qu'il fût un héros; **I don't ~ he'll agree ◊ I ~ he won't agree** cela m'étonnerait qu'il soit d'accord, je ne pense pas qu'il sera d'accord, je suppose qu'il ne sera pas d'accord; **I ~ so** probablement, je suppose que oui; **I don't ~ so ◊ I ~ not** je ne (le) pense *or* crois pas, probablement pas; **do you ~ we could get together for dinner some evening?** accepteriez-vous de dîner avec moi un soir?, pensez-vous que nous pourrions dîner ensemble un soir?; **wouldn't you ~ he'd be sorry?** n'auriez-vous pas pensé qu'il le regretterait? **c** (*modal use in pass* = "*ought*") **to be ~d to do sth** être censé faire qch; **she was ~d to telephone this morning** elle était censée *or* elle devait téléphoner ce matin; **he isn't ~d to know** il n'est pas censé le savoir; **you're not ~d to do that** il ne vous est pas permis de faire cela; **what's that ~d to mean?** qu'est-ce que tu veux dire par là? **d** (*in imperative* = "*I suggest*") **~ we go for a walk!** et si nous allions nous promener?; **~ I tell him myself?** et si c'était moi qui le lui disais? **e** (*prp used as conj* = "*if*") **supposing** si (+ *indic*), à supposer que (+ *subj*), supposé que (+ *subj*); **supposing he can't do it?** et s'il ne peut pas le faire?, et à supposer *or* et supposé qu'il ne puisse le faire?; **even supposing that ...** à supposer même que ... (+ *subj*); **always supposing that ...** en supposant que ... (+ *subj*), en admettant que ... (+ *subj*) **f** (= *presuppose*) supposer; **that ~s unlimited resources** cela suppose des ressources illimitées

2 VI **you'll come, I ~?** vous viendrez, j'imagine *or* je suppose?; **don't spend your time supposing, do something!** ne passe pas ton temps à faire des suppositions, fais quelque chose!

supposed [sə'pəʊzd] ADJ **a** (= *so-called*) prétendu, soi-disant *inv*; **the ~ benefits of an expensive education** les prétendus avantages d'une éducation coûteuse **b** (= *presumed*) supposé → **suppose**

supposedly [sə'pəʊzɪdlɪ] ADV soi-disant; **he had ~ gone to France** il était soi-disant allé en France; **~ safe chemicals** des produits chimiques soi-disant sans danger; **did he go? — ~!** est-ce qu'il y est allé? — soi-disant!; **~, his last words were ...** ses dernières paroles auraient été ...

supposing [sə'pəʊzɪŋ] CONJ → **suppose 1e**

supposition [ˌsʌpə'zɪʃən] N supposition *f*, hypothèse *f*; **it is pure ~** c'est une pure supposition; **on the ~ that ...** à supposer que ... (+ *subj*), dans la supposition que ... (+ *subj*); **on this ~** dans cette hypothèse

suppositional [ˌsʌpə'zɪʃənəl], **suppositious** [ˌsʌpə'zɪʃəs] ADJ hypothétique

supposititious [sə,pɒzɪ'tɪʃəs] ADJ supposé, faux (fausse *f*), apocryphe

suppository [sə'pɒzɪtərɪ] N suppositoire *m*

suppress [sə'pres] VT [+ *abuse, crime*] supprimer, mettre fin à; [+ *revolt*] réprimer, étouffer; [+ *one's feelings*] réprimer, refouler; [+ *yawn*] réprimer; [+ *scandal, facts, truth*] étouffer; [+ *newspaper, publication*] interdire; [+ *evidence*] faire disparaître, supprimer; (*Psych*) refouler; (*Med*) [+ *symptoms*] supprimer; (*Elec, Rad etc*) antiparasiter; (* = *silence*) [+ *heckler etc*] faire taire; **to ~ a cough/sneeze etc** se retenir de *or* réprimer une envie de tousser/d'éternuer *etc*

suppressant [sə'presnt] N **appetite ~** anorexigène *m*

suppression [sə'preʃən] N **a** [*of document, evidence, information, human rights*] suppression *f*; [*of revolt, protest, movement*] répression *f*; [*of democracy*] étouffement *m*; **the ~ of dissidents/minorities** la répression des dissidents/minorités **b** (*Psych*) [*of emotion*] refoulement *m* **c** (*Med*) inhibition *f* **d** (*Elec, Rad etc*) antiparasitage *m*

suppressive [sə'presɪv] ADJ répressif

suppressor [sə'presə'] N (*Elec etc*) dispositif *m* antiparasite

suppurate ['sʌpjʊəreɪt] VI suppurer

suppuration [ˌsʌpjʊə'reɪʃən] N suppuration *f*

supra... ['suːprə] PREF supra..., sur...

supranational [ˌsuːprə'næʃənl] ADJ supranational

suprarenal [ˌsuːprə'riːnl] ADJ surrénal

suprasegmental [ˌsuːprəsəg'mentl] ADJ (*Ling*) suprasegmental

supremacist [sʊ'preməsɪst] N personne *f* qui croit en la suprématie d'un groupe (*or* d'une race *etc*), suprémaciste *mf*

supremacy [sʊ'preməsɪ] N suprématie *f* (**over** sur) → **white**

supreme [sʊ'priːm] ADJ (*all senses*) suprême; (*Rel*) **the Supreme Being** l'Être *m* suprême; (*Mil*) **Supreme Commander** commandant *m* en chef *or* suprême, généralissime *m*; (*Can Jur, US Jur*) **Supreme Court** Cour *f* suprême; **to make the ~ sacrifice** faire le sacrifice de sa vie → **reign, soviet**

supremely [sʊ'priːmlɪ] ADV suprêmement

supremo [sʊ'priːməʊ] N (*Brit*) grand chef *m*

Supt. (*Brit Police*) ABBR = **Superintendent**

sura ['sʊərə] N sourate *f*

surcharge ['sɜːtʃɑːdʒ] **1** N (= *extra payment, extra load, also Elec, Post* = *overprinting*) surcharge *f*; (= *extra tax*) surtaxe *f*; **import ~** surtaxe *f* à l'importation **2** [sɜː'tʃɑːdʒ] VT surcharger, surtaxer

surd [sɜːd] **1** ADJ (*Math*) irrationnel; (*Ling*) sourd **2** N (*Math*) quantité *f* *or* nombre *m* irrationnel(le); (*Ling*) sourde *f*

▼ **sure** [ʃʊə'] **1** ADJ **a** (= *reliable, safe etc*) [*aim, shot, marksman, judgement, method, friend, footing*] sûr; [*solution, remedy*] sûr, infaillible; [*facts*] sûr, indubitable; [*success*] assuré, certain **b** (= *definite, indisputable*) sûr, certain; **it is ~ that he will come ◊ he is ~ to come** il est certain qu'il viendra, il viendra, c'est sûr; **it is not ~ that he will come ◊ he is not ~ to come** il n'est pas sûr *or* certain qu'il vienne; **it's not ~ yet** ça n'a encore rien de sûr; **it's ~ to rain** il va pleuvoir à coup sûr *or* c'est sûr et certain*; **be ~ to tell me ◊ be ~ and tell me** ne manquez pas de me le dire; **you're ~ of a good meal** un bon repas vous est assuré; **he's ~ of success** il est sûr *or* certain de réussir; **you can't be ~ of him** vous ne pouvez pas être sûr de lui; **I want to be ~ of seeing him** je veux être sûr *or* certain de le voir; **to make ~ of a seat** s'assurer (d')une place; **to make ~ of one's facts** vérifier *or* s'assurer de ce qu'on avance; **better get a ticket beforehand and make ~** il vaut

mieux prendre un billet à l'avance pour plus de sûreté *or* pour être sûr*; **did you lock it? — I think so but I'd better make ~** l'avez-vous fermé à clé? — je crois, mais je vais vérifier *or* m'en assurer; **I've made ~ of having enough coffee for everyone** j'ai veillé à ce qu'il y ait assez de café pour tout le monde; **nothing is ~ in this life** dans cette vie on n'est sûr de rien; **~ thing!*** oui bien sûr!, d'accord!; **he is, to be ~, rather tactless** il manque de tact, c'est certain; **well, to be ~!*** bien, ça alors!; **he'll leave for ~** il partira sans aucun doute; **and that's for ~*** ça ne fait aucun doute; **I'll find out for ~** je me renseignerai pour savoir exactement ce qu'il en est; **do you know for ~?** êtes-vous absolument sûr *or* certain?; **I'll do it next week for ~** je le ferai la semaine prochaine sans faute **c** (= *positive, convinced*) sûr (**of** de), certain; **I'm or I feel ~ I've seen him** je suis sûr *or* certain de l'avoir vu; **I'm ~ he'll help us** je suis sûr qu'il nous aidera; **I'm not ~** je ne suis pas sûr *or* certain (**that** que + *subj*); **I'm not ~ how/why/when** *etc* je ne sais pas très bien comment/pourquoi/quand *etc*; **I'm not ~ (if) he can** je ne suis pas sûr *or* certain qu'il puisse; **I'm ~ I didn't mean to** je ne l'ai vraiment pas fait exprès; **he says he did it but I'm not so ~ (about that)** il dit que c'est lui qui l'a fait mais je n'en suis pas si sûr (que ça); **I'm going alone! — I'm not so ~ about that *or* don't be so ~ about that!** j'irai seul! — ne le dis pas si vite!; **to be/feel ~ of o.s.** être/se sentir sûr de soi

2 ADV **a** (*esp US* = *certainly*) pour sûr*; **he can ~ play the piano** pour sûr* en tout cas, il sait jouer du piano; **he was ~ drunk ◊ he ~ was drunk** il était drôlement soûl; **will you do it? — ~!** le ferez-vous? — bien sûr *or* pour sûr!* **b** **~ enough** (*confirming*) effectivement, en effet; (*promising*) assurément, sans aucun doute; **~ enough, he did come** comme je l'avais (*or* on l'avait *etc*) bien prévu, il est venu; **and ~ enough he did arrive** et effectivement *or* en effet il est arrivé; **~ enough*, I'll be there** j'y serai sans faute; **it's petrol, ~ enough** c'est effectivement *or* bien de l'essence, c'est de l'essence en effet; **~ enough!** assurément!; (*US*) **he ~ enough made a hash of that*** pour sûr qu'il a tout gâché* **c** **as ~ as** aussi sûr que; **as ~ as my name's Smith** aussi sûr que je m'appelle Smith; **as ~ as fate ◊ as ~ as anything ◊ as ~ as guns* ◊ as ~ as eggs is eggs*** aussi sûr que deux et deux font quatre

3 COMP ► **sure-enough*** ADJ (*US* = *real, actual*) réel ► **sure-fire*** ADJ certain, infaillible ► **sure-footed** ADJ (*lit*) au pied sûr; (*fig* = *skilful*) **to be ~-footed** faire preuve de doigté ► **sure-footedly** ADV d'un pied sûr

surely ['ʃʊəlɪ] ADV **a** (*expressing confidence: assuredly*) sûrement, certainement; (*expressing incredulity*) tout de même; **~ we've met before?** je suis sûr que nous nous sommes déjà rencontrés; **~ he didn't say that!** il n'a pas pu dire ça, tout de même!; **there is ~ some mistake** il doit sûrement *or* certainement y avoir quelque erreur; **~ you can do something to help?** il doit bien y avoir quelque chose que vous puissiez faire pour aider; **~ you didn't believe him?** vous ne l'avez pas cru, j'espère; **~ to God*, ~ or to goodness*, you know that!** mais bon sang tu devrais bien le savoir!*; **it must rain soon, ~** il va bien pleuvoir, tout de même; **that's ~ not true** ça ne peut pas être vrai, ça m'étonnerait que ce soit vrai; **~ not!** pas possible!; (*US* = *with pleasure*) **~!** bien volontiers! **b** (= *inevitably*) sûrement, à coup sûr; **justice will ~ prevail** la justice prévaudra sûrement **c** [*advance, move*] (= *safely*) sûrement; (= *confidently*) avec assurance → **slowly**

► **LANGUAGE IN USE:** **suppose** 6.2, 26.3 **sure** 6.2, 15.1, 16.1

sureness ['ʃʊənɪs] N (= *certainty*) certitude *f*; (= *sure-footedness*) sûreté *f*; (= *self-assurance*) assurance *f*, sûreté *f* de soi; [*of judgement, method, footing, grip*] sûreté *f*; [*of aim, shot*] justesse *f*, précision *f*; **the ~ of his touch** sa sûreté de main

surety ['ʃʊərətɪ] N **a** (*Jur*) (= *money*) caution *f*; (= *person*) caution *f*, garant(e) *m(f)*; **to go** or **stand ~ for sb** se porter caution or garant pour qn; **in his own ~ of £1,000** après avoir donné une sûreté personnelle de 1 000 livres **b**†† certitude *f*; **of a ~** certainement

surf [sɜːf] **1** N (*NonC*) (= *waves*) vagues *fpl* déferlantes, ressac *m*; (= *foam*) écume *f*; (= *spray*) embrun *m* **2** VI (*also* **go ~ing**) surfer, faire du surf **3** VT [+ *waves*] surfer sur; **to ~ the Net*** surfer sur Internet, surfer sur le net **4** COMP ► **surf boat** N surf-boat *m*

surface ['sɜːfɪs] **1** N **a** [*of earth, sea, liquid, object etc*] surface *f*; **under the ~** [*of sea, lake etc*] sous l'eau; **to come** or **rise to the ~** remonter à la surface; (*fig*) faire surface, se faire jour; **to break ~** [*submarine*] faire surface; [*diver*] réapparaître; **on the ~** (*Naut*) en surface; (*Min: also* **at the ~**) au jour, à la surface; (*fig*) à première vue, au premier abord; **on the ~ of the table** sur la surface de la table; **his faults are all on the ~** il a des défauts mais il a bon fond; (*fig*) **I can't get below the ~ with him** je n'arrive pas à le connaître vraiment or à aller au-delà des apparences avec lui; (*fig*) **prejudices just below** or **beneath the ~** préjugés prêts à refaire surface or à se faire jour; **the road ~ is icy** la chaussée est verglacée; **social unrest, never far below the ~ ...** les troubles sociaux, toujours prêts à éclater ... **b** (*Math*) (= *area*) surface *f*; (= *side: of solid*) côté *m*, face *f*

2 ADJ **a** [*tension*] superficiel (*also fig*); (*Naut*) [*vessel etc*] de surface; (*Min*) [*work*] au jour, à la surface; (*fig*) **it's only a ~ reaction** ce n'est qu'une réaction superficielle **b** [*Phon, Gram*] de surface

3 VT **a** [+ *road*] revêtir (**with** de); [+ *paper*] calandrer, glacer **b** (*Naut*) [+ *submarine, object, wreck*] amener à la surface

4 VI [*swimmer, diver, whale*] revenir or remonter à la surface; [*submarine*] faire surface; (*fig* = *emerge*) [*news, feeling etc*] faire surface, se faire jour; (* *fig*) (*after absence*) réapparaître; (*after hard work*) faire surface

5 COMP ► **surface area** N (*Math etc*) surface *f*, superficie *f* ► **surface grammar** N grammaire *f* de surface ► **surface mail** N (*Post*) courrier *m* par voie de terre; (*by sea*) courrier *m* maritime; **by ~ mail** par voie de terre; (*by sea*) par voie maritime ► **surface noise** N (*on record player*) grésillements *mpl* ► **surface structure** N structure *f* de surface ► **surface-to-air** ADJ (*Mil*) sol-air *inv* ► **surface-to-surface** ADJ (*Mil*) sol-sol *inv* ► **surface workers** NPL (*Min*) personnel *m* qui travaille au jour à la surface

surfboard ['sɜːfbɔːd] **1** N planche *f* de surf **2** VI surfer

surfboarder ['sɜːf,bɔːdəʳ] N = **surfer**

surfboarding ['sɜːf,bɔːdɪŋ] N = **surfing**

surfcasting ['sɜːf,kɑːstɪŋ] N (*US Sport*) pêche *f* au lancer en mer (*depuis le rivage*)

surfeit ['sɜːfɪt] **1** N excès *m* (**of** de); (*NonC* = *satiety*) satiété *f*; **to have a ~ of ...** avoir une indigestion de ... (*fig*); **there is a ~ of ...** il y a par trop de ... **2** VT **to be ~ed with pleasure** être repu de plaisir

surfer ['sɜːfəʳ] N surfeur *m*, -euse *f*; (*: *on internet*) internaute *mf*

surfing ['sɜːfɪŋ] N surf *m* → **surf 2**

surfride ['sɜːfraɪd] VI surfer

surfrider ['sɜːf,raɪdəʳ] N = **surfer**

surfriding ['sɜːf,raɪdɪŋ] N = **surfing**

surge [sɜːdʒ] **1** N (*gen*) mouvement *m* puissant; [*of rage, fear, enthusiasm*] vague *f*, montée *f*; (*Elec*) saute *f* de courant; (*fig: in sales etc*) afflux *m*; **the ~ of the sea** la houle; **he felt a ~ of anger** il a senti la colère monter en lui; **there was a ~ of sympathy for him** il y a eu un vif mouvement or une vague de sympathie pour lui; **the ~ of people around the car** la foule qui se pressait autour de la voiture; **he was carried along by the ~ of the crowd** il était porté par le mouvement de la foule

2 VI **a** [*waves*] s'enfler; [*flood, river*] déferler; **the sea ~d against the rocks** la houle battait or heurtait les rochers; **the surging sea** la mer houleuse; **the ship ~d at anchor** le bateau amarré était soulevé par la houle; (*Elec*) **the power ~d suddenly** il y a eu une brusque surtension de courant; **the blood ~d to his cheeks** le sang lui est monté or lui a reflué au visage; **anger ~d (up) within him** la colère monta en lui **b** [*crowd, vehicles etc*] déferler; **to ~ in/out** *etc* entrer/sortir *etc* à flots; **they ~d round the car** ils se pressaient autour de la voiture; **they ~d forward** ils se sont lancés en avant; (*fig*) **a surging mass of demonstrators** une foule déferlante de manifestants

surgeon ['sɜːdʒən] **1** N chirurgien *m*; **she is a ~** elle est chirurgien; **a woman ~** une femme chirurgien → **dental**, **house**, **veterinary** **2** COMP ► **surgeon general** N (*pl* **surgeons general**) (*Mil*) médecin *m* général; (*US Admin*) ministre *m* de la Santé

surgery ['sɜːdʒərɪ] **1** N **a** (*NonC* = *skill, study, operation*) chirurgie *f*; **it is a fine piece of ~** le chirurgien a fait du beau travail; **to have ~** se faire opérer → **plastic** **b** (*Brit* = *consulting room*) cabinet *m* (de consultation); (*Brit* = *interview*) consultation *f*; **come to the ~ tomorrow** venez à mon cabinet demain, venez à la consultation demain; **when is his ~?** à quelle heure sont ses consultations?, à quelle heure consulte-t-il?; **during his ~** pendant ses heures de consultation; **there is an afternoon ~** il consulte l'après-midi **2** COMP ► **surgery hours** NPL heures *fpl* de consultation

surgical ['sɜːdʒɪkəl] **1** ADJ [*operation, intervention, treatment*] chirurgical; [*instruments*] chirurgical, de chirurgie **2** COMP ► **surgical appliance** N appareil *m* orthopédique ► **surgical cotton** N coton *m* hydrophile ► **surgical dressing** N pansement *m* ► **surgical shock** N choc *m* opératoire ► **surgical spirit** N (*Brit*) alcool *m* à 90 (degrés) ► **surgical strike** N (*Mil*) frappe *f* chirurgicale

surgically ['sɜːdʒɪkəlɪ] ADV chirurgicalement

Surinam [,sʊərɪˈnæm] N le Surinam

Surinamese [,sʊərɪnæˈmiːz] **1** ADJ surinamais **2** N Surinamais(e) *m(f)*

surliness ['sɜːlɪnɪs] N caractère *m* or air *m* revêche or maussade or renfrogné

surly ['sɜːlɪ] ADJ revêche, maussade, renfrogné, bourru

surmise ['sɜːmaɪz] **1** N conjecture *f*, hypothèse *f*; **it was nothing but ~** c'était entièrement conjectural **2** [sɜːˈmaɪz] VT conjecturer, présumer (**from sth** d'après qch); **to ~ that ...** (= *infer*) conjecturer que ..., présumer que ...; (= *suggest*) émettre l'hypothèse que ...; **I ~d as much** je m'en doutais

surmount [sɜːˈmaʊnt] VT **a** (*Archit etc*) surmonter; **~ed by a statue** surmonté d'une statue **b** (= *overcome*) [+ *obstacle, difficulties, problems*] surmonter, venir à bout de

surmountable [sɜːˈmaʊntəbl] ADJ surmontable

surname ['sɜːneɪm] **1** N nom *m* de famille; **name and ~** nom et prénoms **2** VT **~d Jones** nommé or dénommé Jones, dont le nom de famille est Jones

surpass [sɜːˈpɑːs] VT [+ *person*] surpasser (**in** en); [+ *hopes, expectations*] dépasser; (*also iro*) **to ~ o.s.** se surpasser (*also iro*)

surpassing [sɜːˈpɑːsɪŋ] ADJ incomparable, sans pareil

surplice ['sɜːpləs] N surplis *m*

surpliced ['sɜːplɪst] ADJ en surplis

surplus ['sɜːpləs] **1** N (*pl* **surpluses**) (*Comm, Econ, gen*) surplus *m*, excédent *m*; (*Fin*) boni *m*, excédent *m*; **a tea ~** un surplus or un excédent de thé **2** ADJ (*gen*) [*food, boxes etc*] en surplus; (*Comm, Econ*) en surplus, excédentaire; (*Fin*) de boni, excédentaire; **it is ~ to (our) requirements** cela excède nos besoins; **~ copies** [*of book, document etc*] exemplaires *mpl* de passe; **~ stock** surplus *mpl*, stocks *mpl* excédentaires; **American ~ wheat** excédent *m* or surplus *m* de blé américain; **his ~ energy** son surcroît d'énergie **3** COMP ► **surplus store** N magasin *m* de surplus

surprise [səˈpraɪz] **1** N (*NonC*) (= *emotion*) surprise *f*, étonnement *m*; (= *event etc*) surprise *f*; **much to my ◊ to my great ~** à ma grande surprise, à mon grand étonnement; **he stopped in ~** il s'est arrêté sous l'effet de la surprise, étonné il s'est arrêté; **to take by ~** [+ *person*] surprendre, prendre au dépourvu; (*Mil*) [+ *fort, town*] prendre par surprise; **a look of ~** un regard surpris or traduisant la surprise; **imagine my ~ when ...** imaginez quel a été mon étonnement or quelle a été ma surprise quand ...; **what a ~!** quelle surprise!; **~, ~!** (*when surprising sb*) surprise!; (*iro*) comme par hasard (*iro*); **to give sb a ~** faire une surprise à qn, surprendre qn; **it was a lovely/nasty ~ for him** cela a été pour lui une agréable/mauvaise surprise; **it came as a ~ (to me) to learn that ...** j'ai eu la surprise d'apprendre que ...

2 ADJ [*defeat, gift, visit, decision*] inattendu, inopiné; **~ attack** attaque *f* par surprise, attaque *f* brusquée

3 VT **a** (= *astonish*) surprendre, étonner; **he was ~d to hear that ...** il a été surpris or étonné d'apprendre que ..., cela l'a surpris or étonné d'apprendre que ...; **I shouldn't be ~d if it snowed** cela ne m'étonnerait pas qu'il neige (*subj*); **don't be ~d if he refuses** ne soyez pas étonné or surpris s'il refuse, ne vous étonnez pas s'il refuse; **it's nothing to be ~d at** cela n'a rien d'étonnant, ce n'est pas or guère étonnant; **I'm ~d at you!** je ne m'attendais pas à cela de vous!, cela me surprend de votre part!; **it ~d me that he agreed** j'ai été étonné or surpris qu'il accepte (*subj*), je ne m'attendais pas à ce qu'il accepte (*subj*); (*iro*) **go on, ~ me!** allez, étonne-moi!; **he ~d me into agreeing to do it** j'ai été tellement surpris que j'ai accepté de le faire → **surprised** **b** (= *catch unawares*) [+ *army, sentry*] surprendre, attaquer par surprise; [+ *thief*] surprendre, prendre sur le fait; (*gen*) surprendre

surprised [səˈpraɪzd] ADJ surpris, étonné; **you'd be ~ how many people ...** si tu savais combien de gens ...; **he'll surely be on time — you'd be ~!** il sera sûrement à l'heure — n'y compte pas! → **surprise**

surprising [səˈpraɪzɪŋ] ADJ surprenant, étonnant; **it is ~ that ...** il est surprenant or étonnant que ... (+ *subj*)

surprisingly [səˈpraɪzɪŋlɪ] ADV [*big, sad etc*] étonnamment, étrangement; **you look ~ cheerful for someone who ...** vous m'avez l'air de bien bonne humeur pour quelqu'un qui ...; **~ enough, ...** chose étonnante, ...; **not ~ he didn't come** comme on pouvait s'y attendre il n'est pas venu, il n'est pas venu, ce qui n'a rien d'étonnant

surreal [səˈrɪəl] ADJ surréaliste (*fig*)

surrealism [səˈrɪəlɪzəm] N surréalisme *m*

surrealist [səˈrɪəlɪst] ADJ, N surréaliste *mf*

surrealistic [sə‚rɪəˈlɪstɪk] ADJ surréaliste

surrender [səˈrendəʳ] **1** VI (*Mil*) se rendre (**to** à), capituler (**to** devant) ; **to ~ to the police** se livrer à la police, se constituer prisonnier ; (*fig*) **to ~ to despair** s'abandonner *or* se livrer au désespoir

2 VT **a** (*Mil*) [+ *town, hill*] livrer (**to** à) **b** [+ *firearms*] rendre (**to** à) ; [+ *stolen property, documents, photos*] remettre (**to** à) ; [+ *insurance policy*] racheter ; [+ *lease*] céder ; [+ *one's rights, claims, powers, liberty*] renoncer à, abdiquer ; [+ *hopes*] abandonner ; (*fig*) **to ~ o.s. to despair/to the delights of sth** s'abandonner *or* se livrer au désespoir/aux plaisirs de qch

3 N **a** (*Mil etc*) reddition *f* (**to** à), capitulation *f* (**to** devant) ; **no ~!** on ne se rend pas ! → **unconditional b** (= *giving up*) [*of firearms, stolen property, documents*] remise *f* (**to** à) ; [*of one's rights, claims, powers, liberty*] rachat *m* ; [*of one's rights, claims, powers, liberty*] renonciation *f* (**of** à), abdication *f* (**of** de, **to** en faveur de) ; [*of hopes*] abandon *m* ; [*of lease*] cession *f* ; (= *return*) restitution *f* (**of** de, **to** à)

4 COMP ▸ **surrender value** N (*Insurance*) valeur *f* de rachat

surreptitious [‚sʌrəpˈtɪʃəs] ADJ [*entry, removal*] subreptice, clandestin, [*movement, gesture*] furtif

surreptitiously [‚sʌrəpˈtɪʃəslɪ] ADV [*enter, remove*] subrepticement, clandestinement ; [*move*] furtivement, sournoisement (*pej*)

surrogacy [ˈsʌrəgəsɪ] N (*in childbearing*) maternité *f* de substitution

surrogate [ˈsʌrəgɪt] **1** N **a** (*gen: frm*) substitut *m*, représentant *m* **b** (*Psych*) substitut *m* **c** (*Brit: also* ~ **bishop**) *évêque auxiliaire à qui l'on délègue le pouvoir d'autoriser les mariages sans publication de bans* **d** (*US* = *judge*) *juge chargé de l'homologation de testaments etc* **2** ADJ [*pleasure etc*] de remplacement **3** [ˈsʌrəgeɪt] VI (*be a surrogate mother*) être mère porteuse *or* mère de substitution **4** COMP ▸ **surrogate mother** N (*Genetics*) mère *f* porteuse, mère *f* de substitution ; (*Psych*) substitut *m* maternel ▸ **surrogate motherhood** N maternité *f* de substitution

surround [səˈraund] **1** VT entourer ; (*totally*) cerner, encercler ; **~ed by** entouré de ; (*Mil, Police etc*) **you are ~ed** vous êtes cerné *or* encerclé ; (*fig*) **to ~ o.s. with friends/allies** s'entourer d'amis/d'alliés **2** N bordure *f*, encadrement *m* ; [*of fireplace*] entourage *m* ; (*Brit: on floor: also* ~**s**) bordure *f* (*entre le tapis et le mur*) **3** **surrounds** NPL (= *surroundings*) cadre *m* **4** COMP ▸ **surround sound** N (*Cine*) son *m* surround

surrounding [səˈraundɪŋ] **1** ADJ [*streets, countryside, villages*] alentour *inv*, environnant ; **Liège and the ~ area** Liège et ses alentours *or* environs ; (*Med*) **the ~ tissue is healthy** les tissus autour sont sains **2** **surroundings** NPL (= *surrounding country*) alentours *mpl*, environs *mpl* ; (= *setting*) cadre *m*, décor *m* ; **the ~s of Glasgow are picturesque** les alentours *or* les environs de Glasgow sont pittoresques ; **he found himself in ~s strange to him** il s'est retrouvé dans un cadre *or* décor qu'il ne connaissait pas ; **animals in their natural ~s** des animaux dans leur cadre naturel

surtax [ˈsɜːtæks] N (*gen*) surtaxe *f* ; (= *income tax*) tranche *f* supérieure de l'impôt sur le revenu ; **to pay ~** être dans les tranches supérieures d'imposition

surtitles [ˈsɜː‚taɪtlz] NPL surtitres *mpl*

surveillance [sɜːˈveɪləns] N surveillance *f* ; **to keep sb under ~** surveiller qn ; **under constant ~** sous surveillance continue

survey [ˈsɜːveɪ] **1** N **a** (= *comprehensive view*) [*of countryside, prospects, development etc*] vue *f* générale *or* d'ensemble (**of** de) ; **he gave a gen-**eral ~ **of the situation** il a fait un tour d'horizon de la situation, il a passé la situation en revue

b (= *investigation, study*) [*of reasons, prices, situation, sales, trends*] enquête *f* (**of** sur), étude *f* (**of** de) ; **to carry out** *or* **make a ~** enquêter sur, faire une étude de ; **~ of public opinion** sondage *m* d'opinion

c (*Surv: of land, site etc*) (= *act*) levé *m* ; (= *report*) levé *m* → **aerial, ordnance**

d (*Brit: in housebuying*) (= *act*) expertise *f* ; (= *report*) (rapport *m* d')expertise *f*

2 [sɜːˈveɪ] VT **a** (= *look around at*) [+ *countryside, view, crowd*] embrasser du regard ; [+ *prospects, trends*] passer en revue ; **he ~ed the scene with amusement** il regardait la scène d'un œil amusé

b (= *examine, study*) [+ *ground before battle etc*] inspecter ; [+ *developments, needs, prospects*] enquêter sur, faire une étude de ; **the Prime Minister ~ed the situation** le Premier ministre a fait un tour d'horizon de *or* a passé en revue la situation ; **the book ~s the history of the motorcar** le livre passe en revue *or* étudie dans les grandes lignes l'histoire de l'automobile

c (*Surv*) [+ *site, land*] faire le levé de ; (*Brit*) [+ *house, building*] inspecter, examiner ; [+ *country, coast*] faire le levé topographique de ; [+ *seas*] faire le levé hydrographique de

3 COMP ▸ **survey course** N (*US Univ*) cours *m* d'initiation ▸ **survey ship** N navire *m* de recherche hydrographique

surveying [sɜːˈveɪɪŋ] **1** N **a** (*NonC* = *action*) [*of site, land*] levé *m* ; [*of house*] expertise *f* ; [*of country, coast*] levé *m* topographique ; [*of seas*] levé *m* hydrographique **b** (= *science, occupation*) [*of site, land*] arpentage *m* ; [*of house*] expertise *f* ; [*of country, coast*] topographie *f* ; [*of seas*] topographie *f* marine, hydrographie *f* **2** COMP [*instrument*] d'arpentage ; [*studies*] de topographie

surveyor [sɜːˈveɪəʳ] N (*Brit*) [*of property, buildings etc*] expert *m* ; [*of land, site*] (arpenteur *m*) géomètre *m* ; [*of country, coastline*] topographe *mf* ; [*of seas*] hydrographe *mf* → **quantity**

survival [səˈvaɪvəl] **1** N **a** (= *act*) survie *f* (*also Jur, Rel*) ; (= *relic*) [*of custom, beliefs etc*] survivance *f*, vestige *m* ; **the ~ of the fittest** (*lit*): (*in evolution*) la lutte pour la vie ; (*fig*) la loi du plus fort **2** COMP ▸ **survival bag** N ≈ couverture *f* de survie ▸ **survival course** N cours *m* de survie ▸ **survival kit** N trousse *f* de survie

survivalist [səˈvaɪvəlɪst] N *écologiste extrême vivant en autarcie pour pouvoir survivre à une éventuelle catastrophe planétaire*

survive [səˈvaɪv] **1** VI [*person*] survivre (**on** avec) ; [*house, jewellery, book, custom*] survivre, subsister ; **he ~d to tell the tale** il a survécu et a pu raconter ce qui s'était passé ; **only three volumes ~** il ne reste *or* il ne subsiste plus que trois tomes ; (*iro*) **you'll ~!** vous n'en mourrez pas ! ; **they don't eat/earn enough to ~ on** il ne mangent/gagnent pas assez pour survivre **2** VT [+ *person*] survivre à ; [+ *injury, disease*] réchapper de ; [+ *fire, accident, experience, invasion*] survivre à, réchapper de ; **he is ~d by a wife and two sons** sa femme et deux fils lui survivent

surviving [səˈvaɪvɪŋ] ADJ [*spouse, children*] survivant ; (*Fin: after merger*) **~ company** société *f* absorbante

survivor [səˈvaɪvəʳ] N survivant(e) *m(f)* ; [*of accident*] survivant(e) *m(f)*, rescapé(e) *m(f)* ; (*fig*) [*of regime, earlier time*] rescapé(e) *m(f)* ; [*of abuse*] ancienne victime *f* ; **he's a real ~!** il surmonte toutes les crises !

sus* [sʌs] (*Brit*) **1** N (ABBR = **suspicion**) **~ law** loi *f* autorisant à interpeller des suspects à discrétion **2** VT = **suss**

Susan [ˈsuːzn] N Suzanne *f*

susceptibility [sə‚septəˈbɪlɪtɪ] N (= *sensitiveness*) émotivité *f*, sensibilité *f* ; (= *touchiness*) susceptibilité *f* ; (*Med*) prédisposition *f* (**to** à) ; **his ~ to hypnosis** la facilité avec laquelle on l'hypnotise ; **his susceptibilities** ses cordes *fpl* sensibles

susceptible [səˈseptəbl] ADJ **a** (*Med, Bot: to disease*) prédisposé (**to** à) ; (= *impressionable*) émotif ; (= *touchy*) susceptible ; (= *able to be affected*) **~ to sb's influence** sensible à l'influence de qn ; **~ to flattery/to (the) cold** sensible à la flatterie/au froid ; **~ to advertising** influençable par la publicité **b** (*frm* = *capable*) **~ of** *or* **to change/measurement/resolution** susceptible d'être modifié/mesuré/résolu

sushi [ˈsuːʃɪ] **1** N (*NonC*) sushi *m* **2** COMP ▸ **sushi bar** N petit restaurant *m* de sushi ▸ **sushi restaurant** N restaurant *m* de sushi

suspect [ˈsʌspekt] **1** N suspect(e) *m(f)* ; (*fig*) **the usual ~s** les suspects *mpl* habituels **2** ADJ suspect **3** [səˈspekt] VT **a** soupçonner (**that** que) ; [+ *person*] soupçonner, suspecter (**of doing** de faire *or* d'avoir fait) ; [+ *ambush, swindle*] flairer, soupçonner ; **I ~ him of being the author** [*of book etc*] je le soupçonne d'en être l'auteur ; [*of anonymous letter*] je le soupçonne *or* je le suspecte d'en être l'auteur ; **he ~s nothing** il ne se doute de rien **b** (= *think likely*) soupçonner, imaginer ; **I ~ he knows who did it** je soupçonne *or* j'ai dans l'idée *or* j'ai le sentiment qu'il sait qui est le coupable ; **I ~ed as much** je m'en doutais ; **he'll come, I ~** il viendra, j'imagine **c** (= *have doubts about*) douter de ; **I ~ the truth of what he says** je doute de la vérité de ce qu'il dit

suspend [səˈspend] **1** VT **a** (= *hang*) suspendre (**from** à) ; **to be ~ed in sth** [*particles etc*] être en suspension dans qch ; **a column of smoke hung ~ed in the still air** une colonne de fumée flottait dans l'air immobile **b** (= *stop temporarily, defer etc*) [+ *publication*] suspendre, surseoir ; [+ *decision, payment, regulation, meetings, discussions*] suspendre ; [+ *licence, permission*] retirer provisoirement ; [+ *bus service*] interrompre provisoirement ; **to ~ judgement** suspendre son jugement **c** [+ *employee, office holder, officer etc*] suspendre (**from** de) ; (*Scol, Univ*) exclure temporairement **2** COMP ▸ **suspended animation** N (*fig hum*) **to be in a state of ~ed animation** ne donner aucun signe de vie ▸ **suspended sentence** N (*Jur*) condamnation *f* avec sursis ; **he received a ~ed sentence of six months in jail** il a été condamné à six mois de prison avec sursis

suspender [səˈspendəʳ] **1** N (*Brit*) (*for stockings*) jarretelle *f* ; (*for socks*) fixe-chaussette *m* **2** **suspenders** NPL (*US* = *braces*) bretelles *fpl* **3** COMP ▸ **suspender belt** N (*Brit*) porte-jarretelles *m inv*

suspense [səˈspens] N **a** (*NonC*) incertitude *f*, attente *f* ; (*in book, film, play*) suspense *m* ; **we waited in great ~** nous avons attendu haletants ; **to keep sb in ~** tenir qn en suspens, laisser qn dans l'incertitude ; [*film*] tenir qn en suspens *or* en haleine ; **to put sb out of (his) ~** mettre fin à l'incertitude *or* à l'attente de qn ; **the ~ is killing me!*** ce suspense me tue ! (*also iro*) **b** (*Admin, Jur*) **to be** *or* **remain in ~** être (laissé) *or* rester en suspens **2** COMP ▸ **suspense account** N (*Accounts*) compte *m* d'ordre

suspenseful [səˈspensful] ADJ plein de suspense

suspension [səˈspenʃən] **1** N **a** (*NonC*) (= *interruption*) [*of decision, payment, constitution, talks*] suspension *f* ; [*of licence, permission*] retrait *m* provisoire ; [*of programme, service*] interruption *f* provisoire ; [*of democracy*] abandon *m* provisoire ; (*Literat*) ~ **of disbelief** acceptation *f* des invraisemblances **b** (= *debarment*) [*of employee, official, player*] suspension *f* ; [*of pupil, student*] renvoi *m* or exclusion *f* temporaire **c** (*Jur*) [*of sentence*] sursis *m* **d** (*Aut*) suspension *f* **e** (*Chem, Phys*) suspension *f* (**of** de) ; **in** ~ en suspension **2** COMP ▶ **suspension bridge** N pont *m* suspendu ▶ **suspension file** N dossier *m* suspendu (*dans un tiroir*) ▶ **suspension points** NPL (*Typ*) points *mpl* de suspension

suspensory [səsˈpensərɪ] ADJ [*ligament*] suspenseur (*m only*) ; [*bandage*] de soutien

suspicion [səsˈpɪʃən] N **a** soupçon *m* ; (*NonC*) soupçon(s) *m(pl)* ; **an atmosphere laden with** ~ une atmosphère chargée de soupçons ; **above** or **beyond** ~ au-dessus or à l'abri de tout soupçon ; **under** ~ considéré comme suspect ; **he was regarded with** ~ on s'est montré soupçonneux à son égard ; (*Jur*) **to arrest sb on** ~ arrêter qn sur des présomptions ; **on** ~ **of murder** sur présomption de meurtre ; **I had a** ~ **that he wouldn't come back** je soupçonnais or quelque chose me disait or j'avais le sentiment qu'il ne reviendrait pas ; **I had no** ~ **that ...** je ne me doutais pas du tout que ... ; **I had (my)** ~**s about that letter** j'avais mes doutes quant à cette lettre ; **I have my** ~**s about it** j'ai des doutes là-dessus, cela me semble suspect ; **he was right in his** ~ **that ...** il avait raison de soupçonner que ..., c'est à juste titre qu'il soupçonnait que ... **b** (*fig* = *trace, touch*) soupçon *m*

suspicious [səsˈpɪʃəs] ADJ **a** (= *distrustful*) [*person, attitude, look*] méfiant, soupçonneux ; **you've got a** ~ **mind!** tu es très méfiant or soupçonneux ! ; **minds might think that ...** des esprits soupçonneux pourraient croire que ... ; **to be** ~ **of sb/sth** se méfier de qn/qch ; **to be** ~ **about sb/sth** avoir des soupçons sur qn/qch ; **to be** ~ **that ...** soupçonner que ... ; **to become** or **grow** ~ commencer à se méfier **b** (= *causing suspicion*: also ~-**looking**) [*person, object, action, death*] suspect ; **in** ~ **circumstances** dans des circonstances suspectes

suspiciously [səsˈpɪʃəslɪ] ADV **a** (= *with suspicion*) [*examine, glance, ask*] avec méfiance **b** (= *causing suspicion*) [*behave, act*] de manière suspecte ; ~ **similar** d'une ressemblance suspecte ; ~ **high/low prices** des prix étrangement élevés/bas ; **it looks** ~ **like measles** ça a tout l'air d'être la rougeole ; **it sounds** ~ **as though he ...** il y a tout lieu de soupçonner qu'il ... ; **he arrived** ~ **early** c'est louche qu'il soit arrivé si tôt

suspiciousness [səsˈpɪʃəsnɪs] N (*NonC*) **a** (*feeling suspicion*) caractère *m* soupçonneux or méfiant **b** (*causing suspicion*) caractère *m* suspect

suss* [sʌs] VT (*Brit*) **to** ~ (**out**) [+ *situation, plan*] piger‡ ; **I can't** ~ **him out** je n'arrive pas à le cerner ; **he'll** ~ **you (out) straight away** il va tout de suite comprendre ton jeu ; **I've** ~**ed it out** ◊ **I've got it** ~**ed** j'ai pigé‡

sussed* [sʌst] ADJ (*Brit*) [*person*] branché*

sustain [səsˈteɪn] VT **a** [+ *weight, beam etc*] supporter ; [+ *body*] nourrir, sustenter† ; [+ *life*] maintenir ; (*Mus*) [+ *note*] tenir, soutenir ; [+ *effort, role*] soutenir ; [+ *pretence*] poursuivre, prolonger ; [+ *assertion, theory*] soutenir, maintenir ; [+ *charge*] donner des preuves à l'appui de ; **that food won't** ~ **you for long** ce n'est pas cette nourriture qui va vous donner beaucoup de forces ; (*Jur*) **objection** ~**ed** ≈ (objection *f*) accordée ; (*Jur*) **the court** ~**ed his claim** or ~**ed him in his claim** le tribunal a fait droit à sa revendication → **sustained b** (= *suffer*) [+ *attack*] subir ; [+ *loss*] éprouver, essuyer ; [+ *damage*] subir, souffrir ; [+ *injury*] recevoir ; **he** ~**ed concussion** il a été commotionné

sustainable [səsˈteɪnəbl] ADJ **a** (*Econ*) [*rate, growth*] viable ; [*energy, source, forest, devel-*

opment] durable ; [*resource*] renouvelable **b** [*argument*] tenable

sustained [səsˈteɪnd] ADJ [*effort, attack*] soutenu, prolongé ; [*applause*] prolongé ; (*Econ*) ~ **growth** expansion *f* soutenue

sustaining [səsˈteɪnɪŋ] **1** ADJ [*food*] consistant, substantiel **2** COMP ▶ **sustaining pedal** N (*Mus*) pédale *f* forte ▶ **sustaining program** N (*US Rad, TV*) émission *f* non sponsorisée

sustenance [ˈsʌstɪnəns] N (*NonC*) **a** (= *nourishing quality*) valeur *f* nutritive ; (= *food and drink*) alimentation *f*, nourriture *f* ; **there's not much** ~ **in melon** le melon n'est pas très nourrissant or nutritif, le melon n'a pas beaucoup de valeur nutritive ; **they depend for** ~ **on ...** ◊ **they get their** ~ **from ...** ils se nourrissent de ... ; **roots and berries were** or **provided their only** ~ les racines et les baies étaient leur seule nourriture, pour toute nourriture ils avaient des racines et des baies **b** (= *means of livelihood*) moyens *mpl* de subsistance

suttee [sʌˈtiː] N (= *widow*) (veuve *f*) sati *f inv* ; (= *rite*) sati *m*

suture [ˈsuːtʃəʳ] N suture *f*

suzerain [ˈsuːzəˌreɪn] N suzerain(e) *m(f)*

suzerainty [ˈsuːzərəntɪ] N suzeraineté *f*

svelte [svelt] ADJ svelte

Svengali [svenˈgɑːlɪ] N *homme aux pouvoirs malfaisants*

SVGA [ˌesviːdʒiːˈeɪ] N (*Comput*) (ABBR = **super video graphics array**) super-VGA *m*

SVQ [ˌesviːˈkjuː] N (ABBR = **Scottish Vocational Qualification**) *qualification professionnelle* → *NVQ*

SW **a** (*Rad*) (ABBR = **short wave**) OC *fpl* **b** (ABBR = **south-west**) S.-O.

swab [swɒb] **1** N (= *mop, cloth*) serpillière *f* ; (*Naut*) faubert *m* ; (*for gun-cleaning*) écouvillon *m* ; (*Med* = *cotton wool etc*) tampon *m* ; (*Med* = *specimen*) prélèvement *m* ; (*Med*) **to take a** ~ **of sb's throat** faire un prélèvement dans la gorge de qn **2** VT **a** (*also* ~ **down**) [+ *floor etc*] nettoyer, essuyer ; (*Naut*) [+ *deck*] passer le faubert sur **b** (*also* ~ **out**) [+ *gun*] écouvillonner ; (*Med*) [+ *wound*] tamponner, essuyer or nettoyer avec un tampon

swaddle [ˈswɒdl] **1** VT (*in bandages*) emmailloter (**in** de) ; (*in blankets etc*) emmitoufler* (**in** dans) ; [+ *baby*] emmailloter, langer **2** COMP ▶ **swaddling bands**, **swaddling clothes** NPL (*liter*) maillot *m*, lange *m*

swag [swæg] N **a** (= *loot*) butin *m* **b** (*Austral*) bal(l)uchon* *m*

swagger [ˈswægəʳ] **1** N air *m* fanfaron ; (= *gait*) démarche *f* assurée ; **to walk with a** ~ marcher en plastronnant or d'un air important **2** VI (*also* ~ **about, ~ along**) plastronner, parader ; **to** ~ **in/out** etc entrer/ sortir etc d'un air fanfaron or en plastronnant **b** (= *boast*) se vanter (**about** de) **3** COMP ▶ **swagger coat** N manteau *m* trois quarts ▶ **swagger stick** N (*Mil*) badine *f*, jonc *m*

swaggering [ˈswægərɪŋ] **1** ADJ [*gait*] assuré ; [*person*] fanfaron, qui plastronne ; [*look, gesture*] fanfaron **2** N (= *strutting*) airs *mpl* plastronnants ; (= *boasting*) fanfaronnades *fpl*

swagman* [ˈswægmæn] N (*pl* -**men**) (*Austral*) ouvrier *m* agricole itinérant

Swahili [swɑːˈhiːlɪ] **1** ADJ swahili, souahéli **2** N (*pl* **Swahili** or **Swahilis**) (*Ling*) swahili *m*, souahéli *m* **3** NPL (= *people*) Swahilis *mpl*, Souahélis *mpl*

swain [sweɪn] N (†† *or liter*) amant† *m*, soupirant† *m*

SWALK [swɔːlk] (ABBR = **sealed with a loving kiss**) doux baisers (*message au dos d'une enveloppe*)

swallow¹ [ˈswɒləʊ] **1** N (*Orn*) hirondelle *f* ■ (*PROV*) **one** ~ **doesn't make a summer** une hi-

rondelle ne fait pas le printemps (*PROV*) **2** COMP ▶ **swallow dive** N (*Brit*) saut *m* de l'ange ▶ **swallow-tailed coat** N (habit *m* à) queue *f* de pie

swallow² [ˈswɒləʊ] **1** N (= *act*) avalement *m* ; (= *amount*) gorgée *f* ; **at** or **with one** ~ [*drink*] d'un trait, d'un seul coup ; [*food*] d'un seul coup **2** VI avaler ; (*with emotion*) **he** ~**ed hard** sa gorge se serra **3** VT **a** [+ *food, drink, pill*] avaler ; [+ *oyster*] gober **b** (*fig*) [+ *story*] avaler, gober ; [+ *insult*] avaler, encaisser* ; [+ *one's anger, pride*] ravaler ; **that's a bit hard to** ~ c'est plutôt dur à avaler ; **they** ~**ed it whole** ils ont tout avalé or gobé

▶ **swallow down** VT SEP avaler

▶ **swallow up** VT SEP (*fig*) engloutir ; **the ground seemed to** ~ **them up** le sol semblait les engloutir ; **he was** ~**ed up in the crowd** il s'est perdu or il a disparu dans la foule ; **the mist** ~**ed them up** la brume les a enveloppés ; **taxes** ~ **up half your income** les impôts engloutissent or engouffrent la moitié de vos revenus

swallowtail (butterfly) [ˈswɒləʊteɪl(ˈbʌtəflaɪ)] N machaon *m*

swam [swæm] VB *pt of* **swim**

swami [ˈswɑːmɪ] N (*pl* **swamies** or **swamis**) pandit *m*

swamp [swɒmp] **1** N marais *m*, marécage *m* **2** VT (= *flood*) inonder ; [+ *boat*] emplir d'eau ; (= *sink*) submerger ; (*fig*) submerger (**with** de) ; (*fig*) **he was** ~**ed with requests/ letters** il était submergé de requêtes/lettres ; **I'm absolutely** ~**ed* (with work)** je suis débordé (de travail) ; (*Ftbl etc*) **towards the end of the game they** ~**ed us** vers la fin de la partie ils ont fait le jeu **3** COMP ▶ **swamp buggy** N (*US*) voiture *f* amphibie ▶ **swamp fever** N paludisme *m*, malaria *f*

swampland [ˈswɒmplænd] N (*NonC*) marécages *mpl*

swampy [ˈswɒmpɪ] ADJ marécageux

swan [swɒn] **1** N cygne *m* ; **the Swan of Avon** le cygne de l'Avon (*Shakespeare*) **2** VI (*Brit*) **he** ~**ned off to London before the end of term** il est parti à Londres sans s'en faire* or il est tranquillement parti à Londres avant la fin du trimestre ; **he's** ~**ning around in Paris somewhere** il se balade* quelque part dans Paris sans s'en faire* **3** COMP ▶ **swan dive** N (*US*) saut *m* de l'ange ▶ **Swan Lake** N (*Ballet*) le Lac des Cygnes ▶ **swan-necked** ADJ [*woman*] au cou de cygne ; [*tool*] en col de cygne ▶ **swan song** N (*fig*) chant *m* du cygne ▶ **swan-upping** N (*Brit*) recensement annuel des cygnes de la Tamise

swank* [swæŋk] **1** N (*NonC*) esbroufe* *f* ; **out of** ~ pour épater*, pour faire de l'esbroufe* **b** († = *person*) esbroufeur* *m*, -euse* *f* **2** VI faire de l'esbroufe*, chercher à épater* or à en mettre plein la vue* ; **to** ~ **about sth** se vanter de qch

swanky* [ˈswæŋkɪ] ADJ huppé*

swannery [ˈswɒnərɪ] N colonie *f* de cygnes

swansdown [ˈswɒnzdaʊn] N (*NonC*) (= *feathers*) (duvet *m* de) cygne *m* ; (*Tex*) molleton *m*

swap* [swɒp] **1** N troc *m*, échange *m* ; **it's a fair** ~ ça se vaut ; (*stamps etc*) ~**s** doubles *mpl* **2** VT échanger, troquer (**A for B** A contre B) ; [+ *stamps, stories*] échanger (**with sb** avec qn) ; **Paul and Martin have** ~**ped hats** Paul et Martin ont échangé leurs chapeaux ; **let's** ~ **places** changeons de place (l'un avec l'autre) ; **I'll** ~ **you!** tu veux échanger avec moi ? ~ **wife 3** VI échanger **4** COMP ▶ **swap meet** N (*US Comm*) rassemblement où l'on vend or troque divers objets usagés ▶ **swap shop** N (*Brit*) lieu ou rassemblement où l'on troque divers objets usagés

▶ **swap over**, **swap round** VT SEP, VI changer de place

SWAPO ['swɑːpəʊ] N (ABBR = **South-West Africa People's Organization**) SWAPO f

sward†† [swɔːd] N gazon m, pelouse f

swarm[1] [swɔːm] [1] N [of bees, flying insects] essaim m; [of ants, crawling insects] fourmillement m, grouillement m; [of people] nuée f, essaim m; (fig) **in a ~** ◊ **in ~s** en masse [2] VI [a] [bees] essaimer [b] [crawling insects] grouiller; **to ~ in/out** etc [people] entrer/sortir etc en masse; **they ~ed round** or **over** or **through the palace** ils ont envahi le palais en masse; **the children ~ed round his car** les enfants s'agglutinaient autour de sa voiture [c] (lit, fig) [ground, town, streets] fourmiller, grouiller (**with** de)

swarm[2] [swɔːm] VT (also ~ **up**) [+ tree, pole] grimper à toute vitesse à (en s'aidant des pieds et des mains)

swarthiness ['swɔːðɪnɪs] N teint m basané or bistré

swarthy ['swɔːðɪ] ADJ [person] à la peau basanée, au teint basané; [complexion] basané

swashbuckler ['swɒʃˌbʌklər] N fier-à-bras m

swashbuckling ['swɒʃˌbʌklɪŋ] ADJ [person] truculent; [film, role] de cape et d'épée

swastika ['swɒstɪkə] N svastika or swastika m; (Nazi) croix f gammée

SWAT [swɒt] (ABBR = **Special Weapons and Tactics**) ~ **team** ≈ GIGN m (groupe d'intervention de la gendarmerie nationale)

swat [swɒt] [1] VT [+ fly, mosquito] écraser; (* = slap) [+ table etc] donner un coup sur, taper sur [2] N [a] **to give a fly a ~** ◊ **to take a ~ at a fly** donner un coup de tapette à une mouche [b] (also **fly ~**) tapette f

swatch ['swɒtʃ] N échantillon m (de tissu)

swath [swɔːθ] N (pl **swaths** [swɔːðz]) = **swathe** 2

swathe [sweɪð] [1] VT (= bind) emmailloter (in de); (= wrap) envelopper (in dans); **~d in bandages** emmailloté de bandages; **~d in blankets** enveloppé or emmitouflé* dans des couvertures [2] N (Agr) andain m; **to cut corn in ~s** couper le blé en javelles; (fig) **to cut a ~ through** [disease, epidemic] décimer; [recession, cutbacks] ravager

swatter ['swɒtər] N (also **fly ~**) tapette f

sway [sweɪ] [1] N (NonC) [a] (= motion) [of rope, hanging object, trees] balancement m, oscillation f; [of boat] balancement m, oscillations fpl; [of tower block, bridge] mouvement m oscillatoire, oscillation f [b] (liter) emprise f, empire m (**over** sur), domination f (**over** de); **to hold ~ over** avoir de l'emprise or de l'empire sur, tenir sous son emprise or son empire or sa domination [2] VI [tree, rope, hanging object, boat] se balancer, osciller; [tower block, bridge] osciller; [train] tanguer; [person] tanguer, osciller; (fig) (= vacillate) osciller, hésiter (liter) (**between** entre); **he stood ~ing (about** or **from side to side** or **backwards and forwards)** il oscillait (sur ses jambes or de droite à gauche or d'arrière en avant), il tanguait; **to ~ in/out** etc (from drink, injury) entrer/sortir etc en tanguant; (regally) entrer/sortir etc majestueusement; **he ~ed towards leniency** il a penché pour la clémence [3] VT [a] [+ hanging object] balancer, faire osciller; [+ hips] rouler, balancer; [wind] balancer, agiter; [waves] balancer, ballotter [b] (= influence) influencer, avoir une action déterminante sur; **these factors finally ~ed the committee** ces facteurs ont finalement influencé le choix or la décision du comité; **I allowed myself to be ~ed** je me suis laissé influencer; **his speech ~ed the crowd** son discours a eu une action déterminante sur la foule [4] COMP ► **sway-back** N ensellure f, lordose f ► **sway-backed** ADJ ensellé

Swazi ['swɑːzɪ] [1] ADJ swazi [2] N Swazi(e) m(f)

Swaziland ['swɑːzɪˌlænd] N le Swaziland

swear [swɛər] (pret **swore**, ptp **sworn**) [1] VT [a] jurer (**on sth** sur qch, **that** que, **to do** de faire); (+ fidelity, allegiance) jurer; **I ~ it!** je le jure!; **to ~ an oath** (solemnly) prêter serment; (= curse) lâcher or pousser un juron; **to ~ (an oath) to do sth** faire (le) serment or jurer de faire qch; (Jur) **to ~ a charge against sb** accuser qn sous serment; **I could have sworn he touched it** j'aurais juré qu'il l'avait touché; **I ~ he said so!** il l'a dit, je vous le jure!, je vous jure qu'il l'a dit!; **I ~ I've never enjoyed myself more** ma parole, je ne me suis jamais autant amusé → **oath, sworn**; → **black** [b] [+ witness, jury] faire prêter serment à; **to ~ sb to secrecy** faire jurer le secret à qn

[2] VI [a] (= take solemn oath etc) (Jur) **do you so ~?** – **I ~** ≈ dites « je le jure » – je le jure; **he swore on the Bible** il a juré sur la Bible; **I ~ by all I hold sacred** je jure sur ce que j'ai de plus sacré; **to ~ to the truth of sth** jurer que qch est vrai; **would you ~ to having seen him?** est-ce que vous jureriez que vous l'avez vu?; **I think he did but I couldn't** or **wouldn't ~ to it** il me semble qu'il l'a fait mais je n'en jurerais pas; **to ~ blind** (Brit) or **up and down** (US) **that …** jurer ses grands dieux que … [b] (= curse) jurer, pester (**at** contre, après); (= blaspheme) jurer, blasphémer; **don't ~!** ne jure pas!, ne sois pas grossier!; **to ~ like a trooper** jurer comme un charretier; **it's enough to make you ~*** il y a de quoi vous faire râler*

► **swear by** VT FUS (fig) **he ~s by vitamin C tablets** il ne jure que par les vitamines C; **I ~ by whisky as a cure for flu** pour moi il n'y a rien de tel que le whisky pour guérir la grippe

► **swear in** VT SEP [+ jury, witness, president etc] assermenter, faire prêter serment à

► **swear off** VT FUS [+ alcohol, tobacco] jurer de renoncer à; **he has sworn off stealing** il a juré de ne plus voler

► **swear out** VT SEP (US Jur) **to ~ out a warrant for sb's arrest** obtenir un mandat d'arrêt contre qn en l'accusant sous serment

swearword ['swɛəwɜːd] N gros mot m, juron m

sweat [swet] [1] N [a] sueur f, transpiration f; (fig: on walls etc) humidité f, suintement m; (= state) sueur(s) f(pl); **by the ~ of his brow** à la sueur de son front; **to be dripping** or **covered with ~** ruisseler de sueur, être en nage; **to be in a ~** (lit) être en sueur, être couvert de sueur; (* fig) avoir des sueurs froides; **he was in a great ~ about it** ça lui donnait des sueurs froides → **cold** [b] (* = piece of work etc) corvée f; **it was an awful ~** on a eu un mal de chien, on en a bavé*; **no ~!** pas de problème! [c] **an old ~** un vétéran, un vieux routier

[2] VI [person, animal] suer (**with, from** de), être en sueur; [walls] suer, suinter; [cheese etc] suer; **he was ~ing profusely** il suait à grosses gouttes; **to ~ like a bull** or **a pig** suer comme un bœuf; (fig) **he was ~ing over his essay*** il suait or transpirait sur sa dissertation

[3] VT [a] [+ person, animal] faire suer or transpirer; (fig) [+ workers] exploiter; **~ed goods** marchandises fpl produites par une main-d'œuvre exploitée; **~ed labour** main-d'œuvre f exploitée [b] **to ~ blood*** (= work hard) suer sang et eau (**over sth** sur qch); (= be anxious) avoir des sueurs froides; **he was ~ing blood over** or **about the exam*** l'examen lui donnait des sueurs froides; (US fig) **don't ~ it!*** calme-toi!, relaxe!*

[4] COMP ► **sweat gland** N glande f sudoripare ► **sweat lodge** N sorte de sauna à usage religieux dans certaines tribus amérindiennes ► **sweat pants** NPL (US) jogging m ► **sweat-stained** ADJ taché or maculé de sueur

► **sweat off** VT SEP **I've ~ed off half a kilo** j'ai perdu un demi-kilo à force de transpirer

► **sweat out** VT SEP [+ cold etc] guérir en transpirant; (fig) **you'll just have to ~ it out*** il faudra t'armer de patience; **they left him to ~ it out*** ils n'ont rien fait pour l'aider

sweatband ['swetbænd] N (in hat) cuir m intérieur; (Sport) bandeau m

sweater ['swetər] [1] N tricot m, pull-over m, pull* m [2] COMP ► **sweater girl** N fille f bien roulée*

sweating ['swetɪŋ] N [of person, animal] transpiration f; (Med) sudation f; [of wall] suintement m

sweats* [swets] NPL (esp US) (tenue f de) jogging m

sweatshirt ['swetʃɜːt] N sweat-shirt m

sweatshop ['swetʃɒp] N atelier où la main-d'œuvre est exploitée

sweatsuit ['swetsuːt] N (US) survêtement m, survêt* m

sweaty ['swetɪ] ADJ [person, body] (= sweating) en sueur; (= sticky) collant de sueur; [hand, skin] moite (de sueur); [hair, clothes] collant de sueur; [smell] de sueur; [place] où l'on sue; **I've got ~ feet** je transpire or sue des pieds; **to get ~** [person] se mettre en sueur

Swede [swiːd] N Suédois(e) m(f)

swede [swiːd] N (esp Brit) rutabaga m

Sweden ['swiːdən] N la Suède

Swedenborgian [ˌswiːdənˈbɔːdʒɪən] ADJ swedenborgien

Swedish ['swiːdɪʃ] [1] ADJ (gen) suédois; [ambassador, embassy, monarch] de Suède [2] N (Ling) suédois m [3] **the Swedish** NPL les Suédois mpl [4] COMP ► **Swedish gymnastics** NPL gymnastique f suédoise ► **Swedish massage** N massage m suédois ► **Swedish mile** N mile m suédois (= 10 km) ► **Swedish movements** NPL = Swedish gymnastics

sweep [swiːp] (vb: pret, ptp **swept**) [1] N [a] (with broom etc) coup m de balai; **to give a room a ~ (out)** donner un coup de balai à or balayer une pièce → **clean** [b] (also **chimney ~**) ramoneur m → **black** [c] (= movement) [of arm] grand geste m; [of sword] grand coup m; [of scythe] mouvement m circulaire; [of net] coup m; [of lighthouse beam, radar beam] trajectoire f; [of tide] progression f irrésistible; (fig) [of progress, events] marche f; **in** or **with one ~** d'un seul coup; **with a ~ of his arm** d'un geste large; **to make a ~ of the horizon** (with binoculars) parcourir l'horizon; [lighthouse beam] balayer l'horizon; **to make a ~ for mines** draguer des mines; **the police made a ~ of the district** la police a ratissé le quartier [d] (= range) [of telescope, gun, lighthouse, radar] champ m; **with a ~ of 180°** avec un champ de 180° [e] (= curve, line) [of coastline, hills, road, river] grande courbe f; (Archit) courbure f, voussure f; [of curtains, long skirt] drapé m; **a wide ~ of meadowland** une vaste étendue de prairie; (Aut, Aviat, Naut etc) **the graceful ~ of her lines** sa ligne aérodynamique or son galbe plein(e) de grâce [f] * ABBR = **sweepstake**

[2] VT [a] [+ room, floor, street] balayer; [+ chimney] ramoner; (Naut) [+ river, channel] draguer; (fig) [waves, hurricane, bullets, searchlights, skirts] balayer; **to ~ a room clean** donner un bon coup de balai dans une pièce; (Naut) **to ~ sth clean of mines** déminer qch; (fig) **he swept the horizon with his binoculars** il a parcouru l'horizon avec ses jumelles; **his eyes/his glance swept the room** il a parcouru la pièce des yeux/du regard; **their fleet swept the seas in search of …** leur flotte a sillonné or parcouru les mers à la recherche de …; **a wave of panic swept the city** un vent de panique a soufflé sur la ville → **broom** [b] [+ dust, snow etc] balayer; (Naut) [+ mines]

draguer, enlever ; **he swept the rubbish off the pavement** il a enlevé les ordures du trottoir d'un coup de balai ; **she swept the snow into a heap** elle a balayé la neige et en a fait un tas ; *(fig)* **to ~ sth under the carpet** *or* **rug** tirer le rideau sur qch ; **to ~ sth off the table on to the floor** faire tomber qch de la table par terre d'un geste large ; **to ~ one's hair off one's face** écarter ses cheveux de son visage ; **to ~ sth into a bag** faire glisser qch d'un geste large dans un sac ; *(fig)* **to ~ everything before one** remporter un succès total, réussir sur toute la ligne ; **the army swept the enemy before them** l'armée a balayé l'ennemi devant elle ; *(fig)* **to ~ the board** remporter un succès complet, tout rafler* ; **the socialists swept the board at the election** les socialistes ont remporté l'élection haut la main ; *(fig)* **he swept the obstacles from his path** il a balayé *or* écarté les obstacles qui se trouvaient sur son chemin ; **the crowd swept him into the square** la foule l'a emporté *or* entraîné sur la place, il a été pris dans le mouvement de la foule et il s'est retrouvé sur la place ; **the wave swept him overboard** la vague l'a jeté par-dessus bord ; **the wind swept the caravan over the cliff** le vent a emporté la caravane et l'a précipitée du haut de la falaise ; **the current swept the boat downstream** le courant a emporté le bateau ; **to be swept off one's feet** *(by wind, flood etc)* être emporté **(by** par) ; *(fig)* être enthousiasmé *or* emballé* **(by** par) ; **the water swept him off his feet** le courant lui a fait perdre pied ; *(fig)* **he swept her off her feet** elle a eu le coup de foudre pour lui ; *(fig)* **this election swept the socialists into office** *or* **power** cette élection a porté les socialistes au pouvoir avec une forte majorité

3 VI **a** (= *pass swiftly*) **to ~ in/out/along** *etc* [*person, vehicle, convoy*] entrer/sortir/avancer *etc* rapidement ; **the car swept round the corner** la voiture a pris le virage comme un bolide ; **the planes went ~ing across the sky** les avions sillonnaient le ciel ; **the rain swept across the plain** la pluie a balayé la plaine ; **panic swept through the city** la panique s'est emparée de la ville ; **plague swept through the country** la peste a ravagé le pays **b** (= *move impressively*) **to ~ in/out/along** *etc* [*person, procession*] entrer/sortir/avancer *etc* majestueusement ; **she came ~ing into the room** elle a fait une entrée majestueuse dans la pièce ; *(fig: Pol)* **to ~ into office** être porté au pouvoir ; **the royal car swept down the avenue** la voiture royale a descendu l'avenue d'une manière imposante ; *(fig)* **the motorway ~s across the hills** l'autoroute s'élance à travers les collines ; **the forests ~ down to the sea** les forêts descendent en pente douce jusqu'au bord de la mer ; **the bay ~s away to the south** la baie décrit une courbe majestueuse vers le sud ; **the Alps ~ down to the coast** les Alpes descendent majestueusement vers la côte

4 COMP ► **sweep hand** N [*of clock etc*] trotteuse *f*
► **sweep along** 1 VI → **sweep 3a, 3b** 2 VT SEP [*crowd, flood, current, gale*] emporter, entraîner ; [+ *leaves*] balayer
► **sweep aside** VT SEP [+ *object, person*] repousser, écarter ; [+ *suggestion, objection*] repousser, rejeter ; [+ *difficulty, obstacle*] écarter
► **sweep away** 1 VI (= *leave*) *(rapidly)* s'éloigner rapidement ; *(impressively)* s'éloigner majestueusement *or* d'une manière imposante → **sweep 3b** 2 VT SEP [+ *dust, snow, rubbish*] balayer ; [*crowd, flood, current, gale*] emporter ; **they swept him away to lunch** ils l'ont entraîné pour aller déjeuner
► **sweep down** VT SEP [+ *walls etc*] nettoyer avec un balai ; [*flood, gale etc*] emporter ; **the river swept the logs down to the sea** les bûches ont flotté sur la rivière jusqu'à la mer
► **sweep off** = **sweep away**

► **sweep out** 1 VI → **sweep 3a, 3b** 2 VT SEP [+ *room, dust, rubbish*] balayer
► **sweep up** 1 VI **a** (*with broom etc*) **to ~ up after sb** balayer les débris *or* les saletés de qn ; **to ~ up after a party** balayer quand les invités sont partis **b** **he swept up to me** *(angrily)* il s'est approché de moi avec furie *or* majestueusement ; *(impressively)* il s'est approché de moi majestueusement ; **the car swept up to the house** *(rapidly)* la voiture a remonté rapidement l'allée jusqu'à la maison ; *(impressively)* la voiture a remonté l'allée jusqu'à la maison d'une manière imposante 2 VT SEP [+ *snow, leaves, dust etc*] balayer ; **she swept up the letters and took them away** elle a ramassé les lettres d'un geste brusque et les a emportées

sweepback ['swiːpbæk] N [*of aircraft wing etc*] flèche *f*

sweeper ['swiːpəʳ] N **a** (= *worker*) balayeur *m* **b** (= *machine*) balayeuse *f* ; (*also* **carpet ~**) balai *m* mécanique ; (= *vacuum cleaner*) aspirateur *m* **c** *(Ftbl)* libéro *m*

sweeping ['swiːpɪŋ] 1 ADJ **a** [*gesture, movement*] grand ; [*curve*] large ; [*glance*] circulaire ; [*coastline*] qui décrit une courbe majestueuse ; [*lawn*] qui descend en pente majestueuse ; [*staircase*] qui descend majestueusement ; [*bow*] profond ; [*skirts*] qui balaie le sol **b** (= *large-scale*) [*change, reorganization*] radical ; [*reduction, cuts, powers*] considérable ; [*victory*] écrasant **c** (= *decisive*) [*victory*] écrasant **d** *(pej)* (= *indiscriminate*) **~ statement/generalization** déclaration *f*/ généralisation *f* à l'emporte-pièce ; **that's pretty ~!** c'est beaucoup dire ! 2 **sweepings** NPL balayures *fpl*, ordures *fpl* ; *(fig)* [*of society etc*] rebut *m*

sweepstake ['swiːpsteɪk] N sweepstake *m*

sweet [swiːt] 1 ADJ **a** (= *not savoury*) [*taste, food, drink*] sucré ; [*smell*] doux (douce *f*), suave ; [*apple, orange*] doux (douce *f*), sucré ; **to taste ~** être sucré ; **to smell ~** avoir une odeur suave ; **I love ~ things** j'adore le sucré *or* les sucreries *fpl* → **sickly, sweet-and-sour** **b** (= *not dry*) [*cider, wine*] doux (douce *f*) → **medium** **c** (= *kind*) [*person, face, smile*] doux (douce *f*) ; **she has such a ~ nature** elle est d'une nature si douce ; **she is a very ~ person** elle est vraiment très gentille ; **you're such a ~ guy!** t'es vraiment un chic type !* ; **that was very ~ of her** c'était très gentil de sa part ; **how ~ of you to think of me!** comme c'est gentil de votre part d'avoir pensé à moi ! ; **to be ~ to sb** être gentil avec qn ; **to keep sb ~** chercher à être dans les petits papiers de qn* ; *(Brit)* **(as) as pie** [*person*] gentil comme tout ; [*situation*] qui marche parfaitement ; **Sweet Jesus!** nom de Dieu !* → **Fanny** **d** (= *cute*) [*child, dog, house, hat*] mignon ; **a ~ old lady** une adorable vieille dame → **sixteen** **e** (= *pleasant*) [*sound, voice, music*] harmonieux, mélodieux ; **revenge is ~!** la vengeance est douce ! ; **the ~ taste of victory/revenge** le goût exquis de la victoire/vengeance ; **the ~ smell of success** la saveur de la gloire, l'ivresse du succès ; **the news was ~ music to my ears** cette nouvelle a été douce à mes oreilles ; **~ dreams!** fais de beaux rêves ! ; **to whisper ~ nothings in sb's ear** conter fleurette à qn → **bittersweet** **f** (= *pure*) [*air, breath*] frais (fraîche *f*) ; [*water*] pur ; **to smell ~** [*air*] être pur ; [*breath*] être frais **g** *(iro)* **he carried on in his own ~ way** il a continué comme il l'entendait ; **he'll do it in his own ~ time** il le fera quand bon lui semblera ; **she went her own ~ way** elle a fait comme il lui plaisait ; **to please one's own ~ self** n'en faire qu'à sa tête ; **at his own ~ will** à son gré

h (* = *attracted*) **to be ~ on sb** avoir le béguin* pour qn
2 N (*esp Brit* = *candy*) bonbon *m* ; (*Brit* = *dessert*) dessert *m* ; *(fig)* **the ~s of success/solitude etc** les délices *fpl* de la réussite/de la solitude *etc* ; **come here, (my) ~** viens ici, mon ange
3 COMP ► **sweet-and-sour** ADJ aigre-doux (aigre-douce *f*) ► **sweet chestnut** N châtaigne *f*, marron *m* ► **sweet herbs** NPL fines herbes *fpl* ► **sweet-natured** ADJ d'un naturel doux ► **sweet pea** N pois *m* de senteur ► **sweet pepper** N piment *m* doux, poivron *m* (vert *or* rouge) ► **sweet potato** N patate *f* douce ► **sweet-scented**, **sweet-smelling** ADJ agréablement parfumé, odoriférant ► **sweet talk** N flagorneries *fpl* ► **sweet-talk** VT flagorner ► **sweet-tempered** ADJ = **sweet-natured** ► **sweet tooth** N **to have a ~ tooth** avoir un faible pour les sucreries ► **sweet trolley** N *(Brit)* chariot *m* des desserts ► **sweet william** N *(Bot)* œillet *m* de poète

sweetbread ['swiːtbred] N ris *m* de veau *or* d'agneau

sweetbriar, **sweetbrier** ['swiːtbraɪəʳ] N églantier *m* odorant

sweetcorn ['swiːtkɔːn] N maïs *m*

sweeten ['swiːtn] 1 VT **a** [+ *coffee, sauce etc*] sucrer ; [+ *air*] purifier ; [+ *room*] assainir **b** *(fig)* [+ *person, sb's temper, task*] adoucir **c** (* : *also* **~ up**) (= *give incentive to*) amadouer ; (= *bribe*) graisser la patte à* → **pill** 2 VI [*person, sb's temper*] s'adoucir

sweetener ['swiːtnəʳ] N **a** (*for coffee, food*) édulcorant *m* **b** (* *fig*) (= *incentive*) carotte* *f* ; (= *bribe*) pot-de-vin *m* ; (= *compensation*) quelque chose *m* pour faire passer la pilule*, lot *m* de consolation

sweetening ['swiːtnɪŋ] N (*NonC* = *substance*) édulcorant *m*

sweetheart ['swiːthɑːt] N petit(e) ami(e) *m(f)*, bien-aimé(e)† *m(f)* ; **yes ~** oui chéri(e) *or* mon ange *or* mon cœur

sweetie* ['swiːtɪ] N **a** (= *person: also* **~-pie**:) **he's/she's a ~** il/elle est chou*, c'est un ange ; **yes ~** oui mon chou* *or* mon ange **b** (*esp Scot* = *candy*) bonbon *m*

sweetish ['swiːtɪʃ] ADJ au goût sucré, douceâtre *(pej)*

sweetly ['swiːtlɪ] ADV **a** (= *kindly*) [*smile, say, answer*] gentiment **b** (= *pleasantly*) [*sing, play*] mélodieusement **c** (= *efficiently*) **the engine is running ~** le moteur marche sans à-coups ; **he hit the ball ~** il a frappé la balle avec un timing parfait **d** (= *scented*) agréablement parfumé, odoriférant

sweetmeat ['swiːtmiːt] N sucrerie *f*, confiserie *f*

sweetness ['swiːtnɪs] N (*to taste*) goût *m* sucré ; (*in smell*) odeur *f* suave ; (*to hearing*) son *m* mélodieux *or* harmonieux ; [*of person, nature, character, expression*] douceur *f* ; *(fig)* **to be all ~ and light** être tout douceur

sweetshop ['swiːtʃɒp] N *(Brit)* confiserie *f* (souvent avec papeterie, journaux et tabac)

swell [swel] (*vb: pret* **swelled**, *ptp* **swollen** *or* **swelled**) 1 N **a** [*of sea*] houle *f* ; **heavy ~** forte houle *f* → **groundswell** **b** (*Mus*) crescendo *m* inv (et diminuendo *m* inv) ; (*on organ*) boîte *f* expressive **c** (†* = *stylish person*) personne *f* huppée*, gandin *m* (*pej*) ; **the ~s** les gens *mpl* huppés*, le gratin* 2 ADJ* **a** (*esp US*† = *stylish, showy*) [*clothes, house, car, restaurant*] chic inv ; [*relatives, friends*] huppé* **b** (*US* = *wonderful*) super* inv ; **I had a ~ time** je me suis super* bien amusé 3 VI **a** (*also* **~ up**) [*balloon, tyre, air bed*] (se) gonfler ; [*sails*] se gonfler ; [*ankle, arm, eye, face*] enfler ; [*wood*] gonfler ; *(fig)* **to ~ (up) with pride** se gonfler d'orgueil ; **to ~ (up) with**

rage/indignation bouillir de rage/ d'indignation **b** (= increase) [river] grossir; [sound, music, voice] s'enfler; [numbers, population, membership] grossir, augmenter; **the numbers soon ~ed to 500** le nombre a vite atteint 500; **the little group soon ~ed into a crowd** le petit groupe est vite devenu une foule; **the murmuring ~ed to a roar** le murmure s'enfla pour devenir un rugissement

4 VT [+ sail] gonfler; [+ sound] enfler; [+ river, lake] grossir; [+ number] grossir, augmenter; **this ~ed the membership/ population to 1,500** ceci a porté à 1 500 le nombre des membres/le total de la population; **a population swollen by refugees** une population grossie par les réfugiés; **a river swollen by rain** une rivière grossie par les pluies, une rivière en crue; **a fifth edition swollen by a mass of new material** une cinquième édition augmentée d'une quantité de matière nouvelle; **to be swollen with pride** être gonflé or bouffi d'orgueil; **to be swollen with rage** bouillir de rage → **swollen**

5 COMP ► **swell box** N (Mus) boîte f expressive

► **swell out** **1** VI [sails etc] se gonfler **2** VT SEP gonfler

► **swell up** VI = swell 3a

swellhead* ['swelhed] N (US) bêcheur* m, -euse* f

swellheaded* [,swel'hedɪd] ADJ bêcheur*

swellheadedness* [,swel'hedɪdnɪs] N vanité f, suffisance f

swelling ['swelɪŋ] **1** N **a** (= bulge, lump) (gen) grosseur f; (on tyre) hernie f; (Med) bosse f, grosseur f **b** (NonC: Med) [of limb, foot, finger, face, jaw] enflure f [of eye, stomach, breasts, tissue, organ] gonflement m; **it's to reduce the ~** c'est pour faire désenfler **c** (NonC) [of balloon, tyre, sails, wood] gonflement m; [of population] accroissement m **2** ADJ [sound, chorus, voices, ankle, eye] qui enfle; [sail] gonflé

swelter ['sweltə'] VI étouffer de chaleur

sweltering ['sweltərɪŋ] ADJ [weather] étouffant; [heat] étouffant, accablant; [day, afternoon] torride; **it's ~** on étouffe (de chaleur)

swept [swept] VB pt, ptp of **sweep**

sweptback [,swept'bæk] ADJ (Aviat) en flèche; [hair] rejeté en arrière

sweptwing aircraft [,sweptwɪŋ'ɛəkrɑːft] N avion m à ailes en flèche

swerve [swɜːv] **1** VI [boxer, fighter] faire un écart; [ball] dévier; [vehicle, ship] faire une embardée; [driver] donner un coup de volant; (fig) dévier (**from** de); **the car ~d away from the lorry on to the verge** la voiture a fait une embardée pour éviter le camion et est montée sur l'accotement; **he ~d round the bollard** il a viré sur les chapeaux de roues autour de la borne lumineuse **2** VT [+ ball] faire dévier; [+ vehicle] faire faire une embardée à **3** N [of vehicle, ship] embardée f; [of boxer, fighter] écart m

swift [swɪft] **1** ADJ rapide; **the river is ~ at this point** le courant (de la rivière) est rapide à cet endroit; **to wish sb a ~ recovery** souhaiter à qn un prompt rétablissement; **they were ~ to act/respond/obey** ils ont été prompts à agir/ réagir/obéir **2** N (Orn) martinet m **3** COMP ► **swift-flowing** ADJ [river] au courant rapide; [current] rapide ► **swift-footed** ADJ (liter) au pied léger

swiftly ['swɪftlɪ] ADV [move, react, walk, spread, become] rapidement, vite; **a ~ flowing river** une rivière au courant rapide; **the company has moved** or **acted ~ to deny the rumours** l'entreprise a réagi promptement or a démenti les rumeurs

swiftness ['swɪftnɪs] N rapidité f

swig* [swɪg] **1** N lampée* f; (larger) coup m; **to take a ~ at a bottle** boire un coup à même la bouteille **2** VT lamper*

► **swig down*** VT SEP avaler d'un trait

swill [swɪl] **1** N **a** (NonC) (for pigs etc) pâtée f; (= garbage, slops) eaux fpl grasses **b** **to give sth a ~ (out** or **down)** = to swill sth (out or down); → **2a** **2** VT **a** (also ~ out, ~ down) [+ floor] laver à grande eau; [+ glass] rincer **b** (also ~ around) [+ liquid] remuer **c** (* = drink) boire avidement, boire à grands traits **3** VI [liquid] remuer

swim [swɪm] (vb: pret **swam**, ptp **swum**) **1** N **to go for a ~** ◊ **to have** or **take a ~** (in sea, lake, river) aller nager or se baigner; (in swimming baths) aller à la piscine; **it's time for our ~** c'est l'heure de la baignade; **after a 2km ~** après avoir fait 2 km à la nage; **Channel ~** traversée f de la Manche à la nage; **it's a long ~** voilà une bonne or longue distance à parcourir à la nage; **I had a lovely ~** ça m'a fait du bien de nager comme ça; (fig) **to be in the ~ (of things)** être dans le mouvement

2 VI **a** [person] nager; (as sport) faire de la natation; [fish etc] nager; **to go ~ming** (in sea, lake, river) aller nager or se baigner; (in swimming baths) aller à la piscine; **to ~ away/ back** [person] s'éloigner/revenir etc à la nage; [fish] s'éloigner/revenir etc; **to ~ across a river** traverser une rivière à la nage; **he swam under the boat** il est passé sous le bateau (à la nage); **to ~ under water** nager sous l'eau; **he had to ~ for it** son seul recours a été de se sauver à la nage or de se jeter à l'eau et de nager; **to ~ against the current** nager contre le courant; (fig) **to ~ against the tide** nager à contre-courant; (fig) **to ~ with the tide** suivre le courant

b (fig) **the meat was ~ming in gravy** la viande nageait or baignait dans la sauce; **her eyes were ~ming (with tears)** ses yeux étaient noyés or baignés de larmes; **the bathroom was ~ming** la salle de bains était inondée; **the room was ~ming round** or **~ming before his eyes** la pièce semblait tourner autour de lui; **his head was ~ming** la tête lui tournait

3 VT [+ race] nager; [+ lake, river] traverser à la nage; **it was first swum in 1900** la première traversée à la nage a eu lieu en 1900; **he can ~ 10km** il peut faire 10 km à la nage; **he can ~ two lengths** il peut nager or faire deux longueurs; **before he had swum ten strokes** avant qu'il ait pu nager dix brasses; **I can't ~ a stroke** je suis incapable de faire une brasse; **can you ~ the crawl?** savez-vous nager or faire le crawl?

swimmer ['swɪmə'] N nageur m, -euse f

swimming ['swɪmɪŋ] **1** N (gen) nage f; (Sport, Scol) natation f **2** COMP ► **swimming bath(s)** N(PL) (Brit) piscine f ► **swimming cap** N bonnet m de bain ► **swimming costume** N (Brit) maillot m (de bain) une pièce ► **swimming crab** N étrille f ► **swimming gala** N compétition f de natation ► **swimming instructor** N maître m nageur ► **swimming pool** N piscine f ► **swimming ring** N bouée f ► **swimming suit** N maillot m (de bain) ► **swimming trunks** NPL maillot m or caleçon m or slip m de bain

swimmingly*† ['swɪmɪŋlɪ] ADV à merveille; **they got on ~** ils se sont entendus à merveille; **everything went ~** tout a marché comme sur des roulettes

swimsuit ['swɪmsuːt] N maillot m (de bain)

swimwear ['swɪmwɛə'] N (NonC) maillots mpl de bain

swindle ['swɪndl] **1** N escroquerie f; **it's a ~** c'est du vol, nous nous sommes fait estamper* or rouler* **2** VT escroquer; **to ~ sb out of his money** ◊ **to ~ sb's money out of him** escroquer de l'argent à qn

swindler ['swɪndlə'] N escroc m

swine [swaɪn] N (pl inv) (Zool) pourceau m, porc m; (‡ fig = person) salaud‡ m; **you ~!‡** espèce de salaud!‡

swineherd†† ['swaɪnhɜːd] N porcher m, -ère f

swing [swɪŋ] (vb: pret, ptp **swung**) **1** N **a** (= movement) balancement m; [of pendulum] (= movement) mouvement m de va-et-vient, oscillations fpl; (= arc, distance) arc m; [of instrument pointer, needle] oscillations fpl; (Boxing, Golf) swing m; **the ~ of the boom sent him overboard** le retour de la bôme l'a jeté par-dessus bord; **he gave the starting handle a ~** il a donné un tour de manivelle; **the golfer took a ~ at the ball** le joueur de golf a essayé de frapper or a frappé la balle avec un swing; **to take a ~ at sb*** décocher or lancer un coup de poing à qn; (fig) **the ~ of the pendulum brought him back to power** le mouvement du pendule l'a ramené au pouvoir; (Pol) **the socialists need a ~ of 5% to win the election** il faudrait aux socialistes un revirement d'opinion en leur faveur de l'ordre de 5% pour qu'ils remportent (subj) l'élection; (Pol) **a ~ to the left** un revirement en faveur de la gauche; (St Ex) **the ~s of the market** les fluctuations fpl or les hauts et les bas mpl du marché

b (= rhythm) [of dance etc] rythme m; [of jazz music] swing m; **to walk with a ~ in one's step** marcher d'un pas rythmé; **music/poetry with a ~ to it** or **that goes with a ~** musique f/ poésie f rythmée or entraînante; (fig) **to go with a ~** [evening, party] marcher du tonnerre*; [business, shop] très bien marcher; **to be in full ~** [party, election, campaign] battre son plein; [business] être en plein rendement, gazer*; **to get into the ~ of** [+ new job, married life etc] s'habituer or se faire à; **to get into the ~ of things** se mettre dans le bain

c (= scope, freedom) **they gave him full ~ in the matter** ils lui ont donné carte blanche en la matière; **he was given full ~ to make decisions** on l'a laissé entièrement libre de prendre des décisions; **he gave his imagination full ~** il a donné libre cours à son imagination

d (= seat for swinging) balançoire f; **to have a ~** se balancer, faire de la balançoire; **to give a child a ~** pousser un enfant qui se balance; (fig) **what you gain on the ~s you lose on the roundabouts** ◊ **(it's) ~s and roundabouts*** ce qu'on gagne d'un côté on le perd de l'autre **e** (also ~ music) swing m

2 VI **a** (= hang, oscillate) [arms, legs] se balancer, être ballant; [object on rope, hammock] se balancer; [pendulum] osciller; (on a swing) se balancer; (= pivot: also ~ round) tourner, pivoter; [person] se retourner, virevolter; **he was left ~ing by his hands** il s'est retrouvé seul suspendu par les mains; **to ~ to and fro** se balancer; **the load swung (round) through the air as the crane turned** comme la grue pivotait la charge a décrit une courbe dans l'air; **the ship was ~ing at anchor** le bateau se balançait sur son ancre; **he swung across on the rope** agrippé à la corde il s'est élancé et a or est passé de l'autre côté; **the monkey swung from branch to branch** le singe se balançait de branche en branche; **he swung up the rope ladder** il a grimpé prestement à l'échelle de corde; **he swung (up) into the saddle** il a sauté en selle; **the door swung open/shut** la porte s'est ouverte/s'est refermée; **he swung (round) on his heel** il a virevolté

b (= move rhythmically) **to ~ along/away etc** avancer/s'éloigner etc d'un pas rythmé or allègre; **the regiment went ~ing past the king** le régiment a défilé au pas cadencé devant le roi; **to ~ into action** [army] se mettre en branle; (fig) passer à l'action; **music that really ~s** musique f qui swingue

c (= change direction: also ~ round) [plane, vehicle] virer; **the convoy swung (round) into the square** le convoi a viré pour aller sur la place; **the river ~s north here** ici la rivière décrit une courbe *or* oblique vers le nord; (*Pol*) **the country has swung to the right** le pays a viré *or* effectué un virage à droite; (*fig*) **to ~ both ways:** marcher à la voile et à vapeur*

d **to ~ at a ball** frapper *or* essayer de frapper une balle avec un swing; **to ~ at sb** décocher *or* lancer un coup de poing à qn; **he swung at me with the axe** il a brandi la hache pour me frapper

e (* = *be hanged*) être pendu; **he'll ~ for it** on lui mettra la corde au cou pour cela; **I'd ~ for him** je le tuerais si je le tenais

f * (= *be fashionable*) être branché*, être dans le vent; **the party was really ~ing** la surprise-partie était du tonnerre* *or* à tout casser*

3 VT **a** (= *move to and fro*) [+ *one's arms, legs, umbrella, hammock*] balancer; [+ *object on rope*] balancer, faire osciller; [+ *pendulum*] faire osciller; [+ *child on swing*] pousser; (= *brandish*) brandir; **he swung his sword above his head** il a fait un moulinet avec l'épée au-dessus de sa tête; **he swung his axe at the tree** il a brandi sa hache pour frapper l'arbre; **he swung his racket at the ball** il a ramené sa raquette pour frapper la balle; **he swung the box (up) on to the roof of the car** il a envoyé la boîte sur le toit de la voiture; **he swung the case (up) on to his shoulders** il a balancé la valise sur ses épaules; **he swung himself across the stream/over the wall** *etc* il s'est élancé et a franchi le ruisseau/et a sauté par-dessus le mur *etc*; **to ~ o.s. (up) into the saddle** sauter en selle; **to ~ one's hips** rouler *or* balancer les hanches, se déhancher; (*Brit fig*) **to ~ the lead*** tirer au flanc* → **room**

b (= *turn: also often* ~ **round**) [+ *propeller*] lancer; [+ *starting handle*] tourner; **to ~ a door open/shut** ouvrir/fermer une porte; **he swung the ship (round) through 180°** il a viré de 180°, il a fait virer (le bateau) de 180°; **he swung the car round the corner** il a viré au coin

c (= *influence*) [+ *election, decision*] influencer; [+ *voters*] faire changer d'opinion; **his speech swung the decision against us** son discours a provoqué un revirement et la décision est allée contre nous; **he managed to ~ the deal*** il a réussi à emporter l'affaire; **to ~ it on sb:** tirer une carotte à qn*, pigeonner qn*

d (*Mus*) [+ *a tune, the classics etc*] jouer de manière rythmée

4 COMP ▶ **swing band** N (*Mus*) orchestre *m* de swing ▶ **swing-bin** N (*Brit*) poubelle *f* à couvercle pivotant ▶ **swing bridge** N pont *m* tournant ▶ **swing door** N porte *f* battante ▶ **swing music** N → **1e** ▶ **swing shift*** N (*US Ind*) (= *period*) période *f* du soir (*pour un travail posté*); (= *workers*) équipe *f* du soir ▶ **swing vote** N (*esp US*) vote *m* décisif; **the Black community will be the ~ vote in the election** le soutien de ces élections dépendra du vote noir ▶ **swing voter** N (*esp US*) électeur dont le vote est décisif pour l'issue d'une élection ▶ **swing-wing** ADJ (*Aviat*) à géométrie variable

▶**swing round** **1** VI [*person*] se retourner, virevolter; [*crane etc*] tourner, pivoter; [*ship, plane, convoy, procession*] virer; [*car, truck*] virer; (*after collision etc*) faire un tête-à-queue; (*fig*) [*voters*] virer de bord; [*opinions*] connaître un revirement → **swing 2a, 2c** **2** VT SEP [+ *object on rope etc*] faire tourner; [+ *sword, axe*] brandir, faire des moulinets avec; [+ *crane etc*] faire pivoter; [+ *car, ship, plane, convoy, procession*] faire tourner *or* virer → **swing 3b**

▶**swing to** VI [*door*] se refermer

swingeing ['swɪndʒɪŋ] ADJ (*Brit*) [*attack*] violent; [*increase*] considérable; [*fine, tax*] fort; [*defeat, majority*] écrasant; **~ cuts** des coupes *fpl* sombres

swinger* ['swɪŋə*] N **he's a ~** (= *with it*) il est branché* *or* dans le vent; (*going to parties*) c'est un partouzard! *or* un noceur*; (*sexually*) il couche à droite et à gauche

swinging ['swɪŋɪŋ] **1** ADJ **a** (= *swaying, rocking*) [*rope, weight, pendulum, legs, hammock*] qui se balance; [*door, shutter*] qui bat; **a ~ weight on the end of a cord** un poids se balançant *or* qui se balance au bout d'une corde; **the bar was full of ~ fists** dans le bar, les coups volaient **b** (= *syncopated*) [*music, rhythm*] entraînant, qui swingue*; **c** (* = *modern, fashionable*) dans le vent **d** (* = *lively, exciting*) [*party etc*] animé; **~ London** le «Swinging London» **2** COMP ▶ **swinging door** N (*US*) = **swing door**; → **swing** ▶ **swinging single*** N (*US*) célibataire qui a de nombreuses aventures sexuelles ▶ **the Swinging Sixties** NPL les folles années *fpl* soixante

swingometer ['swɪŋɒmɪtə*] N (*at election*) indicateur *m* de tendances

swinish: ['swaɪnɪʃ] ADJ dégueulasse:

swipe [swaɪp] **1** N* (*at ball etc*) grand coup *m*; (= *slap*) baffe* *f*; (*lit*) **to take a ~ at** = **to swipe at**; → **3**; (*fig*) **to take a ~ at sb** s'en prendre à *or* attaquer qn (*de façon détournée*) **2** VT **a** (* = *hit*) [+ *ball*] frapper à toute volée; [+ *person*] gifler à toute volée **b** (: = *steal: often hum*) piquer* (**sth from sb** qch à qn) **c** [+ *card*] **you pay by swiping a credit card** on paie avec une carte magnétique **3** VI **to ~ at*** [+ *ball etc*] frapper *or* essayer de frapper à toute volée; [+ *person*] flanquer* une baffe* à **4** COMP ▶ **swipe card** N carte *f* magnétique

swirl [swɜːl] **1** N (*in river, sea*) tourbillon *m*, remous *m*; [*of dust, sand*] tourbillon *m*; [*of smoke*] tourbillon *m*, volute *f*; (*fig*) [*of cream, ice cream etc*] volute *f*; [*of lace, ribbons etc*] tourbillon *m*; **the ~ of the dancers' skirts** le tourbillon *or* le tournoiement des jupes des danseuses **2** VI [*water, river, sea*] tourbillonner, faire des remous *or* des tourbillons; [*dust, sand, smoke, skirts*] tourbillonner, tournoyer **3** VT **to ~ sth along/away** [*river*] entraîner/emporter qch en tourbillonnant; **he ~ed his partner round the room** il a fait tournoyer *or* tourbillonner sa partenaire autour de la salle

swish [swɪʃ] **1** N [*of whip*] sifflement *m*; [*of water, person in long grass*] bruissement *m*; [*of grass in wind*] frémissement *m*, bruissement *m*; [*of tyres in rain*] glissement *m*; [*of skirts*] bruissement *m*, froufrou *m* **2** VT **a** [+ *whip, cane*] faire siffler **b** (: = *beat, cane*) administrer *or* donner des coups de trique à **3** VI [*cane, whip*] siffler, cingler l'air; [*water*] bruire; [*long grass*] frémir, bruire; [*skirts*] bruire, froufrouter **4** ADJ (*Brit** = *grand*) [*hotel, house etc*] chic *inv*; (*pej*) rupin: **b** (*US** = *effeminate*) efféminé

swishy: ['swɪʃɪ] ADJ **a** (*Brit* = *smart*) chic *inv*; (*pej*) rupin: **b** (*US* = *effeminate*) efféminé

Swiss [swɪs] **1** N (*pl inv*) Suisse *m*, Suisse(sse) *f* **2** **the Swiss** NPL les Suisses *mpl* **3** ADJ (*gen*) suisse; [*ambassador, embassy*] de Suisse **4** COMP ▶ **Swiss cheese** N gruyère *ou* emmenthal; (*esp US hum*) **her argument has more holes than ~ cheese** son argument ne tient pas debout ▶ **Swiss cheese plant** N monstera *f* ▶ **Swiss-French** ADJ (= *from French-speaking Switzerland*) suisse romand ♦ N (= *person*) Suisse *mf* romand(e); (= *language*) français *m* de Suisse, suisse *m* romand ▶ **Swiss-German** ADJ (= *from German-speaking Switzerland*) suisse allemand ♦ N (= *person*) Suisse *mf* allemand(e); (= *language*) suisse *m* allemand ▶ **the Swiss Guards** NPL la garde suisse, les suisses *mpl* ▶ **Swiss roll** N (*Brit Culin*) gâteau *m* roulé ▶ **Swiss steak** N (*US Culin*) steak fariné et braisé aux tomates et aux oignons

switch [swɪtʃ] **1** N **a** (*Elec*) (*gen*) bouton *m* électrique, commande *f* (*esp Tech*); (*for lights*) interrupteur *m*, commutateur *m*; [*of car*] (*also* **ignition ~**) contact *m*; (*Elec*) **the ~ was on/off** le bouton était sur la position ouvert/fermé, c'était allumé/éteint

b (*Rail* = *points*) aiguille *f*, aiguillage *m* **c** (= *transfer*) [*of opinion*] (*gen*) changement *m*; (*radical*) revirement *m*, retournement *m*; [*of allegiance*] changement *m*; [*of funds*] transfert *m* (**from** de, **to** en faveur de); **his ~ to Labour** son revirement en faveur des travaillistes; (*Bridge: in bidding*) **the ~ to hearts/ clubs** (le changement de couleur et) le passage à cœur/trèfle; **the ~ of the 8.30 from platform four** le changement de voie du train de 8h 30 attendu au quai numéro quatre; **the ~ of the aircraft from Heathrow to Gatwick because of fog** le détournement sur Gatwick à cause du brouillard de l'avion attendu à Heathrow

d (= *stick*) baguette *f*; (= *cane*) canne *f*; (= *riding crop*) cravache *f*; (= *whip*) fouet *m* **e** [*of hair*] postiche *m*

2 VT **a** (= *transfer*) [+ *one's support, allegiance, attention*] reporter (**from** de, **to** sur); (*Ind*) **to ~ production to another factory** transférer la production dans une autre usine; (*Ind*) **to ~ production to another model** (*cesser de produire l'ancien modèle et*) se mettre à produire un nouveau modèle; **to ~ the conversation to another subject** détourner la conversation, changer de sujet de conversation **b** (= *exchange*) échanger (**A for B** A contre B, **sth with sb** qch avec qn); (*also* ~ **over,** ~ **round**) [+ *two objects, letters in word, figures in column*] intervertir, permuter; (= *rearrange: also* ~ **round**) [+ *books, objects*] changer de place; **we had to ~ taxis when the first broke down** nous avons dû changer de taxi quand le premier est tombé en panne; **to ~ plans** changer de projet; **we have ~ed all the furniture round** nous avons changé tous les meubles de place **c** (*Rail*) aiguiller (**to** sur) **d** (= *change*) **to ~ the oven to "low"** mettre le four sur « doux »; **to ~ the radio/TV to another programme** changer de station/de chaîne → **switch back, switch on e** **to ~ the grass with one's cane** cingler l'herbe avec sa canne; **the cow ~ed her tail** la vache fouettait l'air de sa queue; **he ~ed it out of my hand** il me l'a arraché de la main

3 VI **a** (= *transfer: also* ~ **over**) **Paul ~ed (over) to Conservative** Paul a voté conservateur cette fois; **we ~ed (over) to oil central heating** (nous avons changé et) nous avons maintenant fait installer le chauffage central au mazout; **many have ~ed (over) to teaching** beaucoup se sont recyclés dans l'enseignement **b** [*tail*] battre l'air

4 COMP ▶ **switch-car** N (*for gangster: in escape etc*) voiture-relais *f* ▶ **switch hit** VI (*Baseball*) frapper la balle indifféremment de la main droite ou de la main gauche ▶ **switch-hitter** N (*Baseball*) batteur *m* ambidextre; (*US** = *bisexual*) bisexuel(le) *m(f)*

▶**switch back** **1** VI (*to original plan, product, allegiance*) revenir, retourner (**to** à); (*Rad, TV*) **to ~ back to the other programme** remettre l'autre émission **2** VT SEP **to ~ the oven back to "low"** remettre le four sur « doux »; **to ~ the light back on** rallumer; **to ~ the heater/oven back on** rallumer le radiateur/le four **3** **~back** N, ADJ → **switchback**

▶**switch off** **1** VI **a** (*Elec*) éteindre; (*Rad, TV*) éteindre *or* fermer le poste; (= *lose interest, unwind*) décrocher*; (*fig*) **when the conversation is boring, he just ~es off*** quand la conversation l'ennuie, il décroche* **b** **to ~ off automatically** [*heater, oven etc*] s'éteindre tout seul *or* automatiquement **2** VT SEP [+ *electricity, gas*] éteindre, fermer; [+ *radio, television, heater*] éteindre; [+ *alarm clock, burglar alarm*] arrêter; **to ~ off the light** éteindre (la lumière); (*Rad, TV*) **he ~ed the programme off** il a éteint (le poste); **to ~ off the engine** [*of car*] couper *or* arrêter le moteur; **the oven ~es itself off** le four s'éteint automatiquement;

(*fig*) **he seems to be ~ed off*** **most of the time** il semble être à côté de ses pompes* la plupart du temps

► **switch on** [1] VI [a] (*Elec*) allumer ; (*Rad, TV*) allumer le poste [b] **to ~ on automatically** [*heater, oven etc*] s'allumer tout seul *or* automatiquement [2] VT SEP [+ *gas, electricity*] allumer ; [+ *water supply*] ouvrir ; [+ *radio, television, heater*] allumer, brancher ; [+ *engine, machine*] mettre en marche ; **to ~ on the light** allumer (la lumière) ; (*fig*) **his music ~es me on*** sa musique me branche* ; (*fig*) **to be ~ed on*** (= *up-to-date*), être dans le vent *or* à la page ; (*by drugs*) planer* ; (*sexually*) être excité

► **switch over** [1] VI [a] = **switch 3a** [b] (*TV, Rad*) changer de chaîne/de station ; **to ~ over to the other programme** mettre l'autre chaîne/station [2] VT SEP [a] → **switch 2b** [b] (*TV, Rad*) **to ~ the programme over** changer de chaîne/de station [3] **~over** N → **switchover**

► **switch round** [1] VI [*two people*] changer de place (l'un avec l'autre) [2] VT SEP → **switch 3b**

switchback ['swɪtʃbæk] [1] N (*Brit = road: also at fair*) montagnes *fpl* russes [2] ADJ (= *up and down*) tout en montées et descentes ; (= *zigzag*) en épingles à cheveux

switchblade ['swɪtʃbleɪd] N (*US: also ~ knife*) couteau *m* à cran d'arrêt

switchboard ['swɪtʃbɔːd] [1] N (*Elec*) tableau *m* de distribution ; (*Telec*) standard *m* [2] COMP ► **switchboard operator** N (*Telec*) standardiste *mf*

switcheroo: [,swɪtʃə'ruː] N (*esp US*) volte-face *f inv*, revirement *m* ; **to pull a ~** faire volte-face, effectuer un revirement

switchgear ['swɪtʃgɪəʳ] N (*NonC: Elec*) appareillage *m* de commutation

switchman ['swɪtʃmən] N (*pl* -**men**) (*Rail*) aiguilleur *m*

switchover ['swɪtʃəʊvə] N **the ~ from A to B** le passage de A à B ; **the ~ to the metric system** l'adoption *f* du système métrique

switchyard ['swɪtʃjɑːd] N (*US Rail*) gare *f* de triage

Swithin ['swɪðɪn] N Swithin *or* Swithun *m* ; **St ~'s Day** (jour *m* de) la Saint-Swithin (*15 juillet : pluie de Saint-Swithin, pluie pour longtemps*)

Switzerland ['swɪtsələnd] N la Suisse ; **French-/German-/Italian-speaking ~** la Suisse romande/allemande/italienne

swivel ['swɪvl] [1] N pivot *m*, tourillon *m* [2] VI (*also ~ round*) faire pivoter, faire tourner [3] VI [*object*] pivoter, tourner [4] COMP [*seat, mounting etc*] pivotant, tournant ► **swivel chair** N fauteuil *m* pivotant

► **swivel round** [1] VI pivoter [2] VT SEP = **swivel 2**

swizz: [swɪz] N (*Brit = swindle*) escroquerie *f* ; (= *disappointment*) **what a ~!** on est eu !*, on s'est fait avoir !*

swizzle ['swɪzl] [1] N (*Brit*) = **swizz** [2] COMP ► **swizzle stick** N fouet *m*

swollen ['swəʊlən] [1] VB *ptp of* **swell** [2] ADJ [*limb, foot, finger, face, jaw*] enflé ; [*eye, breasts, tissue, organ*] gonflé ; [*stomach*] ballonné ; [*river, lake, stream*] en crue ; [*population*] accru ; **~ with blood/pus** etc plein de sang/pus etc ; **eyes ~ with tears** *or* **weeping** yeux gonflés de larmes ; **the river was ~ with rain** la rivière était grossie par les crues ; **the capital is ~ with refugees** la capitale est envahie par les réfugiés ; **to have ~ glands** avoir (une inflammation) des ganglions ; (*Brit fig*) **to get a ~ head** attraper la grosse tête* → **swell 3** COMP ► **swollen-headed*** ADJ = **swellheaded**

swoon [swuːn] [1] VI († *or hum* = *faint*) se pâmer† (*also hum*) ; (*fig*) se pâmer d'admiration (**over sb/sth** devant qn/qch) [2] N († *or hum*) pâmoison *f* ; **in a ~** en pâmoison

swoop [swuːp] [1] N [*of bird, plane*] descente *f* en piqué ; (= *attack*) attaque *f* en piqué (**on**

sur) ; [*of police etc*] descente *f*, rafle *f* (**on** dans) ; **at** *or* **in one (fell) ~** d'un seul coup [2] VI (*also ~ down*) [*bird*] fondre, piquer ; [*aircraft*] descendre en piqué, piquer ; [*police etc*] faire une descente ; **the plane ~ed (down) low over the village** l'avion est descendu en piqué au-dessus du village ; **the eagle ~ed (down) on the rabbit** l'aigle a fondu *or* s'est abattu sur le lapin ; **the soldiers ~ed (down) on the terrorists** les soldats ont fondu sur les terroristes

swoosh* [swuːʃ] [1] N [*of water*] bruissement *m* ; [*of stick etc through air*] sifflement *m* ; [*of tyres in rain*] glissement *m* [2] VI [*water*] bruire ; **he went ~ing through the mud** il est passé avec un bruit de boue qui gicle *or* en faisant gicler bruyamment la boue

swop [swɒp] N = **swap**

sword [sɔːd] [1] N épée *f* ; **to wear a ~** porter l'épée ; **to put sb to the ~** passer qn au fil de l'épée ; **to put up one's ~** rengainer son épée, remettre son épée au fourreau ; (*lit, fig*) **to cross ~s with sb** croiser le fer avec qn ; **those that live by the ~ die by the ~** quiconque se servira de l'épée périra par l'épée ; (*fig*) **to turn** *or* **beat one's ~s into ploughshares** forger des socs de ses épées [2] COMP [*scar, wound*] d'épée ► **sword and sorcery** N (*Literat, Cine etc*) genre de romans, films ou jeux électroniques mêlant barbarie et sorcellerie dans un cadre moyenâgeux ► **sword arm** N bras *m* droit ► **sword dance** N danse *f* du sabre ► **sword-point** N **at ~-point** à la pointe de l'épée ► **sword-swallower** N avaleur *m* de sabres

swordfish ['sɔːdfɪʃ] N (*pl inv*) poisson-épée *m*, espadon *m*

swordplay ['sɔːdpleɪ] N **there was a lot of ~ in the film** il y avait beaucoup de duels *or* ça ferraillait dur* dans le film

swordsman ['sɔːdzmən] N (*pl* -**men**) épéiste *m* ; **to be a good ~** être une fine lame

swordsmanship ['sɔːdzmənʃɪp] N (habileté *f* dans le) maniement *m* de l'épée

swordstick ['sɔːdstɪk] N canne *f* à épée

swore [swɔːʳ] VB *pt of* **swear**

sworn [swɔːn] [1] VB *ptp of* **swear** [2] ADJ [*evidence, statement*] donné sous serment ; [*enemy*] juré ; [*ally, friend*] à la vie et à la mort

swot* [swɒt] (*Brit*) [1] N (*pej*) bûcheur *m*, -euse *f* [2] VT bûcher*, potasser* [3] VI bûcher*, potasser* ; **to ~ for an exam** bachoter ; **to ~ at maths** bûcher* *or* potasser* ses maths

► **swot up*** VI, VT SEP **to ~ up (on) sth** potasser* qch

swotting* ['swɒtɪŋ] N bachotage *m* ; **to do some ~** bosser*, bachoter

swum [swʌm] VB *ptp of* **swim**

swung [swʌŋ] [1] VB *pt, ptp of* **swing** [2] COMP ► **swung dash** N (*Typ*) tilde *m*

sybarite ['sɪbəraɪt] N sybarite *mf*

sybaritic [,sɪbə'rɪtɪk] ADJ sybarite

sycamore ['sɪkəmɔːʳ] N sycomore *m*, faux platane *m*

sycophancy ['sɪkəfənsɪ] N flagornerie *f*

sycophant ['sɪkəfənt] N flagorneur *m*, -euse *f*

sycophantic [,sɪkə'fæntɪk] ADJ [*person*] servile, flagorneur ; [*behaviour, laughter*] obséquieux

Sydney ['sɪdnɪ] N Sydney

syllabary ['sɪləbərɪ] N syllabaire *m*

syllabi ['sɪlə,baɪ] NPL *of* **syllabus**

syllabic [sɪ'læbɪk] ADJ syllabique

syllabification [sɪ,læbɪfɪ'keɪʃən] N syllabation *f*

syllabify [sɪ'læbɪfaɪ] VT décomposer en syllabes

syllable ['sɪləbl] N syllabe *f* ; **to explain sth in words of one ~** expliquer qch en petit nègre

syllabub ['sɪləbʌb] N ≈ sabayon *m*

syllabus ['sɪləbəs] N (*pl* **syllabuses** *or* **syllabi**)

(*Scol, Univ*) programme *m* ; **on the ~** au programme

syllogism ['sɪlədʒɪzəm] N syllogisme *m*

syllogistic [,sɪlə'dʒɪstɪk] ADJ syllogistique

syllogize ['sɪlədʒaɪz] VI raisonner par syllogismes

sylph [sɪlf] N sylphe *m* ; (*fig = woman*) sylphide *f*

sylphlike ['sɪlflaɪk] ADJ [*woman*] gracile, qui a une taille de sylphide ; [*figure*] de sylphide

sylvan ['sɪlvən] ADJ (*liter*) sylvestre

Sylvester [sɪl'vestəʳ] N Sylvestre *m*

Sylvia ['sɪlvɪə] N Sylvie *f*

sylviculture ['sɪlvɪkʌltʃəʳ] N sylviculture *f*

symbiosis [,sɪmbɪ'əʊsɪs] N (*also fig*) symbiose *f*

symbiotic [,sɪmbɪ'ɒtɪk] ADJ (*lit, fig*) symbiotique

symbol ['sɪmbəl] N symbole *m*

symbolic(al) [sɪm'bɒlɪk(əl)] ADJ symbolique

symbolically [sɪm'bɒlɪkəlɪ] ADV symboliquement ; **~ important** important sur le plan symbolique

symbolism ['sɪmbəlɪzəm] N symbolisme *m*

symbolist ['sɪmbəlɪst] ADJ, N symboliste *mf*

symbolization [,sɪmbəlaɪ'zeɪʃən] N symbolisation *f*

symbolize ['sɪmbəlaɪz] VT symboliser

symmetric(al) [sɪ'metrɪk(əl)] ADJ (*gen, Geom, Math*) symétrique

symmetrically [sɪ'metrɪkəlɪ] ADV symétriquement, avec symétrie

symmetry ['sɪmɪtrɪ] N symétrie *f*

sympathetic [,sɪmpə'θetɪk] ADJ [a] (= *showing concern*) [*person, smile*] compatissant ; **to be a ~ listener** écouter avec compassion ; **they were ~ but could not help** ils ont compati mais n'ont rien pu faire pour aider ; **to be/feel ~ towards sb** montrer/ressentir de la compassion pour qn [b] (= *kind*) [*person*] bien disposé, bienveillant ; [*response*] favorable [c] (*Literat, Theat, Cine = likeable*) [*character*] sympathique [d] (*Anat, Physiol*) sympathique ; **the ~ nervous system** le système nerveux sympathique

sympathetically [,sɪmpə'θetɪkəlɪ] ADV [a] (= *compassionately*) avec compassion [b] (= *kindly, favourably*) [*listen, consider, portray*] avec bienveillance ; **to be ~ disposed** *or* **inclined to sb/sth** être favorablement disposé envers qn/qch ; **the house has been ~ restored** la maison a été restaurée en respectant son caractère d'origine [c] (*Anat, Physiol*) par sympathie

sympathize ['sɪmpəθaɪz] VI compatir ; **I do ~ with you!** je compatis !, comme je vous comprends ! ; **her cousin called to ~** sa cousine est venue témoigner sa sympathie ; **I ~ with you in your grief** je m'associe *or* je compatis à votre douleur ; **I ~ with you** *or* **what you feel** *or* **what you say** je comprends votre point de vue

sympathizer ['sɪmpəθaɪzəʳ] N [a] (*in adversity*) personne *f* qui compatit ; **he was surrounded by ~s** il était entouré de personnes qui lui témoignaient leur sympathie [b] (*fig: esp Pol*) sympathisant(e) *m(f)* (**with** de)

▼ **sympathy** ['sɪmpəθɪ] [1] N [a] (= *pity*) compassion *f* ; **to feel ~ for** éprouver *or* avoir de la compassion pour ; **to show one's ~ for sb** témoigner sa sympathie à *or* pour qn ; **please accept my (deepest) ~** *or* **sympathies** veuillez agréer mes condoléances [b] (= *fellow feeling*) solidarité *f* (**for** avec) ; **the sympathies of the crowd were with him** il avait le soutien de la foule, la foule était pour lui ; **I have no ~ with lazy people** je n'ai aucune indulgence pour les gens qui sont paresseux ; **to be in ~ with the workers** il est du côté des ouvriers ; **I am in ~ with your proposals but ...** je suis en accord avec *or* je ne désapprouve pas vos propositions mais ... ; **to come out** *or* **strike in ~**

with sb faire grève en solidarité avec qn [2] COMP ► **sympathy strike** N (Ind) grève f de solidarité

symphonic [sɪm'fɒnɪk] [1] ADJ [music, work, piece] symphonique; **a ~ composer** un compositeur de musique symphonique [2] COMP ► **symphonic poem** N poème m symphonique

symphony ['sɪmfənɪ] [1] N symphonie f [2] COMP [concert, orchestra] symphonique ► **symphony writer** N symphoniste mf

symposium [sɪm'pəʊzɪəm] N (pl **symposiums** or **symposia** [sɪm'pəʊzɪə]) (all senses) symposium m

symptom ['sɪmptəm] N (Med, fig) symptôme m, indice m

symptomatic [,sɪmptə'mætɪk] ADJ symptomatique (**of sth** de qch)

synaesthesia, **synesthesia** (US) [,sɪnəs-'θiːzɪə] N (NonC) synesthésie f

synagogue ['sɪnəgɒg] N synagogue f

synapse ['saɪnæps] N (Anat) synapse f

sync* [sɪŋk] N (ABBR = **synchronization**) **in ~** bien synchronisé, en harmonie; (fig: of people) **they are in ~** ils sont en harmonie, le courant passe; **out of ~** mal synchronisé, déphasé

synchro* ['sɪŋkrəʊ] [1] N synchroniseur m [2] COMP ► **synchro gearbox** N boîte f de vitesses synchronisées

synchromesh [,sɪŋkrəʊ'meʃ] (Aut) [1] N synchroniseur m [2] COMP ► **synchromesh gearbox** N boîte f de vitesses synchronisées

synchronic [sɪŋ'krɒnɪk] ADJ (gen) synchrone; (Ling) synchronique

synchronicity [,sɪŋkrə'nɪsɪtɪ] N synchronisme m

synchronism ['sɪŋkrənɪzəm] N synchronisme m

synchronization [,sɪŋkrənaɪ'zeɪʃən] N synchronisation f

synchronize ['sɪŋkrənaɪz] [1] VT synchroniser [2] VI [events] se passer or avoir lieu simultanément; [footsteps etc] être synchronisés; **to ~ with sth** être synchrone avec qch, se produire en même temps que qch [3] COMP ► **synchronized swimming** N (Sport) natation f synchronisée

synchronous ['sɪŋkrənəs] ADJ synchrone

syncline ['sɪŋklaɪn] N synclinal m

syncopate ['sɪŋkəpeɪt] VT syncoper

syncopation [,sɪŋkə'peɪʃən] N (Mus) syncope f

syncope ['sɪŋkəpɪ] N (Ling, Med) syncope f

syncretism ['sɪŋkrɪtɪzəm] N syncrétisme m

syndic ['sɪndɪk] N (= government official) administrateur m, syndic m; (Brit Univ) membre m d'un comité administratif

syndicalism ['sɪndɪkəlɪzəm] N syndicalisme m

syndicalist ['sɪndɪkəlɪst] ADJ, N syndicaliste mf

syndicate ['sɪndɪkɪt] [1] N [a] (Comm etc) syndicat m, coopérative f [b] [of criminals] gang m, association f de malfaiteurs [c] (US Press) agence spécialisée dans la vente par abonnements d'articles, de reportages etc [2] ['sɪndɪkeɪt] VT [a] (Press: esp US) [+ article etc] vendre or publier par l'intermédiaire d'un syndicat de distribution; (Rad, TV) [+ programme] distribuer sous licence; (Press) **~d columnist** journaliste mf d'agence [b] (Fin) **to ~ a loan** former un consortium de prêt; **~d loan** prêt m consortial [c] [+ workers] syndiquer

syndrome ['sɪndrəʊm] N (lit, fig) syndrome m

synecdoche [sɪ'nɛkdəkɪ] N synecdoque f

synergism ['sɪnə,dʒɪsəm] N synergie f

synergy ['sɪnədʒɪ] N synergie f

synesthesia [,sɪnəs'θiːzɪə] N (US) = **synaesthesia**

synod ['sɪnəd] N synode m

synonym ['sɪnənɪm] N synonyme m

synonymous [sɪ'nɒnɪməs] ADJ (lit, fig) synonyme (**with sth** de qch)

synonymy [sɪ'nɒnəmɪ] N synonymie f

synopsis [sɪ'nɒpsɪs] N (pl **synopses** [sɪ'nɒpsiːz]) résumé m, précis m; (Cine, Theat) synopsis m or f

synoptic [sɪ'nɒptɪk] ADJ synoptique

synovial [saɪ'nəʊvɪəl] ADJ (Anat) synovial

syntactic(al) [sɪn'tæktɪk(əl)] ADJ syntaxique

syntagm ['sɪntæm] (pl **syntagms**), **syntagma** [sɪn'tægmə] (pl **syntagmata** [sɪn'tægmətə]) N syntagme m

syntagmatic [,sɪntæg'mætɪk] ADJ syntagmatique

syntax ['sɪntæks] N syntaxe f; (Comput) **~ error** erreur f de syntaxe

synthesis ['sɪnθəsɪs] N (pl **syntheses** ['sɪnθəsiːz]) synthèse f

synthesize ['sɪnθəsaɪz] VT (= combine) synthétiser; (= produce) produire synthétiquement or par une synthèse, faire la synthèse de

synthesizer ['sɪnθəsaɪzəʳ] N synthétiseur m → **speech, voice**

synthetic [sɪn'θetɪk] [1] ADJ [a] (= man-made) [material, chemical, drug, fibre] synthétique [b] (pej = false) [person, behaviour, emotion, taste] artificiel [2] N (gen) produit m synthétique; (Tex) **~s** fibres fpl synthétiques

syphilis ['sɪfɪlɪs] N syphilis f

syphilitic [,sɪfɪ'lɪtɪk] ADJ, N syphilitique mf

syphon ['saɪfən] = **siphon**

Syria ['sɪrɪə] N la Syrie

Syrian ['sɪrɪən] [1] ADJ (gen) syrien; [ambassador, embassy] de Syrie [2] N Syrien(ne) m(f)

syringe [sɪ'rɪndʒ] [1] N seringue f [2] VT seringuer

syrup ['sɪrəp] N (also Med) sirop m; (also **golden ~**) mélasse f raffinée

syrupy ['sɪrəpɪ] ADJ (lit, fig) sirupeux

system ['sɪstəm] [1] N [a] (= structured whole: gen, Anat, Comput, Ling, Med, Pol, Sci, Tech) système m; **a political/economic/social ~** un système politique/économique/social; **nervous ~** système m nerveux; **digestive ~** appareil m digestif; **the railway ~** le réseau de chemin de fer; **the Social Security ~** le régime de la Sécurité sociale; (Comm) **the Bell ~** la compagnie or le réseau Bell; [of rivers] **the St. Lawrence ~** le système fluvial or le réseau hydrographique du Saint-Laurent; (Geog) **the urban ~** la trame urbaine; **it's all ~s go*** ça turbine (un max)ǃ → **feudal** [b] (gen = method, type, process) système m; **new teaching ~s** nouveaux systèmes mpl d'enseignement [c] (= the body) organisme m; **her ~ will reject it** son organisme le rejettera; **it was a shock to his ~** cela a été une secousse pour son organisme, cela a ébranlé son organisme; (fig) (gen) **to get sth out of one's ~** trouver un exutoire à qch; **let him get it out of his ~*** (anger) laisse-le décharger sa bile; (hobby, passion) laisse-le faire — ça lui passera; **he can't get her out of his ~*** il n'arrive pas à l'oublier [d] (= established order) **the ~** le système; **to get round** or **beat** or **buck the ~** trouver le joint (fig); **down with the ~!** à bas le système! [e] (Comput) système m → **operating** [f] (NonC = order) méthode f (NonC); **to lack ~** manquer de méthode

[2] COMP ► **system disk** N (Comput) disque m système ► **system operator** N (Comput) opérateur m du système, serveur m ► **systems analysis** N analyse f fonctionnelle ► **systems analyst** N analyste mf en système ► **systems desk** N pupitre m ► **systems engineer** N ingénieur m système ► **systems programmer** N programmeur m d'étude ► **systems software** N logiciel m de base or d'exploitation

systematic [,sɪstə'mætɪk] ADJ (gen) systématique; [person] méthodique

systematically [,sɪstə'mætɪkəlɪ] ADV systématiquement

systematization [,sɪstəmətaɪ'zeɪʃən] N systématisation f

systematize ['sɪstəmətaɪz] VT systématiser

systemic [sɪ'stemɪk] ADJ [a] (gen) du système; (Anat) du système, de l'organisme; [insecticide] systémique; **~ circulation** circulation f générale; **~ infection** infection f généralisée [b] (Ling) systémique

systole ['sɪstəlɪ] N systole f

T

T, t [tiː] [1] N (= letter) T, t m; **T for Tommy** ≈ T comme Thérèse; **that's it to a T*** c'est exactement cela; **he'd got everything down to a T*** il avait pensé à tout; **it fits him to a T*** ça lui va comme un gant → **dot** [2] COMP ► **T-bar** N (Ski: also **T-bar lift**) téléski m à archets ► **T-bone** N (Culin: also **T-bone steak**) steak m avec un os en T ► **T-junction** N intersection f en T ► **T-shaped** ADJ en forme de T, en équerre ► **T-shirt** N T-shirt or tee-shirt m ► **T-square** N équerre f en T ► **T-stop** N (Phot) diaphragme m

TA [tiːˈeɪ] N [a] (Brit Mil) (ABBR = **Territorial Army**) → **territorial** [b] (US Univ) (ABBR = **teaching assistant**) → **teaching**

ta* [tɑː] EXCL (Brit) merci!

tab¹ [tæb] N (= part of garment) patte f; (= loop on garment etc) attache f; (= label) étiquette f; (on shoelace) ferret m; (= marker: on file etc) onglet m; (esp US* = café check) addition f, note f; **to keep ~s** or **a ~ on*** [+ person] avoir or tenir à l'œil*; [+ thing] garder un œil sur*; (lit, fig) **to pick up the ~*** payer la note or l'addition

tab² [tæb] N [a] (Comput) (ABBR = **tabulator**) **~ key** touche f de tabulation [b] (Drugs*) pilule f, comprimé m [c] ABBR = **tablet a**

tabard ['tæbəd] N tabard m

Tabasco® [təˈbæskəʊ] N Tabasco® m

tabby ['tæbɪ] N (also **~ cat**) chat(te) m(f) tigré(e) or moucheté(e)

tabernacle ['tæbənækl] N tabernacle m; (Rel) **the Tabernacle** le tabernacle

table ['teɪbl] [1] N [a] (= furniture, food on it) table f; (= people at table) tablée f, table f; **ironing/bridge/garden ~** table f à repasser/de bridge/de jardin; **at ~** à table; **to sit down to ~** se mettre à table; **to lay** or **set the ~** mettre la table or le couvert; **to clear the ~** débarrasser la table, desservir; **the whole ~ laughed** toute la tablée or la table a ri; (Parl) **to lay sth on the ~** remettre or ajourner qch; (Parl) **the bill lies on the ~** la discussion du projet de loi a été ajournée; (fig) **to put sth on the ~** (Brit = propose) avancer qch, mettre qch sur la table; (US = post-pone) ajourner or remettre qch; (fig) **he slipped me £5 under the ~*** il m'a passé 5 livres de la main à la main; (fig) **he was nearly under the ~** un peu plus et il roulait sous la table*; **to turn the ~s** renverser les rôles, retourner la situation (**on sb** aux dépens de qn) [b] [of facts, statistics] table f (also Math); [of prices, fares, names] liste f; (Sport: also **league ~**) classement m; **~ of contents** table f des matières; (Math) **the two-times ~** la table de (multiplication par) deux; (Sport) **we are in fifth place in the ~** nous sommes classés cinquièmes, nous sommes cinquièmes au classement → **log²** [c] (Geog) = **tableland** [d] (Rel) **the Tables of the Law** les Tables fpl de la Loi

[2] VT [a] (Brit Admin, Parl = present) [+ motion etc] présenter, soumettre [b] (US Admin, Parl = postpone) [+ motion etc] ajourner; **to ~ a bill** reporter la discussion d'un projet de loi [c] (= tabulate) dresser une liste or une table de; [+ results] classifier

[3] COMP [wine, grapes, knife, lamp] de table ► **Table Bay** N (Geog) la baie de la Table ► **table dancing** N numéro m de strip-tease sur commande ► **table d'hôte** ADJ à prix fixe ♦ (pl **tables d'hôte**) table f d'hôte, repas m à prix fixe ► **table football** N baby-foot m ► **table leg** N pied m de table ► **table linen** N linge m de table ► **table manners** NPL **he has good ~ manners** il sait se tenir à table ► **Table Mountain** N (Geog) la montagne de la Table ► **table napkin** N serviette f (de table) ► **table runner** N chemin m de table ► **table salt** N sel m fin ► **table talk** N (NonC) menus propos mpl ► **table tennis** N ping-pong m, tennis m de table ♦ COMP de ping-pong ► **table-tennis player** N joueur m, -euse f de ping-pong, pongiste mf ► **table turning** N (NonC) spiritisme m, tables fpl tournantes

tableau ['tæbləʊ] N (pl **tableaux** or **tableaus** ['tæbləʊz]) (Theat) tableau m vivant; (fig) tableau m

tablecloth ['teɪblklɒθ] N nappe f

tableland ['teɪbllænd] N (Geog) (haut) plateau m

tablemat ['teɪblmæt] N (of linen etc) napperon m; (heat-resistant) dessous-de-plat m inv

tablespoon ['teɪblspuːn] N cuiller f de service; (= measurement: also **~ful**) cuillerée f à soupe, ≈ 15 ml

tablet ['tæblɪt] N [a] (Pharm) comprimé m, cachet m; (for sucking) pastille f [b] (: stone: inscribed) plaque f (commémorative); (Hist: of wax, slate etc) tablette f [c] [of chocolate] tablette f; **~ of soap** savonnette f [d] (Comput) tablette f

tabletop ['teɪbltɒp] N dessus m de table

tableware ['teɪblwɛəʳ] N (NonC) vaisselle f

tabloid ['tæblɔɪd] [1] N (Press: also **~ newspaper**) tabloïd(e) m, quotidien m populaire [2] ADJ (also **in ~ form**) en raccourci, condensé

▶ TABLOIDS, BROADSHEETS

Il existe deux formats de journaux en Grande-Bretagne : le grand format du type « Le Figaro » en France (**broadsheet**), qui caractérise la presse de qualité (« Times », « Guardian », « Independent », « Daily Telegraph ») et les tabloïdes qui se distinguent par leurs gros titres accrocheurs, leurs articles courts, leurs nombreuses photographies, leurs opinions tranchées et leur goût pour les histoires à scandale. Parmi les titres représentatifs de cette presse à sensation, on peut citer le « Sun », le « Daily Mirror », le « Daily Express » et le « Daily Mail ».

Aux États-Unis, le principal quotidien **broadsheet** est l'édition nationale du « New York

---

Times ». Les tabloïdes américains les plus connus comprennent le « New York Daily News » et le « Chicago Sun-Times ».

---

taboo [təˈbuː] [1] ADJ, N (Rel, fig) tabou m [2] VT proscrire, interdire

tabor ['teɪbəʳ] N tambourin m

tabu [təˈbuː] = **taboo**

tabular ['tæbjʊləʳ] ADJ tabulaire

tabulate ['tæbjʊleɪt] VT [+ facts, figures] mettre sous forme de table; [+ results] classifier; (Typ) mettre en colonnes

tabulation [ˌtæbjʊˈleɪʃən] N [a] (NonC = act) [of information, results] disposition f or présentation f en tableaux [b] (= table) tableau m

tabulator ['tæbjʊleɪtəʳ] N [of typewriter] tabulateur m

tache* [tæʃ] N (Brit) moustache f, bacchantes* fpl

tacheometer [ˌtækɪˈɒmɪtəʳ] N tachéomètre m

tachograph ['tækəɡrɑːf] N (Brit) tachygraphe m

tachometer [tæˈkɒmɪtəʳ] N tachymètre m

tachycardia [ˌtækɪˈkɑːdɪə] N tachycardie f

tachycardiac [ˌtækɪˈkɑːdɪæk] ADJ tachycardique

tachymeter [tæˈkɪmɪtəʳ] N tachéomètre m

tacit ['tæsɪt] ADJ [approval, agreement, admission, understanding] tacite; [knowledge] implicite

tacitly ['tæsɪtlɪ] ADV tacitement

taciturn ['tæsɪtɜːn] ADJ taciturne

taciturnity [ˌtæsɪˈtɜːnɪtɪ] N taciturnité f

Tacitus ['tæsɪtəs] N Tacite m

tack [tæk] [1] N [a] (for wood, linoleum, carpet) broquette f; (for upholstery) semence f; (US: also **thumbtack**) punaise f [b] (Naut) point m de bâti [c] (Naut) bord m, bordée f; **to make a ~** faire or courir or tirer un bord or une bordée; **to be on a port/starboard ~** être bâbord/tribord amures; (fig) **to change ~** changer de cap; **to be on the right/wrong ~** être sur la bonne/mauvaise voie; **to try another ~** essayer une autre tactique [d] (NonC: for horse) sellerie f (articles) [e] (NonC:* = rubbishy things) objets mpl kitsch [2] VT [a] (also **~ down**) [+ wood, lino, carpet] clouer [b] (Sewing) faufiler, bâtir [3] VI (Naut = make a tack) faire or courir or tirer un bord or une bordée; **they ~ed back to the harbour** ils sont rentrés au port en louvoyant

► **tack down** VT SEP (Sewing) maintenir en place au point de bâti → **tack 2a**

► **tack on** VT SEP [a] (Sewing) bâtir, appliquer au point de bâti [b] (fig) ajouter (après coup) (**to** à)

tackiness ['tækɪnɪs] N (NonC) [a] (* = bad taste) [of person, place, film, clothes, remark] vulgarité f [b] (= stickiness) [of glue, paint, surface] viscosité f

tacking ['tækɪŋ] (Sewing) [1] N bâtissage m, faufilure f; **to take out the ~ from sth** défaufiler qch [2] COMP ► **tacking stitch** N point m de bâti

▼ tackle ['tækl] [1] N [a] (NonC) (Naut = ropes, pulleys) appareil m de levage; (gen = gear, equipment) équipement m; **fishing ~** matériel m de pêche [b] (Ftbl, Hockey, Rugby etc = action)

tac(k)le *m*; (*US Ftbl = player*) plaqueur *m* **2** VT **a** (*physically: Ftbl, Hockey, Rugby etc*) saisir à bras-le-corps [+ *thief, intruder*] saisir à bras-le-corps **b** (*verbally*) **I'll ~ him about it at once** je vais lui en parler or lui en dire deux mots tout de suite; **I ~d him about what he had done** je l'ai questionné sur ce qu'il avait fait **c** [+ *task*] s'attaquer à; [+ *problem, question, subject*] aborder, s'attaquer à;* [+ *meal, food*] attaquer*; **he ~d Hebrew on his own** il s'est mis à l'hébreu tout seul

tackroom ['tækrʊm] N sellerie *f*

tacky ['tækɪ] ADJ **a** (* = *tasteless*) [*person, place, film, clothes, remark*] vulgaire **b** (= *sticky*) [*glue*] qui commence à prendre; [*paint, varnish*] pas tout à fait sec; [*surface*] poisseux, collant

taco ['tɑːkəʊ] N (*pl* **tacos**) taco *m*

tact [tækt] N (*NonC*) tact *m*, délicatesse *f*

tactful ['tæktfʊl] ADJ [*person, remark, behaviour*] plein de tact; [*silence*] diplomatique; [*hint, inquiry, reference*] discret (-ète *f*); **that wasn't a very ~ question** cette question n'était pas très diplomatique; **to be ~ (with sb/about sth)** faire preuve de tact (envers qn/à propos de qch); **she was too ~ to say what she thought** elle avait trop de tact pour dire ce qu'elle pensait

tactfully ['tæktfəlɪ] ADV avec tact; **as he so ~ puts it ...** comme il le dit avec tant de tact ...

tactfulness ['tæktfʊlnɪs] N = **tact**

tactic ['tæktɪk] N (*Mil, fig*) tactique *f*; (*NonC: Mil*) **~s** la tactique

tactical ['tæktɪkəl] **1** ADJ (*Mil, fig*) tactique; **a ~ plan** une stratégie; (*Sport*) **to play a brilliant ~ game** jouer avec une habileté tactique hors pair **2** COMP ► **tactical voting** N (*Brit*) vote *m* utile

tactically ['tæktɪkəlɪ] ADV (*Mil, fig*) [*important, disastrous*] d'un or du point de vue tactique, sur le plan tactique; [*use*] tactiquement; **to vote ~** voter utile

tactician [tæk'tɪʃən] N (*Mil, fig*) tacticien *m*

tactile ['tæktaɪl] ADJ **a** (= *physical*) [*person*] qui a le sens tactile développé **b** (= *pleasant to touch*) [*fabric*] agréable au toucher; **the ~ quality of textiles** le toucher des textiles **c** (*through touch*) [*sense, experience*] tactile

tactless ['tæktlɪs] ADJ [*person*] peu délicat, qui manque de tact; [*hint*] grossier; [*inquiry, reference*] indiscret (-ète *f*); [*answer*] qui manque de tact, peu diplomatique (*fig*) [*suggestion*] peu délicat

tactlessly ['tæktlɪslɪ] ADV [*behave*] de façon peu délicate, sans tact or délicatesse; [*say*] de façon peu délicate

tactlessness ['tæktlɪsnɪs] N manque *m* de tact

tad* [tæd] N **a ~ big/small** *etc* un chouïa* grand/petit *etc*

tadpole ['tædpəʊl] N têtard *m*

Tadzhik ['tɑːdʒɪk] **1** ADJ tadjik **2** N **a** Tadjik(e) *m(f)* **b** (*Ling*) tadjik *m*

Tadzhikistan [tɑːˌdʒɪkɪ'stɑːn] N le Tadjikistan

tae kwon do ['taɪ'kwɒn'dəʊ] N taekwondo *m*

taffeta ['tæfɪtə] N (*NonC*) taffetas *m*

taffrail ['tæfreɪl] N (*Naut*) couronnement *m*; (= *rail*) lisse *f* de couronnement

Taffy* ['tæfɪ] N (*also* **Jones**) sobriquet donné à un Gallois

taffy ['tæfɪ] N (*US*) bonbon *m* au caramel; (*Can*) tire *f* d'érable

tag [tæg] **1** N **a** [*of shoelace, cord etc*] ferret *m*; (*on garment etc*) patte *f*, marque *f*; (= *label: also fig*) étiquette *f*; (= *marker: on file etc*) onglet *m*; (= *surveillance device*) bracelet-émetteur *m* de surveillance électronique; **all uniforms must have name ~s** chaque uniforme doit être marqué au nom de son propriétaire → **price b** (= *quotation*) citation *f*; (= *cliché*) cliché *m*, lieu *m* commun; (= *catchword*) slogan *m*; (*Ling*) **~ (question)** question-tag *f* **c** (*NonC = game*) (jeu *m* du) chat *m*

2 VT **a** [+ *garment*] marquer; [+ *bag, box, file*] étiqueter; (*US* *fig*) [+ *car*] mettre un papillon* sur; [+ *driver*] mettre une contravention à **b** (* = *follow*) suivre; [*detective*] filer **c** (= *describe*) [+ *person*] appeler, étiqueter **3** COMP ► **tag day** N (*US*) journée *f* de vente d'insignes (*pour une œuvre*) ► **tag end** N [*of speech, performance, programme etc*] fin *f*; [*of goods for sale*] restes *mpl* ► **tag line** N [*of play*] dernière réplique *f*; [*of poem*] dernier vers *m*

► **tag along** VI suivre le mouvement*; **she left and the children ~ged along behind her** elle est partie et les enfants l'ont suivie; **the others came ~ging along behind** les autres traînaient derrière or étaient à la traîne derrière; **she usually ~s along (with us)** la plupart du temps elle vient avec nous

► **tag on*** **1** VI **to ~ on to sb** coller aux talons de qn*; **he came ~ging on behind** il la traînait derrière **2** VT SEP (*fig*) ajouter (après coup) (**to** à)

► **tag out** VT SEP (*Baseball*) mettre hors jeu

Tagalog [tə'gɑːlɒg] N (*Ling*) tagal *m*, tagalog *m*

tagboard ['tægbɔːd] N (*US*) carton *m* (pour étiquettes)

tagging ['tægɪŋ] N (*also* **electronic ~**: *in penal system*) étiquetage *m* électronique

tagliatelle [ˌtælja'telɪ, ˌtæglɪə'telɪ] N (*NonC*) tagliatelles *fpl*

tagmeme ['tægmiːm] N (*Ling*) tagmème *m*

tagmemics [tæg'miːmɪks] N (*Ling: NonC*) tagmémique *f*

Tagus ['teɪgəs] N Tage *m*

tahini [tɑː'hiːnɪ] N (*NonC*) crème *f* de sésame

Tahiti [tə'hiːtɪ] N Tahiti *f*; **in ~** à Tahiti

Tahitian [tə'hiːʃən] **1** ADJ tahitien **2** N **a** Tahitien(ne) *m(f)* **b** (*Ling*) tahitien *m*

t'ai chi (ch'uan) ['taɪdʒiː('tʃwɑːn)] N tai-chi(-chuan) *m*

tail [teɪl] **1** N **a** [*of animal, aircraft, comet, kite, procession, hair*] queue *f*; [*of shirt*] pan *m*; [*of coat*] basque *f*; [*of ski*] talon *m*; (*lit, fig*) **with his ~ between his legs** la queue entre les jambes; (*fig*) **to keep one's ~ up** ne pas se laisser abattre; **he was right on my ~** (= *following me*) il me suivait de très près; **it is a case of the ~ wagging the dog** c'est une petite minorité qui se fait obéir; **to turn ~ (and run)** prendre ses jambes à son cou → **sting b** [*of coin*] pile *f*; **~s I win!** pile je gagne! **c** (* *hum* = *buttocks*) postérieur* *m*; (*US*) **a piece of ~**** une fille baisable** **d** **to put a ~ on sb** [*detective etc*] faire filer qn **2** **tails*** NPL (*Dress*) queue *f* de pie **3** VT **a*** [+ *suspect etc*] suivre, filer **b** (= *cut tail of animal*) couper la queue à → **top¹ 4** VI **to ~ after sb** suivre qn tant bien que mal **5** COMP ► **tail assembly** N (*Aviat*) dérive *f* ► **tail coat** N queue *f* de pie ► **tail end** N [*of piece of meat, roll of cloth etc*] bout *m*; [*of procession*] queue *f*; [*of storm, debate, lecture*] toutes dernières minutes *fpl*, fin *f* ► **tail feather** N plume *f* rectrice ► **tail lamp, tail light** N (*Aut, Rail etc*) feu *m* arrière *inv* ► **tail-off** N diminution *f* or baisse *f* graduelle ► **tail section** N [*of aeroplane*] arrière *m* ► **tail skid** N (*Aviat*) béquille *f* de queue ► **tail unit** N (*Aviat*) empennage *m*

► **tail away** VI [*sounds*] se taire (peu à peu); [*attendance, interest, numbers*] diminuer, baisser (petit à petit); [*novel*] se terminer en queue de poisson

► **tail back** **1** VI **the traffic ~ed back to the bridge** le bouchon or la retenue remontait jusqu'au pont **2** **~back** N → **tailback**

► **tail off** VI = **tail away** **2** **~-off** N → **tail**

tailback ['teɪlbæk] N (*Brit Aut*) bouchon *m*

tailboard ['teɪlbɔːd] N (*Aut etc*) hayon *m*

-tailed [teɪld] ADJ (*in compounds*) **long-tailed** à la queue longue

tailgate ['teɪlgeɪt] N (*Aut*) hayon *m* (arrière); **to ~ sb** coller au train* de qn

tailhopping ['teɪlhɒpɪŋ] N (*Ski*) ruade *f*

tailor ['teɪlə] **1** N tailleur *m* **2** VT [+ *garment*] façonner; (*fig*) [+ *speech, book, product, service*] adapter (**to, to suit** à, **for** pour); **a ~ed skirt** une jupe ajustée **3** COMP ► **tailor-made** ADJ [*garment*] fait sur mesure; **the building is ~-made for this purpose** le bâtiment est conçu spécialement pour cet usage; **a lesson ~-made for that class** une leçon conçue or préparée spécialement pour cette classe; **the job was ~-made for him** le poste était fait pour lui ► **tailor's chalk** N craie *f* de tailleur ► **tailor's dummy** N mannequin *m*; (*fig pej*) fantoche *m*

tailoring ['teɪlərɪŋ] N (*fig*) [*of product, service*] personnalisation *f*, adaptation *f* (**to** à)

tailor-make ['teɪləmeɪk] VT **the therapist will ~ the session for you** le psychanalyste adaptera la séance à vos besoins; **we can ~ your entire holiday** nous pouvons vous organiser tout un voyage à la carte

tailpiece ['teɪlpiːs] N (*to speech*) ajout *m*; (*to document, book*) appendice *m*; (*to letter*) postscriptum *m*; (*Typ*) cul-de-lampe *m*; [*of violin*] cordier *m*

tailpipe ['teɪlpaɪp] N (*US Aut*) tuyau *m* d'échappement

tailplane ['teɪlpleɪn] N (*Aviat*) stabilisateur *m*

tailspin ['teɪlspɪn] **1** N (*Aviat*) vrille *f*; [*of prices*] chute *f* verticale; (*Aviat*) **to be in a ~** vriller **2** VI tomber en chute libre

tailwind ['teɪlwɪnd] N vent *m* arrière *inv*

taint [teɪnt] **1** VT [+ *meat, food*] gâter; [+ *water*] infecter, polluer; [+ *air, atmosphere*] vicier, infecter, polluer; (*fig liter*) [+ *sb's reputation*] souiller (*fig*) **2** N (*NonC*) infection *f*, souillure *f*; (= *decay*) corruption *f*, décomposition *f*; (*fig: of insanity, sin, heresy*) tare *f* (*fig*), souillure *f* (*fig liter*)

tainted ['teɪntɪd] ADJ **a** (= *tarnished*) [*money*] sale; [*evidence*] entaché de suspicion; [*reputation*] terni, sali; [*action, motive*] impur; **the system is ~ with corruption** le système est entaché de corruption **b** (= *contaminated*) [*food*] (*gen*) abîmé, gâté; (*with chemicals*) pollué; [*meat*] avarié; [*blood*] contaminé; [*water, air, atmosphere*] pollué; [*breath*] chargé; [*drug*] frelaté

Taiwan ['taɪ'wɑːn] N Taïwan *f*; **in ~** à Taïwan

Taiwanese [ˌtaɪwə'niːz] **1** ADJ taïwanais **2** N (*pl inv*) Taïwanais(e) *m(f)*

Tajikistan [tɑːˌdʒiːkɪstɑːn] N le Tadjikistan

take [teɪk]

vb: pret **took**, *ptp* **taken**	
1 NOUN	**4** COMPOUNDS
2 TRANSITIVE VERB	**5** PHRASAL VERBS
3 INTRANSITIVE VERB	

1 NOUN
a Cine, Phot prise *f* de vue(s); (*Recording*) enregistrement *m*
b Fishing, Hunting prise *f*
c US Comm = takings recette *f*; (*fig*) **to be on the ~** se servir* dans la caisse
d esp US* = share part *f*, montant *m* perçu; **the taxman's ~ is nearly 50%** la ponction fiscale s'élève à près de 50%
e * = view point *m* de vue

2 TRANSITIVE VERB
a gen prendre; (= *seize*) prendre, saisir; **to ~ sb's hand** prendre la main de qn; **he took me by the arm** ◊ **he took my arm** il m'a pris (par) le bras; **he took her in his arms** il l'a prise dans ses bras; **to ~ sb by the throat** prendre or saisir qn à la gorge; **I ~ a (size) 12 in dresses** je mets or fais du 42; **I ~ a (size) 5 in shoes** je chausse du 38; **the policeman took his name and address** l'agent a pris or relevé ses nom et adresse; **he ~s "The Times"** il lit le «Times»;

(*Phot*) **he took the cathedral from the square** il a pris la cathédrale vue de la place; (*Phot*) **he ~s a good photo*** il est très photogénique; **to ~ a ticket for a concert** prendre un billet *or* une place pour un concert; **I'll ~ that one** je prends *or* prendrai celui-là; **to ~ a wife†** prendre femme†; **~ your partners for a waltz** invitez vos partenaires et en avant pour la valse; **to ~ sth (up)on o.s.** prendre qch sur soi; **to ~ it (up)on o.s. to do sth** prendre sur soi *or* sous son bonnet de faire qch

b = *extract* prendre (**from sth** dans qch), tirer (**from sth** de qch); (= *remove*) prendre, enlever, ôter (**from sb** à qn); (*without permission*) **to ~ sth from one's pocket** prendre qch dans *or* tirer qch de sa poche; **to ~ sth from a drawer** prendre qch dans un tiroir; **he ~s his examples from real life** il tire ses exemples de la réalité; **I took these statistics from a government report** j'ai tiré ces statistiques d'un rapport gouvernemental

c Math etc = *subtract* soustraire, ôter (**from** de); **he took 10 francs off the price** il a fait un rabais *or* une remise de 10 F sur le prix

d = *capture* (*Mil*) [+ *city, district, hill*] prendre, s'emparer de; (*gen*) [+ *suspect, wanted man*] prendre, capturer; [+ *fish etc*] attraper; (*sexually*) [+ *woman*] prendre; (*Chess*) prendre; [+ *prize*] obtenir, remporter; [+ *degree*] avoir, obtenir; (*Cards*) **to ~ a trick** faire une levée; **my ace took his king** j'ai pris son roi avec mon as; (*Brit*) **the grocer ~s about £500 per day** l'épicier fait à peu près 500 livres de recette par jour, l'épicier vend pour à peu près 500 livres de marchandises par jour → **fancy, prisoner, surprise**

e = *ingest, consume* [+ *food, drink*] prendre; **he ~s sugar in his tea** il prend du sucre dans son thé; **to ~ tea†** with sb prendre le thé avec qn; **to ~ drugs** (= *medicines*) prendre des médicaments; (= *narcotics*) se droguer; **to ~ morphine** prendre de la morphine; (*Med*) **"not to be ~n (internally)"** "à usage externe"; **he took no food for four days** il n'a rien mangé *or* pris pendant quatre jours

f = *occupy* [+ *chair, seat*] prendre, s'asseoir sur; (= *rent*) [+ *house, flat etc*] prendre, louer; **to ~ one's seat** s'asseoir; **is this seat ~n?** cette place est-elle prise *or* occupée?

g = *go by* [+ *bus, train, plane, taxi*] prendre; [+ *road*] prendre, suivre; **~ the first on the left** prenez la première à gauche

h = *negotiate* [+ *bend*] prendre; [+ *hill*] grimper; [+ *fence*] sauter; **he took that corner too fast** il a pris ce virage trop vite

i Scol, Univ (= *sit*) [+ *exam, test*] passer, se présenter à; (= *study*) [+ *subject*] prendre, faire; **what are you taking next year?** qu'est-ce que tu prends *or* fais l'an prochain (comme matière)?

j esp Brit = *teach* [+ *class, students*] faire cours à; **the teacher who took us for economics** le professeur qui nous faisait cours en économie *or* qui nous enseignait l'économie

k = *tolerate* [+ *behaviour, remark etc*] accepter; [+ *alcohol, garlic*] supporter; **he won't ~ that reply from you** il n'acceptera jamais une telle réponse venant de vous; **I'll ~ no nonsense!** on ne me raconte pas d'histoires!; **I'm not taking any!*** je ne marche pas!*; **I can't ~ it any more** je n'en peux plus; **we can ~ it!** on ne se laissera pas abattre!, on (l')encaissera!*; **I can't ~ alcohol** je ne supporte pas l'alcool

l = *have as capacity* contenir, avoir une capacité de; **the bus ~s 60 passengers** l'autobus a une capacité de 60 places; **the hall will ~ 200 people** la salle contient jusqu'à 200 personnes; **the bridge will ~ 10 tons** le pont supporte un poids maximal de 10 tonnes

m = *receive, accept* [+ *gift, payment*] prendre, accepter; [+ *a bet*] accepter; [+ *news*] supporter; **he won't ~ less than £50 for it** il en demande au moins 50 livres; **~ it from me!**

croyez-moi!, croyez-moi sur parole!; (*you can*) ~ **it or leave it** c'est à prendre ou à laisser; **whisky? I can ~ it or leave it*** le whisky? j'aime ça mais sans plus; **she took his death quite well** elle s'est montrée très calme en apprenant sa mort; **she took his death very badly** elle a été très affectée par sa mort; **I wonder how she'll ~ it** je me demande comment elle prendra cela; **you must ~ us as you find us** vous devez nous prendre comme nous sommes; **to ~ things as they come** prendre les choses comme elles viennent*; **you must ~ things as they are** il faut prendre les choses comme elles sont*; (*handing over task etc*) **will you ~ it from here?** pouvez-vous prendre la suite ou la relève?; (*esp US*) **~ five/ten!*** (= *have a break*) repos!

n = *assume* supposer, imaginer; **I ~ it that ...** je suppose *or* j'imagine que ...; **how old do you ~ him to be?** quel âge lui donnez-vous?; **what do you ~ me for?** pour qui me prenez-vous?; **do you ~ me for a fool?** vous me prenez pour un imbécile?; **I took you for a burglar** je vous ai pris pour un cambrioleur; **I took him to be foreign** je le croyais étranger; **to ~ A for B** prendre A pour B, confondre A et B

o = *consider* prendre; **now ~ Ireland** prenons par exemple l'Irlande; **~ the case of ...** prenons *or* prenez le cas de ...; **taking one thing with another ...** tout bien considéré ...

p = *require* prendre, demander; (*Gram*) être suivi de; **it ~s time** cela prend *or* demande du temps; **the journey ~s five days** le voyage prend *or* demande cinq jours; **it took me two hours to do it** ◊ **I took two hours to do it** j'ai mis deux heures (à *or* pour le faire); **~ your time!** prenez votre temps!; **it won't ~ long** cela ne prendra pas longtemps; **that ~s a lot of courage** cela demande beaucoup de courage; **it ~s a brave man to do that** il faut être courageux pour faire cela; **it ~s some doing*** ce n'est pas évident; **it ~s some believing*** c'est à peine croyable; **it took three policemen to hold him down** il a fallu trois agents pour le tenir ■ (*PROV*) **it ~s two to make a quarrel** il faut être au moins deux pour se battre; **he's got what it ~s!*** il est à la hauteur; **he's got what it ~s to do the job** il a toutes les qualités requises pour ce travail

q = *carry* [+ *child, object*] porter, apporter, emporter; [+ *one's gloves, umbrella*] prendre, emporter (avec soi); (= *lead*) emmener, conduire; (= *accompany*) accompagner; **he took her some flowers** il lui a apporté des fleurs; **~ his suitcase upstairs** montez sa valise; **he ~s home £200 a week** il gagne 200 livres net par semaine; **he took her to the cinema** il l'a emmenée au cinéma; **I'll ~ you to dinner** je vous emmènerai dîner; **they took him over the factory** ils lui ont fait visiter l'usine; **I'll ~ sb to hospital** transporter qn à l'hôpital; **he took me home in his car** il m'a ramené *or* raccompagné dans sa voiture; **this road will ~ you to Paris** cette route vous mènera à Paris; **this bus will ~ you to the town hall** cet autobus vous conduira à la mairie; (*fig*) **£20 won't ~ you far these days** de nos jours on ne va pas loin avec 20 livres; (*fig*) **what took you to Lille?** qu'est-ce qui vous a fait aller à Lille?

r = *refer* **to ~ a matter to sb** soumettre une affaire à qn, en référer à qn; **I took it to him for advice** je lui ai soumis le problème pour qu'il me conseille

3 INTRANSITIVE VERB

fire, vaccination, plant cutting etc prendre

4 COMPOUNDS

▶ **take-home pay** N salaire *m* net ▶ **take-up** N (*Brit*) souscription *f*

5 PHRASAL VERBS

▶ **take aback** VT SEP → **aback**

▶ **take after** VT FUS ressembler à, tenir de; **she ~s after her mother** elle ressemble à *or* tient de sa mère

▶ **take against** VT FUS prendre en grippe

▶ **take along** VT SEP [+ *person*] emmener; [+ *camera etc*] emporter, prendre

▶ **take apart** **1** VI [*toy, machine*] se démonter

2 VT SEP [+ *machine, engine, toy*] démonter, désassembler; (* *fig* = *criticize harshly*) [+ *plan, suggestion*] démanteler, démolir*; **I'll ~ him apart*** if **I get hold of him!** si je l'attrape je l'étripe *or* ça va être sa fête!*

▶ **take aside** VT SEP [+ *person*] prendre à part, emmener à l'écart

▶ **take away** **1** VI **it ~s away from its value** cela diminue *or* déprécie sa valeur; **that doesn't ~ away from his merit** cela n'enlève rien à son mérite

2 VT SEP **a** (= *carry or lead away*) [+ *object*] emporter; [+ *person*] emmener; (*on book etc*) **"not to be ~n away"** « à consulter sur place »

b (= *remove*) [+ *object*] prendre, retirer, enlever (**from sb** à qn, **from sth** de qch); [+ *sb's child, wife, sweetheart*] enlever (**from sb** à qn); **she took her children away from the school** elle a retiré ses enfants de l'école

c (*Math*) soustraire, ôter (**from** de); **if you ~ three away from six ...** six moins trois ...

▶ **take back** VT SEP **a** (= *accept back*) [+ *gift, one's wife, husband*] reprendre; **to ~ back a** *or* **one's promise** reprendre sa parole; **she took back all she had said about him** elle a retiré tout ce qu'elle avait dit à son sujet; **I ~ it all back!** je n'ai rien dit!

b (= *return*) [+ *book, goods*] rapporter (**to** à); (= *accompany*) [+ *person*] raccompagner, reconduire (**to** à)

c (= *recall, evoke*) **it ~s me back to my childhood** cela me rappelle mon enfance

▶ **take down** VT SEP **a** [+ *object from shelf etc*] descendre (**from, off** de); [+ *trousers*] baisser; [+ *picture*] décrocher, descendre; [+ *poster*] décoller *or* **peg**

b (= *dismantle*) [+ *scaffolding, tent*] démonter; [+ *building*] démolir

c (= *write etc*) [+ *notes, letter*] prendre; [+ *address, details*] prendre, noter, inscrire

d (*in courtroom*) **~ him down!** qu'on emmène le prisonnier!

▶ **take from** VT FUS = **take away from**; → **take away**

▶ **take in** VT SEP **a** (*into building*) [+ *garden furniture, harvest*] rentrer; [+ *person*] faire entrer

b (*into one's home*) [+ *lodgers*] prendre; [+ *friend*] recevoir; [+ *homeless person, stray dog*] recueillir

c **she ~s in sewing** elle fait *or* prend de la couture à domicile

d (= *make smaller*) [+ *skirt, dress, waistband*] reprendre; (*Climbing*) **to ~ in the slack on a rope** avaler le mou d'une corde

e (= *include, cover*) couvrir, inclure, englober, embrasser; **we cannot ~ in all the cases** nous ne pouvons pas couvrir *or* inclure tous les cas; **this ~s in all possibilities** ceci englobe *or* embrasse toutes les possibilités; (*fig*) **we took in Venice on the way home** nous avons visité Venise sur le chemin du retour; **to ~ in a movie** aller au cinéma

f (= *grasp, understand*) saisir, comprendre; **that child ~s everything in** rien n'échappe à cet enfant; **the children were taking it all in** les enfants étaient tout oreilles; **she couldn't ~ in his death at first** dans les premiers temps elle ne pouvait pas se faire à l'idée de sa mort; **he hadn't fully ~n in that she was dead** il n'avait pas (vraiment) réalisé qu'elle était morte; **he took in the situation at a glance** il a apprécié la situation en un clin d'œil

g (* = *cheat, deceive*) avoir*, rouler*; **I've been ~n in** je me suis laissé avoir*, j'ai été roulé*; **he's easily ~n in** il se fait facilement avoir*; **to be ~n in by appearances** se laisser prendre aux *or* tromper par les apparences; **I was ~n in by his disguise** je me suis laissé prendre à son déguisement

▶ **take off** **1** VI [*person*] partir (**for** pour); [*air-*

craft, career, scheme] décoller; **the plane took off for Berlin** l'avion s'est envolé pour Berlin

2 VT SEP **a** (= remove) [+ garment] ôter, retirer; [+ buttons, price tag, lid] enlever; [+ telephone receiver] décrocher; [+ item on menu, train, bus] supprimer; (= amputate) **they had to ~ his leg off** on a dû l'amputer d'une jambe; (Comm) **he took £5 off** il a baissé le prix de or il a fait un rabais de 5 livres, il a rabattu 5 livres sur le prix; **I'll ~ something off the price for you** je vais vous faire un rabais or une remise (sur le prix); **her new hairstyle ~s five years off her** sa nouvelle coiffure la rajeunit de cinq ans

b (= lead etc away) [+ person, car] emmener; **he took her off to lunch** il l'a emmenée déjeuner; **to ~ sb off to jail** emmener qn en prison; **he was ~n off to hospital** on l'a transporté à l'hôpital; **after the wreck a boat took the crew off** une embarcation est venue sauver l'équipage du navire naufragé; **to ~ o.s. off** s'en aller

c (Brit = imitate) imiter, pasticher

▶**take on** **1** VI **a** [idea, fashion etc] prendre, marcher*

b (Brit* = be upset) s'en faire*

2 VT SEP **a** (= accept etc) [+ work, responsibility] prendre, accepter, se charger de; [+ bet] accepter; [challenger in game/fight] accepter de jouer/de se battre contre; **I'll ~ you on!** (Betting) chiche!; (Sport) je te parie que je te bats!; **he has ~n on more than he bargained for** il n'avait pas compté prendre une si lourde responsabilité; **to agree to ~ a job on** (employment) accepter un poste; (task) accepter de se charger d'un travail

b [+ employee] prendre, embaucher; [+ cargo, passenger] embarquer, prendre; [+ form, qualities] prendre, revêtir

c (= contend with) [+ enemy] s'attaquer à; (= challenge etc) **he took on the whole committee** il s'est attaqué or s'en est pris au comité tout entier

▶**take out** VT SEP **a** (= lead or carry outside) [+ chair etc] sortir; [+ prisoner] faire sortir; **they took us out to see the sights** ils nous ont emmenés visiter la ville; **he took her out to lunch/the theatre** il l'a emmenée déjeuner/au théâtre; **he has often ~n her out** il l'a souvent sortie; **I'm going to ~ the children/dog out** je vais sortir les enfants/le chien

b (from pocket, drawer) prendre **(from, of** dans); (= remove) sortir, retirer, enlever, ôter **(from, of** de); [+ tooth] arracher; [+ appendix, tonsils] enlever; [+ stain] ôter, enlever (**from** de); **~ your hands out of your pockets** sors or enlève or retire tes mains de tes poches; (fig) **that will ~ you out of yourself a bit** cela vous changera les idées; **that sort of work certainly ~s it out of you*** c'est vraiment un travail épuisant; **when he got the sack he took it out on the dog*** quand il a été licencié, il s'est défoulé* sur le chien; **don't ~ it out on me!*** ce n'est pas la peine de t'en prendre à moi!; **don't ~ your bad temper out on me*** ne passe pas ta mauvaise humeur sur moi

c [+ insurance policy] souscrire à, prendre; [+ patent] prendre; [+ licence] se procurer

d (Mil*) [+ target] descendre*, bousiller*

▶**take over** **1** VI [dictator, army, political party] prendre le pouvoir; **to ~ over from sb** prendre la relève or le relais de qn; **let him ~ over** cédez-lui la place

2 VT SEP **a** (= escort or carry across) **he took me over to the island in his boat** il m'a transporté jusqu'à l'île dans son bateau; **will you ~ me over to the other side?** voulez-vous me faire traverser?

b (= assume responsibility for) [+ business, shop] reprendre; [+ sb's debts] prendre à sa charge; **he took over the shop from his father** il a pris la suite de son père dans le magasin; **he took over the job from Paul** il a succédé à Paul (à ce poste); **I took over his duties** je l'ai remplacé

dans ses fonctions; **he took over the leadership of the party when Smith resigned** il a remplacé Smith à la tête du parti après la démission de celui-ci

c (Fin) [+ another company] absorber, racheter; (fig) **the tourists have ~n over Venice** les touristes ont envahi Venise

▶**take to** VT FUS **a** (= conceive liking for) [+ person] se prendre d'amitié pour, sympathiser avec; [+ game, action, study] prendre goût à, mordre à*; **I didn't ~ to the idea** l'idée ne m'a rien dit; **they took to each other at once** ils se sont plu immédiatement; **I didn't ~ to him** il ne m'a pas beaucoup plu

b (= start, adopt) [+ habit] prendre; [+ hobby] se mettre à; **to ~ to drink/drugs** se mettre à boire/à se droguer; **she took to telling everyone ... elle s'est mise à dire à tout le monde ...**

c (= go to) **to ~ to one's bed** s'aliter; **to ~ to the woods** [walker] aller dans la forêt; [hunted man] aller se réfugier or se cacher dans la forêt; (Naut) **to ~ to the boats** abandonner or évacuer le navire → **heel¹**

▶**take up** **1** VI **to ~ up with sb** se lier avec qn, se prendre d'amitié pour qn

2 VT SEP **a** (= lead or carry upstairs, uphill etc) [+ person] faire monter; [+ object] monter

b (= lift) [+ object from ground] ramasser, prendre; [+ carpet] enlever; [+ roadway, pavement] dépaver; [+ dress, hem, skirt] raccourcir; [+ passenger] prendre; (fig: after interruption) [+ one's work, book] reprendre, se remettre à, continuer; [+ conversation, discussion, story] reprendre (le fil de) → **cudgel**

c (= occupy) [+ space] occuper, tenir, prendre; [+ time] prendre, demander; [+ attention] occuper, absorber; **he is very ~n up** il est très pris; **he is quite ~n up with her** il ne pense plus qu'à elle; **he is completely ~n up with his plan** il est tout entier à son projet; **it ~s up too much room** cela prend or occupe trop de place; **it ~s up all my free time** cela (me) prend tout mon temps libre

d (= absorb) [+ liquids] absorber

e (= raise question of) [+ subject] aborder; **I'll ~ that up with him** je lui en parlerai; **I would like to ~ you up on something you said earlier** je voudrais revenir sur quelque chose que vous avez dit précédemment

f (= start, accept) [+ hobby, subject, sport, language] se mettre à; [+ career] embrasser; [+ method] adopter, retenir; [+ challenge] relever; [+ shares] souscrire à; [+ person] (as friend) adopter; (as protégé) prendre en main; **to ~ up one's new post** entrer en fonction; **I'll ~ you up on your promise** je mettrai votre parole à l'épreuve; **I'd like to ~ you up on your offer of free tickets** je voudrais accepter votre offre de places gratuites; **I'll ~ you up on that some day** je m'en souviendrai à l'occasion, un jour je vous prendrai au mot

takeaway ['teɪkəweɪ] **1** N (Brit = food shop) magasin m de plats à emporter **2** COMP ▶ **takeaway food** N plats mpl préparés (à emporter) ▶ **takeaway meal** N repas m à emporter

takedown* ['teɪkdaʊn] ADJ [toy, weapon] démontable

taken ['teɪkən] **1** VB ptp of **take** **2** ADJ **a** [seat, place] pris, occupé **b** **to be very ~ with sb/sth** être très impressionné par qn/qch; **I'm not very ~ with him** il ne m'a pas fait une grosse impression; **I'm quite ~ with** or **by that idea** cette idée me plaît énormément

takeoff ['teɪkɒf] N (Aviat) décollage m; (Gym, Ski) envol m; (fig: Econ etc) démarrage m; (= imitation) imitation f, pastiche m

takeout ['teɪkaʊt] N **a** (US) = **takeaway** **b** (Bridge: also **~ bid**) réponse f de faiblesse

takeover ['teɪkəʊvər] **1** N (Pol) prise f du pouvoir; (Fin) rachat m **2** COMP ▶ **takeover bid** N offre f publique d'achat, OPA f

taker ['teɪkər] N **~s of snuff** les gens qui prisent; **drug-~s** les drogués mpl; **at £50 he found no ~s** il n'a pas trouvé d'acheteurs or trouvé preneur pour 50 livres; **this suggestion found no ~s** cette suggestion n'a été relevée par personne

taking ['teɪkɪŋ] **1** ADJ [person, manners] séduisant; [child] mignon **2** N **a** **it is yours for the ~** tu n'as qu'à (te donner la peine de) le prendre **b** (Mil = capture) prise f **c** (Brit) **~ and driving away a vehicle** vol m de véhicule **3** **takings** NPL (Brit Comm) recette f

talc [tælk], **talcum (powder)** ['tælkəm-(paʊdər)] N talc m

tale [teɪl] N (= story) conte m, histoire f; (= legend) histoire f, légende f; (= account) récit m, histoire f (pej); **"Tales of King Arthur"** « La Légende du Roi Arthur »; **he told us the ~ of his adventures** il nous a fait le récit de ses aventures; **I've heard that ~ before** j'ai déjà entendu cette histoire-là quelque part; **I've been hearing ~s about you** on m'a dit or raconté des choses sur vous; **to tell ~s** (= inform on sb) rapporter, cafarder*; (= to lie) mentir, raconter des histoires*; (fig) **to tell ~s out of school** raconter ce qu'on devrait taire; **he lived to tell the ~** il y a survécu → **fairy, old, tell, woe**

talebearer ['teɪlbɛərər] N rapporteur m, -euse f, mouchard(e) m(f)

talebearing ['teɪlbɛərɪŋ] N rapportage m, cafardage* m

talent ['tælənt] **1** N **a** (= gift) don m, talent m; (NonC) talent m; **to have a ~ for drawing** être doué pour le dessin, avoir un don or du talent pour le dessin; **a writer of great ~** un écrivain de grand talent or très talentueux; **he encourages young ~** il encourage les jeunes talents; **he is looking for ~ amongst the schoolboy players** il cherche de futurs grands joueurs parmi les lycéens **b** (= attractive people) **there's not much ~ here tonight** il n'y a pas grand-chose comme petits lots* ici ce soir **c** (= coin) talent m **2** COMP ▶ **talent competition, talent contest** N talent show ▶ **talent scout** N (Cine, Theat) découvreur m, -euse f or dénicheur m, -euse f de vedettes; (Sport) dénicheur m, -euse f de futurs grands joueurs ▶ **talent show** N concours m d'amateurs ▶ **talent spotter** N = talent scout

talented ['tæləntɪd] ADJ talentueux, doué

taletelling ['teɪltelɪŋ] N = **talebearing**

tali ['teɪlaɪ] NPL of **talus**

talisman ['tælɪzmən] N (pl **talismans**) talisman m

talk [tɔːk] **1** N **a** conversation f, discussion f; (more formal) entretien m; (= chat) causerie f; **during his ~ with the Prime Minister** pendant son entretien avec le Premier ministre; (esp Pol) **~s** discussions fpl; **peace ~s** pourparlers mpl de paix; **the Geneva ~s on disarmament** la conférence de Genève sur le désarmement; **I enjoyed our (little) ~** notre causerie or notre petite conversation m'a été très agréable; **we've had several ~s about this** nous en avons parlé or discuté plusieurs fois; **I must have a ~ with him** (gen) il faut que je lui parle (subj); (warning, threatening etc) j'ai à lui parler; **we must have a ~ some time** il faudra que nous nous rencontrions (subj) un jour pour discuter or causer **b** (= informal lecture) exposé m (**on** sur); (less academic or technical) causerie f (**on** sur); **to give a ~** faire un exposé, donner une causerie (**on** sur); **Mr Jones has come to give us a ~ on ...** M. Jones est venu nous parler de ...; **to give a ~ on the radio** parler à la radio **c** (NonC) propos mpl; (= gossip) bavardage(s) m(pl); (pej) racontars mpl; **the ~ was all about the wedding** les propos tournaient autour du mariage; **you should hear the ~!** si tu savais ce qu'on raconte!; **there is (some) ~ of his returning** (= it is being discussed) il est question qu'il revienne (subj); (= it is being rumoured) on dit qu'il va peut-être revenir, le bruit court qu'il va revenir; **there was no ~ of his resigning** il n'a pas été question qu'il démissionne (subj); **it's common ~ that ...** on dit partout que ..., tout le monde dit que ...; **it's just ~** ce ne sont que des on-dit or des racontars or des bavardages; **there has been a lot of ~ about her** il a beaucoup été question d'elle; (pej) on a raconté beaucoup d'histoires sur elle; **I've heard a lot of ~ about the new factory** j'ai beaucoup entendu parler de la nouvelle usine; **all that ~ about what he was going to do!** toutes ces vaines paroles sur ce qu'il allait faire!; (pej) **he's all ~** c'est un grand vantard or hâbleur; **it was all (big) ~** tout ça c'était du vent*; **she's/it's the ~ of the town** on ne parle que d'elle/de cela → **baby, idle, small**

2 vi (= speak) parler (**about,** of de); (= chatter) bavarder, causer; **he can't ~ yet** il ne parle pas encore; **after days of torture he finally ~ed** après plusieurs jours de torture, il a enfin parlé; **I'll make you ~!** (avec moi) tu vas parler!; **now you're ~ing!*** voilà qui devient intéressant!; **it's easy or all right for him to ~!** il peut parler!; (iro) **look who's ~ing!** ◊ **YOU can ~!*** tu peux parler!*, tu es mal placé pour faire ce genre de remarque!; (fig) **to ~ through one's hat*** or **through a hole in one's head** ◊ **to ~ out of one's arse**** (Brit) débloquer*, dire des conneries**; **he was just ~ing for the sake of ~ing** il parlait pour ne rien dire; **he ~s too much** (too chatty) il parle trop; (indiscreet) il ne sait pas se taire; (Austral) **he can ~ under water** c'est un moulin à paroles; **don't ~ to me like that!** ne me parle pas sur ce ton!; **do what he tells you because he knows what he's ~ing about** fais ce qu'il te demande parce qu'il sait ce qu'il dit; **he knows what he's ~ing about when he's on the subject of cars** il s'y connaît quand il parle (de) voitures; **he doesn't know what he's ~ing about** il ne sait pas ce qu'il dit; **I'm not ~ing about you** ce n'est pas de toi que je parle, il ne s'agit pas de toi; **he was ~ing of** or **about going to Greece** il parlait d'aller en Grèce; **it's not as if we're ~ing about ...** ce n'est pas comme si s'agissait de ...; **you're ~ing about a million dollars** ça coûterait un million de dollars; **they ~ed of** or **about nothing except ...** ils ne parlaient que de ...; **the marriage was much ~ed of in the town** toute la ville parlait du mariage; **his much ~ed-of holiday never happened** ses fameuses vacances ne sont jamais arrivées; **I'm not ~ing to him any more** je ne lui adresse plus la parole, je ne lui cause plus*; **~ing of films, have you seen ...?** en parlant de or à propos de films, avez-vous vu ...?; **~ about a stroke of luck!*** ça tombe (or tombait etc) à pic!* → **big, tough**

b (= converse) parler (**to** à, **with** avec), discuter (**to, with** avec); (more formally) s'entretenir (**to, with** avec); (= chat) causer (**to, with** avec); (= gossip) parler, causer (**about** de), jaser (pej) (**about** sur); **who were you ~ing to?** à qui parlais-tu?; **I saw them ~ing (to each other)** je les ai vus en conversation l'un avec l'autre; **to ~ to o.s.** se parler tout seul; **I'll ~ to you about that tomorrow** je t'en parlerai demain; (threateningly) j'aurai deux mots à te dire là-dessus demain; **it's no use ~ing to you** je perds mon temps avec toi; **we were just ~ing of** or **about you** justement nous parlions de toi; **the Foreign Ministers ~ed about the crisis in China** les ministres des Affaires étrangères se sont entretenus de la crise chinoise; **I have ~ed with him several times** j'ai eu plusieurs conversations avec lui; **try to keep him ~ing** essaie de le faire parler aussi longtemps que possible; **to get o.s. ~ed about** faire parler de soi → **nineteen**

3 vt **a** [+ a language, slang] parler; **to ~ business/politics** parler affaires/politique; **to ~ nonsense** or **rubbish*** or **tripe*** dire n'importe quoi or des conneries**; **he's ~ing sense** c'est la voix de la raison qui parle, ce

qu'il dit est le bon sens même; **~ sense!** ne dis pas n'importe quoi!; **we're ~ing big money/serious crime here*** il s'agit de grosses sommes d'argent/de crimes graves* → **hind²**, **shop, turkey**

b ~ **sb into doing sth** amener qn à or persuader qn de faire qch (à force de paroles); **I managed to ~ him out of doing it** je suis arrivé à le dissuader de le faire (en lui parlant); **she ~ed him into a better mood** elle l'a remis de meilleure humeur en lui parlant; **he ~ed himself into the job** il a si bien parlé qu'on lui a offert le poste; **to ~ sb through sth** bien expliquer qch à qn

4 COMP ► **talk radio** N (NonC) radio qui donne la priorité aux interviews et aux débats ► **talk show** N (Rad) débat m (radiodiffusé); (TV) débat m (télévisé), talk-show m

► **talk away** vi parler or discuter sans s'arrêter, ne pas arrêter de parler; **we ~ed away for hours** nous avons passé des heures à parler or discuter; **she was ~ing away about her plans when suddenly ...** elle était partie à parler de ses projets quand soudain ...

► **talk back** vi répondre (insolemment) (**to sb** à qn)

► **talk down** **1** vi **to ~ down to sb** parler à qn comme à un enfant **2** vt sep **a** (= silence) **they ~ed him down** leurs flots de paroles l'ont réduit au silence **b** (Aviat) [+ pilot, aircraft] aider à atterrir par radio-contrôle **c** [+ suicidal person] persuader de ne pas sauter **d** (= speak ill of) dénigrer **e** (esp Brit: in negotiations) **to ~ sb down** marchander avec qn (pour qu'il baisse son prix); **to ~ wages down** obtenir une baisse des salaires

► **talk on** vi parler or discuter sans s'arrêter, ne pas arrêter de parler; **she ~ed on and on about it** elle en a parlé pendant des heures et des heures

► **talk out** vt sep **a** (= discuss thoroughly) **to ~ it/things out** mettre les choses au clair **b** (Parl) **to ~ out a bill** prolonger la discussion d'un projet de loi jusqu'à ce qu'il soit trop tard pour le voter **c** **to ~ o.s. out** parler jusqu'à l'épuisement

► **talk over** vt sep **a** [+ question, problem] discuter (de), débattre; **let's ~ it over** discutons-en entre nous; **I must ~ it over with my wife first** je dois d'abord en parler à ma femme **b** = **talk round 1**

► **talk round** **1** vt sep (Brit) **to ~ sb round** amener qn à changer d'avis, gagner qn à son avis, convaincre or persuader qn **2** vt fus [+ problem, subject] tourner autour de; **they ~ed round it all evening** ils ont tourné autour du pot toute la soirée

► **talk up** **1** vi (US = speak frankly) ne pas mâcher ses mots **2** vt fus [+ project, book] pousser, vanter; (esp Brit: in negotiations) **to ~ sb up** marchander avec qn pour qu'il offre davantage; **to ~ the price up** obtenir plus d'argent

talkathon ['tɔːkəθən] N (US) débat-marathon m

talkative ['tɔːkətɪv] ADJ bavard

talkativeness ['tɔːkətɪvnɪs] N volubilité f, loquacité f (liter)

talker ['tɔːkər] N **he's a great ~** c'est un grand bavard, il a la langue bien pendue*; **he's a terrible ~** (talks too much) c'est un vrai moulin à paroles

talkie* ['tɔːkɪ] N (Cine) film m parlant; **the ~s** le cinéma parlant → **walkie-talkie**

talking ['tɔːkɪŋ] **1** N bavardage m; **he did all the ~** il a fait tous les frais de la conversation; **that's enough ~!** assez de bavardages!, assez bavardé!; **no ~!** défense de parler!, silence (s'il vous plaît)! **2** ADJ [doll, parrot, film] parlant **3** COMP ► **talking book** N lecture f enregistrée d'un livre ► **talking head** N (TV) présentateur m, -trice f ► **talking point** N sujet m de discussion or de conversation

► **talking shop*** N (Brit) parlot(t)e f
► **talking-to*** N engueulade* f; **to give sb a (good) ~-to** passer un savon à qn*

tall [tɔːl] **1** ADJ **a** (in height) [building, tree, window] haut; **a ~ person** une personne de grande taille; **a ~ man** un homme grand; **a ~ woman/girl** une grande femme/fille; **a ~ boy** un grand garçon; **a ~ glass** un grand verre; **how ~ is this building/that tree?** quelle est la hauteur de ce bâtiment/cet arbre?; **how ~ are you?** combien mesurez-vous?; **he hadn't realized how ~ she was** il ne s'était pas rendu compte qu'elle était aussi grande; **he is six feet ~** ≈ il mesure 1 mètre 80; **a six-foot-~ man** ≈ un homme d'un mètre 80 or mesurant 1 mètre 80; **~ and slim** élancé; **he is ~er than his brother** il est plus grand que son frère; **she's 5cm ~er than me** ◊ **she's ~er than me by 5cm** elle mesure 5 cm de plus que moi; **she is ~er than me by a head** elle me dépasse d'une tête; **she wears high heels to make herself look ~er** elle porte des talons hauts pour se grandir or pour avoir l'air plus grande; **to get** or **grow ~er** grandir

b **that's a ~ order!*** (= difficult) c'est beaucoup demander!

2 ADV **he stands six feet ~** ≈ il mesure bien 1 mètre 80; (US fig) **to stand ~** garder la tête haute; **to walk ~** marcher la tête haute

3 COMP ► **tall ship** N grand voilier m ► **tall story, tall tale** N histoire f à dormir debout

tallboy ['tɔːlbɔɪ] N (Brit) commode f

tallness ['tɔːlnɪs] N [of person] grande taille f; [of building etc] hauteur f

tallow ['tæləʊ] **1** N suif m **2** N ► **tallow candle** N chandelle f

tally ['tælɪ] **1** N (Hist = stick) taille f (latte de bois); (= count) compte m; **to keep a ~ of** (= count) tenir le compte de; (= mark off on list) pointer **2** vi s'accorder (**with** avec), correspondre (**with** à) **3** vt (also ~ **up** = count) compter

tallyho ['tælɪ'həʊ] EXCL, N taïaut m

Talmud ['tælmʊd] N (Rel) Talmud m

Talmudic [tæl'mʊdɪk] ADJ (Rel) talmudique

talon ['tælən] N **a** [of eagle etc] serre f; [of tiger etc, person] griffe f **b** (Archit, Cards) talon m

talus ['teɪləs] N (pl **tali**) astragale m

Tamagotchi® [tæmə'gɒtʃi] N Tamagotchi® m

tamarin ['tæmərɪn] N tamarin m (Zool)

tamarind ['tæmərɪnd] N (= fruit) tamarin m; (= tree) tamarinier m

tamarisk ['tæmərɪsk] N tamaris m

tambour ['tæm,bʊər] N (Archit, Mus) tambour m; (Sewing) métier m or tambour m à broder

tambourine [,tæmbə'riːn] N tambour m de basque, tambourin m

Tamburlaine ['tæmbəleɪn] N Tamerlan m

tame [teɪm] **1** ADJ **a** (= not wild) [animal, bird] apprivoisé; **to become ~(r)** s'apprivoiser; (hum) **let's ask our ~ American*** demandons à notre Américain de service **b** (pej = compliant) [follower] docile **c** (pej = unexciting) [party, match, book] insipide, fade; [place] insipide; **to be ~ stuff** être insipide **2** vt [+ bird, wild animal] apprivoiser; (+ esp lion, tiger] dompter; (fig) [+ passion] maîtriser; [+ person] mater, soumettre

tamely ['teɪmlɪ] ADV [agree, accept, surrender] docilement; **the story ends ~** le dénouement est plat

tamer ['teɪmər] N dresseur m, -euse f; **lion-~** dompteur m, -euse f (de lions), belluaire m

Tamerlane ['tæməleɪn] N Tamerlan m

Tamil ['tæmɪl] **1** N **a** Tamoul(e) or Tamil(e) m(f) **b** (Ling) tamoul or tamil m **2** ADJ tamoul or tamil

taming ['teɪmɪŋ] N (NonC: gen) apprivoisement m; [of circus animals] dressage m, domptage m; **"The Taming of the Shrew"** « La Mégère apprivoisée »

Tammany ['tæmənɪ] N (US Hist) organisation démocrate de New York

tammy* ['tæmɪ], **tam o'shanter** [ˌtæmə-'ʃæntər] N béret m écossais

tamp [tæmp] VT [+ earth] damer, tasser; [+ tobacco] tasser; (in blasting) **to ~ a drill hole** bourrer un trou de mine à l'argile or au sable

Tampax® ['tæmpæks] N Tampax® m

tamper ['tæmpər] [1] VI **to ~ with** [+ machinery, car, brakes, safe etc] toucher à (sans permission); [+ lock] essayer de crocheter; [+ document, text] altérer, fausser, falsifier; [+ accounts] falsifier, fausser, trafiquer; (Jur) [+ evidence] falsifier; (US) [+ jury] soudoyer; [+ sb's papers, possessions] toucher à, mettre le nez dans* [2] COMP ► **tamper-proof** ADJ impossible à falsifier

tampon ['tæmpɒn] N (Med) tampon m

tan [tæn] [1] N (also **suntan**) bronzage m, hâle m; **she's got a lovely ~** elle a un beau bronzage, elle est bien bronzée; **to get a ~** bronzer [2] ADJ brun clair [3] VT [a] [+ skins] tanner; (fig) **to ~ sb's** or **sb's hide (for him)*** tanner le cuir à qn* [b] [sun] [+ sunbather, holidaymaker] bronzer; [+ sailor, farmer etc] hâler; **to get ~ned** bronzer [4] VI bronzer

tandem ['tændəm] [1] N [a] (= bicycle) tandem m [b] (= in collaboration) **to do sth in ~** faire qch en tandem; **to work in ~ with sb** travailler en collaboration en tandem* avec qn [c] (= simultaneously) **to happen in ~** arriver simultanément; **the two systems will run in ~** les deux systèmes seront appliqués simultanément; **in ~ with sth** parallèlement à qch [2] ADV **to ride ~** rouler en tandem

tandoori [tæn'dʊərɪ] (Culin) ADJ, N tandoori or tandouri m inv

tang [tæŋ] N [a] (= taste) saveur f forte (et piquante); (= smell) senteur f or odeur f forte (et piquante); **the salt ~ of the sea air** l'odeur caractéristique de la marée [b] [of file, knife] soie f

tanga ['tæŋgə] N (= briefs) tanga m

Tanganyika [ˌtæŋgə'njiːkə] N le Tanganyika; **Lake ~** le lac Tanganyika

tangent ['tændʒənt] N (Math) tangente f; (fig) **to go off** or **fly off at a ~** partir dans une digression

tangential [tæn'dʒenʃəl] ADJ [a] (= unconnected) [remark, issue] sans rapport [b] (Geom) [line, curve] tangent (**to** à) [c] (Phys) [force] tangentiel

tangentially [tæn'dʒenʃəlɪ] ADV [a] (= indirectly) [relate to, touch on] indirectement [b] (Geom) tangentiellement

tangerine [ˌtændʒə'riːn] [1] N (also **~ orange**) mandarine f [2] ADJ [colour, skirt] mandarine inv; [flavour] de mandarine

tangibility [ˌtændʒɪ'bɪlɪtɪ] N tangibilité f

tangible ['tændʒəbl] ADJ [object, evidence, proof] tangible; [results, benefits] tangible, palpable; [assets] réel; (Fin) **~ net worth** valeur f nette réelle

tangibly ['tændʒəblɪ] ADV [demonstrate, improve] de manière tangible

Tangier [tæn'dʒɪər] N Tanger m

tangle ['tæŋgl] [1] N [of wool, string, rope] enchevêtrement m; (Climbing: in rope) nœud m; [of creepers, bushes, weeds] fouillis m, enchevêtrement m; (fig = muddle) confusion f; **to get into a ~** [string, rope, wool] s'entortiller, s'enchevêtrer; [hair] s'emmêler; (fig) [person, accounts] s'embrouiller; [traffic] se bloquer; **he got into a ~ when he tried to explain** il s'est embrouillé dans ses explications; **I'm in a ~ with the accounts** je suis empêtré dans les comptes; **the whole affair was a hopeless ~** toute cette histoire était affreusement confuse or était affreusement embrouillée

[2] VT (also **~ up**: lit) enchevêtrer, embrouiller, emmêler; **~d** [string, rope, wool] enchevêtré, entortillé; [hair] emmêlé; (fig) [complicated situation, negotiations] embrouillé; (fig) **a ~d web of lies** un inextricable tissu de mensonges; **his tie got ~d up in the machine** sa cravate s'est entortillée dans la machine; (gen) **to get ~d (up) = to get into a tangle** → 1 [3] VI [a] (= become tangled) = **to get into a tangle** (lit senses) → 1 [b] *** to ~ with sb** se frotter à qn, se colleter avec qn*; **they ~d over whose fault it was** ils se sont colletés* sur la question de savoir qui était responsable

tango ['tæŋgəʊ] [1] N (pl **tangos**) tango m [2] VI danser le tango; (fig) **it takes two to ~** il faut être deux

tangy ['tæŋɪ] ADJ piquant

tank [tæŋk] [1] N [a] (= container) (for storage) réservoir m, cuve f; (for rainwater) citerne f; (for gas) réservoir m; [of car] (also **petrol ~**) réservoir m (à essence); (for transporting) réservoir m, cuve f; (esp oil) tank m; (for fermenting, processing etc) cuve f (also Phot); (for fish) aquarium m → **fuel, septic** [b] (Mil) char m (d'assaut or de combat), tank m [2] COMP (Mil) [commander] de char d'assaut or de combat; [brigade] de chars d'assaut or de combat ► **tank car** N (US Rail) wagon-citerne m ► **tank top** N pull-over m sans manches ► **tank town*** N (US fig) petite ville f (perdue), trou* m (fig) ► **tank trap** N (Mil) fossé m antichar ► **tank truck** N (US) camion-citerne m

► **tank along*** VI (esp on road) foncer*, aller à toute allure*

► **tank up** [1] VI (Aut*) faire le plein; (Brit* fig = drink a lot) se soûler la gueule* [2] VT SEP* [+ car etc] remplir d'essence; (Brit fig) **to be ~ed up*** être bituré*; (Brit fig) **to get ~ed up*** se soûler la gueule*

tankard ['tæŋkəd] N chope f, pot m à bière

tanker ['tæŋkər] N (= truck) camion-citerne m; (= ship) pétrolier m, tanker m; (= aircraft) avion m ravitailleur; (Rail) wagon-citerne m

tankful ['tæŋkfʊl] N **a ~ of petrol** un réservoir (plein) d'essence; **a ~ of water** une citerne (pleine) d'eau

tanned [tænd] ADJ [sunbather, holiday-maker] bronzé; (= weatherbeaten) [sailor, farmer] hâlé

tanner¹ ['tænər] N tanneur m

tanner²†* ['tænər] N (Brit) (ancienne) pièce f de six pence

tannery ['tænərɪ] N tannerie f (établissement)

tannic ['tænɪk] [1] ADJ tannique [2] COMP ► **tannic acid** N tannin m

tannin ['tænɪn] N tan(n)in m

tanning ['tænɪŋ] N [a] (also **suntanning**) bronzage m [b] [of hides] tannage m [c] (: fig = beating) raclée* f

Tannoy® ['tænɔɪ] (Brit) [1] N système m de haut-parleurs; **on** or **over the ~** par haut-parleur [2] VT [+ message] annoncer par haut-parleur

tansy ['tænzɪ] N tanaisie f

tantalize ['tæntəlaɪz] VT mettre au supplice (fig), tourmenter (par de faux espoirs)

tantalizing ['tæntəlaɪzɪŋ] ADJ [glimpse] terriblement attrayant; [possibility] terriblement excitant; [offer, smell] terriblement alléchant

tantalizingly ['tæntəlaɪzɪŋlɪ] ADV d'une façon cruellement tentante; **~ slowly** avec une lenteur désespérante

tantalum ['tæntələm] N tantale m

Tantalus ['tæntələs] N Tantale m

tantamount ['tæntəmaʊnt] ADJ **to be ~ to sth** être équivalent à qch; **it's ~ to failure** cela équivaut à un échec

Tantric ['tæntrɪk] ADJ tantrique

tantrum ['tæntrəm] N (also **temper ~**) crise f de colère; **to have** or **throw a ~** piquer une colère

Tanzania [ˌtænzə'nɪə] N la Tanzanie; **United Republic of ~** République f unie de Tanzanie

Tanzanian [ˌtænzə'nɪən] [1] ADJ tanzanien [2] N Tanzanien(ne) m(f)

Tao ['taʊ] N Tao m

Taoism ['taʊɪzəm] N taoïsme m

Taoist ['taʊɪst] ADJ, N taoïste mf

tap¹ [tæp] [1] N [a] (Brit: for water, gas etc) robinet m; (Brit = tap on barrel etc) cannelle f, robinet m; (= plug for barrel) bonde f; **the hot/cold ~** le robinet d'eau chaude/froide; **ale on ~** bière f (à la) pression; **there are funds/ resources on ~** il y a des fonds/des ressources disponibles; **a wealth of information on ~** une mine d'informations à votre disposition or facilement accessibles; **he has £3 million on ~** il dispose de 3 millions de livres [b] (Telec) écoute f téléphonique [c] (also **screw ~**: Tech) taraud m [2] VT [a] [+ telephone, telephone line] mettre or placer sur écoute; **to ~ sb's phone** mettre qn sur écoute; **my phone is being ~ped** mon téléphone est sur écoute [b] (fig) [+ resources, supplies] exploiter, utiliser; **to ~ sb for money*** taper* qn; **they ~ped her for a loan*** ils ont réussi à lui emprunter de l'argent; **to ~ sb for £10*** taper* qn de 10 livres; **to ~ sb for information** soutirer des informations à qn [c] [+ cask, barrel] percer, mettre en perce; [+ pine] gemmer; [+ other tree] inciser; (Elec) [+ current] capter; [+ wire] brancher; **to ~ the rubber from a tree** saigner un arbre pour recueillir le latex [3] COMP ► **tap water** N eau f du robinet

► **tap into** VT FUS (= gain access to) [+ system, network] accéder à; (= exploit) [+ fear, enthusiasm] exploiter

tap² [tæp] [1] N [a] petit coup m, petite tape f; **there was a ~ at the door** on a frappé doucement or légèrement à la porte [b] (NonC: also **~-dancing**) claquettes fpl [2] **taps** NPL (Mil) (= end of the day) (sonnerie f de) l'extinction f des feux; (at funeral) sonnerie f aux morts [3] VI taper (doucement); (repeatedly) tapoter; **to ~ on** or **at the door** frapper doucement à la porte [4] VT taper (doucement); (repeatedly) tapoter; **she ~ped the child on the cheek** elle a tapoté la joue de l'enfant; **he ~ped me on the shoulder** il m'a tapé sur l'épaule; **to ~ in a nail** enfoncer un clou à petits coups; **to ~ one's foot** taper du pied; **he was ~ping an annoying rhythm on his glass** il tapotait sur son verre d'une manière agaçante; **he ~ped his fingers on the steering wheel** il tapotait (sur) le volant [5] COMP ► **tap dance** N claquettes fpl ► **tap-dance** VI faire des claquettes ► **tap-dancer** N danseur m, -euse f de claquettes ► **tap-dancing** N → 1b

► **tap out** VT SEP [a] [+ one's pipe] débourrer [b] [+ signal, code] pianoter; **to ~ out a message in Morse** transmettre un message en morse

tapas ['tæpəs] NPL (Culin) tapas fpl

tape [teɪp] [1] N [a] (gen: of cloth, paper, metal) ruban m, bande f; (for parcels, documents) bolduc m; (also **sticky ~**) scotch® m, ruban m adhésif; (Med) sparadrap m; **the message was coming through on the ~** le message nous parvenait sur la bande (perforée) → **paper, punch¹, red** [b] (Recording, Comput) (= actual tape) bande f magnétique; (= audio cassette) cassette f (audio inv); (= video cassette) cassette f vidéo inv, vidéocassette f; **the ~ is stuck** la bande est coincée; **I'm going to buy a ~** je vais acheter une cassette; (also **video ~**) je vais acheter une cassette vidéo or une vidéocassette; **bring your ~s** apporte tes cassettes; **to get sth down on ~** enregistrer qch; **to make a ~ of a song** enregistrer une chanson c (Sport) fil m (d'arrivée); (at opening ceremonies) ruban m

d (also ~ **measure**) mètre m à ruban; (esp Sewing) centimètre m

e (Sewing) (decorative) ruban m, ganse f; (for binding) extrafort m

2 VT a (also ~ **up**) [+ parcel etc] attacher avec du ruban or du bolduc; (with sticky tape) scotcher*, coller avec du scotch® or du ruban adhésif; **to ~ sb's mouth** bâillonner qn avec du sparadrap; **they ~d her legs and her feet** ils lui ont attaché les jambes et les pieds avec du sparadrap; **he ~d up the hole in the radiator** il a bouché le trou du radiateur avec du scotch® or du ruban adhésif

b (Brit fig) **I've got him ~d*** je sais ce qu'il vaut; **I've got it all ~d*** je sais parfaitement de quoi il retourne; **they had the game/situation ~d*** ils avaient le jeu/la situation bien en main; **he's got the job ~d*** il sait exactement ce qu'il y a à faire

c (= record) [+ song, message] enregistrer (sur bande or au magnétophone); [+ video material] enregistrer; (Scol etc) **~d lesson** leçon f enregistrée sur bande

3 COMP ► **tape deck** N platine f de magnétophone ► **tape drive** N (Comput) dérouleur m de bande magnétique ► **tape head** N tête f de lecture-enregistrement ► **tape machine** N (Brit = tape recorder) magnétophone m ► **tape measure** N mètre m à ruban; (esp Sewing) centimètre m ► **tape-record** VT enregistrer (sur bande) ► **tape recorder** N magnétophone m ► **tape recording** N enregistrement m (sur bande)

► **tape over** (Recording) 1 VT FUS effacer (en enregistrant autre chose) 2 VT SEP **to ~ sth over sth** enregistrer qch sur qch

taper ['teɪpəʳ] 1 N (for lighting) bougie f fine (pour allumer les cierges, bougies etc); (Rel = narrow candle) cierge m 2 VT [+ column, table leg, trouser leg, aircraft wing] fuseler; [+ stick, end of belt] tailler en pointe, effiler; [+ hair] effiler; [+ structure, shape] terminer en pointe 3 VI [column, table leg, trouser leg] finir en fuseau; [stick, end of belt] s'effiler; [hair] être effilé; [structure, outline] se terminer en pointe, s'effiler

► **taper off** 1 VI [sound] se taire peu à peu; [storm] aller en diminuant; [conversation] tomber; **the end ~s off to a point** le bout se termine en pointe; **immigration is expected to ~ off** on s'attend à ce que l'immigration diminue progressivement; **the snow has ~ed off** la neige a presque cessé de tomber; **the president's popularity is ~ing off** la popularité du président est en baisse 2 VT SEP (lit) finir en pointe; (fig) réduire progressivement

tapered ['teɪpəd] ADJ [column, table leg] fuselé, en fuseau; [fingers] fuselé; [trouser leg] en fuseau; [stick] pointu; [hair] effilé; [structure, outline] en pointe

tapering ['teɪpərɪŋ] ADJ [column, fingers] fuselé → **tapered**

tapestry ['tæpɪstrɪ] N tapisserie f; **the Bayeux Tapestry** la tapisserie de Bayeux; **it's all part of life's rich ~** tout cela forme la trame complexe de l'existence, c'est la vie

tapeworm ['teɪpwɜːm] N ténia m, ver m solitaire

tapioca [,tæpɪ'əʊkə] N tapioca m

tapir ['teɪpəʳ] N tapir m

tappet ['tæpɪt] N (Tech) poussoir m (de soupape)

tapping[1] ['tæpɪŋ] N (NonC) a [of pine] gemmage m; [of other trees] incision f; [of electric current] captage m b (Telec) **phone ~** écoutes fpl téléphoniques

tapping[2] ['tæpɪŋ] N (NonC = noise, act) tapotement m; **~ sound** tapotement m

taproom ['tæprʊm] N (Brit) salle f (de bistro(t))

taproot ['tæprʊt] N (Bot) pivot m, racine f pivotante

tar[1] [tɑːʳ] 1 N (NonC) goudron m; (on roads) goudron m, bitume m 2 VT [+ fence etc] goudronner; [+ road] goudronner, bitumer; **~red felt** (= roofing) couverture f bitumée or goudronnée; **to ~ and feather sb** passer qn au goudron et à la plume; (fig) **they're all ~red with the same brush** ils sont tous à mettre dans le même sac*

tar[2]†* [tɑːʳ] N (= sailor) mathurin† m → **jack**

taramasalata [,tærəməsə'lɑːtə] N tarama m

tarantella [,tærən'telə] N tarentelle f

tarantula [tə'ræntjʊlə] N (pl **tarantulas** or **tarantulae** [tə'ræntjʊ,liː]) tarentule f

tarboosh, tarbush [tɑː'buːʃ] N tarbouch(e) m

tardily ['tɑːdɪlɪ] ADV tardivement

tardiness ['tɑːdɪnɪs] N (NonC) (= slowness) lenteur f, manque m d'empressement (**in doing** à faire); (= unpunctuality) manque m de ponctualité

tardy ['tɑːdɪ] 1 ADJ (= late) [response] tardif; (= slow) [progress] lent; **to be ~ in doing sth** faire qch avec du retard 2 COMP ► **tardy slip** N (US Scol) billet m de retard

tare[1] [tɛəʳ] N **~s**†† (= weeds) ivraie f

tare[2] [tɛəʳ] N (Comm = weight) tare f

target ['tɑːgɪt] 1 N (Mil, Sport: for shooting practice, Mil: in attack or mock attack) cible f; (fig = objective) objectif m; **an easy ~** une cible facile; **he was an obvious ~ for his enemies** il constituait une cible évidente pour ses ennemis; **she was the ~ of a violent attack** elle a été victime d'une violente agression; **the ~ of much criticism** la cible or l'objet m de nombreuses critiques; **dead on ~!** pile!; **to be (dead** or **right) on ~** [rocket, missile, bombs etc] suivre (exactement) la trajectoire prévue; (fig) [remark, criticism] mettre (en plein) dans le mille; (in timing etc) être dans les temps; (Comm) [sales] correspondre (exactement) aux objectifs; [forecast] tomber juste; **we're on ~ for sales of £10 million this year** nos ventes devraient correspondre aux objectifs de 10 millions de livres cette année; **the project is on ~ for completion** le projet devrait être fini dans les temps; **they set themselves a ~ of £1,000** ils se sont fixé 1 000 livres comme objectif or un objectif de 1 000 livres; **the ~s for production** les objectifs de production; (Comm) **"on-~ earnings £30,000"** « salaire jusqu'à £30 000 selon résultats »; **our ~ is young people under 20** notre cible or le public ciblé, ce sont les jeunes de moins de 20 ans; **the government met its ~ for reducing unemployment** le gouvernement a réussi à réduire le chômage conformément à ses objectifs; **they were at least 12km off ~** (gen) ils s'étaient écartés de 12 bons kilomètres de leur destination; (Mil: on bombing raid etc) ils étaient à 12 bons kilomètres de leur objectif

2 VT a (Mil etc) [+ enemy troops] prendre pour cible, viser; [+ missile, weapon] pointer, diriger (**on** sur)

b (Comm, TV, Cine = aim at) [+ market, audience etc] cibler, prendre pour cible

c (= direct, send) [+ aid, benefits etc] affecter

3 COMP [date, amount etc] fixé, prévu ► **target area** N (Mil) environs mpl de la cible ► **target group** N groupe m cible inv ► **target language** N langue f cible inv, langue f d'arrivée ► **target practice** N (Mil, Sport) exercices mpl de tir (à la cible) ► **target price** N prix m indicatif or d'objectif ► **target vehicle** N (Space) vaisseau m cible inv

targetable ['tɑːgɪtəbl] ADJ [warhead] dirigeable

targeting ['tɑːgɪtɪŋ] N a (Mil) **the ~ of civilian areas** la prise des quartiers civils pour ci-

ble b (Comm) ciblage m; **the ~ of young people as potential buyers of ...** la prise pour cible des jeunes comme acheteurs potentiels de ...

Tarheel ['tɑːhiːl] 1 N (US) habitant(e) m(f) de la Caroline du Nord 2 COMP ► **the Tarheel State** N la Caroline du Nord

tariff ['tærɪf] 1 N (Econ = taxes) tarif m douanier; (Comm = price list) tarif m, tableau m des prix 2 COMP [concession, quota] tarifaire ► **tariff barrier** N barrière f douanière ► **tariff heading** N (Jur, Fin) position f tarifaire ► **tariff reform** N (Econ) réforme f des tarifs douaniers

tarmac ['tɑːmæk] 1 N a (NonC: esp Brit = substance) **Tarmac**® goudron m b **the ~** (= airport runway) la piste; (= airport apron) l'aire f d'envol 2 VT macadamiser, goudronner

Tarmacadam® [,tɑːmə'kædəm] N = **tarmac 1a**

tarn [tɑːn] N petit lac m (de montagne)

tarnation: [tɑː'neɪʃən] (US dial) 1 EXCL damnation! 2 ADJ fichu* (before n) 3 ADV fichtrement*

tarnish ['tɑːnɪʃ] 1 VT [+ metal] ternir; [+ gilded frame etc] dédorer; [+ mirror] désargenter; (fig) [+ reputation, image, memory] ternir 2 VI se ternir, se dédorer, se désargenter 3 N (NonC) ternissure f, dédorage m, désargentage m

tarot ['tærəʊ] 1 N (NonC) **the ~** le(s) tarot(s) m(pl) 2 COMP ► **tarot card** N tarot m

tarp* [tɑːp] N (US, Austral) ABBR = **tarpaulin b**

tarpaulin [tɑː'pɔːlɪn] N a (NonC) toile f goudronnée b (= sheet) bâche f (goudronnée); (on truck, over boat cargo) prélart m

tarpon ['tɑːpɒn] N tarpon m

tarragon ['tærəgən] 1 N estragon m 2 COMP ► **tarragon vinegar** N vinaigre m à l'estragon

tarring ['tɑːrɪŋ] N goudronnage m

tarry[1] ['tɑːrɪ] ADJ (= like tar) goudronneux, bitumeux; (= covered with tar) plein de goudron; (= smelling of tar) qui sent le goudron

tarry[2] ['tærɪ] VI (liter) (= stay) rester, demeurer; (= delay) s'attarder, tarder

tarsal ['tɑːsəl] ADJ (Anat) tarsien

tarsus ['tɑːsəs] N (pl **tarsi** ['tɑːsaɪ]) tarse m

tart[1] [tɑːt] ADJ a [fruit, flavour] acide, acidulé b [person, remark, comment] acerbe

tart[2] [tɑːt] N a (esp Brit Culin) tarte f; (small) tartelette f; **apple ~** tarte(lette) f aux pommes b (: = prostitute) poule: f, putain: f

► **tart up** VT SEP (Brit pej) [+ house, car] retaper; **to ~ o.s. up** ◊ (= get ~ed up se pomponner; (= get dressed) s'attifer (pej); (= make up) se maquiller excessivement; **she was all ~ed up for** or **to go to the party** elle était toute pomponnée pour aller à la soirée

tartan ['tɑːtən] 1 N tartan m 2 ADJ [garment, fabric] écossais 3 COMP ► **tartan (travelling) rug** N plaid m

Tartar ['tɑːtəʳ] 1 N a Tartare mf or Tatar(e) m(f) b **tartar** tyran m; (woman) mégère f 2 ADJ a (Geog) tartare or tatar b (Culin) **steak tartar(e)** (steak m) tartare m 3 COMP ► **tartar(e) sauce** N (Culin) sauce f tartare

tartar ['tɑːtəʳ] N (NonC: Chem etc) tartre m → **cream**

tartaric [tɑː'tærɪk] ADJ tartrique

tartlet ['tɑːtlɪt] N (Brit) tartelette f

tartly ['tɑːtlɪ] ADV a [say] aigrement, d'une manière acerbe; [observe] d'une manière acerbe b (in taste) **a ~ flavoured tomato sauce** une sauce tomate au goût acide

tartness ['tɑːtnɪs] N a [of flavour, apple] acidité f; [of remark] aigreur f

tarty* ['tɑːtɪ] ADJ [clothes, make-up] vulgaire; **to look ~** faire vulgaire or mauvais genre

Tarzan ['tɑːzən] N Tarzan m

tash* [tæʃ] N = **tache**

task [tɑːsk] **1** N tâche f; (Scol) devoir m; **a hard ~** une lourde tâche; **to take sb to ~** prendre qn à partie, réprimander qn (**for, about** pour) **2** VT **a** [+ sb's brain, patience, imagination] mettre à l'épreuve; [+ sb's strength] éprouver; **it didn't ~ him too much** cela ne lui a pas demandé trop d'effort **b** **to be ~ed with sth** être chargé de qch; **to be ~ed to do sth** or **with doing sth** être chargé de faire qch **3** COMP ► **task force** N (Mil) corps m expéditionnaire; (Police) détachement m spécial

taskmaster ['tɑːskmɑːstə'] N **he's a hard ~** il mène ses subordonnés à la baguette; **duty is a hard ~** le devoir est un maître exigeant

Tasmania [tæz'meɪnɪə] N la Tasmanie

Tasmanian [tæz'meɪnɪən] **1** ADJ tasmanien **2** N Tasmanien(ne) m(f)

Tasman Sea ['tæzmən'siː] N mer f de Tasman

tassel ['tæsəl] N gland m; (= pompon) pompon m

tasselled ['tæsəld] ADJ à glands

Tasso ['tæsəʊ] N le Tasse

taste [teɪst] **1** N **a** (= flavour) goût m, saveur f; **it has an odd ~** cela a un drôle de goût; **it has no ~** cela n'a aucun goût or aucune saveur; **it left a nasty** or **bad ~ (in his mouth)** (lit) ça lui a laissé un mauvais goût or un goût désagréable dans la bouche; (fig) ça lui a laissé un goût amer **b** (NonC = sense, culture etc) goût m (also fig); **sweet to the ~** (au goût) sucré; (fig) **to have (good) ~** avoir du goût, avoir bon goût; **he has no ~** il n'a aucun goût, il a très mauvais goût; **in good/bad ~** de bon/mauvais goût; **in poor** or **doubtful ~** d'un goût douteux; **the house is furnished in impeccable ~** la maison est meublée avec beaucoup de goût; **people of ~** les gens de goût **c** **to have a ~ of sth** (lit) goûter (à) qch; (fig) goûter de qch; **would you like a ~ (of it)?** voulez-vous (y) goûter?; **he had a ~ of the cake** il a goûté au gâteau; **I gave him a ~ of the wine** je lui ai fait goûter le vin; **it gave him a ~ of military life/of the work** cela lui a donné un aperçu de la vie militaire/du travail; **he's had a ~ of prison** il a tâté de la prison; **to give sb a ~ of his own medicine** rendre à qn la monnaie de sa pièce; **to give sb a ~ of the whip** montrer à qn ce qui l'attend s'il ne marche pas droit; **a ~ of happiness** une idée du bonheur; **we got a ~ of his anger** il nous a donné un échantillon de sa colère; **it was a ~ of things to come** c'était un avant-goût de l'avenir **d** (= small amount, trace) **a ~ of** (gen) un (tout) petit peu de; [+ salt etc] une pincée de; [+ vinegar, cream, brandy] une goutte de, un soupçon de **e** (= liking) goût m, penchant m (**for** pour); **is it to your ~?** est-ce que cela vous plaît?; **to have a ~ for ...** avoir le goût or un penchant pour ...; **to acquire** or **develop a ~ for ...** prendre goût à ...; (Culin) **sweeten to ~** sucrer à volonté; **it's a matter of ~** c'est affaire de goût; **there's no accounting for ~** des goûts et des couleurs on ne discute pas; **each to his own ~** ◊ **~s differ** chacun ses goûts; **her novels are too violent for my ~** ses romans sont trop violents à mon goût; **his ~ in music** ses goûts musicaux; **she has expensive ~s** elle a des goûts de luxe; **he has expensive ~s in cars** il a le goût des voitures de luxe **2** VT **a** (= perceive flavour of) sentir (le goût de); **I can't ~ the garlic** je ne sens pas (le goût de) l'ail; **I can't ~ anything when I have a cold** je trouve tout insipide quand j'ai un rhume; **you won't ~ it** tu n'en sentiras pas le goût **b** (= sample) [+ food, drink] goûter à; (esp for first time) goûter de; (= to test quality) goûter; [+ wine] (at table) goûter; (at wine-tasting) déguster; (fig) [+ power, freedom, success] goûter à, connaître; **just ~ this!** goûtez à ça!; **~ the sauce before adding salt** goûtez la sauce avant d'ajouter du sel; **you must ~ my marmalade** je vais vous faire goûter de ma confiture d'oranges; **I haven't ~d salmon for years** ça fait des années que je n'ai pas mangé or goûté de saumon; **I have never ~d snails** je n'ai jamais mangé d'escargots; **he had not ~d food for a week** il n'avait rien mangé depuis une semaine → **wine** **3** VI **it doesn't ~ at all** cela n'a aucun goût; **to ~ bitter** avoir un goût amer; **to ~ good/bad** avoir bon/mauvais goût; **to ~ of** or **like sth** avoir un goût de qch; **it ~s of garlic** ça a un goût d'ail; **it doesn't ~ of anything in particular** cela n'a pas de goût spécial; **it ~s all right to me** d'après moi cela a un goût normal **4** COMP ► **taste bud** N papille f gustative

tasteful ['teɪstfʊl] ADJ de bon goût, d'un goût sûr

tastefully ['teɪstfəlɪ] ADV [decorated, furnished] avec goût; **the sex scenes are very ~ done** les scènes érotiques sont d'un goût exquis; **his ~ modern flat** son appartement moderne agencé avec (beaucoup de) goût

tastefulness ['teɪstfʊlnɪs] N bon goût m, goût m sûr

tasteless ['teɪstlɪs] ADJ [food, medicine] fade; (fig) [ornament, clothes, remark, action] de mauvais goût

tastelessly ['teɪstlɪslɪ] ADV [decorated] sans goût; **~ extravagant** d'une extravagance de très mauvais goût; **~ inappropriate music** une musique mal choisie pour les circonstances; **her ordeal was ~ handled in the press** sa pénible épreuve a été relatée sans aucun tact par la presse

tastelessness ['teɪstlɪsnɪs] N manque m de saveur, fadeur f (pej); [of ornament, dress, remark etc] mauvais goût m

taster ['teɪstə'] N **a** (= person) dégustateur m, -trice f **b** (Brit* = foretaste) avant-goût m; **that is just a ~ of things to come** ce n'est qu'un avant-goût de ce qui se prépare

tastiness ['teɪstɪnɪs] N saveur f agréable, goût m délicieux

tasting ['teɪstɪŋ] N dégustation f

tasty ['teɪstɪ] ADJ **a** (Culin) savoureux **b** (* = interesting) [gossip, news] croustillant **c** (Brit* = sexy) [person] sexy* inv

tat[1] [tæt] **1** VI faire de la frivolité (dentelle) **2** VT faire en frivolité

tat[2]* [tæt] N (NonC: Brit pej = shabby clothes) friperies fpl; (= goods) camelote* f

ta-ta* ['tæ'tɑː] EXCL (Brit) au revoir!, salut!*

tattered ['tætəd] ADJ **a** [clothes, flag] en loques; [book] tout abîmé; [handkerchief, paper, poster] déchiré; [person] déguenillé, loqueteux **b** [reputation] en miettes

tatters ['tætəz] NPL lambeaux mpl, loques fpl; (lit) **in ~** en lambeaux, en loques; (fig) **his confidence was in ~** il avait perdu toute confiance en lui; **the government's reputation was in ~** la réputation du gouvernement était ruinée

tattie* ['tætɪ] N (Scot) patate* f

tatting ['tætɪŋ] N (NonC) frivolité f (dentelle)

tattle ['tætl] **1** VI (= gossip) jaser, cancaner; (= tell secrets) cafarder* **2** N (NonC) bavardage m, commérages mpl

tattler ['tætlə'] N (= man or woman) commère f (pej), concierge* mf (pej)

tattletale ['tætl,teɪl] (US) **1** N commère f (pej), concierge* mf (pej) **2** ADJ (fig) [mark etc] révélateur (-trice f)

tattoo[1] [tə'tuː] **1** VT tatouer **2** N tatouage m

tattoo[2] [tə'tuː] N (Mil: on drum, bugle) retraite f; (Brit Mil = spectacle) parade f militaire; (gen = drumming) battements mpl; **to beat a ~ on the drums** battre le tambour

tattooist [tə'tuːɪst] N tatoueur m, -euse f

tatty[1]* ['tætɪ] ADJ (esp Brit) [clothes, shoes] fatigué; [house, furniture] en mauvais état; [book, poster] en mauvais état, écorné; [plant, paintwork] défraîchi; **to get ~** (gen) s'abîmer; [poster, paint] se défraîchir; **she looked rather ~** elle était plutôt défraîchie

tatty[2]* ['tætɪ] N = **tattie**

taught [tɔːt] VB pt, ptp of **teach**

taunt [tɔːnt] **1** N raillerie f, sarcasme m **2** VT railler (liter), persifler (liter); **to ~ sb with cowardice** taxer qn de lâcheté sur un ton railleur or persifleur; **to ~ sb with racial abuse** accabler qn d'injures racistes; **he ~ed his wife with his affairs** il torturait sa femme en racontant ses infidélités

taunting ['tɔːntɪŋ] **1** N railleries fpl, persiflage m, sarcasmes mpl **2** ADJ railleur, persifleur, sarcastique

tauntingly ['tɔːntɪŋlɪ] ADV d'un ton railleur or persifleur or sarcastique

taupe [təʊp] ADJ, N (couleur f) taupe m inv

Taurean [,tɔː'rɪən] N **to be a ~** être (du) Taureau

tauromachy [,tɔː'ræmækɪ] N (liter) tauromachie f

Taurus ['tɔːrəs] N (Astron) le Taureau; (Astrol) **I'm (a) ~** je suis (du) Taureau

taut [tɔːt] ADJ **a** (= tight, tense) [skin, muscle, rope, person, face, voice] tendu; [lips] crispé; [nerves] à vif; **to hold sth ~** tendre qch; **stretched ~** tendu; **her nerves were (stretched)** → elle avait les nerfs à vif; **his face was ~ with anger** il avait le visage crispé de colère **b** (= firm) [body] ferme; **to be ~** [person] avoir le corps ferme **c** (= well-constructed) [novel, film] bien ficelé*

tauten ['tɔːtn] **1** VT tendre **2** VI se tendre

tautly ['tɔːtlɪ] ADV (lit) [stretch] à fond; (fig) [say] d'une voix tendue or crispée

tautness ['tɔːtnɪs] N tension f (d'un cordage etc)

tautological [,tɔːtə'lɒdʒɪkəl] ADJ tautologique

tautology [tɔː'tɒlədʒɪ] N tautologie f

tavern† ['tævən] N taverne† f, auberge f

tawdriness ['tɔːdrɪnɪs] N [of goods] qualité f médiocre; [of clothes] mauvais goût m tapageur; [of jewellery] clinquant m; (fig) [of motive etc] indignité f

tawdry ['tɔːdrɪ] ADJ **a** (= tacky) [jewellery, clothes] bon marché **b** (= sordid) [affair, story] sordide

tawny ['tɔːnɪ] **1** ADJ [hair, fur, animal] (de couleur) fauve inv; [skin] mordoré; **~ brown** marron inv foncé **2** COMP ► **tawny owl** N hulotte f, chat-huant m ► **tawny port** N porto m tawny

tax [tæks] **1** N (on goods, services) taxe f, impôt m; (also income ~) impôts mpl; **before/after ~** avant/après l'impôt; **half of it goes in ~** on en perd la moitié en impôts; **how much ~ do you pay?** combien d'impôts payez-vous?; **I paid £3,000 in ~ last year** j'ai payé 3 000 livres d'impôts l'an dernier; **free of ~** exempt or exonéré d'impôt; **to put** or **place** or **levy a ~ on sth** taxer or imposer qch; **petrol ~** ◊ **~ on petrol** taxe(s) f(pl) sur l'essence; (fig) **it was a ~ on his strength** cela a mis ses forces à l'épreuve **2** VT **a** [+ goods] taxer, imposer; [+ income, profits, person] imposer; (fig) [+ patience] mettre à l'épreuve; [+ strength] éprouver; **he is very heavily ~ed** il paie beaucoup d'impôts, il est lourdement imposé → **taxing** **b** **to ~ sb with sth** taxer or accuser qn de qch; **to ~ sb with doing** accuser qn de faire (or d'avoir fait) **c** (Brit) **to ~ one's car** acheter la vignette pour sa voiture **3** COMP (system, incentive etc) fiscal ► **tax accountant** N conseiller m fiscal ► **tax adjust-**

ment N redressement *m* fiscal ► **tax allowance** N abattement *m* or dégrèvement *m* fiscal ► **tax authority** N Administration *f* fiscale, Trésor *m* (public) ► **tax avoidance** N évasion *f* fiscale (légale) ► **tax band** N = **tax bracket** ► **tax base** N assiette *f* de l'impôt ► **tax bite** N ponction *f* fiscale, prélèvement *m* fiscal ► **tax bracket** N tranche *f* du barème fiscal or d'impôts ► **tax break** N réduction *f* d'impôt, avantage *m* fiscal ► **tax burden** N charge *f* fiscale ► **tax code** N (*Brit*) code *m* des impôts ► **tax coding** N indice *m* d'abattement fiscal ► **tax-collecting** N perception *f* des impôts ► **tax collector** N percepteur *m* ► **tax credit** N crédit *m* d'impôt ► **tax cut** N réduction *f* des impôts ► **tax-deductible** ADJ déductible des impôts ► **tax demand** N avis *m* d'imposition ► **tax disc** N (*Brit Aut*) vignette *f* (automobile) ► **tax dodge*** N évasion *f* fiscale ► **tax evader** N fraudeur *m*, -euse *f* fiscal(e) ► **tax evasion** N fraude *f*, évasion *f* fiscale ► **tax-exempt** ADJ (*US*) = **tax-free** ► **tax exemption** N exonération *f* d'impôts ► **tax exile** N personne *f* qui fuit le fisc; **to become a ~ exile** s'expatrier pour raisons fiscales ► **tax form** N feuille *f* d'impôts ► **tax-free** ADJ exonéré d'impôts ► **tax haven** N paradis *m* fiscal ► **tax immunity** N immunité *f* fiscale ► **tax incentive** N incitation *f* fiscale ► **tax inspector** N inspecteur *m*, -trice *f* des impôts ► **tax levy** N prélèvement *m* fiscal ► **tax liability** N assujettissement *m* à l'impôt ► **tax net** N **to bring sb/sth within the ~ net** ramener qn/qch dans une fourchette imposable or dans la première tranche imposable ► **tax purposes** NPL **for ~ purposes** pour des raisons fiscales ► **tax rebate** N dégrèvement *m* fiscal ► **tax refugee** N = **tax exile** ► **tax relief** N dégrèvement *m* or allègement *m* fiscal ► **tax return** N (feuille *f* de) déclaration *f* de revenus or d'impôts ► **tax revenue** N recettes *fpl* fiscales ► **tax shelter** N échappatoire *f* fiscale ► **tax year** N exercice *m* fiscal, année *f* fiscale

taxable ['tæksəbl] [1] ADJ [*assets, income, winnings*] imposable [2] COMP ► **taxable amount** N base *f* d'imposition ► **taxable year** N année *f* fiscale, exercice *m* fiscal (*Fin*)

taxation [tæk'seɪʃən] [1] N (*NonC*) (= *act*) taxation *f*; (= *taxes*) impôts *mpl*, contributions *fpl* → **double**, **immune** [2] COMP [*authority, system*] fiscal

taxeme ['tæksi:m] N taxème *m*

taxi ['tæksɪ] [1] N (*pl* **taxis** or **taxies**) taxi *m*; **by ~** en taxi [2] VI (*aircraft*) se déplacer or rouler lentement au sol; **the plane ~ed along the runway** l'avion a roulé sur la piste; **the aircraft ~ed to a standstill** l'avion a roulé sur la piste avant de s'arrêter [b] (= *go by taxi*) aller en taxi [3] COMP [*charges etc*] de taxi ► **taxi dancer** N (*US*) taxi-girl *m* ► **taxi driver** N chauffeur *m* de taxi ► **taxi fare** N (*gen*) tarif *m* de taxi; **I haven't got the ~ fare** je n'ai pas de quoi payer le taxi ► **taxi rank** (*Brit*), **taxi stance** (*esp Scot*), **taxi stand** (*esp US*) N station *f* de taxis

taxicab ['tæksɪkæb] N (*esp US*) taxi *m*

taxidermist ['tæksɪdɜ:mɪst] N empailleur *m*, -euse *f*, naturaliste *mf*

taxidermy ['tæksɪdɜ:mɪ] N empaillage *m*, naturalisation *f*, taxidermie *f*

taximeter ['tæksimi:tə] N taximètre *m*, compteur *m* (de taxi)

taxing ['tæksɪŋ] ADJ (*mentally*) [*problem*] ardu; (*physically*) [*work*] pénible; **physically/emotionally ~** pénible sur le plan physique/affectif

taxiplane ['tæksipleɪn] N (*US Aviat*) avion-taxi *m*

taxiway ['tæksiweɪ] N (*Aviat*) taxiway *m*, piste *f* de déroulement

taxman* ['tæksmæn] N (*pl* **-men**) percepteur *m*

taxonomist [tæk'sɒnəmɪst] N taxonomiste or taxinomiste *mf*

taxonomy [tæk'sɒnəmɪ] N taxonomie or taxinomie *f*

taxpayer ['tækspeɪə'] N contribuable *mf*; **the British ~ has to pay for it** ce sont les contribuables britanniques qui payeront

TB [ti:'bi:] N ABBR = **tuberculosis**

tba [,ti:bi:'eɪ] (ABBR = **to be arranged** or **to be announced**) à préciser

tbs (*pl* **tbs**) , **tbsp** (*pl* **tbsp** or **tbsps**) , **tblsp** (*pl* **tblsp** or **tblsps**) N (ABBR = **tablespoonful**) c. à soupe *f*; **1 ~ vinegar** 1 c. à soupe de vinaigre

TCE [ti:si:'i:] N (ABBR = **ton coal equivalent**) TEC *f*

Tchaikovsky [tʃaɪ'kɒfskɪ] N Tchaïkovski *m*

TD [ti:'di:] N [a] (*Brit*) ABBR = **Territorial Decoration** [b] (*American Ftbl*) ABBR = **touchdown** [c] (*US*) (ABBR = **Treasury Department**) → **treasury**

te [ti:] N (*Mus*) si *m*

tea [ti:] [1] N [a] (= *plant, substance*) thé *m*; **she made a pot of ~** elle a fait du thé; **I wouldn't do it for all the ~ in China** je ne le ferais pour rien au monde; (*fig*) **~ and sympathy** réconfort *m* → **cup** [b] (*esp Brit = meal*) thé *m*; (*for children*) ≈ goûter *m*; **to have ~** prendre le thé; [*children*] goûter → **high** [c] (*herbal*) infusion *f*, tisane *f* → **beef** [2] COMP ► **tea bag** N sachet *m* de thé ► **tea ball** N (*US*) boule *f* or infuseur *m* à thé ► **tea boy** N (*Brit*) jeune employé chargé de préparer le thé ► **tea break** N (*Brit*) pause-thé *f*; **to have a ~ break** faire la pause-thé ► **tea caddy** N boîte *f* à thé ► **tea chest** N caisse *f* (à thé) ► **tea-cloth** N (*Brit*) (*for dishes*) torchon *m* (à vaisselle); (*for table*) nappe *f* (à thé); (*for trolley, tray*) napperon *m* ► **tea cosy** (*Brit*), **tea cozy** (*US*) N couvre-théière *m*, cache-théière *m* ► **tea dance** N thé *m* dansant ► **tea infuser** N (*Brit*) boule *f* or infuseur *m* à thé ► **tea kettle** N (*US*) bouilloire *f* ► **tea lady** N (*Brit*) dame qui prépare le thé pour les employés d'une entreprise ► **tea leaf** N (*pl* **tea leaves**) feuille *f* de thé → **read** ► **tea party** N thé *m* (réception) ► **tea-plant** N arbre *m* à thé ► **tea plate** N petite assiette *f* ► **tea rose** N rose-thé *f* ► **tea service**, **tea set** N service *m* à thé ► **tea strainer** N passe-thé *m inv* ► **tea table** N (*esp Brit*) **they sat at the ~ table** ils étaient assis autour de la table mise pour le thé; **the subject was raised at the ~ table** on en a discuté pendant le thé; **to set the ~ table** mettre la table pour le thé ► **tea-things** NPL **where are the ~-things?** où est le service à thé?; **to wash up the ~-things** faire la vaisselle après le thé ► **tea towel** N (*Brit*) torchon *m* (à vaisselle) ► **tea tray** N plateau *m* (à thé) ► **tea trolley** N (*Brit*) table *f* roulante ► **tea urn** N fontaine *f* à thé ► **tea wagon** N (*US*) = **tea trolley**

teacake ['ti:keɪk] N (*Brit*) petit pain *m* brioché

teacart ['ti:kɑ:t] N (*US*) = **tea trolley** → **tea**

teach [ti:tʃ] (*pret, ptp* **taught**) [1] VT (*gen*) apprendre (**sb sth, sth to sb** qch à qn); (*Scol, Univ etc*) enseigner (**sb sth, sth to sb** qch à qn); **to ~ sb (how) to do** apprendre à qn à faire; **I'll ~ you what to do** je t'apprendrai ce qu'il faut faire; **he ~es French** il enseigne le français; **he taught her French** il lui a appris or enseigné le français; (*US*) **to ~ school** être professeur; **to ~ o.s. (to do) sth** apprendre (à faire) qch tout seul; (*fig*) **I'll ~ you a lesson!** je vais t'apprendre!; **that will ~ him a lesson!** cela lui servira de leçon!; **they could ~ us a thing or two about family values** ils auraient beaucoup à nous apprendre sur les valeurs familiales; **that will ~ you to mind your own business!** ça t'apprendra à te mêler de tes affaires!; **I'll ~ you (not) to speak to me like that!** je vais t'apprendre à me parler sur ce

ton!; **you can't ~ him anything about cars** il n'a rien à apprendre de personne en matière de voitures; **don't (try to) ~ your grandmother to suck eggs!*** on n'apprend pas à un vieux singe à faire des grimaces! ■ (*PROV*) **you can't ~ an old dog new tricks** ce n'est pas à son (or mon *etc*) âge qu'on apprend de nouveaux trucs [2] VI enseigner; **he always wanted to ~** il a toujours eu le désir d'enseigner; **he had been ~ing all morning** il avait fait cours or fait la classe toute la matinée [3] COMP ► **teach-in** N séminaire *m* (sur un thème)

teachability [,ti:tʃə'bɪlɪtɪ] N (*esp US*) aptitude *f* à apprendre

teachable ['ti:tʃəbl] ADJ (*esp US*) [*child*] scolarisable; [*subject, skill*] enseignable, susceptible d'être enseigné

teacher ['ti:tʃə'] [1] N (*in secondary school: also private tutor*) professeur *m*; (*in primary school*) professeur *m* des écoles, instituteur *m*, -trice *f*; (*in special school, prison*) éducateur *m*, -trice *f*; (*gen = member of teaching profession*) enseignant(e) *m(f)*; **she is a maths ~** elle est professeur de maths; **~'s (hand)book** livre *m* du maître; (*collectively*) **the ~s accepted the government's offer** les enseignants ont or le corps enseignant a accepté l'offre du gouvernement; **the ~s' strike/dispute** la grève/le conflit des enseignants → **2** [2] COMP ► **teacher certification** N (*US*) habilitation *f* à enseigner ► **teacher education** N (*US*) formation *f* pédagogique (des enseignants) ► **teacher evaluation** N (*US Scol, Univ*) appréciations *fpl* sur les professeurs (*par les étudiants ou par l'administration*) ► **teacher-pupil ratio** N taux *m* d'encadrement; **a high/low ~-pupil ratio** un fort/faible taux d'encadrement ► **teacher's aide** N (*US*) assistant(e) *m(f)* du professeur (or de l'instituteur) ► **teachers' certificate** N (*US*) = **teacher training certificate** ► **teachers' college** N (*US*) = **teacher training college** ► **teachers' training** N = **teacher training** ► **teachers' training certificate** N = **teacher training certificate** ► **teachers' training college** N = **teacher training college** ► **teacher training** N (*Brit*) formation *f* pédagogique (des enseignants) ► **teacher training certificate** N (*for primary school*) Certificat *m* d'aptitude au professorat des écoles, ≈ CAPE *m*; (*for secondary schools*) ≈ Certificat *m* d'aptitude au professorat de l'enseignement du second degré, ≈ CAPES *m*; (*for secondary technical schools*) ≈ Certificat *m* d'aptitude au professorat de l'enseignement technique, ≈ CAPET *m* ► **teacher training college** N ≈ Institut *m* universitaire de formation des maîtres, ≈ IUFM *m*

teaching ['ti:tʃɪŋ] [1] N [a] (*NonC*) (= *act, profession*) enseignement *m*; **he's got 16 hours ~ a week** il a 16 heures de cours par semaine; **to go into ~** entrer dans l'enseignement; (*Educ*) **Teaching of English as a Foreign Language** (enseignement *m* de l')anglais *m* langue étrangère; (*Educ*) **Teaching of English as a Second Language** enseignement *m* de l'anglais langue seconde; **Teaching of English as a Second or Other Language** enseignement *m* de l'anglais langue seconde ou autre → TEFL, TESL, TESOL, ELT → **team** [b] (*also* **~s**) [*of philosopher, sage etc*] enseignements *mpl* (*liter*) (**on, about** sur) [2] COMP ► **teaching aid** N outil *m* pédagogique ► **teaching aids** NPL matériel *m* pédagogique ► **teaching assistant** N (*US Univ*) étudiant(e) *m(f)* chargé(e) de travaux dirigés ► **teaching certificate** N (*US*) = **teacher training certificate** → **teacher** ► **teaching equipment** N = **teaching aids** ► **teaching hospital** N centre *m* hospitalier universitaire, CHU *m* ► **teaching job, teaching posi-**

tion, teaching post N poste *m* d'enseignant ▶ **teaching practice** N (*Brit*) stage *m* de formation des enseignants ▶ **the teaching profession** N (= *activity*) l'enseignement *m*; (*in secondary schools only*) le professorat; (*teachers collectively*) le corps enseignant, les enseignants *mpl* ▶ **teaching staff** N personnel *m* enseignant, enseignants *mpl*, équipe *f* pédagogique

teacup ['tiːkʌp] N tasse *f* à thé → **read, storm**

teacupful ['tiːkʌpful] N tasse *f*

teahouse ['tiːhaʊs] N maison *f* de thé

teak [tiːk] N teck *or* tek *m*

teal [tiːl] N (*pl* **teal** *or* **teals**) sarcelle *f*

team [tiːm] **1** N (*Sport, gen*) équipe *f*; (*of horses, oxen*) attelage *m*; **football ~** équipe *f* de football; **our research** = notre équipe de chercheurs **2** VT (*also ~ up*) (+ *actor, worker*) mettre en collaboration (**with** avec); (+ *clothes, accessories*) associer (**with** avec) **3** COMP ▶ **team captain** N capitaine *m* ▶ **team games** NPL jeux *mpl* d'équipe ▶ **team leader** N chef *m* d'équipe ▶ **team-mate** N coéquipier *m*, -ière *f* ▶ **team member** N (*Sport*) équipier *m*, -ière *f* ▶ **team spirit** N (*NonC*) esprit *m* d'équipe ▶ **team teaching** N (*NonC*) enseignement *m* en équipe

▶ **team up** **1** VI (*people*) faire équipe (**with** avec, **to do** pour faire); (*colours*) s'harmoniser (**with** avec); (*clothes, accessories, furnishings etc*) s'associer (**with** avec); **he ~ed up with them to get ...** il s'est allié à eux pour obtenir ... **2** VT SEP → **team 2**

teamster ['tiːmstər] N (*US*) routier *m or* camionneur *m* syndiqué

teamwork ['tiːmwɜːk] N (*NonC*) travail *m* d'équipe

teapot ['tiːpɒt] N théière *f*

tear¹ [tɛər] (*vb: pret* **tore**, *ptp* **torn**) **1** N déchirure *f*, accroc *m*; **to make a ~ in sth** déchirer qch; **it has a ~ in it** c'est déchiré, il y a un accroc dedans

2 VT **a** (= *rip*) (+ *cloth, garment*) déchirer, faire un trou *or* un accroc à; (+ *flesh, paper*) déchirer; **to ~ a hole in ...** faire une déchirure *or* un accroc à ..., faire un trou dans ...; **he tore it along the dotted line** il l'a déchiré en suivant le pointillé; **to ~ to pieces** *or* **to shreds** *or* **to bits***** (+ *paper*) déchirer en petits morceaux; (+ *garment*) mettre en pièces *or* lambeaux; (*fig*) (+ *prey*) mettre en pièces; (*fig*) (+ *play, performance*) éreinter; (+ *argument, suggestion*) descendre en flammes**; **to ~ sth loose** arracher qch; **to ~ (o.s.) loose** se libérer; **to ~ open** (+ *envelope*) déchirer; (+ *letter*) déchirer l'enveloppe de; (+ *parcel*) ouvrir en déchirant l'emballage; **clothes torn to rags** vêtements mis en lambeaux; **I tore my hand on a nail** je me suis ouvert la main sur un clou; (*Med*) **to ~ a muscle/ligament** se déchirer un muscle/un ligament; (*fig*) **that's torn it!***** voilà qui flanque tout par terre!**
b (*fig*) **to be torn by war/remorse** *etc* être déchiré par la guerre/le remords *etc*; **to be torn between two things/people** être tiraillé par *or* balancer entre deux choses/personnes; **I'm very much torn** j'hésite beaucoup (entre les deux)
c (= *snatch*) arracher (**from sb** à qn, **out of** *or* **off** *or* **from sth** de qch); **he tore it out of her hand** il le lui a arraché des mains; **he was torn from his seat** il a été arraché de son siège

3 VI **a** (*cloth, paper etc*) se déchirer
b **he tore at the wrapping paper** il a déchiré l'emballage (impatiemment); **he tore at the earth with his bare hands** il a griffé la terre de ses mains nues
c (= *rush*) **to ~ out/down** *etc* sortir/descendre *etc* à toute allure *or* à toute vitesse; **he tore up the stairs** il a monté l'escalier quatre à quatre; **to ~ along the road** (*person*) filer à toute allure le long de la route; (*car*) rouler à toute allure le long de la route; **they tore after him**

ils se sont lancés *or* précipités à sa poursuite; (*fig*) **to ~ into sb***** (= *attack verbally*) s'en prendre violemment à qn; (= *scold*) passer un savon à qn**

4 COMP ▶ **tear-off** ADJ amovible; **~-off calendar** éphéméride *f* ▶ **tear sheet** N feuillet *m* détachable

▶ **tear apart** VT SEP déchirer; (*fig* = *divide*) déchirer; **his love for Julie is ~ing him apart** son amour pour Julie le déchire

▶ **tear away** **1** VI (*person*) partir comme un bolide; (*car*) démarrer en trombe **2** VT SEP (*lit, fig*) arracher (**from sb** à qn, **from sth** de qch); (*fig*) **I couldn't ~ myself away from it/him** je n'arrivais pas à m'en arracher/à m'arracher à lui **3** **~away** N → **tearaway**

▶ **tear down** VT SEP (+ *poster, flag*) arracher (**from** de); (+ *building*) démolir

▶ **tear off** **1** VI = **tear away 1** **2** VT SEP **a** (+ *label, wrapping*) arracher (**from** de); (+ *perforated page, calendar leaf*) détacher (**from** de) → **strip** **b** (= *remove*) (+ *one's clothes*) enlever à la hâte; (+ *sb's clothes*) arracher **c** (** = write hurriedly*) (+ *letter etc*) bâcler**, torcher** **3** **~-off** ADJ → **tear-off**

▶ **tear out** **1** VI → **tear¹ 3c** **2** VT SEP arracher (**from** de); (+ *cheque, ticket*) détacher (**from** de); **to ~ sb's eyes out** arracher les yeux à qn; **to ~ one's hair out** s'arracher les cheveux

▶ **tear up** VT SEP **a** (+ *paper etc*) déchirer, mettre en morceaux *or* en pièces; (*fig*) (+ *contract*) déchirer; (+ *offer*) reprendre **b** (+ *stake, weed, shrub*) arracher; (+ *tree*) déraciner

tear² [tɪər] **1** N larme *f*; **in ~s** en larmes; **there were ~s in her eyes** elle avait les larmes aux yeux; **she had ~s of joy in her eyes** elle pleurait de joie; **near** *or* **close to ~s** au bord des larmes; **to burst** *or* **dissolve into ~s** fondre en larmes; **the memory/thought brought ~s to his eyes** à ce souvenir/cette pensée il avait les larmes aux yeux; **the film/book/experience brought ~s to his eyes** ce film/ce livre/cette expérience lui a fait venir les larmes aux yeux; **it will end in ~s!** ça va finir mal! → **shed²** **2** COMP ▶ **tear bomb** N grenade *f* lacrymogène ▶ **tear duct** N conduit *m* lacrymal ▶ **tear gas** N gaz *m* lacrymogène ▶ **tear-jerker***** N (***) larmoyant; (*mea, plea, story*) larmoyant; **the film/book** *etc* **was a real ~-jerker** c'était un film/roman *etc* tout à fait du genre à faire pleurer dans les chaumières ▶ **tear-stained** ADJ baigné de larmes

tearaway ['tɛərəweɪ] N (*Brit*) casse-cou *m*

teardrop ['tɪədrɒp] N larme *f*

tearful ['tɪəful] ADJ (*face*) plein de larmes; (*eyes, look*) plein de larmes, larmoyant; (*farewell*) larmoyant; (*reunion*) ému; (*plea, story*) éploré; **to be ~** (*person*) (= *about to cry*) être au bord des larmes, avoir envie de pleurer; (= *in tears*) être en larmes; **in a ~ voice** (avec) des larmes dans la voix, d'une voix éplorée; **to feel ~** avoir envie de pleurer; **to become ~** avoir les larmes aux yeux

tearfully ['tɪəfʊlɪ] ADV (*say*) en pleurant; (*admit*) les larmes aux yeux

tearing ['tɛərɪŋ] **1** N déchirement *m* **2** ADJ **a** **~ noise** un bruit de déchirement **b** (*Brit**) **to be in a ~ hurry** être terriblement pressé; **to do sth in a ~ hurry** faire qch à toute vitesse

tearless ['tɪəlɪs] ADJ sans larmes

tearlessly ['tɪəlɪslɪ] ADV sans larmes, sans pleurer

tearoom ['tiːrʊm] N salon *m* de thé

tease [tiːz] **1** N (= *person*) (*gen*) taquin(e) *m(f)*; (*sexual*) allumeur *m*, -euse *f* **2** VT **a** (*playfully*) taquiner; (*cruelly*) tourmenter; (*sexually*) allumer **b** (*Tech*) (+ *cloth*) peigner; (+ *wool*) carder

▶ **tease out** VT SEP **a** (+ *tangle of wool, knots, matted hair*) débrouiller *or* démêler (patiemment); (*fig*) **to ~ something out of sb** tirer les vers du nez à qn **b** (+ *meaning, sense*) dénicher

teasel ['tiːzl] N (*Bot*) cardère *f*; (*Tech*) carde *f*

teaser ['tiːzər] N **a** (= *person*) (*gen*) taquin(e) *m(f)*; (*sexual*) allumeur *m*, -euse *f* **b** (= *problem*) problème *m* (difficile); (= *tricky question*) colle *f*

teashop ['tiːʃɒp] N (*Brit*) salon *m* de thé

teasing ['tiːzɪŋ] **1** N (*NonC*) taquineries *fpl* **2** ADJ taquin

teasingly ['tiːzɪŋlɪ] ADV **a** (*say, ask, hint*) d'un ton taquin, pour me (*or* le *etc*) taquiner; **he looked at me** ~ il m'a regardé d'un air taquin **b** (*sexually*) de façon aguichante; **~ erotic** sexy** et provocant

Teasmade®, Teasmaid® ['tiːzmeɪd] N *machine à faire le thé*

teaspoon ['tiːspuːn] N petite cuiller *f*, cuiller *f* à thé *or* à café

teaspoonful ['tiːspuːnfʊl] N cuillerée *f* à café

teat [tiːt] N (*of animal*) tétine *f*, tette *f*; (*of cow*) trayon *m*; (*of woman*) mamelon *m*, bout *m* de sein; (*Brit*) (*of baby's bottle*) tétine *f*; (= *dummy*) tétine *f*; (*Tech*) téton *m*

teatime ['tiːtaɪm] N (*esp Brit*) l'heure *f* du thé

teazel, teazle ['tiːzl] N = **teasel**

TEC [ˌtiːiːˈsiː] N (*Brit*) (ABBR = **Training and Enterprise Council**) → **training**

tech*** [tek] N **a** (*Brit*) (ABBR = **technical college**) ≈ CET *m* **b** (ABBR = **technology**) → **high**

techie*** ['tekɪ] N (= *technician*) technicien(ne) *m(f)*; (= *technologist*) technologue *mf*; (= *technophile*) crack** *m* en technologie

technetium [tekˈniːʃɪəm] N technétium *m*

technical ['teknɪkəl] **1** ADJ technique; **~ ability** *or* **skill** compétence *f* technique; **~ problems** des problèmes *mpl* techniques *or* d'ordre technique; **for ~ reasons** pour des raisons techniques *or* d'ordre technique; **~ language** langue *f or* langage *m* technique; (*gen*) **it's just a ~ point** c'est un point de détail; (*Jur*) **a judgement quashed on a ~ point** un arrêt cassé pour vice de forme; (*Jur*) **this constitutes a ~ plea of not guilty** cela équivaut (théoriquement) à plaider non coupable

2 COMP ▶ **technical college** N (*Brit*) collège *m* (d'enseignement) technique ▶ **technical drawing** N (*NonC*) dessin *m* industriel ▶ **technical institute** N (*US*) ≈ IUT *m*, ≈ institut *m* universitaire de technologie ▶ **technical knock-out** N (*Boxing*) K.-O. *m* technique ▶ **technical offence** N (*Jur*) quasi-délit *m* ▶ **technical school** N = **technical institute** ▶ **technical sergeant** N (*US Air Force*) sergent-chef *m*

technicality [ˌteknɪˈkælɪtɪ] N **a** (*NonC*) technicité *f* **b** (= *detail*) détail *m* technique; (= *word*) terme *m* technique; (= *difficulty*) difficulté *f* technique; (= *fault*) ennui *m* technique; **I don't understand all the technicalities** certains détails techniques m'échappent **c** (= *formality*) formalité *f*; **she told him victory was just a ~** elle lui a dit que la victoire n'était qu'une simple formalité **d** (*Jur*) **he got off on a ~** il a été acquitté sur un point de procédure

technically ['teknɪkəlɪ] ADV **a** (= *technologically*) (*superior, feasible, perfect, advanced*) sur le plan technique, techniquement; **~, it's a very risky project** sur le plan technique *or* techniquement, c'est un projet très risqué **b** (= *in technical language: also ~ speaking*) en termes techniques; **fats are ~ known as lipids** le terme technique pour désigner les graisses est « lipides »; **he spoke very ~** il s'est exprimé d'une manière très technique **c** (= *in technique*) **a ~ proficient performance/film** une performance/un film d'un bon niveau technique; **~ demanding music** une musique qui exige une bonne technique; **~, this is a very accomplished album** techniquement, c'est un excellent album **d** (= *strictly*) (*illegal, correct*) théoriquement, en théorie; **this was ~ correct, but highly am-**

biguous c'était théoriquement correct, mais extrêmement ambigu ; **you are ~ correct** vous avez raison en théorie ; **~, they aren't eligible for a grant** en principe, ils n'ont pas droit à une bourse ; **~ (speaking) you're right, but ...** en théorie vous avez raison, mais ...

technician [tek'nɪʃən] N technicien(ne) m(f)

Technicolor® ['teknɪˌkʌləʳ] [1] N technicolor® m ; **in ~** en technicolor® [2] ADJ [a] [film] en technicolor® ; **the ~ process** le technicolor® [b] **technicolour** (Brit) ◊ **technicolor** (US) (* = colourful) [description, dream] en technicolor®

technique [tek'ni:k] N technique f ; **he's got good ~** sa technique est bonne

techno ['teknəʊ] (Mus) [1] N techno f [2] ADJ techno inv

techno... ['teknəʊ] PREF techno...

technocracy [tek'nɒkrəsɪ] N technocratie f

technocrat ['teknəʊkræt] N technocrate mf

technocratic [ˌteknə'krætɪk] ADJ technocratique

technological [ˌteknə'lɒdʒɪkəl] ADJ technologique

technologically [ˌteknə'lɒdʒɪklɪ] ADV [advanced, sophisticated, backward] technologiquement, sur le plan technologique ; [possible, feasible] technologiquement ; **~ oriented** axé sur la technologie ; **~, these cars are nothing new** sur le plan technologique, ces voitures n'ont rien de nouveau ; **~ speaking** technologiquement parlant, du point de vue technologique

technologist [tek'nɒlədʒɪst] N technologue mf

technology [tek'nɒlədʒɪ] N technologie f ; (Brit) **Minister/Ministry of Technology** ministre m/ministère m des Affaires technologiques ; **new ~** les nouvelles technologies fpl ; **space/military ~** technologie f de l'espace/militaire ; **computer ~** technologie f informatique ; **communication ~** technologie(s) f(pl) de communication → **high**

technophobe ['teknəʊfəʊb] N technophobe mf

technophobic [ˌteknəʊ'fəʊbɪk] ADJ technophobe

technostructure ['teknəʊˌstrʌktʃəʳ] N technostructure f

techy ['tetʃɪ] ADJ = **tetchy**

tectonic ['tektɒnɪk] ADJ tectonique

tectonics ['tektɒnɪks] N (NonC) tectonique f

Ted [ted] N [a] (dim of **Edward** or **Theodore**) Ted m [b]* = **teddy boy** ; → **teddy**

ted [ted] VT faner

tedder ['tedəʳ] N (= machine) faneuse f ; (= person) faneur m, -euse f

teddy ['tedɪ] [1] N [a] **Teddy** (dim of **Edward** or **Theodore**) Teddy m [b] (= underwear) teddy m [c] (also ~ **bear**) nounours m (baby talk), ours m en peluche [2] COMP ► **teddy boy†** (Brit) ≈ blouson m noir

tedious ['ti:dɪəs] ADJ [task, work, process] fastidieux ; [account, description, film] fastidieux, ennuyeux ; [life, hours, journey, behaviour] assommant ; **such lists are ~ to read** ces listes sont assommantes à lire

tediously ['ti:dɪəslɪ] ADV ► **boring** profondément ennuyeux ; **~ repetitive/juvenile** tellement répétitif/puéril que c'en est lassant ; **a ~ winding road** une route aux lacets qui n'en finissent pas ; **~ long** long et ennuyeux

tediousness ['ti:dɪəsnɪs], **tedium** ['ti:dɪəm] N (NonC) ennui m, caractère m assommant

tee¹ [ti:] → **T**

tee² [ti:] (Golf) [1] N tee m [2] VT [+ ball] placer sur le tee

► **tee off** [1] VI partir du tee [2] VT SEP (US*) (= annoy) embêter*, casser les pieds à* ; (fig = be-

gin) démarrer*

► **tee up** VI placer la balle sur le tee

tee-hee ['ti:'hi:] (vb : pret, ptp **tee-heed**) [1] EXCL hi-hi ! [2] N (petit) ricanement m [3] VI ricaner

teem [ti:m] VI [a] [crowds, insects] grouiller, fourmiller ; [fish, snakes etc] grouiller ; **to ~ with** [river, street etc] grouiller de, fourmiller de ; **his brain ~s with ideas** il déborde d'idées [b] **it was ~ing (with rain) ◊ the rain was ~ing down** il pleuvait à verse or à seaux

teeming ['ti:mɪŋ] ADJ [a] [city, streets] grouillant de monde ; [crowd, hordes, insects] grouillant ; [river] grouillant de poissons [b] **~ rain** pluie f battante or torrentielle

teen* [ti:n] (ABBR = **teenage**) ADJ [movie, magazine] pour ados* ; [fashion, mother, father] ado* f inv ; [pregnancy] chez les ados* ; [crime] juvénile ; [violence] des ados* ; [audience] d'ados* ; **~ boys** ados* mpl ; **~ girls** ados* fpl ; **~ years** adolescence f → **teens**

teenage ['ti:neɪdʒ] ADJ [mother] adolescent ; [pregnancy] chez les adolescents ; [suicide] d'adolescent(s) ; [idol, heart-throb, culture] des adolescents ; [magazine, fashion] pour adolescents ; **to have a ~ crush on sb** avoir une tocade d'adolescent pour qn ; **~ boy** adolescent m ; **~ girl** adolescente f ; **~ years** adolescence f → **teens**

teenaged ['ti:neɪdʒd] ADJ adolescent ; **a ~ boy/girl** un adolescent/une adolescente

teenager ['ti:nˌeɪdʒəʳ] N adolescent(e) m(f)

teens [ti:nz] NPL adolescence f ; **he is still in his ~** il est encore adolescent ; **he is just out of his ~** il a à peine vingt ans ; **he is in his early/late ~** il a un peu plus de treize ans/un peu moins de vingt ans

teensy(-weensy)* ['ti:nzɪ(wi:nzɪ)] ADJ = **teeny 1**

teeny* ['ti:nɪ] [1] ADJ (also ~-**weeny***) minuscule, tout petit ; **a ~ bit embarrassing/jealous** un petit peu gênant/jaloux ; **to be a ~ bit hungover** avoir un petit peu la gueule de bois [2] N (also ~-**bopper***) préado* mf

teepee ['ti:pi:] N = **tepee**

tee-shirt ['ti:ʃɜ:t] N tee-shirt or T-shirt m

teeter ['ti:təʳ] [1] VI [person] chanceler ; [pile] vaciller ; (fig) **to ~ on the edge** or **brink of** être prêt à tomber dans [2] COMP ► **teeter totter** N (US) jeu de bascule

teeth [ti:θ] NPL of **tooth**

teethe [ti:ð] VI faire or percer ses dents

teething ['ti:ðɪŋ] [1] N poussée f des dents [2] COMP ► **teething ring** N anneau m (de bébé qui perce ses dents) ► **teething troubles** NPL (Brit fig) difficultés fpl initiales

teetotal ['ti:'təʊtl] ADJ [person] qui ne boit jamais d'alcool ; [league] antialcoolique

teetotaler ['ti:'təʊtləʳ] N (US) = **teetotaller**

teetotalism ['ti:'təʊtəlɪzəm] N abstention f de toute boisson alcoolique

teetotaller, **teetotaler** (US) ['ti:'təʊtləʳ] N personne f qui ne boit jamais d'alcool

TEFL ['tefl] N (Educ) (ABBR = **Teaching of English as a Foreign Language**) → **teaching**

TEFL, TESL, TESOL, ELT

Les sigles **TEFL** (Teaching of English as a Foreign Language) et **EFL** (English as a Foreign Language) renvoient à l'enseignement de l'anglais langue étrangère dans les pays non anglophones.

Le **TESL** (Teaching of English as a Second Language) concerne l'enseignement de l'anglais langue seconde, c'est-à-dire aux personnes qui vivent dans un pays anglophone mais dont la langue maternelle n'est pas l'anglais. Cet enseignement cherche à prendre en compte l'origine culturelle de l'apprenant ainsi que sa langue maternelle.

TESOL (Teaching of English as a Second or Other Language - enseignement de l'anglais langue

seconde ou autre) est le terme américain pour **TEFL** et **TESL**.

ELT (English Language Teaching) est le terme général qui désigne l'enseignement de l'anglais en tant que langue étrangère ou langue seconde.

Teflon® ['teflɒn] [1] N téflon® m [2] ADJ (* fig = able to avoid blame) **he was the so-called ~ President** on le surnommait « le président Téflon »

tegument ['tegjʊmənt] N tégument m

te-hee ['ti:'hi:] = **tee-hee**

Teheran [tɛə'rɑ:n] N Téhéran

tel. (ABBR = **telephone (number)**) tél

Tel Aviv ['tɛlə'vi:v] N Tel-Aviv

tele... ['telɪ] PREF télé...

telebanking ['telɪˌbæŋkɪn] N télébanque f

telecamera ['telɪˌkæmərə] N caméra f de télévision, télécaméra f

telecast ['telɪkɑ:st] (US) [1] N émission f de télévision [2] VT diffuser

telecommunication ['telɪkəˌmju:nɪ'keɪʃən] [1] N (gen pl) télécommunications fpl → **post³** [2] COMP ► **telecommunications satellite** N satellite m de télécommunication

telecommute ['telɪkəˌmju:t] VI télétravailler

telecommuter* ['telɪkəˌmju:təʳ] N télétravailleur m

telecommuting* ['telɪkəˌmju:tɪŋ] N télétravail m

teleconference ['telɪkɒnfərəns] N téléconférence f

teleconferencing ['telɪkɒnfərənsɪŋ] N téléconférence(s) f(pl)

Telecopier® ['telɪˌkɒpɪəʳ] N télécopieur m

telecopy ['telɪˌkɒpɪ] N télécopie f

telefacsimile [ˌtelɪfæk'sɪmɪlɪ] N télécopie f

telefax ['telɪfæks] N télécopie f

telefilm ['telɪfɪlm] N téléfilm m, film m pour la télévision

telegenic [ˌtelɪ'dʒenɪk] ADJ télégénique

telegram ['telɪgræm] N télégramme m ; (Diplomacy, Press) dépêche f, câble m

telegraph ['telɪgrɑ:f] [1] N télégraphe m [2] VI télégraphier [3] VT [+ message] télégraphier ; (fig) [+ intentions, plans] dévoiler [4] COMP [message, wires] télégraphique ► **telegraph pole**, **telegraph post** N poteau m télégraphique

telegrapher [tɪ'legrəfəʳ] N télégraphiste mf

telegraphese [ˌtelɪgrə'fi:z] N (NonC) style m télégraphique

telegraphic [ˌtelɪ'græfɪk] ADJ (Telec) télégraphique ; (= concise) [writing, notes] en style télégraphique ; **in ~ style** ◊ **with ~ brevity** en style télégraphique

telegraphically [ˌtelɪ'græfɪkəlɪ] ADV en style télégraphique

telegraphist [tɪ'legrəfɪst] N télégraphiste mf

telegraphy [tɪ'legrəfɪ] N télégraphie f

telekinesis [ˌtelɪkɪ'ni:sɪs] N (NonC) télékinésie f

telekinetic [ˌtelɪkɪ'netɪk] ADJ télékinétique

Telemachus [tə'leməkəs] N Télémaque m

telemarketing ['telɪmɑ:kɪtɪŋ] N (Comm) télémarketing m

telemeeting ['telɪˌmi:tɪŋ] N téléréunion f

Telemessage® ['telɪˌmesɪdʒ] N (Brit) télémessage m

telemeter [tɪ'lemɪtəʳ] N télémètre m

telemetric [ˌtelɪ'metrɪk] ADJ télémétrique

telemetry [tɪ'lemɪtrɪ] N télémétrie f

teleological [ˌtelɪə'lɒdʒɪkl] ADJ téléologique

teleology [ˌtelɪ'ɒlədʒɪ] N téléologie f

telepath ['telɪpæθ] N télépathe mf

telepathic [ˌtelɪ'pæθɪk] ADJ [person] télépathe ; [ability, message] télépathique

telepathically [ˌtelɪˈpæθɪkəlɪ] ADV par télépathie

telepathist [tɪˈlepəθɪst] N télépathe *mf*

telepathy [tɪˈlepəθɪ] N télépathie *f*

telephone [ˈtelɪfəʊn] **1** N téléphone *m* ; **on the ~** au téléphone ; **to be on the ~** (= *speaking*) être au téléphone ; (= *be a subscriber*) avoir le téléphone (chez soi)
2 VT (+ *person*) téléphoner à, appeler (au téléphone) ; (+ *message, telegram*) téléphoner (**to** à) ; **~ 772 3200 for more information** pour de plus amples renseignements, appelez le 772 3200
3 VI téléphoner
4 COMP ► **telephone answering machine** N répondeur *m* (téléphonique) ► **telephone banking** N (*NonC*) services *mpl* bancaires par téléphone ► **telephone book** = **telephone directory** ► **telephone booth** N (*US*) = **telephone box** ► **telephone box** N (*Brit*) cabine *f* téléphonique ► **telephone call** N coup *m* de téléphone*, appel *m* téléphonique ► **telephone directory** N annuaire *m* (du téléphone) ► **telephone exchange** N central *m* téléphonique ► **telephone kiosk** = **telephone box** ► **telephone line** N ligne *f* téléphonique ► **telephone message** N message *m* téléphonique ► **telephone number** N numéro *m* de téléphone ► **telephone numbers*** NPL (*fig* = *large sums*) des mille et des cents* *mpl* ► **telephone operator** N standardiste *mf*, téléphoniste *mf* ► **telephone sales** N = **telesales** ► **telephone service** N service *m* des téléphones ► **telephone sex** N (*NonC*) ≈ téléphone *m* rose ; **~ sex line** (ligne *f* de) téléphone *m* rose ► **telephone subscriber** N abonné(e) *m(f)* au téléphone ► **telephone-tapping** N mise *f* sur écoute (téléphonique) ► **telephone wires** NPL fils *mpl* téléphoniques

telephonic [ˌtelɪˈfɒnɪk] ADJ téléphonique

telephonist [tɪˈlefənɪst] N (*esp Brit*) téléphoniste *mf*

telephony [tɪˈlefənɪ] N téléphonie *f*

telephoto [ˈtelɪˌfəʊtəʊ] ADJ **~ lens** téléobjectif *m*

telephotograph [ˌtelɪˈfəʊtəgræf] N téléphotographie *f*

telephotography [ˌtelɪfəˈtɒgrəfɪ] N (*NonC*) téléphotographie *f*

teleport [ˈtelɪpɔːt] VT téléporter

teleportation [ˌtelɪpɔːˈteɪʃən] N télékinésie *f*

teleprint [ˈtelɪˌprɪnt] VT (*Brit*) transmettre par téléscripteur

teleprinter [ˈtelɪˌprɪntəʳ] N (*Brit*) téléscripteur *m*, Télétype® *m*

Teleprompter® [ˈtelɪˌprɒmptəʳ] N (*US, Can*) prompteur *m*, téléprompteur *m*

telesales [ˈtelɪseɪlz] **1** NPL vente *f* par téléphone, télévente *f* **2** COMP ► **telesales department** N service *m* des ventes par téléphone ► **telesales staff** N vendeurs *mpl*, -euses *fpl* par téléphone, télévendeurs *mpl*, -euses *fpl*

telescope [ˈtelɪskəʊp] **1** N (*reflecting*) télescope *m* ; (*refracting*) lunette *f* d'approche, longue-vue *f* ; (*Astron*) lunette *f* astronomique, télescope *m* **2** VI (*railway carriages etc*) se télescoper ; (*umbrella*) se plier ; **parts made to ~** pièces *fpl* qui s'emboîtent **3** VT **a** (+ *cane*) replier **b** (+ *report, ideas*) condenser

telescopic [ˌtelɪˈskɒpɪk] **1** ADJ télescopique **2** COMP ► **telescopic damper** N (*Aut*) amortisseur *m* télescopique ► **telescopic lens** N téléobjectif *m* ► **telescopic sight** N lunette *f*, collimateur *m* ► **telescopic umbrella** N parapluie *m* pliant *or* télescopique

teleshopping [ˈtelɪʃɒpɪŋ] N (*NonC*) téléachat *m*

teletex [ˈtelɪteks] N Télétex® *m*

Teletext® [ˈtelɪtekst] N télétexte® *m*, vidéotex® *m* diffusé

telethon [ˈtelɪθɒn] N (*TV*) téléthon *m*

Teletype® [ˈtelɪtaɪp] **1** VT transmettre par Télétype® **2** N Télétype® *m*

teletypewriter [ˌtelɪˈtaɪpraɪtəʳ] N (*US*) téléscripteur *m*, Télétype® *m*

televangelism [ˌtelɪˈvændʒəlɪzəm] N (*NonC: esp US*) prédication *f* à la télévision

televangelist [ˌtelɪˈvændʒəlɪst] N (*esp US*) télévangéliste *mf*

teleview [ˈtelɪvjuː] VI (*US*) regarder la télévision

televiewer [ˈtelɪˌvjuːəʳ] N téléspectateur *m*, -trice *f*

televiewing [ˈtelɪˌvjuːɪŋ] N (*NonC: watching TV*) la télévision ; **this evening's ~ contains ...** le programme de (la) télévision pour ce soir comprend ...

televise [ˈtelɪvaɪz] VT téléviser

television [ˈtelɪˌvɪʒən] **1** N télévision *f* ; (*also* **~ set**) (poste *m* de) télévision *f*, téléviseur *m* ; **on ~** à la télévision ; **colour ~** télévision *f* (en) couleur
2 COMP (*actor, camera, studio*) de télévision ; (*report, news, serial*) télévisé ; (*film, script*) pour la télévision ► **television broadcast** N émission *f* de télévision ► **television cabinet** N meuble-télévision *m* ► **television licence** N (*Brit*) certificat *m* de redevance télévision ; **to pay one's ~ licence** payer sa redevance télévision ► **television lounge** N (*in hotel etc*) salle *f* de télévision ► **television programme** N émission *f* de télévision ► **television rights** NPL droits *mpl* d'antenne ► **television room** = **television lounge** ► **television screen** N écran *m* de télévision *or* de téléviseur ; **on the ~ screen** sur le petit écran ► **television set** N télévision *f*, téléviseur *m*, poste *m* (de télévision)

televisual [ˌtelɪˈvɪʒjʊəl] ADJ (*Brit*) télévisuel

telework [ˈtelɪwɜːk] VI télétravailler

teleworker [ˈtelɪwɜːkəʳ] N télétravailleur *m*, -euse *f*

teleworking [ˈtelɪwɜːkɪŋ] N télétravail *m*

telex [ˈteleks] **1** N télex *m* **2** VT télexer, envoyer par télex **3** COMP ► **telex operator** N télexiste *mf*

tell [tel] (*pret, ptp* **told**) **1** VT **a** (*gen*) dire (*that* que) ; **~ me your name** dites-moi votre nom ; **I told him how pleased I was** je lui ai dit combien or à quel point j'étais content ; **I told him what/where/how/why** je lui ai dit ce que/où/comment/pourquoi ; **I told him the way to London** ◊ **I told him how to get to London** je lui ai expliqué comment aller à Londres ; **he told himself it was only a game** il s'est dit que ce n'était qu'un jeu ; **I am glad to ~ you that ...** je suis heureux de pouvoir vous dire que ... ; **to ~ sb sth again** répéter or redire qch à qn ; **something ~s me he won't be pleased** quelque chose me dit qu'il ne sera pas content ; **let me ~ you that you are quite mistaken** permettez-moi de vous dire que vous vous trompez lourdement ; **I won't go, I ~ you!** puisque je te dis que je n'irai pas ! ; **I can't ~ you how grateful I am** je ne saurais vous dire à quel point je suis reconnaissant ; **I can't ~ you how glad I was to leave that place** vous ne pouvez pas savoir à quel point j'étais content de quitter cet endroit ; **don't ~ me you've lost it!** tu ne vas pas me dire que or ne me dis pas que tu l'as perdu ! ; **I told you so!** je te l'avais bien dit ! ; **... or so I've been told ...** ou du moins c'est ce qu'on m'a dit ; **I could ~ you a thing or two about him** je pourrais vous en dire long sur lui ; **I'll ~ you what, let's go for a swim!** tiens, si on allait se baigner ! ; **you're ~ing me!** à qui le dis-tu ! ; **you ~ me!** je n'en sais rien !, qu'est-ce que j'en sais !*
b (= *relate*) dire, raconter ; (+ *story, adventure*) raconter (**to** à) ; (+ *a lie, the truth*) dire ; (= *divulge*) (+ *secret*) dire, révéler ; (+ *sb's age*) révéler ; (+ *the future*) prédire ; **to ~ it like it is*** ne pas mâcher ses mots ; **can you ~ the time?** ◊ **can you ~ time?** (*US*) sais-tu lire l'heure ? ; **can you ~ me the time?** peux-tu me dire l'heure (qu'il est) ? ; **clocks ~ the time** les horloges indiquent l'heure ; **that ~s me all I need to know** maintenant je sais tout ce qu'il me faut savoir ; **it ~s its own tale** or **story** ça dit bien ce que ça veut dire ; **the lack of evidence ~s a tale** or **story** le manque de preuve est très révélateur ; **~ me another!*** à d'autres !* ; **his actions ~ us a lot about his motives** ses actes nous en disent long sur ses motifs ; **she was ~ing him about it** elle lui en parlait, elle était en train de le lui raconter ; **~ me about it** (*lit*) raconte-moi ça ; (* *iro*) ne m'en parle pas ; **I told him about what had happened** je lui ai dit or raconté ce qui était arrivé ; **"by J. Smith, as told to W. Jones"** ≈ « par J. Smith, propos recueillis par W. Jones » → **fortune, picture, tale, truth**
c (= *know*) **how can I ~ what he will do?** comment puis-je savoir ce qu'il va faire ? ; **there's no ~ing what he might do/how long the talks could last** impossible de dire or savoir ce qu'il pourrait faire/combien de temps les pourparlers vont durer ; **it was impossible to ~ where the bullet had entered** il était impossible de dire or savoir par où la balle était entrée ; **I couldn't ~ if he had been in a fight or had just fallen** il (m')était impossible de dire or de savoir s'il s'était battu ou s'il était simplement tombé, je n'aurais pas pu dire s'il s'était battu ou s'il était simplement tombé ; **I couldn't ~ how it was done** je ne pourrais pas dire comment ça a été fait ; **no one can ~ what he'll say** personne ne peut savoir ce qu'il dira ; **you can ~ he's clever by the way he talks** on voit bien qu'il est intelligent à la façon dont il parle ; **you can ~ he's joking** on voit bien qu'il plaisante ; **you can't ~ much from his letter** sa lettre n'en dit pas très long
d (= *distinguish*) distinguer, voir ; (= *know*) savoir ; **to ~ right from wrong** distinguer le bien du mal ; **I can't ~ them apart** je ne peux pas les distinguer (l'un de l'autre) ; **I can't ~ the difference** je ne vois pas la différence (**between** entre)
e (= *command*) dire, ordonner (**sb to do** à qn de faire) ; **do as you are told** fais ce qu'on te dit ; **I told him not to do it** je lui ai dit de ne pas le faire, je lui ai défendu de le faire
f (†† = *count*) compter, dénombrer ; **to ~ one's beads** dire or réciter son chapelet → **all**
2 VI **a** parler (**of, about** de) ; (*fig*) **the ruins told of a long-lost civilization** les ruines témoignaient d'une civilisation depuis longtemps disparue ; **his face told of his sorrow** sa douleur se lisait sur son visage
b (= *know*) savoir ; **how can I ~?** comment le saurais-je ? ; **I can't ~** je n'en sais rien ; **who can ~?** qui sait ? ; **you never can ~** on ne sait jamais ; **you can't ~ from his letter** on ne peut pas savoir d'après sa lettre ; **as** or **so far as one can ~** pour autant que l'on sache
c (= *be talebearer*) **I won't ~!** je ne le répéterai à personne ! ; **to ~ on sb*** rapporter or cafarder* contre qn ; **don't ~ on us!*** ne nous dénonce pas !
d (= *have an effect*) se faire sentir (**on sb/sth** sur qn/qch) ; **his influence must ~** son influence ne peut que se faire sentir ; **his age is beginning to ~** il commence à accuser son âge ; **the pressures of her job are beginning to ~ on her** elle commence à accuser le stress de son travail ; **their age and inexperience told against them** leur âge et leur manque d'expérience militaient contre eux

► **tell off 1** VT SEP **a** (* = *reprimand*) gronder, attraper* (**sb for sth** qn pour qch, **for doing sth** pour avoir fait qch) ; **to be told off** se faire attraper* **b** † (= *select etc*) (+ *person*) affecter (**for sth** à qch), désigner (**to do** pour faire); (= *check off*) dénombrer **2** **~ing-off*** N → **telling**

teller ['telə^r] N (*US, Scot Banking*) caissier *m*, -ière *f*; [*of votes*] scrutateur *m*, -trice *f*; (*US Pol*) **~ vote** vote *m* à bulletin secret (*dans une assemblée*) → **storyteller**

telling ['telɪŋ] **1** ADJ **a** (= *revealing*) [*comment, detail, figures, evidence*] révélateur (-trice *f*), éloquent **b** (= *effective*) [*speech, argument, blow*] efficace; **with ~ effect** avec efficacité **2** N (*NonC*) [*of story etc*] récit *m*; **it lost nothing in the ~** c'était tout aussi bien quand on l'entendait raconter; **this story grows in the ~** cette histoire s'enjolive chaque fois qu'on la raconte **3** COMP ► **telling-off** N engueulade* *f*; **to get/give a good ~-off** recevoir/passer un bon savon* (**from** de, **to** à)

telltale ['telteɪl] **1** N rapporteur *m*, -euse *f*, mouchard(e) *m(f)* **2** ADJ [*mark, sign etc*] révélateur (-trice *f*), éloquent

tellurium [te'lʊərɪəm] N tellure *m*

telly* ['telɪ] N (*Brit*) (ABBR = **television**) télé* *f*; **on the ~** à la télé*

Temazepam® [tɪ'mæzɪpæm] N (*pl* **Temazepam** *or* **Temazepams**) tranquillisant délivré sur ordonnance

temerity [tɪ'merɪtɪ] N (*NonC*) audace *f*, témérité *f*

temp* [temp] ABBR = **temporary** **1** N intérimaire *mf*, secrétaire *mf etc* qui fait de l'intérim **2** VI faire de l'intérim, travailler comme intérimaire

temper ['tempə^r] **1** N **a** (*NonC* = *nature, disposition*) tempérament *m*, caractère *m*; (*NonC* = *mood*) humeur *f*; (= *fit of bad temper*) (accès *m or* crise *f* de) colère *f*; **he has a very even ~** il est d'humeur très égale; **he has a good ~** il a bon caractère; **~s became frayed** tout le monde commençait à perdre patience; **~s are running high** les esprits sont échauffés; **to have a hot** *or* **quick ~** être soupe au lait; **to have a nasty** *or* **foul** *or* **vile ~** avoir un sale caractère, avoir un caractère de cochon*; **to have a short ~** être coléreux *or* soupe au lait *inv*; **his short ~ had become notorious** son caractère *or* tempérament coléreux était devenu célèbre; **he had a ~ and could be nasty** il était soupe au lait et pouvait être méchant; **I hope he can control his ~** j'espère qu'il sait se contrôler *or* se maîtriser; **to be in a ~** être en colère (**with sb** contre qn, **over** *or* **about sth** à propos de qch); **to be in a good/ bad ~** être de bonne/mauvaise humeur; **he was in a foul ~** il était d'une humeur massacrante; **he was not in the best of ~s** il n'était pas vraiment de très bonne humeur; **to keep one's ~** garder son calme, se maîtriser; **to lose one's ~** se mettre en colère; **to put sb into a ~** mettre qn en colère; **~, ~!** du calme!, on se calme!; **in a fit of ~** dans un accès de colère; **he flew into a ~** il a explosé *or* éclaté → **tantrum** **b** [*of metal*] trempe *f* **2** VT [+ *metal*] tremper; (*fig*) [+ *effects, rigours, passions*] tempérer (**with** par)

tempera ['tempərə] N (*NonC: Art*) détrempe *f*

temperament ['tempərəmənt] N (*NonC*) **a** (= *nature*) tempérament *m*, nature *f*; **the artistic ~** le tempérament artiste; **his impulsive ~ got him into trouble** son tempérament impulsif *or* sa nature impulsive lui a posé des problèmes **b** (= *moodiness, difficult temperament*) humeur *f* (changeante); **an outburst of ~** une saute d'humeur; **she was given to fits of ~** elle avait tendance à avoir des sautes d'humeur

temperamental [,tempərə'mentl] ADJ **a** (= *unpredictable*) [*person, behaviour*] fantasque; [*horse, machine*] capricieux; **a ~ outburst** une saute d'humeur **b** (= *innate*) [*differences*] de tempérament; [*inclinations, qualities, aversion*] naturel

temperamentally [,tempərə'mentlɪ] ADV **a** (= *unpredictably*) [*behave*] capricieusement **b** (= *by nature*) **~ suited to a job** fait pour un travail du point de vue du caractère; **~, we were not at all compatible** du point de vue du tempérament *or* pour ce qui est du tempérament, nous n'étions pas du tout compatibles

temperance ['tempərəns] **1** N (*NonC*) modération *f*; (*in drinking*) tempérance *f* **2** COMP [*movement, league*] antialcoolique; [*hotel*] où l'on ne sert pas de boissons alcoolisées

temperate ['tempərɪt] **1** ADJ **a** (*Geog, Met*) [*region, climate*] tempéré; [*forest, plant, animal*] de zone tempérée **b** (= *restrained*) [*person*] (*gen*) modéré; (*with alcohol*) qui fait preuve de tempérance; [*lifestyle, reaction, discussion*] modéré; [*attitude*] mesuré; [*character, nature*] mesuré **2** COMP ► **the Temperate Zone** N la zone tempérée

temperature ['temprɪtʃə^r] **1** N température *f*; **a ~ of ...** à une température de ...; **to have a** *or* **be running a ~** avoir de la température *or* de la fièvre; **he was running a high ~** il avait une forte fièvre; **to take sb's ~** prendre la température de qn; **the bombing has raised the political ~** cet attentat à la bombe a fait monter la tension politique → **high** **2** COMP [*change etc*] de température ► **temperature chart** N (*Med*) feuille *f* de température ► **temperature gauge** N indicateur *m* de température

-tempered ['tempəd] ADJ (*in compounds*) **even-tempered** d'humeur égale → **bad**, **good**

tempest ['tempɪst] N (*liter*) tempête *f*, orage *m*; (*fig*) tempête *f*; (*US*) **it was a ~ in a teapot** c'était une tempête dans un verre d'eau

tempestuous [tem'pestjʊəs] ADJ **a** (= *turbulent*) [*relationship, meeting*] orageux; [*period, time*] orageux, agité; [*marriage, career*] tumultueux; [*person*] impétueux, fougueux **b** (*liter*) [*weather, wind, night*] de tempête; [*sea*] houleux; [*waves*] violent

tempestuously [tem'pestjʊəslɪ] ADV (*fig*) avec violence; **the sea crashed ~ against the cliffs** la mer se jetait avec violence contre les falaises

tempi ['tempiː] (*Mus*) NPL of **tempo**

temping ['tempɪŋ] N intérim *m*

Templar ['templə^r] N = **Knight Templar**; → **knight**

template ['templɪt] N **a** (= *pattern: woodwork, patchwork etc*) gabarit *m*; (*fig* = *model*) modèle *m* (**for sth** à la base de qch) **b** (*Constr* = *beam*) traverse *f* **c** (*Comput*) patron *m*

temple¹ ['templ] N (*Rel*) temple *m*; (*Brit Jur*) **the Temple** ≈ le Palais (de Justice)

temple² ['templ] N (*Anat*) tempe *f*

templet ['templɪt] N = **template**

tempo ['tempəʊ] N (*pl* **tempos** *or* (*Mus*) **tempi**) (*Mus, fig*) tempo *m*

temporal ['tempərəl] **1** ADJ **a** (= *relating to time: also Gram, Rel*) temporel **b** (*Anat*) temporal **2** COMP ► **temporal bone** N (*os m*) temporal *m*

temporarily ['tempərərɪlɪ] ADV (*gen*) temporairement, provisoirement; (*shorter time*) pendant un moment

temporary ['tempərərɪ] ADJ [*job, resident, residence, staff*] temporaire; [*accommodation, building, solution, injunction*] provisoire; [*relief, improvement, problem*] passager; [*licence, powers*] à titre temporaire; **~ road surface** revêtement *m* provisoire

temporize ['tempəraɪz] **1** VI **a** temporiser, chercher à gagner du temps; **to ~ between two people** faire accepter un compromis à deux personnes **b** (*pej* = *bend with circumstances*) faire de l'opportunisme **2** VT **"not exactly, sir", ~d Sloan** « pas exactement monsieur », dit Sloan pour gagner du temps

tempt [tempt] VT **a** tenter, séduire; **to ~ sb to do** donner à qn l'envie de faire; **try and ~ her to eat a little** tâchez de la persuader de manger un peu; **may I ~ you to a little more wine?** puis-je vous offrir un petit peu plus de vin?; **I'm very ~ed** c'est très tentant; **I am very ~ed to accept** je suis très tenté d'accepter; **he was ~ed into doing it** il n'a pas pu résister à la tentation de le faire; (*hum*) **don't ~ me!** n'essaie pas de me tenter! → **sorely** **b** (†: *Bible* = *test*) tenter, induire en tentation; (*common usage*) **to ~ Providence** *or* **fate** tenter le sort

temptation [temp'teɪʃən] N tentation *f*; **to put ~ in sb's way** exposer qn à la tentation; **lead us not into ~** ne nous laissez pas succomber à la tentation; **there is a great ~ to assume ...** il est très tentant de supposer ...; **there is no ~ to do so** on n'est nullement tenté de le faire; **she resisted the ~ to buy it** elle a résisté à la tentation de l'acheter; **the many ~s to which you will be exposed** les nombreuses tentations auxquelles vous serez exposé

tempter ['temptə^r] N tentateur *m*

tempting ['temptɪŋ] ADJ [*offer, proposition, target*] tentant; [*food, smell*] appétissant; **it is ~ to say that ...** on est tenté de dire que ...

temptingly ['temptɪŋlɪ] ADV (*with vb*) d'une manière tentante; (*with adj*) **prices are still ~ low** les prix sont toujours bas et cela donne envie d'acheter; **the sea was ~ near** la mer était tout près et c'était bien tentant

temptress ['temptrɪs] N tentatrice *f*

tempura [tem'pʊərə] N (*NonC*) tempura *f*

ten [ten] **1** ADJ dix *m*; **about ~ books** une dizaine de livres; **the Ten Commandments** les dix commandements *mpl* **2** N dix *m inv*; **~s of thousands of ...** des milliers (et des milliers) de ...; **hundreds, ~s and units** les centaines, les dizaines et les unités; **to count in ~s** compter par dizaines; (*fig*) **~ to one he won't come** je parie qu'il ne viendra pas; (*fig*) **they're ~ a penny*** il y en a tant qu'on en veut, il y en a à la pelle*; (*Aut*) **to drive with one's hands at ~ to two** conduire avec les mains à dix heures dix → **number**; *for other phrases see* **six** **3** PRON dix; **there were ~** il y en avait dix; **there were about ~** il y en avait une dizaine **4** COMP ► **ten-cent store** N (*US*) bazar *m* ► **ten-gallon hat** N (*US*) ≈ chapeau *m* de cow-boy ► **ten-metre line** N (*Rugby*) ligne *f* de dix mètres

tenable ['tenəbl] ADJ **a** (= *defensible*) [*argument, view, position*] défendable; **it's just not ~** ça ne peut vraiment pas se défendre **b** (*the position of chairman is ~ for a maximum of three years* la présidence ne peut être occupée que pendant trois ans au maximum

tenacious [tɪ'neɪʃəs] ADJ **a** (= *determined*) [*person*] tenace; [*defence, resistance*] opiniâtre **b** (= *persistent*) [*belief, illness, condition*] tenace, obstiné **c** (= *firm*) [*grip, hold*] solide, ferme **d** (= *retentive*) [*memory*] indéfectible

tenaciously [tɪ'neɪʃəslɪ] ADV [*cling to, hang on, fight*] avec ténacité; [*survive*] obstinément

tenacity [tɪ'næsɪtɪ] N (*NonC*) ténacité *f*

tenancy ['tenənsɪ] **1** N location *f*; **during my ~ of the house** pendant que j'étais locataire de la maison; **to take on the ~ of a house** prendre une maison en location; **to give up the ~ of a house** résilier un contrat de location; **the new law relating to tenancies** la nouvelle loi relative aux locations **2** COMP ► **tenancy agreement** N contrat *m* de location

tenant ['tenənt] **1** N locataire *mf* **2** VT [+ *property*] habiter comme locataire **3** COMP ► **tenant farmer** N métayer *m* ► **tenant in common** N (*Jur*) indivisaire *mf*

tenantry ['tenəntrɪ] N (*NonC: collective*)

(ensemble *m* des) tenanciers *mpl* (d'un domaine)

tench [tentʃ] N (*pl inv*) tanche *f*

tend¹ [tend] VT [+ *sheep, shop*] garder ; [+ *invalid*] soigner ; [+ *machine*] surveiller ; [+ *garden*] entretenir ; [+ *piece of land to grow food*] travailler, cultiver
► **tend to** VT FUS (= *take care of*) s'occuper de → **tend²**

tend² [tend] VI [*person, thing*] avoir tendance (**to do** à faire) ; **to ~ towards** avoir des tendances à, incliner à *or* vers ; **he ~s to be lazy** il a tendance à être paresseux, il est enclin à la paresse ; **he ~s to(wards) fascism** il a des tendances fascistes, il incline au *or* vers le fascisme ; **that ~s to be the case with such people** c'est en général le cas avec des gens de cette sorte ; **I ~ to think that ...** j'incline *or* j'ai tendance à penser que ... ; **it is a grey ~ing to blue** c'est un gris tirant sur le bleu

tendency [ˈtendənsɪ] N tendance *f* ; **to have a ~ to do sth** avoir tendance à faire qch ; **there is a ~ for prices to rise** les prix ont tendance à *or* tendent à augmenter ; (*St Ex*) **a strong upward ~** une forte tendance à la hausse ; **the present ~ to(wards) socialism** les tendances socialistes actuelles

tendentious [tenˈdenʃəs] ADJ tendancieux

tendentiously [tenˈdenʃəslɪ] ADV tendancieusement

tendentiousness [tenˈdenʃəsnɪs] N caractère *m* tendancieux

tender¹ [ˈtendər] N (*Rail*) tender *m* ; (= *boat*) (*for passengers*) embarcation *f* ; (*for supplies*) ravitailleur *m*

tender² [ˈtendər] **1** VT (= *proffer*) [+ *object*] tendre, offrir ; [+ *money, thanks, apologies*] offrir ; **to ~ one's resignation** donner sa démission (**to sb** à qn) ; **"please ~ exact change"** « prière de faire l'appoint » **2** VI (*Comm*) faire une soumission (**for sth** pour qch) **3** N **a** (*Comm*) soumission *f* (à un appel d'offres) ; **to make** *or* **put in a ~ for sth** répondre *or* soumissionner à un appel d'offres pour qch ; **to invite ~s for sth** ◊ **to put sth out to ~** lancer un appel d'offres pour qch, mettre qch en adjudication ; **they won the ~ to build the bridge** ils ont obtenu le marché pour construire le pont **b** (*Fin*) **legal ~** cours *m* légal ; **to be legal ~** avoir cours ; **East German currency is no longer legal ~** les devises est-allemandes n'ont plus cours **4** COMP ► **tender offer** N (*US St Ex*) offre *f* publique d'achat, OPA *f*

tender³ [ˈtendər] **1** ADJ **a** (*gen*) [*person, expression, kiss, voice, word, thoughts, plant, food*] tendre ; [*body, skin*] délicat ; [*gesture*] tendre, plein de tendresse ; [*moment*] de tendresse ; **he gave her a ~ smile** il lui a souri tendrement ; **they were locked in a ~ embrace** ils étaient tendrement enlacés ; **to bid sb a ~ farewell** dire tendrement adieu à qn ; (*iro*) **to leave sb/ sth to the ~ mercies of sb** abandonner qn/ qch aux bons soins de qn
b (= *young*) **at the ~ age of seven** à l'âge tendre de sept ans ; **she left home at a very ~ age** elle a quitté la maison très jeune ; **he was a hardened criminal by the ~ age of 16** c'était un criminel endurci dès l'âge de 16 ans ; **a child of ~ age** *or* **years** un enfant dans l'âge tendre ; **in spite of his ~ years** malgré son jeune âge
c (= *sore*) [*skin, bruise*] sensible ; **~ to the touch** sensible au toucher
d (= *difficult*) [*subject*] délicat

2 COMP ► **tender-hearted** ADJ sensible, compatissant ; **to be ~-hearted** être un cœur tendre ► **tender-heartedness** N (*NonC*) compassion *f*, sensibilité *f* ► **tender loving care** N **what he needs is some ~ loving care** ce dont il a besoin, c'est d'être dorloté

tenderer [ˈtendərər] N soumissionnaire *mf*

tenderfoot [ˈtendəfʊt] N (*pl* **tenderfoots**) novice *mf*, nouveau *m*, nouvelle *f*

tendering [ˈtendərɪŋ] N (*NonC: Comm*) soumissions *fpl*

tenderize [ˈtendəraɪz] VT (*Culin*) attendrir

tenderizer [ˈtendəraɪzər] N (*Culin*) (= *mallet*) attendrisseur *m* ; (= *spices*) épices pour attendrir la viande

tenderloin [ˈtendəlɔɪn] N (= *meat*) filet *m* ; (*US fig*) quartier *m* louche (*où la police est corrompue*)

tenderly [ˈtendəlɪ] ADV [*kiss*] tendrement ; [*touch, say*] avec tendresse

tenderness [ˈtendənɪs] N (*NonC*) **a** (*gen*) tendresse *f* ; [*of skin*] délicatesse *f* ; [*of meat etc*] tendreté *f* **b** (= *soreness*) [*of arm, bruise etc*] sensibilité *f* **c** (= *emotion*) tendresse *f* (**towards** envers)

tendon [ˈtendən] N tendon *m*

tendril [ˈtendrɪl] N (*Bot*) vrille *f*

tenebrous [ˈtenɪbrəs] ADJ (*liter*) ténébreux

tenement [ˈtenɪmənt] N (= *apartment*) appartement *m*, logement *m* ; (*also* **~ house** *or* **building**) immeuble *m*

Tenerife [ˌtenəˈriːf] N Tenerife

tenet [ˈtenət] N principe *m*, doctrine *f*

tenfold [ˈtenfəʊld] **1** ADJ décuple **2** ADV au décuple ; **to increase ~** décupler

Tenn. ABBR = **Tennessee**

tenner [ˈtenər] N (*Brit*) (billet *m* de) dix livres ; (*US*) (billet *m* de) dix dollars

Tennessee [ˌtenɪˈsiː] N le Tennessee ; **in ~** dans le Tennessee

tennis [ˈtenɪs] **1** N (*NonC*) tennis *m* ; **a game of ~** une partie de tennis **2** COMP [*player, racket, club*] de tennis ► **tennis ball** N balle *f* de tennis ► **tennis camp** N (*US*) **to go to ~ camp** faire un stage de tennis ► **tennis court** N (court *m* *or* terrain *m* de) tennis *m inv* ► **tennis elbow** N (*Med*) synovite *f* du coude ► **tennis shoe** N (chaussure *f* de) tennis *m*

tenon [ˈtenən] N tenon *m*

tenor [ˈtenər] **1** N **a** (= *general sense*) [*of speech, discussion*] teneur *f*, substance *f* ; (= *course*) [*of one's life, events, developments*] cours *m* **b** (= *exact wording*) teneur *f* **c** (*Mus*) ténor *m* **2** ADJ (*Mus*) [*voice, part*] de ténor ; [*aria*] pour ténor ; [*recorder, saxophone*] ténor *inv* **3** COMP ► **the tenor clef** N la clef d'ut quatrième ligne

tenpin [ˈtenpɪn] **1** N quille *f* ; (*US*) **~s** = tenpin bowling **2** COMP ► **tenpin bowling** N (*Brit*) bowling *m* (à dix quilles)

tense¹ [tens] N (*Gram*) temps *m* ; **in the present ~** au temps présent

tense² [tens] **1** ADJ [*person, voice, expression, muscles, rope, situation*] tendu ; [*time, period*] de tension ; (*Ling*) [*vowel*] tendu ; **to become ~** [*person*] se crisper ; **things were getting rather ~** l'atmosphère devenait plutôt tendue ; **to make sb ~** rendre qn nerveux ; **in a voice ~ with emotion** d'une voix voilée par l'émotion ; **they were ~ with fear/anticipation** ils étaient crispés de peur/par l'attente **2** VT [+ *muscles*] contracter ; **to ~ o.s.** se contracter **3** VI [*muscles, person, animal*] se contracter
► **tense up** **1** VI se crisper **2** VT **you're all ~d up** tu es tout crispé

tensely [ˈtenslɪ] ADV [*say*] d'une voix tendue ; **they waited/watched ~** ils attendaient/ observaient, tendus

tenseness [ˈtensnɪs] N (*NonC: lit, fig*) tension *f*

tensile [ˈtensaɪl] **1** ADJ [*material*] extensible, élastique **2** COMP ► **tensile load** N force *f* de traction ► **tensile strength** N résistance *f* à la traction ► **tensile stress** N contrainte *f* de traction → **high**

tension [ˈtenʃən] **1** N (*NonC*) tension *f*

2 COMP ► **tension headache** N (*Med*) mal *m* de tête (dû à la tension nerveuse)

tent [tent] **1** N tente *f* **2** VI camper **3** COMP ► **tent peg** N (*Brit*) piquet *m* de tente ► **tent pole, tent stake** N montant *m* de tente ► **tent trailer** N caravane *f* pliante

tentacle [ˈtentəkl] N (*also fig*) tentacule *m*

tentative [ˈtentətɪv] ADJ (= *provisional*) [*agreement, measure, plan, date, enquiry, conclusion*] provisoire ; (= *hesitant*) [*gesture, step, knock*] hésitant ; [*smile, attempt, suggestion*] timide ; **a ~ offer** (*to buy etc*) une offre provisoire ; (*of help etc*) une offre timide

tentatively [ˈtentətɪvlɪ] ADV (= *provisionally*) [*agreed, scheduled, planned, titled*] provisoirement ; (= *hesitantly*) [*smile, say, knock, wave*] timidement ; [*touch*] avec hésitation

tented [ˈtentɪd] **1** ADJ **a** (= *containing tents*) [*field*] couvert de tentes ; [*camp*] de tentes **b** (= *draped*) [*room, ceiling*] à tentures (*partant du centre du plafond*) **2** COMP ► **tented arch** N (*Archit*) ogive *f*

tenterhooks [ˈtentəhʊks] NPL **to be/keep sb on ~** être/tenir qn sur des charbons ardents *or* au supplice

tenth [tenθ] **1** ADJ dixième **2** N dixième *mf* ; (= *fraction*) dixième *m* ; **nine-~s of the book** les neuf dixièmes du livre ; **nine-~s of the time** la majeure partie du temps ; *for other phrases see* **sixth**

tenuity [teˈnjuːɪtɪ] N (*NonC*) ténuité *f*

tenuous [ˈtenjʊəs] ADJ [*link, connection, distinction*] ténu ; [*relationship*] subtil ; [*evidence*] mince ; [*existence*] précaire ; [*position, alliance*] fragile ; [*lead*] faible ; **to have a ~ grasp of sth** avoir une vague idée *or* de vagues notions de qch ; **to have a ~ hold on sb/sth** n'avoir que peu d'emprise sur qn/qch

tenuously [ˈtenjʊəslɪ] ADV de manière ténue

tenure [ˈtenjʊər] **1** N (*Univ*) fait *m* d'être titulaire ; (*feudal*) tenure *f* ; [*of land, property*] bail *m* ; **to have ~** [*employee*] être titulaire ; **to get ~** être titularisé ; **the system of ~** le système des emplois *or* postes permanents ; **the ~ is for two years** la période de jouissance est de deux ans ; **during his ~ of office** pendant qu'il était en fonction → **security** **2** COMP ► **tenure track position** N (*US Univ*) poste *m* avec possibilité de titularisation

tenured [ˈtenjʊəd] ADJ [*professor etc*] titulaire ; **he has a ~ position** il est titulaire de son poste

tepee [ˈtiːpiː] N tipi *m*

tepid [ˈtepɪd] ADJ **a** (*lit*) [*water, coffee*] tiède **b** (*fig*) [*response*] réservé, sans enthousiasme ; [*support*] réservé, mitigé ; [*applause*] sans conviction

tepidity [teˈpɪdɪtɪ] N (*NonC*) tiédeur *f*

tepidly [ˈtepɪdlɪ] ADV (*fig*) [*agree, respond*] sans grand enthousiasme

tepidness [ˈtepɪdnɪs] N (*NonC*) = **tepidity**

tequila [tɪkiːlə] N tequila *f*

Ter (*Brit*) = **Terr**

terbium [ˈtɜːbɪəm] N terbium *m*

tercentenary [ˌtɜːsenˈtiːnərɪ] ADJ, N tricentenaire *m*

tercet [ˈtɜːsɪt] N (*Poetry*) tercet *m* ; (*Mus*) triolet *m*

Teresa [təˈriːzə] N Thérèse *f*

term [tɜːm] **1** N **a** (*gen, Admin, Fin, Jur, Med*) (= *limit*) terme *m* ; (= *period*) période *f*, terme *m* (*Jur*) ; **to put** *or* **set a ~ to sth** mettre *or* fixer un terme à qch ; (*Fin, Med*) **at ~** à terme ; **in the long ~** à long terme → **long-term** ; **in the medium ~** à moyen terme → **medium** ; **in the short ~** dans l'immédiat → **short** ; **during his ~ of office** pendant la période où il exerçait ses fonctions ; **elected for a three-year ~** élu pour une durée *or* période de trois ans ; **~ of imprisonment** peine *f* de prison
b (*Scol, Univ*) trimestre *m* ; (*Jur*) session *f* ; (*Scol, Univ*) **the autumn/spring/summer ~** le

premier/second or deuxième/troisième trimestre; **in (the) ~** ◊ **during (the) ~** pendant le trimestre; **out of (the) ~** pendant les vacances (scolaires or universitaires)

[c] (Math, Philos) terme m; **A expressed in ~s of B** A exprimé en fonction de B; (fig) **in ~s of production we are doing well** sur le plan de la production nous avons de quoi être satisfaits; **he sees art in ~s of human relationships** pour lui l'art est fonction des relations humaines; **to look at sth in ~s of the effect it will have/of how it ...** considérer qch sous l'angle de l'effet que cela aura/de la façon dont cela ...; **we must think in ~s of ...** il faut penser à ...; (= consider the possibility of) il faut envisager (la possibilité de) ...; **price in ~s of dollars** prix m exprimé en dollars

[d] (= conditions) **~s** (gen) conditions fpl; [of contracts etc] termes mpl; (Comm etc) prix m(pl), tarif m; **you can name your own ~s** vous êtes libre de stipuler vos conditions; **on what ~s?** à quelles conditions?; **not on any ~s** à aucun prix, à aucune condition; **they accepted him on his own ~s** ils l'ont accepté sans concessions de sa part; **to compete on equal or the same ~s** rivaliser dans les mêmes conditions or sur un pied d'égalité; **to compete on unequal or unfair ~s** ne pas rivaliser dans les mêmes conditions, ne pas bénéficier des mêmes avantages; **to lay down or dictate ~s to sb** imposer des conditions à qn; **under the ~s of the contract** d'après les termes du contrat; (Jur) **~s and conditions** modalités fpl; **~s of surrender** conditions fpl or termes mpl de la reddition; **it is not within our ~s of reference** cela n'entre pas dans les termes de notre mandat; **~s of sale** conditions fpl de vente; **~s of payment** conditions fpl or modalités fpl de paiement; **credit ~s** conditions fpl de crédit; (Comm) **we offer it on easy ~s** nous offrons des facilités de paiement; **our ~s for full board** notre tarif pension complète; **"inclusive ~s: £20"** « 20 livres tout compris »

[e] **to come to ~s with** [+ person] arriver à un accord avec; [+ problem, situation] accepter

[f] (relationship) **to be on good/bad ~s with sb** être en bons/mauvais termes or rapports avec qn; **they are on the best of ~s** ils sont au mieux, ils sont en excellents termes; **they're on fairly friendly ~s** ils ont des rapports assez amicaux or des relations assez amicales → **equal, nod, speaking**

[g] (= word) terme m; (= expression) expression f; **technical/colloquial ~** terme m technique/familier; **in plain or simple ~s** en termes simples or clairs; **he spoke of her in glowing ~s** il a parlé d'elle en termes très chaleureux → **uncertain**

[2] VT appeler, nommer; **what we ~ happiness** ce que nous nommons or appelons le bonheur; **it was ~ed a compromise** ce fut qualifié de compromis

[3] COMP [exams etc] trimestriel ► **term insurance** N assurance f vie temporaire ► **term paper** N (US Univ) dissertation f trimestrielle

termagant ['tɜːməgənt] N harpie f, mégère f

terminal ['tɜːmɪnl] [1] ADJ [a] (Med) (= incurable) [patient, illness, cancer] en phase terminale; (= final) [stage] terminal; **~ care** soins mpl aux malades en phase terminale; **~ ward** salle f des malades en phase terminale [b] (= insoluble) [problem, crisis, situation] sans issue; **to be in ~ decline or decay** être à bout de souffle [c] (= last) [stage] final [d] (* = utter) [boredom] mortel; [stupidity, workaholic] incurable [e] (Bot, Anat, Ling) terminal [f] (= termly) trimestriel

[2] N [a] (also **air ~**) aérogare f; (for trains, coaches, buses) (gare f) terminus m inv; (Underground = terminus) (gare f) terminus m inv; (Underground: at beginning of line) tête f de li-

gne; **container ~** terminal m de containers; **oil ~** terminal m pétrolier [b] (Elec) borne f [c] (Comput) terminal m; **dumb/intelligent ~** terminal m passif/intelligent

[3] COMP ► **terminal bonus** N (Fin) bonus payé à échéance d'une police d'assurance ► **terminal point, terminal station** N (Rail) terminus m ► **terminal velocity** N (Phys, Aviat) vitesse f finale

terminally ['tɜːmɪnlɪ] ADV [a] (= incurably) **~ ill** condamné, en phase terminale; **the ~ ill** les malades mpl en phase terminale [b] (* = utterly) définitivement; **a ~ boring film** un film à mourir d'ennui

terminate ['tɜːmɪneɪt] [1] VT terminer, mettre fin à, mettre un terme à; [+ contract] résilier, dénoncer [2] VI se terminer, finir (**in** en, par)

termination [ˌtɜːmɪˈneɪʃən] N fin f, conclusion f; [of contract] résiliation f, dénonciation f; (Gram) terminaison f; **~ of employment** licenciement m, résiliation f du contrat de travail; **~ (of pregnancy)** interruption f de grossesse

termini ['tɜːmɪniː] NPL of **terminus**

terminological [ˌtɜːmɪnəˈlɒdʒɪkəl] ADJ terminologique

terminologist [ˌtɜːmɪˈnɒlədʒɪst] N terminologue mf

terminology [ˌtɜːmɪˈnɒlədʒɪ] N terminologie f

terminus ['tɜːmɪnəs] N (pl **terminuses** or **termini**) terminus m inv

termite ['tɜːmaɪt] N termite m, fourmi f blanche

termtime ['tɜːmtaɪm] [1] N (durée f du) trimestre m; **in ~** ◊ **during ~** pendant le trimestre; **out of ~** pendant les vacances (scolaires or universitaires) [2] COMP ► **termtime employment** N (US Univ) emploi m pour étudiant (rémunéré par l'université)

tern [tɜːn] N hirondelle f de mer, sterne f

ternary ['tɜːnərɪ] ADJ ternaire

Terr (Brit) ABBR = **Terrace**

terrace ['terəs] [1] N (Agr, Geol etc) terrasse f; (= raised bank) terre-plein m; (= patio, veranda, balcony, roof) terrasse f; (Brit = row of houses) rangée f de maisons (attenantes les unes aux autres); (Brit Sport) **the ~s** les gradins mpl → **HOUSE** [2] VT [+ hillside] arranger en terrasses; **~d** [garden, hillside] en terrasses; (Brit) [house] en mitoyenneté [3] COMP ► **terrace cultivation** N culture f en terrasses ► **terrace house** N (Brit) maison f en mitoyenneté → **HOUSE**

terracing ['terəsɪŋ] N [a] (Brit Sport) gradins mpl [b] (Agr) (système m de) terrasses fpl

terracotta ['terəˈkɒtə] [1] N terre f cuite [2] COMP (= made of terracotta) en terre cuite; (= colour) ocre brun inv

terra firma ['terəˈfɜːmə] N terre f ferme

terrain [teˈreɪn] N terrain m (sol)

terrapin ['terəpɪn] N tortue f d'eau douce

terrarium [təˈrɛərɪəm] N (for plants) petite serre f; (for animals) terrarium m

terrazzo [teˈrætsəʊ] N sol m de mosaïque

terrestrial [tɪˈrestrɪəl] ADJ [a] [life, event, animal, plant] terrestre [b] (esp Brit TV) [television, channel] hertzien

terrible ['terəbl] ADJ [disease, consequences, mistake, time, weather, food] terrible; [heat] terrible, atroce; [disappointment, cold] terrible, affreux; [experience, act, pain, injury] atroce; [damage, poverty] effroyable; **her French is ~** son français est atroce; **to feel ~** (= guilty) s'en vouloir beaucoup; (= ill) se sentir mal; **to look ~** (= ill) avoir très mauvaise mine; (= untidy) ne pas être beau à voir; **he sounded ~** (= ill etc) (à l'entendre or à sa voix) il avait l'air d'aller très mal; **I've got a ~ memory** j'ai très mauvaise mémoire; **he was having ~ trouble with his homework** il avait un mal fou* à faire

ses devoirs; **to be a ~ bore** être terriblement ennuyeux; **I've been a ~ fool** j'ai été le dernier des imbéciles; **you're going to get in the most ~ muddle** tu vas te retrouver dans une mélasse* effroyable; **it would be a ~ pity if ...** ce serait extrêmement dommage si ...; **it's a ~ shame (that)** c'est vraiment dommage (que (+ subj))

terribly ['terəblɪ] ADV (= very) [important, upset, hard] extrêmement; [difficult, disappointed] terriblement; [sorry] vraiment; [behave] de manière lamentable; [play, sing] terriblement mal; **I'm not ~ good with money** je ne suis pas très doué pour les questions d'argent; **it isn't a ~ good film** ce n'est pas un très bon film; **he doesn't always come across ~ well** il ne passe pas toujours très bien la rampe*; **to suffer ~** souffrir terriblement; **I missed him ~** il me manquait terriblement

terrier ['terɪə'] N [a] terrier m [b] (Brit Mil) **the ~s** la territoriale*, les territoriaux mpl

terrific [təˈrɪfɪk] ADJ [a] (* = excellent) [person, idea, story, news] super* inv; **to do a ~ job** faire un super bon boulot*; **to look ~** être super*; **to have a ~ time** s'amuser comme un fou or une folle; **~!** super! [b] (= very great) [speed] fou (folle f), fantastique; [amount] énorme; [explosion] formidable; [pain] atroce; [strain, pressure, disappointment] terrible; [noise, cold] épouvantable; [heat] épouvantable, effroyable

terrifically* [təˈrɪfɪkəlɪ] ADV [a] (= extremely) terriblement; **to do ~ well** s'en tirer formidablement bien [b] (= very well) [treat, sing, play] formidablement bien

terrify ['terɪfaɪ] VT terrifier; **to ~ sb out of his wits** rendre qn fou de terreur; **to be terrified of ...** avoir une peur folle de ...

terrifying ['terɪfaɪɪŋ] ADJ terrifiant

terrifyingly ['terɪfaɪɪŋlɪ] ADV [high, fragile] terriblement; [shake, wobble] de façon terrifiante

terrine [teˈriːn] N terrine f

territorial [ˌterɪˈtɔːrɪəl] [1] ADJ (Mil, Pol, Zool) territorial; **a ~ animal** un animal au comportement territorial [2] N (Brit Mil) **Territorial** territorial m; **the Territorials** l'armée f territoriale, la territoriale*, les territoriaux mpl [3] COMP ► **the Territorial Army** N (Brit) l'armée f territoriale ► **territorial waters** NPL eaux fpl territoriales

┌─────────────────────┐
│ **TERRITORIAL ARMY** │
└─────────────────────┘

L'armée territoriale (**Territorial Army** ou **TA**) est une organisation britannique de réservistes volontaires. Elle se compose de civils qui reçoivent un entraînement militaire pendant leur temps libre et qui forment un corps d'armée de renfort en cas de guerre ou de crise grave. Ces volontaires sont rémunérés pour leurs services.

territoriality [ˌterɪtɔːrɪˈælɪtɪ] N (Jur, Zool) territorialité f

territory ['terɪtərɪ] N (lit) (= land) territoire m; (fig = area of knowledge, competence etc) secteur m, terrain m; **the occupied territories** les territoires mpl occupés; (fig) **that's his ~** c'est un secteur qu'il connaît bien, il est sur son terrain; **such problems have become familiar ~** ce genre de problème fait désormais partie du paysage quotidien; **the familiar ~ of sex, power and guilt** le domaine familier du sexe, du pouvoir et du sentiment de culpabilité; (lit, fig) **we are definitely in uncharted ~** nous sommes en terrain or en territoire totalement inconnu; **that comes or goes with the ~** ça fait partie du boulot*, ce sont les risques du métier

terror ['terə'] [1] N [a] (NonC = fear) terreur f, épouvante f; **they were living in ~** ils vivaient dans la terreur; **they fled in ~** épouvantés, ils se sont enfuis; **he went or was in ~ of his life** il craignait fort pour sa vie; **to go or live in ~ of**

sb/sth vivre dans la terreur de qn/qch; **I have a ~ of flying** monter en avion me terrifie; **to hold no ~s for sb** ne pas faire peur du tout à qn → **reign** [b] (*Pol*) terreur *f* [c] (= *person*) terreur*; **he was the ~ of the younger boys** il était la terreur des plus petits*; **he's a ~ on the roads*** c'est un danger public sur les routes; **that child is a (real** *or* **little** *or* **holy)** **~*** cet enfant est une vraie (petite) terreur* [2] COMP ► **terror-stricken, terror-struck** ADJ épouvanté

terrorism ['terərɪzəm] N (*NonC*) terrorisme *m*; **an act of ~** un acte de terrorisme

terrorist ['terərɪst] [1] N terroriste *mf* [2] COMP [*attack, group, activities*] terroriste; [*act*] de terrorisme ► **terrorist bombing** N attentat *m* à la bombe

terrorize ['terəraɪz] VT terroriser

terry ['terɪ] N (*also* **~ cloth, ~ towelling**) tissu *m* éponge

terse [tɜːs] ADJ laconique, brusque (*pej*)

tersely ['tɜːslɪ] ADV laconiquement, avec brusquerie (*pej*)

terseness ['tɜːsnɪs] N laconisme *m*, brusquerie *f* (*pej*)

tertiary ['tɜːʃərɪ] [1] ADJ [a] (= *third*) [*effect, source*] tertiaire; **~ industries** entreprises *fpl* du tertiaire [b] (*Educ*) [*institution, level*] d'enseignement supérieur [c] (*Geol*) **Tertiary** tertiaire [2] N (*Geol*) tertiaire *m*; (*Rel*) tertiaire *mf* [3] COMP ► **tertiary college** N (*Brit Scol*) établissement accueillant des élèves de terminale et dispensant une formation professionnelle ► **tertiary education** N enseignement *m* supérieur ► **the Tertiary period** N le tertiaire ► **the tertiary sector** N (*Ind*) le (secteur) tertiaire

Terylene® ['terəliːn] (*Brit*) [1] N tergal® *m* [2] COMP en tergal®

TESL [tesl] N (ABBR = **Teaching of English as a Second Language**) → **teaching**; → TEFL, TESL, TESOL, ELT

TESOL ['tiːsɒl] N (ABBR = **Teaching of English as a Second or Other Language**) → **teaching**; → TEFL, TESL, TESOL, ELT

Tessa ['tesə] N (ABBR = **Tax Exempt Special Savings Account**) *compte de dépôt dont les intérêts sont exonérés d'impôts à condition que le capital reste bloqué*

tessellated ['tesɪleɪtɪd] ADJ en mosaïque

tessellation [ˌtesɪˈleɪʃən] N (*NonC*) mosaïque *f*

tessitura [ˌtesɪˈtʊərə] N tessiture *f*

test [test] [1] N [a] (*gen, Ind, Tech etc*) essai *m*; **the aircraft have been grounded for ~s** l'avion a été retiré de la circulation pour (être soumis à) des essais *or* des vérifications; **to run a ~ on a machine** tester *or* contrôler une machine; **nuclear ~s** essais *mpl* nucléaires [b] (*Med*) (*on blood, urine*) analyse *f*; (*on organ*) examen *m*; (*Pharm, Chem*) analyse *f*, test *m*; **urine ~** analyse *f* d'urine; **to do a ~ for sugar** faire une analyse pour déterminer la présence *or* le taux de glucose; **hearing ~** examen *m* de l'ouïe; **they did a ~ for diphtheria** ils ont fait une analyse pour voir s'il s'agissait de la diphtérie; (*Med*) **he sent a specimen to the laboratory for ~s** il a envoyé un échantillon au laboratoire pour analyses; **they did ~s on the water to see whether ...** ils ont analysé l'eau pour voir si ...; (*Med*) **the Wasserman ~** la réaction Wasserman [c] (*of physical or mental quality, also Psych*) **they are trying to devise a ~ to find suitable security staff** ils essaient de concevoir un test permettant de sélectionner le personnel de gardiennage; **it's a ~ of his strength** cela teste ses forces; **a ~ of strength** une épreuve de force; **a ~ of his powers to survive in ...** une épreuve permettant d'établir s'il pourrait survivre dans ...; **it wasn't a fair ~ of her linguistic abilities** cela n'a pas permis d'évaluer

correctement ses aptitudes linguistiques; **if we apply the ~ of visual appeal** si nous utilisons le critère de l'attrait visuel → **acid, endurance, intelligence** [d] (*Scol, Univ*) (*written*) devoir *m or* exercice *m* de contrôle, interrogation *f* écrite; (*oral*) interrogation *f* orale; **practical ~** épreuve *f* pratique; (*fig*) **to pass the ~** bien se tirer de l'épreuve [e] (*also* **driving ~**) (examen *m* du) permis *m* de conduire; **my ~ is on Wednesday** je passe mon permis mercredi; **to pass/fail one's ~** être reçu/échouer au permis (de conduire) [f] (*NonC*) **to put to the ~** mettre à l'essai *or* à l'épreuve; **to stand the ~** [*person*] se montrer à la hauteur*; [*machine, vehicle*] résister aux épreuves; **it has stood the ~ of time** cela a (bien) résisté au passage du temps [g] (*Sport*) = **test match**

[2] VT [+ *machine, weapon, tool*] essayer; [+ *vehicle*] essayer, mettre à l'essai; [+ *aircraft*] essayer, faire faire un vol d'essai à; (*Comm*) [+ *goods*] vérifier; (*Chem*) [+ *metal, liquid*] analyser; (*Med*) [+ *blood, urine*] faire une (*or* des) analyse(s) de; [+ *new drug etc*] expérimenter; (*Psych*) [+ *person, animal*] tester; (*gen*) [+ *person*] mettre à l'épreuve; [+ *sight, hearing*] examiner; [+ *intelligence*] mettre à l'épreuve, mesurer; [+ *sb's reactions*] mesurer; [+ *patience, nerves*] éprouver, mettre à l'épreuve; **they ~ed the material for resistance to heat** ils ont soumis le matériau à des essais destinés à vérifier sa résistance à la chaleur; **these conditions ~ a car's tyres/strength** ces conditions mettent à l'épreuve les pneus/la résistance d'une voiture; **to ~ metal for impurities** analyser un métal pour déterminer la proportion d'impuretés qu'il contient; **to ~ the water** [*chemist etc*] analyser l'eau; (*for swimming, bathing baby*) tâter (la température de) l'eau, voir si l'eau est bonne; (*fig: Pol etc*) prendre la température d'une assemblée (*or* d'un groupe etc), se faire une idée de la situation; (*Med*) **they ~ed him for diabetes** ils l'ont soumis à des analyses pour établir s'il avait le diabète; **they ~ed the child for hearing difficulties** ils ont fait passer à l'enfant un examen de l'ouïe; **to ~ sb for drugs/alcohol** faire subir un contrôle de dopage/un alcootest® à qn; **they ~ed the children in geography** ils ont fait subir aux enfants une interrogation *or* un exercice de contrôle en géographie; **they ~ed him for the job** ils lui ont fait passer des tests d'aptitude pour le poste

[3] VI **to ~ for sugar** faire une recherche de sucre; **he ~ed positive for drugs** son contrôle de dopage était positif; **he ~ed positive for steroids** les tests *or* les contrôles ont révélé chez lui la présence de stéroïdes; **they were ~ing for a gas leak** ils faisaient des essais pour découvrir une fuite de gaz; (*Telec etc*) **"~ing, ~ing"** ≈ « un, deux, trois »

[4] COMP [*shot etc*] d'essai; [*district, experiment, year*] test *inv* ► **test ban treaty** N (*Nucl Phys, Pol*) traité *m* d'interdiction d'essais nucléaires ► **test bore** N (*of oil*) sondage *m* de prospection ► **test card** N (*Brit TV*) mire *f* ► **test case** N (*Jur*) précédent *m*, affaire *f* qui fait jurisprudence; **the strike is a ~ case** c'est une grève-test ► **test cricket** N (*NonC*) internationaux *mpl* de cricket ► **test data** N (*Comput*) données *fpl* de test ► **test-drill** VI [*oil company*] se livrer à des forages d'essai ► **test drive** N (*of car*) essai *m* sur route ► **test-drive** VT (*by prospective buyer*) essayer; (*by manufacturer*) mettre au banc d'essai, faire un essai sur route à ► **test film** N (*Cine*) bout *m* d'essai ► **test flight** N (*Aviat*) vol *m* d'essai ► **test-fly** VT faire faire un vol d'essai à ► **test gauge** N bande *f* étalon ► **test-market** VT commercialiser à titre expérimental ► **test match** N (*Cricket, Rugby*) match *m* international ► **test paper** N (*Scol*) interrogation *f* écrite; (*Chem*) (papier *m*)

réactif *m* ► **test pattern** N (*US TV*) = **test card** ► **test piece** N (*Mus*) morceau *m* imposé ► **test pilot** N (*Aviat*) pilote *m* d'essai ► **test run** N (*lit*) essai *m*; (*fig*) période *f* d'essai ► **test strip** N bande *f* d'essai ► **test tube** N éprouvette *f* ► **test-tube baby** N bébé-éprouvette *m*

► **test out** VT SEP [+ *machine, weapon, tool*] essayer; [+ *vehicle*] essayer, mettre à l'essai; [+ *aircraft*] essayer, faire faire un vol d'essai à

testament ['testəmənt] N (*all senses*) testament *m*; **the Old/New Testament** l'Ancien/le Nouveau Testament

testamentary [ˌtestəˈmentərɪ] ADJ testamentaire

testator [tesˈteɪtər] N testateur *m*

testatrix [tesˈteɪtrɪks] N testatrice *f*

tester[1] ['testər] N (= *person*) contrôleur *m*, -euse *f*; (= *machine*) appareil *m* de contrôle

tester[2] ['testər] N (*over bed*) baldaquin *m*, ciel *m* de lit

testes ['testiːz] NPL of **testis**

testicle ['testɪkl] N testicule *m*

testicular [tesˈtɪkjʊlər] ADJ testiculaire

testification [ˌtestɪfɪˈkeɪʃən] N déclaration *f or* affirmation *f* solennelle

testify ['testɪfaɪ] [1] VT (*Jur*) témoigner, déclarer *or* affirmer sous serment (**that** que); (*gen*) **as he will ~** comme il en fera foi [2] VI (*Jur*) porter témoignage, faire une déclaration sous serment; **to ~ against/in favour of sb** déposer contre/en faveur de qn; **to ~ to sth** (*Jur*) attester qch; (*gen*) témoigner de qch

testily ['testɪlɪ] ADV [*say*] avec irritation, d'un ton irrité

testimonial [ˌtestɪˈməʊnɪəl] N (= *character reference*) lettre *f* de recommandation; (= *gift*) témoignage *m* d'estime (*offert à qn par ses collègues etc*); (*Sport: also* **~ match**) match en l'honneur d'un joueur; **as a ~ to our gratitude** en témoignage de notre reconnaissance

testimony ['testɪmənɪ] N (*Jur*) témoignage *m*, déposition *f*; (= *statement*) déclaration *f*, attestation *f*; (*frm*) **in ~ whereof** en foi de quoi

testing ['testɪŋ] [1] N [*of vehicle, machine etc*] mise *f* à l'essai; (*Chem, Pharm*) analyse *f*; [*of new drug*] expérimentation *f*; [*of person*] (*gen*) mise *f* à l'épreuve; (*Psych*) test(s) *m(pl)*; [*of sight, hearing*] examen *m*; [*of intelligence, patience etc*] mise *f* à l'épreuve; [*of sb's reactions*] mesure *f*, évaluation *f*; **nuclear ~** essais *mpl* nucléaires [2] ADJ (= *difficult, trying*) éprouvant; **it is a ~ time for us all** c'est une période éprouvante pour nous tous [3] COMP ► **testing bench** N banc *m* d'essai ► **testing ground** N (*lit, fig*) banc *m* d'essai

testis ['testɪs] N (*pl* **testes**) testicule *m*

testosterone [teˈstɒstərəʊn] N testostérone *f*

testy ['testɪ] ADJ irritable, grincheux

tetanus ['tetənəs] [1] N tétanos *m* [2] COMP [*symptom*] tétanique; [*epidemic*] de tétanos; [*vaccine, injection*] antitétanique

tetchily ['tetʃɪlɪ] ADV [*say*] avec irritation, d'un ton irrité

tetchiness ['tetʃɪnɪs] N (*NonC: Brit*) irritabilité *f*

tetchy ['tetʃɪ] ADJ (*Brit*) [*person, mood*] irritable, grincheux; [*comment*] grincheux; [*voice*] irrité

tête-à-tête ['teɪtɑːˈteɪt] [1] ADV en tête à tête, seul à seul [2] N (*pl* **tête-à-tête** *or* **tête-à-têtes**) tête-à-tête *m inv*

tether ['teðər] [1] N longe *f*; (*fig*) **to be at the end of** *or* **to have reached the end of one's ~** (= *annoyed, impatient*) être à bout (de patience or de nerfs); (= *desperate*) être au bout du rouleau [2] VT (*also* **~ up**) [+ *animal*] attacher (**to** à)

tetherball ['teðəbɔːl] (US) N *jeu consistant à frapper une balle attachée à un poteau par une corde afin de l'enrouler autour de ce poteau*

tetrachloride [ˌtetrə'klɔʊraɪd] N tétrachlorure *m*

tetragon ['tetrəgən] N quadrilatère *m*

tetrahedron [ˌtetrə'hiːdrən] N (*pl* **tetrahedrons** *or* **tetrahedra** [ˌtetrə'hiːdrə]) tétraèdre *m*

tetrameter [te'træmɪtər] N tétramètre *m*

Teutonic [tjuː'tɒnɪk] ADJ teutonique

Tex. ABBR = **Texas**

Texan ['teksən] [1] ADJ texan [2] N Texan(e) *m(f)*

Texas ['teksəs] N le Texas; **in ~** au Texas

Tex-Mex [ˌteks'meks] ADJ tex-mex

text [tekst] [1] N (*gen, also Comput*) texte *m* [2] COMP ► **text editor** N (*Comput*) éditeur *m* de texte(s)

textbook ['tekstbʊk] [1] N manuel *m* scolaire, livre *m* scolaire [2] ADJ (*fig*) **a ~ case** *or* **example of ...** un exemple classique *or* typique de ...; (*fig*) **a ~ landing/dive** *etc* un atterrissage/plongeon *etc* modèle

textile ['tekstaɪl] [1] ADJ, N textile *m*; **~s** *or* **the ~ industry** (l'industrie *f*) textile *m*

textual ['tekstjʊəl] [1] ADJ (*gen*) textuel; [*error, differences*] dans le texte [2] COMP ► **textual criticism** N critique *or* analyse *f* de texte

textually ['tekstjʊəlɪ] ADV textuellement, mot à mot

texture ['tekstʃər] N [*of cloth*] texture *f*; [*of minerals, soil*] texture *f*, structure *f*, contexture *f*; [*of skin, wood, paper, silk*] grain *m*; (*fig*) structure *f*, contexture *f*

textured ['tekstʃəd] [1] ADJ [*paint*] granité; **beautifully ~** de belle texture, d'un beau grain; **rough-/smooth-~** d'une texture grossière/fine, d'un grain grossier/fin [2] COMP ► **textured vegetable protein** N fibre *f* végétale protéique

TGIF [ˌtiːdʒiːaɪ'ef] (*hum*) (ABBR = **Thank God it's Friday**) Dieu merci c'est vendredi

TGWU [ˌtiːdʒiːdʌblju'juː] N (*Brit*) (ABBR = **Transport and General Workers' Union**) *syndicat*

Thai [taɪ] [1] ADJ (*gen*) thaïlandais; [*ambassador, embassy, monarch*] de Thaïlande [2] [a] Thaïlandais(e) *m(f)* [b] (*Ling*) thaï *m*

Thailand ['taɪlænd] N la Thaïlande

thalamus ['θæləməs] N (*pl* **thalami** ['θæləmaɪ]) thalamus *m*

thalassemia [θælə'siːmɪə] N thalassémie *f*

thalidomide [θə'lɪdəʊmaɪd] [1] N thalidomide *f* [2] COMP ► **thalidomide baby** N (petite) victime *f* de la thalidomide

thallium ['θælɪəm] N thallium *m*

Thames [temz] N Tamise *f*; (*fig*) **he'll never set the ~ on fire** il n'a pas inventé la poudre *or* le fil à couper le beurre

than [ðæn, (*weak form*) ðən] CONJ [a] que; **I have more ~ you** j'en ai plus que toi; **he is taller ~ his sister** il est plus grand que sa sœur; **he has more brains ~ sense** il a plus d'intelligence que de bon sens; **more unhappy ~ angry** plus malheureux que fâché; **you'd be better going by car ~ by bus** tu ferais mieux d'y aller en voiture plutôt qu'en autobus; **I'd do anything rather ~ admit it** je ferais tout plutôt que d'avouer cela; **no sooner did he arrive ~ he started to complain** il n'était pas plus tôt arrivé *or* il à peine arrivé qu'il a commencé à se plaindre; **it was a better play ~ we expected** la pièce était meilleure que nous ne l'avions prévu [b] (*with numerals*) de; **more/less ~ 20** plus/moins de 20; **less ~ half** moins de la moitié; **more ~ once** plus d'une fois

▼ **thank** [θæŋk] [1] VT [a] remercier, dire merci à (**sb for sth** qn de *or* pour qch, **for doing** de faire, d'avoir fait); **I cannot ~ you enough** je ne saurais assez vous remercier; **do ~ him for me** remerciez-le bien de ma part; **~ goodness*** ◊ **~ heaven(s)*** ◊ **~ God*** Dieu merci; **~ goodness you've done it!*** Dieu merci tu l'as fait!; (*fig*) **you've got him to ~ for that** c'est à lui que tu dois cela; **he's only got himself to ~** il ne peut s'en prendre qu'à lui-même; **he won't ~ you for that!** ne t'attends pas à ce qu'il te remercie *or* te félicite!; **I'll ~ you to mind your own business!** je vous prierai de vous mêler de ce qui vous regarde!

[b] **~ you** merci; **to say ~ you** dire merci; **~ you very much** merci bien (*also iro*), merci beaucoup; **~ you for the book/for helping us** merci pour le livre/de nous avoir aidés; **no ~ you** (*non*) merci; **without so much as a ~ you** sans même dire merci

[2] **thanks** NPL [a] remerciements *mpl*; **with ~s** avec tous mes (*or* nos) remerciements; **with my warmest** *or* **best ~s** avec mes remerciements les plus sincères; **give him my ~s** transmettez-lui mes remerciements, remerciez-le de ma part; **to give ~s to God** rendre grâces à Dieu; **~s be to God!** Dieu soit loué!; **that's all the ~s I get!** c'est comme ça qu'on me remercie!

[b] (= *thank you*) **~s!*** merci!; **~s very much!*** ◊ **~s a lot!*** merci bien (*also iro*), merci beaucoup, merci mille fois; **~s a million*** merci mille fois; **many ~s for all you've done** merci mille fois pour ce que vous avez fait; **many ~s for helping us** merci mille fois de nous avoir aidés; **~s for nothing!*** je te remercie! (*iro*)

[c] **~s to ...** grâce à ...; **~s to you/your brother/his help** *etc* grâce à toi/ton frère/son aide *etc*; **no ~s to you!** ce n'est pas grâce à toi!

[3] COMP ► **thank(s) offering** N action *f* de grâce(s) (*don*) ► **thank-you** N and now a special **~-you to John** et maintenant je voudrais remercier tout particulièrement John; **~-you card** carte *f* de remerciement

thankful ['θæŋkfʊl] ADJ reconnaissant (**to sb à** qn, **for sth** de qch); **I've got so much to be ~ for** je n'ai pas à me plaindre de la vie; **we were ~ for your umbrella!** nous avons vraiment béni votre parapluie!; **to be ~ for small mercies** s'estimer heureux; **to be ~ to sb for doing sth** être reconnaissant à qn d'avoir fait qch; **I was ~ that he hadn't seen me** j'ai été bien content qu'il ne m'ait pas vu; **let's just be ~ that he didn't find out** estimons-nous heureux qu'il ne l'ait pas découvert; **to be ~ to be alive** être content d'être en vie; **he was ~ to sit down** il était content de (pouvoir) s'asseoir; (*before eating*) **for what we are about to receive may the Lord make us truly ~** rendons grâce à Dieu pour le repas que nous allons partager

thankfully ['θæŋkfəlɪ] ADV [a] (= *fortunately*) heureusement; **~, someone had called the police** heureusement, quelqu'un avait appelé la police [b] (= *gratefully*) [*say, accept*] avec gratitude

thankfulness ['θæŋkfʊlnɪs] N (*NonC*) gratitude *f*, reconnaissance *f*

thankless ['θæŋklɪs] ADJ ingrat

thanksgiving ['θæŋks,gɪvɪŋ] N action *f* de grâce(s); (*Can, US*) **Thanksgiving Day** Thanksgiving *m*

┌─────────────────────────┐
│ **THANKSGIVING** │
└─────────────────────────┘

Les festivités de **Thanksgiving** *se tiennent chaque année le quatrième jeudi de novembre, en commémoration de la fête organisée par les Pères pèlerins à l'occasion de leur première récolte sur le sol américain en 1621. C'est l'occasion pour beaucoup d'Américains de se rendre dans leur famille et de manger de la dinde et de la tarte à la citrouille.* → PILGRIM FATHERS

that [ðæt, (*weak form*) ðət]

┌──────────────────────────────────────┐
│ *pl* **those** │
│ [1] DEM ADJECTIVE   [4] CONJUNCTION │
│ [2] DEM PRONOUN   [5] ADVERB │
│ [3] RELATIVE PRONOUN │
└──────────────────────────────────────┘

[1] DEM ADJECTIVE

[a] **unstressed** ce, cet (*before vowel and mute « h » of masc nouns*); cette *f*, ces *mfpl*; **~ noise** ce bruit; **~ man** cet homme; **~ idea** cette idée; **those books** ces livres; **those houses** ces maisons; **what about ~ £20 I lent you?** et ces 20 livres que je t'ai prêtées?

[b] **stressed, or as opposed to this, these** ce ... -là, cet ... -là, cette ... -là, ces ... -là; **I mean THAT book** c'est de ce livre-là que je parle; **I like ~ photo better than this one** je préfère cette photo-là à celle-ci; **but (on) ~ Saturday ...** mais ce samedi-là ...; BUT **at least everyone agreed on THAT point** au moins tout le monde était d'accord là-dessus

♦ **that one** celui-là *m*, celle-là *f*, ceux-là *mpl*, celles-là *fpl*; **which video do you want?** — ~ one quelle vidéo veux-tu? — celle-là; **of all his records, I like ~ one best** de tous ses disques, c'est celui-là que je préfère; **the only blankets we have are those ones there** les seules couvertures que nous ayons sont celles-là; BUT **there's little to choose between this model and ~ one** il n'y a pas grande différence entre ce modèle-ci et l'autre

♦ **that much: I can't carry ~ much** je ne peux pas porter tout ça; **he was at least ~ much taller than me** il me dépassait de ça au moins

[2] DEM PRONOUN

[a] **singular** (= *that thing, event, statement, person etc*) cela, ça, ce

ça is commoner, and less formal than cela; ce is used only as the subject of être.

what's ~? qu'est-ce que c'est que ça?; **do you like ~?** vous aimez ça *or* cela?; **~'s enough!** ça suffit!; **after ~** après ça, après cela; **~'s fine!** c'est parfait!; **~'s what they've been told** c'est ce qu'on leur a dit; **she's not as stupid as (all) ~** elle n'est pas si bête que ça; **~ is (to say) ...** c'est-à-dire ...; **who's ~?** (*gen*) qui est-ce?; (*on phone*) qui est à l'appareil?; **is ~ you Paul?** c'est toi Paul?; **~'s the boy I told you about** c'est le garçon dont je t'ai parlé; BUT **did he go?** — **he did!†** il y est-il allé? — pour sûr!†

♦ **that which** (= *what*) ce qui (*subject of clause*), ce que (*object of clause*); **too much time is spent worrying about ~ which may never happen** on passe trop de temps à s'inquiéter de ce qui peut très bien ne jamais arriver; **this is the opposite of ~ which they claim to have done** c'est le contraire de ce qu'ils disent avoir fait

[b] = **that one, those ones** celui-là *m*, celle-là *f*, ceux-là *mpl*, celles-là *fpl*; **not ~, the other bottle!** pas celle-là, l'autre bouteille!; **a recession like ~** une récession comme celle-là; **a recession like ~ of 1973-74** une récession comme celle de 1973-74; **those over there** ceux-là (*or* celles-là) là-bas; BUT **are those our seats?** est-ce que ce sont nos places?; **those are nice sandals** elles sont belles, ces sandalettes-là

♦ **that which** (= *the one which*) celui qui *m*, celle qui *f*; **the true cost often differs from ~ which is first projected** le coût réel est souvent différent de celui qui était prévu à l'origine

♦ **those which** (= *the ones which*) ceux qui *mpl*, celles qui *fpl*; **those which are here** ceux qui sont ici

♦ **those who** (= *the ones who*) ceux qui *mpl*, celles qui *fpl*; **those who came** ceux qui sont venus; BUT **there are those who say** certains disent, il y a des gens qui disent

[c] SET STRUCTURES

♦ **at that!: and there were six of them at ~!** et en plus ils étaient six!

♦ **by that: what do you mean by ~?** qu'est-ce que vous voulez dire par là?

- **that's it** (= *the job's finished*) ça y est; (= *that's what I mean*) c'est ça; (= *that's all*) c'est tout; (= *I've had enough*) ça suffit
- **that's just it** justement; **sorry, I wasn't thinking — ~'s just it, you never think!** désolé, je ne faisais pas attention — justement, tu ne fais jamais attention!
- **and that's that!** you're not going and ~'s ~! tu n'y vas pas, un point c'est tout!
- **so that's that** alors c'est ça; **so ~'s ~ then, you're leaving?** alors c'est ça, tu t'en vas?; *BUT* **and so ~ was** et les choses en sont restées là
- **with that** sur ce; **with ~ she burst into tears** sur ce, elle a éclaté en sanglots

3 RELATIVE PRONOUN

a qui (*subject of clause*), que (*object of clause*); **the man ~ came to see you** l'homme qui est venu vous voir; **the letter ~ I sent yesterday** la lettre que j'ai envoyée hier; **the girl ~ he met on holiday and later married** la fille qu'il a rencontrée en vacances et (qu'il) a épousée par la suite; *BUT* **and Martin, idiot ~ he is, didn't tell me** et Martin, cet imbécile, ne me l'a pas dit; **fool ~ I am!** idiot que je suis!

b
- **that ... + preposition** lequel *m*, laquelle *f*, lesquels *mpl*, lesquelles *fpl*; **the pen ~ she was writing with** le stylo avec lequel elle écrivait; **the box ~ you put it in** la boîte dans laquelle vous l'avez mis

à + **lequel, lesquels** and **lesquelles** *combines to give* **auquel, auxquels** and **auxquelles**.
the problem ~ we are faced with le problème auquel nous sommes confrontés

When **that** + *preposition refers to people, preposition* + **qui** *can also be used:*
the man ~ she was dancing with l'homme avec lequel *or* avec qui elle dansait; **the children ~ I spoke to** les enfants auxquels *or* à qui j'ai parlé

dont *is used when the French verb takes* de:
the girl/the book ~ I told you about la jeune fille/le livre dont je vous ai parlé; **the only thing ~ he has a recollection of** la seule chose dont il se souvienne *or* souvient

c **= when** où; **the evening ~ we went to the opera** le soir où nous sommes allés à l'opéra; **during the years ~ he'd been abroad** pendant les années où il était à l'étranger; **the summer ~ it was so hot** l'été où il a fait si chaud

4 CONJUNCTION

a que; **he had seen her** il a dit qu'il l'avait vue; **he was speaking so softly ~ I could hardly hear him** il parlait si bas que je l'entendais à peine; **it is natural ~ he should refuse** il est normal qu'il refuse (*subj*); **~ he should behave like this is incredible** c'est incroyable qu'il se conduise ainsi; (*liter*) **~ it should come to this!** quelle tristesse d'en arriver là!; (*liter*) **I didn't respond: oh ~ I had!** je n'ai pas répondu: que ne l'ai-je fait! (*liter*)

que *cannot be omitted in a second clause if it has a different subject:*
he said ~ he was very busy and his secretary would deal with it il a dit qu'il était très occupé et que sa secrétaire s'en occuperait

- **in that** en ce sens, dans la mesure où; **it's an attractive investment in ~ it is tax-free** c'est un investissement intéressant en ce sens qu'il *or* dans la mesure où il est exonéré d'impôts
- **not that** non (pas) que; **not ~ I want to do it** non (pas) que je veuille le faire
  b (*liter, frm* = **so that**) pour que (+ *subj*), afin que (+ *subj*); **those who fought and died ~ we might live** ceux qui se sont battus et (qui) sont morts pour que *or* afin que nous puissions vivre → **so**

5 ADVERB

a **= so** si; **it's not ~ expensive/important/funny/bad** ce n'est pas si cher/important/drôle/mal (que ça); **I couldn't go ~ far** je ne pourrais pas aller si loin; *BUT* **it's ~ high** (*gestu-*

ring) ça fait ça de haut *or* en hauteur, c'est haut comme ça

b *** = so very** tellement; **it was ~ cold!** il faisait tellement froid *or* un de ces froids*!; **when I found it I was ~ relieved!** lorsque je l'ai trouvé, je me suis senti tellement soulagé!

thatch [θætʃ] **1** N (*NonC*) chaume *m*; (*fig*) **his ~ of hair** sa crinière **2** VT [+ *roof*] couvrir de chaume; [+ *cottage*] couvrir en chaume

thatched [θætʃt] ADJ **~ roof** toit *m* de chaume; **~ cottage** chaumière *f*

thatcher [ˈθætʃəʳ] N couvreur *m* (de toits de chaume)

Thatcherism [ˈθætʃəˌrɪzəm] N thatchérisme *m*

Thatcherite [ˈθætʃəˌraɪt] **1** N thatchériste *mf* **2** ADJ thatchériste

thatching [ˈθætʃɪŋ] N (*NonC*) **a** (= *craft*) couverture *f* de toits de chaume **b** (= *material*) chaume *m*

thaw [θɔː] **1** N (*Met*) dégel *m*; (*fig: Pol etc*) détente *f*; (*fig: Econ*) **economic etc ~** assouplissement *m* des restrictions concernant la vie économique **2** VT (*also ~ out*) [+ *ice*] faire dégeler, faire fondre; [+ *snow*] faire fondre; [+ *frozen food*] décongeler, dégeler **3** VI (*also ~ out*) [*ice*] fondre, dégeler; [*snow*] fondre; [*frozen food*] décongeler, dégeler; (*Met*) **it's ~ing** il dégèle; (*fig*) **he began to ~*** (= *get warmer*) il a commencé à se dégeler* *or* à se réchauffer; (= *grow friendlier*) il a commencé à se dégeler* *or* à se dérider

the [ðiː] (*weak form*) [ðə] **1** DEF ART **a** le, la, l' (*before vowel or mute « h »*), les; **of ~ ◊ from ~** du, de la, de l', des; **to ~ ◊ at ~** au, à la, à l', aux; **~ prettiest** le plus joli, la plus jolie, les plus joli(e)s; **~ poor** les pauvres *mpl*
b (*neuter*) **~ good and ~ beautiful** le bien et le beau; **translated from ~ German** traduit de l'allemand; **it is ~ unusual that is frightening** c'est ce qui est inhabituel qui fait peur
c (*with musical instruments*) **to play ~ piano** jouer du piano
d (*with sg noun denoting whole class*) **~ aeroplane is an invention of our century** l'avion est une invention de notre siècle
e (*distributive use*) **50p ~ kilo** 50 pence le kilo; **two dollars to ~ pound** deux dollars la livre; **paid by ~ hour** payé à l'heure; **30 miles to ~ gallon** ≈ 9,3 litres au 100 (km)
f (*with names etc*) **Charles ~ First/Second/Third** Charles premier/deux/trois; **~ Browns** les Brown; **~ Bourbons** les Bourbons
g (*stressed*) **THE Professor Smith** le célèbre professeur Smith; **he's THE surgeon here** c'est lui le grand chirurgien ici; **it's THE restaurant in this part of town** c'est le meilleur restaurant du quartier; **he's THE man for the job** c'est le candidat idéal pour ce poste; **it was THE colour last year** c'était la couleur à la mode l'an dernier; **it's THE book just now** c'est le livre à lire en ce moment
h (*other special uses*) **he's got ~ measles*** il a la rougeole; **well, how's ~ leg?*** eh bien, et cette jambe?* → **cheek**, **sense**
2 ADV **~ more he works ~ more he earns** plus il travaille plus il gagne d'argent; **it will be all ~ more difficult** cela sera d'autant plus difficile; **it makes me all ~ more proud** je n'en suis que plus fier; **he was none ~ worse for it** il ne s'en est pas trouvé plus mal pour ça → **better**[1], **soon**

theatre, theater (*US*) [ˈθɪətəʳ] **1** N **a** (= *place*) théâtre *m*, salle *f* de spectacle; (= *drama*) théâtre *m*; **I like the ~** j'aime le théâtre; **to go to the ~** aller au théâtre *or* au spectacle; **it makes good ~** c'est du bon théâtre
b (= *large room*) salle *f* de conférences; (*Univ etc*) **lecture ~** amphithéâtre *m*, amphi* *m*
c (*Med: also* **operating ~**) salle *f* d'opération; **he is in (the) ~** [*patient*] il est sur la table d'opération; [*surgeon*] il est en salle d'opération

d (*Mil etc*) théâtre *m*; **~ of operations/war** théâtre *m* des opérations/des hostilités
2 COMP (*Theat*) [*programme, ticket*] de théâtre; [*visit*] au théâtre; [*management*] du théâtre; (*Med*) [*staff, nurse*] de la salle d'opération; [*job, work*] dans la salle d'opération ► **theatre company** N (*Theat*) troupe *f* de théâtre ► **theatre-in-the-round** N (*pl* **theatres-in-the-round**) théâtre *m* en rond ► **theatre lover** N amateur *m* de théâtre ► **theatre workshop** N atelier *m* de théâtre

theatregoer [ˈθɪətəˌɡəʊəʳ] N habitué(e) *m(f)* du théâtre

theatreland [ˈθɪətəlænd] N **London's ~** le Londres des théâtres

theatrical [θɪˈætrɪkəl] **1** ADJ **a** (= *dramatic*) [*production*] de théâtre, dramatique; [*world*] du théâtre; [*performance, tradition*] théâtral; **a ~ family** une famille d'acteurs **b** (*US = cinematic*) **films for ~ release** les films qui vont sortir sur les écrans *or* dans les salles **c** (*pej = melodramatic*) [*person, manner, gesture*] théâtral; **there was something very ~ about him** il avait un côté très théâtral **2 theatricals** NPL théâtre *m* (amateur); **he does a lot of (amateur) ~s** il fait beaucoup de théâtre amateur; (*fig pej*) **what were all those ~s about?** pourquoi toute cette comédie? **3** COMP ► **theatrical agent** N agent *m* artistique (*d'un acteur*) ► **theatrical company** N troupe *f* de théâtre ► **theatrical producer** N producteur *m*, -trice *f* de théâtre

theatricality [θɪˌætrɪˈkælɪtɪ] N (*fig pej*) théâtralité *f*

theatrically [θɪˈætrɪkəlɪ] ADV **a** (= *dramatically*) du point de vue théâtral **b** (*in theatres*) [*feature*] sur scène; (*US = in cinemas*) [*release, open*] dans les salles **c** (*pej = melodramatically*) théâtralement

Thebes [θiːbz] N Thèbes

thee †† [ðiː] PRON (*liter, dial*) te; (*before vowel*) t'; (*stressed: after prep*) toi

theft [θeft] N vol *m*

their [ðɛəʳ] POSS ADJ **a** leur *f inv*; **they've broken ~ legs** ils se sont cassé la jambe; (*stressed*) **THEIR house** leur maison à eux (*or* à elles) **b** (*singular usage*) son, sa, ses; **somebody rang — did you ask them ~ name?** quelqu'un a téléphoné — est-ce que tu lui as demandé son nom?

theirs [ðɛəz] POSS PRON **a** le leur, la leur, les leurs; **this car is ~** cette voiture est à eux (*or* à elles) *or* leur appartient *or* est la leur; **this music is ~** cette musique est d'eux; **a friend of ~** un de leurs amis, un ami à eux (*or* à elles)*; **I think it's one of ~** je crois que c'est un(e) des leurs; **your house is better than ~** votre maison est mieux que la leur; **it's no fault of ~** ce n'est pas de leur faute; (*pej*) **that car of ~** leur fichue* voiture; **that stupid son of ~** leur idiot de fils; **the house became ~** la maison est devenue la leur; **no advice of ~ could prevent him ...** aucun conseil de leur part ne pouvait l'empêcher de ...; (*frm*) **it is not ~ to decide** il ne leur appartient pas de décider; **~ is a specialized department** leur section est une section spécialisée
b (*singular usage*) le sien, la sienne, les sien(ne)s; **if anyone takes one that isn't ~** si jamais quelqu'un en prend un qui n'est pas à lui

theism [ˈθiːɪzəm] N théisme *m*

theist [ˈθiːɪst] ADJ, N théiste *mf*

theistic(al) [θiːˈɪstɪk(əl)] ADJ théiste

them [ðem] (*weak form*) [ðəm] **1** PERS PRON PL **a** (*direct*) (*unstressed*) les; (*stressed*) eux *mpl*, elles *fpl*; **I have seen ~** je les ai vu(e)s; **I know her but I don't know ~** je la connais, elle, mais eux (*or* elles) je ne les connais pas; **if I were ~** si j'étais à leur place, si j'étais eux (*or* elles); **it's ~!** ce sont eux (*or* elles)!, les voilà!
b (*indirect*) leur; **I gave ~ the book** je leur ai donné le livre; **I'm speaking to ~** je leur parle
c (*after prep etc*) eux, elles; **I'm thinking of ~**

je pense à eux (or elles); **as for** ~ quant à eux (or elles); **younger than** ~ plus jeune qu'eux (or elles); **they took it with** ~ ils (or elles) l'ont emporté (avec eux or elles)

d (phrases) **both of** ~ tous (or toutes) les deux; **several of** ~ plusieurs d'entre eux (or elles); **give me a few of** ~ donnez-m'en quelques-un(e)s; **every one of** ~ **was lost** ils furent tous perdus, elles furent toutes perdues; **I don't like either of** ~ je ne les aime ni l'un(e) ni l'autre; **none of** ~ **would do it** aucun d'entre eux (or aucune d'entre elles) n'a voulu le faire; **it was very good of** ~ c'était très gentil de leur part; (fig pej) **he's one of** ~* je (or tu) vois le genre!*

2 PERS PRON SG ~ **1**; le, la, lui; **somebody rang — did you ask** ~ **their name?** quelqu'un a téléphoné — est-ce que tu lui as demandé son nom?; **if anyone asks why I took it, I'll tell** ~ ... si jamais quelqu'un demande pourquoi je l'ai pris, je lui dirai ...; **if anyone arrives early ask** ~ **to wait** si quelqu'un arrive tôt, fais-le attendre

thematic [θɪˈmætɪk] ADJ thématique

theme [θiːm] **1** N **a** thème m, sujet m **b** (Mus) thème m, motif m **c** (Ling) thème m **d** (US Scol = essay) rédaction f **2** COMP ▸ **theme park** N parc m à thème ▸ **theme pub** N (Brit) bar m à décor thématique ▸ **theme song** N chanson de la bande originale; (US = signature tune) indicatif m (musical); (fig) refrain m (habituel), leitmotiv m ▸ **theme tune** N air de la bande originale

themed [θiːmd] ADJ (esp Brit) [restaurant, bar, party] à thème

themself* [ðəmˈself] PERS PRON SG (reflexive: direct and indirect) se; (emphatic) lui-même, elle-même f; (after prep) lui m, elle f; **somebody who could not defend** ~ quelqu'un qui ne pouvait se défendre; **somebody who doesn't care about** ~ quelqu'un qui ne prend pas soin de sa propre personne

themselves [ðəmˈselvz] PERS PRON PL (reflexive: direct and indirect) se; (emphatic) eux-mêmes mpl, elles-mêmes fpl; (after prep) eux, elles; **they've hurt** ~ ils se sont blessés, elles se sont blessées; **they said to** ~ ils (or elles) se sont dit; **they saw it** ~ ils l'ont vu eux-mêmes; **they were talking amongst** ~ ils discutaient entre eux; **these computers can reprogram** ~ ces ordinateurs peuvent se reprogrammer automatiquement; **anyone staying here will have to cook for** ~ les gens qui logent ici doivent faire leur propre cuisine; **(all) by** ~ tout seuls, toutes seules

then [ðen] **1** ADV **a** (= at that time) alors, à l'époque; **we had two dogs** ~ nous avions alors deux chiens, nous avions deux chiens à l'époque; **I'm going to London and I'll see him** ~ je vais à Londres et je le verrai à ce moment-là; ~ **and there** ◊ there and ~ sur-le-champ, séance tenante

b (after prep) **from** ~ **on(wards)** dès lors, à partir de cette époque(-là) or ce moment(-là); **before** ~ avant (cela); **by** ~ **I knew** ... à ce moment-là, je savais déjà ...; **I'll have it finished by** ~ je l'aurai fini d'ici là; **since** ~ depuis ce moment-là or cette époque-là or ce temps-là; **between now and** ~ d'ici là; **(up) until** ~ jusque-là, jusqu'alors

c (= next, afterwards) puis, ensuite; **he went first to London** ~ **to Paris** il est allé d'abord à Londres, puis or et ensuite à Paris; **and** ~ **what?** et puis après?; **now this** ~ **that** tantôt ceci, tantôt cela

d (= in that case) alors, donc; ~ **it must be in the sitting room** alors ça doit être au salon; **if you don't want that** ~ **what do you want?** si vous ne voulez pas de ça, alors que voulez-vous donc?; **but** ~ **that means that** ... mais c'est donc que ...; **someone had already warned you** ~? on vous avait donc déjà prévenu?; **now** ~ **what's the matter?** alors qu'est-ce

qu'il y a?

e (= furthermore, and also) et puis, d'ailleurs; **(and)** ~ **there's my aunt** et puis il y a ma tante; ... **and** ~ **it's none of my business** ... et d'ailleurs or et puis cela ne me regarde pas; ... **and** ~ **again** or **but** ~ **he might not want to go** ... remarquez, il est possible qu'il ne veuille pas y aller; ... **and** ~ **again** or **but** ~ **he has always tried to help us** ... et pourtant, il faut dire qu'il a toujours essayé de nous aider

2 ADJ (before n) d'alors, de l'époque; **the** ~ **Prime Minister** le Premier ministre d'alors or de l'époque

thence [ðens] ADV (frm, liter) **a** (= from there) de là, de ce lieu-là; **an idea which influenced Plato, and** ~ **the future of Western thought** une idée qui a influencé Platon, et, partant, l'avenir de la pensée occidentale; **from** ~ de ce lieu **b** (= from that time) dès lors, depuis lors; **three weeks** ~ trois semaines plus tard **c** (= therefore) par conséquent, pour cette raison

thenceforth [ˈðensfɔːθ], **thenceforward** [ˈðensfɔːwəd] ADV (frm) dès lors

theocracy [θɪˈɒkrəsɪ] N théocratie f

theocratic [θɪəˈkrætɪk] ADJ théocratique

theodolite [θɪˈɒdəlaɪt] N théodolite m

theologian [θɪəˈləʊdʒɪən] N théologien(ne) m(f)

theological [θɪəˈlɒdʒɪkəl] **1** ADJ [debate, issue, text] théologique; [training] théologique, en théologie; [student] en théologie **2** COMP ▸ **theological college** N séminaire m, école f de théologie

theology [θɪˈɒlədʒɪ] N théologie f → **liberation**

theorem [ˈθɪərəm] N théorème m

theoretical [θɪəˈretɪkəl] **1** ADJ (also **theoretic**) théorique **2** COMP ▸ **theoretical physicist** N spécialiste mf de physique théorique ▸ **theoretical physics** N physique f théorique

theoretically [θɪəˈretɪkəlɪ] ADV **a** (= in theory) [possible] théoriquement; **he could** ~ **face the death penalty** il encourt théoriquement la peine de mort; **I was,** ~, **a fully-qualified lawyer** j'étais, en théorique, un avocat diplômé **b** (= as theory) [absurd, interesting, ambitious] sur le plan théorique; [analyse, justify] théoriquement; ~, **his ideas are revolutionary** sur le plan théorique, ses idées sont révolutionnaires

theoretician [ˌθɪərəˈtɪʃən], **theorist** [ˈθɪərɪst] N théoricien(ne) m(f)

theorize [ˈθɪəraɪz] **1** VI [scientist, psychologist etc] élaborer une (or des) théorie(s) (about sur); **it's no good just theorizing about it** ce n'est pas la peine de faire des grandes théories là-dessus* **2** VT **to** ~ **that** ... émettre l'hypothèse que ...

theory [ˈθɪərɪ] N théorie f; **in** ~ en théorie

theosophical [θɪəˈsɒfɪkəl] ADJ théosophique

theosophist [θɪˈɒsəfɪst] N théosophe mf

theosophy [θɪˈɒsəfɪ] N théosophie f

therapeutic [ˌθerəˈpjuːtɪk] **1** ADJ (Med) thérapeutique; **I find chopping vegetables very** ~ ça me détend de couper des légumes **2** COMP ▸ **therapeutic community** N communauté f thérapeutique ▸ **therapeutic touch** N forme de thérapeutique manuelle

therapeutical [ˌθerəˈpjuːtɪkəl] ADJ thérapeutique

therapeutics [ˌθerəˈpjuːtɪks] N (NonC) thérapeutique f

therapist [ˈθerəpɪst] N (gen) thérapeute mf → **occupational**

therapy [ˈθerəpɪ] N (gen, also Psych) thérapie f; (fig) **it's good** ~ c'est très thérapeutique

there [ðɛəʳ] **1** ADV **a** (place) y (before vb), là; **we shall soon be** ~ nous y serons bientôt,

nous serons bientôt là, nous serons bientôt arrivés; **put it** ~ posez-le là; **when we left** ~ quand nous en sommes partis, quand nous sommes partis de là; **on** ~ là-dessus; **in** ~ là-dedans; **back** or **down** or **over** ~ là-bas; **he lives round** ~ il habite par là; (further away) il habite par là-bas; **somewhere round** ~ quelque part par là; **here and** ~ çà et là, par-ci par-là; **from** ~ de là; **they went** ~ **and back in two hours** ils ont fait l'aller et retour en deux heures; **to be** ~ **for sb*** (= supportive) être là pour qn; **I've been** ~ **(myself*)** (= I've experienced it) j'ai connu ça (moi-même) → **here**

b ~ **is** il y a, il est (liter); ~ **are** il y a; **once upon a time** ~ **was a princess** il y avait or il était une fois une princesse; ~ **will be dancing later** plus tard on dansera; ~ **is a page missing** il y a une page qui manque; ~ **are three apples left** il reste trois pommes, il y a encore trois pommes; ~ **comes a time when** ... il vient un moment où ...; ~**'s no denying it** c'est indéniable

c (= in existence) **this road isn't meant to be** ~! cette route ne devrait pas exister or être là!; **if the technology is** ~, **someone will use it** si la technologie existe, quelqu'un l'utilisera **d** (other uses) ~**'s my brother!** voilà mon frère!; ~ **are the others!** voilà les autres!; ~ **he is!** le voilà!; ~ **you are** (= I've found you) (ah) vous voilà!; (offering sth) voilà!; **that man** ~ **saw it all** cet homme-là a tout vu; **hey you** ~! hé or ho toi, là-bas!*; **hurry up** ~! eh! dépêchez-vous!; ~**'s my mother calling me** il y a or voilà ma mère qui m'appelle; ~**'s the problem** là est or c'est or voilà le problème; **I disagree with you** ~ là je ne suis pas d'accord avec vous; **you've got me** ~! alors là, ça me dépasse!*; **but** ~ **again, he should have known better** mais là encore, il aurait dû se méfier; **you press this switch and** ~ **you are!** tu appuies sur ce bouton et ça y est!; ~ **you are, I told you that would happen** tu vois, je t'avais bien dit que ça allait arriver; ~ **they go!** les voilà qui partent!; (fig) **I had hoped to finish early, but** ~ **you go** j'espérais finir tôt mais tant pis; (fig) ~ **you go again***, complaining about ... ça y est, tu recommences à te plaindre de ...; (fig) ~ **he goes again!*** ça y est, il recommence!; (fig) **he's all** ~* c'est un malin, il n'est pas idiot; **he's not all** ~* (gen) il est un peu demeuré; [old person] il n'a plus toute sa tête

2 EXCL ~, **what did I tell you?** alors, qu'est-ce que je t'avais dit?; ~, ~, **don't cry!** allons, allons, ne pleure pas!; ~, **drink this** allez or tenez, buvez ceci; ~ **now, that didn't hurt, did it?** voyons, voyons or eh bien, ça n'a pas fait si mal que ça, si?

thereabouts [ˌðɛərəˈbaʊts] ADV (place) par là, près de là, dans le voisinage; (degree etc) à peu près, environ; **£5 or** ~ environ cinq livres, dans les cinq livres

thereafter [ˌðɛərˈɑːftəʳ] ADV (frm) par la suite

thereat [ˌðɛərˈæt] ADV (frm) (place) là; (time) là-dessus

thereby [ˌðɛəˈbaɪ] ADV de cette façon, de ce fait, par ce moyen; (hum) ~ **hangs a tale!** c'est toute une histoire!

therefore [ˈðɛəfɔːʳ] CONJ donc, par conséquent, pour cette raison

therefrom [ˌðɛəˈfrɒm] ADV (frm) de là

therein [ˌðɛərˈɪn] ADV (frm) (= in that regard) à cet égard, en cela; (= inside) (là-)dedans

thereof [ˌðɛərˈɒv] ADV (frm) de cela, en; **he ate** ~ il en mangea

thereon [ˌðɛərˈɒn] ADV (frm) (là-)dessus

there's [ðɛəz] = **there is**, **there has**; → **be**, **have**

thereto [ˌðɛəˈtuː] ADV (frm) y

theretofore [ˌðɛətuˈfɔː] ADV (frm) jusque-là

thereunder [ˌðɛərˈʌndəʳ] ADV (frm) (là) en-dessous

thereupon [ðɛərə'pɒn] ADV (= *then*) sur ce ; (*frm* = *on that subject*) là-dessus, à ce sujet

therewith [ðɛə'wɪð] ADV (*frm*) (= *with that*) avec cela, en outre ; (= *at once*) sur ce

therm [θɜːm] N = *1,055 x 10⁸ joules* ; (*formerly*) thermie *f*

thermal ['θɜːməl] **1** ADJ **a** (*Elec, Phys*) thermique **b** (*Geol, Med*) [*spring, spa, treatment*] thermal **c** [*underwear, socks*] en Thermolactyl® ; **a ~ t-shirt** un T-shirt en Thermolactyl® **2** N (*Met*) courant *m* ascendant (d'origine thermique), ascendance *f* thermique **3** COMP ► **thermal barrier** N barrière *f* thermique ► **thermal baths** NPL thermes *mpl* ► **thermal blanket** N (*for person*) couverture *f* de survie ► **thermal breeder** N réacteur *m* thermique ► **thermal conductivity** N conductivité *f* thermique ► **thermal efficiency** N rendement *m* thermique ► **thermal expansion** N dilatation *f* thermique ► **thermal imager** N imageur *m* thermique ► **thermal imaging** N thermographie *f* ► **thermal imaging equipment** N matériel *m* or appareils *mpl* de thermographie ► **thermal imaging system** N système *m* de thermographie *or* d'imagerie thermique ► **thermal paper** N papier *m* thermosensible ► **thermal power** N énergie *f* thermique ► **thermal power station** N centrale *f* thermique ► **thermal reactor** N réacteur *m* thermique ► **thermal shock** N choc *m* thermique ► **thermal unit** N (*also* **British ~ unit**) *unité de quantité de chaleur* (= *252 calories*)

thermic ['θɜːmɪk] ADJ = **thermal 1a**

thermionic [ˌθɜːmɪ'ɒnɪk] ADJ [*effect, emission*] thermoïonique ; **~ valve** ◊ **~ tube** (*US*) tube *m* électronique

thermionics [ˌθɜːmɪ'ɒnɪks] N thermoïonique *f*

thermo... ['θɜːməʊ] PREF therm(o)...

thermocouple ['θɜːməʊkʌpl] N thermocouple *m*

thermodynamic ['θɜːməʊdaɪ'næmɪk] ADJ thermodynamique

thermodynamics ['θɜːməʊdaɪ'næmɪks] N (*NonC*) thermodynamique *f*

thermoelectric ['θɜːməʊɪ'lektrɪk] ADJ thermoélectrique

thermograph ['θɜːməʊɡrɑːf] N thermographe *m*

thermography [θɜː'mɒɡrəfɪ] N thermographie *f*

thermometer [θə'mɒmɪtəʳ] N thermomètre *m*

thermonuclear ['θɜːməʊ'njuːklɪəʳ] ADJ [*weapon, war, reaction*] thermonucléaire ; **~ strike** attaque *f* nucléaire

thermopile ['θɜːməʊpaɪl] N pile *f* thermoélectrique

thermoplastic ['θɜːməʊ'plæstɪk] N thermoplastique *m*

thermoplasticity [ˌθɜːməʊplæ'stɪsɪtɪ] N (*NonC*) thermoplasticité *f*

Thermopylae [θə'mɒpɪliː] N les Thermopyles *fpl*

Thermos® ['θɜːməs] **1** N thermos® *m or f inv* **2** COMP ► **Thermos flask** N bouteille *f* thermos®

thermosiphon [ˌθɜːməʊ'saɪfən] N thermosiphon *m*

thermostat ['θɜːməstæt] N thermostat *m*

thermostatic [ˌθɜːmə'stætɪk] ADJ thermostatique

thermotherapy [ˌθɜːməʊ'θerəpɪ] N thermothérapie *f*

thesaurus [θɪ'sɔːrəs] N (*pl* **thesauruses** *or* **thesauri** [θɪ'sɔːraɪ]) (*gen*) trésor *m* (*fig*) ; (= *lexicon*) dictionnaire *m* synonymique ; (*Comput*) thesaurus *m*

these [ðiːz] DEM ADJ, PRON *pl of* **this**

theses ['θiːsiːz] NPL *of* **thesis**

Theseus ['θiːsɪəs] N Thésée *m*

thesis ['θiːsɪs] N (*pl* **theses** ['θiːsiːz]) thèse *f*

Thespian ['θespɪən] **1** ADJ (*liter or hum*) dramatique, de Thespis ; **his ~ talents** son talent de comédien **2** N (*liter or hum* = *actor*) comédien(ne) *m(f)*

Thessalonians [ˌθesə'ləʊnɪənz] NPL Thessaloniciens *mpl*

they [ðeɪ] PERS PRON PL **a** ils *mpl*, elles *fpl* ; (*stressed*) eux *mpl*, elles *fpl* ; **~ have gone** ils sont partis, elles sont parties ; **there ~ are!** les voilà ! ; **~ are teachers** ce sont des professeurs ; **THEY know nothing about it** eux, ils n'en savent rien **b** (= *people in general*) on ; **~ say that ...** on dit que ... **c** (*singular usage*) il *m*, elle *f* ; (*stressed*) lui *m*, elle *f* ; **somebody called but ~ didn't give their name** quelqu'un a appelé, mais il *or* elle n'a pas donné son nom

they'd [ðeɪd] = **they had**, **they would** ; → **have**, **would**

they'll [ðeɪl] = **they will** ; → **will**

they're [ðeəʳ] = **they are** ; → **be**

they've [ðeɪv] = **they have** ; → **have**

thiamine ['θaɪəmiːn] N thiamine *f*

thick [θɪk] **1** ADJ **a** (= *fat, heavy, dense*) [*slice, layer, wall, hair, moustache, smoke, sauce, waist*] épais (-aisse *f*) ; [*pile, lenses, coat*] gros (grosse *f*) ; [*lips, nose, wool, string, line, book*] épais (-aisse *f*), gros (grosse *f*) ; [*neck*] épais (-aisse *f*), large ; [*soup, cream, gravy*] épais (-aisse *f*), consistant ; [*beard, forest, vegetation, foliage*] épais (-aisse *f*), touffu ; [*fog*] épais (-aisse *f*), dense ; [*darkness, crowd*] dense ; [*hedge*] (bien) fourni, touffu ; [*honey*] dur ; **to be 5cm ~** avoir 5 cm d'épaisseur ; **a 7cm ~ door** ◊ **a door 7cm ~** une porte de 7 cm d'épaisseur, une porte épaisse de 7 cm ; **how ~ is it?** quelle est son épaisseur ? ; **to become ~(er)** [*sauce, cream*] épaissir ; [*waist*] (s')épaissir ; [*fog, smoke, darkness, vegetation, crowd*] s'épaissir ; **~ snow was falling** la neige tombait à gros flocons ; **he trudged through the ~ snow** il avançait péniblement dans l'épaisse couche de neige ; **the leaves were ~ on the ground** le sol était recouvert d'une épaisse couche de feuilles ; **antique shops are ~ on the ground around here*** il y a pléthore de magasins d'antiquités par ici ; **the air is very ~ in here** ça sent le renfermé ici ; (*Brit*) **to give someone a ~ ear*** tirer les oreilles à qn* → **skin b** **~ with**: **to be ~ with dust** être couvert d'une épaisse couche de poussière ; **the streets are ~ with people** les rues sont noires de monde ; **the streets are ~ with traffic** la circulation est dense dans les rues ; **the water is ~ with weeds** l'eau est envahie par les mauvaises herbes ; **~ with smoke** [*air, atmosphere, room*] enfumé ; **the air is ~ with the smell of burning wood** l'air est imprégné d'une odeur de bois brûlé ; **the air is ~ with rumours** la rumeur enfle ; **the air was ~ with talk of his possible resignation** on parlait partout de son éventuelle démission **c** (*Brit* = *stupid*) [*person*] bête ; **to get sth into one's ~ head** se mettre qch dans le crâne* ; **as ~ as two (short) planks** *or* **as a brick** bête comme ses pieds* ; **as ~ as pigshit**** con comme un balai* *or* comme la lune* **d** (= *unclear*) [*voice*] pâteux ; **a voice ~ with emotion** une voix chargée d'émotion ; **I woke up with a ~ head** (*from alcohol*) je me suis réveillé avec la gueule de bois* ; (*from fatigue*) je me suis réveillé avec le cerveau embrumé **e** (= *strong*) [*accent*] fort **f** (*Brit*†* = *unfair*) **it's** *or* **that's a bit ~** ça, c'est un peu fort* *or* un peu raide* **g** (* = *friendly*) **to be ~ with sb** être copain (copine *f*) avec qn ; **they are very ~** ils sont comme cul et chemise* ; (*pej*) **to be (as) ~ as thieves** s'entendre comme larrons en foire **2** ADV [*cut*] en tranches épaisses ; [*spread*] en couche épaisse ; **the fumes hung ~ over the pitch** il y avait une fumée épaisse au-dessus du terrain ; **the snow still lies ~ on the mountains** il y a encore une épaisse couche de neige sur les montagnes ; **blows/arrows fell ~ and fast** les coups/flèches pleuvaient (de partout) ; **the jokes came ~ and fast** il y a eu une avalanche de plaisanteries ; **redundancies are coming ~ and fast** il y a des licenciements à la pelle ; **the goals came ~ and fast** les buts arrivaient à la pelle ; **to lay it on ~*** forcer un peu la dose* **3** N [*of finger, leg etc*] partie *f* charnue ; **in the ~ of the crowd** au cœur de la foule ; **in the ~ of the fight** au cœur de la mêlée ; **they were in the ~ of it** ils étaient en plein dedans ; **through ~ and thin** à travers toutes les épreuves, contre vents et marées **4** COMP ► **thick-knit** ADJ gros (grosse *f*), en grosse laine ♦ N gros chandail *m*, chandail *m* en grosse laine ► **thick-lipped** ADJ aux lèvres charnues, lippu ► **thick-skinned** ADJ [*orange*] à la peau épaisse ; (*fig*) [*person*] peu sensible ; **he's very ~-skinned** c'est un dur, rien ne le touche ► **thick-skulled*, thick-witted*** ADJ = **thickheaded**

thicken ['θɪkən] **1** VT [+ *sauce*] épaissir, lier **2** VI [*branch, waist etc*] s'épaissir ; [*crowd*] grossir ; [*sauce etc*] épaissir ; (*fig*) [*mystery*] s'épaissir → **plot**

thickener ['θɪkənəʳ] N épaississant *m*

thicket ['θɪkɪt] N fourré *m*, hallier *m* ; (*fig*) [*of ideas, regulations*] maquis *m*

thickhead* ['θɪkhed] N andouille* *f*

thickheaded* [θɪk'hedɪd] ADJ bête, obtus, borné

thickie* ['θɪkɪ] = **thicky**

thickly ['θɪklɪ] ADV **a** (= *densely*) [*wooded, sown, planted, populated*] densément ; **to grow ~** [*hair, fruit*] pousser en abondance ; **the snow fell ~** la neige tombait dru **b** (= *deeply*) [*spread, roll out*] en couche épaisse ; **~ spread with butter** couvert d'une épaisse couche de beurre ; **to sprinkle sth ~ with flour** saupoudrer qch d'une épaisse couche de farine ; **to sprinkle sth ~ with basil** saupoudrer généreusement qch de basilic ; **dust/snow lay ~ everywhere** il y avait une épaisse couche de poussière/de neige partout ; **~ covered with** *or* **in dust** couvert d'une épaisse couche de poussière ; **~ encrusted with mud** incrusté d'une épaisse couche de boue ; **~ carpeted** couvert d'une épaisse moquette ; **the apples with which the grass was ~ strewn** les pommes qui jonchaient l'herbe **c** (= *coarsely*) [*slice*] en tranches épaisses **d** (= *unclearly*) [*say*] d'une voix pâteuse

thickness ['θɪknɪs] N **a** (*NonC*) [*of slice, layer, wall*] épaisseur *f* ; [*of lips, nose, wool, line*] épaisseur *f*, grosseur *f* ; [*of fog, forest*] épaisseur *f*, densité *f* ; [*of hair*] épaisseur *f*, abondance *f* **b** (= *layer*) épaisseur *f* ; **three ~es of material** trois épaisseurs de tissu

thicko* ['θɪkəʊ] N idiot(e) *m(f)*, crétin(e)* *m(f)*

thickset [θɪk'set] ADJ (*and small*) trapu, râblé ; (*and tall*) bien bâti, costaud*

thicky* ['θɪkɪ] N = **thicko**

thief [θiːf] **1** N (*pl* **thieves**) voleur *m*, -euse *f* ■ (*PROV*) **set a ~ to catch a ~** à voleur voleur et demi (*PROV*) ; **stop ~!** au voleur ! → **honour**, **thick 2** COMP ► **thieves' cant** N argot *m* du milieu ► **thieves' kitchen** N repaire *m* de brigands

thieve [θiːv] VTI voler

thievery ['θiːvərɪ] N (*NonC*) vol *m*

thieves [θiːvz] NPL *of* **thief**

thieving ['θiːvɪŋ] **1** ADJ **a*** **those ~ kids** ces petits voleurs ; **keep your ~ hands off!** enlève tes sales pattes de voleur de là !* **b** (*Mus*) **the Thieving Magpie** la Pie voleuse **2** N (*NonC*) vol *m*

thievish† [ˈθiːvɪʃ] ADJ voleur, de voleur

thigh [θaɪ] **1** N cuisse f **2** COMP ▶ **thigh boots** NPL cuissardes fpl

thighbone [ˈθaɪbəʊn] N fémur m

thimble [ˈθɪmbl] N dé m (à coudre)

thimbleful [ˈθɪmblfʊl] N (fig) doigt m, goutte f

thin [θɪn] **1** ADJ **a** (= lean, not thick) [person, face, legs, arms, animal] maigre ; [lips, waist, nose, layer, slice, strip, sheet] mince ; [line, thread, wire] fin ; [cloth, garment] fin, léger ; [book, mattress, wall] peu épais (-aisse f), mince ; ~ **string** petite ficelle ; **a** ~ **stroke** (with pen) un trait mince or fin, un délié ; **to get** ~(**ner**) [person] maigrir ; **as** ~ **as a rake** [person] maigre comme un clou ; (fig) **it's the** ~ **end of the wedge** c'est s'engager sur une pente savonneuse ; (fig) **to be (skating** or **treading) on** ~ **ice** être sur un terrain glissant → **line¹**, **skin**, **wear**

b (= runny) [liquid, oil] fluide, léger ; [soup, sauce, gravy] clair, clairet (pej) ; [paint] peu épais (-aisse f), liquide ; [cream, honey, mud] liquide ; **to make** ~(**ner**) [+ soup, sauce] éclaircir, délayer

c (= not dense) [smoke, fog, cloud] léger ; [air, atmosphere] raréfié ; **to become** ~**ner** [smoke etc] se dissiper ; [air] se raréfier ; **to disappear** or **vanish into** ~ **air** se volatiliser, disparaître (d'un seul coup) sans laisser de traces ; **to appear out of** ~ **air** apparaître comme par magie ; **to produce** or **conjure sth out of** ~ **air** faire apparaître qch comme par magie

d (= sparse) [crowd] épars ; [hair, beard, eyebrows, hedge] clairsemé ; **to become** ~**ner** [crowd, plants, trees, hair] s'éclaircir ; (esp Brit) **to be** ~ **on the ground** être rare ; **good news has been** ~ **on the ground*** lately les bonnes nouvelles se font rares ces derniers temps ; **to be** ~ **on top*** (= balding) être dégarni* ; **to be getting** ~ **on top*** (= balding) se dégarnir*

e (= feeble) [excuse, argument, evidence, plot] peu convaincant ; [script] médiocre ; [smile, majority] faible ; **his disguise was rather** ~ son déguisement a été facilement percé à jour

f [voice] grêle, fluet ; [sound] aigu (-guë f)

g (Fin) [profit] maigre ; **trading was** ~ **today** le marché était peu actif aujourd'hui ; **to have a** ~ **time (of it)*** passer par une période de vaches maigres

2 ADV [spread] en couche fine or mince ; [cut] en tranches fines or minces

3 VT [+ paint] étendre, délayer ; [+ sauce] allonger, délayer ; [+ trees] éclaircir ; [+ hair] désépaissir

4 VI [fog, crowd] se disperser, s'éclaircir ; [numbers] se réduire, s'amenuiser ; **his hair is** ~**ning** ◊ **he's** ~**ning on top*** il perd ses cheveux, il se dégarnit*

5 COMP ▶ **thin-lipped** ADJ aux lèvres minces or fines ; (with rage etc) les lèvres pincées ▶ **thin-skinned** ADJ [orange] à la peau fine ; (fig) [person] susceptible

▶**thin down 1** VI [person] maigrir **2** VT SEP [+ paint] étendre, délayer ; [+ sauce] allonger

▶**thin out 1** VI [crowd, fog] se disperser, s'éclaircir **2** VT SEP [+ seedlings, trees] éclaircir ; [+ numbers, population] réduire ; [+ crowd] disperser ; [+ workforce] réduire, dégraisser

thine [ðaɪn] (†† or liter) **1** POSS PRON le tien, la tienne, les tiens, les tiennes **2** POSS ADJ ton, ta, tes

thing [θɪŋ] N **a** (gen) chose f ; (= object) chose f, objet m ; **surrounded by beautiful** ~**s** entouré de belles choses or de beaux objets ; ~ **of beauty** bel objet m, belle chose f ; **such** ~**s as money, fame ...** des choses comme l'argent, la gloire ... ; **he's interested in ideas rather than** ~**s** ce qui l'intéresse ce sont les idées et non pas les objets ; ~**s of the mind appeal to him** il est attiré par les choses de l'esprit ; **the** ~ **he loves most is his car** ce qu'il aime le plus au monde c'est sa voiture ; **what's that** ~**?** qu'est-ce que c'est que cette chose-là or ce machin-

là* or ce truc-là* ? ; **the good** ~**s in life** les plaisirs mpl de la vie ; **he thinks the right** ~**s** il pense comme il faut ; **she likes sweet** ~**s** elle aime les sucreries fpl ; **you've been hearing** ~**s!** tu as dû entendre des voix !

b (= belongings) ~**s** affaires fpl ; **have you put away your** ~**s?** as-tu rangé tes affaires ? ; **to take off one's** ~**s** se débarrasser de son manteau etc ; **do take your** ~**s off!** débarrassez-vous (donc) ! ; **have you got your swimming** ~**s?** as-tu tes affaires de bain ? ; **have you got any swimming** ~**s?** as-tu ce qu'il faut pour aller te baigner ? ; **where are the first-aid** ~**s?** où est la trousse de secours ?

c (= affair, item, circumstance) chose f ; **I've two** ~**s still to do** j'ai encore deux choses à faire ; **the** ~ **she said!** les choses qu'elle a pu dire ! ; **the next** ~ **to do is ...** ce qu'il y a à faire maintenant c'est ... ; **the best** ~ **would be to refuse** le mieux serait de refuser ; (iro) **that's a fine** or **nice** ~ **to do!** c'est vraiment la chose à faire ! ; **what sort of (a)** ~ **is that to say to anyone?** ça n'est pas une chose à dire (aux gens) ; **the last** ~ **on the agenda** le dernier point à l'ordre du jour ; **you take the** ~ **too seriously** tu prends la chose trop au sérieux ; **you worry about** ~**s too much** tu te fais trop de soucis ; **I must think** ~**s over** il faut que j'y réfléchisse ; **how are** ~**s with you?** et vous, comment ça va ? ; **how's** ~**s?*** comment va ?* ; **as** ~**s are** dans l'état actuel des choses ; ~**s are going from bad to worse** les choses vont de mal en pis ; **since that's how** ~**s are** puisque c'est comme ça, puisqu'il en est ainsi ; **I believe in honesty in all** ~**s** je crois à l'honnêteté en toutes circonstances ; **to expect great** ~**s of sb/sth** attendre beaucoup de qn/qch ; **they were talking of one** ~ **and another** ils parlaient de choses et d'autres ; **taking one** ~ **with another** à tout prendre, somme toute ; **the** ~ **is to know when he's likely to arrive** ce qu'il faut c'est savoir or la question est de savoir à quel moment il devrait en principe arriver ; **the** ~ **is this: ...** voilà de quoi il s'agit : ... ; **the** ~ **is, she'd already seen him** (ce qu'il y a) c'est qu'elle l'avait vu, mais elle l'avait déjà vu ; **it's a strange** ~**, but ...** c'est drôle, mais ... ; **it is one** ~ **to use a computer, quite another to know how it works** utiliser un ordinateur est une chose, en connaître le fonctionnement en est une autre ; **for one** ~**, it doesn't make sense** d'abord or en premier lieu, ça n'a pas de sens ; **and (for) another** ~**, I'd already spoken to him** et en plus, je lui avais déjà parlé ; **it's a good** ~ **I came** heureusement que je suis venu ; **he's on to a good** ~* il a trouvé le filon* ; **it's the usual** ~**, he hadn't checked the petrol** c'est le truc* or le coup* classique, il avait oublié de vérifier l'essence ; **that was a near** or **close** ~ (of accident) vous l'avez (or il l'a etc) échappé belle ; (of result of race, competition etc) il s'en est fallu de peu ; **it's just one of those** ~**s** ce sont des choses qui arrivent ; **it's just one (damn)** ~ **after another*** les embêtements se succèdent ; **I didn't understand a** ~ **of what he was saying** je n'ai pas compris un mot de ce qu'il disait ; **I hadn't done a** ~ **about it** je n'avais strictement rien fait ; **he knows a** ~ **or two** il s'y connaît ; **he's in London doing his own** ~* il est à Londres et fait ce qui lui plaît or chante* ; **she's gone off to do her own** ~* elle est partie chercher sa voie or faire ce qui lui plaît ; **she's got a** ~ **about spiders*** elle a horreur des araignées, elle a la phobie des araignées ; **he's got a** ~ **about blondes*** il a un faible pour les blondes ; **he made a great** ~ **of my refusal*** quand j'ai refusé il en a fait toute une histoire or tout un plat* ; **don't make a** ~ **of it!*** n'en fais pas tout un plat !*, ne monte pas ça en épingle ! ; **he had a** ~* **with her two years ago** il a eu une liaison avec elle il y a deux ans ; **he's got a** ~* **for her** il en pince pour elle* ; **Mr Thing*** rang up Monsieur Chose* or Monsieur Machin* a téléphoné → **equal**, **first**, **such**

d (= person, animal) créature f ; **(you) poor little** ~**!** pauvre petit(e) ! ; **poor** ~**, he's very ill** le pauvre, il est très malade ; **she's a spiteful** ~ c'est une rosse* ; **you horrid** ~**!*** chameau !* ; **I say, old** ~*† dis donc (mon) vieux

e (= best, most suitable etc) thing) **that's just the** ~ **for me** c'est tout à fait or justement ce qu'il me faut ; **just the** ~**!** ◊ **the very** ~**!** (of object) voilà tout à fait or justement ce qu'il me (or nous etc) faut ! ; (of idea, plan) c'est l'idéal ! ; **homeopathy is the** ~ **nowadays** l'homéopathie c'est la grande mode aujourd'hui ; **it's the in** ~* c'est le truc* à la mode ; **that's not the** ~ **to do** cela ne se fait pas ; **it's quite the** ~ **nowadays** ça se fait beaucoup aujourd'hui ; **I don't feel quite the** ~* **today** je ne suis pas dans mon assiette aujourd'hui ; **he looks quite the** ~* **in those trousers** il est très bien or chic avec ce pantalon ; **this is the latest** ~ **in computer games** c'est le dernier cri en matière de jeux électroniques

thingumabob* [ˈθɪŋəmɪbɒb], **thingumajig*** [ˈθɪŋɪmɪdʒɪg], **thingummy(jig)*** [ˈθɪŋəmɪ(dʒɪg)], **thingy*** [ˈθɪŋɪ] N (= object) machin* m, truc* m, bidule* m ; (= person) Machin(e)* m(f), trucmuche* mf

▼**think** [θɪŋk] (vb: pret, ptp **thought**) **1** N* **I'll have a** ~ **about it** j'y penserai ; **to have a good** ~ **about sth** bien réfléchir à qch ; **you'd better have another** ~ **about it** tu ferais bien d'y repenser ; **he's got another** ~ **coming!** il se fait des illusions !, il faudra qu'il y repense (subj) !

2 VI **a** (gen) réfléchir, penser ; ~ **carefully** réfléchissez bien ; ~ **twice before agreeing** réfléchissez-y à deux fois avant de donner votre accord ; ~ **again!** (= reflect on it) repensez-y ! ; (= have another guess) ce n'est pas ça, recommence! ; **let me** ~ que je réfléchisse*, laissez-moi réfléchir ; **to** ~ **ahead** prévoir, anticiper ; **to** ~ **aloud** penser tout haut ; **to** ~ **big** avoir de grandes idées, voir les choses en grand ; (iro) **I don't** ~**!*** ça m'étonnerait !

b (= have in one's thoughts) penser ; (= devote thought to) réfléchir (of, about à) ; **I was** ~**ing about** or **of you yesterday** je pensais à vous hier ; **I** ~ **of you always** je pense toujours à toi ; **what are you** ~**ing about?** à quoi pensez-vous ? ; **I'm** ~**ing of** or **about resigning** je pense à donner ma démission ; **he was** ~**ing of** or **about suicide** il pensait au suicide ; ~ **of a number** pense à un chiffre ; **you can't** ~ **of everything** on ne peut pas penser à tout ; **he's always** ~**ing of** or **about money** ◊ **he** ~**s of** or **about nothing but money** il ne pense qu'à l'argent ; **it's not worth** ~**ing about** ça ne vaut pas la peine d'y penser ; **(you)** ~ **about it!** ◊ ~ **on it!** († or liter) pensez-y !, songez-y ! ; **and to** ~ **of him going there alone!** quand on pense qu'il y est allé tout seul !, (et) dire qu'il y est allé tout seul ! ; **I'll** ~ **about it** j'y penserai, je vais y réfléchir ; **I'll have to** ~ **about it** il faudra que j'y réfléchisse or pense (subj) ; **that's worth** ~**ing about** cela mérite réflexion ; **you've given us so much to** ~ **about** vous nous avez tellement donné matière à réfléchir ; **come to** ~ **of it** ◊ **when you** ~ **about it** en y réfléchissant (bien) ; **I've got too many things to** ~ **of** or **about just now** j'ai trop de choses en tête en ce moment ; **what else is there to** ~ **about?** c'est ce qu'il y a de plus important or intéressant ; **there's so much to** ~ **about** il y a tant de choses à prendre en considération ; **what were you** ~**ing of** or **about!** où avais-tu la tête ? ; **I wouldn't** ~ **of such a thing!** ça ne me viendrait jamais à l'idée ! ; **would you** ~ **of letting him go alone?** vous le laisseriez partir seul, vous ? ; **sorry, I wasn't** ~**ing** pardon, je n'ai pas réfléchi ; **I didn't** ~ **to ask** or **of asking if you ...** je n'ai pas eu l'idée de demander si tu ...

c (= remember, take into account) penser (of à) ; **he** ~**s of nobody but himself** il ne pense qu'à lui ; **he's got his children to** ~ **of** or **about** il faut qu'il pense (subj) à ses enfants ; ~ **of**

the cost of it! rends-toi compte de la dépense!; **to ~ of** or **about sb's feelings** considérer les sentiments de qn; **that makes me ~ of the day when ...** cela me fait penser au or me rappelle le jour où ...; **I can't ~ of her name** je n'arrive pas à me rappeler son nom; **I couldn't ~ of the right word** le mot juste ne me venait pas

d (= *imagine*) **to ~ (of)** imaginer; **~ what might have happened** imagine ce qui aurait pu arriver; **just ~!** imagine un peu!; **(just) ~, we could go to Spain** rends-toi compte, nous pourrions aller en Espagne; **~ of me in a bikini!** imagine-moi en bikini®!; **~ of her as a teacher** considère-la comme un professeur

e (= *devise etc*) **to ~ of** who'll do it; **I was the one who thought of inviting him** c'est moi qui ai eu l'idée de l'inviter; **what will he ~ of next?** qu'est-ce qu'il va encore inventer?; **he has just thought of a clever solution** il vient de trouver une solution astucieuse; **~ of a number** pense à un chiffre

f (= *have as opinion*) penser (**of** de); **to ~ well** or **highly** or **a lot of sb/sth** penser le plus grand bien de qn/qch, avoir une haute opinion de qn/qch; **he is very well thought of in France** il est très respecté en France; **I don't ~ much of him** je n'ai pas une haute opinion de lui; **I don't ~ much of that idea** cette idée ne me dit pas grand-chose; **to ~ better of doing sth** décider à la réflexion de ne pas faire qch; **he thought (the) better of it** il a changé d'avis; **to ~ the best/the worst of sb** avoir une très haute/très mauvaise opinion de qn; **to ~ nothing of doing sth** (= *do as a matter of course*) trouver tout naturel de faire qch; (= *do unscrupulously*) n'avoir aucun scrupule à faire qch; **~ nothing of it!** mais je vous en prie!, mais pas du tout!; **you wouldn't ~ like that if you'd lived there** tu ne verrais pas les choses de cette façon si tu y avais vécu → **fit¹**

3 VT **a** (= *be of opinion, believe*) penser, croire; **I ~ so/not** je pense or crois que oui/non; **what do you ~?** qu'est-ce que tu (en) penses?; **I don't know what to ~** je ne sais (pas) qu'en penser; **I ~ it will rain** je pense or crois qu'il va pleuvoir; **I don't ~ he came** je ne pense or crois pas qu'il soit venu; **I don't ~ he will come** je ne pense pas qu'il vienne or qu'il viendra; **what do you ~ I should do?** que penses-tu or crois-tu que je doive faire?; **I thought so** or **as much!** je m'y attendais!, je m'en doutais!; **I hardly ~ it likely that ...** cela m'étonnerait beaucoup que ... (+ *subj*); **she's pretty, don't you ~?** elle est jolie, tu ne trouves pas?; **what do you ~ of him?** comment le trouves-tu?; **I can guess what you are ~ing** je devine ta pensée; **who do you ~ you are?** pour qui te prends-tu?; **I never thought he'd look like that** je n'aurais jamais cru qu'il ressemblerait à ça; **you must ~ me very rude** vous devez me trouver très impoli; **he ~s he is intelligent** ◊ **he ~s himself intelligent** il se croit or se trouve intelligent; **they are thought to be rich** ils passent pour être riches; **I didn't ~ to see you here** je ne m'attendais pas à vous voir ici → **3d**; **he ~s money the whole time*** il ne s'intéresse qu'à l'argent → **world**

b (= *conceive, imagine*) (s')imaginer; **~ what we could do with that house!** imagine ce que nous pourrions faire de cette maison!; **I can't ~ what he means!** je ne vois vraiment pas ce qu'il veut dire!; **you would ~ he'd have known that already** on aurait pu penser qu'il le savait déjà; **anyone would ~ he owns the place!** il se prend pour le maître des lieux celui-là!; **who would have thought it!** qui l'aurait dit!; **I'd have thought she'd be more upset** j'aurais pensé qu'elle aurait été plus contrariée; **to ~ that she's only ten!** et dire qu'elle n'a que dix ans!, quand on pense qu'elle n'a que dix ans!

c (= *reflect*) penser à; **just ~ what you're doing!** pense un peu à ce que tu fais!; **we must ~**

how we can do it il faut réfléchir à la façon dont nous allons pouvoir le faire; **I was ~ing (to myself) how ill he looked** je me disais qu'il avait l'air bien malade

d (= *remember*) **did you ~ to bring it?** tu n'as pas oublié de l'apporter?; **I didn't ~ to let him know** il ne m'est pas venu à l'idée or je n'ai pas eu l'idée de le mettre au courant

4 COMP ► **think-piece** N (*Press*) article *m* de fond ► **think tank*** N groupe *m* or cellule *f* de réflexion

► **think back** VI repenser (**to** à), essayer de se souvenir or se rappeler (**to** de); **he thought back, and replied ...** il a fait un effort de mémoire, et a répliqué ...

► **think out** VT SEP [+ *problem, proposition*] réfléchir sérieusement à, étudier; [+ *plan*] élaborer, préparer; [+ *answer, move*] réfléchir sérieusement à, préparer; **that needs ~ing out** il faut y réfléchir à fond; **well-thought-out** bien conçu

► **think over** VT SEP [+ *offer, suggestion*] (bien) réfléchir à, peser; **~ things over carefully first** pèse bien le pour et le contre auparavant; **I'll have to ~ it over** il va falloir que j'y réfléchisse

► **think through** VT SEP [+ *plan, proposal*] examiner en détail or par le menu, considérer dans tous ses détails

► **think up** VT SEP [+ *plan, scheme, improvement*] avoir l'idée de; [+ *answer, solution*] trouver; [+ *excuse*] inventer; **who thought up that idea?** qui a eu cette idée?; **what will he ~ up next?** qu'est-ce qu'il va encore bien pouvoir inventer?

thinkable ['θɪŋkəbl] ADJ **it's not ~ that ...** il n'est pas pensable or concevable or imaginable que ... (+ *subj*)

thinker ['θɪŋkə'] N penseur *m*, -euse *f*

thinking ['θɪŋkɪŋ] **1** ADJ [*being, creature, mind*] rationnel; [*machine*] pensant; **to any ~ person, this ...** pour toute personne douée de raison, ceci ...; **the ~ man** l'intellectuel *m*; **the ~ woman's sex symbol** le sex-symbol de l'intellectuelle; **the ~ man's crumpet*** la pin-up pour intellectuel; **the ~ woman's crumpet*** le mâle pour intellectuelle

2 N (= *act*) pensée *f*, réflexion *f*; (= *thoughts collectively*) opinions *fpl* (**on, about** sur); **I'll have to do some (hard) ~ about it** il va falloir que j'y réfléchisse sérieusement; **current ~ on this** les opinions actuelles là-dessus; **to my way of ~** à mon avis; **that may be his way of ~, but ...** c'est peut-être comme ça qu'il voit les choses, mais ... → **wishful**

3 COMP ► **thinking cap** N **to put on one's ~ cap*** cogiter* ► **thinking pattern** N modèle *m* de pensée ► **the thinking process** N le processus de pensée ► **thinking time** N **to give sb some ~ time** donner à qn un peu de temps pour réfléchir, laisser à qn un délai de réflexion

thinly ['θɪnlɪ] ADV **a** [*slice, cut*] en tranches fines or minces **b** [*spread, roll out*] en couche fine or mince; **toast ~ spread with butter** du pain grillé sur lequel on a étalé une fine or mince couche de beurre **c** **to be ~ populated** avoir une population éparse or clairsemée; **~ wooded** peu boisé; **~ scattered** épars; **the meeting was ~ attended** la réunion n'a pas attiré grand monde; **~ spread resources** des ressources disséminées; **a criticism ~ disguised as a compliment** une critique à peine déguisée en compliment; **a ~ veiled accusation** une accusation à peine voilée; **a ~ veiled attempt** une tentative mal dissimulée **d** **to sow seeds ~** faire un semis clair; **to smile ~** avoir un faible sourire

thinner ['θɪnə'] **1** N (*for paint etc*) diluant *m* **2** ADJ *compar of* **thin**

thinness ['θɪnɪs] N (*NonC*) **a** (= *leanness, lack of thickness*) [*of person, legs, arms, face, animal*] maigreur *f*; [*of waist, fingers, nose, layer, slice, strip, paper*] minceur *f*; [*of wall, book,*

clothes*] minceur *f*; [*of thread, wire*] finesse *f*; [*of cloth, garment*] finesse *f*, légèreté *f* **b (= *runniness*) [*of liquid, oil*] légèreté *f*, fluidité *f*; [*of soup, gravy, sauce, paint*] manque *m* d'épaisseur; [*of cream, honey, mud*] consistance *f* liquide **c** [*of smoke, fog, cloud*] légèreté *f*; **the ~ of the air** or **atmosphere** le manque d'oxygène **d** (= *sparseness*) [*of hair, beard, eyebrows, hedge*] aspect *m* clairsemé; **disappointed by the ~ of the crowd** déçu qu'il y ait si peu de monde **e** (= *feebleness*) [*of excuse, evidence, plot, plans, smile, majority*] faiblesse *f*; [*of script*] médiocrité *f* **f** [*of voice*] timbre *m* grêle or fluet; [*of sound*] timbre *m* aigu **g** (*Fin*) [*of profits, margins*] maigreur *f*

third [θɜːd] **1** ADJ troisième; **in the presence of a ~ person** en présence d'une tierce personne or d'un tiers; (*Gram*) **in the ~ person** à la troisième personne; **(it's/it was) ~ time lucky!** la troisième fois sera/a été la bonne!; **the ~ finger** le majeur, le médius; (*US*) **to be a ~ wheel** tenir la chandelle → **5**; *for other phrases see* **sixth**

2 N **a** troisième *mf*; (= *fraction*) tiers *m*; (*Mus*) tierce *f*; *for phrases see* **sixth** **b** (*Univ = degree*) ≈ licence *f* sans mention **c** (*Aut: also ~ gear*) troisième vitesse *f*; **in ~** en troisième

3 **thirds** NPL (*Comm*) articles *mpl* de troisième choix or de qualité inférieure

4 ADV **a** (*in race, exam, competition*) en troisième place or position; **he came** or **was placed ~** il s'est classé troisième **b** (*Rail*) **to travel ~** voyager en troisième **c** = **thirdly**

5 COMP ► **Third Age** N troisième âge *m* ► **third-class** ADJ → **third-class** ► **third degree** N **to give sb the ~ degree*** (= *torture*) passer qn à tabac*; (= *question closely*) cuisiner* qn ► **third-degree burns** NPL (*Med*) brûlures *fpl* du troisième degré ► **the third estate** N le tiers état ► **third party** N (*Jur*) tierce personne *f*, tiers *m*; **~ party (indemnity) insurance** (assurance *f*) responsabilité *f* civile ► **third party, fire and theft** N (*Insurance*) assurance *f* au tiers, vol et incendie ► **third-rate** ADJ de très médiocre qualité ► **Third World** N tiers-monde *m* ♦ ADJ [*poverty etc*] du tiers-monde

third-class ['θɜːd'klɑːs] **1** ADJ **a** (*lit*) de troisième classe; [*hotel*] de troisième catégorie, de troisième ordre; (*Rail*) [*ticket, compartment*] de troisième (classe); (*fig pej*) [*meal, goods*] de qualité très inférieure; (*Rail*) **~ seat** troisième *f*; (*Univ*) **~ degree** → **2** **2** N (*Univ: also ~ degree*) ≈ licence *f* sans mention **3** ADV **a** (*Rail*) **to travel ~** voyager en troisième **b** (*US Post*) tarif *m* « imprimés »

▼ **thirdly** ['θɜːdlɪ] ADV troisièmement, en troisième lieu

thirst [θɜːst] **1** N (*lit, fig*) soif *f* (**for** de); **I've got a real ~ on (me)*** j'ai la pépie* **2** VI (*lit, fig: liter*) avoir soif (**for** de); **~ing for revenge** assoiffé de vengeance; **~ing for blood** altéré or assoiffé de sang

thirstily ['θɜːstɪlɪ] ADV (*lit, fig*) avidement

thirsty ['θɜːstɪ] ADJ **a** [*person, animal, plant*] qui a soif, assoiffé (*liter*); [*land*] qui manque d'eau;* [*car*] qui consomme beaucoup, gourmand*; **to be** or **feel ~** avoir soif; **to make sb ~** donner soif à qn; **it's ~ work!** ça donne soif! **b** (*liter = eager*) **to be ~ for sth** avoir soif de qch, être assoiffé de qch; (*fig*) **to be ~ for sb's blood** vouloir la peau de qn

thirteen ['θɜː'tiːn] **1** N treize *m inv*; *for phrases see* **six** **3** PRON treize; **there are ~** il y en a treize

thirteenth ['θɜː'tiːnθ] **1** ADJ treizième **2** N treizième *mf*; (= *fraction*) treizième *m*; *for phrases see* **sixth**

thirtieth ['θɜ:tɪɪθ] [1] ADJ trentième [2] N trentième *mf*; (= *fraction*) trentième *m*; *for phrases see* **sixth**

thirty ['θɜ:tɪ] [1] ADJ trente *inv*; **about ~ books** une trentaine de livres [2] N trente *m inv*; **about ~** une trentaine; *for other phrases see* **sixty** [3] PRON trente; **there are ~** il y en a trente [4] COMP ► **thirty-second note** N (*US Mus*) triple croche *f* ► **Thirty-Share Index** N (*Brit*) indice des principales valeurs industrielles ► **the Thirty Years' War** N (*Hist*) la guerre de Trente Ans

this [ðɪs] [1] DEM ADJ (*pl* **these**) [a] ce, cet (*before vowel and mute « h »*), cette *f*, ces *pl*; **who is ~ man?** qui est cet homme?; **whose are these books?** à qui sont ces livres?; **these photos you asked for** les photos que vous avez réclamées; **~ week** cette semaine; **~ time last week** la semaine dernière à pareille heure; **~ time next year** l'année prochaine à la même époque; **~ coming week** la semaine prochaine ou qui vient; **it all happened ~ past half-hour** tout est arrivé dans la demi-heure qui vient de s'écouler; **I've been waiting ~ past half-hour** voilà une demi-heure que j'attends, j'attends depuis une demi-heure; **how's ~ hand of yours?** et votre main, comment va-t-elle?; **~ journalist (fellow) you were going out with*** ce journaliste, là, avec qui tu sortais*; **~ journalist came up to me in the street*** il y a un journaliste qui est venu vers moi dans la rue

[b] (*stressed, or as opposed to that, those*) ce ou cet ou cette ou ces ...-ci; **I mean THIS book** c'est de ce livre-ci que je parle; **I like ~ photo better than that one** je préfère cette photo-ci à celle-là; **~ chair (over) here** cette chaise-ci; **the leaf was blowing ~ way and that** la feuille tournoyait de-ci de-là; **she ran that way and ~** elle courait dans tous les sens

[2] DEM PRON (*pl* **these**) [a] ceci, ce; **what is ~?** qu'est-ce que c'est (que ceci)?; **whose is ~?** à qui appartient ceci?; **who's ~?** (*gen*) qui est-ce?; (*on phone*) qui est à l'appareil?; **~ is it** (*gen*) c'est cela; (*agreeing*) exactement, tout à fait; (*before action*) cette fois, ça y est; **~ is my son** (*in introduction*) je vous présente mon fils; (*in photo etc*) c'est mon fils; **~ is the boy I told you about** c'est ou voici le garçon dont je t'ai parlé; (*on phone*) **~ is Glenys Knowles** ici Glenys Knowles, Glenys Knowles à l'appareil; **~ is Tuesday** nous sommes mardi; **but ~ is May** mais nous sommes en mai; **~ is what he showed me** voici ce qu'il m'a montré; **~ is where we live** c'est ici que nous habitons; **I didn't want you to leave like ~!** je ne voulais pas que tu partes comme ça!; **it was like ~ ...** voici comment les choses se sont passées ...; **do it like ~** faites-le comme ceci; **after ~ things got better** après ceci les choses se sont arrangées; **before ~ I'd never noticed him** je ne l'avais jamais remarqué auparavant; **it ought to have been done before ~** cela devrait être déjà fait; **we were talking of ~ and that** nous bavardions de choses et d'autres; **at ~ she burst into tears** sur ce, elle éclata en sanglots; **with ~ he left us** sur ces mots il nous a quittés; **what's all ~ I hear about your new job?** qu'est-ce que j'apprends, vous avez un nouvel emploi?; **they'll be demanding ~, that and the next thing*** ils vont exiger toutes sortes de choses

[b] (*this one*) celui-ci *m*, celle-ci *f*, ceux-ci *mpl*, celles-ci *fpl*; **I prefer that to ~** je préfère celui-là à celui-ci (*ou* celle-là à celle-ci); **how much is ~?** combien coûte celui-ci (*ou* celle-ci)?; **these over here** ceux-ci (*ou* celles-ci); **not these!** pas ceux-ci (*ou* celles-ci)!

[3] ADV **it was ~ long** c'était aussi long que ça; **he had come ~ far** il était venu jusqu'ici; (*in discussions etc*) il avait fait tant de progrès → **much**

thistle ['θɪsl] N chardon *m*

thistledown ['θɪsldaʊn] N duvet *m* de chardon

thistly ['θɪslɪ] ADJ [*ground*] couvert de chardons

thither†† ['ðɪðəʳ] ADV y (*before vb*), là → **hither**

thitherto [ðɪðə'tuː] ADV jusqu'alors

tho(') [ðəʊ] ABBR = **though**

thole¹ [θəʊl] N (*Naut*) tolet *m*

thole²†† [θəʊl] VT (*dial*) supporter

Thomas ['tɒməs] N Thomas *m* → **doubt**

thong [θɒŋ] N [*of whip*] lanière *f*, longe *f*; (*on garment*) lanière *f*, courroie *f*

Thor [θɔːʳ] N (*Myth*) T(h)or *m*

thoraces ['θɔːrə,siːz] NPL of **thorax**

thoracic [θɔː'ræsɪk] ADJ [*muscle, vertebrae, area*] thoracique; **~ spine** vertèbres *fpl* dorsales; **~ surgeon** spécialiste *mf* de chirurgie thoracique

thorax ['θɔːræks] N (*pl* **thoraxes** *or* **thoraces**) thorax *m*

thorium ['θɔːrɪəm] N thorium *m*

thorn [θɔːn] [1] N (= *spike*) épine *f*; (*NonC: also* **hawthorn**) aubépine *f*; (*fig*) **to be a ~ in sb's side** *or* **flesh** être une source d'irritation constante pour qn; **that was the ~ in his flesh** c'était sa bête noire *ou* **rose**² [2] COMP ► **thorn apple** N stramoine *f*, pomme *f* épineuse ► **thorn bush** N buisson *m* épineux

thornback ['θɔːnbæk] N (= *fish: also* **~ ray**) raie *f* bouclée

thornless ['θɔːnlɪs] ADJ sans épines, inerme (*Bot*)

thorny ['θɔːnɪ] ADJ (*lit, fig*) épineux

thorough ['θʌrə] ADJ [a] (= *careful*) [*person, worker*] qui fait les choses à fond; [*work, investigation, preparation, analysis, training*] approfondi; [*review*] complet (-ète *f*); [*consideration*] ample; **a ~ grounding in English** des bases solides en anglais; **to do a ~ job** faire un travail à fond; **to give sth a ~ cleaning/wash** *etc* nettoyer/laver *etc* qch à fond; **to be ~ in doing sth** faire qch à fond [b] (= *deep*) [*knowledge*] approfondi; [*understanding*] profond [c] (= *complete*) **to make a ~ nuisance of o.s.** être totalement insupportable; **to give sb a ~ walloping** donner une bonne raclée à qn; **it's a ~ disgrace** c'est vraiment une honte

thoroughbred ['θʌrəbred] [1] ADJ [*horse*] pur-sang *inv*; [*other animal*] de race [2] N (= *horse*) (cheval *m*) pur-sang *m inv*; (= *other animal*) bête *f* de race; (*fig* = *person*) **he's a real ~** il est vraiment racé, il a vraiment de la classe

thoroughfare ['θʌrəfɛəʳ] N (= *street*) rue *f*; (= *public highway*) voie *f* publique; **"no ~"** « passage interdit »

thoroughgoing ['θʌrə,gəʊɪŋ] ADJ [*examination, revision*] complet (-ète *f*); [*believer*] convaincu; [*hooligan*] vrai (*before n*); [*rogue, scoundrel*] fieffé

thoroughly ['θʌrəlɪ] ADV [a] (= *carefully*) [*examine, wash, mix*] à fond; **~ clean** tout propre, tout à fait propre; **to research sth ~** faire des recherches approfondies sur qch; **to investigate sb/sth ~** faire une enquête approfondie sur qn/qch [b] (= *completely*) [*modern, enjoyable, convinced*] tout à fait, on ne peut plus; [*miserable, unpleasant*] absolument; [*discredited*] complètement; [*deserve, understand*] tout à fait; **he's a ~ nasty piece of work** il est tout ce qu'il y a de plus odieux; **it was ~ boring** c'était on ne peut plus ennuyeux; **I ~ agree** je suis tout à fait d'accord; **I ~ enjoyed myself** j'ai passé d'excellents moments; **we ~ enjoyed our meal** nous avons fait un excellent repas

thoroughness ['θʌrənɪs] N (*NonC*) [*of worker*] minutie *f*; [*of knowledge*] profondeur *f*; **the ~ of his work/research** la minutie qu'il apporte à son travail/sa recherche

those [ðəʊz] DEM ADJ, DEM PRON *pl* of **that**

thou¹† [ðaʊ] PERS PRON (*liter*) tu; (*stressed*) toi

thou²* [θaʊ] N (*pl* **thou** *or* **thous**) ABBR = **thousand, thousandth**

▼ **though** [ðəʊ] [1] CONJ [a] (= *despite the fact that*) bien que (+ *subj*), quoique (+ *subj*); **~ it's raining** bien qu'il pleuve, malgré la pluie; **~ poor they were honest** ils étaient honnêtes bien que *ou* quoique *ou* encore que pauvres [b] (= *even if*) (**even**) **~ I shan't be there I'll think of you** je ne serai pas là mais je n'en penserai pas moins à toi; **strange ~ it may seem** si *ou* pour étrange que cela puisse paraître; (*frm*) **I will do it ~ I (should) die in the attempt** je le ferai, dussé-je y laisser la vie; (*liter*) **what ~ they are poor** malgré *ou* nonobstant (*liter*) leur misère [c] **as ~** comme si; **it looks as ~ ...** il semble que ... (+ *subj*) → **as** [2] ADV pourtant, cependant; **it's not easy ~** ce n'est pourtant pas facile, pourtant ce n'est pas facile; **did he ~!*** ah bon!, tiens tiens!

▼ **thought** [θɔːt] [1] VB *pt, ptp* of **think**

[2] N [a] (*NonC*) (*gen*) pensée *f*; (= *reflection*) pensée *f*, réflexion *f*; (= *daydreaming*) rêverie *f*; (= *thoughtfulness*) considération *f*; **to be lost** *or* **deep in ~** être perdu dans ses pensées; **after much ~** après mûre réflexion; **he acted without ~** il a agi sans réfléchir; **without ~ for** *or* **of himself he ...** sans considérer son propre intérêt il ...; **he was full of ~ for my welfare** il se préoccupait beaucoup de mon bien-être; **you must take ~ for the future** il faut penser à l'avenir; **he took** *or* **had no ~ for his own safety** il n'avait aucun égard pour sa propre sécurité; **to give ~ to sth** bien réfléchir à qch, mûrement réfléchir sur qch; **I didn't give it a moment's ~** je n'y ai pa pensé une seule seconde; **I gave it no more ~** ◊ **I didn't give it another ~** je n'y ai plus pensé; **don't give it another ~** n'y pensez plus; **further ~ needs to be given to these problems** ceci nécessite une réflexion plus approfondie sur les problèmes [b] (= *idea*) pensée *f*, idée *f*; (= *opinion*) opinion *f*, avis *m*; (= *intention*) intention *f*, idée *f*; **it's a happy ~** voilà une idée qui fait plaisir; **to think evil ~s** avoir de mauvaises pensées; **what a ~!*** imagine un peu!; **what a horrifying ~!*** quel cauchemar!; **what a frightening ~!*** c'est effrayant!; **what a lovely ~!*** (= *good idea*) comme ça serait bien!; (= *how thoughtful*) comme c'est gentil!; **what a brilliant ~!*** c'est une idée géniale!; **that's a ~!*** tiens, mais c'est une idée!; **it's only a ~** ce n'est qu'une idée; **the mere ~ of it frightens me** rien que d'y penser *or* rien qu'à y penser j'ai peur; **he hasn't a ~ in his head** il n'a rien dans la tête; **my ~s were elsewhere** j'avais l'esprit ailleurs; **he keeps his ~s to himself** il garde ses pensées pour lui, il ne laisse rien deviner *ou* paraître de ses pensées; **the Thoughts of Chairman Mao** les pensées du président Mao; **contemporary/scientific ~ on the subject** les opinions des contemporains/des scientifiques sur la question; **the ~ of Nietzsche** la pensée de Nietzsche; **I had ~s** *or* **some ~ of going to Paris** j'avais vaguement l'idée *or* l'intention d'aller à Paris; **he gave up all ~(s) of marrying her** il a renoncé à toute idée de l'épouser; **his one ~ is to win the prize** sa seule pensée *or* idée est de remporter le prix; **it's the ~ that counts** c'est l'intention qui compte; **to read sb's ~s** lire (dans) la pensée de qn → **collect**², **penny**, **second**¹ [c] (*adv phrase*) **a ~** un peu, un tout petit peu; **it is a ~ too large** c'est un (tout petit) peu trop grand

[3] COMP ► **thought police** N police *f* de la pensée ► **thought process** N mécanisme *m* de pensée ► **thought-provoking** ADJ qui pousse à la réflexion, stimulant ► **thought-read** VI lire (dans) la pensée de qn ► **thought-reader** N liseur *m*, -euse *f* de pensées; (*fig*) **he's a ~-reader** il lit dans la pensée des gens; **I'm not a ~-reader** je ne suis pas devin ► **thought reading** N divination *f*

par télépathie ► **thought transference** N transmission f de pensée

thoughtful [ˈθɔːtfʊl] ADJ a (= reflective) [person] (by nature) sérieux, réfléchi; (on one occasion) pensif; [mood, face, eyes] pensif; [expression, look] pensif, méditatif; [remark, research] sérieux, réfléchi; [book, article, approach] sérieux; [design] judicieux b (= considerate) [person] prévenant, attentionné; [act, gesture, remark] plein de délicatesse; [invitation, gift] gentil; **how ~ of you!** comme c'est gentil à vous or de votre part!; **it was ~ of him to invite me** c'était gentil à lui or de sa part de m'inviter; **to be ~ of others** être plein d'égards pour autrui

thoughtfully [ˈθɔːtfʊlɪ] ADV a (= reflectively) [say, look at, nod] pensivement b (= considerately) **he ~ booked tickets for us as well** il a eu la prévenance de louer des places pour nous aussi c (= intelligently) [designed, constructed, positioned] judicieusement

thoughtfulness [ˈθɔːtfʊlnɪs] N (NonC) a (= reflectiveness) [of person] (by nature) sérieux m; (on one occasion) air m pensif; [of book, article] sérieux m b (= considerateness) prévenance f

thoughtless [ˈθɔːtlɪs] ADJ a (= inconsiderate) [person] qui manque d'égards or de considération; [act, behaviour, remark] maladroit; **how ~ of you!** tu manques vraiment d'égards or de considération!; **it was ~ of him to tell him)** ce n'était pas très délicat or c'était maladroit de sa part (de le lui dire) b (= unthinking) **to be ~ of the future** ne pas penser à l'avenir

thoughtlessly [ˈθɔːtlɪslɪ] ADV a (= inconsiderately) [act, forget] inconsidérément b (= unthinkingly) [speak] maladroitement, de façon irréfléchie; [embark upon] sans réfléchir

thoughtlessness [ˈθɔːtlɪsnɪs] N (NonC) (= carelessness) étourderie f, légèreté f; (= lack of consideration) manque m de prévenance or d'égards

thousand [ˈθaʊzənd] 1 ADJ mille inv; **a ~ men** mille hommes; **about a ~ men** un millier d'hommes; **a ~ years** mille ans, un millénaire; **a ~ thanks!** mille fois merci!; **two pounds** deux mille livres; (fig) **I've got a ~ and one things to do** j'ai mille et une choses à faire 2 N mille m inv; **a ~ ◊ one** mille; **a or one ~ and one** mille (et) un; **a ~ and two** mille deux; **five ~** cinq mille; **about a ~ (people)** a ~ (people) un millier (de personnes); (Comm) **sold by the ~** vendu par mille; **~s of people** des milliers de gens; **they came in their ~s** ils sont venus par milliers 3 COMP ► **Thousand Island dressing** N sauce salade à base de mayonnaise, de ketchup, de cornichons hachés etc

thousandfold [ˈθaʊzəndfəʊld] 1 ADJ multiplié par mille 2 ADV mille fois autant

thousandth [ˈθaʊzəntθ] 1 ADJ millième 2 N millième mf; (= fraction) millième m

Thrace [θreɪs] N la Thrace

thraldom [ˈθrɔːldəm] N (NonC: liter) servitude f, esclavage m

thrall [θrɔːl] N (liter: lit, fig) (= person) esclave mf; (= state) servitude f, esclavage m; (fig) **to be in ~ to ...** être esclave de ...

thrash [θræʃ] 1 VT a (= beat) rouer de coups, rosser; (as punishment) donner une bonne correction à; (*: Sport etc) battre à plate(s) couture(s), donner une bonne correction à; **they nearly ~ed the life out of him ◊ they ~ed him to within an inch of his life** ils ont failli le tuer à force de coups; (= move wildly) **the bird ~ed its wings (about)** l'oiseau battait or fouettait l'air de ses ailes; **he ~ed his arms/legs (about)** il battait des bras/des jambes c (Agr) = **thresh** 2 VI battre violemment (**against** contre) 3 N a (Brit*: = party) sauterie* f b (Mus: also ~ **metal**) thrash m

► **thrash about, thrash around** 1 VI (= struggle) se débattre; **he ~ed about with his**

stick il battait l'air de sa canne 2 VT SEP [+ one's legs, arms] battre de; [+ stick] agiter → **thrash 1b**

► **thrash out*** VT SEP [+ problem, difficulty] (= discuss) débattre de; (= solve) résoudre; **they managed to ~ it out** ils ont réussi à résoudre le problème

thrashing [ˈθræʃɪŋ] N correction f, rossée* f; (*: Sport also) correction f (fig), dérouillée: f; **to give sb a good ~** rouer qn de coups; (as punishment, also Sport) donner une bonne correction à qn

thread [θred] 1 N a (gen, also Sewing etc) fil m; **nylon ~** fil m de nylon®; (fig) **to hang by a ~** ne tenir qu'à un fil; **the ceasefire is hanging by a ~** le cessez-le-feu ne tient qu'à un fil; **to lose the ~ (of what one is saying)** perdre le fil de son discours; (fig) **to pick up** or **take up the ~ again** retrouver le fil; **to pick up the ~s of one's career** reprendre le cours de sa carrière; **a ~ of light** un (mince) rayon de lumière b [of screw] pas m, filetage m; **screw with left-hand ~** vis f filetée à gauche 2 **threads** NPL (US = clothes) fringues: fpl 3 VT [+ needle, beads] enfiler; **to ~ sth through a needle/over a hook/into a hole** faire passer qch à travers le chas d'une aiguille/par un crochet/par un trou; **to ~ a film on to a projector** monter un film sur un projecteur; **he ~ed his way through the crowd** il s'est faufilé à travers la foule; **the car ~ed its way through the narrow streets** la voiture s'est faufilée dans les petites rues étroites 4 VI a = **to thread one's way**; → 3 b [needle, beads] s'enfiler; [tape, film] passer

threadbare [ˈθredbɛəʳ] ADJ [rug, clothes] râpé, élimé; [room] défraîchi; (fig) [joke, argument, excuse] usé, rebattu

threadlike [ˈθredlaɪk] ADJ filiforme

threadworm [ˈθredwɜːm] N (Med) oxyure m

threat [θret] N (lit, fig) menace f; **to make a ~ against sb** proférer une menace à l'égard de qn; **under (the) ~ of ...** menacé de ...; **it is a grave ~ to civilization** cela constitue une sérieuse menace pour la civilisation, cela menace sérieusement la civilisation

threaten [ˈθretn] 1 VT menacer (**sb with sth** qn de qch, **to do** de faire); **to ~ violence** proférer des menaces de violence; **a species ~ed with extinction ◊ a ~ed species** une espèce en voie de disparition; (fig) **it is ~ing to rain** la pluie menace 2 VI [storm, war, danger] menacer

threatening [ˈθretnɪŋ] 1 ADJ [person, voice, manner, place, weather, clouds, sky] menaçant; [gesture, tone, words] menaçant, de menace; [phone call, letter] de menace; **to find sb ~** se sentir menacé par qn 2 COMP ► **threatening behaviour** N (Jur) tentative f d'intimidation

threateningly [ˈθretnɪŋlɪ] ADV [say] d'un ton menaçant or de menace; [gesticulate] d'une manière menaçante; **~ close** dangereusement près

three [θriː] 1 ADJ trois inv 2 N trois m inv; (Pol) **the Big Three** les trois Grands mpl; (Sport) **let's play (the) best of ~** jouons au meilleur des trois manches; **they were playing (the) best of ~** ils jouaient deux parties et la belle → **two**; for other phrases see **six** 3 PRON trois; **there are ~** il y en a trois 4 COMP ► **3-D** N = **three-D** ► **three-act play** N pièce f en trois actes ► **three-card monte** N (US) = **three-card trick** ► **three-card trick** N bonneteau m ► **three-cornered** ADJ triangulaire ► **three-cornered hat** N tricorne m ► **three-D** N (ABBR = **three dimensions, three-dimensional**) (in) **~-D** [picture] en relief; [film] en trois dimensions ► **three-day event** N (Horse-riding) concours m complet ► **three-day**

eventer N (Horse-riding) cavalier m, -ière f de concours complet ► **three-day eventing** N (Horse-riding) concours m complet ► **three-dimensional** ADJ [object] à trois dimensions, tridimensionnel; [picture] en relief; [film] en trois dimensions ► **three-fourths** (US) = **three-quarters** ► **three-four time** N (Mus) mesure f à trois temps ► **three-legged** ADJ [table] à trois pieds; [animal] à trois pattes ► **three-legged race** N (Sport) course où les concurrents sont attachés deux par deux par la jambe ► **three-line** ADJ → **whip** ► **three-martini lunch*** N (US fig = expense-account lunch) déjeuner m d'affaires (qui passe dans les notes de frais) ► **three-phase** ADJ (Elec) triphasé ► **three-piece suit** N (costume m) trois-pièces m ► **three-piece suite** N salon composé d'un canapé et de deux fauteuils ► **three-pin plug** N → **pin 1b** ► **three-ply** ADJ [wool] à trois fils ► **three-point landing** N (Aviat) atterrissage m trois points ► **three-point turn** N (Aut) demi-tour m en trois manœuvres ► **three-quarter** ADJ [portrait] de trois-quarts; [sleeve] trois-quarts inv ♦ N (Rugby) trois-quarts m inv ► **three-quarters** N trois quarts mpl ♦ ADV **the money is ~-quarters gone** les trois quarts de l'argent ont été dépensés; **~-quarters full/empty** aux trois quarts plein/vide ► **three-ring circus** N (lit) cirque m à trois pistes; (US* fig) véritable cirque* m ► **the three Rs** N la lecture, l'écriture et l'arithmétique ► **three-sided** ADJ [object] à trois côtés, à trois faces; [discussion] à trois ► **three-way** ADJ [split, division] en trois; [discussion] à trois ► **three-wheeler** N (= car) voiture f à trois roues (= tricycle) tricycle m

┌─────────────┐
│ **THREE Rs** │
└─────────────┘

Les **three Rs** (les trois « R ») sont la lecture, l'écriture et l'arithmétique, considérées comme les trois composantes essentielles de l'enseignement. L'expression vient de l'orthographe fantaisiste « reading, riting and rithmetic » pour « reading, writing and arithmetic ».

threefold [ˈθriːfəʊld] 1 ADJ triple 2 ADV **to increase ~** tripler

threepence [ˈθrepəns] N (Brit) trois anciens pence mpl

threepenny [ˈθrepənɪ] (Brit) 1 ADJ à trois pence; (Mus) **the Threepenny Opera** l'Opéra m de quat'sous 2 N (also ~ **bit** or **piece**) ancienne pièce f de trois pence

threescore [ˌθriːˈskɔːʳ] 1 ADJ, N († or liter) soixante m 2 COMP ► **threescore and ten** ADJ, N († or liter) soixante-dix m

threesome [ˈθriːsəm] N (= people) groupe m de trois, trio m; (= game) partie f à trois; **we went in a ~** nous y sommes allés à trois

threnody [ˈθrenədɪ] N (lit) mélopée f; (fig) lamentations fpl

thresh [θreʃ] VT (Agr) battre

thresher [ˈθreʃəʳ] N (= person) batteur m, -euse f (en grange); (= machine) batteuse f

threshing [ˈθreʃɪŋ] N (Agr) 1 N battage m 2 COMP ► **threshing machine** N batteuse f

threshold [ˈθreʃhəʊld] 1 N seuil m, pas m de la porte; **to cross the ~** franchir le seuil; (fig) **on the ~ of ...** au bord or au seuil de ...; (Psych) **above the ~ of consciousness** supraliminaire; **below the ~ of consciousness** subliminaire; **to have a high/low pain ~** avoir un seuil de tolérance à la douleur élevé/peu élevé 2 COMP ► **threshold agreement** N accord m d'indexation des salaires sur les prix ► **threshold policy** N = **threshold wage policy** ► **threshold price** N prix m de seuil ► **threshold wage policy** N politique f d'indexation des salaires sur les prix

threw [θruː] VB pt of **throw**

thrice [θraɪs] ADV trois fois

thrift [θrɪft] [1] N (NonC) économie f [2] COMP ► **thrift shop** N (US) petite boutique d'articles d'occasion gérée au profit d'œuvres charitables

thriftiness [ˈθrɪftɪnɪs] N = thrift

thriftless [ˈθrɪftlɪs] ADJ imprévoyant, dépensier

thriftlessness [ˈθrɪftlɪsnɪs] N (NonC) imprévoyance f

thrifty [ˈθrɪftɪ] ADJ économe

▼ **thrill** [θrɪl] [1] N frisson m; **a ~ of joy** un frisson de joie; **with a ~ of joy he ...** en frissonnant or avec un frisson de joie, il ...; **what a ~!** quelle émotion!; **she felt a ~ as his hand touched hers** un frisson l'a parcourue quand il lui a touché la main; **it gave me a big ~** ça m'a vraiment fait quelque chose!*; **to get a ~ out of doing sth** se procurer des sensations fortes en faisant qch; **the film was packed with** or **full of ~s** c'était un film à sensations; **the ~ of the chase** l'excitation f de la poursuite [2] VT [+ person, audience, crowd] électriser, transporter; **his glance ~ed her** son regard l'a enivrée; **I was ~ed (to bits)!*** j'étais aux anges!*; **I was ~ed to meet him** ça m'a vraiment fait plaisir or fait quelque chose* de le rencontrer [3] VI tressaillir or frissonner (de joie)

thriller [ˈθrɪlə*] N (= novel) roman m à suspense; (= play) pièce f à suspense; (= film) film m à suspense

thrilling [ˈθrɪlɪŋ] ADJ [match, climax, experience] palpitant; [news] saisissant

thrive [θraɪv] (pret throve or thrived, ptp thrived or thriven [ˈθrɪvn]) VI [a] [baby] se développer bien; [person, animal] être florissant de santé; [plant] pousser or venir bien; [business, industry] prospérer; [businessman] prospérer, réussir; **children ~ on milk** le lait est excellent pour les enfants [b] (fig = enjoy) **he ~s on hard work** le travail lui réussit

thriving [ˈθraɪvɪŋ] ADJ [person, animal] en plein épanouissement; [plant] qui prospère (or prospérait); [business, industry, economy, community, businessman] prospère, florissant

throat [θrəʊt] N (external) gorge f; (internal) gorge f, gosier m; **to take sb by the ~** prendre qn à la gorge; **I have a sore ~** j'ai mal à la gorge, j'ai une angine; **he had a fishbone stuck in his ~** il avait une arête de poisson dans le gosier; (fig) **that sticks in my ~** je n'arrive pas à accepter or avaler* ça; (fig) **to thrust** or **ram** or **force** or **shove* sth down sb's ~** imposer qch à qn; **they are always at each other's ~(s)** ils sont toujours à se battre → **clear, cut, frog¹, jump**

throaty [ˈθrəʊtɪ] ADJ [a] (= husky) [voice, laugh] rauque [b] (Med) [cough] guttural; (Brit) **I'm feeling a bit ~*** j'ai mal à la gorge

throb [θrɒb] [1] N [of heart] pulsation f, battement m; [of engine] vibration f; [of drums, music] rythme m (fort); [of pain] élancement m; **a ~ of emotion** un frisson d'émotion [2] VI [heart] palpiter; [voice, engine] vibrer; [drums] battre (en rythme); [pain] lanciner; **a town ~bing with life** une ville vibrante d'animation; **the wound ~bed** la blessure me (or lui etc) causait des élancements; **my head/arm is ~bing** j'ai des élancements dans la tête/dans le bras; **we could hear the music ~bing in the distance** nous entendions au loin le rythme marqué or les flonflons mpl de la musique

throes [θrəʊz] NPL **in the ~ of death** dans les affres de la mort, à l'agonie; **in the ~ of war/disease/a crisis** etc en proie à la guerre/la maladie/une crise etc; **in the ~ of an argument/quarrel/debate** au cœur d'une discussion/d'une dispute/d'un débat; **while he was in the ~ of (writing) his book** pendant qu'il était aux prises avec la rédaction de son livre; **while we were in the ~ of deciding what to do** pendant que nous débattions de ce qu'il fallait faire

thrombocyte [ˈθrɒmbəsaɪt] N thrombocyte m

thrombosis [θrɒmˈbəʊsɪs] N (pl thromboses [θrɒmˈbəʊsiːz]) thrombose f

throne [θrəʊn] [1] N (all senses) trône m; **to come to the ~** monter sur le trône; **on the ~** sur le trône → **power** [2] COMP ► **throne room** N salle f du trône

throng [θrɒŋ] [1] N foule f, multitude f [2] VI affluer, se presser (**towards** vers, **round** autour de, **to see** pour voir) [3] VT **people ~ed the streets** la foule se pressait dans les rues; **to be ~ed (with people)** [streets, town, shops] être grouillant de monde; [room, bus, train] être bondé or comble

thronging [ˈθrɒŋɪŋ] ADJ [crowd, masses] grouillant, pullulant

throttle [ˈθrɒtl] [1] N (Aut, Tech: also ~ valve) papillon m des gaz; (Aut = accelerator) accélérateur m; **to give an engine full ~** accélérer à fond; **at full ~** à pleins gaz; **to open the ~** accélérer, mettre les gaz; **to close the ~** réduire l'arrivée des gaz [2] VT [+ person] étrangler, serrer la gorge de; (fig) étrangler (fig)

► **throttle back, throttle down** [1] VI mettre le moteur au ralenti [2] VT SEP [+ engine] mettre au ralenti

through [θruː]

When **through** is an element in a phrasal verb, eg **break through, fall through, sleep through,** look up the verb.
---

[1] ADV [a] (place, time, process) **the nail went (right) ~** le clou est passé à travers; **just go ~** passez donc; **to let sb ~** laisser passer qn; **you can get a train right ~ to London** on peut attraper un train direct pour Londres; **did you stay all** or **right ~?** es-tu resté jusqu'à la fin?; **we're staying ~ till Tuesday** nous restons jusqu'à mardi; **he slept all night ~** il ne s'est pas réveillé de la nuit; **I know it ~ and ~** je le connais par cœur; **read it (right) ~ to the end** ◊ **read it right** ~ lis-le en entier or jusqu'au bout → **read through**; → **soak through, wet**

[b] **~ and ~: he's a liar ~ and ~** il ment comme il respire; **he's a Scot ~ and ~** il est écossais jusqu'au bout des ongles

[c] (Brit Telec) **to put sb ~ to sb** passer qn à qn; **I'll put you ~ to her** je vous la passe; **you're ~ now** vous avez votre correspondant; **you're ~ to him** il est en ligne

[d] (* = finished) **I'm ~** ça y est (j'ai fini)*; **are you ~?** ça y est (tu as fini)?*; **I'm not ~ with you yet** je n'en ai pas encore fini or terminé avec vous; **are you ~ with that book?** ce livre, c'est fini?, tu n'as plus besoin de ce livre?; **I'm ~ with football!** le football, (c'est) fini!*; **he told me he was ~ with drugs** il m'a dit que la drogue, pour lui, c'était fini; **I'm ~ with you!** (gen) j'en ai marre* de toi!; (in relationship) c'est fini entre nous!; **he told me we were ~** (in relationship) il m'a dit qu'on allait casser* or que c'était fini entre nous

[2] PREP [a] (place, object) à travers; **a stream flows ~ the garden** un ruisseau traverse le jardin or coule à travers le jardin; **the stream flows ~ it** le ruisseau le traverse or coule à travers; **water poured ~ the roof** le toit laissait passer des torrents d'eau; **to go ~ a forest** traverser une forêt; **to get ~ a hedge** passer au travers d'une haie; **they went ~ the train, looking for ...** ils ont fait tout le train, pour trouver ...; **he went ~ the red light** il a grillé le feu rouge; **to hammer a nail ~ a plank** enfoncer un clou à travers une planche; **he was shot ~ the head** on lui a tiré une balle dans la tête; **to look ~ a window/telescope** regarder par une fenêtre/dans un télescope; (of hole, window etc) **go and look ~ it** va voir ce qu'il y a de l'autre côté; **I can hear them ~ the wall** je les entends de l'autre côté du mur; **he has really been ~ it*** il en a vu de dures*; **I'm half-way ~ the book** j'en suis à la moitié du livre; **to speak ~ one's nose** parler du nez

→ **get through, go through, see through**
[b] (time) pendant, durant; **all** or **right ~ his life** ◊ **all his life ~** pendant toute sa vie, sa vie durant; **he won't live ~ the night** il ne passera pas la nuit; (US) **(from) Monday ~ Friday** de lundi (jusqu')à vendredi; **he stayed ~ July** il est resté pendant tout le mois de juillet or jusqu'à la fin de juillet; **he lives there ~ the week** il habite là pendant la semaine
[c] (indicating means, agency) par, par l'entremise or l'intermédiaire de, grâce à, à cause de; **to send ~ the post** envoyer par la poste; **it was ~ him that I got the job** c'est grâce à lui or par son entremise que j'ai eu le poste; **it was all ~ him that I lost the job** c'est à cause de lui que j'ai perdu le poste; **I heard it ~ my sister** je l'ai appris par ma sœur; **~ his own efforts** par ses propres efforts; **it happened ~ no fault of mine** ce n'est absolument pas de ma faute si c'est arrivé; **absent ~ illness** absent pour cause de maladie; **to act ~ fear** agir par peur or sous le coup de la peur; **he was exhausted ~ having walked all the way** il était épuisé d'avoir fait tout le chemin à pied; **~ not knowing the way he ...** parce qu'il ne connaissait pas le chemin il ...

[3] ADJ [carriage, train, ticket] direct; **~ portion** [of train] rame f directe

[4] COMP ► **through street** N (US) rue f prioritaire ► **through traffic** N (on road sign) **"~ traffic"** ≈ « toutes directions »; **all ~ traffic has been diverted** toute la circulation a été détournée ► **through way** N **"no ~ way"** « impasse »

throughout [θruːˈaʊt] [1] PREP [a] (place) partout dans; **~ the world** partout dans le monde, dans le monde entier; **at schools ~ France** dans les écoles de toute la France [b] (time) pendant, durant; **~ his life** durant toute sa vie, sa vie durant; **~ his career/his story** tout au long de sa carrière/son récit [2] ADV (= everywhere) partout; (= the whole time) tout le temps

throughput [ˈθruːpʊt] N (Comput) débit m; (Ind) capacité f de production

throughway [ˈθruːweɪ] N (US) voie f rapide or express

throve [θrəʊv] VB pt of **thrive**

throw [θrəʊ] (vb: pret **threw,** ptp **thrown**) [1] N [of javelin, discus] jet m; (Wrestling) mise f à terre; (Ftbl: also ~-in) remise f en jeu; **give him a ~** laisse-lui la balle etc; (Sport) **it was a good ~** c'était un bon jet; **with one ~ of the ball he ...** avec un seul coup il ...; (in table games) **you lose a ~** vous perdez un tour; (at fair etc) **50p a ~** 50 pence la partie; (fig) **it costs 10 dollars a ~*** ça coûte 10 dollars à chaque fois → **stone**

[2] VT [a] (= cast) [+ object, stone] lancer, jeter (**to, at** à); [+ ball, javelin, discus, hammer] lancer; [+ dice] jeter; **he threw a towel at her** il lui a jeté or envoyé une serviette à la tête; **they were ~ing stones at the cat** ils jetaient or lançaient des pierres au chat; **he threw the ball 50 metres** il a lancé la balle à 50 mètres; **he threw it across the room** il l'a jeté or lancé à l'autre bout de la pièce; (at dice) **to ~ a six** avoir un six; (fig) **to ~ the book at sb*** (in accusing, reprimanding) accabler qn de reproches; (in punishing, sentencing) donner or coller* le maximum à qn; (fig) **to ~ one's hat** or **cap into the ring** se porter candidat, entrer en lice

[b] (= hurl violently) [explosion, car crash etc] projeter; (in fight, wrestling) envoyer au sol (or au tapis); [+ horse rider] démonter, désarçonner; **the force of the explosion threw him into the air/across the room** la force de l'explosion l'a projeté en l'air/à l'autre bout de la pièce; **he was ~n clear of the car** il a été projeté hors de la voiture; **to ~ o.s. to the ground/at sb's feet/into sb's arms** se jeter à terre/aux pieds de qn/dans les bras de qn; **to**

~ **o.s. on sb's mercy** s'en remettre à la merci de qn; (fig) **she really threw herself at him*** elle s'est vraiment jetée à sa tête or dans ses bras; (fig) **he threw himself into the job** il s'est mis or attelé à la tâche avec enthousiasme; **he threw himself into the task of clearing up** il y est allé de tout son courage pour mettre de l'ordre

[c] (= direct) [+ light, shadow, glance] jeter; [+ slides, pictures] projeter; [+ kiss] envoyer (**to à**); [+ punch] lancer (**at à**); **to ~ one's voice** jouer les ventriloques → **light¹**

[d] (= put suddenly, hurriedly) jeter (**into** dans, **over** sur); **to ~ sb into jail** jeter qn en prison; **to ~ a bridge over a river** jeter un pont sur une rivière; **to ~ a question at sb** poser une question à qn à brûle-pourpoint; **to ~ into confusion** [+ person] semer la confusion dans l'esprit de; [+ meeting, group] semer la confusion dans; **it ~s the emphasis on ...** cela met l'accent sur ...; **it threw the police off the trail** cela a dépisté la police; **to ~ open** [+ door, window] ouvrir tout grand; (fig) [+ house, gardens] ouvrir au public; [+ race, competition etc] ouvrir à tout le monde; **to ~ a party*** organiser une petite fête (**for sb** en l'honneur de qn) → **blame, doubt, fit², relief**

[e] [+ switch] actionner

[f] [+ pottery] tourner; [+ silk] tordre

[g] (* = disconcert) déconcerter; **I was quite ~n when he ...** j'en suis resté baba* quand il ...

[h] (Sport* = deliberately lose) [+ match, race] perdre volontairement

[3] COMP ► **throw-in** N (Ftbl) remise f en jeu ► **throw-off** N (Handball) engagement m ► **throw-out** N (Handball) renvoi m de but

► **throw about, throw around** VT SEP [+ litter, confetti] éparpiller; **don't ~ it about or it might break** ne t'amuse pas à le lancer, ça peut se casser; **they were ~ing a ball about** ils jouaient à la balle; (in boat, bus etc) **to be ~n about** être ballotté; **to ~ one's money about** dépenser (son argent) sans compter; (fig) **to ~ one's weight about** faire l'important; **to ~ o.s. about** se débattre

► **throw aside** VT SEP (lit) jeter de côté; (fig) rejeter, repousser

► **throw away** [1] VT SEP [a] [+ rubbish, cigarette end] jeter; (fig) [+ one's life, happiness, health] gâcher; [+ talents] gaspiller, gâcher; [+ sb's affection] perdre; [+ money, time] gaspiller, perdre; [+ chance] gâcher, laisser passer; **to ~ o.s. away** gaspiller ses dons (**on sb** avec qn) [b] (esp Theat) [+ line, remark] = say casually) laisser tomber; (= lose effect of) perdre tout l'effet [2] **~away** ADJ, N → **throwaway**

► **throw back** [1] VT SEP [a] (= return) [+ ball etc] renvoyer (**to** à); [+ fish] rejeter; (fig) [+ image] renvoyer, réfléchir; (fig) **my offer of friendship was ~n back in my face** je lui ai offert mon amitié et il l'a refusée [b] [+ head, hair] rejeter en arrière; [+ shoulders] redresser; **to ~ o.s. back** se (re)jeter en arrière [c] (fig) repousser; (fig) **to be ~n back upon sth** être obligé de se rabattre sur qch [2] **~back** N → **throwback**

► **throw down** VT SEP [+ object] jeter; [+ weapons] déposer; **to ~ o.s. down** se jeter à terre; **to ~ down a challenge** lancer or jeter un défi; **it's really ~ing it down*** (= raining) il pleut à seaux, il tombe des cordes

► **throw in** [1] VI (US) **to ~ in with sb** rallier qn [2] VT SEP [a] [+ object into box etc] jeter; (Ftbl) [+ ball] remettre en jeu; [+ one's cards] jeter (sur la table); (fig) **to ~ in one's hand** or **the sponge** or **the towel*** jeter l'éponge → **lot²** [b] [+ remark, question] interposer; **he threw in a reference to it** il l'a mentionné en passant [c] (fig) (= as extra) en plus; (= included) compris; **with £5 ~n in** avec 5 livres en plus or par-dessus le marché; (= included) **with meals ~n in** (les) repas compris; **if you buy a washing machine they ~ in a packet of soap powder** si vous achetez une machine à laver

ils vous donnent un paquet de lessive en prime; **we had a cruise of the Greek Islands with a day in Athens ~n in** nous avons fait une croisière autour des îles grecques avec en prime un arrêt d'un jour à Athènes

[3] **~-in** N → **throw**

► **throw off** VT SEP [a] (= get rid of) [+ burden, yoke] se libérer de; [+ clothes] enlever or quitter or ôter (en hâte), se débarrasser brusquement de; [+ disguise] jeter; [+ pursuers, dogs] perdre, semer*; [+ habit, tendency, cold, infection] se débarrasser de [b]* [+ poem, composition] faire or écrire au pied levé

► **throw on** VT SEP [+ coal, sticks] ajouter; [+ clothes] enfiler or passer à la hâte; **she threw on some lipstick** elle s'est vite mis or passé un peu de rouge à lèvres

► **throw out** VT SEP [a] jeter dehors; [+ rubbish, old clothes etc] jeter, mettre au rebut; [+ person] (lit) mettre à la porte, expulser; (fig: from army, school etc) expulser, renvoyer; [+ suggestion] rejeter, repousser; (Parl) [+ bill] repousser; (fig) **to ~ out one's chest** bomber la poitrine [b] (= say) [+ suggestion, hint, idea, remark] laisser tomber; [+ challenge] jeter, lancer [c] (= make wrong) [+ calculation, prediction, accounts, budget] fausser [d] (= disconcert) [+ person] désorienter, déconcerter

► **throw over** VT SEP [+ plan, intention] abandonner, laisser tomber*; [+ friend, boyfriend etc] laisser tomber*, plaquer* (**for sb else** pour qn d'autre)

► **throw together** VT SEP [a] (pej = make hastily) [+ furniture, machine] faire à la six-quatre-deux*; [+ essay] torcher; **he threw a few things together and left at once** il a rassemblé quelques affaires or jeté quelques affaires dans un sac et il est parti sur-le-champ [b] (fig: by chance) [+ people] réunir (par hasard); **they had been ~n together** or **fate had ~n them together** le hasard les avait réunis

► **throw up** [1] VI (* = vomit) vomir [2] VT SEP [a] (into air) [+ ball etc] jeter or lancer en l'air; **he threw the ball up** il a jeté la balle en l'air; **he threw the book up to me** il m'a jeté or lancé le livre; **he threw up his hands in despair** il a levé les bras de désespoir [b] (esp Brit = produce, bring to light etc) produire; **the meeting threw up several good ideas** la réunion a produit quelques bonnes idées, quelques bonnes idées sont sorties de la réunion [c] (= reproach) **to ~ sth up to sb** jeter qch à la figure or au visage de qn, reprocher qch à qn [d] (* = vomit) vomir [e] (* = abandon, reject) [+ job, task, studies] lâcher, abandonner; [+ opportunity] laisser passer

throwaway ['θrəʊəweɪ] [1] ADJ [bottle] non consigné; [packaging] perdu; [remark, line] qui n'a l'air de rien [2] N (esp US) [leaflet etc] prospectus m, imprimé m; **the ~ society** la société d'hyperconsommation or du tout-jetable*

throwback ['θrəʊbæk] N [of characteristic, custom etc] **it's a ~ to ...** ça nous (or les etc) ramène à ...

thrower ['θrəʊər] N lanceur m, -euse f → **discus**

throwing ['θrəʊɪŋ] N (Sport) **hammer/javelin ~** le lancer du marteau/du javelin

thrown [θrəʊn] VB ptp of **throw**

thru [θruː] (US) = **through**

thrum [θrʌm] VTI = **strum**

thrupenny* ['θrʌpnɪ] ADJ, N (Brit) = **threepenny**

thruppence* ['θrʌpəns] N (Brit) = **threepence**

thrush¹ [θrʌʃ] N (Orn) grive f

thrush² [θrʌʃ] N (Med) muguet m; (Vet) échauffement m de la fourchette

thrust [θrʌst] (vb: pret, ptp thrust) [1] N [a] (= push) poussée f (also Mil); (= stab: with knife, dagger, stick etc) coup m; (with sword) botte f; (fig = remark) pointe f; (fig) **that was a ~ at you**

ça c'était une pointe dirigée contre vous, c'est vous qui étiez visé → **cut**
[b] (NonC) [of propeller, jet engine, rocket] poussée f; (Archit, Tech) poussée f; (* fig = drive, energy) dynamisme m, initiative f; **the main ~ of his speech** l'idée maîtresse de son discours

[2] VT [a] pousser brusquement or violemment; [+ finger, stick] enfoncer; [+ dagger] plonger, enfoncer (**into** dans, **between** entre); [+ rag etc] fourrer (**into** dans); **he ~ the box under the table** il a poussé la boîte sous la table; **he ~ his finger into my eye** il m'a mis le doigt dans l'œil; **he ~ the letter at me** il m'a brusquement mis la lettre sous le nez; **to ~ one's hands into one's pockets** enfoncer les mains dans ses poches; **he had a knife ~ into his belt** il avait un couteau glissé dans sa ceinture; **he ~ his head through the window** il a mis or passé la tête par la fenêtre; **he ~ the book into my hand** il m'a fourré le livre dans la main; **to ~ one's way** → **3a**
[b] (fig) [+ job, responsibility] imposer (**upon sb** à qn); [+ honour] conférer (**on à**); **some have greatness ~ upon them** certains deviennent des grands hommes sans l'avoir cherché; **I had the job ~ (up)on me** on m'a imposé ce travail; **to ~ o.s. (up)on sb** imposer sa présence à qn

[3] VI [a] (also ~ one's way) **to ~ in/out** etc entrer/sortir en se frayant un passage; **he ~ past me** il m'a bousculé pour passer; **to ~ through a crowd** se frayer un passage dans la foule
[b] (Fencing) allonger une botte

► **thrust aside** VT SEP [+ object, person] écarter brusquement, pousser brusquement à l'écart; (fig) [+ objection, suggestion] écarter or rejeter violemment

► **thrust forward** VT SEP [+ object, person] pousser en avant (brusquement); **to ~ o.s. forward** s'avancer brusquement, se frayer or s'ouvrir un chemin; (fig) se mettre en avant, se faire valoir

► **thrust in** [1] VI (lit: also ~ one's way in) s'introduire de force; (fig = interfere) intervenir [2] VT SEP [+ stick, pin, finger] enfoncer; [+ rag] fourrer dedans*; [+ person] pousser (violemment) à l'intérieur or dedans

► **thrust out** VT SEP [a] (= extend) [+ hand] tendre brusquement; [+ legs] allonger brusquement; [+ jaw, chin] projeter en avant [b] (= push outside) [+ object, person] pousser dehors; **he opened the window and ~ his head out** il a ouvert la fenêtre et passé la tête dehors

► **thrust up** VI [plants etc] pousser vigoureusement

thruster ['θrʌstər] N [a] (pej) **to be a ~** se mettre trop en avant, être arriviste [b] (= rocket) (micro)propulseur m

thrusting ['θrʌstɪŋ] ADJ dynamique, entreprenant; (pej) qui se fait valoir, qui se met trop en avant

thruway ['θruːweɪ] N (US) voie f rapide or express

Thu N ABBR = **Thursday**

Thucydides [θuːˈsɪdɪdiːz] N Thucydide m

thud [θʌd] [1] N bruit m sourd, son m mat; **I heard the ~ of gunfire** j'entendais gronder sourdement les canons [2] VI faire un bruit sourd, rendre un son mat (**on, against** en heurtant); [guns] gronder sourdement; (= fall) tomber avec un bruit sourd; **to ~ in/out** etc [person] entrer/sortir d'un pas lourd

thug [θʌg] N voyou m, gangster m; (at demonstrations) casseur m; (term of abuse) brute f

thuggery ['θʌgərɪ] N (NonC) brutalité f, violence f

thuggish ['θʌgɪʃ] ADJ de voyou(s)

Thule ['θjuːlɪ] N (also ultima ~) Thulé

thulium ['θjuːlɪəm] N thulium m

thumb [θʌm] **1** N pouce m; (fig) **to be under sb's ~** être sous la coupe de qn; **she's got him under her ~** elle le mène par le bout du nez; (fig) **to be all (fingers and) ~s** être très maladroit; **his fingers are all ~s** il est très maladroit (de ses mains); **he gave me the ~s up (sign)*** (all going well) il a levé le pouce pour dire que tout allait bien or en signe de victoire; (to wish me luck) il a levé le pouce en signe d'encouragement; **he gave me the ~s down sign*** il m'a fait signe que ça n'allait pas (or que ça n'avait pas bien marché); (fig) **they gave my proposal the ~s down** ils ont rejeté ma proposition → **finger, rule, twiddle**

2 VT **a** [+ book, magazine] feuilleter; **well ~ed** tout écorné (par l'usage); **to ~ one's nose** faire un pied de nez (**at sb** à qn) **b** * (gen) **to ~ a lift** or **a ride** faire du stop* or de l'auto-stop; **he ~ed a lift to Paris** il est allé à Paris en stop* or en auto-stop; **I managed at last to ~ a lift** je suis enfin arrivé à arrêter or à avoir une voiture

3 COMP ► **thumb index** N répertoire m à onglets; **with ~ index** à onglets ► **thumb print** N empreinte f du pouce

► **thumb through** VT FUS [+ book] feuilleter; [+ card index] consulter rapidement

thumbnail ['θʌmneɪl] **1** N ongle m du pouce **2** ADJ **~ sketch** esquisse f

thumbscrew ['θʌmskru:] N (Tech) vis f à oreilles; (Hist: torture) **~s** poucettes fpl

thumbstall ['θʌmstɔ:l] N poucier m

thumbtack ['θʌmtæk] N (US) punaise f

thump [θʌmp] **1** N (= blow: with fist/stick etc) (grand) coup m de poing/de canne etc; (= sound) bruit m lourd et sourd; **to fall with a ~** tomber lourdement; **to give sb a ~** assener un coup à qn **2** VT (gen) taper sur; [+ door] cogner à, taper à; (esp Brit) **I could have ~ed him!*** je l'aurais giflé or bouffé*! **3** VI **a** cogner, frapper (**on** sur, **at** à); [heart] battre fort; (with fear) battre la chamade; **he was ~ing on the piano** il tapait (comme un sourd) sur le piano, il jouait comme un forcené **b to ~ in/out** etc [person] entrer/sortir etc d'un pas lourd

► **thump out** VT SEP **to ~ out a tune on the piano** marteler un air au piano

thumping ['θʌmpɪŋ] (Brit) **1** ADJ [majority, defeat] écrasant; [losses] énorme; **a ~ headache** un mal de tête carabiné* **2** ADV **~ great** [lorry] gigantesque; [lie] énorme; **her novel is a ~ good read** son roman est vraiment génial*

thunder ['θʌndə'] **1** N (NonC) tonnerre m; [of applause] tonnerre m, tempête f; [of hooves] retentissement m, fracas m; [of passing vehicles, trains] fracas m, bruit m de tonnerre; **there's ~ about** le temps est à l'orage; **there's ~ in the air** il y a de l'orage dans l'air; **I could hear the ~ of the guns** j'entendais tonner les canons; **with a face like ~** le regard noir (de colère) → **black, peal, steal**

2 VI (Met) tonner; [guns] tonner; [hooves] retentir; **the train ~ed past** le train est passé dans un grondement de tonnerre; (liter, fig = be vehement) **to ~ against sth/sb** tonner or fulminer contre qch/qn

3 VT (also ~ **out**) [+ threat, order] proférer d'une voix tonitruante; **"no!" he ~ed** « non ! » tonna-t-il; **the crowd ~ed their approval** la foule a exprimé son approbation dans un tonnerre d'applaudissements et de cris

thunderbolt ['θʌndəbəʊlt] N coup m de foudre; (fig) coup m de tonnerre

thunderclap ['θʌndəklæp] N coup m de tonnerre

thundercloud ['θʌndəklaʊd] N nuage m orageux; (fig) nuage m noir

thunderer ['θʌndərə'] N **the Thunderer** le dieu de la Foudre et du Tonnerre, Jupiter m tonnant

thunderhead ['θʌndəhed] N (esp US Met) tête f de cumulonimbus

thundering ['θʌndərɪŋ] **1** ADV (Brit†*) **a ~ great lie** un énorme mensonge; **this novel is a ~ good read** ce roman est vraiment génial* **2** ADJ **a** (= loud) [waterfall] rugissant; [voice] tonitruant, tonnant; **~ applause** un tonnerre d'applaudissements **b** (= forceful) [question, attack, article] vibrant **c** (Brit†* = great) **to make a ~ nuisance of o.s.** être bougrement† empoisonnant; **in a ~ rage** or **fury** dans une colère noire; **in a ~ temper** d'une humeur massacrante; **it was a ~ success** ça a eu un succès monstre*

thunderous ['θʌndərəs] ADJ **a** (= loud) [ovation, noise] tonitruant; [voice] tonitruant, tonnant; **~ acclaim** or **applause** dans un tonnerre d'applaudissements **b** (= forceful) [speech, attack] vibrant **c** (= angry) **his face was ~** ◊ **he had a ~ look** or **expression on his face** il était blême de rage

thunderstorm ['θʌndəstɔ:m] N orage m

thunderstruck ['θʌndəstrʌk] ADJ (fig) abasourdi, ahuri, stupéfié

thundery ['θʌndərɪ] ADJ [weather] (= stormy) orageux; (= threatening) menaçant; **~ rain** pluies fpl d'orage; **~ showers** averses fpl orageuses

Thur ABBR = **Thursday**

thurible ['θjʊərɪbl] N encensoir m

thurifer ['θjʊərɪfə'] N thuriféraire m

Thurs. ABBR = **Thursday**

Thursday ['θɜ:zdɪ] N jeudi m → **Maundy Thursday**; for phrases see **Saturday**

▼ **thus** [ðʌs] ADV (= consequently) par conséquent; (= in this way) ainsi; **~ far** (= up to here or now) jusqu'ici; (= up to there or then) jusque-là

thusly ['ðʌslɪ] ADV (frm) ainsi

thwack [θwæk] **1** N (= blow) grand coup m; (with hand) claque f, gifle f; (= sound) claquement m, coup m sec **2** VT frapper vigoureusement, donner un coup sec à; (= slap) donner une claque à

thwart[1] [θwɔ:t] VT [+ plan] contrecarrer, contrarier; [+ person] contrecarrer or contrarier les projets de; **to be ~ed at every turn** voir tous ses plans contrariés l'un après l'autre

thwart[2] [θwɔ:t] N (Naut) banc m de nage

thy [ðaɪ] POSS ADJ (††, liter, dial) ton, ta, tes

thyme [taɪm] N thym m; **wild ~** serpolet m

thymus ['θaɪməs] N (pl **thymuses** or **thymi** ['θaɪmaɪ]) thymus m

thyroid ['θaɪrɔɪd] **1** N (also ~ **gland**) thyroïde f **2** ADJ [disorder, hormone, problem, disease] thyroïdien; [cartilage] thyroïde

thyroxin(e) [θaɪ'rɒksɪn] N thyroxine f

thyself [ðaɪ'self] PERS PRON (††, liter, dial) (reflexive) te; (emphatic) toi-même

ti [ti:] N (Mus) si m

tiara [tɪ'ɑ:rə] N [of lady] diadème m; [of Pope] tiare f

Tiber ['taɪbə'] N Tibre m

Tiberias [taɪ'bɪəriæs] N **Lake ~** le lac de Tibériade

Tiberius [taɪ'bɪərɪəs] N Tibère m

Tibet [tɪ'bet] N le Tibet

Tibetan [tɪ'betən] **1** ADJ tibétain **2** N **a** Tibétain(e) m(f) **b** (Ling) tibétain m

tibia ['tɪbɪə] N (pl **tibias** or **tibiae** ['tɪbɪ,i:]) tibia m

tic [tɪk] **1** N tic m (nerveux) **2** COMP ► **tic-tac-toe** N (US) ≈ (jeu m de) morpion m

tich* [tɪtʃ] N (Brit) → **titch**

tichy* ['tɪtʃɪ] ADJ (Brit) → **titchy**

tick[1] [tɪk] **1** N **a** [of clock] tic-tac m **b** (Brit* = instant) instant m; **just a ~!** ◊ **half a ~!** une seconde!, un instant!; **in a ~** ◊ **in a couple of ~s** (= quickly) en moins de deux, en un clin d'œil; **it won't take a ~** or **two ~s** c'est l'affaire d'un instant, il y en a pour une seconde; **I shan't be a ~** j'en ai pour une seconde **c** (esp Brit = mark) coche f; **to put** or **mark a ~ against sth** cocher qch

2 VT (Brit) [+ name, item, answer] cocher; (Scol = mark right) marquer juste; (on form etc) **please ~ where appropriate** cochez la case correspondante

3 VI [clock, bomb etc] faire tic-tac, tictaquer; (fig) **I don't understand what makes him ~*** il est un mystère pour moi; **I wonder what makes him ~*** je me demande comment il fonctionne

4 COMP ► **tick-over** N (Brit Aut) ralenti m ► **tick-tack-toe** N (US) ≈ (jeu m de) morpion m

► **tick away** **1** VI [clock] continuer son tic-tac; [taximeter] tourner; [time] s'écouler **2** VT SEP **the clock ~ed the hours away** la pendule marquait les heures

► **tick by** VI [time] s'écouler

► **tick off** **1** VT SEP **a** (Brit) (lit) [+ name, item] cocher; (fig = enumerate) [+ reasons, factors etc] énumérer **b** (Brit* = reprimand) attraper, passer un savon à* **c** (US* = annoy) embêter*, casser les pieds à* **2** **~ing-off*** N → **ticking**[2]

► **tick over** VI (Brit) [engine] tourner au ralenti; [taximeter] tourner; [business etc] aller or marcher doucement

tick[2] [tɪk] N (Zool) tique f

tick[3]* [tɪk] N (Brit = credit) crédit m; **on ~** à crédit; **to give sb ~** faire crédit à qn

tick[4] [tɪk] N (NonC = cloth) toile f (à matelas); (= cover) housse f (pour matelas)

ticker ['tɪkə'] **1** N **a** (esp US) téléscripteur m, téléimprimeur m **b*** (= watch) tocante* f; (= heart) cœur m, palpitant* m **2** COMP ► **ticker tape** N (NonC) bande f de téléscripteur or téléimprimeur; (US: at parades etc) ≈ serpentin m; (US) **to get a ~ tape welcome** être accueilli par une pluie de serpentins

ticket ['tɪkɪt] **1** N **a** (Aviat, Cine, Rail, Theat etc: for lottery, raffle) billet m; (for bus, tube) ticket m; (Comm = label) étiquette f; (= counterfoil) talon m; (from cash register) ticket m, reçu m; (for cloakroom) ticket m, numéro m; (for left luggage) bulletin m; (for library) carte f; (from pawnshop) reconnaissance f (du mont-de-piété); **to buy a ~** prendre un billet; **coach ~** billet m de car; **admission by ~ only** entrée réservée aux personnes munies d'un billet; (fig) **that's (just) the ~!*** c'est ça!, c'est parfait! → **return, season** **b** (*: for fine) P.-V. m, papillon m; **I found a ~ on the windscreen** j'ai trouvé un papillon sur le pare-brise; **to get a ~ for parking** attraper un P.-V. pour stationnement illégal; **to give sb a ~ for parking** mettre un P.-V. à qn pour stationnement illégal **c** (= certificate) [of pilot] brevet m; **to get one's ~** [ship's captain] passer capitaine **d** (US Pol = list) liste f (électorale); **he is running on the Democratic ~** il se présente sur la liste des démocrates → **straight**

2 VT **a** [+ goods] étiqueter **b** (US) [+ traveller] donner un billet à; **passengers ~ed on these flights** voyageurs en possession de billets pour ces vols **c** (US* = fine) mettre un P.-V. à

3 COMP ► **ticket agency** N (Theat) agence f de spectacles; (Rail etc) agence f de voyages ► **ticket barrier** N (Brit Rail) portillon m (d'accès) ► **ticket collector** N contrôleur m, -euse f ► **ticket holder** N personne f munie d'un billet ► **ticket inspector** N = **ticket collector** ► **ticket machine** N distributeur m de titres de transport ► **ticket office** N bureau m de vente des billets, guichet m ► **ticket of leave**† N (Brit Jur) libération f conditionnelle ► **ticket tout** N → **tout** 1

---

ticking¹ ['tıkıŋ] N (*NonC: Tex*) toile *f* (à matelas)

ticking² ['tıkıŋ] ① N (*of clock*) tic-tac *m* ② COMP ► **ticking-off** N (*Brit*) **to give sb a ~-off** passer un savon à qn*, enguirlander qn ; **to get a ~-off** recevoir un bon savon*, se faire enguirlander

tickle ['tıkl] ① VT (*lit*) [+ *person, dog*] chatouiller, faire des chatouilles* à ; (= *please*) [+ *sb's vanity, palate etc*] chatouiller ; (* = *delight*) [+ *person*] plaire à, faire plaisir à ; (* = *amuse*) amuser, faire rire ; **to ~ sb's ribs** ◊ **to ~ sb in the ribs** chatouiller qn ; **to be ~d to death*** ◊ **to be ~d pink*** être aux anges → **fancy** ② VI chatouiller ③ N chatouillement *m*, chatouilles* *fpl* ; **he gave the child a ~** il a chatouillé l'enfant, il a fait des chatouilles* à l'enfant ; **to have a ~ in one's throat** avoir un chatouillement dans la gorge → **slap**

tickler* ['tıklə'] N (*Brit*) (= *question, problem*) colle* *f* ; (= *situation*) situation *f* délicate *or* épineuse

tickling ['tıklıŋ] ① N chatouillement *m*, chatouille(s)* *f(pl)* ② ADJ [*sensation*] de chatouillement ; [*blanket*] qui chatouille ; [*cough*] d'irritation

ticklish ['tıklıʃ], **tickly*** ['tıklı] ADJ ⓐ (*sensation*] de chatouillement ; [*blanket*] qui chatouille ; [*cough*] d'irritation ; **to be ~** [*person*] être chatouilleux ⓑ (= *touchy*) [*person, sb's pride*] chatouilleux ; (= *difficult*) [*situation, problem, task*] épineux, délicat

ticktack ['tıktæk] ① N (*Racing*) langage *m* gestuel (*des bookmakers*) ② COMP ► **ticktack man** N (*pl* **ticktack men**) (*Brit*) aide *m* de bookmaker

ticktock ['tık'tɒk] N (*of clock*) tic-tac *m*

ticky-tacky* ['tıkı,tækı] (*US*) ① ADJ [*building*] moche* *f* ② N (*NonC* = *building material*) matériaux *mpl* de mauvaise qualité ; (= *goods*) pacotille *f*, camelote *f*

tidal ['taıdl] ① ADJ [*forces, effects, waters, conditions, atlas*] des marées ; [*river, estuary*] qui a des marées ② COMP ► **tidal barrage** N barrage *m* coupant l'estuaire ► **tidal basin** N bassin *m* de marée ► **tidal energy**, **tidal power** N énergie *f* marémotrice, houille *f* bleue ► **tidal power station** N usine *f* marémotrice ► **tidal wave** N (*lit*) raz-de-marée *m inv* ; (*fig*) [*of people*] raz-de-marée *m inv* ; (*fig*) [*of enthusiasm, protest, emotion*] immense vague *f*

tidbit ['tıdbıt] N (*esp US*) = **titbit**

tiddler* ['tıdlə'] N (*Brit*) (= *stickleback*) épinoche *f* ; (= *tiny fish*) petit poisson *m* ; (= *small person*) demi-portion* *f* ; (= *small child*) mioche* *mf* ; **30 years ago the company was a mere ~** il y a 30 ans, cette entreprise n'était qu'un poids plume

tiddly* ['tıdlı] ADJ (*Brit*) ⓐ (= *drunk*) pompette*, éméché* ; **to get ~** s'enivrer ⓑ (= *small*) minuscule

tiddlywinks ['tıdlıwıŋks] N jeu *m* de puce

tide [taıd] ① N marée *f* ; **at high/low ~** à marée haute/basse ; **the ~ is on the turn** la mer est étale ; **the ~ turns at 3 o'clock** la marée commence à monter (*or* à descendre) à 3 heures ; (*fig*) **the ~ has turned** la chance a tourné ; (*fig*) **to go with the ~** suivre le courant ; (*fig*) **to go against the ~** aller à contre-courant ; **the ~ of events** le cours *or* la marche des événements ; **the rising ~ of public impatience** l'exaspération grandissante et généralisée du public → **time** ② VT **to ~ sb over a difficulty** dépanner qn lors d'une difficulté, tirer qn d'embarras provisoirement ; **it ~d him over till payday** ça lui a permis de tenir *or* l'a dépanné en attendant d'être payé ③ COMP ► **tide table** N échelle *f* des marées ► **tide over** VT SEP **to ~ sb over** permettre à qn de tenir, dépanner qn

...tide ['taıd] N (*in compounds*) saison *f* ; **Eastertide** (la saison de) Pâques *m* → **Whitsun(tide)**

tideland ['taıdlænd] N laisse *f*

tideline ['taıdlaın], **tidemark** ['taıdmɑːk] N laisse *f* de haute mer, ligne *f* de (la) marée haute ; (*esp Brit hum: on neck, in bath*) ligne *f* de crasse

tidewater ['taıdwɔːtə'] N (*Brit*) (eaux *fpl* de) marée *f* ; (*US*) côte *f*

tideway ['taıdweı] N (= *channel*) chenal *m* de marée ; (= *tidal part of river*) section *f* (d'un cours d'eau) soumise à l'influence des marées ; (= *current*) flux *m*

tidily ['taıdılı] ADV [*arrange, fold*] soigneusement, avec soin ; [*write*] proprement ; **she is always ~ dressed** elle est toujours correctement vêtue *or* toujours mise avec soin ; **try to dress more ~** tâche de t'habiller plus correctement *or* d'apporter plus de soin à ta tenue

tidiness ['taıdınıs] N (*NonC*) [*of room, drawer, desk, books*] ordre *m* ; [*of handwriting, schoolwork*] propreté *f* ; **what I like about him is his ~** ce que j'aime chez lui, c'est son sens de l'ordre ; **the ~ of his appearance** sa tenue soignée

tidings ['taıdıŋz] NPL (*liter*) nouvelle(s) *f(pl)*

tidy ['taıdı] ① ADJ ⓐ (= *neat*) [*house, room, drawer, desk*] bien rangé ; [*garden*] bien entretenu ; [*clothes, hair*] net, soigné ; [*appearance, schoolwork*] soigné ; [*handwriting, pile, stack*] net ; [*person*] (*in appearance*) soigné ; (*in character*) ordonné ; **to keep one's room ~** avoir une chambre bien rangée, toujours bien ranger sa chambre ; **try to make your writing tidier** tâche d'écrire plus proprement ; **to look ~** (*person*) avoir une apparence soignée ; [*room*] être bien rangé ; **to make o.s. ~** remettre de l'ordre dans sa toilette ; **to have a ~ mind** avoir l'esprit méthodique ⓑ (* = *sizeable*) [*sum, amount*] coquet*, joli* ; [*profit*] joli* ; [*income, speed*] bon ; **it cost a ~ bit** *or* **a ~ penny** ça a coûté une jolie* *or* coquette* somme ; **it took a ~ bit of his salary** ça lui a pris une bonne partie de son salaire ② N vide-poches *m inv* ③ VT (*also ~ up*) [+ *drawer, cupboard, books, clothes*] ranger, mettre de l'ordre dans ; [+ *desk*] ranger, mettre de l'ordre sur ; **to ~ o.s. (up)** remettre de l'ordre dans sa toilette ; **to ~ (up) one's hair** arranger sa coiffure, remettre de l'ordre dans sa coiffure ④ COMP ► **tidy-out***, **tidy-up*** N **to have a ~-out** *or* **~-up** faire du rangement ; **to give sth a (good) ~-out** *or* **~-up** ranger qch à fond ► **tidy away** VT SEP (*Brit*) ranger ► **tidy out** ① VT SEP [+ *cupboard, drawer*] vider pour y mettre de l'ordre ② N → **tidy** ► **tidy up** ① VI (= *tidy room etc*) (tout) ranger ; (= *tidy o.s.*) s'arranger ② VT SEP = **tidy 3** ③ **~up*** N → **tidy**

tie [taı] ① N ⓐ (= *cord etc*) [*of garment, curtain*] attache *f* ; [*of shoe*] lacet *m*, cordon *m* ; (*fig* = *bond, link*) lien *m* ; (*fig* = *restriction*) entrave *f* ; (*fig*) **the ~s of blood** les liens du sang ; **family ~s** (= *links*) liens *mpl* de famille *or* de parenté ; (= *responsibilities*) attaches *fpl* familiales ; **she finds the children a great ~** avec les enfants elle n'est pas libre → **old** ⓑ (= *necktie*) cravate *f* → **black, white** ⓒ (*esp Sport* = *draw*) égalité *f* (de points) ; (= *drawn match*) match *m* nul ; (= *drawn race/competition*) course *f*/concours *m* dont les vainqueurs sont ex æquo ; **the match ended in a ~** ◊ **the result (of the match) was a ~** les deux équipes ont fait match nul ; (*Scol, Sport etc*) **there was a ~ for second place** il y avait deux ex æquo en seconde position ; **the election ended in a ~** les candidats ont obtenu le même nombre de voix ⓓ (*Sport* = *match*) match *m* de championnat → **cup** ⓔ (*Mus*) liaison *f*

ⓕ (*Archit*) tirant *m*, entrait *m* ⓖ (*US Rail*) traverse *f* ② VT ⓐ (= *fasten*) attacher ; [+ *shoelace, necktie, rope*] attacher, nouer ; [+ *parcel*] attacher, ficeler ; [+ *ribbon*] nouer, faire un nœud à ; [+ *shoes*] lacer ; **to ~ sb's hands** (*lit*) attacher *or* lier les mains de *or* à qn ; (*fig*) lier les mains de *or* à qn ; (*lit, fig*) **his hands are ~d** il a les mains liées ; (*lit, fig*) **to be ~d hand and foot** avoir pieds et poings liés ; **to ~ sth in a bow** ◊ **to ~ a bow in sth** faire un nœud avec qch ; **to ~ a knot in sth** faire un nœud à qch ; **to get ~d in knots** [*rope etc*] faire des nœuds ; (*fig*) **to get ~d in knots*** ◊ **to ~ o.s. in knots*** s'embrouiller ; (*fig*) **to ~ sb in knots*** embrouiller qn ; **to ~ the knot*** (= *get married*) se marier → **apron** ⓑ (= *link*) lier (**to** à) ; (= *restrict*) restreindre, limiter ; (*Mus*) lier ; **the house is ~d to her husband's job** la maison est liée au travail de son mari ; **I'm ~d to the house/my desk all day** je suis retenu *or* cloué à la maison/mon bureau toute la journée ; **are we ~d to this plan?** sommes-nous obligés de nous en tenir à ce projet ? ③ VI ⓐ [*shoelace, necktie, rope*] se nouer ⓑ (= *draw*) (*Sport etc*) faire match nul ; (*in competition*) être ex æquo ; (*in election*) obtenir le même nombre de voix ; (*Sport*) **we ~d (with them)** four-all nous avons fait match nul quatre partout ; (*in race, exam, competition*) **they ~d for first place** ils ont été premiers ex æquo ④ COMP ► **tie-break** N (*Tennis*) tie-break *m* ; (*in quiz/game*) question *f*/épreuve *f* subsidiaire ► **tie clasp**, **tie clip** N fixe-cravate *m* ► **tie-dye** VT nouer-lier-teindre (*méthode consistant à isoler certaines parties du tissu en le nouant ou en le liant*) ► **tie-in** N (= *link*) lien *m*, rapport *m* (**with** avec) ; (*US Comm* = *sale*) vente *f* jumelée *or* par lots ; (*US Comm* = *article*) lot *m* ♦ ADJ [*sale*] jumelé ► **tie-on** ADJ [*label*] à œillet ► **tie-rod** N (*Archit, Aut*) tirant *m* ► **tie-tack** N (*US*) épingle *f* de cravate ► **tie-up** N (= *connection*) lien *m* (**with** avec, **between** entre) ; (*Fin* = *merger*) fusion *f* (**with** avec, **between** entre) ; (*Comm* = *joint venture between two companies*) accord *m*, entente *f*, association *f*, lien *m* (**with** avec, **between** entre) ; (*US* = *stoppage*) interruption *f*, arrêt *m* ; (= *traffic*) embouteillage *m* ► **tie back** ① VT SEP [+ *curtains*] retenir par une embrasse, attacher sur les côtés ; [+ *hair*] nouer (en arrière) ② **~back** N → **tieback** ► **tie down** VT SEP [+ *object, person, animal*] attacher ; (*fig*) **he didn't want to be ~d down** il ne voulait pas perdre sa liberté ; **to ~ sb down to a promise** obliger qn à tenir sa promesse ; **can you ~ him down to these conditions?** pouvez-vous l'astreindre à ces conditions ? ; **we can't ~ him down to a date/a price** nous n'arrivons pas à lui faire fixer une date/un prix ; **I shan't ~ you down to 6 o'clock** il n'est pas nécessaire que ce soit à 6 heures ; **I don't want to ~ myself down to going** je ne veux pas m'engager à y aller *or* me trouver contraint d'y aller ► **tie in** ① VI ⓐ (= *be linked*) être lié (**with** à) ; **it all ~s in with what they plan to do** tout est lié à ce qu'ils projettent de faire ; **this fact must ~ in somewhere** ce fait doit bien avoir un rapport quelque part ⓑ (= *be consistent*) correspondre (**with** à), concorder, cadrer (**with** avec) ; **it doesn't ~ in with what I was told** ça ne correspond pas à *or* ça ne cadre pas avec *or* ça ne concorde pas avec ce que l'on m'a dit ② VT SEP **I'm trying to ~ that in with what he said** j'essaie de voir la liaison *or* le rapport entre ça et ce qu'il a dit ; **can you ~ the visit in with your trip to London?** pouvez-vous combiner la visite et *or* avec votre voyage à Londres ? ③ **~-in** N → **tie** ► **tie on** ① VT SEP [+ *label etc*] attacher (avec une ficelle) ; (*fig*) **to ~ one on*** (= *get drunk*) se cuiter*, se soûler* ② **~-on** ADJ → **tie**

►**tie together** VT SEP [+ *objects, people*] attacher ensemble
►**tie up** 1 VI (*Naut*) accoster
2 VT SEP a (= *bind*) [+ *parcel*] ficeler ; [+ *prisoner*] attacher, ligoter ; (= *tether*) [+ *boat, horse*] attacher (**to** à) ; (*fig*) **there are a lot of loose ends to ~ up** il y a encore beaucoup de points de détail à régler ; (*fig*) **to get (o.s.) all ~d up*** (= *muddled*) s'embrouiller, s'emmêler les pinceaux*
b [+ *capital, money*] immobiliser
c (*fig* = *conclude*) [+ *business deal*] conclure ; **it's all ~d up now** tout est réglé maintenant, c'est une chose réglée maintenant, nous avons (*or* il a *etc*) tout réglé
d (* = *occupy*) **he is ~d up all tomorrow** il est pris *or* occupé toute la journée de demain ; **he is ~d up with the manager** il est occupé avec le directeur ; **we are ~d up for months to come** nous avons un emploi du temps très chargé pour les mois qui viennent ; **he's rather ~d up with a girl in Dover** une jeune fille de Douvres l'accapare en ce moment
e (= *link*) **this company is ~d up with an American firm** cette compagnie a des liens avec *or* est liée à une firme américaine ; **his illness is ~d up* with the fact that his wife has left him** sa maladie est liée au fait que sa femme l'a quitté
f (*US* = *obstruct, hinder*) [+ *traffic*] obstruer, entraver ; [+ *production, sales*] arrêter momentanément ; [+ *project, programme*] entraver ; **to get ~d up** [*traffic*] se bloquer ; [*production, sales*] s'arrêter ; [*project, programme*] être suspendu
3 **~up** N → **tie**

tieback ['taɪbæk] N (= *cord, rope for curtain*) embrasse *f* ; (= *curtain itself*) rideau *m* bonne femme

tiebreaker ['taɪbreɪkər] N = **tie-break** ; → **tie**

tied [taɪd] ADJ a *pt of* **tie** b (*Sport* = *equal*) **to be ~** être à égalité *or* ex aequo c (*Mus*) [*note*] lié d (*Brit*) **~ cottage** logement *m* de fonction (*d'ouvrier agricole etc*) ; **it's a ~ house** [*pub*] ce pub ne vend qu'une marque de bière e (*Fin*) [*loan*] conditionnel f (= *restricted*) **she is very ~ by the children** elle est très prise par ses enfants → **tie up**

tiepin ['taɪpɪn] N épingle *f* de cravate

tier [tɪər] 1 N (*in stadium, amphitheatre*) gradin *m* ; (= *level*) niveau *m* ; (= *part of cake*) étage *m* ; (*Theat*) **grand ~** balcon *m* ; (*Theat*) **upper ~** seconde galerie *f* ; **to arrange in ~s** (*gen*) étager, disposer par étages ; [+ *seating*] disposer en gradins ; **to rise in ~s** s'étager ; **a three-~ system** un système à trois niveaux 2 VT [+ *seats*] disposer en gradins ; **~ed seating** places *fpl* assises en gradins *or* en amphithéâtre ; **three-~ed cake** ≈ pièce *f* montée à trois étages ; **a ~ed skirt/dress** une jupe/robe à volants

Tierra del Fuego [tɪˌerədel'fweɪgəʊ] N la Terre de Feu

tiff [tɪf] N prise *f* de bec*

tiffin† ['tɪfɪn] N (*Brit*) repas *m* de midi

tig [tɪg] N = **tag 1c**

tiger ['taɪgər] 1 N tigre *m* (*also fig*) ; **she fought like a ~** elle s'est battue comme une tigresse ; (*fig*) **he has a ~ by the tail** il a déclenché quelque chose dont il n'est plus maître 2 COMP ► **tiger economy** N (*also* **Asian ~ economy**) tigre *m* asiatique ► **tiger lily** N lis *m* tigré ► **tiger moth** N écaille *f* (*papillon*) ► **tiger's-eye** N œil *m* de tigre

tigereye ['taɪgəraɪ] N = **tiger's-eye** ; → **tiger**

tight [taɪt] 1 ADJ a (= *close-fitting*) [*clothes*] serré ; [*shoes, belt*] qui serre ; **too ~** [*clothes, shoes, belt*] trop juste *or* serré ; **it should be fairly ~ over the hips** cela se porte relativement ajusté sur les hanches → **skintight**
b (= *taut*) [*rope*] raide, tendu ; [*skin*] tendu ; [*knot, weave, knitting*] serré ; **to pull ~** [+ *knot*] serrer ; [+ *string*] tirer sur ; **to stretch ~** [+

fabric, sheet] tendre, tirer sur ; [+ *skin*] étirer ; **as ~ as a drum** tendu comme un tambour ; **to keep a ~ rein on sth** surveiller qch de près ; **to keep a ~ rein on sb** (= *watch closely*) surveiller qn de près ; (= *be firm with*) tenir la bride haute *or* serrée à qn ; **to keep a ~ rein on o.s.** se contenir
c (= *firm, fixed*) [*screw, nut, bolt, lid*] serré ; [*tap, drawer*] dur ; [*grip*] solide ; **screw the lid firmly on the jar to ensure a ~ seal** vissez bien le couvercle pour que le bocal soit fermé hermétiquement ; **to keep a ~ lid on** [+ *emotions*] contenir ; [+ *story*] mettre sous le boisseau ; **he clasped me to his chest in a ~ embrace** il m'a serré (fort) contre lui ; (*lit*) **to have** *or* **keep a ~ hold of sth** serrer fort qch ; (*lit*) **to keep a ~ hold of sb** bien tenir qn ; (*fig*) **to have a ~ grip on sth** avoir qch bien en main ; (*fig*) **to keep a ~ grip on sth** surveiller qch de près → **airtight, skintight, watertight**
d (= *tense, constricted*) [*voice, face*] tendu ; [*lips, throat*] serré ; [*mouth*] aux lèvres serrées ; [*smile*] pincé ; [*muscle*] tendu, contracté ; [*stomach*] noué ; **his mouth was set in a ~ line** il avait les lèvres serrées ; **there was a ~ feeling in his chest** (*from cold, infection*) il avait les bronches prises ; (*from emotion*) il avait la gorge serrée ; **it was a ~ squeeze in the lift** on était affreusement serrés dans l'ascenseur
e (= *compact*) [*group*] compact ; **to curl up in a ~ ball** se recroqueviller complètement ; **~ curls** boucles *fpl* serrées ; (= *close-knit*) **a ~ federation of states** une fédération d'États solidaires ; **a small, ~ knot of people** un petit groupe étroitement lié
f (= *strict*) [*schedule, budget*] serré ; [*restrictions, control*] strict, rigoureux ; [*security*] strict ; **it'll be a bit ~, but we should make it in time** ce sera un peu juste mais je crois que nous arriverons à temps ; **financially things are a bit ~** nous sommes un peu justes*
g (= *sharp*) [*bend, turn*] serré
h (= *close-fought*) [*competition*] serré ; [*match*] disputé
i (= *in short supply*) **to be ~** [*money, space*] manquer ; [*resources*] être limité ; [*credit*] être (res)serré ; **things were ~** l'argent manquait
j (= *difficult*) [*situation*] difficile ; **to be in a ~ corner** *or* **spot** être dans le pétrin*
k (* = *drunk*) soûl* ; **to get ~** se soûler*
l (* = *stingy*) radin* ; **to be ~ with one's money** être près de ses sous*
m (*Mus**) [*band*] bien synchro*
2 ADV (*hold, grasp*) bien, solidement ; [*squeeze*] très fort ; [*shut, fasten, tie, screw*] bien ; [*seal*] hermétiquement ; **don't fasten** *or* **tie it too ~** ne le serrez pas trop (fort) ; **to pack sth ~** bien emballer *or* empaqueter qch ; **packed ~ (with sth)** plein à craquer (de qch) ; **sit ~!** ne bouge pas ! ; **sleep ~!** dors bien ! ; **hold ~!** accroche-toi ! ; **she held ~ to Bernard's hand** elle s'est accrochée à la main de Bernard ; (*fig*) **to hold ~** (= *wait*) s'accrocher ; **all we can do is hold ~ and hope things get better** la seule chose que nous puissions faire c'est nous accrocher et espérer que les choses s'amélioreront ; **she held ~ to her assertion** elle a maintenu ce qu'elle disait
3 **tights** NPL (*esp Brit*) collant(s) *m(pl)*
4 COMP ► **tight-arsed:** (*Brit*), **tight-assed:** (*US*) ADJ [*person, behaviour*] coincé* ► **tight end** N (*US Ftbl*) ailier *m* ► **tight-fisted** ADJ avare, radin*, pingre ► **tight-fitting** ADJ [*garment*] ajusté, collant ; [*lid, stopper*] qui ferme bien ► **tight-knit** ADJ (*fig*) [*community*] très uni ► **tight-lipped** ADJ **to maintain a ~-lipped silence, to be very ~-lipped** ne pas desserrer les lèvres *or* les dents (**about sth** au sujet de qch) ; (*from anger etc*) **he stood there ~-lipped** il se tenait là avec un air pincé ; **in ~-lipped disapproval** d'un air désapprobateur

tighten ['taɪtn] 1 VT (*also* **~ up**) [+ *rope*] tendre ; [+ *coat, skirt, trousers*] ajuster, rétrécir ; [+

screw, wheel, grasp, embrace] resserrer ; [+ *legislation, restrictions, regulations, control*] renforcer ; (*Econ*) [+ *credit*] resserrer ; (*lit, fig*) **to ~ one's belt** se serrer la ceinture 2 VI (*also* **~ up**) [*rope*] se tendre, se raidir ; [*screw, wheel*] se resserrer ; [*restrictions, regulations*] être renforcé
►**tighten up** 1 VI a = **tighten 2** b (*fig*) **to ~ up on security/immigration** devenir plus strict *or* sévère en matière de sécurité/ d'immigration ; **the police are ~ing up on shoplifters** la police renforce la lutte contre les voleurs à l'étalage 2 VT SEP → **tighten 1**

tightening ['taɪtnɪŋ] N [*of muscles*] contraction *f* ; [*of screw, wheel, grasp, embrace*] resserrement *m* ; [*of security, control, legislation, restrictions, regulations*] renforcement *m* ; [*of sanctions, system*] durcissement *m* ; **the ~ of his grip on her hand** la pression plus forte qu'il a exercée sur sa main ; (*Econ*) **~ of credit** resserrement *m* du crédit

tightly ['taɪtlɪ] ADV a (= *firmly*) [*close, bind, wrap*] bien ; **to hold a rope ~** bien tenir une corde ; **to hold sb's hand ~** serrer la main de qn ; **to hold sb ~** serrer qn contre soi ; **to hold a letter ~** serrer une lettre dans sa main ; **~-closed eyes** les paupières serrées ; **~ fitting** [*clothing*] moulant ; (= *tautly*) **~ stretched** (très) tendu ; (= *densely*) **~ packed (with sth)** [*bus, room, shelf*] plein à craquer (de qch) ; **the ~ packed crowds** les gens serrés comme des sardines* b (= *rigorously*) **to be ~ controlled** faire l'objet d'un contrôle rigoureux ; **~ knit** [*community*] très uni

tightness ['taɪtnɪs] N [*of dress, trousers*] étroitesse *f* ; [*of screw, lid, drawer*] dureté *f* ; [*of restrictions, control*] rigueur *f*, sévérité *f* ; **he felt a ~ in his chest** il sentait sa gorge se serrer

tightrope ['taɪtrəʊp] 1 N corde *f* raide, fil *m* ; (*fig*) **to be on** *or* **walking a ~** être *or* marcher sur la corde raide 2 COMP ► **tightrope walker** N funambule *mf*

tightwad: ['taɪtwɒd] N (*US*) radin(e)* *m(f)*, grippe-sou *m*

tigress ['taɪgrɪs] N tigresse *f*

Tigris ['taɪgrɪs] N Tigre *m*

tikka ['tiːkə] N **chicken/lamb ~** poulet *m*/ mouton *m* tikka

tilde ['tɪldə] N tilde *m*

tile [taɪl] 1 N (*on roof*) tuile *f* ; (*on floor, wall, fireplace*) carreau *m* ; (*Brit fig*) **to be out on the ~s*** () **to spend** *or* **have a night on the ~s*** faire la noce* *or* la bombe* ; (*fig*) **he's got a ~ loose:** il lui manque une case* 2 VT [+ *roof*] couvrir de tuiles ; [+ *floor, wall, fireplace*] carreler ; **~d** [*roof*] en tuiles ; [*floor, room etc*] carrelé

tiling ['taɪlɪŋ] N a (= *tiles collectively*) [*of roof*] tuiles *fpl* ; [*of floor, wall*] carrelage *m*, carreaux *mpl* b (= *activity, skill*) [*of roof*] pose *f* des tuiles ; [*of floor, wall etc*] carrelage *m*

till[1] [tɪl] = **until**

till[2] [tɪl] N caisse *f* (enregistreuse) ; (*old-fashioned type*) tiroir-caisse *m* ; (= *takings*) caisse *f* ; **pay at the ~** payez à la caisse ; (*fig*) **to be** *or* **get caught** *or* **found with one's hand** *or* **fingers in the ~** être pris sur le fait *or* en flagrant délit

till[3] [tɪl] VT (*Agr*) labourer

tillage ['tɪlɪdʒ] N (= *activity*) labour *m*, labourage *m* ; (= *land*) labour *m*, guéret *m*

tiller[1] ['tɪlər] N (*Agr*) laboureur *m*

tiller[2] ['tɪlər] N (*Naut*) barre *f* (du gouvernail)

tilt [tɪlt] 1 N a (= *tip, slope*) inclinaison *f* ; **it has a ~ to it** () **it's on a ~** the ~ c'est incliné, ça penche b (*Hist*) (= *contest*) joute *f* ; (= *thrust*) coup *m* de lance ; (*fig*) **to have a ~ at ...** décocher des pointes à ... ; (**at**) **full ~** à toute vitesse, à fond de train c (*fig* = *inclination*) nouvelle orientation *f* (**towards sth** vers qch) 2 VT (*also* **~ over**) [+ *object, one's head*] pencher, incliner ; [+ *backrest*] incliner ; **to ~ one's hat over one's eyes** rabattre son chapeau sur les yeux ; **to ~ one's chair (back)** se balancer sur sa chaise ③ VI ⓐ (gen) s'incliner ; (also ~ **over**) pencher, être incliné ⓑ (Hist) jouter (**at** contre) → **windmill** ④ COMP ► **tilt-top table** N table f à plateau inclinable

tilted ['tɪltɪd] ADJ penché, incliné

tilth [tɪlθ] N (= soil) couche f arable ; (= tilling) labourage m

timber ['tɪmbə'] ① N ⓐ (NonC) (= wood) bois m d'œuvre, bois m de construction ; (= trees collectively) arbres mpl, bois m ; **~!** attention (à l'arbre qui tombe)!, gare! ; **land under ~** futaie f, terre f boisée (pour l'abattage) ⓑ (= beam) madrier m, poutre f ; (Naut) membrure f ② VT (+ tunnel etc) boiser ; **~ed** [house] en bois ; [land, hillside] boisé ► **half** ③ COMP [fence etc] en bois ► **timber-framed** ADJ à charpente de bois ► **timber line** N limite f de la forêt ► **timber merchant** N (Brit) marchand m de bois, négociant m en bois ► **timber wolf** N loup m gris

timbering ['tɪmbərɪŋ] N (NonC) boisage m

timberland ['tɪmbəlænd] N (NonC) exploitation f forestière

timberyard ['tɪmbəjɑːd] N (Brit) dépôt m de bois

timbre ['tæmbrə, 'tɪmbə'] N (gen, also Phon) timbre m

timbrel ['tɪmbrəl] N tambourin m

Timbuktu [,tɪmbʌk'tuː] N (lit, fig) Tombouctou m

time [taɪm]

① NOUN	③ COMPOUNDS
② TRANSITIVE VERB	

① NOUN

For a long time see long.

ⓐ gen temps m ; **~ and space** le temps et l'espace ; **~ flies** le temps passe vite or file ; **~ will show if ...** l'avenir dira si ..., on saura avec le temps si ... ; **in ~ ◊ with ~ ◊ as ~ goes** (or went) by avec le temps, à la longue ; **I've enough ~ and I have the ~ to go there** j'ai le temps d'y aller ; **we've got plenty of ~ ◊ we've all the ~ in the world** nous avons tout notre temps ; **have you got ~ to wait for me?** est-ce que tu as le temps de m'attendre? ; **he spent all/half his ~ reading** il passait tout son temps/ la moitié de son temps à lire ; **we mustn't lose any ~** il ne faut pas perdre de temps ; **I had to stand for part** or **some of the ~** j'ai dû rester debout une partie du temps ; **it works okay some of the ~** ça marche parfois or quelquefois ; **he spends the best part of his ~ in London** il passe la plus grande partie de son temps or le plus clair de son temps à Londres ; **half the ~ she's drunk** la moitié du temps elle est ivre ; **at this point in ~** à l'heure qu'il est, en ce moment ; **from ~ out of mind** de temps immémorial ; **my ~ is my own** mon temps m'appartient ; **free ~ ◊ ~ off** temps libre ; **he'll tell you in his own good ~** il vous le dira quand bon lui semblera ; **in your own ~** en prenant votre temps ; **he was working against ~ to finish it** il travaillait d'arrache-pied pour le terminer à temps ; **it is only a matter** or **question of ~** ce n'est qu'une question de temps ; **~ will tell** l'avenir le dira ■ (PROV) **~ is money** le temps c'est de l'argent (PROV) ■ (PROV) **there's a ~ and a place for everything** il y a un temps pour tout (PROV) ■ (PROV) **~ and tide wait for no man** on ne peut pas arrêter le temps

♦ **all the time** (= always) tout le temps ; (= all along) depuis le début ; **I have to be on my guard all the ~** je dois tout le temps être sur mes gardes ; **the letter was in my pocket all the ~** la lettre était dans ma poche depuis le début ; **all the ~ he knew who had done it** il savait depuis le début qui avait fait le coup

♦ **for all time** pour toujours

♦ **for the time being** pour l'instant

♦ **in good time** (= with time to spare) en avance ; **he arrived in good ~ for the start of the**

match il est arrivé en avance pour le début du match ; **let me know in good ~** prévenez-moi suffisamment à l'avance ; **all in good ~!** chaque chose en son temps!

♦ **to make time to do sth** trouver le temps de faire qch ; **however busy you are, you must make ~ to relax** même si vous êtes très pris, il est important que vous trouviez le temps de vous détendre

♦ **to take time**: **it takes ~ to change people's ideas** ça prend du temps de changer les idées des gens ; **things take ~ to change** les choses ne changent pas du jour au lendemain ; **it took me a lot of ~ to prepare this** j'ai mis beaucoup de temps à préparer ça ; **take your ~** prenez votre temps ; **take your ~ over it!** mettez-y le temps qu'il faudra! ; (fig) **it took me all my ~ to convince her** j'ai eu toutes les peines du monde à la convaincre

♦ **to take time out to do sth** (gen) trouver le temps de faire qch ; (during studies) interrompre ses études pour faire qch ; **some women managers can't afford to take ~ out to have a baby** certaines femmes cadres ne peuvent pas se permettre d'interrompre leur carrière pour avoir un enfant

♦ **to find/have** etc **time for**: **I can't find ~ for the garden** je n'arrive pas à trouver le temps de m'occuper du jardin ; **I've no ~ for that sort of thing** (lit) je n'ai pas le temps de faire ce genre de chose ; (fig) je ne supporte pas ce genre de choses ; **I've no ~ for people like him** je ne supporte pas les types* comme lui ; **I've got a lot of ~* for him** je trouve que c'est un type très bien* ; **it didn't leave him much ~ for sleeping** ça ne lui a guère laissé le temps de dormir ⓑ **= period, length of time for a ~** pendant un (certain) temps ; **what a (long) ~ you've been!** vous y avez mis le temps!, il vous en a fallu du temps! ; **he did it in half the ~** il l'a fait deux fois plus vite or en deux fois moins de temps que vous ; **he is coming in two weeks' ~** il vient dans deux semaines ; (frm) **within the agreed ~** dans les délais convenus ; (US) **to buy sth on ~** acheter qch à tempérament ; (Sport) **what ~ did he do it in?** il a fait quel temps? ; **the winner's ~ was 12 seconds** le temps du gagnant était de 12 secondes ; (US) **to make ~** (= hurry) se dépêcher ; (US) **he's making ~ with her** il la drague*

♦ **a short time** peu de temps ; **a short ~ later** peu (de temps) après ; **for a short ~ we thought that ...** pendant un moment nous avons pensé que ... ; **in a short ~ all the flowers had gone** peu de temps après toutes les fleurs étaient fanées

♦ **in no time**: **in no ~ at all ◊ in next to no ~ ◊ in less than no ~** en un rien de temps, en moins de deux*

♦ **some time**: **I waited for some ~** j'ai attendu assez longtemps or pas mal de temps* ; **I waited for some considerable ~** j'ai attendu très longtemps ; **after some little ~** au bout d'un certain temps ; **some ~ ago** il y a déjà un certain temps ; **that was some ~ ago** ça fait longtemps de cela ; **it won't be ready for some ~ (yet)** ce ne sera pas prêt avant un certain temps ; **some ~ before the war** quelque temps avant la guerre ; **some ~ next year/in 2003** dans le courant de l'année prochaine/de l'année 2003

ⓒ **= period worked** **to work full ~** travailler à plein temps or à temps plein → **full** ; **we get paid ~ and a half on Saturdays** le samedi, nous sommes payés une fois et demie le tarif normal ; **Sunday working is paid at double ~** les heures du dimanche sont payées double ; **in the firm's ◊ in company** pendant les heures de service ; **in** or (US) **on one's own ~** après les heures de service

ⓓ **= day, era** temps m ; **in Gladstone's ~** du temps de Gladstone ; **~ was when one could ...** il fut un temps où l'on pouvait ... ; **in my ~ it was all different** de mon temps c'était complè-

tement différent ; **he is ahead of** or **in advance of** or **before his ◊ he was born before his ~** il est en avance sur son temps ; **to keep up with** or **move with the ~s** [person] vivre avec son temps ; [company, institution] (savoir) évoluer ; **to be behind the ~s** être vieux jeu* inv ; **I've seen some strange things in my ~** j'ai vu des choses étranges dans ma vie ; **that was before my ~** (= before I was born) je n'étais pas encore né, c'était avant ma naissance ; (= before I came here) je n'étais pas encore là ; **to die before one's ~** mourir avant l'âge ; **in ~(s) of peace** en temps de paix ; **in medieval ~s** à l'époque médiévale ; **~s are hard** les temps sont durs ; **those were tough ~s** la vie n'était pas facile en ce temps-là ; **the ~s we live in** l'époque où nous vivons ; **it was a difficult ~ for all of us** cela a été une période difficile pour nous tous

ⓔ **= experience** **they lived through some terrible ~s in the war** ils ont connu des moments terribles pendant la guerre ; **to have a poor** or **rough** or **bad** or **thin** or **tough* ~ (of it)** en voir de dures* ; **what great ~s we've had!** c'était le bon temps! ; **to have a good ~ (of it)** bien s'amuser! ; **to have the ~ of one's life** s'amuser follement*

ⓕ **by clock** heure f ; **what is the ~? ◊ what ~ is it?** quelle heure est-il? ; **what ~ do you make it? ◊ what do you make the ~?** quelle heure avez-vous? ; **what ~ is he arriving?** à quelle heure est-ce qu'il arrive? ; **have you got the right ~?** est-ce que vous avez l'heure exacte or juste? ; **the ~ is 4.30** il est 4 heures et demie ; **your ~ is up** (in exam, prison visit etc) c'est l'heure ; (in game) votre temps est écoulé ; (fig) **it sent the president a clear message: your ~ is up** pour le Président, le message était clair : vos jours sont comptés ; **he looked at the ~** il a regardé l'heure ; **that watch keeps good ~** cette montre est toujours à l'heure ; **at this ~ of (the) night** à cette heure de la nuit ; **at any ~ of the day or night** à n'importe quelle heure du jour ou de la nuit ; **at any ~ during school hours** pendant les heures d'ouverture de l'école ; **open at all ~s** ouvert à toute heure ; (Brit: in pub) **~ gentlemen please!** on ferme! ; (US) **it's midnight by Eastern ~** il est minuit, heure de la côte est ; **it was 6 o'clock Paris ~** il était 6 heures, heure de Paris ; **it's ~ for lunch** c'est l'heure du déjeuner ; **it's ~ to go** c'est l'heure de partir, il est temps de partir ; **it's ~ I was going ◊ it's ~ for me to go** il est temps que j'y aille ; **it's (about) ~ somebody taught him a lesson** il est grand temps que quelqu'un lui donne (subj) une leçon

♦ **preposition + time**: **ahead of ~** en avance ; **(and) about ~ too!** ce n'est pas trop tôt! ; (Brit) **not before ~!** ce n'est pas trop tôt! ; **behind ~** en retard ; **just in ~ (for sth/to do sth)** juste à temps (pour qch/pour faire qch) ; **on ~** à l'heure ; **the trains are on time** or **up to time ◊ the trains are running to ~** les trains sont à l'heure

♦ **the time of day**: **to pass the ~ of day** bavarder un peu, échanger quelques mots (**with sb** avec qn) ; **I wouldn't give him the ~ of day** je ne lui adresserais pas la parole

ⓖ **= moment, point of time** moment m ; **there are ~s when I could hit him** il y a des moments où je pourrais le gifler ; **when the ~ comes** quand le moment viendra ; **when the ~ is right** quand le moment sera venu ; **his ~ is drawing near** or **approaching** son heure or sa fin est proche ; **his ~ has come** son heure est venue ; **to choose one's ~** choisir son moment ; **come (at) any ~** venez quand vous voudrez ; **he may come (at) any ~** il peut arriver d'un moment à l'autre ; **it may happen any ~ now** cela peut arriver d'un moment à l'autre ; **at the** or **that ~** à ce moment-là ; **at this ~** en ce moment ; **at the present ~** en ce moment, actuellement ; **at this particular ~** à ce moment précis ; **at (any) one ~** à un moment donné ; **at all ~s** à tous moments ; **I could hit him at** ~s il y a des moments où je pourrais le gifler ; **I have at no** ~ **said that** je n'ai jamais dit cela ; **at** ~s par moments ; **he came at a very inconvenient** ~ il est arrivé au mauvais moment, il a mal choisi son moment ; **(in) between** ~s entre-temps ; **by the** ~ **I had finished**, it was dark le temps que je termine (subj) il faisait nuit ; **by this** or **that** ~ **she was exhausted** elle était alors épuisée ; **you must be cold by this** ~ vous devez avoir froid maintenant ; **by this** ~ **next year** l'année prochaine à la même époque ; **this is no** or **not the** ~ **for quarrelling** ce n'est pas le moment de se disputer ; **from** ~ **to** ~ de temps en temps ; **from that** ~ or **this** ~ **on he** ... à partir de ce moment il ... ; **from this** ~ **on I shall do what you tell me** désormais or dorénavant je ferai ce que tu me diras ; **some** ~s ... at other ~s des fois ... des fois ; **at this** ~ **of year** à cette époque de l'année ; **this** ~ **tomorrow** demain à cette heure-ci ; **this** ~ **last year** l'année dernière à cette époque-ci ; **this** ~ **last week** il y a exactement une semaine ; **now's the** ~ **to do it** c'est le moment de le faire ; **the** ~ **has come for us to leave** il est temps que nous partions (subj) ; **the** ~ **has come to decide** ... il est temps de décider ... ; **now's your** or **the** ~ **to tell him** c'est maintenant que vous devriez le lui dire

h = **occasion** fois f ; **this** ~ cette fois ; **(the) next** ~ vous la prochaine fois que vous viendrez ; **every** or **each** ~ chaque fois ; **several** ~s plusieurs fois ; **at various** ~s **in the past** plusieurs fois déjà ; **at other** ~s en d'autres occasions ; ~ **after** ◊ ~s **without number** ◊ ~ **and** (~) **again** maintes et maintes fois ; **(the) last** ~ la dernière fois ; **the previous** ~ ◊ **the** ~ **before** la fois d'avant ; **come back some other** ~ revenez une autre fois ; **the** ~s **I've told him that!** je le lui ai dit je ne sais combien de fois! ; **the** ~s **I've wished that** ... combien de fois n'ai-je souhaité que ... ; **some** ~ or **other I'll do it** je le ferai un jour ou l'autre ; **I remember the** ~ **when he told me about it** je me rappelle le jour où il me l'a dit ; **it costs £3 a** ~ **to do a load of washing** ça coûte trois livres pour faire une lessive ; **one at a** ~ un(e) par un(e) ; **for weeks at a** ~ pendant des semaines entières

i multiplying fois f ; **two** ~s **three is six** deux fois trois (font) six ; ~s **as big as** ... ◊ **ten** ~s **the size of** ... dix fois plus grand que ; **it's worth ten** ~s **as much** ça vaut dix fois plus → **times**

j Mus etc measure f ; **in** ~ en mesure (to, with avec) ; **in** ~ **to the music** en mesure avec la musique ; **to be out of** ~ ne pas être en mesure (with avec) ; **to keep** ~ rester en mesure

2 TRANSITIVE VERB

a = **choose time of** [+ visit] choisir le moment de ; **it was** ~d **to begin at** ... le commencement était prévu pour ... ; **you** ~d **that perfectly!** c'est tombé à point nommé!, vous ne pouviez pas mieux choisir votre moment! ; **well-**~d [remark, entrance] tout à fait opportun, qui tombe à point nommé ; [stroke] exécuté avec un bon timing ; **the invasion was carefully** ~d l'invasion a été soigneusement minutée ; **they are timing the bomb alerts to cause maximum disruption** ils font en sorte que ces alertes à la bombe provoquent le maximum de perturbations

b = **count time of** [+ race, runner, worker etc] chronométrer ; [+ programme, ceremony, piece of work] minuter ; **to** ~ **sb over 1,000 metres** chronométrer (le temps de) qn sur 1 000 mètres ; ~ **how long it takes you** notez le temps qu'il vous faut pour le faire ; **to** ~ **an egg** minuter la cuisson d'un œuf

3 COMPOUNDS

► **time and motion study** N (Ind) étude f des cadences ► **time bomb** N bombe f à retardement ► **time capsule** N capsule f témoin (devant servir de document historique) ► **time card** N (Ind) carte f de pointage ► **time check** N (Rad) rappel m de l'heure

► **time clock** N (Ind etc = machine itself) pointeuse f ► **time-consuming** ADJ qui prend beaucoup de temps ► **time delay** N délai m ► **time-delay** ADJ [mechanism, safe] à délai d'ouverture ► **time deposit** N (US Fin) dépôt m à terme ► **time difference** N décalage m horaire ► **time discount** N (US Comm) remise f pour paiement anticipé ► **time draft** N (US Fin) effet m à terme ► **time exposure** N (Phot) temps m de pose ► **time-filler** N façon f de tuer le temps ► **time frame** N délais mpl ► **time fuse** N détonateur m à retardement ► **time-honoured** ADJ consacré (par l'usage) ► **time-lag** N (between events) décalage m, retard m ; (between countries) décalage m horaire ► **time-lapse photography** N (Cine) accéléré m ► **time limit** N (= restricted period) limite f de temps ; (for abortion) délai m légal ; (Jur) délai m de forclusion ; (= deadline) date f limite ; **to put** or **set a** ~ **limit on sth** fixer une limite de temps or un délai pour qch ; **within the** ~ **limit** dans les délais (impartis) ; **without a** ~ **limit** sans limitation de temps ► **time loan** N (US Fin) emprunt m à terme ► **time lock** N fermeture f commandée par une minuterie ► **time machine** N (Sci Fi) machine f à remonter le temps ► **time-out** N (esp US) (Sport) temps m mort ; (Chess) temps m de repos ► **time-saver** N **it is a great** ~-**saver** ça fait gagner beaucoup de temps ► **time-saving** ADJ qui fait gagner du temps ♦ N économie f or gain m de temps ► **time-serving** ADJ (pej) opportuniste ♦ N opportunisme m ► **time-share** VT (Comput) utiliser or exploiter en temps partagé ; [+ holiday home] avoir en multipropriété ♦ N maison f (or appartement m) en multipropriété ► **time-sharing** N (Comput) (exploitation f or travail m en temps partagé ; [of holiday home] multipropriété f ► **time sheet** N (Ind etc) feuille f de présence ► **time signal** N (Rad) signal m horaire ► **time signature** N (Mus) indication f de la mesure ► **time slice** N (Comput) tranche f de temps ► **time span** N période f de temps ► **time study** N = **time and motion study** ► **time switch** N [of electrical apparatus] minuteur m ; (for lighting) minuterie f ► **time travel** N (Sci Fi) voyage m dans le temps ► **time trial** N (Motor Racing, Cycling) course f contre la montre, contre-la-montre m inv ► **time warp** N distorsion f spatiotemporelle ; **it's like going into** or **living in a** ~ **warp** on a l'impression d'avoir fait un bond en arrière (or en avant) dans le temps or d'avoir fait un bond dans le passé (or le futur) ► **time-waster** N (pej) **to be a** ~-**waster** [person] faire perdre du temps ; [activity] être une perte de temps ; (in advert) "no ~ wasters" « pas sérieux s'abstenir » ► **time-wasting** ADJ qui fait perdre du temps ♦ N perte f de temps ► **time zone** N fuseau m horaire

timekeeper ['taɪmkiːpər] N (= watch) montre f ; (= stopwatch) chronomètre m ; (Sport = official) chronométreur m, -euse f officiel(le) ; **to be a good** ~ [person] être toujours à l'heure

timekeeping ['taɪmkiːpɪŋ] N (Sport) chronométrage m ; (at work) **I'm trying to improve my** ~ j'essaie d'être plus ponctuel

timeless ['taɪmlɪs] ADJ [quality, appeal] intemporel ; [beauty] intemporel, éternel

timeliness ['taɪmlɪnɪs] N (NonC) à-propos m, opportunité f

timely ['taɪmlɪ] ADJ [reminder, arrival] opportun ; [intervention] opportun, qui tombe à point nommé ; [event, warning] qui tombe à point nommé

timepiece ['taɪmpiːs] N (= watch) montre f ; (= clock) horloge f

timer ['taɪmər] N (Culin etc) minuteur m ; (with sand in it) sablier m ; (on machine, electrical device etc) minuteur m ; (Aut) distributeur m d'allumage → **old**

times* taɪmz VT (= multiply) multiplier

timescale ['taɪmskeɪl] N durée f, période f ; **our** ~ **for this project is 10 to 15 years** nous nous situons dans une perspective de 10 à 15 ans

timeserver ['taɪmsɜːvər] N (pej) opportuniste mf

timetable ['taɪmteɪbl] 1 N (Rail etc) (indicateur m) horaire m ; (Scol) emploi m du temps ; (Ftbl: also **fixtures** ~) calendrier m des rencontres 2 VT (Brit) [+ visit, course] établir un emploi du temps pour

timeworn ['taɪmwɔːn] ADJ [stones etc] usé par le temps ; [idea] rebattu

timid ['tɪmɪd] ADJ (= shy) timide ; (= unadventurous) timoré, craintif ; (= cowardly) peureux

timidity [tɪ'mɪdɪtɪ] N (NonC) (= shyness) timidité f ; (= unadventurousness) caractère m timoré or craintif ; (= cowardice) caractère m peureux

timidly ['tɪmɪdlɪ] ADV (= shyly) timidement ; (= unadventurously) craintivement ; (= in cowardly way) peureusement

timidness ['tɪmɪdnɪs] N = **timidity**

timing ['taɪmɪŋ] 1 N **a** [of musician etc] sens m du rythme ; **a good comedian depends on his (sense of)** ~ un bon comédien doit minuter très précisément son débit ; **the actors'** ~ **was excellent throughout the play** le minutage des acteurs était excellent tout au long de la pièce ; ~ **is very important in formation flying** la synchronisation est capitale dans les vols en formation ; **the** ~ **of the demonstration** la date et l'heure de la manifestation ; **he arrived just when we were sitting down to the table: I had to admire his** ~ il est arrivé au moment précis où l'on se mettait à table : il ne pouvait pas tomber plus mal **b** réglage m de l'allumage ; (Aut) **to set the** ~ régler l'allumage **c** (Ind, Sport) chronométrage m 2 COMP ► **timing device**, **timing mechanism** N [of bomb etc] mouvement m d'horlogerie ; [of electrical apparatus] minuteur m

Timor ['tiːmɔːr, 'taɪmɔːr] N Timor ; **in** ~ à Timor

timorous ['tɪmərəs] ADJ [person] timoré, craintif ; [reform] frileux, timide ; [speech] timoré

timorously ['tɪmərəslɪ] ADV craintivement

Timothy ['tɪməθɪ] N Timothée m

timothy ['tɪməθɪ] N (Bot) fléole f des prés

timpani ['tɪmpənɪ] NPL timbales fpl

timpanist ['tɪmpənɪst] N timbalier m

tin [tɪn] 1 N **a** (NonC) étain m ; (= tin plate) fer-blanc m **b** (esp Brit = can) boîte f (en fer-blanc) ; ~ **of salmon** boîte f de saumon **c** (for storage) boîte f (de fer) ; **cake** ~ boîte f à gâteaux **d** (Brit Culin) (= mould: for cakes etc) moule m ; (= dish: for meat etc) plat m ; **cake** ~ moule m à gâteau ; **meat** or **roasting** ~ plat m à rôtir 2 VT (= put in tins) [+ food etc] mettre en boîte(s) or en conserve → **tinned b** (= coat with tin) étamer 3 COMP (= made of tin) en étain, d'étain ; (= made of tin plate) en or de fer-blanc ► **tin can** N boîte f (en fer-blanc) ► **tin ear*** N (Mus) **he has a** ~ **ear** il n'a pas d'oreille ► **tin god** N (fig) (little) ~ **god** idole f de pacotille ► **tin hat** N casque m ► **tin lizzie*** N (= car) vieille guimbarde* f ► **tin mine** N mine f d'étain ► **tin-opener** N (Brit) ouvre-boîte m ► **Tin Pan Alley** N (Mus, fig) le monde du showbiz ► **tin plate** N (NonC) fer-blanc m ► **tin soldier** N soldat m de plomb ► **tin whistle** N flûtiau m

tincture ['tɪŋktʃər] 1 N (Pharm) teinture f ; (fig) nuance f, teinte f ; ~ **of iodine** teinture f d'iode 2 VT (lit, fig) teinter (**with** de)

tinder ['tɪndər] N (NonC) (in tinderbox) amadou m; (= small sticks) petit bois m (NonC); **as dry as ~** sec (sèche f) comme de l'amadou

tinderbox ['tɪndəbɒks] N briquet m (à amadou); (fig: esp Pol) poudrière f

tine [taɪn] N [of fork] dent f, fourchon m; [of antler] andouiller m

tinfoil ['tɪnfɔɪl] N (NonC) papier m (d')aluminium, papier m alu*

ting [tɪŋ] **1** N tintement m **2** VI tinter **3** VT faire tinter **4** COMP ► **ting-a-ling** N [of telephone, doorbell] dring m; [of handbell, tiny bells] drelin m

tinge [tɪndʒ] (lit, fig) **1** N teinte f, nuance f **2** VT teinter (**with** de)

tingle ['tɪŋgl] **1** VI (= prickle) picoter, fourmiller; (fig = thrill) vibrer, frissonner; **her face was tingling** le visage lui picotait or lui cuisait; **her cheeks were tingling with cold** le froid lui piquait or lui brûlait des joues; **my fingers are tingling** j'ai des picotements or des fourmis dans les doigts; **the toothpaste makes my tongue ~** le dentifrice me pique la langue; **he was tingling with impatience** il brûlait d'impatience **2** N (= sensation) picotement m, fourmillement m; (= thrill) frisson m; (= sound) **to have a ~ in one's ears** avoir les oreilles qui tintent

tingling ['tɪŋglɪ] **1** N (NonC) = **tingle 2** **2** ADJ [sensation, effect] de picotement, de fourmillement; **to have ~ fingers** avoir des picotements or des fourmillements dans les doigts

tingly ['tɪŋglɪ] ADJ [sensation] de picotement, de fourmillement; **my arm is** or **feels ~** j'ai des fourmis or des fourmillements dans le bras

tinker ['tɪŋkər] **1** N **a** (esp Brit: gen) romanichel(le) m(f) (often pej); (specifically mending things) rétameur m (ambulant); (†* = child) polisson(ne) m(f); (fig) **it's not worth a ~'s cuss** or **~'s damn** ça ne vaut pas tripette* or un clou*; **I don't care** or **give a ~'s cuss** or **~'s damn** je m'en soucie comme de l'an quarante; **~, tailor, soldier, sailor ...** comptine enfantine **b** **to have a ~ (with)*** bricoler* **2** VI **a** (also **~ about**) bricoler, s'occuper à des bricoles; **she was ~ing (about) with the car** elle bricolait la voiture; **stop ~ing with that watch!** arrête de tripoter* cette montre! **b** (fig) **to ~ with** [+ contract, wording, report etc] (= change) faire des retouches à, remanier; (dishonestly) tripatouiller*

tinkle ['tɪŋkl] **1** VI tinter **2** VT faire tinter **3** N **a** tintement m; (Brit Telec) **to give sb a ~*** passer un coup de fil à qn* **b** (* baby talk = passing water) pipi* m

tinkling ['tɪŋklɪŋ] **1** N (NonC) tintement m **2** ADJ [bell] qui tinte; [stream] qui clapote, qui gazouille

tinned [tɪnd] ADJ (Brit) [fruit, tomatoes, salmon] en boîte, en conserve; **~ goods** or **food** conserves fpl

tinnitus [tɪ'naɪtəs] N acouphène m

tinny ['tɪnɪ] ADJ (pej) [sound, taste] métallique; **~ piano** casserole* f, mauvais piano m; **it's such a ~ car** quelle camelote*, cette voiture

tinpot* ['tɪnpɒt] ADJ (esp Brit) [car, bike] qui ne vaut pas grand-chose, en fer-blanc; [dictator, government] fantoche, de pacotille; **a ~ little town** un petit bled*

tinsel ['tɪnsəl] N **a** (NonC) guirlandes fpl de Noël (argentées) **b** (fig pej) clinquant m

Tinseltown* ['tɪnsəltaʊn] N Hollywood

tinsmith ['tɪnsmɪθ] N ferblantier m

tint [tɪnt] **1** N teinte f, nuance f; (for hair) shampooing m colorant → **flesh 2** VT teinter (**with** de); **to ~ one's hair** se faire un shampooing colorant

tintinnabulation ['tɪntɪˌnæbjʊ'leɪʃən] N tintinnabulement m

Tintoretto [ˌtɪntə'retəʊ] N le Tintoret

tiny ['taɪnɪ] ADJ [object] tout petit, minuscule; [person, child, minority] tout petit; **a ~ little man/baby** un tout petit bonhomme/bébé; **a ~ amount of sth** une tout petite quantité de qch

tip¹ [tɪp] **1** N (= end) [of stick, pencil, ruler, wing, finger, nose] bout m; [of sword, knife, asparagus] pointe f; [of iceberg, mountain] pointe f, cime f; [of ski] pointe f, spatule f; [of tongue] pointe f (also Phon), bout m; (metal etc end piece) [of shoe] bout m, pointe f; [of cigarette] bout m; [of filter tip] bout m (filtre); [of umbrella, cane] embout m; [of billiard cue] procédé m; **from ~ to toe** de la tête aux pieds; **he stood on the ~s of his toes** il s'est dressé sur la pointe des pieds; **he touched it with the ~ of his toe** il l'a touché du bout de l'orteil; (fig) **I've got it on** or **it's on the ~ of my tongue** je l'ai sur le bout de la langue; **it was on the ~ of my tongue to tell her what I thought of her** j'étais à deux doigts de lui dire ce que je pensais d'elle; (fig) **it's just the ~ of the iceberg** ce n'est que la partie visible de l'iceberg, ça n'est rien comparé au reste → **fingertip**, **wing**

2 VT (= put tip on) mettre un embout à; (= cover tip of) recouvrir le bout de; (Brit) **~ped cigarettes** cigarettes fpl (à bout) filtre inv; **~ped with steel** ◊ **steel-~ped** ferré, qui a un embout de fer

tip² [tɪp] **1** N **a** (= money) pourboire m; (in restaurant) **the ~ is included** le service est compris **b** (= hint, information) suggestion f, tuyau* m; (= advice) conseil m; (Racing) tuyau* m; **"~s for the handyman"** « les trucs du bricoleur »; **that horse is a hot ~ for the 3.30** ce cheval a une première chance dans la course de 15 h 30; **take my ~** suivez mon conseil **c** (= tap) tape f, petit coup m

2 VT **a** (= reward) donner un pourboire à; **he ~ped the waiter 5 francs** il a donné 5 F de pourboire au serveur **b** (Racing, gen) pronostiquer; **to ~ the winner** pronostiquer le cheval gagnant; **he ~ped Blue Streak for the 3.30** il a pronostiqué la victoire de Blue Streak dans la course de 15 h 30; **to ~ sb the wink* about sth** filer un tuyau* à qn sur qch; (Brit fig) **they are ~ped to win the next election** on pronostique qu'ils vont remporter les prochaines élections; (Brit) **Paul was ~ped for the job** on avait pronostiqué que Paul serait nommé **c** (= tap, touch) toucher (légèrement), effleurer; **to ~ one's hat to sb** mettre or porter la main à son chapeau pour saluer qn

3 COMP ► **tip-off** N **to give sb a ~-off** (gen) prévenir qn, donner or filer un tuyau* à qn; (Police) donner* qn

► **tip off** **1** VT SEP (gen) donner or filer un tuyau* à (**about sth** sur qch); [+ police] prévenir or avertir (par une dénonciation) **2** **~-off** N → **tip²**

tip³ [tɪp] **1** N (Brit) (for rubbish) décharge f, dépotoir m; (for coal) terril m; (* fig = untidy place) (véritable) dépotoir m

2 VT (= incline, tilt) pencher, incliner; (= overturn) faire basculer, renverser; (= pour, empty) [+ liquid] verser (**into** dans, **out of** de); [+ load, sand, rubbish] déverser, déposer; [+ clothes, books etc] déverser (**into** dans, **out of** de); **he ~ped the water out of the bucket** il a vidé le seau; **to ~ sb off his chair** renverser or faire basculer qn de sa chaise; **they ~ped him into the water** ils l'ont fait basculer or tomber dans l'eau; **the car overturned and they were ~ped into the roadway** la voiture s'est retournée et ils se sont retrouvés sur la chaussée; **to ~ the scales at 90kg** peser 90 kg; (fig) **to ~ the scales** or **balance** faire pencher la balance (**in sb's favour** en faveur de qn, **against sb** contre qn); (US) **to ~ one's hand*** or **one's mitt*** dévoiler son jeu (involontairement)

3 VI **a** (= incline) pencher, être incliné; (= overturn) se renverser, basculer; (Brit) **"no ~ping" ◊ "~ping prohibited"** « défense de déposer des ordures »

b **it's ~ping with rain*** il pleut des cordes

4 COMP ► **tip-cart** N tombereau m ► **tip-up seat** N (in theatre etc) siège m rabattable, strapontin m; (in taxi, underground etc) strapontin m ► **tip-up truck** N camion m à benne (basculante)

► **tip back**, **tip backward(s)** **1** VI [chair] se rabattre en arrière; [person] se pencher en arrière, basculer (en arrière) **2** VT SEP [+ chair] rabattre or faire basculer (en arrière)

► **tip down*** VTI (= raining) **it's ~ping (it) down** il pleut des cordes

► **tip forward(s)** **1** VI [chair] se rabattre en avant; [person] se pencher en avant **2** VT SEP [+ chair] rabattre or faire basculer (en avant); [+ car seat] rabattre (en avant)

► **tip out** VT SEP [+ liquid, contents] vider; [+ load] décharger, déverser; **they ~ped him out of his chair/out of bed** ils l'ont fait basculer de sa chaise/du lit

► **tip over** **1** VI (= tilt) pencher; (= overturn) basculer **2** VT SEP faire basculer

► **tip up** **1** VI [table etc] (= tilt) pencher, être incliné; (= overturn) basculer; [box, jug] se renverser; [seat] se rabattre; [truck] basculer **2** VT SEP (= tilt) [+ table etc] incliner; [+ jug, box] pencher, incliner; [+ person] faire basculer **3** **~-up** ADJ → **tip³**

tipcat ['tɪpkæt] N (jeu m du) bâtonnet m

tipper ['tɪpər] N **a** (= vehicle) camion m à benne (basculante); (= back of vehicle) benne f (basculante) **b** (giving money) **he is a good** or **big ~** il a le pourboire facile

tippet ['tɪpɪt] N (also fur ~) étole f (de fourrure)

Tipp-Ex® ['tɪpeks] **1** N Tipp-Ex® m **2** VT **to tippex sth (out)** tippexer qch, effacer qch au Tipp-Ex®

tipple ['tɪpl] **1** VI picoler* **2** N (hum) **gin is his ~** ce qu'il préfère boire c'est du gin

tippler ['tɪplər] N picoleur* m, -euse* f

tippy-toe* ['tɪpɪtəʊ] N, VI (US) = **tiptoe**

tipsily ['tɪpsɪlɪ] ADV [walk] en titubant légèrement; **... he said ~ ...** dit-il un peu ivre

tipstaff ['tɪpstɑːf] N (Brit Jur) huissier m

tipster ['tɪpstər] N (Racing) pronostiqueur m

tipsy ['tɪpsɪ] **1** ADJ éméché*, pompette*; **to get ~** devenir pompette* **2** COMP ► **tipsy cake** N (Brit) sorte de baba au rhum

tiptoe ['tɪptəʊ] **1** N **on ~** sur la pointe des pieds **2** VI **to ~ in/out** etc entrer/sortir etc sur la pointe des pieds

tiptop* ['tɪp'tɒp] ADJ de premier ordre, excellent, de toute première qualité

tirade [taɪ'reɪd] N diatribe f

tiramisu [ˌtɪrəmɪ'suː] N tiramisu m

tire¹ ['taɪər] N (US) = **tyre**

tire² ['taɪər] **1** VT fatiguer; (= weary) fatiguer, lasser **2** VI se fatiguer, se lasser; **he ~s easily** il se fatigue vite, il est vite fatigué; **he never ~s of telling us how ...** il ne se lasse jamais de nous dire comment ...

► **tire out** VT SEP épuiser; **to be ~d out** être épuisé

tired ['taɪəd] ADJ **a** (= weary) [person, eyes] fatigué; [movement, voice] las (lasse f); **to get** or **grow ~** se fatiguer; (hum euph) **~ and emotional** (= drunk) ivre **b** (= bored) **to be ~ of sb/sth** en avoir assez de qn/qch; **to get ~ of sb/sth** commencer à en avoir assez de qn/qch; **to be ~ of doing sth** en avoir assez de faire qch; **to be ~ of sb doing sth** en avoir assez que qn fasse qch → **sick** **c** (= old) **our ~ old car** notre vieille voiture qui ne marche plus bien; **a ~ lettuce leaf** une feuille de laitue défraîchie **d** (pej = hackneyed) [cliché, topic] rebattu; [excuse] rebattu, éculé

tiredly ['taɪədlɪ] ADV [*reply*] d'une voix fatiguée ; [*walk*] d'un pas lourd, avec une démarche fatiguée

tiredness ['taɪədnɪs] N fatigue *f*

tireless ['taɪəlɪs] ADJ [*person*] infatigable (**in sth** dans qch) ; [*work, efforts*] inlassable

tirelessly ['taɪəlɪslɪ] ADV infatigablement, inlassablement

tiresome ['taɪəsəm] ADJ [*person, behaviour, noise*] pénible ; **it's a ~ business going to all these meetings** c'est une corvée que d'aller à toutes ces réunions ; **it is ~ to have to wait** c'est ennuyeux d'avoir à attendre

tiresomeness ['taɪəsəmnɪs] N [*of task*] caractère *m* ennuyeux ; **the ~ of her behaviour** son attitude agaçante

tiring ['taɪərɪŋ] ADJ fatigant

tiro ['taɪərəʊ] N = **tyro**

Tirol [tɪ'rəʊl] N = **Tyrol**

tisane [tɪ'zæn] N tisane *f*

tissue ['tɪʃuː] 1 N (= *cloth*) tissu *m*, étoffe *f* ; (*Anat, Bio*) tissu *m* ; (= *paper handkerchief*) mouchoir *m* en papier, kleenex® *m* ; (*also* **toilet ~**) papier *m* hygiénique ; (*fig* = *web, mesh*) tissu *m*, enchevêtrement *m* ; **a ~ of lies** un tissu de mensonges 2 COMP ▶ **tissue culture** N (*Bio*) culture *f* de tissus ▶ **tissue paper** N (*NonC*) papier *m* de soie

tit[1] [tɪt] N (*Orn*) mésange *f* → **blue**

tit[2] [tɪt] N **~ for tat!** un prêté pour un rendu ! ; **I'll give him ~ for tat** je lui rendrai la pareille, je lui revaudrai ça ; **~-for-tat killings/reprisals** meurtres *mpl* en riposte *or* en représailles/ représailles *fpl* en riposte

tit[3]: [tɪt] N **a** (= *breast*) nichon: *m*, néné* *m* ; **to get on sb's ~s**:: taper sur le système à qn* **b** (= *idiot*) abruti(e): *m(f)*, con(ne): *m(f)*

Titan ['taɪtən] N (*also fig*: **titan**) Titan *m*

titanic [taɪ'tænɪk] ADJ **a** [*struggle*] titanesque **b** [*acid*] titanique, de titane ; [*iron ore*] titanifère

titanium [tɪ'teɪnɪəm] N titane *m*

titbit ['tɪtbɪt] N (*esp Brit*) [*of food*] friandise *f*, bon morceau *m* ; [*of gossip*] potin *m* ; (*in newspaper*) entrefilet *m* croustillant ; (= *snack with drinks*) **~s** amuse-gueule *mpl* ; (*in telling news etc*) **I've saved the ~ for the end** j'ai gardé le détail le plus croustillant pour la fin

titch* [tɪtʃ] N (*Brit*) microbe* *m*

titchy* ['tɪtʃɪ] ADJ (*Brit*) minuscule

titfer: ['tɪtfə'] N (*Brit = hat*) galurin *m*

tithe [taɪð] N dîme *f*

Titian ['tɪʃən] 1 N Titien *m* 2 ADJ **titian** blond vénitien *inv*

titillate ['tɪtɪleɪt] VT titiller, émoustiller

titillation [ˌtɪtɪ'leɪʃən] N titillation *f*

titivate ['tɪtɪveɪt] 1 VI se pomponner, se bichonner 2 VT bichonner, pomponner

title ['taɪtl] 1 N **a** [*of person*] titre *m* ; **what ~ should I give him?** comment dois-je l'appeler ? ; **I don't know his exact ~** je ne connais pas son titre exact ; **George III gave him a ~** Georges III lui a conféré un titre *or* l'a anobli ; **this earned him the ~ of "King of the Ring"** cela lui a valu le titre de « roi du ring » **b** (*Sport*) titre *m* ; **to win/hold the ~** remporter/détenir le titre ▶ **world** **c** [*of book etc*] titre *m* ; **under the ~ of ...** sous le titre de ... **d** (*Cine, TV*) **the ~s** (= *credit titles*) le générique ; (= *subtitles*) les sous-titres *mpl* **e** (*Jur*) droit *m*, titre *m* (**to sth** à qch) 2 VT [+ *book etc*] intituler 3 COMP ▶ **title deed** N titre *m* (constitutif) de propriété ▶ **title fight** N (*Boxing*) match *m* de championnat ▶ **title holder** N (*Sport*) détenteur *m*, -trice *f or* tenant(e) *m(f)* du titre ▶ **title page** N page *f* de titre ▶ **title role** N (*Cine, Theat*) rôle-titre *m* ▶ **title track** N chanson-titre *f*

titled ['taɪtld] ADJ [*person*] titré

titmouse ['tɪtmaʊs] N (*pl* **-mice**) mésange *f*

titrate ['taɪtreɪt] VT titrer (*Chem*)

titter ['tɪtə'] 1 VI rire sottement (**at** de), glousser 2 N gloussement *m*, petit rire *m* sot

tittle ['tɪtl] 1 N (*Typ*) signe *m* diacritique ; (= *particle*) brin *m*, iota *m* → **jot** 2 COMP ▶ **tittle-tattle** N (*NonC*) cancans *mpl*, potins *mpl* ♦ VI cancaner, jaser

titty: ['tɪtɪ] N néné: *m* ; **tough ~** *or* **titties!** pas de pot !*

titular ['tɪtjʊlə'] ADJ [*ruler, leader, power*] nominal ; [*possessions, estate*] titulaire

Titus ['taɪtəs] N Tite *m*

tizzy*, **tizz*** ['tɪzɪ] N affolement* *m*, panique* *f* ; **to be in/get into a ~** être/se mettre dans tous ses états

TLC [ˌtiːel'siː] (ABBR = **tender loving care**) → **tender**

TLS [ˌtiːel'es] N (*Brit*) (ABBR = **Times Literary Supplement**) *magazine littéraire*

TM [tiː'em] N (ABBR = **transcendental meditation**) → **transcendental** **b** (ABBR = **trademark**) MD

TN ABBR = **Tennessee**

TNT [ˌtiːen'tiː] N (ABBR = **trinitrotoluene**) TNT *m*

---

to [tuː, *(weak form)* tə]

1 PREPOSITION	3 COMPOUNDS
2 ADVERB	

1 PREPOSITION

When **to** *is the second element in a phrasal verb, eg* **apply to**, **set to**, *look up the verb. When* **to** *is part of a set combination, eg* **nice to**, **of help to**, **to my mind**, **to all appearances**, *look up the adjective or noun.*

a direction, movement à

à + le = au, **à + les = aux**.

he went to the door il est allé à la porte ; **to go to school** aller à l'école ; **we're going to the cinema** on va au cinéma ; **she's gone to the toilet** elle est allée aux toilettes ; *BUT* **he came over to where I was standing** il est venu jusqu'à moi ; **to go to town** aller en ville
• **to it** (= *there*) y ; **I liked the exhibition, I went to it twice** j'ai aimé l'exposition, j'y suis allé deux fois

b = towards vers ; **he walked slowly to the door** il s'est dirigé lentement vers la porte ; **he turned to me** il s'est tourné vers moi

c home, workplace chez ; **let's go to Christine's (house)** si on allait chez Christine ? ; **we're going to my parents' for Christmas** nous allons passer Noël chez mes parents ; **to go to the doctor('s)** aller chez le docteur

d with geographical names
• **to** + *fem country/area etc* en

Countries etc that end in **e** *are usually feminine.*
to England/France en Angleterre/France ; **to Brittany/Provence/Andalusia** en Bretagne/Provence/Andalousie ; **to Sicily/Crete** en Sicile/Crète ; **to Louisiana/Virginia** en Louisiane/Virginie ; **ambassador to France** ambassadeur en France

en is also used with masc countries beginning with a vowel:
to Iran/Israel en Iran/Israël

• **to** + *masc country/area* au ; **to Japan/Kuwait** au Japon/Koweït ; **to the Sahara/Kashmir** au Sahara/Cachemire

• **to** + *pl country/group of islands* aux ; **to the United States/the West Indies** aux États-Unis/ Antilles

• **to** + *town/island without article* à ; **to London/ Lyons** à Londres/Lyon ; **to Cuba/Malta** à Cuba/ Malte ; **on the way to Paris** en allant à Paris ; *BUT* **to le Havre** au Havre ; **is this the road to Newcastle?** est-ce que c'est la route de Newcastle ? ; **it is 90km to Paris** (= *from here to*)

nous sommes à 90 km de Paris ; (= *from there to*) c'est à 90 km de Paris ; **boats to and from Calais** les bateaux *mpl* à destination ou en provenance de Calais ; **planes to Heathrow** les vols *mpl* à destination de Heathrow

◆ **to** + *masc state/region/county* dans ; **to Texas/ Ontario** dans le Texas/l'Ontario ; **to Poitou/ Berry** dans le Poitou/le Berry ; **to Sussex/ Yorkshire** dans le Sussex/le Yorkshire

dans is also used with many départements:
to the Drôme/the Var dans la Drôme/le Var

e = up to jusqu'à ; **to count to 20** compter jusqu'à 20 ; **I didn't stay to the end** je ne suis pas resté jusqu'à la fin ; **from morning to night** du matin (jusqu')au soir ; *BUT* **it's correct to within a millimetre** c'est exact au millimètre près ; **from Monday to Friday** du lundi au vendredi ; **there were 50 to 60 people** il y avait de (de) 50 à 60 personnes, il y avait entre 50 et 60 personnes

f expressing indirect object à ; **to give sth to sb** donner qch à qn ; **"to my wife Anne"** « à ma femme, Anne » ; **we have spoken to the children about it** nous en avons parlé aux enfants

When a relative clause ends with **to**, *a different word order is required in French:*
the man I sold it to l'homme à qui *or* auquel je l'ai vendu

When translating **to** + *pronoun, look up the pronoun. The translation depends on whether it is stressed or unstressed.*
he was speaking to me il me parlait ; **he was speaking to ME** c'est à moi qu'il parlait

g in time phrases 20 (minutes) to two deux heures moins 20 ; **it's (a) quarter to/ten to** il est moins le quart/moins dix

h in ratios A is to B as C is to D A est à B ce que C est à D ; **the odds against it happening are a million to one** il y a une chance sur un million que ça se produise ; **he got a big majority (twenty votes to seven)** il a été élu à une large majorité (vingt voix contre sept) ; **they won by four (goals) to two** ils ont gagné quatre (buts) à deux ; **three men to a cell** trois hommes par cellule ; **200 people to the square km** 200 habitants au km carré ; **how many kilometres does it do to the litre?** combien consomme-t-elle de litres aux cent (kilomètres) ? ; **six francs to the dollar** six francs pour un dollar ; (*Math*) **three to the fourth** ◊ **three to the power four** trois (à la) puissance quatre

i = concerning that's all there is to it (= *it's easy*) ce n'est pas plus difficile que ça ; **you're not going, and that's all there is to it** (= *it's definite*) tu n'iras pas, un point c'est tout ; (*Comm*) **"to repairing cooker: 1,000 francs"** « remise en état d'une cuisinière : 1 000 F » ; (*Comm*) **"to services rendered"** « pour services rendus »

j = of de ; **the key to the front door** la clé de la porte d'entrée ; **assistant to the manager** adjoint *m* du directeur ; **wife to Mr Milton** épouse *f* de M. Milton ; *BUT* **he has been a good friend to us** il a été vraiment très gentil avec nous

k to my delight/surprise/shame à ma grande joie/surprise/honte

l infinitive to be être ; to eat manger ; **they didn't want to go** ils ne voulaient pas y aller ; **she refused to listen** elle n'a pas voulu écouter

A preposition may be required with the French infinitive, depending on what precedes it: look up the verb or adjective.
he refused to help me il a refusé de m'aider ; **we're ready to go** nous sommes prêts à partir ; **it was very good of him to come at such short notice** c'était très gentil de sa part de venir si rapidement

The French verb may take a clause, rather than the infinitive:
he was expecting me to help him il s'attendaient à ce que je l'aide

m infinitive expressing purpose pour; **well, to sum up** ... alors, pour résumer ...; **we are writing to inform you** ... nous vous écrivons pour vous informer que ...; **they have come to help us** ils sont venus pour nous aider

n to avoid repetition of vb

to is not translated when it stands for the infinitive: **he'd like me to come, but I don't want to** il voudrait que je vienne mais je ne veux pas; **I'll try to** j'essaierai; **yes, I'd love to** oui, volontiers; **I didn't mean to** je ne l'ai pas fait exprès; **I forgot to** j'ai oublié

o in exclamations **and then to be let down like that!** et tout ça pour que l'on nous laisse tomber comme ça!; **and to think he didn't mean a word of it!** et dire que pour lui ce n'étaient que des paroles en l'air!

2 ADVERB
= shut **to push the door to** entrouvrir la porte (en la poussant); **when the door is to** quand la porte est entrouverte

3 COMPOUNDS
► **-to-be** ADJ (*in compounds*) futur; **husband-to-be** futur mari *m* → **mother** ► **to-do*** N (*pl* **to-dos**) **he made a great to-do about lending me the car** il a fait toute une histoire pour me prêter la voiture; **she made a great to-do about it** elle en a fait tout un plat*; **what a to-do!** quelle histoire!, quelle affaire! ► **to-ing and fro-ing** N allées et venues *fpl*

toad [təʊd] **1** N crapaud *m* (*also fig*) **2** COMP ► **toad-in-the-hole** N (*Brit Culin*) *saucisses cuites au four dans de la pâte à crêpes*

toadstool ['təʊdstuːl] N champignon *m* vénéneux

toady ['təʊdɪ] **1** N flagorneur *m*, -euse *f*, lèche-bottes* *mf inv* **2** VI être flagorneur; **to ~ to sb** flagorner qn, flatter qn bassement, lécher les bottes de qn*

toadying ['təʊdɪɪŋ], **toadyism** ['təʊdɪɪzəm] N (*NonC*) flagornerie *f*

toast [təʊst] **1** N **a** (*NonC: Culin*) pain *m* grillé, toast *m*; **you've burnt the ~** tu as laissé brûler le pain *or* les toasts; **a piece** *or* **slice of ~** une tartine grillée, un (morceau de) toast, une rôtie *f*; **sardines on ~** sardines *fpl* sur toast *or* sur canapé; (*fig*) **you've got him on ~*** vous le tenez → **warm**
b (*= drink, speech*) toast *m*; **to drink a ~ to sb** porter un toast à qn *or* en l'honneur de qn, boire à la santé *or* au succès de qn; **they drank his ~ in champagne** ils lui ont porté un toast au champagne; **here's a ~ to all who** ... levons nos verres en l'honneur de tous ceux qui ...; **to propose** *or* **give a ~ to sb** porter un toast à qn *or* en l'honneur de qn; **she was the ~ of the town** elle était la coqueluche *or* la vedette de la ville
2 VT **a** [+ *bread etc*] griller (*faire*); **~ed cheese** toast *m* au fromage; (*fig*) **he was ~ing himself/his toes by the fire** il se chauffait/se rôtissait les pieds auprès du feu
b (*= propose toast to*) porter un toast à; (*= drink toast to*) [+ *person*] boire à la santé de *or* au succès de, porter un toast à; [+ *event, victory*] arroser (**with a**)
3 COMP ► **toasting fork** N fourchette *f* à griller le pain ► **toast rack** N porte-toasts *m inv*

toaster ['təʊstər] N grille-pain *m inv* (*électrique*)

toastie ['təʊstɪ] N ≈ croque-monsieur *m*

toastmaster ['təʊstmɑːstər] N animateur *m* pour réceptions et banquets

toasty ['təʊstɪ] **1** ADJ* bien chaud **2** N = **toastie**

tobacco [tə'bækəʊ] **1** N (*pl* **tobaccos** *or* **tobaccoes**) tabac *m* **2** COMP (*leaf, smoke, plantation, company*) de tabac; [*pouch*] à tabac; [*industry*] du tabac ► **tobacco jar** N pot *m* à

tabac ► **tobacco plant** N (*pied m de*) tabac *m* ► **tobacco planter** N planteur *m* de tabac

tobacconist [tə'bækənɪst] N (*esp Brit*) marchand(e) *m(f)* de tabac, buraliste *mf*; **~'s (shop)** (bureau *m or* débit *m* de) tabac *m*

Tobago [tə'beɪgəʊ] N Tobago → **Trinidad**

toboggan [tə'bɒgən] **1** N toboggan *m*, luge *f*; (*Sport*) luge *f* **2** VI (*also* **go ~ing**) faire du toboggan *or* de la luge; (*Sport*) luger; **he ~ed down the hill** il a descendu la colline en toboggan *or* en luge **3** COMP [*race*] de luge ► **toboggan run** N piste *f* de luge

toby jug ['təʊbɪ,dʒʌg] N chope *f* à effigie humaine

toccata [tə'kɑːtə] N toccata *f*

tocsin ['tɒksɪn] N tocsin *m*

tod: [tɒd] N (*Brit*) **on one's ~** tout seul (toute seule *f*)

today [tə'deɪ] **1** ADV **a** (*= this day*) aujourd'hui; **it rained all (day)*** il a plu toute la journée aujourd'hui; **later ~** plus tard dans la journée; **early ~** aujourd'hui de bonne heure; **earlier ~** en début de journée; (*Brit*) **~ week** ◊ **a week ~** aujourd'hui en huit; **I met her a week ago ~** ça fait une semaine aujourd'hui que je l'ai rencontrée; **what day is it ~?** quel jour sommes-nous aujourd'hui?; **what date is it ~?** on est le combien aujourd'hui?; **money! it's here ~ gone tomorrow** l'argent, ça va ça vient! (*fig*) **here ~, gone tomorrow fashion fads** des modes éphémères; **a lot of staff can be here ~, gone tomorrow** beaucoup d'employés peuvent arriver un jour et repartir le lendemain
b (*= nowadays*) aujourd'hui, de nos jours; **young people ~ have it easy** les jeunes d'aujourd'hui se la coulent douce*; **you can't sack anyone ~ without a good reason** aujourd'hui on ne peut renvoyer personne sans motif valable
2 N **a** aujourd'hui *m*; **what day is ~?** quel jour sommes-nous aujourd'hui?; **~ is Friday** aujourd'hui c'est vendredi; **what is ~'s date?** quelle est la date aujourd'hui?; **~ is the 4th** aujourd'hui c'est le 4; **~ is very wet** il pleut beaucoup aujourd'hui; **~ was a bad day for me** aujourd'hui ça a été une mauvaise journée pour moi; **~'s paper** le journal d'aujourd'hui
b (*= these days*) aujourd'hui *m*; **the writers of ~** les écrivains d'aujourd'hui

toddle ['tɒdl] **1** VI **a** [*child*] **to ~ in/out** *etc* entrer/sortir *etc* à pas hésitants; **he has begun to ~** ◊ **he is just toddling** il fait ses premiers pas **b** (* *hum*) (*= go*) aller; (*= stroll*) se balader*; (*= leave: also* **~ off**) se sauver*, se trotter*
2 N (*hum*) **to go for a ~:** aller faire un petit tour *or* une petite balade*

toddler ['tɒdlər] N tout(e) petit(e) *m(f)* (*qui commence à marcher*), bambin* *m*; **he's only a ~** il est encore tout petit; **she has one baby and one ~** elle a un bébé et un petit qui commence juste à marcher

toddy ['tɒdɪ] N ≈ grog *m*

todger: ['tɒdʒər] N (*Brit*) quéquette: *f*

TOE [tiːəʊ'iː] N (ABBR = **ton oil equivalent**) TEP *f* (*abrév de tonne équivalent pétrole*)

toe [təʊ] **1** N (*Anat*) orteil *m*, doigt *m* de pied; [*of sock, shoe*] bout *m*; **big/little ~** gros/petit orteil *m*; (*lit, fig*) **to tread** *or* **step on sb's ~s** marcher sur les pieds de qn; (*fig*) **to keep sb on his ~s** forcer qn à rester vigilant *or* alerte; (*fig*) **that will keep you on your ~s!** ça t'empêchera de t'endormir!, ça te fera travailler!; (*Brit hum*) **to turn up one's ~s*** (*= die*) passer l'arme à gauche; (*esp US fig*) **to go** *or* **stand ~ to ~ with sb** affronter qn; **there are scenes in the film that make your ~s curl** il y a des scènes dans ce film qui donnent la chair de poule → **tip¹**, **top¹**
2 VT (*= touch/push*) toucher/pousser du bout de l'orteil; **to ~ the line** *or* (*US*) **mark** (*in race*)

se ranger sur la ligne de départ; (*fig*) se mettre au pas, se plier; (*Pol*) **to ~ the party line** ne pas s'écarter de *or* suivre la ligne du parti
3 COMP ► **toe clip** N (*Cycling*) cale-pied *m inv* ► **toe-piece** N (*Ski*) butée *f*

toecap ['təʊkæp] N **reinforced ~** bout *m* renforcé (*de chaussure*)

-toed [təʊd] ADJ (*in compounds*) **three-toed** à trois orteils

TOEFL N (ABBR = **Test of English as a Foreign Language**) *examen d'anglais pour les étudiants étrangers voulant étudier dans des universités anglo-saxonnes*

toehold ['təʊhəʊld] N (*lit*) prise *f* (pour le pied); (*fig*) **to have a ~ in** ... avoir un pied dans ...

toenail ['təʊneɪl] N ongle *m* de l'orteil *or* du pied

toerag: ['təʊræg] N (*Brit*) sale con(ne): *m(f)*

toff: [tɒf] N (*Brit*) aristo: *mf*, dandy* *m*

toffee ['tɒfɪ] **1** N caramel *m* (au beurre); (*fig*) **he can't do it for ~*** il n'est pas fichu* de le faire **2** COMP ► **toffee-apple** N pomme *f* caramélisée ► **toffee-nosed:** ADJ (*Brit pej*) bêcheur*, qui fait du chiqué*

tofu ['təʊ,fuː, 'tɒ,fuː] N tofu *m*, fromage *m* de soja

tog* [tɒg] (*Brit*) **1** VT **to ~ up** *or* **out** nipper*, fringuer:; **to be all ~ged up** *or* **out (in one's best clothes)** être bien fringué: *or* sapé* **2** N (*Brit Measure*) indice d'isolation thermique d'une couette ou d'une couverture **3** **togs** NPL fringues: *fpl*

toga ['təʊgə] N toge *f*

together [tə'geðər]

*When **together** is an element in a phrasal verb, eg **bring together**, **get together**, **sleep together**, look up the verb.*

1 ADV **a** ensemble; **I've seen them ~** je les ai vus ensemble; (*fig*) **we're in this ~** nous sommes logés à la même enseigne; (*fig pej*) **they were both in it ~** ils avaient partie liée tous les deux; **you must keep ~** vous devez rester ensemble, vous ne devez pas vous séparer; **tie the ropes ~** nouez les cordes; **with what you bought yesterday that makes** ... avec ce que vous avez acheté hier ça fait ...; **(taken) ~ with the previous figures, these show that** ... ces chiffres, considérés conjointement avec les précédents, indiquent que ...; **he, ~ with his colleagues, accepted** ... lui, ainsi que ses collègues, a accepté ...; **if you look at the reports ~** si vous considérez les rapports conjointement; **they belong ~** [*objects*] ils vont ensemble; [*people*] ils sont faits l'un pour l'autre → **bang together**, **gather together**, **live together**
b (*= simultaneously*) en même temps, simultanément; [*sing, play, recite*] à l'unisson; **the shots were fired ~** les coups de feu ont été tirés simultanément *or* en même temps; **they both stood up ~** ils se sont tous les deux levés en même temps; **don't all speak ~** ne parlez pas tous à la fois; **all ~ now!** (*shouting, singing*) tous en chœur maintenant!; (*pulling*) (oh!) hisse!; (*Mus*) **you're not ~** vous n'êtes pas à l'unisson
c (*= continuously*) **for days/weeks ~** (*pendant*) des jours entiers/des semaines entières; **for five weeks ~** (*pendant*) cinq semaines de suite *or* d'affilée
d (* *fig*) **to get it ~** ◊ **to get one's act ~** s'organiser; **let's get it ~** il faut qu'on s'organise, il faut qu'on essaie d'y voir plus clair; **she's got it ~** c'est quelqu'un d'équilibré
2 ADJ (* *= well adjusted*) [*person*] équilibré; **a ~ person** quelqu'un d'équilibré

togetherness [tə'geðənɪs] N (*NonC*) (*= unity*) unité *f*; (*= friendliness*) camaraderie *f*

toggle ['tɒgl] **1** N (*Naut*) cabillot *m*; (*on garment*) bouton *m* de duffel-coat **2** COMP ► **toggle joint** N (*Tech*) genouillère *f*

► **toggle key** N (*Comput*) touche *f* à bascule ► **toggle switch** N (*Elec*) interrupteur *m* à bascule

Togo ['təʊgəʊ] N le Togo

toil¹ [tɔɪl] **1** N (*NonC*) travail *m*, labeur *m* (*liter*) **2** VI **a** (= *work hard: also* ~ **away**) travailler dur (**at, over** à, **to do** pour faire), peiner (**at, over** sur, **to do** pour faire) **b** (= *move with difficulty*) **to ~ along/up** *etc* [*person, animal, vehicle*] avancer/monter *etc* péniblement *or* avec peine

toil² [tɔɪl] N (*fig liter* = *snare, net*) **~s** rets *mpl*; (*fig*) **in the ~s of ...** dans les rets de ...

toilet ['tɔɪlɪt] **1** N **a** (= *lavatory*) toilettes *fpl*, W.-C. *mpl*; "**Toilets**" « Toilettes »; **to go to the ~** aller aux toilettes *or* aux W.-C.; **to put sth down the ~** jeter qch dans la cuvette des cabinets **b** (= *dressing etc*, *dress*) toilette *f* **2** COMP ► **toilet bag** N trousse *f* de toilette ► **toilet bowl** N cuvette *f* (des cabinets) ► **toilet case** N = **toilet bag** ► **toilet humour** N (*pej*) humour *m* scatologique ► **toilet paper** N papier *m* hygiénique ► **toilet requisites** NPL (*Comm*) articles *mpl* de toilette ► **toilet roll** N rouleau *m* de papier hygiénique ► **toilet seat** N siège *m or* lunette *f* des cabinets *or* W.-C. *or* toilettes ► **toilet soap** N savonnette *f*, savon *m* de toilette ► **toilet table** N table *f* de toilette ► **toilet tissue** N = **toilet paper** ► **toilet-train** VT **to ~-train a child** apprendre à un enfant à être propre ► **toilet training** N apprentissage *m* de la propreté ► **toilet water** N eau *f* de toilette

toiletries ['tɔɪlɪtrɪz] NPL articles *mpl* de toilette

toilette [twɑː'let] N = **toilet 1b**

toilsome ['tɔɪlsəm] ADJ (*liter*) pénible, épuisant

toke [təʊk] N (*Drugs*) bouffée *f*

▼ **token** ['təʊkən] **1** N **a** (= *sign, symbol*) marque *f*, témoignage *m*, gage *m*; (= *keepsake*) souvenir *m*; (= *metal disc: for travel, telephone etc*) jeton *m*; (= *voucher, coupon*) bon *m*, coupon *m*; (*also* **gift ~**) bon-cadeau *m*; **milk ~** bon *m* de lait; **as a ~ of** *or* **in ~ of** en témoignage de, en gage de; (*fig*) **by the same ~** de même → **book, record** **b** (*Ling*) occurrence *f* **2** ADJ [*payment, wage, strike, resistance, military presence*] symbolique; [*attempt, effort, appearance*] pour la forme; (*pej*) [*woman etc*] de service; **a ~ gesture** un geste symbolique; **I was the ~ pensioner on the committee** j'étais le retraité alibi *or* le retraité de service au comité; **she said she's not just a ~ woman** elle a dit qu'elle n'était pas simplement une femme alibi **3** COMP ► **token vote** N (*Parl*) vote *m* de crédits (*dont le montant n'est pas définitivement fixé*)

tokenism ['təʊkənɪzəm] N politique *f* de pure forme

Tokyo ['təʊkjəʊ] N Tokyo

told [təʊld] VB *pt, ptp of* **tell**

Toledo [tɒ'leɪdəʊ] N Tolède

tolerable ['tɒlərəbl] ADJ **a** (= *bearable*) tolérable, supportable **b** (= *adequate*) assez bon; **the food is ~** on y mange passablement, on n'y mange pas trop mal

tolerably ['tɒlərəblɪ] ADV [*good, comfortable, happy*] relativement; **~ well** relativement bien; **he plays ~ (well)** il joue passablement, il joue relativement bien

tolerance ['tɒlərəns] N (*gen*) tolérance *f*, indulgence *f*; (*Med, Tech*) tolérance *f*

tolerant ['tɒlərənt] ADJ **a** (= *sympathetic*) [*person, society, attitude*] tolérant (**of sb/sth** à l'égard de qn/qch); (*Phys, Med*) ~ **of heat** résistant à la chaleur; **~ to light/a toxin** résistant à la lumière/à une toxine; **to be ~ to a drug** tolérer un médicament

tolerantly ['tɒlərəntlɪ] ADV [*smile*] avec indulgence; [*listen*] patiemment

▼ **tolerate** ['tɒləreɪt] VT [+ *heat, pain*] supporter; [+ *insolence, injustice*] tolérer, supporter; (*Med, Tech*) tolérer

toleration [,tɒlə'reɪʃən] N (*NonC*) tolérance *f*

toll¹ [təʊl] **1** N (= *tax, charge*) péage *m*; (*fig*) **the war took a heavy ~ of** *or* **among the young men** la guerre a fait beaucoup de victimes parmi les jeunes, les jeunes ont payé un fort tribut à la guerre; **it took (a) great ~ of his strength** cela a sérieusement ébranlé *or* sapé ses forces; **it took a ~ of his savings** cela a fait un gros trou dans ses économies; **we must reduce the accident ~ on the roads** il nous faut réduire le nombre des victimes de la route; **the ~ of dead and injured has risen** le nombre des morts et des blessés a augmenté **2** COMP ► **toll bridge** N pont *m* à péage ► **toll call** N (*US Telec*) appel *m* longue distance ► **toll charge** N péage *m* ► **toll-free** ADV (*US Telec*) sans payer la communication ♦ ADJ gratuit; **~-free number** ≈ numéro *m* vert ► **toll road** N route *f* à péage → ROADS

toll² [təʊl] **1** VI [*bell*] sonner; **for whom the bell ~s** pour qui sonne le glas **2** VT [+ *bell, the hour*] sonner; [+ *sb's death*] sonner le glas pour

tollbar ['təʊlbɑːʳ] N barrière *f* de péage

tollbooth ['təʊlbuːð] N poste *m* de péage

tolley ['tɒlɪ] N (= *marble*) calot *m*

tollgate ['təʊlgeɪt] N = **tollbar**

tollhouse ['təʊlhaʊs] N maison *f* de péagiste

tollkeeper ['təʊlkiːpəʳ] N péagiste *mf*

tollway ['təʊlweɪ] N = **toll road**; → **toll¹**

Tolstoy ['tɒlstɔɪ] N Tolstoï *m*

Tom [tɒm] **1** N **a** (*dim of* **Thomas**) Thomas *m*; (*fig*) **(any) ~, Dick or Harry** n'importe qui, le premier venu → **peep¹** **b** (*US pej: also* **Uncle ~**) Oncle Tom *m*, bon nègre *m* **2** COMP ► **Tom Thumb** N Tom-Pouce *m*; (*in French tale*) le Petit Poucet

tom [tɒm] **1** N matou *m* **2** COMP ► **tom cat** N (= *cat*) matou *m*; (*US* = *man*) coureur *m* de jupons, cavaleur* *m*

tomahawk ['tɒməhɔːk] N tomahawk *m*, hache *f* de guerre

tomato [tə'mɑːtəʊ, (*US*) tə'meɪtəʊ] **1** N (*pl* **tomatoes**) (= *fruit, plant*) tomate *f* **2** COMP ► **tomato juice** N jus *m* de tomate ► **tomato ketchup** N ketchup *m* ► **tomato paste** N = **tomato purée** ► **tomato plant** N tomate *f* ► **tomato purée** N purée *f* de tomates ► **tomato sauce** N sauce *f* tomate ► **tomato soup** N soupe *f* de tomates

tomb [tuːm] N tombeau *m*, tombe *f*

tombac, tombak ['tɒmbæk] N (*NonC*) tombac *m*, laiton *m*

tombola [tɒm'bəʊlə] N (*Brit*) tombola *f*

tomboy ['tɒmbɔɪ] N garçon *m* manqué

tomboyish ['tɒmbɔɪɪʃ] ADJ de garçon manqué

tomboyishness ['tɒmbɔɪɪʃnɪs] N (*NonC*) manières *fpl* de garçon manqué

tombstone ['tuːmstəʊn] N pierre *f* tombale, tombe *f*

tome [təʊm] N tome *m*, gros volume *m*

tomfool ['tɒm'fuːl] ADJ absurde, idiot

tomfoolery ['tɒm'fuːlərɪ] N (*NonC*) niaiserie(s) *f(pl)*, âneries *fpl*

Tommy ['tɒmɪ] **1** N (*dim of* **Thomas**) Thomas *m*; (*Brit Mil*: *also* **tommy**) tommy* *m*, soldat *m* britannique **2** COMP ► **Tommy gun** N mitraillette *f*

tommyrot† ['tɒmɪrɒt] N (*NonC*) bêtises *fpl*, âneries *fpl*

tomography [tə'mɒgrəfɪ] N tomographie *f*

tomorrow [tə'mɒrəʊ] **1** ADV demain; **all (day) ~** toute la journée (de) demain; **late ~** tard demain; **early ~** demain de bonne heure; **~ lunchtime** demain à midi; **I met her a**

week ago ~ ça fera une semaine demain que je l'ai vue; **he'll have been here a week ~** demain cela fera huit jours qu'il est là; **see you ~** à demain; **what day will it be ~?** quel jour sera-t-on *or* serons-nous demain?; **what date will it be ~?** on sera le combien demain? → **today** **2** N **a** demain *m*; **what day will ~ be?** quel jour serons-nous demain?; **~ will be Saturday** demain ce sera samedi; **what date will ~ be?** quelle est la date de demain?; **~ will be the 5th** demain ce sera le 5; **I hope ~ will be dry** j'espère qu'il ne pleuvra pas demain; **~ will be a better day for you** demain les choses iront mieux pour vous; **~ never comes** demain n'arrive jamais; **~ is another day!** ça ira peut-être mieux demain!; **~'s paper** le journal de demain **b** (= *the future*) **the writers of ~** les écrivains *mpl* de demain *or* de l'avenir; **like ~ as if there was no ~** [*spend, drive*] sans se soucier du lendemain; [*eat, drink*] comme si c'était la dernière fois; **brighter ~s** des lendemains qui chantent **3** COMP ► **tomorrow afternoon** ADV demain après-midi ► **tomorrow evening** ADV demain soir ► **tomorrow morning** ADV demain matin ► **tomorrow week*** ADV (*Brit*) demain en huit

tomtit ['tɒmtɪt] N mésange *f*

tomtom ['tɒmtɒm] N tam-tam *m*

ton [tʌn] **1** N **a** (= *weight*) tonne *f* (*Brit* = 1016,06 kg; *Can, US etc* = 907,20 kg) **metric ~** tonne *f* (= 1 000 kg); **a seven-~ truck** un camion de sept tonnes; (*fig*) **it weighs a ~** c'est une ~ **weight** ça pèse une tonne; (*fig*) **~s of** beaucoup de, des tas de* **b** (*Naut*) (*also* **register ~**) tonneau *m* (= 2,83 m³); (*also* **displacement ~**) tonne *f*; **a 60,000-~ steamer** un paquebot de 60 000 tonnes **c** (‡ = *hundred*) **a ~** cent; (*Aut etc*) **to do a ~ (up)**‡ faire du cent soixante à l'heure **2** COMP ► **ton-up boys**†‡ NPL (*Brit* = *motorcyclists*) motards* *mpl*, fous *mpl* de la moto

tonal ['təʊnl] **1** ADJ **a** (= *vocal*) [*range, contrast*] tonal; **~ quality** tonalité *f* **b** (*in colour*) [*range, contrast*] de tons **2** COMP ► **tonal music** N musique *f* tonale ► **tonal value** N (*Phot*) tonalité *f*

tonality [təʊ'nælɪtɪ] N tonalité *f*

tondo ['tɒndəʊ] N (*pl* **tondi** ['tɒndiː]) tondo *m*

tone [təʊn] **1** N (*in sound: also* Ling, Mus) ton *m*; (*Telec: also of radio, record player etc*) tonalité *f*; [*of answering machine*] signal *m* sonore, bip *m* (sonore); [*of musical instrument*] sonorité *f*; **to speak in low ~s** *or* **in a low ~** parler à voix basse *or* doucement; **to speak in angry ~s** ◊ **to speak in an angry ~** (of voice) parler sur le ton de la colère; **don't speak to me in that ~ (of voice)!** ne me parlez pas sur ce ton!; **in friendly ~s** ◊ **in a friendly ~** sur un ton amical; (*on answering machine*) **after the ~** après le bip *or* le signal sonore; (*Ling*) **rising/falling ~** ton *m* montant/descendant → **dialling, engaged** **b** (*in colour*) ton *m*; **two-~** en deux tons **c** (= *general character*) ton *m*; **what was the ~ of his letter?** quel était le ton de sa lettre?; **we were impressed by the whole ~ of the school** nous avons été impressionnés par la tenue générale de l'école; (*Fin*) **the ~ of the market** la tenue du marché; **to raise/lower the ~ of sth** rehausser/rabaisser le ton de qch **d** (*NonC* = *class, elegance*) classe *f*; **it gives the restaurant ~** ◊ **it adds ~ to the restaurant** cela donne de la classe au restaurant **e** (*Med, Physiol: of muscles etc*) tonus *m*, tonicité *f* **2** VI [*colour*] s'harmoniser (**with** avec) **3** COMP ► **tone arm** N [*of record player*] bras *m* de lecture ► **tone colour** N (*Mus*) timbre *m* ► **tone control (knob)** N [*of record player etc*] bouton *m* de tonalité ► **tone-deaf** ADJ

to be ~-deaf ne pas avoir d'oreille ► **tone deafness** N manque *m* d'oreille ► **tone language** N (*Ling*) langue *f* à tons ► **tone poem** N poème *m* symphonique ► **tone row, tone series** N (*Mus*) série *f* (de notes)

► **tone down** VT SEP [+ *colour*] adoucir; [+ *sound*] baisser; (*fig*) [+ *criticism, effect*] atténuer, adoucir; [+ *language*] atténuer, modérer; [+ *policy*] modérer, mettre en sourdine

► **tone in** VI s'harmoniser (**with** avec)

► **tone up** VT SEP [+ *muscles, the system*] tonifier

-toned [təʊnd] ADJ (*in compounds*) **flesh-toned** couleur chair *inv*; **high-toned** [*style, book etc*] prétentieux; **sepia-toned** couleur sépia *inv*; **warm-toned** [*colour, skin*] au tons chauds

toneless [ˈtəʊnlɪs] ADJ [*voice*] blanc (blanche *f*), sans timbre

tonelessly [ˈtəʊnlɪslɪ] ADV d'une voix blanche or sans timbre

toner [ˈtəʊnəʳ] N [a] (*for photocopier, printer*) encre *f*, toner *m* [b] (*for skin*) (lotion *f*) tonique *m*

Tonga [ˈtɒŋə] N Tonga, les Tonga *fpl*

tongs [tɒŋz] NPL (*also* **pair of ~**) pinces *fpl*; (*for coal*) pincettes *fpl*; (*for sugar*) pince *f* (à sucre); (*also* **curling ~**) fer *m* (à friser) → **hammer**

tongue [tʌŋ] N [1] [a] (*Anat, Culin*) langue *f*; [*of shoe*] languette *f*; [*of bell*] battant *m*; (*fig: of flame, land, also on tool, machine etc*) langue *f*; **to put out** or **stick out one's ~** tirer la langue (**at sb** à qn); **his ~ was hanging out** [*dog, person*] il tirait la langue; **to give ~** [*hounds*] donner de la voix; (*fig*) **to lose/find one's ~** perdre/retrouver sa langue; **with his ~ in his cheek** ◊ **~ in cheek** ironiquement, en plaisantant; **he held his ~ about it** il a tenu sa langue; **hold your ~!** taisez-vous!; **I'm going to let him feel** or **give him the rough side of my ~†** je vais lui dire ma façon de penser; **keep a civil ~ in your head!** tâchez d'être plus poli!; (*fig*) **I can't get my ~ round it** je n'arrive pas à le prononcer correctement → **cat, loosen, slip, tip[1], wag[1]** [b] (= *language*) langue *f*; (*Rel*) **to speak in ~s** parler de nouvelles langues → **mother** [2] VT (*Mus*) [+ *note*] attaquer en coup de langue [3] COMP ► **tongue-and-groove** N (*Carpentry*) → **tongue-and-groove** ► **tongue depressor** N (*Med*) abaisse-langue *m* ► **tongue-in-cheek** ADJ [*remark etc*] ironique → **1** ► **tongue-lashing*** N **to give sb a ~-lashing** sonner les cloches à qn*; **to get a ~-lashing** se faire remonter les bretelles* ► **tongue-tied** ADJ (*fig*) muet (*fig*); **~-tied from shyness** rendu muet par la timidité, trop timide pour parler ► **tongue twister** N phrase *f* (or nom *m* etc) très difficile à prononcer

tongue-and-groove [ˈtʌŋɡənˈɡruːv] [1] N (*also* **~ boarding** or **strips**) planches *fpl* à rainure et languette; **~ joint** assemblage *m* à rainure et languette [2] VT [+ *wall*] revêtir de planches à rainure et languette

-tongued [tʌŋd] ADJ (*in compounds*) qui a la langue ...; **sharp-tongued** qui a la langue acérée

tonguing [ˈtʌŋɪŋ] N (*Mus*) (technique *f* du) coup *m* de langue

tonic [ˈtɒnɪk] [1] ADJ [a] (= *reviving*) [*bath, properties, drink*] tonifiant; [*effect*] tonique [b] (*Mus, Ling*) tonique [2] N [a] (*Med*) tonique *m*, fortifiant *m*; (*lit, fig*) **you need a ~** il vous faut un bon tonique; (*fig*) **it was a real ~ to see him** cela m'a vraiment remonté le moral de le voir [b] (*also* **~ water, Indian ~**) ≈ Schweppes® *m*; **gin and ~** gin-tonic *m* [c] (*Mus*) tonique *f* [3] COMP ► **tonic sol-fa** N (*Mus*) solfège *m* ► **tonic water** N (*also* **Indian ~ water**) tonic *m*, ≈ Schweppes® *m* → **2b** ► **tonic wine** N vin *m* tonique

tonicity [tɒˈnɪsɪtɪ] N tonicité *f*

tonight [təˈnaɪt] ADV, N (*before bed*) ce soir; (*during sleep*) cette nuit

tonnage [ˈtʌnɪdʒ] N (*Naut: all senses*) tonnage *m*

tonne [tʌn] N tonne *f*

tonneau [ˈtʌnəʊ] N (*pl* **tonneaus** or **tonneaux** [ˈtʌnəʊz]) (*Aut: also* **~ cover**) bâche *f* (*de voiture de sport*)

-tonner [ˈtʌnəʳ] N (*in compounds*) **a ten-tonner** (= *truck*) un (camion de) dix tonnes

tonometer [təʊˈnɒmɪtəʳ] N (*Mus*) diapason *m* de Scheibler; (*Med*) tonomètre *m*

tonsil [ˈtɒnsl] N amygdale *f*; **to have one's ~s out** or **removed** être opéré des amygdales

tonsillectomy [ˌtɒnsɪˈlektəmɪ] N amygdalectomie *f*

tonsillitis [ˌtɒnsɪˈlaɪtɪs] N (*NonC*) angine *f*, amygdalite *f*; **he's got ~** il a une angine, il a une amygdalite (*frm*)

tonsorial [tɒnˈsɔːrɪəl] ADJ (*hum*) de barbier

tonsure [ˈtɒnʃəʳ] [1] N tonsure *f* [2] VT tonsurer

tontine [tɒnˈtiːn] N tontine *f*

Tony [ˈtəʊnɪ] N [a] (*dim of* **Anthony**) Antoine *m* [b] (*Theat*) (*pl* **Tonys** or **Tonies**) (*also* **~ award**) Tony *m* (*oscar du théâtre décerné à Broadway*)

too [tuː] ADV [a] (= *excessively*) trop, par trop (*liter*); **it's ~ hard for me** c'est trop difficile pour moi; **it's ~ hard for me to explain** c'est trop difficile pour que je puisse vous l'expliquer; **that case is ~ heavy to carry** cette valise est trop lourde à porter; **it's ~ heavy for me to carry** c'est trop lourd à porter pour moi; **he's ~ mean to pay for it** il est trop pingre pour le payer; **that's ~ kind of you!** vous êtes vraiment trop aimable!; **I'm not ~ sure about that** je n'en suis pas très certain; **~ true!*** ◊ **~ right!*** que oui!*, et comment!*; **it's just ~-~!*** en voilà un chichi!* → **good, many, much, none**
[b] (= *also*) aussi; (= *moreover*) en plus, par-dessus le marché, de plus; **I went ~** moi aussi j'y suis allé; **you ~ can own a car like this** vous aussi vous pouvez être le propriétaire d'une voiture comme celle-ci; **HE can swim ~** lui aussi sait nager; **he can SWIM ~** il sait nager aussi, il sait aussi or également nager; **they asked for a discount ~!** et en plus or et par-dessus le marché ils ont ont demandé un rabais!; **and then, ~, there's the question of ...** et puis il y a également la question de ...

took [tʊk] VB *pt of* **take**

tool [tuːl] [1] N (*gen, Tech*) outil *m* (de travail); (*fig = book etc*) outil *m*, instrument *m*; **set of ~s** panoplie *f* d'outils; **garden ~s** outils *mpl* or ustensiles *mpl* de jardinage; (*lit, fig*) **these are the ~s of my trade** voilà les outils de mon métier; **he was merely a ~ of the revolutionary party** il n'était que l'outil or l'instrument du parti révolutionnaire; (*fig*) **a ~ in the hands of ...** un instrument dans les mains de ... → **down[1], machine, workman** [2] VT (*gen*) travailler, ouvrager; [+ *silver*] ciseler; [+ *leather*] repousser [3] VI (*Aut*) **to ~ along/past*** rouler/ passer tranquillement or pépère* [4] COMP ► **tool maker** N (*Ind*) outilleur *m* ► **tool making** N (*Ind*) montage *m* et réglage *m* des machines-outils

► **tool up** [1] VT SEP (*Ind*) équiper, outiller [2] VI [*factory etc*] s'équiper, s'outiller; (*fig*) se préparer

toolbag [ˈtuːlbæɡ] N trousse *f* à outils

toolbox [ˈtuːlbɒks] N boîte *f* à outils

toolcase [ˈtuːlkeɪs] N (= *bag*) trousse *f* à outils; (= *box*) caisse *f* à outils

toolchest [ˈtuːltʃest] N coffre *m* à outils

tooled [tuːld] ADJ (*gen*) ouvragé; [*silver*] ciselé; [*leather*] repoussé; [*book cover*] en cuir repoussé

toolhouse [ˈtuːlhaʊs] N = **toolshed**

tooling [ˈtuːlɪŋ] N (*on book-cover etc*) repoussé *m*; (*on silver*) ciselure *f*

toolkit [ˈtuːlkɪt] N trousse à outils; (*Comput*) valise *f*

toolroom [ˈtuːlruːm] N (*Ind*) atelier *m* d'outillage

toolshed [ˈtuːlʃed] N cabane *f* à outils

toot [tuːt] [1] N [*of car horn*] coup *m* de klaxon®; [*of whistle*] coup *m* de sifflet; [*of trumpet, flute*] note *f* (brève) [2] VI [*car horn*] klaxonner; (*on whistle*) donner un coup de sifflet; (*on trumpet, flute*) jouer une note [3] VT (*Aut*) **to ~ the horn** klaxonner

tooth [tuːθ] [1] N (*pl* **teeth**) [*of person, animal, comb, saw etc*] dent *f*; **front ~** dent *f* de devant; **back ~** molaire *f*; **to have a ~ out** or (*esp US*) **pulled** se faire arracher une dent; (*US*) **selling a car these days is like pulling teeth** c'est pratiquement impossible de vendre une voiture en ce moment; **to have a ~ capped** se faire poser une couronne; **to cut a ~** [*child*] percer une dent; **he is cutting teeth** il fait ses dents; (*fig*) **to cut one's teeth on sth** se faire les dents sur qch; **to mutter sth between one's teeth** or **between clenched teeth** grommeler qch entre ses dents; **to set** or **grit one's teeth** serrer les dents; **to bare** or **show one's teeth** montrer les dents; **in the teeth of the wind** contre le vent; **in the teeth of the opposition** en dépit de or malgré l'opposition; **~ and nail** avec acharnement, farouchement; (*fig*) **to get one's teeth into sth** se mettre à fond à qch, se mettre à faire qch pour de bon; **there's nothing you can get your teeth into** [*food etc*] ce n'est pas très substantiel; (*fig*) il n'y a rien de substantiel or solide; (*fig*) **the legislation has no teeth** la législation est impuissante; (*fig*) **to give a law teeth** renforcer le pouvoir d'une loi; (*fig*) **to cast** or **throw sth in sb's teeth** jeter qch à la tête de qn, reprocher qch à qn; **to be fed up** or **sick to the (back) teeth of sth‡** en avoir marre* or ras le bol‡ de qch → **chatter, edge, long[1]**
[2] COMP ► **tooth decay** N (*NonC*) carie *f* dentaire ► **the Tooth Fairy** N ≈ la petite souris ► **tooth powder** N poudre *f* dentifrice

toothache [ˈtuːθeɪk] N mal *m* or rage *f* de dents; **to have ~** avoir mal aux dents

toothbrush [ˈtuːθbrʌʃ] [1] N brosse *f* à dents [2] COMP ► **toothbrush moustache** N moustache *f* en brosse

toothcomb [ˈtuːθkəʊm] N (*also* **fine ~**) → **fine[2]**

toothed [tuːθt] ADJ [*wheel, leaf*] denté

-toothed [tuːθt] ADJ (*in compounds*) **big-toothed** aux grandes dents

toothless [ˈtuːθlɪs] ADJ [a] (= *without teeth*) [*person, smile, grin*] édenté; [*mouth, gums*] sans dents [b] (*fig* = *powerless*) [*organization*] sans pouvoir, sans influence; [*law, agreement, treaty*] qui n'a pas de poids; **a ~ tiger** un tigre de papier

toothpaste [ˈtuːθpeɪst] N (pâte *f*) dentifrice *m*

toothpick [ˈtuːθpɪk] N cure-dent *m*

toothsome [ˈtuːθsəm] ADJ savoureux, succulent

toothy [ˈtuːθɪ] ADJ [*person*] à grandes dents; **to be ~** avoir de grandes dents; **he flashed me a ~ grin** or **smile** il m'a gratifié d'un sourire tout en dents

tootle [ˈtuːtl] [1] N [*of trumpet, flute, car-horn*] notes *fpl* (brèves); (= *tune*) petit air *m* [2] VI [a] (= *toot: Aut*) klaxonner, corner; (*Mus*) jouer un petit air [b] (*Aut*) **to ~ along/past** etc* rouler/passer etc gaiement or sans s'en faire* [3] VT [+ *trumpet, flute etc*] jouer un peu de

toots‡ [tʊts] N ma belle*

tootsie⁑, tootsy⁑ [ˈtʊtsɪ] N 〔a〕 (= *toe*) doigt *m* de pied; (= *foot*) peton* *m*, pied *m* 〔b〕 (= *girl*) jolie nana⁑ *f*; **hi ~!** salut ma belle!*

---

top¹ [tɒp]

1	NOUN	5	TRANSITIVE VERB
2	PLURAL NOUN	6	COMPOUNDS
3	ADVERB	7	PHRASAL VERBS
4	ADJECTIVE		

1 NOUN

〔a〕 **= highest point** [*of mountain*] sommet *m*, cime *f*; [*of tree*] faîte *m*, cime *f*; [*of hill, head*] sommet *m*, haut *m*; [*of ladder, stairs, page, wall, cupboard*] haut *m*; [*of wave*] crête *f*; [*of box, container*] dessus *m*; [*of list, table, classification*] tête *f*; (= *surface*) surface *f*; **it's near the ~ of the pile** c'est vers le haut de la pile; **to come or rise or float to the ~** remonter à la surface, surnager; **the ~ of the milk** la crème du lait; **six lines from the ~ of page seven** sixième ligne à partir du haut de la page sept; (*fig*) **from ~ to toe** ◊ allons du haut de ses toes de la tête aux pieds; **he's talking off the ~ of his head*** il dit n'importe quoi; **I'm saying that off the ~ of my head*** je dis ça sans savoir exactement; (*Ir*) **the ~ of the morning to you!** je vous souhaite bien le bonjour!; (*Brit Aut*) **in ~ = in top gear** → 6; (*indicating status*) **to get to or reach the ~** arriver en haut *or* (*gen*) réussir, aller loin; (*in hierarchy etc*) arriver en haut de l'échelle; **it's ~ of the pops this week** c'est en tête du hit-parade *or* numéro un au hit-parade cette semaine; **the men at the ~** les dirigeants *mpl*, les responsables *mpl*, ceux qui sont au pouvoir; **the men at the ~ don't care about it** en haut lieu ils ne s'en soucient guère

• **at the top of** [+ *hill, mountain*] au sommet de; [+ *stairs, ladder, building, page*] en haut de; [+ *list, division, league*] en tête de; [+ *street etc*] en haut de, au bout de; [+ *garden*] au fond de; [+ *profession, career*] au faîte de; **he was sitting at the ~ of the table** il était assis en tête de la table *or* à la place d'honneur; **it's at the ~ of the pile** c'est en haut *or* au sommet de la pile; (*fig*) **at the ~ of the pile*** *or* **heap*** en haut de l'échelle; (*Scol*) **to be at the ~ of the class** être premier de la classe

• **on (the) top (of): on ~ of it** ◊ **on (the) ~** dessus; **it's the one on (the) ~** c'est celui du dessus; **take the plate on the ~** prends l'assiette du dessus; (*fig*) **he came out on ~** il a eu le dessus; **there was a thick layer of cream on ~ of the cake** il y avait une épaisse couche de crème sur le gâteau; **to live on ~ of each other** vivre les uns sur les autres; **in such a small flat the children are always on ~ of us** dans un appartement si petit, les enfants sont toujours dans nos jambes; **to be on ~ of the world** être aux anges; **to be on ~ of one's form** être au sommet de sa forme; **he's on ~ of things now*** il s'en sort très bien *or* il domine bien la situation maintenant; (*after breakdown, bereavement*) il a repris le dessus maintenant; **things are getting on ~ of her*** elle est dépassée par les événements, elle ne sait plus où donner de la tête; (*fig*) **the lorry was right on ~ of the car in front** le camion touchait presque la voiture de devant; **by the time I saw the car, it was practically on ~ of me** quand j'ai vu la voiture elle était pratiquement sur moi; **he's bought another car on ~ of the one he's got already** il a acheté une autre voiture en plus de celle qu'il a déjà; **then on ~ of all that he refused to help us** et puis par-dessus le marché il a refusé de nous aider

• **from top to bottom** [*redecorate*] complètement, du sol au plafond; [*clean*] de fond en comble; [*cover*] entièrement; [*divide, split*] [+ *political party*] profondément; [*search a person*] de la tête aux pieds; [*search a house*] de fond en comble; **the system is rotten from ~ to bottom** le système tout entier est pourri

• **over the top** (*Mil*) **to go over the ~** monter à l'assaut; (*esp Brit: indicating exaggeration*) **to be**

over the ~ [*film, book*] dépasser la mesure; [*person*] en faire trop*, exagérer; [*act, opinion*] être excessif

〔b〕 **= upper part, section** [*of car etc*] toit *m*; [*of bus*] étage *m* supérieur, impériale *f*; [*of turnip, carrot, radish*] fanes *fpl*; (*on box etc*) **"~"** « haut »; (*on bus*) **seats on ~** places *fpl* à l'étage supérieur; **we saw London from the ~ of a bus** nous avons vu Londres du haut d'un bus; **let's go up on ~** (*in bus*) allons en haut; (*in ship*) allons sur le pont; **the table ~ is made of oak** le plateau de la table est en chêne; **the ~ of the table is scratched** le dessus de la table est rayé; **he hasn't got much up ~*** (= *he is bald*) il a le crâne déplumé*; **she hasn't got much up ~*** (= *she is stupid*) ce n'est pas une lumière*; (= *she is flat-chested*) elle est plate comme une limande* *or* une planche à repasser*

〔c〕 *of garment, pyjamas, bikini* haut *m*; **I want a ~ to go with this skirt** je voudrais un haut qui aille avec cette jupe

〔d〕 **= cap, lid** [*of box*] couvercle *m*; [*of bottle, tube*] bouchon *m*; [*of pen*] capuchon *m*

2 tops* NPL **he's (the) ~s** il est champion*

3 tops ADV **= max** à tout casser*

4 ADJECTIVE

〔a〕 **= highest** [*shelf, drawer*] du haut; [*floor, storey*] dernier; **the ~ coat** [*of paint*] la dernière couche; **the ~ corridor of the main building** le corridor du haut dans le bâtiment principal; **at the ~ end of the scale** en haut de l'échelle; **a car at the ~ end of the range** une voiture haut de gamme; **the ~ layer of skin** la couche supérieure de la peau; (*Mus*) **the ~ note** la note la plus haute; **the ~ step** la dernière marche (en haut)

〔b〕 **in rank etc** **~ management** cadres *mpl* supérieurs; **the ~ men in the party** les dirigeants *mpl* du parti; (*Scol*) **in the ~ class** (*secondary school*) ≈ en terminale; (*primary*) ≈ en cours moyen deuxième année; (= *top stream*) dans le premier groupe

〔c〕 **= best, leading** **he was the ~ student in English** (= *the best*) c'était le meilleur étudiant en anglais; **he was a ~ student in English** (= *one of the best*) c'était l'un des meilleurs étudiants en anglais; (= *leading*) **~ executives** cadres *mpl* supérieurs; **he was Italy's ~ scorer in the World Cup** c'était le meilleur buteur de l'équipe d'Italie pendant la coupe du monde; **one of the ~ pianists** un des plus grands pianistes; **a ~ job** ◊ **one of the ~ jobs** un des postes les plus prestigieux; (*Scol*) **he was** *or* **came ~ in maths** il a été premier en maths; (*Scol*) **the ~ mark** la meilleure note; (*fig*) **~ marks for efficiency** vingt sur vingt pour l'efficacité

〔d〕 **= farthest** **the ~ end of the garden** le fond du jardin; **the ~ end of the field** l'autre bout *m* du champ; **the ~ right-hand corner** le coin en haut à droite

〔e〕 **= maximum** **the vehicle's ~ speed** la vitesse maximale du véhicule; **at ~ speed** à toute vitesse; **a matter of ~ priority** une question absolument prioritaire; **~ prices** prix *mpl* élevés; **we pay ~ price(s) for old clocks** nous offrons les meilleurs prix pour les vieilles horloges

5 TRANSITIVE VERB

〔a〕 **= remove top from** [+ *tree*] étêter, écimer; [+ *plant*] écimer; [+ *radish, carrot etc*] couper *or* enlever les fanes de; (*Brit*) **to ~ and tail fruit** préparer des fruits (*en les équeutant etc*)

〔b〕 ⁑ **= behead** [+ *person*] couper le cou à*

〔c〕 ⁑ **= kill** [+ *person*] buter⁑; **to ~ o.s.** se flinguer*

〔d〕 **= form top of** surmonter; **~ped by a dome** surmonté d'un dôme

〔e〕 **= exceed** dépasser; **we have ~ped last year's sales figures** nous avons dépassé les chiffres des ventes de l'année dernière; **the fish ~ped 10kg** le poisson pesait *or* faisait plus de 10 kg; **to ~ sb in height** dépasser qn en hau-

teur; **the event that ~ped it was ...** l'événement qui a éclipsé cela était ...; **amazing! I'm sure nobody can ~ that** incroyable! je suis sûr que personne ne peut faire mieux; **and to ~ it all ...** et pour couronner le tout ...; **that ~s the lot!*** c'est le bouquet!*

〔f〕 **= pass top of** [+ *hill*] franchir le sommet de; [+ *ridge*] franchir

〔g〕 **= be at top of** [+ *pile*] être au sommet de; [+ *list*] être en tête de *or* à la tête de; (*Theat*) **to ~ the bill** être en tête d'affiche, tenir la vedette

6 COMPOUNDS

► **top banana⁑** N (*US*) (*gen*) gros bonnet* *m*, grosse légume* *f*; (*Theat*) comique *m* principal ► **top boots** NPL bottes *fpl* à revers ► **top brass*** N (*fig*) huiles* *fpl* ► **top-class** ADJ de première classe ► **top copy** N original *m* ► **top dog*** N (*esp US*) **he's ~ dog around here** c'est lui qui commande ici *or* qui fait la pluie et le beau temps ici ► **top dollar*** N (*esp US*) **to pay ~ dollar for sth** payer qch au prix fort ► **top-down** ADJ [*approach, management*] directif ► **top drawer** N **he's out of the ~ drawer** il fait partie du gratin* ► **top-drawer*** ADJ (*socially*) de la haute*, de haute volée; (*in quality, achievement*) de tout premier rang ► **top-dress** VT (*Agr*) ► **top dressing** N fumure *f* en surface ► **top gear** N (*Brit Aut*) **in ~ gear** (*four-speed box*) en quatrième; (*five-speed box*) en cinquième ► **top hand*** N (*US*) collaborateur *m* de premier plan ► **top hat** N (chapeau *m*) haut-de-forme *m* ► **top-hatted** ADJ en (chapeau) haut-de-forme ► **top-heavy** ADJ [*structure etc*] trop lourd du haut, déséquilibré; (*fig*) [*business, administration*] où l'encadrement est trop lourd ► **top-hole†⁑** ADJ (*Brit*) épatant*†*, bath† * ► **top-level** ADJ [*meeting, talks, discussion*] au plus haut niveau; [*decision*] pris au plus haut niveau *or* au sommet ► **top-liner*** N (*Brit Theat*) (artiste *mf* en) tête *f* d'affiche ► **top-loader, top-loading washing machine** N lave-linge *m* à chargement par le haut ► **top-of-the-line, top-of-the-range** ADJ haut de gamme *inv* ► **top-ranked** ADJ [*player, team*] du plus haut niveau ► **top-ranking** ADJ (*très*) haut placé ► **top-secret** ADJ ultrasecret (-ète *f*), top secret (-ète *f*) ► **top-security wing** N [*of prison*] quartier *m* de haute sécurité ► **top-shelf** ADJ (*Brit*) [*magazine, material*] de charme ► **the top ten** NPL (*Mus*) les dix premiers *mpl* du Top ► **the top thirty** NPL le Top 30 ► **top-up** N (*Brit*) **can I give you a ~-up?** je vous en ressers?; (*Aut*) **the battery/oil needs a ~-up** il faut remettre de l'eau dans la batterie/remettre de l'huile ◊ ADJ **~-up loan** prêt *m* complémentaire

7 PHRASAL VERBS

► **top off** 〔1〕 VI (= *reach peak*) [*sales, production etc*] atteindre son (*or* leur) niveau le plus élevé

〔2〕 VT SEP terminer, compléter; **we ~ped off the meal with a glass of cognac** nous avons terminé le repas par un verre de cognac

► **top out** VI (*Constr*) terminer le gros œuvre; (*Comm*) [*rate, cost*] plafonner, atteindre son niveau le plus élevé

► **top up** (*Brit*) 〔1〕 VI [*driver etc*] **to ~ up with oil** remettre *or* rajouter de l'huile

〔2〕 VT SEP [+ *cup, glass*] remplir (à nouveau); [+ *car battery*] remettre de l'eau dans; **I've ~ped up the petrol in your tank** j'ai rajouté *or* remis de l'essence dans votre réservoir; **I've ~ped up your coffee** je vous ai remis du café; **her parents ~ up her grant** ses parents lui donnent de l'argent en complément de sa bourse; **can I ~ you up?*** je vous en remets?

top² [tɒp] N (= *toy*) toupie *f* → **sleep**, **spinning**

topaz [ˈtəʊpæz] N topaze *f*

topcoat [ˈtɒpkəʊt] N 〔a〕 [*of paint*] dernière couche *f* 〔b〕 (*Dress*) pardessus *m*, manteau *m*

tope† [təʊp] VI picoler

topee ['təʊpiː] N casque m colonial

toper† ['təʊpəʳ] N grand buveur m

topflight* [tɒp'flaɪt] ADJ de premier ordre, excellent

topiary ['təʊpɪərɪ] [1] N (NonC) art m topiaire [2] COMP ► **topiary garden** N jardin m d'arbres taillés architecturalement

topic ['tɒpɪk] [1] N [of essay, speech] sujet m; (for discussion) sujet m de discussion, thème m; (esp Brit Scol = project) dossier m; (Ling) thème m [2] COMP ► **topic sentence** N (US Gram) phrase f d'introduction

topical ['tɒpɪkəl] ADJ [issue, theme] d'actualité; [humour, joke] axé sur l'actualité; **a ~ reference** une allusion à l'actualité

topicality [ˌtɒpɪ'kælɪtɪ] N (NonC) actualité f

topknot ['tɒpnɒt] N [of hair] toupet m, houppe f; [of ribbons etc] coque f; [of bird's feathers] aigrette f

topless ['tɒplɪs] [1] ADJ [woman, dancer, model] aux seins nus; [beach] où l'on peut avoir les seins nus; [sunbathing, dancing] seins nus; **photographs showing her ~** des photographies la montrant seins nus [2] ADV [sunbathe, pose, dance] (les) seins nus; **to go ~** se mettre seins nus, faire du topless* [3] COMP ► **topless bar** N bar m topless* ► **topless swimsuit** N monokini m

topmast ['tɒpmɑːst] N (Naut) mât m de hune

topmost ['tɒpməʊst] ADJ le plus haut

topnotch* [tɒp'nɒtʃ] ADJ = **topflight**

topographer [tə'pɒgrəfəʳ] N topographe mf

topographic(al) [ˌtɒpə'græfɪk(l)] ADJ topographique

topography [tə'pɒgrəfɪ] N topographie f

topological [ˌtɒpə'lɒdʒɪkəl] ADJ topologique

topology [tə'pɒlədʒɪ] N topologie f

topper* ['tɒpəʳ] N [a] (= hat) (chapeau m) haut-de-forme m [b] (US) **the ~ was that ...** le comble or le plus fort, c'est que ...

topping ['tɒpɪŋ] [1] ADJ (Brit†*) du tonnerre†* [2] N (for pizza) garniture f; (NonC) **chocolate/orange ~** crème f au chocolat/à l'orange (dont on nappe un dessert); **dessert with a ~ of whipped cream** dessert m nappé de crème fouettée

topple ['tɒpl] [1] VI (= lose balance) [person] basculer, perdre l'équilibre; [pile] basculer; (= fall: also **~ over**, **~ down**) [person] tomber; [pile etc] s'effondrer, se renverser; [empire, dictator, government] tomber; **to ~ over a cliff** tomber du haut d'une falaise [2] VT SEP [+ object] faire tomber, renverser; [+ government, ruler] renverser, faire tomber

TOPS [tɒps] N (Brit) (ABBR = **Training Opportunities Scheme**) programme de recyclage professionnel

topsail ['tɒpseɪl] N (Naut) hunier m

topside ['tɒpsaɪd] [1] N (Brit Culin) gîte m (à la noix); (Naut) accastillage m [2] ADJ (US*) [official etc] haut placé, de haut niveau [3] ADV **to go ~** monter sur le pont supérieur

topsider* ['tɒpsaɪdəʳ] N (US) huile* f, personnage m haut placé

topsoil ['tɒpsɔɪl] N terre f; (Agr) couche f arable

topspin ['tɒpspɪn] N (Tennis) lift m

topsy-turvy ['tɒpsɪ'tɜːvɪ] ADJ, ADV sens dessus dessous, à l'envers; **to turn everything ~** tout mettre sens dessus dessous, tout bouleverser or chambouler*; **everything is ~** tout est sens dessus dessous; (fig) c'est le monde à l'envers or renversé

toque [təʊk] N toque f

tor [tɔːʳ] N butte f (rocheuse)

Torah ['tɔːrə] N Torah f, Thora f

torch [tɔːtʃ] [1] N (flaming) torche f, flambeau m (also fig); (Brit: electric) lampe f de poche, lampe f or torche f électrique; **the house went**

up like a ~ la maison s'est mise à flamber comme du bois sec; **to carry the ~ of** or **for democracy/progress** porter le flambeau de la démocratie/du progrès; **to hand on the ~** passer or transmettre le flambeau; (fig) **he still carries a ~ for her*** il en pince toujours pour elle* → **Olympic** [2] VT **to ~ sth** mettre le feu à qch [3] COMP ► **torch singer** N (US) chanteur m, -euse f réaliste ► **torch song** N chanson f d'amour mélancolique

torchbearer ['tɔːtʃbɛərəʳ] N porteur m, -euse f de flambeau or de torche

torchlight ['tɔːtʃlaɪt] N **by ~** à la lueur des flambeaux (or d'une lampe de poche); **~ procession** retraite f aux flambeaux

tore [tɔːʳ] VB pt of **tear**[1]

toreador [ˈtɒrɪədɔːʳ] N toréador m

torero [tə'rɛərəʊ] N torero m

torment ['tɔːment] [1] N tourment m (liter), supplice m; **to be in ~** être au supplice; **the ~s of jealousy** les affres fpl de la jalousie; **to suffer ~s** souffrir le martyre [2] [tɔː'ment] VT [+ person] tourmenter; [+ animal] martyriser; (fig) **to ~ o.s.** se tourmenter, se torturer; **~ed by jealousy** torturé or rongé par la jalousie

tormentor [tɔː'mentəʳ] N persécuteur m, -trice f; (stronger) bourreau m

torn [tɔːn] VB ptp of **tear**[1]

tornado [tɔː'neɪdəʊ] N (pl **tornados** or **tornadoes**) tornade f

Toronto [tə'rɒntəʊ] N Toronto

torpedo [tɔː'piːdəʊ] [1] N (pl **torpedoes**) (= weapon, fish) torpille f [2] VT (lit, fig) torpiller [3] COMP ► **torpedo attack** N **to make a ~ attack** attaquer à la torpille ► **torpedo boat** N torpilleur m, vedette f lance-torpilles ► **torpedo tube** N (tube m) lance-torpilles m inv

torpid ['tɔːpɪd] ADJ [person] apathique, torpide (liter); [film] très lent; [book] au développement très lent; (Zool) [animal] dans un état de torpeur; **he has a rather ~ intellect** intellectuellement, il n'est pas très vif

torpidity [tɔː'pɪdɪtɪ], **torpor** ['tɔːpəʳ] N torpeur f, engourdissement m

torque [tɔːk] [1] N (Phys) force f de torsion; (Mechanics) couple m; (Hist = collar) torque m [2] COMP ► **torque converter** N (Aut) convertisseur m de couple ► **torque spanner**, **torque wrench** N clef f dynamométrique

torrent ['tɒrənt] N (lit, fig) torrent m; **the rain was coming down in ~s** il pleuvait à torrents

torrential [tɒ'renʃəl] ADJ torrentiel

torrid ['tɒrɪd] [1] ADJ [a] (= hot) [climate, heat, sun] torride [b] (= passionate) [love affair, romance] torride, passionné; [passion] torride, ardent; **~ love scenes** des scènes érotiques torrides [2] COMP ► **the Torrid Zone** N (Geog) la zone intertropicale

torsi ['tɔːsɪ] NPL of **torso**

torsion ['tɔːʃən] [1] N torsion f [2] COMP ► **torsion balance** N balance f de torsion ► **torsion bar** N barre f de torsion

torso ['tɔːsəʊ] N (pl **torsos** or (rare) **torsi**) (Anat) torse m; (Sculp) buste m

tort [tɔːt] [1] N (Jur) acte m délictuel or quasi délictuel [2] COMP ► **torts lawyer** N (US Jur) avocat spécialisé en droit civil

tortilla [tɔː'tiːə] [1] N tortilla f [2] COMP ► **tortilla chip** N chip de maïs épicée

tortoise ['tɔːtəs] N tortue f

tortoiseshell ['tɔːtəʃel] [1] N écaille f (de tortue) [2] COMP [ornament, comb] en or d'écaille; [spectacles] à monture d'écaille ► **tortoiseshell butterfly** N papillon m grande tortue ► **tortoiseshell cat** N chat m écaille et blanc

tortuous ['tɔːtjʊəs] ADJ [road, process, negotiations, history, methods, argument] tortueux;

[language, essay, logic] contourné, alambiqué; [style, sentence] tarabiscoté

torture ['tɔːtʃəʳ] [1] N torture f, supplice m; **to put sb to (the) ~** torturer qn, faire subir des tortures à qn; (fig) **it was sheer ~!** c'était un vrai supplice! [2] VT (lit) torturer; (fig) torturer, mettre à la torture or au supplice; [+ senses etc] mettre au supplice; [+ language] écorcher; [+ meaning] dénaturer; [+ tune] massacrer; (fig) **to ~ o.s.** se torturer; **~d by doubt** torturé or tenaillé par le doute [3] COMP ► **torture chamber** N chambre f de torture

torturer ['tɔːtʃərəʳ] N tortionnaire m, bourreau m

torturous ['tɔːtʃərəs] ADJ atroce, abominable

Tory ['tɔːrɪ] (Pol) [1] N tory m, conservateur m, -trice f [2] ADJ [party, person, policy] tory inv, conservateur (-trice f)

Toryism ['tɔːrɪzəm] N (Pol) torysme m

tosh‡ [tɒʃ] N (Brit: NonC) bêtises fpl, blagues fpl; **~!** allons (donc)!

toss [tɒs] [1] N [a] (= throw) lancement m; (by bull) coup m de cornes; (from horse) **to take a ~** faire une chute, être désarçonné; **with a ~ of his head** d'un mouvement brusque de la tête; (Brit) **I don't give a ~‡** je m'en contrefous‡, j'en ai rien à branler‡‡ (**about** de) [b] [of coin] coup m de pile ou face; (Sport: at start of match) tirage m au sort; **they decided it by the ~ of a coin** ils l'ont décidé à pile ou face; **to win/lose the ~** (gen) gagner/perdre à pile ou face; (Sport) gagner/perdre au tirage au sort → **argue** [2] VT [+ ball, object] lancer, jeter (**to** à); (Brit) [+ pancake] faire sauter; [+ salad] retourner, remuer; [+ head, mane] rejeter en arrière; [bull] projeter en l'air; [horse] désarçonner, démonter; **to ~ sb in a blanket** faire sauter qn dans une couverture; (Culin) **~ in butter** ajoutez un morceau de beurre et remuez; **they ~ed a coin to decide who should stay** ils ont joué à pile ou face pour décider qui resterait; **I'll ~ you for it** on le joue à pile ou face; **the sea ~ed the boat against the rocks** la mer a projeté or envoyé le bateau sur les rochers; **the boat was ~ed by the waves** le bateau était agité or ballotté par les vagues → **caber** [3] VI [a] (also **~ about**, **~ around**) [person] s'agiter; [plumes, trees] se balancer; [boat] tanguer; **he was ~ing (about** or **around) in his sleep** il s'agitait dans son sommeil, son sommeil était agité; **he was ~ing and turning all night** il n'a pas arrêté de se tourner et se retourner toute la nuit [b] (also **~ up**) jouer à pile ou face; **let's ~ (up) for it** on le joue à pile ou face; **they ~ed (up) to see who would stay** ils ont joué à pile ou face pour savoir qui resterait [4] COMP ► **toss-up** N [of coin] coup m de pile ou face; **it was a ~-up between the theatre and the cinema** le théâtre ou le cinéma, ça nous (or leur etc) était égal or c'était kif-kif*; **it's a ~-up whether I go or stay** que je parte ou que je reste (subj), c'est un peu à pile ou face

► **toss about**, **toss around** [1] VI → **toss 3a** [2] VT SEP [+ boat etc] ballotter, faire tanguer; [+ plumes, branches] agiter

► **toss aside** VT SEP [+ object] jeter de côté; (fig) [+ person, helper] repousser; [+ suggestion, offer] rejeter, repousser; [+ scheme] rejeter

► **toss away** VT SEP jeter

► **toss back** VT SEP [+ ball, object] renvoyer; [+ hair, mane] rejeter en arrière; (fig) **they were ~ing ideas back and forth** ils échangeaient toutes sortes d'idées

► **toss off** [1] VI (‡‡ = masturbate) se branler‡‡ [2] VT SEP [a] [+ drink] lamper, avaler d'un coup; [+ essay, letter, poem] écrire au pied levé, torcher (pej) [b] (‡‡ = masturbate) branler‡‡, faire une branlette à‡‡; **to ~ o.s. off** se branler‡‡

► **toss out** VT SEP [+ rubbish] jeter; [+ person]

mettre à la porte, jeter dehors
► **toss over** VT SEP lancer; **~ it over!** envoie!, lance!
► **toss up** 1 VI → **toss 3b** 2 VT SEP [+ *object*] lancer, jeter (**into the air** en l'air) 3 **~-up** N → **toss**

tosser ['tɒsə^r] N (*Brit*) branleur** *m*

tosspot ['tɒspɒt] N a = **tosser** b (††* = *drunkard*) riboteur†† *m*, -euse†† *f*

tot¹ [tɒt] N a (= *child: also* **tiny ~**) tout(e) petit(e) *m(f)*, bambin *m* b (*esp Brit* = *drink*) **a ~ of whisky** un petit verre de whisky; **just a ~** juste une goutte *or* une larme

tot²* [tɒt] (*esp Brit*) 1 VT (*also* **~ up**) additionner, faire le total de 2 VI **it ~s up to £25** ça fait 25 livres en tout, ça se monte *or* ça s'élève à 25 livres; **I'm just ~ting up** je fais le total

total ['təʊtl] 1 ADJ [*amount, number, war, ban, eclipse, silence*] total; [*lack*] total, complet (-ète *f*); [*failure*] complet (-ète *f*); [*effect, policy*] global; **a ~ cost of over £3,000** un coût total de plus de 3 000 livres; **a ~ population of 650,000** une population totale de 650 000 habitants; **the ~ losses/sales/debts** le total des pertes/ventes/dettes; **it was a ~ loss** on a tout perdu; **her commitment to the job was** = elle s'investissait complètement dans son travail; **to get on in business you need** = **commitment** pour réussir en affaires, il faut s'engager à fond; **to be in ~ ignorance of sth** être dans l'ignorance la plus complète de qch, ignorer complètement qch; **they were in ~ disagreement** ils étaient en désaccord total; **a ~ stranger** un parfait inconnu; **~ abstinence** abstinence *f* totale
2 N a (*montant m*) total *m*; **it comes to a ~ of £30** ◊ **the ~ comes to £30** le total s'élève à 30 livres, cela fait 30 livres au total → **grand, sum**
b **in ~** au total
3 VT a (= *add: also* **~ up**) [+ *figures, expenses*] totaliser, faire le total de
b (= *amount to*) s'élever à; **that ~s £50** cela fait 50 livres (en tout), cela s'élève à 50 livres; **the class ~led 40** il y avait 40 élèves en tout dans la classe
c (*esp US* = *wreck*) [+ *car*] bousiller*, démolir
4 COMP ► **total allergy syndrome** N allergie *f* généralisée ► **total recall** N (*Psych*) remémoration *f* totale; **to have ~ recall** se souvenir de tout; **to have ~ recall of sth** se souvenir clairement de qch → **abstainer**

totalitarian [ˌtəʊtælɪ'tɛərɪən] ADJ, N totalitaire *mf*

totalitarianism [ˌtəʊtælɪ'tɛərɪənɪzəm] N totalitarisme *m*

totality [təʊ'tælɪtɪ] N totalité *f*

totalizator ['təʊtəlaɪzeɪtə^r] N a (= *adding etc machine*) (appareil *m*) totalisateur *m*, machine *f* totalisatrice b (*esp Brit Betting*) pari *m* mutuel

totalize ['təʊtəlaɪz] VT totaliser, additionner

totalizer ['təʊtəlaɪzə^r] N = **totalizator**

totally ['təʊtəlɪ] ADV [*convinced, innocent, unacceptable, different, opposed, unheard of*] totalement; [*ignore*] totalement, complètement; **to destroy sth ~** détruire qch totalement *or* complètement

tote¹* [təʊt] 1 N ABBR = **totalizator** b 2 VT (*US*) **to ~ up** additionner 3 COMP ► **tote board** N (*Racing*) tableau *m* totalisateur

tote² [təʊt] 1 VT (* = *carry*) [+ *gun, object*] porter; **I ~d it around all day** je l'ai trimballé* toute la journée 2 COMP ► **tote bag** N (sac *m*) fourre-tout* *m inv*

totem ['təʊtəm] N totem *m*; **~ pole** mât *m* totémique

totemic [təʊ'temɪk] ADJ totémique

totter ['tɒtə^r] VI [*person*] (*from weakness*) chanceler; (*from tiredness, drunkenness*) titu-

ber; [*object, column, chimney stack*] chanceler, vaciller; (*fig*) [*government*] chanceler; **to ~ in/out** *etc* entrer/sortir *etc* en titubant *or* d'un pas chancelant

tottering ['tɒtərɪŋ], **tottery** ['tɒtərɪ] ADJ chancelant

totty ['tɒtɪ] N (*NonC: Brit*) gonzesses* *fpl*; **a nice piece of ~** une belle gonzesse*

toucan ['tuːkən] N toucan *m*

touch [tʌtʃ]

1 NOUN	4 COMPOUNDS
2 TRANSITIVE VERB	5 PHRASAL VERBS
3 INTRANSITIVE VERB	

1 NOUN
a = *sense of touch* toucher *m*; **Braille is read by ~** le braille se lit au toucher; **soft to the ~** doux au toucher; **the cold ~ of marble** la froideur du marbre
b = *act of touching* contact *m*, toucher *m*; [*of instrumentalist, typist*] toucher *m*; [*of artist*] touche *f*; **the slightest ~ might break it** le moindre contact pourrait le casser; **I felt a ~ on my arm** j'ai senti qu'on me touchait le bras; **at the ~ of her hand, he ...** au contact de sa main, il ...; **with the ~ of a finger** d'une simple pression du doigt; **at the ~ of a button** *or* **switch** en appuyant sur un bouton; **she felt the ~ of the wind on her cheek** elle sentait la caresse du vent sur sa joue; **he altered it with a ~ of the brush/pen** il l'a modifié d'un coup de pinceau/d'un trait de plume; **to have a light ~** [*pianist*] avoir un toucher léger; [*writer, actor*] faire preuve de finesse; **you've got the right ~ with him** vous savez vous y prendre avec lui
c fig = *characteristic* **it has the ~ of genius** cela porte le sceau du génie; **he lacks the human** *or* **personal ~** il est trop impersonnel *or* froid, il manque de chaleur humaine; **it's the human** *or* **personal ~ that makes his speeches so successful** c'est la note personnelle qui fait que ses discours ont tant de succès; **that's the Gordon ~** c'est typique de Gordon, c'est du Gordon tout craché*
d = *detail* détail *m*; **small ~es, such as flowers, can transform a room** de petits détails, par exemple des fleurs, peuvent transformer une pièce; (*lit, fig*) **to put the final** *or* **finishing ~(es) to sth** ◊ **to give sth the final** *or* **finishing ~(es)** mettre la dernière main à qch
e = *small amount* **it's a ~ (too) expensive** c'est un petit peu (trop) cher, c'est un poil* trop cher
► **a touch of**: **a ~ of colour/gaiety/humour** une touche de couleur/de gaieté/d'humour; **a ~ of sadness** une pointe de tristesse; **there's a ~ of spring in the air** ça sent le printemps; **tonight there'll be a ~ of frost in places** il y aura un peu de gel cette nuit par endroits; **he got a ~ of the sun** il a pris un petit coup de soleil; **to have a ~ of flu** être un peu grippé; **to have a ~ of rheumatism** faire un peu de rhumatisme; **it needs a ~ of paint** il faudrait y passer une petite couche de peinture
f = *contact, communication*
► **to be in touch with sb** être en contact *or* en rapport *or* en relation avec qn; **I'll be in ~!** je t'écrirai! (*or* je te téléphonerai!)
► **to keep in touch with sb** rester en contact *or* en rapport *or* en relation avec qn; **keep in ~!** tiens-nous au courant!, écris de temps en temps!
► **to get in touch with sb** prendre contact avec qn; (*by phone*) joindre qn; **you can get in ~ with me at this number** vous pouvez me joindre à ce numéro; **you ought to get in ~ with the police** vous devriez prendre contact avec la police
► **to put sb in touch with**: **I'll put you in ~ with him** je vous mettrai en rapport *or* en relation avec lui
► **to lose touch**: **to lose ~ with sb** perdre contact avec qn; **they lost ~ (with each other)**

long ago il y a bien longtemps qu'ils ne sont plus en relation *or* en rapport; **to have lost ~ with sb** avoir perdu le contact avec qn; **to lose ~ with reality** *or* **the facts** perdre le sens des réalités; **to have lost ~ with the political situation** ne plus être au courant de la situation politique; **he has lost ~ with what is going on** il n'est plus dans le coup*
♦ **to be out of touch** (= *not up to date*) **he's completely out of ~** il n'est plus dans le coup*; **I'm out of ~ with the latest political developments** je ne suis pas au courant des derniers développements en matière politique; (= *isolated*) **we're very much out of ~ here** nous sommes coupés de tout ici
g Ftbl, Rugby touche *f*; **the ball went into ~** le ballon est sorti en touche; **it's in ~** il y a touche; **to kick for ~** ◊ **to kick the ball into ~** botter *or* envoyer le ballon en touche; (*fig*) **to kick sth into ~** mettre qch au placard
h : *borrowing* **he's made a ~** il a tapé* quelqu'un; **he's good for a ~** ◊ **he's an easy** *or* **soft ~** (= *will lend money*) il est toujours prêt à se laisser taper*
i = *person one can persuade, exploit* **he's a soft ~** il se laisse faire; **Mr Wilson is no soft ~** M. Wilson n'est pas du genre à se laisser faire
2 TRANSITIVE VERB
a = *come into contact with* toucher; **"do not ~ the goods"** «ne touchez pas les *or* aux marchandises»; **he ~ed it with his finger** il l'a touché du doigt; **he ~ed her arm** il lui a touché le bras; **his hand ~ed mine** sa main a touché la mienne; (*fig*) **they can't ~ you if you don't break the law** ils ne peuvent rien contre vous *or* rien vous faire si vous respectez la loi; **to ~ one's hat to sb** saluer qn en portant la main à son chapeau; **I can ~ the bottom** je peux toucher le fond, j'ai pied; **the ship ~ed the bottom** le bateau a touché le fond; (*Aviat*) **to ~ ground** atterrir; **their land ~es ours** leur terre touche à *or* est contiguë à la nôtre; **the ship ~ed Bordeaux** le bateau a fait escale à Bordeaux; (*fig*) **to ~ base** se mettre à jour *or* au courant; **clouds ~ed with pink** nuages *mpl* à reflets roses
b = *tamper with* toucher à; **don't ~ that switch!** ne touchez pas à ce bouton!; **I didn't ~ it!** je n'y ai pas touché!; **the burglars didn't ~ the safe** les cambrioleurs n'ont pas touché au coffre-fort; **I didn't ~ him!** je ne l'ai pas touché!
c = *damage* **the frost ~ed the plants** la gelée a abîmé les plantes; **the fire didn't ~ the paintings** l'incendie a épargné les tableaux
d = *deal with* (*in exam*) **I didn't ~ the third question** je n'ai pas touché à la troisième question; **he won't ~ anything illegal** si c'est illégal il n'y touchera pas; **water won't ~ these stains** l'eau n'agira pas sur ces taches; **he scarcely ~ed the problem of racism** il a à peine abordé le problème du racisme
e + *food, drink* (*gen neg*) toucher à; **he didn't ~ his meal** il n'a pas touché à son repas; **I never ~ onions** je ne mange jamais d'oignons; **I won't ~ gin** je ne bois jamais de gin
f = *equal, rival* valoir, égaler; **her cooking doesn't** *or* **can't ~ yours** sa cuisine est loin de valoir la tienne; **there's nobody to ~ him as a pianist** ◊ **nobody can ~ him as a pianist** il est inégalable *or* sans égal comme pianiste; **there's nothing to ~ hot whisky for a cold** rien ne vaut un grog au whisky pour guérir un rhume
g = *concern* toucher, concerner; **it ~es us all closely** cela nous touche *or* nous concerne tous de très près; **if it ~es the national interest** s'il y va de l'intérêt national
h = *move emotionally* toucher; **we were very ~ed by your letter** nous avons été très touchés par votre lettre
i *esp Brit* = *reach* [+ *level, speed*] atteindre
j *: for money* **to ~ sb for a loan** taper* qn; **I ~ed him for £10** je l'ai tapé* de 10 livres

3 INTRANSITIVE VERB
a gen toucher; **don't ~!** n'y touchez pas!, ne touchez pas!; (on notice) **"do not ~"** «défense de toucher»
b = come into contact with [hands, ends etc] se toucher; [lands, gardens, areas] se toucher, être contigus
c speaking, writing (fig) **to ~ (up)on a subject** aborder un sujet
4 COMPOUNDS
► **touch-and-go** N **it's ~-and-go with him** il est entre la vie et la mort; **it was ~-and-go whether she did it** elle a été à deux doigts de ne pas le faire; **it was ~-and-go until the last minute** l'issue est restée incertaine jusqu'au bout ► **touch football** N variante du jeu à treize, sans plaquages ► **touch judge** N (Rugby) juge m de touche ► **touch-sensitive** ADJ [screen] tactile; [key] à effleurement ► **touch-tone** ADJ [telephone] à touches ► **touch-type** VI taper sans regarder le clavier ► **touch-typing** N dactylographie f (sans regarder le clavier) ► **touch-typist** N dactylo* f qui tape sans regarder le clavier
5 PHRASAL VERBS
► **touch at** VT FUS (Naut) mouiller à or dans le port de, faire escale à
► **touch down** **1** VI **a** (Aviat, Space) (on land) atterrir; (on sea) amerrir; (on moon) alunir
b (US Ftbl) marquer un touch-down; (behind one's own goal-line) aplatir (la balle) dans son en-but
2 VT SEP (Rugby etc) **to ~ the ball down** marquer un essai; (behind one's own goal-line) aplatir (la balle) dans son en-but
► **touch off** VT SEP [+ fuse, firework] faire partir; [+ mine etc] faire exploser; [+ explosion] déclencher; (fig) [+ crisis, riot] déclencher; [+ reaction, scene, argument] provoquer, déclencher
► **touch up** VT SEP **a** [+ painting, photo] retoucher
b (‡ sexually) peloter‡

touchdown ['tʌtʃdaʊn] N (Aviat, Space) (on land) atterrissage m; (on sea) amerrissage m; (on moon) alunissage m; (American Ftbl) essai m

touché [tu:'ʃeɪ] EXCL (Fencing) touché!; (fig) très juste!

touched [tʌtʃt] ADJ **a** (= moved) touché (**by sth** par qch); **b** (* = mad) toqué*, timbré*

touchiness ['tʌtʃɪnɪs] N (NonC) susceptibilité f

touching ['tʌtʃɪŋ] **1** ADJ touchant **2** PREP concernant, touchant† (also liter)

touchingly ['tʌtʃɪŋlɪ] ADV [speak, write] d'une manière touchante; **~ naïve** d'une touchante naïveté; **~, she has supported him throughout this ordeal** chose touchante, elle l'a soutenu tout au long de cette épreuve

touchline ['tʌtʃlaɪn] N (Ftbl etc) (ligne f de) touche f

touchpaper ['tʌtʃpeɪpə'] N papier m nitraté; (fig) **to light the (blue) ~** mettre le feu aux poudres

touchstone ['tʌtʃstəʊn] N (lit, fig) pierre f de touche

touchwood ['tʌtʃwʊd] N amadou m

touchy ['tʌtʃɪ] ADJ (= easily annoyed) [person] susceptible (**about sth** sur la question or le chapitre de qch); (= delicate) [subject, issue] délicat

touchy-feely* ['tʌtʃɪfi:lɪ] ADJ [person] qui aime le contact physique, démonstratif

tough [tʌf] **1** ADJ **a** (= strong) [cloth, steel, leather, garment etc] solide, résistant; (pej) [meat] dur, coriace; (hum: of meat etc) **it's as ~ as old boots** c'est de la semelle
b [person] (= strong) (physically) robuste, résistant; (mentally) solide, endurant; **you have to be ~ to do that kind of work** il faut être so-

lide pour faire ce genre de travail; **he's a ~ businessman** il est dur en affaires; (hum) **as ~ as old boots*** coriace
c [person] (= hard in character) dur, tenace; [criminal, gangster] endurci; **as ~ as nails** dur à cuire; **he is a ~ man to deal with** il ne fait pas souvent de concessions; **~ guy** dur m; (pej) **they're a ~ lot** ◊ **they're ~ customers** ce sont des durs à cuire*; **to get ~ with sb*** (commencer à) se montrer dur envers qn
d (= hard) [resistance, struggle, opposition] acharné, âpre; [journey, task] rude, pénible; [obstacle] rude, sérieux; [problem] épineux; [regulations] sévère; [conditions] dur; [neighbourhood] dur; **it's ~ when you have kids** c'est dur quand on a des enfants; **it's ~ work** c'est un travail difficile, ce n'est pas de la tarte*; **rugby is a ~ game** le rugby est un jeu rude; **to take a ~ line on sth** [person] être très strict sur qch; [government] se montrer inflexible sur qch; **to take a ~ line with sb** se montrer inflexible or très ferme avec qn; **it took ~ talking to get them to agree to the deal** il a fallu d'âpres négociations pour qu'ils acceptent (subj) de conclure cette affaire
e (* = unfortunate) **that's ~** c'est vache*; **to have a ~ time of it*** en voir de dures*; **it was ~ on the others** c'était vache* pour les autres; **~ luck** déveine* f, manque m de pot*; **~ luck!** (pity) pas de veine!, manque de pot!*; (you'll have to put up with it) tant pis pour vous!; **that's ~ luck on him** il n'a pas de veine or de pot*; **~ shit!**‡ démerdez-vous!‡, tant pis pour vous!
2 N* dur m
3 ADV **to talk** or **act ~** jouer au dur
4 VT (fig) **to ~ it out*** (= hold out) tenir bon, faire front; (= rough it) vivre à la dure
5 COMP ► **tough love*** N (esp US) fermeté f affectueuse ► **tough-minded** ADJ inflexible ► **tough-mindedness** N inflexibilité f

toughen ['tʌfn] (also ~ **up**) **1** VT [+ metal, glass, cloth, leather] rendre plus solide, renforcer; [+ person] endurcir, aguerrir; [+ conditions] rendre plus sévère; **~ed glass** verre m trempé **2** VI [metal, glass, cloth, leather] devenir plus solide; [person] s'endurcir, s'aguerrir; [conditions, regulations] devenir plus sévère

toughie* ['tʌfɪ] N **a** (= question) **that's a ~** ça, c'est une colle* **b** (= person) dur(e) m(f)

toughly ['tʌflɪ] ADV [speak, answer] durement, sans ménagement; [fight, oppose] avec acharnement, âprement; **it is ~ made** c'est du solide

toughness ['tʌfnɪs] N (NonC) **a** [of person] (= hardiness) résistance f, endurance f; (= determination) ténacité f; **mental ~** force f de caractère **b** (= roughness) [of person, school] dureté f; [of sport, game] rudesse f **c** (= durability) [of material] résistance f, solidité f; [of skin] dureté f **d** [of meat] dureté f **e** (= difficulty) [of life, situation, choice, question] difficulté f; [of resistance, competition] âpreté f; [of task, work, conditions, journey] dureté f **f** (= harshness) [of policy, measure] sévérité f

toupee ['tu:peɪ] N postiche m

tour ['tʊə'] **1** N (= journey) voyage m, périple m; (by team, actors, musicians etc) tournée f; (by premier, visiting statesman etc) visite f officielle, tournée f de visites; [of town, factory, museum etc] visite f, tour m; (also **package ~**) voyage m organisé; (also **day ~**) excursion f; (Hist) **the Grand Tour** le tour de l'Europe; **they went on a ~ of the Lake District** ils ont fait un voyage or un périple dans la région des Lacs; **we went on** or **made a ~ of the Loire castles** nous avons visité les châteaux de la Loire; **they went on a ~ to Spain** ils sont allés en voyage organisé or ils ont fait un voyage organisé en Espagne; **the ~ includes three days in Venice** le voyage comprend trois jours à Venise; **to go on a ~ round the world** faire le

tour du monde; **to go on a walking/cycling ~** faire une randonnée à pied/en bicyclette; (sign on bus) **"on ~"** «excursion»; (Sport, Theat etc) **to go on ~** faire une tournée; **to be on ~** être en tournée; (Theat etc) **to take a company on ~** emmener une troupe en tournée; **to take a play on ~** donner une pièce en tournée; **~ of inspection** tournée f d'inspection; (Mil etc) **~ of duty** période f de service → **conduct**
2 VT [+ district, town, exhibition, museum, factory] visiter; **they are ~ing France** ils visitent la France, ils font du tourisme en France; (Sport, Theat) ils sont en tournée en France; **the play is ~ing the provinces** la pièce tourne en province or est en tournée en province
3 VI **to go ~ing** voyager, faire du tourisme; **they went ~ing in Italy** ils sont allés visiter l'Italie, ils ont fait du tourisme en Italie
4 COMP ► **tour director** N (US) accompagnateur m, -trice f ► **tour guide** N (= person) guide m, accompagnateur m, -trice f ► **tour manager** N (Sport, Mus) directeur m de tournée ► **tour operator** N (Brit) (= travel agency) tour-opérateur m, voyagiste m; (= bus company) compagnie f de cars

tour de force ['tʊədəfɔ:s] N (pl **tours de force**) (= action, performance etc) exploit m, prouesse f; (= novel, film etc) chef-d'œuvre m

tourer ['tʊərə'] N (= car) voiture f de tourisme; (= caravan) caravane f

Tourette('s) syndrome [tʊə'ret(s)-ˌsɪndrəʊm] N maladie f de Gilles de La Tourette

touring ['tʊərɪŋ] **1** N (NonC) tourisme m, voyages mpl touristiques **2** ADJ [team] en tournée; **~ car** voiture f de tourisme; (Theat) **~ company** (permanently) troupe f ambulante; (temporarily) troupe f en tournée **3** COMP ► **touring bindings** NPL (Ski) fixations fpl de randonnée

tourism ['tʊərɪzəm] N tourisme m

tourist ['tʊərɪst] **1** N touriste mf; **"Tourists' Guide to London"** «Guide touristique de Londres»; (Sport = touring team) **the ~s** les visiteurs mpl, l'équipe f en tournée **2** ADV [travel] en classe touriste **3** COMP [class, ticket] touriste inv; [season] des touristes ► **tourist agency** N agence f de tourisme ► **tourist bureau** N = **tourist information (centre)** ► **tourist class** N classe f touriste ♦ ADJ, ADV en classe touriste ► **tourist court** N (US) motel m ► **tourist home** N (US) maison particulière dans laquelle des chambres sont louées aux touristes ► **tourist information (centre)**, **tourist (information) office** N office m de tourisme, syndicat d'initiative ► **tourist trade** N tourisme m ► **tourist traffic** N flot m or afflux m de touristes (en voiture) ► **tourist trap** N piège m à touristes

touristy* ['tʊərɪstɪ] ADJ (pej) [place] (trop) touristique; [shop] pour touristes

tournament ['tʊənəmənt] N (Hist, gen) tournoi m; **chess/tennis ~** tournoi m d'échecs/de tennis

tourney ['tʊənɪ] N (Hist) tournoi m

tourniquet ['tʊənɪkeɪ] N (Med) tourniquet m, garrot m

tousle ['taʊzl] VT [+ hair] ébouriffer; [+ clothes] chiffonner, friper, froisser; [+ bed, bedclothes] mettre en désordre

tousled ['taʊzld] ADJ [hair] ébouriffé; [person, appearance] échevelé

tout [taʊt] **1** N (gen) vendeur m ambulant; (for custom) racoleur m; (for hotels) rabatteur m; (Racing) pronostiqueur m; (Brit: also **ticket ~**) revendeur m de billets (au marché noir) **2** VT [+ wares] vendre (avec insistance); (Brit) [+ tickets] revendre (au marché noir) **3** VI racoler; (Racing) vendre des pronostics (esp Brit) **to ~ for custom** racoler les clients; (esp Brit) **the taxi drivers were ~ing for the hotels** les chauffeurs de taxi racolaient des clients pour les hôtels

► **tout about**, **tout (a)round** VT SEP [+ *goods*] vendre (avec insistance); **he has been ~ing those books about for weeks*** ça fait des semaines qu'il essaie de caser* ces livres

tow¹ [təʊ] **1** N **a** (= *act*) remorquage *m*; (= *line*) câble *m* de remorquage; (= *vehicle etc towed*) véhicule *m* en remorque; (*lit*) **to give sb a ~** ◊ **to have sb in ~** remorquer qn; (*fig*) **he had a couple of girls in ~*** il avait deux filles dans son sillage; **to be on ~** (*Brit*) *or* **in ~** (*US*) être en remorque; (*sign*) **"on ~"** « véhicule en remorque »; **to take a car in ~** prendre une voiture en remorque **b** (*also* **ski ~**) téléski *m*, tire-fesses* *m* **2** VT [+ *boat, vehicle*] remorquer (**to, into** jusqu'à); [+ *caravan, trailer*] tirer, tracter; [+ *barge*] haler **3** COMP ► **tow bar** N barre *f* de remorquage ► **tow car** N (*esp US*) chariot-remorque *m* ► **towing-line**, **towing-rope** N câble *m* de remorque ► **towing-truck** N dépanneuse *f* ► **tow-start** N (*Aut*) **to give sb a ~-start** faire démarrer qn en le remorquant ► **tow truck** N (*US*) dépanneuse *f*

► **tow away** VT SEP [+ *vehicle*] remorquer; [*police*] emmener en fourrière

tow² [təʊ] **1** N (*Tex*) filasse *f*, étoupe *f* (blanche) **2** COMP ► **tow-haired**, **tow-headed** ADJ aux cheveux (blond) filasse, blond filasse

towage ['təʊɪdʒ] N remorquage *m*

toward(s) [tə'wɔ:d(z)] PREP **a** (*of direction*) vers, du côté de, dans la direction de; **if he comes ~ you** s'il vient vers vous *or* dans votre direction *or* de votre côté; **his back was ~ the door** il tournait le dos à la porte; (*fig*) **we are moving ~ a solution/war** etc nous nous acheminons vers une solution/la guerre *etc*; **they have begun negotiations ~ an agreement on ...** ils ont entamé des négociations en vue d'un accord sur ...; **he is saving ~ a new car** il fait des économies pour (acheter) une nouvelle voiture; **I'll put the prize money ~ a new car** le prix servira à m'acheter une nouvelle voiture; **all donations will go ~ a new roof** tous les dons serviront à l'achat d'un nouveau toit **b** (*of time*) vers; **~ 10 o'clock** vers *or* sur le coup de 10 heures, sur les 10 heures; **~ the end of the century** vers la fin du siècle **c** (*of attitude*) envers, à l'égard de; **his attitude ~ them** son attitude envers eux *or* à leur égard; **my feelings ~ him** mes sentiments à son égard *or* envers lui *or* pour lui

towaway zone ['təʊəweɪzəʊn] N (*US Aut*) zone *f* de stationnement interdit (sous peine de mise en fourrière)

towboat ['təʊbəʊt] N remorqueur *m*

towel ['taʊəl] **1** N serviette *f* (de toilette); (*also* **dish ~**, **tea ~**) torchon *m*; (*for hands*) essuie-mains *m*; (*for glasses*) essuie-verres *m*; (*also* **sanitary ~**) serviette *f* hygiénique → **bath** **2** VT frotter avec une serviette; **to ~ o.s. dry** *or* **down** se sécher *or* s'essuyer avec une serviette **3** COMP ► **towel rail** N porte-serviettes *m* inv ► **towel ring** N anneau *m* porte-serviettes

towelling ['taʊəlɪŋ] **1** N **a** (*NonC*) tissu *m* éponge **b** (*rubbing with towel*) **to give sb a ~ (down)** frictionner qn avec une serviette **2** COMP [*robe etc*] en *or* de tissu éponge

tower ['taʊəʳ] **1** N tour *f*; **the Tower of Babel** la tour de Babel; **the Tower of London** la tour de Londres; **church ~** clocher *m*; **water ~** château *m* d'eau; (*fig*) **he is a ~ of strength** il est ferme comme un roc, c'est un roc; **he proved a ~ of strength to me** il s'est montré un soutien précieux pour moi **2** VI [*building, mountain, cliff, tree*] se dresser de manière imposante; **I saw him ~ing in the doorway** j'ai vu sa silhouette imposante dans l'embrasure de la porte; **the new block of flats ~s above** *or* **over the church** le nouvel immeuble écrase l'église; **he ~ed over her** elle était toute petite

à côté de lui; (*fig*) **he ~s above** *or* **over his colleagues** il domine de très haut ses collègues **3** COMP ► **tower block** N (*Brit*) immeuble-tour *m*, tour *f* (d'habitation)

► **tower up** VI [*building, cliff etc*] se dresser de manière imposante, s'élever très haut

towering ['taʊərɪŋ] ADJ **a** (= *tall*) [*building*] imposant par sa hauteur; [*cliff, tree*] imposant **b** (= *great*) [*achievement, performance*] grandiose; [*genius, ambition*] hors du commun; [*figure*] dominant; **to be a ~ presence** être une figure particulièrement imposante; **in a ~ rage** dans une colère noire

towline ['təʊlaɪn] N = **towing-line**; → **tow¹**

town [taʊn] **1** N ville *f*; **he lives in (a) ~** il habite en ville *or* à la ville; **she lives in a little ~** elle habite (dans) une petite ville; **there is more work in the ~ than in the country** il y a plus de travail en ville *or* à la ville qu'à la campagne; **guess who's in ~!** devine qui vient d'arriver en ville!; **he's out of ~** il n'est pas là, il est en déplacement; (*US*) **he's from out of ~** il n'est pas d'ici, il est étranger à la ville; **to go (in)to ~** ◊ **to go downtown** aller en ville; **to go up to ~** (*gen*) monter en ville; (*to London*) monter à Londres; **the whole ~ is talking about it** toute la ville en parle; (*Univ*) **~ and gown** les citadins *mpl* et les étudiants *mpl*; **a ~ country** une ville de province; **we're going out on the ~** on va faire une virée en ville*; (*fig*) **to have a night on the ~*** faire la noce* *or* la bombe*; (*fig*) **he really went to ~ on that essay*** il a mis le paquet* pour cette dissertation; **they went to ~ on their daughter's wedding*** ils n'ont pas fait les choses à moitié pour le mariage de leur fille → **man, new, talk** **2** COMP ► **town-and-country planning** N aménagement *m* du territoire ► **town centre** N centre-ville *m* ► **town clerk** N ≈ secrétaire *mf* de mairie ► **town council** N conseil *m* municipal ► **town councillor** N, -ère *f* municipal(e) ► **town crier** N (*Hist*) crieur *m* public ► **town-dweller** N citadin(e) *m(f)* ► **town hall** N ≈ mairie *f*, hôtel *m* de ville ► **town house** N (*gen*) maison *f* de ville; (= *terraced house*) maison *f* mitoyenne; (*more imposing*) hôtel *m* particulier ► **town life** N vie *f* urbaine ► **town meeting** N (*US*) assemblée *f* générale des habitants d'une localité ► **town planner** N (*Brit*) urbaniste *mf* ► **town planning** N (*Brit*) urbanisme *m*

townee*, **townie*** [taʊ'ni:] N (*pej*) pur citadin *m*; (*Univ*) citadin *m*

townscape ['taʊnskeɪp] N paysage *m* *or* panorama *m* urbain

townsfolk ['taʊnzfəʊk] N = **townspeople**

township ['taʊnʃɪp] N commune *f*, municipalité *f*; (*in South Africa*) township *m* *or* *f*

townsman ['taʊnzmən] N (*pl* -**men**) citadin *m*, habitant *m* de la ville (*or* des villes); **my fellow townsmen** mes concitoyens *mpl*

townspeople ['taʊnzpi:pl] NPL citadins *mpl*, habitants *mpl* de la ville (*or* des villes)

townswoman ['taʊnzwʊmən] N (*pl* -**women**) citadine *f*, habitante *f* de la ville (*or* des villes)

towpath ['təʊpɑ:θ] N chemin *m* de halage

towrope ['təʊrəʊp] N = **towing-rope**; → **tow¹**

toxaemia, **toxemia** (*US*) [tɒk'si:mɪə] N toxémie *f*

toxic ['tɒksɪk] **1** ADJ toxique (**to sb/sth** pour qn/qch) **2** COMP ► **toxic shock syndrome** N syndrome *m* du choc toxique ► **toxic waste** N déchets *mpl* toxiques

toxicological [ˌtɒksɪkə'lɒdʒɪkəl] ADJ toxicologique

toxicologist [ˌtɒksɪ'kɒlədʒɪst] N toxicologue *mf*

toxicology [ˌtɒksɪ'kɒlədʒɪ] N toxicologie *f*

toxin ['tɒksɪn] N toxine *f*

toxoplasmosis [ˌtɒksəʊplæz'məʊsɪs] N toxoplasmose *f*

toy [tɔɪ] **1** N jouet *m* **2** VI **to ~ with** [+ *object, pen, sb's affections*] jouer avec; [+ *idea, scheme*] caresser; **to ~ with one's food** manger du bout des dents, chipoter, picorer **3** COMP [*house, truck, stove, railway*] miniature, [*trumpet*] d'enfant ► **toy boy*** N (*Brit fig*) gigolo* *m* ► **toy car** N petite voiture *f* ► **toy dog** N (*fig*) petit chien *m* d'appartement ► **toy maker** N fabricant *m* de jouets ► **toy poodle** N caniche *m* nain ► **toy soldier** N petit soldat *m* ► **toy train** N petit train *m*; (*electric*) train *m* électrique

toybox ['tɔɪbɒks], **toychest** ['tɔɪtʃest] N coffre *m* à jouets

toyshop ['tɔɪʃɒp] N magasin *m* de jouets

toytown ['tɔɪtaʊn] ADJ (*esp Brit pej*) [*politics, revolutionary etc*] de pacotille; **~ money** monnaie *f* de singe

tpi [ti:pi:'aɪ] N (*Comput*) (ABBR = **tracks per inch**) pistes *fpl* par pouce

trace¹ [treɪs] **1** N **a** (*gen*) trace *f*; **there were ~s of the cave having been lived in** il y avait des traces d'habitation dans la grotte; **the police could find no ~ of the thief** la police n'a trouvé aucune trace du voleur; **~s of an ancient civilization** la trace *or* les vestiges *mpl* d'une ancienne civilisation; **there is no ~ of it now** il n'en reste plus trace maintenant; **we have lost all ~ of them** nous avons complètement perdu leur trace; **~s of arsenic in the stomach** traces d'arsenic dans l'estomac; **to vanish/sink without (a) ~** disparaître/sombrer sans laisser de traces; **without a ~ of ill-feeling** sans la moindre rancune **b** (*US* = **trail**) piste *f* **2** VT **a** (= *draw*) [+ *curve, line etc*] tracer; (*with tracing paper etc*) décalquer **b** (= *follow trail of*) suivre la trace de; (*and locate*) [+ *person*] retrouver, dépister; [+ *object*] retrouver; **ask the police to help you ~ him** demandez à la police de vous aider à le retrouver; **they ~d him as far as Paris but then lost him** ils ont pu suivre sa trace jusqu'à Paris mais l'ont perdu par la suite; **I can't ~ your file at all** je ne trouve pas (de) trace de votre dossier; **I can't ~ his having been in touch with us** je n'ai aucune indication *or* mention du fait qu'il nous ait contactés **3** COMP ► **trace element**, **trace mineral** N oligoélément *m*

► **trace back 1** VI (*esp US*) **this ~s back to the loss of ...** ceci est imputable à la perte de ... **2** VT SEP **to ~ back one's ancestry** *or* **descent** *or* **family to ...** faire remonter sa famille à ..., établir que sa famille remonte à ...; **they ~d the murder weapon back to a shop in Leeds** ils ont réussi à établir que l'arme du crime provenait d'un magasin de Leeds; **we ~d him back to Paris, then the trail ended** (en remontant la filière) nous avons retrouvé sa trace à Paris mais là, la piste s'est perdue; **this may be ~d back to the loss of ...** ceci peut être attribué à *or* est attribuable *or* imputable à la perte de ...

► **trace out** VT SEP tracer

trace² [treɪs] N [*of harness*] trait *m* → **kick**

traceable ['treɪsəbl] ADJ **it is ~** on peut le retrouver

tracer ['treɪsəʳ] N (= *person*) traceur *m*, -euse *f*; (= *instrument*) roulette *f*, traçoir *m*; (*Biochem*) traceur *m*; (*also* **~ bullet**) balle *f* traçante; (*also* **~ shell**) obus *m* traçant

tracery ['treɪsərɪ] N (*NonC: Archit*) réseau *m* (de fenêtre ajourée); [*of veins on leaves*] nervures *fpl*; [*of frost on window etc*] dentelles *fpl*

trachea [trə'kɪə] N (*pl* **tracheas** *or* **tracheae** [træ'ki:i:]) trachée *f*

tracheotomy [ˌtrækɪ'ɒtəmɪ] N trachéotomie *f*

trachoma [træ'kəʊmə] N trachome *m*

tracing ['treɪsɪŋ] [1] N (NonC) (= process) calquage m; (= result) calque m [2] COMP ▶ **tracing paper** N papier m calque inv, papier m à décalquer

track [træk] [1] N [a] (= mark, trail, also Climbing) trace f; [of animal, person] trace f, piste f; [of tyres, wheels] trace f; [of boat] sillage m; (= route) trajectoire f; **the hurricane destroyed everything in its** ~ l'ouragan a tout détruit sur son passage; **a** ~ **of muddy footprints across the floor** des traces de pas boueuses sur le plancher; **to follow in sb's** ~**s** (lit) suivre qn à la trace; (fig) suivre les traces de qn, marcher sur les traces de qn; **to be on sb's** ~**(s)** être sur la piste de qn; **he had the police on his** ~**(s)** la police était sur sa piste; **they got on to his** ~ **very quickly** ils ont très vite trouvé sa piste; **to put** or **throw sb off the** ~ désorienter qn; **to cover (up)** or **hide one's** ~**s** (lit) couvrir sa marche; (fig) couvrir sa marche, brouiller les pistes; (fig) **to be on** ~ être sur la bonne voie; **to get the economy back on** ~ remettre l'économie sur les rails; (fig) **to be on the right** ~ être sur la bonne voie; **to put sb on the right** ~ mettre qn dans la bonne voie; (fig) **to be on the wrong** ~ ◊ **to be off the** ~ faire fausse route; (fig) **you're away off the** ~! vous êtes tout à fait à côté!, vous n'y êtes pas du tout!; (fig) **to change** ~ changer de cap; **to keep** ~ **of** [+ spacecraft etc] suivre; (fig) [+ events] suivre la marche or le fil de; [+ developments, situation] suivre, rester au courant de; **they kept** ~ **of him till they reached the wood** ils ont suivi sa trace jusqu'au bois; **I kept** ~ **of her until she got married** je suis resté en contact avec elle or au courant de ce qu'elle faisait jusqu'à son mariage; **I've lost** ~ **of what he's doing** je ne suis plus au courant de ce qu'il fait; **to lose** ~ **of** [+ spacecraft etc] perdre; (fig) [+ developments, situation] ne plus suivre, ne plus être au courant de; [+ events] perdre le fil de; **they lost** ~ **of him in the woods** ils ont perdu sa trace une fois arrivés au bois; **I lost** ~ **of her after the war** j'ai perdu tout contact avec elle or je l'ai perdue de vue après la guerre; **don't lose** ~ **of him** (lit) ne perdez pas sa trace; (fig) ne le perdez pas de vue; **I've lost** ~ **of those books** je ne sais plus or j'ai oublié où sont ces livres; **to lose all** ~ **of time** perdre la notion du temps; **keep** ~ **of the time** n'oubliez pas l'heure; **I've lost** ~ **of what he is saying** j'ai perdu le fil de ce qu'il dit, je ne suis plus ce qu'il dit; (fig = leave) **to make** ~**s*** se sauver*; **we must be making** ~**s*** il faut qu'on se sauve* (subj); **he made** ~**s for the hotel*** il a filé à l'hôtel → **inside, stop**
[b] (= path) chemin m, sentier m; **sheep** ~ piste f à moutons; **mule** ~ chemin m or sentier m muletier → **beaten, cart, dirt**
[c] (Rail) voie f (ferrée), rails mpl; **to leave the** ~**(s)** quitter les rails, dérailler; **to cross the** ~ traverser la voie; **single-** ~ **line** ligne f à voie unique; **to change** ~**s** changer de voie; (esp US fig) **to live on the wrong side of the** ~**s** vivre dans les quartiers pauvres → **one**
[d] (Sport) piste f; **motor-racing** ~ autodrome m; **dog-racing** ~ cynodrome m → **racetrack**
[e] (NonC) athlétisme m
[f] [of electronic tape, CD, computer disk] piste f; [of long-playing record] plage f; (= piece of music) morceau m; **four-** ~ **tape** bande f à quatre pistes → **soundtrack**
[g] (Aut) (= tyre tread) chape f; (= space between wheels) écartement m; (also **caterpillar** ~) chenille f
[h] (US Scol) groupe m de niveau; **divided into five** ~**s** répartis en cinq groupes de niveau; **the top/middle/bottom** ~ la section forte/moyenne/faible
[2] **tracks*** NPL (Drugs) marques fpl de piqûres
[3] VT [+ animal] suivre à la piste or à la trace de; [+ person, vehicle] suivre à la trace de; [+ hurricane, rocket, spacecraft, comet]

suivre la trajectoire de; **to** ~ **dirt over the floor** laisser des traces sales sur le plancher
[4] VI [camera] faire un travelling
[5] COMP ▶ **track and field athletes** NPL athlètes mfpl ▶ **track and field athletics** N athlétisme m ▶ **track athletics** N (Sport) athlétisme m sur piste ▶ **track event** N (Sport) épreuve f sur piste ▶ **tracking device** N dispositif m de pistage ▶ **tracking shot** N (Cine) travelling m ▶ **tracking station** N (Space) station f d'observation (de satellites) ▶ **track lighting** N rampe f de spots ▶ **track maintenance** N (Rail) entretien m de la voie ▶ **track meet** N (US Sport) réunion f sportive sur piste ▶ **track race** N (Sport) course f sur piste ▶ **track racing** N (Sport) courses fpl sur piste ▶ **track record** N (fig) **to have a good** ~ **record** avoir fait ses preuves; **to have a poor** ~ **record** avoir eu de mauvais résultats ▶ **track rod** N (Brit) barre f de connexion ▶ **track shoe** N chaussure f de course ▶ **track shot** N (Cine) travelling m ▶ **track system** N (US Scol) système m de répartition des élèves par niveaux

▶ **track down** VT SEP [+ animal, wanted man] traquer et capturer; [+ lost object, lost person, reference, quotation] (finir par) retrouver or localiser

trackball ['trækbɔːl] N (Comput) boule f roulante

tracked [trækt] ADJ [vehicle] à chenilles

tracker ['trækər] [1] N (Hunting) traqueur m; (gen) poursuivant m(f) [2] COMP ▶ **tracker dog** N chien m policier (dressé pour retrouver les gens)

tracklayer ['trækleɪər] N (US Rail) = **trackman**

trackless ['træklɪs] ADJ [forest, desert] sans chemins; [vehicle] sans chenilles

trackman ['trækmən] N (pl **-men**) (US Rail) responsable m de l'entretien des voies

tracksuit ['træksuːt] N (Brit) survêtement m

trackwalker ['trækwɔːkər] N (US Rail) = **trackman**

tract¹ [trækt] [1] N [a] [of land, water] étendue f; [of coal etc] gisement m; (US = housing estate) lotissement m; **vast** ~**s of wilderness** de vastes zones fpl or étendues désertiques [b] (Anat) **digestive** ~ appareil m or système m digestif [2] COMP ▶ **tract house** N (US) pavillon m (dans un lotissement)

tract² [trækt] N (= pamphlet) tract m; (Rel) traité m

tractable ['træktəbl] ADJ [person] accommodant, souple; [animal] docile; [material] malléable; [problem] soluble

Tractarian [træk'tɛərɪən] ADJ, N (Rel) tractarien m, -ienne f

Tractarianism [træk'tɛərɪənɪzəm] N (Rel) tractarianisme m

traction ['trækʃən] [1] N (NonC: all senses) traction f; (Tech) **electric/steam** ~ traction f électrique/à vapeur [2] COMP ▶ **traction engine** N locomobile f

tractive ['træktɪv] ADJ de traction

tractor ['træktər] [1] N tracteur m [2] COMP ▶ **tractor drive** N (Comput) dispositif m d'entraînement à picots ▶ **tractor driver** N conducteur m, -trice f de tracteur ▶ **tractortrailer** N (US) semi-remorque m

trad* [træd] ADJ (esp Brit Mus) ABBR = **traditional**

tradable ['treɪdəbl] ADJ (esp US Econ, Fin) commercialisable

trade [treɪd] [1] N [a] (NonC = commerce) commerce m, affaires fpl; (illegal) trafic m; (Econ) **overseas** ~ commerce m extérieur; **it's good for** ~ ça fait marcher le commerce; **the fur** ~ l'industrie f de la fourrure; **the wool** ~ ◊ **the** ~ **in wool** le commerce de la laine; **he's in the wool** ~ il est négociant en laine; **the drug** ~ ◊ **the** ~ **in drugs** le marché de la drogue; **they do a lot of** ~ **with ...** ils font

beaucoup d'affaires avec ...; ~ **has been good** or **brisk** les affaires ont été bonnes, le commerce a bien marché; **to do a good** or **brisk** or **roaring** ~ vendre beaucoup (**in** de); **Board of Trade** (Brit) ◊ **Department of Trade** (US) ministère m du Commerce; (Brit) **Secretary (of State) for Trade and Industry** ministre m (du Commerce et) de l'Industrie; **President of the Board of Trade** ◊ **Minister of Trade** ministre m du Commerce; (Brit) **Department of Trade and Industry** ≈ ministère m (du Commerce et) de l'Industrie → **rag¹, tourist**
[b] (= job, skill) métier m; **she wants him to learn a** ~ elle veut qu'il apprenne un métier; **he is a butcher by** or **to*** ~ il est boucher de son métier or de son état; **he's a doctor by** ~ il est médecin de son état; **to put sb to a** ~† mettre qn en apprentissage; (lit, fig) **he's in the** ~ il est du métier; (lit, fig) **as we say in the** ~ comme on dit dans le jargon du métier, pour employer un terme technique; **known in the** ~ **as ...** que les gens du métier appellent ...; **special discounts for the** ~ remises spéciales pour les membres de la profession → **stock, tool, trick**
[c] = **trade wind**; → **4**
[d] (esp US = swap) échange m; **to do a** ~ **with sb for sth** faire l'échange de qch avec qn

[2] VI [a] [firm, country, businessman] faire le commerce (**in** de), commercer, avoir or entretenir des relations commerciales (**with** avec); **he** ~**s as a wool merchant** il est négociant en laine; (fig) **to** ~ **(up)on sb's kindness** abuser de la gentillesse de qn
[b] (US: of private individual) faire ses achats (**with** chez, à), être client(e) (**with** chez)
[c] (St Ex) [currency, commodity] **to be trading at** se négocier à → **cease**
[d] (= exchange) échanger, troquer (**with sb** avec qn)

[3] VT (= exchange) **to** ~ **A for B** échanger or troquer A contre B; **I** ~**d my penknife with him for his marbles** je lui ai donné mon canif en échange de ses billes

[4] COMP (gen) [exchanges, visits] commercial; (Publishing) [press, publications] professionnel, spécialisé ▶ **trade agreement** N accord m commercial ▶ **trade association** N association f commerciale ▶ **trade barriers** NPL barrières fpl douanières ▶ **trade bill** N effet m de commerce ▶ **trade cycle** N (Econ) cycle m économique ▶ **trade deficit** N balance f (commerciale) déficitaire, déficit m extérieur ▶ **Trade Descriptions Act** N (Brit) loi protégeant les consommateurs contre la publicité et les appellations mensongères ▶ **trade discount** N remise f au détaillant ▶ **trade fair** N foire (-exposition) f commerciale ▶ **trade figures** NPL (Econ) résultats mpl (financiers) ▶ **trade gap** N déficit m commercial or de la balance commerciale ▶ **trade-in** N (Comm) reprise f; **he took my old machine as a** ~**-in** il m'a repris ma vieille machine; ~**-in allowance** reprise f; ~**-in price** prix m à la reprise; ~**-in value** valeur f à la reprise ▶ **trade journal** N revue f professionnelle ▶ **trade mission** N mission f commerciale ▶ **trade name** N (= product name) nom m de marque; (= company name) raison f sociale ▶ **trade-off** N (= exchange) échange m (**between** entre); (balancing) compromis m, concessions fpl mutuelles ▶ **trade paper** N = **trade journal** ▶ **trade plate** N (Aut) ≈ plaque f d'immatriculation provisoire ▶ **trade price** N prix m de gros ▶ **trade returns** NPL (Econ) = **trade figures** ▶ **trade route** N route f commerciale ▶ **trade school** N collège m technique ▶ **trade secret** N (Comm, Ind, also fig) secret m de fabrication ▶ **trades union** N = **trade union** ▶ **the Trades Union Congress** N (Brit) la confédération des syndicats britanniques ▶ **trades unionism** N = **trade unionism** ▶ **trades unionist** N = **trade unionist** ▶ **trade union** N syndicat m; ~**(s) union**

membership adhésion *f* à un syndicat ; (= *number of members*) nombre *m* de syndiqués ▸ **trade unionism** N syndicalisme *m* ▸ **trade unionist** N syndicaliste *mf* ▸ **trade talks** NPL (*Pol etc*) négociations *fpl* commerciales ▸ **trade war** N guerre *f* commerciale ▸ **trade wind** N (*Geog*) (vent *m*) alizé *m*
▸ **trade down** VI to ~ **down to a smaller house/car** vendre sa maison/voiture pour en acheter une moins chère
▸ **trade in** VT SEP [+ *car, television etc*] faire reprendre ; **I've ~d it in for a new one** je l'ai fait reprendre quand j'en ai acheté un nouveau
▸ **trade off** 1 VT SEP a (= *balance*) **to ~ off A against B** accepter que A compense B b (= *exchange*) **to ~ off one thing against** or **for another** échanger or troquer une chose contre une autre 2 ~**-off** → **trade**
▸ **trade up** VI to ~ **up to a bigger house/car** vendre sa maison/voiture pour en acheter une plus chère

trademark ['treɪdmɑːk] 1 N marque *f* (de fabrique) 2 VT [+ *product, goods*] apposer une marque sur ; [+ *symbol, word*] déposer ; **registered** ~ marque *f* déposée

trader ['treɪdər] N a commerçant(e) *m(f)*, marchand(e) *m(f)* ; (*bigger*) négociant(e) *m(f)* ; (*also* **street** ~) vendeur *m*, -euse *f* de rue ; (*US St Ex*) contrepartiste *mf* ; **wool** ~ négociant *m* en laine → **slave** b (= *ship*) navire *m* marchand or de la marine marchande

tradescantia [ˌtrædəsˈkæntɪə] N tradescantia *m*

tradesman ['treɪdzmən] 1 N (*pl* **-men**) commerçant *m* ; (= *skilled worker*) ouvrier *m* qualifié 2 COMP ▸ **tradesman's entrance**, **tradesmen's entrance** N entrée *f* de service or des fournisseurs

tradespeople ['treɪdzpiːpl] NPL commerçants *mpl*

tradeswoman ['treɪdzwʊmən] N (*pl* **-women**) commerçante *f* ; (= *skilled worker*) ouvrière *f* qualifiée

trading ['treɪdɪŋ] 1 N (*NonC*) (*in shops, business*) commerce *m*, affaires *fpl* ; (*on larger scale*) commerce *m*, négoce *m* ; (*between countries*) commerce *m*, échanges *mpl* (commerciaux) ; (*St Ex*) transactions *fpl*, opérations *fpl* ; (*St Ex*) ~ **was brisk yesterday** l'activité *f* a été soutenue hier 2 COMP [*port, centre*] de commerce ▸ **trading capital** N capital *m* engagé, capital *m* de roulement ▸ **trading company** N société *f* d'import-export ▸ **trading estate** N (*Brit*) zone *f* artisanale et commerciale ▸ **trading nation** N nation *f* commerçante ▸ **trading partner** N partenaire *mf* commercial(e) ▸ **trading post** N (*esp Can, US*) comptoir *m* (commercial) ▸ **trading profits** NPL (*Fin, Ind*) ~ **profits for last year** bénéfices *mpl* réalisés pour l'exercice de l'année écoulée ▸ **trading stamp** N timbre-prime *m* ▸ **trading standards** NPL normes *fpl* de conformité ▸ **trading standards office** N ≈ Direction *f* de la consommation et de la répression des fraudes

tradition [trəˈdɪʃən] N tradition *f* ; **according to** ~ selon la tradition ; **it's in the (best)** ~ **of ...** c'est dans la (plus pure) tradition de ... ; ~ **has it that ...** la tradition veut que ... ; **it is a ~ that ...** il est de tradition que ... (+ *subj*) ; **the** ~ **that ...** la tradition selon laquelle or qui veut que ...

traditional [trəˈdɪʃənl] 1 ADJ traditionnel ; **it is** ~ (**for sb**) **to do sth** il est de tradition (pour qn) de faire qch ; **to be** ~ **in one's approach to sth** avoir une approche traditionnelle de qch or une attitude traditionnelle face à qch ; **the clothes which are** ~ **to his country** les vêtements traditionnels de son pays 2 COMP ▸ **traditional medicine** N médecine *f* traditionnelle

traditionalism [trəˈdɪʃnəlɪzəm] N traditionalisme *m*

traditionalist [trəˈdɪʃnəlɪst] ADJ, N traditionaliste *mf*

traditionally [trəˈdɪʃnəlɪ] ADV (*gen*) traditionnellement ; ~ **made** à l'ancienne

traduce [trəˈdjuːs] VT (*frm*) calomnier, diffamer

Trafalgar [trəˈfælgər] N **Battle of** ~ bataille *f* de Trafalgar

traffic ['træfɪk] (*vb: pret, ptp* **trafficked**) 1 N (*NonC*) a (*Aut*) circulation *f* ; (*Aviat, Naut, Rail, Telec*) trafic *m* ; **road** ~ circulation *f* routière ; **rail** ~ trafic *m* ferroviaire ; (*Aut*) **holiday** ~ circulation *f* des grands départs (or des grands retours), rush *m* des vacances ; (*Aut*) **the** ~ **is heavy/light** il y a beaucoup de/très peu de circulation ; **the build-up** or **backlog of** ~ **extends to the bridge** le bouchon s'étire jusqu'au pont ; (*Aut*) ~ **out of/into Paris** la circulation dans le sens Paris-province/province-Paris ; ~ **coming into London should avoid Putney Bridge** il est recommandé aux automobilistes se rendant à Londres d'éviter Putney Bridge ; ~ **in and out of Heathrow Airport** le trafic à destination et en provenance de l'aéroport de Heathrow ; (*Naut*) ~ **in** or **using the Channel** trafic or navigation *f* en Manche → **tourist** b (= *trade*) commerce *m* (**in** de) ; (*pej*) trafic *m* (**in** de) ; **the drug** ~ le trafic de la drogue or des stupéfiants
2 VI **to ~ in sth** faire le commerce or le trafic (*pej*) de qch
3 COMP ▸ **traffic calming** N *mesures de ralentissement de la circulation en ville* ▸ **traffic circle** N (*US*) rond-point *m*, carrefour *m* giratoire ▸ **traffic control** N (*Aut*) prévention *f* routière ; (*Aviat, Naut, Rail*) contrôle *m* du trafic ▸ **traffic controller** N (*Aviat*) contrôleur *m*, -euse *f* de la navigation aérienne, aiguilleur *m* du ciel ▸ **traffic control tower** N (*Aviat*) tour *f* de contrôle ▸ **traffic cop*** N (*esp US*) **traffic policeman** ▸ **traffic court** N (*US Jur*) *tribunal où sont jugées les infractions au code de la route* ▸ **traffic diversion** N déviation *f* ▸ **traffic duty** N **to be on** ~ **duty** [*policeman*] faire la circulation ▸ **traffic holdup** N bouchon *m* (*de circulation*) ▸ **traffic island** N refuge *m* (*pour piétons*) ; (*in centre of roundabout*) terre-plein *m* central ▸ **traffic jam** N embouteillage *m*, bouchon *m* ▸ **traffic lights** NPL feux *mpl* de signalisation ; **to go through the** ~ **lights at red** passer au rouge, griller le feu rouge ; **the** ~ **lights were (at) green** le feu était (au) vert ▸ **traffic offence** N (*Jur*) infraction *f* au code de la route ▸ **traffic pattern** N (*Aviat*) couloir *m* or position *f* d'approche ▸ **traffic police** N (*speeding etc*) police *f* de la route ; (*points duty etc*) police *f* de la circulation ▸ **traffic policeman** N (*pl* **traffic policemen**) ≈ agent *m* de police ; (*on points duty*) agent *m* de la circulation ▸ **traffic regulations** NPL réglementation *f* de la circulation ▸ **traffic sign** N panneau *m* de signalisation, poteau *m* indicateur ; **international** ~ **signs** signalisation *f* routière internationale ▸ **traffic signals** NPL = **traffic lights** ▸ **traffic warden** N (*Brit*) contractuel(le) *m(f)*

trafficator† ['træfɪkeɪtər] N (*Brit*) flèche *f* (de direction)†

trafficker ['træfɪkər] N trafiquant(e) *m(f)* (**in** en)

tragedian [trəˈdʒiːdɪən] N (= *writer*) auteur *m* tragique ; (= *actor*) tragédien *m*

tragedienne [trəˌdʒiːdɪˈɛn] N tragédienne *f*

tragedy ['trædʒɪdɪ] N (*gen, Theat*) tragédie *f* ; **the** ~ **of it is that ...** ce qui est tragique, c'est que ... ; **it is a ~ that ...** il est tragique que ... (+ *subj*)

tragic ['trædʒɪk] ADJ [*accident, death, victim, expression, hero*] tragique ; ~ **actor** tragédien(ne) *m(f)* ; **it is ~ that ...** il est tragique que ... (+ *subj*)

tragically ['trædʒɪkəlɪ] ADV tragiquement

tragicomedy ['trædʒɪˈkɒmɪdɪ] N (*pl* **tragicomedies**) tragicomédie *f*

tragicomic ['trædʒɪˈkɒmɪk] ADJ tragicomique

trail [treɪl] 1 N a [*of blood, smoke*] traînée *f* ; **a long ~ of refugees** une longue file or colonne de réfugiés ; **to leave a ~ of destruction** tout détruire sur son passage ; **his illness brought a series of debts in its ~** sa maladie a amené dans son sillage une série de dettes → **vapour** b (= *tracks: gen*) trace *f* ; (*Hunting*) piste *f*, trace(s) *f(pl)* (*lit, fig*) **to be on the ~ of sb** être sur la piste de qn ; **I'm on the ~ of that book you want** j'ai trouvé trace or j'ai retrouvé la trace du livre que vous voulez → **hot** c (= *path, road*) sentier *m*, chemin *m* → **blaze²**, **nature** d (*Ski, Climbing*) trace *f* ; (*cross country skiing*) piste *f* de fond ; **to break a ~** faire la trace, tracer
2 VT a (= *follow*) suivre la piste de ; (*fig = lag behind*) être dépassé par b (= *drag, tow*) [+ *object on rope, toy cart etc*] tirer, traîner ; (*Aut*) [+ *caravan, trailer, boat*] tirer, tracter ; **he was ~ing his schoolbag behind him** il traînait son cartable derrière lui ; **the children ~ed dirt all over the carpet** les enfants ont couvert le tapis de traces sales ; **to ~ one's fingers through** or **in the water** laisser traîner ses doigts dans l'eau ; **don't ~ your feet!** ne traîne pas les pieds ! c (*Mil*) [+ *rifle etc*] porter à la main d (= *announce as forthcoming*) donner un avant-goût de e (*Hort*) **to ~ a plant over a fence** etc faire grimper une plante par-dessus une clôture etc
3 VI a [*object*] traîner ; [*plant*] ramper ; **your coat is ~ing in the mud** ton manteau traîne dans la boue ; **smoke ~ed from the funnel** une traînée de fumée s'échappait de la cheminée ; (*fig*) (*Sport*) **they were ~ing by 13 points** ils étaient en retard de 13 points ; (*Ftbl*) **they are ~ing at the bottom of the league** ils traînent en bas de division b **to ~ along/in/out** etc (= *move in straggling line*) passer/entrer/sortir etc à la queue leu leu or en file ; (= *move wearily*) passer/entrer/sortir etc en traînant les pieds
4 COMP ▸ **trail bike*** N moto *f* de motocross ▸ **trail mix** N mélange *m* de fruits secs
▸ **trail away**, **trail off** VI [*voice, music*] s'estomper

trailblazer ['treɪlbleɪzər] N (*fig*) pionnier *m*, -ière *f*

trailblazing ['treɪlbleɪzɪŋ] ADJ (*fig*) (in)novateur (-trice *f*)

trailbreaker ['treɪlbreɪkər] N (*esp US*) = **trailblazer**

trailer ['treɪlər] 1 N a (*behind car, van, truck*) remorque *f* ; (*esp US* = *caravan*) caravane *f* b (*Cine, TV*) bande-annonce *f* c (*Phot* = *end of film roll*) amorce *f* (en fin d'un rouleau) 2 COMP ▸ **trailer camp**, **trailer court**, **trailer park** N (*US*) camp *m* de caravaning ▸ **trailer tent** N tente-caravane *f*

trailing ['treɪlɪŋ] 1 ADJ [*plant*] grimpant 2 COMP ▸ **trailing edge** N (*Aviat*) bord *m* de fuite ▸ **trailing geranium** N géranium-lierre *m*

train [treɪn] 1 N a (*Rail*) train *m* ; (*in Underground*) rame *f*, métro *m* ; **to go by** ~ prendre le train ; **to go to London by** ~ prendre le train pour aller à Londres, aller à Londres en train or par le train ; **to travel by** ~ voyager par le train or en train ; **on** or **in the** ~ dans le train ; **to transport by** ~ transporter par voie ferroviaire → **express**, **freight**, **slow** b (= *procession*) file *f* ; (= *entourage*) suite *f*, équipage m; [of camels] caravane f, file f; [of mules] train m, file f; [of vehicles] cortège m, file f; **he arrived with 50 men in his ~** il arriva avec un équipage de 50 hommes; (fig) **the war brought famine in its ~** la guerre amena la famine dans son sillage or entraîna la famine → **baggage**

c [= line, series] suite f, série f; [of gunpowder] traînée f; **in an unbroken ~** en succession ininterrompue; **a ~ of events** une suite d'événements; **it broke** or **interrupted his ~ of thought** cela est venu interrompre le fil de sa or ses pensée(s); **I've lost my ~ of thought** je ne retrouve plus le fil de ma or mes pensée(s); (esp Brit fig) **it is in ~** c'est en préparation, c'est en marche; (esp Brit) **to set sth in ~** mettre qch en marche or en mouvement **d** [of dress, robe] traîne f **e** (Tech) train m; **~ of gears** train m de roues d'engrenage

2 VT **a** (= instruct) [+ person, engineer, doctor, nurse, teacher, craftsman, apprentice] former; [+ employee, soldier] former, instruire; (Sport) [+ player] entraîner, préparer; [+ animal] dresser; [+ voice] travailler; [+ ear, mind, memory] exercer; **he is ~ing someone to take over from him** il forme son successeur; (also **house-~**) **to ~ a puppy/child** apprendre à un chiot/à un enfant à être propre; **to ~ an animal to do sth** apprendre à or dresser un animal à faire qch; **to ~ sb to do sth** apprendre à qn à faire qch; (professionally) former qn à faire qch, préparer qn à faire qch; **to ~ o.s. to do sth** s'exercer à or s'exercer à faire qch; **to ~ sb in a craft** apprendre un métier à qn, préparer qn à un métier; **he was ~ed in weaving** or **as a weaver** il a reçu une formation de tisserand; **to ~ sb in the use of sth** or **to use sth** apprendre à qn à utiliser qch, instruire qn dans le maniement de qch; **where were you ~ed?** où avez-vous reçu votre formation? → **trained**

b (= direct) [+ gun, camera, telescope] braquer (**on** sur); **to ~ a plant along a wall** faire grimper une plante le long d'un mur

3 VI **a** recevoir une or sa formation; (Sport) s'entraîner (**for** pour), se préparer (**for** pour); **to ~ as** or **~ to be a teacher/secretary** etc recevoir une formation de professeur/de secrétaire etc; **where did you ~?** où avez-vous reçu votre formation?

b (Rail = go by train) aller en train

4 COMP (Ind) [dispute, strike etc] des cheminots, des chemins de fer ► **train crash** N accident m de chemin de fer; (more serious) catastrophe f ferroviaire ► **train ferry** N ferry-boat m ► **train oil** N huile f de baleine ► **train service** N **there is a very good ~ service to London** les trains pour Londres sont très fréquents; **there is an hourly ~ service to London** il y a un train pour Londres toutes les heures; **do you know what the ~ service is to London?** connaissez-vous l'horaire des trains pour Londres? ► **train set** N train m électrique (jouet) ► **train spotter** N (Brit) passionné(e) m(f) de trains; (* pej = nerd) crétin(e)* m(f) ► **train-spotting** N (Brit) **to go ~-spotting** observer les trains (pour identifier les divers types de locomotives) ► **train-workers** NPL employés mpl des chemins de fer, cheminots mpl

► **train up** VT SEP (Brit) former

trainband ['treɪnbænd] N (Brit Hist) ancienne milice britannique

trainbearer ['treɪnbɛərəʳ] N dame f or demoiselle f d'honneur; (little boy) page m

trained [treɪnd] ADJ [person] (= skilled) qui a reçu une formation; (= qualified) qualifié; [nurse] qualifié, diplômé; [teacher] habilité à enseigner; [soldier, gymnast] entraîné; [animal] dressé; [mind] exercé; **he is not ~ at all** (gen) il n'a reçu aucune formation professionnelle; [soldier, gymnast] il n'a reçu aucun entraînement; **she has a ~ voice** elle a

pris des leçons de chant; **to the ~ eye/ear** pour un œil exercé/une oreille exercée; **it is obvious to a ~ observer that ...** il est évident pour un observateur averti que ...; **to be ~ for sth** (gen) avoir reçu une formation pour qch; [soldier, gymnast] être entraîné pour qch; **he isn't ~ for this job** il n'a pas la formation pour ce poste; **we need a ~ person for the job** il nous faut une personne qualifiée pour ce travail; **well-~** (gen) qui a reçu une bonne formation; [soldier, gymnast] bien entraîné; [servant] stylé; [child] bien élevé; [animal] bien dressé; (hum) **she's got her husband well ~** son mari est bien dressé

trainee [treɪ'niː] **1** N (gen) stagiaire mf; (US Police, Mil etc) jeune recrue f; **sales/management ~** stagiaire mf de vente/de direction **2** ADJ (gen) stagiaire, en stage; (in trades) en apprentissage; **~ typist** dactylo* f stagiaire; **~ hairdresser** apprenti(e) coiffeur m, -euse f

traineeship [treɪ'niːʃɪp] N stage m, stage m d'emploi-formation

trainer ['treɪnəʳ] **1** N **a** [of athlete, football team, racehorse] entraîneur m; (Cycling etc) soigneur m; (in circus) dresseur m, -euse f; [of lions, tigers] dompteur m, -euse f **b** (Aviat) (= flight simulator) simulateur m de vol; (also **~ aircraft**) avion-école m **2** **trainers** NPL (Brit) tennis fpl or mpl; (high-tops) baskets mpl

▼ **training** ['treɪnɪŋ] **1** N [of person, engineer, doctor, nurse, teacher, craftsman] formation f; [of employee, soldier] formation f, instruction f; (Sport) entraînement m, préparation f; [of animal] dressage m; (Sport) **to be out of ~** avoir perdu la forme; (Sport) **to be in ~** (= preparing o.s.) être en cours d'entraînement or de préparation; (= on form) être en forme; (Sport) **to be in ~ for sth** s'entraîner pour or se préparer à qch; **staff ~** formation f du personnel; **he has had some secretarial ~** il a suivi quelques cours de secrétariat; **it is good ~** c'est un bon apprentissage or entraînement → **teacher, toilet, voice**

2 COMP ► **Training and Enterprise Council** N (Brit) organisme de formation et d'aide à la création d'entreprises ► **training camp** N camp m d'entraînement ► **training centre** N (gen) centre m de formation; (Sport) centre m (d'entraînement) sportif ► **training college** N (gen) école f spécialisée or professionnelle; **teacher ~ college** → **teacher 2** ► **training course** N stage m de formation ► **training ground** N (Sport, fig) terrain m d'entraînement ► **training manual** N manuel m or cours m d'instruction ► **Training Opportunities Scheme** N (Brit) programme de recyclage professionnel ► **training plane** N avion-école m ► **training scheme** N programme m de formation or d'entraînement ► **training ship** N navire-école m ► **training shoe** N = **trainer 2** ► **training wheels** NPL (US) [of bicycle] stabilisateurs mpl

trainman ['treɪnmən] N (pl **-men**) (US Rail) cheminot m

traipse* [treɪps] VI **to ~ in/out** etc entrer/sortir etc d'un pas traînant or en traînassant*; **they ~d in wearily** ils sont entrés en traînant les pieds; **to ~ around** or **about** se balader*, déambuler; **we've been traipsing about the shops all day** nous avons traîné or traînassé* dans les magasins toute la journée

trait [treɪt] N trait m (de caractère)

traitor ['treɪtəʳ] N traître(sse) m(f); **to be a ~ to one's country/to a cause** trahir sa patrie/une cause; (Mil, Pol) **to turn ~** passer à l'ennemi

traitorous ['treɪtərəs] ADJ traître (traîtresse f), déloyal, perfide

traitorously ['treɪtərəslɪ] ADV traîtreusement, perfidement, en traître (or en traîtresse)

traitress ['treɪtrɪs] N traîtresse f

trajectory [trə'dʒɛktərɪ] N trajectoire f

tram [træm] N **a** (Brit: also **~car**) tram(way) m; **to go by ~** prendre le tram **b** (Min) berline f, benne f roulante

tramline ['træmlaɪn] N (Brit) **a** = **tramway** **b** (Tennis) **~s** lignes fpl de côté

trammel ['træməl] **1** VT entraver **2** **trammels** NPL entraves fpl

tramp [træmp] **1** N **a** (= sound) **the ~ of feet** le bruit de pas **b** (= hike) randonnée f (à pied), excursion f; **to go for a ~** (aller) faire une randonnée or une excursion; **after a ten-hour ~** après dix heures de marche; **it's a long ~** c'est long à faire à pied **c** (= vagabond) clochard(e) m(f), vagabond(e) m(f) **d** (esp US pej = woman) **she's a ~*** elle est coureuse* **e** (also **~ steamer**) tramp m **2** VI **a** (= along (= hike) poursuivre son chemin à pied; (= walk heavily) marcher d'un pas lourd; [soldiers etc] marteler le pavé or la route; **to ~ up and down** faire les cent pas; **he was ~ing up and down the platform** il arpentait le quai d'un pas lourd **3** VT **to ~ the streets** battre le pavé; **I ~ed the town looking for the church** j'ai parcouru la ville à pied pour trouver l'église

► **tramp down, tramp in** VT SEP tasser du pied

trample ['træmpl] **1** VT **to ~ (underfoot)** [+ sth on ground etc] piétiner, fouler aux pieds; (fig) [+ person, conquered nation] fouler aux pieds, bafouer; [+ sb's feelings] bafouer; [+ objections etc] passer outre à; **he ~d the stone into the ground** il a enfoncé du pied la pierre dans le sol; **he was ~d by the horses** il a été piétiné par les chevaux **2** VI **to ~ in/out** etc entrer/sortir etc d'un pas lourd; (lit, fig) **to ~ on** = **to trample (underfoot)**; → **1 3** N (= act: also **trampling**) piétinement m; (= sound) bruit m de pas

trampoline ['træmpəlɪn] **1** N trampoline m **2** VI (also **to go trampolining**) faire du trampoline

tramway ['træmweɪ] N (Brit) (= rails) voie f de tramway; (= route) ligne f de tramway

trance [trɑːns] N (Hypnosis, Rel, Spiritualism etc) transe f; (Med) catalepsie f; (fig = ecstasy) transe f, extase f; **to go** or **fall into a ~** entrer en transe; (Med) tomber en catalepsie; **to put sb into a ~** [hypnotist] faire entrer qn en transe

tranche [trɑːnʃ] N (Econ etc) tranche f

trannie, tranny ['trænɪ] N (pl **trannies**) **a*** ABBR = **transistor (radio)** **b** (Phot*) ABBR = **transparency b c** (‡ = transvestite) travelo‡ m

tranquil ['træŋkwɪl] ADJ [person, expression, atmosphere, way of life, sleep, morning] paisible, serein; [countryside, water, river, beauty] paisible

tranquillity, tranquility (also US) [træŋ'kwɪlɪtɪ] N tranquillité f, calme m

tranquillize, tranquilize (also US) ['træŋkwɪlaɪz] VT (Med) mettre sous tranquillisants

tranquillizer, tranquilizer (also US) ['træŋkwɪlaɪzəʳ] **1** N tranquillisant m, calmant m **2** COMP ► **tranquillizer dart** N (for gun) seringue f sédative; (for blowpipe) fléchette f enduite de sédatif

trans. ABBR = **transitive, transport(ation), translation, translator, transfer(red)**

trans... [trænz] PREF trans...; **the Trans-Canada Highway** la route transcanadienne

transact [træn'zækt] VT [+ business] traiter, régler, faire

transaction [træn'zækʃən] N (gen) opération f, affaire f; (Econ, Fin, St Ex) transaction f; **we have had some ~s with that firm** nous avons fait quelques opérations or quelques affaires avec cette société; **cash ~** opération f au comptant; **the ~s of the Royal Society** (= proceedings) les travaux mpl de la Royal Society; (= minutes) les actes mpl de la Royal Society

transactional [træn'zækʃənl] ADJ transactionnel; (Psych) **~ analysis** analyse f transactionnelle

transalpine ['trænz'ælpaɪn] ADJ transalpin

transatlantic ['trænzət'læntɪk] ADJ [flight, crossing, phone call, liner] transatlantique; [style, upbringing] d'Outre-Atlantique; (Brit = American) américain

transceiver [træn'siːvəʳ] N (Rad) émetteur-récepteur m

transcend [træn'send] VT [+ belief, knowledge, description] transcender, dépasser; (= excel over) surpasser; (Philos, Rel) transcender

transcendence [træn'sendəns], **transcendency** [træn'sendənsɪ] N transcendance f

transcendent [træn'sendənt] ADJ (frm) transcendant

transcendental [,trænsen'dentl] [1] ADJ transcendantal [2] COMP ► **transcendental meditation** N méditation f transcendantale

transcendentalism [,trænsen'dentəlɪzəm] N transcendantalisme m

transcontinental ['trænz,kɒntɪ'nentl] ADJ transcontinental

transcribe [træn'skraɪb] VT (gen, Phon) transcrire

transcript ['trænskrɪpt] N (gen) transcription f; (US Univ) (copie f de) dossier m complet de la scolarité

transcription [træn'skrɪpʃən] N (gen, Phon) transcription f; (Phon) **narrow/broad ~** transcription f étroite/large

transduce [trænz'djuːs] VT transformer, convertir

transducer [trænz'djuːsəʳ] N (also Comput) transducteur m

transduction [trænz'dʌkʃən] N transduction f

transect [træn'sekt] VT sectionner (transversalement)

transept ['trænsept] N transept m

transfer [træns'fɜːʳ] [1] VT [a] (= move) [+ employee, civil servant, diplomat] transférer, muter (**to** à); [+ soldier, player, prisoner] transférer (**to** à); [+ passenger] transférer (**to** à), transborder; [+ object, goods] transférer (**to sb** à qn, **to a place** à un lieu), transporter (**to a place** dans un lieu), transmettre (**to sb** à qn); (notice) business **~red to** [office] bureaux mpl transférés à; [shop] magasin m transféré à [b] (= hand over) [+ power] faire passer (**from** de, **to** à); [+ ownership] transférer (**from** de, **to** à); [+ money] virer (**from** de, **to, into** à, sur); [+ vote] reporter (**to** sur); **to ~ one's affection to sb** reporter son or ses affection(s) sur qn [c] (= copy) [+ design, drawing] reporter, décalquer (**to** sur) [d] (Brit Telec) **to ~ the charges** téléphoner en PCV; (Brit Telec) **~red charge call** communication f en PCV; **I'm ~ring you now** [telephone operator] je vous mets en communication maintenant

[2] VI [employee, civil servant, diplomat] être transféré or muté (**to** à); [soldier, player, prisoner, offices] être transféré (**to** à); (US Univ = change universities) faire un transfert (pour une autre université); (Univ etc) **he's ~red from Science to Geography** il ne fait plus de science, il s'est réorienté en géographie; **to ~ from one train/plane** etc **to another** être transféré or transbordé d'un train/avion etc à un autre; **we had to ~ to a bus** nous avons dû changer et prendre un car

[3] ['trænsfɜːʳ] N [a] (= move) (gen) transfert m; [of employee, diplomat] transfert m, mutation f; [of soldier, player, prisoner] transfert m; [of passenger] transfert m, transbordement m; [of object, goods] transfert m, transport m; (Ftbl etc) **to ask for a ~** demander un transfert [b] (= handover) [of money] virement m; (Pol) [of power] passation f; (Jur = document) transfert m, translation f (Jur); **to pay sth by bank ~** payer qch par virement bancaire; (Jur) **~ of ownership** transfert m de propriété (**from** de, **to** à); (Jur) **application for ~ of proceed-**

ings demande f de renvoi devant une autre juridiction [c] (= picture, design etc) (rub-on type) décalcomanie f; (stick-on) autocollant m; (sewn-on) décalque m [d] (Transport: also ~ **ticket**) billet m de correspondance

[4] ['trænsfɜːʳ] COMP ► **transfer desk** N guichet m de transit ► **transfer fee** N (Ftbl etc) indemnité f transfert ► **transfer list** (Brit: Ftbl) liste f des transferts; **to be on the ~ list** être sur la liste des transferts ► **transfer lounge** N salle f de transit ► **transfer passenger** N passager m en transit ► **transfer season** N (Ftbl) période f des transferts ► **transfer student** N (US Univ) étudiant(e) m(f) venant d'une autre université ► **transfer tax** N (Fin) droit m de mutation

transferable [træns'fɜːrəbl] [1] ADJ [a] [ticket] transmissible, qui n'est pas nominatif; (on ticket) **"not ~"** «ne peut être ni cédé ni échangé»; **the prize is not ~ to another person** le prix est strictement personnel [b] [skills] réutilisable [2] COMP ► **transferable vote** N voix f reportée (sur un second candidat)

transferee [,trænsfɜː'riː] N (Jur) cessionnaire mf, bénéficiaire mf

transference ['trænsfərəns] N (NonC) [a] = transfer 3; → **thought** [b] (Psych) transfert m

transferor, **transferrer** [træns'fɜːrəʳ] N (Jur) cédant(e) m(f)

transfiguration [,trænsfɪgə'reɪʃən] N (gen, also Rel) transfiguration f

transfigure [træns'fɪgəʳ] VT transfigurer

transfix [træns'fɪks] VT (lit) transpercer; (fig) **to be** or **stand ~ed** être cloué sur place; **to be ~ed with horror** être cloué au sol d'horreur, être paralysé par l'horreur

transform [træns'fɔːm] [1] VT (gen) transformer, métamorphoser (**into** en); (Chem, Elec, Math, Phys) convertir, transformer (**into** en); (Gram) transformer (**into** en); **to ~ o.s. into ...** ◊ **to be ~ed into ...** se transformer en ... [2] ['trænsfɔːm] N (US Ling) transformation f

transformation [,trænsfə'meɪʃən] N (NonC = change: also Elec, Math, Phys, Ling) transformation f (**into sth** en qch); **to have undergone a complete ~** être complètement métamorphosé

transformational [,trænsfə'meɪʃənl] ADJ (Ling) transformationnel

transformer [træns'fɔːməʳ] [1] N (Elec) transformateur m [2] COMP ► **transformer station** N poste m de transformation

transfuse [træns'fjuːz] VT (Med, fig) transfuser

transfusion [træns'fjuːʒən] N (Med, fig) transfusion f; **blood ~** transfusion f sanguine or de sang; **to give sb a ~** faire une transfusion à qn

transgenic [trænz'dʒenɪk] ADJ transgénique

transgress [træns'gres] [1] VT transgresser, enfreindre, violer [2] VI pécher

transgression [træns'greʃən] N (= sin) péché m, faute f; (NonC) transgression f

transgressor [træns'gresəʳ] N [of law etc] transgresseur m (liter); (Rel = sinner) pécheur m, -eresse f

tranship [træn'ʃɪp] VT = **transship**

transhipment [træn'ʃɪpmənt] N = **transshipment**

transience ['trænzɪəns] N caractère m éphémère or transitoire

transient ['trænzɪənt] [1] ADJ (frm) [pain] passager, [fashion, relationship] éphémère; [population] fluctuant; **of a ~ nature** passager [2] N (US: in hotel etc) client(e) m(f) de passage

transistor [træn'zɪstəʳ] N (Elec) transistor m; (also ~ **radio**, ~ **set**) transistor m

transistorize [træn'zɪstəraɪz] VT transistoriser; **~d** transistorisé, à transistors

transit ['trænzɪt] [1] N (NonC) (gen) transit m; (Astron) passage m; **in ~** en transit [2] COMP [goods, passengers] en transit; [documents, port, visa] de transit ► **transit camp** N (Mil etc) camp m volant ► **transit lounge** N (Aviat) salle f de transit ► **Transit van**® N (Brit) camionnette f

transition [træn'zɪʃən] [1] N transition f (**from** de, **to** à) [2] COMP [period] de transition

transitional [træn'zɪʃənl] [1] ADJ [period, arrangement, government, measures] de transition, transitoire; [costs] de transition [2] COMP ► **transitional relief** N (Brit) dégrèvement fiscal accordé lors de la première phase d'application d'une augmentation d'impôt ou de taxe

transitive ['trænzɪtɪv] ADJ [verb, use] transitif; [sentence] à verbe transitif

transitively ['trænzɪtɪvlɪ] ADV transitivement

transitivity [,trænzɪ'tɪvɪtɪ] N (Gram) transitivité f

transitory ['trænzɪtərɪ] ADJ [romance, peace] éphémère; [state] transitoire, passager; **the ~ nature of political success** la nature transitoire du succès politique

Transkei [træn'skaɪ] N le Transkei

translatable [trænz'leɪtəbl] ADJ traduisible

translate [trænz'leɪt] [1] VT [a] (gen, Ling, also Comput) traduire (**from** de, **into** en); **how do you ~ "weather"?** quelle est la traduction de « weather »?, comment traduit-on « weather »?; **the word is ~d as ...** le mot se traduit par ...; **which when ~d means ...** ce que l'on peut traduire par ...; (fig) **to ~ ideas into actions** passer des idées aux actes; **the figures, ~d in terms of hours lost, mean ...** exprimés or traduits en termes d'heures perdues, ces chiffres signifient ... [b] (Rel) [+ bishop, relics] transférer; (= convey to heaven) ravir [2] VI [person] traduire; [word, book] se traduire; **it won't ~** c'est intraduisible

translation [trænz'leɪʃən] N [a] traduction f (**from** de, **into** en); (Scol etc) version f; **the poem loses in ~** le poème perd à la traduction; **it is a ~ from the Russian** c'est traduit du russe [b] (Rel) [of bishop] translation f; [of relics] transfert m; (= conveying to heaven) ravissement m

translator [trænz'leɪtəʳ] N (= person) traducteur m, -trice f; (= machine) traducteur m; (Comput: also ~ **program**) programme m de traduction

transliterate [trænz'lɪtəreɪt] VT translit(t)érer

transliteration [,trænzlɪtə'reɪʃən] N translittération f

translucence [trænz'luːsns] N translucidité f

translucent [trænz'luːsnt], **translucid** [trænz'luːsɪd] ADJ translucide

transmigrate ['trænzmaɪ'greɪt] VI [soul] transmigrer; [people] émigrer

transmigration [,trænzmaɪ'greɪʃən] N [of soul] transmigration f; [of people] émigration f

transmissible [trænz'mɪsəbl] ADJ transmissible

transmission [trænz'mɪʃən] [1] N (gen) transmission f; (US = gearbox) boîte f de vitesses [2] COMP ► **transmission cable** N (Aut) câble m de transmission ► **transmission shaft** N arbre m de transmission

transmit [trænz'mɪt] [1] VT (gen, Aut, Med, Phys etc) transmettre; (Rad, Telec, TV) diffuser → **sexually** [2] VI (Rad, Telec, TV) émettre, diffuser

transmitter [trænz'mɪtəʳ] N [a] (Rad) émetteur m [b] (in telephone) capsule f microphonique [c] (= transmitting device) transmetteur m

transmitting [trænz'mɪtɪŋ] [1] ADJ (Telec) [set, station] émetteur (-trice f) [2] N (gen, Med, Phys) = **transmission 1**

transmogrify [trænz'mɒgrɪfaɪ] VT (hum) métamorphoser, transformer (**into** en)

transmutable [trænz'mju:təbl] ADJ transmuable or transmutable

transmutation [ˌtrænzmju:'teɪʃən] N transmutation f

transmute [trænz'mju:t] VT transmuer or transmuter (**into** en)

transom ['trænsəm] N **a** (= crosspiece) traverse f, imposte f **b** (US: in window) vasistas m

transonic [træn'sɒnɪk] ADJ = **transsonic**

transparency [træns'pærənsɪ] N **a** (NonC: also fig) transparence f **b** (Brit Phot) diapositive f; (for overhead projector) transparent m; **colour ~** diapositive f en couleur

transparent [træns'pærənt] ADJ **a** (= see-through) [object, substance, material, skin] transparent; **~ to light** transparent **b** (= obvious) [honesty] manifeste, évident; **it is ~ that ...** il est visible or évident que ...; **~ to sb** évident pour qn; **he's so ~** il est si transparent **c** [system, institution] transparent **d** (pej = blatant) [lie, device, tactics, attempt] patent, flagrant

transparently [træns'pærəntlɪ] ADV manifestement, visiblement; **~ obvious** or **clear** tout à fait clair

transpierce [træns'pɪəs] VT transpercer

transpiration [ˌtrænspɪ'reɪʃən] N transpiration f

transpire [træns'paɪər] **1** VI **a** (impers vb) (= become known) s'ébruiter, transpirer; (= happen) se passer, arriver; **it ~d that ...** on a appris par la suite que ... **b** (Bot, Physiol) transpirer **2** VT transpirer

transplant [træns'plɑ:nt] **1** VT [+ plant, population] transplanter; (Med) transplanter, greffer; [+ seedlings etc] repiquer **2** ['trænsplɑ:nt] N (Med) transplantation f, greffe f; **he's had a heart ~** on lui a fait une greffe du cœur or une transplantation cardiaque

transplantation [ˌtrænsplɑ:n'teɪʃən] N (NonC) **a** (Med) transplantation f **b** (Hort, Agr) (gen) transplantation f; (= planting out) [of rice, bedding plants, herbs] repiquage m **c** [= transfer] [of culture, ideology] transfert m

transponder [træn'spɒndər] N transpondeur m

transport ['trænspɔ:t] **1** N **a** [of goods, parcels etc] transport m; **road/rail ~** transport m par route/par chemin de fer; **by road ~** par route; **by rail ~** par chemin de fer; (Brit) **Minister/Department of Transport** ministre m/ministère m des Transports; **have you got any ~ for this evening?*** tu as une voiture pour ce soir? **b** (esp Mil = ship/plane/train) navire m/avion m/train m de transport **c** (fig) [of delight etc] transport m; [of fury etc] accès m **2** [træns'pɔ:t] VT (lit, fig) transporter **3** COMP [costs, ship, plane etc] de transport; [system, dispute, strike] des transports ► **transport café** N (Brit) routier m, restaurant m de routiers ► **Transport Police** N (Brit) ≈ police f des chemins de fer

transportable [træns'pɔ:təbl] ADJ transportable

transportation [ˌtrænspɔ:'teɪʃən] N (= act of transporting) transport m; (US = means of transport) moyen m de transport; [of criminals] transportation f; (US) **Secretary/Department of Transportation** ministre m/ministère m des Transports

transporter [træns'pɔ:tər] N (Mil = vehicle, ship) transport m; (= plane) avion m de transport; (= car transporter) (Aut) camion m pour transport d'automobiles; (Rail) wagon m pour transport d'automobiles

transpose [træns'pəuz] VT **a** (= move: also Mus) transposer; **transposing instrument** instrument m transpositeur **b** (= reverse, reorder) transposer, intervertir

transposition [ˌtrænspə'zɪʃən] N transposition f

transputer [træns'pju:tər] N (Comput) transputeur m

transsexual [trænz'seksjʊəl] N transsexuel(le) m(f)

transsexualism [trænz'seksjʊəlɪzəm] N transsexualisme m

transship [træns'ʃɪp] VT transborder

transshipment [træns'ʃɪpmənt] N transbordement m

trans-Siberian [ˌtrænzsaɪ'bɪərɪən] ADJ transsibérien

transsonic [trænz'sɒnɪk] ADJ transsonique

transubstantiate [ˌtrænsəb'stænʃɪeɪt] VT transsubstantier

transubstantiation ['trænsəbˌstænʃɪ'eɪʃən] N transsubstantiation f

Transvaal ['trænzvɑ:l] N (the) ~ le Transvaal

transversal [trænz'vɜ:səl] (Geom) **1** ADJ transversal **2** N (ligne f) transversale f

transversally [trænz'vɜ:səlɪ] ADV transversalement

transverse ['trænzvɜ:s] **1** ADJ **a** (gen, Geom) [arch, beam] transversal **b** [muscle] transverse, transversal **2** N (gen) partie f transversale; (Geom) axe m transversal **3** COMP ► **transverse colon** N (Anat) côlon m transverse ► **transverse engine** N (Aut) moteur m transversal ► **transverse flute** N (Mus) flûte f traversière

transversely [trænz'vɜ:slɪ] ADV transversalement

transvestism [trænz'vestɪzəm] N travestisme m

transvestite [trænz'vestaɪt] N travesti(e) m(f)

Transylvania [ˌtrænsɪl'veɪnɪə] N la Transylvanie

trap [træp] **1** N **a** (gen) piège m; (also **gin ~**) collet m; (= covered hole) trappe f; (fig) piège m, traquenard m; **lion ~** piège m à lions; (lit, fig) **to set** or **lay a ~** tendre un piège (**for sb** à qn); (lit, fig) **to catch in a ~** prendre au piège; **we were caught like rats in a ~** nous étions faits comme des rats; (fig) **he fell into the ~** il est tombé dans le piège; **to fall into the ~ of doing sth** commettre l'erreur classique de faire qch; **it's a ~** c'est un piège → **mantrap, mousetrap, speed** **b** (also **~ door**) trappe f (also Theat); (in greyhound racing) box m de départ; (Shooting) ball-trap m; (in drainpipe) siphon m; (‡ = mouth) gueule‡ f; **shut your ~!**‡ ta gueule!‡; **keep your ~ shut (about it)**‡ ferme ta gueule‡ (là-dessus) **c** (= carriage) charrette f anglaise, cabriolet m **2** **traps** NPL (= luggage) bagages mpl **3** VT **a** (lit, fig = snare) [+ animal, person] prendre au piège; **they ~ped him into admitting that ...** il est tombé dans leur piège et a admis que ... **b** (= immobilize, catch, cut off) [+ person, vehicle, ship] bloquer, immobiliser; [+ gas, liquid] retenir; [+ object] coincer (**in sth** dans qch); **20 miners were ~ped** 20 mineurs étaient bloqués or murés (au fond); **~ped by the flames** cerné par les flammes; **the climbers were ~ped on a ledge** les alpinistes étaient bloqués sur une saillie; **to ~ one's finger in the door** se coincer or se pincer le doigt dans la porte; (Sport) **to ~ the ball** bloquer le ballon **4** COMP ► **trap door** N trappe f

trapeze [trə'pi:z] **1** N trapèze m (de cirque) **2** COMP ► **trapeze artist** N trapéziste mf, voltigeur m, -euse f

trapezium [trə'pi:zɪəm] N (pl **trapeziums** or **trapezia** [trə'pi:zɪə]) trapèze m (Math)

trapezius [trə'pi:zɪəs] N (pl **trapeziuses**) (muscle m) trapèze m

trapezoid ['træpɪzɔɪd] **1** N trapèze m (Math) **2** ADJ trapézoïdal

trapper ['træpər] N trappeur m

trappings ['træpɪŋz] NPL (for horse) harnachement m; (= dress ornaments) ornements mpl; (fig) **shorn of all its ~** débarrassé de toutes ses fioritures; (fig) **if you look beneath the ~** si on regarde derrière la façade; **with all the ~ of kingship** avec tout le cérémonial afférent à la royauté; **all the ~ of success** tous les signes extérieurs du succès

Trappist ['træpɪst] **1** N trappiste m **2** ADJ de la Trappe

trapse* [treɪps] VI = **traipse**

trapshooting ['træpˌʃu:tɪŋ] N ball-trap m

trash [træʃ] **1** N **a** (esp US = refuse) ordures fpl **b** (pej = worthless thing) camelote* f; (= nonsense) inepties fpl; (‡ pej = people) racaille f (NonC); (fig) **this is ~** ça ne vaut rien (du tout); (esp goods) c'est de la camelote*; (message, letter, remark etc) c'est de la blague*; **he talks a lot of ~** il ne raconte que des inepties, ce qu'il dit c'est de la blague*; **they're just ~**‡ [people] c'est de la racaille; **he's ~**‡ c'est un moins que rien → **white** **2** VT* **a** (= vandalize) saccager **b** (= criticize) débiner*, dénigrer **3** VI (US*) commettre des actes de vandalisme **4** COMP ► **trash can** N (US) poubelle f ► **trash heap** N (lit) tas m d'ordures, dépotoir m; (fig) **the ~ heap of history** les oubliettes or la poubelle de l'histoire

trasher* ['træʃər] N (US) vandale mf

trashy ['træʃɪ] ADJ [novel, play, film, pop group, ideas] nul* (nulle* f); **~ goods** camelote* f

Trasimene ['træzɪmi:n] N **Lake ~** le lac Trasimène

trattoria [ˌtrætə'ri:ə] N trattoria f

trauma ['trɔ:mə] **1** N (pl **traumas** or **traumata** ['trɔ:mətə]) (Med, Psych) trauma m; (fig) traumatisme m **2** COMP ► **trauma center** N (US Med) service m de traumatologie

traumatic [trɔ:'mætɪk] ADJ (Med) traumatique; [experience, effect, event, relationship] traumatisant; **it is ~ to lose one's job** c'est traumatisant de perdre son travail → **post-traumatic stress disorder**

traumatism ['trɔ:mətɪzəm] N traumatisme m

traumatize ['trɔ:mətaɪz] VT traumatiser

traumatized ['trɔ:mətaɪzd] ADJ traumatisé

travail †† ['træveɪl] **1** N labeur m; (in childbirth) douleurs fpl de l'enfantement **2** VI peiner; (in childbirth) être en couches

travel ['trævl] **1** VI **a** (= journey) voyager; **they have ~ed a lot** ils ont fait beaucoup de voyages; **they have ~ed a long way** ils sont venus de loin; (fig) ils ont fait beaucoup de chemin; **he is ~ling in Spain just now** il est en voyage en Espagne en ce moment; **as he was ~ling across France** pendant qu'il voyageait à travers la France; **to ~ through a region** traverser une région; (= visit) visiter or parcourir une région; **to ~ round the world** faire le tour du monde; **to ~ light** voyager avec peu de bagages; **I like ~ling by car** j'aime voyager en voiture; **he ~s to work by car** il va au travail en voiture; **he was ~ling on a passport/a ticket which ...** il voyageait avec un passeport/un billet qui ...; **it ~s well** [food, wine] ça supporte bien le voyage **b** (Comm†) voyager, être représentant; **he ~s for a Paris firm** il voyage pour or il représente une société parisienne; **he ~s in soap** il est représentant en savon **c** (= move, go) [person, animal, vehicle] aller; [object] aller, passer; [machine part, bobbin, piston etc] se déplacer; **to ~ at 80km/h** faire du 80 km/h; **you were ~ling too fast** vous rouliez trop vite; **he was really ~ling!*** il roulait drôlement vite!*; **this car can certainly ~*** cette voiture est vraiment rapide; **light ~s at (a speed of) ...** la vitesse de la lumière est de ...; **news ~s fast** les nouvelles se propagent or circulent vite; **the news ~led to Rome** la nouvelle s'est propagée jusqu'à Rome; **the boxes ~ along a moving belt** les boîtes passent sur une or se déplacent le long d'une chaîne; **this part ~s 3cm** cette pièce se déplace de 3 cm or a une course de 3 cm; *(fig)* **his eyes ~led over the scene** son regard se promenait or il se menait son regard sur le spectacle; **her mind ~led over recent events** elle a revu en esprit les événements récents

2 VT **to ~ a country/district** parcourir un pays/une région; **they ~ the road to London every month** ils font la route de Londres tous les mois; **a much-~led road** une route très fréquentée; **they ~led 300km** ils ont fait or parcouru 300 km

3 N *allowance, expenses* le(s) voyage(s) *m(pl)*; **to be fond of ~** aimer voyager, aimer les voyages; **~ was difficult in those days** les voyages étaient difficiles or il était difficile de voyager à l'époque; **~ broadens the mind** les voyages ouvrent l'esprit

b **~s** voyages *mpl*; **his ~s in Spain** ses voyages en Espagne; **he's off on his ~s again** il repart en voyage; **if you meet him on your ~s** *(lit)* si vous le rencontrez au cours de vos voyages; *(fig hum)* si vous le rencontrez au cours de vos allées et venues

c *of machine part, piston etc* course *f*

4 COMP *allowance, expenses* de déplacement; *scholarship* de voyage(s) ► **travel agency** N agence *f* de voyages or de tourisme ► **travel agent** N agent *m* de voyages ► **travel book** N récit *m* de voyage ► **travel brochure** N dépliant *m* or brochure *f* touristique ► **travel bureau** N = travel agency ► **travel card** N *(Brit)* carte *f* de transport; *(= documentary)* documentaire *m* touristique ► **travel film** N film *m* or *(= documentary)* documentaire *m* touristique ► **travel insurance** N assurance *f* voyage ► **travel organization** N organisme *m* de tourisme ► **travel-sick** ADJ **to be ~-sick** avoir le mal des transports ► **travel sickness** N mal *m* des transports ► **travel-sickness pill** N comprimé *m* contre le mal des transports ► **travel-stained** ADJ sali par le(s) voyage(s) ► **travel voucher** N bon *m* de voyage ► **travel-weary, travel-worn** ADJ fatigué par le(s) voyage(s)

travelator ['trævəleɪtə'] N tapis *m* or trottoir *m* roulant

travelled, traveled *(US)* ['trævld] ADJ *person* *(also* **well-~, much-~, widely ~**) qui a beaucoup voyagé; **a well-~** or **much-~ road** une route très fréquentée → **travel**

traveller, traveler *(US)* ['trævlə'] **1** N voyageur *m*, -euse *f*; *(†: also* **commercial ~**) voyageur *m* or représentant *m* de commerce, VRP *m*; *(Comm)* **he is a ~ in soap** il est représentant en savon **2** **travellers** NPL *(Brit = gypsies)* gens *mpl* du voyage **3** COMP ► **traveler's check** N *(US)* = **traveller's cheque** ► **traveller's cheque** N chèque *m* de voyage, traveller's chèque *m* ► **traveller's joy** N *(Bot)* clématite *f* des haies

travelling, traveling *(US)* ['trævlɪŋ] **1** N *(NonC)* voyage(s) *m(pl)* **2** ADJ *actor, musician, circus, theatre company* itinérant, ambulant; *exhibition* itinérant; *crane* mobile; **the ~ public** les gens qui se déplacent; **England's 5,000 ~ fans** les 5000 supporters qui suivent l'équipe d'Angleterre **3** COMP *bag, rug, scholarship* de voyage; *expenses, allowance* de déplacement ► **travelling clock** N réveil *m* or pendulette *f* de voyage ► **travelling library** N bibliobus *m* ► **travelling people** NPL *(Brit)* gens *mpl* du voyage ► **travelling salesman** N *(pl* **travelling salesmen**) *(Comm)* voyageur *m* de commerce, VRP *m*

travelogue, travelog *(US)* ['trævəlɒg] N *(= talk)* compte rendu *m* de voyage; *(= film)* documentaire *m* touristique; *(= book)* récit *m* de voyage

traverse ['trævəs] **1** VT *(gen, Climbing, Ski)* traverser; *searchlights* balayer **2** VI *(Climbing, Ski)* faire une traversée, traverser **3** N *(= line)* transversale *f*; *(= crossbar, crossbeam; also across rampart, trench etc)* traverse *f*; *(Archit)* galerie *f* transversale; *(Climbing, Ski)* traversée *f*

travesty ['trævɪstɪ] **1** N *(Art, Literat etc)* parodie *f*, pastiche *m*; *(pej)* parodie *f*, simulacre *m*; *(pej)* **it was a ~ of freedom/peace** c'était un simulacre de liberté/de paix; **it was a ~ of justice** c'était un simulacre or une parodie de justice **2** VT être un travestissement de

trawl [trɔːl] **1** N *(also* **~ net**) chalut *m*; *(fig = search)* recherche *f* **2** VI pêcher au chalut; **to ~ for herring** pêcher le hareng au chalut; *(fig)* **to ~ for sth** être en quête de qch **3** VT *+ net* traîner, tirer; *(fig)* **to ~ a place/the papers for sth** ratisser un endroit/éplucher les journaux à la recherche de qch

trawler ['trɔːlə'] **1** N *(= ship, man)* chalutier *m* **2** COMP ► **trawler fisherman** N *(pl* **trawler fishermen**) pêcheur *m* au chalut ► **trawler owner** N propriétaire *m* de chalutier

trawling ['trɔːlɪŋ] N *(NonC)* chalutage *m*, pêche *f* au chalut

tray [treɪ] N *(for carrying things)* plateau *m*; *(for storing things: box-type)* boîte *f* *(de rangement)*; *(basket-type)* corbeille *f* *(de rangement)*; *(drawer-type)* tiroir *m*; *of eggs* *(also in chocolate box)* plaque *f*, plateau *m* → **ashtray, ice**

traycloth ['treɪklɒθ] N napperon *m*

treacherous ['tretʃərəs] ADJ **a** *(= disloyal)* *person, action, intentions* traître (traîtresse *f*), perfide; **to be ~ to sb** trahir qn **b** *(= perilous)* *weather conditions, road* traître (traîtresse *f*), dangereux; *waters, river, current, tide, sands* traître (traîtresse *f*); *journey* périlleux **c** *(= unreliable)* *memory* défaillant

treacherously ['tretʃərəslɪ] ADV traîtreusement, perfidement; **the roads are ~ slippery** les routes sont dangereusement glissantes

treachery ['tretʃərɪ] N traîtrise *f*, déloyauté *f*

treacle ['triːkl] *(Brit)* **1** N *(also* **black ~**) mélasse *f* **2** COMP ► **treacle pudding** N pudding *m* à la mélasse raffinée ► **treacle tart** N tarte *f* à la mélasse raffinée

treacly ['triːklɪ] ADJ *substance, liquid, sentimentality* sirupeux; *voice* onctueux

tread [tred] *(vb: pret* **trod**, *ptp* **trodden**) **1** N **a** *(NonC)* *(= footsteps)* pas *mpl*; *(= sound)* bruit *m* de pas **b** *of tyre* bande *f* de roulement; *of stair* giron *m*; *of shoe* semelle *f*; *(= belt over tractor etc wheels)* chenille *f* **2** VI marcher; **to ~ on sth** mettre le pied sur qch, marcher sur qch; *(deliberately)* **he trod on the cigarette end** il a écrasé le mégot du pied; *(fig)* **to ~ on sb's heels** suivre or serrer qn de près, talonner qn; *(lit, fig)* **to ~ carefully** or **softly** or **warily** avancer avec précaution, y aller doucement → **toe** **3** VT *+ path, road* suivre, parcourir *(à pied)*; **he trod the streets looking for somewhere to live** il a erré dans les rues or il a battu le pavé à la recherche d'un logis; **to ~ sth underfoot** fouler qch aux pieds, piétiner qch; **to ~ grapes** fouler du raisin; **~ the earth (in** or **down) round the roots** tassez la terre du pied autour des racines; **he trod his cigarette end into the mud** il a enfoncé du pied son mégot dans la boue; **you're ~ing mud into the carpet** tu mets or tu étales de la boue sur le tapis; *(pret, ptp* **treaded**) **to ~ water** *(lit, fig)* faire du surplace; **well-trodden path** *(lit)* sentier *m* bien tracé; *(fig)* sentier *m* battu; *(Theat†† or liter)* **to ~ the boards** monter sur les planches, faire du théâtre; *(†† or liter)* **to ~ a measure** *(= dance)* danser **4** COMP ► **tread pattern** N *(Aut)* sculptures *fpl*

► **tread down** VT SEP tasser or presser du pied; **the grass was trodden down** l'herbe avait été piétinée or foulée
► **tread in** VT SEP *+ root, seedling* consolider en tassant la terre du pied

treadle ['tredl] **1** N pédale *f* **2** VI actionner la pédale **3** COMP *machine* à pédale

treadmill ['tredmɪl] N *(= mill)* trépigneuse *f*; *(Hist = punishment)* manège *m* de discipline; *(for exercise)* tapis *m* de jogging; *(fig)* **he hated the ~ of life in the factory** il détestait la morne or mortelle routine du travail d'usine

Treas. ABBR = **Treasurer**

treason ['triːzn] N trahison *f*; **high ~** haute trahison *f*

treasonable ['triːzənəbl] ADJ qui relève de la trahison, traître (traîtresse *f*); **it was ~ to do such a thing** un tel acte relevait de la trahison

treasure ['treʒə'] **1** N trésor *m* *(also fig)*; **~s of medieval art** les trésors *mpl* or les joyaux *mpl* de l'art médiéval; **she's a ~** *(gen)* elle est adorable; *(of servant etc)* c'est une perle; **yes my ~** oui mon trésor **2** VT **a** *(= value greatly)* *+ object, sb's friendship, opportunity etc* tenir beaucoup à, attacher une grande valeur à; **this is my most ~d possession** c'est ce que je possède de plus précieux **b** *(= keep carefully: also* **~ up**) *+ object, money, valuables* garder précieusement, prendre grand soin de; *+ memory, thought* conserver précieusement, chérir **3** COMP ► **treasure chest** N *(lit)* malle *f* au trésor; *(fig)* **a ~ chest of information/of useful advice** une mine de renseignements/de conseils utiles ► **treasure-house** N *(lit)* trésor *m* *(lieu)*; *(fig: of library, museum etc)* mine *f*, trésor *m*; **she's a real ~-house of information** c'est une mine de science, c'est une mine d'érudition ► **treasure hunt** N chasse *f* au trésor ► **treasure-trove** N *(NonC)* trésor *m*; *(fig = valuable collection)* mine *f*; *(fig = rich source)* mine *f* d'or

treasurer ['treʒərə'] N trésorier *m*, -ière *f* *(d'une association etc)*

treasury ['treʒərɪ] **1** N **a** **the Treasury** la Trésorerie, ≈ le ministère des Finances; *(US)* **Secretary/Department of the Treasury** ministre *m*/ministère *m* des Finances **b** *(= place)* trésorerie *f*; *(fig = book)* trésor *m* **2** COMP ► **Treasury bench** N *(Brit Parl)* banc *m* des ministres ► **Treasury bill, Treasury bond** N *(US)* ≈ bon *m* du Trésor ► **Treasury Department** N *(US)* ministère *m* des Finances ► **Treasury note** N ≈ bon *m* du Trésor ► **Treasury Secretary** N *(US)* ministre *m* des Finances

┌─────────────┐
│ **TREASURY** │
└─────────────┘
*En Grande-Bretagne, **Treasury** (ou « Her/His Majesty's **Treasury** ») est le nom donné au ministère des Finances, et le ministre porte traditionnellement le nom de chancelier de l'Échiquier (Chancellor of the Exchequer). Il a sa résidence au 11, Downing Street, non loin de celle du Premier ministre.*

*Aux États-Unis, le ministère correspondant est le « Department of **Treasury** », qui a en outre la responsabilité des services secrets chargés d'assurer la garde du président.*

treat [triːt] **1** VT **a** *(gen)* traiter; *+ object, theme, suggestion* traiter, examiner; **to ~ sb well** bien traiter qn, bien agir or se conduire envers qn; **to ~ sb badly** mal agir or se conduire envers qn, traiter qn fort mal; **to ~ sb like a child** traiter qn comme un enfant; **to ~ sb like dirt** or **a dog** traiter qn comme un chien; **he ~ed me as though I was to blame** il s'est conduit envers moi comme si c'était ma faute; **you should ~ your mother with more respect** vous devriez montrer plus de respect envers votre mère; **you should ~ your books with more care** tu devrais faire plus attention *or* prendre plus de soin de tes livres; **the article ~s the problems of race relations with fresh insight** cet article aborde les problèmes des rapports interraciaux d'une façon originale; **he ~s the subject very objectively** il traite le sujet avec beaucoup d'objectivité; **he ~ed the whole thing as a joke** il a pris tout cela à la plaisanterie

b [+ *wood, soil, substance*] traiter (**with sth** à qch); (*Med*) traiter, soigner (**sb for sth** qn pour qch); **they ~ed him/the infection with penicillin** ils l'ont soigné/ont soigné l'infection à la pénicilline

c (= *pay for etc*) **to ~ sb to sth** offrir *or* payer* qch à qn; **to ~ o.s. to sth** s'offrir *or* se payer* qch; **I'll ~ you to a drink** je t'offre *or* te paie* un verre

2 VI **a** (= *negotiate*) **to ~ with sb** traiter avec qn (**for sth** pour qch); **to ~ for peace** engager des pourparlers en vue de la paix

b (= *discuss*) **to ~ of** [*book, article etc*] traiter (de)

3 N **a** (= *pleasure*) plaisir *m*; (= *outing*) sortie *f*; (= *present*) cadeau *m*; **I've got a ~ for you** j'ai une bonne surprise pour toi; **what a ~!** quelle aubaine!, chouette* alors!; **it's a ~ in store** c'est un plaisir à venir; **it was a great ~ (for us) to see them again** ça nous a vraiment fait plaisir de les revoir, ça a été une joie de les revoir; **what would you like as a ~ for your birthday?** qu'est-ce qui te ferait plaisir pour ton anniversaire?; **it is a ~ for her to go out to a meal** elle se fait une joie de *or* c'est tout un événement* pour elle de dîner en ville; **let's give the children a ~** faisons (un) plaisir *or* une gâterie aux enfants, gâtons un peu les enfants; **I want to give her a ~** je veux lui faire plaisir; **to give o.s. a ~** s'offrir un petit extra, s'offrir quelque chose; **the school ~ was a visit to the seaside** la fête de l'école a consisté en une excursion au bord de la mer; **to stand ~** inviter; **to stand sb a ~** (*gen*) offrir *or* payer* quelque chose à qn; (*food, drink only*) régaler* qn; **this is to be my ~** c'est moi qui offre *or* qui paie*; (*food, drink only*) c'est moi qui régale*

b (*Brit*: *adv phrase*) **a ~** à merveille; **the garden is coming on a ~** le jardin avance à merveille; **the plan worked a ~** le projet a marché comme sur des roulettes

treatable ['tri:təbl] ADJ [*illness*] soignable, qui se soigne

treatise ['tri:tɪz] N (*Literat*) traité *m* (**on** de)

treatment ['tri:tmənt] **1** N (*gen, Chem etc*) traitement *m*; (*Med*) traitement *m*, soins *mpl*; **his ~ of his parents/the dog** la façon dont il traite ses parents/le chien; **his ~ of this subject in his book** la façon dont il traite ce sujet dans son livre; **he got very good ~ there** (*gen*) il a été très bien traité là-bas; (*Med*) il a été très bien soigné là-bas; **to give sb preferential ~** accorder à qn un traitement préférentiel *or* un régime de faveur; **he needs medical ~** il a besoin de soins médicaux *or* d'un traitement; **they refused him ~** ils ont refusé de le soigner; **he is having (a course of) ~ for kidney trouble** il suit un traitement *or* il est sous traitement pour ennuis rénaux; (*fig*) **to give sb the ~** en faire voir de toutes les couleurs* à qn → **respond 2** COMP ► **treatment room** N (*Med*) salle *f* de soins

treaty ['tri:tɪ] **1** N **a** traité *m* (**with** avec, **between** entre); (*Pol*) **to make a ~ with sb** conclure *or* signer un traité avec qn **b** (*NonC*) **to sell a house by private ~** vendre une maison par accord privé **2** COMP ► **treaty obligations** NPL obligations *fpl* conventionnelles

treble ['trebl] **1** ADJ **a** (= *triple*) triple; **a ~ whisky** un triple whisky; **the amount is in ~ figures** le montant dépasse la centaine *or* se

chiffre en centaines **b** (*Mus*) [*voice*] de soprano (*de jeune garçon*); [*part*] pour soprano **2** N **a** (*Mus*) (= *part*) soprano *m*; (= *singer*) soprano *mf* **b** (*Recording*) aigus *mpl* **c** (= *drink*) triple *m* **d** (*Darts*) triple *m* **e** (*Brit Sport* = *three victories*) triplé *m* **3** ADV **it expanded to ~ its size** sa taille a triplé; **rents that were ~ their current levels** des loyers qui étaient trois fois plus élevés que ceux d'aujourd'hui **4** VTI tripler **5** COMP ► **the treble chance** N (*in football pools*) méthode de pari au loto sportif ► **treble clef** N (*Mus*) clé *f* de sol ► **treble recorder** N (*Mus*) flûte *f* à bec alto

trebly ['treblɪ] ADV triplement, trois fois plus

tree [tri:] (*vb*: *pret, ptp* **treed**) **1** N **a** arbre *m*; **cherry ~** cerisier *m*; (*Bible*) **the ~ of life** l'arbre *m* de vie; (*Bible*) **the ~ of knowledge of good and evil** l'arbre *m* de la science du bien et du mal; (*Rel*††) **the ~** (= *the Cross*) l'arbre *m* de la Croix; **money doesn't grow on ~s** l'argent ne tombe pas du ciel; **people like that don't grow on ~s** les gens comme ça ne courent pas les rues; (*Brit fig*) **to be at** *or* **to have reached the top of the ~** être arrivé en haut de l'échelle (*fig*); (*fig*) **to be up a ~** être dans le pétrin; **he's out of his ~** (= *crazy*) il est cinglé*; (*through drugs, alcohol*) il est défoncé* → **apple, bark¹, bark², family, plum b** (*also* **shoe ~**) embauchoir *m*; (*cobbler's last*) forme *f* **c** (*Ling*) arbre *m* **d** [*of saddle*] arçon *m* (de la selle) **2** VT forcer à se réfugier dans un arbre **3** COMP ► **tree-covered** ADJ boisé ► **tree creeper** N grimpereau *m* ► **tree diagram** N (*Ling*) représentation *f* en arbre ► **tree fern** N fougère *f* arborescente ► **tree frog** N rainette *f* ► **tree hugger** N (*esp US pej hum*) écolo* *mf* ► **tree house** N cabane *f* construite dans un arbre ► **tree lawn** N (*US*) platebande *f* plantée d'arbres (*entre la rue et le trottoir*) ► **tree line** N limite *f* des arbres ► **tree-lined** ADJ bordé d'arbres ► **tree of heaven** N (*Bot*) ailante *m* ► **tree-runner** N (= *bird*) sittelle *f* ► **tree surgeon** N arboriculteur *m*, -trice *f* (qui s'occupe du traitement des arbres malades) ► **tree surgery** N arboriculture *f* (spécialisée dans le traitement des arbres malades) ► **tree trunk** N tronc *m* d'arbre

treeless ['tri:lɪs] ADJ sans arbres

treetop ['tri:tɒp] N sommet *m or* cime *f* d'un arbre; **in the ~s** au sommet *or* à la cime des arbres

trefoil ['trefɔɪl] **1** N (*Archit, Bot*) trèfle *m* **2** COMP ► **trefoil leaf** N feuille *f* de trèfle

trek [trek] **1** VI **a** (= *go slowly*) cheminer, avancer avec peine; (*as holiday: also* **to go ~king**) faire du trekking *or* de la randonnée; (= *go on long, difficult journey*) faire un périple; (*Hist* = *go on oxcart*) voyager en char à bœufs → **pony b** (* = *walk*) se traîner; **I had to ~ over to the library** il a fallu que je me traîne (*subj*) jusqu'à la bibliothèque **2** N (= *hike*) trekking *m*, randonnée *f*; (= *long, difficult journey*) périple *m*; (= *leg of journey*) étape *f*; (*by oxcart*) voyage *m* en char à bœufs; (* = *walk*) balade* *f*; **it was quite a ~* to the hotel** il y avait un bon bout de chemin* jusqu'à l'hôtel

Trekkie ['trekɪ] N fan *mf* de Star Trek

trekking ['trekɪŋ] N trekking *m*, randonnée *f*; **to go ~** faire du trekking *or* de la randonnée; **to go on a ~ holiday** partir en vacances faire de la randonnée

trellis ['trelɪs] **1** N treillis *m*; (*tougher*) treillage *m*; (*NonC: also* **~work**) treillage *m* **2** VT treillisser, treillager

tremble ['trembl] **1** VI trembler; (*with excitement, passion*) frémir, frissonner; [*voice*] (*with fear, anger*) trembler; (*with age*) chevroter; (*with passion*) vibrer, frissonner; [*hands, legs, lips, object, building, ground*] trembler; [*engine, ship, train*] trépider; **to ~ with fear** trembler *or*

frissonner de peur; **to ~ with cold** trembler de froid, grelotter; **to ~ with anger** trembler de colère; **to ~ with excitement/passion** frémir *or* frissonner d'excitation/de passion; **to ~ at the thought of sth** frémir à la pensée de qch; **I ~ to think what might have happened** je frémis à la pensée de ce qui aurait pu arriver; **what will he do next? — I ~ to think!** qu'est-ce qu'il va encore faire? — j'en frémis d'avance!; **her employees ~d at the mere mention of her name** la simple mention de son nom faisait frémir ses employés; **to ~ in one's shoes** être dans ses petits souliers

2 N [*of person*] tremblement *m*; (*with excitement, passion*) frémissement *m*, frissonnement *m*; (*with age*) tremblotement *m*; [*of voice*] (*with fear, anger*) tremblement *m*; (*with age*) chevrotement *m*; (*with passion*) vibration *f*, frissonnement *m*; [*of hands, legs, lips, building, ground*] tremblement *m*; [*of engine, ship, train*] trépidations *fpl*; **to be all of a ~** trembler comme une feuille

trembling ['tremblɪŋ] → **tremble 1** **1** ADJ [*person*] tremblant; (*with age*) tremblotant; (*with excitement, passion*) frémissant, frissonnant; [*voice*] (*with fear, anger*) tremblant; (*with age*) chevrotant; (*with excitement, passion*) vibrant; [*hands, legs, lips, object, building, ground*] tremblant; [*engine, ship, train*] trépidant **2** N (*NonC*) tremblement *m* → **fear**

tremendous [trə'mendəs] ADJ **a** (= *great, enormous*) [*amount, number, effort, shock, pleasure, potential*] énorme; [*feeling, relief, progress, success, courage, loss*] énorme, immense; [*help, support, achievement, opportunity*] extraordinaire; [*storm, heat, blow, explosion, noise*] épouvantable, terrible; [*speed*] fou (folle *f*); [*victory*] foudroyant; **she taught me a ~ amount** elle m'a énormément appris; **a ~ sense of loyalty** un sens très poussé de la loyauté; **there was a ~ crowd at the meeting** il y avait un monde fou à la réunion **b** (* = *excellent*) [*person*] génial*, super* *inv*; [*goal, food*] super* *inv*; **she has done a ~ job** elle a accompli un travail remarquable; **we had a ~ time*** on s'est drôlement bien amusés*

tremendously [trə'mendəslɪ] ADV [*important*] extrêmement; [*exciting*] terriblement; [*improve, vary*] considérablement; [*help*] énormément; **they've done ~ well** ils s'en sont extrêmement bien tirés

tremolo ['tremələʊ] N (*Mus*) trémolo *m*

tremor ['tremə'] N tremblement *m* → **earth**

tremulous ['tremjʊləs] ADJ (*liter*) **a** (= *timid*) [*person*] craintif; [*smile*] timide, incertain **b** (= *trembling*) [*person*] tremblant; (*with age*) tremblotant; (*with excitement, passion*) frémissant, frissonnant; [*voice*] (*with fear, anger*) tremblant; (*with age*) chevrotant; (*with excitement, passion*) vibrant; [*handwriting*] tremblé; [*hands*] tremblant; [*request*] formulé d'une voix tremblante

tremulously ['tremjʊləslɪ] ADV (*liter*) [*say, answer, suggest*] (= *timidly*) craintivement; (= *in trembling voice*) (*with fear, anger*) en tremblant, d'une voix tremblante; (*with age*) en chevrotant; (*with excitement, passion*) en frémissant, en frissonnant; [*smile*] d'une façon incertaine, timidement

trench [trentʃ] **1** N tranchée *f* (*also Mil*); (*wider*) fossé *m*; **he fought in the ~es** il était dans les tranchées *or* a fait la guerre des tranchées **2** VT (= *dig trenches in*) creuser une *or* des tranchée(s) dans; (*Mil* = *surround with trenches*) [+ *one's position etc*] retrancher **3** VI creuser une *or* des tranchée(s) **4** COMP ► **trench coat** N trench-coat *m* ► **trench fever** N (*Med*) fièvre *f* des tranchées, rickettsiose *f* ► **trench knife** N (*pl* **trench knives**) couteau *m* (à double tranchant) ► **trench warfare** N (*NonC: Mil*) guerre *f* de tranchées

trenchant ['trentʃənt] ADJ [view] tranchant; [criticism, statement] incisif; [person] catégorique (on or about sth sur qch)

trenchantly ['trentʃəntlɪ] ADV d'un ton incisif

trencher ['trentʃəʳ] N tranchoir m

trencherman ['trentʃəmæn] N (pl -men) **he is a good** or **great** or **hearty ~** il a un sacré coup de fourchette*

trend [trend] **1** N (= tendency) tendance f (**towards** à); (Geog) [of coast, river, road] direction f, orientation f; (= fashion) mode f, vogue f; (Fin etc) **upward/downward ~** tendance f à la hausse/à la baisse; **there is a ~ towards doing/away from doing** on a tendance à faire/à ne plus faire; **the latest ~s in swimwear** la mode la plus récente en maillots de bain; **the ~ of events** le cours or la tournure des événements; **to set a ~** donner le ton; (= fashion) lancer une mode; **to buck the ~** aller or agir à contre-courant; **~s in popular music** les tendances fpl de la musique populaire → **market, reverse 2** VI **to ~ northwards/southwards** etc [river, road] se diriger vers le nord/le sud etc; **to ~ towards sth** [events, opinions] tendre vers qch

trendiness* ['trendɪnɪs] N côté m branché

trendsetter ['trendsetəʳ] N (= person) personne f qui donne le ton (or qui lance une mode)

trendsetting ['trendsetɪŋ] **1** N innovation f **2** ADJ innovateur (-trice f), qui donne le ton (or lance une mode)

trendy* ['trendɪ] **1** ADJ [person, clothes, restaurant, ideas] branché*; [opinions, behaviour, religion] à la mode; **he's got quite a ~ image** il fait très branché*; **it's no longer ~ to smoke** fumer n'est plus considéré comme branché* **2** N branché(e)* m(f)

trepan [trɪ'pæn] **1** VT [+ metal plate etc] forer; (Med) trépaner **2** N (for quarrying etc) foreuse f, trépan m; (Med) trépan m

trephine [tre'fi:n] (Med) **1** VT trépaner **2** N trépan m

trepidation [,trepɪ'deɪʃən] N (= fear) vive inquiétude f; (= excitement) agitation f

trespass ['trespəs] **1** N a (NonC Jur = illegal entry) entrée f non autorisée b (††, Rel = sin) offense f, péché m; **forgive us our ~es** pardonnez-nous nos offenses **2** VI a entrer sans permission; **"no ~ing"** «entrée interdite», «propriété privée»; **you're ~ing** vous êtes dans une propriété privée; **to ~ on** [+ sb's land] s'introduire or se trouver sans permission dans or sur; (fig) [+ sb's hospitality, time] abuser de; [+ sb's privacy] s'ingérer dans; [+ sb's rights] empiéter sur b †† **to ~ against** (Rel) [+ person] offenser; [+ law] enfreindre; (Rel) **as we forgive them that ~ against us** comme nous pardonnons à ceux qui nous ont offensés

trespasser ['trespəsəʳ] N a intrus(e) m(f) (dans une propriété privée); **"~s will be prosecuted"** «défense d'entrer sous peine de poursuites» b (††, Rel = sinner) pécheur m, -eresse f

tress [tres] N (liter) boucle f de cheveux; **~es** chevelure f

trestle ['tresl] **1** N tréteau m, chevalet m **2** COMP ► **trestle bridge** N pont m sur chevalets ► **trestle table** N table f à tréteaux

trews [tru:z] NPL pantalon m écossais (étroit)

tri... [traɪ] PREF tri...

Triad ['traɪæd] N (in China) Triade f

triad ['traɪæd] N (gen) triade f; (Mus) accord m parfait

trial ['traɪəl] **1** N a (Jur) (= proceedings) procès m; (NonC) jugement m; **the ~ lasted a month** le procès a duré un mois; **famous ~s** procès mpl or causes fpl célèbres; **a new ~ was ordered** la révision du procès a été demandée; **at the ~ it emerged that ...** au cours du procès or à l'audience il est apparu que ...; **during his ~ he claimed that ...** pendant son procès il a affirmé que ...; **~ by jury** jugement m par jury; (fig) **~ by media** or **television** jugement par les médias; **to be** or **go on ~** passer en jugement or en justice; **to put sb on ~** faire passer qn en jugement → 1b; **to be sent for ~** être traduit en justice (**to** devant), être inculpé; **to be on ~ for theft** être jugé pour vol; **he was on ~ for his life** il encourait la peine de mort; **to bring sb to ~** faire passer qn en jugement or en justice; **to come up for ~** [case] passer au tribunal; [person] passer en jugement; **to stand (one's) ~** passer en jugement (**for sth** pour qch, **for doing** pour avoir fait) → **commit** b (= test) [of machine, vehicle, drug] essai m; **~s** (Ftbl) match m de sélection; (Athletics) épreuve f de sélection; **sheepdog ~s** concours m de chiens de berger; **horse ~s** concours m hippique; **~ of strength** épreuve f de force; **to have a ~ of strength with sb** lutter de force avec qn, se mesurer à qn; **by (a system of) ~ and error** par tâtonnements, en tâtonnant; **it was all ~ and error** on a procédé uniquement par tâtonnements; **to take sb/sth on ~** prendre qn/qch à l'essai; **to be on ~** [machine, method, employee] être à l'essai; **to give sb a ~** mettre qn à l'essai c (= hardship) épreuve f; (= nuisance) souci m; **the ~s of old age** les afflictions fpl or les vicissitudes fpl de la vieillesse; **the interview was a great ~** l'entrevue a été une véritable épreuve or a été très éprouvante; **he is a ~ to his mother** il est un souci perpétuel pour sa mère, il donne beaucoup de soucis à sa mère; **what a ~ you are!** ce que tu es agaçant or exaspérant! → **tribulation**

2 VT (= test) tester

3 COMP [flight, period etc] d'essai; [offer, marriage] à l'essai ► **trial attorney** N (US Jur) avocat(e) m(f) qui plaide à l'audience ► **trial balance** N (Fin) balance f d'inventaire ► **trial balloon** N (US lit, fig) ballon m d'essai ► **trial basis** N **on a ~ basis** à titre d'essai ► **trial court** N (US, Can) cour f jugeant en première instance ► **trial division** N (US, Can Jur) division f or tribunal m de première instance ► **trial judge** N (US) juge m d'instance ► **trial jury** N (US Jur) jury m (de jugement) ► **trial lawyer** N (US Jur) ≈ avocat(e) m(f) ► **trial run** N [of machine etc] essai m; (fig) période f d'essai, répétition f

triangle ['traɪæŋgl] N (Math, Mus, fig) triangle m; (= drawing instrument) équerre f → **eternal**

triangular [traɪ'æŋgjʊləʳ] ADJ triangulaire

triangulate [traɪ'æŋgjʊleɪt] VT trianguler

triangulation [traɪ,æŋgjʊ'leɪʃən] N triangulation f

Triassic [traɪ'æsɪk] **1** ADJ (Geol) [period] triasique **2** N trias m

triathlon [traɪ'æθlən] N triathlon m

tribal ['traɪbəl] ADJ tribal; **the ~ elders** les anciens mpl de la tribu (or des tribus); **~ people** membres mpl d'une tribu; **they are a ~ people** ils vivent en tribu; **divided on** or **along ~ lines** divisé selon des clivages tribaux

tribalism ['traɪbəlɪzəm] N tribalisme m

tribe [traɪb] N (gen, Bot, Zool) tribu f; (* fig) tribu f, smala* m; **the twelve Tribes of Israel** les douze tribus d'Israël

tribesman ['traɪbzmən] N (pl -men) membre m d'une (or de la) tribu

tribo... ['traɪbəʊ] PREF tribo...; **~electricity** tribo-électricité f

tribulation [,trɪbjʊ'leɪʃən] N affliction f, souffrance f; (**trials and**) **~s** tribulations fpl; **in times of ~** en période d'adversité, en temps de malheurs

tribunal [traɪ'bju:nl] N (gen, Jur, fig) tribunal m; **~ of inquiry** commission f d'enquête

tribune ['trɪbju:n] N (= platform) tribune f (also fig); (Hist, gen = person) tribun m

tributary ['trɪbjʊtərɪ] **1** ADJ tributaire **2** N (= river) affluent m; (= state, ruler) tributaire m

tribute ['trɪbju:t] N tribut m, hommage m; (esp Hist = payment) tribut m; **to pay ~ to ...** (= honour) payer tribut à ..., rendre hommage à ...; (Hist etc) payer (le) tribut à ...; **it is a ~ to his generosity that nobody went hungry** qu'aucun n'ait souffert de la faim témoigne de sa générosité → **floral**

trice [traɪs] **1** N **in a ~** en un clin d'œil, en moins de deux* or de rien **2** VT (Naut: also ~ **up**) hisser

Tricel® ['traɪsel] **1** N Tricel® m **2** COMP [shirt etc] de or en Tricel®

tricentenary [,traɪsen'ti:nərɪ], **tricentennial** [,traɪsen'tenɪəl], N tricentenaire m; **~ celebrations** fêtes fpl du tricentenaire

triceps ['traɪseps] N (pl triceps or tricepses) triceps m

trick [trɪk] **1** N a (= dodge, ruse) ruse f, astuce f; (= prank, joke, hoax) tour m, blague* f; [of conjurer, juggler, dog etc] tour m; (= special skill) truc m; **it's a ~ to make you believe ...** c'est une ruse pour vous faire croire ...; **he got it all by a ~** il a tout obtenu par une ruse or un stratagème or une combine*; **he'll use every ~ in the book to get what he wants** il ne reculera devant rien pour obtenir ce qu'il veut, pour lui, tous les moyens sont bons; **that's the oldest ~ in the book** c'est le coup classique; **a dirty** or **low** or **shabby** or **nasty ~** un sale tour, un tour de cochon*; **to play a ~ on sb** jouer un tour à qn, faire une farce à qn; **my eyesight is playing ~s with** or **on me** ma vue me joue des tours; **his memory is playing him ~s** sa mémoire lui joue des tours; **a ~ of the trade** une ficelle du métier; **it's a ~ of the light** c'est une illusion d'optique; **he's up to his (old) ~s again** il fait de nouveau des siennes*; **how's ~s?*** alors, quoi de neuf?; (fig) **he knows a ~ or two*** c'est un petit malin; **I know a ~ worth two of that*** je connais un tour or un truc* bien meilleur encore que celui-là; **that will do the ~*** ça fera l'affaire; **I'll soon get the ~ of it*** je vais vite prendre le pli; (esp US) **~ or treat!** donnez-moi quelque chose ou je vous joue un tour! → HALLOWEEN; **to turn ~s** [prostitute] faire des passes* → **bag, card'**, conjuring b (= peculiarity) particularité f; (= habit) habitude f, manie f; (= mannerism) tic m; **he has a ~ of scratching his ear when puzzled** il a le tic de se gratter l'oreille quand il est perplexe; **he has a ~ of arriving just when I'm making coffee** il a le don d'arriver or le chic* pour arriver au moment où je fais du café; **this horse has a ~ of stopping suddenly** ce cheval a la manie de s'arrêter brusquement; **these things have a ~ of happening just when you don't want them to** ces choses-là se produisent comme par magie or ont le don de se produire juste quand on ne le veut pas; **history has a ~ of repeating itself** l'histoire a le don de se répéter c (Cards) levée f, pli m; **to take a ~** faire une levée or un pli; (fig) **he never misses a ~** rien ne lui échappe

2 VT (= hoax, deceive) attraper, rouler*; (= swindle) escroquer; **I've been ~ed!** on m'a eu or roulé!*; **to ~ sb into doing** amener qn à faire par la ruse; **to ~ sb out of sth** obtenir qch de qn or soutirer qch à qn par la ruse

3 COMP ► **trick cushion** etc N attrape f ► **trick-cyclist** N cycliste-acrobate mf; (Brit*. = psychiatrist) psy* mf, psychiatre mf ► **trick photograph** N photographie f truquée ► **trick photography** N truquage m photographique ► **trick question** N question-piège f ► **trick rider** N (on horse) voltigeur m, -euse f (à cheval) ► **trick riding** N voltige f (à cheval)

►**trick out**, **trick up** VT SEP parer (**with** de); **the ladies ~ed out in all their finery** les dames sur leur trente et un or tout endimanchées

trickery ['trɪkərɪ] N (NonC) ruse f, supercherie f; **by ~** par ruse

trickiness ['trɪkɪnɪs] N (NonC) **a** (= difficulty) [of task] difficulté f, complexité f; [of problem, question] caractère m épineux; [of situation] caractère m délicat **b** (pej = slyness) [of person] roublardise f

trickle ['trɪkl] **1** N [of water, blood etc] filet m; **the stream has shrunk to a mere ~** le ruisseau n'est plus qu'un filet d'eau; **a ~ of people** quelques (rares) personnes fpl; **there was a ~ of news from the front line** il y avait de temps en temps des nouvelles du front; **there was a steady ~ of offers/letters** les offres/les lettres arrivaient en petit nombre mais régulièrement **2** VI [water etc] (= drop slowly) couler or tomber goutte à goutte; (= flow slowly) dégouliner; **tears ~d down her cheeks** les larmes coulaient or dégoulinaient le long de ses joues; **the rain ~d down his neck** la pluie lui dégoulinait dans le cou; **the stream ~d along over the rocks** le ruisseau coulait faiblement sur les rochers; (fig) **to ~ in/out/away** etc [people] entrer/sortir/s'éloigner etc petit à petit; (Ftbl) **the ball ~d into the net** le ballon a roulé doucement dans le filet; **money ~d into the fund** les contributions au fonds arrivaient lentement; **money ~d out of his account** son compte se dégarnissait lentement (mais régulièrement), une succession de petites sorties (d'argent) dégarnissait lentement son compte; **letters of complaint are still trickling into the office** quelques lettres de réclamation continuent à arriver de temps en temps au bureau **3** VT [+ liquid] faire couler goutte à goutte, faire dégouliner or dégoutter (**into** dans, **out of** de) **4** COMP ► **trickle charger** N (Elec) chargeur m à régime lent ► **trickle-down theory** N (Econ) théorie économique selon laquelle l'argent des plus riches finit par profiter aux plus démunis

►**trickle away** VI [water etc] s'écouler doucement or lentement or goutte à goutte; [money etc] disparaître or être utilisé peu à peu → **trickle 2**

trickster ['trɪkstər] N **a** (dishonest) filou m → **confidence** **b** (= magician etc) illusionniste mf

tricksy* ['trɪksɪ] ADJ [person] (= mischievous) filou*; (= scheming) retors

tricky ['trɪkɪ] ADJ **a** (= difficult) [task] difficile, délicat; [problem, question] délicat, épineux; [situation] délicat; **it is ~ to know how to respond** il est difficile de savoir comment réagir; **warts can be ~ to get rid of** il est parfois difficile de se débarrasser des verrues; **it's ~ for me to give you an answer now** il m'est difficile de vous répondre immédiatement **b** (pej) (= sly) [person] retors; **he's a ~ customer** c'est un roublard; (= difficult, touchy) il n'est pas commode

tricolo(u)r ['trɪkələr] N (drapeau m) tricolore m

tricorn ['traɪkɔːn] **1** ADJ à trois cornes **2** N tricorne m

trictrac ['trɪktræk] N trictrac m

tricuspid [traɪ'kʌspɪd] ADJ tricuspide

tricycle ['traɪsɪkl] N tricycle m

trident ['traɪdənt] N trident m

tridentine [traɪ'dentaɪn] ADJ tridentin

tridimensional [ˌtraɪdɪ'menʃənl] ADJ tridimensionnel, à trois dimensions

tried-and-tested ['traɪdəndˈtestɪd], **tried-and-trusted** ['traɪdəndˈtrʌstɪd] ADJ éprouvé, qui a fait ses preuves; **to be tried and tested** or **trusted** avoir fait ses preuves; **select a cou-**

ple of ingredients and add them to a ~ recipe of your own choisissez un ou deux ingrédients et intégrez-les à une recette que vous connaissez bien

triennial [traɪ'enɪəl] **1** ADJ triennal; (Bot) trisannuel **2** N (Bot) plante f trisannuelle

triennially [traɪ'enɪəlɪ] ADV tous les trois ans

Trier [trɪər] N Trèves

trier ['traɪər] N (Brit) **to be a ~** être persévérant, ne pas se laisser rebuter

Trieste [triː'est] N Trieste

trifle ['traɪfl] **1** N **a** bagatelle f; **it's only a ~** [object, sum of money etc] c'est une bagatelle, c'est bien peu de chose; [remark] c'est une vétille, il n'y a pas de quoi fouetter un chat; **he worries over ~s** il se fait du mauvais sang pour un rien; **£5 is a mere ~** 5 livres est une bagatelle or c'est trois fois rien; **he bought it for a ~** il l'a acheté pour une bouchée de pain or trois fois rien **b** (adv phrase) **a ~** un peu, un rien, un tantinet*; **it's a ~ difficult** c'est un peu or un tantinet difficile **c** (Culin) ≈ diplomate m **2** VI **to ~ with** [+ person, sb's affections, trust etc] traiter à la légère, se jouer de; **he's not to be ~d with** il ne faut pas le traiter à la légère; **to ~ with one's food** manger du bout des dents, chipoter

►**trifle away** VT SEP [+ time] perdre; [+ money] gaspiller

trifler ['traɪflər] N (pej) fantaisiste mf, fumiste mf

trifling ['traɪflɪŋ] ADJ insignifiant

trifocal [traɪ'fəʊkəl] **1** ADJ à triple foyer, trifocal **2** N (= lens) verre m à triple foyer; **~s** lunettes fpl à triple foyer or trifocales

trifoliate [traɪ'fəʊlɪɪt] ADJ à trois feuilles, trifolié

triforium [traɪ'fɔːrɪəm] N (pl **triforia** [traɪ'fɔːrɪə]) triforium m

triform ['traɪfɔːm] ADJ à or en trois parties

trigger ['trɪgər] **1** N [of gun] détente f, gâchette f; [of bomb] dispositif m d'amorce, détonateur m; [of tool] déclic m; **to press** or **pull** or **squeeze the ~** appuyer sur la détente or la gâchette; **he's quick** or **fast on the ~** (lit) il n'attend pas pour tirer; (fig) il réagit vite **2** VT (also **~ off**) [+ explosion, alarm] déclencher; [+ bomb] amorcer; [+ revolt] déclencher, provoquer; [+ protest] soulever; [+ reaction] provoquer **3** COMP ► **trigger finger** N index m ► **trigger-happy*** ADJ [person] à la gâchette facile, prêt à tirer pour un rien; (fig) [nation etc] prêt à presser le bouton or à déclencher la guerre pour un rien ► **trigger price** N prix m minimum à l'importation

trigonometric(al) [ˌtrɪgənəˈmetrɪk(əl)] ADJ trigonométrique

trigonometry [ˌtrɪgəˈnɒmɪtrɪ] N trigonométrie f

trigram ['traɪgræm] N trigramme m

trigraph ['traɪgræf] N trigramme m

trike* [traɪk] N ABBR = **tricycle**

trilateral [ˌtraɪ'lætərəl] ADJ trilatéral

trilby ['trɪlbɪ] N (Brit: also **~ hat**) chapeau m mou

trilingual [ˌtraɪ'lɪŋgwəl] ADJ trilingue

trilith ['traɪlɪθ] N trilithe m

trilithic [traɪ'lɪθɪk] ADJ en forme de trilithe

trilithon [traɪ'lɪθɒn, 'traɪlɪθɒn] N = **trilith**

trill [trɪl] **1** N (Mus: also of bird) trille m; (Ling) consonne f roulée **2** VI (Mus: also of bird) triller **3** VT (gen) triller; **"come in" she ~ed** « entrez » roucoula-t-elle **b** (Phon) **to ~ one's r's** rouler les r; **~ed r** r roulé or apical

trillion ['trɪljən] N (Brit) trillion m; (US) billion m; (* fig) **there are ~s of places I want to go** il y a des milliers d'endroits où j'aimerais aller

trilogy ['trɪlədʒɪ] N trilogie f

trim [trɪm] **1** ADJ **a** (= neat) [garden, house, village, ship] bien tenu, coquet; [appearance,

person, clothes] net, soigné; [beard, moustache] bien taillé **b** (= slim) [person, figure] svelte, mince; [waist] mince

2 N **a** (NonC) (= condition) état m, ordre m; **in (good) ~** [garden, house etc] en (bon) état or ordre; [person, athlete] en (bonne) forme; (US) **to be in fighting ~** être en pleine forme; **to get into ~** se remettre en forme; **to get things into ~** mettre de l'ordre dans les choses; (Naut) **the ~ of the sails** l'orientation f des voiles **b** (= cut: at hairdressers) coupe f (d')entretien; **to have a ~** se faire rafraîchir les cheveux, se faire faire une coupe d'entretien; **to give sth a ~ = to trim sth**; → **3a** **c** (around window, door) moulures fpl; [of car] (inside) aménagement m intérieur; (outside) finitions fpl extérieures; (on dress etc) garniture f; **car with blue (interior) ~** voiture f à habillage intérieur bleu

3 VT **a** (= cut) [+ beard] tailler, couper légèrement; [+ hair] rafraîchir; [+ wick, lamp] tailler, moucher; [+ branch, hedge, roses] tailler (légèrement); [+ piece of wood, paper] couper les bords de, rogner; **to ~ one's nails** se rogner or se couper les ongles; **to ~ the edges of sth** couper or rogner les bords de qch; **to ~ the ragged edge off sth** ébarber qch **b** (= reduce) **to ~ costs** réduire les dépenses; **to ~ the workforce** dégraisser* les effectifs, faire des dégraissages* **c** (= decorate) [+ hat, dress] garnir, orner (**with** de); [+ Christmas tree] décorer (**with** de); **to ~ the edges of sth with sth** border qch de qch; (US) **to ~ a store window** composer or décorer une vitrine de magasin **d** [+ boat, aircraft] équilibrer; [+ sail] gréer, orienter; (fig) **to ~ one's sails** réviser ses positions, corriger le tir

►**trim away** VT SEP enlever aux ciseaux (or au couteau or à la cisaille)

►**trim down** VT SEP [+ wick] tailler, moucher

►**trim off** VT SEP = **trim away**

trimaran ['traɪmərən] N trimaran m

trimester [trɪ'mestər] N trimestre m

trimmer ['trɪmər] N **a** (= beam) linçoir or linsoir m **b** (for trimming timber) trancheuse f (pour le bois); (for hair, beard) tondeuse f **c** (Elec) trimmer m, condensateur m ajustable (d'équilibrage) **d** (= person adapting views; pej) opportuniste mf

trimming ['trɪmɪŋ] N **a** (on garment, sheet etc) parement m; (= braid etc) passementerie f (NonC); (fig) **it's £100 without the ~s** c'est 100 livres sans les extras **b** (Culin) garniture f, accompagnement m; **roast beef and all the ~s** du rosbif avec la garniture habituelle **c** (pl) **~s** (= pieces cut off) chutes fpl, rognures fpl **d** (esp US = defeat) raclée* f, défaite f **e** (= cutting back) réduction f, élagage m; [of staff] compression f, dégraissage* m

trimness ['trɪmnɪs] N [of garden, boat, house] aspect m net or soigné; **the ~ of his appearance** son aspect soigné or coquet or pimpant; **the ~ of her figure** la sveltesse de sa silhouette

trimphone® ['trɪmfəʊn] N appareil m (téléphonique) compact

trinary ['traɪnərɪ] ADJ trinaire

Trinidad ['trɪnɪdæd] N (l'île f de) la Trinité; **~ and Tobago** Trinité-et-Tobago

Trinidadian [ˌtrɪnɪ'dædɪən] **1** ADJ de la Trinité, trinidadien **2** N habitant(e) m(f) de la Trinité, Trinidadien(ne) m(f)

trinitrotoluene [traɪˌnaɪtrəʊ'tɒljuːiːn] N trinitrotoluène m

trinity ['trɪnɪtɪ] **1** N trinité f; (Rel) **the Holy Trinity** la Sainte Trinité **2** COMP ► **Trinity Sunday** N la fête de la Trinité ► **Trinity term** N (Univ) troisième trimestre m (de l'année universitaire)

trinket ['trɪŋkɪt] N (= knick-knack) bibelot m, babiole f (also pej); (= jewel) colifichet m (also pej); (on chain) breloque f

trinomial [traɪ'nəʊmɪəl] N (Math) trinôme m

trio ['triːəʊ] N trio m

triode ['traɪəʊd] N (Elec) triode f

triolet ['triːəʊlɪt] N triolet m

trip [trɪp] **1** N **a** (= journey) voyage m; (= excursion) excursion f; **he's (away) on a ~** il est (parti) en voyage; **we did the ~ in ten hours** nous avons mis dix heures pour faire le trajet; **there are cheap ~s to Spain** on organise des voyages à prix réduit en Espagne; **we went on** or **took a ~ to Malta** nous sommes allés (en voyage) à Malte; **we took** or **made a ~ into town** nous sommes allés en ville; **he does the ~ to Scotland a week** il va en Écosse trois fois par semaine; **I don't want another ~ to the shops today** je ne veux pas retourner dans les magasins aujourd'hui; **after four ~s to the kitchen he ...** après être allé quatre fois à la cuisine, il ... → **business, coach, day, round**
b (Drugs*) trip* m; **to be on a ~** faire un trip*; **to have a bad ~** faire un trip* qui tourne mal
c (= stumble) faux pas m; (in wrestling etc) croche-pied m, croc-en-jambe m; (fig = mistake) faux pas m
2 VI **a** (= stumble: also ~ **up**) trébucher (**on, over** contre, sur), buter (**on, over** contre), faire un faux pas; **he ~ped and fell** il a trébuché or il a fait un faux pas et il est tombé
b (go lightly and quickly) **to ~ along/in/out** etc marcher/entrer/sortir etc d'un pas léger or sautillant; **the words came ~ping off her tongue** elle l'a dit sans la moindre hésitation
c (: on drugs) être en plein trip:
3 VT **a** (make fall: also ~ **up**) faire trébucher; (deliberately) faire un croche-pied or un croc-en-jambe à; **I was ~ped (up)** on m'a fait un croche-pied or un croc-en-jambe
b (Tech) [+ mechanism] déclencher, mettre en marche
c **to ~ the light fantastic** †* (= dance) danser
4 COMP ► **trip hammer** N marteau m à bascule or à soulèvement ► **trip switch** N (Elec) télérupteur m
► **trip over** VI trébucher, faire un faux pas
► **trip up 1** VI **a** = **trip 2a b** (fig) faire une erreur, gaffer* **2** VT SEP faire trébucher; (deliberately) faire un croche-pied or un croc-en-jambe à; (fig: in questioning etc) prendre en défaut, désarçonner (fig)

tripartite [ˌtraɪ'pɑːtaɪt] ADJ (gen) tripartite; [division] en trois parties

tripe [traɪp] N (NonC) **a** (Culin) tripes fpl
b (esp Brit* = nonsense) bêtises fpl, inepties fpl; **what absolute ~!** quelles bêtises!, quelles foutaises!*; **it's a lot of ~** tout ça c'est de la foutaise*; **this book is ~** ce livre est complètement inepte

triphase ['traɪfeɪz] ADJ (Elec) triphasé

triphthong ['trɪfθɒŋ] N triphtongue f

triplane ['traɪˌpleɪn] N triplan m

triple ['trɪpl] **1** ADJ triple (gen before n); **the Triple Alliance** la Triple-Alliance; **the Triple Entente** la Triple-Entente; (Mus) **in ~ time** à trois temps; **they require ~ copies of every document** ils demandent trois exemplaires de chaque document **2** N (= amount, number) triple m **3** ADV trois fois plus que **4** VTI tripler **5** COMP ► **triple combination therapy** N trithérapie f ► **triple-digit** (US) ADJ (gen) à trois chiffres; [inflation] supérieur ou égal à 100% ► **triple glazing** N triple vitrage m ► **triple jump** N (Sport) triple saut m ► **triple jumper** N (Sport) spécialiste mf du triple saut

triplet ['trɪplɪt] N (Mus) triolet m; (Poetry) tercet m; (people) **~s** triplé(e)s m(f)pl

triplex ['trɪpleks] **1** ADJ triple **2** N® (Brit) **Triplex (glass)** triplex® m, verre m sécurit®

triplicate ['trɪplɪkɪt] **1** ADJ en trois exemplaires **2** N **a** **in ~** en trois exemplaires **b** (= third copy) triplicata m

triploid ['trɪplɔɪd] ADJ triploïde

triply ['trɪplɪ] ADV triplement

tripod ['traɪpɒd] N trépied m

Tripoli ['trɪpəlɪ] N Tripoli

tripos ['traɪpɒs] N (Cambridge Univ) examen m pour le diplôme de BA

tripper ['trɪpəʳ] N (Brit) touriste mf, vacancier m, -ière f; (on day trip) excursionniste mf

trippy* ['trɪpɪ] ADJ psychédélique

triptych ['trɪptɪk] N triptyque m

tripwire ['trɪpwaɪəʳ] N fil m de détente

trireme ['traɪriːm] N trirème f

trisect [traɪ'sekt] VT diviser en trois parties (égales)

Tristan ['trɪstən] N Tristan m

trisyllabic ['trɪsɪ'læbɪk] ADJ trisyllabe, trisyllabique

trisyllable [ˌtraɪ'sɪləbl] N trisyllabe m

trite [traɪt] ADJ [subject, design, idea, film] banal; [person] qui dit des banalités; **a ~ remark** une banalité, un lieu commun

tritely ['traɪtlɪ] ADV banalement

triteness ['traɪtnɪs] N (NonC) banalité f

tritium ['trɪtɪəm] N tritium m

triton ['traɪtn] N (all senses) triton m; **Triton** Triton m

tritone ['traɪtəʊn] N (Mus) triton m

triturate ['trɪtʃəreɪt] VT triturer, piler

trituration [ˌtrɪtʃə'reɪʃən] N trituration f, pilage m

triumph ['traɪʌmf] **1** N (= victory) triomphe m, victoire f; (= success) triomphe m; (= emotion) sentiment m de triomphe; (Roman Hist) triomphe m; **in ~** en triomphe; **it was a ~ for ...** cela a été un triomphe or un succès triomphal pour ...; **it is a ~ of man over nature** c'est le triomphe de l'homme sur la nature; **his ~ at having succeeded** sa satisfaction triomphante d'avoir réussi **2** VI (lit, fig) triompher (**over** de)

triumphal [traɪ'ʌmfəl] **1** ADJ triomphal **2** COMP ► **triumphal arch** N arc m de triomphe

triumphalism [traɪ'ʌmfəlɪzəm] N triomphalisme m

triumphalist [traɪ'ʌmfəlɪst] ADJ, N triomphaliste mf

triumphant [traɪ'ʌmfənt] ADJ **a** (= victorious) victorieux, triomphant; **to emerge ~** sortir victorieux **b** (= exultant) [person, team, smile, wave, mood] triomphant; [return, homecoming, celebration] triomphal; **to be** or **prove a ~ success** être un triomphe

triumphantly [traɪ'ʌmfəntlɪ] ADV [say, answer, announce] triomphalement, d'un ton triomphant; [look at, smile] d'un air triomphant; [return, march] triomphalement; **he returned ~ in 1997** son retour, en 1997, a été triomphal; **he waved ~** il a fait un geste de triomphe; **to be ~ successful** remporter un succès triomphal

triumvirate [traɪ'ʌmvɪrɪt] N triumvirat m

triune ['traɪjuːn] ADJ (Rel) trin

trivet ['trɪvɪt] N (over fire) trépied m, chevrette f; (on table) dessous-de-plat m inv

trivia ['trɪvɪə] NPL bagatelles fpl, futilités fpl, fadaises fpl; **pub ~ quiz** jeu-concours qui a lieu dans un pub

trivial ['trɪvɪəl] **1** ADJ [matter, sum, reason, offence, detail] insignifiant; [remark] futile; [film, book, news] banal, sans intérêt; **a ~ mistake** une faute sans gravité, une peccadille **2** COMP ► **Trivial Pursuit**® N Trivial Pursuit® m

triviality [ˌtrɪvɪ'ælɪtɪ] N **a** (NonC = trivial nature) [of matter, sum, reason, offence, detail] caractère m insignifiant; [of remark] futilité f; [of film, book, news] banalité f, manque m d'intérêt **b** (= trivial thing) bagatelle f

trivialization [ˌtrɪvɪəlaɪ'zeɪʃən] N banalisation f

trivialize ['trɪvɪəlaɪz] VT banaliser

trivially ['trɪvɪəlɪ] ADV de façon banalisée

triweekly ['traɪ'wiːklɪ] **1** ADV (= three times weekly) trois fois par semaine; (= every three weeks) toutes les trois semaines **2** ADJ [event, visit] qui se produit trois fois par semaine (or toutes les trois semaines)

trochaic [trə'keɪɪk] ADJ trochaïque

trochee ['trəʊkiː] N trochée m

trod [trɒd] VB pt of **tread**

trodden ['trɒdn] VB ptp of **tread**

troglodyte ['trɒglədaɪt] N troglodyte m; (fig pej) homme m des cavernes

troika ['trɔɪkə] N (also Pol) troïka f

troilism ['trɔɪlɪzəm] N (Brit: frm) triolisme m

Troilus ['trɔɪləs] N **~ and Cressida** Troïlus m et Cressida f

Trojan ['trəʊdʒən] **1** ADJ (Hist, Myth) troyen **2** N Troyen(ne) m(f); **to work like a ~** travailler comme un forçat **3** COMP ► **Trojan Horse** N (lit, fig) cheval m de Troie ► **Trojan War** N **the ~ War** or **Wars** la guerre de Troie

troll [trəʊl] N troll m

trolley ['trɒlɪ] **1** N (esp Brit) (for luggage) chariot m (à bagages); (two-wheeled) diable m; (for shopping) poussette f; (in supermarket) chariot m, caddie® m; (also **tea ~**) table f roulante, chariot m à desserte; (in office) chariot m à boissons; (for stretcher etc) chariot m; (in mine, quarry etc) benne f roulante; (Rail) wagonnet m; (on tramcar) trolley m; (US = tramcar) tramway m, tram m; (Brit) **to be/go off one's ~** avoir perdu/perdre la boule **2** COMP ► **trolley bus** N trolleybus m ► **trolley car** N (US) tramway m, tram m ► **trolley line** N (US) (= rails) voie f de tramway; (= route) ligne f de tramway ► **trolley pole** N perche f de trolley

trollop ['trɒləp] N traînée: f

trombone [trɒm'bəʊn] N trombone m (Mus)

trombonist [trɒm'bəʊnɪst] N tromboniste mf

troop [truːp] **1** N [of people] bande f, groupe m; [of animals] bande f, troupe f; [of scouts] troupe f; (Mil or cavalry) escadron m; (Mil) **~s** troupes fpl **2** VI **to ~ in/past** etc entrer/passer etc en bande or en groupe; **they all ~ed over to the window** ils se sont tous allés s'attrouper près de la fenêtre **3** VT (Brit Mil) **to ~ the colour** faire la parade du drapeau; **~ing the colour** (= ceremony) le salut au drapeau (le jour de l'anniversaire officiel de la Reine) **4** COMP (movements etc) de troupes ► **troop carrier** N (Aut, Naut) transport m de troupes; (Aviat) avion m de transport militaire ► **troop train** N train m militaire

trooper ['truːpəʳ] N (Mil) soldat m de cavalerie; (US = state trooper) ≈ CRS m → **swear**

troopship ['truːpʃɪp] N transport m (navire)

trope [trəʊp] N trope m

trophy ['trəʊfɪ] **1** N (Hunting, Mil, Sport, also fig) trophée m **2** COMP ► **trophy wife*** N (pl **trophy wives**) épouse que le mari exhibe comme signe extérieur de réussite

tropic ['trɒpɪk] **1** N tropique m; **Tropic of Cancer/Capricorn** tropique m du Cancer/du Capricorne; **in the ~s** sous les tropiques **2** ADJ (liter) = **tropical**

tropical ['trɒpɪkəl] **1** ADJ (lit, fig) tropical; **the heat was ~** il faisait une chaleur tropicale **2** COMP ► **tropical medicine** N médecine f tropicale ► **tropical storm** N orage m tropical

tropism ['trəʊpɪzəm] N tropisme m

troposphere [ˈtrɒpəsfɪəʳ] N troposphère f

Trot* [trɒt] N (pej) (ABBR = **Trotskyist**) trotskard* m, trotskiste mf

trot [trɒt] **1** N **a** (= pace) trot m; **to go at a ~** [horse] aller au trot, trotter; [person] trotter; **to go for a ~** (aller) faire du cheval **b** (fig) **five days/whiskies etc on the ~*** cinq jours/ whiskies etc de suite or d'affilée; **he is always on the ~*** il court tout le temps, il n'a pas une minute de tranquillité; **to keep sb on the ~** ne pas accorder une minute de tranquillité à qn **c** (= diarrhoea) **to have the ~s**ᵇ (= diarrhoea) avoir la courante*; **2** VI [horse] trotter; [person] trotter, courir; **to ~ in/past** etc [person] entrer/passer etc au trot or en courant **3** VT [+ horse] faire trotter

▶ **trot along** VI **a** = **trot over b** = **trot away**

▶ **trot away**, **trot off** VI partir or s'éloigner (au trot or en courant), filer*

▶ **trot out** VT SEP [+ excuses, reasons] débiter; [+ names, facts etc] réciter d'affilée

▶ **trot over**, **trot round** VI aller, courir; **he ~ted over** or **round to the grocer's** il a fait un saut or a couru chez l'épicier

troth †† [trəʊθ] N promesse f, serment m; **by my ~** pardieu† → **plight²**

Trotsky [ˈtrɒtskɪ] N Trotski m

Trotskyism [ˈtrɒtskɪɪzəm] N trotskisme m

Trotskyist [ˈtrɒtskɪɪst], **Trotskyite** [ˈtrɒtskɪaɪt] ADJ, N trotskiste mf

trotter [ˈtrɒtəʳ] N **a** (= horse) trotteur m, -euse f **b** (Brit Culin) **pig's/sheep's ~s** pieds mpl de porc/de mouton

trotting [ˈtrɒtɪŋ] N (Sport) trot m; **~ race** course f de trot

troubadour [ˈtruːbədɔːʳ] N troubadour m

trouble [ˈtrʌbl] **1** N **a** (NonC = difficulties, unpleasantness) ennuis mpl; **to be in ~** avoir des ennuis; **you're in ~ now** ce coup-ci tu as des ennuis or tu as des problèmes; **he's in ~ with the boss** il a des ennuis avec le patron; **to get into ~ (with sb)** s'attirer des ennuis (avec qn); **he got into ~ for doing that** il a eu or il s'est attiré des ennuis pour (avoir fait) cela; **to get sb into ~** causer des ennuis à qn, mettre qn dans le pétrin*; (euph) **to get a girl into ~*** mettre une (jeune) fille dans une position intéressante (euph); **to get sb/get (o.s.) out of ~** tirer qn/se tirer d'affaire; **to make ~** causer des ennuis (for sb à qn); **you're making ~ for yourself** tu t'attires des ennuis; **I don't want any ~** je ne veux pas d'ennuis; **it's asking for ~** c'est se chercher des ennuis; **he goes around looking for ~** il cherche les ennuis; **he'll give you ~** il vous donnera du fil à retordre; **here comes ~!*** aïe! des ennuis en perspective → **mean¹**

b (NonC = bother, effort) mal m, peine f; **it's no ~** cela ne me dérange pas; **it's no ~ to do it properly** ce n'est pas difficile de le faire comme il faut; **it's not worth the ~** cela ne or n'en vaut pas la peine; **he/it is more ~ than he/it is worth** ça ne vaut pas la peine de s'embêter avec lui/ça; **nothing is too much ~ for her** elle se dévoue or se dépense sans compter; **I had all that ~ for nothing** je me suis donné tout ce mal pour rien; **you could have saved yourself the ~** tu aurais pu t'éviter cette peine; **he went to enormous ~ to help us** il s'est donné un mal fou or il s'est mis en quatre pour nous aider; **to go to the ~ of doing** ◊ **to take the ~ to do** se donner la peine or le mal de faire; **he went to** or **took a lot of ~ over his essay** il s'est vraiment donné beaucoup de mal pour sa dissertation, il s'est vraiment beaucoup appliqué à sa dissertation; **to put sb to some ~** déranger qn; **I don't want to put you to the ~ of writing** je ne veux pas qu'à cause de moi vous vous donniez (subj) le mal d'écrire; **I'm putting you to** or **giving you a lot of ~** je vous donne beaucoup de mal, je vous dérange beaucoup; **it's no ~ at all!** je vous en prie!, ça ne me dérange pas du tout!

c (= difficulty, problem) ennui m, problème m; (= nuisance) ennui m; **what's the ~?** qu'est-ce qu'il y a?, qu'est-ce qui ne va pas?, qu'est-ce que tu as?; **that's (just) the ~!** c'est ça l'ennui!; **the ~ is that ...** l'ennui or le problème (c')est que ...; **the ~ with you is that you can never face the facts** l'ennui or le problème avec toi c'est que tu ne regardes jamais les choses en face; **the carburettor is giving us ~** nous avons des problèmes or des ennuis de carburateur; **the technician is trying to locate the ~** le technicien essaie de localiser la panne or le problème; **there has been ~ between them ever since** depuis, ils s'entendent mal; **he caused ~ between them** il a semé la discorde entre eux; **I'm having ~ with my eldest son** mon fils aîné me donne des soucis or me cause des ennuis; **the child is a ~ to his parents** l'enfant est un souci pour ses parents; **that's the least of my ~s** c'est le cadet de mes soucis; **he had ~ in tying his shoelace** il a eu du mal à attacher son lacet; **did you have any ~ in getting here?** est-ce que vous avez eu des difficultés or des problèmes en venant?; **now your ~s are over** vous voilà au bout de vos peines; **his ~s are not yet over** il n'est pas encore au bout de ses peines, il n'est pas encore sorti de l'auberge; **family ~s** ennuis mpl domestiques or de famille; **money ~s** soucis mpl or ennuis mpl d'argent or financiers; (Med) **I have back ~** ◊ **my back is giving me ~** j'ai mal au dos, mon dos me fait souffrir; **kidney/chest ~** ennuis mpl rénaux/ pulmonaires; (Aut) **we've got engine ~** nous avons des ennuis de moteur, il y a quelque chose qui ne vas pas dans le moteur → **heart**

d (= political, social unrest) troubles mpl, conflits mpl; **there's been a lot of ~ in prisons lately** il y a beaucoup de troubles or de nombreux incidents dans les prisons ces derniers temps; (Ir Hist) **the Troubles** les conflits en Irlande du Nord; **labour ~s** conflits mpl du travail; **there's ~ at the factory** ça chauffe* à l'usine

2 VT **a** (= worry) inquiéter; (= inconvenience) gêner; (= upset) troubler; **to be ~d by anxiety** être sujet à des angoisses; **to be ~d by pain** avoir des douleurs; **his eyes ~ him** il a des problèmes d'yeux; **do these headaches ~ you often?** est-ce que vous souffrez souvent de ces maux de tête?; **to be ~d with rheumatism** souffrir de rhumatismes; **there's one detail that ~s me** il y a un détail qui me gêne; **nothing ~s him** il ne se fait jamais de souci → **troubled**

b (= bother) déranger; **I am sorry to ~ you** je suis désolé de vous déranger; **don't ~ yourself!** ne vous dérangez pas!, ne vous tracassez pas!; **he didn't ~ himself to reply** il ne s'est pas donné la peine de répondre; **may I ~ you for a light?** puis-je vous demander du feu?; **I'll ~ you to show me the letter!** vous allez me faire le plaisir de me montrer la lettre!; **I shan't ~ you with the details** je vous ferai grâce des détails, je vous passerai les détails

3 VI se déranger; **please don't ~!** ne vous dérangez pas!, ne vous donnez pas cette peine-là!; **don't ~ about me** ne vous faites pas de souci pour moi; **to ~ to do sth** se donner la peine or le mal de faire qch

4 COMP ▶ **trouble-free** ADJ [period, visit] sans ennuis or problèmes or soucis; [car] qui ne tombe jamais en panne; [university] non contestataire ▶ **trouble spot** N point m chaud or névralgique

troubled [ˈtrʌbld] ADJ **a** (= worried) [person, expression] inquiet (-ète f), préoccupé; [mind, look, voice] inquiet (-ète f) **b** (= disturbed, unstable) [life, sleep] agité; [relationship, marriage] tourmenté; [area, country, region] en proie à des troubles; [company, industry] en difficulté; **financially ~** en proie à des difficultés financières; **in these ~ times** en cette époque troublée → **oil, fish**

troublemaker [ˈtrʌblmeɪkəʳ] N fauteur m, -trice f de troubles, perturbateur m, -trice f

troublemaking [ˈtrʌblmeɪkɪŋ] **1** N comportement m perturbateur **2** ADJ perturbateur (-trice f)

troubleshoot [ˈtrʌblˌʃuːt] VI (gen, also Ind, Pol) (intervenir pour) régler un problème; (stronger) (intervenir pour) régler une crise; (Tech, Aut) localiser une panne

troubleshooter [ˈtrʌblˌʃuːtəʳ] N (gen) expert m (appelé en cas de crise); [of conflict] médiateur m; (Tech, Aut) expert m

troubleshooting [ˈtrʌblˌʃuːtɪŋ] N (gen) (= fixing problems) dépannage m; (Aut, Elec, Engineering = locating problems) diagnostic m; **most of my job is ~** l'essentiel de mon travail consiste à régler les problèmes

troublesome [ˈtrʌblsəm] ADJ [person] pénible; [pupil, tenant] difficile, à problèmes; [question, issue, problem, period] difficile; [task] difficile, pénible; [request] gênant, embarrassant; [cough, injury] gênant, incommodant; **his back is ~** il a des problèmes de dos; **to be ~ to** or **for sb** poser des problèmes à qn

troublous [ˈtrʌbləs] ADJ (liter) trouble, agité

trough [trɒf] N **a** (= depression) dépression f, creux m; (between waves) creux m; (= channel) chenal m; (fig) point m bas; (Met) **~ of low pressure** dépression f, zone f dépressionnaire **b** (= drinking trough) abreuvoir m; (= feeding trough) auge f; (= kneading trough) pétrin m

trounce [traʊns] VT (= thrash) rosser, rouer de coups; (Sport = defeat) écraser, battre à plate(s) couture(s)

troupe [truːp] N (Theat) troupe f

trouper [ˈtruːpəʳ] N (Theat) membre m d'une troupe de théâtre en tournée; (fig) **an old ~** un vieux de la vieille

trouser [ˈtraʊzəʳ] (esp Brit) **1 trousers** NPL pantalon m; **a pair of ~s** un pantalon; **long ~s** pantalon m long; **short ~s** culottes fpl courtes → **wear 2** COMP ▶ **trouser clip** N pince f à pantalon ▶ **trouser leg** N jambe f de pantalon ▶ **trouser press** N presse f à pantalons ▶ **trouser suit** N (Brit) tailleur-pantalon m

trousseau [ˈtruːsəʊ] N (pl **trousseaus** or **trousseaux** [ˈtruːsəʊz]) trousseau m (de jeune mariée)

trout [traʊt] **1** N (pl **trout** or **trouts**) truite f **2** COMP ▶ **trout fisherman** N (pl **trout fishermen**) pêcheur m de truites ▶ **trout fishing** N pêche f à la truite ▶ **trout rod** N canne f à truite, canne f spéciale truite ▶ **trout stream** N ruisseau m à truites

trove [trəʊv] N → **treasure**

trow †† [traʊ] VTI croire

trowel [ˈtraʊəl] N (Constr) truelle f; (for gardening) déplantoir m → **lay on**

Troy [trɔɪ] N Troie f

troy [trɔɪ] N (also **~ weight**) troy m, troy-weight m, poids m de Troy

truancy [ˈtruːənsɪ] N (Scol) absentéisme m (scolaire); **he was punished for ~** il a été puni pour avoir manqué les cours or pour s'être absenté

truant [ˈtruːənt] **1** N (Scol) élève mf absentéiste or absent(e) sans autorisation; **to play ~** manquer les cours, faire l'école buissonnière; **he's playing ~ from the office today** (il n'est pas au bureau aujourd'hui,) il fait l'école buissonnière **2** ADJ (liter) [thought] vagabond **3** COMP (US) ▶ **truant officer** N fonctionnaire chargé de faire respecter les règlements de la scolarisation

truce [truːs] N trêve f; **to call a ~** conclure une trêve

Trucial [ˈtruːʃəl] ADJ **~ States** États mpl de la Trêve

truck¹ [trʌk] **1** N **a** (NonC) (= barter) troc m, échange m; (= payment) paiement m en nature ; (fig) **to have no ~ with ...** refuser d'avoir affaire à ... b (US = vegetables) produits mpl etc maraîchers 2 COMP ► **truck farm** N (US) jardin m potager ► **truck farmer** N maraîcher m, -ère f ► **truck farming** N culture f maraîchère ► **truck garden** N = **truck farm**

truck² [trʌk] 1 N (esp US = lorry) camion m ; (Brit Rail) wagon m à plateforme, truck m ; (= luggage handcart) chariot m à bagages ; (two-wheeled) diable m 2 VTI (esp US) camionner 3 COMP ► **truck stop** N (US) routier m, restaurant m de routiers

truckage ['trʌkɪdʒ] N (US) camionnage m

truckdriver ['trʌkdraɪvəʳ] N (esp US) camionneur m, routier m

trucker ['trʌkəʳ] N a (esp US = truck driver) camionneur m, routier m b (US = market gardener) maraîcher m

trucking ['trʌkɪŋ] N (US) camionnage m

truckle ['trʌkl] 1 VI s'humilier, s'abaisser (**to** devant) 2 COMP ► **truckle bed** N (Brit) lit m gigogne inv

truckload ['trʌkləʊd] N camion m (cargaison)

truckman ['trʌkmən] N (pl **-men**) (US) = **truck-driver**

truculence ['trʌkjʊləns] N brutalité f, agressivité f

truculent ['trʌkjʊlənt] ADJ agressif

truculently ['trʌkjʊləntlɪ] ADV brutalement, agressivement

trudge [trʌdʒ] 1 VI **to ~ in/out/along** etc entrer/sortir/marcher etc péniblement or en traînant les pieds ; **we ~d round the shops** nous nous sommes traînés de magasin en magasin ; **he ~d through the mud** il pataugeait (péniblement) dans la boue 2 VT **to ~ the streets/the town** se traîner de rue en rue/ dans toute la ville etc 3 N marche f pénible

▼ **true** [truː] 1 ADJ a (= correct, accurate) [story, news, rumour, statement] vrai ; [description, account, report] fidèle ; [copy] conforme ; [statistics, measure] exact ; **it is ~ that ...** il est vrai que ... (+ indic) ; **is it ~ that ...?** est-il vrai que ... (+ indic or subj) ? ; **it's not ~ that ...** il n'est pas vrai que ... (+ indic or subj) ; **can it be ~ that ...?** est-il possible que ... (+ subj) ? ; **is it ~ about Vivian?** est-ce vrai, ce que l'on dit à propos de Vivian ? ; **it is ~ to say that ...** il est vrai que ... ; **this is particularly ~ of ...** cela s'applique particulièrement à ... ; **that's ~!** c'est vrai ! ; **too ~!** ça c'est bien vrai !, je ne le fais pas dire ! ; **unfortunately this is only too ~** or **all too ~** malheureusement, ce n'est que trop vrai ; **to make sth come ~** faire que qch se réalise, réaliser qch ; **the same is ~ of** or **holds ~ for** il en va de même pour ; **he's got so much money it's not ~!*** (= incredible) c'est incroyable ce qu'il est riche ! → **good, ring²** b (= real, genuine) (gen) vrai, véritable ; [cost] réel ; **in Turkey you will discover the ~ meaning of hospitality** en Turquie, vous découvrirez le vrai or véritable sens de l'hospitalité ; **in the ~ sense (of the word)** au sens propre (du terme) ; **he has been a ~ friend to me** il a été un vrai or véritable ami pour moi ; (hum) **spoken like a ~ Englishman!** (= well said!) voilà qui est bien dit ! ; **I certify that this is a ~ likeness of Frances Elisabeth Dodd** je certifie que cette photographie représente bien Frances Elisabeth Dodd ; **to hide one's ~ feelings** cacher ses sentiments (profonds) ; **to discover one's ~ self** découvrir son véritable moi ; **~ love** (= real love) le grand amour ; († = sweetheart) bien-aimé(e)† m(f) ; **to find ~ love (with sb)** connaître le grand amour (avec qn) ; **he taught maths but his ~ love was philosophy** il enseignait les maths, mais sa vraie passion était la philosophie ■ (PROV) **the course of ~ love never did run smooth** un grand amour ne va pas toujours sans encombre ; **the one ~ God** le seul vrai Dieu, le seul Dieu véritable

c (= faithful) fidèle (**to sb/sth** à qn/qch) ; **to be ~ to one's word/to oneself** être fidèle à sa promesse/à soi-même ; **twelve good men and ~** douze hommes parfaitement intègres (représentant le jury d'un tribunal) ; **~ to life** (= realistic) réaliste ; **~ to form** or **type, he ...** comme on pouvait s'y attendre, il ..., fidèle à ses habitudes, il ... ; **to run ~ to form** or **type** [project etc] se dérouler comme on pouvait s'y attendre

d (= straight, level) [surface, join] plan, uniforme ; [wall, upright] d'aplomb ; [beam] droit ; [wheel] dans l'axe

e (Mus) [voice, instrument, note] juste

2 N **out of ~** [upright, wall] pas d'aplomb ; [beam] tordu, gauchi ; [surface] gondolé ; [join] mal aligné ; [wheel] voilé, faussé

3 ADV [aim, sing] juste ; **to breed ~** se reproduire selon le type parental ; **tell me ~** †† dis-moi la vérité ; **you speak ~r than you know** vous ne croyez pas si bien dire → **ring²**

4 VT [+ wheel] centrer

5 COMP ► **true-blue*** ADJ [Conservative, Republican] pur jus* ; [Englishman, Australian] jusqu'au bout des ongles ► **true-born** ADJ véritable, vrai, authentique ► **true-bred** ADJ de race pure, racé ► **the True Cross** N la vraie Croix ► **true-false test** N questionnaire m or test m du type « vrai ou faux » ► **true-hearted** ADJ loyal, sincère ► **true-life*** ADJ vrai, vécu ► **true north** N le nord géographique

truffle ['trʌfl] N truffe f

trug [trʌg] N (Brit) corbeille f de jardinier

truism ['truːɪzəm] N truisme m

truly ['truːlɪ] ADV a (= genuinely) vraiment, véritablement ; **a ~ terrible film** un film vrai-ment mauvais ; **I am ~ sorry (for what happened)** je suis sincèrement or vraiment désolé (de ce qui s'est passé) ; **he's a ~ great writer** c'est véritablement un grand écrivain ; **he did say so, ~ (he did)!** il l'a dit, je te jure !* ; **really and ~?*** vraiment ?, vrai de vrai ? ; **I'm in love, really and ~ in love** je suis amoureux, éperdument amoureux b (faithfully) [reflect] fidèlement c (= truthfully) [answer, tell] franchement ; **tell me ~** dis-moi la vérité ; (letter ending) **yours ~** je vous prie d'agréer l'expression de mes sentiments respectueux or (man to woman) de mes très respectueux hommages ; **nobody knows it better than yours ~*** personne ne le sait mieux que votre humble serviteur

trump¹ [trʌmp] 1 N (Cards) atout m ; **spades are ~s** atout pique ; **what's ~(s)?** quel est l'atout ? ; **the three of ~(s)** le trois d'atout ; (fig) **he had a ~ up his sleeve** il avait un atout en réserve ; (fig) **he was holding all the ~s** il avait tous les atouts dans son jeu ; (Brit fig) **to come up** or **turn up ~s*** (= succeed) mettre dans le mille ; (= come at the right moment) tomber à pic* → **no** 2 VT (Cards) couper, prendre avec un atout ; (fig) **to ~ sb's ace** faire encore mieux que qn 3 COMP ► **trump card** N (fig) carte f maîtresse, atout m

► **trump up** VT SEP [+ charge, excuse] forger or inventer (de toutes pièces)

trump² [trʌmp] N (liter) trompette f ; **the Last Trump** la trompette du Jugement (dernier)

trumpery ['trʌmpərɪ] 1 N (NonC) (= showy trash) camelote* f (NonC) ; (= nonsense) bêtises fpl 2 ADJ (= showy) criard ; (= paltry) insignifiant, sans valeur

trumpet ['trʌmpɪt] 1 N a (= instrument) trompette f b (= player) (in orchestra) trompettiste mf ; (Mil etc = trumpeter) trompette m c (= trumpet-shaped object) cornet m → **ear** d [of elephant] barrissement m 2 VI [elephant] barrir 3 VT trompeter 4 COMP ► **trumpet blast** N coup m or sonnerie f de trompette ► **trumpet call** N (lit) = **trumpet blast** ; (fig) appel m vibrant (**for** pour)

trumpeter ['trʌmpɪtəʳ] N trompette m

trumpeting ['trʌmpɪtɪŋ] N [of elephant] barrissement(s) m(pl)

truncate [trʌŋ'keɪt] VT (gen, Comput) tronquer

truncating [trʌŋ'keɪtɪŋ] N (Comput) troncation f

truncheon ['trʌntʃən] N (= weapon) matraque f ; (Brit: for directing traffic) bâton m (d'agent de police)

trundle ['trʌndl] 1 VT (= push/pull/roll) pousser/traîner/faire rouler bruyamment 2 VI **to ~ in/along/down** entrer/passer/descendre lourdement or bruyamment 3 COMP ► **trundle bed** N (US) lit m gigogne

trunk [trʌŋk] 1 N a (Anat, Bot) tronc m ; [of elephant] trompe f ; (= luggage) malle f ; (US Aut) coffre m, malle f 2 **trunks** NPL (for swimming) slip m or maillot m de bain ; (underwear) slip m (d'homme) → **subscriber** 3 COMP ► **trunk call** N (Brit Telec) communication f interurbaine ► **trunk curl** N (Gym) = **sit-up** ; → **sit** ► **trunk line** N (Telec) inter m, téléphone m interurbain ; (Rail) grande ligne f ► **trunk road** N (Brit) (route f) nationale f → ROADS

trunnion ['trʌnɪən] N tourillon m

truss [trʌs] 1 N [of hay etc] botte f ; [of flowers, fruit on branch] grappe f ; (Constr) ferme f ; (Med) bandage m herniaire 2 VT [+ hay] botteler ; [+ chicken] trousser ; (Constr) armer, renforcer

► **truss up** VT SEP [+ prisoner] ligoter

▼ **trust** [trʌst] 1 N a (NonC = faith, reliance) confiance f (**in** en) ; **position of ~** poste m de confiance ; **breach of ~** abus m de confiance ; **to have ~ in sb/sth** avoir confiance en qn/ qch ; **to put** or **place (one's) ~ in sb/sth** faire confiance or se fier à qn/qch ; **to take sth on ~** accepter qch de confiance or les yeux fermés ; **you'll have to take what I say on ~** il vous faudra me croire sur parole ; **he gave it to me on ~** (= without payment) il me l'a donné sans me faire payer tout de suite

b (Jur) fidéicommis m ; **to set up a ~ for sb** instituer un fidéicommis à l'intention de qn ; **to hold sth/leave money in ~ for one's children** tenir qch/faire administrer un legs par fidéicommis à l'intention de ses enfants

c (= charge, responsibility) **to give sth into sb's ~** confier qch à qn ; **while this is in my ~, I ...** aussi longtemps que j'en ai la charge or la responsabilité, je ...

d (Comm, Fin) trust m, cartel m → **brain, investment, unit**

2 VT a (= believe in, rely on) [+ person, object] avoir confiance en, se fier à ; [+ method, promise] se fier à ; **don't you ~ me?** tu n'as pas confiance (en moi) ? ; **he is not to be ~ed** on ne peut pas lui faire confiance ; **you can ~ me** vous pouvez avoir confiance en moi ; **you can ~ me with your car** tu peux me confier ta voiture, tu peux me prêter ta voiture en toute confiance ; **he's not to be ~ed with a knife** il ne serait pas prudent de le laisser manipuler un couteau ; **can we ~ him to do it?** peut-on compter sur lui pour le faire ? ; **the child is too young to be ~ed on the roads** l'enfant est trop petit pour qu'on le laisse (subj) aller dans la rue tout seul ; **I can't ~ him out of my sight** j'ai si peu confiance en lui que je ne le quitte pas des yeux ; (iro) **~ you!** ça ne m'étonne pas de toi !, (pour) ça on peut te faire confiance ! ; (iro) **~ him to break it!*** pour casser quelque chose on peut lui faire confiance ! ; **he can be ~ed to do his best** on peut être sûr qu'il fera de son mieux ; **you can't ~ a word he says** impossible de croire deux mots de ce qu'il raconte ; **I wouldn't ~ him as far as I can throw him*** je n'ai aucune confiance en lui

b (= entrust) confier (**sth to sb** qch à qn)

c (= hope) espérer (**that** que) ; **I ~ not** j'espère que non

3 VI **to ~ in sb** se fier à qn, s'en remettre à qn ; **let's ~ to luck** or **to chance** essayons tout de même, tentons notre chance, tentons le coup* ; **I'll have to ~ to luck to find the house** il faudra que je m'en remette à la chance pour trouver la maison

4 COMP ► **trust account** N (Banking) compte m en fidéicommis ► **trust company** N société f de gestion ► **trust fund** N fonds m en fidéicommis ► **trust hospital** N (Brit) hôpital qui a choisi l'autonomie par rapport aux autorités locales ► **trust territory** N (Pol) territoire m sous tutelle

trustbuster ['trʌstbʌstər] N (US) fonctionnaire chargé de faire appliquer la loi antitrust

trusted ['trʌstɪd] ADJ [friend, servant] en qui on a confiance ; [method] éprouvé → **tried-and-trusted**

trustee [trʌs'tiː] **1** N **a** (Jur) fidéicommissaire m, curateur m, -trice f ; (Jur, Fin) **~ in bankruptcy** ≈ syndic m de faillite **b** [of institution, school] administrateur m, -trice f ; **the ~s** le conseil d'administration **c** (US Univ) membre m du conseil d'université **2** COMP ► **Trustee Savings Bank** N (Brit) ≈ Caisse f d'épargne

trusteeship [trʌs'tiːʃɪp] N **a** (Jur) fidéicommis m, curatelle f **b** [of institution etc] poste m d'administrateur ; **during his ~** pendant qu'il était administrateur

trustful ['trʌstfʊl] ADJ = **trusting**

trustfully ['trʌstfəlɪ] ADV avec confiance

trusting ['trʌstɪŋ] ADJ confiant ; **a ~ relationship** une relation basée sur la confiance

trustingly ['trʌstɪŋlɪ] ADV en toute confiance

trustworthiness ['trʌst,wɜːðɪnɪs] N (NonC) [of person] loyauté f, fidélité f ; [of statement] véracité f

trustworthy ['trʌst,wɜːðɪ] ADJ [person] digne de confiance ; [report, account] fidèle, exact

trusty ['trʌstɪ] **1** ADJ (†† an hum) fidèle ; **his ~ steed** son fidèle coursier **2** N (in prison) détenu bénéficiant d'un régime de faveur

truth [truːθ] **1** N (pl **truths** [truːðz]) **a** (NonC) vérité f ; **you must always tell the ~** il faut toujours dire la vérité ; **to tell you the ~** or **to ~ tell, he ...** à vrai dire or à dire vrai, il ... ; **the ~ of it is that ...** la vérité c'est que ... ; **there's no ~ in what he says** il n'y a pas un mot de vrai dans ce qu'il dit ; **there's some ~ in that** il y a du vrai dans ce qu'il dit (or dans ce que vous dites etc) ■ PROV **~ will out** la vérité finira (toujours) par se savoir ; (Jur) **the ~, the whole ~ and nothing but the ~** la vérité, toute la vérité et rien que la vérité ; **the honest ~** la pure vérité, la vérité vraie* ; **the plain unvarnished ~** la vérité toute nue, la vérité sans fard ; **in (all) ~** en vérité, à vrai dire ; **~ is stranger than fiction** la réalité dépasse la fiction **b** vérité f → **home 2** COMP ► **truth drug** N sérum m de vérité

truthful ['truːθfʊl] ADJ **a** (= honest) [person] qui dit la vérité ; **he's a very ~ person** il dit toujours la vérité ; **he was not being entirely ~** il ne disait pas entièrement la vérité **b** (= true) [answer, statement] exact ; [portrait, account] fidèle

truthfully ['truːθfəlɪ] ADV honnêtement

truthfulness ['truːθfʊlnɪs] N (NonC) véracité f

try [traɪ] **1** N **a** (= attempt) essai m, tentative f ; **to have a ~** essayer (**at doing** de faire) ; **to give sth a ~** essayer qch ; **it was a good ~** il a (or tu as etc) vraiment essayé ; **it's worth a ~** cela vaut le coup d'essayer ; **to do sth at the first ~** faire qch du premier coup ; **after three tries he gave up** il a abandonné après trois tentatives **b** (Rugby) essai m ; **to score a ~** marquer un essai

2 VT **a** (= attempt) essayer, tâcher (**to do** de faire) ; (= seek) chercher (**to do** à faire) ; **~ to eat** or **~ and eat some of it** essaie or tâche d'en

manger un peu ; **he was ~ing to understand** il essayait de or tâchait de or cherchait à comprendre ; **it's ~ing to rain** il a l'air de vouloir pleuvoir* ; **I'll ~ anything once** je suis toujours prêt à faire un essai ; (warning) **just you ~ it!** essaie donc un peu !, essaie un peu pour voir !* ; **you've only tried three questions** vous avez seulement essayé de répondre à trois questions ; **have you ever tried the high jump?** as-tu déjà essayé le saut en hauteur ? ; **to ~ one's best** or **one's hardest** faire de son mieux, faire tout son possible (**to do** pour faire) ; **to ~ one's hand at sth/at doing** s'essayer à qch/à faire

b (= sample, experiment with) [+ method, recipe, new material, new car] essayer ; **have you tried these olives?** avez-vous goûté à or essayé ces olives ? ; **won't you ~ me for the job?** vous ne voulez pas me faire faire un essai ? ; **have you tried aspirin?** avez-vous essayé (de prendre) de l'aspirine ? ; **~ pushing that button** essayez de presser ce bouton ; **I tried three hotels but they were all full** j'ai essayé trois hôtels mais ils étaient tous complets ; **to ~ the door** essayer d'ouvrir la porte ; **~ this for size** (gen) essaie ça pour voir ; (when suggesting sth) écoute un peu ça

c (= test, put strain on) [+ person, sb's patience, strength, endurance] mettre à l'épreuve, éprouver ; [+ vehicle, plane] tester ; [+ machine, gadget] tester, mettre à l'essai ; [+ eyes, eyesight] fatiguer ; **to ~ one's strength against sb** se mesurer à qn ; **to ~ one's wings** essayer de voler de ses propres ailes ; **to ~ one's luck** tenter sa chance, tenter le coup ; **this material has been tried and tested** ce tissu a subi tous les tests ; **he was tried and found wanting** il ne s'est pas montré à la hauteur, il n'a pas répondu à ce qu'on attendait de lui ; **they have been sorely tried** ils ont été durement éprouvés → **well²**

d (Jur) [+ person, case] juger ; **to ~ sb for theft** juger qn pour vol ; (Mil) **he was tried by court-martial** il est passé en conseil de guerre

3 VI essayer ; **~ again!** recommence !, refais un essai ! ; **just you ~!** essaie donc un peu !, essaie un peu pour voir !* ; **I didn't even ~ (to)** je n'ai même pas essayé ; **I couldn't have done that (even) if I'd tried** je n'aurais pas pu faire cela même si j'avais voulu ; **to ~ for a job/a scholarship** essayer d'obtenir un poste/une bourse ; **it wasn't for lack** or **want of ~ing that he ...** ce n'était pas faute d'avoir essayé qu'il ...

4 COMP ► **try-on*** N **it's a ~-on** c'est du bluff

► **try on 1** VT SEP **a** [+ garment, shoe] essayer ; **~ this on for size** [+ garment] essayez cela pour voir si c'est votre taille ; [+ shoe] essayez cela pour voir si c'est votre pointure **b** (Brit*) **to ~ it on with sb** essayer de voir jusqu'où l'on peut pousser qn ; (sexually) faire des avances à qn ; **he's ~ing it on** il essaie de voir jusqu'où il peut aller ; **he's ~ing it on to see how you'll react** il essaie de voir comment tu vas réagir ; **don't ~ anything on!** ne fais pas le malin ! **2** **~-on** N → **try**

► **try out 1** VT SEP [+ machine, new material] essayer, faire l'essai de ; [+ new drug, new recipe, method, solution] essayer ; [+ new teacher, employee etc] mettre à l'essai ; **~ it out on the cat first** essaie d'abord de voir quelle est la réaction du chat **2** **~-out** N → **tryout**

► **try over** VT SEP (Mus) essayer

trying ['traɪɪŋ] ADJ [person] difficile, fatigant ; [experience, time] éprouvant

tryout ['traɪaʊt] N (= trial) essai m ; (Sport) épreuve f de sélection ; (Theat) audition f

tryst †† [trɪst] N **a** (= meeting) rendez-vous m (d'amour) **b** (also **~ing place**) lieu m de rendez-vous (d'amour)

tsar [zaːʳ] N tsar m

tsarevitch ['zaːrəvɪtʃ] N tsarévitch m

tsarina [zaːˈriːnə] N tsarine f

tsarist ['zaːrɪst] N, ADJ tsariste mf

tsetse fly ['tsetsɪflaɪ] N mouche f tsé-tsé inv

tsp. (pl tsp. or tsps.) (ABBR = **teaspoon(ful)** c. f à café

TSS N = **toxic shock syndrome**; → **toxic**

tsunami [tsʊˈnaːmɪ] N tsunami m

TT N (ABBR = **teetotal, teetotaller b** (ABBR = **tuberculin tested**) → **tuberculin**

TU [tiːˈjuː] N (ABBR = **Trade(s) Union**) → **trade**

tub [tʌb] **1** N (gen, also in washing machine) cuve f ; (for washing clothes) baquet m ; (for flowers) bac m ; (also **bathtub**) tub m ; (in bathroom) baignoire f ; (* = boat) sabot* m, rafiot* m ; (for cream etc) (petit) pot m **2** COMP ► **tub-thumper** N (Brit fig) orateur m démagogue ► **tub-thumping** N (NonC) démagogie f ♦ ADJ démagogique

tuba ['tjuːbə] N (pl **tubas** or (frm) **tubae** ['tjuːbiː]) tuba m

tubby* ['tʌbɪ] ADJ rondelet, dodu

tube [tjuːb] **1** N (gen, Anat, Telec, TV) tube m ; (for tyre) chambre f à air ; (Brit) **the ~** (= the Underground) le métro ; (Brit) **to go by ~** prendre le métro ; (US = television) **the ~*** la télé* ; **to go down the ~s*** tourner en eau de boudin*, partir en couille✱ (fig) → **inner 2** COMP ► **tube station** N (Brit) station f de métro

tubeless ['tjuːblɪs] ADJ [tyre] sans chambre à air

tuber ['tjuːbəʳ] N (Bot, Anat) tubercule m

tubercle ['tjuːbɜːkl] N (Anat, Bot, Med) tubercule m

tubercular [tjʊˈbɜːkjʊləʳ] **1** ADJ (Anat, Bot, Med) tuberculeux ; **~ patients** les tuberculeux mpl **2** COMP ► **tubercular meningitis** N (Med) méningite f tuberculeuse

tuberculin [tjʊˈbɜːkjʊlɪn] N tuberculine f ; **~-tested cows** vaches fpl tuberculinisées ; **~-tested milk** ≈ lait m certifié

tuberculosis [tjʊˌbɜːkjʊˈləʊsɪs] N tuberculose f ; **he's got ~** il a la tuberculose ; **~ sufferer** tuberculeux m, -euse f

tuberculous [tjʊˈbɜːkjʊləs] ADJ = **tubercular**

tubing ['tjuːbɪŋ] N (NonC) (= tubes collectively) tubes mpl, tuyaux mpl ; (= substance) tube m, tuyau m ; **rubber ~** tube m or tuyau m en caoutchouc

tubular ['tjuːbjʊləʳ] **1** ADJ tubulaire **2** COMP ► **tubular bells** NPL (Mus) carillon m ► **tubular steel** N tubes mpl métalliques or d'acier ► **tubular steel chair** N chaise f tubulaire

tubule ['tjuːbjʊl] N (Anat) tube m

TUC [tiːjuːˈsiː] N (Brit) (ABBR = **Trades Union Congress**) → **trade**

tuck [tʌk] **1** N **a** (Sewing) rempli m ; **to put** or **take a ~ in sth** faire un rempli dans qch **b** (NonC: Brit Scol = food) boustifaille✱ f **2** VT **a** (gen) mettre ; **to ~ a blanket round sb** envelopper qn dans une couverture ; **he ~ed the book under his arm** il a mis or rangé le livre sous son bras ; **he ~ed his shirt into his trousers** il a rentré sa chemise dans son pantalon ; **he was sitting with his feet ~ed under him** il avait les pieds repliés sous lui **b** (Sewing) faire un rempli dans **3** VI **a** **to ~ into a meal*** attaquer un repas **4** COMP ► **tuck-in*** N bon repas m, festin m (hum) ; **they had a (good) ~-in** ils ont vraiment bien mangé ► **tuck-shop** N (Brit Scol) petite boutique où les écoliers peuvent acheter des pâtisseries, des bonbons etc

► **tuck away** VT SEP **a** (= put away) mettre, ranger ; **~ it away out of sight** cache-le ; **the hut is ~ed away among the trees** la cabane se cache or est cachée or est perdue parmi les arbres **b** (* = eat) bouffer✱

► **tuck in 1** VI (Brit* = eat) (bien) boulotter* ; **~ in!** allez-y, mangez ! **2** VT SEP [+ shirt, flap, stomach] rentrer ; [+ bedclothes] border ; **to ~ sb in** border qn **3** **~-in*** N → **tuck**

▶**tuck under** VT SEP [+ *flap*] rentrer
▶**tuck up** VT SEP [+ *skirt, sleeves*] remonter; [+ *hair*] relever; [+ *legs*] replier; (*Brit*) **to ~ sb up (in bed)** border qn (dans son lit)

tuckbox ['tʌkbɒks] N (*Brit Scol*) boîte *f* à provisions

tucker[1] ['tʌkəʳ] N **a** (*Dress*††) fichu *m* → **bib b** (*: = food*) bouffe* *f*

tucker[2]* ['tʌkəʳ] VT (*US*) fatiguer, crever*; **~ed (out)*** crevé*, vanné*

Tudor ['tjuːdəʳ] ADJ (*Archit*) Tudor *inv*; [*period*] des Tudors → **stockbroker**

Tue(s). ABBR = **Tuesday**

Tuesday ['tjuːzdɪ] N mardi *m* → **shrove**; *for phrases see* **Saturday**

tufa ['tjuːfə] N tuf *m* calcaire

tuffet ['tʌfɪt] N [*of grass*] touffe *f* d'herbe; (= *stool*) (petit) tabouret *m*

tuft [tʌft] N touffe *f*; (*Orn*) **~ of feathers** huppe *f*, aigrette *f*; **~ of hair** (*on top of head*) épi *m*; (*anywhere on head*) touffe *f* de cheveux

tufted ['tʌftɪd] **1** ADJ [*grass*] en touffe; [*eyebrows*] broussailleux; [*bird, head*] huppé **2** COMP ▶ **tufted duck** N (fuligule *m*) morillon *m*

tug [tʌg] **1** N **a** (= *pull*) (petite) saccade *f*, (petit) coup *m*; **to give sth a ~** tirer sur qch; **I felt a ~ at my sleeve/on the rope** j'ai senti qu'on me tirait par la manche/qu'on tirait sur la corde; (*fig*) **parting with them was quite a ~** les quitter a été un vrai déchirement **b** (*also* **~boat**) remorqueur *m* **2** VT (= *pull*) [+ *rope, sleeve etc*] tirer sur; (= *drag*) tirer, traîner; (*Naut*) remorquer; **to ~ sth up/down** faire monter/faire descendre qch en le tirant *or* traînant **3** VI tirer fort *or* sec (**at, on** sur) **4** COMP ▶ **tug-of-love** N lutte acharnée entre les parents d'un enfant pour en avoir la garde ▶ **tug-of-war** N (*Sport*) tir *m* à la corde; (*fig*) lutte *f* (acharnée *or* féroce)

tuition [tjuˈɪʃən] **1** N (*NonC*) cours *mpl*; **private ~** cours *mpl* particuliers (**in** de) **2** COMP ▶ **tuition fees** NPL (*Scol etc*) frais *mpl* de scolarité

tulip ['tjuːlɪp] N tulipe *f*; **~ tree** tulipier *m*

tulle [tjuːl] N tulle *m*

tum* [tʌm] N (*Brit*) ventre *m*, bide* *m*

tumble ['tʌmbl] **1** N **a** (= *fall*) chute *f*, culbute *f*; [*of acrobat etc*] culbute *f*, cabriole *f*; **to have** *or* **take a ~** faire une chute *or* une culbute; (*fig*) **they had a ~ in the hay** ils ont folâtré dans le foin **b** (= *confused heap*) amas *m*; **in a ~** en désordre **2** VI **a** (= *fall*) dégringoler, tomber; (= *trip*) trébucher (**over** sur); [*river, stream*] descendre en cascade; [*prices*] chuter, dégringoler; (*fig*) [*person, ruler*] faire la culbute; [*acrobat etc*] faire des culbutes *or* des cabrioles; **he ~d out of bed** il est tombé du lit → **2b**; **to ~ head over heels** faire la culbute, culbuter; **to ~ downstairs** culbuter *or* dégringoler dans l'escalier; **he ~d over a chair** il a trébuché sur une chaise; **he ~d over the cliff/into the river** il est tombé du haut de la falaise/dans la rivière; **the clothes ~d out of the cupboard** la pile de vêtements a dégringolé quand on a ouvert le placard; **the tumbling waters of the Colorado River** les eaux tumultueuses du Colorado; (*Brit fig*) **to ~ into war/depression** basculer dans la guerre/la dépression **b** (= *rush*) se jeter; **he ~d into bed** il s'est jeté au lit; **he ~d out of bed** il a bondi hors du lit; **they ~d out of the car** ils ont déboulé de la voiture **c** (*Brit* fig = *realize*) **to ~ to sth** réaliser* qch; **then I ~d (to it)** c'est là que j'ai pigé* **3** VT [+ *pile, heap*] renverser, faire tomber; [+ *hair*] ébouriffer; [+ *books, objects*] jeter en tas *or* en vrac; **~d** [*room*] en désordre; [*bed*] défait; [*clothes*] chiffonné

4 COMP ▶ **tumble-dry** VT faire sécher dans le sèche-linge ▶ **tumble dryer** N sèche-linge *m*

▶**tumble about**, **tumble around** **1** VI [*puppies, children*] gambader, s'ébattre; [*acrobat*] cabrioler **2** VT SEP [+ *books, objects*] mélanger

▶**tumble down** **1** VI [*person*] faire une chute *or* une culbute, culbuter; **to be tumbling down** [*building etc*] tomber en ruine **2** **~down** ADJ → **tumbledown**

▶**tumble out** **1** VI [*objects, contents*] tomber en vrac, s'éparpiller **2** VT SEP [+ *objects, contents*] faire tomber en vrac

▶**tumble over** **1** VI culbuter **2** VT SEP renverser, faire tomber

tumbledown ['tʌmbldaʊn] ADJ en ruine, délabré

tumbler ['tʌmbləʳ] **1** N (= *glass*) verre *m* (droit); (*of plastic, metal*) gobelet *m*; (*in lock*) gorge *f* (de serrure); (*also* **tumble dryer**) tambour *m or* séchoir *m* (à linge) à air chaud; (*Tech etc = revolving drum*) tambour *m* rotatif; (= *acrobat*) acrobate *mf*; (= *pigeon*) pigeon *m* culbutant **2** COMP ▶ **tumbler switch** N (*Elec*) interrupteur *m* à bascule

tumbleweed ['tʌmblwiːd] N (espèce *f* d')amarante *f*

tumbrel ['tʌmbrəl], **tumbril** ['tʌmbrɪl] N tombereau *m*

tumefaction [ˌtjuːmɪˈfækʃən] N tuméfaction *f*

tumescent [tjuːˈmesnt] ADJ tumescent

tumid ['tjuːmɪd] ADJ (*Med*) tuméfié; (*fig*) ampoulé

tummy* ['tʌmɪ] **1** N ventre *m* **2** COMP ▶ **tummy tuck** N plastie *f* abdominale; **to have a ~ tuck** se faire retendre le ventre

tummyache* ['tʌmɪeɪk] N mal *m* de ventre

tumour, **tumor** (*US*) ['tjuːməʳ] N tumeur *f*

tumuli ['tjuːmjʊlaɪ] NPL of **tumulus**

tumult ['tjuːmʌlt] N (= *uproar*) tumulte *m*; (*emotional*) émoi *m*; **in (a) ~** dans le tumulte; (*emotionally*) en émoi

tumultuous [tjuːˈmʌltjʊəs] ADJ [*events, period*] tumultueux; [*welcome, reception*] enthousiaste; [*applause*] frénétique; **the ~ changes in Eastern Europe** les bouleversements en Europe de l'Est

tumultuously [tjuːˈmʌltjʊəslɪ] ADV tumultueusement

tumulus ['tjuːmjʊləs] N (*pl* **tumuli**) tumulus *m*

tun [tʌn] N fût *m*, tonneau *m*

tuna ['tjuːnə] N (*pl* **tuna** *or* **tunas**) (*also* **~ fish**) thon *m* → **blue**, **long**[1]

tundra ['tʌndrə] N toundra *f*

tune [tjuːn] **1** N **a** (= *melody*) air *m*; **he gave us a ~ on the piano** il nous a joué un air au piano; **there's not much ~ to it** ce n'est pas très mélodieux; **to the ~ of** [*sing*] sur l'air de; [*march, process*] aux accents de; (*fig*) **repairs to the ~ of £300** des réparations atteignant la coquette somme de 300 livres; (*fig*) **to change one's ~** ◊ **to sing another** *or* **a different ~** changer de discours *or* de chanson*; (*fig*) **to call the ~** (= *give orders*) commander; (= *take decisions*) décider → **dance b** (*NonC*) **to be in ~** [*instrument*] être accordé; [*singer*] chanter juste; **to be out of ~** [*instrument*] être désaccordé; [*singer*] chanter faux; **to sing/play in ~** chanter/jouer juste; **to sing/play out of ~** chanter/jouer faux; (*fig*) **to be in/out of ~ with ...** être en accord/désaccord avec ... **2** VT (*Mus*) accorder; (*Rad, TV: also* **~ in**) régler (**to** sur); (*Aut*) régler, mettre au point; (*Rad*) **you are ~d (in) to ...** vous êtes à l'écoute de ... → **stay**[1] **3** COMP ▶ **tune-up** N (*Aut*) réglage *m*, mise *f* au point

▶**tune in** (*Rad, TV*) **1** VI se mettre à l'écoute (**to** de); **~ in again tomorrow** soyez de nou-

veau à l'écoute demain; **thousands ~d in** des milliers de gens se sont mis à l'écoute **2** VT SEP (*Rad, TV*) régler (**to** sur); **predatory fish are ~d in to all movement in the sea around them** les poissons prédateurs captent les ondes émises par tout mouvement dans la mer; (*fig = aware of*) **to be ~d in to ...** (*gen*) être à l'écoute de ...; **to be ~d in to new developments** être au fait des derniers développements; (*fig*) **he is/isn't ~d in:** il est/n'est pas dans la course* → **tune 2**

▶**tune out*** (*fig*) **1** VI faire la sourde oreille **2** VT SEP ne pas faire attention à, faire la sourde oreille à

▶**tune up 1** VI (*Mus*) accorder son (*or* ses) instrument(s) **2** VT SEP (*Mus*) accorder; (*Aut*) mettre au point **3** **~up** N → **tune**

tuneful ['tjuːnfʊl] ADJ [*music, instrument, voice*] mélodieux

tunefully ['tjuːnfəlɪ] ADV mélodieusement

tunefulness ['tjuːnfʊlnɪs] N [*of music, instrument, voice*] caractère *m* mélodieux

tuneless ['tjuːnlɪs] ADJ peu mélodieux, discordant

tunelessly ['tjuːnlɪslɪ] ADV [*sing, play*] faux

tuner ['tjuːnəʳ] **1** N (= *person*) accordeur *m*; (*Rad: also* **stereo ~**) syntoniseur *m*, syntonisateur *m* (*Can*); (= *knob*) bouton *m* de réglage → **piano 2** COMP ▶ **tuner amplifier** N amplituner *m*

tungsten ['tʌŋstən] N (*NonC*) tungstène *m*; **~ lamp/steel** lampe *f*/acier *m* au tungstène

tunic ['tjuːnɪk] N tunique *f*

tuning ['tjuːnɪŋ] **1** N (*Mus*) accord *m*; (*Rad, TV*) réglage *m*; (*Aut*) réglage(s), mise *f* au point **2** COMP ▶ **tuning fork** N (*Mus*) diapason *m* ▶ **tuning key** N (*Mus*) accordoir *m* ▶ **tuning knob** N (*Rad etc*) bouton *m* de réglage

Tunis ['tjuːnɪs] N Tunis

Tunisia [tjuːˈnɪzɪə] N la Tunisie

Tunisian [tjuːˈnɪzɪən] **1** ADJ (*gen*) tunisien; [*ambassador, embassy*] de Tunisie **2** N Tunisien(ne) *m(f)*

tunnel ['tʌnl] **1** N (*gen, Rail*) tunnel *m*; (*Min*) galerie *f*; **to make a ~ to tunnel 2** VI [*people, rabbits etc*] percer *or* creuser un *or* des tunnel(s) *or* des galeries (**into** dans, **under** sous); **to ~ in/out** etc entrer/sortir etc en creusant un tunnel **3** VT percer *or* creuser un *or* des tunnel(s) dans; **a mound by rabbits** un monticule dans lequel les lapins ont percé *or* creusé des galeries; **shelters ~led out of the hillside** des abris creusés à flanc de colline; **to ~ one's way in** etc → **to tunnel in**; → **2** COMP ▶ **tunnel effect** N (*Phys*) effet *m* tunnel ▶ **tunnel vision** N (*Opt*) rétrécissement *m* du champ visuel; (*fig*) **to have ~ vision** avoir des œillères

tunny ['tʌnɪ] N (*pl* **tunny** *or* **tunnies**) = **tuna**

tuppence ['tʌpəns] N (ABBR = **twopence**) deux pence *mpl*; (*fig*) **it's not worth ~*** ça ne vaut pas un radis*; **I don't care ~*** je m'en fiche (comme de l'an quarante)*

tuppenny† ['tʌpənɪ] ADJ (= *twopenny*) à deux pence; **a ~ bit** une pièce de deux pence; (*Brit*) **I don't give a ~ damn*** je m'en contrefiche*; **she doesn't give a ~ damn for** *or* **about ...** elle se contrefiche de ...*

tuppenny-ha'penny† * ['tʌpənɪˈheɪpnɪ] ADJ (*fig = insignificant*) de quatre sous, à la noix*

turban ['tɜːbən] **1** N turban *m* **2** VT **~ed** [*person, head*] enturbanné

turbid ['tɜːbɪd] ADJ (*frm: lit, fig*) turbide

turbidity [tɜːˈbɪdɪtɪ] N (*frm*) turbidité *f* (*frm*)

turbine ['tɜːbaɪn] N turbine *f*; **steam/gas ~** turbine *f* à vapeur/à gaz

turbo ['tɜːbəʊ] N = **turbofan**; (*Aut*) **~ engine** moteur *m* turbo

turbo... ['tɜːbəʊ] PREF turbo...

turbocharged ['tɜːbəʊˌtʃɑːdʒd] ADJ **~ engine** moteur *m* turbo

turbofan [ˌtɜːbəʊˈfæn] N (= *fan*) turbofan *m*; (*also* ~ **engine**) turbofan *m*, turboventilateur *m*

turbogenerator [ˌtɜːbəʊˈdʒenəˌreɪtəʳ] N turbogénérateur *m*

turbojet [ˈtɜːbəʊˌdʒet] N (*also* ~ **engine**) turboréacteur *m*; (*also* ~ **aircraft**) avion *m* à turboréacteur

turboprop [ˈtɜːbəʊˌprɒp] N (*also* ~ **engine**) turbopropulseur *m*; (*also* ~ **aircraft**) avion *m* à turbopropulseur

turbosupercharger [ˌtɜːbəʊˈsuːpəˌtʃɑːdʒəʳ] N turbocompresseur *m* de suralimentation

turbot [ˈtɜːbət] N (*pl* **turbot** *or* **turbots**) turbot *m*

turbulence [ˈtɜːbjʊləns] N (*NonC*) turbulence *f* (*also Aviat*); (*of waves, sea*) agitation *f*

turbulent [ˈtɜːbjʊlənt] ADJ [a] (= *choppy*) [*water, sea*] agité, turbulent (*liter*); ~ **air/water** turbulences *fpl* [b] (= *troubled*) [*time, period*] agité; [*history, events, career*] tumultueux; [*crowd, person, personality, mood*] turbulent [c] (*liter = disorderly, troublesome*) [*person*] turbulent

turd ** [tɜːd] N merde** *f*; (= *person*) con* *m*, couillon* *m*

tureen [təˈriːn] N soupière *f*

turf [tɜːf] [1] N (*pl* **turfs** *or* **turves**) [a] (*NonC* = *grass*) gazon *m*; (*one piece*) motte *f* de gazon; (*NonC* = *peat*) tourbe *f*; (*Sport*) turf *m* [b]* [*of gang etc*] territoire *m* or secteur *m* réservé; **to be on the ~*** [*prostitute*] faire le trottoir* [2] VT [a] (*also* ~ **over**) [+ *land*] gazonner [b] (*Brit**) [+ *throw*] balancer*, jeter; (= *push*) pousser; (= *put*) mettre, flanquer* [3] COMP ► **turf accountant** N (*Brit*) bookmaker *m*

► **turf in*** VT SEP (*Brit*) [+ *objects*] balancer* dedans; (*fig = give up*) **he ~ed it all in*** il a tout plaqué*

► **turf out*** VT SEP (*Brit*) [+ *objects*] sortir; (= *throw away*) bazarder*; [+ *person*] flanquer à la porte*, virer*; [+ *suggestion*] démolir*

Turgenev [tɜːˈɡeɪnɪv] N Tourgueniev *m*

turgid [ˈtɜːdʒɪd] ADJ [a] (*lit = swollen*) turgide [b] (*fig = stodgy, lifeless*) [*style, essay etc*] indigeste; [*language*] lourd [c] (*fig = pompous*) [*style, essay, language etc*] ampoulé

Turin [tjʊəˈrɪn] N Turin *m*; **the ~ Shroud** le saint suaire de Turin

Turk [tɜːk] N Turc *m*, Turque *f*; (*fig: esp Pol*) **young ~** jeune Turc *m*

Turkey [ˈtɜːkɪ] N la Turquie

turkey [ˈtɜːkɪ] [1] N (*pl* **turkey** *or* **turkeys**) [a] dindon *m*, dinde *f*; (*Culin*) dinde *f*; (*US fig*) **to talk ~*** parler net or franc; (*esp Brit*) **it would be like ~s voting for Christmas** cela reviendrait à signer son arrêt de mort → **cold** [b] (*esp US: Cine, Theat** = *flop*) four** *m* [c] [a] (= *awkward person*) balourd *m* [2] COMP ► **turkey buzzard** N vautour *m* aura ► **turkey cock** N dindon *m* ► **turkey shoot** N (*fig*) combat *m* inégal

Turkish [ˈtɜːkɪʃ] [1] ADJ turc (turque *f*); [*ambassador, embassy*] de Turquie; [*teacher*] de turc; **as thin as a ~ cat** maigre comme un clou [2] N (*Ling*) turc *m* [3] COMP ► **Turkish bath** N bain *m* turc ► **Turkish coffee** N café *m* turc ► **Turkish Cypriot** ADJ chypriote turc (turque *f*) ♦ N (= *person*) Chypriote *m(f)* turc (turque *f*) ► **Turkish delight** N (*NonC: Culin*) loukoum *m* ► **Turkish towel** N serviette *f* éponge *inv* ► **Turkish towelling** N (*NonC*) tissu *m* éponge (*NonC*)

Turkmen [ˈtɜːkmen] [1] ADJ turkmène [2] N [a] Turkmène *mf* [b] (*Ling*) turkmène *m*

Turkmenia [tɜːkˈmiːnɪə] N la Turkménie

Turkmenistan [ˌtɜːkmenɪsˈtɑːn] N le Turkménistan

turmeric [ˈtɜːmərɪk] N (*NonC*) curcuma *m*, safran *m* des Indes

turmoil [ˈtɜːmɔɪl] N agitation *f*, trouble *m*; (*emotional*) trouble *m*, émoi *m*; **everything was in (a) ~** c'était le bouleversement or le chambardement* le plus complet

turn [tɜːn]

[1] NOUN	[4] COMPOUND
[2] TRANSITIVE VERB	[5] PHRASAL VERBS
[3] INTRANSITIVE VERB	

[1] **NOUN**

[a] = *movement: of wheel, handle etc* tour *m*; **to give sth a ~** tourner qch (une fois); **to give a screw a ~** donner un tour de vis; **with a ~ of his head he could see ...** en tournant la tête il voyait ...

[b] = *bend* (*in road etc*) tournant *m*, virage *m*; (*Ski*) virage *m*; **to make a ~** [*person, vehicle, road*] tourner; [*ship*] virer de bord; **"no left ~"** « défense de tourner à gauche »; **take the next ~ on the left** prenez la prochaine route (*or* rue) à gauche; **the economy may at last be on the ~** l'économie pourrait enfin se redresser

♦ **to take a turn (for)**: **to take a ~ for the worse** s'aggraver; **to take a ~ for the better** s'améliorer; **the patient took a ~ for the worse/better** l'état du malade s'est aggravé/amélioré; **things took a new ~** les choses ont pris une nouvelle tournure; **events took a tragic ~** les événements ont pris un tour ou une tournure tragique

[c] = *walk* tour *m*; **to go for** *or* **take a ~ in the park** aller faire un tour dans le parc

[d] * = *attack* crise *f*, attaque *f*; **he had one of his ~s last night** il a eu une nouvelle crise *or* attaque la nuit dernière; **she has giddy** *or* **dizzy ~s** elle a des vertiges

[e] = *fright* coup* *m*; **it gave me quite a ~** ◊ **it gave me a nasty ~** ça m'a fait un sacré coup*

[f] = *action* **to do sb a good ~** rendre un service à qn; **to do sb a bad ~** jouer un mauvais tour à qn ■ (*PROV*) **one good ~ deserves another** un prêté pour un rendu (*PROV*)

[g] = *act: esp Brit* numéro *m*; **to do a ~** faire un numéro

[h] *Mus* doublé *m*

[i] *in game, queue, series* tour *m*; **it's your ~** c'est votre tour, c'est à vous; **it's your ~ to play** (c'est) à vous de jouer; **whose ~ is it?** (*gen*) c'est à qui le tour?; (*in game*) c'est à qui de jouer?, c'est à qui le tour?; **wait your ~** attendez votre tour; **to take ~s at doing sth** ◊ **to take it in ~(s) to do sth** faire qch à tour de rôle; **take it in ~s!** chacun son tour!; **to take ~s at the wheel** se relayer au volant; **shall I take a ~ at the wheel?** est-ce que tu veux que je conduise un peu?

[j] *Culin* done to a ~ à point

[k] *SET STRUCTURES*

♦ **at every turn** à tout instant

♦ **by turns** (= *alternately*) tantôt ... tantôt ... ; (= *one after another*) à tour de rôle; **he was by ~s optimistic and despairing** il était tantôt optimiste, tantôt désespéré, il était tour à tour optimiste et désespéré; **the pictures are by ~s shocking, charming and cheeky** ces photos sont tantôt choquantes, tantôt pleines de charme et de malice; **my sister and I visit our mother by ~s** ma sœur et moi rendons visite à notre mère à tour de rôle

♦ **in turn** (= *one after another*) à tour de rôle; (= *then*) à mon (*or* son, notre, leur *etc*) tour; **they answered in ~** ils ont répondu à tour de rôle, ils ont répondu chacun (à) leur tour; **and they, in ~, said ...** et, à leur tour, ils ont dit ... ; **he told a colleague, who in ~ told a reporter** il l'a dit à un collègue qui à son tour en a parlé à un journaliste

♦ **out of turn** **I don't want to speak out of ~ but I think that ...** je ne devrais peut-être pas dire cela mais je pense que ...

♦ **turn (and turn) about** à tour de rôle; they

share responsibilities ~ and ~ about ils sont responsables à tour de rôle

♦ **turn of** + *noun*: **at the ~ of the century** au début du siècle; (*Mil*) **~ of duty** tour *m* de garde or de service; **this was a surprising ~ of events** c'était là quelque chose de tout à fait inattendu; **to be of** *or* **have a scientific ~ of mind** avoir l'esprit scientifique; **to be of a pragmatic/of an analytic ~ of mind** avoir l'esprit pratique/l'esprit d'analyse; **to have an original ~ of mind** avoir une tournure d'esprit originale; **~ of phrase** tournure *f*, tour *m* de phrase; **to have a good ~ of speed** avoir une bonne pointe de vitesse; **at the ~ of the year** en fin d'année

[2] **TRANSITIVE VERB**

For **turn** + *adverb/preposition combinations see also phrasal verbs.*

[a] + *handle, knob, screw, key, wheel* tourner; (*mechanically*) faire tourner; **~ it to the left** tournez-le vers la gauche; **what ~s the wheel?** qu'est-ce qui fait tourner la roue?; (*Aut*) **he ~ed the wheel sharply** il a donné un brusque coup de volant; **you can ~ it through 90°** on peut le faire pivoter de 90°; **~ the key in the lock** tourne la clé dans la serrure

[b] + *page* tourner; (*also fig*) **to ~ the page** tourner la page

[c] + *mattress, pillow, collar, soil, steak, record* retourner; **to ~ one's ankle** se tordre la cheville; **it ~s my stomach** cela me soulève le cœur, cela m'écœure

[d] = *change position of, direct* [+ *car, object*] tourner (*towards* vers); [+ *gun, hose, searchlight*] braquer (**on sb** sur qn); [+ *thoughts, attention*] tourner, diriger (*towards* vers); **~ the knob to "high"** tournez le bouton jusqu'à « maximum »; **~ the switch to "on"** mettez l'interrupteur en position « marche »; **~ it to "wash"** mettez-le en position « lavage »; **~ your face this way** tourne-toi de ce côté-ci; **to ~ the lights low** baisser les lumières; **without ~ing a hair** sans sourciller, sans broncher; **already in her first film she ~ed a few heads** déjà dans son premier film, on l'avait remarquée; **he ~ed his steps southward** il dirigea ses pas vers le sud; **they ~ed his argument against him** ils ont retourné son raisonnement contre lui; **they ~ed him against his father** ils l'ont monté contre son père

[e] = *deflect* [+ *blow*] parer, détourner; **nothing will ~ him from his purpose** rien ne l'écartera *or* ne le détournera de son but

[f] = *shape* [+ *wood*] tourner

[g] = *reach* [*age, time*] **as soon as he ~ed 18** dès qu'il a eu 18 ans; **he has** *or* **is ~ed 40** il a plus de 40 ans; **it's ~ed 3 o'clock** il est 3 heures passées

[h] = *transform* changer, transformer (*into* en); (= *translate*) traduire (*into* en); (*Brit Sport*) **his goal ~ed the game** son but a changé la physionomie du match *or* a changé la donne; **she ~ed him into a frog** elle l'a changé *or* transformé en grenouille; **they ~ed the land into a park** ils ont transformé le terrain en parc; **the experience ~ed him into a misogynist** cette expérience a fait de lui un misogyne; **an actor ~ed writer** un acteur devenu écrivain; **~ your talents into hard cash** transformez vos talents en espèces sonnantes et trébuchantes; **to ~ a book into a play/film** adapter un livre pour la scène/à l'écran; **she ~ed her dreams into reality** elle a réalisé ses rêves; **to ~ the milk (sour)** faire tourner le lait; **to ~ sth black** noircir qch; **it ~ed him green with envy** il en était vert de jalousie

[3] **INTRANSITIVE VERB**

[a] = *move round* [*handle, knob, wheel, screw, key*] tourner; [*person*] se tourner (**to, towards** vers); (*right round*) se retourner; **~ to face me** tourne-toi vers moi; **he ~ed and saw me** il s'est retourné et m'a vu; **he ~ed to me and smiled** il s'est tourné vers moi et a souri; **he ~ed to look at me** il s'est retourné pour me re-

garder; **he ~ed to lie on his other side** il s'est
retourné de l'autre côté; **his stomach ~ed at
the sight** le spectacle lui a retourné l'estomac
or soulevé le cœur; **he would ~ in his grave if he
knew** ... il se retournerait dans sa tombe s'il
savait ...
- ♦ **to turn on sth** [+ *hinge, axis*] tourner sur
qch; **the earth ~s on its axis** la terre tourne sur
son axe; (= *depend*) **it all ~s on whether he has
the money** tout dépend s'il a l'argent ou non;
the plot ~s on a question of mistaken identity
l'intrigue repose sur une erreur d'identité
→ **5**
  b = *move in different direction* [*person, vehicle*]
  tourner; [*aircraft*] changer de cap; (= *reverse
  direction*) faire demi-tour; [*ship*] virer; [*road,
  river*] faire un coude; [*wind*] tourner; [*tide*]
  changer de direction; (*Mil*) **right~!** demi-tour,
  droite!; **~ first right** prenez la première à droite; **they ~ed and came back** ils ont fait demi-
  tour et sont revenus sur leurs pas; **the car ~ed
  at the end of the street** (= *turned round*) la voiture a fait demi-tour au bout de la rue; (=
  turned off) la voiture a tourné au bout de la
  rue; (*Aut*) **there's nowhere to ~** il n'y a pas
  d'endroit où faire demi-tour; **the car ~ed into
  a side street** la voiture a tourné dans une rue
  transversale; **our luck has ~ed** la chance a
  tourné pour nous; (*Brit Sport*) **the game ~ed after half-time** la physionomie du match a
  changé après la mi-temps; (*fig*) **he didn't know
  which way to ~** il ne savait plus où donner de
  la tête; **where can I ~ for money?** où pourrais-
  je trouver de l'argent?
- ♦ **to turn against sb** se retourner contre qn
- ♦ **to turn to sb** (*lit*) se tourner vers qn; (*for
  help*) s'adresser à qn; **he ~ed to me for advice** il
  s'est adressé à moi pour me demander
  conseil; **our thoughts ~ to those who** ... nos
  pensées vont à ceux qui ...
- ♦ **to turn to sth** **~ to page 214** voir page 214;
  to ~ (to the) left tourner à gauche; (= *resort*) se
  tourner vers qch; **farmers are increasingly ~ing
  to organic methods** les agriculteurs se
  tournent de plus en plus vers une agriculture
  biologique; **he ~ed to drink** il s'est mis à boire
  → **3c**
  c = *become*
- ♦ **turn** + *adjective*: **to ~ nasty/dangerous/pale** devenir méchant/dangereux/pâle; **to ~ professional** passer professionnel; **to ~ Catholic** se
  convertir au catholicisme; **the weather has
  ~ed cold** le temps s'est rafraîchi
- ♦ **to turn into** + *noun* devenir; **he ~ed into a
  frog** il se changea *or* se transforma en grenouille; **the whole thing ~ed into a nightmare**
  ça a dégénéré en cauchemar, c'est devenu un
  véritable cauchemar
- ♦ **to turn to** + *noun*: **his admiration ~ed to scorn**
  son admiration se changea en *or* fit place au
  mépris; **his love ~ed to hatred** son amour se
  changea en haine *or* fit place à la haine; **to ~
  to stone** se changer en pierre; **his knees ~ed to
  water** *or* **jelly** ses jambes se sont dérobées sous
  lui → **3b**
  d = *change* [*weather*] changer; [*milk*] tourner; [*leaves*] jaunir
4 COMPOUNDS
- ▸ **turn signal** N (*US Aut*) clignotant *m*
5 PHRASAL VERBS
- ▸ **turn about**, **turn around** **1** VI [*person*] se
  retourner; [*vehicle*] faire demi-tour; [*object,
  wind*] tourner; (*Mil*) **about ~!** demi-tour!
  2 VT SEP **a** (*lit*) tourner dans l'autre sens
  b (= *change mind, tactics*) **to ~ sb around** faire
  changer d'avis à qn; **to ~ things around**
  renverser la situation → **turn round**
- ▸ **turn aside** **1** VI (*lit, fig*) se détourner (**from**
  de)
  2 VT SEP détourner
- ▸ **turn away** **1** VI se détourner (**from** de)
  2 VT SEP **a** [+ *head, face*] tourner; [+ *eyes,
  gun*] détourner; **he ~ed his thoughts away from**

the problem il efforçait de ne plus penser à ce
problème
  b (= *send away*) [+ *spectator*] refuser l'entrée
  à; [+ *immigrants*] refouler; [+ *applicants*] refuser; [+ *offer*] refuser, rejeter; **they're ~ing business** *or* **customers away** ils refusent des clients
- ▸ **turn back** **1** VI **a** [*traveller*] rebrousser chemin, faire demi-tour; [*vehicle*] faire demi-
  tour; (= *reverse a decision*) faire marche arrière; **the government cannot ~ back now** le gouvernement ne peut pas faire marche arrière
  maintenant; **there is no ~ing back** on ne peut
  pas retourner en arrière
  b **to ~ back to page 100** revenir à la page 100
  2 VT SEP **a** (= *fold, bend*) [+ *bedclothes, collar*]
  rabattre
  b (= *send back*) [+ *person, vehicle*] faire faire
  demi-tour à; [+ *demonstrators*] faire refluer
  c [+ *clock*] retarder; (*hands of clock*) reculer;
  (*fig*) **we can't ~ the clock back** on ne peut pas
  revenir en arrière; **it has ~ed the clock back ten
  years** cela nous a fait revenir dix ans en arrière
- ▸ **turn down** **1** VT SEP **a** (= *fold, bend*) [+
  collar] rabattre; **to ~ down the corner of the
  page** corner la page; **to ~ down the bed** rabattre les draps
  b (= *reduce*) [+ *gas, heat, lighting, radio, music*]
  baisser
  c (= *refuse*) [+ *offer, suggestion, suitor*] rejeter,
  repousser; [+ *candidate, volunteer*] refuser
  d (= *place upside down*) [+ *playing card*] retourner (face contre table)
  2 VI (= *decrease*) [*rate, level*] baisser
- ▸ **turn in** **1** VI **a** **to ~ in to a driveway** [*car,
  person*] tourner dans une allée
  b (* = *go to bed*) aller se coucher
  2 VT SEP **a** **to ~ in the ends of sth** rentrer les
  bouts de qch
  b (= *hand over*) [+ *wanted man*] livrer (à la
  police); [+ *stolen goods*] restituer; **to ~ o.s. in**
  se rendre, se livrer à la police
  c (= *submit*) [+ *report*] faire, soumettre
  d (*esp US* = *surrender, return*) [+ *borrowed
  goods, equipment*] rendre (**to** à)
  3 VT FUS (*Sport*) **to ~ in a good performance**
  [*player, team*] bien se comporter
- ▸ **turn off** **1** VI **a** [*person, vehicle*] tourner
  b **to ~ off automatically** [*heater, oven etc*]
  s'éteindre automatiquement
  2 VT FUS [+ *road*] quitter; **they decided to ~
  off the motorway** ils décidèrent de quitter l'autoroute
  3 VT SEP **a** [+ *water, tap*] fermer; [+ *radio,
  television*] éteindre; [+ *electricity, gas*] éteindre,
  fermer; [+ *water, electricity*] (*at main*) couper;
  [+ *heater*] éteindre, fermer; **he ~ed the programme off** (*Rad*) il a éteint la radio; (*TV*) il a
  éteint la télé; **to ~ off the light** éteindre (la lumière); **to ~ off the engine** arrêter *or* couper le
  moteur; **the oven ~s itself off** le four s'éteint
  tout seul *or* automatiquement
  b (* = *repel*) rebuter; **aggressive men ~ me off**
  les hommes agressifs me rebutent; **what ~s
  teenagers off science?** qu'est-ce qui, dans les
  sciences, rebute les adolescents?
- ▸ **turn on** **1** VI **a** [*heater, oven etc*] **to ~ on
  automatically** s'allumer automatiquement
  b (*TV*) **millions of viewers ~ on at 6 o'clock** des
  millions de téléspectateurs allument la télé à
  6 heures
  2 VT FUS (= *attack*) attaquer; **the dog ~ed on
  him** le chien l'a attaqué; **they ~ed on him and
  accused him of treachery** ils s'en sont pris à lui
  et l'ont accusé de trahison
  3 VT SEP **a** [+ *tap*] ouvrir; [+ *water*] faire couler; [+ *gas, electricity, radio, television, heater*]
  allumer; [+ *engine, machine*] mettre en marche; **to ~ on the light** allumer (la lumière);
  **when you arrive, you will need to ~ on the elec-
  tricity and gas** lorsque vous arriverez, il va
  falloir brancher l'électricité et le gaz; **to ~ on
  the charm*** faire du charme

  b (* = *excite*) exciter; **she ~s him on** elle l'excite; **this music ~s me on!** cette musique me
  fait quelque chose*; **to be ~ed on** (*sexually*)
  être excité (**by** par); **some men are ~ed on by
  power** il y a des hommes que le pouvoir excite → **turn 3**
- ▸ **turn out** **1** VI **a** (*from bed*) se lever; (*from
  house*) sortir; **not many people ~ed out to see
  her** peu de gens sont venus la voir
  b **to ~ out of a driveway** [*car, person*] sortir
  d'une allée
  c **his toes ~ out** il a les pieds en canard
  d (= *be found*) s'avérer; **it ~ed out that she
  had not seen her** il s'est avéré qu'elle ne l'avait
  pas vue; **it ~ed out to be true** cela s'est avéré
  juste; **it ~ed out to be wrong** cela s'est avéré
  faux; **it ~ed out to be harder than we thought**
  cela s'est avéré plus difficile que l'on ne
  pensait; **he ~ed out to be an excellent neighbour** il s'est avéré être un très bon voisin
  e (= *happen*) se passer; **it all depends how
  things ~ out** tout dépend de la façon dont les
  choses vont se passer; **everything will ~ out all
  right** tout finira bien; **as it ~ed out, nobody
  came** en fin de compte personne n'est venu
  f **it ~ed out nice** [*weather*] il a fait beau en fin
  de compte
  2 VT SEP **a** [+ *light*] éteindre; [+ *gas*] éteindre, fermer
  b **to ~ one's toes out** marcher en canard
  c (= *empty out*) [+ *pockets, suitcase*] vider; [+
  room, cupboard] nettoyer à fond; [+ *cake, jelly*]
  démouler (**on to** sur); (= *expel*) [+ *person*] mettre à la porte; [+ *tenant*] expulser; **they ~ed
  him out of the house** ils l'ont mis à la porte; **to
  ~ sb out of his job** renvoyer qn
  d [+ *troops, police*] envoyer
  e (= *produce*) [+ *goods*] fabriquer, produire;
  the college ~s out good teachers le collège
  forme de bons professeurs
  f **to be well ~ed out** être élégant
- ▸ **turn over** **1** VI **a** [*person*] se retourner; [*car
  etc*] se retourner, faire un tonneau; [*boat*] se
  retourner, chavirer; **she ~ed over and went
  back to sleep** elle s'est retournée et s'est
  rendormie; **my stomach ~ed over** (*at gruesome
  sight*) j'ai eu l'estomac retourné; (*from fright*)
  mon sang n'a fait qu'un tour; (*Aut*) **the engine
  was ~ing over** le moteur tournait au ralenti
  b (= *change channel*) changer de chaîne; (=
  turn page) tourner la page; (*in letter etc*) **please
  ~ over** (*abbr* PTO) tournez s'il vous plaît (*abbr*
  TSVP)
  2 VT SEP **a** [+ *page*] tourner; [+ *mattress, patient, earth, playing card, plate, tape*] retourner;
  to ~ over an idea in one's mind retourner une
  idée dans sa tête, ressasser une idée
  b (= *hand over*) [+ *object, papers*] rendre; [+
  person] livrer (**to** à)
  c (= *give up*) [+ *job, responsibility*] déléguer
  3 VT FUS **the firm ~s over £10,000 a week** l'entreprise réalise un chiffre d'affaires de 10 000
  livres par semaine
- ▸ **turn over to** VT FUS **the land has been ~ed
  over to sugar production** les terres sont
  maintenant consacrées à la production de sucre
- ▸ **turn round** **1** VI **a** [*person*] se retourner; (=
  change direction) [*person, vehicle*] faire demi-
  tour; (= *rotate*) [*object*] tourner; **to ~ round
  and round** tourner sur soi-même; **~ round and
  look at me** retourne-toi et regarde-moi; **he
  ~ed round and came back** il a fait demi-tour et
  est revenu sur ses pas; (*fig*) **he ~ed round and
  said he was leaving** il a subitement annoncé
  qu'il partait
  b (= *improve*) [*business, economy*] se redresser
  c [*ship, plane*] (= *unload, reload and leave*) décharger, recharger et repartir
  2 VT SEP **a** [+ *one's head*] tourner; [+ *object*]
  tourner, retourner; [+ *person*] faire demi-tour à;
  [+ *ship, aircraft*] faire faire demi-tour à; **he ~ed
  the car round** il a fait demi-tour; (= *unload and
  reload*) **to ~ a ship/plane round** décharger et re-

charger un bateau/avion ; (Comm) **to ~ an order** exécuter une commande [b] (= make successful) [+ business, economy] redresser ; (= rephrase) [+ sentence, idea] reformuler ; **to ~ things round** renverser la situation ; **if you ~ed this round a bit it would be very funny** si vous formuliez cela un peu différemment, ce pourrait être très drôle ; (= change mind, tactics) **to ~ sb round** faire changer qn d'avis

► **turn up** [1] VI [a] (= arrive) arriver ; [playing card] sortir ; **something will ~ up** on va bien trouver quelque chose ; **I've lost my job — something will ~ up (for you)** j'ai perdu mon poste — tu finiras bien par trouver quelque chose ; **don't worry about your ring, I'm sure it will ~ up (again)** ne t'en fais pas pour ta bague, je suis sûr que tu finiras par la retrouver ; **to ~ up again** [person] réapparaître → **trump**[1] [b] **his nose ~s up at the end** il a le nez retroussé or en trompette [c] [prices] remonter ; **profits ~ed up in the last quarter** les bénéfices ont remonté au dernier trimestre [2] VT SEP [a] [+ collar] relever ; [+ sleeve] retrousser, relever ; **to have a ~ed-up nose** avoir le nez retroussé or en trompette [b] (= disgust) **it really ~s me up*** ça me dégoûte [b] (= dig up) [+ buried object] déterrer ; (= find) [+ lost object, reference, evidence] trouver ; **a survey ~ed up more than 3,000 people suffering from ...** une enquête a révélé que plus de 3 000 personnes souffraient de ... [c] [+ radio, television] mettre plus fort ; **to ~ up the sound** monter le son or volume ; **when the sugar has dissolved, ~ up the heat** une fois le sucre dissous, faites cuire à feu plus vif ; (fig) **to ~ up the heat** accentuer la pression

turnabout ['tɜːnəbaʊt] N (lit, fig) volte-face f inv

turnaround ['tɜːnəraʊnd] N (lit, fig) volte-face f inv ; (= place for turning vehicle) endroit m pour manœuvrer ; (= unloading time etc) [of plane, truck] rotation f ; [of ship] estarie f, starie f ; **~ time** (Comm) [of order] temps m d'exécution ; (Comput) temps m de retournement ; **the ~ time for our trucks is three hours** nos camions opèrent des rotations de trois heures

turncoat ['tɜːnkəʊt] N renégat(e) m(f)

turndown ['tɜːndaʊn] [1] N [a] [of sales, rate, tendency] fléchissement m, (tendance f à la) baisse f [b] (= rejection) refus m [2] ADJ [flap] à rabattre ; **~ collar** col m rabattu

turner ['tɜːnər] N tourneur m

turnery ['tɜːnərɪ] N atelier m de tournage

turning ['tɜːnɪŋ] [1] N [a] (= side road) route f (or rue f) latérale ; (= fork) embranchement m ; (= bend in road, river) coude m ; **take the second ~ on the left** prenez la deuxième à gauche [b] (NonC: Tech) tournage m [2] COMP ► **turning circle** N (Aut) rayon m de braquage ► **turning lathe** N (Tech) tour m ► **turning point** N (fig) **he was at a ~ point in his career** il était à un tournant de sa carrière ; **that was the ~ point in her life** ce fut le moment décisif de sa vie

turnip ['tɜːnɪp] N navet m

turnkey ['tɜːnkiː] [1] N geôlier m, -ière f [2] COMP ► **turnkey factory** N usine f clés en main

turn-off ['tɜːnɒf] N [a] (Aut) embranchement m (où il faut tourner) [b] **it's a (real) ~!*** c'est vraiment à vous rebuter ! ; (stronger) c'est vraiment à vous dégoûter !* ; (also sexually) c'est vraiment pas sexy !*

turn-on: ['tɜːnɒn] N **it's a (real) ~!** c'est excitant !

turnout ['tɜːnaʊt] N [a] (= attendance) assistance f ; **what sort of a ~ was there?** combien y avait-il de gens (dans l'assistance) ? ; **there was a good ~** beaucoup de gens sont venus ; **~ at the polls** ◊ **voter ~** (taux

m de) participation f électorale ; **a high/low ~ at the polls** un fort/faible taux de participation électorale [b] (= clean-out) nettoyage m ; **to have a good ~ of a room/cupboard** nettoyer une pièce/un placard à fond [c] (Ind = output) production f [d] (Dress) tenue f

turnover ['tɜːnəʊvər] N [a] (Comm etc) [of stock, goods] rotation f ; [of shares] mouvement m ; (= total business done) chiffre m d'affaires ; **a profit of £4,000 on a ~ of £40,000** un bénéfice de 4 000 livres pour un chiffre d'affaires de 40 000 livres ; **he sold them cheaply hoping for a quick ~** il les a vendus bon marché pour les écouler rapidement [b] [of staff, workers] renouvellement m, rotation f ; **there is a high** or **rapid (rate of) ~ in that firm** cette maison connaît de fréquents changements or renouvellements de personnel [c] (Culin) chausson m ; **apple ~** chausson m aux pommes

turnpike ['tɜːnpaɪk] N (= barrier) barrière f de péage ; (US = road) autoroute f à péage → **ROADS**

turnround ['tɜːnraʊnd] N = **turnaround**

turnstile ['tɜːnstaɪl] N tourniquet m

turntable ['tɜːnteɪbl] N [of record player] platine f ; (for trains, cars etc) plaque f tournante ; **~ ladder** échelle f pivotante

turn-up ['tɜːnʌp] N [a] (Brit) [of trousers] revers m [b] **that was a ~ (for the books)!*** ça a été une belle surprise !

turpentine ['tɜːpəntaɪn] N (essence f de) térébenthine f ; **~ substitute** white-spirit m

turpitude ['tɜːpɪtjuːd] N turpitude f

turps* [tɜːps] N ABBR = **turpentine**

turquoise ['tɜːkwɔɪz] [1] N (= stone) turquoise f ; (= colour) turquoise m [2] ADJ (= made of turquoise) de turquoise(s) ; (in colour) turquoise inv ; **blue/green ~** bleu/vert turquoise

turret ['tʌrɪt] [1] N (Archit, Mil, Phot, Tech) tourelle f [2] COMP ► **turret gun** N canon m de tourelle

turreted ['tʌrɪtɪd] ADJ à tourelles

turtle ['tɜːtl] [1] N (= stone) turquoise tortue f marine ; (fig) **to turn ~** chavirer, se renverser → **mock** [2] COMP ► **turtle soup** N consommé m à la tortue

turtledove ['tɜːtldʌv] N tourterelle f

turtleneck ['tɜːtlnek] N (Brit: also **~ sweater**) (pull-over m à) encolure f montante or col m cheminée ; (US) (pull-over m à) col m roulé

Tuscan ['tʌskən] [1] ADJ toscan [2] N [a] Toscan(e) m(f) [b] (Ling) toscan m

Tuscany ['tʌskənɪ] N la Toscane

tush† [tʌʃ] EXCL bah !

tusk [tʌsk] N défense f (d'éléphant etc)

tusker ['tʌskər] N éléphant m (or sanglier m etc) adulte (qui a ses défenses)

tussle ['tʌsl] [1] N (= struggle) lutte f (for pour) ; (= scuffle) mêlée f ; **to have a ~ with sb** (physically) en venir aux mains avec qn ; (verbally) avoir une prise de bec* avec qn [2] VI se battre (with sb avec qn, for sth pour qch) ; **to ~ over sth** se disputer qch

tussock ['tʌsək] N touffe f d'herbe

tut [tʌt] (also **~~**) [1] EXCL allons allons !, allons donc ! [2] VI **he (~~)tutted at the idea** à cette idée il a eu une exclamation désapprobatrice

Tutankhamen [ˌtuːtənˈkɑːmen], **Tutankhamun** [ˌtuːtənkɑːˈmuːn] N Toutankhamon m

tutelage ['tjuːtɪlɪdʒ] N tutelle f

tutelary ['tjuːtɪlərɪ] ADJ tutélaire

tutor ['tjuːtər] [1] N (= private teacher) professeur m (particulier) (in en) ; (full-time) précepteur m, -trice f ; (Brit Univ) directeur m, -trice f d'études ; (Brit Scol: also **form ~**) professeur m principal ; (in prison) éducateur m, -trice f [2] VT donner des leçons particulières or des cours particuliers à ; **to ~ sb in Latin** donner des cours particuliers de latin à qn

[3] COMP ► **tutor group** N (Brit Scol) classe f ► **tutor period** N (Brit Scol) cours m avec le professeur principal (en début de journée) ► **tutor room** N (Brit Scol) salle f de classe (affectée à une classe particulière)

tutorial [tjuːˈtɔːrɪəl] [1] ADJ [a] (= teaching) [work, duties] d'enseignement ; [staff] enseignant ; [guidance, support] pédagogique [b] (Univ) **~ work** travaux mpl dirigés ; **~ essay** exposé m ; **~ duties** encadrement m des travaux dirigés ; **~ group** groupe m de travaux dirigés [2] N (Univ) travaux mpl dirigés (in de)

tutoring ['tjuːtərɪŋ] N cours mpl particuliers (in de) ; (remedial) cours mpl de soutien (in de)

tutti-frutti ['tʊtɪ'frʊtɪ] N (pl **tutti-fruttis**) (= ice-cream) plombières f, cassate f

tutu ['tuːtuː] N tutu m

Tuvalu [tuːˈvɑːluː] N Tuvalu

tuwhit-tuwhoo [təˈwɪttəˈwuː] N hou-hou m

tuxedo [tʌkˈsiːdəʊ], **tux*** ['tʌks] N (esp US) smoking m

TV [ˌtiːˈviː] [1] N (ABBR = **television**) télé f → **television** [2] COMP ► **TV dinner** N plateau-repas m, plateau-télé m

TVEI [ˌtiːviːiːˈaɪ] N (Brit) (ABBR = **technical and vocational educational initiative**) plan de formation pour les jeunes

TVP [ˌtiːviːˈpiː] N (ABBR = **textured vegetable protein**) → **textured**

twaddle ['twɒdl] N (NonC) âneries fpl, fadaises fpl

twain [tweɪn] NPL **the ~**†† les deux ; **and never the ~ shall meet** et les deux sont inconciliables

twang [twæŋ] [1] N [of wire, string] son m (de corde pincée) ; (= tone of voice) ton m nasillard, nasillement m ; **to speak with a ~** nasiller, parler du nez ; **he has an American ~** il a le nasillement américain dans la voix [2] VT [+ guitar] pincer les cordes de, gratter de [3] VI [wire, bow] vibrer

twangy ['twæŋɪ] ADJ [noise] de corde pincée ; [voice, tone] nasillard

'twas†† [twɒz] = **it was** ; → **be**

twat: [twæt] N [a] (= genitals) con* m [b] (pej = person) pauvre con(ne): m(f)

tweak [twiːk] [1] VT [a] (= pull) [+ sb's ear, nose] tordre ; [+ rope etc, sb's hair] tirer (d'un coup sec) [b] (* = alter slightly) modifier légèrement [2] N [a] (= pull) coup m sec ; **to give sth a ~ = to tweak sth** ; → 1 [b] (* = small alteration) petite modification f

twee [twiː] ADJ (Brit pej) [picture, design, decor] cucul* ; [remark, poem] mièvre, gentillet ; [person] chichiteux* ; [house, cottage] mignonnet

tweed [twiːd] [1] N tweed m [2] **tweeds** NPL (= suit) costume m de tweed [3] COMP [jacket etc] de en tweed

tweedy ['twiːdɪ] ADJ [a] (* gen pej) **he's rather ~** il fait un peu bourgeois campagnard, il a le style gentleman-farmer ; **she's one of these ~ ladies** elle est du style bourgeoise campagnarde [b] (= resembling tweed) façon tweed inv

'tween [twiːn] PREP (liter) = **between**

tweeny†* ['twiːnɪ] N (Brit) bonne f

tweet [twiːt] [1] N (also **tweet-tweet**) gazouillis m, gazouillement m, pépiement m [2] VI gazouiller, pépier

tweeter ['twiːtər] N haut-parleur m aigu, tweeter m

tweeze* [twiːz] VT [+ eyebrows etc] épiler

tweezers ['twiːzəz] NPL (also **pair of ~**) pince f fine, pince f à épiler

twelfth [twelfθ] [1] ADJ douzième ; **Twelfth Night** la fête des Rois, l'Épiphanie f [2] N douzième mf ; (= fraction) douzième m ; for phrases see **sixth** [3] COMP ► **twelfth man** N (pl **twelfth men**) (Brit Cricket) remplaçant m

twelve [twelv] [1] ADJ douze *inv* [2] N douze *m inv* → **o'clock**; *for phrases see* **six** [3] PRON douze; **there are ~** il y en a douze [4] COMP ► **twelve-tone** ADJ (*Mus*) dodécaphonique

twelvemonth†† [ˈtwelvmʌnθ] N année *f*, an *m*

twentieth [ˈtwentɪɪθ] [1] ADJ vingtième [2] N vingtième *mf*; (= *fraction*) vingtième *m*; *for phrases see* **sixth**

twenty [ˈtwentɪ] [1] ADJ vingt *inv*; **about ~ books** une vingtaine de livres [2] N vingt *m*; **about ~** une vingtaine; *for other phrases see* **sixty** [3] PRON vingt; **there are ~** il y en a vingt [4] COMP ► **twenty-first** N (= *birthday*) vingt et unième anniversaire *m*; (= *birthday party*) **I'm having my ~-first on Saturday** je fête mes 21 ans *or* mon 21ᵉ anniversaire samedi ► **twenty-four hours** NPL (= *whole day*) vingt-quatre heures *fpl*; (*open etc*) **~-four hours a day** vingt-quatre heures sur vingt-quatre; (*Comm*) **~-four hour service** service jour et nuit, service 24 heures sur 24; **a ~-four hour strike** une grève de vingt-quatre heures ► **twenty-one** N (*Cards*) vingt-et-un *m* (*jeu*) ► **twenty-twenty vision** N **to have ~-~ vision** avoir dix dixièmes à chaque œil ► **twenty-two metre line** N (*Rugby*) ligne *f* des vingt-deux mètres

twerp‡ [twɜːp] N andouille‡ *f*, idiot(e) *m(f)*

twice [twaɪs] ADV deux fois; **~ a week** ◊ **~ weekly** deux fois par semaine; **~ as much** ◊ **~ as many** deux fois plus; **~ as much space** deux fois plus de place; **~ as long (as)** deux fois plus long (que); **she is ~ your age** elle a deux fois votre âge, elle a le double de votre âge; **the national average** le double de *or* deux fois la moyenne nationale; **~ two is four** deux fois deux font quatre; (*fig*) **he didn't have to be asked ~** il ne s'est pas fait prier; **he's ~ the man you are** il vaut beaucoup mieux que toi → **once, think**

twiddle [ˈtwɪdl] [1] VT [+ *knob*] tripoter, manier; (*fig*) **to ~ one's thumbs** se tourner les pouces [2] VI **to ~ with sth** jouer avec *or* tripoter qch [3] N **to give sth a ~** donner plusieurs petits tours à qch

twig¹ [twɪg] N brindille *f*, petite branche *f*

twig²∗ [twɪg] VTI (*Brit* = *understand*) piger∗, comprendre

twilight [ˈtwaɪlaɪt] [1] N (= *evening*) crépuscule *m* (*also fig*); (= *morning*) aube *f* naissante; **at ~** (*evening*) au crépuscule, à la tombée du jour; (*morning*) à l'aube naissante; **in the ~** dans la semi-obscurité *or* la pénombre [2] COMP ► **twilight world** N monde *m* nébuleux ► **twilight zone** N (*fig*) zone *f* floue

twilit [ˈtwaɪlɪt] ADJ [*sky, landscape, place*] crépusculaire, de crépuscule

twill [twɪl] N (*Tex*) sergé *m*

'twill [twɪl] = **it will**; → **will**

twin [twɪn] [1] N jumeau *m*, -elle *f* → **identical, Siamese**
[2] ADJ [*brother, sister, towers, peaks*] jumeau (-elle *f*); **~ boys** jumeaux *mpl*; **~ girls** jumelles *fpl*; **with ~ propellers/taps** avec deux hélices/robinets; **plane with ~ engines** (avion *m*) bimoteur *m*; **they're ~ souls** ce sont deux âmes sœurs; **the ~ concepts of liberty and equality** les concepts inséparables de liberté et d'égalité
[3] VT [+ *town etc*] jumeler (**with** avec)
[4] COMP ► **twin-bedded room** N (*Brit*: *in hotel*) chambre *f* à deux lits ► **twin beds** NPL lits *mpl* jumeaux ► **twin bill**∗ N (*US*) (*Sport*) programme *m* de deux matchs; (*Cine*) programme *m* de deux longs métrages ► **twin-cylinder** ADJ à deux cylindres ♦ N moteur *m* à deux cylindres ► **twin-engined** ADJ bimoteur ► **twin room** N = **twin-bedded room** ► **twin-screw** ADJ à deux hélices ► **twin town** N (*Brit*) ville *f* jumelée ► **twin-track** ADJ

[*approach, process, strategy*] double ► **twin-tub** N machine *f* à laver à deux tambours

twine [twaɪn] [1] N (*NonC*) ficelle *f* [2] VT (= *weave*) tresser; (= *roll*) entortiller, enrouler (**round** autour de); **she ~d her arms round his neck** elle lui a enlacé le cou de ses bras [3] VI [*plant, coil*] s'enrouler (**round** autour de); [*river, road*] serpenter, zigzaguer

twinge [twɪndʒ] N **a ~ (of pain)** un élancement, un tiraillement; **a ~ of conscience** *or* **remorse** *or* **guilt** un (petit) remords; **to feel a ~ of remorse/shame** éprouver un certain remords/une certaine honte; **to feel a ~ of regret** *or* **sadness** avoir un pincement au cœur

twining [ˈtwaɪnɪŋ] ADJ [*plant*] volubile (*Bot*)

twinkle [ˈtwɪŋkl] [1] VI [*star, lights*] scintiller, briller; [*eyes*] briller, pétiller [2] N [*of star, lights*] scintillement *m*; [*of eyes*] éclat *m*, pétillement *m*; **... he said with a ~ (in his eye)** ... dit-il avec un pétillement (malicieux) dans les yeux; **he had a ~ in his eye** il avait les yeux pétillants; **in a ~** ◊ **in the ~ of an eye** en un clin d'œil

twinkling [ˈtwɪŋklɪŋ] [1] ADJ [*star, light*] scintillant; [*eyes*] pétillant [2] N **in the ~ of an eye** en un clin d'œil

twinning [ˈtwɪnɪŋ] N [*of towns*] jumelage *m*

twinset [ˈtwɪnset] N (*Brit*) twin-set *m*; (*Brit*) **she's rather ~ and pearls**∗ elle fait très BCBG

twirl [twɜːl] [1] N [*of body*] tournoiement *m*; [*of dancer*] pirouette *f*; (*in writing*) fioriture *f*; **to give sth a ~** → **to twirl sth**; → 3 [2] VI (*also ~ round*) [*cane, lasso, dancer*] tournoyer; [*handle, knob*] pivoter [3] VT (*also ~ round*) [+ *cane, lasso*] faire tournoyer; [+ *knob, handle*] faire pivoter; [+ *moustache*] tortiller

twirler∗ [ˈtwɜːlər] N (*US*) majorette *f*

twirp‡ [twɜːp] N = **twerp**

twist [twɪst] [1] N [a] (= *action*) torsion *f*; (*Med*) entorse *f*, foulure *f*; **to give a ~ to** [+ *knob, handle*] faire pivoter, faire tourner; [+ *wire*] tordre; [+ *one's ankle*] se tordre, se fouler; **he put a ~ on the ball** il a imprimé une rotation à la balle; **with a quick ~ (of the wrist)** d'un rapide tour de poignet
[b] (= *coil*) rouleau *m*; (*in road*) tournant *m*, virage *m*; (*in river*) coude *m*; (*in wire, flex, cord*) tortillon *m*; (*fig*) [*of events*] tournure *f*; [*of meaning*] distorsion *f*; **a ~ of yarn** une torsade *or* un cordonnet de fil; **sweets in a ~ of paper** des bonbons dans un tortillon de papier *or* une papillote; **a ~ of lemon** un zeste de citron; **the road is full of ~s and turns** la route est pleine de tournants *or* de virages, la route fait des zigzags; **the story has an unexpected ~ to it** l'histoire comporte un coup de théâtre; **he gave a new ~ to this old plot** il a donné un tour nouveau à cette vieille intrigue; (*fig*) **to get (o.s.) into a ~**∗ ◊ **to get one's knickers in a ~**∗ (= *get annoyed*) s'énerver; (= *get confused*) s'emmêler les pinceaux∗; (*fig*) **to go round the ~**∗ devenir dingue∗, perdre la boule∗; **to drive sb round the ~**∗ faire tourner qn en bourrique∗
[c] (‡ = *cheat*) **what a ~!** on s'est fait avoir!∗; **it's a ~!** c'est de la triche!∗
[d] (= *dance*) twist *m*; **to do the ~** twister
[2] VT [a] (= *interweave*) [+ *threads, strands, ropes, wires*] entortiller, tresser; (= *turn round on itself*) [+ *thread, rope, wire, one's handkerchief*] tordre; (= *coil*) enrouler (**round** autour de); (= *turn*) [+ *knob, handle*] tourner; [+ *top, cap*] tourner, visser; (= *deform*) [+ *metal etc*] tordre, déformer; (*fig*) [+ *meaning*] fausser; [+ *words*] déformer; **to get ~ed** [*rope etc*] s'entortiller; **he ~ed the strands into a cord** il a entortillé *or* tressé les fils pour en faire une corde; **he ~ed the paper into a ball** il a tire-bouchonné le papier pour en faire une boule; **you've ~ed it out of shape** tu l'as déformé en le tordant, tu l'as tordu; **~ the cap clockwise** vissez la capsule dans le sens des aiguilles d'une montre; **to ~ the top off a jar**

dévisser le couvercle d'un bocal (pour l'enlever); **to ~ one's ankle** se tordre *or* se fouler la cheville; **to ~ one's neck** se tordre le cou, attraper le torticolis; **to ~ sb's arm** (*lit*) tordre le bras à qn; (*fig*) forcer la main à qn; **she can ~ him round her little finger** elle le mène par le bout du nez; **he ~ed his mouth scornfully** il eut un rictus méprisant; **limbs ~ed by arthritis** des membres tordus par l'arthrite; **his face was ~ed with pain/rage** ses traits étaient tordus par la douleur/la fureur; **you're ~ing everything I say** tu déformes tout ce que je dis → **twisted**
[b] (‡ = *cheat*) rouler∗, avoir∗
[3] VI [a] [*flex, rope etc*] s'entortiller, s'enrouler; [*socks, trousers*] tirebouchonner; [*one's ankle etc*] se tordre; **to ~ round sth** s'entortiller autour de qch; **the road ~s (and turns) through the valley** la route zigzague *or* serpente à travers la vallée; **the motorbike ~ed through the traffic** la moto louvoyait *or* zigzaguait parmi la circulation
[b] (= *dance the twist*) twister
[4] COMP ► **twist grip** N [*of motorcycle*] poignée *f* d'accélération; (= *gear change*) poignée *f* de changement de vitesses
► **twist about, twist around** VI [*rope etc*] tortiller; [*road etc*] serpenter, zigzaguer
► **twist off** [1] VI **the top ~s off** le couvercle se dévisse [2] VT SEP [+ *branch*] enlever en tordant; [+ *bottle-top*] enlever en dévissant
► **twist out** [1] VI **he ~ed out of their grasp** il s'est dégagé de leur étreinte [2] VT SEP [+ *object*] enlever en tournant
► **twist round** [1] VI [*road etc*] serpenter, zigzaguer; [*person*] se retourner [2] VT SEP [+ *rope, wire*] enrouler; [+ *knob, handle*] tourner; [+ *top, cap*] tourner, visser; [+ *one's head, chair*] tourner
► **twist up** [1] VI [*ropes etc*] s'entortiller, s'emmêler; [*smoke*] monter en volutes [2] VT SEP [+ *ropes, threads*] entortiller, emmêler

twisted [ˈtwɪstɪd] ADJ [a] (= *damaged, tangled*) [*key, rod, metal, beam, wreckage*] tordu; [*wrist, ankle*] foulé; [*wire, rope, flex, cord, strap*] entortillé; (*Med*) **~ bowel** volvulus *m* intestinal [b] (= *of twisted construction*) [*rope, cable*] tressé; [*barley-sugar etc*] torsadé [c] (= *deformed, distorted*) [*tree, branch*] tordu; [*limb*] difforme; [*features, smile*] crispé [d] (= *warped*) [*person, mind, logic*] tordu → **bitter**

twister∗ [ˈtwɪstər] N [a] (*Brit* = *crook*) escroc *m* (*lit, fig*) [b] (*US* = *tornado*) tornade *f*

twisting [ˈtwɪstɪŋ] [1] N (*gen*) torsion *f*; [*of meaning*] déformation *f* [2] ADJ [*path*] sinueux, en zigzag

twisty [ˈtwɪstɪ] ADJ [*lane, river*] tortueux

twit¹ [twɪt] VT (= *tease*) taquiner (**about, with** sur, à propos de)

twit²∗ [twɪt] N (*esp Brit* = *fool*) idiot(e) *m(f)*, crétin(e) *m(f)*

twitch [twɪtʃ] [1] N (= *nervous movement*) tic *m*; (= *pull*) coup *m* sec, saccade *f*; **I've got a ~ in my eyelid** j'ai l'œil qui saute; **he has a (nervous) ~ in his cheek** il a un tic à la joue; **with one ~ (of his hand) he freed the rope** il a dégagé la corde d'une saccade; **he gave the rope a ~** il a tiré d'un coup sec sur la corde; **a ~ of the whip** un (petit) coup de fouet [2] VI [a] [*person, animal, hands*] avoir un mouvement convulsif; (*permanent condition*) avoir un tic; [*face, mouth, cheek, eyebrow, muscle*] se convulser, se contracter (convulsivement); [*dog's nose etc*] remuer, bouger [b] (*fig* = *be nervous*) s'agiter [3] VT [*rope etc*] donner un coup sec, donner un coup sec à; **he ~ed it out of her hands** il le lui a arraché des mains; **the cat ~ed its nose/its ears** le nez/les oreilles du chat a/ont remué *or* bougé
► **twitch away** VT SEP arracher d'un petit geste (**from sb** à qn)

twitcher∗ [ˈtwɪtʃər] N ornithologue *mf* amateur

twitchy* ['twɪtʃɪ] ADJ [a] (= *twitching*) agité [b] (= *nervous, jumpy*) [*person, animal*] nerveux ; [*stock market*] fébrile ; **it's a good car but the handling is rather ~** c'est une bonne voiture mais elle a une tenue de route plutôt sautillante

twitter ['twɪtər] [1] VI [*bird*] gazouiller, pépier ; [*person*] (= *chatter*) parler avec agitation (**about** de), jacasser (*pej*) (**about** sur) ; (= *be nervous*) s'agiter (nerveusement) [2] N [*of birds*] gazouillis *m*, pépiement *m* ; (*fig*) **to be in a ~ (about sth)*** être dans tous ses états (à cause de qch)

'twixt [twɪkst] PREP (†† *or liter*) = **betwixt**

two [tu:] [1] ADJ deux *inv* → **mind**
[2] N deux *m inv* ; **to cut sth in ~** couper qch en deux ; **~ by ~** deux par deux, deux à deux ; **in ~s** par deux ; **in ~s and threes** deux ou trois à la fois, par petits groupes ; **they're ~ of a kind** ils se ressemblent (tous les deux) ; (*fig*) **to put ~ and ~ together*** faire le rapport (entre deux *or* plusieurs choses) ; **~'s company** on est mieux à deux ; **~'s company, three's a crowd** quand il y a trois personnes, il y en a une de trop → **one** ; *for other phrases see* **six**
[3] PRON deux ; **there are ~** il y en a deux
[4] COMP ► **two-bit*** ADJ (*esp US pej*) de pacotille ► **two-bits** NPL (*US*) 25 cents *mpl* ► **two-by-four*** ADJ (*US fig*) (= *small*) exigu (-uë *f*) ; (= *unimportant*) minable ► **two-chamber system** N (*Parl*) bicaméralisme *m* ► **two-colour process** N (*Phot*) bichromie *f* ► **two-cycle** ADJ (*US*) = **two-stroke** ► **two-cylinder** ADJ [*car*] à deux cylindres ► **two-door** ADJ [*car*] à deux portes ► **two-edged** ADJ (*lit, fig*) à double tranchant ► **two-faced** ADJ (*fig*) hypocrite ► **two-fisted*** ADJ (*US*) vigoureux, costaud* ► **two-four time** N (*NonC: Mus*) (mesure *f* à) deux-quatre *m inv* ; **in ~-four time** à deux-quatre ► **two-handed** ADJ [*sword*] à deux mains ; [*saw*] à deux poignées ; [*card game*] à deux joueurs ► **two-horse race** N **the election was a ~-horse race** dans ces élections, seuls deux des candidats avaient des chances de gagner ► **two-legged** ADJ bipède ► **two-party** ADJ (*Pol*) bipartite ► **two-phase** ADJ (*Elec*) diphasé ► **two-piece** N **~-piece (suit)** (*man's*) costume *m* (deux-pièces) ; (*woman's*) tailleur *m* ; **~-piece (swimsuit)** deux-pièces *m inv*, bikini® *m* ► **two-pin plug** N → **pin 1b** ► **two-ply** ADJ [*cord, rope*] à deux brins ; [*wool*] à deux fils ; [*wood*] à deux épaisseurs ► **two-seater** ADJ à deux places ◆ N (= *car*) voiture *f* à deux places ; (= *plane*) avion *m* à deux places ► **two-sided** ADJ (*fig*) **this is a ~-sided problem** ce problème peut être appréhendé de deux façons ► **two-star** N (*Brit: also* **~-star petrol**) (essence *f*) ordinaire *f* ► **two-storey** ADJ à deux étages ► **two-stroke** ADJ (*Aut*) **~-stroke (engine)** moteur *m* à deux temps, deux-temps *m inv* ; **~-stroke mixture** mélange *m* deux-temps ; **~-stroke fuel** carburant *m* pour moteur à deux-temps ► **two-tier financing** N (*Fin*) financement *m* à deux étages ► **two-time*** VT tromper, être infidèle à ◆ ADJ (*US*) **~-time loser*** (= *crook etc*) repris de de justice ; (= *divorcee*) homme *m* (*or* femme *f*) deux fois divorcé(e) ► **two-timer*** N (*gen*) traître(sse) *m(f)* ; (*in marriage*) mari *m* (*or* femme *f*) infidèle ► **two-tone** ADJ (*in colour*) de deux tons ; (*in sound*) à deux tons ► **two-way** ADJ (*Elec*) [*switch*] à deux directions ; [*street*] à double sens ; [*traffic*] dans les deux sens ; [*exchange, negotiations*] bilatéral ; **~-way mirror** miroir *m* sans tain ; **~-way radio** émetteur-récepteur *m* ► **two-wheeler** N deux-roues *m inv*

twoccing* ['twɒkɪŋ] N (*NonC: Brit*) vol *m* de voiture

twofer* ['tu:fər] N (*US*) deux articles *mpl* pour le prix d'un

twofold ['tu:fəʊld] [1] ADJ double [2] ADV **to increase ~** doubler

twopence ['tʌpəns] N (*Brit*) deux pence *mpl* → **tuppence**

twopenny ['tʌpənɪ] [1] ADJ (*Brit*) à *or* de deux pence [2] COMP ► **twopenny-halfpenny*** ADJ (*fig*) de rien du tout*, de quatre sous ► **twopenny piece** N pièce *f* de deux pence

twosome ['tu:səm] N (= *people*) couple *m* ; (= *game*) jeu *m or* partie *f* à deux ; **we went in a ~** nous y sommes allés à deux

'twould †† [twʊd] = **it would** ; → **would**

TX ABBR = **Texas**

tycoon [taɪˈkuːn] N (**business** *or* **industrial**) **~** gros *or* important homme *m* d'affaires ; **oil ~** magnat *m or* roi *m* du pétrole

tyke* [taɪk] N (= *dog*) cabot *m* (*pej*) ; (= *child*) môme *mf*

tympana ['tɪmpənə] NPL *of* **tympanum**

tympani ['tɪmpənɪ] N = **timpani**

tympanic [tɪmˈpænɪk] ADJ **~ membrane** tympan *m*

tympanist ['tɪmpənɪst] N = **timpanist**

tympanum ['tɪmpənəm] N (*pl* **tympanums** *or* **tympana**) (*Anat, Archit, Zool*) tympan *m* ; (*Mus*) timbale *f*

type [taɪp] [1] N [a] (*gen, Bio, Sociol etc*) type *m* ; (= *sort*) genre *m* ; (= *make of machine, coffee etc*) marque *f* ; [*of aircraft, car*] modèle *m* ; **books of all ~s** des livres de toutes sortes *or* de tous genres ; **a new ~ of plane** ◊ **a new ~ plane*** un nouveau modèle d'avion ; **a gruyère-~ cheese** un fromage genre gruyère* ; **what ~ do you want?** vous en (*or* le *or* la *etc*) voulez de quelle sorte ? ; **what ~ of car is it?** quel modèle de voiture est-ce ? ; **what ~ of man is he?** quel genre *or* type d'homme est-ce ? ; **what ~ of dog is he?** qu'est-ce que c'est comme (race de) chien ? ; **you know the ~ of thing I mean** vous voyez (à peu près) ce que je veux dire ; **he's not that ~ of person** ce n'est pas son genre ; **I know his ~!** je connais les gens de son genre *or* espèce ; (= *person*) **a queer ~*** un drôle de numéro* ; **he's not my ~*** il n'est pas mon genre* ; **it's my ~ of film** c'est le genre de film que j'aime *or* qui me plaît → **true**
[b] (= *typical example*) type *m* (même), exemple *m* même ; **to deviate from the ~** s'éloigner du type ancestral ; **she was the very ~ of English beauty** c'était le type même *or* l'exemple même de la beauté anglaise → **revert**
[c] (*Ling*) (*gen*) type *m* ; (*also* **word-~**) vocable *m*
[d] (*Typ*) (= *one letter*) caractère *m* ; (= *letters collectively*) caractères *mpl*, type *m* ; **to set ~** composer ; **to set sth (up) in ~** composer qch ; **in ~** composé ; **to keep the ~ set up** conserver la forme ; **in large/small ~** en gros/petits caractères ; **in italic ~** en italiques → **bold**
[2] VT [a] [+ *blood sample etc*] classifier ; (*Theat etc*) **he is now ~d as the kindly old man** on ne lui donne plus que les rôles de doux vieillard ; (*Theat*) **I don't want to be ~d** je ne veux pas me cantonner dans un (seul) rôle
[b] [+ *letter etc*] taper (à la machine)
[3] VI [*typist etc*] taper à la machine ; **"clerk: must be able to ~"** « employé(e) de bureau connaissant la dactylo »
[4] COMP ► **type-cast** ADJ (*Theat etc*) **to be ~-cast as ...** être enfermé dans le rôle de ...
► **type in** VT SEP taper (à la machine)
► **type out** VT SEP [a] [+ *notes, letter*] taper (à la machine) [b] [+ *error*] effacer à la machine
► **type over** VT SEP = **type out b**
► **type up** VT SEP [+ *notes*] taper (à la machine)

typecasting ['taɪpkɑːstɪŋ] N **to avoid ~** éviter les stéréotypes

typeface ['taɪpfeɪs] N (*Typ*) œil *m* de caractère

typescript ['taɪpskrɪpt] N (*NonC*) manuscrit

m or texte *m* dactylographié, tapuscrit *m* (*Tech*)

typeset ['taɪpset] VT composer

typesetter ['taɪpsetər] N (= *person*) compositeur *m*, -trice *f* ; (= *machine*) linotype *f*, composeuse *f*

typesetting ['taɪpsetɪŋ] N (*NonC*) composition *f*

typewrite ['taɪpraɪt] VT taper (à la machine)

typewriter ['taɪpraɪtər] N machine *f* à écrire

typewriting ['taɪpraɪtɪŋ] N dactylographie *f*

typewritten ['taɪprɪtən] ADJ tapé (à la machine), dactylographié

typhoid ['taɪfɔɪd] [1] N (*also* **~ fever**) (fièvre *f*) typhoïde *f* [2] COMP [*symptom, victim*] de la typhoïde ; [*inoculation*] antityphoïdique ► **Typhoid Mary*** N (*US fig*) source *f* d'infection

typhoon [taɪˈfuːn] N typhon *m*

typhus ['taɪfəs] N typhus *m*

typical ['tɪpɪkəl] ADJ [*day, behaviour, example*] typique (**of** de) ; [*price*] habituel ; **the ~ Frenchman** le Français type *or* moyen ; **a ~ Frenchman** un Français typique ; **he's a ~ teacher** c'est le type même du professeur ; **with ~ modesty, he ...** avec la modestie qui le caractérise, il ... ; **it was ~ of our luck that it was raining** avec la chance qui nous caractérise, il a plu ; **Louisa is ~ of many young women who ...** Louisa est un exemple typique de ces nombreuses jeunes femmes qui ... ; **that's ~ of him** c'est bien de lui ; **that's ~ of Paul** ça, c'est Paul tout craché !

typically ['tɪpɪkəlɪ] ADV (*with adj*) typiquement ; **he is ~ English** il est typiquement anglais, c'est l'Anglais type ; **it's ~ French to do that** c'est très *or* bien français de faire ça ; **~, he arrived late** comme d'habitude, il est arrivé en retard

typify ['tɪpɪfaɪ] VT [*behaviour, incident, object*] être caractéristique de ; [*person*] avoir le type même de

typing ['taɪpɪŋ] [1] N (*NonC*) [a] (= *skill*) dactylo *f*, dactylographie *f* ; **to learn ~** apprendre à taper (à la machine), apprendre la dactylo *or* la dactylographie [b] **there were several pages of ~ to read** il y avait plusieurs pages dactylographiées à lire [2] COMP [*lesson, teacher*] de dactylo, de dactylographie ► **typing error** N faute *f* de frappe ► **typing paper** N papier *m* machine ► **typing pool** N bureau *m or* pool *m* de(s) dactylos ; **he works in the ~ pool** il est dactylo au pool ; **to send sth to the ~ pool** envoyer qch à la dactylo* ► **typing speed** N **his ~ speed is 60** il tape 60 mots à la minute

typist ['taɪpɪst] N dactylo *mf*, dactylographe *mf* → **shorthand**

typo ['taɪpəʊ] N (= *error*) coquille *f* (typographique)

typographer [taɪˈpɒɡrəfər] N typographe *mf*

typographic(al) [ˌtaɪpəˈɡræfɪk(əl)] ADJ typographique ; **typographical error** erreur *f* typographique, coquille *f*

typography [taɪˈpɒɡrəfɪ] N typographie *f*

typological [ˌtaɪpəˈlɒdʒɪkəl] ADJ typologique

typology [taɪˈpɒlədʒɪ] N typologie *f*

tyrannic(al) [tɪˈrænɪk(əl)] ADJ tyrannique

tyrannically [tɪˈrænɪkəlɪ] ADV tyranniquement

tyrannicide [tɪˈrænɪsaɪd] N (= *act*) tyrannicide *m* ; (= *person*) tyrannicide *mf*

tyrannize ['tɪrənaɪz] [1] VI **to ~ over sb** tyranniser qn [2] VT tyranniser

tyrannosaur [tɪˈrænəsɔː] N tyrannosaure *m*

tyrannosaurus [tɪˌrænəˈsɔːrəs] N (*also* **~ rex**) tyrannosaure *m*, Tyrannosaurus rex *m*

tyrannous ['tɪrənəs] ADJ tyrannique

tyrannously ['tɪrənslɪ]   ADV tyranniquement

tyranny ['tɪrənɪ] N tyrannie *f*

tyrant ['taɪrənt] N tyran *m*

Tyre [taɪəʳ] N Tyr

tyre ['taɪəʳ]   (*Brit*)   1   N pneu *m* → spare 2   COMP ► **tyre gauge** N manomètre *m* (pour pneus) ► **tyre lever** N démonte-pneu *m* ► **tyre pressure** N pression *f* des pneus ► **tyre valve** N valve *f* (de gonflage)

tyremaker ['taɪəmeɪkəʳ]   N fabricant *m* de pneus

tyro ['taɪrəʊ] N novice *mf*, débutant(e) *m(f)*

Tyrol [tɪ'rəʊl] N **(the)** ~ le Tyrol

Tyrolean [,tɪrə'liː(ə)n], **Tyrolese** [,tɪrə'liːz] 1   ADJ tyrolien ; (*Climbing*) ~ **traverse** tyrolienne *f* 2   N Tyrolien(ne) *m(f)*

Tyrrhenian [tɪ'riːnɪən]   ADJ ~ **Sea** mer *f* Tyrrhénienne

tzar [zɑːʳ] N = tsar

tzarina [zɑː'riːnə]   N = tsarina

tzarist ['zɑːrɪst] N, ADJ = tsarist

tzetze fly ['tsetsɪflaɪ] N = tsetse fly

U

U, u [juː] **1** N **a** (= letter) U, u m; **U for Uncle** ≈ U comme Ursule **b** (Brit Cine) (ABBR = **Universal**) ≈ tous publics; **it's a U film** c'est un film pour tous publics **2** ADJ (Brit†* = upper-class) [word, accent, behaviour] distingué **3** COMP ► **U-bend** N (in pipe) coude m; (Brit: in road) coude m, virage m en épingle à cheveux ► **U-boat** N sous-marin m allemand ► **U-shaped** ADJ en (forme de) U ► **U-turn** N (Aut) demi-tour m; (fig) revirement m, volte-face f (on au sujet de); (Aut) **"no U-turns"** « défense de faire demi-tour »; (fig) **to make a U-turn on sth** faire volte-face au sujet de qch

UAE [ˌjuːeɪˈiː] N (ABBR = **United Arab Emirates**) → **united**

UAW [ˌjuːeɪˈdʌblju] N (US) (ABBR = **United Automobile Workers**) syndicat

UB40 [ˌjuːbiːˈfɔːtɪ] N (Brit: formerly) (ABBR = **Unemployment Benefit 40**) carte de demandeur d'emploi

ubiquitous [juːˈbɪkwɪtəs] ADJ omniprésent

ubiquity [juːˈbɪkwɪtɪ] N omniprésence f

UCAS [ˈjuːkæs] N (Brit) (ABBR = **Universities and Colleges Admissions Service**) → **university**

UCCA [ˈʌkə] N (Brit: formerly) (ABBR = **Universities Central Council on Admissions**) service central des inscriptions universitaires; **~ form** N dossier m d'inscription universitaire

UDA [ˌjuːdiːˈeɪ] N (Brit) (ABBR = **Ulster Defence Association**) → **Ulster**

UDC [ˌjuːdiːˈsiː] N (Brit Local Govt: formerly) (ABBR = **Urban District Council**) → **urban**

udder [ˈʌdə] N pis m, mamelle f

UDI [ˌjuːdiːˈaɪ] N (Brit Pol) (ABBR = **unilateral declaration of independence**) → **unilateral**

UDR [ˌjuːdiːˈɑː] N (Brit) (ABBR = **Ulster Defence Regiment**) → **Ulster**

UEFA [juːˈeɪfə] N (Ftbl) (ABBR = **Union of European Football Associations**) UEFA f

UFO [ˈjuːˈfəʊ, ˈjuːfəʊ] N (ABBR = **unidentified flying object**) ovni m

ufologist [juːˈfɒlədʒɪst] N ufologue mf

ufology [juːˈfɒlədʒɪ] N ufologie f

Uganda [juːˈɡændə] N l'Ouganda m

Ugandan [juːˈɡændən] **1** ADJ ougandais **2** N Ougandais(e) m(f)

UGC [ˌjuːdʒiːˈsiː] N (Brit: formerly) (ABBR = **University Grants Committee**) → **university**

ugh [ɜːh] EXCL pouah!

ugli [ˈʌɡlɪ] N (pl **uglis** or **uglies**) tangelo m

uglify [ˈʌɡlɪfaɪ] VT enlaidir, rendre laid

ugliness [ˈʌɡlɪnɪs] N (NonC) laideur f

ugly [ˈʌɡlɪ] ADJ **a** [person, appearance, face, building, word] laid; [wound, scar] vilain (before n); **as ~ as sin** moche* comme un pou, laid comme un singe; (fig) **~ duckling** vilain petit canard m **b** (fig = unpleasant) [habit] sale; **he gave me an ~ look** il m'a regardé d'un sale œil; **to be in an ~ mood** [person] être d'une humeur massacrante or exécrable; (crowd) être menaçant; **the ~ truth** l'horrible vérité f; **to grow** or **turn ~** [person] se faire menaçant, montrer les

dents; **things** or **the mood turned ~ when ...** les choses ont mal tourné or ont pris une mauvaise tournure quand ...; **the whole business is taking an ~ turn** l'affaire prend une sale tournure; **the situation looks ~** la situation est affreuse; **it is an ~ sight** ce n'est pas beau à voir; **there were ~ scenes** il y a eu des scènes terribles; **an ~ rumour** de vilains bruits mpl; **"blackmail" is an ~ word** « chantage » est un vilain mot

UHF [ˌjuːeɪtʃˈef] N (ABBR = **ultrahigh frequency**) UHF f

uh-huh* [ˈʌˌhʌ] EXCL (= yes) oui oui

UHT [ˌjuːeɪtʃˈtiː] ADJ (ABBR = **ultra heat treated**) [milk etc] UHT inv, longue conservation inv

uh-uh* [ˈʌˌʌ] EXCL (warning) hé!

UK [juːˈkeɪ] N (ABBR = **United Kingdom**) le Royaume-Uni; **in the UK** au Royaume-Uni; **the UK government** le gouvernement du Royaume-Uni; **a UK citizen** un citoyen du Royaume-Uni

uke* [juːk] N ABBR = **ukulele**

Ukraine [juːˈkreɪn] N **(the)** ~ l'Ukraine f; **in (the)** ~ en Ukraine

Ukrainian [juːˈkreɪnɪən] **1** ADJ ukrainien **2** N **a** (= person) Ukrainien(ne) m(f) **b** (Ling) ukrainien m

ukulele [ˌjuːkəˈleɪlɪ] N guitare f hawaïenne

ULC [ˌjuːelˈsiː] N (US) (ABBR = **ultra-large carrier**) superpétrolier m

ulcer [ˈʌlsə] N **a** (Med) ulcère m; **to get an ~** attraper un ulcère **b** (fig) plaie f

ulcerate [ˈʌlsəreɪt] **1** VT ulcérer **2** VI s'ulcérer

ulcerated [ˈʌlsəreɪtɪd] ADJ ulcéreux

ulceration [ˌʌlsəˈreɪʃən] N ulcération f

ulcerative [ˈʌlsəˌreɪtɪv] ADJ ulcératif

ulcerous [ˈʌlsərəs] ADJ **a** (= having ulcers) ulcéreux; (= causing ulcers) ulcératif

ullage [ˈʌlɪdʒ] N (Customs) manquant m

'ullo* [əˈləʊ] EXCL (Brit) = **hello**

ulna [ˈʌlnə] N (pl **ulnas** or **ulnae** [ˈʌlniː]) cubitus m

Ulster [ˈʌlstə] **1** N **a** (Hist) l'Ulster m **b** (= Northern Ireland) l'Irlande f du Nord **c** (= coat) **ulster** gros pardessus m **2** COMP de l'Ulster or de l'Irlande du Nord ► **Ulster Defence Association** N organisation paramilitaire protestante en Irlande du Nord ► **Ulster Defence Regiment** N section de l'armée britannique en Irlande du Nord ► **Ulster Volunteer Force** N organisation paramilitaire protestante en Irlande du Nord

Ulsterman [ˈʌlstəmən] N (pl **-men**) habitant m or natif m de l'Ulster

Ulsterwoman [ˈʌlstəwʊmən] N (pl **-women**) habitante f or native f de l'Ulster

ulterior [ʌlˈtɪərɪə] ADJ ultérieur (-eure f); **~ motive** motif m secret, arrière-pensée f

ultimata [ˌʌltɪˈmeɪtə] NPL of **ultimatum**

ultimate [ˈʌltɪmɪt] **1** ADJ **a** (= final, eventual) [aim, destiny, solution] final; [decision, result, outcome] final, définitif; [victory, defeat] final,

ultime; [control, authority] suprême; (Mil, fig) **the ~ deterrent** l'ultime moyen m de dissuasion; (Mil, fig) **the ~ weapon** l'arme f suprême; **the ~ beneficiary/loser is ...** en fin de compte, le bénéficiaire/le perdant est ...; **he came to the ~ conclusion that ...** il a finalement conclu que ...; **death is the ~ sacrifice** la mort est le sacrifice suprême or l'ultime sacrifice; **to make the ~ sacrifice** faire le sacrifice de sa vie **b** (= best, most effective) suprême; **we have produced the ~ sports car** nous avons fabriqué le nec plus ultra de la voiture de sport; **the ~ insult** l'insulte f suprême; **the ~ (in) luxury/generosity** le summum du luxe/de la générosité; **the ~ (in) selfishness/bad manners** le comble de l'égoïsme/de l'impolitesse **c** (= basic) [principle, cause, truth] fondamental, premier; (Gram) **~ constituent** constituant m ultime **d** (= furthest: gen) le plus éloigné, le plus distant; [boundary of universe] le plus reculé; [ancestor] le plus éloigné; **the ~ origins of man** les origines fpl premières de l'homme; **the ~ frontiers of knowledge** les confins mpl du savoir **2** N **the ~ in comfort** le summum du confort, le fin du fin en matière de confort, le nec plus ultra du confort

ultimately [ˈʌltɪmɪtlɪ] ADV **a** (= finally, eventually) en fin de compte; **to ~ do sth** finir par faire qch; **he was ~ successful/unsuccessful** il a finalement réussi/échoué; **it may ~ be possible** ça sera peut-être possible, en fin de compte **b** (= when all is said and done) [responsible] en définitive; **it ~ depends on you** en définitive or en fin de compte cela dépend de vous

ultimatum [ˌʌltɪˈmeɪtəm] N (pl **ultimatums** or **ultimata**) ultimatum m; **to deliver** or **issue an ~** adresser un ultimatum (**to** à)

ultimo [ˈʌltɪməʊ] ADV (Comm) du mois dernier; **the 25th ~** le 25 du mois dernier

ultra... [ˈʌltrə] PREF ultra..., hyper...*; **~sensitive** ultrasensible, hypersensible; **~right-wing** d'extrême droite; **~fashionable** du tout dernier cri; **~rich** richissime

ultrahigh [ˈʌltrəˈhaɪ] ADJ **~ frequency** ultrahaute fréquence f

ultralight [ˈʌltrəˈlaɪt] **1** ADJ ultraléger **2** N (Aviat) ULM m, ultraléger m motorisé

ultramarine [ˌʌltrəməˈriːn] ADJ, N (bleu) outremer m inv

ultramodern [ˈʌltrəˈmɒdən] ADJ ultramoderne

ultramontane [ˌʌltrəˈmɒnteɪn] ADJ, N ultramontain(e) m(f)

ultramontanism [ˌʌltrəˈmɒntɪnɪzəm] N ultramontanisme m

ultrashort [ˈʌltrəˈʃɔːt] ADJ ultracourt

ultrasonic [ˌʌltrəˈsɒnɪk] **1** ADJ ultrasonique **2** N (NonC) **~s** science f des ultrasons

ultrasound [ˈʌltrəsaʊnd] **1** N (NonC) ultrasons mpl; **to have ~** avoir une échographie

[2] COMP [equipment, machine] à ultrasons ► **ultrasound examination**, **ultrasound scan** N échographie f ► **ultrasound scanner** N appareil m à échographie

ultraviolet [ˌʌltrə'vaɪəlɪt] ADJ ultraviolet; (Med) **to have ~ treatment** se faire traiter aux rayons ultraviolets; **~ radiation** rayons mpl ultraviolets

ultra vires [ˌʌltrə'vaɪəriːz] ADV, ADJ (Jur) au-delà des pouvoirs

ululate ['juːljʊleɪt] VI [owl] (h)ululer; [dog] hurler

ululation [ˌjuːljʊ'leɪʃən] N hululement m; (in Arab context) youyou m

Ulysses [juːˈlɪsiːz] N Ulysse m

um [ʌm] [1] INTERJ euh [2] VI **to um and err*** se tâter*, hésiter; **after a lot of umming and erring*, he decided to buy it** après beaucoup d'hésitations il se décida à l'acheter

umber ['ʌmbər] ADJ, N (terre f d')ombre f, terre f de Sienne → **burnt**

umbilical [ʌmbɪ'laɪkəl] [1] ADJ ombilical [2] COMP ► **umbilical cord** N cordon m ombilical

umbilicus [ʌmbɪ'laɪkəs] N (pl **umbilici** [ˌʌmbə'laɪsaɪ]) ombilic m, nombril m

umbrage ['ʌmbrɪdʒ] N (NonC) ombrage m (fig), ressentiment m; **to take ~** prendre ombrage, se froisser (**at** de)

umbrella [ʌm'brelə] [1] N [a] (gen) parapluie m; (against sun) parasol m; **to put up/put down an ~** ouvrir/fermer un parapluie; **golf ~** parapluie m de golf; **beach or sun ~** parasol m; (Mil) **air ~** écran m de protection aérienne; (fig) **under the ~ of ...** sous les auspices or l'égide de ... [b] [of jellyfish] ombrelle f [2] ADJ **~ body or organization** organisme m qui en chapeaute plusieurs autres; **an ~ term** un terme général [3] COMP ► **umbrella pine** N parasol m ► **umbrella stand** N porte-parapluies m inv

Umbria ['ʌmbrɪə] N l'Ombrie f

Umbrian ['ʌmbrɪən] [1] ADJ ombrien [2] N Ombrien(ne) m(f)

umlaut ['ʊmlaʊt] N [a] (NonC = vowel change) inflexion f vocalique [b] (= diaeresis) tréma m; (in German) umlaut m

ump* [ʌmp] N (US) = **umpire**

umpire ['ʌmpaɪər] [1] N (gen) arbitre m; (Tennis) juge m de chaise [2] VT arbitrer [3] VI servir d'arbitre, être l'arbitre

umpteen* ['ʌmptiːn] ADJ beaucoup de, je ne sais combien de; **I've told you ~ times** je te l'ai dit je ne sais combien de fois or trente-six fois or cent fois; **he had ~ books** il avait je ne sais combien de livres or des quantités de livres

umpteenth* ['ʌmptiːnθ] ADJ (é)nième

UN [juːˈen] N (ABBR = **United Nations**) ONU f

'un* [ən] PRON (= one) **he's a good ~** c'est un brave type*; **she's a good ~** c'est une fille bien; **little ~** petiot(e)* m(f)

un... [ʌn] PREF dé..., dés..., dis..., in..., mal...

unabashed [ʌnə'bæʃt] ADJ [person] nullement décontenancé (**by** par); [love, desire, admiration] dont on n'a pas honte; [greed] sans mesure, sans bornes; **he's an ~ romantic** c'est un romantique et il n'en a pas honte or il ne s'en cache pas; **"yes" he said** « oui » dit-il sans se décontenancer or sans perdre contenance

unabated [ʌnə'beɪtɪd] ADJ (gen) **to remain** or **continue ~** rester inchangé; **the fighting continued ~ well into the next day** les combats ont continué le lendemain avec la même intensité; **with ~ interest** avec toujours autant d'intérêt; **his ~ enthusiasm for the scheme** l'enthousiasme qu'il continuait à exprimer pour ce projet

unabbreviated [ʌnə'briːvɪeɪtɪd] ADJ non abrégé, sans abréviation

▼ **unable** [ʌn'eɪbl] ADJ **to be ~ to do sth** (gen) ne (pas) pouvoir faire qch; (= not know how to) ne pas savoir faire qch; (= be incapable of) être incapable de faire qch; (= be prevented from) être dans l'impossibilité de faire qch, ne pas être en mesure de faire qch

unabridged ['ʌnə'brɪdʒd] ADJ intégral, non abrégé; **~ edition/version** édition f/version f intégrale

unaccented ['ʌnæk'sentɪd], **unaccentuated** ['ʌnæk'sentjʊeɪtɪd] ADJ [voice, speech] sans accent; [syllable] inaccentué, non accentué, atone

unacceptable ['ʌnək'septəbl] ADJ [offer, suggestion] inacceptable; [amount, degree, extent, level] inadmissible; **it's quite ~ that we should have to do this** il est inadmissible que nous devions faire cela; **the ~ face of capitalism** la face honteuse du capitalisme

unacceptably ['ʌnək'septəblɪ] ADV [dangerous] à un point inacceptable or inadmissible; **the cost was ~ high** le coût était si élevé que c'était inacceptable; **~ poor living conditions** des conditions fpl de vie inacceptables or inadmissibles; **an ~ violent programme** un film d'une violence inacceptable or inadmissible; **he suggested, quite ~, doing it later** il a suggéré de le faire plus tard, ce qui était tout à fait inacceptable or inadmissible

unaccommodating ['ʌnə'kɒmədeɪtɪŋ] ADJ (= disobliging) désobligeant; (= not easy to deal with) peu accommodant

unaccompanied ['ʌnə'kʌmpənɪd] ADJ [person, child, luggage] non accompagné; (Mus) [singing] sans accompagnement, a cappella; [instrument] seul

unaccomplished [ʌnə'kʌmplɪʃt] ADJ [a] (frm = unfinished) [work, task, journey] inaccompli, inachevé; [project, desire] inaccompli, non réalisé [b] (= untalented) [person] sans talents; [performance] médiocre

unaccountable [ʌnə'kaʊntəbl] ADJ [a] (= inexplicable) inexplicable, sans raison apparente [b] **to be ~ to** [+ person, official, organization] ne pas être responsable devant

unaccountably [ʌnə'kaʊntəblɪ] ADV **an ~ successful film** un film au succès inexplicable; **~ popular** d'une popularité inexplicable; **he felt ~ depressed** il se sentait déprimé sans savoir pourquoi; **the messenger was ~ delayed** le messager a été retardé sans raison apparente; **he felt sorry for her** sans comprendre pourquoi, il la plaignait

unaccounted [ʌnə'kaʊntɪd] ADJ **~ for: two passengers are still ~ for** deux passagers sont toujours portés disparus or n'ont toujours pas été retrouvés; **£5 is still ~ for** il manque encore 5 livres; **this is ~ for in the report** ceci n'est pas expliqué dans le rapport

unaccustomed [ʌnə'kʌstəmd] ADJ inaccoutumé, inhabituel; **to be ~ to (doing) sth** ne pas avoir l'habitude de (faire) qch; **~ as I am to public speaking ...** n'ayant pas l'habitude de prendre la parole en public ...

unacknowledged [ʌnək'nɒlɪdʒd] ADJ [letter] dont on n'a pas accusé réception; [mistake, help, services] non reconnu (publiquement); [child] non reconnu

unacquainted [ʌnə'kweɪntɪd] ADJ **to be ~ with the facts** ignorer les faits, ne pas être au courant des faits; **she is ~ with poverty** elle ne sait pas ce que c'est que la pauvreté, elle ne connaît pas la pauvreté; **to be ~ with sb** ne pas avoir fait la connaissance de qn; **they are ~** ils ne se connaissent pas

unadaptable [ʌnə'dæptəbl] ADJ inadaptable, peu adaptable

unadapted [ʌnə'dæptɪd] ADJ mal adapté, inadapté (**to** à)

unaddressed [ʌnə'drest] ADJ sans adresse, qui ne porte pas d'adresse

unadjusted [ˌʌnə'dʒʌstɪd] ADJ non corrigé; **seasonally ~ employment figures** statistiques fpl du chômage non corrigées des variations saisonnières

unadopted [ˌʌnə'dɒptɪd] ADJ **many children remain ~** beaucoup d'enfants ne trouvent pas de parents adoptifs

unadorned [ˌʌnə'dɔːnd] ADJ sans ornement, tout simple; (fig) [truth] pur, tout nu; **beauty ~** la beauté sans artifice or sans fard

unadulterated [ˌʌnə'dʌltəreɪtɪd] ADJ pur, naturel; [food, wine] non frelaté; (fig) [bliss, nonsense] pur (et simple)

unadventurous [ˌʌnəd'ventʃərəs] ADJ [person, career, design, theatre production] conventionnel, conservateur (-trice f); **where food is concerned, he is very ~** il est très conservateur dans ses goûts culinaires

unadventurously [ˌʌnəd'ventʃərəslɪ] ADV [dressed, decorated] de façon conventionnelle; [choose, decide] par manque d'audace or d'imagination

unadvertised [ʌn'ædvətaɪzd] ADJ [meeting, visit] sans publicité, discret (-ète f)

unadvised [ʌnəd'vaɪzd] ADJ [a] (= lacking advice) [person] qui n'a pas reçu de conseils [b] (= ill-advised) [person] malavisé, imprudent; [measures] inconsidéré, imprudent

unaesthetic [ʌniːs'θetɪk] ADJ inesthétique, peu esthétique

unaffected [ʌnə'fektɪd] ADJ [a] (= sincere) [person] naturel, simple; [behaviour] non affecté; [style] sans recherche, simple [b] (= unchanged) non affecté; **~ by damp/cold** non affecté par l'humidité/le froid, qui résiste à l'humidité/au froid; **~ by heat** inaltérable à la chaleur; **our plans were ~ by the strike** nos plans sont restés inchangés malgré la grève; **they are ~ by the new legislation** ils ne sont pas affectés or touchés par la nouvelle législation; **he was quite ~ by her sufferings** ses souffrances ne l'ont pas touché or l'ont laissé froid; **he remained ~ by all the noise** il était indifférent à tout ce bruit

unaffectedly [ʌnə'fektɪdlɪ] ADV [behave] sans affectation; [dress] simplement; **her outfit was ~ stylish** sa tenue était à la fois simple et chic

unaffiliated [ʌnə'fɪlɪeɪtɪd] ADJ non affilié (**to** à)

unafraid [ʌnə'freɪd] ADJ sans peur, qui n'a pas peur; **to be ~ of (doing) sth** ne pas avoir peur de (faire) qch

unaided [ʌn'eɪdɪd] [1] ADV [walk, stand] tout(e) seul(e); [breathe] sans aide extérieure; **to reach the North Pole ~** atteindre le pôle Nord par ses propres moyens; **she brought up six children ~** elle a élevé six enfants toute seule [2] ADJ **his ~ work** le travail qu'il a fait tout seul or sans être aidé; **by his own ~ efforts** par ses propres efforts or moyens

unaired [ʌn'eəd] ADJ non aéré

unalike [ʌnə'laɪk] ADJ peu ressemblant; **to be ~** ne pas se ressembler; **the two children are so ~** les deux enfants se ressemblent si peu

unalloyed [ʌnə'lɔɪd] ADJ [happiness] sans mélange, parfait; [metal] non allié

unalterable [ʌn'ɒltərəbl] ADJ [rule] invariable, immuable; [fact] certain; [emotion, friendship] inaltérable

unalterably [ʌn'ɒltərəblɪ] ADV [change, affect] de façon permanente; [opposed] définitivement; **~ wicked** foncièrement méchant

unaltered [ʌn'ɒltəd] ADJ inchangé, non modifié; **his appearance was ~** physiquement il n'avait pas changé

unambiguous ['ʌnæm'bɪgjʊəs] ADJ [statement, wording] non ambigu (-guë f), non équivoque, clair; [order, thought] clair

unambiguously ['ʌnæm'bɪgjʊəslɪ] ADV [say, condemn, support] sans ambiguïté, sans équivoque ; **he gave an ~ affirmative answer** il a répondu sans ambiguïté par l'affirmative

unambitious [ˈʌnæmˈbɪʃəs] ADJ [person] sans ambition, peu ambitieux ; [plan] modeste

un-American [ˈʌnəˈmerɪkən] ADJ **a** (pej = anti-American) antiaméricain **b** (not typical) peu or pas américain

unamiable [ʌnˈeɪmɪəbl] ADJ désagréable, peu aimable

unamused [ˈʌnəˈmjuːzd] ADJ qui n'est pas amusé ; **the story left her ~** l'histoire ne l'a pas amusée du tout, elle n'a pas trouvé l'histoire amusante du tout

unanimity [ˌjuːnəˈnɪmɪtɪ] N (NonC) unanimité f

unanimous [juːˈnænɪməs] ADJ [group, decision] unanime ; **the committee was ~ in its condemnation of this** or **in condemning this** les membres du comité ont été unanimes pour or à condamner cela, les membres du comité ont condamné cela à l'unanimité ; **it was accepted by a ~ vote** cela a été voté à l'unanimité

unanimously [juːˈnænɪməslɪ] ADV [vote, elect] à l'unanimité ; [agree, pass] unanimement, à l'unanimité ; [condemn] unanimement ; **~ favourable** unanimement favorable ; **the album received ~ good reviews** or **was ~ praised** l'album a fait l'unanimité

unannounced [ˈʌnəˈnaʊnst] **1** ADJ [visitor, visit] imprévu ; **to pay an ~ visit to sb** rendre visite à qn sans prévenir ; (in more formal situations) rendre visite à qn sans se faire annoncer ; **the President paid an ~ visit to the Swiss capital** le Président a effectué une visite-surprise dans la capitale helvétique **2** ADV [arrive, enter, turn up] sans prévenir ; (in more formal situations) sans se faire annoncer

unanswerable [ʌnˈɑːnsərəbl] ADJ [question] à laquelle il est impossible de répondre ; [argument] irréfutable, incontestable

unanswered [ʌnˈɑːnsəd] ADJ [letter, request, question] (qui reste) sans réponse ; [problem, puzzle] non résolu ; [criticism, argument] non réfuté ; [prayer] inexaucé ; (Jur) [charge] irréfuté ; **her letter remained ~** sa lettre est restée sans réponse ; **there was a pile of ~ letters on his desk** sur son bureau, il y avait une pile de lettres en attente or une pile de lettres auxquelles il n'avait pas (encore) répondu

unappealing [ˈʌnəˈpiːlɪŋ] ADJ peu attirant, peu attrayant

unappetizing [ʌnˈæpɪtaɪzɪŋ] ADJ (lit, fig) peu appétissant

unappreciated [ˈʌnəˈpriːʃɪeɪtɪd] ADJ [person] méconnu, incompris ; [offer, help] non apprécié

unappreciative [ˈʌnəˈpriːʃɪətɪv] ADJ [audience] froid, indifférent ; **to be ~ of sth** ne pas apprécier qch, rester indifférent à qch

unapproachable [ˈʌnəˈprəʊtʃəbl] ADJ d'un abord difficile, inabordable

unarguable [ʌnˈɑːgjʊəbl] ADJ incontestable

unarguably [ʌnˈɑːgjʊəblɪ] ADV incontestablement

unarmed [ˈʌnˈɑːmd] **1** ADJ [person] non armé ; [ship, plane] sans armes ; **he is ~** il n'est pas armé **2** ADV sans armes **3** COMP ► **unarmed combat** N combat m à mains nues

unashamed [ˈʌnəˈʃeɪmd] ADJ [pleasure, delight, admiration] non déguisé ; [greed, luxury] dont on n'a pas honte ; **he was quite ~ about it** il n'en éprouvait pas la moindre honte or gêne ; **he was an ~ admirer of Mussolini** il admirait Mussolini et ne s'en cachait pas

unashamedly [ˈʌnəˈʃeɪmɪdlɪ] ADV [say, cry] sans aucune gêne ; **~ romantic** qui ne cache pas son romantisme ; **~ luxurious** d'un luxe sans complexes ; **he was ~ delighted about it** il en était réjoui et ne s'en cachait pas ; **he**

was ~ **selfish/a liar** c'était un égoïste/un menteur et il ne s'en cachait pas

unasked [ˈʌnˈɑːskt] **1** ADJ [question] non formulé ; **significant questions will go ~** certaines questions importantes ne seront pas posées ; **this was ~ for** on ne l'avait pas demandé **2** ADV **she did it ~** elle l'a fait sans qu'on le lui ait demandé or de son propre chef ; **he came in ~** il est entré sans y avoir été invité

unaspirated [ˈʌnˈæspəreɪtɪd] ADJ (Phon) non aspiré

unassailable [ˌʌnəˈseɪləbl] ADJ [fortress] imprenable ; [position, reputation] inattaquable ; [argument, reason] irréfutable, inattaquable ; **he is quite ~ on that point** ses arguments sont irréfutables sur ce point, on ne peut pas l'attaquer sur ce point

unassisted [ˈʌnəˈsɪstɪd] **1** ADV tout seul, sans aide **2** ADJ tout seul

unassuming [ˈʌnəˈsjuːmɪŋ] ADJ sans prétentions, modeste

unassumingly [ˈʌnəˈsjuːmɪŋlɪ] ADV modestement, sans prétentions

unattached [ˈʌnəˈtætʃt] ADJ [part etc] non attaché (**to** a), libre (**to** de) ; (fig) [person, group] indépendant (**to** de) ; (= not married etc) libre, sans attaches ; (Jur) non saisi

unattainable [ˈʌnəˈteɪnəbl] ADJ [place, objective, person] inaccessible

unattended [ˈʌnəˈtendɪd] ADJ **a** (= not looked after) [shop, machine, luggage] (laissé) sans surveillance ; [child] sans surveillance, (tout) seul ; **do not leave your luggage ~** ne laissez pas vos bagages sans surveillance ; **~ to** négligé **b** (= unaccompanied) [king etc] seul, sans escorte

unattractive [ˈʌnəˈtræktɪv] ADJ [appearance, house, idea] peu attrayant, peu séduisant ; [person, character] déplaisant, peu sympathique

unattractiveness [ˈʌnəˈtræktɪvnɪs] N (NonC) manque m d'attrait or de beauté

unattributed [ˈʌnəˈtrɪbjuːtɪd] ADJ [quotation, remark] non attribué ; [source] non cité, non indiqué

unauthenticated [ˈʌnɔːˈθentɪkeɪtɪd] ADJ [evidence] non établi ; [signature] non authentifié

unauthorized [ˈʌnˈɔːθəraɪzd] ADJ (gen) non autorisé, (fait) sans autorisation ; **this was ~** cela a été fait sans autorisation ; **~ absence** absence f irrégulière ; (Jur) **~ signature** signature f usurpatoire

unavailable [ˈʌnəˈveɪləbl] ADJ [funds] indisponible ; (Comm) [article] épuisé, qu'on ne peut se procurer ; [person] indisponible, qui n'est pas disponible or libre ; **the Minister was ~ for comment** le ministre s'est refusé à toute déclaration

unavailing [ˈʌnəˈveɪlɪŋ] ADJ [effort] vain, inutile ; [remedy, method] inefficace

unavailingly [ˈʌnəˈveɪlɪŋlɪ] ADV en vain, sans succès

unavoidable [ˈʌnəˈvɔɪdəbl] ADJ inévitable ; **it is ~ that ...** il est inévitable que ... (+ subj)

unavoidably [ˈʌnəˈvɔɪdəblɪ] ADV inévitablement ; **he was ~ delayed** or **detained** il n'a pu éviter d'être retardé

unaware [ˈʌnəˈwɛər] ADJ **to be ~ of sth** ignorer qch, ne pas être conscient de qch, ne pas avoir conscience de qch ; **to be ~ that ...** ignorer que ..., ne pas savoir que ... ; **"stop" he said, ~ of the danger** « arrête » dit-il, ignorant or inconscient du danger ; **I was not ~ that ...** je n'étais pas sans savoir que ... ; **he is politically quite ~** il n'a aucune conscience politique, il n'est pas politisé

unawareness [ˈʌnəˈwɛənɪs] N ignorance f

unawares [ˈʌnəˈwɛəz] ADV **a** (= by surprise) à l'improviste, au dépourvu ; **to catch** or **take sb ~** prendre qn à l'improviste or au dé-

pourvu **b** (= without realizing) inconsciemment, par mégarde

unbacked [ˈʌnˈbækt] ADJ (Fin) à découvert

unbalance [ʌnˈbæləns] **1** VT déséquilibrer **2** N déséquilibre m

unbalanced [ˈʌnˈbælənst] ADJ **a** (physically) mal équilibré ; (mentally) déséquilibré ; **his mind was ~** il était déséquilibré **b** (Fin) [account] non soldé

unban [ˈʌnˈbæn] VT **to ~ an organization** lever l'interdiction frappant une organisation

unbandage [ˈʌnˈbændɪdʒ] VT [+ limb, wound] débander ; [+ person] ôter ses bandages or ses pansements à

unbaptized [ˈʌnbæpˈtaɪzd] ADJ non baptisé

unbar [ˈʌnˈbɑːr] VT [+ door] débarrer, enlever la barre de

unbearable [ʌnˈbɛərəbl] ADJ insupportable

unbearably [ʌnˈbɛərəblɪ] ADV [sad, painful, loud] insupportablement ; **it's ~ hot/cold today** aujourd'hui il fait une chaleur/un froid insupportable

unbeatable [ˈʌnˈbiːtəbl] ADJ imbattable

unbeaten [ˈʌnˈbiːtn] ADJ [army, player, team] invaincu ; [record, price] non battu

unbecoming [ˈʌnbɪˈkʌmɪŋ] ADJ [garment] peu seyant, qui ne va or ne sied pas ; (fig) [behaviour] malséant, inconvenant

unbeknown(st) [ˈʌnbɪˈnəʊn(st)] ADJ, ADV **~ to ...** à l'insu de ... ; **~ to me** à mon insu

unbelief [ˈʌnbɪˈliːf] N (also Rel) incrédulité f ; **in ~ ◊ with an air of ~** d'un air incrédule

unbelievable [ˌʌnbɪˈliːvəbl] ADJ incroyable ; **it is ~ that ...** il est incroyable que ... (+ subj)

unbelievably [ˌʌnbɪˈliːvəblɪ] ADV [beautiful, stupid, selfish etc] incroyablement ; **to be ~ lucky/successful** avoir une chance/un succès incroyable ; **~, he refused** aussi incroyable que cela puisse paraître, il a refusé

unbeliever [ˈʌnbɪˈliːvər] N (also Rel) incrédule mf

unbelieving [ˈʌnbɪˈliːvɪŋ] ADJ (also Rel) incrédule

unbelievingly [ˈʌnbɪˈliːvɪŋlɪ] ADV d'un air incrédule

unbend [ˈʌnˈbend] (pret, ptp **unbent**) **1** VT [+ pipe, wire] redresser ; [+ person] se détendre ; **he unbent enough to ask me how I was** il a daigné me demander comment j'allais

unbending [ʌnˈbendɪŋ] ADJ non flexible, rigide ; (fig) [person, attitude] inflexible, intransigeant

unbent [ʌnˈbent] VB pt, ptp of **unbend**

unbias(s)ed [ʌnˈbaɪəst] ADJ impartial

unbidden [ʌnˈbɪdn] ADV (liter) **she did it ~** elle l'a fait de son propre chef or sans qu'on le lui ait demandé ; **he came in ~** il est entré sans y avoir été invité ; **the phrase sprang ~ to her mind/lips** l'expression lui est venue spontanément à l'esprit/aux lèvres

unbind [ˈʌnˈbaɪnd] (pret, ptp **unbound**) VT (= free) délier ; (= untie) dénouer, défaire ; (= unbandage) débander → **unbound**

unbleached [ˈʌnˈbliːtʃt] ADJ [linen] écru ; [hair] non décoloré ; [flour] non traité

unblemished [ʌnˈblemɪʃt] ADJ (lit, fig) sans tache

unblinking [ʌnˈblɪŋkɪŋ] ADJ [person] imperturbable, impassible ; **he gave me an ~ stare ◊ he looked at me with ~ eyes** il m'a regardé sans ciller

unblinkingly [ʌnˈblɪŋkɪŋlɪ] ADV [stare] sans ciller

unblock [ˈʌnˈblɒk] VT [+ sink, pipe] déboucher ; [+ road, harbour, traffic] dégager

unblushing [ʌnˈblʌʃɪŋ] ADJ effronté, éhonté

unblushingly [ʌnˈblʌʃɪŋlɪ] ADV sans rougir ; (fig) effrontément

unbolt ['ʌn'bəʊlt] VT [+ *door*] déverrouiller, tirer le verrou de ; [+ *beam*] déboulonner

unborn ['ʌn'bɔːn] ADJ **the ~ child** le fœtus ; **generations yet ~** les générations *fpl* futures *or* à venir

unbosom [ʌn'bʊzəm] VT **to ~ o.s. to sb** ouvrir son cœur à qn, se confier à qn

unbound ['ʌn'baʊnd] 1 VB *pt, ptp of* **unbind** 2 ADJ [*prisoner, hands, feet*] non lié ; [*seam*] non bordé ; [*book*] broché, non relié ; [*periodical*] non relié

unbounded [ʌn'baʊndɪd] ADJ [*joy, gratitude*] sans borne, illimité ; [*conceit, pride*] démesuré ; [*ignorance*] sans fond

unbowed ['ʌn'baʊd] ADJ (*fig*) insoumis, invaincu ; **with head ~** la tête haute

unbreakable ['ʌn'breɪkəbl] ADJ incassable ; (*fig*) [*promise, treaty*] sacré

unbreathable ['ʌn'briːðəbl] ADJ irrespirable

unbribable ['ʌn'braɪbəbl] ADJ incorruptible, qui ne se laisse pas acheter

unbridgeable ['ʌn'brɪdʒəbl] ADJ (*fig*) **an ~ gap** *or* **gulf** une divergence irréconciliable

unbridled [ʌn'braɪdld] ADJ (*fig*) débridé, déchaîné, effréné

unbroken [ʌn'brəʊkən] ADJ [a] (= *intact*) [*crockery, limb*] non cassé ; [*seal*] intact, non brisé ; [*skin*] intact, non déchiré ; [*ice*] intact ; [*record*] non battu ; [*promise*] tenu ; **his spirit remained ~** il ne se découragea pas [b] (= *continuous*) [*series, silence, sleep*] ininterrompu ; (*Aut*) **~ line** ligne *f* continue ; **descended in an ~ line from Edward II** qui descend en ligne directe d'Édouard II ; **she was in government for ten ~ years** elle a été au gouvernement pendant dix années de suite ; **a whole morning of ~ sunshine** une matinée entière de soleil sans nuages [c] [*horse*] indompté [d] [*voice*] qui n'a pas mué

unbuckle [ʌn'bʌkl] VT déboucler

unbundle [ʌn'bʌndl] VT [a] (*gen*) séparer, dégrouper [b] (*Fin*) (*after a buyout*) vendre par appartements ; (= *price into separate items*) détailler, tarifer séparément

unburden [ʌn'bɜːdn] VT [+ *conscience*] soulager ; [+ *heart*] épancher ; **to ~ o.s.** s'épancher (**to sb** avec qn), se livrer (**to sb** à qn) ; **to ~ o.s. of sth** se décharger de qch

unburied ['ʌn'berɪd] ADJ non enterré, non enseveli

unbusinesslike [ʌn'bɪznəslaɪk] ADJ [*trader, dealer*] qui n'a pas le sens des affaires, peu commerçant ; [*transaction*] irrégulier ; (*fig*) [*person*] qui manque de méthode *or* d'organisation ; [*report*] peu méthodique

unbutton ['ʌn'bʌtn] VT [+ *shirt, coat, trousers etc*] déboutonner ; [+ *button*] défaire

uncalled-for [ʌn'kɔːldfɔːʳ] ADJ [*criticism*] injustifié ; [*remark*] déplacé ; **that was quite ~** c'était tout à fait déplacé

uncannily [ʌn'kænɪlɪ] ADV étrangement ; **to look ~ like sb/sth** ressembler étrangement à qn/qch

uncanny [ʌn'kænɪ] ADJ [*sound*] mystérieux, étrange ; [*atmosphere, silence*] étrange ; [*mystery, event, question, resemblance, accuracy, knack*] troublant ; **it's ~ how he does it** je ne m'explique vraiment pas comment il fait cela

uncap [ʌn'kæp] VT [+ *bottle*] décapsuler

uncapped ['ʌn'kæpt] ADJ (*Brit Sport*) [*player*] (*for country*) qui n'a pas encore été sélectionné en équipe nationale ; (*for university*) qui n'a pas encore été sélectionné dans l'équipe de son université

uncared-for ['ʌn'kɛədfɔːʳ] ADJ [*garden, building*] négligé, (laissé) à l'abandon ; [*appearance*] négligé, peu soigné ; [*child*] laissé à l'abandon, délaissé

uncaring [ʌn'kɛərɪŋ] ADJ insensible, indifférent

uncarpeted [ʌn'kɑːpɪtɪd] ADJ sans tapis

uncashed [ʌn'kæʃəd] ADJ [*cheque*] non encaissé

uncatalogued ['ʌn'kætəlɒgd] ADJ qui n'a pas été catalogué

uncaught ['ʌn'kɔːt] ADJ [*criminal*] qui n'a pas été appréhendé *or* pris

unceasing [ʌn'siːsɪŋ] ADJ incessant, continu, continuel

unceasingly [ʌn'siːsɪŋlɪ] ADV sans cesse

uncensored ['ʌn'sensəd] ADJ [*letter*] non censuré ; [*film, book*] non censuré, non expurgé

unceremonious ['ʌn,serɪ'məʊnɪəs] ADJ brusque

unceremoniously ['ʌn,serɪ'məʊnɪəslɪ] ADV [a] (= *without ceremony*) [*bury*] sans cérémonie [b] (= *abruptly*) [*eject*] brusquement

▼ uncertain [ʌn'sɜːtn] ADJ [*person*] incertain, qui n'est pas sûr *or* certain ; [*voice, smile, steps*] mal assuré, hésitant ; [*age, date, weather*] incertain ; [*result, effect*] incertain, aléatoire ; [*temper*] inégal ; **it is ~ whether ...** il n'est pas certain *or* sûr que ... (+ *subj*) ; **he is ~ (as to) whether ...** il ne sait pas au juste si ... (+ *indic*), il n'est pas sûr que ... (+ *subj*) ; **to be ~ about sth** être incertain de qch, ne pas être certain *or* sûr de qch, avoir des doutes sur qch ; **he was ~ about what he was going to do** il était incertain de ce qu'il allait faire, il ne savait pas au juste ce qu'il allait faire ; **in no ~ terms** sans ambages, en des termes on ne peut plus clairs

uncertainly [ʌn'sɜːtnlɪ] ADV [*say*] d'une manière hésitante ; [*stand*] avec hésitation ; [*smile, laugh, look at*] d'un air hésitant

uncertainty [ʌn'sɜːtntɪ] N incertitude *f*, doute(s) *m(pl)* ; **in order to remove any ~** pour dissiper des doutes éventuels ; **in view of this ~** *or* **these uncertainties** en raison de l'incertitude dans laquelle nous nous trouvons *or* de ces incertitudes

uncertificated ['ʌn'sɜːtɪfɪkeɪtɪd] ADJ (*gen*) non diplômé ; [*secondary teacher*] non certifié

uncertified ['ʌn'sɜːtɪfaɪd] ADJ [*document etc*] non certifié ; (*US*) **~ teacher** ≈ maître *m* auxiliaire

unchain ['ʌn'tʃeɪn] VT (*fig*) [+ *passions, reaction*] déchaîner ; (*lit*) [+ *dog*] lâcher

unchallengeable ['ʌn'tʃælɪndʒəbl] ADJ indiscutable, incontestable

unchallenged ['ʌn'tʃælɪndʒd] 1 ADJ [*authority, position, superiority*] incontesté, indiscuté ; [*master, champion*] incontesté ; [*action, policy, statement*] non contesté ; [*argument, comment*] non relevé ; (*Jur*) [*juror, witness*] non récusé 2 ADV [a] (= *without being opposed*) **to go ~** [*authority, position*] ne pas être contesté, ne pas être discuté ; [*person, action*] ne pas rencontrer d'opposition, ne pas être contesté ; [*policy, statement*] ne pas être contesté ; [*argument, comment*] ne pas être relevé ; [*juror, witness*] ne pas être récusé ; **to leave sb ~** [+ *leader*] ne pas contester qn ; [+ *candidate*] ne pas s'opposer à qn ; **she couldn't let that go ~** elle ne pouvait pas laisser passer cela sans protester [b] (= *without being stopped*) **to do sth ~** [*person*] faire qch sans être arrêté ; **he slipped ~ through the enemy lines** il a passé au travers des lignes ennemies sans être interpellé

unchangeable [ʌn'tʃeɪndʒəbl] ADJ [*person, system, fact*] immuable

unchanged ['ʌn'tʃeɪndʒd] ADJ inchangé

unchanging [ʌn'tʃeɪndʒɪŋ] ADJ qui ne change pas, immuable

uncharacteristic [,ʌnkærɪktə'rɪstɪk] ADJ [*behaviour, emotion, smile*] qui ne lui (*or* leur *etc*) ressemble (*or* ressemblait) pas ; [*mistake*] qui n'est pas caractéristique ; **it is ~ of** *or* **for him (to do that)** cela ne lui ressemble pas (de faire cela), ce n'est pas son genre (de faire cela)

uncharacteristically [,ʌnkærɪktə'rɪstɪklɪ] ADV **~ rude/generous** d'une grossièreté/générosité peu caractéristique ; **she was ~ silent** elle était silencieuse, ce qui ne lui ressemblait pas ; **he behaved ~** il s'est comporté d'une façon qui ne lui ressemblait pas ; **~, he had overlooked an important detail** il avait laissé passer un détail important, ce qui ne lui ressemblait pas *or* n'était pas son genre

uncharged ['ʌn'tʃɑːdʒd] ADJ (*Elec*) non chargé ; (*Jur*) non accusé ; [*gun*] non chargé

uncharitable [ʌn'tʃærɪtəbl] ADJ peu indulgent, peu charitable

uncharitably [ʌn'tʃærɪtəblɪ] ADV [*think*] avec peu d'indulgence, peu charitablement ; [*say, describe*] avec peu d'indulgence, de manière peu charitable

uncharted ['ʌn'tʃɑːtɪd] ADJ [a] (*lit* = *unmapped*) [*area, sea*] dont on n'a (*or* n'avait) pas dressé la carte ; (= *not on map*) [*island*] qui ne figure (*or* figurait) sur aucune carte [b] (*fig* = *unknown*) **a largely ~ area of medical science** un domaine de la médecine largement inexploré ; **these are ~ waters** *or* **this is ~ territory (for sb)** c'est un terrain inconnu (pour qn) ; **to be in/enter ~ waters** *or* **territory** être/pénétrer en terrain inconnu

unchaste ['ʌn'tʃeɪst] ADJ lascif

unchecked ['ʌn'tʃekt] 1 ADJ [a] (= *unrestrained*) [*growth, power*] non maîtrisé, non contenu ; [*emotion, anger*] non réprimé [b] (= *not verified*) [*data, statement*] non vérifié ; [*typescript*] non relu 2 ADV **to go ~** [*expansion, power*] ne pas être maîtrisé *or* contenu ; [*anger, aggression*] ne pas être réprimé ; **if the spread of AIDS continues ~ ...** si on ne fait rien pour empêcher la propagation du sida ... ; (*Mil*) **they advanced ~ for several kilometres** ils ont fait plusieurs kilomètres sans rencontrer d'obstacle

unchivalrous ['ʌn'ʃɪvəlrəs] ADJ peu galant, discourtois

unchristian ['ʌn'krɪstjən] ADJ peu chrétien, contraire à l'esprit chrétien

uncial ['ʌnsɪəl] 1 ADJ oncial 2 N onciale *f*

uncircumcised ['ʌn'sɜːkəmsaɪzd] ADJ incirconcis

uncivil ['ʌn'sɪvɪl] ADJ [*person, behaviour*] impoli (**to sb** avec qn), incivil (*liter*) (**to sb** avec qn) ; **it would be ~ to refuse** il serait impoli de refuser ; **it was very ~ of you to behave like that** ça a été très impoli de votre part de vous comporter ainsi

uncivilized ['ʌn'sɪvɪlaɪzd] ADJ [a] (= *primitive*) [*people, country*] non civilisé [b] (= *socially unacceptable*) [*conditions, activity*] inacceptable ; [*person, behaviour*] grossier ; **what an ~ thing to do!** quelle grossièreté ! ; **how ~ of him!** comme c'est grossier de sa part ! [c] (* = *early*) **at an ~ time** *or* **hour** à une heure impossible* *or* indue ; **sorry to wake you at this ~ hour** désolé de vous réveiller à cette heure indue ; **what an ~ time to ring up!** ce n'est pas une heure pour téléphoner !

uncivilly ['ʌn'sɪvɪlɪ] ADV impoliment, incivilement (*liter*)

unclad ['ʌn'klæd] ADJ (*liter*) sans vêtements, nu

unclaimed ['ʌn'kleɪmd] ADJ [*property, prize, body*] non réclamé ; **to go ~** ne pas être réclamé

unclasp ['ʌn'klɑːsp] VT [+ *necklace*] défaire, dégrafer ; [+ *hands*] ouvrir

unclassed ['ʌn'klɑːst] ADJ non classé

unclassified ['ʌn'klæsɪfaɪd] 1 ADJ [a] (= *not sorted*) [*items, papers, waste, football results*] non classé [b] (= *not secret*) [*information, document*] non classifié, non (classé) secret 2 COMP ► **unclassified degree** N (*Brit Univ*) licence sans mention accordée lorsque toutes les épreuves n'ont pas été passées ► **unclassified road** N route *f* non classée

uncle [ˈʌŋkl] N oncle m; (in child's language) **yes ~** oui tonton*, oui mon oncle; (US fig) **to say** or **cry ~*** s'avouer vaincu; **Uncle Sam** l'oncle m Sam; (pej) **Uncle Tom** bon nègre m → **Dutch**

unclean [ʌnˈkliːn] ADJ a (= dirty) [person, hands, room] sale b (= impure) [person, animal, activity, thoughts] impur c (= diseased: traditionally said by lepers: also hum) **"~, ~!"** «ne vous approchez pas, je suis contagieux!»

unclear [ʌnˈklɪəʳ] ADJ a (= not obvious, confusing) [reason, motive, message, details, instructions, policy] qui n'est pas clair, obscur; [result, outcome] incertain; **it is ~ whether/who/why** etc ... on ne sait pas bien si/qui/pourquoi etc ...; **it's ~ to me whether/who/why** etc ... on ne sait pas bien si/qui/pourquoi etc ...; **her purpose remains ~** on ne sait toujours pas très bien où elle veut en venir b (= indistinct) [picture, image] qui n'est pas net, flou; [handwriting] qui n'est pas net; [answer, words] indistinct c (= unsure) **I'm ~ on this point** je ne sais pas vraiment à quoi m'en tenir là-dessus, pour moi, ce point n'est pas clair; **I'm ~ whether you agree or not** je ne suis pas sûr de comprendre si vous êtes d'accord ou pas

unclench [ʌnˈklentʃ] VT desserrer

unclimbed [ʌnˈklaɪmd] ADJ [mountain, peak] vierge

uncloak [ʌnˈkləʊk] VT (fig) [+ person] démasquer; [+ mystery, plot] dévoiler

unclog [ʌnˈklɒg] VT [+ pipe] déboucher; [+ wheel] débloquer

unclothe [ʌnˈkləʊð] VT déshabiller, dévêtir

unclothed [ʌnˈkləʊðd] ADJ (frm) [person] dévêtu; [body] dévêtu, nu

unclouded [ʌnˈklaʊdɪd] ADJ [sky] sans nuages, dégagé; [liquid] clair, limpide; (fig) [happiness] sans nuages, parfait; [future] sans nuages

uncoil [ʌnˈkɔɪl] 1 VT dérouler 2 VI se dérouler

uncollectable [ʌnkəˈlektəbl] ADJ [tax] impossible à percevoir

uncollected [ʌnkəˈlektɪd] ADJ [tax] non perçu; [bus fare] non encaissé; [luggage, lost property] non réclamé; [refuse] non ramassé, non enlevé

uncoloured, uncolored (US) [ʌnˈkʌləd] ADJ a (= colourless) [glass, plastic, liquid] non coloré; [hair] non teint b (= unbiased) [account, description, judgement] non faussé (**by sth** par qch)

uncombed [ʌnˈkəʊmd] ADJ [hair, wool] non peigné

un-come-at-able* [ʌnkʌmˈætəbl] ADJ inaccessible

uncomely [ʌnˈkʌmlɪ] ADJ [person] laid, peu joli; [clothes] peu seyant

uncomfortable [ʌnˈkʌmfətəbl] ADJ a (= feeling physical discomfort) **to be** or **feel ~** [person] (in chair, bed, room) ne pas être à l'aise; **are you ~ there?** vous n'êtes pas à l'aise?; **you look rather ~** vous avez l'air plutôt mal à l'aise

b (= causing physical discomfort) [position, chair, shoes, journey] inconfortable; [heat] incommodant

c (= feeling unease) [person] mal à l'aise (**with sb** avec qn); **~ doing sth** mal à l'aise de faire qch; **~ about sth/about doing sth** mal à l'aise à propos de qch/à l'idée de faire qch; **to be ~ with the idea of (doing) sth** être mal à l'aise à l'idée de (faire) qch; **I was ~ with the whole business** toute cette affaire me mettait mal à l'aise; **to make sb ~** mettre qn mal à l'aise

d (= causing unease) [silence] pesant; [situation] inconfortable; [afternoon, feeling] désagréable; [truth, fact] gênant; **to have an ~ feeling that ...** avoir la désagréable impression que ...; **the situation is ~ for her** cette situation la met mal à l'aise; **to make life ~ for sb** mener la vie dure à qn; **to make things ~ for sb** créer des ennuis à qn; **to put sb in an ~ position** mettre qn dans une situation inconfortable; **to have an ~ time** passer un mauvais quart d'heure; (longer) connaître des moments difficiles

uncomfortably [ʌnˈkʌmfətəblɪ] ADV a (= unpleasantly) [tight] trop; **I'm feeling ~ full** je me sens (l'estomac) lourd; **the room was ~ hot** il faisait dans cette pièce une chaleur incommodante, il faisait trop chaud dans la pièce; **to be ~ aware that ...** être désagréablement conscient du fait que ...; **my knees were ~ close to the steering wheel** mes genoux étaient tout près du volant, ce qui me gênait, j'avais les genoux si près du volant que ça me gênait; **the deadline is drawing ~ close** la date limite se rapproche de façon inquiétante b (= awkwardly) [sit] inconfortablement; [dressed] de façon inconfortable; **he shifted ~** il était mal à l'aise et n'arrêtait pas de changer de position c (= uneasily) [say, look at] avec gêne

uncommitted [ʌnkəˈmɪtɪd] ADJ a (= undecided) [voter, delegate] indécis; [country] non engagé; **to remain ~** rester neutre, ne pas s'engager; **I was still ~ to the venture** je ne m'étais pas encore engagé sur ce projet; **she is ~ on policy on this issue** elle n'a pas de position arrêtée sur la politique à suivre/sur cette question b (= unallocated) [space] libre; [resources] disponible, non affecté c (= half-hearted) [performance] sans conviction; [attitude] indifférent

uncommon [ʌnˈkɒmən] 1 ADJ (= rare) [name, species, disease] rare; [intelligence, beauty] peu commun, singulier; **a not ~ problem/sight** un problème/un spectacle qui n'est pas rare; **she was late for work, a not ~ occurrence** elle était en retard au travail, chose qui arrivait assez fréquemment; **he had a slight nosebleed, a not ~ occurrence for him** il saignait légèrement du nez, ce qui lui arrivait assez fréquemment; **it is not ~ to hear this** il n'est pas rare d'entendre cela; **it is not ~ for this to happen** il n'est pas rare que cela arrive (subj) 2 ADV† moult†† (also hum)

uncommonly [ʌnˈkɒmənlɪ] ADV a († = exceptionally) [gifted, pretty, hot] exceptionnellement, singulièrement b (= rarely) [encountered] rarement; **such crimes are not ~ committed by minors** il n'est pas rare que des mineurs commettent (subj) ce genre de crime

uncommunicative [ʌnkəˈmjuːnɪkətɪv] ADJ peu communicatif; **on this issue he proved very ~** sur cette question il s'est montré très peu communicatif or très réservé

uncomplaining [ʌnkəmˈpleɪnɪŋ] ADJ qui ne se plaint pas

uncomplainingly [ʌnkəmˈpleɪnɪŋlɪ] ADV sans se plaindre

uncompleted [ʌnkəmˈpliːtɪd] ADJ inachevé

uncomplicated [ʌnˈkɒmplɪkeɪtɪd] ADJ [person, relationship] qui n'est pas compliqué; [method, view, plot] simple; [pregnancy] sans complications

uncomplimentary [ʌnˌkɒmplɪˈmentərɪ] ADJ peu flatteur

uncomprehending [ʌnˌkɒmprɪˈhendɪŋ] ADJ [rage, horror, astonishment] plein d'incompréhension; **to give sb an ~ look** regarder qn sans comprendre; **he stood there, quite ~** il restait là, sans rien comprendre; **she gave a polite but ~ smile** elle a souri poliment, mais sans comprendre

uncomprehendingly [ʌnˌkɒmprɪˈhendɪŋlɪ] ADV sans comprendre

uncompromising [ʌnˈkɒmprəmaɪzɪŋ] ADJ [person] sans compromis; [attitude, message, demand, honesty, sincerity, film] sans complaisance; **to be ~ in refusing** or **in one's refusal (to do sth)** refuser catégoriquement (de faire qch)

uncompromisingly [ʌnˈkɒmprəmaɪzɪŋlɪ] ADV [say] sans concession(s); [intellectual, austere, modern] résolument; **~ loyal** d'une loyauté totale or absolue

unconcealed [ʌnkənˈsiːld] ADJ [delight, anger, frustration, annoyance] non dissimulé; [object] non caché, non dissimulé

unconcern [ʌnkənˈsɜːn] N (= calm) calme m; (in face of danger) sang-froid m; (= lack of interest) indifférence f, insouciance f

unconcerned [ʌnkənˈsɜːnd] ADJ a (= uninterested) **to be ~** [person] ne pas se sentir concerné (**about** or **with sth** par qch) b (= unworried) [person] insouciant; **he went on speaking, ~** il a continué à parler sans se laisser troubler; **to be ~ that ...** ne pas se soucier du fait que ...; **to be ~ about sth** ne pas se soucier de qch; **to be ~ by sth** ne pas s'inquiéter de qch

unconcernedly [ʌnkənˈsɜːnɪdlɪ] ADV sans s'inquiéter

unconditional [ʌnkənˈdɪʃənl] 1 ADJ [surrender, offer, bail] sans condition(s), inconditionnel; [love, support] inconditionnel 2 COMP ► **unconditional discharge** N (Jur) dispense f de peine inconditionnelle

unconditionally [ʌnkənˈdɪʃnəlɪ] ADV sans conditions

unconfined [ʌnkənˈfaɪnd] ADJ [space] illimité, sans bornes; [animal] en liberté

unconfirmed [ʌnkənˈfɜːmd] ADJ [report, rumour] non confirmé; **the rumours remain ~** ces rumeurs n'ont toujours pas été confirmées

uncongenial [ʌnkənˈdʒiːnɪəl] ADJ [person, company] peu sympathique (**to sb** à qn); [work, surroundings] peu agréable (**to sb** à qn)

unconnected [ʌnkəˈnektɪd] ADJ a (= unrelated) [events, facts, languages] sans rapport; **a series of ~ events** une série d'événements sans rapport entre eux; **the two incidents were ~** il n'y avait pas de rapport entre ces deux incidents; **the two events were not ~** les deux événements n'étaient pas sans rapport; **to be ~ with** or **to sth** ne pas avoir de rapport avec qch, être sans rapport avec qch b (= unstructured) [thoughts, ideas, utterances] décousu; **a stream of ~ one-liners** une suite de bons mots sans rapport entre eux c (= physically separated) séparé (**to sth** de qch); **the island of Borneo, ~ to the Malay peninsula** l'île de Bornéo, séparée de la péninsule malaise d (Elec) [wire, plug] déconnecté; [appliance] débranché

unconquerable [ʌnˈkɒŋkərəbl] ADJ [army, nation, mountain] invincible; [difficulty] insurmontable; [tendency] irrépressible, incorrigible

unconquered [ʌnˈkɒŋkəd] ADJ [land] qui n'a pas été conquis; [mountain] invaincu

unconscionable [ʌnˈkɒnʃnəbl] ADJ (frm) a (= disgraceful) [liar] éhonté; [behaviour, crime] inadmissible; **it is ~ that ...** il est inadmissible que ...; **it would be ~ to allow that** il serait inadmissible de permettre cela; **it is ~ for them to do such a thing** il est inadmissible qu'ils fassent une chose pareille b (= excessive) [amount, delays, demands] déraisonnable; **to be an ~ time doing sth** prendre un temps déraisonnable à faire qch

unconscionably [ʌnˈkɒnʃnəblɪ] ADV (frm) déraisonnablement, excessivement; **you took an ~ long time over it** vous y avez passé beaucoup trop de temps

unconscious [ʌnˈkɒnʃəs] 1 ADJ a (Med) [person] inconscient, sans connaissance; **I was ~ for a few moments** je suis resté inconscient or sans connaissance pendant quelques instants; **to become ~** perdre connaissance; **to beat sb ~** battre qn jusqu'à lui faire perdre connaissance; **to knock sb ~** assommer qn b (= *unaware*) **to be ~ of sth** ne pas être conscient de qch; **he is ~ of his arrogance** il ne se rend pas compte de son arrogance c (*esp Psych*) [*desire, humour, bias*] inconscient; **on an ~ level** au niveau de l'inconscient; **the ~ mind** l'inconscient *m* 2 N (*Psych*) inconscient *m*

unconsciously [ʌnˈkɒnʃəslɪ] ADV [*copy, imitate, offend*] inconsciemment, sans s'en rendre compte; [*expect, resent*] inconsciemment; **~ jealous** inconsciemment jaloux; **he made an ~ funny remark** il a fait une remarque amusante sans s'en rendre compte

unconsciousness [ʌnˈkɒnʃəsnɪs] N (*NonC*) a (*Med*) perte *f* de connaissance; (*specifically fainting*) évanouissement *m* b (= *unawareness*) inconscience *f*

unconsidered [ˈʌnkənˈsɪdəd] ADJ a (= *hasty*) [*comment, decision, action*] inconsidéré b (= *unfancied*) [*horse*] dont on fait (*or* faisait) peu de cas

unconstitutional [ˈʌnˌkɒnstɪˈtjuːʃənl] ADJ inconstitutionnel, anticonstitutionnel; **to declare** *or* **rule sth ~** déclarer que qch est inconstitutionnel *or* anticonstitutionnel

unconstitutionally [ˈʌnˌkɒnstɪˈtjuːʃnəlɪ] ADV inconstitutionnellement, anticonstitutionnellement

unconstrained [ˈʌnkənˈstreɪnd] ADJ [*person*] non contraint, libre; [*behaviour*] aisé

unconsummated [ˈʌnˈkɒnsʌmeɪtəd] ADJ [*marriage, relationship etc*] non consommé

uncontested [ˈʌnkənˈtestɪd] ADJ incontesté; (*Parl*) [*seat*] non disputé, remporté sans opposition

uncontrollable [ˈʌnkənˈtrəʊləbl] ADJ [*person, behaviour, epidemic, inflation*] incontrôlable; [*desire, urge, emotion*] irrépressible; [*animal, situation, change*] impossible à maîtriser; [*bleeding*] impossible à arrêter; **~ fits of rage** emportements *mpl* incontrôlables; **he burst into ~ laughter** il a été pris d'un fou rire; **~ shivering** tremblements *mpl* incontrôlables; **to have an ~ temper** ne pas savoir se contrôler

uncontrollably [ˈʌnkənˈtrəʊləblɪ] ADV [*spread, increase*] de façon incontrôlable; [*cry, shake*] sans pouvoir s'arrêter; **to laugh ~** avoir le fou rire; **the fire raged ~** l'incendie faisait rage et ne pouvait être maîtrisé; **to swerve ~** faire une embardée incontrôlable

uncontrolled [ˈʌnkənˈtrəʊld] ADJ [*person, behaviour, anger, inflation*] incontrôlé; [*emotion, desire*] non réprimé; [*crying, sobbing*] non contenu; [*situation*] non maîtrisé; [*spending*] effréné

uncontroversial [ˈʌnˌkɒntrəˈvɜːʃəl] ADJ qui ne prête pas à controverse, non controversable

unconventional [ˈʌnkənˈvenʃənl] ADJ [*person, behaviour*] original, non conformiste; [*appearance, film, life*] original; [*method, opinion*] original, non conventionnel; [*education, upbringing*] non conventionnel

unconventionality [ˈʌnkənˌvenʃəˈnælɪtɪ] N originalité *f*, caractère *m* peu conventionnel

unconventionally [ˈʌnkənˈvenʃnəlɪ] ADV de manière peu conventionnelle

unconverted [ˈʌnkənˈvɜːtɪd] ADJ (*Fin, Rel, gen*) non converti

unconvinced [ˈʌnkənˈvɪnst] ADJ [*person*] qui n'est pas convaincu (**by sb/sth** par qn/qch, **of sth** de qch); [*tone*] sans conviction; **to be ~ that ...** ne pas être convaincu que ...; **to remain ~** n'être toujours pas convaincu

unconvincing [ˈʌnkənˈvɪnsɪŋ] ADJ peu convaincant

unconvincingly [ˈʌnkənˈvɪnsɪŋlɪ] ADV [*speak, argue*] de manière peu convaincante

uncooked [ˈʌnˈkʊkt] ADJ cru

uncool [ˈʌnˈkuːl] ADJ pas cool*

uncooperative [ˈʌnkəʊˈɒpərətɪv] ADJ peu coopératif

uncooperatively [ˈʌnkəʊˈɒpərətɪvlɪ] ADV de façon peu coopérative

uncoordinated [ˈʌnkəʊˈɔːdɪneɪtɪd] ADJ a (= *clumsy*) [*person*] mal coordonné b (= *lacking organization*) [*action*] qui manque de coordination

uncork [ˈʌnˈkɔːk] VT déboucher, enlever le bouchon de

uncorrected [ˈʌnkəˈrektɪd] ADJ non corrigé

uncorroborated [ˈʌnkəˈrɒbəreɪtɪd] ADJ non corroboré, sans confirmation

uncorrupted [ˈʌnkəˈrʌptɪd] ADJ non corrompu

uncountable [ˈʌnˈkaʊntəbl] 1 ADJ a (= *innumerable*) innombrable, incalculable b (*Ling*) **~ noun** nom *m* non dénombrable 2 N (*Ling*) nom *m* non dénombrable

uncounted [ˈʌnˈkaʊntɪd] ADJ qui n'a pas été compté; (*fig = innumerable*) innombrable

uncouple [ˈʌnˈkʌpl] VT [+ *carriage*] dételer; [+ *train, engine*] découpler; [+ *trailer*] détacher

uncouth [ˈʌnˈkuːθ] ADJ [*person, manners*] grossier, fruste; [*behaviour, remark*] grossier

uncover [ʌnˈkʌvəʳ] VT découvrir

uncovered [ʌnˈkʌvəd] ADJ a (= *without a cover*) découvert; **the stands are ~** les tribunes ne sont pas couvertes; **to leave sth ~** ne pas couvrir qch; **to leave a wound ~** laisser une plaie à l'air b (*Fin*) [*advance*] à découvert; [*cheque*] sans provision; **~ balance** découvert *m*

uncritical [ˈʌnˈkrɪtɪkəl] ADJ [*person*] peu critique; [*attitude, approach, report*] non critique; [*acceptance, support, adulation*] sans réserves; **to be ~ of sb/sth** manquer d'esprit critique à l'égard de qn/qch

uncritically [ˈʌnˈkrɪtɪkəlɪ] ADV [*accept, support*] sans réserves; [*report*] sans faire preuve d'esprit critique

uncross [ˈʌnˈkrɒs] VT décroiser

uncrossed [ˈʌnˈkrɒst] ADJ décroisé; [*cheque*] non barré

uncrowded [ˈʌnˈkraʊdɪd] ADJ où il n'y a pas trop de monde

uncrowned [ˈʌnˈkraʊnd] ADJ [*king, queen*] non couronné, sans couronne; **the ~ world champion** le champion du monde non encore sacré; (*fig*) **the ~ king of sth** le roi sans couronne de qch

uncrushable [ˈʌnˈkrʌʃəbl] ADJ [*fabric, dress*] infroissable; **he's quite ~** il ne se laisse jamais abattre

UNCTAD, Unctad [ˈʌŋktæd] N (ABBR = **United Nations Conference on Trade and Development**) CNUCED *f*

unction [ˈʌŋkʃən] N (*all senses*) onction *f*

unctuous [ˈʌŋktjʊəs] ADJ [*person, behaviour, tone*] mielleux, onctueux

unctuously [ˈʌŋktjʊəslɪ] ADV (*pej*) onctueusement, avec onction

unctuousness [ˈʌŋktjʊəsnɪs] N (*NonC: pej*) manières *fpl* onctueuses

uncultivated [ˈʌnˈkʌltɪveɪtɪd] ADJ a (*Agr*) [*land*] inculte b (= *uncultured*) [*person, mind*] inculte; [*voice, accent*] qui manque de raffinement

uncultured [ˈʌnˈkʌltʃəd] ADJ [*person*] inculte; [*voice, accent*] qui manque de raffinement

uncurl [ˈʌnˈkɜːl] 1 VT [+ *wire, snake*] dérouler; [+ *one's legs*] déplier; [+ *one's fingers*] étendre; **to ~ o.s.** [*person, cat*] s'étirer; **he ~ed himself from his chair** il s'est étiré et s'est levé de sa chaise 2 VI [*snake etc*] se dérouler

uncut [ˈʌnˈkʌt] ADJ a (= *still growing*) [*grass, tree, hair, nails*] non coupé; [*hedge, beard*] non taillé; [*crops*] sur pied; **to leave sth ~** ne pas couper qch b (= *not faceted*) [*diamond, sapphire*] non taillé c (= *unabridged*) [*film, play,*

novel] intégral, sans coupures; **to show a film ~** montrer un film dans sa version intégrale; **the ~ "Peer Gynt"** la version intégrale de « Peer Gynt » d (= *pure*) [*heroin, cocaine*] pur e (* = *not circumcised*) [*man, penis*] qui n'est pas circoncis

undamaged [ʌnˈdæmɪdʒd] ADJ [*goods, vehicle, building*] non endommagé, intact; [*plant*] non endommagé, intact; [*limb*] non atteint; [*reputation*] intact; (*Psych*) non affecté

undamped [ʌnˈdæmpt] ADJ (*fig*) [*enthusiasm, courage*] non refroidi, intact

undated [ʌnˈdeɪtɪd] ADJ non daté

undaunted [ʌnˈdɔːntɪd] ADJ **he carried on ~** il a continué sans se laisser démonter; **he was ~ by their threats** il ne se laissait pas intimider *or* démonter par leurs menaces

undeceive [ʌndɪˈsiːv] VT (*frm*) détromper, désabuser (*liter*)

undecided [ʌndɪˈsaɪdɪd] ADJ [*person*] indécis (**about** *or* **on sth** à propos de qch); [*question*] non résolu; [*weather*] incertain; **to remain ~** [*person*] demeurer indécis; **that is still ~** cela n'a pas encore été décidé; **I am ~ whether to go or not** je n'ai pas décidé si j'irai ou non

undeclared [ʌndɪˈklɛəd] ADJ (*Customs*) non déclaré

undefeated [ʌndɪˈfiːtɪd] ADJ invaincu

undefended [ʌndɪˈfendɪd] ADJ a (*Mil etc*) sans défense, non défendu b (*Jur*) [*suit*] où on ne se présente pas de défense, où le défendeur s'abstient de plaider

undefiled [ʌndɪˈfaɪld] ADJ (*liter: lit, fig*) pur, sans tache; **~ by any contact with ...** qui n'a pas été contaminé *or* souillé par le contact de ...

undefined [ʌndɪˈfaɪnd] ADJ [*word, condition*] non défini; [*sensation etc*] indéterminé, vague

undelete [ʌndɪˈliːt] VT (*Comput*) restaurer

undelivered [ʌndɪˈlɪvəd] ADJ non remis, non distribué; **"if ~ return to sender"** « en cas d'absence, prière de renvoyer à l'expéditeur »

undemanding [ʌndɪˈmɑːndɪŋ] ADJ [*person, work, book, film*] peu exigeant

undemocratic [ʌndeməˈkrætɪk] ADJ antidémocratique

undemonstrative [ʌndɪˈmɒnstrətɪv] ADJ réservé, peu démonstratif

undeniable [ʌndɪˈnaɪəbl] ADJ indéniable, incontestable

▼ **undeniably** [ʌndɪˈnaɪəblɪ] ADV incontestablement, indéniablement; **it is ~ true that ...** il est incontestable *or* indiscutable que ...

undenominational [ʌndɪˌnɒmɪˈneɪʃənl] ADJ non confessionnel

undependable [ʌndɪˈpendəbl] ADJ [*person*] peu fiable, sur qui on ne peut compter; [*information*] peu sûr; [*machine*] peu fiable

under [ˈʌndəʳ] 1 ADV a (= *beneath*) au-dessous, en dessous; **he stayed ~ for three minutes** (= *underwater*) il est resté sous l'eau pendant trois minutes; (= *under anaesthetic*) il est resté sous l'effet de l'anesthésie *or* il est resté anesthésié pendant trois minutes; (*Comm etc*) **as ~** comme ci-dessous; **he lifted the rope and crawled ~** il a soulevé la corde et il est passé dessous en rampant → **down¹**, **go under** b (= *less*) au-dessous; **children of 15 and ~** les enfants de moins de 16 ans; **ten degrees ~** dix degrés au-dessous de zéro

2 PREP a (= *beneath*) sous; **~ the table/sky/umbrella** sous la table/le ciel/le parapluie; **he came out from ~ the bed** il est sorti de dessous le lit; **the book slipped from ~ his arm** le livre a glissé de sous son bras; **it's ~ there** c'est là-dessous; **~ it** dessous; **he went and sat ~ it** il est allé s'asseoir dessous; **to stay ~ water** rester sous l'eau; **~ the microscope** au microscope → **breath**, **cover**, **wing** b (= *less than*) moins de; (*in series, rank, scale*

etc) au-dessous de; **to be ~ age** être mineur → **underage; children ~ 15** enfants *mpl* au-dessous de *or* de moins de 15 ans; **the ~-15s** *etc* les moins de 15 *etc* ans; **it sells at ~ £10** cela se vend à moins de 10 livres; **there were ~ 50 of them** il y en avait moins de 50; **any number ~ ten** un chiffre au-dessous de dix; **in ~ two hours** en moins de deux heures; **those ~ the rank of captain** ceux au-dessous du grade de capitaine

[c] (*gen, Pol: in system*) sous; **~ the Tudors** sous les Tudor; (*Mil etc*) **to serve ~ sb** servir sous les ordres de qn; **he had 50 men ~ him** il avait 50 hommes sous ses ordres; **~ the command of ...** sous les ordres de ...; **to study ~ sb** [*undergraduate*] suivre les cours de qn; [*postgraduate*] faire des recherches *or* travailler sous la direction de qn; [*painter, composer*] être l'élève de qn; **this department comes ~ his authority** cette section relève de sa compétence

[d] (*with names*) sous; **~ an assumed name** sous un faux nom; **you'll find him ~ "plumbers" in the phone book** vous le trouverez sous « plombiers » dans l'annuaire → **circumstance, control, impression, obligation, plain**

[e] (*Comput*) sous; **to run ~ Windows®** fonctionner sous Windows®

[f] (*Jur*) **~ sentence of death** condamné à mort

[g] (*Agr*) **~ wheat** en blé

[h] (= *according to*) selon; **~ French law** selon la législation française; **~ the terms of the contract** selon *or* suivant les termes du contrat; **~ his will** selon son testament; **~ article 25** en vertu de *or* conformément à l'article 25

[3] COMP ► **under-the-counter*** ADJ → **under-the-counter**

[4] PREF [a] (= *below*) sous- → **underfloor, undersea**
[b] (= *insufficiently*) sous-; **~nourished** sous-alimenté; **~used/appreciated** *etc* qui n'est pas assez utilisé/apprécié *etc* → **undercharge, undercooked**
[c] (= *junior*) sous-; **~-gardener** aide-jardinier *m* → **under-secretary**

underachieve [ˌʌndərəˈtʃiːv] VI (*Scol*) être sous-performant, obtenir des résultats décevants

underachiever [ˌʌndərəˈtʃiːvə] N (*Scol*) élève *mf* sous-performant(e) *or* qui obtient des résultats décevants

underage [ˌʌndərˈeɪdʒ] ADJ [*person*] mineur; **~ drinking** consommation *f* d'alcool par les mineurs

underarm [ˈʌndərɑːm] [1] ADV (*Sport etc*) [*throw, bowl*] par en-dessous [2] ADJ [a] [*throw etc*] par en-dessous [b] [*deodorant*] pour les aisselles; [*hair*] des aisselles, sous les bras; **~ odour** odeur *f* de transpiration (des aisselles)

underbade [ˌʌndəˈbeɪd] VB *pt of* **underbid**

underbelly [ˈʌndəbelɪ] N (*Anat*) bas-ventre *m*; (*fig*) **the (soft) ~** le point vulnérable

underbid [ˌʌndəˈbɪd] (*pret* **underbade** *or* **underbid**, *ptp* **underbidden** *or* **underbid**) VTI (*Bridge: also* **~ one's hand**) annoncer au-dessous de sa force

underbody [ˈʌndəbɒdɪ] N (*Aut*) dessous *m* de caisse

underbrush [ˈʌndəbrʌʃ] N (*NonC: US*) sous-bois *m inv*, broussailles *fpl*

undercapitalized [ˌʌndəˈkæpɪtəlaɪzd] ADJ **to be ~** [*businessman*] ne pas disposer de fonds suffisants; [*project*] ne pas être doté de fonds suffisants

undercarriage [ˈʌndəkærɪdʒ] N (*Aviat*) train *m* d'atterrissage

undercharge [ˌʌndəˈtʃɑːdʒ] VT ne pas faire payer assez à; **he ~d me by £2** il aurait dû me faire payer 2 livres de plus

underclass [ˈʌndəklɑːs] N (*in society*) classe *f* (sociale) très défavorisée

underclassman [ˈʌndəˈklɑːsmən] N (*pl* **-men**) (*US Univ*) étudiant *m* de première *or* deuxième année

underclothes [ˈʌndəkləʊðz] NPL, **underclothing** [ˈʌndəkləʊðɪŋ] N (*NonC*) = **underwear**

undercoat [ˈʌndəkəʊt] N [*of paint*] couche *f* de fond; (*US Aut*) couche *f* antirouille (du châssis)

undercoating [ˈʌndəkəʊtɪŋ] N (*NonC: US Aut*) couche *f* antirouille (du châssis)

undercooked [ˌʌndəˈkʊkt] ADJ pas assez cuit

undercover [ˌʌndəˈkʌvə] ADJ secret (-ète *f*), clandestin; **~ agent** agent *m* secret; **~ policeman** policier *m* en civil

undercurrent [ˈʌndəˌkʌrənt] N (*in sea*) courant *m* (sous-marin); (*fig: feeling etc*) courant *m* sous-jacent

undercut [ˌʌndəˈkʌt] (*pret, ptp* **undercut**) [1] VT [a] (*Comm* = *sell cheaper than*) [+ *competitor*] vendre moins cher que [b] (*fig, esp Econ* = *undermine, reduce*) [+ *the dollar, incomes*] réduire la valeur de; **inflation ~s spending power** l'inflation réduit le pouvoir d'achat [c] (*Sport*) [+ *ball*] couper [2] N (*Culin*) (morceau *m* de) filet *m*

underdeveloped [ˌʌndədɪˈveləpt] ADJ (*Econ*) sous-développé; [*heart, lungs etc of foetus*] qui n'est pas complètement développé *or* formé; (*Phot*) insuffisamment développé

underdog [ˈʌndədɒg] N **the ~** (*in game, fight*) le perdant (*or* la perdante); (= *predicted loser*) celui (*or* celle) qui on donne perdant(e); (*economically, socially*) l'opprimé *m*

underdone [ˌʌndəˈdʌn] ADJ [*food*] pas assez cuit; (*Brit*) [*steak etc*] saignant

underdressed [ˌʌndəˈdrest] ADJ **to be ~** ne pas être assez bien habillé

underemphasize [ˌʌndərˈemfəsaɪz] VT ne pas donner l'importance nécessaire à

underemployed [ˌʌndərɪmˈplɔɪd] ADJ [*person, equipment, building*] sous-employé; [*resources*] sous-exploité; **I'm ~ half the time** bien souvent je suis sous-employé *or* je ne suis pas assez occupé

underemployment [ˌʌndərɪmˈplɔɪmənt] N [*of person, equipment, building*] sous-emploi *m*; [*of resources*] sous-exploitation *f*

underestimate [ˌʌndərˈestɪmɪt] [1] N sous-estimation *f* [2] VT [ˌʌndərˈestɪmeɪt] [+ *size, numbers, strength*] sous-estimer; [+ *person*] sous-estimer, mésestimer

underestimation [ˌʌndərestɪˈmeɪʃən] N sous-estimation *f*

underexpose [ˌʌndərɪksˈpəʊz] VT (*Phot*) sous-exposer

underexposed [ˌʌndərɪksˈpəʊzd] ADJ (*Phot*) sous-exposé

underexposure [ˌʌndərɪksˈpəʊʒə] N (*Phot*) sous-exposition *f*

underfed [ˌʌndəˈfed] [1] VB *pt, ptp of* **underfeed** [2] ADJ sous-alimenté

underfeed [ˌʌndəˈfiːd] (*pret, ptp* **underfed**) VT sous-alimenter

underfeeding [ˌʌndəˈfiːdɪŋ] N sous-alimentation *f*

underfelt [ˈʌndəfelt] N [*of carpet*] thibaude *f*

underfinanced [ˌʌndəfaɪˈnænst] ADJ **to be ~** [*businessman*] ne pas disposer de fonds suffisants; [*project etc*] ne pas être doté de fonds suffisants

underfloor [ˈʌndəflɔː] ADJ (*gen*) [*pipes etc*] qui se trouve sous le plancher *or* le sol; **~ heating** chauffage *m* par le plancher *or* par le sol

underflow [ˈʌndəfləʊ] N (*in sea*) courant *m* (sous-marin); (*fig: feeling etc*) courant *m* sous-jacent

underfoot [ˈʌndəˈfʊt] ADV (*gen*) sous les pieds; **to crush** *or* **trample sth ~** fouler qch aux pieds; **it is wet ~** le sol est humide

underfunded [ˌʌndəˈfʌndɪd] ADJ **to be ~** [*businessman*] ne pas disposer de fonds suffisants; [*project etc*] ne pas être doté de fonds suffisants

underfunding [ˌʌndəˈfʌndɪŋ] N insuffisance *f* de financement

undergarment [ˈʌndəgɑːmənt] N sous-vêtement *m*

undergo [ˈʌndəˈgəʊ] (*pret* **underwent**, *ptp* **undergone** [ˈʌndəˈgɒn]) VT [+ *test, change, modification, operation, medical examination*] subir; [+ *suffering*] éprouver; [+ *medical treatment*] suivre; **it is ~ing repairs** c'est en réparation

undergrad* [ˈʌndəgræd] N, ADJ (*esp Brit*) = **undergraduate**

undergraduate [ˌʌndəˈgrædjʊɪt] (*esp Brit*) [1] N étudiant(e) *m(f)* (qui prépare la licence) [2] ADJ [*life, circles*] étudiant, estudiantin; [*room, income*] d'étudiant; [*grant*] d'études; [*opinion*] des étudiants; [*course*] pour étudiants de licence

underground [ˈʌndəgraʊnd] [1] ADJ [a] [*work*] sous terre, souterrain; [*explosion, cable*] souterrain; **~ car park** parking *m* souterrain; **~ railway** métro *m*; (*fig: US Hist: for slaves*) **the ~ railroad** filière clandestine pour aider les esclaves noirs à fuir le Sud [b] (*fig*) [*organization*] clandestin, secret (-ète *f*); [*press*] clandestin; (*Art, Cine*) underground *inv*, d'avant-garde; (*fig*) **~ movement** mouvement *m* clandestin; (*in occupied country*) résistance *f* [2] ADV sous (la) terre; [*fig*] clandestinement, secrètement; **it is 3 metres ~** c'est à 3 mètres sous (la) terre; **to go ~** [*wanted man*] entrer dans la clandestinité; [*guerilla*] prendre le maquis [3] N (*Brit* = *railway*) métro *m*; **by ~** en métro; **the ~** (*Mil, Pol etc*) la résistance; (*Art etc*) mouvement *m* underground *or* d'avant-garde

undergrowth [ˈʌndəgrəʊθ] N (*NonC*) broussailles *fpl*, sous-bois *m inv*

underhand [ˌʌndəˈhænd], **underhanded** (*US*) [ˌʌndəˈhændɪd] ADJ (*pej*) sournois; **~ trick** fourberie *f*

underhandedly [ˌʌndəˈhændɪdlɪ] ADV (*pej*) sournoisement

underinsure [ˌʌndərɪnˈʃʊə] VT sous-assurer; **to be ~d** être sous-assuré, ne pas être suffisamment assuré

underinvest [ˌʌndərɪnˈvest] VI (*Econ, Fin*) sous-investir

underinvestment [ˌʌndərɪnˈvestmənt] N (*Econ, Fin*) sous-investissement *m*

underlain [ˌʌndəˈleɪn] VB *ptp of* **underlie**

underlay [ˌʌndəˈleɪ] [1] VB *pt of* **underlie** [2] N [ˈʌndəleɪ] (*esp Brit*) [*of carpet*] thibaude *f*

underlie [ˌʌndəˈlaɪ] (*pret* **underlay**, *ptp* **underlain**) VT être à la base de, sous-tendre

▼ **underline** [ˌʌndəˈlaɪn] VT (*lit, fig*) souligner

underling [ˈʌndəlɪŋ] N (*pej*) subalterne *m*, sous-fifre* *m inv* (*pej*)

underlining [ˈʌndəlaɪnɪŋ] N (*NonC*) soulignage *m*, soulignement *m*

underlip [ˈʌndəlɪp] N lèvre *f* inférieure

underlying [ˌʌndəˈlaɪɪŋ] ADJ (*gen, Gram, Jur*) sous-jacent

undermanned [ˌʌndəˈmænd] ADJ en sous-effectif

undermentioned [ˌʌndəˈmenʃənd] ADJ (*cité*) ci-dessous

undermine [ˌʌndəˈmaɪn] VT [a] (*lit*) [+ *cliffs*] miner, saper [b] (*fig*) [+ *influence, power, authority*] saper, ébranler; [+ *health*] miner, user; [+ *effect*] amoindrir

undermost [ˈʌndəməʊst] ADJ le plus bas

underneath [ˌʌndəˈniːθ] [1] PREP sous, au-dessous de; **stand ~ it** mettez-vous dessous; **from ~ the table** de dessous la table [2] ADV (en) dessous; **the one ~** celui d'en dessous [3] ADJ d'en dessous [4] N dessous *m*

► **LANGUAGE IN USE:** underline 26.1

undernourish [ˌʌndəˈnʌrɪʃ] VT sous-alimenter

undernourished [ˌʌndəˈnʌrɪʃt] ADJ sous-alimenté

undernourishment [ˌʌndəˈnʌrɪʃmənt] N sous-alimentation f

underoccupied [ˌʌndərˈɒkjʊpaɪd] ADJ [person] qui n'a pas assez à faire

underpaid [ˌʌndəˈpeɪd] 1 VB pt, ptp of **underpay** 2 ADJ sous-payé

underpants [ˈʌndəpænts] NPL slip m

underpart [ˈʌndəpɑːt] N partie f inférieure

underpass [ˈʌndəpɑːs] N (for cars) passage m inférieur (de l'autoroute); (for pedestrians) passage m souterrain

underpay [ˌʌndəˈpeɪ] (pret, ptp **underpaid**) VT sous-payer

underperform [ˌʌndəpəˈfɔːm] VI (St Ex) mal se comporter, faire une contre-performance; **the stock has ~ed on the Brussels stock market** le titre ne s'est pas comporté comme il aurait dû à la Bourse de Bruxelles

underpin [ˌʌndəˈpɪn] VT [a] [+ wall] étayer; [+ building] reprendre en sous-œuvre [b] (fig) **the philosophy that ~s his work** la philosophie sur laquelle son œuvre est fondée

underpinning [ˌʌndəˈpɪnɪŋ] N (Constr) étayage m; [of building] reprise f en sous-œuvre; (fig) bases fpl

underplay [ˌʌndəˈpleɪ] VT (gen) minimiser, réduire l'importance de; **he rather ~ed it** il n'a pas insisté là-dessus, il a minimisé la chose; (Theat) **to ~ a role** jouer un rôle avec beaucoup de retenue

underpopulated [ˌʌndəˈpɒpjʊleɪtɪd] ADJ sous-peuplé

underprice [ˌʌndəˈpraɪs] VT mettre un prix trop bas à

underpriced [ˌʌndəˈpraɪst] ADJ [goods] en vente à un prix inférieur à sa vraie valeur; **at £8 this wine is ~** à 8 livres, ce vin n'est pas assez cher

underpricing [ˌʌndəˈpraɪsɪŋ] N tarification f trop basse

underprivileged [ˌʌndəˈprɪvɪlɪdʒd] 1 ADJ défavorisé 2 **the underprivileged** NPL les défavorisés mpl

underproduce [ˌʌndəprəˈdjuːs] VTI (Econ, Ind) sous-produire

underproduction [ˌʌndəprəˈdʌkʃən] N (Econ, Ind) sous-production f

underqualified [ˈʌndəˈkwɒlɪfaɪd] ADJ sous-qualifié (**for** pour)

underrate [ˌʌndəˈreɪt] VT [+ size, numbers, strength] sous-estimer; [+ person] sous-estimer, méconnaître

underrated [ˌʌndəˈreɪtɪd] ADJ [play, book, actor] sous-estimé, méconnu; **he's very ~** on ne l'estime pas à sa juste valeur

underreact [ˌʌndəriːˈækt] VI réagir mollement

underreaction [ˌʌndəriːˈækʃən] N réaction f molle

underripe [ˌʌndəˈraɪp] ADJ [fruit] vert, qui n'est pas mûr; [cheese] qui n'est pas fait

underscore [ˌʌndəˈskɔːʳ] VT (lit) souligner; (fig) souligner, mettre en évidence

underscoring [ˌʌndəˈskɔːrɪŋ] N (NonC) (lit) [of text, words] soulignage m; (fig) insistance f (**of** sur)

undersea [ˈʌndəsiː] ADJ sous-marin

underseal [ˈʌndəsiːl] (Brit Aut) 1 VT [+ car] traiter contre la rouille (au niveau du châssis) 2 N couche f antirouille (du châssis)

undersealing [ˈʌndəsiːlɪŋ] N (Brit Aut) couche f antirouille (du châssis)

under-secretary [ˌʌndəˈsekrətrɪ] 1 N sous-secrétaire mf 2 COMP ▶ **Under-Secretary of State** N sous-secrétaire mf d'État

undersell [ˌʌndəˈsel] (pret, ptp **undersold**) VT [a] (= undercut) [+ competitor] vendre moins

---

cher que [b] (fig) **to ~ o.s.** ne pas savoir se mettre en valeur or se vendre*

undersexed [ˌʌndəˈsekst] ADJ (= having a low sex drive) de faible libido; **to be ~** avoir une faible libido

undershirt [ˈʌndəʃɜːt] N (US) maillot m de corps

undershoot [ˌʌndəˈʃuːt] (pret, ptp **undershot**) VT (Aviat) **to ~ the runway** atterrir avant d'atteindre la piste

undershorts [ˈʌndəʃɔːts] NPL (US) caleçon m

undershot [ˌʌndəˈʃɒt] 1 VB pt, ptp of **undershoot** 2 ADJ [water wheel] à aubes

underside [ˈʌndəsaɪd] N dessous m

undersigned [ˈʌndəsaɪnd] ADJ, N (Jur, frm) soussigné(e) m(f); **I, the ~, declare ...** je soussigné(e) déclare ...

undersized [ˌʌndəˈsaɪzd] ADJ de (trop) petite taille, trop petit

underskirt [ˈʌndəskɜːt] N jupon m

undersling [ˌʌndəˈslʌŋ] ADJ [car] surbaissé

undersoil [ˈʌndəsɔɪl] N sous-sol m (Agr)

undersold [ˌʌndəˈsəʊld] VB pt, ptp of **undersell**

underspending [ˌʌndəˈspendɪŋ] N (Admin) fait m de ne pas dépenser entièrement les crédits disponibles

understaffed [ˌʌndəˈstɑːft] ADJ en sous-effectif

▼ **understand** [ˌʌndəˈstænd] (pret, ptp **understood**) 1 VT [a] [+ person, words, meaning, painting, difficulty, action, event etc] comprendre; **I can't ~ his attitude** je n'arrive pas à comprendre son attitude; **that's what I can't ~** voilà ce que je ne comprends pas or ce qui me dépasse; **I can't ~ it!** je ne comprends pas!; **I can't ~ a word of it** je n'y comprends rien; **I don't ~ the way she behaved/reacted** je ne comprends pas or je ne m'explique pas son comportement/sa réaction; **as I ~ it,** ... si je comprends bien, ...; **this can be understood in several ways** cela peut se comprendre de plusieurs façons; **that is easily understood** c'est facile à comprendre, cela se comprend facilement; **do you ~ why/how/what?** est-ce que vous comprenez pourquoi/comment/ce que?; **I can't ~ his agreeing to do it** je n'arrive pas à comprendre or je ne m'explique pas qu'il ait accepté de le faire; **to make o.s. understood** se faire comprendre; **do I make myself understood?** est-ce que je me fais bien comprendre?; **that's quite understood!** c'est entendu!; **I quite ~ that you don't want to come** je comprends très bien que vous n'ayez pas envie de venir; **it must be understood that ...** il faut (bien) comprendre que ...; (frm) **it being understood that your client is responsible** à condition que votre client accepte (subj) la responsabilité
[b] (= believe) (croire) comprendre; **I understood we were to be paid** j'ai cru comprendre que nous devions être payés; **I ~ you are leaving today** il paraît que vous partez aujourd'hui, si je comprends bien vous partez aujourd'hui; **she refused — so I ~** elle a refusé — c'est ce que j'ai cru comprendre; (frm: in business letter etc) **we confirm our reservation and we ~ (that) the rental will be ...** nous confirmons notre réservation, étant entendu que la location s'élèvera à ...; **am I to ~ that ...?** dois-je comprendre que ...?; **she is understood to have left the country** ◊ **it is understood that she has left the country** il paraît qu'elle a quitté le pays, elle aurait quitté le pays; **he let it be understood that ...** il a donné à entendre or a laissé entendre que ...; **we were given to ~ that ...** on nous a donné à entendre que ..., on nous a fait comprendre que ...
[c] (= imply, assume) [+ word etc] sous-entendre; **to be understood** [arrangement, price, date] ne pas être spécifié; (Gram) être sous-entendu; **it was understood that he**

---

would pay for it (= it was assumed) on présumait qu'il le paierait; (= it was agreed) il était entendu qu'il le paierait
[d] (= relate to, empathize with) comprendre; **my wife doesn't ~ me** ma femme ne me comprend pas

2 VI comprendre; **now I ~!** je comprends or j'y suis maintenant!; **there's to be no noise, (do you) ~!** or **is that understood?** pas de bruit, c'est bien compris or tu entends!; **he was a widower, I ~** il était veuf, si j'ai bien compris or si je ne me trompe (pas)

▼ **understandable** [ˌʌndəˈstændəbl] ADJ [a] (= intelligible) [person, speech] compréhensible, intelligible [b] (= justifiable) [behaviour] compréhensible; [pride, sorrow] compréhensible, naturel; **it is ~ that ...** on comprend or il est normal que ... (+ subj); **that's ~** ça se comprend

understandably [ˌʌndəˈstændəblɪ] ADV [a] (= intelligibly) [speak, explain] d'une façon compréhensible [b] (= naturally, of course) naturellement; (= rightly) à juste titre; **~, he refused** il a refusé, naturellement or comme on pouvait s'y attendre or et ça se comprend; **he's ~ angry** il est furieux, et à juste titre or et ça se comprend

understanding [ˌʌndəˈstændɪŋ] 1 ADJ [person] compréhensif (**about** à propos de); [smile, look] compatissant, bienveillant
2 N [a] (NonC) compréhension f; **his ~ of the problems/of children** sa compréhension des problèmes/des enfants, sa faculté de comprendre les problèmes/les enfants; **he had a good ~ of the problems** il comprenait bien les problèmes; **it is my ~ that ...** d'après ce que j'ai compris, ...; **the age of ~** l'âge m de discernement; **it's beyond ~** cela dépasse l'entendement
[b] (= agreement) accord m; (= arrangement) arrangement m; **to come to an ~ with sb** s'entendre or s'arranger avec qn; **the president has an ~ with the military commanders** le président s'est entendu avec les chefs militaires; **there is an ~ between us that ...** il est entendu entre nous que ...; **on the ~ that ...** à condition que ... (+ subj)
[c] (NonC: = concord) entente f, bonne intelligence f; **this will encourage ~ between our nations** ceci favorisera l'entente entre nos nations

understandingly [ˌʌndəˈstændɪŋlɪ] ADV avec bienveillance, en faisant preuve de compréhension

understate [ˌʌndəˈsteɪt] VT minimiser, réduire l'importance de

understated [ˌʌndəˈsteɪtɪd] ADJ (gen) discret (-ète f); [fashion detail] discret (-ète f), d'une élégance discrète; **an ~ black dress** une petite robe noire toute simple

understatement [ˈʌndəˌsteɪtmənt] N affirmation f en dessous de la vérité; (Ling) litote f; **to say he is clever is rather an ~** c'est peu dire qu'il est intelligent; **that's an ~** c'est peu dire, le terme est faible; **that's the ~ of the year!*** c'est bien le moins qu'on puisse dire!

understeer [ˈʌndəˌstɪəʳ] VI braquer insuffisamment

understood [ˌʌndəˈstʊd] VB pt, ptp of **understand**

understudy [ˈʌndəstʌdɪ] (Theat) 1 N doublure f 2 VT [+ actor] doubler; [+ part] doubler un acteur dans

undersubscribed [ˌʌndəsəbˈskraɪbd] (St Ex) ADJ non couvert, non entièrement souscrit

undertake [ˌʌndəˈteɪk] (pret **undertook**, ptp **undertaken**) 1 VT [+ task] entreprendre; [+ duty] se charger de; [+ responsibility] assumer; [+ obligation] contracter; **to ~ to do sth** promettre or se charger de faire qch, s'engager à faire qch 2 VTI (Brit Aut*) dépasser du mauvais côté

---

undertaker [ˈʌndəteɪkəʳ] N (*Brit*) entrepreneur *m or* ordonnateur *m* des pompes funèbres ; **the ~'s** les pompes *fpl* funèbres, le service des pompes funèbres

undertaking [ˌʌndəˈteɪkɪŋ] N **a** (= *task, operation*) entreprise *f* ; **it is quite an ~ (to do** or **doing)** ce n'est pas une mince affaire (que de faire) **b** (= *promise*) promesse *f*, engagement *m* ; **to give an ~** promettre (**that** que, **to do** de faire) ; **I can give no such ~** je ne peux rien promettre de la sorte **c** [ˈʌndəˌteɪkɪŋ] (*NonC: Brit Aut:**) dépassement *m* du mauvais côté **d** [ˈʌndəˌteɪkɪŋ] (*NonC: Brit = arranging funerals*) pompes *fpl* funèbres

undertax [ˌʌndəˈtæks] VT [+ *goods*] taxer insuffisamment ; **he was ~ed by £5,000** on lui a fait payer 5 000 livres d'impôts de moins qu'on ne l'aurait dû

under-the-counter* [ˌʌndəðəˈkaʊntəʳ] ADJ clandestin, en douce ; **it was all very ~** tout se faisait sous le manteau *or* en sous-main → **counter¹**

underthings* [ˈʌndəθɪŋz] NPL dessous *mpl*

undertone [ˈʌndətəʊn] N **a** **to say sth in an ~** dire qch à mi-voix **b** (= *suggestion, hint*) sous-entendu *m* ; **political/racial/sexual ~s** sous-entendus *mpl* politiques/raciaux/sexuels ; **there are no sinister ~s to his comments** il n'y a aucun sous-entendu sinistre dans ses commentaires ; **an ~ of criticism** des critiques voilées *or* sous-jacentes **c** [*of perfume, taste, colour*] nuance *f* ; **brown with pinkish ~s** marron avec des nuances de rose

undertook [ˌʌndəˈtʊk] VB *pt of* **undertake**

undertow [ˈʌndətəʊ] N **a** (*lit*) courant *m* sous-marin (*provoqué par le retrait de la vague*) **b** (*fig*) tension *f*

underuse [ˌʌndəˈjuːz] **1** VT = **underutilize** **2** [ˌʌndəˈjuːs] N = **underutilization**

underused [ˌʌndəˈjuːzd] ADJ = **underutilized**

underutilization [ˌʌndəjuːtɪlaɪˈzeɪʃən] N [*of potential, talent, resources, land*] sous-exploitation *f* ; [*of space, facilities, equipment*] sous-utilisation *f*, sous-emploi *m*

underutilize [ˌʌndəˈjuːtɪlaɪz] VT [+ *potential, talent, resources, land*] sous-exploiter ; [+ *space, facilities, equipment*] sous-utiliser, sous-employer

underutilized [ˌʌndəˈjuːtɪlaɪzd] ADJ [*potential, talent, resources, land*] sous-exploité ; [*space, facilities, equipment*] sous-utilisé, sous-employé

undervalue [ˌʌndəˈvæljuː] VT [+ *help, contribution*] sous-estimer ; [+ *person*] sous-estimer, mésestimer

undervalued [ˌʌndəˈvæljuːd] ADJ [*person, helper, help, contribution*] sous-estimé ; **this house is ~** cette maison vaut plus que son prix ; **it's ~ by about £1,000** cela vaut environ 1 000 livres de plus

undervest [ˈʌndəvest] N maillot *m* de corps

underwater [ˌʌndəˈwɔːtəʳ] **1** ADJ sous-marin **2** ADV sous l'eau

underway, **under way** [ˌʌndəˈweɪ] ADJ **to be ~** (*Naut*) faire route, être en route ; (*fig*) [*talks, search, process, campaign*] être en cours ; **the investigation is now ~** l'enquête est en cours ; **to get ~** (*Naut*) appareiller, lever l'ancre ; [*talks, conference, campaign, festival*] démarrer ; [*process, reforms, programme*] être mis en œuvre

underwear [ˈʌndəwɛəʳ] N (*NonC*) sous-vêtements *mpl* ; (*women's only*) dessous *mpl*, lingerie *f* (*NonC*)

underweight [ˌʌndəˈweɪt] ADJ **a** [*person*] **to be ~** ne pas peser assez, être trop maigre ; **she's 20lb ~** elle pèse 9 kilos de moins qu'elle ne devrait **b** [*goods*] d'un poids insuffisant ; **it's 50 grams ~** il manque 50 grammes

underwent [ˌʌndəˈwent] VB *pt of* **undergo**

underwhelming [ˌʌndəˈwelmɪŋ] ADJ (*hum*) décevant

underwired [ˌʌndəˈwaɪəd] ADJ [*bra*] à armature

underworld [ˈʌndəwɜːld] **1** N **a** (*Myth = hell*) **the ~** les enfers *mpl* **b** (*criminal*) **the ~** le milieu, la pègre **2** COMP [*organization, personality*] du milieu ; [*connections*] avec le milieu ; [*attack*] organisé par le milieu

underwrite [ˌʌndəˈraɪt] (*pret* **underwrote**, *ptp* **underwritten**) VT **a** (*Insurance*) [+ *policy*] réassurer ; [+ *risk*] assurer contre, garantir ; [+ *amount*] garantir [*St Ex*] [+ *share issue*] garantir (une *or* l'émission de) **c** (*Comm, Fin*) [+ *project, enterprise*] soutenir *or* appuyer (financièrement) **d** (= *support*) [+ *decision, statement etc*] soutenir, souscrire à

underwriter [ˈʌndəˌraɪtəʳ] N **a** (*Insurance*) assureur *m* **b** (*St Ex*) syndicataire *mf*

underwritten [ˌʌndəˈrɪtn] VB *ptp of* **underwrite**

underwrote [ˌʌndəˈrəʊt] VB *pt of* **underwrite**

undeserved [ˌʌndɪˈzɜːvd] ADJ immérité

undeservedly [ˌʌndɪˈzɜːvɪdlɪ] ADV [*reward, punish*] à tort, indûment ; [*be rewarded, punished*] sans l'avoir mérité, indûment

undeserving [ˌʌndɪˈzɜːvɪŋ] ADJ [*person*] peu méritant ; [*cause*] peu méritoire ; **~ of sth** indigne de qch, qui ne mérite pas qch

undesirable [ˌʌndɪˈzaɪərəbl] **1** ADJ peu souhaitable ; (*stronger*) indésirable ; **it is ~ that ...** il est peu souhaitable que ... (+ *subj*) ; (*Admin, Jur*) **~ alien** étranger *m*, -ère *f* indésirable **2** N indésirable *mf*

undetected [ˌʌndɪˈtektɪd] ADJ non décelé, non détecté ; **to go ~** passer inaperçu, ne pas être repéré ; **to do sth ~** faire qch sans se faire repérer

undetermined [ˌʌndɪˈtɜːmɪnd] ADJ (= *unknown*) indéterminé, non connu ; (= *uncertain*) irrésolu, indécis

undeterred [ˌʌndɪˈtɜːd] ADJ non découragé ; **to carry on ~** continuer sans se laisser décourager

undeveloped [ˌʌndɪˈveləpt] ADJ [*fruit, intelligence, part of body*] qui ne s'est pas développé ; [*film*] non développé ; [*land, resources*] non exploité

undeviating [ʌnˈdiːvɪeɪtɪŋ] ADJ [*path*] droit ; [*policy, course*] constant

undiagnosed [ˌʌnˈdaɪəgnəʊzd] ADJ (*lit, fig*) non diagnostiqué

undid [ʌnˈdɪd] VB *pt of* **undo**

undies* [ˈʌndɪz] NPL dessous *mpl* ; (*women's only*) lingerie *f* (*NonC*)

undigested [ˌʌndaɪˈdʒestɪd] ADJ non digéré

undignified [ʌnˈdɪgnɪfaɪd] ADJ qui manque de dignité ; **how ~!** quel manque de dignité !

undiluted [ˌʌndaɪˈluːtɪd] ADJ **a** (*lit*) [*concentrate*] non dilué **b** (*fig*) [*pleasure*] sans mélange ; [*nonsense*] pur

undiminished [ˌʌndɪˈmɪnɪʃt] ADJ non diminué

undimmed [ʌnˈdɪmd] ADJ **a** (*in brightness*) [*lamp*] qui n'a pas été mis en veilleuse ; [*car headlight*] qui n'est pas en code ; [*colour, metal*] non terni **b** (*liter*) [*sight*] aussi bon qu'auparavant **c** (*fig*) [*enthusiasm, passion, ambition*] aussi fort qu'avant ; [*beauty*] non terni ; **with ~ optimism** avec toujours autant d'optimisme ; **her optimism is ~** elle est toujours aussi optimiste ; **my memory of it is ~** je m'en souviens avec précision

undiplomatic [ˌʌnˌdɪpləˈmætɪk] ADJ [*person*] peu diplomate ; [*action, answer*] peu diplomatique

undipped [ʌnˈdɪpt] ADJ [*car headlight*] qui n'est pas en code

undiscerning [ˌʌndɪˈsɜːnɪŋ] ADJ qui manque de discernement

undischarged [ˌʌndɪsˈtʃɑːdʒd] ADJ [*bankrupt*] non réhabilité ; [*debt*] non acquitté, impayé

undisciplined [ʌnˈdɪsɪplɪnd] ADJ indiscipliné

undisclosed [ˌʌndɪsˈkləʊzd] ADJ non révélé, non divulgué

undiscovered [ˌʌndɪsˈkʌvəd] ADJ (= *not found*) non découvert ; (= *unknown*) inconnu ; **the treasure remained ~ for 700 years** le trésor n'a été découvert que 700 ans plus tard

undiscriminating [ˌʌndɪsˈkrɪmɪneɪtɪŋ] ADJ qui manque de discernement

undisguised [ˌʌndɪsˈgaɪzd] ADJ (*lit, fig*) non déguisé

undismayed [ˌʌndɪsˈmeɪd] ADJ imperturbable

undisputed [ˌʌndɪsˈpjuːtɪd] ADJ incontesté

undistinguished [ˌʌndɪsˈtɪŋgwɪʃt] ADJ (*in character*) médiocre, quelconque ; (*in appearance*) peu distingué

undisturbed [ˌʌndɪsˈtɜːbd] **1** ADJ **a** (= *untouched*) [*papers, clues*] non dérangé, non déplacé ; (= *uninterrupted*) [*sleep*] non troublé, paisible **b** (= *unworried*) non inquiet (-ète *f*), calme ; **he was ~ by the news** la nouvelle ne l'a pas inquiété **2** ADV [*work, play, sleep*] sans être dérangé

undivided [ˌʌndɪˈvaɪdɪd] ADJ **a** (= *wholehearted*) [*admiration*] sans réserve, sans partage ; **to require sb's ~ attention** exiger toute l'attention *or* l'attention pleine et entière de qn **b** (= *not split*) [*country, institution*] uni ; (*Jur*) [*property*] indivis

undo [ˈʌnˈduː] (*pret* **undid**, *ptp* **undone**) VT [+ *button, garment, knot, parcel, box, knitting*] défaire ; [+ *good effect*] détruire, annuler ; [+ *mischief, wrong*] réparer ; (*Comput*) annuler ; **he was undone by his own ambition** c'est son ambition qui l'a perdu ; **they were undone by a goal from Barnes** ils ont été battus grâce à un but de Barnes → **undone**

undocumented [ʌnˈdɒkjʊmentɪd] ADJ **a** [*event*] sur lequel on ne possède pas de témoignages **b** (*US*) [*person*] sans papiers

undoing [ʌnˈduːɪŋ] N (*NonC*) ruine *f*, perte *f* ; **that was his ~** c'est ce qui l'a perdu, c'est ce qui a causé sa perte

undomesticated [ˌʌndəˈmestɪkeɪtɪd] ADJ **a** [*animal*] non domestiqué **b** [*person*] qui n'aime pas les tâches ménagères

undone [ˈʌnˈdʌn] **1** VB *ptp of* **undo** **2** ADJ [*button, garment, knot, parcel*] défait ; [*task*] non accompli ; **to come ~** se défaire ; **to leave sth ~** ne pas faire qch ; (†† *or hum*) **I am ~!** je suis perdu !

undoubted [ʌnˈdaʊtɪd] ADJ indubitable, indéniable

▼**undoubtedly** [ʌnˈdaʊtɪdlɪ] ADV indubitablement, sans aucun doute

undramatic [ˌʌndrəˈmætɪk] ADJ peu dramatique

undreamed-of [ʌnˈdriːmdɒv], **undreamt-of** [ʌnˈdremtɒv] ADJ (= *unhoped for*) inespéré ; (= *unsuspected*) insoupçonné, qui dépasse l'imagination

undress [ʌnˈdres] **1** VT déshabiller ; **to get ~ed** se déshabiller → **undressed 2** VI se déshabiller **3** N **in a state of ~** (*gen*) en petite tenue ; (*also Mil*) (*in civilian clothes*) en civil ; (*in plain uniform*) en simple uniforme

undressed [ʌnˈdrest] **1** VB *pret, ptp of* **undress 2** ADJ **a** [*salad*] non assaisonné **b** [*wound*] non pansé → **dress**

undrinkable [ʌnˈdrɪŋkəbl] ADJ (= *unpalatable*) imbuvable ; (= *poisonous*) non potable

undue [ʌnˈdjuː] ADJ (*gen*) excessif ; [*anger, haste etc*] excessif ; **I hope this will not cause you ~ inconvenience** j'espère que cela ne vous dérangera pas trop *or* pas outre mesure

undulate [ˈʌndjʊleɪt] VI onduler, ondoyer

undulating [ˈʌndjʊleɪtɪŋ] ADJ [*movement*] ondoyant, onduleux ; [*line*] sinueux, onduleux ; [*countryside*] vallonné

undulation [ˌʌndjʊˈleɪʃən] N ondulation *f*, ondoiement *m*

undulatory [ˈʌndjʊlətrɪ] ADJ ondulatoire

unduly [ʌnˈdjuːlɪ] ADV trop, excessivement; **he was not ~ worried** il ne s'inquiétait pas trop *or* pas outre mesure

undying [ʌnˈdaɪɪŋ] ADJ *(fig)* éternel

unearned [ʌnˈɜːnd] ADJ a *(gen)* [*praise, reward*] immérité b *(Fin)* **~ income** rentes *fpl*; **~ increment** plus-value *f*

unearth [ʌnˈɜːθ] VT déterrer; *(fig)* déterrer, découvrir

unearthly [ʌnˈɜːθlɪ] ADJ *(gen)* surnaturel, mystérieux; *(threatening)* [*silence*] lugubre; (* *fig*) impossible*; **at some ~ hour** à une heure indue

unease [ʌnˈiːz] N malaise *m*, gêne *f* (**at, about** devant)

uneasily [ʌnˈiːzɪlɪ] ADV (= *ill-at-ease*) avec gêne; (= *worriedly*) avec inquiétude; **to sleep ~** (= *fitfully*) mal dormir; (= *restlessly*) dormir d'un sommeil agité

uneasiness [ʌnˈiːzɪnɪs] N *(NonC)* inquiétude *f*, malaise *m* (**at, about** devant)

uneasy [ʌnˈiːzɪ] ADJ [*calm, peace, truce*] troublé, difficile; [*silence*] gêné; [*sleep, night*] agité; [*conscience*] pas tranquille; [*person*] (= *ill-at-ease*) mal à l'aise, gêné; (= *worried*) inquiet (-ète *f*) (**at, about** devant, de), anxieux; **to grow** *or* **become ~ about sth** commencer à s'inquiéter au sujet de qch; **I have an ~ feeling that he's watching me** j'ai l'impression déconcertante qu'il me regarde; **I had an ~ feeling that he would change his mind** je ne pouvais m'empêcher de penser qu'il allait changer d'avis

uneatable [ʌnˈiːtəbl] ADJ immangeable

uneaten [ʌnˈiːtn] ADJ non mangé, non touché

uneconomic(al) [ʌnˌiːkəˈnɒmɪk(əl)] ADJ [*machine, car*] peu économique; [*work, method*] peu économique, peu rentable; **it is ~ to do that** il n'est pas économique *or* rentable de faire cela

unedifying [ʌnˈedɪfaɪɪŋ] ADJ peu édifiant

unedited [ʌnˈedɪtɪd] ADJ [*film*] non monté; [*essays, works*] non édité; [*tape*] non mis au point

uneducated [ʌnˈedjʊkeɪtɪd] ADJ [*person*] sans instruction; [*letter, report*] informe, plein de fautes; (= *badly written*) mal écrit; [*handwriting*] d'illettré; [*speech, accent*] populaire

unemotional [ʌnɪˈməʊʃənl] ADJ (= *having little emotion*) peu émotif, flegmatique; (= *showing little emotion*) [*person, voice, attitude*] qui ne montre *or* ne trahit aucune émotion, impassible; [*reaction*] peu émotionnel; [*description, writing*] neutre, sans passion

unemotionally [ʌnɪˈməʊʃnəlɪ] ADV de façon impassible, sans trahir d'émotion

unemployable [ʌnɪmˈplɔɪəbl] ADJ incapable de travailler

unemployed [ʌnɪmˈplɔɪd] 1 ADJ [*person*] au chômage, sans travail *or* emploi; [*machine, object*] inutilisé, dont on ne se sert pas; *(Fin)* [*capital*] qui ne travaille pas; **~ person** chômeur *m*, -euse *f*; *(esp Admin)* demandeur *m* d'emploi; *(Econ)* **the numbers ~** les inactifs *mpl* 2 **the unemployed** NPL les chômeurs *mpl*, les sans-travail *mpl*; *(esp Admin)* les demandeurs *mpl* d'emploi; **the young ~** les jeunes *mpl* sans emploi *or* au chômage

unemployment [ʌnɪmˈplɔɪmənt] 1 N *(NonC)* chômage *m*; **to reduce** *or* **cut ~** réduire le chômage *or* le nombre des chômeurs; **~ has risen** le chômage *or* le nombre des chômeurs a augmenté 2 COMP ► **unemployment benefit** N *(Brit: formerly)* allocation *f* (de) chômage ► **unemployment compensation** N *(US)* → **unemployment benefit** ► **unemployment figures** NPL chiffres *mpl* du chômage, nombre *m* des chômeurs ► **unemployment line** N *(US)* **to join the ~ line(s)** se retrouver au chômage

► **unemployment rate** N **an ~ rate of 10%** *or* **of 1 in 10** un taux de chômage de 10%

unencumbered [ʌnɪnˈkʌmbəd] ADJ non encombré (**with** de)

unending [ʌnˈendɪŋ] ADJ interminable, sans fin

unendurable [ʌnɪnˈdjʊərəbl] ADJ insupportable, intolérable

unenforceable [ʌnɪnˈfɔːsəbl] ADJ [*law etc*] inapplicable

unengaged [ʌnɪnˈgeɪdʒd] ADJ libre

un-English [ʌnˈɪŋglɪʃ] ADJ peu anglais, pas anglais

unenlightened [ʌnɪnˈlaɪtnd] ADJ peu éclairé, rétrograde

unenterprising [ʌnˈentəpraɪzɪŋ] ADJ [*person*] peu entreprenant, qui manque d'initiative; [*policy, act*] qui manque d'audace *or* de hardiesse

unenthusiastic [ˈʌnɪnˌθuːzɪˈæstɪk] ADJ peu enthousiaste; **you seem rather ~ about it** ça n'a pas l'air de vous enthousiasmer *or* de vous emballer*

unenthusiastically [ˈʌnɪnˌθuːzɪˈæstɪkəlɪ] ADV sans enthousiasme

unenviable [ʌnˈenvɪəbl] ADJ peu enviable

unequal [ʌnˈiːkwəl] ADJ a (= *not the same*) [*size, opportunity, work*] inégal; (= *inegalitarian*) [*system*] inégalitaire b (= *inadequate*) **to be ~ to a task** ne pas être à la hauteur d'une tâche

unequalled [ʌnˈiːkwəld] ADJ [*skill, enthusiasm, footballer, pianist*] inégalé, sans égal; [*record*] inégalé

unequally [ʌnˈiːkwəlɪ] ADV inégalement

unequivocal [ˌʌnɪˈkwɪvəkəl] ADJ sans équivoque; **he gave him an ~ "no"** il lui a opposé un « non » catégorique *or* sans équivoque

unequivocally [ˌʌnɪˈkwɪvəkəlɪ] ADV sans équivoque

unerring [ʌnˈɜːrɪŋ] ADJ [*judgement, accuracy*] infaillible; [*aim, skill, blow*] sûr

unerringly [ʌnˈɜːrɪŋlɪ] ADV infailliblement; **they ~ chose the most promising projects** ils choisissaient infailliblement les projets les plus porteurs; **she ~ made the connection** elle n'a pas manqué d'établir le rapport

UNESCO [juːˈneskəʊ] N *(ABBR = **United Nations Educational, Scientific and Cultural Organization**)* UNESCO *f*

unescorted [ˌʌnesˈkɔːtɪd] ADJ, ADV a *(Mil, Naut)* sans escorte b (= *unaccompanied by a partner*) sans partenaire, non accompagné

unessential [ˌʌnɪˈsenʃəl] ADJ non essentiel, non indispensable

unesthetic [ˌʌnɪːsˈθetɪk] ADJ = **unaesthetic**

unethical [ʌnˈeθɪkəl] ADJ *(gen)* moralement contestable, contraire à l'éthique; (= *contrary to professional code of conduct: Med etc*) contraire à la déontologie

unethically [ʌnˈeθɪkəlɪ] ADV *(gen)* [*behave, act, obtain*] de façon immorale *or* moralement contestable; (= *against professional code of conduct*) de façon contraire à la déontologie

uneven [ʌnˈiːvən] ADJ a (= *not flat or straight*) [*surface*] raboteux, inégal; [*path*] cahoteux; [*ground*] accidenté; [*teeth*] irrégulier; **the wall is ~** le mur n'est pas droit b (= *irregular*) [*pace, rate, breathing, pulse*] irrégulier; [*colour*] inégalement réparti; *(Aut)* **the engine sounds ~** il y a des à-coups dans le moteur, le moteur ne tourne pas rond c (= *inconsistent*) [*quality, performance, acting*] inégal d (= *unfair*) [*distribution, contest, competition*] inégal e [*number*] impair

unevenly [ʌnˈiːvənlɪ] ADV a (= *irregularly*) [*move, spread, develop*] de façon irrégulière b (= *unequally*) [*share, distribute*] inégalement; **the two armies were ~ matched** les deux armées n'étaient pas de force égale

unevenness [ʌnˈiːvənnɪs] N *(NonC)* a [*of surface, path, ground*] inégalité *f*, aspérités *fpl* b [*of motion, breathing, pace, rate, pulse*] irrégularité *f*; [*of colour*] répartition *f* inégale c (= *inconsistency*) [*of quality, performance, acting, writing, film*] caractère *m* inégal d (= *inequality*) [*of sharing out, distribution*] inégalité *f*

uneventful [ˌʌnɪˈventfʊl] ADJ [*day, meeting, journey*] sans incidents, peu mouvementé; [*life*] calme, tranquille; [*career*] peu mouvementé

uneventfully [ˌʌnɪˈventfʊlɪ] ADV [*take place, happen*] sans incidents, sans histoires

unexceptionable [ˌʌnɪkˈsepʃnəbl] ADJ irréprochable

unexceptional [ˌʌnɪkˈsepʃənl] ADJ qui n'a rien d'exceptionnel

unexciting [ˌʌnɪkˈsaɪtɪŋ] ADJ [*time, life, visit*] peu passionnant, peu intéressant; [*food*] ordinaire

unexpected [ˌʌnɪksˈpektɪd] ADJ [*arrival*] inattendu, inopiné; [*result, change, success, happiness*] inattendu, imprévu; **it was all very ~** on ne s'y attendait pas du tout

unexpectedly [ˌʌnɪksˈpektɪdlɪ] ADV alors qu'on ne s'y attend (*or* attendait *etc*) pas, subitement; **to arrive ~** arriver à l'improviste *or* inopinément

unexpired [ˌʌnɪksˈpaɪəd] ADJ non expiré, encore valide

unexplained [ˌʌnɪksˈpleɪnd] ADJ inexpliqué

unexploded [ˌʌnɪksˈpləʊdɪd] ADJ non explosé, non éclaté

unexploited [ˌʌnɪksˈplɔɪtɪd] ADJ inexploité

unexplored [ˌʌnɪksˈplɔːd] ADJ inexploré

unexposed [ˌʌnɪksˈpəʊzd] ADJ *(Phot)* [*film*] vierge

unexpressed [ˌʌnɪksˈprest] ADJ inexprimé

unexpurgated [ʌnˈekspɜːgeɪtɪd] ADJ *(frm)* non expurgé, intégral

unfading [ʌnˈfeɪdɪŋ] ADJ *(fig)* [*hope*] éternel; [*memory*] impérissable, ineffaçable

unfailing [ʌnˈfeɪlɪŋ] ADJ [*supply*] inépuisable, intarissable; [*zeal*] inépuisable; [*optimism*] inébranlable; [*remedy*] infaillible

unfailingly [ʌnˈfeɪlɪŋlɪ] ADV infailliblement, immanquablement

unfair [ʌnˈfeər] 1 ADJ [*person, comment, criticism, trial*] injuste (**to sb** envers qn, à l'égard de qn); [*decision, arrangement, deal*] injuste (**to sb** envers qn, à l'égard de qn), inéquitable; [*competition, play, tactics, practices*] déloyal; **you're being ~** vous êtes injuste; **it's ~ that ...** il n'est pas juste *or* il est injuste que ... (+ *subj*); **it is ~ to expect her to do that** il n'est pas juste d'attendre qu'elle fasse cela; **it is ~ of her to do so** il est injuste qu'elle agisse ainsi, ce n'est pas juste de sa part d'agir ainsi; **to have an ~ advantage over sb/sth** être injustement avantagé par rapport à qn/qch 2 COMP ► **unfair dismissal** N licenciement *m* abusif

unfairly [ʌnˈfeəlɪ] ADV [*treat, judge, compare*] injustement; [*decide*] arbitrairement; [*play*] déloyalement; **he was ~ dismissed** il a été victime d'un licenciement abusif

unfairness [ʌnˈfeənɪs] N [*of person, decision, arrangement, deal, advantage, comment, criticism*] injustice *f*; [*of trial*] caractère *m* arbitraire; [*of competition, tactics, practices*] caractère *m* déloyal

unfaithful [ʌnˈfeɪθfʊl] ADJ infidèle (**to** à)

unfaithfully [ʌnˈfeɪθfəlɪ] ADV infidèlement, avec infidélité

unfaithfulness [ʌnˈfeɪθfʊlnɪs] N infidélité *f*

unfaltering [ʌnˈfɔːltərɪŋ] ADJ [*step, voice*] ferme, assuré

unfalteringly [ʌnˈfɔːltərɪŋlɪ] ADV [*speak*] d'une

voix ferme *or* assurée; [*walk*] d'un pas ferme *or* assuré

unfamiliar [ˈʌnfəˈmɪljəʳ] ADJ [*place, sight, person, subject*] inconnu; **to be ~ with sth** mal connaître qch, ne pas bien connaître qch

unfamiliarity [ˈʌnfəˌmɪliˈærɪtɪ] N (*NonC*) aspect *m* étrange *or* inconnu

unfashionable [ˈʌnˈfæʃnəbl] ADJ [*dress, subject*] démodé, passé de mode; [*district, shop, hotel*] peu chic *inv*; **it is ~ to speak of ...** ça ne se fait plus de parler de ...

unfasten [ˈʌnˈfɑːsn] VT [+ *garment, buttons, rope*] défaire; [+ *door*] ouvrir, déverrouiller; [+ *bonds*] défaire, détacher; (= *loosen*) desserrer

unfathomable [ʌnˈfæðəməbl] ADJ (*lit, fig*) insondable

unfathomed [ʌnˈfæðəmd] ADJ (*lit, fig*) insondé

unfavourable, **unfavorable** (*US*) [ʌnˈfeɪvərəbl] ADJ [*conditions, report, impression, outlook, weather*] défavorable; [*moment*] peu propice, inopportun; [*terms*] désavantageux; [*wind*] contraire

unfavourably, **unfavorably** (*US*) [ʌnˈfeɪvərəblɪ] ADV défavorablement; **I was ~ impressed** j'ai eu une impression défavorable; **to regard sth ~** être défavorable *or* hostile à qch

unfazed* [ʌnˈfeɪzd] ADJ imperturbable; **it left him quite ~** il n'a pas bronché

unfeasible [ʌnˈfiːzəbl] ADJ irréalisable

unfeeling [ʌnˈfiːlɪŋ] ADJ insensible, impitoyable

unfeelingly [ʌnˈfiːlɪŋlɪ] ADV sans pitié, impitoyablement

unfeigned [ʌnˈfeɪnd] ADJ non simulé, sincère

unfeignedly [ʌnˈfeɪnɪdlɪ] ADV sincèrement, vraiment

unfeminine [ʌnˈfemɪnɪn] ADJ peu féminin

unfettered [ʌnˈfetəd] ADJ (*liter: lit, fig*) sans entrave; **~ by** libre de

unfilial [ʌnˈfɪljəl] ADJ (*frm*) peu filial

unfilled [ʌnˈfɪld] ADJ [*post, vacancy*] à pourvoir, vacant

unfinished [ʌnˈfɪnɪʃt] ADJ [*task, essay*] inachevé, incomplet (-ète *f*); **I have three ~ letters** j'ai trois lettres à finir; **we have some ~ business (to attend to)** nous avons une affaire (*or* des affaires) à régler; **the Unfinished Symphony** la Symphonie inachevée; **it looks rather ~** [*piece of furniture, craft work etc*] c'est mal fini, la finition laisse à désirer

unfit [ʌnˈfɪt] ①⃞ ADJ ⓐ (= *not physically fit*) qui n'est pas en forme; **he was ~ to drive** il n'était pas en état de conduire; **he is ~ for work** il n'est pas en état de reprendre le travail; **~ for military service** inapte au service militaire; **the doctor declared him ~ for the match** le docteur a déclaré qu'il n'était pas en état de jouer ⓑ (= *incompetent*) inapte, impropre (**for** à, **to do** à faire); (= *unworthy*) indigne (**to do** de faire); **he is ~ to be a teacher** il ne devrait pas enseigner; **~ for habitation** ◊ **~ to live in** inhabitable; **~ for consumption** impropre à la consommation; **~ to eat** (= *unpalatable*) immangeable; (= *poisonous*) non comestible; **~ for publication** impropre à la publication, impubliable; **road ~ for lorries** route impraticable pour les camions ②⃞ VT (*frm*) rendre inapte (**for** à, **to do** à faire)

unfitness [ʌnˈfɪtnɪs] N ⓐ (= *ill health*) incapacité *f* ⓑ (= *unsuitability*) inaptitude *f* (**for** à, **to do** à faire)

unfitted [ʌnˈfɪtɪd] ADJ (*frm*) inapte (**for** à, **to do** à faire)

unfitting [ʌnˈfɪtɪŋ] ADJ (*frm*) [*language, behaviour*] peu *or* guère convenable, inconvenant; [*ending, result*] mal approprié

unfix [ʌnˈfɪks] VT détacher, enlever; (*Mil*) [+ *bayonets*] remettre

unflagging [ʌnˈflægɪŋ] ADJ [*person, devotion, patience*] infatigable, inlassable; [*enthusiasm*] inépuisable; [*interest*] soutenu jusqu'au bout

unflaggingly [ʌnˈflægɪŋlɪ] ADV infatigablement, inlassablement

unflappability* [ˌʌnflæpəˈbɪlɪtɪ] N (*NonC*) calme *m*, flegme *m*

unflappable* [ʌnˈflæpəbl] ADJ imperturbable, flegmatique

unflattering [ʌnˈflætərɪŋ] ADJ [*person, remark, photo, portrait*] peu flatteur; **he was very ~ about it** ce qu'il en a dit n'avait rien de flatteur *or* n'était pas flatteur; **she wears ~ clothes** elle porte des vêtements qui ne la mettent guère en valeur *or* qui ne l'avantagent guère

unflatteringly [ʌnˈflætərɪŋlɪ] ADV d'une manière peu flatteuse

unfledged [ʌnˈfledʒd] ADJ (*fig*) [*person, organization, movement*] qui manque d'expérience, novice

unflinching [ʌnˈflɪntʃɪŋ] ADJ [*support, loyalty*] indéfectible; [*determination*] à toute épreuve; [*expression, determination*] stoïque; **she was ~ in her determination to succeed** elle était absolument déterminée à réussir

unflinchingly [ʌnˈflɪntʃɪŋlɪ] ADV stoïquement, sans broncher

unflyable [ʌnˈflaɪəbl] ADJ [*plane*] qu'on ne peut pas faire voler

unfocu(s)sed [ˌʌnˈfəʊkəst] ADJ ⓐ [*camera*] pas mis au point; [*gaze, eyes*] dans le vague ⓑ (*fig*) [*aims, desires etc*] flou, vague

unfold [ʌnˈfəʊld] ①⃞ VT ⓐ (*lit*) [+ *napkin, map, blanket*] déplier; [+ *wings*] déployer; **to ~ a map on a table** étaler une carte sur une table; **to ~ one's arms** décroiser les bras ⓑ (*fig*) [+ *plans, ideas*] exposer; [+ *secret*] dévoiler, révéler ②⃞ VI [*flower*] s'ouvrir, s'épanouir; [*view, countryside*] se dérouler, s'étendre; [*story, film, plot*] se dérouler

unforced [ʌnˈfɔːst] ADJ [*smile, laugh*] naturel; (*Sport*) **~ error** faute *f* directe

unforeseeable [ˌʌnfɔːˈsiːəbl] ADJ imprévisible

unforeseen [ˈʌnfɔːˈsiːn] ADJ imprévu

unforgettable [ˈʌnfəˈgetəbl] ADJ (*gen*) inoubliable; (*for unpleasant things*) impossible à oublier

unforgettably [ˈʌnfəˈgetəblɪ] ADV **~ beautiful/clear** d'une beauté/clarté inoubliable; **~ ugly/dirty** d'une laideur/saleté frappante

unforgivable [ˌʌnfəˈgɪvəbl] ADJ impardonnable

unforgivably [ˌʌnfəˈgɪvəblɪ] ADV [*behave*] d'une manière impardonnable; **he was ~ rude** il a été d'une grossièreté impardonnable; **she was ~ late** elle est arrivée avec un retard impardonnable

unforgiven [ˌʌnfəˈgɪvən] ADJ non pardonné

unforgiving [ˈʌnfəˈgɪvɪŋ] ADJ implacable, impitoyable

unforgotten [ˈʌnfəˈgɒtn] ADJ inoublié

unformed [ʌnˈfɔːmd] ADJ informe

unforthcoming [ˈʌnfɔːˈθkʌmɪŋ] ADJ [*reply, person*] réticent (**about** sur); **he was very ~ about it** il s'est montré très réticent à ce propos, il s'est montré peu disposé à en parler

unfortified [ʌnˈfɔːtɪfaɪd] ADJ (*Mil*) sans fortifications, non fortifié

unfortunate [ʌnˈfɔːtʃənɪt] ①⃞ ADJ [*person*] malheureux, malchanceux; [*coincidence*] malheureux, fâcheux; [*circumstances*] triste; [*event*] fâcheux, malencontreux; [*incident, episode*] fâcheux, regrettable; [*remark*] malheureux, malencontreux; **it is most ~ that ...** il est très malheureux *or* regrettable que ... (+ *subj*); **how ~!** quel dommage!; **he has been ~** il n'a pas eu de chance ②⃞ N malheureux *m*, -euse *f*

▼ **unfortunately** [ʌnˈfɔːtʃənɪtlɪ] ADV malheureusement, par malheur; **an ~ worded remark** une remarque formulée de façon malheureuse *or* malencontreuse

unfounded [ʌnˈfaʊndɪd] ADJ [*rumour, allegation, belief*] dénué de tout fondement, sans fondement; [*criticism*] injustifié

unframed [ʌnˈfreɪmd] ADJ [*picture*] sans cadre

unfreeze [ʌnˈfriːz] (*pret* **unfroze**, *ptp* **unfrozen**) ①⃞ VT ⓐ (*lit*) dégeler ⓑ (*Econ, Fin*) débloquer ②⃞ VI dégeler

unfreezing [ʌnˈfriːzɪŋ] N (*Econ, Fin*) [*of prices, wages*] déblocage *m*

unfrequented [ˈʌnfrɪˈkwentɪd] ADJ peu fréquenté

unfriendliness [ʌnˈfrendlɪnɪs] N (*NonC*) froideur *f* (**towards** envers)

unfriendly [ʌnˈfrendlɪ] ADJ [*person, reception*] froid; [*attitude, behaviour, act, remark*] inamical; (*stronger*) hostile; **to be ~ to(wards) sb** manifester de la froideur *or* de l'hostilité envers qn

unfrock [ʌnˈfrɒk] VT défroquer

unfroze [ʌnˈfrəʊz] VB *pt of* **unfreeze**

unfrozen [ʌnˈfrəʊzn] VB *ptp of* **unfreeze**

unfruitful [ʌnˈfruːtfʊl] ADJ ⓐ (*lit*) stérile, infertile ⓑ (*fig*) infructueux

unfruitfully [ʌnˈfruːtfʊlɪ] ADV (*fig*) en vain, sans succès

unfulfilled [ˈʌnfʊlˈfɪld] ADJ [*promise*] non tenu; [*ambition, prophecy*] non réalisé; [*desire*] insatisfait; [*condition*] non rempli; **to feel ~** [*person*] se sentir frustré, éprouver un sentiment d'insatisfaction

unfulfilling [ˈʌnfʊlˈfɪlɪŋ] ADJ peu satisfaisant; **he finds it ~** ça ne le satisfait pas pleinement

unfunny* [ʌnˈfʌnɪ] ADJ qui n'est pas drôle, qui n'a rien de drôle

unfurl [ʌnˈfɜːl] ①⃞ VT déployer ②⃞ VI se déployer

unfurnished [ʌnˈfɜːnɪʃt] ADJ non meublé

ungainliness [ʌnˈgeɪnlɪnɪs] N (*NonC*) gaucherie *f*

ungainly [ʌnˈgeɪnlɪ] ADJ gauche, disgracieux

ungallant [ʌnˈgælənt] ADJ peu *or* guère galant, discourtois

ungenerous [ʌnˈdʒenərəs] ADJ ⓐ (= *miserly*) peu généreux, parcimonieux ⓑ (= *uncharitable*) mesquin, méchant

ungentlemanly [ʌnˈdʒentlmənlɪ] ADJ peu *or* guère galant, discourtois

un-get-at-able* [ˈʌngetˈætəbl] ADJ inaccessible

ungird [ʌnˈgɜːd] (*pret, ptp* **ungirt**) VT détacher

unglazed [ʌnˈgleɪzd] ADJ [*door, window*] non vitré; [*picture*] qui n'est pas sous verre; [*pottery*] non vernissé, non émaillé; [*photograph*] mat; [*cake*] non glacé

unglued [ʌnˈgluːd] ADJ (*gen*) sans colle; (*US fig*) **to come ~*** [*person*] flancher*, craquer*

ungodliness [ʌnˈgɒdlɪnɪs] N (*NonC*) impiété *f*

ungodly [ʌnˈgɒdlɪ] ADJ ⓐ (* = *unreasonable*) [*noise*] impossible*; **at some ~ hour** à une heure impossible* *or* indue ⓑ († = *sinful*) [*person, action, life*] impie, irréligieux

ungovernable [ʌnˈgʌvənəbl] ADJ ⓐ (*Pol*) [*people, country*] ingouvernable ⓑ (*liter* = *uncontrollable*) [*rage, hatred, longing*] incontrôlable; [*desire, passion*] irrépressible; **to have an ~ temper** ne pas savoir se contrôler *or* se maîtriser

ungracious [ʌnˈgreɪʃəs] ADJ [*person*] peu aimable; [*remark, gesture*] désobligeant; **it would be ~ to refuse** on aurait mauvaise grâce à refuser

ungraciously [ʌnˈgreɪʃəslɪ] ADV avec mauvaise grâce

ungrammatical [ˌʌngrəˈmætɪkəl] ADJ incorrect, non grammatical, agrammatical

► **LANGUAGE IN USE:** **unfortunately** 12.3, 18.2, 25.2, 26.3

ungrammatically [ˌʌngrəˈmætɪkəlɪ] ADV incorrectement

ungrateful [ʌnˈgreɪtfʊl] ADJ [person] ingrat (**towards sb** envers qn); **to be ~ for sth** ne pas montrer de gratitude pour qch

ungratefully [ʌnˈgreɪtfʊlɪ] ADV avec ingratitude

ungrudging [ˈʌnˈgrʌdʒɪŋ] ADJ [person, contribution] généreux; [help] donné sans compter; [praise, gratitude] très sincère

ungrudgingly [ʌnˈgrʌdʒɪŋlɪ] ADV [give] généreusement; [help] de bon cœur, sans compter

unguarded [ʌnˈgɑːdɪd] ADJ [a] (= unprotected) [place] sans surveillance; **to leave a place ~** laisser un endroit sans surveillance [b] (Tech) [machine] sans protection [c] (= open, careless) [person, comment] spontané, irréfléchi; **in an ~ moment** dans un moment d'inattention

unguardedly [ʌnˈgɑːdɪdlɪ] ADV [say] sans réfléchir

unguent [ˈʌngwənt] N onguent m

ungulate [ˈʌngjʊleɪt] [1] ADJ ongulé [2] N animal m ongulé; **~s** les ongulés mpl

unhallowed [ʌnˈhæləʊd] ADJ (liter) non consacré, profane

unhampered [ˈʌnˈhæmpəd] ADJ [progress] aisé; [access] libre; **to operate ~ by the police** opérer sans être gêné par la police; **trade ~ by tax regulations** commerce m non entravé par la réglementation fiscale

unhand [ʌnˈhænd] VT (†† or hum) lâcher

unhandy [ʌnˈhændɪ] ADJ gauche, maladroit

unhappily [ʌnˈhæpɪlɪ] ADV [a] (= miserably) [look at, go] d'un air malheureux; [say] d'un ton malheureux; **to be ~ married** avoir fait un mariage malheureux [b] (= unfortunately) malheureusement; **~, things didn't work out as planned** malheureusement, les choses ne se sont pas passées comme prévu; **~ for him, he ...** malheureusement pour lui, il ...

unhappiness [ʌnˈhæpɪnɪs] N (NonC) tristesse f, chagrin m

unhappy [ʌnˈhæpɪ] ADJ [a] (= sad) [person, expression, marriage] malheureux; **I had an ~ time at school** j'ai été malheureux à l'école [b] (= discontented) [person] mécontent (**with or about sb/sth** de qn/qch, **at sth** de qch); **to be ~ at doing sth or to do sth** être mécontent de faire qch [c] (= worried) [person] inquiet (-ète f) (**with or about sb/sth** au sujet de qn/qch, **at sth** au sujet de qch); **we are ~ about the decision** cette décision ne nous satisfait pas; **I am or feel ~ about leaving him alone** je n'aime pas (l'idée de) le laisser seul [d] (= regrettable) [experience, episode] malheureux; [situation, circumstances] regrettable; [coincidence] malheureux, fâcheux; **this ~ state of affairs** cette situation regrettable or déplorable or fâcheuse [e] (= unfortunate) [person] malheureux; [place] affligé [f] (frm = unsuitable) [remark] malheureux, malencontreux; **an ~ choice of words** un choix de mots malheureux or malencontreux

unharmed [ʌnˈhɑːmd] ADJ [person, animal] indemne; [thing] intact, non endommagé

unharness [ʌnˈhɑːnɪs] VT dételer (**from** de)

UNHCR N (ABBR = United Nations High Commission for Refugees) HCR m

unhealthy [ʌnˈhelθɪ] ADJ [a] (= harmful) [environment, habit, curiosity, relationship] malsain [b] (= unwell) [person, company, economy] en mauvaise santé [c] (= ill-looking) [person, appearance, skin] maladif

unheard [ʌnˈhɜːd] [1] ADJ [a] (ignored) **to go ~** [person, plea, request] être ignoré; **she condemned him** elle l'a condamné sans l'avoir entendu [b] (= not heard) **his cries went ~** personne n'a entendu ses cris; **a previously ~ opera** un opéra qui est présenté pour la pre-

mière fois [2] COMP ► **unheard-of** ADJ inouï, sans précédent

unhedged [ʌnˈhedʒd] ADJ (esp US) [venture, bet] hasardeux, à découvert

unheeded [ʌnˈhiːdɪd] ADJ [person, plea, warning] ignoré; **to go ~** être ignoré; **it must not go ~** il faut en tenir compte, il faut y prêter attention

unheeding [ʌnˈhiːdɪŋ] ADJ (frm) insouciant (**of** de), indifférent (**of** à); **they passed by ~** ils sont passés à côté sans faire attention

unhelpful [ʌnˈhelpfʊl] ADJ [person] peu serviable; [remark, advice] inutile; [attitude] peu coopératif; [book, computer] qui n'apporte (or apportait) rien d'utile; **he didn't want to seem ~** il voulait avoir l'air serviable; **I found that very ~** ça ne m'a pas aidé du tout; **it is ~ to do sth** ça n'avance pas à grand-chose de faire qch

unhelpfully [ʌnˈhelpfʊlɪ] ADV [behave] de manière peu coopérative; [say, suggest] sans apporter quoi que ce soit d'utile

unhelpfulness [ʌnˈhelpfʊlnɪs] N (NonC) [of person] manque m de serviabilité; [of remark, advice, book, computer] inutilité f

unheralded [ˈʌnˈherəldɪd] ADJ [a] (= unannounced) [arrival, resignation] non annoncé; **to be ~** ne pas être annoncé; **to arrive ~** arriver sans être annoncé [b] (= unacclaimed) [player, artist] méconnu

unhesitating [ʌnˈhezɪteɪtɪŋ] ADJ [response] immédiat; [trust, generosity] spontané; [person, courage, belief] résolu

unhesitatingly [ʌnˈhezɪteɪtɪŋlɪ] ADV sans hésiter, sans hésitation

unhindered [ˈʌnˈhɪndəd] ADJ [progress] sans obstacles, sans encombre; [movement] libre, sans encombre; **to go ~** passer sans rencontrer d'obstacles or sans encombre; **he worked ~** il a travaillé sans être dérangé (**by** par)

unhinge [ʌnˈhɪndʒ] VT enlever de ses gonds, démonter; (fig) [+ mind] déranger; [+ person] déséquilibrer

unhinged [ˈʌnˈhɪndʒd] ADJ [person, mind] déséquilibré; [passion, ranting] délirant

unhip [ʌnˈhɪp] ADJ ringard*

unhitch [ʌnˈhɪtʃ] VT [+ rope] décrocher, détacher; [+ horse] dételer

unholy [ʌnˈhəʊlɪ] ADJ [a] (= sinful) [activity] impie; [pleasure] inavouable; [alliance] contre nature [b] (* = terrible) [mess, row] sans nom; [noise] impossible*

unhook [ʌnˈhʊk] VT [a] (= take off hook) [+ picture from wall etc] décrocher (**from** de) [b] (= undo) [+ garment] dégrafer

unhoped-for [ʌnˈhəʊptfɔːʳ] ADJ inespéré

unhopeful [ʌnˈhəʊpfʊl] ADJ [prospect, start] peu prometteur; [person] pessimiste, qui n'a guère d'espoir

unhorse [ʌnˈhɔːs] VT désarçonner, démonter

unhurried [ʌnˈhʌrɪd] ADJ [pace, atmosphere, activity] tranquille; [reflection] tranquille, paisible; [movement] sans précipitation; [person] paisible; **to be ~** ne pas être pressé; **to have an ~ journey** faire un voyage sans se presser; **in an ~ way** sans se presser

unhurriedly [ʌnˈhʌrɪdlɪ] ADV [walk] sans se presser, tranquillement; [speak] sans précipitation, posément, en prenant son temps

unhurt [ʌnˈhɜːt] ADJ indemne

unhygienic [ˌʌnhaɪˈdʒiːnɪk] ADJ non hygiénique; **it is ~ to do that** ce n'est pas hygiénique de faire ça

uni* [ˈjuːnɪ] N (ABBR = university) fac* f; **at ~** en fac*

uni... [ˈjuːnɪ] PREF uni..., mono...

unicameral [ˌjuːnɪˈkæmərəl] ADJ (Parl) monocaméral

UNICEF [ˈjuːnɪsef] N (ABBR = United Nations Children's Fund) UNICEF f

unicellular [ˈjuːnɪˈseljʊləʳ] ADJ unicellulaire

unicorn [ˈjuːnɪkɔːn] N licorne f

unicycle [ˈjuːnɪˌsaɪkl] N monocycle m

unidentifiable [ˌʌnaɪˈdentɪˌfaɪəbl] ADJ non identifiable

unidentified [ˈʌnaɪˈdentɪfaɪd] [1] ADJ non identifié [2] COMP ► **unidentified flying object** N objet m volant non identifié

unidirectional [ˈjuːnɪdɪˈrekʃənl] ADJ unidirectionnel

unification [ˌjuːnɪfɪˈkeɪʃən] N unification f

unified field theory [ˈjuːnɪfaɪdˌfiːld'θɪərɪ] N théorie f unitaire

uniform [ˈjuːnɪfɔːm] [1] N uniforme m; **in ~** en uniforme; (Mil etc) **in full ~** en grand uniforme; **out of ~** [policeman, soldier] en civil; [schoolboy] en habits de tous les jours; (Police) **the ~s*** les policiers mpl en tenue [2] ADJ [rate, standards, shape, size] identique; **~ in shape/size** ◊ **of a ~ shape/size** de la même forme/taille, de forme/taille identique; **a sky of ~ colour** un ciel de couleur uniforme; **to make sth ~** [+ rate, standards, colour] uniformiser qch; [+ shape, size] normaliser qch [3] COMP [trousers, shirt etc] d'uniforme ► **uniform resource locator** N (Comput) URL m (adresse de site Web)

uniformed [ˈjuːnɪfɔːmd] [1] ADJ [guard, chauffeur, schoolchild] en uniforme; [soldier, police officer] en uniforme, en tenue; [organization] où l'on porte un uniforme [2] COMP ► **uniformed branch** N (Police) (catégorie f du) personnel m en tenue

uniformity [ˌjuːnɪˈfɔːmɪtɪ] N (NonC) uniformité f

uniformly [ˈjuːnɪfɔːmlɪ] ADV uniformément

unify [ˈjuːnɪfaɪ] VT unifier

unifying [ˈjuːnɪfaɪɪŋ] ADJ [factor, force, theme, principle etc] unificateur (-trice f); **the struggle has had a ~ effect on all Blacks** cette lutte a réussi à unifier tous les Noirs

unilateral [ˈjuːnɪˈlætərəl] [1] ADJ unilatéral [2] COMP ► **unilateral declaration of independence** (Brit Pol) N déclaration f unilatérale d'indépendance ► **unilateral disarmament** N désarmement m unilatéral, **unilateral nuclear disarmament** ♦ N désarmement m nucléaire unilatéral

unilateralism [ˈjuːnɪˈlætərəlɪzəm] N adhésion f au désarmement unilatéral, unilatéralisme m; **American ~ on trade** l'habitude f américaine de prendre des décisions unilatérales en ce qui concerne le commerce

unilateralist [ˈjuːnɪˈlætərəlɪst] [1] N partisan m du désarmement unilatéral [2] ADJ [policy] unilatéral; [party] favorable au désarmement nucléaire unilatéral

unilaterally [ˈjuːnɪˈlætərəlɪ] ADV unilatéralement

unimaginable [ˌʌnɪˈmædʒnəbl] ADJ inimaginable (**to sb** pour qn)

unimaginably [ˈʌnɪˈmædʒnəblɪ] ADV incroyablement

unimaginative [ˌʌnɪˈmædʒnətɪv] ADJ [person, film] sans imagination; [food, playing] sans originalité; **to be ~** [person, film] manquer d'imagination; [food, playing] manquer d'originalité

unimaginatively [ˈʌnɪˈmædʒnətɪvlɪ] ADV d'une manière peu imaginative, sans imagination

unimaginativeness [ˈʌnɪˈmædʒnətɪvnɪs] N manque m d'imagination

unimpaired [ˈʌnɪmˈpɛəd] ADJ [mental powers, prestige] intact; [quality] non diminué; **his eyesight/hearing was ~** sa vue/son ouïe n'avait pas diminué; **their faith remains ~** leur foi reste toujours aussi forte; **to be ~ by sth** ne pas souffrir de qch

unimpeachable [ˌʌnɪmˈpiːtʃəbl] ADJ (frm) [source] sûr; [evidence] incontestable, irrécusable; [integrity] impeccable; [character, reputation, conduct, honesty] irréprochable

unimpeded [ˈʌnɪmˈpiːdɪd] 1 ADJ [access] libre; [view] dégagé 2 ADV sans entraves

unimportant [ˈʌnɪmˈpɔːtənt] ADJ [person] insignifiant; [issue, detail] sans importance, insignifiant; **it's quite ~** ça n'a aucune espèce d'importance, c'est sans importance

unimposing [ˈʌnɪmˈpəʊzɪŋ] ADJ peu imposant, peu impressionnant

unimpressed [ˈʌnɪmˈprest] ADJ [a] (= unaffected) **to be ~ (by** or **with sb/sth)** (by person, sight, size, plea) ne pas être impressionné (par qn/qch); **I was ~** ça ne m'a pas impressionné; **Wall Street has been ~** Wall Street est resté calme; **he remained ~** ça ne lui a fait ni chaud ni froid [b] (= unconvinced) **to be ~ (by** or **with sb/sth)** (by person, explanation, argument) ne pas être convaincu (par qn/qch); **I was ~** ça ne m'a pas convaincu

unimpressive [ˈʌnɪmˈpresɪv] ADJ [person] terne, très quelconque; [building, amount] très quelconque; [sight, result, performance] médiocre; [argument] peu convaincant

unimproved [ˈʌnɪmˈpruːvd] ADJ [condition] qui ne s'est pas amélioré, inchangé; [land, pasture] non amendé; **many houses remained ~** beaucoup de maisons n'avaient pas fait l'objet de réfections

unincorporated [ˌʌnɪnˈkɔːpəreɪtɪd] ADJ non incorporé (**in** dans); (Comm, Jur) non enregistré

uninfluential [ˌʌnɪnfluˈenʃəl] ADJ sans influence, qui n'a pas d'influence

uninformative [ˈʌnɪnˈfɔːmətɪv] ADJ [report, document, account] qui n'apprend rien; **he was very ~** il ne nous (or leur etc) a rien appris d'important

uninformed [ˈʌnɪnˈfɔːmd] 1 ADJ [person, organization] mal informé (**about sb/sth** sur qn/qch), mal renseigné (**about sb/sth** sur qn/qch); [comment, rumour, opinion] mal informé; **the ~ observer** l'observateur m non averti 2 **the uninformed** NPL le profane

uninhabitable [ˈʌnɪnˈhæbɪtəbl] ADJ inhabitable

uninhabited [ˈʌnɪnˈhæbɪtɪd] ADJ inhabité

uninhibited [ˈʌnɪnˈhɪbɪtɪd] ADJ [person, behaviour] sans inhibitions; [emotion, impulse, desire] non refréné; [dancing] sans retenue; **to be ~ by sth/in** or **about doing sth** ne pas être gêné par qch/pour faire qch

uninitiated [ˈʌnɪnˈɪʃɪeɪtɪd] 1 ADJ non initié (**into sth** à qch); **to the ~ eye** aux yeux du profane; **to the ~ reader** pour le lecteur non averti 2 **the uninitiated** NPL (Rel) les profanes mpl; (gen) les non-initiés mpl, le profane

uninjured [ˈʌnˈɪndʒəd] ADJ indemne; **he was ~ in the accident** il est sorti indemne de l'accident; **luckily, everyone escaped ~** heureusement, tout le monde s'en est sorti indemne

uninspired [ˈʌnɪnˈspaɪəd] ADJ [person] sans manque d'inspiration; [book, film] sans imagination, fade; [food] sans originalité

uninspiring [ˈʌnɪnˈspaɪərɪŋ] ADJ [person, book, film] terne; [choice] médiocre; [view] sans intérêt; **it was an ~ match** le match n'a pas été passionnant

uninsured [ˈʌnɪnˈʃʊəd] ADJ non assuré (**against** contre)

unintelligent [ˈʌnɪnˈtelɪdʒənt] ADJ [person, comment] inintelligent; [behaviour, tactics] dépourvu d'intelligence; [book, film] sans intelligence

unintelligible [ˈʌnɪnˈtelɪdʒəbl] ADJ inintelligible (**to sb** pour qn)

unintelligibly [ˈʌnɪnˈtelɪdʒəblɪ] ADV [mutter, yell] de façon inintelligible

unintended [ˈʌnɪnˈtendɪd], **unintentional** [ˈʌnɪnˈtenʃənl] ADJ involontaire; **it was quite ~** ce n'était pas fait exprès

unintentionally [ˈʌnɪnˈtenʃənəlɪ] ADV involontairement

uninterested [ʌnˈɪntrɪstɪd] ADJ indifférent; **to be ~ in sb/sth** ne pas être intéressé par qn/qch; **he seems ~ in his son** il ne semble pas s'intéresser à son fils

uninteresting [ʌnˈɪntrɪstɪŋ] ADJ [person, place, book, activity] inintéressant; [offer] sans intérêt, dépourvu d'intérêt

uninterrupted [ˈʌnˌɪntəˈrʌptɪd] ADJ ininterrompu; **to continue ~** continuer sans interruption; **~ by advertisements** sans coupures publicitaires; **to have an ~ view of sth** avoir une très bonne vue or une vue dégagée sur qch

uninterruptedly [ˈʌnˌɪntəˈrʌptɪdlɪ] ADV sans interruption

uninvited [ˈʌnɪnˈvaɪtɪd] ADJ [visitor] sans invitation; [question, sexual advances] mal venu; [criticism] gratuit; **an ~ guest** une personne qui n'a pas été invitée or qui s'invite; **to arrive ~** arriver sans invitation, s'inviter; **to do sth ~** faire qch sans y être invité

uninviting [ˈʌnɪnˈvaɪtɪŋ] ADJ peu attirant, peu attrayant; [food] peu appétissant

union [ˈjuːnjən] 1 N [a] (gen, also Pol) union f; (= marriage) union f, mariage m; **postal/customs ~** union f postale/douanière; (US) **the Union** les États-Unis mpl; **Union of Soviet Socialist Republics** Union f des républiques socialistes soviétiques; **Union of South Africa** Union f sud-africaine; (Univ) **the (Student** or **Students') Union** (= organization) syndicat étudiant; (= building) locaux de l'association d'étudiants; **in perfect ~** en parfaite harmonie; **in ~ there is strength** l'union fait la force (PROV) → **state** [b] (Ind: also **trade ~**, US: also **labor ~**) syndicat m; **~s and management** ≈ les partenaires mpl sociaux; **to join a ~** adhérer à un syndicat, se syndiquer; **to join the Union of Miners** adhérer au Syndicat des mineurs; **to belong to a ~** faire partie d'un syndicat, être membre d'un syndicat [c] (Tech: for pipes etc) raccord m 2 COMP (Ind) [card, leader, movement] syndical; [headquarters] du syndicat; [factory etc] syndiqué ► **union catalogue** N catalogue m combiné (de plusieurs bibliothèques) ► **union dues** NPL cotisation f, syndicale ► **Union Jack** N Union Jack m inv ► **union member** N (Ind) membre m du syndicat, syndiqué(e) m(f) ► **union membership** N (Ind: members collectively) membres mpl du or des syndicat(s); (= number of members) effectifs mpl du or des syndicat(s) → **membership** ► **union rate** N (Ind) tarif m syndical ► **union school** N (US) lycée dont dépendent plusieurs écoles appartenant à un autre secteur ► **union shop** N (US) atelier m d'ouvriers syndiqués ► **union suit** N (US) combinaison f

unionism [ˈjuːnjənɪzəm] N (Ind) syndicalisme m; (Pol) unionisme m

unionist [ˈjuːnjənɪst] N [a] (Ind: also **trade ~**) membre m d'un syndicat, syndiqué(e) m(f); **the militant ~s** les syndicalistes mpl, les militants mpl syndicaux [b] (in Ir, US etc: Pol) unioniste mf

unionization [ˌjuːnjənaɪˈzeɪʃən] N syndicalisation f

unionize [ˈjuːnjənaɪz] (Ind) 1 VT syndiquer 2 VI se syndiquer

uniparous [juːˈnɪpərəs] ADJ (Zool) unipare; (Bot) à axe principal unique

unique [juːˈniːk] 1 ADJ [a] (= one of a kind) unique (**among** parmi); **~ to sb/sth** propre à qn/qch; **his own ~ style** son style inimitable, son style bien à lui [b] (= exceptional) exceptionnel; **rather** or **fairly ~** assez exceptionnel 2 COMP ► **unique selling point**, **unique selling proposition** N avantage m unique

uniquely [juːˈniːklɪ] ADV particulièrement; **~ placed to do sth** particulièrement bien placé pour faire qch

uniqueness [juːˈniːknɪs] N caractère m unique or exceptionnel

unisex [ˈjuːnɪseks] ADJ [clothes, hair salon] unisexe; [hospital ward] mixte

UNISON [ˈjuːnɪsn] N (Brit) syndicat

unison [ˈjuːnɪsn, ˈjuːnɪzn] N (gen, also Mus) unisson m; **in ~** [sing] à l'unisson; **"yes" they said in ~** « oui » dirent-ils en chœur or tous ensemble; **to act in ~** agir de concert

unit [ˈjuːnɪt] 1 N [a] (gen, Admin, Elec, Math, Mil etc) unité f; (Univ etc) module m, unité f de valeur; **administrative/linguistic/monetary ~** unité f administrative/linguistique/monétaire; **~ of length** unité f de longueur → **thermal** [b] (= complete section, part) élément m; [of textbook] chapitre m; **compressor ~** groupe m compresseur; (Elec) **generative ~** groupe m électrogène; **you can buy the kitchen in ~s** vous pouvez acheter la cuisine par éléments → **kitchen, sink²** [c] (= buildings) locaux mpl; (= offices) bureaux mpl; (for engineering etc) bloc m; (for sport, activity) centre m; (looking after the public) service m; **assembly/operating ~** bloc m de montage/opératoire; **X-ray ~** service m de radiologie; **sports ~** centre m sportif; **the library/laboratory ~** la bibliothèque/les laboratoires mpl; **the staff accommodation ~** les logements mpl du personnel [d] (= group of people) unité f; (in firm) service m; **research ~** unité f or service m de recherches; (Sociol) **family ~** groupe m familial 2 COMP ► **unit furniture** N (NonC) mobilier m par éléments ► **unit-linked policy** N (Brit Insurance) assurance-vie avec participation aux bénéfices d'un fonds commun de placement ► **unit of account** N [of European Community] unité f de compte ► **unit price** N prix m unitaire ► **unit rule** N (US Pol) règlement selon lequel la délégation d'un État vote en bloc suivant la majorité de ses membres ► **unit trust** N (Brit Fin) ≈ fonds m commun de placement; (= company) société f d'investissement à capital variable, SICAV f

Unitarian [ˌjuːnɪˈtɛərɪən] ADJ, N (Rel) unitaire mf, unitarien(ne) m(f)

Unitarianism [ˌjuːnɪˈtɛərɪənɪzəm] N (Rel) unitarisme m

unitary [ˈjuːnɪtərɪ] ADJ unitaire

unite [juːˈnaɪt] 1 VT [a] (= join) [+ countries, groups] unir; (= marry) unir, marier; **to ~ A and B** unir A et B; **to ~ A with B** unir A à B [b] (= unify) [+ party, country] unifier 2 VI s'unir (**with sth** à qch, **with sb** à or avec qn, **against** contre, **in doing, to do** pour faire); **women of the world ~!** femmes du monde entier, unissez-vous !

united [juːˈnaɪtɪd] 1 ADJ [country, opposition] uni; **~ in their belief that ...** unis dans la conviction que ...; **~ in opposing sth** unis dans leur opposition à qch; **~ by a common interest** unis par un intérêt commun; **a ~ effort** un effort commun; **their ~ efforts** leurs efforts conjugués; **to present a** or **put on a ~ front (to sb)** présenter un front uni (face à qn); **to take a ~ stand against sb/sth** adopter une position commune contre qn/qch ■ (PROV) **~ we stand, divided we fall** l'union fait la force (PROV) 2 COMP ► **the United Arab Emirates** NPL les Émirats mpl arabes unis ► **the United Arab Republic** N la République arabe unie ► **the United Kingdom (of Great Britain and Northern Ireland)** N le Royaume-Uni (de Grande-Bretagne et d'Irlande du Nord) →

GREAT BRITAIN, UNITED KINGDOM ▶ **United Nations (Organization)** NPL (Organisation *f* des) Nations *fpl* unies ▶ **United Service Organization** N (*US*) organisation venant en aide aux militaires américains, en particulier lors de leurs déplacements ou séjours à l'étranger ▶ **the United States (of America)** NPL les États-Unis *mpl* (d'Amérique)

unity ['ju:nɪtɪ] N unité *f*; (*fig*) harmonie *f*, accord *m*; (*Theat*) **~ of time/place/action** unité *f* de temps/de lieu/d'action unanime ■ (*PROV*) **~ is strength** l'union fait la force (*PROV*); **to live in ~** vivre en harmonie (**with** avec)

Univ. (ABBR = **University**) univ.

univalent ['ju:nɪ'veɪlənt] ADJ univalent

univalve ['ju:nɪvælv] [1] ADJ univalve [2] N mollusque *m* univalve

universal [,ju:nɪ'vɜ:səl] [1] ADJ [*acceptance, approval, condemnation*] unanime; [*language, remedy, beliefs*] universel; **~ access to medical care** l'accès de tous aux soins médicaux; **a ~ health-care system** un système de soins médicaux pour tous; **to win ~ acclaim** être acclamé par tous; **to have a ~ appeal** être apprécié de tous; **he's a ~ favourite** tout le monde l'adore; **a ~ truth** une vérité universelle; **its use has become ~** son usage est devenu universel; **to make sth ~** rendre qch universel [2] N (*Philos*) universel *m*; (*Philos, Ling*) **~s** universaux *mpl* [3] COMP ▶ **universal joint** N (joint *m* de) cardan *m* ▶ **Universal Product Code** N (*US Comm*) code-barres *m* ▶ **universal suffrage** N suffrage *m* universel ▶ **universal time** N temps *m* universel

universality [,ju:nɪvɜ:'sælɪtɪ] N (*NonC*) universalité *f*

universalize [,ju:nɪ'vɜ:səlaɪz] VT universaliser, rendre universel

universally [,ju:nɪ'vɜ:səlɪ] ADV [*accepted, welcomed, condemned*] universellement; [*popular, true, available*] partout; **~ liked/admired** aimé/admiré de tous; **~ praised** loué par chacun or tout le monde

universe ['ju:nɪvɜ:s] N univers *m*; **he's the funniest writer in the ~** c'est l'écrivain le plus amusant qui existe

university [,ju:nɪ'vɜ:sɪtɪ] [1] N université *f*; **to be at/go to ~** être/aller à l'université; **to study at ~** faire des études universitaires; **a place at ~** ◊ **a ~ place** une place à l'université → **open, residence** [2] COMP [*degree, town, library*] universitaire; [*professor, student*] d'université ▶ **Universities and Colleges Admissions Service** N (*Brit*) service central des inscriptions universitaires ▶ **Universities Central Council on Admissions** N (*Brit: formerly*) service central des inscriptions universitaires ▶ **university education** N he has a ~ education il a fait des études universitaires ▶ **university entrance** N entrée *f* à l'université; **~ entrance examination** (*gen*) examen *m* d'entrée à l'université; (*competitive*) concours *m* d'entrée à l'université ▶ **University Grants Committee** N (*Brit: formerly*) ancienne commission gouvernementale responsable de la dotation des universités ▶ **university hospital** N centre *m* hospitalier universitaire

unjust [ʌn'dʒʌst] ADJ injuste (**to sb** envers qn); **it is ~ to do sth** il est injuste de faire qch

unjustifiable [ʌn'dʒʌstɪfaɪəbl] ADJ injustifiable

unjustifiably [ʌn'dʒʌstɪfaɪəblɪ] ADV [*criticize, increase*] de façon injustifiable; **~ high levels of taxation** des taux d'imposition d'un niveau injustifiable; **~ pessimistic** d'un pessimisme injustifiable

unjustified [ʌn'dʒʌstɪfaɪd] ADJ [a] (= *unfair*) [*action, attack, reputation*] injustifié [b] (*Typ*) non justifié

unjustly [ʌn'dʒʌstlɪ] ADV injustement

unkempt ['ʌn'kempt] ADJ [*person, appearance, clothes*] négligé; [*hair*] mal peigné; [*beard*] peu soigné; [*grass, garden, park*] mal entretenu

unkind [ʌn'kaɪnd] ADJ [a] (= *nasty*) [*person, remark, behaviour*] désagréable, peu aimable; **she never has an ~ word to say about anyone** elle n'a jamais un mot désagréable pour qui que ce soit; **it would be ~ to say that ...** il serait peu aimable de dire que ...; **to be ~ to sb** ne pas être aimable avec qn [b] (= *adverse*) [*fate*] cruel (**to sb** envers qn); [*climate*] rude; **the weather was ~ to us** le temps s'est montré peu clément pour nous [c] (*Sport*) [*bounce*] malheureux

unkindly [ʌn'kaɪndlɪ] [1] ADV [*behave*] désagréablement, de façon désagréable or peu aimable; [*say*] désagréablement, sans aménité; [*describe*] sans aménité; **to speak ~ of sb** dire des choses désagréables or peu aimables au sujet de qn; **don't take it ~ if ...** ne soyez pas offensé si ..., ne le prenez pas en mauvaise part si ...; **to take ~ to sth** accepter qch difficilement [2] ADJ [*person, remark*] désagréable, peu aimable; [*climate*] rude; **in an ~ way** de façon désagréable or peu aimable

unkindness [ʌn'kaɪndnɪs] N [a] (*NonC*) [*of person, behaviour*] manque *m* de gentillesse or d'amabilité; (*stronger*) méchanceté *f*; [*of words, remark*] malveillance *f*; [*of fate*] cruauté *f*; [*of weather*] rigueur *f* [b] (= *act of unkindness*) méchanceté *f*, action *f* or parole *f* méchante

unknot [ʌn'nɒt] VT dénouer, défaire (le nœud de)

unknowable ['ʌn'nəʊəbl] ADJ (*esp liter*) inconnaissable

unknowing ['ʌn'nəʊɪŋ] ADJ **to be the ~ victim of sb/sth** être la victime de qn/qch sans le savoir; **to be the ~ cause of sth** être la cause de qch à son insu or sans le savoir; **to be an ~ accomplice in** or **to sth** être le complice de qch à son insu or sans le savoir; **... he said, all ~ ...** dit-il, sans savoir ce qui se passait

unknowingly ['ʌn'nəʊɪŋlɪ] ADV sans le savoir, à mon (*or* son *etc*) insu

unknown ['ʌn'nəʊn] [1] ADJ inconnu; **his real name is ~ (to me)** son vrai nom (m')est inconnu; **she hoped to remain ~ to the authorities** elle espérait que les autorités ne s'apercevraient pas de son existence; **a species ~ to science** une espèce inconnue des scientifiques; **~ to me, he ...** à mon insu, il ..., sans que je le sache, il ...; **~ to him, the plane had crashed** l'avion s'était écrasé, ce qu'il ignorait; **some ~ person** un inconnu; (*lit, fig*) **it is ~ territory (for them)** c'est un territoire inconnu (pour eux); (*Jur*) **murder by person or persons ~** meurtre *m* dont on ignore l'auteur ou les auteurs; **Jill Brown, whereabouts ~** Jill Brown, dont on ignore où elle se trouve actuellement [2] N [a] **the ~** (*Philos, gen*) l'inconnu *m*; (*Math, fig*) l'inconnue *f*; **voyage into the ~** voyage *m* dans l'inconnu; **in space exploration there are many ~s** dans l'exploration de l'espace il y a de nombreuses inconnues [b] (= *person, actor etc*) inconnu(e) *m(f)*; **they chose an ~ for the part of Macbeth** ils ont choisi un inconnu pour jouer le rôle de Macbeth [3] COMP ▶ **unknown factor** N inconnue *f* ▶ **unknown quantity** N (*Math, fig*) inconnue *f*; **he's an ~ quantity** il représente une inconnue ▶ **the Unknown Soldier, the Unknown Warrior** N le Soldat inconnu

unlace ['ʌn'leɪs] VT délacer, défaire (le lacet de)

unladen ['ʌn'leɪdn] ADJ [*ship*] à vide; **~ weight** poids *m* à vide; **to weigh 5 tonnes ~** peser 5 tonnes à vide

unladylike ['ʌn'leɪdɪlaɪk] ADJ [*girl, woman*] mal élevée, qui manque de distinction; [*manners,*

behaviour] peu distingué; **it's ~ to yawn** une jeune fille bien élevée ne bâille pas

unlamented ['ʌnlə'mentɪd] ADJ non regretté; **he died ~** on ne pleura pas sa mort

unlatch ['ʌn'lætʃ] VT ouvrir, soulever le loquet de

unlawful ['ʌn'lɔ:fʊl] [1] ADJ [*act*] illégal, illicite; [*marriage*] illégitime; **by ~ means** par des moyens illégaux [2] COMP ▶ **unlawful assembly** N rassemblement *m* illégal ▶ **unlawful entry** N effraction *f* ▶ **unlawful killing** N homicide *m* volontaire (*sans préméditation*) ▶ **unlawful possession** N détention *f* illégale ▶ **unlawful wounding** N coups *mpl* et blessures *fpl* (*sans préméditation*)

unlawfully ['ʌn'lɔ:fəlɪ] ADV illégalement, illicitement

unleaded ['ʌn'ledɪd] [1] ADJ [*petrol*] sans plomb [2] N (*also* **~ petrol**) essence *f* sans plomb

unlearn ['ʌn'lɜ:n] (*pret, ptp* **unlearned** or **unlearnt**) VT désapprendre

unlearned [1] VB pt, ptp of **unlearn** [2] ADJ ignorant, illettré

unleash [ʌn'li:ʃ] VT [+ *dog*] détacher, lâcher; [+ *hounds*] découpler; (*fig*) [+ *anger etc*] déchaîner, déclencher

unleavened ['ʌn'levnd] ADJ [*bread*] sans levain, azyme (*Rel*); (*fig*) **~ by humour** qui n'est pas égayé par le moindre trait d'humour

unless [ən'les] CONJ à moins que ... (ne) (+ *subj*), à moins de (+ *infin*); **I'll take it, ~ you want it** je vais le prendre, à moins que vous (ne) le vouliez; **take it, ~ you can find another** prenez-le, à moins que vous n'en trouviez un autre; **I won't do it ~ you phone me** je ne le ferai que si tu me téléphones; **I won't go ~ you do** je n'irai que si tu y vas toi aussi; **~ I am mistaken** à moins que (ne) me trompe, si je ne me trompe (pas); **~ I hear to the contrary** sauf avis contraire, sauf contrordre; (*Admin, Comm, Pharm etc*) **~ otherwise stated** sauf indication contraire

unlettered ['ʌn'letəd] ADJ illettré

unliberated ['ʌn'lɪbəreɪtɪd] ADJ [*woman etc*] qui n'est pas libéré or émancipé

unlicensed ['ʌn'laɪsənst] ADJ [*activity*] illicite, non autorisé; [*vehicle*] sans vignette; (*Brit*) **~ premises** établissement *m* qui n'a pas de licence or de débit de boissons

unlikable [ʌn'laɪkəbl] ADJ = **unlikeable**

unlike ['ʌn'laɪk] [1] ADJ dissemblable (*also Math, Phys*), différent; **they are quite ~** ils ne se ressemblent pas du tout [2] PREP **~ his brother, he ...** à la différence de or contrairement à son frère, il ...; **it's so ~ him to say something like that** ça lui ressemble si peu de dire une chose pareille; **how ~ George!** on ne s'attendait pas à ça de la part de George!; **Glasgow is quite ~ Edinburgh** Glasgow ne ressemble pas du tout à Édimbourg; **she is ~ him in every way, except for her dark eyes** elle ne lui ressemble pas du tout, si ce n'est ses yeux sombres; **the portrait is quite ~ him** ce portrait ne lui ressemble pas, ce portrait est très peu ressemblant

unlikeable ['ʌn'laɪkəbl] ADJ [*person*] peu sympathique; [*town, thing*] peu agréable

unlikelihood [ʌn'laɪklɪhʊd], **unlikeliness** [ʌn'laɪklɪnɪs] N (*NonC*) improbabilité *f*

▼**unlikely** [ʌn'laɪklɪ] ADJ [*happening, outcome*] peu probable, improbable; [*explanation*] invraisemblable; [*friendship, candidate, setting*] inattendu; **an ~ place to find ...** un endroit où l'on ne s'attend (or s'attendait) guère à trouver ...; **they're such an ~ couple** ils forment un couple si invraisemblable; **she was wearing the most ~ hat** elle avait un chapeau complètement invraisemblable; **in the ~ event of war** dans le cas improbable où une guerre éclaterait; **in the ~ event that ...** au cas improbable où ...; **in the ~ event of his ac-**

cepting au cas improbable où il accepterait ; **it is ~ that she will come** ◊ **she is ~ to come** il est improbable *or* peu probable qu'elle vienne, il y a peu de chances pour qu'elle vienne ; **it is ~ to be settled** cela ne risque guère d'être réglé ; **she is ~ to succeed** elle a peu de chances de réussir ; **that is ~ to happen** il y a peu de chances que ça se produise ; **it is most** ~ c'est fort *or* très improbable ; **it is not ~ that …** il est assez probable que … (+ *subj*), il se pourrait bien que … (+ *subj*)

unlimited [ʌnˈlɪmɪtɪd] **1** ADJ [*amount, number, use*] illimité ; [*patience*] sans limite(s), sans bornes ; **~ opportunities** des possibilités *fpl* illimitées ; **they had ~ time** ils avaient tout le temps qu'ils voulaient ; **a ticket that allows ~ travel on buses** un ticket qui permet d'effectuer un nombre illimité de trajets en autobus **2** COMP ► **unlimited liability** N (*Comm, Fin, Jur*) responsabilité *f* illimitée

unlined [ʌnˈlaɪnd] ADJ **a** [*garment, curtain*] sans doublure **b** [*face*] sans rides ; [*paper*] uni, non réglé

▼ **unlisted** [ʌnˈlɪstɪd] **1** ADJ qui ne figure pas sur une liste ; (*St Ex*) non inscrit à la cote ; (*US Telec*) qui ne figure pas dans l'annuaire, ≈ qui est sur la liste rouge ; (*US Telec*) **to go ~** ≈ se faire mettre sur la liste rouge **2** COMP ► **unlisted building** N (*Brit*) édifice *m* non classé

unlit [ʌnˈlɪt] ADJ **a** (= *not burning*) [*cigarette, pipe, fire*] non allumé **b** (= *dark*) [*place*] non éclairé ; [*vehicle*] sans feux

unload [ʌnˈləʊd] **1** VT [+ *ship, cargo, truck, rifle, washing machine*] décharger ; (*fig* = *get rid of*) se débarrasser de, se défaire de ; **to ~ sth on (to) sb** se décharger de qch sur qn **2** VI [*ship, truck*] être déchargé, déposer son chargement

unloaded [ʌnˈləʊdɪd] ADJ [*gun*] qui n'est pas chargé ; [*truck, ship*] qui est déchargé

unloading [ʌnˈləʊdɪŋ] N déchargement *m*

unlock [ʌnˈlɒk] **1** VT **a** [+ *door, box*] ouvrir ; **the door is ~ed** la porte n'est pas fermée à clé **b** (*fig*) [+ *heart*] ouvrir ; [+ *mystery*] résoudre ; [+ *secret*] révéler **2** VI [*lock, box, door*] s'ouvrir

unlooked-for [ʌnˈlʊktfɔːʳ] ADJ inattendu, imprévu

unloose [ʌnˈluːs], **unloosen** [ʌnˈluːsn] VT [+ *rope*] relâcher, détendre ; [+ *knot*] desserrer ; [+ *prisoner*] libérer, relâcher ; [+ *grasp*] relâcher, desserrer

unlovable [ʌnˈlʌvəbl] ADJ désagréable

unloved [ʌnˈlʌvd] ADJ mal aimé

unlovely [ʌnˈlʌvlɪ] ADJ déplaisant

unloving [ʌnˈlʌvɪŋ] ADJ [*person*] peu affectueux ; [*marriage*] sans amour

unluckily [ʌnˈlʌkɪlɪ] ADV malheureusement, par malheur ; **~ for him** malheureusement pour lui ; **the day started ~** la journée a commencé sous le signe de la malchance

unluckiness [ʌnˈlʌkɪnɪs] N manque *m* de chance, malchance *f*

unlucky [ʌnˈlʌkɪ] ADJ **a** (= *unfortunate*) [*person*] qui n'a pas de chance, malchanceux ; [*coincidence, event*] malencontreux ; [*choice, defeat, loser, victim*] malheureux ; [*moment*] mal choisi, mauvais ; [*day*] de malchance ; **he is always** ~ il n'a jamais de chance ; **he tried to get a seat but he was** ~ il a essayé d'avoir une place mais il n'y est pas arrivé ; **he was just ~** il n'a simplement pas eu de chance ; **how ~ for you!** vous n'avez pas de chance !, ce n'est pas de chance pour vous ! ; **to be ~ in one's choice of sth** ne pas avoir de chance en choisissant qch ; **to be ~ at cards** ne pas avoir de chance aux cartes ; **to be ~ in love** ne pas avoir de chance en amour ; **it was ~ (for her) that her husband should walk in just then** elle a eu la malchance que son mari soit entré à cet instant précis ; **she was ~ enough to lose her credit card** elle a eu la malchance de perdre sa carte de crédit ; **he was ~ not to score a**

second goal il n'a pas eu de chance de ne pas marquer un deuxième but ; **to be ~ with the weather** ne pas avoir de chance avec le temps **b** (= *bringing bad luck*) [*number, colour, action, object*] qui porte malheur ; [*omen*] néfaste, funeste ; **it is ~ to break a mirror** ça porte malheur de casser un miroir ; **~ for some!** ça porte malheur !

unmade [ʌnˈmeɪd] **1** VB *pt, ptp* of **unmake** **2** ADJ [*bed*] défait ; (*Brit*) (= *unsurfaced*) [*road*] non goudronné ; (= *hypothetical*) **his new album could be the soundtrack to an ~ movie** son nouvel album pourrait être la musique d'un futur film

un-made-up [ʌnmeɪdˈʌp] ADJ [*face, person*] non maquillé, sans maquillage

unmake [ʌnˈmeɪk] (*pret, ptp* **unmade**) VT défaire ; (= *destroy*) détruire, démolir

unman [ʌnˈmæn] VT (*liter*) faire perdre courage à, émasculer (*fig*)

unmanageable [ʌnˈmænɪdʒəbl] ADJ [*number, size, proportions*] écrasant ; [*problem*] impossible à régler ; [*system, situation*] impossible à gérer, ingérable ; [*hair*] impossible à coiffer, rebelle ; [*person*] impossible ; [*animal*] incontrôlable

unmanly [ʌnˈmænlɪ] ADJ indigne d'un homme ; **it is ~ to cry** les hommes, ça ne pleure pas

unmanned [ʌnˈmænd] ADJ **a** (= *automatic*) [*vehicle, aircraft, flight*] sans équipage ; [*spacecraft*] inhabité ; [*lighthouse*] sans gardien ; [*level-crossing*] automatique, non gardé **b** (= *without staff*) [*station*] sans personnel ; [*border post*] qui n'est pas gardé, sans gardes ; [*position, work station*] inoccupé ; **the machine was left ~ for ten minutes** il n'y a eu personne aux commandes de la machine pendant dix minutes ; **the telephone was left ~** il n'y avait personne pour répondre au téléphone *or* pour prendre les communications ; **he left the desk ~** il a quitté son guichet → **unman**

unmannerliness [ʌnˈmænəlɪnɪs] N (*NonC*) manque *m* de savoir-vivre, impolitesse *f*

unmannerly [ʌnˈmænəlɪ] ADJ mal élevé, impoli, discourtois

unmapped [ʌnˈmæpt] ADJ dont on n'a pas établi *or* dressé la carte

unmarked [ʌnˈmɑːkt] ADJ **a** (= *unscathed*) [*person, face*] qui n'a pas de marque **b** (= *anonymous*) [*grave*] sans nom ; [*police car*] banalisé ; [*container*] qui ne porte pas d'étiquette ; [*envelope, door*] qui ne porte pas de nom **c** [*Educ*] [*essay etc*] non corrigé **d** (*Sport*) [*player*] démarqué **e** (*Ling*) non marqué

unmarketable [ʌnˈmɑːkɪtəbl] ADJ invendable

unmarriageable [ʌnˈmærɪdʒəbl] ADJ immariable

unmarried [ʌnˈmærɪd] **1** ADJ [*person*] célibataire, qui n'est pas marié ; [*couple*] non marié **2** COMP ► **unmarried mother** N mère *f* célibataire

unmask [ʌnˈmɑːsk] **1** VT (*lit, fig*) démasquer **2** VI ôter son masque

unmatched [ʌnˈmætʃt] ADJ [*ability, beauty*] sans pareil, sans égal ; **~ by any rival** sans rival ; **facilities ~ by any other European city** des installations *fpl* sans pareilles *or* égales dans les autres grandes villes européennes ; **~ for quality** d'une qualité inégalée

unmeant [ʌnˈment] ADJ qui n'est pas voulu, involontaire

unmemorable [ʌnˈmemərəbl] ADJ [*book, film etc*] qui ne laisse pas un souvenir impérissable ; **an ~ face** un visage quelconque *or* le genre de visage que l'on oublie facilement

unmentionable [ʌnˈmenʃnəbl] **1** ADJ [*object*] qu'il est préférable de ne pas mentionner ; [*word*] qu'il est préférable de ne pas prononcer ; **it is ~** il est préférable de ne

pas en parler **2** **unmentionables**† NPL (*hum*) sous-vêtements *mpl*, dessous *mpl*

unmerciful [ʌnˈmɜːsɪfʊl] ADJ impitoyable, sans pitié (**towards** envers)

unmercifully [ʌnˈmɜːsɪfəlɪ] ADV impitoyablement

unmerited [ʌnˈmerɪtɪd] ADJ immérité

unmet [ʌnˈmet] ADJ [*needs, demands*] insatisfait ; [*condition*] qui n'a pas été satisfait ; **his demands went ~** ses exigences n'ont pas été satisfaites, on n'a pas répondu à ses exigences

unmethodical [ʌnmɪˈθɒdɪkəl] ADJ peu méthodique

unmindful [ʌnˈmaɪndfʊl] ADJ **~ of** oublieux de

unmissable* [ʌnˈmɪsəbl] ADJ (*Brit*) [*programme, film*] à ne pas rater ; **his new film is ~** son nouveau film est un must*

unmistakable [ʌnmɪsˈteɪkəbl] ADJ [*voice, sound, smell, style*] caractéristique, qu'on ne peut pas ne pas reconnaître ; **to send an ~ message to sb that …** faire comprendre clairement à qn que … ; **to bear the ~ stamp of sth** porter la marque indubitable de qch ; **to show ~ signs of sth** montrer des signes indubitables de qch

unmistakably [ʌnmɪsˈteɪkəblɪ] ADV indubitablement

unmitigated [ʌnˈmɪtɪgeɪtɪd] ADJ (*frm*) [*disaster, failure, success*] total ; [*nonsense, folly*] pur ; [*delight, admiration*] non mitigé ; **he is an ~ scoundrel/liar** c'est un fieffé coquin/menteur

unmixed [ʌnˈmɪkst] ADJ pur, sans mélange

unmolested [ʌnməˈlestɪd] ADV [*slip through, pass by etc*] sans encombre ; [*live, sleep*] sans être dérangé, en paix ; **to be left ~** [*person*] être laissé en paix, être laissé tranquille

unmortgaged [ʌnˈmɔːgɪdʒd] ADJ libre d'hypothèques, non hypothéqué

unmotivated [ʌnˈməʊtɪveɪtɪd] ADJ immotivé, sans motif

unmounted [ʌnˈmaʊntɪd] ADJ **a** (= *without horse*) sans cheval, à pied **b** (= *without mounting*) [*gem*] non serti, non monté ; [*picture, photo*] non monté *or* collé sur carton ; [*stamp*] non collé dans un album

unmourned [ʌnˈmɔːnd] ADJ non regretté ; **he died ~** on ne pleura pas sa mort

unmoved [ʌnˈmuːvd] ADJ indifférent (**by sth** à qch) ; **he was ~ by her tears** il est resté indifférent à ses larmes

unmusical [ʌnˈmjuːzɪkəl] ADJ [*person*] peu musicien, qui n'a pas d'oreille ; [*sound, rendition*] peu mélodieux, peu harmonieux

unmuzzle [ʌnˈmʌzl] VT (*lit, fig*) démuseler

unnam(e)able [ʌnˈneɪməbl] ADJ innommable

unnamed [ʌnˈneɪmd] ADJ **a** (= *anonymous*) [*person, source*] dont le nom n'a pas été divulgué ; [*author, donor*] anonyme **b** (= *having no name*) [*baby, comet, star*] qui n'a pas reçu de nom

unnatural [ʌnˈnætʃrəl] **1** ADJ **a** (= *unusual*) [*calm, silence*] anormal ; **it is not ~ that …** il n'est pas anormal que … (+ *subj*) ; **it is not ~ to think that …** il n'est pas anormal de penser que … ; **it is not ~ for sb to think that …** il n'est pas anormal que qn pense (*subj*) que … ; **it is ~ for her to be so pleasant** ça ne lui ressemble pas d'être aussi aimable **b** (= *abnormal, unhealthy*) [*practice, vice, love*] contre nature ; **it's supposedly ~ for women not to want children** il est soi-disant contre nature pour une femme de ne pas vouloir d'enfants **c** (= *affected*) [*smile, voice*] forcé, qui manque de naturel ; [*manner*] affecté, forcé, qui manque de naturel **2** COMP ► **unnatural death** N (*Jur*) mort *f* non naturelle ► **unnatural practices** NPL pratiques *fpl* contre nature

unnaturally [ʌnˈnætʃrəlɪ] ADV **a** (= *unusually*) [*loud, quiet*] anormalement ; **he was ~ silent** il était anormalement silencieux; **it was ~ silent** un silence anormal régnait; **not ~ we were worried** bien entendu, nous étions inquiets, nous étions naturellement inquiets [b] (= *affectedly*) [*speak, smile*] d'une manière affectée *or* forcée

unnavigable [ˈʌnˈnævɪɡəbl] ADJ non navigable

unnecessarily [ʌnˈnesɪsərɪlɪ] ADV [*cruel, difficult, complicated*] inutilement; [*suffer, alarm, worry*] inutilement, pour rien; **~ violent** d'une violence gratuite; **he is ~ strict** il est plus sévère que cela n'est nécessaire

unnecessary [ʌnˈnesɪsərɪ] ADJ (*gen*) inutile, qui n'est pas nécessaire; [*violence*] gratuit; **to cause ~ suffering to sb** faire souffrir inutilement *or* gratuitement qn; **to use ~ force** faire usage de la force plus qu'il n'est nécessaire; **they made a lot of ~ fuss** ils ont fait beaucoup d'histoires pour rien; **it is ~ to do sth** il n'est pas nécessaire de faire qch; **it is ~ for sb to do sth** il n'est pas nécessaire que qn fasse qch; **it is ~ to add that ...** (il est) inutile d'ajouter que ...

unneighbourly, unneighborly (*US*) [ˈʌnˈneɪbəlɪ] ADJ qui n'agit pas en bon voisin, peu sociable; **this ~ action** cette action mesquine de la part de mon (*or* son *etc*) voisin

unnerve [ʌnˈnɜːv] VT troubler, perturber

unnerved [ʌnˈnɜːvd] ADJ troublé, perturbé

unnerving [ʌnˈnɜːvɪŋ] ADJ troublant, perturbant

unnervingly [ʌnˈnɜːvɪŋlɪ] ADV **~ quiet/calm** d'un calme/sang-froid troublant *or* perturbant

unnoticed [ˈʌnˈnəʊtɪst] ADJ inaperçu; **to be ~ (by sb)** ne pas être remarqué (par qn); **to do sth ~** faire qch sans se faire remarquer; **to go** *or* **pass ~ (by sb)** passer inaperçu (de qn); **to enter/leave ~ (by sb)** entrer/partir sans se faire remarquer (par qn)

unnumbered [ˈʌnˈnʌmbəd] ADJ [a] (= *not numbered*) [*page, ticket, seat*] non numéroté; [*house*] sans numéro [b] (*liter* = *countless*) innombrable

UNO [ˈjuːnəʊ] N (ABBR = **United Nations Organization**) ONU *f*

unobjectionable [ˈʌnəbˈdʒekʃnəbl] ADJ [*thing*] acceptable; [*person*] à qui on ne peut rien reprocher

unobservant [ˈʌnəbˈzɜːvənt] ADJ peu observateur (-trice *f*), peu perspicace

unobserved [ˈʌnəbˈzɜːvd] ADJ [a] (= *unnoticed*) **to be ~ (by sb)** ne pas être remarqué (par qn); **to go ~ (by sb)** passer inaperçu (de qn); **to enter/leave ~ (by sb)** entrer/partir sans se faire remarquer (par qn) [b] (= *unwatched*) **he imagined that he was ~** il s'imaginait qu'on ne l'observait pas

unobstructed [ˈʌnəbˈstrʌktɪd] ADJ [*pipe*] non bouché, non obstrué; [*path, road*] dégagé, libre; **the driver has an ~ view to the rear** le conducteur a une excellente visibilité à l'arrière

unobtainable [ˈʌnəbˈteɪnəbl] ADJ [a] (= *unavailable*) **basic necessities were often ~** il était souvent impossible de se procurer l'essentiel [b] (= *unrealizable*) [*goal, objective*] irréalisable [c] (*Telec*) **his number was ~** son numéro était impossible à obtenir [d] (*sexually*) inaccessible

unobtrusive [ˈʌnəbˈtruːsɪv] ADJ discret (-ète *f*)

unobtrusively [ˈʌnəbˈtruːsɪvlɪ] ADV discrètement

unoccupied [ˈʌnˈɒkjʊpaɪd] ADJ [a] (= *empty*) [*house*] inoccupé, inhabité; [*offices, factory*] vide; [*room, seat, table*] inoccupé; [*post*] vacant [b] (*Mil*) [*France, zone*] libre [c] (= *not busy*) [*person*] désœuvré, inoccupé

unofficial [ˈʌnəˈfɪʃəl] [1] ADJ [a] (= *informal*) [*visit, tour*] privé, non officiel; **in an ~ capacity** à titre privé *or* non officiel [b] (= *de facto*) [*leader, spokesperson*] non officiel [c] (= *unconfirmed*) [*report, results*] officieux [2] COMP ► **unofficial strike** N grève *f* sauvage

unofficially [ˈʌnəˈfɪʃəlɪ] ADV [a] (= *informally*) [*ask, tell, report*] en privé, de façon non officielle; [*visit*] à titre privé, à titre non officiel; **they were ~ engaged** ils étaient officieusement fiancés; **he was working ~ for the CIA** il travaillait de façon non officielle pour la CIA [b] (= *off the record*) [*say*] officieusement; **~, he supports the proposals** officieusement *or* en privé, il soutient ces propositions; **officially, I'm in favour of it, ~, I have my doubts** officiellement, je suis pour, personnellement, j'ai des doutes

unopened [ˈʌnˈəʊpənd] ADJ [*bottle, packet, mail*] qui n'a pas été ouvert; **the book was or lay ~** le livre n'avait pas été ouvert; **to send a letter back ~** renvoyer une lettre sans l'avoir ouverte; **to leave sth ~** laisser qch fermé

unopposed [ˈʌnəˈpəʊzd] ADJ (*Parl, gen*) sans opposition; (*Mil*) sans rencontrer de résistance; (*Parl*) **the bill was given an ~ second reading** le projet de loi a été accepté sans opposition à la deuxième lecture

unorganized [ˈʌnˈɔːɡənaɪzd] ADJ (*gen, Bio, Ind*) inorganisé; (= *badly organized*) [*event etc*] mal organisé; [*essay*] qui manque d'organisation; [*person*] qui ne sait pas s'organiser, qui manque d'organisation

unoriginal [ʌnəˈrɪdʒɪnəl] ADJ [*person, work*] qui manque d'originalité, peu original; [*style, remark*] banal; [*idea*] peu original, banal

unorthodox [ˈʌnˈɔːθədɒks] ADJ [a] (= *unconventional*) [*person, behaviour, method*] peu orthodoxe; [*views, ideas*] non orthodoxe [b] (*Rel*) hétérodoxe

unostentatious [ˈʌnˌɒstənˈteɪʃəs] ADJ discret (-ète *f*), sans ostentation, simple

unostentatiously [ˈʌnˌɒstənˈteɪʃəslɪ] ADV discrètement, sans ostentation

unpack [ˈʌnˈpæk] [1] VT [a] [+ *suitcase*] défaire; [+ *belongings*] déballer; **to get ~ed** déballer ses affaires [b] (*fig*) [+ *idea, problem*] analyser [2] VI défaire sa valise, déballer ses affaires

unpacking [ˈʌnˈpækɪŋ] N (*NonC*) déballage *m*; **to do one's ~** déballer ses affaires

unpaid [ˈʌnˈpeɪd] ADJ [*staff, worker, overtime*] non rémunéré; [*work*] non rémunéré, non rétribué; [*leave, tax*] non payé; [*bill, debt, rent*] impayé; **~ volunteer** bénévole *mf*; **to work ~** travailler à titre bénévole *or* sans être rémunéré

unpalatable [ʌnˈpælɪtəbl] ADJ [a] (*in taste*) [*food*] qui n'a pas bon goût [b] (= *difficult*) [*truth*] désagréable à entendre; [*fact*] désagréable; [*choice*] désagréable à faire; [*idea*] difficile à accepter; **to be ~ to sb** être désagréable à qn

unparalleled [ʌnˈpærəleld] ADJ [*opportunity, prosperity, event*] sans précédent; [*collection, success*] hors pair; [*beauty, wit*] incomparable, sans égal; **~ in the history of ...** sans précédent dans l'histoire de ...

unpardonable [ʌnˈpɑːdnəbl] ADJ (*frm*) [*behaviour*] impardonnable, inexcusable; [*sin*] impardonnable; **it is ~ to treat people so badly** c'est impardonnable *or* inexcusable de traiter les gens aussi mal; **it's ~ of him to have taken it** c'est impardonnable de sa part de l'avoir pris

unpardonably [ʌnˈpɑːdnəblɪ] ADV inexcusablement; **~ rude** d'une impolitesse impardonnable *or* inexcusable

unparliamentary [ˈʌnˌpɑːləˈmentərɪ] ADJ [*behaviour, language*] inadmissible au parlement

unpatented [ˈʌnˈpeɪtntɪd] ADJ [*invention*] non breveté

unpatriotic [ˈʌnˌpætrɪˈɒtɪk] ADJ [*person*] peu patriote; [*act, speech*] antipatriotique

unpatriotically [ˈʌnˌpætrɪˈɒtɪkəlɪ] ADV avec antipatriotisme

unpaved [ˈʌnˈpeɪvd] ADJ non pavé

unperceived [ˈʌnpəˈsiːvd] ADJ inaperçu

unperforated [ˈʌnˈpɜːfəreɪtɪd] ADJ non perforé

unperturbed [ˈʌnpəˈtɜːbd] ADJ imperturbable; **he was ~ by this failure** cet échec ne l'a pas perturbé; **~ by this failure, he ...** sans se laisser perturber par cet échec, il ...

unpick [ˈʌnˈpɪk] VT [+ *seam*] découdre, défaire; [+ *stitch*] défaire; (*Brit fig*) [+ *plan, policy*] attaquer (*fig*)

unpin [ˈʌnˈpɪn] VT détacher (**from** de); [+ *sewing, one's hair*] enlever les épingles de

unplaced [ˈʌnˈpleɪst] ADJ (*Sport*) [*horse*] non placé; [*athlete*] non classé

unplanned [ˈʌnˈplænd] ADJ [*occurrence*] imprévu; [*baby*] non prévu

unplasticized [ˈʌnˈplæstɪsaɪzd] ADJ **~ polyvinyl chloride** chlorure *m* de polyvinyle non plastifié

unplayable [ˈʌnˈpleɪəbl] ADJ [a] (*Tennis, Cricket* = *unstoppable*) [*shot, ball, ace*] imparable [b] (*Snooker* = *obstructed*) [*ball*] injouable [c] (= *unbeatable*) [*person*] imbattable [d] (*Mus*) injouable

unpleasant [ʌnˈpleznt] ADJ désagréable

unpleasantly [ʌnˈplezntlɪ] ADV [a] (= *disagreeably*) [*hot, salty*] désagréablement [b] (= *in an unfriendly way*) [*say, laugh, behave*] de façon déplaisante

unpleasantness [ʌnˈplezntnɪs] N [*of experience, person*] caractère *m* désagréable; [*of place, house*] aspect *m* *or* caractère *m* déplaisant; (= *quarrelling*) friction *f*, dissension *f*; **there has been a lot of ~ recently** il y a eu beaucoup de frictions *or* dissensions ces temps derniers; **after that ~ at the beginning of the meeting ...** après cette fausse note au début de la réunion ...

unpleasing [ʌnˈpliːzɪŋ] ADJ (*frm*) déplaisant

unplug [ˈʌnˈplʌɡ] VT (*Elec*) débrancher

unplugged [ˈʌnˈplʌɡd] ADJ (*Mus*) sans sono*

unplumbed [ˈʌnˈplʌmd] ADJ (*liter*) [*depth, mystery*] non sondé

unpoetic(al) [ˈʌnpəʊˈetɪk(əl)] ADJ peu poétique

unpolished [ˈʌnˈpɒlɪʃt] ADJ [a] (*lit*) [*furniture*] non ciré, non astiqué; [*floor, shoes*] non ciré; [*glass*] dépoli; [*silver*] non fourbi; [*diamond*] non poli [b] (*fig*) [*person*] qui manque d'éducation *or* de savoir-vivre; [*manners*] peu raffiné; [*style*] qui manque de poli

unpolluted [ˈʌnpəˈluːtɪd] ADJ [a] (*lit*) [*air, water, beach*] non pollué [b] (*fig*) [*mind*] non contaminé, non corrompu

unpopular [ˈʌnˈpɒpjʊləʳ] ADJ impopulaire (**with sb** auprès de qn)

unpopularity [ˈʌnˌpɒpjʊˈlærɪtɪ] N (*NonC*) impopularité *f*

unpopulated [ˈʌnˈpɒpjʊleɪtɪd] ADJ inhabité

unpractical [ˈʌnˈpræktɪkəl] ADJ [*method, project, suggestion*] qui n'est pas pratique; [*tool*] peu pratique

unpractised, unpracticed (*US*) [ˈʌnˈpræktɪst] ADJ [*person*] inexpérimenté, inexpert; [*movement etc*] inexpert, inhabile; [*eye, ear*] inexercé

unprecedented [ʌnˈpresɪdəntɪd] ADJ sans précédent

unpredictability [ˈʌnprɪˌdɪktəˈbɪlɪtɪ] N imprévisibilité *f*

unpredictable [ˈʌnprɪˈdɪktəbl] ADJ [*person, behaviour, consequences*] imprévisible; [*weather*] incertain

unpredictably [ˈʌnprɪˈdɪktəblɪ] ADV [*behave*]

de façon imprévisible; **~ violent** d'une violence imprévisible

unprejudiced [ʌn'predʒʊdɪst] ADJ [*person*] impartial, sans parti pris, sans préjugés; [*decision, judgement*] impartial, sans parti pris

unpremeditated [ʌn'priː'medɪteɪtɪd] ADJ non prémédité

unprepared [ʌnprɪ'peəd] ADJ **a** (= *unready*) **to be ~ (for sth/to do sth)** [*person*] ne pas être préparé (à qch/à faire qch), ne pas être prêt (pour qch/à faire qch); **I was ~ for the exam** je n'avais pas suffisamment préparé l'examen; **he set out quite ~** il est parti sans aucune préparation *or* sans (s'y) être du tout préparé; **he was ~ for the news** la nouvelle l'a pris au dépourvu *or* l'a surpris; **to catch sb ~** prendre qn au dépourvu **b** (= *unwilling*) **to be ~ to do sth** [*person*] ne pas être disposé à faire qch **c** (= *unrehearsed*) [*speech*] improvisé; [*test, translation*] sans préparation

unpreparedness [ʌnprɪ'peərɪdnɪs] N (*NonC*) manque *m* de préparation, impréparation *f*

unprepossessing [ʌn,priːpə'zesɪŋ] ADJ [*person, appearance*] peu avenant

unpresentable [ʌnprɪ'zentəbl] ADJ [*person, thing*] qui n'est pas présentable

unpretentious [ʌnprɪ'tenʃəs] ADJ sans prétention(s)

unpriced [ʌn'praɪst] ADJ [*goods*] dont le prix n'est pas marqué

unprincipled [ʌn'prɪnsɪpld] ADJ [*person*] peu scrupuleux, sans scrupules; [*behaviour, act*] peu scrupuleux

unprintable [ʌn'prɪntəbl] ADJ **a** (= *unpublishable*) [*article*] impubliable **b** (*gen hum* = *shocking*) [*story*] racontable; [*words, comment*] que la décence interdit de reproduire *or* répéter; **her reply was ~** la décence m'interdit de répéter sa réponse

unprivileged [ʌn'prɪvɪlɪdʒd] ADJ (*gen*) défavorisé; (*Econ*) économiquement faible

unproductive [ʌnprə'dʌktɪv] ADJ **a** (= *ineffective*) [*meeting, discussion*] stérile, improductif; [*factory, work, worker*] improductif **b** (*Agr*) [*land, soil*] improductif **c** (*Fin*) [*capital*] improductif

unprofessional [ʌnprə'feʃənl] **1** ADJ [*person, behaviour, attitude*] peu professionnel; **to behave in a totally ~ manner** manquer totalement de professionnalisme; **it was ~ of her (to say that)** c'était un manque de professionnalisme de sa part (que de dire cela) **2** COMP ► **unprofessional conduct** N manquement *m* aux devoirs de la profession

unprofitable [ʌn'prɒfɪtəbl] ADJ **a** (= *uneconomic*) [*business, industry, route*] peu rentable **b** (= *fruitless*) [*argument, activity, day*] stérile

unprofitably [ʌn'prɒfɪtəblɪ] ADV sans profit

unpromising [ʌn'prɒmɪsɪŋ] ADJ peu prometteur

unpromisingly [ʌn'prɒmɪsɪŋlɪ] ADV de façon peu prometteuse

unprompted [ʌn'prɒmptəd] **1** ADJ [*remark, offer etc*] non sollicité **2** ADV **he did it ~** il l'a fait sans que rien ne lui soit demandé

unpronounceable [ʌnprə'naʊnsəbl] ADJ imprononçable

unprotected [ʌnprə'tektɪd] **1** ADJ **a** (= *defenceless*) [*person*] sans défense; [*place*] non protégé; **to leave sb/sth ~** laisser qn/qch sans protection; **to be ~ by the law** ne pas être protégé par la loi **b** (= *not covered*) [*skin, plants*] qui n'est pas protégé; [*eyes, wood*] sans protection; **to be ~ from the sun** ne pas être protégé du soleil **2** COMP ► **unprotected intercourse, unprotected sex** N rapports *mpl* sexuels non protégés

unproven [ʌn'pruːvən, ʌn'prəʊvən], **unproved** [ʌn'pruːvd] ADJ **a** (= *not proved*) [*allegation, charge*] sans preuves; (*lit, fig*) **the charge remains ~** cette accusation n'est tou-

jours pas fondée **b** (= *not tested*) [*person, technology*] qui n'a pas (encore) fait ses preuves

unprovided-for [ʌnprə'vaɪdɪd,fɔː] ADJ [*person*] sans ressources

unprovoked [ʌnprə'vəʊkt] ADJ [*attack, aggression, violence*] sans provocation; **he was ~** on ne l'avait pas provoqué; **he said that ~** il a dit ça sans avoir été provoqué

unpublishable [ʌn'pʌblɪʃəbl] ADJ impubliable

unpublished [ʌn'pʌblɪʃt] ADJ inédit

unpunctual [ʌn'pʌŋktjʊəl] ADJ peu ponctuel, qui n'est jamais à l'heure

unpunctuality [ʌn'pʌŋktjʊ'ælɪtɪ] N (*NonC*) manque *m* de ponctualité

unpunished [ʌn'pʌnɪʃt] ADJ impuni; **to go** *or* **remain ~** rester impuni

unputdownable* [ʌn,pʊt'daʊnəbl] ADJ **Grossmith's latest novel is ~** le dernier roman de Grossmith se lit tout d'une traite *or* d'une seule traite

unqualified [ʌn'kwɒlɪfaɪd] ADJ **a** (= *without qualifications*) [*person, staff, pilot*] non qualifié; [*engineer, doctor, teacher*] non diplômé; **he is ~ for the job** (= *has no paper qualifications*) il n'a pas les diplômes requis pour ce poste; (= *unsuitable*) il n'a pas les qualités requises pour ce poste; **he is ~ to do it** il n'est pas qualifié pour le faire; **I feel ~ to judge** je ne me sens pas qualifié pour en juger **b** (= *unmitigated*) [*success*] total; [*disaster*] complet; [*acceptance, support, approval*] inconditionnel, sans réserve; [*admiration*] sans réserve; [*praise*] non mitigé, sans réserve; **an ~ "yes"/"no"** « oui »/« non » inconditionnel **c** (*Gram*) [*noun*] non qualifié

unquenchable [ʌn'kwentʃəbl] ADJ (*lit, fig*) insatiable

unquenched [ʌn'kwentʃt] ADJ [*fire*] non éteint; [*desire*] inassouvi; **~ thirst** soif *f* non étanchée; (*fig*) soif *f* inassouvie

unquestionable [ʌn'kwestʃənəbl] ADJ incontestable, indiscutable

▼ **unquestionably** [ʌn'kwestʃənəblɪ] ADV incontestablement, indiscutablement

unquestioned [ʌn'kwestʃənd] ADJ (= *unchallenged*) incontesté, indiscuté

unquestioning [ʌn'kwestʃənɪŋ] ADJ [*belief, faith, obedience*] inconditionnel, absolu; [*support, acceptance, devotion*] total; [*loyalty, love*] absolu; **an ~ supporter of ...** un(e) inconditionnel(le) de ...

unquestioningly [ʌn'kwestʃənɪŋlɪ] ADV [*obey, accept*] de façon inconditionnelle

unquiet [ʌn'kwaɪət] **1** ADJ [*person, mind*] inquiet (-ète *f*), tourmenté; [*times*] agité, troublé **2** N inquiétude *f*, agitation *f*

unquote [ʌn'kwəʊt] ADV (*in dictation*) fermez les guillemets; (*in report, lecture*) fin de citation → **quote**

unquoted [ʌn'kwəʊtɪd] ADJ (*St Ex*) non coté

unravel [ʌn'rævəl] **1** VT [+ *material*] effiler, effilocher; [+ *knitting*] défaire; [+ *threads*] démêler; [+ *mystery*] débrouiller, éclaircir; [+ *plot*] dénouer **2** VI [*knitting*] se défaire; (*fig*) [*plan, system*] aller à vau-l'eau

unread [ʌn'red] ADJ [*book, newspaper, magazine*] qui n'a pas été lu; **I returned the book ~** j'ai rendu le livre sans l'avoir lu; **I left the letter ~** je n'ai pas lu la lettre; **the book lay ~ on the table** le livre est resté sur la table sans avoir été lu

unreadable [ʌn'riːdəbl] ADJ [*book, handwriting, data*] illisible

unreadiness [ʌn'redɪnɪs] N (*NonC*) impréparation *f*

unready [ʌn'redɪ] ADJ mal préparé, qui n'est pas prêt; **he was ~ for what happened next** il ne s'attendait pas à ce qui est arrivé ensuite, ce qui est arrivé ensuite l'a pris au dépourvu

unreal [ʌn'rɪəl] ADJ **a** (= *not real*) [*situation, world*] irréel; [*flowers*] faux (fausse *f*) **b*** (= *excellent*) formidable*; (*pej* = *unbelievable*) incroyable; **you're ~!** t'es incroyable !*

unrealistic [ʌnrɪə'lɪstɪk] ADJ [*person, expectations, demands*] peu réaliste, irréaliste; [*goal, target, deadline*] irréaliste; **it is ~ to expect that ...** il n'est pas réaliste de penser que ...

unrealistically [ʌnrɪə'lɪstɪkəlɪ] ADV [*high, low, optimistic*] excessivement, exagérément; [*assume*] de façon peu réaliste, de façon irréaliste

unreality [ʌnrɪ'ælɪtɪ] N (*NonC*) irréalité *f*

unrealizable [ʌnrɪə'laɪzəbl] ADJ irréalisable

unrealized [ʌn'rɪːlaɪzd] ADJ [*plan, ambition*] qui n'a pas été réalisé; [*objective*] qui n'a pas été atteint

unreason [ʌn'rɪːzn] N (*NonC*) déraison *f*, manque *m* de bon sens

unreasonable [ʌn'rɪːznəbl] **1** ADJ [*person, suggestion, expectations, demands*] déraisonnable; [*price, amount*] exagéré, excessif; **he is being ~** il n'est pas raisonnable; **at this ~ hour** à cette heure indue; **it is ~ to do that** il est déraisonnable de faire cela; **it was ~ for her to reject your offer** il était déraisonnable de sa part de rejeter votre offre **2** COMP ► **unreasonable behaviour** N (*gen*) conduite *f* déraisonnable; (*Jur*) **divorce on grounds of ~ behaviour** divorce *m* pour violation grave ou renouvelée des devoirs du mariage

unreasonableness [ʌn'rɪːznəblnɪs] N (*NonC*) [*of person*] attitude *f* déraisonnable; [*of demand, price*] caractère *m* exagéré *or* excessif

unreasonably [ʌn'rɪːznəblɪ] ADV [*high*] excessivement, exagérément; [*act, refuse*] de façon déraisonnable; **to take an ~ long time** prendre un temps exagéré; **quite ~, I can't stand him** c'est tout à fait irraisonné, mais je ne le supporte pas; **not ~, she had supposed he would help** elle avait de bonnes raisons de supposer qu'il l'aiderait

unreasoning [ʌn'rɪːznɪŋ] ADJ [*panic, anger, action*] irraisonné; [*person*] irrationnel; [*child*] qui n'est pas en âge de raisonner

unreclaimed [ʌn'rɪːkleɪmd] ADJ [*land*] (*from forest*) non défriché; (*from sea*) non asséché

unrecognizable [ʌn'rekəgnaɪzəbl] ADJ [*person, voice, place*] méconnaissable (**to sb** pour qn); **the wreck was ~ as an aircraft** l'épave de l'avion était méconnaissable

unrecognized [ʌn'rekəgnaɪzd] ADJ **a** (= *unnoticed*) [*phenomenon, condition, efforts*] qui n'est pas reconnu; [*value, worth, talent*] méconnu; **to go ~** [*person, phenomenon, condition*] passer inaperçu; [*hard work, talent*] ne pas être reconnu; **he walked ~ down the street** il a descendu la rue (à pied) sans être reconnu *or* sans que personne ne le reconnaisse **b** (*Pol*) [*government, party, country*] non reconnu

unreconstructed [ʌnrɪːkən'strʌktɪd] ADJ (*pej*) [*person, system, idea, policy*] sclérosé; **an ~ male chauvinist** un macho invétéré

unrecorded [ʌnrɪː'kɔːdɪd] ADJ **a** (= *unreported*) [*crime, incident*] non signalé; [*decision*] non enregistré; [*species*] non répertorié, non classé; **to go ~** [*crime, incident*] ne pas être signalé; [*decision*] ne pas être enregistré; [*species*] ne pas être répertorié ou classé **b** [*piece of music*] non enregistré

unredeemed [ʌnrɪː'diːmd] ADJ [*object from pawn*] non dégagé; [*debt*] non remboursé, non amorti; [*bill*] non honoré; [*mortgage*] non purgé; [*promise*] non tenu; [*obligation*] non rempli; [*sinner*] non racheté; [*fault*] non réparé; [*failing*] non racheté, non compensé (*by par*)

unreel [ʌn'rɪəl] **1** VT [+ *film*] dérouler; [+ *thread*] dérouler, dévider; [+ *fishing line*] dérouler, lancer **2** VI se dérouler, se dévider

unrefined [ʌnrɪː'faɪnd] ADJ **a** (= *not processed*) [*food, sugar, cereal*] non raffiné; [*oil*] brut, non raffiné [b] (*pej = vulgar*) [*person*] peu raffiné

unreflecting [ˌʌnrɪˈflektɪŋ] ADJ [a] [*person*] irréfléchi, impulsif; [*act, emotion*] irraisonné [b] [*surface*] non réfléchissant

unreformed [ˌʌnrɪˈfɔːmd] ADJ [*person*] non amendé; [*institution*] non réformé

unregarded [ˌʌnrɪˈgɑːdɪd] ADJ dont on ne tient pas compte, dont on ne fait pas cas; **his generosity went quite ~** sa générosité est passée inaperçue

unregistered [ʌnˈredʒɪstəd] ADJ [*birth*] non déclaré; [*car*] non immatriculé; (*Post*) non recommandé

unregretted [ˌʌnrɪˈgretɪd] ADJ [*person, act, words*] que l'on ne regrette pas; **he died ~** on ne pleura pas sa mort

unrehearsed [ˌʌnrɪˈhɜːst] ADJ [*question, reply*] spontané; [*speech*] improvisé; [*performance*] qui n'a pas été répété; [*performer*] qui n'a pas répété

unrelated [ˌʌnrɪˈleɪtɪd] ADJ [a] (= *unconnected*) [*incident, event, case*] sans rapport; **to be ~ to sth** n'avoir aucun rapport avec qch [b] (= *from different families*) **they are ~ to each other** ils n'ont aucun lien de parenté, ils ne sont pas parents; **he is ~ to me** il n'a pas de lien de parenté avec moi, nous n'avons aucun lien de parenté

unrelenting [ˌʌnrɪˈlentɪŋ] ADJ [*pressure, criticism*] incessant; [*violence*] continuel; [*pain, pace*] tenace; [*sun, rain*] implacable

unreliability [ˌʌnrɪˌlaɪəˈbɪlɪtɪ] N (*NonC*) [*of person, machine*] manque *m* de fiabilité

unreliable [ˌʌnrɪˈlaɪəbl] ADJ [*person, service, machine, data, news*] peu fiable; [*weather*] incertain; **he's very ~** il n'est vraiment pas fiable, on ne peut vraiment pas compter sur lui; **my watch is ~** ma montre n'est pas très fiable

unrelieved [ˌʌnrɪˈliːvd] ADJ [*gloom, monotony*] constant, permanent; [*anguish*] constant, permanent; [*boredom, tedium*] mortel; [*pain*] que rien ne soulage; **~ grey/black** gris/noir uniforme; **the heat was ~ by any breeze** aucune brise ne venait atténuer la chaleur; **a bare landscape ~ by any trees** un paysage nu dont aucun arbre ne rompait la monotonie

unremarkable [ˌʌnrɪˈmɑːkəbl] ADJ [*person, face, place*] sans rien de remarquable, quelconque; [*fact*] anodin; **he would be ~ in a crowd** on ne le remarquerait pas dans une foule

unremarked [ˌʌnrɪˈmɑːkt] ADJ [*fact*] que personne ne remarque; **he stood there, ~** il est resté là sans que personne ne le remarque; **to go** or **pass ~** passer inaperçu

unremitting [ˌʌnrɪˈmɪtɪŋ] ADJ [*hostility, hatred*] implacable; [*gloom*] persistant; [*struggle*] sans relâche; [*kindness, help, effort*] inlassable, infatigable; **it was ~ toil** on a travaillé sans relâche

unremittingly [ˌʌnrɪˈmɪtɪŋlɪ] ADV [*hostile*] implacablement; [*continue, work*] sans relâche, inlassablement; [*rain*] sans arrêt, sans interruption; **~ cheerful** d'une inaltérable gaieté

unremunerative [ˌʌnrɪˈmjuːnərətɪv] ADJ peu rémunérateur (-trice *f*), mal payé; (*fig*) peu fructueux, peu rentable

unrepaid [ˌʌnrɪˈpeɪd] ADJ [*loan*] non remboursé

unrepealed [ˌʌnrɪˈpiːld] ADJ non abrogé

unrepeatable [ˌʌnrɪˈpiːtəbl] ADJ [*offer, bargain*] unique, exceptionnel; [*comment*] trop grossier pour être répété; **what she said is ~** je n'ose répéter ce qu'elle a dit

unrepentant [ˌʌnrɪˈpentənt] ADJ impénitent; **to be** or **remain ~ (about sth)** ne pas manifester le moindre repentir (quant à qch)

unreported [ˌʌnrɪˈpɔːtɪd] ADJ [*crime, attack,*

accident etc] non signalé; **to go ~** [*crime etc*] ne pas être signalé

unrepresentative [ˈʌnˌreprɪˈzentətɪv] ADJ non représentatif (**of sth** de qch)

unrepresented [ˈʌnˌreprɪˈzentɪd] ADJ non représenté

unrequited [ˌʌnrɪˈkwaɪtɪd] ADJ non partagé

unreserved [ˌʌnrɪˈzɜːvd] ADJ [a] (= *wholehearted*) [*apology, praise, support*] sans réserve [b] (= *unbooked*) [*seat, table*] non réservé

unreservedly [ˌʌnrɪˈzɜːvɪdlɪ] ADV sans réserve

unresisting [ˌʌnrɪˈzɪstɪŋ] ADJ [*person*] qui ne résiste pas, soumis; [*attitude, obedience*] soumis

unresolved [ˌʌnrɪˈzɒlvd] ADJ [a] (= *unsolved*) [*problem, issue, dispute*] non résolu, irrésolu; [*question*] qui reste sans réponse [b] (*Mus*) [*chord*] sans résolution

unresponsive [ˌʌnrɪsˈpɒnsɪv] ADJ [a] (= *passive*) [*person*] **to be ~ to sth** ne pas réagir à qch [b] [*car, engine, steering*] qui répond mal

unrest [ʌnˈrest] N (*NonC*) agitation *f*; (*stronger*) troubles *mpl*

unrestrained [ˌʌnrɪˈstreɪnd] ADJ [a] (= *unchecked*) [*joy, laughter, language*] sans retenue; [*violence*] effréné; [*use, growth*] sans frein; **to be ~ by sth** [*person*] ne être bridé par qch; **to be ~ in one's views** exprimer ses opinions sans retenue [b] (= *not held physically*) [*car passenger*] sans ceinture; [*patient*] sans entraves; [*prisoner*] sans liens, sans entraves

unrestrainedly [ˌʌnrɪˈstreɪnɪdlɪ] ADV sans retenue

unrestricted [ˌʌnrɪˈstrɪktɪd] ADJ [a] (= *unlimited*) [*use, right, travel*] sans restriction(s); **to have ~ access to sth** avoir libre accès à qch [b] (= *unobstructed*) **all seats have an ~ view** toutes les places ont une vue parfaitement dégagée

unrevealed [ˌʌnrɪˈviːld] ADJ non révélé

unrewarded [ˌʌnrɪˈwɔːdɪd] ADJ non récompensé; **to be** or **go ~** ne pas être récompensé

unrewarding [ˌʌnrɪˈwɔːdɪŋ] ADJ [a] (= *unfulfilling*) [*work, job, activity*] peu gratifiant, ingrat; [*relationship*] peu satisfaisant, qui n'apporte pas grand-chose [b] (*financially*) [*work, job*] peu rémunérateur (-trice *f*)

unrighteous [ʌnˈraɪtʃəs] [1] ADJ impie† (*also liter*) [2] **the unrighteous** NPL les impies† *mpl* (*also liter*)

unrighteousness [ʌnˈraɪtʃəsnɪs] N (*NonC*) impiété *f*

unripe [ʌnˈraɪp] ADJ pas mûr

unrivalled, unrivaled (*US*) [ʌnˈraɪvəld] ADJ [*knowledge, experience, collection*] incomparable; [*reputation, success*] sans égal; [*opportunity*] unique; **to be ~ in sth** ne pas avoir son pareil pour qch; **her work is ~ in its quality** son travail est d'une qualité incomparable

unroadworthy [ˈʌnrəʊdˌwɜːðɪ] ADJ [*car*] qui n'est pas en état de rouler

unrobe [ʌnˈrəʊb] [1] VI [a] [*judge etc*] se dévêtir, se dépouiller de ses vêtements (*de cérémonie*) [b] (*frm = undress*) se déshabiller [2] VT [a] [+ *judge etc*] dépouiller de ses vêtements (*de cérémonie*), dévêtir [b] (*frm = undress*) déshabiller

unroll [ʌnˈrəʊl] [1] VT dérouler [2] VI se dérouler

unromantic [ˈʌnrəʊˈmæntɪk] ADJ [*place, landscape, words*] peu romantique; [*person*] terre à terre, peu romantique

unrope [ʌnˈrəʊp] VI (*Climbing*) se décorder

UNRRA [ˌjuːenɑːrɑːˈreɪ] N (*formerly*) (ABBR = **United Nations Relief and Rehabilitation Administration**) UNRRA *f*

unruffled [ʌnˈrʌfld] ADJ [a] (= *calm, unflustered*) [*person, voice*] imperturbable; **to be ~ (by sth)** ne pas être perturbé (par qch) [b] (= *smooth*) [*water*] lisse, sans rides; [*hair*]

non défait; [*bedclothes, sheets*] lisse, sans un pli

unruled [ʌnˈruːld] ADJ [*paper*] uni, non réglé

unruly [ʌnˈruːlɪ] ADJ [*child, pupil*] indiscipliné, turbulent; [*employee, behaviour, hair*] indiscipliné; [*crowd, mob, element*] indiscipliné, incontrôlé

unsaddle [ʌnˈsædl] [1] VT [a] [+ *horse*] desseller [b] (= *unseat*) [+ *rider*] désarçonner [2] COMP ► **unsaddling enclosure** N (*Brit*) enclos d'un champ de course où l'on deselle les chevaux et où sont remis certains trophées

unsafe [ʌnˈseɪf] [1] ADJ [a] (= *dangerous*) [*structure, machine*] dangereux, peu sûr; [*activity, product, level*] dangereux; [*street, method*] peu sûr; [*working conditions*] risqué; [*water*] non potable; **the car is ~ to drive** cette voiture est dangereuse à conduire, il est dangereux de conduire cette voiture; **the country is ~ to visit** le pays n'est pas sûr (pour les touristes), il est dangereux de se rendre dans ce pays; **it is ~ to go there at night** il est dangereux or il n'est pas prudent d'y aller la nuit; **~ to eat** ◊ **~ for human consumption** impropre à la consommation; **to declare a house ~ for habitation** déclarer une maison insalubre [b] (= *in danger*) [*person*] en danger [c] (*Jur = dubious*) [*evidence, conviction, verdict*] douteux; **~ and unsatisfactory** contestable et révisable [2] COMP ► **unsafe sex** N rapports *mpl* sexuels non protégés

unsaid [ʌnˈsed] [1] VB *pt, ptp* of **unsay** [2] ADJ inexprimé, passé sous silence; **much was left ~** on a passé beaucoup de choses sous silence; **some things are better left ~** il y a des choses qu'il vaut mieux taire

unsalable [ʌnˈseɪləbl] ADJ (*US*) = **unsaleable**

unsalaried [ʌnˈsælərɪd] ADJ non rémunéré

unsaleable, unsalable (*US*) [ʌnˈseɪləbl] ADJ invendable

unsalted [ʌnˈsɔːltɪd] ADJ (*gen*) sans sel, non salé; [*butter*] sans sel, doux (douce *f*)

unsanitary [ʌnˈsænɪtərɪ] ADJ (*esp US*) insalubre

unsatisfactory [ˈʌnˌsætɪsˈfæktərɪ] ADJ [*situation, method, answer, relationship*] peu satisfaisant; [*accommodation, product*] qui laisse à désirer; **it is ~ that ...** il n'est pas satisfaisant que ... (+ *subj*)

unsatisfied [ʌnˈsætɪsfaɪd] ADJ [a] [*person*] (*gen, sexually*) insatisfait (**with sb/sth** de qn/qch); (*stronger*) mécontent (**with sb/sth** de qn/qch); **to be left ~** rester sur sa faim [b] (= *unfulfilled*) [*need, desire, urge*] insatisfait, inassouvi; [*demand, curiosity*] insatisfait; [*hunger, appetite*] non apaisé

unsatisfying [ʌnˈsætɪsfaɪɪŋ] ADJ [*work, book, relationship, result*] peu satisfaisant; [*food*] qui n'apaise pas la faim

unsaturated [ʌnˈsætʃəreɪtɪd] ADJ non saturé; **~ fat** corps *mpl* gras insaturés

unsavoury, unsavory (*US*) [ʌnˈseɪvərɪ] ADJ [*person*] peu recommandable; [*district*] peu recommandable, louche; [*reputation*] douteux; [*remark*] de mauvais goût; [*habit, fact, incident*] déplaisant; [*food*] peu ragoûtant; [*smell*] plutôt déplaisant; **an ~ business** une sale affaire; **he's a rather ~ character** c'est un personnage assez peu recommandable

unsay [ʌnˈseɪ] (*pret, ptp* **unsaid**) VT se dédire de; **you can't ~ it now** tu ne peux plus te rétracter or te dédire → **unsaid**

unscathed [ʌnˈskeɪðd] ADJ [a] (= *uninjured*) [*person, place*] indemne; **to emerge** or **escape ~ (from sth)** sortir indemne (de qch); **to leave sb/sth ~** épargner qn/qch [b] (= *unaffected*) [*person, company*] non affecté; **to emerge** or **escape ~ from sth** sortir sans dommage de qch

unscented [ʌnˈsentɪd] ADJ non parfumé

unscheduled [ʌnˈʃedjuːld] ADJ imprévu

unscholarly [ˈʌnˈskɒləlɪ] ADJ [*person*] peu érudit, peu savant ; [*work*] qui manque d'érudition

unschooled [ˈʌnˈskuːld] ADJ [*person*] qui n'a pas d'instruction ; [*horse*] qui n'a pas été dressé ; ~ **in** qui n'a rien appris de, ignorant en matière de *or* pour ce qui est de

unscientific [ˈʌnˌsaɪənˈtɪfɪk] ADJ [*approach, survey, practice*] peu scientifique ; [*sample*] sans valeur scientifique ; **he was ~ in his approach** sa démarche n'était pas scientifique ; **their methods are ~** leurs méthodes ne sont pas scientifiques

unscramble [ˈʌnˈskræmbl] VT (*Telec*) désembrouiller ; (*TV*) décoder, décrypter

unscratched [ˈʌnˈskrætʃt] ADJ [*surface*] non rayé, intact ; [*person*] indemne, sain et sauf

unscrew [ˈʌnˈskruː] **1** VT dévisser **2** VI se dévisser

unscripted [ˈʌnˈskrɪptɪd] ADJ [*speech, remark*] improvisé, non préparé d'avance ; (*Rad, TV*) [*programme*] improvisé

unscrupulous [ʌnˈskruːpjʊləs] ADJ sans scrupules

unscrupulously [ʌnˈskruːpjʊləslɪ] ADV [*behave*] sans scrupule(s), peu scrupuleusement ; **to be ~ ambitious** être arriviste

unscrupulousness [ʌnˈskruːpjʊləsnɪs] N (*NonC*) [*of person*] manque *m* de scrupules

unseal [ˈʌnˈsiːl] VT (= *open*) ouvrir, décacheter ; (= *take seal off*) desceller

unseasonable [ʌnˈsiːznəbl] ADJ [*clothes, food*] hors de saison ; **the weather is ~** ce n'est pas un temps de saison

unseasonably [ʌnˈsiːznəblɪ] ADV ~ **warm/cold/mild weather** un temps exceptionnellement chaud/froid/doux pour la saison ; **it was ~ warm/cold** il faisait exceptionnellement chaud/froid pour la saison

unseasoned [ˈʌnˈsiːznd] ADJ [*timber*] vert, non conditionné ; [*food*] non assaisonné

unseat [ˈʌnˈsiːt] VT **a** [+ *rider*] désarçonner **b** [+ *Member of Parliament*] faire perdre son siège à, sortir

unseaworthy [ˈʌnˈsiːˌwɜːðɪ] ADJ qui n'est pas en état de naviguer *or* ne répond pas aux normes de navigabilité

unsecured [ˈʌnsɪˈkjʊəd] ADJ (*Fin*) sans garantie

unseeded [ˈʌnˈsiːdɪd] ADJ (*Tennis etc*) non classé

unseeing [ˈʌnˈsiːɪŋ] ADJ **he stared, ~, out of the window** il regardait par la fenêtre, le regard perdu dans la vague *or* les yeux dans le vague ; (*fig*) **to gaze at sth with ~ eyes** regarder qch sans le voir

unseemliness [ʌnˈsiːmlɪnɪs] N (*NonC: frm*) inconvenance *f*

unseemly [ʌnˈsiːmlɪ] ADJ (*frm*) inconvenant ; **it is ~ for teachers to swear** il est inconvenant pour un professeur de jurer

unseen [ˈʌnˈsiːn] **1** ADJ **a** (= *not previously seen*) [*film, photos, diaries*] inédit, que l'on n'a jamais vu ; **by the public** que le public n'a jamais vu → **sight b** (= *not visible*) [*person, hand, power*] invisible **c** (*esp Brit: Scol, Univ*) [*exam paper*] non préparé ; **~ translation = 3a** **2** ADV [*enter, leave, escape*] sans être vu (**by sb** par qn) ; **to remain ~** ne pas être vu **3** N **a** (*esp Brit: Scol, Univ*) version *f* (*sans préparation*) **b** **the ~** le monde occulte

unselfconscious [ˈʌnˌselfˈkɒnʃəs] ADJ naturel ; **he was very ~ about it** cela ne semblait nullement le gêner

unselfconsciously [ˈʌnˌselfˈkɒnʃəslɪ] ADV avec naturel, sans la moindre gêne

unselfish [ˈʌnˈselfɪʃ] ADJ [*person*] généreux, désintéressé ; [*act, love*] désintéressé ; (*Sport*) [*player*] qui a l'esprit d'équipe

unselfishly [ʌnˈselfɪʃlɪ] ADV [*act, behave*] généreusement, de façon désintéressée ; (*Sport*) [*play*] avec un bon esprit d'équipe

unselfishness [ˈʌnˈselfɪʃnɪs] N (*NonC*) [*of person*] générosité *f* ; [*of act*] désintéressement *m*, générosité *f*

unsentimental [ˈʌnˈsentɪmentl] ADJ [*person*] peu sentimental, qui ne fait pas de sentiment ; [*attitude*] non sentimental ; [*story, language*] qui ne donne pas dans la sensiblerie ; **to be ~ about sth** [*person*] ne pas se montrer sentimental à propos de qch ; [*story*] ne pas donner dans la sensiblerie à propos de qch

unserviceable [ˈʌnˈsɜːvɪsəbl] ADJ inutilisable, hors d'état de fonctionner

unsettle [ˈʌnˈsetl] VT [+ *person, weather*] perturber ; [+ *stomach*] déranger

unsettled [ˈʌnˈsetld] ADJ **a** (= *uncertain*) [*situation, market*] instable ; [*future*] incertain ; [*weather*] changeant, instable **b** (= *restless*) [*person, life*] perturbé ; **to feel ~** être perturbé ; **he feels ~ in his job** il ne se sent pas vraiment à l'aise dans son travail **c** (= *unresolved*) [*issue*] non résolu ; [*conflict*] non réglé ; **to leave matters ~** laisser les choses en suspens ; **the question remains ~** la question n'est toujours pas réglée, la question reste en suspens **d** (= *uninhabited*) [*place*] inhabité, sans habitants **e** (*Fin*) [*account*] impayé **f** (*Med*) [*stomach*] dérangé

unsettling [ˈʌnˈsetlɪŋ] ADJ [*experience, influence, question, book, film, music*] perturbant ; [*news, atmosphere*] troublant ; **to have an ~ effect on sb/sth** avoir un effet perturbateur sur qn/qch ; **it is ~ to know he could be watching me** ça me perturbe de savoir qu'il pourrait être en train de me regarder ; **they found it ~ to have their mother living with them** ils trouvaient perturbant que leur mère vive avec eux

unsex [ˈʌnˈseks] VT faire perdre sa masculinité (*or* féminité) à ; (= *make impotent*) rendre impuissant

unsexed [ˈʌnsekst] ADJ ~ **chicks** poussins *mpl* dont on n'a pas déterminé le sexe

unshackle [ˈʌnˈʃækl] VT ôter les fers à, désenchaîner ; (*fig*) émanciper, libérer

unshaded [ˈʌnˈʃeɪdɪd] ADJ **a** (= *without lampshade*) [*bulb, light*] sans abat-jour **b** (= *in sunlight*) [*place*] non ombragé, en plein soleil **c** (*Art, Geom*) [*area*] non hachuré

unshak(e)able [ʌnˈʃeɪkəbl] ADJ inébranlable

unshak(e)ably [ʌnˈʃeɪkəblɪ] ADV [*certain*] absolument ; **he's ~ confident** il a une confiance inébranlable en lui-même ; **to be ~ confident that ...** être absolument certain que ... ; **~ committed to a cause** entièrement acquis à une cause

unshaken [ˈʌnˈʃeɪkn] ADJ **a** (= *unchanged*) **to be** *or* **remain ~** [*conviction, belief, faith*] ne pas être ébranlé ; [*confidence*] ne pas être ébranlé *or* entamé ; **to be ~ in one's belief that ...** ne pas se laisser ébranler dans sa conviction que ... **b** (= *not worried*) **to be ~** [*person*] ne pas être secoué (**by sth** par qch)

unshaven [ˈʌnˈʃeɪvn] ADJ non rasé

unsheathe [ˈʌnˈʃiːð] VT [+ *sword*] dégainer ; [*cat, tiger*] [+ *claws*] sortir

unship [ˈʌnˈʃɪp] VT [+ *cargo*] décharger, débarquer

unshockable [ˈʌnˈʃɒkəbl] ADJ **he is (completely) ~** rien ne le choque

unshod [ˈʌnˈʃɒd] ADJ [*horse*] qui n'est pas ferré ; [*person*] déchaussé, pieds nus

unshrinkable [ˈʌnˈʃrɪŋkəbl] ADJ irrétrécissable (au lavage)

unsighted [ˈʌnˈsaɪtɪd] ADJ **a** (= *unseen*) qui n'est pas en vue, que l'on n'a pas vu **b** (= *unable to see sth*) **the goalkeeper was ~ by a defender** le gardien de but a eu la vue cachée par un défenseur

unsightliness [ʌnˈsaɪtlɪnɪs] N (*NonC*) aspect *m* disgracieux, laideur *f*

unsightly [ʌnˈsaɪtlɪ] ADJ disgracieux ; **to look ~** être disgracieux ; ~ **facial hair** poils *mpl* disgracieux sur le visage ; **he has an ~ scar on his face** une cicatrice lui dépare le visage

unsigned [ˈʌnˈsaɪnd] ADJ **a** (= *without signature*) [*letter, article, contract*] non signé ; ~ **by sb** sans la signature de qn ; **the treaty remains ~ by the US** le traité n'a toujours pas été signé par les États-Unis **b** (*Mus*) [*band, singer*] qui n'est pas sous contrat avec une maison de disques

unsinkable [ˈʌnˈsɪŋkəbl] ADJ insubmersible ; (*esp Pol: fig*) inattaquable

unskilful, unskillful (*US*) [ˈʌnˈskɪlfʊl] ADJ (= *clumsy*) maladroit ; (= *inexpert*) malhabile, inexpert

unskilfully, unskillfully (*US*) [ˈʌnˈskɪlfəlɪ] ADV (= *clumsily*) avec maladresse ; (= *inexpertly*) malhabilement

unskilled [ˈʌnˈskɪld] **1** ADJ **a** (*Ind*) [*work, labour, job*] ne nécessitant pas de qualification professionnelle **b** (= *not skilful*) [*person, driver*] inexpérimenté ; **to be ~ in sth** ne pas s'y connaître en qch ; **to be ~ in the use of sth** ne pas savoir bien se servir de qch ; **to be ~ in** *or* **at doing sth** ne pas être habile à faire qch **2** COMP ▸ **unskilled worker** N ouvrier *m*, -ière *f* spécialisé(e), OS *mf*

unskimmed [ˈʌnˈskɪmd] ADJ [*milk*] non écrémé, entier

unsmiling [ʌnˈsmaɪlɪŋ] ADJ [*face*] sans sourire ; [*expression*] sérieux ; **he remained ~** il restait sans sourire, il ne souriait pas ; **he stared at her, ~** il l'a dévisagée sans sourire

unsmilingly [ʌnˈsmaɪlɪŋlɪ] ADV sans sourire

unsociability [ˈʌnˌsəʊʃəˈbɪlɪtɪ] N (*NonC*) insociabilité *f*

unsociable [ʌnˈsəʊʃəbl] ADJ **a** (*pej* = *unfriendly*) [*person*] peu sociable ; **I'm feeling rather ~ this evening** je n'ai pas tellement envie de voir des gens ce soir **b** = **unsocial**

unsocial [ʌnˈsəʊʃəl] ADJ **to work ~ hours** travailler en dehors des heures normales

unsold [ˈʌnˈsəʊld] ADJ [*goods, tickets, holidays*] invendu ; ~ **stock** stock *m* d'invendus ; **to be left** *or* **remain ~** ne pas être vendu

unsoldierly [ʌnˈsəʊldʒəlɪ] ADJ [*behaviour, emotion*] indigne d'un soldat ; [*appearance*] peu militaire, peu martial ; [*person*] qui n'a pas l'esprit *or* la fibre militaire

unsolicited [ˈʌnsəˈlɪsɪtɪd] ADJ [*mail, phone call, advice*] non sollicité ; (*Fin*) [*offer, bid*] spontané ; (*US: on customs declarations*) "~ **gift**" « cadeau »

unsolvable [ʌnˈsɒlvəbl] ADJ insoluble, impossible à résoudre

unsolved [ˈʌnˈsɒlvd] ADJ [*mystery*] non résolu, inexpliqué ; [*crime*] non éclairci ; [*problem, crossword clue*] non résolu

unsophisticated [ˈʌnsəˈfɪstɪkeɪtɪd] ADJ [*person, behaviour, tastes, film*] simple ; [*method, device*] simpliste ; **an ~ wine** un petit vin sans prétention ; **financially ~** [*person*] sans grande expérience de la finance, peu versé dans la finance ; **a technically ~ photographer** un photographe sans grande technique

unsought [ˈʌnˈsɔːt] ADJ (*also* ~-**for**) non recherché, non sollicité

unsound [ˈʌnˈsaʊnd] ADJ **a** (= *unreliable*) [*person, advice, evidence*] douteux ; [*reasoning, judgement, argument, claim*] mal fondé, douteux ; [*view, conviction*] mal fondé ; [*decision*] peu sensé, peu judicieux ; [*company*] peu solide ; [*investment*] peu sûr ; [*player*] peu compétent ; **educationally/ecologically ~** contestable sur le plan éducatif/écologique ; **ideologically/politically ~** idéologiquement/politiquement douteux ; **the book is ~ on some points** ce livre est douteux sur certains points **b** (= *in poor condition*) [*building, teeth, gums*] en mauvais état ; [*health, constitution*] mauvais; [*heart, lungs*] en mauvaise santé c (*Psych, Jur*) **psychologically ~** psychologiquement malsain; (*Jur*) **to be of ~ mind** ne pas jouir de toutes ses facultés mentales

unsparing [ʌnˈspɛərɪŋ] ADJ a (= *lavish*) prodigue (**of** de), généreux; **to be ~ in one's efforts to do sth** ne pas ménager ses efforts pour faire qch; **the report was ~ in its criticism** le rapport n'a pas été avare de critiques b (= *cruel*) impitoyable, implacable

unsparingly [ʌnˈspɛərɪŋlɪ] ADV [*give*] généreusement, avec prodigalité; [*work*] inlassablement

unspeakable [ʌnˈspiːkəbl] ADJ [*act, object, horror, food*] innommable; [*pain, cruelty*] indescriptible

unspeakably [ʌnˈspiːkəblɪ] ADV effroyablement

unspecifically [ˌʌnspəˈsɪfɪkəlɪ] ADV [*talk etc*] en restant dans le vague, sans entrer dans les détails

unspecified [ʌnˈspesɪfaɪd] ADJ non spécifié, non précisé

unspectacular [ˌʌnspekˈtækjʊləʳ] ADJ qui n'a rien de remarquable or d'exceptionnel

unspent [ʌnˈspent] ADJ [*money, funds*] non dépensé, qui reste

unspoiled [ʌnˈspɔɪld], **unspoilt** [ʌnˈspɔɪlt] ADJ [*countryside, beauty, view, village*] préservé; [*child*] qui reste naturel; **~ by** non gâché par; **he remained ~ by his great success** malgré son grand succès il restait aussi simple qu'avant

unspoken [ʌnˈspəʊkən] ADJ [*words, hope*] inexprimé; [*criticism, message*] implicite; [*agreement, rule, bond*] tacite

unsporting [ʌnˈspɔːtɪŋ], **unsportsmanlike** [ʌnˈspɔːtsmənlaɪk] ADJ (*gen, Sport*) déloyal; **to be ~** (= *not play fair*) être déloyal, ne pas jouer franc jeu; (= *be bad loser*) être mauvais joueur; **that's very ~ of you** ce n'est pas très chic de votre part

unspotted [ʌnˈspɒtɪd] ADJ (*liter. lit, fig*) sans tache, immaculé

unstable [ʌnˈsteɪbl] ADJ (*all senses*) instable

unstained [ʌnˈsteɪnd] ADJ (= *not coloured*) [*furniture, floor*] non teinté; (= *clean*) [*garment, surface*] immaculé, sans tache; [*reputation*] non terni, sans tache

unstamped [ʌnˈstæmpt] ADJ [*letter*] non affranchi, non timbré; [*document, passport*] non tamponné

unstated [ʌnˈsteɪtɪd] ADJ inexprimé

unstatesmanlike [ʌnˈsteɪtsmənlaɪk] ADJ peu diplomatique

unsteadily [ʌnˈstedɪlɪ] ADV [*get up, walk*] de façon mal assurée; [*say*] d'une voix mal assurée

unsteadiness [ʌnˈstedɪnɪs] N (*NonC*) a (= *shakiness*) [*of hands*] tremblement m; [*of gait, voice*] manque m d'assurance; **to experience some ~ on one's feet** avoir du mal à tenir sur ses jambes b (= *instability*) [*of ladder, structure*] manque m de stabilité c (= *irregularity*) [*of progress, course, rhythm*] irrégularité f

unsteady [ʌnˈstedɪ] ADJ a (= *shaky*) [*person, voice, legs, gait*] mal assuré; **to be ~ on one's feet** (*gen*) ne pas être solide sur ses jambes; (*from drink*) tituber, chanceler b (= *unsecured*) [*ladder, structure*] instable c (= *irregular*) [*progress, course, rhythm*] irrégulier d (= *unreliable*) [*person*] inconstant

unstick [ʌnˈstɪk] (*pret, ptp* **unstuck**) [1] VT décoller; **to come unstuck** [*stamp, notice*] se décoller;* [*plan*] tomber à l'eau; **he certainly came unstuck* over that scheme** il s'est vraiment planté* avec ce projet [2] VI se décoller

unstinted [ʌnˈstɪntɪd] ADJ [*praise*] sans réserve; [*generosity*] sans bornes; [*efforts*] illimité, incessant

unstinting [ʌnˈstɪntɪŋ] ADJ [*help*] sans faille; [*support, praise*] sans réserve; [*kindness, gener-*

osity] sans bornes; [*efforts*] infatigable; [*work*] inlassable; **to be ~ in one's praise (of sb/sth)** ne pas tarir d'éloges (sur qn/qch); **he was ~ in his efforts** il ne ménageait pas ses efforts; (*frm*) **~ of sth** [*person*] prodigue de qch

unstitch [ʌnˈstɪtʃ] VT défaire; **to come ~ed** se découdre

unstop [ʌnˈstɒp] VT [+ *sink*] déboucher, désobstruer; [+ *bottle*] déboucher, décapsuler

unstoppable [ʌnˈstɒpəbl] ADJ [*momentum, progress, rise*] irrépressible; [*force*] irrésistible; [*shot*] que rien ne peut arrêter; **the advance of science is ~** on ne peut arrêter les progrès de la science; **the Labour candidate seems ~** il semble que rien ne puisse arrêter le candidat travailliste

unstrap [ʌnˈstræp] VT **to ~ A from B** détacher A de B, défaire les sangles qui attachent A à B

unstressed [ʌnˈstrest] ADJ [*syllable*] inaccentué, atone

unstring [ʌnˈstrɪŋ] (*pret, ptp* **unstrung**) VT [+ *violin, racket*] enlever or détendre les cordes de; [+ *beads*] désenfiler; (*fig*) [+ *person*] démoraliser

unstructured [ʌnˈstrʌktʃəd] ADJ a (= *loosely organized*) [*method, programme, meeting*] non structuré b (*Dress*) [*jacket*] déstructuré

unstrung [ʌnˈstrʌŋ] [1] VB *pt, ptp of* **unstring** [2] ADJ [*violin, racket*] dont on a enlevé les cordes, dont les cordes sont détendues; (*fig*) démoralisé

unstuck [ʌnˈstʌk] VB *pt, ptp of* **unstick**

unstudied [ʌnˈstʌdɪd] ADJ naturel, spontané

unsubdued [ˌʌnsəbˈdjuːd] ADJ (*lit, fig*) indompté

unsubsidized [ʌnˈsʌbsɪdaɪzd] ADJ non subventionné, qui ne reçoit pas de subvention

unsubstantial [ˌʌnsəbˈstænʃəl] ADJ [*structure*] peu solide, léger; [*meal*] peu substantiel, peu nourrissant; [*argument*] peu solide, sans substance; [*evidence*] insuffisant

unsubstantiated [ˌʌnsəbˈstænʃɪeɪtɪd] ADJ [*rumour*] sans fondement; [*story*] non confirmé; [*claim*] non fondé; [*allegation*] sans preuves; **these reports remain ~** ces informations ne sont toujours pas confirmées

unsubtle [ʌnˈsʌtl] ADJ lourd

unsuccessful [ˌʌnsəkˈsesfʊl] ADJ [*attempt*] sans succès, infructueux; [*campaign, operation, career*] sans succès; [*efforts, negotiations, search*] infructueux; [*firm*] qui ne prospère pas; [*candidate, marriage, outcome*] malheureux; [*writer, book*] qui n'a pas de succès; **to be ~** [*person*] ne pas réussir; **I tried to speak to him but I was ~** j'ai essayé de lui parler mais sans succès; **to be ~ in an exam** échouer à or rater un examen; **they were ~ in their efforts** leurs efforts ont été infructueux; **he is ~ in everything he does** rien ne lui réussit; **to be ~ in doing sth** ne pas réussir à faire qch; **to prove ~** [*search, negotiations*] ne mener à rien; **we regret to inform you that your application for the post has been ~** nous regrettons de ne pouvoir donner suite à votre candidature au poste concerné; **after three ~ attempts** après trois tentatives infructueuses

unsuccessfully [ˌʌnsəkˈsesfəlɪ] ADV sans succès

unsuitability [ˌʌnˌsuːtəˈbɪlɪtɪ] N **the ~ of the candidate** l'inaptitude du candidat; **they talked about her ~ for the job** ils ont évoqué le fait qu'elle ne convenait pas pour le poste

unsuitable [ʌnˈsuːtəbl] ADJ [*place, time, food, climate*] qui ne convient pas; [*person*] (= *inappropriate*) qui ne convient pas; (= *not respectable*) peu recommandable; [*book*] peu recommandable; [*moment*] inopportun; [*action, reply, example, device*] inopportun, peu approprié; [*language, attitude*] inconvenant; [*colour, size*] qui ne va pas; [*job, land*] inapproprié;

[*accommodation*] qui ne convient pas; [*clothes*] (= *inappropriate*) inadapté; (= *not respectable*) non convenable; **he is ~ to be the leader of the party** ce n'est pas l'homme qu'il faut pour diriger le parti; **he is ~ for the post** il ne convient pas pour ce poste; **land that is entirely ~ for agriculture/growing wheat** terrain qui ne se prête pas du tout à l'agriculture/à la culture du blé; **his shoes were totally ~ for walking in the country** ses chaussures étaient totalement inadaptées pour la randonnée; **to be ~ for sb** (= *inappropriate*) ne pas convenir à qn; (= *not respectable*) être déconseillé à qn; **an ~ wife for a clergyman** une femme peu recommandable pour un pasteur; **~ for children** déconseillé aux enfants; **the building was totally ~ as a museum space** ce bâtiment ne se prêtait absolument pas à servir de musée; **the equipment proved ~** l'équipement s'est avéré inadapté

unsuitably [ʌnˈsuːtəblɪ] ADV **~ dressed** (= *inappropriately*) habillé de façon inadaptée; (= *not respectably*) habillé de façon inconvenante; **to be ~ qualified for sth** ne pas avoir les qualifications requises pour qch

unsuited [ʌnˈsuːtɪd] ADJ **~ to sth** [*person*] inapte à qch; [*thing*] inadapté à qch; **Mary and Neil are ~ (to each other)** Mary et Neil ne sont pas faits l'un pour l'autre; **to be ~ to** or **for doing sth** ne pas être fait pour faire qch; **to be ~ for sth** ne pas être fait pour qch; **the horse was ~ for the fast ground** le cheval n'était pas fait pour ce terrain dur

unsullied [ˌʌnˈsʌlɪd] ADJ (*liter*) [*reputation*] sans tache; **she possessed an innocence ~ by contact with the world** elle était d'une innocence que la fréquentation du monde n'avait pas entachée; **a town ~ by modern development** une ville préservée des atteintes de l'urbanisme moderne

unsung [ʌnˈsʌŋ] ADJ [*hero, heroine, achievement*] méconnu

unsupported [ˌʌnsəˈpɔːtɪd] ADJ a (= *unsubstantiated*) [*allegation, accusation*] sans preuves; [*claim, statement, hypothesis*] infondé; **~ by evidence** non étayé par des preuves b (= *without backup*) [*troops*] sans soutien; [*expedition*] sans appui; (*Pol*) [*candidate*] sans appui, sans soutien (**by sb** de la part de qn); (*financially*) [*mother*] sans soutien financier; **~ by troops** sans l'appui de troupes c (*physically*) **to walk/stand ~** [*person*] marcher/se tenir debout sans soutien d (*Archit, Constr*) [*structure, wall*] sans support

unsure [ʌnˈʃʊəʳ] ADJ a (= *doubtful*) **I'm ~** je n'en suis pas sûr, je suis dans l'incertitude; **to be ~ about** or **of sb/sth** ne pas être sûr de qn/qch; **to be ~ about doing sth** ne pas savoir exactement si l'on va faire qch, ne pas être certain de faire qch; **to be ~ about** or **of how to do sth** ne pas trop savoir or ne pas être sûr de savoir comment faire qch; **she is ~ what to do/how to reply** elle ne sait pas trop quoi faire/comment répondre, elle n'est pas sûre de savoir quoi faire/comment répondre; **the police are ~ what caused the violence** la police ne s'explique pas vraiment les raisons de cette violence; **they're ~ when he'll return** ils ne savent pas bien quand il rentrera; **she was ~ where she was** elle ne savait pas au juste où elle se trouvait; **he was ~ where to begin** il ne savait pas trop par où commencer; **he was ~ whether he would be able to do it** il n'était pas sûr de pouvoir le faire; **she was ~ whether to laugh or cry** elle ne savait pas trop si elle devait rire ou pleurer b (= *lacking confidence*) [*person*] mal assuré; **to be ~ of o.s.** ne pas être sûr de soi; **this made him ~ of himself** cela l'a fait douter (de lui) c (= *unreliable*) [*memory*] peu fidèle

unsurmountable [ˌʌnsəˈmaʊntəbl] ADJ insurmontable

unsurpassable [ˈʌnsəˈpɑːsəbl] ADJ insurpassable

unsurpassed [ˈʌnsəˈpɑːst] ADJ qui n'a jamais été dépassé; **to remain ~** rester inégalé

unsurprising [ˈʌnsəˈpraɪzɪŋ] ADJ pas surprenant; **it is ~ that ...** il n'est pas surprenant que ... (+ subj)

unsurprisingly [ˈʌnsəˈpraɪzɪŋlɪ] ADV **~, he left immediately** comme on pouvait s'y attendre, il est parti tout de suite; **not ~, he did it rather well** contrairement à toute attente, il l'a plutôt bien fait

unsuspected [ˈʌnsəsˈpektɪd] ADJ a (= unforeseen) [problem, skill, cause] insoupçonné b (= not under suspicion) [person] qui n'éveille pas de soupçons

unsuspecting [ˈʌnsəsˈpektɪŋ] ADJ sans méfiance; **and he, quite ~, said ...** et lui, sans la moindre méfiance, dit ...

unsuspicious [ˈʌnsəsˈpɪʃəs] ADJ a (= feeling no suspicion) peu soupçonneux, peu méfiant b (= arousing no suspicion) qui n'a rien de suspect, qui n'éveille aucun soupçon; **~-looking** tout à fait ordinaire

unsweetened [ˈʌnˈswiːtnd] ADJ [tea, coffee] sans sucre, non sucré; [yoghurt, soya milk] non sucré; [fruit juice] sans sucre ajouté

unswerving [ʌnˈswɜːvɪŋ] ADJ [support, commitment] indéfectible; [loyalty] à toute épreuve; [faith, devotion, resolve] inébranlable; [policy] inflexible; **to be ~ in one's belief in sth** avoir une foi inébranlable en qch

unswervingly [ʌnˈswɜːvɪŋlɪ] ADV **loyal** d'une loyauté à toute épreuve; **to hold ~ to one's course** poursuivre inébranlablement son but, ne pas se laisser détourner de son but

unsympathetic [ˈʌnˌsɪmpəˈθetɪk] ADJ a (= uncaring) [person, attitude, treatment] peu compatissant (**to sb** envers qn), indifférent; **~ to sb's needs/problems** indifférent aux besoins/problèmes de qn; (= hostile) **~ to sth** [+ cause, idea] hostile à qch; [+ aim] peu sensible à qch b (= unlikeable) [character] antipathique; [portrayal] peu flatteur

unsympathetically [ˈʌnˌsɪmpəˈθetɪkəlɪ] ADV sans compassion

unsystematic [ˈʌnˌsɪstɪˈmætɪk] ADJ [work, reasoning] peu systématique, peu méthodique

unsystematically [ˈʌnˌsɪstɪˈmætɪkəlɪ] ADV sans système, sans méthode

untainted [ˈʌnˈteɪntɪd] ADJ (lit) [food] non contaminé; [water, air] pur; (fig) [reputation] intact, sans tache; [person, mind] non corrompu (**by** par), pur

untam(e)able [ˈʌnˈteɪməbl] ADJ [bird, wild animal] inapprivoisable; [large or fierce animal] non dressable

untamed [ˈʌnˈteɪmd] ADJ a (= uncultivated) [landscape, environment] sauvage; [vegetation] sauvage, luxuriant; [beauty] sauvage, farouche b (= uninhibited) [person] sauvage, indompté; [passion] dévorant, fougueux c (= undomesticated) [animal] qui n'est pas apprivoisé

untangle [ˈʌnˈtæŋgl] VT [+ rope, wool, hair] démêler; [+ mystery] débrouiller, éclaircir; [+ plot] dénouer

untanned [ˈʌnˈtænd] ADJ a [hide] non tanné b [person] non bronzé

untapped [ˈʌnˈtæpt] ADJ inexploité

untarnished [ˈʌnˈtɑːnɪʃt] ADJ (lit, fig) non terni, sans tache

untasted [ˈʌnˈteɪstɪd] ADJ [food, delights] auquel on n'a pas goûté; **the food lay ~ on the plate** le repas restait dans l'assiette; **he left the meal ~** il n'a pas goûté au repas

untaught [ˈʌnˈtɔːt] ADJ a (= uneducated) sans instruction, ignorant; (= natural, innate) [skill, gift] inné, naturel

untaxable [ˈʌnˈtæksəbl] ADJ [income] non imposable; [goods] exempt de taxes

---

untaxed [ˈʌnˈtækst] ADJ [goods] exempt de taxes, non imposé; [income] non imposable, exempté d'impôts; [car] sans vignette

unteachable [ˈʌnˈtiːtʃəbl] ADJ [person] à qui on ne peut rien apprendre; [pupil] réfractaire à tout enseignement; [subject] impossible à enseigner, qui ne se prête pas à l'enseignement

untempered [ˈʌnˈtempəd] ADJ [steel] non revenu

untenable [ˈʌnˈtenəbl] ADJ [theory, argument, opinion] indéfendable; [position, situation] intenable

untenanted [ˈʌnˈtenəntɪd] ADJ inoccupé, sans locataire(s)

untended [ˈʌnˈtendɪd] ADJ (= unwatched) sans surveillance; (= unmaintained) [garden etc] mal entretenu

untested [ˈʌnˈtestɪd] ADJ a (= untried) [drug, method] non testé; [theory] non vérifié; [system, weapon, device] non testé, non essayé b (= inexperienced) [person] inexpérimenté

unthinkable [ʌnˈθɪŋkəbl] 1 ADJ a (= inconceivable) impensable, inconcevable; **it is ~ that ...** il est impensable or inconcevable que ... (+ subj); **it would be ~ to do that** il serait impensable or inconcevable de faire cela; **it would be ~ for her to do that** il serait impensable or inconcevable qu'elle fasse cela b (= unbearable) insupportable 2 N **the ~** l'impensable m, l'inconcevable m

unthinking [ˈʌnˈθɪŋkɪŋ] ADJ [person, behaviour] irréfléchi; [child] étourdi; [action, remark] irréfléchi, inconsidéré; [obedience] aveugle; **she drove on, ~** elle a continué sa route sans réfléchir

unthinkingly [ˈʌnˈθɪŋkɪŋlɪ] ADV [behave] sans réfléchir; **~ cruel** d'une cruauté inconsciente

unthought-of [ˈʌnˈθɔːtɒv] ADJ auquel on n'a pas pensé or songé

unthread [ˈʌnˈθred] VT [+ needle, pearls] désenfiler

untidily [ʌnˈtaɪdɪlɪ] ADV [work] sans méthode, sans ordre; [write, dress] sans soin; **his books lay ~ about the room** ses livres étaient étalés en désordre dans toute la pièce

untidiness [ʌnˈtaɪdɪnɪs] N (NonC) [of room] désordre m; [of dress, person] aspect m débraillé; (in habits) manque m d'ordre

untidy [ʌnˈtaɪdɪ] ADJ (in appearance) [room, desk, clothes, hair] en désordre; [person, appearance, garden] négligé; [writing] peu soigné; [work] brouillon; (in habits) [person] désordonné; **in an ~ heap** or **pile** empilé en désordre

untie [ʌnˈtaɪ] VT [+ knot] défaire; [+ string, shoelaces] dénouer, défaire; [+ shoes] défaire or dénouer les lacets de; [+ parcel] défaire, ouvrir; [+ prisoner, hands] délier, détacher; [+ bonds] défaire, détacher

until [ənˈtɪl] 1 PREP jusqu'à; **~ such time as ...** (in future) jusqu'à ce que ... (+ subj), en attendant que ... (+ subj); (in past) avant que ... (+ subj); **~ the next day** jusqu'au lendemain; **from morning ~ night** du matin (jusqu')au soir; **~ now** jusqu'ici, jusqu'à maintenant; **~ then** jusque-là; **not ~** (in future) jusqu'à (in past) ne ... que; **it won't be ready ~ tomorrow** ce ne sera pas prêt avant demain; **he didn't leave ~ the following day** il n'est parti que le lendemain; **it will be ready on Saturday, ~ when we must ...** ce sera prêt samedi et en attendant nous devons ...; **the work was not begun ~ 1986** ce n'est qu'en 1986 que les travaux ont commencé; **I had heard nothing of it ~ five minutes ago** j'en ai seulement entendu parler or j'en ai entendu parler pour la première fois il y a cinq minutes

2 CONJ (in future) jusqu'à ce que (+ subj), en attendant que (+ subj); (in past) avant que (+ subj); **wait ~ I come** attendez que je vienne; **~**

---

they built the new road avant qu'ils (ne) fassent la nouvelle route; **~ they build the new road** en attendant qu'ils fassent la nouvelle route; **he laughed ~ he cried** il a ri aux larmes; **not ~** (in future) pas avant que ... (ne) (+ subj), tant que ... ne (+ indic) pas; (in past) tant que ... ne ... (+ indic) pas; **he won't come ~ you invite him** il ne viendra pas avant que vous (ne) l'invitiez or avant d'être invité, il ne viendra pas tant que vous ne l'inviterez pas; **they did nothing ~ we came** ils n'ont rien fait tant que nous n'avons pas été là; **do nothing ~ I tell you** ne faites rien avant que je (ne) vous le dise or tant que je ne vous l'aurai pas dit; **do nothing ~ you get my letter** ne faites rien avant d'avoir reçu ma lettre; **wait ~ you get my letter** attendez d'avoir reçu ma lettre; **don't start ~ I come** ne commencez pas avant que j'arrive (subj), attendez-moi pour commencer

untilled [ˈʌnˈtɪld] ADJ non labouré

untimely [ʌnˈtaɪmlɪ] ADJ [death] prématuré; [arrival, return, visit] intempestif; [remark, action] déplacé, inopportun; [pregnancy, rain] inopportun, qui arrive au mauvais moment; **to meet** or **come to an ~ end** [person, project] connaître une fin prématurée

untiring [ʌnˈtaɪərɪŋ] ADJ [campaigner, fighter] infatigable, inlassable; [enthusiasm, work, efforts] inlassable; **to be ~ in one's efforts (to do sth)** ne pas ménager ses efforts (pour faire qch)

untiringly [ʌnˈtaɪərɪŋlɪ] ADV inlassablement

untitled [ʌnˈtaɪtld] ADJ a [painting] sans titre b [person] qui n'a pas de titre

unto [ˈʌntʊ] PREP (liter) = **to, towards**

untogether* [ˌʌntəˈgeðə] ADJ [person] **to be ~** (= disorganized) ne pas être au point*; (= unstable) être paumé*

untold [ʌnˈtəʊld] ADJ a (= indescribable, incalculable) [damage] indescriptible; [misery, suffering] indicible, indescriptible; [worry] indicible; [riches, losses] incalculable; [amounts] inestimable; [varieties] innombrable; **to save ~ numbers of lives** sauver d'innombrables vies; **~ millions of years ago** il y a des millions et des millions d'années b (= not recounted) [story] jamais raconté; [secret] jamais dévoilé or divulgué; **that story remains ~** cette histoire n'a encore jamais été racontée; **to leave sth ~** passer qch sous silence

untouchable [ʌnˈtʌtʃəbl] 1 ADJ a (in India) [person] de la caste des intouchables; [caste] des intouchables; (fig) **to be treated as ~** être traité en paria b (= unattainable, unpunishable) [person, aura, air] intouchable c (= inviolable) [right] intangible d (= unrivalled) [player, performer] imbattable 2 N (in India) intouchable mf, paria m; (fig) paria m

untouched [ˈʌnˈtʌtʃt] ADJ a (= undamaged) [building, constitution] intact; [person] indemne b (= unaffected) **~ by sth** non affecté par qch c (= not eaten or drunk) **he left his meal/coffee ~** il n'a pas touché à son repas/café; **his meal/coffee lay ~ on the table** il a laissé son repas/café sur la table sans y avoir touché

untoward [ˌʌntəˈwɔːd] ADJ fâcheux; **nothing ~ happened** il ne s'est rien passé de fâcheux

untraceable [ˈʌnˈtreɪsəbl] ADJ [person] introuvable; [note, bill] dont il ne reste aucune trace

untrained [ˈʌnˈtreɪnd] ADJ [person, worker] (= inexperienced) sans expérience; (= unqualified) non qualifié; [soldier, gymnast] non entraîné, sans entraînement; [pianist] sans entraînement; [voice] non travaillé; [mind] non formé; [horse, dog] non dressé; **to the ~ eye/ear** pour un œil inexercé/une oreille inexercée; **to be ~ for** or **in sth** (gen) ne pas être formé à qch; [soldier, gymnast] ne pas être entraîné à qch

untrammelled, **untrammeled** (US) [ʌn'træməld] ADJ (frm) [person, life] sans contraintes; [authority] sans limites; **to be ~ by any anxieties** n'être retenu par aucune appréhension; **~ by family ties** non entravé par des liens familiaux; **~ by superstitions** libre de toute superstition

untranslatable [ˌʌntrænz'leɪtəbl] ADJ intraduisible

untravelled, **untraveled** (US) [ʌn'trævld] ADJ a [road] peu fréquenté b [person] qui n'a pas voyagé

untreated [ʌn'triːtɪd] ADJ a (Med) [patient] non traité; [illness, wound] non soigné b (= unprocessed) [sewage, wood, cotton] non traité (**with sth** à qch)

untried [ʌn'traɪd] ADJ a (= untested) [product, drug, method] non testé; [theory] non vérifié; [system, weapon, device] non testé, non essayé b (= inexperienced) [person] qui n'a pas été mis à l'épreuve c (Jur) [prisoner] en détention provisoire; [case] non encore jugé; **he was condemned ~** il a été condamné sans procès

untrodden [ʌn'trɒdn] ADJ (liter) [path] peu fréquenté; [region, territory] inexploré, vierge; [snow] non foulé, vierge

untroubled [ʌn'trʌbld] ADJ a (= serene) [person] serein; [face, sleep] paisible; [life] tranquille; (= not worried) **to be ~ by sth** ne pas être affecté or troublé par qch; **to be ~ by an accusation** ne pas être ébranlé or ne pas se laisser démonter par une accusation; **she is ~ by inconsistencies** les incohérences ne l'inquiètent pas or la gênent pas b (= unaffected) **to be ~ by injury** [footballer etc] ne pas être blessé c (= unharassed) **to be ~ by sb/sth** ne pas être dérangé par qn/qch

untrue [ʌn'truː] ADJ a (= inaccurate) [story, belief, claim] faux (fausse f); **it is ~ (to say) that ...** il est faux (de dire) que ... b (liter = unfaithful) **~ to sb** [lover] infidèle à qn; **to be ~ to one's principles/word/responsibilities** manquer or faillir à ses principes/sa parole/ses responsabilités

untrustworthy [ʌn'trʌst,wɜːðɪ] ADJ [person] indigne de confiance; [witness] récusable; [book] auquel on ne peut se fier; [evidence, results] douteux

untruth [ʌn'truːθ] N (pl untruths [ʌn'truːðz]) contrevérité f; (stronger) mensonge m; (NonC) fausseté f

untruthful [ʌn'truːθʊl] ADJ [person] menteur; [statement, claim, answer] mensonger; **to be ~** [person] mentir

untruthfully [ʌn'truːθəlɪ] ADV de façon mensongère

untruthfulness [ʌn'truːθʊlnɪs] N (NonC) fausseté f, caractère m mensonger

untuneful [ʌn'tjuːnfʊl] ADJ peu harmonieux

untutored [ʌn'tjuːtəd] ADJ [person] sans instruction; [work] spontané; [taste] non formé, qui n'a pas été formé; **he is completely ~** il n'a aucune instruction; **to the ~ eye/ear** pour un œil inexercé/une oreille inexercée; **to be ~ in sth** ne pas avoir reçu d'instruction en qch

untwine [ʌn'twaɪn] VT défaire, détortiller

untwist [ʌn'twɪst] VT (= untangle) [+ rope, threads, wool] démêler, détortiller; (= straighten out) [+ flex, rope] détordre; (= unravel) [+ rope, wool] défaire; (= unscrew) [+ bottle-top] dévisser

untypical [ʌn'tɪpɪkəl] ADJ peu typique, peu caractéristique (**of** de); **it's ~ of him** ça ne lui ressemble pas, ce n'est pas son genre

unusable [ʌn'juːzəbl] ADJ inutilisable

unused [ʌn'juːzd] ADJ a (= not utilized) [land, building, goods, potential] inutilisé; [clothes] jamais porté; [bank notes] non usagé; [food] non consommé; (Ling) inusité b [ʌn'juːst] (= unaccustomed) **to be ~ to (doing) sth** ne pas

être habitué à (faire) qch, ne pas avoir l'habitude de (faire) qch; **I am quite ~ to it now** j'en ai tout à fait perdu l'habitude, je n'en ai plus du tout l'habitude

unusual [ʌn'juːʒʊəl] ADJ [name] peu commun, insolite or d'inhabituel; [measure, occurrence, circumstances, gift, number] inhabituel; [case] étrange; [person, place] étonnant; **nothing ~ about this** à quelque chose d'insolite or d'inhabituel; **a man of ~ intelligence** un homme d'une intelligence exceptionnelle; **it is ~ to see this** il est rare de voir cela; **it is ~ for him to be early** il est rare qu'il arrive (subj) de bonne heure; **it's not ~ for him to be late** or (frm) **that he should be late** il n'est pas rare qu'il soit en retard; **it is ~ that ...** il est rare que ... (+ subj); **this was ~ for me** c'était inhabituel pour moi

unusually [ʌn'juːʒʊəlɪ] ADV [large, quiet, cheerful] exceptionnellement; **~ early/well** exceptionnellement tôt/bien; **she woke, ~ (for her), a little after midnight** contrairement à son habitude, elle s'est réveillée peu après minuit; **~ for a film of this era, it ...** chose rare pour un film de cette époque, il ...

unutterable [ʌn'ʌtərəbl] ADJ (frm) [sadness, joy, boredom, relief] indicible; [nonsense] effarant; [fool] fini

unutterably [ʌn'ʌtərəblɪ] ADV (frm) [sad] indiciblement; [ugly]; [boring] mortellement; **~ tired** mort de fatigue

unvaried [ʌn'vɛərɪd] ADJ uniforme, monotone (pej); **the menu was ~ from one week to the next** le menu ne changeait pas d'une semaine à l'autre

unvarnished [ʌn'vɑːnɪʃt] ADJ a [wood] non verni; [pottery] non vernissé b (fig) [account, description] sans fard; **the ~ truth** la vérité pure et simple, la vérité toute nue

unvarying [ʌn'vɛərɪŋ] ADJ invariable

unvaryingly [ʌn'vɛərɪŋlɪ] ADV invariablement

unveil [ʌn'veɪl] VT dévoiler

unveiling [ʌn'veɪlɪŋ] N dévoilement m; (= ceremony) inauguration f

unventilated [ʌn'ventɪleɪtɪd] ADJ sans ventilation

unverifiable [ʌn'verɪfaɪəbl] ADJ invérifiable

unverified [ʌn'verɪfaɪd] ADJ non vérifié

unversed [ʌn'vɜːst] ADJ **~ in** peu versé dans

unvoiced [ʌn'vɔɪst] ADJ a [opinion, sentiment] inexprimé b (Phon) [consonant] non voisé, sourd

unwaged [ʌn'weɪdʒd] NPL 1 **the unwaged** (Brit Admin = the unemployed) les sans-emploi mpl; **special rates for the ~** des tarifs spéciaux pour les sans-emploi 2 ADJ [person, work] non rémunéré

unwanted [ʌn'wɒntɪd] ADJ [food, possessions] dont on ne veut plus; [pet] dont on ne veut plus, dont on veut se séparer; [advice] inopportun, malvenu; [telephone call, attention] inopportun; [visitor] indésirable; [pregnancy, birth, child] non désiré; [fat] dont on veut se débarrasser; [effect] indésirable; **to feel ~** se sentir rejeté; **she rejected his ~ advances** elle a repoussé ses avances; **to remove ~ hair** s'épiler

unwarlike [ʌn'wɔːlaɪk] ADJ peu belliqueux

unwarrantable [ʌn'wɒrəntəbl] ADJ [intrusion, interference etc] injustifiable; **it is quite ~ that ...** il est tout à fait injustifiable que ... (+ subj)

unwarrantably [ʌn'wɒrəntəblɪ] ADV de façon injustifiable

unwarranted [ʌn'wɒrəntɪd] ADJ injustifié

unwary [ʌn'wɛərɪ] ADJ [visitor, reader] non averti; [driver] non vigilant, qui n'est pas sur ses gardes; [investor] trop confiant

unwashed [ʌn'wɒʃt] 1 ADJ [hands, object] non lavé; [person] qui ne s'est pas lavé 2 N (hum) **the great ~*** la populace (pej)

unwavering [ʌn'weɪvərɪŋ] ADJ [devotion, faith, resolve] inébranlable; [defender] inconditionnel; [gaze] fixe; [voice] ferme; [concentration] qui ne faiblit pas; **to be ~ in one's support for sth** apporter un soutien inébranlable or indéfectible à qch; **to be ~ in one's opposition to sth** être inflexiblement opposé à qch

unwaveringly [ʌn'weɪvərɪŋlɪ] ADV [follow, continue] inébranlablement; [say] fermement; [gaze] fixement

unweaned [ʌn'wiːnd] ADJ non sevré

unwearable [ʌn'wɛərəbl] ADJ [clothes, colour] pas mettable

unwearied [ʌn'wɪərɪd] ADJ pas fatigué

unwearying [ʌn'wɪərɪŋ] ADJ infatigable

unwed† [ʌn'wed] ADJ = **unmarried**

unweighting [ʌn'weɪtɪŋ] N (Ski) allègement m

unwelcome [ʌn'welkəm] ADJ [visitor, gift, attention] importun; [fact, thought] gênant; [news, publicity, surprise] fâcheux; [reminder] malvenu; **to make sb feel ~** donner à qn l'impression qu'il est indésirable or qu'il est de trop; **the money was not ~** l'argent était le bienvenu

unwelcoming [ʌn'welkəmɪŋ] ADJ [person, behaviour] inamical; [place] peu accueillant

unwell [ʌn'wel] ADJ souffrant; **to feel ~** ne pas se sentir bien

unwholesome [ʌn'həʊlsəm] ADJ [food, smell, air, habits, thoughts] malsain; **to have an ~ interest in sb/sth** éprouver un intérêt malsain pour qn/qch

unwieldy [ʌn'wiːldɪ] ADJ a (= difficult to handle) [suitcase] difficile à manier; [tool, weapon] peu maniable, difficile à manier b (= difficult to manage) [system, structure, bureaucracy] pesant, lourd; [name] compliqué

unwilling [ʌn'wɪlɪŋ] ADJ a (= disinclined) **to be ~** [person] être réticent; **to be ~ to do sth** (= disinclined) ne pas être disposé à faire qch; (= refusing) ne pas vouloir faire qch, refuser de faire qch; **to be ~ for sb to do sth/for sth to happen** ne pas vouloir que qn fasse qch/que qch se produise b (= reluctant) [victim] non consentant; [accomplice, conscript] malgré soi; [partner] involontaire; **he was an ~ participant in the affair** il se trouvait involontairement impliqué dans l'affaire, il se trouvait impliqué dans l'affaire malgré lui; **she gave me her ~ assistance** elle m'a aidé à contrecœur

unwillingly [ʌn'wɪlɪŋlɪ] ADV à contrecœur

unwillingness [ʌn'wɪlɪŋnɪs] N (NonC) **his ~ to help is surprising** il est étonnant qu'il ne soit pas disposé à aider

unwind [ʌn'waɪnd] (pret, ptp unwound) 1 VT dérouler 2 VI a [+ thread] se dérouler b (* fig = relax) se détendre, se relaxer

unwisdom [ʌn'wɪzdəm] N (NonC) manque m de bon sens, imprudence f

unwise [ʌn'waɪz] ADJ [person] imprudent, malavisé (liter); [investment, decision, remark] peu judicieux, imprudent; **it was an ~ thing to say** ce n'était pas très judicieux de dire ça; **it would be ~ to expect too much** il ne serait pas raisonnable de s'attendre à trop; **I thought it ~ to travel alone** j'ai pensé qu'il serait imprudent de voyager seul; **it would be ~ (for or of him) to refuse** il serait peu judicieux or malavisé (de sa part) de refuser; **you would be ~ to do that** vous seriez imprudent or malavisé de faire cela, il serait inconsidéré or peu judicieux de votre part de faire cela

unwisely [ʌn'waɪzlɪ] ADV [act, behave] imprudemment; **~, she agreed to go** imprudemment, elle a accepté d'y aller

unwitting [ʌn'wɪtɪŋ] ADJ [involvement] involontaire; **I was your ~ accomplice** j'ai été ton complice sans m'en rendre compte; **to be an ~ victim of sth** être sans le savoir la victime de qch ; **to be the ~ instrument** or **tool of sb/sth** être l'instrument inconscient de qn/qch

unwittingly [ʌn'wɪtɪŋlɪ] ADV [cause, reveal] involontairement

unwomanly [ʌn'wʊmənlɪ] ADJ peu féminin

unwonted [ʌn'wəʊntɪd] ADJ (frm) inhabituel

unworkable ['ʌn'wɜːkəbl] ADJ [a] [proposal, plan, suggestion] irréalisable ; [law] inapplicable [b] [substance, land] impossible à travailler ; [mine] inexploitable

unworldly ['ʌn'wɜːldlɪ] ADJ [a] (= unmaterialistic) [person] détaché de ce monde [b] (= naïve) [person, attitude] naïf (naïve f) (**about sth** en ce qui concerne qch) [c] (= not of this world) [beauty] céleste, qui n'est pas de ce monde ; [silence] surnaturel

unworn [ʌn'wɔːn] ADJ [garment] qui n'a pas été porté

unworthiness [ʌn'wɜːðɪnɪs] N manque m de mérite

unworthy [ʌn'wɜːðɪ] ADJ [activity] peu digne d'intérêt, sans grand intérêt ; [feeling] sans noblesse ; **I feel so ~!** je me sens si indigne ! ; **~ to do sth** indigne de faire qch ; **it is ~ to behave like that** il est indigne de se comporter ainsi ; **~ of sb/sth** indigne de qn/qch ; **it is ~ of comment** ce n'est pas digne de commentaire ; **to feel ~ of having sth** se sentir indigne d'avoir qch

unwound ['ʌn'waʊnd] VB pt, ptp of **unwind**

unwounded ['ʌn'wuːndɪd] ADJ non blessé, indemne

unwrap ['ʌn'ræp] VT défaire, ouvrir

unwritten ['ʌn'rɪtn] [1] ADJ [a] [Literat] [novel, article] qui reste à écrire, qui n'a pas encore été écrit, (= transmitted orally) [song, folk tale] non écrit [b] (= tacit) [rule, agreement] tacite ; **it is an ~ law** or **rule that ...** il est tacitement admis que ... [2] COMP ► **unwritten law** N (Jur) droit m coutumier

unyielding [ʌn'jiːldɪŋ] ADJ [person] inflexible, qui ne cède pas ; [substance] très dur, très résistant ; [structure] rigide

unyoke ['ʌn'jəʊk] VT dételer

unzip ['ʌn'zɪp] VT ouvrir (la fermeture éclair® de) ; **can you ~ me?** peux-tu défaire ma fermeture éclair® ?

---

up [ʌp]

[1]	PREPOSITION	[5]	INTRANSITIVE VERB
[2]	ADVERB	[6]	TRANSITIVE VERB
[3]	NOUN	[7]	COMPOUNDS
[4]	ADJECTIVE		

When **up** *is the second element in a phrasal verb, eg* **come up, throw up, walk up,** *look up the verb. When it is part of a set combination, eg* **the way up, close up,** *look up the other word.*

[1] PREPOSITION

to be up a tree/up a ladder être dans un arbre/sur une échelle ; **up north** dans le nord ; **their house is up that road** ils habitent dans cette rue ; **she climbed slowly up the stairs** elle monta lentement les escaliers ; **put your tissue up your sleeve** mets ton mouchoir dans ta manche ; **further up the page** plus haut sur la même page ; **up yours!**✶ va te faire mettre !✶ → **halfway**

[2] ADVERB

[a] indicating direction, position **up there** là-haut ; **he lives five floors up** il habite au cinquième étage ; **up above** au-dessus ; **up above sth** au-dessus de qch

When used with a preposition, **up** *is often not translated.*

the ladder was up against the wall l'échelle était (appuyée) contre le mur → h ; **this puts it up among the 20 most popular Web sites** cela en fait l'un des 20 sites Web les plus populaires ; **up at the top of the tree** en haut or au sommet de l'arbre ; **he's up at the top of the class** il est dans les premiers (de sa classe) ;

we're up for the day nous sommes ici pour la journée → h ; **he's up from Birmingham** il arrive de Birmingham ; **the rate has risen sharply, up from 3% to 5%** le taux a enregistré une forte hausse, passant de 3 % à 5 % ; **the people three floors up from me** les gens qui habitent trois étages au-dessus de chez moi ; **he threw the ball up in the air** il a jeté le ballon en l'air ; **up in the mountains** dans les montagnes ; **up in London à Londres** ; **up in Scotland** en Écosse ; **he's up in Leeds for the weekend** il est allé or monté à Leeds pour le week-end ; **the temperature was up in the forties** il faisait plus de quarante degrés ; **from up on the hill** (du haut) de la colline ; **up on deck** sur le pont ; **the monument is up on the hill** le monument se trouve en haut de la colline ; **it's up on top** c'est en haut ; **up on top of the cupboard** en haut du placard ; **the bed was up on end** le lit était debout contre le mur ; **prices are up on last year's** les prix sont en hausse par rapport à or sur (ceux de) l'année dernière ; **I was on my way up to London** j'allais à Londres, j'étais en route pour Londres → h

[b] = upwards **from £20 up** à partir de 20 livres ; **from (the age of) 13 up** à partir de (l'âge de) 13 ans ; **from his youth up** dès son plus jeune âge

[c] indicating advantage **Chelsea were three (goals) up** Chelsea menait par trois buts ; **we were 20 points up on them** nous avions 20 points d'avance sur eux

[d] [Jur] **to be** or **come up before Judge Blair** [accused person] comparaître devant le juge Blair ; [case] être jugé par le juge Blair

[e] in running order **first/next up: first up was Tess Buxton, who sang ...** il y eut tout d'abord Tess Buxton, qui chanta ... ; **next up to the microphone was John French** John French a été le prochain à prendre le micro, ensuite, c'est John French qui a pris le micro

[f] = in total **I'll play you 100 up** le premier qui a 100 points gagne

[g] US Culin✶ **a bourbon (straight) up** un bourbon sec ; **two fried eggs, up** deux œufs sur le plat

[h] SET STRUCTURES

♦ **to be up against sth** (fig = facing) **to be up against difficulties** se heurter à des difficultés ; **you don't know what you're up against!** tu ne sais pas ce qui t'attend ! ; **he's up against stiff competition** il est confronté à des concurrents redoutables ; **he's up against a very powerful politician** il a contre lui un homme politique très puissant ; **we're really up against it** ça ne va pas être facile

♦ **up and down: he travelled up and down the country** il parcourait le pays ; **people up and down the country are saying ...** partout dans le pays les gens disent ... ; **he walked up and down (the street)** il faisait les cent pas (dans la rue) ; **I've been up and down (the stairs) all evening** je n'ai pas arrêté de monter et descendre les escaliers toute la soirée

♦ **to be up for sth** (= seeking) **a third of the Senate is up for re-election** un tiers du Sénat doit être renouvelé ; **are you up for it?** ✶ (= willing) tu es partant ?✶ ; (= fit) tu vas pouvoir le faire ?, tu te sens d'attaque✶ ?

♦ **up to** (= as far as) jusqu'à ; **up to now** jusqu'ici, jusqu'à maintenant ; **up to here** jusqu'ici, jusqu'à maintenant ; **up to there** jusque-là ; **up to and including chapter five** jusqu'au chapitre cinq inclus ; **to be up to one's knees/waist in water** avoir de l'eau jusqu'aux genoux/jusqu'à la taille ; **to count up to 100** compter jusqu'à 100 ; [BUT] **what page are you up to?** à quelle page en êtes-vous ?

♦ **to be up to a job** or **task** (= capable of) **she's not up to the job** or **task** elle n'est pas à la hauteur ; **is he up to doing research?** est-il ca-

pable de faire de la recherche ? ; **the directors weren't up to running a modern company** les directeurs n'étaient pas capables de diriger une entreprise moderne

♦ **to feel** or **be up to sth** (= strong enough for) **are you feeling up to going for a walk?** est-ce que tu te sens d'attaque pour faire une promenade ? ; **I just don't feel up to it** je ne m'en sens pas le courage ; **he really isn't up to going back to work yet** il n'est vraiment pas en état de reprendre le travail

♦ **to be up to sth**✶ (pej = doing) **what is he up to?** qu'est-ce qu'il fabrique ?✶, qu'est-ce qu'il peut bien faire ? ; **he's up to something** il manigance or mijote✶ quelque chose ; **what have you been up to?** qu'est-ce que tu as manigancé or fabriqué✶ ? ; **what are you up to with those secateurs?** qu'est-ce que tu fabriques✶ avec ce sécateur ? ; **he's up to no good** il mijote✶ un mauvais coup ; (hum) **what have you been up to lately?** qu'est-ce que tu deviens ?

♦ **to be up to a standard/to much** (= equal to) **it isn't up to his usual standard** il peut faire bien mieux que cela ; (Brit) **it's not up to much**✶ ça ne vaut pas grand-chose

♦ **to be up to sb** (= depend on) **it's up to you to decide** c'est à vous de voir or de décider ; **it's up to you whether you go** c'est à toi de voir si tu veux y aller ; **shall I do it? — it's up to you** je le fais ? — comme vous voulez or à vous de voir ; **if it were up to me ...** si ça ne tenait qu'à moi ... ; **it's up to us to see this doesn't happen again** nous devons faire en sorte que cela ne se répète pas

♦ **to be up with sb** (= equal to) **he was up with the leaders** il était dans les premiers ; **she's right up there with the jazz greats** elle se classe parmi les plus grands interprètes de jazz ; **I'm up with the top two or three in maths** je suis dans les deux ou trois premiers en maths

♦ **up with ...!: up with United!** allez United !

[3] NOUN

♦ **to be on the up (and up)**✶ (Brit = improving) **he's on the up (and up)** il fait son chemin ; **it's on the up and up** ça s'améliore

♦ **on the up and up**✶ (US = honest) réglo✶, légal ; **he insisted the scheme was completely on the up and up** il a insisté sur le fait que ce programme était tout à fait réglo✶ or légal

♦ **ups and downs** (fig: in life, health etc) des hauts mpl et des bas mpl ; **after many ups and downs** après bien des hauts et des bas, après un parcours en dents de scie ; **his career had its ups and downs** il a connu des hauts et des bas dans sa carrière, sa carrière a connu des hauts et des bas

[4] ADJECTIVE

[a] = out of bed **to be up** être levé, être debout inv ; **(get) up!** debout !, levez-vous ! ; **we were up at seven** nous étions levés or debout à sept heures ; **I was still up at midnight** j'étais encore debout à minuit ; **he's always up early** il se lève toujours tôt or de bonne heure ; **I was up late this morning** je me suis levé tard ce matin ; **I was up late last night** je me suis couché tard hier soir ; **he was up all night writing the essay** il a passé toute la nuit sur cette dissertation ; **she was up all night because the baby was ill** elle n'a pas fermé l'œil de la nuit parce que le bébé était malade

[b] = raised **the blinds were up** les stores n'étaient pas baissés ; **he sat in the car with the windows up** il était assis dans la voiture avec les vitres fermées ; **with his head up (high)** la tête haute ; (on parcel) **"this side up"** « haut » ; **hands up, everyone who knows the answer** levez le doigt or la main si vous connaissez la réponse ; **several children had their hands up** plusieurs enfants levaient le doigt or la main, plusieurs enfants avaient la main levée ; (to gunman) **hands up!** haut les mains !

[c] = risen **when the sun was up** après le lever du soleil ; **the tide is up** c'est marée haute ; **the**

river is up le niveau de la rivière est monté ; *(Parl)* **the House is up** la Chambre ne siège pas

d = installed, built

Whichever verb is implicit in English is usually made explicit in French.

we've got the curtains/pictures up at last nous avons enfin posé les rideaux/accroché les tableaux ; **the scaffolding is now up** les échafaudages sont maintenant en place ; **the new building isn't up yet** le nouveau bâtiment n'est pas encore construit ; **the tent isn't up yet** la tente n'est pas encore montée ; **look, the flag is up!** regarde, le drapeau est hissé ! ; **the notice about the outing is up** on a mis une affiche à propos de l'excursion

e = mounted **to be up** être à cheval ; **a horse with Smith up** un cheval monté par Smith

f = increased **to be up** [*prices, salaries, numbers, temperature*] être en hausse, avoir augmenté (**by** de) ; [*water level*] avoir monté (**by** de) ; **petrol is up again** l'essence a encore augmenté ; **shares are up in London this morning** la Bourse de Londres est en hausse ce matin ; **tourism is up** le tourisme est en hausse, le nombre de touristes a augmenté ; **the standard is up** le niveau s'améliore ; **it is up on last year** c'est en hausse *or* ça a augmenté par rapport à l'an dernier

g = finished **his leave/visit is up** sa permission/sa visite est terminée ; **it is up on the 20th** ça se termine *or* ça finit le 20 ; **when three days were up** au bout de trois jours ; **time's up!** c'est l'heure ! → **game**[1]

h * = wrong **what's up?** qu'est-ce qui ne va pas ? ; **what's up with him?** qu'est-ce qu'il a ?, qu'est-ce qui lui prend ? ; **what's up with the car?** qu'est-ce qui ne va pas avec la voiture ? ; **what's up with your leg?** qu'est-ce qui t'es arrivé à la jambe ?* ; **there's something up with Paul** il y a quelque chose qui ne tourne pas rond* chez Paul ; **I know there's something up** (= *happening*) (je sais qu')il se passe quelque chose ; (= *amiss*) (je sais qu')il y a quelque chose qui ne va pas

i Brit = being worked on **the road is up** la route est en travaux

j indicating anger **his blood is up** il est fou de colère ; **his temper is up** il est en colère

k = elated **to be up*** être en forme

l Brit Univ **when I was up*** quand j'étais étudiant *or* à la Fac*

m Brit Rail **the up train** le train pour Londres ; **the up platform** le quai du train pour Londres

n SET STRUCTURES

♦ **up and about**: **she was up and about at 7 o'clock** elle était debout dès 7 heures ; **to be up and about again** [*sick person*] être de nouveau sur pied

♦ **to be up and down**: **he was up and down all night** il n'a pas arrêté de se lever toute la nuit ; **sit down for a bit, you've been up and down all evening** assieds-toi un moment, tu n'as pas arrêté (de) toute la soirée ; **he's been rather up and down recently** (= *sometimes depressed*) il a eu des hauts et des bas récemment → **7**

♦ **up and running** (*Comput* = *functioning*) opérationnel ; **to be up and running** (*Comput*) être opérationnel ; [*project, system*] être en route ; (*Comput, gen*) **to get sth up and running** mettre qch en route

♦ **to be (well) up in sth** (= *informed*) s'y connaître en qch ; **I'm not very up in molecular biology** je ne m'y connais pas beaucoup en biologie moléculaire ; **he's well up in local issues** il s'y connaît bien en affaires locales, il connaît bien ce qui touche aux affaires locales

5 INTRANSITIVE VERB

a **he upped and hit him*** (= *jumped up*) il a bondi et l'a frappé

b **one day he just upped and left*** un jour il est parti comme ça

6 TRANSITIVE VERB

a * = raise [+ *prices, wages, pressure*] augmenter ; [+ *tempo*] accélérer ; **stores upped sales by 60%** les magasins ont augmenté leurs ventes de 60%

b * *Naut* **to up anchor** lever l'ancre

7 COMPOUNDS

▶ **up-and-coming** ADJ [*politician, businessman, actor*] plein d'avenir, qui monte ; [*rival*] qui monte ▶ **up-and-down** ADJ [*movement*] de va-et-vient ; (*fig*) [*business*] qui a des hauts et des bas ; [*progress, career*] en dents de scie ▶ **up-and-under** N (*Rugby*) chandelle *f*, up and under *m* ▶ **up-and-up** ADJ = up and up ; → **3** ▶ **up-bow** N (*Mus*) poussé *m* ▶ **up-current, up-draft** (*US*) N (*Aviat*) courant *m* (d'air) ascendant ▶ **up-front** ADJ → up-front ▶ **up-to-date** ADJ → up-to-date ▶ **up-to-the-minute** ADJ [*news*] en temps réel

upbeat ['ʌpbiːt] **1** ADJ* optimiste ; (*Mus*) enlevé **2** N (*Mus*) levé *m*

upbraid [ʌp'breɪd] VT (*frm*) réprimander ; **to ~ sb for doing sth** reprocher à qn de faire (*or* d'avoir fait) qch

upbringing ['ʌpbrɪŋɪŋ] N éducation *f* ; **he owed his success to his ~** il devait son succès à l'éducation qu'il avait reçue *or* à la manière dont il avait été élevé ; **I had a strict ~** j'ai été élevé d'une manière stricte, j'ai reçu une éducation stricte ; **to have a Christian ~** avoir une éducation chrétienne ; **I had a Jewish ~** j'ai été élevé dans la tradition juive

upchuck: ['ʌptʃʌk] VI (*esp US*) dégueuler:

upcoming ['ʌpkʌmɪŋ] ADJ imminent, prochain

upcountry [ʌp'kʌntrɪ] **1** ADV **we went ~ by train** nous sommes allés vers l'intérieur du pays ou dans l'arrière-pays en train ; **the nearest town was 100km ~** la ville la plus proche était à 100 km à l'intérieur du pays ou dans l'arrière-pays **2** ADJ **natives in ~ villages** les habitants *mpl* des villages de l'intérieur du pays *or* de l'arrière-pays ; **he was away on an ~ trip** il était parti en voyage vers l'intérieur du pays ou dans l'arrière-pays

update [ʌp'deɪt] **1** VT (*gen, also Comput*) mettre à jour ; **to ~ sb on sth** mettre qn au courant de qch **2** ['ʌpdeɪt] N mise *f* à jour ; (*Comput*) [*of software package*] actualisation *f*, update *m*

upend [ʌp'end] VT **a** [+ *box etc*] mettre debout **b** (*fig*) [+ *system etc*] renverser, bouleverser, chambouler*

upfront [ʌp'frʌnt] ADJ **a** (* = *frank*) [*person, attitude*] franc (franche *f*) (**with sb** avec qn) ; **to be ~ about sth** ne rien cacher de qch **b** (= *paid in advance*) [*payment*] réglé d'avance ; [*cost*] à payer d'avance

up front [ʌp'frʌnt] ADV **a** (= *in advance*) [*pay, charge*] d'avance **b** (*esp US* * = *frankly*) franchement, ouvertement

upgrade ['ʌpgreɪd] **1** N rampe *f*, montée *f* ; [*of software*] nouvelle version *f* ; [*of hardware*] extension *f* ; [*of memory*] augmentation *f* de la capacité ; (*fig*) **to be on the ~** [*sales*] être en hausse ; (*Racing*) **Omar is on the ~** les performances d'Omar ne cessent de s'améliorer **2** ['ʌpgreɪd] ADV (*US*) = uphill **1 3** [ʌp'greɪd] VT **a** (= *improve*) améliorer ; (= *modernize*) moderniser ; (*Comput*) [+ *software*] mettre à jour, acheter une nouvelle version de ; [+ *memory*] augmenter **b** (= *raise, promote*) [+ *employee*] promouvoir ; [+ *job, post*] revaloriser ; (*Travel*) **to ~ a passenger** surclasser un passager ; **I have been ~d** (*Mil, Admin*) je suis monté en grade ; (*in company*) j'ai eu une promotion ; **he was ~d to head of department** il a été promu chef de section

upgradeable ['ʌpgreɪdəbl] ADJ (*Comput*) extensible

upheaval [ʌp'hiːvəl] N **a** (*NonC*) (*gen*) bouleversement *m* ; (*esp Pol*) perturbations *fpl* ; (= *moving things around: in home, office etc*) branle-bas *m*, remue-ménage *m* ; **it caused a lot of ~** cela a tout perturbé **b** (= *disturbing event*) crise *f* ; (*stronger*) cataclysme *m* **c** (*Geol*) soulèvement *m*

upheld ['ʌp'held] VB *pt, ptp* of uphold

uphill **1** [ʌp'hɪl] ADV **a** **to go ~** [*road*] monter ; **the car went ~** la voiture a monté la côte ; **my car doesn't go ~ very well** ma voiture a du mal à monter les côtes ; **a car engine uses more fuel when going ~** une voiture consomme plus d'essence en montée **b** (*Ski*) en amont **2** ['ʌp'hɪl] ADJ **a** (= *up gradient*) **~ walk/stretch** montée *f* ; **the ~ walk back home** la remontée vers la maison ; (*lit*) **it was ~ all the way** c'était tout en montée, ça montait tout du long ; **a race over an ~ route** une course en montée **b** (= *difficult*) [*work, task*] pénible, ardu ; **it's an ~ battle** *or* **struggle (trying to find a job/flat)** c'est une tâche pénible *or* ce n'est pas évident* (d'essayer de trouver un emploi/un appartement) ; **we're fighting an ~ battle against corruption** nous luttons tant bien que mal contre la corruption ; **it was ~ all the way (trying to convince him)** ça a été toute une histoire (pour le convaincre) **c** (*Ski*) **~ ski** ski *m* amont *inv*

uphold [ʌp'həʊld] (*pret, ptp* upheld) VT [+ *institution, person*] soutenir, donner son soutien à ; [+ *law*] faire respecter, maintenir ; (*Jur*) [+ *verdict*] confirmer, maintenir

upholder [ʌp'həʊldə'] N défenseur *m*

upholster [ʌp'həʊlstə'] VT recouvrir ; (*fig hum*) **she is fairly well ~ed*** elle est assez bien rembourrée*

upholsterer [ʌp'həʊlstərə'] N tapissier *m*

upholstery [ʌp'həʊlstərɪ] N **a** (= *covering*) (*cloth*) tissu *m* d'ameublement ; (*leather*) cuir *m* ; (*in car*) garniture *f* **b** (*NonC* = *trade*) tapisserie *f* (*art, métier*)

upkeep ['ʌpkiːp] N [*of family, house, car, garden*] entretien *m* ; **~ (costs)** frais *mpl* d'entretien

upland ['ʌplənd] **1** N (*also* **~s**) hautes terres *fpl*, hauteurs *fpl*, plateau(x) *m(pl)* **2** ADJ [*farm, farmer*] des hautes terres ; [*farming*] en altitude ; [*grassland, lake*] d'altitude ; **~ areas** les hautes terres *fpl* ; **~ pastures** pâturages *mpl* de montagne, alpages *mpl*

uplift **1** ['ʌplɪft] N (= *edification*) sentiment *m* d'élévation morale *or* spirituelle ; **an ~ in the economy** un redressement de l'économie **2** [ʌp'lɪft] VT **a** (*fig: spiritually, emotionally*) [+ *soul*] élever ; [+ *person*] édifier, inspirer ; **we were all ~ed by their heroic example** leur héroïsme nous a tous édifiés *or* inspirés ; **art was created to ~ the mind and the spirit** l'art a été créé pour élever l'esprit et l'âme **b** (= *improve living conditions of*) améliorer le cadre de vie de **3** COMP ▶ **uplift bra** N soutien-gorge *m* pigeonnant

uplifted [ʌp'lɪftɪd] ADJ **a** (= *raised*) [*arm, face*] levé **b** (= *edified*) **to feel ~ (by sth)** se sentir grandi (par qch)

uplifting [ʌp'lɪftɪŋ] ADJ inspirant, qui réchauffe le cœur

uplighter ['ʌp,laɪtə'] N applique *f* murale (*qui dirige la lumière en hauteur*)

upmarket [ʌp'mɑːkɪt] ADJ (*esp Brit*) [*goods, car*] haut de gamme *inv* ; [*newspaper*] sérieux ; [*area*] select*

upmost ['ʌpməʊst] = uppermost

upon [ə'pɒn] PREP sur ; **~ the table** sur la table ; **~ the death of his son** à la mort de son fils ; **~ hearing this** en entendant cela ; **~ my word!*** †* ma parole ! → **on 2, once**

upper ['ʌpə'] **1** ADJ [*floor, part, limit*] supérieur (-eure *f*) ; [*teeth*] du haut ; **properties at the ~**

end of the market les propriétés *fpl* dans la tranche supérieure du marché; **to have the ~ hand** avoir le dessus; **to gain** *or* **get the ~ hand** prendre le dessus; **the ~ reaches of the Seine** la haute Seine; **in ~ reaches of the river** en amont de la rivière; **the ~ shelf** l'étagère *f* supérieure *or* du dessus; **the ~ shelf** une des étagères supérieures; **the temperature is in the ~ thirties** la température dépasse trente-cinq degrés; **an ~ window** une fenêtre de l'étage supérieur *or* du dessus

[2] N [a] *(of shoe)* empeigne *f*; *(fig)* **to be (down) on one's ~s*** manger de la vache enragée, être dans la purée*

[b] *(US Rail*)* couchette *f* supérieure

[c] *(* = drug, pill)* stimulant *m*, excitant *m*

[3] COMP ► **the upper arm** N le haut du bras ► **the upper atmosphere** N les couches *fpl* supérieures de l'atmosphère ► **the upper back** N le haut du dos ► **the upper body** N la partie supérieure du corps ► **upper case** N *(Typ)* haut *m* de casse; **in ~ case** en capitales ► **upper-case** ADJ **~-case letter** majuscule *f*, capitale *f*; **~-case "h"** « h » majuscule ► **Upper Chamber** N = **Upper House** ► **upper circle** N *(Brit Theat)* deuxième balcon *m* ► **upper class** N haute société *f* ► **upper-class** ADJ aristocratique, de la haute société ► **upper classes** NPL = **upper class** ► **the upper crust*** *(fig)* le gratin* ► **upper-crust*** ADJ aristocratique, aristo* ► **upper deck** N *(of bus)* étage *m* supérieur; *(Naut)* (= *part of ship*) pont *m* supérieur; (= *personnel*) **the ~ deck*** les officiers *mpl* ► **Upper Egypt** N la Haute-Égypte ► **the Upper House** N *(Parl)* *(gen)* la Chambre haute; *(in Brit)* la Chambre des lords; *(in France, in the US)* le Sénat ► **upper income bracket** tranche *f* supérieure de revenus; **people in the ~ income brackets** les gens *mpl* faisant partie de la tranche supérieure de revenus ► **upper jaw** N mâchoire *f* supérieure ► **upper lip** N lèvre *f* supérieure ► **stiff** ► **upper management** N cadres *mpl* supérieurs ► **upper middle class** N haute bourgeoisie *f* ► **the upper ranks** NPL *(Mil, Admin)* les grades *mpl* supérieurs; *(fig)* les rangs *mpl* supérieurs ► **the Upper Rhine** N le cours supérieur du Rhin ► **upper school** N *(Scol: gen)* grandes classes *fpl*; *(Scol Admin = top section)* (classe *f* de) terminale *f* ► **upper sixth** N *(Brit Scol: also ~ sixth form)* (classe *f* de) terminale *f* ► **Upper Volta** N la Haute-Volta

upperclassman [ˌʌpə'klɑːsmən] N *(pl* **-men**) *(US Univ)* étudiant *m* de troisième *or* quatrième année

uppercut [ˈʌpəkʌt] N *(Boxing)* uppercut *m*

uppermost [ˈʌpəməʊst] [1] ADJ [a] (= *topmost*) [*leaves, branches*] du haut; [*floor*] le dernier *or* la dernière; **the patterned side should be ~** le côté à motifs doit être sur le dessus [b] (= *paramount*) **it is the question of sovereignty which has been ~ at the negotiations** c'est la question de la souveraineté qui a dominé les négociations; **my career is ~ on my agenda** ma carrière est ce qui compte le plus; **safety was ~ in his mind** il pensait avant tout à la sécurité; **there were two thoughts ~ in my mind** deux pensées me préoccupaient en priorité [2] ADV [*turn, lie*] vers le haut; **place your hands on your knees, palms ~** posez les mains sur les genoux, paumes vers le haut

uppish†* [ˈʌpɪʃ] ADJ *(Brit)* = **uppity** b

uppity* [ˈʌpɪtɪ] ADJ [a] (= *awkward*) [*person*] difficile; **to get ~** monter sur ses grands chevaux; **to get ~ with sb/about sth** s'énerver après qn/après qch [b] *(Brit†* = snobbish)* [*person*] bêcheur*; **an ~ man/woman** un bêcheur*/une bêcheuse*; **to get ~ with sb** traiter qn de haut

upraised [ʌp'reɪzd] ADJ [*hand, arm, palm etc*] levé

uprate [ʌp'reɪt] ADJ **~ tax brackets** tranches *fpl* les plus imposées

upright [ˈʌpraɪt] [1] ADJ [a] (= *vertical*) [*person, posture*] droit; **to be ~** [*person*] se tenir droit; **in an ~ position** debout; **put your seat in an ~ position** redressez le dossier de votre siège [b] (= *honest*) [*person*] droit, probe *(liter)* [2] ADV [*stand, sit, stay*] droit; [*place*] verticalement; **to walk ~** [*person*] marcher debout; [*quadruped*] marcher sur ses pattes de derrière; **to pull o.s. ~** se redresser → **bolt** [3] N [a] *(of door, window)* montant *m*, pied-droit *m* *(Archit)*; *(of goal-post)* montant *m* de but [b] (= *piano*) piano *m* droit [4] COMP ► **upright freezer** N congélateur-armoire *m* ► **upright piano** N piano *m* droit ► **upright vacuum cleaner** N aspirateur-balai *m*

uprightly [ˈʌp,raɪtlɪ] ADV honnêtement, avec droiture

uprightness [ˈʌp,raɪtnɪs] N *(NonC)* honnêteté *f*, droiture *f*

uprising [ˈʌpraɪzɪŋ] N soulèvement *m*, insurrection *f*, révolte *f* (**against** contre)

upriver [1] [ʌp'rɪvə'] ADV [*be*] en amont (**from** de); [*swim*] vers l'amont; [*swim*] contre le courant [2] [ˈʌprɪvə'] ADJ d'amont

uproar [ˈʌprɔːʳ] N tumulte *m*; **this caused an ~** ◊ **at this there was (an) ~** (= *shouting*) cela a déclenché un véritable tumulte; (= *protesting*) cela a déclenché une tempête de protestations; **the hall was in (an) ~** (= *shouting*) le tumulte régnait dans la salle; (= *protesting*) toute la salle protestait bruyamment; (= *disturbance*) la plus vive agitation régnait dans la salle; **the meeting ended in (an) ~** la réunion s'est terminée dans le tumulte

uproarious [ʌp'rɔːrɪəs] ADJ [a] (= *noisy*) [*meeting*] agité; [*laughter*] tonitruant [b] (= *hilarious*) [*comedy, occasion*] hilarant

uproariously [ʌp'rɔːrɪəslɪ] ADV [*laugh*] aux éclats; **~ funny** désopilant

uproot [ʌp'ruːt] VT *(lit, fig)* déraciner

upsa-daisy* [ˈʌpsə,deɪzɪ] EXCL *(baby talk)* allez, hop!

upscale* [ˈʌpˈskeɪl] ADJ *(US)* classe*

▼ **upset** [ʌp'set] *(pret, ptp* **upset**) [1] VT [a] (= *overturn*) [+ *cup etc*] renverser; [+ *boat*] faire chavirer; (= *spill*) [+ *milk, contents*] renverser, répandre; *(fig)* **that ~ the applecart*** ça a tout fichu par terre*, ça a chamboulé* tous mes *(or* ses *etc)* projets

[b] *(fig)* [+ *plan, timetable*] déranger, bouleverser; [+ *system*] déranger; [+ *calculation*] fausser; [+ *stomach, digestion*] déranger; [+ *person*] (= *offend*) vexer; (= *grieve*) faire de la peine à; (= *annoy*) contrarier; **don't ~ yourself** ne vous tracassez pas, ne vous en faites pas; **now you've ~ him** maintenant il est vexé; **on-ions always ~ my digestion** *or* **my stomach** les oignons me rendent malade, je ne supporte pas les oignons

[2] ADJ [a] [*person*] (= *annoyed, offended*) vexé (**about sth** par qch); (= *distressed*) troublé (**about sth** par qch); (= *stronger*) bouleversé (**about sth** par qch); **he's ~ that you didn't tell him** (= *offended*) il est vexé que vous ne lui ayez rien dit; **my mother is ~ that I lost the money** ma mère est contrariée que j'ai perdu l'argent; **he was ~ about losing** (= *annoyed*) il était vexé d'avoir perdu; **she was ~ about him leaving** son départ l'a peinée; **to get ~** (= *annoyed*) se vexer; (= *distressed*) être peiné *or* être bouleversé; **don't get ~!** ne le prends pas mal!

[b] *(Med)* [*stomach*] dérangé; **to have an ~ stomach** avoir l'estomac dérangé

[3] [ˈʌpset] N (= *upheaval*) désordre *m*, remue-ménage *m*; *(in plans etc)* bouleversement *m*, changement *m* soudain (**in** de); *(emotional)* chagrin *m*; (* = *quarrel*) brouille *f*;

to have a stomach ~ avoir l'estomac dérangé, avoir une indigestion

[4] [ˈʌpset] COMP ► **upset price** N *(esp US: at auction)* mise *f* à prix

upsetting [ʌp'setɪŋ] ADJ [*experience, incident, feeling*] pénible, bouleversant; **it is ~ to see such terrible things** il est perturbant de voir des horreurs pareilles; **it is ~ for him to talk about the incident** il lui est pénible de parler de cet incident; **the incident was very ~ for me** cet incident m'a bouleversé

upshot [ˈʌpʃɒt] N aboutissement *m*; **the ~ of it all was ...** le résultat de tout cela a été ...; **in the ~** à la fin, en fin de compte

upside [ˈʌpsaɪd] [1] N *(also* **up side** = *positive aspect*) avantage *m*; **on the ~** pour ce qui est des avantages, côté avantages* [2] COMP ► **upside down** ADV à l'envers; **to hang ~ down** [*person*] être suspendu la tête en bas; [*picture*] être à l'envers; **to read (sth) ~ down** lire (qch) à l'envers; **to turn sth ~ down** *(box, bottle)* retourner qch; *(fig)* (= *disorganize*) *(house, room, drawer)* mettre qch sens dessus dessous; *(plans)* faire tomber qch à l'eau, faire échouer qch; **my world** *or* **life (was) turned ~ down** ma vie a été bouleversée ► **upside-down** ADJ (= *inverted*) [*picture, flag, shape*] à l'envers; [*box, car*] retourné; **in an** *or* **the ~-down position** à l'envers; *(fig = topsy-turvy)* **an ~-down world** un monde à l'envers ► **upside-down cake** N *gâteau renversé*; **pineapple ~-down cake** gâteau *m* renversé sur lit d'ananas

upstage [ʌp'steɪdʒ] [1] ADV *(Theat)* dans le lointain, à l'arrière-plan; **~ centre/left/right** à l'arrière-plan au centre/à gauche/à droite [2] ADJ *(Theat)* vers le fond de la scène [3] VT éclipser, souffler la vedette à

upstairs [ʌp'steəz] [1] ADV [a] (= *to a higher floor*) **to go ~** monter; **to run ~** monter l'escalier *or* les escaliers en courant; **to take sb/sth ~** monter qn/qch; **I was taken ~ to a room on the second floor** on m'a emmené dans une pièce au deuxième étage → **kick** [b] (= *on floor above*) *(in two-storey building)* en haut, à l'étage; *(in multi-storey building)* à l'étage au-dessus; **from ~** *(in two-storey building)* d'en haut, de l'étage; *(in multi-storey building)* de l'étage au-dessus; **the people/flat ~** les gens *mpl*/l'appartement *m* du dessus; **the room ~** *(in two-storey building)* la pièce d'en haut *or* à l'étage; *(in multi-storey building)* la pièce à l'étage au-dessus; *(fig hum)* **he hasn't got much ~*** il n'en a pas lourd dans la caboche*

[2] N* **the house has no ~** la maison est de plain-pied *or* n'a pas d'étage; **the ~ belongs to another family** l'étage *m* appartient à une autre famille

[3] [ˈʌpsteəz] ADJ [a] (= *on a higher floor*) [*room, flat, window*] *(in two-storey building)* à l'étage; *(in multi-storey building)* en haut [b] (= *on the floor above*) [*flat, neighbour*] du dessus

upstanding [ʌp'stændɪŋ] ADJ [a] (= *respectable*) [*person*] droit, probe *(liter)*; **a fine young man** un jeune homme très bien [b] *(frm = erect)* [*person*] bien droit; [*animal*] dressé (de toute sa hauteur) [c] *(frm)* **be ~** (= *stand up*) levez-vous

upstart [ˈʌpstɑːt] N parvenu(e) *m(f)*, arriviste *mf*

upstate [ʌp'steɪt] *(US)* [1] ADV [*go*] vers l'intérieur *(d'un État des États-Unis)*; [*be*] à l'intérieur [2] ADJ de l'intérieur; **~ New York** le nord de l'État de New York

upstream [ˈʌp'striːm] [1] ADV [*be*] en amont (**from sth** de qch); [*sail*] vers l'amont; **to swim ~** [*fish*] remonter le courant; [*person*] nager contre le courant [2] ADJ en amont, d'amont; **~ industries** industries *fpl* en amont

upstretched [ʌpˈstretʃt] ADJ **with arms ~** les bras tendus en l'air

upstroke [ˈʌpstrəʊk] N (*with pen*) délié m ; [*of piston etc*] course f ascendante

upsurge [ˈʌpsɜːdʒ] N [*of feeling*] vague f, accès m ; [*of interest*] renaissance f, recrudescence f, regain m

upswept [ˌʌpˈswept] ADJ a (*Aut, Aviat*) profilé b [*hair*] relevé sur la tête

upswing [ˈʌpswɪŋ] N (*lit*) mouvement m ascendant, montée f ; (*fig*) amélioration f notable ; (*Econ*) redressement m, reprise f (**in** de)

upsy-daisy* [ˈʌpsə,deɪzɪ] EXCL = **upsa-daisy**

uptake [ˈʌpteɪk] N a (= *understanding*) **to be quick on the ~*** avoir l'esprit vif, comprendre or saisir vite ; **to be slow on the ~*** être lent à comprendre or à saisir b (*Tech* = *intake*) consommation f c (*Marketing etc* = *interest, acceptance*) **the ~ on the new product** l'intérêt suscité par le nouveau produit

up-tempo [ˈʌptempəʊ] ADJ (*Mus*) au rythme enlevé

upthrust [ˈʌpθrʌst] N (*gen, Tech*) poussée f ascendante ; (*Geol*) soulèvement m

uptight* [ʌpˈtaɪt] ADJ a (= *tense*) [*person*] tendu ; **he was ~ about the meeting** il était tendu à cause de la réunion ; **he seemed ~ about me being there** ma présence semblait le rendre nerveux ; **to get ~** devenir nerveux ; **to feel ~** être tendu b (= *annoyed*) [*person*] énervé (**about sth** par qch) ; **to get ~ (about sth)** s'énerver (à propos de qch) c (= *inhibited*) [*person*] refoulé, complexé ; **~ about sex** refoulé, coincé* ; **to be** or **feel ~ about doing sth** être mal à l'aise à l'idée de faire qch

uptime [ˈʌp,taɪm] N [*of machine, computer*] temps m or durée f de fonctionnement

up-to-date [ˌʌptəˈdeɪt] ADJ a (= *updated*) [*report, file*] à jour b (= *most recent*) [*report, assessment, information*] très (or le plus) récent c (= *modern*) [*building, course*] moderne ; [*attitude, person*] moderne, dans le vent, à la page → **date¹**

uptorn [ʌpˈtɔːn] ADJ [*tree*] déraciné, arraché

uptown [ʌpˈtaʊn] (*US*) 1 ADV [*live*] dans les quartiers chics ; [*go*] vers les quartiers chics 2 ADJ des quartiers chics ; **~ New York** les quartiers mpl chics de New York

uptrend [ˈʌptrend] N reprise f ; **to be on an** or **the ~** (*gen*) être en hausse ; [*market*] être à la hausse

upturn [ʌpˈtɜːn] 1 VT retourner, mettre à l'envers ; (= *overturn*) renverser ; **~ed nose** nez m retroussé 2 [ˈʌptɜːn] N amélioration f (**in** de)

UPVC [ˌjuːpiːviːˈsiː] N (ABBR = **unplasticized polyvinyl chloride**) PVC m dur, PVC m non plastifié

UPW [ˌjuːpiːˈdʌblju] N (*Brit*) (ABBR = **Union of Post Office Workers**) syndicat

upward [ˈʌpwəd] 1 ADJ a (= *rising, increasing*) [*trend, movement, revision*] à la hausse ; **the dollar resumed its ~ climb** le dollar a recommencé à monter ; **~ spiral** spirale f ascendante ; **to be on an ~ trend** (*gen*) être à la hausse ; [*market*] être en hausse ; [*economy*] reprendre b (= *to higher place*) [*motion, grove, look*] vers le haut ; [*slope*] ascendant ; **~ climb** ascension f ; **~ gradient** pente f ascendante ; **~ movement** [*of hand*] mouvement m vers le haut ; [*of needle, mercury*] mouvement m ascendant ; [*of plane, rocket*] mouvement m ascensionnel 2 ADV (*esp US*) = **upwards** 3 COMP ► **upward (social) mobility** N ascension f sociale

upwardly mobile [ˌʌpwədlɪˈməʊbaɪl] (*Sociol*) 1 ADJ **to be ~** monter dans l'échelle sociale 2 **the upwardly mobile** NPL ceux qui montent dans l'échelle sociale

upwards [ˈʌpwədz], **upward** (*esp US*) [ˈʌpwəd] ADV a (= *towards higher place*) [*look*] en haut,

vers le haut ; **to climb/slope ~** monter ; **the road sloped gently ~** la route montait en pente douce ; **naked from the waist ~** torse nu inv b (= *face up*) **place your hands palm ~ on your knees** placez les mains sur les genoux, paumes vers le haut ; **dead rats floated bellies ~** des rats morts flottaient le ventre en l'air ; **lie face ~ on the floor** allongez-vous par terre sur le dos ; **lay the book face ~** posez le livre face en dessus c (= *to higher level*) **prices are heading ~** les prix sont en hausse ; **costs continue to spiral ~** les coûts continuent leur spirale ascendante ; **to be revised ~** être révisé à la hausse d **... and ~** (= *and above*): **this book suits age three years and ~** ce livre convient aux enfants à partir de trois ans ; **prices range from £250,000 and ~** la gamme des prix part de 250 000 livres e (= *starting from*) **prices from 10 francs ~** prix mpl à partir de 10 francs ; **from childhood ~** dès ma (*or* ta *or* sa *etc*) jeunesse, dès l'enfance f **~ of** (= *more than*) plus de ; **to cost ~ of £100,000** coûter plus de 100 000 livres

upwind [ˈʌpwɪnd] 1 ADV [*move*] contre le vent ; **to be ~ (of sb/sth)** être au vent or dans le vent (par rapport à qn/qch) ; **the west of the city is ~ of the smell of industry** à l'ouest de la ville, le vent éloigne l'odeur des usines 2 ADJ au vent

uraemia [jʊˈriːmɪə] N urémie f

uraemic [jʊˈriːmɪk] ADJ urémique

Ural [ˈjʊərəl] N **the ~ Mountains, the ~s** les monts mpl Oural, l'Oural m

uranalysis [ˌjʊərəˈnælɪsɪs] N (*pl* **uranalyses** [ˌjʊərəˈnælɪsiːz]) (*Med*) analyse f d'urine

uranium [jʊəˈreɪnɪəm] 1 N uranium m 2 COMP ► **uranium-bearing** ADJ [*rock*] uranifère

Uranus [jʊəˈreɪnəs] N (*Myth*) Uranus m ; (*Astron*) Uranus f

urban [ˈɜːbən] 1 ADJ [*area, population, life, motorway, warfare, problems, poverty*] urbain ; [*land*] en zone urbaine ; [*workers, poor*] des villes ; [*poverty*] dans les villes 2 COMP ► **urban aid** N aide f pour les zones urbaines défavorisées ► **urban blight** N dégradation f urbaine ► **urban centre** N (= *town*) centre m urbain ; (= *town centre*) centre-ville m ► **urban clearway** N (*Brit Transport*) voie f urbaine à stationnement interdit ► **urban conservation area** N zone f urbaine protégée ► **urban decay** N dégradation f urbaine ► **urban development** N aménagement m urbain ► **urban development zone** N ≈ zone f à urbaniser en priorité, ≈ ZUP f ► **urban district council** N (*Brit Local Govt: formerly*) conseil m de district urbain ► **urban dweller** N (*frm*) habitant(e) m(f) des villes ► **urban guerrilla** N guérillero m urbain ► **the Urban League** N (*in US*) association américaine d'aide aux Noirs vivant dans des quartiers défavorisés ► **urban legend** N légende f urbaine ► **urban migration** N exode m rural ► **urban myth** N = **urban legend** ► **urban planner** N urbaniste mf ► **urban planning** N urbanisme m ► **urban renewal** N rénovations fpl urbaines ► **urban sprawl** N (= *phenomenon*) expansion f urbaine tentaculaire ; (= *area*) ville f tentaculaire ► **urban studies** NPL études fpl d'urbanisme

urbane [ɜːˈbeɪn] ADJ [*person*] urbain (*liter*), courtois ; [*wit*] raffiné ; [*charm*] discret (-ète f) ; **his ~ manner** sa courtoisie

urbanely [ɜːˈbeɪnlɪ] ADV [*say, smile*] courtoisement

urbanite [ˈɜːbənaɪt] N (*US*) citadin(e) m(f)

urbanity [ɜːˈbænɪtɪ] N (*NonC*) urbanité f, courtoisie f

urbanization [ˌɜːbənaɪˈzeɪʃən] N urbanisation f

urbanize [ˈɜːbənaɪz] VT urbaniser

urchin [ˈɜːtʃɪn] N polisson(ne) m(f), garnement m → **sea, street**

Urdu [ˈʊəduː] N ourdou m

urea [ˈjʊərɪə] N urée f

uremia [jʊˈriːmɪə] N = **uraemia**

ureter [jʊˈriːtəʳ] N uretère m

urethra [jʊˈriːθrə] N (*pl* **urethras** or **urethrae** [jʊˈriːθriː]) urètre m

urge [ɜːdʒ] 1 N forte envie f (**to do sth** de faire qch) ; **to feel** or **have an** or **the ~ to do sth** éprouver une forte envie de faire qch ; **he had a strong ~ for revenge** il avait soif de vengeance → **sex** 2 VT [+ *person*] pousser (**to do** à faire), conseiller vivement (**to do** de faire) ; [+ *caution, remedy, measure*] conseiller vivement, recommander avec insistance ; [+ *excuse*] faire valoir ; [+ *point*] insister sur ; **to ~ restraint/caution on sb** recommander vivement la retenue/la prudence à qn ; **to ~ sb back/in/out etc** insister vivement pour que qn revienne/entre/sorte (*subj*) *etc* ; **to ~ patience** prêcher la patience ; **I ~ you to write at once** je ne saurais trop vous conseiller d'écrire immédiatement ; **I ~d him not to go** je lui ai vivement déconseillé d'y aller ; **he needed no urging** il ne s'est pas fait prier ; **to ~ that sth (should) be done** recommander vivement que qch soit fait ; **"do it now!" he ~d** « faites-le tout de suite ! » insista-t-il ; **he ~d acceptance of the report** il a vivement recommandé l'acceptation du rapport

► **urge on** VT SEP [+ *horse*] talonner ; [+ *person*] faire avancer ; [+ *troops*] pousser en avant, faire avancer ; (*fig*) [+ *worker*] presser ; [+ *work*] activer, hâter ; (*Sport*) [+ *team*] encourager, animer ; **to ~ sb on to (do) sth** inciter qn à (faire) qch

urgency [ˈɜːdʒənsɪ] N (*NonC*) [*of case etc*] urgence f ; [*of tone, entreaty*] insistance f ; **a matter of ~** une affaire urgente ; **there's no ~** ce n'est pas urgent, cela ne presse pas ; **with a note of ~ in his voice** avec insistance

urgent [ˈɜːdʒənt] ADJ [*matter, help, message, need*] urgent, pressant ; [*medical attention*] d'urgence ; [*appeal, voice, desire*] pressant ; [*priority*] absolu ; **the matter needs ~ attention** c'est urgent ; **he demands an ~ answer** il exige qu'on lui réponde immédiatement ; **her tone was ~** son ton était insistant ; **I must talk to you, it's ~** il faut que je vous parle, c'est urgent ; **how ~ is it?** est-ce que c'est très urgent ? ; **is it ~?** c'est (vraiment) urgent ? ; **it's not ~** ce n'est pas urgent, ça ne presse pas ; **the letter was marked "~"** la lettre portait la mention « urgent » ; **it is ~ that he should go** il doit y aller de toute urgence ; **it is ~ for us to complete this task** il est urgent que nous accomplissions cette tâche

urgently [ˈɜːdʒəntlɪ] ADV [*need, request, appeal, seek*] d'urgence ; [*say*] d'un ton insistant ; **courier ~ required** on recherche or nous recherchons de toute urgence un coursier ; **he wants to talk to you ~** il veut vous parler de toute urgence

uric [ˈjʊərɪk] ADJ urique

urinal [ˈjʊərɪnl] N (= *place*) urinoir m ; (*in street*) vespasienne f ; (= *receptacle*) urinal m

urinalysis [ˌjʊərɪˈnælɪsɪs] N (*pl* **urinalyses** [ˌjʊərɪˈnælɪsiːz]) = **uranalysis**

urinary [ˈjʊərɪnərɪ] 1 ADJ [*system, complaint, infection, flow*] urinaire ; [*retention*] d'urine 2 COMP ► **urinary tract** N appareil m urinaire, voies fpl urinaires

urinate [ˈjʊərɪneɪt] VI uriner

urine [ˈjʊərɪn] N urine f

URL [ˌjuːɑːrˈel] N (*Comput*) (ABBR = **uniform resource locator**) URL m

urn [ɜːn] N a (= *vase etc*) urne *f*; (*also* **funeral ~**) urne *f* (funéraire) b (*also* **tea ~, coffee ~**) grosse bouilloire électrique

urogenital [ˌjʊərəʊˈdʒenɪtl] ADJ urogénital

urological [ˌjʊərəʊˈlɒdʒɪkl] ADJ urologique

urologist [jʊəˈrɒlədʒɪst] N urologue *mf*

urology [jʊəˈrɒlədʒɪ] N urologie *f*

Ursa [ˈɜːsə] N (*Astron*) **~ Major/Minor** la Grande/Petite Ourse

urticaria [ˌɜːtɪˈkɛərɪə] N urticaire *f*

Uruguay [ˈjʊərəgwaɪ] N l'Uruguay *m*

Uruguayan [ˌjʊərəˈgwaɪən] 1 ADJ uruguayen, de l'Uruguay 2 N Uruguayen(ne) *m(f)*

US [juːˈes] N (ABBR = **United States**) **the ~** les USA *mpl*, les ÉU(A) *mpl*; **in the US** aux USA, aux États-Unis; **the US Army/government** l'armée/le gouvernement des États-Unis

us [ʌs] PERS PRON a nous; **he hit us** il nous a frappés; **give it to us** donnez-le-nous; **in front of us** devant nous; **let us** *or* **let's go!** allons-y!; **younger than us** plus jeune que nous; **both of us** nous deux, tous (*or* toutes) les deux; **several of us** plusieurs d'entre nous; **he is one of us** il est des nôtres; **as for us English, we …** nous autres Anglais, nous …; **we took the books with us** nous avons emporté les livres b (*Brit* = *me*) me, moi; **give us a bit!** donne-m'en un morceau!, donne-moi-z-en!*; **give us a look!** fais voir!

USA [juːesˈeɪ] N a (ABBR = **United States of America**) **the ~** les USA *mpl*, les ÉUA *mpl* b (ABBR = **United States Army**) armée de terre des États-Unis

usable [ˈjuːzəbl] ADJ [*equipment, facility, space*] utilisable (**for sth** pour qch); [*information, evidence, skill*] utilisable, exploitable (**for sth** pour qch); **in ~ condition** [*equipment*] en état de marche; **land ~ for agriculture** terres *fpl* cultivables; **no longer ~** hors d'usage

USAF [juːeseɪˈef] N (ABBR = **United States Air Force**) armée de l'air des États-Unis

usage [ˈjuːzɪdʒ] N (NonC) a (= *custom*) usage *m*, coutume *f* b (*Ling*) usage *m* c (= *treatment*) [*of tool, machine, chair etc*] utilisation *f*; [*of person*] traitement *m*; **it's had some rough ~** ça a été malmené, on s'en est mal servi

usance [ˈjuːzəns] N (*Fin*) usance *f*

USCG [juːessiːˈdʒiː] N (ABBR = **United States Coast Guard**) garde *f* côtière américaine

USDA [juːesdiːˈeɪ] N (ABBR = **United States Department of Agriculture**) → **agriculture**

USDAW [juːesdiːeɪˈdʌblju] N (*Brit*) (ABBR = **Union of Shop Distributive and Allied Workers**) syndicat

USDI [juːesdiːˈaɪ] N (ABBR = **United States Department of the Interior**) → **interior**

use

1	NOUN	4	INTRANSITIVE VERB
2	TRANSITIVE VERB	5	PHRASAL VERBS
3	AUXILIARY VERB		

1 [juːs] NOUN

a NonC = **act of using** emploi *m*, utilisation *f*; **the ~ of steel in industry** l'emploi de l'acier dans l'industrie; **to learn the ~ of sth** apprendre à se servir de qch; **care is necessary in the ~ of chemicals** il faut prendre des précautions quand on utilise des produits chimiques; **to improve with ~** s'améliorer à l'usage

♦ **for use**: directions **for ~** mode *m* d'emploi; **for your (own) personal ~** à votre usage personnel; **"for the ~ of teachers only"** (*book, equipment*) « à l'usage des professeurs seulement »; (*car park, room*) « réservé aux professeurs »; **to keep sth for one's own ~** réserver qch à son usage personnel; **for ~ in case of emergency** à utiliser en cas d'urgence; **fit for ~** en état de servir; **ready for ~** prêt à servir *or* à l'emploi; **for general/household ~** à usage général/domestique; **for ~ in schools/the home** destiné à être utilisé dans les écoles/à la maison; (*Med*) **for external ~ only** à usage externe

♦ **in use** [*machine*] en usage, utilisé; [*word*] en usage, usité; **in general ~** d'usage *or* d'emploi courant; **it is in daily ~** on s'en sert tous les jours; **no longer in ~** ◊ **now out of ~** [*machine*] qui n'est plus utilisé; [*word*] qui ne s'emploie plus, inusité

♦ **into use**: **to put sth into ~** commencer à se servir de qch; **these machines came into ~ in 1975** on a commencé à utiliser ces machines en 1975

♦ **out of use**: **to go** *or* **fall out of ~** tomber en désuétude; **it's gone out of ~** on ne l'emploie plus; (*on machine, lift etc*) **"out of ~"** « en panne »

♦ **to make use of** se servir de, utiliser; **to make good ~ of sth** [+ *machine, time, money*] faire bon usage de qch, tirer parti de qch; [+ *opportunity, facilities*] mettre qch à profit, tirer parti de qch

♦ **to put to use** [+ *money, equipment*] utiliser; [+ *knowledge, experience*] mettre à profit; [+ *idea, theory*] mettre en application; **I absorb ideas and put them to ~** j'absorbe les idées et je les mets en application; **to put sth to good ~** [+ *machine, time, money*] faire bon usage de qch, tirer parti de qch; [+ *opportunity, facilities*] mettre qch à profit, tirer parti de qch

b = **way of using** emploi *m*, utilisation *f*; **a new ~ for …** un nouvel usage de …; **it has many ~s** cela a beaucoup d'emplois; **I'll find a ~ for it** je trouverai un moyen de m'en servir, j'en trouverai l'emploi; **I've no further ~ for it** je n'en ai plus besoin; **I've no ~ for that sort of behaviour!*** je n'ai que faire de ce genre de conduite!; **I've no ~ for him at all!*** il m'embête!*

c = **usefulness** utilité *f*; **this tool has its ~s** cet outil a son utilité; **he has his ~** il est utile par certains côtés; **what's the ~ of all this?** à quoi sert tout ceci?; **oh, what's the ~?*** à quoi bon?; **what's the ~ of telling him not to, he never takes any notice** à quoi bon lui dire de s'arrêter, il n'écoute jamais; **I've told him fifty times already, what's the ~?*** je le lui ai dit trente-six fois déjà, pour ce que ça a servi!

♦ **to be of use** servir, être utile (**for sth, to sth** à qch, **to sb** à qn); **is this (of) any ~ to you?** est-ce que cela peut vous être utile *or* vous servir?; **can I be (of) any ~?** puis-je être *or* me rendre utile?; **a lot of ~ that will be to you!*** ça te fera une belle jambe!*

♦ **to be (of) no use** ne servir à rien; **this is no ~ any more** ce n'est plus bon à rien; **he's no ~** il est incapable, il est nul; **he's no ~ as a goalkeeper** il est nul comme gardien de but; **you're no ~ to me if you can't spell** vous ne m'êtes d'aucune utilité si vous faites des fautes d'orthographe; **there's** *or* **it's no ~ protesting** inutile de protester; **it's no ~ trying to reason with him** cela ne sert à rien d'essayer de le raisonner, on perd son temps à essayer de le raisonner; **it's no ~*, he won't listen** ça ne sert à rien *or* c'est inutile, il ne veut rien entendre

d NonC = **ability to use, access** usage *m*; **to have the ~ of a garage** avoir l'usage d'un garage, avoir un garage à sa disposition; **with ~ of kitchen** avec usage de la cuisine; **he gave me the ~ of his car** il a mis sa voiture à ma disposition; **to have lost the ~ of one's arm** avoir perdu l'usage d'un bras; **to have the full ~ of one's faculties** jouir de toutes ses facultés

e Ling = **sense** emploi *m*, acception *f*

f frm = **custom** coutume *f*, habitude *f*; (*Rel, Sociol*) usage *m*; **this has long been his ~** telle est son habitude depuis longtemps

2 [juːz] TRANSITIVE VERB

a = **make use of** [+ *object, tool*] se servir de, utiliser; [+ *force, discretion*] user de; [+ *opportunity*] profiter de; [+ *method, means*] employer; [+ *drugs*] prendre; [+ *sb's name*] faire usage de; **he ~d a knife to open it** il s'est servi d'un couteau pour l'ouvrir; **it is ~d for opening bottles** on s'en sert pour ouvrir les bouteilles; **are you using this?** vous servez-vous de ceci?, avez-vous besoin de ceci?; **have you ~d a gun before?** vous êtes-vous déjà servi d'un fusil?; **the money is to be ~d to build a new hospital** l'argent servira à construire un nouvel hôpital *or* à la construction d'un nouvel hôpital; **he ~d his shoe as a hammer** il s'est servi de sa chaussure comme marteau; **I ~ that as a table** ça me sert de table; **ointment to be ~d sparingly** crème *f* à appliquer en couche fine; **I don't ~ my French much** je ne me sers pas beaucoup de mon français; **I don't want to ~ the car** je ne veux pas prendre la voiture; **he said I could ~ his car** il a dit que je pouvais me servir de *or* prendre sa voiture; **no longer ~d** [*tools, machine, room*] qui ne sert plus; [*word*] qui ne s'emploie plus, tombé en désuétude; **he wants to ~ the bathroom** il veut aller aux toilettes; **someone is using the bathroom** il y a quelqu'un dans la salle de bains; **~ your head** *or* **brains!*** réfléchis un peu!, tu as une tête, c'est pour t'en servir!; **~ your eyes!** ouvre l'œil!; **I feel I've just been ~d** j'ai l'impression qu'on s'est servi de moi; **I could ~ a drink!*** je prendrais bien un verre!; **the house could ~ a lick of paint!*** une couche de peinture ne ferait pas de mal à cette maison! → **used**

b = **use up** utiliser (tout); **this car ~s too much petrol** cette voiture consomme trop d'essence; **have you ~d all the paint?** avez-vous utilisé toute la peinture?; **you can ~ (up) the leftovers in a soup** vous pouvez utiliser les restes pour faire une soupe

c † = **treat** [+ *person*] traiter; **to ~ sb well** bien traiter qn; **he was badly ~d** on a mal agi envers lui, on a abusé de sa bonne volonté

3 [juːz] AUXILIARY VERB

I ~d to see her every week je la voyais toutes les semaines; **I ~d to swim every day** j'allais nager *or* j'avais l'habitude d'aller nager tous les jours; **I ~d not** *or* **I ~(d)n't*** *or* **I didn't ~* to smoke** (autrefois) je ne fumais pas; **what ~d he to do** (*frm*) *or* **what did he ~ to do* on Sundays?** qu'est-ce qu'il faisait (d'habitude) le dimanche?; **things aren't what they ~d to be** les choses ne sont plus ce qu'elles étaient

4 [juːz] INTRANSITIVE VERB

Drugs* se droguer

5 [juːz] PHRASAL VERBS

► **use up** VT SEP [+ *food*] consommer entièrement, finir; [+ *objects, ammunition, one's strength, resources, surplus*] épuiser; [+ *money*] dépenser; **to ~ up the scraps** utiliser les restes; **it is all ~d up** il n'en reste plus → **use 2b**

used [juːzd] 1 ADJ a (= *not fresh*) [*handkerchief, cup*] qui a servi, sale; [*tissue, sanitary towel, needle, condom*] usagé; [*stamp*] oblitéré; [*engine oil*] usé b (= *second-hand*) [*car, equipment*] d'occasion; [*clothing*] usagé; (*fig hum*) **would you buy a ~ car from this man?** feriez-vous confiance à cet homme? c (*after adv = employed*) **commonly/frequently ~** couramment/fréquemment utilisé d [juːst] (= *accustomed*) **to be ~ to sth** être habitué à qch, avoir l'habitude de qch; **I'm ~ to her now** je me suis habitué à elle maintenant; **to be ~ to doing sth** être habitué à faire qch, avoir l'habitude de faire qch; **he was ~ to being given orders** il avait l'habitude qu'on lui donne des ordres, il était habitué à ce qu'on lui donne des ordres; **to get ~ to sb/sth** s'habituer à qn/qch; **you'll soon get ~ to it** vous vous y ferez vite, vous vous y habituerez vite; **to get ~ to doing sth** prendre l'habitude de faire qch; **to get ~ to sb** *or* **sb's doing sth** s'habituer à ce que qn fasse qch; **I'm ~ to her interrupting me** j'ai l'habitude qu'elle m'interrompe (subj), je suis habitué à ce qu'elle m'interrompe (subj)

2 COMP ► **used-car salesman** N (pl **used-car salesmen**) vendeur m de voitures d'occasion

usedn't ['juːsnt] = **used not**; → **use 3**

useful ['juːsful] ADJ **a** (= handy, helpful) utile (**for, to sb** à qn); ~ **addresses** adresses fpl utiles; **that knife will come in ~*** ce couteau pourra être utile; **to be ~ for (doing) sth** être utile pour faire qch; **to perform a ~ function** jouer un rôle utile, être utile; **these drugs are ~ in treating cancer** ces médicaments sont utiles dans le traitement du cancer; **he's a ~ man to know** c'est un homme qu'il est utile de compter parmi ses relations; **that's ~ to know** or **a ~ thing to know** c'est bon à savoir; **this machine has reached the end of its ~ life** cette machine a fait son temps; **this machine has a ~ life of ten years** cette machine peut servir dix ans; **this work is not serving any ~ purpose** ce travail ne sert pas à grand-chose; (iro) **that's ~!** nous voilà bien avancés!; **it is ~ to know a foreign language** il est utile de connaître une langue étrangère; **it would be ~ for me to have that information** il me serait utile d'avoir ces renseignements

b (Brit* = good) **to be ~ with one's hands** être habile de ses mains; **he's quite ~ with his fists** il sait se servir de ses poings

usefully ['juːsful] ADV utilement; **is there anything the government can ~ do?** y a-t-il quelque chose que le gouvernement puisse faire?; **you might ~ do a bit of preparatory reading** il vous serait peut-être utile de faire quelques lectures préparatoires; **his time could be more ~ spent** or **employed** il pourrait employer son temps de façon plus utile or plus utilement

usefulness ['juːsfulnɪs] N (NonC) utilité f → **outlive**

useless ['juːslɪs] ADJ **a** (= not useful) [person, action, information, tool] inutile (**to sb** pour qn, **against sth** pour qch); [arm, leg, hand] inerte; [life] vide; **our efforts proved ~** nos efforts ont été vains; **shouting is ~** il est inutile de crier, ce n'est pas la peine de crier; **a car is ~ without wheels** une voiture sans roues ne sert à rien; **worse than ~*** plus qu'inutile; **it is ~ to complain** il ne sert à rien de se plaindre; **it is ~ for you to complain** il est inutile que vous vous plaigniez **b** (* = incompetent) [teacher, player, school] nul* (nulle* f) (**at sth** en qch, **at doing sth** quand il s'agit de faire qch)

uselessly ['juːslɪslɪ] ADV inutilement; **his arm hung ~ by his side** son bras pendait, inutile, le long de son corps; **he stood around ~** il est resté là à ne rien faire

uselessness ['juːslɪsnɪs] N (NonC) **a** [of tool, advice etc] inutilité f; [of remedy] inefficacité f **b*** [of person] incompétence f

usen't ['juːsnt] = **used not**; → **use 3**

user ['juːzə'] **1** N **a** [of public service, telephone, road, train, dictionary] usager m; [of machine, tool] utilisateur m, -trice f; [of electricity, gas] usager m, utilisateur m, -trice f; [of Comput] utilisateur m, -trice f; **car ~** automobiliste mf; **computer ~s** ceux qui utilisent un ordinateur, utilisateurs mpl d'ordinateurs

b (Drugs) usager m, consommateur m; **heroin ~** consommateur m, -trice f d'héroïne

2 COMP ► **user-definable, user-defined** N (Comput) touche f définissable par l'utilisateur ► **user-friendliness** N (Comput) convivialité f; [of machine, dictionary etc] facilité f d'utilisation ► **user-friendly** ADJ (Comput) convivial; (gen) facile à utiliser; **we want to make the store more ~-friendly for shoppers** nous voulons rendre le magasin plus accueillant pour les clients ► **user group** N groupe m d'usagers ► **user name** N (Comput) nom m de l'utilisateur, nom m d'utilisateur ► **user's guide** N guide m (de l'utilisateur)

USES [ˌjuːesiːˈes] N (ABBR = **United States Employment Service**) → **employment**

USGS [ˌjuːesdʒiːˈes] N (ABBR = **United States Geological Survey**) → **geological**

usher ['ʌʃə'] **1** N (in law courts etc) huissier m; (= doorkeeper) portier m; (at public meeting) membre m du service d'ordre; (in theatre, church) placeur m **2** VT **to ~ sb out/along** etc faire sortir/avancer etc qn; **to ~ sb into a room** introduire or faire entrer qn dans une salle; **to ~ sb to the door** reconduire qn à la porte

►**usher in** VT SEP [+ person] introduire, faire entrer; (fig) [+ period, season] inaugurer, commencer; **it ~s in a new era** cela annonce or inaugure une nouvelle époque, cela marque le début d'une ère nouvelle; **it ~ed in a new reign** cela inaugura un nouveau règne, ce fut l'aurore d'un nouveau règne; **the spring was ~ed in by storms** le début du printemps fut marqué par des orages

usherette [ˌʌʃəˈret] N (Cine, Theat) ouvreuse f

USIA [ˌjuːesaɪˈeɪ] N (ABBR = **United States Information Agency**) service officiel fournissant des informations sur les États-Unis à l'étranger

USM [ˌjuːesˈem] N (ABBR = **United States Mint**) hôtel de la Monnaie des États-Unis

USMC [ˌjuːesemˈsiː] N (ABBR = **United States Marine Corps**) corps m des marines (des États-Unis)

USN [ˌjuːesˈen] N (ABBR = **United States Navy**) marine de guerre des États-Unis

USO [ˌjuːesˈəʊ] N (US) (ABBR = **United Service Organization**) organisation venant en aide aux militaires américains, en particulier lors de leurs déplacements à l'étranger

USP [ˌjuːesˈpiː] N (ABBR = **unique selling point**) → **unique**

USPHS [ˌjuːespiːeɪtˈes] N (ABBR = **United States Public Health Service**) → **public**

USS [ˌjuːesˈes] N ABBR = **United States Ship** (or **Steamer**)

USSR [ˌjuːeses'ɑː'] N (ABBR = **Union of Soviet Socialist Republics**) URSS f; **in the ~** en URSS

usu. ABBR = **usual(ly)**

usual ['juːʒʊəl] **1** ADJ **a** (= customary) [method, excuse, address, rules] habituel; [price] habituel, courant; [word] usuel, courant; **as is ~ with such machines, it broke down** elle est tombée en panne, ce qui arrive souvent avec ce genre de machine; **as is ~ on these occasions** comme il est d'usage en ces occasions; **it wasn't his ~ car** ce n'était pas la voiture qu'il prenait d'habitude; **he was sitting in his ~ chair** il était assis dans sa chaise habituelle; **in the ~ place** à l'endroit habituel; **his ~ practice was to rise at six** son habitude était de or il avait l'habitude de se lever à six heures; **her ~ routine** son train-train m quotidien; **what did you do on holiday? — oh, the ~ stuff*** qu'est-ce que tu as fait pendant les vacances? — oh, la même chose que d'habitude; **with his ~ tact** avec son tact habituel, avec le tact qui le caractérise; **more than ~** plus que d'habitude or d'ordinaire; **to get up earlier than ~** se lever plus tôt que d'habitude; **it's the ~ thing** c'est comme d'habitude; **he said the ~ things about ...** il a dit ce qu'on dit d'habitude à propos de ...; **come at the ~ time** venez à l'heure habituelle; **7 o'clock is my ~ time to get up** d'habitude, je me lève à 7 heures; **it's ~ to ask first** il est d'usage or il est poli de demander d'abord; **it is ~ for soldiers to wear a uniform** les soldats portent traditionnellement un uniforme; **it's quite ~ for this to happen** ça arrive souvent, ça n'a rien d'inhabituel; **it wasn't ~ for him to arrive early** ce n'était pas dans ses habitudes d'arriver en avance; **it was ~ for her to drink a lot** elle avait l'habitude de boire beaucoup, c'était dans ses habitudes de boire beaucoup; **the journey took four hours instead of the ~ two**

le voyage a pris quatre heures au lieu des deux heures habituelles; **it was not the ~ type of holiday** c'étaient des vacances pas comme les autres; **to do sth in the ~ way** faire qch de la manière habituelle; **she welcomed us in her ~ friendly way** elle nous a accueillis chaleureusement, comme à son habitude → **channel, crowd, self, sense, suspect**

b ~ (= as always) comme d'habitude; **he arrived late as ~** il est arrivé en retard comme d'habitude; **he's late — as ~!** il est en retard — comme d'habitude!; **for her it's just life as ~** pour elle, la vie continue (comme avant); **to carry on as ~** continuer comme d'habitude; **"business as ~"** «horaires d'ouverture habituels»; **it is business as ~ (for them)** (lit) les affaires continuent (pour eux); (fig) la vie continue (pour eux); **as per ~*** comme d'habitude

2 N (* = drink) **you know my ~** vous savez ce que je prends d'habitude; **the ~ please!** comme d'habitude, s'il vous plaît!

usually ['juːʒʊəlɪ] ADV d'habitude, généralement; **more than ~ depressed/busy/hungry** plus déprimé/occupé/affamé que d'habitude; **~, a simple explanation is enough** d'habitude or généralement, une simple explication suffit

usufruct ['juːzjʊfrʌkt] N (Jur) usufruit m

usufructuary [ˌjuːzjʊˈfrʌktjʊərɪ] (Jur) **1** N usufruitier m, -ière f **2** ADJ usufruitier

usurer ['juːʒərə'] N usurier m, -ière f

usurious [juːˈzjʊərɪəs] ADJ usuraire

usurp [juːˈzɜːp] VT usurper

usurpation [ˌjuːzɜːˈpeɪʃən] N (NonC) usurpation f

usurper [juːˈzɜːpə'] N usurpateur m, -trice f

usurping [juːˈzɜːpɪŋ] ADJ usurpateur (-trice f)

usury ['juːʒʊrɪ] N (NonC: Fin) usure f

UT ABBR = **Utah**

Utah ['juːtɑː] N l'Utah m; **in ~** dans l'Utah

utensil [juːˈtensl] N ustensile m → **kitchen**

uteri ['juːtəraɪ] NPL of **uterus**

uterine ['juːtəraɪn] ADJ utérin

uterus ['juːtərəs] N (pl **uteri**) utérus m

utilitarian [ˌjuːtɪlɪˈtɛərɪən] **1** ADJ **a** (= practical) [view, approach, object] utilitaire **b** (= functional) [furniture, building, style] fonctionnel **c** (Philos) utilitaire **2** N utilitariste mf

utilitarianism [ˌjuːtɪlɪˈtɛərɪənɪzəm] N (NonC) utilitarisme m

utility [juːˈtɪlɪtɪ] **1** N **a** (NonC) utilité f **b** (also **public ~**) service m public **2** ADJ [clothes, furniture] fonctionnel; [goods, vehicle] utilitaire **3** COMP ► **utility player** N (Sport) joueur m, -euse f polyvalent(e) ► **utility room** N pièce où l'on range les appareils ménagers, les provisions etc ► **utility software** N (Comput) logiciel m utilitaire

utilizable ['juːtɪˌlaɪzəbl] ADJ utilisable

utilization [ˌjuːtɪlaɪˈzeɪʃən] N (NonC) [of resources] utilisation f, exploitation f; [of facility, technique] utilisation f; [of land, space, skill] exploitation f

utilize ['juːtɪlaɪz] VT [+ object, facilities, equipment] utiliser, se servir de; [+ situation, resources, talent, person] tirer parti de, exploiter; [+ space] utiliser, tirer parti de

utmost ['ʌtməʊst] **1** ADJ **a** (= greatest) [restraint, difficulty, determination] le plus grand or la plus grande, extrême; **of (the) ~ importance (to sb/sth)** de la plus haute importance (pour qn/qch); **it is of (the) ~ importance that ...** il est de la plus haute importance que ... (+ subj); **with the ~ possible care** avec le plus grand soin possible; **an undertaking of the ~ danger** une entreprise des plus dangereuses; **a matter of (the) ~ urgency** une affaire de la plus extrême urgence **b** (= furthest) [limits] extrême **2** N **to do one's ~** faire tout son possible; **to do one's ~ to do sth** faire tout son possible pour faire qch; **to the ~** au plus haut degré *or* point; **at the ~** au maximum, tout au plus

Utopia [juːˈtəʊpɪə] N utopie f

Utopian [juːˈtəʊpɪən] **1** ADJ utopique **2** N utopiste mf

Utopianism [juːˈtəʊpɪənɪzəm] N utopisme m

utricle [ˈjuːtrɪkl] N utricule m

Uttar Pradesh [ˈʊtəˈprɑːdeʃ] N l'Uttar Pradesh m

utter¹ [ˈʌtəʳ] ADJ [lack, failure, disaster] complet (-ète f), total; [incompetence] total; [contempt, disregard, silence, sincerity] absolu, total; [fool, rogue, liar] parfait (before n); [disgust, despair, hopelessness, frustration, stupidity] profond; [futility, misery] extrême; [madness] pur; **to my ~ amazement, I succeeded** à ma plus grande stupéfaction, j'ai réussi; **with ~ conviction** avec une conviction inébranlable; **what ~ nonsense!** c'est complètement absurde!;

she's talking complete and ~ rubbish* elle dit n'importe quoi; **he's a complete and ~ fool/bastard**** etc c'est un imbécile/salaud* etc fini

utter² [ˈʌtəʳ] VT [+ word] prononcer, proférer; [+ cry] pousser; [+ threat, insult] proférer; [+ libel] publier; (Jur) [+ counterfeit money] émettre, mettre en circulation; **he didn't ~ a word** il n'a pas dit un seul mot, il n'a pas soufflé mot

utterance [ˈʌtərəns] N **a** (= remark etc) paroles fpl, déclaration f **b** (NonC) [of facts, theory] énonciation f; [of feelings] expression f; **to give ~ to** exprimer **c** (style of speaking) élocution f, articulation f **d** (Ling) énoncé m

utterly [ˈʌtəlɪ] ADV [untrue, destroy, transform] complètement, totalement; [impossible] tout à fait; [convince] entièrement; **he failed ~** il a complètement or totalement échoué; **he ~ failed to impress them** il ne leur a fait absolument aucun effet; **to be ~ without talent/malice** être dénué de tout talent/toute méchanceté

uttermost [ˈʌtəməʊst] = **utmost**

UV [juːˈviː] ADJ (ABBR = **ultraviolet**) UV

UVA, UV-A [ˌjuːviːˈeɪ] ADJ UVA inv; **~ rays** (rayons mpl) UVA mpl

UVB, UV-B [ˌjuːviːˈbiː] ADJ UVB inv; **~ rays** (rayons mpl) UVB mpl

UVF [ˌjuːviːˈef] N (Brit) (ABBR = **Ulster Volunteer Force**) → **Ulster**

uvula [ˈjuːvjʊlə] N (pl **uvulas** or **uvulae**) luette f, uvule f

uvular [ˈjuːvjʊləʳ] ADJ (Anat, Phon) uvulaire; **~ r** r grasseyé

uxorious [ʌkˈsɔːrɪəs] ADJ excessivement dévoué à sa femme

uxoriousness [ʌkˈsɔːrɪəsnɪs] N (NonC) dévotion f excessive à sa femme

Uzbek [ˈʊzbek] **1** ADJ ouzbek f inv **2** N **a** (= person) Ouzbek mf **b** (Ling) ouzbek m

Uzbekistan [ˌʌzbekɪˈstɑːn] N l'Ouzbékistan m

V

V, v [viː] **1** **a** (= *letter*) V, v *m*; **V for Victor** ◊ **V for Victory** ≈ V comme Victor; (*Brit*) **to stick the Vs up to sb.** ≈ faire un bras d'honneur à qn **b** (ABBR = **vide**) (= *see*) V, voir **c** (ABBR = **versus**) contre **d** (*esp Bible*) ABBR = **verse** **e** ABBR = **very** **2** COMP ► **V and A*** N (*Brit*) = **Victoria and Albert Museum** *musée londonien des arts décoratifs* ► **V-chip** N verrou *m* électronique ► **V-neck** N décolleté *m* en V *or* en pointe ► **V-necked** ADJ à encolure en V *or* en pointe ► **V-shaped** ADJ (en forme de) V ► **V-sign** N **a** (*for victory*) **to give the V-sign** faire le V de la victoire **b** (*in Brit*) geste obscène, ≈ bras *m* d'honneur; **to give sb the V-sign** ≈ faire un bras d'honneur à qn

VA [viːˈeɪ] N **a** (*US*) (ABBR = **Veterans Administration**) → **veteran** **b** ABBR = **Virginia**

Va. ABBR = **Virginia**

vac¹* [væk] N (*Brit Univ*) (ABBR = **vacation**) vacances *fpl* (universitaires)

vac²* [væk] N (*esp Brit*) (ABBR = **vacuum cleaner**) → **vacuum**

vacancy [ˈveɪkənsɪ] N **a** (*in hotel etc*) chambre *f* libre, **"no vacancies"** « complet »; **have you any vacancies for August?** est-ce qu'il vous reste des chambres (libres) pour le mois d'août? **b** (= *job*) poste *m* vacant *or* libre, vacance *f*; **"no vacancies"** « pas d'embauche »; **a short-term ~** un poste temporaire; **"~ for a typist"** « nous recherchons une dactylo », « nous cherchons une dactylo »; **we have a ~ for an editor** nous avons un poste de rédacteur à pourvoir, nous cherchons un rédacteur; **we have a ~ for an enthusiastic sales manager** nous cherchons un directeur des ventes motivé; **to fill a ~** [*employer*] pourvoir un poste vacant; [*employee*] être nommé à un poste vacant; **we are looking for someone to fill a ~ in our sales department** nous cherchons à pourvoir un poste vacant dans notre service de ventes **c** (*NonC* = *emptiness*) vide *m* **d** (*NonC* = *blankness*) esprit *m* vide, stupidité *f*

vacant [ˈveɪkənt] **1** ADJ **a** (= *unoccupied*) [*land, building*] inoccupé; [*hotel room, table, parking space*] libre; [*seat, hospital bed*] libre, disponible; [*post, job*] vacant, à pourvoir; **to fall ~** [*post*] se libérer; **a ~ space** un espace libre; (*Ind*) **a ~ post** un poste vacant *or* à pourvoir; (*Univ etc: on course*) **a ~ place** une place libre *or* disponible; (*Press*) **"situations ~"** « offres d'emploi »; (*Jur*) **with ~ possession** avec libre possession, avec jouissance immédiate **b** (= *stupid*) ahuri; [*expression, look, stare*] (= *blank*) absent, sans expression; [*mind*] vide **2** COMP ► **vacant lot** N (*esp US*) (*gen*) terrain *m* inoccupé; (*for sale*) terrain *m* à vendre

vacantly [ˈveɪkəntlɪ] ADV **a** (= *absently*) [*look, stare, gaze*] d'un air absent; **to gaze ~ into space** fixer le vide, avoir le regard perdu dans le vide **b** [*look, stare, gaze, smile, say*] (= *stupidly*) d'un air ahuri; (= *blankly*) d'un air absent

vacate [vəˈkeɪt] VT (*frm*) [+ *room, seat, job*] quitter; **to ~ a house** quitter une maison; **to ~ one's post** démissionner; **this post will soon be ~d** ce poste sera bientôt vacant *or* à pourvoir; **to ~ the premises** vider les lieux

vacation [vəˈkeɪʃən] **1** N **a** (*US*) vacances *fpl*; **on ~** en vacances; **on his ~** pendant ses vacances; **to take a ~** prendre des vacances; **where are you going for your ~?** où allez-vous passer vos vacances? **b** (*Brit Univ*) vacances *fpl*; (*Jur*) vacations *fpl or* vacances *fpl* judiciaires → **long¹** **2** VI (*US*) passer des (*or* ses *etc*) vacances **3** COMP ► **vacation course** N cours *mpl* de vacances ► **vacation trip** N voyage *m* de vacances; **to go on a ~ trip** partir en vacances

vacationer [vəˈkeɪʃənə], **vacationist** [vəˈkeɪʃənɪst] (*US*) N vacancier *m*, -ière *f*

vaccinate [ˈvæksɪneɪt] VT vacciner (**against** contre); **to get ~d** se faire vacciner; **have you been ~d against ...?** est-ce que vous êtes vacciné contre ...?

vaccination [ˌvæksɪˈneɪʃən] N vaccination *f* (**against** contre); **smallpox/polio** *etc* **~** vaccination *f* contre la variole/la polio *etc*; **to have a ~ against ...** se faire vacciner contre ...

vaccine [ˈvæksiːn] N vaccin *m*; (*Comput*) logiciel *m* antivirus; **polio ~** vaccin *m* contre la polio; **~-damaged** victime de réactions provoquées par un vaccin

vacillate [ˈvæsɪleɪt] VI hésiter (**between** entre); **she ~d so long over accepting that ...** elle s'est demandé si longtemps si elle allait accepter ou non que ...

vacillating [ˈvæsɪleɪtɪŋ] **1** ADJ indécis, hésitant **2** N (*NonC*) hésitations *fpl*, indécision *f*

vacillation [ˌvæsɪˈleɪʃən] N indécision *f*

vacua [ˈvækjʊə] NPL of **vacuum**

vacuity [væˈkjuːɪtɪ] N vacuité *f*; **vacuities** (= *silly remarks*) niaiseries *fpl*, remarques *fpl* stupides

vacuous [ˈvækjʊəs] ADJ (*frm*) [*person, film, book*] inepte; [*comment, remark*] inepte, creux; [*look, stare*] vide; [*expression*] vide, niais; [*smile, face*] niais; [*life*] vide de sens

vacuum [ˈvækjʊm] **1** N **a** (*pl* **vacuums** *or* (*frm*) **vacua**) (*Phys*) vacuum *m*; (*fig*) vide *m*; **in a ~** dans le vide → **nature** **b** (*gen*) vide *m*; **their departure left a ~** leur départ a laissé un (grand) vide; **a cultural ~** un vide culturel **c** (*also* ~ **cleaner**) aspirateur *m*; **to give sth a ~** = **to vacuum sth**; → **2** **2** VT (*also* **~-clean**) [+ *carpet*] passer à l'aspirateur; [+ *room*] passer l'aspirateur dans **3** COMP [*brake, pump, tube*] à vide ► **vacuum aspiration** N (*Med* = *abortion*) IVG *f* par aspiration ► **vacuum bottle** N (*US*) = **vacuum flask** ► **vacuum cleaner** N aspirateur *m* ► **vacuum extraction** N (*Med* = *birth*) accouchement *m* par ventouse ► **vacuum flask** N (*Brit*) bouteille *f* thermos®, thermos® *m or f inv* ► **vacuum-packed** ADJ emballé sous vide

---

pidly) d'un air ahuri; (= *blankly*) d'un air absent

vade mecum [ˈvɑːdɪˈmeɪkʊm] N vademecum *m inv*

vagabond [ˈvægəbɒnd] **1** N vagabond(e) *m(f)*; (= *tramp*) chemineau *m*, clochard(e) *m(f)* **2** ADJ [*life*] errant, de vagabondage; [*thoughts*] vagabond; [*habits*] irrégulier

vagary [ˈveɪgərɪ] N caprice *m*

vagi [ˈveɪdʒaɪ] NPL of **vagus**

vagina [vəˈdʒaɪnə] N (*pl* **vaginas** *or* **vaginae** [vəˈdʒaɪniː]) vagin *m*

vaginal [vəˈdʒaɪnəl] **1** ADJ vaginal **2** COMP ► **vaginal discharge** N pertes *fpl* blanches ► **vaginal dryness** N sécheresse *f* vaginale ► **vaginal intercourse** N (*NonC*) (rapports *mpl* sexuels avec) pénétration *f* vaginale ► **vaginal smear** N frottis *m* (vaginal)

vaginismus [ˌvædʒɪˈnɪzməs] N (*Med*) vaginisme *m*

vagrancy [ˈveɪgrənsɪ] N (*also Jur*) vagabondage *m*

vagrant [ˈveɪgrənt] **1** N vagabond(e) *m(f)*; (= *tramp*) clochard(e) *m(f)*; (*Jur*) vagabond(e) *m(f)* **2** ADJ [*person*] vagabond

vague [veɪg] ADJ **a** (= *unclear*) [*person, idea, gesture, plan, feeling, instructions, reply, promise*] vague; [*description, memory, impression*] vague, flou; [*shape, outline*] flou, imprécis; **I had a ~ idea** *or* **feeling she would come** j'avais comme le sentiment *or* comme une idée* qu'elle viendrait; **he was ~ about the time he would be arriving at** (= *didn't say exactly*) il n'a pas (bien) précisé l'heure de son arrivée; (= *didn't know exactly*) il n'était pas sûr de l'heure à laquelle il arriverait; **I'm still very ~ about all this** ça n'est pas encore très clair dans mon esprit; **I'm still very ~ about how it happened** je ne sais pas encore très bien comment ça s'est passé; **I'm very ~ about French history** je ne m'y connais pas très bien en histoire de France **b** (= *absent-minded*) [*person*] distrait; **he's always rather ~** il est toujours distrait *or* dans la lune; **she's getting rather ~ these days** elle ne s'y retrouve plus très bien *or* elle perd un peu la tête maintenant; **to look ~** avoir l'air vague *or* distrait; **to have a ~ look in one's eyes** avoir l'air vague

vaguely [ˈveɪglɪ] ADV **a** (= *unclearly*) [*say, describe, remember, resemble, understand*] vaguement; **~ familiar/disappointed** vaguement familier/déçu; **to be ~ aware of sth** être vaguement conscient de qch; **a ~ defined set of objectives** un ensemble d'objectifs pas bien définis; **to be ~ reminiscent of sth** rappeler vaguement qch; **a ~ worded agreement** un accord libellé dans des termes vagues **b** (= *absently*) [*look, nod*] d'un air distrait; [*smile*] d'un air vague

vagueness [ˈveɪgnɪs] N **a** [*of question, account, memory, wording, language*] manque *m* de précision; [*of statement, proposal*] imprécision *f*, flou *m*; [*of feeling, sensation*] caractère *m* imprécis, vague *m*; [*of photograph etc*] manque *m* de netteté **b** (= *absent-mindedness*) distraction *f*; **his ~ is very annoy-**

ing c'est agaçant qu'il soit si distrait *or* tête en l'air*

vagus ['veɪɡəs] N (*pl* **vagi**) (*also* **~ nerve**) nerf *m* vague *or* pneumogastrique

vain [veɪn] ADJ [a] (= *fruitless, empty*) [*attempt, effort, plea, hope, promise*] vain (*before n*); [*threat*] en l'air [b] (*pej = conceited*) [*person*] vaniteux; **to be ~ about one's appearance** tirer vanité de son apparence, être vain [c] **in ~** (= *unsuccessfully*) [*try, wait, search for*] en vain, vainement; (= *pointlessly*) [*die, suffer*] pour rien; **it was all in ~** cela n'a servi à rien, c'était inutile *or* en vain; **all his** (*or* **my** *etc*) **efforts were in ~** c'était peine perdue; **I looked for him in ~: he had already left** j'ai eu beau le chercher, il était déjà parti; **to take God's** *or* **the Lord's name in ~** blasphémer; (*hum*) **is someone taking my name in ~?** on parle de moi?

vainglorious [veɪn'ɡlɔːrɪəs] ADJ (*liter*) orgueilleux, vaniteux

vainglory [veɪn'ɡlɔːrɪ] N (*NonC: liter*) orgueil *m*, vanité *f*

vainly ['veɪnlɪ] ADV [a] (= *to no effect*) [*try, seek, believe, hope*] en vain, vainement [b] (= *conceitedly*) vaniteusement, avec vanité

valance ['væləns] N (*above curtains*) cantonnière *f*; (*round bed frame*) tour *m or* frange *f* de lit; (*round bed canopy*) lambrequin *m*

vale [veɪl] N (*liter*) val *m* (*liter*), vallée *f*; (*fig*) **this ~ of tears** cette vallée de larmes

valediction [ˌvælɪ'dɪkʃən] N [a] (= *farewell*) adieu(x) *m(pl)* [b] (*US Scol*) discours *m* d'adieu

valedictorian [ˌvælɪdɪk'tɔːrɪən] N (*US Scol*) major *m* de la promotion (*qui prononce le discours d'adieu*)

valedictory [ˌvælɪ'dɪktərɪ] [1] ADJ (*frm*) d'adieu [2] N (*US Scol*) discours *m* d'adieu

valence ['veɪləns] N [a] (*esp US*) = **valency** [b] (*Bio*) atomicité *f*

Valencia [bɑˈlenθjɑ] N Valence (*en Espagne*)

valency ['veɪlənsɪ] N (*Chem*) valence *f*

valentine ['væləntaɪn] N [a] **Valentine** Valentin(e) *m(f)*; (**St) Valentine's Day** la Saint-Valentin [b] (*also* **~ card**) carte *f* de la Saint-Valentin; **"will you be my ~?"** « c'est toi que j'aime » (*écrit sur une carte*)

valerian [vəˈlɪərɪən] N valériane *f*

valet ['væleɪ] [1] N [a] (= *person: in hotel or household*) valet *m* de chambre [b] (= *rack for clothes*) valet *m* [2] ['vælɪt] VT [+ *man*] servir comme valet de chambre; [+ *clothes*] entretenir; [+ *car*] nettoyer [3] COMP ► **valet parking** N service *m* de garage des voitures

valetudinarian [ˌvælɪˌtjuːdɪ'nɛərɪən] ADJ, N valétudinaire *mf*

Valhalla [vælˈhælə] N Walhalla *m*

valiant ['væljənt] ADJ (*liter*) [*person*] vaillant (*liter*), valeureux (*liter*); [*effort, attempt, fight*] courageux

valiantly ['væljəntlɪ] ADV vaillamment

valid ['vælɪd] ADJ [a] (= *reasonable, acceptable*) [*argument, reason, excuse, claim, objection, interpretation*] valable; [*question*] pertinent; **fashion is a ~ form of art** la mode est une forme d'art à part entière; **it is not ~ to derive such conclusions from the data** il n'est pas valable de tirer de telles conclusions de ces données [b] (= *in force*) [*ticket, passport, licence, contract*] valable, valide; **~ for three months** valable *or* valide pendant trois mois; **no longer ~** périmé

validate ['vælɪdeɪt] VT [+ *document, course, diploma*] valider; [+ *theory, argument, claim*] prouver la justesse de; [+ *results*] confirmer; (*Comput*) valider

validation [ˌvælɪ'deɪʃən] N (*NonC*) [a] [*of claim, document etc*] validation *f* [b] (*Psych = approval*) approbation *f*

validity [vəˈlɪdɪtɪ] N [*of document, claim*] validité *f*; [*of argument*] justesse *f*

valise [vəˈliːz] N sac *m* de voyage; (*Mil*) sac *m* (de soldat)

Valium® ['vælɪəm] N Valium® *m*; **to be on ~** être sous Valium

Valkyrie ['vælkɪrɪ] N Walkyrie *or* Valkyrie *f*; **the ride of the ~s** la chevauchée des Valkyries

valley ['vælɪ] N vallée *f*, val *m* (*liter*); (*small, narrow*) vallon *m*; **the Thames/Rhône** *etc* **~** la vallée de la Tamise/du Rhône *etc*; **the Loire ~** la vallée de la Loire; (*between Orléans and Tours*) le Val de Loire → **lily**

valor ['vælər] N (*US*) = **valour**

valorous ['vælərəs] ADJ (*liter*) valeureux (*liter*)

valour, valor (*US*) ['vælər] N (*liter*) courage *m*, bravoure *f*

valuable ['væljʊəbl] [1] ADJ [*jewellery, antique*] de (grande) valeur; [*information, advice, lesson, contribution, ally, resources, time*] précieux; [*experience*] très utile; **~ possessions** objets *mpl* de valeur; **thank you for granting me so much of your ~ time** je vous remercie de m'avoir accordé autant de votre temps précieux [2] **valuables** NPL objets *mpl* de valeur; **all her ~s were stolen** on lui a volé tous ses objets de valeur

valuation [ˌvæljʊ'eɪʃən] N [a] [*of house, property, painting etc*] estimation *f*; (*by expert*) expertise *f*; (= *value decided upon*) estimation *f*; **to have a ~ done** faire évaluer *or* estimer quelque chose; **what is the ~?** à combien est-ce évalué *or* estimé?; **an independent ~ of the company** une évaluation indépendante de cette société [b] [*of person, sb's character, work etc*] appréciation *f*; **his rather low ~ of the novel** son opinion peu favorable du roman

valuator ['væljʊeɪtər] N expert *m* (*en estimations de biens mobiliers*)

value ['væljuː] [1] N [a] (*gen*) valeur *f*; (= *usefulness, worth*) valeur *f*, utilité *f*; **her training has been of no ~ to her** sa formation ne lui a servi à rien; **to set good ~ on sth** attacher *or* accorder une grande valeur à qch; **to have rarity ~** avoir de la valeur de par sa rareté; **the film has great entertainment ~** c'est un film très divertissant; **the invention never had anything more than novelty ~** cette invention n'a jamais été autre chose qu'un gadget → **shock** [b] (= *worth in money*) valeur *f*; **the large packet is the best ~** le grand paquet est le plus avantageux; **it's good ~ (for money)** on en a pour son argent, le rapport qualité-prix est bon (*esp Comm*); **to get good ~ for money** en avoir pour son argent; **to be of great ~** valoir cher; **of little ~** de peu de valeur; **of no ~** sans valeur; **to gain (in)** ~ prendre de la valeur; **to have ~** avoir de la valeur; **to increase in ~** prendre de la valeur; **increase in ~** hausse *f* ou augmentation *f* de valeur; **to lose (in)** ~ se déprécier; **loss of ~** perte *f* ou diminution *f* de valeur, dépréciation *f*; **he paid the ~ of the cup he broke** il a remboursé (le prix de) la tasse qu'il a cassée; **to put** *or* **place a ~ on sth** évaluer qch; **to put** *or* **place a ~ of £20 on sth** évaluer *or* estimer qch à 20 livres; **what ~ do you put on this?** à quelle valeur estimez-vous cela?, combien pensez-vous que cela vaut?; **to put** *or* **set too high/too low a ~ on sth** surestimer/sous-estimer qch; **to put** *or* **set a low ~ on sth** attacher peu de valeur à qch; **goods to the ~ of £100** marchandises *fpl* d'une valeur de 100 livres; **a cheque to the ~ of £100** un chèque (d'un montant) de 100 livres → **street** [c] (= *moral worth*) [*of person*] valeur *f*, mérite *m*; **to put** *or* **place a high ~ on sth** attacher beaucoup d'importance à qch; **what ~ do you put on this?** quelle valeur accordez-vous *or* attribuez-vous à cela?; **to put** *or* **place a high ~ on doing sth** attacher beaucoup d'importance à faire qch; **he places a high ~ on educating his children** il attache beaucoup d'importance à l'éducation de ses enfants [d] (*Math, Mus, Painting, Phon*) valeur *f*

[2] **values** NPL (= *attitudes, moral standards*) valeurs *fpl* → **production, Victorian**

[3] VT [a] (= *estimate worth of*) [+ *house, jewels, painting*] évaluer, estimer (**at** à); (*by expert*) expertiser; **the house was ~d at £80,000** la maison a été évaluée *or* estimée à 80 000 livres; **he had it ~d** il l'a fait expertiser [b] (= *appreciate, esteem*) [+ *friendship*] apprécier; [+ *comforts*] apprécier, faire grand cas de; [+ *liberty, independence*] tenir à; **if you ~ your life/eyes/freedom** si vous tenez à la vie/à vos yeux/à votre liberté; **we ~ your opinion** votre avis nous importe beaucoup; **he is someone we all ~** nous l'apprécions tous beaucoup

[4] COMP ► **value added tax** N (*Brit: abbr* **VAT**) taxe *f* sur la valeur ajoutée (*abbr* **TVA**) ► **value judg(e)ment** N (*fig*) jugement *m* de valeur

valued ['væljuːd] ADJ [*friend, customer, contribution*] précieux; [*employee, commodity*] apprécié; [*colleague*] estimé

valueless ['væljʊlɪs] ADJ sans valeur

valuer ['væljʊər] N (*Brit*) expert *m* (*en estimations de biens mobiliers*)

valve [vælv] N [a] (*Anat*) valvule *f*; (*Bot, Zool*) valve *f*; (*Tech*) [*of machine*] soupape *f*, valve *f*; [*of air chamber, tyre*] valve *f*; [*of musical instrument*] piston *m*; **inlet/outlet ~** soupape *f* d'admission/d'échappement; **exhaust ~** clapet *m* d'échappement; (*Mus*) **horn/trombone** cor *m*/trombone *m* à pistons → **safety, suction** [b] (*Elec, Rad: also* **thermionic ~**) lampe *f*

valvular ['vælvjʊlər] ADJ valvulaire

vamoose [vəˈmuːs] VI filer*, décamper*; **~!** fiche le camp!*

vamp¹ [væmp] [1] N (= *woman*) vamp *f* [2] VT vamper* [3] VI jouer la femme fatale

vamp² [væmp] [1] VT (= *repair*) rafistoler; (*Mus*) improviser [2] VI (*Mus*) improviser des accompagnements [3] N [*of shoe*] devant *m*

vampire ['væmpaɪər] [1] N (*lit, fig*) vampire *m* [2] COMP ► **vampire bat** N (*Zool*) vampire *m*

vampirism ['væmpaɪərɪzəm] N vampirisme *m*

van¹ [væn] N [a] (*Aut*) (*smallish*) camionnette *f*, fourgonnette *f*; (*large*) camion *m*, fourgon *m* → **removal** [b] (*Brit Rail*) fourgon *m* → **guard, luggage** [c]* (ABBR = **caravan**) caravane *f*; (*gipsy's*) roulotte *f* [2] COMP ► **van-boy** N livreur *m* ► **van-driver** N chauffeur *m* de camion ► **van-man** N (*pl* **van-men**) = **vanboy** ► **van pool** N (*US*) covoiturage *m* en minibus

van² [væn] N ABBR = **vanguard**

vanadium [vəˈneɪdɪəm] N vanadium *m*

Vancouver [væn'kuːvər] N Vancouver [2] COMP ► **Vancouver Island** N l'île *f* de Vancouver

vandal ['vændl] N [a] (= *hooligan*) vandale *mf* [b] (*Hist*) **Vandal** Vandale *mf*

vandalism ['vændəlɪzəm] N vandalisme *m*; **cultural ~** vandalisme *m* culturel

vandalistic [ˌvændə'lɪstɪk] ADJ destructeur (-trice *f*), de vandale

vandalize ['vændəlaɪz] VT vandaliser, saccager

Van Diemen's Land† [ˌvænˈdiːmənzlænd] N la Terre de Van Diemen

vane [veɪn] N [*of windmill*] aile *f*; [*of propeller*] pale *f*; [*of turbine*] aube *f*; [*of quadrant etc*] pinnule *f*, lumière *f*; [*of feather*] barbe *f*; (*also* **weather~**) girouette *f*

vanguard ['vænɡɑːd] N [a] (*Mil, Naut*) avant-garde *f*; **in the ~ (of)** en tête (de) [b] (*fig*) avant-garde *f*; **in the ~ of progress** à l'avant-garde *or* à la pointe du progrès

vanilla [vəˈnɪlə] [1] N (= *spice, flavour*) vanille *f* [2] COMP [*cream, ice*] à la vanille ► **vanilla essence** N extrait *m* de vanille ► **vanilla pod** N gousse *f* de vanille ► **vanilla sugar** N sucre *m* vanillé

vanillin [vəˈnɪlɪn] N vanilline *f*

vanish ['vænɪʃ] [1] VI (gen) disparaître (from de); [fears] se dissiper; **to ~ without trace** disparaître sans laisser de traces; **to ~ into thin air*** se volatiliser; **he ~ed into the countryside** il a disparu dans la campagne; **he/it had ~ed from sight** il/cela avait disparu, il/cela était introuvable; **he/it has ~ed from the face of the earth** il/cela a disparu sans laisser de traces; **Julie ~ed from outside her home** Julie a disparu de devant chez elle; **he ~ed into the distance** il s'est évanoui dans le lointain; **he said goodbye and ~ed into the house** il a dit au revoir et il est rentré précipitamment dans la maison [2] COMP ► **vanishing act*** N (fig) **to do a ~ing act** s'éclipser* ► **vanishing cream†** N crème f de beauté ► **vanishing point** N point m de fuite ► **vanishing trick** N tour m de passe-passe

vanished ['vænɪʃt] ADJ disparu

vanitory unit ['vænɪtərɪ'juːnɪt] N = **vanity unit**; → **vanity**

vanity ['vænɪtɪ] [1] N (NonC) [a] (= conceit) vanité f; **I may say without ~** je peux dire sans (vouloir) me vanter [b] (= worthlessness) vanité f, futilité f; **all is ~** tout est vanité [2] COMP ► **vanity basin** N = **vanity unit** ► **vanity box, vanity case** N mallette f pour affaires de toilette, vanity-case m ► **vanity mirror** N (in car etc) miroir m de courtoisie ► **vanity plate** N (esp US Aut) plaque f d'immatriculation personnalisée ► **vanity press** N (Publishing) maison f d'édition à compte d'auteur ► **vanity publishing** N (NonC) publication f à compte d'auteur ► **vanity unit** N sous-vasque f

───────────────

VANITY PLATE

En Grande-Bretagne comme aux États-Unis, les automobilistes s'intéressent particulièrement aux immatriculations qui forment des mots ou contiennent leurs initiales. Ces plaques, appelées personalized number plates *en Grande-Bretagne et* vanity plates *aux États-Unis, se vendent souvent très cher. Par exemple, on peut imaginer qu'un homme s'appelant James Allan Gordon souhaite acquérir à n'importe quel prix la plaque d'immatriculation « JAG 1 ».*

───────────────

vanquish ['væŋkwɪʃ] VT (liter) vaincre

vanquisher ['væŋkwɪʃə'] N (liter) vainqueur m

vantage ['vɑːntɪdʒ] [1] N avantage m, supériorité f [2] COMP ► **vantage ground** N (Mil) position f stratégique or avantageuse ► **vantage point** N (fig) position f avantageuse, bonne place f

Vanuatu ['vænuːˌætuː] N **(the Republic of) ~** (la République de) Vanuatu

vapid ['væpɪd] ADJ (frm) [remark, conversation, book, song] insipide; [person] ahuri; [smile] mièvre; [style] plat

vapidity [væ'pɪdɪtɪ] N [of conversation] insipidité f; [of style] platitude f

vapor ['veɪpə'] (US) = **vapour**

vaporization [ˌveɪpəraɪ'zeɪʃən] N vaporisation f

vaporize ['veɪpəraɪz] [1] VT vaporiser [2] VI se vaporiser

vaporizer ['veɪpəraɪzə'] N (gen, Chem) vaporisateur m; (Med: for inhalation) inhalateur m; (for perfume) atomiseur m

vaporous ['veɪpərəs] ADJ (liter) [a] (= full of vapour) [air, cloud, heat] vaporeux (liter) [b] (fig = indistinct) vague

vapour, vapor (US) ['veɪpə'] [1] N [a] (Phys: also mist etc) vapeur f; (on glass) buée f [b] **to have the ~s†** avoir des vapeurs† [2] VI (US† = boast) fanfaronner [3] COMP ► **vapour bath** N bain m de vapeur ► **vapour trail** N (Aviat) traînée f de condensation

variability [ˌveərɪə'bɪlɪtɪ] N variabilité f

variable ['veərɪəbl] [1] ADJ [amount, quality, content] variable; [weather] variable, incertain, changeant; [mood] changeant; [work] de qualité inégale [2] N (gen) variable f [3] COMP ► **variable pitch propeller** N hélice f à pas variable ► **variable type** N (Comput) type m de variable

variance ['veərɪəns] N [a] (= disagreement) désaccord m, différend m; **to be at ~** (= in disagreement) être en désaccord; **to be at ~ with sb about sth** avoir un différend avec qn sur qch; **this is at ~ with what he said earlier** cela ne correspond pas à or cela contredit ce qu'il a dit auparavant [b] (= variation) variation f [c] (Math) variance f [d] (Jur) différence f, divergence f; **there is a ~ between the two statements** les deux dépositions ne s'accordent pas or ne concordent pas

variant ['veərɪənt] [1] N (gen, Ling etc) variante f; **spelling ~** variante f orthographique [2] ADJ [method] autre [3] COMP ► **variant form** N (Ling) variante f (orthographique) ► **variant reading** N variante f ► **variant spelling** N = **variant form**

variation [ˌveərɪ'eɪʃən] N (gen, Bio, Chem, Met, Mus, Phys) variation f; (in opinions, views) fluctuation(s) f(pl), changements mpl

varicoloured, varicolored (US) ['veərɪˌkʌləd] ADJ multicolore, bigarré; (fig) divers

varicose ['værɪkəʊs] [1] ADJ [ulcer, eczema] variqueux [2] COMP ► **varicose vein** N varice f; **to have ~ veins** avoir des varices

varied ['veərɪd] ADJ [diet, career, work, programme etc] varié; [reasons, opportunities, talents etc] varié, divers

variegated ['veərɪgeɪtɪd] ADJ [a] (= mottled) [plant, leaf, plumage] panaché; [colour] moucheté; [markings] de couleurs différentes [b] (= varied) [assortment] varié

variegation [ˌveərɪ'geɪʃən] N bigarrure f, diaprure f (liter)

variety [və'raɪətɪ] [1] N [a] (NonC = diversity) variété f (in dans), diversité f; **children like ~** les enfants aiment la variété or ce qui est varié; **it lacks ~** ça n'est pas assez varié; **they have increased in number and ~** ils sont devenus plus nombreux et plus variés ■ (PROV) **~ is the spice of life** il faut de tout pour faire un monde [b] (= assortment, range) **a wide** or **great ~ of ...** un grand nombre de ...; **dolphins produce a ~ of noises** les dauphins émettent différents bruits or un certain nombre de bruits; **for a ~ of reasons** pour diverses raisons; **it offers a ~ of careers** cela offre un grand choix de carrières [c] (Bio = subdivision) variété f; **new plant ~** obtention f or nouveauté f végétale [d] (= type, kind) type m, espèce f; **many varieties of socialist(s)** de nombreux types (différents) de socialistes, de nombreuses espèces (différentes) de socialistes; **books of the paperback ~** des livres du genre livre de poche [e] (NonC: Theat) variétés fpl [2] COMP (Theat) [actor, artiste etc] de variétés, de music-hall ► **variety meats** NPL (US Culin) abats mpl (de boucherie) ► **variety show** N (Theat) spectacle m de variétés or de music-hall; (Rad, TV) émission f de variétés ► **variety store** N (US) ≈ Prisunic m ► **variety theatre** N (théâtre m de) variétés fpl ► **variety turn** N (Brit) numéro m (de variétés or de music-hall)

varifocal ['veərɪ'fəʊkl] [1] ADJ progressif [2] **varifocals** NPL lunettes fpl à verres progressifs

variola [və'raɪələ] N variole f

various ['veərɪəs] ADJ [a] (= differing) divers (before n), différent; **at ~ times of day** à différents moments de la journée; **the ~ meanings of a word** les différents sens d'un mot; **his excuses are many and ~** ses excuses sont nombreuses et variées [b] (= several) divers, plusieurs; **I phoned her ~ times** je lui ai téléphoné à plusieurs reprises; **there are ~ ways of doing it** il y a plusieurs manières de le faire

variously ['veərɪəslɪ] ADV **he was ~ known as John, Johnny or Jack** il était connu sous divers noms: John, Johnny ou Jack; **the crowd was ~ estimated at two to seven thousand** le nombre de personnes a été estimé entre deux et sept mille selon les sources

varlet† ['vɑːlɪt] N (pej) sacripant†† m

varmint* ['vɑːmɪnt] N (= scoundrel) polisson(ne) m(f), vaurien(ne) m(f)

varnish ['vɑːnɪʃ] [1] N (lit, fig) vernis m; (on pottery) vernis m, émail m → **nail, spirit** [2] VT [+ furniture, painting] vernir; [+ pottery] vernisser; **to ~ one's nails** se vernir les ongles; (fig) **to ~ the truth** maquiller la vérité

varnishing ['vɑːnɪʃɪŋ] [1] N vernissage m [2] COMP ► **varnishing day** N (Art) (jour m du) vernissage m

varsity ['vɑːsɪtɪ] [1] N [a] (Brit†* = university) fac* f [b] (US Univ Sport) équipe f de première catégorie (représentant un établissement d'enseignement) [2] COMP ► **varsity match** N match entre les universités d'Oxford et de Cambridge ► **varsity sports** NPL (US) sports pratiqués entre équipes de différents établissements scolaires

vary ['veərɪ] [1] VI varier; **to ~ with the weather** changer selon le temps; **to ~ from sth** différer de qch; **opinions ~ on this point** les opinions varient sur ce point [2] VT [+ programme, menu] varier; [+ temperature] faire varier; (directly) varier

varying ['veərɪɪŋ] ADJ [amounts] variable; [shades] différent; **of ~ abilities** de compétences variées; **of ~ ages** de différents âges; **to ~ degrees** à des degrés variables; **with ~ degrees of success** avec plus ou moins de succès; **for ~ periods of time** pendant des périodes plus ou moins longues; **of ~ sizes** de différentes tailles

vascular ['væskjʊlə'] ADJ vasculaire

vas deferens ['væs'defə,renz] N (pl vasa deferentia ['veɪsə,defə'renʃɪə]) (Anat) canal m déférent

vase [vɑːz] N vase m; **flower ~** vase m à fleurs

vasectomy [væ'sektəmɪ] N vasectomie f; **to have a ~** subir une vasectomie

Vaseline® ['væsɪliːn] [1] N vaseline® f [2] VT enduire de vaseline®

vasoconstrictor [ˌveɪzəʊkən'strɪktə'] N vasoconstricteur m

vasodilator [ˌveɪzəʊdaɪ'leɪtə'] N vasodilatateur m

vasomotor [ˌveɪzəʊ'məʊtə'] ADJ vasomoteur (f -trice)

vassal ['væsəl] N (Hist, fig) vassal m

vassalage ['væsəlɪdʒ] N vassalité f, vasselage m

vast [vɑːst] ADJ [quantity, amount, building, reserve] vaste (before n), énorme; [area, size, organization, army] vaste, immense; [knowledge, experience] vaste, grand; **at ~ expense** à grands frais; **to a ~ extent** dans une très large mesure; **a ~ improvement on sth** une nette amélioration par rapport à qch; **the ~ majority** la grande majorité; **~ sums (of money)** des sommes folles

vastly ['vɑːstlɪ] ADV [different] extrêmement; [superior] largement, nettement; [overrate, increase, improve] considérablement

vastness ['vɑːstnɪs] N immensité f

VAT [viːeɪ'tiː, væt] [1] N (Brit) (ABBR = **value added tax**) TVA f [2] COMP ► **VAT man*** N (pl **VAT men**) inspecteur des impôts chargé du contrôle de la TVA ► **VAT-registered** ADJ enregistré à la TVA ► **VAT return** N formulaire m de déclaration de la TVA

vat [væt] N cuve f, bac m

Vatican ['vætɪkən] [1] N Vatican *m* [2] COMP [*policy etc*] du Vatican ► **Vatican City** N la cité du Vatican ► **the Vatican Council** N le concile du Vatican

vaudeville ['vəʊdəvɪl] (*esp US*) [1] N spectacle *m* de variétés *or* de music-hall [2] COMP [*show, singer*] de variétés, de music-hall

vaudevillian [ˌvəʊdə'vɪlɪən] (*US*) [1] N (= *writer*) auteur *m* de variétés ; (= *performer*) acteur *m*, -trice *f* de variétés [2] ADJ de variétés

vaudevillist ['vəʊdəvɪlɪst] N (*US*) = **vaudevillian 1**

vault[1] [vɔːlt] N [a] (*Archit*) voûte *f* ; (*liter*) **the ~ of heaven** la voûte céleste [b] (*Anat*) voûte *f* ; **cranial ~** voûte *f* crânienne [c] (= *cellar*) cave *f* [d] (*in bank*) (= *strongroom*) chambre *f* forte ; (= *safe deposit box room*) salle *f* des coffres ; **it's lying in the ~s of the bank** c'est dans les coffres de la banque [e] (= *burial chamber*) caveau *m* ; **interred in the family ~** inhumé dans le caveau de famille

vault[2] [vɔːlt] [1] VI (*gen*) sauter ; (*Pole Vaulting*) sauter (à la perche) ; (*Gym*) sauter ; **to ~ over sth** sauter qch (d'un bond) → **pole**[1] [2] VT (*gen*) sauter d'un bond [3] N saut *m*

vaulted ['vɔːltɪd] ADJ [*roof, ceiling*] en voûte ; [*room, hall*] voûté

vaulting[1] ['vɔːltɪŋ] N (*Archit*) voûte(s) *f(pl)*

vaulting[2] ['vɔːltɪŋ] [1] N (*Sport*) exercice *m or* pratique *f* du saut [2] COMP ► **vaulting horse** N cheval *m* d'arçons

vaunt [vɔːnt] VT (*liter*) (= *boast about*) vanter ; (= *praise*) vanter, faire l'éloge de ; **much ~ed** tant vanté

VC [viː'siː] N [a] (*Brit*) (ABBR = **Victoria Cross**) → **Victoria** [b] (*Univ*) (ABBR = **vice-chancellor**) → **vice-** [c] (*US: in Vietnam*) ABBR = **Vietcong**

VCR [ˌviːsiː'ɑːʳ] N (ABBR = **video cassette recorder**) → **video**

VD [viː'diː] N (*Med*) (ABBR = **venereal disease**) → **venereal**

VDT [ˌviːdiː'tiː] N (ABBR = **visual display terminal**) → **visual**

VDU [ˌviːdiː'juː] N (*Comput*) (ABBR = **visual display unit**) → **visual**

VE Day [viː'iːdeɪ] N anniversaire de la victoire des alliés en 1945

┌─ **VE DAY** ─┐

La Grande-Bretagne et les États-Unis commémorent le 8 mai la victoire alliée de 1945 en Europe. C'est le **VE Day** (*Victory in Europe Day*). *La victoire sur le Japon,* **VJ Day** (*Victory over Japan Day*), *est commémorée le 15 août.*

veal [viːl] [1] N veau *m* → **fillet** [2] COMP [*stew, cutlet*] de veau ► **veal crate** N box pour l'élevage des veaux de batterie

vector ['vektəʳ] [1] N [a] (*Bio, Math*) vecteur *m* [b] (*Aviat*) direction *f* [2] VT (*Aviat*) radioguider [3] COMP (*Math*) vectoriel

vectorial [vek'tɔːrɪəl] ADJ vectoriel

veep⁎ [viːp] N (*US: from VP*) = **vice-president** ; → **vice-**

veer [vɪəʳ] [1] VI [a] [*wind*] (= *change direction*) tourner, changer de direction ; [*ship*] virer (de bord) ; [*car, road*] virer ; **to ~ to the north** se diriger vers le nord *or* au nord ; **the car ~ed off the road** la voiture a quitté la route ; **to ~ (off) to the) left/right** virer à gauche/droite [b] (= *change etc*) changer ; **he ~ed round to my point of view** changeant d'opinion il s'est rallié à mon point de vue ; **he ~ed off** *or* **away from his subject** il s'est éloigné de son sujet ; **her feelings for him ~ed between tenderness and love** les sentiments qu'elle lui portait oscillaient entre la tendresse et l'amour [2] VT [a] (*Naut*) [+ *cable*] filer [b] [+ *ship, car*] faire virer

veg⁎ [vedʒ] N (ABBR = **vegetables**) légumes *mpl*
► **veg out**⁎ VI glander⁎

vegan ['viːgən] N, ADJ végétalien(ne) *m(f)*

veganism ['viːgənɪzəm] N végétalisme *m*

vegeburger ['vedʒɪ,bɜːgəʳ] N hamburger *m* végétarien

vegetable ['vedʒtəbl] [1] N [a] légume *m* ; **early ~s** primeurs *fpl* [b] (*generic term* = *plant*) végétal *m*, plante *f* [c] (*fig pej* = *brain-damaged etc person*) épave *f* [2] COMP [*oil, matter*] végétal ► **vegetable dish** N plat *m* à légumes, légumier *m* ► **vegetable garden** N (jardin *m*) potager *m* ► **vegetable kingdom** N règne *m* végétal ► **vegetable knife** N (*pl* **vegetable knives**) couteau-éplucheur *m* ► **vegetable marrow** N (*esp Brit*) courge *f* ► **vegetable patch** N carré *m* de légumes ► **vegetable salad** N salade *f or* macédoine *f* de légumes ► **vegetable slicer** N coupe-légumes *m inv* ► **vegetable soup** N soupe *f* aux *or* de légumes

vegetarian [ˌvedʒɪ'tɛərɪən] ADJ, N végétarien(ne) *m(f)*

vegetarianism [ˌvedʒɪ'tɛərɪənɪzəm] N végétarisme *m*

vegetate ['vedʒɪteɪt] VI (*lit*) végéter ; (*fig*) végéter, moisir⁎

vegetated ['vedʒɪteɪtɪd] ADJ couvert de végétation ; **sparsely/densely ~** couvert d'une végétation clairsemée/dense

vegetation [ˌvedʒɪ'teɪʃən] N (*NonC*) végétation *f*

vegetative ['vedʒɪtətɪv] [1] ADJ végétatif ; **~ growth** croissance *f* de la végétation [2] COMP ► **vegetative coma** N coma *m* dépassé → **persistent**

veggie⁎ ['vedʒɪ] N, ADJ [a] ABBR = **vegetarian** [b] (*esp US*) ABBR = **vegetable 1a**

veggieburger ['vedʒɪ,bɜːdəʳ] N = **vegeburger**

vehemence ['viːɪməns] N [*of person, opposition, denial, tone*] véhémence *f* ; [*of criticism, attack, protest, dislike*] violence *f*

vehement ['viːɪmənt] ADJ [*person, opposition, denial, tone*] véhément ; [*criticism, attack, protest, dislike*] véhément, violent ; [*speech*] véhément, passionné ; [*gesture, condemnation*] vif

vehemently ['viːɪməntlɪ] ADV [*deny, say*] avec véhémence (*liter*) ; [*reject, oppose*] avec véhémence, violemment ; [*attack, curse*] violemment ; [*shake one's head*] vigoureusement ; **~ anti-European** violemment antieuropéen

vehicle ['viːɪkl] N [a] (*Aut, Rail etc*) véhicule *m* ; (*very large*) engin *m* ; **"closed to ~s"** « interdit à la circulation » ; **"authorized ~s only"** « accès réservé aux véhicules autorisés » ► **commercial** [b] (*Chem, Art, Pharm etc, also fig*) véhicule *m* ; **a ~ of** *or* **for communication** un véhicule de la communication ; **her art was a ~ for her political beliefs** son art lui servait à véhiculer ses convictions politiques

vehicular [vɪ'hɪkjʊləʳ] ADJ (*frm*) [*access*] des véhicules ; [*homicide*] commis en conduisant ; **~ deaths** décès *mpl* dus aux accidents de la route ; **~ traffic** circulation *f* (routière)

veil [veɪl] [1] N (*gen*) voile *m* ; (*on hat*) voilette *f* ; (*fig*) voile *m* ; (*Rel*) **to take the ~** prendre le voile ; (*fig liter*) **beyond the ~** dans l'au-delà ; **to be wearing a ~** être voilé ; (*fig*) **to draw/throw a ~ over** mettre/jeter un voile sur ; **under the ~ of ...** sous le voile de ... ; **~ of mist** voile *m* de brume [2] VT voiler, couvrir d'un voile ; (*fig*) [+ *truth, facts*] voiler ; [+ *feelings*] voiler, dissimuler ; **the clouds ~ed the moon** les nuages voilaient la lune

veiled [veɪld] ADJ (*lit, fig*) [*woman, face, criticism, reference, threat, warning, attack*] voilé ; **~ in black** voilé de noir ; (*liter*) **~ in shadow** plongé dans l'ombre ; (*liter*) **~ mountains** des montagnes *fpl* voilées (*liter*)

veiling ['veɪlɪŋ] N (*on hat etc*) voilage *m* ; (*fig*) [*of truth, facts*] dissimulation *f*

vein [veɪn] N [a] (*in body, insect wing*) veine *f* ; (*in leaf*) nervure *f* ; (*suicide*) **to open a ~** s'ouvrir les veines ; **he has French blood in his ~s** il a du sang français dans les veines → **varicose** [b] (*in stone etc: gen*) veine *f* ; (*of ore etc*) filon *m*, veine *f* ; **there's a ~ of truth in what he says** il y a un fond de vérité dans ce qu'il dit ; **a ~ of racism/scepticism** un fond de racisme/scepticisme ; **a ~ of humour runs through her writing** il y a un humour sous-jacent dans tous ses textes [c] (= *style etc*) style *m* ; (= *mood*) esprit *m* ; **in a humorous/revolutionary etc ~** dans un esprit humoristique/révolutionnaire etc ; **in the same ~** ◊ **in a similar ~** dans la même veine ; **in a more realistic ~** dans un style plus réaliste

veined [veɪnd] ADJ [*hand, marble*] veiné ; [*stone*] marbré ; [*leaf*] nervuré ; **blue-~ cheese** fromage *m* à pâte persillée ; **pink flowers ~ with red** des fleurs *fpl* roses veinées de rouge ; **rocks ~ with cracks** rochers *mpl* tout fissurés

veining ['veɪnɪŋ] N [*of marble*] veinures *fpl* ; [*of stone*] marbrures *fpl* ; [*of leaf*] nervures *fpl* ; [*of marble-effect paper*] dessin *mpl* marbrés

veinule ['veɪnjuːl] N veinule *f*

vela ['viːlə] NPL of **velum**

velar ['viːləʳ] ADJ vélaire

Velcro® ['velkrəʊ] N velcro® *m*

veld(t) [velt] N veld(t) *m*

vellum ['veləm] [1] N vélin *m* [2] COMP [*binding*] de vélin ► **vellum paper** N papier *m* vélin

velocipede [və'lɒsɪpiːd] N vélocipède *m*

velocity [vɪ'lɒsɪtɪ] N vélocité *f*, vitesse *f*

velodrome ['viːlə,drəʊm] N vélodrome *m*

velour(s) [və'lʊəʳ] N (*for clothes*) velours *m* rasé ; (*for upholstery*) velours *m* épais

velum ['viːləm] N (*pl* **vela**) (*Anat*) voile *m* du palais

velvet ['velvɪt] [1] N [a] (*gen*) velours *m* → **black, iron** [b] (*US = unearned income*) bénéfice *m* non salarial [2] COMP [*dress*] de velours ► **Velvet Revolution** N révolution *f* de velours

velveteen ['velvɪtiːn] N veloutine *f*

velvety ['velvɪtɪ] ADJ [*surface, texture, material*] velouteux, velouté ; [*sauce, voice*] velouté

vena cava ['viːnə'keɪvə] N (*pl* **venae cavae** ['viːniː'keɪviː]) veine *f* cave

venal ['viːnl] ADJ vénal

venality [viː'nælɪtɪ] N vénalité *f*

vend [vend] VT (*Jur*) vendre

vendee [ven'diː] N (*Jur*) acquéreur *m*

vendetta [ven'detə] N vendetta *f*

vending ['vendɪŋ] [1] N vente *f* [2] COMP ► **vending machine** N distributeur *m* automatique

vendor ['vendəʳ] N [a] (*gen*) marchand(e) *m(f)* ; **ice-cream etc ~** marchand(e) *m(f)* de glaces etc → **newsvendor, street** [b] (= *machine*) distributeur *m* automatique [c] ['vendɔːʳ] (*Jur*) vendeur *m*

veneer [və'nɪəʳ] [1] N placage *m* ; (*fig*) apparence *f*, vernis *m* ; **with** *or* **under a ~ of** sous un vernis de [2] VT plaquer

venerable ['venərəbl] [1] ADJ vénérable [2] COMP ► **the Venerable Bede** N Bède *m* le Vénérable

venerate ['venəreɪt] VT vénérer

veneration [ˌvenə'reɪʃən] N vénération *f*

venereal [vɪ'nɪərɪəl] [1] ADJ vénérien [2] COMP ► **venereal disease** N maladie *f* vénérienne, MST *f*

venereology [vɪ,nɪərɪ'ɒlədʒɪ] N vénérologie *f*

venery ['venərɪ] N [a] (*liter* = *hunting*) vénerie *f* [b] († = *debauchery*) débauche *f*

Venetia [vɪ'niːʃə] N (*Hist*) la Vénétie

Venetian [vɪ'niːʃən] [1] ADJ vénitien, de Venise [2] N Vénitien(ne) *m(f)* [3] COMP

▶ **Venetian blind** N store m vénitien

▶ **Venetian glass** N cristal m de Venise

Veneto [ˈvɛːnɪtəʊ] N **(the)** ~ la Vénétie

Venezuela [ˌveneˈzweɪlə] N le Venezuela

Venezuelan [ˌveneˈzweɪlən] [1] ADJ vénézuélien [2] N Vénézuélien(ne) m(f)

vengeance [ˈvendʒəns] N vengeance f; **to
take ~ (up)on ...** se venger de or sur ...; **to
take ~ for ...** tirer vengeance de ...; (fig) **with a
~ pour de bon***

vengeful [ˈvendʒfʊl] ADJ vengeur (-eresse f)

venial [ˈviːnɪəl] ADJ (also Rel) véniel

veniality [ˌviːnɪˈælɪtɪ] N caractère m véniel

Venice [ˈvenɪs] N Venise

venire [vɪˈnaɪrɪ] N (US Jur) liste f des jurés assi-
gnés

venireman [vɪˈnaɪərɪmən] N (pl -**men**) (US Jur)
juré m nommé par assignation

venison [ˈvenɪsən] N venaison f

venom [ˈvenəm] N (lit, fig) venin m

venomous [ˈvenəməs] ADJ (lit, fig) venimeux;
(fig) ~ **tongue** langue f de vipère

venomously [ˈvenəməslɪ] ADV (say) sur un ton
venimeux; **to glare ~ at sb** lancer des regards
venimeux à qn

venous [ˈviːnəs] ADJ (Anat, Bot) veineux

vent [vent] [1] N (for gas, liquid) (= hole) orifice
m; (= pipe) conduit m; (in chimney) tuyau m;
(of volcano) cheminée f; (in barrel) trou m; (in
coat) fente f; (fig) **to give ~ to** [+ feelings]
donner or laisser libre cours à [2] VT [+ barrel
etc] pratiquer un trou dans; (fig) [+ one's anger
etc] décharger (**on** sur) [3] COMP ▶ **vent
glass** N (Aut) déflecteur m

ventilate [ˈventɪleɪt] VT [a] [+ room, lungs, pa-
tient] aérer, ventiler; [+ tunnel] ventiler; [+
blood] oxygéner [b] (fig) [+ question] livrer à la
discussion; [+ grievance] étaler au grand jour

ventilation [ˌventɪˈleɪʃən] [1] N ventilation f
[2] COMP ▶ **ventilation shaft** N conduit m
d'aération or de ventilation

ventilator [ˈventɪleɪtər] N (Med) respirateur m;
(in room) ventilateur m; (Aut: also ~ **window**)
déflecteur m

ventricle [ˈventrɪkl] N ventricule m

ventriloquism [venˈtrɪləkwɪzəm] N ventriloquie f

ventriloquist [venˈtrɪləkwɪst] [1] N ventriloque mf [2] COMP ▶ **ventriloquist's dummy**
N poupée f de ventriloque

ventriloquy [venˈtrɪləkwɪ] N ventriloquie f

venture [ˈventʃər] [1] N (= project) entreprise f,
projet m; (also **business** ~) entreprise f; **it was
a risky ~** c'était une entreprise assez risquée or
assez hasardeuse; **the success of his first
artistic/film** etc ~ le succès de sa première entreprise artistique/cinématographique etc; **all
his business ~s failed** toutes les entreprises en
matière de commerce or toutes ses tentatives
commerciales ont échoué; **this is a new ~ in
publishing** ceci constitue quelque chose de
nouveau or un coup d'essai en matière d'édition; **at a ~**† au hasard

[2] VT [+ life, fortune, reputation] risquer; [+
opinion] hasarder; [+ explanation, estimate] hasarder, avancer; **when I asked him that, he ~d
a guess** quand je lui ai posé la question, il a
hasardé or avancé une réponse; **to ~ to do**
oser faire, se permettre de faire; **he ~d the
opinion that ...** il a hasardé une opinion selon
laquelle ...; **I ~d to write to you** j'ai pris la liberté de vous écrire; **... but he did not ~ to
speak ...** mais il n'a pas osé parler ■ (PROV)
nothing ~d nothing gained qui ne risque rien
n'a rien (PROV)

[3] VI s'aventurer, se risquer; **to ~ in/out/
through** etc se risquer à entrer/sortir/traverser
etc; **to ~ out of doors** se risquer à sortir; **to ~
into town/into the forest** s'aventurer or se hasarder dans la ville/dans la forêt; **they ~d on**

a programme of reform ils ont essayé de mettre sur pied or d'entreprendre un ensemble de
réformes; **when we ~d on this** quand nous
avons entrepris cela, quand nous nous
sommes lancés là-dedans

[4] COMP ▶ **venture capital** N (Econ) capital
m risque ▶ **venture capitalist** N (Econ) spécialiste mf du capital risque ▶ **Venture
Scout** N (Brit) ≈ scout m de la branche aînée,
≈ routier m, -ière f

▶ **venture forth** VI (liter) se risquer à sortir

venturesome [ˈventʃəsəm] ADJ [person] aventureux, entreprenant; [action] risqué, hasardeux

venue [ˈvenjuː] N (gen) lieu m (de rendez-
vous); (Jur) lieu m du procès, juridiction f;
the ~ of the meeting is ... la réunion aura lieu
à ...

Venus [ˈviːnəs] [1] N (Astron, Myth) Vénus f
[2] COMP ▶ **Venus fly-trap** N (Bot) dionée f

Venusian [vɪˈnjuːzɪən] ADJ vénusien

veracious [vəˈreɪʃəs] ADJ véridique

veracity [vəˈræsɪtɪ] N véracité f

veranda(h) [vəˈrændə] N véranda f

verb [vɜːb] [1] N (Gram) verbe m ▶ **auxiliary**
[2] COMP ▶ **verb phrase** N syntagme m
verbal

verbal [ˈvɜːbəl] [1] ADJ [a] (gen) [attack, agreement, support, statement, reasoning, promise]
verbal; [confession] oral; ~ **dexterity** facilité f
de parole, aisance f verbale; ~ **memory** mémoire f auditive; **to have good/poor ~ skills**
bien/mal s'exprimer [b] (Gram) verbal [2] N
(US Jur*) aveux mpl faits oralement (et servant
de témoignage dans un procès) [3] COMP
▶ **verbal abuse** N (NonC) violence f verbale,
injures fpl

verbalize [ˈvɜːbəlaɪz] VT [+ feelings etc] traduire
en paroles, exprimer

verbally [ˈvɜːbəlɪ] ADV [threaten, attack, communicate, express, agree] verbalement; **to abuse
sb ~** injurier qn; **to be ~ abusive** tenir des
propos injurieux; **to be ~ and physically
abused** être victime de coups et injures or
d'agressions verbales et physiques

verbatim [vɜːˈbeɪtɪm] [1] ADV [quote, repeat]
textuellement, mot pour mot; [translate] mot
à mot, littéralement [2] ADJ [translation] mot à
mot; [quotation] mot pour mot; **he gave me a
~ report of what was said** il m'a rapporté textuellement ce qui a été dit

verbena [vɜːˈbiːnə] N (= genus) verbénacées
fpl; (= plant) verveine f

verbiage [ˈvɜːbɪɪdʒ] N verbiage m

verbless [ˈvɜːblɪs] ADJ sans verbe

verbose [vɜːˈbəʊs] ADJ verbeux, prolixe

verbosely [vɜːˈbəʊslɪ] ADV avec verbosité,
verbeusement

verbosity [vɜːˈbɒsɪtɪ] N verbosité f

verdant [ˈvɜːdənt] ADJ (liter) verdoyant

verdict [ˈvɜːdɪkt] N [a] (Jur) verdict m → **bring
in, guilty** [b] (of doctor, electors, press etc)
verdict m; **to give one's ~ about** or **on** se prononcer sur

verdigris [ˈvɜːdɪɡrɪs] ADJ, N vert-de-gris m inv

verdure [ˈvɜːdjʊər] N (liter) verdure f

verge [vɜːdʒ] N [a] (Brit: of road) bas-côté m,
accotement m; **the car mounted the ~** la voiture est montée sur le bas-côté or l'accotement; **to pull over onto the ~** s'arrêter sur le
bas-côté; (Aut) **"soft ~s"** « accotement non stabilisé »

[b] (= edge) (gen) bord m; (round flowerbed)
bordure f en gazon; [of forest] orée f

[c] **on the ~ of doing sth** sur le point de faire
qch; **on the ~ of ruin/despair/a nervous breakdown** au bord de la ruine/du désespoir/de la
dépression nerveuse; **on the ~ of sleep** or **of
falling asleep** sur le point de s'endormir; **on
the ~ of tears** au bord des larmes, sur le point
de pleurer; **on the ~ of a discovery** à la veille

d'une découverte; **on the ~ of retirement/old
age** au seuil de la retraite/vieillesse; **people
living on the ~ of starvation** les gens que menace la famine, les gens qui risquent de mourir de faim

▶ **verge on** VT FUS friser, frôler; **the plot ~s on
the ridiculous** l'intrigue frise or frôle le ridicule; **disappointment verging on despair** une
déception frisant or frôlant le désespoir; **a
fury that ~d on madness** une fureur proche de
la folie; **she was verging on madness** elle frôlait la folie; **he's verging on bankruptcy** il est
au bord de la faillite; **she is verging on fifty**
elle frise la cinquantaine

verger [ˈvɜːdʒər] N (Rel) bedeau m; (ceremonial)
huissier m à verge

Vergil [ˈvɜːdʒɪl] N Virgile m

Vergilian [vəˈdʒɪlɪən] ADJ virgilien

verifiability [ˌverɪfaɪəˈbɪlɪtɪ] N vérifiabilité f

verifiable [ˈverɪfaɪəbl] ADJ vérifiable

verification [ˌverɪfɪˈkeɪʃən] N (= check) vérification f, contrôle m; (= proof) vérification
f

verifier [ˈverɪfaɪər] N (Comput) vérificatrice f

verify [ˈverɪfaɪ] VT [+ statements, information,
spelling] vérifier; [+ documents] contrôler

verily†† [ˈverɪlɪ] ADV en vérité

verisimilitude [ˌverɪsɪˈmɪlɪtjuːd] N vraisemblance f

veritable [ˈverɪtəbl] ADJ véritable, vrai (before
n)

verity [ˈverɪtɪ] N (liter) vérité f

vermicelli [ˌvɜːmɪˈselɪ] N (NonC) vermicelle(s)
m(pl)

vermicide [ˈvɜːmɪsaɪd] N vermicide m

vermifugal [ˈvɜːmɪfjuːɡəl] ADJ vermifuge

vermifuge [ˈvɜːmɪfjuːdʒ] N vermifuge m

vermilion [vəˈmɪljən] ADJ, N vermillon m inv

vermin [ˈvɜːmɪn] NPL (= animals) animaux mpl
nuisibles; (= insects) vermine f (NonC), parasites mpl; (pej = people) vermine f (NonC), racaille f (NonC), parasites mpl

verminous [ˈvɜːmɪnəs] ADJ [person, clothes]
pouilleux, couvert de vermine; [disease]
vermineux

Vermont [vɜːˈmɒnt] N le Vermont; **in ~** dans
le Vermont

vermouth [ˈvɜːməθ] N vermout(h) m

vernacular [vəˈnækjʊlər] [1] N [a] (Ling) (= native speech) langue f vernaculaire; (= jargon)
jargon m; **the ~ of advertising** le jargon de la
publicité; **in the ~** (= in local language) en
langue vernaculaire; (= not in Latin) en langue
vulgaire [b] (Archit) architecture f vernaculaire
or locale; **in the local ~** dans le style local
[2] ADJ [language] vernaculaire; [crafts, furnitu-
re] du pays; [architecture, style] vernaculaire,
local; [building] de style local

vernal [ˈvɜːnl] [1] ADJ (liter) printanier
[2] COMP ▶ **the vernal equinox** N l'équinoxe m de printemps

Verona [vəˈrəʊnə] N Vérone f

veronica [vəˈrɒnɪkə] N [a] (= plant) véronique
f [b] (= name) **Veronica** Véronique f

verruca [veˈruːkə] N (pl verrucae or verrucas
[veˈruːsiː]) (esp Brit) verrue f (gén plantaire)

Versailles [veəˈsaɪ] N Versailles

versatile [ˈvɜːsətaɪl] ADJ [person] aux talents
variés, plein de ressources; [mind] souple;
[tool, vehicle, software] à usages multiples, polyvalent

versatility [ˌvɜːsəˈtɪlɪtɪ] N [of person] variété f
de talents; [of mind] souplesse f; **his ~** ses talents variés, sa polyvalence

verse [vɜːs] [1] N [a] (= stanza) [of poem] strophe f; [of song] couplet m [b] (NonC = poetry)
poésie f, vers mpl; **in ~** en vers → **blank, free**
[c] [of Bible, Koran] verset m → **chapter**
[2] COMP [drama etc] en vers

versed [vɜːst] ADJ (*also* **well-~**) versé (**in** dans) ; **not (well-)versed** peu versé

versification [ˌvɜːsɪfɪ'keɪʃən] N versification *f*, métrique *f*

versifier ['vɜːsɪfaɪəʳ] N (*pej*) versificateur *m*, -trice *f* (*pej*)

versify ['vɜːsɪfaɪ] **1** VT versifier, mettre en vers **2** VI faire des vers

version ['vɜːʃən] N **a** (= *account*) version *f* ; (= *interpretation*) interprétation *f* ; **his ~ of events** sa version des faits **b** (= *variant*) [*of text*] version *f*, variante *f* ; [*of car*] modèle *m* **c** (= *translation*) version *f*, traduction *f* → **authorized**

verso ['vɜːsəʊ] N verso *m*

versus ['vɜːsəs] PREP **a** (*in comparison*) par opposition à ; **the arguments about public ~ private ownership** les arguments pour ou contre la propriété privée ; **the question of electricity ~ gas for cooking** la question de l'électricité par rapport au gaz *or* de l'électricité comparée au gaz pour la cuisine **b** (*Sport*) contre ; **the England ~ Spain match** le match Angleterre-Espagne **c** (*in dispute, competition*) **it's management ~ workers** c'est la direction contre les ouvriers, la direction s'oppose aux ouvriers ; **the 1960 Nixon ~ Kennedy election** l'élection qui en 1960 a opposé Nixon à Kennedy **d** (*Jur*) **Jones ~ Smith** Jones contre Smith ; (*in Brit*) **Rex/Regina ~ Smith** le Roi/la Reine contre Smith (*formule utilisée pour un procès engagé par l'État contre un particulier*) ; (*in US*) **the People ~ Smith** l'État contre Smith

vertebra ['vɜːtɪbrə] N (*pl* **vertebras** *or* **vertebrae** ['vɜːtɪbriː]) vertèbre *f*

vertebral ['vɜːtɪbrəl] ADJ vertébral

vertebrate ['vɜːtɪbrət] ADJ, N vertébré *m*

vertex ['vɜːteks] N (*pl* **vertexes** *or* **vertices**) (*gen*, *Geom*) sommet *m* ; (*Anat*) vertex *m*

vertical ['vɜːtɪkəl] **1** ADJ [*surface, line, axis, cliff, stripes*] vertical ; **a ~ drop** un à-pic ; **a ~ power structure** une structure du pouvoir verticale **2** N verticale *f* ; **out of** *or* **off the ~** décalé par rapport à *or* écarté de la verticale **3** COMP ► **vertical analysis** N (*Comm*) analyse *f* verticale ► **vertical integration** N (*Econ*) intégration *f* verticale ► **vertical mobility** N (*Sociol*) mobilité *f* verticale ► **vertical planning** N planification *f* verticale ► **vertical take-off aircraft** N avion *m* à décollage vertical

vertically ['vɜːtɪkəlɪ] ADV [*hold, move, run, divide*] verticalement ; [*rise, descend, drop*] verticalement, à la verticale ; (*gen hum*) **~ challenged** de taille au-dessous de la moyenne ; (*Econ*) **~ integrated** à intégration verticale

vertices ['vɜːtɪsɪz] NPL *of* **vertex**

vertigines [vɜː'tɪdʒɪˌniːz] NPL *of* **vertigo**

vertiginous [vɜː'tɪdʒɪnəs] ADJ (*frm*) vertigineux

vertigo ['vɜːtɪgəʊ] N (*pl* **vertigoes** *or* **vertigines**) vertige *m* ; **to suffer from ~** avoir des vertiges

verve [vɜːv] N verve *f*, brio *m*

very ['verɪ] **1** ADV **a** (= *extremely*) très ; **~ amusing** très amusant ; **to be ~ careful** faire très attention ; **I am ~ cold/hot** j'ai très froid/chaud ; **are you tired? — ~/not ~** êtes-vous fatigué ? — très/pas très ; **~ well written/made** très bien écrit/fait ; **I'm ~ sorry** je suis vraiment désolé ; **~ well, if you insist** très bien, si vous insistez ; **~ little** très peu ; **~ little milk** très peu de lait ; **it is not ~ likely** ce n'est pas très probable, c'est peu probable ; **I'm not ~ good at explaining myself** je ne sais pas toujours très bien me faire comprendre, j'ai un peu de mal à me faire comprendre ; **his accent is ~ French** il a un accent très français ; **Jane looks ~ pregnant** la grossesse de Jane paraît très avancée ; (*Rel*) **the Very Reverend ...** le Très Révérend ... ; (*Rad*) **~ high frequency** (*ondes fpl*) très haute fréquence *f* ; (*Elec*) **~ high/low frequency** très haute/basse fréquence *f*

b (= *absolutely*) (*of the*) **~ best quality** de toute première qualité ; **~ last/first** tout dernier/premier ; **she is the ~ cleverest in the class** elle est de loin la plus intelligente de la classe ; **give it to me tomorrow at the ~ latest** donnez-le-moi demain au plus tard *or* demain dernier délai ; **at midday at the ~ latest** à midi au plus tard ; **at the ~ most/least** tout au plus/moins ; **to be in the ~ best of health** être en excellente santé ; **they are the ~ best of friends** ils sont les meilleurs amis du monde

c ~ **much** beaucoup, bien ; **thank you ~ much** merci beaucoup ; **I liked it ~ much** je l'ai beaucoup aimé ; **he is ~ much better** il va beaucoup mieux ; **~ much bigger** beaucoup *or* bien plus grand ; **~ much respected** très respecté ; **he is ~ much the more intelligent of the two** il est de beaucoup *or* de loin le plus intelligent des deux ; **he doesn't work ~ much** il ne travaille pas beaucoup, il travaille peu ; **he is ~ much like his father** il tient beaucoup de son père, il ressemble beaucoup à son père ; (= *emphatic "yes"*) **~ much so!** absolument !

d (*for emphasis*) **the ~ same day** le jour même, ce jour-là ; **the ~ same hat** exactement le même chapeau ; **the ~ next day** le lendemain même, dès le lendemain ; **the ~ next shop we come to** le prochain magasin ; **the ~ next person to do this was ...** la personne qui a fait cela tout de suite après était ... ; **as soon as I heard the news, I took the ~ next train** dès que j'ai entendu la nouvelle, j'ai sauté dans le premier train ; **the ~ latest technology** la toute dernière technologie ; **the ~ last page of the book** la toute dernière page du livre → **next** ; → **own**

2 ADJ **a** (= *precise, exact*) même ; **that ~ day/moment** ce jour/cet instant même ; **on the ~ spot** à l'endroit même *or* précis ; **in this ~ house** dans cette maison même ; **his ~ words** ses propos mêmes ; **the ~ thing/man I need** tout à fait *or* justement la chose/l'homme qu'il me faut ; **the ~ thing!** (= *what I need*) c'est justement ce qu'il me faut ! ; (*of suggestion, solution*) c'est idéal ! ; **to catch sb in the ~ act (of stealing)** prendre qn en flagrant délit (de vol)

b (= *extreme*) tout ; **at the ~ end** [*of play, year*] tout à la fin ; [*of garden, road*] tout au bout ; **at the ~ back** tout au fond ; **to the ~ end** jusqu'au bout ; **in the ~ depths of the sea/forest** au plus profond de la mer/la forêt ; **in the ~ heart of France** au cœur même de la France

c (= *mere*) seul ; **the ~ word** le mot seul, rien que le mot ; **the ~ thought of ...** la seule pensée de ..., rien que de penser à ... ; **the ~ idea!** quelle idée alors !

d (*for emphasis*) **his ~ life was in danger** sa propre vie était en danger ; **democracy is the ~ basis of British politics** la démocratie est le fondement même de la politique en Grande-Bretagne ; **before my ~ eyes** sous mes propres yeux ; **you're the ~ person I wanted to see** c'est justement vous que je voulais voir

e (*liter*) **he is a ~ rascal** *or* **the veriest rascal** c'est un fieffé coquin

Very light [ˈvɪərɪlaɪt] N (*Mil*) fusée *f* éclairante

Very pistol [ˈvɪərɪpɪstl] N pistolet *m* lance-fusées

vesicle ['vesɪkl] N vésicule *f*

vespers ['vespəz] N vêpres *fpl*

vessel ['vesl] N **a** (*Naut*) navire *m*, bâtiment *m* **b** (*Anat, Bot*) vaisseau *m* → **blood** **c** (*liter* = *receptacle*) récipient *m* ; **drinking ~** vaisseau† *m*

vest¹ [vest] **1** N **a** (*Brit*) (= *undergarment*) tricot *m* de corps ; (*also* ~ **top**) débardeur *m* **b** (*US*) gilet *m* **2** COMP ► **vest pocket** N (*US*) poche *f* de gilet ► **vest-pocket** ADJ (*US*) [*calculator etc*] de poche ; (*fig* = *tiny*) minuscule ► **vest top** N → **1a**

vest² [vest] **1** VT (*frm*) **to ~ sb with sth** ◊ **to ~ sth in sb** investir qn de qch, assigner qch à qn ; **the authority ~ed in me** l'autorité dont je suis investi **2** COMP ► **vested interest** N **to have a ~ed interest in** (*gen*) s'intéresser tout particulièrement à ; (*financially*) [+ *business, company*] être directement intéressé dans ; [+ *market, development of business*] être directement intéressé à ; **to have a ~ed interest in doing sth** avoir tout intérêt à faire qch ; **he has a ~ed interest in the play as his daughter is acting in it** il s'intéresse tout particulièrement à cette pièce car sa fille y joue ; (*Comm, Fin, Jur*) **~ed interests** droits *mpl* acquis

vestal virgin [ˌvestl'vɜːdʒɪn] N vestale *f*

vestibular [ve'stɪbjʊləʳ] ADJ (*Anat*) vestibulaire

vestibule ['vestɪbjuːl] N **a** (= *entrance*) [*of house, hotel*] vestibule *m*, hall *m* d'entrée ; [*of church*] vestibule *m* **b** (*Anat*) vestibule *m*

vestige ['vestɪdʒ] N **a** (= *trace, remnant*) vestige *m* ; **~s of past civilizations** vestiges *mpl* de civilisations disparues ; (*fig*) **not a ~ of truth/commonsense** pas un grain de vérité/de bon sens ; **a ~ of hope** un reste d'espoir **b** (*Anat, Bio* = *organ*) organe *m* rudimentaire *or* atrophié ; **the ~ of a tail** une queue rudimentaire *or* atrophiée

vestigial [ves'tɪdʒɪəl] ADJ **a** (*frm* = *remaining*) [*traces*] résiduel ; **~ remains** vestiges *mpl* **b** (*Bio*) [*organ, limb*] vestigial

vesting ['vestɪŋ] N (*Insurance*) acquisition *f* de droits

vestment ['vestmənt] N [*of priest*] vêtement *m* sacerdotal ; (= *ceremonial robe*) habit *m* de cérémonie

vestry ['vestrɪ] N **a** (= *part of church*) sacristie *f* **b** (= *meeting*) assemblée *f* paroissiale, conseil *m* paroissial

vesture ['vestʃəʳ] N (*NonC: liter*) vêtements *mpl*

Vesuvius [vɪ'suːvɪəs] N le Vésuve

vet [vet] **1** N **a** ABBR = **veterinary surgeon**, **veterinarian** **b** (*esp US**) (ABBR = **veteran**) ancien combattant *m* **2** VT (*esp Brit*) [+ *text*] corriger, revoir ; [+ *figures, calculations, job applications*] vérifier ; [+ *papers*] contrôler ; [+ *report*] (= *check*) vérifier le contenu de ; (= *approve*) approuver ; **wage claims are ~ted by the union** les revendications salariales doivent d'abord recevoir l'approbation du syndicat ; **his wife ~s his contracts** sa femme vérifie *or* contrôle ses contrats ; **the purchases are ~ted by a committee** les achats doivent d'abord être approuvés par un comité ; **the director ~ted him for the job** le directeur a soigneusement examiné sa candidature avant de l'embaucher ; **we have ~ted him thoroughly** nous nous sommes renseignés de façon approfondie à son sujet ; **visa applications/applicants are carefully ~ted** les demandes/demandeurs de visa sont soigneusement filtré(e)s

vetch [vetʃ] N vesce *f*

veteran ['vetərən] **1** N **a** (*gen*) vétéran *m* **b** (*Mil: also* **war ~**) ancien combattant *m* **2** ADJ **a** (= *experienced*) chevronné, expérimenté ; **she is a ~ campaigner for women's rights** elle fait campagne depuis longtemps pour les droits de la femme ; **a ~ car** une voiture d'époque (*avant 1919*) ; **a ~ teacher/golfer** *etc* un vétéran de l'enseignement/du golf *etc* **3** COMP ► **Veterans Administration** N (*US*) ministère *des anciens combattants* ► **Veterans Day** N (*US*) le onze novembre (*anniversaire de l'armistice*)

veterinarian [ˌvetərɪ'nɛərɪən] N (*esp US*) vétérinaire *mf*

veterinary ['vetərɪnərɪ] **1** ADJ [*medicine, science, care, practice, hospital*] vétérinaire ; [*expert*] en médecine vétérinaire **2** COMP ► **veterinary surgeon** N (*Brit*) vétérinaire *mf*

▼ veto ['viːtəʊ] **1** N (pl **vetoes**) (= act, decision) veto m; **the power of ~** le droit de veto; **to use one's ~** exercer son droit de veto; **to put a ~ on sth** mettre son veto à qch **2** VT (Pol etc, also fig) mettre or opposer son veto à

vetting ['vetɪŋ] N [of text] correction f, révision f; [of job application, figures] vérification f; [of candidate] enquête f approfondie; [of papers] contrôle m → **positive, security**

vex [veks] VT contrarier, fâcher

vexation [vek'seɪʃən] N (NonC) contrariété f, tracas m

vexatious [vek'seɪʃəs] ADJ [thing] contrariant, ennuyeux; [person] tracassier, contrariant

vexed [vekst] ADJ **a** (= annoyed) [person, voice, frown, expression] contrarié; **~ with sb** fâché contre qn; **to become** or **get ~** se fâcher **b** (= difficult) [question, issue] délicat, épineux

vexing ['veksɪŋ] ADJ **a** (= annoying) [thing] contrariant, ennuyeux; [person] tracassier, contrariant **b** (= difficult) [problem] délicat; [question, issue] délicat, épineux

VG [viː'dʒiː] (Scol etc) (ABBR = **very good**) TB, très bien

VGA [ˌviːdʒiː'eɪ] **1** N ABBR = **video graphics array 2** COMP ► **VGA card** N carte f VGA

vgc (ABBR = **very good condition**) tbe, très bon état

VHF [ˌviːeɪtʃ'ef] N (ABBR = **very high frequency**) VHF f

VHS [ˌviːeɪtʃ'es] N (ABBR = **video home system**) VHS m

VI (ABBR = **Virgin Islands**) → **virgin**

via ['vaɪə] PREP **a** (lit = by way of) via, par; **a ticket to Vienna ~ Frankfurt** un billet pour Vienne via Francfort; **the journey takes nine hours ~ Ostend** le voyage prend neuf heures via Ostende or (si l'on passe) par Ostende; **you should go ~ Paris** vous devriez passer par Paris; **we went home ~ the pub** nous sommes passés par le pub or nous nous sommes arrêtés au pub avant de rentrer **b** (fig = by way of) par; **his rent is paid to his landlord ~ an estate agent** il paie son loyer à son propriétaire par l'intermédiaire d'une agence immobilière **c** (= by means of) au moyen de; **the launch was detected ~ a satellite** le lancement a été détecté au moyen d'un satellite; **she works from home, ~ e-mail** elle travaille à domicile au moyen du courrier électronique

viability [ˌvaɪə'bɪlɪtɪ] N [of company, business, product] viabilité f; [of project, scheme] viabilité f, chances fpl de réussite

viable ['vaɪəbl] ADJ **a** (= feasible) [alternative, option, solution, company, product] viable; [project, method] viable, qui a des chances de réussir; [future] durable, solide; **it's not a ~ proposition** ce n'est pas viable **b** (Bio) [foetus] viable

viaduct ['vaɪədʌkt] N viaduc m

vial ['vaɪəl] N (liter) fiole f; (Pharm) ampoule f

viands ['vaɪəndz] NPL (liter) aliments mpl

viaticum [vaɪ'ætɪkəm] N (pl **viaticums** or **viatica** [vaɪ'ætɪkə]) viatique m

vibes* [vaɪbz] NPL **a** (ABBR = **vibrations**) (from band, singer) atmosphère f, ambiance f; (between individuals) **I get good ~ from her** elle me fait bonne impression; **the ~ are wrong** ça ne gaze pas* **b** ABBR = **vibraphone**

vibrancy ['vaɪbrənsɪ] N [of person, language] vivacité f; [of voice] résonance f; [of city] animation f, vie f; [of performance] caractère m très vivant; [of economy, community] dynamisme m, vitalité f; [of speech] vigueur f; [of light, colours] éclat m

vibrant ['vaɪbrənt] ADJ **a** (= lively) [person, language] vivant, vif; [city] vivant, animé; [performance] vivant; [economy, community, personality] dynamique; [culture] plein de vitalité; [voice, tones] vibrant (**with sth** de qch); **the street was ~ with activity** la rue débordait

d'activité **b** (= bright) [colour, red, green] éclatant; [light] vif

vibraphone ['vaɪbrəfəʊn] N vibraphone m

vibrate [vaɪ'breɪt] **1** VI (= quiver) vibrer (**with** de); (= resound) retentir (**with** de); (fig) frémir, vibrer (**with** de) **2** VT faire vibrer

vibration [vaɪ'breɪʃən] N vibration f

vibrato [vɪ'brɑːtəʊ] (Mus) **1** N vibrato m **2** ADV avec vibrato

vibrator [vaɪ'breɪtəʳ] N **a** (Elec) vibrateur m **b** (= massager, also sexual) vibromasseur m

vibratory ['vaɪbrətərɪ] ADJ vibratoire

viburnum [vaɪ'bɜːnəm] N viorne f

vicar ['vɪkəʳ] **1** N (in Church of England) pasteur m (de l'Église anglicane); **good evening ~** bonsoir pasteur **2** COMP ► **vicar apostolic** N vicaire m apostolique ► **vicar general** (pl **vicars general**) grand vicaire m, vicaire m général ► **the Vicar of Christ** N le vicaire de Jésus-Christ

vicarage ['vɪkərɪdʒ] N presbytère m (de l'Église anglicane)

vicarious [vɪ'keərɪəs] ADJ **a** (= indirect) [experience] vécu par procuration; **to get ~ satisfaction/pleasure from** or **out of sth** (re)tirer de la satisfaction/du plaisir de qch par procuration **b** (frm = for another) [liability, responsibility] assumé pour quelqu'un d'autre; **the ~ suffering of Christ** les souffrances que le Christ subit pour autrui **c** (frm = delegated) délégué; **to give ~ authority to sb** déléguer son autorité à qn

vicariously [vɪ'keərɪəslɪ] ADV **a** [live, enjoy, experience] par procuration **b** (frm) [authorize] par délégation, par procuration

vice¹ [vaɪs] **1** N **a** (NonC = depravity, corruption) vice m **b** (= evil characteristic) vice m; (less strong) défaut m **2** COMP ► **vice den** N (= gambling den) maison f de jeux; (= brothel) maison f close ► **vice girl** N prostituée f ► **vice ring** N réseau m de prostitution ► **Vice Squad** N (Police) brigade f des mœurs

vice², **vise** (US) [vaɪs] N (Tech) étau m → **grip**

vice³ [vaɪs] PREP (frm) à la place de

vice- [vaɪs] **1** PREF vice- **2** COMP ► **vice-admiral** N vice-amiral m d'escadre ► **vice-captain** N (Sport) capitaine m adjoint ► **vice-chairman** N (pl **vice-chairmen**) vice-président(e) m(f) ► **vice-chairmanship** N vice-présidence f ► **vice-chancellor** N (Univ) ≈ président(e) m(f) d'université; (Jur) vice-chancelier m ► **vice-consul** N vice-consul m ► **vice-premier** N Premier ministre m adjoint ► **vice-presidency** N vice-présidence f ► **vice-president** N vice-président(e) m(f); **Vice-President Smith** (Pol) le vice-président Smith ► **vice-presidential** ADJ (Pol) vice-présidentiel ► **vice-presidential candidate** N (Pol) candidat(e) m(f) à la vice-présidence ► **vice-principal** N (Scol: gen) directeur m, -trice f adjoint(e); (of lycée) censeur m; (of collège) principal(e) m(f) adjoint(e) ► **vice-regal** ADJ de or du vice-roi

viceroy ['vaɪsrɔɪ] N vice-roi m

vice versa ['vaɪsɪ'vɜːsə] ADV **and/or ~** et/ou vice versa; **rather than ~** plutôt que l'inverse

vicinity [vɪ'sɪnɪtɪ] N (= nearby area) voisinage m, environs mpl; (= closeness) proximité f; **in the ~** dans les environs, à proximité; **in the ~ of the town** aux alentours de la ville, à proximité de la ville; **it's something in the ~ of £100** c'est aux alentours de 100 livres; **in the immediate ~** dans les environs immédiats; **the immediate ~ of the town** les abords mpl de la ville

vicious ['vɪʃəs] **1** ADJ [person, attack, temper] brutal; [animal] méchant; [horse] vicieux; [look] haineux, méchant; [criticism, remark] acerbe, méchant; [campaign] virulent; **to have a ~ tongue** être mauvaise langue, avoir une langue de vipère **2** COMP ► **vicious**

circle N cercle m vicieux; **to be caught in a ~ circle** être pris dans un cercle vicieux ► **vicious cycle** N cycle m infernal

viciously ['vɪʃəslɪ] ADV (= violently) [attack, stab] brutalement; [beat, strike] brutalement, violemment; (= nastily) [say, think, criticize] méchamment

viciousness ['vɪʃəsnɪs] N [of person, attack, temper] brutalité f; [of criticism, remark, campaign] méchanceté f; [of dog] agressivité f; **a horse renowned for its ~** un cheval connu pour être vicieux; **everyone feared the ~ of his tongue** tout le monde craignait sa langue acérée or acerbe

vicissitude [vɪ'sɪsɪtjuːd] N vicissitude f

victim ['vɪktɪm] **1** N (lit, fig) victime f; **the accident/bomb ~s** les victimes f de l'accident/de l'explosion; **many of the Nazi ~s ◊ many of the ~s of the Nazis** de nombreuses victimes des Nazis; **to be the** or **a ~ of ...** être victime de ...; **to fall (a) ~ to ...** devenir la victime de ...; (fig: to sb's charms etc) succomber à ... **2** COMP ► **Victim Support** N (Brit) organisme d'aide aux victimes de crimes

victimization [ˌvɪktɪmaɪ'zeɪʃən] N (actes mpl de) persécution f; **the dismissed worker alleged ~** l'ouvrier licencié a prétendu être victime de persécution; **the result was further ~** ceci a mené à d'autres actes de persécution; **there must be no ~ of strikers** on ne doit pas exercer de représailles contre les grévistes

victimize ['vɪktɪmaɪz] VT persécuter; (Ind: after strike) exercer des représailles sur; **to be ~d** être victime de persécutions

victimless ['vɪktɪmlɪs] ADJ **~ crime** délit m sans victimes

victor ['vɪktəʳ] N vainqueur m; **to emerge the ~ over sb** remporter la victoire sur qn

Victoria [vɪk'tɔːrɪə] **1** N **a** (= name) Victoria f; (= Australian state) le Victoria; **Lake ~** le lac Victoria **b** (= carriage) **victoria** victoria f **2** COMP ► **Victoria Cross** N (Brit Mil: abbr VC) Croix f de Victoria (la plus haute décoration militaire) ► **(the) Victoria Falls** NPL les chutes fpl Victoria

Victorian [vɪk'tɔːrɪən] **1** N victorien(ne) m(f) **2** ADJ (= 19th century) [house, furniture] victorien, de l'époque victorienne; (= strict, puritan) [person, values] victorien; [attitude] d'un puritanisme victorien

---

VICTORIAN

L'adjectif victorien qualifie la Grande-Bretagne sous le règne de la reine Victoria (1837-1901).

Les attitudes ou qualités victoriennes sont celles considérées comme caractéristiques de cette époque: attachement à la respectabilité sociale, moralité stricte et répressive, absence d'humour, bigoterie et hypocrisie. Les valeurs victoriennes sont parfois invoquées par les gens qui regrettent l'évolution de la société contemporaine et prônent un retour au dépassement de soi, à la décence, au respect de l'autorité et à l'importance de la famille.

Victoriana [vɪkˌtɔːrɪ'ɑːnə] N (NonC) objets mpl victoriens, antiquités fpl victoriennes

victorious [vɪk'tɔːrɪəs] ADJ [person, army, team, campaign] victorieux; [shout] de victoire

victoriously [vɪk'tɔːrɪəslɪ] ADV victorieusement

victory ['vɪktərɪ] N victoire f; **to gain** or **win a ~ over ...** remporter une victoire sur ...; **he led the party to ~** il a mené le parti à la victoire → **winged**

victual ['vɪtl] **1** VT approvisionner, ravitailler **2** VI s'approvisionner, se ravitailler **3** **victuals**† NPL victuailles fpl, vivres mpl

victualler ['vɪtləʳ] N fournisseur m (de provisions) → **license**

vicuña [vaɪ'kjuːnə] N (= animal, wool) vigogne f

vid* [vɪd] N (ABBR = **video**) vidéo ƒ (film)

vide ['vɪdeɪ] IMPERS VB (frm) voir, cf

videlicet [vɪ'diːlɪset] ADV (frm) c'est-à-dire, à savoir

video ['vɪdɪəʊ] **1** N **a** (NonC) vidéo ƒ; (= machine) magnétoscope m; (= cassette) cassette ƒ vidéo inv, vidéocassette ƒ; (= film) vidéo ƒ; **I've got it on ~** je l'ai en vidéo; **get a ~ for tonight** loue une (cassette) vidéo pour ce soir; **to make a ~ of sth** ◊ **to record sth on ~** (with video recorder) enregistrer qch au magnétoscope; (with camcorder) faire une vidéo de qch **b** (US = television) télévision ƒ, télé* ƒ **2** VT (from TV) enregistrer (sur magnétoscope); (with camcorder) faire une vidéo de, filmer **3** COMP (= on video) [film, entertainment] en vidéo; [facilities] vidéo inv; (US = on television) [film etc] télévisé ▸ **video arcade** N salle ƒ de jeux vidéo ▸ **video art** N art m vidéo inv ▸ **video camera** N caméra ƒ vidéo inv ▸ **video cassette** N vidéocassette ƒ, cassette ƒ vidéo ▸ **video cassette recorder** N magnétoscope m ▸ **video cassette recording** N enregistrement m en vidéo or sur magnétoscope ▸ **video clip** N clip m vidéo inv ▸ **video club** N vidéoclub m ▸ **video conference** N visioconférence ƒ, vidéoconférence ƒ ▸ **video conferencing** N (système m de) visioconférence ƒ or vidéoconférence ƒ ▸ **video diary** N (TV) vidéo ƒ amateur (qui passe à la télévision) ▸ **video disk** N vidéodisque m ▸ **video disk player** N lecteur m de vidéodisques ▸ **video film** N film m vidéo inv ▸ **video frequency** N vidéofréquence ƒ ▸ **video game** N jeu m vidéo inv ▸ **video library** N vidéothèque ƒ ▸ **video nasty*** N (cassette ƒ) vidéo ƒ à caractère violent (or pornographique) ▸ **video piracy** N piratage m de vidéocassettes ▸ **video player** N magnétoscope m ▸ **video recorder** N = **video cassette recorder** ▸ **video recording** N = **video cassette recording** ▸ **video rental** N location ƒ de vidéocassettes ◊ ADJ [shop, store] de location de vidéocassettes; **the ~ rental business** la location de vidéocassettes ▸ **video screen** N écran m vidéo inv ▸ **video shop** N vidéoclub m ▸ **video surveillance** N vidéosurveillance ƒ ▸ **video tape** N bande ƒ vidéo inv; (= cassette) vidéocassette ƒ ▸ **video tape recorder** N = **video cassette recorder** ▸ **video tape recording** N = **video cassette recording** ▸ **video wall** N mur m d'écrans (vidéo)

videophone ['vɪdɪəʊfəʊn] N visiophone m

videotape ['vɪdɪəʊteɪp] VT = **video 2**

Videotex® ['vɪdɪəʊteks] N vidéotex® m

videotext ['vɪdɪəʊtekst] N vidéotex® m

vie [vaɪ] VI rivaliser; **to ~ with sb for sth** rivaliser avec qn pour (obtenir) qch, disputer qch à qn; **to ~ with sb in doing** rivaliser avec qn pour faire; **they ~d with each other in their work** ils travaillaient à qui mieux mieux

Vienna [vɪ'enə] **1** N Vienne **2** COMP (gen) viennois, de Vienne ▸ **Vienna roll** N (Culin) pain m viennois

Viennese [,vɪə'niːz] **1** ADJ viennois **2** N (pl inv) Viennois(e) m(f)

Vietcong, Viet Cong [,vjet'kɒŋ] **1** N (= group) Vietcong or Viêt-cong m; (= individual: pl inv) Vietcong or Viêt-cong m **2** ADJ vietcong or viêt-cong inv

Vietnam, Viet Nam ['vjet'næm] N le Vietnam or Viêt-nam; **North/South ~** le Vietnam or Viêt-nam du Nord/du Sud; **the ~ war** la guerre du Vietnam or Viêt-nam

Vietnamese [,vjetnə'miːz] **1** ADJ vietnamien; **North/South ~** nord-/sud-vietnamien **2** N **a** (pl inv) Vietnamien(ne) m(f); **North/South ~** Nord-/Sud-Vietnamien(ne) m(f) **b** (Ling) vietnamien m **3** **the Vietnamese** NPL les Vietnamiens mpl

▼ **view** [vjuː] **1** N **a** (= ability to see) vue ƒ; **it blocks the ~** ça bouche la vue, on ne peut pas voir; **he has a good ~ of it from his window** de sa fenêtre, il le voit bien; **the ship came into ~** le navire est apparu; **I came in ~ of the lake** je suis arrivé en vue du lac; **hidden from ~** caché aux regards; **the cameraman had a job keeping the plane in ~** le caméraman avait du mal à ne pas perdre l'avion de vue; **if your hands are often in ~ ...** si vos mains sont souvent en évidence ..., si on voit souvent vos mains ...; **in full ~ of thousands of people** devant des milliers de gens, sous les yeux de milliers de gens; **in full ~ of the house** devant la maison; **the pictures are on ~** les tableaux sont exposés; **the house will be on ~ tomorrow** on pourra visiter la maison demain; **to keep sth out of ~** cacher qch (aux regards); **exposed to ~** exposé aux regards; **it is lost to ~** on ne le voit plus; **the house is within ~ of the sea** de la maison, on voit la mer; **all the people within ~** tous ceux qu'on pouvait voir **b** (= sight, prospect) vue ƒ, panorama m; **there is a wonderful ~ from here** d'ici la vue or le panorama est magnifique; **the ~ from the top** la vue or le panorama d'en haut; **a trip to see the ~s** une excursion pour admirer les belles vues; **room with a sea ~** or **a ~ of the sea** chambre ƒ avec vue sur la mer; **a good ~ of the sea** une belle vue de la mer; **a ~ over the town** une vue générale de la ville; **a back/front ~ of the house** la maison vue de derrière/devant; **this is a side ~** c'est une vue latérale; **I got a side ~ of the church** j'ai vu l'église de côté; **it will give you a better ~** vous verrez mieux comme ça **c** (= photo etc) vue ƒ, photo ƒ; **50 ~s of Paris** 50 vues or photos de Paris; **I want to take a ~ of the palace** je veux photographier le palais **d** (= opinion) opinion ƒ; **her ~s on politics/education** ses opinions politiques/sur l'éducation; **an exchange of ~s** un échange de vues or d'opinions; **in my ~** à mon avis; **that is my ~** voilà mon opinion or mon avis là-dessus; **my personal ~ is that he ...** à mon avis, il ..., personnellement, je pense qu'il ...; **it's just a personal ~** ce n'est qu'une opinion personnelle; **the Government ~ is that one must ...** selon le gouvernement or dans l'optique gouvernementale, on doit ...; **the generally accepted ~ is that he ...** selon l'opinion généralement répandue, il ...; **each person has a different ~ of democracy** chacun comprend la démocratie à sa façon; **one's ~ of old age changes** les idées que l'on se fait de la vieillesse évoluent; **I cannot accept this ~** je trouve cette opinion or cette façon de voir les choses inacceptable; **I've changed my ~ on this** j'ai changé d'avis là-dessus; (in exam question) **give reasons for your ~s** justifiez votre réponse; **I have no strong ~s on that** je n'ai pas d'opinion bien arrêtée or précise là-dessus; **to hold ~s on sth** avoir un avis or une opinion sur qch; **to hold** or **take the ~ that ...** estimer que ..., considérer que ...; **we don't take that ~** nous avons une opinion différente là-dessus; **I take a similar ~** je partage cet avis; **he takes a gloomy/optimistic ~ of society** il a une image pessimiste/optimiste de la société; **to take a dim** or **poor ~ of sth** avoir une bien mauvaise opinion de qch → **point** **e** (= way of looking at sth) vue ƒ; **an idealistic ~ of the world** une vue or une vision idéaliste du monde; **a general** or **an overall ~ of the problem** une vue d'ensemble or générale du problème; **a clear ~ of the facts** une idée claire des faits **f** **in ~ of: in ~ of his refusal** étant donné son refus, vu son refus; **in ~ of this** ceci étant; **in ~ of the fact that ...** étant donné que ..., vu que ... **g** (= intention) **with this (aim** or **object) in ~** dans ce but, à cette fin; **with the ~ of doing** ◊ **with a ~ to doing** en vue de faire, afin de faire; **negotiations with a ~ to a permanent solution** des négociations en vue d'une solution permanente; **what end has he in ~?** quel est son but?; **he has in ~ the purchase of the house** il envisage d'acheter la maison; **I don't teach only with the exams in ~** je ne pense pas uniquement aux examens quand je fais mes cours; **he has the holiday in ~ when he says ...** il pense aux vacances quand il dit ...

2 VT **a** (= look at, see) voir; **London ~ed from the air** Londres vu d'avion **b** (= inspect, examine) examiner, inspecter; [+ slides, microfiches] visionner; [+ object for sale] inspecter; [+ castle] visiter; (in house-buying) [+ house, flat] visiter **c** (TV) regarder, visionner; **we have ~ed a video recording of the incident** nous avons regardé or visionné un enregistrement vidéo de l'incident **d** (= think of, understand) considérer, envisager; **to ~ sb/sth as ...** considérer qn/qch comme ...; **it can be ~ed in many different ways** on peut l'envisager or l'examiner sous plusieurs angles; **how do you ~ that?** qu'est-ce que vous en pensez?, quelle est votre opinion là-dessus?; **he ~s it very objectively** il l'envisage de façon très objective; **the management ~ed the scheme favourably** la direction a été favorable au projet; **they ~ the future with alarm** ils envisagent l'avenir avec inquiétude

3 VI (TV) regarder la télévision

Viewdata® ['vjuːdeɪtə] N ≈ minitel® m

viewer ['vjuːəʳ] N **a** (TV) téléspectateur m, -trice ƒ **b** (for slides) visionneuse ƒ **c** = **viewfinder**

viewership ['vjuːəʃɪp] N (US TV) **to score a good** or **a wide ~** obtenir un bon indice d'écoute

viewfinder ['vjuːfaɪndəʳ] N (Phot) viseur m

viewing ['vjuːɪŋ] **1** N **a** (TV) visionnage m; **there's no good ~ tonight** il n'y a rien de bon à la télévision ce soir; **your ~ for the weekend** vos programmes du week-end; **tennis makes excellent ~** le tennis est un sport qui passe très bien à la télévision or qui est très télégénique **b** (in house-buying) **"early ~ essential"** « à visiter aussi tôt que possible » **c** (= watching) observation ƒ **2** COMP (Astron etc) [conditions] d'observation; (TV) [patterns] d'écoute; [habits] des téléspectateurs ▸ **viewing audience** N (TV) téléspectateurs mpl ▸ **viewing figures** NPL (TV) nombre m de téléspectateurs, taux m d'écoute ▸ **viewing gallery** N (in building) galerie ƒ ▸ **viewing public** N (TV) téléspectateurs mpl ▸ **viewing time** N (TV) heure ƒ d'écoute; **at peak** or **prime ~ time** aux heures de grande écoute

viewphone ['vjuːfəʊn] N visiophone m

viewpoint ['vjuːpɔɪnt] N (lit, fig) point m de vue

vigil ['vɪdʒɪl] N (gen) veille ƒ; (by sickbed, corpse) veillée ƒ; (Rel) vigile ƒ; (Pol) manifestation ƒ silencieuse; **to keep ~ over sb** veiller qn; **a long ~** une longue veille, de longues heures sans sommeil; (Pol) **to hold a ~** manifester en silence

vigilance ['vɪdʒɪləns] N vigilance ƒ

vigilant ['vɪdʒɪlənt] ADJ [person] vigilant; **to remain ~** rester vigilant; **to escape sb's ~ eye** échapper à l'œil vigilant de qn; **to keep a ~ eye on sb/sth** rester vigilant en ce qui concerne qn/qch

vigilante [,vɪdʒɪ'læntɪ] N membre m d'un groupe d'autodéfense; **~ group** groupe m d'autodéfense or de légitime défense

vigilantism [,vɪdʒɪ'læntɪzəm] N (pej) attitude et méthodes caractéristiques des groupes d'autodéfense

vigilantly ['vɪdʒɪləntlɪ] ADV avec vigilance, attentivement

vignette [vɪ'njet] N (in books) vignette ƒ; (Art,

Phot) portrait *m* en buste dégradé ; (= *character sketch*) esquisse *f* de caractère

vigor ['vɪɡə'] N (*US*) = **vigour**

vigorous ['vɪɡərəs] ADJ [*exercise, defence, denial, debate, campaign, opponent, advocate*] énergique ; [*person, opposition, growth*] vigoureux

vigorously ['vɪɡərəslɪ] ADV [*nod, shake hands, defend, oppose, protest*] énergiquement ; [*exercise, shake, beat, deny*] vigoureusement ; **to campaign ~** faire une campagne énergique ; **boil the beans ~ for twenty minutes** faites bouillir les haricots à feu vif pendant vingt minutes

vigour, **vigor** (*US*) ['vɪɡə'] N (= *physical or mental strength*) vigueur *f*, énergie *f* ; (= *health*) vigueur *f*, vitalité *f* ; (*sexual*) vigueur *f*

Viking ['vaɪkɪŋ] [1] ADJ [*art, customs etc*] viking ; **~ ship** drakkar *m* [2] N Viking *mf*

vile [vaɪl] ADJ [a] (= *base, evil*) [*action, traitor, crime, conditions, language*] infâme, ignoble [b] (= *unpleasant*) [*person*] exécrable ; [*food, drink, play*] exécrable, abominable ; [*smell, taste*] abominable, infect ; **what ~ weather!** quel temps infect *or* abominable ! ; **to be in a ~ temper** *or* **mood** être d'une humeur massacrante

vilely ['vaɪllɪ] ADV [a] (= *basely, evilly*) [*treat, exploit, seduce*] de façon ignoble ; [*swear*] de façon odieuse ; **~ offensive** d'une grossièreté ignoble [b] (= *unpleasantly*) **~ coloured** aux couleurs exécrables

vileness ['vaɪlnɪs] N vilenie *f*, bassesse *f*

vilification [,vɪlɪfɪ'keɪʃən] N diffamation *f*

vilify ['vɪlɪfaɪ] VT diffamer

villa ['vɪlə] N (*in town*) pavillon *m* (*de banlieue*) ; (*in country*) maison *f* de campagne ; (*by sea*) villa *f*

village ['vɪlɪdʒ] [1] N village *m* [2] COMP [*well*] du village ► **village green** N pré *m* communal ► **village hall** N (*Brit*) salle *f* des fêtes ► **village idiot** N idiot *m* du village ► **village school** N école *f* de *or* du village, école *f* communale

villager ['vɪlɪdʒə'] N villageois(e) *m(f)*

villain ['vɪlən] N (= *scoundrel*) scélérat *m*, vaurien *m* ; (*in drama, novel*) traître(sse) *m(f)* ; (* = *rascal*) coquin(e) *m(f)* ; (* = *criminal*) bandit *m* ; (*fig*) **he's the ~ (of the piece)** c'est lui le coupable

villainous ['vɪlənəs] ADJ [a] (= *evil*) [*person, character, action, conduct*] ignoble, infâme ; **~ deed** infamie *f* [b] (* = *unpleasant*) [*coffee, weather*] abominable, infect

villainously ['vɪlənəslɪ] ADV d'une manière ignoble

villainy ['vɪlənɪ] N infamie *f*, bassesse *f*

...ville [vɪl] N, ADJ (*in compounds*) **squaresville** les ringards❉ ; **it's dullsville** on s'ennuie vachement❉

villein ['vɪlɪn] N (*Hist*) vilain(e) *m(f)*, serf *m*, serve *f*

villus ['vɪləs] N (*pl* **villi** ['vɪlaɪ]) villosité *f*

vim❋ [vɪm] N (*NonC*) énergie *f*, entrain *m* ; **full of ~** plein d'entrain

vinaigrette [,vɪneɪ'ɡret] N (*Culin*) vinaigrette *f*

Vincent ['vɪnsənt] N Vincent *m*

vindaloo [,vɪndə'luː] N type de curry très épicé

vindicate ['vɪndɪkeɪt] VT [a] [+ *person*] (= *prove innocent*) donner raison à ; (*Jur*) innocenter ; **this ~d him** (= *proved him right*) cela a prouvé qu'il avait eu raison [b] [+ *opinion, action, decision*] justifier ; [+ *rights*] faire valoir

vindication [,vɪndɪ'keɪʃən] N justification *f*, défense *f* ; **in ~ of** en justification de, pour justifier

vindictive [vɪn'dɪktɪv] ADJ vindicatif (**towards sb** à l'égard de qn)

vindictively [vɪn'dɪktɪvlɪ] ADV par vengeance

vindictiveness [vɪn'dɪktɪvnɪs] N caractère *m* vindicatif

---

vine [vaɪn] [1] N (*producing grapes*) vigne *f* ; (= *climbing plant*) plante *f* grimpante *or* rampante ; (*fig*) **to wither** *or* **die on the ~** avorter (*fig*) [2] COMP [*leaf, cutting*] de vigne ► **vine grower** N viticulteur *m*, -trice *f*, vigneron(ne) *m(f)* ► **vine-growing** N viticulture *f* ; **~-growing district** région *f* viticole ► **vine harvest** N vendange(s) *f(pl)*

vinegar ['vɪnɪɡə'] N vinaigre *m* → **cider**, **oil**

vinegary ['vɪnɪɡərɪ] ADJ [a] (= *like vinegar*) [*wine*] qui a un goût de vinaigre ; [*smell, taste*] de vinaigre, vinaigré ; [*food*] acide ; **the sauce tastes too ~** la sauce est trop vinaigrée [b] (= *sour-tempered*) [*person*] acariâtre ; [*remark*] acide, acerbe

vinery ['vaɪnərɪ] N (= *hothouse*) serre *f* où l'on cultive la vigne ; (= *vineyard*) vignoble *m*

vineyard ['vɪnjəd] N vignoble *m*

viniculture ['vɪnɪkʌltʃə'] N viticulture *f*

vino❋ ['viːnəʊ] N pinard *m*, vin *m*

vinous ['vaɪnəs] ADJ vineux

vintage ['vɪntɪdʒ] [1] N [a] [*of wine*] (= *season*) vendanges *fpl* ; (= *year*) année *f*, millésime *m* ; (= *harvesting*) vendange(s) *f(pl)*, récolte *f* ; **what ~ is this wine?** ce vin est de quelle année ? ; **1966 was a good ~** 1966 était une bonne année *or* un bon millésime ; **the 1972 ~** le vin de 1972 [b] (= *era*) époque *f* ; **he wanted to meet people of his own ~** il voulait rencontrer des gens de sa génération [2] ADJ [a] (= *choice*) [*champagne, port*] millésimé → [3] [b] (= *classic*) [*comedy, drama*] classique ; **the book is ~ Grisham** ce livre est du Grisham du meilleur cru [c] (* = *very old*) [*object*] très ancien, antique [3] COMP ► **vintage car** N voiture *f* d'époque (*construite entre 1919 et 1930*) ► **vintage wine** N grand vin *m*, vin de grand cru ► **vintage year** N (*gen, for wine*) **a ~ year for Burgundy** une bonne année pour le bourgogne

vintner ['vɪntnə'] N (= *merchant*) négociant *m* en vins ; (= *wine-maker*) viticulteur *m*, -trice *f*, vigneron(ne) *m(f)*

vinyl ['vaɪnɪl] [1] N vinyle *m* [2] COMP [*tiles*] de *or* en vinyle ; [*paint*] vinylique

viol ['vaɪəl] N viole *f* ; **~ player** violiste *mf*

viola[1] [vɪ'əʊlə] [1] N (*Mus*) alto *m* [2] COMP ► **viola da gamba** N viole *f* de gambe ► **viola d'amore** N viole *f* d'amour ► **viola player** N altiste *mf*

viola[2] [vɪ'əʊlə] N (= *flower*) (sorte *f* de) pensée *f* ; (= *genus*) violacée *f*

violate ['vaɪəleɪt] VT [a] (= *disobey*) [+ *law, rule, agreement*] violer, enfreindre ; [+ *the Commandments*] violer, transgresser [b] (= *show disrespect for*) [+ *principles, honour*] bafouer ; [+ *human rights, civil rights*] violer ; [+ *public order, property, frontier*] ne pas respecter [c] (= *disturb*) [+ *peace*] troubler, perturber ; **to ~ sb's privacy** (*in room etc*) déranger le repos de qn ; [*detective, reporter etc*] (*in private life*) déranger qn dans sa vie privée [d] (= *desecrate*) [+ *place*] violer, profaner ; [+ *tomb*] violer [e] († *or liter* = *rape*) violer, violenter†

violation [,vaɪə'leɪʃən] N [a] (= *failure to respect*) [*of human rights, law, agreement, sanctions, grave*] violation *f* ; **in ~ of sth** en violation de qch ; **he was in ~ of his contract** il contrevenait aux clauses de son contrat [b] (*US* = *minor offence*) infraction *f* ; (*on parking meter*) dépassement *m* ; **a minor traffic ~** une infraction mineure au code de la route [c] († *or liter* = *rape*) viol *m*

violator ['vaɪəleɪtə'] N [a] (*gen*) violateur *m* [b] (*esp US Jur* = *offender*) contrevenant *m* ; **~s will be prosecuted** toute violation fera l'objet de poursuites

violence ['vaɪələns] N violence *f* ; **by ~** par la violence ; **a climate of ~** un climat de violence ; **we are witnessing an escalation of ~** nous assistons à une escalade de la violence ; **~ erupted when ...** ◊ **there was an outbreak of**

~ when ... de violents incidents *mpl* ont éclaté quand ... ; **racial ~** violence *f* raciste ; **all the ~ on the screen today** toute la violence *or* toutes les scènes de violence à l'écran aujourd'hui ; **terrorist ~** actes *mpl* de violence terroristes ; **police ~** violence *f* policière ; **act of ~** acte *m* de violence ; (*Jur*) **crime of ~** voie *f* de fait ; (*Jur*) **robbery with ~** vol *m* avec coups et blessures ; **to do ~ to sb/sth** faire violence à qn/qch

violent ['vaɪələnt] ADJ (*gen*) violent ; [*scenes*] de violence ; [*pain*] vif, aigu (-guë *f*) ; [*dislike*] vif ; [*indigestion*] fort ; [*halt, change*] brutal ; [*colour, red*] criard ; **to be ~ with sb** se montrer violent avec qn, user de violence avec qn ; **to turn ~** [*demonstration*] tourner à la violence ; [*person*] devenir violent ; (*lit, fig*) **a ~ attack** une violente attaque ; **to die a ~ death** mourir de mort violente ; **to meet a ~ end** connaître une fin brutale ; **to have a ~ temper** être sujet à des colères violentes ; **to be in a ~ temper** être dans une colère noire *or* dans une rage folle

violently ['vaɪələntlɪ] ADV [*attack, criticize, tremble*] violemment ; [*react*] violemment, avec violence ; [*act*] de façon violente ; [*say*] avec violence, sur un ton très violent ; [*swerve, brake*] brusquement ; [*change*] brutalement ; **opposed to sth** violemment opposé à qch ; **~ anti-communist** violemment anticommuniste ; **to behave ~** se montrer violent ; **to fall ~ in love with sb** tomber follement *or* éperdument amoureux de qn ; **to disagree ~** être en profond désaccord ; **to die ~** mourir de mort violente ; **~ angry** dans une violente colère *or* une colère noire ; **to be ~ ill** *or* **sick** être pris de violentes nausées

violet ['vaɪəlɪt] [1] N (*Bot*) violette *f* ; (= *colour*) violet *m* [2] ADJ violet

violin [,vaɪə'lɪn] [1] N violon *m* → **first** [2] COMP [*sonata, concerto*] pour violon ► **violin case** N étui *m* à violon ► **violin player** N violoniste *mf*

violinist [,vaɪə'lɪnɪst] N violoniste *mf*

violist [vɪ'əʊlɪst] N (*US*) altiste *mf*

violoncellist [,vaɪələn'tʃelɪst] N violoncelliste *mf*

violoncello [,vaɪələn'tʃeləʊ] N violoncelle *m*

VIP [,viːaɪ'piː] ABBR = **very important person** [1] N VIP❋ *m inv*, personnalité *f* (de marque) [2] COMP [*visitor*] de marque ► **VIP lounge** N (*in airport*) salon *m* d'accueil (*réservé aux personnages de marque*) ► **VIP treatment** N **to give sb/get the ~ treatment** traiter qn/être traité comme un VIP❋ *or* une personnalité de marque

viper ['vaɪpə'] N (*Zool, fig*) vipère *f*

viperish ['vaɪpərɪʃ] ADJ de vipère (*fig*)

virago [vɪ'rɑːɡəʊ] N (*pl* **viragoes** *or* **viragos**) mégère *f*, virago *f*

viral ['vaɪərəl] ADJ viral

Virgil ['vɜːdʒɪl] N Virgile *m*

virgin ['vɜːdʒɪn] [1] N (*fille f*) vierge *f*, puceau *m* ; **she is a ~** elle est vierge ; **he is a ~** il est vierge *or* puceau ; (*Astrol, Astron, Rel*) **the Virgin** la Vierge ; **the Virgin Mary** la Vierge Marie [2] ADJ [*person, snow, forest, soil, wool, page*] vierge ; [*freshness, sweetness*] virginal ; (*lit, fig*) **~ territory** terre *f* vierge [3] COMP ► **virgin birth** N (*Bio*) parthénogenèse *f* ; (*in Christianity*) **the Virgin Birth** la conception virginale ► **the Virgin Islands** NPL les îles *fpl* Vierges ► **virgin olive oil** N huile *f* d'olive vierge ► **the Virgin Queen** N Élisabeth Ière

virginal ['vɜːdʒɪnl] [1] ADJ [*woman*] d'une pureté virginale ; [*purity, innocence*] virginal ; **dressed in ~ white** vêtu de blanc virginal [2] N (*Mus*) virginal *m*

Virginia [və'dʒɪnjə] [1] N la Virginie ; **in ~** en Virginie [2] COMP ► **Virginia creeper** N (*Brit*) vigne *f* vierge ► **Virginia tobacco** N Virginie *m*, tabac *m* blond

Virginian [vəˈdʒɪnjən] **1** ADJ de Virginie **2** N Virginien(ne) *m(f)*

virginity [vɜːˈdʒɪnɪtɪ] N virginité *f*; **to lose one's ~** perdre sa virginité

Virgo [ˈvɜːgəʊ] N (*Astron*) la Vierge; (*Astrol*) **I'm (a) ~** je suis de la Vierge

Virgoan [vɜːˈgəʊən] N **to be a ~** être (de la) Vierge

virgule [ˈvɜːgjuːl] N (*US Typ*) barre *f* oblique

virile [ˈvɪraɪl] ADJ (*lit, fig*) viril (virile *f*)

virility [vɪˈrɪlɪtɪ] N virilité *f*

virologist [ˌvaɪəˈrɒlədʒɪst] N virologiste *mf*

virology [ˌvaɪəˈrɒlədʒɪ] N virologie *f*

virtual [ˈvɜːtjʊəl] **1** ADJ **a** (= *near*) quasi-; **a ~ certainty** une quasi-certitude; **a ~ impossibility** une quasi-impossibilité; **a ~ monopoly** un quasi-monopole; **to come to a ~ halt** *or* **standstill** en arriver à un arrêt quasi complet *or* total; **she was a ~ prisoner/recluse/stranger** elle était quasiment prisonnière/recluse/étrangère **b** (*Comput*) virtuel **2** COMP ► **virtual memory** N (*Comput*) mémoire *f* virtuelle ► **virtual reality** N (*Comput*) réalité *f* virtuelle; **~-reality computer** ordinateur *m* à réalité virtuelle; **~-reality helmet** casque *m* à réalité virtuelle; **~-reality system** système *m* de réalité virtuelle

virtuality [vɜːtjʊˈælɪtɪ] N virtualité *f*

virtually [ˈvɜːtjʊəlɪ] ADV (= *almost*) pratiquement, quasiment; (*Comput*) de façon virtuelle; **he started with ~ nothing** il est parti de presque rien

virtue [ˈvɜːtjuː] N **a** (= *good quality*) vertu *f*; **to make a ~ of necessity** faire de nécessité vertu **b** (*NonC* = *chastity*) vertu *f*, chasteté *f*; **a woman of easy ~†** une femme de petite vertu **c** (= *advantage*) mérite *m*, avantage *m*; **this set has the ~ of being portable** ce poste a l'avantage d'être portatif; **it has the ~ of clarity** ça a l'avantage d'être clair *or* de la clarté; **he has the ~ of being easy to understand** il a le mérite d'être facile à comprendre; **there is no ~ in doing that if it is unnecessary** il n'y a aucun mérite à faire cela si ce n'est pas nécessaire; **this method has no ~s over the others** cette méthode n'a pas d'avantages particuliers par rapport aux autres **d** **in** *or* **by ~ of** en vertu de, en raison de; **by ~ of the fact that ...** en vertu *or* en raison du fait que ...; **by ~ of being British, he ...** en vertu *or* en raison du fait qu'il était britannique, il ... **e** (*NonC* = *power*) **healing ~** pouvoir *m* thérapeutique

virtuosity [ˌvɜːtjʊˈɒsɪtɪ] N virtuosité *f*

virtuoso [ˌvɜːtjʊˈəʊzəʊ] **1** N (*pl* **virtuosos** *or* **virtuosi** [ˌvɜːtjʊˈəʊziː]) (*esp Mus*) virtuose *mf*; **a violin ~** un(e) virtuose du violon **2** ADJ [*performance*] de virtuose; **a ~ violinist** un(e) virtuose du violon

virtuous [ˈvɜːtjʊəs] **1** ADJ vertueux **2** COMP ► **virtuous circle** N cercle *m* vertueux

virtuously [ˈvɜːtjʊəslɪ] ADV vertueusement

virulence [ˈvɪrʊləns] N virulence *f*

virulent [ˈvɪrʊlənt] ADJ [*disease, poison, hatred, attack, speech, critic*] virulent; [*colour, green, purple*] criard

virulently [ˈvɪrʊləntlɪ] ADV [*attack, oppose*] (*also Med*) avec virulence; [*opposed, anti-Semitic*] violemment

virus [ˈvaɪərəs] N (*pl* **viruses**) (*Med, Comput*) virus *m*; **rabies ~** virus *m* de la rage *or* rabique; **the AIDS ~** le virus du sida; **~ disease** maladie *f* virale *or* à virus

visa [ˈviːzə] **1** N (*pl* **visas**) **a** (*in passport*) visa *m* (*de passeport*); **entrance/exit ~** visa *m* d'entrée/de sortie; **to get an Egyptian ~** obtenir un visa pour l'Égypte **b** (= *credit card*) **Visa® (card)** carte *f* Visa®, ≈ Carte bleue® *f* **2** VT viser

visage [ˈvɪzɪdʒ] N (*liter*) visage *m*, figure *f*

vis-à-vis [ˈviːzævɪː] **1** PREP [+ *person*] vis à vis de; [+ *thing*] par rapport à, devant; **~ the West** vis à vis de l'Occident **2** N (= *person placed opposite*) vis-à-vis *m*; (= *person of similar status*) homologue *mf*

viscera [ˈvɪsərə] NPL viscères *mpl*

visceral [ˈvɪsərəl] ADJ (*liter*) [*hatred, dislike*] (*also Anat*) viscéral; [*thrill, pleasure*] brut

viscid [ˈvɪsɪd] ADJ visqueux (*lit*)

viscose [ˈvɪskəʊs] **1** N viscose *f* **2** ADJ visqueux (*lit*)

viscosity [vɪsˈkɒsɪtɪ] N viscosité *f*

viscount [ˈvaɪkaʊnt] N vicomte *m*

viscountcy [ˈvaɪkaʊntsɪ] N vicomté *f*

viscountess [ˈvaɪkaʊntɪs] N vicomtesse *f*

viscounty [ˈvaɪkaʊntɪ] N = **viscountcy**

viscous [ˈvɪskəs] ADJ visqueux, gluant

vise [vaɪs] N (*US*) = **vice²**

visé [ˈviːzeɪ] N (*US*) = **visa 1a**

visibility [ˌvɪzɪˈbɪlɪtɪ] N visibilité *f*; **good/poor** *or* **low ~** bonne/mauvaise visibilité *f*; **~ is down to** *or* **is only 20 metres** la visibilité ne dépasse pas 20 mètres

visible [ˈvɪzəbl] **1** ADJ **a** (= *detectable*) [*effect, damage, sign, result, effort*] visible; [*impatience*] visible, manifeste; **to become ~** apparaître; **there is no ~ difference** il n'y a pas de différence notable *or* visible; **it serves no ~ purpose** on n'en voit pas vraiment l'utilité; **the barn wasn't ~ from the road** la grange n'était pas visible depuis la route; **it was not ~ to a passer-by** un passant ne pouvait pas l'apercevoir; **~ to the naked eye** visible à l'œil nu; (*Jur*) **with no ~ means of support** sans ressources apparentes **b** (= *prominent*) [*person, minority*] en vue **2** COMP ► **visible exports** NPL exportations *fpl* visibles ► **visible light** N (*Phys*) lumière *f* visible ► **visible panty line** N (*hum*) slip qui se devine sous un vêtement

visibly [ˈvɪzəblɪ] ADV [*shocked, upset, moved, angry*] manifestement, visiblement; [*relax, shake, flinch*] visiblement

Visigoth [ˈvɪzɪgɒθ] N Wisigoth *m*

vision [ˈvɪʒən] **1** N **a** (*NonC*) vision *f*, vue *f*; (*fig* = *foresight*) vision *f*, prévoyance *f*; **his ~ is very bad** sa vue est très mauvaise; **within/outside one's range of ~** à portée de/hors de vue; (*fig*) **a man of great ~** un homme qui voit loin; **his ~ of the future** sa vision de l'avenir → **field b** (*in dream, trance*) vision *f*, apparition *f*; **it came to me in a ~** j'en ai eu une vision; **to have** *or* **see ~s** avoir des visions; **to have ~s of wealth** avoir des visions de richesses; **she had ~s of being drowned** elle s'est vue noyée **2** VT (*US*) envisager **3** COMP ► **vision mixer** N (*Cine, TV*) (= *machine*) mixeur *m* (d'images); (= *person*) **"~ mixer: Alexander Anderson"** «mixage: Alexander Anderson » ► **vision-mixing** N (*Cine, TV*) mixage *m* (d'images)

visionary [ˈvɪʒənərɪ] ADJ, N visionnaire *mf*

visit [ˈvɪzɪt] **1** N (= *call, tour: also Med*) visite *f*; (= *stay*) séjour *m*; **to pay a ~ to** [+ *person*] rendre visite à; [+ *place*] aller à; (*fig*) **to pay a ~*** aller au petit coin*; **to be on a ~ to** [+ *person*] être en visite chez; [+ *place*] faire un séjour à; **he went on a two-day ~ to Paris** il est allé passer deux jours à Paris; **I'm going on a ~ to Glasgow next week** j'irai à Glasgow la semaine prochaine; **on a private/an official ~** en visite privée/officielle; **his ~ to Paris lasted three days** son séjour à Paris a duré trois jours **2** VT **a** (= *go and see*) [+ *person*] aller voir, rendre visite à; [+ *doctor, solicitor*] aller voir, aller chez; [+ *sick person*] (*gen*) aller voir; [*priest, doctor etc*] [+ *patient*] visiter; [+ *town*] aller à, faire un petit tour à; [+ *museum, zoo*] aller à; [+ *theatre*] aller à **b** (= *go and stay with*) [+ *person*] faire un séjour chez; (= *go and stay in*) [+ *town, country*]

faire un séjour à (*or* en) **c** (= *formally inspect*) [+ *place*] inspecter, faire une visite d'inspection à; [+ *troops*] passer en revue; (*Jur*) **to ~ the scene of the crime** se rendre sur les lieux du crime **d** († = *inflict*) [+ *person*] punir (**with** de); **to ~ the sins of the fathers upon the children** punir les enfants pour les péchés de leurs pères **3** VI **a** **I'm just ~ing** je suis de passage **b** (*US* = *chat*) bavarder
► **visit with** VT FUS (*US*) [+ *person*] passer voir

visitation [ˌvɪzɪˈteɪʃən] N **a** (*by official*) visite *f* d'inspection; [*of bishop*] visite *f* pastorale; (*hum*) **we had a ~ from her** elle nous a fait l'honneur de sa visite, elle nous a honorés de sa présence; (*Rel*) **the Visitation of the Blessed Virgin Mary** la Visitation de la Vierge **b** (= *calamity*) punition *f* du ciel

visiting [ˈvɪzɪtɪŋ] **1** N **I find ~ a nuisance** cela m'ennuie de faire des visites **2** COMP [*friends*] de passage; [*lecturer etc*] invité, de l'extérieur ► **visiting card** N (*Brit*) carte *f* de visite ► **visiting fireman*** N (*pl* **visiting firemen**) (*US fig: iro*) visiteur *m* de marque ► **visiting hours** NPL heures *fpl* de visite ► **visiting nurse** N (*US*) infirmière *f* à domicile ► **visiting professor** N (*Univ*) professeur *m* associé ► **visiting rights** NPL droit *m* de visite ► **visiting teacher** N (*US*) ≈ visiteuse *f* scolaire ► **visiting team** N (*Sport*) visiteurs *mpl* ► **visiting terms** NPL **I know him but I'm not on ~ terms with him** je le connais, mais nous ne nous rendons pas visite ► **visiting time** N = **visiting hours**

visitor [ˈvɪzɪtəʳ] **1** N **a** (= *guest*) invité(e) *m(f)*; **to have a ~** avoir de la visite; **to have ~s** avoir des visites *or* de la visite; **we've had a lot of ~s** nous avons eu beaucoup de visites; **have your ~s left?** est-ce que tes invités sont partis?; (*fig iro*) **we seem to have had a ~ during the night** on dirait qu'on a eu de la visite cette nuit! **b** (= *client*) (*in hotel*) client(e) *m(f)*; (*at exhibition*) visiteur *m*; (= *tourist*) visiteur *m*; **~s to London** visiteurs *mpl* de passage à Londres; **~s to the castle** les personnes *fpl* visitant le château → **health, passport, prison** **2** COMP ► **visitor centre** N accueil *m* des visiteurs (*sur un site historique avec exposition, diaporama, cafétéria etc*) ► **visitors' book** N livre *m* d'or ► **visitors' gallery** N (*Parl etc*) tribune *f* du public ► **visitor's tax** N taxe *f* de séjour

visor [ˈvaɪzəʳ] N visière *f* → **sun**

VISTA [ˈvɪstə] N (*US*) (ABBR = **Volunteers in Service to America**) *organisme américain chargé de l'aide aux personnes défavorisées*

vista [ˈvɪstə] N (= *view*) vue *f*; (= *survey*) (*of past*) vue *f*, image *f*; (*of future*) perspective *f*, horizon *m*; (*fig*) **to open up new ~s** ouvrir de nouveaux horizons *or* de nouvelles perspectives

visual [ˈvɪzjʊəl] **1** ADJ visuel; **the ~ cortex of the brain** l'aire du cortex cérébral contrôlant la vision; **within ~ range** à portée de vue; **she's a very ~ person** c'est une visuelle **2** **visuals** NPL (= *display material*) support(s) *m(pl)* visuel(s); [*of video game, film etc*] images *fpl* **3** COMP ► **visual aid** N support *m* visuel ► **visual artist** N plasticien(ne) *m(f)* ► **the visual arts** NPL les arts *mpl* plastiques ► **visual display terminal, visual display unit** N console *f*, écran *m* ► **visual field** N (*Opt*) champ *m* de vision

visualization [ˌvɪzjʊəlaɪˈzeɪʃən] N visualisation *f*

visualize [ˈvɪzjʊəlaɪz] VT **a** (= *recall*) [+ *person, sb's face*] se représenter, évoquer **b** (= *imagine*) [+ *sth unknown*] s'imaginer; [+ *sth unknown*] se représenter; **try to ~ a million pounds** essayez de vous imaginer un million de livres; **I ~d him working at his desk** je me le suis représenté travaillant à son bureau **c** (= *foresee*) envisager, prévoir; **we do not ~ many**

changes nous n'envisageons pas beaucoup de changements

visually ['vɪzjʊəlɪ] ADV [attractive] visuellement; [stunning, exciting] d'un point de vue visuel; [judge] de visu; **~ handicapped** or **impaired** malvoyant; **the ~ handicapped** or **impaired** les malvoyants mpl; **~, it's a very impressive film** d'un point de vue visuel, c'est un film très impressionnant

vital ['vaɪtl] **1** ADJ **a** (= crucial) [part, component, element, information] vital, essentiel; [question, matter] vital, fondamental; [supplies, resources] vital; [ingredient, factor, role] essentiel, fondamental; [link] essentiel; [importance] capital; **your support is ~ to us** votre soutien est vital or capital pour nous; **such skills are ~ for survival** de telles techniques sont indispensables à la survie; **it is ~ to do** il est vital or essentiel de faire; **it is ~ for you to come** ◊ **it is ~ that you (should) come** il faut absolument que vous veniez (subj) **b** (= dynamic) [person, institution] énergique; **~ spark** étincelle f de vie **c** (Physiol) [organ, force, functions] vital; **~ parts** organes mpl vitaux **2** N **the ~s** (Anat) les organes mpl vitaux; (fig) les parties fpl essentielles **3** COMP ► **vital signs** NPL (Med) signes mpl vitaux; (fig) signes mpl de vitalité; **his ~ signs are normal** ses fonctions vitales sont normales; **he shows no ~ signs** il ne donne aucun signe de vie ► **vital statistics** NPL (Sociol) statistiques fpl démographiques; (Brit) [of woman] mensurations fpl

vitality [vaɪ'tælɪtɪ] N (lit, fig) vitalité f

vitalize ['vaɪtəlaɪz] VT (lit) vivifier; (fig) mettre de la vie dans, animer

vitally ['vaɪtəlɪ] ADV **a** (= crucially, greatly) [necessary] absolument; [interested, concerned] au plus haut point; [affect] de façon cruciale; **~ important** d'une importance capitale; **it is ~ important that I talk to her** il est absolument indispensable que or il faut absolument que je lui parle (subj); **~ urgent** des plus urgents; **~ needed foreign investment** investissements mpl étrangers dont on a un besoin vital; **~, he was still willing to compromise** fait essentiel or capital, il était toujours prêt à envisager un compromis **b** (= intensely) **she is so ~ alive** elle est tellement débordante de vitalité; **traditions that are ~ alive** traditions fpl qui restent des plus vivaces; **music which remains ~ fresh** musique f qui conserve une intense fraîcheur

vitamin ['vɪtəmɪn] **1** N vitamine f; **~ A/B** etc vitamine A/B etc; **with added ~s** vitaminé **2** COMP [content] en vitamines ► **vitamin deficiency** N carence f en vitamines ► **vitamin deficiency disease** N avitaminose f ► **vitamin-enriched** ADJ vitaminé ► **vitamin pill** N comprimé m de vitamines ► **vitamin-rich** ADJ riche en vitamines ► **vitamin tablet** N = **vitamin pill**

vitaminize ['vɪtəmɪnaɪz] VT incorporer des vitamines dans; **~d food** nourriture f vitaminée

vitiate ['vɪʃɪeɪt] VT (all senses) vicier

viticulture ['vɪtɪkʌltʃər] N viticulture f

vitreous ['vɪtrɪəs] **1** ADJ **a** [china, rock, electricity] vitré; [enamel] vitrifié **b** (Anat) vitré **2** COMP ► **vitreous body** N (corps m) vitré m ► **vitreous humour** N humeur f vitrée

vitrifaction [ˌvɪtrɪ'fækʃən], **vitrification** [ˌvɪtrɪfɪ'keɪʃən] N vitrification f

vitrify ['vɪtrɪfaɪ] **1** VT vitrifier **2** VI se vitrifier

vitriol ['vɪtrɪəl] N (Chem, fig) vitriol m

vitriolic [ˌvɪtrɪ'ɒlɪk] **1** ADJ [attack, speech] au vitriol; [abuse, outburst] venimeux; [criticism] venimeux, au vitriol **2** COMP ► **vitriolic acid**† N (Chem) vitriol† m

vitriolize ['vɪtrɪəlaɪz] VT vitrioler

vitro ['vɪtrəʊ] → **in vitro**

vituperate [vɪ'tjuːpəreɪt] (frm) **1** VT injurier, vitupérer contre **2** VI vitupérer

vituperation [vɪˌtjuːpə'reɪʃən] N (frm) vitupérations fpl

vituperative [vɪ'tjuːpərətɪv] ADJ (frm) [remark] injurieux; [attack, abuse, critic] virulent; **a ~ man/woman** un vitupérateur/une vitupératrice (liter); **to be ~ about sb** vitupérer contre qn

Vitus ['vaɪtəs] N → **saint**

viva¹ ['viːvə] **1** EXCL vive! **2** N vivat m

viva² ['vaɪvə] N (Brit Univ) épreuve f orale, oral m

vivacious [vɪ'veɪʃəs] ADJ [woman, personality] plein de vivacité

vivaciously [vɪ'veɪʃəslɪ] ADV [say, laugh] avec vivacité

vivacity [vɪ'væsɪtɪ] N vivacité f; (in words) verve f

vivarium [vɪ'vɛərɪəm] N (pl **vivariums** or **vivaria** [vɪ'vɛərɪə]) vivarium m; (for fish, shellfish) vivier m

viva voce [ˌvaɪvə'vəʊsɪ] **1** ADJ oral, verbal **2** ADV de vive voix, oralement **3** N (Brit Univ) épreuve f orale, oral m

vivid ['vɪvɪd] ADJ [colour, imagination] vif; [memory] très net, vif; [dream] pénétrant; [description, language] vivant, coloré; [account] vivant; [example, comparison, demonstration] frappant; **in ~ detail** avec des détails saisissants; **to be a ~ reminder that ...** rappeler de façon saisissante que ...

vividly ['vɪvɪdlɪ] ADV [remember, recall] très nettement or distinctement; [describe, portray, express] de façon vivante; [illustrate, demonstrate] de façon frappante; **~ coloured** aux couleurs vives

vividness ['vɪvɪdnɪs] N [of colour] vivacité f, éclat m; [of light] éclat m, clarté f; [of memory] netteté f; [of description] caractère m très vivant; [of dream] clarté f; [of style] clarté f, vigueur f

vivify ['vɪvɪfaɪ] VT vivifier, ranimer

viviparous [vɪ'vɪpərəs] ADJ vivipare

vivisect [ˌvɪvɪ'sekt] VT pratiquer la vivisection sur, viviséquer

vivisection [ˌvɪvɪ'sekʃən] N vivisection f

vivisectionist [ˌvɪvɪ'sekʃənɪst], **vivisector** ['vɪvɪsektər] N (= scientist) vivisecteur m, -trice f; (= supporter) partisan(e) m(f) de la vivisection

vixen ['vɪksn] N **a** (Zool) renarde f **b** (= woman) mégère f

viz [vɪz] ADV (ABBR = **vide licet**) (= namely) c.-à-d., c'est-à-dire

vizier [vɪ'zɪər] N vizir m

VJ Day ['viː'dʒeɪdeɪ] N anniversaire de la victoire des alliés sur le Japon en 1945 → VE DAY

VLF [viːel'ef] N (ABBR = **very low frequency**) → **very**

VLSI N (Comput) (ABBR = **very large-scale integration**) intégration f à très grande échelle

vocab* ['vəʊkæb] ABBR = **vocabulary**

vocable ['vəʊkəbl] N vocable m

vocabulary [vəʊ'kæbjʊlərɪ] N (gen) vocabulaire m; (in textbook) (bilingual) lexique m, vocabulaire m; (technical) lexique m, glossaire m

vocal ['vəʊkəl] **1** ADJ **a** (= using voice: also Anat) vocal; (Mus) **~ score** partition f vocale; **~ training** = **voice training**; **to be ~** (= outspoken) [opposition, protest] vif; **a ~ minority** une minorité bruyante; **he was very ~ during the meeting** il n'a pas hésité à prendre la parole pendant la réunion; **to be ~ in one's displeasure** exprimer énergiquement son déplaisir; **to be ~ in supporting sth** prendre énergiquement parti pour qch; **to become more** or **increasingly ~** [person] se faire de plus en plus entendre; **public discontent was increasingly ~** de plus en plus les gens exprimaient leur mécontentement **2** N (Mus) **~(s)** chant m; **featuring Chrissie Hynde on ~s** avec Chrissie

Hynde au chant; **backing ~s** chœurs mpl **3** COMP ► **vocal c(h)ords**, **vocal folds** NPL cordes fpl vocales

vocalic [vəʊ'kælɪk] ADJ vocalique

vocalisation [ˌvəʊkəlaɪ'zeɪʃən] N vocalisation f

vocalist ['vəʊkəlɪst] N chanteur m, -euse f (dans un groupe)

vocalize ['vəʊkəlaɪz] **1** VT **a** [+ one's opinions] exprimer **b** (Ling) [+ consonant] vocaliser; [+ text] écrire en marquant des points-voyelles **2** VI (Ling) se vocaliser; (Mus) vocaliser, faire des vocalises

vocally ['vəʊkəlɪ] ADV **a** (Mus) [perfect, impressive, difficult etc] du point de vue vocal; **a ~ superb cast** des chanteurs extraordinaires; **~, it's a very simple song** la mélodie de cette chanson est très simple **b** (= outspokenly) **to support/oppose sth ~** exprimer énergiquement son soutien/opposition à qch; **to be ~ anti-feminist** exprimer énergiquement ses opinions antiféministes

vocation [vəʊ'keɪʃən] N (Rel etc) vocation f; **to have a ~ for teaching** avoir la vocation de l'enseignement

vocational [vəʊ'keɪʃənl] **1** ADJ [training, education, subject, qualifications, skills] technique et professionnel; **~ course** (= period) stage m de formation professionnelle; (= subject) filière f technique et professionnelle **2** COMP ► **vocational guidance** N orientation f professionnelle ► **vocational school** N (in US) ≈ lycée m technique

vocationally [vəʊ'keɪʃənlɪ] ADV **~ oriented courses** cours mpl à orientation professionnelle; **~ relevant subjects** matières fpl d'intérêt professionnel; **to train sb ~** donner à qn une formation professionnelle

vocative ['vɒkətɪv] **1** N vocatif m; **in the ~** au vocatif **2** ADJ vocatif; **~ case** vocatif m; **~ ending** désinence f du vocatif

vociferate [vəʊ'sɪfəreɪt] VI vociférer, brailler*

vociferation [vəʊˌsɪfə'reɪʃən] N vocifération f

vociferous [vəʊ'sɪfərəs] ADJ véhément; **~ in one's opposition to sth** véhément dans son opposition à qch; **to be ~ in one's criticism of sb/sth** critiquer qn/qch avec véhémence; **to be ~ in demanding one's rights** réclamer ses droits avec véhémence

vociferously [vəʊ'sɪfərəslɪ] ADV (frm) avec véhémence

vodka ['vɒdkə] N vodka f

vogue [vəʊg] **1** N vogue f, mode f; **moustaches were the ~ or in ~ then** les moustaches étaient alors en vogue or à la mode; **to be all the ~** faire fureur; **to come into ~** devenir à la mode; **to go out of ~** passer de mode; **the ~ for ...** la vogue or la mode de ...; **the current ~ for mini-skirts** la vogue que connaissent actuellement les minijupes **2** ADJ à la mode, en vogue

voice [vɔɪs] **1** N **a** (gen) voix f; (pitch, quality) voix f, ton m; **in a deep ~** d'une voix grave; **at the top of one's ~** à tue-tête; **to raise/lower one's ~** élever/baisser la voix; **keep your ~ down** ne parle pas trop fort; **to say sth in a low ~** dire qch à voix basse; **he likes the sound of his own ~** il aime s'écouter parler; **his ~ has broken** il a mué, sa voix a mué; **a ~ could be heard at the back of the room** on entendait une voix au fond de la salle; **they acclaimed him with one ~** ils ont été unanimes à l'acclamer; **to give ~ to sth** exprimer qch; **the ~ of reason** la voix de la raison; **the ~ of God** la voix de Dieu; **he is a ~ (crying) in the wilderness** il prêche dans le désert → **find, lose, loud**

b (fig = opinion, influence) **there were no dissenting ~s** il n'y a pas eu d'opposition; **to have a ~ in the matter** avoir son mot à dire, avoir voix au chapitre; **his wife has no ~ in their business affairs** sa femme n'a pas son mot à dire dans leurs affaires; **can't I have a ~ in this?** est-ce que je peux avoir mon mot à dire?; **Egypt is an important ~ in Arab politics** l'Égypte joue un rôle déterminant dans la politique des pays arabes; **France retains an influential ~ in African affairs** la France a gardé une position d'influence en Afrique

c (Mus) voix f; **tenor/bass ~** voix f de ténor/de basse; **a piece for ~ and piano** un morceau pour voix et piano; **a piece for three soprano ~s** un morceau pour trois sopranos; **to be in good ~** être en voix; **he has a lovely tenor ~** il a une belle voix-de ténor

d (Gram) voix f; **active/passive ~** voix f active/passive; **in the active/passive ~** à l'actif/au passif

e (NonC: Phon) voix f

f (Theat) **~s off** voix fpl dans les coulisses

2 VT **a** (= express) [+ feelings, opinion] exprimer, formuler; [+ concern, support, fear] exprimer; **to ~ (one's) opposition to sth** s'élever contre qch

b (Ling) [+ consonant] sonoriser; **~d consonant** consonne f sonore or voisée

c (Mus) accorder

3 COMP ▶ **voice-activated** ADJ à commande vocale ▶ **voice box** N (Anat) larynx m ▶ **voice mail** N messagerie f vocale ▶ **voice-over** N (TV) (commentaire m en) voix f off ▶ **voice parts** NPL (Mus) parties fpl vocales ▶ **voice production** N diction f, élocution f ▶ **voice range** N registre m de la voix ▶ **voice recognition** N reconnaissance f vocale ▶ **voice synthesis** N synthèse f vocale ▶ **voice synthesizer** N synthétiseur m vocal ▶ **voice training** N [of actor etc] cours mpl de diction or d'élocution; [of singer] cours mpl de chant ▶ **voice vote** N (US Pol etc) vote m par acclamation

voiced [vɔɪst] ADJ (Phon) [consonant] voisé, sonore

voiceless ['vɔɪslɪs] ADJ **a** (= mute) [person] (gen) sans voix, aphone; (Med) aphone **b** (= disenfranchised) [minority] silencieux **c** (Phon) [consonant, sound] non voisé, sourd

voiceprint ['vɔɪsprɪnt] N empreinte f vocale

voicing ['vɔɪsɪŋ] N (Phon) sonorisation f, voisement m

void [vɔɪd] **1** N (lit, fig) vide m; (fig) **an aching ~** un grand vide; **to fill the ~** combler le vide **2** ADJ **a** (Jur = invalid) [agreement] nul (nulle f); **to declare sth ~** annuler qch → **null b** (frm = empty) vide; **~ of** [ornament, charm, talent, qualities, imagination] dépourvu de; [scruples, compassion, good sense, meaning] dénué de **c** (Cards) **his spades were ~** he was **~ in spades** il n'avait pas de pique **3** VT **a** (= remove) évacuer (**from** de) **b** (Med) (= excrete) évacuer; (= vomit) vomir **c** (Jur = invalidated) annuler

voile [vɔɪl] N voile m (Tex)

Voivodina, **Vojvodina** ['vɔɪvə'diːnə] N la Voïvodine or Vojvodine

vol. ABBR = **volume**

volatile ['vɒlətaɪl] ADJ **a** (Chem) volatil **b** (fig = uncertain) [situation, atmosphere, relationship, market] instable; [person, personality] versatile

volatility [ˌvɒlə'tɪlɪtɪ] N **a** (Chem) volatilité f **b** (= uncertainty) [of situation, atmosphere, relationship, market] inconstance f; [of person, personality] versatilité f

volatilize [vɒ'lætəlaɪz] **1** VT volatiliser **2** VI se volatiliser, s'évaporer

vol-au-vent ['vɒləʊ,vɑ̃ː, 'vɒlə,vɒn] N vol-au-vent m; **chicken/mushroom ~** vol-au-vent m au poulet/aux champignons

volcanic [vɒl'kænɪk] ADJ (lit, fig) volcanique

volcano [vɒl'keɪnəʊ] N (pl **volcanoes** or **volcanos**) volcan m

vole[1] [vəʊl] N (Zool) campagnol m → **water**

vole[2] [vəʊl] (Cards) **1** N vole f **2** VI faire la vole

Volga ['vɒlgə] N Volga f

volition [vɒ'lɪʃən] N volition f, volonté f; **of one's own ~** de son propre gré

volley ['vɒlɪ] **1** N **a** (Mil) volée f, salve f; [of stones] grêle f **b** (fig) [of insults] bordée f, torrent m; [of questions] feu m roulant; [of applause] salve f; **to fire a ~** tirer une salve **c** (Sport) volée f; **half ~** demi-volée f **2** VT (Sport) [+ ball] reprendre de volée, attraper à la volée **3** VI **a** (Mil) tirer par salves **b** (Sport) renvoyer une volée

volleyball ['vɒlɪbɔːl] **1** N volley(-ball) m **2** COMP ▶ **volleyball player** N volleyeur m, -euse f

volleyer ['vɒlɪə'] N (Tennis) volleyeur m, -euse f

volt [vəʊlt] **1** N volt m **2** COMP ▶ **volt meter** N voltmètre m

voltage ['vəʊltɪdʒ] N voltage m, tension f; **high/low ~** haute/basse tension f

voltaic [vɒl'teɪɪk] ADJ voltaïque

volte-face ['vɒlt'fɑːs] N (pl inv) volte-face f inv; (lit, fig) **to perform a ~** faire volte-face

volubility [ˌvɒljʊ'bɪlɪtɪ] N volubilité f, loquacité f

voluble ['vɒljʊbl] ADJ volubile

volubly ['vɒljʊblɪ] ADV avec volubilité, volubilement

volume ['vɒljuːm] **1** N **a** (= book) volume m; (= one in a set) volume m, tome m; **~ one/two** tome m premier/second; **~ three/four** etc tome m trois/quatre etc; **in six ~s** en six volumes; **a two-~ dictionary** un dictionnaire en deux volumes; (fig) **to write ~s** écrire des volumes; (fig) **to speak** or **say ~s** en dire long (**about** sur)

b (= size, bulk: Phys) volume m; **the gas expanded to twice its original ~** le gaz s'est dilaté et a doublé de volume; **your hair needs more ~** il faut redonner du volume à vos cheveux; **production ~** volume m de la production; **the ~ of imports/exports** le volume des importations/exportations; **the ~ of protest has increased since ...** les protestations ont pris de l'ampleur depuis ...

c (= capacity) [of tank, container] capacité f

d (= loudness) volume m, puissance f; (Rad, TV) **to turn the ~ up/down** augmenter/diminuer le volume

2 volumes NPL (gen) **~s of** énormément de; **~s of work** énormément de travail; **~s of smoke** des nuages mpl de fumée

3 COMP ▶ **volume control** N (Rad, TV) bouton m de réglage du volume

volumetric [ˌvɒljʊ'metrɪk] ADJ volumétrique

voluminous [və'luːmɪnəs] ADJ volumineux

voluntarily ['vɒləntərɪlɪ] ADV **a** (= willingly) volontairement **b** (= without payment) [work] bénévolement, à titre bénévole

voluntarism ['vɒləntərɪzəm] N bénévolat m

voluntary ['vɒləntərɪ] **1** ADJ **a** (= not compulsory, spontaneous) [subscription, contribution, redundancy, repatriation, movement] volontaire; [confession, statement] volontaire, spontané; [attendance, course] facultatif; [pension scheme] à contribution volontaire; [agreement] librement consenti; **on a ~ basis** à titre volontaire **b** (= unpaid, charitable) [group, service] bénévole; **~ helper** bénévole mf; **~ help** (= assistance) aide f bénévole; **on a ~ basis** à titre bénévole

2 N (Mus, Rel) morceau m d'orgue

3 COMP ▶ **voluntary agency**, **voluntary body** N organisation f bénévole ▶ **voluntary euthanasia** N euthanasie f volontaire ▶ **voluntary liquidation** N (Comm, Fin) dépôt m de bilan; **to go into ~ liquidation** déposer son bilan; **they put the company into ~ liquidation** l'entreprise a déposé son bilan ▶ **voluntary manslaughter** N (Jur) homicide m volontaire ▶ **voluntary organization** N

organisation f bénévole ▶ **voluntary school** N (Brit) école f libre ▶ **the voluntary sector** N les organisations fpl bénévoles, le secteur associatif; **he works in the ~ sector** il travaille pour une organisation bénévole or dans le secteur associatif ▶ **Voluntary Service Overseas** N (Brit) ≈ coopération f technique ▶ **voluntary work** N travail m bénévole, bénévolat m; **she does ~ work (in a hospital)** elle travaille comme bénévole (dans un hôpital) ▶ **voluntary worker** N bénévole mf

volunteer [ˌvɒlən'tɪə'] **1** N (gen, Mil) volontaire mf; (= voluntary helper) bénévole mf; **to ask for** or **call for ~s** demander des volontaires

2 ADJ **a** (= having offered to do sth) [group] de volontaires; [person] volontaire

b (= unpaid) [helper etc] bénévole

3 VT [+ money] donner or offrir de son plein gré; [+ information] fournir (spontanément); **they ~ed five pounds a week to the fund** ils ont offert une contribution hebdomadaire au fonds de cinq livres; **they ~ed to carry it all back** ils ont offert de tout remporter; **"there were seven of them" he ~ed** « ils étaient sept » dit-il spontanément

4 VI (Mil) s'engager comme volontaire (**for** dans); (gen) **to ~ for sth** s'offrir or se proposer pour (faire) qch

5 COMP ▶ **Volunteers in Service to America** N organisme américain chargé de l'aide aux personnes défavorisées ▶ **the Volunteer State** N le Tennessee

voluptuous [və'lʌptjʊəs] ADJ voluptueux; **she has a ~ figure** elle est bien faite

voluptuously [və'lʌptjʊəslɪ] ADV [move, stretch] voluptueusement; **her ~ curved body** son corps aux rondeurs voluptueuses; **his lips were ~ full** il avait une bouche sensuelle

voluptuousness [və'lʌptjʊəsnɪs] N volupté f, sensualité f

volute [və'luːt] N (Archit) volute f

voluted [və'luːtɪd] ADJ (Archit) en volute

vomit ['vɒmɪt] **1** N vomissement m, vomi m **2** VT (lit, fig) vomir; (liter) **to ~ out** or **up** or **forth** vomir **3** VI vomir

vomiting ['vɒmɪtɪŋ] N vomissements mpl

voodoo ['vuːduː] **1** ADJ vaudou inv **2** N vaudou m **3** VT envoûter

voracious [və'reɪʃəs] ADJ [appetite, person, animal] vorace; [reader, collector] avide; **to be a ~ eater** être vorace

voraciously [və'reɪʃəslɪ] ADV [eat, devour] voracement, avec voracité; [read] avec avidité

voracity [vɒ'ræsɪtɪ] N (lit, fig) voracité f

vortex ['vɔːteks] N (pl **vortexes** or **vortices** ['vɔːtɪsiːz]) (lit) vortex m, tourbillon m; (fig) tourbillon m

vorticism ['vɔːtɪˌsɪzəm] N (Art) vorticisme m

votary ['vəʊtərɪ] N (liter) fervent(e) m(f) (**of** de)

vote [vəʊt] **1** N **a** (= ballot) vote m; **to put sth to the ~** mettre qch au vote; **the matter was settled by ~** on a réglé la question en la mettant au vote; **to take a ~** (gen) voter (**on** sur); (Admin, Pol) procéder au vote (**on** sur); **they took a ~ on whether to sell the company** ils ont voté pour décider s'ils allaient (ou non) vendre l'entreprise; **after the ~** après le scrutin; **~ of censure** or **no confidence** motion f de censure; **to pass a ~ of censure** voter une motion de censure; **~ of confidence** vote m de confiance; **to ask for a ~ of confidence** réclamer un vote de confiance; **to pass a ~ of confidence (in)** voter la confiance (à); **(to move a) ~ of thanks** (faire un) discours m de remerciement

b (= franchise) droit m de vote; **to give the ~ to the under twenty-ones** accorder le droit de vote au moins de vingt et un ans; **one man one ~** ≈ suffrage m universel, ≈ une seule voix par électeur; **~s for women!** le droit de vote pour les femmes!

c (= *vote cast*) voix *f*, vote *m*; **to give one's ~ to ...** donner sa voix à ..., voter pour ...; **to win ~s** gagner des voix; **to count the ~s** compter les voix *or* les votes; (*Pol*) dépouiller le scrutin; **he has my ~** je voterai pour lui; **~ for/against sth** voix *f* pour/contre qch; **elected by a majority ~** élu au vote majoritaire; **they won by a two-thirds ~** ils ont remporté les deux tiers des voix

d (= *body of voters*) électorat *m*; **the Jewish/ Scottish ~** l'électorat *m* juif/écossais; **to lose/ court the Catholic ~** perdre le soutien de/ courtiser l'électorat catholique; **he'll win/lose the Massachusetts ~** il va remporter/perdre le Massachusetts; (*Pol*) **the Labour ~** les voix *fpl* travaillistes → **casting**, **floating**

2 VT a (= *approve*) [+ *bill*, *treaty*] voter; **the committee ~d to request a subsidy** le comité a voté une demande d'une subvention

b (= *elect*) élire; **he was ~d chairman** il a été élu président; (*fig*) **the group ~d her the best cook** le groupe l'a proclamée la meilleure cuisinière

c (= *propose*) **I ~ we go to the cinema***je propose que l'on aille au cinéma

3 VI voter (**for** pour, **against** contre), donner sa voix (**for sb** à qn, **for sth** pour qch); (*in general election etc*) aller aux urnes, voter; **the country ~s in three weeks** les élections ont lieu dans trois semaines; **to ~ Socialist** voter socialiste; **to ~ for the Socialists** voter pour les socialistes; **~ (for) Harris!** votez Harris!; **to ~ for sth** voter pour *or* en faveur de qch; (*Parl*) **to ~ for a bill** voter une loi; **to ~ on sth** mettre qch au vote; (*fig*) **to ~ with one's feet***(= *go elsewhere*) partir en signe de mécontentement, montrer son désaccord en partant; **people are voting with their feet***le verdict de l'opinion publique est clair

4 COMP ► **vote-catching***ADJ (*pej*) électoraliste ► **vote-loser***N **it's a ~-loser (for us)** ça risque de nous faire perdre des voix, c'est un point mort pour nous ► **vote-winner***N atout *m* électoral; **they hope it will be a ~-winner for them** ils espèrent que cela leur fera gagner des voix

► **vote down** VT SEP rejeter (*par le vote*)

► **vote in** VT SEP [+ *law*] adopter, voter; [+ *person*] élire

► **vote out** VT SEP [+ *amendment*] rejeter; [+ *MP, chairman etc*] ne pas réélire, sortir*; **he was ~d out (of office)** il n'a pas été réélu; **he was ~d out by a large majority** il a été battu à une forte majorité; **the electors ~d the Conservative government out** les électeurs ont rejeté le gouvernement conservateur

► **vote through** VT SEP [+ *bill, motion*] voter, ratifier

voter ['vəʊtə'] 1 N électeur *m*, -trice *f* 2 COMP ► **voter registration** N (*US Pol*) inscription *f* sur les listes électorales ► **voter registration card** N carte *f* d'électeur → **turnout**

voting ['vəʊtɪŋ] 1 N (*NonC*) vote *m*, scrutin

m; **the ~ went against him** le vote lui a été défavorable; **the ~ took place yesterday** le scrutin a eu lieu hier 2 COMP ► **voting booth** N isoloir *m* ► **voting machine** N (*US*) machine *f* pour enregistrer les votes ► **voting paper** N bulletin *m* de vote ► **voting precinct** N (*US Pol*) circonscription *f* électorale ► **voting rights** NPL droit *m* de vote ► **voting share** N (*Fin*) action *f* avec droit de vote

votive ['vəʊtɪv] ADJ votif

vouch [vaʊtʃ] VI **to ~ for sb/sth** se porter garant de qn/qch, répondre de qn/qch; **to ~ for the truth of sth** garantir la vérité de qch

voucher ['vaʊtʃə'] N a (= *coupon*: *for cash, meals, petrol*) bon *m* → **luncheon** b (= *receipt*) reçu *m*, récépissé *m*; (*for debt*) quittance *f*

vouchsafe [vaʊtʃ'seɪf] VT (*frm*) [+ *reply*] accorder; [+ *help, privilege*] accorder, octroyer; **to ~ to do sth** accepter gracieusement de faire qch; (*pej*) condescendre à faire qch; **it is not ~d to everyone to understand such things** il n'est pas donné à tout le monde de comprendre ce genre de choses; **he has not ~d an answer** il n'a pas jugé bon de nous donner une réponse

vow [vaʊ] 1 N vœu *m*, serment *m*; **to take a ~** faire vœu (**to do** de faire, **of sth** de qch); **the ~s which he took when ...** les vœux qu'il a faits quand ...; (*Rel*) **to take one's ~s** prononcer ses vœux; **to make a ~ = to vow**; → **2**; **~ of celibacy** vœu *m* de célibat; **to take a ~ of chastity** faire vœu de chasteté; **to take a ~ of obedience (to)** (*Rel*) faire vœu d'obéissance (à); (*Hist*) jurer obéissance (à); **she swore a ~ of secrecy** elle a juré *or* elle a fait le serment de ne rien divulguer → **break** 2 VT a (*publicly*) jurer (**to do** de faire, **that** que); [+ *obedience, loyalty etc*] faire vœu de; **to ~ vengeance on sb** jurer de se venger de qn b (*to oneself*) se jurer (**to do** de faire, **that** que); **he ~ed (to himself) that he would remain there** il s'est juré d'y rester

vowel ['vaʊəl] 1 N voyelle *f* 2 COMP [*system, sound*] vocalique ► **vowel shift** N mutation *f* vocalique

vox pop*[ˌvɒks'pɒp] N micro-trottoir *m*

voyage ['vɔɪɪdʒ] 1 N (*Naut*) voyage *m* par mer, traversée *f*; (*fig*) voyage *m*; **to go on a ~** partir en voyage (par mer); **the ~ across the Atlantic** la traversée de l'Atlantique; **the ~ out** le voyage d'aller; **the ~ back** *or* **home** le voyage de retour; **on the ~ out/home** à l'aller/au retour; **a ~ of discovery** un voyage d'exploration 2 VT (*Naut*) traverser, parcourir 3 VI (*Naut*) voyager par mer; **to ~ across** traverser

voyager ['vɔɪədʒə'] N (= *traveller*) passager *m*, -ère *f*, voyageur *m*, -euse *f*; (*Hist* = *explorer*) navigateur *m*

voyageur [ˌvɔɪə'dʒɜː] N (*Can Hist*) trappeur ou batelier etc assurant la liaison entre différents comptoirs

voyeur [vwa:'jɜː'] N voyeur *m*

voyeurism ['vwa:jɜːˌrɪzəm] N voyeurisme *m*

voyeuristic [ˌvwa:jɜː'rɪstɪk] ADJ [*behaviour*] de voyeur; [*activity*] qui frise le voyeurisme; [*film, book*] qui sombre dans le voyeurisme

VP [viː'piː] N (*US*) (ABBR = **Vice-President**) → **vice-**

VPL*N (ABBR = **visible panty line**) → **visible**

VR [viː'ɑː'] N (ABBR = **virtual reality**) → **virtual**

vroom [vru:m] EXCL vroum!

vs (ABBR = **versus**) VS, contre

VSO [ˌviːes'əʊ] N (*Brit*) (ABBR = **Voluntary Service Overseas**) → **voluntary**

VSOP [ˌviːesəʊ'piː] (ABBR = **Very Special Old Pale**) (*brandy, port*) VSOP

VT ABBR = **Vermont**

Vt. ABBR = **Vermont**

VTOL [ˌviːti:əʊ'el] ABBR = **vertical takeoff and landing** N a ~ (**aircraft**) ADAV *m*, VTOL *m* b (= *technique*) décollage *m* et atterrissage *m* verticaux

Vulcan ['vʌlkən] N (*Myth*) Vulcain *m*

vulcanite ['vʌlkənaɪt] N ébonite *f*

vulcanization [ˌvʌlkənar'zeɪʃən] N vulcanisation *f*

vulcanize ['vʌlkənaɪz] VT vulcaniser

vulcanologist [ˌvʌlkə'nɒlədʒɪst] N volcanologue *mf*

vulcanology [ˌvʌlkə'nɒlədʒɪ] N volcanologie *f*

vulgar ['vʌlgə'] 1 ADJ a (= *impolite*) vulgaire; **it is ~ to talk about money** il est vulgaire de parler d'argent b (*Ling* = *vernacular*) [*language, tongue*] vulgaire 2 COMP ► **vulgar fraction** N (*Math*) fraction *f* ordinaire ► **Vulgar Latin** N latin *m* vulgaire

vulgarian [vʌl'gɛərɪən] N (*pej*) personne *f* vulgaire, parvenu(e) *m(f)*

vulgarism ['vʌlgərɪzəm] N a (= *uneducated expression*) vulgarisme *m* b (= *swearword*) gros mot *m*, grossièreté *f*

vulgarity [vʌl'gærɪtɪ] N vulgarité *f*, grossièreté *f*

vulgarization [ˌvʌlgəraɪ'zeɪʃən] N vulgarisation *f*

vulgarize ['vʌlgəraɪz] VT a (*frm* = *make known*) vulgariser, populariser b (= *make coarse*) rendre vulgaire

vulgarly ['vʌlgəlɪ] ADV a (= *generally*) vulgairement, communément b (= *coarsely*) vulgairement, grossièrement

Vulgate ['vʌlgɪt] N Vulgate *f*

vulnerability [ˌvʌlnərə'bɪlɪtɪ] N vulnérabilité *f*

vulnerable ['vʌlnərəbl] ADJ vulnérable (**to sth** à qch); **to find sb's ~ spot** trouver le point faible de qn

vulture ['vʌltʃə'] N (*lit, fig*) vautour *m*; (*Orn*) **black ~** moine *m*

vulva ['vʌlvə] N (*pl* **vulvas** *or* **vulvae** ['vʌlviː]) vulve *f*

vying ['vaɪɪŋ] N rivalité *f*, concurrence *f*

W

W, w ['dʌblju] N a (= letter) W, w m; **W for Willie** ≈ W comme William b (ABBR = **watt**) W c (ABBR = **west**) O., ouest

W. ABBR = **Wales, Welsh**

WA ABBR = **Washington**

wacko* ['wækəʊ] 1 ADJ = **wacky** 2 N cinglé(e)* m(f)

wacky* ['wæki] 1 ADJ loufoque* 2 COMP ► **wacky baccy*** N (Brit: hum) herbe* f (marijuana)

wad [wɒd] 1 N a (= plug, ball) [of cloth, paper] tampon m; [of putty, chewing gum] boulette f; [for gun] bourre f; [of straw] bouchon m; **a ~ of cotton wool** un tampon d'ouate; **a ~ of tobacco** (uncut) une carotte de tabac; (for chewing) une chique de tabac b (= bundle, pile) [of papers, documents] tas m, pile f; (tied together) liasse f; [of banknotes] liasse f c **~s** or **a ~ of cash*** (= lots of money) des paquets mpl de fric* 2 VT a (also **~ up**) [+ paper, cloth, cotton wool] faire un tampon de; [+ putty, chewing gum] faire une boulette de b [+ garment] doubler d'ouate, ouater; [+ quilt] rembourrer c (also **~ up**) [+ hole, crack] boucher avec un tampon or une boulette

wadding ['wɒdɪŋ] N (NonC) (= raw cotton or felt: also for gun) bourre f; (gen: for lining or padding) rembourrage m, capiton m; (for garments) ouate f

waddle ['wɒdl] 1 VI [duck] se dandiner; [person] se dandiner, marcher comme un canard; **to ~ in/out/across** etc entrer/sortir/traverser etc en se dandinant 2 N dandinement m

wade [weɪd] 1 VI a (= paddle) **to go wading** barboter; **to ~ through water/mud/long grass** avancer or marcher dans l'eau/la boue/l'herbe haute; **he ~d ashore** il a regagné la rive à pied; **to ~ across a river** traverser une rivière à gué b (* = advance with difficulty) **to ~ through a crowd** se frayer un chemin à travers une foule; **I managed to ~ through his book** je suis (péniblement) venu à bout de son livre; **it took me an hour to ~ through your essay** il m'a fallu une heure pour venir à bout de votre dissertation; **he was wading through his homework** il s'échinait sur ses devoirs c (= attack) **to ~ into sb*** (physically) se jeter or tomber or se ruer sur qn; (verbally) tomber sur qn, prendre qn à partie 2 VT [+ stream] passer or traverser à gué
► **wade in*** VI (in fight/argument etc) se mettre de la partie (dans une bagarre/dispute etc)

wader ['weɪdə'] N a (= boot) cuissarde f, botte f de pêcheur b (= bird) échassier m

wadge [wɒdʒ] N = **wodge**

wadi ['wɒdɪ] N (pl **wadies**) oued m

wading ['weɪdɪŋ] 1 N (NonC) barbotage m, pataugeage m 2 COMP ► **wading bird** N échassier m ► **wading pool** N (US) petit bassin m

wafer ['weɪfə'] 1 N a (Culin) gaufrette f; (Rel) hostie f; (= seal) cachet m (de papier rouge) b (Comput, Elec) tranche f; **silicon ~** tranche f de silicium 2 COMP ► **wafer-thin** ADJ mince comme du papier à cigarette or comme une pelure d'oignon

wafery ['weɪfəri] ADJ = **wafer-thin**; → **wafer**

waffle[1] ['wɒfl] 1 N (Culin) gaufre f 2 COMP ► **waffle iron** N gaufrier m

waffle[2]* ['wɒfl] (Brit) 1 N (NonC) (when speaking) verbiage m; (in book, essay) remplissage m, délayage m; **there's too much ~ in this essay** il y a trop de remplissage or de délayage dans cette dissertation 2 VI (when speaking) parler pour ne rien dire; (in book, essay) faire du remplissage or du délayage; **he was waffling on about ...** il parlait interminablement de ...

waffler* ['wɒflə'] N (Brit) personne f qui fait du verbiage

waft [wɑːft] 1 VT [+ smell, sound] porter, apporter; (also **~ along**) [+ boat] faire avancer, pousser; [+ clouds] faire glisser or avancer 2 VI [sound, smell] flotter 3 N [of air, scent] (petite) bouffée f

wag[1] [wæg] 1 VT [animal] [+ tail] remuer; **the dog ~ged its tail (at me)** le chien a remué la queue (en me voyant); **he ~ged his finger/his pencil at me** il a agité le doigt/son crayon dans ma direction; **to ~ one's head** hocher la tête 2 VI [tail] remuer; (excitedly) frétiller; (fig) **his tongue never stops ~ging** il a la langue bien pendue, il ne s'arrête jamais de bavarder; (fig) **tongues are ~ging** les langues vont bon train, ça fait jaser; **the news set tongues ~ging** la nouvelle a fait marcher les langues or a fait jaser (les gens) 3 N [of tail] remuement m; (excitedly) frétillement m; **with a ~ of its tail** en remuant la queue

wag[2]† [wæg] N (= joker) plaisantin m, farceur m, -euse f

wage [weɪdʒ] 1 N salaire m, paie or paye f; [of domestic servant] gages mpl; **weekly/hourly ~** salaire m hebdomadaire/horaire; **I've lost two days' ~s** j'ai perdu deux jours de salaire or de paie; **his week's ~s** son salaire or sa paye de la semaine; **his ~ is** or **his ~s are £250 per week** il touche un salaire de 250 livres par semaine; **he gets a good ~** il est bien payé, il a un bon salaire; (Bible) **the ~s of sin is death** la mort est le salaire du péché → **living** 2 VT **to ~ war** faire la guerre (**against** à, contre); **to ~ a campaign** faire campagne (**against** contre), mener une campagne (**for** pour) 3 COMP ► **wage bargaining** N (NonC) négociations fpl salariales ► **wage bill** N = **wages bill** ► **wage claim** N = **wages claim** ► **wage clerk** N = **wages clerk** ► **wage demand** N = **wages claim** ► **wage differential** N écart m salarial or de salaires ► **wage drift** N dérapage m salarial, dérive f des salaires ► **wage earner** N salarié(e) m(f); **she is the family ~ earner** c'est elle qui fait vivre la famille or qui est le soutien de la famille; **we are both ~ earners** nous gagnons tous les deux notre vie ► **wage freeze** N = **wages freeze** ► **wage increase** N augmentation f or hausse f de salaire ► **wage packet** N (esp Brit) (lit) enveloppe f de paie; (fig) paie or paye f ► **wage-price spiral** N spirale f prix-salaires ► **wage-push inflation** N inflation f par les salaires ► **wage rates** NPL niveau m des salaires ► **wage restraint** N limitation f des salaires ► **wage rise** N = **wage increase** ► **wages bill** N masse f salariale ► **wage scale** N échelle f des salaires ► **wages claim** N (Brit) revendication f salariale ► **wages clerk** N employé(e) m(f) au service de la paie, ≈ aide-comptable mf ► **wage settlement** N = **wages settlement** ► **wages freeze** N blocage m des salaires ► **wage slave** N (hum) **I'm a ~ slave** je ne suis qu'un pauvre salarié ► **wage slip** N = **wages slip** ► **wage spread** N (US) éventail m des salaires ► **wages settlement** N accord m salarial ► **wages slip** N bulletin m de salaire, fiche f de paie ► **wage worker** N (US) = **wage earner**

waged [weɪdʒd] ADJ [person] salarié

wager ['weɪdʒə'] 1 VT parier (**on** sur, **that** que) 2 N pari m; **to lay a ~** faire un pari

waggish† ['wægɪʃ] ADJ badin, facétieux

waggishly† ['wægɪʃlɪ] ADV [say] d'une manière facétieuse, d'un ton facétieux or badin; [smile] avec facétie

waggle ['wægl] 1 VT [+ pencil, branch] agiter; [+ loose screw, button] faire jouer; [+ one's toes, fingers, ears] remuer; [+ loose tooth] faire bouger; **he ~d his finger at me** il a agité le doigt dans ma direction; **to ~ one's hips** tortiller des hanches 2 VI [toes, fingers, ears] remuer; [tail] remuer; (excitedly) frétiller; **his hips ~d as he walked** il tortillait des hanches en marchant

waggon ['wægən] N (esp Brit) = **wagon**

Wagnerian [vɑːg'nɪərɪən] ADJ wagnérien

wagon ['wægən] 1 N (horse- or ox-drawn) chariot m; (= truck) camion m; (Brit Rail) wagon m (de marchandises); (US: also **station ~**) break m; (US = police van) **the ~*** le panier à salade*; (fig) **to go/be on the ~*** ne plus/ne pas boire (d'alcool), se mettre/être au régime sec; **he's off the ~ (again)*** il s'est remis à boire; (fig) **to circle the ~s ◊ to pull one's ~s in a circle** se serrer les coudes (pour faire front) → **station** 2 COMP ► **wagon train** N (US Hist) convoi m de chariots

wagoner ['wægənə'] N roulier m, charretier m

wagonette [,wægə'net] N break† m (hippomobile)

wagonload ['wægənləʊd] N (Agr) charretée f; (Rail) wagon m

wagtail ['wægteɪl] N (Orn) hochequeue m, lavandière f

wah-wah pedal ['wɑːwɑː,pedl] N (Mus) pédale f wah-wah

waif [weɪf] N enfant mf misérable; (homeless) enfant m(f) abandonné(e); **~s and strays** enfants mpl abandonnés

wail [weɪl] 1 N [of person, wind] gémissement m, plainte f; [of baby] vagissement m; [of siren] hurlement m ; **to give a ~** pousser un gémissement or un vagissement, gémir, vagir [2] VI [person] gémir, pousser un or des gémissement(s) ; (= cry) pleurer ; (= whine) pleurnicher ; [baby] vagir ; [wind] gémir ; [siren] hurler ; [bagpipes etc] gémir

wailing ['weɪlɪŋ] [1] N (NonC) [of person, wind] gémissements mpl, plaintes fpl ; (= whining) pleurnicheries fpl ; [of baby] vagissements mpl ; [of siren] hurlement m ; [of bagpipes] gémissement m [2] ADJ [voice, person] gémissant ; [sound] plaintif [3] COMP ► **the Wailing Wall** le mur des Lamentations

wain [weɪn] N (liter) chariot m ; (Astron) **Charles's Wain** le Chariot de David, la Grande Ourse

wainscot ['weɪnskət] N lambris m (en bois)

wainscot(t)ing ['weɪnskətɪŋ] N lambrissage m (en bois)

waist [weɪst] [1] N [a] (Anat, Dress) taille f ; **he put his arm round her ~** il l'a prise par la taille ; **she measures 70cm round the ~** elle fait 70 cm de tour de taille ; **they were stripped to the ~** ils étaient nus jusqu'à la ceinture, ils étaient torse nu ; **he was up to the** or **his ~ in water** l'eau lui arrivait à la ceinture or à mi-corps [b] (= narrow part) [of jar, vase etc] étranglement m, resserrement m ; [of violin] partie f resserrée de la table [c] (US) (= blouse) corsage m, blouse f ; (= bodice) corsage m, haut m [2] VT [+ jacket etc] cintrer [3] COMP ► **waist measurement**, **waist size** N tour m de taille ► **waist slip** N jupon m

waistband ['weɪstbænd] N ceinture f

waistcoat ['weɪskəʊt] N (Brit) gilet m

-waisted ['weɪstɪd] ADJ (in compounds) **to be slim-waisted** avoir la taille fine ; **high-/low-waisted dress** robe f à taille haute/basse → **shirtwaist**

waistline ['weɪstlaɪn] N taille f ; (hum) **I've got to think of my ~** je dois faire attention à ma ligne

wait [weɪt] [1] N [a] attente f ; **you'll have a three-hour ~** vous aurez trois heures d'attente or à attendre ; **it was a long ~** il a fallu attendre longtemps, l'attente a été longue ; (= pause: on coach journey etc) **there is a half-hour ~ at Leeds** il y a un arrêt d'une demi-heure or une demi-heure d'arrêt à Leeds ; **there was a 20-minute ~ between trains** il y avait 20 minutes de battement or d'attente entre les trains ; **during the ~ between the performances** pendant le battement or la pause entre les représentations ; **to be** or **lie in ~ for** [huntsman, lion] guetter ; [bandits, guerrillas] dresser un guet-apens or une embuscade à ; **the journalists lay in ~ for him as he left the theatre** les journalistes l'attendaient (au passage) à sa sortie du théâtre or le guettaient à sa sortie du théâtre [b] (Brit) **the ~s** les chanteurs mpl de Noël (qui vont de porte en porte)

[2] VI [a] attendre ; **to ~ for sb/sth** attendre qn/qch ; **to ~ for sb to leave** attendre le départ de qn, attendre que qn parte ; **we ~ed and ~ed** nous avons attendu à n'en plus finir ; **to keep sb ~ing** faire attendre qn ; **don't keep us ~ing** ne te fais pas attendre, ne nous fais pas attendre ; **I was kept ~ing in the corridor** on m'a fait attendre dans le couloir, j'ai fait le pied de grue dans le couloir ; **to ~ until sb leaves** attendre que qn parte ; **~ till you're old enough** attends d'être assez grand ; **can you ~ till 10 o'clock?** pouvez-vous attendre jusqu'à 10 heures ? ; **parcel ~ing to be collected** colis m en souffrance ; (Comm) **"repairs while you ~"** « réparations minute » ; (Comm) **they do it while you ~** ils le font pendant que vous attendez
[b] (fig) **just you ~!** tu vas voir ce que tu vas voir! ; **just ~ till your father finds out!** attends un peu que ton père apprenne ça! ; **all that can ~ till tomorrow** tout cela peut attendre

jusqu'à demain ; **I just can't ~ for next Saturday!** je meurs d'impatience or d'envie d'être à samedi prochain! ; (longingly) **I can't ~ to see him again!** je meurs d'envie de le revoir! ; **I can't ~ for the day when this happens** je rêve du jour où cela arrivera ; **the Conservatives can't ~ to reverse this policy** les conservateurs brûlent de révoquer cette politique ; (Brit) **~ for it!*** (= order to wait) attendez! ; (= guess what) devinez quoi!* ; ~ → **4** ; **we'll have to ~ and see** il va falloir attendre, il va falloir voir venir ; **~ and see what happens next** attendez voir ce qui va se passer ; **that was worth ~ing for** cela valait la peine d'attendre ; **everything comes to he who ~s** tout vient à point à qui sait attendre (PROV)
[c] servir ; **to ~ (at table)** servir à table, faire le service

[3] VT [a] [+ signal, orders, one's turn] attendre ; **I ~ed two hours** j'ai attendu (pendant) deux heures ; **could you ~ a moment?** vous pouvez patienter un moment ? ; **~ a moment** or **a minute** or **a second!** (attendez) un instant or une minute! ; (interrupting, querying) minute! ; **to ~ one's moment** or **chance (to do sth)** attendre son heure (pour faire qch)) ; (esp US) **we'll ~ lunch for you** nous vous attendrons pour nous mettre à table
[b] (esp US) **to ~ table** servir à table, faire le service

[4] COMP ► **wait-and-see tactics** NPL (Pol etc) attentisme m ► **wait-listed** ADJ (Travel) **to be ~-listed on a flight** être sur la liste d'attente d'un vol

► **wait about**, **wait around** VI attendre ; (= loiter) traîner ; **to ~ about for sb** attendre qn, faire le pied de grue pour qn ; **the job involves a lot of ~ing about** on perd beaucoup de temps à attendre dans ce métier ; **you can't expect him to ~ about all day while you ...** tu ne peux pas exiger qu'il traîne (subj) toute la journée en t'attendant pendant que tu ...

► **wait behind** VI rester ; **to ~ behind for sb** rester pour attendre qn

► **wait in** VI (esp Brit) rester à la maison (for sb pour attendre qn)

► **wait on** VT FUS [a] [servant, waiter] servir ; **I'm not here to ~ on him!** je ne suis pas sa bonne or son valet de chambre! ; **she ~s on him hand and foot** elle est aux petits soins pour lui [b] (frm) = **wait upon** [c] (Scot, N Engl) attendre ; **I'm ~ing on him finishing** j'attends qu'il finisse ; **~ on!** attends!

► **wait out** VT SEP **to ~ it out** patienter

► **wait up** VI (= not go to bed) ne pas se coucher, veiller ; **we ~ed up till 2 o'clock** nous avons veillé or attendu jusqu'à 2 heures, nous ne nous sommes pas couchés avant 2 heures ; **she always ~s up for him** elle attend toujours qu'il rentre (subj) pour se coucher, elle ne se couche jamais avant qu'il ne soit rentré ; **don't ~ up (for me)** couchez-vous sans m'attendre ; **you can ~ up to see the programme** tu peux te coucher plus tard pour regarder l'émission

► **wait upon** VT FUS [a] (frm) [ambassador, envoy etc] présenter ses respects à [b] = **wait on a**

waiter ['weɪtə'] N garçon m de café, serveur m ; **~!** Monsieur or garçon, s'il vous plaît ! → **dumbwaiter**, **head**, **wine**

waiting ['weɪtɪŋ] [1] N (NonC) attente f ; (on road sign) **"no ~"** « arrêt interdit » ; **all this ~!** ce qu'on attend!, dire qu'il faut attendre si longtemps! ; (frm) **to be in ~ on sb** être attaché au service de qn → **lady** [2] ADJ qui attend [3] COMP ► **waiting game** N (fig) **to play a ~ game** (gen) attendre son heure ; (in diplomacy, negotiations etc) mener une politique d'attente, se conduire en attentiste ► **waiting list** N liste f d'attente ► **waiting room** N salle f d'attente

waitress ['weɪtrɪs] [1] N serveuse f ; **~!** Made-

moiselle (or Madame), s'il vous plaît ! [2] VI travailler comme serveuse

waitressing ['weɪtrɪsɪŋ] N (NonC) travail m de serveuse

waive [weɪv] VT (Jur) (= relinquish) [+ one's claim, right, privilege] renoncer à, ne pas insister sur ; (= relax) [+ condition, age limit] ne pas insister sur ; (= abolish) [+ sb's rights] abolir

waiver ['weɪvə'] N [of law] dérogation f (of à) ; [of requirement] (= abolition) annulation f (of de) ; (= relaxing) dispense f (of de) ; [of right] (= relinquishing) renonciation f (of à) ; (= abolition) abolition f (of de) ; (Insurance) clause f de renonciation ; **to sign a ~ (of responsibility)** signer une décharge ; **tax/visa ~** exemption f d'impôts/de visa

wake¹ [weɪk] N [of ship] sillage m, eaux fpl ; (fig) **in the ~ of the storm/unrest/dispute** à la suite de l'orage/des troubles/du conflit ; **in the ~ of the army** dans le sillage or sur les traces de l'armée ; **the war brought famine in its ~** la guerre a amené la famine dans son sillage ; **to follow in sb's ~** marcher sur les traces de qn or dans le sillage de qn

wake² [weɪk] (vb: pret **woke**, **waked**, ptp **waked**, **woken**, **woke**) [1] N [a] (over corpse) veillée f mortuaire
[b] (N Engl) **Wakes (Week)** semaine de congé annuel dans le nord de l'Angleterre

[2] VI (also **~ up**) se réveiller, s'éveiller (from de) ; **~ up!** réveille-toi! ; (fig) **~ up (to yourself)!*** (= think what you're doing) tu ne te rends pas compte! ; (US) **~ up and smell the coffee!*** arrête de rêver! ; **to ~ from sleep** se réveiller, s'éveiller ; **to ~ (up) from a nightmare** (lit) se réveiller d'un cauchemar ; (fig) sortir d'un cauchemar ; **she woke (up) to find them gone** en se réveillant or à son réveil elle s'est aperçue qu'ils étaient partis ; **he woke up (to find himself) in prison** il s'est réveillé en prison ; **he woke up to find himself rich** à son réveil il était riche ; (fig) **to ~ (up) to sth** prendre conscience de or se rendre compte de qch ; **to ~ (up) from one's illusions** revenir de ses illusions ; (fig) **he suddenly woke up and started to work hard** (= stirred himself) il s'est tout à coup réveillé or remué et s'est mis à travailler dur ; (fig) **he suddenly woke up and realized that ...** (= understood) tout à coup ses yeux se sont ouverts et il s'est rendu compte que ...

[3] VT (also **~ up**) [+ person] réveiller (from de), tirer du sommeil ; (fig) [+ memories] (r)éveiller, ranimer ; [+ desires] éveiller ; **a noise that would ~ the dead** un bruit à réveiller les morts ; (fig) **he needs something to ~ him up** il aurait besoin d'être secoué

[4] COMP ► **wake-up call** N [a] (Telec) réveil m téléphonique, mémo appel m [b] (esp US = warning) avertissement m

wakeful ['weɪkfʊl] ADJ [a] (= unable to sleep) éveillé ; **I had a ~ night** (awake part of night) je n'ai pratiquement pas dormi de la nuit, j'ai mal dormi ; (didn't sleep at all) j'ai passé une nuit blanche, je n'ai pas dormi de la nuit [b] (frm = vigilant) [person] vigilant

wakefulness ['weɪkfʊlnɪs] N [a] (= sleeplessness) insomnie f [b] (frm = watchfulness) vigilance f

waken ['weɪkən] VTI = **wake²**

waker ['weɪkə'] N **to be an early ~** se réveiller tôt

wakey-wakey* ['weɪkɪ'weɪkɪ] EXCL réveillez-vous!, debout !

waking ['weɪkɪŋ] [1] ADJ **in one's ~ hours** pendant les heures de veille ; **he devoted all his ~ hours to ...** il consacrait chaque heure de sa journée à ... ; **~ or sleeping, he ...** (qu'il soit) éveillé ou endormi, il ... [2] N (état m de) veille f ; **between ~ and sleeping** dans un (état de) demi-sommeil ③ COMP ► **waking dream** N rêve m éveillé

Waldorf salad [ˌwɔːldɔːfˈsæləd] N (Culin) salade f Waldorf (composée de pommes, noix, céleri et mayonnaise)

wale [weɪl] N (US) = **weal**¹

Wales [weɪlz] N le pays de Galles; **in ~** au pays de Galles; **North/South ~** le Nord/le Sud du pays de Galles; (Brit) **Secretary of State for ~** ministre m des Affaires galloises → **prince**

walk [wɔːk] ① N ⓐ (= stroll) promenade f; (= ramble) randonnée f; **to go for a country ~** faire une promenade à la campagne; **to go for a ~ ◊ to take** or **have a ~** se promener, faire une promenade; (shorter) faire un tour; **let's have a** or **go for a little ~** promenons-nous un peu, allons faire un petit tour; **he had a long ~** il a fait une grande promenade; **we went on a long ~ to see the castle** nous avons fait une excursion (à pied) pour visiter le château; **on their ~ to school** en allant à l'école (à pied), sur le chemin de l'école; **on their ~ home** en rentrant chez eux (à pied); **the Post Office is on my ~ home (from work)** le bureau de poste est sur mon chemin quand je rentre chez moi (du travail); **to take sb for a ~** emmener qn se promener or en promenade; **to take the dog for a ~** promener le chien; **to do a 10-km ~** faire une promenade de 10 km; **the house is ten minutes' ~ from here** la maison est à dix minutes de marche d'ici or à dix minutes à pied d'ici; **it's only a short ~ to the shops** il n'y a pas loin à marcher jusqu'aux magasins, il n'y a pas loin pour aller aux magasins; **(go) take a ~!*** fous le camp!‡, dégage!*; (US fig) **in a ~*** (= easily) [win] dans un fauteuil*; [do sth] les doigts dans le nez* → **sponsor**

ⓑ (= gait) démarche f, façon f de marcher; **I knew him by his ~** je l'ai reconnu à sa démarche or à sa façon de marcher

ⓒ (= pace) he slowed down to a ~ il a ralenti pour aller au pas; **you've got plenty of time to get there at a ~** vous avez tout le temps pour y arriver sans courir; **she set off at a brisk ~** elle est partie d'un bon pas

ⓓ (= path, route: in country) chemin m, sentier m; (= avenue) avenue f, promenade f; **a coastal ~** un chemin côtier; **there's a nice ~ by the river** il y a un joli chemin or sentier le long de la rivière, il y a une jolie promenade à faire le long de la rivière; (fig) **people from all ~s** or **every ~ of life** des gens de tous (les) horizons

ⓔ (US: also **sidewalk**) trottoir m

ⓕ (Sport = walking race) épreuve f de marche

② VI ⓐ (gen) marcher; (= not run) aller au pas, ne pas courir; **I haven't ~ed since the accident** je n'ai pas (re)marché depuis l'accident; **I can't ~ as I used to** je ne marche plus mes jambes d'autrefois; **to learn to ~** [baby, injured person] apprendre à marcher; **to ~ across the road** traverser la route; **you should always ~ across the road** on ne doit jamais traverser la rue en courant; **to ~ across/down** etc traverser/descendre etc (à pied or sans courir); **to ~ up/down the stairs** (gen = went up/down) il a monté/descendu l'escalier; (= didn't run) il a monté/descendu l'escalier sans courir; **he was up and down** il marchait de long en large, il faisait les cent pas; **don't ~ on the grass** ne marchez pas sur la pelouse; (on sign) «pelouse interdite»; **to ~ with a stick/with crutches** marcher avec une canne/des béquilles, marcher à l'aide d'une canne/de béquilles; **I'll ~ with you** je vais vous accompagner; **to ~ in one's sleep** être somnambule, marcher en dormant; **she was ~ing in her sleep** elle marchait en dormant; (fig) **you must learn to ~ before you can run** avant de vouloir courir il faut savoir marcher; **~, don't run** ne cours pas; (US: at pedestrian crossing) **"~/don't ~"** «(piétons) traversez/attendez»

ⓑ (= not ride or drive) aller à pied; (= go for a

walk) se promener, faire une promenade; **they ~ed all the way to the village** ils ont fait tout le chemin à pied jusqu'au village; **I always ~ home** je rentre toujours à pied; **shall we ~ a little?** si nous faisions quelques pas?, si nous marchions un peu?; (longer walk) si nous nous promenions un peu?; **they were out ~ing** ils étaient partis se promener (à pied)

ⓒ [ghost] apparaître

ⓓ * (fig hum) [object] disparaître, se volatiliser; **my pen seems to have ~ed** mon stylo a disparu or s'est volatilisé

ⓔ (* = be acquitted) être acquitté

③ VT ⓐ [+ distance] faire à pied; **he ~s 5km every day** il fait 5 km (de marche) à pied par jour; **you can ~ it in a couple of minutes** vous y serez en deux minutes à pied, à pied vous en avez pour deux minutes; **he ~ed it in ten minutes** il l'a fait à pied en dix minutes, il lui a fallu dix minutes à pied; (fig) **he ~ed it*** (= it was easy) cela a été un jeu d'enfant pour lui

ⓑ [+ town etc] parcourir; **to ~ the streets** se promener dans les rues; (to fill in time) flâner dans les rues; (from poverty) errer dans les rues, battre le pavé; [prostitute] faire le trottoir; **he ~ed the town looking for a dentist** il a parcouru la ville en tous sens à la recherche d'un dentiste; **they ~ed the countryside in search of ...** ils ont battu la campagne à la recherche de ...; **I've ~ed this road many times** j'ai pris cette route (à pied) bien des fois

ⓒ (= cause to walk) [+ dog] promener; [+ horse] conduire à pied; **to ~ sb in/out** etc faire entrer/sortir etc qn; **to ~ sb home** raccompagner qn (chez lui or elle); **he seized my arm and ~ed me across the room** il m'a pris par le bras et m'a fait traverser la pièce; **I had to ~ my bike home** j'ai dû pousser mon vélo jusqu'à la maison; **to ~ a cooker/chest of drawers across a room** pousser une cuisinière/une commode petit à petit d'un bout à l'autre d'une pièce (en la faisant pivoter d'un pied sur l'autre); **the nurse ~ed him down the ward to exercise his legs** l'infirmier l'a fait marcher or se promener dans la salle pour qu'il s'exerce (subj) les jambes; **they ~ed him off his feet** ils l'ont tellement fait marcher qu'il ne tenait plus debout; **I ~ed him round Paris** je l'ai promené dans Paris; **I ~ed him round the garden to show him the plants** je lui ai fait faire le tour du jardin pour lui montrer les plantes; **I ~ed him round the garden till he was calmer** je me suis promené avec lui dans le jardin jusqu'à ce qu'il se calme (subj); **I'll ~ you to the station** je vais vous accompagner (à pied) à la gare; **he ~ed her to her car** il l'a raccompagnée jusqu'à sa voiture

④ COMP ► **walk-in** ADJ [wardrobe, cupboard, larder] de plain-pied; **in ~ condition** [flat, house] habitable immédiatement ► **walk-on part** N (Theat) rôle m de figurant(e), figuration f ► **walk-through** N (Theat etc) répétition f technique ► **walk-up** N (US) (= house) immeuble m sans ascenseur; (= apartment) appartement m dans un immeuble sans ascenseur

► **walk about** ① VI = **walk around** ② **~about*** N → **walkabout**

► **walk across** VI (over bridge etc) traverser; **to ~ across to sb** s'approcher de qn, se diriger vers qn

► **walk around** VI se promener; **within two days of the accident, she was ~ing around** deux jours après l'accident, elle marchait de nouveau; **stand up and ~ around a little to see how the shoes feel** levez-vous et faites quelques pas pour voir comment vous vous sentez dans ces chaussures

► **walk away** ① VI partir; **to ~ away from sb** s'éloigner de qn, quitter qn; **he ~ed away with the wrong coat** il s'est trompé de manteau en partant; **to ~ away from an accident** (= be unhurt) sortir indemne d'un acci-

dent; (fig) **to ~ away with sth** (= win easily) gagner or remporter qch haut la main; **I did the work but he ~ed away with all the credit** c'est moi qui ai fait tout le travail et c'est lui qui a reçu tous les éloges ② **~away*** N → **walkaway**

► **walk back** VI (= come back) revenir; (= go back) retourner; (= go home) rentrer; (specifically on foot) revenir or rentrer or retourner à pied

► **walk in** ① VI entrer; **who should ~ in but Paul!** et qui entre sur ces entrefaites? Paul!; **they just ~ed in and took all my money** ils sont entrés et ont pris tout mon argent; **he just ~ed in and gave me the sack** il est entré sans crier gare et m'a annoncé qu'il me mettait à la porte; **he just ~ed in on me!** il est entré sans prévenir! ② **~-in** ADJ → **walk**

► **walk into** VT FUS ⓐ [+ trap, ambush] tomber dans; **you really ~ed into that one!*** tu es vraiment tombé or tu as vraiment donné dans le panneau!; **he wondered what he had ~ed into** il se demandait dans quelle galère* il s'était laissé entraîner ⓑ (= hit against) [+ person, lamppost, table] se cogner à ⓒ (= find easily) [+ job] trouver sans problème or facilement

► **walk off** ① VI ⓐ = **walk away 1** ⓑ (= steal) **to ~ off with sth*** barboter* or faucher* qch ② VT SEP [+ excess weight] perdre en marchant; **to ~ off a headache** prendre l'air or faire une promenade pour se débarrasser d'un mal de tête

► **walk off with*** VT FUS = **walk away with** → **walk away**

► **walk on** VI (Theat) être figurant(e), jouer les utilités

► **walk out** ① VI (= go out) sortir; (= go away) partir; (as protest) partir (en signe de protestation); (= go on strike) se mettre en grève; (fig) **you can't ~ out now!** tu ne peux pas partir comme ça!, tu ne peux pas tout laisser tomber* comme ça!; **her husband has ~ed out** son mari l'a quittée or plaquée*; **they ~ed out of the meeting** ils ont quitté la réunion (en signe de protestation) ② **~out** N → **walkout**

► **walk out on*** VT FUS [+ boyfriend, business partner] laisser tomber*, plaquer*

► **walk out with†** VT FUS (Brit = court) fréquenter†

► **walk over** ① VI passer (à pied), faire un saut (à pied); **I'll ~ over tomorrow morning** j'y passerai or j'y ferai un saut (à pied) demain matin; **he ~ed over to me and said ...** il s'est approché de moi et a dit ... ② VT FUS* ⓐ (= defeat easily) battre haut la main ⓑ (= treat badly: also = all over) marcher sur les pieds de; **she lets him ~ all over her** elle se laisse marcher sur les pieds (sans jamais lui faire de reproche) ③ **~over** N → **walkover**

► **walk through** ① VT FUS (Theat) répéter les mouvements de ② **~-through** N → **walk**

► **walk up** ① VI (= go upstairs etc) monter; (= approach) s'approcher (**to sb** de qn); (at fair etc) **~ up, ~ up!** approchez, approchez!; **I saw the car and ~ed up to it** j'ai vu la voiture et m'en suis approché ② **~-up** N → **walk**

walkabout [ˈwɔːkəbaʊt] N (Austral) voyage m (d'un aborigène) dans le bush; (Brit) [president, celebrity] bain m de foule; **to go on (a) ~** (Austral = go for a walk) partir se balader* dans le bush; (Brit) [president, celebrity] prendre un bain de foule; (fig hum) **to go ~*** [object] disparaître, se volatiliser

walkathon* [ˈwɔːkəθɒn] N (US) marathon m (de marche)

walkaway* [ˈwɔːkəweɪ] N (US: also **victory** or **win**) victoire f facile

walker [ˈwɔːkəʳ] ① N ⓐ (esp Sport) marcheur m, -euse f; (for pleasure) promeneur m, -euse f; **I'm not a great ~** je ne suis pas un grand marcheur; **he's a fast ~** il marche vite → **sleepwalker, streetwalker** ⓑ (= support frame) (for invalid) déambulateur m; (for babies) trotte-bébé *m* [2] COMP ► **walker-on** N (*Theat*) figurant(e) *m(f)*, comparse *mf*

walkies* ['wɔːkɪz] N (*Brit*) **to go ~** (*lit*) aller se promener; (*fig*) disparaître

walkie-talkie ['wɔːkɪ'tɔːkɪ] N talkie-walkie *m*

walking ['wɔːkɪŋ] [1] N [a] (*NonC*) marche *f* à pied, promenade(s) *f(pl)* (à pied) → **sleepwalking**
[b] (*Sport*) marche *f* (athlétique); (*Basketball*) marcher *m*
[2] ADJ ambulant; (*Mil*) **the ~ wounded** les blessés *mpl* capables de marcher; **he's a ~ encyclopedia** c'est une encyclopédie ambulante *or* vivante; **he is a ~ miracle** c'est un miracle ambulant, il revient de loin
[3] COMP ► **walking-boot** N chaussure *f* de randonnée *or* de marche ► **walking distance** N **it is within ~ distance (of the house)** on peut facilement y aller à pied (de la maison); **five minutes' ~ distance away** à cinq minutes de marche ► **walking frame** N déambulateur *m* ► **walking holiday** N **we had a ~ holiday in the Tyrol** pour nos vacances nous avons fait de la marche dans le Tyrol ► **walking pace** N **at (a) ~ pace** au pas ► **walking papers*** NPL (*US*) **to give sb his ~ papers** renvoyer qn, mettre *or* flanquer* qn à la porte ► **walking race** N épreuve *f* de marche ► **walking shoe** N chaussure *f* de marche ► **walking stick** N canne *f* ► **walking tour, walking trip** N **to be on a ~ tour** *or* **trip** faire une randonnée à pied (de plusieurs jours)

Walkman® ['wɔːkmən] N Walkman® *m*, baladeur *m*, somnambule *m* (*Can*)

walkout ['wɔːkaʊt] N (= *strike*) grève *f* surprise; (*from meeting, lecture etc*) départ *m* (en signe de protestation); **to stage a ~** [*workers*] faire une grève surprise; [*students, delegates etc*] partir (en signe de protestation)

walkover ['wɔːkəʊvər] N (*Racing*) walk-over *m inv*; (*fig*) **it was a ~!** [*game*] c'était une victoire facile!; [*exam*] c'était un jeu d'enfant!, c'était simple comme bonjour!; (*Sport*) **it was a ~ for Moore*** Moore a gagné haut la main

walkway ['wɔːkweɪ] N (*Brit*) sentier *m* pédestre; (*US*) passage *m* pour piétons, cheminement *m* piéton

Walkyrie [væl'kɪərɪ] N Walkyrie *f*

wall [wɔːl] [1] N (*gen*) mur *m*; (*interior: also of trench, tunnel*) paroi *f*; (*round garden, field*) mur *m* (de clôture); (*round city, castle etc*) murs *mpl*, remparts *mpl*; (*Anat*) paroi *f*; (*of tyre*) flanc *m*; (*fig*) [*of mountains*] mur *m*, muraille *f*; [*of smoke, fog*] mur *m*; **within the (city) ~s** dans les murs, dans la ville; **the north ~ of the Eiger** la face nord *or* la paroi nord de l'Eiger; **they left only the bare ~s standing** ils n'ont laissé que les murs; (*Econ*) **a high tariff ~** une barrière douanière élevée; **~s have ears** les murs ont des oreilles; **to go over the ~** [*prisoner*] s'évader, se faire la belle*; (*fig*) **to go to the ~** [*person*] perdre la partie; (= *go bankrupt*) faire faillite; [*plan, activity*] être sacrifié; **it's always the weakest to the ~** ce sont toujours les plus faibles qui écopent*; (*fig*) **he had his back to the ~** ◊ **he was up against the ~** il avait le dos au mur, il était acculé; **to get sb up against the ~** ◊ **to drive** *or* **push sb to the ~** acculer qn, mettre qn au pied du mur; (*fig*) **to bang** *or* **knock** *or* **beat one's head against a (brick) ~** se taper la tête contre les murs; (*fig*) **to come up against a (blank) ~** ◊ **to come up against a stone** *or* **brick ~** se heurter à un mur; **to drive** *or* **send sb up the ~*** rendre qn dingue* *or* fou → **Berlin, great, off, party**
[2] VT [+ *garden*] entourer d'un mur, construire un mur autour de; [+ *city*] fortifier, entourer de murs *or* de remparts; **~ed garden** jardin *m* clos; **~ed town** ville *f* fortifiée
[3] COMP [*decoration, clock, map*] mural ► **wall bars** NPL espalier *m* (pour exercices de gymnasti-

que) ► **wall chart** N planche *f* murale ► **wall cupboard** N placard *m* mural *or* suspendu ► **wall lamp, wall light** N applique *f* ► **wall lighting** N éclairage *m* par appliques ► **wall-mounted** ADJ [*clock, phone*] mural ► **wall socket** N (*Elec*) prise *f* (murale). ► **Wall Street** N (*US*) Wall Street *m* ► **wall to wall** ADV **to carpet sth ~ to ~** recouvrir qch de moquette ► **wall-to-wall** ADJ **~-to-~ carpet(ing)** moquette *f*; (*fig*) **it got ~-to-~ coverage** on ne parlait que de ça (dans les médias); (*fig*) **there were ~-to-~ people** l'endroit était bondé

►**wall in** VT SEP [+ *garden etc*] entourer d'un mur

►**wall off** VT SEP [+ *plot of land*] séparer par un mur

►**wall up** VT SEP [+ *doorway, window*] murer, condamner; [+ *person, relics*] murer, emmurer

wallaby ['wɒləbɪ] N (*pl* **wallabies** *or* **wallaby**) wallaby *m*

wallah ['wɒlə] N (*Hist: in India*) **the laundry** *etc* **~** le préposé au blanchissage *etc*

wallboard ['wɔːlbɔːd] N (*US*) panneau *m* de revêtement

wallcovering ['wɔːlkʌvərɪŋ] N revêtement *m* mural

wallet ['wɒlɪt] N portefeuille *m*; (*of pilgrim etc*) besace *f*

walleye ['wɔːlaɪ] N (= *squint*) strabisme *m* divergent

walleyed ['wɔːlaɪd] ADJ atteint de strabisme divergent

wallflower ['wɔːlflaʊər] N (*Bot*) giroflée *f*; (*fig*) **to be a ~** faire tapisserie

Walloon [wɒ'luːn] [1] ADJ wallon [2] N [a] Wallon(ne) *m(f)* [b] (*Ling*) wallon *m*

wallop* ['wɒləp] [1] N (= *slap*) torgnole* *f*; (*with fist*) gnon* *m*; (*in accident*) coup *m*; (*sound*) fracas *m*, boucan* *m*; **to give sb a ~** flanquer une beigne* *or* une torgnole* à qn; **~!** vlan!; **it hit the floor with a ~** vlan! c'est tombé par terre [2] VT [+ *person*] flanquer une beigne* *or* une torgnole* à; [+ *ball, object*] taper sur, donner un *or* des grand(s) coup(s) dans [3] ADV **~ into the wall** il est rentré* en plein dans le mur

walloping* ['wɒləpɪŋ] [1] ADJ sacré* (*before n*); **~ big** vachement grand*; **a ~ £100 million** la somme astronomique de 100 millions de livres [2] N raclée* *f*, rossée* *f*; **to give sb a ~** (= *punish*) flanquer une raclée* *or* une rossée* à qn; (*Sport etc* = *beat*) enfoncer* qn, battre qn à plate(s) couture(s)

wallow ['wɒləʊ] [1] VI [*person, animal*] se vautrer (**in** dans); [*ship*] être ballotté; (*fig*) (*in vice, sin*) se vautrer (**in** dans); (*in self-pity etc*) se complaire (**in** à) [2] N [a] (= *pool, bog etc*) mare *f* bourbeuse [b] (*in bath*) **to have a ~*** se prélasser

wallpaper ['wɔːlpeɪpər] [1] N papier *m* peint [2] VT tapisser (de papier peint) [3] COMP ► **wallpaper music*** N (*pej*) musique *f* d'ascenseur (*pej*) *or* de supermarché (*pej*)

wally* ['wɒlɪ] N (*Brit*) andouille* *f*

walnut ['wɔːlnʌt] [1] N noix *f*; (*also ~ tree*) noyer *m*; (*NonC* = *wood*) noyer *m* [2] COMP [*table etc*] de *or* en noyer; [*cake*] aux noix; [*oil*] de noix

Walpurgis Night [væl'pʊəgɪsnaɪt] N la nuit de Walpurgis

walrus ['wɔːlrəs] [1] N (*pl* **walruses** *or* **walrus**) morse *m* (*Zool*) [2] COMP ► **walrus moustache** N moustache *f* à la gauloise

Walter Mitty [,wɔːltə'mɪtɪ] N **he's something of a ~ (character)** il vit dans un monde imaginaire

waltz [wɔːls] [1] N valse *f*; (*US fig*) **it was a ~!** c'était du gâteau* *or* de la tarte!* [2] VI valser, danser la valse; (*fig*) **to ~ in/out** *etc* (*gaily*) entrer/sortir *etc* d'un pas joyeux *or* dansant; (*brazenly*) entrer/sortir *etc* avec désinvolture;

she ~ed in without even knocking* elle a fait irruption sans même frapper; **he ~ed off with the prize*** il a gagné le prix haut la main; **he ~ed* into the job** il n'a pas eu besoin de se fouler* pour obtenir ce poste [3] VT **he ~ed her round the room** il l'a entraînée dans une valse tout autour de la pièce; (*fig: in delight etc*) il s'est mis à danser de joie avec elle

►**waltz through*** VT FUS [+ *exam*] être reçu les doigts dans le nez*; [+ *competition, match*] gagner les doigts dans le nez*

waltzer ['wɔːlsər] N [a] (= *dancer*) valseur *m*, -euse *f* [b] (*at fairground*) Mont-Blanc *m*

wampum ['wɒmpəm] N [a] (= *beads*) wampum *m* [b] (*US** = *money*) pognon* *m*, fric* *m*

WAN [wæn] N (*Comput*) (ABBR = **wide area network**) → **wide**

wan [wɒn] ADJ [*face, light, sky*] blême, blafard; [*person*] au visage blême *or* blafard; [*smile*] pâle (*de person*) avoir le visage blême *or* blafard; **to grow ~** [*light, sky*] blêmir

wand [wɒnd] N [*of conjurer, fairy*] baguette *f* (magique); [*of usher, steward, sheriff*] verge *f*, bâton *m*; (*Comput*) crayon *m* optique, photostyle *m*

wander ['wɒndər] [1] N tour *m*, balade* *f*; **to go for a ~ around the town/the shops** aller faire un tour en ville/dans les magasins
[2] VI [a] [*person*] errer, aller sans but; (*for pleasure*) flâner; [*thoughts*] errer, vagabonder; [*river, road*] serpenter, faire des méandres; **he ~ed through the streets** il errait *or* allait sans but dans les rues; **his gaze ~ed round the room** son regard errait dans la pièce [b] (= *stray*) s'égarer; **to ~ from the point** *or* **subject** s'écarter du sujet; **his eyes ~ed from the page** son regard distrait s'est écarté de la page; **his thoughts ~ed back to his youth** ses pensées se sont distraitement reportées à sa jeunesse; **his attention ~ed** il était distrait, il n'arrivait pas à fixer son attention *or* à se concentrer; **sorry, my mind was ~ing** excusez-moi, j'étais distrait; **to ~ back to the day when ...** il repensa par hasard au jour où ...; (*pej*) **his mind is ~ing** ◊ **his wits are ~ing** ◊ **he's ~ing*** (*from fever*) il délire, il divague; (*from old age*) il divague, il déraille*; **don't take any notice of what he says, he's just ~ing*** ne faites pas attention à ce qu'il dit, il radote [c] (= *go casually*) **to ~ in/out/away** *etc* entrer/sortir/partir *etc* d'un pas nonchalant; **they ~ed round the shop** ils ont flâné dans le magasin; **let's ~ down to the café** allons tranquillement au café
[3] VT parcourir au hasard, errer dans; (*for pleasure*) flâner dans; **to ~ the streets** aller au hasard des rues, errer dans les rues; **to ~ the hills/the countryside** se promener au hasard *or* errer dans les collines/dans la campagne; **to ~ the world** courir le monde, rouler sa bosse*

►**wander about, wander around** VI (*aimlessly*) errer, aller sans but; [*animals*] errer; (*leisurely*) **to ~ about the town/the streets** errer dans la ville/dans les rues; **we ~ed around looking in the shop windows** nous avons flâné en faisant du lèche-vitrine

►**wander off** VI partir; (= *get lost*) s'égarer; **he ~ed off the path** il s'est écarté du chemin

wanderer ['wɒndərər] N vagabond(e) *m(f)* (*also pej*); (*hum*) **the ~'s returned!** tiens, un revenant!

wandering ['wɒndərɪŋ] [1] ADJ [*person, gaze*] errant; [*imagination, thoughts*] vagabond; [*band*] itinérant; [*tribe*] nomade; [*river, road*] qui serpente, en lacets; **a ~ way of life** une vie errante; **to have a ~ eye** reluquer les filles*; **to have ~ hands** avoir les mains baladeuses [2] **wanderings** NPL (= *journeyings*) pérégrinations *fpl*, voyages *mpl*; (*fig: in speech etc*) divagations *fpl*; **her ~s in Europe and Africa** ses pérégrinations en Europe et en Afrique, ses voyages à travers l'Europe et l'Afrique [3] COMP ► **wandering Jew** N (*Bot*) misère *f*;

(*Myth*) **the Wandering Jew** le Juif errant ► **wandering minstrel** N ménestrel *m*

wanderlust ['wɒndəlʌst] N envie *f* de voir le monde, bougeotte* *f*

wane [weɪn] **1** VI [*moon*] décroître; [*enthusiasm, interest, emotion*] diminuer; [*strength, reputation, popularity, empire*] décliner, être en déclin **2** N **to be on the ~** = **to wane**; → **1**

wangle* ['wæŋgl] VT (= *get*) se débrouiller pour avoir, resquiller*; **to ~ sth for sb** se débrouiller pour obtenir qch pour qn; **can you ~ me a free ticket?** est-ce que tu peux m'avoir *or* te débrouiller pour m'obtenir un billet gratuit?; **I'll ~ it somehow** je me débrouillerai pour arranger ça, je goupillerai* ça; **he ~d £10 out of his father** il a soutiré 10 livres à son père

wangling* ['wæŋglɪŋ] N (*NonC*) système D* *m*, carottage* *m*, resquille* *f*

waning ['weɪnɪŋ] **1** N (*NonC*) [*of moon*] décroissement *m*; [*of popularity, influence*] déclin *m* **2** ADJ [*moon*] à son déclin; [*enthusiasm, interest*] qui diminue; [*strength, reputation, popularity, empire*] déclinant, qui baisse

wankⁿⁿ [wæŋk] (*Brit*) **1** VI se branlerⁿⁿ, se faire une branletteⁿⁿ **2** N **a** **to have a ~** = **to wank**; → **1 b** (*NonC* = *nonsense*) foutaise* *f*

wankerⁿⁿ ['wæŋkəʳ] N (*Brit fig*) branleurⁿⁿ *m*

wankyⁿⁿ ['wæŋkɪ] ADJ péteux*

wanly ['wɒnlɪ] ADV **a** (= *weakly*) [*smile*] faiblement; [*say*] mollement **b** (= *faintly*) [*shine*] avec une lueur blafarde *or* blême

wanna* ['wɒnə] = **want to**

wannabe* ['wɒnəbiː] **1** N **an Elvis ~** un type qui joue les Elvis* **2** ADJ **a ~ Elvis** un type qui joue les Elvis*; **a ~ writer** quelqu'un qui rêve de devenir écrivain

wanness ['wɒnnɪs] N [*of person, complexion*] pâleur *f*

▼ **want** [wɒnt] **1** N **a** (*NonC* = *lack*) manque *m*; **for ~ of ...** faute de ..., par manque de ...; **for ~ of anything better** faute de mieux; **for ~ of anything better to do** faute d'avoir quelque chose à faire; **for ~ of something to do he ...** comme il n'avait rien à faire il ..., par désœuvrement il ...; **it wasn't for ~ of trying that he ...** ce n'était pas faute d'avoir essayé qu'il ...; **there was no ~ of enthusiasm** ce n'était pas l'enthousiasme qui manquait **b** (*NonC* = *poverty, need*) besoin *m*; **to be or live in ~** être dans le besoin, être nécessiteux†; **to be in ~ of sth** avoir besoin de qch **c** (*gen pl* = *requirement, need*) **~s** besoins *mpl*; **his ~s are few** il a peu de besoins; **it fills** *or* **meets a long-felt ~** cela comble enfin cette lacune

2 VT **a** (= *wish, desire*) vouloir, désirer (**to do** faire); **what do you ~?** que voulez-vous?, que désirez-vous?; **what do you ~ with** *or* **of him?** qu'est-ce que vous lui voulez?; **what do you ~ to do tomorrow?** qu'est-ce que vous avez envie de faire demain?, qu'est-ce que vous voulez *or* désirez faire demain?; **I don't ~ to!** je n'en ai pas envie!; (*more definite*) je ne veux pas!; **all I ~ is a good night's sleep** tout ce que je veux, c'est une bonne nuit de sommeil; **he ~s success/popularity** il veut *or* désire le succès/la popularité; **I ~ your opinion on this** je voudrais votre avis là-dessus; **what does he ~ for that picture?** combien veut-il *or* demande-t-il pour ce tableau?; **I ~ you to tell me ...** je veux que tu me dises ...; **I ~ the car cleaned** je veux qu'on nettoie (*subj*) la voiture; **I always ~ed a car like this** j'ai toujours voulu *or* souhaité avoir une voiture comme ça; **I ~ed** *or* **I was ~ing to leave** j'avais envie de partir; **to ~ in/out*** vouloir entrer/sortir; (*fig*) **he ~s out*** il ne veut plus continuer, il veut laisser tomber*; **you're not ~ed here** on n'a pas besoin de vous ici, on ne veut pas de vous ici; **I know when I'm not ~ed!*** je me rends compte que je suis de trop;

where do you ~ this table? où voulez-vous (qu'on mette) cette table?; (*fig*) **you've got him where you ~ him** vous l'avez coincé*, vous le tenez à votre merci; (*iro*) **you don't ~ much!** il n'en faut pas beaucoup pour vous faire plaisir *or* vous satisfaire! (*iro*); (*sexually*) **to ~ sb** désirer qn

b (= *seek, ask for*) demander; **the manager ~s you in his office** le directeur veut vous voir *or* vous demande dans son bureau; **you're ~ed on the phone** on vous demande au téléphone; **to be ~ed by the police** être recherché par la police; **"good cook ~ed"** « recherchons cuisinier ou cuisinière qualifié(e) » → **wanted**

c (*gen Brit*) (= *need*) [*person*] avoir besoin de; [*task*] exiger, réclamer; (* = *ought*) devoir (**to do** faire); **we have all we ~** nous avons tout ce qu'il nous faut; **just what I ~(ed)!** exactement ce qu'il me faut!; **you ~ a bigger hammer if you're going to do it properly** tu as besoin de *or* il te faut un plus gros marteau pour faire cela correctement; **what do you ~ with a house that size?** pourquoi as-tu besoin d'une *or* veux-tu une maison aussi grande?; **such work ~s good eyesight** un tel travail exige *or* nécessite une bonne vue; **the car ~s cleaning** la voiture a besoin d'être lavée, il faudrait laver la voiture; **your hair ~s combing** tu as besoin d'un coup de peigne, il faudrait que tu te peignes (*subj*), tu devrais te peigner; **that child ~s a smacking** cet enfant a besoin d'une *or* mérite une bonne fessée; **you ~ to be careful with that!*** fais attention avec ça!, fais gaffe* avec ça!; **you ~ to see his new boat!*** tu devrais voir son nouveau bateau!

d (= *lack*) **he ~s talent** il manque de talent, le talent lui fait défaut; **this shirt ~s a button** il manque un bouton à cette chemise; **the carpet ~s 5cm to make it fit** il manque 5 cm pour que le tapis soit de la bonne dimension; **it ~ed only his agreement** il ne manquait que son accord; **it ~s 12 minutes to midnight†** dans 12 minutes il sera minuit

3 VI (= *be in need*) être dans le besoin, être nécessiteux; (= *lack*) **to ~ for sth** manquer de qch, avoir besoin de qch; **they ~ for nothing** il ne leur manque rien, ils ne manquent de rien, ils n'ont besoin de rien → **waste**

4 COMP ► **want ad** N (*US Press*) petite annonce *f*

wanted ['wɒntɪd] **1** ADJ **a** (*Police*) [*criminal*] recherché; **America's most ~ man** le criminel le plus recherché de toute l'Amérique; **"~ (for murder)"** « recherché (pour meurtre) »; **"~: dead or alive"** « recherché: mort ou vif »; **a "~" poster** un avis de recherche → **want 2b** **b** (*Press*) **"~"** « cherche »; **"wanted: good cook"** « recherchons cuisinier ou cuisinière qualifié(e) » → **want 2b 2** COMP ► **wanted list** N liste *f* de personnes recherchées

wanting ['wɒntɪŋ] **1** ADJ (= *deficient*) **to be ~ in sth** manquer de qch; **the necessary funds were ~** les fonds nécessaires faisaient défaut, il manquait les fonds nécessaires; **the end of the poem is ~** (= *missing*) il manque la fin du poème, la fin du poème manque; (= *deficient*) la fin du poème est faible; **to find sth ~** trouver que qch laisse à désirer; **to find sb ~** trouver que qn ne fait pas l'affaire; **to be found ~** [*person, thing*] ne pas faire l'affaire; **to prove ~** se révéler insuffisant **2** PREP (= *without*) sans; (= *minus*) moins

wanton ['wɒntən] **1** ADJ **a** (*pej* = *gratuitous*) [*destruction, violence, cruelty*] gratuit; [*killer*] qui tue sans raison **b** († *pej* = *dissolute*) [*woman, behaviour*] dévergondé **c** (*liter* = *playful*) [*person, behaviour, breeze*] capricieux **d** (*liter* = *luxuriant*) [*growth, weeds*] luxuriant, exubérant **2** N† libertin *m*, femme *f* légère

wantonly ['wɒntənlɪ] (*pej*) ADV **a** (= *gratuitously*) [*destroy, violate*] gratuitement; **~ cruel** d'une cruauté gratuite **b** († = *dissolutely*) [*behave, desire*] de façon dévergondée

wantonness ['wɒntənnɪs] N (*NonC*) **a** (= *gratuitousness*) [*of destruction, violence, cruelty*] gratuité *f* **b** († *pej* = *dissoluteness*) [*of person, behaviour*] dévergondage *m*

war [wɔːʳ] **1** N guerre *f*; **to be at ~** être en (état de) guerre (**with** avec); **to go to ~** [*country*] entrer en guerre (**against** contre, **over** à propos de); **to go (off) to ~** [*soldier*] partir pour la guerre, aller à la guerre; (*Mil, also fig*) **to make ~ on** faire la guerre à; **~ of attrition** guerre *f* d'usure; **the Wars of the Roses** la guerre des Deux-Roses; **the Great War** la Grande Guerre, la guerre de 14 *or* de 14-18; **the ~ to end all ~s** la der des ders*; **the (American) War of Independence** la guerre de Sécession; **the period between the ~s** (= *1918-39*) l'entre-deux-guerres *m inv*; (*Mil, fig*) **to carry** *or* **take the ~ into the enemy's camp** passer à l'attaque, prendre l'offensive; (*fig*) **it was ~ to the knife** *or* **the death between them** c'était une lutte à couteaux tirés entre eux; (*fig*) **~ of words** guerre *f* de paroles; (*fig*) **you've been in the ~s again*** tu t'es encore fait amocher* *or* estropier → **cold, nerve, state**

2 VI faire la guerre (**against** à)

3 COMP [*conditions, debt, crime, criminal, orphan, widow, wound, zone*] de guerre ► **war baby** N enfant *m* de la guerre ► **war bond** N (*US Hist*) titre *m* d'emprunt de guerre (*pendant la Deuxième Guerre mondiale*) ► **war bride** N mariée *f* de la guerre ► **war cabinet** N (*Pol*) cabinet *m* de guerre ► **war chest** N (*Pol*) caisse *f* spéciale (*d'un parti politique pour les élections*) ► **war clouds** NPL (*fig*) signes *mpl* avant-coureurs de la guerre ► **war correspondent** N (*Press, Rad, TV*) correspondant(e) *m(f)* de guerre ► **war cry** N cri *m* de guerre ► **war dance** N danse *f* guerrière ► **the War Department** N (*US*) = **the War Office** ► **the war-disabled** NPL les mutilé(e)s *m(f)pl* *or* invalides *mfpl* de guerre ► **war fever** N psychose *f* de guerre ► **war footing** N **on a ~ footing** sur le pied de guerre ► **war games** NPL (*Mil: for training*) kriegspiel *m*; (*Mil = practice manoeuvres*) manœuvres *fpl* militaires; (= *board games, computer games etc*) jeux *mpl* de stratégie militaire, wargames *mpl* ► **war grave** N tombe *f* de soldat (*mort au champ d'honneur*) ► **war hero** N héros *m* de la guerre ► **war lord** N chef *m* militaire, seigneur *m* de la guerre ► **war memorial** N monument *m* aux morts ► **the War Office** N (*Brit*) le ministère de la Guerre ► **war paint** N peinture *f* de guerre (*des Indiens*); (*fig hum* = *make-up*) maquillage *m*, peinturlurage *m* (*pej*) ► **war record** N **what is his ~ record?** comment s'est-il comporté *or* qu'a-t-il fait pendant la guerre?; **he has a good ~ record** ses états de service pendant la guerre sont tout à fait honorables ► **war-torn** ADJ déchiré par la guerre ► **war-weariness** N lassitude *f* de la guerre ► **war-weary** ADJ las (*lasse f*) de la guerre ► **war whoop** N (*US*) cri *m* de guerre ► **the war-wounded** NPL les blessés *mpl* de guerre

warble¹ ['wɔːbl] N **a** (= *abscess*) [*of cattle*] var(r)on *m* **b** (*on horse's back*) callosité *f*

warble² ['wɔːbl] **1** N (= *sound*) gazouillis *m*, gazouillements *mpl* **2** VI [*bird*] gazouiller; [*person*] roucouler; [*telephone*] sonner **3** VT (*also ~ out*) chanter en gazouillant

warbler ['wɔːbləʳ] N **a** (= *bird*) fauvette *f*, pouillot *m* **b** (*hum* = *singer*) chanteur *m*, -euse *f* (*à la voix de casserole*)

warbling ['wɔːblɪŋ] N gazouillis *m*, gazouillement(s) *m(pl)*

ward [wɔːd] **1** N **a** [*of hospital*] salle *f*; (*separate building*) pavillon *m*; [*of prison*] quartier *m* **b** (*Brit Local Govt*) section *f* électorale **c** (*Jur = person*) pupille *mf*; **~ of court** pupille *mf* sous tutelle judiciaire; **in ~** sous tutelle judiciaire → **watch²** **2** COMP ► **ward heeler** N (*US Pol: pej*) agent *m or* courtier *m* électoral

► **ward round** N (*Med*) visite *f* (*de médecin hospitalier*) ► **ward sister** N (*Brit Med*) infirmière *f* en chef (*responsable d'une salle ou d'un pavillon*)

►**ward off** VT SEP [+ *blow, danger*] parer, éviter; [+ *illness*] éviter

...ward [wəd] SUF = **...wards**

warden ['wɔːdn] N [*of institution*] directeur *m*, -trice *f*; [*of city, castle*] gouverneur *m*; [*of park, game reserve*] gardien *m*, -ienne *f*; [*of youth hostel*] responsable *mf*; (*Brit* = *prison warder*) surveillant(e) *m(f)* de prison; (*US* = *prison governor*) directeur *m*, -trice *f*; [*of student residence etc*] directeur *m*, -trice *f* de résidence universitaire; (*Brit: on hospital board etc*) membre *m* du conseil d'administration; (*Brit: also* **air-raid ~**) préposé(e) *m(f)* à la défense passive; (*also* **traffic ~**) contractuel(le) *m(f)*; (*Brit*) **Warden of the Cinque Ports** gouverneur *m* des Cinq Ports → **churchwarden, fire**

warder ['wɔːdəʳ] N [a] (*esp Brit*) gardien *m* or surveillant *m* (de prison) [b] (*esp US*) (*in building*) concierge *m*; (*in museum*) gardien *m* (de musée)

wardress ['wɔːdrɪs] N (*esp Brit*) gardienne *f* or surveillante *f* (de prison)

wardrobe ['wɔːdrəʊb] [1] N [a] (= *cupboard*) (*gen*) armoire *f*, (*for hanging only*) penderie *f* [b] (= *clothes*) garde-robe *f*; (*Theat*) costumes *mpl*; (*Cine, Theat*) **Miss Lilly's ~ by ...** costumes *mpl* de Mlle Lilly par ..., habillée par ... [2] COMP ► **wardrobe mistress** N (*Theat*) costumière *f* ► **wardrobe trunk** N malle-penderie *f*

wardroom ['wɔːdrʊm] N (*Naut*) carré *m*

...wards [wədz] SUF vers, dans la or en direction de; **townwards** vers la ville, dans la or en direction de la ville → **backwards, downwards**

wardship ['wɔːdʃɪp] N (*NonC*) tutelle *f*

ware ['wɛə] [1] N (*NonC*) articles *mpl*; **kitchenware** articles *mpl* de cuisine; **tableware** articles *mpl* pour la table; **crystalware** articles *mpl* en cristal; **silverware** argenterie *f* → **hardware** [2] **wares** NPL (= *goods*) marchandises *fpl*

warehouse ['wɛəhaʊs] [1] N (*pl* **warehouses** ['wɛə,haʊzɪz]) entrepôt *m* [2] ['wɛəhaʊz] VT entreposer, mettre en magasin [3] COMP ► **warehouse club** N (*esp US Comm*) grande surface qui, pour une adhésion annuelle, vend ses produits en vrac à prix réduits

warehouseman ['wɛəhaʊsmən] N (*pl* -**men**) magasinier *m*

warehousing ['wɛəhaʊzɪŋ] N (*Comm*) entreposage *m*

warfare ['wɔːfɛə] N (*NonC*) (*Mil*) guerre *f* (*NonC*); (*fig*) lutte *f* (**against** contre); **class ~** lutte *f* des classes

warhead ['wɔːhed] N ogive *f*; **nuclear ~** ogive *f* or tête *f* nucléaire

warhorse ['wɔːhɔːs] N cheval *m* de bataille; (*fig*) **an old ~** un vétéran

warily ['wɛərɪlɪ] ADV [*watch, ask, say*] avec méfiance; (*fig*) **to tread ~** y aller avec méfiance

wariness ['wɛərɪnɪs] N (*NonC*) [*of person*] méfiance *f* (**about** or **of** of sth à l'égard de qch); ~ **about doing sth** méfiance *f* à faire qch; **the ~ of his manner** sa méfiance, son attitude *f* méfiante

Warks ABBR = **Warwickshire**

warlike ['wɔːlaɪk] ADJ guerrier, belliqueux

warlock ['wɔːlɒk] N sorcier *m*

warm [wɔːm] [1] ADJ [a] [*liquid, object, air, climate, temperature, summer, day, night*] (assez) chaud; **the water is just ~** l'eau est juste chaude or n'est pas très chaude; **I can't stand ~ coffee, I like it really hot** je déteste le café juste chaud, je l'aime brûlant; **this room is quite ~** il fait (assez) chaud dans cette pièce; **leave the dough in a ~ place to rise** laissez lever la pâte dans un endroit chaud; **it's too ~**

► **LANGUAGE IN USE**: **warn** 2.3

in here il fait trop chaud ici; **it's nice and ~ in here** il fait bon or agréablement chaud ici; **a ~ oven** un four moyen; **the iron/oven is ~** le fer/four est (assez) chaud; **a nice ~ fire** un bon feu; **it's ~** ◊ **the weather is ~** il fait bon; **in ~ weather** par temps chaud; **during the ~er months** pendant les mois où il fait moins froid; **to keep sth ~** tenir qch au chaud; **it's ~ work** c'est un travail qui donne chaud; **I am ~** j'ai (assez) chaud; **the body was still ~ when it was found** le corps était encore chaud quand on l'a trouvé; **to get sth ~** (ré)chauffer qch; **to get** or **grow ~** [*water, object*] chauffer; [*person*] se réchauffer; **come and get ~ by the fire** venez vous (ré)chauffer auprès du feu; (*in guessing etc games*) **you're getting ~(er)!** tu chauffes!; **keep me ~** tiens-moi chaud; **keep him ~** (*sick person*) ne le laissez pas prendre froid; **this scarf keeps me ~** cette écharpe me tient chaud; **you've got to keep yourself ~** surtout ne prenez pas froid; **I'm as ~ as toast*** je suis bien au chaud

[b] (= *cosy*) [*clothes, blanket*] chaud

[c] (*fig*) [*colour, shade*] chaud; [*voice, tone, feelings*] chaud, chaleureux; [*greeting, welcome, congratulations, encouragement*] cordial, chaleureux; [*apologies, thanks*] vif; [*applause*] chaleureux, enthousiaste; [*supporter, admirer*] ardent, chaud; **the lamp gives out a ~ glow** cette lampe donne un éclairage chaud; **to get a ~ reception (from sb)** être chaudement or chaleureusement reçu (par qn); **he gave me a ~ smile** il m'a adressé un sourire chaleureux; **they have a very ~ relationship** ils ont beaucoup d'affection l'un pour l'autre; **she is a very ~ person** ◊ **she has a very ~ nature** elle est très chaleureuse (de nature); **to have a ~ heart** avoir beaucoup de cœur; **she felt a ~ glow inside when she heard the news** la nouvelle lui a (ré)chauffé le cœur; (*in letter*) **"with ~est wishes"** « avec mes vœux les plus sincères »

[2] N* **to give sth a ~** (ré)chauffer qch; **come and have a ~ by the fire** viens te (ré)chauffer près du feu; **come inside and sit in the ~** entrez vous asseoir au chaud

[3] VT [a] (*also* ~ **up**) [+ *person, room*] réchauffer; [+ *water, food*] (ré)chauffer, faire (ré)chauffer; [+ *coat, slippers*] (ré)chauffer; **to ~ o.s.** se réchauffer; **to ~ one's feet/hands** se réchauffer les pieds/les mains; **to ~ o.s. at the fire** se (ré)chauffer auprès du feu

[b] (*fig*) **the news ~ed my heart** la nouvelle m'a (ré)chauffé le cœur → **cockle**

[4] VI [a] (*also* ~ **up**) [*person*] se (ré)chauffer; [*water, food*] chauffer; [*room, bed*] se réchauffer, devenir plus chaud; [*weather*] se réchauffer

[b] (*fig*) **to ~ to an idea** s'enthousiasmer peu à peu pour une idée; **I ~ed to him** je me suis pris de sympathie pour lui; **to ~ to one's theme** or **subject** se laisser entraîner par son sujet, traiter son sujet avec un enthousiasme grandissant

[5] COMP ► **warm-blooded** ADJ (*Zool*) à sang chaud; (*fig*) (*gen*) sensible; (*sexually*) qui a le sang chaud ► **warm front** N (*Met*) front *m* chaud ► **warm-hearted** ADJ chaleureux, affectueux ► **warm-up*** N (*Sport*) échauffement *m*; (*Rad, Theat, TV etc*) mise *f* en train ♦ ADJ [*exercise, routine, stretches*] d'échauffement ► **warm-ups** NPL (*US*) survêtement *m*

►**warm over, warm through** VT SEP [+ *food*] faire (ré)chauffer

►**warm up** [1] VI [a] = **warm 4a** [b] [*engine, car*] se réchauffer; [*athlete, dancer*] s'échauffer [c] (*fig*) [*discussion*] s'échauffer, s'animer; [*audience*] devenir animé; **the party was ~ing up** la soirée commençait à être pleine d'entrain, la soirée chauffait*; **things are ~ing up** ça commence à s'animer or à chauffer* [2] VT SEP [a] = **warm 3a** [b] [+ *engine, car*] faire chauffer [c] (*fig*) [+ *discussion*] animer; (*Theat*

etc) [+ *audience*] mettre en train [3] ~**-up*** N → **warm**

warming ['wɔːmɪŋ] [1] ADJ [*drink, food*] qui réchauffe [2] COMP ► **warming pan** N bassinoire *f* ► **warming-up exercises** NPL exercices *mpl* d'échauffement

warmly ['wɔːmlɪ] ADV [a] [*dress*] chaudement; ~ **tucked up in bed** bordé bien au chaud dans son lit; **the sun shone ~** le soleil était agréablement chaud [b] (*fig*) [*recommend*] chaudement; [*greet, smile*] chaleureusement; [*thank, applaud*] avec chaleur, chaleureusement; [*say, speak of*] avec chaleur

warmonger ['wɔː,mʌŋgə] N belliciste *mf*

warmongering ['wɔː,mʌŋgərɪŋ] [1] ADJ belliciste [2] N (*NonC*) propagande *f* belliciste

warmth [wɔːmθ] N (*NonC: lit, fig*) chaleur *f*; **they huddled together for ~** ils se sont serrés l'un contre l'autre pour se tenir chaud; **it was good to be in the ~ again** cela faisait du bien d'être de nouveau au chaud; **for extra ~, wear a wool jumper** pour avoir plus chaud, portez un pull-over en laine; **she greeted us with great ~** elle nous a accueillis avec beaucoup de chaleur or très chaleureusement

▼ **warn** [wɔːn] VT prévenir, avertir (**of** de, **that** que); **to ~ the police** alerter la police; **you have been ~ed!** vous êtes averti or prévenu!; **to ~ sb against doing sth** or **not to do sth** conseiller à qn de ne pas faire qch, déconseiller à qn de faire qch; **to ~ sb off** or **against sth** mettre qn en garde contre qch, déconseiller qch à qn

warning ['wɔːnɪŋ] [1] N (= *act*) avertissement *m*; (*in writing*) avis *m*, préavis *m*; (= *signal: also Mil*) alerte *f*, alarme *f*; (*Met*) avis *m*; **it fell without ~** c'est tombé subitement; **they arrived without ~** ils sont arrivés à l'improviste or sans prévenir; **he left me without ~** il m'a quitté sans prévenir; **let this be a ~ to you** que cela vous serve d'avertissement; **thank you for the ~** merci de m'avoir prévenu or averti; **there was a note of ~ in his voice** il y avait une mise en garde dans le ton qu'il a pris; **to take ~ from sth** tirer la leçon de qch; **his employer gave him a ~ about lateness** son patron lui a donné un avertissement à propos de son manque de ponctualité; **to give a week's ~** prévenir huit jours à l'avance, donner un préavis de huit jours; **I gave you due** or **fair ~ (that ...)** je vous avais bien prévenu (que ...); (*Met*) **gale/storm ~** avis *m* de grand vent/de tempête; (*Mil*) **four minute ~** alerte *f* de quatre minutes

[2] ADJ [*glance, cry*] d'avertissement; **... he said in a ~ tone** or **voice** ... dit-il pour mettre en garde

[3] COMP ► **warning device** N dispositif *m* d'alarme, avertisseur *m* ► **warning light** N voyant *m* (avertisseur), avertisseur *m* lumineux ► **warning notice** N avis *m*, avertissement *m* ► **warning shot** N (*gen, Mil*) tir *m* de sommation; (*Naut, also fig*) coup *m* de semonce ► **warning sign** N panneau *m* avertisseur ► **warning triangle** N (*Aut*) triangle *m* de présignalisation

warningly ['wɔːnɪŋlɪ] ADV [*say*] sur un ton d'avertissement; [*shake one's head*] en signe d'avertissement

warp [wɔːp] [1] N [a] (*Tex*) chaîne *f*; (*fig* = *essence, base*) fibre *f* [b] (= *distortion*) (*in wood*) gauchissement *m*, voilure *f*; (*in metal*) voilure *f*; (*Recording*) voile *m* (d'un disque) → **time** [2] VT [a] (*lit*) [+ *wood*] gauchir, voiler; [+ *metal, aircraft wing, tennis racket*] voiler [b] (*fig*) [+ *judgement*] fausser, pervertir; [+ *mind, character, person*] pervertir; **he has a ~ed mind** ◊ **his mind is ~ed** il a l'esprit tordu; **he has a ~ed sense of humour** il a un sens de l'humour morbide; **he gave us a ~ed account of ...** il nous a fait un récit tendancieux de ... [3] VI [a] (*lit*) [*ruler, board, wood*] gauchir;

[*wheel, metal plate*] se voiler; [*mechanism*] se fausser [b] [*person, institution*] se pervertir

warpath ['wɔ:pæθ] N (*fig*) **to be on the ~** être sur le sentier de la guerre, chercher la bagarre*

warplane ['wɔ:pleɪn] N avion *m* militaire *or* de guerre

warrant ['wɒrənt] [1] N [a] (*NonC = justification*) justification *f*, droit *m*; **he has no ~ for saying so** il ne s'appuie sur rien pour justifier cela [b] (*Comm, Fin etc = certificate*) (*for payment or services*) bon *m*; (= *guarantee*) garantie *f*; (*Customs*) warrant *m*; (= *guarantee*) garantie *f*; (*Customs*) warrant *m*; (*Mil*) brevet *m*; (*Jur, Police*) mandat *m*; (*Jur*) **there is a ~ out against him** ◊ **there is a ~ out for his arrest** il y a un mandat d'arrêt contre lui, un mandat d'arrêt a été délivré contre lui; (*to police officer*) **do you have a ~?** vous avez un mandat (de perquisition)? → **death, search** [2] VT [a] (= *justify*) [+ *action, assumption, reaction, behaviour*] justifier, légitimer; **the facts do not ~ it** les faits ne le justifient pas [b] (= *guarantee*) garantir; **I'll ~ you he won't come back** je te garantis *or* je suis sûr qu'il ne va pas revenir; **he won't come here again in a hurry, I'll ~ (you)!*** il ne reviendra pas de sitôt, tu peux me croire! [3] COMP ► **warrant card** N (*Brit Police*) carte *f* de police ► **warrant officer** N (*Mil*) adjudant *m* (*auxiliaire de l'officier*) ► **warrant sale** N (*Scot Jur*) vente *f* forcée *or* judiciaire

warrantable ['wɒrəntəbl] ADJ justifiable, légitime

warranted ['wɒrəntɪd] ADJ [a] (= *justified*) [*action, fears, charges*] justifié [b] (= *guaranteed*) [*goods*] garanti

warrantee [,wɒrən'ti:] N (*Jur*) créancier *m*, -ière *f*

warranter, warrantor ['wɒrəntə'] N (*Jur*) garant(e) *m(f)*, débiteur *m*, -trice *f*

warranty ['wɒrəntɪ] N autorisation *f*, droit *m*; (*Comm, Jur*) garantie *f*

warren ['wɒrən] N [a] (*also* **rabbit ~**) terriers *mpl*, garenne *f* [b] (*fig = building*) labyrinthe *m*; **a ~ of little streets** un dédale *or* un labyrinthe de petites rues

warring ['wɔ:rɪŋ] ADJ [*nations*] en guerre; (*fig*) [*interests*] contradictoire, contraire; [*ideologies*] en conflit, en opposition

warrior ['wɒrɪə'] N guerrier *m*, -ière *f* → **unknown**

Warsaw ['wɔ:sɔ:] [1] N Varsovie [2] COMP ► **Warsaw Pact** N pacte *m* de Varsovie; **the ~ Pact countries** les pays *mpl* du pacte de Varsovie

warship ['wɔ:ʃɪp] N navire *m* *or* vaisseau *m* de guerre

wart [wɔ:t] [1] N (*Med*) verrue *f*; (*Bot*) excroissance *f*; (*on wood*) loupe *f*; (*fig*) **~s and all** avec tous ses défauts [2] COMP ► **wart hog** N phacochère *m*

wartime ['wɔ:taɪm] [1] N (*NonC*) temps *m* de guerre; **in ~** en temps de guerre [2] COMP en temps de guerre

warty ['wɔ:tɪ] ADJ couvert de verrues, verruqueux

wary ['weərɪ] ADJ [*person*] prudent, sur ses gardes; [*voice, look, manner*] prudent; **to be ~ about sb/sth** se méfier de qn/qch; **to be ~ of doing sth** hésiter beaucoup à faire qch; **to keep a ~ eye on sb/sth** avoir l'œil sur qn/qch, surveiller qn/qch de près

was [wɒz] VB *pt of* **be**

wash [wɒʃ] [1] N [a] **to give sth a ~** (*gen*) laver qch; [+ *paintwork, hair, walls*] lessiver qch; **to give one's hands/hair/face a ~** se laver les mains/les cheveux/le visage; **to have a ~** se laver; **to have a quick ~** se débarbouiller, faire un brin de toilette; **to have a ~ and brush-up** faire sa toilette; **it needs a ~** cela a besoin d'être lavé, il faut laver cela; **your face needs a ~** il faut

que tu te laves (*subj*) la figure *or* que tu te débarbouilles (*subj*) [b] (= *laundry*) **I do a big ~ on Mondays** je fais une grande lessive le lundi, le lundi est mon jour de grande lessive; **put your jeans in the ~** (= *ready to be washed*) mets tes jeans au lavage; **your shirt is in the ~** (= *being washed*) ta chemise est à la lessive; **the colours ran in the ~** cela a déteint à la lessive *or* au lavage; **to send sheets to the ~** envoyer des draps au blanchissage *or* à la laverie; (*fig*) **it will all come out in the ~*** (= *be known*) on finira bien par savoir ce qu'il en est; (= *be all right*) ça finira par se tasser* *or* s'arranger → **car** [c] [*of ship*] sillage *m*, remous *m*; (= *sound*) [*of waves etc*] clapotis *m* [d] (= *layer of paint: for walls etc*) badigeon *m*; **to give the walls a blue ~** badigeonner les murs en *or* de bleu → **whitewash** [e] (*Art*) lavis *m*; **to put a ~ on a drawing** laver un dessin [f] (*Pharm*) solution *f* → **eyewash, mouthwash** [g] (*Brit Geog*) **the Wash** le golfe du Wash [2] VT [a] (*gen*) laver; [+ *paintwork, walls*] lessiver; **to ~ o.s.** [*person*] se laver; [*cat*] faire sa toilette; **to ~ one's hair** se laver les cheveux; **to ~ one's hands/feet/face** se laver les mains/les pieds/le visage; **to ~ a child's face** laver le visage d'un enfant, débarbouiller un enfant; **he ~ed the dirt off his hands** il s'est lavé les mains (pour en enlever la saleté); **to ~ the dishes** faire la vaisselle; **to ~ the clothes** faire la lessive; **can you ~ this fabric?** (= *is it washable*) ce tissu est-il lavable?; **~ this garment at 40°/in hot water** lavez ce vêtement à 40°/à l'eau chaude; **to ~ sth with detergent** nettoyer qch avec du détergent; (*fig*) **to ~ one's hands of sth** se laver les mains de qch; (*fig*) **to ~ one's hands of sb** se désintéresser de qn → **clean** [b] [*river, sea, waves*] (= *flow over*) baigner; **the Atlantic ~es its western shores** la côte ouest est baignée par l'Atlantique; **to ~ sth ashore** (*onto coast*) rejeter qch sur le rivage; (*onto riverbank*) rejeter qch sur la rive; **to be ~ed out to sea** être emporté par la mer, être entraîné vers le large; **to be ~ed overboard** être emporté par une vague; **it was ~ed downstream** le courant l'a entraîné *or* emporté [c] (= *paint*) **to ~ walls with distemper** passer des murs au badigeon, peindre des murs à la détrempe; **to ~ brass with gold** couvrir du cuivre d'une pellicule d'or [d] (*Min*) [+ *earth, gravel, gold, ore*] laver; (*Chem*) [+ *gas*] épurer [3] VI [a] (= *have a wash*) [*person*] se laver; [*cat*] faire sa toilette; (= *do the laundry*) laver, faire la lessive; **he ~ed in cold water** il s'est lavé à l'eau froide; **this garment ~es/doesn't ~ very well** ce vêtement se lave très facilement/ne se lave pas très facilement [b] (*Brit* fig) **that just won't ~!** on ne le prend pas!; **that excuse won't ~ with him** cette excuse ne prendra pas *or* ne marchera pas avec lui, on ne lui fera pas avaler cette excuse [c] [*waves, sea, flood, river*] **to ~ against** [+ *cliffs, rocks*] baigner; [+ *lighthouse, boat*] clapoter contre; **to ~ over sth** balayer qch; **to ~ ashore** être rejeté sur le rivage [d] (*fig = flow*) **let the music ~ over you** laisse-toi bercer par la musique; **a wave of nausea ~ed through her** il a été prise d'une nausée soudaine; **a wave of anger ~ed through her** elle a senti monter une bouffée de colère; **relief ~ed over his face** il a soudain eu l'air profondément soulagé; **a wave of sadness/tiredness ~ed over him** il a soudain ressenti une profonde tristesse/une grande fatigue; **her explanation/words just ~ed over me** son explication a/ses paroles ont glissé sur moi [4] COMP ► **wash-and-wear** ADJ [*clothes, fabric*] facile à entretenir ► **wash drawing** N (*Art*) (dessin *m* au) lavis *m* ► **wash-hand basin** N lavabo *m* ► **wash house** N lavoir *m*

► **wash leather** N (*Brit*) peau *f* de chamois ► **wash load** N charge *f* (de linge) ► **wash-out*** N (= *event*) fiasco *m*, désastre *m*; (= *person*) zéro* *m*, nullité* *f* ► **wash-wipe** N (*Aut*) (*on window*) lave-glace *m inv*; (*on headlamp*) essuie-phares *mpl*

► **wash away** [1] VI s'en aller *or* partir au lavage [2] VT SEP [a] [+ *stain*] enlever *or* faire partir au lavage; (*fig*) [+ *sins*] laver; **the rain ~ed the mud away** la pluie a fait partir la boue [b] [*river, current, sea*] (= *carry away*) emporter, entraîner; [+ *footprints etc*] balayer, effacer; **the boat was ~ed away** le bateau a été emporté; **the river ~ed away part of the bank** la rivière a emporté une partie de la rive

► **wash down** [1] VT SEP [a] [+ *deck, car*] laver (à grande eau); [+ *wall*] lessiver [b] [+ *medicine, pill*] faire descendre (**with** avec); [+ *food*] arroser (**with** de) [c] [*rain, flood, river*] emporter, entraîner [2] **~down** N → **washdown**

► **wash in** VT SEP [*sea, tide*] rejeter (sur le rivage)

► **wash off** [1] VI (*from clothes*) s'en aller *or* partir au lavage; (*from walls*) partir au lessivage; **it won't ~ off** ça ne s'en va pas, ça ne part pas; (*from hands*) **it will ~ off** ça partira quand tu te laveras (*or* je me laverai *etc*) les mains [2] VT SEP (*from clothes*) faire partir au lavage; (*from wall*) faire partir en lessivant

► **wash out** [1] VI [a] [*stain*] s'en aller *or* partir au lavage; [*dye, colours*] passer au lavage; **this stain won't ~ out** cette tache ne s'en va pas *or* ne part pas [b] (*US*) **he ~ed out of university*** il s'est fait recaler aux examens de la fac* [2] VT SEP [a] (= *remove*) [+ *stain*] enlever *or* faire partir au lavage [b] (= *rinse*) [+ *bottle, pan*] laver; (*lit*) **to ~ one's mouth out** se faire un bain de bouche; **~ your mouth out (with soap and water)!** tu devrais avoir honte de dire des choses pareilles! [c] (*fig = spoil*) perturber; (* = *cancel*) rendre impossible; (*by rain*) **the match was ~ed out** (= *prevented*) le match a été annulé *or* n'a pas eu lieu à cause de la pluie; (= *halted*) la pluie a perturbé *or* interrompu le match; **to be/look/feel ~ed out*** (= *tired*) être/avoir l'air/se sentir complètement lessivé* [d] (*fig*) **~ed-out** (= *pale*) [*colour*] délavé [3] **~-out*** N → **wash**

► **wash through** VT SEP [+ *clothes*] laver rapidement, passer à l'eau

► **wash up** [1] VI [a] (*Brit* = *wash dishes*) faire *or* laver la vaisselle [b] (*US* = *have a wash*) se débarbouiller, faire un brin de toilette [2] VT SEP [a] (*Brit*) [+ *plates, cups*] laver; **to ~ up the dishes** faire *or* laver la vaisselle [b] [*sea, tide*] rejeter (sur le rivage); [*river*] rejeter (sur la berge) [c] (*gen pass:** = *finish*) **to be (all) ~ed up** [*plan, scheme, marriage etc*] être fichu*, être tombé à l'eau*; **Paul and Anne are all ~ed up** tout est fini entre Paul et Anne [d] (*US* = *tired etc*) **to be/feel/look ~ed up** être/se sentir/avoir l'air lessivé* [3] **~ing-up** N, ADJ → **washing**

washable ['wɒʃəbl] ADJ lavable, lessivable

washbag ['wɒʃbæg] N trousse *f* de toilette

washbasin ['wɒʃbeɪsn] N (*Brit*) (= *handbasin*) lavabo *m*; (= *bowl*) cuvette *f*

washboard ['wɒʃbɔ:d] N planche *f* à laver

washbowl ['wɒʃbəʊl] N cuvette *f*

washcloth ['wɒʃklɒθ] N (*esp US*) ≈ gant *m* de toilette

washday ['wɒʃdeɪ] N jour *m* de lessive

washdown ['wɒʃdaʊn] N **to give sth a ~** laver qch à grande eau

washer ['wɒʃə'] [1] N [a] (*Tech*) rondelle *f*, joint *m*; (*in tap*) rondelle *f* [b] (= *washing machine*) machine *f* à laver, lave-linge *m inv*; (*Aut: for windscreen*) lave-glace *m inv* → **dishwasher, windscreen** [2] COMP ► **washer-dryer** N lave-linge *m* séchant

washerwoman ['wɒʃəwʊmən] N (*pl* **-women**) lavandière *f*, laveuse *f* (de linge)

washing ['wɒʃɪŋ] [1] N [a] (= *act*) [*of car*] lavage *m*; [*of clothes*] (*gen*) lessive *f*; (*professionally cleaned*) blanchissage *m*; [*of walls*] lessivage *m*

→ **brainwashing**

[b] (*NonC* = *clothes*) linge *m*, lessive *f*; **to do the ~** faire la lessive, laver le linge; **to hang out the ~** étendre le linge *or* la lessive; **the dirty ~** le linge sale → **dirty**

[2] COMP ► **washing day** N jour *m* de lessive ► **washing line** N corde *f* à linge ► **washing machine** N machine *f* à laver, lave-linge *m inv* ► **washing powder** N (*Brit*) lessive *f* (en poudre), détergent *m* (en poudre) ► **washing soda** N cristaux *mpl* de soude ► **washing-up** N (*Brit*) vaisselle *f* (à laver); **to do the ~-up** faire or laver la vaisselle; **look at all that ~-up!** regarde tout ce qu'il y a comme vaisselle à faire *or* à laver! ► **washing-up bowl** N bassine *f*, cuvette *f* ► **washing-up liquid** N produit *m* pour la vaisselle ► **washing-up water** N eau *f* de vaisselle

Washington ['wɒʃɪŋtən] N (= *city*) Washington; (= *state*) le Washington; **in ~** (**State**) dans le Washington

washrag ['wɒʃræg] N (*US*) ≈ gant *m* de toilette

washroom ['wɒʃrʊm] N toilettes *fpl*

washstand ['wɒʃstænd] N table *f* de toilette

washtub ['wɒʃtʌb] N (*for clothes*) baquet *m*, bassine *f*

washy ['wɒʃɪ] ADJ = **wishy-washy**

wasn't ['wɒznt] = **was not**; → **be**

wasp [wɒsp] [1] N guêpe *f*; **~'s nest** guêpier *m* [b] (*US**) (ABBR = **White Anglo-Saxon Protestant**) **Wasp** *or* **WASP** wasp *mf* (*Anglo-Saxon blanc et protestant*) [2] COMP ► **wasp-waisted** ADJ à la taille de guêpe

waspish ['wɒspɪʃ] ADJ grincheux, hargneux

waspishly ['wɒspɪʃlɪ] ADV avec hargne

wassail †† ['wɒseɪl] [1] N (= *festivity*) beuverie *f*; (= *drink*) bière *f* épicée [2] VI faire ribote†

wast †† [wɒst] VB *2nd pers sg pret of* **be**

wastage ['weɪstɪdʒ] [1] N [a] (*NonC*) [of resources, energy, food, money] gaspillage *m*; [of time] gâchage *m*; (as part of industrial process etc) déperdition *f*; (= amount lost from container) fuites *fpl*, pertes *fpl*; (= rejects) déchets *mpl*; **a great ~ of human resources** un grand gaspillage de ressources humaines; **water/energy ~** gaspillage *m* d'eau/d'énergie; **the amount of ~ that goes on in large establishments** le gaspillage or le gâchis qui se produit dans les grands établissements → **waste**; → **natural** [b] (= *wasting away*) [of muscles, tissue] atrophie *f*; **muscle ~** atrophie *f* musculaire [2] COMP ► **wastage rate** N **the ~ rate among students/entrants to the profession** le pourcentage d'étudiants qui abandonnent en cours d'études/de ceux qui abandonnent en début de carrière

waste [weɪst] [1] N [a] (*NonC*) [of resources, energy, food, money] gaspillage *m*; [of time] perte *f*; **to go to ~** être gaspillé, se perdre inutilement; [land] tomber en friche, être à l'abandon; **there's too much ~ in this firm** il y a trop de gaspillage dans cette compagnie; **we must reduce the ~ in the kitchens** nous devons diminuer le gaspillage or le gâchis dans les cuisines; **what a ~!** quel gaspillage!; **it's a ~ of effort** c'est un effort inutile; **it's a ~ of human resources** c'est un gaspillage de ressources humaines; **it's a ~ of money to do that** on gaspille de l'argent en faisant cela, on perd de l'argent à faire cela; **that machine was a ~ of money** cela ne valait vraiment pas la peine d'acheter cette machine, on a vraiment fichu de l'argent en l'air* en achetant cette machine; (*lit*) **~ of space** perte *f* de place; (*fig*) **it's/he's a ~ of space*** c'est/il est nul*; **it's a ~ of time** c'est une perte de temps, c'est du temps perdu; **it's a ~ of time doing that** on perd son temps à faire or en faisant cela; **it's a ~ of time and energy** c'est peine perdue; **it's a ~ of breath** c'est perdre sa salive, c'est dépenser sa salive pour rien [b] (*NonC* = *waste material*) (*US*: also *~s*) (gen)

(= *water*) eaux *fpl* sales or usées; **household** *or* **kitchen ~** ordures *fpl* (ménagères); **industrial/nuclear/metal ~** déchets *mpl* industriels/nucléaires/de métal; **toxic/radioactive ~** déchets *mpl* toxiques/radioactifs → **cotton**

[c] (often pl = expanse) terres *fpl* désolées, désert *m*; (in town) terrain *m* vague; **~s or a ~ of snow and ice** une étendue de neige et de glace

[2] ADJ (*liter*) **to lay sth to ~** ◊ **to lay ~ to sth** ravager qch, dévaster qch

[3] VT [a] [+ resources, food, electricity, energy etc] gaspiller; [+ time] perdre; [+ opportunity] perdre, laisser passer; **I ~d a whole day on that journey/trying to find it** j'ai perdu toute une journée avec ce voyage/à essayer de le trouver; **she didn't want to ~ a single minute of sunshine** elle ne voulait pas perdre une seule minute de soleil; **nothing is ~d in this firm** il n'y a aucun gaspillage or il n'y a aucun gâchis dans cette entreprise; **his attempts to convince her were ~d** il a essayé en vain de la convaincre, ses efforts pour la convaincre ont été vains; **you're wasting your breath!** tu dépenses ta salive pour rien!, tu perds ton temps!; **I won't ~ my breath discussing that** je ne vais pas perdre mon temps or me fatiguer à discuter cela; **~d effort** des efforts *mpl* inutiles or vains; **we tried to make him listen, but our efforts were ~d** nous avons essayé de le forcer à écouter, mais en pure perte or en vain; **I wouldn't like you to have a ~d journey** je ne voudrais pas que vous vous déplaciez pour rien; **a ~d life** une vie gâchée; **the ~d years of his life** les années gâchées de sa vie; **to ~ one's money** gaspiller son argent (**on sth** pour qch, **on doing** pour faire); **she's wasting her talents** elle gaspille ses dons, elle n'exploite pas ses talents; **you're wasting your time trying** tu perds ton temps à essayer; **to ~ no time in doing** ne pas perdre de temps à faire; **a vote for him is a ~d vote** voter pour lui, c'est gaspiller votre voix; **the sarcasm was ~d on him** il n'a pas compris or saisi le sarcasme; **caviar is ~d on him** il ne sait pas apprécier le caviar

[b] (* = *kill*) zigouiller*, supprimer

[4] VI [food, goods, resources] se perdre; **you mustn't let it ~** il ne faut pas le laisser perdre ■ (*PROV*) **~ not want not** il n'y a pas de petites économies

[5] COMP ► **waste disposal unit**, **waste disposer** N broyeur *m* à ordures ► **waste ground** N terrain *m* vague ► **Waste Land** N (*Literat*) **"The Waste Land"** « la Terre désolée » → **wasteland** ► **waste management** N gestion *f* des déchets ► **waste material**, **waste matter** N (also *Physiol*) déchets *mpl* ► **waste pipe** N (tuyau *m* de) vidange *f* ► **waste products** NPL (*Ind*) déchets *mpl* industriels; (*Physiol*) déchets *mpl* (de l'organisme) ► **waste water** N eaux *fpl* usées

► **waste away** VI dépérir; (*iro*) **you're not exactly wasting away!** tu ne fais pas vraiment peine à voir or pitié! (*iro*)

wastebasket ['weɪstbɑːskɪt] N corbeille *f* à papier

wastebin ['weɪstbɪn] N (*Brit*) (= *wastebasket*) corbeille *f* à papier; (in kitchen) poubelle *f*, boîte *f* à ordures

wasted ['weɪstɪd] ADJ [a] [limb] (= *emaciated*) décharné; (= *withered*) atrophié ► **by disease** (= *emaciated*) décharné par la maladie; (= *withered*) atrophié par la maladie [b] (* = *exhausted*) [person] lessivé*, crevé* [c]‡ (on drugs) défoncé‡; (on alcohol) bourré‡; **to get ~** (on drugs) se défoncer*; (on alcohol) se bourrer‡ (la gueule)

wasteful ['weɪstfʊl] ADJ [person] gaspilleur; [process] peu économique, peu rentable; ► **expenditure** gaspillage *m*, dépenses *fpl* excessives or inutiles; **~ habits** gaspillage *m*; **to be ~**

of sth [person] gaspiller qch; [method, process] mal utiliser qch

wastefully ['weɪstfʊlɪ] ADV **to use sth ~** gaspiller qch; **to spend money ~** gaspiller son argent

wastefulness ['weɪstfʊlnɪs] N (*NonC*) [of person] manque *m* d'économie; [of process] manque *m* de rentabilité

wasteland ['weɪstlænd] N (gen) terres *fpl* à l'abandon or en friche; (in town) terrain *m* vague; (in countryside) désert *m*; **a piece of ~** un terrain vague

wastepaper [ˌweɪst'peɪpə^r] [1] N vieux papiers *mpl* [2] COMP ► **wastepaper basket** N = **wastebasket**

waster* ['weɪstə^r] N [a] (= *good-for-nothing*) propre *mf* à rien [b] (= *spendthrift*) dépensier *m*, -ière *f*

wasting ['weɪstɪŋ] ADJ [disease] qui ronge, qui mine

wastrel † ['weɪstrəl] N [a] (= *spendthrift*) dépensier *m*, -ière *f*, panier *m* percé [b] (= *good-for-nothing*) propre *mf* à rien

watch[1] [wɒtʃ] [1] N montre *f*; **by my ~** à ma montre → **stopwatch**, **wrist** [2] COMP [chain, glass] de montre ► **watch pocket** N gousset *m* ► **watch strap** N = **watchband**

watch[2] [wɒtʃ] [1] N (*NonC*) (= *vigilance*) vigilance *f*; (= *act of watching*) surveillance *f*; **to keep** *or* **be on ~** faire le guet; **to keep (a) close ~ on** *or* **over sb/sth** surveiller qn/qch de près or avec vigilance; **to set a ~ on sth/sb** faire surveiller qch/qn; (*frm*) **to keep ~ and ward over sth** surveiller qch avec vigilance; **to be under ~** être sous surveillance; **to be on ~** (Mil etc) monter la garde; (gen) faire le guet; **to be on the ~ for sb/sth** guetter qn/qch; **to be on the ~ for danger** être sur ses gardes (dans l'éventualité d'un danger); **to be on the ~ for bargains** être à l'affût des bonnes affaires

[b] (*Naut* = period of duty) quart *m*; **to be on ~** être de quart; (fig:† or liter) **the long ~es of the night** les longues nuits sans sommeil → **dogwatch**

[c] (= group of men) (Mil) garde *f*; (Naut) quart *m*; (= one man) (Mil) sentinelle *f*; (Naut) homme *m* de quart; (Naut) **the port ~** les bâbordais *mpl*; **the starboard ~** les tribordais *mpl*; (Hist) **the ~** le guet, la ronde → **officer**

[2] VT [a] [+ event, match, programme, TV, ceremony] regarder; [+ person] regarder, observer; (= spy on) surveiller, épier; [+ suspect, suspicious object, house, car] surveiller; [+ expression, birds, insects etc] observer; [+ notice board, small ads etc] consulter régulièrement; [+ political situation, developments] surveiller, suivre de près; **~ me** ◊ **~ what I do** regarde-moi (faire), regarde ce que je fais; **~ how he does it** regarde or observe comment il s'y prend; **~ the soup to see it doesn't boil over** surveille la soupe pour qu'elle ne déborde (subj) pas; **to ~ sb do** *or* **doing sth** regarder qn faire qch; **it's about as exciting as ~ing grass grow** or **~ing paint dry** c'est ennuyeux comme la pluie; **to ~ sb like a hawk** surveiller qn de (très) près; **have you ever ~ed an operation?** avez-vous déjà vu une opération or assisté à une opération?; **we are being ~ed** (gen) on nous surveille or épie; (by police, detective etc) on nous surveille; **to ~ sb's movements** [neighbour] épier les allées et venues de qn; [police, detective] surveiller les allées et venues de qn; **he needs ~ing** il faut le surveiller, il faut l'avoir à l'œil; **~ tomorrow's paper** ne manquez pas de lire le journal de demain ■ (*PROV*) **a ~ed pot never boils** plus on attend une chose, plus elle se fait attendre; **"~ this space"** « histoire à suivre », « à suivre » → **bird** [b] (Mil etc = guard) monter la garde devant, garder; (= take care of) [+ child, dog] surveiller; s'occuper de; [+ luggage, shop] surveiller, garder

c (= *be careful of, mind*) faire attention à; **~ that knife!** (fais) attention avec ce couteau!; **~ that branch!** (fais) attention à la branche!; **~ your head!** attention à ta tête!; **to ~ one's step** (*lit*) faire attention *or* regarder où on met les pieds; (*fig*) se surveiller; (*fig*) **~ your step!** ◊ **~ how you go!** ◊ **~ yourself!** (*fais*) attention!, fais gaffe!*; **we'll have to ~ the money carefully** il faudra que nous fassions attention à *or* surveillions nos dépenses; **to ~ sb's interests** veiller sur les intérêts de qn, prendre soin des intérêts de qn; **I must ~ the *or* my time as I've got a train to catch** il faut que je surveille (*subj*) l'heure car j'ai un train à prendre; **he works well but does tend to ~ the clock** il travaille bien mais il a tendance à surveiller la pendule; **to ~ what one says** faire attention à ce que l'on dit; **~ what you're doing!** fais attention (à ce que tu fais)!; **~ it!** (*warning*) attention!, fais gaffe!*; (*threat*) attention!, gare à toi!; **~ your language!** surveille ton langage!; **~ you don't burn yourself** fais attention *or* prends garde de ne pas te brûler; **~ (that) he does all his homework** veillez à ce qu'il fasse *or* assurez-vous qu'il fait tous ses devoirs

d (= *look for*) [+ *opportunity*] guetter; **he ~ed his chance and slipped out** il a guetté *or* attendu le moment propice et s'est esquivé

3 VI regarder; (= *be on guard*) faire le guet, monter la garde; (*Rel etc* = *keep vigil*) veiller; (= *pay attention*) faire attention; **he has only come to ~** il est venu simplement pour regarder *or* simplement en spectateur; **to ~ by sb's bedside** veiller au chevet de qn; **to ~ over** [+ *person*] surveiller; [+ *thing*] surveiller, garder; [+ *sb's rights, safety*] protéger, surveiller; **somebody was ~ing at the window** quelqu'un regardait à la fenêtre; **to ~ for sth/sb** (= *wait for*) guetter qch/qn; (= *be careful of*) faire attention à qch/qn; **he's ~ing to see what you're going to do** il attend pour voir ce que vous allez faire; **~ and you'll see how it's done** regarde et tu vas voir comme cela se fait; **he'll be here soon, just (you) ~** attends, il sera bientôt là → **brief**

4 COMP ► **Watch Committee** N (*Brit Hist*) *comité veillant au maintien de l'ordre dans une commune* ► **watch night service** N (*Rel*) ≈ messe *f* de minuit de la Saint-Sylvestre

► **watch out** VI (= *keep a look-out*) faire le guet; (*fig* = *take care*) faire attention, prendre garde; **~ out for the signal** guettez *or* attendez le signal; **~ out!** attention!, fais gaffe!*; (*as menace*) attention!, gare à toi!; **~ out for cars when crossing the road** faites attention *or* prenez garde aux voitures en traversant la rue; **to ~ out for thieves** faire attention aux voleurs; **~ out for trouble if ...** préparez-vous *or* attendez-vous à des ennuis si ...

watchable ['wɒtʃəbl] ADJ [*programme, film*] qui se laisse regarder

watchband ['wɒtʃbænd] N bracelet *m* de montre

watchdog ['wɒtʃdɒg] **1** N (*lit*) chien *m* de garde; (*fig*) (*official*) observateur *m*, -trice *f* officiel(le); (*unofficial*) gardien(ne) *m(f)* **2** VT (*US**) [+ *events, developments*] suivre de près **3** COMP [*group etc*] qui veille ► **watchdog committee** N comité *m* de surveillance

watcher ['wɒtʃə'] N (= *observer*) observateur *m*, -trice *f*; (*spy, hostile*) guetteur *m*; (= *spectator*) spectateur *m*, -trice *f*; (= *onlooker*) curieux *m*, -euse *f*; (*Pol*) **China ~** spécialiste *mf* des questions chinoises; **Kremlin ~** kremlinologue *mf* → **bird**

watchful ['wɒtʃfʊl] ADJ vigilant, attentif; **to keep a ~ eye on sth/sb** garder qch/qn à l'œil, avoir l'œil sur qch/qn; **under the ~ eye of ...** sous l'œil vigilant de ...

watchfully ['wɒtʃfʊlɪ] ADV avec vigilance

watchfulness ['wɒtʃfʊlnɪs] N vigilance *f*

watchmaker ['wɒtʃmeɪkə'] N horloger *m*, -ère *f*

watchmaking ['wɒtʃmeɪkɪŋ] N horlogerie *f*

watchman ['wɒtʃmən] N (*pl* **-men**) (*gen*) gardien *m*; (*also* **night ~**) veilleur *m* gardien *m* de nuit

watchtower ['wɒtʃtaʊə'] N tour *f* de guet

watchword ['wɒtʃwɜːd] N (= *password*) mot *m* de passe; (*fig* = *motto*) mot *m* d'ordre

water ['wɔːtə'] **1** N **a** (*NonC: gen*) eau *f*; **I'd like a drink of ~** je voudrais de l'eau *or* un verre d'eau; **to turn on the ~** (*at mains*) ouvrir l'eau; (*from tap*) ouvrir le robinet; **hot and cold (running) ~ in all rooms** eau courante chaude et froide dans toutes les chambres; **the road is under ~** la route est inondée, la route est recouverte par les eaux; **the road/field was under three inches of ~** la route/le champ disparaissait sous 10 cm d'eau; **to swim under ~** nager sous l'eau; **to go by ~** voyager par bateau; **the island across the ~** l'île de l'autre côté de l'eau; **we spent an afternoon on the ~** nous avons passé un après-midi sur l'eau; **at high/low ~** (= *tide*) à marée haute/basse, à mer pleine/basse; **to take in** *or* **make ~** [*ship*] faire eau; **it won't hold ~** [*container, bucket*] cela n'est pas étanche, l'eau va fuir; (*fig*) [*plan, suggestion, excuse*] cela ne tient pas debout, cela ne tient pas la route; (*fig*) **a lot of ~ has passed under the bridge since then** il est passé beaucoup d'eau sous les ponts depuis ce temps-là; (*fig*) **that's (all) ~ under the bridge** tout ça c'est du passé; **he spends money like ~** il jette l'argent par les fenêtres, l'argent lui fond dans les mains; (*fig*) **it's like ~ off a duck's back*** ça glisse comme de l'eau sur les plumes *or* les ailes d'un canard; **lavender/rose ~** eau *f* de lavande/de rose → **deep, firewater, fish**

b (*Med, Physiol*) **to pass ~** uriner; **her ~s broke** (*in labour*) elle a perdu les eaux; **~ on the knee** épanchement de synovie; **~ on the brain** hydrocéphalie *f* → **feel**

2 **waters** NPL [*of spa, lake, river, sea*] eaux *fpl*; **to take** *or* **drink the ~s** prendre les eaux, faire une cure thermale; **in French ~s** dans les eaux (territoriales) françaises; **the ~s of the Rhine** l'eau *or* les eaux du Rhin → **territorial**

3 VI [*eyes*] larmoyer, pleurer → **mouth**

4 VT [+ *plant, garden*] arroser; [+ *animals*] donner à boire à, faire boire; **the river ~s the whole province** le fleuve arrose *or* irrigue toute la province

5 COMP [*pressure, pipe, vapour*] d'eau; [*pump, mill*] à eau; [*plant etc*] aquatique; (*Ind*) [*dispute, strike*] des employés de l'eau ► **water bailiff** N garde-pêche *m* ► **water bed** N matelas *m* d'eau ► **water beetle** N gyrin *m*, tourniquet *m* ► **water bird** N oiseau *m* aquatique ► **water biscuit** N craquelin *m* ► **water blister** N (*Med*) ampoule *f*, phlyctène *f* ► **water boatman** N (*pl* **water boatmen**) (*Zool*) notonecte *m or f* ► **water bomb** N bombe *f* à eau ► **water bottle** N (*gen: plastic*) bouteille *f* (en plastique); [*of soldier*] bidon *m*; [*of cyclist, peasant*] bidon *m*; (*smaller*) gourde *f* → **hot** ► **water buffalo** N buffle *m* d'eau, buffle *m* d'Asie; (*Malaysian*) karbau *m*, kérabau *m* ► **water butt** N (*Brit*) citerne *f* (à eau de pluie) ► **water cannon** N canon *m* à eau ► **water carrier** N (= *person*) porteur *m*, -euse *f* d'eau; (= *container*) bidon *m* à eau; (*Astrol, Astron*) **the Water Carrier** le Verseau ► **water cart** N (*for streets*) arroseuse *f* (municipale); (*for selling*) voiture *f* de marchand d'eau ► **water chestnut** N macle *f*, châtaigne *f* d'eau ► **water clock** N horloge *f* à eau ► **water closet** N (*abbr* **WC**) cabinet(s) *m(pl)*, waters *mpl*, W.-C. *mpl* ► **water-cooled** ADJ à refroidissement par eau ► **water-cooler** N distributeur *m* d'eau réfrigérée ► **water-cooling** N refroidissement *m* par eau ► **water-cracker** N (*US*) = **water biscuit** ► **water diviner** N

sourcier *m*, -ière *f*, radiesthésiste *mf* ► **water divining** N art *m* du sourcier, radiesthésie *f* ► **water filter** N filtre *m* à eau ► **water fountain** N (*for drinking*) fontaine *f*, distributeur *m* d'eau fraîche; (*decorative*) jet *m* d'eau ► **water-free** ADJ sans eau, anhydre ► **water gas** N gaz *m* à l'eau ► **water glass** N **a** (= *tumbler*) verre *m* à eau **b** (*Chem*) verre *m* soluble ► **water gun** N (*US*) = **water pistol** ► **water heater** N chauffe-eau *m inv* ► **water hen** N poule *f* d'eau ► **water hole** N point *m* d'eau, mare *f* ► **water ice** N (*Brit Culin*) sorbet *m*, glace *f* à l'eau ► **water jacket** N (*Aut etc*) chemise *f* d'eau ► **water jump** N (*Racing*) rivière *f*, brook *m* ► **water level** N (*gen*) niveau *m* de l'eau; (*Aut*) [*of radiator*] niveau *m* d'eau ► **water lily** N nénuphar *m* ► **water main** N conduite *f* (principale) d'eau ► **water meadow** N (*esp Brit*) prairie *f* souvent inondée, noue *f* ► **water meter** N compteur *m* d'eau ► **water nymph** N naïade *f* ► **water pistol** N pistolet *m* à eau ► **water polo** N water-polo *m* ► **water power** N énergie *f* hydraulique, houille *f* blanche ► **water purifier** N (= *device*) épurateur *m* d'eau; (= *tablet*) cachet *m* pour purifier l'eau ► **water-rail** N (= *bird*) râle *m* (d'eau) ► **water rat** N rat *m* d'eau ► **water rate** N (*Brit*) taxe *f* sur l'eau ► **water-repellent** ADJ hydrofuge, imperméable ► **water-resistant** ADJ [*ink etc*] qui résiste à l'eau, indélébile; [*material*] imperméable ► **water-ski** N ski *m* nautique (*objet*) ♦ VI (*also* **go ~-skiing**) faire du ski nautique ► **water-skier** N skieur *m*, -euse *f* nautique ► **water-skiing** N (*NonC*) ski *m* nautique (*sport*) ► **water slide** N toboggan *m* (de piscine) ► **water snake** N serpent *m* d'eau ► **water softener** N adoucisseur *m* d'eau ► **water-soluble** ADJ soluble dans l'eau, hydrosoluble (*Chem*) ► **water sports** NPL sports *mpl* nautiques; (‡ = *sexual practices*) ondinisme *m* ► **water supply** N (*for town*) approvisionnement *m* en eau, distribution *f* des eaux; (*for building*) alimentation *f* en eau; (*for traveller*) provision *f* d'eau; **the ~ supply was cut off** on avait coupé l'eau ► **water system** N (*Geog*) réseau *m* hydrographique; (*for building, town*) = **water supply** ► **water table** N (*Geog*) nappe *f* phréatique, niveau *m* hydrostatique ► **water tank** N réservoir *m* d'eau, citerne *f* ► **water tower** N château *m* d'eau ► **water vole** N rat *m* d'eau ► **water wings** NPL bouée *f*, flotteurs *mpl* de natation ► **water worker** N (*Ind*) employé *m* du service des eaux

► **water down** VT SEP [+ *milk, wine*] couper (d'eau), baptiser*; (*fig*) [+ *story*] édulcorer; [+ *effect*] atténuer, affaiblir

waterborne ['wɔːtəbɔːn] ADJ flottant; [*boats*] à flot; [*goods*] transporté par voie d'eau; [*disease*] d'origine hydrique

watercolour, watercolor (*US*) ['wɔːtəˌkʌlə'] **1** N **a** (= *painting*) aquarelle *f* **b** (= *paint*) **~s** couleurs *fpl* à l'eau *or* pour aquarelle; **painted in ~s** peint à l'aquarelle **2** ADJ à l'aquarelle

watercolourist, watercolorist (*US*) ['wɔːtəˌkʌlərɪst] N aquarelliste *mf*

watercourse ['wɔːtəkɔːs] N cours *m* d'eau

watercress ['wɔːtəkres] N cresson *m* (de fontaine)

watered ['wɔːtəd] **1** ADJ **a** [*milk etc*] coupé d'eau **b** [*silk etc*] moiré **2** COMP ► **watered-down** ADJ (*lit*) [*milk, wine etc*] coupé d'eau; (*fig*) [*version, account*] édulcoré ► **watered silk** N (*Tex*) soie *f* moirée ► **watered stock** N (*US*) (= *cattle*) bétail *m* gorgé d'eau (avant la pesée); (*St Ex*) actions *fpl* gonflées (sans raison)

waterfall ['wɔːtəfɔːl] N chute *f* d'eau, cascade *f*

waterfowl ['wɔːtəfaʊl] N (*sg*) oiseau *m* d'eau; (*collective pl*) gibier *m* d'eau

waterfront ['wɔːtəfrʌnt] N (*at docks*) quais *mpl*; (= *sea front*) front *m* de mer

Watergate ['wɔːtəgeɪt] N Watergate *m*

watering ['wɔːtərɪŋ] **1** N [*of plants, streets*] arrosage *m*; [*of fields, region*] irrigation *f*; **frequent ~ is needed** il est conseillé d'arroser fréquemment **2** COMP ► **watering can** N arrosoir *m* ► **watering hole** N (*for animals*) point *m* d'eau; (* *fig*) bar *m* ► **watering place** N (*for animals*) point *m* d'eau; (= *spa*) station *f* thermale, ville *f* d'eaux; (= *seaside resort*) station *f* balnéaire; (*fig hum*) bar *m*

waterless ['wɔːtəlɪs] ADJ [*area*] sans eau; **to be ~** être dépourvu d'eau

waterline ['wɔːtəlaɪn] N (*Naut*) ligne *f* de flottaison; (*left by tide, river*) = **watermark**

waterlogged ['wɔːtəlɒgd] ADJ [*land, pitch*] détrempé; [*wood*] imprégné d'eau; [*shoes*] imbibé d'eau

Waterloo [ˌwɔːtəˈluː] N Waterloo *m*; **the Battle of ~** la bataille de Waterloo; (*fig*) **to meet one's ~** essuyer un revers irrémédiable

waterman ['wɔːtəmən] N (*pl* **-men**) batelier *m*

watermark ['wɔːtəmɑːk] N (*in paper*) filigrane *m*; (*left by tide*) laisse *f* de haute mer; (*left by river*) ligne *f* des hautes eaux; (*on wood, on surface*) marque *f* or tache *f* d'eau; **above/below the ~** au-dessus/au-dessous de la laisse de haute mer or de la ligne des hautes eaux

watermelon ['wɔːtəmelən] N pastèque *f*, melon *m* d'eau

waterproof ['wɔːtəpruːf] **1** ADJ [*material*] imperméable; [*watch*] étanche; [*mascara*] résistant à l'eau; **~ sheet** (*for bed*) alaise *f*; (*tarpaulin*) bâche *f* **2** N (*Brit*) imperméable *m* **3** VT imperméabiliser

waterproofing ['wɔːtəpruːfɪŋ] N (*NonC*) (= *process*) imperméabilisation *f*; (= *quality*) imperméabilité *f*

watershed ['wɔːtəʃed] N (*Geog*) ligne *f* de partage des eaux; (*fig*) moment *m* critique or décisif, grand tournant *m*; (*Brit TV*) heure à *partir de laquelle les chaînes de télévision britanniques peuvent diffuser des émissions réservées aux adultes*

waterside ['wɔːtəsaɪd] **1** N bord *m* de l'eau **2** ADJ [*flower, insect*] du bord de l'eau; [*landowner*] riverain; **at** or **by the ~** au bord de l'eau, sur la berge; **along the ~** le long de la rive

waterspout ['wɔːtəspaʊt] N (*on roof etc*) (tuyau *m* de) descente *f*; (*Met*) trombe *f*

watertight ['wɔːtətaɪt] ADJ **a** [*container*] étanche; **~ compartment** compartiment *m* étanche; **in ~ compartments** séparé par des cloisons étanches **b** (*fig*) [*excuse, plan, argument*] inattaquable, indiscutable

waterway ['wɔːtəweɪ] N voie *f* navigable

waterweed ['wɔːtəwiːd] N élodée *f*

waterwheel ['wɔːtəwiːl] N roue *f* hydraulique

waterworks ['wɔːtəwɜːks] NPL (= *system*) système *m* hydraulique; (= *place*) station *f* hydraulique; (*fig pej*) **to turn on the ~*** (= *cry*) se mettre à pleurer à chaudes larmes or comme une Madeleine*; (*Brit Med: euph*) **to have something wrong with one's ~*** avoir des ennuis de vessie

watery ['wɔːtərɪ] ADJ **a** (= *like, containing water*) [*fluid, discharge, solution*] aqueux **b** (*pej* = *containing excessive water*) [*tea, coffee*] trop léger; [*beer*] trop aqueux; [*soup, sauce*] trop clair; [*taste*] d'eau; [*paint, ink*] trop liquide, trop délayé; [*ground*] détrempé, saturé d'eau **c** (= *producing water*) [*eyes*] humide **d** (= *insipid*) [*smile, sun, light*] faible; [*sky, moon*] délavé **e** (= *pale*) [*colour*] pâle **f** (= *relating to water*) aquatique; **a ~ world of streams and fountains** un monde aquatique de cours d'eau et de fontaines; **the ~ depths** les profondeurs *fpl* aquatiques; (*liter*) **to go to a ~ grave** être enseveli dans les eaux (*liter*)

watt [wɒt] N (*Elec*) watt *m*

wattage ['wɒtɪdʒ] N (*Elec*) puissance *f* or consommation *f* en watts

wattle ['wɒtl] N **a** (*NonC* = *woven sticks*) clayonnage *m*; **~ and daub** clayonnage *m* enduit de torchis **b** [*of turkey, lizard*] caroncule *f*; [*of fish*] barbillon *m*

wave [weɪv] **1** N **a** (*at sea*) vague *f*, lame *f*; (*on lake*) vague *f*; (*on beach*) rouleau *m*; (*on river, pond*) vaguelette *f*; (*in hair*) ondulation *f*, cran *m*; (*on surface*) ondulation *f*; [*of dislike, enthusiasm, strikes, protests etc*] vague *f*; (*liter*) **the ~s** les flots *mpl*, l'onde *f*; (*fig*) **to make ~s** créer des remous; **her hair has a natural ~ (in it)** ses cheveux ondulent naturellement; (*Mil*) **the first ~ of the attack** la première vague d'assaut; **to come in ~s** [*people*] arriver par vagues; [*explosions etc*] se produire par vagues; (*Cine etc: fig*) **the new ~** la nouvelle vague → **crime, heatwave, permanent**
b (*Phys, Rad, Telec etc*) onde *f*; **long ~** grandes ondes *fpl*; **medium/short ~** ondes *fpl* moyennes/courtes → **light[1], long[1], medium, shock[1], shortwave, sound[1]**
c (= *gesture*) geste *m* or signe *m* de la main; **he gave me a cheerful ~** il m'a fait un signe joyeux de la main; **with a ~ of his hand** d'un geste or signe de la main, en agitant la main
2 VI **a** [*person*] faire signe de la main; [*flag*] flotter (au vent); [*branch, tree*] être agité; [*grass, corn*] onduler, ondoyer; **to ~ to sb** (*in greeting*) saluer qn de la main, faire bonjour (or au revoir) de la main à qn; (*as signal*) faire signe à qn (**to do** de faire)
b [*hair*] onduler, avoir un or des cran(s)
3 VT **a** [+ *flag, handkerchief*] agiter; (*threateningly*) [+ *stick, sword*] brandir; **to ~ one's hand to sb** faire signe de la main à qn; **he ~d the ticket at me furiously** il a agité vivement le ticket sous mon nez; **to ~ goodbye to sb** dire au revoir de la main à qn, agiter la main en signe or guise d'adieu (à qn); **he ~d his thanks** il a remercié d'un signe de la main, il a agité la main en signe or guise de remerciement; **to ~ sb back/through/on** *etc* faire signe à qn de reculer/de passer/d'avancer *etc*; **he ~d the car through the gates** il a fait signe à la voiture de franchir les grilles
b [+ *hair*] onduler
4 COMP ► **wave energy** N énergie *f* des vagues ► **wave guide** N (*Elec*) guide *m* d'ondes ► **wave mechanics** N (*NonC: Phys*) mécanique *f* ondulatoire ► **wave power** N énergie *f* des vagues

►**wave about, wave around** VT SEP [+ *object*] agiter dans tous les sens; **to ~ one's arms about** gesticuler, agiter les bras dans tous les sens

►**wave aside, wave away** VT SEP [+ *person, object*] écarter or éloigner d'un geste; [+ *objections*] écarter (d'un geste); [+ *offer, sb's help etc*] rejeter or refuser (d'un geste)

►**wave down** VT SEP **to ~ down a car** faire signe à une voiture de s'arrêter

►**wave off** VT SEP faire au revoir de la main à

waveband ['weɪvbænd] N (*Rad*) bande *f* de fréquences

wavelength ['weɪvleŋkθ] N (*Phys*) longueur *f* d'ondes; (*fig*) **we're not on the same ~** nous ne sommes pas sur la même longueur d'ondes*

wavelet ['weɪvlɪt] N vaguelette *f*

waver ['weɪvəʳ] VI [*flame, shadow*] vaciller, osciller; [*voice*] trembler, trembloter; [*courage, loyalty, determination*] vaciller, chanceler; [*support*] devenir hésitant; [*person*] (= *weaken*) lâcher pied, flancher*; (= *hesitate*) hésiter (**between** entre); **he ~ed in his resolution** sa résolution chancelait; **he is beginning to ~** il commence à lâcher pied or à flancher*

waverer ['weɪvərəʳ] N indécis(e) *m(f)*, irrésolu(e) *m(f)*

wavering ['weɪvərɪŋ] **1** ADJ **a** [*light, shadow*] vacillant; **his ~ steps** ses pas hésitants **b** (*fig*)

[*person*] indécis; [*support*] hésitant; [*loyalty, determination*] chancelant; [*voice*] mal assuré **2** N (*NonC* = *hesitation*) hésitations *fpl*

wavy ['weɪvɪ] **1** ADJ [*hair, surface, edge*] ondulé; [*line*] onduleux **2** COMP ► **wavy-haired** ADJ aux cheveux ondulés

wax[1] [wæks] **1** N (*NonC*) cire *f*; (*for skis*) fart *m*; (*in ear*) cérumen *m*, (bouchon *m* de) cire *f* → **beeswax, sealing[2]** **2** VT [+ *floor, furniture*] cirer, encaustiquer; [+ *skis*] farter; [+ *shoes, moustache*] cirer; [+ *thread*] poisser; [+ *car*] lustrer; **to ~ one's legs** s'épiler les jambes à la cire **3** COMP [*candle, doll, seal, record*] de or en cire ► **wax bean** N (*US*) haricot *m* beurre *inv* ► **waxed cotton** N coton *m* huilé ► **waxed jacket** N veste *f* de or en coton huilé ► **waxed paper** N papier *m* paraffiné or sulfurisé ► **wax museum** N (*esp US*) musée *m* de cire ► **wax paper** N = **waxed paper**

wax[2] [wæks] VI [*moon*] croître; **to ~ and wane** [*feelings, issues etc*] croître et décroître; († or *hum*) **to ~ merry/poetic** etc devenir d'humeur joyeuse/poétique *etc*; **to ~ eloquent** déployer toute son éloquence (**about, over** à propos de); **he ~ed lyrical about Louis Armstrong** il est devenu lyrique quand il a parlé de Louis Armstrong → **enthusiastic**

waxen ['wæksən] ADJ (*liter* = *like wax*) [*complexion, face*] cireux; († = *made of wax*) de or en cire

waxing ['wæksɪŋ] N (*gen*) cirage *m*; [*of skis*] fartage *m*

waxwing ['wækswɪŋ] N (= *bird*) jaseur *m*

waxwork ['wækswɜːk] N **a** (= *figure*) personnage *m* en cire **b** (*pl inv: Brit*) **~s** (= *museum*) musée *m* de cire

waxy ['wæksɪ] ADJ [*substance, texture, consistency*] cireux; [*complexion, face, colour*] cireux; [*potato*] ferme

---

way [weɪ]

1 NOUN	**3** COMPOUNDS
2 ADVERB	

1 NOUN
a (= *route*) chemin *m*; **to ask the** or **one's ~** demander son chemin (**to** pour aller à); **we went the wrong ~** nous avons pris le mauvais chemin, nous nous sommes trompés de chemin; **a piece of bread went down the wrong ~** j'ai (or il a *etc*) avalé une miette de pain de travers; **to go the long ~ round** prendre le chemin le plus long or le chemin des écoliers*; **we met several people on** or **along the ~** nous avons rencontré plusieurs personnes en chemin; **to go the same ~ as sb** (*lit*) aller dans la même direction que qn; (*fig*) suivre les traces or l'exemple de qn, marcher sur les traces de qn; (*fig*) **he has gone the ~ of his brothers** il a suivi le même chemin que ses frères; **they went their own ~s** or **their separate ~s** (*lit*) ils sont partis chacun de leur côté; (*fig*) chacun a suivi son chemin; (*fig*) **she knows her ~ around** or **about** elle sait se débrouiller; **to lose the** or **one's ~** se perdre, s'égarer; **to make one's ~ towards ...** se diriger vers ...; **he had to make his own ~ in Hollywood** il a dû se battre pour réussir à Hollywood

♦ **the/one's way to:** can you tell me the **~ to** the tourist office? pouvez-vous m'indiquer le chemin or la direction du syndicat d'initiative?; **the shortest** or **quickest ~ to Leeds** le chemin le plus court pour aller à Leeds; **the ~ to success** le chemin du succès; **I know the** or **my ~ to** the station je connais le chemin de la gare, je sais comment aller à la gare

♦ **on the/one's way (to):** on the or my **~ here** I saw ... en venant (ici) j'ai vu ...; **you pass it on your ~ home** vous passez devant en rentrant chez vous; **he's on his ~** il arrive; **I must be on my ~** il faut que j'y aille; **to start** or **go on one's ~** s'en aller; **with that, he went on his ~** sur ce, il s'en est allé; **on the** or **our ~ to London we met ...** en allant à Londres nous avons rencontré ...; **it's on the ~ to the station** c'est sur le chemin de la gare; **he is on the ~ to great things** il a un avenir brillant devant lui; **to be (well) on the** or one's **~ to success/victory** etc être sur la voie du succès/de la victoire etc

◆ **to be on the way** (= to be expected) être prévu; **more snow is on the ~** d'autres chutes de neige sont prévues; **she's got twins, and another baby on the ~*** elle a des jumeaux, et un bébé en route*

◆ **the/one's way back**: **the ~ back to the station** le chemin pour revenir à la gare; **on the** or his **~ back he met ...** au retour or sur le chemin du retour or en revenant il a rencontré ...; **he made his ~ back to the car** il est retourné (or revenu) vers la voiture

◆ **the/one's way down**: **I don't know the ~ down** je ne sais pas par où on descend; **I met her on the** or my **~ down** je l'ai rencontrée en descendant; **inflation is on the ~ down** l'inflation est en baisse

◆ **the way forward**: **the ~ forward is ...** l'avenir, c'est ...; **they held a meeting to discuss the ~ forward** ils ont organisé une réunion pour discuter de la marche à suivre; **is monetary union the ~ forward?** l'union monétaire est-elle la bonne voie or la voie du progrès?

◆ **the/one's way in**: **we couldn't find the ~ in** nous ne trouvions pas l'entrée; **I met her on the** or my **~ in** je l'ai rencontrée à l'entrée; (fig) **it's on the ~ in** [fashion etc] c'est à la mode

◆ **the/one's way out**: **can you find your own ~ out?** pouvez-vous trouver la sortie tout seul?; **I'll find my own ~ out** ne vous dérangez pas, je trouverai (bien) la sortie; **you'll see it on the** or **your ~ out** vous le verrez en sortant; (fig) **he tried to talk his ~ out of it** il a essayé de s'en sortir avec de belles paroles; (fig) **there's no other ~ out** il n'y a pas d'autre solution; **there is no ~ out of this difficulty** il n'y a pas moyen d'éviter cette difficulté; **it's on the ~ out** [fashion etc] ce n'est plus vraiment à la mode, c'est out*

◆ **the/one's way up**: **I don't know the ~ up** je ne sais pas par où on monte; **all the ~ up** jusqu'en haut, jusqu'au sommet; **I met him on the** or my **~ up** je l'ai rencontré en montant; **I was on my ~ up to see you** je montais vous voir; **unemployment is on the ~ up** le chômage est en hausse

◆ **a/no way round**: **we're trying to find a ~ round it** nous cherchons un moyen de contourner or d'éviter ce problème; **there's no ~ round this difficulty** il n'y a pas moyen de contourner cette difficulté

[b] **= path** **their ~ was blocked by police** la police leur barrait le passage; **to push** or **force one's ~ through a crowd** se frayer un chemin or un passage à travers une foule; **to hack** or **cut one's ~ through the jungle** se frayer un chemin à la machette dans la jungle; **to crawl/ limp** etc **one's ~ to the door** ramper/boiter etc jusqu'à la porte; **they live over** or **across the ~*** ils habitent en face

◆ **in the/sb's way**: **to be in the ~** (lit) bloquer or barrer le passage; (fig) gêner; **am I in the** or **your ~?** (lit) est-ce que je vous empêche de passer?; (fig) est-ce que je vous gêne?; **he put me in the ~ of one or two good bargains*** il m'a indiqué quelques bonnes affaires; **to put difficulties in sb's ~** créer des difficultés à qn

◆ **out of the/sb's way**: **it's out of the ~ over there** ça ne gêne pas là-bas; **to get out of the ~** s'écarter; **(get) out of the** or my **~!** pousse-toi!, laisse-moi passer!; **could you get your foot out of the ~?** tu peux pousser or retirer ton pied?; **as soon as I've got the exams out of the ~*** dès que les examens seront finis; **keep matches out of children's ~** ne laissez pas les allumettes à la portée des enfants; **to keep out of sb's ~** éviter qn; **keep (well) out of his ~ today!** ne te mets pas sur son chemin aujourd'hui!; **he kept well out of the ~** il a pris soin de rester à l'écart; **the village is quite out of the ~** le village est vraiment à l'écart or isolé; **to put sth out of the ~** ranger qch; **he wants his wife out of the ~*** il veut se débarrasser de sa femme; **I'll take you home, it's not out of my ~** je vous ramènerai, c'est sur mon chemin; **that would be nice, but don't go out of your ~** ce serait bien mais ne vous dérangez pas; (fig) **to go out of one's ~ to do sth** se donner du mal pour faire qch; **he went out of his ~ to help us** il s'est donné du mal pour nous aider; (fig) **it's nothing out of the ~** cela n'a rien de spécial or d'extraordinaire, c'est très quelconque

◆ **to make way (for)**: **to make ~ for sb** faire place à qn, s'écarter pour laisser passer qn; (fig) laisser la voie libre à qn; **they made ~ for the ambulance** ils se sont écartés or rangés pour laisser passer l'ambulance; (fig) **to make ~ for sth** ouvrir la voie à qch; **this made ~ for a return to democracy** ceci a ouvert la voie à la restauration de la démocratie; **make ~!†** place!†

[c] *** = area** **there aren't many parks round our ~** il n'y a pas beaucoup de parcs par chez nous; **round this ~** par ici; **I'll be down** or **round your ~ tomorrow** je serai près de chez vous demain; **it's out** or **over Oxford ~** c'est du côté d'Oxford

[d] **= distance** **a short ~ up the road** à quelques pas; **to be some ~ off** être assez loin; **a little ~ away** or **off** pas très loin; **he stood some ~ off** il se tenait à l'écart; **is it far? — yes, it's a good*** or **quite a* ~** — oui, il y a un bon bout de chemin*; **it's a good* ~ to London** il y a un bon bout de chemin* jusqu'à Londres; **to be a long ~ away** or **off** être loin; **it's a long ~ from here** c'est loin d'ici; **he's a long ~ from home** il est loin de chez lui; **that's a long ~ from the truth** c'est loin d'être vrai; **a long ~ off I could hear ...** j'entendais au loin ...; **is it finished? — not by a long ~!** est-ce terminé? — loin de là or loin s'en faut!; **it was our favourite by a long ~** c'était de loin celui que nous préférions; (fig) **they've come a long ~** ils ont fait du chemin; **the roots go a long ~ down** les racines sont très profondes; **we've got a long ~ to go** (lit) nous avons beaucoup de chemin à faire; (fig) (= still far from our objective) nous ne sommes pas au bout de nos peines; (= not got enough) nous sommes encore loin du compte; **to go a long ~ round** faire un grand détour; **he makes a little go a long ~** il tire le meilleur parti de ce qu'il a; **a little praise goes a long ~*** un petit compliment de temps à autre, ça aide*; **this spice is expensive, but a little goes a long ~** cette épice est chère mais on n'a pas besoin d'en mettre beaucoup; (iro) **I find a little goes a long ~ with rap music*** le rap, c'est surtout à petites doses que je l'apprécie; **it should go a long ~/some ~ towards paying the bill** cela devrait couvrir une grande partie/une partie de la facture; **it should go a long ~/some ~ towards improving relations between the two countries** cela devrait améliorer considérablement/contribuer à améliorer les rapports entre les deux pays

◆ **all the way** (= the whole distance) **he had to walk all the ~ (to the hospital)** il a dû faire tout le chemin à pied (jusqu'à l'hôpital); **there are street lights all the ~** il y a des réverbères tout le long du chemin; **it rained all the ~** il a plu pendant tout le chemin; **he talked all the ~ to the theatre** il a parlé pendant tout le chemin jusqu'au théâtre; **I'm with you all the ~*** (= entirely agree) je suis entièrement d'accord avec vous; **I'll be with you all the ~** (= will back you up) je vous soutiendrai jusqu'au bout; **to go all the ~ with sb*** coucher* avec qn; **to go all the ~*** passer à l'acte, concrétiser*

[e] **= direction** **are you going my ~?** est-ce que vous allez dans la même direction que moi?; **he never looked my ~** il n'a pas fait attention à moi; **this ~** par ici; **turn this ~ for a moment**

tourne-toi par ici un moment; **"this ~ for** or **to the cathedral"** « vers la cathédrale »; **he went that ~** il est parti par là; **which ~ did he go?** par où est-il passé?, dans quelle direction est-il parti?; (fig) **she didn't know which ~ to look** elle ne savait pas où se mettre; **which ~ do we go from here?** (lit) par où allons-nous maintenant?, quel chemin prenons-nous maintenant?; (fig) qu'allons-nous faire maintenant?; (fig) **everything's going his ~*** just now tout lui réussit en ce moment; **if the chance comes your ~*** si jamais vous en avez l'occasion; **I'll try and put some work your ~*** j'essayerai de t'avoir du travail; (lit, fig) **he looked the other ~** il a regardé ailleurs, il a détourné les yeux; **cars parked every which ~*** des voitures garées n'importe comment or dans tous les sens

◆ **this way and that**: **the leaves were blowing this ~ and that** les feuilles tournoyaient de-ci de-là; **he ran this ~ and that** il courait dans tous les sens

[f] **= footpath** **the Pennine/North Wales W~** le chemin de grande randonnée des Pennines/ du nord du pays de Galles

[g] **= side** **your jersey is the right/wrong ~ out** ton pull est à l'endroit/à l'envers; **have I got this dress the right ~ round?** est-ce que j'ai bien mis cette robe à l'endroit?; **turn the rug the other ~ round** tourne le tapis dans l'autre sens; **he didn't hit her, it was the other ~ round** ce n'est pas lui qui l'a frappée, c'est le contraire; (on box) **"this ~ up"** « haut »; **the right ~ up** dans le bon sens; **the wrong ~ up** à l'envers

[h] **= part** **the region/loot was split three ~s** la région/le butin a été divisé(e) en trois; **a three-~ discussion** une discussion à trois participants; **a four-~ radio link-up** une liaison radio à quatre voies

[i] **= manner** façon f, manière f; **(in) this/that ~** comme ceci/cela, de cette façon, de cette manière; **what an odd ~ to behave!** quelle drôle de manière or façon de se comporter!, quel drôle de comportement!; **to do sth the right/ wrong ~** bien/mal faire qch; **he had to do it, but there's a right and a wrong ~ of doing everything*** il était obligé de le faire mais il aurait pu y mettre la manière; **he said it in such a ~ that ...** il l'a dit sur un tel ton or d'une telle façon que ...; **do it your own ~** fais comme tu veux or à ta façon; **I did it my ~** je l'ai fait à ma façon; **he insisted I did it his ~** il a insisté pour que je suive sa méthode or pour que je le fasse à sa façon; **he is amusing in his (own) ~** il est amusant à sa façon; **he has his own ~ of doing things** il a une façon bien à lui de faire les choses; **in every ~ possible** ◊ **in every possible ~** [help] par tous les moyens possibles; **to try in every ~ possible** or **in every possible ~ to do sth** faire tout son possible pour faire qch; **every** or **any which ~ (one can)*** de toutes les manières possibles; (esp US) **~ to go!** bravo!; (of sb's death) **what a ~ to go!** (terrible) c'est vraiment triste de partir ainsi; (good) il (or elle) a eu une belle mort; **that's the ~ the money goes** c'est comme ça que l'argent file; **that's just the ~ he is** il est comme ça, c'est tout; **whatever ~ you look at it** quelle que soit la façon dont on envisage la chose; **leave it the ~ it is** laisse-le comme il est; **the ~ things are going we shall have nothing left** au train où vont les choses, il ne nous restera plus rien; **it's just the ~ things are** c'est la vie!

◆ **in a small/big way**: **in a small ~ he contributed to ...** à sa manière, il a contribué à ...; **in his own small ~ he helped a lot of people** à sa manière, il a aidé beaucoup de gens; **in a small ~ it did make a difference** cela a quand même fait une différence; **he furthered her career in a big ~*** il a beaucoup contribué à faire progresser sa carrière; **he does things in a big ~*** il fait les choses en grand*; **soccer is taking off in the States in a big ~*** le football connaît un vé-

ritable essor aux États-Unis
- **no way!*** pas question!; no ~ am I doing that (il n'est) pas question que je fasse ça; I'm not paying, no ~! je refuse de payer, non!; will you come? — no ~! tu viens? — pas question or sûrement pas!; there's no ~ that's champagne! ce n'est pas possible que ce soit du champagne!
- **one way or another/the other** (= somehow) d'une façon ou d'une autre; everyone helped one ~ or another tout le monde a aidé d'une façon ou d'une autre; (= either way) it doesn't matter one ~ or the other ça n'a aucune importance; two days one ~ or the other won't make much difference* deux jours de plus ou de moins ne changeront pas grand-chose
- [I] = method, technique méthode f, solution f; the best ~ is to put it in the freezer for ten minutes la meilleure méthode or solution, c'est de le mettre au congélateur pendant dix minutes, le mieux, c'est de le mettre au congélateur pendant dix minutes; that's the ~ to do it voilà comment il faut faire or s'y prendre; that's quite the wrong ~ to go about it ce n'est pas comme ça qu'il faut s'y prendre or qu'il faut le faire; that's the ~! voilà, c'est bien or c'est ça!
- **to have a way with**: he has a ~ with people il sait s'y prendre avec les gens; he has got a ~ with cars il s'y connaît en voitures; to have a ~ with words (= be eloquent) manier les mots avec bonheur; (pej) avoir du bagou*; she has a (certain) ~ with her* elle a un certain charme
- [k] = means moyen m; we'll find a ~ to do or of doing it nous trouverons bien un moyen de le faire ∎ (PROV) love will find a ~ l'amour finit toujours par triompher
- **by way of** (= via) par; (= as) en guise de; (= so as to) pour, afin de; (= by means of) au moyen de; he went by ~ of Glasgow il est passé par Glasgow; "I'm superstitious", she said by ~ of explanation «je suis superstitieuse», dit-elle en guise d'explication; it was by ~ of being a joke c'était une plaisanterie; I did it by ~ of discovering what ... je l'ai fait pour découvrir or afin de découvrir ce que ...; by ~ of lectures, practicals and tutorials au moyen de cours magistraux, de travaux pratiques et de travaux dirigés
- [l] = situation, state, nature that's always the ~ c'est toujours comme ça; that's always the ~ with him c'est toujours comme ça or toujours pareil avec lui; it was this ~ ... (= happened like this) ça s'est passé comme ça ...; in the ordinary ~ of things d'ordinaire, normalement; it's the ~ of the world! ainsi va le monde!; things are in a bad ~* ça va mal; he is in a bad ~* il va mal; the car is in a very bad ~* la voiture est en piteux état; she was in a terrible ~* (physically) elle était dans un état lamentable; (= agitated) elle était dans tous ses états
- [m] = habit to get into/out of the ~ of doing sth prendre/perdre l'habitude de faire qch; that's not my ~ ce n'est pas mon genre, je ne suis pas comme ça; it's not my ~ to flatter people ce n'est pas mon genre or dans mes habitudes de flatter les gens; don't be offended, it's just his ~ ne vous vexez pas, il est comme ça, c'est tout; it's only his (little) ~ il est comme ça; he has an odd ~ of scratching his chin when he laughs il a une drôle de façon or manière de se gratter le menton quand il rit; I know his little ~s je connais ses petites habitudes or ses petits travers; they didn't like his pretentious ~s ils n'aimaient pas ses manières prétentieuses; I love her funny little ~s j'adore sa manière bien à elle de faire les choses; to mend or improve one's ~s s'amender; she is very precise in her ~s elle porte une attention maniaque aux détails; Spanish ~s ◊ the ~s of the Spanish les coutumes fpl or mœurs fpl espagnoles
- [n] = respect, particular in some ~s à certains égards; in many ~s à bien des égards; in more ~s than one à plus d'un titre; can I help you in

any ~? puis-je vous aider en quoi que ce soit?, puis-je faire quelque chose pour vous aider?; does that in any ~ explain it? est-ce là une explication satisfaisante?; he's in no ~ or not in any ~ to blame ce n'est vraiment pas de sa faute; not in any ~! pas le moins du monde!; I offended her, without in any ~ intending to do so je l'ai vexée tout à fait involontairement; he's right in a or one ~ il a raison dans un certain sens; she's good/bad/clever etc that ~* elle est bonne/mauvaise/douée etc pour ce genre de choses
- **by way of** ◊ **in the way of** (= as regards) what is there by ~ or in the ~ of kitchen utensils? qu'est-ce qu'il y a comme ustensiles de cuisine?
- **by the way** → by
- [o] = desire to get one's own ~ n'en faire qu'à sa tête; to want one's own ~ vouloir imposer sa volonté; I won't let him have things all his own ~ je ne vais pas le laisser faire tout ce qu'il veut; Arsenal had it all their own ~ in the second half* Arsenal a complètement dominé la deuxième mi-temps; (hum) to have or get one's wicked or evil ~ with sb (= seduce) parvenir à ses fins avec qn
- [p] = possibility there are no two ~s about it il n'y a pas à tortiller*; (Racing) each ~ gagnant ou placé; you can't have it both or all ~s il faut choisir
- [q] Naut = speed to gather/lose ~ prendre/perdre de la vitesse
- 2 ADVERB
- [a] = far ~ over there là bas, au loin; ~ down below tout en bas; ~ up in the sky très haut dans le ciel; ~ out to sea loin au large; you're ~ out* in your calculations tu t'es trompé de beaucoup dans tes calculs
- [b] * = very much très; I had to plan ~ in advance j'ai dû m'y prendre très longtemps à l'avance; it's ~ too big c'est beaucoup trop grand; ~ above average bien au-dessus de la moyenne; it's ~ past your bedtime ça fait longtemps que tu devrais être au lit
- 3 COMPOUNDS
- ► **way of life** N mode m de vie; the French ~ of life le mode de vie des Français, la vie française; (fig) such shortages are a ~ of life de telles pénuries sont monnaie courante or font partie de la vie de tous les jours ► **the Way of the Cross** N (Rel) le chemin de la Croix ► **way-out*** ADJ excentrique; ~-out! super!*, formidable! ► **way port** N port m intermédiaire ► **ways and means** NPL moyens mpl (of doing de faire) ► **Ways and Means Committee** N (US Pol) commission des finances de la Chambre des représentants (examinant les recettes) ► **way station** N (US Rail) petite gare f; (fig = stage) étape f ► **way train** N (US) omnibus m

waybill ['weɪbɪl] N (Comm) récépissé m
wayfarer ['weɪ͵fɛərə] N voyageur m, -euse f
wayfaring ['weɪ͵fɛərɪŋ] N voyages mpl
waylay ['weɪ'leɪ] (pret, ptp **waylaid**) VT [a] (= attack) attaquer, assaillir [b] (= speak to) arrêter au passage
wayside ['weɪsaɪd] [1] N bord m or côté m de la route; along the ~ le long de la route; by the ~ au bord de la route; (liter) to fall by the ~ (= err, sin) quitter le droit chemin; (fig) to fall or go by the ~ [competitor, contestant] (= drop out) abandonner; (= be eliminated) être éliminé; [project, plan] tomber à l'eau; [marriage] se solder par un échec; [company] connaître l'échec; it went by the ~ on a dû laisser tomber*; his diet soon fell or went by the ~ il a vite oublié son régime; two actors fell by the ~ during the making of the film (= gave up) deux acteurs ont abandonné pendant le tournage du film; (= were sacked) deux acteurs ont été renvoyés pendant le tournage du film; a lot of business opportunities are

going by the ~ on perd de nombreuses occasions de faire des affaires
2 COMP [plant, café] au bord de la route
wayward ['weɪwəd] ADJ [a] (= wilful) [person] qui n'en fait qu'à sa tête; [horse, behaviour] rétif; (= capricious) versatile; (= unfaithful) her ~ husband son mari volage [b] (gen hum = unmanageable) [hair] rebelle; [satellite, missile] incontrôlable
waywardness ['weɪwədnɪs] N (NonC) (= stubbornness) entêtement m; (= capriciousness) inconstance f
WBA ['dʌbljuːbiː'eɪ] N (ABBR = World Boxing Association) WBA f
WC ['dʌbljuː'siː] N (ABBR = water closet) W.-C. or WC mpl
we [wiː] PERS PRON (pl: unstressed, stressed) nous; **we went to the pictures** nous sommes allés or on est allé* au cinéma; **as we say in England** comme on dit (chez nous) en Angleterre; **we all make mistakes** tout le monde peut se tromper; **we French** nous autres Français; **we teachers understand that** ... nous autres professeurs, nous comprenons que ...; **we three have already discussed it** nous en avons déjà discuté tous les trois; **"we agree"** said the king «nous sommes d'accord» dit le roi → royal
w/e (ABBR = week ending) ~ **28 Oct** semaine terminant le 28 octobre
WEA ['dʌbljuːiː'eɪ] N (in Brit) (ABBR = Workers' Educational Association) association d'éducation populaire
weak [wiːk] [1] ADJ [a] (= debilitated) (gen) faible; [immune system] affaibli; to grow ~(er) [person] s'affaiblir, devenir plus faible; [structure, material] faiblir; [voice] faiblir, devenir plus faible; to have a ~ heart être cardiaque, avoir le cœur fragile; to have ~ lungs or a ~ chest avoir les poumons fragiles; (lit) to have a ~ stomach avoir l'estomac fragile; (fig) to have a ~ stomach être impressionnable; to have ~ eyesight avoir la vue faible, avoir une mauvaise vue; to have a ~ chin/mouth avoir le menton fuyant/la bouche veule; ~ from or with hunger affaibli par la faim; he was ~ from or with fright la peur lui coupait les jambes; to feel ~ with desire se sentir défaillir sous l'effet du désir; to feel ~ with relief trembler rétrospectivement; his knees felt ~ ◊ he went ~ at the knees (from fright) ses genoux se dérobaient sous lui; (from fatigue, illness etc) il avait les jambes molles or comme du coton*; (hum) he went ~ at the knees at the sight of her il s'est senti défaillir quand il l'a vue; to be ~ in the head* être faible d'esprit, être débile*; ~ point or spot point m faible; (fig) the ~ link in the chain le point faible; (US) the ~ sister* le faiblard* (or la faiblarde*) (dans un groupe) → constitution, sex, wall
[b] (= poor, unconvincing) [essay, script, plot, novel, excuse, argument, evidence] faible; [actor, acting] médiocre; to give a ~ performance [actor, dancer, athlete] faire une prestation médiocre; [currency] mal se comporter; [company] avoir de mauvais résultats; the economy has begun a ~ recovery l'économie connaît une faible reprise; to give a ~ smile avoir un faible sourire; he is ~ in maths il est faible en maths; French is one of his ~er subjects le français est une de ses matières faibles, le français n'est pas son fort*
[c] (= not powerful) [army, country, team, government, political party, economy, currency, demand] faible; the government is in a very ~ position le gouvernement est dans une très mauvaise position or n'est pas du tout en position de force; you're too ~ with her tu te montres trop faible envers elle; to grow ~(er) [influence, power] baisser, diminuer; [economy] s'affaiblir; [currency, demand] faiblir, s'affaiblir

d [*coffee, tea*] léger; [*solution, mixture, drug, lens, spectacles, magnet*] faible; (*Elec*) [*current*] faible

2 the weak NPL les faibles *mpl*

3 COMP ► **weak-kneed*** ADJ (*fig*) mou (molle *f*), lâche, faible ► **weak-minded** ADJ (= *simple-minded*) faible or simple d'esprit; (= *indecisive*) irrésolu ► **weak verb** N (*Gram*) verbe *m* faible ► **weak-willed** ADJ faible, velléitaire

weaken ['wi:kən] **1** VI [*person*] (*in health*) s'affaiblir; (*in resolution*) faiblir, flancher*; (= *relent*) se laisser fléchir; [*structure, material*] faiblir, commencer à fléchir; [*voice*] faiblir, baisser; [*influence, power*] baisser, diminuer; [*country, team*] faiblir; (*St Ex*) [*prices*] fléchir; (*St Ex*) **the price of tin has ~ed further** le cours de l'étain a de nouveau faibli or a accentué son repli **2** VT [+ *person*] (*physically*) affaiblir, miner; (*morally, politically*) affaiblir; [+ *join, structure, material*] abîmer; [+ *heart, muscles, eyesight*] affaiblir; [+ *country, team, government*] affaiblir, rendre vulnérable; [+ *defence, argument, evidence*] affaiblir, enlever du poids or de la force à; [+ *coffee, solution, mixture*] couper, diluer; (*Econ*) [+ *the pound, dollar*] affaiblir, faire baisser

weakening ['wi:kənɪŋ] **1** N [*of health, resolution*] affaiblissement *m*; [*of structure, material*] fléchissement *m*, fatigue *f* **2** ADJ [*effect*] affaiblissant, débilitant; [*disease, illness*] débilitant, qui mine

weakling ['wi:klɪŋ] N (*physically*) gringalet *m*, mauviette *f*; (*morally etc*) faible *mf*, poule *f* mouillée

weakly ['wi:klɪ] **1** ADV **a** (= *feebly*) [*move, smile, speak*] faiblement; **his heart was beating ~** son cœur battait faiblement **b** (= *irresolutely*) [*say, protest*] mollement **2** ADJ [*person*] chétif

weakness ['wi:knɪs] N **a** (*NonC: lit, fig* = *lack of strength*) [*of person, argument, signal, currency*] faiblesse *f*; [*of industry, economy, regime*] fragilité *f*; (*fig*) **to negotiate from a position of ~** négocier dans une position d'infériorité **b** (= *weak point*) [*of person, system, argument*] point *m* faible **c** (*NonC: pej, Psych*) [*of person, character*] faiblesse *f*; **a sign of ~** un signe de faiblesse **d** (= *defect*) [*of structure, material*] défaut *m* **e** (*NonC* = *fragility*) [*of structure, material*] défauts *mpl* **f** (= *penchant*) [*of person*] faible *m* (**for sth** pour qch); **a ~ for sweet things** un faible pour les sucreries

weal¹ [wi:l] N (*esp Brit: on skin*) zébrure *f*

weal²†† [wi:l] N bien *m*, bonheur *m*; **the common ~** le bien public; **~ and woe** le bonheur et le malheur

weald†† [wi:ld] N (= *wooded country*) pays *m* boisé; (= *open country*) pays *m* découvert

wealth [welθ] **1** N **a** (*NonC*) (= *fact of being rich*) richesse *f*; (= *money, possessions, resources*) richesses *fpl*, fortune *f*; (= *natural resources etc*) richesse(s) *f(pl)*; **a man of great ~** un homme très riche; **the ~ of the oceans** les richesses *fpl* or les riches ressources *fpl* des océans; **the mineral ~ of a country** les richesses *fpl* minières d'un pays **b** (*fig* = *abundance*) **a ~ of ideas** une profusion or une abondance d'idées; **a ~ of experience/talent** énormément d'expérience/de talent; **a ~ of information** or **detail about sth** une mine de renseignements sur qch; **the lake is home to a ~ of species** ce lac abrite une faune et une flore très riches **2** COMP ► **wealth tax** N (*Brit*) impôt *m* sur la fortune

wealthy ['welθɪ] **1** ADJ [*person, family*] fortuné; [*country*] riche **2 the wealthy** NPL les riches *mpl*

wean [wi:n] **1** VT sevrer; **to ~ a baby (onto solids)** sevrer un bébé; (*fig: from bad habits etc*) **to ~ sb off cigarettes/alcohol** aider qn à arrêter de fumer/de boire; **to ~ o.s. off**

cigarettes/chocolate/alcohol apprendre à se passer de cigarettes/de chocolat/d'alcool; **I ~ed her off the idea of going to Greece** je l'ai dissuadée de partir en Grèce; **I'm trying to ~ her onto more adult novels** j'essaie de lui faire lire des romans plus adultes; (*fig*) **to be ~ed on sth** être nourri de qch (*fig*) **2** [weɪn] N (*Scot* = *baby, young child*) petit(e) *m(f)*

weaning ['wi:nɪŋ] N (*lit, fig*) [*of baby, addict*] sevrage *m*

weapon ['wepən] N (*lit, fig*) arme *f*; **~ of offence/defence** arme *f* offensive/défensive

weaponry ['wepənrɪ] N (*NonC: collective*) (*gen* = *arms*) armes *fpl*; (*Mil*) matériel *m* de guerre, armements *mpl*

wear [wɛəʳ] (*vb: pret* **wore**, *ptp* **worn**) **1** N (*NonC*) **a** (= *clothes collectively*) vêtements *mpl*; **children's/summer/ski ~** vêtements *mpl* pour enfants/d'été/de ski; **it is compulsory ~ for officers** le port en est obligatoire pour les officiers; **what is the correct ~ for these occasions?** quelle est la tenue convenable pour de telles occasions?, qu'est-ce qui est de mise en de telles occasions? → **footwear**, **sportswear** **b** (= *act of wearing*) **clothes for everyday ~** vêtements *mpl* pour tous les jours; **it's suitable for everyday ~** on peut le porter tous les jours; **clothes for evening ~** tenue *f* de soirée; **for evening ~, dress the outfit up with jewellery** pour le soir, agrémentez cette tenue de bijoux; **clothes for informal** or **casual ~** des vêtements *mpl* décontractés **c** (= *use*) usage *m*; (= *deterioration through use*) usure *f*; **this material will stand up to a lot of ~** ce tissu résistera bien à l'usure; **this carpet has seen** or **had some hard ~** ce tapis a beaucoup servi; **there is still some ~ left in it** (*garment, shoe*) c'est encore mettable; (*carpet, tyre*) cela fera encore de l'usage; **he got four years' ~ out of it** cela lui a fait or duré quatre ans; **it has had a lot of ~** c'est très usagé, cela a été beaucoup porté or utilisé; **fair** or **normal ~ and tear** usure *f* normale; **the ~ and tear on the engine** l'usure du moteur; **to show signs of ~** [*clothes, shoes*] commencer à être défraîchi or fatigué; [*carpet*] commencer à être usé; [*tyres, machine*] commencer à être fatigué or usagé; (*US*) **~ resistant** inusable → **worse**

2 VT **a** [+ *garment, flower, sword, watch, spectacles, disguise*] porter; [+ *beard, moustache*] porter, avoir; [+ *bandage, plaster, tampon, sanitary towel*] avoir; **he was ~ing a hat** il avait or il portait un chapeau; **I never ~ a hat** je ne mets or porte jamais de chapeau; **people rarely ~ hats now** les chapeaux ne se portent plus guère aujourd'hui; **he was ~ing nothing but a bath towel** il n'avait qu'une serviette de bain sur lui; **he was ~ing nothing but a pair of socks** il n'avait pour tout vêtement qu'une paire de chaussettes; **what shall I ~?** qu'est-ce que je vais mettre?; **I've nothing to ~** ◊ **I haven't got a thing to ~*** je n'ai rien à me mettre; **she had nothing to ~ to a formal dinner** elle n'avait rien à se mettre pour un dîner habillé; **I haven't worn it for ages** cela fait des siècles que je ne l'ai pas mis or porté; **they don't ~ (a) uniform at her school** on ne porte pas d'uniforme dans son école; **cyclists should always ~ a helmet** les cyclistes devraient toujours porter or mettre un casque; **she was ~ing blue** elle était en bleu; **what the well-dressed woman is ~ing this year** ce que la femme élégante porte cette année; **he ~s good clothes** il s'habille bien; **she was ~ing a bandage on her arm** elle avait le bras bandé; **she ~s her hair long** elle a les cheveux longs; **she ~s her hair in a bun** elle porte un chignon; **she usually ~s her hair up** (*in ponytail, plaits etc*) elle s'attache généralement les cheveux; (*in a bun*) elle relève généralement ses cheveux en chignon; **to ~ lipstick/moisturizer** *etc* (se) mettre du rouge à lèvres/de la crème

hydratante *etc*; **to ~ perfume** se parfumer, (se) mettre du parfum; **she was ~ing perfume** elle s'était parfumée, elle s'était mis du parfum; **she was ~ing make-up** elle (s')était maquillée; (*fig*) **she's the one who ~s the trousers** or (*esp US*) **the pants** c'est elle qui porte la culotte* or qui commande **b** (*fig*) [+ *smile*] arborer; [+ *look*] avoir, afficher; **she wore a frown** elle fronçait les sourcils; **he wore a look** or **an air of satisfaction** ◊ **he wore a satisfied look on his face** son visage exprimait la satisfaction, il affichait or avait un air de satisfaction; **she ~s her age** or **her years well** elle se porte bien son âge, elle est encore bien pour son âge **c** (= *rub etc*) [+ *clothes, fabric, stone, wood*] user; [+ *groove, path*] creuser peu à peu; **to ~ a hole in sth** trouer or percer peu à peu qch, faire peu à peu un trou dans or à qch; **the rug was worn thin** or **threadbare** le tapis était usé jusqu'à la corde or complètement râpé; **worn with care** usé or rongé par les soucis → **worn; → frazzle, work d** (*Brit** = *tolerate, accept*) tolérer; **he won't ~ that** il n'acceptera jamais (ça), il ne marchera pas*; **the committee won't ~ another £100 on your expenses** vous ne ferez jamais avaler au comité 100 livres de plus pour vos frais*

3 VI **a** (= *deteriorate with use*) [*garment, fabric, stone, wood*] s'user; **these trousers have worn at the knees** ce pantalon est usé aux genoux; **to ~ into holes** se trouer peu à peu; **the rock has worn smooth** la roche a été polie par le temps; **the material has worn thin** le tissu est râpé; **the rug has worn thin** or **threadbare** le tapis est usé jusqu'à la corde or complètement râpé; (*fig*) **that excuse has worn thin!** cette excuse ne prend plus!; **my patience is ~ing thin** je suis presque à bout de patience; **their optimism is starting to ~ thin** ils commencent à perdre leur optimisme; **that joke is starting to ~ a bit thin!** cette plaisanterie commence à être éculée!, cette plaisanterie n'est plus vraiment drôle! **b** (= *last*) [*clothes, carpet, tyres etc*] faire de l'usage, résister à l'usure; **that dress/carpet has worn well** cette robe/ce tapis a bien résisté à l'usure or a fait beaucoup d'usage; (*fig*) **a theory/friendship that has worn well** une théorie/amitié qui a résisté à l'épreuve du temps; **she has worn well*** elle est bien conservée **c** **to ~ to its end** or **to a close** [*day, year, sb's life*] tirer à sa fin

► **wear away 1** VI [*wood, metal*] s'user; [*cliffs, rock etc*] être rongé or dégradé; [*inscription, design*] s'effacer **2** VT SEP [+ *wood, metal*] user; [+ *cliffs, rock*] ronger, dégrader; [+ *inscription, design*] effacer

► **wear down 1** VI [*heels, pencil etc*] s'user; [*resistance, courage*] s'épuiser **2** VT SEP [+ *materials*] user; [+ *patience, strength*] user, épuiser; [+ *courage, resistance*] miner; **the hard work was ~ing him down** le travail l'usait or le minait; **constantly being criticized ~s you down** ça (vous) mine d'être constamment critiqué; **I had worn myself down by overwork** je m'étais usé or épuisé en travaillant trop; **the unions managed to ~ the employers down and get their demands met** les syndicats ont réussi à faire céder les employeurs et à obtenir ce qu'ils demandaient

► **wear off 1** VI [*colour, design, inscription*] s'effacer, disparaître; [*pain*] disparaître, passer; [*anger, excitement*] s'apaiser, passer; [*effects*] se dissiper, disparaître; [*anaesthetic, magic*] se dissiper; **the novelty has worn off** cela n'a plus l'attrait de la nouveauté **2** VT SEP effacer par l'usure, faire disparaître

► **wear on** VI [*day, year, winter etc*] avancer; [*battle, war, discussions etc*] se poursuivre; **as the years wore on** à mesure que les années passaient, avec le temps

►**wear out** [1] VI [clothes, material, machinery] s'user; [patience, enthusiasm] s'épuiser [2] VT SEP [a] [+ shoes, clothes] user; [+ one's strength, reserves, materials, patience] épuiser [b] [= exhaust] [+ person, horse] épuiser; **to ~ one's eyes out** s'user les yeux or la vue; **to ~ o.s. out** s'épuiser, s'exténuer (**doing** à faire); **to be worn out** être exténué or éreinté [3] **worn-out** ADJ → **worn**

►**wear through** [1] VT SEP trouer, percer [2] VI se trouer (par usure)

wearable ['wɛərəbl] ADJ [clothes] mettable, portable; [shoes] mettable; [colour] facile à porter

wearer ['wɛərəʳ] N porteur m, euse f; **denture/spectacle/contact lens ~s** les porteurs mpl de dentier/de lunettes/de lentilles; **he's not really a tie ~** ce n'est pas vraiment son style de porter la cravate; **this device can improve the ~'s hearing considerably** cet appareil peut considérablement améliorer l'audition (de l'utilisateur); **special suits designed to protect the ~ from the cold** des combinaisons spéciales conçues pour protéger (l'utilisateur) du froid; **direct from maker to ~** directement du fabricant au client

wearied ['wɪərɪd] ADJ [person, animal, smile, look] las (lasse f); [sigh] de lassitude; **~ by sth** las de qch

wearily ['wɪərɪlɪ] ADV [say, smile, look at, nod] d'un air las, avec lassitude; [sigh, think, move] avec lassitude

weariness ['wɪərɪnɪs] N (NonC) (physical) lassitude f, fatigue f; (mental) lassitude f (**with sth** à l'égard de qch), abattement m → **war, world**

wearing ['wɛərɪŋ] ADJ [person, job] fatigant, lassant; **it's ~ on one's nerves** ça met les nerfs à rude épreuve

wearisome ['wɪərɪsəm] ADJ (frm) (= tiring) lassant, fatigant; (= boring) ennuyeux, lassant, fastidieux; (= frustrating) frustrant

weary ['wɪərɪ] ADJ [a] (= tired) las (lasse f); **to be ~ of (doing) sth** être las de (faire) qch; **~ of life** las de vivre; **~ with walking** las d'avoir marché; **to grow ~** [person, animal] se lasser; [eyes] devenir las; **to grow ~ of (doing) sth** se lasser de (faire) qch → **world** [b] (liter) [months, miles, wait] épuisant; **I made my ~ way back home** je suis rentré, épuisé [2] VI se lasser (**of** sth de qch, **of doing** de faire) [3] VT (= tire) fatiguer, lasser; (= try patience of) lasser, agacer, ennuyer (**with** à force de) → **wearied**

weasel ['wiːzl] [1] N (pl **weasel** or **weasels**) belette f; (fig pej = person) fouine f (fig pej) [2] VI (US*: also **~-word**) (speaking) s'exprimer de façon ambiguë or équivoque; **to ~ out of sth** (= extricate o.s.) se sortir or se tirer de qch en misant sur l'ambiguïté; (= avoid it) éviter qch en misant sur l'ambiguïté [3] COMP ► **weasel words** NPL (fig) paroles fpl ambiguës or équivoques

weather ['wɛðəʳ] [1] N temps m; **what's the ~ like?** ◊ **what's the ~ doing?*** quel temps fait-il?; **it's fine/bad ~** il fait beau/mauvais; **summer ~** temps m d'été or estival; **in this ~** par ce temps, par un temps comme ça; **in hot/cold/wet/stormy ~** par temps chaud/froid/humide/orageux; **in good ~** par beau temps; **to be under the ~*** être mal fichu*, ne pas être dans son assiette → **heavy, wet** [2] VT [a] (= survive) [+ tempest, hurricane] essuyer; (fig) [+ crisis] survivre à, réchapper à; **to ~ a storm** (lit) essuyer une tempête; (fig) tenir le coup; **can the company ~ the recession?** l'entreprise peut-elle survivre à or surmonter la récession? [b] (= expose to weather) [+ wood etc] faire mûrir; **~ed rocks** rochers mpl exposés aux intempéries; **rocks ~ed by rain and wind** rochers mpl érodés par la pluie et par le vent [3] VI [wood] mûrir; [rocks] s'éroder

[4] COMP [knowledge, map, prospects] météorologique; [conditions, variations] atmosphérique; (Naut) [side, sheet] du vent ► **weather-beaten** ADJ [person, face] hâlé, tanné; [building] dégradé par les intempéries; [stone] érodé or usé par les intempéries ► **weatherbound** ADJ immobilisé or retenu par le mauvais temps ► **Weather Bureau** N (US) = **Weather Centre** ► **Weather Centre** N (Brit) Office m national de la météorologie ► **weather chart** N carte f du temps, carte f météorologique ► **weather check** N (bref) bulletin m météo inv ► **weather cock** N girouette f ► **weather eye** N (fig) **to keep a ~ eye on sth** surveiller qch; (fig) **to keep one's ~ eye open** veiller au grain (fig) ► **weather forecast** N prévisions fpl météorologiques, météo* f (NonC) ► **weather forecaster** N météorologue mf, météorologiste mf ► **weather girl*** N présentatrice f météo inv ► **weather report** N bulletin m météo(rologique), météo* f (NonC) ► **weather ship** N navire m météo inv ► **weather station** N station f or observatoire m météorologique ► **weather strip** N bourrelet m (pour porte etc) ► **weather vane** N = **weather cock** ► **weather-worn** ADJ = **weather-beaten**

weatherboard(ing) ['wɛðəbɔːd(ɪŋ)] N (NonC) planches fpl à recouvrement

weatherman* ['wɛðəmæn] N (pl **-men**) météorologue m; (on TV) présentateur m météo inv

weatherproof ['wɛðəpruːf] [1] ADJ [clothing] imperméable; [house] étanche [2] VT [+ clothing] imperméabiliser; [+ house] rendre étanche

weave [wiːv] (vb: pret **wove**, ptp **woven**) [1] N tissage m; **loose/tight ~** tissage m lâche/serré; **a cloth of English ~** du drap tissé en Angleterre [2] VT [+ threads, cloth, web] tisser; [+ strands] entrelacer; [+ basket, garland, daisies] tresser; (fig) [+ plot] tramer, tisser; [+ story] inventer, bâtir; **to ~ flowers into one's hair** entrelacer des fleurs dans ses cheveux; **to ~ details into a story** introduire or incorporer des détails dans une histoire; **to ~ one's way** → **3b** [3] VI [a] (Tex etc) tisser [b] (pret, ptp gen **weaved**) (also **~ one's** or **its way**) [road, river, line] serpenter; **to ~ (one's way) through the crowd** se faufiler à travers la foule; **the drunk ~d (his way) across the room** l'ivrogne a titubé or zigzagué à travers la pièce; **the car was weaving (its way) in and out through the traffic** la voiture se faufilait or se glissait à travers la circulation; **the boxer was weaving in and out skilfully** le boxeur esquivait les coups adroitement; **to ~ in and out of the trees** zigzaguer entre les arbres; (fig) **let's get weaving!†*** allons, remuons-nous!

weaver ['wiːvəʳ] N (= person) tisserand(e) m(f); (also **~ bird**) tisserin m

weaving ['wiːvɪŋ] [1] N (NonC) [of threads, cloth, web] tissage m; [of basket, garland, daisies] tressage m; [of strands] entrelacement m; [of plot] élaboration f [2] COMP ► **weaving mill** N (atelier m de) tissage m

web [web] [1] N [a] (= fabric) tissu m; [of spider] toile f; (between toes etc) [of animals etc] palmure f; [of humans] palmature f; (fig) [of lies etc] tissu m [b] (Comput) **the (World Wide) Web** le Web [2] COMP ► **web(bed) feet, web(bed) toes** NPL **to have ~(bed) feet** or **toes** [animal] être palmipède, avoir les pieds palmés; [human] avoir une palmature ► **web-footed** ADJ **to be ~-footed** = **to have web(bed) feet**

webbing ['webɪŋ] N (NonC) [a] (= fabric) toile f; (on chair: also Mil) sangles fpl [b] (on bird's, animal's foot) palmure f; (on human foot) palmature f

website ['websaɪt] N (Comput) site m Web

we'd [wiːd] = **we had, we should, we would;** → **have, should, would**

wed [wed] (pret **wedded**, ptp **wedded, wed**) [1] VT [a] (= marry) épouser, se marier avec; [priest] marier; **to be ~ to get** se marier [b] (fig) → **wedded** [2] VI† se marier

Wed. ABBR = **Wednesday**

wedded ['wedɪd] ADJ [a] (frm = married) [person, couple] marié; [life] conjugal; **~ bliss** bonheur m conjugal; **his (lawful or lawfully) ~ wife** sa légitime épouse; **do you take this woman to be your lawful(ly) ~ wife?** voulez-vous prendre cette femme pour épouse? [b] (= committed) **to be ~ to sth** [+ idea] être profondément attaché à qch; [+ cause] être entièrement dévoué à qch; **he is ~ to his work** il est marié avec son travail, il ne vit que pour son travail [c] (= allied) **to be ~ to sth** être allié à qch; **he advocates change ~ to caution** il prône le changement allié à la prudence; **his cunning, ~ to ambition, led to ...** sa ruse, alliée à l'ambition, a conduit à ...

wedding ['wedɪŋ] [1] N (= ceremony) mariage m, noces fpl; **silver/golden ~** noces fpl d'argent/d'or; **they had a quiet ~** ils se sont mariés dans l'intimité, le mariage a été célébré dans l'intimité; **they had a church ~** ils se sont mariés à l'église → **civil** [2] COMP [cake, night] de noces; [present] de mariage, de noces; [invitation] de mariage; [ceremony, march] nuptial ► **wedding anniversary** N anniversaire m de mariage ► **wedding band** N = **wedding ring** ► **wedding breakfast** N (Brit) lunch m de mariage; (less elegant) repas m de noces ► **wedding day** N **her/my/their ~ day** le jour de son/mon/leur mariage ► **wedding dress, wedding gown** N robe f de mariée ► **wedding guest** N invité(e) m(f) (à un mariage) ► **wedding reception** N réception f de mariage ► **wedding ring** N alliance f, anneau m de mariage ► **wedding vows** NPL vœux mpl de mariage

wedeln ['veɪdln] (Ski) [1] VI godiller [2] N godille f

wedge [wedʒ] [1] N [a] (for holding sth steady: under wheel etc, also Golf) cale f; (for splitting wood, rock) coin m; (fig) **that drove a ~ between them** cela a creusé un fossé entre eux → **thin** [b] (= piece) [of cake, cheese, pie etc] (grosse) part f, (gros) morceau m [c] (Ski) chasse-neige m; (Climbing) coin m de bois [2] **wedges** NPL (= wedge-heeled shoe) chaussures fpl à semelles compensées [3] VT (= fix) [+ table, wheels] caler; (= stick, push) enfoncer (**into** dans, **between** entre); **to ~ a door open/shut** maintenir une porte ouverte/fermée à l'aide d'une cale; **the door was ~d** on avait mis une cale à la porte; **he ~d the table leg to hold it steady** il a calé le pied de la table (pour la stabiliser); **to ~ a stick into a crack** enfoncer un bâton dans une fente; **I can't move this, it's ~d** je n'arrive pas à le faire bouger, c'est coincé; **she was sitting on the bench, ~d between her mother and her aunt** elle était assise sur le banc, coincée entre sa mère et sa tante [4] COMP ► **wedge-heeled** ADJ à semelles compensées ► **wedge-shaped** ADJ en forme de coin ► **wedge-soled** ADJ = **wedge-heeled**

►**wedge in** [1] VI [person] se glisser [2] VT SEP (into case, box etc) [+ object] faire rentrer, enfoncer; (into car, onto seat etc) [+ person] faire rentrer; [+ several people] entasser; **to be ~d in** être coincé

wedlock ['wedlɒk] N (NonC) mariage m; **to be born out of ~** être (un) enfant naturel

Wednesday ['wenzdeɪ] N mercredi m → **ash²**; for phrases see **Saturday**

Weds. ABBR = **Wednesday**

wee¹ [wiː] ADJ [a] (esp Scot or *) petit; **when I was a ~ boy** quand j'étais petit; **a ~ bit un**

tout petit peu **b** **the ~ small hours (of the morning)** les premières heures du matin (*de 1 à 4 h du matin*)

wee²* ['wiː] (*baby talk*) **1** N pipi* *m*; **to have a ~** faire pipi* **2** VI faire pipi*

weed [wiːd] **1** N **a** mauvaise herbe *f*; (* *pej* = *person*) mauviette *f*; (‡ = *marijuana*) herbe* *f*; (*hum*) **the ~*** le tabac **b** **(widow's) ~s** vêtements *mpl* de deuil; **in widow's ~s** en deuil **2** VT désherber; (= *hoe*) sarcler **3** COMP ► **weed-killer** N désherbant *m*, herbicide *m*

► **weed out** VT SEP [+ *plant*] enlever, arracher; (*fig*) [+ *weak candidates*] éliminer (**from** de); [+ *troublemakers*] expulser (**from** de); [+ *old clothes, books*] trier et jeter

weedhead* ['wiːdhed] N (*Drugs*) consommateur *m*, -trice *f* de marijuana

weeding ['wiːdɪŋ] N (*NonC*) désherbage *m*; (*with hoe*) sarclage *m*; **I've done some ~** j'ai un peu désherbé

weedy ['wiːdɪ] ADJ **a** (*Bot, Hort*) [*flowerbed, land*] couvert de mauvaises herbes; [*river, pond*] envahi par les herbes **b** (*Brit* pej* = *scrawny*) [*person*] chétif (*pej*), malingre (*pej*)

week [wiːk] N semaine *f*; **what day of the ~ is it?** quel jour de la semaine sommes-nous?; **this ~** cette semaine; **next/last ~** la semaine prochaine/dernière; **the ~ before last** l'avant-dernière semaine; **the ~ after next** pas la semaine prochaine, celle d'après; **by the end of the ~ he had ...** à la fin de la semaine il avait ...; **in the middle of the ~** vers le milieu *or* dans le courant de la semaine; **twice a ~** deux fois par semaine; **this time next ~** dans huit jours à la même heure; **this time last ~** il y a huit jours à la même heure; **today ~*** (*Brit*) ◊ **a ~ today** aujourd'hui en huit; **tomorrow ~*** (*Brit*) ◊ **a ~ tomorrow** demain en huit; **yesterday ~*** (*Brit*) ◊ **a ~ yesterday** il y a eu une semaine hier; **Sunday ~*** (*Brit*) ◊ **a ~ on Sunday** dimanche en huit; **every ~** chaque semaine; **two ~s ago** il y a deux semaines, il y a quinze jours; **in a ~** (= *a week from now*) dans une semaine; (= *in the space of a week*) en une semaine; **in a ~'s time** d'ici une semaine, dans une semaine; **in three ~s' time** dans *or* d'ici trois semaines; **~ in ~ out** ◊ **~ after ~** semaine après semaine; **it lasted (for) ~s** cela a duré des semaines (et des semaines); **the first time etc in ~s** la première fois *etc* depuis des semaines; **the ~ ending 6 May** la semaine qui se termine le 6 mai; **he owes her three ~s' rent** il lui doit trois semaines de loyer; **paid by the ~** payé à la semaine; **the working ~** la semaine de travail; **a 36-hour ~** une semaine (de travail) de 36 heures; **a three-day ~** une semaine (de travail) de trois jours; **a ~'s wages** le salaire hebdomadaire *or* de la *or* d'une semaine → **Easter**

weekday ['wiːkdeɪ] **1** N jour *m* de semaine, jour *m* ouvrable (*esp Comm*); **(on) ~s** en semaine, les jours ouvrables (*esp Comm*) **2** COMP [*activities, timetable*] de la semaine

weekend [wiːk'end] **1** N week-end *m*; **(at) ~s** pendant le(s) week-end(s); **what are you doing at the ~?** qu'est-ce que tu vas faire pendant le week-end?; **we're going away for the ~** nous partons en week-end; **to take a long ~** prendre un week-end prolongé; **they had Tuesday off so they made a long ~ of it** comme ils ne devaient pas travailler mardi ils ont fait le pont **2** VI passer le week-end **3** COMP [*visit, programme*] de *or* du week-end ► **weekend bag**, **weekend case** N sac *m* de voyage ► **weekend cottage** N maison *f* de campagne

weekender ['wiːk'endə'] N personne *f* partant (*or* partie) en week-end; **the village is full of ~s** le village est plein de gens venus pour le week-end

weekly ['wiːklɪ] **1** ADJ [*magazine, meeting, wage, rainfall*] hebdomadaire; [*hours*] par se-

maine **2** ADV [*meet, attend, play*] chaque semaine; [*sell*] par semaine; **twice/three times ~** deux/trois fois par semaine; **paid ~** payé à la semaine; **on a ~ basis** [*pay*] à la semaine; (= *every week*) chaque semaine, toutes les semaines; **we meet ~ on Thursdays** nous nous rencontrons tous les jeudis **3** N (= *magazine*) hebdomadaire *m*

weeknight ['wiːknaɪt] N soir *m* de semaine

weenie* ['wiːnɪ] N (*US Culin*) = **wienie**

weensy* ['wiːnzɪ] ADJ (*US*) = **weeny 1**

weeny* ['wiːnɪ] (*Brit*) **1** ADJ tout petit; **it was a ~ bit embarrassing** c'était un tout petit peu gênant **2** COMP ► **weeny-bopper*** N préado* *mf*

weep [wiːp] (*pret, ptp* **wept**) **1** VI **a** (= *cry*) [*person*] verser des larmes, pleurer; **to ~ for** *or* **with joy** pleurer de joie; **to ~ for sb/sth** pleurer qn/qch; **to ~ over sth** pleurer *or* se lamenter sur qch; **she wept to see him leave** elle a pleuré de le voir partir; **I could have wept!** j'en aurais pleuré! **b** [*walls, sore, wound*] suinter **2** VT [+ *tears*] verser, répandre; **to ~ tears of joy/fury/despair** verser des larmes *or* pleurer de joie/de colère/de désespoir → **bucket 3** N* **to have a good ~** pleurer un bon coup; **to have a little ~** pleurer un peu, verser quelques larmes

weeping ['wiːpɪŋ] **1** N (*NonC*) larmes *fpl*; **we heard the sound of ~** on entendait quelqu'un qui pleurait **2** ADJ [*person*] qui pleure; [*walls, sore, wound*] suintant; **~ willow** saule *m* pleureur

weepy ['wiːpɪ] **1** ADJ [*person*] à la larme facile; [*eyes, voice, mood, song*] larmoyant; [*film*] mélo*, sentimental; **to feel ~** [*person*] avoir envie de pleurer, se sentir au bord des larmes **2** N (*Brit* = *film, book*) mélo* *m*, film *m* (*or* livre *m*) sentimental

weever* ['wiːvə'] N (= *fish*) vive *f*

weevil ['wiːvəl] N charançon *m*

wee-wee* ['wiːwiː] N, VI = **wee²**

weft [weft] N (*Tex*) trame *f*

weigh [weɪ] **1** VT (*lit, fig*) peser; **to ~ o.s.** se peser; **to ~ sth in one's hand** soupeser qch; **it ~s 9 kilos** ça pèse 9 kilos; **how much** *or* **what do you ~?** combien est-ce que vous pesez?; **to ~ one's words (carefully)** peser ses mots; **to ~ (up) A against B** mettre en balance A et B; **to ~ (up) the pros and cons** peser le pour et le contre; **the advantages must be ~ed against the possible risks** il faut mettre en balance les avantages et les risques éventuels **b** (*Naut*) **to ~ anchor** lever l'ancre **2** VI [*object, responsibilities*] peser (**on** sur); **this box ~s quite heavy** cette boîte pèse assez lourd; **the fear of cancer ~s on her** *or* **on her mind all the time** la peur du cancer la tourmente constamment, elle vit constamment avec la peur du cancer; **there's something ~ing on her mind** quelque chose la préoccupe *or* la tracasse; **the divorce laws ~ heavily against men** les lois sur le divorce sont nettement en défaveur des hommes; **economic considerations ~ed heavily in their decision** les considérations économiques ont beaucoup pesé dans leur décision **3** COMP ► **weigh-in** N (*Sport*) pesage *m* ► **weighing machine** NPL (*gen*) balance *f*; (*for heavy loads*) bascule *f* ► **weighing scales** NPL balance *f*

► **weigh down 1** VI peser *or* appuyer de tout son poids (**on sth** sur qch); (*fig*) **this sorrow ~ed down on her** ce chagrin la rongeait *or* la minait **2** VT SEP faire plier *or* ployer, courber; (*fig*) accabler, tourmenter; **the fruit ~ed the branch down** la branche ployait *or* pliait sous le poids des fruits; **he was ~ed down with parcels** il pliait sous le poids des paquets; **to be ~ed down by** *or* **with responsibilities** être accablé *or* surchargé de responsabilités; **to be ~ed**

down with fears être en proie à toutes sortes de peurs

► **weigh in 1** VI **a** [*boxer, jockey etc*] se faire peser; **to ~ in at 70 kilos** peser 70 kilos avant l'épreuve; **the hippopotamus ~s in at* an impressive 1.5 tonnes** l'hippopotame fait le poids imposant de 1,5 tonnes **b** (*fig* = *contribute*) intervenir; **he ~ed in with more money** il est intervenu en apportant davantage d'argent; **he ~ed in with his opinion** il est intervenu en donnant son opinion **2** VT SEP [+ *boxer, jockey*] peser (*avant le match ou la course*) **3** ~**in** N → **weigh**

► **weigh out** VT SEP [+ *sugar etc*] peser

► **weigh up** VT SEP (= *consider*) examiner, calculer; (= *compare*) mettre en balance (**A with B, A against** A et B); **to ~ up A with** *or* **against B** mettre en balance A et B; (*Brit* = *assess*) [+ *person, the opposition*] juger, sonder; **I'm ~ing up whether to go or not** je me tâte pour savoir si j'y vais ou non → **weigh 1a**

weighbridge ['weɪbrɪdʒ] N pont-bascule *m*

weight [weɪt] **1** N **a** (*NonC*) poids *m*; (*Phys: relative weight*) pesanteur *f*; (*Phys*) **atomic ~** poids *m* atomique; **it is sold by ~** cela se vend au poids; **what is your ~?** combien pesez-vous?, quel poids faites-vous?; **my ~ is 60 kilos** je pèse 60 kilos; **it is 3 kilos in ~** ça pèse 3 kilos; **they are the same ~** ils font le même poids; **~ when empty** poids *m* à vide; (*fig*) **it's/she's worth its/her ~ in gold** cela/elle vaut son pesant d'or; **to put on** *or* **gain ~** grossir, prendre du poids; **to lose ~** maigrir, perdre du poids; **he put** *or* **leaned his full ~ on the handle** il a pesé *or* appuyé de tout son poids sur la poignée; **he put his full ~ behind the blow** il a frappé de toutes ses forces; **to move** *or* **shift one's ~ from one foot to the other** se balancer d'un pied sur l'autre; **he shifted his ~ to the other foot/onto his elbow** il fit porter son poids sur son autre pied/sur son coude; (*fig*) **to throw one's ~** *or* **to put all one's ~ behind sth/sb** apporter personnellement tout son soutien à qch/à qn; **feel the ~ of this box!** soupesez-moi cette boîte!; **what a ~ (it is)!** que c'est lourd!; **he looks as if he's carrying the ~ of the world on his shoulders** on dirait qu'il porte toute la misère du monde sur ses épaules → **pull, throw about b** (*fig*) [*of argument, words, public opinion, evidence*] poids *m*, force *f*; [*of worry, responsibility, years, age*] poids *m*; **to attach** *or* **lend** *or* **give ~ to sth** donner du poids à qch; **to carry ~** [*argument, factor*] avoir du poids (**with** pour); [*person*] avoir de l'influence; **we must give due ~ to his arguments** nous devons donner tout leur poids à ses arguments → **mind c** (*for scales, on clock etc*) poids *m* → **paperweight, put 2** VT **a** lester → **weighted b** (= *assign value to*) pondérer **3** COMP ► **weight lifter** N (*Sport*) haltérophile *mf* ► **weight lifting** N haltérophilie *f* ► **weight limit** N limitation *f* de poids ► **weight loss** N (*NonC*) perte *f* de poids ► **weights and measures** NPL poids et mesures *mpl* ► **weights and measures inspector** N inspecteur *m* des poids et mesures ► **weight-train** VI faire de la musculation ► **weight training** N musculation *f* (*avec des poids*) ► **weight watcher** N he's a ~ watcher (= *actively slimming*) il suit un régime amaigrissant; (= *figure-conscious*) il surveille son poids

► **weight down** VT SEP [+ *papers, tablecloth etc*] retenir *or* maintenir avec un poids

weighted ['weɪtɪd] ADJ **a** (= *biased*) **~ in sb's favour** *or* **towards sb** favorable à qn; **~ in favour of/against sb** favorable/défavorable à qn; **the situation was heavily ~ in his favour/against him** la situation lui était nettement favorable/défavorable **b** (= *made heavier*) [*diving belt*] lesté **2** COMP ► **weighted average** N moyenne *f* pondérée

weightiness ['weɪtɪnɪs] N (NonC) [of argument, matter] poids m; [of responsibility] importance f

weighting ['weɪtɪŋ] N **a** (on salary) indemnité f, allocation f; **London ~** indemnité f de vie chère à Londres **b** (Scol) coefficient m; (Econ) coefficient m, pondération f

weightless ['weɪtlɪs] ADJ [astronaut, falling object] en état d'apesanteur; [conditions] d'apesanteur; **in a ~ environment** en apesanteur; **to feel ~** se sentir léger comme l'air

weightlessness ['weɪtlɪsnɪs] N apesanteur f

weighty ['weɪtɪ] ADJ **a** (frm = serious) [matter, problem] grave, important; [argument, reason] de poids; [burden, responsibility] lourd **b** (liter = heavy) [tome, volume] lourd; [load] pesant, lourd

Weimar ['vaɪmɑːr] **1** N Weimar **2** COMP ► **the Weimar Republic** N la république de Weimar

weir [wɪər] N barrage m

weird [wɪəd] ADJ **a** (* = peculiar) [person, object, behaviour, coincidence] bizarre, étrange; **it felt ~ going back there** ça faisait bizarre d'y retourner; **the ~ thing is that ...** ce qu'il y a de bizarre c'est que ...; **lots of ~ and wonderful* species** plein d'espèces étranges et merveilleuses **b** (= eerie) [sound, light] surnaturel, mystérieux

weirdly ['wɪədlɪ] ADV **a** (* = peculiarly) [behave, dress] bizarrement **b** (= eerily) [glow] mystérieusement, de façon surnaturelle; [sing] de façon surnaturelle

weirdness ['wɪədnɪs] N étrangeté f

weirdo: ['wɪədəʊ] N (pej) cinglé(e)* m(f)

Welch† [weltʃ] ADJ = **Welsh**

welch [weltʃ] VI = **welsh**

▼**welcome** ['welkəm] **1** ADJ **a** (= gladly accepted) **to be ~** [person] être le (or la) bienvenu(e); **he'll/you'll always be ~ here** il sera/tu seras toujours le bienvenu ici; **some members were more ~ than others** certains membres étaient plus appréciés que d'autres; **he's not ~ here any more** sa présence ici est devenue indésirable; **I didn't feel very ~** je n'ai pas vraiment eu l'impression d'être le bienvenu; **to make sb ~** faire bon accueil à qn; **they really make you feel ~** on y est vraiment bien accueilli; (fig) **to roll out** or **put out the ~ mat for sb*** se donner du mal pour recevoir qn; (esp US: answer to thanks) **you're ~!** je vous en prie!, de rien!; (giving permission) **you're ~ to try** je vous en prie, essayez; (iro) libre à vous d'essayer; **you're ~ to use my car** vous pouvez emprunter ma voiture si vous voulez; **she's ~ to visit any time** elle est toujours la bienvenue; **a lounge which guests are ~ to use** un salon que les hôtes sont invités à utiliser; **I don't use it any more, so you're ~ to it** je ne m'en sers plus, alors profitez-en; **he wants the job? he's ~ to it!** il veut le poste? eh bien, qu'il le prenne!; **he's ~ to her!** qu'il se débrouille avec elle!

b (= appreciated) [food, drink, change, visitor] bienvenu; [decision, reminder, interruption] opportun; **she was a ~ sight** nous avons été (or il a été etc) heureux de la voir; **it was ~ news** nous avons été (or il a été etc) heureux de l'apprendre; **it was a ~ gift** ce cadeau m'a (or lui a etc) fait bien plaisir; **it was a ~ relief** ça m'a (or l'a etc) vraiment soulagé; **to make a ~ return** faire un retour apprécié

2 EXCL **~!** soyez le bienvenu (or la bienvenue etc)!, bienvenue!; **~ home!** bienvenue!; **~ back!** bienvenue!, content de vous (or te) revoir!; **~ to our house!** bienvenue chez nous!; (on notice) **"~ to England"** « bienvenue en Angleterre »

3 N accueil m; **to bid sb ~** souhaiter la bienvenue à qn; **to give sb a warm ~** faire un accueil chaleureux à qn; **they gave him a great ~** ils lui ont fait fête; **words of ~** paroles

fpl d'accueil, mots mpl de bienvenue; **what sort of a ~ will this product get from the housewife?** comment la ménagère accueillera-t-elle ce produit? → **outstay**

4 VT [+ person, delegation, group of people] (= greet, receive) accueillir; (= greet warmly) faire bon accueil à, accueillir chaleureusement; (= bid welcome) souhaiter la bienvenue à; [+ sb's return, news, suggestion, change] se réjouir de; **he ~d me in** il m'a chaleureusement invité à entrer; (TV etc) **please ~ Tony Brennan!** veuillez accueillir Tony Brennan!; **we would ~ your views on ...** nous serions heureux de connaître votre point de vue or opinion sur ...; **I'd ~ a cup of coffee** je prendrais volontiers une tasse de café, je ne dirais pas non à une tasse de café → **open**

► **welcome back** VT SEP **they ~d him back after his journey** ils l'ont accueilli chaleureusement or ils lui ont fait fête à son retour (de voyage)

welcoming ['welkəmɪŋ] ADJ [person, smile, place] accueillant; [atmosphere] chaleureux; [banquet, ceremony, speech] d'accueil; (lit, fig) **~ party** or **committee** comité m d'accueil; **to be ~ to sb** [person] être accueillant avec qn, faire bon accueil à qn; [atmosphere, place] paraître accueillant à qn

weld [weld] **1** N soudure f **2** VT [+ metal, rubber, seam, join] souder; (also **~ together**) [+ pieces, parts] souder, assembler; (fig) [+ groups, parties] cimenter l'union de; **to ~ sth on to sth** souder qch à qch; **the hull is ~ed throughout** la coque est complètement soudée; (fig) **he ~ed them (together) into a united party/ team** il en a fait un parti cohérent/une équipe soudée **3** VI souder

welder ['weldər] N (= person) soudeur m; (= machine) soudeuse f

welding ['weldɪŋ] **1** N (NonC) (Tech) soudage m; (fig) [of parties] union f; [of ideas] amalgame m **2** COMP [process] de soudure, de soudage ► **welding torch** N chalumeau m

welfare ['welfeər] **1** N **a** (gen) bien m; (= comfort) bien-être m; (US) aide f sociale; **the nation's ~ ◊ ~ of all** le bien public or de tous; **the physical/spiritual ~ of the young** la santé physique/morale des jeunes; **I'm anxious about his ~** je suis inquiet à son sujet; **to look after sb's ~** avoir la responsabilité de qn → **child**

b **public/social ~** assistance f publique/ sociale; **to be on ~** toucher les prestations sociales, recevoir l'aide sociale; **to live on ~** vivre des prestations sociales

2 COMP [milk, meals] gratuit ► **welfare benefits** NPL avantages mpl sociaux ► **welfare centre** N centre m d'assistance sociale ► **welfare check** N (US) chèque m d'allocations ► **welfare hotel** N (US) foyer où sont hébergés temporairement les bénéficiaires de l'aide sociale ► **welfare mother** N (US) mère seule qui bénéficie de l'aide sociale ► **welfare officer** N assistant(e) m(f) social(e) ► **welfare payments** NPL prestations fpl sociales ► **welfare services** NPL services mpl sociaux ► **welfare state** N État-providence m; **the establishment of the Welfare State in Great Britain** l'établissement de l'État-providence en Grande-Bretagne; **thanks to the Welfare State** grâce à la sécurité sociale et autres avantages sociaux ► **welfare work** N travail m social ► **welfare worker** N assistant(e) m(f) social(e), travailleur m, -euse f social(e)

welfarism ['welfeərɪzəm] N (US Pol) théorie f de l'État-providence

welfarist ['welfeərɪst] ADJ, N (US Pol) partisan m de l'État-providence

welfarite* ['welfeəraɪt] N (US pej) assisté(e) m(f)

well¹ [wel] **1** N (for water, oil) puits m; [of staircase, lift] cage f; (= shaft between buildings) puits m, cheminée f; (Brit Jur) barreau m; (fig) **this book is a ~ of information** ce livre est une mine de renseignements → **inkwell, oil** **2** VI

(also **~ up**) [tears, emotion] monter; **tears ~ed (up) in her eyes** les larmes lui montèrent aux yeux; **anger ~ed (up) within him** la colère sourdit (liter) or monta en lui **3** COMP ► **well-digger** N puisatier m ► **well water** N eau f de puits

► **well out** VI [spring] sourdre; [tears, blood] couler (from de)

▼**well²** [wel] **1** ADV (compar **better**, superl **best**) **a** (= satisfactorily, skilfully etc) [behave, sleep, eat, treat, remember] bien; **he sings as ~ as he plays** il chante aussi bien qu'il joue; **he sings as ~ as she does** il chante aussi bien qu'elle; **to live ~** vivre bien; **~ done!** bravo!, très bien!; **~ played!** bien joué!; **everything is going ~** tout va bien; **the evening went off very ~** la soirée s'est très bien passée; **to do ~ in one's work** bien réussir dans son travail; **to do ~ at school** bien marcher à l'école; **he did very ~ for an eight-year-old** il s'est bien débrouillé pour un enfant de huit ans; **he did quite ~** il ne s'en est pas mal sorti, il ne s'est pas mal débrouillé; **the patient is doing ~** le malade est en bonne voie; **he did ~ after the operation but ...** il s'est bien rétabli après l'opération mais ...; **you did ~ to come at once** vous avez bien fait de venir tout de suite; **you would do ~ to think about it** tu ferais bien d'y penser; **to do as ~ as one can** faire de son mieux; **he did himself ~** il ne s'est privé de rien; **to do ~ by sb** bien agir or être généreux envers qn; **you're ~ out of it!** c'est une chance que tu n'aies plus rien à voir avec cela (or lui etc)!; **how ~ I understand!** comme je vous (or le etc) comprends!; **I know the place ~** je connais bien l'endroit; **(and) ~ I know it!** je le sais bien!, je ne le sais que trop!

b (intensifying = very much, thoroughly) bien; **it was ~ worth the trouble** cela valait bien le dérangement or la peine de se déranger; **he is ~ past** or **over fifty** il a largement dépassé la cinquantaine; **it's ~ past 10 o'clock** il est bien plus de 10 heures; **~ over 1,000 people** plus de 1 000 personnes; **it continued ~ into 1996** cela a continué pendant une bonne partie de 1996; **~ above ...** bien au-dessus de ...; (esp Brit) **~ and truly** bel et bien; **he could ~ afford to pay for it** il avait largement les moyens de le payer; **lean ~ forward** penchez-vous bien en avant; (Brit = very) **~ dodgy/ annoyed** etc** super* louche/contrarié etc

c (= with good reason, with equal reason) **you may ~ be surprised to learn that ...** vous serez sans aucun doute surpris d'apprendre que ...; **one might ~ ask why** on pourrait à juste titre demander pourquoi; **you might ~ ask!** belle question!, c'est vous qui me le demandez!; **you could ~ refuse to help them** vous pourriez à juste titre refuser de les aider; **he couldn't very ~ refuse** il ne pouvait guère refuser; **we may as ~ begin now** autant (vaut) commencer maintenant, nous ferions aussi bien de commencer maintenant; **you might (just) as ~ say that ...** autant dire que ...; **you may as ~ tell me the truth** autant me dire la vérité, tu ferais aussi bien de me dire la vérité; **shall I go? — you may** or **might as ~** j'y vais? — tant qu'à faire, allez-y!*; **we might (just) as ~ have stayed at home** autant valait rester à la maison, nous aurions aussi bien fait de rester à la maison; **she apologized, as ~ she might** elle a présenté ses excuses, comme il se devait; **she apologized — and ~ she might!** elle a présenté ses excuses — c'était la moindre des choses! → **pretty**

d (= in addition) **as ~** (= also) aussi; (= on top of all that) par-dessus le marché; **I'll take those as ~!** je prendrai ceux-là aussi; **and it rained as ~!** et par-dessus le marché il a plu!; **by night as ~ as by day** de jour comme de nuit, aussi bien de jour que de nuit; **as ~ as his dog he has two rabbits** en plus de son chien il a deux lapins; **on bikes as ~ as in cars**

à vélo aussi bien qu'en voiture, à vélo comme en voiture; **I had Paul with me as ~ as Lucy** j'avais Paul aussi en même temps que Lucy; **all sorts of people, rich as ~ as poor** toutes sortes de gens, tant riches que pauvres `e` (= *positively*) **to think/speak ~ of** penser/dire du bien de `f` **to leave ~ alone** laisser les choses telles qu'elles sont ■ (*PROV*) **let** or **leave ~ alone** le mieux est l'ennemi du bien (*PROV*)

`2` EXCL (*surprise*) tiens!, eh bien!; (*relief*) ah bon!, eh bien!; (*resignation*) enfin!; (*dismissively*) bof!*; (*resuming after interruption*) **~, as I was saying ...** donc, comme je disais ..., je disais donc que ...; (*hesitation*) **~ ...** c'est que ...; **he has won the election! — ~, ~(, ~)!** il a été élu! — tiens, tiens!; **~? eh bien?, et alors?; ~, who would have thought it?** eh bien! qui l'aurait cru?; **~ I never!*** ◊ **~, what do you know!*** pas possible!, ça par exemple!; **I intended to do it — ~, have you?** j'avais l'intention de le faire — et alors?; **~, what do you think of it?** eh bien! vous en dites-vous?; **~, here we are at last!** eh bien! nous voilà enfin!; **~, there's nothing we can do about it** enfin, on n'y peut rien; **~, you may be right** qui sait, vous avez peut-être raison; **~ then** (bon) d'accord; **you know Paul? ~, he's getting married** vous connaissez Paul? eh bien il se marie; **are you coming? — ~, I've got a lot to do here** vous venez? — c'est que ... j'ai beaucoup à faire ici

`3` ADJ (*compar, superl* **best**) `a` bien, bon; **all is not ~ with her** il y a quelque chose qui ne va pas, elle traverse une mauvaise passe; **it's all very ~ to say that** c'est bien beau or joli de dire cela; **that's all very ~ but ...** ◊ **that's all ~ and good but ...** tout ça c'est bien joli or beau mais ...; **if you want to do it, ~ and good** si vous voulez le faire je ne vois pas d'inconvénient; (*Mil*) **all's ~!** tout va bien! ■ (*PROV*) **all's ~ that ends well** tout est bien qui finit bien (*PROV*)

`b` (= *healthy*) **how are you? — very ~, thank you** comment allez-vous? — très bien, merci; **I hope you're ~** j'espère que vous allez bien; **to feel ~** se sentir bien; **to get ~** se remettre; **get ~ soon!** remets-toi vite!; **people who are ~ do not realize that ...** les gens qui se portent bien or qui sont en bonne santé ne se rendent pas compte que ...

`c` (= *cautious*) **it** or **we would be ~ to start early** on ferait bien de partir tôt; **it is as ~ to remember** il y a tout lieu de se rappeler; **it's as ~ not to offend her** il vaudrait mieux ne pas la froisser; **it would be just as ~ for you to stay** vous feriez tout aussi bien de rester

`d` (= *lucky*) **it's ~ for you that nobody saw you** heureusement pour vous qu'on ne vous a pas vu, vous avez de la chance or c'est heureux pour vous qu'on ne vous ait pas vu

`4` PREF **~-** bien; **~-chosen/dressed** bien choisi/habillé → **6**

`5` N **I wish you ~!** je vous souhaite de réussir!, bonne chance!; **somebody who wishes you ~** quelqu'un qui vous veut du bien

`6` COMP ► **well-adjusted** ADJ (*gen*) [*person*] posé, équilibré; (*to society, school*) bien adapté ► **well-advised** ADJ [*action, decision*] sage, prudent; **you would be ~-advised to leave** vous auriez (tout) intérêt à partir ► **well-aimed** ADJ [*shot*] bien ajusté; [*remark*] qui porte ► **well-appointed** ADJ [*house, room*] bien aménagé ► **well-argued** ADJ [*case, report*] bien argumenté ► **well-assorted** ADJ bien assorti ► **well-attended** ADJ [*meeting, lecture*] qui attire beaucoup de monde, qui a du succès; [*show, play*] couru ► **well-baby clinic** N (*Brit*) *centre prophylactique et thérapeutique pour nouveau-nés* ► **well-balanced** ADJ [*person, diet, argument*] (bien) équilibré; [*paragraph, sentence*] bien construit ► **well-behaved** ADJ [*child*] sage, qui se conduit

bien; [*animal*] obéissant ► **well-being** N bien-être *m* ► **well-born** ADJ bien né, de bonne famille ► **well-bred** ADJ (= *of good family*) de bonne famille; (= *courteous*) bien élevé; [*animal*] de bonne race ► **well-built** ADJ [*building*] bien construit, solide; [*person*] bien bâti, costaud* ► **well-chosen** ADJ bien choisi; **in a few ~-chosen words** en quelques mots bien choisis ► **well-cooked** ADJ (*gen*) [*food, meal*] bien cuisiné; (= *not rare*) [*meat*] bien cuit ► **well-defined** ADJ [*colours, distinctions*] bien défini; [*photo, outline*] net; [*problem*] bien défini, précis ► **well-deserved** ADJ bien mérité ► **well-developed** ADJ (*Anat*) bien développé; [*person*] bien fait; [*plan*] bien développé; [*argument, idea*] bien exposé ► **well-disposed** ADJ bien disposé (**towards** envers) ► **well-documented** ADJ [*case, work*] bien documenté; **his life is ~-documented** on a beaucoup de renseignements or documents sur sa vie ► **well-dressed** ADJ bien habillé, bien vêtu ► **well-earned** ADJ bien mérité ► **well-educated** ADJ cultivé, instruit ► **well-endowed** ADJ (*euph*) [*man*] bien membré; [*woman*] à la poitrine généreuse ► **well-equipped** ADJ bien équipé; (*esp with tools*) [*person*] bien outillé; [*factory*] bien équipé, doté d'un équipement important; **to be ~-equipped to do** [*person*] avoir ce qu'il faut pour faire; [*factory*] être parfaitement équipé pour faire ► **well-favoured**†† ADJ beau (belle *f*) ► **well-fed** ADJ bien nourri ► **well-fixed*** ADJ (*US*) **to be ~-fixed** (= *well-to-do*) être nanti, vivre dans l'aisance; **we're ~-fixed for food** nous avons largement assez à manger ► **well-formed** ADJ (*Ling*) bien formé, grammatical ► **well-formedness** N (*Ling*) grammaticalité *f* ► **well-founded** ADJ [*suspicion*] bien fondé, légitime ► **well-groomed** ADJ [*person*] soigné; [*hair*] bien coiffé; [*horse*] bien pansé ► **well-grounded** ADJ [*suspicion, belief, rumour*] bien fondé, légitime; **our students are ~-grounded in grammar/physics** nos étudiants ont de solides connaissances or bases en grammaire/physique ► **well-heeled*** ADJ nanti, fort à l'aise ► **well-hung*** ADJ [*man*] bien monté* ► **well-informed** ADJ bien renseigné (**about** sur); (= *knowledgeable*) [*person*] instruit; (*Pol, Press*) **~-informed circles** les milieux *mpl* bien informés ► **well-intentioned** ADJ bien intentionné ► **well-judged** ADJ [*remark, criticism*] bien vu, judicieux; [*shot, throw*] bien ajusté; [*estimate*] juste ► **well-kept** ADJ [*house, garden*] bien entretenu, bien tenu; [*hands, nails*] soigné; [*hair*] bien entretenu; [*secret*] bien gardé ► **well-knit** ADJ (*fig*) [*person, body*] bien bâti; [*arguments, speech*] bien enchaîné; [*scheme*] bien conçu ► **well-known** ADJ (= *famous*) bien connu, célèbre; **it's a ~-known fact that ...** tout le monde sait que ... ► **well-liked** ADJ très apprécié ► **well-lined** ADJ **to have ~-lined pockets** avoir de gros moyens, être cousu d'or* ► **well-loved** ADJ très aimé ► **well-made** ADJ bien fait ► **well-managed** ADJ bien mené ► **well-man clinic** N (*Brit*) *centre prophylactique et thérapeutique pour hommes* ► **well-mannered** ADJ qui a de bonnes manières, bien élevé ► **well-meaning** ADJ [*person*] bien intentionné; [*remark, action*] fait avec les meilleures intentions ► **well-meant** ADJ fait avec les meilleures intentions ► **well-nigh** ADV (*liter*) presque ► **well-nourished** ADJ bien nourri ► **well-off** ADJ (= *rich*) **to be ~-off** vivre dans l'aisance, être riche; **the less ~-off** ceux qui ont de petits moyens; (= *fortunate*) **you don't know when you're ~-off** tu ne connais pas ton bonheur; **she's ~-off without him** elle est mieux sans lui ► **well-oiled** ADJ (*lit*) bien graissé; (* = *drunk*) pompette* ► **well-padded*** ADJ (*hum*) [*person*] rembourré ► **well-paid** ADJ bien payé, bien rémunéré ► **well-preserved** ADJ [*building, person*] bien conservé ► **well-read**

ADJ cultivé ► **well-respected** ADJ très respecté or considéré ► **well-rounded** ADJ [*style*] harmonieux; [*sentence*] bien tourné ► **well-spent** ADJ [*time*] bien employé, bien utilisé; [*money*] utilement dépensé → **money** ► **well-spoken** ADJ [*person*] qui parle bien, qui a une élocution soignée; [*words*] bien choisi, bien trouvé; **she's very ~-spoken of** elle est très appréciée ► **well-stocked** ADJ [*shop, fridge*] bien approvisionné; [*river, lake*] bien empoissonné ► **well-tempered** ADJ (*Mus*) **the Well-Tempered Clavier** le Clavier or Clavecin bien tempéré ► **well-thought-of** ADJ [*person*] (bien) considéré, dont on a bonne opinion; [*thing*] bien considéré, très apprécié ► **well-thought-out** ADJ bien conçu ► **well-thumbed** ADJ [*book*] lu et relu ► **well-timed** ADJ [*remark, entrance*] tout à fait opportun, tombé à point nommé; [*blow*] bien calculé ► **well-to-do** ADJ nanti ► **well-tried** ADJ [*method*] éprouvé, qui a fait ses preuves ► **well-trodden** ADJ **to follow a ~-trodden path** (*lit*) suivre un chemin fréquenté; (*fig*) suivre les sentiers battus ► **well-turned** ADJ [*phrase*] bien tourné; [*leg*] bien fait ► **well-wisher** N ami(e) *m(f)*; (*unknown*) ami(e) *m(f)* or admirateur *m*, -trice *f* inconnu(e); (*Pol* = *supporter*) sympathisant(e) *m(f)*; **he got many letters from ~-wishers** il a reçu de nombreuses lettres d'encouragement ► **well-woman clinic** N (*Brit*) *centre prophylactique et thérapeutique pour femmes* ► **well-worn** ADJ [*carpet, clothes*] usagé; (*fig*) [*phrase, expression*] éculé, rebattu; (*fig*) **to follow a ~-worn path** suivre les sentiers battus ► **well-written** ADJ bien écrit

we'll [wi:l] = **we shall, we will**; → **shall, will**

wellhead ['welhed] N (*lit, fig*) source *f*

Wellington ['welɪŋtən] N (*in NZ*) Wellington

wellington ['welɪŋtən] N (*Brit: also* ~ **boot**) botte *f* de caoutchouc

Wellsian ['welzɪən] ADJ de Wells

wellspring ['welsprɪŋ] N = **wellhead**

welly* ['welɪ] N (*pl* **wellies**) (*Brit*) ~ **boots** ◊ **wellies** bottes *fpl* de caoutchouc; (*Brit*) **give it some ~!*** allez, du nerf!*

Welsh [welʃ] `1` ADJ (*gen*) gallois; [*teacher*] de gallois `2` N (*Ling*) gallois *m* `3` **the Welsh** NPL les Gallois *mpl* `4` COMP ► **Welsh dresser** N (*Brit*) vaisselier *m* ► **Welsh Nationalism** N (*Pol*) nationalisme *m* gallois ► **Welsh Nationalist** N nationaliste *mf* gallois(e) ► **the Welsh Office** N (*Brit Pol*) le ministère des Affaires galloises ► **Welsh rabbit, Welsh rarebit** N (*Culin*) toast *m* au fromage

welsh* [welʃ] VI **to ~ on a promise** manquer à une promesse; **they ~ed on the agreement** ils n'ont pas respecté l'accord

Welshman ['welʃmən] N (*pl* **-men**) Gallois *m*

Welshwoman ['welʃwʊmən] N (*pl* **-women**) Galloise *f*

welt [welt] N (= *weal*) marque *f* de coup, zébrure *f*; [*of shoe*] trépointe *f*

welter ['weltər] `1` N [*of objects, words, ideas*] fatras *m*; **a ~ of conflicting interests** un tourbillon d'intérêts contradictoires; **in a ~ of blood** dans un bain de sang; **in a ~ of mud** dans un véritable bourbier `2` VI (*in blood*) baigner; (*in mud*) se vautrer, se rouler

welterweight ['weltəweɪt] (*Boxing*) `1` N poids *m* welter `2` COMP [*champion, fight*] poids welter *inv*

wen [wen] N loupe *f*, kyste *m* sébacé; (*fig*) **the Great Wen** Londres

wench [wentʃ] († *or hum*) `1` N jeune fille *f*, jeune femme *f* `2` VI **to go ~ing** courir le jupon

wend [wend] VT **to ~ one's way** aller son chemin, s'acheminer (**to, towards** vers); **to ~ one's way back from** s'en revenir de

Wendy house ['wendɪ,haʊs] N (*Brit*) maison *f* miniature (*pour enfants*)

went [went] VB *pt of* **go**

wept [wept] VB *pret ptp of* **weep**

were [wɜːʳ] VB *pt of* **be**

we're [wɪəʳ] = **we are**; → **be**

weren't [wɜːnt] = **were not**; → **be**

werewolf [ˈwɪəʳwʊlf] N (*pl* **werewolves** [ˈwɪə-wʊlvz]) loup-garou *m*

wert†† [wɜːt] VB *2nd pers sg pret of* **be**

Wesleyan [ˈwezlɪən] [1] N disciple *m* de Wesley [2] ADJ de Wesley, wesleyen; ~ **Methodists** méthodistes *mpl* wesleyens

west [west] [1] N ouest *m*; **to the ~ (of)** à l'ouest (de); **in the ~ of Scotland** dans l'ouest de l'Écosse; **a house facing west** ~ une maison exposée à l'ouest; **to veer to the ~◊ to go into the ~** [*wind*] tourner à l'ouest; **the wind is in the ~** le vent est à l'ouest; **the wind is (coming** *or* **blowing) from the ~** le vent vient *or* souffle de l'ouest; **to live in the ~** habiter dans l'ouest; **the West** (*Pol*) l'Occident *m*, l'Ouest *m*; (*US Geog*) l'Ouest *m* → **wild**

[2] ADJ [*coast, wing*] ouest *inv*; ~ **wind** vent *m* d'ouest; **on the ~ side** du côté ouest; **a room with a ~ aspect** une pièce exposée à l'ouest; (*Archit*) ~ **transept/door** transept *m*/portail *m* ouest; **in ~ Devon** dans l'ouest du Devon; **in ~ Leeds** dans les quartiers ouest de Leeds; **in the ~ Atlantic** dans l'Atlantique ouest → **4**

[3] ADV [*go, travel, fly*] vers l'ouest, en direction de l'ouest; [*be, lie*] à l'ouest; **go ~ till you get to Crewe** allez en direction de l'ouest jusqu'à Crewe; **we drove ~ for 100km** nous avons roulé vers l'ouest pendant 100 km; (*fig*) **to go ~*** [*thing*] être fichu* *or* perdu; [*person*] passer l'arme à gauche*; **further ~** plus à l'ouest; **to sail due ~** aller droit vers l'ouest; (*Naut*) avoir le cap à l'ouest; ~ **by south** ouest quart sud-ouest

[4] COMP ► **West Africa** N l'Afrique *f* occidentale ► **West African** ADJ de l'Afrique occidentale, ouest-africain ♦ N habitant(e) *m(f)* de l'Afrique occidentale ► **the West Bank** N la Cisjordanie ► **West Berlin** N (*Hist*) Berlin-Ouest ► **West Berliner** N (*Hist*) habitant(e) *m(f)* de Berlin-Ouest ► **the West Country** N (*Brit*) le sud-ouest de l'Angleterre ► **the West End** N (*in London*) le West End (*centre touristique et commercial de Londres*) ► **West Ender** N (*in London*) habitant(e) *m(f)* du West End ► **west-facing** ADJ exposé *or* orienté à l'ouest *or* au couchant ► **West German** ADJ allemand de l'Ouest ► **West Germany** N l'Allemagne *f* de l'Ouest ► **West Indian** ADJ antillais ♦ N Antillais(e) *m(f)* ► **the West Indies** NPL les Antilles *fpl*; (*Hist*) les Indes *fpl* occidentales ► **west-north-west** N ouest-nord-ouest *m* ♦ ADJ (de l' *or* à l')ouest-nord-ouest *inv* ♦ ADV vers l'ouest-nord-ouest ► **West Point** N (*US*) école *f* militaire, ≈ Saint-Cyr ► **west-south-west** N ouest-sud-ouest *m* ♦ ADJ (de l' *or* à l')ouest-sud-ouest *inv* ♦ ADV vers l'ouest-sud-ouest ► **West Virginia** N la Virginie-Occidentale; **in West Virginia** en Virginie-Occidentale

westbound [ˈwestbaʊnd] ADJ, ADV [*traffic, vehicles*] (se déplaçant) en direction de l'ouest; [*carriageway*] ouest *inv*; **to be ~ on the M8** être sur la M8 en direction de l'ouest

westerly [ˈwestəlɪ] [1] ADJ [*wind*] de l'ouest; [*situation*] à l'ouest, au couchant; **in a ~ direction** en direction de l'ouest, vers l'ouest; **longitude** longitude *f* ouest *inv*; ~ **aspect** exposition *f* à l'ouest *or* au couchant [2] ADV vers l'ouest

western [ˈwestən] [1] ADJ (de l')ouest *inv*; **in ~ France** dans l'ouest de la France; **the ~ coast** la côte ouest *or* occidentale; **house with a ~ outlook** maison *f* exposée à l'ouest; ~ **wall** mur *m* ouest; **Western Europe** Europe *f* occidentale; **the Western Church** l'Église *f* d'Occident, l'Église *f* latine → **country** [2] N (= *film*)

western *m*; (= *novel*) roman-western *m*

[3] COMP ► **Western Australia** N l'Australie-Occidentale *f* ► **the Western Isles** NPL (*Brit*) les Hébrides *fpl* ► **Western omelet** N (*US Culin*) omelette *f* au jambon avec oignons et poivrons ► **western roll** N (*Sport*) (saut *m* en) rouleau *m* ► **the Western Sahara** N le Sahara occidental ► **Western Samoa** N les Samoa *fpl* (occidentales) ► **western writer** N écrivain *m* de (romans-)westerns

westerner [ˈwestənəʳ] N homme *m* *or* femme *f* de l'ouest, habitant(e) *m(f)* de l'ouest; (*Pol*) Occidental(e) *m(f)*

westernization [ˌwestənaɪˈzeɪʃən] N occidentalisation *f*

westernize [ˈwestənaɪz] VT occidentaliser; **to become ~d** s'occidentaliser

westernmost [ˈwestənməʊst] ADJ le plus à l'ouest

Westminster [ˈwestˌmɪnstəʳ] N (*Brit*) Westminster *m* (*le Parlement britannique*)

westward [ˈwestwəd] [1] ADJ [*route*] en direction de l'ouest; [*slope*] exposé à l'ouest; **in a ~ direction** en direction de l'ouest, vers l'ouest [2] ADV (*also* **~s**) vers l'ouest

wet [wet] [1] ADJ [a] [*object, grass, clothes, towel, swimsuit, nappy, baby*] mouillé, humide; (*stronger*) trempé; [*cement, plaster, paint, ink*] frais (fraîche *f*); [*sand, hair*] mouillé; **to be ~ to the skin** *or* ~ **through** être trempé jusqu'aux os; ~ **with blood** trempé de sang; ~ **with sweat** humide de sueur; (*stronger*) trempé de sueur; **cheeks ~ with tears** joues baignées de larmes; ~ **with dew** humide de rosée; **to get ~** se mouiller; **to get one's feet ~** (*lit*) se mouiller les pieds; (*US fig*) s'y mettre, se lancer; **don't get your shoes ~** ne mouille pas tes chaussures; **don't come into the house with ~ feet** n'entre pas (dans la maison) avec les pieds mouillés; **it grows in ~ places** ça pousse dans les endroits humides; **a ~ patch** une tache d'humidité; **the roads are very ~** les routes sont très humides *or* mouillées; **the road is slippery when ~** la chaussée est glissante par temps de pluie; (*notice*) **"~ paint"** « attention, peinture fraîche »; (*fig*) **he's still ~ behind the ears*** (= *immature*) si on lui pressait le nez il en sortirait du lait*; (= *inexperienced*) il manque d'expérience → **soaking, wringing**

[b] (*of weather*) **it** *or* **the weather is ~** le temps est pluvieux, il pleut; **it's going to be ~** le temps est à la pluie, il va pleuvoir; **a ~ day** un jour de pluie, un jour pluvieux; **on ~ days** les jours de pluie; **it's a very ~ climate** c'est un climat très humide *or* pluvieux; **in ~ weather** quand le temps est pluvieux, par temps humide *or* pluvieux; **the ~ season** la saison des pluies; **it's been a very ~ winter/summer/ weekend** l'hiver/l'été/le week-end a été très humide *or* pluvieux; (*Met*) **it's been one of the wettest Junes on record** c'est un des mois de juin les plus pluvieux que l'on ait connus; ~ **snow** neige *f* fondue

[c] (*Brit* = *spineless*) **he's really ~*** c'est un chiffe molle

[d] (*Brit Pol*) [*Tory politician, policy*] gauchisant

[e] (*in US* = *against prohibition*) [*town, state*] où la vente des boissons alcoolisées est autorisée

[f] (*US fig* = *quite wrong*) **you're all ~!*** tu te fiches complètement dedans!*, tu te fourres le doigt dans l'œil!*

[2] N [a] **the ~** (= *rain*) la pluie; (= *damp*) l'humidité *f*; **it got left out in the ~** il est resté dehors sous la pluie *or* à l'humidité; **my car doesn't start in the ~** ma voiture ne démarre pas par temps de pluie; **the road surface is slippery, especially in the ~** la chaussée est glissante, surtout par temps de pluie; **come in out of the ~** ne restez pas sous la pluie, entrez

[b] (* *pej* = *spineless person*) chiffe *f* molle

[c] (*Brit Pol**) gauchisant(e) *m(f)* (du parti

conservateur)

[3] VT [a] mouiller; **to ~ one's lips** se mouiller les lèvres; (*fig*) **to ~ one's whistle** †* boire un coup*, en siffler un*

[b] (= *urinate*) **to ~ the bed** mouiller le lit; (*lit*) **to ~ o.s.** *or* **one's pants** mouiller sa culotte; **to ~ o.s.** *or* **one's pants* (laughing)** rire à en faire pipi* dans sa culotte

[4] COMP ► **wet bar** N (*US*) petit bar avec eau courante ► **wet blanket** N (*fig*) rabat-joie *mf inv* ► **wet dock** N (*Naut*) bassin *m* à flot ► **wet dream** N pollution *f* *or* éjaculation *f* nocturne ► **wet fish** N poisson *m* frais ► **the wet look** N (*Fashion*) le look brillant ► **wet-nurse** N nourrice *f* ♦ VT servir de nourrice à, élever au sein ► **wet rot** N (*NonC*) pourriture *f* humide (du bois) ► **wet shave** N rasage *m* au rasoir mécanique ► **wet wipe** N serviette *f* rafraîchissante

wetback‡ [ˈwetbæk] N (*US pej*) ouvrier *m* agricole mexicain (*entré illégalement aux États-Unis*)

wether [ˈweðəʳ] N bélier *m* châtré, mouton *m*

wetlands [ˈwetlændz] NPL (*esp US*) zones *fpl* humides

wetly [ˈwetlɪ] ADV [a] (= *damply*) **her hair clung ~ to her head** ses cheveux mouillés étaient plaqués sur sa tête; **she kissed him ~ on the mouth** elle lui donna un baiser mouillé sur la bouche [b] (= *feebly*) [*smile*] mollement

wetness [ˈwetnɪs] N [a] humidité *f*; **the ~ of the weather** le temps pluvieux [b] (*Brit Pol*) **they suspected him of political ~** ils le soupçonnaient de tendances gauchisantes

wetsuit [ˈwetsuːt] N combinaison *f* *or* ensemble *m* de plongée

wetting [ˈwetɪŋ] N [a] (*gen*) **to get a ~** se faire arroser; **to give sth/sb a ~** arroser qch/qn [b] (= *incontinence*) incontinence *f* d'urine; (*also* **bed-~**) énurésie *f* nocturne

WEU (ABBR = **Western European Union**) UEO *f*

we've [wiːv] = **we have**; → **have**

whack [wæk] [1] N [a] (= *blow*) grand coup *m*; (= *sound*) coup *m* sec, claquement *m*; **to give sth/sb a ~** donner un grand coup à qch/qn; **~!** vlan!; (*esp US*) **out of ~‡** détraqué, déglingué* [b] (* = *attempt*) **to have a ~ at doing** essayer de faire; **I'll have a ~ at it** je vais tenter le coup* [c] (*Brit** = *share*) part *f*; **you'll get your ~** tu auras ta part; **to pay one's ~** payer sa part; **to pay top** *or* **the full ~ for sth** payer qch plein pot*; **you'll get £15,000 a year, top ~** tu auras 15 000 livres par an, grand maximum* [2] VT [+ *thing, person*] donner un (*or* des) grand(s) coup(s) à; (= *spank*) fesser;* (= *defeat*) donner une raclée* à, flanquer une déculottée* *or* une dérouillée* à

whacked* [wækt] ADJ (*Brit fig* = *exhausted*) crevé*, claqué*

whacking [ˈwækɪŋ] [1] N (= *spanking*) fessée *f*; (= *beating*: *lit, fig*) raclée* *f*; **to give sb/sth a ~** = **to whack sb/sth**; → **whack** [2] ADJ (*esp Brit**: *also* **~ big, ~ great**) énorme

whacko* [ˌwæˈkəʊ] ADJ, N = **wacko**

whacky‡ [ˈwækɪ] ADJ = **wacky**

whale [weɪl] [1] N (*pl* **whales** *or* **whale**) [a] (= *animal*) baleine *f* [b] (*phrases*) **we had a ~ of a time*** on s'est drôlement* bien amusé; **a ~ of a difference*** une sacrée* différence; **a ~ of a lot of*** ... vachement* de ..., une sacrée* quantité de ... [2] VI **to go whaling** aller à la pêche à la baleine, aller pêcher la baleine [3] COMP ► **whale calf** N baleineau *m* ► **whale oil** N huile *f* de baleine ► **whale watching** N **to go ~ watching** aller regarder les baleines

whaleboat [ˈweɪlbəʊt] N (*Naut*) baleinière *f*

whalebone [ˈweɪlbəʊn] N fanon *m* de baleine; (*Dress*) baleine *f*

whaler [ˈweɪləʳ] N (= *person*) pêcheur *m* de baleine; (= *ship*) baleinier *m*

whaling ['weɪlɪŋ] ① N (NonC) pêche f à la baleine ② COMP [industry] baleinier ► **whaling ship** N baleinier m ► **whaling station** N port m baleinier

wham [wæm] EXCL vlan !

whammy ['wæmɪ] N (US) mauvais sort m, poisse* f ; **double/triple ~*** double/triple coup m dur*

whang [wæŋ] ① N bruit m retentissant ② VT donner un coup dur et sonore à ③ VI faire un bruit retentissant

wharf [wɔːf] N (pl **wharfs** or **wharves**) quai m (pour marchandises)

wharfage ['wɔːfɪdʒ] N (NonC) droits mpl de quai

wharves [wɔːvz] NPL of **wharf**

---

what [wɒt]

| ① ADJECTIVE | |
| ② PRONOUN | ③ COMPOUNDS |

① ADJECTIVE

[a] in questions and indirect speech quel m, quelle f, quels mpl, quelles fpl ; **~ sort of music do you like?** quel genre de musique aimes-tu ? ; **~ time is it?** quelle heure est-il ? ; **~ flavours do you want?** quels parfums voulez-vous ? ; **~ subjects did you choose?** quelles matières as-tu choisies ? ; **she told me ~ colour it was** elle m'a dit de quelle couleur c'était ; **they asked me ~ kind of films I liked** ils m'ont demandé quel genre de films j'aimais ; **he told me ~ time it was** il m'a dit quelle heure il était, il m'a donné l'heure

[b] = all the I gave him ~ money/coins I had je lui ai donné tout l'argent/toutes les pièces que j'avais ; **~ savings we had are now gone** le peu d'économies que nous avions s'est maintenant envolé ; **I will give you ~ information we have** je vais vous donner toutes les informations dont nous disposons ; **they packed ~ few belongings they had** ils ont rassemblé le peu qui leur appartenait ; **I gave ~ little help I could** j'ai aidé comme j'ai pu ; I gave her ~ comfort I could je l'ai réconfortée comme j'ai pu ; I gave them ~ advice I could je les ai conseillés comme j'ai pu

[c] exclamations

◆ **what a ...!**: **~ an idiot!** quel imbécile ! ; **~ a nice surprise!** quelle bonne surprise ! ; **~ a ridiculous suggestion!** quelle suggestion ridicule ! ; **~ a beautiful boat!** quel beau bateau ! ; **~ a nightmare!** quel cauchemar ! ; **~ a nuisance!** quelle barbe !*, c'est vraiment ennuyeux ! ; **~ a lot of people!** que de monde ! ; (iro) **~ an excuse!** drôle d'excuse !

◆ **what** + plural/uncount noun: **~ fools we were!** quels imbéciles nous faisions !, nous étions vraiment bêtes ! ; **~ lovely hair you've got!** quels jolis cheveux tu as !

② PRONOUN

[a] used alone, or in emphatic position quoi ; **~?** I didn't get that quoi ? tu peux répéter ? ; **I've forgotten something — ~?** j'ai oublié quelque chose — quoi ? ; **you told him WHAT?** quoi ! qu'est-ce que vous lui avez dit ? ; **it's WHAT?** c'est quoi ? ; **he's getting married — ~!** il se marie — quoi !, il se marie — non ! ; **~! you expect me to believe that!** quoi ! et tu penses que je vais croire ça !, tu ne penses quand même pas que je vais croire ça ! ; BUT **it's getting late, ~?**†* (esp Brit: seeking confirmation) il se fait tard, n'est-ce pas ?

quoi is used with a preposition, if the French verb requires one.
I've just thought of something — ~? je viens de penser à quelque chose — à quoi ? ; **I've just remembered something — ~?** je viens de me souvenir de quelque chose — de quoi ?

◆ **you what?*** (Brit) (expressing surprise) c'est pas vrai !* ; (= what did you say?) hein ?*

[b] subject in direct questions qu'est-ce qui ; **~'s happened?** qu'est-ce qui s'est passé ? ; **~'s**

bothering you? qu'est-ce qui te préoccupe ? ; **~'s for lunch/dinner?** qu'est-ce qu'il y a pour déjeuner/dîner ? ; BUT **~ is his address?** quelle est son adresse ? ; **~'s the French for "pen"?** comment dit-on « pen » en français ? ; **~ is this called?** comment ça s'appelle ? ; **~'s money if you have no time to spend it?** à quoi bon avoir de l'argent si on n'a pas le temps de le dépenser ?

When asking for a definition or explanation, qu'est-ce que c'est que is often used.
~ is a lycée polyvalent? qu'est-ce que c'est qu'un lycée polyvalent ?, c'est quoi, un lycée polyvalent ? ; **~ are capers?** qu'est-ce que c'est les câpres ?, c'est quoi, les câpres ? ; **~'s that noise?** quel est ce bruit ?, c'est quoi, ce bruit ?

◆ **what's that?** (asking about sth) qu'est-ce que c'est que ça ? ; (= what did you say) comment ?, qu'est-ce que tu as dit ?

[c] object in direct questions qu'est-ce que, que, quoi (after prep)

The object pronoun que is more formal than qu'est-ce que and requires inversion of verb and pronoun.
~ did you do? qu'est-ce que vous avez fait ?, qu'avez-vous fait ? ; **~ can we do?** qu'est-ce qu'on peut faire ?, que peut-on faire ?

A subject pronoun may become the object when translated.
~ does it matter? qu'est-ce que ça peut bien faire ? ; **~'s it to you?*** qu'est-ce que cela peut vous faire ?

The French preposition cannot be separated from the pronoun.
~ does he owe his success to? à quoi doit-il son succès ? ; **~ were you talking about?** de quoi parliez-vous ?

[d] = which in particular quel m, quelle f, quels mpl, quelles fpl ; **~ are the commonest mistakes students make?** quelles sont les erreurs les plus courantes des étudiants ? ; **~'s the best time to call?** quel est le meilleur moment pour vous joindre ? ; **~ are the advantages?** quels sont les avantages ?

[e] = how much combien ; **~ will it cost?** combien est-ce que ça va coûter ?, ça va coûter combien ? ; **~ does it weigh?** combien est-ce que ça pèse ? ; **~ do 2 and 2 make?** combien font 2 et 2 ?

[f] in indirect questions ce qui (subject of vb), ce que (object of vb) ; **I wonder ~ will happen** je me demande ce qui va se passer ; **I wonder ~ they think** je me demande ce qu'ils pensent ; **he asked me ~ she said** il m'a demandé ce qu'elle avait dit ; **I don't know ~ that building is** je ne sais pas ce que c'est que ce bâtiment

If the French verb takes a preposition, what is translated by quoi.
tell us ~ you're thinking about dites-nous à quoi vous pensez ; **I wonder ~ they need** je me demande de quoi ils ont besoin ; **I wonder ~ they are expecting** je me demande à quoi ils s'attendent

quoi is used when what ends the sentence.
I don't know who's doing ~ je ne sais pas qui fait quoi

[g] in relative clauses (= that which) ce qui (subject of vb), ce que (object of vb), ce dont (object of vb taking « de »), ce à quoi (object of verb taking « à ») ; **~ is done is done** ce qui est fait est fait ; **the hotel isn't ~ it was** l'hôtel n'est plus ce qu'il était ; **~ I don't understand is ...** ce que je ne comprends pas c'est ... ; **say ~ you like, ...** vous pouvez dire ce que vous voulez, ... ; **~ I need is** ... ce dont j'ai besoin c'est ... ; **it wasn't ~ I was expecting** ce n'était pas ce à quoi je m'attendais ; **do ~ you like** fais ce que tu veux, fais comme tu veux

When what = the ones which, the French pronoun is generally plural.
I've no clothes except ~ I'm wearing je n'ai d'autres vêtements que ceux que je porte

[h] SET STRUCTURES

◆ **and I don't know what (all)**: **they raped, pillaged and I don't know ~ (all)** ils ont violé, pillé et je ne sais quoi encore ; **it was full of cream, jam, chocolate and I don't know ~** c'était plein de crème, de confiture, de chocolat et je ne sais trop quoi

◆ **and what is** + adjective/adverb: **and ~'s more** et qui plus est ; **and ~ is worse** et ce qui est pire ; **and, ~ was more surprising, there was ...** et, plus surprenant encore, il y avait ...

◆ **and what have you*** ◊ **and what not*** et cetera

◆ **or what?**: **are you coming/do you want it or ~?** tu viens/tu le veux ou quoi ? ; **I mean, is this sick, or ~?*** il faut vraiment être malade !* ; **is this luxury or ~?*** c'est le grand luxe !

◆ **tell you what**: **tell you ~, let's stay here another day** j'ai une idée : si on restait un jour de plus ?

◆ **what about**: **~ about Robert?** et Robert ? ; **~ about people who haven't got cars?** et les gens qui n'ont pas de voiture (alors) ? ; **~ about the danger involved?** et les risques que l'on encourt ? ; **~ about lunch, shall we go out?** qu'est-ce qu'on fait à midi, on va au restaurant ? ; **your car ... — ~ about it?*** ta voiture ... — qu'est-ce qu'elle a ma voiture ? ; **~ about going to the cinema?** si on allait au cinéma ?

◆ **what for?** pourquoi ? ; **~ did you do that for?** pourquoi avez-vous fait ça ? → 3

◆ **what if** et si ; **~ if this doesn't work out?** et si ça ne marchait pas ? ; **~ if he says no?** et s'il refuse ? ; **~ if it rains?** et s'il pleut ?

◆ **what of**: but **~ of the country's political leaders?** et les dirigeants politiques du pays ?, qu'en est-il des dirigeants politiques du pays ? ; **~ of it?*** et alors ?

◆ **what's what**: **he knows ~'s ~** il s'y connaît, il connaît son affaire ; **you should try my job, then you'd really see ~'s ~** tu devrais faire mon travail et alors tu comprendrais ; **I've done this job long enough to know ~'s ~** je fais ce travail depuis assez longtemps pour savoir de quoi il retourne* ; **I'll show them ~'s ~** je vais leur montrer de quel bois je me chauffe*

◆ **what with**: **~ with the stress and lack of sleep, I was in a terrible state** entre le stress et le manque de sommeil, j'étais dans un état lamentable ; **~ with one thing and another** avec tout ça ; **~ with the suitcase and his bike he could hardly ...** avec la valise et son vélo, il pouvait à peine ...

◆ **not but what**: **not but ~ that wouldn't be a good thing** non que ce soit une mauvaise chose

③ COMPOUNDS

► **what-d'ye-call-her*** N Machine* f ► **what-d'ye-call-him*** N Machin* m, Machin Chouette* m ► **what-d'ye-call-it*** N machin* m, truc* m, bidule* m ► **what-for*** N **to give sb ~-for** passer un savon à qn* ► **what-ho!**†* EXCL ohé bonjour ! ► **what's-her-name*** N = what-d'ye-call-her ► **what's-his-name*** N = what-d'ye-call-him ► **what's-it** N = what-d'ye-call-it ; **Mr What's-it*** Monsieur Machin (Chose)* ► **what's-its-name*** N = what-d'ye-call-it

---

what'er [wɒt'ɛər] (liter) = **whatever**

▼ **whatever** [wɒt'evər] ① ADJ [a] (gen) **~ book you choose** quel que soit le livre que vous choisissiez (subj) ; **any box of ~ size** n'importe quelle boîte quelle qu'en soit la taille ; **give me ~ money you've got** donne-moi (tout) ce que tu as comme argent ; **he agreed to make ~ repairs might prove necessary** il a accepté de faire toutes les réparations qui s'avéreraient nécessaires ; **you'll have to change ~ plans you've made** quoi que vous ayez prévu, il vous faudra changer vos plans

b (*: *emphatic interrog*) **~ books have you been reading?** qu'est-ce que vous êtes allé lire?, vous avez lu de drôles de livres!*; **~ time is it?** quelle heure peut-il bien être?

2 ADV **~ the weather** quel que soit le temps (qu'il fasse); **~ the news from the front, they ...** quelles que soient les nouvelles du front, ils ...; **I'll take anything ~ you can spare** je prendrai tout ce dont vous n'avez pas besoin (quoi que ce soit); **I've no money ~** je n'ai pas un sou, je n'ai pas le moindre argent; **there's no doubt ~ about it** cela ne fait pas le moindre doute *or* pas l'ombre d'un doute; **nothing ~** rien du tout, absolument rien; **did you see any? — none ~!** tu en as vu? — non, absolument aucun!; **in no case ~ shall we agree to see ...** en aucun cas nous n'accepterons de voir ...; **has he any chance ~?** a-t-il la moindre chance?

3 PRON **a** (= *no matter what*) quoi que (+ *subj*); **~ happens** quoi qu'il arrive (*subj*); **~ you (may) find** quoi que vous trouviez (*subj*); **~ it may be** quoi que ce soit; **~ he may mean** quel que soit ce qu'il veut dire; **~ it** *or* **that means** *or* **may mean** *or* **meant** quel que soit le sens du mot (*or* de la phrase *etc*); (*hum, iro*) maintenant, allez savoir ce que ça veut dire; **I'll pay ~ it costs** je paierai ce que ça coûtera; **~ it costs, get it** achète-le quel qu'en soit le prix; **~ he said before, he won't now do it** quoi qu'il ait dit auparavant, il ne le fera pas maintenant

b (= *anything that*) tout ce que; **do ~ you please** faites ce que vous voulez *or* voudrez; **we shall do ~ seems necessary** nous ferons le nécessaire; **Monday or Tuesday, ~ suits you best** lundi ou mardi, ce qui *or* le jour qui vous convient le mieux; **~ you say, sir** comme monsieur voudra; (*iro*) **I tell you I'm ill! — ~ you say** je te dis que je suis malade! — bien sûr, puisque tu le dis (*iro*)

c (*: *emphatic interrog*) **~ did you do?** qu'est-ce que vous êtes allé faire?; **~ did you say that for?** pourquoi êtes-vous allé dire ça?

d (= *other similar things*) **the books and the clothes and ~** les livres et les vêtements et tout ça *or* et que sais-je encore

whatnot ['wɒtnɒt] N **a** (= *furniture*) étagère *f* **b*** = **what-d'ye-call-it**; → **what c** (= *and other things*) **and ~*** et ainsi de suite, et tout ce qui s'ensuit

whatsoever (*emphatic*) [ˌwɒtsəʊˈevər], **whatsoe'er** (*liter*) [ˌwɒtsəʊˈeər] = **whatever**

wheat [wiːt] **1** N (*NonC*) blé *m*, froment *m*; (*fig*) **to separate** *or* **divide the ~ from the chaff** séparer le bon grain de l'ivraie **2** COMP [*flour*] de blé, de froment; [*field*] de blé, à blé ► **wheat sheaf** N gerbe *f* de blé

wheatear ['wiːtɪər] N (= *bird*) traquet *m* (motteux)

wheaten ['wiːtn] ADJ de blé, de froment

wheatgerm ['wiːtdʒɜːm] N (*NonC*) germes *mpl* de blé

wheatmeal ['wiːtmiːl] N farine *f* complète; **~ bread** ≈ pain *m* de campagne

wheedle ['wiːdl] VT cajoler, câliner; **to ~ sth out of sb** obtenir *or* tirer qch de qn par des cajoleries *or* des câlineries; **to ~ sb into doing sth** cajoler *or* câliner qn pour qu'il fasse qch, amener qn à force de cajoleries *or* câlineries à faire qch

wheedling ['wiːdlɪŋ] **1** ADJ câlin, enjôleur **2** N cajolerie(s) *f(pl)*, câlinerie(s) *f(pl)*

wheel [wiːl] **1** N **a** (*gen*) roue *f*; (*smaller*) [*of trolley, toy etc*] roulette *f*; (*of ship*) volant *m*; (= *steering wheel*) volant *m*; (= *spinning wheel*) rouet *m*; (= *potter's wheel*) tour *m* (de potier); (*in roulette etc*) roue *f*; (*Hist* = *torture instrument*) roue *f*; **at the ~** (*of car*) au volant; (*of ship*) à la barre; **to take the ~** (*of ship*) prendre le gouvernail; (*of car*: *also* **to get behind the ~**) se

mettre au volant; (*Aut*) **to change a ~** changer une roue; (*Hist*) **to break sb on the ~** rouer qn → **shoulder, spoke**[1]

b (*in fig phrases*) **the ~s of government/of justice** les rouages *mpl* du gouvernement/de l'institution judiciaire; **the ~s of justice are moving** *or* **turning very slowly** la justice suit son cours avec beaucoup de lenteur; **to oil** *or* **grease the ~s** huiler les rouages; **there are ~s within ~s** c'est plus compliqué que ça ne paraît, il y a toutes sortes de forces en jeu; **the ~ has come full circle** la boucle est bouclée; **it was hell on ~s*** c'était l'enfer; (*US fig*) **a third** *or* **fifth ~** la cinquième roue du carrosse → **reinvent**

c (* = *car*) (**set of**) **~s** bagnole* *f*; **have you got ~s?** vous êtes motorisé?*

d (*Mil* = *turn*) **to make a right/left ~** effectuer une conversion à droite/à gauche

2 VT **a** [+ *barrow, pushchair*] pousser, rouler; [+ *bed, cycle*] pousser; [+ *child*] pousser (dans un landau *etc*); **to ~ a trolley into/out of a room** rouler *or* pousser un chariot dans/hors d'une pièce; **they ~ed the sick man over to the window** ils ont poussé le malade (dans son fauteuil roulant *or* sur son lit roulant) jusqu'à la fenêtre

b (* *fig* = *bring*) **he ~ed out an enormous box** il a sorti une boîte énorme; **~ him in!** amenez-le!; **the government have ~ed out their usual pre-election tax cuts** le gouvernement a ressorti ses réductions d'impôt, comme il en a l'habitude à la veille des élections; **he ~ed out his usual arguments** il a sorti* ses arguments habituels; **spokesmen were ~ed out to deny these rumours** on a fait venir des porte-parole pour démentir ces rumeurs

3 VI **a** (*also* **~ round**) [*birds*] tournoyer; [*windmill sails etc*] tourner (en rond); [*person*] se retourner (brusquement), virevolter; (*Mil*) effectuer une conversion; [*procession*] tourner; (*Mil*) **right ~!** à droite!

b (*fig*) **he's always ~ing and dealing*** il est toujours en train de manigancer quelque chose *or* de chercher des combines*

4 COMP ► **wheel brace** N (*Aut*) clef *f* en croix ► **wheel clamp** N sabot *m* (de Denver) ► **wheel gauge** N (*Aut*) écartement *m* des essieux ► **wheel horse** N (*US fig*) cheval *m* de labour (*fig*) ► **wheel of fortune** N roue *f* de la fortune

wheelbarrow ['wiːlbærəʊ] N brouette *f*

wheelbase ['wiːlbeɪs] N (*Aut*) empattement *m*

wheelchair ['wiːltʃeər] **1** N fauteuil *m* roulant; **"~ access"** «accès aux handicapés»; (*hum*) **when I'm in a ~ ...** quand je serai dans un *or* en fauteuil roulant **2** COMP ► **wheelchair Olympics**† N Jeux *mpl* olympiques handisports

wheeled [wiːld] ADJ [*object*] à roues, muni de roues; **three-~** à trois roues

wheeler ['wiːlər] N (*pej*) **~-(and-)dealer*** magouilleur* *m*, -euse* *f*; (= *businessman*) affairiste *m*; (*pej*) **~-dealing*** = **wheeling and dealing**; → **wheeling**

-wheeler ['wiːlər] N (*in compounds*) **four-wheeler** voiture *f* à quatre roues → **two**

wheelhouse ['wiːlhaʊs] N (*Naut*) timonerie *f*

wheelie* ['wiːlɪ] **1** N **to do a ~** faire une roue arrière **2** COMP ► **wheelie bin*** N (*Brit*) poubelle *f* à roulettes

wheeling ['wiːlɪŋ] N (*pej*) **~ and dealing*** magouilles* *fpl*, combines* *fpl*; **there has been a lot of ~ and dealing*** over the choice of candidate le choix du candidat a donné lieu à toutes sortes de combines *or* de magouilles*

wheelspin ['wiːlspɪn] N (*Aut*) patinage *m*

wheelwright ['wiːlraɪt] N charron *m*

wheeze [wiːz] **1** N **a** respiration *f* bruyante *or* sifflante **b** (*Brit*)* (* = *scheme*) truc* *m*, combine* *f* **c** (*US* * = *saying*) dicton *m*, adage

m **2** VI (*person*) (= *breathe noisily*) respirer bruyamment; (= *breathe with difficulty*) avoir du mal à respirer; [*animal*] souffler **3** VT (*also* **~ out**) **"yes", he ~d** «oui», dit-il d'une voix rauque; **the old organ ~d out the tune** le vieil orgue a joué le morceau dans un bruit de soufflerie

wheezy ['wiːzɪ] ADJ [*person*] poussif, asthmatique; [*voice*] d'asthmatique; [*animal*] poussif; [*organ etc*] asthmatique (*fig*)

whelk [welk] N bulot *m*, buccin *m*

whelp [welp] **1** N (= *animal*) petit(e) *m(f)*; (*pej* = *youth*) petit morveux *m* **2** VI (*of animals*) mettre bas

---

when [wen]

1 ADVERB	**3** NOUN
2 CONJUNCTION	

1 ADVERB

quand

Note the various ways of asking questions in French:

~ does the term start? quand commence le trimestre?, quand est-ce que le trimestre commence?; **~ did it happen?** quand cela s'est-il passé?, ça s'est passé quand?; **~ was penicillin discovered?** quand la pénicilline a-t-elle été découverte?; **~ was the Channel Tunnel opened?** quand a-t-on ouvert le tunnel sous la Manche?; **~ would be the best time to phone?** quand est-ce je pourrais rappeler?; **~'s the wedding?** à quand le mariage?, quand doit avoir lieu le mariage?

There is no inversion after **quand** *in indirect questions.*

I don't know ~ I'll see him again je ne sais pas quand je le reverrai; **did he say ~ he'd be back?** a-t-il dit quand il serait de retour?; **let me know ~ you want your holidays** faites-moi savoir quand *or* à quelle date vous désirez prendre vos congés

If **when** *means* what time/date, *a more specific translation is often used.*

~ does the train leave? à quelle heure part le train?; **~ do you finish work?** à quelle heure est-ce tu quittes le travail?; **~ is your birthday?** quelle est la date de ton anniversaire?, c'est quand, ton anniversaire?; **~ do the grapes get ripe?** vers quelle date *or* quand est-ce que les raisins sont mûrs?

♦ **say when!*** (*pouring drinks etc*) vous m'arrêterez ...

2 CONJUNCTION

a = *at the time that* quand, lorsque; **everything looks nicer ~ the sun is shining** tout est plus joli quand *or* lorsque le soleil brille

If the **when** *clause refers to the future, the future tense is used in French.*

I'll do it ~ I have time je le ferai quand j'aurai le temps; **let me know ~ she comes** faites-moi savoir quand elle arrivera; **~ you're older, you'll understand** quand tu seras plus grand, tu comprendras; **go ~ you like** partez quand vous voulez *or* voudrez

en + *present participle may be used, if the subject of both clauses is the same, and the verb is one of action.*

she burnt herself ~ she took the dish out of the oven elle s'est brûlée en sortant le plat du four; **he blushed ~ he saw her** il a rougi en la voyant

♦ **when** + *noun*: **~ a student at Oxford, she ...** lorsqu'elle était étudiante à Oxford, elle ...; **~ a child, he ...** enfant, il ...

♦ **when** + *adjective*: **my father, ~ young, had a fine tenor voice** quand mon père était jeune il avait une belle voix de ténor; **~ just three years old, he was ...** à trois ans il était déjà ...; **the floor is slippery ~ wet** le sol est glissant quand *or* lorsqu'il est mouillé

♦ **when** + *-ing*: **you should take your passport**

with you ~ **changing money** munissez-vous de votre passeport lorsque *or* quand vous changez de l'argent; **take care** ~ **opening the tin** faites attention lorsque *or* quand vous ouvrez la boîte, faites attention en ouvrant la boîte

♦ *day/time/moment* + **when** où; **on the day** ~ **I met him** le jour où je l'ai rencontré; **at the time** ~ **I should have been at the station** à l'heure où j'aurais dû être à la gare; **at the very moment** ~ **I was about to leave** juste au moment où j'allais partir; **one day** ~ **the sun was shining** un jour que *or* où le soleil brillait; **it was one of those days** ~ **everything is quiet** c'était un de ces jours où tout est calme; **there are times** ~ **I wish I'd never met him** il y a des moments où je souhaiterais ne l'avoir jamais rencontré; *BUT* **this is a time** ~ **we must speak up for our principles** c'est dans un moment comme celui-ci qu'il faut défendre nos principes

[b] = **which is when** **he arrived at 8 o'clock,** ~ **traffic is at its peak** il est arrivé à 8 heures, heure à laquelle la circulation est la plus intense; **in August,** ~ **peaches are at their best** en août, époque où les pêches sont les plus savoureuses; **it was in spring,** ~ **the snow was melting** c'était au printemps, à la fonte des neiges

[c] = **the time when** **he told me about** ~ **you got lost in Paris** il m'a raconté le jour *or* la fois* où vous vous êtes perdu dans Paris; **now is** ~ **I need you most** c'est maintenant que j'ai le plus besoin de vous; **that's** ~ **the programme starts** c'est l'heure à laquelle l'émission commence; **that's** ~ **Napoleon was born** c'est l'année où Napoléon est né; **that's** ~ **you ought to try to be patient** c'est dans ces moments-là qu'il faut faire preuve de patience; **that was** ~ **the trouble started** c'est alors que les ennuis ont commencé

[d] = **after** quand, une fois que; ~ **you read the letter you'll know why** quand vous lirez la lettre vous comprendrez pourquoi; ~ **they left, I felt relieved** quand ils sont partis, je me suis senti soulagé; ~ **you've been to Greece you realize how ...** quand *or* une fois qu'on est allé en Grèce, on se rend compte que ...; ~ **he had made the decision, he felt better** il se sentit soulagé une fois qu'il eut pris une décision; ~ **(it is) finished the bridge will measure ...** une fois terminé, le pont mesurera ...; *BUT* ~ **they had left he telephoned me** après leur départ il m'a téléphoné

[e] = **each time that, whenever** quand; **I take aspirin** ~ **I have a headache** je prends un cachet d'aspirine quand j'ai mal à la tête; ~ **it rains I wish I were back in Italy** quand il pleut je regrette l'Italie

[f] = **whereas** alors que; **he thought he was recovering,** ~ **in fact ...** il pensait qu'il était en voie de guérison alors qu'en fait ...

[g] = **if** **how can I be self-confident** ~ **I look like this?** comment veux-tu que j'aie confiance en moi en étant comme ça?; **how can you understand** ~ **you won't listen?** comment voulez-vous comprendre si vous n'écoutez pas?; **what's the good of trying** ~ **I know I can't do it?** à quoi bon essayer, si *or* puisque je sais que je ne peux pas le faire

[h] = **and then** quand; **he had just sat down** ~ **the phone rang** il venait juste de s'asseoir quand le téléphone a sonné; **I was about to leave** ~ **I remembered ...** j'étais sur le point de partir quand je me suis rappelé ...; *BUT* **I had only just got back** ~ **I had to leave again** à peine venais-je de rentrer que j'ai dû repartir

[3] NOUN
I want to know the ~ **and the how of all this** je veux savoir quand et comment tout ça est arrivé

---

whence [wens] ADV, CONJ (*liter*) d'où

whenever [wen'evəʳ], **whene'er** (*liter*) [wen-ˈɛəʳ] [1] CONJ [a] (= *at whatever time*) quand;

---

come ~ **you wish** venez quand vous voulez *or* voudrez; **you may leave** ~ **you're ready** vous pouvez partir quand vous serez prêt

[b] (= *every time that*) quand, chaque fois que; **come and see us** ~ **you can** venez nous voir quand vous le pouvez; ~ **I see a black horse I think of Jenny** chaque fois que je vois un cheval noir je pense à Jenny; ~ **it rains the roof leaks** chaque fois qu'il pleut le toit laisse entrer l'eau; ~ **people ask him he says ...** quand on lui demande il dit ...; ~ **you touch it it falls over** on n'a qu'à le toucher et il tombe

[2] ADV* mais quand donc; ~ **did you do that?** mais quand donc est-ce que vous avez fait ça?; **last Monday, or** ~ lundi dernier, ou je ne sais quand; **I can leave on Monday, or Tuesday, or** ~ je peux partir lundi, ou mardi, ou un autre jour *or* ou n'importe quand

whensoever (*emphatic*) [ˌwensəʊ'evəʳ], **whensoe'er** (*liter*) [ˌwensəʊ'ɛəʳ] = **whenever**

where [wɛəʳ] [1] ADV (= *in or to what place*) où; ~ **do you live?** où habitez-vous?; ~ **are you going (to)?** où allez-vous?; ~**'s the theatre?** où est le théâtre?; ~ **are you from?** ◊ ~ **do you come from?** d'où venez-vous?, vous venez d'où?; ~ **have you come from?** d'où est-ce que vous arrivez?, vous arrivez d'où?; **you saw him near** ~? vous l'avez vu près d'où?; ~ **have you got to in the book?** où est-ce que vous en êtes de votre livre?; (*fig*) ~ **do I come into it?** qu'est-ce que je viens faire dans tout ça?, quel est mon rôle dans tout ça?; ~**'s the difference?** où voyez-vous une différence?; **I wonder** ~ he is je me demande où il est; **I don't know** ~ **I put it** je ne sais pas où je l'ai mis; **don't eat that, you don't know** ~ **it's been** ne mangez pas cela, vous ne savez pas où ça a traîné; ~ **would we be if ...?** où serions-nous si ...?

[2] CONJ [a] (*gen*) (là) où; **stay** ~ **you are** restez (là) où vous êtes; **there is a garage** ~ **the two roads intersect** il y a un garage au croisement des deux routes; **Lyons stands** ~ **the Saône meets the Rhône** Lyon se trouve au confluent de la Saône et du Rhône; **there is a school** ~ **our house once stood** il y a une école là où *or* à l'endroit où se dressait autrefois notre maison; **go** ~ **you like** allez où vous voulez *or* voudrez; **it is coldest** ~ **there are no trees for shelter** c'est là où il n'y a pas d'arbre pour s'abriter (du vent) qu'il fait le plus froid; **I'm at the stage** ~ **I could ...** j'en suis au point où je pourrais ...; **my book is not** ~ **I left it** mon livre n'est pas là ou à l'endroit où je l'avais laissé; **it's not** ~ **I expected to see it** je ne m'attendais pas à le voir là; **he ran towards** ~ **the bus had crashed** il a couru vers l'endroit où le bus avait eu l'accident; **I told him** ~ **he could stick his job:** je lui ai dit où il pouvait se le mettre son boulot:

[b] (= *in which, at which etc*) où; **the house** ~ **he was born** la maison où il est né, sa maison natale; **in the place** ~ **there used to be a church** à l'endroit où il y avait une église; **England is** ~ **you'll find this sort of thing most often** c'est en Angleterre que vous trouverez le plus fréquemment cela

[c] (= *the place that*) là que; **this is** ~ **the car was found** c'est là qu'on a retrouvé la voiture; **this is** ~ **we got to in the book** c'est là que nous en sommes du livre; **that's** ~ **you're wrong!** c'est là que vous vous trompez!, voilà votre erreur!; **so that's** ~ **my gloves have got to!** voilà où sont passés mes gants!; (= *when*) **that's** ~ *or* **there's*** ~ **things started to go wrong** c'est là que les choses se sont gâtées; **this is** ~ *or* **here's*** ~ **you've got to make your own decision** là il faut que tu décides (*subj*) tout seul; **that's** ~ **I meant** c'est là que je voulais dire; **he went up to** ~ **she was sitting** il s'est approché de l'endroit où elle était assise; **I walked past** ~ **he was standing** j'ai dépassé l'endroit où il se tenait; **from** ~ **I'm standing I can see ...** d'où *or* de là où je suis je

---

peux voir ...

[d] (= *wherever*) là où; **you'll always find water** ~ **there are trees** vous trouverez toujours de l'eau là où il y a des arbres; ~ **there is kindness, you will find ...** là où il y a de la gentillesse, vous trouverez ...

[e] (= *whereas*) alors que; **he walked** ~ **he could have taken the bus** il est allé à pied alors qu'il aurait pu prendre le bus; **he walked** ~ **I would have taken the bus** il est allé à pied alors que *or* tandis que moi j'aurais pris le bus

[3] N **I want to know the** ~ **and the why of it** je veux savoir où et pourquoi c'est arrivé

whereabouts ['wɛərəbaʊts] [1] ADV où (donc); ~ **did you put it?** où (donc) l'as-tu mis? [2] N **to know sb's/sth's** ~ savoir où est qn/qch; **his** ~ **are unknown** personne ne sait où il se trouve

whereafter [ˌwɛər'æftəʳ] CONJ (*frm*) après quoi

▼ **whereas** [wɛər'æz] CONJ (= *while*) alors que, tandis que; (= *in view of the fact that*) attendu que, considérant que; (= *although*) bien que (+ *subj*), quoique (+ *subj*)

whereat [wɛər'æt] ADV (*liter*) sur quoi, après quoi, sur ce

whereby [wɛə'baɪ] PRON (*frm*) par quoi, par lequel (*or* laquelle *etc*), au moyen duquel (*or de* laquelle *etc*)

wherefore†† ['wɛə,fɔːʳ] [1] CONJ (= *for that reason*) et donc, et pour cette raison → **why** [2] ADV (= *why*) pourquoi

wherein [wɛər'ɪn] [1] INTERROG ADV†† où, dans quoi [2] CONJ (*frm*) où, dans quoi

whereof [wɛər'ɒv] ADV, PRON (*frm, liter*) de quoi, dont, duquel (*or de* laquelle *etc*)

whereon [wɛər'ɒn] PRON (*frm, liter*) sur quoi, sur lequel (*or* laquelle *etc*)

wheresoever (*emphatic*) [ˌwɛəsəʊ'evəʳ], **wheresoe'er** (*liter*) [ˌwɛəsəʊ'ɛəʳ] = **wherever**

whereto [wɛə'tuː] ADV (*frm*) et dans ce but, et en vue de ceci

whereupon [ˌwɛərə'pɒn] ADV sur quoi, après quoi

wherever [wɛər'evəʳ] [1] CONJ [a] (= *no matter where*) où que (+ *subj*); ~ **I am I'll always remember** où que je sois, je n'oublierai jamais; ~ **you go I'll go too** où que tu ailles *or* partout où tu iras, j'irai; **I'll buy it** ~ **it comes from** je l'achèterai d'où que cela provienne *or* quelle qu'en soit la provenance; ~ **it came from, it's here now!** peu importe d'où cela vient, c'est là maintenant!

[b] (= *anywhere*) (là) où; **sit** ~ **you like** asseyez-vous (là) où vous voulez; **go** ~ **you please** allez où bon vous semblera; **we'll go** ~ **you wish** nous irons (là) où vous voudrez; **he comes from Barcombe,** ~ **that is** il vient d'un endroit qui s'appellerait Barcombe

[c] (= *everywhere*) partout où; ~ **you see this sign, you can be sure that ...** partout où vous voyez ce signe, vous pouvez être sûr que ...; ~ **there is water available** partout où il y a de l'eau

[2] ADV* mais où donc; ~ **did you get that hat?** mais où donc avez-vous déniché* ce chapeau?; **I bought it in London or Liverpool or** ~ je l'ai acheté à Londres, Liverpool ou Dieu sait où

wherewith [wɛə'wɪθ] ADV (*frm, liter*) avec quoi, avec lequel (*or* laquelle *etc*)

wherewithal ['wɛəwɪðɔːl] N moyens *mpl*, ressources *fpl* nécessaires; **he hasn't the** ~ **to buy it** il n'a pas les moyens de l'acheter

whet [wet] VT [a] [+ *tool*] aiguiser, affûter [b] [+ *desire, appetite, curiosity*] aiguiser, stimuler

whether ['weðəʳ] CONJ [a] si; **I don't know** ~ **it's true or not** ◊ **I don't know** ~ **or not it's true** je ne sais pas si c'est vrai ou non; **you must tell him** ~ **you want him (or not)** il faut que tu lui dises si oui ou non tu as besoin de lui; **I**

don't know ~ to go or not je ne sais pas si je dois y aller ou non ; **it is doubtful ~ ...** il est peu probable que ... (+ *subj*) ; **I doubt ~ ...** je doute que ... (+ *subj*) ; **I'm not sure ~ ...** je ne suis pas sûr si ... (+ *indic*) *or* que ... (+ *subj*) **[b]** que (+ *subj*) ; **~ it rains or (~ it) snows I'm going out** qu'il pleuve ou qu'il neige (*subj*) je sors ; **~ you go or not ◊ ~ or not you go** que tu y ailles ou non **[c]** soit ; **~ today or tomorrow** soit aujourd'hui soit demain ; **~ before or after** soit avant soit après ; **~ with a friend to help you or without** avec ou sans ami pour vous aider ; **I shall help you ~ or no** de toute façon *or* quoi qu'il arrive (*subj*) je vous aiderai

whetstone ['wetstəʊn] N pierre *f* à aiguiser

whew* [hwju:] EXCL (*relief, exhaustion*) ouf ! ; (*surprise, admiration*) fichtre !*

whey [weɪ] N petit-lait *m*

which [wɪtʃ] **[1]** ADJ **[a]** (*in questions etc*) quel ; **~ card did he take?** quelle carte a-t-il prise ?, laquelle de ces cartes a-t-il prise ? ; **I don't know ~ book he wants** je ne sais pas quel livre il veut ; **~ one?** lequel (*or* laquelle) ? ; **~ one of you?** lequel (*or* laquelle) d'entre vous ? ; **~ Campbell do you mean?** de quel Campbell parlez-vous ? **[b]** **~ case** auquel cas ; **he spent a week here, during ~ time ...** il a passé une semaine ici au cours de laquelle ... **[2]** PRON **[a]** (*in questions etc*) lequel *m*, laquelle *f* ; **~ is the best of these maps?** ◊ **~ of these maps is the best?** quelle est la meilleure de ces cartes ?, laquelle de ces cartes est la meilleure ? ; **~ have you taken?** lequel *m* (*or* laquelle *f*) avez-vous pris(e) ? ; **~ of you two is taller?** lequel de vous deux est le plus grand ?, qui est le plus grand de vous deux ? ; **~ are the ripest apples?** quelles sont les pommes les plus mûres ?, quelles pommes sont les plus mûres ? ; **~ would you like?** lequel aimeriez-vous ? ; **~ of you are married?** lesquels d'entre vous sont mariés ? ; **~ of you owns the red car?** lequel d'entre vous est le propriétaire de la voiture rouge ? **[b]** (= *the one or ones that*) (*subject*) celui *m* (*or* celle *f or* ceux *mpl or* celles *fpl*) qui ; (*object*) celui etc que ; **I don't mind ~ you give me** vous pouvez me donner celui que vous voudrez (ça m'est égal) ; **I don't mind ~** ça m'est égal ; **show me ~ is the cheapest** montrez-moi celui qui est le moins cher ; **I can't tell** *or* **I don't know ~ is** je ne peux pas les distinguer ; **I can't tell ~ key is** je ne sais pas à quoi correspondent ces clés *or* quelle clé ouvre quelle porte ; **tell me ~ are the Frenchmen** dites-moi lesquels sont les Français ; **I know ~ I'd rather have** je sais celui que je préférerais ; **ask him ~ of the books he'd like** demandez-lui parmi tous les livres lequel il voudrait **[c]** (= *that*) (*subject*) qui ; (*object*) que ; (*after prep*) lequel *m* (*or* laquelle *f or* lesquels *mpl or* lesquelles *fpl*) ; **the book ~ is on the table** le livre qui est sur la table ; **the apple ~ you ate** la pomme que vous avez mangée ; **the house towards ~ she was going** la maison vers laquelle elle se dirigeait ; **the film of ~ he was speaking** le film dont il parlait ; **opposite ~** en face duquel (*or* de laquelle etc) ; **the book ~ I told you about** le livre dont je vous ai parlé ; **the box ~ you put it in** la boîte dans laquelle vous l'avez mis **[d]** (= *and that*) (*subject*) ce qui ; (*object*) ce que ; (*after prep*) quoi ; **he said he knew her, ~ is true** il a dit qu'il la connaissait, ce qui est vrai ; **she said she was 40, ~ I doubt very much** elle a dit qu'elle avait 40 ans, ce dont je doute beaucoup ; **you're late, ~ reminds me ...** vous êtes en retard, ce qui me fait penser ... ; **... upon ~ he left the room** ... sur quoi *or* sur ce elle a quitté la pièce ; **... of ~ more later** ... ce dont je reparlerai plus tard, ... mais je reviendrai là-dessus plus tard ; **from ~ we deduce that ...** d'où *or* et de là nous déduisons

que ... ; **after ~ we went to bed** après quoi nous sommes allés nous coucher

whichever [wɪtʃ'evər] **[1]** ADJ **[a]** (= *that one which*) **~ method is most successful should be chosen** on devrait choisir la méthode garantissant les meilleurs résultats, peu importe laquelle ; **take ~ book you like best** prenez le livre que vous préférez, peu importe lequel ; **I'll have ~ apple you don't want** je prendrai la pomme que *or* dont vous ne voulez pas ; **keep ~ one you prefer** gardez celui que vous préférez ; **go by ~ route is the most direct** prenez la route la plus directe, peu importe laquelle ; **do it in ~ way you can** faites-le comme vous pourrez **[b]** (= *no matter which*) (*subject*) quel que soit ... qui (+ *subj*) ; (*object*) quel que soit ... que (+ *subj*) ; **~ dress you wear** quelle que soit la robe que tu portes ; **~ book is left** quel que soit le livre qui reste ; **~ book is chosen** quel que soit le livre choisi ; (*fig*) **~ way you look at it** de quelque manière que vous le considériez (*subj*) **[2]** PRON **[a]** (= *the one which*) (*subject*) celui *m* qui, celle *f* qui ; (*object*) celui *m* que, celle *f* que ; **~ is best for him** celui *m* (*or* celle *f*) qui lui convient le mieux ; **~ you choose will be sent to you at once** celui *m* (*or* celle *f*) que vous choisirez vous sera expédié(e) immédiatement ; **~ of the books is selected** quel que soit le livre qui sera sélectionné ; **choose ~ is easiest** choisissez (celui qui est) le plus facile ; **on Thursday or Friday, ~ is more convenient** jeudi ou vendredi, le jour qui vous conviendra le mieux ; **A or B, ~ is the greater** A ou B, à savoir le plus grand des deux ; **at sunset or 7pm, ~ is the earlier** au coucher du soleil ou à 19 heures au plus tard, selon la saison **[b]** (= *no matter which one*) (*subject*) quel *m* que soit celui qui (+ *subj*), quelle *f* que soit celle qui (+ *subj*) ; (*object*) quel *m* que soit celui que (+ *subj*), quelle *f* que soit celle que (+ *subj*) ; **~ of the two books he chooses, it won't make a lot of difference** quel que soit le livre qu'il choisira, cela ne fera pas beaucoup de différence ; **~ of the methods is chosen, it can't affect you much** quelle que soit la méthode choisie, ça ne changera pas grand-chose pour vous

whiff [wɪf] **[1]** N **[a]** (= *puff*) [*of smoke, hot air*] bouffée *f* ; **a ~ of garlic** une bouffée d'ail ; **a ~ of seaweed** une odeur d'algues ; **one ~ of this is enough to kill you** il suffit de respirer ça une fois pour mourir ; **I caught a ~ of gas** j'ai senti l'odeur du gaz ; **take a ~ of this!*** renifle ça ! **[b]** (= *bad smell*) **what a ~!*** qu'est-ce que ça pue *or* fouette* ! **[c]** (*fig = hint*) [*of scandal*] parfum *m*, odeur *f* ; [*of corruption*] odeur *f* ; **a case which had a ~ of espionage about it** une affaire qui sentait l'espionnage **[2]** VI* sentir mauvais

whiffy* ['wɪfɪ] ADJ qui sent mauvais

Whig [wɪg] ADJ, N (*Pol Hist*) whig *m*

while [waɪl] **[1]** CONJ **[a]** (= *during the time that*) pendant que ; **it happened ~ I was out of the room** c'est arrivé pendant que *or* alors que j'étais hors de la pièce ; **can you wait ~ I telephone?** pouvez-vous attendre pendant que je téléphone ? ; **she fell asleep ~ reading** elle s'est endormie en lisant ; **~ you're away I'll write some letters** pendant ton absence *or* pendant que tu seras absent j'écrirai quelques lettres ; **don't drink ~ on duty** ne buvez pas pendant le service ; **"heels repaired ~ you wait"** « ressemelage minute » ; **~ you're up you could close the door** pendant que *or* puisque tu es debout tu pourrais fermer la porte ; **and ~ you're about it ...** et pendant que vous y êtes ... **[b]** (= *as long as*) tant que ; **~ there's life there's hope** tant qu'il y a de la vie il y a de l'espoir ; **it won't happen ~ I'm here** cela n'arrivera pas tant que je serai là ; **~ I live I shall make sure that ...** tant que *or* aussi longtemps

que je vivrai je ferai en sorte que ... **[c]** (= *although*) quoique (+ *subj*), bien que (+ *subj*) ; **~ I admit he is sometimes right ...** tout en admettant *or* quoique j'admette qu'il ait quelquefois raison ... ; **~ there are a few people who like that sort of thing ...** bien qu'il y ait un petit nombre de gens qui aiment ce genre de chose ... **[d]** (= *whereas*) alors que, tandis que ; **she sings quite well, ~ her sister can't sing a note** elle ne chante pas mal alors que *or* tandis que sa sœur ne sait pas chanter du tout

[2] N **[a]** **a ~** quelque temps ; **a short ~** ◊ **a little ~** un moment, un instant ; **for a little ~** pendant un petit moment ; **a long ~** ◊ **a good ~** (assez) longtemps, pas mal de temps ; **after a ~** quelque temps après, au bout de quelque temps ; **let's stop for a ~** arrêtons-nous un moment ; (*longer*) arrêtons quelque temps ; **for a ~ I thought ...** j'ai pensé un moment ... ; (*longer*) pendant quelque temps j'ai pensé ... ; **it takes quite a ~ to ripen** cela met assez longtemps à mûrir ; **once in a ~** (une fois) de temps en temps ; **(in) between ~s** entre-temps → **worthwhile** **[b]** **he looked at me (all) the ~ or the whole ~** il m'a regardé pendant tout ce temps-là **[3]** COMP ▶ **while-you-wait heel repairs** NPL ressemelage *m* minute *inv*

▶ **while away** VT SEP (*faire*) passer

whiles [waɪlz] ADV (*esp Scot, dial*) quelquefois, de temps en temps

whilst [waɪlst] CONJ (*esp Brit*) = **while 1**

whim [wɪm] N caprice *m*, lubie *f* ; **to be subject to sb's ~s/to the ~s of the economy** être livré aux caprices de qn/de l'économie ; **it's just a (passing) ~** c'est une lubie qui lui (*or* te etc) passera ; **he gives in to her every ~** il lui passe tous ses caprices ; **to cater** *or* **pander to sb's ~s/sb's every ~** satisfaire les caprices/tous les petits caprices de qn ; **as the ~ takes him** comme l'idée lui prend ; **at** *or* **on ~** sur un coup de tête

whimper ['wɪmpər] **[1]** N gémissement *m*, geignement *m* ; **... he said with a ~** ... gémit-il, pleurnicha-t-il (*pej*) ; (*fig*) **without a ~** sans se plaindre **[2]** VI [*person, baby*] gémir, pleurnicher (*pej*) ; [*dog*] gémir, pousser de petits cris plaintifs **[3]** VT **"no", he ~ed** « non », gémit-il *or* pleurnicha-t-il (*pej*)

whimpering ['wɪmpərɪŋ] **[1]** N geignements *mpl*, gémissements *mpl* **[2]** ADJ [*tone, voice*] larmoyant, pleurnicheur (*pej*) ; [*person, animal*] qui gémit faiblement

whimsical ['wɪmzɪkəl] ADJ [*person*] fantasque ; [*smile, look*] curieux ; [*humour*] original ; [*idea, story*] saugrenu, fantaisiste

whimsicality [,wɪmzɪ'kælɪtɪ] N **[a]** (*NonC*) [*of person*] caractère *m* fantasque ; [*of idea, story*] caractère *m* fantaisiste *or* saugrenu ; [*of smile, look*] caractère *m* curieux **[b]** **whimsicalities** idées *fpl* (*or* actions *fpl* etc) bizarres *or* saugrenues

whimsically ['wɪmzɪkəlɪ] ADV [*say, suggest*] de façon saugrenue ; [*smile, look*] étrangement, curieusement ; [*muse, ponder*] malicieusement

whimsy ['wɪmzɪ] N (= *whim*) caprice *m*, fantaisie *f* ; (*NonC* = *whimsicality*) caractère *m* fantaisiste

whim-whams* ['wɪmwæmz] NPL (*US*) trouille* *f*, frousse* *f*

whin [wɪn] N (*Bot*) ajonc *m*

whine [waɪn] **[1]** N [*of person, child, dog*] gémissement *m* (prolongé) ; [*of bullet, shell, siren, machine*] plainte *f* stridente *or* monocorde ; (*fig = complaint*) plainte *f* ; **... he said with a ~** ... se lamenta-t-il, ... dit-il d'une voix geignarde ; **it's another of his ~s about taxes** le voilà encore en train de se plaindre *or* de geindre* à propos de ses impôts **[2]** VI [*person, dog*] geindre, gémir ; [*siren*] gémir ; [*engine*] vrombir ; (*fig = complain*) se lamenter, se plaindre; *(fig)* **to ~ about sth** se lamenter sur qch, se plaindre à propos de qch; **don't come whining to me about it** ne venez pas vous plaindre à moi; **it's just a scratch: stop whining** ce n'est qu'une égratignure: arrête de geindre* *or* **"it's happened again", he ~d** « ça a recommencé », se lamenta-t-il *or* dit-il d'une voix geignarde

whinge* ['wɪndʒ] *(Brit)* **1** VI geindre* *(pej)* **(about** à propos de); **stop ~ing** arrête de geindre* *or* de te plaindre **2** N **he was having a real ~** il n'arrêtait pas de geindre*; **he was having a ~ about the price of cigarettes** il râlait* à propos du prix des cigarettes

whingeing* ['wɪndʒɪŋ] *(Brit)* **1** ADJ geignard, plaintif **2** N gémissements *mpl*, plaintes *fpl*

whinger* ['wɪndʒəʳ] N geignard(e)* *m(f)*

whining ['waɪnɪŋ] **1** N *[of person, child]* gémissements *mpl* (continus), pleurnicheries *fpl*; *[of dog]* gémissements *mpl*; *(fig = complaining)* plaintes *fpl* continuelles **2** ADJ **a** *[person, child]* pleurnicheur; *[dog]* gémissant; *(fig = complaining)* *[person, voice]* geignard **b** *(= high-pitched)* **a ~ sound** *or* **noise** une plainte aiguë

whinny ['wɪnɪ] **1** N hennissement *m* **2** VI hennir

whip [wɪp] **1** N **a** fouet *m*; *(also* **riding ~)** cravache *f*
b *(Parl)* *(= person)* whip *m*, parlementaire chargé de la discipline dans son parti; *(Brit = summons)* convocation *f*; **three-line ~** convocation *f* d'un député *(impliquant sa présence obligatoire et le respect des consignes de vote)*
c *(Culin = dessert)* crème *f or* mousse *f* instantanée
2 VT **a** *[+ person, animal, child]* fouetter; **the rain ~ped her face** la pluie lui cinglait *or* fouettait la figure; **to ~ sb into a frenzy** mettre qn hors de ses gonds
b *(Culin)* *[+ cream]* fouetter, battre au fouet; *[+ egg white]* battre en neige
c *(* fig)* *(= defeat)* battre à plates coutures; *(= criticize severely)* critiquer vivement, éreinter
d *(* = seize)* **to ~ sth out of sb's hands** enlever brusquement *or* vivement qch des mains de qn; **he ~ped a gun out of his pocket** il a brusquement sorti un revolver de sa poche; **he ~ped the letter off the table** il a prestement fait disparaître la lettre qui était sur la table
e *(Brit* = *steal)* faucher*, piquer*; **somebody's ~ped my watch!** quelqu'un m'a fauché* *or* piqué* ma montre!
f *[+ cable, rope]* surlier; *(Sewing)* surfiler
3 VI **to ~ along/away** *etc* filer/partir *etc* à toute allure *or* comme un éclair; **to ~ back** revenir brusquement; **the wind ~ped through the trees** le vent fouettait les branches des arbres; **the rope broke and ~ped across his face** la corde a cassé et lui a cinglé le visage
4 COMP ▸ **whip hand** N *(fig)* **to have the ~ hand** être le maître, avoir le dessus; **to have the ~ hand over sb** avoir la haute main sur qn ▸ **whipped cream** N crème *f* fouettée ▸ **whip-round*** N *(Brit)* collecte *f*; **to have a ~-round for sb/sth*** faire une collecte pour qn/qch

▸ **whip away 1** VI → whip 3 **2** VT SEP *(= remove quickly)* *[person]* enlever brusquement *or* vivement, faire disparaître; *[wind etc]* emporter brusquement

▸ **whip in 1** VI **a** *[person]* entrer précipitamment *or* comme un éclair **b** *(Hunting)* être piqueur **2** VT SEP **a** *(Hunting)* *[+ hounds]* ramener, rassembler; *(Parl)* *[+ members voting]* battre le rappel de; *(fig)* *[+ voters, supporters]* rallier **b** ~ **in the cream** incorporez la crème avec un fouet

▸ **whip off** VT SEP *[+ garment etc]* ôter *or* enlever en quatrième vitesse*; *[+ lid, cover]* ôter brusquement

▸ **whip on** VT SEP *[+ garment etc]* enfiler en

quatrième vitesse* **b** *(= urge on)* *[+ horse]* cravacher

▸ **whip out 1** VI *[person]* sortir précipitamment **2** VT SEP *[+ knife, gun, purse]* sortir brusquement *or* vivement **(from** de)

▸ **whip over*** VI = whip round 1b

▸ **whip round 1** VI **a** *(= turn quickly)* *[person]* se retourner vivement; *[object]* pivoter brusquement **b** *(* = pop round)* **he's just ~ped round to the grocer's** il est juste allé faire un saut à l'épicerie; **~ round to your aunt's and tell her ...** va faire un saut *or* cours chez ta tante lui dire ... **2** ~**-round*** N → whip

▸ **whip through** VT FUS *[+ book]* parcourir rapidement; *[+ homework, task]* expédier, faire en quatrième vitesse*

▸ **whip up** VT SEP **a** *[+ emotions, enthusiasm, indignation]* attiser; *[+ support, interest]* stimuler **b** *[+ cream, egg whites]* fouetter, battre au fouet **c** *(* = prepare)* **to ~ up a meal** préparer un repas en vitesse; **can you ~ us up something to eat?** est-ce que vous pourriez nous faire à manger *or* nous préparer un morceau* en vitesse? **d** *(= snatch up)* saisir brusquement

whipcord ['wɪpkɔːd] N *(Tex)* whipcord *m*

whiplash ['wɪplæʃ] **1** N **a** *(= blow from whip)* coup *m* de fouet **b** *(in car accident)* coup *m* du lapin*, syndrome *m* cervical traumatique; *(fig)* **he felt the ~ of fear** il fut saisi d'une peur cinglante **2** COMP ▸ **whiplash injury** N *= injury to the neck* traumatisme *m* cervical

whipper-in [ˌwɪpər'ɪn] N *(pl* **whippers-in)** *(Hunting)* piqueur *m*

whippersnapper† ['wɪpəˌsnæpəʳ] N *(hum)* freluquet *m*

whippet ['wɪpɪt] N whippet *m*

whipping ['wɪpɪŋ] **1** N *(as punishment)* correction *f*; **to give sb a ~** fouetter qn, donner le fouet à qn, donner des coups de fouet à qn **2** COMP ▸ **whipping boy** N *(fig)* souffre-douleur *m inv* ▸ **whipping cream** N *(Culin)* crème *f* fraîche *(à fouetter)* ▸ **whipping post** N poteau auquel on attachait les personnes condamnées à être fouettées ▸ **whipping top** N toupie *f*

whippoorwill ['wɪpˌpʊəˌwɪl] N engoulevent *m* d'Amérique du Nord

whippy ['wɪpɪ] ADJ souple

whir [wɜːʳ] = whirr

whirl [wɜːl] **1** N **a** *[of leaves, papers, smoke]* tourbillon *m*, tournoiement *m*; *[of sand, dust, water]* tourbillon *m*; *(fig)* **a ~ of parties and dances** un tourbillon de réceptions et de soirées dansantes; **the whole week was a ~ of activity** nous n'avons *(or* ils n'ont *etc)* pas arrêté de toute la semaine; **the social ~** le tourbillon de la vie mondaine; **her thoughts/emotions were in a ~** tout tourbillonnait dans sa tête; **my head is in a ~** la tête me tourne; *(fig)* **to give sth a ~*** essayer qch **2** VI **a** *(= spin: also* **~ round)** *[leaves, papers, smoke, dancers]* tourbillonner, tournoyer; *[sand, dust, water]* tourbillonner; *[wheel, merry-go-round, spinning top]* tournoyer; **they ~ed past us in the dance** ils sont passés près de nous en tourbillonnant pendant la danse; **the leaves ~ed down** les feuilles tombaient en tourbillonnant; **my head is ~ing** la tête me tourne; **her thoughts/emotions were ~ing** tout tourbillonnait dans sa tête/son cœur **b** *(= move rapidly)* **to ~ along** aller à toute vitesse *or* à toute allure; **to ~ away** *or* **off** partir à toute vitesse *or* à toute allure **3** VT *[wind]* *[+ leaves, smoke]* faire tourbillonner, faire tournoyer; *[+ dust, sand]* faire tourbillonner; **he ~ed his sword round his head** il a fait tournoyer son épée au-dessus de sa tête; **they ~ed me up to Liverpool to visit Mary** ils m'ont embarqué* pour aller voir Mary à Liverpool

▸ **whirl round 1** VI *(= turn suddenly)* *[person]* se retourner brusquement, virevolter; *[revolving*

chair *etc]* pivoter → **whirl 2a** **2** VT SEP **a** *[wind]* *[+ leaves, smoke]* faire tourbillonner, faire tournoyer; *[+ dust, sand]* faire tourbillonner **b** *[+ sword, object on rope etc]* faire tournoyer; *[+ revolving chair etc]* faire pivoter

whirligig ['wɜːlɪgɪg] N **a** *(= toy)* moulin *m* à vent; *(= merry-go-round)* manège *m*; *(of events etc)* tourbillon *m* *(liter)* **b** *(also* **~ beetle)** tourniquet *m*, gyrin *m*

whirlpool ['wɜːlpuːl] **1** N tourbillon *m* **2** COMP ▸ **whirlpool bath** N bain *m* à remous

whirlwind ['wɜːlwɪnd] **1** N tornade *f*, trombe *f* → sow² **2** ADJ *(fig)* éclair *inv*

whirlybird* ['wɜːlɪbɜːd] N *(US)* hélico* *m*, hélicoptère *m*

whirr [wɜːʳ] **1** VI *[bird's wings, insect's wings]* bruire; *[cameras, machinery]* ronronner; *(louder)* vrombir; *[propellers]* vrombir; **the helicopter went ~ing off** l'hélicoptère est parti en vrombissant **2** N *[of bird's wings, insect's wings]* bruissement *m* *(d'ailes)*; *[of machinery]* ronronnement *m*; *(louder)* vrombissement *m*; *[of propellers]* vrombissement *m*

whisk [wɪsk] **1** N **a** *(also* **egg ~)** fouet *m* *(à œufs)*; *(rotary)* batteur *m* à œufs **b** *(= movement)* **give the mixture a good ~** bien battre le mélange; **with a ~ of his tail, the horse ...** d'un coup de queue, le cheval ... **2** VT **a** *(Culin: gen)* battre au fouet; *[+ egg whites]* battre en neige; ~ **the eggs into the mixture** incorporez les œufs dans le mélange avec un fouet *or* en remuant vigoureusement **b** **he ~ed its tail** le cheval fouettait l'air de sa queue **c** **to ~ sth out of sb's hands** enlever brusquement *or* vivement qch des mains de qn; **she ~ed the baby out of the pram** elle a sorti brusquement le bébé du landau; **he ~ed it out of his pocket** il l'a brusquement sorti de sa poche; **he ~ed me round the island in his sports car** il m'a fait faire le tour de l'île à toute allure dans sa voiture de sport; **the lift ~ed us up to the top floor** l'ascenseur nous a emportés à toute allure jusqu'au dernier étage; **he was ~ed into a meeting** on l'a brusquement entraîné dans une réunion; **he ~ed her off to meet his mother** il l'a emmenée illico* faire la connaissance de sa mère **3** VI **to ~ along/in/out** *etc* filer/entrer/sortir *etc* à toute allure; **I ~ed into the driveway** je me suis précipité dans l'allée; **she ~ed past the photographers into the hotel** elle est passée en trombe *or* à toute allure devant les photographes et s'est précipitée dans l'hôtel; **he ~ed through the pile of letters on his desk** il a parcouru rapidement la pile de lettres qui était sur son bureau

▸ **whisk away** VT SEP *[+ flies]* chasser; *(fig = remove)* *[+ object]* faire disparaître

▸ **whisk off** VT SEP *[+ flies]* chasser; *[+ lid, cover]* ôter brusquement; *[+ garment]* enlever *or* ôter en quatrième vitesse*; **they ~ed me off to hospital** ils m'ont emmené à l'hôpital sur le champ → whisk 2c

▸ **whisk together** VT SEP *(Culin)* mélanger en fouettant *or* avec un fouet

▸ **whisk up** VT SEP *(Culin)* fouetter → whisk 2c

whisker ['wɪskəʳ] N *[of animal]* moustaches *fpl*; *[of person]* poil *m*; **~s** *(also* **side ~s)** favoris *mpl*; *(= beard)* barbe *f*; *(= moustache)* moustache(s) *f(pl)*; **he won the race by a ~** il s'en est fallu d'un cheveu *or* d'un poil* qu'il ne perde la course; *(fig)* **they came within a ~ of being ...** il s'en est fallu d'un cheveu qu'ils ne soient ...

whiskered ['wɪskəd] ADJ *[man, face]* *(= with side whiskers)* qui a des favoris; *(= with beard)* barbu; *(= with moustache)* moustachu; *[animal]* qui a des moustaches

whiskery ['wɪskərɪ] ADJ *[man, old woman]* au visage poilu; *[face]* poilu

whiskey (Ir, US), **whisky** (Brit, Can) ['wɪskɪ]
[1] N whisky m; **a ~ and soda** un whisky soda
→ **sour** [2] COMP [flavour] de whisky

whisper ['wɪspə'] [1] VI [person] chuchoter, parler à voix basse; [leaves, water] chuchoter, murmurer; **to ~ to sb** parler or chuchoter à l'oreille de qn, parler à voix basse à qn; **it's rude to ~** c'est mal élevé de chuchoter à l'oreille de quelqu'un; **you'll have to ~** il faudra que vous parliez (subj) bas
[2] VT chuchoter, dire à voix basse (**sth to sb** qch à qn, **that** que); **he ~ed a word in my ear** il m'a dit or soufflé quelque chose à l'oreille; **"where is she?" he ~ed** «où est-elle?» dit-il à voix basse or murmura-t-il; (fig) **it is (being) ~ed that ...** le bruit court que ..., on dit que ...
→ **sweet**
[3] N (= low tone) chuchotement m; [of wind, leaves, water] murmure m, bruissement m; (fig = rumour) bruit m, rumeur f; **I heard a ~** j'ai entendu un chuchotement, j'ai entendu quelqu'un qui parlait à voix basse; **a ~ of voices** des chuchotements; **to say/answer in a ~** dire/répondre à voix basse; **to speak in a ~** or **~s** parler bas or à voix basse; **her voice scarcely rose above a ~** sa voix n'était guère qu'un murmure; (fig) **not a ~ to anyone!** n'en soufflez mot à personne!; (fig) **I've heard a ~ that he isn't coming back** j'ai entendu dire qu'il ne reviendrait pas; **there is a ~ (going round) that ...** le bruit court que ..., on dit que ...

whispering ['wɪspərɪŋ] [1] ADJ [person] qui chuchote, qui parle à voix basse; [leaves, wind, stream] qui chuchote, qui murmure; **~ voices** des chuchotements mpl [2] N [of voice] chuchotement m; [of leaves, wind, stream] bruissement m, murmure m; (= gossip) médisances fpl, (= rumours) rumeurs fpl insidieuses; (fig) **there has been a lot of ~ about them** toutes sortes de rumeurs insidieuses ont couru sur leur compte [3] COMP
► **whispering campaign** N (fig) campagne f diffamatoire (insidieuse) ► **whispering gallery** N galerie f à écho

whist [wɪst] [1] N (Brit) whist m [2] COMP
► **whist drive** N tournoi m de whist

whistle ['wɪsl] [1] N [a] (= sound) (made with mouth) sifflement m; (= jeering) sifflet m; (made with a whistle) coup m de sifflet; [of factory] sirène f (d'usine); **the ~s of the audience** (= booing) les sifflets mpl du public; (= cheering) les sifflements mpl d'admiration du public; **to give a ~** (gen) siffler; (= blow a whistle) donner un coup de sifflet
[b] [of train, kettle, blackbird] sifflement m
[c] (= object) sifflet m; (Mus: also **penny ~**) chalumeau m; **a blast on a ~** un coup de sifflet strident; **the referee blew his ~** l'arbitre a donné un coup de sifflet or a sifflé; **the referee blew his ~ for half-time** l'arbitre a sifflé la mi-temps; (fig) (= inform on) **to blow the ~ on sb*** dénoncer qn; **to blow the ~ on sth*** tirer la sonnette d'alarme sur qch, dénoncer qch; **he blew the ~ (on it)** (= informed on it) il a dévoilé le pot aux roses*; (= put a stop to it) il y a mis le holà
[2] VI [a] [person] siffler; (tunefully, light-heartedly) siffloter; (= blow a whistle) donner un coup de sifflet, siffler; **the audience booed and ~d** les spectateurs ont hué et sifflé; **the audience cheered and ~d** les spectateurs ont manifesté leur enthousiasme par des acclamations et des sifflements; **he strolled along whistling (away)** il flânait en sifflotant gaiement; **he ~d at me to stop** il a sifflé pour que je m'arrête (subj); **the boy was whistling at all the pretty girls** le garçon sifflait toutes les jolies filles; **the crowd ~d at the referee** la foule a sifflé l'arbitre; **he ~d to his dog** il a sifflé son chien; **he ~d for a taxi** il a sifflé un taxi; **the referee ~d for a foul** l'arbitre a sifflé une faute; (fig) **he can ~ for it!*** il peut se

brosser!*, il peut toujours courir!*; (fig) **he's whistling in the dark** or **in the wind** il dit ça pour se rassurer, il essaie de se donner du courage
[b] [bird, bullet, wind, kettle, train] siffler; **the cars ~d by us** les voitures passaient devant nous à toute allure; **an arrow ~d past his ear** une flèche a sifflé à son oreille
[3] VT [+ tune] siffler; (casually, light-heartedly) siffloter; **to ~ a dog back/in** etc siffler un chien pour qu'il revienne/entre (subj) etc
[4] COMP ► **whistle blower*** N (fig) dénonciateur m, -trice f, personne f qui tire la sonnette d'alarme ► **whistle-stop** → **whistle-stop**
► **whistle up*** VT SEP (fig) dégoter*; **he ~d up four or five people to give us a hand** il a dégoté* quatre ou cinq personnes prêtes à nous donner un coup de main; **can you ~ up another blanket or two?** vous pouvez dégoter* or dénicher* encore une ou deux couvertures?

whistle-stop ['wɪsl,stɒp] [1] N visite f éclair inv (dans une petite ville au cours d'une campagne électorale) [2] ADJ **he made a ~ tour of Virginia** il a fait à toute allure le tour de la Virginie; (US) **a ~ town** une petite ville or un petit trou* (où le train s'arrête) [3] VI (US) faire une tournée électorale

Whit [wɪt] [1] N la Pentecôte [2] COMP [holiday etc] de Pentecôte ► **Whit Monday** N le lundi de Pentecôte ► **Whit Sunday** N le dimanche de Pentecôte ► **Whit Week** N la semaine de Pentecôte

whit [wɪt] N (frm) **there was not a ~** or **no ~ of truth in it** il n'y avait pas un brin de vérité là-dedans; **he hadn't a ~ of sense** il n'avait pas un grain de bon sens; **it wasn't a ~ better after he'd finished** quand il a eu terminé ce n'était pas mieux du tout; **I don't care a ~** ça m'est profondément égal, je m'en moque complètement

white [waɪt] [1] ADJ [a] blanc (blanche f); **to go** or **turn ~** (with fear, anger) blêmir, pâlir; [hair] blanchir; [object] devenir blanc, blanchir; **to be ~ with fear/rage** être blanc or blême de peur/rage; **he went ~ with fear** il a blêmi or pâli de peur; (as) **~ as a ghost** pâle comme la mort; (as) **~ as a sheet** pâle comme un linge; **as ~ as snow** blanc comme (la) neige; **this detergent gets the clothes whiter than ~** cette lessive lave encore plus blanc; **the public likes politicians to be whiter-than-~** les gens aiment que les hommes politiques soient irréprochables
[b] (racially) [person, face, skin, race] blanc (blanche f); **a white man** un Blanc; **a white woman** une Blanche; **the white South Africans** les Blancs mpl d'Afrique du Sud; **white supremacy** la suprématie de la race blanche → 4
[2] N [a] (= colour) blanc m; (= whiteness) blancheur f; **to be dressed in ~** être vêtu de blanc; **his face was a deathly ~** son visage était d'une pâleur mortelle; **the sheets were a dazzling ~** les draps étaient d'une blancheur éclatante; (Mil etc) **don't fire till you see the ~s of their eyes** ne tirez qu'au dernier moment → **black**
[b] [of egg, eye] blanc m
[c] (*: also **~ wine**) blanc m
[d] **White** (= person of White race) Blanc m, Blanche f → **poor**
[3] **whites** NPL (= linen etc) **the ~s** le (linge) blanc; (= clothes) **tennis ~s** tenue f de tennis
[4] COMP ► **white blood cell** N globule m blanc ► **white bread** N pain m blanc ► **white Christmas** N Noël m sous la neige ► **white coat** N blouse f blanche ► **white coffee** N (Brit) (gen) café m au lait; (in café: when ordering) café m crème ► **white-collar** ADJ **a ~-collar job** un emploi de bureau; **~-collar union** syndicat m d'employé(e)s de bu-

reau or de cols blancs ► **white-collar crime** N (NonC = illegal activities) criminalité f en col blanc; **~-collar worker** employé(e) m(f) de bureau, col m blanc ► **white corpuscle** N globule m blanc ► **whited sepulchre** N (fig) sépulcre m blanchi, hypocrite mf ► **white dwarf** N (Astron) naine f blanche ► **white elephant** N (fig) (= ornament) objet m superflu; (= scheme, project, building) gouffre m (financier); **it's a ~ elephant** c'est tout à fait superflu, on n'en a pas besoin ► **white elephant stall** N étalage m de bibelots ► **white-faced** ADJ blême, pâle ► **white feather** N (fig) **to show the ~ feather** manquer de courage ► **white flag** N drapeau m blanc ► **white fox** N (= animal) renard m polaire; (= skin, fur) renard m blanc ► **white frost** N gelée f blanche ► **white gold** N or m blanc ► **white goods** NPL (Comm) (= domestic appliances) appareils mpl ménagers; (= linens) (linge m) blanc m ► **white-haired** ADJ [person] aux cheveux blancs; [animal] à poil blanc, aux poils blancs ► **white-headed** ADJ [person] aux cheveux blancs; [bird] à tête blanche; (fig) **the ~-headed boy** l'enfant m chéri ► **white heat** N (Phys) chaude f blanche, chaleur f d'incandescence; **to raise metal to a ~ heat** chauffer un métal à blanc; **the indignation of the crowd had reached ~ heat** l'indignation de la foule avait atteint son paroxysme ► **white hope** N (fig) **to be the ~ hope of ...** être le grand espoir de ... ► **white horse** N (at sea) = **whitecap** ► **white-hot** ADJ chauffé à blanc ► **the White House** N (US) la Maison-Blanche ► **white knight** N (St Ex) chevalier m blanc ► **white-knuckle** ADJ (= terrifying) terrifiant; **~-knuckle ride** manège m qui décoiffe* or qui fait dresser les cheveux sur la tête ► **white lead** N blanc m de céruse ► **white lie** N pieux mensonge m ► **white light** N (Phys) lumière f blanche ► **white line** N (on road) ligne f blanche ► **white-livered** ADJ (fig liter) poltron, couard ► **white magic** N magie f blanche ► **white meat** N viande f blanche ► **white meter** N (Elec) compteur m bleu; **~ meter heating** chauffage m par accumulateur ► **the White Nile** N le Nil Blanc ► **white noise** N (Acoustics) bruit m blanc ► **White-Out®** N (US) Tipp-Ex® m ► **white owl** N harfang m, chouette f blanche ► **white paper** N (Parl) livre m blanc (on sur) ► **white pepper** N poivre m blanc ► **white plague** N (US = tuberculosis) tuberculose f pulmonaire ► **white rabbit** N lapin m blanc ► **white raisin** N (US) raisin m sec de Smyrne ► **white rhino***, **white rhinoceros** N rhinocéros m blanc ► **White Russia** N la Russie Blanche ► **White Russian** (Geog, Hist, Pol) ADJ russe blanc (russe blanche f) ♦ N Russe m blanc, Russe f blanche ► **white sale** N (Comm) vente f de blanc ► **white sapphire** N saphir m blanc ► **white sauce** N (savoury) sauce f blanche; (sweet) crème f pâtissière (pour le plum-pudding de Noël) ► **the White Sea** N la mer Blanche ► **white settler** N (Hist) colon m blanc; (fig pej = incomer) citadin arrogant qui va s'installer à la campagne ► **white shark** N requin m blanc ► **white slavery**, **the white slave trade** N la traite des blanches ► **white spirit** N (Brit) white-spirit m ► **white stick** N [of blind person] canne f blanche ► **white-tailed eagle** N orfraie f, pygargue m ► **white tie** N (= tie) nœud m papillon blanc; (= suit) habit m ► **white-tie** ADJ **it was a ~-tie affair** l'habit était de rigueur; **to wear ~-tie** être en tenue de soirée; **a ~-tie dinner** un dîner chic or habillé ► **white trash*** N (NonC: US pej) racaille f blanche ► **white water** N (esp Sport) eau f vive ► **white-water rafting** N rafting m ► **white wedding** N mariage m en blanc ► **white whale** N baleine f blanche ► **white wine** N vin m blanc ► **white witch** N femme qui pratique la magie blanche

whitebait ['waɪtbeɪt] N blanchaille f; (Culin) petite friture f

whiteboard ['waɪtbɔːd] N tableau m blanc

whitecap ['waɪtkæp] N (at sea) mouton m

Whitehall ['waɪt,hɔːl] N (Brit) Whitehall m (siège des ministères et des administrations publiques)

whiten ['waɪtn] VTI blanchir

whitener ['waɪtnər] N (for coffee etc) succédané m de lait en poudre; (for clothes) agent m blanchissant

whiteness ['waɪtnɪs] N (NonC) [a] (= colour) [of teeth, snow, cloth] blancheur f [b] (racial) appartenance f à la race blanche [c] (= paleness) [of person, face] blancheur f, pâleur f

whitening ['waɪtnɪŋ] N (NonC) [a] (= act) [of linen] blanchiment m, décoloration f; [of hair] blanchissement m; [of wall etc] blanchiment m [b] (substance: for shoes, doorsteps etc) blanc m

whiteout ['waɪtaʊt] N visibilité f nulle (à cause de la neige ou du brouillard)

whitethorn ['waɪtθɔːn] N (Bot) aubépine f

whitethroat ['waɪtθrəʊt] N (= Old World warbler) grisette f; (= American sparrow) moineau m d'Amérique

whitewall tyre, whitewall tire (US) ['waɪtwɔːltaɪər] N (Aut) pneu m à flanc blanc

whitewash ['waɪtwɒʃ] [1] N [a] (NonC: for walls etc) lait m ou blanc m de chaux [b] (fig) the article in the paper was nothing but a ~ of ... l'article du journal ne visait qu'à blanchir ... [c] (Sport*) raclée* f [2] VT [a] [+ wall etc] blanchir à la chaux, chauler [b] (fig) [+ sb's reputation, actions] blanchir; [+ incident] étouffer; they tried to ~ the whole episode ils ont essayé d'étouffer l'affaire [c] (Sport*) écraser complètement*

whitewood ['waɪtwʊd] N bois m blanc

whitey* ['waɪtɪ] N (esp US pej) (= individual) Blanc m, Blanche f; (= Whites collectively) les Blancs mpl

whither ['wɪðər] ADV (liter) où; (in headlines, titles etc) "~ the Government now?" « où va le gouvernement? »

whiting¹ ['waɪtɪŋ] N (pl whiting) (= fish) merlan m

whiting² ['waɪtɪŋ] N (NonC: for shoes, doorsteps etc) blanc m

whitish ['waɪtɪʃ] ADJ blanchâtre

whitlow ['wɪtləʊ] N panaris m

Whitsun ['wɪtsn] N → Whit

Whitsun(tide) ['wɪtsn(taɪd)] N les fêtes fpl de (la) Pentecôte, la Pentecôte

whittle ['wɪtl] VT [+ piece of wood] tailler au couteau; to ~ sth out of a piece of wood ◊ to ~ a piece of wood into sth tailler qch au couteau dans un morceau de bois
► **whittle away** [1] VI to ~ away at sth tailler qch au couteau [2] VT SEP → whittle down
► **whittle down** VT SEP [a] [+ wood] tailler [b] (fig) [+ costs, amount] amenuiser, réduire; [+ proposal] revoir à la baisse; he had ~d eight candidates down to two sur les huit candidats, il en avait retenu deux

whiz(z) [wɪz] [1] N [a] (= sound) sifflement m [b]* champion/ m, as m; a computer/ marketing/financial ~ un as de l'informatique/du marketing/des finances; he's a ~ at tennis/cards c'est un as du tennis/des jeux de cartes; she's a real ~ with a paintbrush elle se débrouille comme un chef* avec un pinceau [c] (NonC:* = amphetamine) amphés* fpl [2] VI filer à toute allure or comme une flèche; to ~ or go whizzing through the air fendre l'air (en sifflant); (in car) to ~ along/past etc filer/ passer etc à toute vitesse or à toute allure; bullets whizzed by les balles sifflaient; I'll just ~ over to see him* je file* le voir; she whizzed off* to Hong Kong on business elle a filé* à Hong-Kong pour affaires

[3] VT [a]* (= throw) lancer, filer*; (= transfer quickly) apporter; he whizzed it round to us as soon as it was ready il nous l'a apporté or passé dès que ça a été prêt [b] (also ~ up: in blender) mixer

[4] COMP ► **whiz(z)-bang***: N (Mil = shell) obus m; (= firework) pétard m ◆ ADJ (US = excellent) du tonnerre* ► **whiz(z) kid*** N she's a real ~ kid at maths elle a vraiment la bosse* des maths

WHO [,dʌblju:eɪtʃ'əʊ] N (ABBR = **World Health Organization**) OMS f

who [huː] [1] PRON [a] (interrog: also used instead of "whom" in spoken English) (qui est-ce) qui; (after prep) qui; ~'s there? qui est là?; ~ are you? qui êtes-vous?; ~ has the book? (qui est-ce) qui a le livre?; ~ does he think he is? il se prend pour qui?, pour qui il se prend?; ~ came with you? (qui est-ce) qui est venu avec vous?; ~ should it be but Robert! c'était Robert, qui d'autre!; I don't know ~'s ~ in the office je ne connais pas très bien les gens au bureau; you remind me of somebody! — ~? vous me rappelez quelqu'un! — qui donc?; ~(m) did you see? vous avez vu qui?, qui avez-vous vu?; ~(m) do you work for? pour qui travaillez-vous?; ~(m) did you speak to? à qui avez-vous parlé?, vous avez parlé à qui?; ~'s the book by? le livre est de qui?; ~(m) were you with? vous étiez avec qui?; (indignantly) ~ is he to tell me ...? de quel droit est-ce qu'il me dit ...?; you-know-~ said ... qui vous savez a dit ...; WHO can't? tu es incapable de chanter — ah bon! tu crois ça! [b] (rel) qui; my aunt ~ lives in London ma tante qui habite à Londres; he ~ wishes to object must do so now quiconque désire élever une objection doit le faire maintenant; those ~ can swim ceux qui savent nager; (Bible) ~ is not with me is against me celui qui or quiconque n'est pas pour moi est contre moi [2] COMP ► **"Who's Who"** N ≈ « Bottin Mondain »

whoa [wəʊ] EXCL [a] (also ~ there) ho!, holà! [b] (in excitement, triumph) ouah!*

who'd [huːd] = who had, who would; → who

whodun(n)it* [,huː'dʌnɪt] N roman m (or film m or feuilleton m etc) policier (à énigme), polar* m

whoe'er [huː'ɛər] (liter) PRON = whoever

whoever [huː'ɛvər] PRON (also used instead of "whomever" in spoken English) [a] (= anyone that) quiconque; ~ wishes may come with me quiconque le désire peut venir avec moi; you can give it to ~ wants it vous pouvez le donner à qui le veut or voudra; ~ finds it can keep it quiconque or celui qui le trouvera pourra le garder; ~ gets home first does the cooking celui qui rentre le premier prépare à manger, le premier rentré à la maison prépare à manger; ~ said that was an idiot celui qui a dit ça était un imbécile; ask ~ you like demandez à qui vous voulez or voudrez [b] (= no matter who) ~ you are, come in! qui que vous soyez, entrez!; ~ he plays for next season ... quelle que soit l'équipe dans laquelle il jouera la saison prochaine ... [c] (*: interrog: emphatic) qui donc; ~ told you that? qui donc vous a dit ça?, qui a bien pu vous dire ça?; ~ did you give it to? vous l'avez donné à qui?

whole [həʊl] [1] ADJ [a] (= entire) (+ sg n) tout, entier; (+ pl n) entier; along its ~ length sur toute sa longueur; villages were destroyed des villages entiers ont été détruits; the ~ road was like that toute la route était comme ça; the ~ world le monde entier; he used a ~ notebook il a utilisé un carnet entier; he swallowed it ~ il l'a avalé tout entier; the pig was roasted ~ le cochon a été rôti tout entier; we waited a ~ hour nous avons attendu une heure entière or toute une heure; it rained

(for) three ~ days il a plu trois jours entiers; but the ~ man eludes us mais l'homme tout entier reste un mystère pour nous; is that the ~ truth? est-ce que c'est bien toute la vérité?; but the ~ point of it was to avoid that mais tout l'intérêt de la chose était d'éviter cela; with my ~ heart de tout mon cœur; he took the ~ lot* il a pris le tout; the ~ lot of you* vous tous, tous tant que vous êtes; it's a ~ lot* better c'est vraiment beaucoup mieux; there are a ~ lot* of things I'd like to tell her il y a tout un tas de choses que j'aimerais lui dire; to go the ~ hog* aller jusqu'au bout des choses, ne pas faire les choses à moitié; (US) to go (the) ~ hog* for sb/sth essayer par tous les moyens de conquérir qn/d'obtenir qch → 3 [b] (= intact, unbroken) intact, complet (-ète f); not a glass was left ~ after the party il ne restait pas un seul verre intact après la fête; keep the egg yolks ~ gardez les jaunes entiers; he has a ~ set of Dickens il a une série complète des œuvres de Dickens; to our surprise he came back ~ à notre grande surprise il est revenu sain et sauf; the seal on the letter was still ~ le sceau sur la lettre était encore intact; (US fig) made out of ~ cloth inventé de toutes pièces; his hand was made ~†† (= healed) sa main a été guérie [2] N [a] (= the entire amount of) the ~ of the morning toute la matinée; the ~ of the time tout le temps; the ~ of the apple was bad la pomme tout entière était gâtée; the ~ of Paris was snowbound Paris était complètement bloqué par la neige; the ~ of Paris was talking about it dans tout Paris on parlait de ça; nearly the ~ of our output this year presque toute notre production or presque la totalité de notre production cette année; he received the ~ of the amount il a reçu la totalité de la somme; on the ~ dans l'ensemble [b] (= complete unit) tout m; four quarters make a ~ quatre quarts font un tout or un entier; the ~ may be greater than the sum of its parts le tout peut être plus grand que la somme de ses parties; the estate is to be sold as a ~ la propriété doit être vendue en bloc; considered as a ~ the play was successful, although some scenes ... dans l'ensemble, la pièce était réussie, bien que certaines scènes ... [3] COMP ► **whole-hog*** ADJ (esp US) [support] sans réserve(s), total; [supporter] acharné, ardent (before n) ◆ ADV jusqu'au bout → 1a ► **whole-hogger*** N (esp US) to be a ~-hogger (gen) se donner entièrement à ce qu'on fait; (Pol) être jusqu'au-boutiste ► **whole milk** N lait m entier ► **whole note** N (Mus) ronde f ► **whole number** N (Math) nombre m entier ► **whole step** N (US Mus) = **whole tone** ► **whole tone** N ton m entier

wholefood(s) ['həʊlfuːd(z)] (Brit) [1] N(PL) aliments mpl complets [2] COMP ► **wholefood restaurant** N restaurant m diététique

wholegrain ['həʊlgreɪn] ADJ [bread, flour, rice] complet (-ète f)

wholehearted [,həʊl'hɑːtɪd] ADJ [approval, admiration] sans réserve; [supporter] inconditionnel; they made a ~ attempt to do ... ils ont mis tout leur enthousiasme à faire ...

wholeheartedly [,həʊl'hɑːtɪdlɪ] ADV [accept, approve, support] sans réserve; to agree ~ être entièrement or totalement d'accord

wholemeal ['həʊlmiːl] ADJ (Brit) [flour, bread] complet (-ète f)

wholeness ['həʊlnɪs] N complétude f

wholesale ['həʊlseɪl] [1] N (NonC: Comm) (vente f en) gros m; at or by ~ en gros [2] ADJ [a] (Comm) [price, trade] de gros [b] (= indiscriminate) [slaughter, destruction] systématique; [change] gros (grosse f); [reform, rejection] en bloc; [privatisation] complet (-ète f); there has been ~ sacking of unskilled workers il y a eu des licenciements en masse parmi les manœuvres ③ ADV **a** (*Comm*) [*buy, sell*] en gros; **I can get it for you ~** je peux vous le faire avoir au prix de gros **b** (= *indiscriminately*) [*slaughter, destroy*] systématiquement; [*sack*] en masse; [*reject, accept*] en bloc ④ COMP ► **wholesale dealer, wholesale merchant** N grossiste *mf*, marchand(e) *m(f)* en gros ► **wholesale price index** N indice *m* des prix de gros ► **wholesale trader** N = **wholesale dealer**

wholesaler ['həʊseɪləʳ] N (*Comm*) grossiste *mf*, marchand(e) *m(f)* en gros

wholesaling ['həʊseɪlɪŋ] N (*NonC*) commerce *m* de gros

wholesome ['həʊlsəm] ADJ [*food, life, thoughts, book, person*] sain; [*air, climate*] sain, salubre; [*exercise, advice*] salutaire

wholesomeness ['həʊlsəmnɪs] N [*of food, life, thoughts, book, person*] caractère *m* sain; [*of air, climate*] salubrité *f*

wholewheat ['həʊlwiːt] ADJ [*flour, bread*] complet (-ète *f*)

wholism ['həʊlɪzəm] N = **holism**

wholistic [həʊ'lɪstɪk] ADJ = **holistic**

who'll [huːl] = **who will, who shall**; → **who**

wholly ['həʊlɪ] ① ADV [*unacceptable, unreliable*] totalement; [*satisfactory*] totalement, tout à fait; [*approve, trust, justify*] entièrement; **I'm not ~ convinced** je n'en suis pas totalement or tout à fait convaincu ② COMP ► **wholly-owned subsidiary** N (*Jur, Econ*) filiale *f* à cent pour cent

whom [huːm] PRON **a** (*interrog: often replaced by "who" in spoken English*) qui; **~ did you see?** qui avez-vous vu?; **when was the photo taken and by ~?** quand est-ce que la photo a été prise et par qui?; **with ~?** avec qui? **to ~?** à qui? → **who 1a b** (*rel*) **my aunt, ~ I love dearly** ma tante, que j'aime tendrement; **those ~ he had seen recently** ceux qu'il avait vus récemment; **the man to ~ ...** l'homme à qui ..., l'homme auquel ...; **the man of ~ ...** l'homme dont ...; **the woman with ~ he had an affair** la femme avec qui il a eu une liaison; **my daughters, both of ~ are married** mes filles, qui sont toutes les deux mariées; (*liter*) **~ the gods love the young** ceux qui sont aimés des dieux meurent jeunes

whomever [huːm'evəʳ] PRON *accusative case of* **whoever**

whomp* [wɒmp] (*US*) ① VT (= *hit*) cogner*; (= *defeat*) enfoncer* ② N bruit *m* sourd

whomping* ['wɒmpɪŋ] ADJ (*US: also* **~ big, ~ great**) énorme

whomsoever [huːmsəʊ'evəʳ] PRON (*emphatic*) *accusative case of* **whosoever**

whoop [huːp] ① N cri *m* (de joie, de triomphe); (*Med*) toux *f* coquelucheuse, toux *f* convulsive (de la coqueluche); **with a ~ of glee/triumph** avec un cri de joie/de triomphe ② VI pousser des cris; (*Med*) avoir des quintes de toux coquelucheuse ③ VT **to ~ it up**†* faire la noce* *or* la bombe* ④ COMP ► **whooping cough** N coqueluche *f*

whoopee [wʊ'piː] ① EXCL hourra!, youpi! ② N **to make ~**†* faire la noce* *or* la bombe* ③ COMP ► **whoopee cushion*** N coussin(-péteur) *m* de farces et attrapes

whoops [wuːps] EXCL (*also* **~-a-daisy**) (*avoiding fall etc*) oups!, houp-là!; (*lifting child*) houp-là!, hop-là!

whoosh [wuːʃ] ① EXCL zoum! ② N **the ~ of sledge runners in the snow** le bruit des patins de luges glissant sur la neige, le glissement des patins de luges sur la neige ③ VI **the car ~ed past** la voiture est passée à toute allure dans un glissement de pneus

whop‡ [wɒp] VT (= *beat*) rosser*; (= *defeat*) battre à plate(s) couture(s)

whopper* ['wɒpəʳ] N (*car/parcel/nose etc*) voiture *f*/colis *m*/nez *m* etc énorme; (= *lie*) mensonge *m* énorme

whopping ['wɒpɪŋ] ① ADJ* [*lie, loss*] énorme; **to win a ~ 89 per cent of the vote** remporter les élections avec une écrasante majorité de 89 pour cent; **a ~ $31 billion** la somme énorme de 31 milliards de dollars ② ADV **~ great** *or* **big*** énorme ③ N* raclée* *f*

whore [hɔːʳ] ① N (‡ *pej*) putain* *f* ② VI (*lit: also* **go whoring**) courir la gueuse, se débaucher; (*fig liter*) **to ~ after sth** se prostituer pour obtenir qch

who're ['huːəʳ] = **who are**; → **who**

whorehouse‡ ['hɔːˌhaʊs] N bordel* *m*

whoremonger† ['hɔːˌmʌŋgəʳ] N fornicateur *m*; (= *pimp*) proxénète *m*, souteneur *m*

whorish‡ ['hɔːrɪʃ] ADJ de putain‡, putassier‡*

whorl [wɜːl] N [*of fingerprint*] volute *f*; [*of spiral shell*] spire *f*; [*of flower*] verticille *m*; **~s of meringue/cream** des tortillons *mpl* de meringue/crème

whortleberry ['wɜːtlbərɪ] N myrtille *f*

who's [huːz] = **who is, who has**; → **who**

whose [huːz] ① POSS PRON à qui; **~ is this?** à qui est ceci?; **I know ~ it is** je sais à qui c'est; **~ is this hat?** à qui est ce chapeau?; **here's a lollipop each — let's see ~ lasts longest!** voici une sucette chacun — voyons celle de qui durera le plus longtemps! ② POSS ADJ **a** (*interrog*) à qui, de qui; **~ hat is this?** à qui est ce chapeau?; **~ son are you?** de qui êtes-vous le fils?; **~ book is missing?** c'est le livre de qui qui manque?, qui n'a pas (*or* n'a pas remis *etc*) son livre?; **~ fault is it?** à qui la faute? **b** (*rel use*) dont, de qui; **the man ~ hat I took** l'homme dont j'ai pris le chapeau; **the boy ~ sister I was talking to** le garçon à la sœur duquel *or* à la sœur de qui je parlais; **those ~ passports I've got here** ceux dont j'ai les passeports ici

whosever [huːz'evəʳ] POSS PRON = **of whomever**; → **whoever**; **~ book you use, you must take care of it** peu importe à qui est le livre dont tu te sers, il faut que tu en prennes soin

whosoever (*emphatic*) [ˌhuːsəʊ'evəʳ], **whosoe'er** (*liter*) [ˌhuːsəʊ'eəʳ] PRON = **whoever**

who've [huːv] = **who have**; → **who**

▼ **why** [waɪ] ① ADV pourquoi; **~ did you do it?** pourquoi l'avez-vous fait?; **I wonder ~ he left her** je me demande pourquoi il l'a quittée; **I wonder ~** je me demande pourquoi; **he told me ~ he did it** il m'a dit pourquoi il l'a fait *or* la raison pour laquelle il l'a fait; **~ not?** pourquoi pas?; **~ not phone her?** pourquoi ne pas lui téléphoner?; **~ ask her when you don't have to?** pourquoi le lui demander quand vous n'êtes pas obligé de le faire? ② EXCL (*esp US*†) eh bien!, tiens!; **~, what's the matter?** eh bien, qu'est-ce qui ne va pas?; **~, it's you!** tiens, c'est vous!; **~, it's quite easy!** voyons donc, ce n'est pas difficile! ③ CONJ **the reasons ~ he did it** les raisons pour lesquelles il l'a fait; **there's no reason ~ you shouldn't try again** il n'y a pas de raison (pour) que tu n'essaies (*subj*) pas de nouveau; **that's (the reason) ~** voilà pourquoi; **that is ~ I never spoke to him again** c'est pourquoi je ne lui ai jamais reparlé ④ N **the ~(s) and (the) wherefore(s)** le pourquoi et le comment; **the ~ and (the) how** le pourquoi et le comment

whyever* [waɪ'evəʳ] ADV (*interrog: emphatic*) pourquoi donc; **~ did you do that?*** pourquoi donc est-ce que vous avez fait ça?

WI [ˌdʌblju:'aɪ] N **a** (*Brit*) (ABBR = **Women's Institute**) → **woman b** ABBR = **Wisconsin c** (ABBR = **West Indies**) → **west**

wibbly-wobbly* [ˌwɪblɪ'wɒblɪ] ADJ = **wobbly**

wick [wɪk] N mèche *f*; (*Brit fig*) **he gets on my ~*** il me tape sur le système*, il me court sur le haricot*

wicked ['wɪkɪd] ADJ **a** (= *immoral*) [*person*] méchant, mauvais; [*behaviour, act, deed*] vilain (*before n*); [*system, policy, attempt, world*] pernicieux; **that was a ~ thing to do!** c'était vraiment méchant (de faire ça)!; **a ~ waste** un scandaleux gâchis → **rest b** (= *nasty*) [*comment*] méchant; **to have a ~ temper** avoir mauvais caractère **c** (= *naughty*) [*grin, look, suggestion*] malicieux; [*sense of humour*] plein de malice; **a ~ cake/pudding** un gâteau/dessert à vous damner **d** (* = *skilful*) **that was a ~ shot!** quel beau coup!; **he plays a ~ game of draughts** il joue super bien* aux dames **e** (* = *excellent*) super* *inv*; **I've just won again: ~!** je viens encore de gagner: super!*

wickedly ['wɪkɪdlɪ] ADV **a** (= *immorally*) [*behave*] méchamment; **a ~ destructive child** un enfant méchant et destructeur; **a ~ cruel act** un acte méchant et cruel; **he ~ destroyed ...** méchamment, il a détruit ... **b** (= *naughtily*) [*grin, look at, suggest*] malicieusement; **~ funny** drôle et caustique; **~ seductive** malicieusement séducteur (-trice *f*); **a ~ rich pudding** un dessert terriblement *or* méchamment* riche **c** (* = *skilfully*) [*play*] comme un chef*, super bien*

wickedness ['wɪkɪdnɪs] N [*of behaviour, order, decision, person*] méchanceté *f*, cruauté *f*; [*of murder*] horreur *f*, atrocité *f*; [*of look, smile, suggestion*] malice *f*; [*of waste*] scandale *m*

wicker ['wɪkəʳ] ① N (*NonC*) (= *substance*) osier *m*; (= *objects: also* **~work**) vannerie *f* ② COMP (*also* **~work**) [*basket, chair*] d'osier, en osier

wicket ['wɪkɪt] N **a** (= *door, gate*) (petite) porte *f*, portillon *m*; (*for bank teller etc*) guichet *m* **b** (*Cricket*) (= *stumps*) guichet *m*; (= *pitch between them*) terrain *m* (entre les guichets); **to lose/take a ~** perdre/prendre un guichet → **losing, sticky** ② COMP ► **wicket-keeper** N (*Cricket*) gardien *m* de guichet

wickiup ['wɪkiˌʌp] N (*US*) hutte *f* de branchages

widdershins ['wɪdəʃɪnz] ADV (*esp Scot*) = **withershins**

wide [waɪd] ① ADJ **a** (= *broad*) [*road, river, strip*] large; [*margin*] grand; [*garment*] large, ample; [*ocean, desert*] immense, vaste; [*circle, gap, space*] large, grand; (*fig*) [*knowledge*] vaste, très étendu; [*choice, selection*] grand, considérable; [*survey, study*] de grande envergure; **how ~ is the room?** quelle est la largeur de la pièce?; **it is 5 metres ~** cela a *or* fait 5 mètres de large; **the ~ Atlantic** l'immense *or* le vaste Atlantique; **no one/nowhere in the whole ~ world** personne/nulle part au monde; **she stared, her eyes ~ with fear** elle regardait, les yeux agrandis de peur *or* par la peur; **mouth ~ with astonishment** bouche *f* bée de stupeur; **a man with ~ views** *or* **opinions** un homme aux vues larges; **he has ~ interests** il a des goûts très éclectiques; **in the widest sense of the word** au sens le plus général *or* le plus large du mot; **it has a ~ variety of uses** cela se prête à une grande variété d'usages **b** (= *off target*) **the shot/ball/arrow was ~** le coup/la balle/la flèche est passé(e) à côté; **it was ~ of the target** c'était loin de la cible → **mark²** ② ADV [*aim, shoot, fall*] loin du but; **the bullet went ~** la balle est passée à côté; **he flung the door ~** il a ouvert la porte en grand; **they are set ~ apart** [*trees, houses, posts*] ils sont largement espacés; [*eyes*] ils sont très écartés; **he stood with his legs ~ apart** il se tenait debout les jambes très écartées; **to open one's eyes ~** ouvrir grand les yeux *or* ses yeux en grand; (*at dentist's*) **"open ~!"** « ouvrez grand! »; **~ open** [*door, window*] grand ouvert; **the race was still ~ open** l'issue de la course était encore indécise ; **he left himself ~ open to criticism** il a prêté le flanc à la critique ; **to blow sth ~ open** (= *change completely*) révolutionner qch ; **he threatened to blow the operation ~ open** (= *reveal secret*) il a menacé de tout révéler sur l'opération → **far**

3 COMP ► **wide-angle lens** N (*Phot*) objectif *m* grand-angulaire, objectif *m* grand angle *inv* ► **wide area network** N (*Comput*) grand réseau *m* ► **wide-awake** ADJ (*lit*) bien or tout éveillé ; (*fig*) éveillé, alerte ► **wide-bodied aircraft, wide-body aircraft** N avion *m* à fuselage élargi, gros-porteur *m* ► **wide boy**‡ N (*Brit pej*) arnaqueur* *m* ► **wide-eyed** ADJ (*in naïveté*) aux yeux grands ouverts or écarquillés ; (*in fear, surprise*) aux yeux écarquillés ♦ ADV les yeux écarquillés ; **in ~-eyed amazement** les yeux écarquillés par la stupeur ► **wide-mouthed** ADJ [*river*] à l'embouchure large ; [*cave*] avec une vaste entrée ; [*bottle*] au large goulot ; [*bag*] large du haut ► **wide-ranging** ADJ [*mind, report, survey*] de grande envergure ; [*interests*] divers, variés ► **wide screen** N (*Cine*) écran *m* panoramique

-wide [waɪd] ADJ, ADV (*in compounds*) → **countrywide, nationwide**

widely ['waɪdlɪ] ADV a (= *generally*) [*available*] généralement ; [*used, regarded, expected*] largement ; [*known*] bien ; **it is ~ believed that ...** on pense communément or généralement que ... ; **~-held opinions** opinions *fpl* très répandues b (= *much*) [*travel, vary*] beaucoup ; [*scatter, spread*] sur une grande étendue ; **~ different** extrêmement différent ; **the trees were ~ spaced** les arbres étaient largement espacés ; **the talks ranged ~** les pourparlers ont porté sur des questions très diverses ; **to be ~ read** [*author, book*] être très lu ; [*reader*] avoir beaucoup lu ; **she is ~ read in philosophy** elle a beaucoup lu d'ouvrages de philosophie c (= *broadly*) **to smile ~** avoir un large sourire

widen ['waɪdn] 1 VT [+ *circle, gap, space*] élargir, agrandir ; [+ *road, river, strip, garment*] élargir ; [+ *margin*] augmenter ; [+ *knowledge*] accroître, élargir ; [+ *survey, study*] élargir la portée de ; (*in election, race etc*) **to ~ one's lead over sb** accroître son avance sur qn 2 VI (*also* **~ out**) s'élargir, s'agrandir

wideness ['waɪdnɪs] N largeur *f*

widespread ['waɪdspred] ADJ a [*availability*] courant b [*arms*] en croix ; [*wings*] déployé ; [*belief, opinion*] très répandu ; [*confusion*] général

widgeon ['wɪdʒən] N canard *m* siffleur

widget* ['wɪdʒɪt] N (= *device*) gadget *m* ; (= *thingummy*) truc* *m*, machin* *m*

widow ['wɪdəʊ] 1 N veuve *f* ; **~ Smith**† la veuve Smith ; **she's a golf ~** elle ne voit jamais son mari qui est toujours à jouer au golf, son mari la délaisse pour aller jouer au golf → **grass, mite, weed** 2 VT **to be ~ed** [*man*] devenir veuf ; [*woman*] devenir veuve ; **she was ~ed in 1989** elle est devenue veuve en 1989, elle a perdu son mari en 1989 ; **she has been ~ed for ten years** elle est veuve depuis dix ans ; **he lives with his ~ed mother** il vit avec sa mère qui est veuve 3 COMP ► **widow's benefit** N ► **widow's pension** ► **widow's peak** N pousse *f* de cheveux en V sur le front ► **widow's pension** N (*Admin*) ≈ allocation *f* de veuvage ► **widow's walk** N (*US*) belvédère *m* (*construit sur le faîte d'une maison côtière*)

widower ['wɪdəʊər] N veuf *m*

widowhood ['wɪdəʊhʊd] N veuvage *m*

width [wɪdθ] N a (*NonC*) [*of road, river, strip, bed, ocean, desert, gap, space, margin*] largeur *f* ; [*of garment*] ampleur *f* ; [*of circle*] largeur *f*, diamètre *m* ; **what is the ~ of the room?** quelle est la largeur de la pièce ?, quelle largeur a la pièce ? ; **it is 5 metres in ~** ◊ **its ~ is 5 metres** ◊ **it**

has a **~ of 5 metres** cela a or fait 5 mètres de large ; **measure it across its ~** prends la mesure en largeur b [*of cloth*] largeur *f*, lé *m* ; **you'll get it out of one ~** une largeur or un lé te suffira

widthways ['wɪdθweɪz], **widthwise** ['wɪdθwaɪz] ADV en largeur

wield [wiːld] VT a [+ *sword, axe, pen, tool*] manier ; (= *brandish*) brandir b [+ *power, authority, control*] exercer

wiener* ['wiːnə] (*US*) 1 N saucisse *f* de Francfort 2 COMP ► **wiener schnitzel** ['viːnə'ʃnɪtsəl] N escalope *f* viennoise

wienie* ['wiːnɪ] N (*US*) saucisse *f* de Francfort

wife [waɪf] (*pl* **wives**) 1 N a (= *spouse*) femme *f* ; (*esp Admin*) épouse *f* ; (= *married woman*) femme *f* mariée ; **his second ~** sa deuxième or seconde femme, la femme qu'il a (*or avait etc*) épousée en secondes noces ; **the farmer's/ butcher's ~** la fermière/bouchère *etc* ; **the ~:** la patronne* ; **he decided to take a ~** † il a décidé de se marier or de prendre femme† ; **to take sb to ~** † prendre qn pour femme ; **wives whose husbands have reached the age of 65** les femmes *fpl* mariées dont les maris ont atteint 65 ans ; **"The Merry Wives of Windsor"** « Les Joyeuses Commères de Windsor » → **working** b († *dial* = *woman*) bonne femme* *f* ; **she's a poor old ~** c'est une pauvre vieille → **old** 2 COMP ► **wife-batterer, wife-beater** N homme *m* qui bat sa femme ► **wife's equity** N (*US Jur*) part *f* de la communauté revenant à la femme en cas de divorce ► **wife-swapping** N échangisme *m* ; **~-swapping party** partie *f* carrée

wifely† ['waɪflɪ] ADJ de bonne épouse

wig [wɪg] N (*gen*) perruque *f* ; (= *hairpiece*) postiche *m* ; (‡ = *hair*) tignasse* *f*

wigeon ['wɪdʒən] N = **widgeon**

wigging†‡ ['wɪgɪŋ] N (*Brit* = *scolding*) attrapade‡ *f*, réprimande *f* ; **to give sb a ~** passer un savon* à qn ; **to get a ~** se faire enguirlander*

wiggle ['wɪgl] 1 VT [+ *pencil, stick*] agiter ; [+ *toes*] agiter, remuer ; [+ *loose screw, button, tooth*] faire jouer ; **to ~ one's hips** tortiller des hanches ; **my finger hurts if you ~ it like that** j'ai mal quand vous me tortillez le doigt comme ça ; **he ~d his finger at me warningly** il a agité l'index dans ma direction en guise d'avertissement 2 VI [*loose screw etc*] branler ; [*tail*] remuer, frétiller ; [*rope, snake, worm*] se tortiller ; **she ~d across the room** elle a traversé la pièce en se déhanchant or en tortillant des hanches 3 N **to walk with a ~** marcher en se déhanchant, marcher en tortillant des hanches ; **to give sth a ~ = to wiggle sth**; → **1**

wiggly ['wɪglɪ] ADJ [*snake, worm*] qui se tortille ; **a ~ line** un trait ondulé

wight†† [waɪt] N être *m*

wigmaker ['wɪgmeɪkə] N perruquier *m*, -ière *f*

wigwam ['wɪgwæm] N wigwam *m*

wilco ['wɪlˌkəʊ] EXCL (*Telec*) message reçu !

wild [waɪld] 1 ADJ a [*animal, plant, tribe, man, land, countryside*] sauvage ; **~ beast** (*gen*) bête *f* sauvage ; (= *dangerous*) bête *f* féroce ; **~ goat** chèvre *f* sauvage ; (= *uncultivated*) **it was growing ~** ça poussait à l'état sauvage ; **the plant in its ~ state** la plante à l'état sauvage ; **a ~ stretch of coastline** une côte sauvage ; (*US*) **~ and woolly*** fruste, primitif ; (*fig*) **to sow one's ~ oats** jeter sa gourme†, faire les quatre cents coups ; **~ horses wouldn't make me tell you** je ne te le dirais pour rien au monde → **3** ; → **rose²**, **run**, **strawberry** b (= *rough*) [*wind*] violent, furieux ; [*sea*] démonté ; **in ~ weather** par gros temps ; **it was a ~ night** la tempête faisait rage cette nuit-là c (= *unrestrained*) [*appearance*] farouche ; [*laughter, anger, evening, party*] fou (*folle f*) ; [*idea, plan*] fou (*folle f*), extravagant ; [*imagi-*

nation, enthusiasm*] débordant, délirant ; [*life*] de bâtons de chaise* ; **his hair was ~ and uncombed** il avait les cheveux en bataille ; **there was ~ confusion at the airport** la confusion la plus totale régnait à l'aéroport ; **he took a ~ swing at his opponent** il a lancé le poing en direction de son adversaire ; **he had a ~ look in his eyes** il avait une lueur sauvage or farouche dans les yeux ; **he was ~ in his youth** ◊ **he had a ~ youth** il a fait les quatre cents coups dans sa jeunesse ; **a whole gang of ~ kids** toute une bande de casse-cou ; **to have a ~ night out (on the town)** sortir faire la fête* ; **we had some ~ times together** nous avons fait les quatre cents coups ensemble ; (= *tough*) **those were ~ times** les temps étaient durs, la vie était rude en ce temps-là ; **he had some ~ scheme for damming the river** il avait un projet complètement fou or abracadabrant pour barrer le fleuve ; **there was a lot of ~ talk about ...** on a avancé des tas d'idées folles au sujet de ... ; **they made some ~ promises** ils ont fait quelques promesses folles or extravagantes ; **that is a ~ exaggeration** c'est une énorme exagération ; **to make a ~ guess** risquer or émettre à tout hasard une hypothèse (**at sth** sur qch) d (= *excited*) comme fou (*folle f*) ; (= *enthusiastic*) fou (*folle f*), dingue* (**about** de) ; **to be ~ about sb/sth*** être dingue* de qn/qch ; **I'm not ~ about it*** ça ne m'emballe* pas beaucoup ; **he was ~ with joy** il ne se tenait plus de joie ; **he was ~ with anger/indignation** il était fou de rage/d'indignation ; **the audience went ~ (with delight)** le public a hurlé de joie ; **his fans went ~ when he appeared** la folie a gagné ses fans* quand il est apparu ; **the dog went ~ when he saw his owner** le chien est devenu comme fou quand il a vu son maître ; **it's enough to drive you ~!*** c'est à vous rendre dingue !*

2 N **the call of the ~** l'appel *m* de la nature ; (= *natural habitat*) **in the ~** dans la nature, à l'état sauvage ; **this plant grows in the ~** cette plante existe à l'état sauvage ; **he went off into the ~s** il est parti vers des régions sauvages or reculées ; **he lives in the ~s of Alaska** il vit au fin fond de l'Alaska ; (*fig*) **we live out in the ~s** nous habitons en pleine brousse

3 COMP ► **wild boar** N sanglier *m* ► **wild child** N a (*wayward*) noceur* *m*, -euse* *f* b (*living in wilds*) enfant *mf* sauvage ► **wild duck** N canard *m* sauvage ► **wild-eyed** ADJ (= *mad*) au regard fou ; (= *grief-stricken*) aux yeux hagards ► **wild flowers** NPL fleurs *fpl* des champs, fleurs *fpl* sauvages ► **wild-goose chase** N **he sent me off on a ~-goose chase** il m'a fait courir partout pour rien ► **wild rabbit** N lapin *m* de garenne ► **wild rice** N riz *m* sauvage ► **the Wild West** N (*US*) le Far West ► **Wild West show** N (*US*) spectacle *m* sur le thème du Far West

wildcard ['waɪldkɑːd] N (*Comput*) caractère *m* joker or de remplacement ; (*fig*) élément *m* imprévisible

wildcat ['waɪldˌkæt] 1 N (*pl* **wildcats** or **wildcat**) a (= *animal*) chat *m* sauvage ; (*fig* = *person*) personne *f* féroce b (= *oil well*) forage *m* de prospection 2 ADJ (*US* = *unsound*) [*scheme, project*] insensé ; (*financially*) financièrement douteux 3 VI (*for oil*) entreprendre un forage dans un terrain vierge 4 COMP ► **wildcat strike** N (*Ind*) grève *f* sauvage

wildcatter* ['waɪldˌkætə] N (= *striker*) gréviste *mf* ; (*Fin*) spéculateur *m*

wildebeest ['wɪldɪbiːst] N (*pl* **wildebeests** or **wildebeest**) gnou *m*

wilderness ['wɪldənɪs] N (*gen*) étendue *f* déserte, région *f* reculée or sauvage ; (*Bible, also fig*) désert *m* ; (= *overgrown garden*) jungle *f* ; **a ~ of snow and ice** de vastes étendues de neige et de glace ; **a ~ of empty seas** une mer vaste et désolée ; **a ~ of streets/ruins** un désert de rues/de ruines ; (*Bible*) **to preach in the ~** prêcher dans le désert ; (*fig*) **to be in the ~** faire sa traversée du désert ; **this garden is a ~** ce jardin est une vraie jungle

wildfire ['waɪldfaɪəʳ] N feu *m* or incendie *m* de forêt ; **to spread like ~** se répandre comme une traînée de poudre

wildfowl ['waɪldfaʊl] N (*one bird*) oiseau *m* sauvage ; (*collectively*) oiseaux *mpl* sauvages ; (*Hunting*) gibier *m* à plumes

wildfowling ['waɪldfaʊlɪŋ] N **to go ~** chasser (le gibier à plumes)

wildlife ['waɪldlaɪf] [1] N faune *f* et flore *f* ; **he's interested in ~** il s'intéresse à la faune et à la flore ; **the ~ of Central Australia** la faune et la flore d'Australie centrale [2] COMP ► **wildlife park, wildlife sanctuary** N réserve *f* naturelle

wildly ['waɪldlɪ] ADV [a] (= *excitedly*) [*applaud*] frénétiquement ; [*gesticulate, wave*] furieusement ; [*talk*] avec beaucoup d'agitation ; [*protest*] violemment ; [*behave*] de façon extravagante ; **to cheer ~** pousser des acclamations frénétiques ; **to look ~ around** jeter des regards éperdus autour de soi [b] (= *violently, frantically*) **her heart was beating ~** son cœur battait violemment or à se rompre ; **he hit out ~** il lançait des coups dans tous les sens or au hasard ; **they were rushing about ~** ils se précipitaient dans tous les sens ; **the wind blew ~** le vent soufflait violemment ; **the storm raged ~** la tempête faisait rage [c] (= *at random*) [*shoot*] au hasard ; **you're guessing ~** tu dis ça tout à fait au hasard [d] (= *extremely*) [*optimistic, excited, happy*] follement ; [*vary*] de façon aberrante ; **I'm not ~ pleased* about it** ce n'est pas que ça me fasse très plaisir

wildness ['waɪldnɪs] N [*of land, countryside, scenery*] aspect *m* sauvage ; [*of tribe, people*] sauvagerie *f* ; [*of wind, sea*] fureur *f*, violence *f* ; [*of appearance*] désordre *m* ; [*of imagination*] extravagance *f* ; [*of enthusiasm*] ferveur *f* ; **the ~ of the weather** le sale temps qu'il fait

wiles [waɪlz] NPL artifices *mpl*, manège *m* ; (*stronger*) ruses *fpl*

wilful, willful (*US*) ['wɪlfʊl] ADJ [a] (= *deliberate*) [*misconduct, destruction, ignorance*] délibéré ; [*murder, damage*] volontaire [b] (= *obstinate*) [*person*] têtu, obstiné

wilfully, willfully (*US*) ['wɪlfəlɪ] ADV [a] (= *deliber- ately*) délibérément [b] (= *obstinately*) obstinément

wilfulness, willfulness (*US*) ['wɪlfʊlnɪs] N [*of person*] obstination *f*, entêtement *m* ; [*of action*] caractère *m* délibéré or intentionnel

wiliness ['waɪlɪnɪs] N ruse *f* (*NonC*), astuce *f* (*NonC*)

will [wɪl] [1] MODAL AUX VB (*neg* **will not** *often abbr to* **won't**) [a] (*used to form future tense*) **he ~ speak** il parlera ; (*near future*) il va parler ; **don't worry, he ~ come** ne vous inquiétez pas, il ne manquera pas de venir or il viendra sans faute ; **you'll regret it some day** tu le regretteras un jour ; **we ~ come too** nous viendrons (nous) aussi ; **you won't lose it again, ~ you?** tu ne le perdras plus, n'est-ce pas ? ; **you ~ come to see us, won't you?** vous viendrez nous voir, n'est-ce pas ? ; **~ he come too? — yes he ~** est-ce qu'il viendra (lui) aussi ? — oui ; **I'll go with you — (oh) no you won't!** je vais vous accompagner — non, certainement pas ! ; **they'll arrive tomorrow — ~ they?** ils arriveront demain — ah bon or c'est vrai ? ; **I don't think he'll do it tomorrow** je ne pense pas qu'il le fasse demain ; (*in commands*) **you ~ speak to no one** ne parlez à personne, vous ne parlerez à personne ; **~ you be quiet!** veux-tu (bien) te taire ! [b] (*indicating conjecture*) **that ~ be the taxi** ça doit être le taxi, c'est or voilà sans doute le

taxi ; **that ~ have been last year, I suppose** je suppose que c'était l'année dernière ; **she'll be about forty** elle doit avoir quarante ans environ ; **she'll have forgotten all about it by now** elle aura tout oublié à l'heure qu'il est [c] (*indicating willingness*) **I ~ help you** je vous aiderai, je veux bien vous aider ; **~ you help me? — yes I ~/no I won't** tu veux m'aider ? — oui je veux bien/non je ne veux pas ; **if you'll help me I think we can do it** si vous voulez bien m'aider je crois que nous y arriverons ; **won't you come with us?** vous ne voulez pas venir (avec nous) ? ; **~ you have a cup of coffee?** voulez-vous or prendrez-vous un petit café ? ; **won't you have a drink?** vous prendrez bien un verre ? ; (*in requests*) **~ you please sit down!** voulez-vous vous asseoir, s'il vous plaît ! ; **just a moment, ~ you?** un instant, s'il vous plaît ; (*in marriage service*) **I ~** oui ; **I ~ see him!** on ne m'empêchera pas de le voir ! ; **I won't have it!** je ne tolère pas ça !, je n'admets pas ça ! ; **the window won't open** la fenêtre ne s'ouvre pas or ne veut pas s'ouvrir ; (*frm*) **do what you ~** faites ce que vous voulez or comme vous voulez ; (*frm*) **come when you ~** venez quand vous voulez ; (*frm*) **look where you ~** regardez où bon vous semble [d] (*indicating habit, characteristic*) **he ~ sit for hours doing nothing** il reste assis pendant des heures à ne rien faire ; **this bottle ~ hold one litre** cette bouteille contient un litre or fait le litre ; **the car ~ do 150km/h** cette voiture fait du 150 km/h ; **he ~ talk all the time!** il ne peut pas s'empêcher or s'arrêter de parler ! ; **if you ~ make your speeches so long, you can hardly blame people for not listening** si vous persistez à faire des discours aussi longs, il ne faut pas vraiment vous étonner si les gens n'écoutent pas ; **he ~ annoy me by leaving his socks lying all over the place** il m'énerve à toujours laisser traîner ses chaussettes partout ; **I ~ call him Richard, though his name's actually Robert** il faut toujours que je l'appelle (*subj*) Richard bien qu'en fait il s'appelle Robert ; **boys ~ be boys** il faut (bien) que jeunesse se passe (*PROV*)

[2] (*pret, ptp* **willed**) VT [a] (*frm* = *wish, intend*) vouloir (**that** que + *subj*) ; **God has ~ed it so** Dieu a voulu qu'il en soit ainsi ; **it is as God ~s** c'est la volonté de Dieu ; **you must ~ it really hard if you wish to succeed** pour réussir il faut le vouloir très fort ; **to ~ sb's happiness** vouloir le bonheur de qn

[b] (= *urge by willpower*) **he was ~ing her to accept** il l'adjurait intérieurement d'accepter ; **he ~ed himself to stand up** il fit un suprême effort pour se mettre debout

[c] (*Jur* = *leave in one's will*) léguer (**sth to sb** qch à qn)

[3] N [a] (= *faculty*) volonté *f* ; (= *wish*) volonté *f*, désir *m* ; **he has a ~ of his own** il sait ce qu'il veut ; **he has a strong ~** il a beaucoup de volonté ; **a ~ of iron ◊ an iron ~** une volonté de fer ; **to have a weak ~** manquer de volonté ; **the ~ to live** la volonté de survivre ■ (*PROV*) **where there's a ~ there's a way** vouloir c'est pouvoir (*PROV*) ; **the ~ of God** la volonté de Dieu, la volonté divine ; **it is the ~ of the people that ...** la volonté du peuple est que ... (+ *subj*) ; (*frm*) **what is your ~?** quelle est votre volonté ? ; (*frm*) **it is my ~ that he should leave** je veux qu'il parte ; (*Rel*) **thy ~ be done** que ta volonté soit faite ; **at ~** (= *as much as you like*) à volonté ; (= *whenever you like*) quand vous le voulez ; **to choose/borrow** *etc* **at ~** choisir/ emprunter *etc* à volonté ; **you are free to leave at ~** vous êtes libre de partir quand vous voulez ; **to do sth against one's ~** faire qch à son corps défendant or à contre-cœur ; **with the best ~ in the world** avec la meilleure volonté du monde ; **to work with a ~** travailler avec détermination or ardeur → **free, goodwill, ill, sweet**

[b] (*Jur*) testament *m* ; **the last ~ and testament of ...** les dernières volontés de ... ; **he left it to me in his ~** il me l'a légué par testament, il me l'a laissé dans son testament

willful *etc* ['wɪlfʊl] ADJ (*US*) = **wilful** *etc*

William ['wɪljəm] N Guillaume *m* ; **~ the Conqueror** Guillaume le Conquérant ; **~ of Orange** Guillaume d'Orange ; **~ Tell** Guillaume Tell

willie* ['wɪlɪ] [1] N (*Brit*) zizi* *m* [2] **the willies** NPL **to have the ~s** avoir les chocottes* *fpl*, avoir la trouille* ; **it gives me the ~s** ça me donne les chocottes*, ça me fout la trouille* ; **he gives me the ~s** il me fout la trouille*

willing ['wɪlɪŋ] [1] ADJ [a] (= *prepared*) **to be ~ to do sth** être prêt or disposé à faire qch, bien vouloir faire qch ; **he wasn't very ~ to help** il n'était pas tellement prêt or disposé à aider ; **I was quite ~ for him to come** j'étais tout à fait prêt or disposé à ce qu'il vienne ; **will you help us? — I'm perfectly ~** voulez-vous nous aider ? — bien volontiers → **god, ready, spirit** [b] (= *eager*) [*audience, participant*] enthousiaste ; [*helper, worker, partner*] plein de bonne volonté ; **~ hands helped him to his feet** des mains secourables se tendirent et l'aidèrent à se lever ; **there were plenty of ~ hands** il y avait beaucoup d'offres d'assistance ; **he's very ~** il est plein de bonne volonté [c] (= *voluntary*) [*help, sacrifice*] volontaire [2] N **to show ~** faire preuve de bonne volonté [3] COMP ► **willing horse*** N (= *person*) bonne âme *f* (qui se dévoue toujours)

willingly ['wɪlɪŋlɪ] ADV [a] (= *readily*) [*accept, work*] de mon (or ton, son *etc*) plein gré ; **can you help us? — ~!** peux-tu nous aider ? — volontiers ! [b] (= *voluntarily*) volontairement ; **did he do it ~ or did you have to make him?** l'a-t-il fait de lui-même or volontairement ou bien vous a-t-il fallu le forcer ?

willingness ['wɪlɪŋnɪs] N bonne volonté *f* ; (= *enthusiasm*) empressement *m* (**to do** à faire) ; **I don't doubt his ~, just his competence** ce n'est pas sa bonne volonté que je mets en doute mais sa compétence ; **I was grateful for his ~ to help** je lui étais reconnaissant de bien vouloir m'aider or de son empressement à m'aider ; **in spite of the ~ with which she agreed** malgré la bonne volonté qu'elle a mise à accepter, malgré son empressement à accepter

will-o'-the-wisp ['wɪlðə'wɪsp] N (*lit, fig*) feu follet *m*

willow ['wɪləʊ] [1] N (= *tree*) saule *m* ; (= *wood*) (bois *m* de) saule *m* (*NonC*) ; (*for baskets etc*) osier *m* ; (*fig* = *cricket/baseball bat*) **the ~*** la batte (de cricket/de baseball) → **pussy, weeping** [2] COMP [*bat etc*] de or en saule ; [*basket*] d'osier, en osier ► **willow pattern** N motif chinois dans les tons bleus ; **~ pattern china** porcelaine *f* à motif chinois ► **willow warbler** N (*Orn*) pouillot *m* fitis

willowherb ['wɪləʊhɜːb] N (*Bot*) épilobe *m*

willowy ['wɪləʊɪ] ADJ [*person*] svelte, élancé

willpower ['wɪlpaʊəʳ] N volonté *f*

willy* ['wɪlɪ] N = **willie 1**

willy-nilly ['wɪlɪ'nɪlɪ] ADV [a] (= *willingly or not*) bon gré mal gré [b] (= *at random*) au hasard

wilt[1] †† [wɪlt] VB *2nd person sg of* **will 1**

wilt[2] [wɪlt] [1] VI [*flower*] se faner, se flétrir ; [*plant*] se dessécher, mourir ; [*person*] (= *grow exhausted*) s'affaiblir ; (= *lose courage*) fléchir, être pris de découragement ; [*effort, enthusiasm etc*] diminuer ; **the guests began to ~ in the heat of the room** la chaleur de la pièce commençait à incommoder les invités ; **business confidence has visibly ~ed** la confiance des milieux d'affaires a visiblement diminué ; **United visibly ~ed under Liverpool's onslaught in the semi-final** United a manifestement flanché en demi-finale face à l'assaut de Liverpool ; **demand for household goods has ~ed with the collapse of the housing market** la demande en biens d'équipement ménager a fléchi avec l'effondrement du marché immobilier ; **I ~ed into my chair** je me suis effondré dans mon fauteuil

2 VT [+ *flower*] faner, flétrir ; [+ *plant, leaves*] dessécher

Wilts [wɪlts] ABBR = **Wiltshire**

wily ['waɪlɪ] ADJ (*gen pej*) [*person*] rusé, malin (-igne *f*) ; **a ~ trick** une astuce ; **he's a ~ old devil** or **bird** or **fox ◊ he's as ~ as a fox** il est rusé comme un renard

wimp* [wɪmp] N (*pej*) mauviette *f*, poule *f* mouillée

►**wimp out**: VI se dégonfler

wimpish* ['wɪmpɪʃ] (*pej*) ADJ [*behaviour*] de mauviette ; **a ~ young man** une jeune mauviette ; **his ~ friend** sa mauviette d'ami ; **he's so ~!** c'est une telle mauviette ! ; **stop being so ~!** cesse de faire la mauviette !

wimpishly* ['wɪmpɪʃlɪ] ADV [*say*] misérablement ; [*behave*] comme une mauviette

wimple ['wɪmpl] N guimpe *f*

wimpy* ['wɪmpɪ] ADJ = **wimpish**

win [wɪn] (*vb*: *pret, ptp* **won**) **1** N (*Sport etc*) victoire *f* ; **another ~ for Scotland** une nouvelle victoire pour l'Écosse ; **it was a convincing ~ for France** la victoire revenait indiscutablement à la France ; **to have a ~** gagner ; **to back a horse for a ~** jouer un cheval gagnant

2 VI **a** (*in war, sport, competition etc*) gagner, l'emporter ; **to ~ by a length** gagner or l'emporter d'une longueur ; **go in and ~!** vas-y et ne reviens pas sans la victoire ! ; **he was playing to ~** il jouait pour gagner ; **who's ~ning?** qui est-ce qui gagne ? ; **to ~ hands down*** gagner les doigts dans le nez*, gagner haut la main ; (*esp in race*) arriver dans un fauteuil ; (*US Sport*) **~, place and show** gagnant, placé et troisième ; (*in reluctant agreement*) **you ~!** soit ! tu as gagné ! ; **I (**or **you etc) (just) can't ~** j'ai (or on a etc) toujours tort

b **to ~ free** or **loose** se dégager (**from sth** de qch)

3 VT **a** (= *gain victory in*) [+ *war, match, competition, bet, race*] gagner ; **to ~ the day** (*Mil*) remporter la victoire ; (*gen*) l'emporter

b (= *compete for and get*) [+ *prize*] gagner, remporter ; [+ *victory*] remporter ; [+ *scholarship*] obtenir ; [+ *sum of money*] gagner ; **he won it for growing radishes** il l'a gagné or remporté or eu pour sa culture de radis ; **he won £5 (from her) at cards** il (lui) a gagné 5 livres aux cartes ; **his essay won him a trip to France** sa dissertation lui a valu un voyage en France

c (= *obtain etc*) [+ *fame, fortune*] trouver ; [+ *sb's attention*] capter, captiver ; [+ *sb's friendship*] gagner ; [+ *sb's esteem*] gagner, conquérir ; [+ *sympathy, support, admirers, supporters*] s'attirer ; [+ *coal, ore etc*] extraire (**from** de) ; **to ~ friends** se faire des amis ; **to ~ a name** or **a reputation (for o.s.)** se faire un nom or une réputation (**as** en tant que) ; **this won him the friendship of ...** ceci lui a gagné or valu l'amitié de ... ; **this won him the attention of the crowd** ça lui a valu l'attention de la foule ; **this manoeuvre won him the time he needed** cette manœuvre lui a valu d'obtenir le délai dont il avait besoin ; **to ~ sb's love/respect** se faire aimer/respecter de qn ; **to ~ sb to one's cause** gagner or rallier qn à sa cause ; **to ~ a lady** or **a lady's hand (in marriage)†** obtenir la main d'une demoiselle

d (= *reach*) [+ *summit, shore, goal*] parvenir à, arriver à ; **he won his way to the top of his profession** il a durement gagné sa place au sommet de sa profession

►**win back** VT SEP [+ *cup, trophy*] reprendre (**from** à) ; [+ *gaming loss etc*] recouvrer (**from** sur), reprendre (**from** à) ; [+ *land*] reconquérir (**from** sur) ; [+ *sb's favour, support, esteem, one's girlfriend etc*] reconquérir ; **I won the money back from him** j'ai repris l'argent qu'il m'avait gagné

►**win out** VI **a** l'emporter, gagner **b** = **win through**

►**win over**, **win round** VT SEP [+ *person*] convaincre, persuader ; [+ *voter*] gagner à sa cause ; **I won him over to my point of view** je l'ai gagné à ma façon de voir ; **the figures won him over to our way of thinking** les statistiques l'ont fait se rallier à notre façon de voir ; **I won him over eventually** j'ai fini par le convaincre or le persuader ; **to ~ sb over to doing sth** convaincre or persuader qn de faire qch

►**win through** VI y arriver, finir par réussir ; **you'll ~ through all right!** tu y arriveras !, tu finiras par réussir ! ; (*in competition etc*) **he won through to the second round** il a gagné le premier tour

wince [wɪns] **1** VI (= *flinch*) tressaillir ; (= *grimace*) grimacer (de douleur) ; **he ~d at the thought/at the sight** cette pensée/ce spectacle l'a fait tressaillir or grimacer ; **he ~d as I touched his injured arm** il a tressailli sous l'effet de la douleur or il a grimacé de douleur lorsque j'ai touché son bras blessé ; (*fig*) **without wincing** sans broncher or sourciller **2** N (= *flinch*) tressaillement *m*, crispation *f* ; (= *grimace*) grimace *f* (de douleur or dégoût etc) ; **to give a ~** = **to wince** ; → **1**

winceyette [ˌwɪnsɪˈet] N (*NonC: Brit*) flanelle *f* de coton

winch [wɪntʃ] **1** N treuil *m* **2** VT **to ~ sth up/down** etc monter/descendre etc qch au treuil ; **they ~ed him out of the water** ils l'ont hissé hors de l'eau au treuil

Winchester ['wɪntʃɪstə] N **~ (rifle)**® (carabine *f*) Winchester *f* ; (*Comput*) **~ disk** disque *m* Winchester

wind¹ [wɪnd] **1** N **a** vent *m* ; **high ~** grand vent *m*, vent *m* violent or fort ; **following ~** vent *m* arrière ; **the ~ is rising/dropping** le vent se lève/tombe ; **the ~ was in the east** le vent venait de l'est or était à l'est ; **where is the ~?** which way is the ~? d'où vient le vent ? ; **to go/run like the ~** aller/filer comme le vent ; (*Naut*) **between ~ and water** près de la ligne de flottaison ; (*Naut*) **to run before the ~** avoir or courir vent arrière ; (*fig*) **to take the ~ out of sb's sails** couper l'herbe sous le pied de qn ; **to see how the ~ blows** or **lies** (*lit*) voir d'où vient le vent ; (*fig*) prendre le vent, voir d'où vient le vent ; **the ~ of change is blowing** le vent du changement souffle ; **there's something in the ~** il y a quelque chose dans l'air, il se prépare quelque chose ; **to get ~ of sth** avoir vent de qch ; **he threw caution to the ~s** il a fait fi de toute prudence† (*also frm*) ; (*US fig*) **she was left twisting** or **swinging in the ~** on l'a laissée dans le pétrin* → **ill, north, sail**

b (= *breath*) souffle *m* ; **he has still plenty of ~** il a encore du souffle ; **he had lost his ~** il avait perdu le souffle or perdu haleine ; **to knock the ~ out of sb** [*blow*] couper la respiration or le souffle à qn ; [*fighter*] mettre qn hors d'haleine ; [*fall, exertion*] essouffler qn, mettre qn hors d'haleine ; (*lit*) **to get one's ~ back** reprendre (son) souffle, reprendre haleine ; (*fig*) **give me time to get my ~ back!** laisse-moi le temps de souffler or de me retourner ! ; (*Brit*) **to put the ~ up sb*** flanquer la frousse* à qn ; (*Brit*) **to get/have the ~ up*** avoir la frousse* (**about** à propos de) → **second¹, sound²**

c (*NonC: Med* = *flatulence*) gaz *mpl* ; **the baby has got ~** le bébé a des gaz ; **to break ~** lâcher un vent ; **to bring up ~** avoir un renvoi

d (*Mus*) **the instruments** *mpl* à vent

2 VT **a** **to ~ sb** [*blow etc*] couper la respiration or le souffle à qn ; [*fighter*] mettre qn hors d'haleine ; [*fall, exertion*] essouffler qn, mettre qn hors d'haleine ; **he was ~ed by the blow ◊ the blow ~ed him** le coup lui a coupé le souffle or la respiration ; **he was quite ~ed by the climb** l'ascension l'avait essoufflé or mis hors d'haleine ; **I'm only ~ed** j'ai la respiration coupée, c'est tout

b [+ *horse*] laisser souffler **c** (*Hunting* = *scent*) avoir vent de **d** **to ~ a baby** faire faire son rot* or son renvoi à un bébé

3 COMP [*erosion etc*] éolien ► **wind-bells** NPL = **wind-chimes** ► **wind-borne** ADJ [*seeds, pollen*] transporté or porté par le vent ► **wind-chill (factor)** N (facteur *m* de) refroidissement *m* dû au vent ; **a ~-chill factor of 10°** une baisse de 10° due au vent ► **wind-chimes** NPL carillon *m* éolien ► **wind deflector** N (*Aut*) déflecteur *m* ► **wind farm** N éoliennes *fpl*, parc *m* d'éoliennes ► **wind gauge** N anémomètre *m* ► **wind generator** N aérogénérateur *m* ► **wind instrument** N (*Mus*) instrument *m* à vent ► **wind machine** N (*Theat, Cine*) machine *f* à vent ► **wind power** N énergie *f* éolienne ► **wind tunnel** N (*Phys*) tunnel *m* aérodynamique ; (*fig*) **there was a ~ tunnel between the two tower blocks** il y avait un fort courant d'air entre les deux tours

wind² [waɪnd] (*pret, ptp* **winded** or **wound**) VT **to ~ the horn** sonner du cor ; (*Hunting*) sonner de la trompe

wind³ [waɪnd] (*vb*: *pret, ptp* **wound**) **1** N **a** (= *bend: in river etc*) tournant *m*, coude *m* **b** (= *action of winding*) **to give one's watch a ~** remonter sa montre ; **give the handle another ~** or **two** donne un ou deux tours de manivelle de plus

2 VT **a** (= *roll*) [+ *thread, rope etc*] enrouler (**on** sur, **round** autour de) ; (= *wrap*) envelopper (**in** dans) ; **to ~ wool (into a ball)** enrouler de la laine (pour en faire une pelote) ; **~ this round your head** enroule-toi ça autour de la tête ; **with the rope wound tightly round his waist** la corde bien enroulée autour de la taille, la corde lui ceignant étroitement la taille ; **she wound a shawl round the baby ◊ she wound the baby in a shawl** elle a enveloppé le bébé dans un châle ; **to ~ one's arms round sb** enlacer qn ; **the snake/rope wound itself round a branch** le serpent/la corde s'est enroulé(e) autour d'une branche ; **he slowly wound his way home** il s'en revint lentement chez lui, il prit lentement le chemin du retour → **3**

b [+ *clock, watch, toy*] remonter ; [+ *handle*] donner un (or des) tour(s) de

3 VI (*also* **~ its way**) **to ~ along** [*river, path*] serpenter, faire des zigzags ; **the road ~s through the valley** la route serpente à travers la vallée, la route traverse la vallée en serpentant ; **the procession wound through the town** la procession a serpenté à travers la ville ; **the line of cars wound slowly up the hill** la file de voitures a lentement gravi la colline en serpentant ; **to ~ up/down** [*path etc*] monter/descendre en serpentant or en zigzags ; [*stairs, steps*] monter/descendre en tournant ; **to ~ round sth** [*snake, ivy etc*] s'enrouler autour de qch

►**wind back** VT SEP [+ *tape, film*] rembobiner

►**wind down** **1** VI **a** → **wind³ 3 b** (* = *relax*) se détendre, se relaxer **c** (*fig*) **to be ~ing down** [*event*] tirer à sa fin ; [*energy, enthusiasm, interest*] diminuer, être en perte de vitesse **2** VT SEP **a** (*on rope/winch etc*) faire descendre (avec une corde/avec un treuil etc) **b** [+ *car window*] baisser **c** (*fig*) [+ *department, service etc*] réduire progressivement (en vue d'un démantèlement éventuel)

►**wind forward** VT SEP = **wind on**

►**wind off** VT SEP dérouler, dévider

►**wind on** VT SEP enrouler

►**wind up** **1** VI **a** → **wind³ 3 b** [*meeting, discussion*] se terminer, finir (**with** par) ; (*in debate*) **he wound up for the Government** c'est lui qui a résumé la position du gouvernement dans le discours de clôture ; (*Jur*) **Mr Paul Herbert wound up for the prosecution/defence** M. Paul Herbert a conclu pour la partie civile/pour la défense

c * they wound up stranded in Rotterdam ils ont fini *or* ils se sont retrouvés bloqués à Rotterdam ; **he wound up as a doctor** il a fini médecin ; **he wound up with a fractured skull** il s'est retrouvé avec une fracture du crâne

2 VT SEP **a** [+ *object on rope/winch etc*] faire monter (au bout d'une corde/avec un treuil *etc*) ; (*fig = end*) [+ *meeting, speech*] terminer, clore (**with** par) ; (*Comm*) [+ *business*] liquider ; **to ~ up one's affairs** liquider ses affaires ; (*Banking*) **to ~ up an account** clôturer un compte

b [+ *car window*] monter, fermer

c [+ *watch etc*] remonter ; (*fig*) **to be wound up*** (= *tense*) être tendu *or* crispé (**about** à propos de) ; **it gets me all wound up (inside)*** ça me retourne*

d (*Brit = tease person*) faire marcher*

3 ~ing-up N → **winding**

4 ~-up* N (*Brit = practical joke*) blague *f*, bobard* *m*

windbag* ['wɪndbæg] N (*fig pej*) moulin *m* à paroles

windblown ['wɪndbləʊn] ADJ [*person, hair*] ébouriffé par le vent ; [*tree*] fouetté par le vent

windbreak ['wɪndbreɪk] N (= *tree, fence etc*) brise-vent *m* ; (*for camping etc*) pare-vent *m inv*

Windbreaker® ['wɪndbreɪkər] N = **windcheater**

windburn ['wɪndbɜːn] N (*Med*) brûlure *f* épidermique (due au vent)

windcheater ['wɪndtʃiːtər] N (*Brit*) anorak *m* léger, coupe-vent *m inv*

winder ['waɪndər] N **a** [*of watch etc*] remontoir *m* **b** (*for car windows*) lève-glace *m*, lève-vitre *m* **c** (*for thread etc*) dévidoir *m* ; (= *person*) dévideur *m*, -euse *f*

windfall ['wɪndfɔːl] **1** N (*lit*) fruit(s) *m(pl)* tombé(s) (*sous l'effet du vent*) ; (*fig*) aubaine *f*, manne *f* (tombée du ciel) **2** COMP ► **windfall profit** N bénéfices *mpl* exceptionnels ► **windfall tax** N taxe *f* exceptionnelle sur les bénéfices (*des entreprises privatisées*)

windflower ['wɪndflaʊər] N anémone *f* des bois

winding ['waɪndɪŋ] **1** ADJ [*road, path*] sinueux, tortueux ; [*river*] sinueux, qui serpente ; [*stairs, staircase*] tournant **2** N **a** (*NonC*) [*of thread, rope*] enroulement *m* ; [*of clock, watch, toy*] remontage *m* ; (*onto bobbin*) bobinage *m* **b** ~(**s**) [*of road*] zigzags *mpl* ; [*of river*] méandres *mpl* **3** COMP ► **winding-sheet**† N linceul *m* ► **winding-up** [*of meeting, account*] clôture *f* ; [*of business, one's affairs*] liquidation *f* ; (*Jur, Fin*) ~-up **arrangements** concordat *m*

windjammer ['wɪndʒæmər] N **a** (*Naut*) grand voilier *m* (de la marine marchande) **b** (*Brit = windcheater*) anorak *m* léger, coupe-vent *m inv*

windlass ['wɪndləs] N guindeau *m*, treuil *m*

windless ['wɪndlɪs] ADJ [*day*] sans vent ; [*air*] immobile

windmill ['wɪndmɪl] N moulin *m* à vent ; (*fig*) **to tilt at** *or* **fight ~s** se battre contre des moulins à vent ; (*Volleyball*) ~ **service** service *m* balancier

window ['wɪndəʊ] **1** N **a** (*gen, also Comput*) fenêtre *f* ; (*in car, train*) vitre *f*, glace *f* ; (*also ~ pane*) vitre *f*, carreau *m* ; (*stained-glass*) vitrail *m* ; (*larger*) verrière *f* ; [*of shop*] vitrine *f*, devanture *f* ; (*more modest*) étalage *m* ; [*of café etc*] vitrine *f* ; (*in post office, ticket office etc*) guichet *m* ; (*in envelope*) fenêtre *f* ; **I saw her at the ~** je l'ai vue à la fenêtre ; **don't lean out of the ~** ne te penche pas par la fenêtre ; (*in train, car etc*) ne te penche pas en dehors ; **to look/ throw** *etc* **out of the ~** regarder/jeter *etc* par la fenêtre ; (*in car etc*) regarder/jeter *etc* dehors ; (*fig*) **to go** *or* **fly** *or* **disappear out of the ~** s'évanouir, se volatiliser ; **well, there's another**

plan out the ~!* eh bien voilà encore un projet de fichu* *or* qui tombe à l'eau ; **the ~s look out onto fields** les fenêtres donnent sur *or* ont vue sur des champs ; **to break a ~** casser une vitre *or* un carreau ; **to clean the ~s** nettoyer *or* laver les vitres *or* les carreaux ; **to put sth in the ~** mettre qch en vitrine *or* à la devanture ; (*Comm*) **I saw it in the ~** j'ai vu ça à l'étalage *or* à la devanture *or* en vitrine ; (*Comm*) **the ~s are lovely at Christmas time** les vitrines sont très belles au moment de Noël ; (*Comm*) **in the front of the ~** sur le devant de la vitrine ; **there is perhaps a ~ of opportunity to change ...** nous avons peut-être maintenant la possibilité de changer ...

b (*Space: also* **launch ~**) fenêtre *f* *or* créneau *m* de lancement

2 COMP ► **window box** N jardinière *f* ► **window cleaner** N (= *person*) laveur *m*, -euse *f* de vitres *or* de carreaux ; (= *substance*) produit *m* à nettoyer les vitres *or* les carreaux ► **window-cleaning** N **to do the ~-cleaning** faire les vitres *or* carreaux ► **window display** N devanture *f*, vitrine *f* (de magasin) ► **window dresser** N (*Comm*) étalagiste *mf* ► **window dressing** N (*Comm*) composition *f* d'étalage ; **she is learning ~ dressing** elle fait des études d'étalagiste ; (*fig pej*) **it's just ~ dressing** ce n'est qu'une façade ► **window envelope** N enveloppe *f* à fenêtre ► **window frame** N châssis *m* (de fenêtre) ► **window glass** N (*NonC*) verre *m* (*utilisé pour les vitres*) ► **window ledge** N = **window-sill** ► **window pane** N vitre *f*, carreau *m* ► **window seat** N (*in room*) banquette *f* (située sous la fenêtre) ; (*in vehicle*) place *f* côté fenêtre ► **window shade** N (*US*) store *m* ► **window-shopper** N **she's a great ~-shopper** elle adore faire du lèche-vitrines ► **window-shopping** N lèche-vitrines *m* ; **to go ~-shopping** faire du lèche-vitrines ► **window winder** N (*Aut*) lève-glace *m*, lève-vitre *m*

windowsill ['wɪndəʊsɪl] N (*inside*) appui *m* de fenêtre ; (*outside*) rebord *m* de fenêtre

windpipe ['wɪndpaɪp] N (*Anat*) trachée *f*

windproof ['wɪndpruːf] **1** ADJ protégeant du vent, qui ne laisse pas passer le vent **2** VT protéger du *or* contre le vent

windscreen ['wɪndskriːn] (*esp Brit Aut*) **1** N pare-brise *m inv* **2** COMP ► **windscreen washer** N lave-glace *m* ► **windscreen wiper** N essuie-glace *m*

windshield ['wɪndʃiːld] N (*US*) = **windscreen**

windsleeve ['wɪndsliːv], **windsock** ['wɪndsɒk] N manche *f* à air

windstorm ['wɪndstɔːm] N vent *m* de tempête

windsurf ['wɪndsɜːf] VI (*also* **go ~ing**) faire de la planche à voile

windsurfer ['wɪndsɜːfər] N **a** (= *person*) (véli)planchiste *mf* **b** (= *board*) planche *f* à voile

windsurfing ['wɪndsɜːfɪŋ] N planche *f* à voile (*sport*)

windswept ['wɪndswept] ADJ venteux, battu par les vents, balayé par le(s) vent(s)

windward ['wɪndwəd] **1** ADJ qui est au vent *or* contre le vent, qui est du côté du vent ; (*Geog*) **the Windward Islands** les îles *fpl* du Vent **2** ADV au vent **3** N côté *m* du vent ; **to look to ~** regarder dans la direction du vent ; **to get to ~ of sth** se mettre contre le vent par rapport à qch

windy ['wɪndɪ] **1** ADJ **a** (= *blustery*) [*day*] de vent ; **it's** *or* **the weather's ~ today** il y a du vent aujourd'hui ; **wet and ~ weather** la pluie et le vent **b** (= *windswept*) [*place*] balayé par les vents, venteux **c** (* = *pompous*) [*person*] ronflant ; [*phrases, speech*] ronflant, pompeux ; **a ~ old bore** un vieux raseur sentencieux **d** (*Brit*†* = *scared*) **to be ~ (about sth)** avoir la frousse* (à propos de qch) ; **to get ~ (about sth)** paniquer (à propos

de qch) **2** COMP ► **the Windy City** N (*US*) Chicago → CITY NICKNAMES

wine [waɪn] **1** N vin *m* ; **elderberry ~** vin *m* de sureau

2 VT **to ~ and dine sb** emmener qn faire un dîner bien arrosé

3 VI **to ~ and dine** faire un dîner bien arrosé

4 COMP [*bottle, cellar*] à vin ; [*colour*] lie de vin *inv* *or* lie-de-vin *inv* ► **wine bar** N bar *m* à vin(s) ► **wine-bottling** N mise *f* en bouteilles (du vin) ► **wine box** N cubitainer® *m* ► **wine cask** N fût *m*, tonneau *m* (à vin) ► **wine-coloured** ADJ lie de vin *inv*, lie-de-vin *inv* ► **wine cooler** N (= *device*) rafraîchisseur *m* (à vin), seau *m* à rafraîchir ; (= *drink*) boisson à base de vin, de jus de fruit et d'eau gazeuse ► **wine grower** N viticulteur *m*, -trice *f* (vigneron(ne) *m(f)*) ► **wine growing** N viticulture *f*, culture *f* de la vigne ♦ ADJ [*district, industry*] vinicole, viticole ► **wine gum** N (*Brit*) boule *f* de gomme ► **wine list** N carte *f* des vins ► **wine merchant** N (*Brit*) marchand(e) *m(f)* de vin ; (*on larger scale*) négociant(e) *m(f)* en vins ► **wine press** N pressoir *m* (à vin) ► **wine rack** N casier *m* à bouteilles (de vin) ► **wine taster** N (= *person*) dégustateur *m*, -trice *f* (de vins) ; (= *cup*) tâte-vin *m inv*, taste-vin *m inv* ► **wine tasting** N dégustation *f* (de vins) ► **wine vinegar** N vinaigre *m* de vin ► **wine waiter** N sommelier *m*

winebibber ['waɪnbɪbər] N grand(e) buveur *m*, -euse *f* (de vin), bon(ne) buveur *m*, -euse *f*

wined up* ['waɪndʌp] ADJ (*US*) bourré‡, noir*

wineglass ['waɪnglɑːs] N verre *m* à vin

winery ['waɪnərɪ] N (*US*) établissement *m* vinicole

wineshop ['waɪnʃɒp] N boutique *f* du marchand de vin

wineskin ['waɪnskɪn] N outre *f* à vin

wing [wɪŋ] **1** N **a** (*gen, Zool: also of plane*) aile *f* ; **to be on the ~** être en vol, voler ; **to shoot a bird on the ~** tirer un oiseau au vol ; **to take ~** [*bird*] prendre son vol, s'envoler ; (*fig, liter*) **his heart took ~** son cœur s'emplit de joie ; **to take sb under one's ~** prendre qn sous son aile ; **to be under sb's ~** être sous l'aile (*protectrice*) de qn ; **on the ~s of fantasy** sur les ailes de l'imagination ; **fear lent** *or* **gave him ~s** la peur lui donnait des ailes ; **on a ~ and a prayer** à la grâce de Dieu → clip², spread

b (*Pol*) aile *f* ; **on the left/right ~ of the party** sur l'aile gauche/droite du parti

c (*Sport = person*) ailier *m*, aile *f* ; ~ (**three-quarter**) trois-quarts aile *f* ; **left/right ~** ailier *m* gauche/droit ; **he plays (on the) left ~** il est ailier gauche

d (*Brit: of car*) aile *f* ; [*of armchair*] oreille *f*, oreillard *m*

e [*Aviat = insignia*] ~**s** insigne *m* (de pilote) ; **to earn** *or* **win** *or* **get one's ~s** devenir pilote (*dans l'armée de l'air*)

f [*of building, mansion*] aile *f*

g [*of organization etc*] aile *f* ; **the political ~ of the IRA** l'aile *f* politique de l'IRA

2 **the wings** NPL (*Theat*) les coulisses *fpl*, la coulisse ; **to stand** *or* **stay in the ~s** (*Theat*) se tenir dans les coulisses ; (*fig*) rester dans la (*or* les) coulisse(s) ; (*fig*) **to wait in the ~s for sb to do sth** attendre dans la *or* les coulisse(s) que qn fasse qch

3 VT **a** (= *wound*) [+ *bird*] blesser *or* toucher (à l'aile) ; [+ *person*] blesser au bras (*or* à la jambe *etc*)

b (*liter*) **to ~ an arrow at sth** darder une flèche en direction de qch ; **to ~ one's way** = **to wing** ; → **4**

c [*actor, speaker etc*] **to ~ it*** improviser

4 VI (= *wing one's way*) voler ; **they ~ed over the sea** ils ont survolé la mer

5 COMP ► **wing case** N (*Zool*) élytre *m* ► **wing chair** N bergère *f* à oreilles ► **wing collar** N col *m* cassé ► **wing commander** N

(Aviat) lieutenant-colonel m (de l'armée de l'air) ► **wing flap** N (Aviat) aileron m ► **wing-footed** ADJ (liter) aux pieds ailés ► **wing-forward** N (Rugby) ailier m ► **wing mirror** N (Brit Aut) rétroviseur m latéral ► **wing nut** N papillon m, écrou m à ailettes ► **wing three-quarter** N (Rugby) trois-quarts aile m ► **wing tip** N extrémité f de l'aile

wingback ['wɪŋˌbæk] N (Sport) ailier m offensif

wingding: ['wɪŋˌdɪŋ] N (US = party) fête f, boum* f

winge* ['wɪndʒ] VI = **whinge**

winged [wɪŋd] ADJ [creature, goddess, statue] ailé; **Mercury, the ~ messenger of the gods** Mercure, le messager des dieux aux pieds ailés; **the Winged Victory of Samothrace** la Victoire de Samothrace

-winged ADJ (in compounds) **white-winged** aux ailes blanches

winger ['wɪŋə'] N (Sport) ailier m; (Pol) **left-/right-~** sympathisant(e) m(f) de gauche/droite, homme m (or femme f) de gauche/droite

wingless ['wɪŋlɪs] ADJ sans ailes; [insect] aptère

wingspan ['wɪŋspæn], **wingspread** ['wɪŋspred] N envergure f

wink [wɪŋk] [1] N clin m d'œil; (= blink) clignement m; **to give sb a ~** faire un clin d'œil à qn; **with a ~** en clignant de l'œil; **in a ~** ◊ (as) **quick as a** ◊ **in the ~ of an eye** en un clin d'œil; **I didn't get a ~ of sleep*** je n'ai pas fermé l'œil (de la nuit) → **forty, sleep, tip²** [2] VI [person] faire un clin d'œil (**to, at** à); (= blink) cligner des yeux; [star, light] clignoter; (fig) **to ~ at sth** fermer les yeux sur qch; **they were willing to ~ at corruption within the prison service** ils étaient prêts à fermer les yeux sur la corruption dans le service pénitentiaire [3] VT **to ~ one's eye** faire un clin d'œil (**at sb** à qn); **to ~ a tear back** or **away** cligner de l'œil pour chasser une larme

winker ['wɪŋkə'] N (Brit Aut) clignotant m

winking ['wɪŋkɪŋ] [1] ADJ [light, signal] clignotant [2] N clins mpl d'œil; (= blinking) clignements mpl d'yeux; **it was as easy as ~*** c'était simple comme bonjour

winkle ['wɪŋkl] [1] N (Brit) bigorneau m [2] VT **to ~ sth out of sth/sb** extirper qch de qch/qn [3] COMP ► **winkle pickers*** NPL (Brit = shoes) chaussures fpl pointues

winnable ['wɪnəbl] ADJ gagnable

winner ['wɪnə'] N [a] (= victor: in fight, argument) vainqueur m; (Sport) gagnant(e) m(f), vainqueur m; (in competitions etc) lauréat(e) m(f), gagnant(e) m(f); (horse/car/essay etc) (cheval m/voiture f/composition f etc) gagnant(e) m(f); (Sport = winning goal) but m de la victoire; (= winning shot) coup m de la victoire; **to be the ~** gagner; (Tennis) **that ball was a ~** cette balle était imparable*; **his latest CD/show is a ~*** son dernier CD/spectacle va faire un malheur*; (fig) **he's a ~!*** il est sensass!*†; **I think he's on to a ~** (= will win) je crois qu'il va gagner; (= has chosen winner) je crois qu'il a tiré le bon numéro → **pick** [b] (gen pl = beneficiary) gagnant(e) m(f) (fig); **the ~s will be the shareholders** ce sont les actionnaires qui seront les gagnants

winning ['wɪnɪŋ] [1] ADJ [a] [person, dog, car etc] gagnant; [blow, stroke, shot etc] décisif, de la victoire; **the ~ goal came in the last five minutes** le but de la victoire a été marqué dans les cinq dernières minutes [b] (= captivating) [person] charmant, adorable; [smile, manner] charmeur, engageant; **the child has ~ ways** ◊ **the child has a ~ way with him** cet enfant a une grâce irrésistible [2] **winnings** NPL (Betting etc) gains mpl [3] COMP ► **winning post** N poteau m d'arrivée

winningly ['wɪnɪŋlɪ] ADV d'une manière charmeuse, d'un air engageant

Winnipeg ['wɪnɪpeg] N Winnipeg

winnow ['wɪnəʊ] VT [+ grain] vanner; (liter) **to ~ truth from falsehood** démêler le vrai du faux

winnower ['wɪnəʊə'] N (= person) vanneur m, -euse f; (= machine) tarare m

wino: ['waɪnəʊ] N poivrot* m, ivrogne mf

winsome ['wɪnsəm] ADJ [person] avenant; [smile] gracieux, charmant; [charm] délicieux

winsomely ['wɪnsəmlɪ] ADV d'une manière séduisante, d'un air engageant

winsomeness ['wɪnsəmnɪs] N (NonC) charme m, séduction f

winter ['wɪntə'] [1] N hiver m; **in ~** en hiver; **in the ~ of 1996** pendant l'hiver de 1996; **"A Winter's Tale"** « Conte d'hiver » [2] VI hiverner, passer l'hiver [3] VT [+ animals] hiverner [4] COMP [weather, day, residence] d'hiver, hivernal; [activities, temperatures] hivernal ► **winter clothes** NPL vêtements mpl d'hiver ► **winter depression** N spleen m hivernal ► **winter holidays** NPL vacances fpl d'hiver ► **Winter Olympics** NPL (Sport) Jeux mpl olympiques d'hiver ► **winter resident** N (= person) hivernant(e) m(f) ► **the winter season** N la saison d'hiver ► **winter sleep** N sommeil m hibernal, hibernation f ► **winter sports** NPL sports mpl d'hiver

wintergreen ['wɪntəˌgriːn] N (Bot) gaulthérie f; **oil of ~** essence f de wintergreen

winterize ['wɪntəraɪz] VT (US) préparer pour l'hiver

winterkill ['wɪntəˌkɪl] (US) [1] VT [+ plant] tuer par le gel [2] VI être tué par le gel

wintertime ['wɪntəˌtaɪm] [1] N hiver m; **in (the) ~** en hiver [2] COMP [staff, visitors, food etc] en hiver

wintry ['wɪntrɪ] ADJ [a] (Met) [weather, day, sky, sun] d'hiver; **in ~ conditions** par temps d'hiver; **~ conditions on the roads** difficultés fpl de circulation dues à l'hiver [b] (= unfriendly) [person, smile] glacial (**with sb** avec qn)

wipe [waɪp] [1] N coup m de torchon (or d'éponge etc); **to give sth a ~** donner un coup de torchon (or d'éponge etc) à qch [2] VT [a] [+ table, dishes, floor] essuyer (**with** avec); **to ~ one's hands/face/eyes** s'essuyer les mains/le visage/les yeux (**on** sur, **with** avec); **to ~ one's feet** (with towel, on mat) s'essuyer les pieds; **to ~ one's nose** se moucher; **to ~ one's bottom** s'essuyer; **he ~d the glass dry** il a essuyé le verre; **to ~ the blackboard** effacer or essuyer or nettoyer le tableau; (fig) **to ~ the slate clean** passer l'éponge, tout effacer (fig); **to ~ the floor with sb*** réduire qn en miettes* [b] (Comput, TV, Recording etc) [+ tape, disk, video] effacer; **to ~ sth from a tape** etc effacer qch sur une bande etc [3] COMP ► **wipe-out** N (= destruction) destruction f, annihilation f; (Windsurfing etc) chute f, gamelle* f

► **wipe at** VT FUS essuyer; **to ~ at one's eyes** s'essuyer les yeux

► **wipe away** VT SEP [+ tears] essuyer; [+ marks] effacer

► **wipe down** VT SEP [+ surface, wall etc] essuyer

► **wipe off** VT SEP effacer; **that will ~ the smile** or **grin off her face!*** après ça on va voir si elle a toujours le sourire!

► **wipe out** [1] VT SEP [a] [+ container] bien essuyer; [+ writing, error etc] effacer; (fig) [+ insult] laver; [+ debt] amortir; [+ the past, memory] oublier, effacer; **to ~ out an old score** régler une vieille dette (fig) [b] (= annihilate) [+ town, people, army] anéantir [c] (= opposing team) écraser; **to ~ sb out*** [person] régler son compte à qn; [event, news] anéantir qn [2] **~-out** N → **wipe**

► **wipe up** [1] VI essuyer la vaisselle [2] VT SEP essuyer

wiper ['waɪpə'] [1] N (= cloth) torchon m; (Aut) essuie-glace m inv [2] COMP ► **wiper blade** N (Aut) balai m d'essuie-glace

wire [waɪə'] [1] N [a] (NonC = substance) fil m (métallique or de fer); (Elec) fil m (électrique); (= piece of wire) fil m; (= snare) collet m, lacet m; (also ~ **fence**) grillage m, treillis m métallique; **to pull ~s for sb** exercer son influence pour aider qn, pistonner qn; **they got their ~s crossed*** il y a eu malentendu, ils se sont mal compris; (US) **to work** etc **down to the ~*** travailler etc jusqu'au bout or jusqu'au dernier moment; (esp US fig: of competition) **to go down to the ~*** entrer dans sa phase finale; (US fig) **to come in** or **get in (just) under the ~*** arriver de justesse → **barbed, live²** [b] (US = telegram) télégramme m [c] (Police = hidden microphone) micro m caché [2] **wires*** NPL (US = spectacles) lunettes fpl à monture d'acier [3] VT [a] (also ~ **up**) [+ opening, fence] grillager; [+ flowers, beads] monter sur fil de fer; (Elec) [+ house] faire l'installation électrique de; [+ circuit] installer; **to ~ sth to sth** relier or rattacher qch à qch (avec du fil de fer); (Elec) brancher qch sur qch, relier qch à qch; **to ~ a room (up) for sound** sonoriser une pièce; **he was ~d for sound:** (= wearing hidden microphone) il avait un micro sur lui; **it's all ~d (up) for television** l'antenne (réceptrice or émettrice) de télévision est déjà installée; **to be ~d** (for cable TV) être raccordé; (= bugged) être équipé de micros cachés; (US fig) **~d-up:** (= tense) surexcité, tendu [b] (US = telegraph) télégraphier (**to** à) [4] VI (US) télégraphier [5] COMP [object, device] de or en fil de fer ► **wire brush** N brosse f métallique ► **wire-cutters** NPL cisailles fpl, pinces fpl coupantes ► **wire-drawer, wire-drawing machine** N étireuse f ► **wire gauge** N calibre m (pour fils métalliques) ► **wire gauze** N toile f métallique ► **wire glass** N (US) verre m armé ► **wire-haired terrier** N terrier m à poils durs ► **wire mesh** N (NonC) treillis m métallique, grillage m ► **wire netting** N = **wire mesh** ► **wire-puller*** N (US) **he's a ~-puller** il n'hésite pas à se faire pistonner* or à faire jouer le piston* ► **wire-pulling*** N (US) le piston*; **to do some ~-pulling for sb** pistonner* qn ► **wire rope** N câble m métallique ► **wire service** N (US Press) agence f de presse (utilisant des téléscripteurs) ► **wire wool** N (Brit) paille f de fer

► **wire together** VT SEP [+ objects] attacher (avec du fil de fer)

► **wire up** VT SEP = **wire 3a**

wireless † ['waɪəlɪs] (esp Brit) [1] N télégraphie f sans fil, TSF† f; **to send a message by ~** envoyer un sans-fil; **they were communicating by ~** ils communiquaient par sans-fil; **on the ~** à la TSF†; **to listen to the ~** écouter la TSF† [2] COMP [station, programme] radiophonique ► **wireless message** N radiogramme m, radio m, sans-fil m ► **wireless operator** N radiotélégraphiste mf, radio m ► **wireless room** N cabine f radio inv ► **wireless set** N poste m de TSF† ► **wireless telegraph, wireless telegraphy** N télégraphie f sans fil, TSF† f, radiotélégraphie f ► **wireless telephone** N téléphone m sans fil ► **wireless telephony** N téléphonie f sans fil, radiotéléphonie f

wireman ['waɪəmən] N (pl **-men**) (US) câbleur m

wiretap ['waɪətæp] [1] VI mettre un (or des) téléphone(s) sur écoute [2] VT mettre sur écoute [3] N écoute f téléphonique

wiretapping ['waɪətæpɪŋ] N écoutes fpl téléphoniques

wireworks ['waɪəwɜːks] N (NonC) tréfilerie f

wiring ['waɪərɪŋ] N (NonC: Elec) (in building) installation f (électrique); [of appliance] circuit m électrique; **to have the ~ redone** faire refaire l'installation électrique (**in** de)

wiry ['waɪərɪ] ADJ [a] (= *thin*) [*person*] au physique maigre et nerveux; [*body*] maigre et nerveux [b] (= *coarse*) [*hair, grass*] rêche

Wis ABBR = **Wisconsin**

Wisconsin [wɪs'kɒnsɪn] N le Wisconsin; **in ~** dans le Wisconsin

wisdom ['wɪzdəm] [1] N (NonC) [*of person*] sagesse *f*; [*of action, remark*] prudence *f* [2] COMP ► **wisdom tooth** N dent *f* de sagesse

▼**wise**[1] ['waɪz] [1] ADJ [a] (= *prudent*) [*person, words, decision*] sage; [*action, choice, investment*] judicieux; **a ~ man** un sage; **a ~ move** une sage décision; **to grow ~r with age** s'assagir avec l'âge or en vieillissant; **to be ~ after the event** avoir raison après coup; **how ~ of you!** vous avez eu bien raison!; **it wasn't very ~ (of you) to tell him that** ce n'était pas très judicieux (de lui dire ça) or de lui dire ça; **it would be ~ to accept** il serait judicieux d'accepter; **you'd be ~ to accept** il serait judicieux que vous acceptiez (*subj*); **he was ~ enough to refuse** il a eu la sagesse de refuser; **the ~st thing to do is to ignore him** le plus judicieux or sage est de l'ignorer → **word**
[b] (* = *aware, informed*) **to get ~** piger*; **to be** or **get ~ to sb** voir clair dans le jeu de qn; **to be** or **get ~ to sth** piger* qch; **I was fooled once, but then I got ~** j'ai été échaudé une fois, mais j'ai retenu la leçon; **get ~!** réveille-toi!; **I'm ~ to that one now** j'ai compris le truc*; **to put sb ~ (to sth)** ouvrir les yeux de qn (sur qch), mettre qn au courant (de qch); **I'm none the ~r** ◊ **I'm no ~r** (= *don't understand*) ça ne m'avance pas beaucoup, je ne suis pas plus avancé; **nobody will be any the ~r** (= *won't find out*) personne n'en saura rien
[2] COMP ► **wise guy*** N petit malin* *m* ► **the Wise Men** NPL (*Bible: also* **the Three Wise Men**) les Rois *mpl* mages

►**wise up*** [1] VI **to ~ up (to sth)** réaliser* (qch); **people finally seem to be wising up (to what is going on)** les gens semblent enfin réaliser* (ce qui se passe); **~ up!** réveille-toi! [2] VT SEP **to ~ sb up** ouvrir les yeux de qn (**to**, **about** de); **to get ~d up about sth** être mis au parfum* de qch

wise[2] [waɪz] N (*frm*) **in no ~** aucunement, en aucune façon or manière; **in this ~** ainsi, de cette façon or manière

...wise [waɪz] ADV (*in compounds*) [a] (*: specifying point of view*) question*, côté*; **healthwise he's fine but moneywise things aren't too good** question* or côté* santé ça va, mais question* or côté* argent ça pourrait aller mieux [b] (*specifying direction, position*) à la manière de, dans le sens de *etc* → **clockwise, lengthways**

wiseacre ['waɪzeɪkəʳ] N (*pej*) puits *m* de science (*iro*)

wisecrack ['waɪzkræk] [1] N vanne* *f* [2] VI balancer or sortir une (or des) vanne(s)*; **"need any help?" he ~ed** «vous avez besoin de mes services?» ironisa-t-il

wisely ['waɪzlɪ] ADV [a] (= *prudently*) [*use, spend*] avec sagesse; [*behave*] judicieusement; **you have chosen ~** votre choix a été sage or judicieux; **~, he turned down their first offer** il a eu la sagesse de refuser leur première proposition [b] (= *sagely*) [*nod, say etc*] d'un air entendu

▼**wish** [wɪʃ] [1] VT [a] (= *desire*) souhaiter, désirer; **I ~ that you ...** (+ *cond*) je voudrais que vous ...; **I ~ to be told when he comes** je souhaite or désire être informé de sa venue; **I ~ to be alone** je souhaite or désire or voudrais être seul; **he did not ~ it** il ne le souhaitait or désirait pas; **what do you ~ him to do?** que voudriez-tu or souhaites-tu or désires-tu qu'il fasse?; **I ~ I'd gone with you** j'aurais bien voulu vous accompagner, je regrette de ne pas vous avoir accompagné; **I ~ you had left with him** j'aurais bien voulu que tu sois parti avec lui, je regrette que tu ne sois

pas parti avec lui; **I ~ I hadn't said that** je regrette d'avoir dit cela; **I ~ you'd stop talking!** tu ne peux donc pas te taire!; **I only ~ I'd known about that before!** si seulement j'avais su ça avant!, comme je regrette de n'avoir pas su ça avant!; **I ~ I could!** si seulement je pouvais!; **I ~ to heaven* he hadn't done it!** si seulement il ne l'avait pas fait!; **I ~ it weren't so** si seulement il pouvait ne pas en être ainsi
[b] (= *desire for sb else*) souhaiter, vouloir; (= *bid*) souhaiter; **he doesn't ~ her any ill** or **harm** il ne lui veut aucun mal; **I ~ you well** or **I ~ you (good) luck in what you're trying to do** je vous souhaite de réussir dans ce que vous voulez faire; (*iro*) **I ~ you well of it!** ◊ **I ~ you luck of it!** je te souhaite bien du plaisir!; **he ~ed us (good) luck as we left** il nous a souhaité bonne chance au moment de partir; **~ me luck!** souhaite-moi bonne chance!; **to ~ sb good morning** dire bonjour à qn, souhaiter or donner le bonjour à qn† (*also hum*); **to ~ sb good-bye** dire au revoir à qn; **to ~ sb a happy birthday** souhaiter bon anniversaire à qn; **I ~ you every happiness** je vous souhaite d'être très heureux!; **he ~ed us every happiness** il nous a exprimé ses souhaits de bonheur
[c] (* *fig*) **the bike was ~ed on (to) me** je n'ai pas pu faire autrement que d'accepter le vélo; **the job was ~ed on (to) me** c'est un boulot qu'on m'a collé*; **I wouldn't ~ that on anybody** or **my worst enemy** c'est quelque chose que je ne souhaiterais pas à mon pire ennemi; **I wouldn't ~ him on anybody** je ne souhaiterais sa présence à personne; **I got her kids ~ed on (to) me for the holiday** elle m'a laissé ses gosses sur les bras pendant les vacances*
[2] VI faire un vœu; **you must ~ as you eat it** il faut faire un vœu en le mangeant; **to ~ for sth** souhaiter qch; **I ~ed for that to happen** j'ai souhaité que cela se produise; **she's got everything she could ~ for** elle a tout ce qu'elle peut désirer; **what more could you ~ for?** que pourrais-tu souhaiter de plus?; **it's not everything you could ~ for** ce n'est pas l'idéal
[3] N [a] (= *desire, will*) désir *m*; **what is your ~?** que désirez-vous?; (*liter or hum*) **your ~ is my command** vos désirs sont pour moi des ordres; **it has always been my ~ to do that** j'ai toujours désiré faire or eu envie de faire cela; **he had no great ~ to go** il n'avait pas grande envie d'y aller; **to go against sb's ~es** contrecarrer les désirs de qn; **he did it against my ~es** il l'a fait contre mon gré
[b] (= *specific desire*) vœu *m*, souhait *m*; **to make a ~** faire un vœu; **the fairy granted him three ~es** la fée lui accorda trois souhaits; **his ~ came true** ◊ **his ~ was granted** ◊ **he got his ~** son vœu or souhait s'est réalisé; **you shall have your ~** ton souhait sera réalisé or te sera accordé, ton vœu sera exaucé
[c] (= *greeting*) **give him my good** or **best ~es** (*in conversation*) faites-lui mes amitiés; (*in letter*) transmettez-lui mes meilleures pensées; **he sends his best ~es** (*in conversation*) il vous fait ses amitiés; (*in letter*) il vous envoie ses meilleures pensées; **best ~es** or **all good ~es for a happy birthday** tous mes (or nos) meilleurs vœux pour votre anniversaire; **(with) best ~es for a speedy recovery/your future happiness** tous mes (or nos) vœux de prompt rétablissement/de bonheur; **(with) best ~es for Christmas and the New Year** (nos) meilleurs vœux pour Noël et la nouvelle année; **(with) best ~es to both of you on your engagement** meilleurs vœux (de bonheur) à tous deux à l'occasion de vos fiançailles; **(with) best ~es for a happy holiday** je vous souhaite (or nous vous souhaitons) d'excellentes vacances; (*in letter*) **with best ~es from** ◊ **with all good ~es from** bien amicalement; **the Queen sent a message of good ~es on Independence Day** la reine a envoyé des vœux pour le jour de l'Indépendance; **they**

came to offer him their best ~es on the occasion of ... ils sont venus lui offrir leurs meilleurs vœux pour ...
[4] COMP ► **wish fulfilment** N (*Psych*) accomplissement *m* d'un désir ► **wish list** N liste *f* de souhaits; **what is your ~ list?** quels sont vos souhaits?; **top of my ~ list** mon souhait le plus cher

wishbone ['wɪʃbəʊn] N (*Orn*) bréchet *m*, fourchette *f*; (*Sport*) wishbone *m*

wishful ['wɪʃfʊl] ADJ **to be ~ to do** or **of doing** (*frm*) avoir envie de faire; **he hopes he'll be released from prison next month, but that's just ~ thinking!** il espère être libéré de prison le mois prochain, mais il prend ses désirs pour des réalités!; **all this is pure ~ thinking on our part** là, nous prenons vraiment nos désirs pour des réalités, ce ne sont que des vœux pieux; **it is ~ thinking to expect it to be warm in March** il ne faut pas rêver*, il ne fera pas chaud en mars

wishy-washy* ['wɪʃɪˌwɒʃɪ] ADJ (*pej*) [*person, answer*] mou (molle *f*); [*style*] mou (molle *f*), fadasse*; [*speech, taste*] fadasse*; [*colour*] fadasse*, délavé; [*statement, phrase*] qui manque de fermeté

wisp [wɪsp] N [*of straw*] brin *m*; [*of hair*] fine mèche *f*; [*of thread*] petit bout *m*; [*of smoke*] mince volute *f*; **a little ~ of a girl** une fillette menue

wispy ['wɪspɪ] ADJ [*hair, beard, moustache*] fin et clairsemé; [*bit of straw*] fin; [*cloud*] léger; **traces of ~ smoke** maigres filets *mpl* de fumée

wistaria [wɪs'tɛərɪə], **wisteria** [wɪs'tɪərɪə] N glycine *f*

wistful ['wɪstfʊl] ADJ [*person, look, song, mood, smile, sigh, voice*] mélancolique, nostalgique; **to feel ~ (about sth)** se sentir plein de nostalgie (à la pensée de qch)

wistfully ['wɪstfəlɪ] ADV [*look, smile, sigh*] avec mélancolie or nostalgie

wistfulness ['wɪstfʊlnɪs] N [*of person*] caractère *m* mélancolique; [*of look, smile, voice*] nostalgie *f*, mélancolie *f*, regret *m*

wit[1] [wɪt] VI (*frm, also Jur*) **to ~ ...** à savoir ..., c'est à dire ...

wit[2] [wɪt] N [a] (= *intelligence*) **~(s)** esprit *m*, intelligence *f*; **mother ~** or **native ~** bon sens *m*, sens *m* commun; **he hadn't the ~** or **he hadn't enough ~ to hide the letter** il n'a pas eu l'intelligence or la présence d'esprit de cacher la lettre; **to have your ~s about you** avoir de la présence d'esprit; **you'll need (to have) all your ~s about you if you're to avoid being seen** tu vas devoir faire très attention or être très vigilant pour éviter d'être vu; **keep your ~s about you!** restez attentif!; **use your ~s!** sers-toi de ton intelligence!; **it was a battle of ~s (between them)** ils jouaient au plus fin; **he lives by** or **on his ~s** il vit d'expédients; **to collect** or **gather one's ~s** rassembler ses esprits; **the struggle for survival sharpened his ~s** la lutte pour la vie aiguisait ses facultés; **he was at his ~s' end** il ne savait plus que faire, il ne savait plus à quel saint se vouer; **I'm at my ~s' end to know what to do** je ne sais plus du tout ce que je dois faire; **to be/go out of one's ~s** être/devenir fou; **she was nearly out of her ~s with worry about him** elle était folle d'inquiétude pour lui
[b] (*NonC* = *wittiness*) esprit *m*; **the book is full of ~** le livre est très spirituel or est plein d'esprit; **he has a ready** or **pretty ~** il a beaucoup d'esprit, il est très spirituel; **in a flash of ~ he said ...** obéissant à une inspiration spirituelle il a dit ...; **this flash of ~ made them all laugh** ce trait d'esprit les a tous fait rire
[c] (= *person*) homme *m* d'esprit, femme *f* d'esprit; (*Hist, Literat*) bel esprit *m*

witch [wɪtʃ] [1] N sorcière *f*; (*fig*) (= *charmer*) ensorceleuse *f*, magicienne *f*; (*fig pej*) **she's an old ~** c'est une vieille sorcière; **~es' sabbath**

sabbat *m* (de sorcières) ② COMP ► **witch doctor** N sorcier *m* (*de tribu*) ► **witch-elm** N = **wych-elm** ► **witches' brew** N (*lit*) brouet *m* de sorcière ; (*fig*) mélange *m* explosif ► **witch hazel** N hamamélis *m* ► **witch hunt** N (*esp Pol: fig*) chasse *f* aux sorcières ► **witching hour** N the ~ing hour of midnight minuit, l'heure fatale, minuit, l'heure du crime (*hum*) ► **witch's brew** N = **witches' brew**

witchcraft ['wɪtʃkrɑːft] N sorcellerie *f*

witchery ['wɪtʃərɪ] N sorcellerie *f* ; (*fig = fascination*) magie *f*, envoûtement *m*

with [wɪð, wɪθ]

① PREPOSITION	② COMPOUNDS

① PREPOSITION

When **with** *is part of a set combination, eg* **good with**, **pleased with**, **to agree with**, *look up the other word.*

a avec ; **I was ~ her** j'étais avec elle ; **come ~ me!** viens avec moi ! ; **he had an argument ~ his brother** il s'est disputé avec son frère ; **the trouble ~ Paul is that ...** l'ennui avec Paul, c'est que ... ; **he walks ~ a stick** il marche avec une canne ; **be patient ~ her** sois patient avec elle

The pronoun is not translated in the following, where **it** *and* **them** *refer to things:*
he's gone ~ it il est parti avec ; **take my gloves, I can't drive ~ them** on prends mes gants, je ne peux pas conduire avec

Note the verbal construction in the following examples:
that problem is always ~ us ce problème n'est toujours pas résolu ; **she had her umbrella ~ her** elle avait emporté son parapluie

♦ **to be with sb** (*lit*) être avec qn ; (= *understand*) suivre qn ; **I'm ~ you** (= *understand*) je vous suis ; **sorry, I'm not ~ you** désolé, je ne vous suis pas ; (= *paying attention*) **are you ~ us, Laura?** tu nous suis, Laura ? ; (= *attend to*) **I'll be ~ you in a minute** je suis à vous dans une minute ; (= *support*) **I'm ~ you all the way** je suis à fond avec vous

♦ **to be with it*** [*person*] être dans le vent*

♦ **to get with it*** : **get ~ it!** (= *pay attention*) réveille-toi !, secoue-toi ! ; (= *face facts*) redescends sur terre !

b = **on one's person** sur ; **I haven't got any money ~ me** je n'ai pas d'argent sur moi

c = **in the house of, working with** chez ; **she was staying ~ friends** elle habitait chez des amis ; **he lives ~ his aunt** il habite chez or avec sa tante ; **he's ~ IBM** il travaille chez IBM ; [BUT] **a scientist ~ ICI** un chercheur de ICI ; **I've been ~ this company for seven years** cela fait sept ans que je travaille pour cette société

d [*in descriptions* = *that has, that have*] **the man ~ the beard** l'homme à la barbe ; **the boy ~ brown eyes** le garçon aux yeux marron ; **the house ~ the green shutters** la maison aux volets verts ; **I want a coat ~ a fur collar** je veux un manteau avec un col de fourrure ; **passengers ~ tickets** voyageurs *mpl* munis de or en possession de billets ; **patients ~ cancer** les personnes atteintes d'un cancer ; **only people ~ good incomes can afford such holidays** seules les personnes qui ont un bon salaire peuvent s'offrir de telles vacances ; **a car ~ the latest features** une voiture équipée des derniers perfectionnements techniques

e cause de ; **she was sick ~ fear** elle était malade de peur ; **he was shaking ~ rage** il tremblait de rage ; **the hills are white ~ snow** les montagnes sont blanches de neige

f = **in spite of** malgré ; **~ all his faults I still like him** je l'aime bien malgré tous ses défauts ; **~ all his intelligence, he still doesn't understand** malgré toute son intelligence, il ne comprend toujours pas ; **~ all that he is still the best we've got** malgré tout, c'est encore le meilleur homme que nous ayons

g manner avec ; **he did it ~ great care** il l'a fait avec beaucoup de précautions ; **I'll do it ~ pleasure** je le ferai avec plaisir ; [BUT] **... he said ~ a smile** ... dit-il en souriant ; **she took off her shoes ~ a sigh** elle a retiré ses chaussures en soupirant ; **I found the street ~ no trouble at all** je n'ai eu aucun mal à trouver la rue ; **she turned away ~ tears in her eyes** elle s'est détournée, les larmes aux yeux ; **~ my whole heart** de tout mon cœur

h circumstances **~ the price of petrol these days ...** au prix où est l'essence de nos jours ... ; **~ these words he left us** sur ces mots, il nous a quittés ; **~ the approach of winter** à l'approche de l'hiver ; **~ the elections no one talks anything but politics** avec les élections, on ne parle plus que politique ; **I couldn't see him ~ so many people there** il y avait tellement de monde que je ne l'ai pas vu ; **~ so much happening it was difficult to ...** il se passait tellement de choses qu'il était difficile de ...

♦ **with that : ~ that, he closed the door** sur ce or là-dessus, il a fermé la porte

② COMPOUNDS
► **with-profits** ADJ (*Fin*) [*policy*] avec participation aux bénéfices

withal †† [wɪˈðɔːl] ADV en outre, de plus

withdraw [wɪθˈdrɔː] (*pret* **withdrew**, *ptp* **withdrawn**) **①** VT [+ *person, hand, money, application, troops*] retirer (**from** de) ; [+ *permission, help*] retirer (**from** à) ; [+ *ambassador, representative*] rappeler ; [+ *accusation, opinion, suggestion, statement*] retirer, rétracter ; [+ *claim*] retirer, renoncer à ; [+ *order*] annuler ; (*Med*) [+ *drugs*] arrêter ; (*Comm*) [+ *goods*] retirer de la vente ; (*Fin*) [+ *banknotes*] retirer de la circulation ; (*Jur*) **to ~ a charge** retirer une accusation ; **to ~ one's penis** se retirer (**from** de)

② VI **a** (= *move away*) [*troops*] se replier (**from** de) ; [*person*] se retirer ; (*Mil*) **to ~ to a new position** se replier ; **he withdrew a few paces** il a reculé de quelques pas ; **she withdrew into her bedroom** elle s'est retirée dans sa chambre ; **to ~ into o.s.** se replier sur soi-même

b (= *retract offer, promise etc*) se rétracter, se dédire

c [*candidate, competitor, participant*] se retirer, se désister (**from** de, **in favour of sb** en faveur de qn) ; **you can't ~ now, we've practically achieved our goal** tu ne peux plus te retirer maintenant, nous avons pratiquement atteint notre but ; **I ~ from the game** je me retire de la partie, j'abandonne ; **they threatened to ~ from the talks** ils ont menacé de se retirer des négociations or de quitter la table des négociations

d (= *retract penis*) se retirer

withdrawal [wɪθˈdrɔːəl] **①** N **a** (*NonC*) (= *removal*) [*of money, application, troops, product*] retrait *m* (**from sth** de qch) ; [*of services*] suppression *f* ; **his party has announced its ~ of support for the government** son parti a annoncé qu'il retirait son soutien au gouvernement ; **the ~ of American diplomats from the area** le rappel des diplomates américains dans la région ; **the army's ~ to new positions** le repli de l'armée sur de nouvelles positions ; (*Fin: from bank etc*) **to make a ~** effectuer un retrait

b (*NonC* = *retraction*) [*of remark, allegation*] rétractation *f*

c (= *resigning*) [*of member, participant, candidate*] désistement *m* (**from sth** de qch) ; [*of athlete*] retrait *m* (**from sth** de qch)

d (*NonC: Psych*) repli *m* sur soi-même (**from sb/sth** par rapport à qn/qch), rétraction *f*

e (*NonC: after addiction*) (état *m* de) manque *m*, syndrome *m* de sevrage ; **alcohol/caffeine ~** l'état *m* de manque dû à l'arrêt de la consommation d'alcool/de café ; **to be in** or **suffering from ~** être en (état de) manque

f (*as contraception*) coït *m* interrompu

② COMP ► **withdrawal method** N méthode *f* du coït interrompu ► **withdrawal slip** N (*Banking*) bordereau *m* de retrait ► **withdrawal symptoms** NPL symptômes *mpl* de (l'état de) manque ; **to suffer** or **experience** or **have ~ symptoms** être en (état de) manque

withdrawn [wɪθˈdrɔːn] **①** VB *ptp of* **withdraw ②** ADJ (= *reserved*) [*person*] renfermé

withdrew [wɪθˈdruː] VB *pt of* **withdraw**

withe [wɪθ] N = **withy**

wither ['wɪðər] **①** VI [*plant*] se flétrir, se faner ; [*person, limb*] (*from illness*) s'atrophier ; (*from age*) se ratatiner ; (*fig*) [*beauty*] se faner ; [*hope, love, enthusiasm*] s'évanouir **②** VT [+ *plant*] flétrir, faner ; [+ *limb*] atrophier, ratatiner ; [+ *beauty*] faner ; [+ *hope etc*] détruire petit à petit ; **he ~ed her with a look** il l'a regardée avec un profond mépris, son regard méprisant lui a donné envie de rentrer sous terre

► **wither away** VI [*plant*] se dessécher, mourir ; [*hope etc*] s'évanouir ; [*organization*] disparaître

withered ['wɪðəd] ADJ **a** (= *dried-up*) [*flower, leaf, plant*] flétri, fané ; [*fruit*] desséché, ridé ; (*fig*) [*person*] desséché, ratatiné **b** [*liter = atrophied*] [*arm, leg, hand*] atrophié

withering ['wɪðərɪŋ] **①** N **a** [*of plant*] dépérissement *m* **b** (*liter*) [*of limb*] atrophie *f* **c** [*of beauty*] déclin *m* ; [*of hope, love, enthusiasm*] évanouissement *m* **②** ADJ [*remark, criticism, contempt, scorn, irony*] cinglant ; [*tone, smile, look*] profondément méprisant ; [*heat*] desséchant ; **to give sb a ~ look** jeter à qn un regard profondément méprisant ; **to launch a ~ attack on sb** lancer une attaque violente contre qn

witheringly ['wɪðərɪŋlɪ] ADV [*say, reply*] d'un ton plein de mépris ; [*look at*] avec mépris

withers ['wɪðəz] NPL garrot *m* (*du cheval*)

withershins ['wɪðəʃɪnz] ADV (*dial* = *anticlockwise*) dans le sens inverse des aiguilles d'une montre

withhold [wɪθˈhəʊld] (*pret*, *ptp* **withheld** [wɪθˈheld]) VT [+ *money from pay etc*] retenir (**from sth** de qch) ; [+ *payment, decision*] remettre, différer ; [+ *one's consent, permission, one's help, support*] refuser (**from sb** à qn) ; [+ *facts, truth, news*] cacher, taire (**from sb** à qn) ; **~ing tax** retenue *f* à la source ; **he withheld his tax in protest against ...** il a refusé de payer ses impôts pour protester contre ...

within [wɪˈðɪn] **①** ADV dedans, à l'intérieur ; **from ~** de l'intérieur

② PREP **a** (= *inside*) à l'intérieur de ; **~ the box** à l'intérieur de la boîte ; **~ it** à l'intérieur ; **~ (the boundary of) the park** à l'intérieur du parc, dans les limites du parc ; **here ~ the town** à l'intérieur même de la ville ; **~ the city walls** intra-muros, dans l'enceinte de la ville ; **a voice ~ him said ...** une voix en lui disait ...

b (= *within limits of*) **to be ~ the law** être dans (les limites de) la légalité ; **to live ~ one's income** or **means** vivre selon ses moyens ; **~ the range of the guns** à portée de(s) canon(s) ; **the coast was ~ sight** la côte était en vue ; **they were ~ sight of the town** ils étaient en vue de la ville ; (*fig*) **he was ~ reach** or **sight of his goal** il touchait au but → **call, province, reach**

c (*in measurement, distances*) **~ a kilometre of the house** à moins d'un kilomètre de la maison ; **we were ~ a mile of the town** nous étions à moins d'un mille de la ville ; **correct to ~ a centimetre** correct à un centimètre près → **inch**

d (*in time*) **~ a week of her visit** (= *after*) moins d'une semaine après sa visite ; (= *before*) moins d'une semaine avant sa visite ; **I'll be back ~ an hour** or **the hour** je serai de retour d'ici une heure ; **they arrived ~ minutes (of our call)** ils sont arrivés très peu de temps après (notre appel) ; **he returned ~ the week** il est revenu avant la fin de la semaine ; **~ two years from now** d'ici deux ans ; **"use ~ three**

days of opening" «se conserve trois jours après ouverture»; (*Comm*) **~ a period of four months** dans un délai de quatre mois; **~ the stipulated period** dans les délais stipulés → **living**

[3] ADJ (*Jur*) **the ~ instrument** le document ci-inclus

without [wɪð'aʊt]

*When **without** is an element in a phrasal verb, eg do without, go without, look up the verb.*

[1] ADV† à l'extérieur, au dehors; **from ~** de l'extérieur, de dehors

[2] PREP [a] (= *lacking*) sans; **~ a coat** sans manteau; **~ a coat or hat** sans manteau ni chapeau; **he went off ~ it** il est parti sans (le prendre); **~ any money** sans argent, sans un ou le sou*; **he is ~ friends** il n'a pas d'amis; **with or ~ sugar?** avec ou sans sucre?; **~ so much as a phone call** sans même un malheureux coup de fil; **~ a doubt** sans aucun doute; **~ doubt** sans doute; **not ~ some difficulty** non sans difficulté; **do it ~ fail** ne manquez pas de le faire, faites-le sans faute; **he was quite ~ shame** il n'avait aucune honte; **~ speaking, he ...** sans parler, il ...; **~ anybody knowing** sans que personne le sache; **to go ~ sth** ◊ **to do ~ sth** se passer de qch

[b] (†† = *outside*) au *or* en dehors de, à l'extérieur de

withstand [wɪθ'stænd] (*pret, ptp* **withstood** [wɪθ'stʊd]) VT résister à

withy [wɪðɪ] N brin *m* d'osier

witless [wɪtlɪs] ADJ stupide; **to scare sb ~*** faire une peur bleue à qn; **I was scared ~*** j'étais mort de peur; **to be bored ~*** s'ennuyer à mourir

witness [wɪtnɪs] [1] N [a] (*Jur etc* = *person*) témoin *m*; (*Jur*) **~ for the defence/prosecution** témoin *m* à décharge/à charge; **to lead a ~** poser des questions tendancieuses à un témoin; **there were three ~es to this event** trois personnes ont été témoins de cet événement, cet événement a eu trois témoins; **he was a ~ to or of this incident** il a été témoin de cet incident; **often children are ~ to violent events** les enfants sont souvent témoins de violences; **the ~es to his signature** les témoins certifiant sa signature; **in front of two ~es** en présence de deux témoins; (*Jur*) **to call sb as ~** citer qn comme témoin; (*Jur*) **"your ~"** «le témoin est à vous» → **eyewitness**

[b] (*esp Jur* = *evidence*) témoignage *m*; **in ~ of** en témoignage de; **in ~ whereof** en témoignage de quoi, en foi de quoi; **to give ~ on behalf of/against** témoigner en faveur de/contre, rendre témoignage pour/contre; **to bear or be ~ to sth** témoigner de qch; (*fig*) **his poems bear ~ to his years spent in India** ses poèmes témoignent de ses années passées en Inde; **her clothes were ~ to her poverty** ses vêtements témoignaient de sa pauvreté; **he has his good points, ~ his work for the blind** il a ses bons côtés, témoin *or* comme le prouve ce qu'il fait pour les aveugles; **~ the case of ...** témoin le cas de ...

[2] VT [a] (= *see*) [+ *attack, murder, theft*] être témoin de; [+ *fight, rape*] être témoin de, assister à; **did anyone ~ the theft?** quelqu'un a-t-il été témoin du vol?; **the accident was ~ed by several people** plusieurs personnes ont été témoins de l'accident

[b] (*fig*) (= *see*) voir; (= *notice*) [+ *change, improvement*] remarquer; (*fig*) **a building/a century which has ~ed ...** un bâtiment/un siècle qui a vu ...; **1989 ~ed the birth of a new world order** 1989 a vu l'avènement d'un nouvel ordre mondial; **Americans are generous people, ~ the increase in charitable giving** les Américains sont généreux, témoin l'augmentation des dons aux associations caritatives

[c] (*esp Jur*) [+ *document*] attester *or* certifier l'authenticité de; **to ~ sb's signature** certifier la signature de qn

---

[3] VI (*Jur*) **to ~ to sth** témoigner de qch; **he ~ed to having seen the accident** il a témoigné avoir vu l'accident; **to ~ against sb** témoigner contre qn

[4] COMP ► **witness box** (*Brit*), **witness stand** (*US*) N barre *f* des témoins; **in the ~ box** *or* **stand** à la barre

-witted [wɪtɪd] ADJ (*in compounds*) à l'esprit ...; **quick-witted** à l'esprit vif → **slow**

witter* [wɪtə^r] VI (*Brit*) **to ~ on about sth** dégoiser* sur qch; **stop ~ing (on)** arrête de parler pour ne rien dire

witticism [wɪtɪsɪzəm] N mot *m* d'esprit, bon mot *m*

wittily [wɪtɪlɪ] ADV avec esprit *or* humour; **"only on Fridays", he said ~** «seulement le vendredi» dit-il avec esprit *or* humour; **the film was well acted and ~ written** le film était bien joué et écrit avec esprit *or* humour

wittiness [wɪtɪnɪs] N (*NonC*) esprit *m*, humour *m*

wittingly [wɪtɪŋlɪ] ADV (*frm*) sciemment, en connaissance de cause

witty [wɪtɪ] ADJ [*person, speaker, remark*] spirituel, plein d'esprit; [*conversation, story, speech, script*] plein d'esprit; **a ~ remark** un mot d'esprit, une remarque pleine d'esprit

wives [waɪvz] NPL *of* **wife**

wiz [wɪz] N (*US*) as *m*, crack* *m*

wizard [wɪzəd] N magicien *m*, enchanteur *m*; **he is a financial ~** il a le génie de la finance, c'est un magicien de la finance; **he is a ~ with a paintbrush** c'est un champion* *or* un as du pinceau; **he's a ~ with numbers** il est très doué pour les chiffres; **he's a ~ at chess** c'est un as *or* un crack* des échecs; (*Brit*) **~!**†* au poil!*

wizardry [wɪzədrɪ] N (*NonC*) magie *f*; (*fig*) génie *m*; **a piece of technical ~** une merveille d'ingéniosité technique; **this evidence of his financial ~** cette preuve de son génie en matière financière; **£600,000 worth of electronic ~** une merveille de l'électronique valant 600 000 livres

wizened [wɪznd] ADJ [*person*] desséché, ratatiné; [*face, hands*] flétri

wk ABBR = **week**

WLTM* VT (ABBR = **would like to meet**) souhaite rencontrer, cherche

WO [ˌdʌblju:'əʊ] N (*Mil*) (ABBR = **warrant officer**) → **warrant**

woad [wəʊd] N guède *f*

woah [wəʊ] EXCL = **whoa**

wobble [wɒbl] [1] VI [a] [*jelly, hand, pen, voice*] trembler; [*cyclist, object about to fall, pile of rocks*] vaciller; [*tightrope walker, dancer*] chanceler; [*table, chair*] branler, être bancal; [*compass needle*] osciller; [*wheel*] avoir du jeu; **the table was wobbling** la table branlait; **this table ~s** cette table est bancale; **the cart ~d through the streets** la charrette bringuebalait *or* cahotait dans les rues [b] (* *fig* = *hesitate*) hésiter (**between** entre) [2] VT faire vaciller

wobbly [wɒblɪ] ADJ (= *shaky*) [*table, chair*] bancal; [*jelly*] qui tremble; [*tooth*] qui bouge; [*wheel*] qui a du jeu; [*hand, voice*] tremblant; [*bottom, thighs*] gros (grosse *f*) et flasque; **his legs are a bit ~** ◊ **he's a bit ~ on his legs** il flageole un peu sur ses jambes; **she was still a bit ~ after her illness** elle se sentait toujours un peu patraque* après sa maladie; **a ~ line*** une ligne qui n'est pas droite; **to be ~ = to wobble;** → **wobble 1** [b] (* = *dodgy*) [*organization, economy, sector*] fragile [2] [a] **to throw a ~*** piquer une crise* [b] (*US Hist*) **the Wobblies*** mouvement syndicaliste du début du 20e siècle

wodge [wɒdʒ] N (*Brit*) gros morceau *m*

woe [wəʊ] N malheur *m*; († *or hum*) **~ is me!** pauvre de moi!; **~ betide the man who ...** malheur à celui qui ...; **he told me his ~s and his tale of ~** il m'a fait le récit de ses

---

malheurs; **it was such a tale of ~ that ...** c'était une litanie si pathétique que ...

woebegone [wəʊbɪˌgɒn] ADJ (*liter*) désolé, abattu

woeful [wəʊfʊl] ADJ [a] (*liter = tragic*) [*person*] malheureux; [*news, story, sight*] tragique, terrible [b] (= *appalling, dire*) [*ignorance, inability, track-record*] lamentable, déplorable

woefully [wəʊfəlɪ] ADV [a] (*liter*) [*look*] d'un air affligé; [*say*] d'un ton affligé [b] (= *appallingly*) [*inadequate, underfunded etc*] terriblement; **to be ~ ignorant of politics/science** *etc* être d'une ignorance crasse en matière de politique/science *etc*; **~ inefficient** terriblement inefficace; **the hospital is ~ lacking in modern equipment** cet hôpital manque cruellement de matériel moderne, le matériel moderne fait cruellement défaut à cet hôpital; **modern equipment is ~ lacking** on manque cruellement de matériel moderne, le matériel moderne fait cruellement défaut

wog.* [wɒg] N (*Brit pej*) (= *African*) bougnoule.* *mf*; (= *Mediterranean*) métèque.* *m*

wok [wɒk] N wok *m*

woke [wəʊk] VB *pt of* **wake²**

woken [wəʊkn] VB *ptp of* **wake²**

wold [wəʊld] N haute plaine *f*, plateau *m*

wolf [wʊlf] [1] N (*pl* **wolves**) loup *m*; **she-~** louve *f*; **a ~ in sheep's clothing** un loup déguisé en agneau; **that will keep the ~ from the door** cela nous (*or* les *etc*) mettra au moins à l'abri du besoin; (*fig*) **to throw sb to the wolves** jeter qn dans la fosse aux lions; (*to the press*) jeter qn en pâture aux journalistes → **cry, lone** [2] VT (*also ~ down*) engloutir [3] COMP ► **wolf call** N (*US*) = **wolf whistle** ► **wolf cub** N (*also Scouting*†) louveteau *m* ► **wolf pack** N meute *f* de loups ► **wolf whistle** N (*fig*) sifflement *m* admiratif (*à l'adresse d'une fille*); **he gave a ~ whistle** il a sifflé la fille (*or* les filles)

wolfhound [wʊlfhaʊnd] N chien-loup *m*

wolfish [wʊlfɪʃ] ADJ vorace

wolfishly [wʊlfɪʃlɪ] ADV voracement

wolfram [wʊlfrəm] N wolfram *m*, tungstène *m*

wolfsbane [wʊlfsbeɪn] N (*Bot*) aconit *m*

wolverine [wʊlvəri:n] [1] N [a] (*Zool*) glouton *m*, carcajou *m* [b] (*US*) **Wolverine** habitant(e) *m(f)* du Michigan [2] COMP ► **the Wolverine State** N (*US*) le Michigan

wolves [wʊlvz] NPL *of* **wolf**

woman [wʊmən] (*pl* **women**) [1] N [a] femme *f*; **~ is a mysterious creature** la femme est une créature mystérieuse; **she's the ~ for the job** c'est la femme qu'il (nous *or* leur *etc*) faut pour ce travail; **she's her own ~** elle est son propre maître; **a ~ of the world** une femme du monde; **Paul and all his women** Paul et toutes ses maîtresses; **the ~ must be mad*** cette femme doit être folle; **~ to ~** entre femmes; **look here, my good ~**† écoutez, chère Madame; (*hum = wife*) **the little ~.** ma (*or* sa *etc*) légitime.*; **the other ~** (= *lover*) la maîtresse; **young ~**† jeune femme *f*; **a ~ of letters** une femme de lettres; **she belongs to a women's group** elle est membre d'un groupe féministe; (*Press*) **women's page** la page des lectrices; **women's rights** les droits *mpl* de la femme; **women's suffrage** le droit de vote pour les femmes; **women's team** équipe *f* féminine ■ (*PROV*) **a ~'s place is in the home** la place d'une femme est au foyer ■ (*PROV*) **a ~'s work is never done** on trouve toujours à faire dans une maison

[b] (= *cleaner*) femme *f* de ménage; **I've got a ~ who comes in three times a week** j'ai une femme de ménage qui vient trois fois par semaine

[2] ADJ **he's got a ~ music teacher** son professeur de musique est une femme; **~ friend** amie *f*; **~ worker** ouvrière *f*; **women doctors think that ...** les femmes médecins pensent

que ...; **women often prefer women doctors** les femmes préfèrent souvent les femmes médecins

3 COMP ► **woman driver** N conductrice *f*; **women drivers are often maligned** on dit souvent du mal des femmes au volant ► **woman-hater** N misogyne *mf* ► **woman police constable** N (*Brit*) femme *f* agent de police ► **Women's Centre** N ≈ centre *m* d'accueil de femmes ► **Women's Institute** N (*Brit*) *association de femmes de tendance plutôt traditionaliste* ► **Women's Lib**†* N = Women's (Liberation) Movement ► **Women's Libber**†* N féministe *mf* ► **women's liberation** N la libération de la femme ► **Women's (Liberation) Movement** N mouvement *m* de libération de la femme, MLF *m* ► **women's refuge** N refuge *m* pour femmes battues ► **women's room** N (*US*) toilettes *fpl* pour dames ► **women's studies** NPL (*Univ*) *étude des rôles sociologique, historique et littéraire de la femme*

womanhood ['wʊmənhʊd] N (*NonC* = *feminine nature*) féminité *f*; **to reach ~** devenir femme

womanish ['wʊmənɪʃ] ADJ (*pej*) efféminé

womanize ['wʊmənaɪz] VI courir les femmes

womanizer ['wʊmənaɪzəʳ] N coureur *m* de jupons

womankind ['wʊmənkaɪnd] N les femmes *fpl*

womanliness ['wʊmənlɪnɪs] N (*NonC*) féminité *f*, caractère *m* féminin

womanly ['wʊmənlɪ] ADJ [*figure, bearing*] féminin; [*behaviour*] digne d'une femme

womb [wuːm] **1** N utérus *m*, matrice *f*; (*fig*) (*of nature*) sein *m*; (*of earth*) sein *m*, entrailles *fpl* **2** COMP ► **womb-leasing** N location *f* d'utérus, pratique *f* des mères porteuses

wombat ['wɒmbæt] N wombat *m*, phascolome *m*

women ['wɪmɪn] NPL *of* **woman**

womenfolk ['wɪmɪnfəʊk] NPL les femmes *fpl*

won [wʌn] VB *pt, ptp of* **win**

▼ **wonder** ['wʌndəʳ] **1** N **a** (*NonC* = *admiration*) émerveillement *m*; (= *astonishment*) étonnement *m*; **to be lost in ~** être émerveillé *or* ébloui; **he watched, lost in silent ~** il regardait en silence, émerveillé *or* ébloui; **the sense of ~ that children have** la faculté d'être émerveillé qu'ont les enfants; **... he said in ~** ... dit-il tout étonné **b** (= *sth wonderful*) prodige *m*, miracle *m*; **the ~ of electricity** le miracle de l'électricité; **the ~s of science/medicine** les prodiges *mpl or* les miracles *mpl* de la science/de la médecine; **the Seven Wonders of the World** les sept merveilles *fpl* du monde; **to be a nine-day** *or* **one-day** *or* **seven-day ~** ne pas faire long feu; **he promised us ~s** il nous a promis monts et merveilles; (*iro*) **~s will never cease** c'est un miracle!, cela tient du miracle! (*iro*); **the ~ of it all is that ...** le plus étonnant dans tout cela c'est que ...; **it's a ~ that he didn't fall** c'est un miracle qu'il ne soit pas tombé; **it's a ~ to me that ...** je n'en reviens pas que ... (+ *subj*); **it's a ~ how they were able to get these jobs** on se demande par quel miracle ils ont réussi à obtenir ces postes; **no ~ he came late** ◊ **it's no ~ (that) he came late** ce n'est pas étonnant qu'il soit arrivé en retard *or* s'il est arrivé en retard; **no ~!** cela n'a rien d'étonnant!, pas étonnant!*; **it's little** *or* **small ~ that ...** il n'est guère étonnant que ... (+ *subj*) → **nine, work**

2 VI **a** (= *marvel*) (*in astonishment*) s'étonner; (*in admiration*) s'émerveiller; **the shepherds ~ed at the angels** les bergers s'émerveillaient devant les anges; **I ~ at your rashness** votre audace m'étonne *or* me surprend; **I ~ (that) you're still able to work** je ne sais pas comment vous faites pour travailler encore; **I ~ (that) he didn't kill you** cela m'étonne qu'il ne vous ait pas tué; **do you ~**

or **can you ~ at it?** est-ce que cela vous étonne?; **he'll be back, I shouldn't ~**†* cela ne m'étonnerait pas qu'il revienne **b** (= *reflect*) penser, songer; **his words set me ~ing** ce qu'il a dit m'a donné à penser *or* m'a laissé songeur; **it makes you ~** cela donne à penser; **I was ~ing about what he said** je pensais *or* songeais à ce qu'il a dit; **I'm ~ing about going to the pictures** j'ai à moitié envie d'aller au cinéma; **he'll be back — I ~!** il reviendra — je me le demande!

3 VT se demander; **I ~ who he is** je me demande qui il est, je serais curieux de savoir qui il est; **I ~ what to do** je ne sais pas quoi faire; **I ~ where to put it** je me demande où (je pourrais) le mettre; **he was ~ing whether to come with us** il se demandait s'il allait nous accompagner; **I ~ why!** je me demande pourquoi!

4 COMP ► **wonder-worker** N **he is a ~-worker** il accomplit de vrais miracles; **this drug/treatment is a ~-worker** c'est un remède/un traitement miracle

wonderful ['wʌndəfʊl] ADJ **a** (= *excellent*) merveilleux; **it's ~ to see you** je suis si heureux de te voir; **we had a ~ time** c'était merveilleux **b** (= *astonishing*) étonnant, extraordinaire; **the human body is a ~ thing** le corps humain est quelque chose d'étonnant *or* d'extraordinaire

wonderfully ['wʌndəfəlɪ] ADV **a** (*with adj, adv*) merveilleusement; **the weather was ~ warm** il a fait merveilleusement chaud; **it works ~ well** ça marche merveilleusement bien *or* à merveille; **he looks ~ well** il a très bonne mine **b** (*with vb: gen*) merveilleusement bien; [*succeed, function, go with*] à merveille; **I slept ~** j'ai merveilleusement bien dormi; **my cousins get on ~** mes cousins s'entendent à merveille

wondering ['wʌndərɪŋ] ADJ **a** (= *astonished*) étonné; (= *thoughtful*) songeur, pensif

wonderingly ['wʌndərɪŋlɪ] ADV (= *with astonishment*) avec étonnement, d'un air étonné; (= *thoughtfully*) songeusement, pensivement

wonderland ['wʌndəlænd] N pays *m* des merveilles, pays *m* merveilleux → **Alice**

wonderment ['wʌndəmənt] N = **wonder 1a**

wonderstruck ['wʌndəstrʌk] ADJ (*liter*) frappé d'étonnement, émerveillé

wondrous ['wʌndrəs] (*liter*) **1** ADJ **a** (= *excellent*) merveilleux **b** (= *amazing*) extraordinaire **2** ADV **a** (= *excellently*) merveilleusement; **~ well** merveilleusement bien **b** (= *amazingly*) extraordinairement

wondrously ['wʌndrəslɪ] ADV (*liter*) = **wondrous 2**

wonga‡ ['wɒŋə] N (*Brit*) pèze‡ *m*, pognon‡ *m*

wonk* ['wɒŋk] N (*US*) bosseur* *m*, -euse* *f* → **policy**¹

wonky* ['wɒŋkɪ] ADJ (*Brit*) **a** (= *wobbly*) [*chair, table*] bancal **b** (= *crooked*) de traviole*, de travers **c** (= *defective*) détraqué*; **to go ~** [*car, machine*] se déglinguer; [*TV picture*] se dérégler; **he's feeling rather ~ still** il se sent encore un peu patraque* *or* vaseux*

won't [wəʊnt] = **will not**; → **will**

wont [wəʊnt] (*frm*) **1** ADJ **to be ~ to do sth** avoir coutume de faire qch; **as he was ~ to do** comme il avait coutume de faire, comme à son habitude **2** N coutume *f*, habitude *f* (**to do** de faire); **as was my ~** ainsi que j'en avais l'habitude, comme de coutume

wonted ['wəʊntɪd] ADJ (*frm*) habituel, coutumier

woo [wuː] VT [+ *woman*] faire la cour à, courtiser; (*fig*) [+ *influential person*] rechercher les faveurs de; [+ *voters, audience*] chercher à plaire à; [+ *fame, success*] rechercher; (*fig*) **he ~ed them with promises of ...** il cherchait à s'assurer leurs faveurs *or* à leur plaire en leur promettant ...

wood [wʊd] **1** N **a** (*NonC* = *material*) bois *m*; (*fig*) **to touch ~** ◊ **to knock on ~** (*US*) toucher du bois; **touch ~!*** ◊ **knock on ~!*** (*US*) touchons *or* je touche du bois; (*fig*) **he can't see the ~ for the trees** il se perd dans les détails → **deadwood, hardwood, softwood b** (= *forest*) bois *m*; **~s** bois *mpl*; **a pine/beech ~** un bois de pins/hêtres, une pinède/hêtraie; (*fig*) **we're out of the ~(s) now** on est au bout du tunnel maintenant; **we're not out of the ~(s) yet** on n'est pas encore tiré d'affaire *or* sorti de l'auberge* → **neck c** (= *cask*) **drawn from the ~** tiré au tonneau; **aged in the ~** vieilli au tonneau; **wine in the ~** vin *m* au tonneau **d** (*Mus*) **the ~s** les bois *mpl* **e** (*Golf*) bois *m*; (*Bowls*) boule *f*; (*Golf*) **a number 2 ~** un bois 2

2 COMP [*floor, object, structure*] de bois, en bois; [*fire*] de bois; [*stove*] à bois ► **wood alcohol** N esprit-de-bois *m*, alcool *m* méthylique ► **wood anemone** N anémone *f* des bois ► **wood block** N (*Art*) bois *m* de graveur ► **wood-burning stove** N poêle *m* à bois ► **wood carving** N (*NonC*) (= *act*) sculpture *f* sur bois; (= *object*) sculpture *f* en bois ► **wood engraving** N gravure *f* sur bois ► **wood nymph** N (*Myth*) dryade *f*, nymphe *f* des bois ► **wood pulp** N pâte *f* à papier ► **wood shavings** NPL copeaux *mpl* (de bois) ► **wood trim** N (*US*) boiseries *fpl* ► **wood wool** N (*NonC*) copeaux *mpl* de bois

woodbine ['wʊdbaɪn] N chèvrefeuille *m*

woodchip ['wʊdtʃɪp] N (*NonC*) (= *chips of wood*) copeaux *mpl* de bois; (= *board*) aggloméré *m*; (*also* **~ wallpaper**) papier peint parsemé de petits morceaux de bois

woodchuck ['wʊdtʃʌk] N marmotte *f* d'Amérique

woodcock ['wʊdkɒk] N (*Orn*) bécasse *f* des bois

woodcraft ['wʊdkrɑːft] N (*NonC*) (*in forest*) connaissance *f* de la forêt; (= *handicraft*) art *m* de travailler le bois

woodcut ['wʊdkʌt] N gravure *f* sur bois

woodcutter ['wʊdkʌtəʳ] N bûcheron *m*, -onne *f*

woodcutting ['wʊdkʌtɪŋ] N (*Art*) (= *act, object*) gravure *f* sur bois; (*in forest*) abattage *m* des arbres

wooded ['wʊdɪd] ADJ boisé; **heavily** *or* **thickly** *or* **densely ~** très boisé

wooden ['wʊdn] **1** ADJ **a** (*lit* = *made of wood*) en bois; **a ~ floor** un parquet **b** (*fig* = *unnatural*) [*acting, performance*] qui manque de naturel; [*actor, performer*] peu naturel **2** COMP ► **wooden-headed** ADJ idiot, imbécile ► **wooden Indian**‡ N (*US pej* = *constrained*) personne *f* raide comme la justice; (= *dull*) personne *f* terne *or* ennuyeuse ► **wooden leg** N jambe *f* de bois ► **wooden nickel**‡ N (*US fig*) objet *m* sans valeur; **to try to sell sb ~ nickels*** essayer de rouler qn ► **wooden spoon** N (*also Rugby*) cuiller *f* de *or* en bois

woodenly ['wʊdnlɪ] ADV [*act, speak*] avec raideur; [*look at, stare*] d'un air impassible

woodland ['wʊdlænd] **1** N (*NonC*) région *f* boisée, bois *mpl* **2** COMP [*flower etc*] des bois; [*path*] forestier

woodlark ['wʊdlɑːk] N (*Orn*) alouette *f* des bois

woodlouse ['wʊdlaʊs] N (*pl* **woodlice** ['wʊdlaɪs]) cloporte *m*

woodman ['wʊdmæn] N (*pl* **-men**) forestier *m*

woodpecker ['wʊdpekəʳ] N (*Orn*) pic *m*

woodpigeon ['wʊdpɪdʒən] N (*Orn*) (pigeon *m*) ramier *m*

woodpile ['wʊdpaɪl] N tas *m* de bois → **nigger**

woodshed ['wʊdʃed] N bûcher *m* (*abri*)

► LANGUAGE IN USE: **wonder** 2.2, 16.1

woodsman ['wʊdzmən] N (pl **-men**) (US) = **woodman**

woodsy ['wʊdzɪ] ADJ (US) [countryside] boisé; [flowers etc] des bois

woodwind ['wʊdwɪnd] N (Mus) (one instrument) bois m; (collective pl) bois mpl

woodwork ['wʊdwɜːk] N **a** (craft, school subject) (= carpentry) menuiserie f; (= cabinetmaking) ébénisterie f **b** (in house) (= beams etc) charpente f; (= doors, skirting boards, window frames etc) boiseries fpl; (fig pej) **to come** or **crawl out of the ~*** sortir de son trou **c** (Ftbl*) bois mpl, poteaux mpl (de but)

woodworm ['wʊdwɜːm] N ver m du bois; **the table has got ~** la table est vermoulue or piquée des vers

woody ['wʊdɪ] **1** ADJ **a** [plant, stem, texture] ligneux; [odour] de bois **b** (= wooded) [countryside] boisé **2** COMP ► **woody nightshade** N douce-amère f

wooer† ['wuːə'] N prétendant m

woof¹ [wʊf] N (Tex) trame f

woof² [wʊf] **1** N [of dog] aboiement m; **~, ~!** ouah, ouah! **2** VI aboyer

woofer ['wʊfə'] N haut-parleur m grave, woofer m

wooftah⁚ ['wʊftə], **woofter⁚** ['wʊftə'] N (Brit pej) tapette* f (pej)

wool [wʊl] **1** N laine f; **he was wearing ~** il portait de la laine or des lainages; **a ball of ~** une pelote de laine; **knitting/darning ~** laine f à tricoter/repriser; **this sweater is all ~** or **pure ~** ce pull-over est en pure laine; (US fig) **all ~ and a yard wide*** authentique, de première classe; **to pull the ~ over sb's eyes** duper qn → **dye, steel** **2** COMP [cloth] de laine; [dress] en or de laine ► **wool fat** N suint m ► **wool-gathering** N (fig) rêvasserie f; **to be** or **go ~-gathering** être dans les nuages, rêvasser ► **wool-grower** N éleveur m, -euse f de moutons à laine ► **wool-lined** ADJ doublé laine ► **wool merchant** N négociant(e) m(f) en laine, lainier m, -ière f ► **wool shop** N magasin m de laines ► **wool trade** N commerce m de la laine

woolen ['wʊlən] (US) = **woollen**

wooliness ['wʊlɪnɪs] N (US) = **woolliness**

woollen, woolen (US) ['wʊlən] **1** ADJ [garment] en laine; [cloth] de laine; **~ cloth** or **material** lainage m, étoffe f de laine; **~ goods** lainages mpl; **the ~ industry** l'industrie f lainière **2** **woollens** NPL lainages mpl

woolliness, wooliness (US) ['wʊlɪnɪs] N **a** [of material, garment, sheep, animal's coat] aspect m laineux **b** (fig = vagueness) [of ideas, thinking, essay, book, speech] caractère m confus or nébuleux; [of person] côté m nébuleux

woolly, wooly (US) ['wʊlɪ] **1** ADJ **a** [material, garment, animal] laineux; [hair] laineux **b** (also **~-headed, ~-minded**) [ideas, thinking, essay, book, speech] confus, nébuleux; [person] nébuleux; (pej) **~ liberals** les libéraux mpl aux idées confuses → **wild** **2** N (Brit* = jersey etc) tricot m, pull m; **woollies*** ◊ **woolies*** (US) lainages mpl; **winter woollies*** lainages mpl d'hiver **3** COMP ► **woolly bear*** N (= caterpillar) oursonne f, chenille f de l'écaille martre ► **woolly mammoth** N mammouth m laineux ► **woolly pully*** N pull m ► **woolly rhinoceros** N rhinocéros m laineux

Woolsack ['wʊlsæk] N **the ~** (Brit Parl) siège du grand chancelier d'Angleterre à la Chambre des lords

woolshed ['wʊlʃed] N lainerie f

wooly ['wʊlɪ] (US) = **woolly**

woops* [wʊps] EXCL = **whoops**

woozy* ['wuːzɪ] ADJ dans les vapes*; **I feel a bit ~** je suis un peu dans les vapes*

wop⁚ [wɒp] N (pej = Italian) Rital⁚ m

Worcester(shire) sauce ['wʊstə(ʃə)sɔːs] N sauce épicée au soja et au vinaigre

Worcs N ABBR = **Worcestershire**

▼ **word** [wɜːd]

1 NOUN	**3** COMPOUNDS
2 TRANSITIVE VERB	

1 NOUN

a gen mot m; (spoken) mot m, parole f; [of song etc] **~s** paroles fpl; **the written/spoken ~** ce qui est écrit/dit; **what's the ~ for "banana" in German?** ◊ **what's the German ~ for "banana"?** comment dit-on « banane » en allemand?; **there's no such ~ as "impossible"** impossible n'est pas français; **he won't hear a ~ against her** il n'admet absolument pas qu'on la critique (subj); **I didn't breathe a ~** je n'ai pas soufflé mot; **in ~ and deed** en parole et en fait; **... or ~s to that effect** ... ou quelque chose de ce genre; **I remember every ~ he said** je me souviens de ce qu'il a dit mot pour mot, je me souviens absolument de tout ce qu'il a dit; **those were his very ~s** ce sont ses propres paroles, c'est ce qu'il a dit mot pour mot or textuellement; **angry ~s** mots mpl prononcés sous le coup de la colère; **big ~s!*** toujours les grands mots!; **a man of few ~s** un homme peu loquace; **fine ~s** de belles paroles fpl; (iro) **fine ~s!** belles paroles!; **I can't find (the) ~s (to tell you ...)** je ne trouve pas les mots (pour vous dire ...); **there are no ~s to describe how I felt** il n'y a pas de mot pour expliquer ce que je ressentais; **he could find no ~s to express his misery** il ne trouvait pas de mot pour exprimer sa tristesse; **it's too stupid for ~s** c'est vraiment trop stupide; **from the ~ go** dès le début or le commencement; **I can't get a ~ out of him** je ne peux pas en tirer un mot; **tell me in your own ~s** dites-le-moi à votre façon; **in the ~s of Racine** comme le dit Racine, selon les mots de Racine; **I can't put my thoughts/feelings into ~s** je ne trouve pas les mots pour exprimer ce que je pense/ressens; **by** or **through ~ of mouth** de bouche à oreille → **3**; **in other ~s** autrement dit; **to put in a (good) ~ for sb** dire or glisser un mot en faveur de qn; **don't put ~s into my mouth!** ne me faites pas dire ce que je n'ai pas dit!; **you took the ~s right out of my mouth** c'est exactement ce que j'allais dire; **with these ~s, he sat down** sur ces mots il s'est assis; **without a ~, he left the room** il a quitté la pièce sans dire un mot

♦ **to have a word (with sb)** (= speak to) **can I have a ~?*** puis-je vous dire un mot (en privé)?, auriez-vous un moment?; **I'll have a ~ with him about it** je lui en toucherai un mot, je vais lui en parler; **I had a ~ with him about it** je lui en ai touché un mot, je lui en ai parlé brièvement; **I want (to have) a ~ with you** j'ai à vous parler; (Brit) **to have a ~ in sb's ear** glisser un mot à l'oreille de qn

♦ **to have words with sb** (= rebuke) dire deux mots à qn; (= quarrel) avoir des mots avec qn, se disputer avec qn

♦ **to say a word: I never said a ~** je n'ai rien dit du tout, je n'ai pas ouvert la bouche; **Mr Martin will now say a few ~s** M. Martin va maintenant prendre la parole or dire quelques mots; **he didn't say a ~ about it** il n'en a pas soufflé mot; **nobody had a good ~ to say about him** personne n'a trouvé la moindre chose à dire en sa faveur

♦ **a word/words of: a ~ of advice** un petit conseil; **a ~ of thanks** un mot de remerciement; **I'll give you a ~ of warning** je voudrais vous mettre en garde; **after these ~s of warning** après cette mise en garde

♦ **in a word** en un mot

♦ **in so** or **as many words: I told him in so** or **as many ~s that ...** je le lui ai carrément dit que ..., sans y aller par quatre chemins, je le lui ai dit que ...; **he didn't say so in so many** or **as many ~s** il ne l'a pas dit explicitement, ce n'est pas exactement ce qu'il a dit

♦ **word for word** [repeat, copy out] mot pour mot, textuellement; [translate] mot à mot, littéralement; [review, go over] mot par mot → **3**

♦ **a/the word for it**: **the French have a ~ for it** les Français ont un mot pour dire cela; **boring is not the ~ for it!** ennuyeux, c'est le moins que l'on puisse dire!; **"negligent" is a better ~ for it** « négligent » serait plus juste or serait plus près de la vérité; **"murder"? that's not quite the (right) ~ (for it)** « meurtre » ? ce n'est pas tout à fait le mot (qui convient); **she disappeared, there's no other ~ for it** or **that's the only ~ for it** elle a disparu, c'est bien le mot or on ne peut pas dire autrement

b = **advice** conseil m; **a ~ to new fathers** quelques conseils aux nouveaux pères; **a ~ to the wise** un bon conseil

c NonC = **news, message** nouvelles fpl; **she's waiting for ~ from headquarters** elle attend des nouvelles du siège central; **~ came from headquarters that ...** le quartier général nous (or leur etc) a fait dire or nous (or les etc) a prévenus que ...; **~ came that ...** on a appris que ...; **to send ~ that ...** faire savoir or faire dire que ...; **there's no ~ from John yet** on est toujours sans nouvelles de John; **the purpose of his mission is to bring back ~ of enemy manoeuvres** le but de sa mission est de rapporter des renseignements sur les manœuvres de l'ennemi → **leave**

d = **rumour** **~ has it** or **the ~ is that** he has left le bruit court qu'il est parti; **if ~ got out about his past, there'd be a scandal** si l'on apprenait certaines choses sur son passé, cela ferait un scandale

e = **promise, assurance etc** parole f, promesse f; **~ of honour** parole f d'honneur; **it was his ~ against mine** c'était sa parole contre la mienne; **his ~ is his bond** il n'a qu'une parole; **to break one's ~** manquer à sa parole; **to give one's ~ to sb/that** donner sa parole (d'honneur) à qn/que; **I give you my ~ (on** or **for it)** je vous donne ma parole (là-dessus); **you have my ~ (of honour)** vous avez ma parole (d'honneur); **to go back on one's ~** revenir sur sa parole; **he is as good as his ~** on peut le croire sur parole; **he was as good as his ~** il a tenu parole; **I've only got her ~ for it** c'est elle qui le dit, je n'ai aucune preuve; **to hold sb to his ~** contraindre qn à tenir sa promesse; **to keep one's ~** tenir (sa) parole; **a man of his ~** un homme de parole; **my ~!*** ◊ **upon my ~!†** ma parole!; **to take sb at his ~** prendre qn au mot; **you'll have to take his ~ for it** il vous faudra le croire sur parole; **take my ~ for it, he's a good man** c'est un brave homme, croyez-moi

f = **command** (mot m d')ordre m; **the ~ of command** l'ordre m; **his ~ is law** c'est lui qui fait la loi, sa parole fait loi; **he gave the ~ to advance** il a donné l'ordre d'avancer

g Rel **the Word** (= logos) le Verbe; (= the Bible, the Gospel: also **the Word of God**) le Verbe (de Dieu), la parole de Dieu

h Comput mot m

2 TRANSITIVE VERB

[+ document, protest] (spoken or written) formuler; (written) rédiger, libeller (Admin); **he had ~ed the letter very carefully** il avait choisi les termes de sa lettre avec le plus grand soin; **well ~ed** bien tourné; **I don't know how to ~ it** je ne sais pas comment le formuler

3 COMPOUNDS

► **word association** N (Psych) association f de mots ► **word-blind†** ADJ dyslexique ► **word-blindness†** N dyslexie f ► **word class** N (Gram) catégorie f grammaticale ► **word formation** N (Ling) formation f des mots ► **word-for-word** ADJ mot pour mot; **a ~-for-~ translation** une traduction littérale or mot à mot ► **word game** N jeu m de lettres ► **word list** N (in exercise etc) liste f de mots; (in dictionary) nomenclature f ► **word-of-**

mouth ADJ verbal, oral ► **word order** N (Gram) ordre m des mots ► **word-perfect** ADJ **to be ~-perfect in sth** savoir qch sur le bout des doigts ► **word picture** N **to give a ~ picture of sth** faire une description vivante de qch ► **word processing** N traitement m de texte ; **~ processing package** logiciel m de traitement de texte ► **word processor** N traitement m de texte ► **word-type** N (Ling) vocable m ► **word wrap** N (Comput) retour m (automatique) à la ligne

wordbook ['wɜːdbʊk] N lexique m, vocabulaire m

wordcount ['wɜːdkaʊnt] N (Comput) comptage m, nombre m de mots

wordiness ['wɜːdɪnɪs] N verbosité f

wording ['wɜːdɪŋ] N [of letter, speech, statement] termes mpl, formulation f ; [of official document] libellé m ; **the ~ of the last sentence is clumsy** la dernière phrase est maladroitement exprimée or formulée ; **the ~ is exceedingly important** le choix des termes est extrêmement important ; **change the ~ slightly** changez quelques mots (ici et là) ; **a different ~ would make it less ambiguous** ce serait moins ambigu si on l'exprimait autrement

wordless ['wɜːdlɪs] ADJ a (= silent) [anguish, admiration] muet ; **he watched her in ~ admiration** il la regardait, muet d'admiration b (= without words) inarticulé ; **a ~ cry/shriek** un cri/hurlement inarticulé

wordlessly ['wɜːdlɪslɪ] ADV sans prononcer un mot

wordplay ['wɜːdpleɪ] N (= pun) jeu m de mots ; (NonC = puns) jeux mpl de mots

wordsmith ['wɜːdsmɪθ] N manieur m de mots ; **he's a skilled ~** il sait tourner ses phrases ; (stronger) il a le génie des mots

wordy ['wɜːdɪ] ADJ [person, style] verbeux ; [document] au style verbeux

wore [wɔːʳ] VB pt of wear

▼ **work** [wɜːk]

1 NOUN	4 COMPOUNDS	
2 INTRANSITIVE VERB	5 PHRASAL VERBS	
3 TRANSITIVE VERB		

1 NOUN

a NonC: gen travail m ; **to start ~** ◊ **to set to ~** se mettre au travail ; **I've got some more ~ for you** j'ai encore du travail pour vous ; **he does his ~ well** il travaille bien, il fait du bon travail ; **she put a lot of ~ into it** elle y a consacré beaucoup de travail ; **there's still a lot of ~ to be done on it** il reste encore beaucoup à faire ; **I'm trying to get some ~ done** j'essaie de travailler ; **~ has begun on the new bridge** (= building it) on a commencé la construction du nouveau pont ; **you'll have your ~ cut out** ça ne va pas être facile ; **domestic ~** travaux mpl domestiques ; **office ~** travail m de bureau ; **~ in progress** travaux mpl en cours ; **it's women's ~** c'est un travail de femme ; **it's quite easy ~** ce n'est pas un travail difficile ; **good ~!** (= well done!) bien travaillé !, bravo ! ; **it's good ~** c'est du bon travail ; **it's hot ~** ça donne chaud ; (iro) **nice ~ if you can get it!*** c'est une bonne planque !* ; **to make short or quick ~ of sth** faire qch très rapidement ; **he did useful ~ in the Ministry of Transport** il a fait du bon travail au ministère des Transports → **works**

♦ **to be at work** (= working) travailler, être au travail ; **he was at ~ on another picture** il travaillait sur un autre tableau ; (= operating) **there are subversive forces at ~ here** des forces subversives sont à l'œuvre → **1b**

b = employment, place of employment travail m ; **he's looking for ~** il cherche du travail ; (US) **"~ wanted"** « demandes d'emploi » ; **to go to ~** aller au travail ; **on her way to ~** en allant à son travail ; **where is his (place of) ~?** où travaille-t-il ?

♦ **at work** (= at place of work) au travail ; **he's at ~ at the moment** il est au travail en ce moment ; **accidents at ~** les accidents mpl du travail

♦ **in work**: those in **~** les actifs mpl ; **he is in regular ~** il a un emploi régulier

♦ **out of work**: **to be out of ~** être au chômage or sans emploi ; **an increase in the numbers out of ~** une augmentation du nombre des demandeurs d'emploi or des chômeurs ; **to put or throw sb out of ~** mettre qn au chômage ; **this decision threw a lot of people out of ~** cette décision a fait beaucoup de chômeurs ; **600 men were thrown out of ~** 600 hommes ont été licenciés or ont perdu leur emploi

♦ **off work**: **he's off ~ today** il n'est pas allé (or venu) travailler aujourd'hui ; **he has been off ~ for three days** il est absent depuis trois jours ; **a day off ~** un jour de congé ; **I'll have to take time off ~** il va falloir que je prenne une journée (or une matinée etc) de congé

c = product œuvre f ; **the ~s of God** l'œuvre f de Dieu ; **his life's ~** l'œuvre f de sa vie ; **his ~ will not be forgotten** son œuvre passera à la postérité ; **it's obviously the ~ of a professional** c'est manifestement l'œuvre d'un professionnel or du travail de professionnel ; **this is the ~ of a madman** c'est l'œuvre d'un fou

d Art, Literat, Mus etc œuvre f ; (= book on specific subject) ouvrage m ; **the complete ~s of Shakespeare** les œuvres fpl complètes de Shakespeare ; **Camus' last ~** la dernière œuvre de Camus ; **a ~ on Joyce** un ouvrage sur Joyce ; **this ~ was commissioned by ...** cette œuvre a été commandée par ... ; **~s of fiction/reference** ouvrages mpl de fiction/référence ; **he sells a lot of his ~** ses tableaux (or ses livres etc) se vendent bien

2 INTRANSITIVE VERB

For work + preposition/adverb combinations see also phrasal verbs.

a gen travailler ; **to ~ hard** travailler dur ; (Ind) **to ~ to rule** faire la grève du zèle ; **he is ~ing at his German** il travaille à son allemand ; **he has always ~ed for/against a reform** il a toujours lutté pour/contre une telle réforme ; **he ~s in education/publishing** il travaille dans l'enseignement/l'édition ; **he prefers to ~ in wood/clay** il préfère travailler le bois/l'argile ; **he prefers to ~ in oils** il préfère la peinture à l'huile or travailler à la peinture à l'huile ; **he ~ed on the car all morning** il a travaillé sur la voiture toute la matinée ; **he's ~ing on his memoirs** il travaille à ses mémoires ; **have you solved the problem?** — **we're ~ing on it** avez-vous résolu le problème ? — on y travaille ; (fig) **I've been ~ing on him but haven't yet managed to persuade him** j'ai bien essayé de le convaincre, mais je n'y suis pas encore parvenu ; **the police are ~ing on the case** la police enquête sur l'affaire ; **they are ~ing on the principle that ...** ils partent du principe que ... ; **there are not many facts/clues to ~ on** il y a peu de faits/d'indices sur lesquels travailler ; **to ~ towards sth** œuvrer pour qch ; **we are ~ing towards equality of opportunity** nous œuvrons pour l'égalité des chances ; **we are ~ing towards a solution/an agreement** nous essayons de parvenir à une solution/un accord

b = function, be effective [mechanism, watch, machine, car, switch, scheme, arrangement] marcher, fonctionner ; [drug, medicine] agir, faire effet ; [yeast] fermenter ; **the lift isn't ~ing** l'ascenseur ne marche pas or est en panne ; **it ~s off the mains/on electricity/off batteries** ça marche sur (le) secteur/à l'électricité/avec des piles ; (hum) **my brain doesn't seem to be ~ing today** je n'ai pas les idées très claires aujourd'hui ; **the spell ~ed** le charme a fait son effet ; **it just won't ~** ça ne marchera pas or jamais ; **that ~s both ways** c'est à double tranchant ; **this may ~ in our favour** ça pourrait jouer en notre faveur

c = pass **she ~ed methodically down the list** elle a suivi la liste de façon méthodique ; **water has ~ed through the roof** de l'eau s'est infiltrée par le toit

d = move [face, mouth] se contracter, se crisper

3 TRANSITIVE VERB

a = cause to work [+ person, staff] faire travailler ; [+ mechanism, lever, pump] actionner ; [+ machine] faire marcher ; **I don't know how to ~ the video** je ne sais pas comment faire marcher le magnétoscope ; **he ~s his staff too hard** il fait trop travailler son personnel, il surmène son personnel ; **the machine is ~ed by solar energy** cette machine marche or fonctionne à l'énergie solaire

♦ **to work o.s.**: **he ~s himself too hard** il se surmène ; **he's ~ing himself to death** il se tue à la tâche

b = bring about [+ miracle] faire, accomplir ; [+ change] apporter ; **to ~ wonders** or **marvels** [person] faire des merveilles ; [drug, medicine, action, suggestion] faire merveille

c * = arrange for **he has managed to ~ his promotion** il s'est débrouillé pour obtenir de l'avancement ; **can you ~ it so she can come too?** pouvez-vous faire en sorte qu'elle vienne aussi ? ; **I'll ~ it if I can** si je peux m'arranger pour le faire, je le ferai

d = exploit resources of [+ mine, land] exploiter ; **this rep ~s the south-east** ce représentant couvre le Sud-Est

e = manoeuvre **he ~ed the rope gradually through the hole** il est parvenu à faire passer progressivement la corde dans le trou, il s'est employé à enfoncer progressivement la corde dans le trou ; **he ~ed his hands free** il est parvenu à libérer ses mains ; **to ~ sth loose** parvenir à desserrer qch ; **he ~ed the lever up and down** il a actionné le levier plusieurs fois ; **she ~ed the hook carefully out of the cloth** avec précaution, elle s'employa à retirer l'hameçon du tissu ; **he ~ed the crowd (up) into a frenzy** il a réussi à déchaîner la foule

♦ **to work one's way**: **he ~ed his way along the edge of the cliff** il a longé prudemment le bord de la falaise ; **rescuers ~ing their way towards the trapped men** les sauveteurs se fraient un passage jusqu'aux hommes qui sont bloqués ; **he ~ed his way up from nothing** il est parti de rien ; **he ~ed his way up to the top of his firm** il a gravi un à un tous les échelons de la hiérarchie de son entreprise ; **he ~ed his way up from office boy to managing director** il est devenu PDG après avoir commencé comme garçon de bureau ; **to ~ one's way through college** travailler pour payer ses études

f = make, shape [+ metal, wood, leather] travailler ; [+ dough, clay] travailler, pétrir ; [+ object] façonner (out of dans) ; (= sew) coudre ; (= embroider) [+ design etc] broder ; (Culin) **~ the butter and sugar together** mélangez bien le beurre et le sucre

4 COMPOUNDS

► **work area** N coin m de travail, bureau m ► **work camp** N (= prison) camp m de travail forcé ; (voluntary) chantier m de travail (bénévole) ► **work ethic** N éthique f du travail, déontologie f ► **work experience** N (gen) expérience f professionnelle ; (for students) stage m professionnel ► **work file** N (Comput) fichier m de travail ► **work-in** N (Ind) grève avec occupation des locaux et appropriation des moyens de production ► **work load** N charge f de travail ; **his ~ load is too heavy** il a trop de travail ; **they were discussing ~ loads** ils discutaient de la répartition du travail ► **work of art** N œuvre f d'art ► **work permit** N permis m de travail ► **work prospects** NPL [of course, training] débouchés mpl ;

[of student] perspectives fpl ► **work-rule** N (US Ind) = work-to-rule ► **work-sharing** N partage m du travail ► **work space** N = work area ► **work station** N poste m de travail ► **work-study student** N (US Univ) étudiant(e) m(f) ayant un emploi rémunéré par l'université ► **work surface** N = worktop ► **work-to-rule** N (Brit Ind) grève f du zèle ► **work week** N semaine f de travail; (US) a ~ week of 38 hours une semaine de 38 heures ► **work-worn** ADJ [hands] usé par le travail

5 PHRASAL VERBS

►**work away** VI they ~ed away all day ils n'ont pas arrêté de toute la journée; she was ~ing away at her embroidery elle était absorbée par sa broderie

►**work down** VI [stockings etc] glisser

►**work in 1** VI a [dust, sand] s'introduire b (= fit in) she ~s in with us as much as possible elle collabore avec nous autant que possible; this doesn't ~ in with our plans to reorganize the department cela ne cadre pas or ne concorde pas avec nos projets de réorganisation du service; that'll ~ in very well ça cadrera très bien

2 VT SEP a [+ finger, hook, lever, blade] introduire petit à petit, enfoncer; [+ reference, quotation] glisser, introduire; (fig) [+ subject] s'arranger pour mentionner; we'll ~ in a mention of it somewhere on s'arrangera pour le mentionner quelque part; he ~ed the incident into his speech il s'est arrangé pour parler de l'incident dans son discours b (= amalgamate) incorporer; ~ the flour in gradually incorporez la farine petit à petit

►**work off 1** VI [nut, handle etc] se desserrer **2** VT SEP a [+ debt, obligation] travailler pour s'acquitter de b [+ one's surplus fat] se débarrasser de; [+ weight] éliminer; [+ anger] passer, assouvir; to ~ off one's energy dépenser son surplus d'énergie; jogging helps ~ off stress le jogging aide à évacuer le stress or à décompresser*; he ~ed it all off gardening il s'est défoulé* en faisant du jardinage

►**work out 1** VI a [plan, arrangement] marcher; [puzzle, problem] se résoudre; it's all ~ing out as planned tout se déroule comme prévu; things didn't ~ out (well) for her les choses ont plutôt mal tourné pour elle; their marriage didn't ~ out leur couple n'a pas marché*; it will ~ out all right in the end tout finira (bien) par s'arranger; how did it ~ out in the end? comment ça s'est terminé?; it hasn't ~ed out that way les choses se sont passées autrement b [amount] what does the total ~ out at? ça fait combien en tout?; it ~s out (at) £50 per child il faut compter 50 livres par enfant c (= exercise) faire de la musculation

2 VT SEP a (= figure out) [+ problem, puzzle, equation] résoudre; [+ answer, total] trouver; [+ code] déchiffrer; [+ plan, scheme, idea] élaborer, mettre au point; [+ settlement] parvenir à; I'll have to ~ it out (gen) il faut que j'y réfléchisse; (counting) il faut que je calcule; who ~ed all this out? qui a combiné tout ça?; I had the whole design ~ed out in my mind j'avais déjà tout conçu dans ma tête; can you ~ out where we are on the map? peux-tu trouver où nous sommes sur la carte?; he finally ~ed out why she'd gone il a fini par comprendre pourquoi elle était partie; I can't ~ it out ça me dépasse; I can't ~ him out* je n'arrive pas à comprendre comment il fonctionne b (= exhaust resources of) [+ mine, land] épuiser c [+ notice] she has to ~ out her notice elle doit respecter le délais de préavis d (= get rid of) don't try and ~ out your frustration on me! ne t'en prends pas à moi parce que tu te sens frustré!; he stood up in order to ~ out his impatience il se mit debout pour calmer son impatience

►**work over*** VT SEP (= beat up) tabasser*,

---

passer à tabac*

►**work round** VI (= move gradually) tourner; his tie had ~ed round to the back of his neck sa cravate avait tourné et lui pendait dans le dos; the wind has ~ed round to the south le vent a tourné au sud petit à petit; to ~ round to sth (in conversation, negotiations) aborder qch; you'll have to ~ round to that subject tactfully il faudra que vous abordiez (subj) ce sujet avec tact; what are you ~ing round to? où voulez-vous en venir?

►**work through** VT FUS (Psych = resolve emotionally) assumer

►**work up 1** VI a events were ~ing up to a crisis une crise se préparait; the book ~s up to a dramatic ending le roman s'achemine progressivement vers un dénouement spectaculaire; (in conversation etc) I knew they were ~ing up to something je savais qu'ils préparaient quelque chose; I thought he was ~ing up to asking me for a divorce je croyais qu'il préparait le terrain pour demander le divorce; what is he ~ing up to? où veut-il en venir? b [skirt, sleeve] remonter

2 VT SEP a (= rouse) he ~ed the crowd up into a frenzy il a déchaîné l'enthousiasme de la foule; to get ~ed up s'énerver; he ~ed himself up into a rage il s'est mis dans une colère noire b (= prepare) [+ article, drawings] préparer c (= develop) [+ trade, business] développer; he ~ed this small firm up into a major company il a réussi à faire de cette petite société une grande entreprise; (Comm) he's trying to ~ up a connection in Wales il essaie d'établir une tête de pont au pays de Galles; I ~ed up an appetite/thirst carrying all those boxes ça m'a mis en appétit/m'a donné soif de porter toutes ces caisses; I can't ~ up much enthusiasm for the plan j'ai du mal à m'enthousiasmer pour ce projet; can't you ~ up a little more interest in it? tu ne pourrais pas t'y intéresser un peu plus?

-work [wɜːk] N (in compounds) **cement-work** le ciment; **lattice-work** le treillis

workable ['wɜːkəbl] ADJ a [scheme, arrangement, solution, suggestion, plan, projet] viable, réalisable; [agreement, settlement, compromise] viable; it's just not ~ cela ne marchera jamais b (= malleable) [metal, dough] facile à travailler c (= exploitable) [land, mine] exploitable

workaday ['wɜːkədeɪ] ADJ [object, tastes, surroundings] ordinaire; [concerns, chores] de tous les jours; the ~ world la vie de tous les jours

workaholic* [ˌwɜːkə'hɒlɪk] N bourreau m de travail

workbag ['wɜːkbæg] N sac m à ouvrage

workbasket ['wɜːkbɑːskɪt] N (Sewing) corbeille f à ouvrage

workbench ['wɜːkbentʃ] N établi m

workbook ['wɜːkbʊk] N (= exercise book) cahier m d'exercices; (= manual) manuel m; (= work record book) cahier m de classe

workbox ['wɜːkbɒks] N (Sewing) boîte f à ouvrage

workday ['wɜːkdeɪ] (esp US) **1** ADJ = workaday **2** N a of eight hours une journée de travail de huit heures; **Saturday is a ~** (gen) on travaille le samedi; (Comm) le samedi est un jour ouvrable

worker ['wɜːkə'] **1** N a (gen, Ind, Agr etc) travailleur m, -euse f; **woman ~** travailleuse f; he's a good ~ il travaille bien; he's a fast ~ (lit) il travaille vite; (* fig) c'est un tombeur* or un don Juan; all the ~s in this industry tous ceux qui travaillent dans cette industrie; (Ind) **management and ~s** patronat m et ouvriers mpl; **we rely on volunteer ~s** nous dépendons de travailleurs bénévoles; **office ~**

---

employé(e) m(f) de bureau; **research ~** chercheur m, -euse f

2 COMP ► **worker ant** N (fourmi f) ouvrière f ► **worker bee** N (abeille f) ouvrière f ► **worker director** N (Ind) ouvrier m faisant partie du conseil d'administration ► **worker participation** N (Ind) participation f des travailleurs ► **worker priest** N prêtre-ouvrier m ► **Workers' Educational Association** N (Brit) ≈ Association f d'éducation populaire

workfare ['wɜːkfeə'] N système où les chômeurs doivent participer à des programmes de création d'emplois pour avoir droit aux allocations

workforce ['wɜːkfɔːs] N [of region, country] travailleurs mpl; [of company] personnel m; (= manual workers) main-d'œuvre f

workhorse ['wɜːkhɔːs] N (lit, fig) cheval m de labour

workhouse ['wɜːkhaʊs] N (Brit Hist) hospice m; (US Jur) maison f de correction

working ['wɜːkɪŋ] **1** ADJ a (= to do with work) [clothes, lunch, dinner, group] de travail; [partner, population] actif; the ~ class la classe ouvrière → **4**; (Pol) (collectively) the ~ classes le prolétariat; (Brit) a ~ day of eight hours une journée de travail de huit heures; (Brit) **Saturday is a ~ day** (gen) on travaille le samedi; (Comm) le samedi est un jour ouvrable; **good ~ environment** bonnes conditions fpl de travail; **~ expenses** [of mine, factory] frais mpl d'exploitation; [of salesman] frais mpl; **during or in ~ hours** pendant les heures de travail; (gen) **~ life** vie f active; **she spent most of her ~ life abroad** elle a passé la plus grande partie de sa vie active à l'étranger; **a long and strenuous ~ life** une longue vie de labeur; (Ind, Sociol etc) the ~ man will not accept ... les travailleurs n'accepteront pas ...; he's an ordinary ~ man c'est un simple travailleur; he's a ~ man now il travaille maintenant, il gagne sa vie maintenant; (Brit) ~ party (gen) groupe m de travail; (grander) commission f d'enquête; (= squad: of soldiers) escouade f; a ~ wife une femme mariée qui travaille; she is an ordinary ~ woman c'est une simple travailleuse; she is a ~ woman (= economically active) elle travaille, elle gagne sa vie; (Comm, Press, Sociol etc) the ~ woman la femme qui travaille → **order** b (= operational) ~ capital fonds mpl de roulement; (Comput) ~ disk disque m de travail; ~ drawing épure f; ~ hypothesis hypothèse f de travail; (Pol etc) to have a ~ majority avoir une majorité suffisante; to build or form a ~ partnership (Ind) établir de bons rapports; (emotionally) parvenir à une bonne relation de couple c (= functioning) [model] qui marche

2 N (NonC) travail m; [of machine etc] fonctionnement m; [of yeast] fermentation f; [of mine, land] exploitation f; [of metal, wood, leather] travail m; [of clay, dough] travail m, pétrissage m; (Sewing) couture f; (= embroidery) broderie f

3 **workings** NPL (= mechanism) mécanisme m; [of government, organization] rouages mpl; (Min) chantier m d'exploitation; **I don't understand the ~s of her mind** je ne comprends pas ce qui se passe dans sa tête

4 COMP ► **working-class** ADJ [origins, background, accent, suburb] ouvrier, prolétarien; **he is ~-class** il appartient à la classe ouvrière ► **working dog** N chien adapté, de par sa race ou son dressage, à des tâches utilitaires ► **working girl** N (euph) professionnelle* f (euph) ► **working holiday** N (Brit) vacances mises à profit pour effectuer une activité rémunérée ► **working men's club** N (Brit) ≈ foyer m d'ouvriers ► **working relationship** N relations fpl or rapports mpl de travail; **to have a good ~ relationship (with sb)** avoir de bonnes relations or bons rapports de travail (avec qn) ► **working title** N titre m provisoire

► **working vacation** N (US) = **working holiday**

workman ['wɜːkmən] (pl **-men**) N a (gen, Comm, Ind etc) ouvrier m ∎ (PROV) **a bad ~ blames his tools** les mauvais ouvriers ont toujours de mauvais outils (PROV); **workmen's compensation** pension f d'invalidité (pour ouvriers) b **to be a good ~** bien travailler, avoir du métier

workmanlike ['wɜːkmənlaɪk] ADJ [person, attitude] professionnel; [object, product, tool] bien fait, soigné; (fig) [attempt] sérieux; **it was a ~ essay** c'était une dissertation honnête or bien travaillée; **he made a ~ job of it** il a fait du bon travail; **he set about it in a very ~ way** il s'y est pris comme un vrai professionnel

workmanship ['wɜːkmənʃɪp] N [of craftsman] métier m, maîtrise f; [of artefact] exécution f or fabrication f soignée; **this example of his ~** cet exemple de son savoir-faire; **a chair of fine ~** une chaise faite avec art; **a superb piece of ~** un or du travail superbe

workmate ['wɜːkmeɪt] N camarade mf de travail

workmen ['wɜːkmən] NPL of **workman**

workout ['wɜːkaʊt] N (Sport) séance f d'entraînement

workpeople ['wɜːkpiːpl] NPL travailleurs mpl, ouvriers mpl

workplace ['wɜːkpleɪs] N lieu m de travail

workroom ['wɜːkrʊm] N salle f de travail

works [wɜːks] 1 N (pl inv) a (Brit Ind etc) (= factory) usine f; (= processing plant etc) installations fpl; **gasworks** usine f à gaz; **steelworks** aciérie f; **irrigation ~** installations f d'irrigation, barrage m; **price ex ~** prix m sortie d'usine b (Admin, Mil) travaux mpl; [of clock, machine etc] mécanisme m; (Rel) œuvres fpl; **each man will be judged by his ~** chaque homme sera jugé selon ses œuvres c **the (whole) ~*** (= the lot) tout le tremblement*, tout le tralala*; (US) **to put in the ~*** sortir le grand jeu → **public, spanner** 2 COMP [entrance, car park, canteen] de l'usine; [car] de l'entreprise; (as opposed to staff) des ouvriers ► **works committee, works council** N comité m d'entreprise ► **works manager** N directeur m, -trice f de l'usine

workshop ['wɜːkʃɒp] N (lit, fig) atelier m

workshy ['wɜːkʃaɪ] ADJ fainéant, tire-au-flanc* inv

worktable ['wɜːkteɪbl] N table f de travail

worktop ['wɜːktɒp] N plan m de travail

world [wɜːld] 1 N a (gen, Geog etc) monde m; **the most powerful nation in the ~** la nation la plus puissante du monde; **the English-speaking ~** le monde anglophone; **to be alone in the ~** être seul au monde; **the ancient ~** le monde antique, l'antiquité f; **a citizen of the ~** un citoyen du monde; **it's not the end of the ~** ça pourrait être bien pire; **the ~ we live in** le monde où nous vivons; (fig) **he lives in a ~ of his own ◊ he lives in another ~** il vit dans un monde à lui; **all over the ~ ◊ (all) the ~ over** dans le monde entier; **to go round the ~ ◊ to go on a trip round the ~ or a round-the-~ trip** faire le tour du monde, voyager autour du monde; **a round-the-~ cruise** une croisière autour du monde; **to see the ~** voir du pays, courir le monde; **since the ~ began ◊ since the beginning of the ~** depuis que le monde est monde; **it is known throughout the ~** c'est connu dans le monde entier, c'est universellement connu → **dead, fire, lead¹, new, old, old-world** b (emphatic phrases) **what/where/why/how in the ~ ...?** que/où/pourquoi/comment diable* ...?; **where in the ~ has he got to?** où a-t-il bien pu passer?, où diable* est-ce qu'il a passé?; **nowhere in the ~ ◊ nowhere in the**

whole (wide) ~ nulle part au monde; **I wouldn't do it for (anything in) the ~ ◊ nothing in the ~ would make me do it** je ne le ferais pour rien au monde, je ne le ferais pas pour tout l'or du monde; **they were ~s apart** (gen) ils n'avaient rien en commun, tout les séparait; (in opinion) ils étaient diamétralement opposés; **there's a ~ of difference between Paul and Richard** il y a un monde entre Paul et Richard; **it was for all the ~ as if ...** c'était exactement or tout à fait comme si ...; **I'd give the ~ to know ...** je donnerais tout au monde pour savoir ...; **it did him a ~ of good** ça lui a fait énormément de bien or un bien fou*; **it's what he wants most in (all) the ~** c'est ce qu'il veut plus que tout au monde; **in the whole (wide) ~ you won't find a better man than he is** nulle part au monde vous ne trouverez un meilleur homme que lui; **she means the ~ to him** elle est tout pour lui; **she thinks the ~ of him** elle ne jure que par lui; **I'm the ~'s worst cook** il n'y a pas pire cuisinier que moi

c (= this life) monde m; (Rel: as opposed to spiritual life) siècle m, monde m; (Rel) **the ~, the flesh and the devil** les tentations fpl du monde, de la chair et du diable; (Rel) **without end** dans les siècles des siècles; **he's gone to a better ~** il est parti pour un monde meilleur; **the next ~ ◊ the ~ to come** l'au-delà m, l'autre monde m; **he's not long for this ~** il n'en a plus pour longtemps (à vivre); **in this ~** ici-bas, en ce (bas) monde; (Rel) **in the ~** dans le siècle; **to bring a child into the ~** mettre un enfant au monde; **to come into the ~** venir au monde, naître; (fig) **it's out of this ~*** c'est extraordinaire, c'est sensationnel* → **best, other**

d (= domain, environment) monde m, univers m; **in the ~ of music** dans le monde de la musique; **the ~ of dreams** l'univers m or le monde des rêves; **the ~ of nature** la nature; **in the ~ of tomorrow** dans le monde de demain; **the business/sporting ~** le monde des affaires/du sport, les milieux mpl d'affaires/sportifs; **in the university/political/financial ~** dans les milieux universitaires/politiques/financiers; **his childhood was a ~ of hot summers and lazy days** son enfance était un univers d'étés brûlants et de journées oisives; **in an ideal or a perfect ~** dans un monde idéal; **in the best of all possible ~s** dans le meilleur des mondes (possibles)

e (= society) monde m; **the Rockefellers/Mr Smiths etc of this ~** des gens comme les Rockefeller/M. Smith etc; **you know what the ~ will say if ...** tu sais ce que les gens diront si ...; **he had the ~ at his feet** il avait le monde à ses pieds; **you have to take the ~ as you find it** il faut prendre le monde comme il est or les choses comme elles sont; **he has come down in the ~** il a connu des jours meilleurs; **to go up in the ~** faire du chemin (fig); **on top of the ~*** (= happy) aux anges; (= healthy) en pleine forme; **to make one's way in the ~** faire son chemin dans le monde; **the ~ and his wife** absolument tout le monde, tout le monde sans exception → **man**

2 COMP [power, war, proportions] mondial; [record, tour] du monde; [language] universel ► **World Bank** N Banque f mondiale ► **world-beater*** N (fig = person) champion(ne) m(f); **it's going to be a ~-beater!** ça va faire un tabac!* ► **World Boxing Association** N World Boxing Association f (association américaine de boxe) ► **world champion** N (Sport) champion(ne) m(f) du monde ► **world championship** N championnat m du monde ► **world-class** ADJ [player, team etc] de niveau international; [statesman, politician] de carrure internationale ► **World Council of Churches** N Conseil m œcuménique des Églises ► **World Court** N (Jur) Cour f internationale de justice

► **World Cup** N (Ftbl) Coupe f du monde ► **World Fair** N (Comm) Exposition f internationale ► **world-famous** ADJ de renommée mondiale, célèbre dans le monde entier ► **World Health Organization** N Organisation f mondiale de la santé ► **World Heritage Site** N site m inscrit sur la liste du patrimoine mondial ► **world leader** N (Pol, Comm) leader m mondial; **Clari UK is a ~ leader in agrochemicals** Clari UK est un leader mondial en matière de produits chimiques agricoles ► **world music** N world music f ► **world scale** N **on a ~ scale** à l'échelle mondiale ► **World Series** N (US Baseball) championnat m national de baseball ► **World Service** N (Brit Rad) service m international de la BBC ► **world-shaking, world-shattering** ADJ renversant ► **World title** N (Sport) titre m de champion du monde; (Boxing) **the World title fight** le championnat du monde ► **World Trade Organization** N Organisation f mondiale du commerce ► **world-view** N vision f du monde ► **World War One** N la Première Guerre mondiale ► **World War Two** N la Deuxième or Seconde Guerre mondiale ► **world-weariness** N dégoût m du monde ► **world-weary** ADJ las (lasse f) du monde ► **world-wide** ADJ mondial, universel ◆ ADV [be known] mondialement, universellement; [travel] à travers le monde, partout dans le monde ► **the World Wide Web** N (Comput) le Web

worldliness ['wɜːldlɪnɪs] N [of person] attachement m aux biens de ce monde; (Rel) mondanité f

worldly ['wɜːldlɪ] 1 ADJ a (= earthly) [matters] de ce monde; [pleasures, wealth] de ce monde, temporel; [success] matériel; **his ~ goods** ses biens mpl temporels; **to put aside ~ things** renoncer aux choses de ce monde b (pej = materialistic) [person, attitude] matérialiste c (= experienced) [person] qui a l'expérience du monde; [manner] qui démontre une expérience du monde 2 COMP ► **worldly-minded** ADJ matérialiste ► **worldly-wisdom** N expérience f du monde ► **worldly-wise** ADJ qui a l'expérience du monde

worm [wɜːm] 1 N (gen = earthworm etc) ver m (de terre); (in fruit etc) ver m; (= maggot) asticot m; (Med) ver m; (fig = person) minable* mf; (Med) **to have ~s** avoir des vers; (fig) **the ~ has turned** il en a eu (or j'en ai eu etc) assez de se (or me etc) faire marcher dessus; (fig) **the ~ in the apple or bud** le ver dans le fruit (fig); **you ~!*** misérable! → **bookworm, glow-, silkworm**

2 VT a (= wriggle) **to ~ o.s. or one's way along/down/across etc** avancer/descendre/traverser etc à plat ventre or en rampant; **he ~ed his way through the skylight** il a réussi en se tortillant à passer par la lucarne; (fig) **he ~ed his way into our group** il s'est insinué or immiscé dans notre groupe; (pej) **to ~ one's way into sb's affections** gagner insidieusement l'affection de qn b (= extract) **to ~ sth out of sb** soutirer qch à qn; **I'll ~ it out of him somehow** je m'arrangerai pour lui tirer les vers du nez c (= to rid of worms) [+ dog, cat, person] soigner pour ses vers or contre les vers 3 COMP ► **worm-cast** N déjections fpl de ver ► **worm drive** N (Tech) transmission f à vis sans fin; (Comput) unité f à disques inscriptibles une seule fois ► **worm-eaten** ADJ [fruit] véreux; [furniture] mangé aux vers, vermoulu ► **worm gear** N (Tech) engrenage m à vis sans fin ► **worm(ing) powder** N (Vet) poudre f vermifuge ► **worm's eye view*** N (Phot, Cine) contre-plongée f; (fig) **a ~'s eye view of what is going on** un humble aperçu de ce qui se passe

wormhole ['wɜːmhəʊl] N trou m de ver

wormlike ['wɜ:mlaɪk] ADJ vermiculaire, vermiforme

wormwood ['wɜ:mwʊd] N armoise f

wormy* ['wɜ:mɪ] ADJ (= worm-eaten) [fruit] véreux; [furniture] vermoulu, mangé aux vers

worn [wɔ:n] [1] VB ptp of **wear** [2] ADJ [garment, carpet, tyre, step, hands] usé; [face] las (lasse f); **to look ~** [person] avoir l'air las → **wear** [3] COMP ► **worn-out** ADJ [garment, carpet, tyre] usé jusqu'à la corde; [tool, machine part] complètement usé; [person] épuisé, éreinté; [idea] éculé, rebattu → **wear**

worried ['wʌrɪd] ADJ inquiet (-ète f); **she is ~ about her future** elle s'inquiète pour son avenir; **I'm ~ about her health** sa santé m'inquiète, je suis inquiet pour sa santé; **to get ~** s'inquiéter; **I was ~ that he would find out the truth** j'avais peur qu'il découvre (subj) la vérité; **~ sick** or **stiff*** fou d'inquiétude; **where do you want to go? — wherever, I'm not ~*** où veux-tu aller? — n'importe, ça m'est égal; **you had me ~ (for a minute)** tu m'as fait peur → **worry**; **~ to death**

worrier ['wʌrɪə'] N anxieux m, -euse f, inquiet m, -ète f; **he's a dreadful ~** c'est un éternel inquiet

worrisome ['wʌrɪsəm] ADJ préoccupant

worry ['wʌrɪ] [1] N souci m; **the ~ of having to find the money** le souci d'avoir à trouver l'argent; **he hasn't any worries** il n'a pas de soucis; **to make o.s. sick with ~** se faire un sang d'encre, se ronger les sangs (about, over au sujet de, pour); **that's the least of my worries** c'est le cadet de mes soucis; **what's your ~?*** qu'est-ce qui ne va pas?; **he's a constant ~ to his parents** il est un perpétuel souci pour ses parents; **it's a great ~ to us all** ◊ **it's causing us a lot of ~** cela nous cause or nous donne beaucoup de souci(s); **what a ~ it all is!** tout ça n'est que du souci!

[2] VI ⓐ se faire du souci, s'inquiéter (**about, over** au sujet de, pour); **don't ~ about me** ne vous inquiétez pas or ne vous en faites pas pour moi; **she worries about her health** sa santé la tracasse; **I've got enough to ~ about without that (as well)** j'ai déjà assez de soucis (comme ça); **there's nothing to ~ about** il n'y a aucune raison de s'inquiéter or s'en faire; (iro) **I should ~!*** je ne vois pas pourquoi je m'en ferais!*; **I'll punish him if I catch him at it, don't you ~!*** je le punirai si je l'y prends, (ne) t'en fais pas!*; **not to ~!** tant pis, ce n'est pas grave!

ⓑ **to ~ at sth = to worry sth**; → **3c**

[3] VT ⓐ (= make anxious) inquiéter, tracasser; **it worries me that he should believe ...** cela m'inquiète qu'il puisse croire ...; **the whole business worries me to death*** j'en suis fou d'inquiétude; **don't ~ yourself about it** ne t'en fais pas or ne t'inquiète pas or ne te tracasse pas pour ça; **don't ~ your head!** ne vous mettez pas martel en tête!; **she worried herself sick over it all** elle s'est rendue malade à force de se faire du souci pour tout ça, elle s'est rongé les sangs à propos de tout ça; **what's ~ing you?** qu'est-ce qui te tracasse? → **worried**

ⓑ (= bother) déranger; **the cold doesn't ~ me** le froid ne me dérange pas

ⓒ [dog etc] [+ bone, rat, ball] prendre entre les dents et secouer, jouer avec; [+ sheep] harceler; **he kept ~ing the loose tooth with his tongue** il n'arrêtait pas d'agacer avec sa langue la dent qui bougeait

[4] COMP ► **worry beads** NPL ≈ komboloï m ► **worry line*** N ride f (causée par l'inquiétude)
► **worry along** VI continuer à se faire du souci
► **worry at** VT FUS [+ problem] ressasser

worrying ['wʌrɪɪŋ] [1] ADJ inquiétant [2] N ~ **does no good** il ne sert à rien de se faire du souci; **all this ~ has aged him** tout le souci qu'il s'est fait l'a vieilli → **sheep**

worse [wɜ:s] [1] ADJ compar of **bad** and **ill** ⓐ (in quality) [news, weather, smell, result] plus mauvais (**than** que), pire (**than** que); **your essay is ~ than his** votre dissertation est pire or plus mauvaise que la sienne; **his essay is bad but yours is ~** sa dissertation est mauvaise mais la vôtre est pire; **I can't remember a ~ harvest** je ne me rappelle pas une plus mauvaise récolte; **I'm bad at English, but ~ at maths** je suis mauvais en anglais et pire en maths; **business is ~ than ever** les affaires vont plus mal que jamais; **it** or **things could be ~!** ça pourrait être pire!; **things couldn't be ~** ça ne pourrait pas aller plus mal; **~ things have happened!** ◊ **~ things happen at sea!*** (hum) on a vu pire!; **there are ~ things (than being unemployed)** il y a pire (que d'être au chômage); **there's nothing ~ than ...** il n'y a rien de pire que ...; **it looks ~ than it is** ça n'est pas aussi grave que ça en a l'air; **~ luck!*** hélas!; **and, what's ~, ...** et, qui pis est ...; **to get** or **grow ~** [situation, conditions] empirer, se détériorer; [weather, climate] être de pire en pire, se dégrader; [food, smell] être de plus en plus mauvais, être de pire en pire; [memory] empirer; **things will get ~ before they get better** les choses ne sont pas près d'aller mieux or de s'améliorer; **wait, it gets ~** ... attends, il y a pire ...; **to get ~ and ~** ne faire qu'empirer; **that would just make things or matters ~** cela ne ferait qu'aggraver les choses; **you've only made matters or things or it ~** tu n'as fait qu'aggraver la situation or qu'envenimer les choses; **he made matters ~ (for himself) by refusing** il a aggravé son cas en refusant; **and, to make matters or things ~, he ...** et pour ne rien arranger, il ... → **bad**

ⓑ (in behaviour) pire; **you're ~ than he is!** tu es pire que lui!; **he was always arrogant, but he's even ~ now** il a toujours été arrogant, mais il est encore pire maintenant; **he is getting ~** il ne s'améliore pas or s'arrange pas

ⓒ (in health) **to be ~** aller plus mal; **to feel ~** se sentir moins bien or plus mal; **to get** or **grow ~** aller plus mal

ⓓ (= more harmful) **smoking is (even) ~ for you than cholesterol** le tabac est (encore) plus mauvais or nocif pour la santé que le cholestérol

ⓔ (= more intense, serious) [noise, pressure, pain, stress] pire; **to get** or **grow ~** empirer; **the rain was getting ~** la pluie s'intensifiait

ⓕ **the ~ for sth: he's none the ~ for it** il ne s'en porte pas plus mal; **he's none the ~ for his fall** sa chute ne lui a pas fait trop de mal; **the house would be none the ~ for a coat of paint** une couche de peinture ne ferait pas de mal à cette maison; **it will be the ~ for you if ...** c'est vous qui serez perdant si ...; **so much the ~ for him!** tant pis pour lui!; **to be the ~ for drink** (= tipsy) être éméché, (= drunk) être ivre; **to look the ~ for wear*** [clothes, shoes] être vraiment défraîchi or fatigué; [carpet] être vraiment usé; **he was (looking) somewhat the ~ for wear*** il n'était pas très frais

[2] ADV compar of **badly** and **ill** ⓐ (in quality, behaviour) [sing, play] plus mal; **he did it ~ than you did** il l'a fait plus mal que toi; **that child behaves ~ and ~** cet enfant se conduit de plus en plus mal; **in spite of all those lessons, I played ~ than ever** malgré toutes ces leçons, j'ai joué plus mal que jamais; **you might or could do ~** vous pourriez faire pire; **you might do ~ than to accept** accepter n'est pas ce que vous pourriez faire de pire; **~, the food was running out** pire (encore), les vivres s'épuisaient; **and, ~, ...** et, qui pis est, ...; **now I'm ~ off than before** maintenant, je suis moins bien loti qu'avant

ⓑ (= more intensely, seriously) **it's raining ~ than ever** il pleut plus fort que jamais; **she hates me ~ than before** elle me déteste encore plus qu'avant; **it hurts ~ than ever** ça fait plus mal que jamais; **the ~ hit** or **~ affected areas** les régions fpl les plus touchées

ⓒ **the ~ for sth: I like him none the ~ for that** je ne l'en apprécie pas moins pour ça; **I won't think any the ~ of you for it** tu ne baisseras pas pour autant dans mon estime

[3] N pire m; **I have ~ to tell you** je ne vous ai pas tout dit, il y a pire encore; **there's ~ to come** le pire est à venir; **~ followed** ensuite cela a été pire; **there has been a change for the ~** (gen) il y a eu une détérioration très nette de la situation; (in medical patient) il y a eu une aggravation très nette de son état → **bad**

worsen ['wɜ:sn] [1] VI [situation, conditions, weather] empirer, se détériorer, se dégrader; [sb's state, health] empirer, s'aggraver; [illness] s'aggraver; [chances of success] diminuer, se gâter; [relationship] se détériorer, se dégrader [2] VT empirer, rendre pire

worsening ['wɜ:snɪŋ] [1] N [of situation, conditions, weather, relations, quality] détérioration f, dégradation f; [of health, crisis] aggravation f [2] ADJ [situation, weather, health, quality] qui empire, qui se détériore; [crisis] qui empire

worship ['wɜ:ʃɪp] [1] N ⓐ (Rel, also of money, success etc) culte m; (gen: of person) adoration f, culte m; **form of ~** liturgie f; (Rel) **place of ~** lieu m de culte; (Christian) église f; (Rel) **hours of ~** heures fpl des offices → **hero** ⓑ (esp Brit: in titles) **His Worship (the Mayor)** Monsieur le maire; **Your Worship** (to Mayor) Monsieur le Maire; (to magistrate) Monsieur le Juge [2] VT (Rel) [+ God, idol etc] rendre un culte à; (gen) vouer un culte à; [+ money, success etc] avoir le culte de; **he ~ped the ground she walked on** il vénérait jusqu'au sol qu'elle foulait; **she had ~ped him for years** elle lui avait voué un culte pendant des années [3] VI (Rel) faire ses dévotions; (fig) **to ~ at the altar of power/fame** avoir le culte du pouvoir/de la renommée, vouer un culte au pouvoir/à la renommée

worshipful ['wɜ:ʃɪpfʊl] ADJ ⓐ (frm = reverential) révérencieux (liter) ⓑ (esp Brit: in titles) **the Worshipful Company of Goldsmiths** l'honorable compagnie f des orfèvres; **the Worshipful Mayor of ...** Monsieur le maire de ...

worshipper, worshiper (US) ['wɜ:ʃɪpə'] N (Rel, fig) adorateur m, -trice f; (in church) **~s** fidèles mpl

worst [wɜ:st] [1] ADJ (superl of **bad** and **ill**) **the ~ ...** le (or la) plus mauvais(e) ..., le (or la) pire ...; **the ~ film I've ever seen** le plus mauvais film que j'aie jamais vu; **he was the ~ student in the class** c'était le plus mauvais élève de la classe; **the ~ thing about men is ...** ce qu'il y a de pire chez les hommes c'est que ...; **the ~ thing about living on your own is ...** ce qu'il y a de pire quand on vit seul, c'est ...; **come on, what's the ~ thing that could happen?** allons, on a vu pire!; **that's the ~ kind of arrogance** c'est la pire sorte d'arrogance; (US fig) **in the ~ way*** désespérément; **of all the children, he's (the) ~** de tous les enfants, c'est le pire; **it was the ~ thing he ever did** c'est la pire chose qu'il ait jamais faite; **it was the ~ winter for 20 years** c'était l'hiver le plus rude depuis 20 ans; **my ~ fears were confirmed (when ...)** mes pires craintes se sont confirmées (quand ...); **that was his ~ mistake** cela a été son erreur la plus grave or sa plus grave erreur; **the ~ victims of inflation are the old** les plus grandes victimes de l'inflation sont les personnes âgées, les personnes les plus touchées par l'inflation sont les personnes âgées

[2] ADV (superl of **badly** and **ill**) le plus mal; **they all sing badly but he sings ~ of all** ils chantent tous mal mais c'est lui qui chante le plus mal de tous; **he came off ~** c'est lui qui s'en est le plus mal sorti; **the ~ off** le (or la) plus mal loti(e); **~ of all, ...** pire que tout, ...; **that boy behaved ~ of all** ce garçon a été le

pire de tous; **it's my leg that hurts ~ of all** c'est ma jambe qui me fait le plus mal; **the ~-dressed man in England** l'homme *m* le plus mal habillé d'Angleterre; **the ~ hit** *or* **~ affected areas** les régions *fpl* les plus touchées

3 N pire *m*, pis *m* (*liter*) **the ~ that can happen** le pire chose *or* le pire qui puisse arriver; **the ~ is yet to come** il faut s'attendre à pire, on n'a pas encore vu le pire; **the ~ was yet to come** le pire devait arriver ensuite, on n'avait pas encore vu le pire; **the ~ hasn't come to the ~ yet** ce pourrait encore être pire, la situation n'est pas désespérée; **if the ~ comes to the ~** (*Brit*) ◊ **if ~ comes to ~** (*US*) en mettant les choses au pis, même en envisageant le pire; **at (the) ~** au pire; **to be at its** (*or* **their**) **~** [*crisis, storm, winter, epidemic*] être à son (*or* leur) paroxysme; [*situation, conditions, relationships*] n'avoir jamais été aussi mauvais; **things** *or* **matters were at their ~** les choses ne pouvaient pas aller plus mal; **at the ~ of the storm/epidemic** au plus fort de l'orage/de l'épidémie; **the ~ of it is that ...** le pire c'est que ....; **... and that's not the ~ of it!** ... et il y a pire encore!; **that's the ~ of being ...** (ça) c'est l'inconvénient d'être ...; **the ~ of both worlds** tous les inconvénients à la fois; **it brings out the ~ in me** ça réveille en moi les pires instincts; **do your ~!** vous pouvez toujours essayer!; **to get the ~ of it** *or* **of the bargain*** être le perdant → **think**

4 VT (*frm*) battre, avoir la supériorité sur; **to be ~ed** avoir le dessous

5 COMP ► **worst-case** ADJ [*hypothesis, projection, guess*] le (*or* la) plus pessimiste; **the ~-case scenario** le pire qui puisse arriver, le pire scénario ► **the worst off** ADJ le (*or* la) plus mal loti(e)

worsted ['wʊstɪd] **1** N worsted *m* **2** COMP [*suit etc*] en worsted

▼ **worth** [wɜːθ] **1** N **a** (= *value*) valeur *f*; **what is its ~ in today's money?** ça vaut combien en argent d'aujourd'hui?; **its ~ in gold** sa valeur (en) or; **a book/man** *etc* **of great ~** un livre/homme *etc* de grande valeur; **I know his ~** je sais ce qu'il vaut; **he showed his true ~** il a montré sa vraie valeur *or* ce dont il était capable

b (= *quantity*) **he bought £2 ~ of sweets** il a acheté pour 2 livres de bonbons; **50 pence ~, please** (pour) 50 pence s'il vous plaît → **money**

2 ADJ **a** (= *equal in value to*) **to be ~** valoir; **the book is ~ £10** le livre vaut 10 livres; **it can't be ~ that!** ça ne peut pas valoir autant!; **what** *or* **how much is it ~?** ça vaut combien?; **I don't know what it's ~ in terms of cash** je ne sais pas combien ça vaut en argent *or* quel prix ça pourrait aller chercher; **how much is the old man ~?*** à combien s'élève la fortune du vieux?; **he's ~ millions** sa fortune s'élève à plusieurs millions; **it's ~ a great deal** ça a beaucoup de valeur, ça vaut cher; **it's ~ a great deal to me** ça a beaucoup de valeur pour moi; **Swiss chocolate is dearer but it's ~ every penny** le chocolat suisse est plus cher mais on en a pour son argent; **what is his friendship ~ to you?** quel prix attachez-vous à son amitié?; **it's more than my life is ~ to do that** pour rien au monde je ne peux me permettre de faire cela; **it's as much as my job is ~ to show him that** lui montrer ça est un coup à perdre mon emploi*; **it's not ~ the paper it's written on** ça ne vaut pas le papier sur lequel c'est écrit; **this pen is ~ ten of any other make** ce stylo en vaut dix d'une autre marque; **one Scotsman's ~ three Englishmen** un Écossais vaut trois Anglais; **tell me about it — what's it ~ to you?!*** dites-moi — vous donneriez combien pour le savoir?*; **I'll give you my opinion for what it's ~** je vais vous donner mon avis, vous en ferez ce que vous voudrez; **he was running/shouting for all he**

was ~ il courait/criait comme un perdu *or* de toutes ses forces; **to try for all one is ~ to do sth** faire absolument tout son possible pour faire qch

b (= *deserving, meriting*) **it's ~ the effort** ça mérite qu'on fasse l'effort; **it was well ~ the trouble** ça valait bien le dérangement *or* la peine qu'on se dérange (*subj*); **it's not ~ the time and effort involved** c'est une perte de temps et d'effort; **it's ~ reading/having** *etc* ça vaut la peine d'être lu/d'en avoir un *etc*; **it's not ~ having** ça ne vaut rien*; **that's ~ knowing** c'est bon à savoir; **it's ~ thinking about** ça mérite réflexion; **it's ~ going to see the film just for the photography** rien que pour la photographie le film mérite *or* vaut la peine d'être vu ■ (*PROV*) **if a job's ~ doing, it's ~ doing well** si un travail vaut la peine d'être fait, autant le faire bien; **it's ~ it** ça vaut la peine *or* le coup*; **will you go? — is it ~ it?** tu iras? — est-ce que ça en vaut la peine?; **life isn't ~ living** la vie ne vaut pas la peine d'être vécue; **she/it makes (my) life ~ living** elle/cela *etc* est ma raison de vivre; **the museum is ~ a visit** le musée vaut la visite; **it is ~ while to study the text** on gagne à étudier le texte, c'est un texte qui mérite d'être étudié; **it would be ~ (your) while to go and see him** vous gagneriez à aller le voir; **it's not ~ (my) while waiting for him** je perds (*or* perdrais) mon temps à l'attendre; **it's not ~ while** ça ne vaut pas le coup*; **it wasn't ~ his while to take the job** il ne gagnait rien à accepter l'emploi, ça ne valait pas le coup* qu'il accepte (*subj*) l'emploi; **I'll make it ~ your while*** je vous récompenserai de votre peine, vous ne regretterez pas de l'avoir fait

worthily ['wɜːðɪlɪ] ADV dignement

worthiness ['wɜːðɪnɪs] N **a** (= *deservingness, merit*) [*of person, work, cause*] mérite *m* ► **airworthiness, creditworthiness b** (= *association with vegetarianism/green issues*) les prétendus mérites *mpl* du végétarisme/de l'écologie

worthless ['wɜːθlɪs] ADJ [*object, advice, asset*] qui n'a aucune valeur, sans valeur; [*person*] bon à rien

worthlessness ['wɜːθlɪsnɪs] N [*of object, advice*] absence *f* totale de valeur; [*of effort*] inutilité *f*; [*of person*] absence *f* totale de qualités

worthwhile [wɜːθ'waɪl] ADJ [*visit*] qui en vaut la peine; [*book*] qui mérite d'être lu; [*film*] qui mérite d'être vu; [*work, job, occupation, life, career*] utile, qui a un sens; [*contribution*] notable; [*cause*] louable, digne d'intérêt; **he is a ~ person to go and see** c'est une personne qu'on gagne à aller voir; **I want the money to go to someone ~** je veux que l'argent aille à quelqu'un qui le mérite *or* à une personne méritante

worthy ['wɜːðɪ] **1** ADJ **a** (= *deserving, meritorious*) [*person*] méritant; [*motive, aim, effort*] louable; **a ~ winner** un digne gagnant; **it's for a ~ cause** c'est pour une bonne *or* noble cause; **to be ~ of sth/qn** être digne de qn/qch; **to be ~ to do sth** être digne de faire qch, mériter de faire qch; **he found a ~ opponent** *or* **an opponent ~ of him (in Jones)** il a trouvé (en Jones) un adversaire digne de lui; **it is ~ of note that ...** il est intéressant de remarquer que ...; **they have no hospital ~ of the name** ils n'ont pas d'hôpital digne de ce nom **b** (*iro = earnest*) [*person*] brave (*before n*) **2** N (= *respectable citizen*) notable *m*; (*hum iro*) brave homme *m*, brave femme *f*; **a Victorian ~** un notable de l'époque victorienne; (*hum iro*) **the village worthies** les dignes *or* braves habitants *mpl* du village

wot [wɒt] **1** VTI *~* sais, sait; **God ~** Dieu sait **2** (*Brit*) = **what**

Wotan ['vəʊtɑːn] N Wotan *m*

wotcha‡ ['wɒtʃə], **wotcher‡** ['wɒtʃəʳ] EXCL (*Brit*) salut!

would [wʊd] **1** MODAL AUX VB *cond of* **will** (*neg* **would not** *often abbr to* **wouldn't**) **a** (*used to form conditional tenses*) **he ~ do it if you asked him** il le ferait si vous le lui demandiez; **he ~ have done it if you had asked him** il l'aurait fait si vous le lui aviez demandé; **I wondered if you'd come** je me demandais si vous viendriez *or* si vous alliez venir; **I thought you'd want to know** j'ai pensé que vous aimeriez le savoir; **who ~ have thought it?** qui l'aurait pensé?; **you'd never guess** *or* **know she had false teeth** jamais on ne croirait qu'elle a de fausses dents; **so it ~ seem** c'est bien ce qu'il semble; **you ~ think she had enough to do without ...** on pourrait penser qu'elle a assez à faire sans ...

b (*indicating willingness*) **I said I ~ do it** je lui ai dit que je le ferais *or* que je voulais bien le faire; **he wouldn't help me** il ne voulait pas m'aider, il n'a pas voulu m'aider; **the car wouldn't start** la voiture ne voulait pas démarrer *or* n'a pas voulu* démarrer; **the door wouldn't shut** la porte ne fermait pas *or* ne voulait pas* fermer; **if you ~ come with me, I'd go to see him** si vous vouliez bien m'accompagner, j'irais le voir; **what ~ you have me do?** que voulez-vous que je fasse?; **~ you like some tea?** voulez-vous du thé?; **~ you like to go for a walk?** voulez-vous faire une promenade?, est-ce que vous aimeriez faire une promenade?; (*in requests*) **~ you please leave!** voulez-vous partir, s'il vous plaît!; (*frm*) **~ you be so kind** *or* **good as to tell him** auriez-vous l'amabilité *or* la gentillesse de le lui dire; **~ you mind closing the window please** voulez-vous fermer la fenêtre, s'il vous plaît

c (*indicating habit, characteristic*) **he ~ always read the papers before dinner** il lisait toujours *or* il avait l'habitude de lire les journaux avant le dîner; **50 years ago the streets ~ be empty on Sundays** il y a 50 ans, les rues étaient vides le dimanche; **you ~ go and tell her!** c'est bien de toi d'aller le lui dire!*, il a fallu que tu ailles le lui dire!; **you ~!** c'est bien de toi!*, ça m'étonne pas de toi!; **it ~ have to rain!** il pleut, naturellement!, évidemment il fallait qu'il pleuve!

d (*expressing preferences*) **I wouldn't have a vase like that in my house** je n'aurais pas ce vase chez moi!; **I ~ never marry in church** je ne me marierais jamais à l'église

e (*indicating conjecture*) **it ~ have been about 8 o'clock when he came** il devait être 8 heures à peu près quand il est venu, il a dû venir vers 8 heures; **he ~ have been about fifty if he'd lived** il aurait eu la cinquantaine s'il avait vécu; **he'd be about 50, but he doesn't look it** il doit avoir dans les 50 ans, mais il ne les fait pas*; **I saw him come out of the shop — when ~ this be?** je l'ai vu sortir du magasin — quand est-ce que c'était?

f (*giving advice*) **I wouldn't worry, if I were you** à ta place, je ne m'inquiéterais pas; **I ~ wait and see what happens first** à ta place j'attendrais de voir ce qui se passe

g (*subjunctive uses: liter*) **~ to God she were here!** plût à Dieu qu'elle fût ici!; **~ that it were not so!** si seulement cela n'était pas le cas!; **~ I were younger!** si seulement j'étais plus jeune!

2 COMP ► **would-be** ADJ **~-be poet/teacher** personne *f* qui veut être poète/professeur; (*pej*) prétendu *or* soi-disant poète *m*/professeur *m*

wouldn't ['wʊdnt] = **would not**; → **would**

would've ['wʊdəv] = **would have**; → **would**

wound[1] [wuːnd] **1** N (*lit, fig*) blessure *f*; (*esp Med*) plaie *f*; **bullet/knife ~** blessure *f* causée par une balle/un couteau; **he had three bullet ~s in his leg** il avait reçu trois balles dans la jambe; **chest/head ~** blessure *f* *or* plaie *f* à la poitrine/tête; **the ~ is healing up** la plaie se cicatrise; (*fig*) **to open** *or* **re-open old ~s** rouvrir de vieilles plaies → **lick**, **salt** [2] VT (*lit, fig*) blesser; **he ~ed in the leg** il s'était blessé à la jambe; **he had been ~ed in combat** il avait été blessé au combat; **the bullet ~ed him in the shoulder** la balle l'a atteint *or* l'a blessé à l'épaule; **her feelings were** *or* **she was ~ed by this remark** elle a été blessée par cette remarque; **he was deeply ~ed by their disloyalty** il a été profondément blessé par leur traîtrise → **wounded**

wound² [waʊnd] VB *pt, ptp of* **wind²**, **wind³**

wounded [ˈwuːndɪd] [1] ADJ (*lit, fig*) [*person, pride, feelings*] blessé; **seriously ~** gravement *or* grièvement blessé; **a ~ man** un blessé; **a ~ woman** une blessée; **there were six dead and fifteen ~** il y a eu six morts et quinze blessés [2] **the wounded** NPL les blessés *mpl* → **walking**, **war**

wounding [ˈwuːndɪŋ] ADJ (*fig*) [*remark, insult*] blessant

wove [waʊv] VB *pt of* **weave**

woven [ˈwaʊvən] VB *ptp of* **weave**

wow* [waʊ] [1] EXCL sensass!† *, terrible!* [2] N **it's a ~!** c'est sensationnel* *or* terrible!* [b] (*Acoustics*) pleurage *m*, baisse *f* de hauteur du son [3] VT (* = *make enthusiastic*) emballer*

WP [ˌdʌbljuːˈpiː] [a] (ABBR = **weather permitting**) si le temps le permet, si les conditions météorologiques le permettent [b] (ABBR = **word processing**) → **word** [c] (ABBR = **word processor**) → **word**

WPC [ˌdʌbljuːpiːˈsiː] N (*Brit*) (ABBR = **Woman Police Constable**) → **woman**

wpm (ABBR = **words per minute**) mots/minute

WRAC [ræk] N (*Brit*) (ABBR = **Women's Royal Army Corps**) section féminine de l'armée

wrack¹ [ræk] VT = **rack¹ 2**

wrack² [ræk] N = **rack²**

wrack³ [ræk] N (= *seaweed*) varech *m*

WRAF [wæf] N (*Brit*) (ABBR = **Women's Royal Air Force**) section féminine de l'armée de l'air

wraith [reɪθ] N apparition *f*, spectre *m*; **~-like** spectral

wrangle [ˈræŋgl] [1] N querelle *f*; **legal/financial/political ~s** querelles *fpl* juridiques/financières/politiques; **the ~s within the party** les conflits au sein du parti [2] VI se quereller; **they were wrangling over** *or* **about who should pay** ils se querellaient pour savoir qui allait payer

wrangler [ˈræŋglər] N (*Cambridge Univ*) ≈ major *m*; (*US* = *cowboy*) cow-boy *m*

wrangling [ˈræŋglɪŋ] N (= *quarrelling*) disputes *fpl*

wrap [ræp] [1] N [a] (= *shawl*) châle *m*; (= *stole, scarf*) écharpe *f*; (= *cape*) pèlerine *f*; (= *housecoat etc*) peignoir *m*; (= *rug, blanket*) couverture *f*; **~s** (= *outdoor clothes*) vêtements *mpl* chauds
[b] (= *outer covering: on parcel etc*) emballage *m*; (*fig*) **to keep a scheme under ~s** ne pas dévoiler un projet; (*fig*) **when the ~s come off** quand le voile est levé; (*fig*) **to take the ~s off sth** dévoiler qch
[c] (*fig: Cine*) **it's a ~*** c'est dans la boîte* [2] VT (= *cover*) envelopper (**in** dans); (= *pack*) [*+ parcel, gift*] emballer, empaqueter (**in** dans); (= *wind*) [*+ tape, bandage*] enrouler (**round** autour de); (*Culin*) **~ the chops in foil** enveloppez les côtelettes dans le papier d'aluminium; **chops ~ped in foil** côtelettes *fpl* en papillotes; (*in gift shop*) **shall I ~ it for you?** c'est pour offrir?, je vous fais un paquet-cadeau?; **she ~ped the child in a blanket** elle a enveloppé l'enfant dans une couverture; **~ the rug round your legs** enroulez la couverture autour de vos jambes, enveloppez vos jambes dans la couverture; **he ~ped his arms round her** il l'a enlacée; (*fig*) **he ~ped* the car round a lamppost** il s'est payé* un lampadaire; **~ped**

bread/cakes *etc* pain *m*/gâteaux *mpl etc* préemballé(s) *or* préempaqueté(s); (*fig*) **the town was ~ped in mist** la brume enveloppait la ville; **the whole affair was ~ped in mystery** toute l'affaire était enveloppée *or* entourée de mystère → **giftwrap**
[3] COMP ► **wrap-up*** N (*US*) (= *summary*) résumé *m*; (= *concluding event*) conclusion *f*, aboutissement *m*

► **wrap up** [1] VI [a] (= *dress warmly*) s'habiller chaudement, s'emmitoufler; **~ up well!** couvrez-vous bien!
[b] (*Brit** = *be quiet*) la fermer*, la boucler*; **~ up!** la ferme!*, boucle-la!*
[2] VT SEP [a] [*+ object*] envelopper (**in** dans); [*+ parcel*] emballer, empaqueter (**in** dans); [*+ child, person*] (*in rug etc*) envelopper; (*in clothes*) emmitoufler; **~ yourself up well!** couvrez-vous bien!
[b] (*fig = conceal one's intentions*) dissimuler; **he ~ped up his meaning in unintelligible jargon** il a enveloppé *or* noyé ce qu'il voulait dire dans un jargon tout à fait obscur; **tell me straight out, don't try to ~ it up*** dis-le-moi carrément, n'essaie pas de me dorer la pilule
[c] (*fig = engrossed*) **to be ~ped up in one's work** être absorbé par son travail; **to be ~ped up in sb** penser constamment à qn; **he is quite ~ped up in himself** il ne pense qu'à lui-même; **they are ~ped up in each other** ils vivent entièrement l'un pour l'autre, ils n'ont d'yeux que l'un pour l'autre
[d] (* = *conclude*) [*+ deal*] conclure; **he hopes to ~ up his business there by Friday evening** il espère conclure *or* régler ce qu'il a à y faire d'ici vendredi soir; **let's get all this ~ped up** finissons-en avec tout ça; **he thought he had everything ~ped up** il pensait avoir tout arrangé *or* réglé; (*esp US fig*) **to ~ up the evening's news** résumer les informations de la soirée
[3] **~up** N → **wrap**

wraparound [ˈræpəraʊnd], **wrapover** [ˈræpəʊvər] ADJ **~ skirt/dress** jupe *f*/robe *f* portefeuille *inv*

wrapper [ˈræpər] N [a] [*of sweet, chocolate bar*] papier *m*; [*of parcel*] papier *m* d'emballage; [*of newspaper for post*] bande *f*; [*of book*] jaquette *f*, couverture *f* [b] (*US* = *garment*) peignoir *m*

wrapping [ˈræpɪŋ] [1] N [*of parcel*] papier *m* (d'emballage); [*of sweet, chocolate*] papier *m* [2] COMP ► **wrapping paper** N (= *brown paper*) papier *m* d'emballage; (= *decorated paper*) papier *m* cadeau

wrapround rear window [ˈræpraʊndrɪəˈwɪndəʊ] N (*Aut*) lunette *f* arrière panoramique

wrath [rɒθ] N (*liter*) colère *f*, courroux *m* (*liter*)

wrathful [ˈrɒθfʊl] ADJ (*liter*) courroucé (*liter*)

wrathfully [ˈrɒθfəlɪ] ADV (*liter*) avec courroux (*liter*)

wreak [riːk] VT [*+ one's anger etc*] assouvir (**upon sb** sur qn); **to ~ vengeance** *or* **revenge** assouvir une vengeance (**on sb** sur qn); **~ing destruction along the way** détruisant tout sur son passage

wreath [riːθ] N (*pl* **wreaths** [riːðz]) [*of flowers*] guirlande *f*, couronne *f*; (*also* **funeral ~**) couronne *f*; [*of smoke*] volute *f*, ruban *m*; [*of mist*] nappe *f*; **laurel ~** couronne *f* de laurier; (*ceremony*) **the laying of ~s** le dépôt de gerbes *fpl* au monument aux morts

wreathe [riːð] [1] VT [a] (= *garland*) [*+ person*] couronner (**with** de); [*+ window etc*] orner (**with** de); (*fig*) **a valley ~d in mist** une vallée frangée de brume; **hills ~d in cloud** collines *fpl* dont les sommets disparaissent dans les nuages; **his face was ~d in smiles** son visage était rayonnant [b] (= *entwine*) [*+ flowers*] enrouler (**round** autour de) [2] VI [*smoke*] **to ~ upwards** s'élever en tournoyant

wreck [rek] [1] N [a] (= *wrecked ship*) épave *f*, navire *m* naufragé; (= *act, event*) naufrage *m*; (*of plans, ambitions*) effondrement *m*; (*of hopes*) effondrement *m*, anéantissement *m*; **to be saved from the ~** réchapper du naufrage; **the ~ of the Hesperus** le naufrage de l'Hesperus; **sunken ~s in the Channel** des épaves englouties au fond de la Manche; **the ship was a total ~** le navire a été entièrement perdu
[b] (*esp US* = *accident: Aut, Aviat, Rail*) accident *m*; **he was killed in a car ~** il a été tué dans un accident de voiture
[c] (= *wrecked train/plane/car etc*) train *m*/avion *m*/voiture *f etc* accidenté(e), épave *f*; (= *building*) ruines *fpl*, décombres *mpl*; **the car was a complete ~** la voiture était bonne à mettre à la ferraille *or* à envoyer à la casse
[d] (= *person*) épave *f*; **he was a ~** c'était une épave; **he looks a ~** on dirait une loque, il a une mine de déterré; **a ~ of humanity** ◊ a human ~ une épave, une loque humaine
[2] VT [a] [*+ ship*] provoquer le naufrage de; [*+ train, plane, car*] [*bomb, terrorist, accident*] détruire; [*driver, pilot*] démolir; [*+ building*] démolir; [*+ mechanism*] détraquer; [*+ furniture etc*] casser, démolir; **to be ~ed** [*ship, sailor*] faire naufrage; **the plane was completely ~ed** il n'est resté que des débris de l'avion; **in his fury he ~ed the whole house** dans sa rage il a tout démoli *or* cassé dans la maison
[b] (*fig*) [*+ marriage, friendship*] briser, être la ruine de; [*+ career*] briser; [*+ plans, health*] ruiner; [*+ hopes, ambitions*] ruiner, anéantir; [*+ negotiations, discussions*] faire échouer; **this ~ed his chances of success** cela a anéanti ses chances de succès; **it ~ed my life** cela a brisé ma vie, ma vie en a été brisée

wreckage [ˈrekɪdʒ] N (*NonC*) [a] (= *wrecked ship, car, plane*) épave *f*; (= *pieces from this*) débris *mpl*; [*of building*] décombres *mpl*; (*Aviat, Rail*) **~ was strewn over several kilometres** les débris étaient disséminés sur plusieurs kilomètres; (*fig*) **things look black but we must try to save** *or* **salvage something from the ~** la situation est sombre mais il faut essayer de sauver les meubles* [b] (= *act*) [*of ship*] naufrage *m*; [*of train*] déraillement *m*; (*fig*) [*of hopes, ambitions, plans*] anéantissement *m*

wrecked [rekt] ADJ [a] [*ship*] naufragé; [*train, car*] complètement démoli, accidenté [b] [*plan*] anéanti [c]* [*person*] (= *exhausted*) vidé*; (= *drunk*) bourré*

wrecker [ˈrekər] N [a] (*gen*) destructeur *m*, démolisseur *m*; (*Hist: of ships*) naufrageur *m* [b] (*in salvage*) (= *person*) sauveteur *m* (d'épave); (= *boat*) canot *m or* bateau *m* sauveteur; (= *truck*) dépanneuse *f* [c] (*US*) (*in demolition*) [*of buildings*] démolisseur *m*; [*of cars*] (= *person*) casseur *m*, épaviste *mf*; (= *business*) casse *f*

wrecking [ˈrekɪŋ] [1] N (= *act*) [*of ship*] naufrage *m*; [*of train*] déraillement *m*; (*fig*) [*of hopes, ambitions, plans*] anéantissement *m* [2] COMP ► **wrecking ball** N boulet *m* de démolition ► **wrecking bar** N pied-de-biche *m* ► **wrecking crane** N (*Rail*) grue *f* de levage

wren [ren] N [a] (= *bird*) roitelet *m*, troglodyte *m* [b] (*Brit Navy*) **Wren** Wren *f* (auxiliaire féminine de la marine royale britannique)

wrench [rentʃ] [1] N [a] (= *tug*) mouvement *m* violent de torsion; **he gave the handle a ~** il a tiré de toutes ses forces sur la poignée
[b] (*fig: emotional*) déchirement *m*; **the ~ of parting** le déchirement de la séparation; **it was a ~ when she saw him leave** cela a été un déchirement quand elle l'a vu partir
[c] (*Med*) entorse *f*
[d] (= *tool*) clé *f* (à écrous), tourne-à-gauche *m inv*; (*Aut: for wheels*) clé *f* en croix; (*US fig*) **to throw a ~ into the works** mettre des bâtons dans les roues; **to throw a ~ into the economy** porter un coup très dur à l'économie → **monkey**

[2] VT [a] (+ *handle etc*) tirer violemment sur ; **to ~ sth (away) from sb** *or* **from sb's grasp** arracher qch des mains de qn ; **to ~ sth off** *or* **out** *or* **away** arracher qch ; **he ~ed himself free** il s'est dégagé d'un mouvement brusque ; **to ~ a box open** ouvrir de force une boîte
[b] (*Med*) **to ~ one's ankle**† se tordre la cheville

wrest [rest] VT [+ *object*] arracher violemment (**from sb** des mains de qn) ; [+ *secret, confession*] arracher (**from sb** à qn) ; [+ *power, leadership, title*] ravir (*liter*) (**from sb** à qn) ; **he managed to ~ a living**† **from the poor soil** à force de travail et de persévérance, il a réussi à tirer un revenu de ce sol pauvre

wrestle ['resl] [1] VI lutter (corps à corps) (**with sb** contre qn) ; (*Sport*) catcher (**with sb** contre qn) ; (*Graeco-Roman*) lutter ; (*fig*) **to ~ with** [+ *problem, one's conscience, sums, device*] se débattre avec ; [+ *difficulties*] se débattre contre, se colleter avec ; [+ *temptation, illness, disease*] lutter contre ; **the pilot ~d with the controls** le pilote se débattait avec les commandes ; (*fig*) **she was wrestling with her suitcases** elle peinait avec ses valises, elle se débattait avec ses valises [2] VT [+ *opponent*] lutter contre ; **to ~ sb to the ground** terrasser qn [3] N lutte *f* ; **to have a ~ with sb** lutter avec qn

wrestler ['reslə*r*] N (*Sport*) catcheur *m*, -euse *f* ; (*Graeco-Roman*) lutteur *m*, -euse *f*

wrestling ['resliŋ] [1] N (*Sport*) catch *m* ; (*Sport*) **Graeco-Roman** ~ lutte *f* gréco-romaine [2] COMP ► **wrestling hold** N prise *f* de catch *or* de lutte ► **wrestling match** N match *m* *or* rencontre *f* de catch *or* de lutte

wretch [retʃ] N (*unfortunate*) pauvre diable *m* ; (*pej*) scélérat(e)† *m(f)* (*also liter*), misérable *mf* ; (*hum*) affreux *m*, -euse *f*, misérable *mf* ; **he's a filthy ~*** c'est un salaud* ; **you ~!** misérable ! ; **cheeky little ~!** petit polisson !, petit misérable !

wretched ['retʃid] ADJ [a] [*person*] (= *penniless*) misérable ; (= *unhappy*) malheureux ; [*animal*] malheureux ; [*life, slum, conditions*] misérable ; **in ~ poverty** dans une misère noire ; **the ~ plight of the refugees** la situation épouvantable des réfugiés [b] (†* = *dreadful*) [*weather, pay*] minable ; **what ~ luck!** quelle déveine !* ; **I was feeling ~** (= *ill*) je me sentais vraiment mal ; (= *unhappy*) j'étais très malheureux ; **I feel ~ about it** (= *guilty, ashamed*) j'en ai vraiment honte [c] (*: *expressing annoyance*) satané*, misérable† ; **where did I put my ~ keys?** où ai-je mis mes satanées* clés ? ; **the ~ woman!** la misérable !†, maudite femme ! ; **that ~ man's late again!** cet espèce d'olibrius†* est encore en retard !

wretchedly ['retʃidli] ADV [a] (= *miserably*) [*live*] misérablement ; [*weep, apologize*] misérablement, pitoyablement ; [*say, explain*] d'un ton pitoyable ; **~ poor** misérable ; **~ unhappy** terriblement malheureux ; **to be ~ paid** recevoir un salaire de misère [b] († = *dreadfully*) [*play, sing, treat*] lamentablement

wretchedness ['retʃidnis] N [a] (= *extreme poverty*) misère *f* ; (= *unhappiness*) extrême tristesse *f*, détresse *f* ; (= *shamefulness*) [*of amount, wage, sum*] caractère *m* dérisoire *or* pitoyable ; [*of act, behaviour*] mesquinerie *f* ; **his ~ at the thought of having to tell her the news** la détresse qu'il éprouvait à la pensée de devoir lui apprendre la nouvelle [b] (= *poor quality*) [*of meal, hotel, weather*] extrême médiocrité *f*, caractère *m* minable *or* pitoyable

wrick [rik] [1] VT (*Brit*) **to ~ one's ankle** se tordre la cheville ; **to ~ one's neck** attraper un torticolis [2] N entorse *f* ; (*in neck*) torticolis *m*

wriggle ['rigl] [1] N **with a ~ he freed himself** il s'est dégagé en se tortillant *or* en se contorsionnant ; **to give a ~ = to wriggle** ; → **2**
[2] VI [*worm, snake, eel*] se tortiller ; [*fish*] frétiller ; [*person*] gigoter*, se trémousser ; (*in embarrassment*) se tortiller ; (*squeamishly*)

frissonner, tressaillir ; (*excitedly*) frétiller ; **to ~ along/down** *etc* avancer/descendre *etc* en se tortillant ; **the fish ~d off the hook** le poisson a réussi à se détacher de l'hameçon, le poisson frétillait tellement qu'il s'est détaché de l'hameçon ; **she managed to ~ free** elle a réussi à se dégager en se tortillant *or* en se contorsionnant ; **he ~d through the hole in the hedge** il s'est faufilé *or* s'est glissé dans le trou de la haie (en se tortillant) ; **do stop wriggling (about)!** arrête de te trémousser *or* de gigoter* comme ça !

[3] VT **to ~ one's toes/fingers** remuer *or* tortiller les orteils/les doigts ; **to ~ one's way along** *etc* = **to wriggle along** ; → **2**

► **wriggle about**, **wriggle around** VI [*worm, snake, eel*] se tortiller ; [*fish, tadpole*] frétiller ; [*person*] gigoter*, se trémousser → **wriggle 2**

► **wriggle out** VI [a] (*lit*) [*worm etc*] sortir ; [*person*] se dégager ; **the snake ~d out of the cage** le serpent a rampé hors de la cage ; **the fish ~d out of my hand** le poisson m'a glissé des mains *or* m'a glissé entre les doigts [b] (*fig*) **to ~ out of a difficulty** esquiver une difficulté ; **to ~ out of a task/responsibility** se dérober à une tâche/responsabilité ; **he'll manage to ~ out of it somehow** il trouvera bien un moyen de s'esquiver *or* de se défiler*

wriggler ['riglə*r*] N [a] **he's a dreadful ~** [*child etc*] il n'arrête pas de gigoter*, il ne se tient jamais tranquille [b] (= *mosquito larva*) larve *f* de moustique

wriggly ['rigli] ADJ [*worm, eel, snake*] qui se tortille ; [*fish*] frétillant ; [*child*] remuant, qui gigote* *or* se trémousse

wring [riŋ] (*vb*: *pret, ptp* **wrung**) [1] N **to give clothes a ~** essorer des vêtements
[2] VT [a] (= *squeeze, twist*) serrer, tordre ; **to ~ a chicken's neck** tordre le cou à un poulet ; **if I catch you doing that, I'll ~ your neck!*** si je te prends à faire ça, je te tords le cou !* ; **to ~ one's hands** se tordre les mains (de désespoir) ; **he wrung my hand** ◊ **he wrung me by the hand** il m'a serré longuement la main ; (*fig*) **a story to ~ one's heart** une histoire à vous fendre le cœur [b] (*also* **~ out**) [+ *wet clothes, rag, towel*] essorer ; [+ *water*] extraire, exprimer (**from sth** de qch) ; (*on label*) **"do not ~"** « ne pas essorer » ; **~ a cloth out in cold water and apply to the forehead** faites une compresse avec un linge mouillé dans de l'eau froide et appliquez-la sur le front [c] (*fig* = *extort*: *also* **~ out**) arracher, extorquer ; **they wrung a confession/the truth from** *or* **out of him** ils lui ont arraché une confession/la vérité ; **he wrung £10 out of me** il m'a extorqué *or* soutiré 10 livres ; **I'll ~ it out of him!** je vais lui tirer les vers du nez !, je vais le faire parler ! ; **they managed to ~ out of him what had happened** ils sont arrivés non sans peine à lui faire dire *or* avouer ce qui s'était passé

► **wring out** VT SEP [a] = **wring 2b, 2c** [b] (= *exhausted*) **to be wrung out*** être lessivé* *or* vidé*

wringer ['riŋə*r*] N essoreuse *f* (à rouleaux) ; **to put sth through the ~** essorer qch (à la machine) ; (*fig*) **to go** *or* **be put through the ~*** passer un mauvais quart d'heure ; **to put sb through the ~** passer qn à la moulinette*

wringing ['riŋiŋ] ADJ (*also* **~ wet**) [*garment*] trempé, à tordre* ; [*person*] trempé jusqu'aux os

wrinkle ['riŋkl] [1] N [a] (*on skin, fruit*) ride *f* ; (*in socks, cloth, rug etc*) pli *m* [b]* (= *tip*) tuyau* *m* ; (= *good idea*) combine* *f* [2] VT (*also* **~ up**) [+ *skin*] rider ; [+ *forehead*] plisser ; [+ *nose*] froncer ; [+ *fruit*] rider, ratatiner ; [+ *rug, sheet*] plisser, faire des plis dans [3] VI [*sb's brow*] se plisser, se contracter ; [*nose*] se plisser, se froncer ; [*rug*] faire des plis ; [*socks*] être en accordéon

► **wrinkle down** VI [*socks, stockings*] tomber en accordéon
► **wrinkle up** [1] VI [*skirt, sweater*] remonter en faisant des plis ; [*rug*] faire des plis ; [*sb's brow, nose*] se plisser [2] VT SEP = **wrinkle 2**

wrinkled ['riŋkld] ADJ [*person, skin, face, neck*] ridé ; [*brow, nose*] plissé, froncé ; [*apple*] ridé, ratatiné ; [*shirt, skirt, sheet, rug*] qui fait des plis ; [*stocking, sock*] en accordéon

wrinkly ['riŋkli] [1] ADJ = **wrinkled** [2] **wrinklies** NPL (*Brit pej* = *old people*) les vioques* *mpl*

wrist [rist] [1] N poignet *m* [2] COMP ► **wrist joint** N articulation *f* du poignet ► **wrist loop** N (*Climbing*) dragonne *f* ► **wrist watch** N montre-bracelet *f*

wristband ['ristbænd] N [*of shirt*] poignet *m* ; [*of watch*] bracelet *m*

wristlet ['ristlit] [1] N bracelet *m* (de force) [2] COMP ► **wristlet watch** N montre-bracelet *f*

writ[1] [rit] [1] N (*Jur*) acte *m* judiciaire ; (*for election*) lettre officielle émanant du président de la Chambre des communes, demandant qu'on procède à des élections ; **to issue a ~ against sb** assigner qn (en justice) ; **to issue a ~ for libel against sb** assigner qn en justice pour diffamation ; **to serve a ~ on sb** ◊ **to serve sb with a ~** assigner qn [2] COMP ► **writ of attachment** N commandement *m* de saisie ► **writ of execution** N titre *m* exécutoire ► **writ of habeas corpus** N ordre *m* (écrit) d'habeas corpus ► **writ of subpoena** N assignation *f* *or* citation *f* (en justice)

writ[2]†† [rit] [a] VB *pt, ptp* of **write** [b] (*liter*) **~ large** (= *very obvious*) en toutes lettres (*fig*) ; (= *exaggerated*) poussé à l'extrême

▼**write** [rait] (*pret* **wrote**, *ptp* **written**) [1] VT [a] (*gen*) écrire ; [+ *list*] faire, écrire ; [+ *prescription, certificate*] rédiger ; [+ *bill, cheque*] faire ; **did I ~ that?** j'ai écrit ça, moi ? ; **you must print, not ~ your name** il ne faut pas écrire votre nom en cursive mais en caractères d'imprimerie ; (*liter*) **it is written "thou shalt not kill"** il est écrit «tu ne tueras point» ; **he had "policeman" written all over him*** cela sautait aux yeux *or* crevait les yeux qu'il était de la police ; (*US fig*) **that's all she wrote** c'est tout ce qu'il y a à dire [b] [+ *book, essay, letter, poem*] écrire ; [+ *music, opera*] écrire, composer ; **you could ~ a book about all that is going on here** on pourrait écrire *or* il y aurait de quoi écrire un livre sur tout ce qui se passe ici [c] (*US* = *write letter to*) écrire ; **can you ~ me when you get there?** tu peux m'envoyer un mot *or* m'écrire quand tu seras arrivé ? [d] (*Comput*) [+ *program, software etc*] écrire, rédiger → **read**
[2] VI [a] (*gen*) écrire ; **he can read and ~** il sait lire et écrire ; **~ on both sides of the paper** écrivez des deux côtés de la feuille ; **as I ~, I can see ...** en ce moment même, je peux voir ... ; **this pen ~s well** ce stylo écrit bien [b] (*as author*) **he had always wanted to ~** il avait toujours voulu écrire *or* être écrivain ; **he ~s for a living** il est écrivain de métier *or* de profession ; **he ~s about social policy** il écrit sur les *or* il traite des questions de politique sociale ; **he ~s for "The Times"** il écrit dans le «Times» ; **he ~s on foreign policy for "The Guardian"** il écrit des articles de politique étrangère dans le «Guardian» ; **what shall I ~ about?** sur quoi est-ce que je vais écrire ? [c] (= *correspond*) écrire (**to** à) ; **he wrote to tell us that ...** il (nous) a écrit pour nous dire que ... ; (= *send off for*) **~ for our brochure** demandez notre brochure ; **I've written for a form** j'ai écrit pour leur demander un formulaire → **write** [d] (*Comput*) **to ~ to a file** modifier un fichier
[3] COMP ► **write-in** N (*US Pol*) (= *insertion of name*) inscription *f* ; (= *name itself*) nom *m* inscrit ► **write-off** N → **write-off** ► **write-**

► **LANGUAGE IN USE:** **write** 21.1, 21.2

protected ADJ (*Comput*) protégé contre l'écriture ► **write-protect notch** N (*Comput*) encoche *f* de protection contre l'écriture ► **write-up** N → **write-up**

► **write away** VI (= *send off*) écrire (**to** à); **to ~ away for** [+ *information, application form, details*] écrire pour demander; [+ *goods*] commander par lettre

► **write back** VI répondre (*par lettre*)

► **write down** VT SEP [a] écrire; (= *note*) noter; (= *put in writing*) mettre par écrit; **~ it down at once or you'll forget** écrivez-le *or* notez-le tout de suite sinon vous allez oublier; **~ all your ideas down and send them to me** mettez toutes vos idées par écrit et envoyez-les-moi; **it was all written down for posterity** c'était tout consigné pour la postérité [b] (*Comm* = *reduce price of*) réduire le prix de

► **write in** [1] VI **listeners are invited to ~ in with their suggestions** nos auditeurs sont invités à nous envoyer leurs suggestions; **a lot of people have written in to complain** beaucoup de gens nous ont écrit pour se plaindre; **to ~ in for sth** écrire pour demander qch [2] VT SEP [+ *word, item on list etc*] insérer, ajouter; (*US Pol*) [+ *candidate's name*] inscrire; **to ~ sth in to an agreement** *or* **contract** (*at the outset*) stipuler qch dans un contrat; (*add*) ajouter qch à un contrat [3] **~in** N → **write**

► **write off** [1] VI = **write away** [2] VT SEP [a] (= *write quickly*) [+ *letter etc*] écrire en vitesse *or* d'une traite [b] [+ *debt*] annuler; (*fig*) considérer comme perdu *or* gâché, faire une croix* sur; **they wrote off £20,000** ils ont passé 20 000 livres aux profits et pertes; (*Comm*) **the operation was written off as a total loss** ils ont décidé de mettre un terme à l'opération qui se révélait une perte sèche; (*fig*) **I've written off the whole thing as a dead loss** j'en ai fait mon deuil*, j'ai fait une croix dessus*; (*fig*) **we've written off the first half of the term** nous considérons la première moitié du trimestre comme perdue *or* gâchée; (*fig*) **he had been written off as a failure** on avait décidé qu'il ne ferait jamais rien de bon; **they had written off all the passengers (as dead)** ils tenaient tous les passagers pour morts; **the insurance company decided to ~ off his car** la compagnie d'assurances a décidé que la voiture était irréparable; **he wrote his car off* in the accident** il a complètement bousillé* sa voiture dans l'accident, après l'accident, sa voiture était bonne pour la casse*; **the boat was completely written off*** le bateau a été complètement détruit *or* réduit à l'état d'épave [3] **~off** N → **write-off**

► **write out** VT SEP [a] [+ *one's name and address, details etc*] écrire; [+ *list*] faire, écrire; [+ *prescription*] rédiger; [+ *bill, cheque*] faire [b] (= *copy*) [+ *notes, essay etc*] recopier, mettre au propre; [+ *recipe*] copier; **~ out the words three times each** copiez chaque mot trois fois [c] (*TV, Rad*) [+ *character*] retirer (de la distribution *or* du générique); **she was written out of the series after a year** elle a cessé de figurer au générique de la série) au bout d'un an

► **write up** [1] VI = **write away** [2] VT SEP [a] [+ *notes, diary*] mettre à jour; (= *write report on*) [+ *happenings, developments*] faire un compte rendu de; (= *record*) (*Chem etc*) [+ *experiment*] rédiger; (*Archeol etc*) [+ *one's findings*] consigner; **he wrote up the day's events in the ship's log** il a inscrit *or* consigné dans le journal de bord les événements de la journée; **he wrote up his visit in a report** il a rendu compte de sa visite dans un rapport; **she wrote it up for the local paper** elle en a fait le compte rendu pour le journal local [b] (= *praise*) écrire un article élogieux (*or* une lettre élogieuse) sur [3] **~up** N → **write-up**

write-off ['raɪtɒf] N (*Comm*) perte *f* sèche; (*Fin: tax*) déduction *f* fiscale; **to be a ~** [*car*] être irréparable, être bon pour la casse*; [*project,*

operation] n'avoir abouti à rien, n'avoir rien donné; **the afternoon was a ~** l'après-midi n'a été qu'une perte de temps

writer ['raɪtə'] [1] N (*of letter, book etc*) auteur *m*; (*as profession*) écrivain *m*, auteur *m*; **the (present) ~ believes ...** l'auteur croit ...; **a thriller ~** un auteur de romans policiers; **he is a ~** il est écrivain, c'est un écrivain; **to be a good ~** (*of books*) être un bon écrivain, écrire bien; (*in handwriting*) écrire bien, avoir une belle écriture; **to be a bad ~** (*of books*) écrire mal, être un mauvais écrivain; (*in handwriting*) écrire mal *or* comme un chat → **hack²**, **letter** [b] (*Comput: of program etc*) auteur *m* [2] COMP ► **writer's block** N hantise *f* de la page blanche ► **writer's cramp** N crampe *f* des écrivains ► **Writer to the Signet** N (*Scot Jur*) notaire *m*

write-up ['raɪtʌp] N (*gen, also Comput*) description *f*; (= *review*) [*of play etc*] compte rendu *m*, critique *f*; (= *report*) [*of event etc*] compte rendu *m*, exposé *m*; **there's a ~ about it in today's paper** il y a un compte rendu là-dessus dans le journal d'aujourd'hui; **the play got a good ~** la pièce a eu de bonnes critiques

writhe [raɪð] VI se tordre; **it made him ~** (*in pain*) cela le fit se tordre de douleur; (*from disgust*) il en frémit de dégoût; (*from embarrassment*) il ne savait plus où se mettre; **he ~d under the insult** il frémit sous l'injure

► **writhe about**, **writhe around** VI (*in pain*) se tordre dans des convulsions; (*to free o.s.*) se contorsionner en tous sens

writing ['raɪtɪŋ] [1] N [a] (*NonC* = *handwriting, sth written*) écriture *f*; **there was some ~ on the page** il y avait quelque chose d'écrit sur la page; **I could see the ~ but couldn't read it** je voyais bien qu'il y avait quelque chose d'écrit mais je n'ai pas pu le déchiffrer; **I can't read your ~** je n'arrive pas à déchiffrer votre écriture; **in his own ~** écrit de sa main; (*esp Brit fig*) **he has seen the ~ on the wall** il mesure la gravité de la situation; (*esp Brit fig*) **the ~ is on the wall** la catastrophe est imminente [b] (*NonC* = *written form*) écrit *m*; **I'd like to have that in ~** j'aimerais avoir cela par écrit; **get his permission in ~** obtenez sa permission par écrit; **evidence in ~ that ...** preuve *f* par écrit *or* littérale que ...; **to put sth in ~** mettre qch par écrit [c] (*NonC* = *occupation of writer*) **he devoted his life to ~** il a consacré sa vie à son œuvre d'écrivain; **~ is his hobby** écrire est son passe-temps favori; **he earns quite a lot from ~** ses écrits lui rapportent pas mal d'argent [d] (= *output of writer*) écrits *mpl*, œuvres *fpl*; **there is in his ~ evidence of a desire to ...** on trouve dans ses écrits la manifestation d'un désir de ...; **the ~s of H. G. Wells** les œuvres *fpl* de H. G. Wells [e] (*NonC* = *act*) **he's learning reading and ~** il apprend à lire et à écrire; **~ is a skill which must be learned** écrire est un art qui s'apprend; **the ~ of this book took ten years** écrire ce livre a pris dix ans [2] COMP ► **writing case** N (*Brit*) écritoire *m* ► **writing desk** N secrétaire *m* (*bureau*) ► **writing pad** N bloc *m* de papier à lettres, bloc-notes *m* ► **writing paper** N papier *m* à lettres ► **writing room** N (*in hotel etc*) salon *m* d'écriture ► **writing table** N bureau *m*

written ['rɪtn] [1] VB *ptp* of **write** [2] ADJ [*test, agreement, constitution etc*] écrit; [*permission, confirmation*] par écrit; **~ evidence** (*gen, Hist*) documents *mpl*; (*Jur*) documents *mpl* écrits; (*Jur*) **~ proof** preuves *fpl* écrites; **her ~ English is excellent** son anglais est excellent à l'écrit; **Somali has been a ~ language for over 25 years** le somali est une langue écrite depuis plus de 25 ans; **the power of the ~ word** le pouvoir de l'écrit → **face**, **hand**

WRNS [renz] N (*Brit*) (ABBR = **Women's Royal Naval Service**) service des auxiliaires féminines de la marine royale britannique

▼ **wrong** [rɒŋ]

[1] ADJECTIVE	[4] TRANSITIVE VERB
[2] ADVERB	[5] COMPOUNDS
[3] NOUN	

[1] ADJECTIVE

[a] = **mistaken, incorrect** [*guess*] erroné; [*answer, solution, calculation, sum, musical note*] faux (fausse *f*); **the letter has the ~ date on it** ils *etc* se sont trompés de date sur la lettre; **I'm in the ~ job** je ne suis pas fait pour ce travail, ce n'est pas le travail qu'il me faut; (*also hum*) **he's got the ~ kind of friends** il a de mauvaises fréquentations; **that's the ~ kind of plug** ce n'est pas la prise qu'il faut; **she married the ~ man** elle n'a pas épousé l'homme qu'il lui fallait; **you've got** *or* **picked the ~ man if you want someone to mend a fuse** vous tombez mal si vous voulez quelqu'un qui puisse réparer un fusible; **you've put it back in the ~ place** vous ne l'avez pas remis à la bonne place *or* là où il fallait; **it's the ~ road for Paris** ce n'est pas la bonne route pour Paris; (*fig*) **you're on the ~ road** *or* **track** vous faites fausse route; **to say the ~ thing** dire ce qu'il ne faut pas dire, faire un impair; **he got all his sums ~** toutes ses opérations étaient fausses; **the accountant got his sums ~*** le comptable a fait une erreur *or* s'est trompé dans ses calculs; **he told me the ~ time** il ne m'a pas donné la bonne heure; **it happened at the ~ time** c'est arrivé au mauvais moment; **he got on the ~ train** il s'est trompé de train, il n'a pas pris le bon train; **the ~ use of drugs** l'usage abusif des médicaments

• **to be wrong**: **my clock/watch is ~** ma pendule/ma montre n'est pas à l'heure; **you're quite ~** vous vous trompez, vous avez tort; **I was ~ about him** je me suis trompé sur son compte; **he was ~ in deducing that ...** il a eu tort de déduire que ...

• **to get sth wrong**: **you've got your facts ~** ce que vous avancez est faux; **he got the figures ~** il s'est trompé dans les chiffres; **they got it ~ again** ils se sont encore trompés; (*iro*) **how ~ can you get!** comme on peut se tromper!

[b] = **bad** mal *inv*; (= *unfair*) injuste; **it is ~ to lie** ◊ **lying is ~** c'est mal de mentir; **it is ~ for her to have to beg** ◊ **it is ~ that she should have to beg** il est injuste qu'elle soit obligée de mendier; **you were ~ to hit him** ◊ **it was ~ of you to hit him** tu n'aurais pas dû le frapper, tu as eu tort de le frapper

[c] = **exceptionable** **there's nothing ~ with hoping that ...** il n'y a pas de mal à espérer que ...; **what's ~ with going to the cinema?** quel mal y a-t-il à aller au cinéma?; **there's nothing ~ with** *or* **in (doing) that** il n'y a rien à redire à cela

[d] = **amiss** qui ne va pas; **something's ~** *or* **there's something ~ (with it)** il y a quelque chose qui ne va pas; **something's ~** *or* **there's something ~ with him** il y a quelque chose qui ne va pas chez lui; **something's ~ with my leg** j'ai quelque chose à la jambe; **something's ~ with my watch** ma montre ne marche pas comme il faut; **there's something ~ somewhere** il y a quelque chose qui cloche* là-dedans; **something was very ~** quelque chose n'allait vraiment pas; **there's nothing ~** tout va bien; **nothing ~, I hope?** tout va bien *or* pas d'ennuis, j'espère?; **there's nothing ~ with it** (*theory, translation*) c'est tout à fait correct; [+ *method, plan*] c'est tout à fait valable; [+ *machine, car*] ça marche très bien; **there's nothing ~ with him** il va très bien; **he's ~ in the head*** il a le cerveau dérangé *or* fêlé*

• **what's wrong?** qu'est-ce qui ne va pas?; **what's ~ with you?** qu'est-ce que tu as?; **what's ~ with your arm?** qu'est-ce que vous avez au bras?; **what's ~ with the car?** qu'est-ce qu'elle a, la voiture?

2 ADVERB
[answer, guess] mal ; **you're doing it all ~** vous vous y prenez mal ; **you did ~ to refuse** vous avez eu tort de refuser ; **you've spelt it ~** vous l'avez mal écrit ; **you thought ~** tu t'es trompé ; **she took me up ~*** elle n'a pas compris ce que je voulais dire

◆ **to get sb/sth wrong** : **you've got the sum ~** vous vous êtes trompé dans votre calcul, vous avez fait une faute de calcul ; **you've got it all ~** (= *misunderstood*) vous n'avez rien compris ; **don't get me ~*** comprends-moi bien ; **you've got me all ~*** (= *misunderstood my meaning*) tu n'as rien compris à ce que je t'ai dit ; (= *misunderstood what I'm like*) tu te trompes complètement à mon sujet

◆ **to go wrong** (*in directions*) se tromper de route ; (*in calculations, negotiations etc*) se tromper, faire une faute or une erreur ; (*morally*) mal tourner ; [*plan*] mal tourner ; [*business deal etc*] tomber à l'eau ; [*machine, car*] tomber en panne ; [*clock, watch etc*] se détraquer ; **you can't go ~** (*in directions*) vous ne pouvez pas vous perdre or vous tromper ; (*in method etc*) c'est simple comme bonjour ; (*in choice of job, car etc*) (de toute façon) c'est un bon choix ; **you can't go ~ with this brand** vous ferez le bon choix en achetant cette marque ; **you won't go far ~ if you ...** vous ne pouvez guère vous tromper si vous ... ; **something went ~ with the gears** quelque chose s'est détraqué dans l'embrayage ; **something must have gone ~** il a dû arriver quelque chose ; **nothing can go ~ now** tout doit marcher comme sur des roulettes maintenant ; **everything went ~ that day** tout est allé mal or de travers ce jour-là

3 NOUN
a = **evil** mal *m* ; **to do ~** mal agir ; (*fig*) **he can do no ~ in her eyes** tout ce qu'il fait est bien à ses yeux or trouve grâce à ses yeux → **right**

b = **injustice** injustice *f*, tort *m* ; **he suffered great ~** il a été la victime de graves injustices ; **to right a ~** réparer une injustice ■ (*PROV*) **two ~s don't make a right** on ne répare pas une injustice par une autre (injustice) ; **you do me**

~ in thinking †... vous me faites tort en pensant †... ; **he did her ~†** il a abusé d'elle
c **to be in the ~** être dans son tort, avoir tort ; **to put sb in the ~** mettre qn dans son tort

4 TRANSITIVE VERB
faire du tort à, faire tort à† ; **you ~ me if you believe ...** vous êtes injuste envers moi si vous croyez ... ; **a ~ed wife** une femme trompée

5 COMPOUNDS
► **wrong-foot** VT (*Ftbl, Tennis*) prendre à contre-pied ; (*Brit fig*) prendre au dépourvu
► **wrong-headed** ADJ [*person*] buté ; [*idea, view, approach*] aberrant

wrongdoer ['rɒŋ,duːəʳ] N malfaiteur *m*, -trice *f*

wrongdoing ['rɒŋ,duːɪŋ] N (*NonC*) méfaits *mpl*

wrongful ['rɒŋfʊl] **1** ADJ (*frm*) injustifié **2** COMP ► **wrongful arrest** N (*Jur*) arrestation *f* arbitraire ► **wrongful dismissal** N (*Ind*) licenciement *m* abusif ► **wrongful trading** N (*Jur*) opérations *fpl* frauduleuses

wrongfully ['rɒŋfəlɪ] ADV à tort

wrongly ['rɒŋlɪ] ADV **a** (= *incorrectly*) [*answer, guess, translate, interpret, position, insert, calculate*] mal ; [*spell, price, install*] incorrectement ; [*believe, attribute, state, accuse, convict, imprison*] à tort ; **~ accused of murder/of doing sth** faussement accusé or accusé à tort de meurtre/d'avoir fait qch ; **the handle has been put on ~** le manche n'a pas été mis comme il fallait or a été mal mis ; **she was ~ dressed for the occasion** sa tenue n'était pas adaptée à la circonstance → **rightly b** (= *wrongfully*) [*treat*] injustement

wrongness ['rɒŋnɪs] N (= *incorrectness*) [*of answer*] inexactitude *f* ; (= *injustice*) injustice *f* ; (= *evil*) immoralité *f*

wrote [rəʊt] VB *pt of* **write**

wrought [rɔːt] **1** VB †† *pret, ptp of* **work** (*liter*) **the destruction ~ by the floods** les ravages provoqués par l'inondation ; **the damage the hurricane had ~ on Florida** les dégâts que l'ou-ragan avait provoqués en Floride ; **the changes ~ by time** les changements apportés par le temps **2** ADJ [*silver*] ouvré **3** COMP
► **wrought iron** N fer *m* forgé ► **wrought-iron** ADJ [*gate, decoration*] en fer forgé
► **wrought-ironwork** N ferronnerie *f*
► **wrought-up** ADJ [*person*] très tendu

wrung [rʌŋ] VB *pt, ptp of* **wring**

WRVS [,dʌbljuːɑːviːˈes] N (*Brit*) (ABBR = **Women's Royal Voluntary Service**) *service d'auxiliaires bénévoles au service de la collectivité*

wry [raɪ] ADJ [*person, smile, remark*] ironique ; [*wit*] empreint d'ironie ; **to listen/look on with ~ amusement** écouter/regarder d'un air amusé et narquois ; **a ~ sense of humour** un sens de l'humour empreint d'ironie ; **to make a ~ face** faire la grimace ; **a ~ comedy** une comédie pleine d'ironie

wryly ['raɪlɪ] ADV [*say, think*] avec ironie ; **to smile ~** avoir un sourire ironique ; **~ amusing** amusant et ironique

WS [,dʌbljuːˈes] N (*Scot Jur*) (ABBR = **Writer to the Signet**) → **writer**

wt ABBR = **weight**

wuss: [wʌs] N (*esp US*) mauviette* *f*

WV ABBR = **West Virginia**

WWF N (ABBR = **Worldwide Fund for Nature**) WWF *m*

WWI (ABBR = **World War One**) → **world**

WWII (ABBR = **World War Two**) → **world**

WWW N (*Comput*) (ABBR = **World Wide Web**) **the ~** le Web

WY ABBR = **Wyoming**

wych-elm ['wɪtʃˈelm] N orme *m* blanc or de montagne

wynd [waɪnd] N (*Scot*) venelle *f*

Wyoming [waɪˈəʊmɪŋ] N le Wyoming ; **in ~** dans le Wyoming

WYSIWYG ['wɪzɪwɪg] N (*Comput*) (ABBR = **what you see is what you get**) WYSIWYG *m*, ce que l'on voit est ce que l'on obtient, tel écran tel écrit

X

X, x [eks] *(vb: pret, ptp* **x-ed, x'ed)** ① N (= *letter*) X, x *m*; *(Math, fig)* x; *(at end of letter = kiss)* bises *fpl*; *(several kisses)* grosses bises *fpl*; **X for X-ray** ≈ X comme Xavier; **he signed his name with an X** il a signé d'une croix *or* en faisant une croix; **for x years** pendant x années; **Mr X** Monsieur X; **X marks the spot** l'endroit est marqué d'une croix → **X-ray** ② VT marquer d'une croix ③ COMP ▶ **x-axis** N axe *m* des x ▶ **X-certificate** *(Brit Cine: formerly)* classé X, ≈ interdit aux moins de 18 ans ▶ **X-chromosome** N chromosome *m* X ▶ **X-rated** ADJ *(fig)* [*book, language etc*] obscène, porno*; *(US Cine)* classé X, ≈ interdit aux moins de 17 ans

xenon ['zenɒn] N xénon *m*

xenophobe ['zenəfəʊb] ADJ, N xénophobe *mf*
xenophobia [ˌzenə'fəʊbɪə] N xénophobie *f*
xenophobic [ˌzenə'fəʊbɪk] ADJ xénophobe
Xenophon ['zenəfən] N Xénophon *m*
xerography [zɪə'rɒgrəfɪ] N xérographie *f*
Xerox® ['zɪərɒks] ① N (= *machine*) photocopieuse *f*; (= *reproduction*) photocopie *f* ② VT (faire) photocopier, prendre *or* faire une photocopie de, copier* ③ VI se faire *or* se laisser photocopier
Xerxes ['zɜːksiːz] N Xerxès *m*
XL [ˌek'sel] (ABBR = **extra large**) XL
Xmas ['eksməs, 'krɪsməs] N ABBR = **Christmas**
X-ray ['eks,reɪ] ① N (= *ray*) rayons *mpl* X; (= *photograph*) radiographie *f*, radio* *f*; **to have an ~** se faire radiographier, se faire faire une

radio* ② VT [+ *heart, lungs, object*] radiographier, faire une radio de*; [+ *person*] radiographier, faire une radio à* ③ COMP radioscopique, radiographique ▶ **X-ray diagnosis** N radiodiagnostic *m* ▶ **X-ray examination** N examen *m* radioscopique, radio* *f* ▶ **X-ray photo, X-ray picture** N (*on film*) radiographie *f*, radio* *f*; (*on screen*) radioscopie *f*, radio* *f* ▶ **X-ray treatment** N radiothérapie *f*
xylograph ['zaɪləgrɑːf] N xylographie *f*
xylographic [ˌzaɪlə'græfɪk] ADJ xylographique
xylography [zaɪ'lɒgrəfɪ] N xylographie *f*
xylophone ['zaɪləfəʊn] N xylophone *m*
xylophonist [zaɪ'lɒfənɪst] N joueur *m* de xylophone

Y

Y, y [waɪ] **1** N (= *letter*) Y, y *m*; **Y for Yellow** ≈ Y comme Yvonne; **Y-shaped** en (forme d')Y **2** COMP ► **y-axis** N axe *m* des y ► **Y-chromosome** N chromosome *m* Y ► **Y-fronts**® NPL (*Brit*) slip *m* (ouvert)

yacht [jɒt] **1** N (*luxury motorboat*) yacht *m*; (*with sails*) voilier *m* **2** VI **to go ~ing** faire de la navigation de plaisance, faire du bateau **3** COMP ► **yacht club** N yacht-club *m* ► **yacht race** N course *f* à la voile *or* de voile

yachting [ˈjɒtɪŋ] **1** N navigation *f* de plaisance, voile *f* **2** COMP [*enthusiast*] de la voile, de la navigation de plaisance; [*cruise*] en yacht; [*magazine*] de navigation de plaisance ► **yachting cap** N casquette *f* de marin ► **yachting club** N yacht-club *m* ► **yachting event** N = **yachting regatta** ► **the yachting fraternity** N les plaisanciers *mpl* ► **yachting regatta** N régate *f* ► **yachting trip** N sortie *f* en mer

yachtsman [ˈjɒtsmən] N (*pl* **-men**) (*in race, professional*) navigateur *m*; (*amateur*) plaisancier *m*

yachtswoman [ˈjɒtswʊmən] N (*pl* **-women**) (*in race, professional*) navigatrice *f*; (*amateur*) plaisancière *f*

yack• [jæk], **yackety-yak**• [ˈjækɪtɪjæk] (*pej*) **1** VI caqueter, jacasser **2** N caquetage *m*

yah [jɑː] **1** EXCL **a** (= *yes*) ouais!• **b** (*defiance: also* ~ **boo**) na! **2** COMP ► **yah-boo politics** N politique *f* de provocation

yahoo [jɑːˈhuː] N butor *m*, rustre *m*

yak¹ [jæk] N (*Zool*) yak *m* or yack *m*

yak²• [jæk] = **yackety-yak**; → **yack**

Yakuza [jəˈkuːzə] **1** N (= *person*) yakusa *m* (*pl inv*) **2 the Yakuza** NPL (= *organization*) les yakusa *mpl* **3** COMP ► **Yakuza boss** N chef *m* yakusa

Yale® [jeɪl] N (*also* ~ **lock**) serrure *f* à barillet *or* à cylindre

y'all• [jɔːl] PRON (*US*) vous (autres)

yam [jæm] N **a** (= *plant, tuber*) igname *f* **b** (*US* = *sweet potato*) patate *f* douce

yammer• [ˈjæmə] VI jacasser

yang [jæŋ] N (*Philos*) yang *m*

Yangtze [ˈjæŋksɪ] N Yang-Tsê Kiang *m*

Yank• [jæŋk] **1** ABBR = **Yankee 1** ADJ amerloque•, ricain• (*pej*) **2** N Amerloque• *mf*, Ricain(e)• *m(f)* (*pej*)

yank [jæŋk] **1** N coup *m* sec, saccade *f* **2** VT tirer d'un coup sec
► **yank off**• VT SEP (= *detach*) arracher *or* extirper (d'un coup sec)
► **yank out**• VT SEP arracher *or* extirper (d'un coup sec)

Yankee• [ˈjæŋkɪ] **1** N (*Hist*) Yankee *mf*; (*esp pej*) yankee *mf* **2** ADJ yankee (*f inv*); ~ **Doodle** chanson populaire de la Révolution américaine

┌── **YANKEE** ──┐

yap [jæp] (*pej*) **1** VI [*dog*] japper;• [*person*] jacasser **2** N jappement *m*

yapping [ˈjæpɪŋ] (*pej*) **1** ADJ [*dog*] jappeur; [*person*] jacasseur **2** N [*of dog*] jappements *mpl*; [*of person*] jacasserie *f*

yappy• [ˈjæpɪ] ADJ [*dog*] jappeur

Yarborough [ˈjɑːbrə] N (*Bridge etc*) main ne contenant aucune carte supérieure au neuf

yard¹ [jɑːd] N **a** yard *m* (91,44 *cm*), ≈ mètre *m*; **one ~ long** long d'un yard, ≈ long d'un mètre; **20 ~s away (from us)** à une vingtaine de mètres (de nous); **he can't see a ~ in front of him** il ne voit pas à un mètre devant lui; **to buy cloth by the ~** ≈ acheter de l'étoffe au mètre; **how many ~s would you like?** ≈ quel métrage désirez-vous?; (*fig*) **a word a ~ long** un mot qui n'en finit plus; **an essay ~s long** une dissertation-fleuve; **with a face a ~ long** faisant une tête longue comme ça; **sums by the ~** des calculs à n'en plus finir; **to give sb the whole nine ~s**• y mettre le paquet• **b** (*Naut*) vergue *f*

yard² [jɑːd] **1** N **a** [*of farm, hospital, prison, school etc*] cour *f*; (*surrounded by the building: in monastery, hospital etc*) préau *m*; **backyard** arrière-cour *f* → **farmyard b** (= *work-site*) chantier *m*; (*for storage*) dépôt *m*; **builder's/ shipbuilding ~** chantier *m* de construction/de construction(s) navale(s); **coal/contractor's ~** dépôt *m* de charbon/de matériaux de construction → **dockyard, goods c** (*Brit*) **the Yard** ◊ **Scotland Yard** Scotland Yard *m*; **to call in the Yard** demander l'aide de Scotland Yard **d** (*US*) (= *garden*) jardin *m*; (= *field*) champ *m* **e** (= *enclosure for animals*) parc *m* → **stockyard 2** COMP ► **yard sale** N (*US*) vente *f* d'objets usagés (*chez un particulier*) → CAR-BOOT SALE, GARAGE SALE

yardage [ˈjɑːdɪdʒ] N longueur *f* en yards, ≈ métrage *m*

yardarm [ˈjɑːdɑːm] N (*Naut*) les extrémités *d*'une vergue

yardbird• [ˈjɑːdbɜːd] N (*US*) (= *soldier*) bidasse *m* empoté• (*qui est souvent de corvée*); (= *convict*) taulard• *m*

Yardie• [ˈjɑːdɪ] N (*Brit*) membre d'une organisation criminelle d'origine jamaïquaine

yardmaster [ˈjɑːdmɑːstə] N (*US Rail*) chef *m* de triage

yardstick [ˈjɑːdstɪk] N (*fig*) mesure *f*

yarmulke [ˈjɑːmʊlkə] N kippa *f*

yarn [jɑːn] **1** N **a** fil *m*; (*Tech: for weaving*) filé *m*; **cotton/nylon** *etc* ~ fil *m* de coton/de nylon® *etc* **b** (= *tale*) longue histoire *f* → **spin 2** VI raconter *or* débiter des histoires

yarrow [ˈjærəʊ] N mille-feuille *f*, achillée *f*

yashmak [ˈjæʃmæk] N litham *m*

yaw [jɔː] VI (*Naut*) (*suddenly*) faire une embardée, embarder; (*gradually*) dévier de la route; (*Aviat, Space*) faire un mouvement de lacet

yawl [jɔːl] N (*Naut*) (= *sailing boat*) yawl *m*; (= *ship's boat*) yole *f*

yawn [jɔːn] **1** VI **a** [*person*] bâiller; **to ~ with boredom** bâiller d'ennui **b** [*chasm etc*] s'ouvrir **2** VT **to ~ one's head off** bâiller à se décrocher la mâchoire; **"no", he ~ed** «non», dit-il en bâillant **3** N bâillement *m*; **to give a ~** bâiller; **the film is one long ~**• ce film est ennuyeux de bout en bout → **stifle**

yawning [ˈjɔːnɪŋ] **1** ADJ [*chasm*] béant; [*person*] qui bâille **2** N bâillements *mpl*

yawp [jɔːp] (*US*) **1** N **a** (• = *yelp*) braillement• *m*; **to give a ~** brailler• **b** (• = *chatter*) papotage *m*; **to have a ~** bavasser• (*pej*) **2** VI **a** (• = *yelp*) brailler• **b** (• = *chatter*) bavasser• (*pej*)

yaws [jɔːz] N (*Med*) pian *m*

yd ABBR = **yard**

ye¹ [jiː] PERS PRON (††, *liter, dial*) vous; **ye gods!**• grands dieux!•, ciel! (*hum*)

ye² †† [jiː] DEF ART (= *the*) ancienne forme écrite

yea [jeɪ] **1** ADV **a** (*frm* = *yes*) oui; **to say ~ to sth** dire oui à qch; **or nay** oui ou non **b** († = *indeed*) en vérité **2** N oui *m*; **the ~s and the nays** les voix *fpl* pour et les voix *fpl* contre, les oui *mpl* et les non *mpl*

yeah• [jɛə] PARTICLE ouais•, oui; (*iro*) **oh ~?** et puis quoi encore?; (*iro*) **~, (that'll be) right!** c'est ça!, tu parles!•

year [jɪə] **1** N **a** an *m*, année *f*; **next ~** l'an *m* prochain, l'année *f* prochaine; **last ~** l'an dernier, l'année *f* dernière; **this ~** cette année; **they intend to complete the project when the conditions are right: this ~, next ~, sometime, never?** ils prévoient d'achever le projet quand les conditions seront propices: mais combien de temps faudra-t-il attendre?; **document valid one ~** document *m* valable (pendant) un an; **taking one ~ with another** ◊ **taking the good ~s with the bad** bon an mal an; **a ~ (ago) last January** il y a eu un an au mois de janvier (dernier); **a ~ in January** ◊ **a ~ next January** il y aura un an en janvier (prochain); **it costs £500 a ~** cela coûte 500 livres par an; **he earns £15,000 a ~** il gagne 15 000 livres par an; **three times a ~** trois fois par an *or* l'an; **all the ~ round** toute l'année; **as (the) ~s go (or went) by** au cours *or* au fil des années; **~ in, ~ out** année après année; **over the ~s** au cours *or* au fil des années; **~ by ~** d'année en année; **to pay by the ~** payer à l'année; **every ~** ◊ **each ~** tous les ans, chaque année; **every other ~** ◊ **every second ~** tous les deux ans; **~s (and ~s•) ago** il y a (bien) des années; **for ~s together** *or* **on end**• plusieurs années de suite; **they have not met for ~s** ils ne se sont pas vus depuis des années; **I haven't laughed so much for** *or* **in**•

~s ça fait des années que je n'ai pas autant ri ; **I haven't seen him for** *or* **in* ~s** ça fait des années *or* des lustres* que je ne l'ai (pas) vu ; (*fig*) **it took us ~s* to find the restaurant** il (nous) a fallu un temps fou pour trouver le restaurant ; **from ~ to ~** d'année en année ; **from one ~ to the next** d'une année à l'autre ; **from ~('s) end to ~('s) end** d'un bout de l'année à l'autre ; (*frm*) **in the ~ of grace** *or* **of Our Lord 1492** en l'an de grâce 1492 ; **in the ~ 1869** en 1869 ; **in the ~ two thousand** en l'an deux mille ; **a friend of 30 ~s' standing** un ami de 30 ans *or* que l'on connaît (*or* connaissait *etc*) depuis 30 ans → **after, donkey, New Year, old**

b (*referring to age*) **he is six ~s old** *or* **six ~s of age** il a six ans ; **in his fortieth ~** dans sa quarantième année ; **from his earliest ~s** dès son âge le plus tendre ; **he looks old for his ~s** il fait *or* paraît plus vieux que son âge ; **young for his ~s** jeune pour son âge ; **she is very active for (a woman of) her ~s** elle,est très active pour (une femme de) son âge ; **well on in ~s** d'un âge avancé ; **to get on in ~s** prendre de l'âge ; (*liter*) **to grow in ~s** avancer en âge ; **it's put ~s on me!** cela m'a vieilli de vingt ans !, cela m'a fait prendre un coup de vieux* ; **changing your hairstyle can take ten ~s off you** changer de coiffure peut vous rajeunir de dix ans ; **it's taken ~s off my life!** cela m'a vieilli de vingt ans ! ; **I feel ten ~s younger** j'ai l'impression d'avoir dix ans de moins *or* d'avoir rajeuni de dix ans

c (*Scol, Univ*) année *f* ; **he is first in his ~** il est le premier de son année ; **she was in my ~ at school/university** elle était de mon année au lycée/à l'université ; **he's in (the) second ~** (*Univ*) il est en deuxième année ; (*secondary school*) ≈ il est en cinquième ; **the academic ~ 1997/98** l'année *f* universitaire 1997/98 ; (*Brit = pupil*) **the first ~s to study French and Spanish** ≈ les élèves de sixième étudient le français et l'espagnol

d (*Prison*) an *m* ; **he got ten ~s** il en a pris pour dix ans*, on l'a condamné à dix ans de prison ; **sentenced to 15 ~s' imprisonment** condamné à 15 ans de prison

e [*of coin, stamp, wine*] année *f*

f (*Fin*) **financial ~** exercice *m* financier ; **tax ~** exercice *m* fiscal, année *f* fiscale

2 COMP ► **year end** N (*Comm, Fin*) clôture *f* *or* fin *f* de l'exercice ; ► **end report/accounts** rapport *m*/comptes *mpl* de fin d'exercice ► **year head** N (*Brit Scol*) conseiller *m*, -ère *f* (principal(e)) d'éducation ► **year-long** ADJ qui dure toute une année ► **year-round** ADJ [*resident, population*] qui réside toute l'année ; [*work*] qui dure toute l'année ; [*facilities*] ouvert toute l'année ► **year tutor** N (*Brit Scol*) = **year head**

yearbook ['jɪəbʊk] N annuaire *m* (*d'une université, d'un organisme etc*)

yearling ['jɪəlɪŋ] **1** N animal *m* d'un an ; (= *racehorse*) yearling *m* **2** ADJ (âgé) d'un an

yearly ['jɪəlɪ] **1** ADJ annuel **2** ADV **a** (= *every year*) chaque année, tous les ans ; **twice ~** deux fois par an ; **twice-~** semestriel **b** (= *per year*) [*produce, spend*] par an

yearn [jɜːn] VI **a** (= *feel longing*) languir (**for, after** après), aspirer (**for, after** à) ; **to ~ for home** avoir la nostalgie de chez soi *or* du pays ; **to ~ to do** avoir très envie *or* mourir d'envie de faire, aspirer à faire **b** (= *feel tenderness*) s'attendrir, s'émouvoir (**over** sur)

yearning ['jɜːnɪŋ] **1** N désir *m* ardent *or* vif (**for, after de, to do** de faire), envie *f* (**for, after** de, **to do** de faire), aspiration *f* (**for, after** vers, **to do** à faire) **2** ADJ [*desire*] vif, ardent ; [*look*] plein de désir *or* de tendresse

yearningly ['jɜːnɪŋlɪ] ADV (= *longingly*) avec envie, avec désir ; (= *tenderly*) avec tendresse, tendrement

yeast [jiːst] **1** N (*NonC*) levure *f* ; **dried ~** le-

vure *f* déshydratée **2** COMP ► **yeast extract** N extrait *m* de levure de bière

yeasty ['jiːstɪ] ADJ [*flavour, taste, smell*] de levure ; [*bread*] qui sent la levure ; (= *frothy*) écumeux

yec(c)h‡ [jek] EXCL (*US*) berk *or* beurk !

yegg‡ [jeg] N (*US: also* **~man**) cambrioleur *m*, casseur‡ *m*

yeh* [jeə] = **yeah**

yell [jel] **1** N hurlement *m*, cri *m* ; **a ~ of fright** un hurlement *or* un cri d'effroi ; **a ~ of pain** un hurlement *or* un cri de douleur ; **a ~ of alarm/dismay** un cri d'inquiétude/de désarroi ; **to give** *or* **let out a ~** pousser un hurlement *or* un cri ; (*US Univ*) **college ~** ban *m* d'étudiants **2** VI (*also* **~ out**) hurler (**with** de) ; **to ~ at sb** crier après qn ; **to ~ with pain** hurler de douleur **3** VT (*also* **~ out**) hurler ; **"stop it!", he ~ed** « arrêtez ! » hurla-t-il ; **to ~ abuse** hurler des injures

yelling ['jelɪŋ] **1** N hurlements *mpl*, cris *mpl* **2** ADJ hurlant

yellow ['jeləʊ] **1** ADJ **a** (*in colour*) [*object etc*] jaune ; [*hair, curls*] blond ; **to go** *or* **turn** *or* **become** *or* **grow ~** devenir jaune, jaunir → **2, canary**

b (*fig pej* = *cowardly*) lâche ; **there was a ~ streak in him** il y avait un côté lâche en lui

2 N (*also of egg*) jaune *m*

3 VI jaunir

4 VT jaunir ; **paper ~ed with age** papier *m* jauni par le temps

5 COMP ► **yellow-belly‡** N (*pej*) froussard(e)* *m(f)*, trouillard(e)‡ *m(f)* ► **yellow brick road** N (*fig*) voie *f* du succès ► **yellow card** N (*Ftbl*) carton *m* jaune ► **yellow-dog contract** N (*US Ind Hist*) contrat *m* interdisant de se syndiquer (*aujourd'hui illégal*) ► **yellow fever** N (*Med*) fièvre *f* jaune ► **yellow flag** N (*Naut*) pavillon *m* de quarantaine ► **yellow jack*** N (*Naut*) = **yellow flag** ► **yellow jersey** N maillot *m* jaune ► **yellow line** N (*Aut*) ligne *f* jaune ; **double ~ lines** bandes jaunes indiquant l'interdiction de stationner ► **yellow metal** N (= *gold*) métal *m* jaune ; (= *brass*) cuivre *m* jaune ► **yellow ochre** N ocre *f* jaune ► **Yellow Pages®** NPL (*Telec*) pages *fpl* jaunes ► **the yellow peril†** N (*Pol*) le péril jaune ► **yellow press†** N (*Press*) presse *f* à sensation ► **yellow rain** N (*Ind, Ecol*) pluie *f* jaune ► **the Yellow River** N le fleuve Jaune ► **the Yellow Sea** N la mer Jaune ► **yellow soap** N savon *m* de Marseille ► **yellow spot** N (*Anat*) tache *f* jaune ► **yellow wagtail** N (*Orn*) bergeronnette *f* flavéole

yellowhammer ['jeləʊˌhæmər] N (*Orn*) bruant *m* jaune

yellowish ['jeləʊɪʃ] ADJ tirant sur le jaune, jaunâtre (*pej*) ; **~ brown** d'un brun tirant sur le jaune, brun jaunâtre *inv* (*pej*) ; **~ green** d'un vert tirant sur le jaune, vert jaunâtre *inv* (*pej*)

yellowness ['jeləʊnɪs] N (*NonC*) **a** (= *colour*) [*of object*] couleur *f* jaune, jaune *m* ; [*of skin*] teint *m* jaune ; (* *pej* = *cowardice*) lâcheté *f*, trouillardise‡ *f*

yellowy ['jeləʊɪ] ADJ = **yellowish**

yelp [jelp] **1** N [*of dog*] jappement *m* ; [*of fox, person*] glapissement *m* **2** VI japper, glapir

yelping ['jelpɪŋ] **1** N [*of dog*] jappement *m* ; [*of fox, person*] glapissement *m* **2** ADJ [*dog*] jappeur ; [*fox, person*] glapissant

Yemen ['jemən] N **(the) ~** le Yémen ; **North/South ~** le Yémen du Nord/Sud

Yemeni ['jemənɪ], **Yemenite** ['jemənaɪt] **1** ADJ (*gen*) yéménite ; [*ambassador, embassy*] du Yémen ; **North/South ~** yéménite *or* du Yémen du Nord/Sud **2** N Yéménite *mf* ; **North/South ~** Yéménite *mf* du Nord/Sud

yen¹ [jen] N (*pl inv* = *money*) yen *m*

yen²* [jen] N désir *m* intense, grande envie *f* (**for** de) ; **to have a ~ to do** avoir (grande) envie de faire

yenta* ['jentə] N (*US pej*) commère *f*

yeoman ['jəʊmən] (*pl* **-men**) **1** N **a** (*Hist* = *freeholder*) franc-tenancier *m* **b** (*Brit Mil*) cavalier *m* → **yeomanry 2** COMP ► **yeoman farmer** N (*Hist*) franc-tenancier *m* ; (*modern*) propriétaire *m* exploitant ► **Yeoman of the Guard** N (*Brit*) hallebardier *m* de la garde royale ► **yeoman service** N (*fig*) **to do** *or* **give ~ service** rendre des services inestimables

yeomanry ['jəʊmənrɪ] N (*NonC*) **a** (*Hist*) (classe *f* des) francs-tenanciers *mpl* **b** (*Brit Mil*) régiment de cavalerie (*volontaire*)

yeomen ['jəʊmən] NPL of **yeoman**

yep* [jep] PARTICLE ouais*, oui

yer‡ [jɜːʳ] PRON = **your**

yes [jes] **1** PARTICLE (*answering affirmative question*) oui ; (*answering neg question*) si ; **do you want some? — ~!** en voulez-vous ? — oui ! ; **don't you want any? — ~ (I do)!** vous n'en voulez pas ? — (mais) si ! ; **to say ~** dire oui ; **he says ~ to everything** il dit oui à tout ; **~ of course** ◊ certainly mais oui ; **~ and no** oui et non ; (*contradicting*) **oh ~, you did say that** si si *or* mais si, vous avez bien dit cela ; **~?** (*awaiting further reply*) (ah) oui ?, et alors ? ; (*answering knock at door*) oui ?, entrez ! ; **waiter! — ~ sir?** garçon ! — (oui) Monsieur ? ; (*in triumph*) **~!*** ouah !* **2** N oui *m inv* ; **he gave a reluctant ~** il a accepté de mauvaise grâce **3** COMP ► **yes man** N (*pl* **yes men**) (*pej*) béni-oui-oui* *m inv* (*pej*) ; **he's a ~ man** il dit amen à tout ► **yes-no question** N (*Ling*) question *f* fermée

yeshiva(h) [jeˈʃiːvə] N (*pl* **yeshiva(h)s** *or* **jeshivoth** [jeˈʃiːvɒt]) yeshiva *f*

yesterday ['jestədeɪ] **1** ADV **a** (*lit*) (= *day before today*) hier ; **it rained ~** il a plu hier ; **all (day) ~** toute la journée d'hier ; **late ~** hier dans la soirée ; **he arrived only ~** il n'est arrivé qu'hier ; **a week from ~** dans une semaine à compter d'hier ; **the news was announced a week ago** ~ il y avait une semaine hier que la nouvelle avait été annoncée ; **I had to have it by ~** *or* **no later than ~** il fallait que je l'aie hier au plus tard ; (*hum*) **when do you need it by? — ~!** il vous le faut pour quand ? — hier ! (*hum*) → **born, day**

b (*fig* = *in the past*) hier, naguère ; **towns which ~ were villages** des villes qui étaient hier *or* naguère des villages

2 N **a** (*lit* = *day before today*) hier *m* ; **~ was the second** c'était hier le deux ; **~ was Friday** c'était hier vendredi ; **~ was very wet** il a beaucoup plu hier ; **~ was a bad day for him** la journée d'hier s'est mal passée pour lui ; **the day before ~** avant-hier *m* ; **where's ~'s newspaper?** où est le journal d'hier ?

b (*fig*) (= *the past*) hier *m*, passé *m* ; **the great men of ~** tous les grands hommes du passé *or* d'hier ; (*liter*) **all our ~s** tout notre passé

3 COMP ► **yesterday afternoon** ADV hier après-midi ► **yesterday evening** ADV hier (au) soir ► **yesterday morning** ADV hier matin ► **yesterday week*** ADV (*Brit*) il y a eu huit jours hier

yesternight†† ['jestəˈnaɪt] N, ADV la nuit dernière, hier soir

yesteryear ['jestəˈjɪəʳ] N (*esp liter*) les années *fpl* passées ; **the cars/hairstyles/fashions of ~** les voitures *fpl*/coiffures *fpl*/modes *fpl* d'antan

▼ **yet** [jet] **1** ADV **a** (= *by this time: with neg*) **not ~** pas encore ; **they haven't (as) ~ returned** ◊ **they haven't returned (as) ~** ils ne sont pas encore de retour ; **they hadn't (as) ~ managed to do it** ils n'étaient pas encore arrivés à le faire ; **no one has come (as) ~** personne n'est encore arrivé ; **no one had come (as) ~** jusqu'alors *or* jusque-là personne n'était (encore) venu ; **we haven't come to a**

decision ~ nous ne sommes pas encore parvenus à une décision ; **I don't think any decision has been reached as** ~ je ne pense pas qu'on soit déjà parvenu à une décision ; **are you coming? — not just** ~ est-ce que vous venez ? — pas tout de suite ; **don't come in (just)** ~ n'entrez pas tout de suite or pas pour l'instant ; **I needn't go (just)** ~ je n'ai pas besoin de partir tout de suite ; **that won't happen (just)** ~ ◊ **that won't happen (just)** ~ **awhile(s)*** ça n'est pas pour tout de suite ; (hum) **you ain't seen nothing** ~* vous n'avez encore rien vu

b (= already: in questions) déjà ; **have you had your lunch** ~? avez-vous déjà déjeuné ? ; **I wonder if he's come** ~ je me demande s'il est déjà arrivé or s'il est arrivé maintenant ; **must you go just** ~? faut-il que vous partiez (subj) déjà ?

c (= so far: with superl) jusqu'à présent, jusqu'ici ; **she's the best teacher we've had** ~ c'est le meilleur professeur que nous ayons eu jusqu'à présent or jusqu'ici ; **the greatest book** ~ **written** le plus grand livre qui ait jamais été écrit

d (= still) encore ; **he may come** ~ or ~ **come** il peut encore venir ; **he could come** ~ il pourrait encore venir ; **his plan may** ~ **fail** son plan peut encore échouer ; **we'll make a footballer of you** ~ nous finirons pas faire un footballeur de toi ; (gen hum) **there is hope for me** ~ tout n'est pas perdu pour moi ; **I'll speak to her** ~ je finirai bien par lui parler ; **I'll do it** ~ j'y arriverai bien quand même ; **he has** ~ **to learn** il a encore à apprendre, il lui reste à apprendre ; **I have** ~ **to see one** je n'en ai encore jamais vu ; **Mr Lea has** ~ **is** ~ **to score** Lea n'a pas encore marqué de points ; **his guilt is** ~ **to be proved** sa culpabilité reste à prouver ; **there were revelations** ~ **to come** des révélations devaient encore arriver ; (liter) **she is** ~ **alive** or **alive** ~ elle est encore vivante, elle vit encore ; **for all I know he is there** ~ autant que je sache il est encore or toujours là

e (= from now) **we've got ages** ~ nous avons encore plein de temps ; **it'll be ages** ~ **before she's ready** il va encore lui falloir des heures pour se préparer ; **we'll wait for five minutes** ~ nous allons attendre encore cinq minutes ; **it won't be dark for half an hour** ~ il ne fera pas nuit avant une demi-heure ; **I'll be here for a (long) while** ~ or **for a long time** ~ je resterai ici encore un bon bout de temps ; **he won't be here for a (long) while** ~ or **for a long time** ~ il ne sera pas ici avant longtemps ; **for some time** ~ pour encore pas mal de temps ; **not for some time** ~ pas avant un certain temps ; **they have a few days** ~ ils ont encore or il leur reste encore quelques jours ; **there's another bottle** ~ il reste encore une bouteille

f (= even: with compar) ~ **more people** encore plus de gens ; **he wants** ~ **more money** il veut encore plus or encore davantage d'argent ; **this week it's been work, work and** ~ **more work** cette semaine, ça a été du travail, encore du travail et toujours plus de travail ; ~ **louder shouts** des cris encore plus forts ; **these remains date back** ~ **further** ces vestiges remontent à encore plus longtemps ; **the latest results were better/worse** ~ les tout derniers résultats étaient encore meilleurs/pires ; ~ **again** ◊ once more une fois de plus ; **she was** ~ **another victim of racism** c'était une victime de plus du racisme ; **another arrived and** ~ **another** il en est arrivé un autre et encore un autre

g (frm) **not he nor** ~ **I** ni lui ni moi ; **I do not like him nor** ~ **his sister** je ne les aime ni lui ni sa sœur, je ne l'aime pas et sa sœur non plus or et sa sœur pas davantage ; **they did not come nor** ~ **(even) write** ils ne sont pas venus et ils n'ont pas même pas écrit

2 CONJ (= however) cependant, pourtant ; (= nevertheless) toutefois, néanmoins ; **(and)** ~

everyone liked her (et) pourtant or néanmoins tout le monde l'aimait, mais tout le monde l'aimait quand même ; **(and)** ~ **I like the house** (et) malgré tout or (et) pourtant or (et) néanmoins j'aime bien la maison ; **it's strange** ~ **true** c'est vrai étrange mais pourtant vrai or mais vrai tout de même

yeti ['jɛtɪ] N yéti or yeti m

yew [juː] 1 N a (also ~ **tree**) if m b (= wood) (bois m d')if m 2 COMP [bow etc] en bois d'if

YHA [ˌwaɪeɪtʃ'eɪ] N (ABBR = **Youth Hostels Association**) auberges de jeunesse du pays de Galles et de l'Angleterre, ≈ FUAJ f

Yid: [jɪd] N (pej) youpin(e)** m(f) (pej)

Yiddish ['jɪdɪʃ] 1 ADJ yiddish inv 2 N (Ling) yiddish m

yield [jiːld] 1 N [of land, farm, field, tree, industry, mine] production f ; (per unit) rendement m ; [of oil well] débit m ; [of labour] produit m, rendement m ; [of tax] recettes fpl ; [of business, shares] rapport m, rendement m ; ~ **per hectare/year** etc rendement à l'hectare/l'année etc ; **the** ~ **of this land/orchard** etc **is** ... ce terrain/verger etc produit ...

2 VT a (= produce, bring in) [earth, mine, oil well] produire ; [farm, field, land, orchard, tree] rendre, produire, rapporter ; [labour, industry] produire ; [business, investments, tax, shares] rapporter ; **to** ~ **a profit** rapporter un profit or un bénéfice ; **that land** ~s **no return** cette terre ne rend pas ; (Fin) **shares** ~**ing high interest** actions fpl à gros rendement or d'un bon rapport ; **shares** ~**ing 10%** actions fpl qui rapportent 10% ; **to** ~ **results** donner or produire des résultats ; **this** ~**ed many benefits** bien des bénéfices en ont résulté

b (= surrender, give up) [+ ground, territory] céder ; [+ fortress, territory] abandonner (**to** à) ; [+ ownership, rights] céder (**to** à), renoncer à (**to** en faveur de) ; [+ control] renoncer à (**to** en faveur de) ; (Mil, fig) **to** ~ **ground to sb** céder du terrain à qn ; (fig) **to** ~ **the floor to sb** laisser la parole à qn ; **to** ~ **a point to sb** concéder un point à qn, céder à qn sur un point ; (esp US Aut) **to** ~ **the right of way to sb** céder le passage à qn ; (frm) **to** ~ **obedience/thanks to sb** rendre obéissance/grâces à qn (frm)

3 VI a (= give produce, bring in revenue) [farm, field, land, orchard, tree] rendre ; [business, investments, tax, shares] rapporter ; [labour, industry, mine, oil well] produire ; **a field that** ~s **well** un champ qui donne un bon rendement, un champ qui rend bien ; **land that** ~s **poorly** une terre qui rend peu or mal, une terre à faible rendement

b (= surrender, give in) céder (**to** devant, à), se rendre (**to** à) ; **we shall never** ~ nous ne céderons jamais, nous ne nous rendrons jamais ; **they begged him but he would not** ~ ils l'ont supplié mais il n'a pas cédé or il ne s'est pas laissé fléchir ; (Mil etc) **they** ~**ed to us** ils se rendirent à nous ; **to** ~ **to force** céder devant or à des forces supérieures ; **to** ~ **to superior forces** céder devant or à des forces supérieures ; **to** ~ **to superior numbers** céder au nombre ; **to** ~ **to reason** se rendre à la raison ; **to** ~ **to an impulse** céder à une impulsion ; **to** ~ **to sb's entreaties** céder aux prières or instances de qn ; **to** ~ **to sb's threats** céder devant les menaces de qn ; **to** ~ **to sb's argument** se rendre aux raisons de qn ; **the disease** ~**ed to treatment** le traitement est venu à bout de la maladie ; **to** ~ **to temptation** céder or succomber à la tentation ; (liter) **he** ~**ed to nobody in courage** il ne le cédait à personne pour le courage (liter) ; **I** ~ **to nobody in my admiration for** ... personne plus que moi n'admire ...

c (= collapse, give way) [branch, door, ice, rope] céder ; [beam] céder, fléchir ; [floor, ground] s'affaisser ; [bridge] céder, s'affaisser ; **to** ~ **under pressure** céder à la pression

d (US Aut) céder le passage

►**yield up** VT SEP (esp liter) [+ secrets] livrer ; **to**

~ **o.s. up to temptation** céder or succomber à la tentation ; **to** ~ **up the ghost** rendre l'âme

yielding ['jiːldɪŋ] 1 ADJ a (fig) [person] complaisant, accommodant b (lit = soft, flexible) [floor, ground, surface] mou (molle f), élastique ; [branch] qui cède 2 N (NonC = surrender) [of person] soumission f ; [of town, fort] reddition f, capitulation f ; [of right, goods] cession f

yike(s)* [jaɪk(s)] EXCL (esp US) mince !*

yin [jɪn] N (Philos) yin m ; ~**-yang symbol** symbole m du yin et du yang

yip [jɪp] (US) = **yelp**

yipe(s)* [jaɪp(s)] EXCL (esp US) = **yike(s)**

yippee: [jɪ'piː] EXCL hourra !

YMCA [ˌwaɪemsiː'eɪ] N (ABBR = **Young Men's Christian Association**) YMCA m

yo: [jəʊ] EXCL (esp US) salut !*

yob: ['jɒb] N (Brit pej) loubard* m

yobbish* ['jɒbɪʃ] ADJ (Brit pej) [behaviour] de loubard* ; **a** ~ **young man** un jeune loubard*

yobbo: ['jɒbəʊ] N (Brit) = **yob**

yock: [jɒk] (US) 1 N gros rire m, rire m gras 2 VT **to** ~ **it up** rigoler*, s'esclaffer

yod [jɒd] N (Phon) yod m

yodel ['jəʊdl] 1 VT jodler or iodler, faire des tyroliennes 2 N (= song, call) tyrolienne f

yoga ['jəʊɡə] N yoga m

yoghurt ['jəʊɡət] = **yogurt**

yogi ['jəʊɡɪ] N (pl **yogis** or **yogin** ['jəʊɡɪn]) yogi m

yogic flying [ˌjəʊɡɪk'flaɪɪŋ] N lévitation pratiquée par les adeptes d'une forme de yoga

yogurt ['jəʊɡət] 1 N yaourt m, yogourt m 2 COMP ► **yogurt-maker** N yaourtière f

yo-heave-ho ['jəʊhiːv'həʊ] EXCL (Naut) oh hisse !

yoke [jəʊk] 1 N a (for oxen) joug m ; (for carrying pails) palanche f, joug m ; (on harness) support m de timon b (fig = dominion) joug m ; **the** ~ **of slavery** le joug de l'esclavage ; **the communist** ~ le joug communiste ; **to come under the** ~ **of** tomber sous le joug de ; **to throw off** or **cast off the** ~ secouer le joug c (pl inv = pair) attelage m ; **a** ~ **of oxen** une paire de bœufs d [of dress, blouse] empiècement m e (Constr) [of beam] moise f, lien m ; (Tech) bâti m, carcasse f 2 VT (also ~ **up**) [+ oxen] accoupler ; [+ ox tree] mettre au joug ; [+ pieces of machinery] accoupler ; (fig: also ~ **together**) unir ; **to** ~ **oxen (up) to the plough** atteler des bœufs à la charrue 3 COMP ► **yoke oxen** NPL bœufs mpl d'attelage

yokel ['jəʊkəl] N (pej) rustre m, péquenaud m

yolk [jəʊk] 1 N (Bio) vitellus m ; (Culin) jaune m (d'œuf) 2 COMP ► **yolk sac** N (Bio) membrane f vitelline

Yom Kippur [ˌjɒmkɪ'pʊər] N Yom Kippour m

yomp: [jɒmp] VI (Mil) crapahuter

yon [jɒn] ADJ (††, liter, dial) = **yonder 2**

yonder ['jɒndər] 1 ADV († or dial) là(-bas) ; **up** ~ là-haut ; **over** ~ là-bas ; **down** ~ là-bas en bas 2 ADJ (liter) ce ...-là, ce ... là-bas ; **from** ~ **house** de cette maison-là, de cette maison là-bas

yonks* [jɒŋks] NPL (Brit) **for** ~ très longtemps ; **I haven't seen him for** ~ ça fait une éternité or une paye* que je ne l'ai pas vu

yoof* [juːf] N (hum) = **youth**

yoo-hoo* ['juːˈhuː] EXCL ohé !, hou hou !

YOP (Brit: formerly) N (ABBR = **Youth Opportunities Programme**) → **youth**

yore [jɔːr] N (liter) **of** ~ d'antan (liter), (d')autrefois ; **in days of** ~ au temps jadis

Yorks [jɔːks] ABBR = **Yorkshire**

Yorkshire ['jɔːkʃər] 1 N le Yorkshire 2 COMP ► **Yorkshire pudding** N (Brit Culin) pâte à *crêpe cuite qui accompagne un rôti de bœuf* ▶ **Yorkshire terrier** N yorkshire-terrier *m*

you [juː] 1 PERS PRON a (*subject*) tu, vous, vous (*pl*); (*object or indirect object*) te, vous, vous (*pl*); (*stressed and after prep*) toi, vous, vous (*pl*); ~ **are very kind** vous êtes très gentil; **I'll see ~ soon** je te *or* je vous verrai bientôt, on se voit bientôt; **this book is for ~** ce livre est pour toi *or* vous; **she is younger than ~** elle est plus jeune que toi *or* vous; ~ **and yours** toi et les tiens, vous et les vôtres; **all of ~** vous tous; **all ~ who came here** vous tous qui êtes venus ici; ~ **who know him** toi qui le connais, vous qui le connaissez; ~ **French** vous autres Français; ~ **two wait here!** attendez ici, vous deux!; **now ~ say something** maintenant à toi *or* à vous de parler; ~ **and I will go together** toi *or* vous et moi, nous irons ensemble; **there ~ are!** (= *you've arrived*) te *or* vous voilà!; **there ~ are* ◊ there ~ go!*** (= *have this*) voilà!; **if I were ~** (si j'étais) à ta *or* votre place, si j'étais toi *or* vous; **between ~ and me** (*lit*) entre toi *or* vous et moi; (= *in secret*) entre nous, de toi *or* vous à moi; ~ **fool (~)!** imbécile (que tu es)!, espèce d'imbécile!; ~ **darling!** tu es un amour!; **it's** ~ c'est toi *or* vous; **I like the uniform, it's very ~*** j'aime bien ton uniforme, c'est vraiment ton style *or* ça te va parfaitement; ~ **there!** toi *or* vous là-bas!; **never ~ mind*** (= *don't worry*) ne t'en fais pas*, ne vous en faites pas*; (= *it's not your business*) ça ne te *or* vous regarde pas, mêle-toi de tes *or* mêlez-vous de vos affaires; **don't ~ go away** ne pars pas, toi!, ne partez pas, vous!; **there's a fine house for ~** en voilà une belle maison!; **that's Australia for ~!*** qu'est-ce que tu veux, c'est ça l'Australie!; (†† *or hum*) **sit ~ down** assieds-toi, asseyez-vous b (= *one, anyone*) (*nominative*) on; (*accusative, dative*) vous, te; ~ **never know ◊** ~ **never can tell** on ne sait jamais; ~ **never know your (own) luck** on ne connaît jamais son bonheur *or* sa chance; ~ **go towards the church** vous allez *or* on va vers l'église; **fresh air does ~ good** l'air frais vous *or* te fait du bien 2 COMP ▶ **you-all*** PRON (*US*) vous (autres) ▶ **you-know-who*** N qui tu sais, qui vous savez

you'd [juːd] = **you had, you would**; → **have, would**

you'll [juːl] = **you will**; → **will**

young [jʌŋ] 1 ADJ [*person, tree, country*] jeune; [*vegetable, grass*] nouveau (nouvelle *f*), nouvel (*m before vowel*); [*appearance, smile*] jeune, juvénile; **he is ~ for his age** il paraît *or* fait plus jeune que son âge; **he is very ~ for this job** il est bien jeune pour ce poste; **that dress is too ~ for her** cette robe fait trop jeune pour elle; **children as ~ as seven** des enfants de pas plus de sept ans; **I'm not as ~ as I was** je n'ai plus vingt ans ■ (*PROV*) **you're only ~ once** jeunesse n'a qu'un temps (*PROV*); ~ **at heart** jeune de cœur; **to die ~** mourir jeune → **hopeful**; **to marry ~** se marier jeune; **he is three years ~er than you** il a trois ans de moins que vous, il est votre cadet de trois ans; ~ **Mr Brown** le jeune M. Brown; **Mr Brown the ~er** (*as opposed to his father*) M. Brown fils; **Pitt the Younger** le second Pitt; **Pliny the Younger** Pline le Jeune; **in my ~ days** dans ma jeunesse, dans mon jeune temps; **in my ~er days** quand j'étais plus jeune; **they have a ~ family** ils ont de jeunes enfants; ~ **France** la jeune génération en France; **the ~(er) generation** la jeune génération, la génération montante; ~ **lady** (*unmarried*) jeune fille *f*, demoiselle *f*; (*married*) jeune femme *f*; **listen to me, ~ man**

écoutez-moi, jeune homme; **her ~ man**† son amoureux, son petit ami; **the ~ moon** la nouvelle lune; **the night is ~** (*liter*) la nuit n'est pas très avancée; (* *hum*) on a toute la nuit devant nous; **he has a very ~ outlook** il a des idées très jeunes; ~ **people** les jeunes *mpl*; **you ~ hooligan!** petit *or* jeune voyou! 2 NPL a (= *people*) ~ **and old** les (plus) jeunes *mpl* comme les (plus) vieux *mpl*, tout le monde; **the ~** les jeunes *mpl*; **books for the ~** livres *mpl* pour les jeunes b [*of animal*] petits *mpl*; **cat with ~** (= *pregnant*) chatte *f* pleine; (= *with kittens*) chatte *f* et ses petits 3 COMP ▶ **young blood** N (*fig*) sang *m* nouveau *or* jeune ▶ **Young Conservative** N (*Brit Pol*) jeune membre *m* du parti conservateur ▶ **young-looking** ADJ qui a (*or* avait *etc*) l'air jeune; **she's very ~-looking** elle a l'air très jeune ▶ **young offender** N (*Brit Jur*) jeune délinquant(e) *m(f)* ▶ **young offenders institution** N (*Brit Jur*) centre *m* de détention pour mineurs ▶ **young wine** N vin *m* vert

youngish ['jʌŋɪʃ] ADJ assez jeune

youngster ['jʌŋstər] N (= *boy*) jeune garçon *m*, jeune *m*; (= *child*) enfant *mf*

your [jɔːr] POSS ADJ ~ ton, ta, tes, votre, vos; ~ **book** ton *or* votre livre; **YOUR book** ton livre à toi, votre livre à vous; ~ **table** ta *or* votre table; ~ **friend** ton ami(e), votre ami(e); ~ **clothes** tes *or* vos vêtements; **this is the best of ~ paintings** c'est ton *or* votre meilleur tableau; **give me ~ hand** donne-moi *or* donnez-moi ta main; **you've broken ~ leg!** tu t'es cassé la jambe! → **majesty, worship** b (= *one's*) son, sa, ses, ton *etc*, votre *etc*; **you give him ~ form and he gives you ~ pass** on lui donne son formulaire et il vous remet votre laissez-passer; **exercise is good for ~ health** l'exercice est bon pour la santé c (* = *typical*) ton *etc*, votre *etc*; **so these are ~ country pubs?** alors c'est ça, vos bistro(t)s* de campagne?; ~ **ordinary** *or* **average Englishman will always prefer ...** l'Anglais moyen préférera toujours ...

you're [jʊər] = **you are**; → **be**

yours [jɔːz] POSS PRON le tien, la tienne, les tiens, les tiennes, le vôtre, la vôtre, les vôtres; **this is my book and that is ~** voici mon livre et voilà le tien *or* le vôtre; **this book is ~** ce livre est à toi *or* à vous, ce livre est le tien *or* le vôtre; **is this poem ~?** ce poème est-il de toi *or* de vous?; **when will the house be** *or* **become ~?** quand entrerez-vous en possession de la maison?; **she is a cousin of ~** c'est une de tes *or* de vos cousines; **that is no business of ~** cela ne te *or* vous regarde pas, ce n'est pas ton *or* votre affaire; **it's no fault of ~** ce n'est pas de votre faute (à vous); (*Comm*) ~ **of the 10th inst.** votre honorée du 10 courant (*Comm*); **no advice of ~ could prevent him** aucun conseil de votre part ne pouvait l'empêcher; (*frm*) **it is not ~ to decide** ce n'est pas à vous de décider, il ne vous appartient pas de décider; ~ **is a specialized department** votre section est une section spécialisée; **how's that thesis of ~* getting on?** et cette thèse, comment ça avance?*; **where's that husband of ~?*** où est passé ton mari?; (*pej*) **that dog of ~*** ton *or* votre fichu* chien; **that stupid son of ~*** ton *or* votre idiot de fils; **that temper of ~*** ton sale caractère; (*buying drinks*) **what's ~?*** qu'est-ce que tu prends *or* vous prenez? → **affectionately, ever, truly, you**

yourself [jɔːˈself] PERS PRON (*pl* **yourselves** [jɔːˈselvz]) (*reflexive: direct and indirect*) te, vous, vous (*pl*); (*after prep*) toi, vous, vous (*pl*); (*emphatic*) toi-même, vous-même, vous-mêmes (*pl*); **have you hurt ~?** tu t'es fait mal?, vous vous êtes fait mal?; **are you enjoying ~?** tu t'amuses bien?, vous vous amu-

sez bien?; **were you talking to ~?** tu te parlais à toi-même?, tu parlais tout seul?, vous vous parliez à vous-même?, vous parliez tout seul?; **you never speak about ~** tu ne parles jamais de toi, vous ne parlez jamais de vous; **you ~ told me ◊ you told me ~** tu me l'as dit toi-même, vous me l'avez dit vous-même; **(all) by ~** tout seul; **did you do it by ~?** tu l'as *or* vous l'avez fait tout seul?; **you will see for ~** tu verras toi-même, vous verrez vous-même; **someone like ~** quelqu'un comme vous; **people like yourselves** des gens comme vous; **how's ~?** et toi, comment (ça) va?*; **how are you? — fine, and ~?*** comment vas-tu? — très bien, et toi?; **you haven't been ~ lately** (= *not behaving normally*) tu n'es pas dans ton état normal *or* vous n'êtes pas dans votre état normal ces temps-ci; (= *not looking well*) tu n'es pas dans ton assiette *or* vous n'êtes pas dans votre assiette ces temps-ci → **among(st)**

youth [juːθ] 1 N a (*NonC*) jeunesse *f*; **in (the days of) my ~** dans ma jeunesse, au temps de ma jeunesse; **in early ~** dans la première *or* prime jeunesse; **he has kept his ~** il est resté jeune; **he was enchanted with her ~ and beauty** sa jeunesse et sa beauté l'enchantaient ■ (*PROV*) ~ **will have its way** *or* **its fling** il faut que jeunesse se passe (*PROV*) → **first** b (*pl* **youths** [juːðz]) (= *young man*) jeune homme *m*; ~**s** jeunes gens *mpl* 2 NPL (= *young people*) jeunesse *f*, jeunes *mpl*; **she likes working with (the) ~** elle aime travailler avec les jeunes; **the ~ of a country** la jeunesse d'un pays; **the ~ of today are very mature** les jeunes d'aujourd'hui sont très mûrs, la jeunesse aujourd'hui est très mûre 3 COMP de jeunes, de jeunesse ▶ **youth club** N maison *f* de jeunes ▶ **youth custody** N (*Brit Jur*) éducation *f* surveillée; **to be sentenced to 18 months' ~ custody** être condamné à 18 mois d'éducation surveillée ▶ **youth hostel** N auberge *f* de jeunesse ▶ **youth leader** N animateur *m*, -trice *f* de groupes de jeunes ▶ **Youth Opportunities Programme** N (*Brit: formerly*) programme en faveur de l'emploi des jeunes ▶ **youth orchestra** N orchestre *m* de jeunes ▶ **Youth Training Scheme** N (*Brit: formerly*) ≈ pacte *m* national pour l'emploi des jeunes ▶ **youth worker** N éducateur *m*, -trice *f*

youthful ['juːθfʊl] ADJ [*person, looks, face, skin*] jeune; [*mistake, adventure*] de jeunesse; [*quality, freshness, idealism, enthusiasm*] juvénile; **she looks ~** elle a l'air jeune; **a ~-looking 49-year-old** un homme/une femme de 49 ans, jeune d'allure; **he's a ~ 50** il porte allègrement ses 50 ans

youthfully ['juːθfʊlɪ] ADV ~ **exuberant** d'une exubérance juvénile; **his face was ~ smooth** son visage était doux comme une peau de bébé

youthfulness ['juːθfʊlnɪs] N jeunesse *f*; ~ **of appearance** air *m* jeune *or* de jeunesse

you've [juːv] = **you have**; → **have**

yow [jaʊ] EXCL aïe!

yowl [jaʊl] 1 N [*of person, dog*] hurlement *m*; [*of cat*] miaulement *m* 2 VI [*person, dog*] hurler (**with, from** de); [*cat*] miauler

yowling ['jaʊlɪŋ] N [*of person, dog*] hurlements *mpl*; [*of cat*] miaulements *mpl*

yo-yo ['jəʊjəʊ] 1 N (*pl* **yo-yos**) a yoyo® *m* b (*US* = *fool*) ballot* *m*, poire* *f* 2 VI (= *fluctuate*) fluctuer (considérablement)

yr ABBR = **year**

YTS [ˌwaɪtiːˈes] N (*Brit: formerly*) (ABBR = **Youth Training Scheme**) → **youth**

ytterbium [ɪˈtɜːbɪəm] N ytterbium *m*

yttrium ['ɪtrɪəm] N yttrium *m*

yuan [juːˈæn] N (*pl inv*) yuan *m*

yucca ['jʌkə] N yucca *m*

yuck• [jʌk] EXCL berk *or* beurk!, pouah!

yucky• ['jʌkɪ] ADJ dégueulasse‡, dégoûtant

Yugoslav ['ju:gəʊ'slɑːv] ① ADJ (*gen*) yougoslave; [*ambassador, embassy*] de Yougoslavie ② N Yougoslave *mf*

Yugoslavia ['ju:gəʊ'slɑːvɪə] N la Yougoslavie

Yugoslavian ['ju:gəʊ'slɑːvɪən] ADJ = **Yugoslav**

yuk• [jʌk] EXCL = **yuck**

yukky• ['jʌkɪ] ADJ = **yucky**

Yukon ['ju:kɒn] ① N **(the)** ~ le Yukon ② COMP ► **(the) Yukon Territory** N le (territoire de) Yukon

Yule [ju:l] ① N († *or liter*) Noël *m* ② COMP ► **Yule log** N bûche *f* de Noël

Yuletide ['ju:ltaɪd] N († *or liter*) (époque *f* de) Noël *m*

yummy• ['jʌmɪ] ① ADJ [*food*] délicieux ② EXCL miam-miam!•

yum-yum‡ ['jʌm'jʌm] EXCL = **yummy 2**

yup• [jʌp] EXCL (*esp US*) ouais•, oui

yuppie• ['jʌpɪ] ① N (ABBR = **young upwardly-mobile** *or* **urban professional**) yuppie *mf* ② COMP [*car, clothes*] de yuppie; [*bar, restaurant, area*] de yuppies ► **yuppie flu**• N (*pej*)

syndrome *m* de la fatigue chronique, encéphalomyélite *f* myalgique

yuppiedom• ['jʌpɪdəm] N monde *m* or univers *m* des yuppies

yuppified• ['jʌpɪˌfaɪd] ADJ [*bar, restaurant, area, flat*] transformé en bar (*or* restaurant *etc*) de yuppies; **he is becoming more and more ~** il se transforme de plus en plus en yuppie

yuppy• ['jʌpɪ] N = **yuppie**

YWCA [,waɪdʌbljʊsiː'eɪ] N (ABBR = **Young Women's Christian Association**) YWCA *m*

Z

Z, z [zed, (US) ziː] ⒈ N (= letter) Z, z m ; **Z for Zebra** ≈ Z comme Zoé ⒉ COMP ► **z-axis** N axe m des z ► **Z-bed** N (Brit) lit m de camp

Zacharias [ˌzækəˈraɪəs] N Zacharie m

zaftig: [ˈzɑːftɪk] ADJ (US) joli et bien en chair

Zaïre [zɑːˈiːər] N (= country) le Zaïre

Zaïrean, Zaïrian [zɑːˈiːərɪən] ⒈ ADJ zaïrois ⒉ N Zaïrois(e) m(f)

Zambese, Zambezi [zæmˈbiːzɪ] N Zambèze m

Zambia [ˈzæmbɪə] N la Zambie

Zambian [ˈzæmbɪən] ⒈ ADJ zambien ⒉ N Zambien(ne) m(f)

zany [ˈzeɪnɪ] ⒈ ADJ loufoque* ⒉ N (Theat Hist) bouffon m, zanni m

Zanzibar [ˈzænzɪbɑːr] N Zanzibar

zap* [zæp] ⒈ EXCL paf !, vlan ! ⒉ VT ⒜ (= destroy) [+ town] ravager, bombarder ; [+ person] supprimer, descendre* ⒝ (= delete) [+ word, data] supprimer ⒞ (TV) **to ~ the TV channels** zapper ⒟ (= send quickly) **I'll ~ it out to you straight away** je vais vous l'expédier tout de suite ⒊ VI ⒜ (= move quickly) [car] foncer ; **we had to ~ down to London** nous avons dû filer à Londres à toute vitesse ; **to ~ along** [car] foncer ; **we're going to have to ~ through the work to get it finished in time** il va falloir que nous mettions la gomme* pour finir le travail à temps ⒝ (TV) **to ~ through the channels** zapper

zapped: [zæpt] ADJ (= exhausted) crevé:, vanné:

zapper* [ˈzæpər] N (TV = remote control) télécommande f

zappy: [ˈzæpɪ] ADJ [person, style] qui a du punch ; [car] rapide, qui fonce or gaze*

Zarathustra [ˌzærəˈθuːstrə] N Zarathoustra m or Zoroastre m

zeal [ziːl] N (NonC) ⒜ (= religious fervour) zèle m, ferveur f ⒝ (= enthusiasm) zèle m, empressement m (for à) ; **in her ~ to do** dans son empressement à faire

zealot [ˈzelət] N ⒜ fanatique mf, zélateur m, -trice f (liter) (for de) ⒝ (Jewish Hist) **Zealot** zélote m

zealotry [ˈzelətrɪ] N fanatisme m

zealous [ˈzeləs] ADJ [person] zélé ; [effort] diligent ; **he is ~ for the cause** il défend sa cause avec zèle ; **to be ~ in doing sth** montrer de l'empressement à faire qch

zealously [ˈzeləslɪ] ADV avec zèle

zebra [ˈzebrə, ˈziːbrə] (pl zebras or zebra) ⒈ N zèbre m ⒉ COMP ► **zebra crossing** N (Brit) passage m pour piétons ► **zebra stripes** NPL zébrures fpl ; **with ~ stripes** zébré

zebu [ˈziːbuː] N zébu m

Zechariah [ˌzekəˈraɪə] N = **Zacharias**

zed [zed], **zee** (US) [ziː] N (la lettre) z m

Zeitgeist [ˈzaɪtgaɪst] N esprit m de l'époque

Zen [zen] ⒈ N Zen m ⒉ COMP ► **Zen Buddhism** N bouddhisme m zen ► **Zen Buddhist** N bouddhiste mf zen

zenana [zeˈnɑːnə] N zénana m

zenith [ˈzenɪθ] N (Astron) zénith m ; (fig) zénith m, apogée m ; **at the ~ of his power** à l'apogée de son pouvoir ; **the ~ of Perugia's influence** l'apogée de l'influence de Pérouse ; **with this success, he reached the ~ of his glory** avec ce succès, il a atteint l'apogée de sa gloire

Zephaniah [ˌzefəˈnaɪə] N Sophonie m

zephyr [ˈzefər] N zéphyr m

zeppelin [ˈzeplɪn] N zeppelin m

zero [ˈzɪərəʊ] (pl zeros or zeroes) ⒈ N ⒜ (= point on scale) zéro m ; **15 degrees below ~** 15 degrés au-dessous de zéro ; **his chances of success sank to ~** ses chances de réussite se réduisirent à néant or zéro ; **snow reduced visibility to near ~** à cause de la neige, la visibilité était quasi nulle

⒝ (= cipher, numeral etc) zéro m ; **row of ~s** série f de zéros

⒉ COMP [tension, voltage] nul (nulle f) ► **zero altitude** N (Aviat) altitude f zéro ; **to fly at ~ altitude** voler en rase-mottes, faire du rase-mottes ► **zero-base** VT (US fig) [+ question, issue] reprendre à zéro, réexaminer point par point ► **zero-gravity, zero-G***** N apesanteur f ► **zero growth** N (Econ) taux m de croissance zéro, croissance f économique zéro ► **zero hour** N (Mil) l'heure f H ; (fig) le moment critique or décisif ► **the zero option** N (Pol) l'option f zéro ► **zero point** N point m zéro ► **zero population growth** N croissance f démographique nulle ► **zero-rated** ADJ (for VAT) exempt de TVA, non assujetti à la TVA ► **zero-rating** N exemption f de TVA, non-assujettissement m à la TVA ► **zero-sum** ADJ (US) [bargaining, thinking] à somme nulle ; **~-sum game** jeu m à somme nulle ► **zero tolerance** N politique f d'intransigeance ► **zero-tolerance** ADJ **~-tolerance policing** politique f d'intransigeance en matière de maintien de l'ordre

► **zero in** VI **to ~ in on sth** (= move in on) se diriger droit vers or sur qch ; (= identify) mettre le doigt sur qch, identifier qch ; (= concentrate on) se concentrer sur qch ; (= criticize) **he ~ed in on those who ...** il s'en est pris tout particulièrement à ceux qui ...

┌──────┐
│ ZERO │
└──────┘

« Zéro » se dit **zero** en anglais américain, mais en anglais britannique, l'emploi de ce terme est réservé aux sciences et aux mathématiques (notamment pour exprimer les températures et les graduations).

Le terme « **nought** » s'utilise en Grande-Bretagne dans les nombres décimaux, par exemple « nought point nought seven » pour dire « 0,07 », mais aussi dans les notations : ainsi, « nought out of ten » veut dire « 0 sur 10 ». Les Américains comme les Britanniques disent « oh » pour indiquer des numéros de carte de crédit ou de téléphone : par exemple, « oh one four one » pour « 0141 ». Dans les scores de matchs en Grande-Bretagne, on dit « nil ». « Liverpool a gagné par cinq buts à zéro » se dira ainsi « Liver-

pool won five nil ». L'équivalent américain est « nothing » (terme parfois employé familièrement par les Britanniques) ou, sous une forme plus familière, « zip » : « nous avons gagné par sept buts à zéro » se dira « we won seven-zip ».

---

zest [zest] N (NonC) ⒜ (= gusto) entrain m ; **to fight with ~** combattre avec entrain ; **he ate it with great ~** il l'a mangé avec grand appétit ; **~ for life** or **living** goût m de la vie, appétit m de vivre ; **he lost his ~ for winning** il a perdu son désir de gagner ⒝ (fig) saveur f, piquant m ; **her books are thrilling, full of ~** ses livres sont palpitants et savoureux ; **it adds ~ to the story** cela donne une certaine saveur or du piquant à l'histoire ⒞ (Culin) [of orange, lemon] zeste m

zestful [ˈzestfʊl] ADJ plein d'entrain, enthousiaste

zestfully [ˈzestfʊlɪ] ADV avec entrain or enthousiasme

zesty [ˈzestɪ] ADJ [wine] piquant

Zetland [ˈzetlənd] N (formerly) les Zetland fpl

Zeus [zjuːs] N Zeus m

zidovudine [zaɪˈdɒvjuˌdiːn] N zidovudine f

ZIFT [zɪft] N (ABBR = **Zygote Intrafallopian Transfer**) fivète f

ziggurat [ˈzɪgʊræt] N ziggourat f

zigzag [ˈzɪgzæg] ⒈ N zigzag m ⒉ ADJ [path, road, course, line] en zigzag ; [pattern, design] à zigzags ⒊ ADV en zigzag ⒋ VI zigzaguer, faire des zigzags ; **to ~ along** avancer en zigzaguant ; **to ~ out/through** etc sortir/traverser etc en zigzaguant

zilch: [zɪltʃ] N que dalle: ; **these shares are worth ~** ces actions valent que dalle: ; **Mark knows ~ about art** Mark connaît que dalle: à l'art

zillion* [ˈzɪljən] ADJ, N (pl zillions or zillion) **a ~ dollars** des millions mpl et des millions mpl de dollars ; **~s of problems** ◊ **a ~ problems** des tas mpl de problèmes

Zimbabwe [zɪmˈbɑːbwɪ] N le Zimbabwe

Zimbabwean [zɪmˈbɑːbwɪən] ⒈ ADJ zimbabwéen ⒉ N Zimbabwéen(ne) m(f)

Zimmer® [ˈzɪmər] N (Brit: also **~ frame**) déambulateur m

zinc [zɪŋk] ⒈ N (NonC) zinc m ⒉ COMP [plate, alloy] de zinc ; [roof] zingué ► **zinc blende** N blende f (de zinc) ► **zinc chloride** N chlorure m de zinc ► **zinc dust** N limaille f de zinc ► **zinc ointment** N pommade f à l'oxyde de zinc ► **zinc oxide** N oxyde m de zinc ► **zinc-plating** N zingage m ► **zinc sulphate** N sulfate m de zinc ► **zinc white** N blanc m de zinc

zine*, 'zine* [ziːn] N (= magazine) magazine m ; (= fanzine) fanzine m

zing [zɪŋ] ⒈ N ⒜ (= noise of bullet) sifflement m ⒝ (NonC* = energy) entrain m ⒉ VI [bullet, arrow] siffler ; **the bullet ~ed past his ear** la balle lui a sifflé à l'oreille ; **the cars ~ed past** les voitures sont passées en trombe*

zinnia ['zɪnɪə] N zinnia *m*

Zion ['zaɪən] N Sion

Zionism ['zaɪənɪzəm] N sionisme *m*

Zionist ['zaɪənɪst] [1] ADJ sioniste [2] N sioniste *mf*

zip [zɪp] [1] N [a] (*Brit: also* ~ **fastener**) fermeture *f* éclair®, fermeture *f* à glissière ; **pocket with a** ~ poche *f* à fermeture éclair®, poche *f* zippée* [b] (= *sound of bullet*) sifflement *m* [c] (*NonC* = energy*) entrain *m*, élan *m* ; **put a bit of** ~ **into it** activez-vous ! [d] (‡ = *nothing*) que dalle‡ ; **I know** ~ **about it** je n'en sais *or* j'y connais que dalle‡ → ZERO [2] VT [a] (= *close*: *also* ~ **up**) [+ *dress, bag*] fermer avec une fermeture éclair® *or* à glissière [b] **she** ~**ped open her dress/bag** *etc* elle a ouvert la fermeture éclair® *or* à glissière de sa robe/de son sac *etc* [3] VI **to** ~ **in/out/past/up** *etc* [*car, person*] entrer/sortir/passer/monter *etc* comme une flèche [4] COMP ► **zip code** N (*US Post*) code *m* postal ► **zip fastener** N = **zip 1a** ► **zip gun** N (*US*) pistolet *m* rudimentaire (*à ressort ou à élastique*) ► **zip-on** ADJ à fermeture éclair®

► **zip on** [1] VI s'attacher avec une fermeture éclair® *or* fermeture à glissière [2] VT SEP attacher avec une fermeture éclair® *or* fermeture à glissière [3] ~**-on** ADJ → **zip**

► **zip up** [1] VI → **zip 3** [2] VT SEP **can you** ~ **me up?** tu peux m'aider avec la fermeture éclair® ? → **zip 2a**

zipper ['zɪpəʳ] N (*esp US*) = **zip 1a**

zippy‡ ['zɪpɪ] ADJ [*person*] plein d'entrain *or* d'allant

zircon ['zɜːkən] N zircon *m*

zirconium [zɜːˈkəʊnɪəm] N zirconium *m*

zit‡ [zɪt] N bouton *m*

zither ['zɪðəʳ] N cithare *f*

zloty ['zlɒtɪ] N (*pl* **zlotys** *or* **zloty**) zloty *m*

zodiac ['zəʊdɪæk] N zodiaque *m* → **sign**

zodiacal [zəʊˈdaɪəkəl] ADJ du zodiac ; ~ **light** lumière *f* zodiacale

zoftig‡ ['zɒftɪg] ADJ = **zaftig**

zombie ['zɒmbɪ] N (*lit*) zombie *m*, zombi *m* ; (* *fig pej*) automate *mf*, mort(e) *m(f)* vivant(e)

zonal ['zəʊnl] ADJ zonal

zone ['zəʊn] [1] N [a] (*gen, Astron, Geog, Math etc*) zone *f* ; (= *subdivision of town*) secteur *m* ; **it lies within the** ~ **reserved for ...** cela se trouve dans la zone or le secteur réservé(e) à ... → **battle, danger, time** [b] (*US: also* **postal delivery** ~) zone *f* (postale) [2] VT [a] (= *divide into zones*) [+ *area*] diviser en zones ; [+ *town*] diviser en secteurs [b] **this district has been** ~**d for industry** c'est une zone réservée à l'implantation industrielle [3] COMP ► **zone defence**, **zone defense** (*US*) N (*Sport*) défense *f* de zone ► **zone therapy** N (*Med*) réflexothérapie *f*

zoning ['zəʊnɪŋ] N répartition *f* en zones

zonked‡ [zɒŋkt] ADJ (*also* ~ **out**) (= *exhausted*) vanné* ; (*from drugs*) défoncé* ; (*US = drunk*) bourré*

zoo [zuː] [1] N zoo *m* [2] COMP ► **zoo keeper** N gardien(ne) *m(f)* de zoo

zoological [ˌzəʊəˈlɒdʒɪkəl] [1] ADJ zoologique [2] COMP ► **zoological gardens** NPL jardin *m* zoologique

zoologist [ˌzəʊˈɒlədʒɪst] N zoologiste *mf*

zoology [zəʊˈɒlədʒɪ] N zoologie *f*

zoom [zuːm] [1] N [a] (= *sound*) vrombissement *m*, bourdonnement *m* [b] (*Aviat* = *upward flight*) montée *f* en chandelle [c] (*Phot: also* ~ **lens**) zoom *m* [2] VI [a] [*engine*] vrombir, bourdonner [b] **to** ~ **away/through** *etc* démarrer/traverser *etc* en trombe* ; **the car** ~**ed past us** la voiture est passée en trombe* [c] (*Aviat*) [*plane*] monter en chandelle

► **zoom in** VI (*Cine, TV*) faire un zoom (**on** sur)

► **zoom out** VI (*Cine, TV*) faire un zoom arrière

zoomorphic [ˌzəʊəˈmɔːfɪk] ADJ zoomorphe

zoophyte ['zəʊə‚faɪt] N zoophyte *m*

zoot-suit* ['zuːtsuːt] N costume *m* zazou

zoot-suiter* ['zuːtsuːtəʳ] N zazou *m*

Zoroaster [ˌzɒrəʊˈæstəʳ] N Zoroastre *m or* Zarathoustra *m*

Zoroastrianism [ˌzɒrəʊˈæstrɪənɪzəm] N zoroastrisme *m*

zouk [zuːk] N (*Mus*) zouk *m*

zucchini [zuːˈkiːnɪ] N (*pl* **zucchini** *or* **zucchinis**) (*US*) courgette *f*

Zuider Zee ['zaɪdəˈziː] N Zuiderzee *m*

Zulu ['zuːluː] [1] ADJ zoulou *f inv* [2] N [a] Zoulou *mf* [b] (*Ling*) zoulou *m*

Zululand ['zuːluːlænd] N le Zoulouland

Zürich ['zjʊərɪk] N Zurich ; **Lake** ~ le lac de Zurich

zwieback ['zwiːbæk] N (*US*) biscotte *f*

zygote ['zaɪgəʊt] N zygote *m*

APPENDICES

ANNEXES

The French Verb

Le Verbe Français

FORMATION OF COMPOUND TENSES OF FRENCH VERBS

Most verbs form their compound tenses using the verb *avoir*, except in the reflexive form. Simple tenses of the auxiliary are followed by the past participle to form the compound tenses shown below (the verb *avoir* is given as an example):

AVOIR

COMPOUND TENSES OF VERBS

PRESENT		
	j'	**ai**
	tu	**as**
	il	**a**
	nous	**avons**
	vous	**avez**
	ils	**ont**

= **PERFECT**

(*chanter* = il **a chanté**)
(*boire* = il **a bu**)
(*avoir* = il **a eu**)
(*être* = il **a été**)

IMPERFECT		
	j'	**avais**
	tu	**avais**
	il	**avait**
	nous	**avions**
	vous	**aviez**
	ils	**avaient**

= **PLUPERFECT**

(il **avait chanté**, il **avait bu**,
il **avait eu**, il **avait été**)

FUTURE		
	j'	**aurai**
	tu	**auras**
	il	**aura**
	nous	**aurons**
	vous	**aurez**
	ils	**auront**

= **FUTURE PERFECT**

(il **aura chanté**, il **aura bu**,
il **aura eu**, il **aura été**)

CONDITIONAL (PRESENT)		
	j'	**aurais**
	tu	**aurais**
	il	**aurait**
	nous	**aurions**
	vous	**auriez**
	ils	**auraient**

+ PAST PARTICIPLE

(chanté) (bu) (eu) (été)

= **PAST CONDITIONAL**
(this tense is rarely studied but the forms are not rare)

(il **aurait chanté**, il **aurait bu**,
il **aurait eu**, il **aurait été**)

PAST HISTORIC		
	j'	**eus**
	tu	**eus**
	il	**eut**
	nous	**eûmes**
	vous	**eûtes**
	ils	**eurent**

= **PAST ANTERIOR**
(rare as a spoken form)

(il **eut chanté**, il **eut bu**,
il **eut eu**, il **eut été**)

IMPERATIVE	
	aie
	ayons
	ayez

= **PAST IMPERATIVE** (rare)

(**aie chanté**, **aie bu**, **aie eu**, **aie été**)

PRESENT PARTICIPLE	
	ayant

= **SECOND FORM OF PAST PARTICIPLE**

(**ayant chanté**, **ayant bu**,
ayant eu, **ayant été**)

SUBJUNCTIVE (PRESENT)		
	que j'	**aie**
	que tu	**aies**
	qu'il	**ait**
	que nous	**ayons**
	que vous	**ayez**
	qu'ils	**aient**

= **PAST SUBJUNCTIVE**
(rare as spoken form)

(qu'il **ait chanté**, qu'il **ait bu**,
qu'il **ait eu**, qu'il **ait été**)

SUBJUNCTIVE (IMPERFECT) (rare)		
	que j'	**eusse**
	que tu	**eusses**
	qu'il	**eût**
	que nous	**eussions**
	que vous	**eussiez**
	qu'ils	**eussent**

= **PLUPERFECT SUBJUNCTIVE**
(very rare, even in the written form)

(qu'il **eût chanté**, qu'il **eût bu**,
qu'il **eût eu**, qu'il **eût été**)

conjugation 1 — **ARRIVER:** regular verbs ending in **-er**

INDICATIVE

PRESENT

j'arrive
tu arrives
il arrive
nous arrivons
vous arrivez
ils arrivent

IMPERFECT

j'arrivais
tu arrivais
il arrivait
nous arrivions
vous arriviez
ils arrivaient

PAST HISTORIC

j'arrivai
tu arrivas
il arriva
nous arrivâmes
vous arrivâtes
ils arrivèrent

FUTURE

j'arriverai [aʀiv(ə)ʀɛ]
tu arriveras
il arrivera
nous arriverons [aʀiv(ə)ʀɔ̃]
vous arriverez
ils arriveront

PERFECT

je suis arrivé
tu es arrivé
il est arrivé
nous sommes arrivés
vous êtes arrivés
ils sont arrivés

PLUPERFECT

j'étais arrivé
tu étais arrivé
il était arrivé
nous étions arrivés
vous étiez arrivés
ils étaient arrivés

PAST ANTERIOR

je fus arrivé
tu fus arrivé
il fut arrivé
nous fûmes arrivés
vous fûtes arrivés
ils furent arrivés

FUTURE PERFECT

je serai arrivé
tu seras arrivé
il sera arrivé
nous serons arrivés
vous serez arrivés
ils seront arrivés

SUBJUNCTIVE

PRESENT

que j'arrive
que tu arrives
qu'il arrive
que nous arrivions
que vous arriviez
qu'ils arrivent

IMPERFECT

que j'arrivasse
que tu arrivasses
qu'il arrivât
que nous arrivassions
que vous arrivassiez
qu'ils arrivassent

PAST

que je sois arrivé
que tu sois arrivé
qu'il soit arrivé
que nous soyons arrivés
que vous soyez arrivés
qu'ils soient arrivés

PLUPERFECT

que je fusse arrivé
que tu fusses arrivé
qu'il fût arrivé
que nous fussions arrivés
que vous fussiez arrivés
qu'ils fussent arrivés

CONDITIONAL

PRESENT

j'arriverais [aʀivʀɛ]
tu arriverais
il arriverait
nous arriverions [aʀivəʀjɔ̃]
vous arriveriez
ils arriveraient

PAST I

je serais arrivé
tu serais arrivé
il serait arrivé
nous serions arrivés
vous seriez arrivés
ils seraient arrivés

PAST II

je fusse arrivé
tu fusses arrivé
il fût arrivé
nous fussions arrivés
vous fussiez arrivés
ils fussent arrivés

IMPERATIVE	PRESENT	PAST
	arrive	sois arrivé
	arrivons	soyons arrivés
	arrivez	soyez arrivés

PARTICIPLE	PRESENT	PAST
	arrivant	arrivé, ée
		étant arrivé

INFINITIVE	PRESENT	PAST
	arriver	être arrivé

NB The verbs *jouer, tuer* etc. are regular: e.g. *je joue, je jouerai ; je tue, je tuerai.*

conjugation 1 (reflexive form) — **SE REPOSER:** regular verbs ending in **-er**

INDICATIVE

PRESENT
je me repose
tu te reposes
il se repose
nous nous reposons
vous vous reposez
ils se reposent

IMPERFECT
je me reposais
tu te reposais
il se reposait
nous nous reposions
vous vous reposiez
ils se reposaient

PAST HISTORIC
je me reposai
tu te reposas
il se reposa
nous nous reposâmes
vous vous reposâtes
ils se reposèrent

FUTURE
je me reposerai
tu te reposeras
il se reposera
nous nous reposerons
vous vous reposerez
ils se reposeront

PERFECT
je me suis reposé
tu t'es reposé
il s'est reposé
nous nous sommes reposés
vous vous êtes reposés
ils se sont reposés

PLUPERFECT
je m'étais reposé
tu t'étais reposé
il s'était reposé
nous nous étions reposés
vous vous étiez reposés
ils s'étaient reposés

PAST ANTERIOR
je me fus reposé
tu te fus reposé
il se fut reposé
nous nous fûmes reposés
vous vous fûtes reposés
ils se furent reposés

FUTURE PERFECT
je me serai reposé
tu te seras reposé
il se sera reposé
nous nous serons reposés
vous vous serez reposés
ils se seront reposés

SUBJUNCTIVE

PRESENT
que je me repose
que tu te reposes
qu'il se repose
que nous nous reposions
que vous vous reposiez
qu'ils se reposent

IMPERFECT
que je me reposasse
que tu te reposasses
qu'il se reposât
que nous nous reposassions
que vous vous reposassiez
qu'ils se reposassent

PAST
que je me sois reposé
que tu te sois reposé
qu'il se soit reposé
que nous nous soyons reposés
que vous vous soyez reposés
qu'ils se soient reposés

PLUPERFECT
que je me fusse reposé
que tu te fusses reposé
qu'il se fût reposé
que nous nous fussions reposés
que vous vous fussiez reposés
qu'ils se fussent reposés

CONDITIONAL

PRESENT
je me reposerais
tu te reposerais
il se reposerait
nous nous reposerions
vous vous reposeriez
ils se reposeraient

PAST I
je me serais reposé
tu te serais reposé
il se serait reposé
nous nous serions reposés
vous vous seriez reposés
ils se seraient reposés

PAST II
je me fusse reposé
tu te fusses reposé
il se fût reposé
nous nous fussions reposés
vous vous fussiez reposés
ils se fussent reposés

IMPERATIVE

PRESENT	PAST
repose-toi	unused
reposons-nous	
reposez-vous	

PARTICIPLE

PRESENT	PAST
se reposant	s'étant reposé

INFINITIVE

PRESENT	PAST
se reposer	s'être reposé

conjugation 2 — **FINIR:** regular verbs ending in **-ir**

INDICATIVE

PRESENT

je finis
tu finis
il finit
nous finissons
vous finissez
ils finissent

IMPERFECT

je finissais
tu finissais
il finissait
nous finissions
vous finissiez
ils finissaient

PAST HISTORIC

je finis
tu finis
il finit
nous finîmes
vous finîtes
ils finirent

FUTURE

je finirai
tu finiras
il finira
nous finirons
vous finirez
ils finiront

PERFECT

j'ai fini
tu as fini
il a fini
nous avons fini
vous avez fini
ils ont fini

PLUPERFECT

j'avais fini
tu avais fini
il avait fini
nous avions fini
vous aviez fini
ils avaient fini

PAST ANTERIOR

j'eus fini
tu eus fini
il eut fini
nous eûmes fini
vous eûtes fini
ils eurent fini

FUTURE PERFECT

j'aurai fini
tu auras fini
il aura fini
nous aurons fini
vous aurez fini
ils auront fini

SUBJUNCTIVE

PRESENT

que je finisse
que tu finisses
qu'il finisse
que nous finissions
que vous finissiez
qu'ils finissent

IMPERFECT

que je finisse
que tu finisses
qu'il finît
que nous finissions
que vous finissiez
qu'ils finissent

PAST

que j'aie fini
que tu aies fini
qu'il ait fini
que nous ayons fini
que vous ayez fini
qu'ils aient fini

PLUPERFECT

que j'eusse fini
que tu eusses fini
qu'il eût fini
que nous eussions fini
que vous eussiez fini
qu'ils eussent fini

CONDITIONAL

PRESENT

je finirais
tu finirais
il finirait
nous finirions
vous finiriez
ils finiraient

PAST I

j'aurais fini
tu aurais fini
il aurait fini
nous aurions fini
vous auriez fini
ils auraient fini

PAST II

j'eusse fini
tu eusses fini
il eût fini
nous eussions fini
vous eussiez fini
ils eussent fini

IMPERATIVE

PRESENT	PAST
finis	aie fini
finissons	ayons fini
finissez	ayez fini

PARTICIPLE

PRESENT	PAST
finissant	fini, ie
	ayant fini

INFINITIVE

PRESENT	PAST
finir	avoir fini

conjugations 3 to 8

		INDICATIVE			
		1st person — present — 3rd person		imperfect	past historic
3	**placer**	je place [plas] nous plaçons [plasɔ̃]	il place ils placent	je plaçais	je plaçai

NB Verbs in **-ecer** (e.g. *dépecer*) are conjugated like **placer** and **geler**. Verbs in **-écer** (e.g. *rapiécer*) are conjugated like **céder** and **placer**.

	bouger	je bouge [buʒ] nous bougeons [buʒɔ̃]	il bouge ils bougent	je bougeais nous bougions	je bougeai

NB Verbs in **-éger** (e.g. *protéger*) are conjugated like **bouger** and **céder**.

4	**appeler**	j'appelle [apɛl] nous appelons [ap(ə)lɔ̃]	il appelle ils appellent	j'appelais	j'appelai
	jeter	je jette [ʒɛt] nous jetons [ʒ(ə)tɔ̃]	il jette ils jettent	je jetais	je jetai

5	**geler**	je gèle [ʒɛl] nous gelons [ʒ(ə)lɔ̃]	il gèle ils gèlent	je gelais nous gelions [ʒəljɔ̃]	je gelai
	acheter	j'achète [aʃɛt] nous achetons [aʃ(ə)tɔ̃]	il achète ils achètent	j'achetais [aʃtɛ] nous achetions	j'achetai

Also verbs in **-emer** (e.g. *semer*), **-ener** (e.g. *mener*), **-eser** (e.g. *peser*), **-ever** (e.g. *lever*) etc.
NB Verbs in **-ecer** (e.g. *dépecer*) are conjugated like **geler** and **placer**.

6	**céder**	je cède [sɛd] nous cédons [sedɔ̃]	il cède ils cèdent	je cédais nous cédions	je cédai

Also verbs in **-é** + consonant(s) + **-er** (e.g. *célébrer, lécher, déléguer, préférer* etc.).
NB Verbs in **-éger** (e.g. *protéger*) are conjugated like **céder** and **bouger**. Verbs in **-écer** (e.g. *rapiécer*) are conjugated like **céder** and **placer**.

7	**épier**	j'épie [epi] nous épions [epjɔ̃]	il épie ils épient	j'épiais nous épiions [epijɔ̃]	j'épiai
	prier	je prie [pʀi] nous prions [pʀijɔ̃]	il prie ils prient	je priais nous priions [pʀijjɔ̃]	je priai

8	**noyer**	je noie [nwa] nous noyons [nwajɔ̃]	il noie ils noient	je noyais nous noyions [nwajjɔ̃]	je noyai

Also verbs in **-uyer** (e.g. *appuyer*).
N.B. **Envoyer** has in the future tense : *j'enverrai*, and in the conditional : *j'enverrais*.

	payer	je paie [pɛ] or je paye [pɛj] nous payons [pɛjɔ̃]	il paie or il paye ils paient or ils payent	je payais nous payions [pɛjjɔ̃]	je payai

Also all verbs in **-ayer**.

irregular verbs ending in **-er**

future	CONDITIONAL present	SUBJUNCTIVE present	IMPERATIVE present	PARTICIPLES present past
je placerai [plasʀɛ]	je placerais	que je place que nous placions	place plaçons	plaçant placé, ée
je bougerai [buʒʀɛ]	je bougerais	que je bouge que nous bougions	bouge bougeons	bougeant bougé, ée
j'appellerai [apɛlʀɛ]	j'appellerais	que j'appelle que nous appelions	appelle appelons	appelant appelé, ée
je jetterai [ʒɛtʀɛ]	je jetterais	que je jette que nous jetions	jette jetons	jetant jeté, ée
je gèlerai [ʒɛlʀɛ]	je gèlerais	que je gèle que nous gelions	gèle gelons	gelant gelé, ée
j'achèterai [aʃɛtʀɛ]	j'achèterais	que j'achète que nous achetions	achète achetons	achetant acheté, ée
je céderai [sedʀɛ ; sɛdʀɛ] [1]	je céderais [1]	que je cède que nous cédions	cède cédons	cédant cédé, ée

1. Actually pronounced as though there were a grave accent on the future and the conditional (*je cèderai, je cèderais*), rather than an acute.

future	CONDITIONAL present	SUBJUNCTIVE present	IMPERATIVE present	PARTICIPLES present past
j'épierai [epiʀɛ]	j'épierais	que j'épie	épie épions	épiant épié, iée
je prierai [pʀiʀɛ]	je prierais	que je prie	prie prions	priant prié, priée
je noierai [nwaʀɛ]	je noierais	que je noie	noie noyons	noyant noyé, noyée
je paierai [pɛʀɛ] or je payerai [pejʀɛ] nous paierons or nous payerons	je paierais or je payerais	que je paie or que je paye	paie or paye payons	payant payé, payée

conjugation 9

INDICATIVE

PRESENT

je vais [vɛ]
tu vas
il va
nous allons [alɔ̃]
vous allez
ils vont [vɔ̃]

IMPERFECT

j'allais [alɛ]
tu allais
il allait
nous allions [aljɔ̃]
vous alliez
ils allaient

PAST HISTORIC

j'allai
tu allas
il alla
nous allâmes
vous allâtes
ils allèrent

FUTURE

j'irai [iʀɛ]
tu iras
il ira
nous irons
vous irez
ils iront

PERFECT

je suis allé
tu es allé
il est allé
nous sommes allés
vous êtes allés
ils sont allés

PLUPERFECT

j'étais allé
tu étais allé
il était allé
nous étions allés
vous étiez allés
ils étaient allés

PAST ANTERIOR

je fus allé
tu fus allé
il fut allé
nous fûmes allés
vous fûtes allés
ils furent allés

FUTURE PERFECT

je serai allé
tu seras allé
il sera allé
nous serons allés
vous serez allés
ils seront allés

SUBJUNCTIVE

PRESENT

que j'aille [aj]
que tu ailles
qu'il aille
que nous allions
que vous alliez
qu'ils aillent

IMPERFECT

que j'allasse [alas]
que tu allasses
qu'il allât
que nous allassions
que vous allassiez
qu'ils allassent

PAST

que je sois allé
que tu sois allé
qu'il soit allé
que nous soyons allés
que vous soyez allés
qu'ils soient allés

PLUPERFECT

que je fusse allé
que tu fusses allé
qu'il fût allé
que nous fussions allés
que vous fussiez allés
qu'ils fussent allés

ALLER

CONDITIONAL

PRESENT

j'irais
tu irais
il irait
nous irions
vous iriez
ils iraient

PAST I

je serais allé
tu serais allé
il serait allé
nous serions allés
vous seriez allés
ils seraient allés

PAST II

je fusse allé
tu fusses allé
il fût allé
nous fussions allés
vous fussiez allés
ils fussent allés

IMPERATIVE	PRESENT	PAST
	va	sois allé
	allons	soyons allés
	allez	soyez allés

PARTICIPLE	PRESENT	PAST
	allant	allé, ée
		étant allé

INFINITIVE	PRESENT	PAST
	aller	être allé

conjugations 10 to 22

		INDICATIVE			
		present		imperfect	past historic
		1st person	3rd person		
10	**haïr**	je hais ['ɛ] nous haïssons [aisɔ̃]	il hait [ɛ] ils haïssent [ais]	je haïssais nous haïssions	je haïs ['ai] nous haïmes
11	**courir**	je cours [kuʀ] nous courons [kuʀɔ̃]	il court ils courent	je courais [kuʀɛ] nous courions	je courus
12	**cueillir**	je cueille [kœj] nous cueillons [kœjɔ̃]	il cueille ils cueillent	je cueillais nous cueillions [kœjjɔ̃]	je cueillis
13	**assaillir**	j'assaille nous assaillons [asajɔ̃]	il assaille ils assaillent	j'assaillais nous assaillions [asajjɔ̃]	j'assaillis
14	**servir**	je sers [sɛʀ] nous servons [sɛʀvɔ̃]	il sert ils servent [sɛʀv]	je servais nous servions	je servis
15	**bouillir**	je bous [bu] nous bouillons [bujɔ̃]	il bout ils bouillent [buj]	je bouillais nous bouillions [bujjɔ̃]	je bouillis
16	**partir**	je pars [paʀ] nous partons [paʀtɔ̃]	il part ils partent [paʀt]	je partais nous partions	je partis
	sentir	je sens [sɑ̃] nous sentons [sɑ̃tɔ̃]	il sent ils sentent [sɑ̃t]	je sentais nous sentions	je sentis
17	**fuir**	je fuis [fɥi] nous fuyons [fɥijɔ̃]	il fuit ils fuient	je fuyais nous fuyions [fɥijjɔ̃]	je fuis nous fuîmes
18	**couvrir**	je couvre nous couvrons	il couvre ils couvrent	je couvrais nous couvrions	je couvris
19	**mourir**	je meurs [mœʀ] nous mourons [muʀɔ̃]	il meurt ils meurent	je mourais [muʀɛ] nous mourions	je mourus
20	**vêtir**	je vêts [vɛ] nous vêtons [vɛtɔ̃]	il vêt ils vêtent [vɛt]	je vêtais nous vêtions	je vêtis [veti] nous vêtîmes
21	**acquérir**	j'acquiers [akjɛʀ] nous acquérons [akeʀɔ̃]	il acquiert ils acquièrent	j'acquérais [akeʀɛ] nous acquérions	j'acquis
22	**venir**	je viens [vjɛ̃] nous venons [v(ə)nɔ̃]	il vient ils viennent [vjɛn]	je venais nous venions	je vins [vɛ̃] nous vînmes [vɛ̃m]

irregular verbs ending in -ir

future	CONDITIONAL present	SUBJUNCTIVE present	IMPERATIVE present	PARTICIPLES present / past
je haïrai ['aɪʀɛ]	je haïrais	que je haïsse	hais haïssons	haïssant haï, haïe ['aɪ]
je courrai [kuʀʀɛ]	je courrais	que je coure	cours courons	courant couru, ue
je cueillerai	je cueillerais	que je cueille	cueille cueillons	cueillant cueilli, ie
j'assaillirai	j'assaillirais	que j'assaille	assaille assaillons	assaillant assailli, ie
je servirai	je servirais	que je serve	sers servons	servant servi, ie
je bouillirai	je bouillirais	que je bouille	bous bouillons	bouillant bouilli, ie
je partirai	je partirais	que je parte	pars partons	partant parti, ie
je sentirai	je sentirais	que je sente	sens sentons	sentant senti, ie
je fuirai	je fuirais	que je fuie	fuis fuyons	fuyant fui, fuie
je couvrirai	je couvrirais	que je couvre	couvre couvrons	couvrant couvert, erte [kuvɛʀ, ɛʀt]
je mourrai [muʀʀɛ]	je mourrais	que je meure	meurs mourons	mourant mort, morte [mɔʀ, mɔʀt]
je vêtirai	je vêtirais	que je vête	vêts vêtons	vêtant vêtu, ue [vɛty]
j'acquerrai [akeʀʀɛ]	j'acquerrais	que j'acquière	acquiers acquérons	acquérant acquis, ise [aki, iz]
je viendrai [vjɛ̃dʀɛ]	je viendrais	que je vienne	viens venons	venant venu, ue

conjugations 23 to 33

		INDICATIVE			
		1st person / present	3rd person	imperfect	past historic
23	**pleuvoir**	(impersonal)	il pleut [plø]	il pleuvait	il plut
24	**prévoir**	je prévois [pʀevwa] nous prévoyons [pʀevwajɔ̃]	il prévoit ils prévoient	je prévoyais nous prévoyions [pʀevwajjɔ̃]	je prévis
25	**pourvoir**	je pourvois nous pourvoyons	il pourvoit ils pourvoient	je pourvoyais nous pourvoyions	je pourvus
26	**asseoir**	j'assieds [asjɛ] nous asseyons [asɛjɔ̃] or j'assois nous assoyons	il assied ils asseyent [asɛj] or il assoit ils assoient	j'asseyais nous asseyions or j'assoyais nous assoyions	j'assis
27	**mouvoir**	je meus [mø] nous mouvons [muvɔ̃]	il meut ils meuvent [mœv]	je mouvais nous mouvions	je mus [my] nous mûmes

NB *Émouvoir* and *promouvoir* have the past participles *ému, e* and *promu, e* respectively.

		INDICATIVE			
28	**recevoir** **devoir**	je reçois [ʀ(ə)swa] nous recevons [ʀ(ə)səvɔ̃]	il reçoit ils reçoivent [ʀəswav]	je recevais nous recevions	je reçus [ʀ(ə)sy]
29	**valoir** **équivaloir** **prévaloir** **falloir**	je vaux [vo] nous valons [valɔ̃] (impersonal)	il vaut ils valent [val] il faut [fo]	je valais nous valions il fallait [falɛ]	je valus il fallut
30	**voir**	je vois [vwa] nous voyons [vwajɔ̃]	il voit ils voient	je voyais nous voyions [vwajjɔ̃]	je vis
31	**vouloir**	je veux [vø] nous voulons [vulɔ̃]	il veut ils veulent [vœl]	je voulais nous voulions	je voulus
32	**savoir**	je sais [sɛ] nous savons [savɔ̃]	il sait ils savent [sav]	je savais nous savions	je sus
33	**pouvoir**	je peux [pø] or je puis nous pouvons [puvɔ̃]	il peut ils peuvent [pœv]	je pouvais nous pouvions	je pus

irregular verbs ending in **-oir**

future	CONDITIONAL present	SUBJONCTIVE present	IMPERATIVE present	PARTICIPLE present past
il pleuvra	il pleuvrait	qu'il pleuve [plœv]	does not exist	pleuvant plu (no feminine)
je prévoirai	je prévoirais	que je prévoie [pʀevwa]	prévois prévoyons	prévoyant prévu, ue
je pourvoirai	je pourvoirais	que je pourvoie	pourvois pourvoyons	pourvoyant pourvu, ue
j'assiérai [asjeʀɛ] or j'asseyerai [asɛjʀɛ] or j'assoirai	j'assiérais or j'assoirais	que j'asseye [asɛj] or que j'assoie [aswa]	assieds asseyons or assois assoyons	asseyant assis, ise or assoyant assis, ise

NB *j'asseyerai* is old-fashioned.

future	CONDITIONAL present	SUBJONCTIVE present	IMPERATIVE present	PARTICIPLE present past
je mouvrai [muvʀɛ]	je mouvrais	que je meuve que nous mouvions	meus mouvons	mouvant mû, mue [my]
je recevrai	je recevrais	que je reçoive que nous recevions	reçois recevons	recevant reçu, ue
				dû, due
je vaudrai [vodʀɛ]	je vaudrais	que je vaille [vaj] que nous valions [valjɔ̃]	vaux valons	valant valu, ue
				équivalu (no feminine)
		que je prévale	does not exist	prévalu (no feminine)
il faudra [fodʀa]	il faudrait	qu'il faille [faj]		does not exist fallu (no feminine)
je verrai [veʀɛ]	je verrais	que je voie [vwa] que nous voyions [vwajjɔ̃]	vois voyons	voyant vu, vue
je voudrai [vudʀɛ]	je voudrais	que je veuille [vœj] que nous voulions [vuljɔ̃]	veux or veuille voulons	voulant voulu, ue
je saurai [soʀɛ]	je saurais	que je sache [saʃ] que nous sachions	sache sachons	sachant su, sue
je pourrai [puʀɛ]	je pourrais	que je puisse [pɥis] que nous puissions	not used	pouvant pu

conjugation 34

INDICATIVE

PRESENT	PERFECT
j'ai [e; ɛ]	j'ai eu
tu as [a]	tu as eu
il a [a]	il a eu
nous avons [avɔ̃]	nous avons eu
vous avez [ave]	vous avez eu
ils ont [ɔ̃]	ils ont eu

IMPERFECT	PLUPERFECT
j'avais	j'avais eu
tu avais	tu avais eu
il avait	il avait eu
nous avions	nous avions eu
vous aviez	vous aviez eu
ils avaient	ils avaient eu

PAST HISTORIC	PAST ANTERIOR
j'eus [y]	j'eus eu
tu eus	tu eus eu
il eut	il eut eu
nous eûmes [ym]	nous eûmes eu
vous eûtes [yt]	vous eûtes eu
ils eurent [yʀ]	ils eurent eu

FUTURE	FUTURE PERFECT
j'aurai [ɔʀɛ]	j'aurai eu
tu auras	tu auras eu
il aura	il aura eu
nous aurons	nous aurons eu
vous aurez	vous aurez eu
ils auront	ils auront eu

SUBJUNCTIVE

PRESENT
que j'aie [ɛ]
que tu aies
qu'il ait
que nous ayons [ɛjɔ̃]
que vous ayez
qu'ils aient

IMPERFECT
que j'eusse [ys]
que tu eusses
qu'il eût [y]
que nous eussions [ysjɔ̃]
que vous eussiez
qu'ils eussent

PAST
que j'aie eu
que tu aies eu
qu'il ait eu
que nous ayons eu
que vous ayez eu
qu'ils aient eu

PLUPERFECT
que j'eusse eu
que tu eusses eu
qu'il eût eu
que nous eussions eu
que vous eussiez eu
qu'ils eussent eu

conjugations 35 to 37

		INDICATIVE			
		1st person / present	2nd and 3rd persons	imperfect	past historic
35	**conclure**	je conclus [kɔ̃kly] nous concluons [kɔ̃klyɔ̃]	il conclut ils concluent	je concluais nous concluions	je conclus

NB **Exclure** is conjugated like **conclure**: past participle *exclu, ue*; **inclure** is conjugated like **conclure** except for the past participle *inclus, use*.

36	**rire**	je ris [ʀi] nous rions [ʀijɔ̃]	il rit ils rient	je riais nous riions [ʀijɔ̃] or [ʀijjɔ̃]	je ris

37	**dire**	je dis [di] nous disons [dizɔ̃]	il dit vous dites [dit] ils disent [diz]	je disais nous disions	je dis

NB **Médire, contredire, dédire, interdire, prédire** are conjugated like **dire** except for the 2nd person plural of the present tense: *médisez, contredisez, dédisez, interdisez, prédisez.*

	suffire	je suffis [syfi] nous suffisons [syfizɔ̃]	il suffit ils suffisent [syfiz]	je suffisais nous suffisions	je suffis

NB **Confire** is conjugated like **suffire** except for the past participle *confit, ite.*

AVOIR

<table>
<tr><td rowspan="3">C
O
N
D
I
T
I
O
N
A
L</td><td>

PRESENT

j'aurais
tu aurais
il aurait
nous aurions
vous auriez
ils auraient

PAST I

j'aurais eu
tu aurais eu
il aurait eu
nous aurions eu
vous auriez eu
ils auraient eu

PAST II

j'eusse eu
tu eusses eu
il eût eu
nous eussions eu
vous eussiez eu
ils eussent eu
</td></tr>
</table>

IMPERATIVE	PRESENT	PAST
	aie [ɛ]	aie eu
	ayons [ɛjɔ̃]	ayons eu
	ayez [eje]	ayez eu

PARTICIPLE	PRESENT	PAST
	ayant	eu, eue [y]
		ayant eu

INFINITIVE	PRESENT	PAST
	avoir	avoir eu

irregular verbs ending in -re

future	CONDITIONAL present	SUBJUNCTIVE present	IMPERATIVE present	PARTICIPLES present past
je conclurai	je conclurais	que je conclue	conclus concluons	concluant conclu, ue
je rirai	je rirais	que je rie	ris rions	riant ri (no feminine)
je dirai	je dirais	que je dise	dis disons dites	disant dit, dite
je suffirai	je suffirais	que je suffise	suffis suffisons	suffisant suffi (no feminine)

conjugations 38 to 48

		INDICATIVE			
		1st person — present	3rd person	imperfect	past historic
38	**nuire**	je nuis [nɥi] nous nuisons [nɥizɔ̃]	il nuit ils nuisent [nɥiz]	je nuisais nous nuisions	je nuisis
		Also the verbs *luire*, *reluire*.			
	conduire	je conduis nous conduisons	il conduit ils conduisent	je conduisais nous conduisions	je conduisis
		Also the verbs *construire*, *cuire*, *déduire*, *détruire*, *enduire*, *induire*, *instruire*, *introduire*, *produire*, *réduire*, *séduire*, *traduire*.			
39	**écrire**	j'écris [ekʀi] nous écrivons [ekʀivɔ̃]	il écrit ils écrivent [ekʀiv]	j'écrivais nous écrivions	j'écrivis
40	**suivre**	je suis [sɥi] nous suivons [sɥivɔ̃]	il suit ils suivent [sɥiv]	je suivais nous suivions	je suivis
41	**rendre**	je rends [ʀɑ̃] nous rendons [ʀɑ̃dɔ̃]	il rend ils rendent [ʀɑ̃d]	je rendais nous rendions	je rendis
		Also the verbs ending in *-andre* (e.g. *répandre*), *-erdre* (e.g. *perdre*), *-ondre* (e.g. *répondre*), *-ordre* (e.g. *mordre*).			
	rompre	je romps [ʀɔ̃] nous rompons [ʀɔ̃pɔ̃]	il rompt ils rompent [ʀɔ̃p]	je rompais nous rompions	je rompis
		Also the verbs *corrompre* and *interrompre*.			
	battre	je bats [ba] nous battons [batɔ̃]	il bat ils battent [bat]	je battais nous battions	je battis
42	**vaincre**	je vaincs [vɛ̃] nous vainquons [vɛ̃kɔ̃]	il vainc ils vainquent [vɛ̃k]	je vainquais nous vainquions	je vainquis
43	**lire**	je lis [li] nous lisons [lizɔ̃]	il lit ils lisent [liz]	je lisais nous lisions	je lus
44	**croire**	je crois [kʀwa] nous croyons [kʀwajɔ̃]	il croit ils croient	je croyais nous croyions [kʀwajjɔ̃]	je crus nous crûmes
45	**clore**	je clos [klo]	il clôt ils closent [kloz] (rare)	je closais (rare)	not applicable
46	**vivre**	je vis [vi] nous vivons [vivɔ̃]	il vit ils vivent [viv]	je vivais nous vivions	je vécus [veky]
47	**moudre**	je mouds [mu] nous moulons [mulɔ̃]	il moud ils moulent [mul]	je moulais nous moulions	je moulus
		NB Most forms of this verb are rare except *moudre*, *moudrai (s)*, *moulu, e*.			
48	**coudre**	je couds [ku] nous cousons [kuzɔ̃]	il coud ils cousent [kuz]	je cousais nous cousions	je cousis [kuzi]

irregular verbs ending in **-re**

future	CONDITIONAL present	SUBJUNCTIVE present	IMPERATIVE present	PARTICIPLES present past
je nuirai	je nuirais	que je nuise	nuis nuisons	nuisant nui (no feminine)
je conduirai	je conduirais	que je conduise	conduis conduisons	conduisant conduit, ite
j'écrirai	j'écrirais	que j'écrive	écris écrivons	écrivant écrit, ite
je suivrai	je suivrais	que je suive	suis suivons	suivant suivi, ie
je rendrai	je rendrais	que je rende	rends rendons	rendant rendu, ue
je romprai	je romprais	que je rompe	romps rompons	rompant rompu, ue
je battrai	je battrais	que je batte	bats battons	battant battu, ue
je vaincrai	je vaincrais	que je vainque	vaincs vainquons	vainquant vaincu, ue
je lirai	je lirais	que je lise	lis lisons	lisant lu, ue
je croirai	je croirais	que je croie	crois croyons	croyant cru, crue
je clorai (rare)	je clorais (rare)	que je close	clos	closant (rare) clos, close
je vivrai	je vivrais	que je vive	vis vivons	vivant vécu, ue
je moudrai	je moudrais	que je moule	mouds moulons	moulant moulu, ue
je coudrai	je coudrais	que je couse	couds cousons	cousant cousu, ue

conjugations 49 to 59

		INDICATIVE			
		present 1st person	present 3rd person	imperfect	past historic
49	**joindre**	je joins [ʒwɛ̃] nous joignons [ʒwaɲɔ̃]	il joint ils joignent [ʒwaɲ]	je joignais nous joignions [ʒwaɲjɔ̃]	je joignis
50	**traire**	je trais [tʀɛ] nous trayons [tʀɛjɔ̃]	il trait ils traient	je trayais nous trayions [tʀɛjjɔ̃]	not applicable
51	**absoudre**	j'absous [apsu] nous absolvons [apsɔlvɔ̃]	il absout ils absolvent [apsɔlv]	j'absolvais nous absolvions	j'absolus [apsɔly] (rare)

NB *Dissoudre* is conjugated like **absoudre**; *résoudre* is conjugated like **absoudre,** but the past historic *je résolus* is current. *Résoudre* has two past participles: *résolu, ue (problème résolu),* and *résous, oute (brouillard résous en pluie* [rare]).

52	**craindre**	je crains [kʀɛ̃] nous craignons [kʀɛɲɔ̃]	il craint ils craignent [kʀɛɲ]	je craignais nous craignions [kʀɛɲjɔ̃]	je craignis
	peindre	je peins [pɛ̃] nous peignons [pɛɲɔ̃]	il peint ils peignent [pɛɲ]	je peignais nous peignions [pɛɲjɔ̃]	je peignis
53	**boire**	je bois [bwa] nous buvons [byvɔ̃]	il boit ils boivent [bwav]	je buvais nous buvions	je bus
54	**plaire**	je plais [plɛ] nous plaisons [plɛzɔ̃]	il plaît ils plaisent [plɛz]	je plaisais nous plaisions	je plus

NB The past participle of **plaire, complaire, déplaire** is generally invariable.

	taire	je tais nous taisons	il tait ils taisent	je taisais nous taisions	je tus
55	**croître**	je croîs [kʀwa] nous croissons [kʀwasɔ̃]	il croît ils croissent [kʀwas]	je croissais nous croissions	je crûs nous crûmes

NB Like **accroître**, the past participle of **décroître** is *décru, e.*

	accroître	j'accrois nous accroissons	il accroît ils accroissent	j'accroissais	j'accrus nous accrûmes
56	**mettre**	je mets [mɛ] nous mettons [metɔ̃]	il met ils mettent [mɛt]	je mettais nous mettions	je mis
57	**connaître**	je connais [kɔnɛ] nous connaissons [kɔnɛsɔ̃]	il connaît ils connaissent [kɔnɛs]	je connaissais nous connaissions	je connus
58	**prendre**	je prends [pʀɑ̃] nous prenons [pʀənɔ̃]	il prend ils prennent [pʀɛn]	je prenais nous prenions	je pris
59	**naître**	je nais [nɛ] nous naissons [nɛsɔ̃]	il naît ils naissent [nɛs]	je naissais nous naissions	je naquis [naki]

NB *Renaître* has no past participle.

irregular verbs ending in **-re**

future	CONDITIONAL present	SUBJUNCTIVE present	IMPERATIVE present	PARTICIPLES present past
je joindrai	je joindrais	que je joigne	joins joignons	joignant joint, jointe
je trairai	je trairais	que je traie	trais trayons	trayant trait, traite
j'absoudrai	j'absoudrais	que j'absolve	absous absolvons	absolvant absous[1], oute [apsu, ut]

1. The past participle forms *absout, dissout*, with a final *t*, are often preferred.

future	CONDITIONAL present	SUBJUNCTIVE present	IMPERATIVE present	PARTICIPLES present past
je craindrai	je craindrais	que je craigne	crains craignons	craignant craint, crainte
je peindrai	je peindrais	que je peigne	peins peignons	peignant peint, peinte
je boirai	je boirais	que je boive que nous buvions	bois buvons	buvant bu, bue
je plairai	je plairais	que je plaise	plais plaisons	plaisant plu (no feminine)
je tairai	je tairais	que je taise	tais taisons	taisant tu, tue
je croîtrai	je croîtrais	que je croisse	croîs croissons	croissant crû, crue
j'accroîtrai	j'accroîtrais	que j'accroisse	accrois accroissons	accroissant accru, ue
je mettrai	je mettrais	que je mette	mets mettons	mettant mis, mise
je connaîtrai	je connaîtrais	que je connaisse	connais connaissons	connaissant connu, ue
je prendrai	je prendrais	que je prenne que nous prenions	prends prenons	prenant pris, prise
je naîtrai	je naîtrais	que je naisse	nais naissons	naissant né, née

conjugation 60 — **FAIRE**

INDICATIVE

PRESENT
je fais [fɛ]
tu fais
il fait
nous faisons [f(ə)zɔ̃]
vous faites [fɛt]
ils font [fɔ̃]

PERFECT
j'ai fait
tu as fait
il a fait
nous avons fait
vous avez fait
ils ont fait

IMPERFECT
je faisais [f(ə)zɛ]
tu faisais
il faisait
nous faisions [fəzjɔ̃]
vous faisiez [fəsje]
ils faisaient

PLUPERFECT
j'avais fait
tu avais fait
il avait fait
nous avions fait
vous aviez fait
ils avaient fait

PAST HISTORIC
je fis
tu fis
il fit
nous fîmes
vous fîtes
ils firent

PAST ANTERIOR
j'eus fait
tu eus fait
il eut fait
nous eûmes fait
vous eûtes fait
ils eurent fait

FUTURE
je ferai [f(ə)ʀɛ]
tu feras
il fera
nous ferons [f(ə)ʀɔ̃]
vous ferez
ils feront

FUTURE PERFECT
j'aurai fait
tu auras fait
il aura fait
nous aurons fait
vous aurez fait
ils auront fait

SUBJUNCTIVE

PRESENT
que je fasse [fas]
que tu fasses
qu'il fasse
que nous fassions
que vous fassiez
qu'ils fassent

IMPERFECT
que je fisse [fis]
que tu fisses
qu'il fît
que nous fissions
que vous fissiez
qu'ils fissent

PAST
que j'aie fait
que tu aies fait
qu'il ait fait
que nous ayons fait
que vous ayez fait
qu'ils aient fait

PLUPERFECT
que j'eusse fait
que tu eusses fait
qu'il eût fait
que nous eussions fait
que vous eussiez fait
qu'ils eussent fait

CONDITIONAL

PRESENT
je ferais [f(ə)ʀɛ]
tu ferais
il ferait
nous ferions [fəʀjɔ̃]
vous feriez
ils feraient

PAST I
j'aurais fait
tu aurais fait
il aurait fait
nous aurions fait
vous auriez fait
ils auraient fait

PAST II
j'eusse fait
tu eusses fait
il eût fait
nous eussions fait
vous eussiez fait
ils eussent fait

IMPERATIVE

PRESENT	PAST
fais	aie fait
faisons	ayons fait
faites	ayez fait

PARTICIPLE

PRESENT	PAST
faisant [f(ə)zɑ̃]	fait
	ayant fait

INFINITIVE

PRESENT	PAST
faire	avoir fait

conjugation 61 — ÊTRE

INDICATIVE

PRESENT

je suis [sɥi]
tu es [ɛ]
il est [ɛ]
nous sommes [sɔm]
vous êtes [ɛt]
ils sont [sɔ̃]

IMPERFECT

j'étais [etɛ]
tu étais
il était
nous étions [etjɔ̃]
vous étiez
ils étaient

PAST HISTORIC

je fus [fy]
tu fus
il fut
nous fûmes
vous fûtes
ils furent

FUTURE

je serai [s(ə)ʀɛ]
tu seras
il sera
nous serons [s(ə)ʀɔ̃]
vous serez
ils seront

PERFECT

j'ai été
tu as été
il a été
nous avons été
vous avez été
ils ont été

PLUPERFECT

j'avais été
tu avais été
il avait été
nous avions été
vous aviez été
ils avaient été

PAST ANTERIOR

j'eus été
tu eus été
il eut été
nous eûmes été
vous eûtes été
ils eurent été

FUTURE PERFECT

j'aurai été
tu auras été
il aura été
nous aurons été
vous aurez été
ils auront été

SUBJUNCTIVE

PRESENT

que je sois [swa]
que tu sois
qu'il soit
que nous soyons [swajɔ̃]
que vous soyez
qu'ils soient

IMPERFECT

que je fusse
que tu fusses
qu'il fût
que nous fussions
que vous fussiez
qu'ils fussent

PAST

que j'aie été
que tu aies été
qu'il ait été
que nous ayons été
que vous ayez été
qu'ils aient été

PLUPERFECT

que j'eusse été
que tu eusses été
qu'il eût été
que nous eussions été
que vous eussiez été
qu'ils eussent été

CONDITIONAL

PRESENT

je serais [s(ə)ʀɛ]
tu serais
il serait
nous serions [səʀjɔ̃]
vous seriez
ils seraient

PAST I

j'aurais été
tu aurais été
il aurait été
nous aurions été
vous auriez été
ils auraient été

PAST II

j'eusse été
tu eusses été
il eût été
nous eussions été
vous eussiez été
ils eussent été

IMPERATIVE	PRESENT	PAST
	sois [swa]	aie été
	soyons [swajɔ̃]	ayons été
	soyez [swaje]	ayez été

PARTICIPLE	PRESENT	PAST
	étant	été [ete]
		ayant été

INFINITIVE	PRESENT	PAST
	être	avoir été

RULES OF AGREEMENT FOR PAST PARTICIPLE

The past participle is a form of the verb which does not vary according to tense or person, but which is more like an adjective, in that it may agree in gender and number with the word to which it refers.

PAST PARTICIPLE AGREEMENT DEPENDING ON USAGE

without auxiliary (adjectival use)	• **agreement** with the word it refers to *une affaire bien partie* (agrees with *affaire*, feminine singular)

with *être*	• **agreement** with the subject of **être** *les hirondelles sont revenues* (agrees with *hirondelles*, feminine plural)
with *avoir*	• **agreement** with the direct object, provided the direct object precedes the past participle *je les ai crus* (agrees with *les*, masculine plural) *la lettre qu'il a écrite* (agrees with *que*, referring back to *lettre*, feminine singular) • **no agreement,** then, in the following cases: *nous avons couru* (no direct object) *elles ont pris la clé* (direct object follows past participle)

with *s'être* as with *être* as with *avoir*	• if the verb is reflexive, the past participle agrees with the subject *ils se sont enrhumés* (agrees with *ils*, masculine plural) • if the reflexive pronoun is the indirect object, any agreement is with the preceding direct object *la bosse qu'il s'est faite* (agrees with *que*, referring back to *bosse*, feminine singular) **no agreement,** then, if the direct object follows the past participle *ils se sont lavé les mains* (the object being *les mains*)

LE VERBE ANGLAIS

THE ENGLISH VERB

L'anglais comprend de nombreux verbes forts ou irréguliers (dont nous donnons la liste ci-dessous, § 7) ainsi que de nombreuses variantes orthographiques (voir au § 8), mais à chacun des temps la conjugaison reste la même pour toutes les personnes sauf pour la troisième personne du singulier au présent de l'indicatif.
Les notes qui suivent se proposent de résumer la structure et les formes du verbe anglais.

1 LE MODE INDICATIF

PRÉSENT	FORMATION	Le présent de l'indicatif a la même forme que l'infinitif présent à toutes les personnes sauf à la troisième personne du singulier, à laquelle vient s'ajouter un *s*, ex. : *he sells.*
	verbes se terminant par une sifflante ou une chuintante	Dans les cas où l'infinitif se termine par une sifflante ou une chuintante on intercale un *e*, ex. : *he kisses, he buzzes, he rushes, he touches.*
	verbes se terminant par consonne + y	Les verbes qui se terminent en consonne + *y* changent cet *y* en *ies* à la troisième personne du singulier, ex. : *he tries, he pities, he satisfies.* REMARQUE. Là où le *y* est précédé d'une voyelle, on applique la règle générale, ex. : *pray — he prays, annoy — she annoys.*
	formes irrégulières	● Le verbe *to be* a des formes irrégulières pour toutes les personnes : *I am, you are, he is, we are, you are, they are.* ● Trois autres verbes ont une forme irrégulière à la troisième personne du singulier : *do he does* *have he has* *go he goes*
IMPARFAIT **PASSÉ SIMPLE** **PARTICIPE PASSÉ**	FORMATION	L'imparfait, le passé simple et le participe passé ont, en anglais, la même forme. On les construit en ajoutant *ed* au radical de l'infinitif, ex. : *paint — I painted — painted.*
	verbes se terminant par un e muet	On ajoute *d* à l'infinitif des verbes qui se terminent par un *e* muet, ex. : *bare — I bared — bared, move — I moved — moved, revise — I revised — revised.*
	verbes irréguliers	Pour les verbes irréguliers, voir la liste ci-dessous, § 7.
TEMPS COMPOSÉS ou PASSÉS	FORMATION	Les temps composés du passé se forment à l'aide de l'auxiliaire *to have* suivi du participe passé.
	PASSÉ COMPOSÉ	Présent de *to have* + participe passé. ex. : *I have painted.*
	PLUS-QUE-PARFAIT	Passé de *to have* + participe passé, ex. : *I had painted.*
FUTUR	FUTUR SIMPLE	Le futur se forme à l'aide de *will* suivi de l'infinitif, ex. : *I will do it.* Dans la langue soignée, on utilise *shall* à la première personne du singulier et du pluriel, ex. : *we shall see to it.*
	FUTUR ANTÉRIEUR	L'auxiliaire *to have* accompagné de *will* (ou de *shall* dans la langue soignée) et du participe passé du verbe conjugué s'emploie pour le futur antérieur, ex. : *I will have finished.*
FORME PROGRESSIVE		Il existe également en anglais, au mode indicatif, une forme progressive qui se forme avec l'auxiliaire *to be*, conjugué au temps approprié et suivi du participe présent, ex. : *I am waiting, we were hoping, they will be leaving, they would still have been waiting, I had been painting all day.* Ce système diffère dans une certaine mesure du système français, qui a parfois comme équivalent la formule « être en train de » suivie de l'infinitif.

2 LE CONDITIONNEL

PRÉSENT	Le conditionnel se forme à l'aide de *would* suivi de l'infinitif,
	  ex. : *I would go.*
	Dans la langue soignée, on utilise *should* à la première personne du singulier et du pluriel,
	  ex. : *we should see it.*

PASSÉ	L'auxiliaire *to have* accompagné de *would* (ou de *should* dans la langue soignée) et du participe passé du verbe conjugué s'emploie pour le conditionnel passé, ex. : *I would have paid.*

3 LE MODE SUBJONCTIF

PRÉSENT	Au présent et à toutes les personnes, le subjonctif a la même forme que l'infinitif, ex. : *(that) I go, (that) she go* etc.
IMPARFAIT	À l'imparfait, *to be* est l'unique verbe qui ait une forme irrégulière. Cette forme est *were* pour toutes les personnes : ex. : *(that) I were, (that) we were* etc.
Emploi	Le subjonctif est peu utilisé en anglais. Il faut cependant noter que le subjonctif s'emploie obligatoirement en anglais dans : *if I were you, were I to attempt it* (l'emploi de *was* étant considéré comme incorrect dans ces expressions, ainsi que dans d'autres expressions analogues). Le subjonctif se rencontre aussi dans l'expression figée *so be it* et dans le langage juridique ou officiel, ex. : *it is agreed that nothing be done, it was resolved that the pier be painted* (quoique *should be done* et *should be painted* soient également corrects).

4 LE MODE IMPÉRATIF

FORMATION	Il n'y a qu'une forme de l'impératif, qui est en fait celle de l'infinitif, ex. : *tell me, come here, don't do that.*

5 LE GÉRONDIF ET LE PARTICIPE PRÉSENT

FORMATION	Le gérondif et le participe présent ont la même forme en anglais. Ils s'obtiennent en ajoutant la désinence *-ing* au radical de l'infinitif, ex. : *washing, sending, passing.* Pour les variantes orthographiques voir paragraphe 8.

6 LA VOIX PASSIVE

FORMATION	La voix passive se forme exactement comme en français avec le temps approprié du verbe *to be* et le participe passé :
	  ex. : *we are forced to, he was killed, they had been injured,*
	    the company will be taken over,
	    it ought to have been rebuilt, were it to be agreed.

7 VERBES FORTS OU IRRÉGULIERS

INFINITIF	PRÉTÉRIT	PARTICIPE PASSÉ	INFINITIF	PRÉTÉRIT	PARTICIPE PASSÉ
abide	abode or abided	abode or abided	fall	fell	fallen
arise	arose	arisen	feed	fed	fed
awake	awoke or awaked	awoken or awaked	feel	felt	felt
be	was, were	been	fight	fought	fought
bear[1]	bore	borne	find	found	found
beat	beat	beaten	flee	fled	fled
become	became	become	fling	flung	flung
beget	begot, begat††	begotten	fly	flew	flown
begin	began	begun	forbid	forbad(e)	forbidden
bend	bent	bent	forget	forgot	forgotten
beseech	besought	besought	forsake	forsook	forsaken
bet	bet or betted	bet or betted	freeze	froze	frozen
bid	bade or bid	bid or bidden	get	got	got, (US) gotten
bind	bound	bound	gild	gilded	gilded or gilt
bite	bit	bitten	gird	girded or girt	girded or girt
bleed	bled	bled	give	gave	given
blow[1]	blew	blown	go	went	gone
break	broke	broken	grind	ground	ground
breed	bred	bred	grow	grew	grown
bring	brought	brought	hang	hung,	hung,
build	built	built		(Jur) hanged	(Jur) hanged
burn	burned or burnt	burned or burnt	have	had	had
burst	burst	burst	hear	heard	heard
buy	bought	bought	heave	heaved,	heaved,
can[1]	could	—		(Naut) hove	(Naut) hove
cast	cast	cast	hew	hewed	hewed or hewn
catch	caught	caught	hide	hid	hidden
chide	chid	chidden or chid	hit	hit	hit
choose	chose	chosen	hold	held	held
cleave[1]	clove or cleft	cloven or cleft	hurt	hurt	hurt
(fendre)			keep	kept	kept
cleave[2]	cleaved	cleaved	kneel	knelt	knelt
(s'attacher)			know	knew	known
cling	clung	clung	lade	laded	laden
come	came	come	lay	laid	laid
cost	cost or costed	cost or costed	lead	led	led
creep	crept	crept	lean	leaned or leant	leaned or leant
cut	cut	cut	leap	leaped or leapt	leaped or leapt
deal	dealt	dealt	learn	learned or learnt	learned or learnt
dig	dug	dug	leave	left	left
dive	dived, (US) dove	dived	lend	lent	lent
do	did	done	let	let	let
draw	drew	drawn	lie[1]	lay	lain
dream	dreamed or dreamt	dreamed or dreamt	light[1+3]	lit or lighted	lit or lighted
drink	drank	drunk	lose	lost	lost
drive	drove	driven	make	made	made
dwell	dwelled or dwelt	dwelled or dwelt	may	might	—
eat	ate	eaten	mean	meant	meant

INFINITIF	PRÉTÉRIT	PARTICIPE PASSÉ	INFINITIF	PRÉTÉRIT	PARTICIPE PASSÉ
meet	met	met	speed	speeded or sped	speeded or sped
mow	mowed	mown or mowed	spell³	spelled or spelt	spelled or spelt
pay	paid	paid	spend	spent	spent
put	put	put	spill	spilled or spilt	spilled or spilt
quit	quit or quitted	quit or quitted	spin	spun or span††	spun
read [riːd]	read [red]	read [red]	spit	spat	spat
rend	rent	rent	split	split	split
rid	rid	rid	spoil	spoiled or spoilt	spoiled or spoilt
ride	rode	ridden	spread	spread	spread
ring²	rang	rung	spring	sprang	sprung
rise	rose	risen	stand	stood	stood
run	ran	run	stave	stove or staved	stove or staved
saw	sawed	sawed or sawn	steal	stole	stolen
say	said	said	stick	stuck	stuck
see	saw	seen	sting	stung	stung
seek	sought	sought	stink	stank	stunk
sell	sold	sold	strew	strewed	strewed or strewn
send	sent	sent	stride	strode	stridden
set	set	set	strike	struck	struck
sew	sewed	sewed or sewn	string	strung	strung
shake	shook	shaken	strive	strove	striven
shave	shaved	shaved or shaven	swear	swore	sworn
shear	sheared	sheared or shorn	sweep	swept	swept
shed	shed	shed	swell	swelled	swollen
shine	shone	shone	swim	swam	swum
shoe	shod	shod	swing	swung	swung
shoot	shot	shot	take	took	taken
show	showed	shown or showed	teach	taught	taught
shrink	shrank	shrunk	tear	tore	torn
shut	shut	shut	tell	told	told
sing	sang	sung	think	thought	thought
sink	sank	sunk	thrive	throve or thrived	thriven or thrived
sit	sat	sat	throw	threw	thrown
slay	slew	slain	thrust	thrust	thrust
sleep	slept	slept	tread	trod	trodden
slide	slid	slid	wake	woke or waked	woken or waked
sling	slung	slung	wear	wore	worn
slink	slunk	slunk	weave	wove or weaved	woven or weaved
slit	slit	slit	weep	wept	wept
smell	smelled or smelt	smelled or smelt	win	won	won
smite	smote	smitten	wind²⁺³	wound	wound
sow	sowed	sowed or sown	wring	wrung	wrung
speak	spoke	spoken	write	wrote	written

REMARQUE. Ne sont pas compris dans cette liste les verbes formés avec un préfixe. Pour leur conjugaison, se référer au verbe de base, ex. : pour *forbear* voir **bear,** pour *understand* voir **stand.**

8 VERBES FAIBLES PRÉSENTANT DES VARIANTES ORTHOGRAPHIQUES

TERMINAISON DES VERBES À L'INFINITIF	VARIANTE ORTHOGRAPHIQUE AU PARTICIPE PASSÉ ET AU GÉRONDIF	EXEMPLE		
		INFINITIF	PARTICIPE PASSÉ	GÉRONDIF
Les verbes se terminant par une seule consonne précédée d'une seule voyelle accentuée	redoublent la consonne devant la désinence *ed* ou *ing*.	sob	sobbed	sobbing
		wed	wedded	wedding
		lag	lagged	lagging
		control	controlled	controlling
		dim	dimmed	dimming
		tan	tanned	tanning
		tap	tapped	tapping
		prefer	preferred	preferring
		pat	patted	patting
		(En revanche *to cook* devient *cooked — cooked* parce qu'il comporte une voyelle longue, et *fear* qui comporte une diphtongue donne *feared — fearing*.)		
Les verbes qui se terminent en *c*	changent le *c* en *ck* devant les désinences *ed* et *ing*.	frolic	frolicked	frolicking
		traffic	trafficked	trafficking
Les verbes terminés par la consonne *l* ou *p* précédée d'une voyelle non accentuée	redoublent la consonne au participe passé et au gérondif en anglais britannique, mais restent inchangés en anglais américain.	grovel	(Brit) grovelled (US) groveled	(Brit) grovelling (US) groveling
		travel	(Brit) travelled (US) traveled	(Brit) travelling (US) traveling
		worship	(Brit) worshipped (US) worshiped	(Brit) worshipping (US) worshiping
		N.B. La même différence existe entre les formes substantivées de ces verbes : (Brit) traveller worshipper (US) traveler worshiper		
Lorsque le verbe se termine par un *e* muet,	le *e* muet disparaît en faveur de la désinence *ed* ou *ing*.	invite	invited	inviting
		rake	raked	raking
		smile	smiled	smiling
		move	moved	moving
		(Le *e* muet se conserve toutefois dans les verbes *dye, singe,* etc. et dans une série peu nombreuse de verbes se terminant en *oe* : *dyeing, singeing, hoeing*.)		
Si le verbe se termine en *y,*	le *y* devient *ied* pour former le prétérit et le participe passé.	worry	worried — worried	Le gérondif de ces verbes est parfaitement régulier, ex. : *worrying, trying,* etc.
		pity	pitied — pitied	
		falsify	falsified — falsified	
		try	tried — tried	
Gérondif des verbes monosyllabiques *die, lie, vie*				dying, lying, vying.

9 VERBES ANGLAIS À PARTICULE

vi	verbe intransitif. ex. : ► **blow off** dans *his hat blew off*.
vt sep	verbe transitif séparable. ex. : ► **blow off** dans *the wind blew off his hat* ou *the wind blew his hat off*. Le complément d'objet du verbe peut se mettre soit après la particule, soit entre les deux éléments du verbe en les séparant. Cette dernière structure est d'ailleurs obligatoire lorsque le complément d'objet est un pronom : *the wind blew it off*.
vt fus	verbe transitif fusionné. ex. : ► **admit to** dans *he admitted to the theft*. Le complément d'objet ne peut jamais s'intercaler entre les deux éléments du verbe, même lorsqu'il s'agit d'un pronom : *he admitted to it*.

REMARQUE. Pour beaucoup de verbes qui indiquent un mouvement ou une direction, les verbes à particule correspondants n'ont pas été dissociés de l'article principal, car ils peuvent être déduits des illustrations fournies. Ainsi, à partir de

crawl [krɔːl]
2 VI a [*animals*] ramper, se glisser ; [*person*] se traîner, ramper ; **to ~ in/out** *etc* entrer/sortir *etc* en rampant *or* à quatre pattes ;

vous pouvez construire : *to crawl across* (traverser en rampant), *to crawl down* (descendre en rampant), etc.

Numbers, Time and Dates

Nombres, Heures et Dates

1 CARDINAL AND ORDINAL NUMBERS
NOMBRES CARDINAUX ET ORDINAUX

Cardinal numbers		Les nombres cardinaux	Ordinal numbers	Les nombres ordinaux
nought	0	zéro		
one	1	(m) un, (f) une	first	(m) premier, (f) -ière
two	2	deux	second	deuxième
three	3	trois	third	troisième
four	4	quatre	fourth	quatrième
five	5	cinq	fifth	cinquième
six	6	six	sixth	sixième
seven	7	sept	seventh	septième
eight	8	huit	eighth	huitième
nine	9	neuf	ninth	neuvième
ten	10	dix	tenth	dixième
eleven	11	onze	eleventh	onzième
twelve	12	douze	twelfth	douzième
thirteen	13	treize	thirteenth	treizième
fourteen	14	quatorze	fourteenth	quatorzième
fifteen	15	quinze	fifteenth	quinzième
sixteen	16	seize	sixteenth	seizième
seventeen	17	dix-sept	seventeenth	dix-septième
eighteen	18	dix-huit	eighteenth	dix-huitième
nineteen	19	dix-neuf	nineteenth	dix-neuvième
twenty	20	vingt	twentieth	vingtième
twenty-one	21	vingt et un	twenty-first	vingt et unième
twenty-two	22	vingt-deux	twenty-second	vingt-deuxième
twenty-three	23	vingt-trois		
thirty	30	trente	thirtieth	trentième
thirty-one	31	trente et un	thirty-first	trente et unième
thirty-two	32	trente-deux		
forty	40	quarante	fortieth	quarantième
fifty	50	cinquante	fiftieth	cinquantième
sixty	60	soixante	sixtieth	soixantième
seventy	70	soixante-dix	seventieth	soixante-dixième
eighty	80	quatre-vingt(s)	eightieth	quatre-vingtième
ninety	90	quatre-vingt-dix	ninetieth	quatre-vingt-dixième
ninety-nine	99	quatre-vingt-dix-neuf		
a (or one) hundred	100	cent	hundredth	centième
a hundred and one	101	cent un	hundred and first	cent unième
a hundred and two	102	cent deux		
a hundred and ten	110	cent dix	hundred and tenth	cent dixième
a hundred and eighty-two	182	cent quatre-vingt-deux		

Cardinal numbers		Les nombres cardinaux	Ordinal numbers	Les nombres ordinaux
two hundred	200	deux cents	two hundredth	deux centième
two hundred and one	201	deux cent un		
two hundred and two	202	deux cent deux		
three hundred	300	trois cents	three hundredth	trois centième
four hundred	400	quatre cents	four hundredth	quatre centième
five hundred	500	cinq cents	five hundredth	cinq centième
six hundred	600	six cents	six hundredth	six centième
seven hundred	700	sept cents	seven hundredth	sept centième
eight hundred	800	huit cents	eight hundredth	huit centième
nine hundred	900	neuf cents	nine hundredth	neuf centième
a (or one) thousand	1,000 French 1 000	mille	thousandth	millième
a thousand and one	1,001 French 1 001	mille un		
a thousand and two	1,002 French 1 002	mille deux		
two thousand	2,000 French 2 000	deux mille	two thousandth	deux millième
ten thousand	10,000 French 10 000	dix mille		
a (or one) hundred thousand	100,000 French 100 000	cent mille		
a (or one) million (see note b)	1,000,000 French 1 000 000	un million (voir note b)	millionth	millionième
two million	2,000,000 French 2 000 000	deux millions	two millionth	deux millionième

NOTES ON USAGE OF THE CARDINAL NUMBERS

[a] To divide the larger numbers clearly, a space or a point is used in French where English places a comma:
    English 1,000   French 1 000 or 1.000
    English 2,304,770 French 2 304 770 or 2.304.770
(This does not apply to dates: see below.)

[b] **1 000 000:** In French, the word *million* is a noun, so the numeral takes *de* when there is a following noun:
    un million de fiches
    trois millions de maisons détruites

[c] **One,** and the other numbers ending in *one*, agree in French with the noun (stated or implied):
    une maison, un employé, il y a cent une personnes.

REMARQUES SUR LES NOMBRES CARDINAUX

[a] Alors qu'un espace ou un point est utilisé en français pour séparer les centaines des milliers, l'anglais utilise la virgule à cet effet ;
    français 1 000 (ou 1.000)   anglais 1,000
  français 2 304 770 (ou 2.304.770) anglais 2,304,770
(Cette règle ne s'applique pas aux dates. Voir ci-dessous.)

[b] En anglais, le mot *million* (ainsi que *mille* et *cent*) n'est pas suivi de *of* lorsqu'il accompagne un nom:
    a million people,
    a hundred houses,
    a thousand people.

NOTES ON USAGE OF THE ORDINAL NUMBERS
REMARQUES SUR LES NOMBRES ORDINAUX

[a] **Abbreviations:** English 1st, 2nd, 3rd, 4th, 5th, etc. French (m) 1er, (f) 1re, 2e, 3e, 4e, 5e and so on.

[b] **First,** and the other numbers ending in *first*, agree in French with the noun (stated or implied):
La première maison, le premier employé, la cent unième personne.

[c] See also the notes on dates, below.
Voir aussi ci-dessous le paragraphe concernant les dates.

2 FRACTIONS   LES FRACTIONS

one half, a half	$\frac{1}{2}$	(m) un demi, (f) une demie
one and a half helpings	$1\frac{1}{2}$	une portion et demie
two and a half kilos	$2\frac{1}{2}$	deux kilos et demi
one third, a third	$\frac{1}{3}$	un tiers
two thirds	$\frac{2}{3}$	deux tiers
one quarter, a quarter	$\frac{1}{4}$	un quart
three quarters	$\frac{3}{4}$	trois quarts
one sixth, a sixth	$\frac{1}{6}$	un sixième
five and five sixths	$5\frac{5}{6}$	cinq et cinq sixièmes
one twelfth, a twelfth	$\frac{1}{12}$	un douzième
seven twelfths	$\frac{7}{12}$	sept douzièmes
one hundredth, a hundredth	$\frac{1}{100}$	un centième
one thousandth, a thousandth	$\frac{1}{1000}$	un millième

3 DECIMALS   LES DÉCIMALES

In French, a comma is written where English uses a point:

Alors que le français utilise la virgule pour séparer les entiers des décimales, le point est utilisé en anglais à cet effet :

English/anglais   French/français

3.56 (three point five six) = 3,56 (trois virgule cinquante-six)
.07 (point nought seven) = 0,07 (zéro virgule zéro sept)

4 NOMENCLATURE   NUMÉRATION

3,684 is a four-digit number
It contains 4 units, 8 tens, 6 hundreds and 3 thousands
The decimal .234 contains 2 tenths, 3 hundredths and 4 thousandths

3.684 est un nombre à quatre chiffres
4 est le chiffre des unités, 8 celui des dizaines, 6 celui des centaines et 3 celui des milliers
la fraction décimale 0,234 contient 2 dixièmes, 3 centièmes et 4 millièmes

5 PERCENTAGES   LES POURCENTAGES

$2\frac{1}{2}\%$ two and a half per cent   Deux et demi pour cent

18% of the people here are over 65   Ici dix-huit pour cent des gens ont plus de soixante-cinq ans

Production has risen by 8%   La production s'est accrue de huit pour cent
(See also the main text of the dictionary.)   *(Voir aussi dans le corps du dictionnaire.)*

6 SIGNS   LES SIGNES

addition sign	+	signe plus, signe de l'addition
plus sign (e.g. + 7 = plus seven)	+	signe plus (ex. : + 7 = plus 7)
subtraction sign	−	signe moins, signe de la soustraction
minus sign (e.g. − 3 = minus three)	−	signe moins (ex. : − 3 = moins 3)
multiplication sign	×	signe de la multiplication
division sign	÷	signe de la division
square root sign	√	signe de la racine carrée
infinity	∞	symbole de l'infini
sign of identity, is equal to	≡	signe d'identité
sign of equality, equals	=	signe d'égalité
is approximately equal to	≈	signe d'équivalence
sign of inequality, is not equal to	≠	signe de non-égalité
is greater than	>	est plus grand que
is less than	<	est plus petit que

7 CALCULATION   LE CALCUL

$8 + 6 = 14$ eight and (or plus) six are (or make) fourteen

huit et (ou plus) six font (ou égalent) quatorze

$15 − 3 = 12$ fifteen take away (or fifteen minus) three equals twelve, three from fifteen leaves twelve

trois ôté de quinze égalent douze, quinze moins trois égalent douze

$3 × 3 = 9$ three threes are nine, three times three is nine

trois fois trois égalent neuf, trois multiplié par trois égalent neuf

$32 ÷ 8 = 4$ thirty-two divided by eight is (or equals) four

trente-deux divisé par huit égalent quatre

$3^2 = 9$ three squared is nine

trois au carré égale neuf

$2^5 = 32$ two to the power of five (or to the fifth) is (or equals) thirty-two

deux à la puissance cinq égale trente-deux

$\sqrt{16} = 4$ the square root of sixteen is four

la racine carrée de seize ($\sqrt{16}$) est quatre

8 TIME   L'HEURE

2 hours 33 minutes and 14 seconds	deux heures trente-trois minutes et quatorze secondes
half an hour	une demi-heure
a quarter of an hour	un quart d'heure
three quarters of an hour	trois quarts d'heure
what's the time?	quelle heure est-il?
what time do you make it?	quelle heure avez-vous?
have you the right time?	avez-vous l'heure exacte?
I make it 2.20	d'après ma montre il est 2 h 20
my watch says 3.37	il est 3 h 37 à ma montre
it's 1 o'clock	il est une heure
it's 2 o'clock	il est deux heures
it's 5 past 4	il est quatre heures cinq
it's 10 to 6	il est six heures moins dix
it's half past 8	il est huit heures et demie
it's a quarter past 9	il est neuf heures et quart
it's a quarter to 2	il est deux heures moins le quart
at 10 a.m.	à dix heures du matin
at 4 p.m.	à quatre heures de l'après-midi
at 11 p.m.	à onze heures du soir
at exactly 3 o'clock, at 3 sharp, at 3 on the dot	à trois heures exactement, à trois heures précises
the train leaves at 19.32	le train part à dix-neuf heures trente-deux
(at) what time does it start?	à quelle heure est-ce que cela commence?
it is just after 3	il est trois heures passées
it is nearly 9	il est presque neuf heures
about 8 o'clock	aux environs de huit heures
at (or by) 6 o'clock at the latest	à six heures au plus tard
have it ready for 5 o'clock	tiens-le prêt pour 5 heures
it is full each night from 7 to 9	c'est plein chaque soir de 7 à 9
"closed from 1.30 to 4.30"	« fermé de 13 h 30 à 16 h 30 »
until 8 o'clock	jusqu'à huit heures
it would be about 11	il était environ 11 heures, il devait être environ 11 heures
it would have been about 10	il devait être environ dix heures
at midnight	à minuit
before midday, before noon	avant midi

9 DATES

NB The days of the week and the months start with a small letter in French: lundi, mardi, février, mars.

the 1st of July, July 1st
the 2nd of May, May 2nd
on June 21st, on the 21st (of) June
on Monday
he comes on Mondays
"closed on Fridays"
he lends it to me from Monday to Friday
from the 14th to the 18th
what's the date?, what date is it today?
today's the 12th
one Thursday in October
about the 4th of July
1978 nineteen (hundred and) seventy-eight

4 B.C., B.C. 4
70 A.D., A.D. 70
in the 13th century
in (or during) the 1930s
in 1940 something

HEADING OF LETTERS:
19th May 1993
(See also the main text of the dictionary.)

LES DATES

N.B. Contrairement au français, les jours de la semaine et les mois prennent une majuscule en anglais : Monday, Tuesday, February, March.

le 1er juillet
le 2 mai
le 21 juin
lundi
il vient le lundi
« fermé le vendredi »
il me le prête du lundi au vendredi
du 14 au 18
quelle est la date d'aujourd'hui ?
aujourd'hui nous sommes le 12
un jeudi en octobre
aux environs du 4 juillet
mille neuf cent soixante-dix-huit, dix-neuf cent soixante-dix-huit

4 av. J.-C.
70 apr. J.-C.
au XIIIe siècle
dans (ou pendant) les années 30
en 1940 et quelques

EN-TÊTE DE LETTRES :
le 19 mai 1993
(Voir aussi dans le corps du dictionnaire.)

WEIGHTS, MEASURES AND TEMPERATURES

POIDS, MESURES ET TEMPÉRATURES

NOTES

1. Metric system

Measures formed with the following prefixes are mostly omitted:

deca-	10 times
hecto-	100 times
kilo-	1000 times
deci-	one tenth
centi-	one hundredth
mil(l)i-	one thousandth

2. US measures

In the US, the same system as that which applies in Great Britain is used for the most part; the main differences are mentioned below.

3. The numerical notations of measures:

Numerical equivalents are shown in standard English notation when they are translations of French measures and in standard French notation when they are translations of English measures;
e.g. 1 millimetre (millimètre) = 0.03937 inch should be read in French as 0,03937 pouce.
e.g. 1 inch (pouce) = 2,54 centimètres should be read in English as 2.54 centimetres.

REMARQUES

1. Le système métrique

La plupart des mesures formées à partir des préfixes suivants ont été omises :

10 fois	*déca-*
100 fois	*hecto-*
1 000 fois	*kilo-*
un dixième	*déci-*
un centième	*centi-*
un millième	*mil(l)i-*

2. Mesures US

Les mesures britanniques sont valables pour les USA dans la majeure partie des cas. Les principales différences sont énumérées ci-dessous.

3. Notation graphique des équivalences de mesures :

Les équivalences sont notées en anglais lorsqu'elles traduisent des mesures françaises et en français lorsqu'elles se rapportent à des mesures anglaises :
ex. 1 millimetre (millimètre) = 0.03937 inch doit se lire en français 0,03937 pouce.
ex. 1 inch (pouce) = 2,54 centimètres doit se lire en anglais 2.54 centimetres.

1 LINEAR MEASURES — MESURES DE LONGUEUR

metric system système métrique	1 millimetre US millimeter	(millimètre)	**mm**	0.03937 inch
	1 centimetre US centimeter	(centimètre)	**cm**	0.3937 inch
	1 metre US meter	(mètre)	**m**	39.37 inches = 1.094 yards
	1 kilometre US kilometer	(kilomètre)	**km**	0.6214 mile (5/8 mile)

French non-metric measures mesures françaises non métriques	1 nautical mile	1 mille marin	= 1 852 mètres
	1 knot	1 nœud	= 1 mille/heure

British system système britannique	1 inch	(pouce)		**in**	2,54 centimètres
	1 foot	(pied)	= 12 inches	**ft**	30,48 centimètres
	1 yard	(yard)	= 3 feet	**yd**	91,44 centimètres
	1 furlong		= 220 yards		201,17 mètres
	1 mile	(mile)	= 1,760 yards	**m** ou **ml**	1,609 kilomètre

surveyors' measures mesures d'arpentage	1 link	= 7.92 inches	=	20,12 centimètres
	1 rod (or pole, perch)	= 25 links	=	5,029 mètres
	1 chain	= 22 yards = 4 rods	=	20,12 mètres

2 SQUARE MEASURES — MESURES DE SUPERFICIE

metric system système métrique	1 square centimetre US square centimeter	(centimètre carré)		cm^2	0.155 square inch
	1 square metre US square meter	(mètre carré)		m^2	10.764 square feet = 1.196 square yards
	1 square kilometre US square kilometer	(kilomètre carré)		km^2	0.3861 square mile = 247.1 acres
	1 are	(are)	= 100 square metres	**a**	119.6 square yards
	1 hectare	(hectare)	= 100 ares	**ha**	2.471 acres

British system système britannique	1 square inch	(pouce carré)		in^2	6,45 cm^2
	1 square foot	(pied carré)	= 144 square inches	ft^2	929,03 cm^2
	1 square yard	(yard carré)	= 9 square feet	yd^2	0,836 m^2
	1 square rod		= 30.25 square yards		25,29 m^2
	1 acre		= 4,840 square yards	**a**	40,47 ares
	1 square mile	(mile carré)	= 640 acres	m^2 ou ml^2	2,59 km^2

3   CUBIC MEASURES — MESURES DE VOLUME

metric system **système métrique**	1 cubic centimetre US cubic centimeter	(centimètre cube)		cm^3	0.061 cubic inch
	1 cubic metre US cubic meter	(mètre cube)		m^3	35.315 cubic feet 1.308 cubic yards
British system **système britannique**	1 cubic inch			in^3	16,387 cm^3
	1 cubic foot	(pied cube)	= 1,728 cubic inches	ft^3	0,028 m^3
	1 cubic yard	(yard cube)	= 27 cubic feet	yd^3	0,765 m^3
	1 register ton	(tonne)	= 100 cubic feet		2,832 m^3

4   MEASURES OF CAPACITY — MESURES DE CAPACITÉ

					Brit	US
metric system **système métrique**	1 litre	(litre)	= 1,000 cubic centimetres	**l**	1.76 pints	2,12 pints
	1 stere	(stère)	= 1 cubic metre	**st**	1.308 cubic yards	
				=	0.22 gallon	0,26 gallon

	British system / système britannique					US measures / mesures US		
(a) liquid **pour liquides**	1 gill			=	0,142 litre	1 US liquid gill		= 0,118 litre
	1 pint (pinte)	= 4 gills	**pt**		0,57 litre	1 US liquid pint	= 4 gills	= 0,473 litre
	1 quart	= 2 pints	**qt**		1,136 litres	1 US liquid quart	= 2 pints	= 0,946 litre
	1 gallon (gallon)	= 4 quarts	**g** ou **gal** ou **gall**		4,546 litres	1 US gallon	= 4 quarts	= 3,785 litres
(b) dry **pour matières** **sèches**	1 peck	= 2 gallons		=	9,087 litres	1 US dry pint		= 0,550 litre
	1 bushel	= 4 pecks		=	36,36 litres	1 US dry quart	= 2 dry pints	= 1,1 litre
	1 quarter	= 8 bushels		=	290,94 litres	1 US peck	= 8 dry quarts	= 8,81 litres
						1 US bushel	= 4 pecks	= 35,24 litres

5 WEIGHTS — POIDS

metric system / système métrique	1 gram or gramme	(gramme)		french **g**	15.4 grains
	1 kilogram or kilogramme	(kilogramme)		Brit **g** or **gr** **kg**	2.2046 pounds
	1 quintal	(quintal)	= 100 kilogrammes	**q**	220.46 pounds
	1 metric ton	(tonne)	= 1 000 kilogrammes	**t**	0.9842 ton

Avoirdupois system / système avoirdupoids

British system / système britannique	1 grain	(grain)		**gr**	0,0648 gramme
	1 drachm or dram		= 27.34 grains	**dr**	1,772 grammes
	1 ounce	(once)	= 16 drachms	**oz**	28,349 grammes
	1 pound	(livre)	= 16 ounces	**lb**	453,59 grammes = 0,453 kilogramme
	1 stone		= 14 pounds	**st**	6,348 kilogrammes
	1 quarter		= 28 pounds		12,7 kilogrammes
	1 hundredweight		= 112 pounds	**cwt**	50,8 kilogrammes
	1 (long) ton	(tonne)	= 2,240 pounds	**t**	1 016,05 kilogrammes

US measures / mesures US	1 (short) hundredweight	= 100 pounds		45,36 kilogrammes
	1 (short) ton	= 2000 pounds,		907,18 kilogrammes

6 TEMPERATURES — TEMPÉRATURES

$59\,°F = (59 - 32) \times \dfrac{5}{9} = 15\,°C$

A rough-and-ready way of converting centigrade to Fahrenheit and vice versa: start from the fact that

10 °C = 50 °F

thereafter for every 5 °C add 9 °F.

Thus :

15 °C = (10 + 5) = (50 + 9) = 59 °F
68 °F = (50 + 9 + 9)
    = (10 + 5 + 5) = 20 °C

$20\,°C = (20 \times \dfrac{9}{5}) + 32 = 68\,°F$

Une manière rapide de convertir les centigrades en Fahrenheit et vice versa : en prenant pour base

10 °C = 50 °F

5 °C équivalent à 9 °F.

Ainsi :

15 °C = (10 + 5) = (50 + 9) = 59 °F
68 °F = (50 + 9 + 9)
    = (10 + 5 + 5) = 20 °C

TABLE DES MATIÈRES

CONTENTS

Introduction	xii
Comment utiliser le dictionnaire	xvii
Prononciation	
Prononciation du français	xxxvi
Prononciation de l'anglais	xxxviii
DICTIONNAIRE FRANÇAIS-ANGLAIS	1-987
Grammaire active de l'anglais	
et du français	1-61
DICTIONNAIRE ANGLAIS-FRANÇAIS	989-2081
Annexes	
Le verbe français	3
Le verbe anglais	25
Nombres, heures et dates	33
Poids, mesures et	
températures	41

Introduction	xiv
Using the dictionary	xvii
Pronunciation	
Pronunciation of French	xxxvi
Pronunciation of English	xxxviii
FRENCH-ENGLISH DICTIONARY	1-987
Language in use: a grammar	
of communication in French	
and English	1-61
ENGLISH-FRENCH DICTIONARY	989-2081
Appendices	
The French verb	3
The English verb	25
Numbers, time and dates	33
Weights, measures	
and temperatures	41

abréviation	abrév, abbr	abbreviated, abbreviation
adjectif	adj	adjective
administration	Admin	administration
adverbe	adv	adverb
agriculture	Agr	agriculture
anatomie	Anat	anatomy
anciennement	anciennt	formerly
antiquité	Antiq	ancient history
approximativement	approx	approximately
archéologie	Archéol, Archeol	archaeology
architecture	Archit	architecture
argot	arg	slang
article	art	article
astrologie	Astrol	astrology
astronomie	Astron	astronomy
attribut	attrib	predicative
audiovisuel	Audiov	audiovisual
australien, Australie	Austral	Australian, Australia
automobile	Aut	automobiles
auxiliaire	aux	auxiliary
aviation	Aviat	aviation
belge, Belgique	Belg	Belgian, Belgium
biologie	Bio	biology
biochimie	Biochem	biochemistry
botanique	Bot	botany
britannique, Grande-Bretagne	Brit	British, Great Britain
canadien, Canada	Can	Canadian, Canada
chimie	Chim, Chem	chemistry
cinéma	Ciné, Cine	cinema
commerce	Comm	commerce
mots composés	comp	compound, in compounds
comparatif	compar	comparative
comptabilité	Comptab	accounting
informatique	Comput	computing
conditionnel	cond	conditional
conjonction	conj	conjunction
construction	Constr	building trade
cuisine	Culin	cookery
défini	déf, def	definite
démonstratif	dém, dem	demonstrative
dialectal, régional	dial	dialect
diminutif	dim	diminutive
direct	dir	direct
écologie	Écol, Ecol	ecology
économie	Écon, Econ	economics
écossais, Écosse	Écos	Scottish, Scotland
enseignement	Éduc, Educ	education
par exemple	eg	for example
électricité, électronique	Élec, Elec	electricity, electronics
épithète	épith	before noun
surtout	esp	especially
et cetera	etc	etcetera
ethnologie	Ethnol	ethnology
euphémisme	euph	euphemism
par exemple	ex	for example
exclamation	excl	exclamation
féminin	f	feminine
figuré	fig	figuratively
finance	Fin	finance
féminin pluriel	fpl	feminine plural
formel, langue soignée	frm	formal language
football	Ftbl	football
fusionné	fus	fused
futur	fut	future
en général, généralement	gén, gen	in general, generally
géographie	Géog, Geog	geography
géologie	Géol, Geol	geology
géométrie	Géom, Geom	geometry
gouvernement	Govt	government
grammaire	Gram	grammar
gymnastique	Gym	gymnastics
suisse, Suisse	Helv	Swiss, Switzerland
héraldique	Hér, Her	heraldry
histoire	Hist	history
horticulture	Hort	horticulture
humoristique	hum	humorous
impératif	impér, imper	imperative
impersonnel	impers	impersonal
imprimerie	Imprim	printing
industrie	Ind	industry
indéfini	indéf, indef	indefinite
indicatif	indic	indicative
indirect	indir	indirect
infinitif	infin	infinitive
inséparable	insep	inseparable
interjection	interj	interjection
interrogatif	interrog	interrogative
invariable	inv	invariable
irlandais, Irlande	Ir	Irish, Ireland
ironique	iro	ironic
irrégulier	irrég, irreg	irregular
droit, juridique	Jur	law, legal
linguistique	Ling	linguistics
littéral, au sens propre	lit	literally
littéraire	liter	literary
littérature	Literat	literature
littéraire	littér	literary
littérature	Littérat	literature
locution	loc	locution